CHILTON'S

IMPORT AUTOMOTIVE SERVICE MANUAL

Publisher Kerry A. Freeman, S.A.E.
Editor-In-Chief Dean F. Morgantini, S.A.E. □ **Managing Editor** David H. Lee, A.S.E., S.A.E.
Senior Editor Richard J. Rivele, S.A.E. □ **Senior Editor** Nick D'Andrea □ **Senior Editor** Ron Webb
Project Manager Peter M. Conti, Jr. □ **Project Manager** Ken Grabowski, A.S.E., S.A.E.
Project Manager Richard T. Smith
Service Editors Lawrence C. Braun, S.A.E., A.S.C., Robert E. Doughten, Jacques Gordon
Michael L. Grady, Ben Greisler, Martin J. Gunther, Steve Horner, Neil Leonard, A.S.E.,
James R. Marotta, Robert McAnally, Steven Morgan, Don Schnell, James B. Steele,
Larry E. Stiles, Jim Taylor, Anthony Tortorici, A.S.E., S.A.E.
Editorial Consultants Edward K. Shea, S.A.E., Stan Stephenson

Manager of Manufacturing John J. Cantwell
Production Manager W. Calvin Settle, Jr., S.A.E
Assistant Production Manager Andrea Steiger
Mechanical Artist Marsha Park Herman
Mechanical Artist Lorraine Martinelli
Special Projects Peter Kaprielyan

Director, Sales & Marketing Donald A. Wright
National Sales Coordinator David H. Flaherty
Regional Sales Managers Joseph Andrews, Jr., Larry W. Marshall, Bruce McCorkle

OFFICERS
President Gary R. Ingersoll
Senior Vice President, Book Publishing & Research Ronald A. Hoxter

CHILTON BOOK COMPANY
ONE OF THE ABC PUBLISHING COMPANIES,
A PART OF CAPITAL CITIES/ABC, INC.
Manufactured in USA ©1991 Chilton Book Company ● Chilton Way, Radnor, Pa. 19089
ISBN 0–8019–8133–6   1234567890 0987654321   ISSN 0742–0307

SAFETY NOTICE

Proper service and repair procedures are vital to the safe, reliable operation of all motor vehicles, as well as the personal safety of those performing repairs. This manual outlines procedures for servicing and repairing vehicles using safe, effective methods. The procedures contain many NOTES, CAUTIONS and WARNINGS which should be followed along with standard safety procedures to eliminate the possibilty of personal injury or improper service which could damage the vehicle or compromise its safety.

It is important to note that the repair procedures and techniques, tools and parts for servicng motor vehicles, as well as the skill and experience of the individual performing the work vary widely. It is not possible to anticipate all of the conceivable ways or conditions under which vehicles may be serviced, or to provide cautions as to all of the possible hazards that may result. Standard and accepted safety precautions and equipment should be used when handling toxic or flammable fluids, and safety goggles or other protection should be used during cutting, grinding, chiseling, prying, or any other process that can cause material removal or projectiles.

Some procedures require the use of tools specially designed for a specific purpose. Before substituting another tool or procedure, you must be completely satisfied that neither your personal safety, nor the performance of the vehicle will be endangered

PART NUMBERS

Part numbers listed in this reference are not recomendations by Chilton for any product by brand name. They are references that can be used with interchange manuals and aftermarket supplier catalogs to locate each brand supplier's discrete part number.

Although information in this manual is based on industry sources and is complete as possible at the time of publication, the possibilty exists that some car manufacturers made later changes which could not be included here. While striving for total accuracy, Chilton Book Company cannot assume responsibility for any errors, changes or omissions that may occur in the compilation of this data.

SERIAL NUMBER IDENTIFICATION

Vehicle Identification Plate

Acura and Sterling vehicle identification numbers are mounted on the left top edge of the instrument panel and are visible from the outside. There is also a vehicle identification number stamped on the center of the firewall in the engine compartment.

Engine Number

The engine serial number is stamped into the right rear side of the engine on the Integra vehicles and front left side of the en- gine on the Legend and Sterling vehicles. The first 5 digits indi- cate the engine model identification. The remaining numbers refer to the production sequence.

Vehicle Identification Label

A vehicle/engine identification label is located under the hood, on the center of the cowl and on the driver's side door pillar.

Transaxle Number

The transaxle serial number is stamped on the top towards the rear of the transaxle/clutch case.

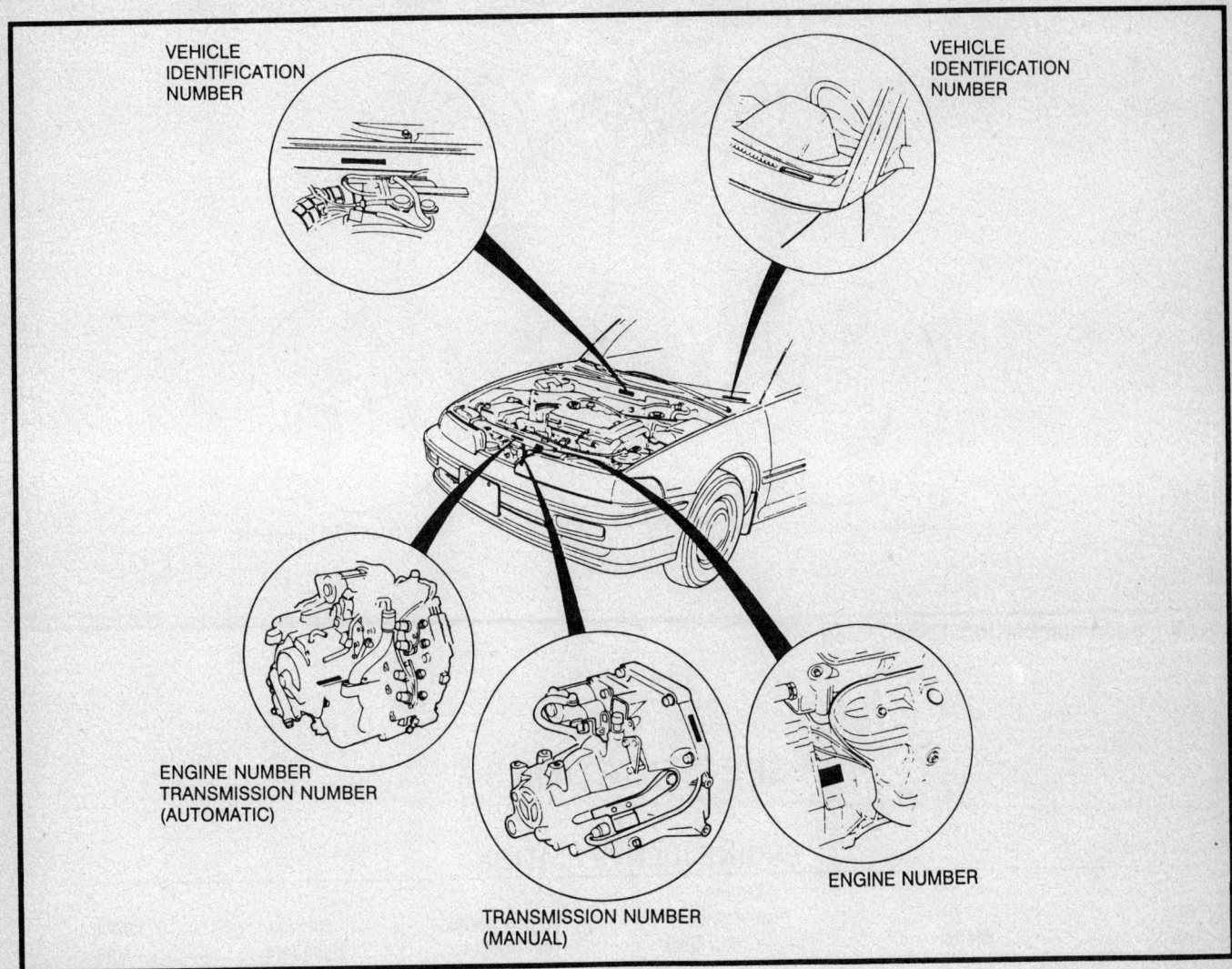

Identification number locations—Legend and Sterling

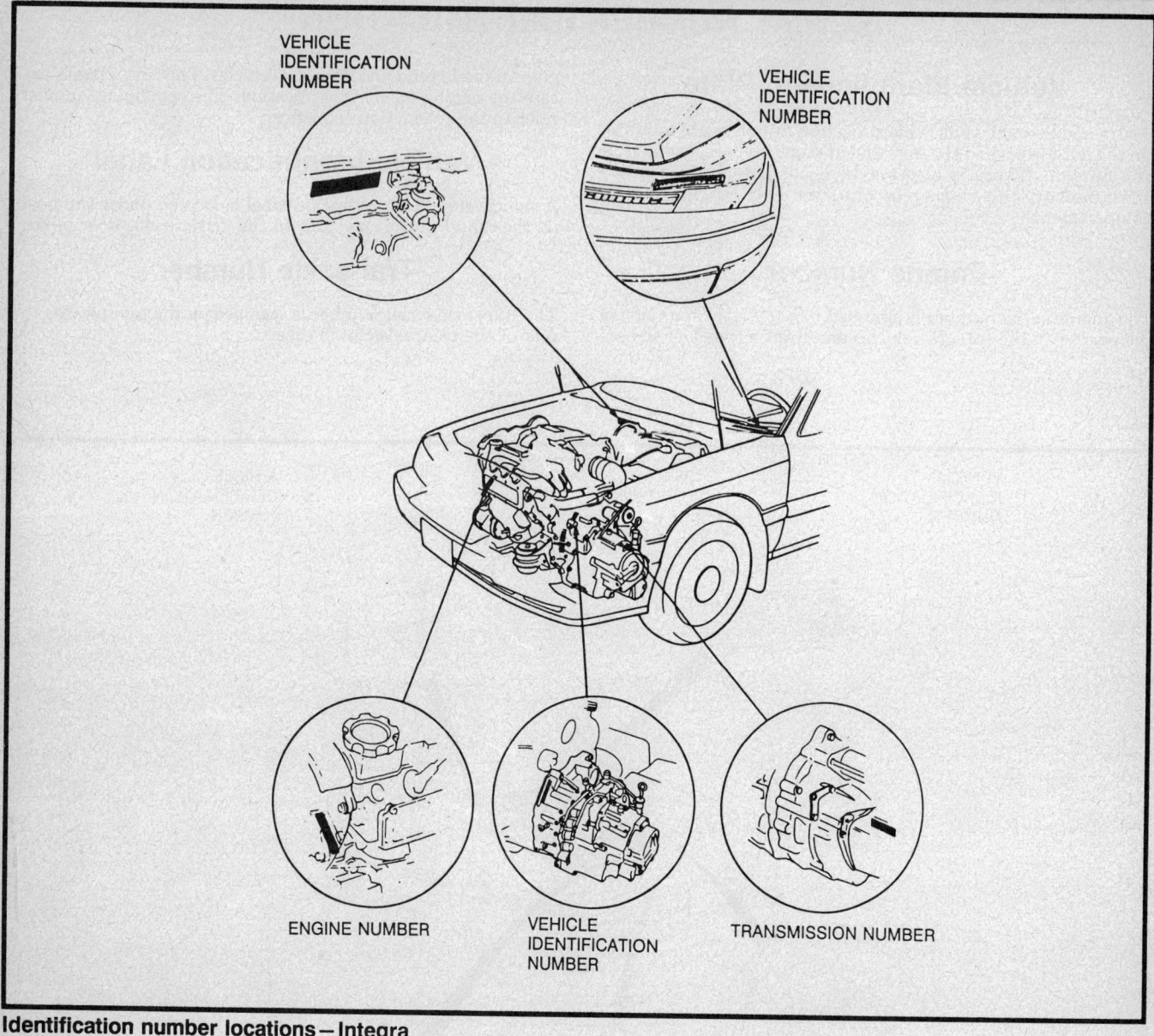

Identification number locations — Integra

SPECIFICATIONS

ENGINE IDENTIFICATION

Year	Model	Engine Displacement cu. in. (cc/liter)	Engine Series Identification	No. of Cylinders	Engine Type
1987	Integra	97 (1590/1.6)	D16A1	4	DOHC 16V
	Legend	152 (2494/2.5)	C25A1	6	OHC V6
	Legend Coupe	163 (2675/2.7)	C27A1	6	OHC V6
	825	152 (2494/2.5)	C25A1	6	OHC V6

ENGINE IDENTIFICATION

Year	Model	Engine Displacement cu. in. (cc/liter)	Engine Series Identification	No. of Cylinders	Engine Type
1988	Integra	97 (1590/1.6)	D16A1	4	DOHC 16V
	Legend	163 (2675/2.7)	C27A1	6	OHC V6
	Legend Coupe	163 (2675/2.7)	C27A1	6	OHC V6
	825	152 (2494/2.5)	C25A1	6	OHC V6
1989	Integra	97 (1590/1.6)	D16A1	4	DOHC 16V
	Legend	163 (2675/2.7)	C27A1	6	OHC V6
	Legend Coupe	163 (2675/2.7)	C27A1	6	OHC V6
	827	163 (2675/2.7)	C27A1	6	OHC V6
1990-91	Integra	112 (1834/1.8)	B18A1	4	DOHC 16V
	Legend	163 (2675/2.7)	C27A1	6	OHC V6
	Legend Coupe	163 (2675/2.7)	C27A1	6	OHC V6
	827	163 (2675/2.7)	C27A1	6	OHC V6

DOHC 16V Double Overhead Camshaft, 16 valve head
OHC Overhead Camshaft

GENERAL ENGINE SPECIFICATIONS

Year	Model	Engine Displacement cu. in. (cc)	Fuel System Type	Net Horsepower @ rpm	Net Torque @ rpm (ft. lbs.)	Bore × Stroke (in.)	Compression Ratio	Oil Pressure @ 3000 rpm
1987	Integra	97 (1590)	PGM-F1	113 @ 6250	99 @ 5500	2.95 × 3.54	9.3:1	60-78
	Legend	152 (2494)	PGM-F1	151 @ 5800	154 @ 4500	3.31 × 2.95	9.0:1	71-82
	Legend Coupe	163 (2675)	PGM-F1	161 @ 5900	162 @ 4500	3.43 × 2.95	9.0:1	71-82
	825	152 (2494)	PGM-F1	151 @ 5800	154 @ 4500	3.31 × 2.95	9.0:1	71-82
1988	Integra	97 (1590)	PGM-F1	113 @ 6250	99 @ 5500	2.95 × 3.54	9.5:1	60-78
	Legend	163 (2675)	PGM-F1	161 @ 5900	162 @ 4500	3.43 × 2.95	9.0:1	71-82
	Legend Coupe	163 (2675)	PGM-F1	161 @ 5900	162 @ 4500	3.43 × 2.95	9.0:1	71-82
	825	152 (2494)	PGM-F1	151 @ 5800	154 @ 4500	3.31 × 2.95	9.0:1	71-82
1989	Integra	97 (1590)	PGM-F1	118 @ 6500	103 @ 5500	2.95 × 3.54	9.5:1	60-78
	Legend	163 (2675)	PGM-F1	161 @ 5900	162 @ 4500	3.43 × 2.95	9.0:1	71-82
	Legend Coupe	163 (2675)	PGM-F1	161 @ 5900	162 @ 4500	3.43 × 2.95	9.0:1	71-82
	827	163 (2675)	PGM-F1	161 @ 5900	162 @ 4500	3.43 × 2.95	9.0:1	71-82
1990-91	Integra	112 (1834)	PGM-F1	130 @ 6000	121 @ 5000	3.19 × 3.50	9.2:1	69-79
	Legend	163 (2675)	PGM-F1	161 @ 5900	162 @ 4500	3.43 × 2.95	9.0:1	71-82
	Legend Coupe	163 (2675)	PGM-F1	161 @ 5900	162 @ 4500	3.43 × 2.95	9.0:1	71-82
	827	163 (2675)	PGM-F1	161 @ 5900	162 @ 4500	3.43 × 2.95	9.0:1	71-82

PGM-F1—Electronic Fuel Injection

TUNE-UP SPECIFICATIONS

Year	Model	Engine Displacement cu. in. (cc)	Spark Plugs Type	Spark Plugs Gap (in.)	Ignition Timing (deg.) MT	Ignition Timing (deg.) AT	Compression Pressure (psi)	Fuel Pump (psi)	Idle Speed (rpm) MT	Idle Speed (rpm) AT	Valve Clearance In.	Valve Clearance Ex.
1987	Integra	97 (1590)	①	0.039–0.043	0 ③	0 ③	164–192	36	750–850	750–850	0.0051–0.0067	0.0059–0.0075
	Legend	152 (2494)	②	0.039–0.043	3B ④	3B ④	135–178	36	670–770	670–770	Hyd.	Hyd.
	Legend Coupe	163 (2675)	②	0.039–0.043	15B ③	15B ③	142–171	36	630–730	630–730	Hyd.	Hyd.
	825	152 (2494)	②	0.039–0.043	3B ④	3B ④	135–178	36	670–770	670–770	Hyd.	Hyd.
1988	Integra	97 (1590)	①	0.039–0.043	12B ⑤	12B ⑤	135–192	36	700–800	650–750	0.0051–0.0067	0.0059–0.0075
	Legend	163 (2675)	②	0.039–0.043	15B ⑤	15B ⑤	142–171	36–41	630–730	630–730	Hyd.	Hyd.
	Legend Coupe	163 (2675)	②	0.039–0.043	15B ⑤	15B ⑤	142–171	36–41	630–730	630–730	Hyd.	Hyd.
	825	152 (2494)	②	0.039–0.043	3B ④	3B ④	135–178	36–41	670–770	670–770	Hyd.	Hyd.
1989	Integra	97 (1590)	①	0.039–0.043	12B ⑤	12B ⑤	135–192	36	700–800	650–750	0.0051–0.0067	0.0059–0.0075
	Legend	163 (2675)	②	0.039–0.043	15B ⑤	15B ⑤	142–171	36–41	630–730	630–730	Hyd.	Hyd.
	Legend Coupe	163 (2675)	②	0.039–0.043	15B ⑤	15B ⑤	142–171	36–41	630–730	630–730	Hyd.	Hyd.
	827	163 (2675)	②	0.039–0.043	15B ⑤	15B ⑤	142–171	36–41	630–730	630–730	Hyd.	Hyd.
1990	Integra	112 (1834)	②	0.039–0.043	16B ⑤	16B ⑤	135–196	35–41	750±50	750±50	0.0060–0.0070	0.0010–0.0080
	Legend	163 (2675)	②	0.039–0.043	15B ⑤	15B ⑤	142–171	36–41	680±50	680±50	Hyd.	Hyd.
	Legend Coupe	163 (2675)	②	0.039–0.043	15B ⑤	15B ⑤	142–171	36–41	680±50	680±50	Hyd.	Hyd.
	827	163 (2675)	②	0.039–0.043	15B ⑤	15B ⑤	142–171	36–41	680±50	680±50	Hyd.	Hyd.
1991	SEE UNDERHOOD SPECIFICATIONS STICKER											

NOTE: The Underhood Specifications sticker often reflects tune-up changes made in production. Sticker figures must be used if they disagree with those in this chart.

MT Manual transmission
AT Automatic transmission
NA Not adjustable
A After Top Dead Center
B Before Top Dead Center
Hyd. Hydraulic valve lash adjusters
① BCPR6EY-11
   BCPR6EY-N11
   Q20PR-U11
② BCPR6E-11
   BCPR6EY-N11
   Q20PR-U11
③ Vacuum advance hoses disconnected. White mark on crankshaft pulley
④ Vacuum advance hoses disconnected. Yellow mark on crankshaft pulley
⑤ Red mark on crankshaft pulley

FIRING ORDER

NOTE: To avoid confusion, always replace spark plug wires one at a time.

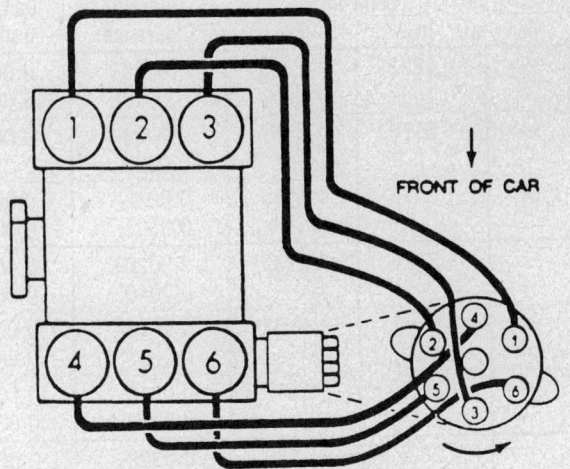

FRONT OF CAR

2494cc and 2675cc Engines
Engine Firing Order: 1–4–2–5–3–6
Distributor Rotation: Counterclockwise

FRONT OF CAR

1590cc and 1843cc Engines
Engine Firing Order: 1–3–4–2
Distributor Rotation: Clockwise

CAPACITIES

Year	Model	Engine Displacement cu. in. (cc)	Engine Crankcase (qts.) with Filter	without Filter	Transmission (pts.) 4-Spd	5-Spd	Auto.	Drive Axle (pts.)	Fuel Tank (gal.)	Cooling System (qts.)
1987	Integra	97 (1590)	4.5	4.0	—	4.8	5.0①	—	13.2	6.0
	Legend	152 (2494)	4.8	4.2	—	4.6	6.8①	—	18.0	9.2
	Legend Coupe	163 (2675)	4.8	4.2	—	4.6	6.8①	—	18.0	9.2
	825	152 (2494)	4.8	4.2	—	4.6	6.8①	—	17.0	9.8
1988	Integra	97 (1590)	4.5	4.0	—	4.8	5.0①	—	13.2	6.0
	Legend	163 (2675)	4.8	4.2	—	4.6	6.8①	—	18.0	9.2
	Legend Coupe	163 (2675)	4.8	4.2	—	4.6	6.8③	—	18.0	9.2
	825	152 (2494)	4.8	4.2	—	4.6	6.8①	—	17.0	9.8
1989	Integra	97 (1590)	4.5	4.0	—	4.8	5.0①	—	13.2	6.0
	Legend	163 (2675)	4.8	4.2	—	4.6	6.8①	—	18.0	9.2
	Legend Coupe	163 (2675)	4.8	4.2	—	4.6	6.8③	—	18.0	9.2
	827	163 (2675)	4.8	4.2	—	4.6	6.8①	—	17.0	9.8
1990–91	Integra	112 (1834)	4.6	4.0	—	4.0	6.0①	—	13.2	6.9
	Legend	163 (2675)	4.8	4.2	—	4.6	6.8①	—	18.0	9.2
	Legend Coupe	163 (2675)	4.8	4.2	—	4.6	6.8①	—	18.0	9.2
	827	163 (2675)	4.8	4.2	—	4.6	6.8①	—	17.0	9.8

① Oil change capacity.

CAMSHAFT SPECIFICATIONS

All measurements given in inches.

Year	Engine Displacement cu. in. (cc)	Journal Diameter 1	2	3	4	5	Lobe Lift In.	Ex.	Bearing Clearance	Camshaft End Play
1987	97 (1590)	—	—	—	—	—	1.2822	1.2733	0.0020–0.0040	0.0020–0.0060
	152 (2494)	—	—	—	—	—	1.5578	1.5561	0.0018–0.0032	0.0020–0.0060
	163 (2675)	—	—	—	—	—	1.5535	1.5515	0.0018–0.0032	0.0020–0.0060
1988	97 (1590)	—	—	—	—	—	1.2822	1.2735	0.0020–0.0040	0.0020–0.0060
	152 (2494)	—	—	—	—	—	1.5578	1.5561	0.0018–0.0032	0.0020–0.0060
	163 (2675)	—	—	—	—	—	1.5535	1.5515	0.0018–0.0032	0.0020–0.0060
1989	97 (1590)	—	—	—	—	—	1.2822	1.2735	0.0020–0.0040	0.0020–0.0060
	163 (2675)	—	—	—	—	—	1.5535	1.5515	0.0018–0.0032	0.0020–0.0060
1990–91	112 (1834)	—	—	—	—	—	1.316	1.308	0.0020–0.0040	0.0020–0.0060
	163 (2675)	—	—	—	—	—	1.5535	1.5515	0.0018–0.0032	0.0020–0.0060

CRANKSHAFT AND CONNECTING ROD SPECIFICATIONS

All measurements are given in inches.

Year	Engine Displacement cu. in. (cc)	Crankshaft Main Brg. Journal Dia.	Main Brg. Oil Clearance	Shaft End-play	Thrust on No.	Connecting Rod Journal Diameter	Oil Clearance	Side Clearance
1987	97 (1590)	2.1644–2.1654	0.0009–0.0017①	0.0040–0.0140	3	1.7707–1.7717	0.0008–0.0015	0.0060–0.0120
	152 (2494)	2.5187–2.5197	0.0009–0.0019	0.0040–0.0140	3	2.0463–2.0472	0.0010–0.0020	0.0060–0.0120
	163 (2675)	2.5187–2.5197	0.0009–0.0019	0.0040–0.0140	3	2.0463–2.0472	0.0010–0.0020	0.0060–0.0120
1988	97 (1590)	2.1644–2.1654	0.0009–0.0017①	0.0040–0.0140	3	1.7707–1.7717	0.0008–0.0015	0.0060–0.0120
	152 (2494)	2.5187–2.5197	0.0009–0.0019	0.0040–0.0140	3	2.0463–2.0472	0.0010–0.0020	0.0060–0.0120
	163 (2675)	2.5187–2.5197	0.0009–0.0019	0.0040–0.0140	3	2.0463–2.0472	0.0010–0.0020	0.0060–0.0120
1989	97 (1590)	2.1644–2.1654	0.0009–0.0017①	0.0040–0.0140	3	1.7707–1.7717	0.0008–0.0015	0.0060–0.0120
	163 (2675)	2.5187–2.5197	0.0009–0.0019	0.0040–0.0140	3	2.0463–2.0472	0.0010–0.0020	0.0060–0.0120
1990–91	112 (1834)	2.1644–2.1651②	0.0009–0.0017③	0.0040–0.0140	3	1.7707–1.7717	0.0008–0.0015	0.0060–0.0120
	163 (2675)	2.5187–2.5197	0.0009–0.0019	0.0040–0.0140	3	2.0463–2.0472	0.0010–0.0020	0.0060–0.0120

① No. 1 oil clearance—0.0012–0.0190
② No. 3 2.1642–2.1651
③ No. 3 0.0012–0.0190

VALVE SPECIFICATIONS

Year	Engine Displacement cu. in. (cc)	Seat Angle (deg.)	Face Angle (deg.)	Spring Test Pressure (lbs.)	Spring Installed Height (in.)	Stem-to-Guide Clearance (in.)		Stem Diameter (in.)	
						Intake	Exhaust	Intake	Exhaust
1987	97 (1590)	45	45	—	—	0.0010–0.0020	0.0020–0.0030	0.2591–0.2594	0.2579–0.2583
	152 (2494)	45	45	—	—	0.0010–0.0020	0.0020–0.0030	0.2591–0.2594	0.2579–0.2583
	163 (2675)	45	45	—	—	0.0010–0.0020	0.0020–0.0030	0.2591–0.2594	0.2579–0.2583
1988	97 (1590)	45	45	—	—	0.0010–0.0020	0.0020–0.0030	0.2591–0.2594	0.2579–0.2583
	152 (2494)	45	45	—	—	0.0010–0.0020	0.0020–0.0030	0.2591–0.2594	0.2579–0.2583
	163 (2675)	45	45	—	—	0.0010–0.0020	0.0020–0.0030	0.2591–0.2594	0.2579–0.2583
1989	97 (1590)	45	45	—	—	0.0010–0.0020	0.0020–0.0030	0.2591–0.2594	0.2579–0.2583
	163 (2675)	45	45	—	—	0.0010–0.0020	0.0020–0.0030	0.2591–0.2594	0.2579–0.2583
1990–91	112 (1834)	45	45	—	—	0.0010–0.0020	0.0020–0.0030	0.2591–0.2594	0.2579–0.2583
	163 (2675)	45	45	—	—	0.0010–0.0020	0.0020–0.0030	0.2591–0.2594	0.2579–0.2583

PISTON AND RING SPECIFICATIONS

All measurements are given in inches.

Year	Engine Displacement cu. in. (cc)	Piston Clearance	Ring Gap			Ring Side Clearance		
			Top Compression	Bottom Compression	Oil Control	Top Compression	Bottom Compression	Oil Control
1987	97 (1590)	0.0004–0.0024	0.0060–0.0140	0.0060–0.0140	0.0080–0.0280	0.0012–0.0024	0.0012–0.0022	—
	152 (2494)	0.0002–0.0013	0.0080–0.0140	0.0080–0.0140	0.0080–0.0280	0.0008–0.0018	0.0008–0.0018	—
	163 (2675)	0.0006–0.0015	0.0080–0.0140	0.0140–0.0190	0.0080–0.0280	0.0006–0.0018	0.0006–0.0018	—
1988	97 (1590)	0.0004–0.0024	0.0060–0.0140	0.0120–0.0180	0.0080–0.0280	0.0012–0.0022	0.0012–0.0022	—
	152 (2494)	0.0002–0.0013	0.0080–0.0140	0.0080–0.0140	0.0080–0.0280	0.0008–0.0018	0.0008–0.0018	—
	163 (2675)	0.0006–0.0015	0.0080–0.0140	0.0140–0.0190	0.0080–0.0280	0.0006–0.0018	0.0006–0.0018	—
1989	97 (1590)	0.0004–0.0024	0.0060–0.0140	0.0120–0.0180	0.0080–0.0280	0.0012–0.0022	0.0012–0.0022	—
	163 (2675)	0.0006–0.0015	0.0080–0.0140	0.0140–0.0190	0.0080–0.0280	0.0006–0.0018	0.0006–0.0018	—
1990–91	112 (1834)	0.0004–0.0016	0.0080–0.0140	0.0160–0.0220	0.0080–0.0280	0.0018–0.0028	0.0018–0.0028	—
	163 (2675)	0.0006–0.0015	0.0080–0.0140	0.0140–0.0190	0.0080–0.0280	0.0006–0.0018	0.0006–0.0018	—

TORQUE SPECIFICATIONS
All readings in ft. lbs.

Year	Engine Displacement cu. in. (cc)	Cylinder Head Bolts	Main Bearing Bolts	Rod Bearing Bolts	Crankshaft Pulley Bolts	Flywheel Bolts	Manifold Intake	Manifold Exhaust	Spark Plugs
1987	97 (1590)	①	40	23	83	②	16	23	13
	152 (2494)	③	④	32	83	⑤	16	⑥	13
	163 (2675)	③	④	33	83	⑤	16	⑥	16
1988	97 (1590)	①	46	23	83	②	16	23	13
	152 (2494)	③	④	32	83	⑤	16	⑥	13
	163 (2675)	③	④	33	83	⑤	16	⑥	16
1989	97 (1590)	①	46	23	119	②	16	23	13
	163 (2675)	③	④	33	83	⑤	16	⑥	16
1990-91	112 (1834)	⑦	56	30	87	⑤	17	23	13
	163 (2675)	③	④	33	123	⑤	16	⑥	16

① Nuts—1st step—22 ft. lbs.
2nd step—48 ft. lbs.
② Manual transaxle—87 ft. lbs.
Automatic transaxle—54 ft. lbs.
③ 1st step—29 ft. lbs.
2nd step—56 ft. lbs.
④ Cap bolt (9mm)—29 ft. lbs.
Cap bridge bolt (11mm)—49 ft. lbs.
Side bolt (10mm)—36 ft. lbs.
⑤ Manual transaxle—76 ft. lbs.
Automatic transaxle—54 ft. lbs.
⑥ 8mm nuts—22 ft. lbs.
10mm nuts—40 ft. lbs.
⑦ 1st step—22 ft. lbs.
2nd step—61 ft lbs.

BRAKE SPECIFICATIONS
All measurements in inches unless noted.

Year	Model	Lug Nut Torque (ft. lbs.)	Master Cylinder Bore	Brake Disc Minimum Thickness	Brake Disc Maximum Runout	Standard Brake Drum Diameter	Minimum Lining Thickness Front	Minimum Lining Thickness Rear
1987	Integra	80	—	①	②	—	0.12	0.06
	Legend	80	—	③	④	—	0.12	0.06
	Legend Coupe	80	—	③	④	—	0.06	0.06
	825	80	—	③	④	—	0.12	0.06
1988	Integra	80	—	①	②	—	0.12	0.06
	Legend	80	—	③	④	—	0.06	0.06
	Legend Coupe	80	—	③	④	—	0.06	0.06
	825	80	—	③	④	—	0.06	0.06
1989	Integra	80	—	①	②	—	0.12	0.06
	Legend	80	—	③	④	—	0.06	0.06
	Legend Coupe	80	—	③	④	—	0.06	0.06
	827	80	—	③	④	—	0.06	0.06
1990-91	Integra	80	—	①	②	—	0.06	0.06
	Legend	80	—	③	④	—	0.06	0.06
	Legend Coupe	80	—	③	④	—	0.06	0.06
	827	80	—	③	④	—	0.06	0.06

① Front—0.67
Rear—0.31
② Front—0.004
Rear—0.006
③ Front—0.75
Rear—0.31
④ Front—0.004
Rear—0.004

WHEEL ALIGNMENT

Year	Model		Caster		Camber		Toe-in (in.)	Steering Axis Inclination (deg.)
			Range (deg.)	Preferred Setting (deg.)	Range (deg.)	Preferred Setting (deg.)		
1987	Integra	Front	$1\frac{3}{16}$P–$3\frac{3}{16}$P	$2\frac{3}{16}$P	$1\frac{1}{2}$N–$\frac{1}{2}$P	$\frac{1}{2}$N	$\frac{1}{32}$N	13
		Rear	—	—	1N–$\frac{1}{2}$N	$\frac{3}{4}$N	$\frac{1}{16}$P	—
	Legend	Front	$1\frac{1}{16}$P–$2\frac{1}{16}$P	$1\frac{11}{16}$P	1N–1P	0	0	NA
		Rear	—	—	1N–1P	0	0	—
	Legend Coupe	Front	$1\frac{1}{16}$P–$2\frac{1}{16}$P	$1\frac{11}{16}$P	1N–1P	0	0	NA
		Rear	—	—	1N–1P	0	0	—
	825	Front	$1\frac{1}{16}$P–$2\frac{1}{16}$P	$1\frac{11}{16}$P	1N–1P	0	0	NA
		Rear	—	—	1N–1P	0	0	—
1988	Integra	Front	$1\frac{3}{16}$P–$3\frac{3}{16}$P	$2\frac{3}{16}$P	$1\frac{1}{2}$N–$\frac{1}{2}$P	$\frac{1}{2}$N	$\frac{1}{32}$N	13
		Rear	—	—	1N–$\frac{1}{2}$N	$\frac{3}{4}$N	$\frac{1}{16}$P	—
	Legend	Front	$1\frac{1}{16}$P–$2\frac{1}{16}$P	$1\frac{11}{16}$P	1N–1P	0	0	NA
		Rear	—	—	1N–1P	0	0	—
	Legend Coupe	Front	$1\frac{1}{16}$P–$2\frac{1}{16}$P	$1\frac{11}{16}$P	1N–1P	0	0	NA
		Rear	—	—	1N–1P	0	0	—
	825	Front	$1\frac{1}{16}$P–$2\frac{1}{16}$P	$1\frac{11}{16}$P	1N–1P	0	0	NA
		Rear	—	—	1N–1P	0	0	—
1989	Integra	Front	$1\frac{3}{16}$P–$3\frac{3}{16}$P	$2\frac{3}{16}$P	$1\frac{1}{2}$N–$\frac{1}{2}$P	$\frac{1}{2}$N	$\frac{1}{32}$N	13
		Rear	—	—	1N–$\frac{1}{2}$N	$\frac{3}{4}$N	$\frac{1}{16}$P	—
	Legend	Front	$1\frac{1}{16}$P–$2\frac{1}{16}$P	$1\frac{11}{16}$P	1N–1P	0	0	NA
		Rear	—	—	1N–1P	0	0	—
	Legend Coupe	Front	$1\frac{1}{16}$P–$2\frac{1}{16}$P	$1\frac{11}{16}$P	1N–1P	0	0	NA
		Rear	—	—	1N–1P	0	0	—
	827	Front	$1\frac{1}{16}$P–$2\frac{1}{16}$P	$1\frac{11}{16}$P	1N–1P	0	0	NA
		Rear	—	—	1N–1P	0	0	—
1990–91	Integra	Front	$1\frac{1}{8}$P–$3\frac{1}{8}$P	$2\frac{1}{8}$P	$1\frac{1}{2}$N–$\frac{1}{2}$P	$\frac{1}{2}$N	$\frac{1}{32}$N	13
		Rear	—	—	1N–$\frac{1}{2}$N	$\frac{3}{4}$N	$\frac{3}{16}$P	—
	Legend	Front	$1\frac{1}{16}$P–$2\frac{1}{16}$P	$1\frac{11}{16}$P	1N–1P	0	0	NA
		Rear	—	—	1N–1P	0	0	—
	Legend Coupe	Front	$1\frac{1}{16}$P–$2\frac{1}{16}$P	$1\frac{11}{16}$P	1N–1P	0	0	NA
		Rear	—	—	1N–1P	0	0	—
	827	Front	$1\frac{1}{16}$P–$2\frac{1}{16}$P	$1\frac{11}{16}$P	1N–1P	0	0	NA
		Rear	—	—	1N–1P	0	0	—

NA—Not Available
N—Negative
P—Positive

ENGINE ELECTRICAL

NOTE: Disconnecting the negative battery cable on some vehicles may interfere with the functions of the on board computer systems and may require the computer to undergo a relearning process, once the negative battery cable is reconnected.

Distributor

Removal

1. Disconnect the negative battery cable. Disconnect the high tension and primary lead wires and the radio condenser wire from the distributor.

2. Label and disconnect the vacuum hoses, if equipped, or the electrical connectors, if equipped, from the distributor.

3. Remove the distributor cap hold-down screws and the distributor cap; move it aside.

4. Using chalk or paint, carefully mark the position of the distributor rotor in relation to the distributor housing and the distributor housing relation to the engine block.

NOTE: This aligning procedure is very important because the distributor must be reinstalled in the exact location from which it was removed.

5. Remove the distributor hold-down bolts and the distributor from the cylinder head.

NOTE: Do not disturb the engine while the distributor is removed, for the timing will be altered.

Installation

1. To install, lubricate the O-ring (Integra) with engine oil, align the tip of the rotor with the mark on the distributor housing.

2. With the rotor and housing aligned, insert the distributor into the engine and align the mark on the housing with the mark on the block, cylinder head or extension housing.

NOTE: The distributor is equipped with a coupling that connects to the camshaft. The lugs at the end of the coupling and it's mating grooves in the end of the camshaft are offset, to prevent installing the distributor 180 degrees out of time.

3. When the distributor is fully seated in the engine, install and tighten the distributor retaining bolts.

4. Align and install the distributor cap, then install the hold-down screws.

5. Connect the vacuum hoses, if equipped, or the electrical connectors, if equipped. Install the high tension and primary wires and the radio condenser wire onto the coil.

6. Start the engine and check the ignition timing. Reconnect the negative battery cable.

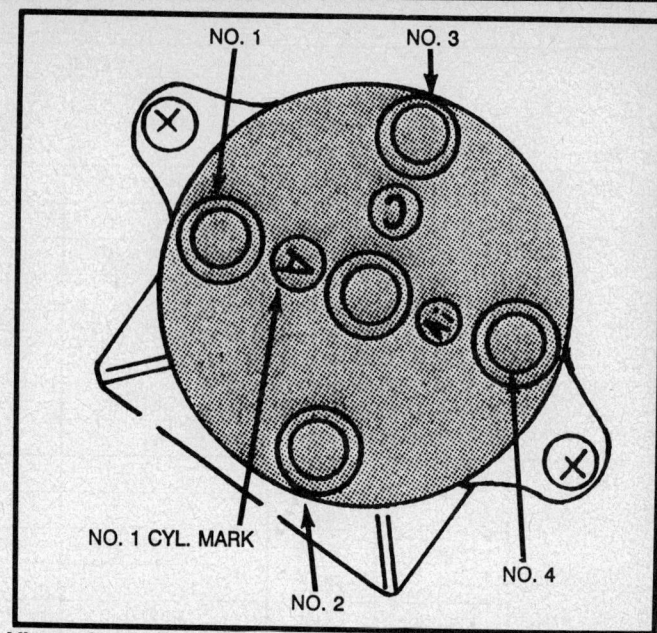

View of the distributor cap—1987 1590cc engine

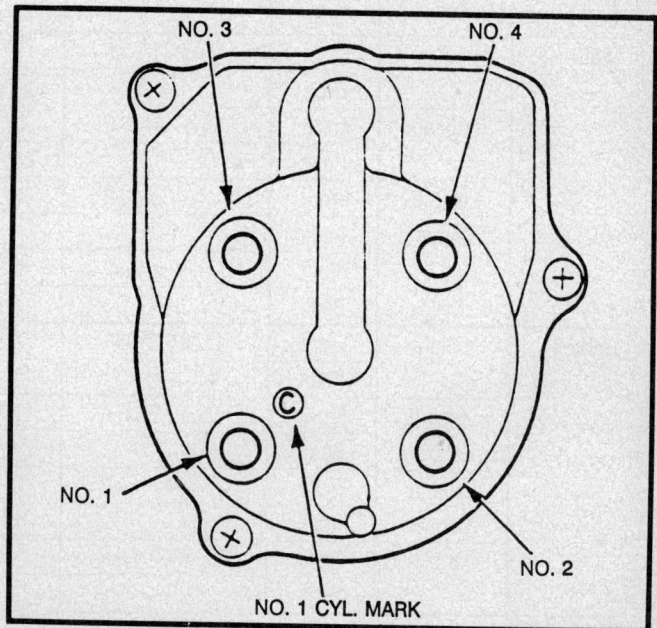

View of the distributor cap—1988–91 1590cc and 1834cc engines

Ignition Timing

The timing marks are located on the crankshaft pulley, with a pointer on the timing belt cover; the 1590cc and 1843cc engine marks are visible from the driver's side of the engine compartment and the 2494cc and 2675cc timing marks are visible from the passengers side of the engine compartment.

In all cases, the timing is checked with the engine warmed to operating temperature, allowing the cooling fan to turn ON, with the engine idling and the transaxle in the N position.

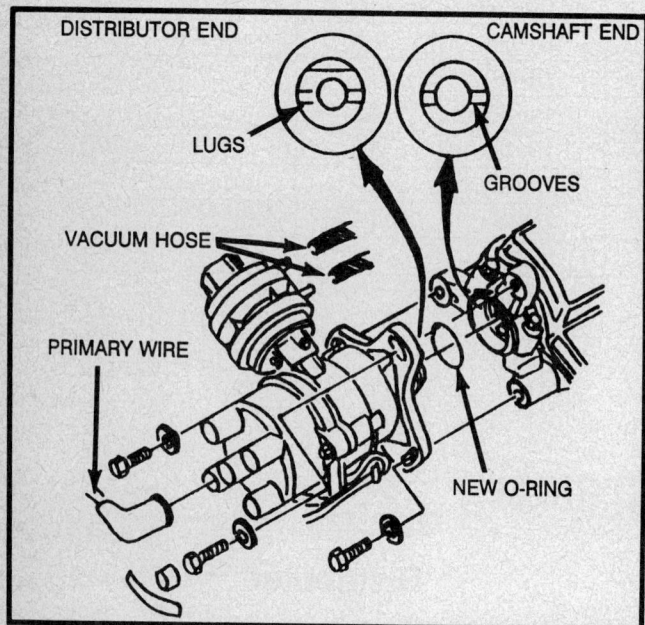

Distributor lug positioning—1590cc and 1843cc engines

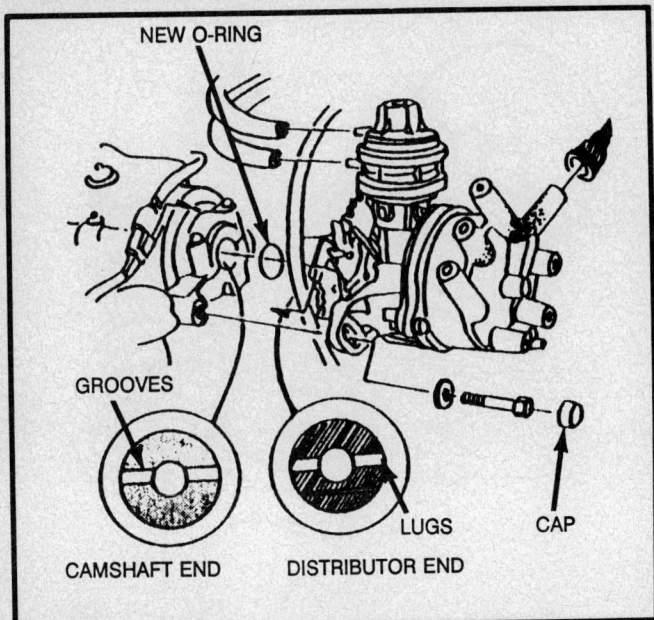

Distributor lug positioning—2499cc and 2675cc engines

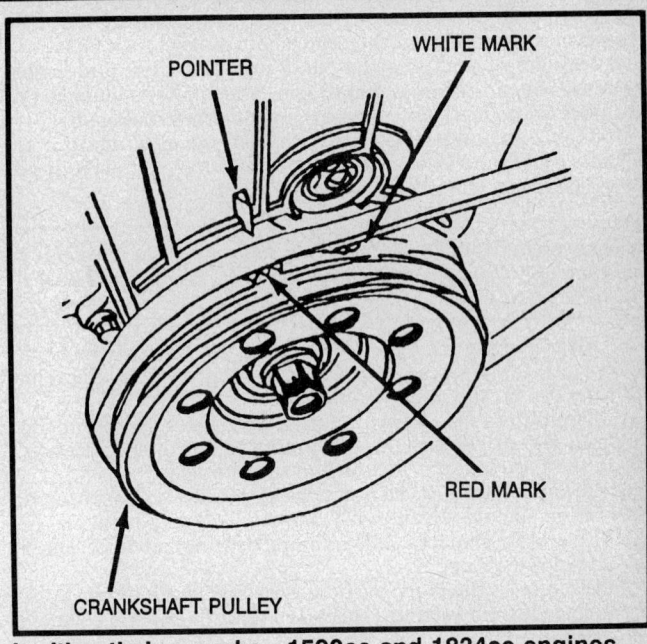

Ignition timing marks—1590cc and 1834cc engines

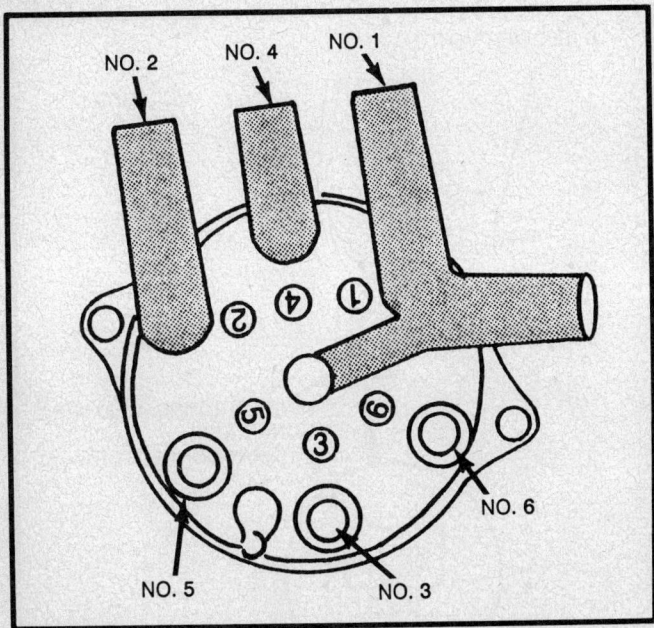

View of the distributor cap—2494cc and 2675cc engines

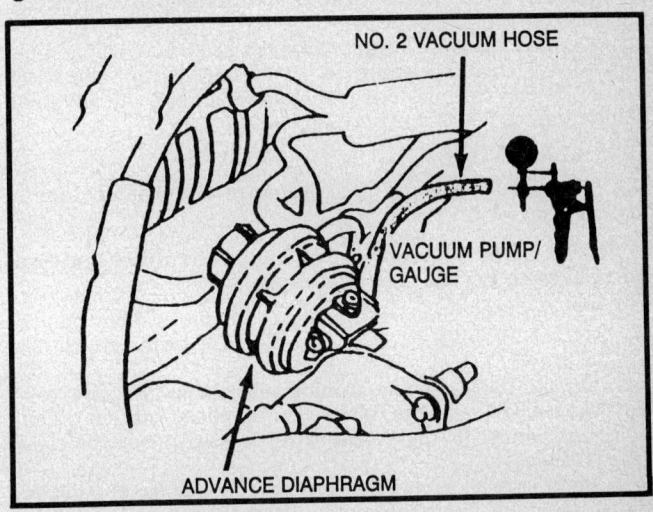

Number 2 vacuum hose

Adjustment

1987 INTEGRA

1. With the engine stopped, connect a tachometer according to the manufacturer's instructions.

NOTE: On some engines, pull back the rubber ignition coil cover to reveal the terminals.

2. Connect a timing light to the engine according to the manufacturer's instructions.

3. Make sure all wires are clear of the cooling fan and hot ex-

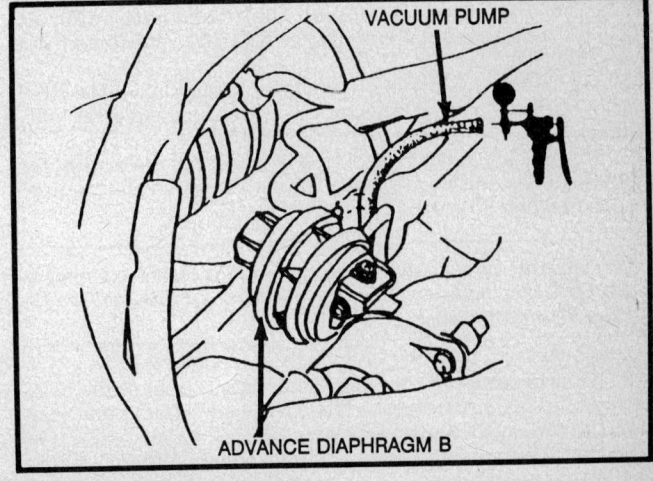

Number 5 vacuum hose

haust manifolds. Start the engine. Point the timing light at the timing mark pointer and the crankshaft pulley.

4. Disconnect and plug the No. 2 and No. 5 vacuum hoses from the vacuum advance diaphragm. The pointer should be on the WHITE mark (−2-2 degrees) on the crankshaft pulley.

5. If necessary, adjust the timing by loosening the distributor adjusting bolts and slowly rotate the distributor, in the required direction, while observing the timing marks.

—— CAUTION ——

Do not grasp the top of the distributor cap while the engine is running it could give off a shock and cause personal injury. Instead, grab the distributor housing to rotate.

6. After making the necessary adjustment, tighten the hold-down bolts, taking care not to disturb the adjustment and reinstall the cap on the upper adjusting bolt.

7. Unplug the No. 2 vacuum hose and check for 20 in. Hg (500mm Hg) of vacuum. If the vacuum is not to specification, check the hose and it's port on the throttle body.

8. Connect the No. 2 vacuum hose to the advance diaphragm. The timing should advance 4–8 degrees, half way between the WHITE and RED marks. If the timing does not advance, check the advance diaphragm.

9. Disconnect the No. 5 vacuum hose and check for vacuum. If the hose has no vacuum, check the ignition control solenoid valve. Rapidly open and release the throttle. The vacuum should momentarily go to 0. If the vacuum does not drop to 0, check the ignition control solenoid valve.

10. Connect the No. 5 vacuum hose to the advance diaphragm. The timing should advance to 10–14 degrees (on the RED mark). If the timing does not advance check the advance diaphragm.

1988–91 INTEGRA

1. Connect a tachometer according to the manufacturer's instructions.

NOTE: On some engines, pull back the rubber ignition coil cover to reveal the terminals.

2. On the 1590cc engine, remove the main fuse box lid and connect the BROWN/BLACK and BROWN terminals with a jumper wire.

3. On the 1834cc engine, using a suitable jumper wire, connect the GREEN and BROWN terminals of the ignition timing adjusting connector (light gray wire) located under the right side of the dash.

4. Make sure all wires are clear of the cooling fan and hot exhaust manifolds. Start the engine. Point the timing light at the timing mark pointer and the crankshaft pulley.

5. On the 1590cc engine, the pointer should be on the RED mark (10–14 degrees BTDC) on the crankshaft pulley at 700–800 rpm (manual transaxle) or 650–750 rpm (automatic transaxle).

6. On the 1834cc engine, the pointer should be on the RED mark (10–16 degrees BTDC) on the crankshaft pulley at 700–800 rpm.

7. If necessary, adjust the timing by loosening the distributor adjusting bolts and slowly rotate the distributor in the required direction while observing the timing marks.

—— CAUTION ——

Do not grasp the top of the distributor cap while the engine is running as it could give off a shock and cause personal injury. Instead, grab the distributor housing to rotate.

8. After making the necessary adjustment, tighten the hold-down bolts, taking care not to disturb the adjustment and reinstall the cap on the upper adjusting bolt.

9. Remove the jumper wire and put the lid on the main fuse box, if necessary.

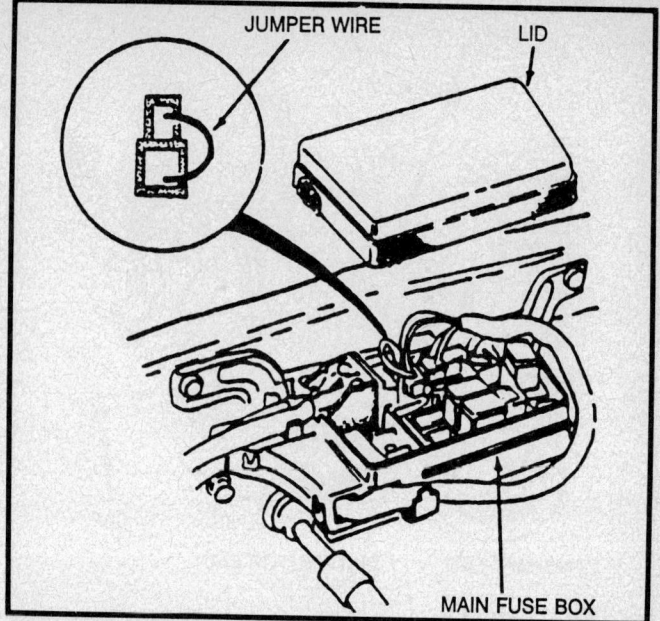

Installing the jumper wire in the main fuse box for ignition timing—1988–89 Integra

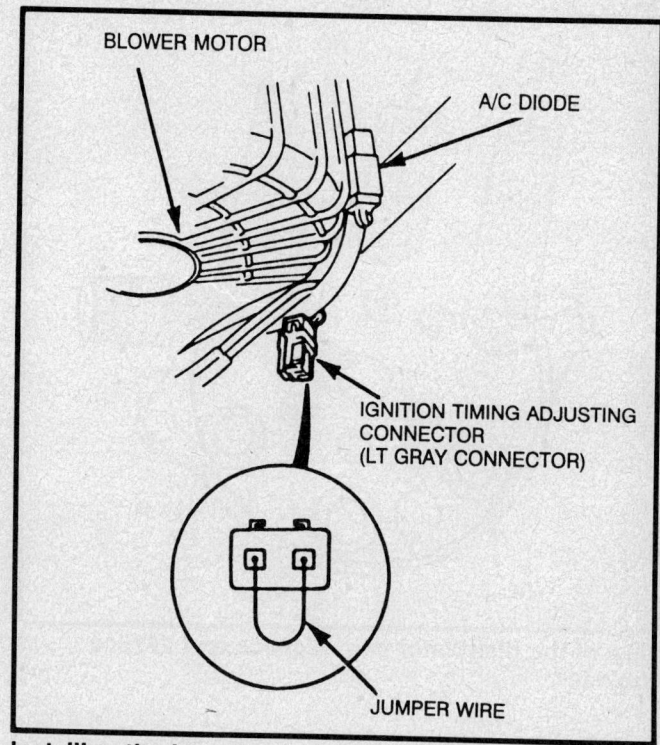

Installing the jumper wire into the ignition timing connector on the 1834cc engine

LEGEND, 825 AND 827

2494cc Engine

1. Disconnect the vacuum hoses from the vacuum advance diaphragm and, while the engine idles, check each hose for vacuum. The No. 4 and No. 11 hoses should both have vacuum. If the No. 11 hose has no vacuum, check the solenoid valve **A**. If the No. 4 hose has no vacuum, check the solenoid valve **B** vacuum hoses disconnected, plug the end of the hoses.

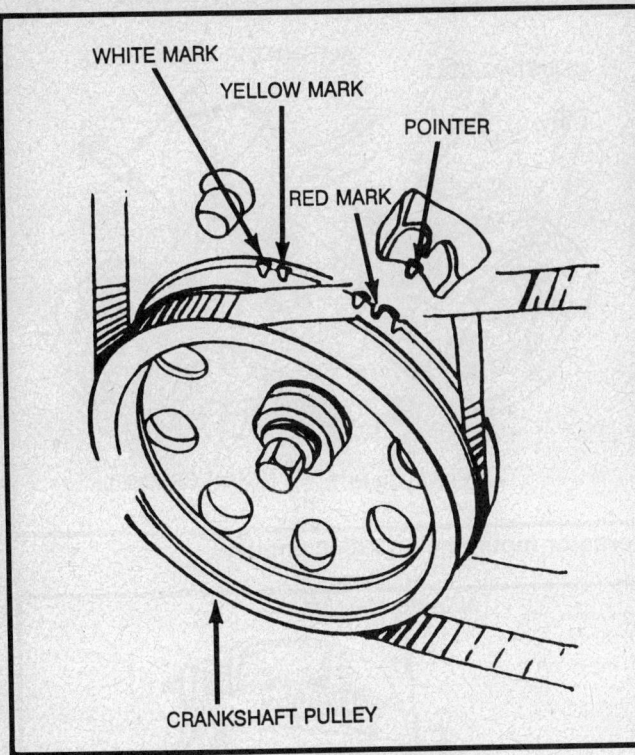

Ignition timing marks—2494cc engine

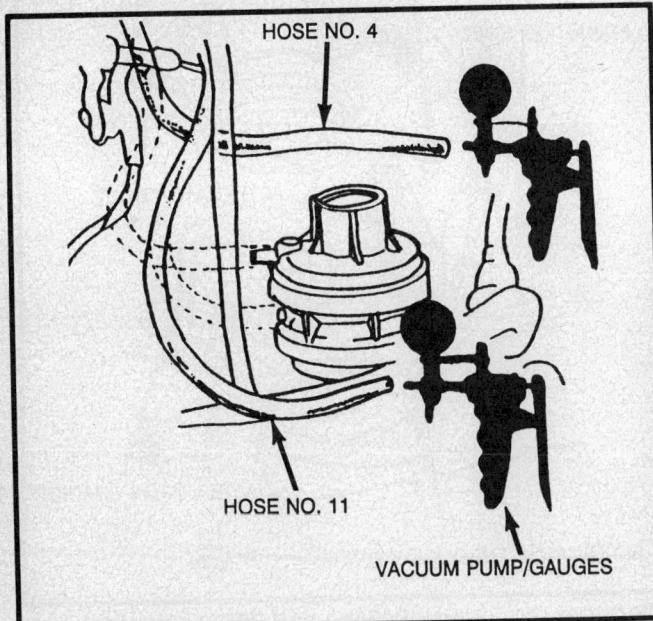

Vaccum hose locations

2. Stop the engine and connect a tachometer according to the manufacturer's instructions.

NOTE: On some vehicles, pull back the rubber ignition coil cover to reveal the terminals.

3. Make sure all wires are clear of the cooling fan and hot exhaust manifolds. Start the engine. Point the timing light at the timing mark pointer and the crankshaft pulley.

4. Adjust the initial timing, if necessary to the following

specification. The pointer should be on the YELLOW mark on the crankshaft pulley (3 degrees BTDC) at 670–770 rpm.

5. If necessary, adjust the timing by loosening the distributor adjusting bolt and slowly rotate the distributor in the required direction while observing the timing marks.

--- **CAUTION** ---

Do not grasp the top of the distributor cap while the engine is running as it could give off a shock and cause personal injury. Instead, grab the distributor housing to rotate.

6. After making the necessary adjustment, tighten the hold-down bolts, taking care not to disturb the adjustment and reinstall the cap on the upper adjusting bolt.

7. Connect the No. 4 and No. 11 vacuum hoses to the vacuum advance and inspect the ignition timing at idle. The ignition timing 21–25 degrees (manual transaxle) RED mark at idle or 16–20 degrees (automatic transaxle) RED mark at idle. If the advance is not to specification, check the advance diaphragm and the distributor advance mechanism.

2675cc Engine

1. Start the engine and warm to normal operating temperatures; the cooling fan should turn ON.

2. Stop the engine and connect a tachometer according to the manufacturer's instructions.

NOTE: On some engines, pull back the rubber ignition coil cover to reveal the terminals.

3. Make sure all wires are clear of the cooling fan and hot exhaust manifolds. Start the engine. Point the timing light at the timing mark pointer and the crankshaft pulley.

4. Adjust the timing, if necessary, to the following specification. The pointer should be on the RED mark on the crankshaft pulley (13–15 degrees BTDC) at 630–730 rpm.

5. If necessary, adjust the timing by turning the adjusting screw on the ignition timing adjuster, in the control box as follows:

a. Remove the control box upper and lower cover.

b. Drill off the rivets, with a $^3/_{16}$ in. drill bit and separate the stay cover from the adjuster.

c. To adjust the timing, turn the adjusting screw (on the adjuster); clockwise to advance or counterclockwise to retard.

d. After adjusting, install the stay cover to the ignition timing adjuster with new rivets and the adjuster to the control box.

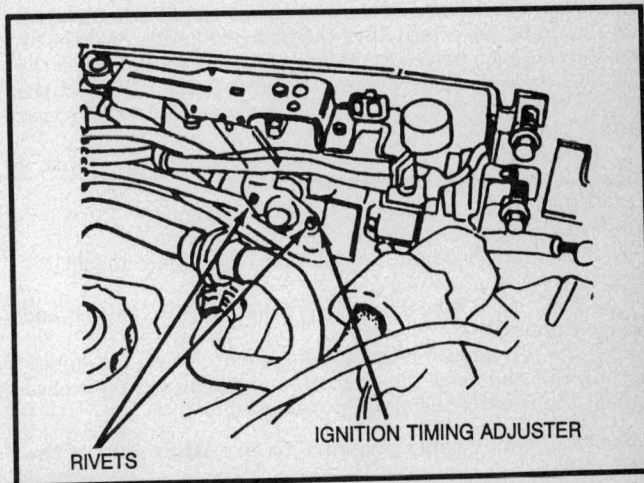

Control box and ignition timing adjuster—2675cc engine

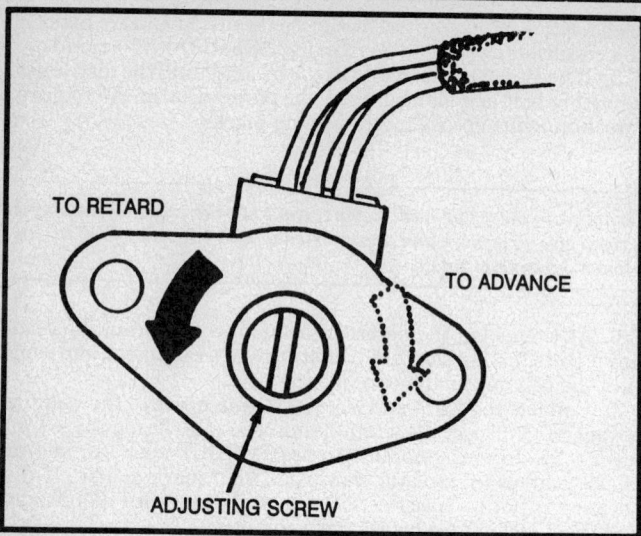

Ignition timing adjuster—2675cc engine

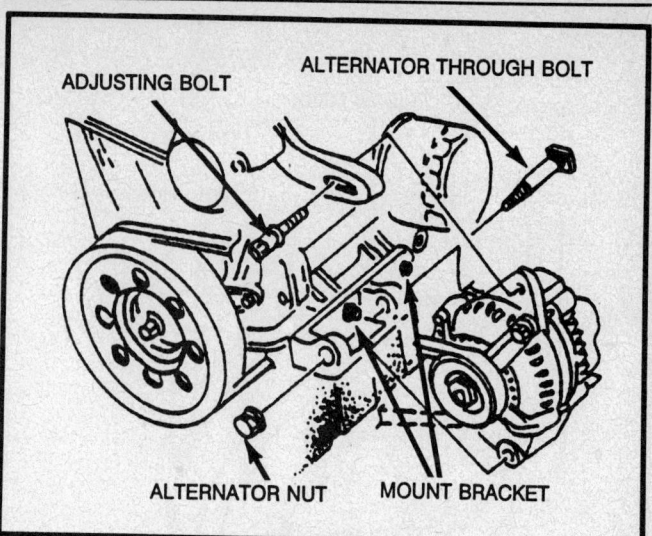

Alternator mounting—1590cc engine

Alternator

Precautions

• Observe the proper polarity of the battery connections by making sure the positive (+) and negative (−) terminal connections are not reversed. Mis-connection will allow current to flow in the reverse direction, resulting in damaged diodes and an overheated wire harness.

• Never ground or short out an alternator or regulator terminals.

• Never operate the alternator with it's or the battery's leads disconnected.

• Always remove the battery or disconnect the output lead while charging it.

• Always disconnect the ground cable when replacing any electrical components.

• Never subject the alternator to excessive heat or dampness if the engine is being steam cleaned.

• Never use arc welding equipment with the alternator connected.

Belt Tension Adjustment

The initial inspection and adjustment to the alternator drive belt should be performed after the first 3000 miles or if the alternator has been moved for any reason; afterward, inspect the belt tension every 30,000 miles. Before adjusting, inspect the belt for cracks or wear; be sure it's surfaces are free of grease and oil.

1. Push down on the belt halfway between pulleys with a force of about 22 lbs. The belt should deflect:

0.25–0.38 in. (7–10mm)—on the 1590cc engine

0.33–0.41 in. (9–11mm)—on the 1834cc engine

0.71–0.87 in. (18–22mm)—on the 1987–88 2494cc and 2675cc engines

0.67–0.77 in. (17.0–19.5mm)—on the 1989–91 2494cc and 2675cc engines.

2. If the belt tension requires adjustment, loosen the adjusting link bolt and move the alternator with a prybar positioned against the front of the alternator housing.

NOTE: Do not apply pressure to any other part of the alternator.

3. After obtaining the proper tension, tighten the adjusting link bolt.

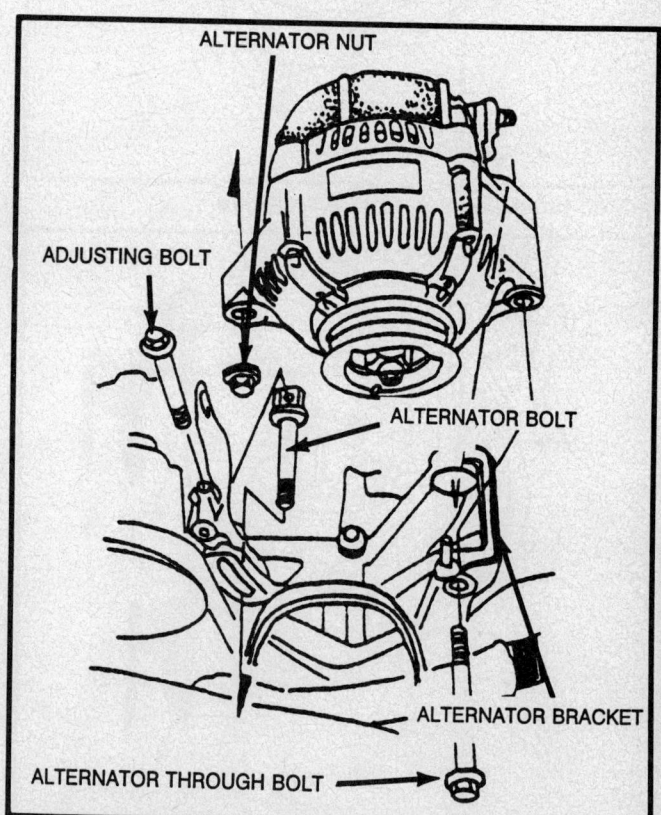

Alternator mounting—2494cc and 2675cc engines

NOTE: Do not over tighten the belt. Damage to the alternator bearings could result.

Removal and Installation

EXCEPT 1990–91 INTEGRA

1. Disconnect the negative (−) battery terminal.

2. Label and disconnect the wires from the plugs on the rear of the alternator.

3. Remove the alternator harness cover, if equipped, the alternator bolts, the V-belt and the alternator.

To install:

4. Position the alternator into the brackets, connect the V-belt and loosely install the bolts.

5. Adjust the alternator belt tension and torque the bolts.

1990–91 INTEGRA

1. Disconnect the negative battery cable.

2. Loosen the left front wheel lugs. Raise and safely support the vehicle.

3. Remove the left front wheel. Raise the locking tab on the spindle nut and remove it using a suitable socket.

4. Remove the damper fork nut and damper pinch bolt. Remove the damper fork.

5. Remove the knuckle-to-lower arm castle nut and separate the lower arm from the knuckle using a suitable puller with the pawls applied to the lower arm.

6. Pull the knuckle outward and remove the halfshaft outboard CV-joint from the knuckle using a suitable plastic mallet.

7. Pry the halfshaft assembly with a suitable tool to force the set ring at the halfshaft end past the groove.

8. Pull the inboard CV-joint and remove the halfshaft and CV-joint out of the intermediate shaft.

NOTE: Do not pull on the driveshaft, as the CV-joint may come apart. Use care when prying out the assembly and pull it straight to avoid damaging the intermediate shaft seals.

9. Disconnect and tag the alternator wire connection from the alternator. Remove the terminal nut and the white wire from the **B** terminal.

10. Loosen the adjusting nut and remove the alternator nut. Remove the alternator belt from the alternator pulley. Remove the lower through bolt and raise the alternator.

11. Remove the 3 mounting bracket bolts and mounting brackets. Remove the adjusting nut and upper through bolt, pull out the alternator.

To install:

12. Position the alternator in the proper position and install the through bolt and adjusting nut. Install the mounting brackets and mounting bracket bolts. Torque to 33 ft. lbs. (45 Nm).

13. Lower the alternator and install the lower through bolt. Install the alternator belt and adjusting nut. Place the proper amount of belt tension on the alternator belt; 0.33–0.41 in. (9–11mm). Torque the adjusting nut to 17 ft. lbs. (24 Nm).

14. Reconnect all the alternator wiring connections to the alternator.

15. Place the CV-joint and halfshaft onto the intermediate shaft. Install a new set ring into the halfshaft groove. Install the inboard end of the driveshaft into the intermediate shaft.

16. Place the steering knuckle back into position and install the lower arm-to-knuckle castle nut. Torque the nut to 40 ft. lbs. (55 Nm).

17. Install the damper fork, pinch bolt and fork nut. Torque the the pinch bolt to 32 ft. lbs. (44 Nm) and the fork nut to 47 ft. lbs. (65 Nm).

18. Install the spindle nut and torque it to 134 ft. lbs. (185 Nm).

19. Place the wheel back onto the vehicle and tighten the lug nuts. Lower the vehicle.

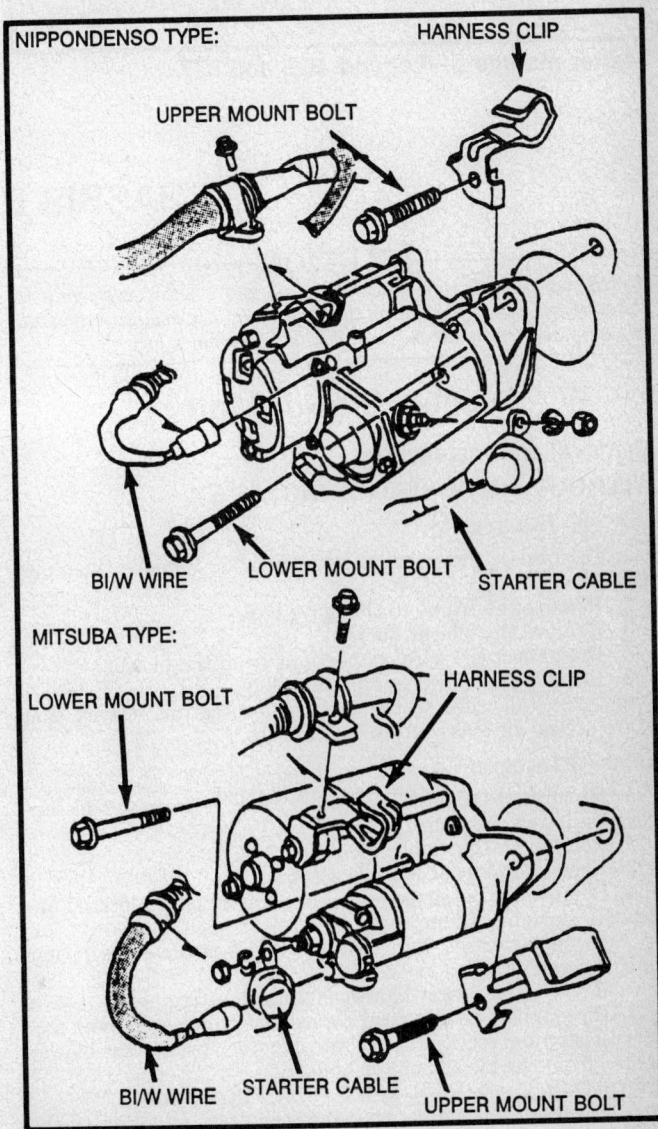

Starter mounting—Integra

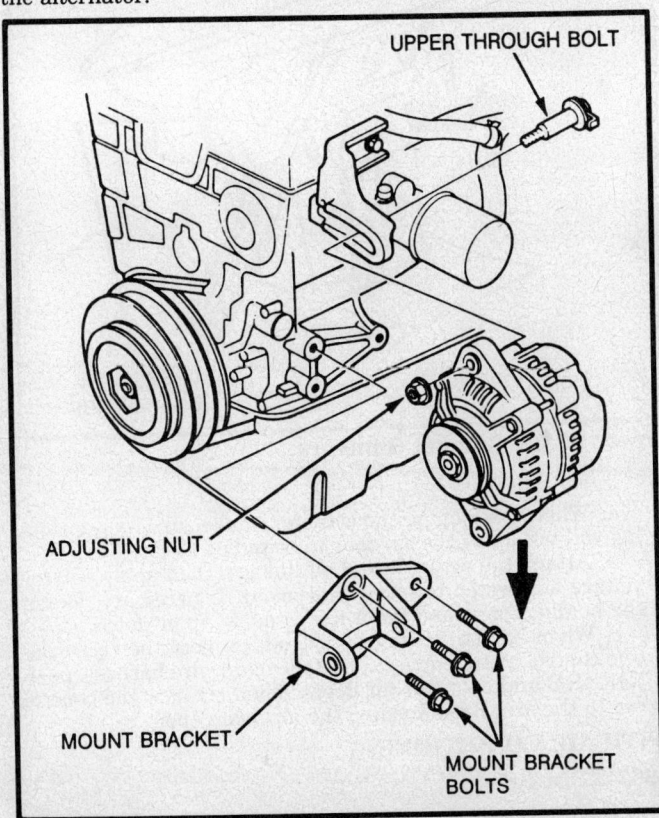

Alternator mounting—1834cc engine

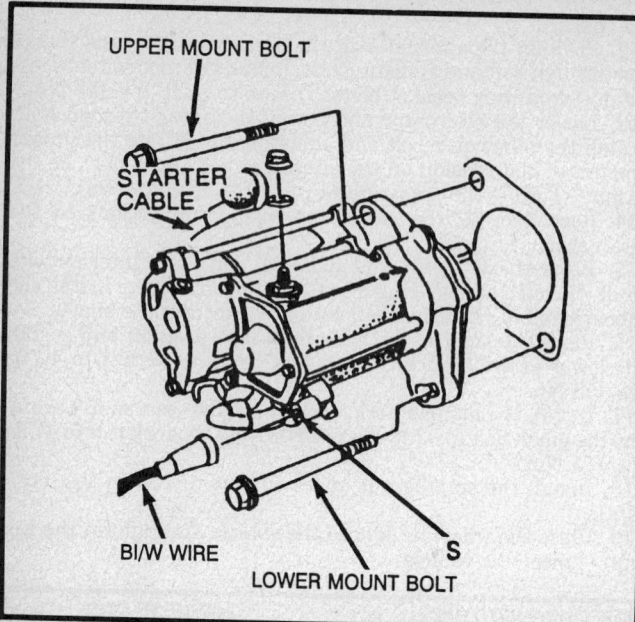

Starter mounting—Legend, 825 and 827

UPPER MOUNT BOLT
STARTER CABLE
BI/W WIRE
LOWER MOUNT BOLT
S

20. Reconnect the negative battery cable.

Starter

Removal and Installation

1. Disconnect the battery negative (−) cable and the starter motor cable from the positive (+) terminal.
2. At the starter motor, remove the wiring harness from the harness clip.
3. Disconnect the wires from the starter solenoid.
4. On the Sterling 827, raise and safely support the vehicle. Remove the left front wheel assembly. Remove the bolts from the left front fender access panel and remove the panel in order to gain access to the starter motor.
5. Remove the starter-to-engine bolts and the starter.

To install:
6. Position the starter to the engine and torque the bolts 32 ft. lbs. (45 Nm). Connect the electrical connectors and wiring harness to the starter.
7. Connect the cables to the battery. Check the starter operation.

CHASSIS ELECTRICAL

CAUTION

On vehicles equipped with an air bag, the negative battery cable must be disconnected, before working on the vehicle. Failure to do so may result in deployment of the air bag and possible personal injury.

Heater Blower Motor

Removal and Installation
WITHOUT AIR CONDITIONING
1987–89 Integra

1. Disconnect the negative battery cable. Remove the glove box.
2. Remove the frame to the glove box.
3. Remove the blower duct.
4. Disconnect the wire connections from the blower.
5. Remove the blower motor assembly.
6. To install, reverse the removal procedures. Check that there are no air leaks in the blower case.

1990–91 Integra

1. Disconnect the negative battery cable. Remove the passenger side lower dashboard cover.
2. Remove the glove box assembly.
3. Remove the front console assembly.
4. Remove the passenger side knee bolster panel, located under the glove box frame.
5. Remove the self tapping screws and remove the heater duct assembly.
6. Remove the heater blower motor mounting bolts.
7. Disconnect the electrical connectors from the blower motor, resistor and recirculation control motor. Remove the blower motor from the blower motor housing.
To install:
8. Reverse the removal procedure and pay attention to the following:

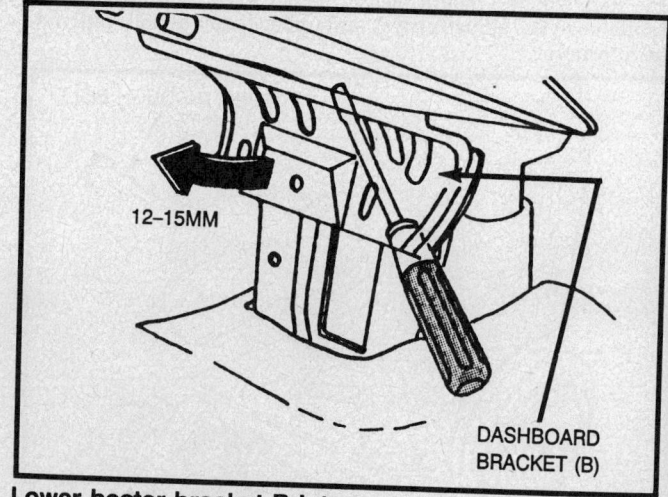

12–15MM
DASHBOARD BRACKET (B)

Lower heater bracket B Integra

  a. When reattaching the actuator, make sure its positioning will not allow the air door to be pulled to far.
  b. Attach the actuator and all linkage, then apply battery voltage and watch the door movement. If necessary, loosen the holding screw and move the actuator up or down.
  c. When adjusting the control rod, connect the recirculation control motor connection to the main wire harness, push **RECIRC** and open the air doors. Then connect the control rod to the arm while holding the air doors open.

WITH AIR CONDITIONING
1987–89 Integra

1. Disconnect the negative battery cable. Remove the glove box.

2. Remove the frame to the glove box and the side frame.

3. Remove the bolts and the retractor control unit with the bracket.

4. Unbolt the dashboard lower bracket **A** from bracket **B** and insert a small prybar to pry a 12–15mm clearance, to ease in the removal of the evaporator.

5. Loosen the sealing band toward the right side.

6. Disconnect the wire connections from the blower.

7. Remove the blower bolts and the blower assembly.

To install:

8. Reverse the removal procedures. Check that there are no air leaks in the blower case.

1990–91 Integra

1. Disconnect the negative battery cable.

2. Discharge the refrigerant from the air conditioning system. Disconnect the receiver line and suction hose from the evaporator assembly. Be sure to cap the open fitting to prevent moisture from entering the system.

3. Remove the passenger side lower dashboard cover.

4. Remove the glove box assembly.

5. Remove the front console assembly.

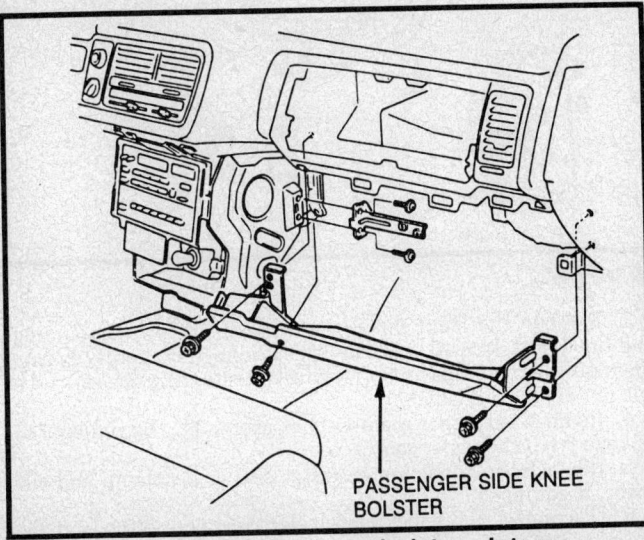

Removing the passenger knee bolster – Integra

PASSENGER SIDE KNEE BOLSTER

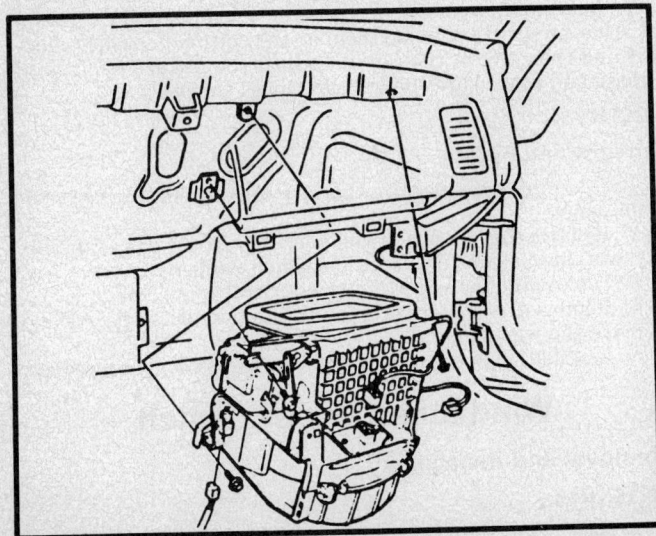

Removing the blower motor housing

6. Remove the passenger side knee bolster panel, located under the glove box frame.

7. Remove the 2 self tapping screws and the air conditioning bands from around the evaporator assembly

8. Disconnect the wire connector from the thermostat switch and pull off the wire harness from the clamps. Remove the evaporator.

9. Remove the self tapping screws and remove the heater duct assembly.

10. Remove the heater blower motor mounting bolts.

11. Disconnect the electrical connectors from the blower motor, resistor and recirculation control motor. Remove the blower motor from the blower motor housing.

To install:

12. Reverse the removal procedure.

13. When reattaching the actuator, make sure its positioning will not allow the air door to pulled to far.

14. Attach the actuator and all linkage, then apply battery voltage and watch the door movement. If necessary, loosen the holding screw and move the actuator up or down.

15. When adjusting the control rod, connect the recirculation control motor connection to the main wire harness, push **RECIRC** and open the air doors. Then connect the control rod to the arm while holding the air doors open.

Legend, 825 and 827

1. Disconnect the negative battery cable.

2. Remove the glove box lower cover screws and the cover.

3. Remove the glove box screws and the glove box.

4. Remove the glove box frame screws, the glove box frame, the clips and the heater duct.

5. Discharge the refrigerant from the air conditioning system.

6. Remove the evaporator as follows:

   a. Disconnect the receiver line and suction hose from the evaporator assembly.

   b. Be sure to cap the open fitting to prevent moisture from entering the system.

   c. Remove the self-tapping screws and the air conditioning bands from around the evaporator assembly.

   d. Disconnect the wire connector from the thermostat switch and pull off the wire harness from the clamps.

   e. Remove the evaporator.

7. Disconnect the wire connectors from the blower.

8. Remove the blower assembly bolts and the assembly.

To install:

9. Reverse the removal procedures. Check that there are no air leaks in the blower case. Recharge the air conditioning system and pay attention to the following procedures.

10. When reattaching the actuator, make sure its positioning will not allow the air door to be pulled to far.

11. Attach the actuator and all linkage, then apply battery voltage and watch the door movement. If necessary, loosen the holding screw and move the actuator up or down.

12. When adjusting the control rod, connect the recirculation control motor connection to the main wire harness, push the **FRESH/RECIRC** switch to **FRESH** and open the air doors. Then connect the control rod to the arm while holding the air doors open.

Windshield Wiper Motor

Removal and Installation

FRONT

1. Remove the negative cable from the battery. Position the wiper arms in a positioned where they are not concealed. On the 1990–91 Integra, pull the lock tab with the wiper arm lifted away from the windshield to release the spring pressure.

2. Open the hood and remove the wiper arm nuts and the wiper arms.

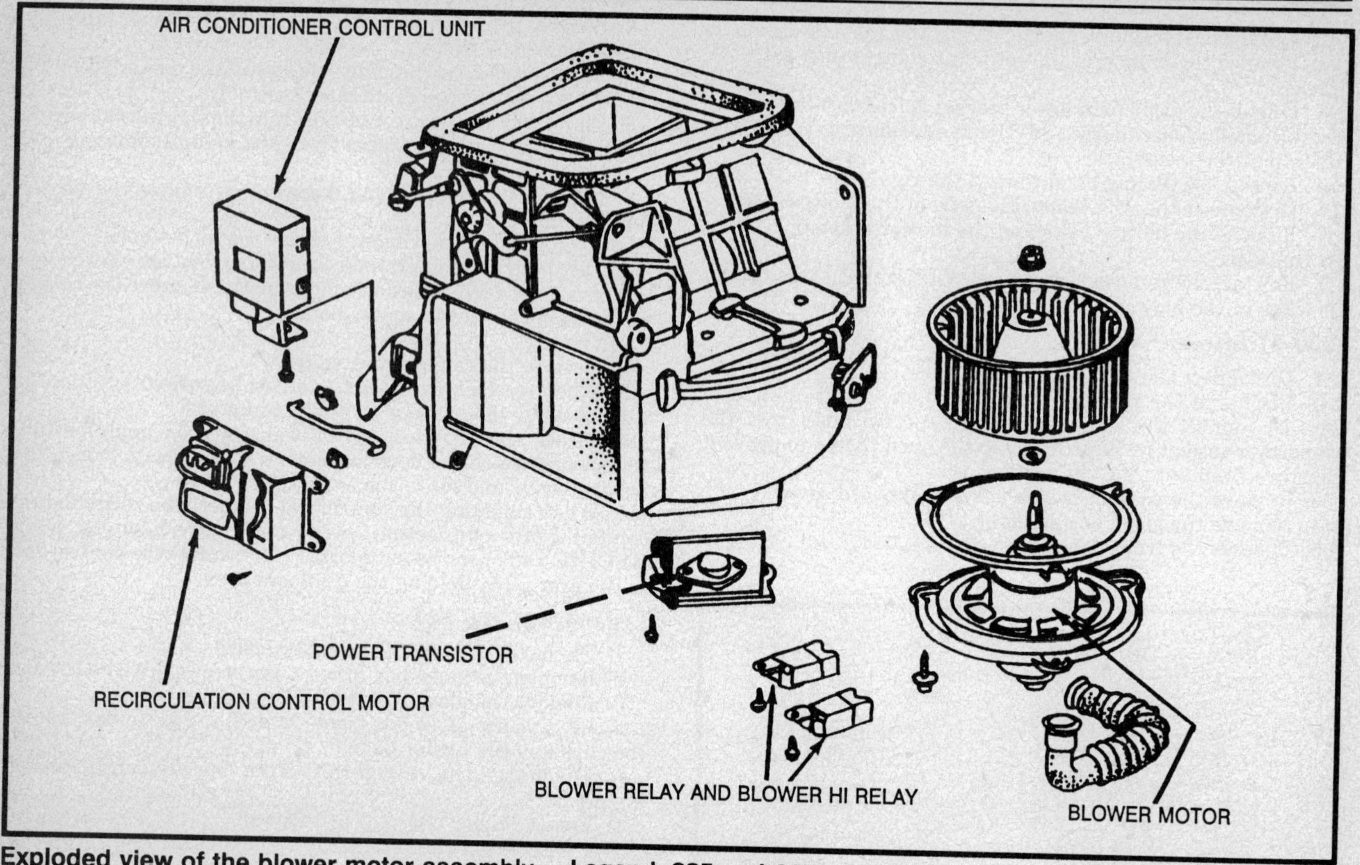

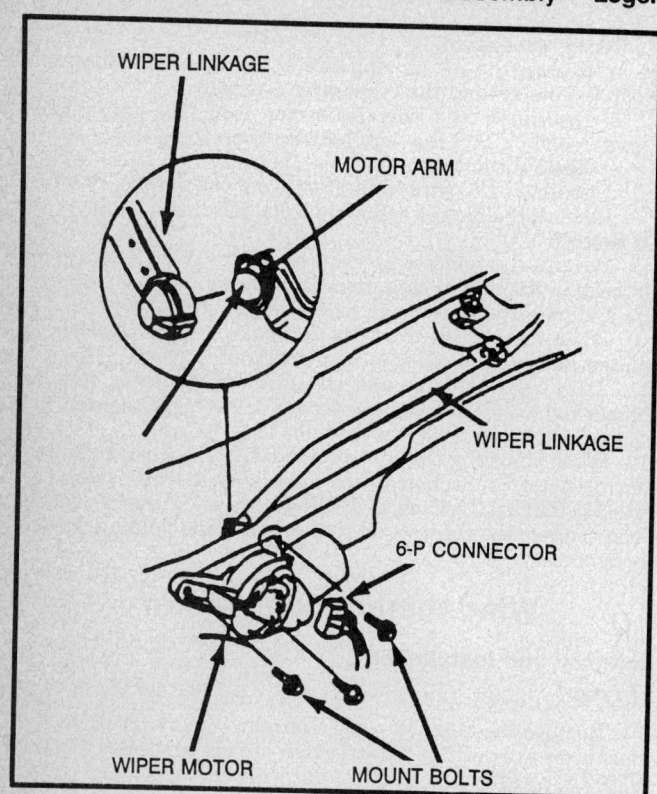

Exploded view of the blower motor assembly— Legend, 825 and 827

AIR CONDITIONER CONTROL UNIT

POWER TRANSISTOR

RECIRCULATION CONTROL MOTOR

BLOWER RELAY AND BLOWER HI RELAY

BLOWER MOTOR

WIPER LINKAGE

MOTOR ARM

WIPER LINKAGE

6-P CONNECTOR

WIPER MOTOR

MOUNT BOLTS

View of the wiper motor replacement—Integra— Legend and Sterling are similar

3. Remove the front air scoop, windshield lower moulding and hood seal, located over the wiper linkage by lightly prying them off the trim clips and removing the retaining screws at the bottom of the windshield.

4. Remove the wiper maintenance grommet. Disconnect the linkage from the wiper motor.

5. Remove the wiper motor water seal cover clamp and the cover, if equipped.

6. Disconnect the wiper motor electrical connector, remove the motor mounting bolts and remove the motor.

To install:

7. Reverse the removal procedures. When installing the wiper arms, be sure to position them on the bottom line of the stopper and then mount the cap nuts. Coat the linkage joints with grease and make sure the linkage moves smoothly.

REAR

Integra and 827

1. Disconnect the negative battery cable. Remove the hatch trim panel.

2. Remove the nut cover, wiper arm nut, wiper arm, cap, special nut, special washer and the cushion rubber.

3. Disconnect the wiper motor electrical connector.

4. Remove the wiper motor mounting nuts with spacers and remove the wiper motor.

5. Installation is the reverse order of the removal procedure.

Windshield Wiper Switch

Removal and Installation

INTEGRA

1. Disconnect the negative battery cable. Remove the steering wheel.

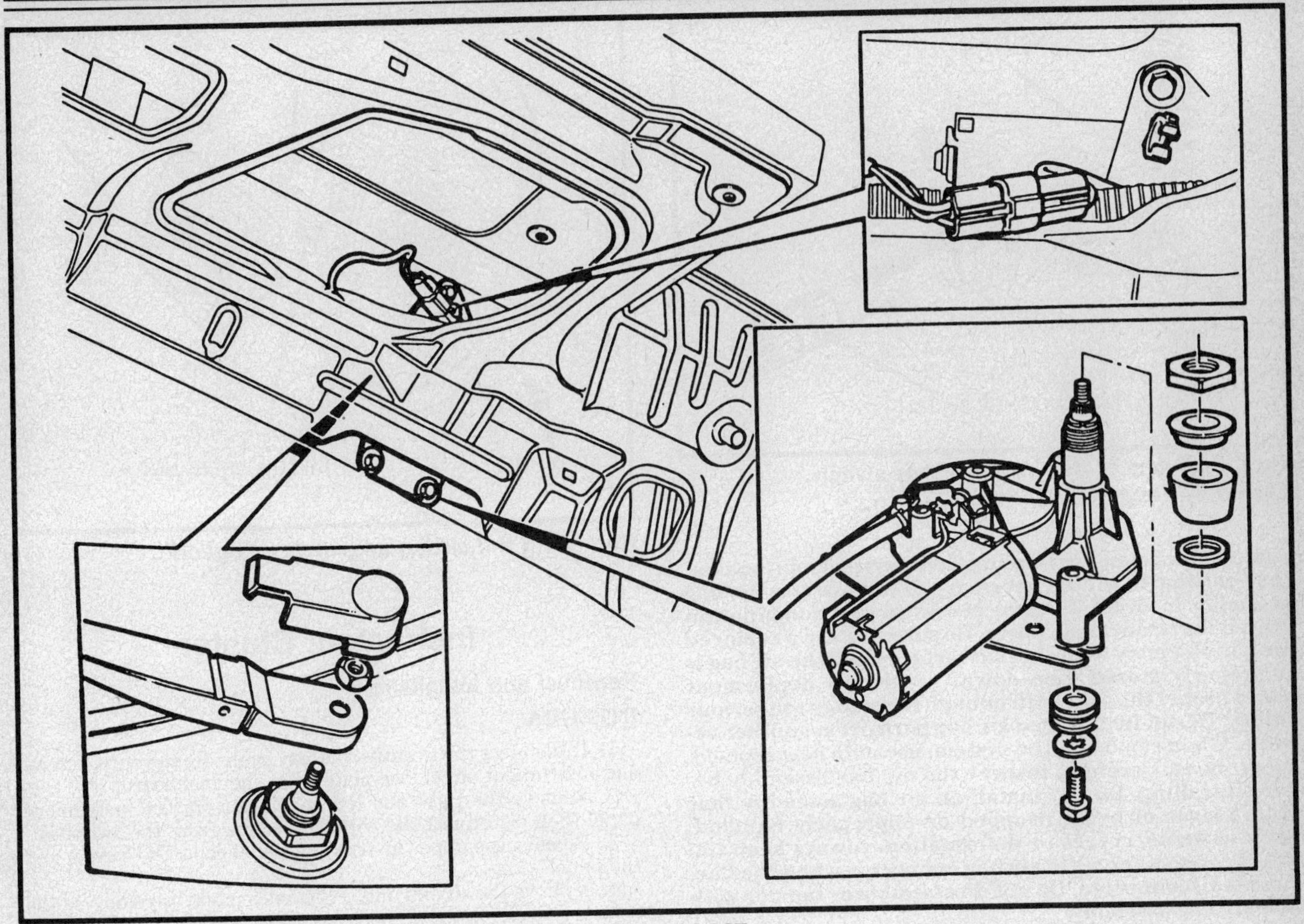

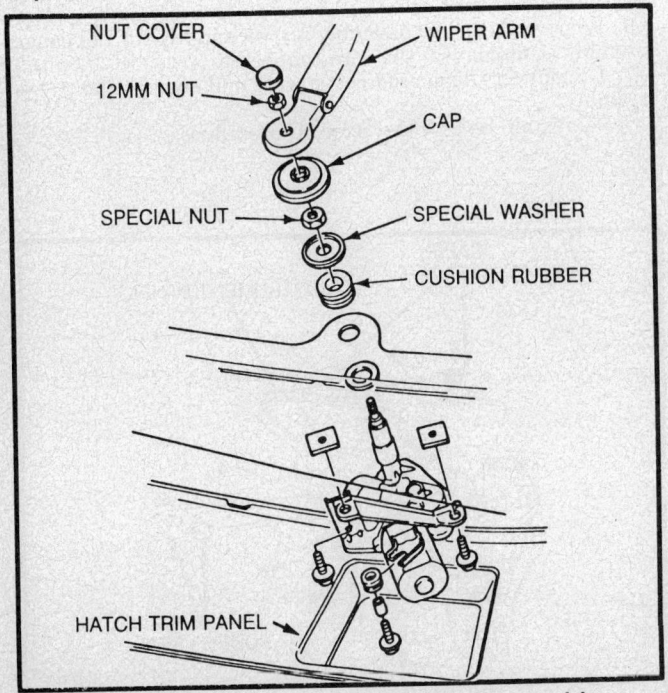

Exploded view of the rear wiper motor assembly — 825 and 827

NUT COVER
WIPER ARM
12MM NUT
CAP
SPECIAL NUT
SPECIAL WASHER
CUSHION RUBBER
HATCH TRIM PANEL

Exploded view of the rear wiper motor assembly — Integra

2. Disconnect the column wiring harness and coupler.

NOTE: Be careful not to damage the steering column or shaft.

3. Remove the turn signal canceling sleeve. Remove the rubber bands, then remove the upper column holder, bending plate and bending plate base, if equipped.

4. Remove the cruise control slip ring, if equipped. Remove the bending plate guide.

5. Remove the combination switch retaining screws and remove the switch.

6. Installation is the reverse of the removal procedures.

1987 LEGEND AND 825

1. Remove the negative cable from the battery.

2. Remove the dashboard lower panel and disconnect the 6-pin and 8-pin connectors from the wiper control unit on the lower panel.

3. Disconnect the 10-pin connector from the wiper/washer switch.

4. Remove the steering wheel, the steering column lower cover and disconnect the 6-pin connector from the wiper position switch.

5. Remove the upper cover from the steering column.

6. Remove the screws and slide the wiper/washer switch out of the housing.

7. To install, reverse the removal procedures.

1988–91 LEGEND, 825 AND 827

NOTE: The 1988–91 Legend and Legend Coupe are

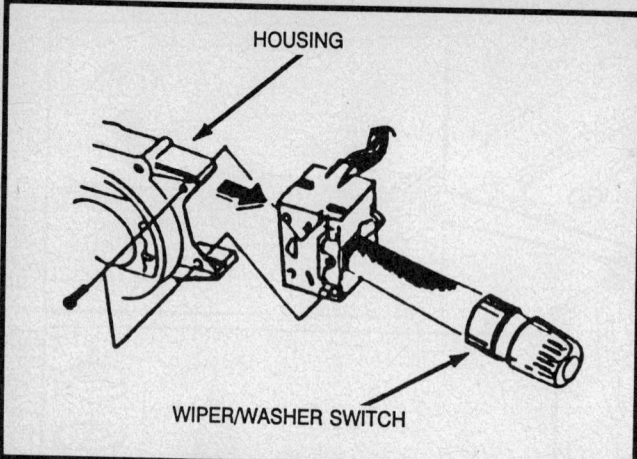

Exploded view of the wiper/washer switch assembly—Legend, 825 and 827

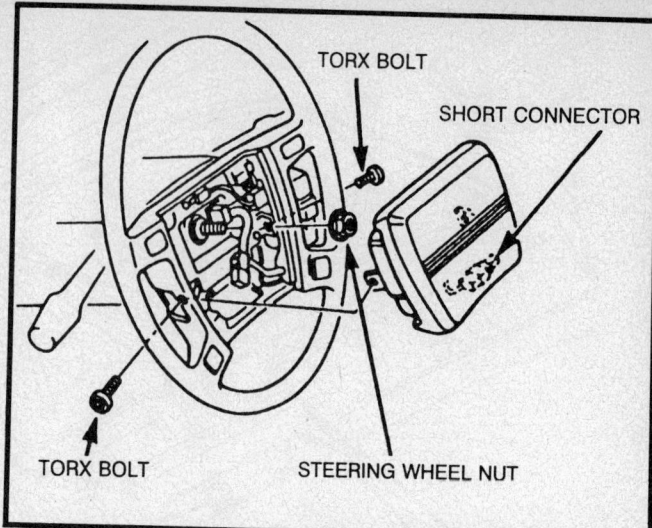

Removing the airbag assembly—Legend

equipped with an Air Bag Restraint system; optional on the Sterling. It will be necessary to remove this air bag assembly in order to gain access to the combination switch for removal purposes. Be sure to store a removed air bag assembly with the pad surface up, if the air bag is improperly stored face down, accidental deployment could propel the unit with enough force to cause serious injury. Do not install used air bag parts from another vehicle. When repairing the system, use only new replacement parts. Carefully inspect the air bag assembly before installing. Do not install an air bag assembly that shows signs of being dropped or improperly handled, such as dents, cracks or deformation. Always keep the short connector on the air bag connector when the harness is disconnected. Do not disassemble or tamper with the air bag assembly.

1. Disconnect both the negative and positive battery cable from the battery.
2. Remove the lower maintenance lid below the air bag and then remove the short connector.
3. Disconnect the connector between the air bag and the cable reel.
4. Connect the short connector to the air bag side of the connector.
5. Remove the left side maintenance lid and the cruise control/set resume switch cover.
6. Insert a T30 Torx® bit and remove the Torx® bolts. Remove the air bag assembly.
7. Remove the dashboard lower panel and disconnect the 6-pin connector from the wiper position switch and the 6-pin and 8-pin connectors from the wiper control unit on the lower panel.
8. Remove the left knee bolster. Disconnect the combination switch connectors.
9. Remove the upper and lower steering column covers.
10. Remove the lighting and wiper switch mounting screws and remove the switches.
To install:
11. Reverse the removal procedures. Be sure to pay attention to the following:
    a. Be sure to install the air bag wiring so it is not pinched or interfering with other parts. Be sure the battery cables are disconnected.
    b. After installing the air bag assembly, turn the ignition switch to the **II** position, the instrument panel air bag light should go on for approximately 8 seconds and then go off.
    c. Confirm operations of horn buttons and cruise control set/resume switch.

Instrument Cluster

Removal and Installation

INTEGRA

1. Disconnect the negative battery cable. Remove the screws and instrument panel face plate from the dashboard.
2. Remove the right and left switches from the instrument panel then disconnect the wire connecters from the switches.
3. Remove the upper instrument panel caps, the screws and the panel.
4. Remove the screws under the holes made by removing the switches.
5. Remove the rubber seal, loosen the column cover screws and the instrument panel.
6. Remove the gauge assembly screws and lift out the gauge assembly to disconnect the wire connectors.
7. Disconnect the speedometer cable and remove the gauge assembly.
8. To install, reverse the removal procedures.

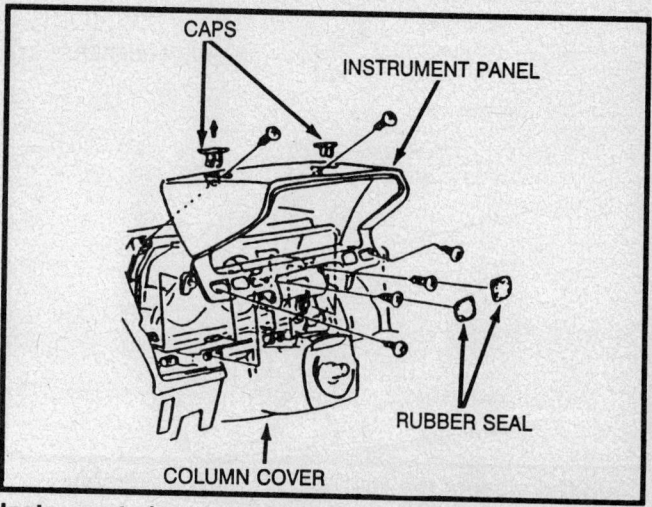

Instrument cluster replacement—Integra

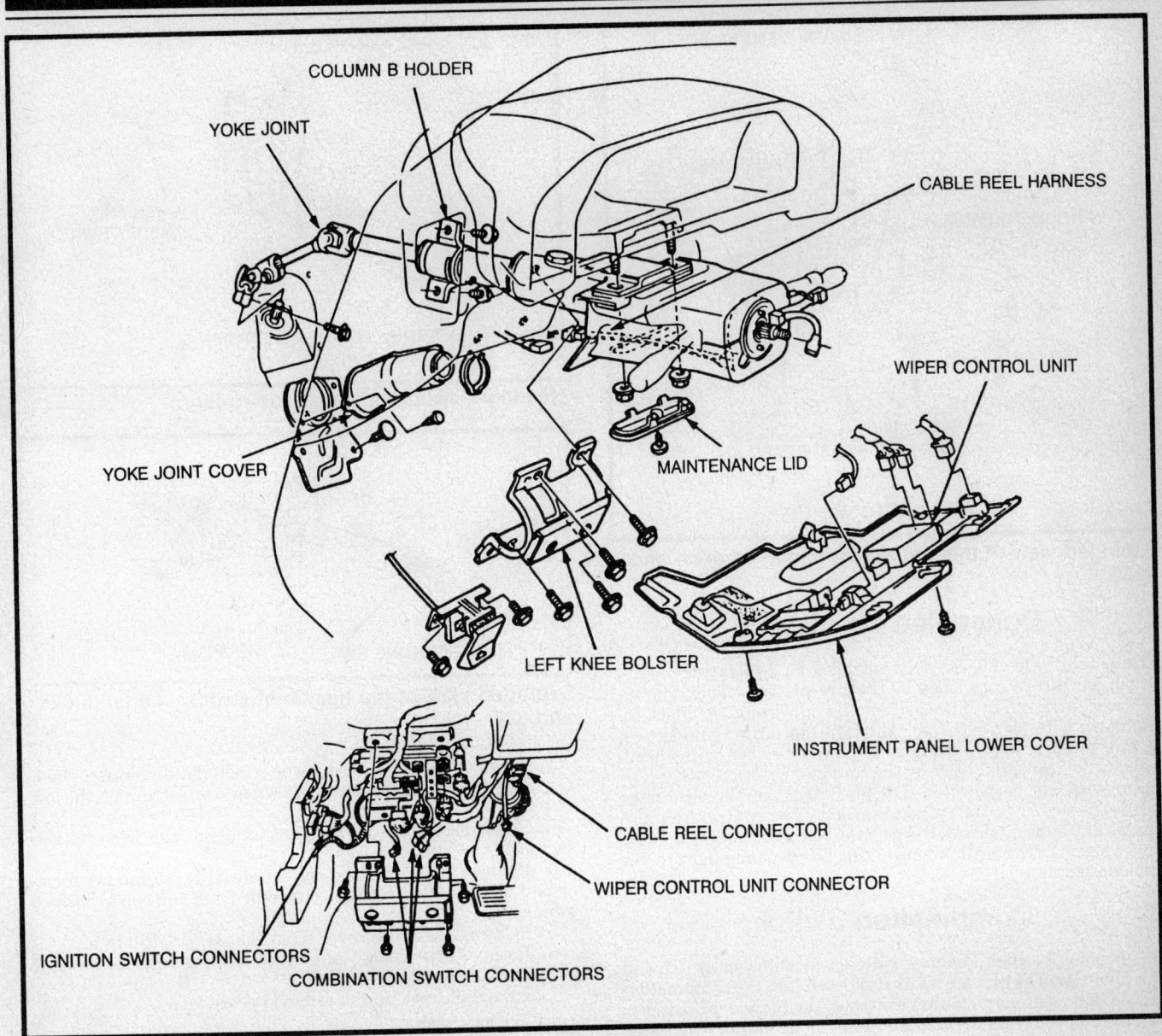

Exploded view of the combination switch removal— **Legend**

LEGEND, 825 AND 827

━━━━━━━━━ **CAUTION** ━━━━━━━━━

The Legend and Legend Coupe LS (Optional on the 825 and 827) are equipped with a Supplemental (air bag) Restraint System (SRS). Improper maintenance, including incorrect removal and installation of related components, can lead to personal injury caused by unintentional activation of the air bag.

1. Disconnect the negative battery cable. Remove the screws and the instrument panel by disconnecting the wire harness.

2. Remove the gauge assembly screws and lift out the gauge assembly to disconnect the wire connectors.

3. Disconnect the speedometer cable and remove the gauge assembly.

4. On the 827 Sterling use the following procedure:

   a. Remove the instrument cluster cover strip screw.

   b. Remove the cluster screws, 3 off the center of the cowl above the instrument cluster, 2 below the drivers vent, 2 below the air conditioning controls and 2 off the rear access of the cowl.

   c. Remove the dashboard retaining clips and disconnect the switch connectors. Remove the air conditioning mode unit, cowl assembly and drivers vent.

   d. Remove the screws from the control switches, disconnect the electrical connectors and remove the instrument cluster.

NOTE: Once the instrument cluster or panel is removed the speedometer may be removed from the back of the instrument cluster by removing the retaining screws and then removing the speedometer assembly. On some vehicles there may be an electric motor attached to the rear of the speedometer, this can be removed separately or as a complete unit.

5. To install, reverse the removal procedures.

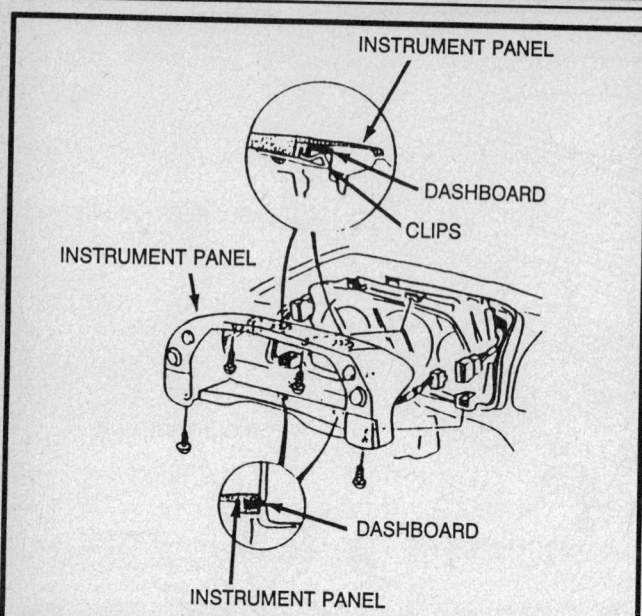

Exploded view of the instrument panel—Legend and 825S

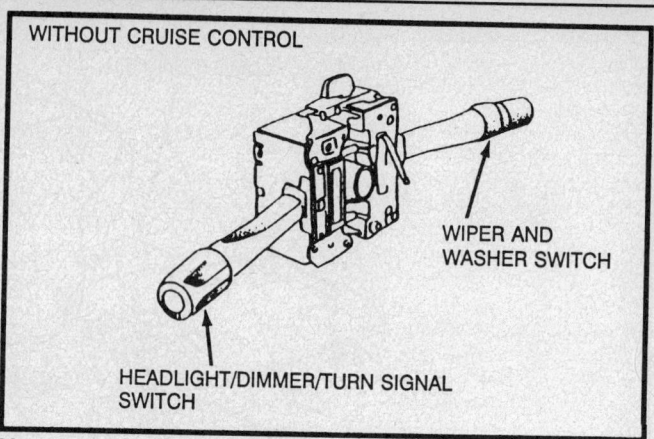

Headlight switch replacement—Integra

Concealed Headlights

The concealed headlights are controlled by 2 retractor motors which are inturn controlled by their respective relays. The relays are energized by power either the up wire (white/black) of the down wire (white/yellow), through the slip ring on the retractor motors. The up wire can be powered either by the headlight switch/control unit or by the retractor switch directly. The down wire can be powered by the control unit by either the headlight switch or the retractor switch. The control unit also senses any abnormality in the way the retractor motors operate and warns the driver by illuminating the warning light in the dash assembly.

Combination Switch

The headlight switch, dimmer switch, wiper/washer switch and the turn signal switch are all incorporated into the combination switch. On some combination switches, the individual switches can be removed from the combination switch. But in most cases the combination switch must be replaced as a complete unit.

Removal and Installation

INTEGRA

1. Disconnect the negative battery cable. Remove the steering wheel.
2. Disconnect the column wiring harness and coupler.

NOTE: Be careful not to damage the steering column or shaft.

3. Remove the turn signal canceling sleeve. Remove the rubber bands, then remove the upper column holder, bending plate and bending plate base, if equipped.
4. Remove the cruise control slip ring, if equipped. Remove the bending plate guide.
5. Remove the combination switch retaining screws and remove the switch.
6. To assemble and install, reverse the removal procedures.

1987 LEGEND, 1987-91 825 AND 827

1. Disconnect the negative battery cable.

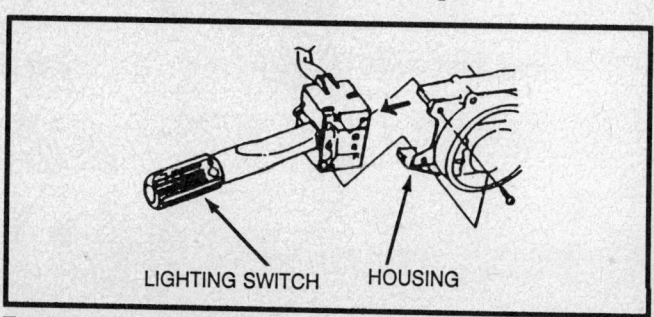

Exploded view of the headlight switch—Legend, 825 and 827

2. Remove the dashboard lower panel and disconnect the 6-pin and 8-pin connectors from the wiper control unit on the lower panel.
3. Disconnect the 10-pin connector from the wiper/washer switch.
4. Remove the steering wheel, the steering column lower cover and disconnect the 6-pin connector from the wiper position switch.
5. Remove the upper cover from the steering column.
6. Remove the screws and slide the combination switch switch off of the column.
7. To install, reverse the removal procedures.

1988-91 LEGEND

NOTE: The 1988-91 Legend and Legend Coupe vehicles are equipped with an Air Bag Restraint system. It may be necessary to remove this air bag assembly in order to gain access to the combination switch for removal purposes. Be sure to store a removed air bag assembly with the pad surface up, if the air bag is improperly stored face down, accidental deployment could propel the unit with enough force to cause serious injury. Do not install used air bag parts from another vehicle. When repairing the system, use only new replacement parts. Carefully inspect the air bag assembly before installing. Do not install an air bag assembly that shows signs of being dropped or improperly handled, such as dents, cracks or deformation. Always keep the short connector on the air bag connector when the harness is disconnected. Do not disassemble or tamper with the air bag assembly.

1. Disconnect both the negative and positive battery cable from the battery.
2. Remove the lower maintenance lid below the air bag and then remove the short connector.

3. Disconnect the connector between the air bag and the cable reel.

4. Connect the short connector to the air bag side of the connector.

5. Remove the left side maintenance lid and the cruise control/set resume switch cover.

6. Insert a T30 Torx® bit and remove the Torx® bolts. Remove the air bag assembly.

7. Remove the dashboard lower panel and disconnect the 6-pin connector from the winter position position switch and the 6-pin and 8-pin connectors from the wiper control unit on the lower panel.

8. Remove the left knee bolster. Disconnect the combination switch connectors.

9. Remove the upper and lower steering column covers.

10. Remove the lighting and wiper switch mounting screws and remove the switches.

To install:

11. Reverse the removal procedures. Be sure to pay attention to the following:

    a. Be sure to install the air bag wiring so it is not pinched or interfering with other parts. Be sure the battery cables are disconnected.

    b. After installing the air bag assembly, turn the ignition switch to the **II** position, the instrument panel air bag light should go on for approximately 8 seconds and then go off.

    c. Confirm operations of horn buttons and cruise control set/resume switch.

Ignition Lock/Switch

Removal and Installation

INTEGRA

1. Disconnect the negative battery cable.

2. Remove the dashboard lower panel, left knee bolster and left kick panel.

3. Remove the steering wheel. Remove the steering column covers.

4. Center punch each of the shear bolts and drill the heads off with a $^3/_{16}$ in. drill bit. Be sure to be careful not to damage the switch body when removing the shear head.

5. Remove the shear bolts from the switch body.

To install:

6. Install the new ignition switch without the key inserted. Loosely tighten the new shear bolts. Make sure the projection of the ignition switch is aligned with the hole in the steering column.

7. Insert the ignition key and check for proper operation of the steering wheel lock and that the ignition key turns freely.

8. Tighten the shear bolts until the heads twist off.

LEGEND, 825 AND 827

1. Disconnect the negative battery cable.

2. Remove the steering column lower cover. Disconnect the ignition switch wire connector from the dash fuse box.

3. Insert the key and place on the **O** position.

4. Remove the 2 screws and replace the base of the switch.

NOTE: The air bag system wire harness is routed near the steering lock assembly. All air bag system wire harness and connectors are colored yellow. Do not use electrical test equipment on these circuits. Be careful not to damage the air bag system wire harness when servicing the steering lock.

5. Remove the steering wheel. Remove the steering column covers.

6. Center punch each of the shear bolts and drill their heads off with a $^3/_{16}$ in. drill bit. Be sure to be careful not to damage the switch body when removing the shear head.

7. Remove the shear bolts from the switch body.

To install:

8. Install the new ignition switch without the key inserted. Loosely tighten the new shear bolts. Make sure the projection of the ignition switch is aligned with the hole in the steering column.

9. Insert the ignition key and check for proper operation of the steering wheel lock and that the ignition key turns freely.

10. Tighten the shear bolts until the heads twist off.

Key Cylinder Replacement

1. Disconnect the negative battery cable and remove the ignition switch assembly.

2. Turn the ignition switch to the **I** position.

3. Push the pin in and remove the key cylinder from the lock body.

To install:

4. Turn the key to the **LOCK** position and align the key cylinder with the lock body.

5. Turn the key almost to the **I** position and insert the key in the cylinder until the pin touches the body.

6. Turn the key to the **I** position, push the pin and insert the key cylinder into the lock body until the pin clicks into place.

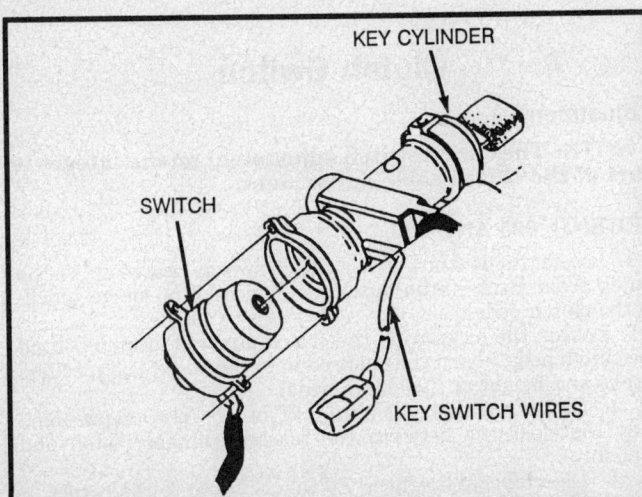

Typical ignition switch replacement

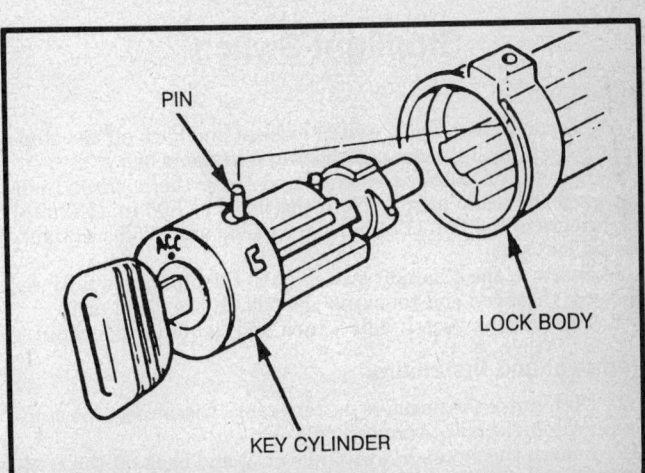

Installing the lock cylinder into the lock body

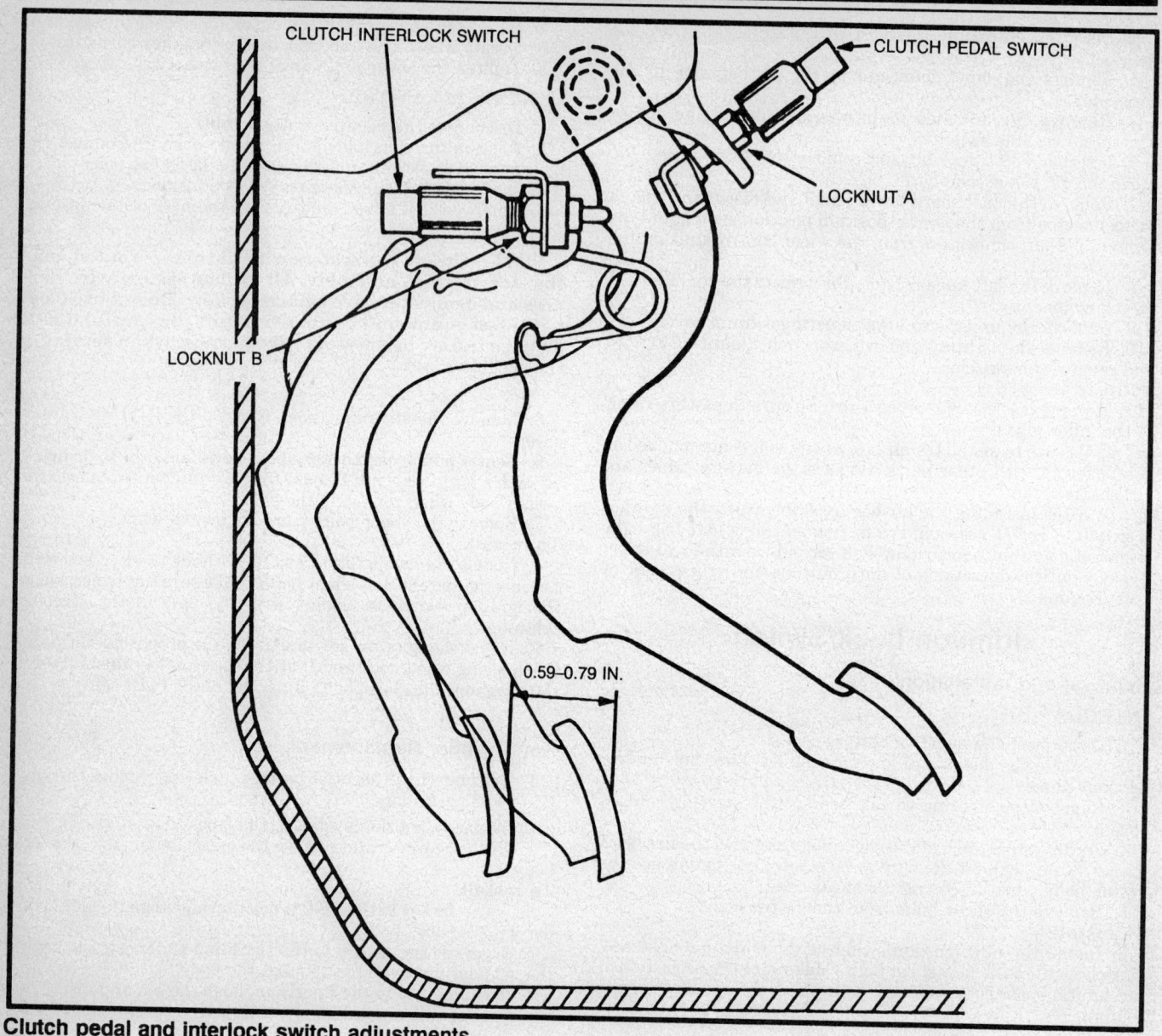

Clutch pedal and interlock switch adjustments

Stoplight Switch

Adjustment

1. Loosen the stoplight switch locknut and back off the stoplight switch until it does not touch the brake pedal.
2. Loosen the pushrod locknut and screw the pushrod in or out until the pedal height (from the floor) is 7.05 in. (179mm) for Integra or 6.69 in. (171mm) for Legend and 825S and tighten the locknut.
3. Screw in the stoplight switch until the plunger is fully depressed; threaded end touching the pad on the pedal arm.
4. Back off the switch half a turn and tighten the locknut.

Removal and Installation

1. Disconnect the negative battery cable. Disconnect the stoplight switch electrical connectors.
2. Loosen the stoplight switch locknut and back off the stoplight switch until it is removed from the brake pedal.
3. Installation is the reverse order of the removal procedure.

Clutch Switch

Adjustment

NOTE: The clutch switch adjustment on the Integra is part of the clutch cable adjustment.

LEGEND, 825 AND 827

1. Loosen the locknut on the clutch switch located above the clutch pedal. Back off the clutch switch until it no longer touches the clutch pedal.
2. Loosen the locknut on the clutch pushrod located behind the clutch pedal. Turn the pushrod in or out to get the specified stroke and height at the clutch pedal.
   a. Clutch pedal play is 0.04–0.28 in. (1–7mm) determined by the clearance between the master cylinder piston and pushrod.
   b. Clutch pedal height is 7.0 in. (179mm) to the carpet.
   c. Clutch pedal stroke is 5–6 in. (140–150mm) stroke at the clutch pedal.

NOTE: The total clutch free-play is 0.35–0.59 in. (9–15mm). If there is no clearance between the master cylinder piston and the pushrod, the release bearing is held against the diaphragm spring, which can result in clutch slippage or other clutch problems.

3. Torque the clutch pushrod locknut to 13 ft. lbs. (18 Nm).
4. Thread the clutch pedal switch in until it contacts the clutch pedal. Turn the switch in further ¼–½ of a turn.
5. Torque the clutch pedal switch locknut to 8 ft. lbs. (10 Nm).
6. Loosen the clutch interlock switch locknut. Measure the clearance between the floor board and the clutch pedal with the clutch pedal fully depressed.
7. Release the clutch pedal 0.59–0.79 in. (15–20mm) from the fully depressed position and hold it there. Adjust the position of the clutch interlock switch so the engine will start with the clutch in this position.
8. Thread the clutch interlock switch in further ¼–½ of a turn. Torque the clutch interlock locknut to 8 ft. lbs. (10 Nm).

Removal and Installation

1. Disconnect the negative battery cable.
2. Remove the instrument panel lower cover and knee bolster, if equipped.
3. Disconnect the electrical connectors from the clutch switch.
4. Loosen the clutch switch locknut and unscrew the switch from the switch mounting.
5. To install, reverse the removal procedure and torque the clutch switch locknut to 8 ft. lbs. (10 Nm).

NOTE: The removal and installation procedure for the clutch interlock switch is the same as the clutch pedal switch.

Fuses Circuit Breakers and Relays

Location
INTEGRA

The Integra fuse/relay box is located in the interior on the drivers side below the dashboard usually next to or behind the left side kick panel. There is also a main fuse box located in the right side of the engine compartment containing two 45 amp and a 65 amp fuse. In addition to these, there is a 10 amp hazard fuse located at the positive battery terminal. There are many relays used on the Integra and some of them are located in the engine fuse box and the interior fuse box. Listed below are some of the other possible relay locations:

Air Conditioning Compressor Relay—located on the left front side of the radiator support.
Air Conditioning Condenser Fan Relay—located on the left front side of the radiator support.
Air Conditioning Radiator Fan Relay—located on the left front side of the radiator support.
Anti-Lock Brake Front Safe Relay—located on the right inner fender panel.
Anti-Lock Brake Motor Relay—located on the right inner fender panel.
Anti-Lock Brake Rear Safe Relay—located on the right inner fender panel.
Day Time Running Light Relay (Canada only)—located behind the right side kick panel.
Fog Light Relay—located on the top of the interior fuse box.
PGM-FI Main Relay—located behind the left side of the instrument panel.
Power Window Relay—located on the top of the interior fuse box.
Rear Defogger Relay—located on the top of the interior fuse box.

Retractable Headlight Relays—located on a relay bracket in the lower right side of the engine compartment.
Starter Relay (Manual Transaxle only)—located behind the radio in the center of the instrument panel.
Sun Roof Relay—located on the top of the interior fuse box.

LEGEND AND LEGEND COUPE

The fuse box is located in the interior on the drivers side below the dashboard usually located next to or behind the left side kick panel. There is also a relay box located in the left side of the engine compartment. There are many relays being used on these vehicles and most of them are located in the engine fuse/relay box and the interior fuse/relay box. Listed below are some of the other possible relay locations:

Air Conditioning Compressor Relay—located on the left front side of the inner fender panel.
Air Conditioning Condenser Fan Relay—located on the right front side of the inner fender panel, near the fuse/relay box.
Air Conditioning Condenser Fan Timer Relay—located on the left front side of the inner fender panel.
Air Conditioning Radiator Fan Relay—located on the right front side of the inner fender panel, near the fuse/relay box.
Air Conditioning Radiator Fan Timer Relay—located on the right front side of the inner fender panel, near the fuse/relay box.
Anti-Lock Brake Front Safe Relay—located on the right inner fender panel, near the battery.
Anti-Lock Brake Rear Safe Relay—located on the right inner fender panel, near the battery.
Blower High Relay—located on the blower motor housing.
Blower Motor Relay—located on the blower motor housing.
Day Time Running Light Relay (Canada only)—located under the drivers side seat.
Power Seat Belt Relays—there is one for both front seats, located under the seats.

825 AND 827

The fuse box is located in the interior on the drivers side below the dashboard usually located next to or behind the left side kick panel. There is also a relay box located in the left side of the engine compartment. There are many relays being used on these vehicles and most of them are located in the engine fuse/relay box and the interior fuse/relay box. Listed below are some of the other possible relay locations:

Air Conditioning Clutch Relay—located in the front corner of the right front inner fender.
Air Conditioning Fan Changeover Relay—located in the engine compartment fuse/relay block.
Anti-Lock Brake System Return Pump Relay—located on the hydraulic modulator.
Anti-Lock Brake System Solenoid Valve Relay—located on the hydraulic modulator.
Blower Motor Relays—located on the blower motor housing.
Cooling Fan Relays—located in the engine compartment fuse/relay block.
Main Relay—located on the left side of the steering wheel, behind instrument panel.
Over-voltage Protection Relay—located in the trunk, next to the ABS control unit.
Power Windows Relay—located in the fuse/relay block located in the passenger compartment.
Wiper Motor Relay—located in the fuse/relay block located in the passenger compartment.

Computers

Location
INTEGRA

Anti-Lock Brake Control Unit (Hatchback)—located in the

top center area of the luggage compartment behind the interior panel.

Anti-Lock Brake Control Unit (Sedan)—located in the left side panel area of the luggage compartment behind the interior panel.

Automatic Shoulder Seat Belt Control Unit—located behind the right side kick panel.

Automatic Transaxle Control Unit—is located behind the left side of the instrument panel.

Cooling Fan Timer Unit—located behind the radio in the center of the instrument panel area.

Cruise Control Unit—located behind the left side of the instrument panel.

Integrated Control Unit—located behind the left side kick panel.

PGM-FI Electronic Control Unit—located on under a protective cover on the drivers side front floorboard area; sometimes under the seat.

Power Door Lock Control Unit—located behind the radio in the center of the instrument panel area.

Retractable Headlight Control Unit—located on the lower left inner fender panel in the engine compartment.

LEGEND AND LEGEND COUPE

Anti-Lock Brake Control Unit—located behind the drivers side rear seat or the panel next to the rear seat.

Automatic Transaxle Control Unit—located under the right side floor panel.

Cooling Fan Control Unit—located under the instrument panel next to the steering column support.

Cooling Fan Timer Unit—located under the right side floor panel.

Dashlight Brightness Control Unit—located on the left side of the center front console.

Information Control Unit—located behind the upper portion of the glove box assembly.

Integrated Control Unit—located on the interior fuse/relay box located under the left side of the instrument panel.

Interlock Control Unit (Automatic Transaxle)—located on the interior fuse/relay box located under the left side of the instrument panel.

PGM-FI Electronic Control Unit—located under a protective cover located on the right front floor board.

Power Window Control Unit—located inside the driver's inner door panel.

Security Control Unit—located on the right rear shock tower.

Supplemental Restraint System Control Unit—located under the left side of the instrument panel.

825 AND 827

Anti-Lock Brake Control Unit—located in the luggage compartment, behind the left side panel.

Anti-Theft Control Unit—located in the center console, above the ashtray assembly.

Central Locking Control Unit—located above the steering column.

Cruise Control Unit—located on the left kick panel, behind the fuse/relay box.

Electronic Control Unit—located under the passenger's seat.

Fuel Injection Control Unit—located under the driver's seat.

Ignition Module—located on the side of the distributor assembly.

Power Door Lock Relay Module—there is one located in each of the rear doors.

Remote Door Lock Reciever Control Unit—located in the headliner, next to the rear view mirror.

Vehicle Condition Monitor—located under the passenger's seat.

Flashers

Location

INTEGRA

The Hazard/Turn Signal Relay, is located either on the interior fuse/relay box or located up behind the left side of the instrument panel.

LEGEND, 825 AND 827

The Hazard/Turn Signal Relay, is located on the interior fuse/relay box, located under the left side of the instrument panel.

Cruise Control

For further information, please refer to "Chilton's Chassis Electronics Service Manual" for additional coverage.

Adjustment

INTEGRA

1. Check that the actuator cable operates smoothly with no binding or sticking.
2. Start the engine and let it warm up to reach normal operating temperature.
3. Measure the amount of movement of the output linkage until the engine speed starts to increase.
4. At first, the output linkage should be located at the full closed position. The free-play should be 43 ± 0.06 inches (11 ± 1.5mm).
5. If the free-play is not within specifications, loosen the locknut and turn the adjusting nut as required.
6. Retighten the locknut and recheck the free-play.

LEGEND, 825 AND 827

1. Check that the actuator cable operates smoothly with no binding or sticking.
2. Start the engine and let it warm up to reach normal operating temperature.
3. Measure the amount of movement of the actuator rod until the cable pulls on the accelerator lever; engine speed starts to increase.
4. The free-play should be 43 ± 0.06 inches (11 ± 1.5mm).
5. If the free-play is not within specifications, loosen the locknut and turn the adjusting nut, as required.

NOTE: If necessary, check the throttle cable free-play and recheck the actuator rod free-play.

6. Retighten the locknut and recheck the free-play.

ENGINE COOLING

Radiator

Removal and Installation

NOTE: When removing the radiator, take care not to damage the core and fins.

1. Disconnect the negative battery cable. Drain the cooling system.

NOTE: On the 825 and 827 vehicles, it may be necessary to raise and safely support the vehicle in order to

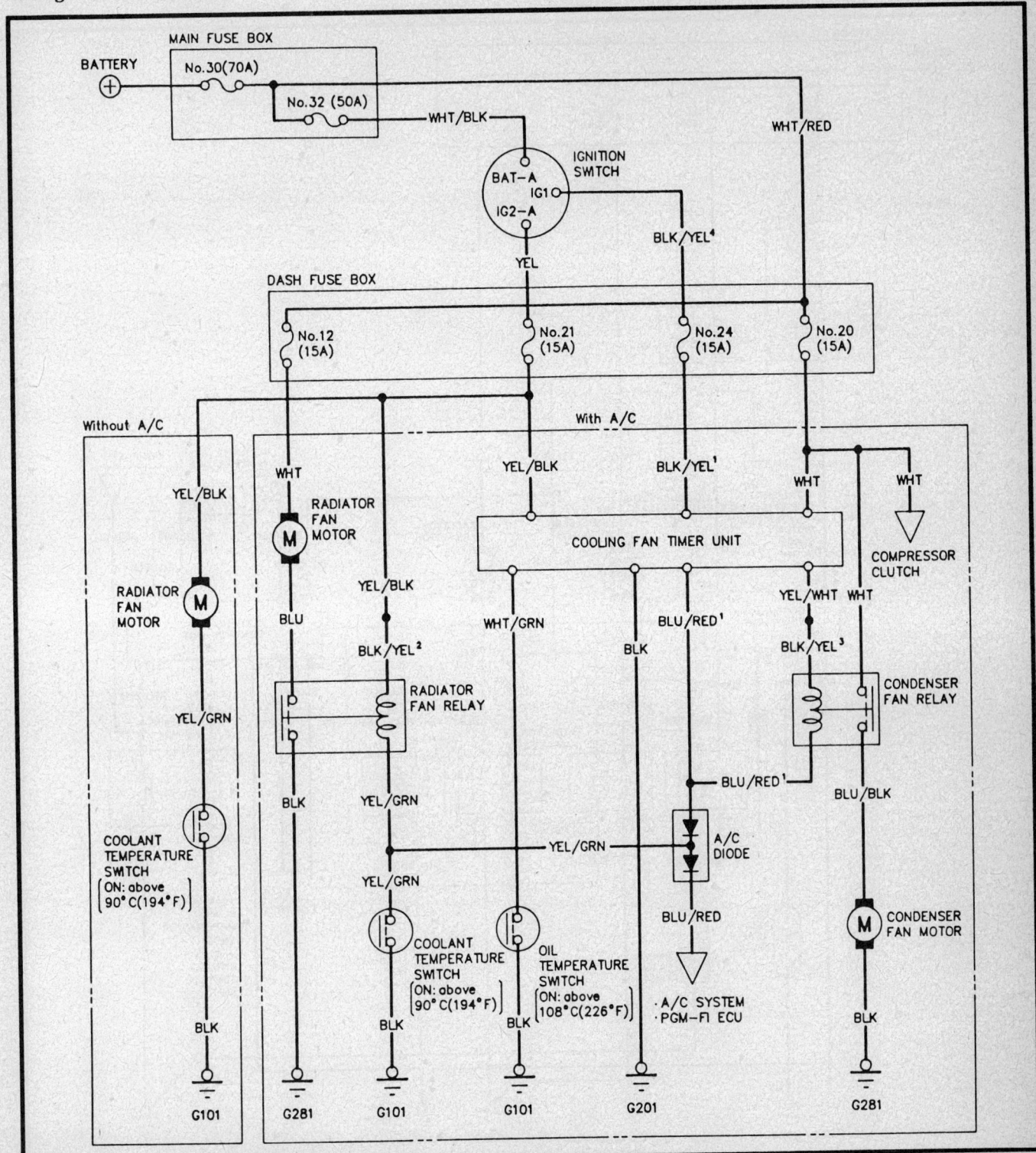

Cooling fan electrical schematic—Integra

remove the front under protection panel to gain access to the lower radiator and shroud mounting bolts.

2. Disconnect the thermo-switch wire and the fan motor wire. Remove the fan shroud, if equipped.

3. Disconnect the upper coolant hose at the upper radiator tank and the lower hose at the water pump connecting pipe. If equipped with an automatic transaxle, disconnect and plug the cooling lines at the bottom of the radiator.

4. Remove the hoses to the coolant reservoir.

5. Remove the radiator bolts and the radiator with the fan attached. The fan can be easily unbolted from the back of the radiator.

6. To install, reverse the removal procedure. Bleed the cooling system.

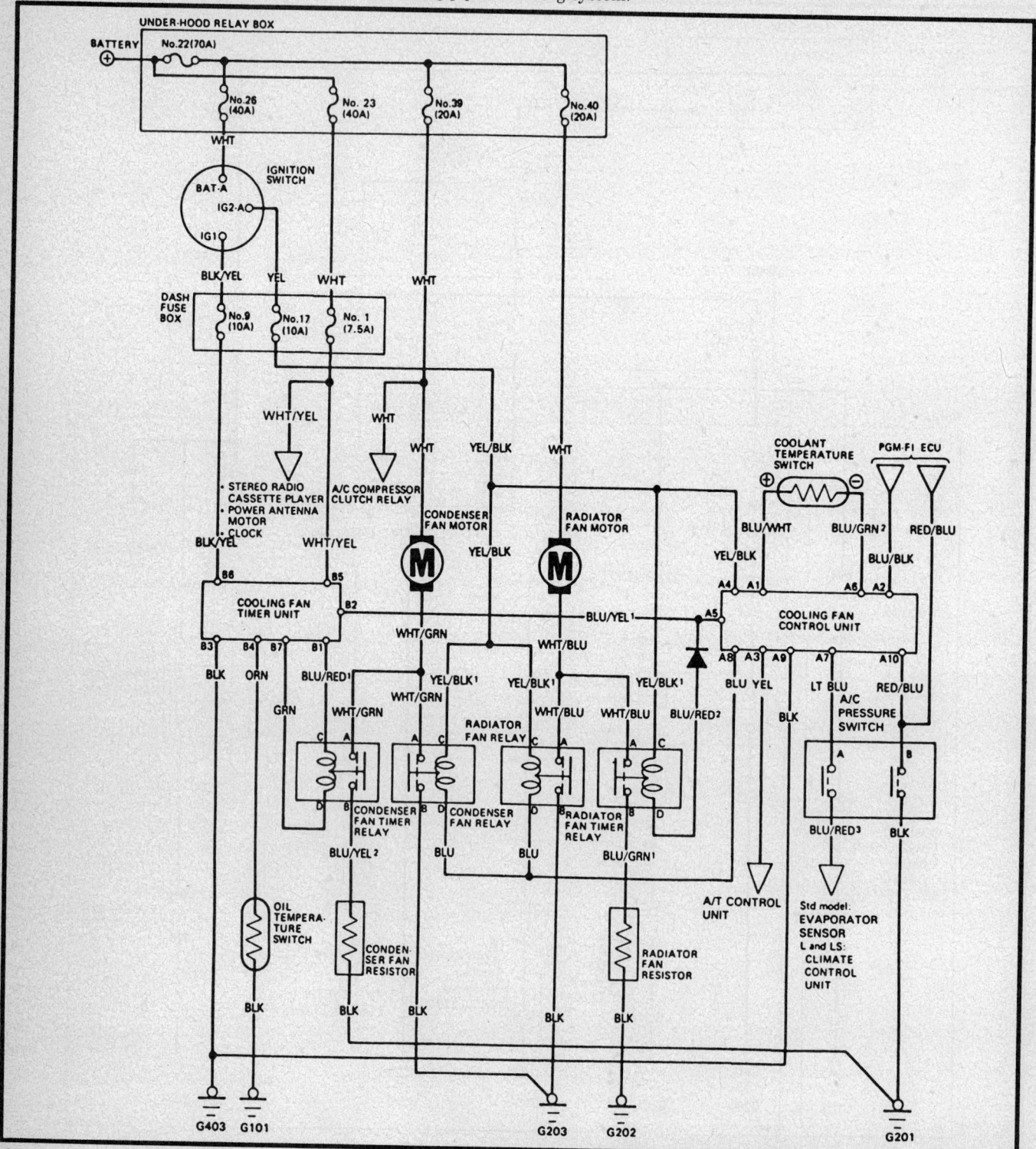

Cooling fan electrical schematic—Legend, 825 and 827 similar

Electric Cooling Fan

Testing

1. Disconnect the electrical connector from the cooling fan motor.
2. Test the cooling fan motor operation by connecting battery positive to the **A** top terminal and negative to the bottom **B** terminal.
3. If the motor fails to run or run smoothly, replace it.

NOTE: This test procedure can also be used on the air conditioning condenser fan motor. Also to test the fan control relay. Check for continuity between the upper left A and lower left B terminals with battery voltage connected to the other 2 terminals. There should be no continuity present when the battery voltage is disconnected. If the relay fails this test, replace it.

Removal and Installation

1. Disconnect the negative battery cable. Disconnect the electrical connection at the cooling fan motor.

NOTE: On the 825 and 827, it may be necessary to raise and safely support the vehicle in order to remove the front under protection panel so as to gain access to the lower cooling fan and shroud mounting bolts.

2. Remove any and all cooling fan wire retaining clips.
3. Remove the radiator fan shroud retaining bolts and remove the shroud assembly from the vehicle.
4. With the radiator fan shroud remove, remove the cooling fan mounting nuts and remove the cooling fan.

NOTE: On some vehicles there may be enough clearance to remove the cooling fan motor from the vehicle without removing the fan shroud.

5. To Install, reverse the removal procedure.

Heater Core

For further information, please refer to "Chilton's Heating and Air Conditioning Manual" for additional coverage.

Removal and Installation
WITHOUT AIR CONDITIONING
Integra

1. Disconnect the negative battery cable. Drain the cooling system.
2. Disconnect the heater hoses at the firewall.

NOTE: Coolant will run out of the heater hoses when disconnected, place a drain pan under them to catch the coolant.

3. Disconnect the heater valve cable from the heater valve.
4. On the Integra, it is necessary to remove the dashboard assembly; this can be done by using the following procedure:
   a. Slide the front seats all the way back. Remove the right and left dashboard lower panels.
   b. Remove the front console.
   c. Remove the driver's side knee bolster. Disconnect the wire harness from the connectors and the fuse box.
   d. Lower the steering column. Disconnect the ground cable to the right of the steering column.
   e. Remove the instrument panel.
   f. Remove the 4 screws, then pull the gauge assembly out half way and disconnect the speedometer cable and connectors.

g. Disconnect the antenna cable, wire connector and loosen the 2 screws, then remove the radio assembly.
   h. Disconnect the shift position switch and the shift lock wire connectors from the dashboard wire harness; automatic transaxle vehicles only.
   i. Remove the clock assembly from the top of the dashboard.
   j. Remove the side defroster garnishes from both ends of the dashboard.
   k. Remove the dashboard mounting bolts. Lift up and remove the dashboard assembly.
5. Remove the heater duct. Remove the heater assembly lower mounting nut.
6. Disconnect the air mix cable from the heater.
7. Disconnect the wire harness connector from the function control motor.
8. Remove the heater bolts and pull the heater assembly away from the body.
9. Remove the self tapping screws and the heater core retaining plate.
10. Pull the heater core from the heater housing.

To install:

11. Reverse the removal procedures.
12. Apply sealant to the grommets.
13. Do not interchange the inlet and outlet hoses.
14. Bleed the cooling system.
15. Connect all cable and adjust them properly.
16. Be sure the dashboard fits onto the body correctly.
17. Before tightening the dashboard bolts, make sure the instrument wires are not pinched and that the dashboard is not interfering with the heater control cable. For ease of installation, remove the gauge assembly from the dash.

Legend, 825 and 827

1. Disconnect the negative battery cable. Drain the cooling system.
2. Disconnect the heater hoses at the firewall.

NOTE: Coolant will run out of the heater hoses when disconnected, place a drain pan under them to catch the coolant.

3. Remove the dashboard as follows:
   a. Disconnect the negative battery cable. Slide the seat all the way to the rear and remove the lower dashboard panel.
   b. Remove the knee bolster and the left air duct.
   c. Remove the hood opener and the center console.
   d. Disconnect the wire harness from the connector holder.
   e. Remove the dash harness ground bolt from the steering column.
   f. Remove the screws and radio panel assembly, then disconnect the wire connectors, antenna cables and wire tie.

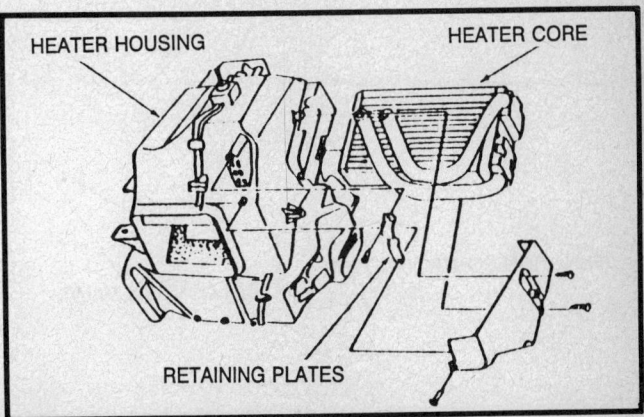

Heater core replacement—Integra

g. Remove the radio assembly, remove the center dash pocket.

h. Lower the steering column. Be sure to remove the ignition key from the lock cylinder.

i. Remove the dashboard mounting bolts.

j. Pull the dashboard straight back and disconnect the speedometer. Remove the dashboard.

4. Disconnect the wire harness and the vacuum hoses.

5. Remove the heater mounting bolts and pull the heater assembly away from the body.

6. Remove the self-tapping screws and the heater core retaining plate.

7. Pull the heater core from the heater housing.

To install:

8. Reverse the removal procedures.

9. Apply sealant to the grommets.

10. Do not interchange the inlet and outlet hoses.

11. Bleed the cooling system.

12. Connect all cables and adjust them properly.

13. Be sure the dashboard fits onto the body correctly.

14. Before tightening the dashboard bolts, make sure the instrument wires are not pinched and that the dashboard is not interfering with the heater control cable. For ease of installation, remove the gauge assembly from the dash.

WITH AIR CONDITIONING

Integra

It may or may not be necessary to remove the evaporator assembly from the under the instrument panel in order to gain access to the heater core housing. This can be determined by the individual technician performing this operation. The following is a procedure on how to remove the heater core housing if the evaporator housing must be removed.

1. Disconnect the negative battery cable.

2. Discharge the refrigerant from the air conditioning system. Disconnect the receiver line and suction hose from the evaporator assembly. Be sure to cap the open fitting to prevent moisture from entering the system.

3. Remove the passenger side lower dashboard cover.

4. Remove the glove box assembly.

5. Remove the front console assembly.

6. Remove the passenger side knee bolster panel, located under the glove box frame.

7. Remove the 2 self tapping screws and the air conditioning bands from around the evaporator assembly.

8. Disconnect the wire connector from the thermostat switch and pull off the wire harness from the clamps. Remove the evaporator.

9. Remove the self-tapping screws and remove the heater duct assembly.

10. Remove the heater core housing.

To install:

11. Reverse the removal procedure. Recharge the air conditioning system and paying attention to the following:

a. When reattaching the actuator, make sure its positioning will not allow the air door to be pulled to far.

b. Attach the actuator and all linkage, then apply battery voltage and watch the door movement. If necessary, loosen the holding screw and move the actuator up or down.

c. When adjusting the control rod, connect the recirculation control motor connection to the main wire harness, push **RECIRC** and open the air doors. Then connect the control rod to the arm while holding the air doors open.

Legend, 825 and 827

— **CAUTION** —

This procedure requires discharging the air conditioning system. This should only be performed with extreme caution and with safety goggles and gloves.

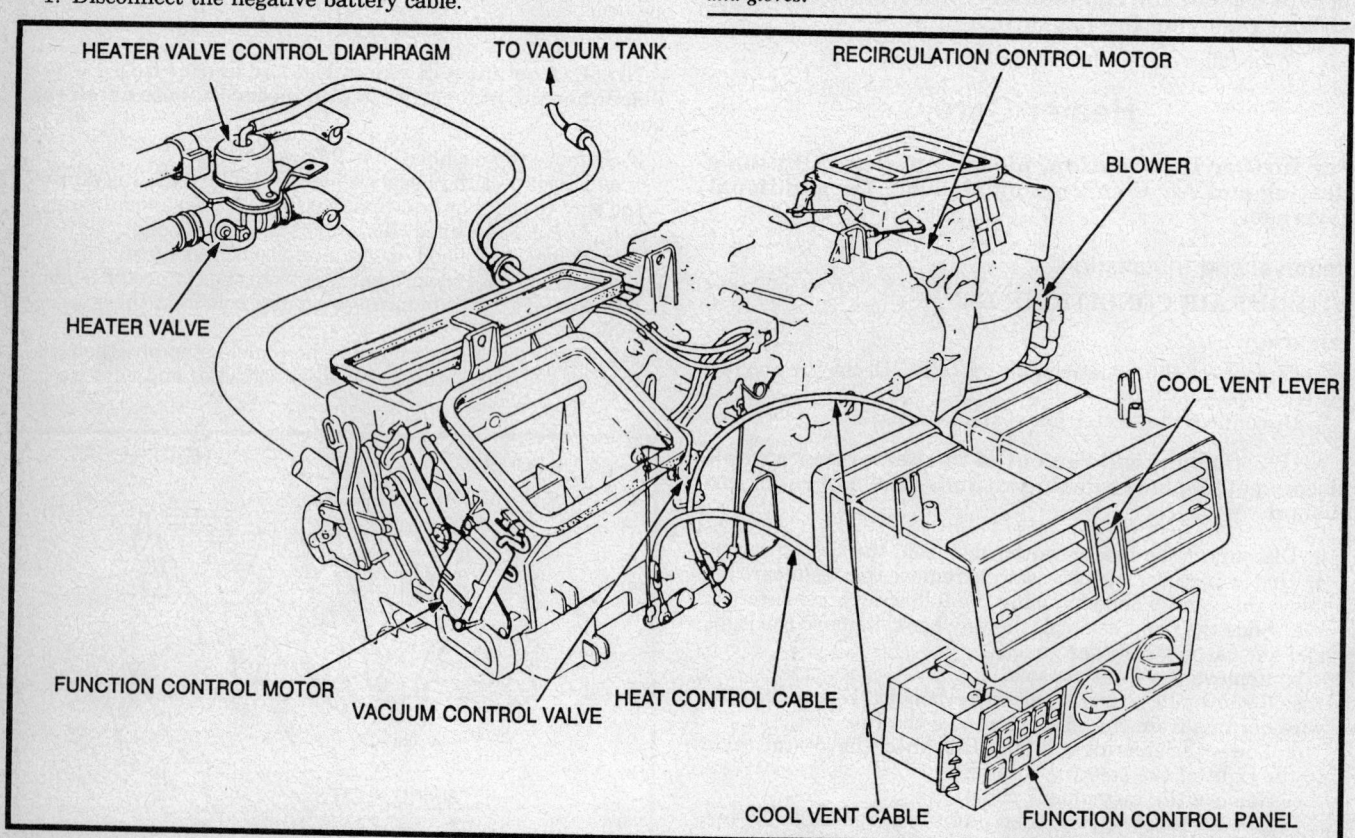

View of the air and heating system components

1. Disconnect the negative battery cable.
2. Remove the glove box lower cover screws and the cover.
3. Remove the glove box screws and the glove box.
4. Remove the glove box frame screws, the glove box frame, the clips and the heater duct.
5. Discharge the refrigerant from the air conditioning system.
6. Remove the evaporator as follows, disconnect the receiver line and suction hose from the evaporator assembly. Be sure to cap the open fitting to prevent moisture from entering the system. Remove the self-tapping screws and the air conditioning bands from around the evaporator assembly. Disconnect the wire connector from the thermostat switch and pull off the wire harness from the clamps. Remove the evaporator.
7. Remove the heater core housing assembly.

To install:

8. Reverse the removal procedures. Check that there are no air leaks in the blower case. Recharge the air conditioning system and paying attention to the following:

a. When reattaching the actuator, make sure its positioning will not allow the air door to pulled to far.

b. Attach the actuator and all linkage, then apply battery voltage and watch the door movement. If necessary, loosen the holding screw and move the actuator up or down.

c. When adjusting the control rod, connect the recirculation control motor connection to the main wire harness, push the **FRESH/RECIRC** switch to **FRESH** and open the air doors. Then connect the control rod to the arm while holding the air doors open.

Water Pump

Removal and Installation

It is necessary to remove the timing belt cover(s) and remove the timing belt from the water pump sprocket. A small amount of weeping from the bleed hole in the water pump is considered normal and no cause for alarm.

1. Remove the timing belt from the water pump drive sprocket.
2. Drain the cooling system to a level below the water pump.
3. Remove the water pump-to-engine bolts and remove together with the drive sprocket.
4. To install, use a new O-ring and reverse the removal procedures. Bleed the cooling system.
5. Refill the cooling system. Start the engine, allow it to reach normal operating temperatures and check for leaks. Check and/or adjust the engine timing.

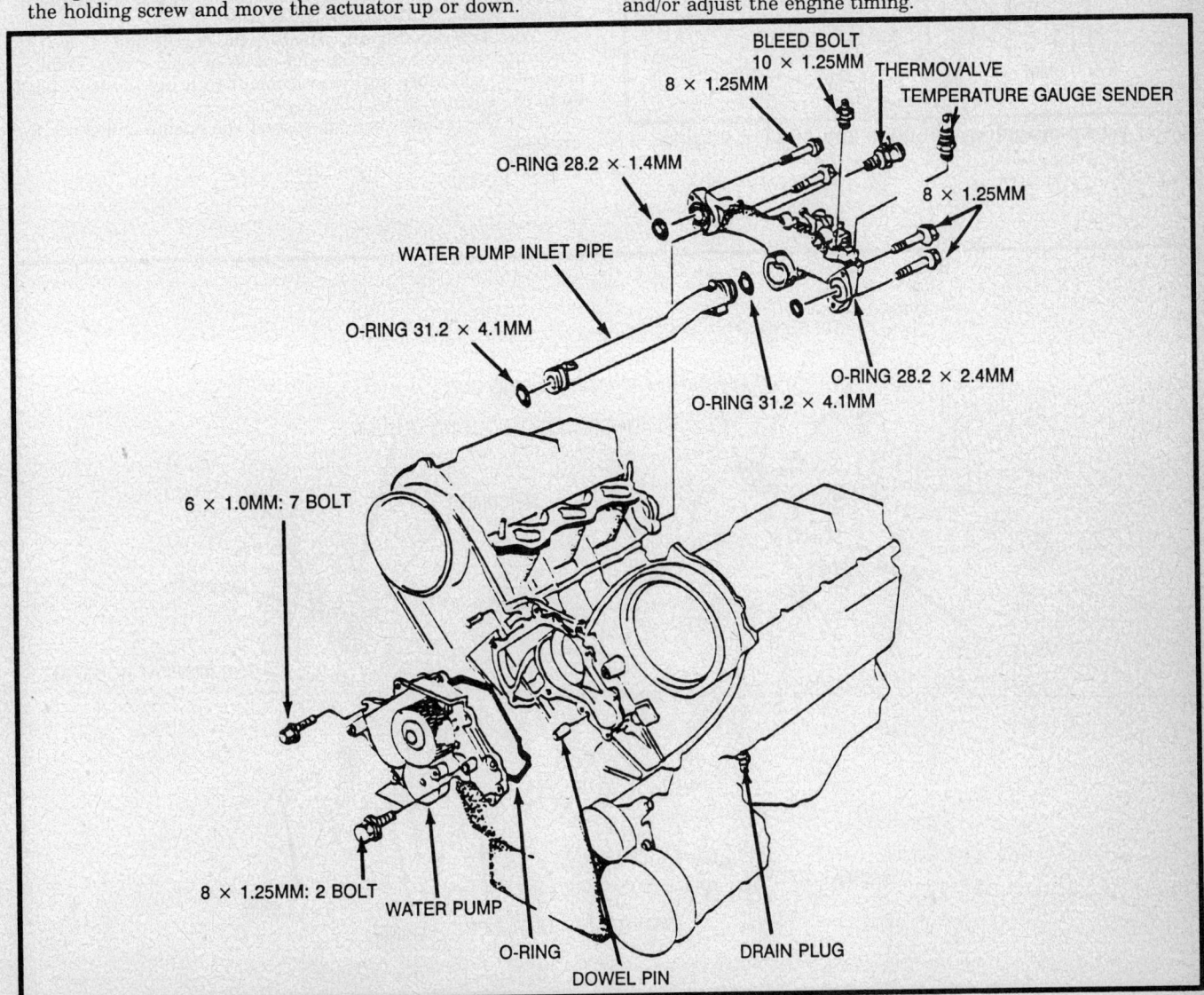

Water pump mounting—2494cc and 2675cc engines

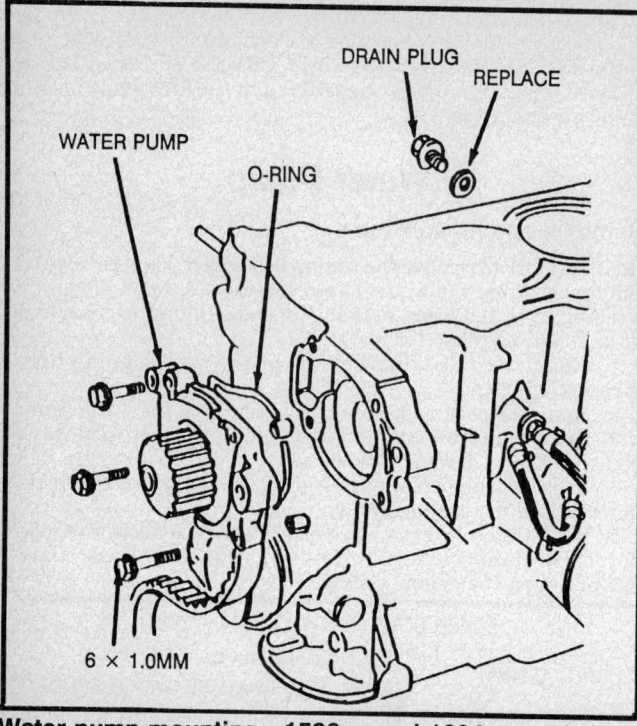

WATER PUMP

DRAIN PLUG

REPLACE

O-RING

6 × 1.0MM

Water pump mounting—1590cc and 1834cc engines

Thermostat

Removal and Installation

The thermostat is located under the thermostat housing.
1. Drain the cooling system to a level below the thermostat housing. Remove the coolant hose(s) attached to the thermostat.
2. Remove the thermostat housing bolts, the housing and the thermostat.
3. Clean the gasket mounting surfaces.
4. To install, use new gaskets and reverse the removal procedures; install the thermostat's spring end toward the engine. Torque both cover bolts to 9 ft. lbs. (12 Nm). Refill and bleed the cooling system.

Cooling System Bleeding

1. Move the temperature selector to the **MAX HEAT**.
2. Fill the coolant reservoir to the **MAX** mark.
3. Loosen the air bleed bolt in the water outlet and refill the radiator to the bottom of the filler neck with antifreeze/coolant. Tighten the bleed bolt as soon as the coolant starts to run out in a steady stream without any air bubbles in it.
4. With the radiator cap off, start the engine and allow it to warm up; the cooling fan should go on at least twice. Then, if necessary, add more antifreeze/coolant to bring the level back up to the bottom of the filler neck.
5. Put the radiator cap on, restart the engine and check for any leaks.

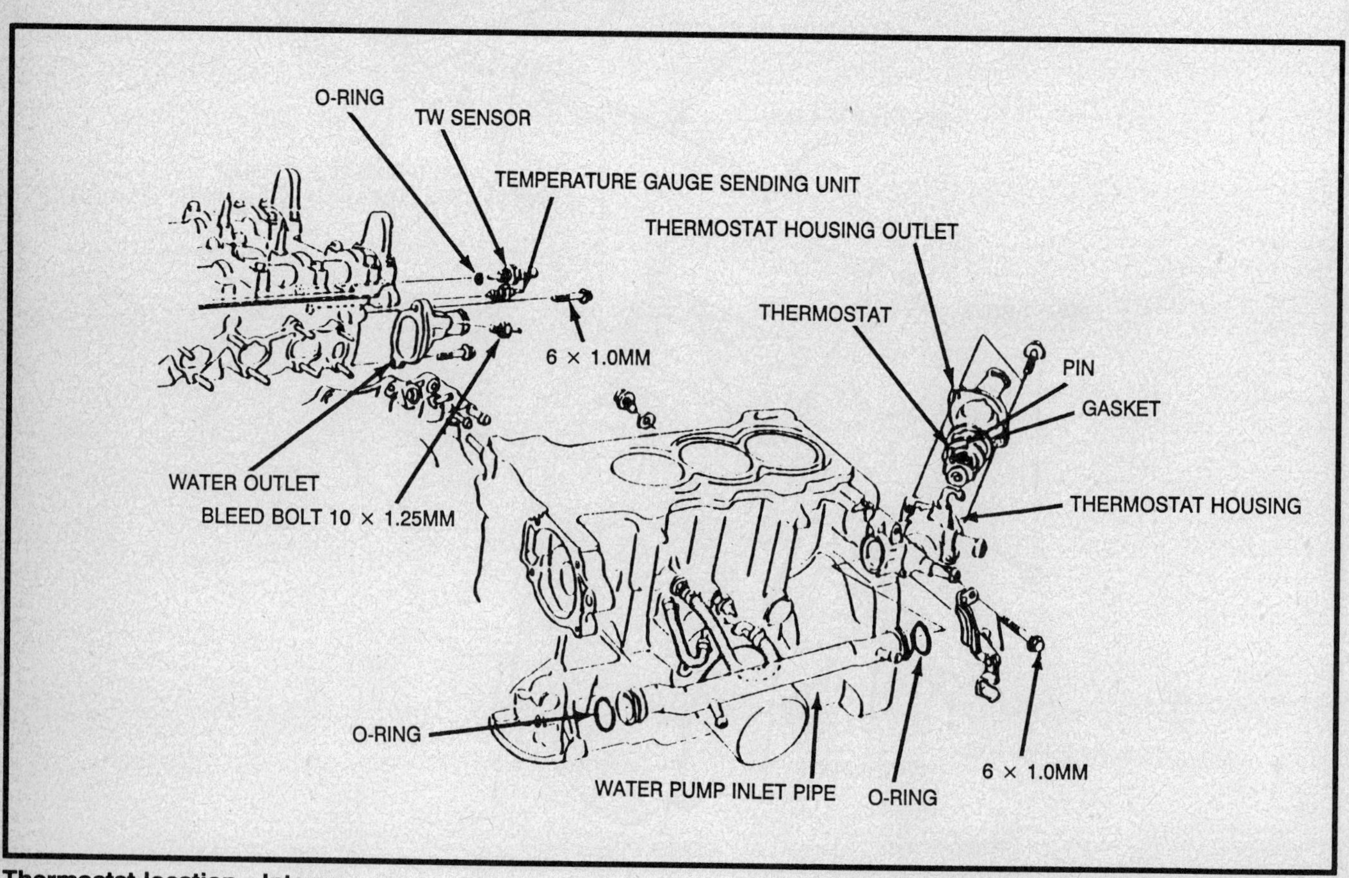

O-RING

TW SENSOR

TEMPERATURE GAUGE SENDING UNIT

THERMOSTAT HOUSING OUTLET

THERMOSTAT

PIN

GASKET

6 × 1.0MM

THERMOSTAT HOUSING

WATER OUTLET

BLEED BOLT 10 × 1.25MM

O-RING

WATER PUMP INLET PIPE

O-RING

6 × 1.0MM

Thermostat location—Integra

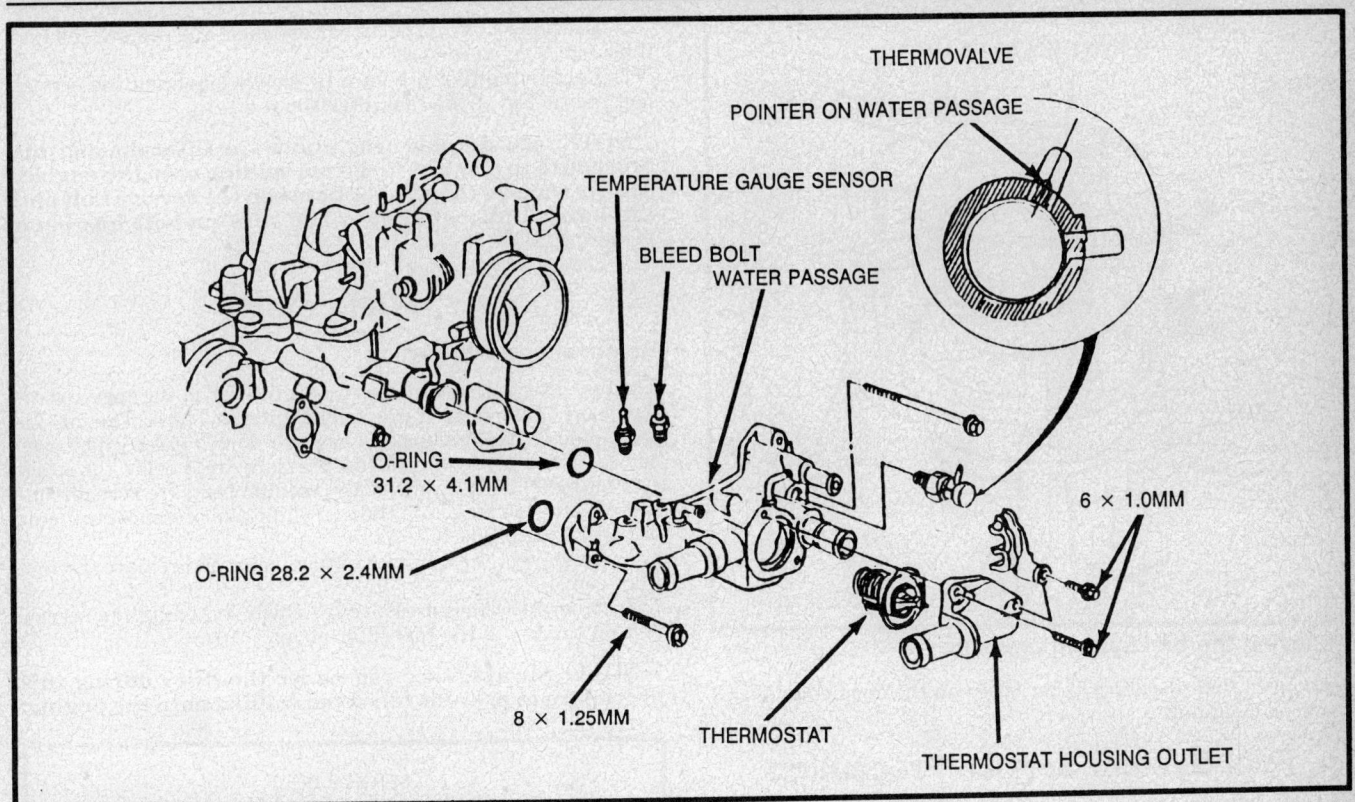

Thermostat location—2494cc and 2675cc engines

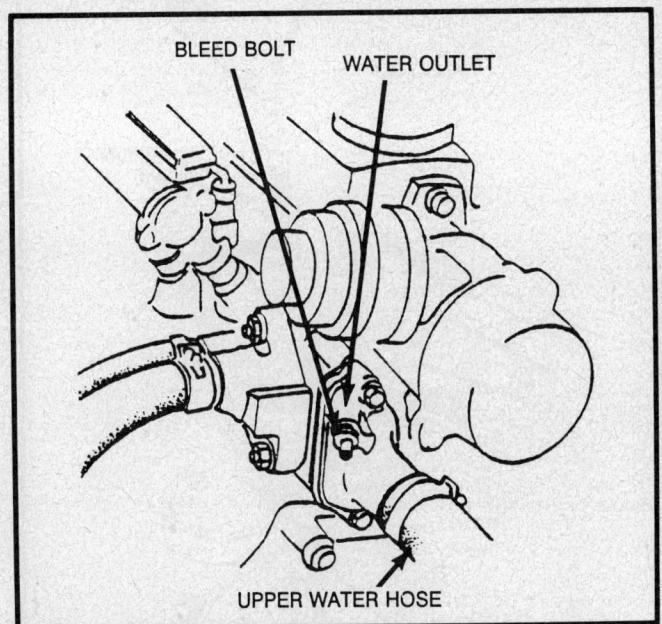

Cooling system bleed bolt location—1590cc and 1834cc engines

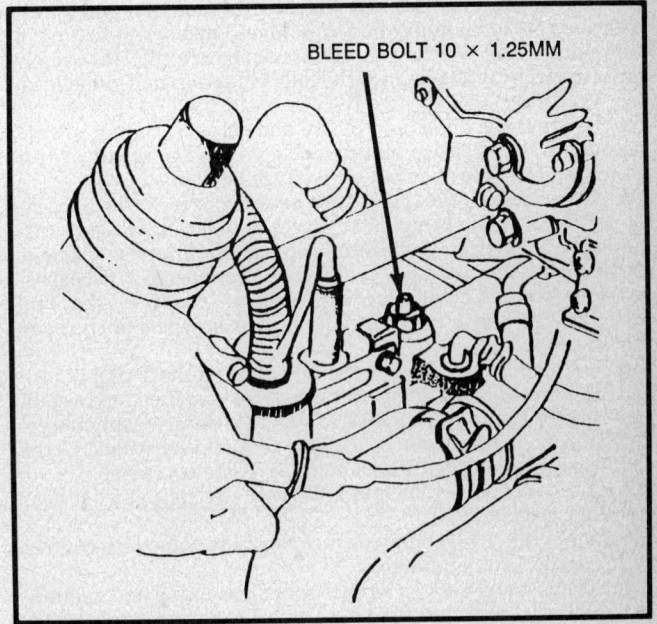

Cooling system bleed bolt location—2494cc and 2675cc engines

FUEL SYSTEM

Both Acura and Sterling use Honda's Programmed Fuel Injection system. This system is a multiport electronic fuel injection system. The PGM-FI system is based on sequential port injection by which each injector is timed to provide the proper

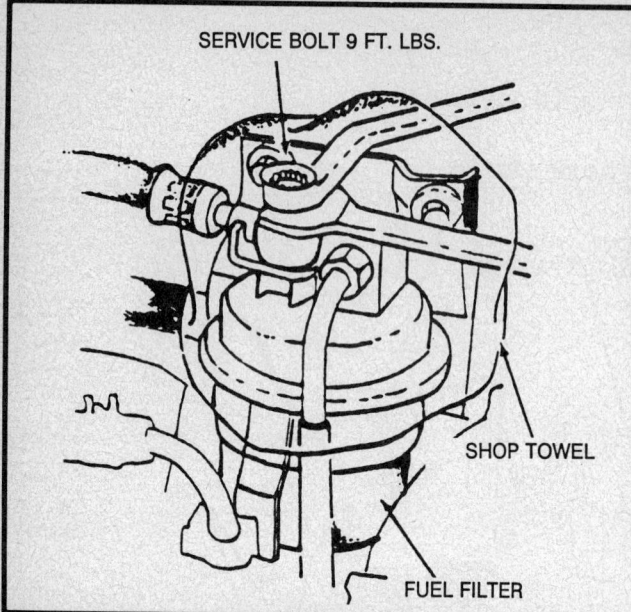

SERVICE BOLT 9 FT. LBS.

SHOP TOWEL

FUEL FILTER

Relieving the fuel system pressure

amount of fuel to each cylinder based on the engine speed and the load condition.

Fuel System Service Precaution

Safety is the most important factor when performing not only fuel system maintenance but any type of maintenance. Failure to conduct maintenance and repairs in a safe manner may result in serious personal injury or death. Maintenance and testing of the vehicle's fuel system components can be accomplished safely and effectively by adhering to the following rules and guidelines.

• To avoid the possibility of fire and personal injury, always disconnect the negative battery cable unless the repair or test procedure requires that battery voltage be applied.
• Always relieve the fuel system pressure prior to disconnecting any fuel system component (injector, fuel rail, pressure regulator, etc.), fitting or fuel line connection. Exercise extreme caution whenever relieving fuel system pressure to avoid exposing skin, face and eyes to fuel spray. Please be advised that fuel under pressure may penetrate the skin or any part of the body that it contacts.
• Always place a shop towel or cloth around the fitting or connection prior to loosening to absorb any excess fuel due to spillage. Ensure that all fuel spillage (should it occur) is quickly removed from engine surfaces. Ensure that all fuel soaked cloths or towels are deposited into a suitable waste container.
• Always keep a dry chemical (Class B) fire extinguisher near the work area.
• Do not allow fuel spray or fuel vapors to come into contact with a spark or open flame.
• Always use a backup wrench when loosening and tightening fuel line connection fittings. This will prevent unnecessary stress and torsion to fuel line piping. Always follow the proper torque specifications.
• Always replace worn fuel fitting O-rings with new. Do not substitute fuel hose or equivalent where fuel pipe is installed.

Relieving Fuel System Pressure

NOTE: Do not smoke while working on the fuel system. Keep open flames or sparks away from the work area. Be sure to relieve fuel pressure while the engine is off.

1. Disconnect the negative battery cable and remove the fuel filler cap.
2. Relieve the fuel pressure by slowly loosening the service bolt on the top of the fuel filter about a turn.

NOTE: Always place rag under the filter during this procedure to prevent fuel from spilling onto the engine. Always replace the washer between the service bolt and the banjo bolt, whenever the service bolt has been loosened.

Fuel Filter

Removal and Installation

The fuel filter is either located on the firewall in the engine compartment or along the frame rail near the fuel tank. The fuel filter should be changed every 4 years or 60,000 miles which ever comes first or whenever the fuel pressure drops below the specified rating (of 36–41 psi with the vacuum pressure hose disconnected) after making sure the fuel pump and pressure regulator are operating properly.

1. Disconnect the negative battery cable and remove the fuel filler cap.
2. Relieve the fuel pressure by slowly loosening the service bolt on the top of the fuel filter about a turn.

NOTE: Always place rag under the filter during this procedure to prevent fuel from spilling onto the engine.

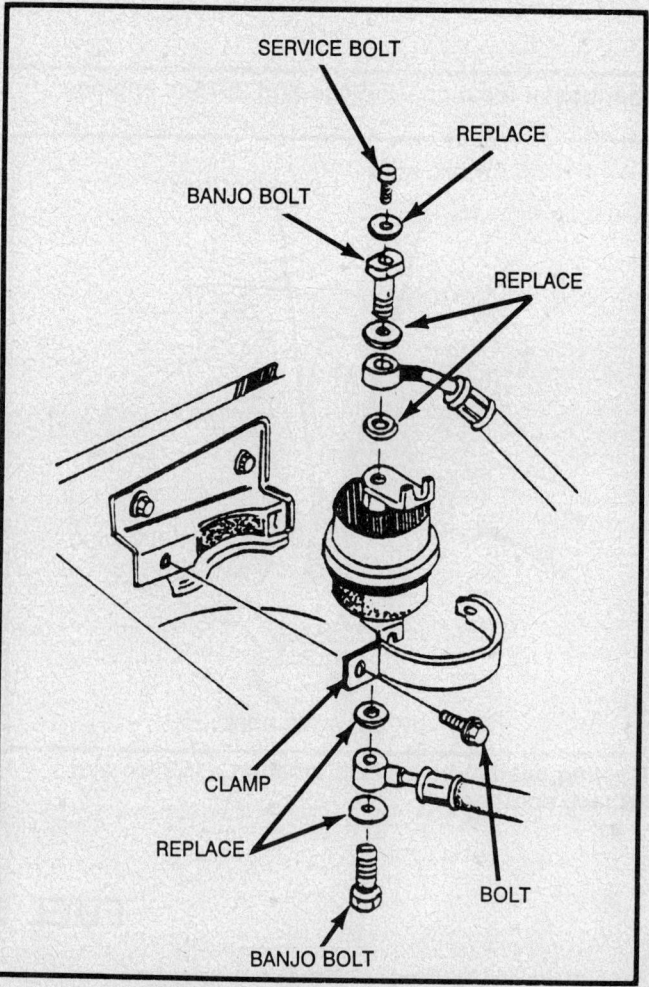

SERVICE BOLT

REPLACE

BANJO BOLT

REPLACE

CLAMP

REPLACE

BOLT

BANJO BOLT

Fuel filter assembly—Integra

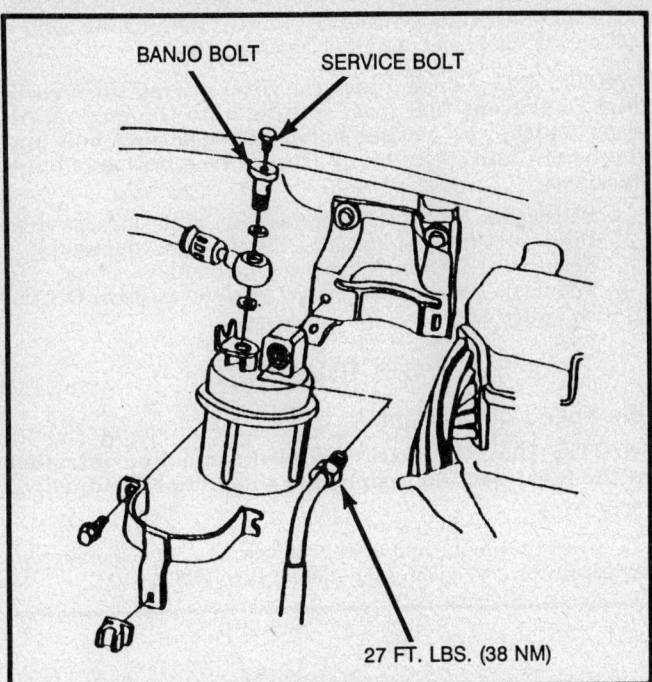

BANJO BOLT   SERVICE BOLT

27 FT. LBS. (38 NM)

Fuel filter assembly—Legend, 825 and 827

Always replace the washer between the service bolt and the banjo bolt, whenever the service bolt has been loosened.

3. Remove the fittings from the fuel filter.
4. Remove the fuel filter clamp and the fuel filter.
5. To assemble, use a new filter, washers and reverse the removal procedures.

Electric Fuel Pump

Pressure Testing

1. Disconnect the negative battery cable and remove the fuel filler cap.
2. Relieve the fuel pressure by slowly loosening the service bolt on the top of the fuel filter about a turn.

NOTE: Always place rag under the filter during this procedure to prevent fuel from spilling onto the engine. Always replace the washer between the service bolt and the banjo bolt, whenever the service bolt has been loosened.

3. Using a fuel pressure gauge, attach it to the top of the fuel filter.
4. Start the engine and measure the fuel pressure with the engine idling and vacuum hose from the pressure regulator disconnected; the fuel pressure should be 35–41 psi. (240–279 kPa).
5. If the fuel pressure is not within specifications, check the fuel pump.
6. If the pressure is higher than specifications, check for a pinched or clogged fuel return hose or faulty pressure regulator.
7. If the pressure is lower than specifications, check for a clogged filter, defective pressure regulator or leakage in the fuel line.
8. After inspection, remove the pressure gauge.
9. To assemble, use a new filter, washers and reverse the removal procedures.

Preliminary Testing

If a problem with the fuel pump is suspected, check that the fuel pump actually runs; when it is **ON** and the fuel filler cap is removed there should be a noise heard from the fuel pump. The fuel pump should run for 2 seconds, when the ignition switch is first turned to the **ON** position. If the pump does not make any noise, check it's operation as follows:

1. On the 1987–89 Integra, raise and safely support the vehicle. Remove the fuel pump cover and disconnect the fuel pump connector.
2. On the 1990–91 Integra, remove the rear seat and disconnect the fuel pump electrical connector. Be sure the ignition switch is in the **OFF** position.
3. On the Legend and Sterling vehicles, remove the fuel pump access cover located in the luggage compartment and disconnect the fuel pump connector.
4. Disconnect the electrical connector from the main fuel pump relay located under the left side of the instrument panel. Connect a jumper wire to the 2 bottom right terminals (black/yellow—yellow/black) of the main fuel pump relay.
5. Check that there is battery voltage available at the fuel pump connector when the ignition switch is turned to the **ON** position; positive probe to the yellow/black wire, negative probe to the black wire.
6. If there is battery voltage available, replace the fuel pump. If there is no voltage available, check the main relay harness and relay assembly.
7. After performing this quick test, the fuel pump can be removed as follows.

Removal and Installation

INTEGRA

1. Disconnect the negative battery cable.
2. Relieve the fuel pressure by slowly loosening the service bolt on the top of the fuel filter about a turn.

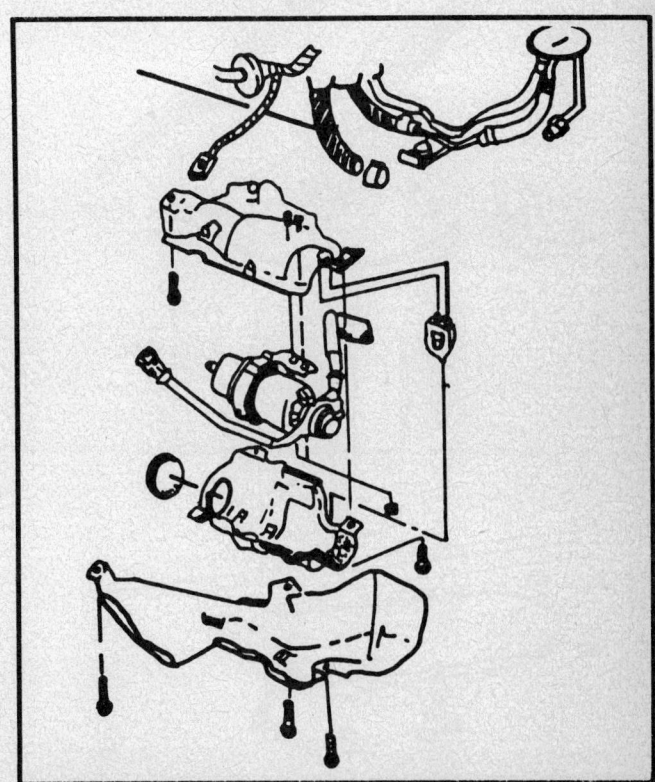

Fuel pump mounting—1987–89 Integra

NOTE: Place a rag under the filter during this procedure to prevent fuel from spilling onto the engine. Always replace the washer between the service bolt and the banjo bolt, whenever the service bolt has been loosened.

3. Raise and safely support the vehicle. Remove the fuel tank drain plug, if equipped, and drain the fuel into a suitable container.

4. Remove the left rear wheel.

5. On the 1990–91 Integra, remove the rear seat and disconnect the fuel pump connector. Remove the 2 way valve cover and hose protector. Disconnect the fuel hoses. Place a suitable jack under the fuel tank. Remove the strap nuts and let the straps fall free. Lower the jack and remove the fuel pump mounting bolts. Remove the fuel pump.

6. On the 1987–89 Integra vehicles, remove the fuel pump cover bolts and the cover.

7. Remove the fuel pump mount bolts and the fuel pump with it's mount.

8. Disconnect the fuel lines and the electrical connectors.

9. Remove the clamp and remove the fuel pump from the mounting bracket.

10. Remove the fuel line and silencer from the pump.

11. To install, reverse the removal procedures. Turn **ON** the ignition switch and check for fuel leaks.

LEGEND, 825 AND 827

1. Disconnect the negative battery cable.

2. Relieve the fuel pressure by slowly loosening the service bolt on the top of the fuel filter about a turn.

NOTE: Place a rag under the filter during this procedure to prevent fuel from spilling onto the engine. Always replace the washer between the service bolt and the banjo bolt, whenever the service bolt has been loosened.

3. Remove the maintenance access cover in the luggage area.

4. Disconnect the fuel lines and the electrical connectors.

5. Remove the fuel pump from the fuel tank.

6. To install, reverse the removal procedures. Turn **ON** the ignition switch and check for fuel leaks.

Fuel Injection

Idle Speed Adjustment

NOTE: The idle mixture is electronically controlled by the fuel injection system and should not be adjusted.

INTEGRA

1. Start the engine and allow it to warm to normal operating temperatures; the cooling fan should turn **ON**.

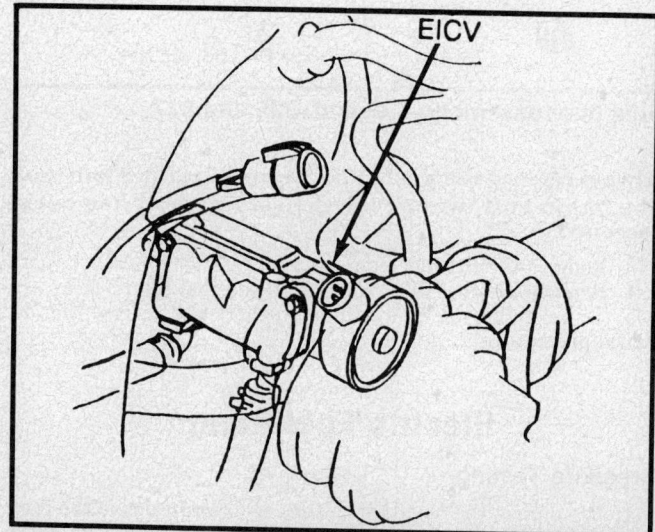

EICV connector—1590cc engine

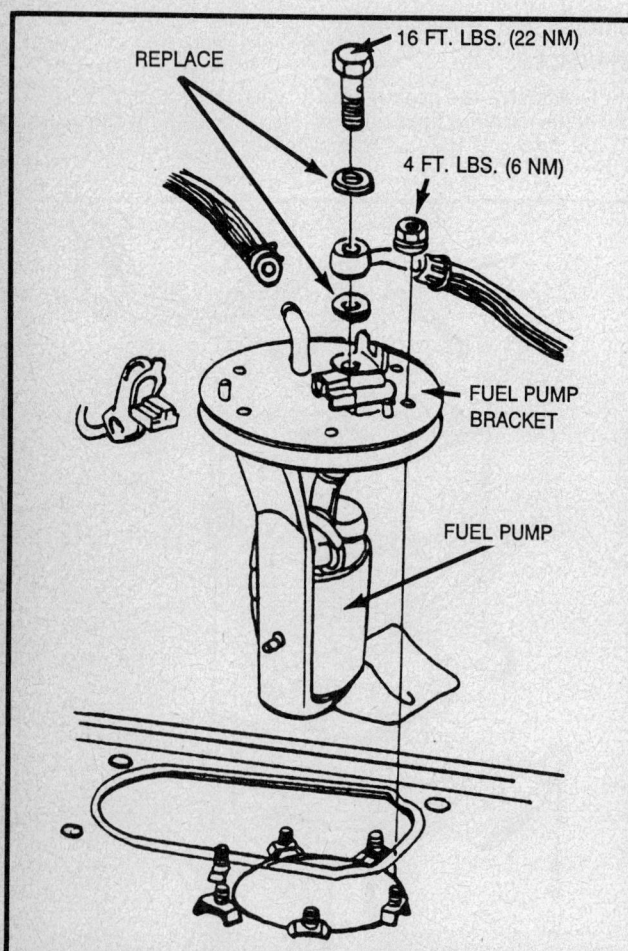

Fuel pump mounting—Legend, 825 and 827

View of the EACV connector—1590cc engine

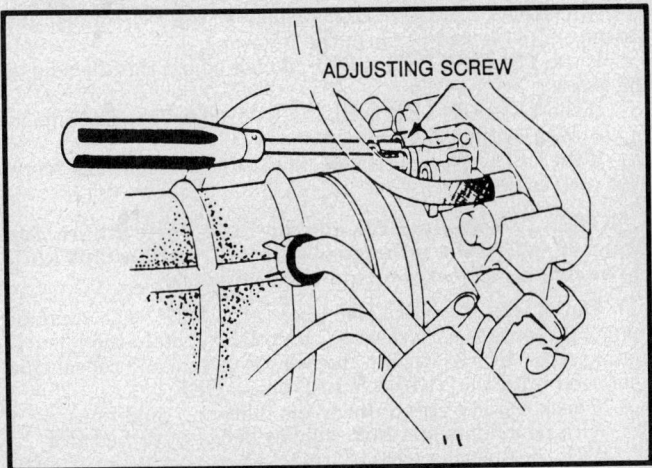

Idle speed adjusting screw—1590cc engine

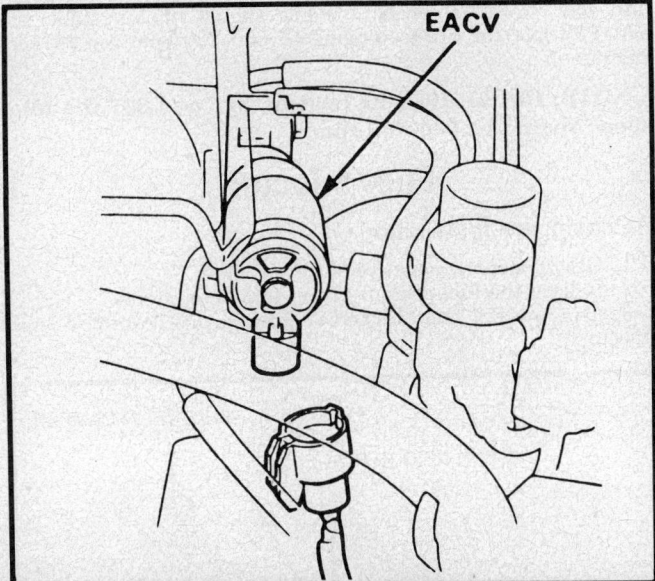

View of the EACV connector—1834cc engine

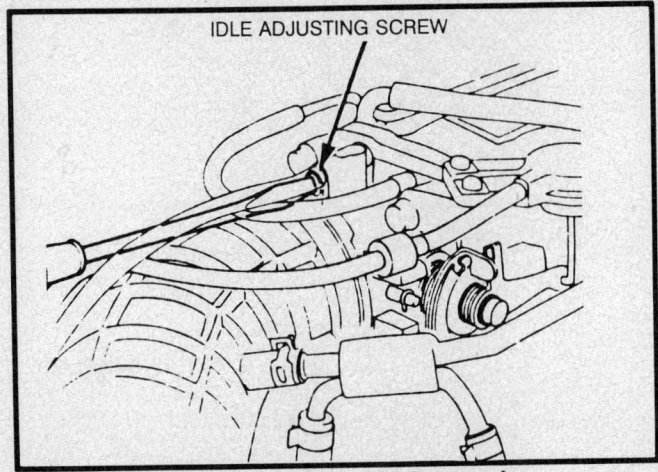

Idle speed adjusting screw—1834cc engine

2. Connect a tachometer to the engine as per the manufacturer's instructions.

3. With the engine idling, disconnect the connector at the **EICV** (1987) or the **EACV** (1988–91).

4. Check the idle speed with the headlights, heater blower, rear window defroster, cooling fan and the air conditioner turned **OFF**. Idle speed should be set to 500–650 rpm. If necessary, adjust the idle speed, by turning the idle adjusting screw on the top of the throttle body.

5. After the adjustment, turn the ignition switch **OFF** and reconnect the connector at the **EICV** or **EACV**.

6. Remove the **HAZARD** fuse in the main fuse/relay box at the battery terminal for at least 10 seconds to reset the ECU memory.

7. Start the engine and allow it to warm to normal operating temperatures; the cooling fan should turn **ON**.

8. Check the idle speed with the headlights, heater blower, rear window defroster, cooling fan and the air conditioner turned **OFF**. Idle speed should be 750–850 rpm for 1987 or 650–750 rpm for 1988–91.

9. Check the idle speed under the following conditions:
   a. With headlights and rear window defogger turned **ON**.
   b. With the air conditioner compressor turned **ON**.
   c. If equipped with an automatic transaxle, shift the transaxle into gear, except **P** or **N**, the idle should remain stable at:
     1987 manual transaxle—750–850 rpm.
     1988–89 manual transaxle—700–800 rpm.
     1988–91 automatic transaxle—650–750 rpm.

10. With the engine idling for a minute, with the fan switch turned on HI and the air conditioner turned **ON**, check the idle speed; it should be:
     1988–91 manual transaxle—700–800 rpm.
     1988–91 automatic transaxle—680–780 rpm.

LEGEND, 825 AND 827

1. Start the engine and allow it to warm to normal operating temperatures; the cooling fan should turn **ON**.

2. Connect a tachometer to the engine, as per the manufacturer's instructions.

3. Set the steering in the forward condition and check the idle speed with the headlights, heater blower, rear window defroster, cooling fan and the air conditioner turned **OFF**; the idle speed should be 670–770 rpm for 2494cc engine or 630–730 rpm for 2675cc engine.

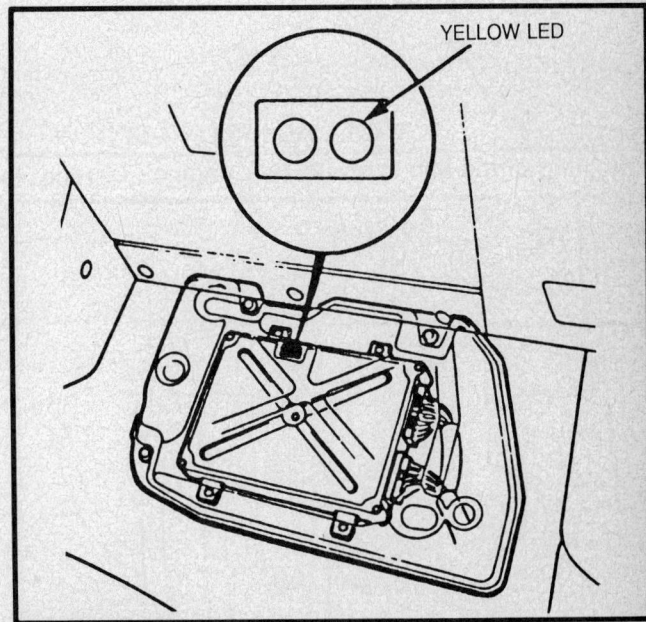

ECU yellow LED location—2494cc and 2675cc engines

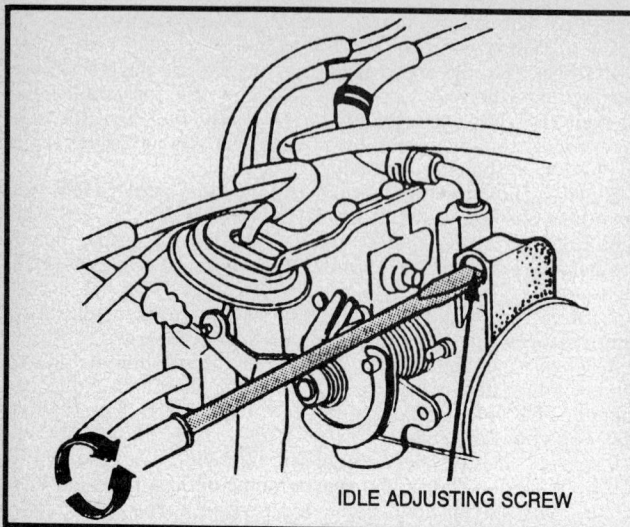

Adjusting of the idle screw 2494cc engine

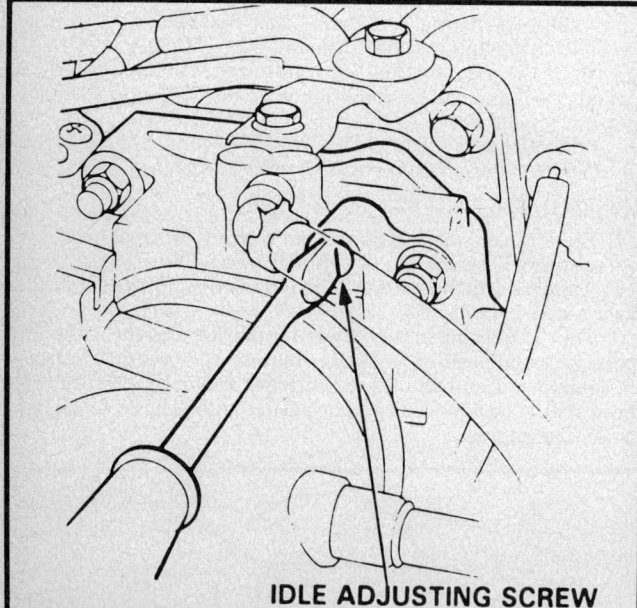

IDLE ADJUSTING SCREW

Adjusting of the idle screw 2675cc engine—Legend

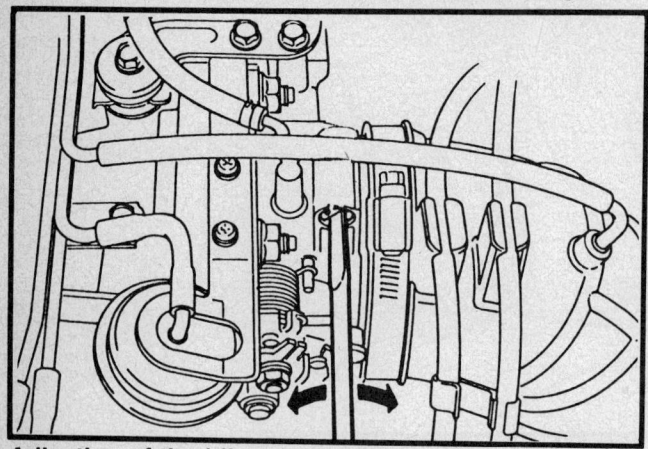

Adjusting of the idle screw 2675cc engine—825 and 827

4. Check the YELLOW LED display at the ECU under the passenger's seat and perform the following:

If the YELLOW LED is **OFF**, do not adjust the idle adjusting screw.

If the YELLOW LED is BLINKING, adjust the idle adjusting screw a ¼ turn clockwise.

If the YELLOW LED is **ON**, adjust the idle adjusting screw a ¼ turn counterclockwise.

NOTE: The yellow LED may be lit at early stages, for example, when the mileage is within 310 miles (500 km). However, no adjustments should be made.

5. Check that the YELLOW LED turns **OFF** after approximately 30 seconds. If it does not turn **OFF**, rotate the idle adjusting screw by a ¼ turn in the same direction and repeat this operation until the YELLOW LED turns **OFF**.

6. Check the idle speed under the following conditions:
With headlights and rear window defogger turned **ON**
With the steering wheel turning
With the air conditioner compressor turned **ON**
If equipped with an automatic transaxle, shift the transaxle into gear, except **P** or **N**, the idle should remain stable at 670–770 rpm for 2494cc engine or 630–730 rpm for 2675cc engine.

NOTE: On the 1990–91 Legend, 825 and 827 the idle speed should be 630–730 rpm.

Fuel Injector

Removal and Installation

1. Disconnect the negative battery cable.
2. Relieve the fuel pressure from the fuel system.
3. Disconnect the electrical connectors from the fuel injectors.

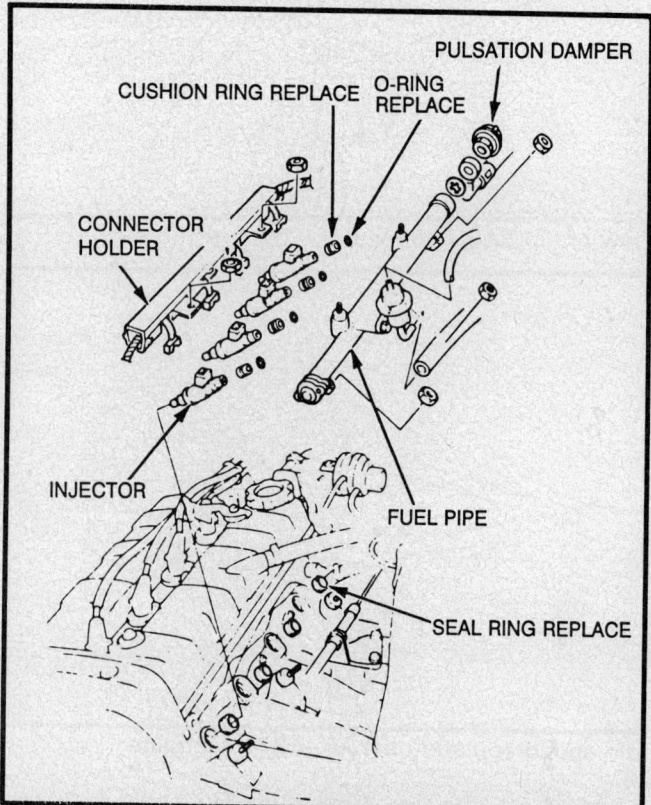

Removing the injector assembly—1590cc engine

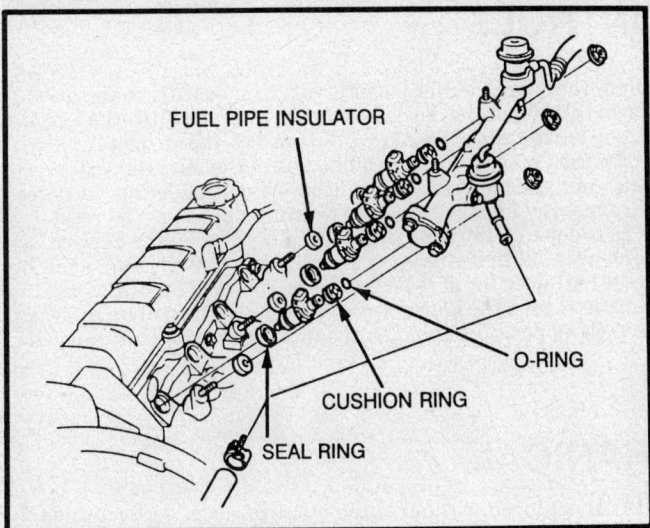

Removing the injector assembly—1834cc engine

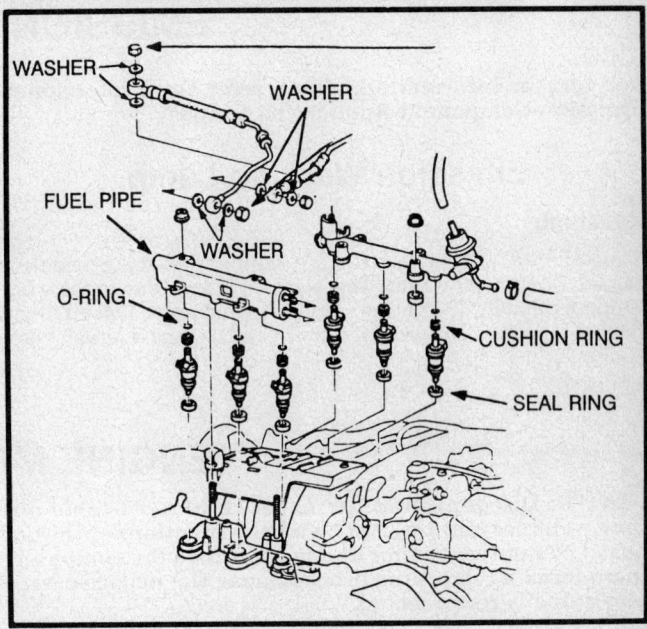

Removing the injector assembly—Legend, 825 and 827

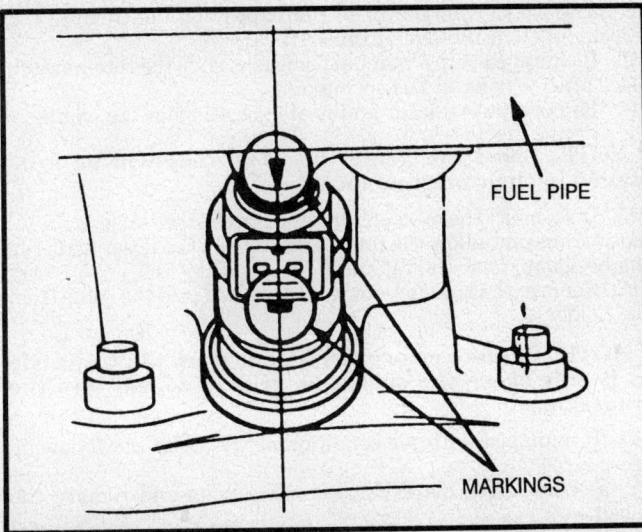

Aligning the fuel injector connector and the fuel pipe

4. Disconnect the vacuum hose and the fuel return hose from the fuel pressure regulator. Be sure to place a shop rag or towel over the hose and tube before disconnecting them.

5. Remove the fuel line and the pulsation damper, if equipped.

6. Remove the connector holder and loosen the retainer nuts of the fuel pipe assembly.

7. Disconnect the fuel pipe assembly and remove the fuel injectors from the intake manifold.

To install:

8. Slide the new cushion rings onto the injectors. Be sure to coat the new O-rings with clean engine oil and put them onto the injectors.

9. Insert the injectors into the fuel pipe first. Coat the new seal rings with clean engine oil and press them into the intake manifold.

10. Install the injectors and fuel pipe assembly into the intake manifold. To prevent damage to the O-rings, install the injectors in the fuel pipe first then install them into the intake manifold.

11. Align the center line on the connector with the mark on the fuel pipe.

12. Install and tighten the retainer nuts. Connect the vacuum hose and the fuel return hose to the pressure regulator.

13. Install the electrical connectors on the fuel injectors.

14. Turn the ignition switch **ON** but do not start the engine. After the fuel pump runs for approximately 2 seconds, the fuel pressure in the fuel line rises. Repeat this 2-3 times, then make the checks for for fuel leakage.

Injector Testing

1. If there is a driveability problem and the injectors are suspected, check the injectors by pulling the electrical connector off of them one at a time with the engine running.

2. If the idle speed drop is almost the same for each cylinder, the injectors are normal. If the idle speed or quality remains the same when a particular injector is disconnected, replace the injector and retest.

3. To check the resistance at the injectors, remove the electrical connector of the injector and measure the resistance between the 2 terminals of the injector. The resistance should be 1.5-2.5 ohms. If the resistance is not within specifications, replace the injector.

4. The injector should make a clicking sound as a sign that the injector is working. This can be checked by using a stethoscope to listen to each injector as the engine is idling.

EMISSION CONTROLS

For further information, please refer to "Professional Emission Component Application Guide".

Emission Warning Lamp

Resetting

Some 1988–91 Acura vehicles, are equipped with a Scheduled Service Due warning light. This warning light is due to come on at approximately 7500 miles to indicate that an oil and oil filter change is needed. However, if a shorter oil change interval is desired, there are 7 different intervals to choose from all the way down to 1500 miles. To choose a new interval, push the Service Reset button and the Arrow button for approximately 3 seconds, then push the Arrow button until the interval desired appears and then push the Set button. After completing the necessary maintenance service, the warning light must be reset.

In order to reset the maintenance light, open the Service Reset button. With the ignition switch in the **ON** position, hold the reset button in for at least 3 seconds. To verify that the reset is complete, turn the ignition switch to the **OFF** position and back to the **ON** position, the maintenance light should not turn ON.

ENGINE MECHANICAL

NOTE: Disconnecting the negative battery cable on some vehicles may interfere with the functions of the on board computer systems and may require the computer to undergo a relearning process, once the negative battery cable is reconnected.

Engine Assembly

Removal and Installation

1987–89 INTEGRA

1. Apply the parking brake and place blocks behind the rear wheels. Raise and safely support the vehicle. Remove the engine and wheel well splash shields.
2. Disconnect the battery cables from the battery; negative cable first. Remove the battery and the battery tray from the engine compartment, if necessary.
3. Using a scratch awl, scribe a line where the hood brackets meet the inside of the hood; this will help realign the hood during the installation. Disconnect and remove the washer fluid tube(s). Remove the hood-to-hinge bolts and the hood.
4. Drain the oil from the engine, the coolant from the radiator and the fluid from the transaxle.

NOTE: Removal of the filler plug or radiator cap will speed the draining process.

5. Remove the following items:
   a. The air flow tube and the air intake duct.
   b. The throttle control cable and/or clutch cable.
   c. The coil wire and ignition primary leads.
   d. The cruise control cable.
6. Relieve the fuel pressure by slowly loosening the service bolt on the top of the fuel filter about a turn.

NOTE: Place a rag under the filter during this procedure to prevent fuel from spilling onto the engine.

7. Disconnect the fuel hose from the fuel filter. Remove the special nut and the fuel hose.
8. Label and disconnect the following items:
   a. The engine compartment sub-harness connector.
   b. The engine secondary cable.
   c. The brake booster vacuum hose.
9. Disconnect the control box connectors. Remove the control boxes from the brackets and allow it hang next to the engine.
10. Loosen the throttle cable locknut and adjusting nut, then, slip the cable end out of the throttle bracket and remove it.
11. Remove the power steering pump-to-bracket bolts and V-belt, then, without disconnecting the hose, move the pump aside.

12. If equipped with an automatic transaxle, perform the following procedures:
    a. Remove the center console.
    b. Move the shift lever to the **R** position and remove the lock pin from the end of the shift cable.
13. If equipped with a manual transaxle, slide the retainer into place after driving in the spring pin.
14. Remove the radiator and heater hoses from the engine.

NOTE: Label the heater hoses so they will be reinstalled in their original locations.

15. Disconnect the oil cooler hoses from the transaxle for automatic transaxle, allow the fluid to drain from the hoses and prop the hoses up, near the radiator.
16. Remove the speedometer cable clip and pull the cable from the holder.

NOTE: Do not remove the holder from the transaxle as it may cause the speedometer gear to fall into the transaxle.

17. If equipped with air conditioning, perform the following procedures:
    a. Loosen the drive belt adjusting bolts and remove the belt.
    b. Remove the compressor-to-bracket bolts and wire it aside onto the front beam.

NOTE: Do not disconnect the air conditioning freon lines. The compressor can be moved without discharging the system.

    c. Remove the lower compressor mounting bracket.
18. Disconnect the alternator wiring harness connector. Remove the adjusting bolt and the alternator belt. Remove the mount bolt, bracket and the alternator.
19.. Using a ball joint puller, separate the ball joint from the front hub.
20. Slowly, lower the floor jack to lower the control arm. Using a small prybar, pry out the inboard CV-joint approximately 13mm in order to release the spring clip from the groove in the differential. Pull the steering knuckle assembly outward. Pull the halfshaft from the transaxle case.
21. Attach an lifting sling to the engine block and raise the engine, to remove the slack from the chain.
22. Remove the rear transaxle mount and the bolts from the front transaxle mount and the engine side mount.
23. Check that the engine and transaxle are free from any hoses or electrical connectors.
24. Slowly raise the engine up and out of the vehicle.
To install:
25. Slowly lower the engine into the vehicle.

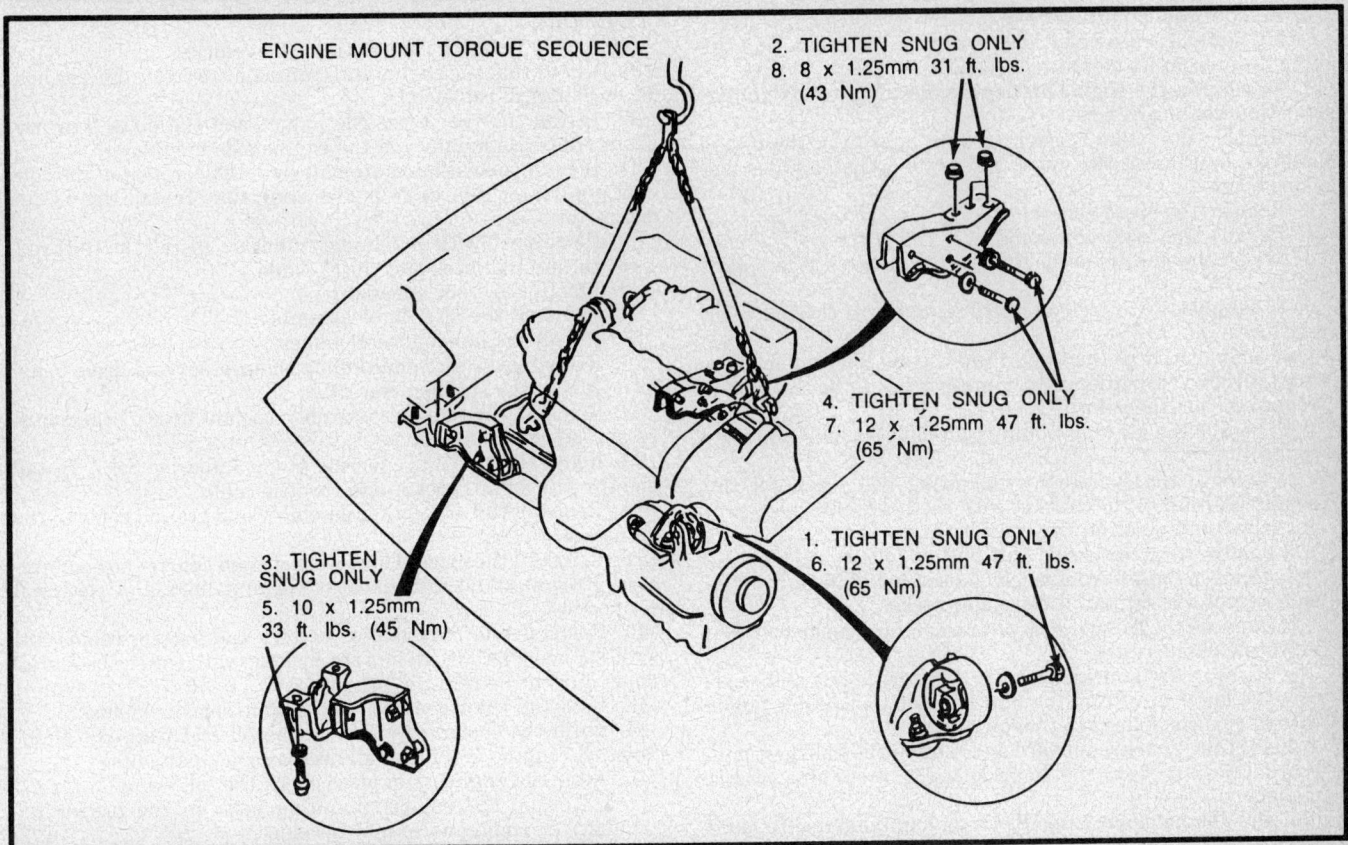

ENGINE MOUNT TORQUE SEQUENCE

2. TIGHTEN SNUG ONLY
8. 8 x 1.25mm 31 ft. lbs.
(43 Nm)

4. TIGHTEN SNUG ONLY
7. 12 x 1.25mm 47 ft. lbs.
(65 Nm)

1. TIGHTEN SNUG ONLY
6. 12 x 1.25mm 47 ft. lbs.
(65 Nm)

3. TIGHTEN SNUG ONLY
5. 10 x 1.25mm 33 ft. lbs. (45 Nm)

View of the engine mount torquing sequence—1987– 89 Integra

26. Check that the engine and transaxle are free from any hoses or electrical connectors.

27. Install the rear transaxle mount and the bolts from the front transaxle mount and the engine side mount.

28. Install the halfshaft assemblies.

29. Reinstall the alternator assembly.

30. Reinstall the air conditioning compressor and drive belts.

31. Install the speedometer cable.

32. Reinstall the radiator assembly, coolant hoses, heater hoses and oil cooler lines.

33. Reinstall the shift lever, cable and center console assembly, if equipped.

34. Reinstall the power steering pump and drive belts. Install the throttle cable bracket and throttle cable.

35. Reinstall the control box brackets and control box connectors. Reconnect all disconnected vacuum lines and electrical connectors.

36. Reinstall the battery box, battery and battery cables. Reinstall the hood, be sure to line the hood up with the scribe marks made during the removal procedure.

37. Install the wheel well and engine splash shields.

38. Refill the coolant system, engine oil and transaxle fluid. Start the engine and make all necessary adjustments.

39. Pay special attention to the following:

   a. Torque the engine mounting bolts in the proper sequence or engine noise may develop.

   b. Be sure the spring clip on the end of each halfshaft clicks into the differential.

NOTE: Always use new spring clips on installation.

   c. Bleed the air from the cooling system.
   d. Adjust the belt tension and the throttle cable tension.
   e. Check the clutch pedal free-play.

1990-91 INTEGRA

1. Apply the parking brake and place blocks behind the rear wheels. Raise and safely support the vehicle. Remove the engine and wheel well splash shields.

2. Disconnect the battery cables from the battery; negative cable first. Remove the battery and the battery tray from the engine compartment, if necessary.

3. Using a scratch awl, scribe a line where the hood brackets meet the inside of the hood; this will help realign the hood during the installation. Disconnect and remove the washer fluid tubes. Remove the hood-to-hinge bolts and the hood.

4. Drain the oil from the engine, the coolant from the radiator and the fluid from the transaxle.

NOTE: Removal of the filler plug or radiator cap will speed the draining process.

5. The air flow tube and the air intake duct.

6. Relieve the fuel pressure. Remove the fuel feed hose from the fuel filter. Be sure to place a shop rag or towel under the fuel hose to prevent the fuel from spraying on the engine.

7. Disconnect the charcoal canister hose from the throttle body. Disconnect the 2 connectors and remove the control bracket from the firewall. Do not remove the vacuum lines from the intake manifold.

8. Remove the ground cable from the transaxle. Disconnect the 2 distributor electrical connectors and remove the distributor. Be sure to make alignment marks on the distributor to help in the installation procedure.

9. Remove the throttle cable by loosening the locknut, then slip the cable end out of the throttle bracket and accelerator linkage. Take care not to bend the cable when removing it. Do not use pliers to remove the cable from the linkage. Always replaced a kinked cable with a new one.

10. Remove the mounting bolts and the V-belt for the power steering pump, then without disconnecting the hoses, pull the pump away from its mounting bracket.

11. Disconnect the engine harness connectors and clamp. Remove the fuel return hose.

12. Remove the brake booster vacuum hose from the intake manifold. Disconnect the upper and lower radiator hoses and heater hoses.

13. Remove the speed sensor.

14. Remove the radiator assembly.

15. If not already removed, remove the driver's side splash shield.

16. If equipped with air conditioning, perform the following procedures:

   a. Only discharge the freon from the air conditioning system, if the air conditioning compressor has to be completely removed from the vehicle.

   b. Loosen the air conditioning belt adjusting bolt and idler pulley nut.

   c. Remove the compressor mounting bolt, then lift the compressor out of the bracket with the hoses attached, support the compressor on the front beam.

17. Remove the driver's side halfshaft as follows:

   a. Remove the left front wheel. Raise the locking tab on the spindle nut and remove it a suitable socket.

   b. Remove the damper fork nut and damper pinch bolt. Remove the damper fork.

   c. Remove the knuckle to lower arm castle nut and separate the lower arm from the knuckle using a suitable puller with the pawls applied to the lower arm.

   d. Pull the knuckle outward and remove the halfshaft outboard CV-joint from the knuckle using a suitable plastic mallet.

   e. Pry the halfshaft assembly with a suitable tool to force the set ring at the halfshaft end past the groove.

   f. Pull the inboard CV-joint and remove the halfshaft and CV-joint out of the intermediate shaft.

NOTE: Do not pull on the driveshaft, as the CV-joint may come apart. Use care when prying out the assembly and pull it straight to avoid damaging the intermediate shaft seals.

18. Disconnect the alternator wiring harness connector. Remove the adjusting bolt and the alternator belt. Remove the mount bolt, bracket and the alternator.

19. Remove the front exhaust pipe assembly.

20. If equipped with a manual transaxle, perform the following procedures:

   a. Remove the clutch cable. Take care not to bend the cable when removing it. Do not use pliers to remove the cable from the linkage. Always replaced a kinked cable with a new one.

   b. Remove the shift lever torque rod and shift rod.

21. If equipped with an automatic transaxle, remove the torque converter cover. Remove the cable holder, cotter pin and control pin, then remove the shift control cable. Take care not to bend the cable when removing it. Do not use pliers to remove the cable from the linkage. Always replaced a kinked cable with a new one.

22. Attach a suitable lifting device to the engine. Raise the engine to remove all the slack from the lifting device.

23. Remove the rear transaxle mount and rear transmission mounting bracket.

24. Remove the front transaxle mount. Remove the side transaxle mounting bracket. Remove the side engine mount.

25. Check that the engine/transaxle assembly is completely free of all vacuum hoses and electrical wires.

26. Slowly raise the engine approximately 6 inches.

27. Raise the engine/transaxle assembly all the way and remove it from the vehicle. Place the engine on a suitable engine stand assembly.

To install:

28. Slowly lower the engine into the vehicle.

29. Check that the engine and transaxle are free from any hoses or electrical connectors.

30. Install the rear transaxle mount and the bolts from the front transaxle mount and the engine side mount.

31. If equipped with an automatic transaxle, reinstall the control pin, cotter pin, cable holder and cable. Install the torque converter cover.

32. If equipped with an manual transaxle, install the shift rod, shift torque rod lever and clutch cable.

33. Install the front exhaust pipe.

34. Reinstall the alternator assembly.

35. Install the halfshaft assemblies.

36. Reinstall the air conditioning compressor and drive belts.

37. Install the speedometer cable.

38. Reinstall the radiator assembly, coolant hoses, heater hoses and oil cooler lines.

39. Reinstall the power steering pump and drive belts. Install the throttle cable bracket and throttle cable.

40. Reinstall the distributor assembly and ground cable to the transaxle.

41. Reinstall the control box brackets and control box connectors. Reconnect all disconnected vacuum lines and electrical connectors.

42. Reinstall the battery box, battery and battery cables. Install the hood, be sure to line the hood up with the scribe marks made during the removal procedure.

43. Reinstall the wheel well and engine splash shields.

44. Refill the coolant system, engine oil and transaxle fluid. Start the engine and make all necessary adjustments.

45. After the engine is in place check the following:

   a. Torque the engine mounting bolts in the proper sequence or engine noise may develop.

   b. Be sure the spring clip on the end of each halfshaft clicks into the differential.

NOTE: Always use new spring clips on installation.

   c. Bleed the air from the cooling system.

   d. Adjust the belt(s) tension and the throttle cable tension.

   e. Check the clutch pedal free-play.

LEGEND, 825 AND 827

1. Apply the parking brake and place blocks behind the rear wheels. Raise and safely support the vehicle.

2. Disconnect both battery cables from the battery. Remove the battery and the battery tray from the engine compartment.

3. Position the hood in the vertical position by removing the open stay mounting bolt on the hood side and fitting it to the mounting hole near the hinge.

4. Remove the air intake tube, air cleaner and resonator tube as an assembly.

5. Remove the splash guard from under the engine.

6. Remove the oil filler cap and drain the engine oil.

NOTE: When replacing the drain plug be sure to use a new washer.

7. Remove the radiator cap, then open the radiator drain petcock and drain the coolant from the radiator.

8. Remove the transaxle filler plug, then remove the drain plug and drain the transaxle.

9. Disconnect the pressure switch wire from the oil filter case.

10. Disconnect the both water hoses from the engine oil cooler.

11. Remove the drain bolt from the oil filter case to drain the oil. Remove the oil filter case from the engine block.

12. Disconnect the upper and lower radiator hoses from the radiator.

13. If equipped with an automatic transaxle, disconnect cooler hose from the bottom of the radiator.

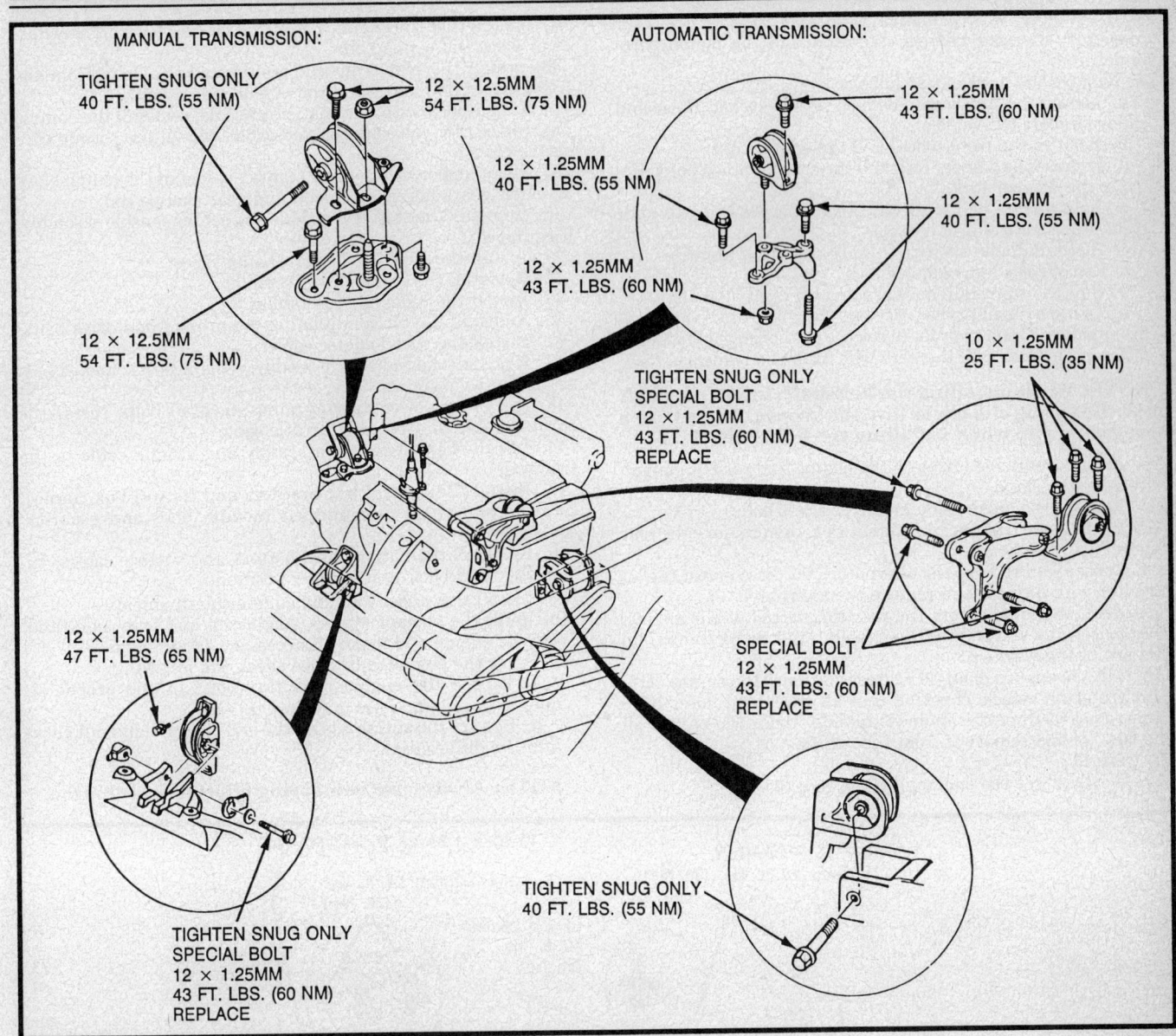

MANUAL TRANSMISSION:

TIGHTEN SNUG ONLY
40 FT. LBS. (55 NM)

12 × 12.5MM
54 FT. LBS. (75 NM)

12 × 1.25MM
40 FT. LBS. (55 NM)

12 × 12.5MM
54 FT. LBS. (75 NM)

12 × 1.25MM
43 FT. LBS. (60 NM)

AUTOMATIC TRANSMISSION:

12 × 1.25MM
43 FT. LBS. (60 NM)

12 × 1.25MM
40 FT. LBS. (55 NM)

TIGHTEN SNUG ONLY
SPECIAL BOLT
12 × 1.25MM
43 FT. LBS. (60 NM)
REPLACE

10 × 1.25MM
25 FT. LBS. (35 NM)

SPECIAL BOLT
12 × 1.25MM
43 FT. LBS. (60 NM)
REPLACE

12 × 1.25MM
47 FT. LBS. (65 NM)

TIGHTEN SNUG ONLY
SPECIAL BOLT
12 × 1.25MM
43 FT. LBS. (60 NM)
REPLACE

TIGHTEN SNUG ONLY
40 FT. LBS. (55 NM)

View of the engine mount torquing sequence—1990– 91 Integra

14. Disconnect the following engine sub-harness connectors from the body side:
   a. Four right side connectors and clamp
   b. Both left side main fuse connectors
   c. Coil wire, primary lead connectors and the condenser connector.
   d. Both ground cables from the cylinder head and the transaxle.
15. Disconnect the connector from the power steering pump and both hoses. Disconnect the hose from the cruise control actuator and the hose from the power brake booster.
16. Using the following procedures relieve the fuel system pressure. Place a shop rag over the fuel filter to absorb any gasoline which may be sprayed on the engine while relieving the pressure. Slowly loosen the service bolt approximately one full turn. This will relieve any pressure in the system. Using a new sealing washer, tighten the service bolt.
17. Disconnect the fuel return hose from the pressure regulator. Remove the banjo nut and the fuel hose.

18. Disconnect the throttle cable from the throttle body and the emission tubes from the control box from the connection stay.
19. Remove the speed sensor from the transaxle.
20. Remove the air conditioning compressor as follows:
   a. Remove the compressor clutch lead wire.
   b. Loosen the belt adjusting bolt.

NOTE: Do not remove the air conditioning hoses. The air conditioning compressor can be moved without discharging the air conditioning system.

   c. Remove the compressor mounting bolts, then lift the compressor out of the bracket with the hoses attached and hang it to the front bulkhead with a piece of wire.
21. Remove the center console. Place the shift lever in **R**, then remove the lock pin from the end of the shift cable. Remove the exhaust pipe from the front and rear manifolds.
22. If equipped with an automatic transaxle, disconnect the control wire from the selector side of the transaxle.

23. If equipped with a manual transaxle, remove the gear change rod, the gear change extension and the clutch slave cylinder.

24. Remove the halfshaft as follows:

a. Loosen the 32mm spindle nuts with a socket. Raise and safely support the vehicle.

b. Remove the front wheel and the spindle nut.

c. Remove the damper fork and the damper pinch bolts. Remove the damper fork.

d. Remove the ball joint bolt and separate the ball joint from lower control arm control.

e. Disconnect the tie rods from the steering knuckles.

f. Remove the sway bar bolts.

g. Pull the front hub outward and off the halfshaft.

h. Using a small prybar, pry out the inboard CV-joint approximately 13mm in order to release the spring clip from the differential, then pull the halfshaft from the transaxle case.

NOTE: When installing the halfshaft, insert the shaft until the spring clip clicks into the groove. Always use a new spring clip when installing the halfshaft.

25. Attach a suitable lifting to the engine and raise it enough to remove the slack.

26. Remove the engine side mount bracket bolts.

27. Remove the front engine mount nut, then remove the rear engine mount nut.

28. Loosen and remove the alternator belt. Disconnect the alternator wire harness and remove the alternator.

29. Remove the bolt from the rear torque rod at the engine, then loosen the bolt in the frame mount and swing the rod up and out of the way.

30. Tilt the engine about 30 degrees and raise the engine carefully from the vehicle checking that all wires and hoses have been removed from the engine/transaxle. Raise the engine all the way up and remove it from the vehicle.

To install:

31. Slowly lower the engine into the vehicle.

32. Check that the engine and transaxle are free from any hoses or electrical connectors.

33. Install the rear transaxle mount and the bolts from the front transaxle mount and the engine side mount.

34. If equipped with automatic transaxle, reinstall the control pin, cotter pin, cable holder and cable. Intsall the torque converter cover.

35. If equipped with manual transaxle, install the clutch slave cylinder, gear change extension and gear change rod.

36. Reinstall the shift lever, cable and center console assembly, if equipped.

37. Install the front and rear exhaust pipes.

38. Reinstall the alternator assembly.

39. Install the halfshaft assemblies.

40. Reinstall the air conditioning compressor and drive belts.

41. Install the speedometer cable.

42. Reinstall the radiator assembly, coolant hoses, heater hoses and oil cooler lines.

43. Install the power steering pump and drive belts. Install the throttle cable bracket and throttle cable.

44. Install the distributor assembly and ground cable to the transaxle.

45. Install the control box brackets and control box connectors. Reconnect all disconnected vacuum lines and electrical connectors.

46. Reinstall the battery box, battery and battery cables. Install the hood back to its proper position.

47. Install the wheel well and engine splash shields.

48. Refill the coolant system, engine oil and transaxle fluid. Start the engine and make all necessary adjustments.

49. After the engine is in place check the following:

a. Torque the engine mounting bolts in the proper sequence or engine noise may develop.

b. Be sure the spring clip on the end of each halfshaft clicks into the differential.

NOTE: Always use new spring clips on installation.

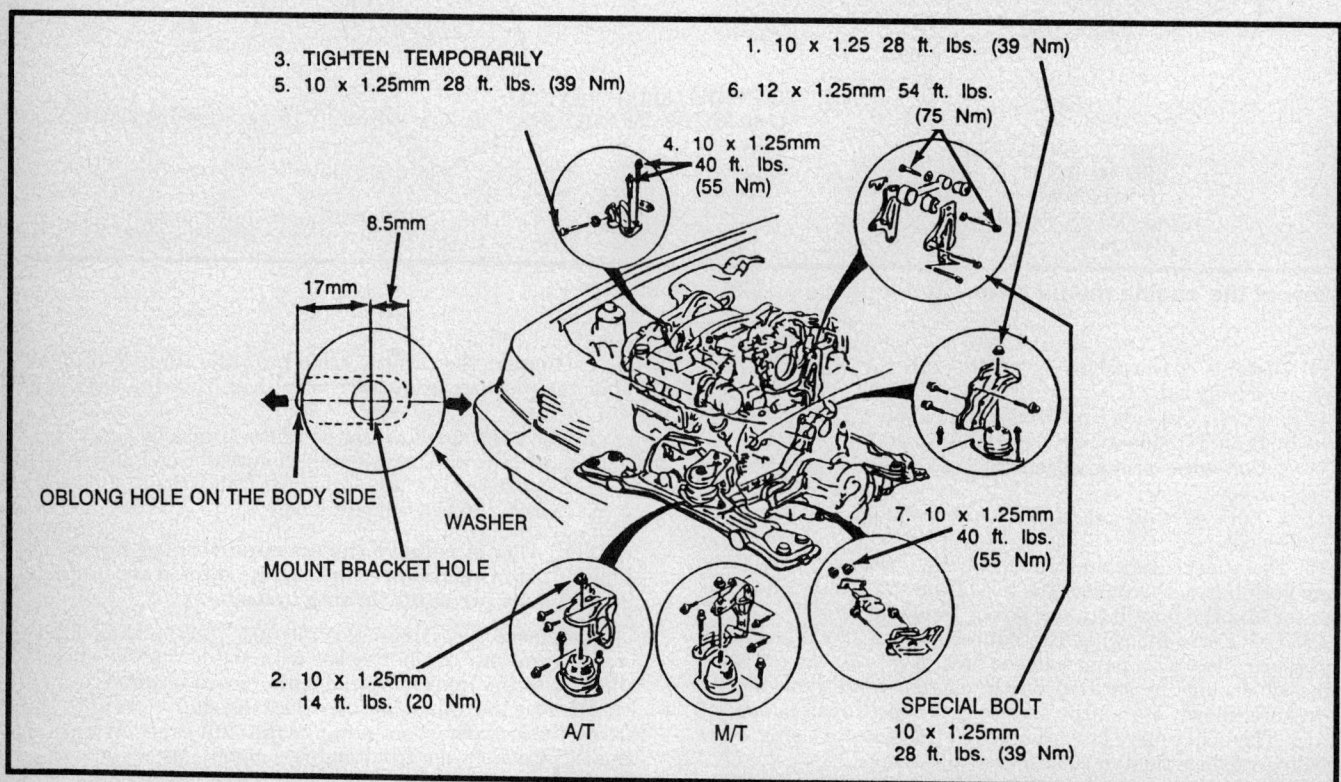

View of the engine mount torquing sequence — Legend, 825 and 827

c. Bleed the air from the cooling system.
d. Adjust the belt(s) tension and the throttle cable tension.
e. Check the clutch pedal free-play.

Cylinder Head

Removal and Installation

1987–89 INTEGRA

NOTE: Cylinder head temperature must be below 100°F.

Before removing the cylinder head check the following:
Inspect the timing belt.
Turn the flywheel so the No. 1 cylinder is at TDC.
Mark all emission hoses before disconnecting them.
1. Disconnect the negative battery cable.
2. Drain the cooling system.
3. Remove the air cleaner:
   a. Remove the air cleaner cover and filter.
   b. Disconnect the hot/cold air intake ducts and remove the air chamber hose.
   c. Remove the air cleaner.

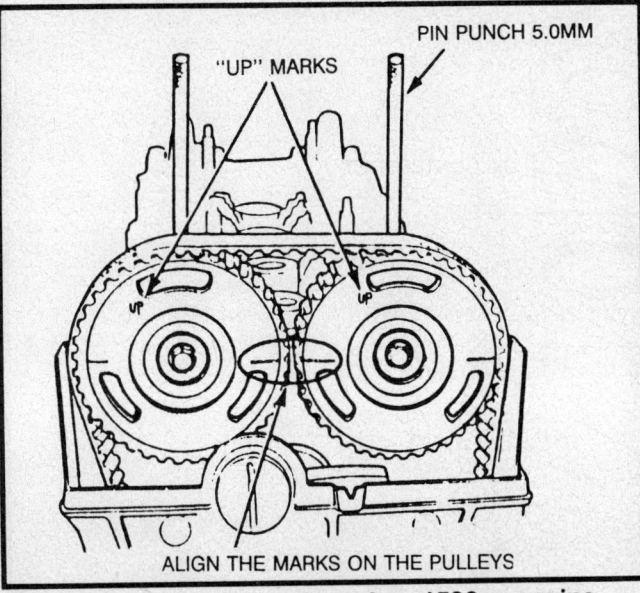

Alignment of the camshaft marks—1590cc engine

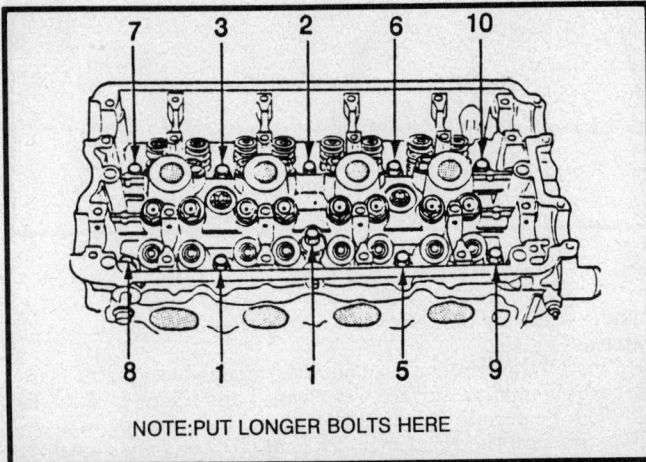

Cylinder head torque sequence—1987 1590cc engine

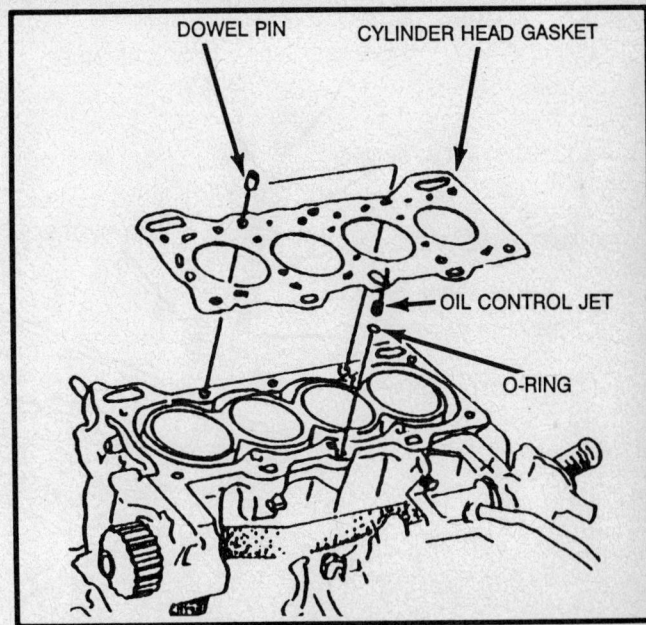

Dowel pin and oil jet control location—1590cc engine

4. Relieve the fuel pressure using the following procedure:
   a. Slowly loosen the service bolt on the top of the fuel filter about a turn.

NOTE: Place a rag under the filter during this procedure to prevent fuel from spilling onto the engine.

   b. Disconnect the fuel return hose from the pressure regulator. Remove the special nut and the fuel hose.
5. Remove the brake booster vacuum tube from the intake manifold.
6. Remove the engine ground wire from the valve cover. Disconnect the throttle cable from the throttle body.
7. Disconnect the spark plug wires from the spark plugs and remove the distributor assembly.
8. Disconnect the hoses from the charcoal canister and from the No. 1 control box at the tubing manifold.
9. If equipped with air conditioning, disconnect the idle control solenoid hoses.
10. Disconnect the upper radiator heater and bypass hoses.
11. Disconnect the engine sub harness connectors and the following couplers from the cylinder head and the intake manifold:
    a. The 4 injector couplers.
    b. The TA sensor connector.
    c. The ground connector.
    d. The TW sensor connector.
    e. The throttle sensor connector.
    f. The crankshaft angle sensor coupler.
    g. The EAVC connector, if equipped.
    h. The CYL sensor connector, if equipped.
12. Remove the thermostat housing-to-intake manifold hose.
13. Disconnect the oxygen sensor coupler.
14. Remove the exhaust manifold bracket, the manifold bolts and the manifold.
15. Remove the bolts from the intake manifold and bracket.
16. Disconnect the breather chamber-to-intake manifold hose.
17. Remove the valve and upper timing belt covers.
18. Loosen the timing belt tensioner adjustment bolt and remove the belt.
19. Remove the lower timing belt cover bolts, the camshaft holder bolts, the camshaft holders, the camshafts and the rocker arms.
20. Remove the cylinder head bolts in the reverse order given in the head bolt torque sequence.

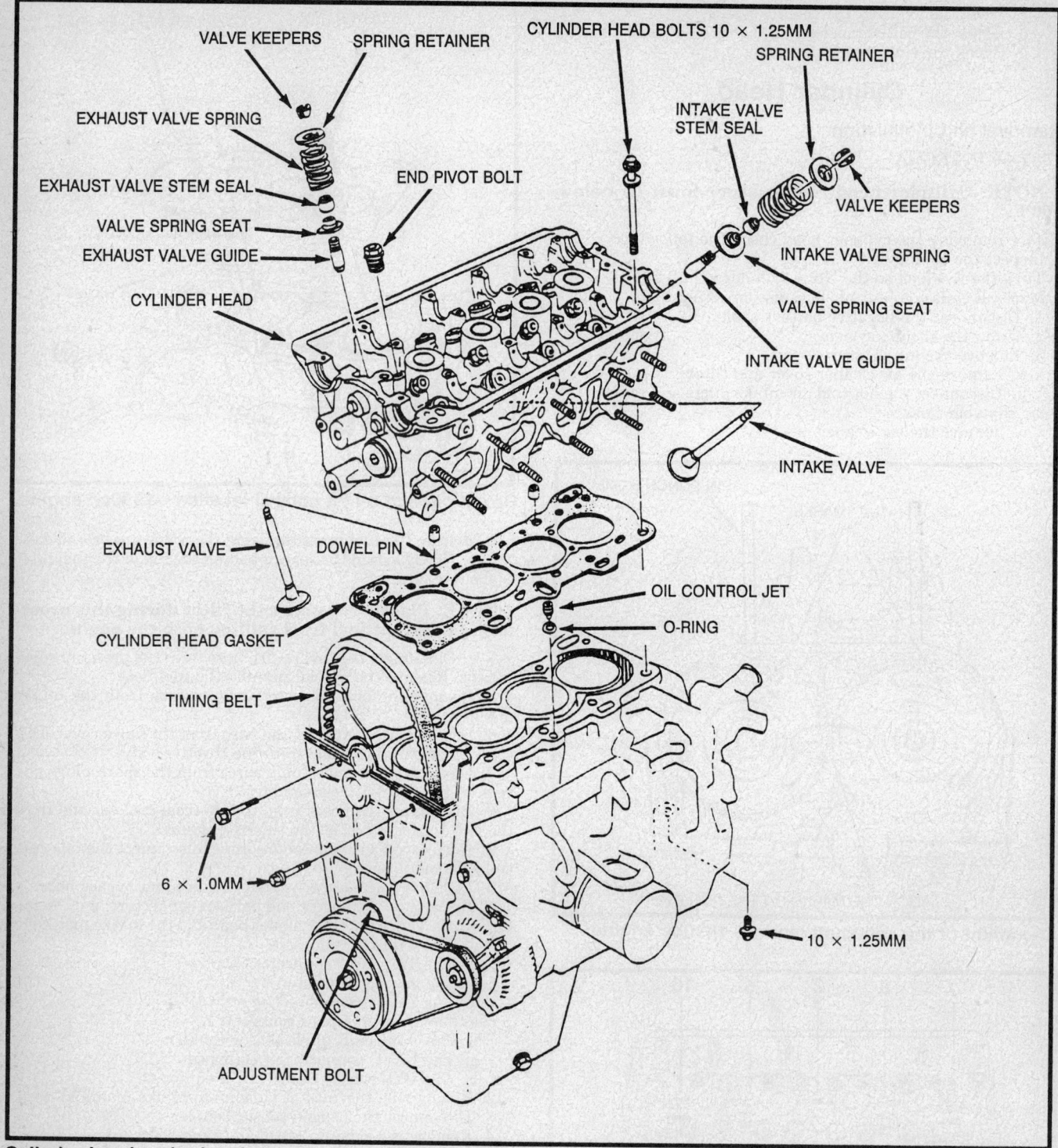

Cylinder head and related components—1590cc engine

Labels (from the diagram):
- VALVE KEEPERS
- SPRING RETAINER
- CYLINDER HEAD BOLTS 10 × 1.25MM
- SPRING RETAINER
- EXHAUST VALVE SPRING
- INTAKE VALVE STEM SEAL
- EXHAUST VALVE STEM SEAL
- END PIVOT BOLT
- VALVE KEEPERS
- VALVE SPRING SEAT
- EXHAUST VALVE GUIDE
- INTAKE VALVE SPRING
- CYLINDER HEAD
- VALVE SPRING SEAT
- INTAKE VALVE GUIDE
- INTAKE VALVE
- EXHAUST VALVE
- DOWEL PIN
- OIL CONTROL JET
- CYLINDER HEAD GASKET
- O-RING
- TIMING BELT
- 6 × 1.0MM
- 10 × 1.25MM
- ADJUSTMENT BOLT

NOTE: Unscrew the bolts ⅓ of a turn each time and repeat the sequence to prevent cylinder head warpage.

21. Carefully, remove the intake manifold from the cylinder head and the cylinder head from the engine.
22. Clean the gasket mounting surfaces.

To install:
23. Use new gaskets and install the intake manifold onto the cylinder head and tighten the bolts in a criss-cross pattern in 2–3 steps.
24. Install the cylinder head onto the engine block, after making sure the mating surface was cleaned and a new gasket was installed. Be sure to pay attention to the following points:
    a. Be sure the No. 1 cylinder is at TDC and the camshaft pulleys UP mark is on the top before positioning the head in place.

b. The cylinder head dowel pins and oil control jet must be aligned.

c. Torque the cylinder head bolts in 2 progressive steps and in the proper sequence. First to 22 ft. lbs. (30 Nm), in sequence, then to 48 ft. lbs. (67 Nm), in the same sequence.

d. Use the longer bolt in the No. 8 for 1987 or No. 9 for 1988–89 position.

25. Make sure the keyways on the camshafts are facing up. The valve locknuts should be loosened and the adjusting screw back off before installation. Replace the rocker arms in their original position.

26. Place the rocker arms on the pivot bolts and the valve stems.

27. Install the camshafts and the camshaft seals with the open side, spring facing upward.

28. Be sure to note the I and E marks that are stamped on the camshaft holders. Do not apply oil to the holder mating surface of the camshaft seals.

29. Apply a liquid gasket to the head of the mating surfaces of the No. 1 and No. 6 camshaft holders then install them, along with No. 2, 3, 4 and 5. Tighten the holders temporarily and make sure the rocker arms are properly positioned on the valve stems.

30. Press in the camshaft seal securely with a suitable seal driver.

31. Tighten each bolt 2 turns at a time to insure that the rockers do not bind on the valves.

32. Install the keys into their groves in the camshafts. To set the No. 1 piston at TDC, align the holes on the camshaft witht he holes in the No. 1 camshaft holders and drive 5.0mm pin punches into the holes.

33. Push the camshaft pulleys onto the camshafts, then torque the retaining bolts to 27 ft. lbs. (38 Nm).

34. Install the timing belt and adjust the timing belt tensioner bolt. Install the lower timing belt cover and bolts.

35. Install the upper timing belt covers and valve covers.

36. Reconnect the breather chamber-to-intake manifold hose.

37. Install the exhaust manifold, the manifold bolts and the manifold bracket.

38. Reconnect all disconnected electrical connections and vacuum lines.

39. Reconnect the upper radiator hose and bypass hoses.

40. Reinstall the distributor assembly and the spark plug wires to the spark plugs.

41. Install the engine ground wire from the valve cover. Reconnect the throttle cable from the throttle body.

42. Reinstall the air cleaner assembly and duct work that goes along with it. Reconnect the negative battery cable.

43. After installation, check to see that all hoses and wires are installed correctly.

44. Refill the coolant system.

45. Adjust the valve clearance. Make all other necessary adjustments

NOTE: It is recommended that after completing the cylinder head removal and installation the engine oil should be changed.

1990–91 INTEGRA

NOTE: Cylinder head temperature must be below 100°F.

Before removing the cylinder head check the following:
Inspect the timing belt.
Turn the flywheel so the No. 1 cylinder is at TDC.
Mark all emission hoses before disconnecting them.
1. Disconnect the negative battery cable.
2. Drain the cooling system.
3. Remove the air cleaner:
a. Remove the air cleaner cover and filter.

b. Disconnect the hot/cold air intake ducts and remove the air chamber hose.

c. Remove the air cleaner.

4. Relieve the fuel pressure by slowly loosen the service bolt on the top of the fuel filter about a turn.

NOTE: Place a rag under the filter during this procedure to prevent fuel from spilling onto the engine.

5. Disconnect the fuel feed line. Remove the vacuum hose, breather hose and air intake hose.

6. Remove the water bypass hose from cylinder head. Remove the charcoal canister hose from the throttle body.

7. Remove the brake booster vacuum hose from the intake manifold. Remove the fuel return hose. Remove the PCV hose.

8. Remove the throttle cable from the throttle body. Take care not to bend the cable when removing it. Do not use pliers to remove the cable from the linkage. Always replaced a kinked cable with a new one.

9. Disconnect the ignition coil connector, TDC and Crankshaft/Cylinder sensor connector from the distributor.

10. Remove and tag the spark plug wirers.

11. Remove the emission control bracket but do not remove the emission hoses.

12. Disconnect the 3 engine harness connectors on the left side of the engine compartment.

13. Disconnect the engine sub-harness connectors from the cylinder head and intake manifold. The connectors are as follows:
a. Four injector connectors.
b. TA sensor connector.
c. Throttle angle sensor connector.
d. EGR valve lift sensor; automatic transaxle only.
e. Ground cable terminal.
f. TW sensor ground.
g. Coolant temperature gauge sender terminal.
h. Oxygen sensor terminal.
i. EACV connector.

14. Remove the upper radiator hose and heater inlet hose from the cylinder head.

15. Remove the power steering belt and power steering pump. Do not disconnect the hoses from the pump.

16. Raise and safely support the vehicle.

17. Remove the left front wheel and then remove the left splash shield.

18. Remove the intake manifold bracket bolts and remove the exhaust manifold upper shroud.

19. Remove the exhaust manifold bracket. Remove front exhaust pipe and remove the exhaust manifold.

20. Remove the valve cover and engine ground cable.

21. Remove the timing belt middle cover. Loosen the timing belt adjusting bolt but do not remove the adjusting bolt and release the timing belt. Be sure to push the tensioner to release tension from the belt then retighten the adjusting bolt.

22. Remove the timing belt from the driven pulleys. Be sure not to crimp or bend the timing belt more then 90 degrees or less then 1 in. (25mm) in diameter.

23. Remove the driven pulleys. Remove the camshaft holder bolts, then remove the camshaft holders, camshafts and rocker arms.

24. Remove the cylinder head bolts and remove the cylinder head. To prevent warpage, unscrew the cylinder head bolts in sequence ⅓ turn at a time, repeat this sequence until all the bolts are loosened.

25. Remove the intake manifold from the cylinder head.
To install:
26. Use new gaskets and install the intake manifold onto the cylinder head and tighten the bolts in a criss-cross pattern in 2–3 steps.

27. Install the cylinder head onto the engine block, after making sure the mating surface was cleaned and a new gasket was installed. Be sure to pay attention to the following points:

a. Be sure the No. 1 cylinder is at TDC and the camshaft pulleys UP mark is on the top before positioning the head in place.

b. The cylinder head dowel pins and oil control jet must be aligned.

c. Torque the cylinder head bolts, in 2 progressive steps: First to 22 ft. lbs. (30 Nm), in sequence, then to 61 ft. lbs. (85 Nm), in the same sequence.

d. Apply engine oil to the cylinder head bolts and washers. Use the longer bolt in the No. 1 and No. 2 positions.

28. Make sure the keyways on the camshafts are facing up. The valve locknuts should be loosened and the adjusting screw back off before installation. Replace the rocker arms in their original position.

29. Place the rocker arms on the pivot bolts and the valve stems.

30. Install the camshafts and the camshaft seals with the open side, spring facing upward.

31. Be sure to note the I and E marks that are stamped on the camshaft holders. Do not apply oil to the holder mating surface of the camshaft seals.

32. Apply a liquid gasket to the head of the mating surfaces of the No. 1 and No. 6 camshaft holders then install them, along with No. 2, 3, 4 and 5. Tighten the holders temporarily and make sure the rocker arms are properly positioned on the valve stems.

33. Press in the camshaft seal securely with a suitable seal driver.

34. Tighten each bolt, 2 turns at a time, to insure that the rockers do not bind on the valves.

35. Install the keys into their groves in the camshafts. To set the No. 1 piston at TDC, align the holes on the camshaft with the holes in the No. 1 camshaft holders and drive 5.0mm pin punches into the holes.

36. Push the camshaft pulleys onto the camshafts, then torque the retaining bolts to 27 ft. lbs. (38 Nm).

37. Install the timing belt and adjust the timing belt tensioner bolt. Install the lower and middle timing belt covers and bolts.

38. Install the valve cover and engine ground cable.

39. Install the exhaust manifold, the manifold bolts, manifold bracket and front exhaust pipe with the exhaust manifold upper shroud.

40. Install the left front wheel splash shield and the left front wheel. Lower the vehicle.

41. Install the power steering pump and drive belt.

42. Reconnect all disconnected electrical connections and vacuum lines.

43. Reconnect the upper radiator hose and heater inlet hose.

44. Reinstall the spark plug wires to the spark plugs.

45. Install the engine ground wire from the valve cover. Reconnect the throttle cable from the throttle body.

46. Reinstall the air cleaner assembly and duct work that goes along with it. Reconnect the negative battery cable.

47. After installation, check to see that all hoses and wires are installed correctly.

48. Refill the coolant system.

49. Adjust the valve clearance. Make all other necessary adjustments

NOTE: It is recommended that after completing the cylinder head removal and installation the engine oil should be changed.

LEGEND, 825 AND 827

NOTE: The cylinder head temperature must be below 100°F.

Before removing the cylinder head check the following:
Inspect the timing belt.
Turn the flywheel so the No. 1 cylinder is at TDC.
Mark all emission hoses before disconnecting them.

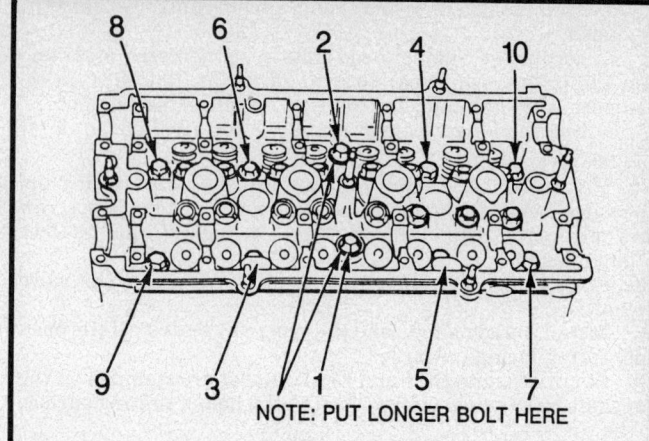

Cylinder head torque sequence—1834cc engine

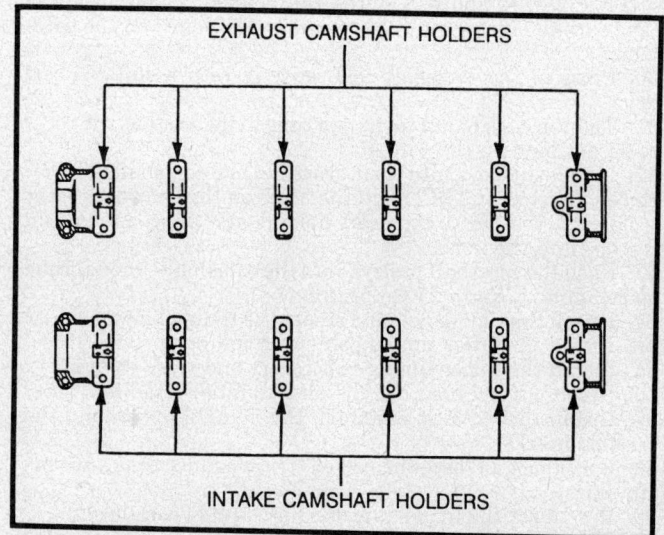

Camshaft holder sequence—1834cc engine

1. Disconnect the battery ground cable.
2. Drain the cooling system.
3. Remove the vacuum hose from the brake booster.
4. Remove the secondary ground cable from the cylinder head and the transaxle housing.
5. Disconnect the radio noise condensor connector, ignition coil wire and the ignition primary connector.
6. Remove the air cleaner cover.
7. Relieve the fuel pressure using the follwoing procedure:

a. Slowly loosen the service bolt on the top of the fuel filter about a turn.

NOTE: Be sure to place a rag under the fuel filter during this procedure to prevent the fuel from spilling onto the engine.

b. Disconnect the fuel return hose from the pressure regulator. Remove the special nut and the fuel hose.

8. Disconnect the throttle cable from the throttle valve.
9. Disconnect the charcoal canister hose from the throttle valve.
10. Disconnect the engine sub harness connectors and the following couplers from the cylinder head and the intake manifold:

a. The 6 injector couplers.
b. The TA sensor connector.
c. The temperature unit connector.

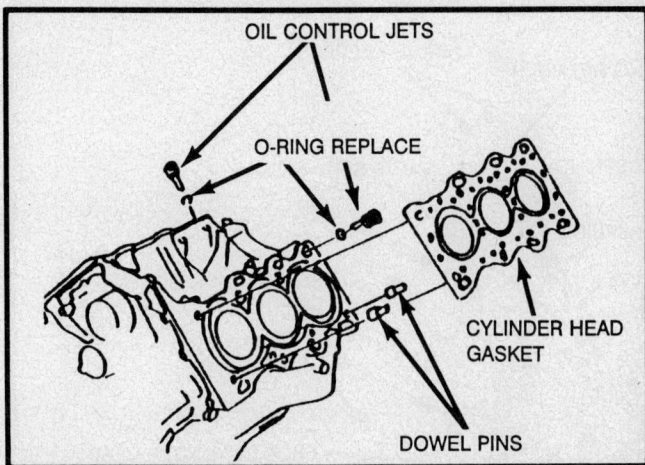

Dowel pin and oil jet control locations—2494cc and 2675cc engine

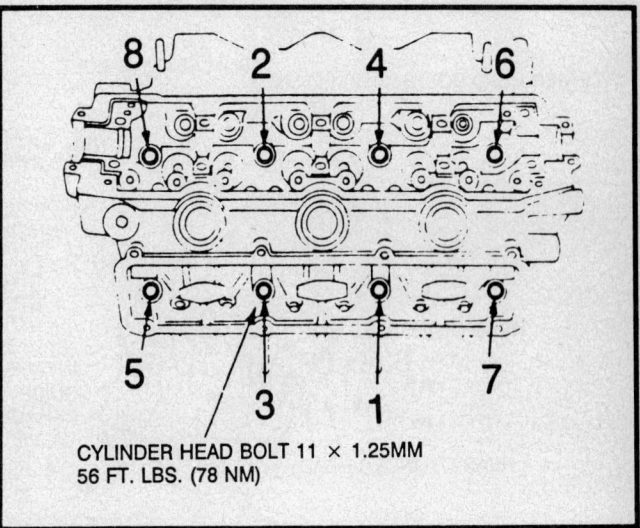

CYLINDER HEAD BOLT 11 × 1.25MM
56 FT. LBS. (78 NM)

Cylinder head bolt torque sequence—1989–91 2675cc engines

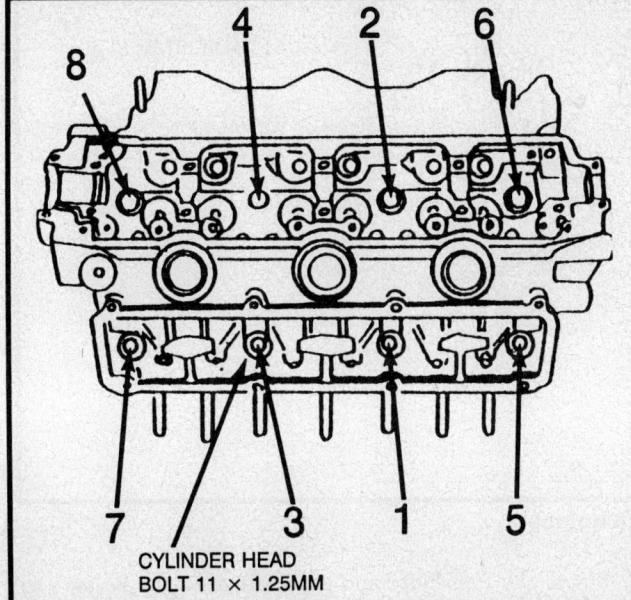

CYLINDER HEAD BOLT 11 × 1.25MM

Cylinder head bolt torque sequence—1987–88 2494cc and 2675cc engines

d. The ground connector from the fuel pipe.
e. The TW sensor connector.
f. The throttle sensor connector.
g. The crankshaft angle sensor coupler.
h. EGR valve connector.
i. The 4 wire harness clamps.
11. Disconnect the oxygen sensor coupler.
12. Disconnect the cooling system hoses from the cylinder head. Remove the hose between the water passage and the intake manifold. Disconnect the connecting pipe to the valve body hose and bypass outlet hose.
13. Disconnect the spark plug wires from the spark plugs and remove the distributor assembly.
14. Remove the intake manifold cover from the intake manifold.
15. Remove the wire harness cover.
16. Remove the alternator pulley cover.
17. Remove the alternator and belt.

18. Remove the power steering pump and disconnect the pump hoses. Also, remove the hose clamp bolt on the body.
19. Disconnect the idle boost solenoid hoses.
20. Remove the cruise control actuator.
21. Remove the exhaust header pipe and pull it clear of the exhaust manifold.
22. Remove the air cleaner base mount bolts and disconnect the hose from the intake manifold to the breather chamber.
23. Remove the air cleaner base from the intake manifold.
24. Remove the EGR tube nuts from the cylinder head.
25. Remove the exhaust manifold cover nuts.
26. Remove the air suction tube nuts from the exhaust manifold and air suction valve.
27. Remove the intake manifold assembly from the cylinder head.
28. Remove the water passage assembly from the front and rear of the cylinder head.
29. Remove the timing belt upper covers.
30. Loosen the tensioner adjustment bolt and remove the timing belt.

NOTE: Advance the crankshaft by 15 degrees before removing the timing belt to prevent interference between the piston and the valve.

31. Remove the front and rear camshaft pulleys using the following procedure:
   a. Before removing the rear pulley, adjust the cam position so no valve is fully open.
   b. Remove the pulley mounting bolts with a universal holder and a double-end wrench. For the rear pulley, first, remove the top 2 bolts and then the remaining bolt.
32. Remove the upper cover back plates.
33. Remove the valve covers and the head side covers.
34. Remove the bearing cap oil pipes, the bearing caps and the camshaft.
35. Remove the intake and exhaust inside rocker arms and pushrods.

NOTE: Label all valve train components to ensure reinstallation in their proper locations.

36. Remove the cylinder head bolts and remove the head.

NOTE: Unscrew the cylinder head bolts ⅓ of a turn in the reverse order of the torque sequence each turn until loose to prevent warpage to the cylinder head.

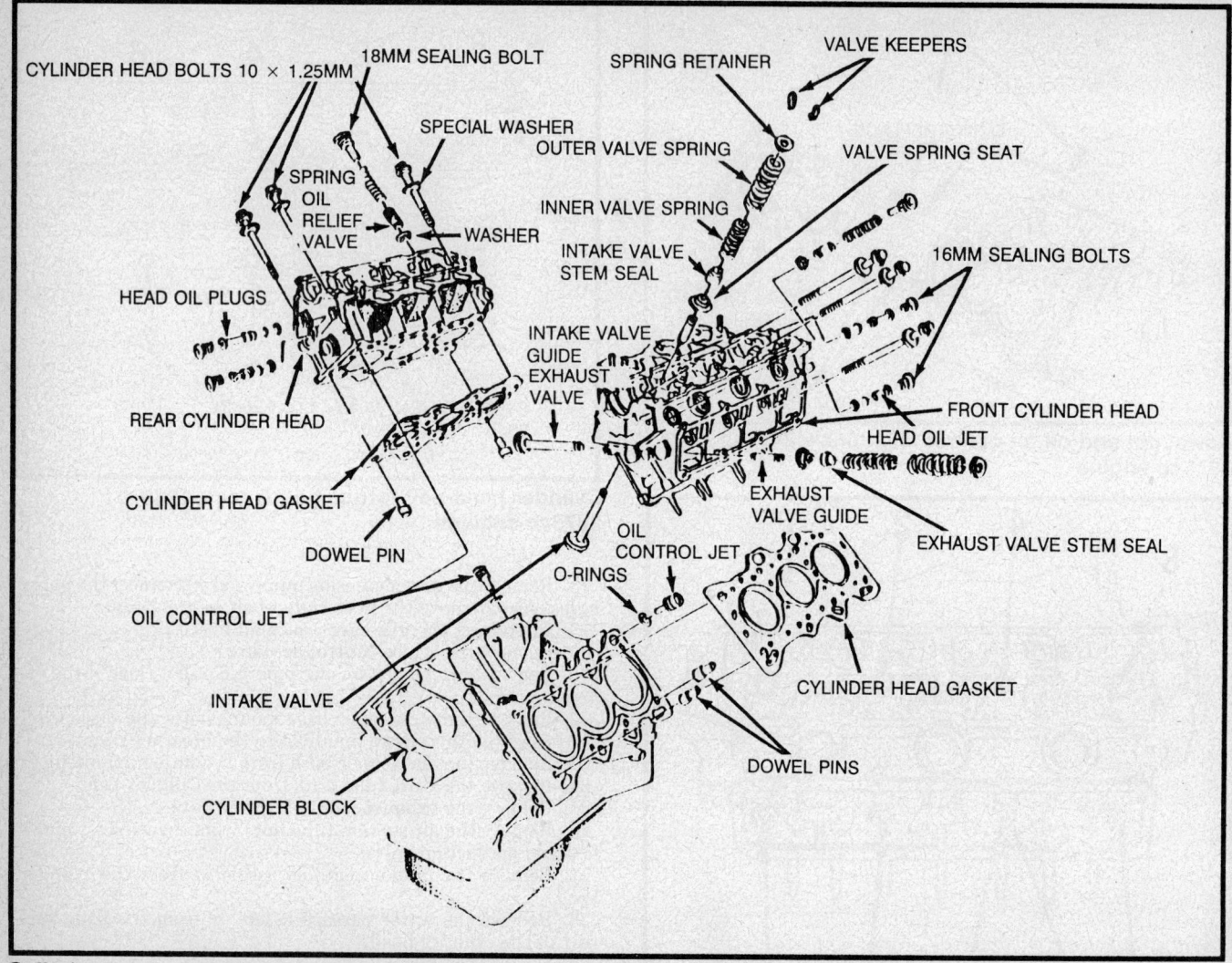

CYLINDER HEAD BOLTS 10 × 1.25MM
18MM SEALING BOLT
SPRING RETAINER
VALVE KEEPERS
SPECIAL WASHER
OUTER VALVE SPRING
VALVE SPRING SEAT
SPRING OIL RELIEF VALVE
WASHER
INNER VALVE SPRING
16MM SEALING BOLTS
HEAD OIL PLUGS
INTAKE VALVE STEM SEAL
INTAKE VALVE GUIDE
EXHAUST VALVE
FRONT CYLINDER HEAD
HEAD OIL JET
REAR CYLINDER HEAD
CYLINDER HEAD GASKET
EXHAUST VALVE GUIDE
EXHAUST VALVE STEM SEAL
DOWEL PIN
OIL CONTROL JET
O-RINGS
OIL CONTROL JET
INTAKE VALVE
CYLINDER HEAD GASKET
CYLINDER BLOCK
DOWEL PINS

Cylinder head and related components—2494cc and 2675cc engines

37. Clean the gasket mounting surfaces.

To install:

38. Use new gaskets and install the exhaust manifold onto the cylinder head and tighten the bolts in a criss-cross pattern in 2–3 steps.

39. Install the cylinder head onto the engine block, after making sure the mating surface was cleaned and a new gasket was installed. Be sure to pay attention to the following points:

    a. Be sure the No. 1 cylinder is at TDC and the camshaft pulleys UP mark is on the top before positioning the head in place.

    b. The cylinder head dowel pins and oil control jet must be aligned.

    c. Torque the cylinder head bolts, in 2 progressive steps: First to 29 ft. lbs. (40 Nm), in sequence, then to 56 ft. lbs. (78 Nm), in the same sequence.

40. Pour engine oil into the cylinder head hydraulic tappet mounting hole, up to the level of the oil path.

41. Install the hydraulic tappet into the cylinder head. Do not rotate the hydraulic tappet while inserting it into the head.

42. Pour engine oil into the oil fillers on the cylinder head.

43. Install the pushrods and rocker arms. Be sure to install each part in its original position. Loosen the rocker arm adjusting screws and locknuts before installation.

44. Install the camshafts and camshaft oil seals. Be sure to take note of the locations of the camshafts; the front camshaft has a groove for driving the distributor.

    a. Make sure the camshaft is mounted parallel with the rocker arm slipper surface.

    b. Advance the crankshaft by 15 degrees from the No. 1 cylinder TDC of compression stroke to prevent interference between the piston and valve.

    c. Place the rear camshaft on the cylinder head at the position where the cam is not pushing the valve.

    d. Preset the oil seal, with its spring side facing inward.

    e. Install the rear camshaft sealing rubber. Do not apply oil to the cam holder side of the oil seal.

45. Apply liquid gasket to the camshaft oil seal mounting surface and on the head contact surface. Temporarily tighten the bearing caps.

46. Carefully, fit the camshaft oil seal until it contacts the bearing cap. Tighten the bolts of the camshaft bearing cap diagonally from the center. Tighten the 6mm bolt last. Make sure the oil seal is properly positioned.

47. Install the upper timing cover plate. Install the camshaft pulley and torque the bolts to 23 ft. lbs. (32 Nm). Install the timing belt.

48. Install the water passage assembly from the front and rear of the cylinder head.

49. Install the intake manifold assembly on the cylinder head.
50. Install the air suction tube nuts to the exhaust manifold and air suction valve.
51. Install the exhaust manifold cover nuts.
52. Install the EGR tube nuts to the cylinder head.
53. Install the air cleaner base to the intake manifold.
54. Install the air cleaner base mount bolts and reconnect the hose from the intake manifold to the breather chamber.
55. Install the exhaust header pipe to the exhaust manifold.
56. Install the cruise control actuator.
57. Reconnect the idle boost solenoid hoses.
58. Install the power steering pump and reconnect the pump hoses. Also, install the hose clamp bolt on the body.
59. Install the alternator and belt.
60. Install the alternator pulley cover.
61. Install the wire harness cover.
62. Install the intake manifold cover to the intake manifold.
63. Install the distributor assembly and reconnect the spark plug wires to the spark plugs.
64. Reconnect the cooling system hoses to the cylinder head. Install the hose between the water passage and the intake manifold. Reconnect the connecting pipe to the valve body hose and bypass outlet hose.
65. Reconnect the oxygen sensor coupler and all disconnected electrical connections.
66. Reconnect the charcoal canister hose to the throttle valve.
67. Reconnect the throttle cable to the throttle valve.
68. Install all disconnected fuel line. Install the air cleaner cover.
69. Install the secondary ground cable to the cylinder head and the transaxle housing.
70. Install the vacuum hose to the brake booster.
71. Refill the cooling system.
72. Reconnect the battery ground cable.
73. Readjust the exhaust valves.
74. After the heads are reassembled, make sure the engine sits for approximately 5 minutes to allow the hydraulic tappets to reach the proper oil level.
75. Remove the spark plugs and crank the engine, feel for compression at each cylinder at the spark plug holes. It may be necessary to crank the engine through several cycles to confirm compression.
76. If any cylinder does not have compression, it may be necessary to disassemble the head and check the suspected tappet.
77. If all cylinders have compression, reinstall the plugs and start the engine.

Valve Lifters

Removal and Installation
LEGEND, 825 AND 827

1. Remove the camshafts from the cylinder heads.
2. With the camshafts removed, remove the rocker arms and the pushrods.
3. Use a suitable valve lifter removal tool and remove the hydraulic tappet (lifter) from the cylinder head hydraulic tappet mounting hole.
4. Use the following steps to inspect the hydraulic tappet (lifter).
   a. Inspect the hydraulic tappet for wear or damage or for a clogged oil hole.
   b. Measure the free length of each hydraulic tappet by attaching the hydraulic tappet bleeder to the tappet. Then push and release the bleeder slowly while in a container filled with 10W–30W engine oil. Be sure to keep the hydraulic tappet upright and below the surface of the oil while pushing and release the bleeder.
   c. Continue operating the bleeder until there are no air bubbles left in the hydraulic tappet.

   d. Remove the hydraulic tappet and try to compress it quickly by hand. Measure the compression stroke with a dial indicator on a surface plate. The standard compression stroke measurement should be 0.0004–0.003 in. (0.01–0.08mm).

To install:

5. Pour engine oil into the cylinder head hydraulic tappet mounting hole, up to the level of the oil path.
6. Install the hydraulic tappet into the cylinder head. Do not rotate the hydraulic tappet while inserting it into the head.
7. Pour engine oil into the oil fillers on the cylinder head.
8. Install the pushrods and rocker arms. Be sure to install each part in its original position. Loosen the rocker arm adjusting screws and locknuts before installation.
9. Install the camshafts and camshaft oil seals. Be sure to take note of the locations of the camshafts; the front camshaft has a groove for driving the distributor. Adjust the exhaust valve clearanace.
10. After the heads are reassembled, make sure the engine sits for approximately 5 minutes to allow the hydraulic tappets to reach the proper oil level.
11. Remove the spark plugs and crank the engine, feel for compression at each cylinder at the spark plug holes. It may be necessary to crank the engine through several cycles to confirm compression.
12. If any cylinder does not have compression, it may be necessary to disassemble the head and check the suspected tappet.
13. If all cylinders have compression, reinstall the plugs and start the engine.

Valve Lash

The Legend, 825 and 827 engines use hydraulic lash adjusters on the intake valves and do not require periodic adjustment; only the exhaust valves need adjustment.

Adjustment
INTEGRA

NOTE: While all valve adjustments must be as accurate as possible, it is better to have the valve adjustment slightly loose than tight, as burned valves may result from overly tight adjustments.

1. Make sure the engine is cold; cylinder head temperature below 100°F.
2. Remove the valve cover.
3. Set the No. 1 cylinder, cylinder closest to the camshaft sprockets, to Top Dead Center (TDC). The word UP should appear at the top and the TDC grooves on the pulley should align with the cylinder head surface. Double check this by checking the position of the distributor rotor. Using chalk or a pencil, mark the No. 1 spark plug wire's position at the distributor cap on the distributor body. Then, remove the cap and make sure the rotor points toward the mark.
4. With the No. 1 cylinder at TDC, adjust the valves of the No. 1 cylinder by performing the following procedures:
   a. Using a flat feeler gauge, for the 1987–89 1590cc engine, 0.0051–0.0067 in. on the intake valves and 0.0059–0.0075 in. on the exhaust valves. Place the feeler gauge between the rocker arm and the valve stem, there should be a slight drag on the feeler gauge.
   b. If there is no drag or if the gauge cannot be inserted, loosen the valve adjusting the screw locknut.
   c. Turn the adjusting screw with a suitable tool to obtain the proper clearance.
   d. Hold the adjusting screw and torque the locknut(s) to 18 ft. lbs.
   e. Recheck the clearance.
5. Turn the crankshaft 180 degrees counterclockwise, the cam pulley will turn 90 degrees. With the No. 3 cylinder at TDC, the distributor rotor should be pointing to the No. 3 plug wire

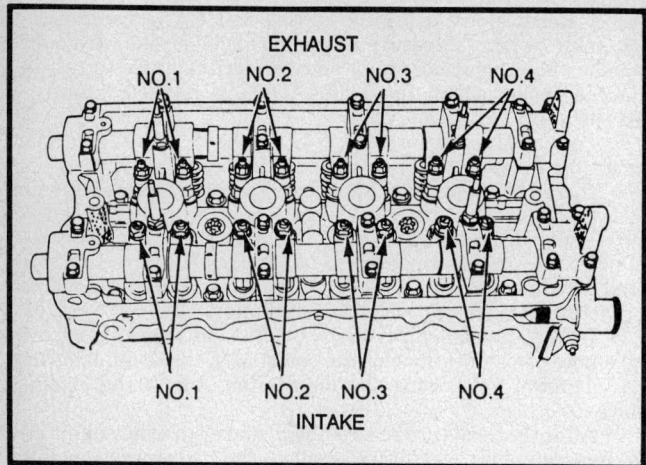

Valve locations—1590cc engine

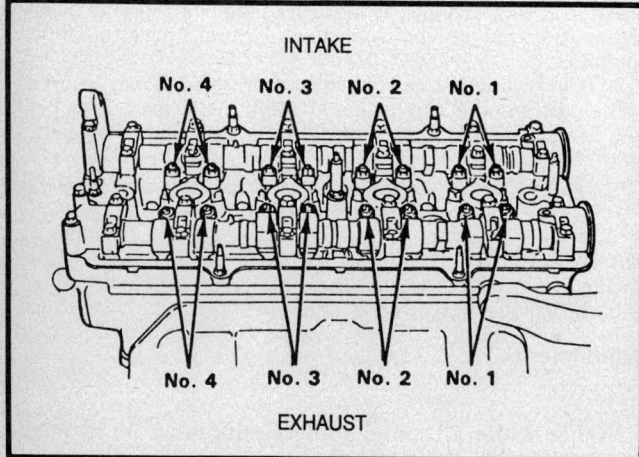

Valve locations—1834cc engine

and the UP marks should be at the exhaust side, adjust the valves on the No. 3 cylinder.

6. Turn the crankshaft 180 degrees counterclockwise, the cam pulley will turn 90 degrees. With the No. 4 cylinder at TDC, both UP marks should be at the bottom and the distributor ro-

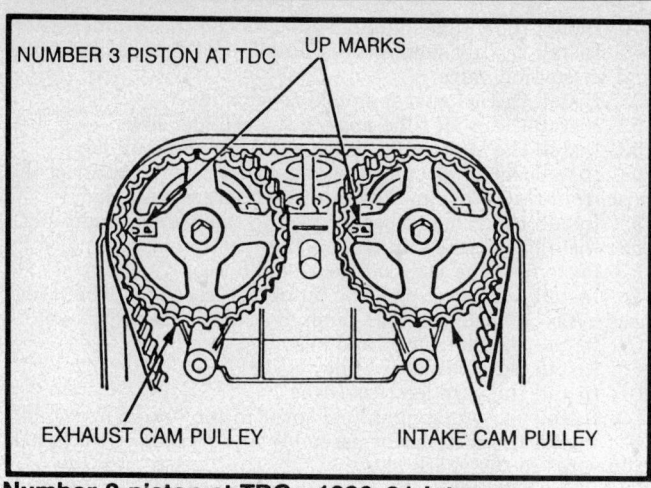

Number 3 piston at TDC—1990–91 Integra

tor pointing to the No. 4 plug wire, adjust the valves on the No. 4 cylinder.

7. Turn the crankshaft 180 degrees counterclockwise. The No. 2 cylinder will now be on TDC, this can be confirmed by the distributor rotor pointing to the No. 2 plug wire and the UP marks should be at the intake side. The valves on the No. 2 cylinder may now be adjusted.

LEGEND, 825 AND 827

This procedure is used to adjust the exhaust valves; the intake valves require no adjustment.

1. Make sure the engine is cold, cylinder head temperature below 100°F.
2. Remove the valve and side head covers.
3. Rotate the crankshaft to position the No. 1 piston on the TDC of it's compression stroke; the camshaft sprockets should be in the upward position, aligned with the timing mark and the crankshaft pulley V-notch should be aligned with the timing pointer on the timing cover.

NOTE: Double check this by checking the position of the distributor rotor. Using chalk or a pencil, mark the No. 1 spark plug wire's position at the distributor cap on the distributor body. Then, remove the cap and make sure the rotor points toward the mark.

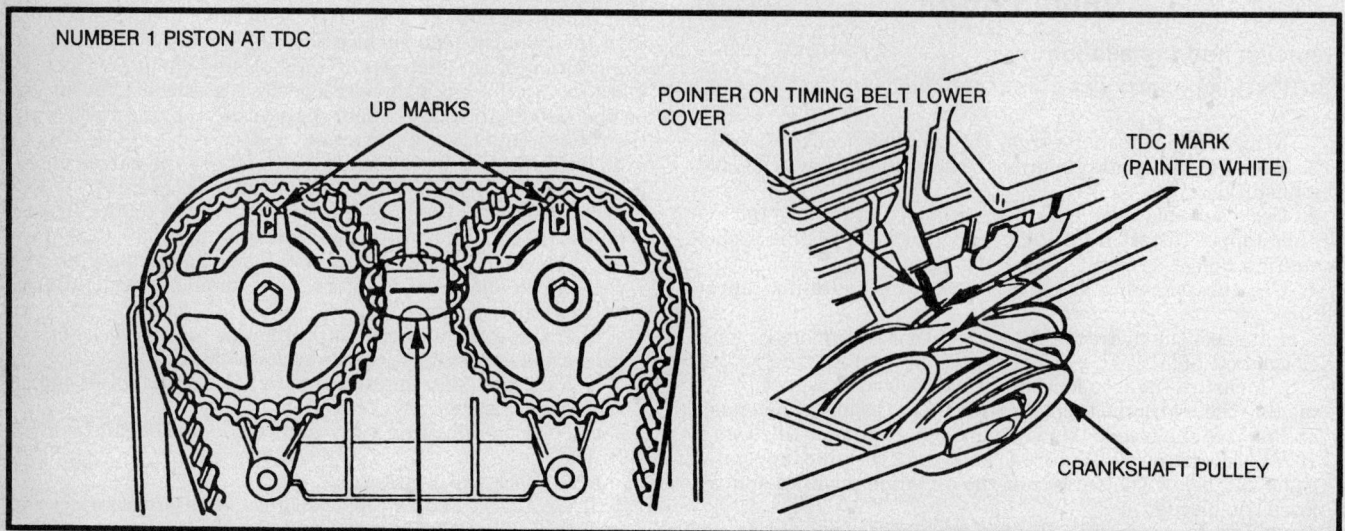

Number 1 piston at TDC—1990–91 Integra

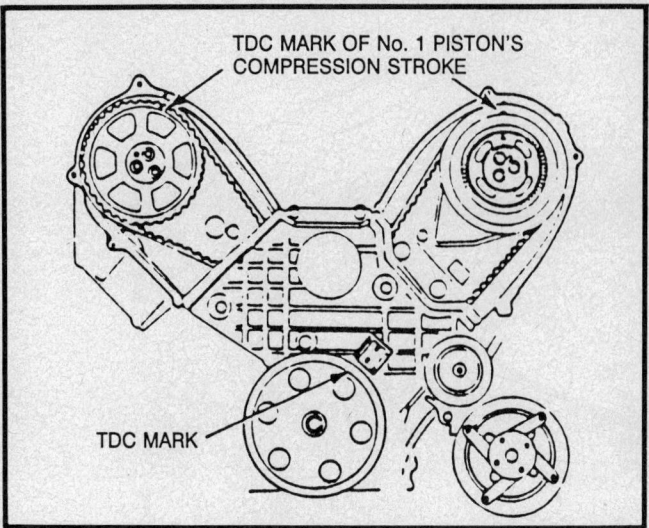

Positioning the camshaft sprockets and crankshaft pulley on the TDC of the No. 1 pistons compression stroke—Legend, 825 and 827

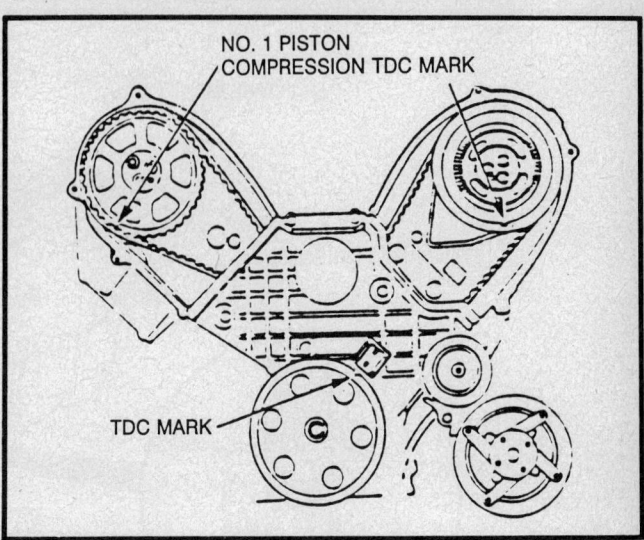

Positioning the camshaft sprockets and crankshaft pulley on the TDC of the No. 5 pistons compression stroke—Legend, 825 and 827

4. To adjust the exhaust valves, perform the following procedures:

    a. Loosen the exhaust valve locknuts on all of the cylinders.

    b. Tighten the adjusting screw of the No. 1 cylinder, until it contacts the valve and tighten it 1½ turns. Tighten the locknut firmly.

    c. Perform the same procedure for the exhaust valves No. 2 and 4.

    d. Rotate the crankshaft 180 degrees and align the crankshaft pulley's V-notch with the timing pointer on the timing cover; the No. 5 piston is at TDC of it's compression stroke.

    e. Tighten the adjusting screw of the No. 5 cylinder, until it contacts the valve and tighten it 1½ turns. Tighten the locknut firmly.

    f. Perform the same procedure for the exhaust valves No. 3 and 6.

5. After adjustment, use new gaskets and install the valve and side head covers.

Rocker Arms/Shafts

Removal and Installation

The rocker arms ride directly against the camshafts and are serviced with the camshaft. The valves are designed to be adjusted after the camshafts are installed.

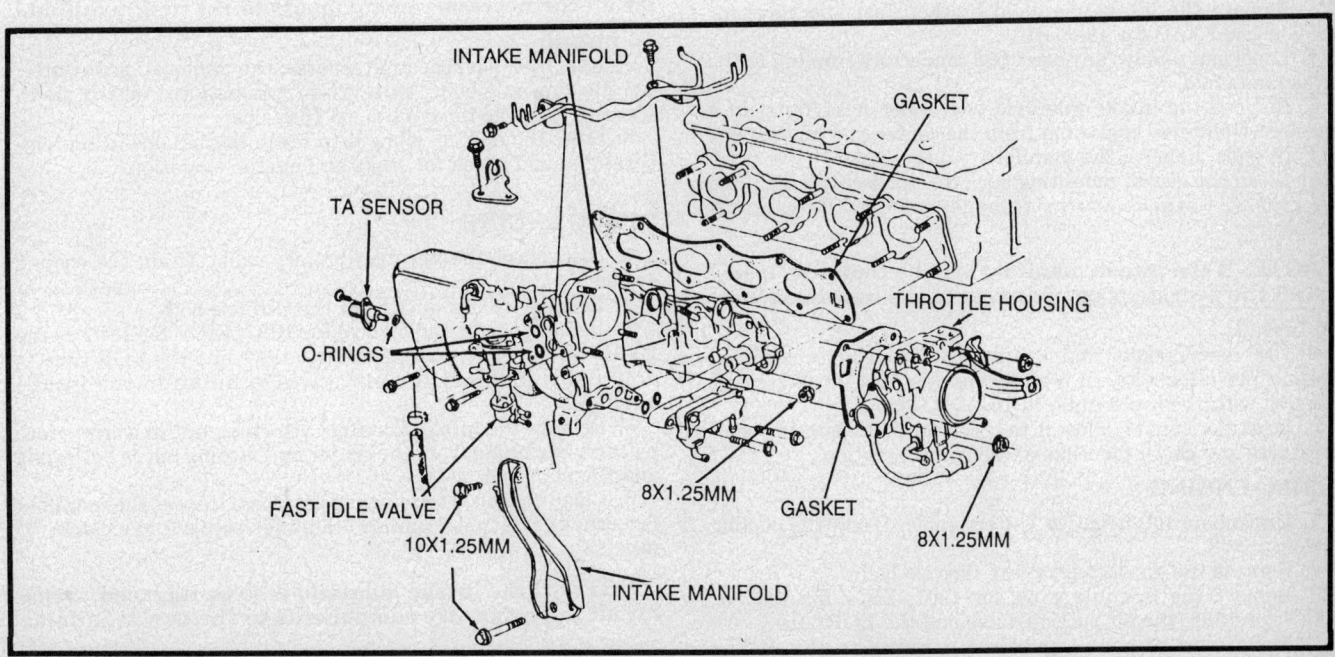

Intake manifold assembly—1590cc engine

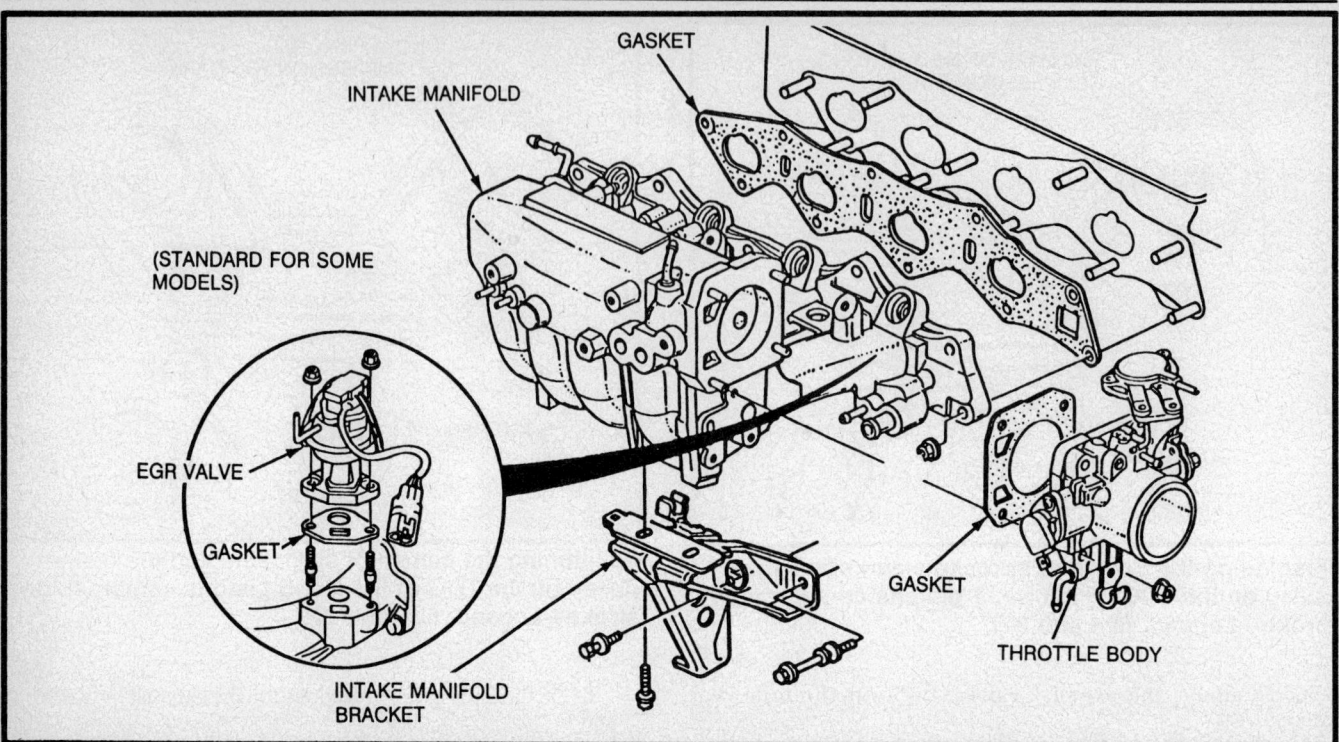

GASKET

INTAKE MANIFOLD

(STANDARD FOR SOME MODELS)

EGR VALVE

GASKET

INTAKE MANIFOLD BRACKET

GASKET

THROTTLE BODY

Intake manifold assembly—1834cc engine

Intake Manifold

Removal and Installation

1590CC AND 1834CC ENGINES

1. Disconnect the negative battery cable. Drain the cooling system.
2. Remove the air duct from the throttle body.
3. Remove the intake manifold bracket, fast idle valve for 1987 or the EVAC for 1988–91.
4. Label and remove any electrical connectors running to the intake manifold.
5. Remove the intake manifold-to-cylinder head nuts, in a criss-cross pattern, beginning from the center and moving out to both ends. Remove the manifold and the gasket.
6. Clean the gasket mounting surfaces. Inspect the manifold for cracks, flatness and/or damage; replace the parts, if necessary.

NOTE: If the intake manifold is to be replaced, transfer all the necessary components to the new manifold.

To install:

7. Use new gaskets and reverse the removal procedures. Torque the nuts/bolts, in a criss-cross pattern, in 2–3 steps, starting with the inner nuts, to 16–17 ft. lbs.
8. Start the engine, allow it to reach normal operating temperatures and check for leaks and engine operation.

2494CC ENGINE

1. Disconnect the negative battery cable. Drain the cooling system.
2. Remove the air duct from the throttle body.
3. Remove the fast idle valve for 1987, EICV for 1987 or EACV for 1988, the air suction valve and the EGR tube.
4. Label and remove any wires running to the intake manifold.

5. Remove the intake manifold attaching nut in a criss-cross pattern, beginning from the center and moving out to both ends and the manifold.
6. Clean the gasket mounting surfaces. Inspect the manifold for cracks, flatness and/or damage; replace the parts, if necessary.

NOTE: If the intake manifold is to be replaced, transfer all the necessary components to the new manifold.

To install:

7. Use new gaskets and reverse the removal procedures. Torque the nuts/bolts, in a criss-cross pattern, in 2–3 steps, starting with the inner nuts, to 16 ft. lbs.
8. Start the engine, allow it to reach normal operating temperatures and check for leaks and engine operation.

2675CC ENGINE

1. Disconnect the negative battery cable. Drain the cooling system.
2. Remove the air duct from the throttle body.
3. Remove the fast idle valve for 1987, EICV for 1987 or the EVAC for 1988–90, the air suction valve and the EGR tube.
4. Label and remove any wires running to the intake manifold.
5. Remove the intake manifold attaching nut in a criss-cross pattern, beginning from the center and moving out to both ends and the manifold.
6. Clean the gasket mounting surfaces. Inspect the manifold for cracks, flatness and/or damage; replace the parts, if necessary.

NOTE. If the intake manifold is to be replaced, transfer all the necessary components to the new manifold.

To install:

7. Use new gaskets and reverse the removal procedures.

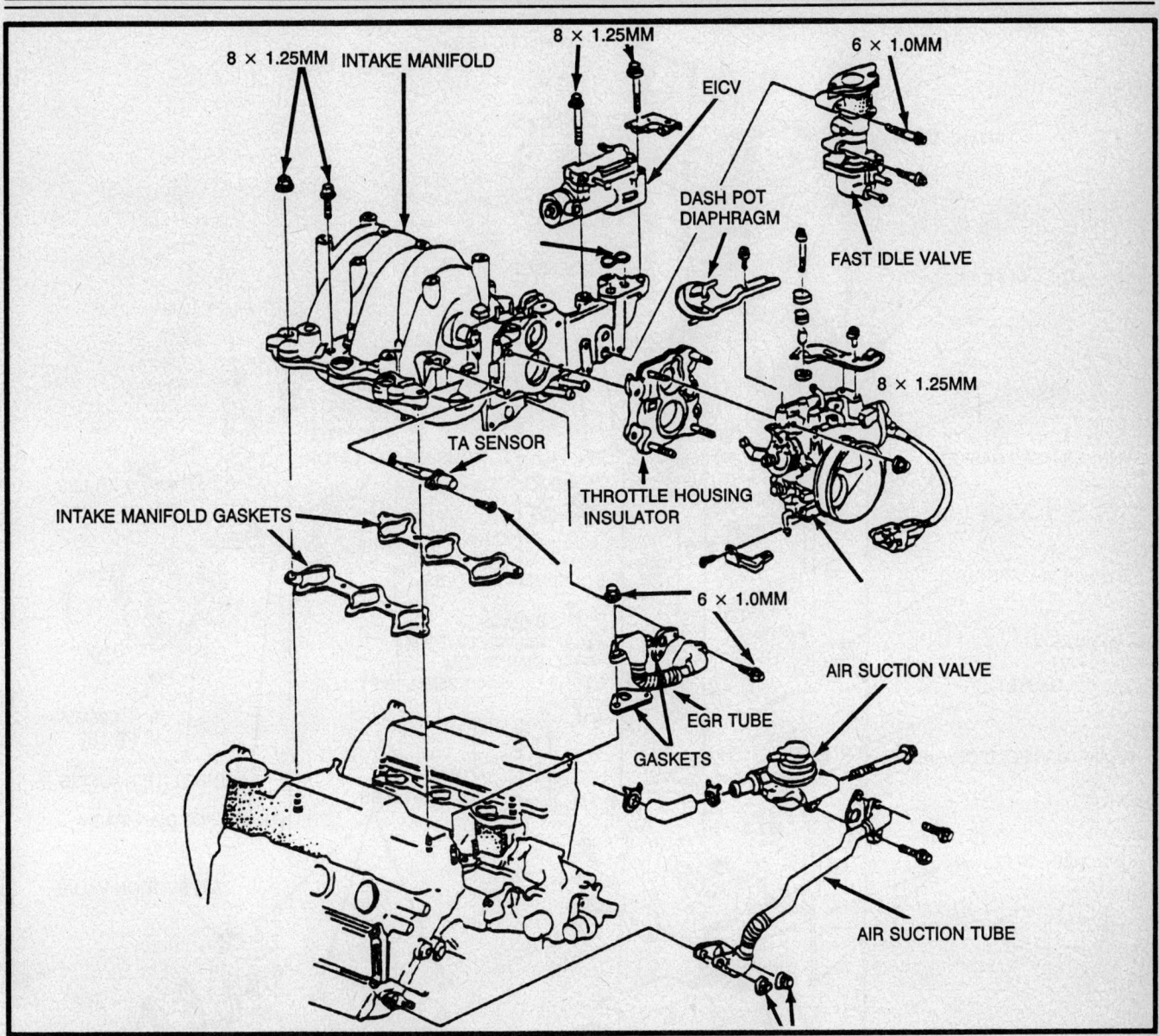

8 × 1.25MM   INTAKE MANIFOLD

8 × 1.25MM

6 × 1.0MM

EICV

DASH POT
DIAPHRAGM

FAST IDLE VALVE

8 × 1.25MM

TA SENSOR

THROTTLE HOUSING
INSULATOR

INTAKE MANIFOLD GASKETS

6 × 1.0MM

AIR SUCTION VALVE

EGR TUBE

GASKETS

AIR SUCTION TUBE

Intake manifold assembly—2494cc engine

Torque the nuts/bolts, in a criss-cross pattern in 2–3 steps, starting with the inner nuts, to 16 ft. lbs.

8. Start the engine, allow it to reach normal operating temperatures and check for leaks and engine operation.

Exhaust Manifold

Removal and Installation

NOTE: Do not perform this operation on a warm or hot engine.

1590CC AND 1834CC ENGINES

1. Disconnect the negative battery cable. Remove the exhaust manifold shroud.
2. Remove the exhaust pipe-to-exhaust manifold nuts.
3. Remove the oxygen sensor, if equipped.
4. Remove the exhaust manifold bracket bolt.
5. Remove the exhaust manifold-to-cylinder head nuts in a criss-cross pattern starting from the center and the manifold.

6. Clean the gasket mounting surfaces. Inspect the manifold for cracks, flatness and/or damage; replace the parts, if necessary.

To install:

7. Use new gaskets and reverse the removal procedures. Torque the manifold nuts in a criss-cross pattern starting from the center, to 23 ft. lbs. and the exhaust pipe-to-manifold nuts to 40 ft. lbs.

8. Start the engine and check for leaks.

2494CC AND 2675CC ENGINES

1. Disconnect the negative battery cable. Remove the exhaust manifold shrouds.
2. Remove the exhaust pipe-to-exhaust manifold nuts.
3. Remove the oxygen sensors.
4. Remove the air suction tube.
5. Remove the exhaust pipe-to-exhaust manifold nuts.
6. Clean the gasket mounting surfaces. Inspect the manifold for cracks, flatness and/or damage; replace the parts, if necessary.

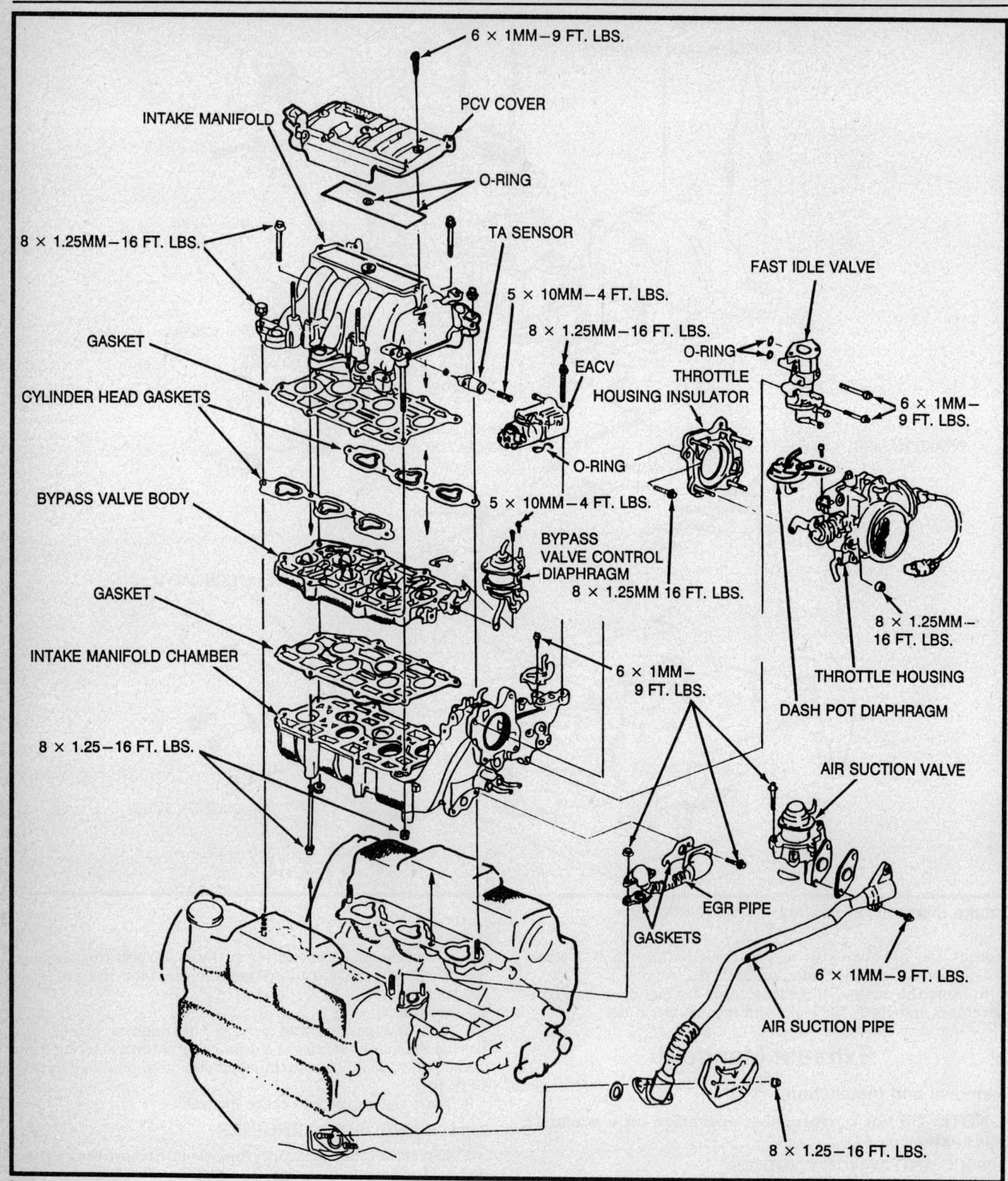

Intake manifold assembly—2675cc engine

6 × 1MM—9 FT. LBS.

PCV COVER

INTAKE MANIFOLD

O-RING

TA SENSOR

FAST IDLE VALVE

8 × 1.25MM—16 FT. LBS.

5 × 10MM—4 FT. LBS.

8 × 1.25MM—16 FT. LBS.

O-RING

EACV

THROTTLE
HOUSING INSULATOR

6 × 1MM—
9 FT. LBS.

GASKET

CYLINDER HEAD GASKETS

O-RING

5 × 10MM—4 FT. LBS.

BYPASS VALVE BODY

BYPASS
VALVE CONTROL
DIAPHRAGM

8 × 1.25MM 16 FT. LBS.

8 × 1.25MM—
16 FT. LBS.

GASKET

6 × 1MM—
9 FT. LBS.

THROTTLE HOUSING

DASH POT DIAPHRAGM

INTAKE MANIFOLD CHAMBER

8 × 1.25—16 FT. LBS.

AIR SUCTION VALVE

EGR PIPE

GASKETS

6 × 1MM—9 FT. LBS.

AIR SUCTION PIPE

8 × 1.25—16 FT. LBS.

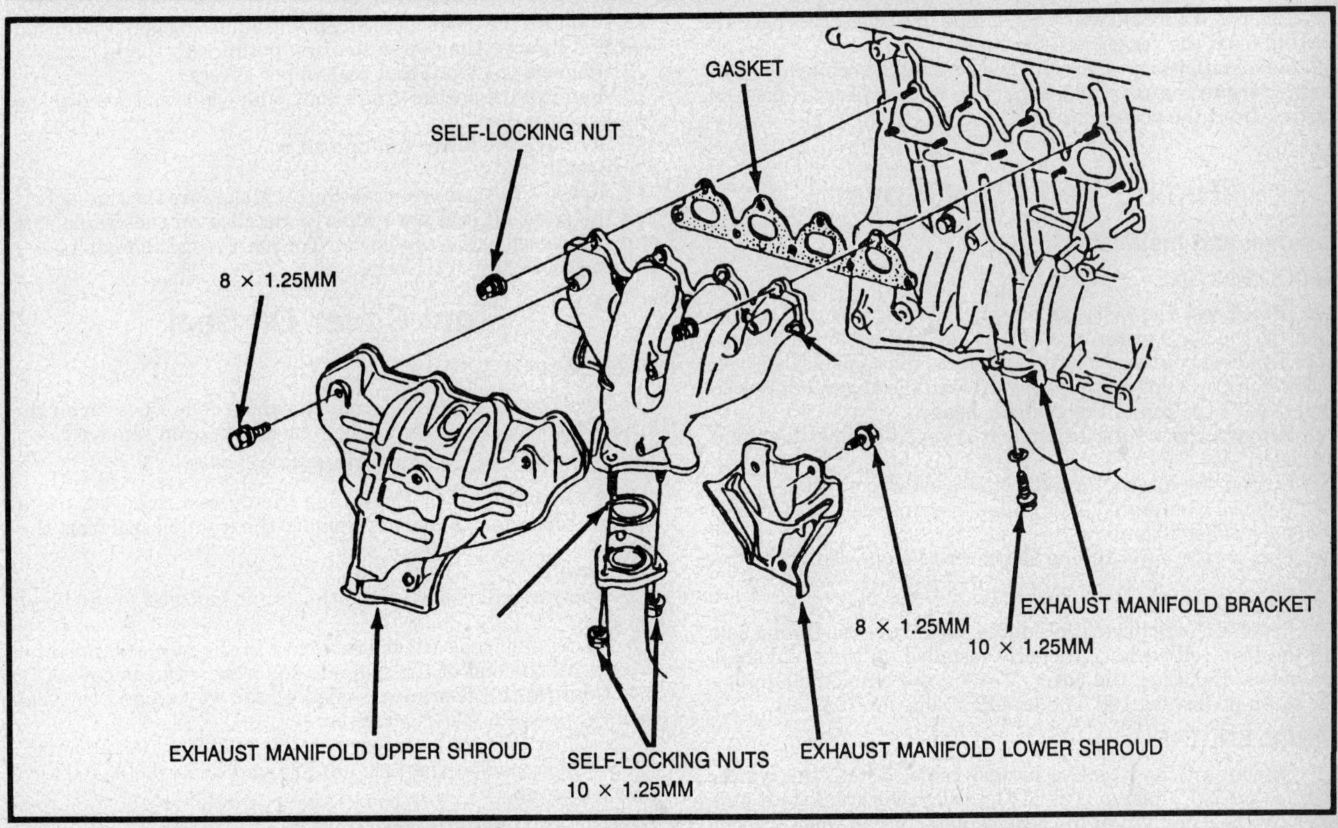

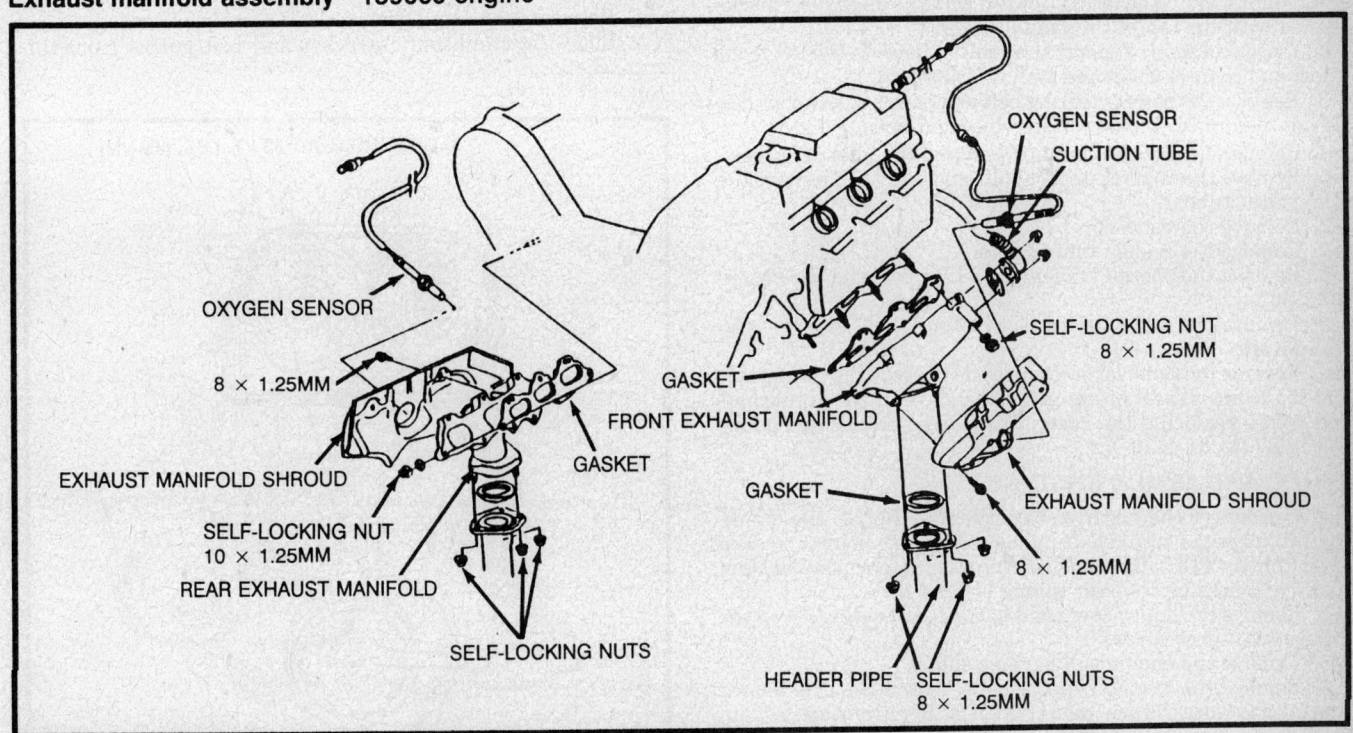

GASKET

SELF-LOCKING NUT

8 × 1.25MM

EXHAUST MANIFOLD BRACKET

8 × 1.25MM

10 × 1.25MM

EXHAUST MANIFOLD UPPER SHROUD

SELF-LOCKING NUTS
10 × 1.25MM

EXHAUST MANIFOLD LOWER SHROUD

Exhaust manifold assembly—1590cc engine

OXYGEN SENSOR
SUCTION TUBE

OXYGEN SENSOR

8 × 1.25MM

SELF-LOCKING NUT
8 × 1.25MM

GASKET

FRONT EXHAUST MANIFOLD

EXHAUST MANIFOLD SHROUD

GASKET

GASKET

SELF-LOCKING NUT
10 × 1.25MM

EXHAUST MANIFOLD SHROUD

REAR EXHAUST MANIFOLD

8 × 1.25MM

SELF-LOCKING NUTS

HEADER PIPE   SELF-LOCKING NUTS
8 × 1.25MM

Exhaust manifold assembly—2494cc and 2675cc engines

7. Remove the exhaust attaching nuts in a criss-cross pattern starting from the center and the manifold.

8. To install, use new gaskets and reverse the removal procedures. Torque the manifold nuts/bolts in a criss-cross pattern starting from the center, to 16 ft. lbs.

Timing Belt Front Cover

Removal and Installation

1590CC ENGINE

1. Disconnect the negative battery cable. Rotate the crankshaft, (so the No. 1 piston is at TDC, to align the crankshaft pulley or flywheel pointer, at top dead center; the camshaft sprockets UP mark should be facing upward with the alignment marks aligned with the top of the cylinder head.

2. Remove the timing belt upper cover-to-engine bolts and the cover.

3. Loosen the alternator and remove the drive belt(s).

4. Remove the crankshaft pulley-to-crankshaft pulley bolt and the crankshaft pulley.

5. Remove the lower timing belt cover-to-engine bolts and the cover.

To install:

6. Reverse the removal procedures. Make sure the timing belt and the front oil seal are properly installed on the crankshaft and before replacing the cover. Torque the crankshaft pulley bolt to 83 ft. lbs. for 1987–88 or 119 ft. lbs. for 1989–91.

1834CC ENGINE

1. Disconnect the negative battery cable. Rotate the crankshaft, so the No. 1 piston is at TDC, to align the crankshaft pulley or flywheel pointer, at top dead center; the camshaft sprockets UP mark should be facing upward with the alignment marks aligned with the top of the cylinder head.

2. Raise and safely support the vehicle. Remove the left front wheel and remove the wheel well splash guard.

3. Remove the power steering belt and power steering pump. Do not disconnect the power steering fluid lines.

4. Remove the air conditioning belt and the alternator belt.

5. Remove the engine support bolts and nut, then remove the side mount rubber.

6. Remove the valve cover.

7. Remove the middle timing cover.

8. Remove the special crankshaft pulley bolt and the crankshaft pulley.

9. Remove the lower timing belt cover.

To install:

10. Reverse the removal procedures. Make sure the timing belt and the front oil seal are properly installed on the crankshaft and before replacing the cover. Torque the crankshaft pulley bolt to 87 ft. lbs. (120 Nm).

2494CC AND 2675CC ENGINES

1. Disconnect the negative battery cable. Rotate the crankshaft to align the crankshaft pulley or flywheel pointer, at Top Dead Center (TDC); the camshaft sprocket notches should align with the marks on the rear timing belt cover.

2. Remove the pulley cover and harness cover from above the timing belt upper cover.

3. Remove the engine sub harness clip.

4. Remove the engine support bolts, loosen the side mount rubber, and raise the side mount bracket. Be sure to use a chain hoist to support the engine.

5. Remove the lower splash guard from under the front of the vehicle.

6. Loosen the air conditioning idle pulley adjusting bolt and remove the air conditioning compressor belt.

7. Remove the alternator adjusting bolt, mounting bolt and remove the alternator with the belt.

8. Remove the power steering pump adjusting bolt, mounting bolt and remove the power steering pump with the belt.

9. Remove the front and rear upper covers.

10. Remove the special crankshaft pulley bolt and remove the crankshaft pulley.

11. Remove the lower timing belt cover.

To install:

12. Reverse the removal procedures. Make sure the timing belt and the front oil seal are properly installed on the crankshaft and before replacing the cover. Torque the crankshaft pulley bolt to 123 ft. lbs. (170 Nm).

Front Cover Oil Seal

Replacement

The front cover oil seal replacement can be done when on all vehicles when the front timing belt cover has been removed.

1590CC AND 1834CC ENGINES

1. With timing cover containing the oil seal removed, use a suitable seal removal tool and remove the front oil seal from the cover.

To install:

2. Apply a light coat of oil to the crankshaft and to the lip of the seal.

3. Using a oil seal driver tool, drive in the new seal into the cover until the end of the seal sits squarely with the cover.

4. Confirm the clearance is good all the way around the seal with the use of a feeler gauge.

   a. Clearance on the Integra – 0.02–0.0003 in. (0.5–0.8mm).

   b. Clearance on the Legend, 825 and 827 – 0.008–0.02 in. (0.2–0.5mm).

2494CC AND 2675CC ENGINES

1. Remove the timing belt.

2. Slide the crankshaft sprocket and belt guides from the crankshaft.

ADJUSTING BOLT 33 FT. LBS. (45 NM)

DIRECTION OF ROTATION

Timing belt adjustment—1590cc and 1834cc engines

3. Using a small prybar, pry the oil seal from the oil pump housing; be careful not to damage the seal's mounting surface.

4. Using a new oil seal, lubricate the seal lips with engine oil. Using a seal drive tool or equivalent, drive the new seal into the oil pump housing until it seats.

5. To complete the installation, reverse the removal procedures. Adjust the timing belt tension. Torque the crankshaft pulley bolt to 83 ft. lbs. for 1987–88 or 123 ft. lbs. for 1989–91.

Timing Belt And Tensioner

Adjustment

1590CC AND 1834CC ENGINES

NOTE: Always adjust the timing belt tension with the engine cold. The tensioner is spring-loaded to apply the proper tension to the belt automatically after making the following adjustments.

1. Turn the crankshaft pulley until the No. 1 piston is at TDC of the compression stroke. This can be determined by observing the valves (all closed) or by feeling for pressure in the spark plug hole (with a compression gauge) as the engine is turned.

2. Loosen the adjusting bolt on the tensioner pulley.

3. Rotate the crankshaft counterclockwise 3 teeth on the camshaft pulley to create tension on the timing belt.

4. Torque the adjusting bolt on the tensioner pulley to 33 ft. lbs. (45 Nm).

5. If the crankshaft pulley broke loose while turning the crank, torque it as follows:

   a. 1987–88 — 83 ft. lbs.
   b. 1989 — 119 ft. lbs.
   c. 1990–91 — 87 ft. lbs.

NOTE: Place the transaxle in gear and set the parking brake before torquing the crankshaft pulley bolt.

2494CC AND 2675CC ENGINES

NOTE: Always adjust the timing belt tension with the engine cold. The tensioner is spring-loaded to apply the proper tension to the belt automatically after making the following adjustments.

1. Turn the crankshaft pulley until No. 1 is at TDC of the compression stroke. This can be determined by observing the valves (all closed) or by feeling for pressure in the spark plug hole (with a compression gauge) as the engine is turned.

2. Rotate the crankshaft clockwise, as viewed from the pulley side of the engine, 9 teeth on the camshaft pulley, the blue mark on the camshaft pulley should match the pointer on the lower cover.

3. Loosen the adjusting bolt to create tension on the timing belt.

4. Torque the adjusting bolt to 31 ft. lbs. (43 Nm).

Removal and Installation

1590CC ENGINE

1. Rotate the crankshaft pulley until No. 1 is at TDC of the compression stroke. This can be determined by observing the valves, all closed, or by feeling for pressure in the spark plug hole, with your thumb or a compression gauge, as the engine is turned.

2. Remove the alternator belt, the power steering belt, if equipped, and the air conditioning belt, if equipped, crankshaft pulley and timing gear cover. Mark the direction of timing belt rotation.

3. Loosen but do not remove, the tensioner adjusting bolt.

4. Slide the timing belt off the camshaft sprockets, crankshaft sprocket and the water pump sprocket; remove it from the engine.

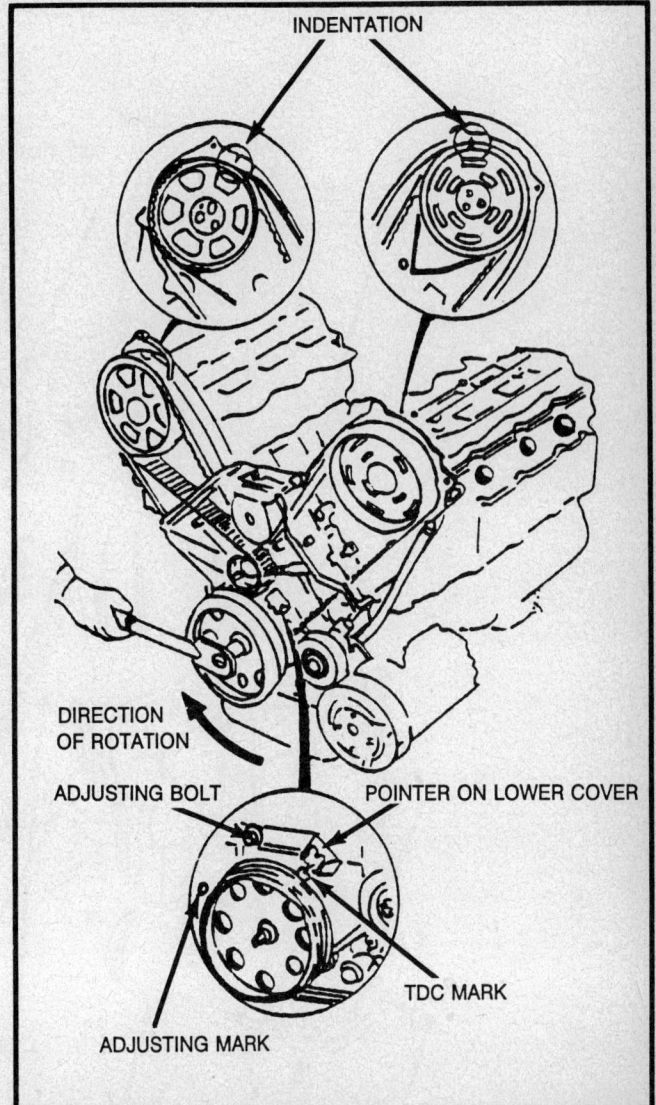

Timing belt adjustment—2494cc and 2675cc engines

5. Remove the tensioner pulley bolt and the pulley.

6. Inspect the timing belt; replace it if it is oil soaked, find source of oil leak also or if it appears worn on the leading edges of the belt teeth.

To install:

7. Reverse the removal procedures. Be sure to position the crankshaft and camshaft timing sprockets in the TDC position.

8. Adjust the timing belt tension.

1834CC ENGINE

1. Rotate the crankshaft, so the No. 1 piston is at TDC, to align the crankshaft pulley or flywheel pointer, at top dead center; the camshaft sprockets UP mark should be facing upward with the alignment marks aligned with the top of the cylinder head.

2. Raise and safely support the vehicle. Remove the left front wheel and remove the wheel well splash guard.

3. Remove the power steering belt and power steering pump. Do not disconnect the power steering fluid lines.

4. Remove the air conditioning belt and the alternator belt.

5. Remove the engine support bolts and nut, then remove the side mount rubber.

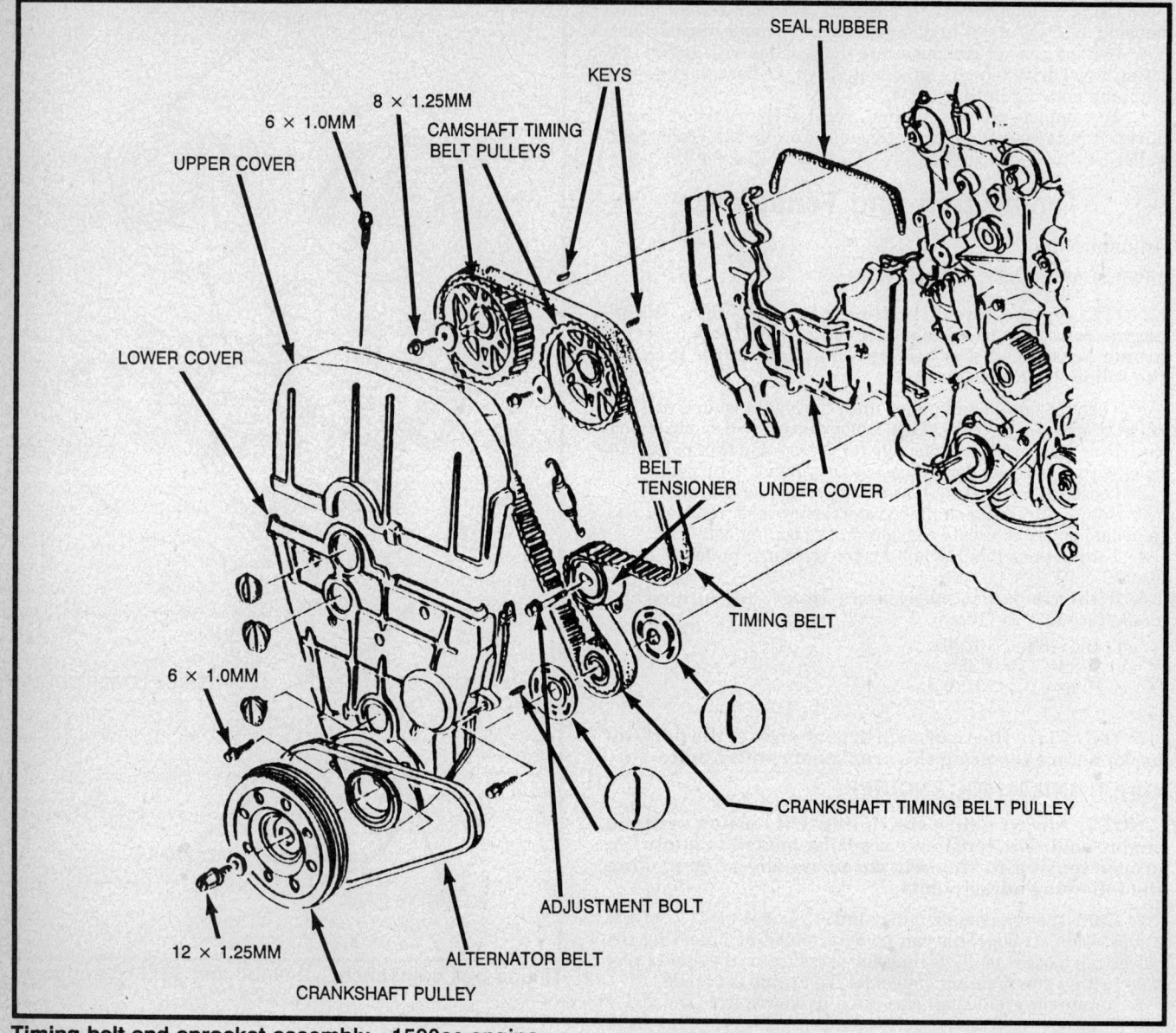

Timing belt and sprocket assembly—1590cc engine

6. Remove the valve cover.
7. Remove the middle timing cover.
8. Remove the special crankshaft pulley bolt and the crankshaft pulley.
9. Remove the lower timing belt cover.
10. Loosen but do not remove the adjusting bolt, push the tensioner to remove tension from the timing belt, then retighten the bolt. Remove the timing belt.

NOTE: Install the timing belt with the No. 1 piston at TDC on its compression stroke. To set the camshafts to the top dead center position for No. 1 cylinder, align the hole in the camshafts with the holes in the No. 1 camshaft holders and drive a 5.0mm pin punches into the holes.

To install:
11. Reverse the order of the removal procedure. Make sure both UP marks on the camshaft sprockets are pointing straight up and that the pointer on the timing belt cover aligns with the

TDC painted mark on the crank pulley.
12. Make sure the timing belt and the front oil seal are properly installed on the crankshaft before replacing the cover. Torque the crankshaft pulley bolt to 87 ft. lbs. (120 Nm).

2494CC AND 2675CC ENGINES

1. Disconnect the negative battery cable. Remove the pulley cover and the harness cover from above the timing belt upper cover.
2. Remove the engine sub-harness clamp.
3. Remove the engine support bolts, loosen the side mount rubber and raise the side mount bracket.

NOTE: A suitable lifting device or chain hoist should be used here to raise and support the engine.

4. Remove the bolts/screws and the lower splash guard.
5. Loosen the air conditioning idle pulley adjusting bolt and remove the compressor belt.

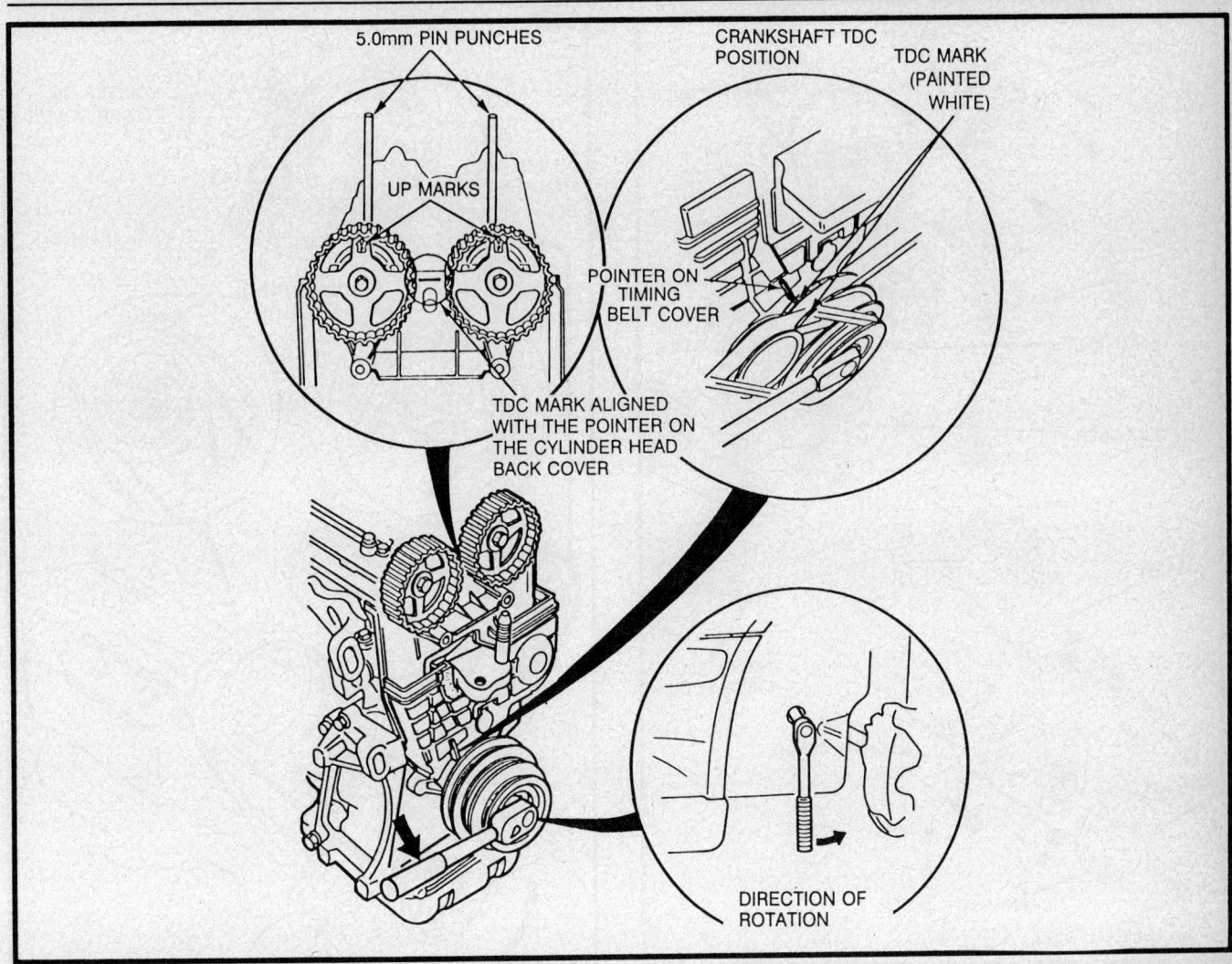

5.0mm PIN PUNCHES

UP MARKS

CRANKSHAFT TDC POSITION

TDC MARK (PAINTED WHITE)

POINTER ON TIMING BELT COVER

TDC MARK ALIGNED WITH THE POINTER ON THE CYLINDER HEAD BACK COVER

DIRECTION OF ROTATION

Timing belt and sprocket assembly—1834cc engine

6. Remove the alternator adjusting bolt, the mounting bolt, the drive belt and the alternator.

7. Remove the power steering pump bolt, the mounting bolt, the drive belt and the power steering pump.

NOTE: During installation be sure to adjust all the belt tensions.

8. Remove the front and rear upper covers.

9. Remove the special bolt and the crankshaft pulley.

10. Remove the lower cover.

11. Loosen the adjusting bolt and remove the timing belt.

12. Remove the adjustment pulley bolt and the pulley. Inspect the timing belt. Replace it, if it is oil soaked, find source of oil leak also, or if it appears worn on the leading edges of the belt teeth.

To install:

13. Reverse the removal procedure. Be sure to install the belt with the arrow facing in the same direction it was facing during removal.

14. Remove all the spark plugs from the engine.

15. Advance the crankshaft by about 15 degrees from the No. 1 cylinder compression TDC. After adjusting the front and rear camshaft pulleys to the No. 1 cylinder compression TDC, return the crankshaft pulley by about 15 degrees again to adjust the TDC position.

NOTE: Fabricate a universal holder to rotate the camshaft driving pulley.

16. To fix the adjusting bolt with the timing belt tensioner at the belt loosening position, perform the following procedures:

  a. Push the tensioner bracket with a suitable tool to loosen the belt tension.

  b. Do not push on the timing belt.

17. To install the timing belt, perform the following procedure.

  a. Install the timing belt in the following sequence; crankshaft pulley, front crankshaft pulley, water pump pulley, tensioner and rear camshaft pulley.

  b. For ease of installation, advance the rear camshaft pulley by about a half a tooth from the TDC position.

18. Loosen the adjusting bolt and retorque it after tensioning the belt.

19. Rotate the crankshaft 5–6 turns clockwise, so the belt may fit in position on the pulleys. Adjust the timing belt tension.

Timing Sprockets

Removal and Installation

1590CC AND 1834CC ENGINES

1. Disconnect the neagtive battery cable. Remove the timing

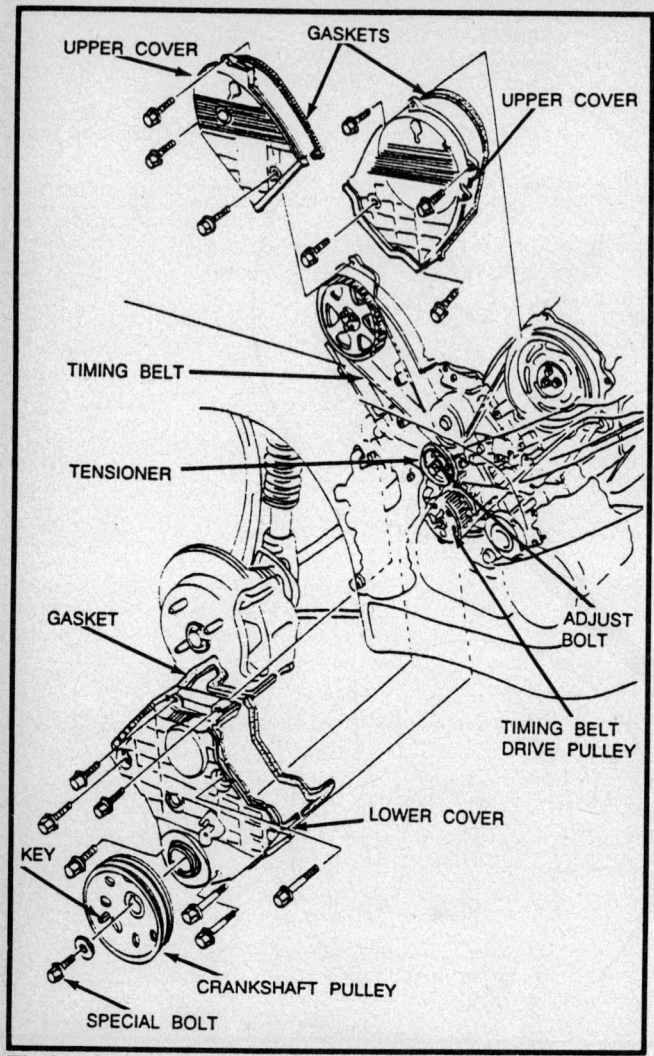

Timing belt and sprocket assembly—2494cc and 2675cc engines

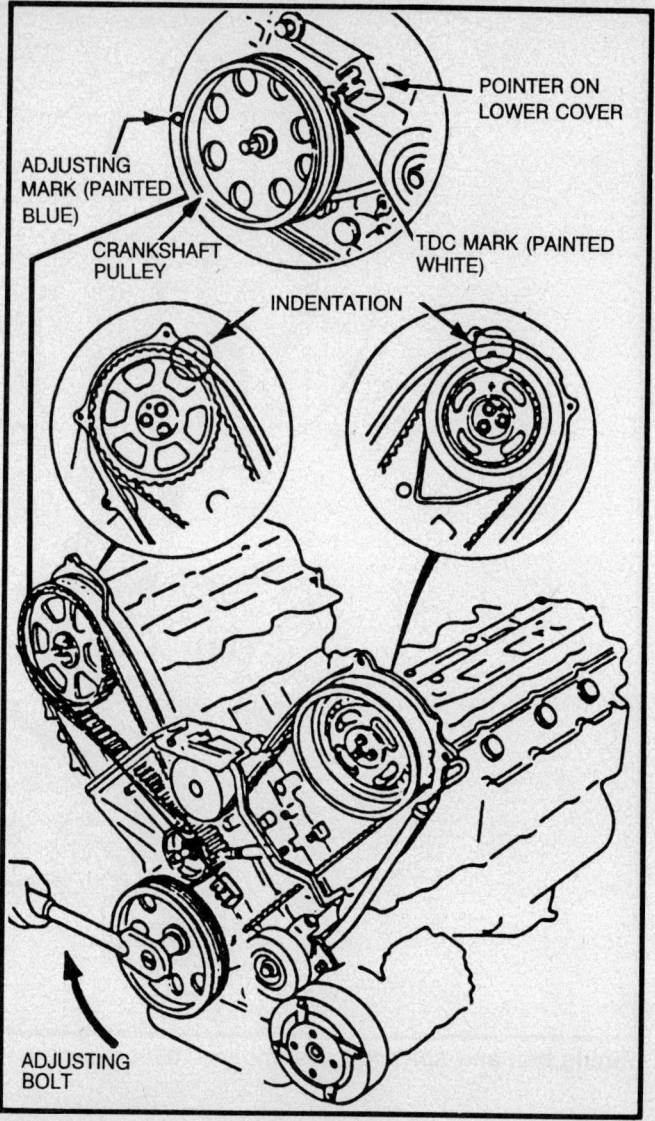

Aligning the timing belts—Legend

belt, the No. 1 cylinder should be on the TDC of it's compression stroke.

2. Align the holes in the No. 1 camshaft bearing holders with the holes in the camshafts. Using 5.0mm pin punches, drive the into the holes to secure the camshafts.

3. Remove the camshaft sprocket-to-camshaft bolts, the washers and the sprockets; remove the sprocket with a pulley remover or a brass hammer.

NOTE: Be careful not to loose the Woodruff® key.

4. Using a dial indicator, loosen the camshaft adjusting screws and check the camshaft endplay; it should be 0.002–0.006 in. (0.05–0.15mm).

NOTE: Inspect the timing belt. Replace it, if it is oil soaked, find source of oil leak also, or if it appears worn on the leading edges of the belt teeth.

To install:

5. Reverse the removal procedure. Torque the camshaft sprocket-to-camshaft bolts to 27 ft. lbs. (38 Nm). Push the camshaft inward and torque the camshaft holder adjusting bolts to 9 ft. lbs. Be sure to position the crankshaft and camshaft timing sprockets in the top dead center position.

NOTE: When installing the timing belt, do not allow oil to come in contact with the belt. Oil will cause the rubber to swell. Be careful not to bend or twist the belt unnecessarily, since it is made of fiberglass. There should be no tools being used that have sharp edges when installing or removing the belt. Be sure to install the belt with the arrow facing in the same direction it was facing during removal.

6. After installing the timing belt, adjust the belt tension.

2494CC AND 2675CC ENGINES

1. Disconnect the negative battery cable. Remove the timing belt.

2. Remove the special bolt and the crankshaft pulley.

3. Remove the lower cover.

4. Loosen the adjusting bolt and remove the timing belt.

5. Remove the adjustment pulley bolt and the pulley. Inspect the timing belt. Replace it, if it is oil soaked, find source of oil leak also, or if it appears worn on the leading edges of the belt teeth.

6. Using a camshaft holding tool or equivalent, secure the

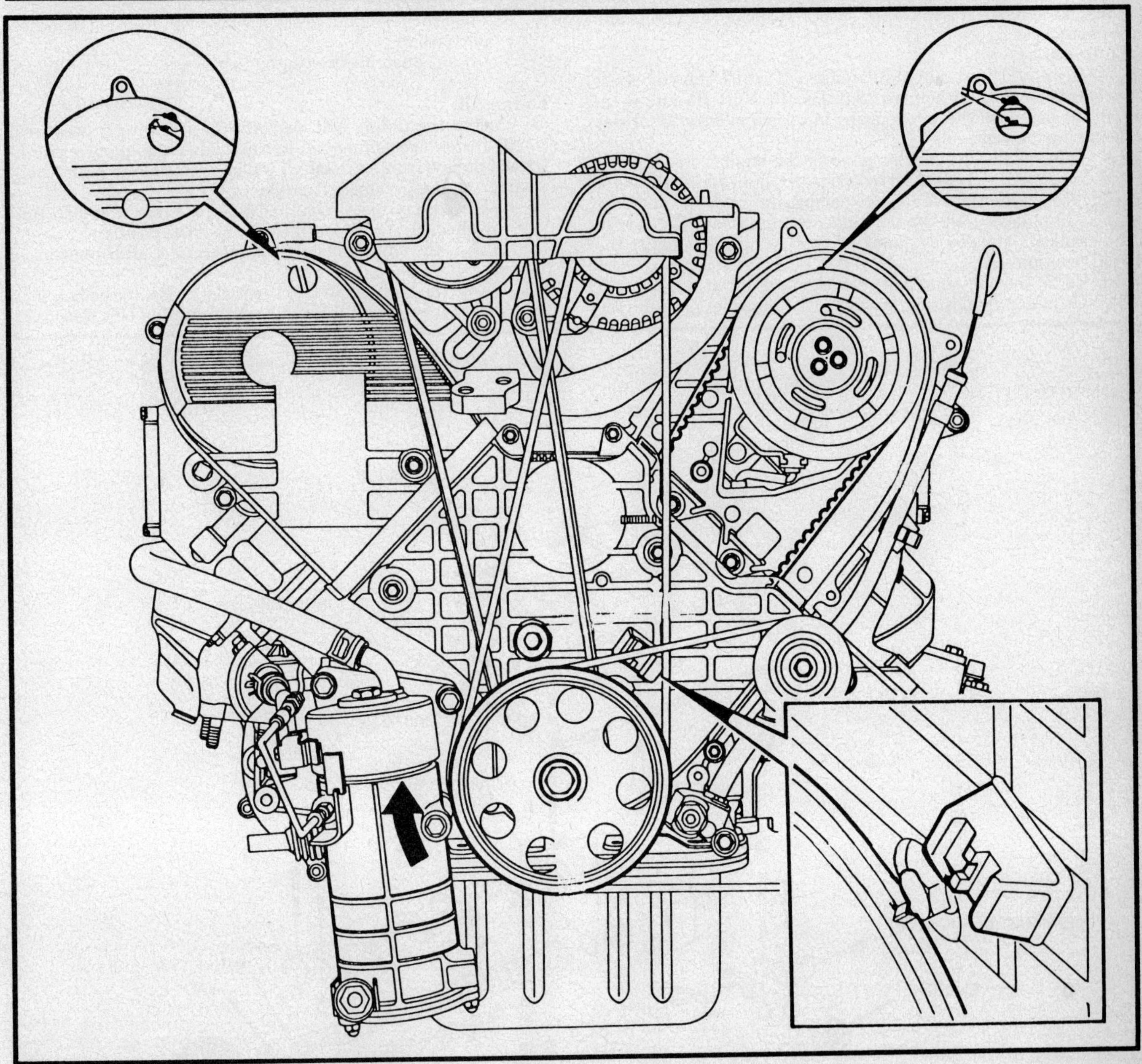

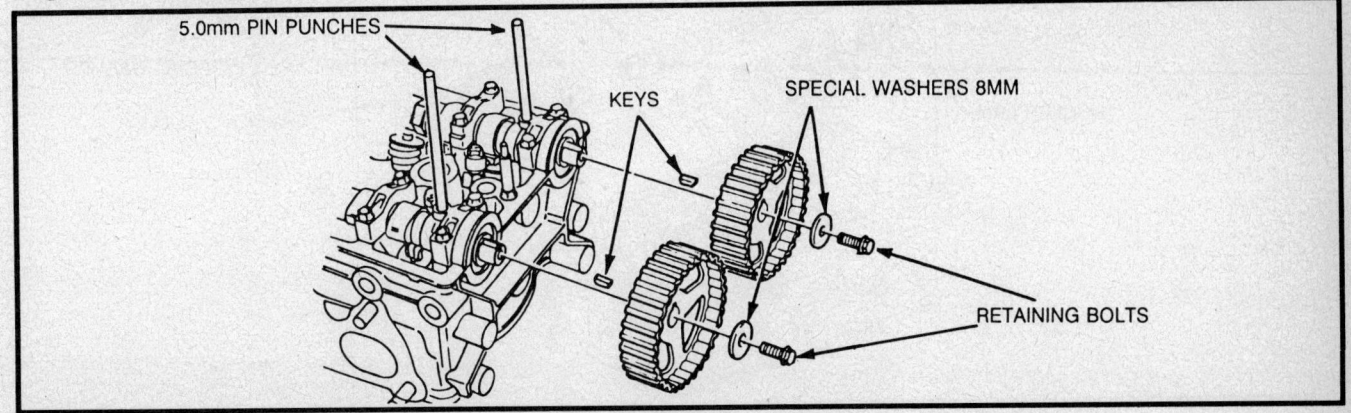

Aligning the timing belts—825 and 827

5.0mm PIN PUNCHES

KEYS

SPECIAL WASHERS 8MM

RETAINING BOLTS

Locking the camshafts into position to remove the sprockets—Integra

camshaft sprockets, remove the sprocket-to-camshaft bolts and the sprockets.

To install:

7. Reverse the removal procedure. Torque the camshaft sprocket-to-camshaft bolts to 23 ft. lbs. (32 Nm). Be sure to install the belt with the arrow facing in the same direction it was facing during removal.

8. Remove all the spark plugs from the engine.

9. Advance the crankshaft by about 15 degrees from the No. 1 cylinder compression TDC. After adjusting the front and rear camshaft pulleys to the No. 1 cylinder compression TDC, return the crankshaft pulley by about 15 degrees again to adjust the TDC position.

10. To fix the adjusting bolt with the timing belt tensioner at the belt loosening position, perform the following procedures:

a. Push the tensioner bracket with a suitable tool to loosen the belt tension.

b. Do not push on the timing belt.

To install:

11. Install the timing belt, perform the following procedures:

a. Install the timing belt in the following sequence; crankshaft pulley, front crankshaft pulley, water pump pulley, tensioner and rear camshaft pulley.

b. For ease of installation, advance the rear camshaft pulley by about a ½ of a tooth from the TDC position.

12. Loosen the adjusting bolt and retorque it after tensioning the belt.

13. Rotate the crankshaft 5–6 turns clockwise, so the belt may fit in position on the pulleys. Adjust the timing belt tension.

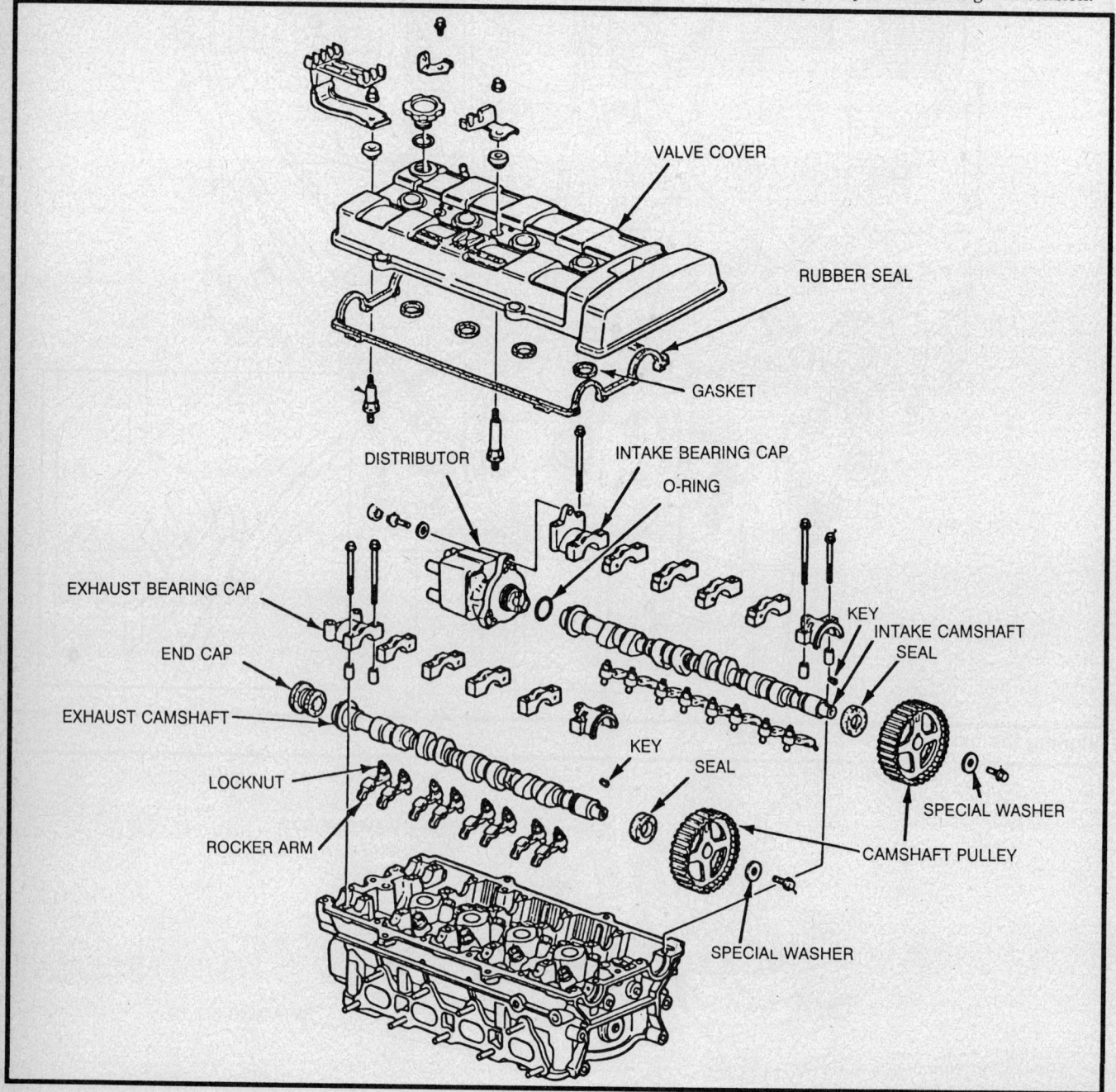

Camshaft installation—1834cc engine

Camshaft

Removal and Installation

1590CC AND 1834CC ENGINES

NOTE: To facilitate installation, make sure the No. 1 piston is at TDC before removal of the camshafts.

1. Disconnect the negative battery cable. Remove the cylinder head before attempting to remove the camshaft.
2. Loosen and remove the camshaft holder bolts, the camshaft holders, the camshafts and the rocker arms.
3. Lift the camshaft from the cylinder head, wipe them clean and inspect the lift ramps. Replace the camshaft(s) if the lobes are pitted, scored or excessively worn.

To install:

4. Check the following before installing the camshafts:
   a. Be certain the keyways on the camshafts are facing UP (No. 1 cylinder at TDC).
   b. The valve locknuts should be loosened and the adjusting screws backed off before installation.
   c. Replace the rocker arms in there original positions.
5. Place the rocker arms on the pivot bolts and the valve stems.
6. Install the camshafts and the camshaft seals with the open side (spring) facing in and observe the following;
   a. The marks I or E are stamped on the camshaft holders.
   b. Do not apply oil to the holder mating surface of the camshaft seals.
7. Apply liquid gasket to the head mating surfaces of the No. 1 and No. 6 camshaft holders then install them along with the No. 2, 3, 4 and 5.
8. Temporarily tighten the camshaft holders while making sure the rocker arms are positioned on the valve stems.
9. Using an oil seal driver tool 07947–SB00100 or equivalent, press new oil seals into the No. 1 camshaft holders.
10. Tighten each bolt 2 turns at a time, in sequence, while checking that the rockers do not bind on the valves.
11. Install the camshaft pulley keys onto the grooves in the camshafts.
12. Push the camshaft pulleys onto the camshafts, then tight the retaining bolts to 27 ft. lbs. (38 Nm).
13. Adjust the valve timing, then check that all tubes, hoses and connectors have been installed correctly.

2494CC AND 2675CC ENGINES

NOTE: To facilitate installation, make sure the No. 1 piston is at TDC before removal of the camshafts.

1. Disconnect the negative battery cable. Remove the cylinder head before attempting to remove the camshaft.
2. Loosen and remove the camshaft bearing cap bolts, then remove the camshaft bearing caps, the camshafts and the rocker arms.
3. Lift the camshaft from the cylinder head, wipe them clean and inspect the lift ramps. Replace the camshaft(s) if the lobes are pitted, scored or excessively worn.

To install:

4. Pour engine oil into the cylinder head hydraulic tappet mounting hole, up to the level of the oil path.
5. Install the hydraulic tappets into the cylinder head while observing the following;
   a. Do not rotate the hydraulic tappet while inserting it.
   b. Carefully, follow the special start-up procedure given below after the head is reassembled to allow the lifters to fill with oil.
6. Pour engine oil into the oil fillers on the cylinder head.
7. Install the pushrod and rocker arms while observing the following;
   a. Install each part in it's original position.
   b. Loosen the rocker arm adjusting screws and locknuts before installation.

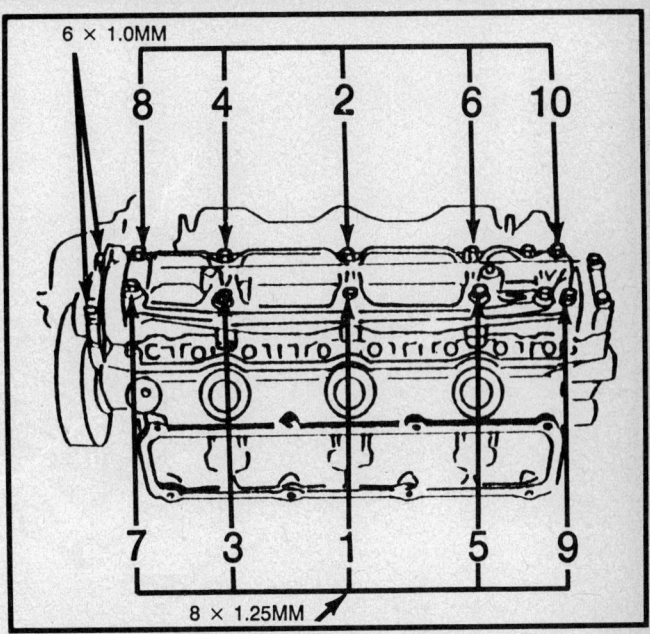

Camshaft tightening sequence—2494cc and 2675cc engines

6 × 1.0MM

8 4 2 6 10

7 3 1 5 9

8 × 1.25MM

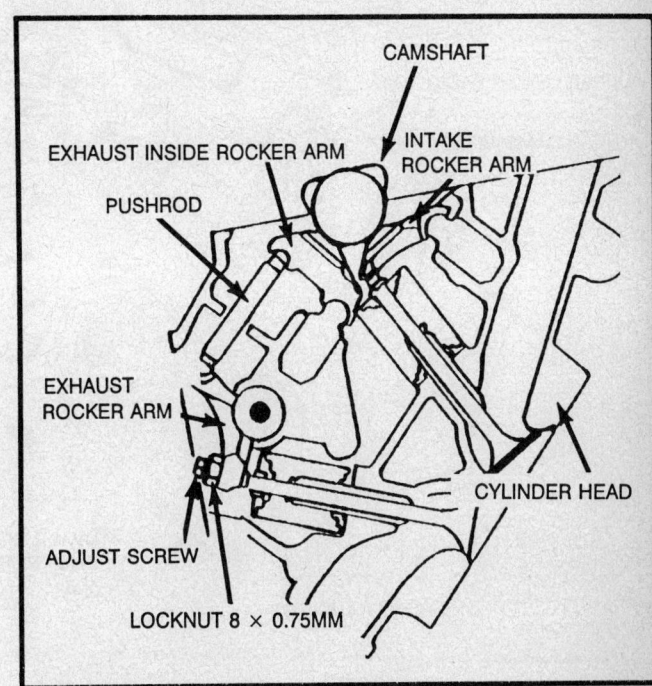

Rocker arm adjustment—2494cc and 2675cc engines

CAMSHAFT

EXHAUST INSIDE ROCKER ARM

INTAKE ROCKER ARM

PUSHROD

EXHAUST ROCKER ARM

CYLINDER HEAD

ADJUST SCREW

LOCKNUT 8 × 0.75MM

8. Install the camshafts and the camshaft oil seals as follows:
   a. Make sure the camshaft is parallel with the rocker arm slipper surface.
   b. Advance the camshaft by 15 degrees from the No. 1 cylinder TDC of the compression stroke to prevent interference between the piston and the valve.
   c. Place the rear camshaft on the cylinder head at the position where the cam is not pushing the valve.
   d. Preset the oil seal with it's spring side facing upward.
   e. Install the rear camshaft sealing rubber.
   f. Do not apply oil to the cam holder side of the oil seal.

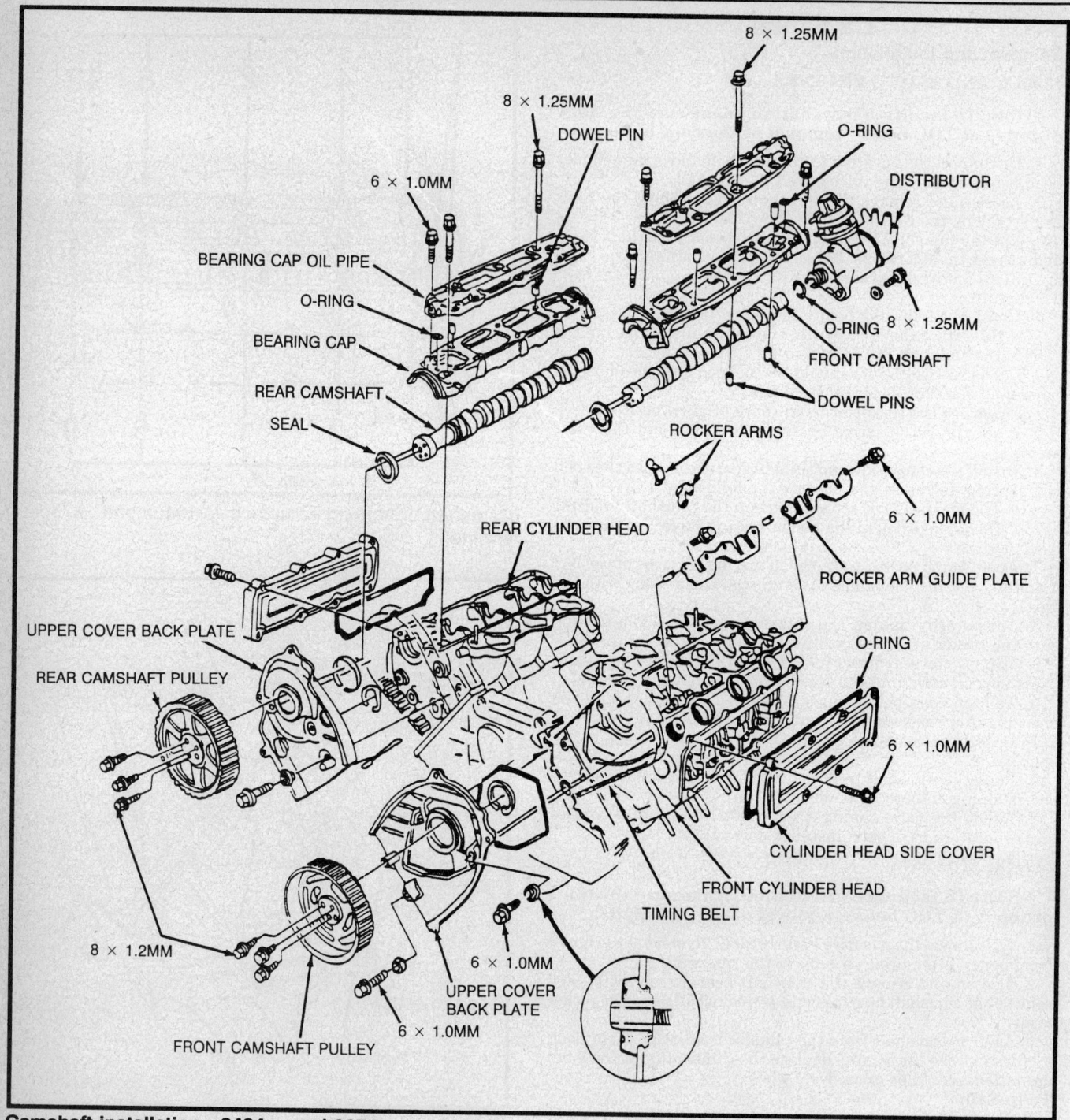

Camshaft installation—2494cc and 2675cc engines

9. Apply liquid gasket sealer to the camshaft oil seal mounting surface and on the head contact surface. Temporarily tighten the bearing caps as shown in the illustration.

10. Carefully, fit the camshaft oil seal until it contacts the bearing cap.

11. Torque the bearing caps diagonally from the center of the head while observing the following;
    a. Torque the 6mm bolts last.
    b. Make sure the oil seal is properly positioned.
    c. Torque the 8mm bolts to 20 ft. lbs. (28 Nm).
    d. Torque the 6mm bolts to 9 ft. lbs. (12 Nm).

12. Install the upper timing belt cover plate.
13. Install the camshaft pulley.
14. Install the timing belt.
15. Adjust the timing belt tension and the valve timing.
16. Adjust the exhaust rocker arm screws as follows;
    a. Adjust the front and rear camshafts at No. 1 TDC of the compression stroke. The No. 1, No. 2 and No. 4 cylinders now have the exhaust valves closed.
    b. Tighten the adjusting screw from the No. 1 cylinder. When screw contact is felt at the valve, tighten the screw 1½ turns. Tighten the locknut firmly.

c. Set the adjusting screws for No. 2 and No. 4 cylinders in the same way as Step b.

d. Rotate the crankshaft pulley 1 turn clockwise, as viewed from the pulleys side, to adjust the TDC of the No. 5 piston's compression stroke. The No. 3, No. 5 and No. 6 cylinders now have the exhaust valves closed.

e. Set the adjusting screws for No. 3 and No. 5 and No. 6 cylinders by tighten the adjusting screws until they contact the valves and tighten them 1½ turns. Tighten the locknut firmly.

17. Install the valve covers and the head side covers. Replace the O-rings for the head side covers.

18. Follow the special start-up procedure given below.

a. After the heads are reassembled, make sure the engine sits for at least 5 minutes to allow the hydraulic tappets to reach the proper oil level.

b. Remove the spark plugs. Have someone crank the engine; feel for compression from each cylinder at the spark plug holes. It may be necessary to crank the engine through several cycles to confirm compression.

c. If any cylinder does not have compression, it may be necessary to disassemble that head and check the suspected tappet.

d. If all cylinders have compression, reinstall the plugs and start the engine.

Camshaft Oil Seal

Replacement

1. Remove the timing sprockets.

2. Using a small prybar, pry the camshaft oil seals from the cylinder heads; be careful not to damage the seal mounting surfaces.

3. Using an oil seal driver tool or equivalent, lubricate the seal lips, apply sealant to the seal housing and drive the new seal into the cylinder head until it seats.

4. To complete the installation, reverse the removal procedures.

Pistons and Connecting Rods

Positioning

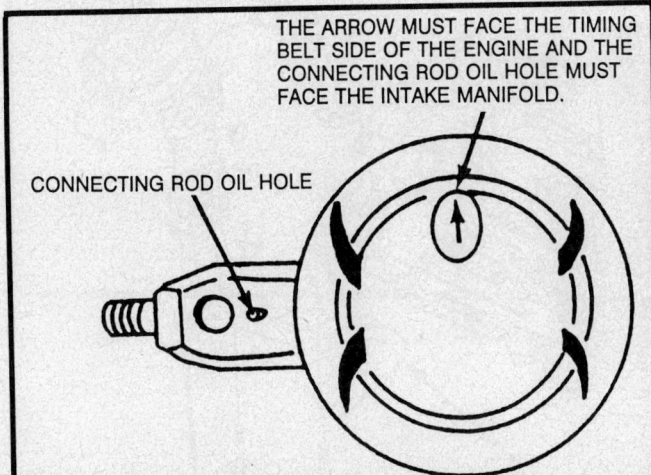

THE ARROW MUST FACE THE TIMING BELT SIDE OF THE ENGINE AND THE CONNECTING ROD OIL HOLE MUST FACE THE INTAKE MANIFOLD.

CONNECTING ROD OIL HOLE

Piston and rod positioning—1590cc engine

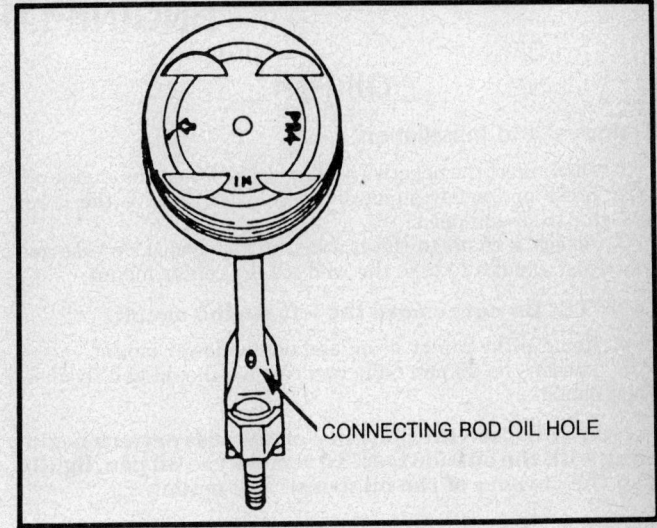

CONNECTING ROD OIL HOLE

Piston and rod positioning—1834cc engine

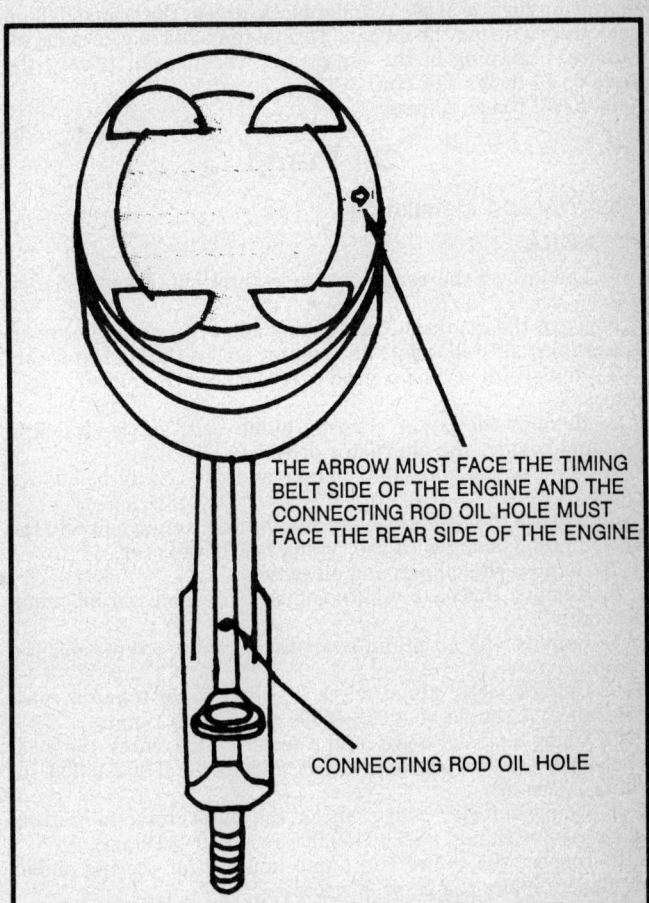

THE ARROW MUST FACE THE TIMING BELT SIDE OF THE ENGINE AND THE CONNECTING ROD OIL HOLE MUST FACE THE REAR SIDE OF THE ENGINE

CONNECTING ROD OIL HOLE

Piston and rod positioning—2494cc and 2675cc engines

ENGINE LUBRICATION

Oil Pan

Removal and Installation

1. Disconnect the negative battery cable. Drain the engine oil.
2. Raise and safely support the vehicle. Remove the lower splash pan, if equipped.
3. Attach a chain to the bracket on the transaxle case and raise just enough to take the load off the center mount.

NOTE: Do not remove the left engine mount.

4. Remove the center beam and engine lower mount.
5. Loosen the oil pan bolts and remove the oil pan flywheel dust shield.

NOTE: Loosen the bolts in a criss-cross pattern beginning with the outside bolt. To remove the oil pan, lightly tap the corners of the oil pan with a mallet.

6. Clean the gasket mounting surfaces.

To install:

7. Reverse the removal procedure. Apply sealant to the entire mounting surface of the cylinder block, except the crankshaft oil seal, before fitting the oil pan. Torque the bolts in a circular sequence, beginning in the center and working out toward the ends to 10 ft. lbs. (14 Nm).
8. Refill the crankcase.

Oil Pump

Removal and Installation

INTEGRA

1. Disconnect the neagtive battery terminal. Remove the oil pan.
2. Turn the crankshaft pulley and align the white groove on the crankshaft pulley with the pointer on the timing belt cover.
3. Remove the cylinder head cover and the timing belt upper cover.
4. Remove the power steering pump belt, air conditioning belt and remove the alternator drive belt.
5. Remove the crankshaft pulley and the timing belt lower cover.
6. Release the belt tensioner, remove the timing belt and the driven pulley along with the timing belt back cover.
7. Remove the oil pan and oil screen.
8. Remove the oil pump-to-engine bolts and the oil pump assembly.
9. Remove the oil pump cover-to-oil pump screws and the cover.
10. Using a feeler gauge, check the inner rotor-to-outer rotor clearance; it should be 0.002–0.006 in. (0.04–0.16mm).
11. Using a straight-edge and a feeler gauge, check the axial clearance on the pump rotor, it should be 0.001–0.003 in. (0.03–0.07mm).
12. Using a feeler gauge, check the outer rotor-to-housing clearance; it should be 0.004–0.007 in. (0.10–0.19mm).
13. Inspect the rotors and pump housing for scoring and/or damage; replace the parts, if necessary.
14. Using a prybar, pry the oil pump from the pump housing.
15. Using the oil seal installer tool or equivalent, drive the new oil seal into the housing until it seats and lubricate the lip with oil.

To install:

16. Check that the oil pump turns freely.
17. Apply a light coat of oil to the seal lip.
18. Install the 2 dowel pins and a new O-ring on the cylinder block.

19. Apply sealant to the cylinder block mating surface of the oil pump and observe the following:
   a. Check the mating surfaces are clean and dry before applying the liquid gasket.
   b. Apply sealant evenly in a narrow bead centered on the mounting surface.
   c. To prevent oil leakage, apply sealant to the inner threads of the bolt holes.
   d. Do not allow the sealant to dry before assembly.
   e. Wait at least 30 minutes after assembly before filling the engine with oil.
20. Install the oil pump to the cylinder block.
21. Install the oil screen.
22. To complete the installation, use new gaskets and reverse of the removal procedures. Torque the oil pump-to-engine bolts to 9 ft. lbs. (12 Nm), the pickup tube-to-engine bolts to 9 ft. lbs. (12 Nm) and the pickup tube-to-oil pump housing bolts to 17 ft. lbs. (24 Nm). Refill the crankcase. Start the engine and check for leaks.

NOTE: On the 1834cc engine, torque the lower 2 pump housing bolts to 17 ft. lbs. (24 Nm), the other pump housing bolts to 8 ft. lbs. (11 Nm) and the pick-up tube to oil pump housing bolts to 8 ft. lbs. (11 Nm).

LEGEND, 825 AND 827

1. Disconnect the negative battery cable. Remove the the oil pan.
2. Rotate the crankshaft pulley and align the timing mark on the crankshaft pulley with the timing mark on the cover, with the No. 1 cylinder at TDC of it's compression stroke.
3. Remove the timing belt upper cover.

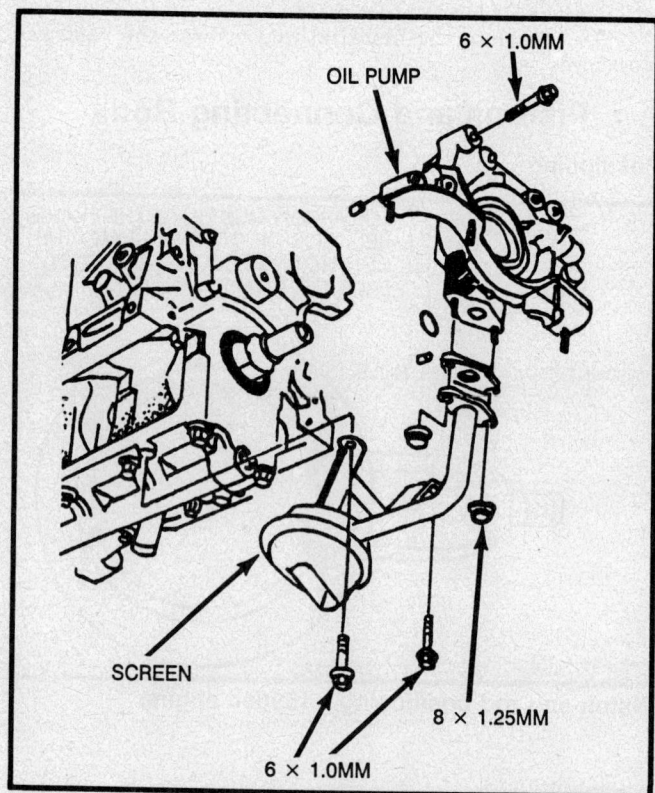

Oil pump mounting housing—1590cc engine—1834cc engine is similar

4. Remove the alternator drive belt, power steering drive belt and the air compressor drive belt.

5. Remove the splash guard.

6. Remove the crankshaft pulley and the timing belt lower cover.

7. Release the belt tensioner, remove the timing belt and the driven pulley.

8. Remove the oil filter assembly.

9. Remove the oil screen and the low level switch, if equipped.

10. Remove the baffle plate.

11. Remove the oil pass pipe and joint.

12. Remove the mounting bolts and the oil pump assembly.

To install:

13. Remove the oil pump cover-to-oil pump screws and the cover.

14. Using a feeler gauge, check the inner rotor-to-outer rotor clearance; it should be 0.002–0.007 in. (0.04–0.018mm).

15. Using a straight-edge and a feeler gauge, check the rotor-to-cover clearance; it should be 0.001–0.003 in. (0.02–0.07mm).

16. Using a feeler gauge, check the outer rotor-to-housing clearance; it should be 0.004–0.007 in. (0.1–0.18mm).

17. Inspect the rotors and pump housing for scoring and the following:

    a. Check the mating surfaces are clean and dry before applying the liquid gasket.

    b. Apply liquid gasket evenly in a narrow bead centered on the mating surface.

    c. To prevent oil leakage, apply sealant to the inner threads of the bolt holes.

    d. Do not allow the sealant to dry before assembly.

    e. Wait at least 30 minutes after assembly before filling the engine with oil.

18. Install the oil pump to the cylinder block; apply sealant to the threads of the 8mm bolt. Torque the oil pump-to-cylinder head bolts to 9 ft. lbs. (12 Nm), the pickup tube-to-engine bolts to 9 ft. lbs. (12 Nm) and the pickup tube-to-oil pump bolts to 9 ft. lbs. (12 Nm).

NOTE: Be sure to torque the 2 longer oil pump housing bolts to 16 ft. lbs. (22 Nm).

19. To complete the installation, reverse the removal procedures. Refill the crankcase. Start the engine and check for leaks.

Front Oil Pump Seal

Replacement

1. Remove the timing belt.

2. Slide the crankshaft sprocket and belt guides from the crankshaft.

3. Using a small prybar, pry the oil seal from the oil pump housing; be careful not to damage the seal's mounting surface.

4. Using a new oil seal, lubricate the seal lips with engine oil. Using a seal drive tool or equivalent, drive the new seal into the oil pump housing until it seats.

5. To complete the installation, reverse the removal procedures. Adjust the timing belt tension. Torque the crankshaft pulley bolt as follows:

    a. 1987–88 Integra—83 ft. lbs.

    b. 1989 Integra—119 ft. lbs.

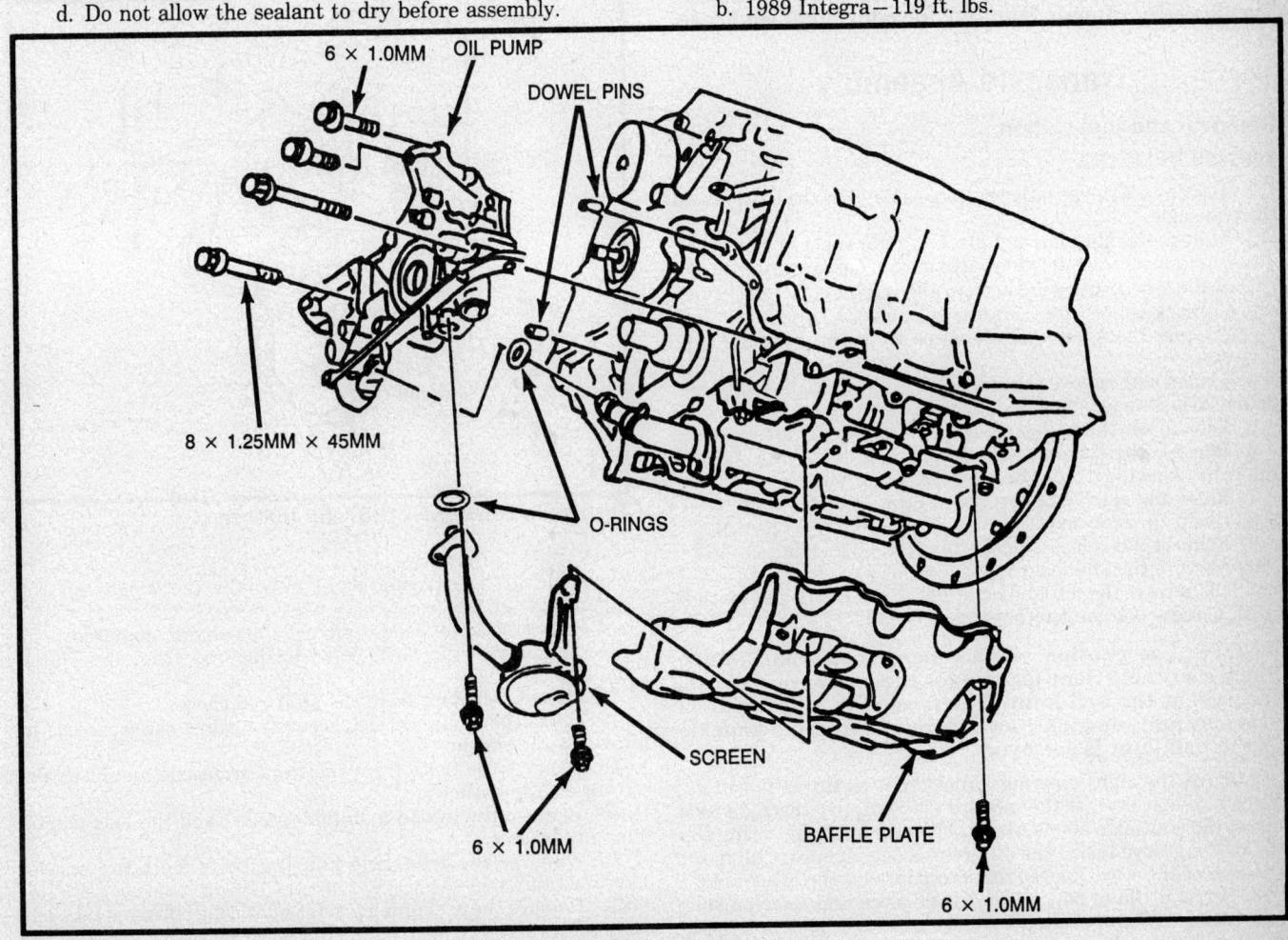

Oil pump mounting housing—2494cc engine and 2675cc engines

c. 1990–91 Integra—87 ft. lbs.
d. 1987–89 Legend and 825—83 ft. lbs.
e. 1990–91 Legend and 827—123 ft. lbs.

Rear Main Bearing Oil Seal

Removal and Installation

1. Remove the oil pan and the transaxle from the vehicle.
2. If equipped with a manual transaxle, perform the following procedures:
   a. Matchmark the pressure plate-to-flywheel.
   b. Insert the clutch alignment tool or equivalent, into the pilot bearing.
   c. Remove the pressure plate-to-flywheel bolts (gradually), the pressure and the clutch plate.
   d. Remove the flywheel-to-crankshaft bolts and the flywheel.
3. If equipped with an automatic transaxle, remove the flexplate-to-flywheel bolts and the flexplate.
4. Remove the rear oil seal housing-to-engine bolts and the gasket.

5. Using a prybar, pry the oil seal from the housing.

To install:

6. Clean the gasket mounting surfaces. Check the flywheel or flexplate for cracks and/or damage; replace it, if necessary.
7. Using an oil seal installation tool or equivalent, drive the new oil seal into the rear oil seal housing until it seats.
8. Using sealant, apply a coat on the gasket mounting surface. Using oil, lubricate the oil seal lips.
9. Reverse the removal procedures. Torque the oil seal housing-to-engine bolts to 9 ft. lbs. (12 Nm); be careful not to damage the oil seal lip.
10. To complete the installation, reverse the removal procedures. Torque the flywheel-to-crankshaft bolts to 54 ft. lbs. (75 Nm) for automatic transaxles or 76 ft. lbs. (105 Nm) for manual transaxles. Refill the crankcase, start the engine and check for leaks.

NOTE: The 1987 1590cc engine had a flywheel torque of 87 ft. lbs. (120 Nm) on the vehicles equipped with a manual transaxle.

MANUAL TRANSAXLE

For further information, please refer to "Professional Transmission Repair Manual" for additional coverage.

Transaxle Assembly

Removal and Installation

1987–89 INTEGRA

1. Disconnect the negative battery cable from the battery and the transaxle.
2. Unlock the steering and place the transaxle in N.
3. Disconnect the following wires in the engine compartment:
   a. Battery positive cable from the starter.
   b. Black/white wire from the solenoid.
   c. Green/black and yellow wires from the back-up light switch.
4. Unclip and remove the speedometer cable at the transaxle; do not disassemble the speedometer gear holder.
5. Disconnect the clutch cable from the release arm.
6. Remove the side and top starter mounting bolts. Loosen the front wheel lug nuts. Remove the front wheels.
7. Raise and safely support the vehicle.
8. Drain the transaxle.
9. Remove the splash shields from the underside.
10. Remove the stabilizer bar.
11. Disconnect the left and right lower ball joints and tie rods ends, using a ball joint remover.

NOTE: Use caution when removing the ball joints. Place a suitable floor jack under the lower control arm securely at the ball joint. Otherwise, the lower control arm may jump suddenly away from the steering knuckle as the ball joint is removed.

12. Turn the right steering knuckle out as far as it will go. Place a prybar against the inboard CV-joint, pry the right axle out of the transaxle about 13mm. This will force the spring clip out of the groove inside the differential gear splines. Pull it out the rest of the way. Repeat this procedure on the other side.
13. Screw a 10mm bolt at the engine block and attach a suitable lifting device of chain hoist and chain to the bolt; attach the other end of the chain on the opposite side, to the engine hanger

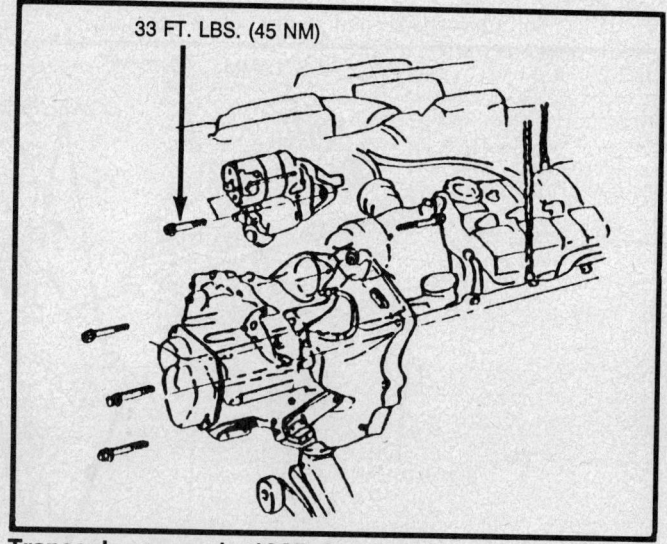

33 FT. LBS. (45 NM)

Transaxle removal—1987–89 Integra

plate and lift the engine slightly to take the weight off the mounts.
14. Disconnect the header pipe at the exhaust manifold.
15. Disconnect the shift lever torque rod from the clutch housing.
16. Remove the bolt from the shift rod clevis.
17. Raise the transaxle jack securely against the transaxle to take up the weight.
18. Remove the bolts from the front transaxle mount at the front engine stiffener.
19. Remove the intake manifold bracket and the rear engine mount bracket.
20. Remove the transaxle housing bolts from the engine torque bracket.
21. Remove the remaining starter mounting bolts and take out the starter.
22. Remove the remaining transaxle mounting bolts.

23. Pull the transaxle away from the engine until it clears the 14mm dowel pins, then lower on the transaxle jack.

24. Separate the mainshaft from the clutch pressure plate and remove the transaxle by lowering the jack.

To install:

25. Install the transaxle on a transaxle jack. Clean and lubricate the clutch release bearing surfaces.

26. Make sure both 14mm dowel pins are installed in the clutch housing.

27. Raise the transaxle high enough to align the dowel pins with the matching holes in the block.

28. Roll the transaxle toward the engine and fit the mainshaft into the clutch disc splines. If the driver's side suspension was left in place, install new spring clips on both axles and carefully insert the left axle into the differential when installing the transaxle.

NOTE: Install new 26mm spring clips on both axles. Make sure the axles fully bottom out. Slide the axle in until the spring clip engages the differential.

29. Push and wiggle the transaxle until it fits flush with the flange.

30. Bolt the transaxle to the engine with the mounting bolts from the engine side. Torque the bolts to 50 ft. lbs. (68 Nm).

31. Install the rear mount bracket on the transaxle housing. Torque the mounting bolts to 47 ft. lbs. (65 Nm).

32. Install the engine torque bracket on the transaxle housing. Torque the mounting bolts to 33 ft. lbs. (45 Nm).

33. Loosely install the bolts for the front of the transaxle mount, then torque them to specifications.

34. Install the starter mounting bolts and torque them to 33 ft. lbs. (45 Nm).

35. Install the intermediate shaft, the right and left halfshaft.

36. Turn the right steering knuckle/axle assembly outward far enough to insert the free end of the axle into the transaxle. Repeat this procedure on the other side.

NOTE: Make sure the axles fully bottom out. Slide the axle in until the spring clip engages the differential.

37. Reconnect the shift rod and the shift lever torque rod.

38. Reconnect the lower arm to the ball joints and torque them to 33 ft. lbs. (45 Nm).

39. Reconnect the tie rod end ball joints and torque them to 33 ft. lbs. (45 Nm).

40. Install the engine and wheelwell splash shields.

41. Reconnect the exhaust header pipe.

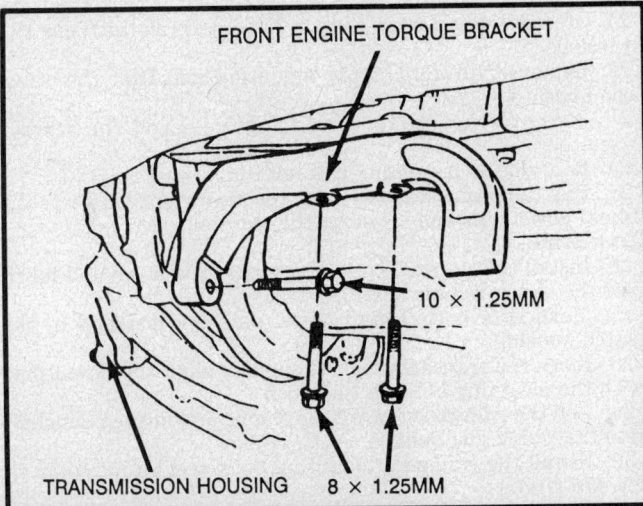

Front transaxle mounting bolt tightening sequence— 1987–89 Integra

42. Install the front wheels, lower the vehicle to the ground and tighten the lug nuts to 80 ft. lbs. (110 Nm).

43. Remove the lifting device from the 10mm bolt on the cylinder head and the engine hanger plate.

44. Install the speedometer cable.

45. Install the transaxle housing bolts and torque them to 33 ft. lbs. (45 Nm).

46. Connect the clutch cable to the release arm, then attach the cable housing end to the transaxle bracket.

47. Connect the engine compartment wiring:
    a. Battery positive cable from the starter.
    b. Black/white wire from the solenoid.
    c. Green/black and yellow wires from the back-up light switch.

48. With the ignition key turned **OFF**, connect the ground cable to the battery and the transaxle.

49. Refill the transaxle with SAE 30, 10W–30, 10W–40 or 20W–40 and adjust the clutch free-play.

50. Check the transaxle for smooth operation.

1990–91 INTEGRA

1. Disconnect the negative first and then the positive battery cables.

2. Remove the 4 battery mounting bolts and remove the battery.

3. Remove the air cleaner case complete with air intake tube. Disconnect the transaxle ground cable.

4. Loosen the clutch cable adjusting nut and disconnect the clutch cable at the release arm, then disconnect from the clutch cable bracket.

5. Disconnect the electrical connectors for the back-up light switch, oxygen sensor and the starter motor cables and wire harness clamp from the starter.

6. Remove the power steering speed sensor with the sensor hose intack.

7. Disconnect the distributor connectors and remove the distributor mounting bolts. Before removing the distributor, be sure to make some alignment marks on the distributor housing and engine to aid in the installation procedure.

8. Raise and safely support the vehicle. Remove the starter.

9. Drain the transaxle oil into a suitable container.

10. Remove the right front splash shield and splash guard. Remove the center beam bolts and remove the center beam.

11. Remove the cotter pin from the lower right ball joint castle nut, remove the nut and using a ball joint separator, remove the ball joint and lower arm.

12. Remove the right damper fork. Remove the right radius rod locknut, then the bolts and remove the right radius arm.

13. Remove the right halfshaft assembly.

14. Remove the cotter pin from the lower left ball joint castle nut, remove the nut and using a ball joint separator, remove the ball joint and lower arm.

15. Remove the left halfshaft from the intermediate shaft. Remove the intermediate shaft bolts and remove the intermediate shaft.

16. Remove the shift rod and shift lever torque rod from the transaxle.

17. Remove the front engine stiffener and the rear engine stiffener. Remove the 4 bolts from the clutch housing cover and remove the cover.

18. Remove the 2 transaxle mount bolts from the engine side.

19. Remove the 2 transaxle mount bolts from the rear engine mount bracket.

20. Remove the side transaxle mount bolt from the underside. Remove the front transaxle mount bolts and mount.

21. Install the bolts into the cylinder head and attach a suitable lifting device or chain hoist to the bolts. Lift the engine slightly to take the load off of the engine mounts.

22. Place a suitable transaxle jack under the transaxle and raise the transaxle enough to take the weight off of the transax-

le mounts. Remove the bolts and nuts that attach the brackets to the side transaxle mounts.

23. Remove the 3 transaxle mount bolts from the transaxle side.

24. Pull the transaxle away from the clutch pressure plate until it clears the mainshaft, then remove the transaxle by lowering the jack.

To install:

25. Install the transaxle on a transaxle jack. Clean and lubricate the clutch release bearing surfaces.

26. Make sure both 14mm dowel pins are installed in the clutch housing.

27. Loosely install the transaxle mount bolts, then torque them to 49 ft. lbs. (68 Nm).

28. Secure the transaxle to the engine with the engine side mounting bolt and torque it to 50 ft. lbs. (68 Nm).

29. Install the transaxle to side transaxle mount. Install the transaxle to the front transaxle mount.

30. Install the transaxle to the rear engine mount bracket.

31. Loosely install the bolt in the front stiffener and then torque then to 17 ft. lbs. (24 Nm).

32. Loosely install the bolt in the rear stiffener and then torque then to 17 ft. lbs. (24 Nm).

33. Remove the transaxle jack. Remove the lifting device by removing the hoist bolts from the cylinder head.

34. Install the shift lever torque rod and shift rod. On reassembly, slide the retainer back into place after driving in the spring pin.

35. Install the intermediate shaft.

36. Install the left halfshaft, then the left ball joint and lower arm.

37. Install the right halfshaft assembly. Be sure to turn the right steering knuckle fully outward and slide the axle into the differential until the spring clip engages the side gear.

38. Install the right radius arm, damper fork bolt and the right ball joint to the lower arm.

39. Install the center beam. Install the right front splash guard and splash shield.

40. Install the starter motor. Install the distributor, be sure to use the alignment marks made earlier in the removal procedure.

41. Connect the starter motor cables and wire harness clamp. Install the power steering speed sensor.

42. Connect the oxygen sensor connector, back-up light connector and connect the clutch cable to the clutch cable bracket, then connect to the release arm.

43. Connect the transaxle ground. Install the air cleaner case complete with the air intake tube.

44. Install the battery base. Refill the transaxle with the recommended transaxle fluid.

45. Install the battery and connect the battery cables.

46. Adjust the clutch free-play. Check the ignition timing and road test the vehicle to be sure the transaxle is operating properly.

LEGEND, 825 AND 827

1. Disconnect the both battery cables from the battery.

2. Disconnect the starter and ground cables.

3. Disconnect the back-up light wires from the engine harness.

4. Loosen the 6mm bolt attaching the harness holder at the side of the transaxle hanger and the release harness from the transaxle.

5. Loosen the 6mm bolts at the side of the battery base and the intake hose band.

6. Remove the air cleaner case assembly along with the intake hose.

7. Remove the 8mm bolts and the clutch slave cylinder with the clutch hose and the pushrod.

NOTE: Do not operate the clutch pedal once the slave cylinder has been removed.

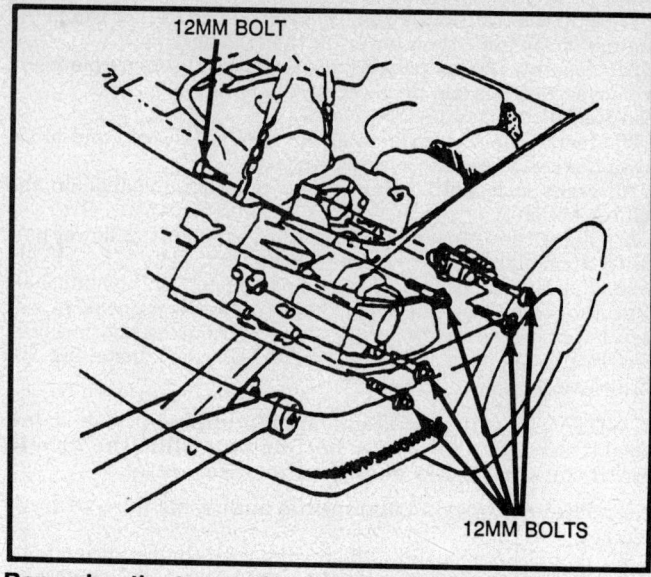

Removing the transaxle—Legend, 825 and 827

8. Remove the 8mm bolts and clutch damper assembly from the transaxle hanger bracket.

9. Remove the power steering speed sensor with the sensor hose intact.

10. Drain the oil from the transaxle.

11. Remove the halfshaft from the vehicle.

12. Remove the bolts securing the intermediate shaft and remove the shaft.

13. Remove the shift rod and the shift extension.

14. Remove the bolts attaching the torque rod bracket to the clutch case.

NOTE: Replace the torque rod bolts whenever loosened or removed.

15. Place a transaxle jack securely beneath the transaxle.

16. Remove the sub frame center beam.

17. Attach a engine support chain with two 10mm bolts to the engine block, 1 on each bank.

18. Lift the engine slightly to take the weight off the mounts.

19. Remove the center stop bracket from the transaxle.

20. Remove the clutch cover.

21. Remove both rear engine mounting bolts from the transaxle.

22. Remove both front engine mounting bolts from the transaxle housing.

23. Remove the starter mounting bolts and the starter assembly.

24. Remove the remaining transaxle mounting bolts.

25. Pull the transaxle away from the engine until it clears the 14mm dowel pins and lower on the transaxle jack.

To install:

26. Install the transaxle on a transaxle jack; clean and lubricate the clutch release bearing surfaces.

27. Make sure both 14mm dowel pins are installed in the clutch housing.

28. Raise the transaxle high enough to align the dowel pins with the matching holes in the block.

29. Roll the transaxle toward the engine and fit the mainshaft into the clutch disc splines.

30. Install the transaxle mounting bolts and torque to 55 ft. lbs. (75 Nm).

31. Install the starter and torque the mounting bolts.

32. Install the front engine mounting bolts and torque to 29 ft. lbs. (40 Nm).

33. Install the rear engine mounting bolts and torque to 29 ft. lbs. (40 Nm).

34. Install the center stopper bracket bolts and torque to 29 ft. lbs. (40 Nm).

35. Install the clutch cover.

36. Install the center beam.

37. Remove the transaxle jack.

38. Install and torque the new torque rod bracket bolts to 29 ft. lbs. (40 Nm).

NOTE: Replace the torque rod bolts whenever loosened or removed.

39. Remove the engine support chain by removing both 10mm bolts.

40. Install the shift rod and shift extension.

41. Install the intermediate shaft with the 8mm bolts. Torque the bolts to 29 ft. lbs. (40 Nm).

42. Install the right and left halfshaft.

43. Install the speed sensor.

44. Install the clutch slave cylinder with the 8mm bolts complete with the hose and pushrod. Torque the bolts to 16 ft. lbs. (22 Nm).

45. Install the clutch damper assembly and the 8mm bolts to the transaxle hanger bracket. Torque the bolts to 16 ft. lbs. (22 Nm).

46. Install the air cleaner assembly and the air intake hose.

47. Install and torque both 6mm bolts at the side of the battery case and tighten the intake hose band.

48. Tighten the 6mm harness holder bolt at the side of the transaxle hanger.

49. Connect the back-up light switch wire to the engine harness.

50. Connect the starter and ground cables.

51. Connect the both battery cables.

52. Refill the transaxle with SAE 10W–30 or 10W–40 and adjust the free-play.

53. Check the transaxle for smooth operation.

Linkage Adjustment

The shift linkage is non-adjustable. However, if the linkage is binding or if there is excessive play, check the linkage bushings and pivot points. Lubricate with light oil or replace worn bushings, as necessary.

CLUTCH

All vehicles use a single dry disc with a diaphragm spring type pressure plate. On the Integra model the clutch is cable operated. However, on the Legend, 825 and 827, a hydraulic master and slave cylinder system is used.

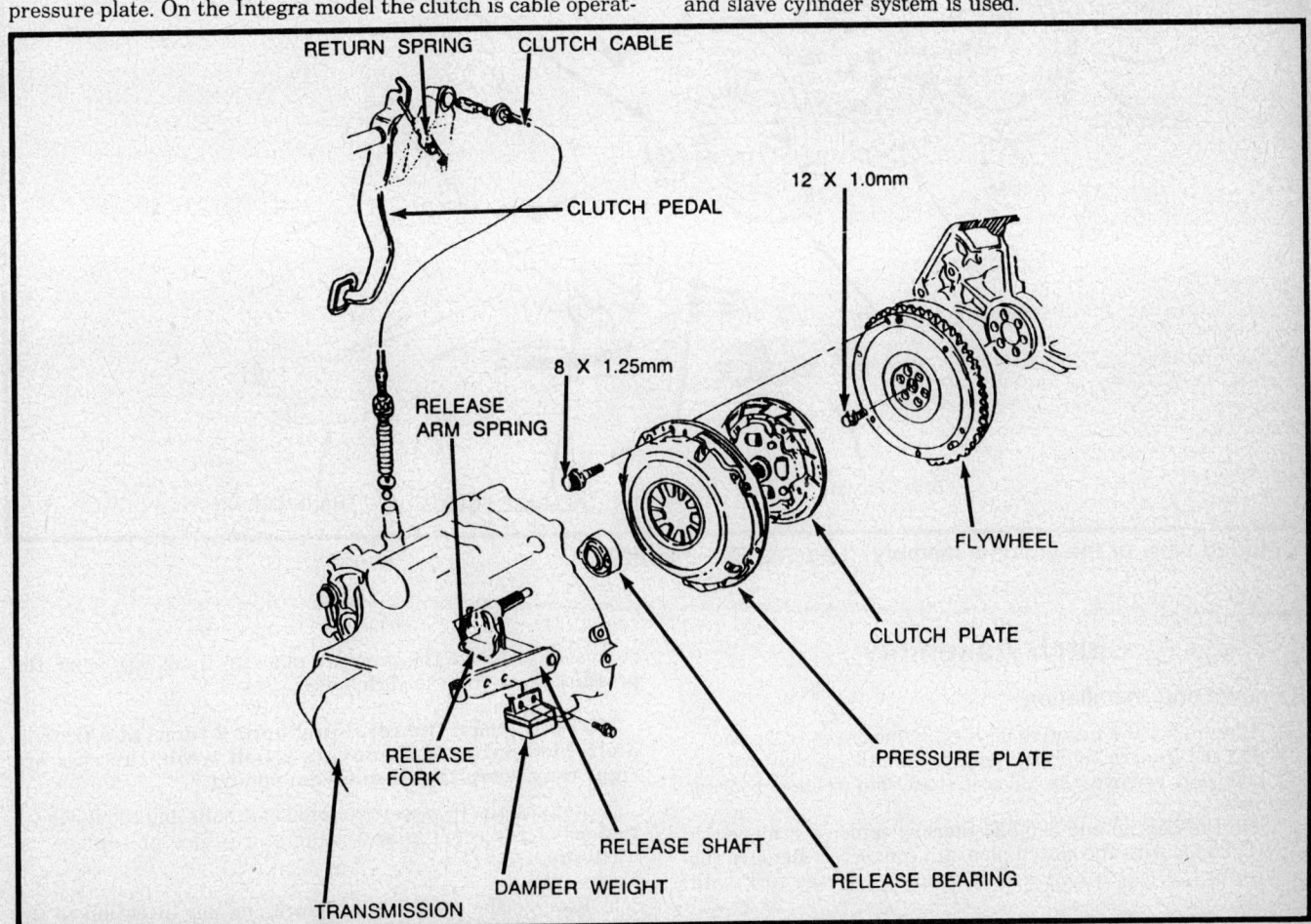

Exploded view of the clutch assembly—Integra

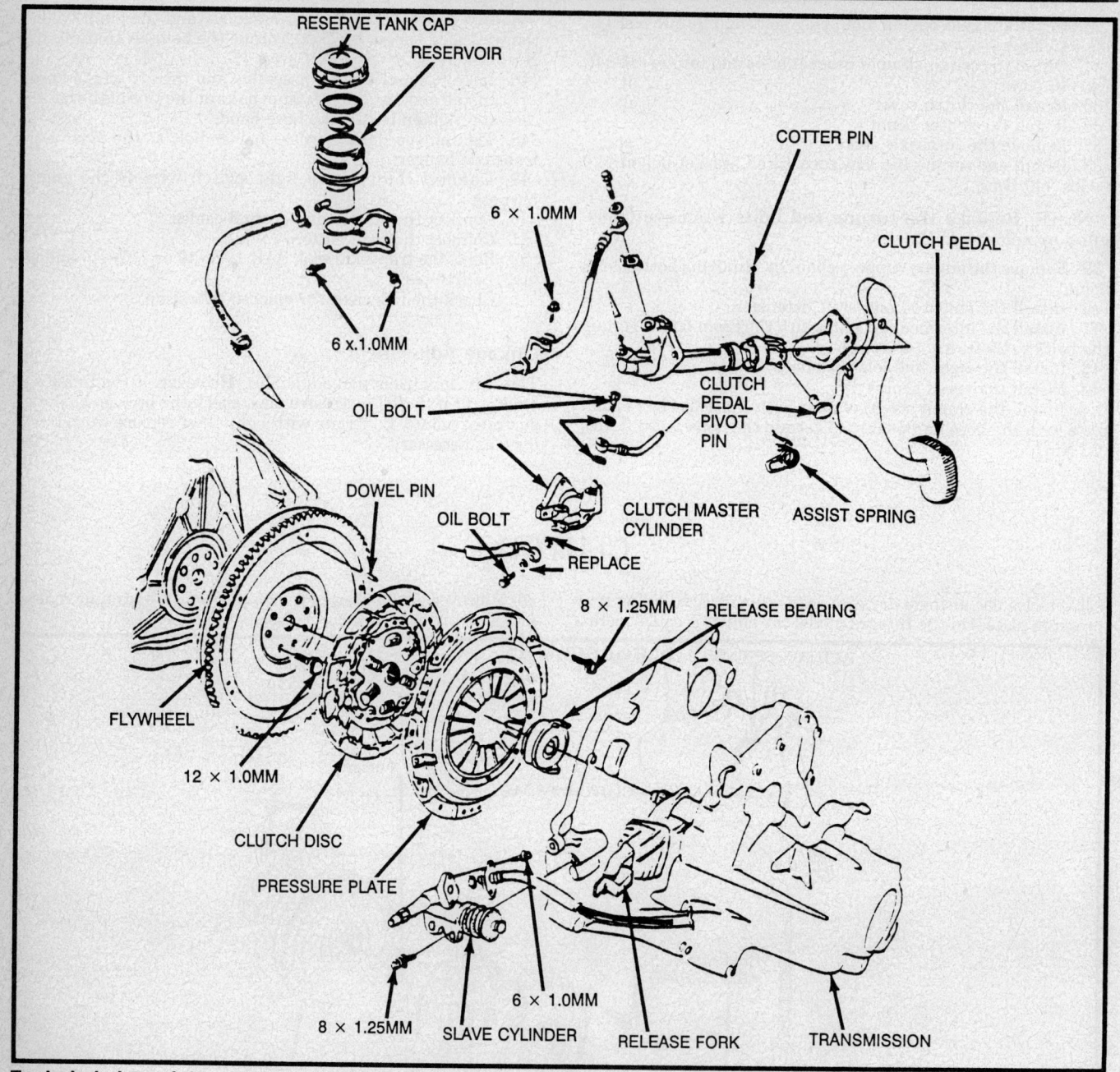

RESERVE TANK CAP
RESERVOIR
COTTER PIN
CLUTCH PEDAL
6 × 1.0MM
6 x.1.0MM
OIL BOLT
CLUTCH PEDAL PIVOT PIN
DOWEL PIN
OIL BOLT
CLUTCH MASTER CYLINDER
ASSIST SPRING
REPLACE
8 × 1.25MM
RELEASE BEARING
FLYWHEEL
12 × 1.0MM
CLUTCH DISC
PRESSURE PLATE
8 × 1.25MM
SLAVE CYLINDER
6 × 1.0MM
RELEASE FORK
TRANSMISSION

Exploded view of the clutch assembly—Legend, 825 and 827

Clutch Assembly

Removal and Installation

1. Disconnect the negative battery. Remove the transaxle.
2. On the Integra vehicles, Remove the release shaft retaining bolt and remove the release shaft and release bearing assembly.
3. On the Legend and 825/827 Sterling vehicles, remove the slave cylinder with the clutch pipe still connected. Remove the boot from the clutch case and remove the release fork with bearing.
4. Matchmark the flywheel and pressure plate for easy reassembly. Install the clutch alignment tool 07974–6890101 or

equivalent, remove the pressure plate-to-clutch disc bolts, the pressure plate and the clutch disc.

NOTE: Loosen the retaining bolts 2 turns at a time in a circular pattern. Removing a bolt while the rest are tight may warp the diaphragm spring.

5. Remove the flywheel-to-crankshaft bolts and the flywheel. Inspect it for scoring and wear and reface or replace, as necessary.

To install:

6. Reverse the removal procedure and pay attention to the following points:
   a. Make sure the flywheel and the end of the crankshaft are

clean before assembly. Torque the flywheel-to-crankshaft bolts to specifications.

b. When installing the pressure plate, align the mark on the outer edge of the flywheel with the alignment mark on the pressure plate. Failure to align these marks will result in imbalance.

c. When torquing the pressure plate bolts, use a pilot shaft to center the friction disc. After centering the disc, tighten the bolts 2 turns at a time, in a criss-cross pattern to avoid warping the diaphragm springs; torque to 19 ft. lbs. (26 Nm).

d. When installing the transaxle, make sure the mainshaft is properly aligned with the disc spline and the aligning pins are in place, before torquing the case bolts.

Pedal Height/Free-Play Adjustment

INTEGRA

1. Adjust the clutch free-play at the release lever by turning the adjusting nut (at the transaxle). The clutch pedal height should be:
   1987—5.67 in. (144mm)
   1988–89—5.87 (149mm)
   1990–91—6.97 (177mm)
2. Make sure there is $\frac{5}{32}$–$\frac{13}{64}$ in. (4.0–5.0mm) of free-play at the tip of the release arm after the adjustment.
3. If equipped with cruise control, turn the adjuster (above the clutch pedal) until the clutch pedal stroke is:
   1987—5.31–5.51 in. (135–140mm)
   1988–89—5.51–5.71 in. (140–145mm)
   1990–91—5.59–5.79 in. (142–147mm)
4. Tighten the locknut securely.

LEGEND, 825 AND 827

Total clutch free-play is 0.35–0.59 in. (9–15mm).
1. Loosen the locknut on the clutch pedal switch.
2. Loosen the locknut on the clutch master cylinder pushrod. Turn the pushrod in or out to obtain the correct stroke and height at the clutch pedal.
   Stroke at pedal—5.7–5.9 in. (145–150mm)
   Clutch pedal height—7.0 in. (179mm) (to floor)
3. Tighten the locknut on the clutch master cylinder pushrod.
4. Screw the clutch pedal switch until it contacts the pedal.
5. Turn the switch another ¼–½ turn. Tighten the locknut.

Clutch Cable

Adjustment

INTEGRA

1. Measure the clutch pedal disengagement height.
2. Measure the clutch pedal free-play.
3. Adjust the clutch pedal free-play by turning the adjusting nut. Be sure there is 0.16–0.20 in. (4.0–5.0mm) free-play at the tip of the release arm after the adjustment.
4. Turn the adjusting bolt right or left to bring the clutch pedal stroke to the proper specification and then tighten the locknut to 16 ft. lbs. (22 Nm).

Removal and Installation

1. Release the clutch cable from the release arm by loosening the adjusting nut to allow enough slack to enable the cable to be removed from the elongated hole in the release arm.
2. From under the dash panel and behind the clutch pedal, remove the clevis pin that retains the clutch cable to the clutch pedal.
3. Remove the clutch cable holder from the firewall. Push the clutch cable through the grommet, if equipped, or squeeze the cable retaining clip and push or pull the cable through the firewall to remove it.

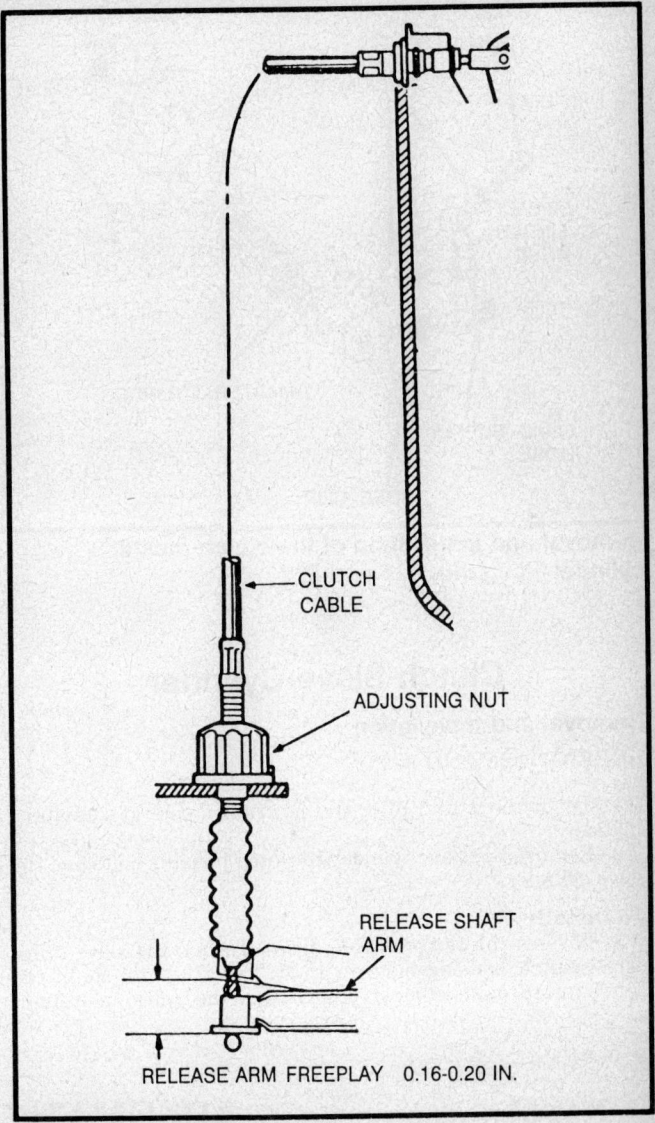

CLUTCH CABLE

ADJUSTING NUT

RELEASE SHAFT ARM

RELEASE ARM FREEPLAY 0.16-0.20 IN.

Adjusting the clutch free-play—Integra

4. To Install; reverse the order of the removal procedure and adjust the clutch cable.

Clutch Master Cylinder

Removal and Installation

LEGEND, 825 AND 827

The clutch master cylinder is located on the firewall in the engine compartment next to the brake master cylinder.
1. From the top of the clutch pedal, remove the cotter pin and pivot pin from the clutch pedal-to-pushrod junction.
2. Disconnect the hydraulic line (banjo bolt) from the clutch master cylinder.
3. Remove the master cylinder-to-firewall nuts and the master cylinder.
4. Disconnect the reservoir hose from the master cylinder by removing the clip.
To install:
5. Reverse the removal procedures. Torque the master cylinder-to-firewall nuts to 16 ft. lbs. (22 Nm). Refill the clutch master cylinder reservoir and bleed the system after installation.

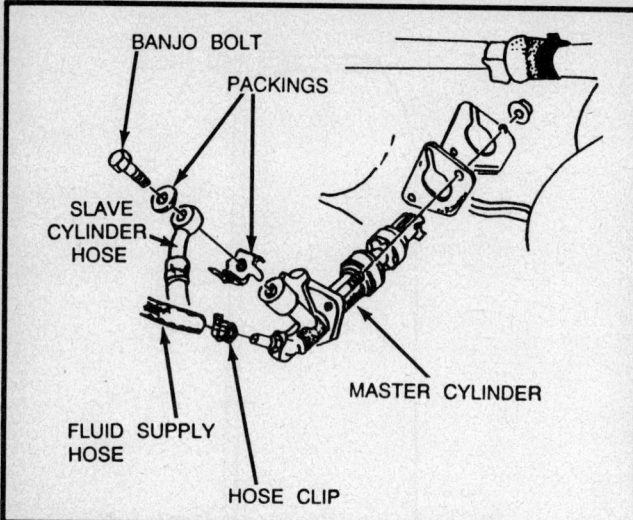

Removal and installation of the clutch master cylinder—Legend, 825 and 827

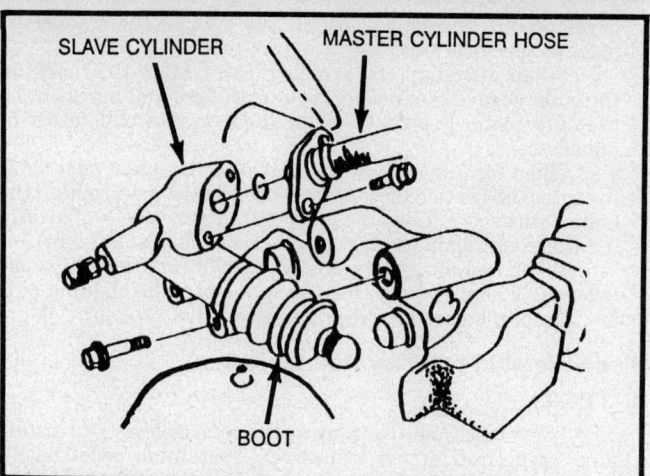

Exploded view of the slave cylinder assembly— Legend, 825 and 827

Clutch Slave Cylinder

Removal and Installation
LEGEND, 825 AND 827

1. Disconnect and plug the hydraulic line at the slave cylinder.
2. Remove the slave cylinder-to-clutch housing bolts and the slave cylinder.

To install:
3. Reverse the removal procedures. Torque the slave cylinder-to-clutch housing bolts to 16 ft. lbs. (22 Nm). Refill the clutch master cylinder reservoir and bleed the hydraulic system.

Hydraulic Clutch System Bleeding
LEGEND, 825 AND 827

The hydraulic system must be bled whenever the system has been leaking or has been dismantled. The bleed screw is located on the slave cylinder.
1. Remove the bleed screw dust cap.
2. Attach a clear hose to the bleed screw. Immerse the other end of the hose in a clear jar ½ filled with brake fluid.
3. Refill the clutch master cylinder with fresh brake fluid.
4. Open the bleed screw slightly and have an assistant slowly depress the clutch pedal. Close the bleed screw when the pedal reaches the end of it's travel. Allow the clutch pedal to return slowly.
5. Repeat Steps 3–4 until all air bubbles are expelled from the system.
6. Discard the brake fluid in the jar. Replace the dust cap. Refill the master cylinder.

AUTOMATIC TRANSAXLE

For further information, please refer to "Professional Transmission Repair Manual" for additional coverage.

Transaxle Assembly

Removal and Installation
1987–89 INTEGRA

1. Disconnect the negative battery cable and the ground cable from the transaxle. Raise and safely support the vehicle.
2. Unlock the steering and place the transaxle in **N**.
3. Disconnect the following wires in the engine compartment:
   a. Battery positive cable from the starter.
   b. Black/white wire from the solenoid.
4. Drain the transaxle.
5. Disconnect the speedometer cable.
6. Disconnect and plug the transaxle cooler hoses; wire them up next to the radiator so the automatic transaxle fluid won't drain out.
7. Remove the center console and disconnect the shift cable by removing the adjusting pin.

8. Unscrew the cable guide bolt and pull out the throttle cable.
9. Remove the right and left halfshaft and intermediate shaft.
10. Screw a 10mm bolt at the cylinder head and attach a suitable lifting device or chain hoist and chain to the bolt; attach the other end of the chain to the engine hanger plate and lift the engine slightly to take the weight off the mounts.
11. Remove transaxle stop bracket, if equipped, the undercover and the engine splash shields.
12. Disconnect the header pipe from the exhaust manifold.
13. Using a transaxle jack, place it under the transaxle and raise it enough to take the weight off the mounts.
14. At the front of the engine bracket, remove the bolts from the front transaxle mount.
15. Remove the rear transaxle mount bracket bolts and the mount.
16. From the front transaxle mount bracket, remove the transaxle housing bolts.
17. Remove the torque converter cover. Matchmark the torque converter-to-driveplate location.
18. Rotate the crankshaft pulley and remove the torque converter-to-driveplate bolts.

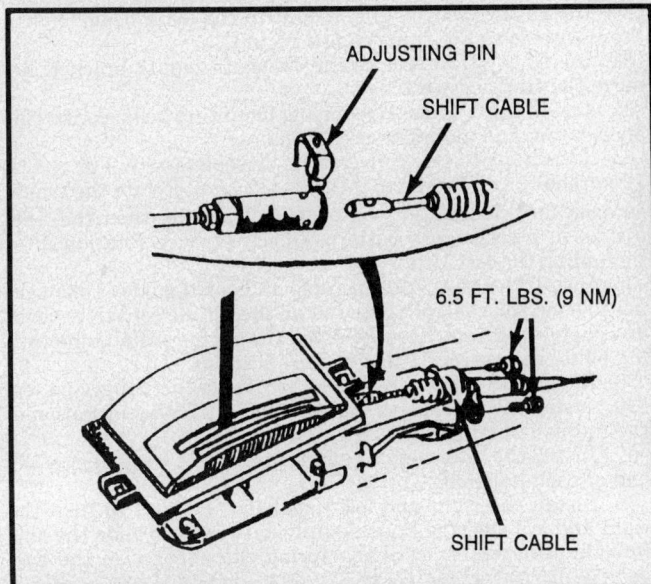

ADJUSTING PIN

SHIFT CABLE

6.5 FT. LBS. (9 NM)

SHIFT CABLE

Shift cable adjusting pin—1987–89 Integra

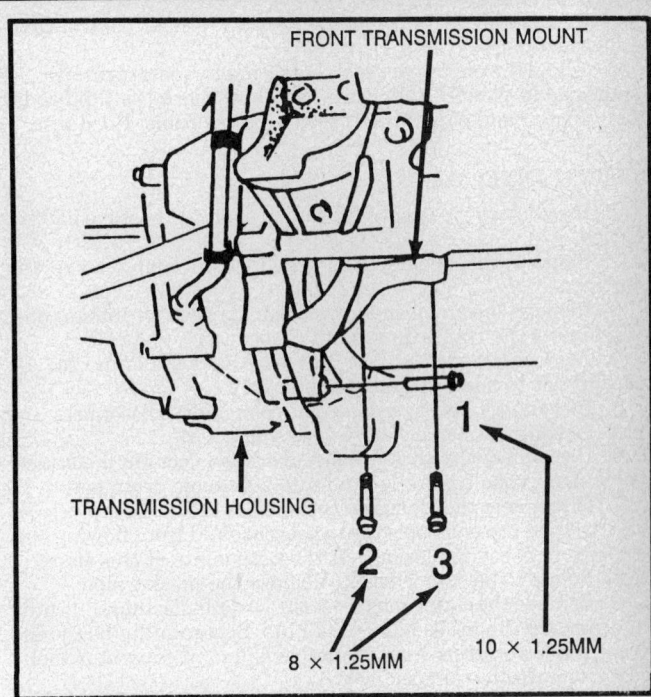

FRONT TRANSMISSION MOUNT

TRANSMISSION HOUSING

8 × 1.25MM

10 × 1.25MM

Front transaxle mount tightening sequence—1987–89 Integra

NOTE: The crankshaft pulley bolt is a right hand thread and may be loosened when the pulley is turned counterclockwise. After removing the driveplate, check that the pulley bolt is torqued properly.

19. Remove the starter bolts and the starter.
20. Remove the remaining transaxle mounting bolts.
21. Pull the transaxle away from the engine until it clears the 14mm dowel pins and lower it on the transaxle jack.
To install:
22. Install the transaxle on a transaxle jack.
23. Make sure both 14mm dowel pins are installed in the torque converter housing.
24. Raise the transaxle high enough to align the dowel pins with the matching holes in the block. Align the torque converter matchmark and the bolt heads with holes in the driveplate.
25. If the driver's side suspension was left in place, install new spring clips on both axles, then carefully insert the left axle into the differential as the transaxle is raised to the engine.

NOTE: Install new 26mm spring clips on both axles. Make sure the axles fully bottom out. Slide the axle in until the spring clip engages the differential.

26. Push and wiggle the transaxle until it fits flush with the flange.
27. Torque the transaxle-to-engine bolts (from the engine side) to 42 ft. lbs. (58 Nm).
28. Attach the torque converter to the driveplate with 12mm bolts and torque to 9 ft. lbs. (12 Nm). Rotate the crankshaft as necessary to torque the bolts to half the torque, then final torque in a criss-cross pattern. Check for free rotation after torquing the last bolt.
29. Install the shift cable.
30. Remove the transaxle jack.
31. Install the torque converter cover plate.
32. Install the rear mount bracket on the transaxle housing. Torque the bolts to 48 ft. lbs. (65 Nm).
33. Install the front transaxle mount bracket. Torque the bolts to 33 ft. lbs. (45 Nm).
34. Loosely install the bolts for the front of the transaxle mount, then torque them to 18 ft. lbs. (24 Nm).
35. Install the transaxle stop bracket, if equipped, and torque the bolts to 33 ft. lbs. (45 Nm). Install the starter mounting bolts and torque them to 33 ft. lbs. (45 Nm).

36. Install the intermediate shaft, the right and left halfshaft.
37. Turn the right steering knuckle/axle assembly outward far enough to insert the free end of the axle into the transaxle. Repeat this procedure on the other side.

NOTE: Make sure the axles fully bottom out. Slide the axle in until the spring clip engages the differential.

38. Reconnect the lower arm to the ball joints and torque them to 33 ft. lbs. (45 Nm).
39. Reconnect the tie rod end ball joints and torque them to 33 ft. lbs. (45 Nm).
40. Install the engine splash shields.
41. Reconnect the exhaust header pipe.
42. Install the front wheels, lower the vehicle to the ground and torque the lug nuts 80 ft. lbs. (110 Nm).
43. Remove the lifting device from the 10mm bolt on the cylinder head and the engine hanger plate.
44. Install the speedometer cable.
45. Install the 3 top transaxle mounting bolts and torque them to 48 ft. lbs. (65 Nm).
46. Connect the cooler hoses and torque the banjo bolts to 21 ft. lbs. (29 Nm).
47. Attach the shift control cable to the shaft lever with the pin and clip, if removed. Check the adjustment.
48. Reinstall the center console.
49. Connect the engine compartment wiring:
   a. Battery positive cable to the starter.
   b. Black/white wire from the solenoid.
   c. Transaxle ground cable.
50. With the ignition key turned **OFF**, connect the ground cable to the battery and the transaxle.
51. Unscrew the dipstick from the top of the transaxle housing and add 2.5 qts. of Dexron® ATF through the hole. Reinstall the dipstick.

NOTE: If the torque converter was replaced, the transaxle fill quantity is 5.7 qts.

52. Start the engine, set the parking brake and shift the trans-

axle through all gears 3 times. Check for proper control cable adjustment.

53. Allow the engine to reach operating temperature with the transaxle in **N** or **P**, then turn it off and check the fluid level.

54. Install and adjust the throttle control cable. Road test.

1990–91 INTEGRA

1. Disconnect the negative first and then the positive battery cables.

2. Remove the 4 battery mounting bolts and remove the battery.

3. Remove the air cleaner case complete with air intake tube. Disconnect the transaxle ground cable.

4. Remove the speed sensor, but leave its hoses connected. Be careful not to bend the speedometer cable.

5. Disconnect the speed pulser connector. Disconnect the lock-up control solenoid valve wire connectors.

6. Disconnect the vacuum hose from the vacuum modulator valve. Drain the transaxle fluid into a suitable drain pan.

7. Disconnect the transaxle cooler lines at the joint pipes. Be sure to turn the ends up so as to prevent fluid from flowing out. Be sure to check for leakage at the hose joints at this time.

8. Remove the center beam. Remove the header pipe.

9. Remove the cotter pins from the lower ball joint castle nuts and remove the lower ball joints nuts. Separate the ball joints from the lower arms with a suitable ball joint separator tool.

10. Remove the damper fork.

11. Pry the right and left halfshafts out of the differential and the intermediate shaft. Pull on the inboard CV-joint and remove the right and left halfshafts.

12. Remove the 3 mounting bolts and lower the bearing support. Remove the intermediate shaft from the differential.

13. Remove the engine splash shield and the right wheelwell splash shield.

14. Remove the right damper pinch bolt, then separate the damper fork and damper.

15. Remove the bolts and nut from the right radius arm and remove the radius arm.

16. Remove the front and rear engine stiffners. Remove the torque converter cover and cable holder.

17. Remove the shift control cable by removing the cotter pin, control pin and control lever roller from the control lever.

18. Remove the shift control cable guide, take care not to bend the control cable.

19. Remove the plug, then remove the driveplate bolts 1 at a time while rotating the crankshaft pulley. Remove the mounting bolt from the front engine mount.

20. Remove the 2 mounting bolts from the rear engine mount bracket. Remove the front and rear transaxle housing mounting bolt.

21. Loosen the differential housing mounting bolt.

22. Attach a a suitable lifting device or chain hoist to the transmission housing hoist bracket and differential housing to engine mounting bolt, then lift the engine slightly to unload the mounts.

23. Place a transaxle jack under the transaxle and raise the transaxle enough to take the weight of the mounts.

24. Remove the front engine mount. Remove the 4 transaxle housing mounting bolts and 2 mount bracket bolts.

25. Pull the transaxle away from the engine until it clears the 14mm dowel pins, then lower down the transaxle jack.

To install:

26. Install the transaxle on a transaxle jack.

27. Make sure both 14mm dowel pins are installed in the torque converter housing.

28. Raise the transaxle high enough to align the dowel pins with the matching holes in the block. Align the torque converter matchmark and the bolt heads with holes in the driveplate.

29. Install the 4 transaxle housing mounting bolts, then install the transaxle to the engine block.

30. Install the front engine mount to the front beam. Install the transaxle to the front engine mount.

31. Install the transaxle to the transaxle mount bracket. Remove the transaxle jack.

32. Install the 2 transaxle housing mounting bolts engine side and rear engine mount bracket bolts.

33. Attach the torque converter to driveplate with 8 (6 × 1 × 12mm) bolts and torque to 9 ft. lbs. (12 Nm). Rotate the crank, as necessary, to tighten the bolts half torque, then the final torque in a criss-cross pattern. Check for free rotation after tightening the last bolt.

34. Install the shift control cable and cable guide. Take care not to bend the control cable. Install the torque converter cover and engine stiffners. Loosely install the engine stiffener mounting bolts, then torque them to specifications.

35. Remove the lifting device by removing the hanger plates.

36. Install the radius arm. Be sure to check for deterioration of the radius rod rubber bushings.

37. Install the intermediate shaft. Install a new set ring on the end of each halfshaft.

38. Install the right and left halfshafts. Be sure to turn the right and left steering knuckle fully outward and slide the axle into the differential until the spring clip engages in the side gear.

39. Install the damper fork. Install the splash shield.

40. Install the damper fork bolts and the ball joint nuts to the lower arms.

41. Install the header pipe and center beam.

42. Install the speed sensor and connect the speed pulser connector.

43. Connect the lock-up control solenoid valve wire connectors. Connect the transaxle oil cooler lines to the joint pipes.

44. Connect the vacuum hose to the modulator. Install the transaxle ground cable.

45. Refill the transaxle with the proper transaxle fluid.

46. Connect the battery cables. Install the air intake hose.

47. Start the engine, set the parking brake and shift the transaxle through all gears 3 times. Check for proper control cable adjustment. Check the ignition timing.

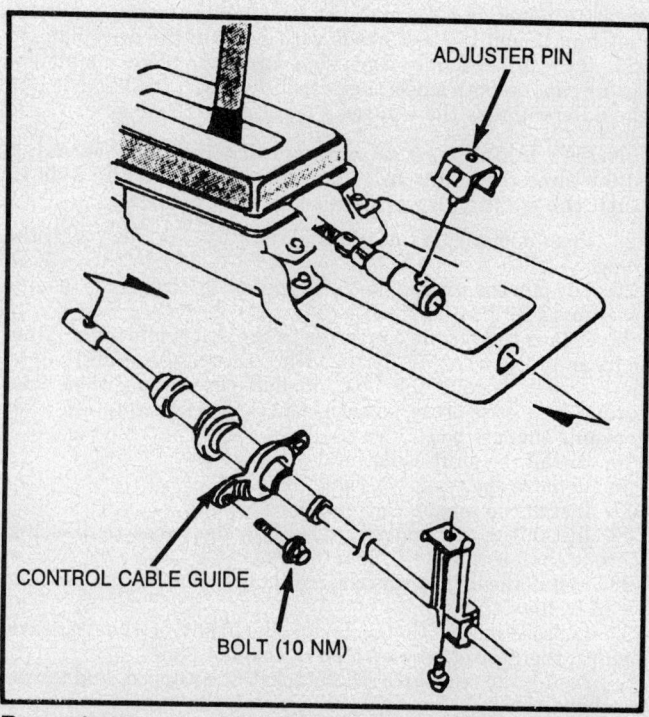

ADJUSTER PIN

CONTROL CABLE GUIDE

BOLT (10 NM)

Removing the control cable—Legend, 825 and 827

48. Allow the engine to reach operating temperature with the transaxle in **N** or **P**, then turn it off and check the fluid level.

49. Road test the vehicle and make sure the transaxle is operating properly.

LEGEND, 825 AND 827

1. Disconnect the negative and positive battery cables from the battery.
2. Disconnect the starter motor and ground cables.
3. Drain the transaxle fluid from the transaxle.
4. Remove the both 6mm bolts located at the side of the battery base and the intake hose band at the throttle body.
5. Remove the air cleaner assembly along with the intake hose.
6. Remove the speedometer gearbox complete with the power steering speed sensor hose.
7. Disconnect the throttle control cable from the transaxle housing.
8. Disconnect and plug the transaxle cooler hoses at the joint pipes; turn the ends up to prevent the transaxle fluid from flowing out.

9. Near the oil cooler pipe bracket, disconnect the lockup control solenoid valve wire connector and the automatic speed pulser wire connector for 1988–90.
10. Remove the center console, pry off the adjuster pin and disconnect the control cable.
11. Remove the control cable guide bolts and pull out the cable assembly; be careful not to bent the cable when removing it.
12. Remove the right/left halfshafts and the intermediate shaft.
13. Remove the torque converter case mounting bolts from the torque rod bracket.
14. Attach a suitable lifting device or chain hoist with 2 bolts and raise the engine slightly to unload the mounts.
15. Remove the front engine mount bolts from the transaxle housing.
16. While holding the locknut, turn off the radius rod.
17. Remove the center beam.
18. Remove the center stopper bracket from the transaxle.
19. Remove the torque converter cover.
20. Place a transaxle jack under the transaxle and raise the transaxle just enough to take the weight off the mounts.

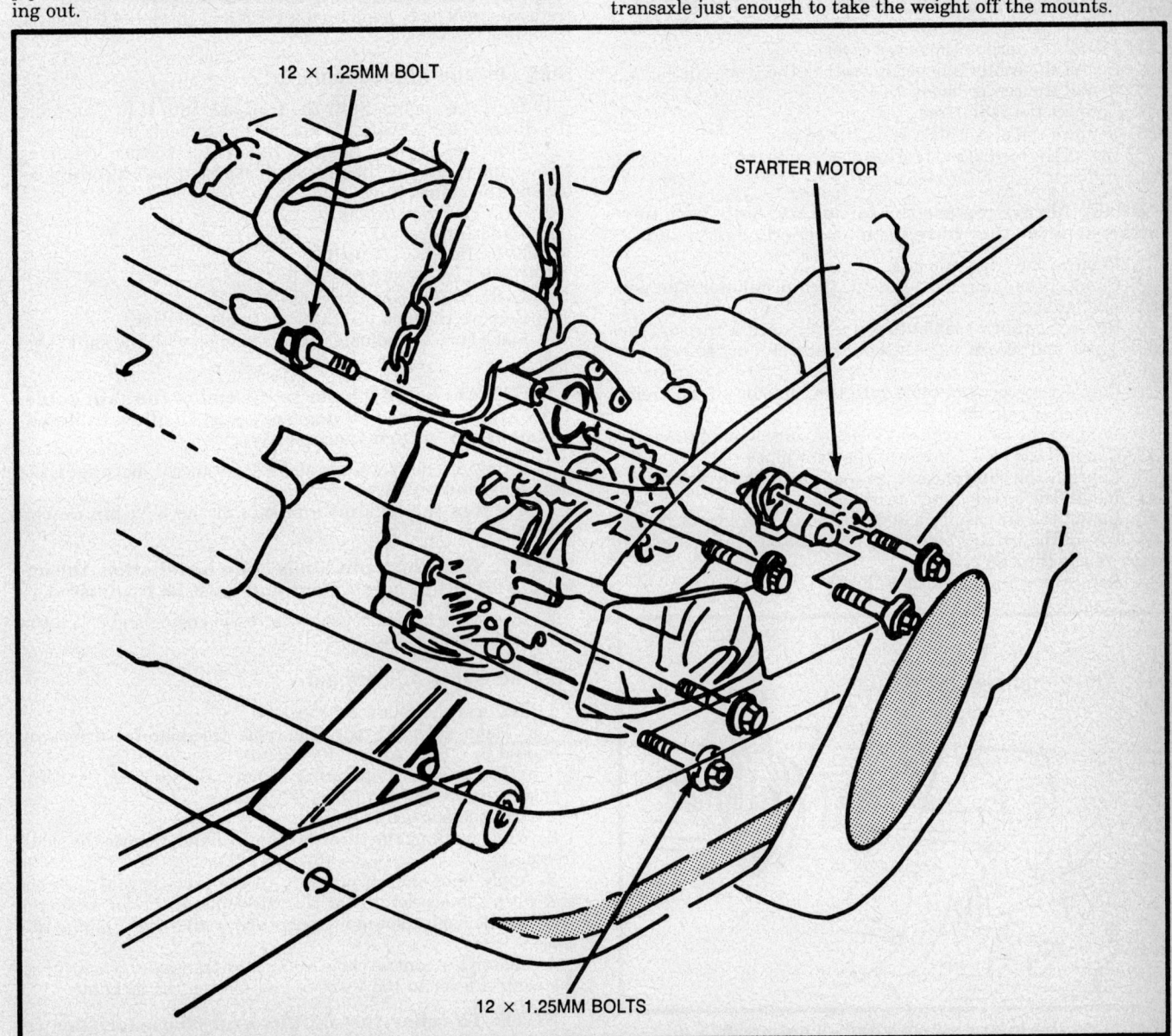

Removing the automatic transaxle—Legend, 825 and 827

21. Remove the both rear engine mount bolts from the transaxle.

22. Matchmark the torque converter-to-driveplate. Remove the plug and the driveplate bolts one at a time while rotating the crankshaft pulley.

23. Remove the starter-to-engine bolts and the starter.

24. Remove the remaining transaxle housing-to-engine bolts.

25. Pull the transaxle away from the engine and lower it from the vehicle.

To install:

26. Install the transaxle on a transaxle jack and raise to engine level.

27. Secure the transaxle to the engine with the mounting bolts.

28. Install the starter motor.

29. Align the matchmarks and attach the torque converter-to-driveplate bolts; torque the bolts to 9 ft. lbs. (12 Nm). Rotate the crank, as necessary, to torque the bolts to ½ torque, the to the final torque, in a criss-cross pattern. Check for free rotation after torquing the last bolt.

30. Install the transaxle to the front engine mount bracket bolts and torque to 29 ft. lbs. (39 Nm).

31. Install the torque converter cover.

32. Install the center stopper bracket to the transaxle.

33. Install the center beam.

34. Connect the radius rod.

35. Remove the chain hoist from the engine.

36. Install the torque rod bracket and torque the bolts to 29 ft. lbs. (40 Nm).

NOTE: Always replace the torque rod bolts with new ones whenever they have been loosened or removed.

37. Remove the transaxle jack.

38. Connect the intermediate shaft, then install the right and left halfshafts.

39. Route the control cables to the center console through the cable guide and secure with the bolt; be careful not to bent the cables.

40. Connect the control cable with the adjuster pin and reinstall the center console.

41. Connect the lockup control solenoid valve wire connectors.

42. Connect the cooler hoses to the joint pipes.

43. Connect the control cable on the throttle body side.

44. Install the speedometer gearbox.

45. Install the air cleaner assembly and the air intake hose.

46. Install the battery base bolts and tighten the intake hose band on the throttle body.

47. Refill the transaxle with ATF.

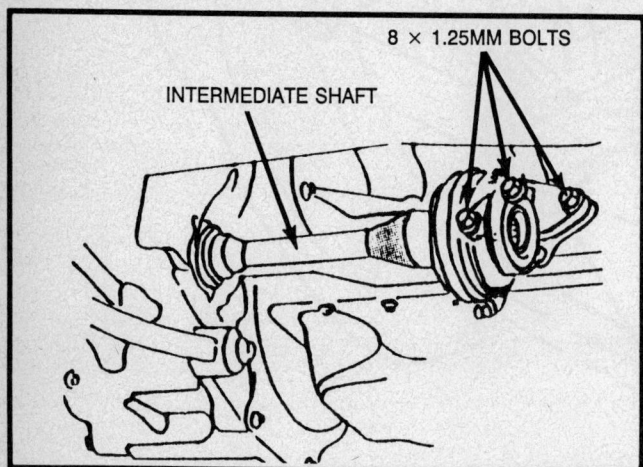

8 × 1.25MM BOLTS

INTERMEDIATE SHAFT

Installing the intermediate shaft—Legend, 825 and 827

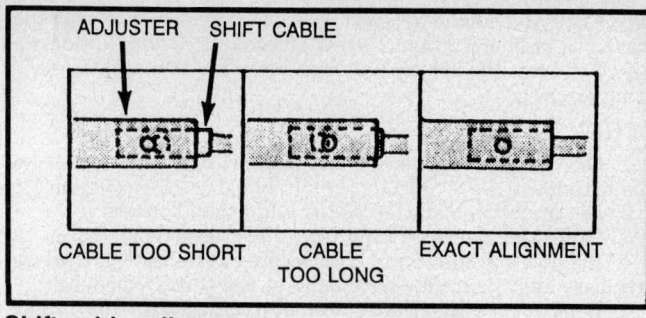

ADJUSTER   SHIFT CABLE

CABLE TOO SHORT   CABLE TOO LONG   EXACT ALIGNMENT

Shift cable adjustment

48. Connect the starter and ground cables.

49. Connect the battery cables.

50. Start the engine, set the parking brake, then shift the transaxle through all gears 3 times. Check for proper control cable adjustment.

51. Allow the engine reach operating temperature with the transaxle in **N** or **P**, then turn it **OFF** and check the fluid level. Road test the vehicle.

Shift Linkage Adjustment

1. Start the engine. Shift the transaxle into **R** to make sure the reverse gear engages. If not, other problems are suspect.

2. Stop the engine. Remove the center console retaining screws and pull away the console to expose the shift control cable and the adjuster.

3. Shift the transaxle into:
1987–88 Integra—**D**
1989–91 Integra—**N** or **R**
1987–88 Legend and 825S—**R**
1989–91 Legend and Sterling—**N** or **R**

4. Remove the lock pin from the cable adjuster.

5. Make sure the adjuster hole is aligned with the shift cable hole.

NOTE: There are 2 holes in the end of the shift cable. They are positioned 90 degrees apart to allow cable adjustments in ¼ turn increments.

6. If they are not perfectly aligned, loosen the locknut on the shift cable and adjust, as required.

7. Tighten the locknut and install the lock pin on the adjuster.

NOTE: If the lock pin binds upon installation, the cable is still out of adjustment and must be readjusted.

8. Install the center console. Start the engine and check the shift lever in all gears.

Throttle Cable Adjustment

1. Perform the following checks:
   a. Make sure the throttle cable free-play is correct; it should be 0.39–0.47 in. (10–12mm).
   b. The engine is operating at normal operating temperatures; the cooling fan turns **ON**.
   c. The idle speed is correct.

2. While working the throttle cable by hand, remove the cable free-play.

3. Apply light thumb pressure to the throttle control lever and work the accelerator or throttle linkage; the lever should move as the engine speed increases above idle, if not, adjust the cable.

4. Loosen the control cable nuts at the transaxle, synchronize the control lever to the throttle and tighten the locknuts.

NOTE: To tailor the shift/lock-up characteristics to the driving expectations, adjust the control cable up to 3mm shorter than the synchronized point.

DRIVE AXLE

Halfshaft

Removal and Installation

The front halfshaft assembly consists of a sub-axle shaft and a halfshaft with 2 universal joints.

A constant velocity ball joint is used for both universal joints, which are factory packed with special grease and enclosed in sealed rubber boots. The outer joint cannot be disassembled except for removal of the boot.

1987–89 INTEGRA

1. Loosen, but do not remove, the front wheel spindle nut with a 32mm socket.
2. Raise and safely support the vehicle.
3. Drain the transaxle.
4. Remove the wheel lug nuts and the wheel.
5. Remove the spindle nut.
6. Using a floor jack to support the lower control arm, remove the lower arm ball joint cotter pin and nut.

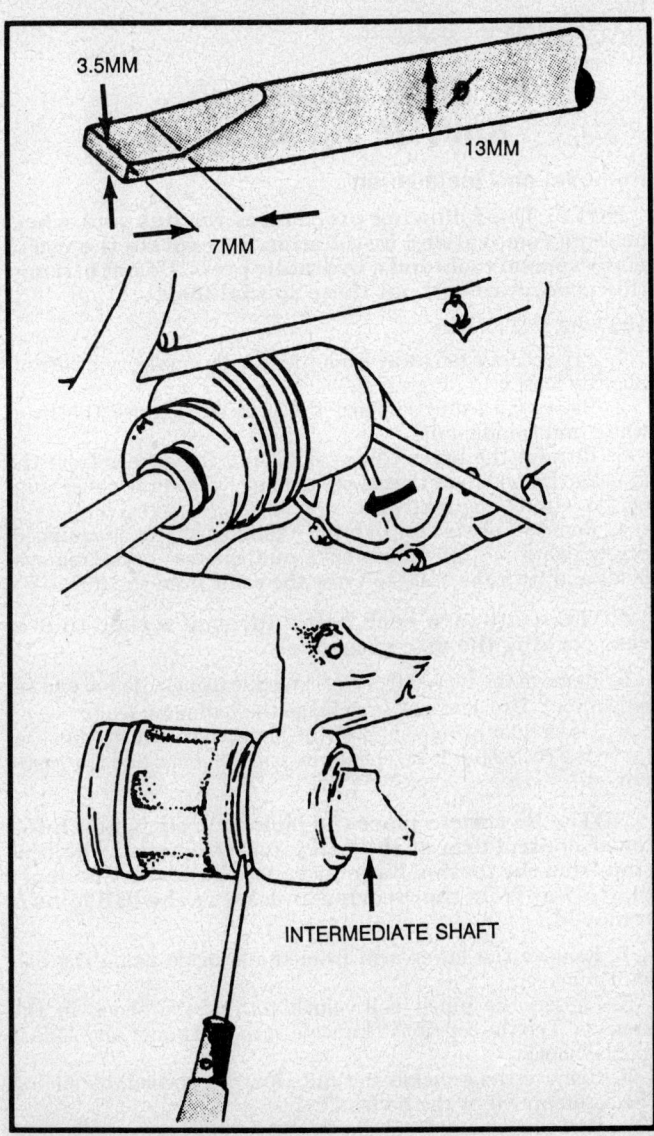

Halfshaft removal—Integra

NOTE: Make sure a floor jack is positioned securely under the lower control arm, at the ball joint. Otherwise, the lower control arm may jump suddenly away from the steering knuckle as the ball joint is removed.

7. Separate the ball joint from the front hub with a ball joint puller.
8. Slowly lower the floor jack to lower the control arm.
9. Using a small prybar with a 3.5 × 7mm tip, pry out the inboard CV-joint approximately ½ in. (12mm) in order to force the spring clip out of the groove in the differential side gears.

NOTE: Be careful not to damage the oil seal. Do not pull on the inboard CV-joint, it may come apart.

10. Pull the halfshaft out of the differential or the intermediate shaft.

To install:

11. Reverse the removal procedure. If either the inboard or outboard joint boot bands have been removed for inspection or disassembly of the joint (only the inboard joint can be disassembled), be sure to repack the joint with a sufficient amount of bearing grease.

NOTE: Make sure the CV-joint sub-axle bottoms so the spring clip may hold the halfshaft securely in the differential/intermediate shaft groove. Always replace the spring clip with a new one!

1990–91 INTEGRA

1. Disconnect the negative battery cable.
2. Loosen the left front wheel lugs. Raise and safely support the vehicle.
3. Remove the left front wheel. Raise the locking tab on the spindle nut and remove it a suitable socket.
4. Remove the damper fork nut and damper pinch bolt. Remove the damper fork.
5. Remove the knuckle to lower arm castle nut and separate the lower arm from the knuckle using a suitable puller with the pawls applied to the lower arm.
6. Pull the knuckle outward and remove the halfshaft outboard CV-joint from the knuckle using a suitable plastic mallet.
7. Pry the halfshaft assembly with a suitable tool to force the set ring at the halfshaft end past the groove.
8. Pull the inboard CV-joint and remove the halfshaft and CV-joint out of the intermediate shaft.

NOTE: Do not pull on the driveshaft, as the CV-joint may come apart. Use care when prying out the assembly and pull it straight to avoid damaging the intermediate shaft seals.

9. To remove the intermediate shaft, remove the 3mm bolts. Lower the bearing support close to the steering gear box and remove the intermediate shaft from the differential. To prevent any damage from the differential oil seal, hold the intermediate shaft horizontal until it is clear of the differential.

To install:

10. Reverse the removal procedure. If either the inboard or outboard joint boot bands have been removed for inspection or disassembly of the joint (only the inboard joint can be disassembled), be sure to repack the joint with a sufficient amount of bearing grease. Always use a new set ring whenever the driveshaft is being installed. Be sure the driveshaft locks in the differential side gear groove and that the CV-joint subaxle bottoms in the differential or the intermediate shaft.

LEGEND, 825 AND 827

1. Loosen the front wheel lug nuts.
2. Raise and safely support the vehicle.
3. Drain the transaxle.

NOTE: It is not necessary to drain the transaxle when the right for 1987 or left for 1988–90 halfshaft is removed.

4. Remove the wheel lug nuts and then the wheel.
5. Raise the locking tab on the spindle nut and remove it with a 36mm socket wrench.
6. Remove the damper fork bolt, the damper pinch bolt and the damper fork.
7. Remove the knuckle-to-lower arm castle nut and separate the lower arm from the knuckle, using a bearing puller tool or equivalent.
8. Pull the knuckle outward and remove the halfshaft outboard joint from the knuckle, using a plastic tipped hammer.
9. Using a small prybar with a 3.5 × 7mm tip, pry out the inboard CV-joint approximately ½ in. (12mm) in order to force the spring clip out of the groove in the differential side gears.

NOTE: Be careful not to damage the oil seal. Do not pull on the inboard CV-joint, it may come apart.

10. Pull the halfshaft out of the differential or the intermediate shaft.

To install:

11. Reverse the removal procedure. If either the inboard or outboard joint boot bands have been removed for inspection or disassembly of the joint (only the inboard joint can be disassembled), be sure to repack the joint with a sufficient amount of bearing grease.

NOTE: Make sure the CV-joint sub-axle bottoms so the spring clip may hold the halfshaft securely in the differential, intermediate shaft groove. Always replace the spring clip with a new one!

Intermediate Shaft

Removal and Installation

1. Drain the oil from the transaxle.
2. Remove the 10mm bolts on the Integra, the 8mm and 10mm bolt on the Legend, 825 and 827.
3. Lower the bearing support close to the steering gearbox and remove the intermediate shaft from the differential.

NOTE: To avoid damage to the differential oil seal, hold the intermediate shaft horizontal until it clears the differential.

4. To install, reverse the removal procedure.

CV-Joint Boot

NOTE: The following procedures are for how to remove the CV-joint boot from the halfshaft once the halfshaft has been removed from the vehicle. If a quick seal boot is to be used, it is recommended that the manufacturers instruction be followed.

Removal and Installation

NOTE: Be sure to mark the roller grooves during disassembly to ensure proper positioning during reassembly. Before disassembly mark the spider gear and the driveshaft so they can be installed in their original positions. The inboard joint must be removed to replace the boots.

1. Remove the halfshaft that requires the boot change.
2. Remove the front and rear boot retaining bands and slide the boots off the halfshaft.

To install:

3. Wrap the spline with vinyl tape to prevent damage to the boots. Install the outboard and inboard boots onto the halfshaft, then remove the vinyl tape.

4. Install the stopper ring onto the driveshaft groove. Also install the dynamic damper at this time, if equipped.
5. Install the spider gear onto the halfshaft by aligning the marks and install it in its original position.
6. Fit the snapring into the halfshaft groove.
7. Pack the outboard joint boot with high quality molybdenum disulfide grease or an equivalent high temperature all purpose bearing grease.
8. Fit the rollers to the spider gear with their high shoulders facing outward. Reinstall the rollers in their original positions on the spider gear.
9. Pack the inboard joint boot with high quality molybdenum disulfide grease or an equivalent high temperature all purpose bearing grease.
10. Fit the inboard joint onto the driveshaft. Hold the driveshaft assembly so the inboard joint points up. to prevent it from falling off.
11. Adjust the length of the driveshafts so the distance from one boot end to the other is 21.0–21.2 in. (533–538mm). Now adjust the boots to halfway between full compression and full extension.
12. Install the new boot bands on the boots and bend both sets of locking tabs. Lightly tap on the locking tabs to ensure a good fit.
13. Reinstall the halfshaft.

Front Wheel Hub, Knuckle and Bearings

Removal and Installation

NOTE: The following procedures for hub and wheel bearing removal and installation necessitate the use of many special tools and a hydraulic press. Do not attempt this procedure without these special tools.

1987–89 INTEGRA

1. Pry the lock tab away from the spindle and loosen the nut. Slightly loosen the lug nuts.
2. Raise and safely support the vehicle. Remove the front wheel and spindle nut.
3. Remove the brake caliper bolts and the caliper from the knuckle. Do not allow the caliper to hang by the brake hose, support it with a length of wire.
4. Remove the disc brake rotor retaining screws, if equipped. Screw two 8 × 1.25 12mm bolts into the disc brake removal holes and turn the bolts to press the rotor from the hub.

NOTE: Only turn each bolt 2 turns at a time to prevent cocking the disc excessively.

5. Remove the tie rod from the knuckle using a tie rod end removal tool. Use care not to damage the ball joint seals.
6. Use a floor jack to support the lower control arm, then, remove the cotter pin from the lower arm ball joint and the castle nut.

NOTE: Be sure to place the jack securely beneath the lower control arm at the ball joint. Otherwise, the tension from the torsion bar may cause the arm to suddenly jump away from the steering knuckle as the ball joint is removed.

7. Remove the lower arm from the knuckle using the ball joint remover.
8. Loosen the pinch bolt which retains the shock in the knuckle. Tap the top of the knuckle with a hammer and slide it off the shock.
9. Remove the knuckle and hub, if still attached, by sliding the assembly off of the halfshaft.
10. Remove the hub from the knuckle using special tools and a hydraulic press.

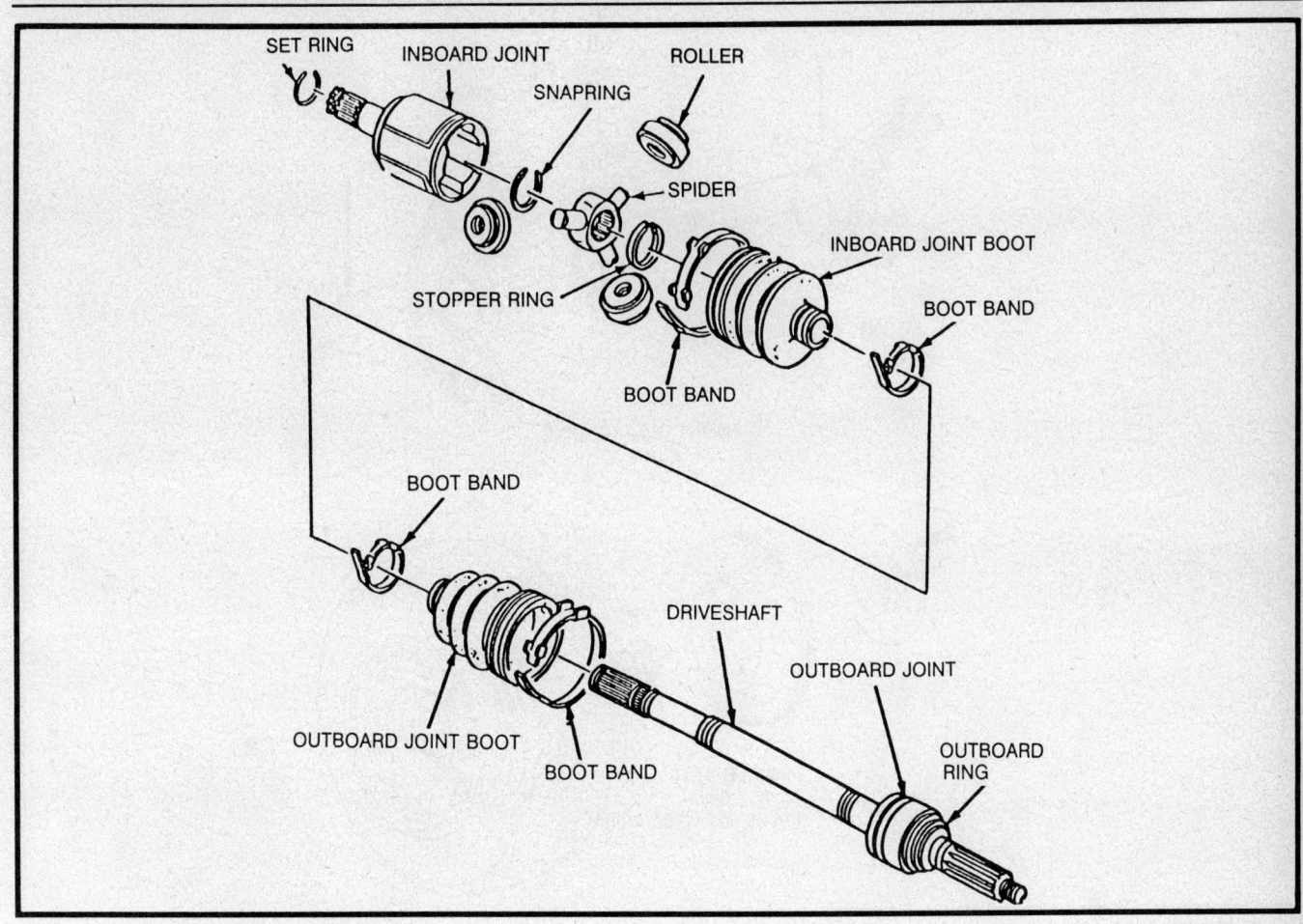

CV-joint boot removal and installation

11. Remove the splash guard and the snapring.
12. Press the bearing outer race out of the knuckle using special tools and a hydraulic press.
13. Remove the outboard bearing inner race from the hub using special tools and a bearing puller.

NOTE: Whenever the wheel bearings are removed, always replace them with a new set of bearings and an outer dust seal.

14. Clean all old grease from the halfshaft and spindles on the vehicle.
15. Remove the old grease from the hub and knuckle and thoroughly dry and wipe clean all components.

To install:
16. Install the bearings, press the bearing outer race into the knuckle using the special tools as used above, plus the installation base tool or equivalent.
17. Install the snapring and the splash guard.
18. Place the hub in the special tool fixture, set the knuckle in position on the press and apply downward pressure.
19. The remaining step are the reverse of the removal procedure. Torque the spindle nut to 134 ft. lbs. (185 Nm). Use a new spindle nut and stake it after torquing.

1990–91 INTEGRA
1. Pry the lock tab away from the spindle and loosen the nut. Slightly loosen the lug nuts.
2. Raise and safely support the vehicle. Remove the front wheel and spindle nut.

3. Remove the brake caliper bolts and the caliper from the knuckle. Do not allow the caliper to hang by the brake hose, support it with a length of wire.
4. Remove the disc brake rotor retaining screws, if equipped. Screw two 8×1.0mm bolts into the disc brake removal holes and turn the bolts to press the rotor from the hub.

NOTE: Only turn each bolt 2 turns at a time to prevent cocking the disc excessively.

5. Remove the cotter pin from the tie rod end and remove the castle nut. Break loose the tie rod ball joint using a suitable ball joint removal tool and lift the tie rod out the steering knuckle.
6. Remove the cotter pin and loosen the lower arm ball joint nut half the length of the joint threads. Separate the ball joint and lower arm using a puller with the pawls applied to the lower arm. Avoid damaging the ball joint thread. If necessary, apply a suitable penetrating type lubricant to loosen the ball joint.
7. Remove the knuckle protector. Remove the cotter pin and remove the upper ball pin nut. Separate the upper ball joint and the knuckle using a suitable ball joint removal tool.
8. Remove the steering knuckle and hub by sliding them off of the halfshaft.
9. Remove the splash guard screws from the knuckle. Separate the hub from the knuckle using a suitable hydraulic press. Be careful not to distort the splash guard. Hold onto the hub to keep it from falling when pressed clear. To prevent damage to the tool make sure the threads are fully engaged before pressing.

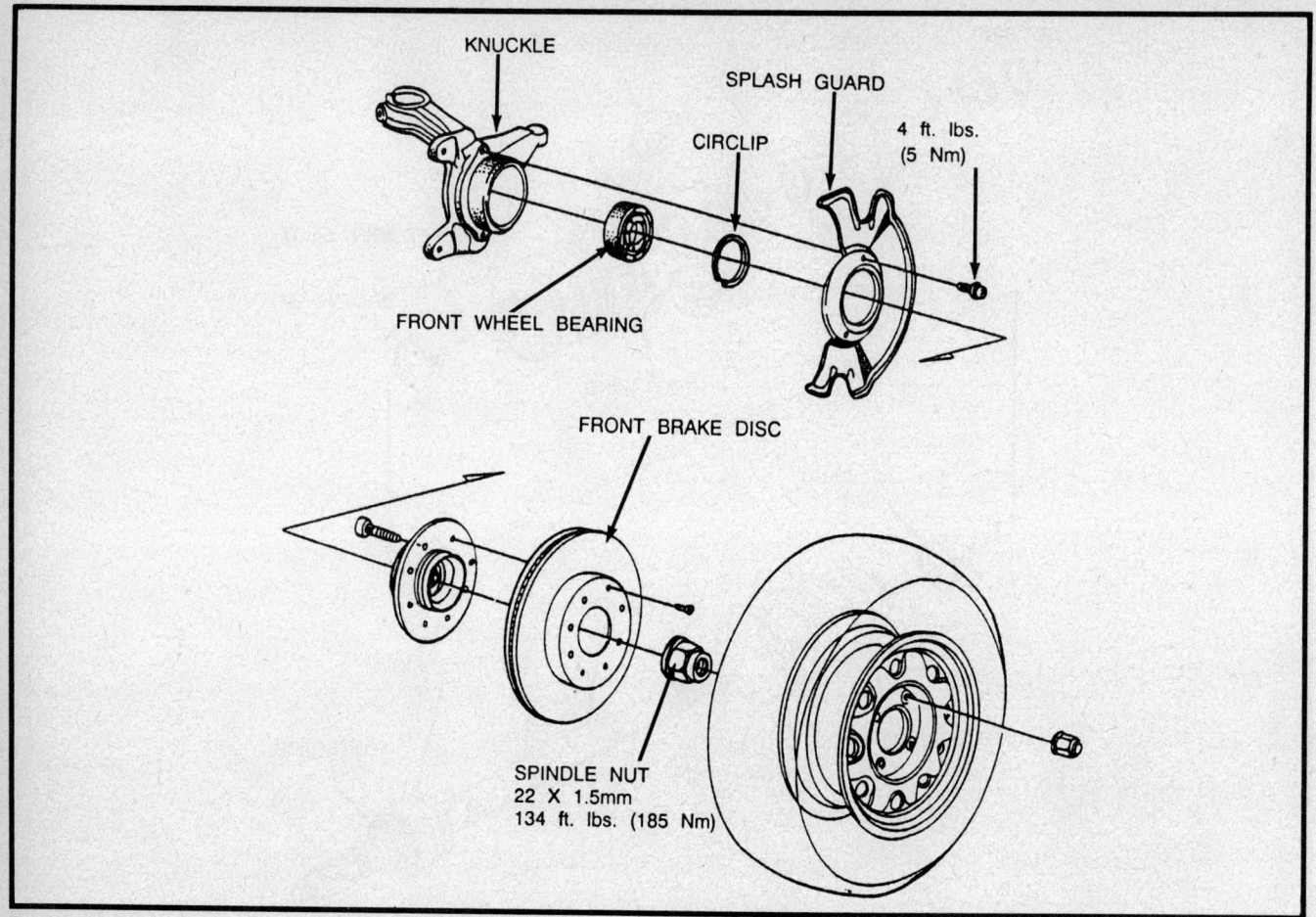

KNUCKLE

SPLASH GUARD

CIRCLIP

4 ft. lbs. (5 Nm)

FRONT WHEEL BEARING

FRONT BRAKE DISC

SPINDLE NUT
22 X 1.5mm
134 ft. lbs. (185 Nm)

Front steering knuckle, hub and bearing assembly—1987–89 Integra

NOTE: **Always replace the bearing with a new one after removal.**

10. Remove the snapring and knuckle ring from the knuckle. Press the wheel bearing out of the knuckle using suitable press tools and a hydraulic press.

11. Remove the outboard bearing inner race from the hub by using a suitable bearing puller.

To install:

12. Remove the old grease from the hub and knuckle and thoroughly dry and wipe clean all components. Press in a new wheel bearing into the hub using suitable hub tools and a hydraulic press. Install the snapring securely in the knuckle groove.

13. Install the splash guard and tighten the screws. Install the shaft into the base with the appropriate size end according to the front hub identification.

14. Place the front hub onto the press and using the suitable press tools, press in the pilot. Set the knuckle in position and press it into the assembly.

15. Install the front knuckle ring onto the steering knuckle.

16. The remaining step are the reverse of the removal procedure. Torque the spindle nut to 134 ft. lbs. (185 Nm). Use a new spindle nut and stake it after torquing.

LEGEND, 825 AND 827

1. Pry the lock tab away from the spindle and loosen the 36mm nut. Slightly loosen the lug nuts.

2. Raise and safely support the vehicle. Remove the front wheel and spindle nut.

3. Remove the bolts retaining the brake caliper and the caliper from the knuckle. Do not allow the caliper to hang by the brake hose, support it with a length of wire.

4. Remove the disc brake rotor retaining screws if equipped. Screw both 8 × 1.25 × 12mm bolts into the disc brake removal holes and turn the bolts to press the rotor from the hub.

NOTE: **Only turn each bolt 2 turns at a time to prevent cocking the disc excessively.**

5. Remove the tie rod from the knuckle using a tie rod end removal tool. Use care not to damage the ball joint seals.

6. Remove the cotter pin from the lower arm ball joint and the castle nut.

7. Remove the lower control arm from the knuckle using the ball joint remover.

8. Remove the cotter pin from the upper arm ball joint and the castle nut.

9. Remove the upper arm from the knuckle using the ball joint remover.

10. Remove the knuckle and hub by sliding the assembly off of the halfshaft.

11. Remove the back splash guard screws from the knuckle.

12. Remove the hub from the knuckle using special tools and a hydraulic press.

13. Remove the splash guard, dust seal, snapring and outer bearing race.

14. Turn the knuckle over, remove the inboard dust seal, bearing and inner race and bearing.

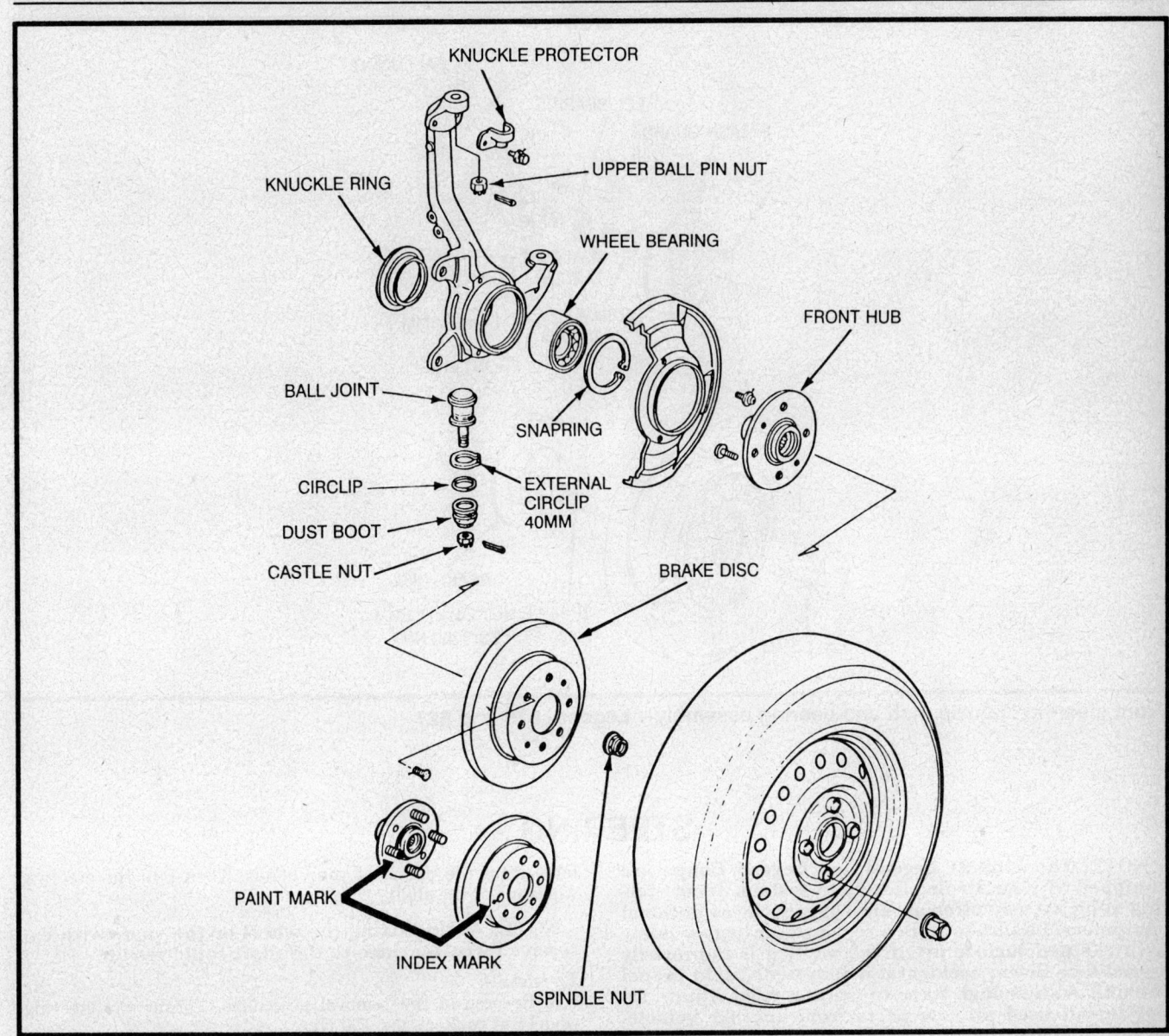

Front steering knuckle, hub and bearing assembly — 1990–91 Integra

15. Press the bearing outer race out of the knuckle using special tools and a hydraulic press.

16. Remove the outboard bearing inner race from the hub using special tools and a bearing puller.

17. Remove the outboard dust seal from the hub.

NOTE: Whenever the wheel bearings are removed, always replace with a new set of bearings and outer dust seal.

18. Clean all old grease from the halfshaft spindles on the vehicle.

19. Remove all old grease from the hub and knuckle and thoroughly dry and wipe clean all components.

To install:

20. Install the bearings, press the bearing outer race into the knuckle using the special tools used as above, plus the installing base tool.

21. Install the outboard ball bearing and inner race in the knuckle.

22. Install the snapring. Pack grease in the groove around the sealing lip of the outboard grease dust seal.

23. Drive the outboard grease seal into the knuckle, using a seal driver and hammer, until it is flush with the knuckle surface.

24. Install the splash guard, turn the knuckle upside down and install the inboard ball bearing and it's inner race.

25. Place the hub in the special tool fixture, set the knuckle in position on the press and apply downward pressure.

26. Pack grease in the groove around the sealing lip of the inboard dust seal.

27. Drive the dust seal into the knuckle using a seal driver.

28. To complete the installation, reverse the removal procedures. Use a new spindle nut and stake it after torquing it to 180 ft. lbs. (250 Nm).

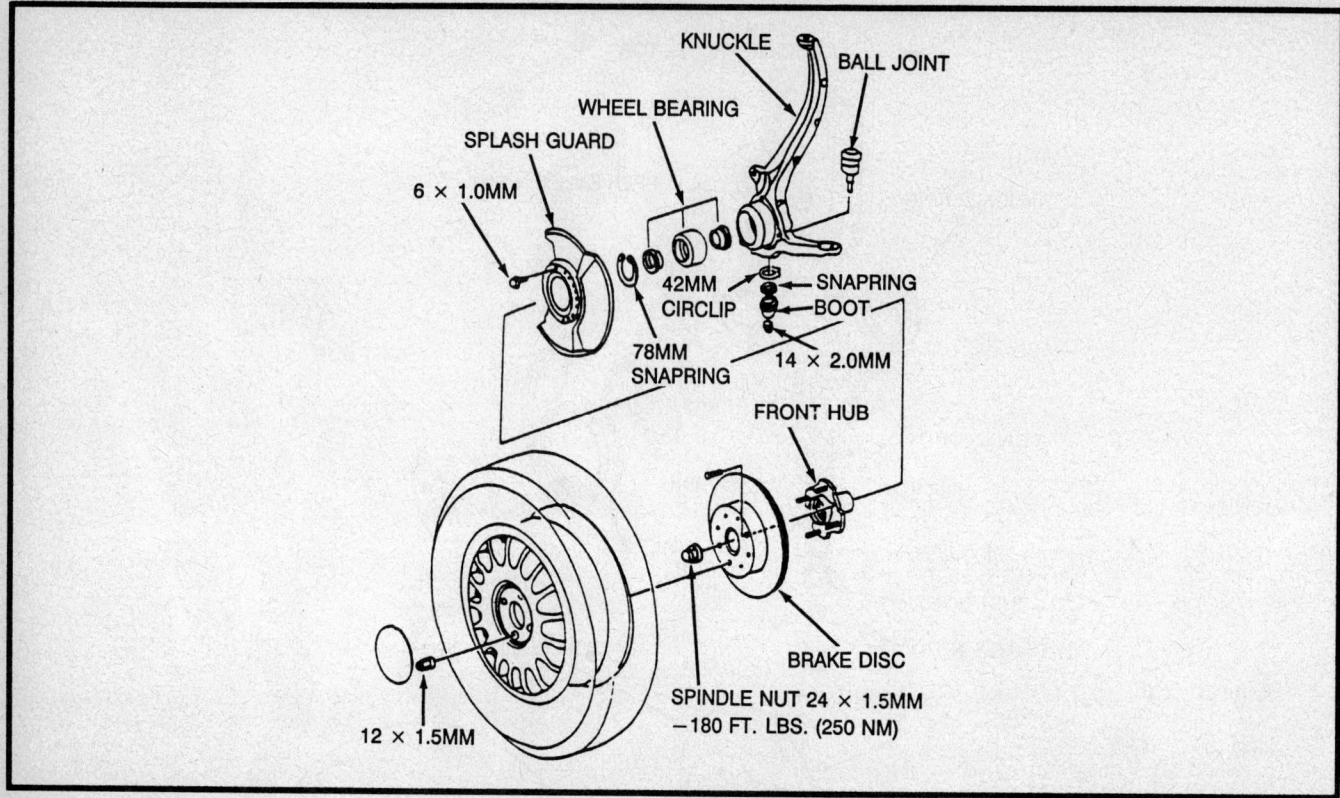

Front steering knuckle, hub and bearing assembly— Legend, 825 and 827

STEERING

NOTE: The 1988–91 Legend and Legend Coupe are equipped with an Air Bag Restraint system. Some Sterling vehicles may offer an air bag system as optional equipment. Be sure to store a removed air bag assembly with the pad surface up, if the air bag is improperly stored face down, accidental deployment could propel the unit with enough force to cause serious injury. Do not install used air bag parts from another vehicle. When repairing the system, use only new replacement parts. Carefully inspect the air bag assembly before installing. Do not install an air bag assembly that shows signs of being dropped or improperly handled, such as dents, cracks or deformation. Always keep the short connector on the air bag connector when the harness is disconnected. Do not disassemble or tamper with the air bag assembly.

Steering Wheel

Removal and Installation

WITHOUT AIR BAG

1. Place the steering wheel in the straight ahead position.
2. Disconnect the negative battery cable. Lift off the steering wheel pad.
3. Remove the steering wheel retaining nut and the horn pad.
4. If equipped with cruise control, remove the cruise control set/resume switch.
5. Gently rock the steering wheel from side to side and gently hit the backside of each of the steering wheel spokes with equal force from the palms of your hands. Then pull the steering wheel off of the shaft.

NOTE: Avoid hitting the wheel or the shaft with excessive force. Damage to the shaft could result.

To install:

6. Reverse of the removal procedure. Torque the steering wheel nut to 36 ft. lbs. (50 Nm).

WITH AIR BAG

CAUTION

On vehicles equipped with an airbag, the negative battery cable must be disconnected, before working on the vehicle. Failure to do so may result in deploymentr of the airbag and possible injury.

1. Disconnect both the negative and positive battery cable from the battery.
2. Remove the lower maintenance lid below the air bag and then remove the short connector.
3. Disconnect the connector between the air bag and the cable reel.
4. Connect the short connector to the air bag side of the connector.
5. Remove the left side maintenance lid and the cruise control/set resume switch cover.
6. Insert a T30 Torx® bit and remove the Torx® bolts. Remove the air bag assembly.

NOTE: Be sure to store the air bag in a safe place with the pad side facing upwards.

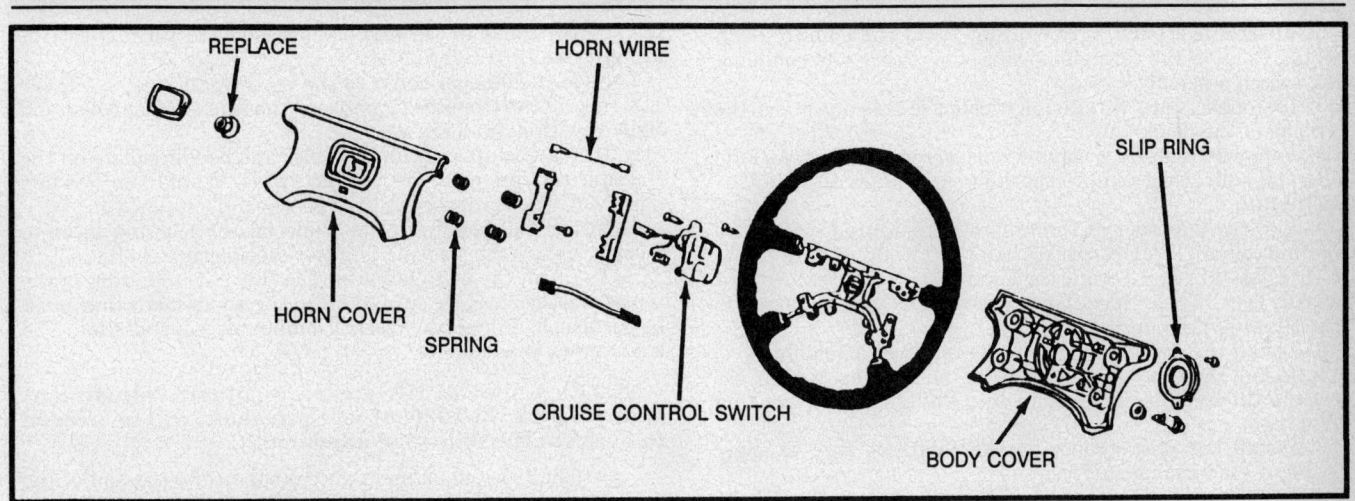

Typical steering wheel assembly

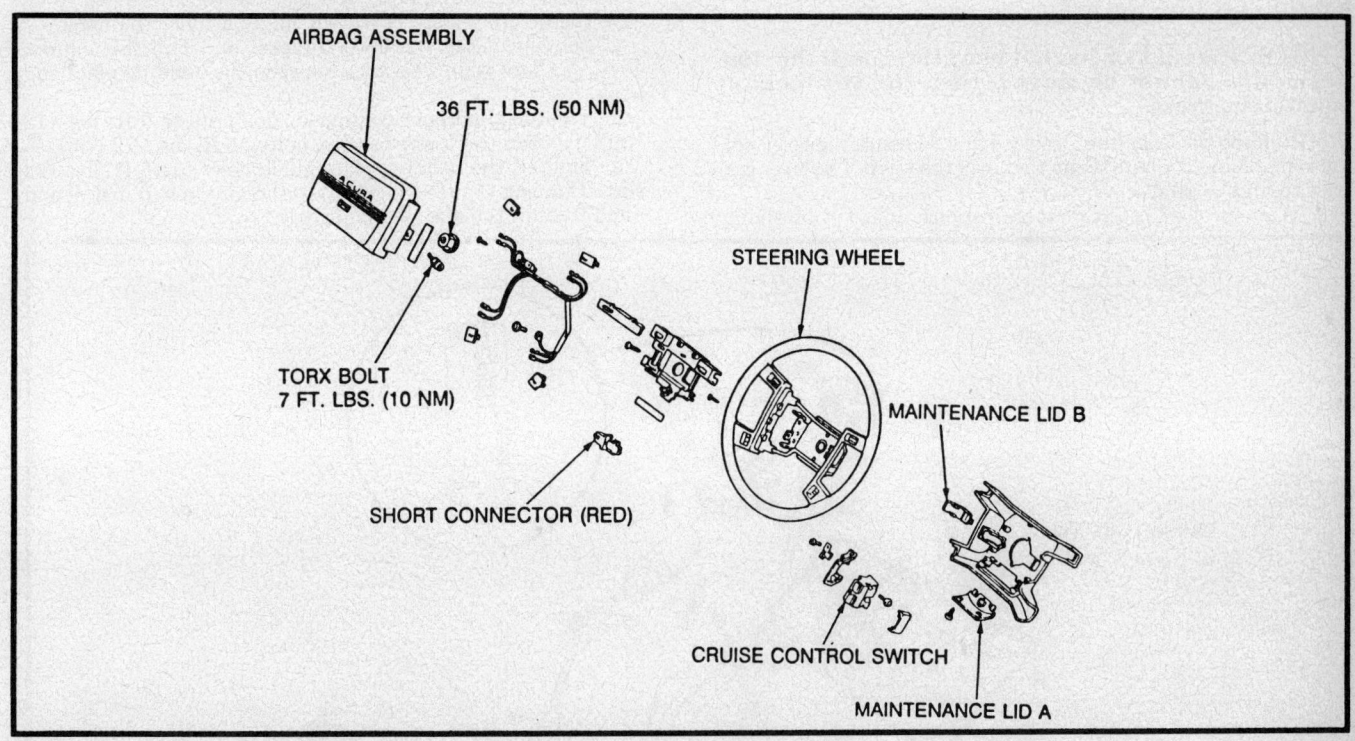

Exploded view of a steering wheel equipped with an airbag assembly

7. Remove the steering wheel retaining nut. Gently hit the backside of each of the steering wheel spokes with equal force with the palms of the hands.

NOTE: Avoid hitting the wheel or the shaft with excessive force. Damage to the shaft could result.

To install:

8. When installing, reverse the order of the removal procedure. Torque the steering wheel nut to 36 ft. lbs. (50 Nm).

9. Using new Torx® screws, torque the air bag to 7 ft. lbs. (10 Nm).

10. After installation, turn the ignition switch **ON** to the **II** position; the instrument panel SRS light should turn **ON** for about 8 seconds and turn **OFF**.

11. Make sure the horn buttons operate and the cruise control set/resume switch is in operation.

Steering Column

Removal and Installation

INTEGRA

1. Remove the steering wheel center pad. Remove the steering wheel shaft nut.

2. Remove the steering wheel by rocking it slightly from side to side and pull steadily with both hands.

3. Remove the right and left lower instrument panel covers. Remove the front console.

4. Remove the driver's side knee bolster from the steering hanger. Remove the steering joint cover.

5. Remove the steering joint bolts and move the joint toward the steering column. Remove the upper and lower steering column covers.

6. Disconnect each wire coupler from the combination switch. Remove the turn signal canceling sleeve and combination switch assembly.

7. Disconnect each wire coupler from the fuse box under the left side of the dash.

8. Remove the steering column holder. Remove the attaching nuts and bolts, then remove the steering column assembly.

To install:

9. Reverse the order of the removal procedure. Torque the steering column support bracket bolts to 9 ft. lbs. (13 Nm) nuts to 16 ft. lbs. (22 Nm). Torque the lower bolt on the steering joint to 16 ft. lbs. (22 Nm). If equipped with tilt steering columns use the following procedures.

10. Install the 10mm washer on the tilt lever assembly.

11. Install the bending plate base on the steering column. Insert the tilt lever assembly shaft into the hole in the bending plate base.

12. Install the spin stopper on the shaft. Be sure to apply grease to each sliding surface.

13. Install the stopper collar over the spin stopper. Install the column hanger spring.

14. Torque the tilt locknut to 5 ft. lbs. (7 Nm) and slide the stopper collar to the tilt locknut side.

NOTE: The tilt lock has left hand threads. If the stopper collar cannot be moved, turn the tilt locknut counterclockwise.

15. Pull the tilt lever knob upward and measure the lever preload at 1.38 in. (35.0mm) from the tip of the knob. The lever preload should be 20 lbs.

16. If the preload is out of specifications, adjust it by sliding the stopper collar to the spin stopper side and turning the tilt locknut one turn right or left.

17. Slide the stopper collar to the tilt locknut side.

18. Install the stopper clip between the spin stopper collar and tighten with a 3mm screw.

19. Install the upper column holder and bending plate on the steering column with the rubber bands. Install the bending plate with the arrow toward the gearbox.

20. Install the bending plate guide on the steering column. Loosely install the steering joint on the steering shaft.

21. To finish the installation process, reverse the order of the removal procedure. Be sure to make the adjustment that must be performed on the tilt steering column after installation. The adjustment is as follows:

NOTE: A special tilt steering column adjustment guide tool 07973–6920001 or equivalent, will be needed to perform the following adjustment.

a. Install the adjustment guide tool on the top end of the steering shaft and turn it as far as it will go.

b. Loosely install the upper column holder and bending plate guide attaching bolts and pull the column down to be sure the bending plate is seated snugly against the hook.

c. Loosely install the lower bracket and pull the column down so there is no clearance between the bending plate and hook.

d. Tighten the upper column holder nuts to 9 ft. lbs. (13 Nm). Tighten the lower bracket bolts 16 ft. lbs. (22 Nm).

e. Tighten the bending plate guide bolts to 16 ft. lbs. (22 Nm). Connect the steering joint to the pinion and install and hand tighten the steering joint bolt.

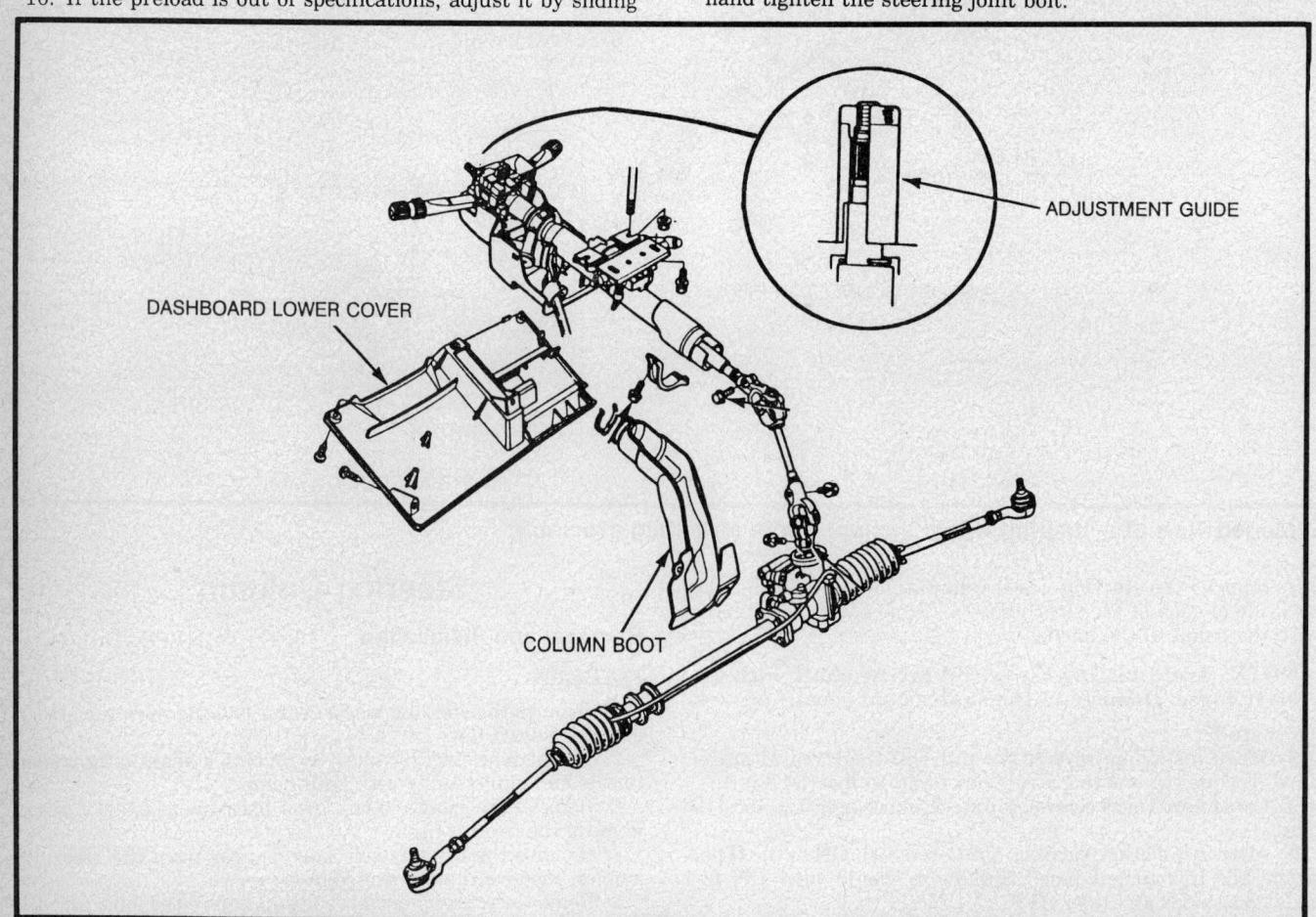

Making the tilt steering column adjustment on the Integra

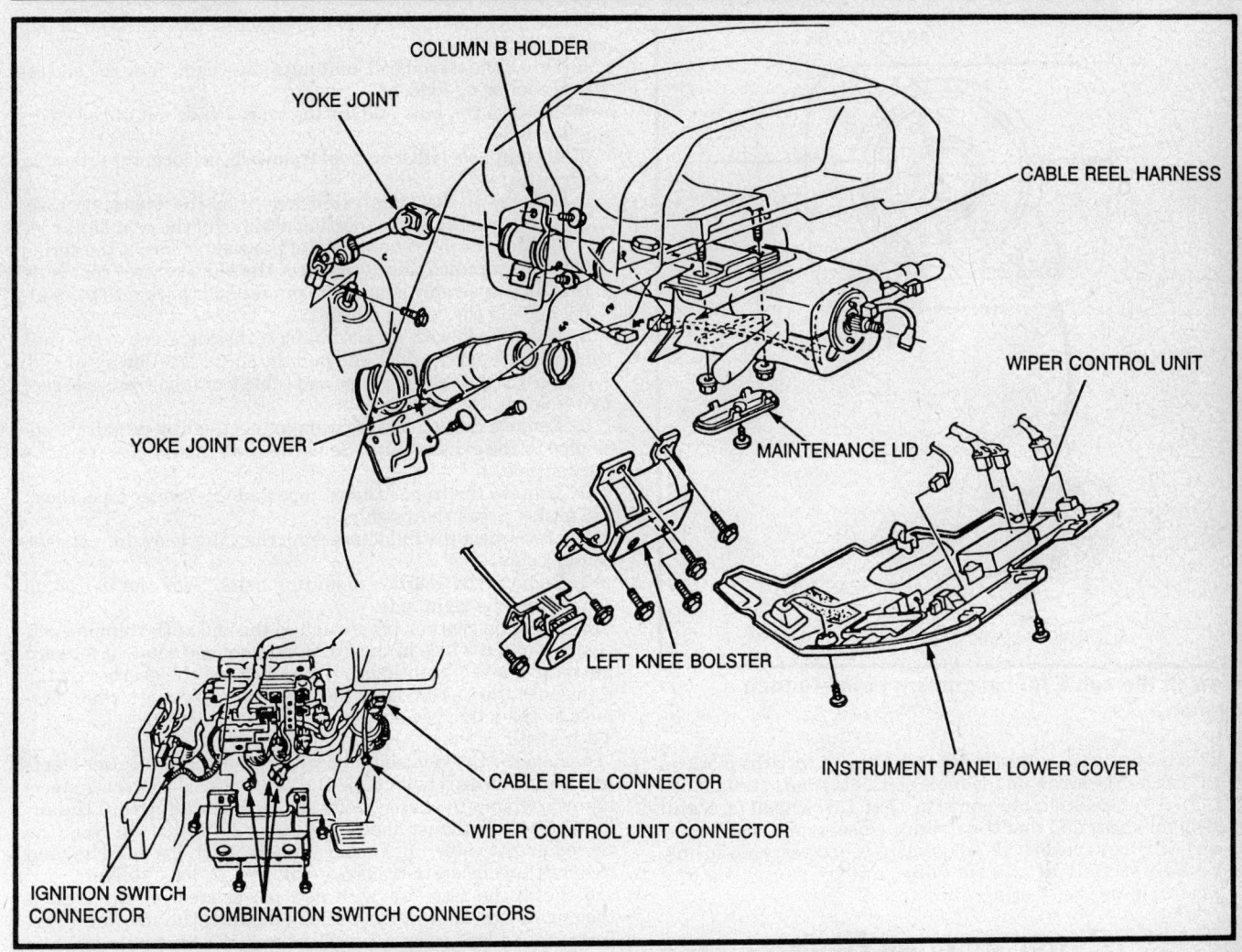

YOKE JOINT

COLUMN B HOLDER

CABLE REEL HARNESS

YOKE JOINT COVER

WIPER CONTROL UNIT

MAINTENANCE LID

LEFT KNEE BOLSTER

INSTRUMENT PANEL LOWER COVER

CABLE REEL CONNECTOR

WIPER CONTROL UNIT CONNECTOR

IGNITION SWITCH CONNECTOR

COMBINATION SWITCH CONNECTORS

Removal and installation of the steering column— Legend—825 and 827 are similar

f. Put the steering joint down and tighten the steering joint bolts to 22 ft. lbs. (30 Nm). Make sure the end adjustment guide bottoms against the turn signal switch as shown.

g. Install the column cover, column boot and dashboard lower panel.

LEGEND, 825 AND 827

1. Disconnect both the negative and positive battery cable from the battery.

2. Remove the lower maintenance lid below the air bag and then remove the short connector.

3. Disconnect the connector between the air bag and the cable reel.

4. Connect the short connector to the air bag side of the connector.

5. Remove the left side maintenance lid and the cruise control/set resume switch cover.

6. Insert a T30 Torx® bit and remove the Torx® bolts. Remove the air bag assembly.

NOTE: Be sure to store the air bag in a safe place with the pad side facing upwards.

7. Remove the steering wheel retaining nut. Gently hit the backside of each of the steering wheel spokes with equal force with the palms of the hands.

NOTE: Avoid hitting the wheel or the shaft with excessive force. Damage to the shaft could result.

8. Disconnect the connectors for the horn, cruise control and release the air bag connector clips. To disconnect the cruise control connector be sure to release both lock tabs on the connector.

9. Remove the yoke joint cover. Remove the instrument panel lower cover then disconnect the wiper control unit connector.

10. Remove the left knee bolster. Remove the column cover's maintenance lid. Disconnect the cable reel harness at the connection located on the underside of the steering column.

11. Remove the rear steering column holder. Remove the steering column mounting nuts.

12. Remove the steering yoke joint bolts and disconnect the yoke joint. Disconnect the harness connectors attached to the column assembly, then remove the column assembly.

To install:

13. Reverse the order of the removal procedure. Paying attention to the following:

a. Before installing the steering wheel, the front wheels should be aligned straight forward.

b. Be sure to install the harness wires so they are not pinched or interfering with other parts.

c. Center the cable reel, by rotating the cable reel clockwise until it stops. Then rotate it counterclockwise (approximately

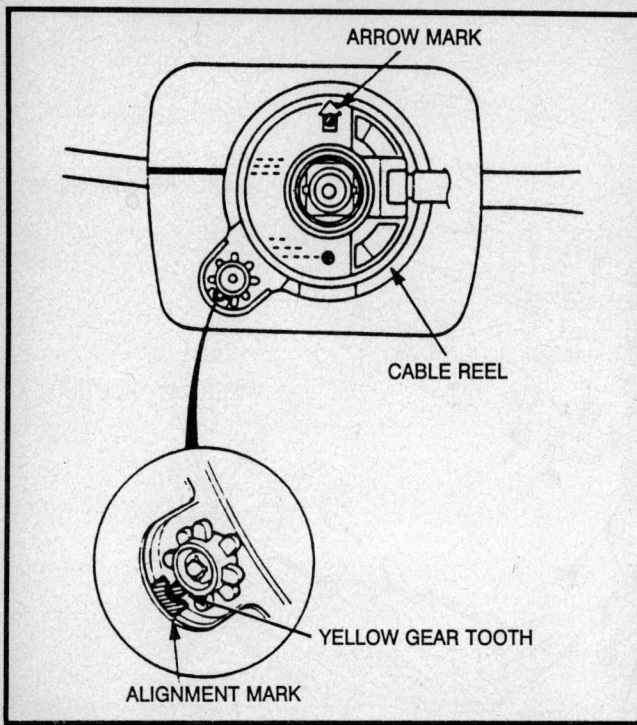

ARROW MARK

CABLE REEL

YELLOW GEAR TOOTH

ALIGNMENT MARK

View of the cable reel alignment point—airbag system

2 turns) until. the yellow gear tooth lines up with the mark on the cover. The arrow on the cable reel lable points straight up.

d. After reassembly confirm that the wheels are still straight ahead and that the steering wheel spoke angle is correct. If minor spoke angle adjustment is necessary, do so only by adjustment of the tie rods, not by removing and repositioning the steering wheel.

Power Steering Rack

Adjustment
INTEGRA

1. Loosen the locknut on the rack guide screw with tool 07916–SA50001 or equivalent.
2. Tighten the guide screw until it compresses the spring against the guide; loosen it, torque it to about 3 ft. lbs. (4 Nm) and back it off about 25 degrees.
3. Torque the locknut to about 18 ft. lbs. (25 Nm) while preventing the guide screw from moving.

LEGEND, 825 AND 827

1. Loosen the locknut on the rack guide screw with tool 07916–SA50001 or equivalent.
2. Tighten the guide screw until it compresses the spring against the guide; loosen it, torque it to about 2 ft. lbs. (3 Nm) and back it off about 20 degrees.
3. Torque the locknut to about 18 ft. lbs. (25 Nm) while preventing the guide screw from moving.

Removal and Installation
INTEGRA

1. Remove the steering joint cover, the steering shaft connector bolts and pull the connector up off the pinion shaft. Drain the power steering fluid and remove the gearbox shield.
2. Raise and safely support the vehicle.
3. Remove the front wheels.

4. Remove the cotter pins and unscrew the tie rod end ball joint nuts halfway.
5. Break the tie rod ball joint nuts loose using a tie rod end removal tool or equivalent.
6. Remove the nuts and lift the tie rod ends out of the steering knuckles.
7. If equipped with a manual transaxle, perform the following procedures:
   a. Remove the shift extension from the transaxle case. Slide the boot at the connecting position of the gear shift rod.
   b. Slide the pin retainer out of the way, drive out the spring pin with a punch and disconnect the shift control rod. Note that on reassembly, install the pin retainer back into place after driving the spring pin in.
8. If equipped with an automatic transaxle, remove the shift cable guide from the floor and pull the shift cable down by hand. Remove the shift cable holder and cable from the transaxle case by removing the clamp.
9. Remove the self locking nuts connecting the exhaust header pipe to the exhaust pipe. Separate the exhaust pipe from the header pipe.
10. Remove the front exhaust pipe and the header pipe. Clean the gasket areas thoroughly.
11. Disconnect the fluid lines from the valve body. Remove the center beam.
12. Remove the gearbox mounting bolts. Slide the tie rod all the way to the right side.
13. Drop the gearbox far enough so the end of the pinion shaft comes out of it's hole in the frame channel and rotate it forward until the shaft is pointing to the rear. Slide the gearbox to the right until the tie rod clears the rear beam, lower it from the vehicle to the left.

To install:
14. Reverse the removal procedures. Torque the power steering gear-to-chassis bolts to 32 ft. lbs. (44 Nm), the power steering gear clamp-to-chassis bolts to 29 ft. lbs. (40 Nm), the exhaust pipe-to-exhaust manifold nuts to 29 ft. lbs. (40 Nm), the tie rod ends-to-steering knuckle nuts to 40 ft. lbs. (55 Nm) and the shift extension-to-transaxle bolt to 7 ft. lbs. (10 Nm).
15. Refill the reservoir with new power steering fluid. Start the engine and allow it run at fast idle, turn the steering wheel from lock-to-lock several times to bleed the air out.
16. Check the fluid again and add, if necessary. Check the system for leaks.

LEGEND, 825 AND 827

1. Remove the steering joint cover and disconnect the steering shaft from the gearbox.
2. Drain the power steering fluid.
3. Remove the gearbox shield.
4. Using cleaning solvent and a brush, clean the control unit, it's lines and the end of the gearbox. Blow dry with compressed air, if possible.
5. Raise and safely support the vehicle.
6. Remove the front wheels.
7. Remove the cotter pins and unscrew the tie rod end ball joint nuts halfway.
8. Break the tie rod ball joint nuts loose, using a tie rod end removal tool or equivalent.
9. Remove the nuts and lift the tie rod ends from the steering knuckles.
10. If equipped with a manual transaxle, perform the following procedures:
    a. Remove the shift extension from the transaxle case.
    b. Disconnect the gearshift rod from the transaxle case by removing the 8mm spring pin.
11. If equipped with an automatic transaxle, remove the shift control cable from the clamp.
12. Remove the center beam bolts and the center beam.

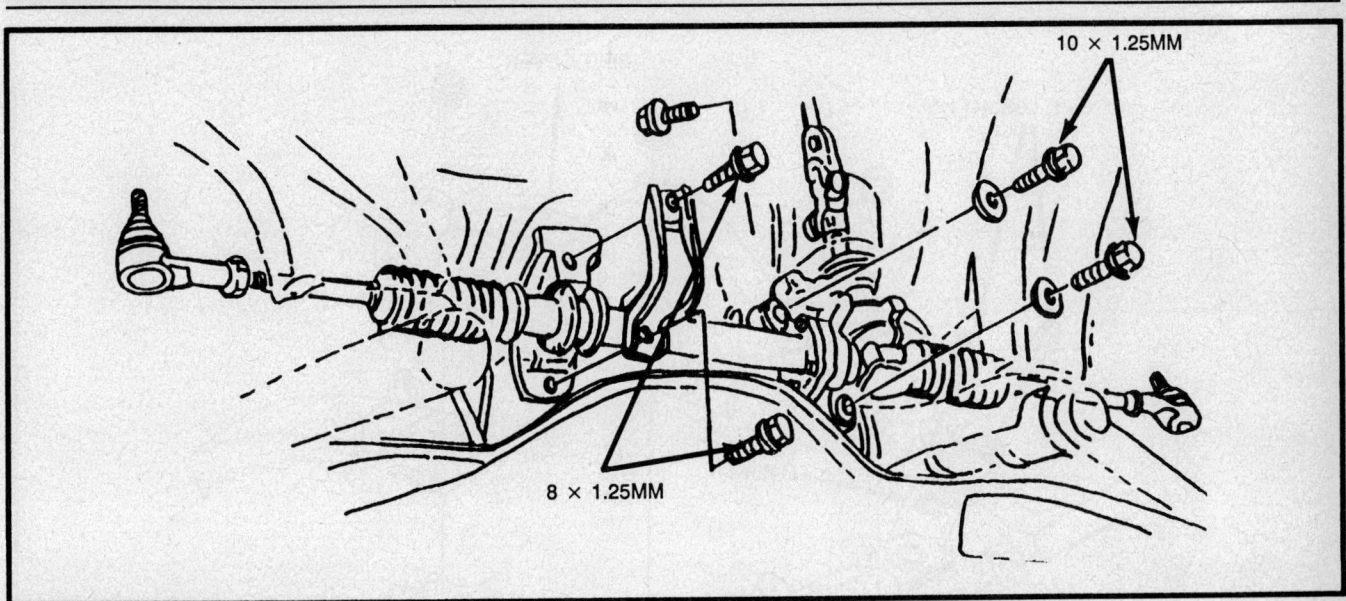

Gearbox mounting—Integra

NOTE: Replace the self-locking nuts retaining the center beam, if worn.

13. Disconnect the exhaust header pipe from the manifold. Replace the exhaust gasket and the self-locking nuts when reinstalling the pipe.
14. Remove the header pipe joint nuts and the header pipe.
15. Disconnect the 4 lines from the control unit.
16. Slide the tie rod all the way to the right side.
17. Slide the gear box right so the left tie rod clears the bottom of the rear beam and remove the gearbox.

To install:

18. Reverse the removal procedures. Torque the power steering gear-to-chassis bolts to 28 ft. lbs. (39 Nm), the exhaust pipe-to-exhaust manifold nuts to 40 ft. lbs. (55 Nm), the exhaust pipe-to-muffler nuts to 25 ft. lbs., the center beam-to-chassis bolts to 37 ft. lbs. (51 Nm), the shift extension-to-transaxle bolt to 7 ft. lbs. (10 Nm) and the tie rod end-to-steering knuckle nut to 32 ft. lbs. (44 Nm).
19. Refill the reservoir with new power steering fluid. Start the engine and allow it to run at fast idle, turn the steering wheel from lock-to-lock several times to bled the air out.
20. Check the fluid again and add, if necessary. Check the system for leaks.

Power Steering Pump

Removal and Installation

1987–89 INTEGRA

1. Disconnect and plug the hoses from the reservoir.
2. Remove the 10mm flange bolts, the belt from the pulley and the pump assembly.

To install:

3. Reverse the removal procedures. Torque the power steering pump-to-engine bolts to 29 ft. lbs. (40 Nm). Be sure to observe the following:
   a. Connect the hoses tightly.
   b. Adjust the belt tension.
   c. Check the fluid level and add, if necessary.
   d. Bleed the air from the system.

1990–91 INTEGRA

1. Drain the power steering fluid. Disconnect the inlet and outlet hoses from the power steering pump and plug them.

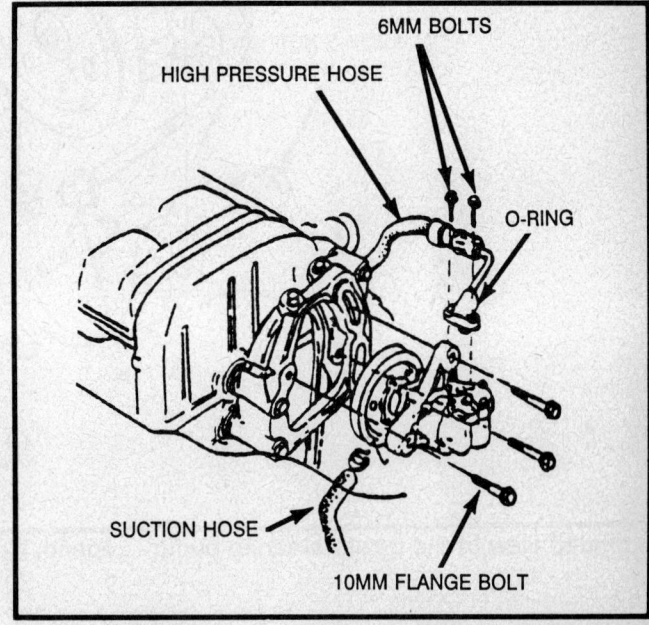

Power steering pump mounting—1987–89 Integra

2. Remove the belt by loosening the adjusting bolts on the pump bracket.
3. Remove the power steering mounting bolts and remove the power steering pump.

To install:

4. Reverse the removal procedures. Torque the power steering pump-to-engine bolts to 17 ft. lbs. (24 Nm). Be sure to observe the following:
   a. Connect the hoses tightly.
   b. Adjust the belt tension.
   c. Check the fluid level and add, if necessary.
   d. Bleed the air from the system.

NOTE: When installing a new or rebuilt pump, check the power steering pump preload in a vise before installing it on the vehicle. Check the pump preload with a torque wrench it should be 3 ft. lbs. (4 Nm).

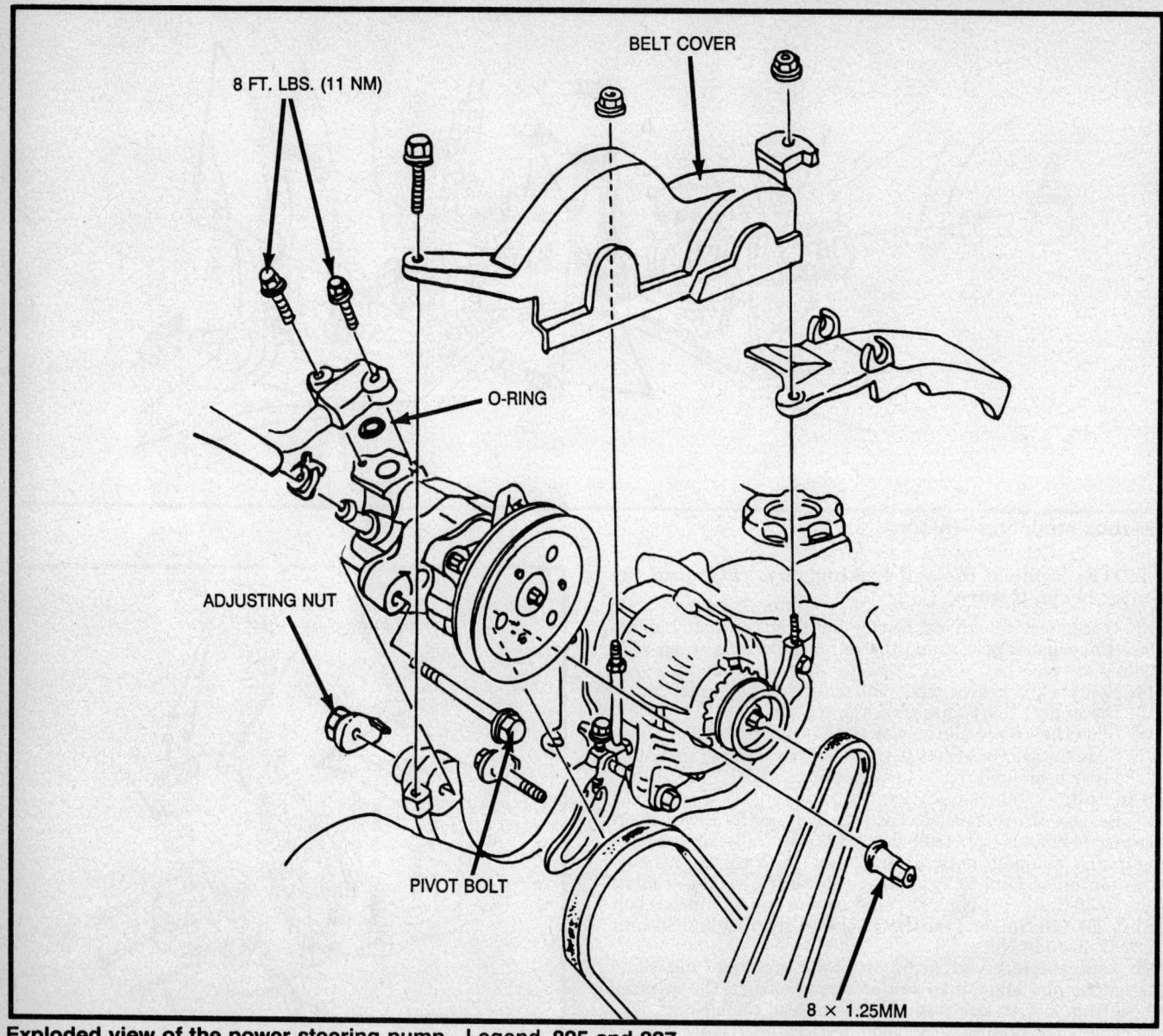

8 FT. LBS. (11 NM)

BELT COVER

O-RING

ADJUSTING NUT

PIVOT BOLT

8 × 1.25MM

Exploded view of the power steering pump—Legend, 825 and 827

LEGEND, 825 AND 827

1. Remove the belt cover.
2. Drain the fluid from the system.
3. Disconnect and plug the inlet/outlet hoses from the pump.
4. Remove the belt by loosening the pump pivot bolt and adjusting nut.
5. Remove the pump assembly nut/bolt and the assembly.

To install:

6. Reverse the removal procedures. Torque the power steering pump-to-bracket bolt to 28 ft. lbs. (39 Nm) and the power steering pump-to-bracket nut to 16 ft. lbs. (22 Nm). Be sure to observe the following:
   a. Refill the reservoir with new fluid to the Upper Level on the reservoir.
   b. Connect the hoses tightly.
   c. Adjust the belt tension.
   d. Bleed the air from the system.
   e. Check the fluid level and add, if necessary.

Belt Adjustment

1. Loosen the adjuster arm bolt.
2. Move the pump toward or away from the engine, until the belt can be depressed approximately ¾–¹⁵⁄₁₆ in. (19–24mm) at the midpoint between both pulleys under moderate thumb pressure. If the tension adjustment is being made on a new belt, the deflection should only be about 11mm, to allow for the initial stretching of the belt.
3. Torque the bolt to 29 ft. lbs. (40 Nm) for Integra or 33 ft. lbs. (45 Nm) for Legend, 825 and 827. Recheck the adjustment.

System Bleeding

1. Raise and safely support the vehicle.
2. Refill the power steering pump reservoir to the full level.
3. Start the engine and turn the steering wheel from lock-to-lock (several times).
4. After the air bubbles have been eliminated from the system, refill the reservoir and lower the vehicle.

Tie Rod Ends

Removal and Installation

INTEGRA

1. Raise and safely support the vehicle. Remove the front wheel.
2. Loosen the tie rod end-to-power steering gear jam nut.
3. Remove the tie rod end-to-steering knuckle cotter pin and nut.
4. Using a tie rod removal tool or equivalent, separate the tie rod end from the steering knuckle.
5. While supporting the power steering rod, remove the tie rod end, be sure to count revolutions required to remove the tie rod end.

To install:

6. Install the new tie rod end, turn it the same amount of revolutions necessary to remove it and tighten the jam nut to 42 ft. lbs. (58 Nm) and the tie rod end-to-steering knuckle nut to 29 ft. lbs. (40 Nm).

LEGEND, 825 AND 827

1. Raise and safely support the vehicle. Remove the front wheels.
2. Remove the cotter pin and the nut from the tie rod end. Use a ball joint remover tool or equivalent, separate the tie rod from the steering knuckle.
3. Disconnect the air tube at the dust seal joint. Remove the tie rod dust seal bellows clamps and move the rubber bellows on the tie rod rack joints.
4. Straighten the tie rod lockwasher tabs at the tie rod-to-rack joint and remove the tie rod by turning it with a wrench.

To install:

5. Reverse the removal procedure. Always use a new tie rod lockwasher during reassembly.
6. Torque the tie rod end-to-power steering gear to 40 ft. lbs. (55 Nm) and the tie rod end-to-steering knuckle nut to 32 ft. lbs. (44 Nm).
7. Fit the locating lugs into the slots on the rack and bend the outer edge of the washer over the flat part of the rod, after the tie rod nut has been properly tightened.

BRAKES

Master Cylinder

Removal and Installation

NOTE: Before removing the master cylinder, cover the body surfaces with fender covers and rags to prevent damage to painted surfaces by brake fluid.

1. Disconnect and plug the brake lines at the master cylinder.
2. Remove the master cylinder-to-power booster bolts and the master cylinder from the vehicle.
3. To install, reverse the removal procedure. Torque the master cylinder-to-power booster bolts to 11 ft. lbs. (15 Nm). Bleed the brake system.

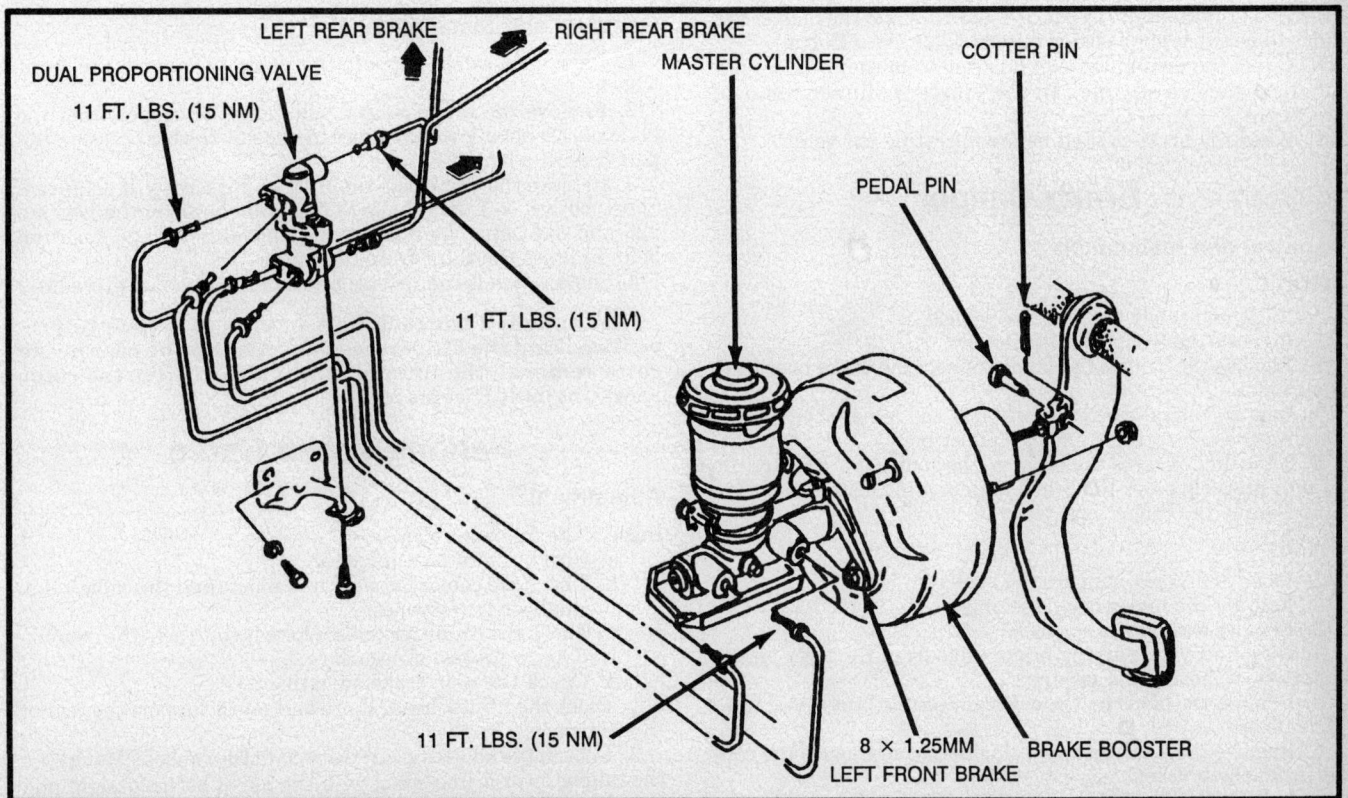

Typical master cylinder and booster assembly

Proportioning Valve

Removal and Installation

1. Disconnect and plug the hydraulic lines from the dual proportioning valve.
2. Remove the proportioning valve-to-bracket bolts and the valve from the vehicle.
3. To install, reverse the removal procedures. Bleed the brake system.

Power Brake Booster

Inspection

A preliminary check of the vacuum booster can be made as follows:

1. Depress the brake pedal several times using normal pressure; make sure the pedal height does not vary.
2. Hold the pedal in the depressed position and start the engine. The pedal should drop slightly.
3. Hold the pedal in the above position and stop the engine. The pedal should stay in the depressed position for approximately 30 seconds.
4. If the pedal does not drop when the engine is started or rises after the engine is stopped, the booster is not functioning properly.

Removal and Installation

1. Disconnect the vacuum hose from the booster.
2. Disconnect and plug the brake lines at the master cylinder.
3. Remove the brake pedal-to-booster link pin and the booster nuts; the pushrod and nuts are located inside the vehicle under the instrument panel.
4. Remove the booster with the master cylinder attached.

To install:

5. Reverse the removal procedure. Torque the power brake booster-to-firewall nuts to 9 ft. lbs. (13 Nm) and the master cylinder-to-power brake booster nuts to 11 ft. lbs. (15 Nm).
6. Check the vacuum booster pushrod-to-master cylinder piston clearance as outlined in the master cylinder removal procedure.
7. Bleed the brake system before operating the vehicle.

Brake Caliper

Removal and Installation

FRONT

1. Raise and safely support the vehicle.
2. Remove the front wheel assembly.
3. Remove the banjo bolt and disconnect the brake hose from the caliper.
4. Remove the caliper retaining bolts and remove the caliper. Remove the pad spring from the caliper body.
5. To install, reverse the order of the removal procedure. Be sure to properly bleed the brake system after installation.
6. Torque the caliper bolt to 24 ft. lbs. (33 Nm).

REAR

1. Raise and safely support the vehicle.
2. Remove the rear wheel assembly.
3. Remove the caliper shield.
4. Disconnect the parking brake cable from the lever on the caliper by removing the lock pin.
5. Remove the banjo bolt and disconnect the brake hose from the caliper.
6. Remove the 2 caliper mounting bolts and remove the caliper from the bracket.
7. To install, reverse the order of the removal procedure. Be sure to properly bleed the brake system after installation.

8. Torque the caliper-to-caliper support bolts to 28 ft. lbs. (39 Nm).

Disc Brake Pads

Removal and Installation

FRONT

1. Raise and safely support the vehicle. Remove the front wheels.
2. Using a prybar, between the brake pad and the caliper, pry the brake caliper away from the vehicle until the piston is fully seated in the caliper.
3. Remove the lower caliper-to-caliper support bolt and swing the caliper upward and away from the disc.
4. Remove the brake pad shim, the brake pad retainers and the pad.
5. Install new brake pads, coated with Molykote® M77, between the pads and shims, the shims and retainers.
6. Lower the calipers of the brake pad assemblies and torque the caliper bolt to 24 ft. lbs. (33 Nm).

REAR

1. Raise and safely support the rear of the vehicle. Remove the rear wheels.
2. Using a prybar, between the brake pad and the caliper, pry the brake caliper away from the vehicle until the piston is fully seated in the caliper.
3. Remove the caliper-to-caliper support bolts and the caliper from the disc.
4. Remove the brake pads and shims.
5. To install, use new brake pads and reverse the removal procedures. Torque the caliper-to-caliper support bolts to 28 ft. lbs. (39 Nm).

Brake Rotor

Removal and Installation

1. Raise and safely support the vehicle. Remove the front wheel.
2. Remove the brake caliper bolts and the caliper from the knuckle. Do not allow the caliper to hang by the brake hose, support it with a length of wire.
3. Remove the disc brake rotor retaining screws, if equipped. Screw both 8 × 1.0mm bolts (8 × 12mm bolts on the Legend, 825 and 827) into the disc brake removal holes and turn the bolts to press the rotor from the hub.
4. Installation is the reverse order of the removal procedure.

NOTE: Only turn each bolt 2 turns at a time to prevent cocking the disc excessively. Also on the rear brake rotor removal, the rotor should slide off after the rotor retaining bolt is removed.

Parking Brake Cable

Adjustment

Inspect the following items:

  a. Check the ratchet for wear.
  b. Check the cables for wear or damage and the cable guide and equalizer for looseness.
  c. Check the equalizer cable where it contracts the equalizer and apply grease, if necessary.
  d. Check the rear brake adjustment.

1. Block the front wheels. Raise and safely support the rear of the vehicle.
2. Loosen the adjusting nut, located in the console. Make sure the caliper lever is in contact with the pin at both the right and left rear calipers.
3. Pull the parking brake lever up a notch.

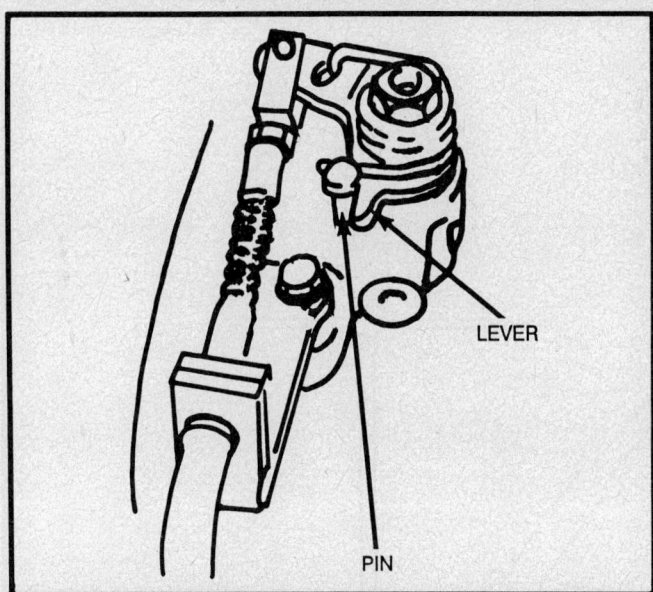

View of the rear brake cable lever — Integra — Legend, 825 and 827 are similar

4. Tighten the adjusting nut until the rear brakes drag slightly.

5. Release the brake lever and make sure the rear brakes do not drag.

6. The rear brakes should be locked when the hand brake lever is pulled; 4–8 notches for 1987–89 Integra, 6–10 notches for 1990–91 Integra or 7–11 notches for Legend and Sterling.

Removal and Installation

1. Remove the adjusting nut from the equalizer mounted on the console and separate the cable from the equalizer.

2. Set the parking brake lever to a fully released position. Raise and support the vehicle safely. Remove the cotter pin from the rear caliper assembly.

3. After removing the cotter pin, pull out the pin which connects the cable and the lever.

4. Detach the cable from the guides at the calipers and remove the cable.

5. To install, reverse the removal procedure, making sure grease is applied to the cable and the guides.

Brake System Bleeding

NOTE: The master cylinder must be full at the start of the bleeding procedure and checked after bleeding each caliper. Add fluid as required. Use only DOT 3 or 4 brake fluid. If a pressure bleeder is not available it will be necessary to have the aid of an assistant to perform this brake bleeding operation.

1. Have an assistant slowly pump the brake pedal several times and then apply a steady pressure to the brake pedal.

2. Attach a bleed hose to the bleed screw and place it into a clear container. Loosen the brake bleed screw at the brake caliper furthest away from the master cylinder (passenger's rear) to allow the air to escape from the system.

3. Repeat this procedure for each brake caliper, until no air bubbles appear in the brake fluid. Use the following brake caliper sequence in order to bleed the brake system properly:

    a. Right rear, passenger's side brake caliper.

    b. Left front, driver's side brake caliper.

    c. Left rear, driver's side brake caliper.

    d. Right front, passenger's side brake caliper.

4. Check the fluid level in the master cylinder and add, if necessary. Road test the vehicle and check the brake performance.

Anti-Lock Brake System Service

Precautions

The anti-lock brake system accumulator contains a high pressure nitrogen gas, do not puncture, expose to flame or attempt to disassemble the accumulator or it may explode and severe personal injury may result.

Relieving Anti-Lock Brake System Pressure

1. Drain the brake fluid from the master cylinder and the modulator reservoir thoroughly.

2. Remove the red cap from the bleeder on the top of the power unit.

3. Install special bleeder T wrench 07HAA-SG00100 or equivalent and turn it out 90 degrees, to collect the high pressure fluid into the reservoir. Turn the special tool out 1 turn to drain the brake fluid thoroughly.

4. Retighten the bleeder screw and discard the fluid. Reinstall the red cap.

Anti-Lock Brake Modulator

Removal and Installation

1. Relieve the accumulator line pressure.

2. Disconnect and plug the lines from the hydraulic modulator.

3. Remove the mounting bolts and the modulator from the vehicle.

4. To install, reverse the removal procedures. Bleed the brake system.

Accumulator Pressure Switch

Removal and Installation

NOTE: The anti-lock brake system accumulator contains a high pressure nitrogen gas, do not puncture, expose to flame or attempt to disassemble the accumulator or it may explode and severe personal injury may result.

1. Relieve the accumulator line pressure.

2. Remove the 3 flange bolts, then remove the accumulator from the accumulator bracket.

3. Secure the accumulator in a suitable vise so the relief plug points straight up.

4. Slowly turn the plug 3½ turns and then wait 3 minutes for all pressure to escape.

5. Remove the plug completely and dispose of the accumulator unit.

6. To install, reverse the order of the removal procedure.

Pulsers/Sensors

Removal and Installation

1. To remove the wheel sensors, it is just a matter of removing the wheel that the sensor must be removed from and remove the the sensor bolts, then remove the sensor.

2. The important part of the wheel sensor removal and installation procedure is the air gap that is necessary when the sensor is installed. Use the following procedure to set the air gap.

    a. Check the pulser/sensor for chipped or damaged teeth.

    b. Measure the air gap between the sensor and pulser all

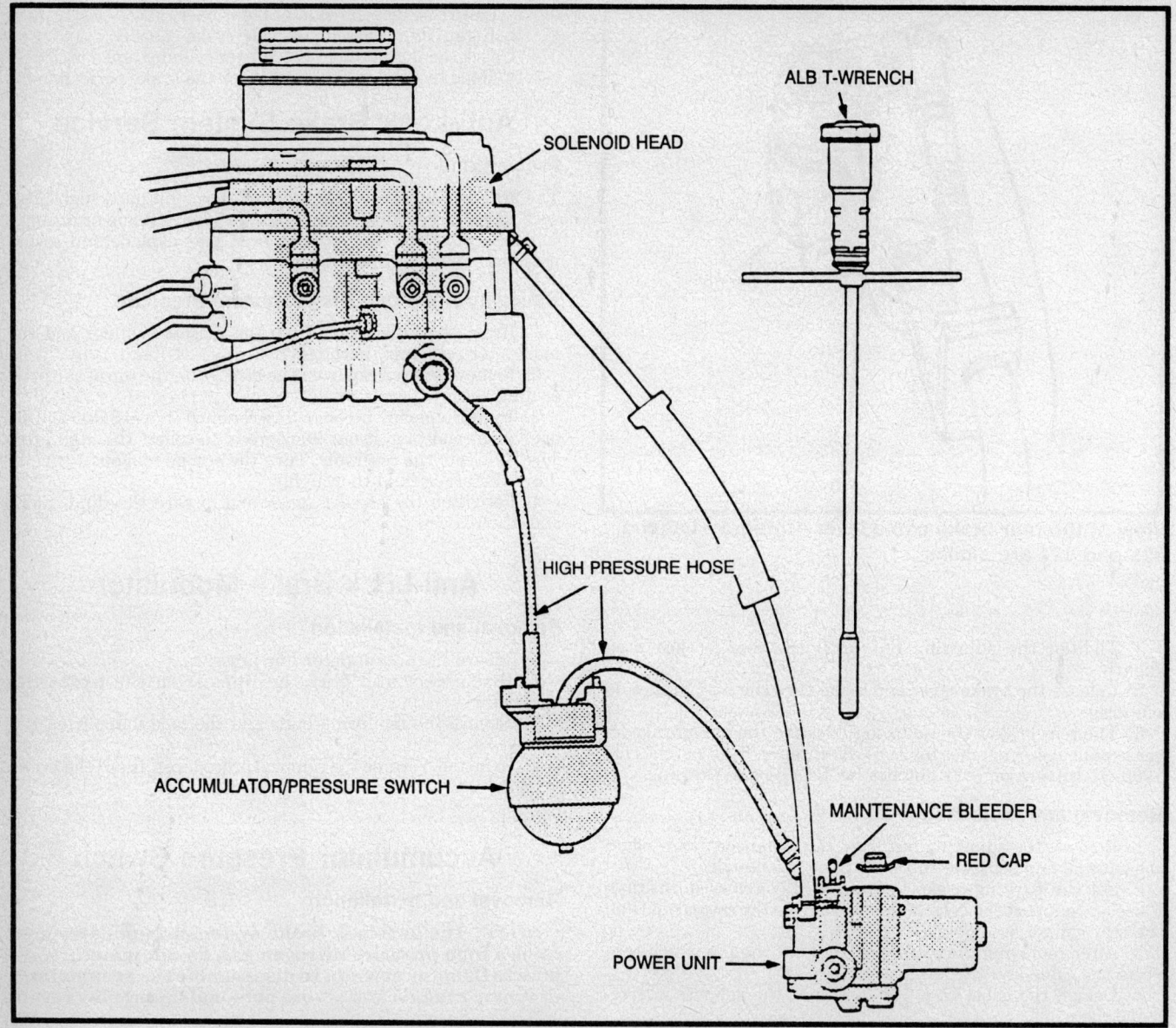

Bleeding the pressure from the anti-lock brake system

the way around while rotating the halfshaft or the hub by hand. The air gap on the both front and rear sensors should be 0.016–0.039 in. (0.4–1.0mm).

c. If the gap exceeds 0.039 in. (1.0mm), the probability is a distorted knuckle which should be replaced.

3. Be careful when installing the sensors to avoid twisting the wires. Use a white line on the wires as a guide. After sensor replacement comfirm the proper operation of the ABS system.

FRONT SUSPENSION

The Integra suspension consists of 2 independent torsion bars and front shock absorbers similar to a front strut assembly but without a spring. Both lower forged radius arms are connected with a stabilizer bar.

The Legend, 825 and 827 use a double wishbone system. The lower wishbone consists of a forged transverse link with a locating stabilizer bar. The lower end of the strut assembly has a fork shape to allow the halfshaft to pass through it. The upper arm is located in the wheel well and is twist mounted, angled forward from it's inner mount, to clear the strut assembly.

Shock Absorbers

Removal and Installation
1987–89 INTEGRA

1. Raise and safely support the vehicle. Remove the front wheels.
2. Remove the brake hose clamp bolt.
3. Place a floor jack beneath the lower control arm to support it.

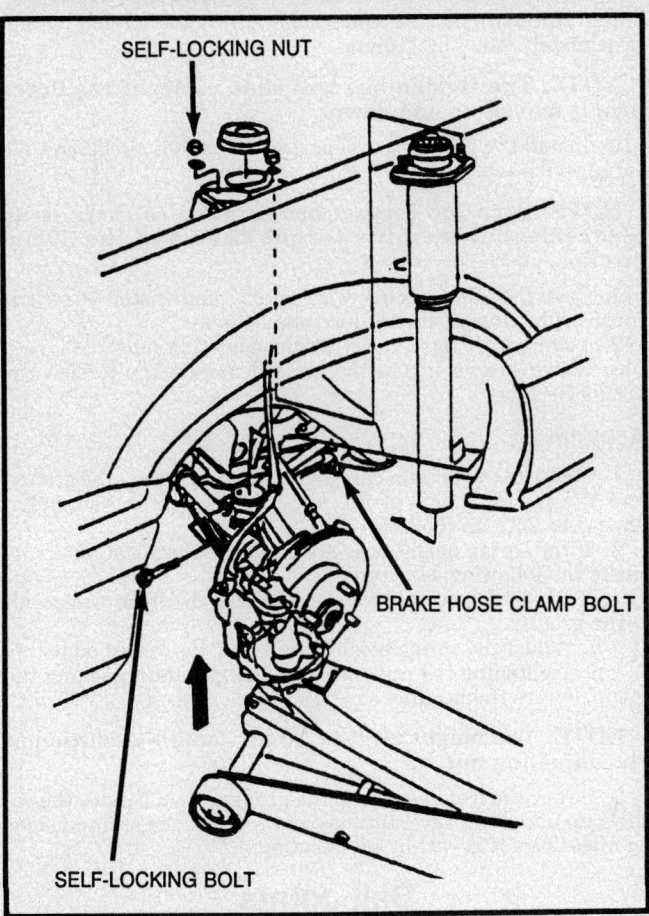

Front shock absorber—Integra

4. Remove the lower shock-to-steering knuckle bolt and slowly lower the jack.

NOTE: Be sure the jack is positioned securely beneath the lower control arm at the ball joint. Otherwise, the tension from the torsion bar may cause the lower control arm to suddenly jump away from the shock absorber as the pinch bolt is removed.

5. Compress the shock absorber by hand, remove the upper locknuts and the shock from the vehicle.
To install:
6. Reverse the removal procedures, taking note of the following:
   a. Use new self locking nuts on the top of the shock assembly and torque to 33 ft. lbs. (45 Nm).
   b. Torque the lower pinch bolt to 47 ft. lbs. (65 Nm).
   c. Install and torque the brake hose clamp to 16 ft. lbs. (22 Nm).

MacPherson Strut

Inspection

1. Check for wear or damage to the bushings and needle bearings.
2. Check for oil leaks from the struts.
3. Check all rubber parts for wear or damage.
4. Bounce the vehicle to check shock absorber effectiveness. The vehicle should continue to bounce for no more than 2 cycles.

Removal and Installation

INTEGRA

1. Raise and safely support the vehicle. Remove the front wheels.
2. Remove the brake hose clamps from the strut (damper).
3. Remove the damper fork bolt and remove the damper fork. Remove the damper by removing the 2 spring washer nuts.
To install:
4. Loosely install the damper on the frame with the aligning tab facing inside.
5. Install the damper fork on the halfshaft and the lower arm. Install the damper in the damper fork so the aligning tab is aligned with the slot in the damper fork. Hand tighten the bolts and nuts.
6. Raise the knuckle with a suitable floor jack until the vehicle just lifts off of the support. The mount base nuts should be tightened with the damper under the vehicle.
7. Tighten the pinch bolt. Secure the damper fork bolt with a new self-locking nut. Torque the locking nut to 47 ft. lbs. (65 Nm) and torque the pinch bolt to 32 ft. lbs. (44 Nm). Install the brake hose clamps with 2 bolts.
8. Secure the damper assembly to the frame with the spring washer nuts.

LEGEND, 825 AND 827

1. Raise and safely support the vehicle. Remove the front wheels.
2. Remove the brake hose clamps from the strut.
3 Remove the strut locking bolt.
4. Remove the strut fork bolt and the strut fork.
5. Remove the strut assembly.

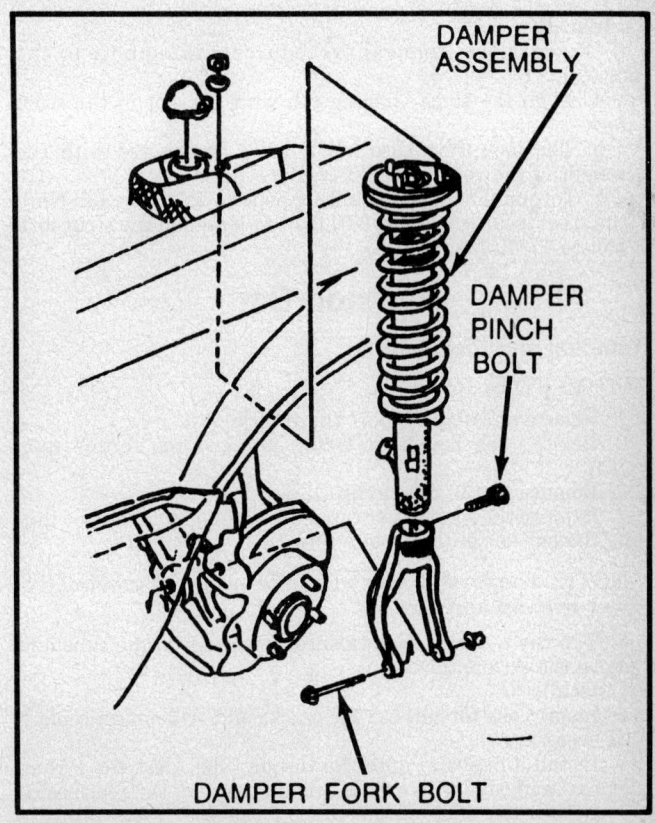

Exploded view of the damper (MacPherson Strut)— Legend, 825 and 827

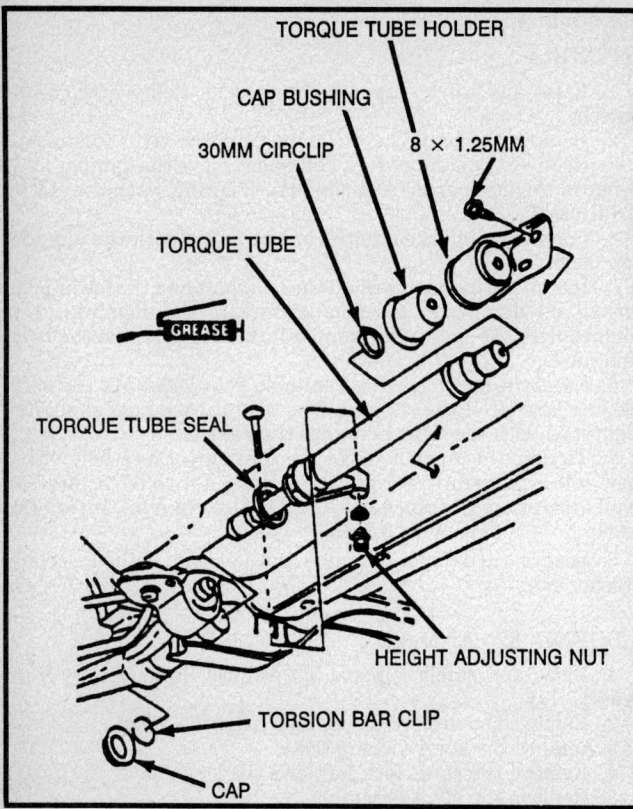

Torsion bar assembly—1987–89 Integra

To install:

6. Reverse the removal procedures, taking note of the following:

a. Align the strut aligning tab with the slot in the sturt fork.

b. The mounting base bolt should be torqued with the weight of the vehicle placed on the strut.

c. Torque the upper mounting bolts to 28 ft. lbs. (39 Nm), the strut locking bolt to 32 ft. lbs. (44 Nm) and the strut fork bolt to 47 ft. lbs. (65 Nm).

Torsion Bar

Removal and Installation

1987–89 INTEGRA

1. Raise and safely support the vehicle.

2. Remove the height adjusting nut and the torque tube holder.

3. Remove the 30mm circlip.

4. Remove the torsion bar cap and the torsion bar clip by tapping the bar out of the torque tube.

NOTE: The torsion bar will slide easier by moving the lower arm up and down.

5. Tap the torsion bar backward, from the torque tube and remove the torque tube.

To install:

6. Inspect the torsion bar for cracks and/or damage; replace it, if necessary.

7. Install a new seal onto the torque tube. Coat the torque tube seal and tube with grease, install them on the rear beam.

8. Grease the ends of the torsion bar and insert into the torque tube from the rear.

9. Align the projection on the torque tube splines with the cutout in the torsion bar splines and insert the torsion bar approximately 0.394 in. (10mm).

NOTE: The torsion bar will slide easier if the lower arm is moved up and down.

10. Install the torsion bar clip, cap, the 30mm circlip and the torque tube cap.

NOTE: Push the torsion bar forward so there is no clearance between the torque tube and the 30mm circlip.

11. Coat the cap bushing with grease and install it on the torque tube. Install the torque tube holder.

12. Temporarily tighten the height adjusting nut.

13. Lower the vehicle to the ground. Adjust the torsion bar spring height.

Adjustment

1. Measure the torsion bar spring height between the ground and the highest point of the wheel arch. The measurement should be 25.7 in. (653mm).

2. If the spring height does not meet the specification above, make the following adjustment.

a. Raise and support the vehicle with the front wheels off the ground.

b. Adjust the spring height by turning the height adjusting nut. Tightening the nut raises the height and loosening the nut lowers the height.

NOTE: The height varies 0.20 in. (5mm)/revolution of the adjusting nut.

3. Lower the front wheels to the ground, then bounce the vehicle up and down several times and recheck the spring height to make sure it is within specifications.

Ball Joints

Inspection

Check ball joint play as follows:

1. Raise and safely support the vehicle.

2. Clamp a dial indicator onto the lower control arm and place the indicator tip on the knuckle, near the ball joint.

3. Place a prybar between the lower control arm and the knuckle. Replace the lower control arm if the play exceeds 0.5mm.

Removal and Installation

1987–89 INTEGRA

The integra is equipped with only a lower ball joint. If the lower ball joint play exceeds 0.05mm, replace the lower ball joint and radius as an assembly.

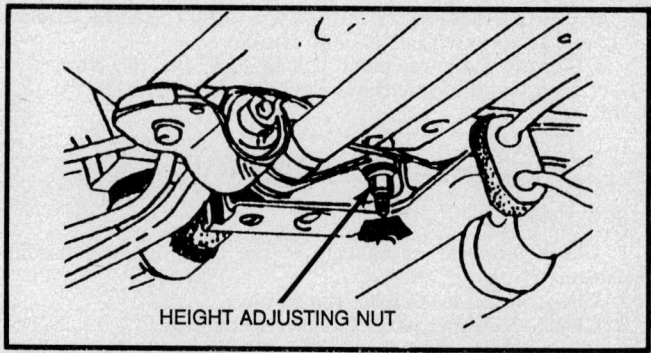

Torsion bar adjustment—1987–89 Integra

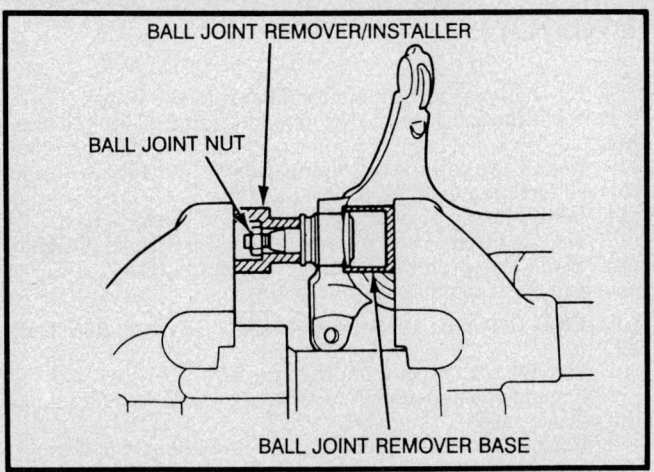

BALL JOINT REMOVER/INSTALLER

BALL JOINT NUT

BALL JOINT REMOVER BASE

Ball joint removing and installation—1990–91 Integra

1990–91 INTEGRA

1. Raise and support the vehicle safely. Remove the front wheel assemblies. Remove the steering knuckle.
2. Remove the boot by prying off the snap ring. Remove the 40 mm clip.
3. Install the special ball joint removal/installtion tool 07965-SB00100 or equivalent, on the ball joint and tighten the ball joint nut.
4. Position the ball joint in this special tool and set this assembly in a vise. Press the ball joint out of the steering knuckle.
To install:
5. Place the ball joint in position by hand. Install the ball joint into the special tool and press in the new ball joint in the vise.
6. Install the 40mm circlip. Adjust the special tool with he adjusting bolt until the end of the tool aligns with the groove on the boot. Slide the clip over the tool and into position.

LEGEND, 825 AND 827

NOTE: This procedure is performed after the removal of the steering knuckle and requires the use of the following special tools or their equivalent: a Acura part 07GAF–SD40330 ball joint removal base, 07GAF–SD40320 ball joint installation base and 07GAG–SD40700 clip guide tool.

1. Raise and support the vehicle safely. Remove the front wheel assemblies. Remove the steering knuckle from the vehicle.
2. Position the ball joint removal tool base or equivalent, on the ball joint, position the assembly in a shop press and press the ball joint from the steering knuckle.
3. Position the new ball joint into the hole of the steering knuckle.
4. Install the ball joint installer tool or equivalent, with the small end facing outward.
5. Position the ball joint installation base tool or equivalent, on the ball joint, position the assembly in a shop press and press the ball joint into the steering knuckle.
6. Seat the snaprring in the groove of the ball joint.
7. Install the boot and snaprring using the clip guide tool.

Radius Arm

Removal and Installation

1987–89 INTEGRA

1. Raise and safely support the vehicle. Remove the front wheels.

2. Place a floor jack beneath the lower control arm and remove the ball joint cotter pin/nut.

NOTE: Be sure to place the jack securely beneath the lower control arm at the ball joint. Otherwise, the tension from the torsion bar may cause the arm to suddenly jump away from the steering knuckle as the ball joint is removed.

3. Using a ball joint remover tool or equivalent, remove the ball joint from the steering knuckle.
4. Remove the radius arm locking nuts and the stabilizer locking nut and separate the radius arm from the stabilizer bar.
5. Remove the lower arm bolts and the radius arm by pulling it down and forward.
To install:
6. Reverse the removal procedures. Tighten all the rubber bushings and damper parts only after the vehicle is placed back on the ground.

Upper Control Arm

Removal and Installation

LEGEND, 825 AND 827

1. Raise and safely support the vehicle. Remove the front wheel.
2. Remove the cotter pin and the upper control arm-to-steering knuckle nut.
3. Using a ball joint removal tool or equivalent, separate the upper control arm from the steering knuckle.
4. Remove the upper control arm-to-chassis nuts, washers and the upper control arm from the vehicle.
To install:
5. Reverse the removal procedures. Torque the upper control arm-to-chassis nuts to 47 ft. lbs. (65 Nm) and the upper control arm ball joint-to-steering knuckle nut to 32 ft. lbs. (42 Nm).

Lower Control Arm

Removal and Installation

LEGEND, 825 AND 827

1. Raise and safely support the vehicle. Remove the front wheels.
2. Disconnect the lower arm ball joint; be careful not to damage the seal.
3. Remove the stabilizer bar brackets, starting with the center brackets.
4. Remove the lower arm ball joint-to-steering knuckle nut. Using a ball joint removal tool, separate the ball joint from the steering knuckle.
5. Remove the radius arm-to-chassis bolt and the arm.
To install:
6. Reverse the removal procedure. Torque the radius arm-to-chassis bolt to 39 ft. lbs. (55 Nm) and the radius arm ball joint-to-steering knuckle nut to 72 ft. lbs. (100 Nm).

REAR SUSPENSION

Shock Absorber

Removal and Installation

1987–88 LEGEND SEDAN AND 825

1. Raise and safely support the rear of the vehicle.
2. Remove the rear wheels.
3. Place a jack under the lower arm and raise slightly.
4. Remove the 8mm nuts from the top of the assembly.
5. Lower the jack.
6. Remove the lower shock pinch bolt.
7. Remove the shock absorber from the hub assembly.

To install:

8. Reverse the removal procedures, torque the upper 8mm bolts to 16 ft. lbs. (22 Nm) and the lower pinch bolt to 47 ft. lbs. (65 Nm).

MacPherson Strut

Removal and Installation

INTEGRA

1. Raise and safely support the rear of the vehicle.
2. Remove the rear wheels.
3. Place a jack under the rear axle beam.
4. Remove the strut maintenance lid and the self locking nut. On the 1990–91 vehicles the maintenance lid is located at the rear seat lining.
5. Lower the jack gradually. Remove the self-locking bolt, rear spring and spring seat.

To install:

6. Fit the upper spring seat into the frame.
7. Install the strut protector on the strut assembly, the dust cover, strut mounting collar and rear spring; temporarily tighten the strut to the axle beam.

8. Fit the inner strut mount rubber into the frame.
9. Raise the axle beam so the damper shaft fits into the frame hole.
10. Install the outer strut mount rubber and washer; torque the self-locking nut to 16 ft. lbs. (22 Nm).
11. Install the strut maintenance lid.
12. Torque the shock on the rear axle beam with the weight of the vehicle placed on the ground. Torque the the strut-to-rear axle beam bolt to 40 ft. lbs. (55 Nm).

LEGEND COUPE, 1989–91 LEGEND SEDAN, 825 AND 827

1. Remove the carpet from the trunk.
2. Remove the upper strut mounting nuts. Raise and support the vehicle safely.
3. Remove the parking brake cable-to-trailing arm clamp.
4. Remove the stabilizer linkage from the trailing arm.
5. Remove the upper arm mounting bolts.
6. Remove the lower strut mounting bolt.
7. Lower the rear suspension and remove the strut assembly.

To install:

8. Lower the rear suspension and position the strut assembly in it's original position.
9. Loosely install the lower strut mounting bolt.
10. Install and torque the strut upper mounting nuts to 16 ft. lbs. (22 Nm) for 1987–88 or 28 ft. lbs. (39 Nm) for 1989–91.
11. Using a floor jack, raise the rear suspension until the weight of the vehicle is on the strut assembly.
12. Torque the strut-to-axle bolt to 47 ft. lbs. (65 Nm).
13. Install the parking brake clamp and the stabilizer linkage on the trailing arm.

Coil Springs

Removal and Installation

1987–88 LEGEND SEDAN AND 825

1. Raise and safely support the rear of the vehicle.

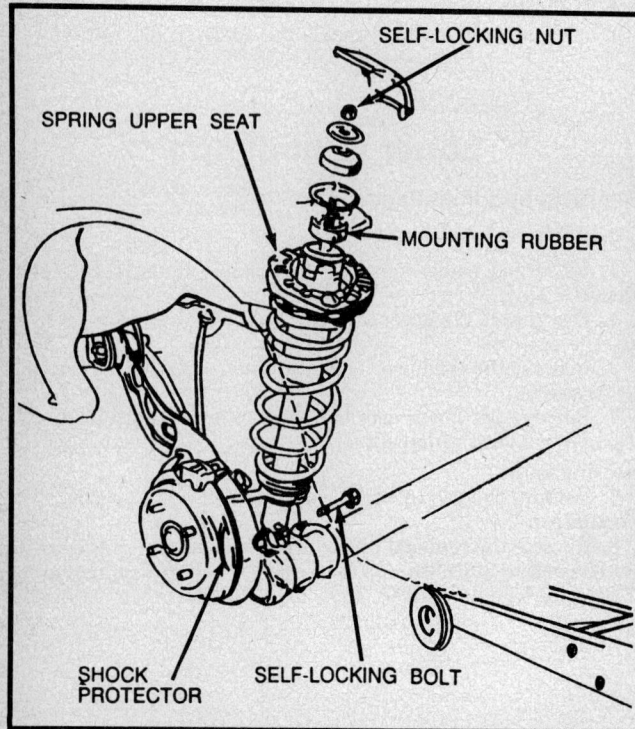

Rear strut assembly – Integra

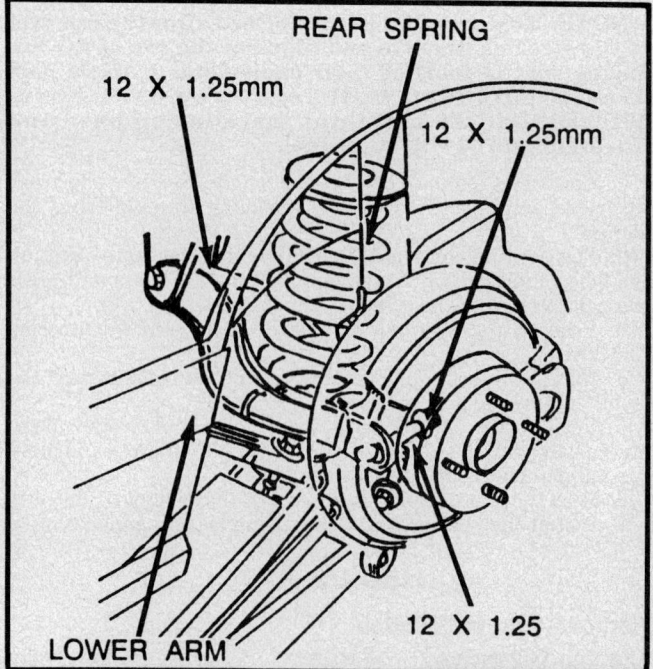

View of the rear spring assembly – 1987–89 Legend, 825 and 827

2. Place a floor jack under the lower arm.
3. Pull out the hub carrier lower bolt.
4. Loosen the lower arm outside bolt.
5. Pull out the lower arm inside bolt.
6. Lower the jack gradually and remove the rear spring.

To install:

7. Reverse the removal procedures. Install the rear spring with the lower end of the spring outside.

8. Torque the lower arm-to-hub carrier nut/bolt to 54 ft. lbs. (75 Nm), with the weight of the vehicle on the ground.

Rear Control Arms

Removal and Installation

LOWER CONTROL ARM

The 1989–91 Legend, 825 and 827 are equipped with 2 lower control arms, **A** and **B**.

1. Raise and safely support the rear of the vehicle.

2. Remove the lower control arms-to-steering knuckle nut/bolt.

3. Remove the lower control arms-to-chassis nuts/bolts and the control arms from the vehicle.

To install:

4. Reverse the removal procedures. Torque the lower control arm **A**-to-chassis nut/bolt to 54 ft. lbs. (75 Nm), the lower control arm **B**-to-chassis nut/bolt to 16 ft. lbs. (22 Nm) and the lower control arms-to-steering knuckle nut/bolts to 47 ft. lbs. (65 Nm).

TRAILING ARM

The 1989–91 Legend, 825 and 827 are equipped with trailing arms.

1. Raise and safely support the rear of the vehicle.

2. Remove the trailing arm-to-steering knuckle nuts.

3. Remove the trailing arm-to-bracket nut/bolt and the trailing arm.

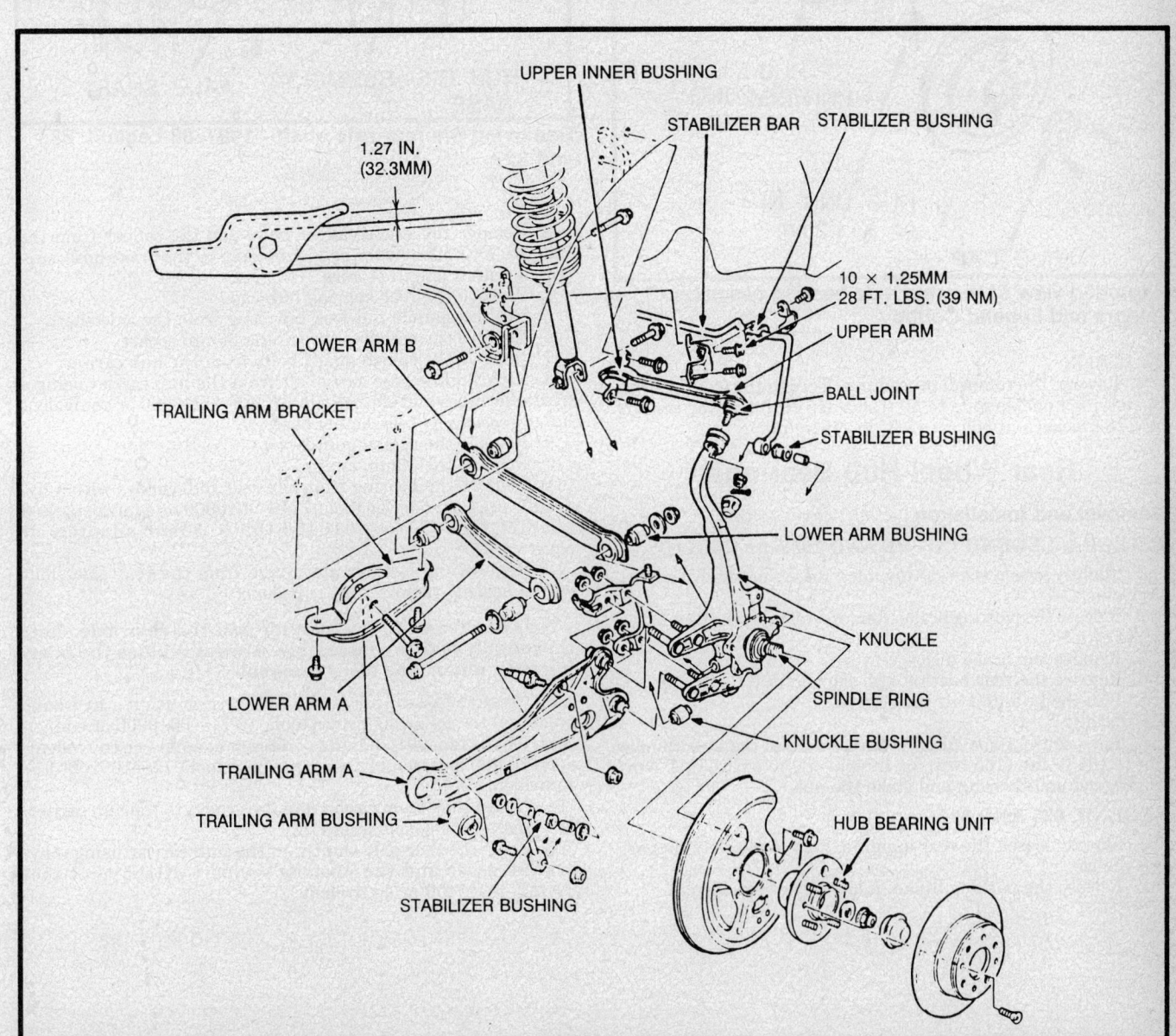

Exploded view of the rear suspension system – Legend, 825 and 827

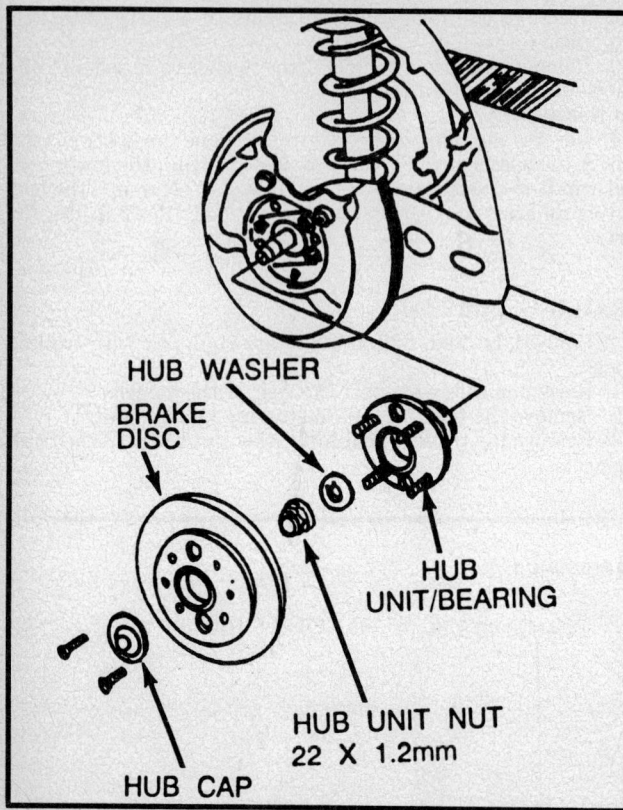

Exploded view of the rear axle bearing assembly—Integra and Legend Coupe

To install:

4. Reverse the removal procedures. Torque the trailing arm-to-steering knuckle nuts to 40 ft. lbs. (55 Nm) and the trailing arm-to-bracket nut/bolt to 47 ft. lbs. (65 Nm).

Rear Wheel Hub Bearings

Removal and Installation

INTEGRA, LEGEND COUPE AND 1989–91 LEGEND

1. Slightly loosen the rear lug nuts. Raise and safely support the vehicle.
2. Release the parking brake. Remove the rear wheels and the brake calipers.
3. Remove the brake disc.
4. Remove the rear bearing hub cap and nut.
5. Pull the hub unit off the spindle.

To install:

6. Reverse the removal procedures. Torque the new spindle nut to 134 ft. lbs. (185 Nm) for Integra or 180 ft. lbs. (250 Nm) for Legend and Sterling and stake the nut.

LEGEND, 825 AND 827

1. Slightly loosen the rear lug nuts. Raise and safely support the vehicle.
2. Release the parking brake. Remove the rear wheels.

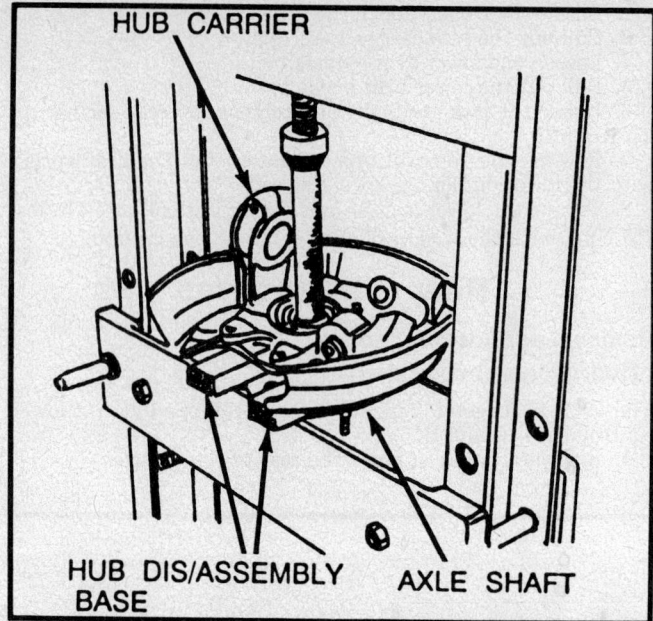

Removing the rear axle shaft—1987–88 Legend, 825 and 827

3. Remove the brake caliper bolts and the caliper from the knuckle. Do not allow the caliper to hang by the brake hose; support it with a length of wire.
4. Remove the rear bearing hub cap.
5. Pry the spindle nut lock tab away from the axle shaft.
6. Remove the spindle nut using a 36mm socket.
7. Remove the splash guard bolts from the hub carrier.
8. Separate the rear axle shaft from the hub carrier using a hydraulic press and special tool 07GAF–SD40700 or equivalent hub disassembly/ reassembly base.
9. Remove the splash guard.
10. Remove the 68mm circlip.
11. Remove the bearing from the rear hub carrier with a hydraulic press and driver tool 07749–0010000 or equivalent, and adapter tool 07746–0010400 (52 × 55mm adapter) or equivalent.
12. Remove the bearing inner race from the rear axle shaft with a bearing remover or equivalent.

NOTE: Clean the hub carrier and the rear axle shaft thoroughly before reassembly. Always replace the bearing with a new one after removal.

13. Press the bearing into the hub carrier using a hydraulic press and the following driver tools; 07749–0010000 or equivalent, tool 07746–0010500 (62 × 68mm adapter) or equivalent, and the hub disassembly/assembly base tool 07965–6920001 or equivalent.
14. Install the 68mm circlip into the groove in the hub carrier.
15. Install the splash guard.
16. Press the rear axle shaft into the hub carrier using a hydraulic press and the bearing support attachment tool 07GAF–SD40400 or equivalent.

SPECIFICATIONS

ENGINE IDENTIFICATION

Year	Model	Engine Displacement cu. in. (cc/liter)	Engine Series Identification	No. of Cylinders	Engine Type
1987	Spider	119.7 (1962/2.0)	AR01544	4	DOHC
	Spider Veloce	119.7 (1962/2.0)	AR01544	4	DOHC
	Graduate	119.7 (1962/2.0)	AR01544	4	DOHC
	Milano	152.1 (2492/2.5)	019.11	6	DOHC
	Milano	180.5 (2959/3.0)	061.24	6	DOHC
1988	Spider	119.7 (1962/2.0)	AR01544	4	DOHC
	Spider Veloce	119.7 (1962/2.0)	AR01544	4	DOHC
	Graduate	119.7 (1962/2.0)	AR01544	4	DOHC
	Milano	152.1 (2492/2.5)	0.19.11	6	DOHC
	Milano	180.5 (2959/3.0)	061.24	6	DOHC
1989	Spider	119.7 (1962/2.0)	AR01544	4	DOHC
	Spider Veloce	119.7 (1962/2.0)	AR01544	4	DOHC
	Graduate	119.7 (1962/2.0)	AR01544	4	DOHC
	Milano	152.1 (2492/2.5)	0.19.11	6	DOHC
	Milano	180.5 (2959/3.0)	061.24	6	DOHC
1990	Spider	119.7 (1962/2.0)	AR01544	4	DOHC
	Spider Veloce	119.7 (1962/2.0)	AR01544	4	DOHC
	Graduate	119.7 (1962/2.0)	AR01544	4	DOHC
1991	Spider	119.7 (1962/2.0)	01588	4	DOHC
	Spider Veloce	119.7 (1962/2.0)	01588	4	DOHC
	164L	180.6 (2959/3.0)	6412T1	6	DOHC
	164S	180.6 (2959/3.0)	6412T2	6	DOHC

GENERAL ENGINE SPECIFICATIONS

Year	Model	Engine Displacement cu. in. (cc)	Fuel System Type	Net Horsepower @ rpm	Net Torque @ rpm (ft. lbs.)	Bore × Stroke (in.)	Compression Ratio	Oil Pressure @ rpm
1987	Spider	119.7 (1962)	EFI	115 @ 5500	118.8 @ 2750	3.31 × 3.48	9.0:1	7–14 @ 900
	Veloce	119.7 (1962)	EFI	115 @ 5500	118.8 @ 2750	3.31 × 3.48	9.0:1	7–14 @ 900
	Graduate	119.7 (1962)	EFI	115 @ 5500	118.8 @ 2750	3.31 × 3.48	9.0:1	7–14 @ 900
	Milano	152.1 (2492)	EFI	157 @ 5600	154.7 @ 4000	3.46 × 2.69	9.0:1	7–11 @ 900
	Milano	180.5 (2959)	EFI	188 @ 5800	159.3 @ 1000	3.66 × 2.85	9.5:1	7–11 @ 900
1988	Spider	119.7 (1962)	EFI	115 @ 5500	118.8 @ 2750	3.31 × 3.48	9.0:1	7–14 @ 900
	Veloce	119.7 (1962)	EFI	115 @ 5500	118.8 @ 2750	3.31 × 3.48	9.0:1	7–14 @ 900
	Graduate	119.7 (1962)	EFI	115 @ 5500	118.8 @ 2750	3.31 × 3.48	9.0:1	7–14 @ 900
	Milano	152.1 (2492)	EFI	157 @ 5600	154.7 @ 4000	3.46 × 2.69	9.0:1	7–11 @ 900
	Milano	180.5 (2959)	EFI	188 @ 5800	159.3 @ 1000	3.66 × 2.85	9.5:1	7–11 @ 900
1989	Spider	119.7 (1962)	EFI	115 @ 5500	118.8 @ 2750	3.31 × 3.48	9.0:1	7–14 @ 900
	Veloce	119.7 (1962)	EFI	115 @ 5500	118.8 @ 2750	3.31 × 3.48	9.0:1	7–14 @ 900
	Graduate	119.7 (1962)	EFI	115 @ 5500	118.8 @ 2750	3.31 × 3.48	9.0:1	7–14 @ 900
	Milano	152.1 (2492)	EFI	157 @ 5600	154.7 @ 4000	3.46 × 2.69	9.0:1	7–11 @ 900
	Milano	180.5 (2959)	EFI	188 @ 5800	159.3 @ 1000	3.66 × 2.85	9.5:1	7–11 @ 900

ALFA ROMEO
GRADUATE • MILANO • SPIDER • 164

GENERAL ENGINE SPECIFICATIONS

Year	Model	Engine Displacement cu. in. (cc)	Fuel System Type	Net Horsepower @ rpm	Net Torque @ rpm (ft. lbs.)	Bore × Stroke (in.)	Compression Ratio	Oil Pressure @ rpm
1990	Spider	119.7 (1962)	EFI	115 @ 5500	118.8 @ 2750	3.31 × 3.48	9.0:1	7–14 @ 900
	Veloce	119.7 (1962)	EFI	115 @ 5500	118.8 @ 2750	3.31 × 3.48	9.0:1	7–14 @ 900
	Graduate	119.7 (1962)	EFI	115 @ 5500	118.8 @ 2750	3.31 × 3.48	9.0:1	7–14 @ 900
1991	Spider	119.7 (1962)	EFI	120 @ 5800	118.7 @ 4200	3.31 × 3.48	9.0:1	7–14 @ 900
	Veloce	119.7 (1962)	EFI	120 @ 5800	118.7 @ 4200	3.31 × 3.48	9.0:1	7–14 @ 900
	164L	180.6 (2959)	EFI	183 @ 5600	191 @ 4400	3.66 × 2.86	9.5:1	11.6 @ 900
	164S	180.6 (2959)	EFI	200 @ 5800	195 @ 4500	3.66 × 2.86	10.0:1	11.6 @ 900

GASOLINE ENGINE TUNE-UP SPECIFICATIONS

Year	Model	Engine Displacement cu. in. (cc)	Spark Plugs Type	Spark Plugs Gap (in.)	Ignition Timing (deg.) MT	Ignition Timing (deg.) AT	Compression Pressure (psi)	Fuel Pump (psi)	Idle Speed (rpm) MT	Idle Speed (rpm) AT	Valve Clearance In.	Valve Clearance Ex.
1987	Spider	119.7 (1962)	RN5C	0.023–0.028	11B	—	NA	33–38	900–1000	—	0.016–0.018	0.018–0.020
	Veloce	119.7 (1962)	RN5C	0.023–0.028	11B	—	NA	33–38	900–1000	—	0.016–0.018	0.018–0.020
	Graduate	119.7 (1962)	RN5C	0.023–0.028	11B	—	NA	33–38	900–1000	—	0.016–0.018	0.018–0.020
	Milano	152.1 (2492)	RN-11YC	0.028–0.031	2B	—	NA	35.6	900–1000	—	0.020	0.010
	Milano	180.5 (2959)	RN-11YC	0.028–0.031	7B	—	NA	35.6	800–900	—	0.020	0.010
1988	Spider	119.7 (1962)	RN5C	0.023–0.028	11B	—	NA	33–38	900–1000	—	0.016–0.018	0.018–0.020
	Veloce	119.7 (1962)	RN53	0.023–0.028	11B	—	NA	33–38	900–1000	—	0.016–0.018	0.018–0.020
	Graduate	119.7 (1962)	RN5C	0.023–0.028	11B	—	NA	33–38	900–1000	—	0.016–0.018	0.018–0.020
	Milano	152.1 (2492)	RN-11YC	0.028–0.031	2B	—	NA	35.6	900–1000	—	0.020	0.010
	Milano	180.5 (2959)	RN-11YC	0.028–0.031	7B	—	NA	35.6	800–900	—	0.020	0.010
1989	Spider	119.7 (1962)	RN5C	0.023–0.028	11B	—	NA	33–38	900–1000	—	0.016–0.018	0.018–0.020
	Veloce	119.7 (1962)	RN5C	0.023–0.028	11B	—	NA	33–38	900–1000	—	0.016–0.018	0.018–0.020
	Graduate	119.7 (1962)	RN5C	0.023–0.028	11B	—	NA	33–38	900–1000	—	0.016–0.018	0.018–0.020
	Milano	152.1 (2492)	RN-11YC	0.028–0.031	2B	—	NA	35.6	900–1000	—	0.020	0.010
	Milano	180.5 (2959)	RN-11YC	0.028–0.031	7B	—	NA	35.6	800–900	—	0.020	0.010
1990	Spider	119.7 (1962)	RN5C	0.023–0.028	11B	11B	NA	42–47	750–850	900–1000	0.016–0.018	0.018–0.020
	Veloce	119.7 (1962)	RN5C	0.023–0.028	11B	11B	NA	42–47	750–850	900–1000	0.016–0.018	0.018–0.020
	Graduate	119.7 (1962)	RN5C	0.023–0.028	11B	11B	NA	42–47	750–850	900–1000	0.016–0.018	0.018–0.020

GASOLINE ENGINE TUNE-UP SPECIFICATIONS

Year	Model	Engine Displacement cu. in. (cc)	Spark Plugs Type	Spark Plugs Gap (in.)	Ignition Timing (deg.) MT	Ignition Timing (deg.) AT	Compression Pressure (psi)	Fuel Pump (psi)	Idle Speed (rpm) MT	Idle Speed (rpm) AT	Valve Clearance In.	Valve Clearance Ex.
1991	Spider	119.7 (1962)	RN5C	0.023–0.028	11B	11B	NA	42–47	750–850	900–1000	0.016–0.018	0.018–0.020
	Veloce	119.7 (1962)	RN5C	0.023–0.028	11B	11B	NA	42–47	750–850	900–1000	0.016–0.018	0.018–0.020
	164L	180.6 (2959)	①	①	NA	NA	NA	42–47	NA	NA	0.019–0.020	0.009–0.010
	164S	180.6 (2959)	①	①	NA	NA	NA	42–47	NA	NA	0.019–0.020	0.009–0.010

NA—Not available
① Factory installed: Golden lodge 2HL, no gap adjustment required

FIRING ORDERS

NOTE: To avoid confusion, always replace spark plug wires one at a time.

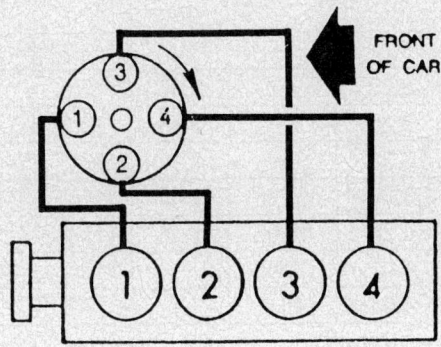

2.0L Engine
Engine Firing Order: 1–3–4–2
Distributor Rotation: Clockwise

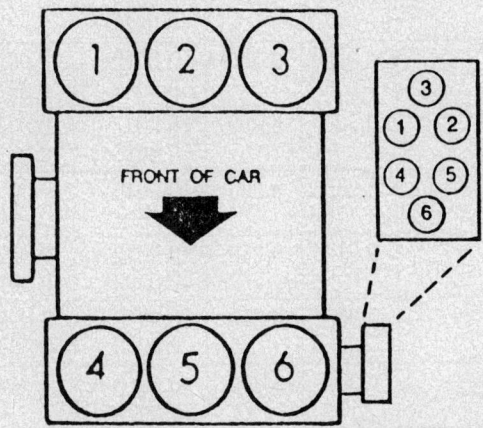

3.0L Engine
Engine Firing Order: 1–4–2–5–3–6
Distributor Rotation: Clockwise

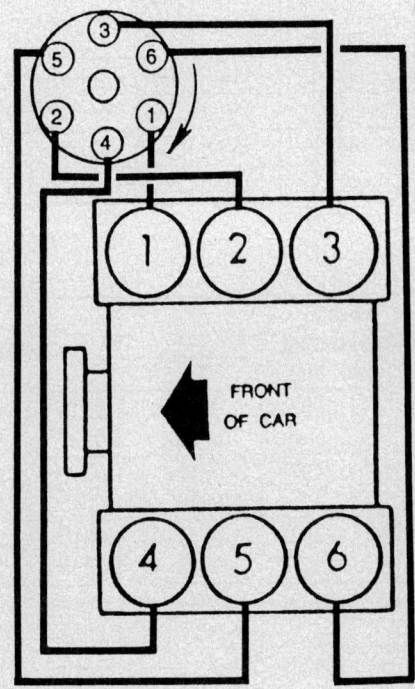

2.5L and 3.0L Engines
Engine Firing Order: 1–4–2–5–3–6
Distributor Rotation: Clockwise

ALFA ROMEO
GRADUATE • MILANO • SPIDER • 164

CAPACITIES

Year	Model	Engine Displacement cu. in. (cc)	Engine Crankcase with Filter	Engine Crankcase without Filter	Transmission (pts.) 4-Spd	Transmission (pts.) 5-Spd	Transmission (pts.) Auto.	Drive Axle (pts.)	Fuel Tank (gal.)	Cooling System (qts.)
1987	Spider	119.7 (1962)	7.7–7.9	7.1	—	3.25	—	2.46	12.2	7.6
	Veloce	119.7 (1962)	7.7–7.9	7.1	—	3.25	—	2.46	12.2	7.6
	Graduate	119.7 (1962)	7.7–7.9	7.1	—	3.25	—	2.46	12.2	7.6
	Milano	152.1 (2492)	7.7–7.9	7.1	—	NA	—	NA	17.7	10.5
	Milano	180.5 (2959)	7.7–7.9	7.1	—	NA	—	NA	17.7	10.5
1988	Spider	119.7 (1962)	7.7–7.9	7.1	—	3.25	—	2.46	12.2	7.6
	Veloce	119.7 (1962)	7.7–7.9	7.1	—	3.25	—	2.46	12.2	7.6
	Graduate	119.7 (1962)	7.7–7.9	7.1	—	3.25	—	2.46	12.2	7.6
	Milano	152.1 (2492)	7.7–7.9	7.1	—	NA	—	NA	17.7	10.5
	Milano	180.5 (2959)	7.7–7.9	7.1	—	NA	—	NA	17.7	10.5
1989	Spider	119.7 (1962)	7.7–7.9	7.1	—	3.25	—	2.46	12.2	7.6
	Veloce	119.7 (1962)	7.7–7.9	7.1	—	3.25	—	2.46	12.2	7.6
	Graduate	119.7 (1962)	7.7–7.9	7.1	—	3.25	—	2.46	12.2	7.6
	Milano	152.1 (2492)	7.7–7.9	7.1	—	NA	—	NA	17.7	10.5
	Milano	180.5 (2959)	7.7–7.9	7.1	—	NA	—	NA	17.7	10.5
1990	Spider	119.7 (1962)	7.7–7.9	7.1	—	3.25	—	2.46	12.2	7.6
	Veloce	119.7 (1962)	7.7–7.9	7.1	—	3.25	—	2.46	12.2	7.6
	Graduate	119.7 (1962)	7.7–7.9	7.1	—	3.25	—	2.46	12.2	7.6
1991	Spider	119.7 (1962)	7.7–7.9	7.1	—	3.25	10.96	2.46	12.2	9.0
	Veloce	119.7 (1962)	7.7–7.9	7.1	—	3.25	10.96	2.46	12.2	9.0
	164L	180.6 (2959)	7.7–7.9	7.1	—	4.0	19.2	—	17.5	10.2
	164S	180.6 (2959)	7.7–7.9	7.1	—	4.0	19.2	—	17.5	10.2

CAMSHAFT SPECIFICATIONS
All measurements given in inches.

Year	Engine Displacement cu. in. (cc)	Journal Diameter 1	Journal Diameter 2	Journal Diameter 3	Journal Diameter 4	Journal Diameter 5	Lobe Lift In.	Lobe Lift Ex.	Bearing Clearance	Camshaft End Play
1987	119.7 (1962)	1.0614–1.0622	1.0614–1.0622	1.0614–1.0622	—	—	0.350	0.350	0.0016–0.0021	NA
	152.1 (2492)	1.0610–1.0618	1.0610–1.0618	1.0610–1.0618	—	—	0.360	0.250	0.0012–0.0033	0.0026–0.0079
	180.5 (2959)	1.0610–1.0618	1.0610–1.0618	1.0610–1.0618	—	—	0.360	0.250	0.0012–0.0033	0.0026–0.0079
1988	119.7 (1962)	1.0614–1.0622	1.0614–1.0622	1.0614–1.0622	—	—	0.350	0.350	0.0016–0.0021	NA
	152.1 (2492)	1.0610–1.0618	1.0610–1.0618	1.0610–1.0618	—	—	0.360	0.250	0.0012–0.0033	0.0026–0.0079
	180.5 (2959)	1.0610–1.0618	1.0610–1.0618	1.0610–1.0618	—	—	0.360	0.250	0.0012–0.0033	0.0026–0.0079
1989	119.7 (1962)	1.0614–1.0622	1.0614–1.0622	1.0614–1.0622	—	—	0.350	0.350	0.0016–0.0021	NA
	152.1 (2492)	1.0610–1.0618	1.0610–1.0618	1.0610–1.0618	—	—	0.360	0.250	0.0012–0.0033	0.0026–0.0079
	180.5 (2959)	1.0610–1.0618	1.0610–1.0618	1.0610–1.0618	—	—	0.360	0.250	0.0012–0.0033	0.0026–0.0079

CAMSHAFT SPECIFICATIONS

All measurements given in inches.

Year	Engine Displacement cu. in. (cc)	Journal Diameter 1	2	3	4	5	Lobe Lift In.	Ex.	Bearing Clearance	Camshaft End Play
1990	119.7 (1962)	1.0614–1.0622	1.0614–1.0622	1.0614–1.0622	—	—	0.430	0.350	0.0016–0.0021	NA
1991	119.7 (1962)	1.0614–1.0622	1.0614–1.0622	1.0614–1.0622	—	—	0.430	0.350	0.0016–0.0021	NA
	180.6 (2959)	1.0610–1.0618	1.0610–1.0618	1.0610–1.0618	—	—	0.360	0.250	0.0012–0.0033	0.0023–0.0079

CRANKSHAFT AND CONNECTING ROD SPECIFICATIONS

All measurements are given in inches.

Year	Engine Displacement cu. in. (cc)	Crankshaft Main Brg. Journal Dia.	Main Brg. Oil Clearance	Shaft End-play	Thrust on No.	Connecting Rod Journal Diameter	Oil Clearance	Side Clearance
1987	119.7 (1962)	①	②	0.0031–0.0104	—	2.1140–2.1145	⑨	0.008–0.012
	152.1 (2492)	③	0.0006–0.0022	0.0031–0.0104	—	2.1854–2.1860	⑧	0.008–0.012
	180.5 (2959)	④	0.0002–0.0018	0.0031–0.0104	—	2.1854–2.1860	⑧	0.008–0.012
1988	119.7 (1962)	①	②	0.0031–0.0104	—	2.1140–2.1145	⑨	0.008–0.012
	152.1 (2492)	③	0.0006–0.0022	0.0031–0.0104	—	2.1854–2.1860	⑧	0.008–0.012
	180.5 (2959)	④	0.0002–0.0018	0.0031–0.0104	—	2.1854–2.1860	⑧	0.008–0.012
1989	119.7 (1962)	①	②	0.0031–0.0104	—	2.1140–2.1145	⑨	0.008–0.012
	152.1 (2492)	③	0.0006–0.0022	0.0031–0.0104	—	2.1854–2.1860	⑧	0.008–0.012
	180.5 (2959)	④	0.0002–0.0018	0.0031–0.0104	—	2.1854–2.1860	⑧	0.008–0.012
1990	119.7 (1962)	①	②	0.0031–0.0104	—	2.1140–2.1145	⑨	0.008–0.012
1991	119.7 (1962)	①	②	0.0031–0.0104	—	2.1140–2.1145	⑨	0.008–0.012
	180.6 (2959)	⑤	⑥	0.0031–0.0104	—	⑦	⑩	0.008–0.012

① Except Crankpin:
Blue—2.3603–2.3607
Red—2.3607–2.3611
Crankpin:
Blue—1.9676–1.9680
Red—1.9680–1.9684

② Except Crankpin:
Blue—0.0002–0.0018
Red—0.0002–0.0019
Crankpin:
Blue—0.0010–0.0024
Red—0.0011–0.0024

③ Except Crankpin:
Blue—2.3603–2.3607
Red—2.3607–2.3610
Crankpin:
Blue—2.0465–2.0468
Red—2.0468–2.0472

④ Except Crankpin:
Blue—2.3607–2.3611
Red—2.3611–2.3614
Crankpin:
Blue—2.0465–2.0468
Red—2.0468–2.0472

⑤ Lt. Blue—2.3607–2.3611
Red—2.3611–2.3615

⑥ Blue—0.0002–0.0019
Red—0.0008–0.0019

⑦ Lt. Blue—2.0465–2.0468
Red—2.0468–2.0472

⑧ Blue—0.0009–0.0024
Red—0.0009–0.0024

⑨ Blue—0.0008–0.0022
Red—0.0009–0.0023

⑩ Blue—0.0009–0.0024
Red—0.0008–0.0023

VALVE SPECIFICATIONS

Year	No. Cylinder Displacement cu. in. (cc)	Seat Angle (deg.)	Face Angle (deg.)	Spring Test Pressure (lbs.)	Spring Installed Height (in.)	Stem-to-Guide Clearance (in.)		Stem Diameter (in.)	
						Intake	Exhaust	Intake	Exhaust
1987	119.7 (1962)	NA	NA	①	③	0.0005–0.0017	0.0016–0.0031	0.3532–0.3538	0.3518–0.3528
	152.1 (2492)	NA	NA	38.2–39.6 @ 1.256	0.93	0.0005–0.0017	0.0016–0.0031	0.3532–0.3538	0.3518–0.3528
	180.5 (2959)	NA	NA	38.2–39.6 @ 1.256	0.93	0.0005–0.0017	0.0018–0.0030	0.3532–0.3538	0.3520–0.3526
1988	119.7 (1962)	NA	NA	①	③	0.0005–0.0017	0.0016–0.0031	0.3532–0.3538	0.3518–0.3528
	152.1 (2492)	NA	NA	38.2–39.6 @ 1.256	0.93	0.0005–0.0017	0.0016–0.0031	0.3532–0.3538	0.3518–0.3528
	180.5 (2959)	NA	NA	38.2–39.6 @ 1.256	0.93	0.0005–0.0017	0.0018–0.0030	0.3532–0.3538	0.3520–0.3526
1989	119.7 (1962)	NA	NA	①	③	0.0005–0.0017	0.0016–0.0031	0.3532–0.3538	0.3518–0.3528
	152.1 (2492)	NA	NA	38.2–39.6 @ 1.256	0.93	0.0005–0.0017	0.0016–0.0031	0.3532–0.3538	0.3518–0.3528
	180.5 (2959)	NA	NA	38.2–39.6 @ 1.256	0.93	0.0005–0.0017	0.0018–0.0030	0.3532–0.3538	0.3520–0.3526
1990	119.7 (1962)	NA	NA	①	③	0.0005–0.0017	0.0016–0.0031	0.3532–0.3538	0.3518–0.3528
1991	119.7 (1962)	NA	NA	②	④	0.0005–0.0017	0.0016–0.0031	0.3532–0.3538	0.3518–0.3528
	180.6 (2959)	45	NA	⑤	⑥	0.0005–0.0017	0.0018–0.0029	0.3532–0.3538	0.3520–0.3525

NA—Not available

① Outer—101.6–105.2 lbs. @ 1.00 in
  Inner—54.8–56.7 lbs. @ 0.93 in.
② Outer—85.3–88.3 @ 1.06 in.
  Inner—49.0–51.1 @ 1.02 in.

③ Outer—1.00 in.
  Inner—0.93 in.
④ Outer—1.06 in.
  Inner—1.02 in.

⑤ Outer—54.6–56.6 @ 1.28 in.
  Inner—28.3–29.2 @ 1.20 in.
⑥ Outer—1.28 in.
  Inner—1.20 in.

PISTON AND RING SPECIFICATIONS

All measurements are given in inches.

Year	No. Cylinder Displacement cu. in. (cc)	Piston Clearance	Ring Gap			Ring Side Clearance		
			Top Compression	Bottom Compression	Oil Control	Top Compression	Bottom Compression	Oil Control
1987	119.7 (1962)	0.0019–0.0020	0.010–0.016	0.012–0.018	0.010–0.016	0.0018–0.0027	0.0018–0.0027	0.0005–0.0017
	152.1 (2492)	0.0016–0.0023	0.012–0.018	0.012–0.018	0.010–0.016	0.0014–0.0026	0.0014–0.0026	0.0010–0.0022
	180.5 (2959)	0.0016–0.0023	0.016–0.026	0.016–0.026	0.012–0.024	0.0014–0.0026	0.0014–0.0026	0.0010–0.0022
1988	119.7 (1962)	0.0019–0.0020	0.010–0.016	0.012–0.018	0.010–0.016	0.0018–0.0027	0.0018–0.0027	0.0005–0.0017
	152.1 (2492)	0.0016–0.0023	0.012–0.018	0.012–0.018	0.012–0.016	0.0014–0.0026	0.0014–0.0026	0.0010–0.0022
	180.5 (2959)	0.0016–0.0023	0.016–0.026	0.016–0.026	0.012–0.024	0.0014–0.0026	0.0014–0.0026	0.0010–0.0022

PISTON AND RING SPECIFICATIONS

All measurements are given in inches.

Year	No. Cylinder Displacement cu. in. (cc)	Piston Clearance	Ring Gap			Ring Side Clearance		
			Top Compression	Bottom Compression	Oil Control	Top Compression	Bottom Compression	Oil Control
1989	119.7 (1962)	0.0019–0.0020	0.010–0.016	0.012–0.018	0.010–0.016	0.0018–0.0027	0.0018–0.0027	0.0005–0.0017
	152.1 (2492)	0.0016–0.0023	0.012–0.018	0.012–0.018	0.010–0.016	0.0014–0.0026	0.0014–0.0026	0.0010–0.0022
	180.5 (2959)	0.0016–0.0023	0.016–0.026	0.016–0.026	0.012–0.024	0.0014–0.0026	0.0014–0.0026	0.0010–0.0022
1990	119.7 (1962)	0.0019–0.0020	0.012–0.020	0.012–0.020	0.010–0.020	0.0018–0.0027	0.0018–0.0027	0.0015–0.0018
1991	119.7 (1962)	0.0019–0.0020	0.012–0.020	0.012–0.020	0.010–0.020	0.0018–0.0027	0.0018–0.0027	0.0015–0.0018
	180.6 (2959)	0.0020–0.0027	0.016–0.026	0.016–0.026	0.012–0.023	0.0014–0.0026	0.0014–0.0026	0.0010–0.0022

TORQUE SPECIFICATIONS

All readings in ft. lbs.

Year	Engine Displacement cu. in. (cc)	Cylinder Head Bolts	Main Bearing Bolts	Rod Bearing Bolts	Crankshaft Pulley Bolts	Flywheel Bolts	Manifold		Spark Plugs
							Intake	Exhaust	
1987	119.7 (1962)	①	33.9–36.1	36.1–38.4	137.9–143.8	81.1–83.3	NA	NA	18.4–25.1
	152.1 (2492)	②	61.9–68.4	39.4–43.5	174.0	83.2	NA	NA	NA
	180.5 (2959)	③	61.9–68.4	39.4–43.5	174.0	83.2	NA	NA	NA
1988	119.7 (1962)	①	33.9–36.1	36.1–38.4	137.9–143.8	81.1–83.3	NA	NA	18.4–25.1
	152.1 (2492)	②	61.9–68.4	39.4–43.5	174.0	83.2	NA	NA	NA
	180.5 (2959)	③	61.9–68.4	39.4–43.5	174.0	83.2	NA	NA	NA
1989	119.7 (1962)	①	33.9–36.1	36.1–38.4	137.9–143.8	81.1–83.3	NA	NA	18.4–25.1
	152.1 (2492)	②	61.9–68.4	39.4–43.5	174.0	83.2	NA	NA	NA
	180.5 (2959)	③	61.9–68.4	39.4–43.5	174.0	83.2	NA	NA	NA
1990	119.7 (1962)	①	33.9–36.1	36.1–38.4	137.9–143.8	81.1–83.3	NA	NA	18.4–25.1
1991	119.7 (1962)	①	33.9–36.1	36.1–38.4	137.9–143.8	81.1–83.3	NA	NA	18.4–25.1
	180.6 (2959)	③	④	39.4–43.5	173.0	84.4	NA	18.8	18.4–25

NA—Not available

① Cold engine—tighten in 2 steps:
1. Lubricate nuts and threads and tighten in sequence to 56.8–58.3 ft. lbs.
2. After 600 miles, with cold engine, slacken nuts one turn, in sequence, lubricate and retighten to 63.4–64.9 ft. lbs.
Warm engine—tighten without slackening to 60.5–61.2 ft. lbs.

② Cold engine—tighten in 2 steps:
1. Tighten to 57.9 ft. lbs.
2. After 600 miles, with cold engine, slacken nuts one turn, in sequence, lubricate and retighten to 65.1 ft. lbs.
③ Cold engine—tighten in 2 steps:
1. Tighten to 65.0–72.3 ft. lbs.

2. After 600 miles, with cold engine, slacken nuts one turn, in sequence, lubricate and retighten to 72.1–79.8 ft. lbs.
④ Main bearing cap to engine block nuts— 62–68.4 ft. lbs.
Main bearing cap locknuts to 14.8–18.5 ft. lbs.

BRAKE SPECIFICATIONS

All measurements in inches unless noted.

Year	Model	Lug Nut Torque (ft. lbs.)	Master Cylinder Bore	Brake Disc		Standard Brake Drum Diameter	Minimum Lining Thickness	
				Minimum Thickness	Maximum Runout		Front	Rear
1987	Spider	72	0.870	①	0.015	—	0.28	0.28
	Milano	72	0.870	②	0.025	—	NA	NA

BRAKE SPECIFICATIONS
All measurements in inches unless noted.

Year	Model	Lug Nut Torque (ft. lbs.)	Master Cylinder Bore	Brake Disc Minimum Thickness	Brake Disc Maximum Runout	Standard Brake Drum Diameter	Minimum Lining Thickness Front	Minimum Lining Thickness Rear
1988	Spider	72	0.870	①	0.015	—	0.28	0.28
	Milano	72	0.870	②	0.025	—	NA	NA
1989	Spider	72	0.870	①	0.015	—	0.28	0.28
	Milano	72	0.870	②	0.025	—	NA	NA
1990	Spider	72	0.870	①	0.015	—	0.28	0.28
1991	Spider	72	0.870	①	0.015	—	0.28	0.28
	164	70–77	0.875	③	0.059	—	0.079	0.079

NA—Not available
① Front—0.42 in.
   Rear—0.30 in.
② Front—0.787 in.
   Rear—0.315 in.
③ Front—0.795 in.
   Rear—0.354 in.

WHEEL ALIGNMENT

Year	Model	Caster Range (deg.)	Caster Preferred Setting (deg.)	Camber Range (deg.)	Camber Preferred Setting (deg.)	Toe-in (in.)	Steering Axis Inclination (deg.)
1987	Spider	1P–2P	$1^1/_2$P	$^3/_{16}$N–$^{13}/_{16}$P	$^5/_{16}$P	$^1/_8$	NA
	Veloce	1P–2P	$1^1/_2$P	$^3/_{16}$N–$^{13}/_{16}$P	$^5/_{16}$P	$^1/_8$	NA
	Graduate	1P–2P	$1^1/_2$P	$^3/_{16}$N–$^{13}/_{16}$P	$^5/_{16}$P	$^1/_8$	NA
	Milano	4P–5P	$4^1/_2$P	1N–0	$^1/_2$N	$^5/_{64}$ out	NA
1988	Spider	1P–2P	$1^1/_2$P	$^3/_{16}$N–$^{13}/_{16}$P	$^5/_{16}$P	$^1/_8$	NA
	Veloce	1P–2P	$1^1/_2$P	$^3/_{16}$N–$^{13}/_{16}$P	$^5/_{16}$P	$^1/_8$	NA
	Graduate	1P–2P	$1^1/_2$P	$^3/_{16}$N–$^{13}/_{16}$P	$^5/_{16}$P	$^1/_8$	NA
	Milano	4P–5P	$4^1/_2$P	1N–0	$^1/_2$N	$^5/_{64}$ out	NA
1989	Spider	1P–2P	$1^1/_2$P	$^3/_{16}$N–$^{13}/_{16}$P	$^5/_{16}$P	$^1/_8$	NA
	Veloce	1P–2P	$1^1/_2$P	$^3/_{16}$N–$^{13}/_{16}$P	$^5/_{16}$P	$^1/_8$	NA
	Graduate	1P–2P	$1^1/_2$P	$^3/_{16}$N–$^{13}/_{16}$P	$^5/_{16}$P	$^1/_8$	NA
	Milano	4P–5P	$4^1/_2$P	1N–0	$^1/_2$N	$^5/_{64}$ out	NA
1990	Spider	1P–2P	$1^1/_2$P	$^3/_{16}$N–$^{13}/_{16}$P	$^5/_{16}$P	$^1/_8$	NA
	Veloce	1P–2P	$1^1/_2$P	$^3/_{16}$N–$^{13}/_{16}$P	$^5/_{16}$P	$^1/_8$	NA
	Graduate	1P–2P	$1^1/_2$P	$^3/_{16}$N–$^{13}/_{16}$P	$^5/_{16}$P	$^1/_8$	NA
1991	Spider	1P–2P	$1^1/_2$P	$^3/_{16}$N–$^{13}/_{16}$P	$^5/_{16}$P	$^1/_8$	NA
	Veloce	1P–2P	$1^1/_2$P	$^3/_{16}$N–$^{13}/_{16}$P	$^5/_{16}$P	$^1/_8$	NA
	164L	2P–$2^2/_3$P	$2^1/_3$P	$1^2/_3$N–$1^2/_3$P	1N	$^1/_8$N	NA
	164S	2P–$2^2/_3$P	$2^1/_3$P	$1^2/_3$N–$1^2/_3$P	1N	$^1/_8$N	NA

NA—Not available

ENGINE ELECTRICAL

NOTE: Disconnecting the negative battery cable on some vehicles may interfere with the functions of the on board computer systems and may require the computer to undergo a relearning process, once the negative battery cable is reconnected.

Distributor

Removal

SPIDER AND MILANO

1. Disconnect the negative battery cable.
2. Remove the distributor cap.
3. Tag and remove all electrical and vacuum lines to the distributor.
4. Mark the relationship of the rotor to the distributor housing and the distributor housing to the engine.
5. Remove the hold-down clamp and remove the distributor.

164 SERIES

1. Disconnect the negative battery cable.
2. Remove the distributor cap or cover.
3. Remove the rotor arm and cap.
4. Remove the 2 bolts and remove the distributor from the cylinder head.

Installation

TIMING NOT DISTURBED

Spider and Milano

1. Install the distributor, aligning the marks made during removal.
2. Install and tighten the hold-down clamp.
3. Install the wires and hoses.
4. Connect the negative battery cable.

164 SERIES

1. Install the distributor, align the shaft as shown, then install the 2 retaining screws.

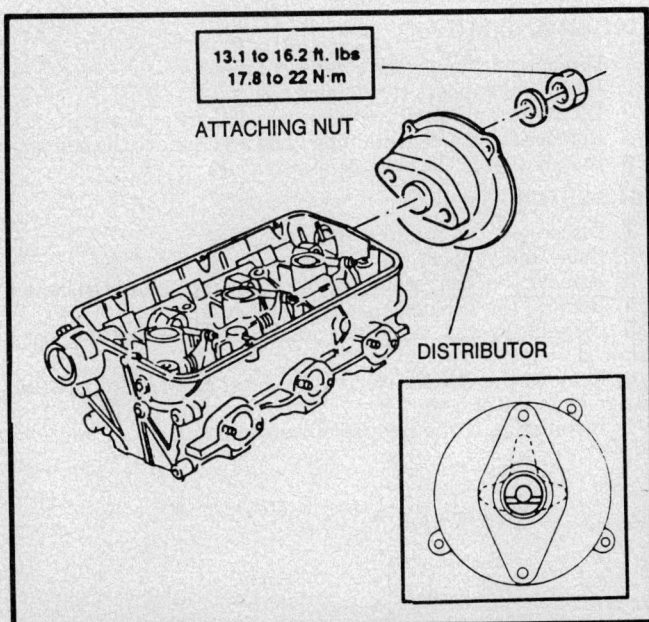

Distributor installation and alignment—model 164

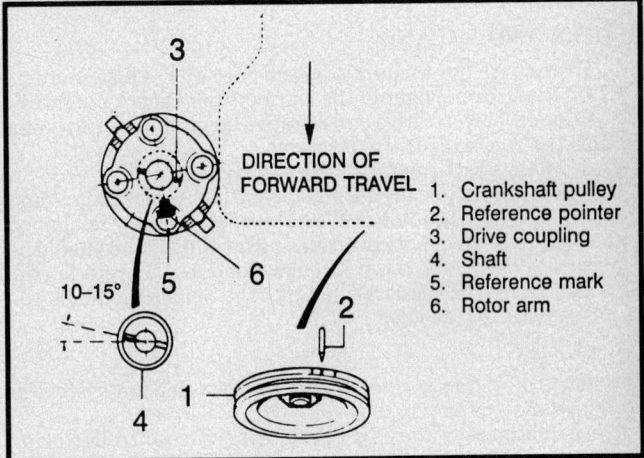

Distributor installation and alignment—Spider

1. Crankshaft pulley
2. Reference pointer
3. Drive coupling
4. Shaft
5. Reference mark
6. Rotor arm

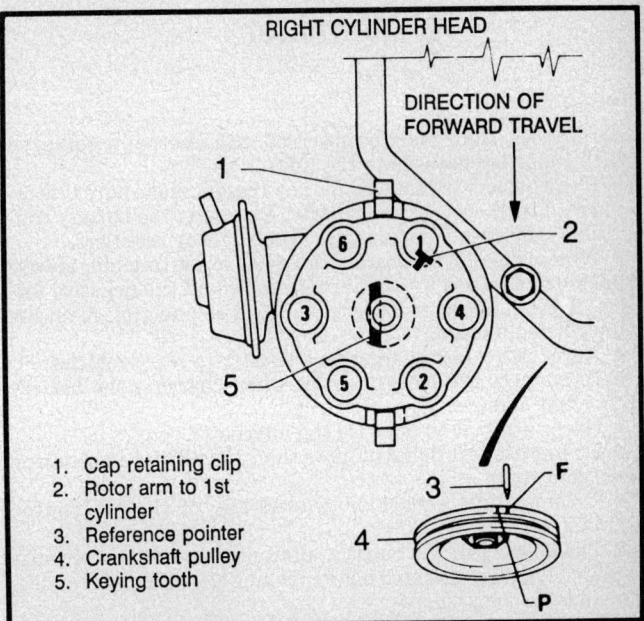

Distributor installation and alignment—Milano

1. Cap retaining clip
2. Rotor arm to 1st cylinder
3. Reference pointer
4. Crankshaft pulley
5. Keying tooth

3. Install the install the rotor, cap and cover.
4. Install the wires and reconnect the battery.

TIMING DISTURBED

Spider and Milano

1. Turn the crankshaft to bring the piston No. 1 on the compression stroke, with both valves closed. The reference mark **F** stamped on the crankshaft pulley, aligns with the reference pointer attached to the water pump.
2. With the cap removed, install the distributor on the front cover. Insert the drive coupling in the groove of the oil pump.
3. Turn the distributor until the reference mark on the edge of the body aligns with the centerline of the rotor arm and tighten the distributor clamp.
4. Install the cap and spark plug wires to the distributor.
5. Connect the negative battery cable.

Ignition Timing

Adjustment

SPIDER AND MILANO

1. Disconnect the vacuum advance hose at the distributor.
2. Connect timing light to the No. 1 cylinder spark plug wire.
3. Connect both positive and negative terminals of the timing light to the related battery terminals.
4. Connect a tachometer to the engine.
5. Run the engine at normal operating temperature and check at idle that the notch **F** on the engine pulley is aligned with the referecnce pin. Correct timing for the Milano should be 1–3 degrees BTDC for the 2.5L engine and 6–8 degrees for the 3.0L engine, at idle. Correct timing for the Spider should be 10–12 degrees BTDC, at idle.

164 SERIES

The ignition system is integrated with the injection system in the Motronic system.

The adjustment of the spark plug advance is controlled using the Motroniic control unit, that supplies a signal directly to the ignition coil, and from there to the distributor.

Alternator

Precautions

Several precautions must be observed with alternator equipped vehicles to avoid damage to the unit.

• If the battery is removed for any reason, make sure it is reconnected with the correct polarity. Reversing the battery connections may result in damage to the one-way rectifiers.
• When utilizing a booster battery as a starting aid, always connect the positive to positive terminals and the negative terminal from the booster battery to a good engine ground on the vehicle being started.
• Never use a fast charger as a booster to start vehicles.
• Disconnect the battery cables when charging the battery with a fast charger.
• Never attempt to polarize the alternator.
• Do not use test lights of more than 12 volts when checking diode continuity.
• Do not short across or ground any of the alternator terminals.
• The polarity of the battery, alternator and regulator must be matched and considered before making any electrical connections within the system.
• Never separate the alternator on an open circuit. Make sure all connections within the circuit are clean and tight.
• Disconnect the battery ground terminal when performing any service on electrical components.
• Disconnect the battery if arc welding is to be done on the vehicle.

Belt Tension Adjustment

SPIDER AND MILANO

1. Belt tension for the Milano should be 33–66 ft. lbs. (147–294 Nm), using a belt tensioning tool and measuring tension at the midpoint of the belt. This is about a 0.63 in. deflection.

2. Belt tension for the Spider should be 17.6 ft. lbs. (78 Nm), using a belt tensioning tool and measuring tension at the midpoint of the belt. This is about a 0.39–0.59 in. deflection.
3. Loosen the adjusting screws on the arm, then loosen the swing bolt. Move the alternator away to increase belt tension.
4. Tighten 1 screw and check the tension.
5. Tighten both screws and the bolt when the correct tension is obtained.

164 SERIES

1. Belt tension should be as follows, using a belt tensioning tool and measuring tension at the midpoint of the belt.
   New belt—90–101 ft. lbs. (400–450 Nm)
   Minimum cold engine—67.5 ft. lbs. (300Nm)
2. Remove the complete right headlight unit.
3. Loosen the securing screws and move the alternator upwards to increase belt tension.
4. Tighten 1 screw and check the tension.
5. Tighten both screws when the correct tension is obtained.
6. Retension the belt as follows:
   a. Run the engine at normal operating temperature for about 10 minutes.
   b. Allow the engine to cool down and recheck the belt tension.
   c. The tension should be 67.5–78.7 ft. lbs. (300–350 Nm).

Removal and Installation

1. Disconnect the negative battery cable.
2. On the Spider it may be necessary to remove the air cleaner assembly.
3. Loosen the adjusting screws on the arm, then loosen the swing bolt. Move the alternator to release the tension and remove the drive belt.
4. Disconnect the electrical connector, remove the alternator retaining bolts and remove the alternator.
5. Installation is the reverse of removal.

Starter

Removal and Installation

SPIDER AND MILANO

1. Disconnect the negative battery cable.
2. Raise and support the vehicle safely.
3. Disconnect all electrical wire connections at the starter.
4. Remove the starter retaining bolts and remove the starter.
5. Installation is the reverse of removal.

164 SERIES

1. Disconnect the negative battery cable.
2. Raise and support the vehicle safely.
3. Remove the front section of the exhaust pipes and gaskets.
4. Remove the exhaust manifold and gaskets.
5. On vehicles with automatic transaxle, disconnect the reaction rod.
6. Remove the starter electrical cables, and retaining bolts and remove the starter.
7. Installation is the reverse of removal.

CHASSIS ELECTRICAL

Heater Blower Motor

Removal and Installation

WITHOUT AIR CONDITIONING

Spider

1. Disconnect the negative battery cable.
2. Drain the cooling system.
3. Remove the rear console, the knee padding, the front console and the side walls of the console below the instrument panel.
4. Remove the the instrument panel.
   a. Remove the glove compartment.
   b. Disconnect the vents and ducts.
   c. Unscrew the 2 wing nuts retaining the instrument panel to the body and remove the instrument panel from the vehicle.
5. Remove the 2 screws and remove the ducts from the heater assembly.
6. Disconnect and plug the heater outlet hose.
7. Working from the engine compartment, disconnect and plug the heater inlet hose.
8. Working from inside the vehicle, remove the nuts securing the heater assembly to the body, disconnect the ground wire from the electric fan and remove the heater unit from the vehicle.

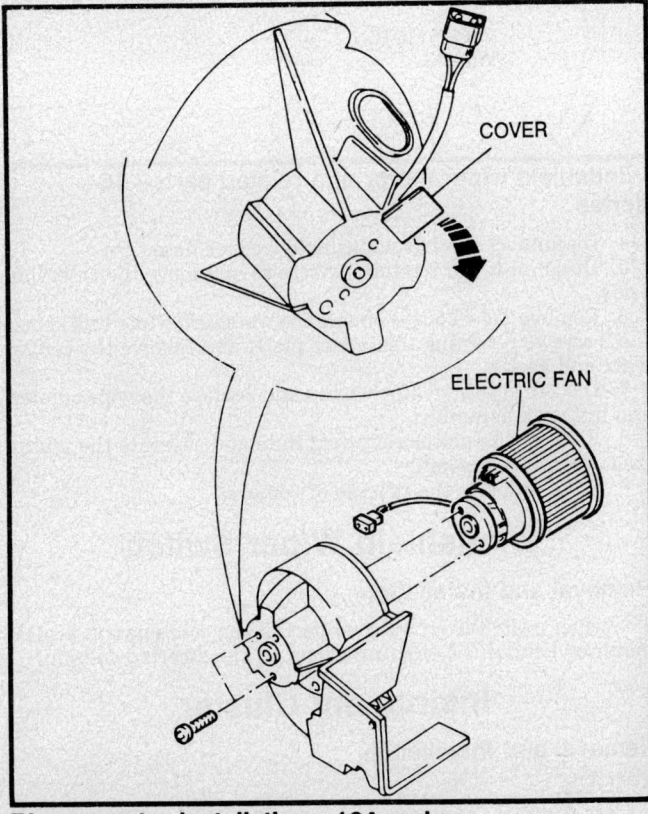

COVER

ELECTRIC FAN

Blower motor installation—164 series

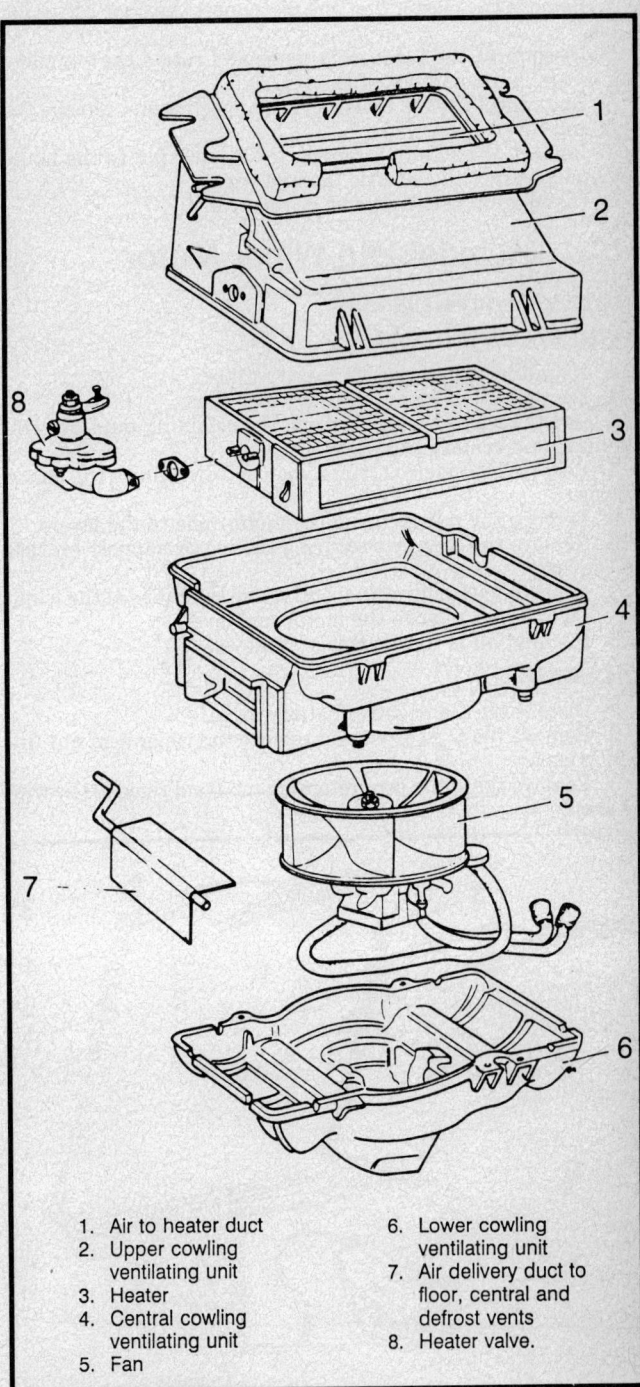

1. Air to heater duct
2. Upper cowling ventilating unit
3. Heater
4. Central cowling ventilating unit
5. Fan
6. Lower cowling ventilating unit
7. Air delivery duct to floor, central and defrost vents
8. Heater valve.

Heater unit—Spider

9. Unscrew the bolts and separate the lower cowling of the heater unit complete with the electric fan.
10. Separate the electric fan from the lower part of the heater case.
11. Installation is the reverse of removal.

WITH AIR CONDITIONING

164 SERIES

1. Disconnect the negative battery cable.

2. Remove the evaporator unit.

3. Disconnect the electric fan connector.

4. Remove the elastic ring and disconnect the door actuating cable.

5. Disconnect the 2 securing tangs and rotate the complete fan assembly up and out of the vehicle.

6. Disconnect the fan housing retaining clips and remove the grill and cover.

7. Remove the screws retaining the electric fan to the housing and separate the electric fan and wiring.

8. Installation is the reverse of removal.

Windshield Wiper Motor

Removal and Installation

SPIDER AND MILANO

1. Disconnect the negative battery cable.

2. Detach the blades from the wiper arms.

3. Lift the wiper arm cover from the retaining nuts, remove the nuts and remove the wiper arms.

4. Remove the external trim screen and disconnect the motor wiring.

5. Remove the nut securing the motor pins to the levers.

6. Remove the 3 screws securing the motor support bracket to the body.

7. Remove the 2 ring nuts securing the lever pins of the windshield wiper and remove the motor and levers.

8. Installation is the reverse of removal.

164 SERIES

1. Disconnect the negative battery cable.

2. Remove the trim cover and remove the wiper arm nut finishing caps.

3. Remove the wiper arm retaining nuts and remove the wiper arms.

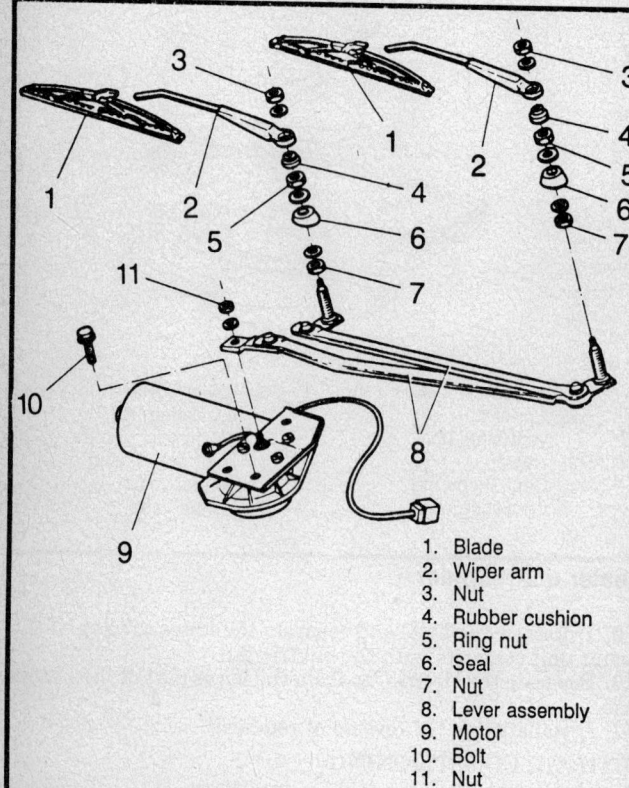

1.	Blade
2.	Wiper arm
3.	Nut
4.	Rubber cushion
5.	Ring nut
6.	Seal
7.	Nut
8.	Lever assembly
9.	Motor
10.	Bolt
11.	Nut

Windshield wiper motor and related parts—Spider

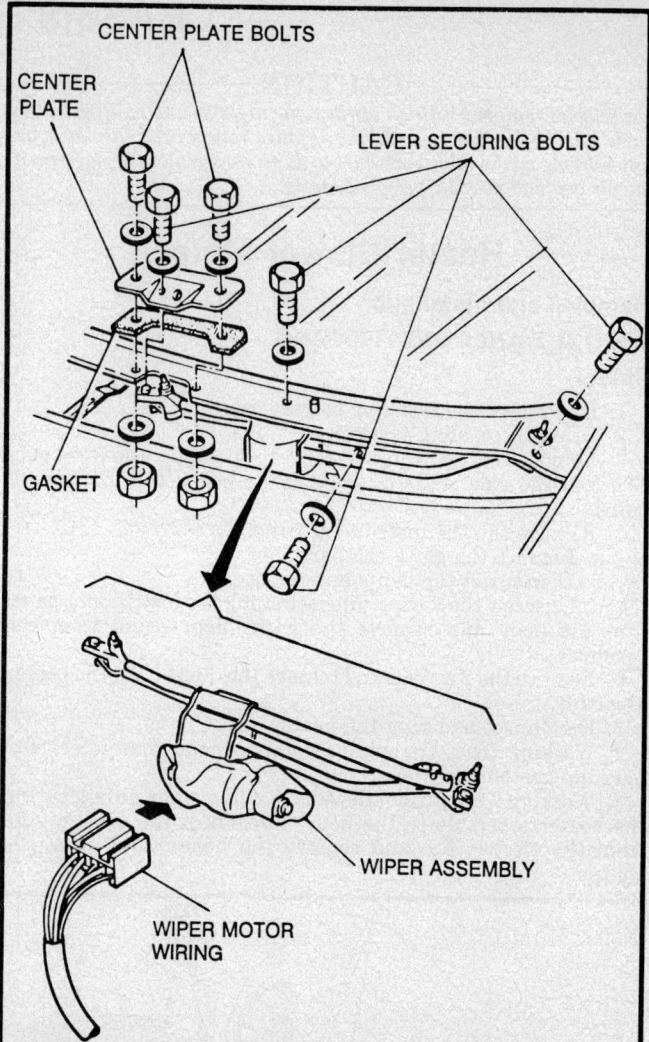

Windshield wiper motor and related parts—164 series

4. Disconnect the left windshield washer hose.

5. Disconnect the 2 retaining screws and move the reservoir aside.

6. Remove the 4 bolts securing the winshield wiper link arms, the 2 screws retaining the center plate, and remove the center plate and gasket.

7. Disconnect the motor wiring and remove the wiper motor and link arm assembly.

8. Remove the motor retaining nuts and separate the motor from the wiper assembly.

9. Installation is the reverse of removal.

Windshield Wiper Switch

Removal and Installation

The wiper switch is an integral part of the combination switch mounted behind the steering wheel on the steering column.

Instrument Cluster

Removal and Installation

SPIDER

1. Disconnect the negative battery cable.

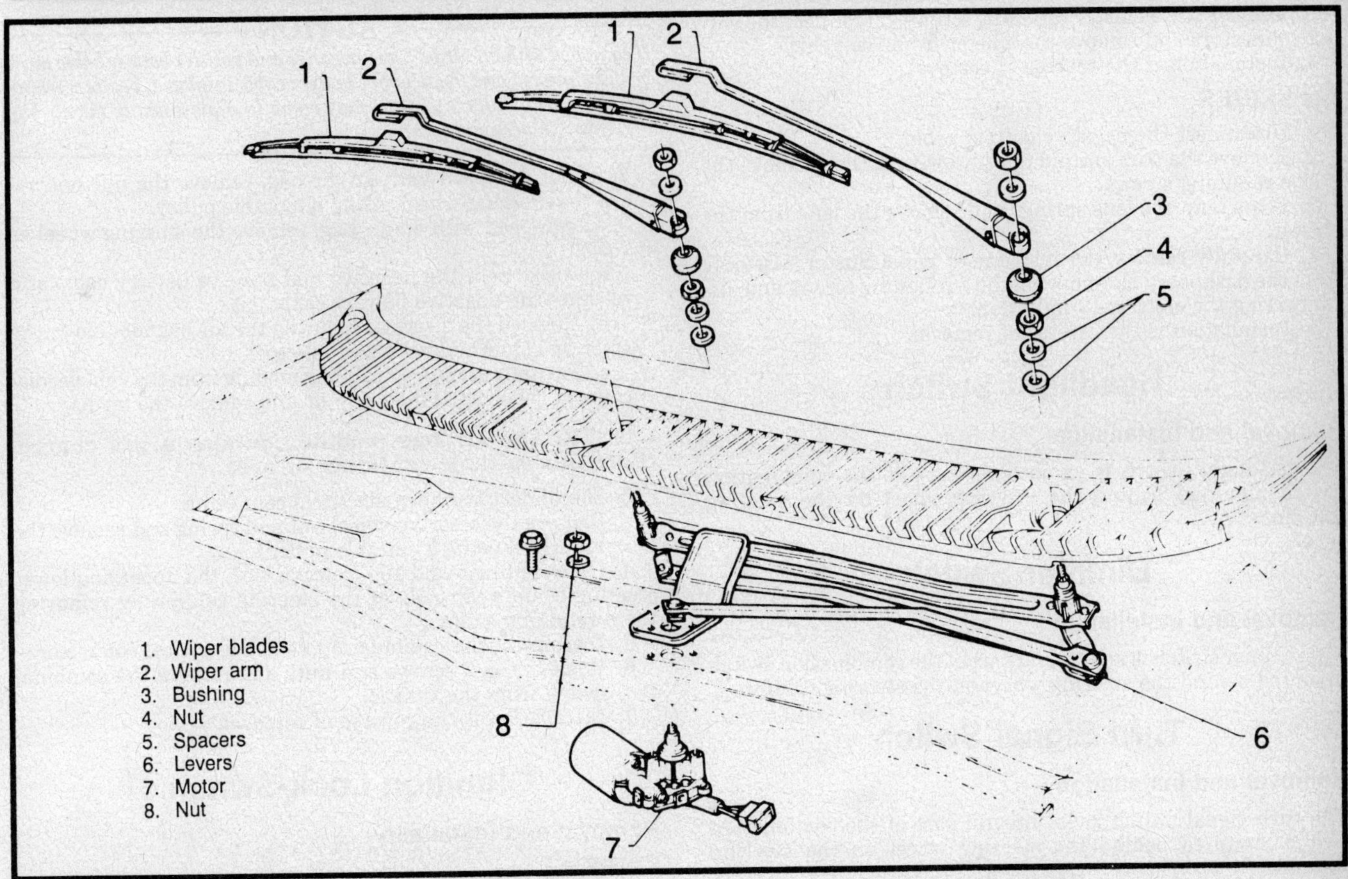

1. Wiper blades
2. Wiper arm
3. Bushing
4. Nut
5. Spacers
6. Levers
7. Motor
8. Nut

Windshield wiper motor and related parts—Milano

2. Remove the left side knee padding.
3. Remove the steering column upper and lower shrouds.
4. Disconnect the cluster wiring connections.
5. Remove the cluster retaining screws and ring nuts and remove the cluster.
6. Installation is the reverse of removal.

MILANO

1. Disconnect the negative battery cable.
2. Remove the instrument panel dashboard.

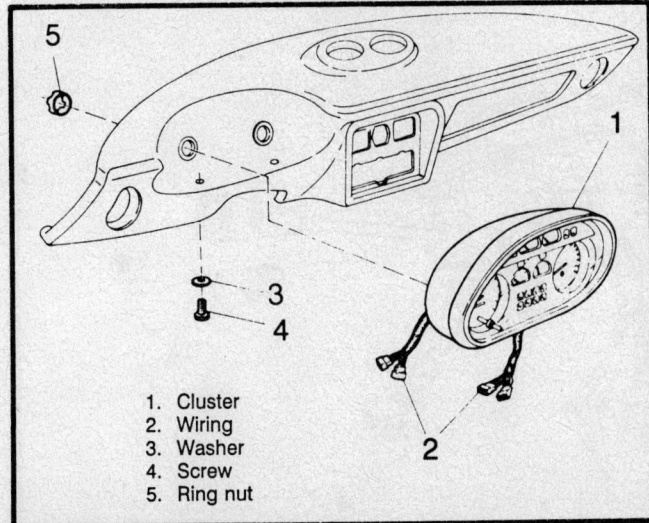

1. Cluster
2. Wiring
3. Washer
4. Screw
5. Ring nut

Instrument cluster—Spider

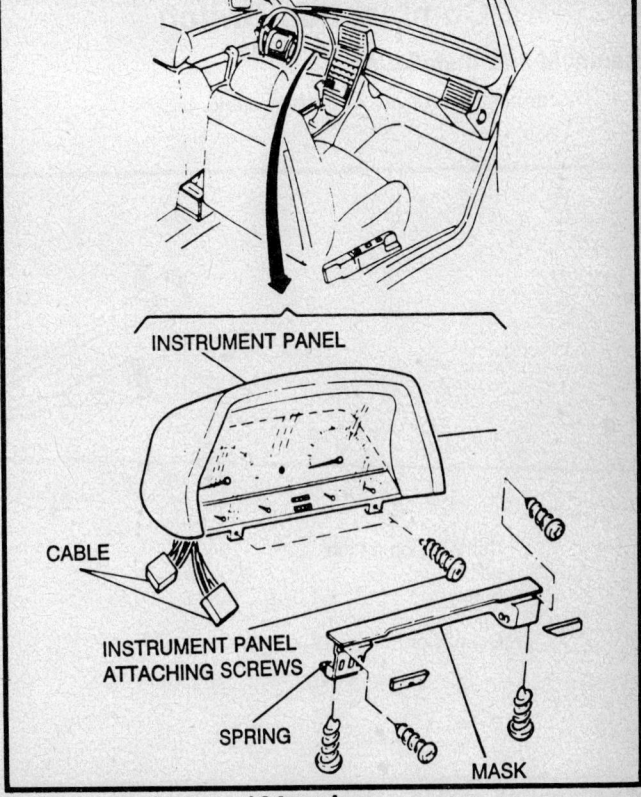

INSTRUMENT PANEL

CABLE

INSTRUMENT PANEL
ATTACHING SCREWS

SPRING

MASK

Instrument cluster—164 series

3. Remove the 5 cluster retaining screws, disconnect the wiring connectors and remove the cluster from the vehicle.

4. Installation is the reverse of removal.

164 SERIES

1. Disconnect the negative battery cable.
2. Remove the trim around the cluster lens, then remove the 4 lens retaining screws.
3. Press onto the lens springs and remove the lens from the cluster.
4. Carefully remove the instrument panel/cluster assembly from the dashboard by removing the 2 retaining screws and disconnecting the electrical connection.
5. Installation is the reverse of removal.

Headlight Switch

Removal and Installation

The headlight switch is an integral part of the combination switch mounted behind the steering wheel on the steering column.

Dimmer Switch

Removal and Installation

The dimmer switch is an integral part of the combination switch mounted behind the steering wheel on the steering column.

Turn Signal Switch

Removal and Installation

The turn signal switch is an integral part of the combination switch mounted behind the steering wheel on the steering column.

Combination Switch

Removal and Installation

1. Disconnect the negative battery cable.

— CAUTION —

If equipped with an air bag, the negative and positive battery cable must be disconnected and the negative battery cable insulated, before working on the vehicle. Failure to do so may result in deployment of the air bag and possible personal injury.

2. If not equipped with an air bag, remove the nut and remove the steering wheel, using a suitable puller.
3. If equipped with an air bag, remove the steering wheel as follows:

   a. Disconnect the negative and positive battery cable and insulate the negative battery cable.

   b. Remove the 2 screws securing the air bag module to the steering column using a suitable tool.

   c. Partially extract the air bag module from the vehicle, disconnect the electrical connector and remove the air bag.

NOTE: The air bag module contains a gas charge. Store in a suitable container or area.

   d. Disconnect the horn electrical connector.

   e. Remove the steering wheel nut and spring and remove the steering wheel using a suitable puller.

4. On the Milano and 164, remove both the upper and lower steering column shrouds of the steering column by removing the 6 retaining screws.
5. Disconnect the combination switch electrical connectors.
6. Remove the 2 screws and nuts and remove the combination switch from the vehicle.
7. Installation is the reverse of removal.

Ignition Lock/Switch

Removal and Installation
SPIDER

1. Place the wheels in a straight-ahead position.
2. Disconnect the negative battery cable.
3. Remove the steering wheel and if equipped with an air bag perform the following:

   a. Disconnect the negative and positive battery cable and insulate the negative battery cable.

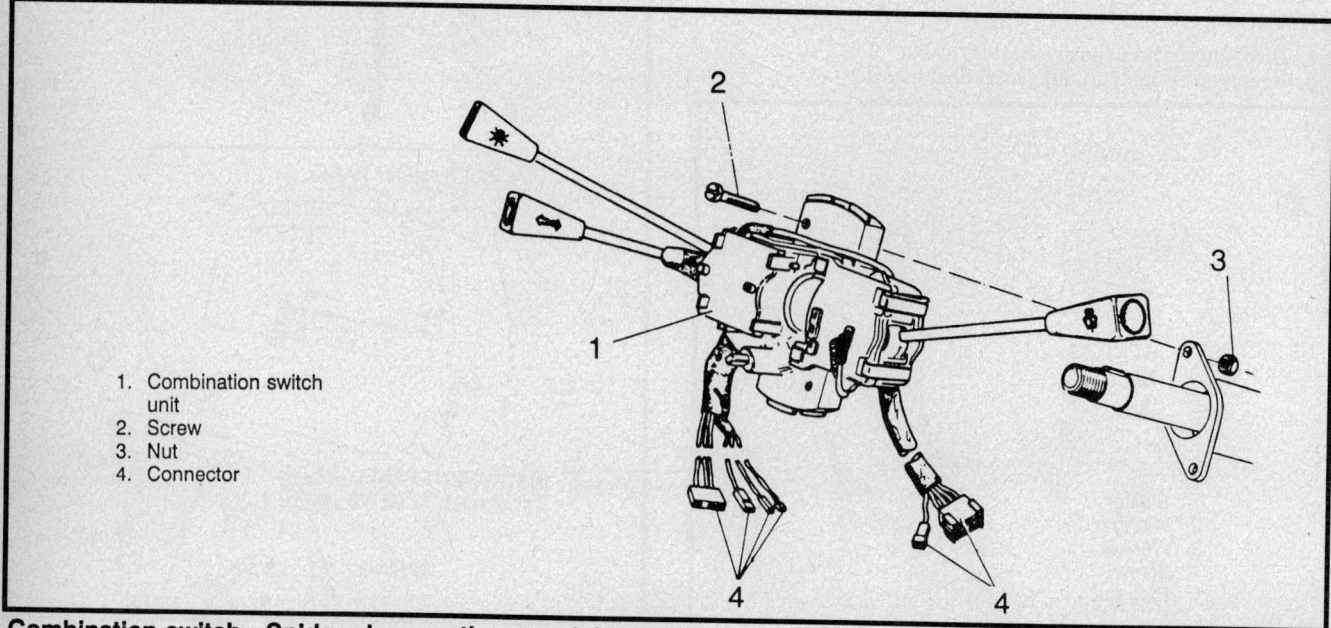

1. Combination switch unit
2. Screw
3. Nut
4. Connector

Combination switch—Spider shown, others models similar

b. Remove the 2 screws securing the air bag module to the steering column using a suitable tool.

c. Partially extract the air bag module from the vehicle, disconnect the electrical connector and remove the air bag.

NOTE: The air bag module contains a gas charge. Store in a suitable container or area.

d. Disconnect the horn electrical connector.

e. Remove the steering wheel nut and spring and remove the steering wheel using a suitable puller.

4. Remove the 2 retaining screws and remove the combination switch without disconnecting the wiring connector.

5. Disconnect the ignition switch/lock electrical connection hanging under the steering column.

6. Remove the 2 bolts retaining the column to the body, remove the upper universal joint screw and remove the steering column from the vehicle.

7. Clamp the steering column in a soft jawed vice.

8. Using a punch, back off the saftey screw and withdraw the steering lock/ignition switch, being careful not to damage the cables.

9. Installation is the reverse of removal.

164 SERIES

1. Disconnect the negative battery cable.
2. Remove the steering column upper and lower shrouds.
3. Using a suitable punch and hammer, remove the switch locking pin.
4. Disconnect the wire connector, working through the fuse holder opening and remove the switch.
5. Installation is the reverse of removal.

Stoplight Switch

Removal and Installation

SPIDER

1. Disconnect the negative battery cable.
2. Remove the knee padding below the instrument panel on the driver's side.
3. Remove the plastic nut attaching the switch to the bracket, below the steering column.
4. Slide the switch off of the bracket and disconnect the wiring connector.
5. Installation is the reverse of removal.

MILANO

The stoplight switch is mounted on a special bracket on the steering column rear support.

1. Disconnect the negative battery cable.
2. Remove the door lock control unit from its seat in the lower side of the dashboard, under the cluster.
3. Working through the glove box opening, remove the plastic retaining nut, disconnect the wiring and remove the switch.
4. Installation is the reverse of removal.

164 SERIES

1. Disconnect the negative battery cable.
2. Working from under the brake pedal, disconnect the switch wiring, loosen the retaining nut and remove the switch from the support.
3. Installation is the reverse of removal.

Fuses, Circuit Breakers and Relays

Location

FUSES

Spider and Milano

There is a main fuse box located under the dashboard, at the driver's side. It can be reached by pulling the release lever on the Spider or turning the knob on the Milano and opening the plastic cover. On a few models, in-line fuses are inserted in the electrical system for some particular loads such as the ABS systems.

164 SERIES

There is a main fuse box and an auxiliary fuse box located under the under the dashboard, at the driver's side. It can be opened by unscrewing the lock knob and opening the plastic cover.

There is an anti-skid fuse located on the right side of the dashboard and may be accessed by rotating the lid lock pin and removing the lid.

The electronics power relay fuse, radio power supply fuse, front seat adjustment fuse, sun roof in-line fuse (164S only) and the shift interlock control unit fuse are located behind the electronic instrument panel, which may have to be removed to gain access.

The engine cooling fan fuse and air conditioner fan fuse are located in the rear of the engine compartment, the automatic transaxle oil fan fuse, horn fuse and the left low beam fuse are located on the driver's side front of the engine compartment and the right low beam light fuse is located on the passenger's side front of the engine compartment.

The rear defogger fuse, anti-theft fuse, rear seat movement fuse, rear seat inhibiter fuse and the controlled dampening suspension relay (164S only), are located in the trunk.

RELAYS

SPIDER

The following relays are located in the main fuse box under the left side of the dashboard:
- Engine cooling fan
- Heated rear window
- Horn relay
- Power windows
- Horn
- Radio
- Electromatic coupling control

MILANO

The following relays are located in the main fuse box under the left side of the dashboard:
- External mirror defrost
- Foglight
- Roof light
- Foglight
- Rear foglight
- Key operated supply

The following relays are located on the driver's side front of the engine compartment:
- Brake fluid level switch
- Horns

The following relays are located on the passenger's side front of the engine compartment:
- Compressor electromagnetic coupling
- Engine cooling fan

164 SERIES

The following relays are inside the engine compartment:
- Right low beam light
- Headlights washer timer
- Fuel pump Motronic relay
- Motronic relay with diode
- Engine cooling fan relay
- Engine cooling fan relay 2nd speed
- Left low beam light
- Horns
- ABS system control unit
- Dome lights
- Brake fluid tank

- Air conditioner fan
- Stop switch
- ABS electric pump
- Automatic transaxle oil cooling fan

The following relays are located behind the glove box on the right hand side of the dashboard.

- Dome light

The following relay is located on the extreme right hand side of the dashboard at the right of the glove box, behind a plastic cover.

- Anti-skid system

The following relays are located behind the instrument panel cluster.

- Radio
- Front window
- Starter motor inhibitor
- High beam light
- Parking light
- Selected gear signal (automatic transaxle) for Motronic control unit
- Turn signal and hazard lights
- Rear window

- Electromagnetic coupling control
- Electronic control units power supply
- Sun roof

The following relays are located on the main fuse box located under the driver's side of the instrument panel, behind a plastic cover.

- Rear fog lights
- Fog lights
- Turn signal lights flasher unit
- Rear power window
- External rear view mirrors demisting
- Sun roof and power seats
- Front power window
- Dome lights

The following relay is located under the center console.

- Left and right power seat

The following relays are located inside the trunk.

- Trunk opener
- Rear window defogger
- Fuel filter lid opening
- Shock absorber solenoid
- Rear seats device enable

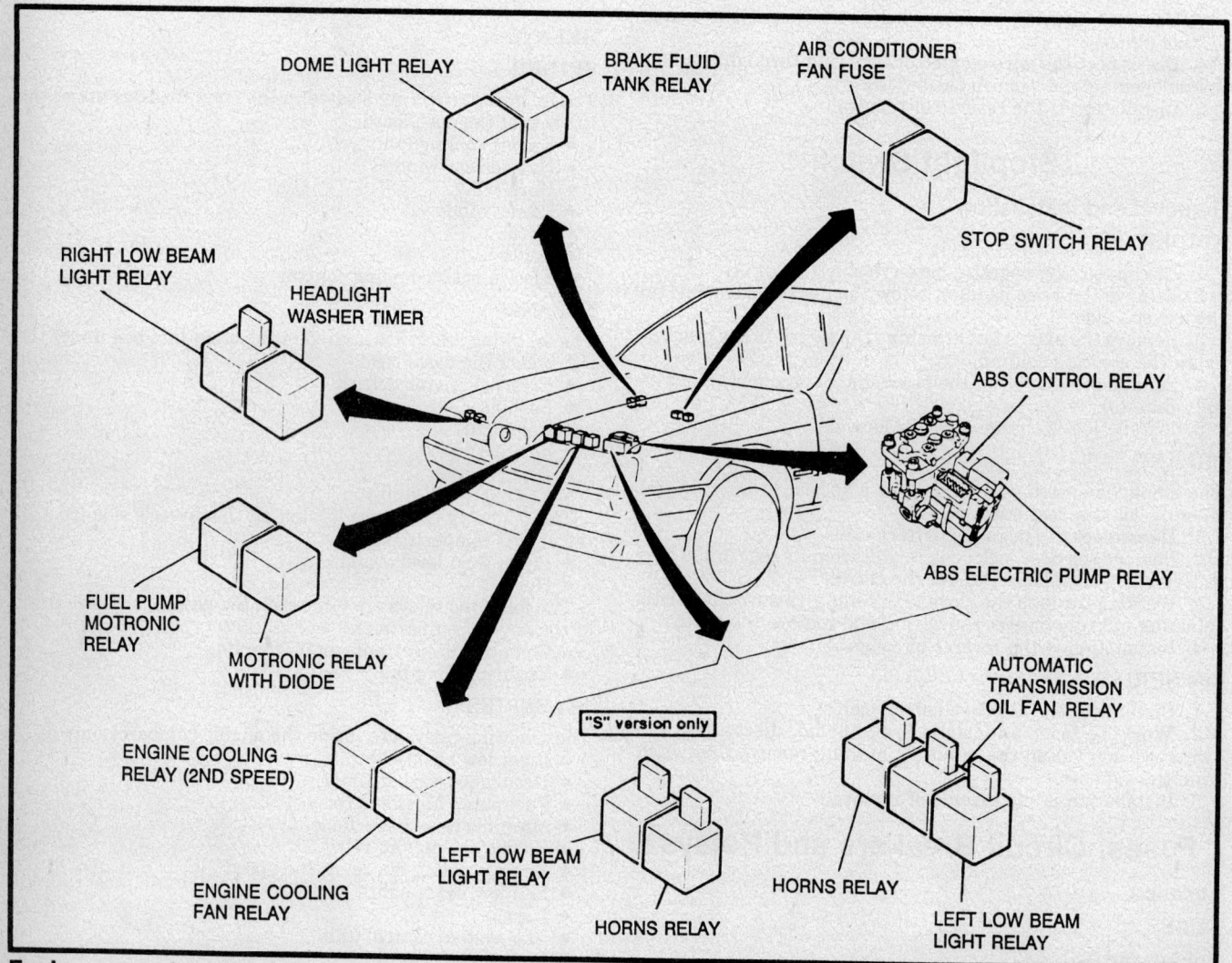

Engine compartment relay location—164 series

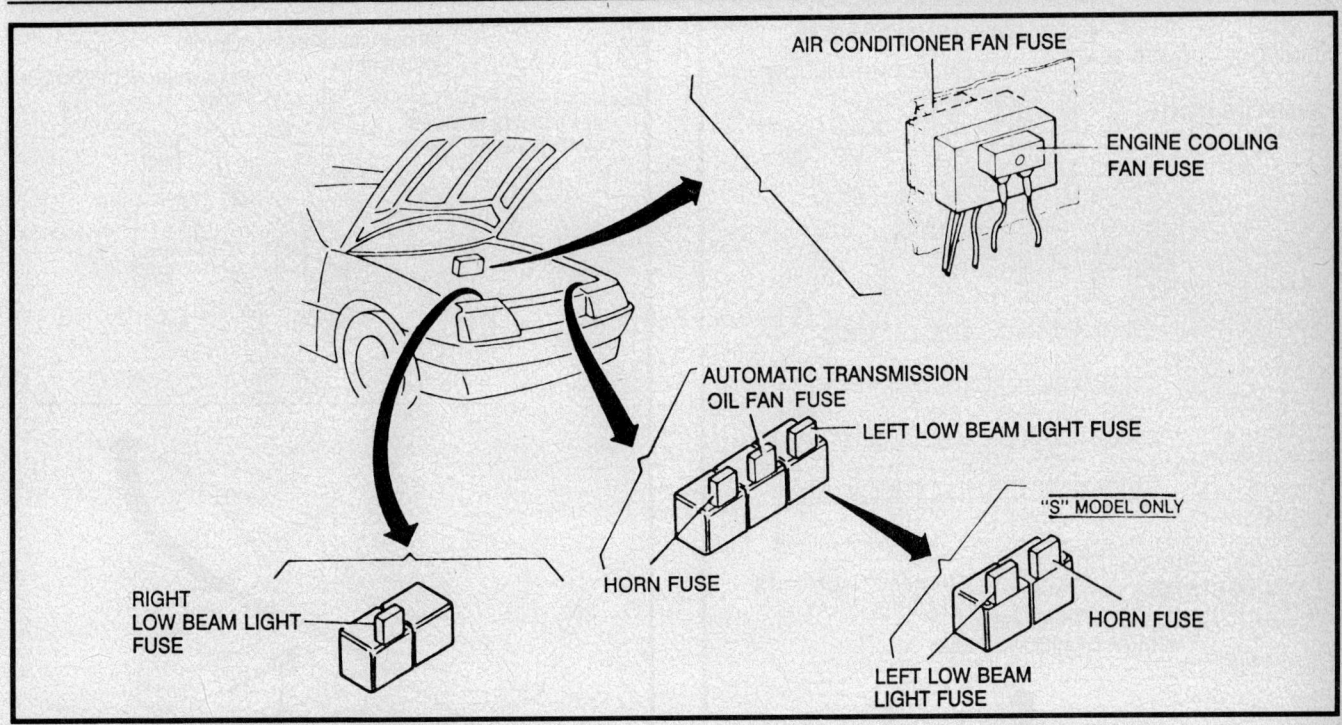

AIR CONDITIONER FAN FUSE

ENGINE COOLING FAN FUSE

AUTOMATIC TRANSMISSION OIL FAN FUSE

LEFT LOW BEAM LIGHT FUSE

"S" MODEL ONLY

HORN FUSE

HORN FUSE

LEFT LOW BEAM LIGHT FUSE

RIGHT LOW BEAM LIGHT FUSE

Underhood relay location—164 series

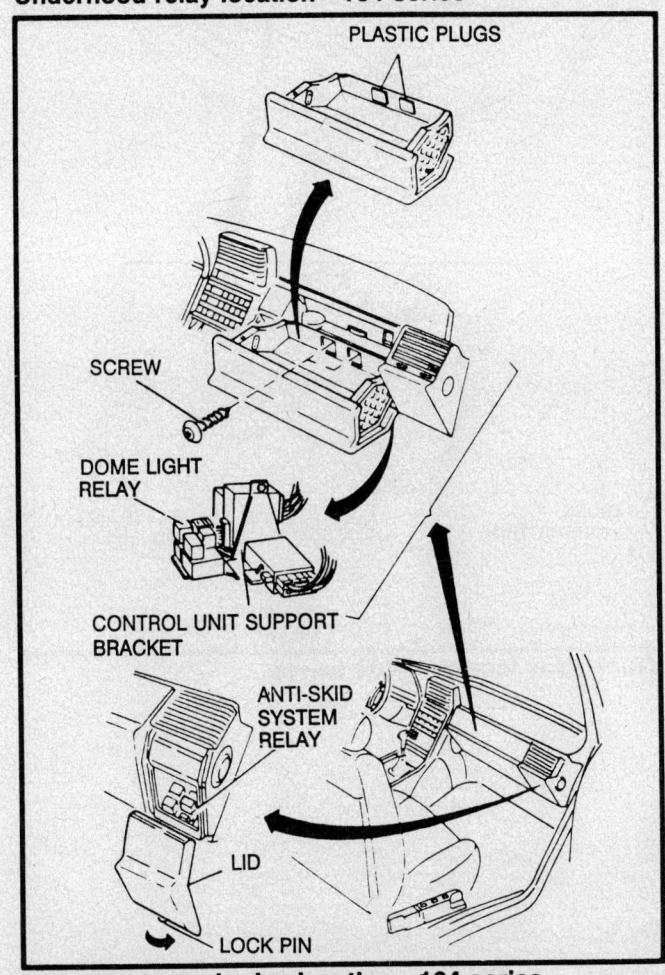

PLASTIC PLUGS

SCREW

DOME LIGHT RELAY

CONTROL UNIT SUPPORT BRACKET

ANTI-SKID SYSTEM RELAY

LID

LOCK PIN

Instrument panel relay location—164 series

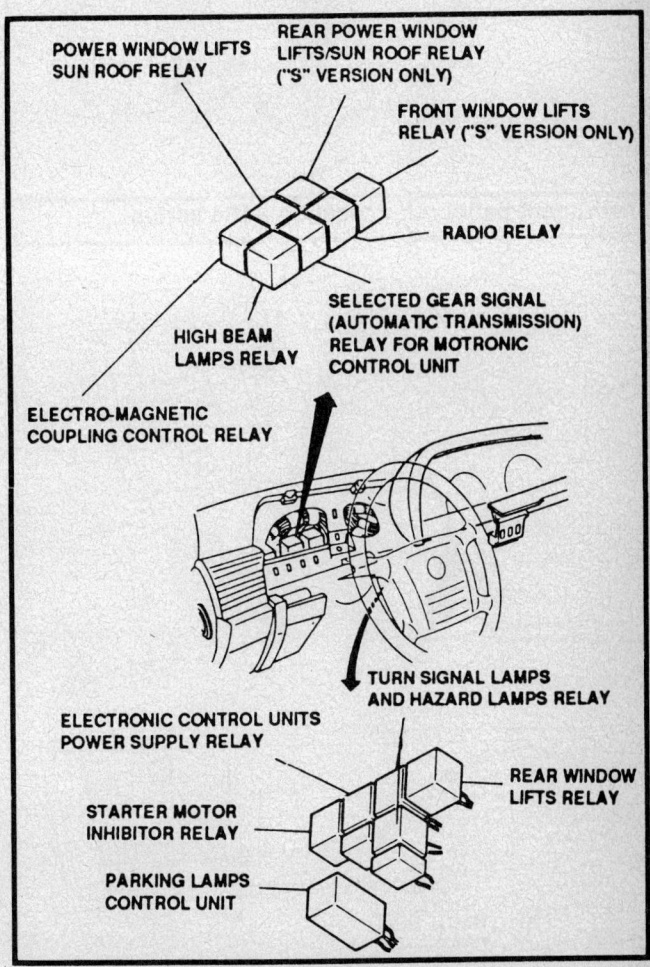

POWER WINDOW LIFTS SUN ROOF RELAY

REAR POWER WINDOW LIFTS/SUN ROOF RELAY ("S" VERSION ONLY)

FRONT WINDOW LIFTS RELAY ("S" VERSION ONLY)

RADIO RELAY

SELECTED GEAR SIGNAL (AUTOMATIC TRANSMISSION) RELAY FOR MOTRONIC CONTROL UNIT

HIGH BEAM LAMPS RELAY

ELECTRO-MAGNETIC COUPLING CONTROL RELAY

TURN SIGNAL LAMPS AND HAZARD LAMPS RELAY

ELECTRONIC CONTROL UNITS POWER SUPPLY RELAY

REAR WINDOW LIFTS RELAY

STARTER MOTOR INHIBITOR RELAY

PARKING LAMPS CONTROL UNIT

Instrument panel relay location—164 series

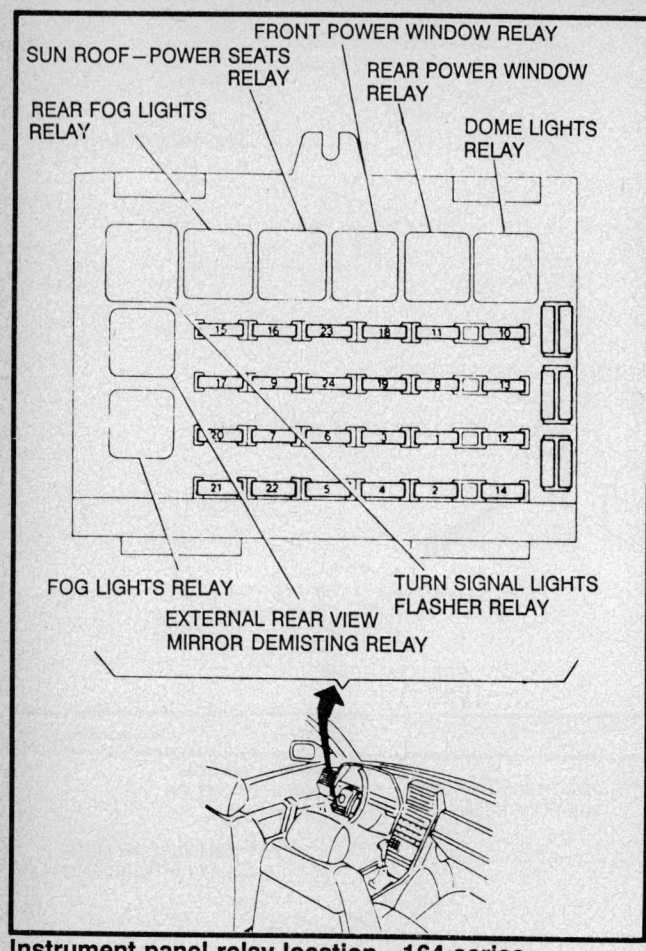

SUN ROOF—POWER SEATS RELAY

REAR FOG LIGHTS RELAY

FRONT POWER WINDOW RELAY

REAR POWER WINDOW RELAY

DOME LIGHTS RELAY

FOG LIGHTS RELAY

EXTERNAL REAR VIEW MIRROR DEMISTING RELAY

TURN SIGNAL LIGHTS FLASHER RELAY

Instrument panel relay location—164 series

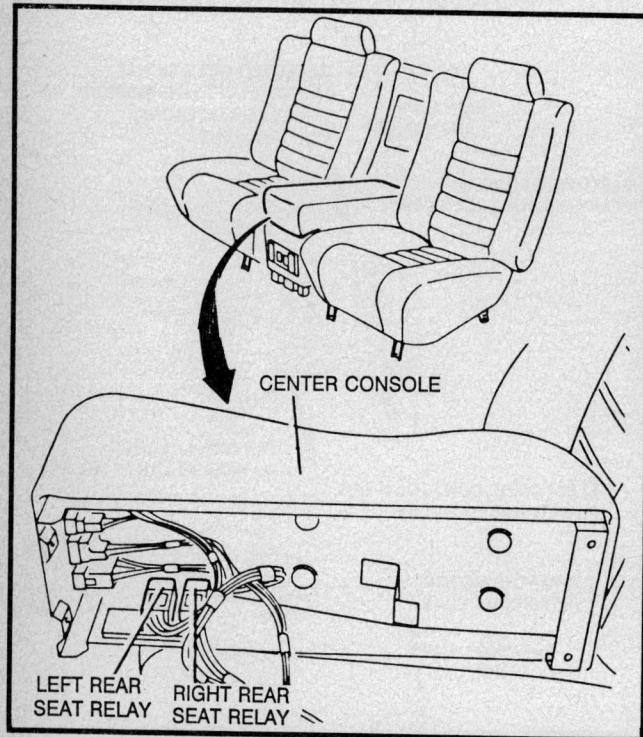

CENTER CONSOLE

LEFT REAR SEAT RELAY

RIGHT REAR SEAT RELAY

Power seat relay location—164 series

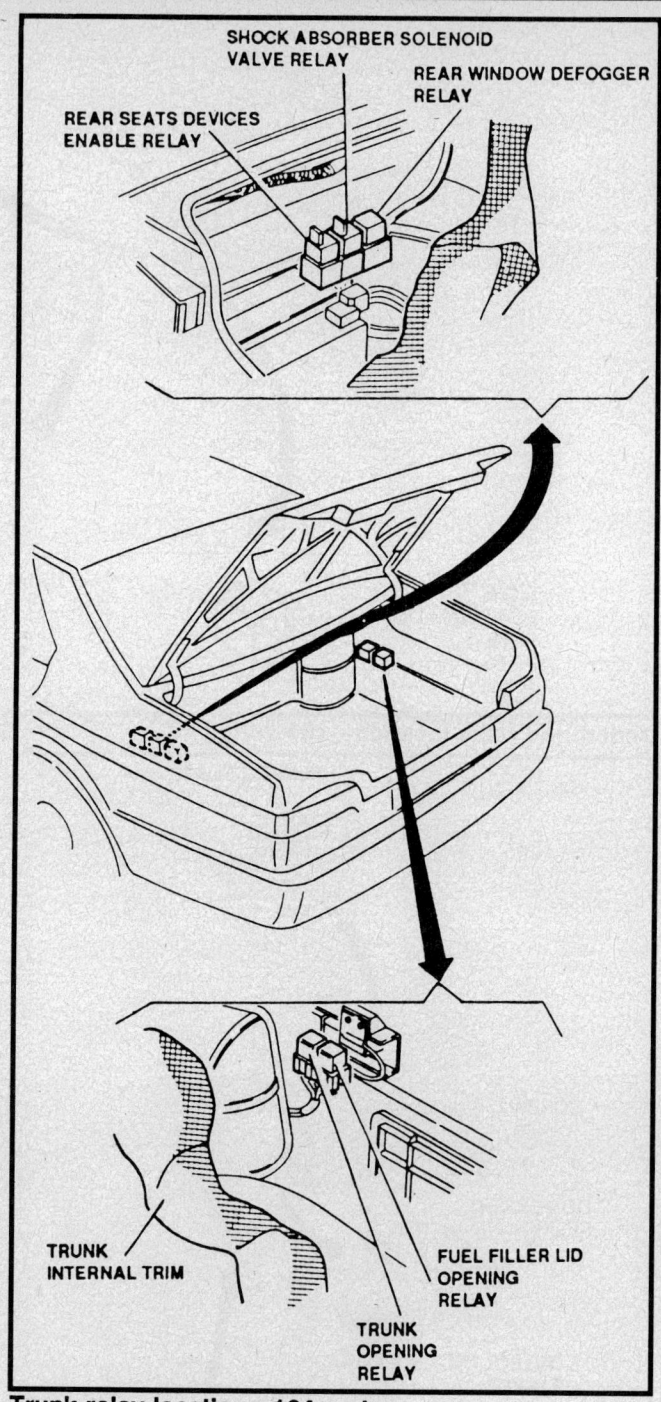

SHOCK ABSORBER SOLENOID VALVE RELAY

REAR WINDOW DEFOGGER RELAY

REAR SEATS DEVICES ENABLE RELAY

TRUNK INTERNAL TRIM

FUEL FILLER LID OPENING RELAY

TRUNK OPENING RELAY

Trunk relay location—164 series

Computers

Location

SPIDER

The Motronic injection control unit is located beneath the rear upholstery, behind the passenger seat.

To gain access to the the ignition ECU unit, tilt both seat backs forward, loosen the luggage compartment floor retainers and remove the luggage compartment floor. The ECU is located behind the trim lining on the right side of the vehicle.

MILANO

The L-Jetronic injection control unit is located in a floor compartment, beneath the passenger side dash panel.

164 SERIES

The Motronic ML 4-1 injection control unit is located behind the trim on the right side of the tunnel. Also found at this location are the ABS, cruise and air bag control units.

Flashers

Location

SPIDER AND MILANO

The turn signal and hazard light flasher is located on the main fuse box located under the driver's side of the instrument panel, behind a plastic cover.

164 SERIES

The turn signal light flasher is located on the main fuse box located under the driver's side of the instrument panel, behind a plastic cover.

The hazard flasher relay is located behind the instrument panel cluster.

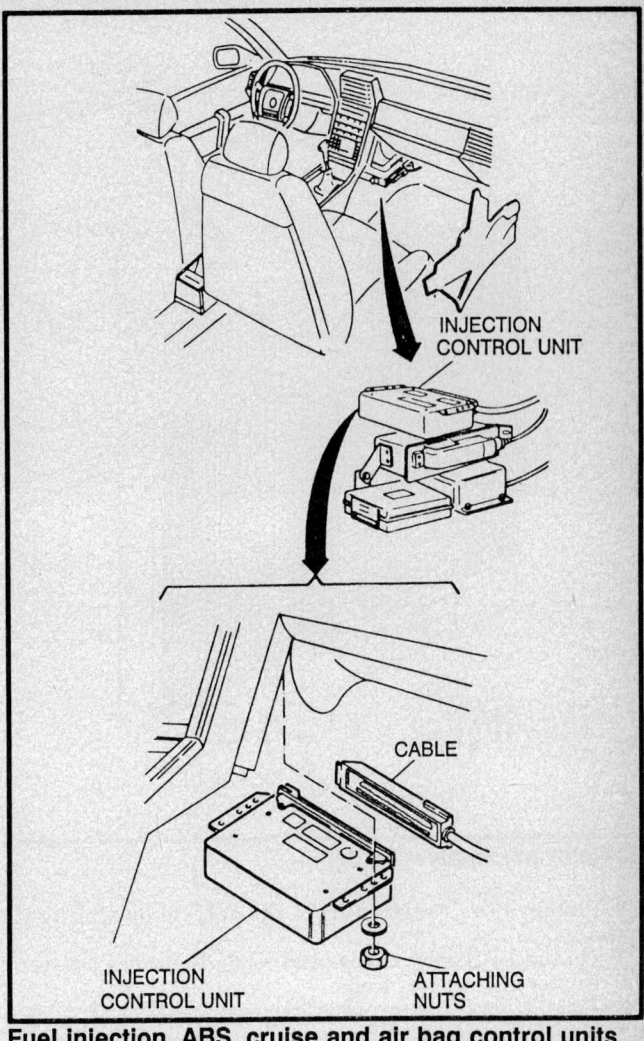

INJECTION CONTROL UNIT

CABLE

INJECTION CONTROL UNIT

ATTACHING NUTS

Fuel injection, ABS, cruise and air bag control units location—164 series

ENGINE COOLING

Radiator

Removal and Installation

SPIDER

1. Disconnect the negative battery cable.
2. Remove the hood and drain the cooling system.
3. Remove the power steering pump and support without disconnecting the fluid lines.
4. Disconnect all coolant lines to the radiator.
5. Disconnect all fan electrical connectors.
6. To facilitate radiator removal, remove the air cleaner assembly.
7. Remove the bolts securing the radiator to the housing and remove the radiator.
8. If necessary, remove the electric fans from the radiator.
9. Installation is the reverse of removal.

MILANO

1. Disconnect the negative battery cable.

2. Drain the cooling system and disconnect all coolant lines to the radiator.
3. Disconnect the radiator fan electrical connectors.
4. Remove the upper radiator retaining bolt and remove the radiator from the vehicle.
5. If necessary, remove the electric fan from the radiator.
6. Installation is the reverse of removal. Make sure the rubber pads are in position between the radiator and the body while installing.

164 SERIES

1. Disconnect the negative battery cable.
2. Drain the cooling system and disconnect all coolant lines to the radiator.
3. Disconnect the hood release cable.
4. Remove the upper cross beam and cover that runs across the top of the radiator.
5. Disconnect the thermal switch connector and the radiator fan electrical connector.

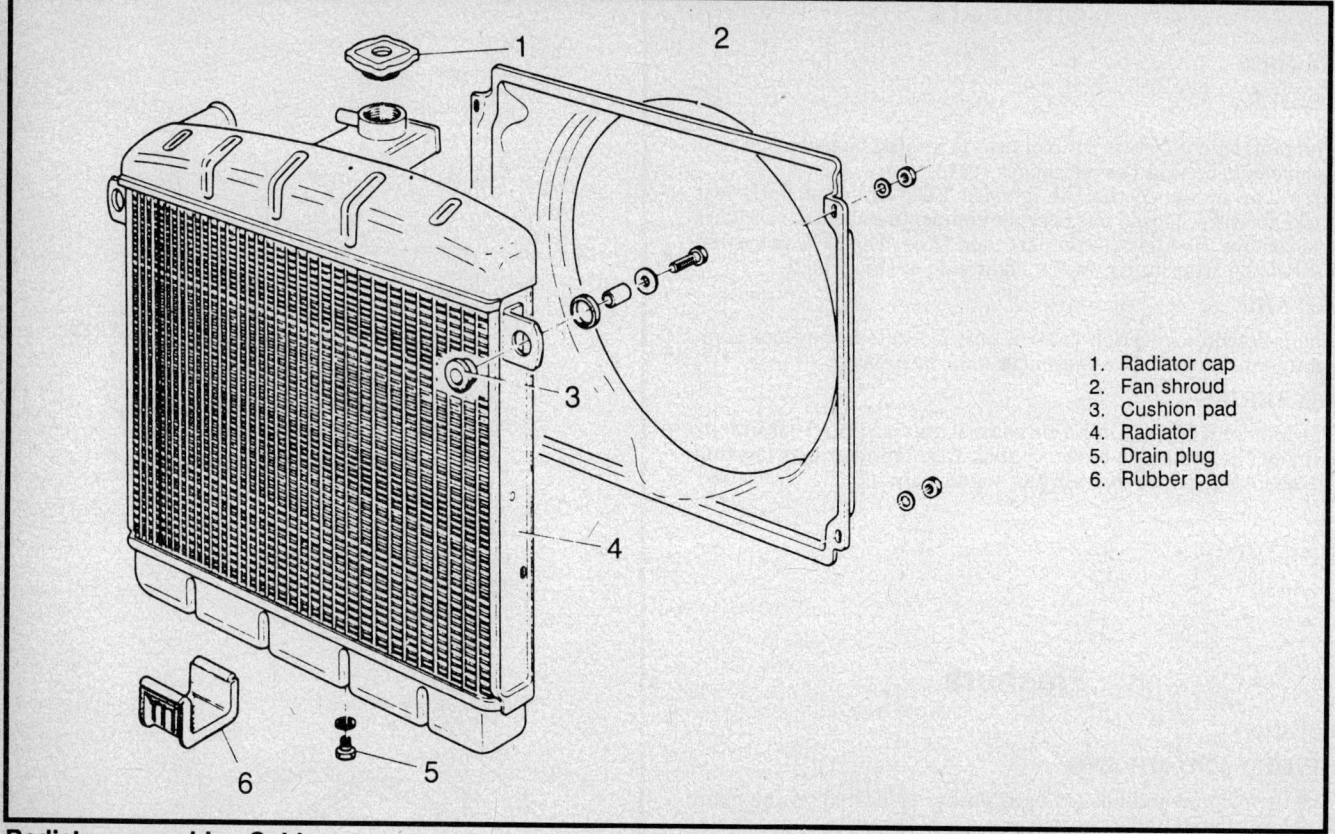

1. Radiator cap
2. Fan shroud
3. Cushion pad
4. Radiator
5. Drain plug
6. Rubber pad

Radiator assembly—Spider

6. Remove the radiator from the vehicle by sliding it upwards.
7. On the 164S only, remove and retain the shims between the radiator and support frame.
8. Installation is the reverse of removal.

Heater Core

For further information, please refer to "Chilton's Heating and Air Conditioning Manual" for additional coverage.

Removal and Installation
WITHOUT AIR CONDITIONING
Spider

1. Disconnect the negative battery cable.
2. Drain the cooling system.
3. Remove the rear console, the knee padding, the front console and the side walls of the console below the instrument panel.
4. Remove the instrument panel.
   a. Remove the glove compartment.
   b. Disconnect the vents and ducts.
   c. Unscrew the 2 wing nuts retaining the instrument panel to the body and remove the instrument panel from the vehicle.
5. Remove the 2 screws and remove the ducts from the heater assembly.
6. Disconnect and plug the heater outlet hose.
7. Working from the engine compartment, disconnect and plug the heater inlet hose.

8. Working from inside the vehicle, remove the nuts securing the heater assembly to the body, disconnect the ground wire from the electric fan and remove the heater unit from the vehicle.
9. Separate the the upper half of the heater case and remove the heater core from the cavity.
10. Installation is the reverse of removal.

WITH AIR CONDITIONING
Spider

1. Disconnect the negative battery cable.
2. Drain the cooling system.
3. Remove the rear console, the knee padding, the front console and the side walls of the console below the instrument panel.
4. Remove the central facing on the instrument panel.
5. Unscrew the bolts securing the lower face of the cooler unit.
6. Disconnect the condensation drain hose from the cooler hose.
7. Remove the screws securing the upper face of the cooler unit.
8. Loosen the clamp attaching the left side air duct to the steering column, then remove the fusebox.
9. Push the cooler unit down and slide the side air hoses out of their vents. Remove the left side air duct from the cooler unit.
10. If necessary, remove the side vents on the instrument panel.
11. Detach the central air hoses from the conveyor box by sliding them out from below.
12. Disconnect all electrical connections from the cooler unit.
13. Disconnect and plug the inlet and outlet hose couplings from the cooler unit.

14. Remove the retaining screw and remove the air conditioning system control unit, located on the rear face from the cooler unit and remove the cooler unit from the vehicle.

15. Remove the instrument panel.
  a. Remove the glove compartment.
  b. Disconnect the vents and ducts.
  c. Unscrew the 2 wing nuts retaining the instrument panel to the body and remove the instrument panel from the vehicle.

16. Remove the 2 screws and remove the ducts from the heater assembly.

17. Disconnect and plug the heater outlet hose.

18. Working from the engine compartment, disconnect and plug the heater inlet hose.

19. Working from inside the vehicle, remove the nuts securing the heater assembly to the body, disconnect the ground wire from the electric fan and remove the heater unit from the vehicle.

20. Separate the the upper half of the heater case and remove the heater core from the cavity.

21. Installation is the reverse of removal. Recharge the air conditioning system.

164 SERIES

1. Disconnect the negative battery cable.
2. Remove the evaporator unit and the electric fan.
3. Move away and lift the the heater core, then disconnect the coolant hoses.
4. Remove the heater core from the vehicle.
5. Installation is the reverse of removal. Refill the cooling system.

Water Pump

Removal and Installation

SPIDER

1. Disconnect the negative battery cable.
2. Drain the cooling system.
3. Remove the air cleaner cover and filter.
4. Remove power steering pump and support, without disconnecting the hydraulic lines.
4. Disconnect the coolant hoses from the radiator.
5. Remove the alternator belt and move the alternator outwards.
6. Loosen the 9 water pump nuts and washers and remove the water pump from the vehicle.
7. Installation is the reverse of removal. Tighten the retaining nuts to 10.3–16.2 ft. lbs. (14–22 Nm).

MILANO

1. Disconnect the negative battery cable and drain the cooling system.
2. Disconnect the coolant hoses.
3. Disconnect the temperature sensor electrical connector.
4. Disconnect the spark plug cables from the timing belt case covers.
5. Loosen and remove all drive belts.
6. Remove the distributor covers and disconnect the related cap; remove the covers on the timing belt case.
7. Engage the transmission 5th speed gear and move the vehicle forward so as to rotate crankshaft in the running direction until notch **P**, marked on the engine pulley is aligned with the reference pin, No. 1 piston at TDC. If the engine is timed, the notches on the camshaft pulleys are aligned with the references on the timing belt cases. Also the middle of the distributor motor arm must be toward the lst cylinder.
8. Remove the retaining bolts, release the fuel return hose and ECU cables from the brackets and remove the cases.
9. Lift the belt tensioner arm and insert a pin into the arm hose to keep the arm itself lifted.

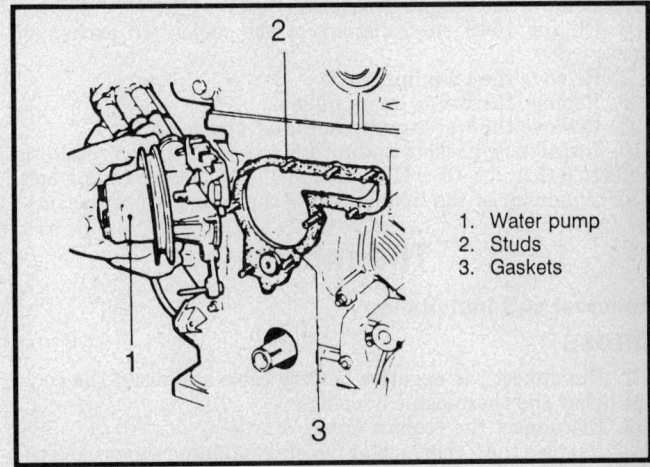

1. Water pump
2. Studs
3. Gaskets

Water pump—Spider

Water pump—Milano

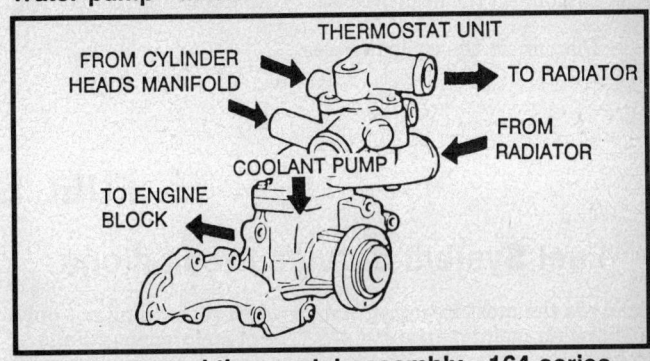

THERMOSTAT UNIT
FROM CYLINDER HEADS MANIFOLD
TO RADIATOR
FROM RADIATOR
COOLANT PUMP
TO ENGINE BLOCK

Water pump and thermostat assembly—164 series

10. Unscrew the nuts loosening the timing belt drive system and remove both the belt and the tightener.

11. Remove the screw which secures the distributor drive pulley and remove the pulley.

12. With the thermostat hoses disconnected, remove the water pump to block retaining bolts and remove the water pump and thermostat as a unit.

13. Remove the 4 retaining bolts and separate the thermostat from the pump, as necessary.

14. Install new gaskets and torque the water pump retaining bolts to 6–7 ft. lbs. (8–9 Nm). Install and adjust the timing belt. The remainder of the installation is the reverse of removal.

164 SERIES

1. Disconnect the negative battery cable and drain the cooling system.
2. Disconnect the coolant lines from the water pump.
3. Disconnect and tag all electrical connections at the water pump.
4. Remove the water pump and air conditioner drive belt.

5. Remove the engine timing belt.

6. On the 164S only, disconnect the coolant/oil exchanger lines.

7. Remove the oil pump pulley.

8. Remove the water pump pulley.

9. Remove the water pump and thermostat unit.

10. Install new gaskets and torque the water pump retaining bolts to 6–7 ft. lbs. (8–9 Nm). Install and adjust the timing belt. The remainder of the installation is the reverse of removal.

Thermostat

Removal and Installation
SPIDER

1. Disconnect the negative battery cable and drain the coolant below the thermostat housing.

2. Disconnect the coolant hoses.

3. Remove the 2 thermostat housing retaining screws and remove the thermostat, housing, thermostat and gasket.

4. To install, clean the mating surfaces and reverse the removal procedure.

MILANO

1. Disconnect the negative battery cable and drain the coolant below the thermostat housing.

2. Disconnect the coolant hoses.

3. Remove the 3 retaining screws and remove the thermostat, gasket and bracket.

4. To install, clean the mating surfces and reverse the removal procedure.

164 SERIES

1. Disconnect the negative battery cable and drain the cooling system.

2. Disconnect the coolant hoses.

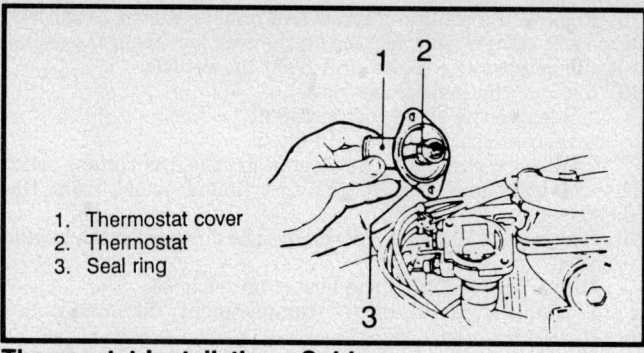

1. Thermostat cover
2. Thermostat
3. Seal ring

Thermostat Installation—Spider

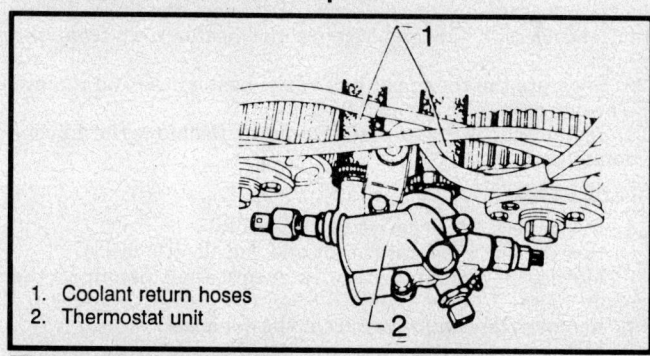

1. Coolant return hoses
2. Thermostat unit

Thermostat unit—Milano

3. Remove the thermostat unit cover and gasket, then the thermostat unit body and gasket.

4. To install, clean the mating surfaces and reverse the removal procedure.

FUEL SYSTEM

Fuel System Service Precautions

Safety is the most important factor when performing not only fuel system maintenance but any type of maintenance. Failure to conduct maintenance and repairs in a safe manner may result in serious personal injury or death. Maintenance and testing of the vehicle's fuel system components can be accomplished safely and effectively by adhering to the following rules and guidelines.

● To avoid the possibility of fire and personal injury, always disconnect the negative battery cable unless the repair or test procedure requires that battery voltage be applied.

● Always relieve the fuel system pressure prior to disconnecting any fuel system component (injector, fuel rail, pressure regulator, etc.), fitting or fuel line connection. Exercise extreme caution whenever relieving fuel system pressure to avoid exposing skin, face and eyes to fuel spray. Please be advised that fuel under pressure may penetrate the skin or any part of the body that it contacts.

● Always place a shop towel or cloth around the fitting or connection prior to loosening to absorb any excess fuel due to spillage. Ensure that all fuel spillage (should it occur) is quickly removed from engine surfaces. Ensure that all fuel soaked cloths or towels are deposited into a suitable waste container.

● Always keep a dry chemical (Class B) fire extinguisher near the work area.

● Do not allow fuel spray or fuel vapors to come into contact with a spark or open flame.

● Always use a backup wrench when loosening and tightening fuel line connection fittings. This will prevent unnecessary stress and torsion to fuel line piping. Always follow the proper torque specifications.

● Always replace worn fuel fitting O-rings with new. Do not substitute fuel hose or equivalent where fuel pipe is installed.

Relieving Fuel System Pressure

1. Start the engine and disconnect the fuel pump, either by disconnecting the fuel pump fuse or relay.

2. Let the engine run until it runs out of fuel.

3. Open the fuel filler cap to relieve any fuel system pressure in the tank.

Fuel Filter

Removal and Installation
SPIDER AND MILANO

1. Relieve the fuel system pressure.

2. Disconnect the negative battery cable.

3. Raise and support the vehicle safely.

4. Wrap an absorbent rag around the hose connections and disconnect the hoses from the filter.

5. Unscrew the clamp bolt and remove the filter from the clamp.

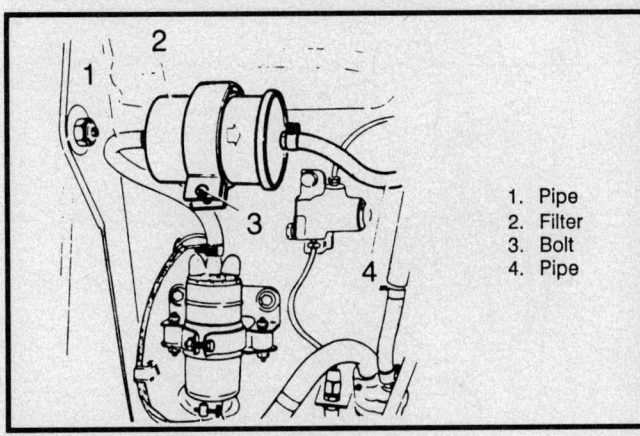

1. Pipe
2. Filter
3. Bolt
4. Pipe

Fuel filter installation—Spider

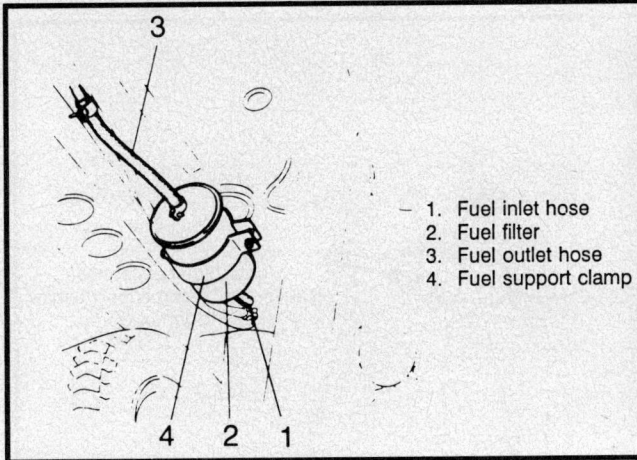

1. Fuel inlet hose
2. Fuel filter
3. Fuel outlet hose
4. Fuel support clamp

Fuel filter installation—Milano

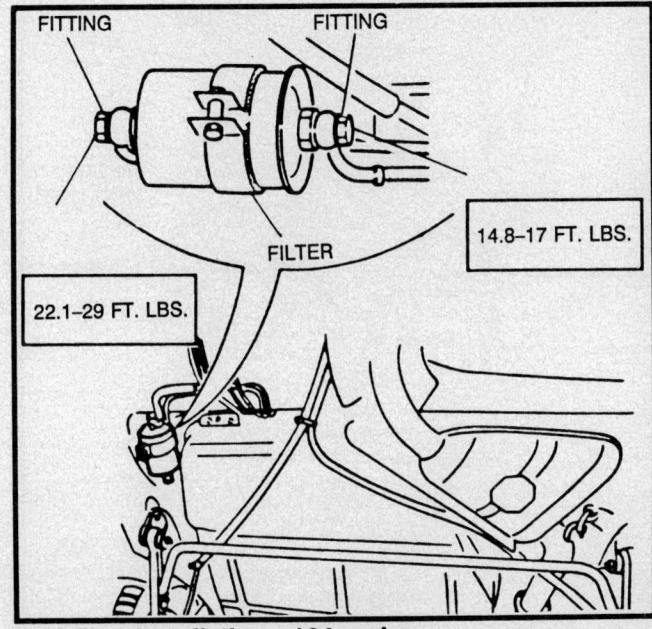

FITTING   FITTING

14.8–17 FT. LBS.

22.1–29 FT. LBS.

FILTER

Fuel filter installation—164 series

6. Install the filter in the correct direction and in the reverse of removal.

164 SERIES

1. Relieve the fuel system pressure.
2. Disconnect the negative battery cable.
3. Raise and support the vehicle safely.
4. Loosen the 2 filter connections, let the fuel drain in a suitable container and close the connections.
5. Loosen the filter retaining clamp and remove the filter from the vehicle.
6. Install the new filter in the correct direction and in the reverse of removal.

Fuel Pump

Pressure Testing

SPIDER

1. Disconnect the fuel inlet hose to the injector fuel inlet manifold.
2. Connect a pressure gauge, through a union tee, at the ends of the inlet line.
3. Detach the hose connecting the pressure regulator to the plenum chamber. This is to prevent any unevenness in the engine rotation, which could cause an incorrect reading.
4. Run the engine at idle and check that the fuel pressure is 32.7–38.4 psi for 1987–90 or 41.2–46.9 psi for 1991.
5. Reconnect the hose to the plenumm chamber. At minimum the pressure should decrease by approximately 7.25 psi and then increase when the throttle valve opens. If not check for leaks in the vacuum hose.
6. With the pressure gauge still connected, pinch the inlet hose immediately after the pressure regulator and verify that the pressure increases up to 43.5 psi for 1987–90 and 58 psi for 1991. Prevent the pressure from exceeding this value.
7. When 43.5 psi for 1987–90 or 58 psi for 1991 is obtained, check for leaks in the unions and lines of the fuel system.
8. If the pressure does not reach 43.5 psi for 1987–90 or 58 psi for 1991 and no leaks are present, check the filter and/or fuel pump functioning.

MILANO AND 164 SERIES

1. Disconnect the fuel inlet hose to the injector fuel inlet manifold.
2. Connect a pressure gauge, through a union tee, at the ends of the inlet line.
3. Detach the hose connecting the pressure regulator to the intake air box. This is to prevent any unevenness in the engine rotation, which could cause an incorrect reading.
4. Run the engine at idle and check that the fuel pressure is 35.6 psi for the Milano and 42–47 psi for the 164.
5. Reconnect the hose to the intake air box. At minimum the pressure should decrease by approximately 7.3 psi and then increase when the throttle valve opens. If not check for leaks in the vacuum hose.
6. With the pressure gauge still connected, pinch the inlet hose immediately after the pressure regulator and verify that the pressure increases up to 36.3 psi for the Milano or 58 psi for the 164 . Prevent the pressure from exceeding this value.
7. When 36.3 psi for the Milano or 58 psi for the 164 is obtained, check for leaks in the unions and lines of the fuel system.
8. If the pressure does not reach 36.3 psi for the Milano or 58 psi for the 164 and no leaks are present, check the filter and/or fuel pump functioning.

Removal and Installation

SPIDER AND MILANO

1. Release the fuel system pressure.
2. Disconnect the negative battery cable.

3. Raise and support the vehicle safely.

4. Working from under the vehicle, disconnect the pump power supply wires.

5. Pinch off the fuel inlet and outlet hoses, using a suitable clamping device and disconnect the hoses from the pump.

6. Loosen the fuel pump retaining clamp and remove the fuel pump from the vehicle.

NOTE: The replacement pump is filled with a protective oil and capped. The oil is immediately burned by the engine and it is not necessary to drain the pump before installation.

7. Installation is the reverse of removal.

164 SERIES

1. Release the fuel system pressure.
2. Disconnect the negative battery cable.
3. Remove the trunk floor trim and access cover.
4. Disconnect all fuel and vapor lines from the pump.
5. Disconnect the fuel pump electrical connections.
6. Remove the 8 fuel pump retaining bolts and remove the pump from the tank.

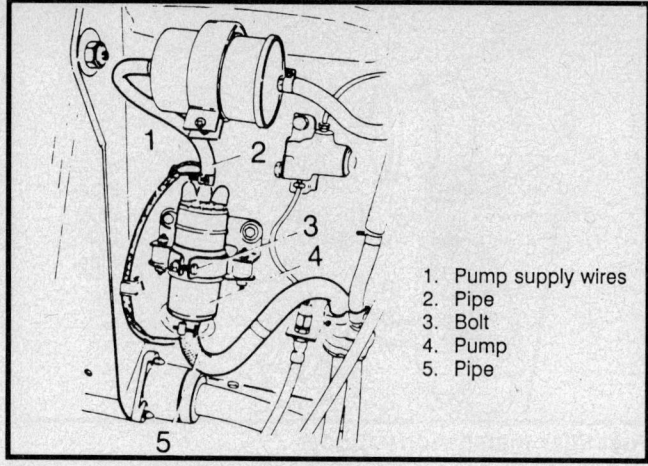

1. Pump supply wires
2. Pipe
3. Bolt
4. Pump
5. Pipe

Fuel pump installation—Spider

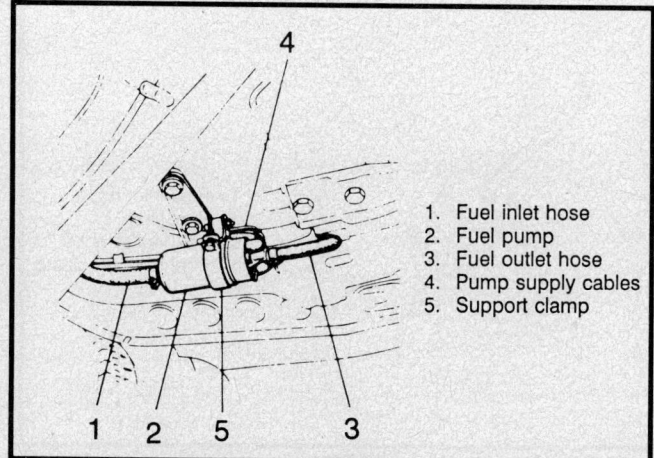

1. Fuel inlet hose
2. Fuel pump
3. Fuel outlet hose
4. Pump supply cables
5. Support clamp

Fuel pump installation—Milano

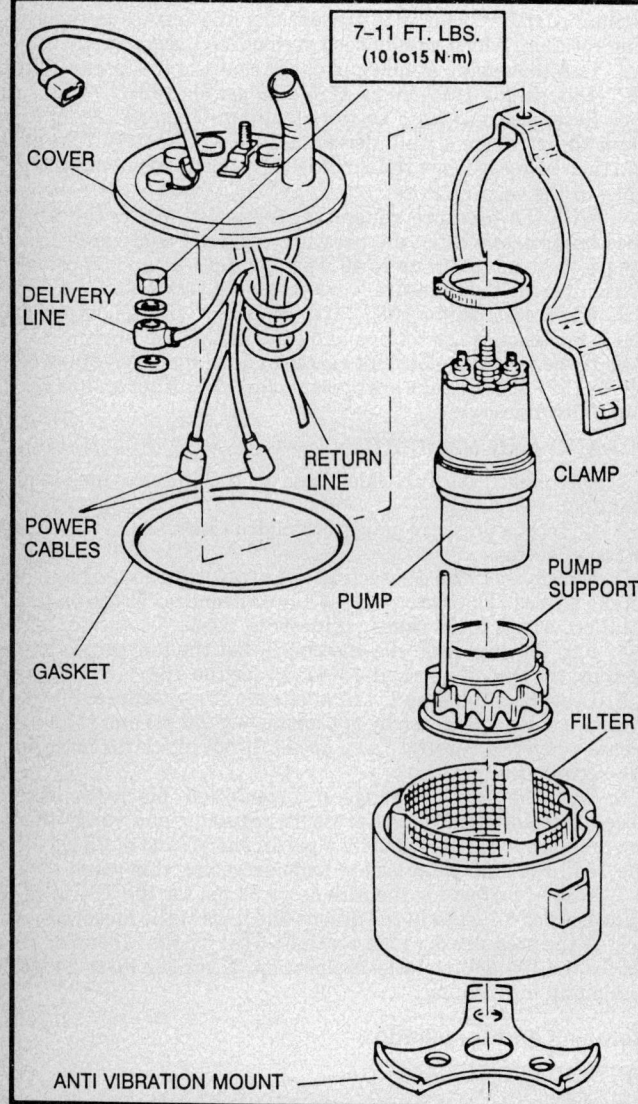

Fuel pump assembly—164 series

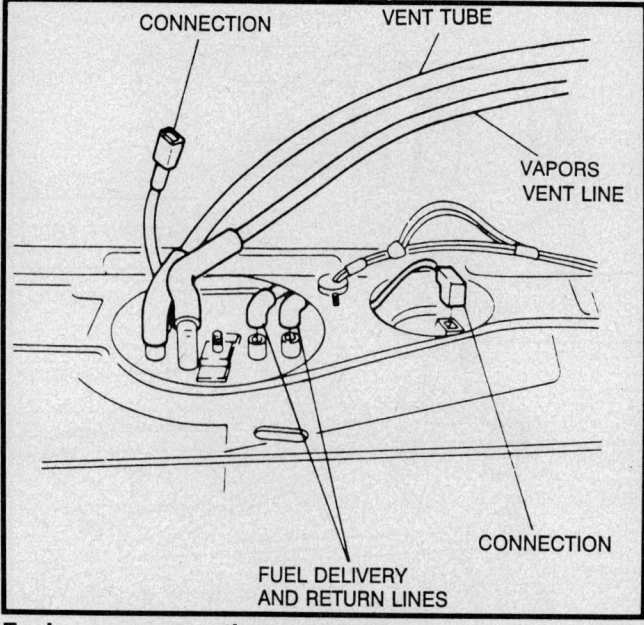

Fuel pump connections—164 series

NOTE: The replacement pump is filled with a protective oil and capped. The oil is immediately burned by the engine and it is not necessary to drain the pump before installation.

7. Installation is the reverse of removal.

Fuel Injection

For further information, please refer to ''Chilton's Electronic Engine Control's Manual'' for additional coverage.

Idle Speed Adjustment

SPIDER

1. Run the engine to normal operating temperature and place the transmission in the **N** position.
2. Loosen the locknut of the idle rpm adjusting device, rotate the control device union until the idle speed is 900–1000 rpm for 1987–89 and 750–850 rpm for 1990–91.
3. Tighten the locknut after the desired idle speed is obtained.

MILANO

1. Run the engine to normal operating temperature and place the transmission in the **N** position.
2. Loosen the locknut and rotate the screw until the idle speed is 900–1000 rpm for the 2.5L engine and 800–900 rpm for the 3.0L engine.

NOTE: Idle speed may differ at higher altitudes.

3. Tighten the locknut after the desired idle speed is obtained.

164 SERIES

An idle speed actuator, located on the throttle body by pass line controls idle speed by exactly determining the quantity of air during any idle condition. The actuator is controlled by the accelerator and the Motronic control unit.

Idle Mixture Adjustment

Idle mixture is electronically controlled and is adjusted automatically.

Fuel Injector

Removal and Installation
SPIDER

1. Release the fuel system pressure.
2. Disconnect the negative battery cable.
3. Remove the rubber air intake hose connected to the air filter.
4. Disconnect the wires from the spark plugs and coil then remove the distributor cap along with the wires.
5. Remove the by-pass hose and the oil vapor return hose from the intake duct.
6. Disconnect the air intake duct from the cam cover and disconnect the end of the duct connected to the throttle body.
7. Disconnect the connectors from the coolant temperature sender.
8. Detach the hose from the throttle body and the hose from the pressure regulator.
9. Disconnect the hoses from the feed manifold and pressure regulator.
10. Remove the nut securing the fuel feed manifold to the support bracket, unscrew the injector securing screws and remove them together with the fuel feed duct.

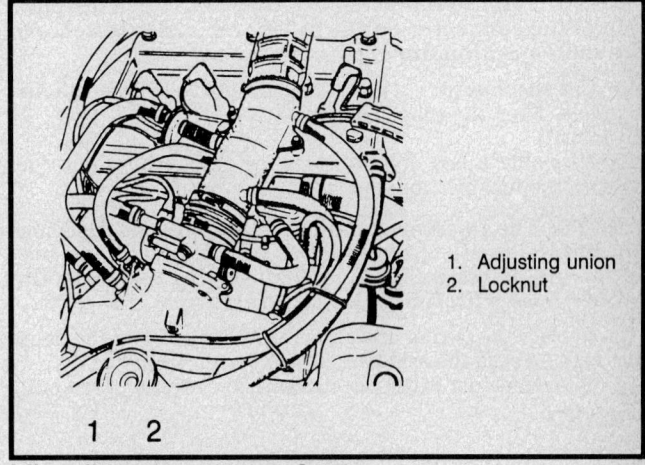

1. Adjusting union
2. Locknut

Idle adjustment screw—Spider

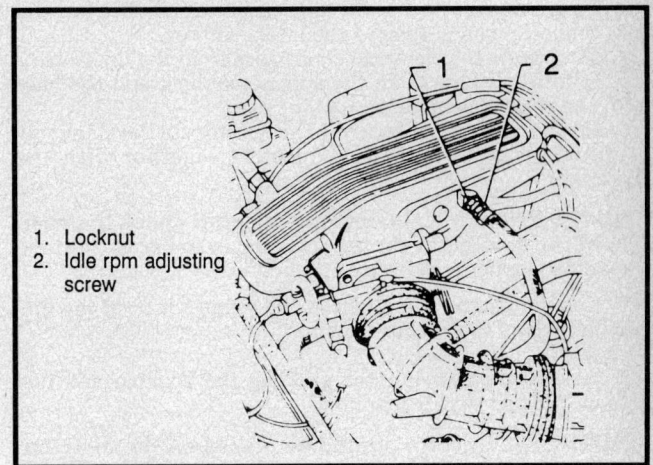

1. Locknut
2. Idle rpm adjusting screw

Idle adjustment screw—Milano

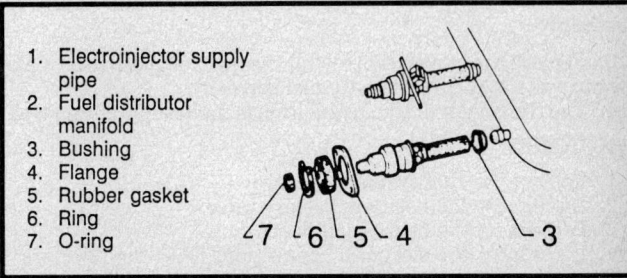

1. Electroinjector supply pipe
2. Fuel distributor manifold
3. Bushing
4. Flange
5. Rubber gasket
6. Ring
7. O-ring

Fuel injector installation—Spider and Milano

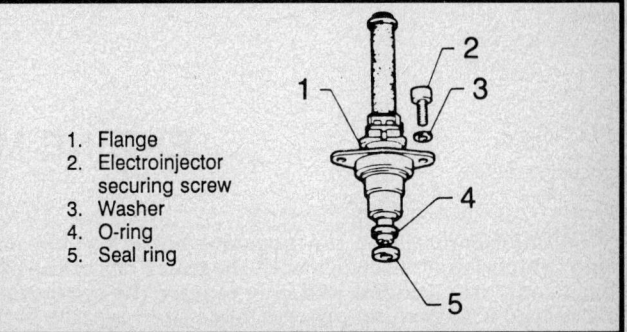

1. Flange
2. Electroinjector securing screw
3. Washer
4. O-ring
5. Seal ring

Fuel injector installation—Spider and Milano

NOTE: Prior to replacing any injector, check the position of the connector on the injector in order to achieve the same position during replacement.

11. Cut the injector supply hose and remove it from the fuel manifold. Keep the rubber bushing.

To install:

12. Assemble a new injector pressing the bushing and fuel hose on the fuel distributor manifold.

NOTE: The injector should be placed on the distributor manifold with the connector facing upwards as noted during disassembly. It is advisable to lubricate the rubber hose with fuel prior to assembly.

13. Replace the O-ring and assemble the injector in the housing, making sure the seal ring is positioned correctly.

14. The remainder of the installation is the reverse of removal.

MILANO

1. Release the fuel system pressure.
2. Disconnect the negative battery cable.
3. Disconnect the duct to the air cleaner, tag all electrical and hose connections and remove the intake air box.
4. Disconnect the electrical connectors from the injectors.
5. Detach the hose from the supply manifold and the hose from the pressure regulator.
6. Remove the screws securing the injectors to the air supply manifolds, then remove the injectors together with the manifold.

NOTE: Prior to replacing any injector, check the position of the connector on the injector in order to achieve the same position during replacement.

7. Cut the injector supply hose and remove it from the fuel manifold. Keep the rubber bushing.

To install:

8. Assemble a new injector pressing the bushing and fuel hose on the fuel supply manifold.

NOTE: The injector should be placed on the distributor manifold with the connector facing the cylinder heads upwards as noted during disassembly. It is advisable to lubricate the rubber hose with fuel prior to assembly.

9. Replace the O-ring and install the injector in its seat, making sure the seal ring is positioned correctly.

10. The remainder of the installation is the reverse of removal.

164 SERIES

1. Release the fuel system pressure.
2. Disconnect the negative battery cable.
3. Disconnect the depression hose.
4. Disconnect the electrical connections from the injectors.
5. Disconnect the fuel delivery and return lines.
6. Disconnect the stub pipes from the intake manifolds and tilt the intake box backward after removal of the securing screws.

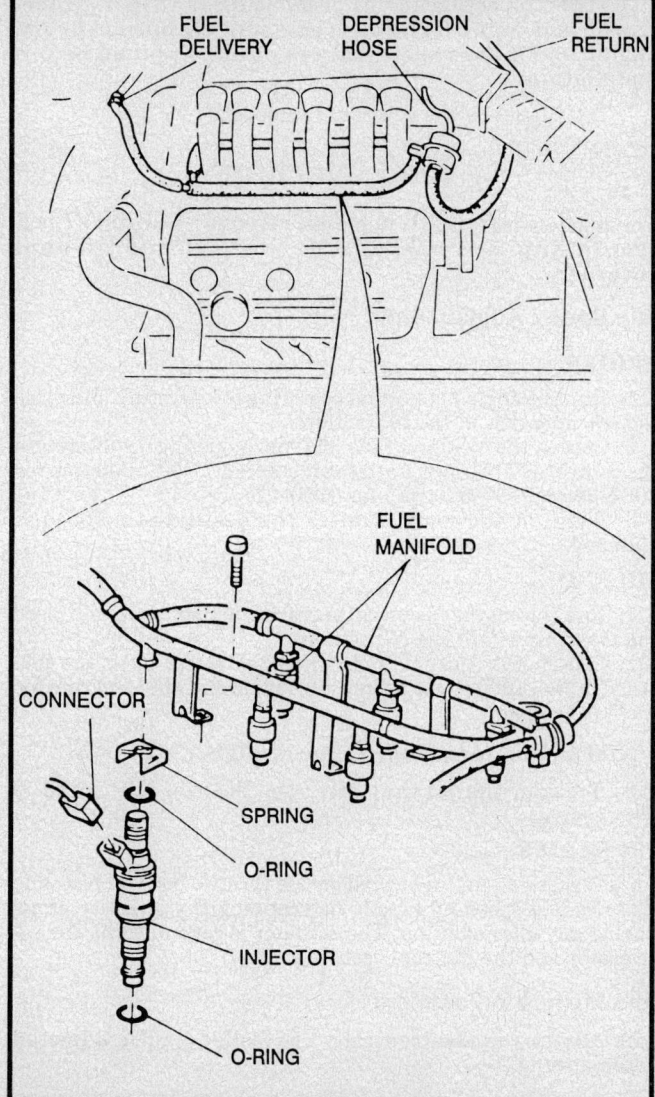

Fuel injector installation—164 series

7. Remove the 4 retaining screws and remove the fuel manifold and injectors.
8. For each injector to be removed, remove the spring securing the injector to the fuel manifold.
9. Remove the injector and the O-ring.
10. Installation is the reverse of removal.

ENGINE MECHANICAL

NOTE: Disconnecting the negative battery cable on some vehicles may interfere with the functions of the on board computer systems and may require the computer to undergo a relearning process, once the negative battery cable is reconnected.

Engine Assembly

Removal and Installation
SPIDER

1. Disconnect the negative battery cable.

2. Remove the hood.

3. Drain the cooling system and remove the radiator and coolant reservoir.

4. Disconnect the coolant return hoses from the water pump and throttle valve to the heater.

5. Disconnect the air flow transmitter cable from the air flow sensor.

6. Remove the rubber duct from the air flow sensor and throttle valve.

7. Release the clips and remove the air cleaner cover along with the air flow sensor, then remove the element underneath.

8. Uncsrew the 3 screws and and remove the air filter support.

9. Disconnect the servo brake vacuum intake hose and the vacuum sensor hose below.

10. Disconnect the idle oil vapor return pipe and the fuel vapor return pipe from the plenum chamber.

11. Detach the canister to rubber duct pipe.

12. Release the fuel system pressure.

13. Carefully disconnect the fuel delivery hose to the injectors from the distribution manifold, following all fuel system safety precautions.

14. Carefully disconnect the fuel return hose from the pressure regulator, following all fuel system safety precautions.

15. Disconnect the accelerator control rod from the throttle opening control.

16. Tag and disconnect all vacuum hoses, and electrical wires that may interfere with engine removal.

NOTE: Slide the injection system electrical wiring out from the upper part of the engine.

17. Discharge the air conditioning system, disconnect the compressor electrical wire from the flywheel connector and disconnect and plug the inlet and outlet refrigerent hoses from the compressor.

18. Remove from both sides the screws securing the upper part of the engine side supports.

19. Remove the cotter pin and unscrew the nut securing the right hand track to the steering box.

20. Raise and support the vehicle safely and drain the engine oil.

21. Disconnect the exhaust pipe to manifold retaining nuts.

22. Lower the vehicle.

23. From inside the passenger compartment, remove the console, clamp and rubber bellows.

24. Unscrew the bolt securing the gear selector rod to the trunnion pivot pin and remove the rod.

25. Disconnect the rear exhaust pipe from the front exhaust pipe.

26. Partially disconnect and bend the shield above the catalytic converter, to gain access to the 6 tie bar to body retaining screws, and remove the tie bar.

27. Scribe marks on the driveshaft and remove the 4 bolts at the flanges.

28. Remove the bolt securing the transmission to the cross bar, unscrew the 4 screws and remove the cross bar and rubber support washers.

29. Uncrew the tachometer cable, the 3 carrier retaining nuts and remove the carrier along with the bracket.

30. Remove the 2 nuts securing the transmission central carrier to the body frame.

31. Remove the bolt and nut retaining the muffler to the body.

32. Disconnect the back up light wiring connection.

33. Using a syringe, empty the hydraulic system tank, disconnect the union, hose and ground wire.

34. Remove from both sides the screws securing the lower part of the engine side supports.

35. Lower the vehicle and attach a suitable engine lifting device to the engine raising U-bolt, provided for this purpose.

36. Carefully raise the engine and transmission assembly from the vehicle and lower to a suitable engine stand.

To install:

37. With a suitable engine lifting device attached to the engine raising U-bolt, provided for this purpose, lower the engine into the vehicle.

38. With the vehicle raised and safely supported, install to both sides the screws securing the lower part of the engine side supports.

39. Connect the union, hose and ground wire and fill the hydraulic system tank.

40. Connect the back up light wiring.

41. Install the bolt and nut retaining the muffler to the body.

42. Install the 2 nuts securing the transmission central carrier to the body frame.

43. Install the carrier and bracket with the 3 retaining nuts and attach the tachometer cable.

44. Install the bolts and rubber support washers securing the transmission cross bar.

45. Install the driveshaft and tighten the 4 bolts at the flanges to 27–29 ft. lbs. (37–39 Nm)

46. Install the 6 tie bar to body retaining screws and reposition and install the shield above the catalytic converter.

47. Reconnect the rear exhaust pipe to the front exhaust pipe.

48. Lower the vehicle.

49. Connect the bolt securing the gear selector rod to the trunnion pivot pin.

50. From inside the passenger compartment, install the console, clamp and rubber bellows.

51. Connect the exhaust pipe to manifold retaining nuts.

52. Install the nut and cotter pin securing the right track to the steering gear.

53. Install to both sides the screws securing the upper part of the engine side supports.

54. Connect the compressor electrical wire to the flywheel connector and unplug and connect the inlet and outlet refrigerent hoses to the compressor. Charge the air conditioning system.

55. Connect all vacuum hoses, and electrical wires that were tagged during removal.

56. Connect the accelerator control rod to the throttle opening control.

57. Connect the fuel delivery hose to the injectors from the distribution manifold and the fuel return hose to the pressure regulator.

58. Attach the canister to rubber duct pipe.

59. Connect the idle oil vapor return pipe and the fuel vapor return pipe to the plenum chamber.

60. Connect the servo brake vacuum intake hose and the vacuum sensor hose.

61. Install the 3 screws retaining the air filter support.

62. Install the air cleaner element and cover along with the air flow sensor.

63. Install the rubber duct to the air flow sensor and throttle valve.

64. Connect the air flow transmitter cable to the air flow sensor.

65. Connect the coolant return hoses to the water pump and throttle valve.

66. Install and fill the coolant reservoir and radiator.

67. Add the engine oil, connect the battery and install the hood.

MILANO

1. Disconnect the terminals from the battery and remove the hood.

2. Drain the engine oil and cooling system.

3. Remove the air cleaner and element.

4. Release the fuel system pressure.

5. Tag and disconnect all vacuum hoses, fuel hoses and electrical wiring that may interfere with engine removal.

6. Disconnect the accelerator control cable.

7. Remove the radiator hoses, radiator and electric fan.

8. Remove the air conditioner compressor drive belt, the 2 compressor bracket to block retaining screws and move the compressor to the right side of the vehicle and support it.

NOTE: If necessary, discharge the air conditioning system and disconnect and plug the hoses and connections.

9. Remove the power steering pump and move aside.
10. Raise and support the vehicle safely.
11. Remove the catalytic converter and exhaust pipe center section.
12. Remove the driveshaft as follows:
   a. Remove the heat proof protective shield.
   b. Remove the center crossmember from the body.
   c. Remove the boot, bolt and and transmission rod.
   d. If necessary, remove the 4 screws supporting the gearbox lever support and move aside.
   e. Remove the flywheel cover.
   f. With the transmission in neutral, rotate the driveshaft, and alternately remove the nuts and bolts that connect it to the engine flywheel.
   g. Remove both screws and disconnect the rear engine support pin from the body.
   h. Remove the screws securing the rear crossmember to the body.
   i. Safely raise the rear axle with a suitable lifting device and remove the driveshaft from the clutch fork.
   j. Lower the rear axle lifting device and remove the driveshaft.
13. Remove the 3 securing screws and remove the bracket from the engine rear support.
14. Remove the nuts securing the lower the part of the side supports.
15. Lower the vehicle and remove the screws securing the upper part of the side support.
16. Attach a suitable engine lifting device to the lifting brackets and remove the engine from the vehicle.

To install:
17. With the engine lifting device attached, center the engine in its compartment, resting it on the 2 side supports, aligning the screw and stud holes.
18. Insert on both sides the screws and lock washers securing the flexible supports to the body.
19. Raise and support the vehicle safely.
20. Insert on both sides the nuts securing the lower part of the flexible supports to the body.
21. Install the engine rear support bracket and retaining screws.
22. Install the driveshaft to the vehicle by reversing Step 12. Tighten the nuts and bolts securing the driveshaft flexible coupling to the engine flywheel and clutch fork to 40.5–42.0 ft. lbs. (55–57 Nm).
23. Install the catalytic converter and exhaust pipe center section.
24. Reinstall the power steering pump and belt. The belt should have a center deflection of 0.51 in.
25. Reinstall the air conditioner compressor and belt. The belt should have a center deflection of 0.55 in.
26. Install the radiator, electric fan and hoses and refill the cooling system.
27. Make all electrical, vacuum and fuel connections which were tagged for identification and disconnected during removal.
28. Add engine oil, connect the battery and install the hood.

164 SERIES

1. Disconnect the negative battery cable.
2. Remove the hood.
3. Drain the cooling system.
4. Using a suitable syringe, empty the power steering fluid reservoir.

5. Remove the 2 air deflectors on each side of the radiator.
6. Disconnect the engine attachment upper link rod.
7. Disconnect the vacuum hoses and electrical connector from the air intake duct and remove the duct, air cleaner cover and filter and box.
8. Release the fuel system pressure.
9. Tag and disconnect all vacuum hoses, fuel hoses and electrical wiring that may interfere with engine removal.
10. Remove the cover from the ABS solenoid valves and disconnect the multiple connector and ground strap. Disconnect ABS solenoids and move to 1 side without disconnecting the rigid tubing lines.
11. Disconnect the engine hood release cable.
12. Disconnect the high voltage cable from the ignition coil.
13. Disconnect the ignition coil and relays bracket from the upper cross beam and move it to 1 side. Remove the upper cross beam.
14. Disconnect the coolant hoses and remove the radiator together with the electric fan.

NOTE: Do not remove or damage the air conditioning condenser and pipes.

15. On the 164S only, remove the shims located between the radiator and support frame.
16. On the 164S only, remove the ABS solenoid valves bracket.
17. On vehicles with manual transaxle, disconnect the hydraulic clutch control. Remove the bracket along with the control cylinder without disconnecting the pipe.
18. On vehicles with automatic transaxle, disconnect the oil cooler lines to the oil radiator and remove the oil radiator.
19. Remove the alternator.
20. Disconnect the accelerator cable.
21. On vehicles with automatic transaxle, disconnect the kickdown cable.
22. On the 164S, remove the engine throttle sensor.
23. Disconnect the electronic injectors cable support bracket.
24. Disconnect the electronic injectors connector.
25 Release the fuel system pressure.
26. Disconnect the fuel vapor and cruise control pipe.
27. Disconnect the fuel pressure regulator control pipe.
28. Carefully disconnect the fuel supply and return lines following all fuel system safety precautions.
29. Disconnect the servo-brake vacuum pipe.
30. Raise and support the vehicle safely.
31. Remove the right front inner fender splash shields.
32. Disconnect the timing belt central protection cover.
33. Disconnect the power steering hoses.
34. Disconnect the right front axle shaft.
35. Remove the left front fender inner splash shield.
36. Disconnect the left axle shaft.
37. Remove the air conditioning compressor without disconnecting the freon lines and lower into the engine compartment.
38. If equipped with manual transaxle, disconnect the gear control rod and reactor rod.
39. If equipped with automatic transaxle, remove the dipstick and plug the opening.
40. If equipped with automatic transaxle, remove the 2 support brackets, then disconnect the automatic gear mount damper.
41. With the vehicle in the raised position and safely supported, remove the front section of the exhaust pipe and gaskets.
42. Disconnect the right front and rear mounts.
43. Place a hydraulic jack under the transaxle.
44. Disconnect and remove the mount on the transaxle side.
45. Connect a suitable lifting device to the engine lifting brackets and carefully lift the engine from the vehicle.

NOTE: Be careful when lifting the engine from the vehicle that all electrical wires, pipes, hoses and ducts have been disconnected and that remaining components in the engine compartment are not damaged.

To install:

46. With a suitable lifting device attached to the engine lifting brackets, carefully lower the engine into the position. Place a hydraulic jack under the transaxle.

47. Install the mount on the transaxle side.

48. Install the right front and rear mounts.

49. With the vehicle in the raised position and safely supported, install the front section of the exhaust pipe and gaskets.

50. If equipped with automatic transaxle, connect the automatic gear mount damper, then install the 2 support brackets.

51. If equipped with automatic transaxle, install the dipstick.

52. If equipped with manual transaxle, connect the gear control rod and reactor rod.

53. Install the air conditioning compressor.

54. Install the left axle shaft the left front fender inner splash shield.

55. Install the right front axle shaft.

56. Connect the power steering hoses.

57. Install the timing belt central protection cover.

58. Install the right front inner fender splash shields.

59. Lower the vehicle and connect the servo-brake vacuum pipe.

60. Connect the fuel supply and return lines and the fuel vapor and cruise control pipe.

61. Connect the fuel pressure regulator control pipe.

62. Connect the electronic injectors cable support bracket.

63. Disconnect the electronic injectors connector.

64. On the 164S, install the engine throttle sensor.

65. On vehicles with automatic transaxle, connect the kickdown cable.

66. Connect the accelerator cable.

67. Install the alternator.

68. On vehicles with automatic transaxle, install the oil radiator and connect the oil cooler lines.

69. On vehicles with manual transaxle, install the hydraulic clutch control.

70. On the 164S only, install the shims located between the radiator and support frame and install the ABS solenoid valves bracket.

71. Install the radiator, radiator hoses and the electric fan.

72. Install the ignition coil and relays bracket to the upper cross beam and install the upper cross beam.

73. Connect the high voltage cable to the ignition coil.

74. Connect the engine hood release cable.

75. Reposition and install the ABS solenoid valves, connect the multiple connector and ground strap and install the cover.

76. Connect all tagged vacuum hoses, fuel hoses and electrical wiring that were disconnected during engine removal.

77. Install the 2 air deflectors on each side of the radiator.

78. Install the engine attachment upper link rod.

79. Install the air cleaner box, filter, cover and intake duct.

80. Refill all fluids; engine oil and coolant and power steering fluid.

81. Reconnect the battery cables and install the hood.

Cylinder Head

Removal and Installation

MILANO

1. Disconnect the negative battery cable.
2. Release the fuel system pressure.
3. Drain the cooling system.
4. Remove the air cleaner assembly and timing belt.

5. Disconnect and tag all vacuum hoses, electrical connections and fuel system components.

6. Disconnect the exhaust pipe and manifold.

7. Remove the screws and washers securing the valve cover to the cylinder head and remove the cover.

8. Remove the packings from the 6 spark plug wells.

9. On the right cylinder head, remove the distributor and extract the gear operating the distributor and oil pump.

10. Remove the 8 nuts and washers securing each cylinder head to the block.

11. Lift the cylinder heads from the block, being careful not to damage the studs.

12. Remove the head gasket from the block and the rings fitted on each cylinder liner.

13. Remove the O-ring for the lubrication duct on each side of the block.

To install:

14. Turn the crankshaft until the number 1 piston of the compression stroke. The notch on the engine pulley is aligned with the mark on the front cover.

15. Install the head gasket to the block and the rings on each cylinder liner.

16. Install the O-ring for the lubrication duct on each side of the block.

17. Using a suitable tool, turn the camshaft of each head until the timing notches are in line with the caps. On the right head the notch corrosponds with the 3rd cap and on the left head it is on the 2nd cap.

18. Install the heads to the block and lubricate the threads of the studs, washers and locknuts with clean engine oil.

19. Install the 8 locknuts and torque in the proper sequence.

    a. On the 2.5L engine, with the engine cold, torque to 56.8–57.3 ft. lbs., then after 600 miles, with the engine cold, slacken the nuts one turn, in sequence, lubricate and retighten to 65.1 ft. lbs.

    b. On the 3.0L engine, with the engine cold, torque to 65.0–72.3 ft. lbs., then after 600 miles, with the engine cold, slacken the nuts one turn, in sequence, lubricate and retighten to 72.1–79.8 ft. lbs.

20. The remainder of the installation is the reverse of removal.

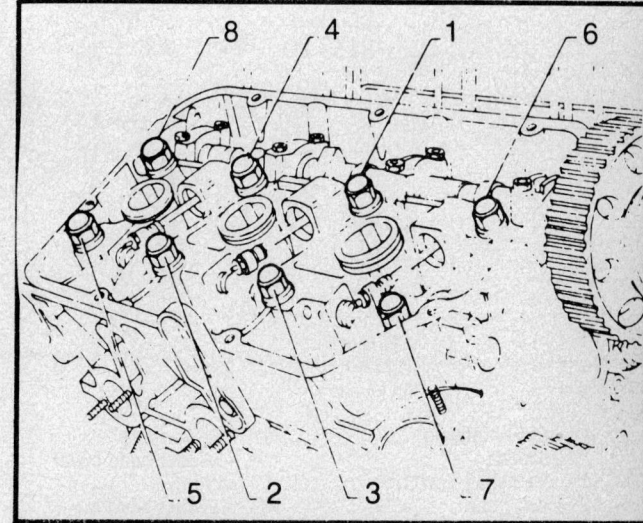

Cylinder head bolt tightening sequence – Milano with the 2.5L and 3.0L engines

1. Oil sump cover
2. Oil sump cover gasket
3. Oil sump
4. Oil sump gasket
5. Front cover gasket
6. Front cover
7. Front cover retaining screws
8. Front oil seal
9. Back-up washer
10. Camshaft drive pulley
11. Crankshaft pulley
12. Spacer
13. Lock washer
14. Crankshaft pulley locknut
15. Hydraulic belt stretcher
16. Locknut
17. Distributor and oil pump drive belt

26. Toothed pulley locknut
27. Toothed pulley hub.
28. Hub retaining screws
29. Seal ring
30. Hub and toothed pulley support
31. Camshaft drive pulley
32. Camshaft drive gear
33. Cylinder head gasket
34. Cylinder head cover gasket
35. Cylinder head cover
36. Plug gasket

43. Lock washer
44. Flywheel to clutch group retaining bolts
45. Oil sump retaining bolts
46. Oil pump
47. Oil pump retaining bolts
48. Oil drain plug

T :
88 Nm
(9 kgm
65.1 ft·lb)
For 3000 engine (061.24)
97.8 to 108.2 Nm
(10 to 11 kgm
72.1 to 79.8 ft·lb)

T : 97 to 117 N·m
(71.6 to 86.1 ft·lb;
9.9 to 11.9 kg·m)

T : 113 N·m
(83.2 ft·lb;
11.5 kg·m)

T : 235 N·m
(173.6 ft·lb;
24 kg·m)

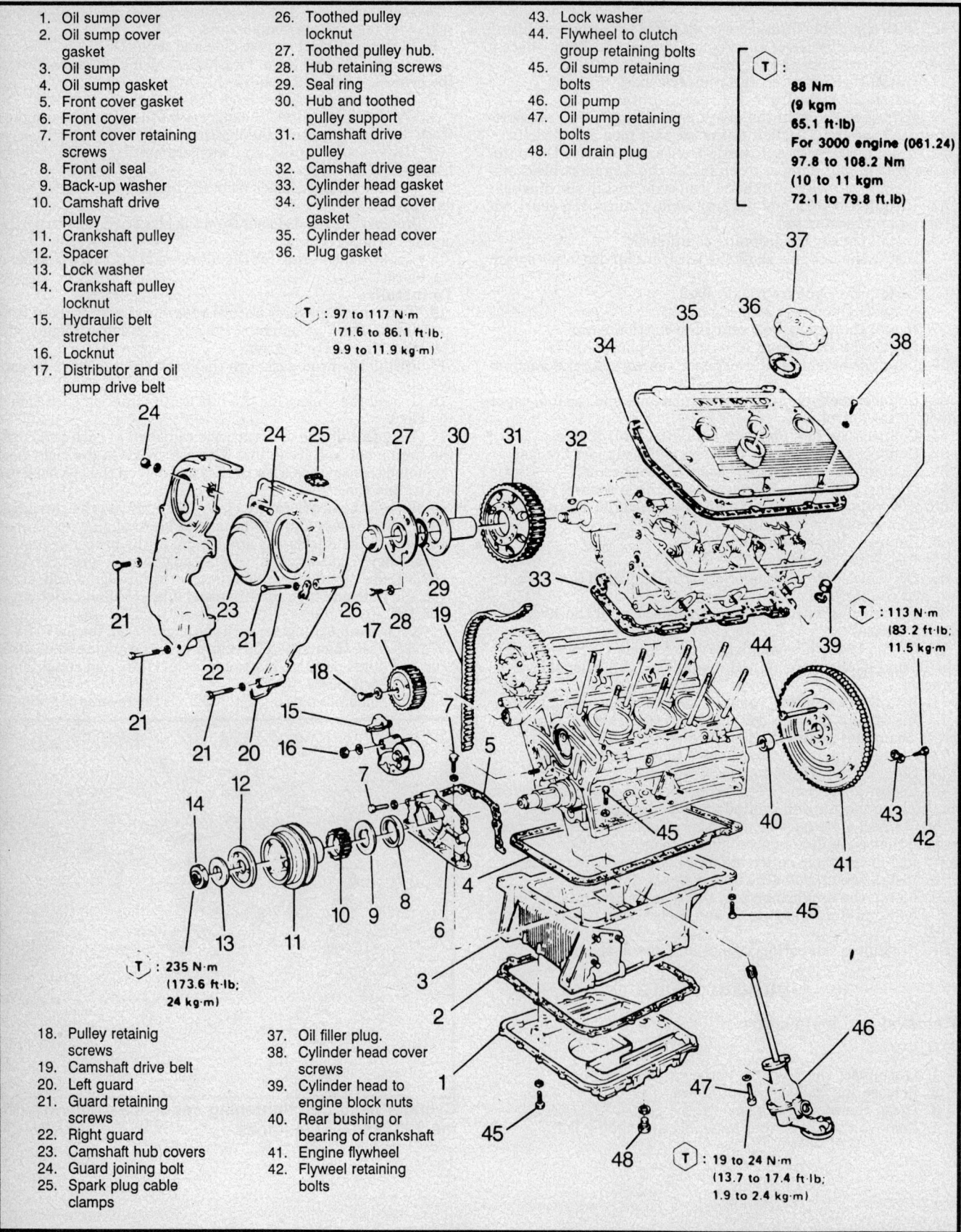

18. Pulley retainig screws
19. Camshaft drive belt
20. Left guard
21. Guard retaining screws
22. Right guard
23. Camshaft hub covers
24. Guard joining bolt
25. Spark plug cable clamps

37. Oil filler plug.
38. Cylinder head cover screws
39. Cylinder head to engine block nuts
40. Rear bushing or bearing of crankshaft
41. Engine flywheel
42. Flywheel retaining bolts

T : 19 to 24 N·m
(13.7 to 17.4 ft·lb;
1.9 to 2.4 kg·m)

Disassembled view of the 2.5L and 3.0L engine — Milano

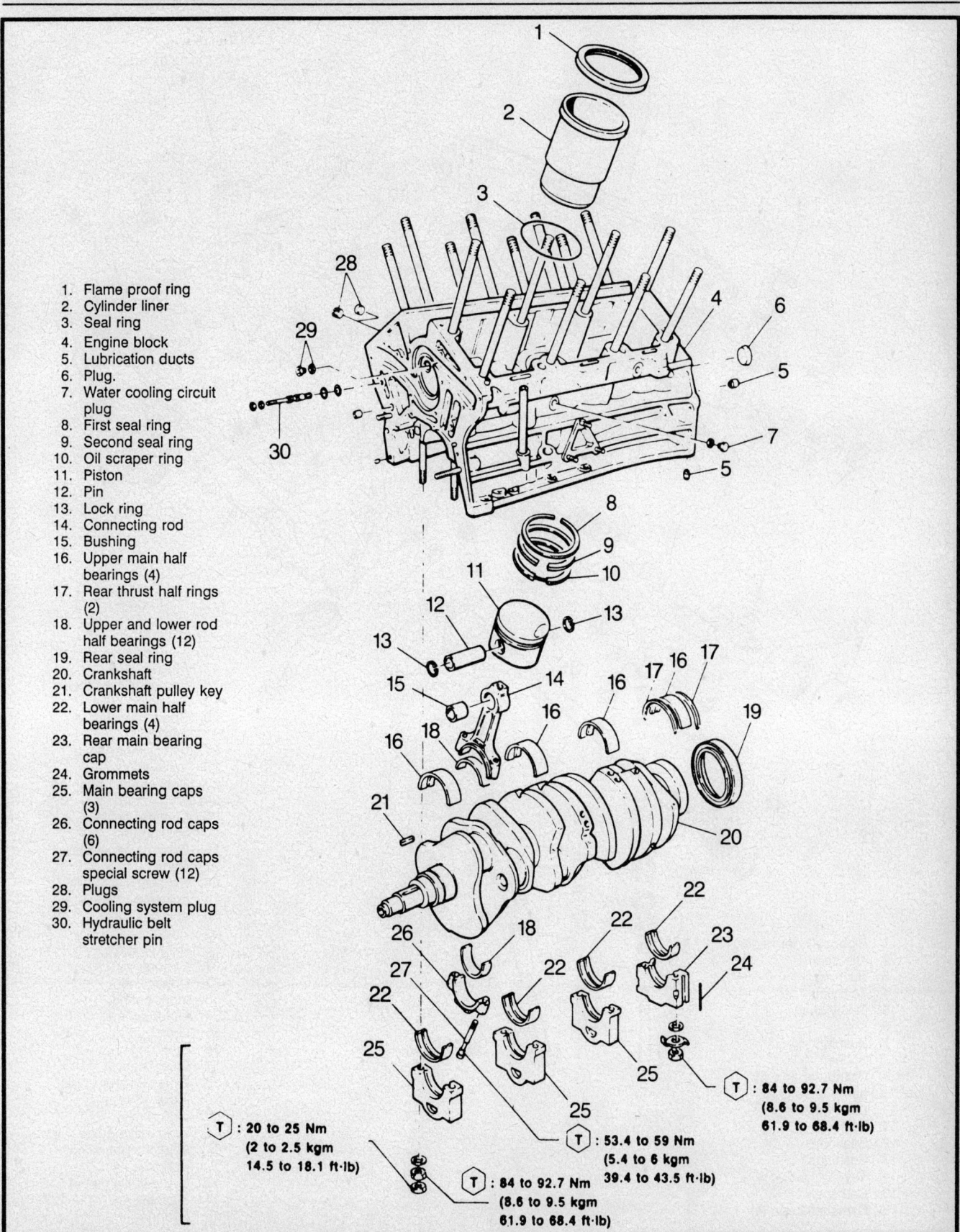

1. Flame proof ring
2. Cylinder liner
3. Seal ring
4. Engine block
5. Lubrication ducts
6. Plug.
7. Water cooling circuit plug
8. First seal ring
9. Second seal ring
10. Oil scraper ring
11. Piston
12. Pin
13. Lock ring
14. Connecting rod
15. Bushing
16. Upper main half bearings (4)
17. Rear thrust half rings (2)
18. Upper and lower rod half bearings (12)
19. Rear seal ring
20. Crankshaft
21. Crankshaft pulley key
22. Lower main half bearings (4)
23. Rear main bearing cap
24. Grommets
25. Main bearing caps (3)
26. Connecting rod caps (6)
27. Connecting rod caps special screw (12)
28. Plugs
29. Cooling system plug
30. Hydraulic belt stretcher pin

Ⓣ : 84 to 92.7 Nm
(8.6 to 9.5 kgm
61.9 to 68.4 ft·lb)

Ⓣ : 20 to 25 Nm
(2 to 2.5 kgm
14.5 to 18.1 ft·lb)

Ⓣ : 53.4 to 59 Nm
(5.4 to 6 kgm
39.4 to 43.5 ft·lb)

Ⓣ : 84 to 92.7 Nm
(8.6 to 9.5 kgm)
61.9 to 68.4 ft·lb)

Disassembled view of the 2.5L and 3.0L engine block—Milano

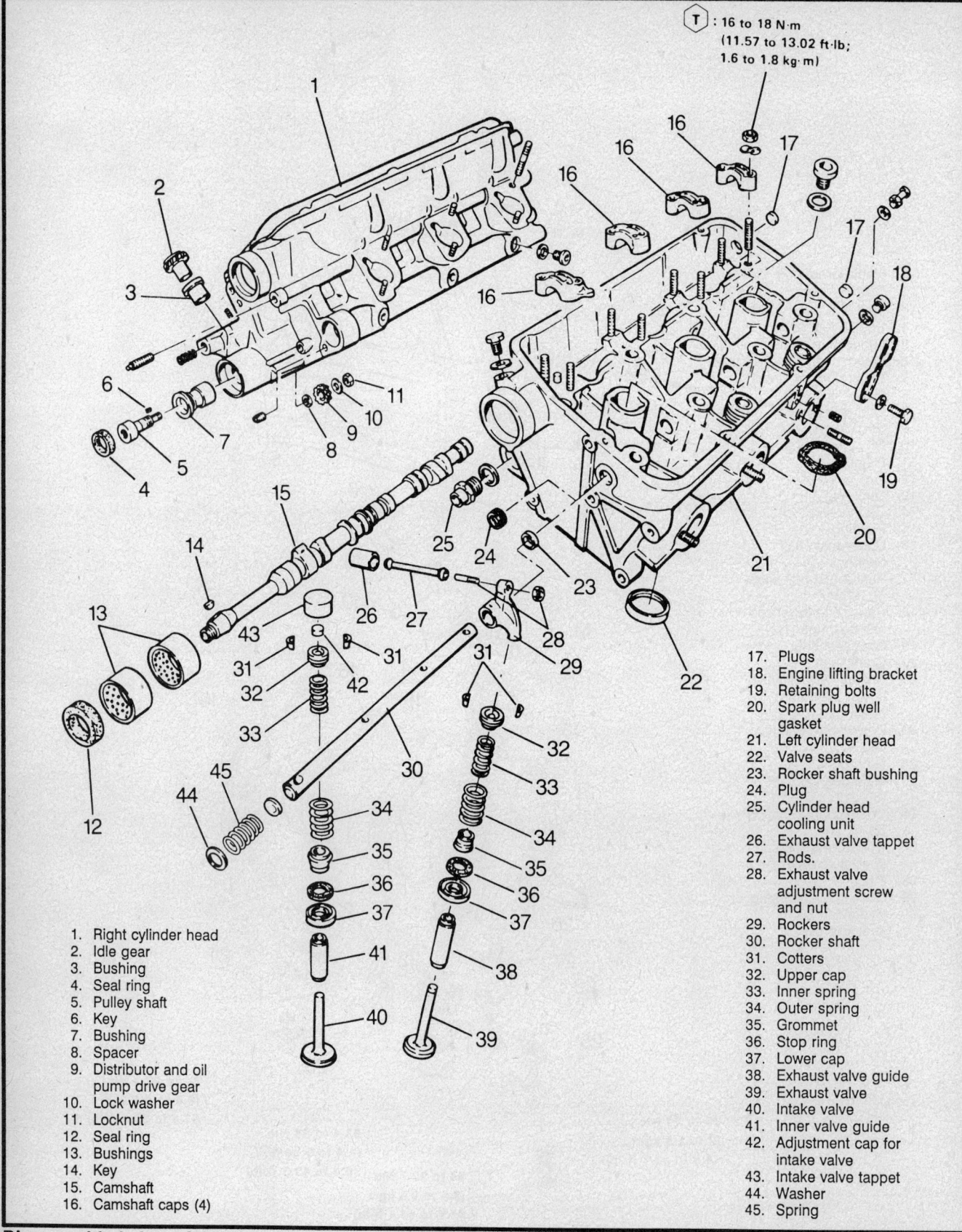

T : 16 to 18 N·m
(11.57 to 13.02 ft·lb;
1.6 to 1.8 kg·m)

1. Right cylinder head
2. Idle gear
3. Bushing
4. Seal ring
5. Pulley shaft
6. Key
7. Bushing
8. Spacer
9. Distributor and oil pump drive gear
10. Lock washer
11. Locknut
12. Seal ring
13. Bushings
14. Key
15. Camshaft
16. Camshaft caps (4)

17. Plugs
18. Engine lifting bracket
19. Retaining bolts
20. Spark plug well gasket
21. Left cylinder head
22. Valve seats
23. Rocker shaft bushing
24. Plug
25. Cylinder head cooling unit
26. Exhaust valve tappet
27. Rods.
28. Exhaust valve adjustment screw and nut
29. Rockers
30. Rocker shaft
31. Cotters
32. Upper cap
33. Inner spring
34. Outer spring
35. Grommet
36. Stop ring
37. Lower cap
38. Exhaust valve guide
39. Exhaust valve
40. Intake valve
41. Inner valve guide
42. Adjustment cap for intake valve
43. Intake valve tappet
44. Washer
45. Spring

Disassembled view of the 2.5L and 3.0L engine cylinder head—Milano

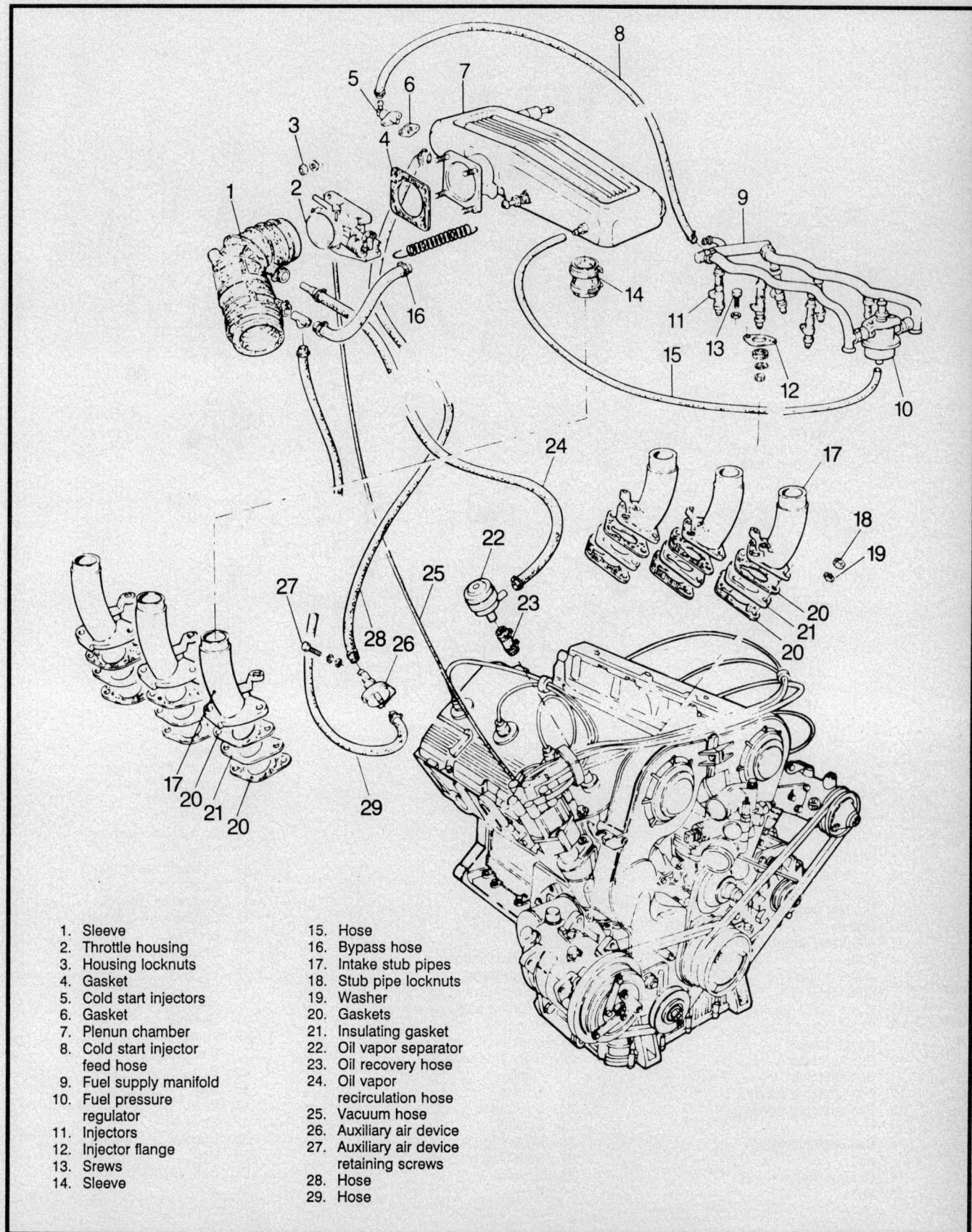

1. Sleeve
2. Throttle housing
3. Housing locknuts
4. Gasket
5. Cold start injectors
6. Gasket
7. Plenun chamber
8. Cold start injector feed hose
9. Fuel supply manifold
10. Fuel pressure regulator
11. Injectors
12. Injector flange
13. Srews
14. Sleeve
15. Hose
16. Bypass hose
17. Intake stub pipes
18. Stub pipe locknuts
19. Washer
20. Gaskets
21. Insulating gasket
22. Oil vapor separator
23. Oil recovery hose
24. Oil vapor recirculation hose
25. Vacuum hose
26. Auxiliary air device
27. Auxiliary air device retaining screws
28. Hose
29. Hose

Disassembled view of the 2.5L and 3.0L engine fuel system components—Milano

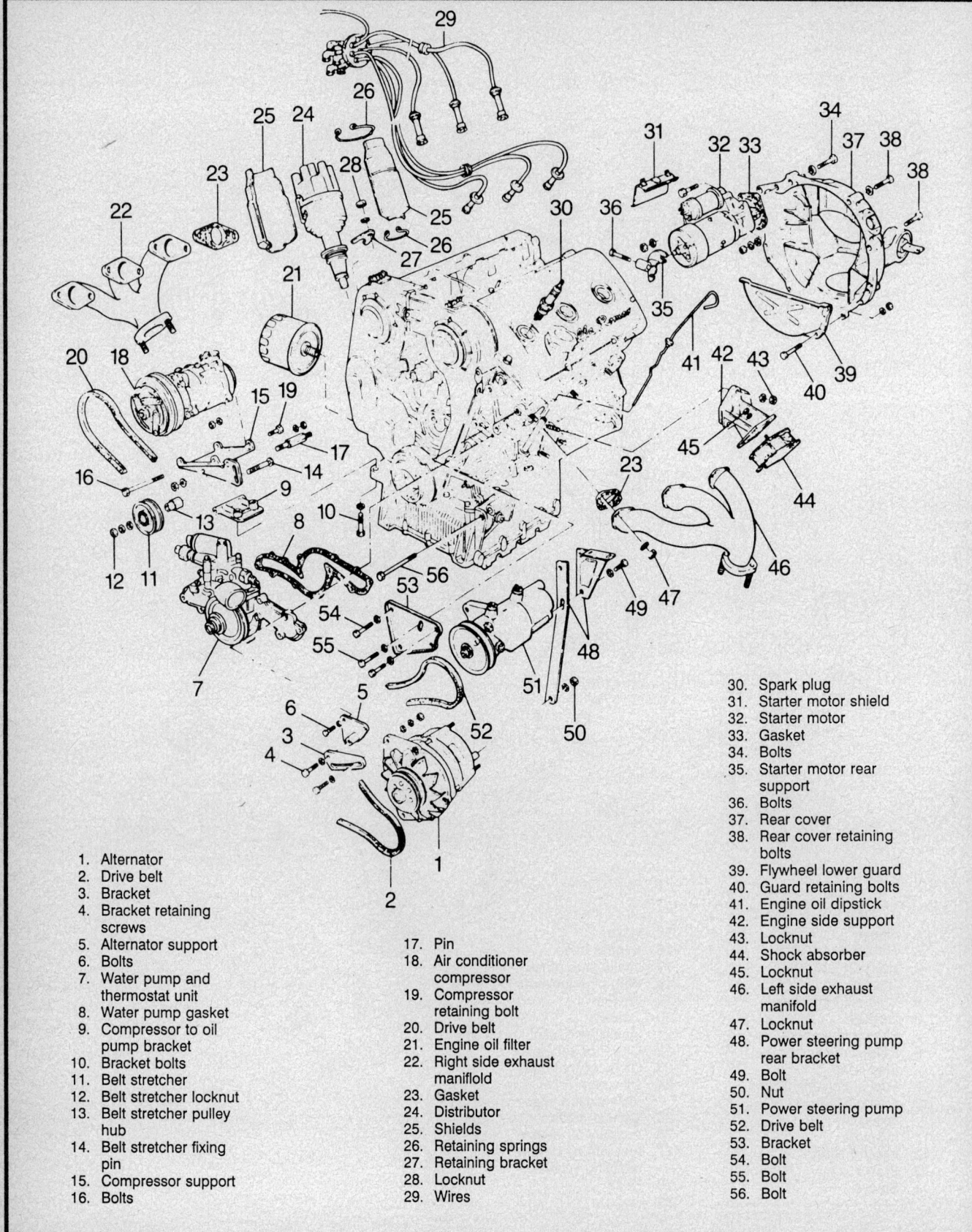

1. Alternator
2. Drive belt
3. Bracket
4. Bracket retaining screws
5. Alternator support
6. Bolts
7. Water pump and thermostat unit
8. Water pump gasket
9. Compressor to oil pump bracket
10. Bracket bolts
11. Belt stretcher
12. Belt stretcher locknut
13. Belt stretcher pulley hub
14. Belt stretcher fixing pin
15. Compressor support
16. Bolts
17. Pin
18. Air conditioner compressor
19. Compressor retaining bolt
20. Drive belt
21. Engine oil filter
22. Right side exhaust manifold
23. Gasket
24. Distributor
25. Shields
26. Retaining springs
27. Retaining bracket
28. Locknut
29. Wires
30. Spark plug
31. Starter motor shield
32. Starter motor
33. Gasket
34. Bolts
35. Starter motor rear support
36. Bolts
37. Rear cover
38. Rear cover retaining bolts
39. Flywheel lower guard
40. Guard retaining bolts
41. Engine oil dipstick
42. Engine side support
43. Locknut
44. Shock absorber
45. Locknut
46. Left side exhaust manifold
47. Locknut
48. Power steering pump rear bracket
49. Bolt
50. Nut
51. Power steering pump
52. Drive belt
53. Bracket
54. Bolt
55. Bolt
56. Bolt

Disassembled view of the 2.5L and 3.0L engine external components—Milano

164 SERIES

Left Side

1. Disconnect the negative battery cable.
2. Release the fuel system pressure.
3. Drain the cooling system.
4. Remove the air cleaner assembly.
5. Rotate the crankshaft and align the timing marks on the camshaft to the marks on the relevant caps. In this position the No. 1 cylinder is at TDC and the hole on the flywheel and the mark engraved on the gearbox cone must be aligned.
6. Lift the hydraulic belt tensioner arm and lock the tightener with tool 1.820.053.000 or equivalent.
7. Loosen the nuts, push the belt tightener downwards to bottom of travel and tighten the upper nut. Remove the timing belt.
8. Disconnect and tag all vacuum hoses, electrical connections and fuel system components.
9. Remove the distributor rotor arm and cover.
10. Disconnect the exhaust pipe and manifold.
11. Remove the screws and washers securing the camshaft cover to the cylinder head and remove the cover.
12. Remove the packings from the 6 spark plug wells.
13. Remove the thermostat unit cover and gasket.
14. Remove the thermostat unit body by disconnecting it from the cooling duct.
15. Prevent rotation of the oil pump drive pulley and unscrew the oil pump drive intermediate gear retaining nut. Remove the washer and the intermediate gear.
16. Remove the 8 nuts and washers securing each cylinder head to the block.
17. Lift the cylinder heads from the block, being careful not to damage the studs.
18. Remove the head gasket from the block and the rings fitted on each cylinder liner.
19. Remove the O-ring for the lubrication duct on each side of the block.
20. Install cylinder liner fixing tool.

To install:

21. Rotate the crankshaft and align the timing marks on the camshaft to the marks on the relevant caps. Make sure each camshaft of each head timing notches are in line with the caps. On the right head the notch corrosponds with the 3rd cap and on the left head it is on cap No. 7. In this position the No. 1 cylinder is at TDC and the hole on the flywheel and the mark engraved on the gearbox cone must be aligned.
22. Remove the liners fixing tool.
23. Install the head gasket to the block and the rings on each cylinder liner.
24. Install the O-ring for the lubrication duct on each side of the block.
25. Install the heads to the block and lubricate the threads of the studs, washers and locknuts with clean engine oil.
26. Install the 8 locknuts and torque in the proper sequence. With the engine cold, torque to 65.0–72.3 ft. lbs., then after 600 miles, with the engine cold, slacken the nuts 1 turn, in sequence, lubricate and retighten to 72.1–79.8 ft. lbs.
27. The remainder of the installation is the reverse of removal.

Right Side

1. Disconnect the negative battery cable.
2. Release the fuel system pressure.
3. Drain the cooling system and disconnect the relevent coolant hoses.
4. Disconnect the oil vapors recirculation pipe and idle speed actuator.
5. Disconnect and tag all vacuum hoses, electrical connections and fuel system components.
6. Disconnect the coolant inlet and outlet pipes from the throttle body.
7. Remove the throttle body cover.
8. Disconnect the accelerator cable.
9. If equipped with automatic transaxle, disconnect the kick down cable.
10. On the 164S, remove the engine throttle sensor.
11. Loosen the 3 attaching screws on the ducts and intake pipes, then remove the air intake box.
12. Remove the 6 intake pipes and gaskets.
13. Remove the camshaft cover cover and gasket.
14. Remove the upper engine link rod.
15. Disconnect the injector from the electronic injectors and remove the fuel manifold with injectors, without disconnecting fuel delivery and return pipes.
16. Clean the spark plug housings and remove the spark plugs. Plug the holes to prevent entry of foreign materials.
17. Remove the upper, center and lower sections of the timing belt cover.
18. Rotate the crankshaft and align the timing marks on the camshaft to the marks on the relevant caps. In this position the No. 1 cylinder is at TDC and the hole on the flywheel and the mark engraved on the gearbox cone must be aligned.
19. Lift the hydraulic belt tensioner arm and lock the tightener with tool 1.820.053.000 or equivalent.
20. Lift the hydraulic belt tensioner arm and lock the tightener with tool 21.820.053.000 or equivalent.
21. Remove the oil pump intermediate gear cap and O-ring.
22. Prevent rotation of the oil pump pulley using tool 1.820.051.000 or equivalent.
23. Remove the oil pump intermediate gear retaining nut, washer and remove the intermediate gear.
24. Loosen the nuts, rotate the belt tightener upwards and lock in this position by retightening the nuts. Remove the timing belt.
25. Remove the front section of the exhaust pipes and gaskets.
26. Remove the exhaust manifold and gaskets.
27. Remove the engine starter heat shield and remove the left front wheel.
28. Disconnect the left axle shaft and move it rearwards.
29. Disconnect the engine mount on the gearbox side after a suitable hydraulic jack has been placed below the oil sump.
30. Carefully remove the complete engine mount on the gearbox side and tilt the engine until the gearbox cone comes in contact with the auxiliary frame.
31. Remove the cylinder head and gasket.

To install:

32. Rotate the crankshaft and align the timing marks on the camshaft to the marks on the relevant caps. Make sure each camshaft of each head timing notches are in line with the caps. On the right head the notch corrosponds with the 3rd cap and on the left head it is on cap No. 7. In this position the No. 1 cylinder is at TDC and the hole on the flywheel and the mark engraved on the gearbox cone must be aligned.
33. Remove the liners fixing tool.
34. Install the head gasket to the block and the rings on each cylinder liner.
35. Install the O-ring for the lubrication duct on each side of the block.
36. Install the heads to the block and lubricate the threads of the studs, washers and locknuts with clean engine oil.
37. Install the 8 locknuts and torque in the proper sequence. With the engine cold, torque to 65.0–72.3 ft. lbs., then after 600 miles, with the engine cold, slacken the nuts 1 turn, in sequence, lubricate and retighten to 72.1–79.8 ft. lbs.
38. The remainder of the installation is the reverse of removal.

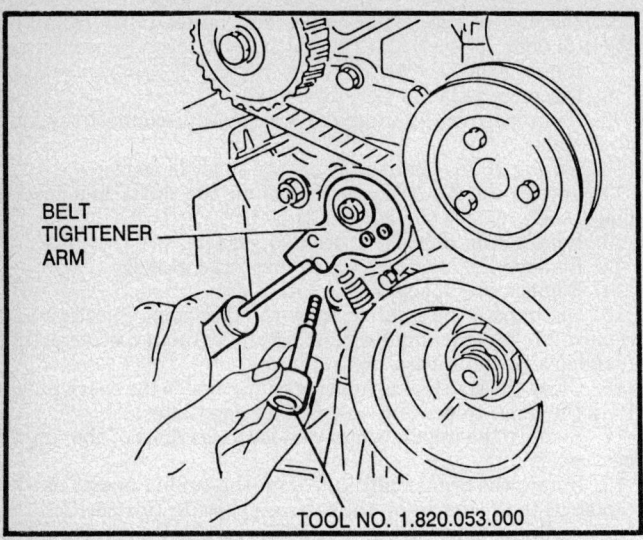

Locking the hydraulic belt tensioner arm—164 series with the 3.0L engine

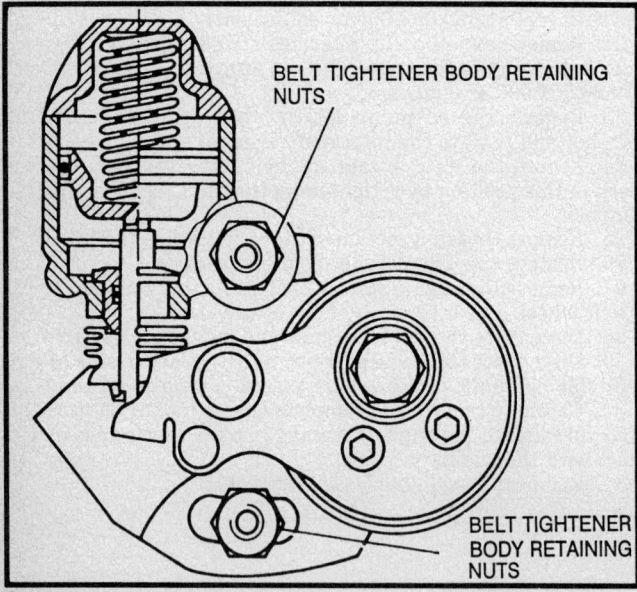

Belt tightener body retaining nuts—164 series with the 3.0L engine

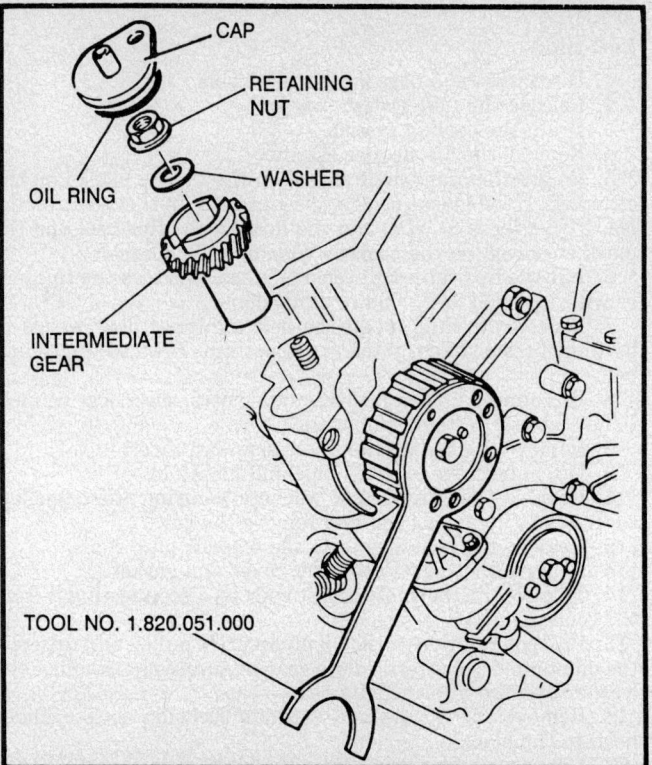

Removing the oil pump intermediate gear—model 164 with the 3.0L engine

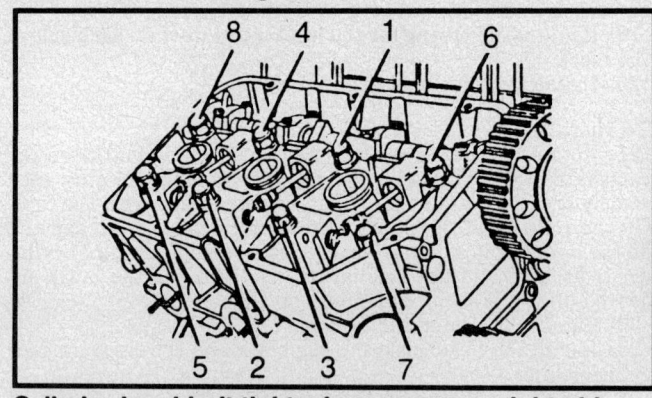

Cylinder head bolt tightening sequence, right side shown—164 series with 3.0L engine

Valve Lash

Adjustment
SPIDER

1. Disconnect the negative battery cable.
2. Disconnect and tag all vacuum hoses, electrical connections and fuel system components to gain access the the camshaft covers.
4. Remove the right and left camshaft covers.
5. Check the valve clearance as follows:
   a. Clean the spark plug housings and remove the spark plugs. Plug the holes to prevent entry of foreign materials.
   b. With the engine cold, check the clearance between the cams rest angle and the top of the valve caps is between 0.0157–0.0177 in. (0.400–0.450mm) for the intake and between 0.0177–0.0197 in. (0.450–0.500mm) for the exhaust.

6. Adjust the valve clearance as follows:
   a. Rotate the crankshaft until the notches on the camshaft are aligned with the notches on the related caps. When in this position, the alignment between the fixed index and the notch **P** on the front pulley must correspond with the No. 1 piston in the TDC position.
   b. Release the chain tightener securing screw, compress the chain downwards so as to overcome the tension load of the chain tightener spring and lock the chain tightener in this position.
   c. Remove the camshaft caps, then remove the complete camshaft and chain and rest on the central part of the head.
   d. Remove the valve bowl and the valve clearance adjusting cap and measure the adjusting cap thickness. Select a new cap of suitable thickness.
   e. Lubricate and install the valve bowel, camshaft and chain.

f. Install the caps on the camshaft following the numbering marked on them and tighten the retaining nuts to 15–16 ft. lbs. (20–22 Nm).

7. Check the chain tensioning as follows:

a. Loosen the chain tightener securing screw.

b. Engage the 5th speed gear, move the vehicle forwards and backwards and while keeping the cahin stretched, lock the chain tightener securing screw.

8. Adjust the timing system as follows:

a. With the 5th speed gear engaged, move the vehicle forwards and backwards until the No. 1 piston is at TDC with the valves closed.

b. Make sure when the cams of cylinder No.1 are outward, the notches on the camshaft pins are aligned with those on the caps.

9. If the notches on the left camshaft (exhaust valves) are not aligned proceed as follows:

a. Lift the edge of the nut clamp and by means of tool A.5.0103 or equivalent, used as a blocking device, loosen the retaining nut securing the gear to the camshaft.

b. Remove the bolt securing gear to the sleeve on the camshaft.

Loosening the chain tightener securing screw—Spider with the 2.0L engine

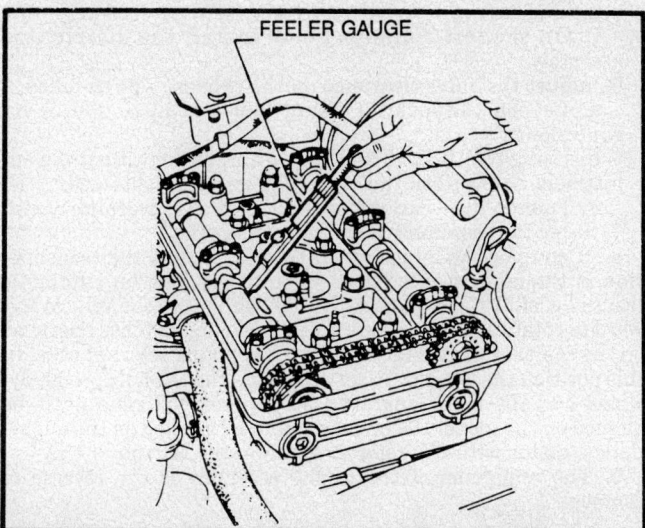

Checking the valve clearance—Spider with the 2.0L engine

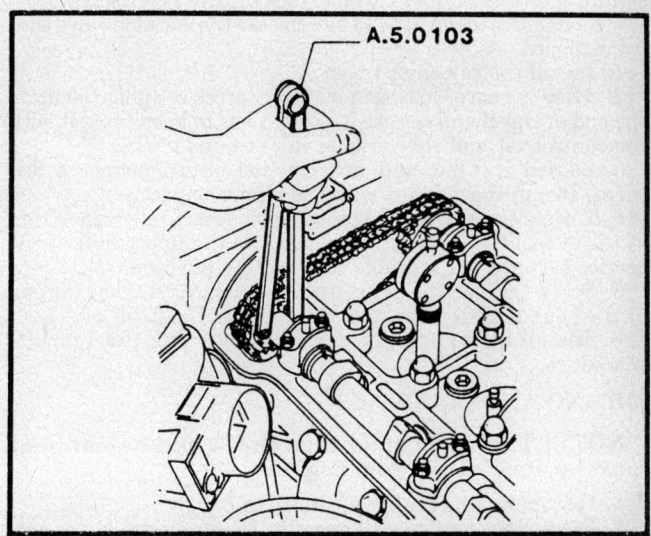

Using tool as a blocking device—Spider with the 2.0L engine

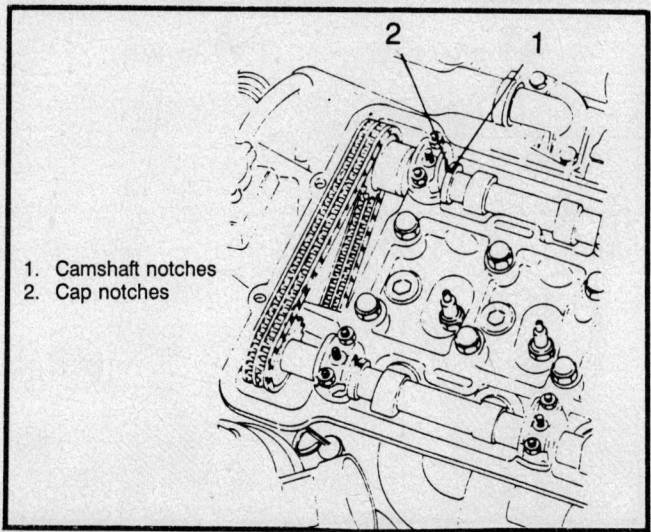

1. Camshaft notches
2. Cap notches

Camshaft and cap notch location—Spider with the 2.0L engine

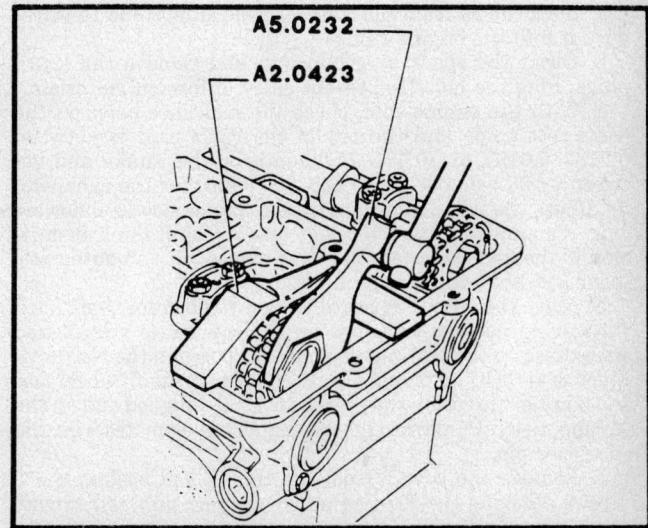

Locking the variable valve timing device—Spider with the 2.0L engine

c. Using tool A.5.0103 or equivalent, as a blocking device, tighten the nut previously loosened.

d. Fit the nut in the aligned holes of the gears, tighten it and bend the clamp on the nut.

10. If the notches on the right camshaft (intake valves), fitted with the variable valve timing device are not aligned, proceed as follows:

a. Lock the variable valve timing device, by means of tool A.2.0423 or equivalent, and loosen the securing nut, using wrench A.5.0232 or equivalent, not further than ⅛ turn.

b. Remove tool A.2.0423 and release the camshaft.

c. Loosen the nut further so the gear is completely disengaged from the front coupling.

d. Rotate the camshaft until the reference notches are aligned.

e. Tighten the nut until the gear is blocked on the front coupling.

f. Block the variable valve timing device, using tool A.2.0423 or equivalent.

g. Tighten the nut, using wrench A.5.0232 or equivalent until a torque of 65–71 ft. lbs. (88–96 Nm) is obtained.

h. Remove tool A.2.0423 and release the variable valve timing device.

11. Install the camshaft cover.

12. After the cover has been installed, press the pushrod up to the end of travel and release it slowly so as to keep contact with the control valve of the variable valve timing device.

13. Loosen the nut and unscrew the electromagnet a few turns. Install the support with the electromagnet.

14. Unscrew the electromagnet further so as to allow insertion of the of tool C.6.0203 or equivalent, via the upper hole of the carrier between the movable core and the pushrod.

15. Screw the electromagnet until the pushrod reaches the end of travel and tighten the nut. Remove tool C.6.0203.

16. Install all remaining parts by reversing the removal procedure.

MILANO AND 164 SERIES

NOTE: The valve clearance check and adjustment must be done with a cold engine.

1. Disconnect the negative battery cable.

2. Disconnect and tag all vacuum hoses, electrical connections and fuel system components to gain access the the camshaft covers.

3. Remove the right and left camshaft covers.

4. Check the valve clearance as follows:

a. Suck the oil from the cylinder head sumps and re-introduce it into the engine sump.

b. Clean the spark plug housings and remove the spark plugs. Plug the holes to prevent entry of foreign materials.

c. With the engine cold, check the clearance between the cams rest angle and the top of the valve caps is between 0.0187–0.0197 in. (0.475–0.500mm) for the intake and between 0.0088–0.0098 in. (0.225–0.250mm) for the exhaust.

5. Adjust the valve clearance on the intake side as follows:

a. If equipped with a manual transaxle, shift the transmission in the highest speed gear. If equipped with an automatic transaxle, shift the transmission in **D**.

b. Move the vehicle forward to rotate the crankshaft until the timing notches engraved on the camshafts are aligned with those on the relevant caps. In this position the No. 1 cylinder is at TDC on the 164 and the hole on the flywheel and the mark engraved on the gearbox cone are aligned and on the Milano, notch **P**, marked on the engine pulley mates with the reference pin.

c. Remove the covers from the timing belt casing, the 3 screws securing the toothed pulley support hub and extract the support hub and seal using a puller.

d. Remove the camshaft caps.

e. On the model 164, on the left cylinder head, remove the

distributor cap, rotor arm and body.

f. Withdraw the camshaft by lifting from the rear end.

g. Withdraw a valve cup and relevant adjustment cap.

h. Check that the clearance between the cams rest angle and the top of the valve caps is between 0.0187–0.0197 in. (0.475–0.500mm). Select a new cap of the proper thickness, lubricate with engine oil and install together with the valve cup. Tighten the cap retaining nuts to 11.8–13.2 ft. lbs. (16–18 Nm).

NOTE: Observe the numbering and arrow engraved on the caps.

i. Rotate the camshaft to align the notches on the camshaft to those engraved on the relevant cap and check the alignment of the flywheel hole with the notch engraved on the gearbox cone on the model 164 and the notch **P**, marked on the engine pulley mates, with the reference pin on the Milano.

j. Install the toothed pulley support hub along with a new seal. Do not tighten the attaching screws at this time.

k. Install the nut retaining the toothed pulley to the camshaft and while keeping the pulley from rotating tighten the lock nut to 71.6–86.3 ft. lbs. (97–117 Nm). Tighten the pulley attaching screws.

l. On the left cylinder head, install the distributor assembly.

6. Adjust the valve clearance on the exhaust side as follows:

a. Loosen the locknut using tool 1.822.016.000 or its equivalent.

b. Using tool 1.822.016.000 or its equivalent, turn the adjustment screw until the correct clearance is obtained.

c. Tighten the locknut and check the valve clearance again.

7. Prior to reassembly align the camshaft.

8. If equipped with a manual transaxle, shift the transmission in the highest speed gear. If equipped with an automatic transaxle, shift the transmission in **D** and move the vehicle forward to rotate the crankshaft until the timing notches engraved on the camshafts are aligned with those on the relevant caps. In this position the No. 1 cylinder is at TDC and the hole on the flywheel and the mark engraved on the gearbox cone must be aligned on the model 164 and the notch **P**, marked on the engine pulley, mates with the reference pin on the Milano.

9. The remainder if the of the assembly is the reverse of removal.

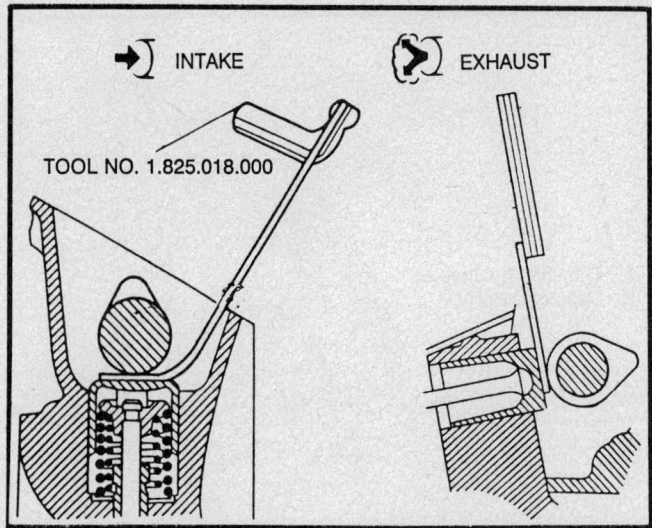

Check the valve clearance with a feeler gauge at these locations—Milano and 164 series

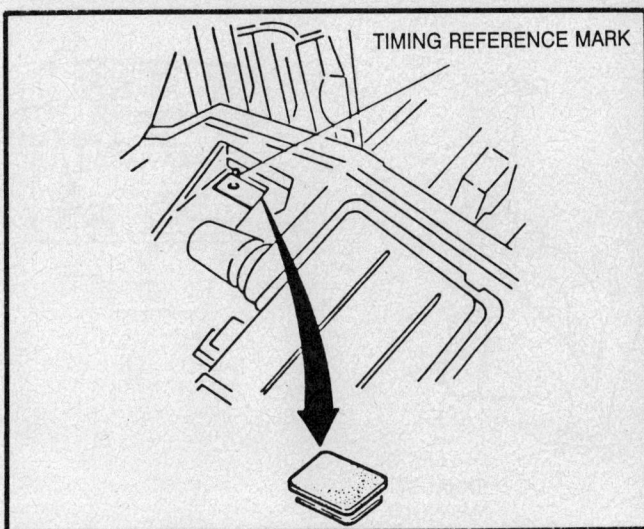

Align the hole on the flywheel with the notch engraved on the gearbox cone—Milano and model 164

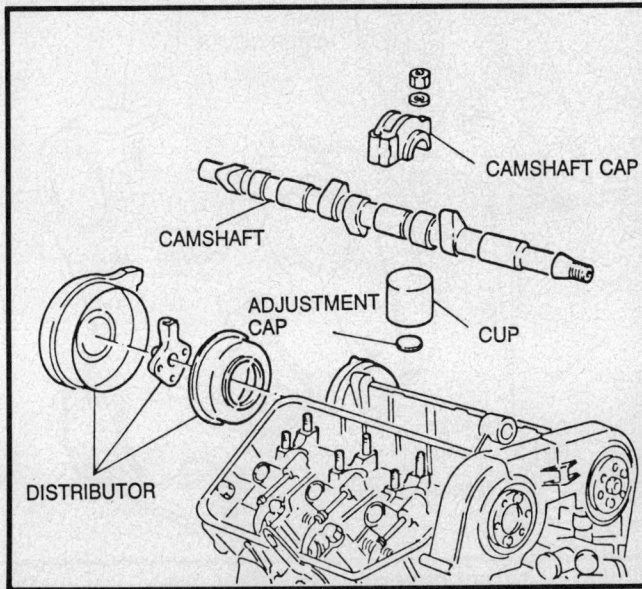

Adjustment cap, left side shown—164 series

Intake Manifold

Removal and Installation

164 SERIES

1. Disconnect the negative battery cable.
2. Remove the air intake box assembly.
   a. Unplug the idle speed actuator.
   b. Disconnect the oil fumes recovery hose.
   c. Disconnect the oil recovery hose.
   d. Unplug the throttle valve min/max opening switch connector.
   e. Disconnect the vacuum pipe for the fuel pressure regulator and the fuel vapors and cruise control hose.
   f. Disconnect the throttle body inlet and outlet coolant hoses.
   g. Remove the throttle body cover.
   h. On the 164S only, remove the engine throttle sensor.
   i. If equipped with automatic transaxle, disconnect the kickdown cable.
   j. Disconnect the vacuum inake hose from the power brake.
   k. Loosen the air intake duct clamps, remove the screws and remove the air intake box assembly.
3. Remove the retaining bolts and remove the air intake pipes.
4. Remove the retaining bolts and remove the intake manifold and gasket.
5. Installation is the reverse of removal.

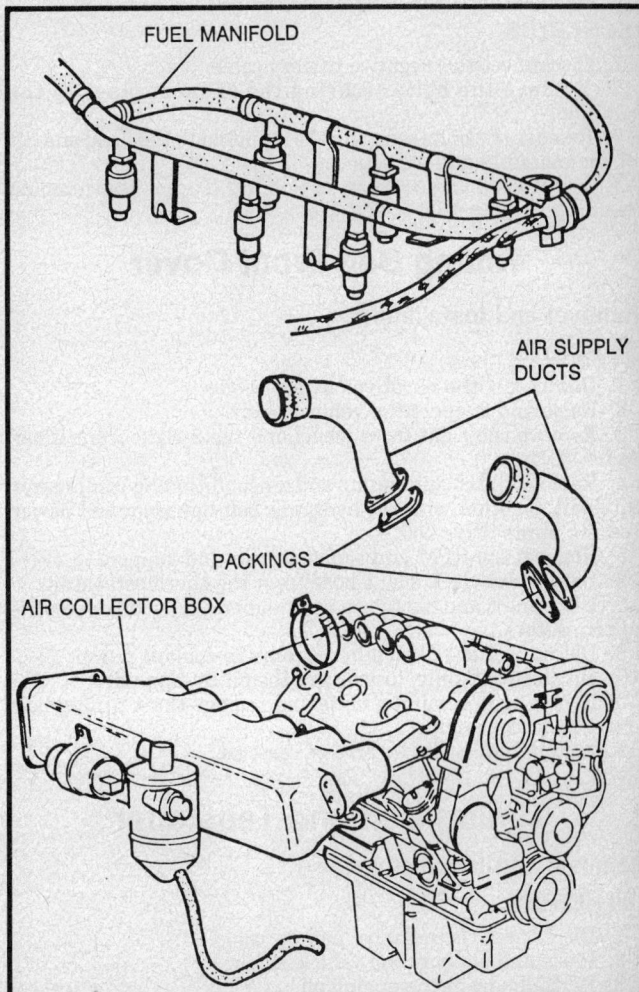

Air collector box and intake ducts—164 series

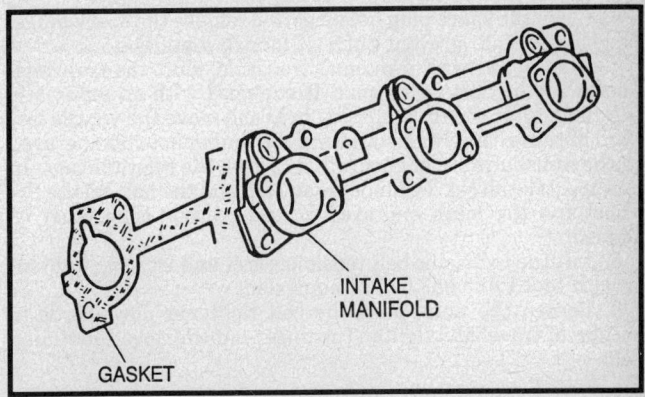

Intake manifold—164 series

Exhaust Manifold

Removal and Installation

SPIDER

1. Disconnect the negative battery cable.
2. Remove the bolts securing the exhaust pipes to the manifold.
3. Remove the bolts securing the manifold to the head and lift off the manifold and gaskets.
4. Installation is the reverse of removal.

164 SERIES

1. Disconnect the negative battery cable.
2. Remove the bolts securing the exhaust pipes to the manifold.
3. Remove the bolts securing the manifold to the head and lift off the manifold and gaskets.
4. Installation is the reverse of removal. Torque the manifold retaining bolts to 18.8 ft. lbs. (25.5 Nm).

Timing Belt Front Cover

Removal and Installation

164 SERIES

1. Disconnect the negative battery cable.
2. Raise and support the vehicle safely.
3. Remove the right front wheel and the 2 right front inner fender skirts.
4. Remove the coolant pump and air conditioning compressor drive belt, together with the hydraulic belt tightener and power steering pump drive belt.
5. Remove the RPM and stroke sensor and support.
6. Disconnect the coolant hose from the thermostat unit.
7. Disconnect and tag the engine temperature sensors electrical connectors.
8. Disconnect the return hose from the coolant pump.
9. On the 164S only, disconnect the oil cooling lines.
10. Remove the retaining bolts and remove the 4 timing belt covers from the engine.
11. Installation is the reverse of removal.

Timing Belt and Tensioner

Removal and Installation

164 SERIES

1. Disconnect the negative battery cable.
2. Raise and support the vehicle safely.
3. Partially drain the engine oil.
4. Remove both camshaft covers.
5. Remove the 4 covers protecting the timing belt.
6. Clean the spark plug housings and remove the spark plugs. Plug the holes to prevent entry of foreign materials.
7. If equipped with a manual transaxle, shift the transmission in the highest speed gear. If equipped with an automatic transaxle, shift the transmission in **D** and move the vehicle forward to rotate the crankshaft until the timing notches engraved on the camshafts are aligned with those on the relevant caps. In this position the No. 1 cylinder is at TDC and the hole on the flywheel and the mark engraved on the gearbox cone must be aligned.
8. Lift the hydraulic belt tensioner arm and lock the tightener with tool 1.820.053.000 or equivalent.
9. Loosen the nuts, push the belt tightener downwards to bottom of travel and tighten the upper nut. Remove the timing belt.

To install:

10. Make sure each camshaft of each head timing notches are

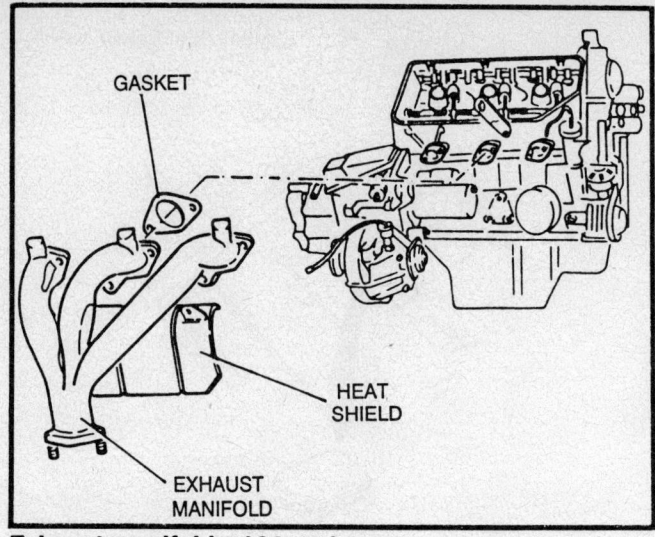
Exhaust manifold—164 series

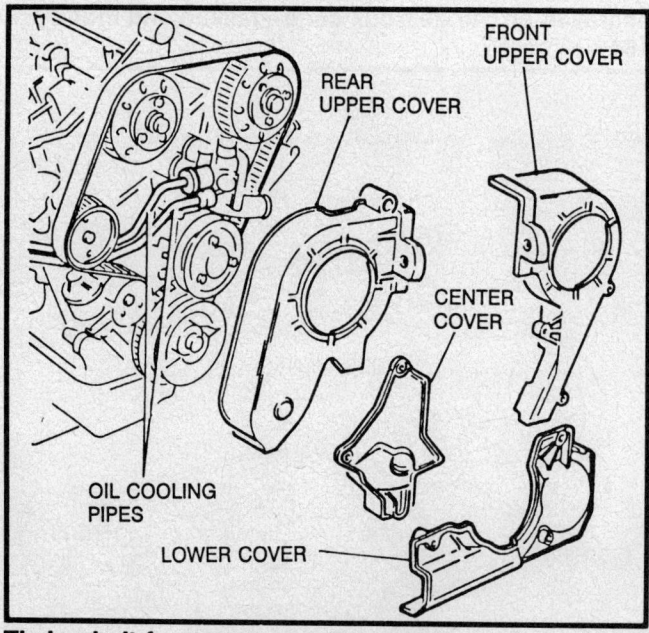
Timing belt front covers—164 series

in line with the caps. On the right head the notch corrosponds with the 3rd cap and on the left head it is on cap No. 7. In this position the No. 1 cylinder is at TDC and the hole on the flywheel and the mark engraved on the gearbox cone must be aligned.

11. Make sure the No. 1 cylinder is at TDC and the hole on the flywheel and the mark engraved on the gearbox cone are be aligned.
12. Install the toothed belt maintaining under pressure the stretched arms and reassemble in the following order:
   • Crankshaft toothed pulley
   • Left cylinder head toothed pulley
   • Right cylinder head toothed pulley
   • Oil pump toothed pulley
   • Belt tightener pulley
13. Loosen the nuts securing the belt tensioners.
14. If equipped with a manual transaxle, shift the transmission in the highest speed gear. If equipped with an automatic transaxle, shift the transmission in **D** and move the vehicle forward to rotate the crankshaft 2 revolutions until the timing

notches engraved on the camshafts are aligned with those on the relevant caps. In this position the No. 1 cylinder is at TDC and the hole on the flywheel and the mark engraved on the gearbox cone must be aligned.

15. keep the belt under tension, press the tightener pulley against the belt and tighten the 2 nuts securing the belt tensioner.

16. Slightly lift the tensioner arm and remove the pin and relaese the tightener arm.

17. The remainder of the installation is the reverse of removal.

Camshaft Sprockets

Removal and Installation

164 SERIES

1. Disconnect the negative battery cable.
2. Remove the timing belt.
3. Using tool 1.820.051.000 torque reactor or equivalent, to hold the sprocket, remove the sprocket attaching nut.
4. Remove the 3 screws attaching the support hub to the sprocket.
5. Using puller 1.821.123.000 and torque reactor 1.820.051.000 or their equivalents, remove the support hub.
6. Remove the seal ring from the hub.
7. Remove the sprocket and oil ring.
8. Installtion is the revrse of removal. Grease and insert the oil seal ring, using tool 1.821.126.000 or equivalent. Tighten the front hub attaching nut to 71.6–80.3 ft. lbs. (97–117 Nm).

Camshaft

Removal and Installation

164 SERIES

1. Disconnect the negative battery cable.
2. Remove the air intake box assembly.
   a. Unplug the idle speed actuator.
   b. Disconnect the oil fumes recovery hose.
   c. Disconnect the oil recovery hose.
   d. Unplug the throttle valve min/max opening switch connector.
   e. Disconnect the vacuum pipe for the fuel pressure regulator and the fuel vapors and cruise control hose.
   f. Disconnect the throttle body inlet and outlet coolant hoses.
   g. Remove the throttle body cover.
   h. On the 164S only, remove the engine throttle sensor.
   i. If equipped with automatic transaxle, disconnect the kickdown cable.
   j. Disconnect the vacuum inake hose from the power brake.
   k. Loosen the air intake duct clamps, remove the screws and remove the air intake box assembly.

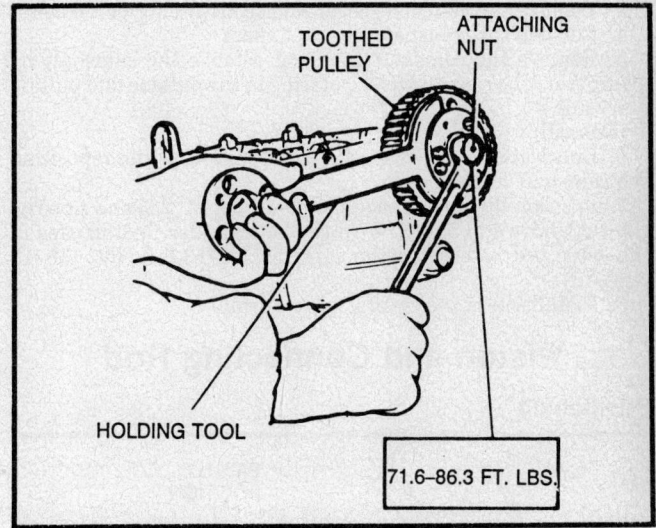

Camshaft sprocket removal—164 series

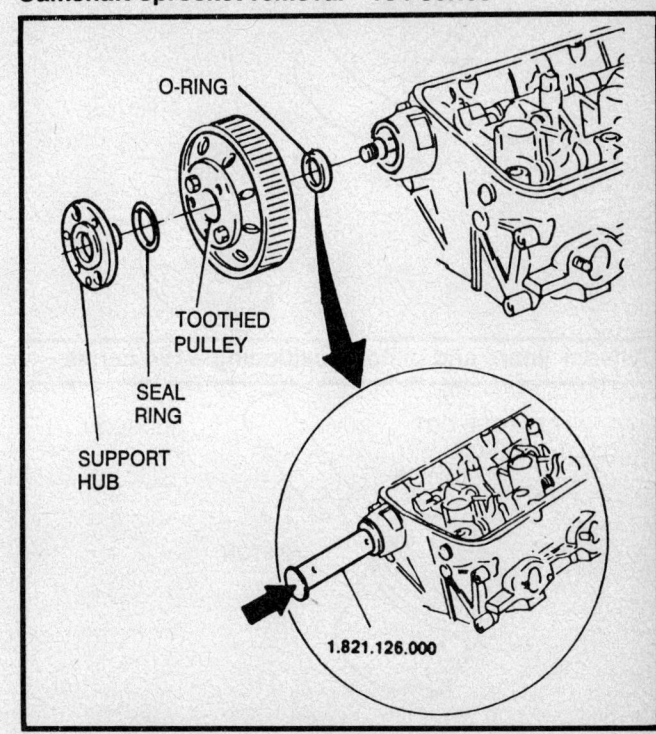

Camsshaft sprocket installation—164 series

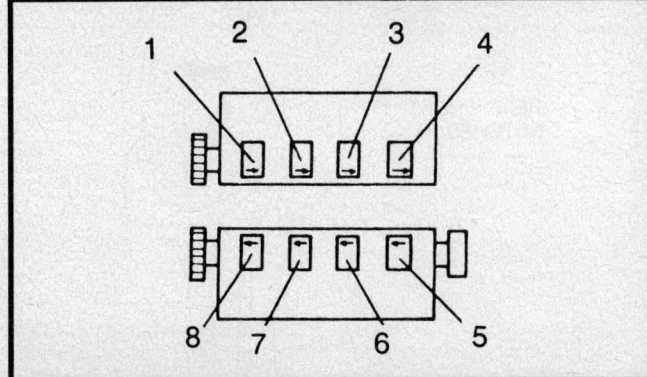

Camshaft cap numbering sequence—164 series

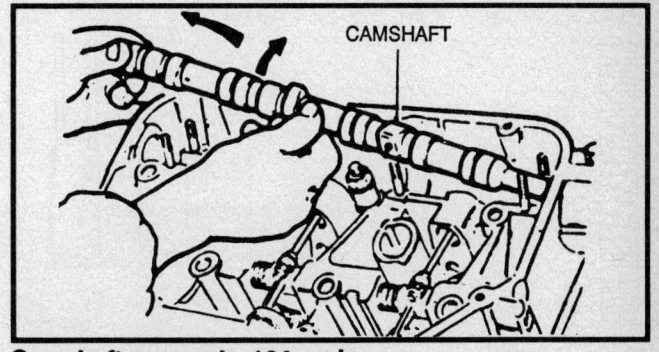

Camshaft removal—164 series

3. Remove the camshaft cover and front timing belt covers.

4. Remove the camshaft sprocket gears.

5. Remove the camshaft caps and remove the camshaft by lifting from the rear end first, rotating to the outside and pulling rearward.

To install:

6. Lubricate the journals with clean engine oil and reposition the camshaft in the head.

7. Position the caps in sequence. Numbers 1, 2, 3 and 4 on the right cylinder and 5, 6, 7, 8 on the left cylinder. Install caps in the same order. Tighten the caps to 11.8–13.2 ft. lbs. (16–18 Nm).

8. Installtion is the reverse of removal.

Piston and Connecting Rod

Positioning

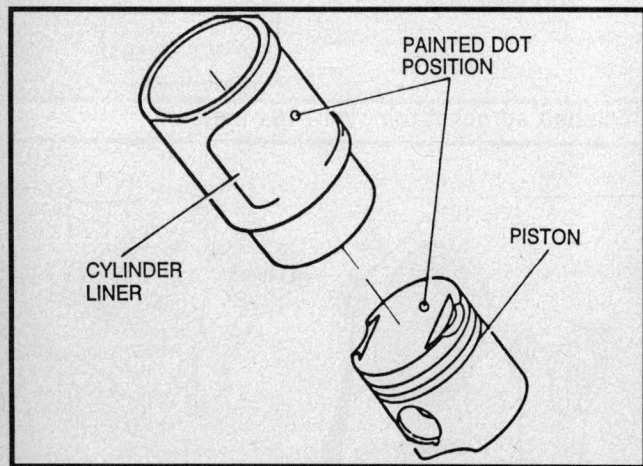

Cylinder liners and piston positioning—164 series

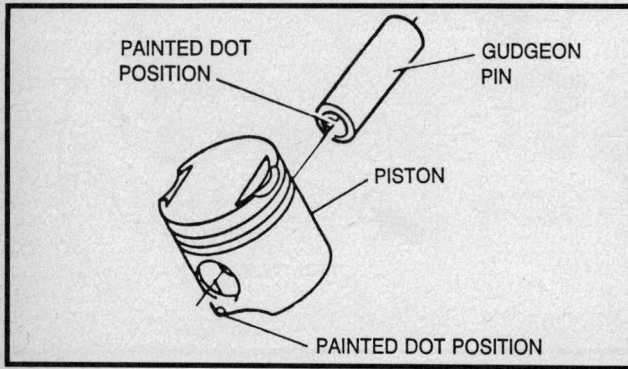

Piston and pins positioning—164 series

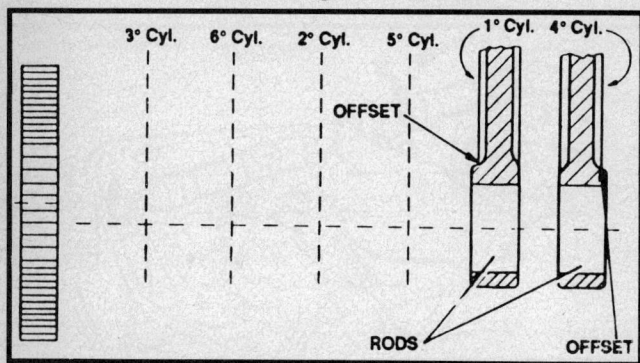

Piston and rods positioning—164 series

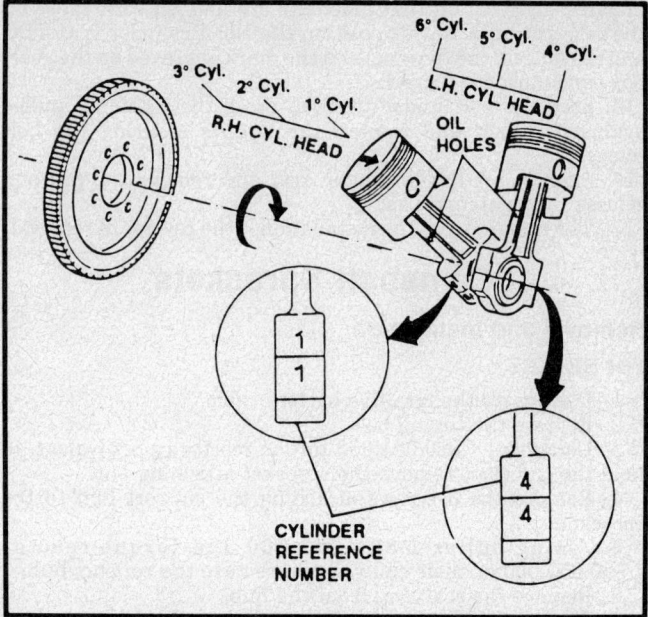

Piston and rods positioning—164 series

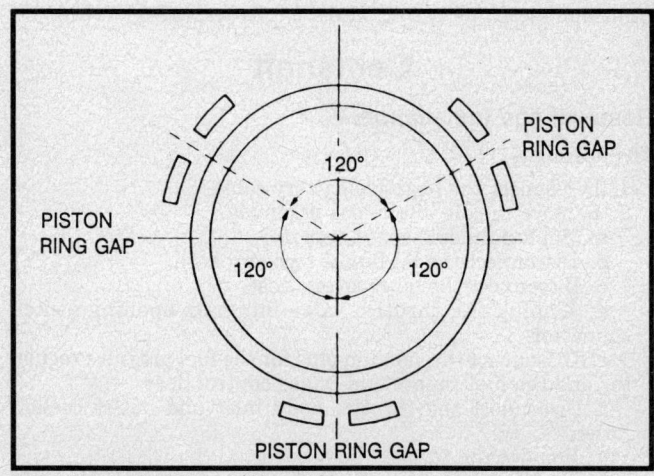

Ring installation—164 series

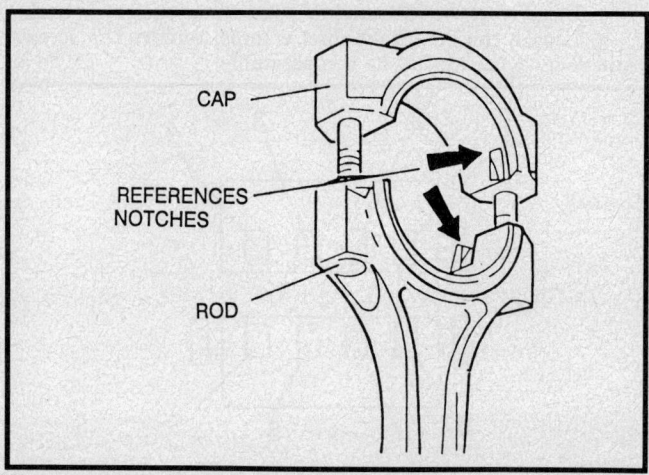

Connecting rod and cap—164 series

ENGINE LUBRICATION

Oil Pan

Removal and Installation

MILANO AND 164 SERIES

1. Raise and support the vehicle safely.
2. On the 164, remove the exhaust pipe.
3. Remove the oil pan attaching screws and remove the oil pan and gasket.
4. Installation is the reverse of removal.

Oil Pump

Removal and Installation

MILANO

1. Raise and support the vehicle safely.
2. Drain the engine oil.
3. Remove the oil pan attaching screws and remove the oil pan and gasket.
4. Reemove the oil pump retaining bolts and remove the oil pump and suction screen.
5. Installation is the reverse of removal. Tighten the oil pump retaining bolts to 13.7–17.4 ft. lbs. (19–24 Nm).

164 SERIES

The oil pump is attached to the lower innner side of the engine block and is driven by a timing toothed belt through a pulley and a shaft.

1. Raise and support the vehicle safely.
2. Drain the engine oil.
3. Remove the exhaust pipe.
4. Remove the oil pan attaching screws and remove the oil pan and gasket.
5. Remove the oil pump retaining bolts and remove the oil pump and suction screen.

MANUAL TRANSMISSION

Transmission Assembly

For further information, please refer to "Professional Transmission Repair Manual" for additional coverage.

Removal and Installation

SPIDER

1. Disconnect the negative battery cable.
2. From inside the passenger compartment, remove the console, clamp and rubber bellows.
3. Unscrew the bolt securing the gear selector rod to the trunnion pivot pin and remove the rod.
4. Raise and support the vehicle safely.
5. Disconnect the rear exhaust pipe from the front exhaust pipe.
6. Partially disconnect and bend the shield above the catalytic converter, to gain access to the 6 tie bar to body retaining screws and remove the tie bar.
7. Scribe marks on the driveshaft and remove the 4 bolts at the flanges.
8. Remove the bolt securing the transmission to the cross bar, unscrew the 4 screws and remove the cross bar and rubber support washers.
9. Uncrew the tachometer cable, the 3 carrier retaining nuts and remove the carrier along with the bracket.
10. Remove the 2 nuts securing the transmission central carrier to the body frame.
11. Remove the bolt and nut retaining the muffler to the body.
12. Disconnect the back up light wiring connection.
13. Using a syringe, empty the hydraulic system tank, disconnect the union, hose and ground wire.
14. Disconnect the electronic ignition system connectors.
15. Safely support the transmission with a suitable lifting device.
16. Uscrew the nuts securing the transmission and clutch assembly to the engine and the 3 bolts securing the starter motor and while securing the washers, slide off the whole assembly.
17. Remove the 3 bolts securing the flexible coupling of the front driveshaft to the transmission output driveshaft fork.
To install:
18. Install the 3 bolts securing the flexible coupling of the front driveshaft to the transmission output driveshaft fork and tighten to 39.8–41.3 ft. lbs. (54–56 Nm).
19. Reposition the whole assembly, using a suitable lifting device and install the nuts securing the transmission and clutch assembly to the engine and the 3 bolts and washers securing the starter motor.
20. Connect the electronic ignition system connectors.
21. Connect the union, hose and ground wire to the hydraulic system tank.
22. Connect the back up light wiring connection.
23. Install the bolt and nut retaining the muffler to the body.
24. Install the 2 nuts securing the transmission central carrier to the body frame and tighten to 72.3–101.1 ft. lbs. (98–137 Nm).
25. Install the 3 carrier retaining nuts and install the carrier along with the bracket. Install the tachometer cable.
26. Install the 4 screws and install the cross bar and rubber support washers.
27. Install the bolt securing the transmission to the cross bar.
28. Install the 4 bolts connecting the driveshaft front and rear flanges, aligning the scribe marks and tighten to 27.3–28.8 ft. lbs. (37–39 Nm).
29. Install the 6 tie bar to body retaining screws and install the tie bar.
30. Connect and bend the shield in place above the catalytic converter.
31. Connect the rear exhaust pipe to the front exhaust pipe.
32. Lower the vehicle and install the bolt securing the gear selector rod to the trunnion pivot pin.
33. From inside the passenger compartment, install the console, clamp and rubber bellows.
34. Connect the negative battery cable.

164 SERIES

1. Disconnect the negative battery cable.
2. Raise and support the vehicle safely.
3. Remove the hood.
4. Remove the front wheels.
5. Disconnect the hoses from the intake duct and the electrical connection from the air flow meter and remove the air filter cover, air flow meter and intake duct assembly.
6. Remove the air filter and canister.

7. Remove the cruise control actuator.

8. Remove the air filter support bracket.

9. Remove the front exhaust pipes and the rear exhaust manifold along with the engine starter shroud.

10. Remove the clutch actuating cylinder and bracket and move aside.

11. Disconnect the backup light switch.

12. On the 164S, disconnect the gearbox sensor electrical connector.

13. Disconnect the ground strap and the odometer sensor.

14. Release the clips and and remove the gear selector cover.

15. On the 164S, remove the left front suspension electrical connector protective cover from the rear fender.

16. Remove the brake caliper and support it aside.

17. Disconnect the left CV-joint from the differential flange.

18. Using tool 1.821.174.000 or equivalent, withdraw the pin from the steering cross tie rod spherical joint and disconnect the spherical joint from the suspension arm.

19. Disconnect the shock absorber, hub and axle shaft as a unit.

20. Remove the flywheel cover.

21. Disconnect the speed engagement control rod.

22. Remove the speed selection rod bracket.

23. Remove the gearbox attaching bolt and install the lifting bracket on the gearbox unit using the bolt.

24. Install an engine support cross beam 1.820.581.000 or equivalent, and engage it to the relevant lifting brackets.

25. Remove the gearbox mount.

26. Drain the oil from the gearbox-differential.

27. Remove the right front inner fender skirt.

28. Disconnect the right axle CV-joint from the intermediate shaft.

29. Remove the bolt securing the intermediate shaft flange to the rear engine mount and withdraw the shaft from the differential.

NOTE: It may be necessary to lift the engine with a column type hydraulic jack.

30. Disconnect the speed selector control rod to gain access to the bolt securing the gearbox mount.

31. Remove the bolts securing the gearbox to the engine, with the exception of bolt "A", which must be left installed.

32. Connect the hook of a suitable hoist and lift the transmission after the bolt "A", has been removed.

33. Remove the solenoid valve group from the support in the

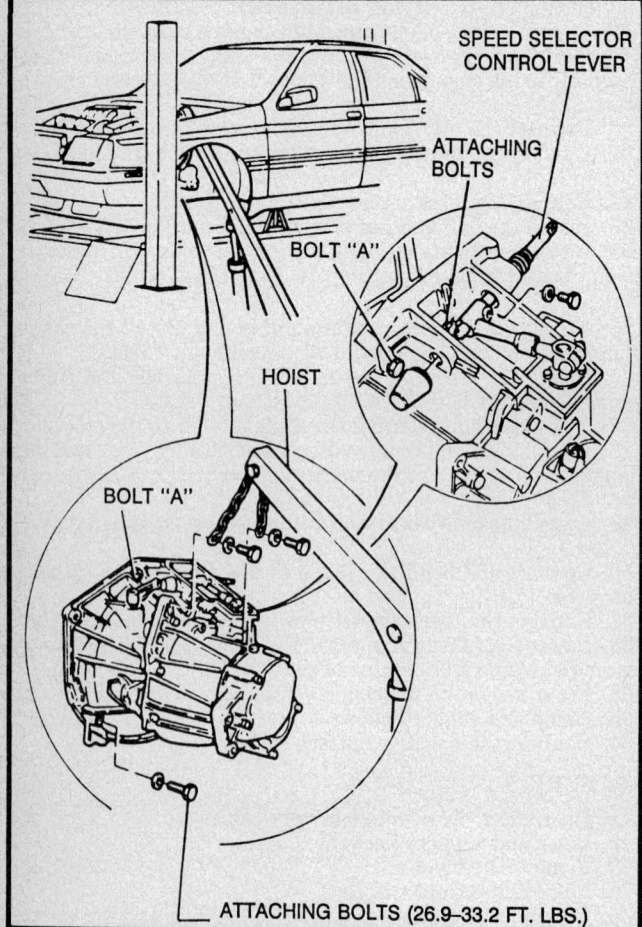

Leave bolt "A" in place before connecting the lifting device, then remove—164 series

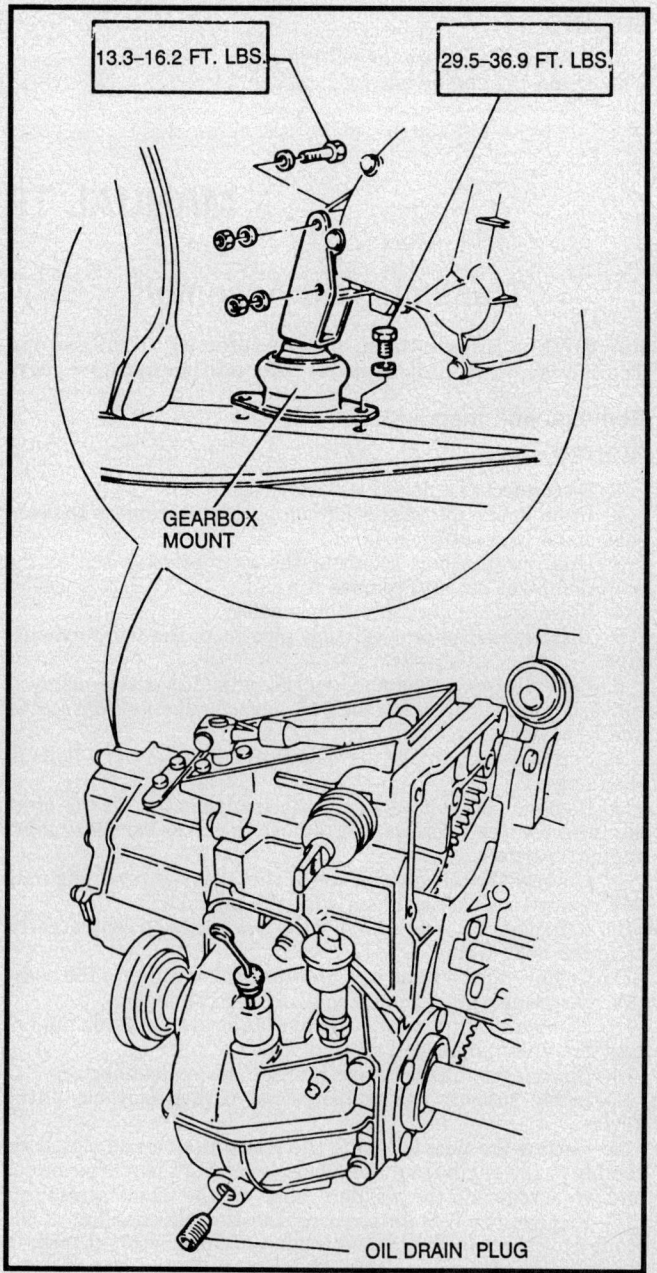

Gearbox mounting—164 series

engine compartment and move aside being careful not to damage the tubes.

34. Remove the solenoid valve group support.
35. Remove the inductive sensor and support.

To install:

36. Install the inductive sensor and support.
37. Install the solenoid valve group support and solenoid valve.
38. Connect the hook of a suitable hoist and reposition the transmission in the vehicle and install the bolts connecting the gearbox to the engine.
39. Connect the speed selector control rod.
40. Install intermediate shaft to the differential and the bolt securing the shaft flange to the rear engine mount.

NOTE: It may be necessary to lift the engine with a column type hydraulic jack.

41. Connect the right axle CV-joint to the intermediate shaft.
42. Install the right front inner fender skirt.
43. Install the gearbox mount.
44. Remove the engine support cross beam 1.820.581.000 or equivalent.
45. Remove the lifting bracket on the gearbox unit, then reinstall the gearbox attaching bolt.
46. Install the speed selection rod bracket.

47. Install the flywheel cover.
48. Connect the shock absorber, hub and axle shaft.
49. Install the pin to the steering cross tie rod spherical joint and suspension arm.
50. Connect the left cv-joint to the differential flange.
51. Install the brake caliper.
52. On the 164S, install the left front suspension electrical connector protective cover to the rear fender.
53. Install the gear selector cover.
54. Connect the ground strap and the odometer sensor.
55. On the 164S, connect the gearbox sensor electrical connector and the backup light switch.
56. Install the clutch actuating cylinder and bracket.
57. Install the front exhaust pipes and the rear exhaust manifold along with the engine starter shroud.
58. Install the air filter support bracket.
59. Install the cruise control actuator.
60. Install the air filter and canister.
61. Install the air flow meter, intake duct and air filter cover assembly and connect the hoses to the intake duct and the electrical connection to the air flow meter.
62. Install the front wheels.
63. Reconnect the battery cable, fill the transmission with the proper lubricant and install the hood.

MANUAL TRANSAXLE

Transaxle Assembly

Removal and Installation

MILANO

1. Disconnect the negative battery cable.
2. Raise and support the vehicle safely.
3. Remove the drive shaft, clutch slave cylinder and disconnect the shift linkage.
4. Remove the 6 front support bolts.
5. Place a support tool A.2.0075 on a transmission jack under the center of the rear axle tube and raise the tube slowly. The front transaxle subassembly will drop away from the vehicle.
6. Position spacer support tool A.2.0268 between the axle side tubes and the vehicle body and remove the transmission jack.
7. Disconnect the front transaxle mounting bolts.
8. Remove the bolts that hold the axle shafts to the stub axle shafts.
9. Remove the rear brake rotors and calipers without disconnecting the fluid lines and support the calipers aside.
10. Place a transaxle support bracket tool R.4.0150 or equivalent, on a transmission jack under the transaxle.
11. Lower the transaxle and remove it from the vehicle.
12. Installation is the reverse of removal.

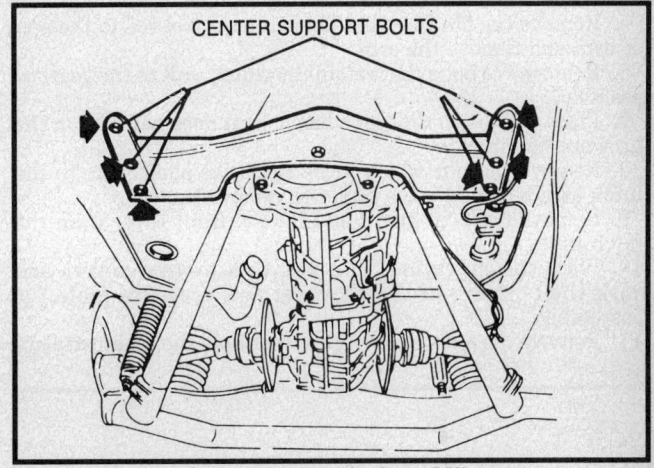
Removing the front support bolts—Milano

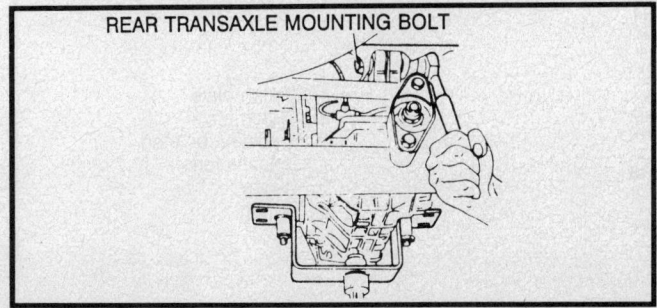
Removing the rear transaxle mounting bolts—Milano

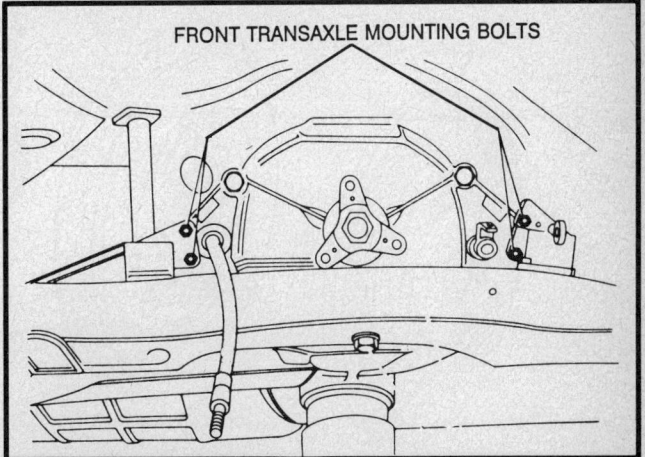
Removing the front transaxle mounting bolts—Milano

CLUTCH

Clutch Assembly

Removal and Installation

SPIDER AND 164 SERIES

1. Disconnect the negative battery cable.
2. Raise and support the vehicle safely.
3. Remove the transmission.
4. Scribe a corresponding marks on the clutch cover and flywheel.
5. Remove the 6 bolts and remove the cover and clutch plate.
6. If necessary, remove the center bushing from the transmission output shaft, the throwout bearing and release fork.

To install:

7. Install the center bushing on the output shaft, if removed.
8. Slide the clutch cover and plate onto a centering tool, and place the the clutch cover and flywheel on the flywheel, aligning the scribed marks.
9. Tighten the retaining bolts diagonally to 15.5–18.4 ft. lbs. (21–35 Nm).
10. Install the throwout bearing and release fork, if removed.
11. Install the transmission.

MILANO

1. Disconnect the negative battery cable.
2. Raise and support the vehicle safely.
3. Remove the transaxle.
4. Remove the clutch fork from the front housing.
5. Remove the pin that that holds the control rod to the sector arm and remove the arm.
6. Remove the bolts that retain the clutch unit to the gearbox assembly.
7. Place the clutch unit on a bench so it does not rest on the throwout bearing.
8. Remove the nut which holds the drive shaft yoke to the clutch assembly and use a puller to remove the yoke.
9. Remove the dust guard and lift the front cover from the clutch unit.
10. Place the clutch unit in a vise with protective jaws and mark the position of the flywheel and pressure plate for reassembly.
11. Remove the bolts and washers that hold the pressure plate

to the flywheel and separate the 2, exposing the clutch plate.
12. Using a puller, remove the pilot bearing from the flywheel shaft.
13. If necessary, remove the flywheel shaft retaining bolts.
14. With the rear pressure plate on the bench, press down on the diaphragm and release the circlip.
15. Remove the circlip, the throwout bearing fastening ring and remove the the throwout bearing from the pressure plate.
16. Remove the Beleville washer from the throwout bearing.
17. If necessary, remove the gear selector dust boot from the

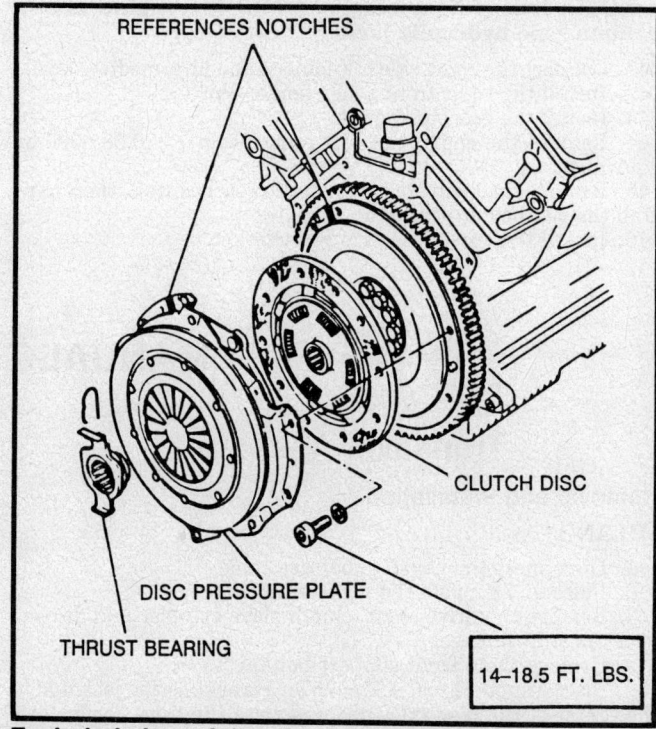

REFERENCES NOTCHES

CLUTCH DISC

DISC PRESSURE PLATE

THRUST BEARING

14–18.5 FT. LBS.

Exploded view of the clutch assembly—164 series

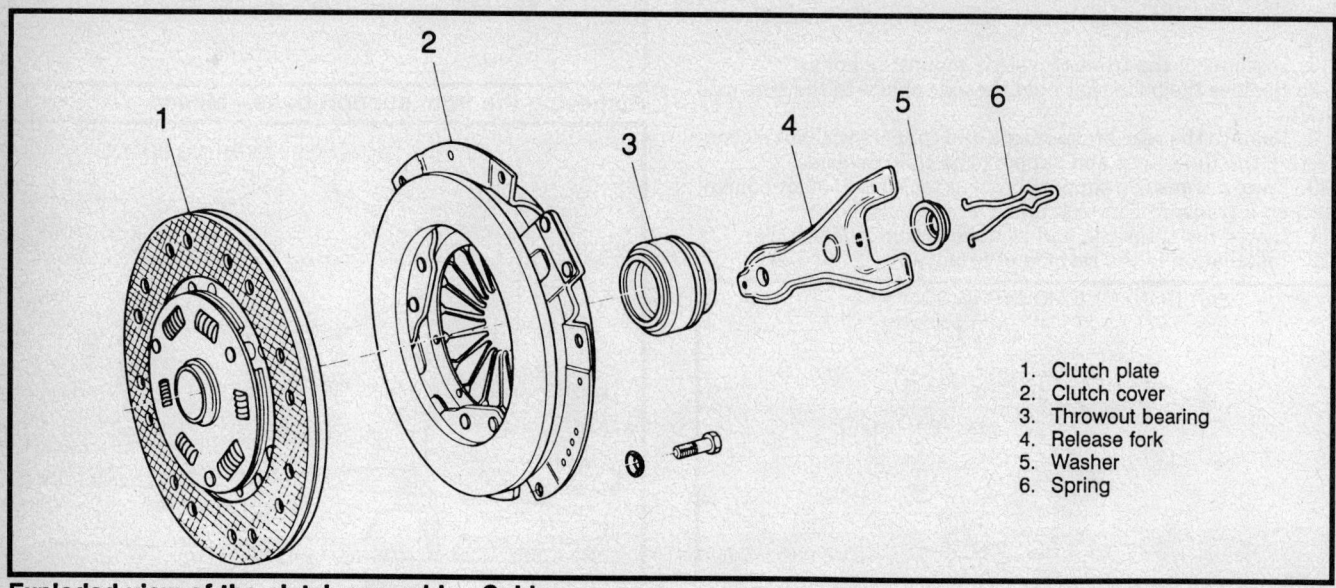

1. Clutch plate
2. Clutch cover
3. Throwout bearing
4. Release fork
5. Washer
6. Spring

Exploded view of the clutch assembly—Spider

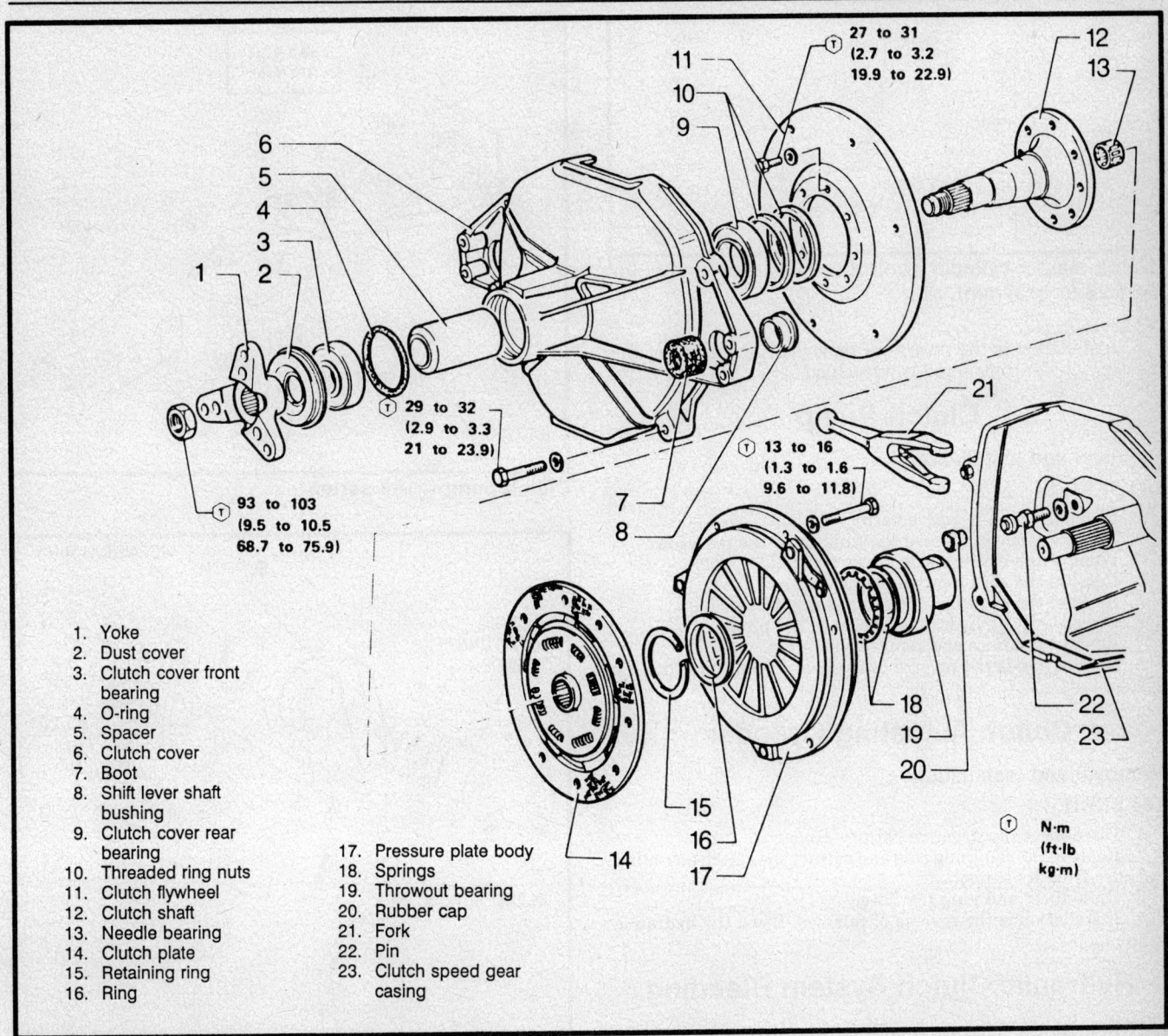

6
5
4
3
2
1

27 to 31
(2.7 to 3.2
19.9 to 22.9)
11
10
9

12
13

29 to 32
(2.9 to 3.3
21 to 23.9)

93 to 103
(9.5 to 10.5
68.7 to 75.9)

7
8

13 to 16
(1.3 to 1.6
9.6 to 11.8)

21

18
19
20

22
23

15
16
17

14

N·m
(ft·lb
kg·m)

1. Yoke
2. Dust cover
3. Clutch cover front bearing
4. O-ring
5. Spacer
6. Clutch cover
7. Boot
8. Shift lever shaft bushing
9. Clutch cover rear bearing
10. Threaded ring nuts
11. Clutch flywheel
12. Clutch shaft
13. Needle bearing
14. Clutch plate
15. Retaining ring
16. Ring
17. Pressure plate body
18. Springs
19. Throwout bearing
20. Rubber cap
21. Fork
22. Pin
23. Clutch speed gear casing

Exploded view of the clutch assembly—Milano

front cover. remove the rear bearing retaining locknuts, the front ball bearing, spacer and O-ring. Use an extractor, to drive the rear ball bearing from the cover.

To install:

18. Use a rear bearing driver tool, and install the clutch cover rear bearing and shoulder washer. Install the retaining ring, making sure it seats correctly.

19. Turn the cover over and install the spacer with the chamfered surface toward the front of the cover, then install the O-ring.

20. Install the clutch cover front bearing.

21. If disassembled, assemble the flywheel and shaft. Apply thread sealing compound and tighten the retaining bolts to 20–23 ft. lbs. (27–31 Nm)

22. Install the pilot bearing in the shaft, using a driver tool.

23. Install the throwout bearing, circlip and fastening ring on the pressure plate.

24. With the flywheel in a vise, use a clutch alignment tool and install the pressure plate and throwout bearing assembly on the flywheel, aligning the marks made during disassembly. Tighten

in the proper sequence to 9.6–11.8 ft. lbs. (13–16 Nm).

25. Remove the clutch alignment tool and place the clutch cover over the flywheel.

26. Install the dust cover, apply a new coating of sealant on the splines and place the yoke on the shaft. Tighten the yoke locknut to 69–76 ft. lbs. (93–103 Nm).

27. Install the shift lever shaft bushings and protective boot.

Clutch Master Cylinder

Removal and Installation

SPIDER

1. Disconnect the negative battery cable.

2. Using a syringe, remove the fluid from the clutch master cylinder reservoir and separate the reservoir from the master cylinder.

3. Disconnect the hydraulic line from the master cylinder.

4. Remove the cotter pin and separate the lever from the fork.

5. Remove the 2 bolts and separate the master cylinder from

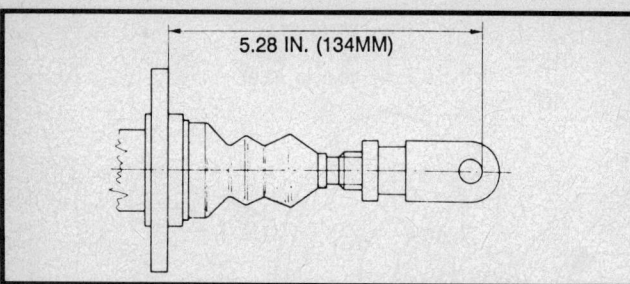

Clutch master cylinder control rod dimension should be 5.28 in. (134mm).

the servo brake.

6. Installation is the reverse of removal. Adjustment of the master cylinder control rod is wrench adjusted. Fill with fluid.

Clutch Pump

Removal and Installation

164 SERIES

1. Disconnect the negative battery cable.
2. Using a syringe, remove the fluid from the reservoir.
3. Remove the driver's side knees protection panel.
4. Remove the clutch pump plastic cover.
5. Remove the cotter pin at the clutch pump-pedal.
6. Disconnect the hydraulic line from the pump.
7. Remove the nuts and remove the pump.
8. Installation is the reverse of removal. Bleed the hydraulic system.

Clutch Actuating Cylinder

Removal and Installation

164 SERIES

1. Disconnect the negative battery cable.
2. Remove the retaining ring and extract the clutch actuating cylinder from its support.
3. Disconnect and plug the hose.
4. Installation is the reverse of removal. Bleed the hydraulic system.

Hydraulic Clutch System Bleeding

1. Remove the filler cap from the reservoir and if necessary top off with fluid.
2. Remove the protective cover from the bleeder valve, connect a hose to the valve and immerse the end of the hose in a transparent container containing fluid.
3. Loosen the bleeder valve and press the clutch pedal down allowing it to return slowly. Repeat until all bubbles have been removed.
4. Press the pedal all the way down, close the bleeder valve, remove the hose and install the cover.
5. Make sure the fluid level is at the correct level.

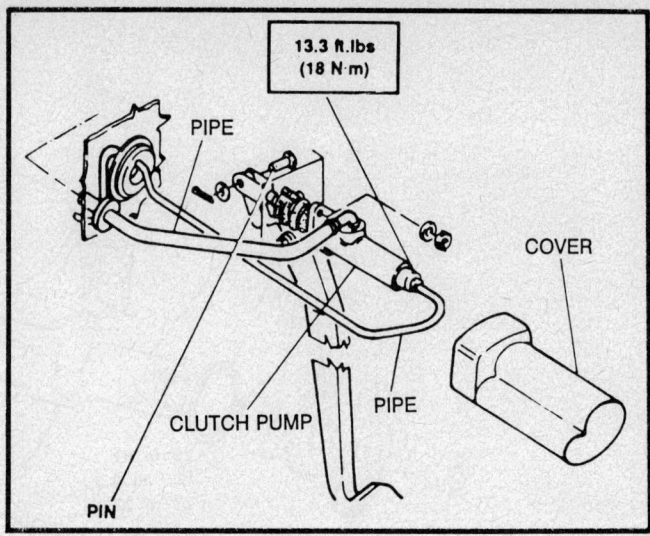

Clutch pump—164 series

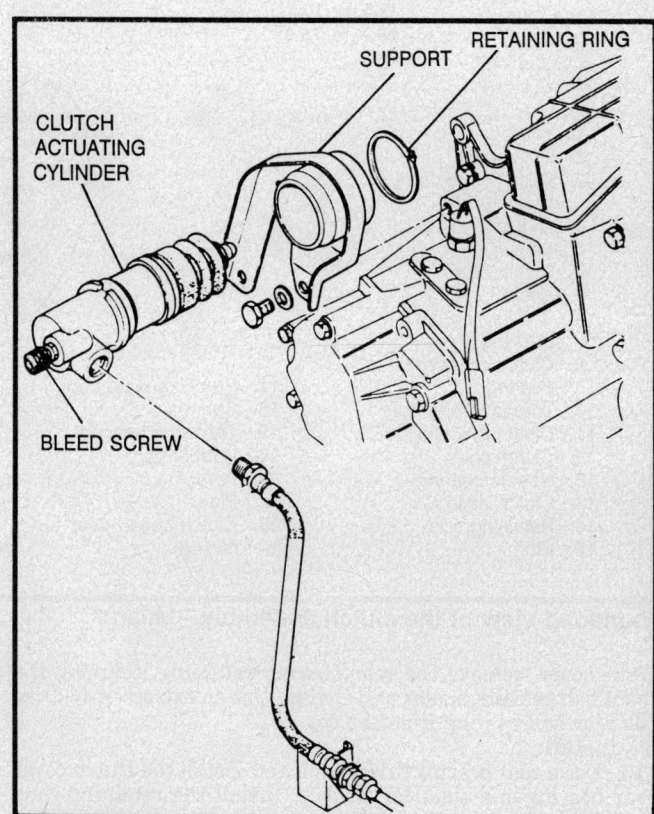

Clutch actuating cylinder—164 series

AUTOMATIC TRANSMISSION

Transmission Assembly

Removal and Installation

SPIDER

1. Disconnect the negative battery cable.
2. From inside the engine compartment, disconnect the lambda probe and remove the dipstick.
3. Remove the plastic shield and disconnect the kickdown cable.
4. Raise and support the vehicle safely.
5. Drain the fluid from the transmission.
6. Disconnect the front exhaust pipe from the manifold and move the entire front exhaust pipe aside.
7. Remove the 4 bolts and remove the transmission housing cover.
8. Remove the 4 bolts that retain the converter to the engine flywheel.
9. Disconnect the 2 hydraulic line fittings.
10. Scribe marks on the driveshaft and remove the 4 bolts at the flanges.
11. Remove the 8 bolts securing the transmission driveshaft cross bar, remove the split pin and pin and free the idler arm from the lever.
12. Remove the bolt securing the transmission to the transmission support cross bar, remove the 4 bolts and remove the cross bar and rubber support washers.
13. Disconnect the speedometer connector.
14. Remove the 2 nuts and bolt that retain the support to the transmission and remove the support together with the bracket.
15. Attach transmission lifting support 1.820.222.000 or equivalent to the transmission, using the 2 nuts on the rear side and the 2 nuts on the front side. Connect a column jack to the tool.
16. Remove the 2 nuts and remove the central transmission support to the body.
17. Lower the transmission assembly slightly and remove the bolts that attach the transmission to the engine.
18. Remove the 3 starter motor attaching bolts and remove the starter motor and shims.
19. Adjust the kickdown cable, release the transmission from the engine and lower the transmission.
20. Remove the 4 bolts securing the flexible coupling of the front driveshaft to the transmission output driveshaft fork.

To install:

21. Install the 4 bolts securing the flexible coupling of the front driveshaft to the transmission output driveshaft fork and tighten to 33–39 ft. lbs. (45–53 Nm).
22. Reposition the whole assembly, using lifting support 1.820.222.000 or equivalent, to the transmission, attaching 2 nuts on the rear side, 2 nuts on the front side and connecting a column jack to the tool.
23. Connect the kickdown cable.
24. Install the starter motor and shims.
25. Raise the transmission assembly slightly and install the bolts that attach the transmission to the engine and tighten to 9.4–10.3 ft. lbs. (12.7–14 Nm).
26. Install the 2 nuts attaching the central transmission support to the body.
27. Remove the transmission lifting and column jack.
28. Install the 2 nuts and bolt that retain the support to the transmission.
29. Connect the speedometer connector.

30. Install the cross bar with the the bolt securing the transmission to the cross bar and the 4 bolts and rubber support washers.
31. Install the 8 bolts securing the driveshaft cross bar, remove the split pin and pin and free the idler arm from the lever.
32. Install the 4 bolts at the front and rear flanges of the transmission shaft.
33. Connect the 2 hydraulic line fittings and tighten to 28–32 ft. lbs. (38–43 Nm).
34. Install the 4 bolts that retain the converter to the engine flywheel and tighten to 15–16 ft. lbs. (20–22 Nm).
35. Install the 4 bolts retaining the transmission housing cover and tighten to 3.5–4.4 ft. lbs. (4.8–6 Nm).
36. Connect the front exhaust pipe to the manifold.
37. Lower the vehicle and connect the kickdown cable and install the plastic shield.
38. From inside the engine compartment, connect the Lambda probe and install the dipstick.
39. Connect the battery cable and fill with transmission fluid.

164 SERIES

1. Disconnect the negative battery cable.
2. Raise and support the vehicle safely.
3. Remove the front wheels.
4. Remove the right side front half fender skirt and the left side front and rear halves.
5. Remove the plug and drain the oil from the differential.
6. Disconnect the lower hose and drain the coolant.
7. Disconnect the hoses from the intake duct and the electrical connection from the air flow meter and remove the air filter cover, air flow meter and intake duct assembly.
8. Remove the air filter support bracket.
9. Disconnect the throttle minimum and maximum opening switch connector.
10. Remove the throttle group cover.
11. Loosen the nuts securing the kick down cable to the bracket on the accelerator control pulley support and disconnect the cable end from the pulley groove.
12. Remove the bolts retaining the upper cross bar and tilt it forward to gain access to the bolts securing the ABS system hydraulic control unit.
13. Disconnect the spark plug cables from the front of the engine and the cable to the coil. Remove the distributor cap and rest it on the engine.
14. Remove the cover from the ABS hydraulic unit relay and disconnect the wiring clamp, the wiring connector, the ground lead and the wire from the transmission oil temperature sensor.
15. Remove the solenoid valve unit from the support and secure it to the distributor without disconnecting the tubes. Remove the support.
16. Remove the front exhaust pipes, the flywheel cover, the engine starter cover and the starter retaining bolts.
17. Remove the left side brake caliper and support it aside.
18. Remove the left side pulse emitting wheel sensor.
19. Disconnect the left CV-joint from the differential flange.
20. Using tool 1.821.169.000 or equivalent, withdraw the track rod ball joint pin from the steering rod.
21. Remove the left side spring and shock absorber.
22. Disconnect the ball joint from the wishbone.
23. Remove the wheel hub, complete with axle driveshaft and brake disc, from the wishbone.
24. Disconnect the halfshaft coupling from the intermediate driveshaft.
25. Remove the clip that secures the speed engagement control cable to the gearbox lever.
26. Remove the speed control engagement control cable bracket.

27. Disconnect the odometer pulse transmitter wire.
28. Remove the oil thermostat valve support.
29. Disconnect the transmission oil tubes to the radiator.
30. Remove the thermostat valve.
31. Remove the converter to flywheel retaining bolts.
32. Remove the bolts securing the intermediate driveshaft flange to the rear engine support and withdraw it from the differential.
33. Position a column jack under the oil pan and slightly lift the engine.
34. Remove the bolts securing the crossbar.
35. Remove the transmission support.
36. Remove the bolts attaching the transmission to the engine.
37. Remove the transmission cover and install, as a replacement, a protective cover 1.820.202.000.
38. Install lifting device 1.820.200.000 or equivalent and remove the transmission using a column type jack or equivalent.

To install:
39. Install lifting device 1.820.200.000 or equivalent and install the transmission using a column type jack or equivalent.
40. Remove the replacement protective transmission cover and install the original transmission cover.
41. Install the bolts attaching the transmission to the engine and tighten to 27–33 ft. lbs. (36.6–45 Nm).
42. Install the transmission support.
43. Install the bolts securing the crossbar.
44. Remove the column jack under the oil pan.
45. Install the bolts securing the intermediate driveshaft flange to the rear engine support.
46. Install the converter to the flywheel and tighten the retaining bolts to 25.4–31.4 ft. lbs. (34.1–42.5 Nm).
47. Install the thermostat valve.
48. Connect the transmission oil tubes to the radiator.
49. Install the oil thermostat valve support.
50. Connect the odometer pulse transmitter wire.
51. Install the speed control engagement control cable bracket.
52. Install the clip that secures the speed engagement control cable to the gearbox lever.
53. Connect the halfshaft coupling to the intermediate driveshaft and tighten the retaining bolts to 34.7–42.8 ft. lbs. (47–58 Nm).
54. Install the wheel hub, complete with axle driveshaft and brake disc, from the wishbone.
55. Connect the ball joint to the wishbone.
56. Install the left side spring and shock absorber unit and tighten the lower retaining bolts to 29.5–36.2 ft. lbs. (40–49 Nm) and the upper nuts to 9–11 ft. lbs. (12–15 Nm).
57. Install the track rod ball joint pin to the steering rod.
58. Connect the left CV-joint to the differential flange and tighten to 37.7–42.8 ft. lbs. (47–58 Nm).
59. Install the left side pulse emitting wheel sensor.
60. Install the left side brake caliper.
61. Install the starter, starter cover, flywheel cover and the front exhaust pipes.
62. Install the solenoid valve unit and support.
63. Connect the ABS hydraulic unit relay wiring clamp, the wiring connector, the ground lead, cover and the wire to the transmission oil temperature sensor.
64. Reinstall the distributor cap and reconnect the spark plug cables and the cable to the coil.
65. Reposition upper crossbar and install the retaining bolts.
66. Connect the cable end to the pulley groove and tighten the nuts securing the kickdown cable to the bracket on the accelerator control pulley support.
67. Install the throttle group cover.
68. Connect the throttle minimum and maximum opening switch connector.
69. Install the air filter support bracket.
70. Install the cruise control actuator.
71. install the air filter and canister.

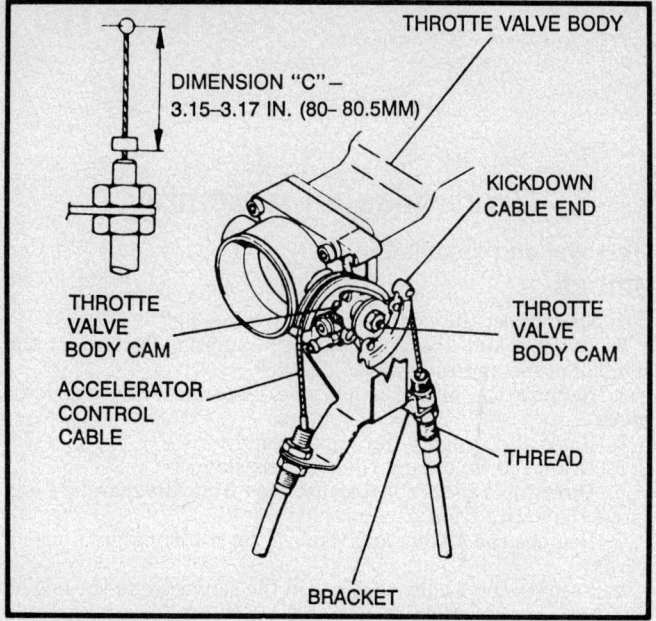

Kickdown cable dimension "C" should be 3.15–3.17 in. (80–80.5mm) – 164 series.

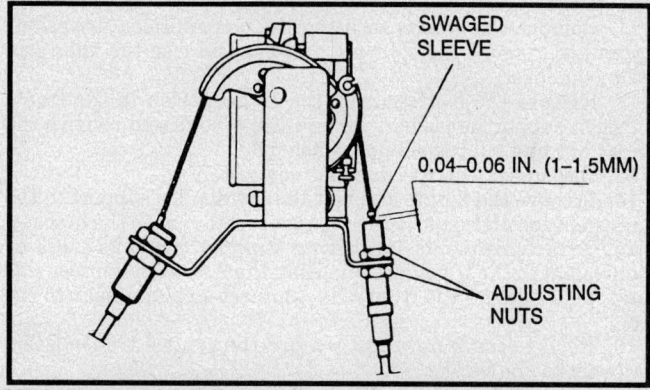

Kickdown cable dimension with accelerator pedal fully released – 164 series.

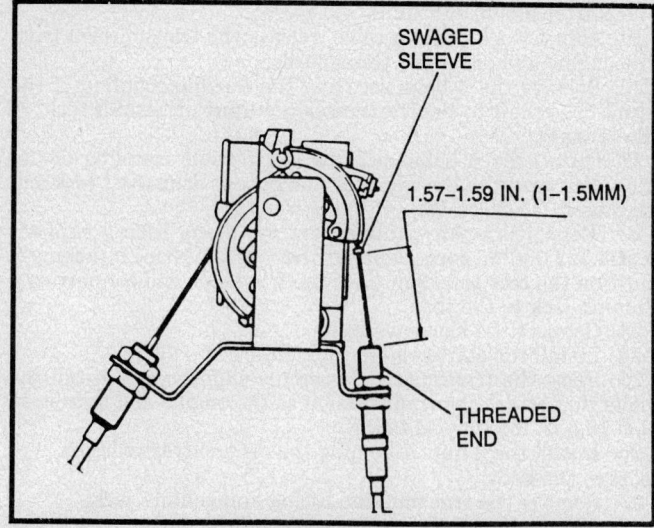

Kickdown cable dimension with accelerator pedal fully depressed – 164 series.

72. Connect the lower coolant hose.
73. Make sure the oil plug is installed in the differential.
74. Install the right side front half fender skirt and the left side front and rear halves.
75. Install the front wheels.
76. Lower the vehicle and connect the negative battery cable.
77. Make sure the kickdown cable is adjusted correctly.

Kickdown Shift Cable Adjustment

164 SERIES

1. Check that dimension **C** is 3.15–3.17 in. (80–80.5mm).
2. Check that all connections are correctly fitted.
3. With the accelerator pedal fully released, check that the

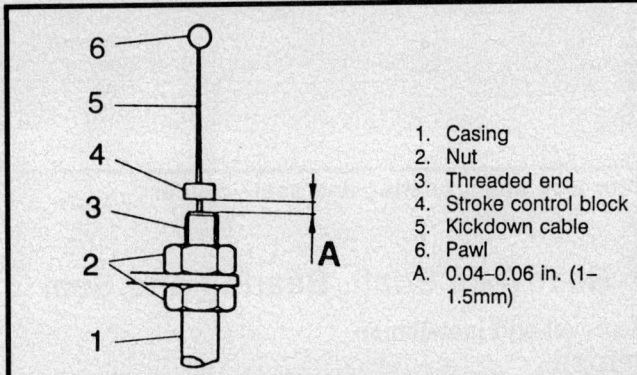

1. Casing
2. Nut
3. Threaded end
4. Stroke control block
5. Kickdown cable
6. Pawl
A. 0.04–0.06 in. (1–1.5mm)

Kickdown cable dimension (rest position) "A" should be 0.04–0.06 in. (1–1.5mm) – Spider

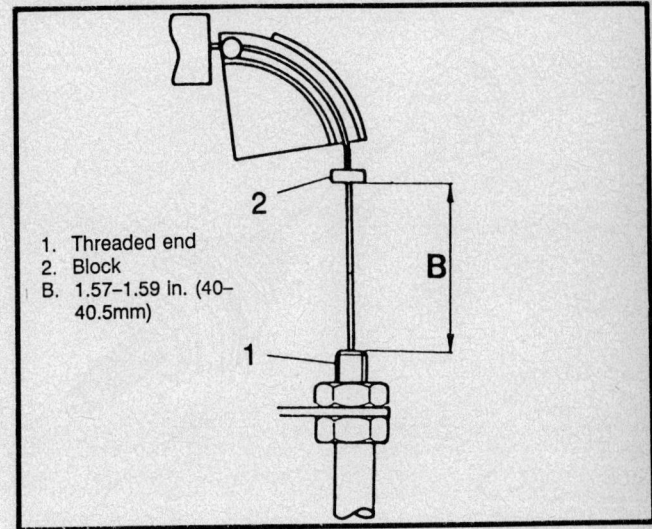

1. Threaded end
2. Block
B. 1.57–1.59 in. (40–40.5mm)

Kickdown cable dimension (insertion position) "B" should be 1.57–1.59 in. (40–40.5mm) – Spider

distance between the cable threaded end and the swaged sleeve is 0.04–0.06 in. (1–1.5mm). Adjust the cable position as necessary with the nut locknut.

4. With the accelerator pedal fully depressed, check that the distance between the cable threaded end and the swaged sleeve is 1.57–1.59 in. (40–40.5mm). To correct, adjust the position of the limit stop, located under the accelerator pedal.

DRIVE AXLE

Halfshaft

Removal and Installation

164 SERIES

Left Side

1. Raise and support the vehicle safely.
2. Remove the front wheel.
3. Remove the front fender skirt.
4. Remove the bolts securing the halfshaft to the to the differential flange.
5. Remove the nut and caulking securing the joint.
6. Installation is the reverse of removal. Use a new gasket and caulking and tighten the retaining bolts to 34.7–42.8 ft. lbs. (47–58 Nm).

Right Side

1. Raise and support the vehicle safely.
2. Remove the front wheel.
3. Remove the front fender skirt.
4. Remove the nut and caulking securing the joint.
5. Remove the bolts securing the halfshaft to the to the intermediate shaft flange and remove the halfshaft.
6. Installation is the reverse of removal. Use a new gasket and caulking and tighten the retaining bolts to 34.7–42.8 ft. lbs. (47–58 Nm).

CV-Boot

Remove and Installation

164 SERIES

Transmission Side

1. Raise and support the vehicle safely.
2. Remove the halfshaft.
3. Remove the clamps securing the boot.
4. Remove the CV-joint and remove the boot.

To install:

5. Repositon a new boot on the shaft and install the CV-joint.
6. Install the retaining ring.
7. Fill the joint and boot with 0.26 lbs. (120 g) of the correct grease.
8. Install the boot retaining clamp.
9. Install the shaft and and lower the vehicle.

Wheel Side

1. Raise and support the vehicle safely.
2. Remove the halfshaft.
3. Lock the shaft in a vice and remove the clamps securing the boot.
4. Using suitable pliers, remove the CV-joint retaining ring and remove the CV-joint using a puller.

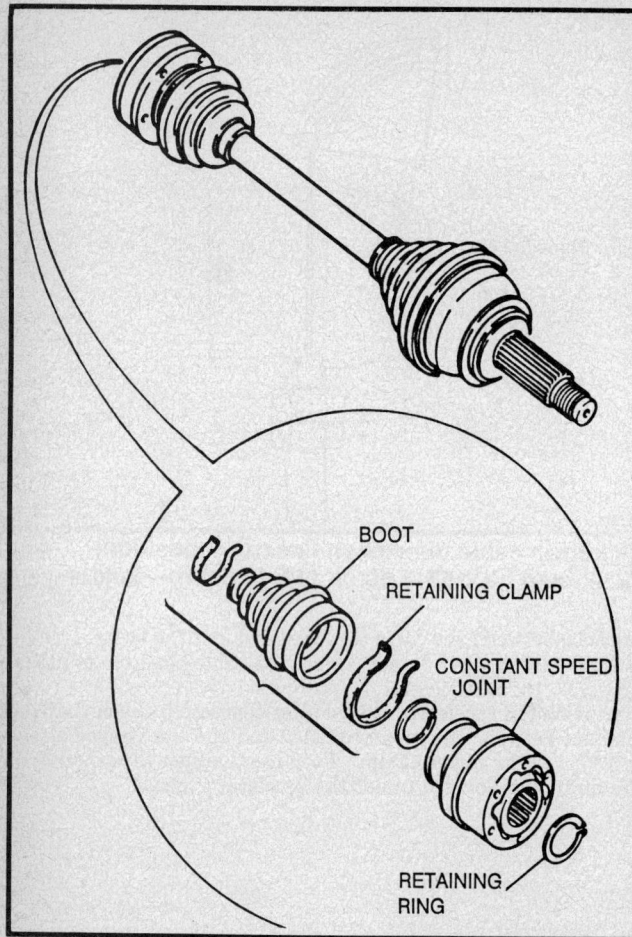

Disassembled view of the transmission side CV-joint and boot—Spider

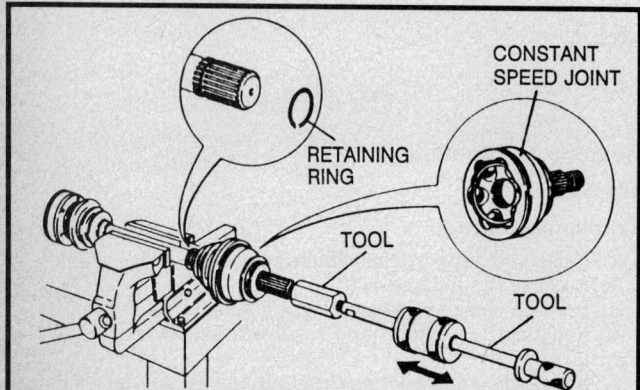

Removal of the CV-joint and boot on the wheel side— Spider

To install:

5. Repositon a new boot on the shaft and install the retaining ring on the axle shaft.
6. Compress the retaining ring with a screw clamp.
7. Position the joint onto the axle shaft, insert it and seat it with a hammer.
8. Fill the joint and boot with 0.26 lbs. (120 g) of the correct grease.
9. Install the boot retaining clamps.
10. Install the shaft and and lower the vehicle.

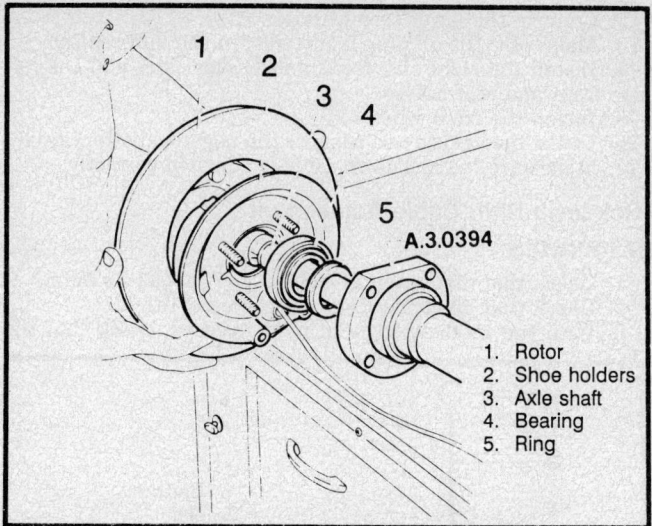

Rear axle shaft, bearing and seal—Spider

1. Rotor
2. Shoe holders
3. Axle shaft
4. Bearing
5. Ring

Rear Axle Shaft, Bearing and Seal

Removal and Installation
SPIDER

1. Raise and support the vehicle safely.
2. Place a column type jack under the differential, raise the vehicle at the rear and remove the wheel.
3. Disconnect the brake line tubing at the caliper.
4. Remove the brake pads and remove the caliper.
5. Remove the 4 nuts holding the splash shield to the axle tube.
6. Slide off the complete axle shaft, brake disc, splash shield assembly.
7. Using a suitable tool, pry the seal ring from the axle tube.
8. Slide the splash shield off the axle shaft.
9. Install tool A.3.0394 or equivalent, to the shoe holders and remove the axle shaft bearing.
10. Remove the nuts holding the tool and slide off the brake disc together with he axle shaft, the shoe holder, bearing and ring.

To install:
11. Slide the shoe holder onto the axle shaft.
12. Using tool A.3.0395 or equivalent and a press, drive the bearing onto the axle shaft.
13. Slide off tool A.3.0395 or equivalent, heat the ring and again using tool A.3.0395 or equivalent and a press, drive the ring until it abuts against the bearing. Allow the ring to cool before removing the tool.
14. The remainder of the installation is the reverse of removal.

Front Wheel Hub, Knuckle/Spindle and Bearings

Removal and Installation
SPIDER

1. Raise and support the vehicle safely.
2. Remove the stabilizer bar.
3. Remove the nut securing the shock absorber to the pin on the lower wishbone. Slide off the shock absorber along with the inner and outer washers.
4. Remove the spring assembly.

NOTE: For removal of the wheel hub and bearings only, it is not necessary to remove the brake caliper or steering knuckle, only the brake pads.

5. Remove the cotter pins and 3 nuts securing the upper wishbone, track rod and the lower wishbone to the steering knuckle.

6. Using tool A.3.0156 or equivalent, disconnect the track rod from the steering knuckle.

7. Using tool A.3.0157 or equivalent, disconnect the lower wishbone from the steering knuckle.

8. Remove the brake fluid from the reservoir and disconnect the brake hose from the front caliper.

NOTE: It may be possible to remove the caliper without disconnecting the hydraulic hose. Carefully secure aside.

9. Remove the steering knuckle along with the wheel hub.

10. Fit the whole assembly in a vice. Use a punch, drive the check pins of the brake pads out and remove the cross spring and pads.

11. Remove the 2 bolts retaining the brake caliper to the steering knuckle.

12. Remove the cover, cotter pin and nut and remove and remove the brake wheel hub disc assembly from the steering knuckle. Retrieve the washer and the internal race of the outer bearing.

13. Remove the 4 nuts and the splash shield and the steering lever.

14. Remove the 2 nuts securing the wheel hub to the brake disc and separate the 2 parts.

15. Using a suitable tool, pry the seal ring from the hub and retrieve the inner race of the inner bearing.

16. Remove the outer races of the bearing.

To install:

17. Lubricate the bearings and the wheel hub internal chamber with suitable grease and reverse the removal procedure.

18. Using tool A.3.0192 or equivalent, driving tool, install the wheel hub seal ring.

19. Reassemble using new self locking nuts. Tighten the steering lever to the steering knuckle bolts to 28.8–32.4 ft. lbs. (39–44 Nm).

20. Lubricate the steering knuckle thread, assemble the brake disc-hub bearing assembly, washers and hub nut. Tighten the hub nut to 14.8–18.4 ft. lbs. (20–25 Nm), while turning the hub at the same time. Loosen the nut and tighten it again to 3.7–7.4 ft. lbs. (5–10 Nm). Unscrew the nut by 90 degrees and insert the cotter pin.

NOTE: If the notch on the nut and the hole in the steering knuckle fail to align, screw the nut to the minimum angle necessary to insert the cotter pin and tap the end of the steering knuckle once with a mallet to settle the bearings and make sure the washer is not stuck.

21. Install the caliper to the steering knuckle and tighten the retaining bolts to 54.6–61.2 ft. lbs. (74–83 Nm).

22. Tighten the upper and lower ball joint to steering knuckle nuts to 54.6–61.2 ft. lbs. (74–83 Nm).

23. Tighten the track bar ball and socket joint nuts to 34.7–39.8 ft. lbs. (47–54 Nm).

MILANO

1. Raise and support the vehicle safely.
2. Disconnect the shock absorber from the lower link.
3. Remove the front stabilizer bar.
4. If equipped with ABS, remove the bolt securing the cable plate to the upper link of the suspension and remove the impulse pick-up and support from the steering knuckle without disconnecting it electrically. Carefully move aside.
5. Position a suitable support jack under the link seats and raise unit.
6. Remove the cotter pin and nut and disconnect the lower link from the steering knuckle using tool A.3.0377 or equivalent.
7. Lower the lift and unload the torsion bar.
8. Remove the brake fluid from the reservoir and disconnect the brake hose from the front caliper.

NOTE: It may be possible to remove the caliper without disconnecting the hydraulic hose. Carefully secure aside.

9. Using tool A.3.0156 or equivalent, disconnect the steering tie rod from the steering knuckle.
10. Using tool A.3.0377 or equivalent, disconnect the upper link from the steering knuckle.

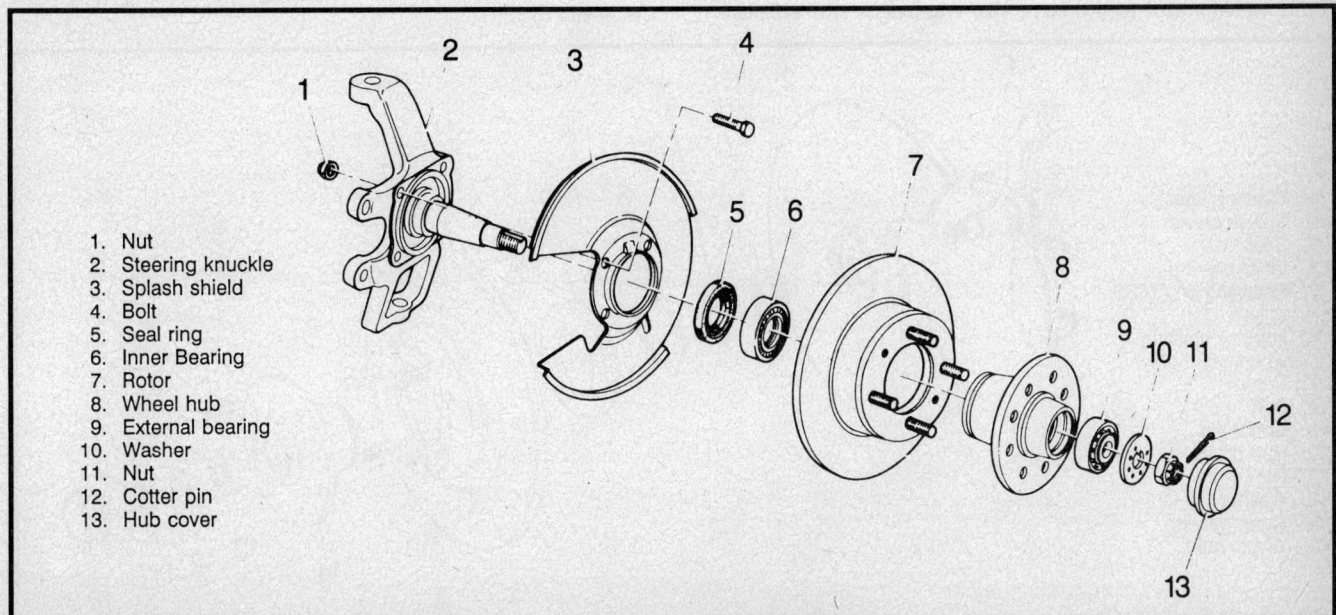

1. Nut
2. Steering knuckle
3. Splash shield
4. Bolt
5. Seal ring
6. Inner Bearing
7. Rotor
8. Wheel hub
9. External bearing
10. Washer
11. Nut
12. Cotter pin
13. Hub cover

Disassembled view of the steering knuckle and and wheel hub—Spider

11. Remove the steering knuckle along with the wheel hub.

12. Fit the whole assembly in a vice. Use a punch, drive the check pins of the brake pads out and remove the cross spring and pads.

13. Remove the brake caliper from the steering knuckle.

14. Remove the cover, cotter pin, nut and washer and remove and remove the brake wheel hub disc assembly from the steering knuckle.

15. Remove the 3 nuts and remove the splash guard.

16. If equipped with ABS, remove the retaining ring and separate the impulse emitting wheel from the wheel hub.

17. Remove the outer bearing from the hub.

18. Remove the 2 nuts securing the wheel hub to the brake disc and separate the 2 parts.

19. Using a suitable tool, pry the seal ring from the hub and remove the inner bearing from the seat.

20. Remove the outer and inner races of the bearing.

To install:

21. Using inserter A.3.0329 or equivalent, with a press, install the inner bearing cup on the hub.

22. Using inserter A.3.0328 or equivalent, with a press, install the outer bearing cup on the hub.

23. Lubricate the bearing cups and pack the hub recess with suitable grease.

NOTE: Do not exceed 1.76 oz. of grease in the hub or leakage could occur.

24. Lubricate and install the hub inner bearing.

25. Install the splash guard and install the brake disc to the hub.

26. On vehicles equipped with ABS, clean and install the impulse emitting wheel on the hub.

27. Lubricate the steering knuckle thread, washer and hub nut. Install the hub on the knuckle and then install the outer bearing. Tighten the hub nut to 14.8–17.7 ft. lbs. (20–24 Nm), while turning the hub at the same time. Loosen the nut and tighten it again to 3.7–7.4 ft. lbs. (5–10 Nm).

28. If not equipped with ABS, unscrew the nut by 90 degrees and insert the cotter pin.

NOTE: If the notch on the nut and the hole in the steering knuckle fail to align, screw the nut to the minimum angle necessary to insert the cotter pin and tap the end of the steering knuckle once with a mallet to settle the bearings and make sure the washer is not stuck.

29. On vehicles equipped with ABS, check the front hub bearing clearance.

    a. Install a dial gauge so it touches the steering knuckle axis and preload the gauge to 0.04 in. (1mm).

    b. Move the wheel hub back and forth and read the clearance on the gauge. The hub bearing clearance should be 0.0008–0.005 in. (0.02–0.12mm).

    c. If the clearance is 0.0008–0.002 in. (0.02–0.06mm), back off the nut until the cotter pin is inserted.

    d. If the clearance is 0.002–0.005 in. (0.06–0.12mm), tighten the nut until the cotter pin is inserted.

    e. Bend the cotter pin back and install the cover.

30. Install the caliper to the steering knuckle and tighten the retaining bolts to 54.6–61.2 ft. lbs. (74–83 Nm).

31. Install the brake pads, cross spring and retaining pins.

32. Position tools A.2.0265 and A.2.0069 or equivalent, and load the torsion bar to connect the steering knuckle to both the lower and upper links.

33. Tighten the upper link ball joint to to steering knuckle nut to 59–66.4 ft. lbs. (80–90 Nm).

34. Tighten the steering link ball joint to knuckle nut to 33.2–40.6 ft. lbs. (45–55 Nm).

35. Tighten the lower ball joint to steering knuckle nuts to 33.2–40.6 ft. lbs. (45–55 Nm).

36. If equipped with ABS, install the impulse pick-up in the reverse order of removal and tighten the impulse pick-up support and cable plate securing nuts and bolts to 6.6–7.4 ft. lbs. (9–10 Nm).

37. If equipped with ABS, use a thickness gauge and check that the air gap between the impulse pick-up and the impulse emitting wheel is 0.03 in. (0.7mm). Turn the adjusting screw to adjust.

164 SERIES

1. Raise and support the vehicle safely.

2. Remove the front wheel and brake caliper.

3. Remove the caulking and remove the spindle locknut.

4. Disconnect the shock absorber strut from the hub carrier (steering knuckle).

5. Using a suitable tool pull out the ball joint from the steering link rod.

6. Using a suitable, extract the suspension control arm ball joint from the hub carrier (steering knuckle).

7. Remove the hub carrier (steering knuckle) together with the brake disc.

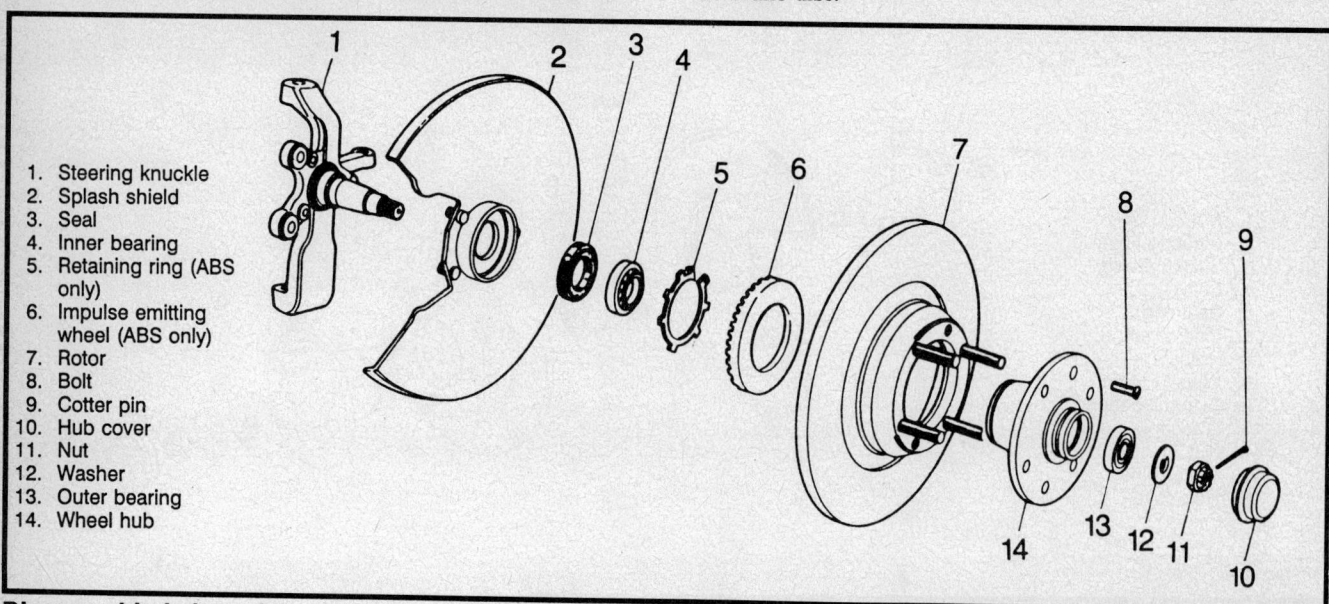

1. Steering knuckle
2. Splash shield
3. Seal
4. Inner bearing
5. Retaining ring (ABS only)
6. Impulse emitting wheel (ABS only)
7. Rotor
8. Bolt
9. Cotter pin
10. Hub cover
11. Nut
12. Washer
13. Outer bearing
14. Wheel hub

Disassembled view of the steering knuckle and and wheel hub—Milano

8. Remove the bracket supporting the brake caliper.

9. If equipped with ABS, remove the inductive sensor and support.

10. Place the hub carrier (steering knuckle) in a vice and remove the snap ring.

11. Using a suitable tool, press the hub from the knuckle.

12. Using a suitable tool, press the bearing from the knuckle.

To install:

13. Using a suitable tool and a press, install bearing to the knuckle, then install the retaining snapring.

14. Using a suitable tool and a press, install hub to the knuckle.

15. The remainder of the installation is the reverse of removal. Tighten the spindle locknut to 262.7–295.2 ft. lbs. (356–400 Nm), the brake caliper retaining bolts to 22.9–28 ft. lbs. (31–38 Nm), ball joint nuts to 36.9–44.3 ft. lbs. (50–60 Nm) and the brake caliper support bracket bolts 38.4–42.8 ft. lbs. (52-58 Nm).

Differential Carrier

Removal and Installation

SPIDER

1. Raise and support the vehicle safely.

2. Remove the plug and drain the oil from the differential.

3. Mark the flanges for references, remove the 4 bolts and separate the transmission and differential flanges.

4. Working from both sides of the rear axle, remove the nut, and slide the link rods of the stabilizer bar from the pins on the trailing arms.

5. Remove the cotter pins and slide out the pins coupling the cables and parking brake brackets.

6. Remove the cotter pin and loosen but do not remove the nut securing the differential to the reaction triangle.

7. Working from both sides of the rear axle, remove the locknut, and nut securing the shock absorber to the trailing arm, re-

trieving the cup and the rubber bushing.

8. Assemble tool A.2.0143, by inserting the pin in the hole in the axle flange. turn the tool sleeve until the tool bracket comes against the spring bushing housing. At this point it is possible to free the pin coupling the trailing arm and axle. Turn the tool sleeve so as to lower the bracket and release the spring.

9. Dismantle the tool, slide off the spring, retrieving the cup and the upper gasket.

10. Remove the brake fluid from the reservoir and disconnect the brake hose at the union.

11. Position a suitable column jack and support under the rear axle.

12. Working from both sides of the rear axle, loosen the 2 upper bolts remove the 2 lower ones and slide off the limit rebound strap.

13. Remove the previously loosened nut securing the differential to the reaction triangle, retrieving the bushing, then move the rear axle towards the right so as to slide off the nut and lower the column jack and entire rear axle assembly.

To install:

14. Installation is the reverse of removal. Pay attention to the following:

a. Lubricate the pin coupling the differential to the reaction triangle using suitable grease.

b. Use an anti-seize compound on the lower pins of the shock absorbers, the lock bolts, trailing arms at the rear axle and the bolts securing the limit rebound straps.

c. Tighten the bolts securing the trailing arms to the rear axle to 79.7–98.1 ft. lbs. (108–133 Nm).

d. Tighten the nuts securing the reaction triangle to the rear axle to 73.8–91.5 ft. lbs. (100–124 Nm).

e. Tighten the nuts securing the link rods of the stabilizer bar to the rear axle to 23.6–25.1 ft. lbs. (32–34 Nm).

f. Tighten the bolts securing the transmission and differential flanges to 27.3–28.8 ft. lbs. (37–39 Nm).

g.Fill the differential with lubricant HD 80W90.

h.Bleed the brake system.

STEERING

Steering Wheel

------------------ **CAUTION** ------------------

On vehicles equipped with an air bag, the negative and positive battery cable must be disconnected and the negative battery cable insulated, before working on the vehicle. Failure to do so may result in deployment of the air bag and possible personal injury.

Removal and Installation

SPIDER

Without Air Bag

1. Disconnect the negative battery cable.

2. Pry off the hub cover by hand.

3. Remove the horn push button screws, disconnect the cable and remove the push button.

4. Straighten out the nut retainer and remove the steering wheel locknut.

5. Remove the steering wheel, using a suitable puller.

6. Installation is the reverse of removal. align the wheel and tighten the locknut to 36.9–40.6 ft. lbs. (50–55 Nm).

With Air Bag

1. Place the wheels in the straight ahead position.

2. Disconnect the negative and positive battery cable and in-

sulate the negative battery cable.

3. Remove the 2 screws securing the air bag module to the steering column using a suitable tool.

4. Partially extract the air bag module, disconnect the electrical connector and remove the air bag.

NOTE: The air bag module contains a gas charge. Store in a suitable container or area.

5. Disconnect the horn electrical connector.

6. Detach the left knee pad.

7. Remove the upper and lower steering column shrouds.

8. Disconnect the horn connections.

9. Remove the steering wheel nut and spring and remove the steering wheel using a suitable puller.

10. Installation is the reverse of removal. Tighten the wheel retaining nut to 20.7–23.6 ft. lbs. (28–32 Nm). If the air bag warning light displays "fault" on the dashboard, reset as follows:

a. While the air bag warning light is flashing, disconnect pin **8B** of the control unit to ground for 2–4 seconds.

b. Reconnect pin **8B** of the control unit to ground for 2–4 seconds.

c. Disconnect pin **8B** of the control unit to ground definitively.

164 SERIES

1. Place the wheels in the straight-ahead position.

2. Disconnect the negative and positive battery cable and insulate the negative battery cable.

3. Remove the 2 screws securing the air bag module to the steering column using a suitable tool.

4. Partially extract the air bag module, disconnect the electrical connector and remove the air bag.

NOTE: The air bag module contains a gas charge. Store in a suitable container or area.

5. Disconnect the horn electrical connector.

6. Remove the steering wheel nut and spring and remove the steering wheel using a suitable puller.

7. Installation is the reverse of removal. Tighten the wheel retaining nut to 12.5–15.5. ft. lbs. (17–21 Nm). If the air bag warning light displays "fault" on the dashboard, reset as follows:

    a. While the air bag warning light is flashing, disconnect pin **8B** of the control unit to ground for 2–4 seconds.

    b. Reconnect pin **8B** of the control unit to ground for 2–4 seconds.

    c. Disconnect pin **8B** of the control unit to ground.

Steering Column

Removal and Installation

SPIDER

Without Air Bag

1. Disconnect the negative battery cable.
2. Pry off the hub cover by hand.
3. Remove the horn push button screws, disconnect the cable and remove the push button.
4. Straighten out the nut retainer and remove the steering wheel locknut.
5. Remove the steering wheel, using a suitable puller.
6. Detach the left knee pad.
7. Remove the upper and lower steering column shrouds.
8. Remove the 2 bolts and slide out the combination switch unit, keeping it connected.
9. Remove the 2 bolts securing the column support to the body and loosen the bolt retaining the steering column support to the steering column tube.
10. Disconnect the anti-theft/ignition switch connector.
11. Raise and support the vehicle safely.
12. Remove the left front wheel and tire assembly.
13. Remove the 3 bolts securing the gearbox to the body. Working from inside the vehicle, lower the steering column support slightly and remove it from the steering column.
14. Installation is the reverse of removal. Tighten the bolts securing the steering box to the body to 37.6–39.1 ft. lbs. (51–53 Nm) and the steering wheel to column nut to 36.9–40.6 ft. lbs. 50–55 Nm).

With Air Bag

1. Place the wheels in the straight-ahead position.
2. Disconnect the negative and positive battery cable and insulate the negative battery cable.
3. Remove the 2 screws securing the air bag module to the steering column using a suitable tool.
4. Partially extract the air bag module from the vehicle, disconnect the electrical connector and remove the air bag.

NOTE: The air bag module contains a gas charge. Store in a suitable container or area.

5. Disconnect the horn electrical connector.
6. Detach the left hand knee pad.
7. Remove the upper and lower steering column shrouds.
8. Disconnect the horn connections.
9. Remove the steering wheel nut and spring and remove the steering wheel using a suitable puller.

10. Remove the 2 retaining bolts and remove the combination switch unit without disconnecting it.

11. Disconnect the steering lock-ignition switch electrical connector.

12. Remove the 2 bolts fastening the steering column to the body, then loosen the upper universal joint screw.

13. Withdraw the whole steering column freeing it from the cardan shaft. save the cardan shaft, if necessary after removing the bolt connecting the lower universal joint to the steering box input shaft.

14. Installation is the reverse of removal. Tighten the bolts securing the steering box to the body to 36–40 ft. lbs. (49–54 Nm) and the steering wheel to column nut to 21–24 ft. lbs. (29–32 Nm).

164 SERIES

1. Place the wheels in the straight ahead position.
2. Disconnect the negative and positive battery cable and insulate the negative battery cable.
3. Remove the 2 screws securing the air bag module to the steering column using a suitable tool.
4. Partially extract the air bag module from the vehicle, disconnect the electrical connector and remove the air bag.

NOTE: The air bag module contains a gas charge. Store in a suitable container or area.

5. Disconnect the horn electrical connector.
6. Remove the steering wheel nut and spring and remove the steering wheel using a suitable puller.
7. Remove the electric contact group after removal of the steering column half cowls, being careful not to damage the reference spring.
8. Remove the knee protection panel.
9. Remove the upper and lower steering column shrouds.
10. Remove the screws retaining the combination switch, leaving it connected to the wiring harness.
11. Remove the relays support plate from the steering column, leaving the wiring harness connected.
12. Disconnect the ground connection from the rear side of the steering column.
13. Remove the plastic protective cover from the clutch pump.
14. Disconnect the electrical connections from the ignition switch and radio inhibitor switch.
15. Remove the steering column support securing bolt, bushing and nut.
16. Loosen the nut and remove the steering wheel adjustment lever.
17. Remove the steering column support assembly recovering key located on the splined part.
18. Remove the upper cover of the intermediate shaft universal joint.
19. Remove the lower cover studs.
20. Remove the bolt securing the intermediate shaft universal joint to the steering box pinion and remove the intermediate shaft.
21. Remove the lower protection cover and slide out the intermediate shaft end from the steering column support.
22. Remove the steering column retaining flange.
23. Slide out the the complete steering column together with the bearing and snapring.
24. Installation is the reverse of removal. Tighten the wheel retaining nut to 12.5–15.5. ft. lbs. (17–21 Nm). If the air bag warning light displays "fault" on the dashboard, reset as follows:

    a. While the air bag warning light is flashing, disconnect pin **8B** of the control unit to ground for 2–4 seconds.

    b. Reconnect pin **8B** of the control unit to ground for 2–4 seconds.

    c. Disconnect pin **8B** of the control unit to ground.

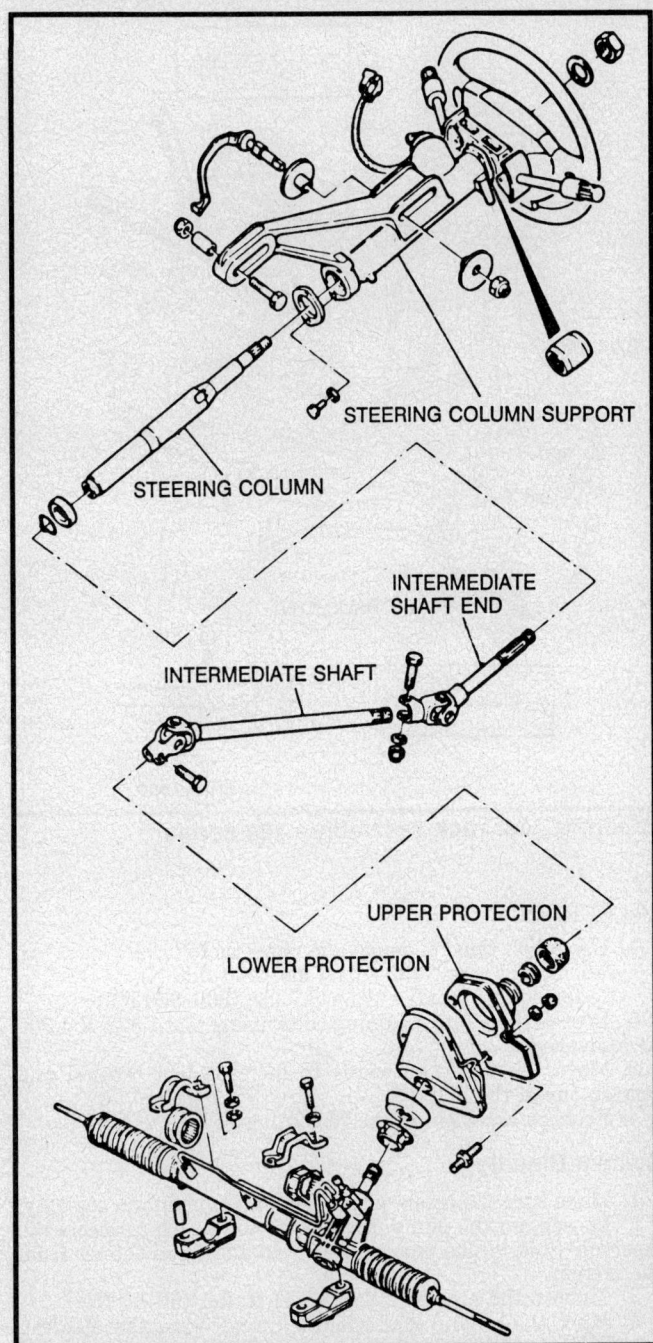

Disassembled view of the steering column—model 164

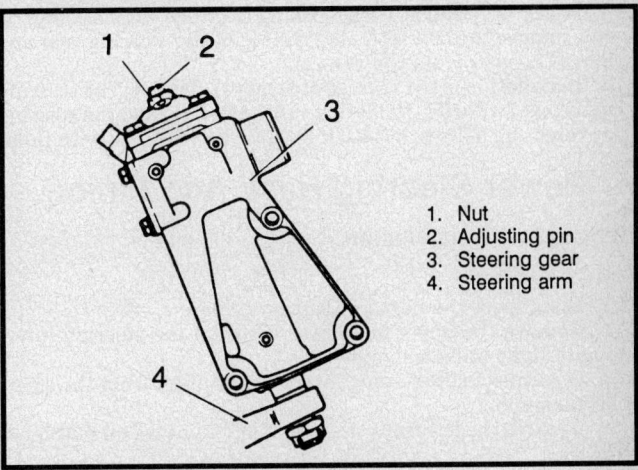

1. Nut
2. Adjusting pin
3. Steering gear
4. Steering arm

Steering gear adjustment—Spider

Manual Steering Gear

Adjustment

SPIDER

1. Straighten out the wheels and disconnect the tie-rods from the steering arm.

2. Unlock the nut and unscrew the pin so as to obtain a high clearance on the arm.

3. If necessary, center the steering by taking the steering wheel to a limit and turning it half as many times as required to take it to the opposite limit.

4. Screw the pin back on gradually until there is no longer angular clearance on the arm.

5. Tighten the pin by ¼–½ turns and while holding it in place, lock the nut to 18.4–21.4 ft. lbs. (25–29 Nm).

6. Reconnect the tie-rods and tighten the nuts to 34.7–39.8 ft. lbs. (47–54 Nm).

Removal and Installation

SPIDER

1. Disconnect the negative battery cable.
2. Disconnect the steering column support.
3. Remove the air filter assembly.
4. Remove the brake pedal assembly.
5. Remove the cotter pin and nut and disconnect the steering arm from the steering gear.
6. Using tool A.3.0119 or equivalent, remove the steering arm from the steering gear output shaft.
7. Working from the engine compartment, remove the steering gear.
8. Installation is the reverse of removal. Tighten the steering arm to gear nut to 90.7–101.1 ft. lbs. (123–137 Nm), the steering gear to body bolts to 37.6–39.1 ft. lbs. (51–53 Nm) and the nut securing the steering wheel to 36.9–40.6 ft. lbs. (50–55 Nm). Adjust the gear as necessary.

Power Steering Gear

Removal and Installation

SPIDER

1. Disconnect the negative battery cable.
2. Remove the fluid from the power steering reservoir.
3. If equipped with fuel injection, disconnect the air cleaner assembly.
4. If equipped with a carburetor, remove the battery and support bracket.
5. Raise and support the vehicle safely.
6. Remove the exhaust manifolds.
7. Disconnect the inlet and return lines to the steering gear.
8. From inside the engine compartment, loosen the bolt which attaches the steering column lower universal joint to the steering gear input shaft.
9. Matchmark the position and remove the cotter pin and nut attaching the steering control arm to the gear output shaft.
10. Using tool A.3.0119 or equivalent, remove the steering arm from the steering gear output shaft.
11. Remove the 2 bolts which fasten the steering gear bottom by loosening the nuts from the wheelhouse.

12. Lower the vehicle, then working from the engine compartment, remove the bolt retaining the top of the steering gear and remove the gear from the vehicle.

13. Installation is the reverse of removal. Tighten the steering arm to gear nut to 94–103 ft. lbs. (127–140 Nm) and the steering gear retaining bolts to 36–40 ft. lbs. (49–54 Nm). Fill with fluid.

Power Steering Rack And Pinion

Removal and Installation

164 SERIES

1. Disconnect the negative battery cable.
2. Remove the upper and lower cover on the steering intermediate shaft universal joint.
3. Disconnect the steering intermediate shaft from the steering gear pinion.
4. Remove the left front wheel and left front wheel rear fender skirt.
5. Remove the fluid from the power steering reservoir.
6. Disconnect the inlet and return lines to the steering gear rack.
7. Using a suitable tool, disconnect the steering tie-rod ball joint on both sides.
8. Remove the steering gear rack bulkhead.
9. Remove the bolts retaining the steering rack assembly to the frame and slide out from the left wheelhouse opening.
10. Measure the distance or amount of threads the tie-rod ends are installed on the link rods, loosen the locknuts and remove the tie-rod ends from the link rods.
11. Installtion is the reverse of removal. Tighten the steering rack assembly retaining bolts to 10.3–16.2 ft. lbs. (14–22 Nm) and the tie-rod end locknut to 29.5–46.5 ft. lbs. (40–63 Nm).

Power Steering Pump

Removal and Installation

SPIDER

1. Disconnect the negative battery cable.
2. Remove the fluid from the power steering reservoir.
3. Disconnect the inlet and return lines to the steering pump.
4. Remove the pump retaining bolts and remove the pump and belt.
5. Installation is the reverse of removal.

164 SERIES

1. Disconnect the negative battery cable.
2. Raise and support the vehicle safely.
3. Remove the right front wheel.
4. Working from inside the right front fender, remove the front protection cover and lift the rear cover that protects the steering pump.
5. Disconnect the hoses from the pump, drain the fluid and plug the holes from which the hoses were connected.
6. Using a suitable tool, remove the bolts located in the tension adjustment holes.
7. Remove the upper retaining bolts and the bolts retaining the pulley.
8. Remove the pulley, drive belt and pump.
9. Installation is the reverse of removal.

Belt Adjustment

SPIDER

1. Use a belt tension gauge and check as follows:
   Assembling a belt – 112–123 lbs. (500–550 N).
   Re-tensioning (cold) – 90–101 lbs. (400–450 N).
2. Loosen the slotted arm retaining and adjusting bolts.
3. Move the pump upward to increase belt tension and tighten the bolts.

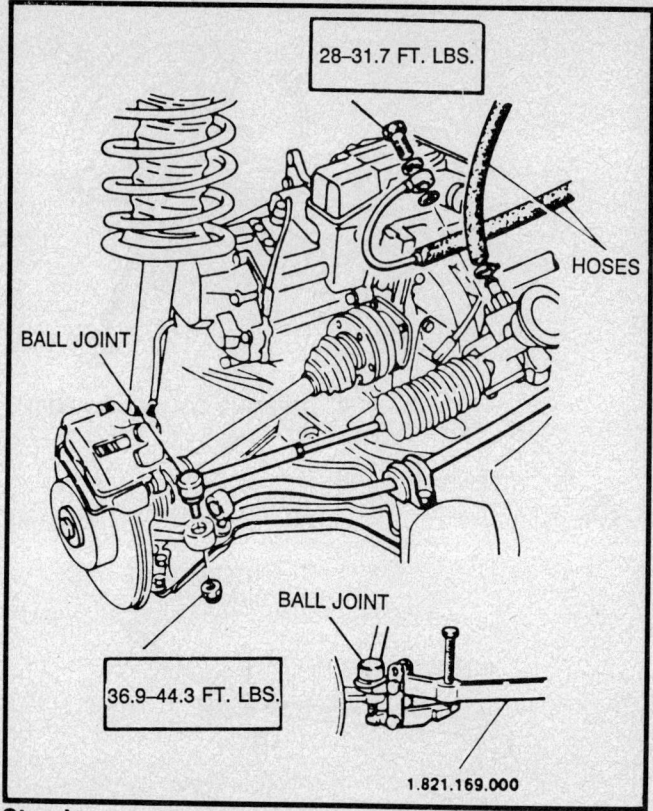

Steering gear rack assembly – 164 series

28–31.7 FT. LBS.

HOSES

BALL JOINT

BALL JOINT

36.9–44.3 FT. LBS.

1.821.169.000

164 SERIES

1. Use a belt tension gauge and check as follows:
   Assembling a belt – 90–101.2 lbs. (400–500 N).
   Re-tensioning (cold) – 67.5–78.7 lbs. (300–350 N).
2. Loosen the pump retaining bolts, using tool 1.822.104.000 or equivalent.
3. Move the pump outwards to increase belt tension and tighten one of the bolts.
4. Recheck and tighten the remaining bolt.

System Bleeding

1. Make sure the reservoir is filled to its maximum capacity.
2. Loosen, on the pump, the pipe fitting which connects the reservoir fluid intake pipe to the pump and bleed the air from the system.
3. Tighten the pipe fitting to 37–41 ft. lbs. (50–55 Nm).
4. Start the engine and while running, turn the steering wheel lock-to-lock several times, then fill the reservoir to the proper level.

Tie Rod Ends

Removal and Installation

SPIDER

1. Raise and support the vehicle safely.
2. Using tool A.3.0156 or equivalent, remove the tie rod ends from the knuckle arms.
3. Installation is the reverse of removal. Tighten the steering arm to gear nut to 90.7–101.1 ft. lbs. (123–137 Nm) and the tie-rod ball and socket joint nuts to 34.7–39.8 ft. lbs. (47–54 Nm).

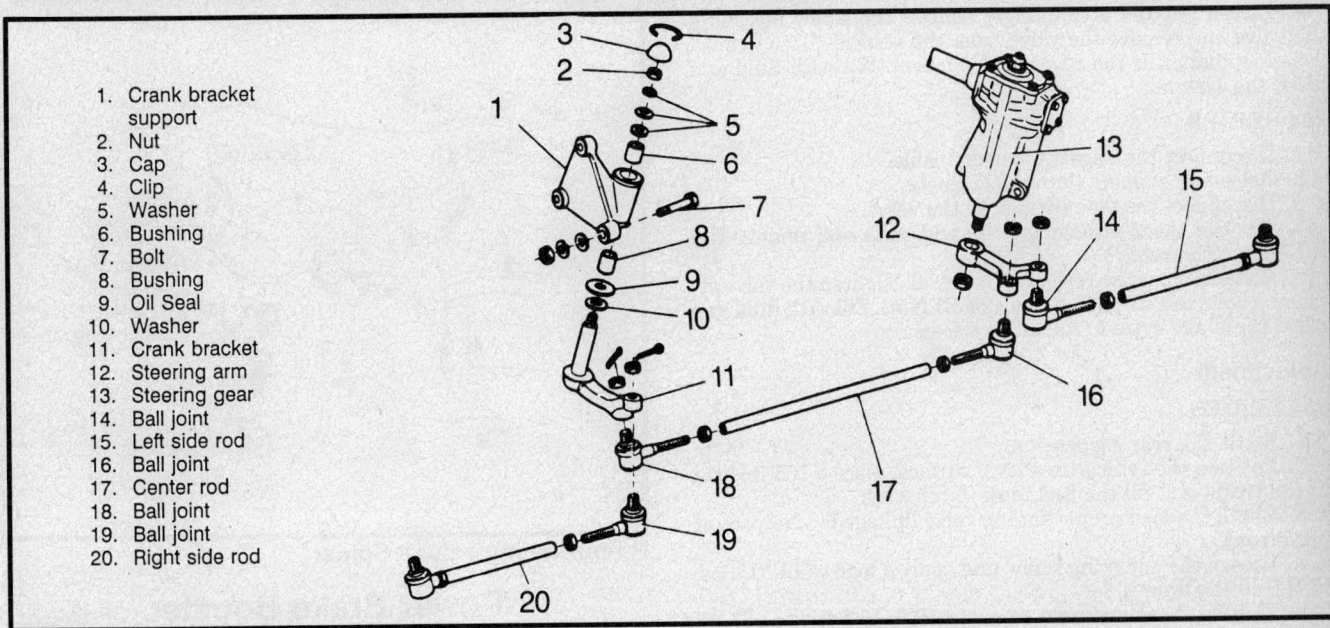

1. Crank bracket support
2. Nut
3. Cap
4. Clip
5. Washer
6. Bushing
7. Bolt
8. Bushing
9. Oil Seal
10. Washer
11. Crank bracket
12. Steering arm
13. Steering gear
14. Ball joint
15. Left side rod
16. Ball joint
17. Center rod
18. Ball joint
19. Ball joint
20. Right side rod

Steering gear and linkage–Spider

164 SERIES

1. Raise and support the vehicle safely.
2. Measure the distance or amount of threads the tie-rod ends are installed on the link rods, loosen the locknuts and remove the tie-rod ends from the link rods.
3. Installation is the reverse of removal. Tighten the tie-rod end locknut to 29.5–46.5 ft. lbs. (40–63 Nm).

BRAKES

Master Cylinder

Removal and Installation

SPIDER

1. Disconnect the negative battery cable.
2. Disconnect the fluid warning light electrical connector.
3. Remove the fluid from the reservoir.
4. Disconnect the the fluid couplings from the master cylinder.
5. Remove the 2 nuts and remove the master cylinder from the power brake booster.
6. Installation is the reverse of removal. Fill with fluid.

MILANO

NOTE: The master cylinder is part of the ABS hydraulic unit assembly and should not be separated. The following procedure is for removal of the hydraulic unit assembly.

1. Discharge the brake system pressure by removing the ignition key and pressing the brake pedal down repeatedly, 20 times, until it sticks.
2. Disconnect the negative battery cable.
3. Remove the windshield washer reservoir.
4. Drain the clutch and brake fluid from the tank by removing the plug and disconnecting the feed hose from the electropump and draining into a container.
5. Loosen the union and disconnect the pipe from the unit.

6. Disconnect and tag all electrical connections.
7. Remove the bolt for the connection of the front wheel impulse pick-up to the hydraulic unit.
8. Disconnect the clutch master cylinder supply hose.
9. Disconnect the unions for all the pipes connected to the hydraulic unit.
10. Working from inside the passenger compartment, disconnect the brake pedal from the piston of the master cylinder.
11. Remove the retaining nuts and remove the hydraulic system from the studs.
12. Installation is the reverse of removal. Bleed the brake system.

164 SERIES

1. Disconnect the negative battery cable.
2. Remove the fluid from the reservoir and remove the reservoir.
3. Disconnect and tag the fluid pipes, remove the attaching nuts and remove the master cylinder from the vehicle.
4. On the 164S, a brake sensor is attached to the master cylinder and may be removed, if necessary.
5. Installation is the reverse of removal. Fill with fluid and bleed the system.

Proportioning Valve

Removal and Installation

SPIDER

1. Disconnect the negative battery cable.
2. Remove the brake fluid from the reservoir.
3. Raise and support the vehicle safely.

4. Disconnect the 2 couplings, remove the screw attaching the valve and remove the valve from the vehicle.

5. Installation is the reverse of removal. Fill with fluid and bleed the system.

164 SERIES

1. Disconnect the negative battery cable.
2. Raise and support the vehicle safely.
3. Disconnect the pipe fittings at the valve.
4. Remove the 2 attaching bolts and nuts and remove the valve from the vehicle.
5. Installation is the reverse of removal. Tighten the valve attaching bolts to 17.7–22.9 ft. lbs. (24–31 Nm). Fill with fluid and bleed the brake system. Adjust as necessary.

Adjustment

164 SERIES

1. Settle the rear suspension.
2. Position the vehicle on a level surface, place a 165 lb. load in the trunk and fill the fuel tank to capacity.
3. Check the load proportioning valve linkage for freedom of movement.
4. Loosen the adjusting screw and apply a load of 11.023 lbs. (5 Kg) to the lever hole.
5. Tighten the adjustment screw to 42.0–46.5 ft. lbs. (57–63 Nm).

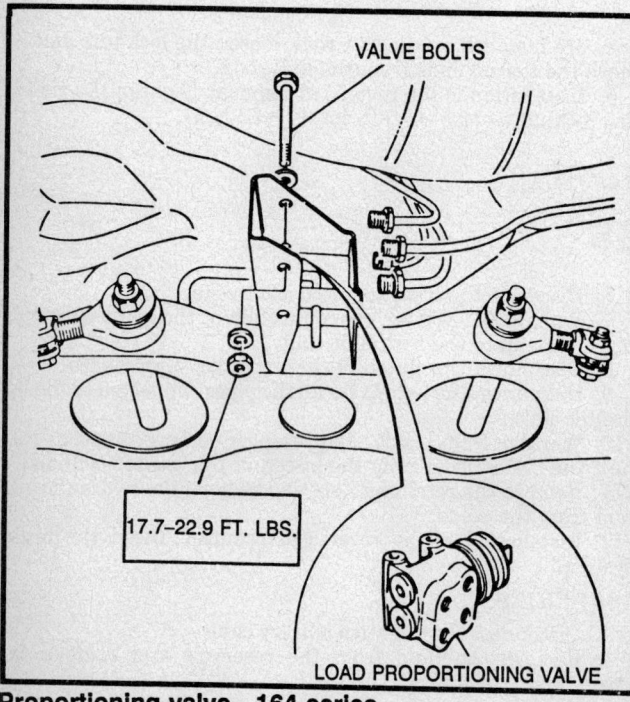

VALVE BOLTS

17.7–22.9 FT. LBS.

LOAD PROPORTIONING VALVE

Proportioning valve—164 series

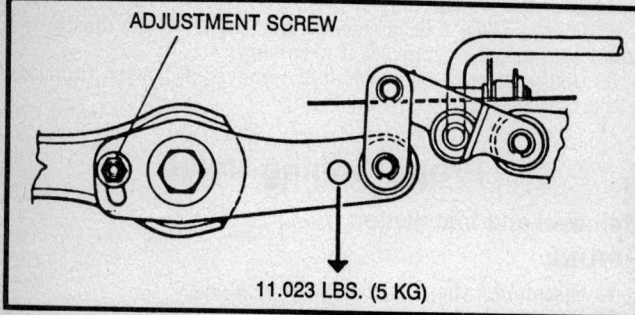

ADJUSTMENT SCREW

11.023 LBS. (5 KG)

Proportioning valve adjustment—164 series

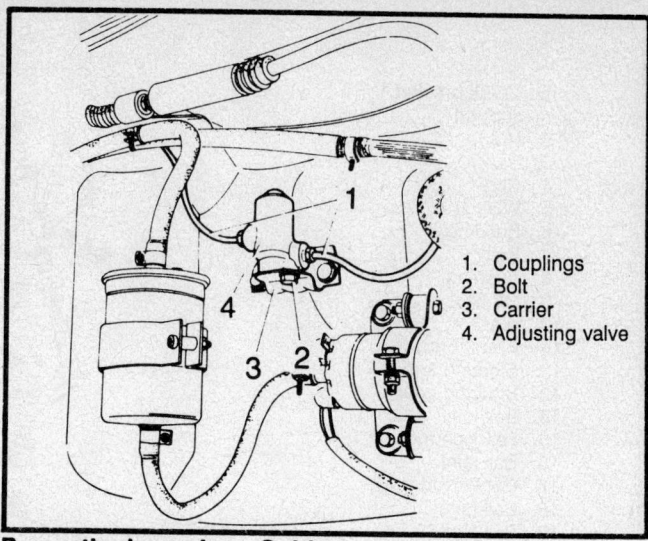

1. Couplings
2. Bolt
3. Carrier
4. Adjusting valve

Proportioning valve—Spider

Power Brake Booster

Removal and Installation

SPIDER

1. Disconnect the negative battery cable.
2. Disconnect the fluid warning light electrical connector.
3. Remove the fluid from the reservoir.
4. Disconnect the the fluid couplings from the master cylinder.
5. Remove the cotter pin, slide off the pin and detatch the lever from the fork.
6. Remove the 2 bolts and separate the clutch master cylinder from the booster.
7. From inside the engine compartment, remove the bolt attaching the booster to the body.
8. Working from inside the passenger compartment, remove the booster to brake pedal fork bolt, the 4 booster retaining nuts and remove the booster from the vehicle.
9. Installation is the reverse of removal. Bleed and fill the brake hydraulic system.

164 SERIES

1. Disconnect the negative battery cable.
2. Disconnect the vacuum inlet hose from the booster.
3. Remove the brake master cylinder.
4. From inside the vehicle, disconnect the brake pedal from the fork.
5. From inside the vehicle, remove the booster retaining nuts and remove the booster from the vehicle.
6. Installation is the reverse of removal. Bleed and fill the brake hydraulic system.

Brake Caliper

Removal and Installation

SPIDER

1. Remove the brake fluid from the reservoir.
2. Raise and support the vehicle safely.
3. Remove the front wheel and remove the brake shoe pads.
4. Disconnect the hydraulic pipe, remove the 2 retaining bolts and remove the caliper.
5. Installation is the reverse of removal. Tighten the caliper to knuckle bolts on the front brakes to 54.6–61.2 ft. lbs. (74–83 Nm) and the caliper to carrier bolts on the rear brakes to 32.5–39.8 ft. lbs. (44–54 Nm). Bleed and fill the hydraulic system.

164 SERIES

Front

1. Raise and support the vehicle safely.
2. Disconnect the fitting and hose from the valance.
3. Disconnect the electrical connection from the wear sensor.
4. Remove the caliper attaching bolt and remove the caliper from the vehicle.
5. Remove the pads and brake caliper mounting bracket, as necessary.
6. Installation is the reverse of removal. Tighten the brake caliper bracket bolts to 38.3–42.8 ft. lbs. (52–58 Nm) and the caliper mounting bolts to 22.9–28 ft. lbs. (31–38 Nm). Bleed the brake system.

Rear

1. Raise and support the vehicle safely.
2. Remove the rear wheel.
3. Disconnect the brake hose at the fitting.
4. Remove the brake caliper attaching bolts, then disconnect the parking brake control cable from the caliper.
5. Remove the pads and brake caliper mounting bracket, as necessary.
6. Installation is the reverse of removal. Tighten the brake caliper bracket bolts to 32.7–36.1 ft. lbs. (44.3–49 Nm) and the caliper mounting bolts to 22.9–25.8 ft. lbs. (31–35 Nm). Bleed the brake system.

Disc Brake Pads

Removal and Installation

SPIDER

1. Remove the brake fluid from the reservoir.
2. Raise and support the vehicle safely and remove the front wheels.
3. Using a punch, remove one of the pins, take out the cross spring, remove the other pin and slide out the pads.
4. Using a suitable tool, push the pistons back in the caliper.
5. Installation is the reverse of removal. Fill the brake fluid reservoir, as necessary.

164 SERIES

Front

1. Raise and support the vehicle safely.
2. Remove some brake fluid from the reservoir.
3. Disconnect the electrical connection from the wear sensor.
4. Remove the caliper attaching bolts and remove the caliper without disconnecting the hose. Support the caliper so as not to put tension on the brake hose.
5. Press manually on the caliper piston until fully in and remove the pads.
6. Installation is the reverse of removal. Tighten the brake caliper mounting bolts to 22.9–28 ft. lbs. (31–38 Nm). Fill with brake fluid, as necessary.

NOTE: Position the pad with the wear sensor on the piston side of the caliper and the relief groove faced towards the rear end of the vehicle.

Rear

1. Raise and support the vehicle safely.
2. Remove some brake fluid from the reservoir.
3. Remove the rear wheels.
4. Remove the brake caliper attaching bolts, and remove the caliper without disconnecting the hose. Support the caliper so as not to put tension on the brake hose.
5. Press manually on the caliper piston until fully in and remove the pads.
6. Installation is the reverse of removal. Tighten the caliper

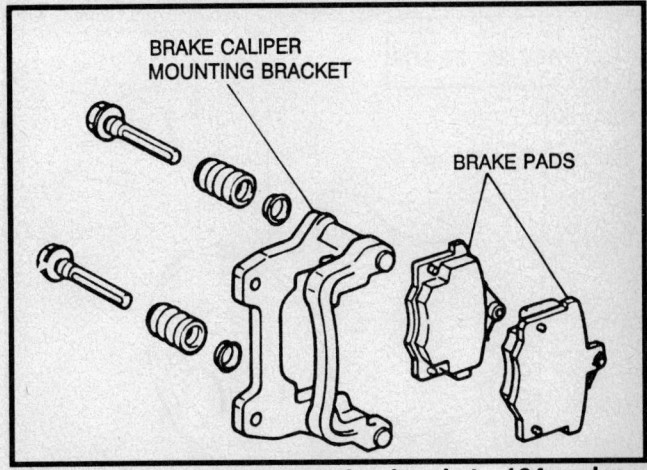

Front brake pads and mounting bracket—164 series

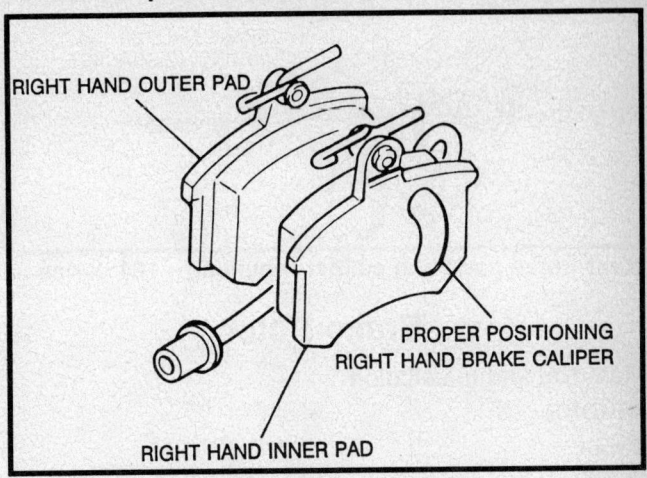

Front brake pad positioning—164 series

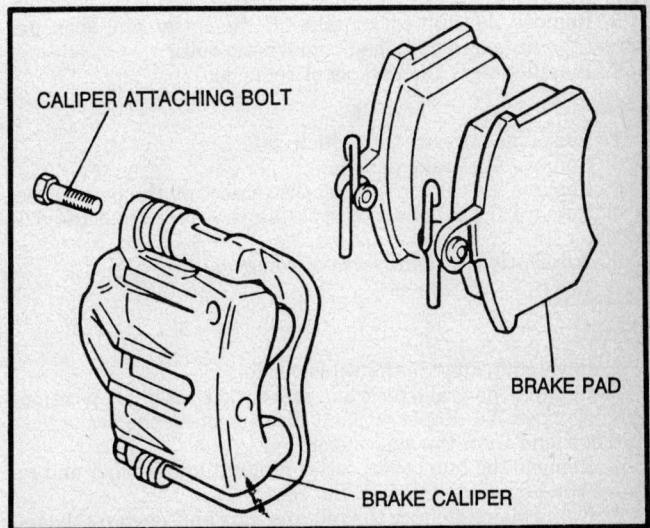

Rear brake pads and caliper—164 series

mounting bolts to 22.9–25.8 ft. lbs. (31–35 Nm). Fill with brake fluid, as necessary.

NOTE: Start the engine and press the brake pedal several times to adjust the parking brake.

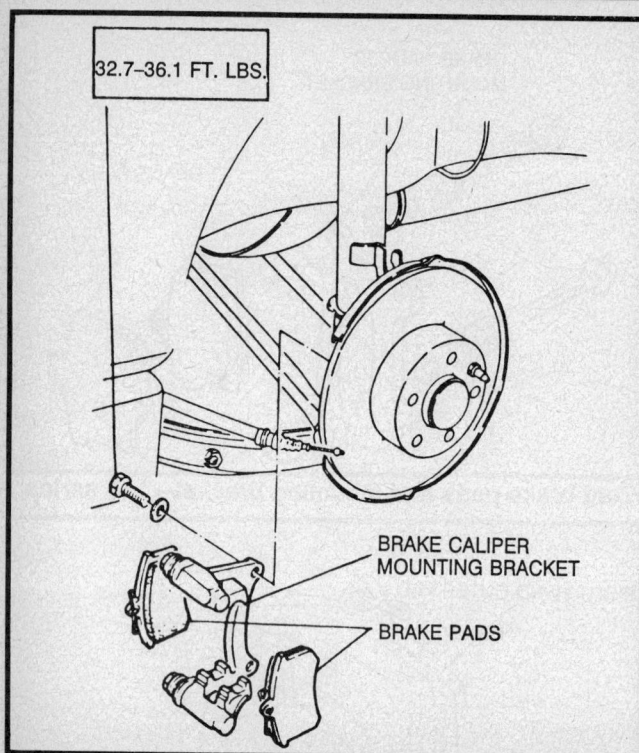

Rear brake pads and caliper mounting—164 series

Brake Rotor

Removal and Installation

SPIDER

Front

1. Raise and support the vehicle safely.
2. Remove the brake pads and mark their assembly position.
3. Remove the hub cover, take off the cotter pin, then unscrew the nuts and bolts and remove the rotor.
4. Installation is the reverse of removal.

Rear

1. Raise and support the vehicle safely.
2. Remove the brake pads.
3. Remove the caliper without disconnecting the brake hose.
4. Remove the 2 bolts and separate the rotor from the axle shaft.
5. Installation is the reverse of removal.

MILANO

Front

1. Raise and support the vehicle safely.
2. Remove the brake pads and mark their assembly position.
3. Remove the caliper without disconnecting the brake hose and suspend from the suspension.
4. Remove the hub cover, cotter pin, nut and washer and remove the hub complete with the rotor.
5. Using pliers, remove the retainer ring and separate the impulse emitting wheel from the hub.
6. Remove the bolts securing the wheel hub to the rotor and separate.
7. Installation is the reverse of removal.

164 SERIES

1. Raise and support the vehicle safely.
2. Remove the caliper and pads without disconnecting the

brake hose and suspend from the suspension.
3. Remove the 2 rotor to hub retaining bolts and remove the rotor.
4. Installation is the reverse of removal. Tighten both rotor retaining bolts to 4.6–9.6 ft. lbs. (6.2–13 Nm).

Parking Brake Cable

Adjustment

SPIDER

1. Make sure the parking brake control lever is in the rest position.
2. Adjust the parking brakes as in the the parking brake shoe removal procedure.
3. Screw the nut until the axial clearance of the cable is zeroed.
4. Activate the parking brake control lever and check that the rear wheels lock.

MILANO

1. Make sure the parking brake control lever is in the rest position.
2. With the brake pad clearance adjusted correctly, adjust the nut at the end of the threaded end of the cable until the axial clearance of the cable is zeroed.
3. Operate the parking brake lever and check that the rear wheels are locked after 4–5 clicks.

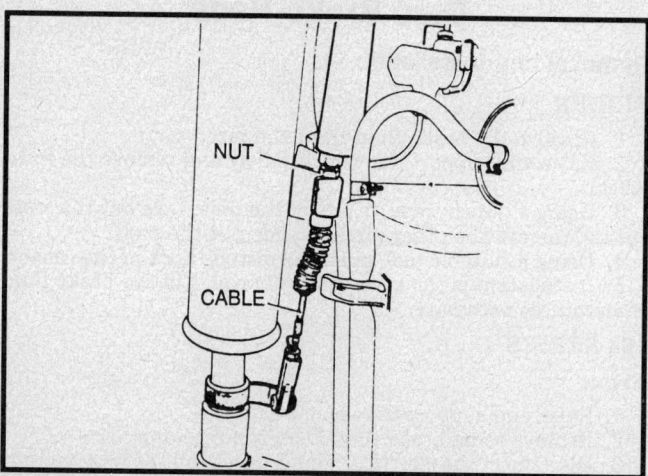

Parking brake cable adjusting nut—Spider

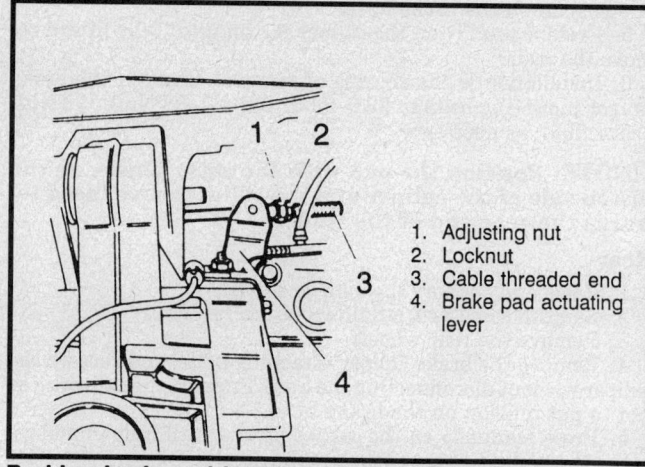

1. Adjusting nut
2. Locknut
3. Cable threaded end
4. Brake pad actuating lever

Parking brake cable adjustment—Milano

164 SERIES

The parking brake adjustment must be carried out only after the brake pads, the cable or caliper have been replaced, since the take-up of the slack is automatic, normally.

1. With the parking brake control cables disconnected from the brake calipers, perform at least 10 hard applications of the brake pedal to allow the automatic slack take-up device to resume the normal operating position.
2. Connect the control cables to the brake calipers.
3. Set the parking brake lever to the 3rd detent.
4. Turn the adjustment nut until the wheels are blocked.
5. Operate the parking brake lever 4–5 times and check that the sector gear does not trip more than 7 teeth and the wheels are free with the control lever in the rest position.

Removal and Installation

SPIDER

1. Raise and support the vehicle safely.
2. Remove the cotter pin, slide out the pin, then release the fork with the cable.
3. Disconnect the cable from the bracket.
4. Remove the cotter pins, slide out the pins and release the driving cables of the brake shoes from the links.
5. Remove the cotter pins, slide off the pins and remove the links with the cable from the outer differential casing.
6. Release the cable casing from the bracket on the right side trailing arm.
7. Installation is the reverse of removal. Perform the parking brake adjustment.

MILANO

1. Raise and support the vehicle safely.
2. Remove the exhaust pipe front and center section.
3. Disconnect the remote control rod from the gear lever and move aside to gain access to parking brake control lever and cable connection.

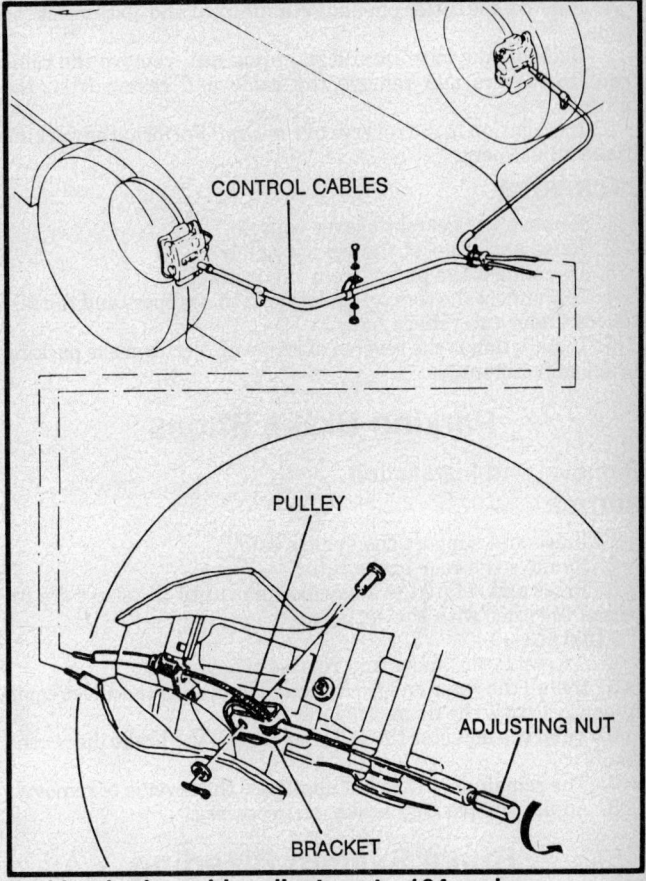

Parking brake cable adjustment—164 series

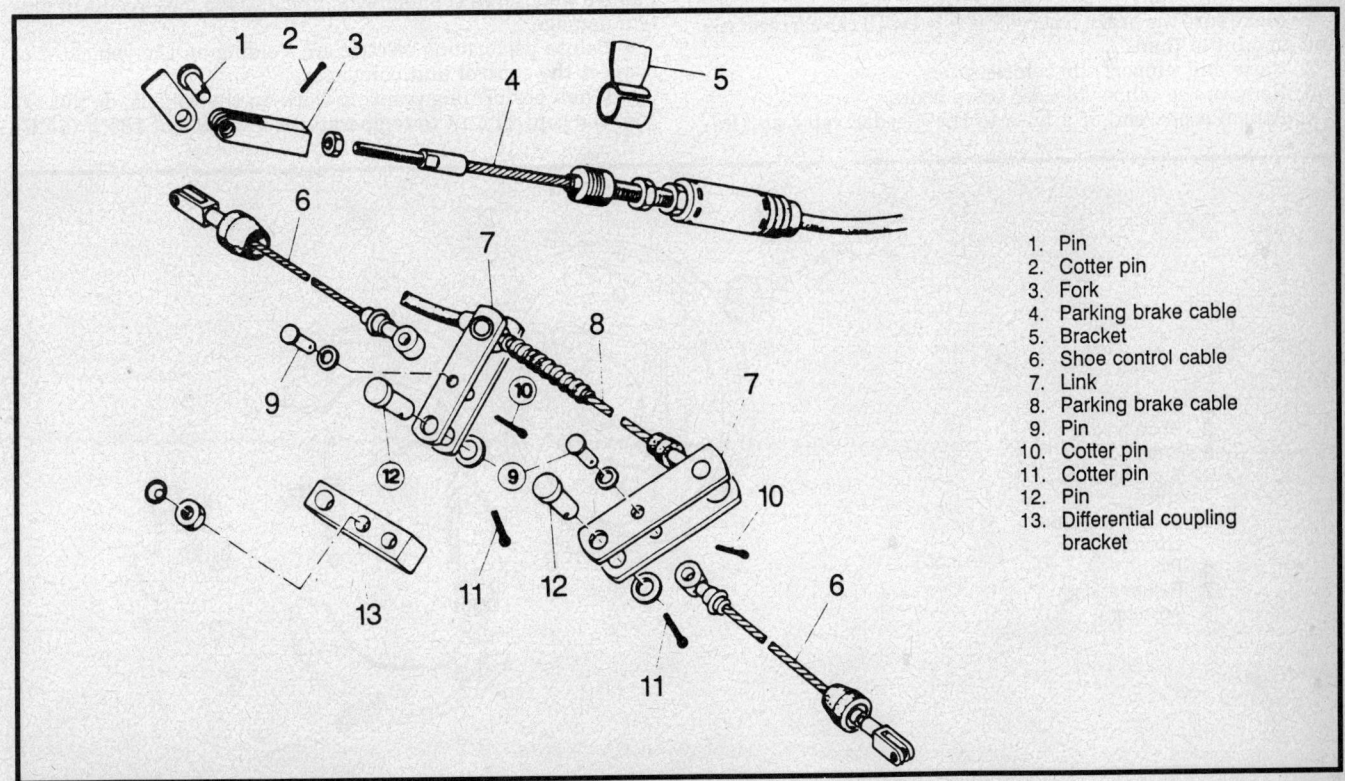

1. Pin
2. Cotter pin
3. Fork
4. Parking brake cable
5. Bracket
6. Shoe control cable
7. Link
8. Parking brake cable
9. Pin
10. Cotter pin
11. Cotter pin
12. Pin
13. Differential coupling bracket

Parking brake cable—Spider

4. Remove the cotter pin and retaining pin and disconnect the cable.

5. Back off the locknut and retaining nut, remove the cable from the levers and remove the cable and casing from the bracket.

6. Installation is the reverse of removal. Perform the parking brake adjustment.

164 SERIES

1. Remove the gearshift lever console.
2. Raise and support the vehicle safely.
3. Disconnect the pulley from the bracket.
4. Disconnect the control cables from the calipers and the fasteners under the vehicle body.
5. Installation is the reverse of removal. Perform the parking brake adjustment.

Parking Brake Shoes

Removal and Installation

SPIDER

1. Raise and support the vehicle safely.
2. Remove the rear brake rotor.
3. Press and rotate the 2 bayonet pins until the shoes are released together with the springs.

To install:

4. Assemble the shoes and release the adjuster.
5. Install the rotor and turn the adjuster until the shoes come in contact with the drum on rotor.
6. Turn the adjuster the other way until the brake disc turns freely.
7. The remainder of the installation is the reverse of removal.
8. Adjust the parking brake, as necessary.

Brake System Bleeding

SPIDER AND 164 SERIES

1. Make sure the brake reservoir is filled with the correct type and amount of fluid.
2. Raise and support the vehicle safely.
3. Remove the caliper bleeder valve boots.
4. Attach a one end of a hose to the bleeder valve and im-

merse the other end in a container of brake fluid.

5. Loosen the bleeder screws and press the brake pedal repeatedly, waiting a few seconds between times. Repeat this operation until the container is totally bubble free, then press the pedal down and lock the bleeder valves.

6. Repeat this operation for all 4 wheels.

MILANO

Front

1. Make sure the brake reservoir is filled with the correct type and amount of fluid.
2. Raise and support the vehicle safely.
3. Remove the caliper bleeder valve boot.
4. Attach a one end of a hose to the bleeder valve and immerse the other end in a container of brake fluid.
5. Loosen the bleeder screws and press the brake pedal repeatedly, waiting a few seconds between times. Repeat this operation until the container is totally bubble free, then press the pedal down and lock the bleeder valves.
6. Repeat this operation for the other front caliper.

Rear

1. Turn the key to **IGNITION** and check for the electropump activation and await disconnection.
2. Raise and support the vehicle safely.
3. Remove the caliper bleeder valve boots.
4. Attach a one end of a hose to the bleeder valves and immerse the other end in a container of brake fluid.
5. Loosen the bleeder screws and keep the brake pedal slightly depressed until the container is totally bubble free, then tighten the the bleeder valves and remove the hoses.
6. Repeat Steps 3–5 to the other rear caliper.

Anti-Lock Brake System Service

Precaution

Failure to observe the following precautions may result in system damage.

• Before performing electric arc welding on the vehicle, disconnect the control unit connectors.

• When performing painting work on the vehicle, do not expose the control unit to temperatures in excess of 185°F (85°C)

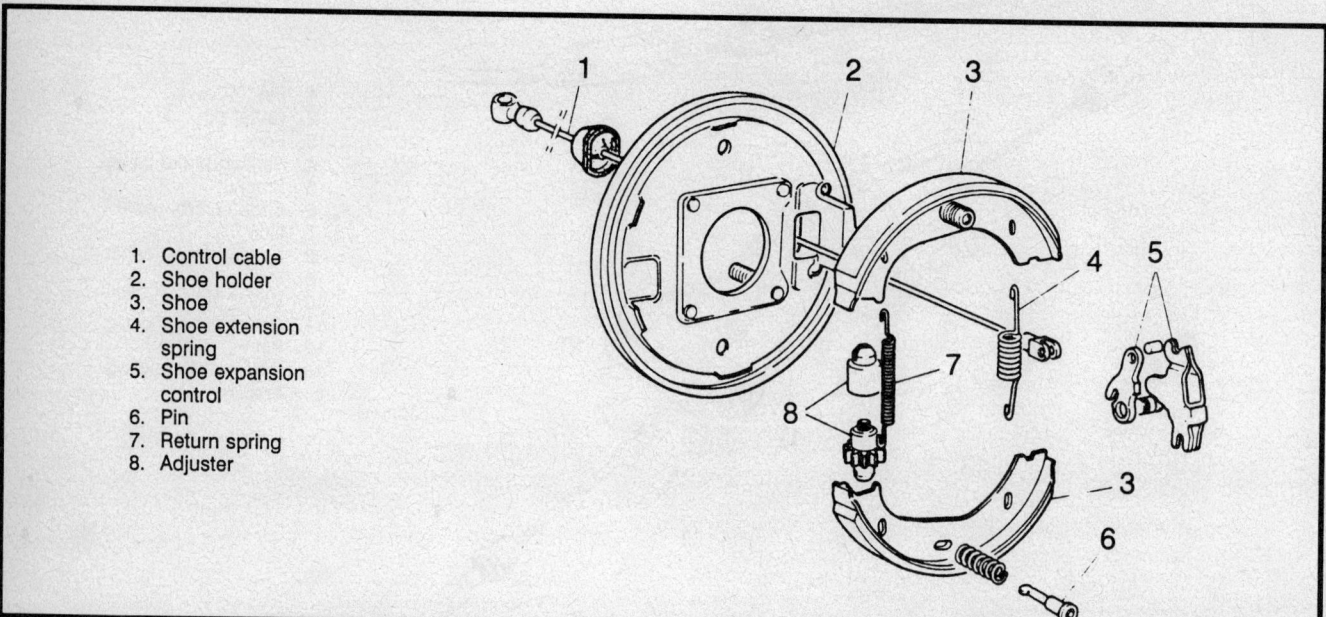

1. Control cable
2. Shoe holder
3. Shoe
4. Shoe extension spring
5. Shoe expansion control
6. Pin
7. Return spring
8. Adjuster

Exploded view of the parking brake shoes–Spider

for longer than 2 hrs. The system may be exposed to temperatures up to 200°F (95°C) for less than 15 min.

• Never disconnect or connect the electronic control unit or electro-hydraulic unit connectors with the ignition switch ON.

• Never disassemble any component of the Anti-Lock Brake System (ABS) which is designated non-servicable; the component must be replaced as an assembly.

• When filling the master cylinder, always use brake fluid which meets Super DOT-4 specifications; petroleum base fluid will destroy the rubber parts.

Relieving Anti-Lock Brake System Pressure

MILANO

Discharge the brake system pressure by removing the ignition key and pressing the brake pedal down repeatedly, 20 times, until it sticks.

Hydraulic Assembly

Removal and Installation

MILANO

1. Discharge the brake system pressure by removing the ignition key and pressing the brake pedal down repeatedly, 20 times, until it sticks.
2. Disconnect the negative battery cable.
3. Remove the windshield washer reservoir.
4. Drain the clutch and brake fluid from the tank by removing the plug and disconnecting the feed hose from the electropump and draining into a container.
5. Loosen the union and disconnect the pipe from the unit.
6. Disconnect and tag all electrical connections.
7. Remove the bolt for the connection of the front wheel impulse pick-up to the hydraulic unit.
8. Disconnect the clutch master cylinder supply hose.
9. Disconnect the unions for all the pipes connected to the hydraulic unit.
10. Working from inside the passenger compartment, disconnect the brake pedal from the piston of the master cylinder.
11. Remove the retaining nuts and remove the hydraulic system from the studs.
12. Installation is the revers of removal. Bleed the brake system.

NOTE: Do not disassemble the electrovalve unit and brake pressure adjusting valve components or separate the master cylinder from the hydraulic unit.

Electropump Unit

Removal and Installation

MILANO

1. Discharge the brake system pressure by removing the ignition key and pressing the brake pedal down repeatedly, 20 times, until it sticks.
2. Disconnect the negative battery cable.
3. Drain the brake and clutch fluid.
    a. Remove the plug from the reservoir tank.
    b. Disconnect and drain the feed hose from the electropump and drain from the tank.
4. Disconnect the connectors from the electric motors and pressure switch.
5. Disconnect the pipe and spring from the electropump unit.
6. Remove the screw securing the electropump unit to the support and remove the electropump from the support by sliding it off the pin.
7. Installation is the reverse of removal. Fill with fluid and bleed the system.

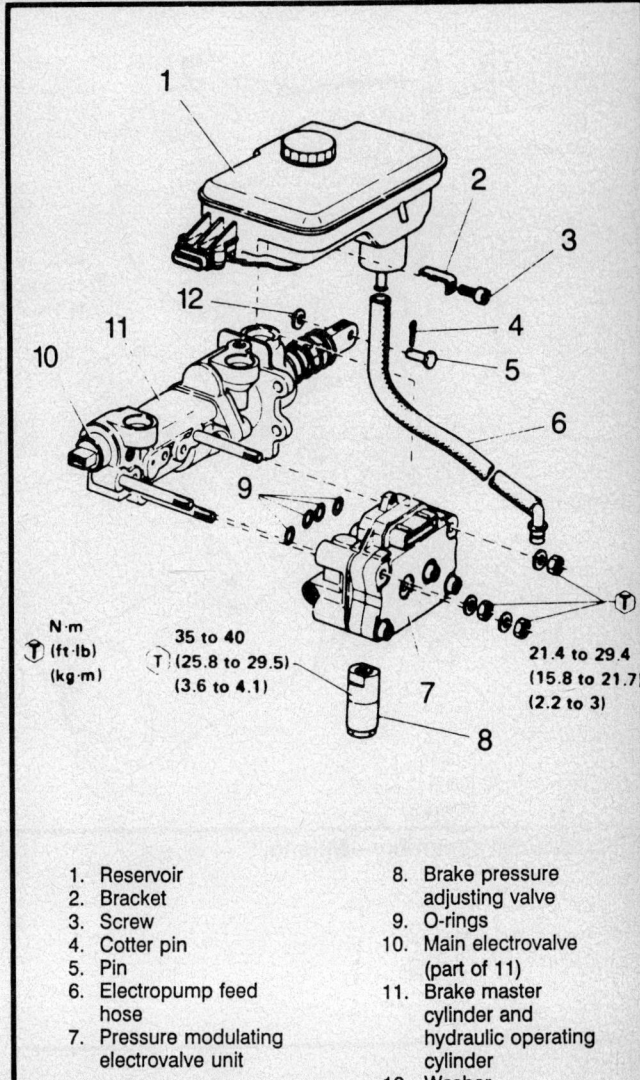

1. Reservoir	8. Brake pressure
2. Bracket	adjusting valve
3. Screw	9. O-rings
4. Cotter pin	10. Main electrovalve
5. Pin	(part of 11)
6. Electropump feed	11. Brake master
hose	cylinder and
7. Pressure modulating	hydraulic operating
electrovalve unit	cylinder
	12. Washer

N·m (ft·lb) (kg·m)

35 to 40 (25.8 to 29.5) (3.6 to 4.1)

21.4 to 29.4 (15.8 to 21.7) (2.2 to 3)

Hydraulic assembly—Milano

Electro-Hydraulic Unit

Removal and Installation

164 SERIES

NOTE: The electro-hydraulic replacement units are supplied fully serviced with brake fluid and with the solenoid valves open. Therefore bleeding and servicing are that of a conventional brake system.

1. Disconnect the negative battery cable.
2. Remove the cover from the relays.
3. Remove the clamp securing the harness and disconnect the harness connector and the ground wire.
4. Disconnect, mark and plug all fluid pipes to the electro-hydraulic unit. Also plug the ports of the electro-hydraulic unit.
5. Remove the electro-hydraulic unit from the support.
6. Installation is the reverse of removal. Fill with fluid and bleed the brake system.

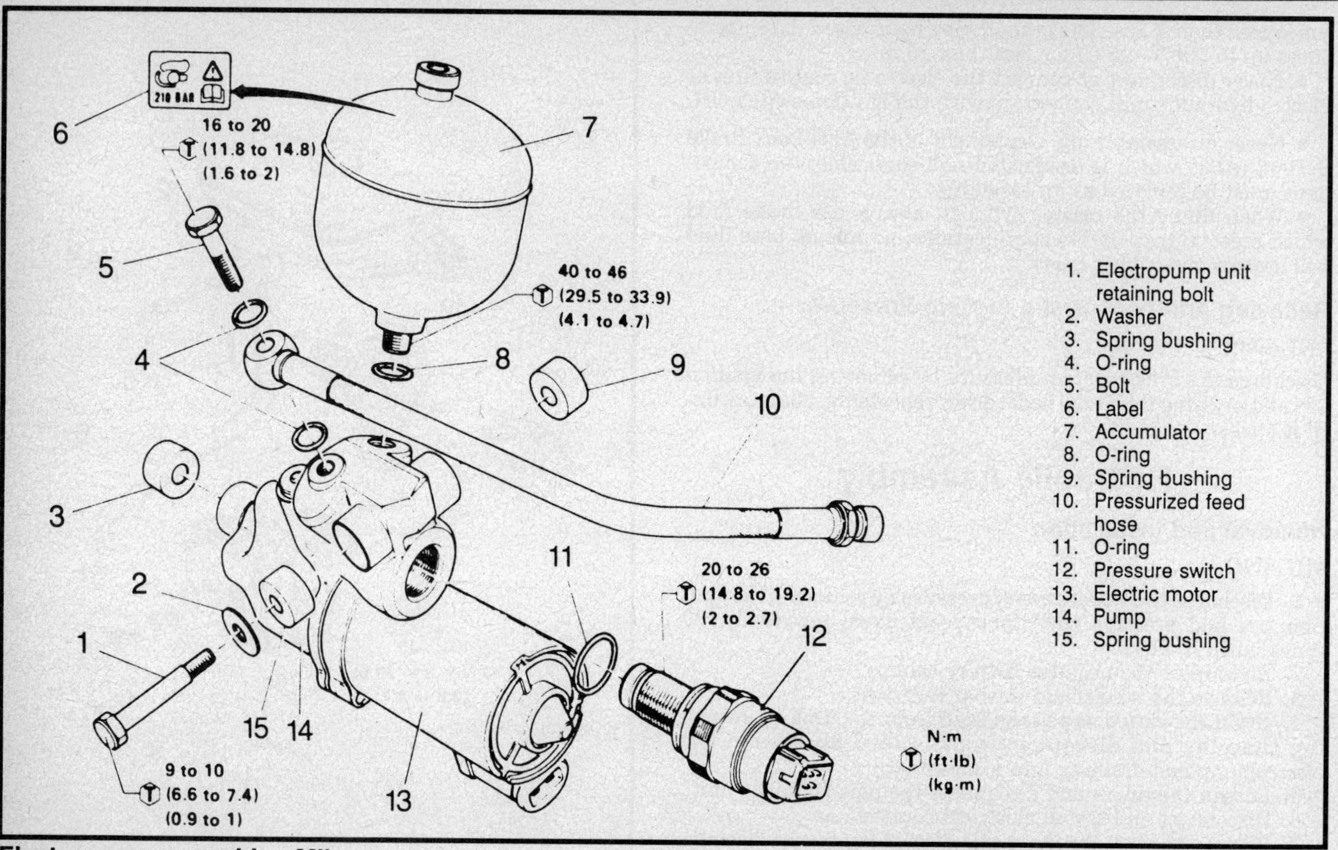

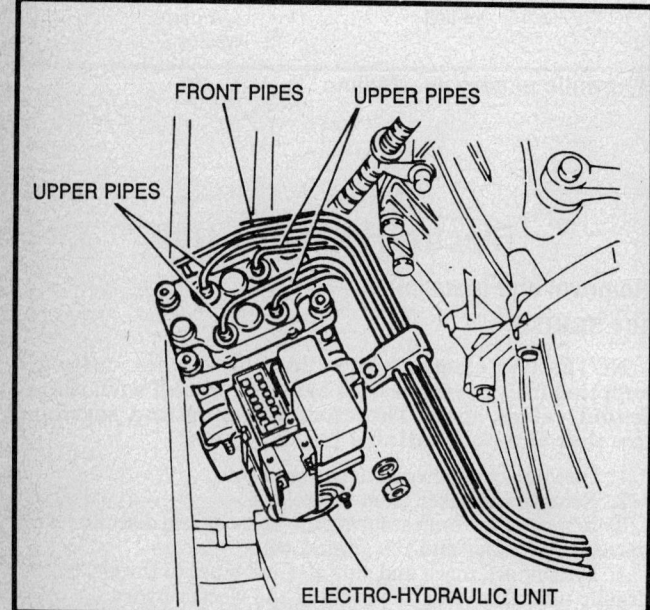

6
16 to 20
(11.8 to 14.8)
(1.6 to 2)

210 BAR

5

4

3

2

1

9 to 10
(6.6 to 7.4)
(0.9 to 1)

15 14

13

7

40 to 46
(29.5 to 33.9)
(4.1 to 4.7)

8

9

10

11

20 to 26
(14.8 to 19.2)
(2 to 2.7)

12

N·m
(ft·lb)
(kg·m)

1. Electropump unit retaining bolt
2. Washer
3. Spring bushing
4. O-ring
5. Bolt
6. Label
7. Accumulator
8. O-ring
9. Spring bushing
10. Pressurized feed hose
11. O-ring
12. Pressure switch
13. Electric motor
14. Pump
15. Spring bushing

Electropump assembly—Milano

FRONT PIPES   UPPER PIPES

UPPER PIPES

ELECTRO-HYDRAULIC UNIT

Electro hydraulic unit fluid pipe connections—model 164

Impulse Pick-Up

Removal and Installation

MILANO

Front

1. Disconnect the negative battery cable.
2. Disconnect the electrical connection of the cable of the front impulse pick-up in the engine compartment.
3. Raise and support the vehicle safely.
4. Remove the bolt securing the cable bracket to the suspension upper link.
5. Remove the bolt securing the impulse pick-up to the support and remove the impulse pick-up.
6. Installation is the reverse of removal. Use a thickness gauge and check that the air gap between the impulse pick-up and the impulse emitting wheel is 0.03 in. (0.7mm). Turn the adjusting screw to adjust.

Rear

1. Disconnect the negative battery cable.
2. Remove the rear seat, raise the sound proof upholstery, then disconnect the electrical connection of the rear impulse pick-up.
3. Raise and support the vehicle safely.
4. Release the impulse pick-up cable from the 3 clips on the axle tube.
5. Remove the bolt securing the impulse pick-up to the support and remove the impulse pick-up.
6. Installation is the reverse of removal. Use a thickness gauge and check that the air gap between the impulse pick-up and the impulse emitting wheel is 0.04 in. (1.1mm). Turn the adjusting screw to adjust.

Inductive Sensor

Removal and Installation
164 SERIES
Front

1. Disconnect the negative battery cable.
2. Disconnect the electrical connector inside of the wheel.
3. Remove the safety lock, retaining bolt and spacer and remove the sensor.

To install:

4. Coat the spacer mounting surface with Shell Retinax grease or its equivalent.
5. Insert a feeler gauge of 0.0084–0.0295 in. (0.25–0.75mm) between the pulse generator and the sensor support.
6. Position the sensor into its support and hand screw the mounting screw.
7. Using a second feeler gauge, measure the distance between the sensor supporting surface and the support, install shims as needed and tighten the sensor attaching screw.

Rear

1. Disconnect the negative battery cable.
2. Raise and support the vehicle safely and remove the wheel.
3. Disconnect the electrical connector located in the trunk.
4. Remove the safety lock, retaining bolt and spacer and remove the sensor.

To install:

5. Coat the spacer mounting surface with Shell Retinax grease or its equivalent.
6. Insert a feeler gauge of 0.0084–0.0295 in. (0.25–0.75mm) between the pulse generator and the sensor support.
7. Position the sensor into its support and hand screw the mounting screw.
8. Using a second feeler gauge, measure the distance between the sensor supporting surface and the support, install shims as needed and tighten the sensor attaching screw.

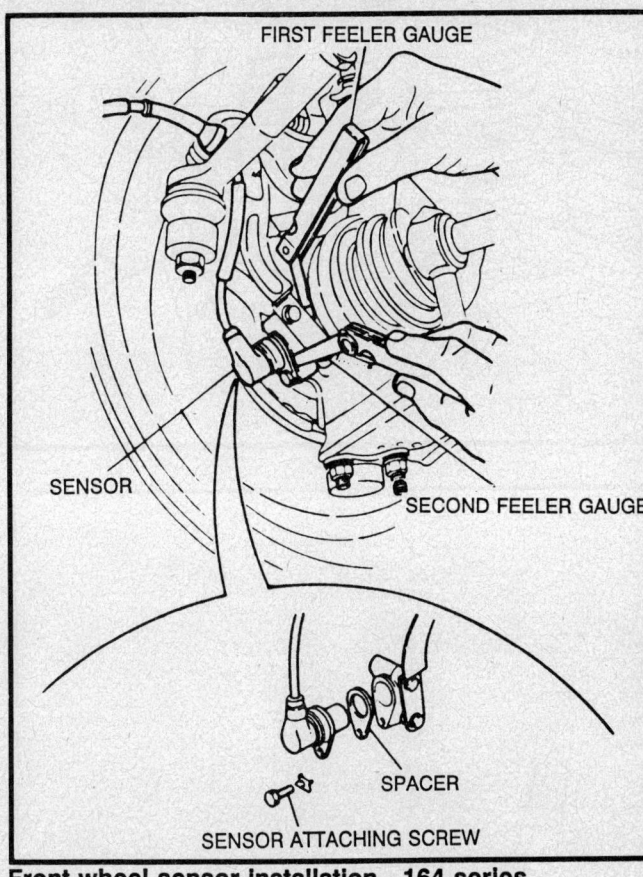

FIRST FEELER GAUGE

SENSOR

SECOND FEELER GAUGE

SPACER

SENSOR ATTACHING SCREW

Front wheel sensor installation—164 series

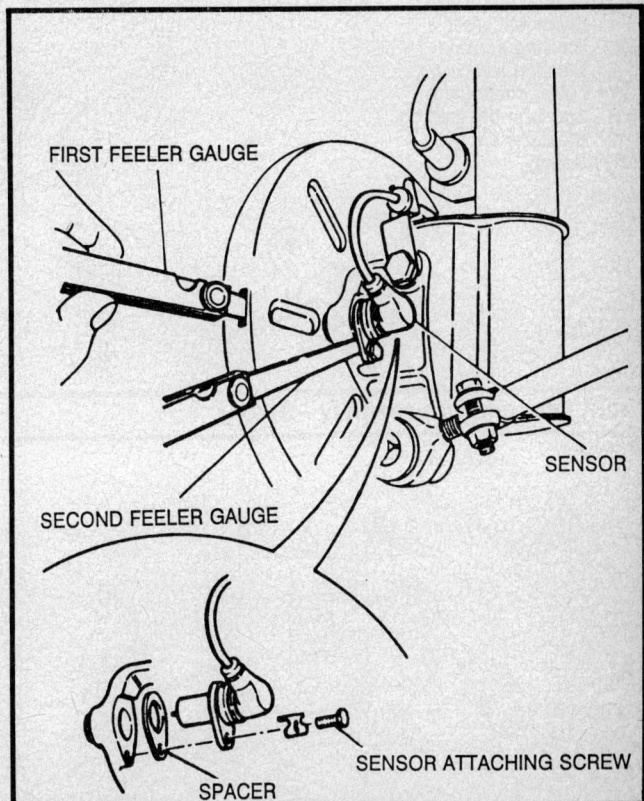

FIRST FEELER GAUGE

SENSOR

SECOND FEELER GAUGE

SPACER

SENSOR ATTACHING SCREW

Rear wheel sensor installation—164 series

FRONT SUSPENSION

Shock Absorbers

Removal and Installation
SPIDER

1. Raise and support the vehicle safely and remove the wheel.
2. Remove the locknut and nut from the top of the shock absorber.
3. Remove the nut securing the shock to the lower wishbone and remove the shock absorber, washers and upper bushings.
4. Installation is the reverse of removal.

MILANO

1. Remove underhood components as necessary to gain access to the shock to body retaining nuts.
2. From the engine compartment, disconnect the upper

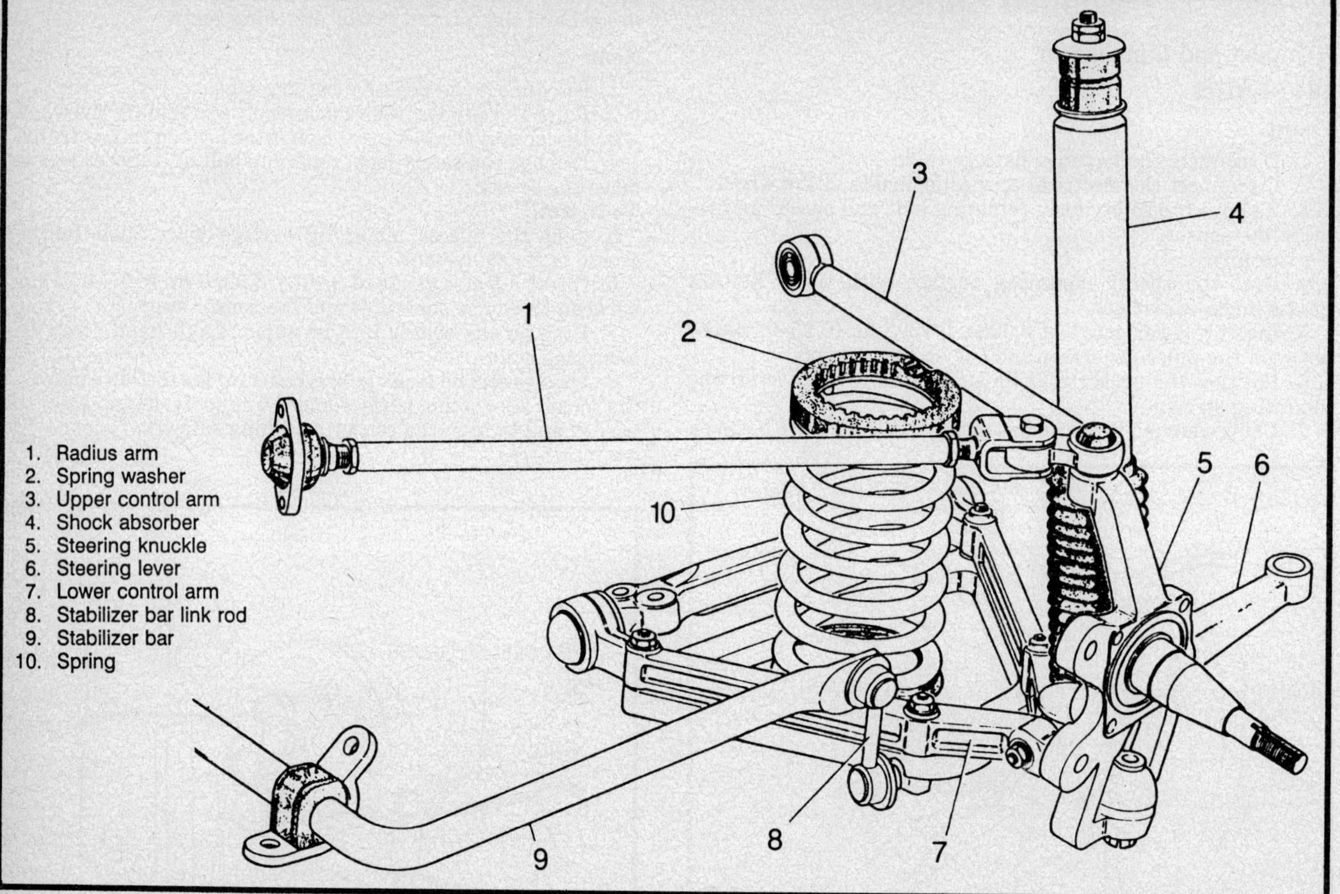

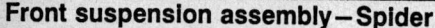

1. Radius arm
2. Spring washer
3. Upper control arm
4. Shock absorber
5. Steering knuckle
6. Steering lever
7. Lower control arm
8. Stabilizer bar link rod
9. Stabilizer bar
10. Spring

Front suspension assembly—Spider

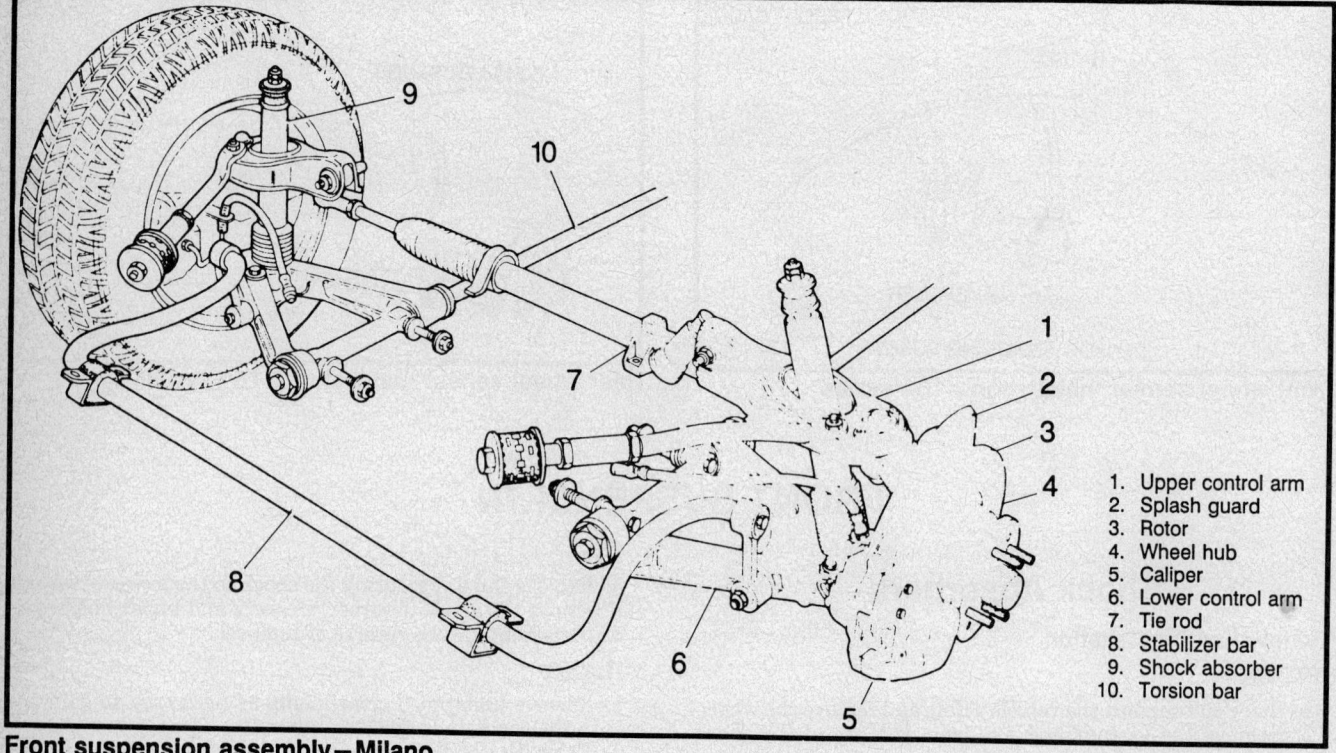

1. Upper control arm
2. Splash guard
3. Rotor
4. Wheel hub
5. Caliper
6. Lower control arm
7. Tie rod
8. Stabilizer bar
9. Shock absorber
10. Torsion bar

Front suspension assembly—Milano

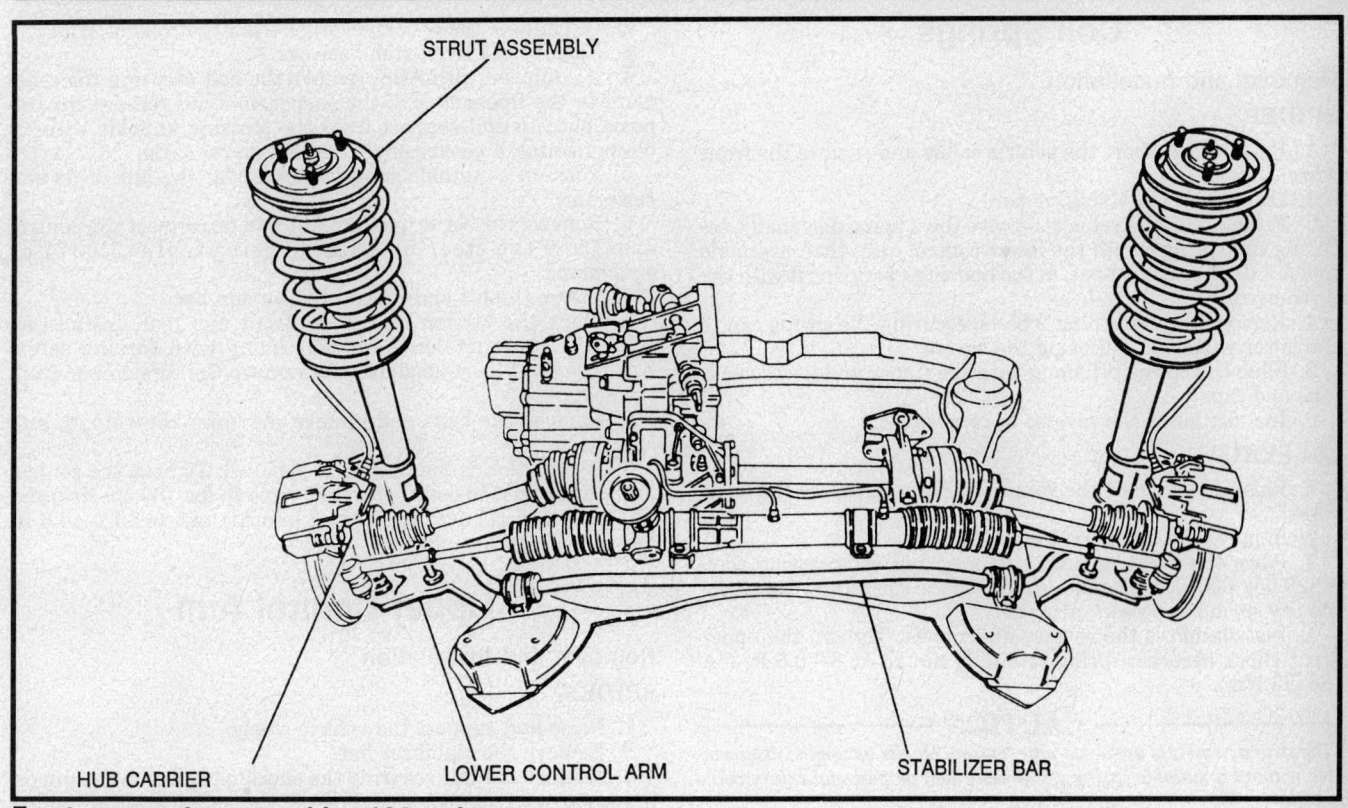

STRUT ASSEMBLY

HUB CARRIER   LOWER CONTROL ARM   STABILIZER BAR

Front suspension assembly—164 series

shock absorber locknut, retaining nut, washers and bushings.

3. Raise and support the vehicle safely.

4. Disconnect the shock absorber to lower control arm retaining bolts and remove the shock absorber.

5. Installation is the reverse of removal. Tighten the shock absorber upper locknut to 17.7–21.4 ft. lbs. (24–29 Nm) and the shock absorber to lower control arm bolt to 18.4–22.9 ft. lbs. (25–31 Nm).

MacPherson Strut

Removal and Installation

164 SERIES

1. Raise and support the vehicle safely and remove the front wheel.

2. Disconnect the lower strut from the hub carrier.

3. Disconnect the 3 upper strut to wheelarch retaining nuts and remove the strut assembly.

4. Installation is the reverse of removal. Tighten the lower strut to hub carrier bolts to 29.5–36.2 ft. lbs. (40–49 Nm) and the upper strut to wheelarch retaining nuts to 8.86–11.1 ft. lbs. (12–15 Nm).

CAUTION

The strut assembly is under extreme tension. Do not attempt to disassemble without a suitable spring compressor tool or personal injury could result.

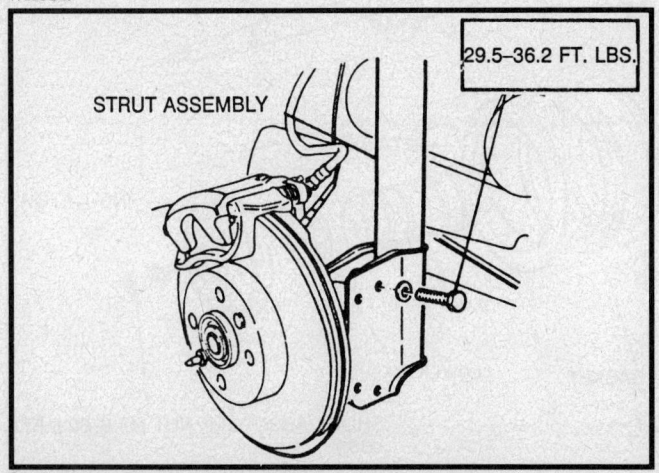

29.5–36.2 FT. LBS.

STRUT ASSEMBLY

Lower strut attaching bolts—164 series

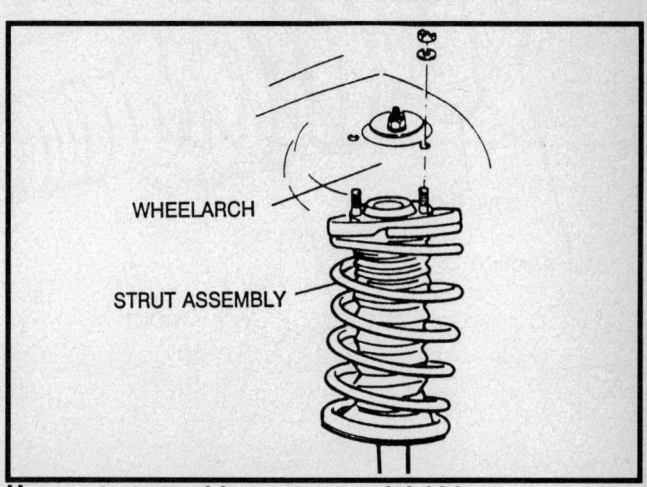

WHEELARCH

STRUT ASSEMBLY

Upper strut attaching nuts—model 164

Coil Springs

Removal and Installation
SPIDER

1. Raise and support the vehicle safely and remove the front wheel.
2. Disconnect the stabilizer bar.
3. From under the vehicle, remove the 2 bolts, diagonally, securing the spring cap to the lower control arm, then assemble tool A.2.0169 or equivalent, in the housings, securing it with the 2 removed bolts.
4. Remove the remaining 2 bolts, securing the spring cap to the lower wishbone, releasing the spring.
5. Slide the spring off along with the upper and lower cushions and cap.
6. Installation is the reverse of removal.

164 SERIES

1. Raise and support the vehicle safely and remove the front wheel.
2. Remove the front strut assembly.
3. Place the strut assembly in a spring compression tool, 1.820.089.000 or equivalent, compress the spring and disassemble the spring and shock absorber.
4. Installation is the reverse of removal. Tighten the upper strut shock absorber/spring retaining nut to 48.8–60.5 ft. lbs. (66–82 Nm).

―――――――――――――― **CAUTION** ――――――――――――――
The strut assembly is under extreme tension. Do not attempt to disassemble without a suitable spring compressor tool or personal injury could result.

Torsion Bars

Removal and Installation
MILANO

1. Raise and support the vehicle safely.

2. Disconnect the shock absorber from the control arm.
3. Remove the front stabilizer bar.
4. If equipped with ABS, remove the bolt securing the cable plate to the upper link of the suspension and remove the impulse pick-up and support from the steering knuckle without disconnecting it electrically. Carefully move aside.
5. Position a suitable support jack under the link seats and raise unit.
6. Remove the cotter pin and nut and disconnect the control arm from the steering knuckle using tool A.3.0377 or equivalent.
7. Lower the lift and unload the torsion bar.
8. Mark the torsion bar at the front and rear, install tool A.3.0374 or equivalent, and nut along with forcing screw A.3.0374/0001 or equivalent, and remove the torsion bar from the seat.
9. Remove the bolts and remove the lower control arm and spacers.
10. Installation is the reverse of removal. Tighten the control arm (lower link) to body bolts to 59–66.4 ft. lbs. (80–90 Nm) and the lower control arm to steering knuckle nut to 33.2–40.6 ft. lbs. (45–55 Nm).

Upper Control Arm

Removal and Installation
SPIDER

1. Raise and support the vehicle safely.
2. Remove the stabilizer bar.
3. Remove the nut securing the shock absorber to the pin on the lower control arm and slide off the shock absorber along with the inner and outer washers.
4. Remove the spring assembly.
5. Remove the cotter pin and nut securing the upper control arm to the steering knuckle, then using tool A.3.0156 or equivalent, disconnect the upper control arm from the knuckle.
6. Remove the bolt connecting the upper control arm to the control arm.
7. Working from inside the engine compartment, remove the

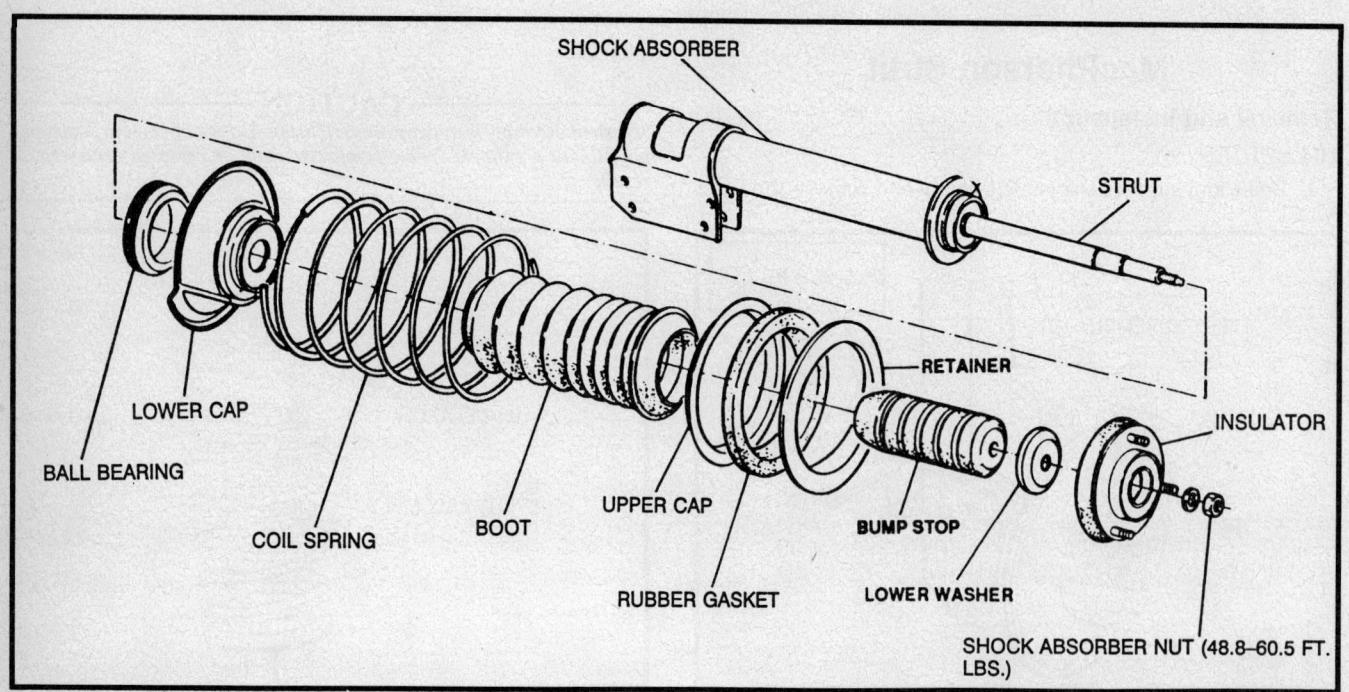

Exploded view of the strut assembly—164 series

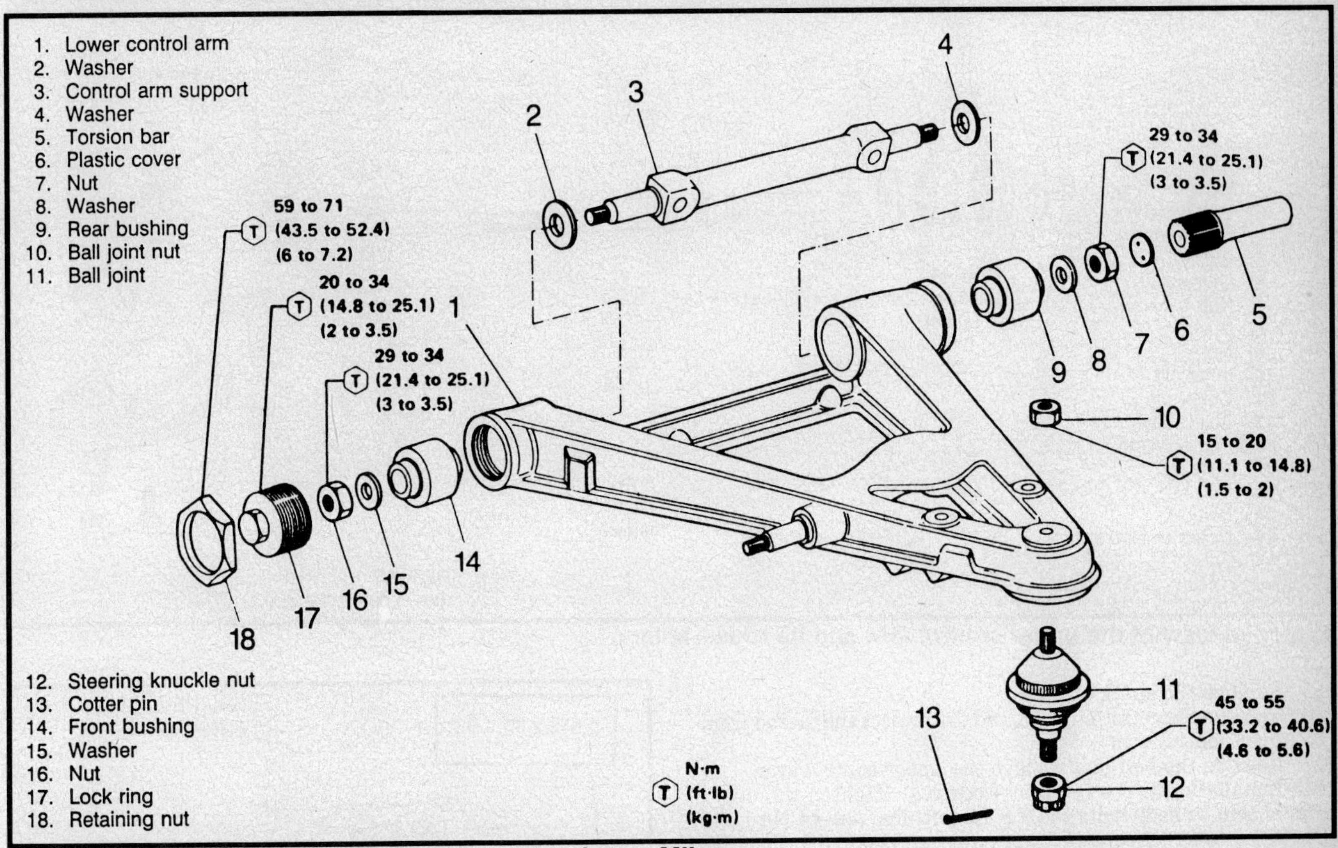

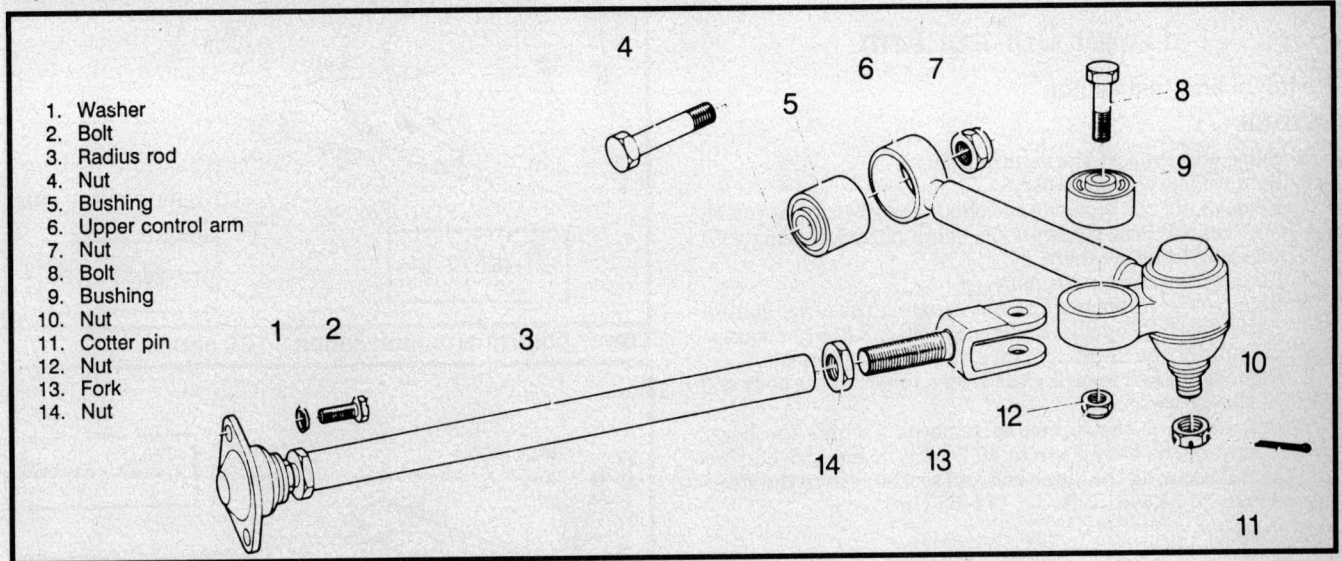

1. Lower control arm
2. Washer
3. Control arm support
4. Washer
5. Torsion bar
6. Plastic cover
7. Nut
8. Washer
9. Rear bushing
10. Ball joint nut
11. Ball joint

(T) 59 to 71 (43.5 to 52.4) (6 to 7.2)

(T) 20 to 34 (14.8 to 25.1) (2 to 3.5)

(T) 29 to 34 (21.4 to 25.1) (3 to 3.5)

(T) 29 to 34 (21.4 to 25.1) (3 to 3.5)

(T) 15 to 20 (11.1 to 14.8) (1.5 to 2)

12. Steering knuckle nut
13. Cotter pin
14. Front bushing
15. Washer
16. Nut
17. Lock ring
18. Retaining nut

(T) 45 to 55 (33.2 to 40.6) (4.6 to 5.6)

N·m
(T) (ft·lb)
(kg·m)

Exploded view of the lower control arm torsion bars—Milano

1. Washer
2. Bolt
3. Radius rod
4. Nut
5. Bushing
6. Upper control arm
7. Nut
8. Bolt
9. Bushing
10. Nut
11. Cotter pin
12. Nut
13. Fork
14. Nut

Exploded view of the upper control arm and radius rod—Spider

bolt securing the upper control arm to the body and remove the upper control arm.

8. Installation is the reverse of removal. Tighten the control arm to the upper control arm bolt to 27.3–33.9 ft. lbs. (37-46 Nm).

MILANO

1. Raise and support the vehicle safely.
2. Disconnect the shock absorber from the lower control arm.
3. Remove the front stabilizer bar.

4. If equipped with ABS, remove the bolt securing the cable plate to the upper control arm of the suspension and remove the impulse pick-up and support from the steering knuckle without disconnecting it electrically. Carefully move aside.

5. Position a suitable support jack under the control arm seats and raise unit.

6. Remove the cotter pin and nut and disconnect the upper control arm from the steering knuckle using tool A.3.0377 or equivalent.

7. Lower the support jack to lower the upper control arm.

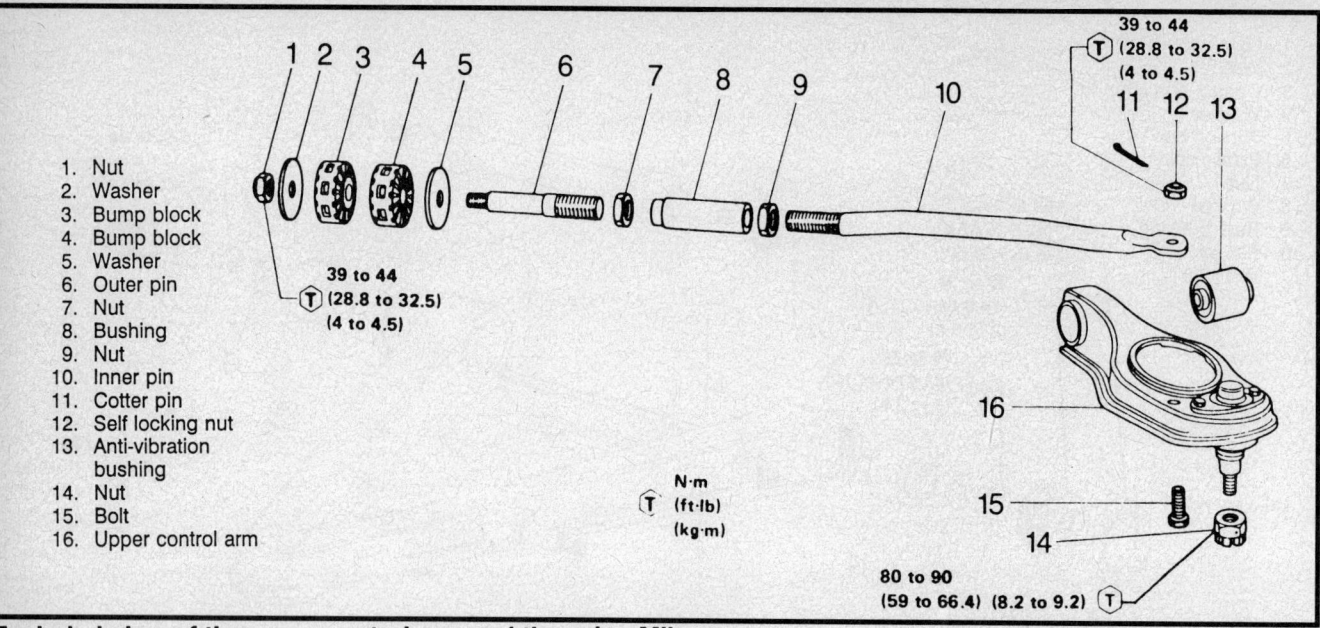

1. Nut
2. Washer
3. Bump block
4. Bump block
5. Washer
6. Outer pin
7. Nut
8. Bushing
9. Nut
10. Inner pin
11. Cotter pin
12. Self locking nut
13. Anti-vibration bushing
14. Nut
15. Bolt
16. Upper control arm

39 to 44 (28.8 to 32.5) (4 to 4.5)

39 to 44 (28.8 to 32.5) (4 to 4.5)

N·m (ft·lb) (kg·m)

80 to 90 (59 to 66.4) (8.2 to 9.2)

Exploded view of the upper control arm and tie rods—Milano

8. Remove the shock absorber.
9. Remove the cotter pin, nut and disconnect the tie rod from the upper control arm.
10. Remove the bolt and remove the upper control arm.
11. Installation is the reverse of removal. Tighten the upper control arm to body bolts to 28.8–32.5 ft. lbs. (39–44 Nm) and the tie rod to upper control arm to nut to 28.8–32.5 ft. lbs. (39–44 Nm).

Lower Control Arm

Removal and Installation

SPIDER

1. Raise and support the vehicle safely.
2. Remove the stabilizer bar.
3. Remove the nut securing the shock absorber to the pin on the lower control arm. Slide off the shock absorber along with the inner and outer washers.
4. Remove the spring assembly.
5. Remove the cotter pin and nut securing the lower control arm to the steering knuckle, then using tool A.3.0157 or equivalent, disconnect the lower control arm from the knuckle.
6. Remove the bolt securing the lever support to the body and remove the entire lever.
7. Installation is the reverse of removal. Tighten the lower control arm to the body bolts to 40.6–42.8 ft. lbs. (55–58 Nm) and the nut securing the lower ball and socket joint to the steering knuckle to 54.6–61.2 ft. lbs. (74–83 Nm).

MILANO

1. Raise and support the vehicle safely.
2. Disconnect the shock absorber from the lower link.
3. Remove the front stabilizer bar.
4. If equipped with ABS, remove the bolt securing the cable plate to the upper link of the suspension and remove the impulse pick-up and support from the steering knuckle without disconnecting it electrically. Carefully move aside.
5. Position a suitable support jack under the link seats and raise unit.
6. Remove the cotter pin and nut and disconnect the lower control arm from the steering knuckle using tool A.3.0377 or equivalent.

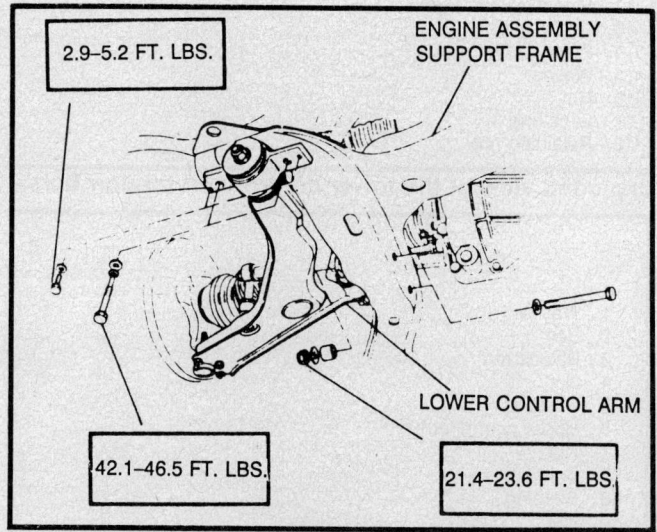

2.9–5.2 FT. LBS. — ENGINE ASSEMBLY SUPPORT FRAME — LOWER CONTROL ARM — 42.1–46.5 FT. LBS. — 21.4–23.6 FT. LBS.

Lower control arm installation—164 series

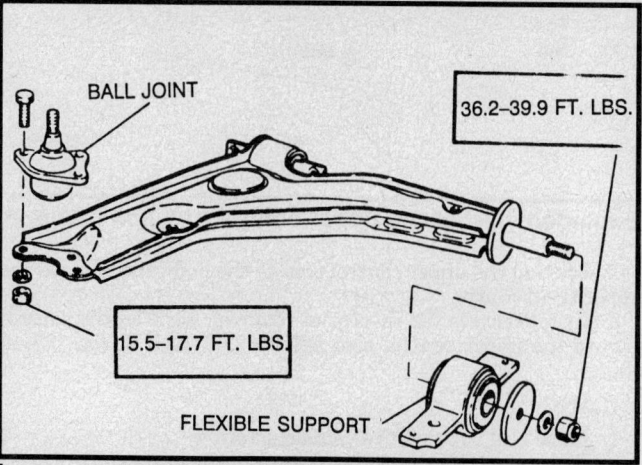

BALL JOINT — 36.2–39.9 FT. LBS. — 15.5–17.7 FT. LBS. — FLEXIBLE SUPPORT

Lower control arm installation—164 series

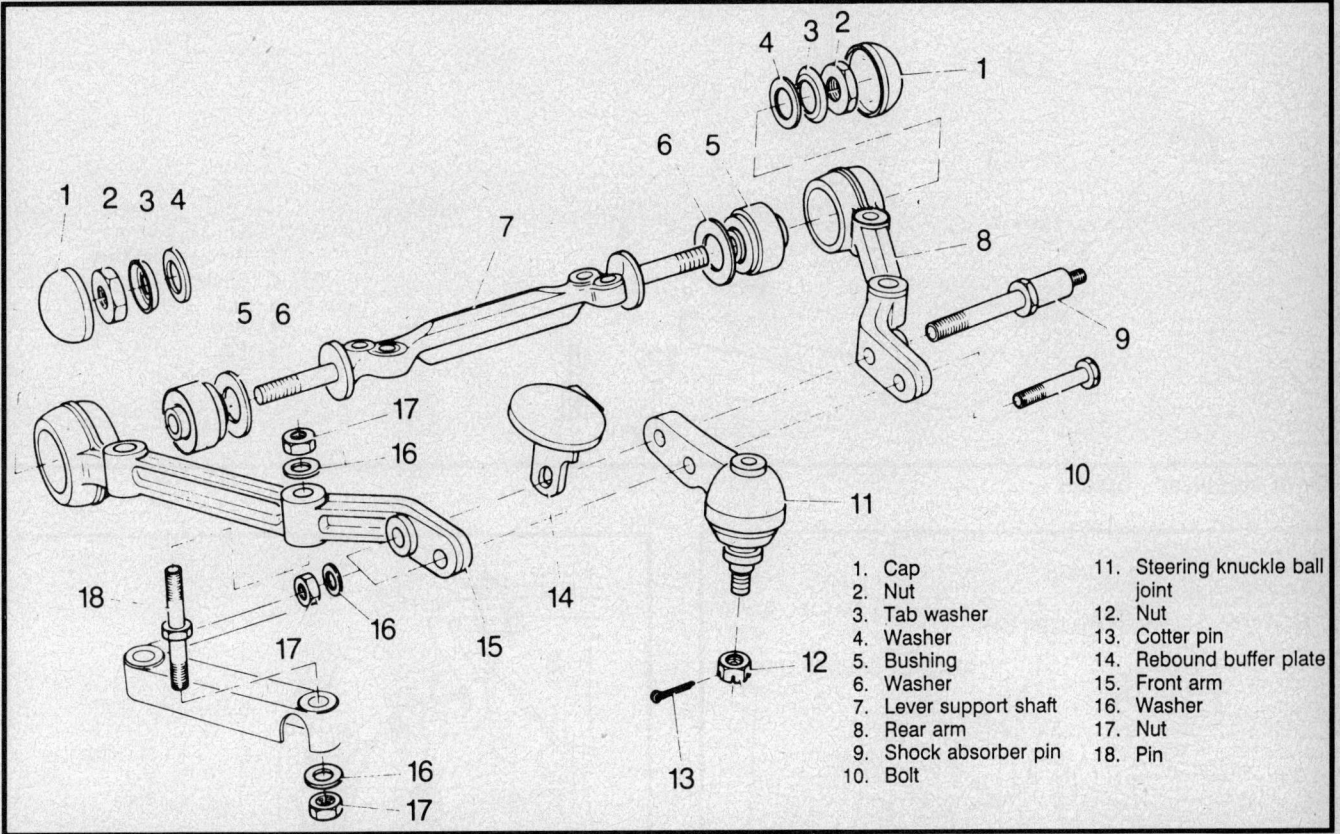

1. Cap
2. Nut
3. Tab washer
4. Washer
5. Bushing
6. Washer
7. Lever support shaft
8. Rear arm
9. Shock absorber pin
10. Bolt
11. Steering knuckle ball joint
12. Nut
13. Cotter pin
14. Rebound buffer plate
15. Front arm
16. Washer
17. Nut
18. Pin

Exploded view of the lower control arm—Spider

7. Lower the lift and unload the torsion bar.
8. Mark the torsion bar at the front and rear, install tool A.3.0374 or equivalent, and nut along with forcing screw A.3.0374/0001 or equivalent, and remove the torsion bar from the seat.
9. Remove the bolts and remove the lower control arm and spacers.
10. Remove the torsion bar from the front.
11. Installation is the reverse of removal. Tighten the control arm to body bolts to 59–66.4 ft. lbs. (80–90 Nm) and the lower control arm to steering knuckle nut to 33.2–40.6 ft. lbs. (45–55 Nm).

164 SERIES

1. Raise and support the vehicle safely and remove the front wheel.
2. Remove the stabilizer arm from the control arm arm.
3. Using a suitable tool, pull out the ball joint from the hub carrier.
4. Remove the bolts and remove the control arm from the engine support frame.
5. Installation is the reverse of removal. Tighten the stabilizer bar nuts to 11.8–14.8 ft. lbs. (16–20 Nm), ball joint-to-hub carrier nut to 36.9–44.3 ft. lbs. (50–60 Nm), control arm-to-engine support frame bolts to 21.4–23.6 ft. lbs. (29–32 Nm) and the control arm front bolts to 42.1–46.5 ft. lbs. (57–63 Nm) for the long bolts and 2.9–5.2 ft. lbs. (4–7 Nm) for the short bolts.

Radius Rod

Removal and Installation
SPIDER

1. Raise and support the vehicle safely.

2. Remove the 2 bolts securing the control arm to the body and the bolt connecting it to the upper control arm.
3. Installation is the reverse of removal. Tighten the 2 bolts securing the control arm to the body to 16.2–19.9 ft. lbs. (22–27 Nm) and the bolt connecting it to the upper control arm to 79.7–98.8 ft. lbs. (108–134 Nm).

Stabilizer Bar

Removal and Installation
SPIDER

1. Raise and support the vehicle safely.
2. Remove the bolts securing the stabilizer bar to the body.
3. Disconnect the stabilizer bar from the link rods leaving the link rods connected to the lower control arm.
4. Installation is the reverse of removal. Tighten the bolts securing the stabilizer bar-to-body to 14.8–16.2 ft. lbs. (20–22 Nm) and the the stabilizer bar-to-link rod nuts to 53.1–59 ft. lbs. (72–80 Nm).

MILANO

1. Raise and support the vehicle safely.
2. Remove the nuts securing the stabilizer connecting rod to the lower control arm.
3. Remove the securing bracket bolts from the stabilizer bar.
4. Remnove the connecting rods from the stabilizer bar using a press.
5. Installation is the reverse of removal. Tighten the nuts securing the stabilizer connecting rod-to-lower control arm to 13.3–17 ft. lbs. (18–23 Nm) and the bracket retaining bolts to 18.4–21.4 ft. lbs. (25–29 Nm).

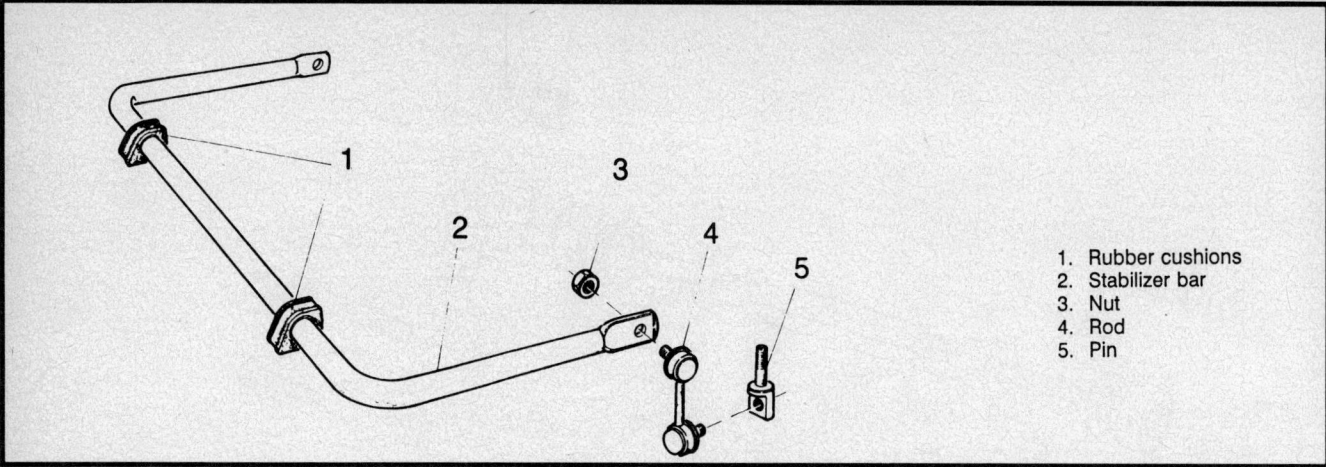

1. Rubber cushions
2. Stabilizer bar
3. Nut
4. Rod
5. Pin

Front stabilizer—Spider

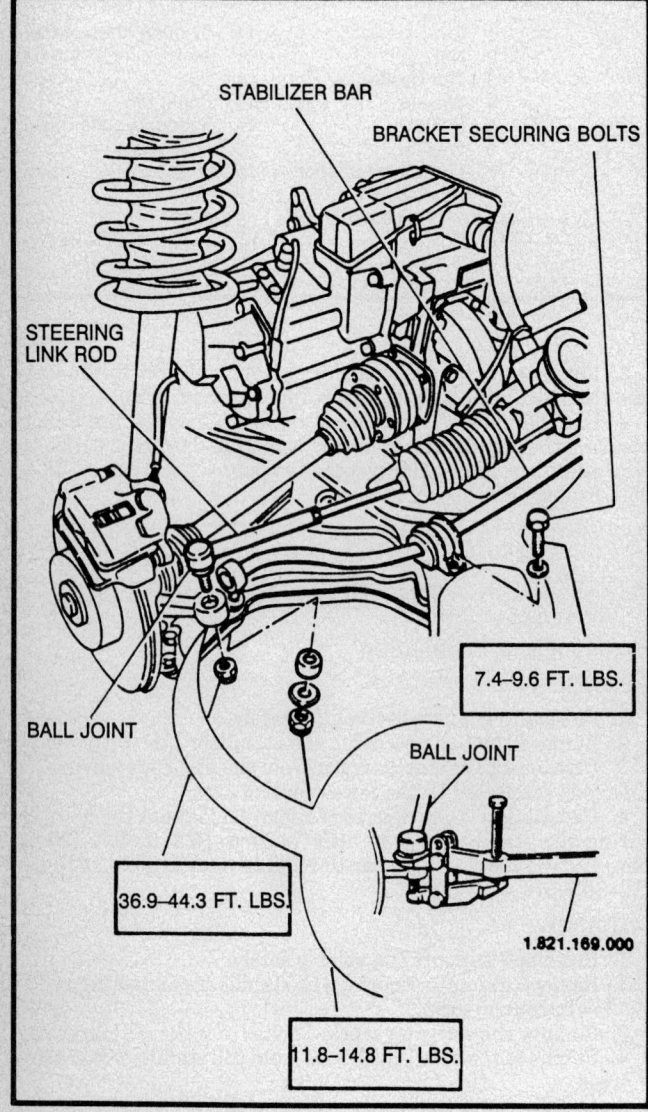

STABILIZER BAR

BRACKET SECURING BOLTS

STEERING LINK ROD

BALL JOINT

BALL JOINT

7.4–9.6 FT. LBS.

36.9–44.3 FT. LBS.

1.821.169.000

11.8–14.8 FT. LBS.

Front stabilizer installation—164 series

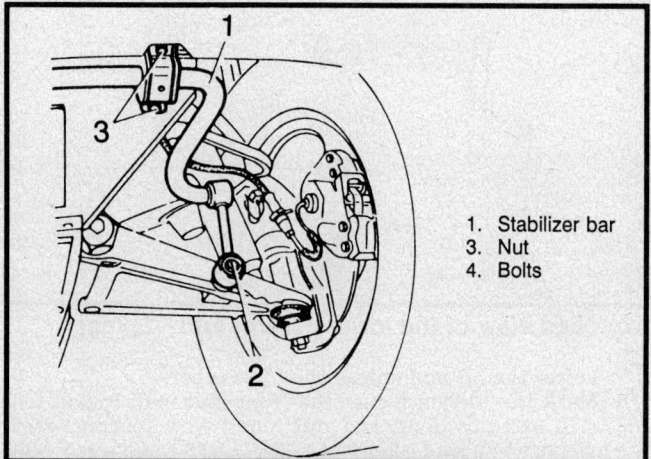

1. Stabilizer bar
3. Nut
4. Bolts

Front stabilizer installation—Milano

164 SERIES

1. Raise and support the vehicle safely and remove the front wheel.
2. Remove the wheel housing rear protection cover.
3. Disconnect the stabilizer bar from the suspension arms.
4. Remove the securing bracket bolts from the stabilizer bar.
5. Using a suitable tool, pull out the ball joint from the steering link rod.
6. Pull out the stabilizer bar from the side of the vehicle where the link rod was disconnected.
7. Installation is the reverse of removal.

Front Wheel Bearings

For front wheel bearing removal and installation and adjustment, please refer to Front Wheel Hub Knuckles and Bearings in the Drive Axle section.

REAR SUSPENSION

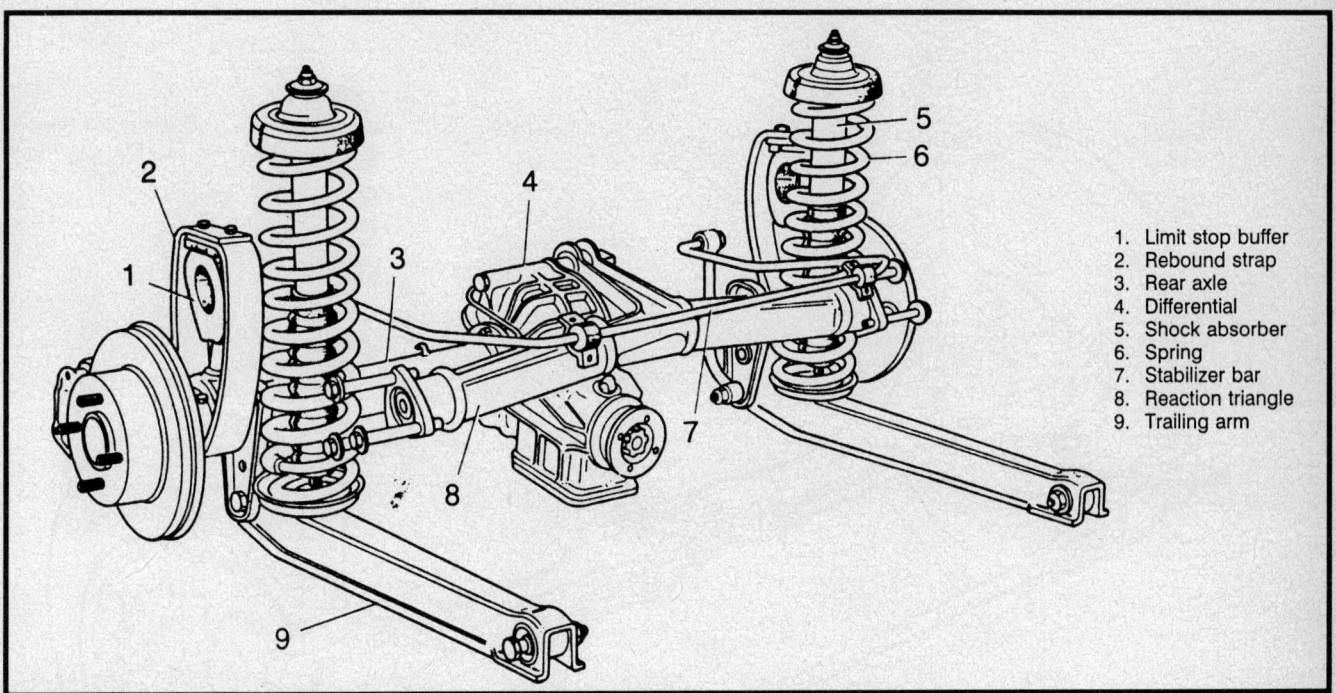

1. Limit stop buffer
2. Rebound strap
3. Rear axle
4. Differential
5. Shock absorber
6. Spring
7. Stabilizer bar
8. Reaction triangle
9. Trailing arm

Rear suspension—Spider

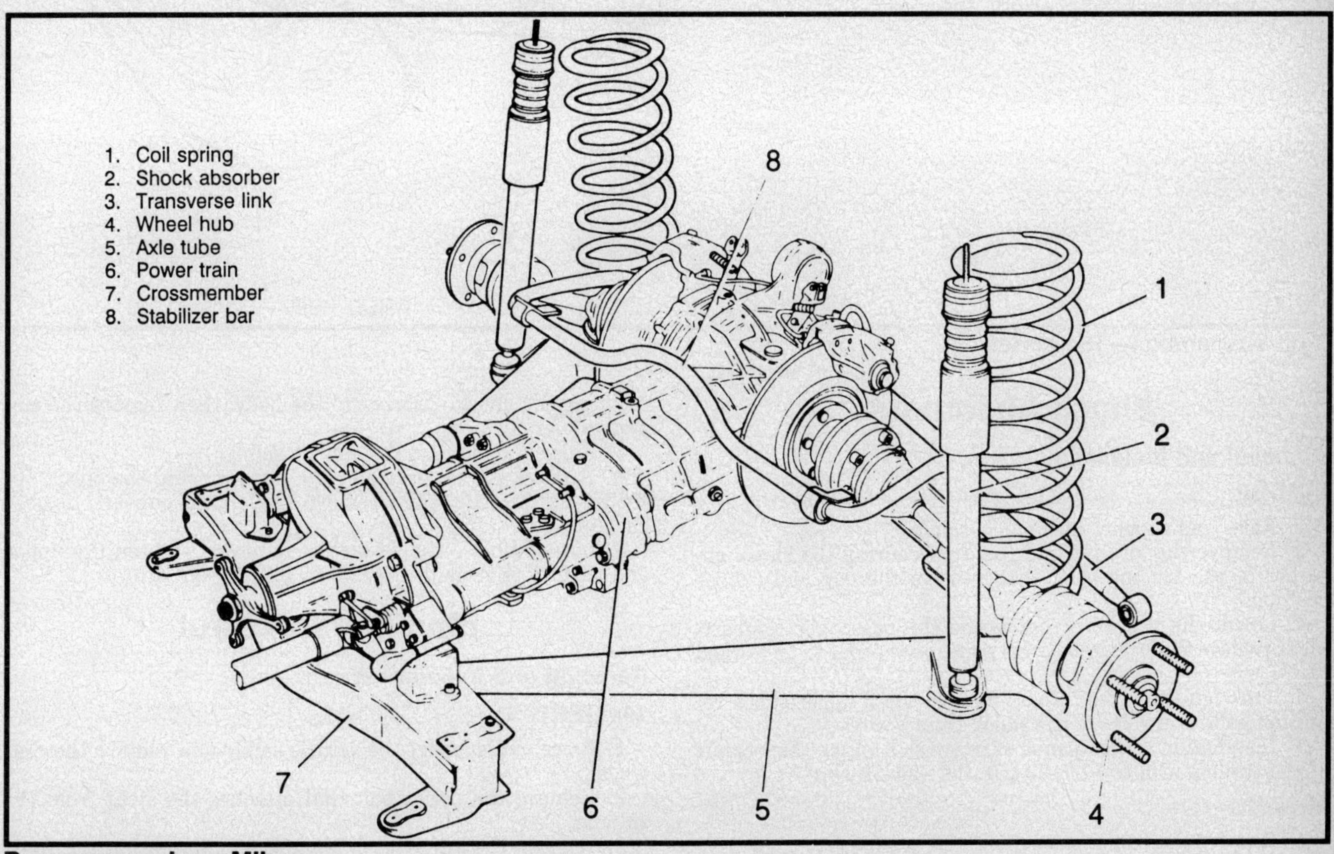

1. Coil spring
2. Shock absorber
3. Transverse link
4. Wheel hub
5. Axle tube
6. Power train
7. Crossmember
8. Stabilizer bar

Rear suspension—Milano

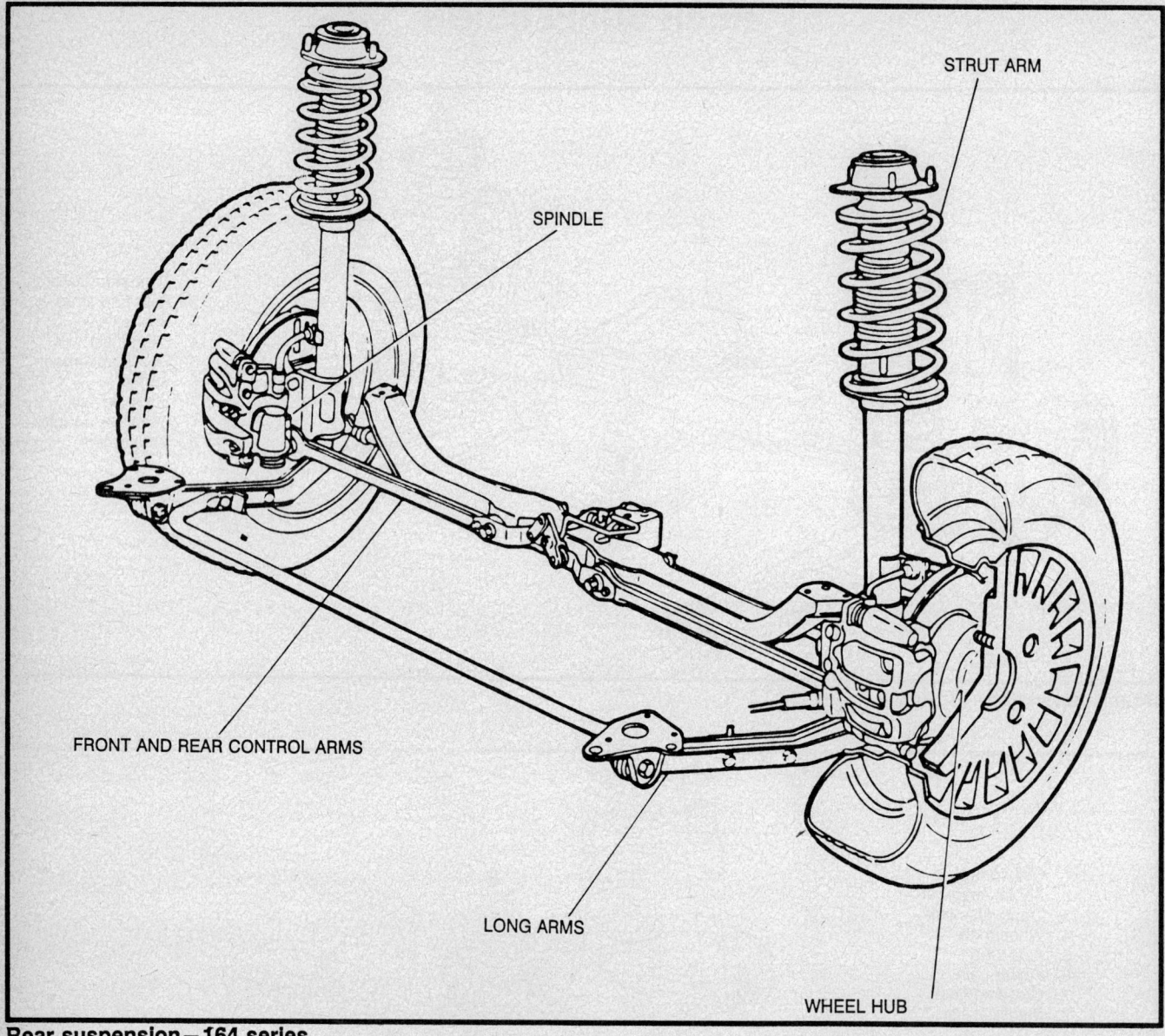

STRUT ARM

SPINDLE

FRONT AND REAR CONTROL ARMS

LONG ARMS

WHEEL HUB

Rear suspension—164 series

Shock Absorbers

Removal and Installation

SPIDER

1. Raise and support the vehicle safely.
2. Remove the locknut and the nut securing the shock absorber to the trailing arm, then remove the cup and rubber cushion.
3. Lower the vehicle. From inside the passenger compartment remove the trim and access panel on the side to be worked on.
4. Through the access panel, remove the 2 upper shock retaining bolts and remove the shock from above.
5. Installation is the reverse of removal. Tighten the locknut at the trailing arm to 17.7–22.1 ft. lbs. (24–30 Nm).

MILANO

1. Remove the rear seat cushion and seat back.
2. Through the access panel, remove the locknut and the nut

securing the shock absorber to the body, then remove the cup and rubber cushion.
3. Raise and support the vehicle safely.
4. Remove the locknut and the nut securing the shock absorber to the axle, then remove the shock, cup and rubber cushion.
5. Installation is the reverse of removal. Tighten the upper and lower lock nuts to 17–19.9 ft. lbs. (23–27 Nm).

MacPherson Strut

Removal and Installation

164 SERIES

1. Raise and support the vehicle safely and remove the rear wheel.
2. Remove the upper bolt that attaches the strut from the spindle.
3. Remove the lower retaining bolt and disconnect the front and rear control arms.

4. Disconnect the upper strut retaining nuts in the trunk and remove the strut assembly from the vehicle.

5. Installation is the reverse of removal. Tighten the upper bolt that attaches the strut to the spindle to 11.4–14 ft. lbs. (15.4–19 Nm) and lower retaining bolts to the front and rear control arms to 42.1–46.5 ft. lbs. (57–63 Nm).

—————————— **CAUTION** ——————————

The strut assembly is under extreme tension. Do not attempt to disassemble without a suitable spring compressor tool or personal injury could result.

Coil Springs

Removal and Installation

SPIDER

1. Raise and support the vehicle safely.
2. Position a column type jack under the differential.
3. Remove the wheel on the side to be worked on.
4. Remove the nut and slide the link rod of the stabilizer bar off the pin on the trailing arm.
5. Remove the locknut and the nut securing the shock absorber to the trailing arm, then remove the cup and rubber cushion.
6. Remove the nut securing the axle to the trailing arm.
7. Assemble tool A.2.0143, by inserting the pin in the hole on the axle flange. Turn the tool sleeve until the tool bracket comes against the spring bushing housing. At this point it is possible to free the pin coupling the trailing arm and axle. Turn the tool sleeve, lower the bracket and release the spring.
8. Remove the tool, slide out the spring, upper cup and gasket.
9. Installation is the reverse of removal. Tighten the trailing arm to axle bolts to 79.7–98.1 ft. lbs. (108–133 Nm) and nuts securing the stabilizer link rods to the axle to 23.6–25.1 ft. lbs. (32–34 Nm).

164 SERIES

1. Raise and support the vehicle safely and remove the front wheel.
2. Remove the front strut assembly.
3. Place the strut assembly in a suitable spring compression tool, such as 1.820.089.000 or equivalent, compress the spring and disassemble the spring and shock absorber.
4. Installation is the reverse of removal. Tighten the upper strut shock absorber/spring retaining nut to 63.5–70.1 ft. lbs. (86–95 Nm).

—————————— **CAUTION** ——————————

The strut assembly is under extreme tension. Do not attempt to disassemble without a suitable spring compressor tool or personal injury could result.

Rear Control Arms

Removal and Installation

164 SERIES

1. Raise and support the vehicle safely.
2. Position a column type jack under the crossmember to support the rear suspension.
3. Remove the load proportioning valve from the crossmember.
4. Remove the crossmember from the body.
5. Remove the nuts securing the valve torsion bar to the front control arms.
6. Disconnect the arms from the crossmember and wheel spindle.

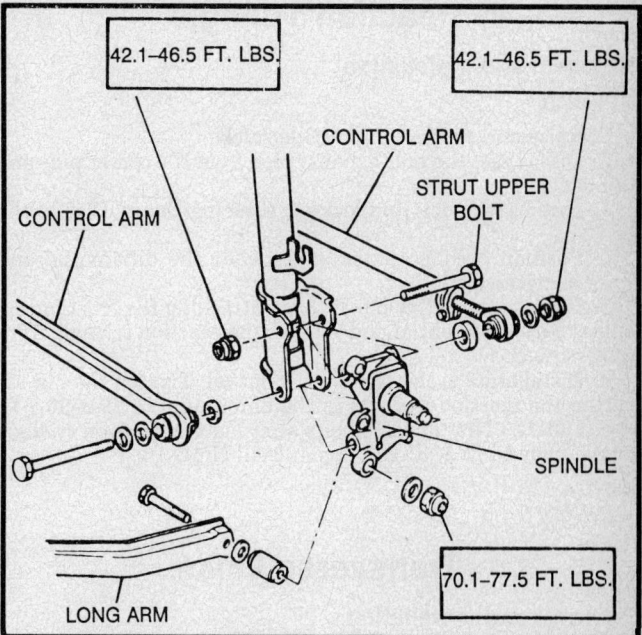

Rear suspension installation details—164 series

To install:

7. Installation is the reverse of removal.
8. Tighten the the nuts securing the valve torsion bar to the front control arms to 42.1–46.5 ft. lbs. (57–63 Nm).
9. Install the 2 spacers in their original position and tighten the nuts securing the control arms to the spindle to 42.1–46.5 ft. lbs. (57–63 Nm).
10. Bleed the brake system.
11. Adjust the load proportioning valve as follows:
  a. Settle the rear suspension.
  b. Position the vehicle on a level surface, place a 165 lb. load in the trunk and fill the fuel tank to capacity.
  c. Check the load proportioning valve linkage for freedom of movement.
  d. Loosen the adjusting screw and apply a load of 11.023 lbs. (5 Kg) to the lever hole.
  e. Tighten the adjustment screw to 42.0–46.5 ft. lbs. (57–63 Nm).

Trailing Arms

Removal and Installation

SPIDER

1. Raise and support the vehicle safely.
2. Position a column type jack under the differential.
3. Remove the wheel on the side to be worked on.
4. Remove the nut and slide the link rod of the stabilizer bar off the pin on the trailing arm.
5. Remove the locknut and the nut securing the shock absorber to the trailing arm, then remove the cup and rubber cushion.
6. Remove the nut securing the axle to the trailing arm.
7. Assemble tool A.2.0143, by inserting the pin in the hole on the axle flange. Turn the tool sleeve until the tool bracket comes against the spring bushing housing. At this point it is possible to free the pin coupling the trailing arm and axle. Turn the tool sleeve, lower the bracket and release the spring tension.
8. Remove the bolt securing the trailing arm at the front of the body.
9. Installation is the reverse of removal. Tighten the bolt securing the trailing arm at the front of the body to 59–72.3 ft. lbs.

Reaction Triangle

Removal and Installation

SPIDER

1. Raise and support the vehicle safely.
2. Disconnect the rear exhaust pipe from the center pipe and the body.
3. Remove the bolt and locknut securing the muffler to the body.
4. Position a column type jack under the differential and raise as necessary.
5. Remove the cotter pin and nut attaching the reaction triangle to the differential and remove the reaction triangle from under the body.
6. Installation is the reverse of removal. Tighten the nut securing the reaction triangle to the differential to 73.8–90.7 ft. lbs. (100–123 Nm) and the bolts securing the reaction triangle to the body to 28.8–33.2 ft. lbs. (39–45 Nm).

Transverse Links

Removal and Installation

MILANO

1. Raise and support the vehicle safely.
2. Remove the bolts and disconnect the transverse links.
3. Using a punch, release the staked area on the nut retaining the rocker to the axle tube.
4. Remove the nut and washer and take off the rocker together with the 2 transverse links from the pin on the axle.
6. Installation is the reverse of removal. Tighten the rocker to axle pin nut to 43.5–72.3 ft. lbs. (59–98 Nm) and the transverse links to rocker and body supports bolts to 28.8–36.1 ft. lbs. (39-49 Nm).

Rear Wheel Hub

Removal and Installation

MILANO

1. Raise and support the vehicle safely and remove the rear wheel.
2. Remove the bolts, washers and plates and uncouple the outer axle shaft.
3. Remove the cotter pin from the wheel shaft and slide off the locknut.
4. Install a suitable tool to prevent the wheel from turning, remove the nut securing the hub to the wheel shaft and slide off the related washer.
5. Assemble tool A.3.0617 on tool A.3.0327 or equivalent, and extract the wheel hub.
6. Installation is the reverse of removal. Tighten the wheel hub nut to 195.5–239 ft. lbs. (265–324 Nm).

164 SERIES

1. Raise and support the vehicle safely and remove the rear wheel.
2. Remove the brake caliper, pads, caliper supporting bracket and rotor.
3. Remove the hub cap and hub retaining nut.
4. Using puller assembly, 1.821.161.000 and 1.821.134.000 or equivalent, extract the complete hub assembly from the vehicle.
5. Installation is the reverse of removal. Tighten the hub retaining nut to 184.5–221.4 ft. lbs. (250–300 Nm).

Rear Axle Assembly

Removal and Installation

MILANO

1. Slacken the rear wheel nuts and raise and support the vehicle safely.
2. If equipped with ABS, perform the following:
   a. Free the rear impulse pick-up cables from the axle tube.
   b. Remove the nuts and remove the impulse pick-ups, complete with supports, from the wheel hubs without disconnecting the electrical connections.
   c. Position the impulse pick-ups safely aside.
3. Install a suitable hydraulic lifting device and support and raise the rear axle.
4. Remove the rear wheels.
5. Remove the exhaust system, as necessary.
6. Remove the transmission remote control rod and isostatic control.
7. Remove the bolts, washers and lock plates and remove the axle shafts.
8. Remove the locknuts, nuts rubber cushions and cups and disconnect the stabilizer bar from the axle tube.
9. Remove the locknuts, nuts rubber cushions and cups and remove the shock absorbers.
10. Remove the bolts and disconnect the transverse links.
11. Lower the hydraulic lift until the coil springs are fully unloaded, then remove the coil springs, pads and seals.
12. Disconnect the speedometer and back-up light switch cables.
13. Support the power train by means of a suitable hydraulic lifting device and support.
14. Remove the bolts attaching the driveshaft joint to the clutch fork.
15. Slacken the center bolt in the axle crossmember and back off the 6 outer crossmember bolts.
16. Lower the power train and remove the center bolt in the crossmember. Remove the remaining bolts and remove the crossmember.
17. Remove the entire axle tube and linkage and install the crossmember to support power train.
18. Installation is the reverse of removal. Tighten the transmission crossmember-to-body bolt to 28.8–32.5 ft. lbs. (39–44 Nm), axle-to-transmission bolts to 64.9–79.7 ft. lbs. (88–108 Nm), transverse links-to-body support bolts to 28.8–36.1 ft. lbs. (39 – 49 Nm). Use a thickness gauge and check that the air gap between the impulse pick-up and the impulse emitting wheel is 0.04 in. (1.1mm). Turn the adjusting screw to adjust.

Rear Axle Spindle

Removal and Installation

164 SERIES

1. Raise and support the vehicle safely and remove the wheel.
2. Remove the rear wheel hub and disc brake protection cover.
3. If equipped with ABS, remove the inductive sensor and spacer.
4. Remove the upper bolt connecting the shock absorber to the spindle.
5. Remove the lower bolt and disconnect the front and rear control arms from the spindle.
6. Disconnect the longitudinal arm from the spindle and remove the spindle.
7. Installation is the reverse of removal. Tighten the bolt connecting the longitudinal arm-to-spindle to 70.1–77.5 ft. lbs. (95–105 Nm) and lower retaining bolts-to-front and rear control arms to 42.1–46.5 ft. lbs. (57–63 Nm).

SERIAL NUMBER IDENTIFICATION

Vehicle Identification Plate

The Vehicle Identification Number (VIN) is located on a plate on top of the instrument panel. The VIN number is visible from outside through the left side of the windshield. The VIN number is also stamped into the upper right corner of the firewall. The vehicle identification plate is mounted on the right front wheel housing.

Engine Number

4 Cylinder Engine

The engine serial number is stamped into the left rear side of the engine block, below the cylinder head, next to the distributor.

5 Cylinder Engine

The engine serial number is stamped into the left rear side of the engine block. In addition to the serial number, an engine code number is stamped into the starter end of the engine block, below the cylinder head mounting surface. This number indicates the original cylinder bore size of the engine.

8 Cylinder Engine

The engine serial number is stamped into the left side of the engine block, just above the power steering hydraulic pump.

Vehicle Identification Label

On all vehicles, a vehicle identification label is located on the inside of the luggage compartment lid.

ENGINE IDENTIFICATION

Year	Model	Engine Displacement cu. in. (cc/liter)	Engine Series Identification	No. of Cylinders	Engine Type
1987	4000 Coupe	136 (2226/2.2)	KX	5	OHC
	4000 S	109 (1780/1.8)	MG	4	OHC
	4000 CS Quattro	136 (2226/2.2)	JT	5	OHC
	5000 CS Turbo	136 (2226/2.2)	MC	5	OHC
	5000 CS Quattro Turbo	136 (2226/2.2)	MC	5	OHC
	5000 CS Quattro Wagon	136 (2226/2.2)	MC	5	OHC
	5000 S	136 (2226/2.2)	MC	5	OHC
	5000 S Wagon	136 (2226/2.2)	MC	5	OHC
	Coupe GT	136 (2226/2.2)	KX	5	OHC
1988	80	121 (1983/2.0)	3A	4	OHC
	80 Quattro	141 (2309/2.3)	NG	5	OHC
	90 ①	121 (1983/2.0)	3A	4	OHC
	90	141 (2309/2.3)	NG	5	OHC
	90 Quattro	141 (2309/2.3)	NG	5	OHC
	5000 CS Turbo	136 (2226/2.2)	MC	5	OHC
	5000 CS Quattro Turbo	136 (2226/2.2)	MC	5	OHC
	5000 CS Quattro Wagon	136 (2226/2.2)	MC	5	OHC
	5000 S	141 (2309/2.3)	NF	5	OHC
	5000 S Wagon	141 (2309/2.3)	NF	5	OHC
	5000 S Quattro	141 (2309/2.3)	NF	5	OHC
1989	80	121 (1983/2.0)	3A	4	OHC
	80 Quattro	141 (2309/2.3)	NG	5	OHC
	90	121 (1983/2.0)	3A	4	OHC
	90	141 (2309/2.3)	NG	5	OHC
	90 Quattro	141 (2309/2.3)	NG	5	OHC
	100	141 (2309/2.3)	NF	5	OHC
	100 Quattro	141 (2309/2.3)	NF	5	OHC
	200	136 (2226/2.2)	MC	5	OHC
	200 Quattro	136 (2226/2.2)	MC	5	OHC

ENGINE IDENTIFICATION

Year	Model	Displacement cu. in. (cc/liter)	Engine Series Identification	No. of Cylinders	Engine Type
1990-91	80	121 (1983/2.0)	3A	4	OHC
	80 Quattro	141 (2309/2.3)	NG	5	OHC
	90	121 (1983/2.0)	3A	4	OHC
	90	141 (2309/2.3)	NG	5	OHC
	90 Quattro	141 (2309/2.3)	NG	5	OHC
	100	141 (2309/2.3)	NF	5	OHC
	100 Quattro	141 (2309/2.3)	NF	5	OHC
	200	136 (2226/2.2)	MC	5	OHC
	200 Quattro	136 (2226/2.2)	MC	5	OHC
	V8 Quattro	220 (3562/3.6)	PT	8	OHC

① With automatic transmission

GENERAL ENGINE SPECIFICATIONS

Year	Model	Engine Displacement cu. in. (cc)	Fuel System Type	Net Horsepower @ rpm	Net Torque @ rpm (ft. lbs.)	Bore × Stroke (in.)	Compression Ratio	Oil Pressure @ rpm
1987	4000 S	109 (1780)	CIS-E	88 @ 5500	101 @ 3000	3.19 × 3.40	8.5:1	29 @ 2000
	4000 Coupe	136 (2226)	CIS-E	110 @ 5500	122 @ 2500	3.19 × 3.40	8.5:1	29 @ 2000
	4000 CS Quattro	136 (2226)	CIS-E	115 @ 5500	126 @ 3000	3.19 × 3.40	8.5:1	29 @ 2000
	5000 S	136 (2226)	CIS-E	110 @ 5500	122 @ 2500	3.19 × 3.40	8.5:1	29 @ 2000
	5000 S Wagon	136 (2226)	CIS-E	110 @ 5500	122 @ 2500	3.19 × 3.40	8.5:1	29 @ 2000
	5000 CS Turbo	136 (2226)	CIS-E	158 @ 5500	166 @ 3000	3.19 × 3.40	7.8:1	29 @ 2000
	5000 Turbo	136 (2226)	CIS-E	160 @ 5500	166 @ 3000	3.19 × 3.40	7.8:1	29 @ 2000
	5000 Quattro Turbo	136 (2226)	CIS-E	158 @ 5500	166 @ 3000	3.19 × 3.40	7.8:1	29 @ 2000
	5000 CS Quattro Wagon	136 (2226)	CIS-E	158 @ 5500	166 @ 3000	3.19 × 3.40	7.8:1	29 @ 2000
	Coupe GT	136 (2226)	CIS-E	110 @ 5500	122 @ 2500	3.19 × 3.40	8.5:1	29 @ 2000
1988	80	121 (1983)	CIS-M	108 @ 5300	121 @ 3250	3.65 × 3.40	10.4:1	29 @ 2000
	80 Quattro	141 (2309)	CIS-E	130 @ 5700	140 @ 4500	3.25 × 3.40	10.0:1	29 @ 2000
	90 ①	121 (1983)	CIS-M	108 @ 5300	121 @ 3250	3.65 × 3.40	10.4:1	29 @ 2000
	90	141 (2309)	CIS-E	130 @ 5700	140 @ 4500	3.25 × 3.40	10.0:1	29 @ 2000
	90 Quattro	141 (2309)	CIS-E	130 @ 5700	140 @ 4500	3.25 × 3.40	10.0:1	29 @ 2000
	5000 CS Turbo	136 (2226)	CIS-E	158 @ 5500	166 @ 3000	3.19 × 3.40	7.8:1	29 @ 2000
	5000 CS Quattro Turbo	136 (2226)	CIS-E	158 @ 5500	166 @ 3000	3.19 × 3.40	7.8:1	29 @ 2000
	5000 CS Quattro Wagon	136 (2226)	CIS-E	158 @ 5500	166 @ 3000	3.19 × 3.40	7.8:1	29 @ 2000
	5000 S	141 (2309)	KE-III	130 @ 5600	140 @ 4000	3.25 × 3.40	10.0:1	29 @ 2000
	5000 S Wagon	141 (2309)	KE-III	130 @ 5600	140 @ 4000	3.25 × 3.40	10.0:1	29 @ 2000
	5000 S Quattro	141 (2309)	KE-III	130 @ 5600	140 @ 4000	3.25 × 3.40	10.0:1	29 @ 2000
1989	80	121 (1983)	CIS	108 @ 5300	121 @ 3200	3.25 × 3.65	10.5:1	29 @ 2000
	80 Quattro	141 (2309)	CIS-EIII	130 @ 5700	140 @ 4500	3.25 × 3.40	10.0:1	29 @ 2000
	90 ①	121 (1983)	CIS	108 @ 5300	121 @ 3200	3.25 × 3.65	10.5:1	29 @ 2000
	90	141 (2309)	CIS-EIII	130 @ 5700	140 @ 4500	3.25 × 3.40	10.0:1	29 @ 2000
	90 Quattro	141 (2309)	CIS-EIII	130 @ 5700	140 @ 4500	3.25 × 3.40	10.0:1	29 @ 2000
	100	141 (2309)	CIS-EIII	130 @ 5700	140 @ 4500	3.25 × 3.40	10.0:1	29 @ 2000
	100 Quattro	141 (2309)	CIS-EIII	130 @ 5700	140 @ 4500	3.25 × 3.40	10.0:1	29 @ 2000
	200	136 (2226)	CIS	162 @ 5500	177 @ 3000	3.19 × 3.40	7.8:1	29 @ 2000
	200 Quattro	136 (2226)	CIS	162 @ 5500	177 @ 3000	3.19 × 3.40	7.8:1	29 @ 2000

GENERAL ENGINE SPECIFICATIONS

Year	Model	Engine Displacement cu. in. (cc)	Fuel System Type	Net Horsepower @ rpm	Net Torque @ rpm (ft. lbs.)	Bore × Stroke (in.)	Compression Ratio	Oil Pressure @ rpm
1990–91	80	121 (1983)	CIS	108 @ 5300	121 @ 3200	3.25 × 3.65	10.5:1	29 @ 2000
	80 Quattro	141 (2309)	CIS-EIII	130 @ 5700	140 @ 4500	3.25 × 3.40	10.0:1	29 @ 2000
	90 ①	121 (1983)	CIS	108 @ 5300	121 @ 3200	3.25 × 3.65	10.5:1	29 @ 2000
	90	141 (2309)	CIS-EIII	130 @ 5700	140 @ 4500	3.25 × 3.40	10.0:1	29 @ 2000
	90 Quattro	141 (2309)	CIS-EIII	130 @ 5700	140 @ 4500	3.25 × 3.40	10.0:1	29 @ 2000
	100	141 (2309)	CIS-EIII	130 @ 5700	140 @ 4500	3.25 × 3.40	10.0:1	29 @ 2000
	100 Quattro	141 (2309)	CIS-EIII	130 @ 5700	140 @ 4500	3.25 × 3.40	10.0:1	29 @ 2000
	200	136 (2226)	CIS	162 @ 5500	177 @ 3000	3.19 × 3.40	7.8:1	29 @ 2000
	200 Quattro	136 (2226)	CIS	162 @ 5500	177 @ 3000	3.19 × 3.40	7.8:1	29 @ 2000
	V8 Quattro	220 (3562)	②	240 @ 5800	245 @ 4000	3.19 × 3.40	10.6:1	NA

NA—Not Available
① With automatic transmission
KE-III—KE-III Jetronic injection
② Bosch Motronic w/2 Knock Sensors

ENGINE TUNE-UP SPECIFICATIONS

Year	Model	Engine Displacement cu. in. (cc)	Spark Plugs Type	Spark Plugs Gap (in.)	Ignition Timing (deg.) MT	Ignition Timing (deg.) AT	Compression Pressure (psi)	Fuel Pump (psi)	Idle Speed (rpm) MT	Idle Speed (rpm) AT	Valve Clearance In.	Valve Clearance Ex.
1987	4000 S	109 (1780)	N8GY	0.031	6B	6B	NA	75–82	800–1000	800–1000	Hyd.	Hyd.
	4000 Coupe	136 (1780)	N8GY	0.032	8B	8B	NA	75–81	750–850	750–850	Hyd.	Hyd.
	4000 CS Quattro	136 (2226)	N8GY	0.032	8B	8B	NA	75–81	750–850	750–850	Hyd.	Hyd.
	5000 S	136 (2226)	N8GY	0.028	6B	6B	NA	75–85	750–850	750–850	Hyd.	Hyd.
	5000 S Wagon	136 (2226)	N8GY	0.028	6B	6B	NA	75–85	750–850	750–850	Hyd.	Hyd.
	5000 CS Turbo	136 (2226)	N8GY	0.028	0	0	NA	84–91	750–850	750–850	Hyd.	Hyd.
	5000 Turbo	136 (2226)	N8GY	0.028	0	0	NA	84–91	750–850	750–850	Hyd.	Hyd.
	5000 Quattro Turbo	136 (2226)	N8GY	0.028	0	0	NA	84–91	750–850	750–850	Hyd.	Hyd.
	5000 CS Quattro Wagon	136 (2226)	N8GY	0.028	6B	6B	NA	75–85	750–850	750–850	Hyd.	Hyd.
	Coupe GT	136 (2226)	N8GY	0.032	8B	8B	NA	75–85	750–850	750–850	Hyd.	Hyd.
1988	80	121 (1983)	NA	0.031	6B	6B	NA	88–94	780–900	780–900	Hyd.	Hyd.
	80 Quattro	141 (2309)	N9BYC	0.031	15B	15B	NA	88–94	720–860	720–860	Hyd.	Hyd.
	90 ①	121 (1983)	NA	0.031	6B	6B	NA	88–94	780–900	780–900	Hyd.	Hyd.
	90	141 (2309)	N9BYC	0.031	15B	15B	NA	88–94	720–860	720–860	Hyd.	Hyd.
	90 Quattro	141 (2309)	N9BYC	0.031	15B	15B	NA	88–94	720–860	720–860	Hyd.	Hyd.

ENGINE TUNE-UP SPECIFICATIONS

Year	Model	Engine Displacement cu. in. (cc)	Spark Plugs Type	Gap (in.)	Ignition Timing (deg.) MT	AT	Com-pression Pressure (psi)	Fuel Pump (psi)	Idle Speed (rpm) MT	AT	Valve Clearance In.	Ex.
1988	100	141 (2309)	N8GY	0.031	15B	15B	NA	88–94	670–770	670–770	Hyd.	Hyd.
	100 Quattro	141 (2309)	N8GY	0.031	15B	15B	NA	88–94	670–770	670–770	Hyd.	Hyd.
	200	136 (2226)	N8GY	0.028	0	0	NA	84–95	750–850	750–850	Hyd.	Hyd.
	200 Quattro	136 (2226)	N8GY	0.028	0	0	NA	84–95	750–850	750–850	Hyd.	Hyd.
	5000 CS Turbo	136 (2226)	N8GY	0.028	0	0	NA	84–95	750–850	750–850	Hyd.	Hyd.
	5000 CS Quattro Turbo	136 (2226)	N8GY	0.028	0	0	NA	84–95	750–850	750–850	Hyd.	Hyd.
	5000 CS Quattro Wagon	136 (2226)	N8GY	0.028	0	0	NA	84–95	750–850	750–850	Hyd.	Hyd.
	5000 S	141 (2309)	N8GY	0.031	15B	15B	NA	88–94	670–770	670–770	Hyd.	Hyd.
	5000 S Wagon	141 (2309)	N8GY	0.031	15B	15B	NA	88–94	670–770	670–770	Hyd.	Hyd.
	5000 S Quattro	141 (2309)	N8GY	0.031	15B	15B	NA	88–94	670–770	670–770	Hyd.	Hyd.
1989	80	121 (1983)	NA	0.031	6B	6B	NA	88–94	780–900	780–900	Hyd.	Hyd.
	80 Quattro	141 (2309)	N9BYC	0.031	15B	15B	NA	88–94	720–860	720–860	Hyd.	Hyd.
	90 ①	121 (1983)	NA	0.031	6B	6B	NA	88–94	780–900	780–900	Hyd.	Hyd.
	90	141 (2309)	N9BYC	0.031	15B	15B	NA	88–94	720–860	720–860	Hyd.	Hyd.
	90 Quattro	141 (2309)	N9BYC	0.031	15B	15B	NA	88–94	720–860	720–860	Hyd.	Hyd.
	100	141 (2309)	N8GY	0.031	15B	15B	160–172	88–94	670–770	670–770	Hyd.	Hyd.
	100 Quattro	141 (2309)	N8GY	0.031	15B	15B	160–172	88–94	670–770	670–770	Hyd.	Hyd.
	200	136 (2226)	N8GY	0.028	①	①	123–144	84–95	750–850	670–770	Hyd.	Hyd.
	200 Quattro	136 (2226)	N8GY	0.028	①	①	123–144	84–95	750–850	670–770	Hyd.	Hyd.
1990–91	80	121 (1983)	NA	0.031	6B	6B	NA	88–94	780–900	780–900	Hyd.	Hyd.
	80 Quattro	141 (2309)	N9BYC	0.031	15B	15B	NA	88–94	720–860	720–860	Hyd.	Hyd.
	90 ①	121 (1983)	NA	0.031	6B	6B	NA	88–94	780–900	780–900	Hyd.	Hyd.
	90	141 (2309)	N9BYC	0.031	15B	15B	NA	88–94	720–860	720–860	Hyd.	Hyd.
	90 Quattro	141 (2309)	N9BYC	0.031	15B	15B	NA	88–94	720–860	720–860	Hyd.	Hyd.

ENGINE TUNE-UP SPECIFICATIONS

Year	Model	Engine Displacement cu. in. (cc)	Spark Plugs Type	Spark Plugs Gap (in.)	Ignition Timing (deg.) MT	Ignition Timing (deg.) AT	Compression Pressure (psi)	Fuel Pump (psi)	Idle Speed (rpm) MT	Idle Speed (rpm) AT	Valve Clearance In.	Valve Clearance Ex.
1990–91	100	141 (2309)	N8GY	0.031	15B	15B	160–172	88–94	670–770	670–770	Hyd.	Hyd.
	100 Quattro	141 (2309)	N8GY	0.031	15B	15B	160–172	88–94	670–770	670–770	Hyd.	Hyd.
	200	136 (2226)	N8GY	0.028	2	2	123–144	84–95	750–850	670–770	Hyd.	Hyd.
	200 Quattro	136 (2226)	N8GY	0.028	2	2	123–144	84–95	750–850	670–770	Hyd.	Hyd.
	V8 Quattro	220 (3562)	②	0.032	—	③	145–189	55–65	—	660–720	Hyd.	Hyd.

B Before top dead center
A After top dead center
Hyd. Hydraulic lash adjusters—no adjustment is necessary.

NA Not available
① Top dead center (not adjustable)
③ Bosch H6DCO

② Timing determined by Electronic Control Unit and cannot be adjusted.

FIRING ORDERS

NOTE: To avoid confusion, always replace spark plug wires one at a time.

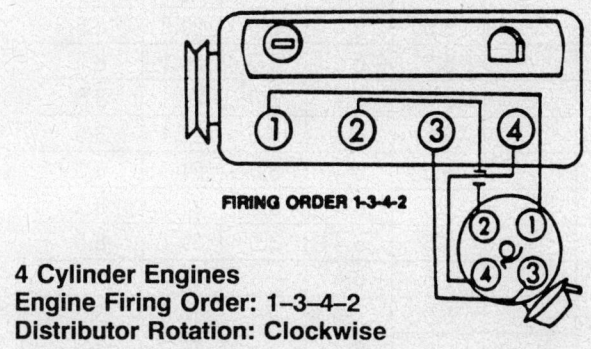

FIRING ORDER 1-3-4-2

4 Cylinder Engines
Engine Firing Order: 1–3–4–2
Distributor Rotation: Clockwise

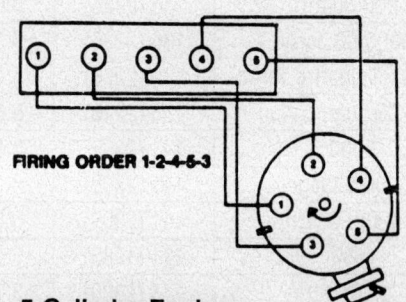

FIRING ORDER 1-2-4-5-3

5 Cylinder Engines
Engine Firing Order: 1–2–4–5–3
Distributor Rotation: Clockwise

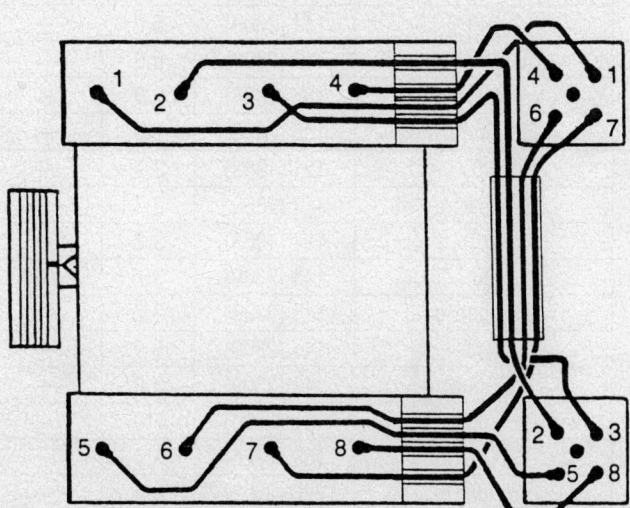

8 Cylinder Engines
Engine Firing Order: 1–5–4–8–6–3–7–2
Distributor Rotation: Clockwise

CAPACITIES

Year	Model	Engine Displacement cu. in. (cc)	Crankcase (qts.) with Filter	Crankcase (qts.) without Filter	Transmission (pts.) 4-Spd	Transmission (pts.) 5-Spd	Transmission (pts.) Auto.	Drive Axle (pts.)	Fuel Tank (gal.)	Cooling System (qts.)
1987	4000 S	109 (1780)	3.5	3.0	—	5.5	6.4	2.2	15.9	7.4
	4000 Coupe	136 (2226)	4.0	3.5	—	5.5	6.4	2.2	15.9	7.4
	4000 CS Quattro	136 (2226)	4.0	3.5	—	5.5	6.4	2.2	15.9	8.6
	5000 S	136 (2226)	5.3	5.0	—	5.4	6.4	3.0	21.0	8.5
	5000 Turbo	136 (2226)	5.0	4.5	—	5.5	6.4	3.0	21.0	8.6
	5000 CS Turbo	136 (2226)	5.3	5.0	—	5.4	6.4	3.0	21.0	8.5
	5000 S Wagon	136 (2226)	5.3	5.0	—	5.4	6.4	3.0	21.0	8.5
	5000 CS Quattro Turbo	136 (2226)	5.3	5.0	—	5.4	6.4	3.0	21.0	8.5
	5000 CS Quattro Wagon	136 (2226)	5.3	5.0	—	5.4	6.4	3.0	21.0	8.5
	Coupe GT	136 (2226)	4.0	3.7	—	5.0	6.4	3.0	15.8	7.4
1988	80	121 (1983)	3.2	3.0	—	5.5	6.4	2.2	18.0	7.4
	80 Quattro	141 (2309)	3.7	3.5	—	5.5	6.4	2.2	18.5	8.5
	90 ①	121 (1983)	3.2	3.0	—	—	6.4	2.2	18.0	7.4
	90	141 (2309)	3.7	3.5	—	5.5	6.4	2.2	18.0	8.5
	90 Quattro	141 (2309)	3.7	3.5	—	5.5	6.4	2.2	18.5	7.4
	100	141 (2309)	5.0	4.5	—	5.5	6.4	3.0	21.1	8.5
	100 Quattro	141 (2309)	5.0	4.5	—	5.5	6.4	3.0	20.6	8.5
	200	136 (2226)	5.0	4.5	—	5.5	6.4	3.0	20.6	8.5
	200 Quattro	136 (2226)	5.0	4.5	—	5.5	6.4	3.0	20.6	8.5
	5000 CS Turbo	136 (2226)	5.3	4.5	—	5.5	6.4	3.0	21.1	8.5
	5000 CS Quattro Turbo	136 (2226)	5.3	4.5	—	5.5	6.4	3.0	21.1	8.5
	5000 CS Quattro Wagon	136 (2226)	5.3	4.5	—	5.5	6.4	3.0	21.1	8.5
	5000 S	141 (2309)	5.3	4.5	—	5.5	6.4	3.0	21.1	8.5
	5000 S Wagon	141 (2309)	5.3	4.5	—	5.5	6.4	3.0	21.1	8.5
	5000 S Quattro	141 (2309)	5.3	4.5	—	5.5	6.4	3.0	21.1	8.5
1989	80	121 (1983)	3.2	—	—	2.5	6.4	—	18	7.4
	80 Quattro	141 (2309)	3.7	—	—	6.0	—	—	18.5	8.5
	90 ①	121 (1983)	3.2	—	—	—	6.4	—	18	7.4
	90	141 (2309)	3.7	—	—	5.0	—	—	18	8.5
	90 Quattro	141 (2309)	3.7	—	—	6.0	—	—	18.5	8.5
	100	141 (2309)	5.0	—	—	5.0	7.0	—	21.1	8.5
	100 Quattro	141 (2309)	5.0	—	—	6.0	—	—	21.1	8.5
	200	136 (2226)	5.0	—	—	5.0	7.0	—	20.6	8.5
	200 Quattro	136 (2226)	5.0	—	—	6.0	—	—	21.1	8.5
1990–91	80	121 (1983)	3.2	—	—	2.5	6.4	—	18	7.4
	80 Quattro	141 (2309)	3.7	—	—	6.0	—	—	18.5	8.5
	90 ①	121 (1983)	3.2	—	—	—	6.4	—	18	7.4
	90	141 (2309)	3.7	—	—	5.0	—	—	18	8.5
	90 Quattro	141 (2309)	3.7	—	—	6.0	—	—	18.5	8.5
	100	141 (2309)	5.0	—	—	5.0	7.0	—	21.1	8.5
	100 Quattro	141 (2309)	5.0	—	—	6.0	—	—	21.1	8.5
	200	136 (2226)	5.0	—	—	5.0	7.0	—	20.6	8.5
	200 Quattro	136 (2226)	5.0	—	—	6.0	—	—	21.1	8.5
	V8 Quattro	220 (3562)	8.4	—	—	—	②	③	21.0	11.0

① Automatic transmission
② Initial fill—20.4 pts.
Oil change—8.0 pts.
③ Front final drive—.75 pts. GL5 90 wt.
Rear final drive—3.60 pts. GL5 90 wt.
Both filled for service life. No oil change.

CRANKSHAFT AND CONNECTING ROD SPECIFICATIONS

All measurements are given in inches.

Year	Engine Displacement cu. in. (cc)	Crankshaft				Connecting Rod		
		Main Brg. Journal Dia.	Main Brg. Oil Clearance	Shaft End-play	Thrust on No.	Journal Diameter	Oil Clearance	Side Clearance
1987	109 (1780)	2.1260	0.0010–0.0030	0.003–0.007	3	1.8110	0.0010–0.0030	0.015
	136 (2226)	2.2818	0.0006–0.0030	0.003–0.007	4	1.8803	0.0006–0.0020	0.016
1988	121 (1983)	2.1268–2.1276	NA	NA	3	1.8827–1.8835	NA	NA
	136 (2226)	2.2818–2.2825	0.0006–0.0030	0.003–0.009	4	1.8487–1.8495	0.0004–0.0020	0.016
	141 (2309)	2.2818–2.2825	0.0010–0.0020	0.003–0.009	4	1.8802–1.8810	0.0004–0.0020	0.016
1989	121 (1983)	2.1268–2.1276	NA	NA	3	1.8827–1.8835	NA	NA
	136 (2226)	2.2818–2.2825	0.0006–0.0030	0.003–0.009	4	1.8487–1.8495	0.0004–0.0020	0.016
	141 (2309)	2.2818–2.2825	0.0010–0.0020	0.003–0.009	4	1.8802–1.8810	0.0004–0.0020	0.016
1990–91	121 (1983)	2.1268–2.1276	NA	NA	3	1.8827–1.8835	NA	NA
	136 (2226)	2.2818–2.2825	0.0006–0.0030	0.003–0.009	4	1.8487–1.8495	0.0004–0.0020	0.016
	141 (2309)	2.2818–2.2825	0.0010–0.0020	0.003–0.009	4	1.8802–1.8810	0.0004–0.0020	0.016
	220 (3562)	NA	NA	NA	NA	NA	NA	NA

NA—Not available

VALVE SPECIFICATIONS

Year	Engine Displacement cu. in. (cc)	Seat Angle (deg.)	Face Angle (deg.)	Spring Test Pressure (lbs.)	Spring Installed Height (in.)	Stem-to-Guide Clearance (in.)		Stem Diameter (in.)	
						Intake	Exhaust	Intake	Exhaust
1987	109 (1780)	45	45	—	—	0.039	0.051	0.3140	0.3130
	136 (2226)	45	45	—	—	0.039	0.051	0.3140	0.3130
1988	121 (1983)	45	45	—	—	0.039	0.051	0.3140	0.3130
	136 (2226)	45	45	—	—	0.039	0.051	0.3140	0.3130
	141 (2309)	45	45	—	—	0.039	0.051	0.3140	0.3130
1989	121 (1983)	45	45	—	—	0.039	0.051	0.3140	0.3130
	136 (2226)	45	45	—	—	0.039	0.051	0.3140	0.3130
	141 (2309)	45	45	—	—	0.039	0.051	0.3140	0.3130
1990–91	121 (1983)	45	45	—	—	0.039	0.051	0.3140	0.3130
	136 (2226)	45	45	—	—	0.039	0.051	0.3140	0.3130
	141 (2309)	45	45	—	—	0.039	0.051	0.3140	0.3130
	220 (3562)	45	45	—	—	0.039	0.051	0.3140	0.3130

NOTE: To measure Stem-to-Guide Clearance, insert new valve into guide until end of valve is flush with end of guide. Use dial indicator to measure valve head movement.

PISTON AND RING SPECIFICATIONS

All measurements are given in inches.

Year	Engine Displacement cu. in. (cc)	Piston Clearance	Ring Gap			Ring Side Clearance		
			Top Compression	Bottom Compression	Oil Control	Top Compression	Bottom Compression	Oil Control
1987	109 (1780)	0.0011	0.012–0.018	0.012–0.018	0.012–0.018	0.0008–0.0020	0.0008–0.0020	0.0008–0.0020
	136 (2226)	0.0011	0.010–0.020	0.010–0.020	0.010–0.020	0.0008–0.0030	0.0008–0.0030	0.0008–0.0030
1988	121 (1983)	0.0011	0.012–0.018	0.012–0.018	0.010–0.018	0.0010–0.0020	0.0010–0.0020	0.0010–0.0020
	136 (2226)	0.0011	0.008–0.020	0.008–0.020	0.010–0.020	0.0010–0.0030	0.0010–0.0030	0.0010–0.0020
	141 (2309)	0.0011	0.008–0.016	0.008–0.016	0.010–0.020	0.0010–0.0030	0.0010–0.0030	0.0010–0.0020
1989	121 (1983)	0.0011	0.012–0.018	0.012–0.018	0.010–0.018	0.0010–0.0020	0.0010–0.0020	0.0010–0.0020
	136 (2226)	0.0011	0.008–0.020	0.008–0.020	0.010–0.020	0.0010–0.0030	0.0010–0.0030	0.0010–0.0020
	141 (2309)	0.0011	0.008–0.016	0.008–0.016	0.010–0.020	0.0010–0.0030	0.0010–0.0030	0.0010–0.0020
1990–91	121 (1983)	0.0011	0.012–0.018	0.012–0.018	0.010–0.018	0.0010–0.0020	0.0010–0.0020	0.0010–0.0020
	136 (2226)	0.0011	0.008–0.020	0.008–0.020	0.010–0.020	0.0010–0.0030	0.0010–0.0030	0.0010–0.0020
	141 (2309)	0.0011	0.008–0.016	0.008–0.016	0.010–0.020	0.0010–0.0030	0.0010–0.0030	0.0010–0.0020
	220 (3562)	NA	NA	NA	NA	NA	NA	NA

NA—Not available

TORQUE SPECIFICATIONS

All readings in ft. lbs.

Year	Engine Displacement cu. in. (cc)	Cylinder Head Bolts	Main Bearing Bolts	Rod Bearing Bolts	Crankshaft Pulley Bolts	Flywheel Bolts	Manifold		Spark Plugs
							Intake	Exhaust	
1987	109 (1780)	①	47	22③	145	54②	22	22	14
	136 (2226)	①	47	22③	253	54②	22	26	14
1988	121 (1983)	①	48	22③	④	74	15	18	14
	136 (2226)	①	48	22③	258	74	22	26	14
	141 (2309)	①	48	22③	258	74	22	26	14
1989	121 (1983)	①	48	22③	④	74	15	18	14
	136 (2226)	①	48	22③	258	74	22	26	14
	141 (2309)	①	48	22③	258	74	22	26	14
1990–91	121 (1983)	①	48	22③	④	74	15	18	14
	136 (2226)	①	48	22③	258	74	22	26	14
	141 (2309)	①	48	22③	258	74	22	26	14
	220 (3562)	⑤	NA	NA	258	74	⑥	18	22

NOTE: Always use new rod bearing bolts.
① In sequence 29 ft. lbs., 43 ft. lbs. and then tighten it a half turn more (180 degrees).
② Models with a built in lug—145 ft. lbs.
③ Plus a quarter turn (90 degrees).
④ In sequence 66 ft. lbs., then a half turn more (180 degrees).
⑤ In sequence 30 ft. lbs., 44 ft. lbs., and then tighten it a half turn more (180 degrees). It is not necessary to retighten head bolts during maintenance service or after repairs.
⑥ Lower manifold to block—7 ft. lbs. Lower manifold to upper manifold—11 ft. lbs.
NA—Not available

BRAKE SPECIFICATIONS

All measurements in inches unless noted

Year	Model	Lug Nut Torque (ft. lbs.)	Master Cylinder Bore	Brake Disc Minimum Thickness	Brake Disc Maximum Runout	Standard Brake Drum Diameter	Minimum Lining Thickness Front	Minimum Lining Thickness Rear
1987	4000 S	80	0.810	0.472	0.002	7.913	0.276②	0.098
	4000 Coupe	80	0.810	0.472	0.002	7.913	0.276②	0.098
	4000 CS Quattro	80	0.810	0.728	0.003	—	③	③
	5000 S	80	0.810	0.787	0.002	9.980	0.051	0.472②
	5000 S Wagon	80	0.810	0.787	0.002	9.980	0.051	0.472②
	5000 CS Turbo	80	0.810	0.807④	0.002	—	③	③
	5000 Turbo	80	0.875	0.807④	0.002	9.980	0.051	0.472②
	5000 Quattro Turbo	80	0.810	0.807④	0.002	—	③	③
	5000 CS Quattro Wagon	80	0.810	0.807④	0.002	—	③	③
	Coupe GT	80	0.810	0.472	0.002	7.894	0.078	0.098
1988	80	81	0.874	0.787⑤	0.002	—	0.078	0.078⑥
	80 Quattro	81	0.874	0.787⑤	0.002	—	0.078	0.078⑥
	90	81	0.874	0.787⑤	0.002	—	0.078	0.078⑥
	90 Quattro	81	0.874	0.787⑤	0.002	—	0.078	0.078⑥
	5000 CS Turbo	81	0.875	0.787⑤	0.002	—	③	0.472②
	5000 CS Quattro Turbo	81	0.875	0.787⑤	0.002	—	③	0.472②
	5000 CS Quattro Wagon	81	0.875	0.787⑤	0.002	—	③	0.472②
	5000 S	81	0.810	0.787⑤	0.002	—	③	0.098
	5000 S Wagon	81	0.810	0.787⑤	0.002	—	③	0.098
	5000 S Quattro	81	0.810	0.787⑤	0.002	—	③	0.098
1989	80	81	0.874	0.787⑤	0.002	—	0.078	0.078
	80 Quattro	81	0.874	0.787⑤	0.002	—	0.078	0.078
	90 ①	81	0.874	0.787⑤	0.002	—	0.078	0.078
	90	81	0.874	0.787⑤	0.002	—	0.078	0.078
	90 Quattro	81	0.874	0.787⑤	0.002	—	0.078	0.078
	100	81	0.874	0.787⑤	0.002	—	③	0.472②
	100 Quattro	81	0.874	0.787⑤	0.002	—	③	0.472②
	200	81	0.874	0.905⑤	0.002	—	③	0.472②
	200 Quattro	81	0.874	0.905⑤	0.002	—	③	0.472②
1990-91	80	81	0.874	0.787⑤	0.002	—	0.078	0.078
	80 Quattro	81	0.874	0.787⑤	0.002	—	0.078	0.078
	90 ①	81	0.874	0.787⑤	Runout	—	0.078	0.078
	90	81	0.874	0.787⑤	0.002	—	0.078	0.078
	90 Quattro	81	0.874	0.787⑤	0.002	—	0.078	0.078
	100	81	0.874	0.787⑤	0.002	—	③	0.472②
	100 Quattro	81	0.874	0.787⑤	0.002	—	③	0.472②
	200	81	0.874	0.905⑤	0.002	—	③	0.472②
	200 Quattro	81	0.874	0.905⑤	0.002	—	③	0.472②
	V8 Quattro	81	1.000	⑦	0.002	—	③	0.280③

NOTE: Minimum lining thickness is as recommended by the manufacturer. Due to variations in state inspection regulations, the minimum allowable thickness may be different than recommended by the manufacturer.

① With ventilated discs—0.768 after refinishing—0.728 discard thickness
② Included backing plate
③ Replace the pads when the indicator on the dash turns on
④ All models with rear disc brakes—Minimum Thickness 0.335
⑤ All models with rear disc brakes minimum thickness 0.315
⑥ 0.275 in. including backing plate
⑦ Front 0.984 Limit 0.906 Rear 0.787 Limit 0.709

AUDI
80 • 90 • 100 • 200 • 4000 • 5000 • COUPE • QUATTRO • V8

WHEEL ALIGNMENT

Year	Model	Caster Range (deg.)	Caster Preferred Setting (deg.)	Camber Range (deg.)	Camber Preferred Setting (deg.)	Toe-in (in.)	Steering Axis Inclination (deg.)
1987	4000 S	$15/16$P–$15/16$P	$17/16$P	$1/6$N–$11/6$N	$2/3$N	$1/12$	—
	4000 Coupe	$15/16$P–$15/16$P	$17/16$P	$1/6$N–$11/6$N	$2/3$N	$1/12$	—
	4000 CS Quattro	$15/16$P–$15/16$P	$17/16$P	$1/6$N–$11/6$N	$2/3$N	$1/12$	—
	5000 S	$11/32$P–$121/32$P	1P	1N–0① ②	$1/2$N	0③ ④	—
	5000 S Wagon	$11/32$P–$121/32$P	1P	1N–0① ②	$1/2$N	0③ ④	—
	5000 CS Turbo	$11/32$P–$121/32$P	1P	1N–0① ②	$1/2$N	0③ ④	—
	5000 Turbo	$11/32$P–$121/32$P	1P	1N–0① ②	$1/2$N	0③ ④	—
	5000 Quattro Turbo	$11/32$P–$121/32$P	1P	1N–0① ②	$1/2$N	0③ ④	—
	5000 CS Quattro Wagon	$11/32$P–$121/32$P	1P	1N–0① ②	$1/2$N	0③ ④	—
	Coupe GT	0P–1P	$1/2$P	$15/32$N–$5/32$N	$21/32$N	$5/64$	—
1988	80	$3/4$P–$13/4$P	$11/4$P	$11/4$N–$1/4$N	$3/4$N	$5/64$	—
	80 Quattro	$3/4$P–$13/4$P	$11/4$P	$113/32$N–$13/32$N	$27/32$N	$5/64$	—
	90	$3/4$P–$13/4$P	$11/4$P	$11/4$N–$1/4$N	$3/4$N	$5/64$	—
	90 Quattro	$3/4$P–$13/4$P	$11/4$P	$113/32$N–$13/32$N	$27/32$N	$5/64$	—
	5000 CS Turbo	$5/32$N–$11/2$P	$27/32$P	1N–0	$1/2$N	0	—
	5000 CS Quattro Turbo	$11/32$P–$121/32$P	1P	1N–0	$1/2$N	$1/64$	—
	5000 CS Quattro Wagon	$11/32$P–$121/32$P	1P	1N–0	$1/2$N	$1/64$	—
	5000 S	$5/32$N–$11/2$P	$27/32$P	1N–0	$1/2$N	0	—
	5000 S Wagon	$5/32$N–$11/2$P	$27/32$P	1N–0	$1/2$N	0	—
	5000 S Quattro	$11/32$P–$121/32$P	1P	1N–0	$1/2$N	$1/64$	—
1989	80	$3/4$P–$13/4$P	$11/4$P	$11/4$N–$1/4$N	$3/4$N	$5/64$	—
	80 Quattro	$3/4$P–$13/4$P	$11/4$P	$113/32$N–$13/32$N	$27/32$N	$5/64$	—
	90	$3/4$P–$13/4$P	$11/4$P	$11/4$N–$1/4$N	$3/4$N	$5/64$	—
	90 Quattro	$3/4$P–$13/4$P	$11/4$P	$113/32$N–$13/32$N	$27/32$N	$5/64$	—
	100	$5/32$N–$11/2$P	$27/32$P	1N–0	$1/2$N	$1/16$N	—
	100 Quattro	$5/32$N–$11/2$P	$27/32$P	1N–0	$1/2$N	$1/16$N	—
	200	$5/32$N–$11/2$P	$27/32$P	1N–0	$1/2$N	$1/16$N	—
	200 Quattro	$5/32$N–$11/2$P	$27/32$P	1N–0	$1/2$N	$1/16$N	—
1990–91	80	$3/4$P–$13/4$P	$11/4$P	$11/4$N–$1/4$N	$3/4$N	$5/64$	—
	80 Quattro	$3/4$P–$13/4$P	$11/4$P	$113/32$N–$13/32$N	$27/32$N	$5/64$	—
	90	$3/4$P–$13/4$P	$11/4$P	$11/4$N–$1/4$N	$3/4$N	$5/64$	—
	90 Quattro	$3/4$P–$13/4$P	$11/4$P	$113/32$N–$13/32$N	$27/32$N	$5/64$	—
	100	$5/32$N–$11/2$P	$27/32$P	1N–0	$1/2$N	$1/16$N	—
	100 Quattro	$5/32$N–$11/2$P	$27/32$P	1N–0	$1/2$N	$1/16$N	—
	200	$5/32$N–$11/2$P	$27/32$P	1N–0	$1/2$N	$1/16$N	—
	200 Quattro	$5/32$N–$11/2$P	$27/32$P	1N–0	$1/2$N	$1/16$N	—
	V8 Quattro	$5/8$N–$17/8$P	$11/4$P	1N–0	$1/2$N	$3/16$N	—

N Negative
P Positive
① Rear axle—$5/6$N–$1/6$N
② Maximum difference between left and right—
Rear Axle—$1/2$N
③ Up to chassis No. EN096669—Rear Axle—
$1/30$P–$5/18$P
④ from chassis No. EN096670—Rear Axle—
$1/30$P–$1/4$P

ENGINE ELECTRICAL

NOTE: Disconnecting the negative battery cable on some vehicles may interfere with the functions of the on board computer systems and may require the computer to undergo a relearning process, once the negative battery cable is reconnected. Never disconnect any electrical connector with the ignition key ON, unless specified in repair procedure or damage to electronic components may result.

Distributor

Removal

1. Disconnect the wiring harness connector from the distributor cap. Note that V8 Quattro vehicles have 2 distributors, driven off the exhaust camshafts.
2. Unclip and remove the distributor cap and static shield with the spark plug wires still attached.
3. Disconnect and tag the vacuum lines at the distributor, if equipped.
4. Note the position of the rotor in relation to the distributor housing. Scribe a mark on the distributor and engine block for installation. Matchmark the tip of the rotor to the engine. Note the approximate position of the vacuum advance unit in relation to the engine.
5. Remove the distributor hold-down bolt and clamp.
6. Lift the distributor assembly from the engine.

Installation

TIMING NOT DISTURBED

1. With the rotor pointing in the same direction as when removed, insert the distributor into the engine.
2. Once the distributor is seated into the engine, line up the marks on the distributor and engine with the metal tip of the rotor.
3. Make sure the vacuum advance unit, if equipped, is pointed in the same direction as it was pointed originally. If the marks on the distributor and the engine are lined up properly, this will be done automatically.
4. Install the distributor hold-down clamp and bolt.
5. Install the distributor cap and static shield.
6. Install the vacuum lines, if equipped.
7. Install the distributor wiring harness connector.
8. Start the engine. Adjust the ignition timing.

TIMING DISTURBED

NOTE: If the engine has been turned or disturbed in any manner while the distributor was removed or if the marks were not drawn, it will be necessary to initially time the engine. Follow the procedure given below.

1. It is necessary to place the No. 1 cylinder in the firing position (TDC) to correctly install the distributor. To locate this position, the ignition timing marks on the flywheel and the clutch housing are used.
2. Remove the spark plug from the No. 1 cylinder. Turn the crankshaft until the piston in the No. 1 cylinder is moving up on the compression stroke. This can be determined by placing a finger over the spark plug hole and feeling the air being forced out of the cylinder. Stop turning the engine when the timing mark on the flywheel is aligned with the lug on the flywheel housing.
3. Remove the timing belt cover.
4. Align the mark on the camshaft sprocket with the upper edge of the drive belt cover or with the upper edge of the valve cover gasket mounting surfaces.
5. On 4 cylinder engines, align the oil pump drive pinion lug so it aligns with the threaded hole.

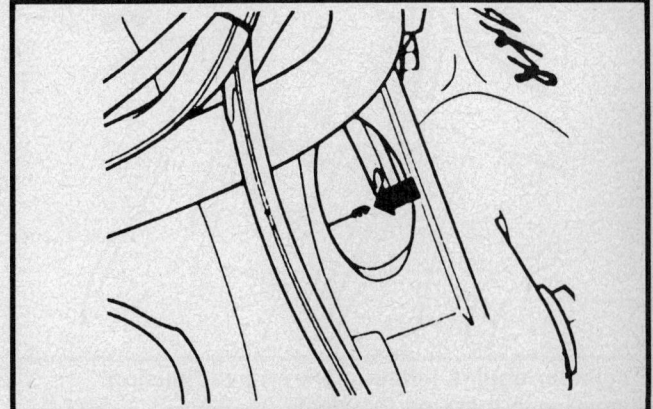

4 cylinder engine timing mark on bell housing aligned with mark on flywheel.

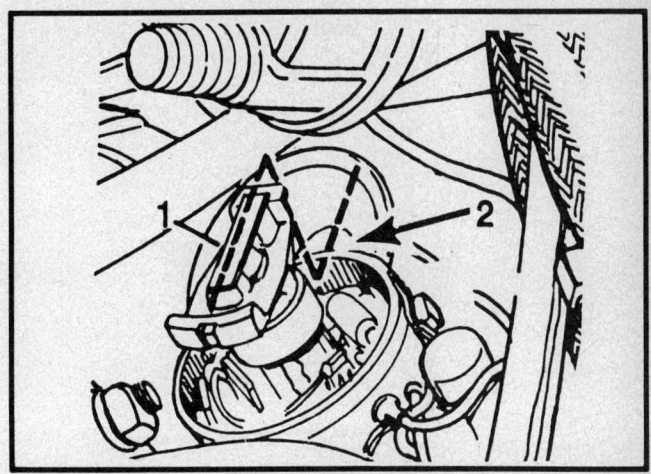

The distributor rotor (1) aligned with the No. 1 cylinder mark (2) on the rim of the distributor body. The dust cap is removed.

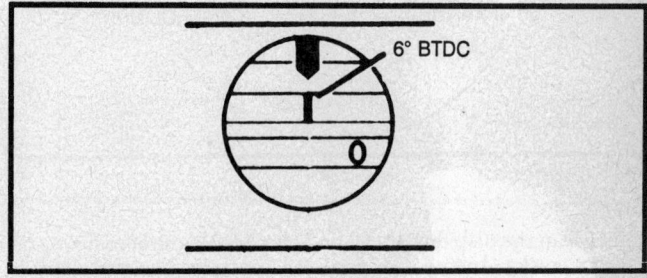

Timing mark alignment—4 cylinder engines

6. Oil the distributor housing lightly where it bears on the cylinder block.
7. Install the distributor so the rotor tip, points to the mark on the distributor housing for the No. 1 cylinder.
8. On 4 cylinder engines, when the distributor shaft has reached bottom, move the rotor back and forth slightly until the drive lug on the oil pump shaft enters the slots cut into the end of the distributor shaft and the distributor assembly slides down into place.

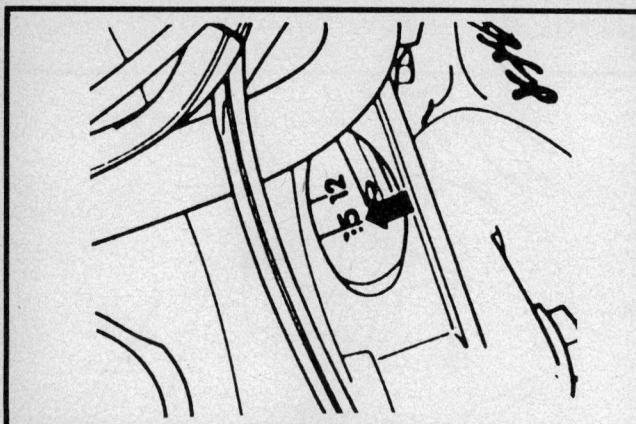

5 cylinder engine timing mark on bell housing, aligned with mark on flywheel.

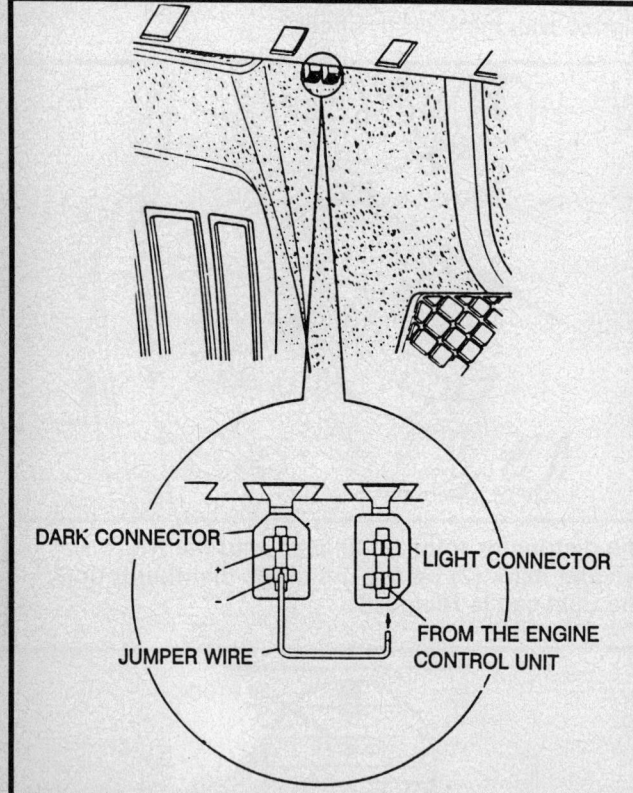

DARK CONNECTOR

LIGHT CONNECTOR

JUMPER WIRE

FROM THE ENGINE CONTROL UNIT

Test connector

9. Clean the distributor cap and check for signs of cracking or carbon tracks. Install the cap and continue the installation procedure.

Ignition Timing

Adjustment

Some tachometers, dwell-meters and oscilloscopes will not work with these ignition systems. Some test equipment may be damaged. Consult the manufacturer of the test equipment if there is any doubt.

NOTE: 1987–89 vehicles have an impedance transformer installed on top of the ignition control unit in

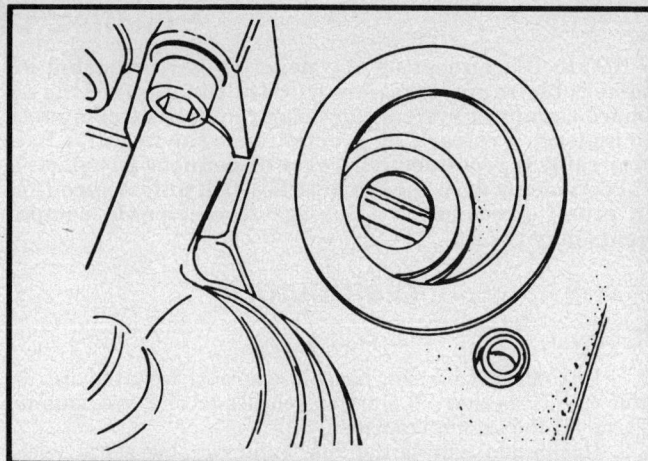

Oil pump driveshaft must be parallel to the crankshaft on 4 cylinder engines.

place of an idle stabilizer as used on previous vehicles. Do not disconnect the transformer when checking the ignition timing.

1988–91 engines are timed by aligning the distributor housing with reference marks. The electronic control unit will retard or advance the timing for each cylinder as required.

NOTE: V8 Quattro vehicles have 2 ignition coils with power stages and 2 distributors. They are both controlled by the Motronic ECU. Each coil and distributor is responsible for providing spark to 4 cylinders. One distributor is mounted on the back of each cylinder head. Both distributors are driven by lugs on the exhaust camshafts. A Hall sender is installed in the distributor mounted on the right cylinder head. The signal from this Hall unit identifies cylinder No. 1 for the start of the sequential fuel injection and cylinder selective knock regulation. Ignition timing is determined by the electronic control unit and cannot be adjusted.

Alternator

Precautions

Several precautions must be observed with alternator equipped vehicles to avoid damage to the unit.

• If the battery is removed for any reason, make sure it is reconnected with the correct polarity. Reversing the battery connections may result in damage to the one-way rectifiers.
• When utilizing a booster battery as a starting aid, always connect the positive to positive terminals and the negative terminal from the booster battery to a good engine ground on the vehicle being started.
• Never use a fast charger as a booster to start vehicles.
• Disconnect the battery cables when charging the battery with a fast charger.
• Never attempt to polarize the alternator.
• Do not use test lamps of more than 12 volts when checking diode continuity.
• Do not short across or ground any of the alternator terminals.
• The polarity of the battery, alternator and regulator must be matched and considered before making any electrical connections within the system.
• Never separate the alternator on an open circuit. Make sure all connections within the circuit are clean and tight.
• Disconnect the battery ground terminal when performing any service on electrical components.

● Disconnect the battery if arc welding is to be done on the vehicle.

Belt Tension Adjustment

The drive belts are correctly tensioned when the longest span of belt between pulleys can be depressed ⅛–½ in. using moderate thumb pressure. To adjust, loosen the slotted adjusting bracket bolt on the alternator. If the alternator hinge bolts are very tight, it may be necessary to loosen them slightly to move the alternator. Move the alternator in or out to obtain the correct tension. Tighten the adjusting bolt when finished.

V-belts under 39 inches in length should deflect about ⅛ inch. Belts over 40 inches long should deflect about ½ inch.

Poly-ribbed belt alignment is especially important on 8 cylinder engines. Check that the poly-ribbed belt between the air conditioner compressor and the hydraulic pump is in alignment front-to-back to prevent damage to the belt. If the 2 toothed belt pulleys are not in alignment, remove the bolts securing the ribbed belt pulley for the hydraulic pump. Using shims, available in sizes 0.020, 0.040 and 0.060 in. (0.5, 1.0 and 1.5mm) adjust the pulleys until they are in alignment. Note that the poly-ribbed belt used on 8 cylinder engines is designed to last the life of the engine.

Removal and Installation

NOTE: If equipped with a 4 cylinder engine, the procedure can be done from the top of the vehicle. If equipped with a 5 cylinder engine, remove and install the alternator from below the vehicle.

1. Disconnect the negative battery cable.
2. Disconnect and tag the alternator wiring. On turbocharged engines, the cold air housing must be removed from the back of the alternator.
3. Remove the pivot bolt from the adjusting bracket.
4. Remove the drive belt.
5. Unbolt and remove the alternator.

NOTE: On some 4 cylinder engines, the top alternator mount has a bushing on the engine side of the mount. Check the condition of the bushing and replace if necessary, before installing the alternator.

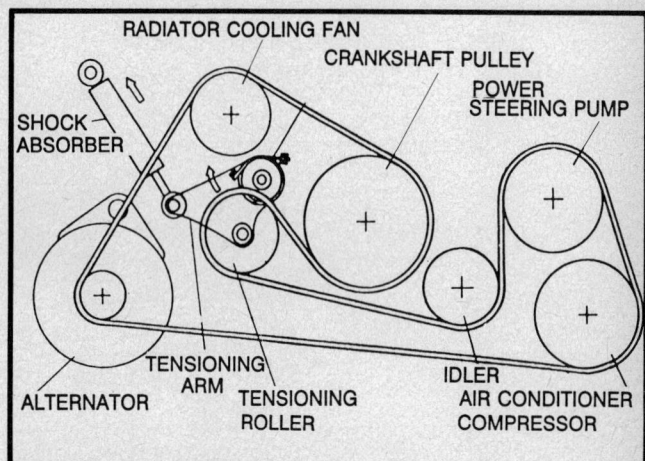

Poly-ribbed belt layout for V8 Quattro

To install:

6. Hold the alternator in position and install the pivot bolts.
7. Install the drive belt and adjusting bolt.
8. Adjust the belt tension.
9. Connect the electrical connections, making sure they are installed in their original locations.
10. Connect the negative battery cable.

Starter

Removal and Installation

1. Disconnect the negative battery cable.
2. Raise and safely support the vehicle.
3. Disconnect and tag the starter wiring.
4. On 4 cylinder engine, remove the starter support bracket bolts. Remove the starter mounting bolts from the rear of the starter.
5. On 5 cylinder engine, 1 bolt goes through the transaxle with a nut on the end of the bolt.
6. Remove the starter from the engine.
7. Installation is the reverse of the removal procedure.

CHASSIS ELECTRICAL

―――――― CAUTION ――――――

On vehicles equipped with an air bag, the negative battery cable must be disconnected, before working on the system. Failure to do so may result in deployment of the air bag and possible personal injury. Never disconnect any electrical connector with the ignition switch turned ON or damage to electronic controlling devices could occur.

NOTE: Before disconnecting the power on any vehicle equipped with a Delta radio, make certain that the radio anti-theft code is recorded.

Heater Blower Motor

Removal and Installation

1987–88 5000, 1989–91 100 AND 200

NOTE: Blower or core removal requires removal and disassembly of the entire unit.

1. Disconnect the negative battery cable.

2. Drain the cooling system.

NOTE: If equipped with air conditioning, the system must be discharged.

3. Discharge the air conditioning system.
4. Disconnect the:
   a. Temperature sensor connector
   b. Evaporator/heater connector clamp
   c. Temperature control cable
   d. Fresh air door vacuum hose
5. Disconnect the main harness connector.
6. Loosen the case retaining strap.
7. Remove the coolant hoses at the heater core tubes.
8. Remove the yellow, green and red vacuum hoses from the heater case.
9. Remove the air duct hoses.
10. Remove the heater case mounting screws, 2 in the passenger compartment, 1 in the engine compartment. Remove the 4 evaporator housing mounting screws in the passenger compartment.

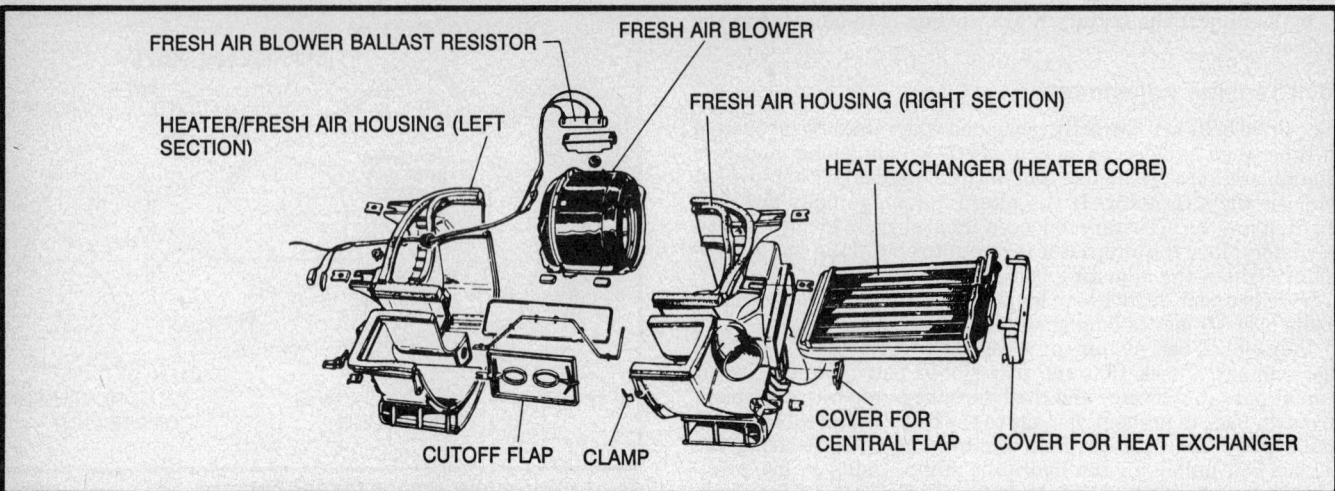

Exploded view of the 4000 heater assembly.

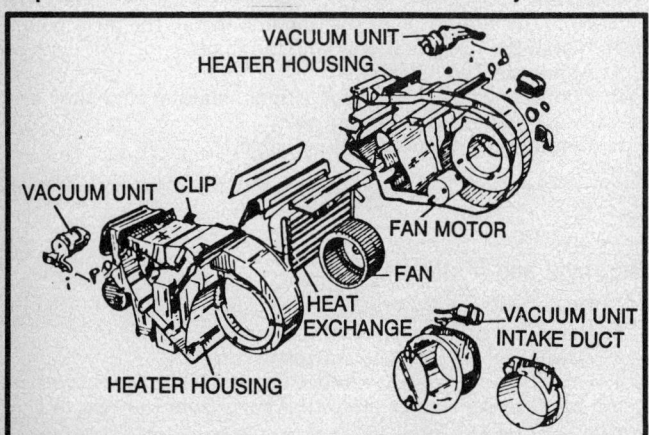

Exploded view of the 100, 200 and 5000 heater assembly.

11. Support the heater/evaporator unit and pull it away from the firewall.

12. Remove the control cable grommet to facilitate case removal.

13. The case halves may be separated by removing the clips at the top and bottom with a small prybar.

14. Remove the blower motor and the heater core from the unit.

15. Installation is the reverse of removal. Replace all sealing material. Evacuate, charge and leak test the system.

─────── **CAUTION** ───────

Freon will freeze any surface it contacts, including skin and eyes. It also turns into a poisonous gas in the presence of an open flame. Wear eye protection and suitable gloves when working on or around the air conditioning system.

4000, COUPE, 80 AND 90

1. Disconnect the negative battery cable.
2. Remove the air plenum from the cowl.
3. Remove the ballast resistor.
4. At the blower motor, disconnect the electrical connector.
5. Remove the blower mounting bolts and the blower from the heater assembly.
6. To install, reverse the removal procedures.

1990–91 V8 QUATTRO

1. Disconnect the negative battery cable.

2. Matchmark hood hinges and remove hood.
3. Remove the windshield wiper assembly.
4. Remove the cap from the engine coolant overflow bottle.
5. Remove the heater retaining band.
6. Remove the vacuum hoses from the vacuum servo motors.
7. Clamp off the heater hoses to the heater core and remove the hoses.
8. Remove the retainers between the body and heater. Remove the heater box.
9. After removing the heater box, remove the blower cooling hose.
10. Remove the lock ring, stop washer and grommet. Remove the blower from the housing.

To install:

11. Before installing the fresh air blower guides, lubricate with petroleum jelly. Install the blower motor using the black electrical connection area only.

12. Installation is the reverse of the removal procedure. When connecting the water hoses, the lower connection on the heater core is connected to the hose going to the water pump.

Windshield Wiper Motor

Removal and Installation

1. Disconnect the negative battery cable and disconnect the wiring harness connector at the motor. Pry off the wiper arms and remove the nuts from the studs in the cowl.

2. Remove the brace-to-body screws. While holding the crank, remove the nut securing the crank to the wiper motor and remove the crank.

3. Remove the bolts securing the wiper motor to the support and remove the motor.

4. Connect the new motor to the wiring harness, run the motor 2 revolutions and turn the wiper switch to the OFF position. The wiper motor should stop in the park position. Remove the linkage followed by the motor.

5. To install, reverse the removal procedures. Make sure the crank is installed in the proper position.

Instrument Cluster

Removal and Installation

4000 AND COUPE

1. Disconnect the negative battery cable.
2. Remove the retaining screws for the instrument cluster cover. Remove the cover and the trim strip.

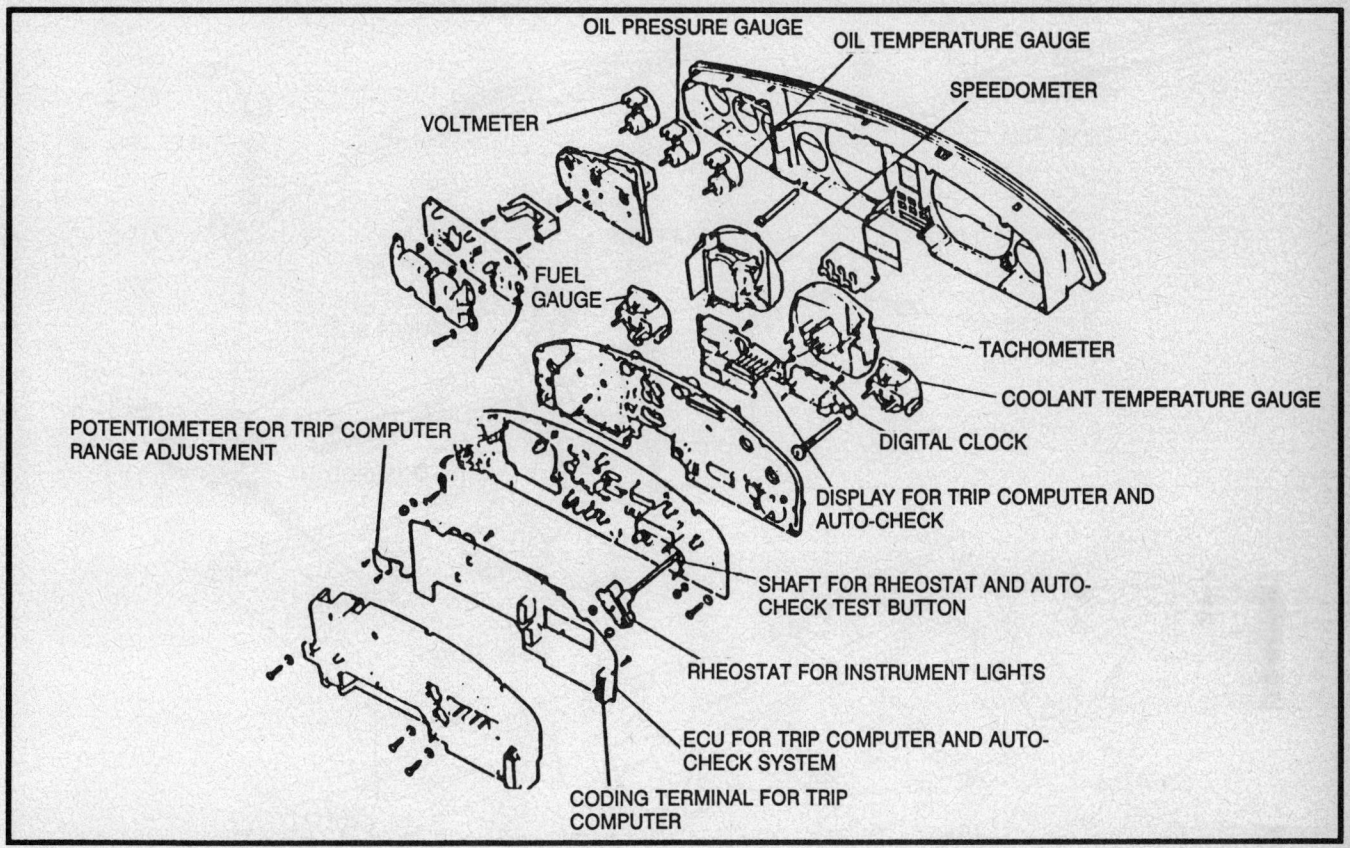

OIL PRESSURE GAUGE
OIL TEMPERATURE GAUGE
VOLTMETER
SPEEDOMETER
FUEL GAUGE
TACHOMETER
POTENTIOMETER FOR TRIP COMPUTER RANGE ADJUSTMENT
COOLANT TEMPERATURE GAUGE
DIGITAL CLOCK
DISPLAY FOR TRIP COMPUTER AND AUTO-CHECK
SHAFT FOR RHEOSTAT AND AUTO-CHECK TEST BUTTON
RHEOSTAT FOR INSTRUMENT LIGHTS
ECU FOR TRIP COMPUTER AND AUTO-CHECK SYSTEM
CODING TERMINAL FOR TRIP COMPUTER

Instrument cluster—typical

3. From the top of the instrument cluster, remove the 4 multi-point connectors.

4. Unscrew the speedometer cable.

5. Remove each switch panel from the side of the instrument cluster.

6. Remove the instrument cluster retaining screws and remove the cluster.

7. Installation is in the reverse order of removal.

1987–88 5000

1. Disconnect the negative battery cable. Pull on the the horn pad and remove the steering wheel.

2. Remove the instrument cluster attaching bolts. Disconnect the speedometer cable at the transaxle.

3. Pull out the instrument cluster and disconnect the speedometer cable at the speedometer head. Disconnect and tag all necessary electrical connectors and remove the instrument cluster.

4. Installation is the reverse order of the removal procedure.

1988–91 80, 90, 100, 200, 5000 AND QUATTRO

1. Disconnect the negative battery cable. Remove the steering wheel. On V8 Quattro vehicles, the instrument cluster is removed after first removing the instrument panel cover. The screws are under the speaker covers and behind the air conditioning outlets, which are removed with long nose pliers.

2. Loosen the clamp on the steering column switch.

3. Pull forward and remove electrical connector.

4. Remove steering column switches.

5. Tilt instrument cluster back and remove the connector retainers.

6. Remove the electrical connectors.

7. Remove the retaining screws for the instrument cluster and remove the instrument cluster.

8. Installation is in the reverse order of removal.

Headlight Switch

Removal and Installation

INSTRUMENT PANEL MOUNTED

1. Remove the instrument cluster cover.

2. Disconnect the wiring harness connector from the headlight switch.

3. Depress the clips on the headlight switch retainer and remove the switch from the instrument cluster.

4. Installation is the reverse order of the removal procedure.

NOTE: On some vehicles the headlight switch could be incorporated with the combination switch. This switch can contain the headlight switch, parking light switch, turn signal switch, low/high beam switch, headlight flasher switch and cruise control switch.

Combination Switch

Removal and Installation

The windshield wiper switch is incorporated with the combination switch located on the steering column. On some vehicles, if the wiper switch has to be replaced, the combination switch must be replaced.

4000, COUPE, 80 AND 90

1. Disconnect the negative battery cable. Pull off the horn pad and remove the steering wheel.

2. Remove the steering column cover. Remove the 3 screws on the turn signal switch.

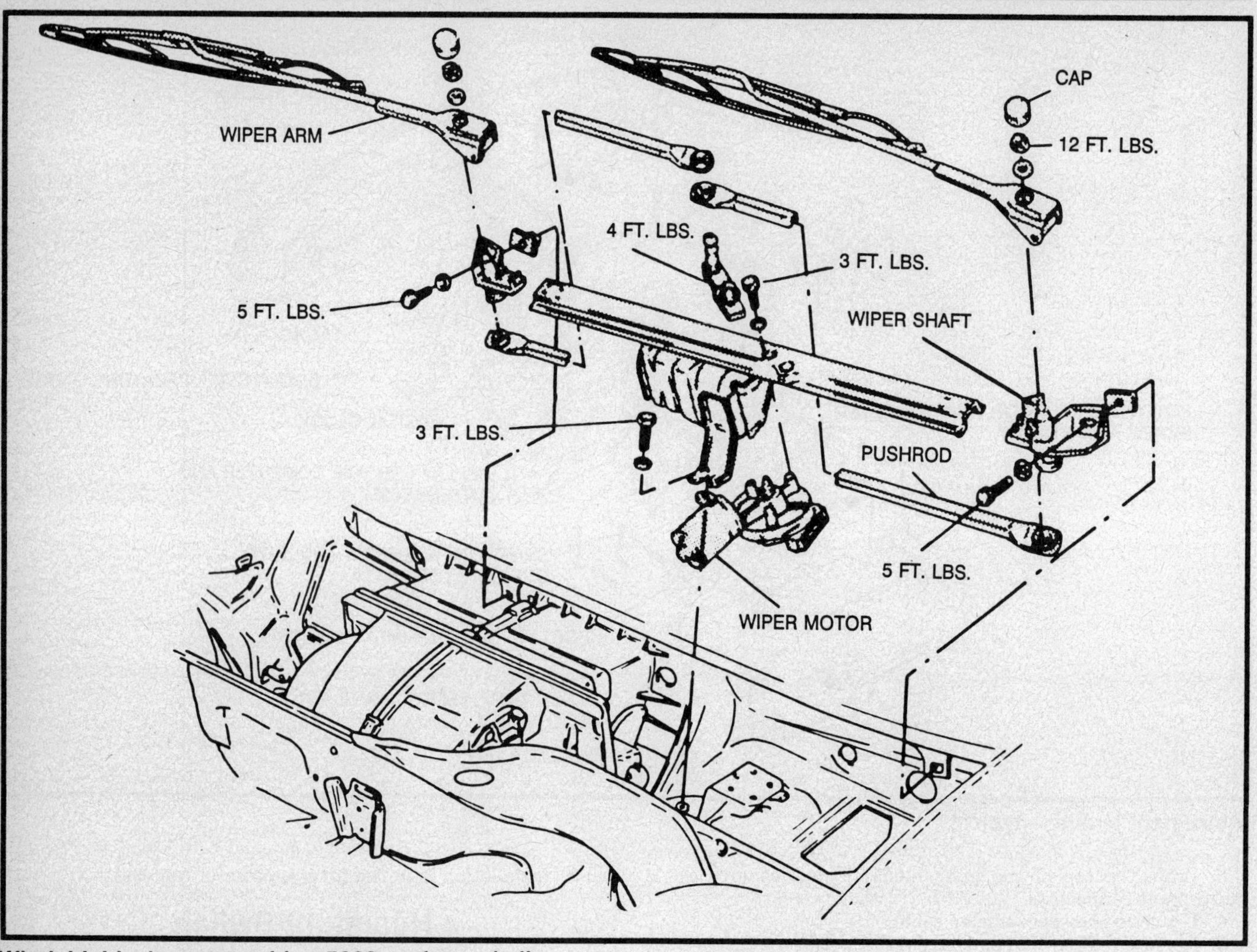

WIPER ARM

CAP

12 FT. LBS.

4 FT. LBS.

3 FT. LBS.

WIPER SHAFT

5 FT. LBS.

3 FT. LBS.

PUSHROD

5 FT. LBS.

WIPER MOTOR

Windshield wiper assembly—5000—others similar

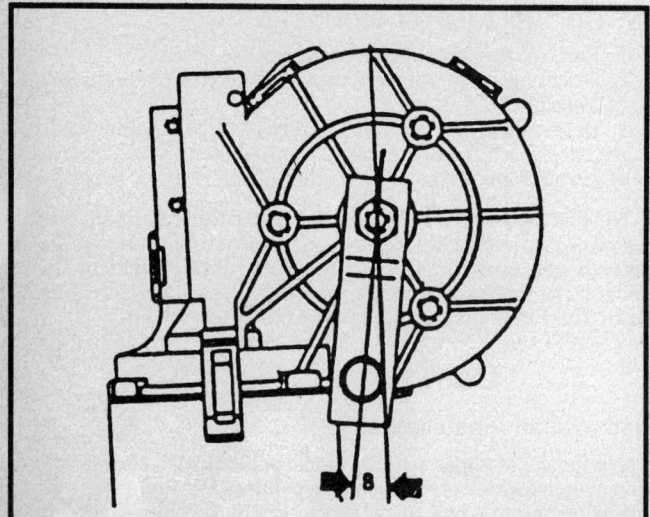

Wiper crank in the park position (at 8 degrees)—4000 and Coupe GT.

3. Pull the turn signal switch and the wiper switch from the column.

4. Installation is the reverse order of the removal procedure.

5000, 100 AND 200

— **CAUTION** —

This vehicle is equipped with a driver's side air bag system. Working around the steering column on this vehicle means caution must be used and proper procedures followed. Always disconnect the negative battery cable and cover the battery terminal. Also, separate the red, single-pin connector marked with the word AIR BAG for the power supply behind the instrument panel.

1. Disconnect the negative battery cable. Remove the steering wheel.

2. Insert a suitable tool into the slot at the bottom of the steering column cover and loosen the screw(s).

3. Pull the switch and the top of the cover assembly off of the steering column. Remove the 2 screws inside the cover to remove the wiper switch from the cover.

4. Installation is the reverse order of the removal procedure.

1990–91 V8 QUATTRO

The windshield wiper/washer switch, hazard flasher switch, intensive washer system switch, headlight wiper/washer switch and on-board computer function switch are built into one steering column mounted combination switch.

CAUTION

This vehicle is equipped with a driver's side air bag system. Working around the steering column on this vehicle means caution must be used and proper procedures followed. Always disconnect the negative battery cable and cover the battery terminal. Also, separate the red, single-pin connector marked with the word AIR BAG for the power supply behind the instrument panel.

1. Disconnect the negative battery cable.

NOTE: Before disconnecting the power on any vehicle equipped with a Delta radio, make certain that the anti-theft code is recorded.

2. Remove the air bag unit or horn bar, by removing the Torx® screws from behind the the steering wheel.
3. Tilt the air bag unit down and remove the air bag connector retaining strap and remove the air bag assembly.
4. Remove the upper steering column trim retaining screws

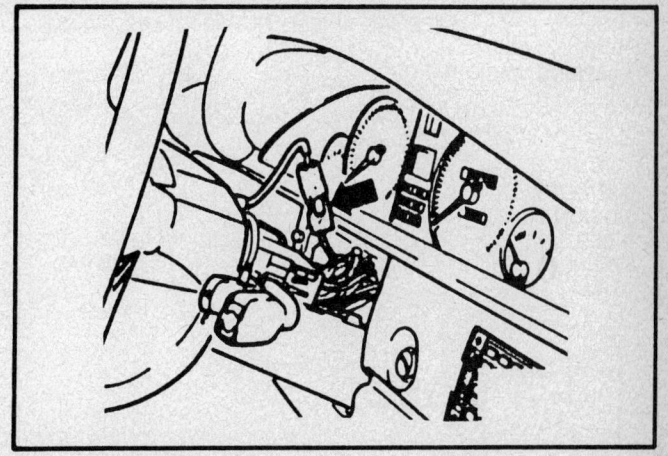

Connector for air bag

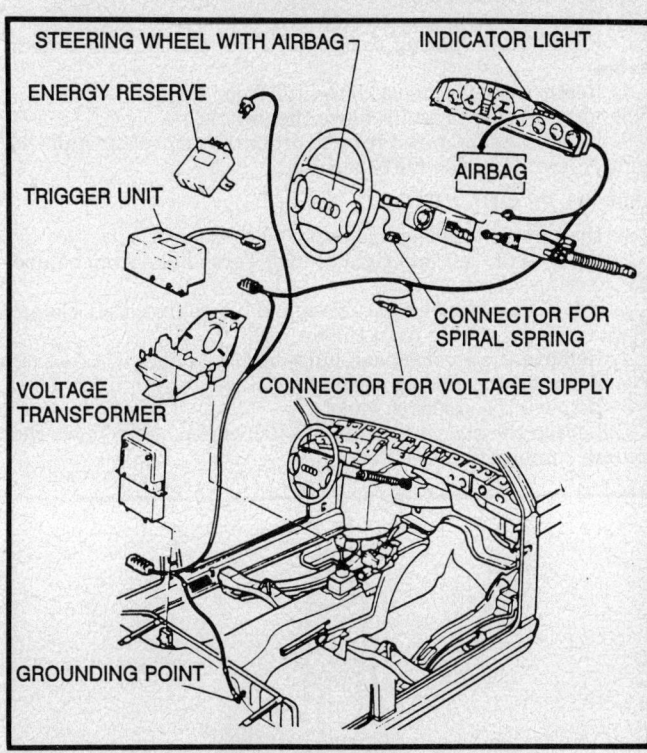

Air bag system—200 shown

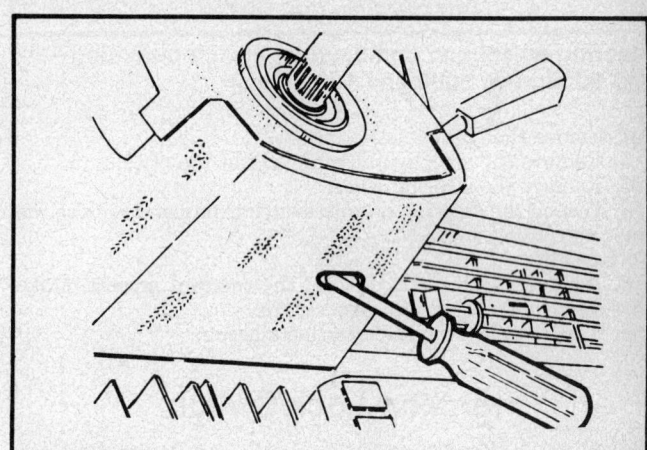

To remove switch housing on the 5000, loosen screw from below

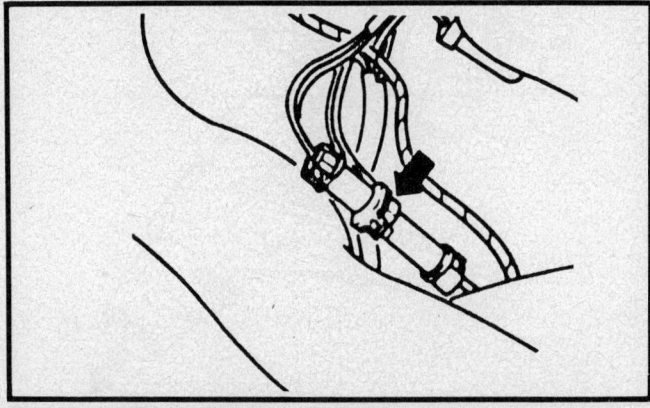

Power connector must be disconnected—steering wheel with air bag

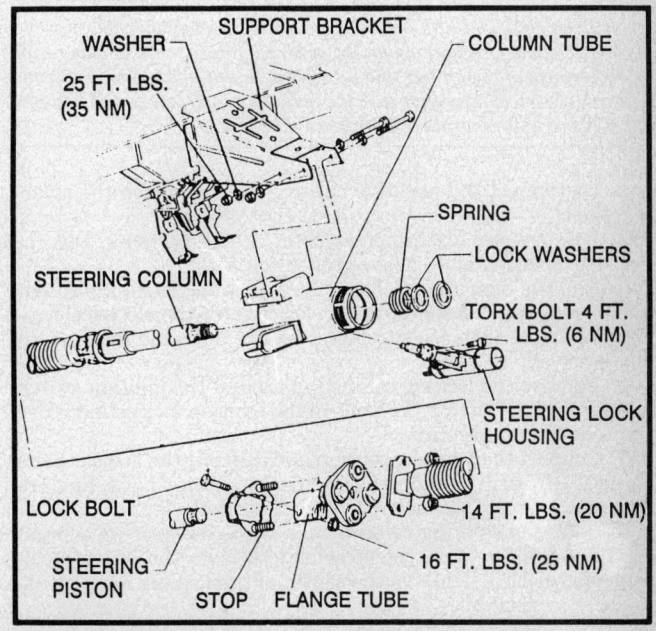

Exploded view of steering column—80 and 90—others similar

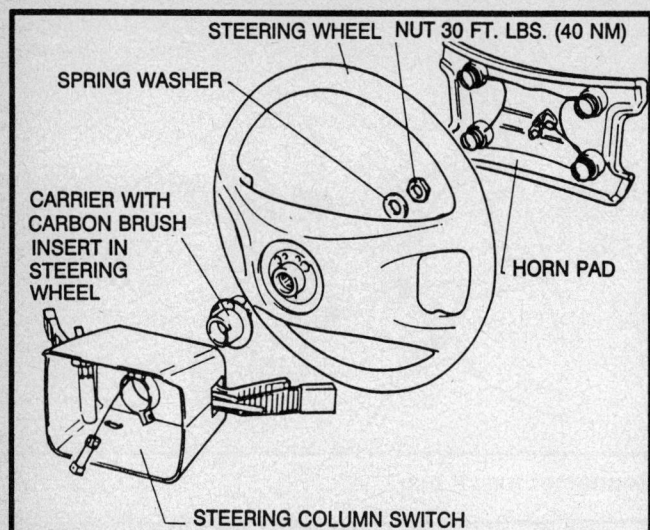

Steering wheel and combination switch mounting—80 and 90 shown; 5000 and 100 similar

and remove the trim.

  5. Remove the air bag unit connector at top of column.

  6. Remove the steering wheel.

  7. Loosen the steering column switch clamp and remove the steering column switches.

To install:

  8. Installation is the reverse of the removal process. Make sure all air bag connections are secure.

  9. Test column switches after installation.

Ignition Lock/Switch

Removal and Installation

1987–88 5000, 1989–91 100 AND 200

CAUTION

On vehicles equipped with an air bag, the negative battery cable must be disconnected, before working on the system. Failure to do so may result in deployment of the air bag and possible personal injury. Never disconnect any electrical connector with the ignition switch turned ON or damage to electronic controlling devices could occur.

---

  1. Disconnect the negative battery cable. Remove the steering wheel.

  2. Remove the instrument cluster attaching bolts. Disconnect the speedometer cable at the transaxle.

  3. Pull the instrument cluster forward and detach the speedometer cable at the speedometer. Disconnect the electrical connectors at the instrument cluster and remove the instrument cluster.

  4. Remove the locking compound around the ignition switch and remove the switch. To remove the ignition lock cylinder use the following procedure.

  5. Support the steering column and drill out the 2 shear bolts using a ⅛ in. drill bit. Loosen the steering column bolts. Remove the left lower dash panel and the left air deflector.

  6. Slide the steering column tube with the steering column downward and remove the steering lock from the steering column clamp. Drill a hole in the center of the locking housing using a ⅛ in. drill bit.

  7. Push the retaining spring in with a suitable punch and remove the lock cylinder.

  8. Installation is the reverse order of the removal procedure.

1987 4000, COUPE, 80 AND 90

  1. Disconnect the negative battery cable.

  2. Remove the steering wheel, the steering column covers and the steering column combination switches.

  3. Pry the lock washer off the steering column and discard it.

  4. Remove the spring and pull off the contact ring.

  5. Unplug the electrical connector.

  6. Unscrew the retaining bolt and slide the ignition switch/steering lock assembly off of the steering column tube.

  7. Installation is in the reverse order of removal. Use a new lock washer.

1988–91 80 AND 90

  1. Disconnect the negative battery cable.

  2. Remove the steering wheel, the steering column covers and the steering column combination switches.

  3. Remove instrument cluster retaining screws.

  4. Tilt the instrument cluster backwards slightly and remove the electrical connectors.

  5. Remove the instrument cluster.

  6. Remove the locking compound from the ignition switch screws.

  7. Remove the electrical connector from switch.

  8. Remove screws and remove the switch.

  9. Installation is in the reverse order of removal. Install the ignition switch in the **OFF** position.

1990–91 V8 QUATTRO

  1. Disconnect the negative battery cable.

  2. Remove the left and right air bag Torx® bolts from behind the steering wheel.

  3. Tilt the air bag unit backward and lift up the safety clamp. Disconnect the wiring from the air bag unit.

  4. Remove the steering column trim top section.

  5. Separate the air bag connector.

  6. Remove the steering wheel.

  7. Loosen the steering column switch clamp and remove the column combination switches.

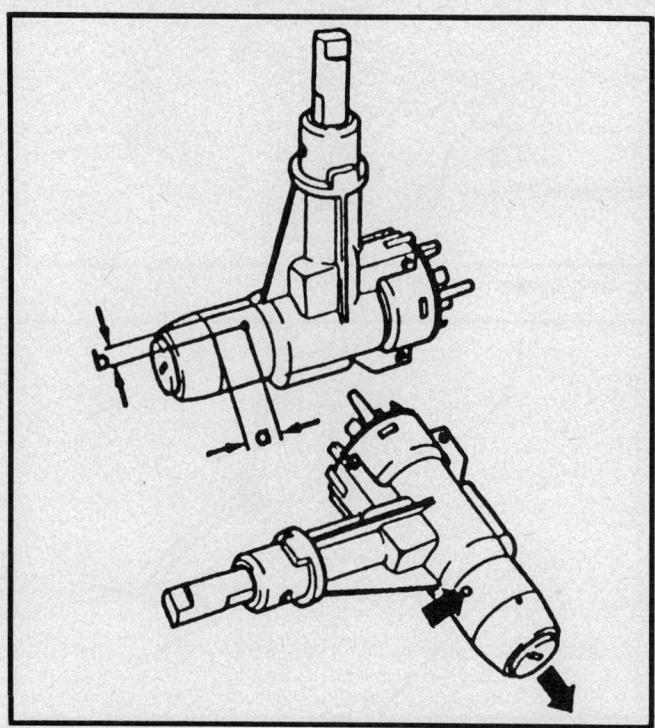

Drill lock housing to remove key cylinder—a = 0.50 in., b = 0.125 in.

8. Remove the instrument cluster and trim under the left side of the instrument panel.

9. Remove the electrical connector from the ignition switch.

10. Remove the locking compound from the switch mounting screws, loosen the screws slightly and pull the ignition switch assembly from the housing. To remove the ignition lock cylinder:

    a. Remove the glove box.

    b. Remove instrument panel crossmember.

    c. Remove lock housing Torx® screw and remove steering lock housing.

    d. Drill one hole, approx. ⅛ in. (3mm) diameter in steering lock housing only 0.080 in. (2mm) deep, 0.50 in. (12.5mm) from the key end. Do not drill too deeply or the lock cylinder will be damaged.

    e. Remove the lock cylinder by pushing in on the retaining spring.

To install:

11. Installation is the reverse of the removal procedure. When installing the lock cylinder, push into the steering lock housing until the retaining spring engages.

12. After installing the ignition switch, apply locking compound to switch mounting screws.

Stoplight Switch

Removal and Installation

1. Disconnect the negative battery cable.

2. Disconnect the stoplight switch wire connector from the switch.

3. If the stoplight switch is located behind the brake pedal, remove the hairpin retainer and outer nylon washer from the pedal pin. Slide the stoplight switch off the brake pedal pin just far enough for the outer side plate of the switch to clear the pin. Remove the switch. Quattro V8 vehicles will have 2 switches on the brake pedal. The stoplight switch is the top switch. It presses into clips on the pedal bracket.

4. If the stoplight switch is located in the master cylinder, use a suitable wrench and remove the switch from the master cylinder.

5. Installation is the reverse order of the removal procedure. If the switch was located in the master cylinder, be sure to top off the master cylinder reservoir and bleed the brake circuit.

Neutral Safety Switch

The neutral safety switch prevents the engine from being started with the transaxle in any position other than **P** or **N**. It also activates the back-up lights. The switch is at the base of the shift lever, inside the floorshift console except on the V8 Quattro.

On this vehicle, a multi-function switch on the transaxle tells the transaxle ECU which selector lever position has been selected by the driver. It also energizes the back-up light relay and sends a signal to the Automatic Shift Lock (ASL) control unit. This prevents the selector lever from being moved from the **P** or **N** positions unless the driver first steps on the foot brake.

Adjustment

1. Remove the 4 screws which hold the console to the floor.

2. Shift into **N**. Remove the 2 screws which hold the shift position indicator plate to the console. Remove the shift knob and the console.

3. Disconnect the red/black electrical leads from the switch.

4. Loosen both switch retaining screws.

5. Using an ohmmeter, adjust the switch so the neutral safety switch contacts are together.

6. Install the electrical connectors. Hold the footbrake while making sure the engine will start only in **N** and **P**. Make sure

the back-up lights operate only in **R**. If the switch does not operate properly, it may have to be moved on its slotted mounting bracket.

7. Replace the console cover when adjustment is complete.

Removal and Installation

1. Remove the 4 screws which hold the console to the floor.

2. Shift into **N**. Remove the 2 screws which hold the shift position indicator plate to the console. Remove the shift knob and the console.

3. Disconnect the switch electrical leads. These are: red/black—neutral safety; black—back-up lights; blue/red—back-up lights. The back-up light wires are at the front.

4. Remove the 2 switch retaining screws. Remove the switch.

5. Install the new switch so the neutral safety switch contacts are together.

6. Install the electrical connectors. Hold the footbrake while making sure the engine will start only in **N** and **P**. Make sure the back-up lights operate only in **R**. If the switch does not operate properly, it may have to be moved on its slotted mounting bracket.

7. Replace the console cover when adjustment is complete.

Fuses, Circuit Breakers and Relays

NOTE: Before disconnecting the power on any vehicle equipped with a Delta radio, make certain that the anti-theft code has been recorded.

Location

Relays are also plugged into the fuse box. The fuse box for all 4000 and Coupe vehicles can be found under the left side of the dashboard, behind the rear panel of the package tray or under the left rear side of the engine compartment. Other vehicles may have the fuse box located under the hood, at the rear of the engine compartment.

V8 Quattro vehicles have the main fuse relay panel located behind the side kick panel cover in the front passenger footwell. An auxiliary relay panel is located under the carpet in the passenger side footwell. This panel also houses the connectors for the factory diagnostic tester.

In the cover of each fuse box and in the Owner's Manual, is a chart that tells which circuit the fuse protects and its correct amperage. The chart also tells to which circuit the relays are connected. Each vehicle may also use in-line fuses for certain circuits; fuel pump, battery, air conditioning and power door locks, if equipped.

FUSE COLOR CODES

The number on the face of the fuse is the amperage rating.

    1. Brown—5–Amp

    2. Red—10–Amp

    3. Blue—15–Amp

    4. Yellow—25–Amp

    5. Green—30–Amp

AUXILIARY RELAY

An auxiliary relay panel, usually located under the left side of the instrument panel may contain additional relays.

Computers

Location

Computers are used in a variety of applications, primarily for engine fuel management. The main computer is located under the instrument panel, generally on the driver's side near the console. A new 4-speed electronically controlled automatic transaxle is now used in the V8 Quattro and is also tied into the computer.

Flashers

Location
Turn signal and hazard flashers are located in the fuse and relay panels.

ENGINE COOLING

Radiator

Removal and Installation
4 CYLINDER ENGINE

NOTE: The 80 and 90 series vehicles use a dual fan electric/belt driven assembly. Replacement is similar to the other 4 cylinder engines.

1. Drain the cooling system.
2. If equipped with air conditioning, remove the grille and detach the condenser from the radiator. Leave refrigerant hoses attached, if possible. If not, safely discharge the air conditioning system.
3. Remove the upper and lower radiator hoses, the expansion tank supply hose and the expansion tank vent hose. Being careful not to crimp them, tie all hoses back aside.
4. Disconnect the wiring at the temperature switch, 2 switches if air conditioned, and the rear of the fan motor.
5. Unscrew the fan shroud retaining bolts and remove the fan, motor and shroud as an assembly.
6. Unscrew the radiator retaining bolts and remove the radiator.
7. Installation is in the reverse order of removal.

EXCEPT 4 CYLINDER ENGINE

1. Drain the cooling system.
2. Remove the 3 pieces of the radiator cowl and the fan motor assembly. Take care in removing the fan motor connectors to avoid bending them.
3. Remove the upper and lower radiator hoses and the coolant tank supply hose.
4. Disconnect the coolant temperature switch located on the lower right side of the radiator.
5. Remove the radiator mounting bolts and lift out the radiator.
6. Installation is the reverse of removal. Torque radiator mounting bolts to 14 ft. lbs. and cowl bolts to 7 ft. lbs.

Electric Cooling Fan

Testing
Factory procedures call for using the factory tester to check the entire system at the instrument panel multi-pin connectors. It is possible to do a basic check of the sensors with an ohmmeter.
1. Check the radiator coolant temperature sensor. It should have a resistance of approximately 360 ohms when cold and 70 ohms when hot.
2. Check the cylinder head coolant temperature sensor. It should also have a resistance of approximately 360 ohms when cold and 70 ohms when hot.
3. If the sensors check out and the electric cooling fan still does not run, check the wiring and connections. Jumper wires with battery voltage can also be connected to the fan motors to test operation.

Removal and Installation
1. Disconnect the battery negative cable.

2. Remove the 3 pieces of the radiator cowl.
3. Remove the fan motor assembly. Take care in removing the fan motor connectors to avoid bending them.
4. Installation is the reverse of the removal process.

Heater Core

For further information, please refer to "Chilton's Heating and Air Conditioning Manual" for additional coverage.

Removal and Installation
EXCEPT V8 QUATTRO

1. Disconnect the negative battery cable.
2. At the radiator, pull off the bottom hose and drain the coolant into a container for reuse.
3. Remove the heater hoses from the heat exchanger.
4. At the heater assembly control valve, disconnect the control wire.
5. Remove the console. Remove the left and the right heater covers from below the dashboard. On 80 and 90 vehicles, remove the instrument panel.
6. Discharge the air conditioning system and remove the refrigerant lines from the evaporator.
7. At the heater control unit, pull off the control knobs.
8. Remove the trim plate from the heater control unit.
9. At the heater control unit, remove the retaining screws and the center cover.
10. Remove the heater air ducts and the heater assembly retaining springs.
11. Remove the air plenum from the cowl and the heater assembly from the vehicle.
12. Separate the heater unit and remove the heater core.
13. Installation is the reverse order of the removal procedure.
14. Refill the cooling system and evacuate and recharge the air conditioning system, if equipped.

V8 QUATTRO

1. Disconnect the negative battery cable.
2. Matchmark hood hinges and remove hood.
3. Remove the windshield wiper assembly.
4. Remove the cap from the engine coolant overflow bottle.
5. Remove the heater retaining band.
6. Remove the vacuum hoses from the vacuum servo motors.
7. Clamp off the heater hoses to the heater core and remove the hoses.
8. Remove the retainers between the body and heater and remove the heater box.
9. Remove the silicone rubber sealant from the heater core inlet/outlet area and separate the housing halves. Remove the heater core from the housing.
To install:
10. Installation is the reverse of the removal procedure. Before installing the fresh air blower guides, lubricate with petroleum jelly.
11. Apply gasket around the heater core without gaps before installing the heater core into the heater box.

12. After installing the heater core, fill the opening between the heater core and the housing with silicone sealant.

13. When connecting the water hoses, make sure the lower connection on the heater core is connected to the hose going to the water pump.

Water Pump

Removal and Installation
4 AND 5 CYLINDER ENGINES

1. Drain the cooling system.
2. Remove the V-belts, timing belt covers. On 5 cylinder engine, remove the timing belt from the water pump.
3. On 4 cylinder engine, remove the water pump pulley retaining bolts and remove the pulley. Remove the pump retaining bolts. Take note of various lengths and locations. Turn the pump slightly and lift from engine block.
4. Always replace the old gasket or O-ring.
5. Installation is the reverse of the removal procedure.
6. Reinstall the timing belt on 5 cylinder engine and properly tension the belt with the water pump.

8 CYLINDER ENGINE

1. Disconnect the negative battery cable.
2. Drain cooling system.
3. Remove the toothed drive belt.
4. Remove the belt tensioner.
5. Remove the 9 Torx® head bolts and remove water pump.
6. Installation is the reverse of the removal process. Always use a new gasket. Torque the water pump bolts to 7 ft. lbs.
7. When refilling the cooling system, fill the expansion tank with new coolant to the maximum mark. Close the expansion tank and warm the engine until the radiator cooling fan cycles.
8. Check the coolant level and if necessary, top off. When the engine is at normal temperature, the level should be slightly over the maximum mark. When the engine is cold, between the maximum and minimum marks.

Thermostat

Removal and Installation
4 CYLINDER ENGINE

The thermostat is located in the lower radiator hose neck on the bottom of the water pump housing.
1. Drain the cooling system.
2. Remove the 2 retaining bolts from the lower water pump neck.

NOTE: It is not necessary to disconnect the lower radiator hose. But removing the hose from the thermostat yoke may ease installation.

3. Move the neck, with the hoses attached, aside.
4. Carefully, pry the thermostat out of the water pump housing.
5. Install with new gasket or O-ring.
6. Install the radiator hose, if removed.

5 CYLINDER ENGINE

The thermostat is located in the lower radiator hose neck, on

the left side of the engine block, behind the water pump housing.
1. Drain the cooling system.
2. Remove the 2 retaining bolts from the lower water pump neck.

NOTE: It is not necessary to disconnect the lower radiator hose. But removing the hose from the thermostat yoke may ease installation.

3. Move the neck, with the hoses attached, aside.
4. Drain the cooling system.
5. Remove the 2 retaining bolts from the lower water pump neck.
6. Carefully, pry the thermostat out of the engine block.
7. Install a new O-ring on the water pump neck.
8. Install the thermostat.

NOTE: When installing the thermostat, the spring end should be pointing toward the engine block.

9. Reposition the water pump neck and tighten the retaining bolts.
10. Install radiator hose, if removed.

8 CYLINDER ENGINE

The thermostat is located at the front right-hand side of the engine below the intake manifold.
1. Drain the cooling system.
2. Remove the 2 retaining bolts from the thermostat housing.

NOTE: It is not necessary to disconnect the lower radiator hose. But removing the hose from the thermostat yoke may ease installation.

3. Remove the thermostat housing.
4. Carefully, pry the thermostat from the engine block.
5. Install the new thermostat with the breather valve at the top or 12 o'clock position. Use a new gasket or O-ring.
6. Install the radiator hose, if removed. Refill with coolant.

Cooling System Bleeding

After working on the cooling system, even to replace the thermostat, the system should be bled. Air trapped in the system will prevent proper filling and leave the radiator coolant level low, causing a risk of overheating.
1. To bleed the system, start with the system cool, the radiator cap off and the radiator filled to about an 1 in. below the filler neck.
2. Start the engine and run it at slightly above normal idle speed. This will insure adequate circulation. If air bubbles appear and the coolant level drops, fill the system with an antifreeze/water mixture to bring the level back to the proper level.
3. Run the engine this way until the thermostat opens. When this happens, coolant will move abruptly across the top of the radiator and the temperature of the radiator will suddenly rise.
4. At this point, air is often expelled and the level may drop quite a bit. Keep refilling the system until the level is near the top of the radiator and remains constant.
5. If equipped with an overflow tank, fill the radiator right up to the filler neck. Replace the radiator filler cap.

FUEL SYSTEM

Fuel System Service Precaution

Safety is the most important factor when performing not only

fuel system maintenance but any type of maintenance. Failure to conduct maintenance and repairs in a safe manner may result in serious personal injury or death. Maintenance and testing of the vehicle's fuel system components can be accomplished safely and effectively by adhering to the following rules and guidelines.

● To avoid the possibility of fire and personal injury, always disconnect the negative battery cable unless the repair or test procedure requires that battery voltage be applied.

● Always relieve the fuel system pressure prior to disconnecting any fuel system component (injector, fuel rail, pressure regulator, etc.), fitting or fuel line connection. Exercise extreme caution whenever relieving fuel system pressure to avoid exposing skin, face and eyes to fuel spray. Please be advised that fuel under pressure may penetrate the skin or any part of the body that it contacts.

● Always place a shop towel or cloth around the fitting or connection prior to loosening to absorb any excess fuel due to spillage. Ensure that all fuel spillage (should it occur) is quickly removed from engine surfaces. Ensure that all fuel soaked cloths or towels are deposited into a suitable waste container.

● Always keep a dry chemical (Class B) fire extinguisher near the work area.

● Do not allow fuel spray or fuel vapors to come into contact with a spark or open flame.

● Always use a backup wrench when loosening and tightening fuel line connection fittings. This will prevent unnecessary stress and torsion to fuel line piping. Always follow the proper torque specifications.

● Always replace worn fuel fitting O-rings with new. Do not substitute fuel hose or equivalent where fuel pipe is installed.

Relieving Fuel System Pressure

Modern fuel injection systems operate under high pressure. This makes it necessary to first relieve the system of pressure before servicing. The pressurized fuel when released may ignite or cause personal injury.

1. Disconnect the power to the fuel pump by removing the relay or the fuel pump fuse which is generally fuse No. 13 on most vehicles. Check the fuse box. The fuse can be removed to keep the fuel pump from running. With the engine operating at idle, wait until the engine stalls from fuel starvation.

2. Remove the negative battery cable.

3. Carefully loosen the fuel line on the control pressure regulator or component to be serviced.

4. Wrap a clean rag around the connection, while loosening, to catch any fuel.

5. After service is complete, discard the fuel soaked rag in the proper manner and reconnect negative battery cable, relay or fuses.

Fuel Filter

Removal and Installation

Most vehicles use a fuel filter mounted under the vehicle, below the fuel tank. An arrow should be on the filter indicating fuel flow direction. Install with arrow pointing to engine. Use care not to mix up fuel supply or return lines. Fuel pressure applied to the return side of the system will cause damage.

In addition, some vehicles use a filter in the engine compartment near the fuel distributor. If equipped, use the following procedure:

1. Make certain to follow precautions and relieve fuel pressure.

2. Disconnect the fuel lines leading into and out of the fuel distributor.

3. Unscrew the filter retaining bracket and remove the filter.

4. Install a new filter in the bracket and reattach bracket to vehicle. Make sure the arrows are pointing in the direction of the fuel flow to the distributor.

5. Reconnect the fuel lines, start the engine and check for leaks.

Electric Fuel Pump

Pressure Testing

NOTE: The fuel tank is pressurized. Do not open the fuel tank cap until after the fuel pump delivery rate has been tested.

NON-TURBOCHARGED

1. Using tool US 4480/3 or equivalent, connect it in place of the fuel pump relay with the switch OFF.

2. Remove the fuel pump cover from the floor of the trunk, on 80 and 90 vehicles raise and safely support vehicle to access the pump.

3. At the fuel pump connecting plug, pull back the rubber cover, leave the plug connected to the pump.

4. Using a voltmeter, connect the probes to terminals 1 and 2 of the fuel pump connector. Turn the fuel pump ON.

5. Check the voltage of the running pump, it should be at least 9.0V. Turn the pump OFF.

6. In the engine compartment, disconnect the fuel line return connection and place it into a graduated container.

7. Turn the fuel pump ON for 30 seconds and measure the quantity of fuel collected, it should be about 46 cu. in. of fuel. If not, check the fuel filter and/or the fuel pump.

TURBOCHARGED

1. Using tool VW 1318 or equivalent, connect between the fuel line at the cold start valve and the lower chamber test connection of the fuel distributor. Position the gauge lever so the valve is open.

2. Remove the fuel pump relay from the fuse panel and install tool US 4480/3 or equivalent. Be certain that it is turned OFF.

3. Remove the electrical connector from the differential pressure regulator.

4. Turn ON the fuel pump, the fuel pressure should be 75–82 psi.

5. If the pressure is below specifications, check the fuel pump delivery quantity.

6. If the fuel pump delivery is within specifications, replace the diaphragm pressure regulator.

7. If the pressure is higher than specifications, disconnect the fuel tank return line from the diaphragm pressure regulator and repeat the test.

8. If the pressure is within specifications, check for a plugged fuel return line.

9. If the pressure is not within specifications, replace the diaphragm pressure regulator.

NOTE: The system pressure is not adjustable.

Removal and Installation

1987 4000

The fuel pump is located at the left rear of the undercarriage.

1. Disconnect the battery negative cable.

2. Raise and safely support vehicle.

3. Disconnect the pump wiring.

4. Disconnect the fuel lines.

5. Unbolt and dismount the pump.

6. Installation is the reverse of removal. Torque the mounting bolts to 14 ft. lbs.

1987–91 100, 5000 AND V8 QUATTRO

The fuel pump is located in the fuel tank.

1. Remove the floor cover from the luggage compartment.

2. Disconnect the negative battery cable and the electrical connector from the fuel gauge sender.

3. Mark and remove the hoses from the fuel gauge sender.

4. A special wrench is available to loosen the fuel gauge sender-to-fuel tank retaining ring. Pull out the fuel gauge fuel pump assembly.

5. From inside the assembly housing, pull off the fuel hoses, detach the electrical connections and remove the gravity vent valve.

6. To install, reverse the removal procedures. Start the engine and check for leaks.

1988–91 80 AND 90

The fuel pump is located under the vehicle on a bracket in front of the fuel tank. The fuel pump assembly is located on the right side of front wheel drive vehicles and on the left side on Quattro vehicles. The 80 and 90 vehicles do not use a separate fuel pump filter. The filter is expected to be a lifetime unit, unless the fuel was contaminated.

1. Make certain to follow precautions and relieve fuel pressure.
2. Disconnect the negative battery cable.
3. Raise and safely support vehicle.
4. Carefully loosen fuel line at fuel pump. Catch excess fuel in a container.
5. Remove fuel pump electrical connectors and remove the fuel pump.
6. Install fuel pump. Connect the fuel lines.
7. Connect the fuel pump electrical connectors.
8. Lower vehicle and connect the negative battery cable.
9. Replace any relays or fuses, that had been removed. Start engine and inspect for fuel leakage.

Fuel Injection

For further information, please refer to "Chilton's Electronic Engine Control's Manual" for additional coverage.

Idle Speed Adjustment

100, 200 AND 5000

The CIS-E system incorporates 2 control units. An Ignition Control Unit (ICU) or Knock Sensor Control Unit (KSCU), on 5000S only, and a Fuel Injection Control Unit (FICU).

The CIS-E system also has self-diagnosis and troubleshooting capabilities. Input and output signals from various sensors, switches and signaling devices are constantly monitored for faults. These faults are stored in the control unit memory. Faults can be displayed by a flashing 4 digit code sequence from an LED light located on the instrument panel.

Idle speed should be 650–790 rpm. The idle speed is not adjustable. If idle speed is not within specification, check for an engine problem such as vacuum leaks, etc. Also, check for a defective differential pressure regulator.

80 AND 90

The CIS Motronic system used on 80 and 90 vehicles uses a single Electronic Control Unit (ECU), located behind the air conditioner evaporator assembly. The ECU controls the fuel delivery, ignition system and operation of the emission control components. The CIS Motronic system also incorporates self-diagnostic capabilities.

The idle speed is maintained between 780–900 rpm. No idle speed adjustments are necessary or possible. The idle stabilizer valve is located between the intake air boot and intake manifold.

V8 QUATTRO

The Motronic fuel injection system used on the V8 Quattro is a self-learning adaptive system that continuously learns using a sophisticated feedback system, that constantly readjusts various control settings. These new values are then stored in the ECU memory. The adaptive system allows the system to compensate for changes in the engine's operating conditions, such as intake leaks, altitude changes or any other system malfunction.

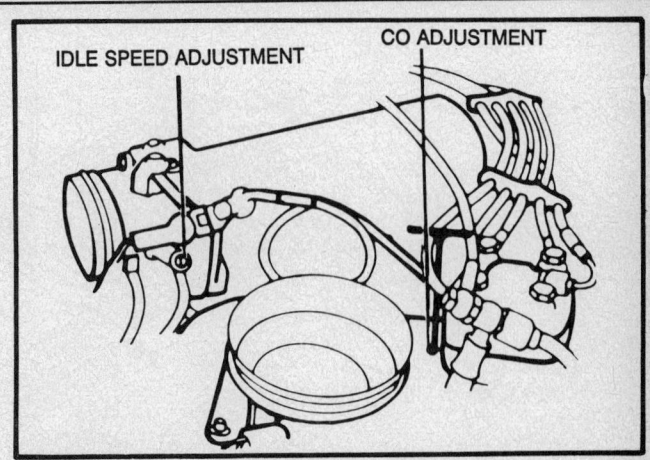

Idle speed and mixture adjustment screws—4 cylinder engines

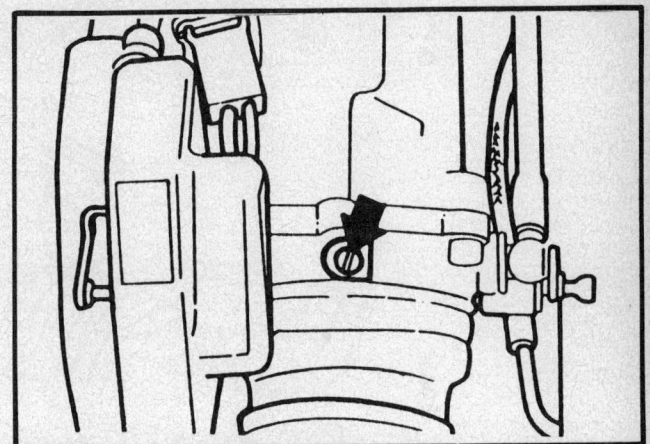

Idle speed adjustment screw—5 cylinder engines

A Hall effect signal from the right side distributor helps the ECU establish a reference point to start the fuel injection process. After the engine is running, the reference sender and speed sensor provide the necessary information to the ECU for ignition and fuel injection.

Both the idle speed and the ignition timing are controlled by the ECU and cannot be adjusted.

Idle Speed Pre-Check

The following procedure should be applicable to all vehicles. Before checking idle speed, the following conditions must be met:
   A. Start and allow engine to reach normal operating temperature.
   B. Check that the throttle valve is in the idle position.
   C. All accessories are OFF.
   D. Fuel pressure gauge not connected.

1. Connect tester with negative lead to ground, positive lead to the remote positive cable connection and the tachometer lead to the No. 1 terminal on the right side of the ignition coil.
2. Start engine and allow to idle. Check idle speed against specification.
3. If specifications are not as indicated, diagnostic work will need to be performed using the vehicle's fault memory.

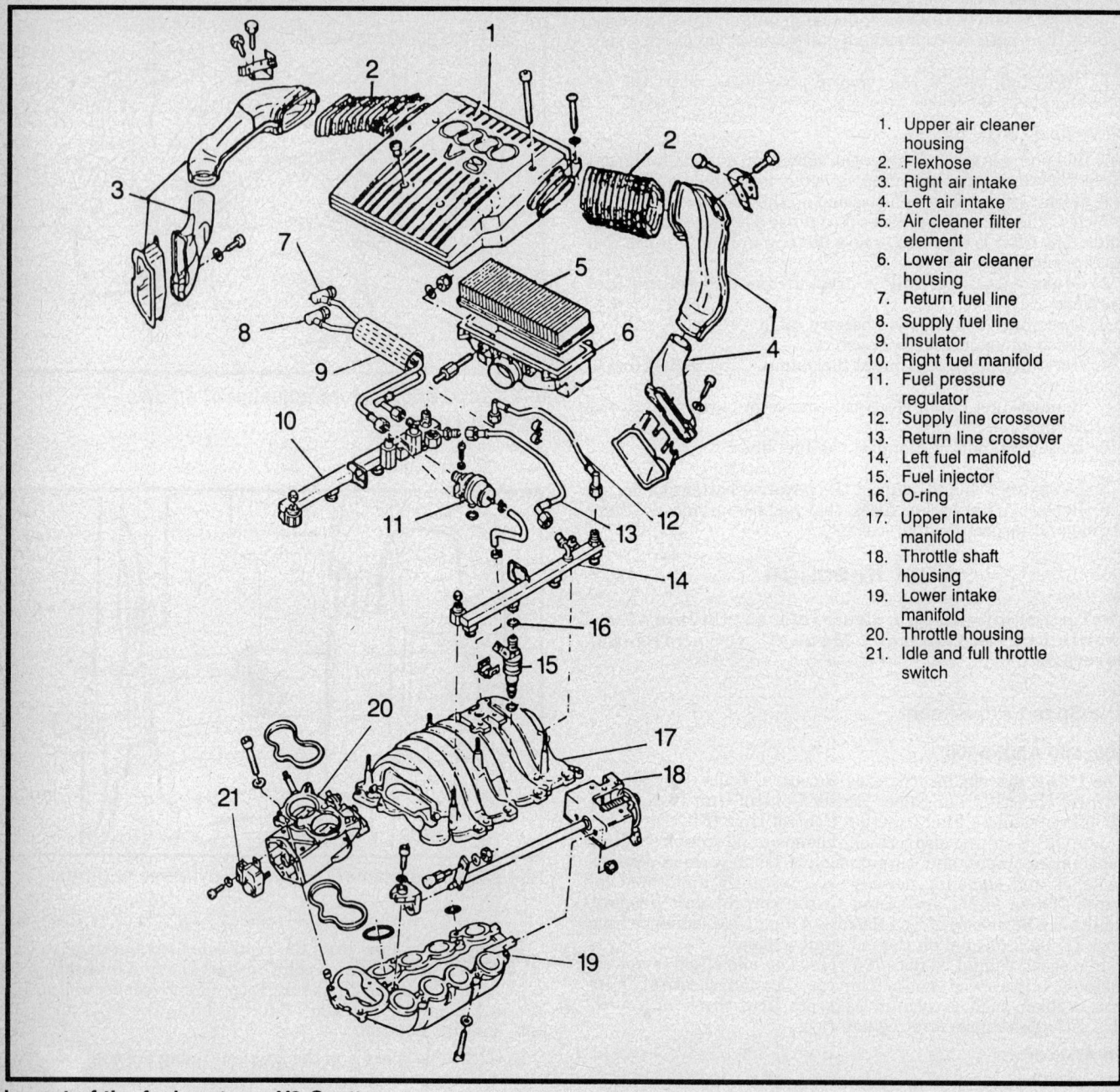

1. Upper air cleaner housing
2. Flexhose
3. Right air intake
4. Left air intake
5. Air cleaner filter element
6. Lower air cleaner housing
7. Return fuel line
8. Supply fuel line
9. Insulator
10. Right fuel manifold
11. Fuel pressure regulator
12. Supply line crossover
13. Return line crossover
14. Left fuel manifold
15. Fuel injector
16. O-ring
17. Upper intake manifold
18. Throttle shaft housing
19. Lower intake manifold
20. Throttle housing
21. Idle and full throttle switch

Layout of the fuel system—V8 Quattro

Fuel Injector

Removal and Installation

1. Disconnect the battery negative cable.
2. Remove the left and right support braces, then the intake air duct.
3. Remove the engine compartment support brace.
4. Remove the upper air cleaner attaching bolts, then the upper air cleaner.
5. Remove the lower air cleaner housing attaching bolts, then push the housing back and lift outward.
6. Remove the upper ventilation hose, then the right fuel rail cable tie.

NOTE: **When assembling, install a new cable tie in the same position and location as the original.**

7. Remove the engine wiring harness support clip attaching bolts, and position the wiring harness aside.
8. Disconnect the throttle valve potentiometer, thermoswitch and idle stabilizer valve electrical connectors.
9. Remove the idle stabilizer valve, then disconnect the vacuum hoses to the carbon canister.
10. Remove the bolts attaching the intake air temperature sensor, then position aside.
11. Disconnect the air mass sensor electrical connectors, then the 2 knock sensor plug connections.
12. Disconnect the fuel return and supply lines, then the pressure regulator vacuum hose.
13. Remove the fuel rail attaching bolts, then the fuel rail and injectors as an assembly.
14. Reverse procedure to install. Use new injector O-rings and coat with fuel before installing.

EMISSION CONTROLS

For further information, please refer to "Professional Emission Component Application Guide".

Emission Warning Lamps

Resetting

OXYGEN SENSOR REMINDER

Vehicles Without On-Board Diagnostics

Every 30,000 miles a maintenance reminder light in the dashboard will come on. This is an indications that the emission systems should be checked and that the oxygen sensor should be replaced.

1. To reset the non-turbocharged vehicles, remove the instrument panel cluster. Remove the switch cover near the **OXS** button. Push the switch to reset the light.

2. On turbocharged vehicles, lift the rear seat and push the button marked **OXS** on the reset box.

3. On the 5000S vehicles, depress the switch below the warning light after removing the housing cover. Place the ignition switch in the **ON** position and verify the reminder light is out.

4. On all other vehicles, trace the speedometer cable to the mileage counter control box, usually located on the left side of the instrument panel. The control box is installed in-line with the cable, press the white button on the control box and check to see that the reminder light has gone out.

1987–88 Vehicles With On-Board Diagnostics

The indicator light comes on whenever a fault develops which could cause the vehicle to fail an exhaust emission test. The light will remain on while driving as long as the fault exists. The light will go out after the fault has been repaired or no longer exists. Once the fault has been corrected, the permanent memory can be cleared the with the following procedures:

1. With the ignition **OFF**, insert a fuse in the top of the fuel pump relay.
2. Turn ignition **ON**.
3. Wait at least 4 seconds, then remove the fuse.
4. Repeat Step 3, 3 times until indicator flashes Code 4443.
5. Reinsert fuse in top of fuel pump relay for 4 seconds.
6. Repeat Step 5, until indicator flashes Code 0000.
7. Reinsert fuse in top of fuel pump relay.
8. Wait at least 10 seconds, then remove fuse.
9. Memory is clear.

1989–91 Vehicles With On-Board Diagnostics

Diagnostic connectors have been added to the driver's side footwell. It is not possible to activate fault memory by means of the fuel pump relay, as in older vehicles. If the indicator light comes on when a fault develops, the light will remain on while driving as long as the fault exists. The light will go out after the fault has been repaired or no longer exists.

ENGINE MECHANICAL

NOTE: Disconnecting the negative battery cable on some vehicles may interfere with the functions of the on board computer systems and may require the computer to undergo a relearning process, once the negative battery cable is reconnected.

Engine Assembly

Removal and Installation

4 CYLINDER ENGINE

1. Matchmark hood and hinges and remove hood. Disconnect the negative battery cable.

2. Remove the 2 grille retaining clips on the top of the grille. Remove the screw on the bottom and remove the grille.

3. Loosen the right and left sides of the air conditioning condenser. Tie the condenser away from the radiator.

4. Remove the rubber air duct from the throttle valve housing.

5. Remove the hose from the air duct to the auxiliary air regulator.

6. Disconnect the fuel lines from the cold start valve and fuel injectors. Cap the end of the fuel lines. Remove the injectors from the cylinder head.

7. Remove the fuel distributor, air flow sensor, fuel injectors and the air cleaner from the vehicle, as an assembly.

8. Remove the front engine mount-to-chassis bolts and remove the mount.

9. Loosen the nuts on the outer half of the crankshaft pulley and remove the V-belt.

────── **CAUTION** ──────

Compressed refrigerant used in the air conditioning system expands and evaporates into the atmosphere at a temperature of −21.7°F or less. This will freeze any surface it comes in contact with, including eyes. In addition, the refrigerant decomposes into a poisonous gas in the presence of flame.

10. Discharge the air conditioning system.
11. Remove all air conditioning lines from the compressor and plug the open connections.
12. Remove the crankcase ventilation hose from the valve cover.
13. Support the air conditioning hoses away from the engine.
14. Remove the air conditioning compressor mounting bolts and remove the compressor.
15. Open the heater control valve all the way.
16. Remove the cap on the expansion tank and drain the cooling system.
17. Remove the upper and lower radiator hoses from the radiator.
18. Disconnect and tag the radiator fan wiring and thermoswitch at the radiator. Remove the radiator with the fan and shroud as an assembly.
19. Remove the power steering pump, if equipped, with hoses attached, move aside and secure to body.
20. If equipped with a manual transaxle, disconnect the clutch cable at the release lever.
21. Disconnect and tag the engine wiring.
22. Remove the control pressure regulator (above the oil filter) from the engine, leaving all the fuel lines connected. Support it aside.
23. Remove the air hose from the back of the alternator, if equipped.
24. Disconnect the blue wire from the alternator at the plug located between the battery and the rear of the engine, if equipped.
25. Remove the charcoal filter hose at the intake air duct.
26. Remove the heater hoses from the engine.
27. Remove the throttle cable from the engine.
28. Disconnect and tag all vacuum hoses at the engine.
29. Remove the hose from the auxiliary regulator to the air inlet duct.
30. Remove the 3 upper engine to transaxle mounting bolts.

31. Remove the right and left engine mount nuts.
32. Raise and support the vehicle safely. Disconnect the exhaust pipe from the exhaust manifold.
33. Remove the flywheel cover plate. If equipped with automatic transaxle, remove the torque converter-to-flywheel mounting bolts.

NOTE: Matchmark the converter to flywheel for installation.

34. Remove the front engine mounting bolts and remove the mount.
35. Disconnect and tag the starter wiring and remove the starter.
36. Remove the 2 lower engine to transaxle mounting bolts.
37. Loosen the right and left engine mount nuts on the subframe.
38. Remove the bolt from the front exhaust pipe support.
39. Support the transaxle.
40. Lift the engine until the weight is taken off of the engine mounts and carefully separate the engine and transaxle.
41. Remove the engine from the vehicle.

To install:
42. Guide the engine assembly into place and secure the engine mounts.
43. Connect the flexplate to the torque converter, then install the starter.
44. Connect the exhaust, lower the vehicle and reconnect all electrical connections and vacuum lines.
45. Connect fresh air ducts, emission hoses, throttle cable and clutch cable, if equipped.
46. Install the power steering pump, coolant hoses and air conditioning lines.
47. Install the accessory drive belts and connect all fuel lines.
48. Install air conditioning condenser, grille. Install and align hood.
49. Tighten the engine-to-transaxle bolts to 40 ft. lbs., starter bolts to 14 ft. lbs. Tighten the cold start valve, pressure control regulator and radiator mounting bolts to 7 ft. lbs. Use a new gasket on the cold start valve when installing.

NOTE: Tighten the engine and subframe mounting bolts while the engine is running at idle. Tighten the front engine mount bolts to 18 ft. lbs. and the right and left engine mount bolts to 25 ft. lbs.

5 CYLINDER ENGINE

With Turbocharger

NOTE: Tag all hoses and wiring during removal, to use as reference during reassembly.

1. Remove the rear seat bottom and disconnect the negative battery cable.
2. Open the heater control valve all the way and drain the cooling system.
3. Remove the fuel injector cooling fan blower motor and intake hose from the engine.
4. Remove the upper radiator cover, grille, bumper strip. Disconnect the wiring harness in bumper for turn signals and headlights. Remove the bumper.
5. Disconnect the electrical connector from the coolant fan. Remove the upper radiator hose from the engine. Remove the radiator-to-expansion tank hose from the tank and the bleeder hose from the auxiliary radiator.
6. Disconnect the wire from the thermo-switch. Remove the radiator mounting bolts, right-side radiator cover and bottom radiator cover.
7. Remove the windshield washer reservoir from the mount and support it aside.

CAUTION

The compressed refrigerant used in the air conditioning system expands and evaporates into the atmosphere at a temperature of −21.7°F or less. This will freeze any surface it comes in contact with, including eyes. In addition, the refrigerant decomposes into a poisonous gas in the presence of flame.

---

8. Following all precautions, discharge the air conditioning system and disconnect the refrigerant hoses from the air conditioning condenser.
9. Remove the radiator and air conditioning condenser together. Remove the air conditioning compressor and mounting bracket from the engine.
10. Remove the power steering pump drive belt from the pump. Remove the pump from the mounts. Leaving the hoses attached, support it aside.
11. Disconnect the coolant hose from the thermostat housing, wires from the oil pressure switch and temperature sender. Disconnect the wire plugs from the control pressure regulator.
12. Remove the control pressure regulator from the engine leave the fuel lines connected. Support it aside.
13. Remove the throttle rod clips and remove the rod from the engine. Remove the injector line holder and remove the fuel injectors from the cylinder head.
14. Disconnect the electrical connector from the cold start valve and remove the valve from the intake manifold. Leave the fuel line connected.
15. At the throttle body, disconnect the electrical connectors from the throttle valve switches and intake air temperature switch.
16. Disconnect the air intake hose. Disconnect the wire from the auxiliary air regulator, pull off the vacuum hoses and disconnect the breaker hose from the engine.
17. At the 2-way valve, remove and tag the vacuum hoses. Remove the thermo-pneumatic valve. Leave the vacuum lines connected and the rpm sensor.
18. Disconnect the speedometer cable from the transaxle.
19. Remove the distributor from the engine.
20. Disconnect and tag the thermo-time switch and overheating warning lamp connectors. Disconnect the heater hoses from the engine.
21. At the left engine mount, disconnect the brake booster from the firewall, with the reservoir and leave the lines connected. On Quattro vehicles, disconnect the differential lock control lights connector. Disconnect the backup light switch wires.
22. Disconnect the tie rods from the steering rack. Disconnect the steering linkage.
23. If equipped with a manual transaxle, remove the clutch slave cylinder from the bell housing. Leave the line attached. Remove the bracket and pin under the transaxle bracket.
24. Disconnect the left engine mount ground strap. Disconnect the vacuum hose from the auxiliary air valve.
25. Remove the air duct from the intercooler and remove the intercooler.
26. Disconnect and tag the electrical connectors from the alternator. Remove the oil cooler. Leave the lines attached. Disconnect and tag the starter wiring.
27. Disconnect the exhaust pipe at the turbocharger. Remove the transaxle cover plates and the right side transaxle mount. Disconnect the halfshafts from the transaxle. On Quattro vehicles, disconnect the driveshaft from the rear of the transaxle.
28. On Quattro vehicles at the transaxle, disconnect the differential lock, remove the front and rear circlips and push back the boot. Disconnect the cable.
29. Remove the left-side transaxle mounting bolt and mounts from both sides.
30. At both front wheels, remove the ball joint pinch bolts. At the subframe, remove the mounting bolts and subframe. Separate the ball joints from the steering knuckle.
31. Install an engine lifting device on the engine. Raise the en-

gine slightly and remove the left and right engine mounts. Lower the engine/transaxle assembly from the vehicle.

32. Raise the front of the vehicle and slide the engine/transaxle assembly from under the vehicle.

33. Separate the engine from the transaxle.

To install:

34. Install the engine assembly and secure the engine mounts.

35. Install the steering joints to the steering knuckles. Install the ball joints with the pinch bolts.

36. Install the exhaust and 4WD differential lock clips, if equipped.

37. Lower the vehicle and install the electrical connections, oil cooler, air ducts and clutch slave cylinder, if equipped.

38. Install the distributor, speedometer cable and all vacuum lines. Connect the throttle body connectors, throttle linkage and fuel injection pressure regulator.

39. Install the radiator and air conditioning condenser. Connect the hoses.

40. Refill the cooling system. Connect the battery negative cable.

Without Turbocharger

NOTE: Tag all hoses and wiring during removal to use as reference during reassembly.

1. Disconnect the negative battery cable.
2. Drain the cooling system.
3. Disconnect the radiator and heater hoses from the engine.
4. Remove the control pressure regulator from the engine, without disconnecting the fuel lines.
5. Remove the cold start valve from the intake manifold, without disconnecting the fuel lines.
6. Pull out the fuel injectors from the cylinder head and support the injectors and fuel lines aside.

NOTE: Protect the fuel injectors and the cold start valve with caps.

7. Loosen the air duct and vacuum hoses from the throttle valve assembly.
8. Remove the air box cover and filter.
9. At the top of the grille, pull the hood latch cable guide off of its bracket.
10. If equipped with air conditioning, proceed with the following procedures:

    a. Remove the 2 clips from the top of the grille and the screw from the bottom. Remove the grille.

    b. Remove the condenser mounting bolts.

    c. Remove the air duct to auxiliary air regulator hose and remove the air duct from the throttle valve housing.

    d. Remove the fuel distributor, air flow sensor, fuel injectors and air box, as a unit.

NOTE: When removing the fuel injectors, leave all of the lines connected and cover the fuel injectors with caps.

    e. Remove the accessory drive belts.

—————————— **CAUTION** ——————————

The compressed refrigerant used in the air conditioning system, expands and evaporates into the atmosphere at a temperature of −21.7°F or less. This will freeze any surface it comes in contact with, including eyes. In addition, the refrigerant decomposes into a poisonous gas in the presence of flame.

————————————————————————————

    f. Discharge the refrigerant from the air conditioning system. Remove and plug the air conditioning hoses, move them away from the engine.

    g. Remove the upper/lower compressor mounting bolts and remove the compressor from the engine.

11. Remove the power steering pump from the engine, leaving the hose connected.
12. Remove the vacuum amplifier.

13. Remove the EGR control valve.
14. Remove the windshield washer reservoir from its holder.
15. Remove the distributor cap and ignition wires. Remove the distributor vacuum hose(s).

NOTE: Tape the distributor dust cap on to prevent it from falling off.

16. Disconnect the throttle linkage from the engine.
17. If equipped with an automatic transaxle, remove the throttle pushrod.
18. Disconnect the oil pressure and water temperature sensor wiring.
19. Remove the exhaust pipe to manifold nuts.
20. Remove the exhaust pipe support bracket from the transaxle.
21. Remove the front engine mount bolts and remove the mount. Disconnect the ground strap on left engine mount, if equipped.
22. Tag and disconnect all wires from the starter and remove the starter.
23. Tag and disconnect all wires leading from the alternator and remove the alternator.
24. If equipped with an automatic transaxle, through the starter mounting hole, remove the torque converter mounting bolts.
25. Remove the lower engine to transaxle mounting bolts.
26. Support the transaxle and lower the vehicle.
27. Remove the upper engine to transaxle mounting bolts.
28. Remove the left engine support bracket.
29. Loosen the right engine bracket from the right engine mount.
30. Lift the engine until the crankshaft V-belt pulley is behind the grille opening.
31. Carefully detach the engine from the transaxle.
32. Remove the engine assembly by turning it to the right while lifting it out.

To install:

33. Install the engine assembly and secure the mounts.
34. Install the starter and connect the wiring.
35. Install the exhaust.
36. Lower the vehicle and connect engine compartment wiring including the oil pressure and water temperature sensor wiring.
37. Connect the throttle linkage. Install the distributor cap and wire, the washer reservoir, power steering pump and EGR valve.
38. Install the air conditioning condenser.
39. Connect fuel lines, pressure regulator and cold start valve.
40. Install the radiator, refill the cooling system. Connect the battery negative cable.
41. Torque the engine-to-transaxle mounting bolts to 43 ft. lbs., the torque converter-to-drive plate bolts to 14 ft. lbs., the starter bolts to 14 ft. lbs., the air conditioner mounting bolts to 29 ft. lbs. and the power steering pump and the control pressure regulator mounting bolts to 14 ft. lbs.

NOTE: Tighten the engine and subframe mounting bolts, while the engine is running at idle, to 32 ft. lbs.

8 CYLINDER ENGINE

The engine is taken out towards the front without the transaxle. All cable ties which have to be released or cut open when removing the engine must be replaced in the same position when the engine is installed.

1. Disconnect the battery negative cable. The battery is under the rear seat.
2. Under the dashboard, remove the retainers and remove left dashboard end cap and the knee protector.
3. Remove the heater duct for the driver-side area, under the dash panel, by removing the right-hand screw and loosening the left-hand clip.
4. Unclip the floor lamp and push it through the opening.

5. Remove the control units with brackets.

6. Open the locking mechanisms on the control unit connectors and disconnect the harness connectors. Lock the connectors so they don't become tangled when removing the cable harness. Pull off connectors 11, 13 and 15. The numbers should be marked on the wiring harness.

7. Remove the connector panel by removing the lower screw, loosening the upper screw and pulling the panel downwards. Press the latch on the butterfly connector lock and slide it sideways to release the connector from the panel.

8. Under the hood, remove the plenum chamber cover and lift up on the rubber grommet on the middle wiring harness. Cut the cable tie and pull the wiring harness carefully out of the passenger compartment and plenum chamber. Open the expansion tank cap for coolant.

9. Raise and safely support vehicle. Remove the sound insulation or under pan.

10. Remove the bolts and nuts holding bumper and bracket, remove the electrical connectors and pull off the bumper towards the front.

11. Drain the coolant from the radiator. Also open the block drains on both sides.

12. Remove the oil cooler hoses from the oil filter housing and the hose from the bottom of the transaxle oil cooler. Remove the bracket for the line on the air conditioner and disconnect the engine ground cable at the engine.

13. Separate the harness for the headlight washing system and air conditioner harness. Disconnect the coolant temperature sensor harness, the cool air duct from the alternator, the coolant hose and hose for headlight washer system.

14. Disconnect the outer half of the air intake elbow for the alternator. Disconnect the wiring from the alternator and starter motor. Unscrew oil filter.

15. Remove the upper bolt on the starter by guiding a 10mm Allen® socket, with extension and flex fitting, through the opening on the transaxle housing over the final drive. Remove starter.

16. Locate and remove the bolts from the front of the subframe, on left and right sides. Remove the bolts securing the exhaust system on the left and right sides.

17. Remove the 4 bolts connecting the bottom of the engine and transaxle.

18. Remove the bolts above and below the long member on the left and right sides. Remove the bolts for the cadmium strip and remove the bolts on fender.

19. Remove the harness connector from the temperature sensor at the front of the air conditioning condenser and disconnect the hood release cable.

20. Open the fuse box on the left side behind the hydraulic reservoir. Disconnect the wire to the fan and the ground wire at the top of the suspension strut. Expose the wiring.

21. Remove the air conditioning dryer with the bracket.

22. Remove the intake manifold bracket on the left and right. Pull out the exchanger. Remove the bar-shaped reinforcement strut.

23. Remove the air conditioning condenser bolts and swivel downward. Wiring should remain connected.

24. Remove the wiring bracket from the top of the transaxle cooler. Remove the water hose from both sides of the engine. Remove the bleeder hose from the expansion tank on the radiator. Remove the front apron.

25. Remove the screws securing the upper part of the air cleaner housing. There are 4 screws on the housing and 3 screws at the rear of the housing.

26. Remove the screws securing the lower part of the air cleaner housing. Press toward the rear and lift out. Remove the right-hand stud from the lower air cleaner housing.

27. Disconnect the carbon canister hose from the front of the engine. Cut both cable ties on the fuel injector. Remove the fuel supply and return lines at the right-hand side and release at left. Turn the fuel lines to the left and lay to one side.

28. Remove the coolant hose to expansion tank. Disconnect the high tension wire and connector on the ignition coil at the left and right. Remove the bolts holding the left coil, cable housing and retaining clip. Watch for the spacer sleeve.

29. Remove the left and right heat shields. Remove the housing for the ignition wire retainer. Disconnect the vacuum line.

30. Remove the screws securing the left and right distributor caps. Wiring remains connected. Using a cable tie, secure the 2 distributor caps aside against the PCV hose.

31. Disconnect the throttle cable by unclipping both retaining clips. Remove the screws securing the throttle cable support bracket. Unscrew both coolant hoses. Disconnect the supporting clamp.

32. Separate both harness connectors from the oxygen sensor. Disconnect the vacuum line to the cruise control system.

33. Remove the transaxle oil fill tube bolt from the engine. Pull the wiring harness through the contact plate and place on the engine.

34. Remove the 6 torque converter bolts through the starter opening.

35. Release the tension on the ribbed drive belt by pulling firmly by hand in the middle at the bottom and inserting a pin through the holes provides in the tensioner bracket. Remove the belt.

36. Remove the bolts holding the air conditioning compressor. Lift the compressor over the strut. The lines remain connected.

37. Remove the bolts for the air conditioning compressor bracket and the hydraulic pump. Watch the guide sleeves. Place the bracket with the hydraulic pump on the long member. The lines remain connected. Note that at installation, fit the lower bolts with the guide sleeves in position and tighten lightly. Then the upper bolts can be installed.

38. Remove the nuts from the left and right engine mountings. Remove the bolts securing the engine support at the front. Take note of the shims. The same thickness shims must be used at installation.

39. Disconnect the engine and transaxle at the top by removing 3 of the 4 bolts. Loosen the fourth bolt but do not remove.

40. Install a suitable lifting sling to the front left-hand side and rear right-hand side.

41. Move in hoist, being careful of the air conditioning compressor. Lift engine carefully. Remove last bolt from the top of the engine and transaxle. Unscrew the engine mounting from the left and right sides and pull the engine out from the front. Lift carefully to prevent damage to the transaxle main shaft, clutch and body.

42. Use care when selecting a suitable engine repair stand. Attaching to some types of stands could cause the engine block to distort and cause any cylinder bore measurements to be inaccurate.

To install:

43. Installation is the reverse of the removal procedure. Note that there are guide sleeves in the engine block for centering the engine and transaxle. Make sure they are installed.

44. Install the engine assembly and secure to the transaxle and engine mounts.

45. Install the air conditioning compressor and power steering pump. Fit the lower bolts with the guide sleeves first. Tighten lightly and then install the top bolts.

46. Install all electrical connectors, hoses and sheet metal heat shields.

47. Install the air conditioning condenser and the small brackets that were removed.

48. Install the oil cooler, radiator and other small connections.

49. Refill the cooling system.

50. Install the interior parts removed.

51. Connect battery negative cable.

52. When installing the wiring harness make sure it is first pushed through the contact plate.

53. Always replace all self-locking nuts. Make sure the exhaust

system is installed free of strain. Check all fluid levels before starting the engine. Check the fluid level in the automatic transaxle.

Cylinder Head

NOTE: Before removing or installing the cylinder head, align the engine timing marks at TDC. Rotate the crankshaft mark away about ¼ turn (BTDC). This will prevent the valves from hitting the piston heads. Be sure to turn the crankshaft to the proper position after cylinder head installation.

Removal and Installation

NOTE: Cylinder head removal should not be attempted unless the engine is cold.

EXCEPT 8 CYLINDER ENGINE

1. Disconnect the negative battery cable.
2. Drain the cooling system.
3. Disconnect the air duct from the throttle valve assembly on all vehicles except the Turbo and Quattro. On the Turbo and Quattro, remove the hose which runs between the air duct and the turbocharger.
4. Disconnect the throttle cable from the throttle valve assembly.
5. Remove the air duct for the injector cooling fan on the Turbo and Quattro.
6. Clean and remove the fuel injectors and all other fuel lines.

NOTE: Protect the fuel injectors and the cold start valve with caps.

7. Tag and disconnect all vacuum and PCV lines.
8. Remove the hose which runs from the intake manifold to the turbocharger on the Turbo and Quattro.
9. Tag and disconnect all electrical lines leading to the cylinder head.
10. Remove the intake manifold.
11. Disconnect all radiator and heater hoses where they are attached to the cylinder head. Position them aside.
12. Tag and remove all spark plug wires.
13. Remove the distributor. To aid installation, scribe a mark on the body of the distributor and the cylinder head.
14. Separate the exhaust manifold from the exhaust pipe.

NOTE: Exhaust pipe detachment differs slightly on the Turbo and Quattro. First the exhaust pipe must be unbolted from the turbocharger. Second, it must be unbolted from the wastegate at the rear of the engine.

15. Disconnect the EGR valve and oxygen sensor from the exhaust manifold.
16. Remove the heat deflector shield.
17. Remove the oil lines (2) from the turbocharger.
18. Remove the exhaust manifold.

NOTE: When removing the exhaust manifold on the Turbo and Quattro, the manifold, turbocharger and wastegate should all be removed as 1 unit.

19. Remove the air hose cover from the back of the alternator.
20. Tag and disconnect all wires coming from the back of the alternator and remove the alternator from the engine.
21. Disconnect and plug the hoses coming from the power steering pump.
22. Remove the power steering pump and the V-belt.
23. Remove the timing belt cover and belt.
24. Remove the valve cover.
25. Loosen the cylinder head bolts in the reverse order of the tightening sequence.
26. Remove the bolts and lift the cylinder head off of the engine.

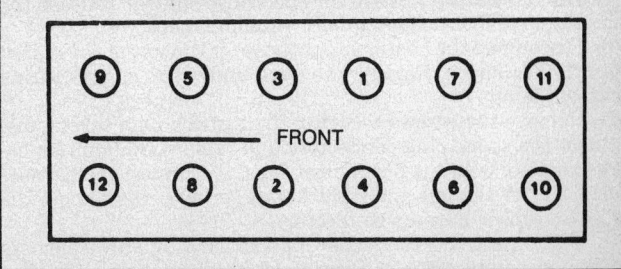

Torque sequence for all 5 cylinder engines

To install:

27. Clean the cylinder head and engine block mating surfaces thoroughly and install the new gasket without any sealing compound. Make sure the words TOP or OBEN are facing UP, when the gasket is installed.
28. Place the cylinder head on the engine block and install bolts No. 8 and 10 first. These holes are smaller and will properly locate the gasket and the head on the engine block.
29. Install the remaining bolts. Tighten them in 3 stages as follows: Step 1 – 29 ft. lbs., Step 2 – 43 ft. lbs. and Step 3 – Tighten ½ turn more (180 degrees).
30. Installation of all other components is in the reverse order of removal.

8 CYLINDER ENGINE

1. Disconnect the negative battery cable. The battery is under the rear seat.
2. Remove the toothed cam drive belt. It should not be necessary to loosen or remove the vibration damper.
3. Open the left and right block drains.
4. Remove the bolts holding the exhaust pipe on both sides.
5. Remove the supply line at the fuel manifold. Remove the fuel return line. Remove the bolt holding the pressure regulator to the fuel manifold. At assembly, press the regulator directly into the seat of the O-ring seal. Do not pull in with bolts.
6. Disconnect the breather hose at the rear of the intake manifold, the vacuum hose and the bolt holding the upper part of the supporting clamp for the engine wiring harness. Remove the mounting bracket for ignition wire holder.

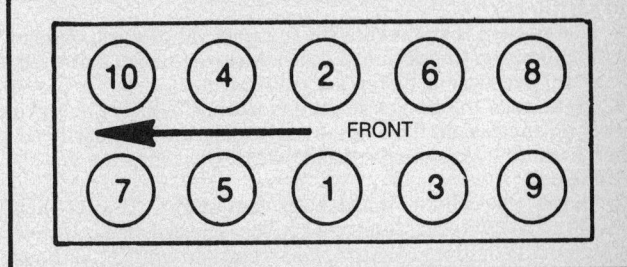

Torque sequence for all 4 cylinder engines

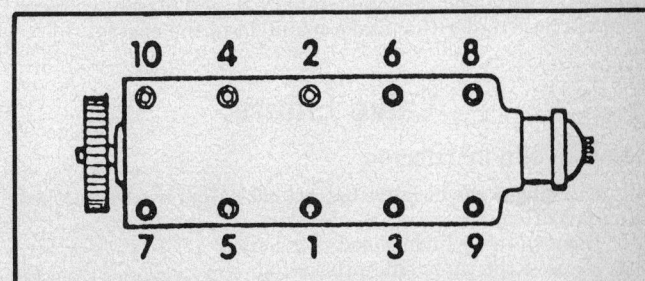

Torque sequence – V8 Quattro

7. Disconnect the linkage for the cruise control. Release the throttle cable by unclipping both retaining clips.

8. Disconnect the heater supply hose for coolant at the rear of the cylinder heads. Release the hose under the engine wiring harness clamp.

9. Remove the screws securing the 2 spark plug covers, disconnect the spark plug connectors and remove the ignition cables complete with the distributor caps. Disconnect the harness connector for the left and right knock sensors. Disconnect the air mass sensor harness connector.

10. Disconnect the connector for the throttle valve harness connector potentiometer. Disconnect the idle stabilizer valve harness connector. Remove the idle stabilizer valve. Remove the hose from the carbon canister.

11. Remove the air temperature sensor. Remove the wiring holder behind the rear toothed belt guard at the right side and, if necessary, also on the left side.

12. Remove the bolts securing the coolant hose holder on the right rear cylinder head. Disconnect the heater supply hose from the cylinder heads by pulling towards the rear.

13. Disconnect the harness connector for the Hall sender on the right cylinder head. If the right cylinder head needs to be removed, disconnect the temperature sensor harness connector on the right cylinder head.

14. Remove the breather hose at the top. Turn the hose with pliers until the retaining lug unlatches. Remove the breather hose on the cylinder head, on the left side at the rear.

15. Remove the bolts securing the fuel rails and lift out complete with injectors and place on plenum chamber. At installation, make sure the O-rings are not damaged. Moisten slightly with fuel.

16. Remove the bolts securing the intake manifold and lift out. Watch the front breather hose under the intake manifold.

17. If it is the left hand cylinder head being removed, unscrew the dipstick guide and pull out. Remove the transaxle oil filler tube bolt.

18. Remove the cylinder head cover. Note that the 2 center mounting bolts are different. The bolt with the longer hexagon fitting must be installed at the rear.

19. If the left cylinder head is being removed, remove the bolts securing the cruise control vacuum unit and bracket. Do not forget the deflector plate during installation.

20. Remove the cylinder head bolts in reverse sequence of tightening. Remove the cylinder head.

To install:

21. Installation is the reverse of the removal process, observing the following. Check that the gasket surface is not distorted. Maximum permissible distortion is 0.004 in.

22. Make sure the gasket surface is clean. Look for the word OBEN on the gasket. This is the top, facing the cylinder head. When installing the cylinder head, watch the centering dowels in the block.

23. Insert the cylinder head bolts hand-tight. Torque in 3 steps. First to 30 ft. lbs., then to 44 ft. lbs. The 3rd step is to give the bolts and additional ½ turn. Use a regular wrench, without stopping. It should not be necessary to retighten the cylinder head bolts during maintenance or after repairs.

24. When installing the intake manifold, first attach the front breather hose under the intake manifold to the engine.

Valve Lifters

Removal and Installation

1. Disconnect the negative battery cable. Remove the toothed camshaft drive belt.

2. Remove the cylinder head cover.

3. Remove the camshaft sprocket.

4. On the 8 cylinder engine, on the exhaust side, remove the intermediate flange and bearing cap for the distributor. Loosen

the bearing cap in front of the chain, plus caps 2 and 3. Loosen bearing caps 1 and 4 alternately and in a diagonal sequence.

5. On the 8 cylinder engine, on the intake side, remove bearing caps 6 and 7. Loosen bearing caps 5 and 8 alternately and in a diagonal sequence.

6. Remove the cam and lift out the valve lifter. If it is to be reused, it must go in the bore from which it was removed.

To install:

7. Installation is the reverse of removal. Before assembly coat the moving parts with clean oil.

8. On the 8 cylinder engine, install the camshafts with the chain so the markings on the chain sprockets are in alignment. Install the bearing caps so the stamped-on numbers can be read from the intake side.

9. Make sure the bearing caps are installed properly. They will cause parts failure if installed backwards. Tighten bearing caps alternately, in a diagonal sequence to 11 ft. lbs.

Valve Lash

Adjustment

All engines are equipped with hydraulic valve lash adjusters that eliminate the need for routine valve lash adjustments. Intermittent valve noise is normal when the engine is cold. If valve noise persists, check the camshaft lobes and/or camshaft followers for wear. Replace if necessary. Do not attempt valve lifter repair. If worn or damaged, replace the complete assembly.

Use care when handling valve lifters. Always place a removed valve lifter on a clean surface with the contact surface or camshaft side, facing downward.

After working on the valve train, carefully turn the engine by hand at least 2 turns to make sure the valves do not strike the pistons when the engine is started. Do not start the engine for 30 minutes after installing new valve lifters or the valves may strike the pistons. The lifter must be allowed to bleed down to proper adjustment.

To check a suspect lifter, use the following procedure:

1. Warm the engine to operating temperature until the radiator fan comes on at least once.

2. Bring the engine to approximately 2500 rpm for 2 minutes. If a lifter is still noisy, shut off engine and remove the cylinder head cover.

3. Turn the crankshaft pulley bolt clockwise until the cam lobes of the cylinder to be checked point upward.

4. Push down against the valve lifter with light pressure using a suitable tool. If the valve lifter can be pushed down more than 0.004 in., replace the lifter.

5. Do not start the engine for 30 minutes after installing new valve lifters or the valves may strike the pistons. The lifter must be allowed to bleed down to proper adjustment.

Intake Manifold

Removal and Installation

4 CYLINDER ENGINE

1. Disconnect the negative battery cable. Relieve the fuel pressure in the system.

2. Disconnect the throttle cable at the throttle valve housing.

3. Disconnect the wiring for the cold start valve and thermo time switch.

4. Disconnect the ground wire from the intake manifold.

5. Remove the fuel line from the cold start valve. Cap the valve and line.

6. Remove the air boot from the throttle valve housing and sensor plate housing.

7. Disconnect and tag the vacuum hoses at the manifold.

8. Remove the fuel injectors from the cylinder head, without disconnecting the fuel lines from the injectors.

9. Remove the control pressure regulator line and move the regulator aside.

10. Remove the 2 straps that connect the intake and exhaust manifolds.

11. Disconnect the CO percentage check tube from the intake manifold.

12. Remove the intake manifold mounting nuts and remove the manifold from the engine.

NOTE: Before loosening the intake manifold mounting nuts, soak the nuts and studs with lubricant. Studs are very difficult to replace with the cylinder head installed on the engine.

To install:

13. Clean the gasket mating surfaces of the engine and intake manifold.

14. Before installation, hold the intake manifold gasket up to the engine and check for proper fit. Trim, if necessary.

15. Install the intake manifold on the cylinder head. Tighten the 6mm nuts to 7 ft. lbs. and the 8mm nuts to 18 ft. lbs.

16. The remainder of the installation is the reverse of the removal procedure.

17. Lubricate the fuel injector O-rings with a drop of engine oil, before installation in the cylinder head.

18. When finished, run the engine and check for leaks.

5 CYLINDER ENGINE

1. Disconnect the negative battery cable.

2. Relieve the fuel system pressure.

3. On non-turbocharged engines, disconnect the air duct from the throttle valve assembly. On turbocharged engines, remove the hose between the air duct and turbocharger.

4. Disconnect the throttle cable and rod from the throttle valve assembly.

5. On turbocharged engines, remove the air duct for the injector cooling fan.

6. Remove the fuel injectors from the cylinder head, with the fuel lines attached.

7. Disconnect the cold start valve wiring and remove the fuel line from the valve.

NOTE: Protect the fuel injectors and cold start valve with caps.

8. Tag and disconnect all vacuum and PCV lines.

9. Tag and disconnect all electrical lines leading to the cylinder head.

10. On turbocharged engines, remove the hose which runs from the intake manifold to the turbocharger; intercooler on the Quattro.

11. Remove the auxiliary air regulator. Remove the air box cover and filter element.

12. Remove the intake manifold mounting nuts and remove the manifold from the engine.

To install:

13. Clean the gasket mating surfaces on the manifold and engine.

14. Using a new gasket, install the manifold on the cylinder head and tighten the nuts to 15 ft. lbs.

15. The remainder of the installation is the reverse of the removal procedure.

16. Always use new gaskets and O-rings where necessary.

17. Check the engine oil level and correct, if necessary.

18. When finished, run the engine and check for leaks.

8 CYLINDER ENGINE

1. Disconnect the negative battery cable.

2. Relieve the fuel system pressure.

3. Remove the 7 bolts retaining the upper part of the air cleaner housing and the 2 bolts securing the lower part. Press the housing towards the rear and lift out.

4. Remove the fuel supply and return lines. Remove the fuel pressure regulator from the fuel rail.

5. Remove the breather hose at the rear of the intake manifold, remove the vacuum hose and the bolt securing the upper part of the engine wiring harness clamp.

6. Disconnect the harness connectors for the left and right knock sensor, the air mass sensor, the potentiometer, the thermo-switch and idle stabilizer valve. Remove the idle stabilizer valve and disconnect the hose to the carbon canister.

7. Remove the air temperature sensor bolts. Remove the breather hose at the top of the cam cover by using pliers to turn the hose until the retaining lug unlatches. Remove the breather on the cylinder head at the left rear.

8. Remove the bolts securing the fuel rails and lift out the rails with the injectors. Place on the plenum chamber.

9. Remove the intake manifold bolts and lift out the manifold. Watch the front breather hose under the intake manifold.

NOTE: There are 2 oil retention valves that must be replaced if they sound noisy on short drives, although the noise may go away on longer drives. To replace these valves, after the intake manifold has been removed, remove the right hand knock sensor and the bolts securing the engine breather cover and lift out the cover along with the bulkhead panel. It may be easier to lift the right side first. Locate the oil retention valves and remove the circlips. Screw a M6 × 50mm bolt with a large washer into the oil retention valve. Remove the valve by prying evenly under the washer.

To install:

10. Installation is the reverse of the the removal procedure. Use care when installing the intake manifold. First install the front breather hose to the engine under the intake manifold.

11. When reinstalling the fuel system parts, use care not to damage any O-rings.

12. When installing the fuel pressure regulator, first press it directly into the seat of the O-ring seal. Do not pull it in with bolts.

Exhaust Manifold

Removal and Installation

NON-TURBOCHARGED ENGINES

Except 8 Cylinder Engine

NOTE: Although not necessary, more working clearance will be found by removing the intake manifold before removing the exhaust manifold. Before starting, soak the manifold studs with lubricant to aid in the removal.

1. Disconnect the negative battery cable. Raise and support the vehicle safely. Disconnect the exhaust pipe from the exhaust manifold.

2. Disconnect the EGR valve and oxygen sensor, from the manifold.

3. Remove the heat deflector shield on 4 cylinder engines.

4. Disconnect the CO probe receptacle tube.

5. Remove the exhaust manifold mounting nuts and remove the manifold from the engine.

To install:

6. Clean the gasket mating surfaces of the manifold and engine.

7. Using a new gasket, install the manifold on the engine and tighten the nuts to 22 ft. lbs.

NOTE: Always replace the old mounting nuts with new brass nuts. Check the condition of the studs before installation. The oxygen sensor, EGR tube, bolts and nuts exposed to high temperatures should receive a light coating of anti-seize compound on the threads before assembly.

8. Connect the exhaust pipe to the manifold, using a new gasket and tighten nuts to 26 ft. lbs.

9. Install and tighten the CO measuring tube to 22 ft. lbs.

10. The remainder of the installation is the reverse of the removal procedure.

11. When finished, run the engine and check for leaks.

8 Cylinder Engine

1. Disconnect negative battery cable.

2. Disconnect the front exhaust pipe at the manifolds.

3. For the left side manifold, unscrew the guide for the dipstick tube and remove.

4. For both the left and right manifolds, remove the bolts securing the exhaust manifolds to the cylinder heads.

5. Remove the manifolds one at a time. Lift up the engine at the edge of the oil pan on the side of the manifold to be removed.

To install:

6. Installation is the reverse of the removal process. Make sure the sealing rings between the exhaust manifold and the cylinder head are installed in such a way that the beading makes contact with the manifold.

7. When installing the dipstick guide, replace the sealing ring.

TURBOCHARGED ENGINE

1. Disconnect the negative battery cable. Remove the hose which runs between the air duct and the turbocharger.

2. If the intake manifold has not been removed, disconnect the hose which runs from the intake manifold to the turbocharger or intercooler.

3. Disconnect the exhaust pipe from the turbocharger.

4. Disconnect the exhaust pipe from the wastegate on the rear of the manifold.

5. Disconnect the EGR valve and the oxygen sensor, if necessary, from the manifold.

6. Remove the oil lines from the turbocharger.

7. Remove the line from the bottom of the turbocharger to the intercooler, if equipped.

NOTE: The manifold, turbocharger and wastegate are removed as 1 unit.

8. Remove the manifold assembly.

9. Installation is the reverse of the removal procedure. Always use new gaskets and O-rings where necessary.

NOTE: The oxygen sensor, EGR tube, bolts and nuts exposed to high temperatures should receive a light coating of anti-seize compound on the threads before assembly.

10. Install and tighten the wastegate nuts to 22 ft. lbs.

11. Tighten the exhaust manifold mounting nuts to 26 ft. lbs.

12. Tighten the exhaust pipe nuts to 26 ft. lbs.

13. Start engine allow to reach normal operating temperature.

14. Check for leaks, and proper engine operation.

Turbocharger

Removal and Installation

1. Disconnect the negative battery cable.

2. Spray all mounting bolts with a lubricant.

3. Relieve the fuel system pressure.

4. Remove the vacuum tube between the intake air boot and turbocharger.

5. Remove the intake boot and crankcase ventilation hose. Remove the hose assembly between the intake manifold and throttle housing.

6. Remove the air box cover and remove the filter element.

7. Remove the right side engine mount heat shield.

8. Remove the oil supply pipe from the turbocharger. Remove the exhaust pipe from the corrugated pipe. Loosen the exhaust pipe at the transaxle mount and catalytic converter.

9. Remove the retaining clamp from the starter housing and sensor air hose.

10. Remove the exhaust pipe from the turbocharger.

11. Remove the alternator support bolt and position the alternator to the side.

12. Remove the oil return pipe from the turbocharger. Remove mounting bolts and turbocharger.

13. Install in the reverse order using new gaskets and O-rings, where necessary.

NOTE: Bolts and nuts exposed to high temperatures should receive a light coating of anti-seize compound on the threads before assembly. After servicing the turbocharger, always replace the engine oil along with the turbocharger filter and engine oil filter.

Turbocharger Wastegate

Removal and Installation

NOTE: Although not necessary, more working clearance will be found by removing the intake manifold before removing the wastegate. Before starting, soak the studs with lubricant to aid in the removal.

1. Disconnect the negative battery cable. Remove the wastegate to exhaust pipe connecting tube. There are 3 bolts on the top and on the bottom.

2. Remove the mounting bolt for the tube leading from the wastegate to the exhaust manifold.

3. Remove the vacuum line from the end of the wastegate.

4. Remove the 4 mounting bolts and remove the wastegate from the exhaust manifold.

5. Installation is in the reverse order of removal.

NOTE: Bolts and nuts exposed to high temperatures should receive a light coating of anti-seize compound on the threads before assembly.

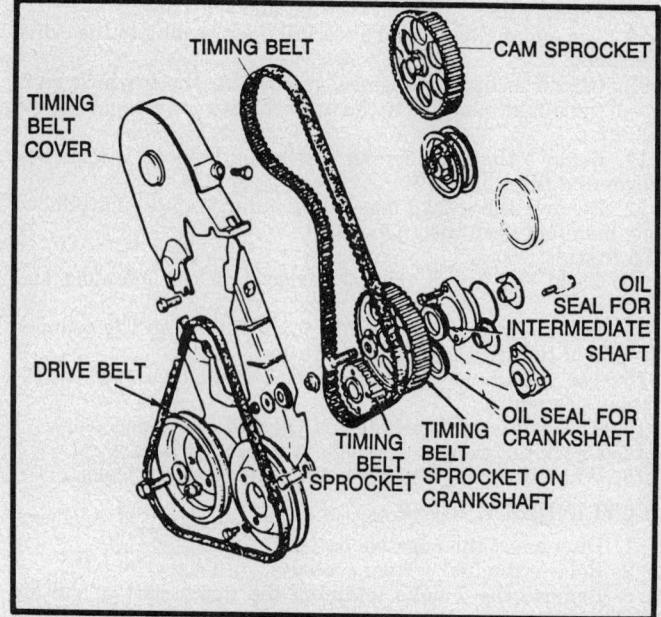

Cam drive 4 cylinder engines

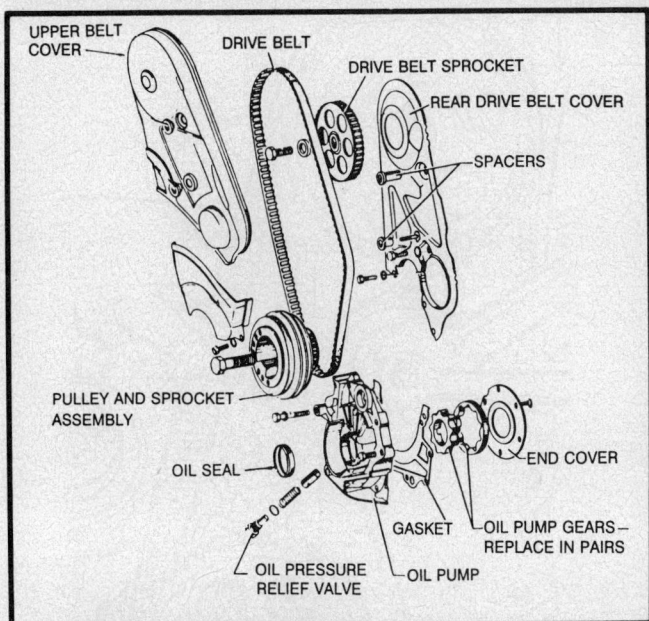

Cam drive 5 cylinder engines

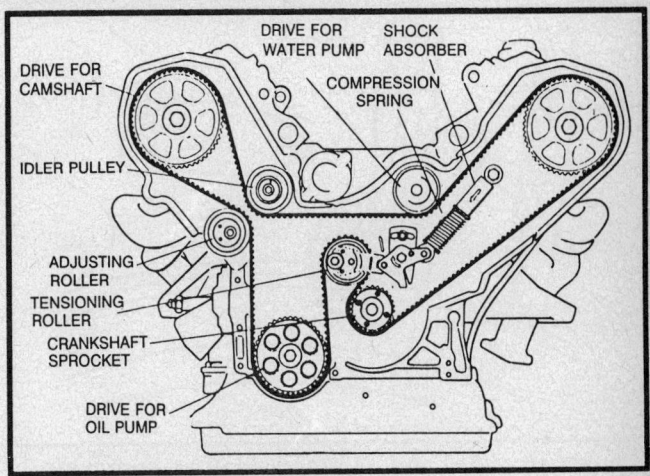

Cam drive 8 cylinder engines

Timing Belt Front Cover

Removal and Installation

4 CYLINDER ENGINE

Upper Cover

1. Disconnect the negative battery cable. Loosen the alternator adjusting bolts, pivot the alternator over and slip the drive belt off.
2. Loosen the air conditioning compressor mounting bolts and remove the drive belt.

3. Remove the valve cover nuts and remove the valve cover and retaining straps.
4. Remove the upper timing belt cover nuts. Note the position of the washers and spacers while removing the cover.
5. Installation is the reverse of the removal procedure.
6. Adjust the drive belt tension when finished.

Lower Cover

1. Disconnect the negative battery cable. Remove the upper timing belt cover.
2. Using the large bolt on the crankshaft sprocket, rotate the engine until the No. 1 cylinder is at TDC of the compression stroke. At this point, both valves for No. 1 cylinder will be closed and the **0** mark on the flywheel will be aligned with the pointer on the bell housing.
3. Remove the crankshaft pulley retaining bolts and loosen the crankshaft sprocket bolt, if the sprocket or rear cover is to be serviced.

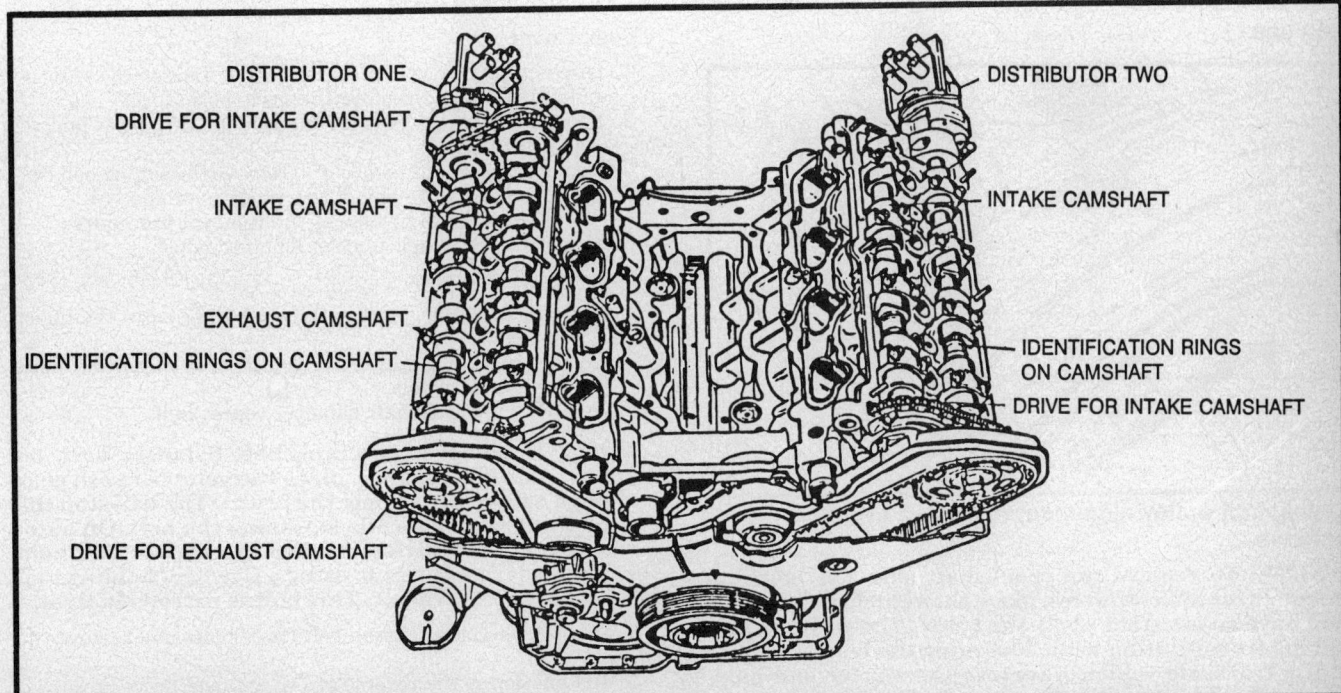

Layout of cam and valve gear for 8 cylinder engine

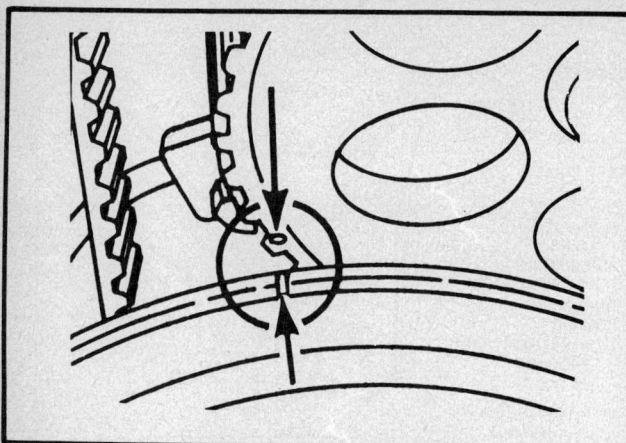

Crankshaft pulley and intermediate shaft sprocket alignment—4 cylinder engines

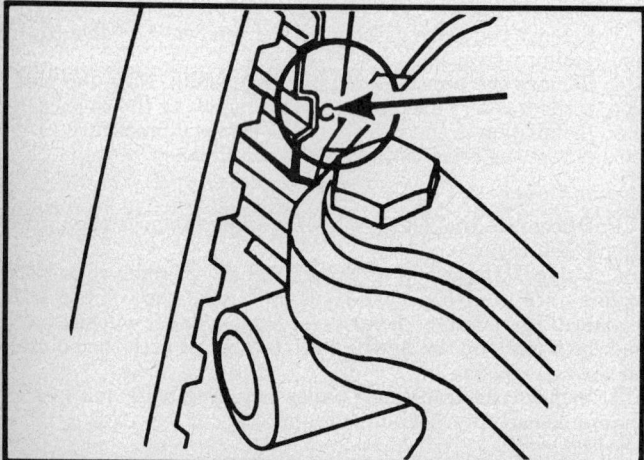

Camshaft sprocket alignment—4 and 5 cylinder engines

Crankshaft pulley alignment marks—5 cylinder engines

NOTE: To remove the crankshaft sprocket bolt, on manual transaxle vehicles, place the vehicle in 5th gear and have an assistant apply the brake. The will stop the engine from rotating while loosening the bolt. On automatic transaxle vehicles, remove the starter and hold the flywheel from turning, using a flywheel holding tool VW 10–201 or equivalent.

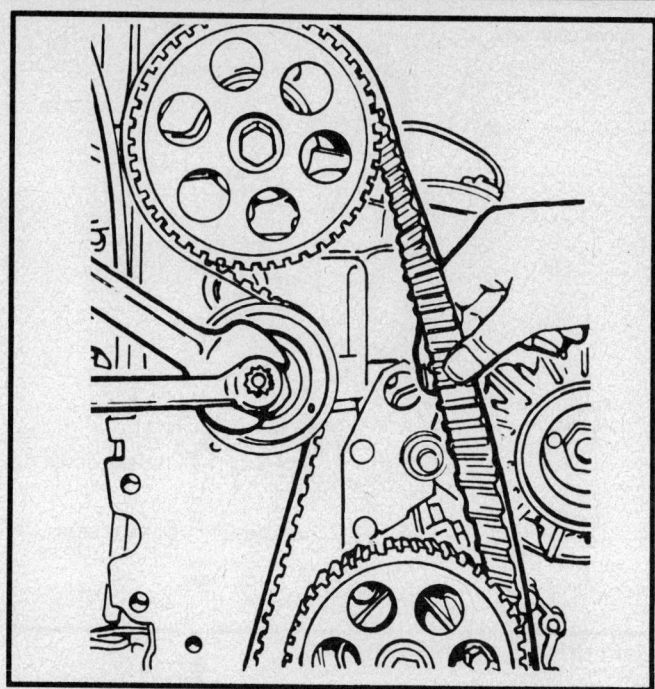

The timing belt is correctly adjusted when it can be twisted 90 degrees with thumb and forefinger

4. Remove the crankshaft pulley.
5. Remove the water pump pulley retaining bolts and remove the pulley.
6. Remove the lower cover retaining nuts and remove the cover. Take care not to lose any of the washers or spacers.
7. Installation is the reverse of the removal procedure.
8. Tighten the crankshaft sprocket bolt to 66 ft. lbs. plus ½ additional turn.

5 CYLINDER ENGINE

Upper Cover

1. Disconnect the negative battery cable. Loosen the alternator adjusting bolts and remove the drive belt.
2. Loosen the power steering pump adjusting bolts and remove the drive belt.
3. Remove the retaining nuts and remove the timing belt cover. Take care not to lose any of the washers or spacers.
4. Installation is the reverse of the removal procedure.
5. Adjust the drive belt tension when finished.

Lower Cover

1. Disconnect the negative battery cable. Remove the upper timing belt cover.
2. Loosen the air conditioning compressor mounting bolts and remove the drive belt.
3. Remove the crankshaft balancer center bolt.

NOTE: To remove the crankshaft balancer bolt, on manual transaxle vehicles, place the vehicle in 5th gear and have an assistant apply the brake. The will stop the engine from rotating while loosening the bolt. On automatic transaxle vehicles, remove the starter and hold the flywheel from turning, using a flywheel holding tool VW 10–201 or equivalent. This bolt is extremely tight.

4. Remove the lower timing belt cover bolts and remove the cover.
5. Installation is the reverse of the removal procedure.
6. Use the same procedure to install the crankshaft center bolt as when removing the bolt. Apply a locking compound on

the bolt threads and tighten the bolt to 258 ft. lbs. in several steps.

7. Adjust the drive belt tension when finished.

8 CYLINDER ENGINE

1. Disconnect the negative battery cable. The battery is under the rear seat.

2. The toothed cam drive belt must first be removed. Remove the coolant expansion tank cap. Raise and safely support vehicle. Remove the sound insulator or lower pan. Drain coolant from radiator.

3. Remove the alternator cooling air duct. Loosen the clip and disconnect the coolant temperature sensor harness connector. Remove the coolant hose.

4. Disconnect the outer half of the air duct at the alternator. Remove the screws securing the wiring at the alternator. Note that the alternator wiring must be bought out at the side, not downward. Otherwise the alternator air duct cannot be mounted.

5. Release tension on the poly-ribbed drive belt and remove the belt in a downward direction by placing a 13mm box wrench on the hexagon guide of the tensioner and pressing the wrench slowly upwards.

6. Remove the alternator mounting bolts and remove the alternator.

7. Working from below, remove the 3 bolts for the toothed belt guard.

8. Remove the bolts securing the bracket for the air intake ducts on the left and right and remove the ducts. Remove the bar-shaped strut brace.

9. Remove the 7 screws securing the upper part of the air cleaner housing, then remove the bolts holding the lower part of the housing. Press towards the rear and lift out.

10. Remove the upper radiator hose and clips.

11. Disconnect the electric fan bolts, lift the fan assembly out and lay to one side, wiring still connected.

12. Remove the bolts securing the supporting clamp for the lower radiator hose and take off the upper part. Disconnect the radiator hose at the thermostat housing. Swing the radiator hose to right at rear.

13. Remove the fan shroud by unscrewing the bolts for the viscous fan at the top. Remove the bolts securing the viscous fan. A 2 pin spanner may be needed to hold the fan hub. Note that this is a left hand thread. Turn to the right to loosen. Lift out the fan and shroud together.

14. Disconnect the engine support at the front. Note any shims. The same thickness shims must be used at installation. Remove the radiator hose. At installation, install the radiator hose first.

15. Loosen the center bolt of the vibration damper by one turn. A special tool may be needed to hold the damper from turning. This bolt was installed to over 250 ft. lbs. torque and will be difficult to remove.

16. Remove the bolts securing the left side toothed belt cover or guard.

17. Remove the lower part of the supporting clamp for the lower radiator hose. Turn the tensioner for the poly-ribbed accessory drive belt in the loosening direction and insert an appropriate size holding pin in the hole hole provided.

18. Remove the bolts securing the right side toothed belt cover, with the exception of the top bolt. Remove the tensioner holding pin. Remove the belt cover top screw and remove the cover or guard. Carefully lift the guard from the bottom to avoid damaging the radiator.

To install:

19. Installation is the reverse of the removal process. The crankshaft damper center bolt must be torque to 258 ft. lbs. A holding tool may be needed to keep the crankshaft from turning.

20. The viscous fan hub uses a left hand thread. Turn right to loosen, left to tighten.

Oil Seal Replacement

CAMSHAFT

Except 8 Cylinder Engine

1. Disconnect the negative battery cable. Set engine to TDC. Make sure crankshaft and cam timing marks are aligned.

2. Remove timing belt.

3. Hold camshaft from turning, and remove cam drive sprocket by tapping from behind. Take care not to loose the cam drive key.

4. Pry out the old oil seal. In some cases it may be easier to remove the front camshaft bearing cap.

To install:

5. Installation is the reverse of the removal procedure. Lubricate the seal lip with clean engine oil. Reinstall the front bearing cap if removed. Torque hold-down nuts to 15 ft. lbs.

6. Use a suitable socket as a driver and tap the new seal into position.

7. Install the cam drive sprocket with the drive key. Check the timing marks. Torque center bolt to 60 ft. lbs.

8. Install cam belt and cover.

8 Cylinder Engine

1. Disconnect the negative battery cable. Remove the toothed timing belt.

2. Remove the camshaft sprockets.

3. Remove the left and right belt guards.

NOTE: The toothed belt guard on the left-hand side contains 2 sealing rings and 1 shaft seal. The toothed belt guard on the right side contains 1 sealing ring and 1 shaft seal. If one shaft seal is leaking, the seals on both sides must be replaced.

4. Drive out the shaft seal.

To install:

5. When driving in the new seals, make sure the shaft seal is flush with the front edge of the belt guard. Replace the sealing rings.

6. Guide the camshaft sprocket into place.

7. Install the cam belt. Check timing marks on crankshaft and cam sprockets.

8. Clean the sealing surface at the rear of the guard and on the cylinder head. After installing the new sealing rings, apply a thin coat of sealant to both surfaces. Install the rear toothed belt cover and torque the bolts to 7 ft. lbs.

CRANKSHAFT

4 Cylinder Engine

1. Disconnect the negative battery cable. Remove timing belt.

2. Remove the crankshaft timing belt sprocket assembly.

3. A special oil seal extractor is recommended to pull the seal from the front cover flange.

4. Install the new seal after lubricating with engine oil. Press the seal in to the stop.

5. Reinstall the crankshaft sprocket and timing belt.

5 Cylinder Engine

The oil seal is a part of the oil pump.

1. Disconnect the negative battery cable. Remove the timing belt.

2. Using a small prybar, pry the oil seal from the oil pump.

3. Clean out the seal seat. Using a new seal, lubricate the lip with engine oil. Using a suitable socket drive the seal into the seal seat.

NOTE: When installing a new seal, be careful not to damage the lip of the seal.

4. Reinstall the timing belt. Torque the crankshaft pulley bolt to 253 ft. lbs.

8 Cylinder Engine

1. Disconnect the negative battery cable. Remove the toothed cam drive belt.
2. Remove the vibration damper.
3. A special oil seal extractor is recommended to pull the seal from the front cover flange.
4. Install the new seal after lubricating with engine oil. Press the seal in only until flush. Note that if the crankshaft shows signs of scoring, press the sealing ring in completely.
5. Reinstall the crankshaft sprocket and timing belt.

Timing Belt and Tensioner

Adjustment

4 CYLINDER ENGINE

1. Holding the large bolt on the tensioner pulley, loosen the small nut and turn the tensioner clockwise to tighten and counterclockwise to loosen.
2. The belt is correctly tensioned when it can be twisted 90 degrees midway between the camshaft and the intermediate shaft drive sprockets.

5 CYLINDER ENGINE

1. Loosen the water pump adjusting bolts and rotate the pump clockwise to tighten and counterclockwise to loosen.
2. The belt is correctly tensioned when it can be twisted 90 degrees midway between the camshaft drive sprocket and the water pump.

8 CYLINDER ENGINE

1. Remove the timing belt covers.
2. Perform the basic setting of the toothed belt tensioner by turning the idler pulley eccentric clockwise. A special turning tool may be needed. Turn the eccentric and measure the shock-absorber shaped damper length. Measure the overall length, not counting the mounting eyes. Measure the length of the barrel. Turn the eccentric until the damper length is 5.11–5.23 in. (130–133mm). Tighten the idler pulley eccentric to 18 ft. lbs.
3. Remove any camshaft and crankshaft locking tool previously installed. Turn engine at least 2 turns. Tighten the vibration damper center bolt to 258 ft. lbs. Check the damper length and if necessary, readjust the idler pulley.
4. Reinstall the cam belt cover.

Removal and Installation

4 CYLINDER ENGINE

1. Disconnect the negative battery cable. Using the large bolt on the crankshaft sprocket, rotate the engine until the No. 1 cylinder is at TDC of the compression stroke. At this point, both valves will be closed and the **0** mark on the flywheel will be aligned with the pointer on the bell housing. If the belt hasn't jumped teeth the timing mark on the rear face of the camshaft sprocket should be aligned with the upper left edge of the valve cover.
2. Remove the upper and lower timing belt covers.
3. While holding the large hex nut on the tensioner pulley, loosen the smaller pulley locknut.
4. Turn the tensioner counterclockwise to relieve the tension on the timing belt.
5. Carefully slide the timing belt off of the sprockets and remove the belt.

To install:
6. If the engine had moved or jumped timing, use the large bolt on the crankshaft sprocket, rotate the engine until the No. 1 cylinder is at TDC of the compression stroke. At this point, both valves will be closed and the **0** mark on the flywheel will be aligned with the pointer on the bell housing. Rotate the camshaft until the timing mark on the rear face of the camshaft sprocket is aligned with the upper left edge of the valve cover.

7. Install the crankshaft pulley and check that the notch on the pulley is aligned with the mark on the intermediate shaft sprocket. If not, rotate the intermediate shaft until they align.

NOTE: If the timing marks are not correctly aligned with the No. 1 piston at TDC of the compression stroke and the belt is installed, valve timing will be incorrect. Poor performance and possible engine damage can result from the improper valve timing.

8. Remove the crankshaft pulley. Note the pulley location on the crankshaft sprocket so it can be replaced in the same position. Hold the large nut on the tensioner pulley and loosen the smaller locknut. Turn the tensioner counterclockwise to loosen and install the timing belt.
9. Slide the timing belt onto the sprockets and adjust the belt tension. The timing belt tension is correct when the belt can be twisted 90 degrees.
10. The remainder of the installation is the reverse of the removal procedure.

5 CYLINDER ENGINE

1. Disconnect the negative battery cable. Using the large bolt on the crankshaft sprocket, rotate the engine until the No. 1 cylinder is at TDC of the compression stroke. Align the TDC mark **0** with the cast mark on the bell housing. If the belt hasn't jumped teeth, the timing mark on the rear face of the camshaft sprocket should be aligned with the upper left edge of the valve cover.
2. Remove the alternator and air conditioner compressor drive belts.
3. Remove the upper and lower timing belt covers.
4. Loosen the water pump bolts only enough to turn the pump clockwise.

NOTE: By loosening the water pump bolts, the coolant may drain from the engine at the water pump. If necessary, drain the cooling system, remove the water pump and reinstall it with a new O-ring.

5. Slide the timing belt off the sprockets.
To install:
6. If necessary, turn the camshaft until the notch on the back of the sprocket is in line with the left side edge of the cylinder head gasket surface.
7. If necessary, align the TDC **0** mark with the with the lug cast on the bell housing.
8. Install the timing belt and turn the water pump counterclockwise to tighten the belt. Tighten the water pump bolts to 15 ft. lbs.

NOTE: The timing belt is correctly tensioned when it can be twisted 90 degrees along with the straight run between the camshaft sprocket and water pump. Belt must not be jammed between the oil pump and sprocket when installing the vibration damper.

9. Install the timing belt covers and tighten the bolts to 7 ft. lbs.
10. Install the alternator and air conditioning compressor belts. These belts are correctly tensioned when they can be depressed ⅜ in. along their longest straight run.

8 CYLINDER ENGINE

1. Disconnect the negative battery cable. The battery is under the rear seat.
2. The toothed cam drive belt must first be removed. Remove the coolant expansion tank cap. Raise and safely support vehicle. Remove the sound insulator or lower pan. Drain coolant from radiator.
3. Remove the alternator cooling air duct. Loosen the clip and disconnect the coolant temperature sensor harness connector. Remove the coolant hose.

4. Disconnect the outer half of the air duct at the alternator. Remove the screws securing the wiring at the alternator.

5. Release tension on the poly-ribbed drive belt and remove the belt in a downward direction, by placing a 13mm box wrench on the hexagon guide of the tensioner and pressing the wrench slowly upwards.

6. Remove the alternator mounting bolts and remove the alternator.

7. Working from below, remove the 3 bolts for the toothed belt guard.

8. Remove the bolts securing the bracket for the air intake ducts on the left and right and remove the ducts. Remove the bar-shaped strut brace.

9. Remove the 7 screws securing the upper part of the air cleaner housing, then remove the bolts holding the lower part of the housing. Press towards the rear and lift out.

10. Remove the upper radiator hose and clips.

11. Disconnect the electric fan bolts, lift the fan assembly out and lay to one side, wiring still connected.

12. Remove the bolts securing the supporting clamp for the lower radiator hose and take off the upper part. Disconnect the radiator hose at the thermostat housing. Swing the radiator hose to the right.

13. Remove the fan shroud by unscrewing the bolts for the viscous fan at the top. Remove the bolts securing the viscous fan. A 2 pin spanner may be needed to hold the fan hub. Note that this is a left hand thread. Turn to the right to loosen. Lift out the fan and shroud together.

14. Disconnect the engine support at the front. Note any shims. The same thickness shims must be used at installation. Remove the radiator hose. At installation, install the radiator hose first.

15. Loosen the center bolt of the vibration damper by one turn. A special tool may be needed to hold the damper from turning. This bolt was installed to over 250 ft. lbs. torque and will be difficult to remove.

16. Remove the bolts securing the left side toothed belt cover or guard.

17. Remove the lower part of the supporting clamp for the lower radiator hose. Turn the tensioner for the poly-ribbed accessory drive belt in the loosening direction and insert an appropriate size holding pin in the hole hole provided.

18. Remove the bolts securing the right side toothed belt cover, with the exception of the top bolt. Remove the tensioner holding pin. Remove the belt cover top screw and remove the cover or guard. Carefully lift the guard from the bottom to avoid damaging the radiator.

19. Disconnect the ignition cables at the coils. Remove both distributor caps. Turn the engine to TDC. It may be necessary to temporarily install the damper to align the timing marks. Check that the distributor rotor is pointing to the mark on the housing. If not, turn the crankshaft 1 additional turn. Remove both distributors.

20. Remove the stop plate at the toothed belt tensioner. Disconnect the shock-absorber shaped damper at the top bolt.

21. Remove the belt from the tensioning idler pulley (with eccentric). Pulley is on right side of engine. Take the belt off both camshaft sprockets.

22. A special holding tool is available that is installed on the back of the camshafts. It fits the locating pin on the distributor flanges. If necessary, use a special hook wrench tool to turn the camshaft until the pins latch into the special holding tool. Secure the special tool with the distributor mounting bolts.

23. At the camshaft sprocket end, loosen the mounting bolts 2 turns. Using a plastic hammer, tap the edge of the camshaft sprockets loose.

NOTE: After the sprockets are removed note the grooves machined in the camshaft ends. Woodruff® keys must not be installed in the camshaft sprocket/camshaft connection. Unlike the other engines, this engine does not use cam keys.

24. Remove the vibration damper which was previously temporarily reinstalled to line up TDC timing marks. A puller can be used. Unscrew 2 opposing bolts of the 4 bolts connecting the vibration damper and toothed belt sprocket. Use a puller in these holes.

25. Remove the toothed belt.

To install:

26. Installation is the reverse of the removal procedure. Before installing a new belt, the rollers and tensioners must be checked for dirt, rough running and ease of rotation. Clean or replace rollers and tensioners, as necessary.

27. Fit the toothed belt at the crankshaft and install the vibration damper with the belt on the crankshaft. Apply thread locking compound to the center bolt and tighten using hand wrench. A holding tool may be required to keep the crankshaft from turning. It is a must to ensure that the TDC mark on the vibration damper is aligned with the TDC pointer before and after tightening the camshaft sprockets.

28. Guide the toothed belt into position and install the idler pulley with eccentric. Only tighten the nut as far as the eccentric can be turned.

29. Tighten the damper top bolt to 18 ft. lbs. Engage the damper to the tensioner lever by pressing the lever downward.

30. Perform the basic setting of the toothed belt tensioner by turning the idler pulley eccentric clockwise. A special turning tool may be needed. Turn the eccentric and measure the damper length. Measure the overall length, not counting the mounting eyes. Measure the length of the barrel. Turn the eccentric until the damper length is 5.11–5.23 in. (130–133mm). Tighten the idler pulley eccentric to 18 ft. lbs. Tighten the camshaft sprockets to 33 ft. lbs.

31. Remove any camshaft and crankshaft locking tool previously installed. Turn engine at least 2 turns. Tighten the vibration damper center bolt to 258 ft. lbs. Check the damper length and if necessary, readjust the idler pulley.

32. The remaining installation for the toothed cam drive belt is performed in reverse order of removal.

Timing Sprockets

Removal and Installation

EXCEPT 8 CYLINDER ENGINE

All timing belt sprockets except 8 cylinder engines, are located by keys on their respective shafts. Each sprocket is retained by a bolt. To remove any or all of the sprockets, first remove the timing belt cover(s) and timing belt.

1. Disconnect the negative battery cable. Remove the center retaining bolt for the sprocket.

2. Pull the sprocket off of the shaft.

3. If the sprocket is sticking on the shaft, use a gear puller or tap lightly with a plastic hammer. Do not hammer on the sprocket or damage may occur.

4. Remove the sprocket, being careful not to lose the key.

5. Installation is in the reverse order of removal.

NOTE: Always check valve timing after removing the drive sprockets.

8 CYLINDER ENGINE

1. Disconnect the negative battery cable. Remove timing cover, toothed timing belt and both distributors. Note that the timing belt drives the exhaust camshaft. A chain from the exhaust cam drives the intake cam.

2. A special holding tool is available that is installed on the back of the camshafts. It fits the locating pin on the distributor flanges. If necessary, use a special hook wrench tool to turn the camshaft until the pins latch into the special holding tool. Secure the special tool with the distributor mounting bolts.

3. At the camshaft sprocket end, loosen the mounting bolts 2 turns. Using a plastic hammer, tap the edge of the camshaft sprockets slightly loose.

NOTE: After the sprockets are removed note the grooves machined in the camshaft ends. Woodruff® keys must not be installed in the camshaft sprocket/camshaft connection. Unlike the other engines, keys are not used.

4. When assembling the sprockets to the camshafts, make sure the timing marks found on the backside of the chain sprockets are still aligned. They should align next to each other at the 3 o'clock and 9 o'clock positions.

Camshaft

Removal and Installation

4 CYLINDER ENGINE

Except 80 and 90

1. Disconnect the negative battery cable. Remove the timing belt from the camshaft sprocket.
2. Remove the PCV line from the valve cover.
3. Remove the valve cover.
4. Remove the camshaft timing belt sprocket.
5. First remove bearing caps No. 1, 3 and 4. Loosen bearing cap No. 2 afterwards.
6. Remove the camshaft from the cylinder head.

To install:

7. Lubricate the camshaft journals, lobes and contact faces of the caps with assembly lube or gear oil before reinstallation.
8. Replace the camshaft oil seal in the cylinder head.
9. Install the bearing caps in the proper order, observing the off-center position.
10. Lightly tighten bearing cap No. 2 before installing bearing caps No. 4, 1 and 3. Tighten all the nuts to 14 ft. lbs.

NOTE: Tighten the bearing caps diagonally. Observe off center bearing position. The numbers on the bearing caps are not always on the same side.

11. Replace the camshaft seal under the No. 1 bearing cap.
12. Installation of the remaining components is in the reverse order of removal. When installing the crankshaft timing belt sprocket, be sure the lug on the sprocket is properly installed into the slot on the crankshaft.

NOTE: Always recheck the valve timing and valve clearance after the camshaft has been removed.

80 and 90

1. Disconnect the negative battery cable. Remove the upper drive belt, vacuum lines to valve cover and valve cover.
2. Using the large bolt on the crankshaft sprocket, rotate the engine until the No. 1 cylinder is at TDC of the compression stroke. At this point, both valves will be closed and the **0** mark on the flywheel will be aligned with the pointer on the bell housing. If the belt hasn't jumped teeth the timing mark on the rear face of the camshaft sprocket should be aligned with the upper left edge of the valve cover.
3. Remove the timing belt from the camshaft sprocket.
4. Remove the camshaft timing belt sprocket, take care not to loose Woodruff® key.
5. First remove bearing caps No. 1 and 3. Bearing cap No. 1 is located at the sprocket. Next remove bearing caps No. 2 and 5, alternately and diagonally. Bearing cap No. 5 is on the opposite end from the cam sprocket. There is no bearing cap No. 4.
6. Remove the camshaft from the cylinder head.

To install:

7. Lubricate the camshaft journals, lobes and contact faces of the caps with assembly lube before reinstallation.
8. Replace the camshaft oil seal in the cylinder head.

NOTE: The bearing caps are offset. Before installing the camshaft, set the bearing caps into position. Check that they are facing in the correct direction. The numbers on the bearing caps are not always on the same side.

9. Install the bearing caps in the proper order, observing the off-center position.
10. Install bearing caps No. 2 and 5 and tighten to 15 ft. lbs.
11. Install bearing caps No. 1 and 3 and tighten to 15 ft. lbs.
12. Mount camshaft sprocket and tighten to 59 ft. lbs.
13. Installation of the remaining components is in the reverse order of removal. When installing the crankshaft timing belt sprocket, be sure the lug on the sprocket is properly installed into the slot.
14. Coat new camshaft seal with oil and press into cylinder head until flush.

NOTE: Always recheck the valve timing and valve clearance after the camshaft has been removed.

5 CYLINDER ENGINE

Except 80 and 90

1. Disconnect the negative battery cable. Remove the upper drive belt cover, valve cover and upper part of intake manifold, if necessary.
2. Using the large bolt on the crankshaft sprocket, rotate the engine until the No. 1 cylinder is at TDC of the compression stroke. Align the TDC mark **0** with the cast mark on the bell housing. If the belt hasn't jumped teeth, the timing mark on the rear face of the camshaft sprocket should be aligned with the upper left edge of the valve cover.
3. Remove the timing belt from the camshaft sprocket. Remove the camshaft sprocket.
4. Diagonally loosen bearing caps No. 2 and 4 and remove the bearing caps.
5. Diagonally loosen bearing caps No. 1 and 3 and remove the bearing caps.
6. Lift the camshaft out of the cylinder head.

To install:

7. When installing, lightly oil the camshaft and bearing journals, with clean engine oil.
8. Position the caps on the same journals from which they were removed.
9. Tighten the nuts of caps 2 and 4 until snug.
10. Tighten all nuts to 15 ft. lbs.
11. Install the camshaft sprocket and timing belt. Install the valve cover. The camshaft sprocket bolt is tightened to 58 ft. lbs.

80 and 90

1. Disconnect the negative battery cable. Remove the upper drive belt cover, valve cover and upper part of intake manifold, if necessary.
2. Using the large bolt on the crankshaft sprocket, rotate the engine until the No. 1 cylinder is at TDC of the compression stroke. Align the TDC mark **0** with the cast mark on the bell housing. If the belt hasn't jumped teeth the timing mark on the rear face of the camshaft sprocket should be aligned with the upper left edge of the valve cover.
3. Remove the timing belt from the camshaft sprocket. Remove the camshaft sprocket.
4. Remove bearing caps No. 1 and 3.
5. Diagonally loosen bearing caps No. 2 and 4 and remove the bearing caps.
6. Lift the camshaft out of the cylinder head.

To install:

7. When installing, lightly oil the camshaft and bearing journals, with clean engine oil.
8. Position the caps on the same journals from which they were removed.

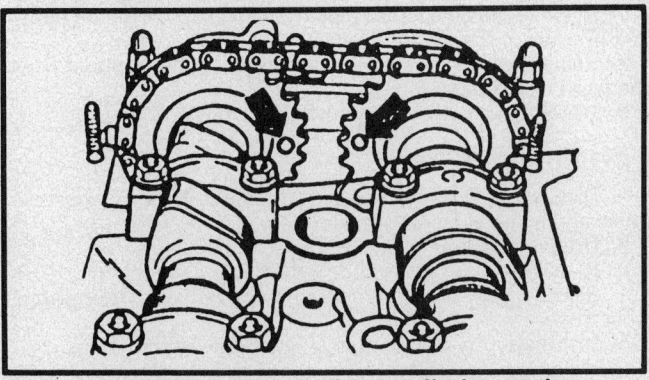

Cam gear alignment marks for 8 cylinder engine

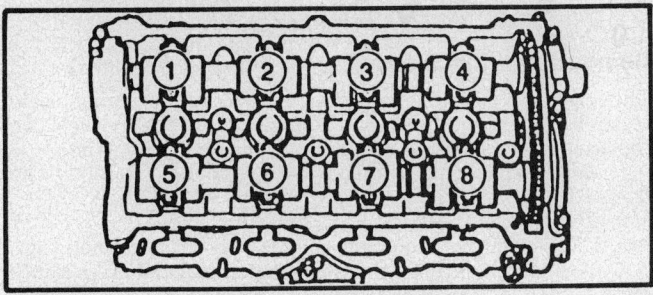

Cam bearing cap tightening sequence

9. Install bearing caps No. 2 and 4. Tighten alternately and diagonally to 15 ft. lbs.

10. Install bearing caps No. 1 and 3 and tighten to 15 ft. lbs.

11. Install the camshaft sprocket and timing belt. Install the valve cover. The camshaft sprocket bolt is tightened to 59 ft. lbs.

8 CYLINDER ENGINE

1. Disconnect the negative battery cable. Remove the toothed camshaft drive belt.

2. Remove the cylinder head cover.

3. Remove the camshaft sprocket.

4. On the exhaust side, remove the intermediate flange and bearing cap for the distributor. All bearing caps that are removed should be marked or identified so they can be installed in the same position. Do not mix bearing caps or install then backwards. Loosen the bearing cap in front of the chain, plus caps No. 2 and 3. Loosen bearing caps No. 1 and 4 alternately and in a diagonal sequence.

5. On the intake side, remove bearing caps No. 6 and 7. Loosen bearing caps No. 5 and 8 alternately and in a diagonal sequence.

6. Remove the cam. If a lifter is removed and is to be reused, it must go in the bore from which it was removed.

To install:

7. Installation is the reverse of removal. Before assembly coat the moving parts with clean oil.

8. Install the camshafts with the chain so the markings on the chain sprockets are in alignment. The marks are on the back side of the chain sprocket. They should face each other at the 3 o'clock and 9 o'clock positions. Install the bearing caps so the stamped-on numbers can be read from the intake side.

9. Make sure the bearing caps are installed properly. They will cause parts failure if installed backwards. Tighten bearing caps alternately in a diagonal sequence to 11 ft. lbs.

Piston and Connecting Rod

Positioning

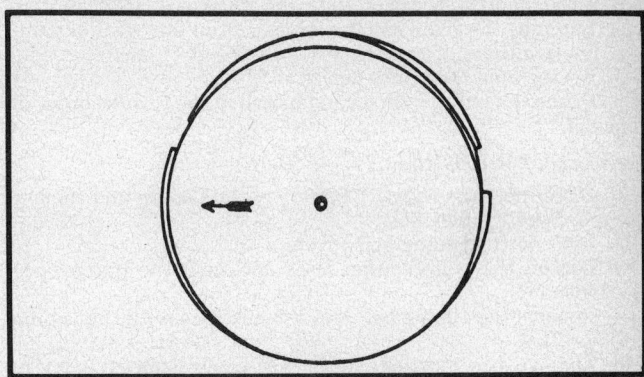

Arrow on piston must face forward

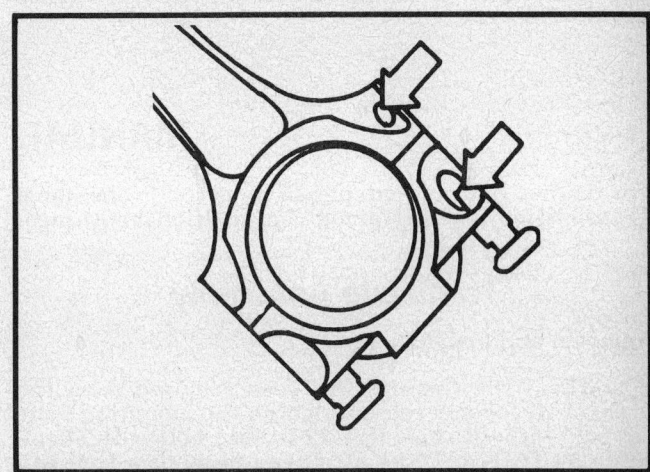

Align the forge marks when assembling the connecting rods and caps

ENGINE LUBRICATION

Oil Pan

Removal and Installation

1. Disconnect the negative battery cable. Raise and support the vehicle safely.

2. Drain the oil from the crankcase. Remove the cover plate from under the engine, if equipped.

3. If necessary, remove the 4 bolts from the subframe and lower the subframe. Remove the oil pan bolts while supporting the pan.

4. Lower the pan from the engine. Discard the gasket. Note that the 8 cylinder engine uses a 2 piece oil pan as well as a honeycomb baffle insert. Both an upper and lower pan gasket will be required.

5. Coat both sides of a new gasket with sealer and install the gasket and oil pan.

6. Tighten the pan bolts to 7 ft. lbs. on 4 cylinder engines and 15 ft. lbs. on 5 cylinder engines. On 8 cylinder engines, tighten

the lower pan-to-upper pan bolts to 14 ft. lbs., and the upper pan-to-block bolts to 18 ft. lbs.

Oil Pump

Removal and Installation

4 CYLINDER ENGINE

1. Disconnect the negative battery cable. Raise and safely support vehicle. Drain the oil and remove the oil pan.
2. Remove the oil pump mounting bolts and pull the pump down and out of the engine.
3. Unscrew the 2 bolts and separate the pump halves.
4. Clean the lower half in solvent.
5. To remove the oil strainer for cleaning, bend out the metal rim of the oil strainer cover plate and remove it.
6. Examine the gears and the driveshaft for any wear or damage. Replace them, if necessary.
7. Reassemble the pump halves.
8. Prime the pump with oil and install in the reverse order of removal.

5 CYLINDER ENGINE

1. Disconnect the negative battery cable. Loosen and remove the crankshaft pulley bolt.
2. Remove the timing belt covers.
3. Loosen the water pump bolts and turn the pump body clockwise.
4. Remove the timing belt and V-belt pulley with the timing belt sprocket.
5. Remove the dipstick. Raise and safely support vehicle. Drain the engine oil.
6. Remove the front bolts on the subframe and remove the oil pan.

7. Remove the oil suction pipe from the base of the oil pump and bracket to the engine block.
8. Remove the oil pump bolts and remove the oil pump from the front of the engine.
9. Installation is the reverse of the removal procedure.

8 CYLINDER ENGINE

1. Disconnect the negative battery cable. Pull out dipstick. Raise and safely support vehicle.
2. Drain engine oil.
3. Remove oil pan bolts and pull off pan assembly.
4. Remove bolts securing oil pump and pull out, disengaging from drive.
5. Installation is the reverse of the removal procedure.

Rear Main Bearing Oil Seal

Removal and Installation

The rear main oil seal is located at the rear of the engine block. It can be found in a housing or flange behind the flywheel. To replace the seal, remove the transaxle or pull the engine.

1. Disconnect the negative battery cable. Remove the transaxle.
2. Remove the flywheel.
3. Using a suitable tool, pry the old seal out of its housing.
4. To install, lightly oil the replacement seal and press it into place.

NOTE: Be careful not to damage the seal or score the crankshaft.

5. Install the flywheel and the transaxle.

MANUAL TRANSAXLE

For further information, please refer to "Professional Transmission Repair Manual" for additional coverage.

Transaxle Assembly

Removal and Installation

NOTE: If the flywheel has been removed from the crankshaft for any reason, tighten the mounting bolts to: bolt without shoulder – 72 ft. lbs.; bolt with shoulder – 54 ft. lbs. Coat all threads with a locking compound.

1987 4000 EXCEPT QUATTRO, 1988-91 80 AND 90 EXCEPT QUATTRO

1. Disconnect the negative battery cable.
2. Unplug the 2 electrical connectors for the back-up lights. They can be found between the ignition coil and the fuel distributor filter.
3. Remove the upper engine-to-transaxle bolts.
4. Detach the speedometer cable from the transaxle.
5. Detach the clutch cable from the clutch lever.
6. Unbolt the exhaust pipe from the exhaust manifold.
7. Unscrew the 3 mounting bolts and remove the center engine mount.
8. Unbolt the front exhaust pipe from the support bracket and unbolt it from the catalytic converter or muffler.
9. Unscrew the 6 screws and remove the left halfshaft from the transaxle. Wire the halfshaft up and aside. Repeat the procedure for the right halfshaft.

10. Remove the cover plate.
11. Tag and disconnect all wires leading to the starter and remove the starter.
12. Remove the bolt from the shift rod coupling.
13. Pry off the linkage coupling with a suitable small prybar.
14. Pull the shift rod coupling off of the shift rod. Place a transaxle jack under the transaxle, support it by lifting up slightly.
15. Loosen the left chassis bolt on the rear transaxle support. Remove the bolts from the right or transaxle side of the support and pivot the support aside.
16. Remove the rubber mounting block.
17. Unscrew 3 bolts and remove the front transaxle support.
18. Remove the lower engine-to-transaxle bolts.
19. Carefully, pry the transaxle apart from the engine and remove it.

To install:
20. Installation is in the reverse order of removal. Note the following:
  a. Make sure all engine to transaxle mounts are correctly aligned and free of tension.
  b. Check for proper adjustment of the gear shift lever.
  c. Secure the bolt on the shift rod coupling with wire.
  d. Tighten the engine-to-transaxle bolts to 40 ft. lbs.
  e. Tighten the halfshaft-to-drive flange bolts to 33 ft. lbs.
  f. Tighten the subframe-to-body bolts to 51 ft. lbs.
  g. Tighten the front transaxle support-to-transaxle bolts to 18 ft. lbs.
  h. Tighten the rubber mount-to-body bolts to 80 ft. lbs.
  i. Tighten the rubber mount-to-transaxle bolts to 40 ft. lbs.

j. Tighten the rubber mount-to-crossmember bolts to 18 ft. lbs.

1987 4000 QUATTRO

1. Disconnect the negative battery cable.
2. Disconnect the rpm sensor.
3. Remove the upper engine-to-transaxle bolts.
4. Disconnect the speedometer cable from the transaxle.
5. Disconnect the tie rod coupling from the steering rack.

NOTE: When removing the tie rod coupling, remove the self-locking nuts first and then the mounting bolts.

6. Disconnect the transaxle switch electrical connector from the transaxle.
7. At the clutch slave cylinder, drive out the lock pin, remove the cylinder leaving the hydraulic line attached and move it aside.
8. Disconnect the shift linkage from the transaxle.
9. Using a suitable hoist or tool, support the engine and remove the left halfshaft from the transaxle.
10. At the rear of the transaxle, disconnect the driveshaft and the differential lock cable.
11. Remove the transaxle cover plate and turn the spindle of the engine support tool to raise the engine.
12. At the right transaxle mount, remove the halfshaft deflector and the transaxle mount.
13. Remove the front exhaust pipe. Disconnect the right halfshaft from the transaxle.
14. At the left side of the transaxle, remove the halfshaft.
15. Place a transaxle support lift tool under the transaxle and secure it to the transaxle.
16. Remove the lower engine-to-transaxle bolts, push the transaxle back and lower it from the vehicle.

NOTE: When removing the transaxle, make sure the halfshafts, driveshaft, tie rods and shift linkage do not interfere.

To install:
17. To install, reverse the removal procedures. Tightening bolts to the following torque:
    a. Torque the engine-to-transaxle bolts to 43 ft. lbs.
    b. Torque the transaxle mounting-to-transaxle bolts to 29 ft. lbs.
    c. Torque the transaxle mount-to-frame bolts to 32 ft. lbs.
    d. Torque the halfshafts-to-transaxle bolts to 33 ft. lbs.
    e. Torque the tie rod coupling-to-steering rack bolts to 29 ft. lbs.
    f. Torque the driveshaft-to-transaxle bolts to 39 ft. lbs.
18. Adjust the shift linkage.

1988–91 80 AND 90 QUATTRO

1. Disconnect the negative battery cable.
2. Remove the 3 upper engine-to-transaxle bolts.

NOTE: Tag all bolts during removal, so all bolts can be replaced in their correct locations, as they are not all the same size.

3. Disconnect the ground strap from the transaxle.
4. Remove the wiring connectors from the speedometer sender and the multi-function switch.
5. Disconnect the wiring for the oxygen sensor and oxygen sensor heating element.
6. Remove the engine protection plate.
7. Disconnect the exhaust pipe from the manifold.
8. Separate the exhaust pipe behind the catalyst and remove the pipe and catalyst.
9. Matchmark and remove the driveshaft.
10. Remove the rear crossmember.
11. Remove the shift rod securing bolt at the transaxle and let the shift rod hang.

12. Remove the transaxle cover plate.
13. Remove the right halfshaft shield.
14. Disconnect the left and right halfshafts, turn the steering to the right lock and tie both shafts up.
15. Remove the clutch slave cylinder.
16. Remove the tie rod coupling from the steering rack and turn wheel to the left.
17. Support the engine.
18. Support the transaxle.
19. Remove the transaxle strut at the left rear and front engine mount.
20. Remove the heat shield from the bonded rubber bushing.
21. Remove the bonded rubber bushing support bracket from the transaxle.
22. Remove the bonded rubber bushing.
23. Remove the bolt from the seatbelt tension in cable guide at the left rear of the transaxle. Position the cables and guide aside.
24. Lower the right rear subframe by loosening the mounting bolts.
25. Remove the remaining transaxle to engine bolts.
26. Remove the transaxle.
To install:
27. Installation is reverse of the removal procedure. When installing the transaxle, make certain alignment bushings are in the cylinder block before reassembly.
28. Press clutch master cylinder in with a lever, until retaining bolt can be installed.

NOTE: A replacement bolt for mounting the clutch slave cylinder is available from Audi, with a pointed tip for easier installation.

29. Tighten subframe mounting bolts to 25 ft. lbs., plus an additional 90 degree turn.
30. Tighten transaxle retaining bolts as follows: Torque the 8mm bolts to 18 ft. lbs., the 10mm bolts to 33 ft. lbs. and the 12mm bolts to 48 ft. lbs.
31. Torque the driveshaft to flange bolts to 33 ft. lbs. and the driveshaft to transaxle and final drive bolts to 40 ft. lbs.
32. Torque the tie rod coupling to steering rack to 33 ft. lbs.

1987–88 5000 EXCEPT QUATTRO

The manual transaxle may be removed with the engine in place.
1. Disconnect the negative battery cable.
2. Remove the air filter, if necessary.
3. Remove the windshield washer bottle.
4. Remove the upper engine-to-transaxle bolts.
5. Raise and safely support the vehicle.
6. Disconnect the speedometer cable from the transaxle.
7. Disconnect all wires and hoses connected to the transaxle.
8. Drive out the clutch slave cylinder lockpin and remove the slave cylinder. Leave the hydraulic line connected.
9. Support the engine, either from above with a hoist or from below with a jack.
10. Remove the heat shield.
11. Remove the lower engine and transaxle splash shield, if equipped.
12. Disconnect the exhaust pipe from the manifold.
13. Remove the right side guard plate.
14. Disconnect the halfshafts from the flanges and support them aside with wires. Disconnect the front-to-rear driveshaft at the rear output shaft on the transaxle and wire it aside.
15. Disconnect the back-up light switch.
16. Pry off the shift and adjusting rods.
17. Remove the lower engine-to-transaxle bolts.
18. Remove the starter.
19. Remove the subframe skid plate.
20. Install a jack under the transaxle and lift it slightly.
21. Remove both transaxle-to-subframe bolts.
22. Remove the right side transaxle bracket.

23. Slide the transaxle back off the locating dowels and remove it from the vehicle.

To install:

24. Installation is the reverse of the removal procedure. Install the transaxle assembly and install the transaxle-to-engine bolts. When installing, place the halfshafts on top of the subframe; tighten the lower bolts first.

25. Install the clutch cylinder, shift rod and exhaust pipe.

26. Tighten the transaxle bracket, subframe and upper bolts. Driveshaft bolts are torqued to 32 ft. lbs.; transaxle bracket bolts to 29 ft. lbs.; subframe support bolts to 29 ft. lbs.; subframe-to-body bolts to 80 ft. lbs. and the transaxle-to-engine bolts to 40 ft. lbs.

27. Install the lower body panel. Connect the oxygen sensor wire, speedometer cable and any other parts in reverse order of removal.

1987–88 5000 QUATTRO, 5000 QUATTRO TURBO AND 4000 QUATTRO COUPE

1. Disconnect the negative battery cable and disconnect the rpm sensor.

2. Remove the upper engine-to-transaxle attaching bolts. Disconnect the speedometer.

3. Disconnect the tie rod coupling from the steering rack, first removing the self locking nuts below the tie rod coupling and second, the mounting bolts.

4. Drive out the clutch slave cylinder lock pin. Remove the clutch slave cylinder leaving the hydraulic lines attached. Disconnect the back-up light switch and shift linkage.

5. Support the engine with a suitable engine hoist. Remove the deflector for the halfshaft and the right transaxle mount. Remove the right transaxle mount.

6. Disconnect the exhaust pipe at the flange and the right halfshaft at the transaxle. Remove the left transaxle mount and disconnect the left halfshaft at the transaxle.

7. On Quattro vehicles, disconnect the driveshaft at the transaxle. Disconnect the differential lock cable and remove the transaxle cover plate.

8. Raise the engine slightly and place a suitable transaxle jack under the transaxle. Remove the lower engine-to-transaxle bolts.

9. Remove the transaxle from under the vehicle. On the Quattro Turbo, remove the transaxle towards the rear of the vehicle, making sure the transaxle clears the halfshafts, tie rods and shift linkage.

To install:

10. Installation is the reverse of the removal procedure. Torque the exhaust pipe flange attaching bolts to 18 ft. lbs. Torque the exhaust pipe-to-transaxle mount attaching bolts to 22 ft. lbs. Torque the tie rod coupling-to-the steering rack attaching bolts and the transaxle mount-to-transaxle attaching bolts to 29 ft. lbs.

11. Torque the transaxle mount-to-subframe attaching bolts and driveshaft attaching bolts to 32 ft. lbs. Torque the engine-to-transaxle mounting bolts to 43 ft. lbs. Torque the halfshaft-to-transaxle mounting bolts to 58 ft. lbs.

1989–91 100

1. Disconnect the negative battery cable.
2. Remove the upper engine-to-transaxle bolts.

NOTE: Tag all bolts during removal, so all bolts can be replaced in their correct locations, as they are not all the same size.

3. Disconnect the ground strap from the transaxle, if equipped.

4. Remove the wiring connectors from the speedometer sender and the multi-function switch.

5. Support the engine.

6. Disconnect the wiring for the oxygen sensor and oxygen sensor heating element.

7. Raise and safely support vehicle. Remove the splash shield, if equipped.

8. Disconnect the exhaust pipe from the manifold.

9. Separate the exhaust pipe behind the catalyst and remove the pipe and catalyst.

10. Remove the bolt for the shift rod at the transaxle and separate.

11. Remove the heat shield from the right inner CV-joint.

12. Remove the halfshafts from the flanges and tie aside.

13. Remove the heat shield for the bonded rubber bushing on the right side.

14. Support the transaxle.

15. Remove the strut at the rear of the transaxle.

16. Remove the clutch slave cylinder. Do not remove the hydraulic line from the slave cylinder.

17. Remove the lower transaxle-to-engine bolts.

18. Pry transaxle back and lower assembly.

19. Remove the transaxle.

To install:

20. Installation is the reverse of the removal procedure. When installing the transaxle, make certain alignment bushings are in the cylinder block before reassembly.

21. Press clutch master cylinder in with a lever, until retaining bolt can be installed.

NOTE: A replacement bolt for mounting the clutch slave cylinder is available from Audi, with a pointed tip for easier installation.

22. Tighten subframe mounting bolts to 25 ft. lbs., plus an additional 90 degree turn.

23. Tighten transaxle retaining bolts as follows: Torque the 8mm bolts to 18 ft. lbs., the 10mm bolts to 33 ft. lbs. and the 12mm bolts to 48 ft. lbs.

24. Torque the halfshaft-to-flange bolts to 33 ft. lbs. and the halfshaft-to-transaxle and final drive bolts to 40 ft. lbs.

25. Torque the tie rod coupling to steering rack to 33 ft. lbs.

1989–91 200

1. Disconnect the negative battery cable.
2. Remove the upper engine to transaxle bolts.
3. Remove the connector for the speedometer sender by pressing in the clips. If equipped with a turbocharger, unscrew the cover plate although it cannot be removed yet.

4. Remove the clip from the clutch slave cylinder and drive out spring pin, if equipped. Remove the bolt securing the clutch slave cylinder to the transaxle and remove the cylinder. Leave the hydraulic line connected.

5. Support the engine. Tie up coolant hoses and cables, as needed.

6. Remove the right side guard plate.

7. Disconnect the halfshafts from the flanges and rest both halfshafts on top of the subframe.

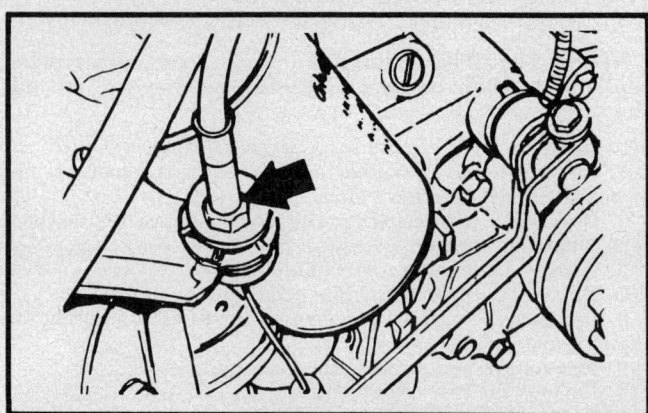

Clutch cable adjustment nut

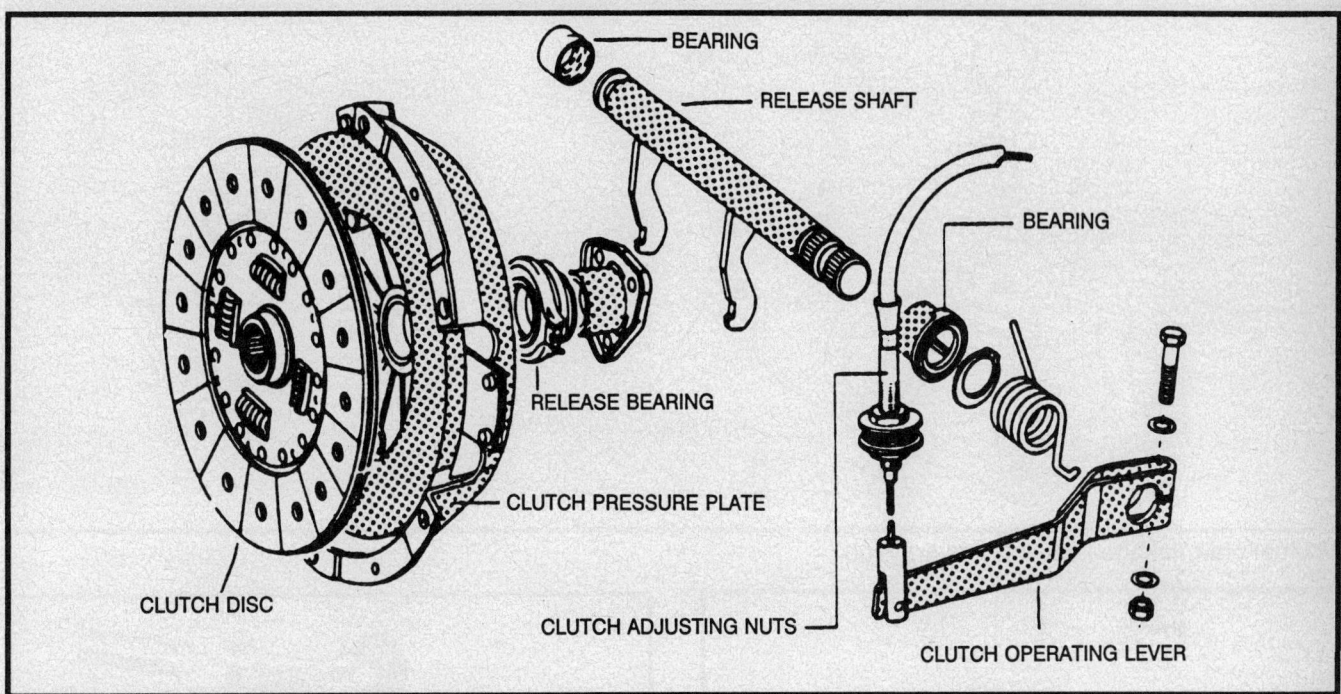

Exploded view of the clutch, 4000—except Quattro

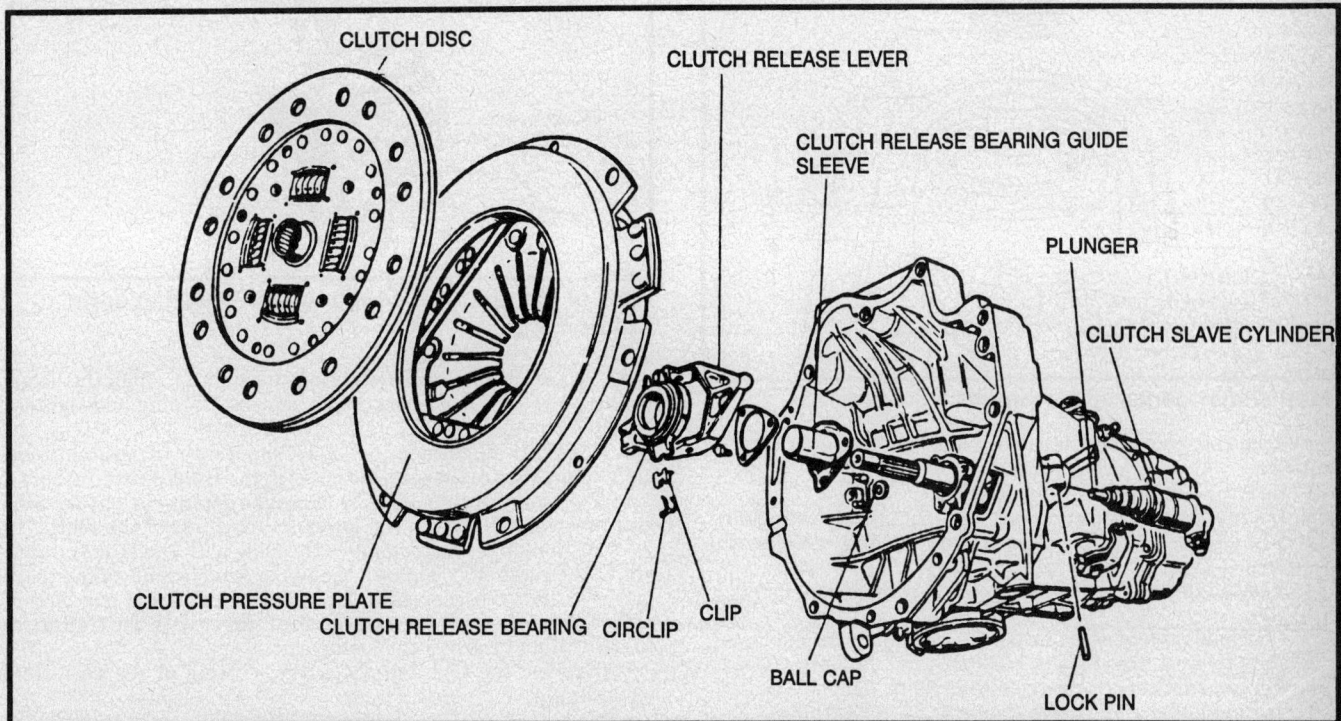

Exploded view of clutch assembly—all 5 cylinder engine, 80 and 90 with 4 cylinder engine

8. Tag and disconnect the wire from the back-up light switch. On Quattro vehicles tag and disconnect vacuum hoses at the servo.

9. Pry off the shift and adjusting rods.

10. Remove the lower engine-to-transaxle bolts.

11. Remove the starter.

12. Remove the guard plate from the subframe.

13. With suitable jack, lift transaxle slightly.

14. Remove both rear subframe mounting bolts.

15. Remove both transaxle support bolts from the subframe.

16. Remove the bracket from the transaxle, push tension system cable and bracket off the retainer on transaxle. The retainer can only be removed with the transaxle out of the vehicle.

17. Remove the right side transaxle bracket.

18. Pull transaxle off dowel sleeves.

19. Lower transaxle and take out from below.

To install:

20. Installation is the reverse of the removal procedure. Before

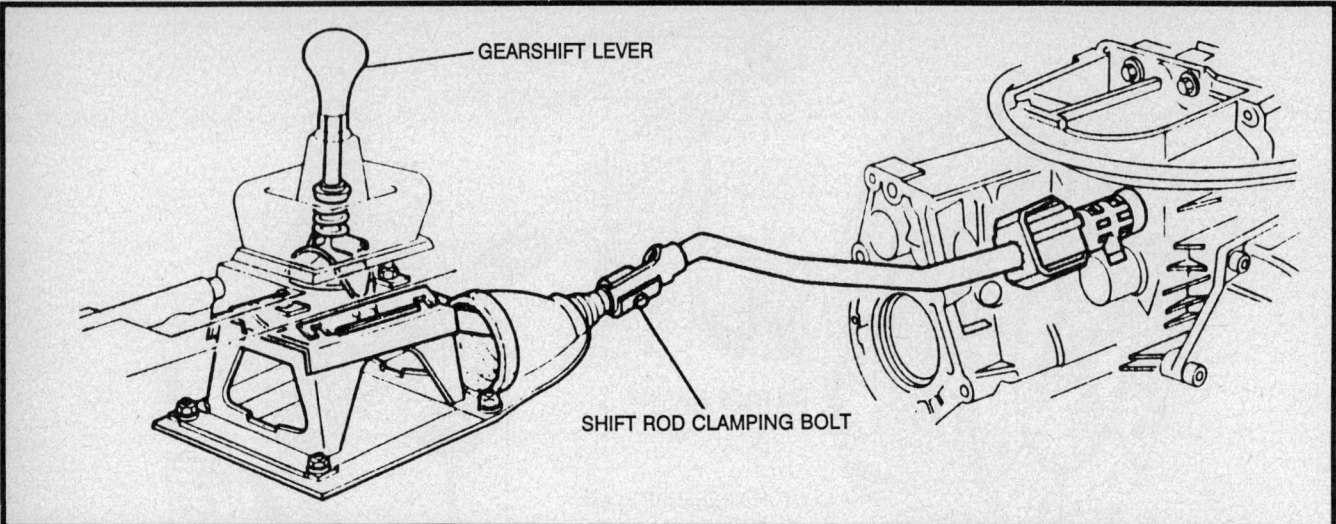

GEARSHIFT LEVER

SHIFT ROD CLAMPING BOLT

Manual shift linkage—80, 90, 100 and 200

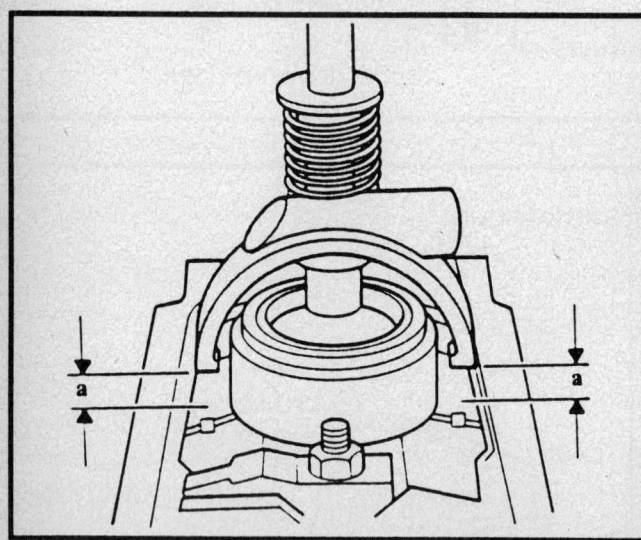

Keep shifter centered for proper adjustment

installing the transaxle, rest both halfshafts on top of the subframe.

21. Lubricate mainshaft splines.
22. Install transaxle onto dowels and install the lower bolts.
23. Install the tensioning system bracket and cable to the transaxle.
24. Tighten the transaxle bracket and subframe upper bolts to 29 ft. lbs.
25. Check alignment of transaxle and torque transaxle-to-engine bolts to 40 ft. lbs.
26. Torque subframe-to-body bolts to 80 ft. lbs.
27. Torque halfshaft-to-drive flange bolts to 58 ft. lbs.

Linkage Adjustments

4000, COUPE, 80 AND 90 VEHICLES EXCEPT QUATTRO

1. Place the shift lever into the neutral position.
2. Working under the vehicle, loosen the clamp nut on the shift rod. Be certain that the shift finger slides freely on the shift rod.
3. Working inside the vehicle, remove the gear shift lever knob and the boot.

View of the shift rod coupling—4000 Sedan and Coupe GT

4. Loosen the shifter base plate bolts slightly. Align the holes in the plate with the holes in the bearing housing and tighten the bolts.
5. Using the alignment tool 3057, slip it over the gearshift lever and make sure the locating pin is in the front centering hole.
6. Position the shift lever to the right detent cut out for 5th and reverse and tighten the lower knurled nut of the tool.
7. At the top of the tool, move the slide with the gear shift lever to the right stop. Tighten the upper knurled nut of the tool.
8. Position the gear shift lever into the left cut-out of the slide. Adjust the shift rod and the shift finger with the transaxle in neutral and tighten the clamp nut.
9. Remove the tool and check the shifting of the gears for smoothness.

5000

1. Remove the gear shift boot.
2. Position the shift lever in neutral.
3. The seam on the plastic stop bracket should line up with the center hole in the curved stop plate. If not, proceed below:

NOTE: On the Quattro, adjust the adjusting rod (center-to-center) to 5.275 in. (134mm) and install the rod.

4. Loosen the 4 bolts at the base of the shifter.
5. Align the holes in the shifter base with the holes in the bearing plate directly below it.

Loosen the clamp nut on the shift rod—4000

6. Tighten the bolts.
7. Loosen the clamp between the front and rear shift rods; the rear shift rod must move freely.
8. Make certain the front shift rod is in the neutral position.
9. Using the shifter locating tool 3048, place it on the stop plate with the shift lever resting in the notch. Tighten the shift rod clamp.

NOTE: On the 1987–88 vehicles, a bearing pin is used. Adjust the projection of this pin to $^{11}/_{16}$ in. The bearing pin is attached to the shift lever lower bearing and faces the rear of the vehicle.

10. Release the shifter and check its operation in all gears.

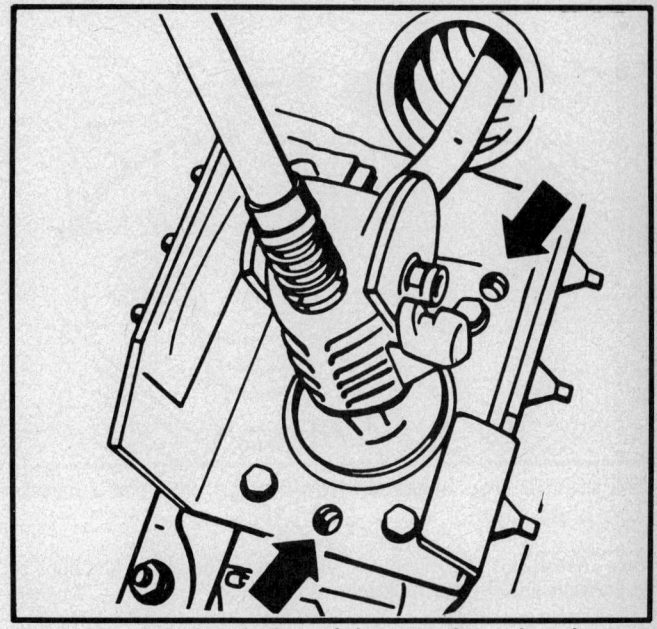

Align the centering holes of the stop lever bearing (arrows), then tighten the bolts on 5000

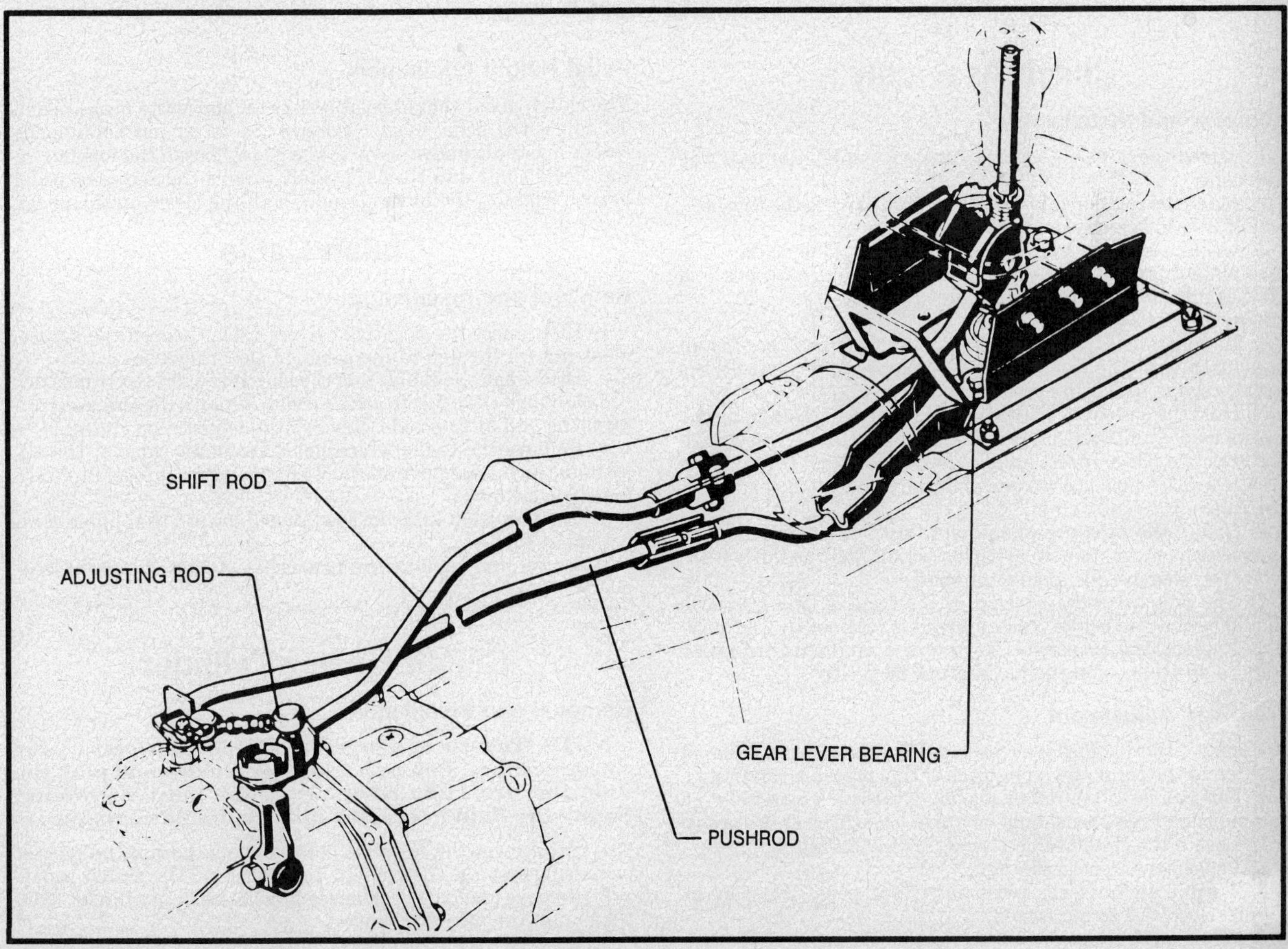

SHIFT ROD

ADJUSTING ROD

GEAR LEVER BEARING

PUSHROD

Linkage adjustment point at the transaxle—5000 5- speed

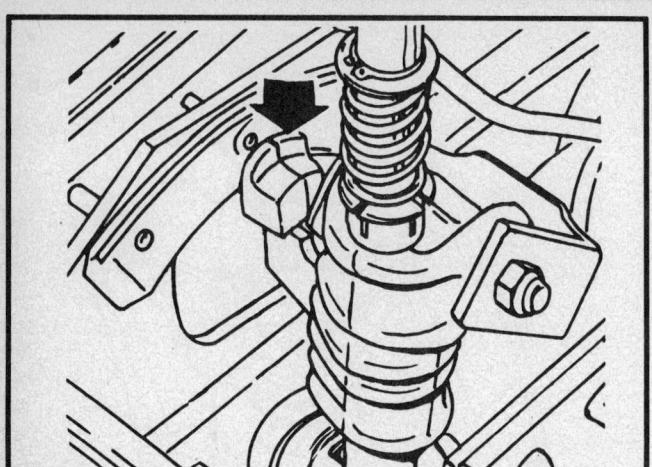

The plastic stop bracket should align with the curved stop plate—5000

11. Install the shifter boot, making sure the top of the boot is in contact with the shift knob.

QUATTRO, QUATTRO TURBO AND QUATTRO COUPE VEHICLES

1. Place the shift lever in neutral. Adjust the length of the adjusting rod so the distance between the center point of the end holes is 5.275 in.
2. Loosen the clamp nut, making sure the shift rod moves freely. Loosen the bolts slightly, align the centering holes of the gear shift lever housing and stop plate and tighten the bolts.
3. Install tool 3048 or equivalent, tighten the clamp nut and remove the tool. Engage 1st gear, press the shaft lever to the left, stop and release the shift lever.
4. Engage 5th gear, press the shaft lever to the right, stop and release the shift lever.
5. If the lever does not spring back approximately the same distance as in Steps 3 and 4, move the gear shift lever housing slightly in the slots sideward.
6. Make sure all gears engage easily without jamming.

100 AND 200

The shift rod is no longer splined on newer vehicles.
1. Loosen the shift rod clamping bolt.
2. Place the gear shift in a vertical position so the dimensions are equal on both sides and retighten shift rod clamp bolt.

CLUTCH

Clutch Assembly

Removal and Installation

1. Disconnect the negative battery cable. Remove the transaxle.
2. Mark the relationship of the pressure plate to the flywheel, only if it is to be reused.
3. Using a suitable tool, lock the flywheel. Unbolt the pressure plate from the flywheel, loosening the bolts alternately, a little at a time, to prevent warpage.
To install:
4. Installation is the reverse of the removal procedure. Install the clutch with the driven plate on the pressure plate so the spring cage is facing the pressure plate.
5. Hold the clutch assembly against the flywheel, aligning the marks made in Step 2 and the dowel pins on the flywheel with the pressure plate. Insert an alignment shaft tool through the pressure plate and the driven plate into the crankshaft pilot bearing.
6. Install the pressure plate bolts finger tight. Tighten the bolts evenly, in rotation, to avoid distortion. Torque the bolts to 18 ft. lbs. Remove the alignment shaft.
7. The clutch release bearing in the front of the transaxle should be checked before reassembly. It is retained by 2 springs.
8. Replace the transaxle. Torque the engine-to-transaxle bolts to 40 ft. lbs. and the halfshaft to 58 ft. lbs.

Free-Play Adjustment

Free-play is the distance that the pedal travels from the released position to the point at which clutch spring pressure can first be felt. This can be measured by placing a yardstick alongside the clutch pedal. Free-play should be $9/16$ in. measured at the pedal.
1. Locate the clutch cable bracket by the oil filter.
2. Loosen the upper cable nut.
3. Turn both nuts clockwise to reduce pedal free-play or counterclockwise to increase it.
4. When adjustment is correct, tighten the upper nut to lock the cable in position.

Pedal Height Adjustment

The clutch pedal should be at rest $3/8$ in. above the brake pedal. To adjust the pedal height, remove the cotter pin holding the clutch master cylinder clevis to the pedal, loosen the locknut on the clevis shaft and turn the shaft to give the required pedal height. Tighten the locknut and install the clevis on the pedal.

Clutch Cable

Removal and Installation

1. Disconnect the negative battery cable. Loosen the adjustment nut on the end of the cable, at the transaxle.
2. Disengage the cable from the clutch arm on the transaxle.
3. Unhook the cable from the pedal. Remove the threaded eye from the end of the cable. Remove the adjustment nut(s).
4. Remove the C-clip which holds the outer cable at the adjustment point. Remove all the washers and bushings, first noting their locations.
5. Pull the cable out from the firewall toward the engine compartment side.
6. Install and connect the new cable. Adjust the pedal free-play.

Clutch Master Cylinder

Removal and Installation

NOTE: The use of a pressure bleeder is necessary for this procedure. Before beginning, remove and plug the fluid line from the reservoir to the master cylinder. Empty the fluid in the line into a suitable container.

1. Disconnect the negative battery cable. Locate the master cylinder under the instrument panel, behind the clutch pedal.
2. Remove and plug the line leading to the slave cylinder from the end of the master cylinder.
3. Remove the circlip and the pin which attaches the clevis to the clutch pedal.

4. Remove the 2 master cylinder mounting bolts from the pedal mounting.

5. Remove and plug the reservoir line. Remove the master cylinder.

6. Installation is in the reverse order of removal. Tighten the master cylinder mounting bolts to 15 ft. lbs.

7. Bleed the clutch system when finished.

Clutch Slave Cylinder

Removal and Installation

1. Disconnect the negative battery cable. Locate the slave cylinder on top of the transaxle housing.

2. Remove the retaining clip from the pin.

3. Drive out the slave cylinder lock pin, using a small punch.

4. Remove and plug the fluid line at the slave cylinder. This step is necessary only if the cylinder is being replaced.

5. Lightly grease the machined surfaces of the transaxle housing and the slave cylinder.

6. Install the fluid line on the slave cylinder. Install the slave cylinder in the transaxle. Install the retaining pin.

7. The remainder of the installation is the reverse of the removal procedure.

8. If the fluid line was removed, bleed the system.

Hydraulic Clutch System Bleeding

The clutch system should be bled using a pressure bleeder. Follow the instructions that come with the bleeder tank, for the proper bleeding procedure. The maximum line pressure must not exceed 36 psi.

AUTOMATIC TRANSAXLE

For further information, please refer to "Professional Transmission Repair Manual" for additional coverage.

Transaxle Assembly

Removal and Installation

089 SERIES TRANSAXLE

1. Disconnect the negative battery cable.

2. Remove the upper engine-to-transaxle bolts. Raise and support the vehicle safely.

3. Using a suitable engine support tool, secure it to the engine and the vehicle.

4. At the front of the engine, remove both top bolts. Remove the starter.

5. Through the starter opening, remove the torque converter to drive plate bolts and remove torque converter cover plate.

6. Clamp off the coolant hoses at the ATF cooler and remove the hoses from the cooler.

7. Remove the speedometer cable from the transaxle.

8. Remove the inner halfshaft-to-transaxle bolts. Using a wire, tie up the halfshafts.

9. At the left control arm, mark the position of the ball joint and remove the ball joint and the support.

10. Place an oil catch pan under the transaxle, remove the oil filler tube from the oil pan and drain the fluid.

11. Remove the exhaust pipe-to-transaxle bracket.

12. Remove the selector cable bracket from the transaxle. At the transaxle shift lever, remove the selector cable circlip and the cable.

13. At the transaxle, remove the accelerator cable bracket and the cable from the operating lever.

14. From the transaxle mount, remove the center bolt. Using the engine support tool, lift the engine slightly.

15. Remove the throttle cable bracket bolts and the bracket.

16. Support the transaxle and lift it slightly. Remove the lower transaxle-to-engine bolts.

17. Separate the engine from the transaxle and lower it from the vehicle. Be sure to secure the torque converter.

To install:

18. Installation is the reverse of the removal procedure. When installing the transaxle, should the torque converter slip off the one-way clutch support, the oil pump shaft could be pulled from the oil pump. This may cause severe damage when bolting the transaxle to the engine.

19. Tighten the engine-to-transaxle bolts to 41 ft. lbs., the subframe bolts to 52 ft. lbs., the torque converter-to-driveplate bolts to 22 ft. lbs., the halfshaft-to-transaxle bolts to 33 ft. lbs., the ball joint to control arm bolts to 48 ft. lbs. and the transaxle mount center bolt to 30 ft. lbs.

20. Refill the transaxle.

21. Adjust the accelerator linkage and align the engine-to-transaxle mounts, if necessary.

ATU 018 SERIES TRANSAXLE

V8 Quattro All Wheel Drive

1. Disconnect the negative battery cable. The battery is under the rear bench seat.

2. Raise and safely support vehicle. Remove the front wheels.

3. Remove the cross struts for the spring strut domes.

4. Remove the air cleaner housing and air cleaner assembly.

5. Remove the supports for the ignition cables and the left and right distributor caps. Remove the throttle cable and support.

6. Disconnect the oxygen sensor and probe heater. Remove the cable clamp for the electrical cables running alongside.

7. Disconnect the 2-pin plug connection at the transaxle bell housing. Disconnect the cable clamp for the wire harness next to the 2-pin plug.

8. Disconnect the retaining strap for the ventilation hose at the firewall.

9. Loosen the transaxle filler pipe on the cylinder head

10. Remove the radiator fan. The left fan can be set aside while still connected.

11. Remove the right engine mounting bolts on the body.

12. Raise and safely support vehicle. Remove the lower engine cover, the crossmember, the front exhaust pipe with catalytic converter and the heat deflector for the driveshaft.

13. Remove the driveshaft by loosening the driveshaft mounting bolts on the transaxle, rear final drive and body.

NOTE: A special driveshaft assembly device or aligning jig is required, tool 3213. This tool keeps the multipiece driveshaft straight and in proper alignment. Attach this jig to the driveshaft and tighten the nuts. Remove the bolts on the transaxle and rear final drive. Support the driveshaft and alignment jig, remove the mounting bolts from the body and carefully lower the the driveshaft from the vehicle. Take note of any shims. Always move and store the driveshaft flat.

14. Detach the selector lever cable and support bracket at the transaxle, and remove the oil filter. Remove the upper bolt on the starter by guiding a 10mm Allen® socket with extension and

flex fitting through the opening, on the transaxle housing, over the final drive. Remove the bolt and take out the starter.

15. Working through the starter opening, remove the 6 torque converter bolts.

16. Remove the mounting bolts on both sides of the transaxle mounting.

17. Attach a lifting hoist to the engine mounting on the left side and lift slighty.

18. Under the vehicle, support the subframe using a suitable transaxle jack. Remove the mounting bolts on the subframe and lower the subframe carefully until it hangs freely. Disconnect the halfshafts from the transaxle and tie up.

19. Drain the transaxle and remove the filler pipe. Unscrew the cooling lines, the retaining clip that holds both lines together and tie to the subframe, aside.

20. Remove the left and right transaxle mounts.

21. Disconnect the eight-pin electrical connector on the transaxle by turning counterclockwise.

22. Disconnect the plug on the speed sensor. Push the locking lever down and remove the plug from the multi-function transaxle switch. Remove the retainers for the electrical wires from the transaxle and unclamp the ventilation hose.

23. Remove the tabs on the seat belt tensioning cables and disconnect the cables.

24. Remove the speed and TDC sensor with heat deflector plate on the engine. Remove the 2 upper engine-to-transaxle bolts.

25. Support the transaxle with a suitable transaxle jack. Remove the remaining engine-to-transaxle connecting bolts and remove the transaxle from the engine. Lower the transaxle carefully and secure the torque converter to keep it from falling out. Use caution not to damage the halfshafts, bolt-on parts or the multi-function switch.

To install:

26. Installation is the reverse of the removal process. If a new replacement transaxle is being installed, the following must be carried out. Transfer the catalytic converter mountings on the left and right side of the housing. Transfer the pipes for the transaxle cooler and the support for the seat belt tensioning cables. Check that both guide sleeves are installed in the engine block at the 2 o'clock and 8 o'clock positions, viewed from the flywheel.

27. Make sure the torque converter is secured and install the transaxle in reverse order. Note that if only the torque converter is replaced, it should be carefully positioned on the free-wheel support and should not be tilted. To engage the splines of the pump shaft, rotate the torque converter forward and backward slightly. The torque converter must be inserted onto the free-wheel support up to the stop.

28. Install the transaxle and make sure the halfshafts, any bolt-on parts and the multi-function switch all work freely.

29. Install and adjust the driveshaft. Align with care. Use the following procedure:

a. With the alignment jig holding the driveshaft straight, set the driveshaft in place.

b. Carefully, measure the distance between the body pan bolt holes and the mounting ears of the center support bracket. This distance should be the same left to right.

c. Five different shims are available: 2, 4, 6, 8 and 10mm. Determine the thickness of the required shims.

d. Push the driveshaft all the way to the rear up to the stop. Mark the position of the center mounting bracket on the floor pan.

e. Push the driveshaft forward all the way and park the position of the center mounting bracket on the floor pan. The center mounting must be midway between these 2 marks.

f. Insert the bolts and shims as determined beforehand and tighten to 15 ft. lbs. Remove the alignment jig.

30. Fill the unit with automatic transaxle fluid.

31. Adjust the selector cable. Check the throttle cable linkage and, if necessary, adjust. Install and tighten all bolts for the lower engine cover. Check engine oil level. Align front end.

32. Tightening torques are:

a. Cross brace to suspension strut domes-to-17 ft. lbs.

b. Engine mounting-to-body to 30 ft. lbs.

c. Torque converter-to-driveplate to 26 ft. lbs.

d. Transaxle mounting-to-subframe to 30 ft. lbs.

e. Transaxle support for mounting-to-transaxle to 30 ft. lbs.

f. Subframe-to-body to 48 ft. lbs. plus ¼ turn.

g. Halfshaft-to-transaxle to 59 ft. lbs.

h. Driveshaft-to-transaxle to 41 ft. lbs.

i. Transaxle-to-engine to 44 ft. lbs.

j. Support for seat belt cables to 30 ft. lbs.

k. Side threaded bushings to 111 ft. lbs.

Shift Linkage Adjustment

The function of this adjustment is to make sure the transaxle is fully engaged in each shift position. If this is not done, the transaxle may be only partially engaged in a certain range position. This would result in severe damage due to slippage.

VEHICLES WITHOUT SHIFTLOCK

Except V8 Quattro

1. Remove the floor console. Place the selector lever in **P**.
2. Loosen the cable clamp nut at the transaxle end.
3. Press the selector lever on the transaxle into the **P** position to the stop.
4. Tighten the clamp nut to 6 ft. lbs. Install the console.

V8 Quattro

1. Position floor shift lever in **P**.
2. Pry the socket off of the transaxle selector lever cable with a suitable prying tool.
3. Position the floor shift lever in **N** as follows: Push the selector knob forward until the final stop **P** is reached, then move from **R** to **N**. Position the selector lever at **N**.
4. Check that the socket on the cable and the ball on the transaxle shift lever are aligned. If they are aligned, attach the selector lever cable to the ball head by hand. It must lock in place.
5. If the socket and ball are not aligned, adjust the selector cable as follows:

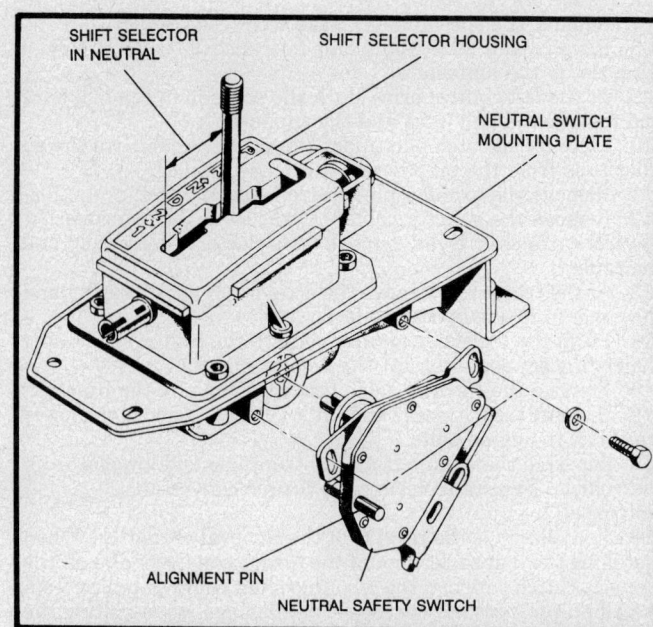

SHIFT SELECTOR IN NEUTRAL — SHIFT SELECTOR HOUSING — NEUTRAL SWITCH MOUNTING PLATE — ALIGNMENT PIN — NEUTRAL SAFETY SWITCH

Automatic transaxle neutral safety switch – 1987–88

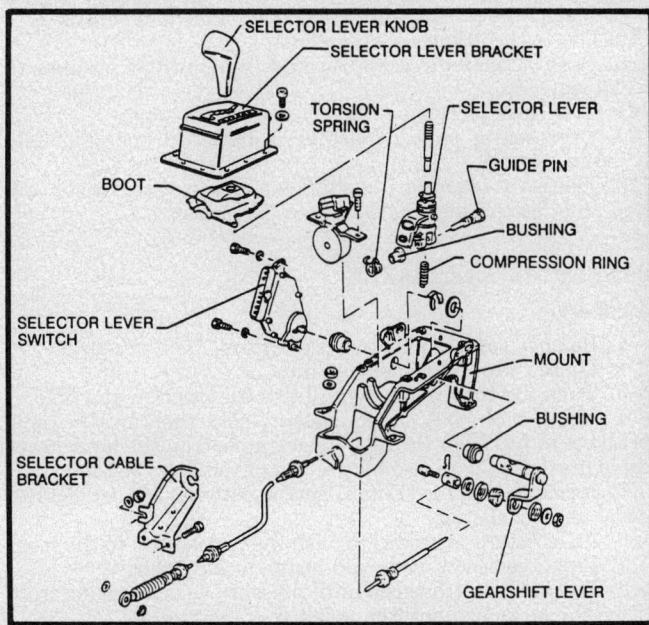

Shiftlock II automatic shifter assembly

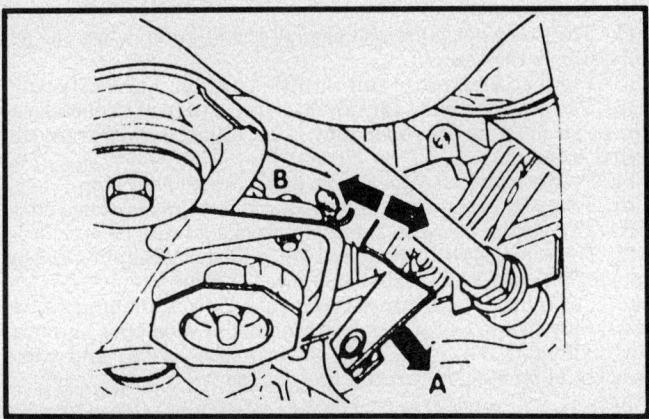

Adjusting transaxle pushrod

   a. Loosen the 2 small bolts on the support bracket of the cable until the bracket can be easily moved.
   b. Push the socket forward or rearward until the head and socket are exactly aligned.
   c. Retighten the bolts on the support bracket. Snap the socket onto the ball head.
   6. Switch ignition to ON.
   7. Depress brake pedal and hold until the end of this checking procedure. Move the selector slowly and check whether the selector lever position display corresponds to the selector lever position. If not, repeat the adjustment or adjust the multi-function switch.

VEHICLES WITH SHIFTLOCK II

1988–1991

The Shiftlock II system is dependent on fuse S12, brake light switch circuit, interior light relay control unit, driver's door switch circuit and vehicle speed.

With ignition switch ON the selector cannot be shifted out of **P** or **N** unless the brake pedal is depressed. At speeds under 3.7 mph, when shifted into **N** the shifter should lock in **N** after 1 second, unless the brake pedal is depressed. At speeds above 3.7 mph the shifter should not lock.

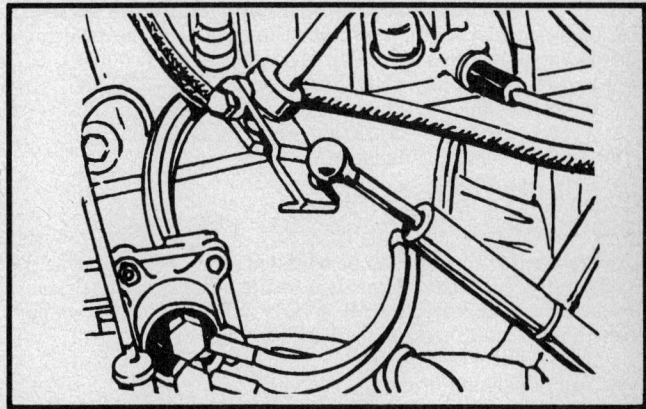

Kickdown detent linkage—typical

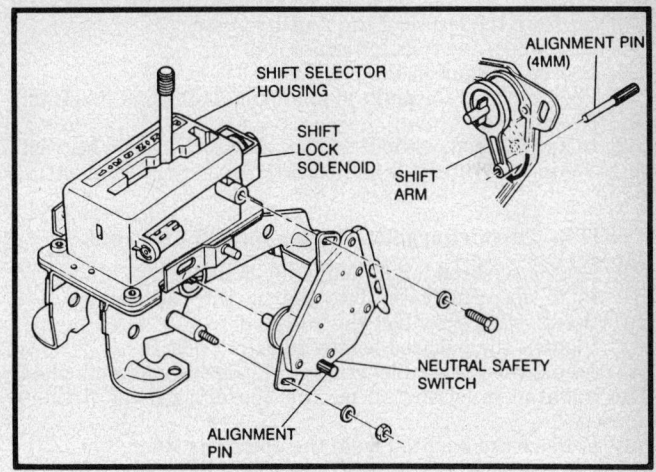

Adjusting neutral safety switch

   1. Adjust the solenoid switch, using a 1mm gauge between the selector lever and solenoid switch. With lever in **R**, push the solenoid against the gauge and tighten to 7 ft. lbs. (0.1 Nm).
   2. Center the lower bore of fork piece and supply voltage to switch. The solenoid pin locks the fork piece.
   3. Install the gear shift lever housing so selector lever is in the **N** position relative to the housing.
   4. Install the shift arm with a 4mm aligning pin through the housing bore.
   5. Shift the selector lever to the **N** position.
   6. Install the selector lever switch so the mount locks into the lever shaft.
   7. Tighten the mounting bolts to 44 in. lbs. (5 Nm).
   8. Remove aligning pin.
   9. Check for correct operation.
   10. If shifter does not function properly, it may be necessary to check the electronic control systems.

Kickdown Switch Adjustment

1987–88 VEHICLES

   1. Position the accelerator pedal in the fully released position.
   2. Check the distance between the pedal lower edge and the pedal stop. Clearance should be 3.0 in.
   3. If not, loosen the lock bolt which holds the cable at the pedal and place the pedal to give the 3 in. clearance. Tighten the lock bolt.
   4. Press the pedal to the full throttle position, but not into the kickdown detent. The kickdown take-up spring should not be compressed and the throttle valve should be wide open.

5. Press the accelerator lever to the stop (kickdown position); the operating lever must contact the stop and the pushrod's kickdown spring must be compressed to:

    a. 1987 4000, 80, 90, transaxle series 087—$^{13}/_{32}$ in.

    b. 1987 4000, 80, 90, transaxle series 089—$^{5}/_{16}$ in.

    c. 1987–88 5000, transaxle series 087—$^{5}/_{16}$ in.

6. Adjust the shift linkage.

087 SERIES TRANSAXLE

1989–91

The accelerator control is to be adjusted so at closed throttle the operating lever on the transaxle is at the no–throttle position. If adjustment is incorrect, shift speeds will be too high at part throttle and main pressure will be too high at idle.

1. Put selector in **P**.
2. Apply parking brake.
3. Adjust accelerator control in idle position with closed throttle.
4. Disconnect the locks on ball sockets and and disconnect the pull rod from the levers of the routing guide.
5. Disconnect the rods for cruise control.
6. Loosen locknut on the pull rod.
7. Position lever for pull rod approximately 0.040 in. (1mm) before stop.
8. Install pull rod, without tension. Ball socket must be twisted to be in line with ball and throttle lever must contact the stop.

NOTE: Turbocharged vehicles have 2 pull rods.

9. Loosen pushrod length adjusting bolt B.
10. Push operating lever into the no throttle position, the throttle valve must contact the idle stop.
11. Tighten the pushrod length adjusting bolt B.
12. Adjust the pushrod length by shifting the adjusting plate. The pushrod must install on the operating lever without tension.
13. Remove the pushrod from the operating lever.
14. Have an assistant depress the accelerator pedal to the stop.
15. Depress the operating lever to the kickdown stop.
16. Using pliers, pull the accelerator pedal cable back and fasten.
17. Check that the operating lever is in contact with the kickdown stop, readjust the pedal cable, if necessary.

18. Install the pushrod onto operating lever and secure.
19. Check throttle lever operation.
20. Push accelerator cable through full throttle position to kickdown stop.
21. Transaxle lever must be in contact with stop.
22. Over center spring must be compressed approximately 0.320 in. (8mm).
23. Release accelerator pedal and install rod to cruise control. Rod must be tension free, adjust as necessary.

089 SERIES TRANSAXLE

1988–91

1. Remove covering for throttle control.
2. Loosen the 2 cable locking nuts.
3. Turn the throttle to the full throttle position and hold.
4. Using tool 3004 or equivalent, hold the throttle cable brackets at full open throttle. Attach an end on the lever lower cable bracket and an end on the end of the hood gas strut.
5. Insert a $^{11}/_{16}$ in. (17mm) spacer between the accelerator pedal and pedal stop.
6. An assistant is needed to push the pedal down to the stop.
7. Pull accelerator cable and install locking clip.
8. Pull cable to transaxle until pressure against spring from transaxle kickdown position is felt.
9. Tighten the nut on cable side against the bracket, next tighten the nut on pivot side against bracket.
10. Remove tool.
11. Throttle lever must rest against the idle stop when the accelerator is released.
12. Press accelerator to full throttle position, not kickdown.
13. The pressure point for full throttle position of the accelerator pedal must be approximately ¾ in. (19mm) away from the pedal stop.
14. Press the accelerator to the pedal (kickdown) stop.
15. Transaxle operating lever must contact the kickdown stop.
16. The spring between the cable brackets must be stressed.
17. For vehicles with cruise control, adjust the coupling rod by moving the ball end 0.039–0.059 in. (1–1.5mm).
18. For vehicles with cruise control the air conditioning switch must only switch ON at kickdown and not at wide-open throttle, approximately $^{3}/_{16}$ in. (2mm) between the switch and cable bracket at wide-open throttle (not kickdown).

DRIVE AXLE

Front Halfshaft

Removal and Installation

4000, COUPE, 80 AND 90

Except Quattro Turbo

NOTE: Never remove or install the axle nut with the wheel off the ground. The vehicle must be resting on the ground for these operations.

1. Remove the halfshaft end nut or bolt.
2. Unbolt and remove the halfshaft-to-transaxle drive flange bolts.
3. Mark the position of the ball joint on the control arm, remove the 2 retaining nuts and remove the ball joint.
4. On 80 and 90, remove the ball joint-to-steering knuckle bolt and separate the knuckle from the ball joint. Remove the mounting bolts for the control arm/stablizer and push control arm downward, if necessary.

NOTE: On 4000 equipped with manual transaxles, only remove the right side ball joint. Use puller 1389 or equivalent, to remove haftshaft, if necessary. Never use heat.

5. Pull the pivot mounting outward and remove the halfshaft.

To install:

6. Installation is the reverse of the removal procedure.
7. When installing the right halfshaft, take care not to damage the boot on the cover plate.
8. Tighten the ball joint-to-control arm/knuckle nuts/bolt to 47 ft. lbs. Tighten the halfshaft flange bolts to 33 ft. lbs.
9. Always use a new self-locking axle nut/bolt and tighten to 167 ft. lbs.
10. Check for proper alignment when finished.

Quattro Turbo

1. With the vehicle on the ground, loosen the halfshaft end nut.

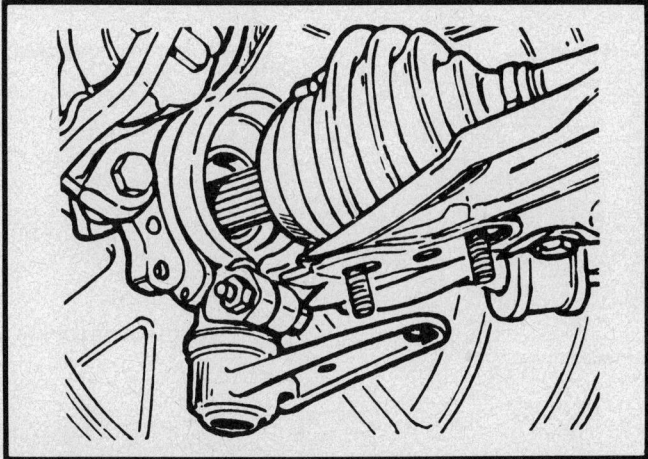

Remove the halfshafts by pivoting the control arm outward

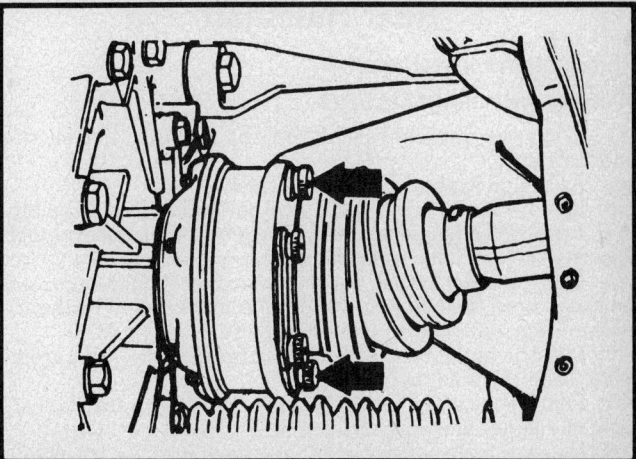

Remove the halfshaft retaining bolts at the transaxle

2. Raise and support the vehicle safely.

3. Remove the end nut and the wheel assembly. Remove the right backing plate.

4. Remove the halfshaft-to-transaxle flange bolts. Support the halfshaft with wire.

5. Using a halfshaft press tool, attach it to the wheel hub and press the halfshaft from the hub.

6. Using the locking compound D-6, apply a ¼ in. bead around the front edge of the spline section of the halfshaft.

NOTE: After applying the locking compound, allow it to dry for at least an hour.

7. To install, reverse the removal procedure. Be sure to replace the inner CV-joint gasket. Tighten the halfshaft-to-transaxle flange bolts to 58 ft. lbs., the halfshaft-to-wheel hub nut to 203 ft. lbs. and the wheel bolts to 80 ft. lbs.

5000, 100 AND 200

Except 100 and 200 Quattro

NOTE: Never remove or install the halfshaft nut with the wheel off the ground. The vehicle must be resting on the ground for these operations. A puller is required for this procedure.

1. Remove the halfshaft end nut.

2. Raise and support the vehicle safely. Remove the wheels.

3. On the right side, remove the halfshaft skid plate.

4. Disconnect the halfshaft from the transaxle. Using wire, support the halfshaft.

5. Using a 4-armed puller mounted on the wheel hub, press the halfshaft out of the hub.

6. Guide the inside end of the shaft up over the transaxle and out of the hub.

7. If equipped with an automatic transaxle, perform the following:

    a. Remove the stabilizer bar clamps.

    b. Remove the ball joint-to-hub bolt. Remove the ball joint from the hub.

    c. Press the halfshaft from the hub.

    d. Swing the suspension strut outward and press the halfshaft from the hub.

8. When installing, make certain that the splines are clean and free of grease. Apply a ¼ in. bead of RTV silicone sealant around the leading edge of the splines. Allow it to harden at least 1 hour. Torque the shaft-to-transaxle bolts to 32 ft. lbs. and the axle nut to 203 ft. lbs.

Quattro Turbo

1. Remove the wheel cover and loosen the lug nuts. Remove the dust cover and the halfshaft nut or through bolt, if equipped.

2. Raise and support the vehicle safely. Remove the lug nuts and wheel assembly. Remove the right backing plate.

3. Disconnect the halfshaft at the transaxle flange and position it aside.

4. Using a suitable puller, press out the stub axle from the hub. Use only a mechanical or hydraulic puller to remove the stub axle. Never use hot air blower or a flame to heat the stub axle.

5. Installation is the reverse of the removal procedure, with the following exceptions:

    a. Replace the gasket on the inner CV-joint.

    b. Make sure the splines on the stub axle and the wheel hub are free of oil, grease and old locking compound.

    c. Apply a bead of suitable locking compound approximately ¹³⁄₆₄ in. wide around the splines and install the stub halfshaft. Allow at least 1 hour for the locking compound to harden.

    d. Tighten the halfshaft to transaxle bolts to 58 ft. lbs. Tighten the lug nuts to 80 ft. lbs. and halfshaft end nut to 207 ft. lbs.

V8 Quattro

1. Remove the wheel cover from the wheel rim. Remove the hexagon through bolt and washer from the halfshaft end. Loosen and tighten only when the vehicle is standing on the wheels.

2. Slightly pull back the wheel speed sensor. Remove both stabilizer bar brackets.

3. Remove the clamp bolt at the steering knuckle and press out the ball joint pivot pin for the lower control arm. Be careful not to damage the joint boot or seal. Never widen the slit in the steering knuckle housing. Use penetrating oil as required.

4. Remove the halfshaft from the transaxle drive flange.

5. Push the strut outward and remove the halfshaft.

To install:

6. Installation is the reverse of the removal procedure. Always use a new gasket at the transaxle drive flange. Pull off the protective film from the replacement gasket and stick to CV-joint.

7. When replacing the ball joint, install the lock bolt with the head facing to the rear of the vehicle. When installing the halfshaft through bolt, always use a new bolt and tighten when the vehicle's weight is on the floor. Torque to 150 ft. lbs., plus ¼ turn.

8. After installing the halfshaft, insert the wheel speed sensor into the housing as far as possible.

Rear Halfshaft

Removal and Installation

4000, 80 AND 90 QUATTRO

1. With the vehicle resting on the ground, loosen the halfshaft nut.
2. Raise and support the vehicle safely.
3. Remove the halfshaft nut, wheel bolts and wheel assembly.
4. Remove the ball joint nut. Using a ball joint removal tool, separate the ball joint from the strut.
5. Using a suitable tool, pry downward on the lower control arm to remove the ball joint from the control arm, if necessary loosen lower control arm mounting bolts.
6. Pull the brake hose and parking brake cable, with grommets, from the holding fixture.
7. Remove the inner halfshaft flange bolts. Separate the shaft from the flange and support it.
8. Using an halfshaft pulling tool, attach it to the wheel hub and press the halfshaft out of the hub.
9. Clean the halfshaft splines of any grease, dirt or locking compound. Using the locking compound D-6, apply a ¼ in. bead around the outer edge of the splines.

NOTE: Allow the locking compound to dry for an hour before installation.

10. To install, use a new inner flange gasket and reverse the removal procedures. Tighten the inner halfshaft flange bolts to 58 ft. lbs., the halfshaft to hub nut to 203 ft. lbs. (4000) or 238 ft. lbs. (80 and 90), the wheel bolts to 80 ft. lbs. and the ball joint nut to 47 ft. lbs.

5000 QUATTRO

1. With the vehicle weight on the ground, loosen the halfshaft end nut.
2. Raise and support the vehicle safely.
3. Remove the halfshaft nut, wheel bolts and wheel assembly.
4. Remove the brake caliper-to-strut retaining bolts and remove the caliper, without disconnecting the line. Using wire, support the caliper.
5. Remove the brake rotor. Remove the inner halfshaft flange bolts and support the halfshaft.

NOTE: When removing the right side halfshaft, remove the fuel tank cover plate first.

6. Remove the transverse link to wheel bearing housing nut and remove the link.
7. Remove the trapezoidal arm to crossmember nut and bolt. Pry the arm downward.
8. Using a halfshaft pulling tool, attach it to the wheel hub and remove the halfshaft from the hub.
9. Clean the halfshaft splines of any grease, dirt or locking compound. Using the locking compound D-6, apply a ¼ in. bead around the outer edge of the splines.

NOTE: Allow the locking compound to dry for an hour before installation.

10. To install, use a new inner flange gasket and reverse the removal procedures.
11. Tighten the halfshaft flange bolts to 58 ft. lbs., the halfshaft to hub nut to 266 ft. lbs., the wheel bolts to 80 ft. lbs., the brake caliper-to-wheel bearing housing bolt to 48 ft. lbs., the trapezoidal arm-to-crossmember nut to 63 ft. lbs. and the transverse link-to-wheel bearing housing nut to 148 ft. lbs.

100 AND 200 QUATTRO

1. With the vehicle weight on the ground, loosen the halfshaft end nut.
2. Raise and support the vehicle safely.
3. Remove the halfshaft nut, wheel bolts and wheel assembly.

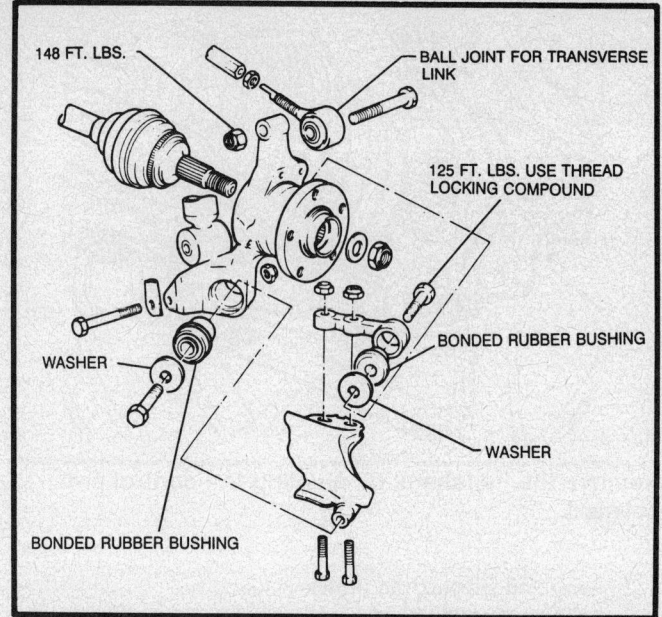

Exploded view of the rear suspension— 5000 CS Turbo Quattro

4. Remove the brake caliper to strut retaining bolts and remove the caliper, without disconnecting the line. Using wire, support the caliper.
5. Remove the brake rotor. Remove the inner halfshaft flange bolts and support the halfshaft.
6. Remove the fuel tank cover plate, if necessary.
7. Remove the transverse link-to-wheel bearing housing nut and remove the link.
8. Remove the trapezoidal arm-to-crossmember nut and bolt. Pry the arm downward.
9. Remove the mounting bolt for suspension strut.
10. Before removing halfshaft, pull speed sensor out of the housing slightly.
11. Press down on wheel bearing housing and remove the halfshaft.
12. Clean the halfshaft splines of any grease, dirt or locking compound.

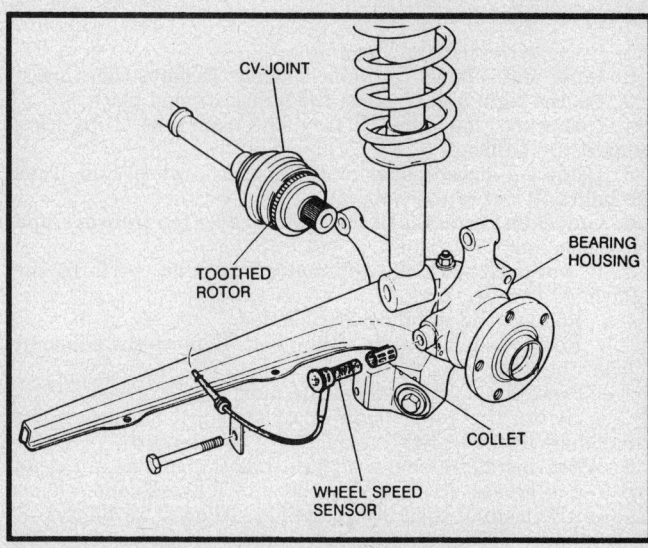

Rear axle speed sensor mounting—200

To install:

13. Use a new inner flange gasket and reverse the removal procedures.

14. Tighten the axleshaft flange bolts to 59 ft. lbs. (80 Nm).

15. Install caliper on housing.

NOTE: Some bolts are self-locking type; it is recommended to always use new self-locking type bolts.

16. Install new bolts and torque to 25 ft. lbs. (35 Nm).

17. Adjustment of parking brake assembly may be necessary.

18. Install the halfshaft bolt and washer assembly, tighten until just snug.

19. Make certain speed sensor sleeve is in place and install speed sensor , by hand, until seated

20. Install wheels.

21. Lower vehicle and torque halfshaft bolts to 147 ft. lbs. (200 Nm) and then tighten halfshaft bolts an additional ¼ turn (90 degrees).

CV-Boot

Removal and Installation

NOTE: Some vehicles are to have the entire halfshaft replaced, not serviced. Always check parts availability before removing CV-boots. If boots are available, use the following procedure.

1. Remove the halfshaft. Always loosen the halfshaft end locking nut or through bolt with the vehicle on the floor.

2. On the inner joint, remove the circlip from the inner CV-joint stub shaft. On a shop press, support the ball hub and press out the shaft. Remove the boot.

3. On the outer joint, spread the circlip and drive the joint off the shaft by tapping lightly with a soft copper or brass drift against the hub.

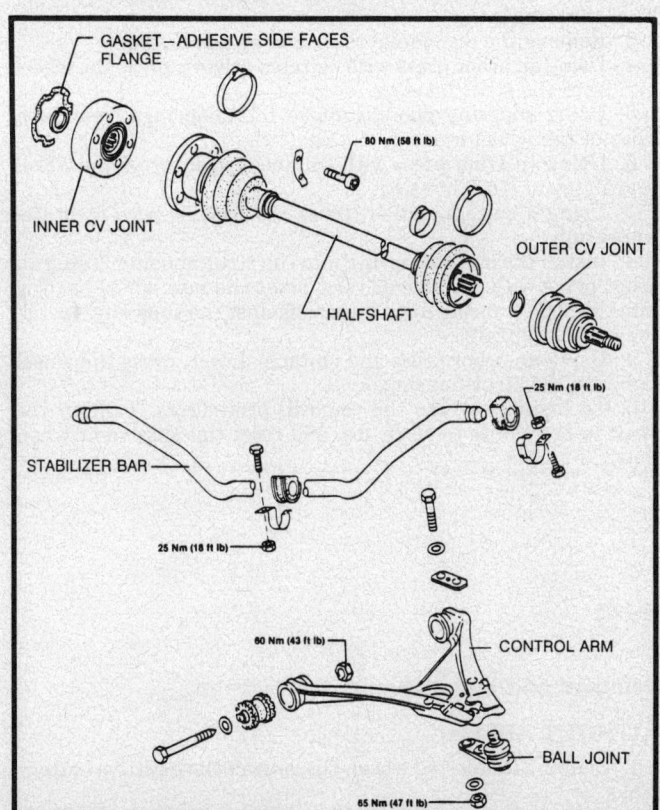

Rear drive axle—Quattro

To install:

4. Installation is the reverse of the removal process. Press the joint onto the shaft until the circlip can be pressed into the groove. The chamfer on the inside diameter of the ball hub splines must face the halfshaft.

5. After applying the correct amount of special lube, usually supplied with the replacement boots, tighten the boot band with an appropriate tool.

Driveshaft and U-Joints

Removal and Installation

QUATTRO

1. Raise and support the vehicle safely.

2. Using a scribing tool, mark the position of the driveshaft to the transaxle flange and the rear differential.

3. Remove the driveshaft flange mounting bolts from both ends and remove the driveshaft from the vehicle. Remove the center bearing bolts.

4. To install reverse the removal procedures. Note that the universal joints are not replaceable. If a universal joint is damaged or worn out, replace the driveshaft assembly.

5. Align scribe marks and install driveshaft.

6. Tighten the driveshaft-to-transaxle/differential flange bolts to 39 ft. lbs. (4000, 80, 90 Quattro) or 33 ft. lbs. (5000, 100, 200 and V8 Quattro) and the driveshaft center bearing to frame bolts to 14 ft. lbs.

Front Wheel Hub, Knuckle and Bearings

Removal and Installation

4000, COUPE, 80 AND 90

NOTE: 80 and 90 vehicles use 2 types of front wheel bearing housing assemblies. A single piece unit that cannot be separated from the strut and a bearing housing that is removable from the strut for service. The repair procedures are similar for both with the exception that the single piece unit housing, if defective, must be replaced as a strut assembly.

1. Raise and safely support vehicle. Remove the halfshafts.

2. Remove the strut housing to body nuts and remove the strut/hub assembly from the vehicle.

3. Remove the brake disc and splash shield.

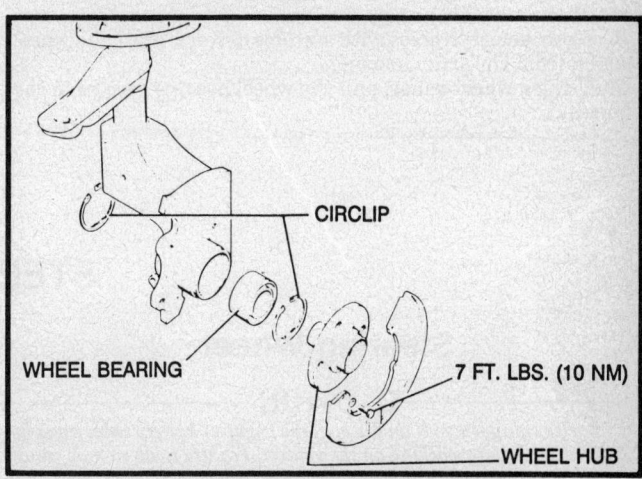

Exploded view of the front hub and bearing

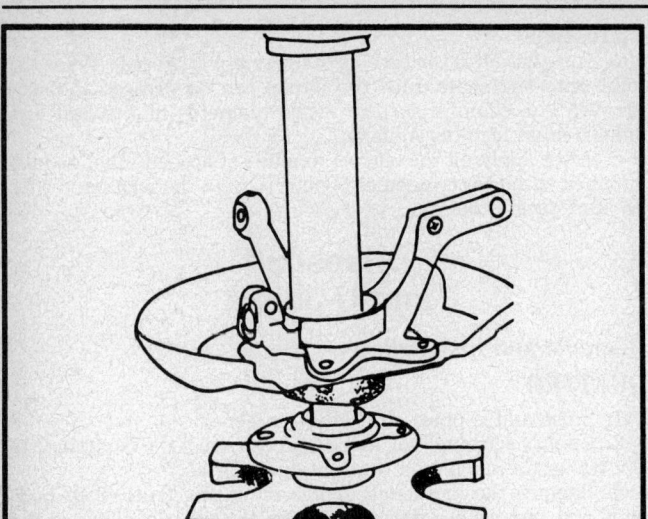

Pressing the hub from the spindle

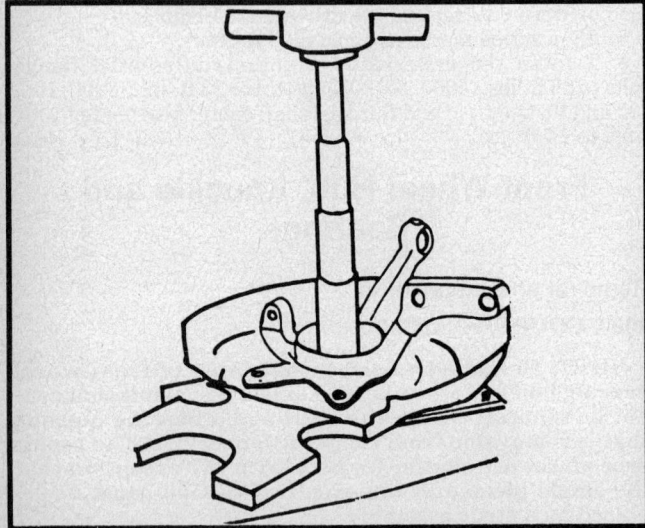

Pressing the bearing from the spindle

4. Using an arbor press with suitable drivers, press the wheel hub from the strut housing.
5. Using snapring pliers, remove the snaprings from both sides of the wheel bearing.
6. Using an arbor press with suitable drivers, press the wheel bearing from the strut housing.
7. Using a wheel puller, pull the wheel bearing race from the wheel hub.

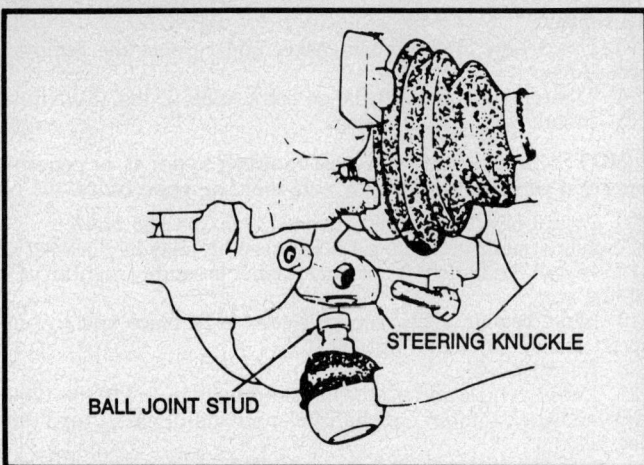

STEERING KNUCKLE

BALL JOINT STUD

Separate the ball joint from the knuckle to remove the axleshaft

8. Place new grease inside the strut housing before installing the new bearing.
9. Using an arbor press and suitable drivers, press the new wheel bearing and wheel hub into the strut housing. Be sure to replace the snaprings.
10. To install the strut and wheel hub assembly, reverse the removal procedures. Tighten the strut to body nuts to 44 ft. lbs.

5000, 100, 200 AND V8 QUATTRO

1. Raise and safely support vehicle. Remove the halfshafts.
2. Remove the strut to vehicle nuts and remove the strut from the vehicle.
3. Remove the disc brake rotor and splash shield.
4. Using an arbor press with suitable drivers, press the wheel hub from the strut housing.
5. Using snapring pliers, remove the snaprings from both sides of the wheel bearing.
6. Using an arbor press with suitable driver, press the wheel bearing from strut housing.
7. Using a suitable puller, press the bearing race from the wheel hub.
8. Install the outer snapring into the strut housing. Using an arbor press with suitable drivers, press the new wheel bearing into the strut housing until it seats against the snapring. Install the inner snapring.
9. Using an arbor press and suitable driver, press the wheel hub into the strut housing.
10. To install, reverse the removal procedures. Tighten the strut to body nuts to 43 ft. lbs. and reset the alignment when finished.

STEERING

Steering Wheel

CAUTION
On vehicles equipped with an air bag, the negative battery cable must be disconnected, before working on the vehicle. Failure to do so may result in deployment of the air bag and personal injury.

Removal and Installation

WITHOUT AIR BAG

1. Center the steering wheel. Disconnect the negative battery cable.
2. Pull off the center horn pad and disconnect the wire. Mark the relationship of the steering wheel to the steering shaft.

3. Remove the steering wheel mounting nut and remove the steering wheel. A steering wheel puller should not be necessary.

4. To install, align the matchmarks and tighten the nut to 30 ft. lbs.

NOTE: Never strike or pound on the steering wheel. The collapsible steering column may be damaged.

WITH AIR BAG

1. Center the steering wheel. Disconnect the negative battery cable.

2. Remove the side trim from center console, disconnect the power supply connector to the air bag.

—————————— CAUTION ——————————

The power connector to the air bag must be disconnected, as the air bag can trigger with the vehicle battery disconnected, due to the use of the energy reserve circuit.

3. Remove the screws for the upper steering column trim and remove the upper trim.

4. Separate the connector for the air bag spiral spring.

5. Remove the air bag Torx® head retaining bolts.

6. Unhook the air bag unit, lift up safety clamp and remove the air bag wiring at the terminal.

7. Remove the steering wheel mounting nut and remove the steering wheel. A steering wheel puller may be necessary.

8. If removing sprial spring, wheel must be straight ahead position. Do not twist spring after removing it.

To install:

9. To install, align the matchmarks and tighten the nut to 30 ft. lbs.

NOTE: Never strike or pound on the steering wheel. The collapsible steering column may be damaged.

10. Reinstall air bag, air bag connector and reinstall Torx® head screws. Torque the Torx® head screws to 53 in. lbs.

11. Install steering column upper trim.

12. Connect air bag system power connector.

13. Install the side trim on center console.

14. Connect the negative battery cable.

Steering Column

Removal and Installation

1. Disconnect the negative battery cable.

2. Remove the steering wheel and steering column switch.

3. Remove the instrument panel by prying out the speaker covers and using long nose pliers to pull out the air conditioning vents for access to the retainer screws.

4. Remove the trim under the instrument panel.

5. Remove the glove box and center console, if necessary, for clearance.

6. Remove the instrument panel crossmember, where used.

7. Disconnect the wiring from the ignition switch.

8. Remove the flange tube pinch bolt from the steering pinion connector.

9. Disconnect the steering column and flange tube from the pinion and remove assembly.

To install:

10. Installation is the reverse of the removal procedure. The pinch bolt should be replaced with a new bolt. Any self-locking nuts should also be replaced with new parts.

Power Steering Rack

Adjustment

1. Position the wheels in the straight-ahead position.

2. On top of the steering gear, loosen the locknut. Turn the adjusting nut until it bottoms against the thrust piece. While holding the adjusting screw, tighten the locknut.

3. If the steering rattles, is too tight or does not center, readjust the adjusting screw.

Removal and Installation

1987 4000, COUPE, 1988–91 80 AND 90

1. Raise and safely support the vehicle.

2. Remove the lower left instrument panel cover, the steering column-to-steering rack clamp bolt and the steering column-to-dash bolts. Remove the steering column from the vehicle.

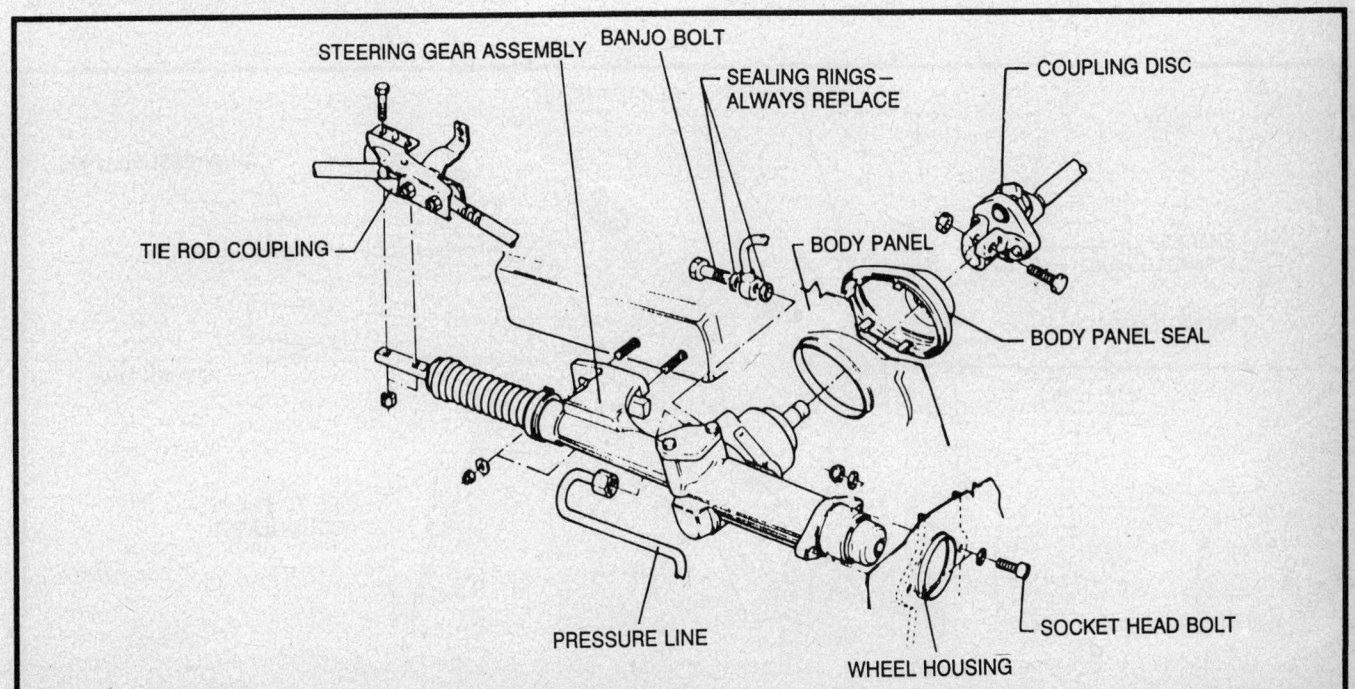

STEERING GEAR ASSEMBLY — BANJO BOLT — SEALING RINGS — ALWAYS REPLACE — COUPLING DISC — TIE ROD COUPLING — BODY PANEL — BODY PANEL SEAL — PRESSURE LINE — WHEEL HOUSING — SOCKET HEAD BOLT

Power steering gear mounting—80 and 90

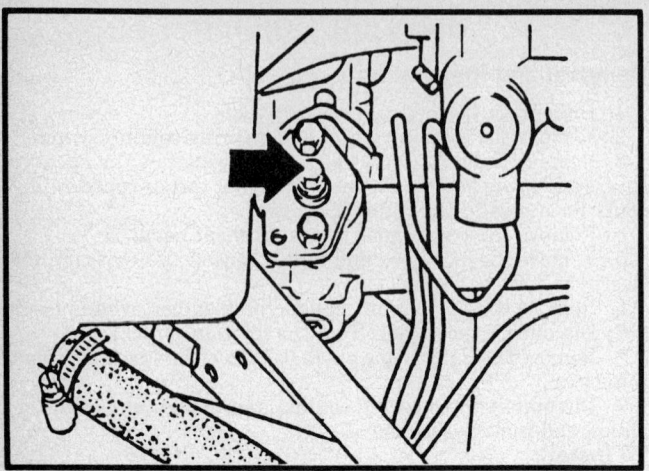

Steering gear adjustment bolt

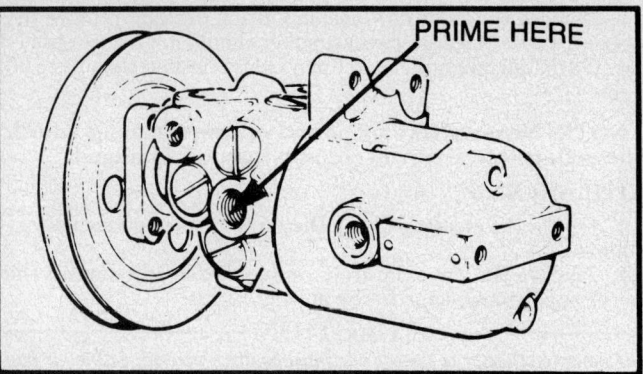

PRIME HERE

Prime the power steering pump with fluid before installing

3. Using a pair of locking pliers, clamp off the fluid return line to the reservoir. Disconnect the fluid pressure line from the steering gear.

4. At the steering column boot, press in on the clips and remove the boot from the panel. From inside the vehicle, remove the fluid return line from the control valve body. On 1988–91 5 cylinder vehicles, push off the dash panel boot and push the boot into the passenger compartment to access the pressure and return line.

5. At the left wheel housing, disconnect the steering rack from the frame.

6. At the steering rack, remove the tie rod coupling locknuts/bolts and the tie rods from the rack. Push the rack back into the steering housing.

7. Disconnect the steering assembly from the firewall. Turn the wheels to the right. Remove the assembly between the left wheel housing and the control arm.

8. To install, reverse the removal procedures. Bleed the hydraulic system.

1987–88 5000, 1989–91 100 AND 200

1. Raise and safely support the vehicle.

2. Pry off the lock plate and remove both tie rod mounting bolts from the steering rack, inside the engine compartment. Pry the tie rods out of the mounting pivot.

3. Remove the lower instrument panel trim.

4. Remove the pressure and return lines from the steering rack control valve body.

5. Remove the shaft clamp bolt, pry off the clip and drive the shaft toward the inside of the vehicle with a brass drift.

6. Remove the steering gear mounting bolts at both ends. There is a single bolt at the right end.

7. Turn the wheels all the way to the right and remove the steering gear through the opening in the right wheel housing.

To install:

8. Temporarily install the tie rod mounting pivot to the rack with both mounting bolts. Remove 1 bolt, install the tie rod and replace the bolt. Do the same on the other tie rod. Make sure to install the lock plate.

9. On all vehicles except the 100 and 200, torque the tie rod to 39 ft. lbs., the mounting pivot bolt to 15 ft. lbs. and the steering

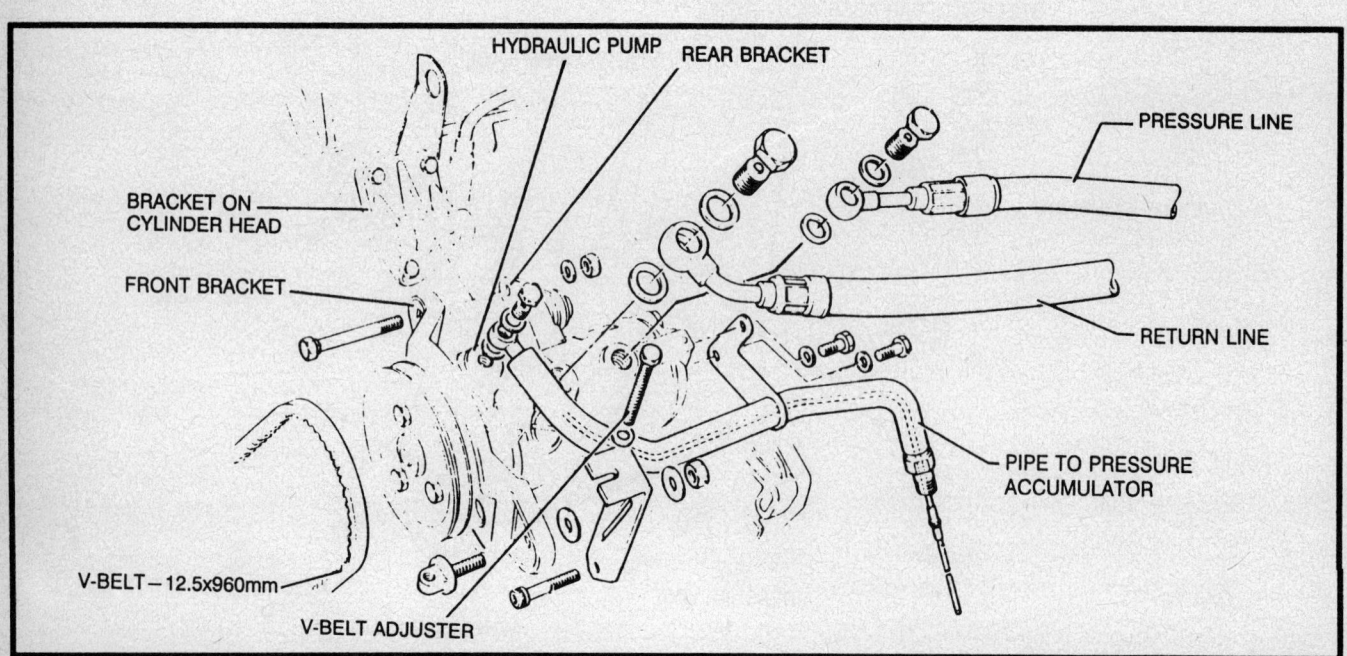

Power steering gear mounting—5000 and 100

HYDRAULIC PUMP REAR BRACKET

PRESSURE LINE

BRACKET ON CYLINDER HEAD

FRONT BRACKET

RETURN LINE

PIPE TO PRESSURE ACCUMULATOR

V-BELT — 12.5x960mm

V-BELT ADJUSTER

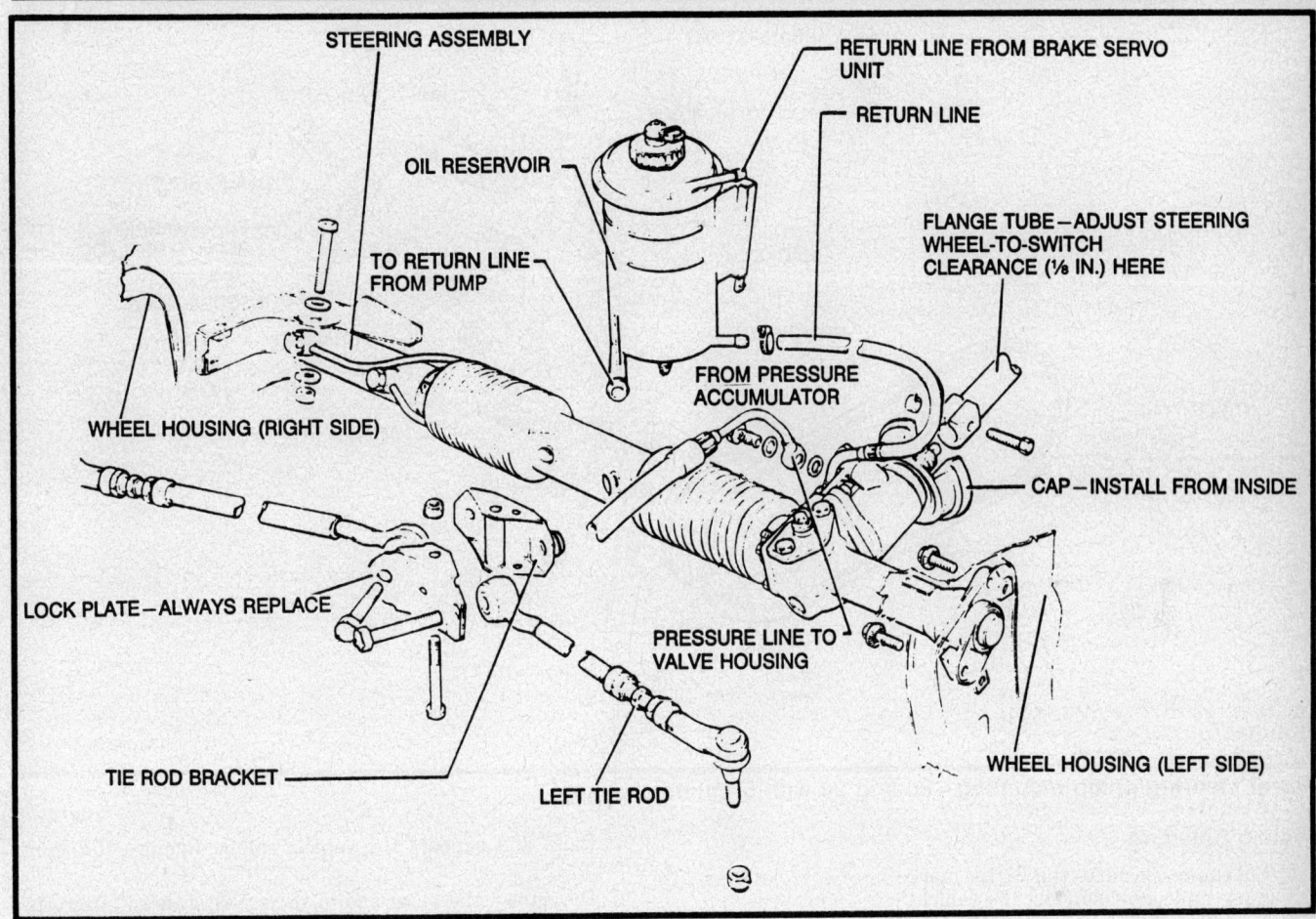

STEERING ASSEMBLY

RETURN LINE FROM BRAKE SERVO UNIT

RETURN LINE

OIL RESERVOIR

FLANGE TUBE—ADJUST STEERING WHEEL-TO-SWITCH CLEARANCE (⅛ IN.) HERE

TO RETURN LINE FROM PUMP

FROM PRESSURE ACCUMULATOR

WHEEL HOUSING (RIGHT SIDE)

CAP—INSTALL FROM INSIDE

LOCK PLATE—ALWAYS REPLACE

PRESSURE LINE TO VALVE HOUSING

WHEEL HOUSING (LEFT SIDE)

TIE ROD BRACKET

LEFT TIE ROD

Power steering pump mounting—5000 and 100

gear-to-body mounting bolts to 15 ft. lbs. On 100 and 200, torque the tie rod to 44 ft. lbs., pivot bolt to 30 ft. lbs. and gear-to-body bolts to 15 ft. lbs.

10. Install hose lines with new O-rings and torque to 30 ft. lbs.
11. Bleed the hydraulic system.

Power Steering Pump

Removal and Installation

EXCEPT V8 QUATTRO

1. Disconnect the negative battery cable. Remove the hoses from the pump. Plug the openings.
2. Remove the belt adjusting bolt, push the pump to 1 side and remove the belt.
3. Support the pump, remove the mounting bolts and lift out the pump.
4. Installation is the reverse. Be sure to fill the pump suction chamber with hydraulic fluid before attaching lines or the pump may be damaged.

V8 QUATTRO

1. Disconnect the battery negative cable.
2. Remove the air duct tube bolt near the engine oil dipstick.
3. Remove the retaining screws and remove the air duct elbow.
4. Remove the retaining bolts and move the radiator fan and motor assembly to one side.
5. Loosen the pump pulley mounting bolts.

6. Place a 13mm wrench on the tensioner bolt and move the wrench upward slowly and firmly until tension on the ribbed belt is released. Remove the drive belt from the idler pulley and take the pulley off the pump. Save any adjustment shims.
7. Clamp off the fluid intake and return lines, remove the lines from the pump and seal the openings. Before removing the banjo bolt take note of the proper installation of the pipe, over the corner of the pump support.
8. Remove the mounting bolts and the front support bracket, then remove the rear pump bolts. Push the pump forward from the support and twist the pump for clearance as it is removed.

To install:

9. Installation is the reverse of the removal process. When installing the pump bolts, install all bolts only finger tight until everything is aligned.
10. Before installing the banjo bolt for the one hydraulic line, make sure the pipe is properly aligned with the pump support. Use new seals.
11. Check the belt and pulley alignment. Shim the pulley, if necessary.

Belt Adjustment

1. Loosen the pump mounting bolts.
2. Turn the pump adjusting bolt until the center of the belt can be depressed ⅜ in. (10mm).
3. After adjustment, tighten the mounting bolts.

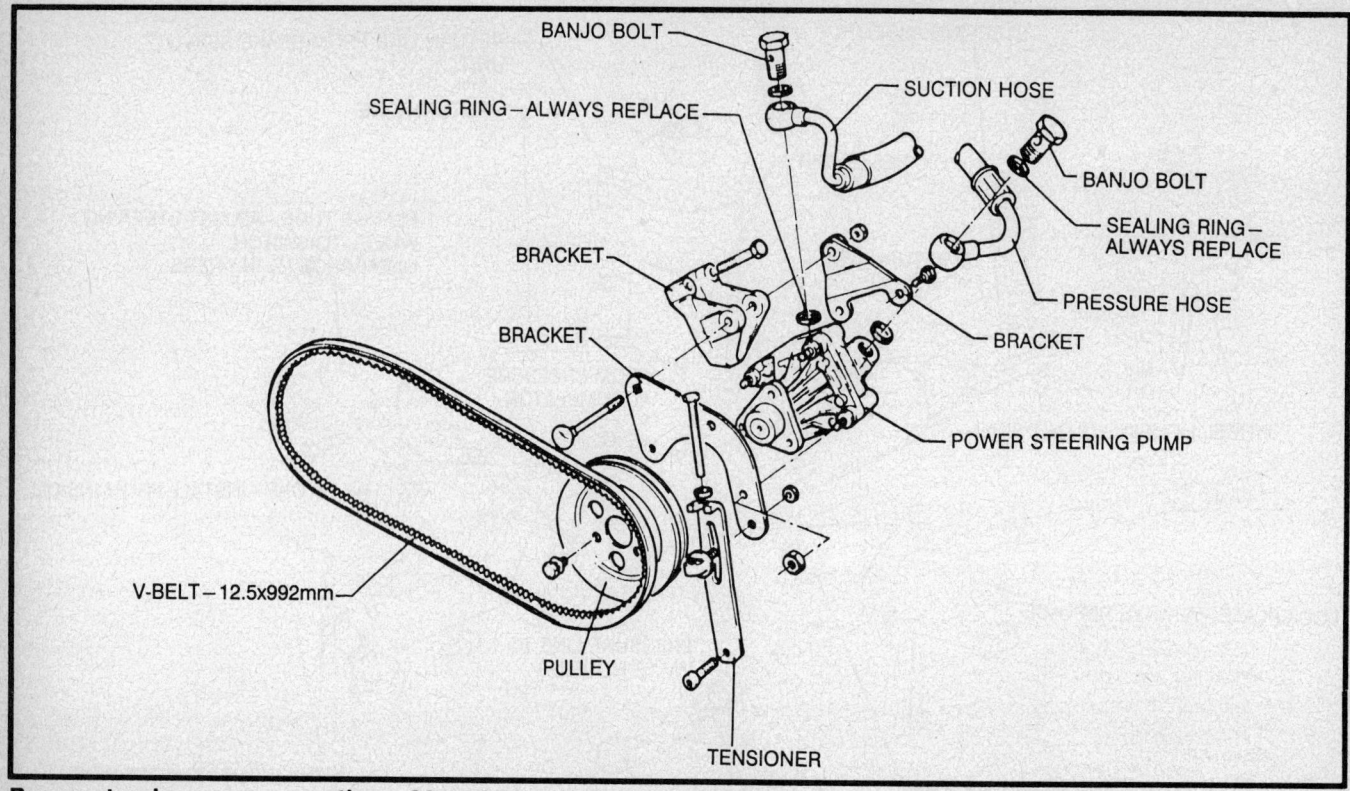

BANJO BOLT

SEALING RING—ALWAYS REPLACE

SUCTION HOSE

BANJO BOLT

SEALING RING—ALWAYS REPLACE

BRACKET

BRACKET

PRESSURE HOSE

BRACKET

POWER STEERING PUMP

V-BELT—12.5x992mm

PULLEY

TENSIONER

Power steering pump mounting—80 and 90 with 5 cylinder engine

System Bleeding

1. Fill the reservoir to the FULL mark.
2. Raise and safely support the vehicle.
3. Turn the steering wheel with the engine not running from lock to lock several times to remove the air from the system.
4. Add fluid to the reservoir until the level is maintained at $1\frac{3}{16}$ in. (30mm) below the FULL mark.
5. Start the engine. As the fluid in the reservoir continues to drop, add fluid to maintain the $1\frac{3}{16}$ in. (30mm) level.

NOTE: When turning the steering wheel, do not use more force than necessary to turn it.

6. Keep bleeding the system until no more air bubbles appear in the reservoir.
7. Turn off the engine and pump the brake pedal at least 20 times.
8. Replenish the fluid to the proper level.

Tie Rod Ends

Removal and Installation

NOTE: A puller or press is required for this procedure.

1. Raise and support the vehicle safely. Remove the front wheels.
2. Disconnect the outer end of the steering tie rod from the steering knuckle by removing the cotter pin and nut and pressing out the tie rod end. A small puller or press is required to free the tie rod end.
3. Under the hood, pry off the lock plate and remove the mounting bolts from both tie rod inner ends. Pry the tie rod out of the mounting pivot.
4. Install the mounting pivot to the rack with both mounting bolts.
5. Remove 1 bolt, install the tie rod and replace the bolt. Do the same on the other tie rod.
6. Make sure to install the lock plate. The inner tie rod end bolts should be torqued to:
   a. 1987 4000, Coupe—32 ft. lbs.
   b. 1987–88 5000—44 ft. lbs.
   c. 1988–91 80 and 90—32 ft. lbs.
   d. 1989–91 100, 200, V8 Quattro—44 ft. lbs.
7. If replacing the adjustable left tie rod, adjust it to the same length as the old one. Check the toe-in.
8. Use new cotter pins or replace self-locking nuts when installing the outer tie rod end.

BRAKES

Master Cylinder

Removal and Installation

1. Disconnect the negative battery cable. Have an assistant hold the brake pedal down about 1½ in. Disconnect the brake lines nearest the firewall.

2. Hold a container under the fitting disconnected in Step 1 and have the assistant release the pedal. The contents of the reservoir will drain into the container. Discard the used fluid.

3. Disconnect the other brake line.
4. Disconnect the stoplight switch and any warning switches from the master cylinder.

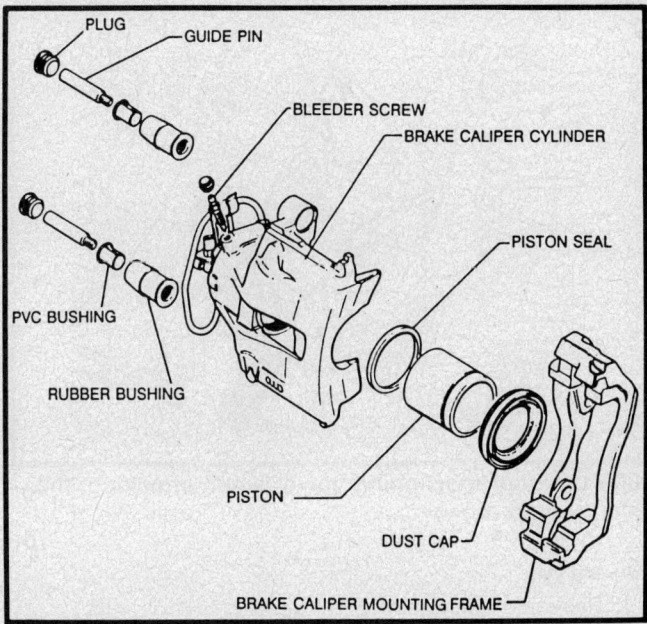

Teves type front brakes

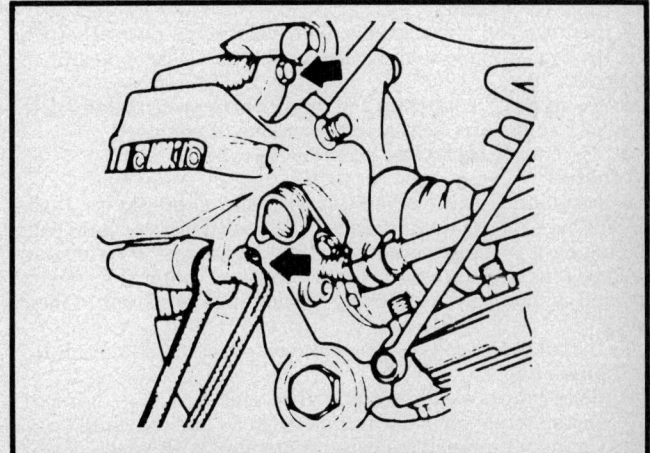

Holding guide pin with open end wrench

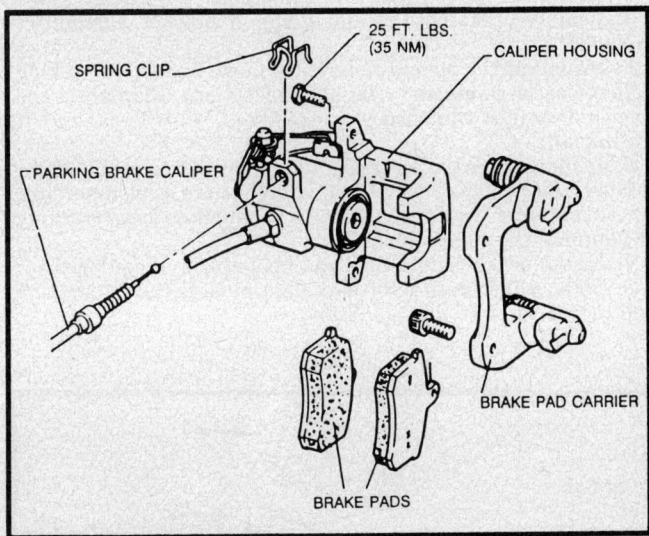

Girling type rear brakes

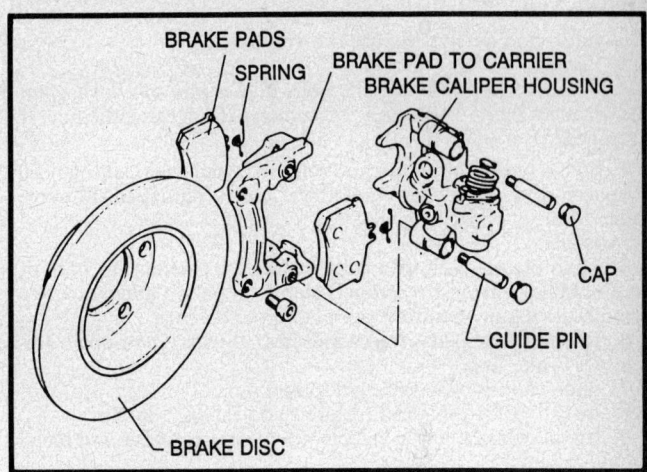

Teves type rear brakes

5. Remove the master cylinder from the power brake unit. Be careful not to loose the sealing ring between the 2 units.
6. Installation is the reverse of removal.
7. Transfer the reservoir from the master cylinder to the new unit.

NOTE: **Bench bleeding master cylinder will speed the on vehicle bleeding procedure. Raise the front or rear of the vehicle, if necessary, to maintain bleeding locations at the highest point in the hydraulic system.**

8. Master cylinder bolt torque is 17 ft. lbs. Fill and bleed the system. There should be a pedal free-play of 0.2 in. Free-play can be adjusted with the linkage, inside.

Proportioning Valve

Removal and Installation

1. Disconnect the negative battery cable. Remove and plug the 4 brake lines leading from the proportioning valve.

2. Disconnect the spring which is attached to the valve and the axle beam.
3. Remove the 2 mounting bolts and remove the valve.

NOTE: **Do not disassemble the valve.**

4. Installation is in the reverse order of removal.
5. Bleed the brake system when finished.

Power Brake Booster

Removal and Installation

1. Remove the master cylinder. Do not disconnect the brake lines.
2. Disconnect the vacuum hose from the power brake booster.
3. From under the dash, disconnect the pushrod from the brake pedal, remove the power brake booster-to-firewall nuts and remove the booster from the vehicle.
4. To install, reverse the removal procedures.

Brake Caliper

Removal and Installation
FRONT
Double Piston Caliper Type

1. Raise and safely support the vehicle.

2. Remove wheels.

3. Remove the lower caliper bolt, hold guide pin with open end wrench, while loosening. Disconnect the wear indicator, if equipped.

4. Swing brake caliper up and remove brake pads, taking note of spacer shims and heat-shield locations, if equipped.

5. Disconnect brake line and remove caliper.

To install:

6. Installation is the reverse of the removal procedure. Push pistons back into caliper. Place old disc pad on piston side of caliper, using a C-clamp centered on old pad across both piston, push pistons back into bore. Make certain to center C-clamp on pad and caliper to avoid cracking or jamming the pistons in their bores.

7. Install brake pads, shims and heat shield, if equipped. Install brake line.

8. Slide caliper over rotor and align pins.

9. Install guide pins and torque to 26 ft. lbs. (35 Nm).

10. Connect the wear indicator and install wheels.

11. Lower vehicle and fill master cylinder. Bleed brake system.

Girling Type

1. Raise and safely support the vehicle.

2. Remove wheels.

3. Remove the lower caliper bolt, hold guide pin with open end wrench, while loosening. Disconnect the wear indicator, if equipped.

4. Swing brake caliper up and remove brake pads, taking note of spacer shims and heat-shield locations, if equipped. Remove brake line.

To install:

5. Push piston back into caliper, using a C-clamp in bore of piston. Make certain to center C-clamp on piston and caliper to avoid cracking or jamming the piston in the bore.

6. Install brake pads, shims and heat shield, if equipped. Reconnect brake line.

7. Slide caliper over rotor and align pins.

8. Install guide pins and torque to 25 ft. lbs. (35 Nm).

9. Install wheels, lower vehicle, fill master cylinder and bleed brake system.

5000 brake proportioning valve; when checking, the lever should move

Teves Type

1. Raise and safely support the vehicle.

2. Remove wheels.

3. Remove guide pin caps and guide pins.

4. Remove brake hose retaining clip or bracket. Disconnect brake line.

5. Swing caliper up and remove. Remove brake pads, taking note of spacer shims and heat-shield locations. Disconnect the wear indicator, if equipped.

To install:

6. Installation is the reverse of the removal process. Push piston back into caliper, using a C-clamp in bore of piston. Make certain to center C-clamp on piston and caliper to avoid cracking or jamming the piston in the bore.

7. Install brake pads, shims and heat shield, if equipped.

8. Slide caliper over rotor and align pins. Install guide pins and torque to 18 ft. lbs. (25 Nm).

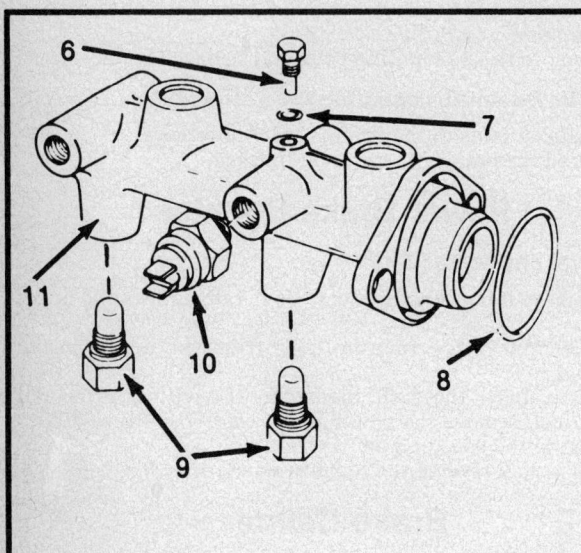

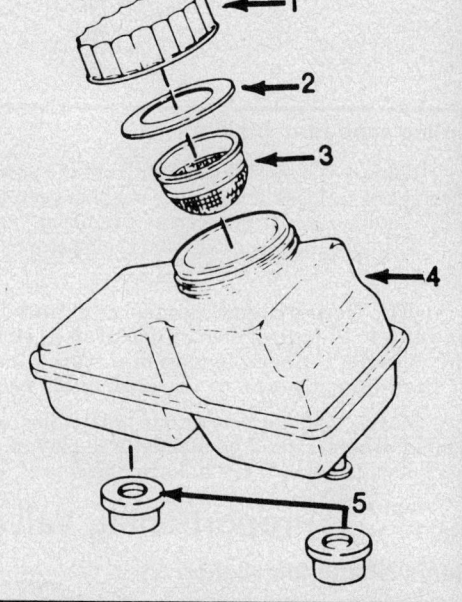

1. Reservoir Cap
2. Washer
3. Filter screen
4. Reservoir
5. Master cylinder plugs
6. Stop screw
7. Stop screw seal
8. Master cylinder seal
9. Residual pressure valves
10. Warning light sender unit
11. Brake master cylinder housing

4000 master cylinder—5000 similar

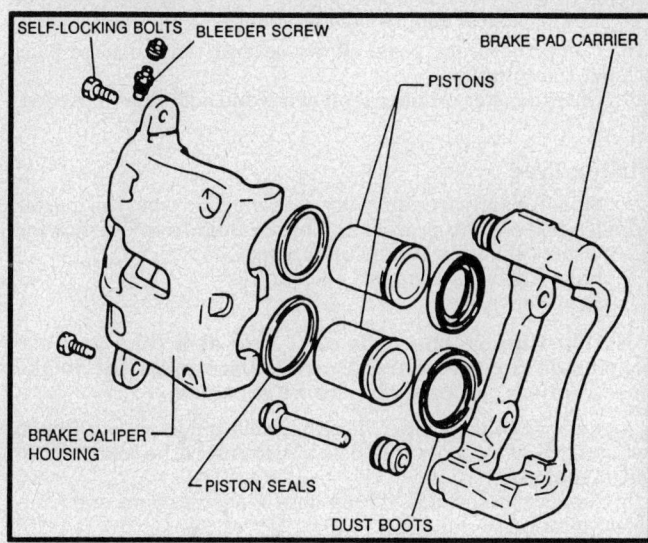

Double piston type caliper

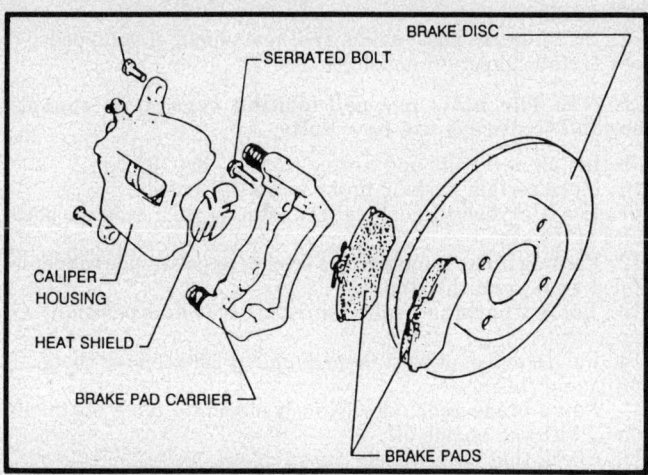

Girling type front brakes

9. Install brake hose and clip.
10. Install wheels.
11. Lower vehicle and fill master cylinder. Bleed brake system.

REAR

Girling Type

1. Raise and safely support the vehicle.
2. Remove wheels.
3. Remove rear brake caliper housing, hold guide pin with open end wrench while loosening bolts. Disconnect the wear indicator, if equipped.
4. Remove brake pads, taking note of spacer shims and heat-shield locations. Disconnect brake line.

To install:
5. Installation is the reverse of the removal procedure. Screw piston into housing by turning is clockwise with a socket head wrench while pushing in firmly.
6. Install brake pads, shims and heat shield, if equipped.
7. Install caliper on housing. Install new bolts and torque to 25 ft. lbs. (35 Nm).

NOTE: The bolts are self-locking type; it is recommended to always use new bolts.

8. Make certain parking brake is free of tension.

9. Use a prybar to push caliper lever against stop on both sides of vehicle.
10. Parking brake is too tight, if lever of opposite side caliper is pulled away from the stop.
11. Loosen parking brake adjusting nut and position, as necessary.
12. Push a tool of at least 6mm diameter between rear hook of spring and roller.
13. Pump brake pedal slowly with moderate force about 40 times, with the engine off.
14. Check that both wheels rotate freely.
15. Remove 6mm tool.
16. Install wheels. Lower vehicle and fill master cylinder. Bleed brake system.

Teves Type

1. Raise the rear of vehicle and safely support on stands.
2. Remove rear wheels.
3. Remove both protective caps. Loosen both guide pins but do not pull out of the rubber boots.
4. Pull caliper housing toward the outside of vehicle by hand. Disconnect brake line.
5. Swing the caliper housing to the rear and remove. Disconnect the wear indicator, if equipped.
6. Remove brake pads, taking note of spacer shims and heat-shield locations.

To install:
7. Installation is the reverse of the removal procedure. Push piston back into caliper, using a C-clamp in bore of piston. Make certain to center C-clamp on piston and caliper to avoid cracking or jamming the piston in the bore.
8. Install brake pads, shims and heat shield, if equipped.
9. Slide caliper over rotor and align pins. Install guide pins and torque to 18 ft. lbs. (25 Nm). Install the protective caps. Reconnect brake line.
10. Make certain parking brake is free of tension.
11. Use a prybar to push caliper lever against stop on both sides of vehicle.
12. Parking brake is too tight, if lever of opposite side caliper is pulled away from the stop.
13. Loosen parking brake adjusting nut and position, as necessary.
14. Push a tool of at least 6mm diameter between rear hook of spring and roller.
15. Pump brake pedal slowly with moderate force about 40 times, with the engine off.
16. Check that both wheels rotate freely.
17. Remove 6mm tool.
18. Install wheels. Lower vehicle and fill master cylinder. Bleed brake system.

Disc Brake Pads

Removal and Installation

FRONT

Double Piston Caliper Type

1. Siphon a sufficient quantity of brake fluid from the master cylinder reservoir to prevent the brake fluid from overflowing the master cylinder when installing pads.
2. Raise and safely support the vehicle.
3. Remove wheels.

NOTE: Change the pads on 1 axle at a time and use other side for reference. Do not disconnect the brake hoses, unless the caliper is to be serviced.

4. Remove the lower caliper bolt, hold guide pin with open end wrench, while loosening. Disconnect the wear indicator, if equipped.

5. Swing brake caliper up and remove brake pads, taking note of spacer shims and heat-shield locations, if equipped.

6. Push pistons back into caliper. Place old disc pad on piston side of caliper, using a C-clamp centered on old pad across both piston, push pistons back into bore. Make certain to center C-clamp on pad and caliper to avoid cracking or jamming the pistons in their bores.

To install:

7. Install brake pads, shims and heat shield, if equipped.
8. Slide caliper over rotor and align pins.
9. Install guide pins and torque to 26 ft. lbs. (35 Nm).
10. Connect the wear indicator and install wheels.
11. Lower the vehicle and fill master cylinder.
12. Pump the brake pedal slowly several time to force pads against the rotors.
13. Check master cylinder level again and add fluid, if needed.

Girling Type

1. Siphon a sufficient quantity of brake fluid from the master cylinder reservoir to prevent the brake fluid from overflowing the master cylinder when installing pads.
2. Raise and safely support the vehicle.
3. Remove wheels.

NOTE: Change the pads on 1 axle at a time and use other side for reference. Do not disconnect the brake hoses, unless the caliper is to be serviced.

4. Remove the lower caliper bolt, hold guide pin with open end wrench, while loosening. Disconnect the wear indicator, if equipped.
5. Swing brake caliper up and remove brake pads, taking note of spacer shims and heat-shield locations, if equipped.
6. Push piston back into caliper, using a C-clamp in bore of piston. Make certain to center C-clamp on piston and caliper to avoid cracking or jamming the piston in the bore.

To install:

7. Install brake pads, shims and heat shield, if equipped.
8. Slide caliper over rotor and align pins.
9. Install guide pins and torque to 25 ft. lbs. (35 Nm).
10. Install wheels.
11. Lower vehicle and fill master cylinder.
12. Pump the brake pedal slowly several time to force pads against the rotors.
13. Check master cylinder level again and add fluid, if needed.

Teves Type

1. Siphon a sufficient quantity of brake fluid from the master cylinder reservoir to prevent the brake fluid from overflowing the master cylinder when installing pads.
2. Raise and safely support the vehicle.
3. Remove wheels.

NOTE: Change the pads on 1 axle at a time and use other side for reference. Do not disconnect the brake hoses, unless the caliper is to be serviced.

4. Remove guide pin caps.
5. Remove guide pins.
6. Remove brake hose retaining clip or bracket.
7. Swing caliper up and secure in position, using a wire. Do not allow caliper to hang from brake hose.
8. Remove brake pads, taking note of spacer shims and heat-shield locations. Disconnect the wear indicator, if equipped.
9. Push piston back into caliper, using a C-clamp in bore of piston. Make certain to center C-clamp on piston and caliper to avoid cracking or jamming the piston in the bore.

To install:

10. Install brake pads, shims and heat shield, if equipped.
11. Slide caliper over rotor and align pins.
12. Install guide pins and torque to 18 ft. lbs. (25 Nm).
13. Install brake hose clip.
14. Install wheels.

15. Lower vehicle and fill master cylinder.
16. Pump the brake pedal slowly several time to force pads against the rotors.
17. Check master cylinder level again and add, fluid if needed.

REAR

Girling Type

1. Siphon a sufficient quantity of brake fluid from the master cylinder reservoir to prevent the brake fluid from overflowing the master cylinder when installing pads.
2. Raise and safely support the vehicle.
3. Remove wheels.

NOTE: Change the pads on 1 axle at a time and use other side for reference. Do not disconnect the brake hoses, unless the caliper is to be serviced.

4. Remove brake caliper housing, hold guide pin with open end wrench while loosening bolts. Disconnect the wear indicator, if equipped.
5. Remove brake pads, taking note of spacer shims and heat-shield locations.
6. Screw piston into housing by turning is clockwise with a socket head wrench while pushing in firmly.

To install:

7. Install brake pads, shims and heat shield, if equipped.
8. Install caliper on housing.

NOTE: The bolts are self-locking type; it is recommended to always use new bolts.

9. Install new bolts and torque to 25 ft. lbs. (35 Nm).
10. Make certain parking brake is free of tension.
11. Use a prybar to push caliper lever against stop on both sides of vehicle.
12. Parking brake is too tight, if lever of opposite side caliper is pulled away from the stop.
13. Loosen parking brake adjusting nut and position, as necessary.
14. Push a tool of at least 6mm diameter between rear hook of spring and roller.
15. Pump brake pedal slowly with moderate force about 40 times, with the engine off.
16. Check that both wheels rotate freely.
17. Remove 6mm tool.
18. Install wheels.
19. Lower vehicle and fill master cylinder.

Teves Type

1. Siphon a sufficient quantity of brake fluid from the master cylinder reservoir to prevent the brake fluid from overflowing the master cylinder when installing pads.
2. Raise and safely support the vehicle.
3. Remove wheels.

NOTE: Change the pads on 1 axle at a time and use other side for reference. Do not disconnect the brake hoses, unless the caliper is to be serviced.

4. Remove both protective caps.
5. Loosen both guide pins but do not pull out of the rubber boots.
6. Pull caliper housing toward the outside of vehicle by hand.
7. Swing the caliper housing to the rear and remove. Do not allow caliper to hang from brake hose. Disconnect the wear indicator, if equipped.
8. Remove brake pads, taking note of spacer shims and heat-shield locations.
9. Push piston back into caliper, using a C-clamp in bore of piston. Make certain to center C-clamp on piston and caliper to avoid cracking or jamming the piston in the bore.

To install:

10. Install brake pads, shims and heat shield, if equipped.

11. Slide caliper over rotor and align pins.
12. Install guide pins and torque to 18 ft. lbs. (25 Nm).
13. Install the protective caps.
14. Make certain parking brake is free of tension.
15. Use a prybar to push caliper lever against stop on both sides of vehicle.
16. Parking brake is too tight, if lever of opposite side caliper is pulled away from the stop.
17. Loosen parking brake adjusting nut and position, as necessary.
18. Push a tool of at least 6mm diameter between rear hook of spring and roller.
19. Pump brake pedal slowly with moderate force about 40 times, with the engine off.
20. Check that both wheels rotate freely.
21. Remove 6mm tool.
22. Install wheels. Refill master cylinder.

Brake Rotor

Removal and Installation

1. Raise and safely support vehicle.
2. Remove wheels.
3. Remove brake caliper.
4. Remove disc rotor.
5. When replacing rotors, always replace in pairs. If machining, watch wear limit. Always machine both sides, never one side only.

Parking Brake Cable

Adjustment

NOTE: Because of the self-adjusting rear brakes, adjustment is only necessary after replacement of any of the brake components.

1. Raise and support the vehicle safely.
2. Release the parking brake lever.
3. Check that the parking brake levers at the rear calipers stay on the stop. If not, loosen the adjusting nut.
4. Depress the brake pedal approximately 40 times and pull the parking brake lever to the 3rd tooth.

NOTE: Always make sure basic adjustment on rear brakes is correct first.

5. Tighten the adjusting nut on the parking brake equalizer bar until the rear wheels can just be turned by hand.
6. Release the brake and check that both wheels rotate freely and that the parking brake levers at the rear calipers stay on the stops.
7. Turn the ignition switch on and check that the brake warning light comes ON when the parking brake is pulled to the first tooth and goes OFF when it is released.

Removal and Installation
ALL VEHICLES

1. Raise and safely support the vehicle. Release the parking brake.
2. Remove the rear brake drums, if not equipped with disc brakes.
3. Disconnect the cable from the shoe assembly by pushing the spring forward and removing the cable from the adjusting arm, if not equipped with disc brakes.
4. Pull the parking brake cable out of its retaining clip on the caliper, if equipped with disc brakes.
5. Remove the cable compensating spring.
6. Back off the equalizer nut and guide the cable through the trailing arms and supports.

7. Installation is the reverse of removal.
8. Adjust, if necessary.

NOTE: When installing the parking brake cables on the Turbo and Quattro, the cable coupling should connect the 2 cables on the right side of the equalizer bar.

Brake System Bleeding

To bleed system, use bottle with transparent hose attached, so brake fluid can be checked for air bubbles. Do not re-use fluid removed from reservoir.
1. Raise and safely support vehicle.
2. Connect bleeder hose and bleed calipers. Have an assistant press the pedal. When in the down position, open the bleeder screw. Close the bleeder screw and press the pedal again. Open the bleeder screw and again allow the air to come out. Repeat at each wheel until the fluid in the container shows no sign of air bubbles.
3. Bleed in the following sequence:
   a. Right rear caliper
   b. Left rear caliper
   c. Right front caliper
   d. Left front caliper
4. Bleed right rear caliper. After bleeding, refill brake fluid reservoir.

Anti-Lock Brake System Service

Precautions

The following precautions should be observed when working on the Anti-lock Brake System (ABS).
● Electrical testing should be done using the factory LED tester. This tester must be used to check out the hydraulic modulator, ABS control unit, wheel speed sensors and ABS wiring harness. It is also necessary to perform the test procedure if the brake lines or brake pressure regulators are replaced because of accident damage.
● Switch the ignition OFF before connecting or disconnecting the ABS control unit connector.
● Disconnect the ABS control unit connector before using electrical welding equipment on the vehicle.
● Disconnect the battery connections before charging the battery or replacing the hydraulic modulator.
● Remove the ABS control unit before drying paint repairs in an oven if the temperature will be more than 185°F. for more than 2 hours.
● Do not use mini-spare tires on vehicles equipped with ABS. Use wheels and tires of matching size on ABS equipped vehicles.
● Do not drive the vehicle with the anti-lock brake tester connected.
● Do not fabricate brake lines. Use only original equipment parts. Brake line flare nuts are to be tightened to 11 ft. lbs. torque.
● Do not repair the hydraulic modulator except when replacing relays. If the hydraulic modulator is defective, it must be replaced.

Relieving Anti-Lock Brake System Pressure

A special factory tool is recommended for ABS system bleed-down. It is set of high and low pressure gauges that is also used for system pressure testing. It is used as follows:
1. Raise and safely support vehicle. Remove one front wheel.
2. Remove the bleeder screw from the caliper.
3. Connect the special tool and install a brake pedal depressor between the brake pedal and the driver's seat.
4. Press the brake pedal until the pressure gauge drops down indicating system pressure has been relieved.

NOTE: If the pressure drops more than 58 psi in 45 seconds, replace the hydraulic modulator. Press the brake pedal until pressure reads 87 psi. If pressure drops more than 14.5 psi in 3 minutes, replace the hydraulic modulator.

Hydraulic Modulator

Removal and Installation

1. Disconnect negative battery cable.
2. Bleed down system pressure.
3. Remove the modulator cover.
4. Remove the harness retainer.
5. Disconnect the hydraulic modulator from the mounting.
6. Unclip the hydraulic fluid reservoir from the mounting.
7. Unscrew the brake lines. Mark the lines so they will be reinstalled in their proper locations. Seal any openings immediately with plugs.

To install:

8. Installation is the reverse of the removal procedure. Refill with DOT 4 brake fluid only.

Wheel Speed Sensors

Removal and Installation

FRONT

The front wheel speed sensor is pressed into the wheel bearing housing, also called a steering knuckle. A sleeve is inserted into a hole in the housing which retains the speed sensor.

1. Raise and safely support vehicle.
2. Remove wheel and tire assembly.
3. Locate the sensor in the side of the housing and pull out. Left and right are identical.
4. To disconnect the wiring, remove the engine lower cover.
5. Unclip the connector from its mount and disconnect sensor.

To install:

6. Installation is the reverse of the removal procedure. Before inserting the retainer sleeve, the opening in the wheel bearing housing should be greased with brake cylinder paste.
7. Press the sleeve in as far as possible.
8. Push the sensor in to stop by hand.

REAR

The rear wheel speed sensor is pressed into the rear wheel bearing housing. A sleeve is inserted into a hole in the front side of the housing which retains the speed sensor.

1. Raise and safely support vehicle.
2. Remove wheel and tire assembly.
3. Locate the sensor in the front side of the rear wheel bearing housing and pull out. Left and right are identical. Unclip the connector and remove sensor.

To install:

4. Installation is the reverse of the removal process. Before inserting the retainer sleeve, the opening in the rear wheel bearing housing should be greased with brake cylinder paste.
5. Press the sleeve in as far as possible.
6. Push the sensor in to stop by hand.

Acceleration Switch

Removal and Installation

The ABS acceleration switch is located under the left rear seat bench. It is a mercury switch activated during deceleration. When braking with ABS the switch helps the braking system provide additional stabilization during braking.

1. Switch the ignition OFF.
2. Remove the mounting screws.
3. Disconnect the wiring.
4. At installation, note that the arrow on the cover must point forward, in the direction of driving.

Electronic Control Unit

Removal and Installation

The ABS electronic control unit is located under the left side of the rear passenger seat.

1. Switch ignition OFF.
2. Raise rear seat and locate ABS control unit. Remove hold down nuts.
3. The ABS control unit plug has locks to secure it. Disconnect by pressing the spring on the narrow end of the plug. To connect, insert the lug of the connector into the adapter and push the connector against the spring. The connector should snap into the lock with a click.

FRONT SUSPENSION

All vehicles use MacPherson struts. The strut unit, steering arm and steering knuckle are all combined in 1 strut assembly. There is no upper control arm.

MacPherson Strut

Removal and Installation

1. Disconnect the negative battery cable. With the vehicle on the ground, remove the front axle nut and loosen the wheel bolts.
2. Raise and support the vehicle safely. Remove the wheel assembly.
3. Remove the brake caliper mounting bolts and disconnect the brake line bracket. Remove speed sensor, if equipped.
4. Remove the brake caliper, with the line still attached and support it aside.
5. Remove disc brake rotor.
6. Remove the ball joint clamp bolt and nut.

7. Remove the tie rod end nut and separate the tie rod end from the strut.
8. If equipped with a stabilizer bar, remove the retaining bolt and remove the stabilizer bar end clamps. Pivot the stabilizer bar downward.
9. Remove the 2 center stabilizer bar clamps and unbolt it from the lower control arm.
10. Pry the lower control arm down and separate the ball joint from the strut, while alternately turning the steering wheel from right to left.
11. Using a suitable hub puller, press the halfshaft out of the hub.
12. On 4000, 80 and 90, support the strut assembly, hold the shock absorber piston rod with an internal socket wrench and remove the retaining nut. Remove the strut assembly from the vehicle.
13. On 5000, 100 and 200, remove the upper strut cover, support the strut assembly and remove the 3 strut retaining nuts. Remove the strut assembly.

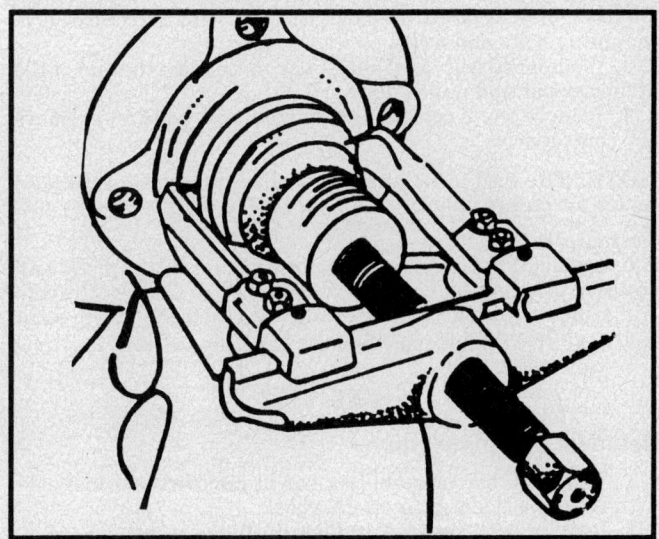

Removing the outer bearing race from the hub

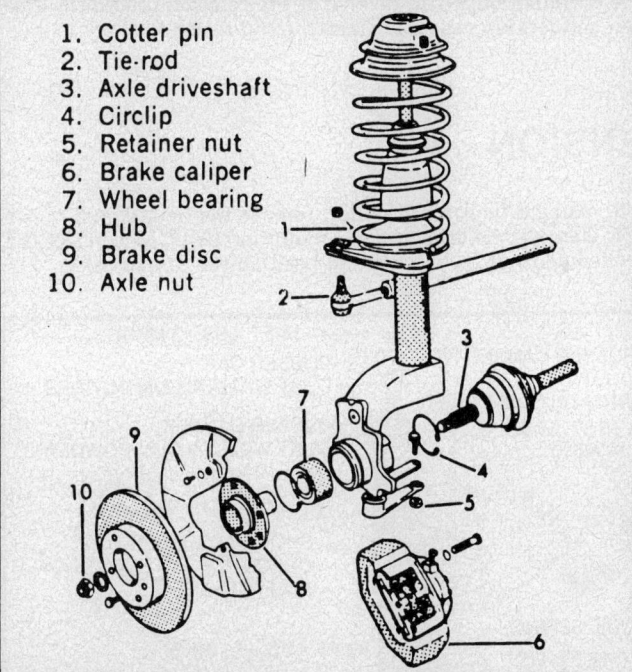

1. Cotter pin
2. Tie-rod
3. Axle driveshaft
4. Circlip
5. Retainer nut
6. Brake caliper
7. Wheel bearing
8. Hub
9. Brake disc
10. Axle nut

4000 front suspension

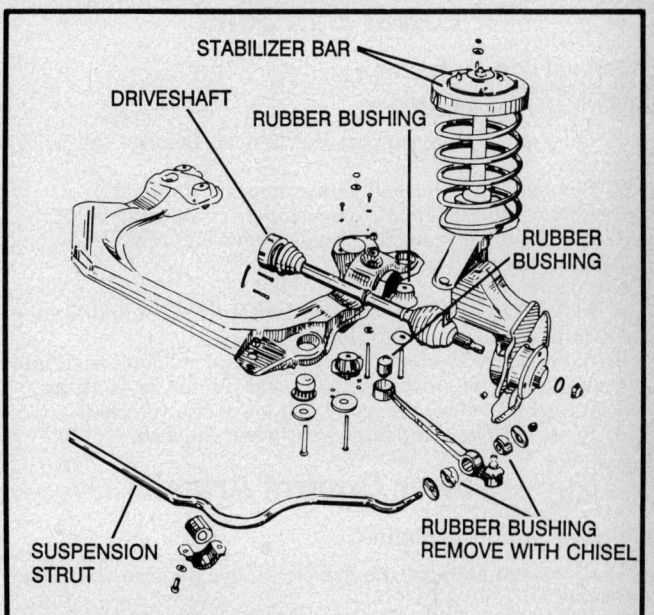

STABILIZER BAR
DRIVESHAFT
RUBBER BUSHING
RUBBER BUSHING
SUSPENSION STRUT
RUBBER BUSHING REMOVE WITH CHISEL

Front suspension—5000

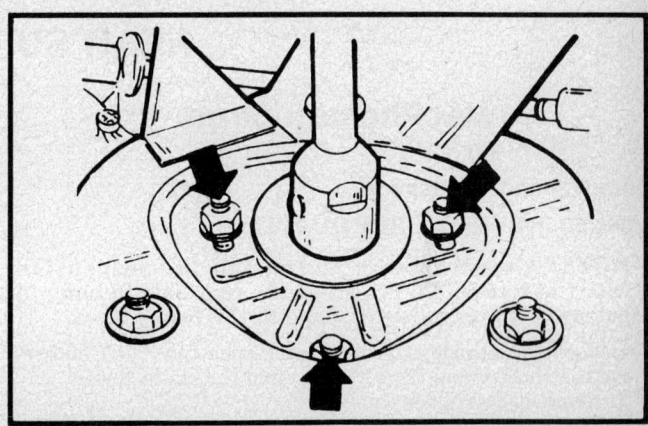

To adjust camber on the 5000, move the strut assembly in the slots of the spring mounting plate

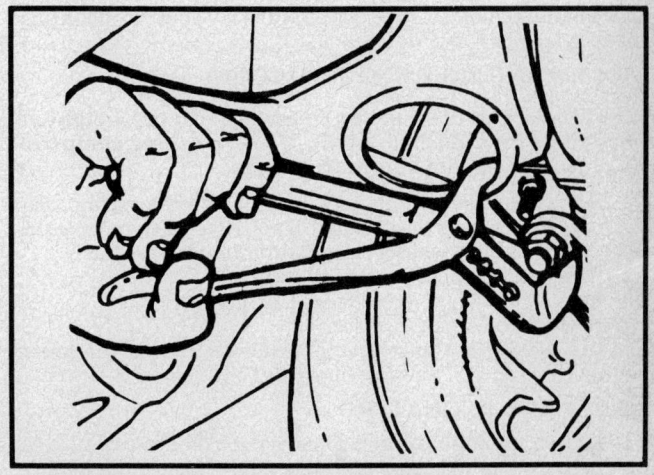

Adjusting the camber on the 4000 and Quattro

To install:

14. Installation is the reverse of the removal procedure. Note the following during installation:

   a. When installing the stabilizer bar, the position is correct if the clamps are difficult to install in the rubber bushings. Attach the clamps loosely, take a short test drive to bring the bushings into the correct position and tighten to 18 ft. lbs.

   b. Tighten the ball joint bolt to 36 ft. lbs. on 4000, 80, 90 or 47 ft. lbs. on 5000 vehicles or 48 ft. lbs., plus an additional ¼ turn (90 degrees) on 100, 200 and V8 Quattro.

   c. Tighten the axleshaft end nut to 167 ft. lbs. on the 4000, 80 and 90 on Quattro and Quattro Turbos and 237 ft. lbs. on all other 5000, 100 and 200 vehicles.

   d. Make certain speed sensor and sleeve are completely seated, by hand.

Lower Ball Joint

Removal and Installation

4000, COUPE, 80 AND 90

1. Raise and safely support the vehicle. Remove the wheel assembly.
2. Remove the lower ball joint clamp nut and bolt.
3. Remove the ball joint to control arm mounting bolts.
4. Pry the lower control arm downward and remove the ball joint from the strut assembly.

To install:

5. Install the new ball joint on the control arm and tighten the mounting bolts to 46 ft. lbs.
6. Slowly allow the lower control arm and ball joint to fit into the strut assembly. Install the bolt and tighten to 48 ft. lbs.
7. Install the wheel assembly and lower the vehicle.
8. Reset the front end alignment when finished.

Lower Control Arms

Removal and Installation

1. Raise and support the vehicle safely. Remove the wheel assembly.
2. Remove the ball joint to strut bolt and nut. Pry and hold the control arm down. Remove the ball joint to control arm mounting bolts and nuts.
3. If equipped with a stabilizer bar, disconnect the end of the stabilizer bar and pull it down.
4. Remove the 2 control arm to subframe bolts and remove the control arm.

NOTE: The ball joint and control arm must be replaced as an assembly.

To install:

5. Installation is in the reverse order of removal. Check control arm bushings for cracking or undue wear. Tighten the control arm-to-subframe bolts to 43 ft. lbs.; the ball joint-to-strut bolt to 46 ft. lbs. and the stabilizer bar bolts to 18 ft. lbs.

Sway Bar

Removal and Installation

1. The sway bar or stabilizer bar is removed and installed with the vehicle standing on its wheels.
2. Remove both sway bar rubber bushing brackets.
3. Disconnect the ends of the sway bar where it goes through the lower control arm and remove.
4. Installation is the reverse of the removal procedure. Use new self-locking nuts and tighten to 80 ft. lbs.

REAR SUSPENSION

MacPherson Struts

Removal and Installation

4000, 80 AND 90 EXCEPT QUATTRO

NOTE: Always remove and install the suspension struts 1 at a time. Do not allow the rear axle to hang in place as this may cause damage to the brake lines.

1. With the vehicle at ground level, open the trunk and remove the sheet metal trim from around the shock tower.
2. Remove the rubber cap.
3. Remove the strut mounting nut.
4. Raise and support the vehicle safely.
5. Remove the lower strut mounting bolt from the axle beam and remove the strut.
6. Installation is the reverse of removal. Torque the upper strut mounting bolt to 14 ft. lbs. and the lower strut mounting bolt to 43 ft. lbs.

5000, 100 AND 200 EXCEPT QUATTRO

NOTE: The struts must be removed with the weight of the vehicle on the rear wheels. If not, a spring compressor must be used on the rear springs.

1. If the vehicle is not on its wheels, install the spring compressor and compress the spring. Do not attempt to remove the shock with the rear wheels raised without a compressor.
2. Remove the upper strut mounting nut.
3. Remove the lower strut mounting nut.
4. Remove the shock absorber.
5. Installation is the reverse of removal. Torque the lower mounts to 66 ft. lbs. and the upper to 14 ft. lbs.

4000, 80 AND 90 QUATTRO

1. Loosen the lug nuts and remove the axle nut cover.
2. Remove the axle nut and raise and support the vehicle safely. Remove the wheels.

3. Using a tie rod end puller, remove the tie rod end.
4. Remove the brake caliper mounting bolts. Disconnect the brake line from its bracket and position the caliper aside.

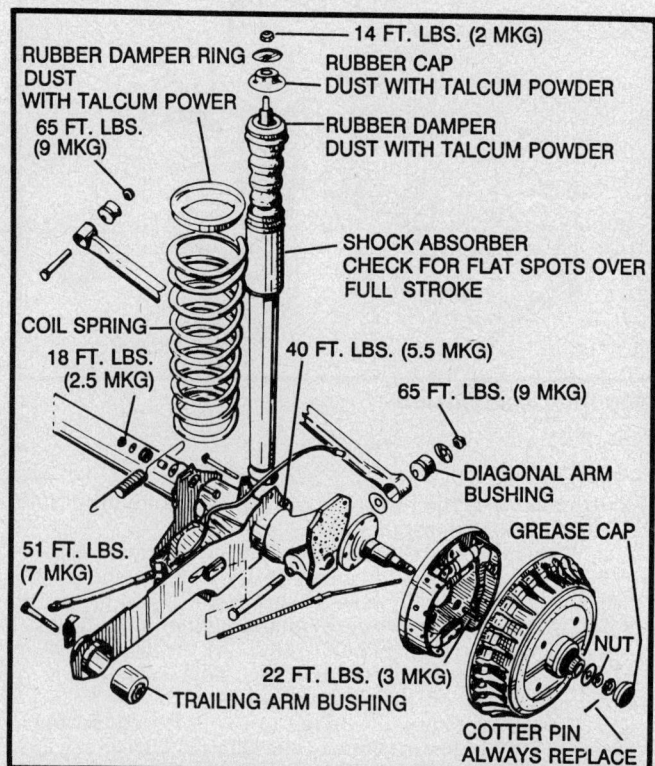

RUBBER DAMPER RING

DUST WITH TALCUM POWER

65 FT. LBS. (9 MKG)

14 FT. LBS. (2 MKG)

RUBBER CAP
DUST WITH TALCUM POWDER

RUBBER DAMPER
DUST WITH TALCUM POWDER

SHOCK ABSORBER
CHECK FOR FLAT SPOTS OVER FULL STROKE

COIL SPRING
18 FT. LBS. (2.5 MKG)

40 FT. LBS. (5.5 MKG)

65 FT. LBS. (9 MKG)

DIAGONAL ARM BUSHING

GREASE CAP

51 FT. LBS. (7 MKG)

NUT

22 FT. LBS. (3 MKG)
TRAILING ARM BUSHING

COTTER PIN
ALWAYS REPLACE

Rear suspension on the 5000, except Quattro—4000 similar

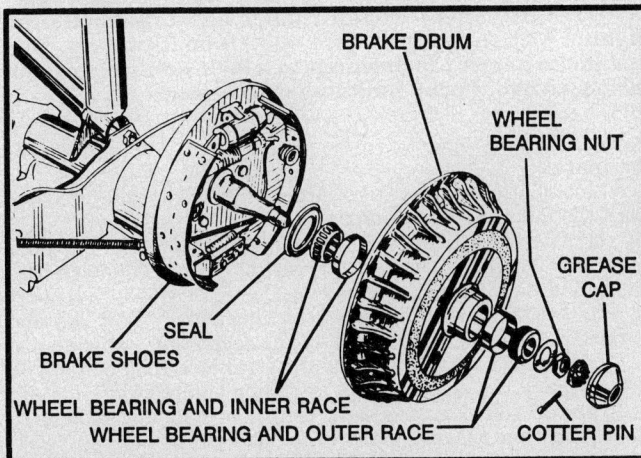

Rear wheel bearing—typical of all vehicles, except Quattro

Labels: BRAKE DRUM, WHEEL BEARING NUT, GREASE CAP, COTTER PIN, WHEEL BEARING AND OUTER RACE, WHEEL BEARING AND INNER RACE, BRAKE SHOES, SEAL

5. Remove the brake disc and the ball joint clamp bolt and pry the ball joint out of the hub.

6. Using a 4 arm puller, press the halfshaft from the strut/wheel hub assembly.

7. Have a helper hold the strut assembly and remove the upper strut mounting nut. Remove the strut.

NOTE: The rear axle assembly must not be under tension while removing the strut.

8. Installation is in the reverse order of removal. Note the following torque figures:

    a. Tie rod nut—29 ft. lbs. (non-Turbo) or 43 ft. lbs. (Turbo).

    b. Axle nut—203 ft. lbs.

    c. Upper strut mounting nut—43 ft. lbs.

    d. Ball joint clamp bolt—54 ft. lbs. (non-Turbo) or 47 ft. lbs. (Turbo).

5000, 100, 200 AND V8 QUATTRO

1. Raise and support the vehicle safely. Remove the wheel assembly.

2. Open the trunk and remove the shock absorber covers, the remove the shock absorber-to-body nuts/bolts.

3. Remove the shock absorber-to-rear wheel knuckle assembly. Remove the shock absorber from the vehicle.

4. To install, reverse the removal procedures. Torque the shock absorber-to-body nuts/bolts to 15 ft. lbs. and the shock absorber-to-rear wheel knuckle assembly bolt to 66 ft. lbs.

Rear Control Arms

Removal and Installation

1987 4000 QUATTRO, 1988–91 80 AND 90 QUATTRO

1. Raise and support the vehicle safely, under the frame and differential.

2. Using a scribing tool, mark the position of the ball joint carrier with the control arm.

3. Remove the ball joint carrier-to-control arm nuts and the lock plate. Separate the ball joint carrier from the control arm.

4. Remove the control arm-to-subframe bolts and the control arm from the vehicle.

5. To install, reverse the removal procedures. Always using new replacement nuts. Torque the control arm-to-subframe bolts to 43 ft. lbs. Check the rear wheel alignment.

1987–88 5000 QUATTRO, 1989–91 100 AND 200 QUATTRO

On these vehicles, the control arm is know as the trapezoidal arm. It is connected to the wheel bearing housing and to 2 separate cross-members. It is recommended to use new self-locking nuts on all applications.

1. Raise and support the vehicle safely, under the frame and differential.

2. Remove the wheel. Along the trapezoidal arm, remove the speed sensor wiring bracket nuts/bolts and the guide.

3. Remove the wheel bearing housing-to-trapezoidal arm front and rear bolts.

4. Remove the trapezoidal arm-to-rear cross-member bolt.

5. At the brake pressure regulator, disconnect the spring.

6. Remove the trapezoidal arm-to-front cross-member nut and the trapezoidal arm from the vehicle.

7. To install, reverse the removal procedures. Torque the trapezoidal arm-to-front crossmember nut to 44 ft. lbs., the trapezoidal arm-to-rear crossmember bolt to 63 ft. lbs., the trapezoidal arm-to-wheel bearing housing bolts to 125 ft. lbs. and the speed sensor guide nut/bolts to 7 ft. lbs. Adjust the rear wheel alignment.

NOTE: Before installing the trapezoidal arm, be sure to coat the fasteners with locking compound.

Rear Wheel Bearings

Removal and Installation

EXCEPT QUATTRO

1. Raise and support the vehicle safely. Remove the wheel assembly.

2. If equipped with disc brakes, remove caliper assembly from rotor. Disconnecting the hydraulic lines or parking brake cable may not be necessary. Suspend caliper with wire do not let caliber hang by brake hose.

3. Pry off the grease cap and remove the cotter pin, nut and washer.

4. Remove the outer bearing.

5. Remove the brake drum or rotor.

6. Remove the bearing inner bearing and seal, using a soft drift or press.

7. Remove the bearing inner and outer race(s) from the drum or rotor, using a soft drift or press.

To install:

8. Clean and inspect mating surfaces for bearing races.

9. Install new races, using soft drift or press.

10. Install new properly greased inner bearing.

11. Install seal.

12. Install drum or rotor, outer bearing, washer, nut and adjust bearing play.

13. Install cotter pin and dust cap.

14. If equipped with disc brakes, install caliper assembly.

15. If hydraulic lines had be removed, install and bleed brakes.

16. If parking brake cable had been remove, install and adjust as necessary.

17. Install the wheel assembly.

18. Lower vehicle and check brakes for proper operation.

Adjustment

EXCEPT QUATTRO

1. Raise and support the vehicle safely.

2. Remove the grease cap.

3. Remove the cotter pin and the locking nut.

4. While turning the wheel, so the wheel bearing does not jam, tighten the adjusting nut firmly.

5. Back the nut off slightly. Using an appropriate tool, try to move the thrust washer with just finger pressure; when the

thrust washer can be moved slightly, the correct adjustment has been met.

6. To install, place new grease in the grease cap and reverse the removal procedure.

Rear Axle Assembly

Removal and Installation

4WD VEHICLES

1. Raise and support the vehicle safely. Remove the wheel assembly. Detach the muffler hanger bands. Lower and support the muffler and tail pipe.

2. Remove the parking brake cable to equalizer nut. Pry the cable sleeve from the bracket. Remove both parking brake cables at the brackets and disconnect the brake hoses at the brake line brackets. Cap all hoses and lines. Vehicles equipped with anti-lock brakes, disconnect the speed sensor.

3. Remove the nuts from the bolts attaching the trailing arms to the body. Do not remove the bolts at this time. On the right side, disconnect the spring from the brake pressure regulator.

4. Remove the bolts attaching the diagonal arms to the axle and remove the bolts attaching the strut to the axle. Slide out the trailing arm to the body attaching bolts and carefully remove the axle from the vehicle.

NOTE: All bolts through rubber bushings should be tighten with the weight of the vehicle on its wheels. This is done to preset the bushings in a level non-stressed position, to avoid poor handling or tire wear.

To install:

5. Installation is the reverse order of the removal procedure, with the following exceptions:

   a. After positioning the axle in the vehicle, install both trailing arm bolts finger tight. Install the wheel and tire assemblies and lower the vehicle.

   b. Torque the trailing arm attaching bolts to 72 ft. lbs. and raise the vehicle so as to install the remaining components.

   c. On 1987 vehicles, torque the strut attaching bolts to 43 ft. lbs. and the diagonal arm attaching bolts to 51 ft. lbs. On 80 and 90 vehicles, torque the control arm mounting bolts to 72 ft. lbs. and the diagonal arm-to- body to 58 ft. lbs. and diagonal arm-to-axle to 66 ft. lbs. On 100, 200 and V8 vehicles, torque the control arm mounting bolts to 72 ft. lbs. and the diagonal arm-to-body to 66 ft. lbs. and diagonal arm-to-axle to 70 ft. lbs.

   d. After the installation procedure has been completed, install the speed sensor, if equipped, bleed the brake system and adjust the parking brake, as necessary.

SERIAL NUMBER IDENTIFICATION

Vehicle Identification Plate

The manufacturer's plate is located in the engine compartment, on the right side inner fender panel or support.

Engine Number

The engine number is located on the left rear side of the engine, above the starter motor.

Vehicle Identification Number

The vehicle identification number is located on a plate, on the drivers side of the instrument panel.

Chassis Number

The chassis number can be found in the engine compartment on the right front inner fender support or facing forward on the right side of the bulkhead. A label is also attached to the upper steering column cover, inside the vehicle.

SPECIFICATIONS

ENGINE IDENTIFICATION

Year	Model	Engine Displacement cu. in. (cc/liter)	Engine Series Identification	No. of Cylinders	Engine Type
1987	325	165 (2693/2.7)	M20B27	6	OHC
	325i	152 (2494/2.5)	M20B25	6	OHC
	528e	165 (2693/2.7)	M20B27	6	OHC
	325iS	152 (2494/2.5)	M20B25	6	OHC
	535i	209 (3428/3.4)	M30B34	6	OHC
	635CSi	209 (3428/3.4)	M30B35MZ	6	OHC
	735i	209 (3428/3.4)	M30B35MZ	6	OHC
	M5	210.6 (3453/3.5)	S38Z	6	DOHC
	M6	210.6 (3453/3.5)	S38Z	6	DOHC
1988	325	165 (2693/2.7)	M20B27	6	OHC
	528e	165 (2693/2.7)	M20B27	6	OHC
	325i	152 (2494/2.5)	M20B25	6	OHC
	325iS	152 (2494/2.5)	M20B25	6	OHC
	325iX	152 (2494/2.5)	M20B25	6	OHC
	535i	209 (3428/3.4)	M30B34	6	OHC
	635CSi	209 (3428/3.4)	M30B35MZ	6	OHC
	L6	209 (3428/3.4)	M30B35MZ	6	OHC
	735i	209 (3428/3.4)	M30B35MZ	6	OHC
	M3	140.4 (2302/2.3)	S14	4	DOHC
	M5	210.6 (3453/3.5)	S38Z	6	DOHC
	M6	210.6 (3453/3.5)	S38Z	6	DOHC
	750iL	304.4 (4988/5.0)	M70	12	OHC
1989	325	165 (2693/2.7)	M20B27	6	OHC
	325i	152 (2494/2.5)	M20B25	6	OHC
	325iS	152 (2494/2.5)	M20B25	6	OHC
	325iX	152 (2494/2.5)	M20B25	6	OHC
	525	152 (2494/2.5)	M20B25	6	OHC
	535i	209 (3428/3.4)	M30B34	6	OHC
	635CSi	209 (3428/3.4)	M30B35MZ	6	OHC

ENGINE IDENTIFICATION

Year	Model	Engine Displacement cu. in. (cc/liter)	Engine Series Identification	No. of Cylinders	Engine Type
1989	L6	209 (3428/3.4)	M30B35MZ	6	OHC
	735i	209 (3428/3.4)	M30B35MZ	6	OHC
	735iL	209 (3428/3.4)	M30B35MZ	6	OHC
	M3	140.4 (2302/2.3)	S14	4	DOHC
	M5	210.6 (3453/3.5)	S38Z	6	DOHC
	M6	210.6 (3453/3.5)	S38Z	6	DOHC
	750iL	304.4 (4988/5.0)	M70	12	OHC
1990–91	318iS	109.6 (1796/1.8)	M42	4	OHC
	325i	152 (2494/2.5)	M20B25	6	OHC
	325iS	152 (2494/2.5)	M20B25	6	OHC
	325iX	152 (2494/2.5)	M20B25	6	OHC
	525i	152 (2494/2.5)	M30B25L	6	OHC
	535i	209 (3430/3.5)	M30B34M	6	OHC
	M3	140 (2302/2.3)	S14B23	4	DOHC
	735i	209 (3430/3.5)	M30B35M	6	·OHC
	735iL	209 (3430/3.5)	M30B35M	6	OHC
	750iL	304 (4988/5.0)	M70	12	OHC

GENERAL ENGINE SPECIFICATIONS

Year	Model	Engine Displacement cu. in. (cc)	Fuel System Type	Net Horsepower @ rpm	Net Torque @ rpm (ft. lbs.)	Bore × Stroke (in.)	Compression Ratio	Oil Pressure @ rpm
1987	325	165 (2693)	EFI	121 @ 4250	170 @ 3250	3.307 × 3.189	9.0:1	71 @ 5000
	528e	165 (2693)	EFI	121 @ 4250	170 @ 3250	3.307 × 3.189	9.0:1	71 @ 5000
	325i	152 (2494)	EFI	167 @ 5800	164 @ 4300	3.307 × 2.953	8.8:1	71 @ 5000
	325iS	152 (2494)	EFI	167 @ 5800	164 @ 4300	3.307 × 2.953	8.8:1	71 @ 5000
	535i	209 (3428)	EFI	182 @ 5400	213 @ 4000	3.62 × 3.38	8.0:1	71 @ 6000
	635CSi	209 (3428)	EFI	208 @ 5700	225 @ 4000	3.62 × 3.38	9.0:1	64 @ 6200
	735i	209 (3428)	EFI	208 @ 5700	225 @ 4000	3.62 × 3.38	9.0:1	64 @ 6200
	M5	210.6 (3453)	EFI	256 @ 6500	239 @ 4500	3.67 × 3.30	9.8:1	71 @ 6900
	M6	210.6 (3453)	EFI	256 @ 6500	239 @ 4500	3.67 × 3.30	9.8:1	71 @ 6900
1988	325	165 (2693)	EFI	121 @ 4250	170 @ 3250	3.307 × 3.189	9.0:1	71 @ 5000
	528e	165 (2693)	EFI	121 @ 4250	170 @ 3250	3.307 × 3.189	9.0:1	71 @ 5000
	325i	152 (2494)	EFI	167 @ 5800	164 @ 4300	3.307 × 2.953	8.8:1	71 @ 6000
	325iS	152 (2494)	EFI	167 @ 5800	164 @ 4300	3.307 × 2.953	8.8:1	71 @ 6000
	325iX	152 (2494)	EFI	167 @ 5800	164 @ 4300	3.307 × 2.953	8.8:1	71 @ 6000
	535i	209 (3428)	EFI	182 @ 5400	213 @ 4000	3.62 × 3.38	8.0:1	71 @ 6100
	635CSi	209 (3428)	EFI	208 @ 5700	225 @ 4000	3.62 × 3.38	9.0:1	64 @ 6200
	L6	209 (3428)	EFI	208 @ 5700	225 @ 4000	3.62 × 3.38	9.0:1	64 @ 6200
	735i	209 (3428)	EFI	208 @ 5700	225 @ 4000	3.62 × 3.38	9.0:1	64 @ 6200
	M3	104.4 (2302)	EFI	194 @ 6750	166 @ 4750	3.67 × 3.30	10.5:1	71 @ 7250
	M5	210.6 (3453)	EFI	256 @ 6500	239 @ 4500	3.67 × 3.30	9.8:1	71 @ 6800
	M6	210.6 (3453)	EFI	256 @ 6500	239 @ 4500	3.67 × 3.30	9.8:1	71 @ 6800

GENERAL ENGINE SPECIFICATIONS

Year	Model	Engine Displacement cu. in. (cc)	Fuel System Type	Net Horsepower @ rpm	Net Torque @ rpm (ft. lbs.)	Bore × Stroke (in.)	Compression Ratio	Oil Pressure @ rpm
1989	325	165 (2693)	EFI	121 @ 4250	170 @ 3250	3.307 × 3.189	9.0:1	71 @ 5000
	325i	152 (2494)	EFI	167 @ 5800	164 @ 4300	3.307 × 2.953	8.8:1	71 @ 6000
	325iS	152 (2494)	EFI	167 @ 5800	164 @ 4300	3.307 × 2.953	8.8:1	71 @ 6000
	325iX	152 (2494)	EFI	167 @ 5800	164 @ 4300	3.307 × 2.953	8.8:1	71 @ 6000
	525i	152 (2494)	EFI	167 @ 5800	164 @ 4300	3.31 × 3.295	8.8:1	71 @ 6000
	535i	209 (3428)	EFI	182 @ 5400	213 @ 4000	3.62 × 3.38	8.0:1	71 @ 6100
	635CSi	209 (3428)	EFI	208 @ 5700	225 @ 4000	3.62 × 3.38	9.0:1	64 @ 6200
	L6	209 (3428)	EFI	208 @ 5700	225 @ 4000	3.62 × 3.38	9.0:1	64 @ 6200
	735i	209 (3428)	EFI	208 @ 5700	225 @ 4000	3.62 × 3.38	9.0:1	64 @ 6200
	735iL	209 (3428)	EFI	208 @ 5700	225 @ 4000	3.62 × 3.38	9.0:1	64 @ 6200
	M3	104.4 (2302)	EFI	194 @ 6750	166 @ 4750	3.67 × 3.30	10.5:1	71 @ 7250
	M5	210.6 (3453)	EFI	256 @ 6500	239 @ 4500	3.67 × 3.30	9.8:1	71 @ 6800
	M6	210.6 (3453)	EFI	256 @ 6500	239 @ 4500	3.67 × 3.30	9.8:1	71 @ 6800
1990-91	318iS	109.6 (1796)	EFI	136 @ 5800	127 @ 4600	NA	NA	NA
	325i	152 (2494)	EFI	168 @ 5800	164 @ 4300	3.31 × 2.95	8.8:1	71 @ 6000
	325iS	152 (2494)	EFI	168 @ 5800	164 @ 4300	3.31 × 2.95	8.8:1	71 @ 6000
	325iX	152 (2494)	EFI	168 @ 5800	164 @ 4300	3.31 × 2.95	8.8:1	71 @ 6000
	525i	152 (2494)	EFI	168 @ 5800	164 @ 4300	3.31 × 2.95	8.8:1	71 @ 6000
	535i	209 (3430)	EFI	208 @ 5700	225 @ 4000	3.62 × 3.39	9.0:1	71 @ 6000
	735i	209 (3430)	EFI	208 @ 5700	225 @ 4000	3.62 × 3.39	9.0:1	64 @ 6200
	735iL	209 (3430)	EFI	208 @ 5700	225 @ 4000	3.62 × 3.39	9.0:1	64 @ 6200
	750iL	304 (4988)	EFI	296 @ 5200	332 @ 4100	3.31 × 2.95	8.8:1	57 @ 6000
	M3	140 (2302)	EFI	192 @ 6750	170 @ 4750	3.68 × 3.31	10.5:1	71 @ 7250

EFI–Electronic Fuel Injection
NA–Not Available

GASOLINE ENGINE TUNE-UP SPECIFICATIONS

Year	Model	Engine Displacement cu. in. (cc)	Spark Plugs Type	Spark Plugs Gap (in.)	Ignition Timing (deg.) MT	Ignition Timing (deg.) AT	Compression Pressure (psi)	Fuel Pump (psi)	Idle Speed (rpm) MT	Idle Speed (rpm) AT	Valve Clearance In.	Valve Clearance Ex.
1987	325	165 (2693)	WR9LS	0.029	①	①	149	33–38	700	700	0.010	0.010
	528e	165 (2693)	WR9LS	0.029	①	①	149	33–38	700	700	0.010	0.010
	325i	152 (2494)	W8LCR	0.029	①	①	149	43	720	720	0.010	0.010
	325iS	152 (2494)	W8LCR	0.029	①	①	149	43	720	720	0.010	0.010
	535i	209 (3428)	WR9LS	0.029	①	①	149	43	800	800	0.012	0.012
	635CSi	209 (3428)	WR9LS	0.029	①	①	149	43	800	800	0.012	0.012
	735i	209 (3428)	WR9LS	0.029	①	①	149	43	800	800	0.012	0.012
	M5	210.6 (3453)	X5DC	0.029	①	①	149	43	800	—	0.013	0.013
	M6	210.6 (3453)	X5DC	0.029	①	①	149	43	800	—	0.013	0.013

GASOLINE ENGINE TUNE-UP SPECIFICATIONS

Year	Model	Engine Displacement cu. in. (cc)	Spark Plugs Type	Gap (in.)	Ignition Timing (deg.) MT	AT	Compression Pressure (psi)	Fuel Pump (psi)	Idle Speed (rpm) MT	AT	Valve Clearance In.	Ex.
1988	325	165 (2693)	WR9LS	0.027	①	①	149	36	720	720	0.010	0.010
	528e	165 (2693)	WR9LS	0.027	①	①	149	36	720	720	0.010	0.010
	325i	152 (2494)	WR9LS	0.027	①	①	149	43	760	760	0.010	0.010
	325iS	152 (2494)	WR9LS	0.027	①	①	149	43	760	760	0.010	0.010
	325iX	152 (2494)	WR9LS	0.027	①	①	149	43	760	760	0.010	0.010
	535i	209 (3428)	WR9LS	0.027	①	①	149	43	800	800	0.012	0.012
	635CSi	209 (3428)	WR9LS	0.027	①	①	149	43	800	800	0.012	0.012
	L6	209 (3428)	WR9LS	0.027	①	①	149	43	800	800	0.012	0.012
	M3	140.4 (2302)	WR9LS	0.027	①	①	149	43	—	—	0.012	0.012
	M5	210.6 (3453)	WR9LS	0.027	①	①	149	43	850	—	0.013	0.013
	M6	210.6 (3453)	WR9LS	0.027	①	①	149	43	850	—	0.013	0.013
	735i	209 (3428)	W8LCR	0.027	①	①	149	43	①	①	0.012	0.012
	750i	304 (4988)	F8LCR	0.027	①	①	176	43	700	700	NA	NA
1989	325	165 (2693)	WR9LS	0.027	①	①	149	36	720	720	0.010	0.010
	325i	152 (2494)	WR9LS	0.027	①	①	149	43	760	760	0.010	0.010
	325iS	152 (2494)	WR9LS	0.027	①	①	149	43	760	760	0.010	0.010
	325iX	152 (2494)	WR9LS	0.027	①	①	149	43	760	760	0.010	0.010
	525i	152 (2494)	WR9LS	0.027	①	①	149	43	760	760	0.010	0.010
	535i	209 (3428)	WR9LS	0.027	①	①	149	43	800	800	0.012	0.012
	635CSi	209 (3428)	WR9LS	0.027	①	①	149	43	800	800	0.012	0.012
	L6	209 (3428)	WR9LS	0.027	①	①	149	43	800	800	0.012	0.012
	M3	140.4 (2302)	WR9LS	0.027	①	①	149	43	—	—	0.012	0.012
	M5	210.6 (3453)	WR9LS	0.027	①	①	149	43	850	—	0.013	0.013
	M6	210.6 (3453)	WR9LS	0.027	①	①	149	43	850	—	0.013	0.013
	735i	209 (3428)	W8LCR	0.027	①	①	149	43	①	①	0.012	0.012
	735iL	209 (3428)	W8LCR	0.027	①	①	149	43	①	①	0.012	0.012
	750iL	304 (4988)	F8LCR	0.027	①	①	176	43	700	700	NA	NA
1990	318iS	109.6 (1796)	FO3DAR	0.032	①	①	142–156	43	NA	NA	NA	NA
	325i	152 (2494)	W8LCR	0.028	①	①	142–156	43	760	760	0.010	0.010
	325iS	152 (2494)	W8LCR	0.028	①	①	142–156	43	760	760	0.010	0.010
	325iX	152 (2494)	W8LCR	0.028	①	①	142–156	43	760	760	0.010	0.010
	525i	152 (2494)	W8LCR	0.028	①	①	143–156	43	800	800	③	③
	535i	209 (3430)	W8LCR	0.028	①	①	143–156	43	800	800	③	③
	725i	209 (3430)	W8LCR	0.028	①	①	142–156	43	800	800	③	③
	735iL	209 (3430)	W8LCR	0.028	①	①	142–156	43	800	800	③	③
	750iL	304 (4988)	F8LCR	0.028	①	①	142–170	43	800	800	③	NA
	M3	140 (2302)	X50L	0.028	①	①	143–156	43	880	880	0.0010–0.0026	0.0010–0.0026
1991						All SEE UNDERHOOD SPECIFICATIONS							

NOTE: The underhood specifications sticker often reflects tune-up changes made in production. Sticker figures must be used if they disagree with those in this chart.

NA Not available
B Before Top Dead Center
① Motronic injection system—controlled by computer, please refer to the underhood sticker for specifications

② 0.010–0.014 COLD
0.012–0.016 HOT
③ 0.012—COLD
0.014—HOT

FIRING ORDERS

NOTE: To avoid confusion, always replace spark plug wires one at a time.

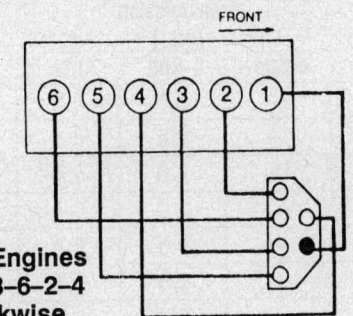

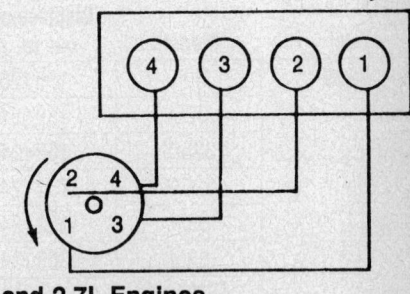

2.5L, 2.7L, 3.4L and 5.0L Engines
Engine Firing Order 1–5–3–6–2–4
Distributor Rotation: Clockwise

2.3L and 2.7L Engines
Engine Firing Order: 1–3–4–2
Distributor Rotation: Counterclockwise

1.8L Engine
Engine Firing Order: 1–3–4–2
Distributorless Ignition System

2.3L Engine
Engine Firing Order: 1–3–4–2
Distributorless Ignition System

CAPACITIES

Year	Model	Engine Displacement cu. in. (cc)	Engine Crankcase (qts.) with Filter	Engine Crankcase (qts.) without Filter	Transmission (pts.) 4-Spd	Transmission (pts.) 5-Spd	Transmission (pts.) Auto.	Drive Axle (pts.)	Fuel Tank (gal.)	Cooling System (qts.)
1987	325	165 (2693)	4.5	4.2	—	2.6	6.4	3.6	15.3	12.7
	528e	165 (2693)	4.5	4.2	—	3.4	6.4	3.8	16.6	11.6
	535i	209 (3428)	6.1	5.3	—	3.4	6.4	4.0	16.6	12.7
	635CSi	209 (3428)	6.1	5.3	—	3.4	6.4	4.0	16.6	12.7
	735i	209 (3428)	6.1	5.3	—	3.4	6.4	3.6	21.4	12.7
	M5	210.6 (3453)	6.1	5.3	—	2.6	6.4	4.0	16.6	12.7
	M6	210.6 (3453)	6.1	5.3	—	2.6	6.4	4.0	16.6	12.7
1988	325	165 (2693)	4.5	4.2	—	2.6	6.4	3.6	16.4	11.6
	325i	152 (2494)	5.0	4.75	—	2.6	6.4	3.6	16.4	11.0
	325iS	152 (2494)	5.0	4.75	—	2.6	6.4	3.6	16.4	11.0
	325iX	152 (2494)	5.0	4.75	—	2.6	6.4①	3.6②	16.4	11.0
	528e	165 (2693)	4.5	4.2	—	3.4	6.4	3.8	16.6	11.6
	535i	209 (3428)	6.1	5.3	—	2.6	6.4	4.0	16.6	11.6
	535iS	209 (3428)	6.1	5.3	—	2.6	6.4	4.0	16.6	12.7
	635CSi	209 (3428)	6.1	5.3	—	3.4	6.4	4.0	16.6	12.7
	L6	209 (3428)	6.1	5.3	—	3.4	6.4	4.0	16.6	12.7
	735i	209 (3428)	6.1	5.3	—	2.6	6.4	4.0	21.4	12.7
	M3	104.4 (2302)	5.0	4.75	—	2.6	6.4	3.6	16.4	12.7
	M5	210.6 (3453)	6.1	5.3	—	2.6	6.4	4.0	14.5	12.7
	M6	210.6 (3453)	6.1	5.3	—	2.6	6.4	4.0	16.6	12.7
	750iL	304 (4988)	7.9	6.8	—	2.6	6.4	4.0	21.4	12.7

BMW
3-SERIES • 5-SERIES • 6-SERIES • 7-SERIES

CAPACITIES

Year	Model	Engine Displacement cu. in. (cc)	Engine Crankcase (qts.) with Filter	without Filter	Transmission (pts.) 4-Spd	5-Spd	Auto.	Drive Axle (pts.)	Fuel Tank (gal.)	Cooling System (qts.)
1989	325	165 (2693)	4.5	4.2	—	2.6	6.4	3.6	16.4	11.6
	325i	152 (2494)	5.0	4.75	—	2.6	6.4	3.6	16.4	11.0
	325iS	152 (2494)	5.0	4.75	—	2.6	6.4	3.6	16.4	11.0
	325iX	152 (2494)	5.0	4.75	—	2.6	6.4①	3.6②	16.4	11.0
	525i	152 (2494)	5.0	4.75	—	2.6	6.4	3.6	16.4	11.0
	535i	209 (3428)	6.1	5.3	—	2.6	6.4	4.0	16.6	11.6
	535iS	209 (3428)	6.1	5.3	—	2.6	6.4	4.0	16.6	12.7
	635CSi	209 (3428)	6.1	5.3	—	3.4	6.4	4.0	16.6	12.7
	L6	209 (3428)	6.1	5.3	—	3.4	6.4	4.0	16.6	12.7
	735i	209 (3428)	6.1	5.3	—	2.6	6.4	4.0	21.4	12.7
	735iL	209 (3428)	6.1	5.3	—	2.6	6.4	4.0	21.4	12.7
	M3	104.4 (2302)	5.0	4.75	—	2.6	—	3.6	14.5	12.7
	M5	210.6 (3453)	6.1	5.3	—	2.6	6.4	4.0	16.6	12.7
	M6	210.6 (3453)	6.1	5.3	—	2.6	—	4.0	16.6	12.7
	750iL	304 (4988)	7.9	6.8	—	2.6	6.4	4.0	21.4	12.7
1990–91	318iS	109.6 (1796)	NA	NA	—	NA	NA	NA	NA	NA
	325i	152 (2494)	5.0	4.75	—	2.6	6.4	3.6	16.4	11.0
	325iS	152 (2494)	5.0	4.75	—	2.6	6.4	3.6	16.4	11.0
	325iX	152 (2494)	5.0	4.75	—	2.6	6.4①	3.6②	16.4	11.0
	525i	152 (2494)	5.0	4.75	—	2.6	6.4	3.6	21.0	11.0
	535i	209 (3430)	6.10	5.30	—	2.6	6.4	4.0	21.0	12.7
	725i	209 (3430)	6.10	5.30	—	2.6	6.4	4.0	21.4	12.7
	735iL	209 (3430)	6.10	5.30	—	2.6	6.4	4.0	21.4	12.7
	750iL	304 (4988)	7.90	6.80	—	2.6	7.4	4.0	24	14.8
	M3	140 (2303)	4.5	4.2	—	2.6	—	3.6	14.5	9.5

NA Not Available
① 325iX Transfer case—1.1
② 325iX Front drive axle—1.5

CRANKSHAFT AND CONNECTING ROD SPECIFICATIONS

All measurements are given in inches.

Year	Engine Displacement cu. in. (cc)	Crankshaft Main Brg. Journal Dia.	Main Brg. Oil Clearance	Shaft End-play	Thrust on No.	Connecting Rod Journal Diameter	Oil Clearance	Side Clearance
1987	152 (2494)	2.3622	0.0012–0.0027	0.030–0.007	4	1.7717	0.0012–0.0028	0.0016
	165 (2693)	2.3622	0.0012–0.0027	0.030–0.007	4	1.7717	0.0012–0.0028	0.0016
	209 (3428)	2.3622	0.0012–0.0027	0.030–0.007	4	1.8898	0.0012–0.0028	0.0016
	210.6 (3453)	2.3622	0.0012–0.0027	0.030–0.007	4	1.88877–1.88940	0.0012–0.0028	0.0016

CRANKSHAFT AND CONNECTING ROD SPECIFICATIONS

All measurements are given in inches.

| Year | Engine Displacement cu. in. (cc) | Crankshaft | | | | Connecting Rod | | |
		Main Brg. Journal Dia.	Main Brg. Oil Clearance	Shaft End-play	Thrust on No.	Journal Diameter	Oil Clearance	Side Clearance
1988	140.4 (2302)	2.1653	0.0012–0.0028	0.0033–0.0068	3	1.88877–1.88940	0.0012–0.0028	0.0016
	152 (2494)	2.3622	0.0012–0.0027	0.0033–0.0068	4	1.7717	0.0012–0.0028	0.0016
	165 (2693)	2.3622	0.0012–0.0027	0.0033–0.0068	4	1.7717	0.0012–0.0028	0.0016
	209 (3428)	2.3622	0.0012–0.0027	0.0033–0.0068	4	1.8898	0.0012–0.0028	0.0016
	210.6 (3453)	2.3622	0.0012–0.0027	0.0033–0.0068	4	1.88877–1.88940	0.0012–0.0028	0.0016
	304 (4988)	2.9521–2.9523	0.0010–0.0030	0.0033–0.0068	—	1.7707–1.7713	0.0006–0.0023	0.0016
1989	140.4 (2302)	2.1653	0.0012–0.0028	0.0033–0.0068	3	1.88877–1.88940	0.0012–0.0028	0.0016
	152 (2494)	2.3622	0.0012–0.0027	0.0033–0.0068	4	1.7717	0.0012–0.0028	0.0016
	165 (2693)	2.3622	0.0012–0.0027	0.0033–0.0068	4	1.7717	0.0012–0.0028	0.0016
	209 (3428)	2.3622	0.0012–0.0027	0.0033–0.0068	4	1.8898	0.0012–0.0028	0.0016
	210.6 (3453)	2.3622	0.0012–0.0027	0.0033–0.0068	4	1.88877–1.88940	0.0012–0.0028	0.0016
	304 (4988)	2.9521–2.9523	0.0010–0.0030	0.0033–0.0068	—	1.7707–1.7713	0.0006–0.0023	0.0016
1990–91	109.6 (1796)	①	NA	0.008–0.016	—	①	0.0008–0.0022	0.0008–0.0020
	140.4 (2302)	2.1653	0.0012–0.0028	0.0033–0.0068	3	1.88877–1.88940	0.0012–0.0028	0.0016
	152 (2494)	2.3622	0.0012–0.0027	0.0033–0.0068	4	1.7717	0.0012–0.0028	0.0016
	209 (3430)	2.3622	0.0012–0.0027	0.0033–0.0068	4	1.88877 1.88940	0.0012–0.0028	0.0016
	304 (4988)	2.9521–2.9523	0.0010–0.0030	0.0033–0.0068	—	1.7707–1.7713	0.0006–0.0023	0.0016

NA Not Available
① One paint stripe—0.010″
   Two paint stripes—0.020″

VALVE SPECIFICATIONS

| Year | Engine Displacement cu. in. (cc) | Seat Angle (deg.) | Face Angle (deg.) | Spring Test Pressure (lbs.) | Spring Installed Height (in.) | Stem-to-Guide Clearance (in.) | | Stem Diameter (in.) | |
						Intake	Exhaust	Intake	Exhaust
1987	152 (2494)	45	45.5	64 @ 148	1.71①	0.031②	0.031②	0.3149	0.3149
	165 (2693)	45	45	NA	NA	0.031②	0.031②	0.275	0.275
	209 (3428)	45	45.5	64 @ 1.48	1.71①	0.031②	0.031②	0.3149	0.3149
	210.6 (3453)	45	NA	NA	NA	0.025②	0.031②	0.276	0.276

VALVE SPECIFICATIONS

Year	Engine Displacement cu. in. (cc)	Seat Angle (deg.)	Face Angle (deg.)	Spring Test Pressure (lbs.)	Spring Installed Height (in.)	Stem-to-Guide Clearance (in.)		Stem Diameter (in.)	
						Intake	Exhaust	Intake	Exhaust
1988	140.4 (2302)	45	NA	NA	NA	0.025②	0.031②	0.276	0.276
	152 (2494)	45	NA	NA	NA	0.031②	0.031②	0.275	0.275
	165 (2693)	45	NA	NA	NA	0.031②	0.031②	0.275	0.275
	209 (3428)	45	NA	NA	NA	0.031②	0.031②	0.315	0.315
	210.6 (3453)	45	NA	NA	NA	0.025②	0.031②	0.276	0.276
	304 (4988)	45	NA	NA	NA	0.020②	0.020②	0.275	0.275
1989	140.4 (2302)	45	NA	NA	NA	0.025②	0.031②	0.276	0.276
	152 (2494)	45	NA	NA	NA	0.031②	0.031②	0.275	0.275
	165 (2693)	45	NA	NA	NA	0.031②	0.031②	0.275	0.275
	209 (3428)	45	NA	NA	NA	0.031②	0.031②	0.315	0.315
	210.6 (3453)	45	NA	NA	NA	0.025②	0.031②	0.276	0.276
	304 (4988)	45	NA	NA	NA	0.020②	0.020②	0.275	0.275
1990–91	109.6 (1796)	NA	NA	NA	NA	NA	NA	NA	NA
	140 (2302)	45	NA	NA	NA	0.025②	0.031②	0.276	0.276
	152 (2494)	45	NA	NA	NA	0.031②	0.031②	0.275	0.275
	209 (3430)	45	NA	NA	NA	0.031②	0.031②	0.275	0.275
	304 (4988)	45	NA	NA	NA	0.031②	0.031②	0.275	0.275

NA Not Available

① A dimension of 1.8110 applies to some springs, depending upon manufacturer. Figure given is free height

② Tilt clearance

PISTON AND RING SPECIFICATIONS

All measurements are given in inches

Year	Engine Displacement cu. in. (cc)	Piston Clearance	Ring Gap			Ring Side Clearance		
			Top Compression	Bottom Compression	Oil Control	Top Compression	Bottom Compression	Oil Control
1987	152 (2494)	0.0004–0.0016	0.0120–0.0200	0.0120–0.0200	0.0100–0.0200	0.0016–0.0028	0.0012–0.0024	0.0008–0.0017
	165 (2693)	0.0004–0.0016	0.0120–0.0200	0.0120–0.0200	0.0100–0.0200	0.0016–0.0028	0.0012–0.0024	0.0008–0.0017
	209 (3428)	0.0008–0.0020	0.0120–0.0200	0.0080–0.0160	0.0100–0.0200	0.0200–0.0320	0.0016–0.0028	0.0008–0.0020
	210.6 (3453)	0.0012–0.0024	0.0120–0.0220	0.0120–0.0220	0.0100–0.0200	0.0024–0.0035	0.0024–0.0035	0.0008–0.0020
1988	140 (2302)	0.0012–0.0024	0.0120–0.0220	0.0120–0.0220	0.0100–0.0200	0.0024–0.0035	0.0024–0.0035	0.0008–0.0020
	152 (2494)	0.0004–0.0016	0.0120–0.0200	0.0120–0.0200	0.0100–0.0200	0.0016–0.0028	0.0012–0.0024	0.0008–0.0017
	165 (2693)	0.0004–0.0016	0.0120–0.0200	0.0120–0.0200	0.0100–0.0200	0.0016–0.0028	0.0012–0.0024	0.0008–0.0017
	209 (3428) ①	0.0008–0.0020	0.0120–0.0200	0.0080–0.0160	0.0100–0.0200	0.0200–0.0320	0.0016–0.0028	0.0008–0.0020
	209 (3428) ②	0.0008–0.0020	0.0080–0.0180	0.0160–0.0260	0.0160–0.0240	0.0016–0.0028	0.0012–0.0024	0.0008–0.0022
	210.6 (3453)	0.0012–0.0024	0.0120–0.0220	0.0120–0.0220	0.0100–0.0200	0.0024–0.0035	0.0024–0.0035	0.0008–0.0020
	304 (4988)	0.0004–0.0013	0.0080–0.0160	0.0080–0.0160	0.0100–0.0200	0.0016–0.0025	0.0012–0.0028	0.0008–0.0022

PISTON AND RING SPECIFICATIONS
All measurements are given in inches

Year	Engine Displacement cu. in. (cc)	Piston Clearance	Ring Gap Top Compression	Bottom Compression	Oil Control	Ring Side Clearance Top Compression	Bottom Compression	Oil Control
1989	140 (2302)	0.0012–0.0024	0.0120–0.0220	0.0120–0.0220	0.0100–0.0200	0.0024–0.0035	0.0024–0.0035	0.0008–0.0020
	152 (2494)	0.0004–0.0016	0.0120–0.0200	0.0120–0.0200	0.0100–0.0200	0.0016–0.0028	0.0012–0.0024	0.0008–0.0017
	165 (2693)	0.0004–0.0016	0.0120–0.0200	0.0120–0.0200	0.0100–0.0200	0.0016–0.0028	0.0012–0.0024	0.0008–0.0017
	209 (3428)①	0.0008–0.0020	0.0120–0.0200	0.0080–0.0160	0.0100–0.0200	0.0200–0.0320	0.0016–0.0028	0.0008–0.0020
	209 (3428)②	0.0008–0.0020	0.0080–0.0180	0.0160–0.0260	0.0160–0.0240	0.0016–0.0028	0.0012–0.0024	0.0008–0.0022
	210.6 (3453)	0.0012–0.0024	0.0120–0.0220	0.0120–0.0220	0.0100–0.0200	0.0024–0.0035	0.0024–0.0035	0.0008–0.0020
	304 (4988)	0.0004–0.0013	0.0080–0.0160	0.0080–0.0160	0.0100–0.0200	0.0016–0.0025	0.0012–0.0028	0.0008–0.0022
1990-91	109.6 (1796)	0.0004–0.0016	0.0080–0.0160	0.0080–0.0160	NA	0.0008–0.0020	0.0008–0.0020	0.0008–0.0022
	140 (2302)	0.0012–0.0024	0.0120–0.0220	0.0120–0.0220	0.0100–0.0200	0.0024–0.0035	0.0024–0.0035	0.0008–0.0020
	152 (2494)	0.0004–0.0016	0.0120–0.0200	0.0120–0.0200	0.0100–0.0200	0.0016–0.0028	0.0012–0.0024	0.0008–0.0017
	209 (3430)	0.0008–0.0020	0.0080–0.0180	0.0160–0.0260	0.0160–0.0240	0.0016–0.0028	0.0012–0.0024	0.0008–0.0020
	304 (4988)	0.0004–0.0013	0.0080–0.0160	0.0008–0.0016	0.0100–0.0200	0.0016–0.0025	0.0012–0.0028	0.0008–0.0022

NA Not Available   ① B34 used in 535i   ② B35 used in 6 and 7 series cars

TORQUE SPECIFICATIONS
All readings in ft. lbs.

Year	Engine Displacement cu. in. (cc)	Cylinder Head Bolts	Main Bearing Bolts	Rod Bearing Bolts	Crankshaft Pulley Bolts	Flywheel Bolts	Intake	Exhaust	Spark Plugs
1987	152 (2494)	①	42–45⑤	②	283–311	71–81	22–24	22–24	15–21
	165 (2693)	①	42–45⑤	②	283–311	71–81	22–24	22–24	15–21
	209 (3428)	④	42–45⑤	38–41	311–325	71–81	22–24	22–24	15–21
	210.6 (3453)	⑥	14.5–17.5⑤	⑦	311–325	71–81	14–17	6.5–7	15–21
1988	140.4 (2302)	⑥	14.5–17.5⑤	⑦	311–325	75.5–76.5	6.5–7.0	6.5–7.0	15–21
	152 (2494)	①	42–45	②	283–311	75.5–76.5	22–24	16–18⑪	15–21
	165 (2693)	①	42–45	②	283–311	75.5–76.5	22–24	16–18⑪	15–21
	209 (3428)	④	42–45	38–41	311–325	75.5–76.5	22–24	16–18⑪	15–21
	210.6 (3453)	⑥	14.5–17.5⑤	⑦	311–325	75.5–76.5	14–17⑩	6.5–7	15–21
	304 (4988)	⑧	⑯	②	311–325	74	16–18	16–18	15–21
1989	140.4 (2302)	⑥	14.5–17.5⑤	⑦	311–325	75.5–76.5	6.5–7.0	6.5–7.0	15–21
	152 (2494)	①	42–45	②	283–311	75.5–76.5	22–24	16–18⑪	15–21
	165 (2693)	①	42–45	②	283–311	75.5–76.5	22–24	16–18⑪	15–21
	209 (3428)	④	42–45	38–41	311–325	75.5–76.5	22–24	16–18⑪	15–21
	210.6 (3453)	⑥	14.5–17.5⑥	⑦	311–325	75.5–76.5	14–17⑩	6.5–7	15–21
	304 (4988)	⑮	⑯	②	311–325	74	16–18	16–18	15–21

TORQUE SPECIFICATIONS
All readings in ft. lbs.

Year	Engine Displacement cu. in. (cc)	Cylinder Head Bolts	Main Bearing Bolts	Rod Bearing Bolts	Crankshaft Pulley Bolts	Flywheel Bolts	Manifold		Spark Plugs
							Intake	Exhaust	
1990-91	109.6 (1796)	⑫	③	②	224	87	NA	NA	17
	140.4 (2302)	⑥	14.5–17.5⑤	⑦	311–325	71–81	6.5–7.0	6.5–7.0	14–22
	152 (2494)①	42–45	②	②	283–311	71–81	22–24	16–18	14–22
	209 (3430)	④	42–45	38–41	311–325	71–81	22–24	16–18	14–22
	304 (4988)	⑧	⑨	②	—	74	14–17	16–18	14–22

NA Not Available
① Step 1—29-33
　Wait 20 minutes
　Step 2—43-47
　Warm engine fully
　Step 3—20°-30°
② Torque to 14.5 ft. lbs.
　Turn 70° angle torque
③ Step 1—17 ft. lbs.
　Step 2—50° angle torque
④ Step 1—42-44
　Wait 20 minutes
　Step 2—57-59

Run engine warm for 25 minutes
Step 3—30°-40° angle torque
⑤ Step 1—Torque to figure shown
　Step 2—Turn 47°-53° angle torque
⑥ Step 1—35-37
　Step 2—57-59
　Wait 15 minutes
　Step 3—71-73
⑦ Step 1—7
　Step 2—21.5
　Step 3—60°-62° angle torque
⑧ Step 1—22
　Wait 15 minutes

Step 2—Turn 120° angle torque
⑨ Step 1—14.5
　Step 2—Turn 70° angle torque
⑩ Applies to (larger) M8 bolts. Torque M6 (smaller) bolts to 6.5-7.0
⑪ Coat the threads of the upper row of bolts with a locking type sealer
⑫ Step 1—24 ft. lbs.
　Step 2—93° angle torque
　Step 3—93° angle torque

ENGINE ELECTRICAL

NOTE: Disconnecting the negative battery cable on some vehicles may interfere with the functions of the on board computer systems and may require the computer to undergo a relearning process, once the negative battery cable is reconnected.

Distributor

Removal

4 CYLINDER ENGINES EXCEPT M3 AND 318iS

1. Disconnect the negative battery cable. On all engines so equipped, remove the weather-proof rubber cap protecting the distributor cap and wires from moisture. Prior to removal, using paint, chalk or a sharp instrument, scribe alignment marks showing the relative position of the distributor body to its mount on the rear of the cylinder head.

2. Mark each spark plug wire with a dab of paint or chalk noting its respective cylinder. It will be easier and faster to install the distributor and get the firing order right if the plug wires are left in the cap.

3. Pull up and disconnect the secondary wire (high tension cable leading from the coil to the center of the distributor cap), and remove the spark plug loom retaining nut(s) from the cylinder head cover. Disconnect the vacuum line(s) from the vacuum advance unit.

4. Disconnect the primary wire (low tension wire running from one of the coil terminals to the side of the distributor) at the distributor. On electronic ignition distributors, disconnect the plug.

5. Disconnect the distributor retaining clasps and lift off the cap and wire assembly. On all engines equipped with a dust cap under the rotor, remove the rotor, remove the dust cap and reinstall the rotor.

6. Now, with the aid of a remote starter switch, "bump" the starter a few times until the No. 1 piston is at TDC of its com-pression stroke. At this time, the notch scribed on the metal tip of the distributor rotor must be aligned with a corresponding notch scribed on the distributor case. Before removing the distributor, make sure these 2 marks coincide.

7. Loosen the clamp bolt at the base of the distributor (where it slides into its mount) and lift the distributor up and out. Notice that the rotor turns clockwise as the distributor is removed. This is because the distributor is gear driven and must be compensated for during installation.

Installation

TIMING NOT DISTURBED

1. To install the distributor, position it in the block. Remember to rotate the rotor approximately 1.4 in. counterclockwise

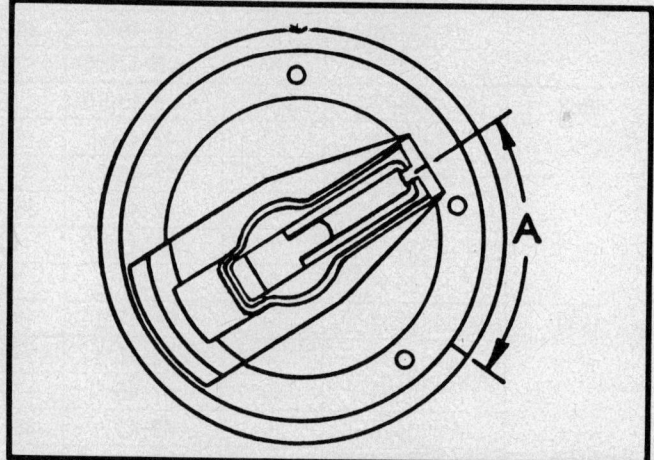

Distance (A) rotor moves from the housing mark during the removal of the electronic distributor.

from the notch scribed in the distributor body. This will ensure that when the distributor is fully seated in its mount, the marks will coincide. Adjust the ignition timing. Tighten the clamp bolt to 8.0 ft. lbs.

2. Reinstall the cap and wires.
3. Connect the negative battery cable.

TIMING DISTURBED

Sometimes, the engine is accidentally turned over while the distributor is removed; in this case, it will be necessary to find TDC position for No. 1 cylinder before installing the distributor. Check the exact position of the crankshaft via the timing marks on the flywheel or front pulley, and obtain exact alignment as indicated by them. Then, proceed to install the distributor.

6 Cylinder Engines and M3 and 318iS Vehicles

NOTE: Most 6 cylinders and the 4 cylinder engine used on the M3 and the 318iS use a distributor which is contained within the engine. Other than distributor cap and rotor removal and installation, no service is possible.

Ignition Timing

Adjustment

1. If equipped with the Motronic control unit, the timing can be checked; however, timing cannot be adjusted. The only cure for improper timing is to replace the control unit. Also, timing must be within a specified range, as the computer changes the timing slightly to allow for various changes in operating condition. In other words, the timing does not have to be right on, but anywhere within the specified range.

2. The engine should be at normal operating temperature and the operation should be performed at normal room temperatures. The engine rpm should be within the specified range under the control of the computer.

3. Look up the control unit number on the unit itself. On 3, 5, and 6 Series vehicles, the unit is in the glove box; on the 7 Series, it is in the right side speaker cutout.

4. Connect a tachometer and a timing light to the engine (the latter to the No. 1 cylinder). Start the engine and check the rpm. If it is not correct, check the idle speed and reset it as necessary. Then, operate the timing light to see if timing is within range. If it is significantly outside the range, the Motronic control unit must be replaced.

Alternator

Precautions

Several precautions must be observed with alternator equipped vehicles to avoid damaging the unit. They are as follows:

● If the battery is removed for any reason, make sure it is reconnected with the correct polarity. Reversing the battery connections may result in damage to the one-way rectifiers.

● When utilizing a booster battery as a starting aid, always connect it as follows: positive to positive, and negative (booster battery) to a good ground on the engine.

● Never use a fast charger as a booster to start vehicles with alternating-current (AC) circuits.

● When servicing the battery with a fast charger, always disconnect the battery cables.

● Never attempt to polarize an alternator.

● Avoid long soldering times when replacing diodes or transistors. Prolonged heat is damaging to alternators.

● Do not use test lamps of more than 12 volts for checking diode continuity.

● Do not short across or ground any of the terminals on the alternator.

● The polarity of the battery, alternator, and regulator must be matched and considered before making any electrical connections within the system.

● Never operate the alternator on an open circuit. Make sure all connections within the circuit are clean and tight.

● Turn off the ignition switch and then disconnect the battery terminals when performing any service on the electrical system or charging the battery.

● Disconnect the battery ground cable if arc welding is to be done on any part of the vehicle.

Belt Tension Adjustment

The fan belt tension is adjusted by moving the alternator on the slack adjuster bracket. The belt tension is adjusted to a deflection of approximately ½ in. under moderate thumb pressure in the middle of its longest span. On many engines, the position of the top of the alternator is adjusted via a bolt that is geared to the bracket. This bolt is turned to position the alternator and determine tension, and then is locked in position with a lock bolt.

Removal and Installation

1. Disconnect the negative battery cable.

2. Disconnect the wires from the rear of the alternator, marking them for later installation. Note that there is a ground wire on some vehicles. On the 735i and 735iL, remove the cap and then disconnect the positive terminal at the junction box on the fender well. On the 325, M3, 635CSi, 735i and 735iL, it may be easier to remove the alternator mounting bolts, turn it, and then remove the wires.

On the M5 and M6:

a. Unscrew the nut and loosen the hose clamp. Pull of the plug. Then, lift out the air cleaner and airflow sensor.

b. Make sure the engine is cool. Place a pan under the radiator and disconnect the lower radiator hose.

c. On the 325, 525, M3 and 528e, remove the airflow sensor and air cleaner, if necessary.

d. On the 735i and 735iL, make sure the engine is cool. Place a pan under the radiator and disconnect the lower radiator hose.

3. Loosen the adjusting and pivot bolts, and remove the belt on those vehicles with a standard mounting system. If the alternator has the tensioning bolt described in Step 4, loosen the lock bolt, turn the tensioning bolt so as to eliminate belt tension and then remove the belt. Remove the bolts and remove the alternator. On the 635CSi, 735i and 735iL, it may be necessary to loosen the fan cowl to get at the mounting bolts. On the 535i and 525i, it may be necessary to disconnect a power steering line that runs near the alternator.

To install:

4. Install the alternator in position and install the retaining bolts.

5. Adjust the belt tension to approximately ⅜ in., measured between the balancer and the alternator pulley.

6. The tensioning bolt on the front of the alternator must be turned so as to tension the belt, using a torque wrench, until the torque is approximately 5 ft. lbs. Then, hold the adjustment with one wrench while tightening the locknut at the rear of the unit. Make sure, if the unit has a ground wire on the alternator, it has been reconnected. On the M5 and M6, 735i and 735iL, make sure to reconnect the radiator hose, refill and bleed the cooling system. On the M5, M6 and 528e securely reinstall the air cleaner and airflow sensor. On the 528e, if the power steering line had to be disconnected, reconnect it securely, refill, and bleed the system.

Starter

Removal and Installation

1. Disconnect the negative battery cable.
2. On 6 cylinder engines with 6 identical intake tubes, it may be necessary to remove No. 6 intake tube for clearance. On 4 cylinder vehicles, remove the intake cowl from the mixture control unit.
On the 325 and the M3:
    a. Remove the air cleaner and airflow sensor. Then, remove the mounting bolts for the bracket for the air collector and remove it.
On the 528e:
    a. Remove the air cleaner and airflow sensor.
    b. Disconnect the electrical leads. Remove the 3 bolts and remove the mounting bracket.
On the 535i and 525i:
    a. Make sure the engine is cool. Drain some coolant from the cooling system and then remove the expansion tank.
On the 635CSi:
    a. Make sure the engine is cool and drain some coolant out. Disconnect the heater hose that is near the starter.
    b. Operate the brake pedal hard 20 times. Disconnect the power steering line that would otherwise prevent access to the starter.
    c. Cut off the straps and remove the solenoid switch insulating cover, located right near the solenoid.
On the M5 and M6:
    a. Remove the exhaust manifold.

    b. Cut off the straps and remove the solenoid switch insulating cover, located right near the solenoid.
3. Remove the starter solenoid wire leads, marking them for later installation, unless they have already been removed. On 4 cylinder vehicles, disconnect the mounting bracket at the block. On the 325 and the M3, drain coolant out of the engine and then disconnect the heater hose located near the starter; also unscrew and remove the coolant pipe if necessary for clearance.

NOTE: Remove the accelerator cable holder on automatic transmission equipped vehicles.

4. Unbolt and remove the starter.

NOTE: On the 525i, 535i, 735i, 735iL, M5 and M6, it may be necessary to use a box wrench with an angled handle to unscrew the main starter mounting bolts. On the 528e and 635CSi, the final mounting bolt must be removed from underneath. On the 325 and M3, the starter must be pulled out from above. On the M3 remove the intake manifold, if neccessry.

To install:

5. Install the starter and install the retaining bolts. Install all removed components on all vehicles.
6. Make sure to reconnect all hoses and refill and bleed the cooling system or power steering system.
7. Where the solenoid switch cover has been unstrapped, reinstall it with new straps to locate it properly for electrical safety.

CHASSIS ELECTRICAL

———— **CAUTION** ————
On vehicles equipped with an air bag, the negative battery cable must be disconnected, before working on the system. Failure to do so may result in deployment of the air bag and possible personal injury.

Heater Blower Motor

Removal and Installation

318iS, 325, 325i, 325iS, 325iX AND M3

1. Disconnect the negative battery cable. The blower is accessible by removing the cover at the top of the firewall in the engine compartment. To remove the cover, pull off the rubber strip, cut off the wire that runs diagonally across the cover, unscrew and remove the bolts, and pull the cover aside.
2. Open the retaining straps, swing them aside, and then remove the blower cover.
3. Pull off both connectors. Disengage the clamp that fastens the assembly in place by pulling the bottom in the direction of the operator. Now, lift out the motor/fan assembly, being careful not to damage the air damper underneath.
4. The installation is the reverse of the removal procedure.

525, 525i, 528e, 535i, 635CSi, M5 AND M6

1. Disconnect the negative battery cable.
2. Remove the rubber insulator from the cowl. Remove the mounting bolts for the cover which is located under the windshield.
3. Push back the 3 retaining tabs and remove the 2 shells that cover the blower wheels.
4. Disconnect the electrical connector for the motor. Unclip the retaining strap for the motor and remove the motor and blower wheels.

5. Replace the motor and blower wheels as an assembly (prebalanced). The motor will fit into the housing only one way. Reverse all procedures to install, making sure the flat surface on the inlet cowls face the body.

735i, 735iL AND 750iL

1. Disconnect the negative battery cable. Pull the rubber cover off the overflow tank for the cooling system. Disconnect the electrical connector and overflow hose from the overflow tank. Then, remove the mounting nuts and put the tank aside without damaging the hose leading to the radiator.
2. Cut the straps for the wiring harness running across the cowl.
3. Remove the mounting screws and remove the blower cover from the cowl.
4. Disconnect the cable and unclip it where it is clipped to the blower cover. Then, open the plastic retainer and take off the cover.
5. Disconnect the electrical connector. Lift off the metal retainer for the blower motor and remove the blower motor.
6. Install a new, prebalanced motor and blower assembly. Install in reverse order.

Windshield Wiper Motor

The electric wiper motor assembly is located under the engine hood, at the top of the cowl panel. A few vehicles have covers over the wiper motor assembly, while others have the motors exposed. Link rods operate the left and right wiper pivot assemblies from a drive crank bolted to the wiper motor output shaft.

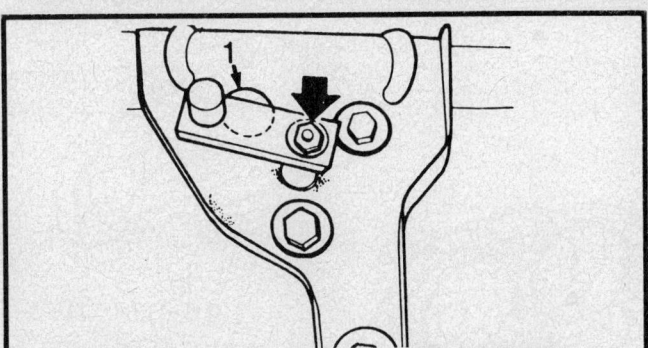

On the 735i and 733i, install the motor crank in the position shown, with the bolt (1) half hidden by the upper edge of the crank.

Removal and Installation

318iS, 325, 325i 325iS, 325iX AND M3

1. Disconnect the negative battery cable. Remove the heater motor, as described above. Remove the bracket bracing the windshield wiper motor, which is now visible.
2. Disconnect the electrical connector for the motor.
3. Lift out the grill located at the top of the cowl and disconnect the linkages to both wiper arms at the left side shaft mounts.
4. Disconnect both wiper arms from their shafts by lifting the cover, unscrewing the nut, and pulling the arm off. Then, remove the cover, nut and washer surrounding the shafts and holding the console in place. Now remove the entire console.
5. With the motor still mounted, remove the nut retaining the linkage to the motor shaft. Then, unbolt and remove the motor from the console.
6. Installation is the reverse of the removal procedure.

528e, 525i, 535i, 635CSi, M5 AND M6

1. Disconnect the negative battery cable. Remove the cowl cover to expose the wiper motor, if equipped.
2. Disconnect the wiper motor crank arm from the motor output shaft by removing the nut and pulling off the crank arm.
3. Remove the motor retaining screws and disconnect the electrical connector.
4. Remove the wiper motor from the vehicle.
5. Reverse the procedure to install the motor.

735i, 735iL AND 750iL

1. Disconnect the negative battery cable. Make sure the wipers are in the parked position. Remove the heater blower. Take off the cover near the blower.
2. Disconnect the heater cable and lift out the linkage. Disconnect the temperature sensor.
3. Disconnect the clips, lift the cowl cover slightly and then remove the fresh air inlet cowls on either side. Then, remove the cover.
4. Unscrew bolts and remove the mounting bracket for the wiper housing. Remove the left wiper arm by pulling up the cover, loosening the pinch bolt, and removing it. Remove the right wiper by pulling up the cover, removing the through bolt and then pulling it off.
5. Lift out the clips and remove the cover for the linkage.
6. Unscrew and remove the nuts fastening the linkage to the cowl. Pull the linkage arms downward and out of the cowl.
7. Mark the relationship between the linkage lever and the motor. Remove the nut and disconnect the linkage at the motor shaft. Disconnect the electrical connector and remove the linkage.

8. Remove the mounting bolts and remove the wiper motor. If installing a new motor, connect the motor and operate it until it reaches parked position; then install the linkage so the shaft lever and linkage link are in a straight line.
To install:
9. Perform the remaining portions of the installation in reverse order, noting these points:
    a. Make sure the wiper arms are pressed all the way onto the linkage shafts so the contact pressure control will work.
    b. Make sure the inlet cowling is installed in proper relation to the blower housing and fresh air flap.

Windshield Wiper Switch

Removal and Installation

1. Disconnect the negative battery cable. Remove the steering wheel. Remove the lower/left instrument panel trim.
2. Remove the screws and remove the lower steering column cover.
3. Push the locking hook for the flasher back and remove the relay, socket facing downward.
4. Take off the upper steering column cover. If the vehicle is equipped with airbags, drive out the pins and lift out the expansion rivet first.
5. Press the retaining hooks inward on both sides, pull the switch out, and then disconnect the electrical connector.
6. Installation is the reverse of removal.

Instrument Cluster

Removal and Installation

1. Disconnect the negative battery cable. Remove the attaching screws and remove the lower instrument panel trim from under the steering column.
2. Remove the mounting nuts for the trim just under the instrument carrier, and remove it.
3. Unscrew the 4 screws underneath and 2 above the instrument carrier, and remove trim that surrounds the instrument carrier.
4. Remove the 2 screws at the top of the carrier, lift it out of the instrument panel, and then disconnect the plugs. To disconnect the combination plug, first pull the sliding clamp off the center.
5. To replace the speedometer, pull the speedometer from the instrument carrier.
6. Installation is the reverse of removal.

Headlight Switch

Removal and Installation

1. Disconnect the negative battery cable. Remove the lower/left trim panel screws and remove the panel.
2. Unscrew the knob from the switch.
3. Pull off the connector plug from behind the dash panel. Pull out the switch from behind and remove it.
4. Install in reverse order.

Combination Switch

Removal and Installation

—————————— **CAUTION** ——————————
On vehicles equipped with an air bag, the negative battery cable must be disconnected, before working on the system. Failure to do so may result in deployment of the air bag and possible personal injury.

1. Instrument carrier
2. Fuel guage
3. Speedometer
4. Tachometer and economy control
5. Temperature gauge
6. LCD control
7. System carrier
8. Light bulb
9. Bulb holder
10. Socket lamp
11. Baseplate

Instrument cluster—525i and 535i

1. Disconnect the negative battery cable. Remove the steering wheel.
2. Remove the lower instrument panel on the left side.
3. Remove the steering column casing lower section.
4. If equipped with airbags, drive out the pins and lift out the expansion rivet. Remove the upper section of the steering column casing.
5. Remove the plug and disconnect the electrical connectors.
6. Push in the retaining hooks on both sides and pull out the switch.
7. The installation is the reverse of the removal procedure.

Ignition Switch

Removal and Installation

1. Disconnect the negative battery cable. Remove the steering wheel.
2. Remove the trim panel on the lower left side.
3. Remove the steering column casing lower section.
4. Press in the retaining hooks on both sides and remove the switch.
5. The installation is the reverse of the removal procedure. Check the position of the ignition switch to the steering wheel lock.

Stoplight Switch

Adjustment

1. Disconnect the negative battery cable. Disconnect the electrical connector to the switch.
2. Loosen the locknut and then turn the switch outward to remove it.
3. Screw the new switch in. Adjust the gap between the pedal and actuator on the switch to 0.197–0.236 in. on the 3 series and 0.236–0.020 in. except 3 series.

4. Tighten the locknut.

Removal and Installation

1. Disconnect the negative battery cable.
2. Remove the lower left side trim panel and disconnect the plug.
3. Press down the brake pedal and pull the plunger and sleeve down completely.
4. Press in the retainers and pull back on the switch.
5. The installation is the reverse of the removal procedure

Neutral Safety Switch

Adjustment

1. Disconnect the leads at the switch terminal.
2. Ground the negative terminal and connect a proper test light to the positive terminal.
3. The test light should light when the gear selector is placed on **P** or **N**.
4. If the switch needs adjusting, unscrew the switch and place thicker shims behind the switch and the transmission housing.

Removal and Installation

1. Disconnect the negative battery cable. Raise and safely support the vehicle.
2. Disconnect the electrical connection at the switch.
3. Remove the switch using the proper tool.
4. The installation is the reverse of the removal procedure.

Fuses, Circuit Breakers and Relays

Location

The fuse box is located under the engine hood on the left side, near the upper strut housing or near the battery.

Various relays are also mounted on the fuse box for easy accessibility.

Computer

Location

The Digital Motor Electronics (DME) unit is located in the engine compartment on the passenger side by the firewall.

Flashers

Location

The flashers are located behind the bottom center of the lower instrument trim panel.

Cruise Control

For further information, please refer to "Chilton's Chassis Electronics Service Manual" for additional coverage.

Adjustment

1. Check the distance between the nipple and the nipple holder with the throttle valve closed and the vehicle in the **N** position.

2. Adjust with a knurled nut, if necessary. The distance should be 0.039–0.059 in. exc. 7 series and 0.039–0.079 in. on the 7 series.

ENGINE COOLING

Radiator

Removal and Installation

1. Disconnect the negative battery cable. Drain the cooling system. On some engines, this requires removing the plug from the bottom radiator tank.
2. If equipped with a coolant expansion tank, remove the cap, disconnect the hose at the radiator and drain the coolant into a clean container. If equipped with a splash guard, remove it.
3. Remove the coolant hoses and disconnect the automatic transmission oil cooler lines and plug their openings as well as the openings in the cooler.
4. Disconnect any of the temperature switch wire connectors.
5. Remove the shroud from the radiator. On some vehicles, this is done by simply pressing plugs toward the rear of the vehicle. On others, there are metal slips that must be pulled upward and off to free the shroud from the radiator. The shroud will remain in the vehicle, resting on the fan on most vehicles. On the 735i and 735iL, remove the fan and shroud together. Make sure to store the fan in a vertical position. The fan must be held stationary with some sort of flat blade cut to fit over the hub and drilled to fit over 2 of the studs on the front of the pulley. Then, unscrew the retaining nut at the center of the fluid drive hub turning it clockwise to remove it because it has left hand threads.
6. If equipped with the M30 B35 engine, remove the fan and shroud; then, spread the retaining clip and pull the oil cooler out to the right. Remove the radiator retaining bolt(s) and lift the radiator from the vehicle.
7. The radiator is installed in the reverse order of removal. Fill and bleed the cooling system.

NOTE: On the M3, there are rubber washers that go on either side of the mounting brackets at the top and that the bottom of the unit is suspended by rubber bushings into which prongs located on the bottom tank will fit. Make sure all parts fit right when the unit is installed.

8. Check that rubber mounts are located so as to effectively isolate the radiator from the chassis, as this will help ensure reliable radiator performance. Note that if the vehicle uses plastic upper and lower radiator tanks and has a radiator drain plug, be careful not to over torque the plugs.
9. Torque engine oil cooler pipes to 18–21 ft. lbs. and transmission cooler pipes to 13–15 ft. lbs.
10. Torque the thermostatic fan hub on the 735i and 735iL to 29–36 ft. lbs.

Heater Core

For further information, please refer to "Chilton's Heating and Air Conditioning Manual" for additional coverage.

Removal and Installation

325, 325i, 325iS, 325iX AND M3

1. Disconnect the negative battery cable. Remove the package tray. Remove bolts and remove the left/lower dish trim panel.
2. Drain the coolant, loosen the bolt and remove the clamp bracing the 2 lines going to the heater core.
3. Remove the left side duct carrying air from the heater to the rear seat duct.
4. Unscrew the bolts and remove the lower heater discharge duct.
5. Unscrew the bolts fastening the water lines from the engine compartment to the lines coming down from the heater core. Remove and discard the O-ring seals.
6. Unscrew the bolts, separate the halves of the core housing, and pull the core out of the housing.
7. Installation is the reverse of removal. Replace the O-ring seals for the water lines.

528e, 635CSi, M5 AND M6

1. Disconnect the negative battery cable. Remove the instrument panel trim at bottom left. Remove the package tray.
2. Carefully, discharge the air conditioning system through the Schrader® valve, and then cap the valve off.
3. Remove the bolts and remove the trim panel underneath the evaporator unit.
4. Remove the tape type insulation. Get caps for the refrigerant lines. Using a backup wrench, disconnect the low and high pressure lines and cap them.
5. Disconnect the electrical connector for the evaporator. Disconnect the temperature sensor plug, accessible from the outside of the evaporator housing.
6. Remove the bolts and then remove the bracket that braces the housing at the firewall. Remove the mounting bolt from either side of the housing.
7. Unclip both fasteners and remove the housing.
8. Move into the engine compartment and remove the rubber insulator from the cowl.
9. Remove the mounting bolts for the cover which is located under the windshield.
10. Remove the mounting nuts for the heater housing located on either side of the blower.

11. Drain the cooling system and disconnect the hoses at the core.

12. Working inside the vehicle, remove the 3 electrical connectors for the heater housing. Pull off the air ducts.

13. Remove the mounting nuts and remove the heater unit.

14. Remove the air duct connections from the housing. Push the retaining bar back and then split and remove the blower shells.

15. Remove the retaining clips from the housing halves and split the housing. Then, remove the core.

To install:

16. To install, reverse the removal procedure, noting the following points:

a. Cement a new rubber seal on the core.

b. Make sure when reassembling the halves of the housing, all the distributor door flap shafts pass through the holes in the housing.

c. Before reconnecting the refrigerant lines, coat the threads with clean refrigerant oil.

d. Refill the cooling system with clean coolant and bleed it.

e. Properly, evacuate and recharge the air conditioning system.

525i, 535i, 735i, 735iL AND 750iL

1. Disconnect the negative battery cable. Drain coolant from the cooling system. Remove the center console.

2. Remove the mounting bolts and remove the right core mounting bracket. Lift out the front blower motor on the 7 series.

3. Remove the core cover screws. Loosen the wire straps and clips and remove the cover.

4. Disconnect the temperature sensor(s).

5. Unscrew the mounting bolts and lift out the heater pipes. Replace the O-rings. Then, lift out the core from the right side.

6. Install in reverse order. Refill and bleed the cooling system.

Water Pump

Removal and Installation

EXCEPT 318iS, 325, 325i, 325iS, 325iX, M3 AND 528e

1. Disconnect the negative battery cable. Drain the cooling system.

2. Remove the fan cowl and fan, if necessary.

3. Remove the drive belt and the pulley. Disconnect the bracket, if necessary.

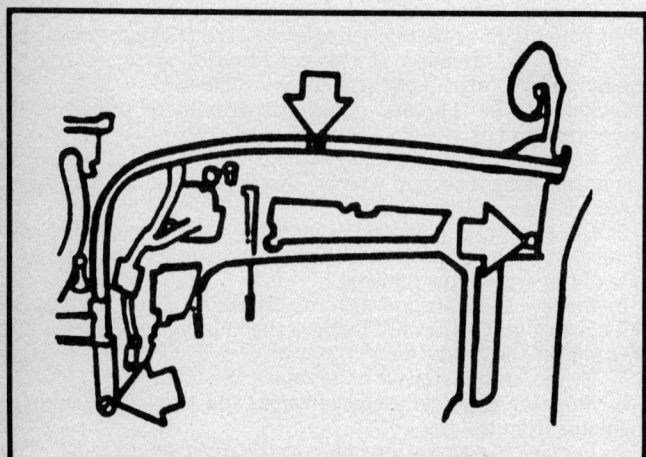

Remove the two arrowed screws to remove the heater core—1987–88 735i

4. Remove the air cleaner with the air flow sensor, if needed.

5. Disconnect the cooling hoses and remove the water pump.

6. The installation is the reverse of the removal procedure.

325, 325i, 325iS, 325iX, M3 AND 528e

1. Disconnect the negative battery cable. Drain the cooling system.

2. Remove the distributor cap and rotor. Remove the inner distributor cap and rubber sealing ring.

3. The fan must be held stationary with some sort of flat blade cut to fit over the hub and drilled to fit over 2 of the studs on the front of the pulley or use the proper tool. Remove the fan coupling nut; left hand thread—turn clockwise to remove.

4. Remove the belt and pulley.

5. Remove the rubber guard and distributor and or upper timing belt cover.

6. Compress the timing tensioner spring and clamp pin with the proper tool.

NOTE: Observe the installed position of the tensioner spring pin on the water pump housing for reinstallation purposes.

7. Remove the water hoses, remove the 3 water pump bolts and remove the pump.

8. Clean the gasket surfaces and use a new gasket.

9. Install the water pump in position. Note the position of the tensioner spring pin.

10. Add coolant and bleed the cooling system.

318iS

1. Disconnect the negative battery cable. Drain the cooling system.

2. Remove the drive belt and the water pump pulley.

3. Remove the pump mounting bolts.

4. Screw 2 bolts into the tapped bores and press the water pump out of the cover uniformly.

5. Lubricate and install a new O-ring.

6. Install the water pump and tighten the bolts to 6.5 ft. lbs.

7. The remainder of the installation is the reverse of the removal procedure.

Thermostat

Removal and Installation

The thermostat is located near the water pump, either on the cylinder head or intake manifold on some vehicles and is located between 2 coolant hose sections on some vehicles.

Always drain some coolant out and save it in a clean container before removing the thermostat. On the M5, M6 engine, the forward (removable) portion of the housing has a hose connected to it. The hose need not be disconnected to remove the housing. On the engine used in the M5, M6, there is a large O-ring seal for the main portion of the housing and a small, O-ring located above it in a small passage. The M20B25 and MB20B27 engines also use a large O-ring which must be replaced with the thermostat. Replace both these seals on all vehicles.

Note that thermostats for 3.5L engines carry an "A" designation. The thermostat for M20B27 and M20B25 engines is smaller in diameter. On all vehicles, except M3, the thermostat is installed with the thermostatic sensing unit facing inward and the cross-band facing outward. Refill and bleed the cooling system.

On the M3, the thermostat is installed in a coolant lines with a 3rd connection that goes to the block. To replace it, first drain coolant and then note the routing of hoses. Loosen all 3 hose clamps and then replace the unit. Refill and bleed the system.

Cooling System Bleeding

With Bleeder Screw on Thermostat Housing

Set the heat valve in the **WARM** position, start the engine and

Bleeding of the cooling system with bleeder screw

bring it to normal operating temperature. Run the engine at fast idle and open the venting screw on the thermostat housing until the coolant comes out free of air bubbles. Close the bleeder screw and refill the cooling system.

Without Bleeder Screw

Fill the cooling system, place the heater valve in the WARM position, close the pressure cap to the second (fully closed) position. Start the engine and bring to normal operating temperature. Carefully release the pressure cap to the first position and squeeze the upper and lower radiator hoses in a pumping action to allow trapped air to escape through the radiator. Recheck the coolant level and close the pressure cap to its second position.

FUEL SYSTEM

Fuel System Service Precautions

Safety is the most important factor when performing not only fuel system maintenance but any type of maintenance. Failure to conduct maintenance and repairs in a safe manner may result in serious personal injury or death. Maintenance and testing of the vehicle's fuel system components can be accomplished safely and effectively by adhering to the following rules and guidelines.

• To avoid the possibility of fire and personal injury, always disconnect the negative battery cable unless the repair or test procedure requires that battery voltage be applied.

• Always relieve the fuel system pressure prior to disconnecting any fuel system component (injector, fuel rail, pressure regulator, etc.), fitting or fuel line connection. Exercise extreme caution whenever relieving fuel system pressure to avoid exposing skin, face and eyes to fuel spray. Fuel under pressure may penetrate the skin or any part of the body that it contacts.

• Always place a shop towel or cloth around the fitting or connection prior to loosening to absorb any excess fuel due to spillage. Ensure that all fuel spillage (should it occur) is quickly removed from engine surfaces. Ensure that all fuel soaked cloths or towels are deposited into a suitable waste container.

Always keep a dry chemical (Class B) fire extinguisher near the work area.

• Do not allow fuel spray or fuel vapors to come into contact with a spark or open flame.

• Always use a backup wrench when loosening and tightening fuel line connection fittings. This will prevent unnecessary stress and torsion to fuel line piping. Always follow the proper torque specifications.

• Always replace worn fuel fitting O-rings with new. Do not substitute fuel hose or equivalent where fuel pipe is installed.

Relieving Fuel System Pressure

To relieve the pressure in the system, first find the fuel pump relay plug, located on the cowl. Unplug the relay, leaving it in a safe position where the connections cannot ground. If necessary, tape the plug in place or tape over the connector prongs with electrical tape. Then, start the engine and operate it until it stalls. Crank the engine for 10 seconds after it stalls to remove any residual pressure.

Fuel Filter

Removal and Installation

EXCEPT M5 AND M6

On filters that are located near the fuel tank, it is necessary to

clamp the fuel lines closed before disconnecting them, or fuel will run out continuously.

1. Disconnect the negative battery cable. Relieve fuel system pressure. Clamp the lines closed if the filter is mounted low, near the fuel tank. Then, loosen the clamps and disconnect the inlet and outlet hoses. Remove the hose clamps or slide them back, well off the connections to make it easier to pull off the hoses, if necessary.

2. The filters will usually be attached to a frame, floor pan or wheel well by a bracket. Loosen the bracket and remove the filter. On the 735 with the M30 B35 engine, remove the phillips head screw clamping the filter inside the mounting band. Note the direction of flow and then remove the filter.

3. Observe the instructions on the inlet and outlet during installation.

M5 AND M6

1. Relieve fuel system pressure. Disconnect the battery ca-

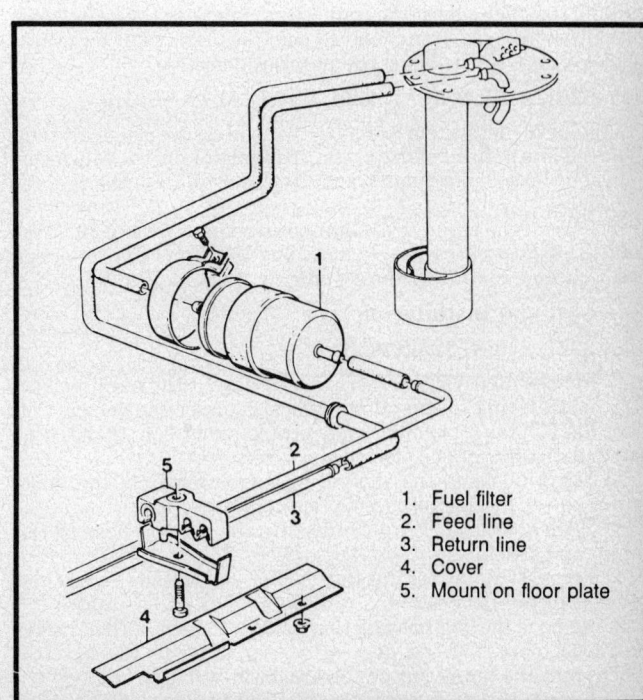

1. Fuel filter
2. Feed line
3. Return line
4. Cover
5. Mount on floor plate

Fuel filter location—525i and 535i

bles. Working under the fuel tank, pull back the protective caps and then unscrew the attaching nuts and pull off the electrical connections for the fuel pump.

2. Pinch off the inlet line to the fuel pump and the outlet from the filter. Then, loosen the clamps and disconnect these 2 hoses.

3. Remove the nut that clamps the fuel line near the pump. Then, remove the bolts which mount the pump and filter to the bottom of the body and remove the assembly.

4. Remove the bolt fastening the halves of the bracket together and remove the filter from the bracket. Loosen the clamp on the inlet side of the filter and disconnect the inlet line, noting the direction of flow (arrow). Remove the rubber bushing in which the filter is mounted, and mount it on the new filter.

5. Install the filter in exact reverse order, making sure all clamps are securely tightened. Operate the engine and check for leaks.

Electric Fuel Pump

Pressure Testing

318iX, 325, 325i, 325iS AND 325iX

1. Relieve fuel system pressure. Tee a pressure gauge into the fuel feed line in front of the pressure regulator.

2. Disconnect the fuel pump relay.

3. Connect a remote starter switch between terminals KL30 and KL87 of the relay. Close the switch and check the pressure. It should be 43 psi. If not, the filter is severely clogged or the fuel pump is defective.

M3

1. Relieve fuel system pressure. Tee a pressure gauge into the fuel return line at the pressure regulator. Then, clamp off the return line so pressure builds up to the maximum level the pump can produce.

2. Remove the trim from the cowl on the right (passenger's side). Then, unplug the fuel pump relay. Connect a remote starter switch between terminals 30 and 87 (left side and top holding the male side of the connector). Energize the switch and check the pressure. It must be 43 psi. Check the filter for excessive clogging. If it is okay, the pump is defective.

525, 525i, 535i, 635CSi, 735i, 735iL, M5 AND M6

1. Relieve fuel system pressure. Tee a pressure gauge into the fuel feed line in front of the pressure regulator on M5, M6, tee in between the cold start valve and the fuel rail. Plug the fuel return hose.

2. Pull off the pump relay. Jumper terminals 87 and 30. Measure the delivery pressure. It should be 43 psi on vehicles except the 735i and 735iL. On these vehicles, it should be 48 psi.

Removal and Installation

325, 325i, 325iS, 325iX AND M3

1. Relieve fuel system pressure. Disconnect the negative battery cable. Going to the pump, which is under the vehicle and near the fuel tank, push back any protective caps, note the routing and disconnect the electrical connector(s).

2. Securely clamp the suction hose (coming from the tank) and plug the discharge hose so no fuel can escape.

3. Open the hose clamp connecting the suction hose to the pump and disconnect it.

4. Remove the attaching nuts which mount the pump and bracket to the floor pan and remove both as an assembly.

5. Remove the bolt passing through the 2 parts of the bracket and also mounting the hose attaching strap to the bracket. Then, pull the pump out of the bracket.

6. Loosen the hose clamp for the discharge hose and disconnect it at the pump. Pull the rubber ring off the pump.

Electric fuel pump assembly—typical

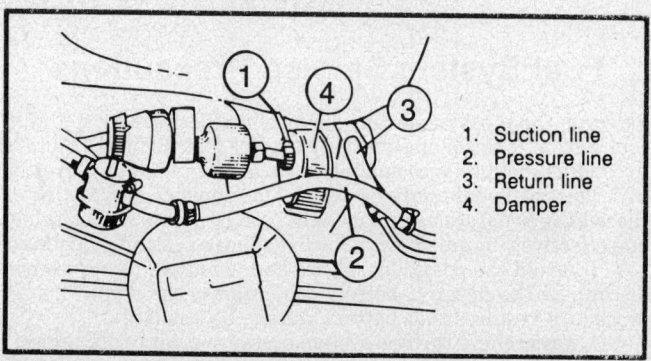

1. Suction line
2. Pressure line
3. Return line
4. Damper

Note the arrangement of the fuel pump, lines, and damper—1987–89 325 series vehicles

7. Note the code number on the pump and make sure to replace it with one of the same number. Inspect all the rubber mounts on the pump mounting bracket and replace any that are cracked or crushed.

8. Install the pump in reverse order. Make sure to unclamp the hoses and then run the engine and check for leaks. Check the fuel system pressure.

ALL 5 SERIES EXCEPT M5

The fuel pump is an electrical unit, delivering fuel through a pressure regulator, to a fuel distributor or a ring-line for the injection valves. The fuel pump is mounted under the vehicle, in the fuel tank, or in the engine compartment.

1. Relieve fuel system pressure. Disconnect the negative battery connector. Push back any protective caps and disconnect the electrical connector(s).

2. If the fuel lines are flexible, pinch them closed with an appropriate tool. Disconnect the fuel lines and plug the ends.

3. Remove the retaining bolts and remove the pump and expansion tank as an assembly.

4. The pump can be separated from the expansion tank after removal.

5. Install the pump in the correct position, be sure to use similar types of hose clamps, if any need replacing. The wrong type clamp can damage the pressure lines.

6. Run the engine and check the fuel lines for leakage. Check the fuel system pressure.

M5 AND M6

1. Disconnect the negative battery cable. Relieve fuel system pressure. Clamp the lines closed if the filter is mounted low, near the fuel tank. Then, loosen the clamps and disconnect the

inlet and outlet hoses. Remove the hose clamps or slide them back, well off the connections to make it easier to pull off the hoses, if necessary.

2. The filters will usually be attached to a frame, floor pan or wheel well by a bracket. Loosen the bracket and remove the filter. Note the direction of flow and then remove the filter.

3. Observe the instructions on the inlet and outlet during installation.

4. Remove the bolt fastening the halves of the bracket together and remove the filter from the bracket. Loosen the clamp on the outlet side of the fuel pump and disconnect the line. Then, slide off the rubber bushing in which the pump is mounted.

5. Check the code number on the side of the pump and make sure the replacement unit carries the same code.

6. Install the pump in exact reverse order, making sure all clamps are securely tightened. Operate the engine and check for leaks.

635CSi, 735i, 735iL AND 750iL

The pump on this vehicle is mounted in the top of the tank along with the fuel level sending unit.

1. Disconnect the negative battery cable. Drain the fuel tank, enough to prevent spillage when removing the pump.

2. Relieve fuel system pressure. Remove the trim panels from the trunk. Then, remove the screws from the cover for the pump/sending unit assembly.

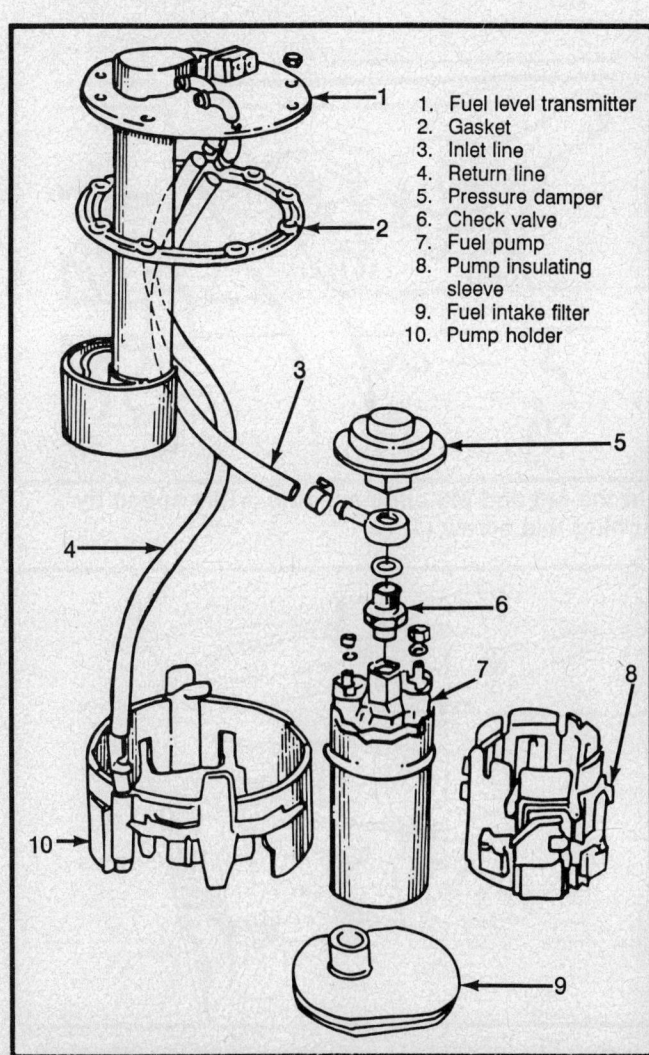

1.	Fuel level transmitter
2.	Gasket
3.	Inlet line
4.	Return line
5.	Pressure damper
6.	Check valve
7.	Fuel pump
8.	Pump insulating sleeve
9.	Fuel intake filter
10.	Pump holder

View of the in-tank fuel pump—735i and 735iL

3. Label the fuel hoses connecting at the top of the pump/sending unit assembly. Unclamp and disconnect the fuel hoses and then plug them.

4. Slide the collar for the electrical connector to one side and then unplug the connector.

5. Remove the mounting screws and remove the pump/sending unit assembly. Replace the gasket.

6. Press the retaining locks for the pump unit inward and slide the pump out of the pump/sending unit assembly.

7. Note the routing of the fuel and electrical lines to the pump from the top of the pump/sending unit assembly. Loosen the hose clamp screws and the screws attaching the electrical connectors to the pump. Disconnect the hose and connector.

8. Unscrew the pressure regulator from the top of the check valve. Then, unscrew the check valve from the top of the pump.

9. Pull the insulating sleeve off the pump. Then, loosen the retaining screw and slide the filter off the pump.

10. Install the pump in reverse order. Be careful to ensure that the 2 retaining locks fasten the pump in place in a secure manner. Operate the engine and check for leaks.

Fuel Injection

For further information, please refer to "Chilton's Electronic Engine Control's Manual" for additional coverage.

Idle Speed and Mixture Adjustment

NOTE: The idle speed and mixture can be adjusted ONLY with the aid of a CO meter. If this tool is not available, do not attempt any of the following procedures. The idle mixture can be adjusted ONLY with the aid of a CO meter on most vehicles. Idle speed is not adjustable on any vehicle with the Motronic control unit except the M5 and M6. If idle speed is incorrect, either the idle valve or the idle control unit must be replaced. See the fuel injection unit repair section.

325, 325i AND 325iS

1. Disconnect the hose, leading from the throttle housing, that goes to the carbon canister. Do not plug the openings. Remove the bolts on either side of the exhaust manifold plug.

2. Remove the plug in the exhaust manifold, install the test nipple part No. 13 0 100 or equivalent and connect the CO tester 13 0 070 or equivalent, into the open nipple.

3. With the engine valve clearances correctly adjusted, ignition timing correct and the engine at operating temperature, measure the CO percentage at idle speed. CO nominal value is 0.2–1.2 percent.

4. If the CO level is within the specified range, disconnect the test unit, replace the plug in the exhaust manifold, and conclude the test. If not, adjust the CO as described below.

5. Turn off the engine and then unplug the oxygen sensor plug. Drill a hole in the anti-tamper plug in the throttle body with special tool 13 1092 or equivalent. Then screw the extractor tool 13 1 094 or equivalent into the hole drilled into the plug and draw the plug out. Finally, use an adjustment tool 13 1 060 or 13 1 100 or equivalent to turn the adjustment, with the engine running, until the CO meets nominal values.

6. When the adjustment is complete, install a new anti-tamper plug, and reconnect the oxygen sensor plug and the carbon canister hose. Also, remove the nipple in the exhaust manifold and replace the plug. Reinstall the exhaust manifold bolts.

528e

1. Pull the canister purge hose off the solenoid, leave it unplugged.

2. Connect the CO meter 13 0 070 or equivalent, to the manifold via the nipple 13 0 100.

3. With the engine valve clearances correctly adjusted, ignition timing correct and the engine at operating temperature, measure the CO percentage at idle speed. CO nominal value is 0.2–1.2 percent.

4. If the CO level is within the specified range, disconnect the test unit, replace the plug in the exhaust manifold, and conclude the test. If not, adjust the CO as described below.

5. Turn off the engine and then unplug the oxygen sensor plug. Drill a hole in the anti-tamper plug in the throttle body with special tool No. 13 1 092 or equivalent. Then screw the extractor tool 13 1 094 or equivalent into the hole drilled into the plug and draw the plug out with the impact mass. Finally, use an adjustment tool 13 1 060 or 13 1 100 or equivalent to turn the adjustment, with the engine running, until the CO meets nominal values.

6. When the adjustment is complete, install a new anti-tamper plug, and reconnect the oxygen sensor plug and the carbon canister hose. Also, remove the nipple in the exhaust manifold and replace the plug. Reconnect the hose to the solenoid.

525i, 535i, 635CSi, 735i, 735iL AND 750iL

1. Make sure the idle speed is correct. The engine must be hot. Disconnect the evaporative emissions canister purge hose at the bottom of the solenoid mounted on the firewall. Leave the openings unplugged.

2. Unscrew the bolts on the exhaust manifold and install a nipple, part No. 13 0 100 or equivalent and connect the CO test unit 13 0 070 or equivalent. CO should be 0.2–1.2 percent. If CO is not within limits, adjust it as described below.

3. Turn off the engine and unplug the oxygen sensor plug. Then, remove the air flow sensor by removing the air cleaner and removing the mounting bolts to separate the airflow sensor from it.

4. Use special tool 13 1 092 or equivalent to remove the anti-tamper plug. Use this tool to drill a hole in the plug and then use 13 1 094 or equivalent to pull it. The second tool should be screwed into the hole already drilled; use the slide hammer to pull the plug out.

5. Once the plug is removed, install the air flow sensor back onto the air cleaner and reinstall the air cleaner. With the engine idling hot and the oxygen sensor plug still disconnected, measure the CO and adjust it with Tool 13 1 060 or 13 1 100 or equivalent. The CO level must meet the nominal value of 0.2–1.2 percent.

6. Once the level is adjusted, stop the engine and reconnect the oxygen sensor plug. Then, remove the air flow sensor, put it on a bench, and install a new anti-tamper plug. Reinstall the airflow sensor and air cleaner. Reconnect the canister purge hose to the solenoid.

M3

NOTE: This test must be performed at essentially sea level altitude. In an area well above sea level, it will be necessary to use a BMW Service tester or equivalent device from another source and run the test with the system's altitude correction box connected.

1. Make sure the engine is at operating temperature and that the air cleaner is in reasonably clean condition. All basic engine tuning factors (spark plug condition and gap, valve adjustment, ignition timing, etc.) must be correct. Turn off all accessories.

2. A special electrical fitting special tool 13 4 010 or equivalent is required to disable the Motronic control system's throttle valve switch. Pull off the electrical connector leading to the throttle valve switch. Then, plug the special tool into the open end of the connector.

3. Adjust the idle speed to specification by turning the screw located just above the "M" on the valve cover Make sure to restore the throttle valve switch when the idle speed is correct.

4. Make sure the engine is in good basic tune, including proper spark plug gap and valve clearances. The engine must be at operating temperature.

On vehicles with no test openings in the exhaust manifold:

a. With a CO meter in the tail pipe, disconnect the oxygen sensor so it no longer influences the mixture produced by the injection system. CO level should be zero. If there is a CO reading, it is necessary to get a special adjusting screw cap remover tool 13 1 011 or equivalent and an adjusting tool 13 1 100 or equivalent.

b. The adjusting screw cap is located on the top surface of the airflow sensor; the adjusting screw is accessible in the aperture underneath. Remove the cap with the cap remover and then turn the adjusting screw slowly to correct the CO value to 0. Reinstall the cap and reconnect the oxygen sensor.

On vehicles with a test opening in the exhaust manifold:

a. Remove the plug in the exhaust manifold and put the probe of the CO meter into the opening. Disconnect the oxygen sensor so it no longer influences the mixture produced by the injection system. CO level should be 0.8–1.2%. If the CO reading is outside the nominal value range, it is necessary to get a special adjusting screw cap remover tool 13 1 011 or equivalent and an adjusting tool 13 1 100 or equivalent.

b. The adjusting screw cap is located on the top surface of the airflow sensor; the adjusting screw is accessible in the ap-

On the M5 and M6 engines, adjust idle speed by turning this screw (1)

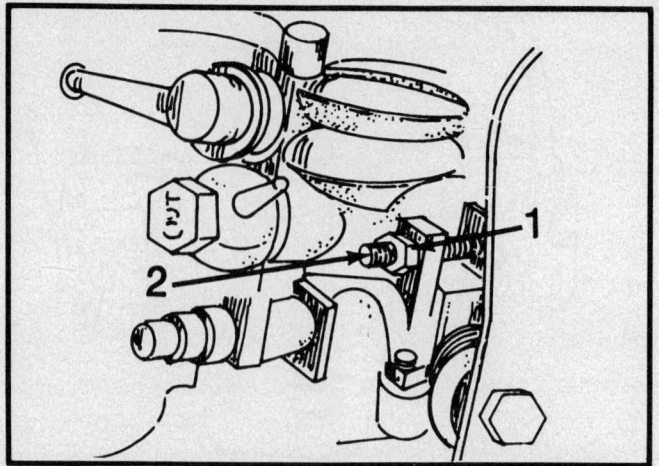

Loosen the locknut (1) and turn the adjusting screw (2) to adjust the idle—diesel engine

erture underneath. Remove the cap with the cap remover and then turn the adjusting screw slowly to correct the CO value to .8–1.2%. Reinstall the cap and reconnect the oxygen sensor.

M5 AND M6

1. Make sure the engine is at operating temperature, and that the air cleaner is in reasonably clean condition. All basic engine tuning factors (spark plug condition and gap, valve adjustment, ignition timing, etc.) must be correct.
2. Adjust the idle speed by turning the screw shown in the illustration.
3. To adjust CO, first remove the cap located at the center of the top surface of the airflow sensor. Use tool 13 1 100 to turn the airflow control screw in the airflow sensor, accessible after the anti-tamper cap is removed. CO must be 0.4–1.2 percent.
4. Install a new cap when CO meets specification.

Fuel Injector

Removal and Installation

EXCEPT 318iS

1. Disconnect the negative battery cable. Remove the hose and plastic caps, if necessary.

2. Remove the plugs, plate and screws from the injector pipe.
3. Push up on the injector pipe until the injectors have cleared the guides on the intake manifold or the throttle valve housing.
4. Pull of the plugs and lift up the retainer. Remove the injectors.
5. Check the O-ring and replace, if necessary. Install in the reverse order of the removal. Start the engine and check for leaks.

318iS

1. Disconnect the negative battery cable. Remove the upper section of the collector.
2. Disconnect the rear brace and remove the injector hose.
3. Remove the holder for the preheater.
4. Remove the screws and lift off the upper section of the intake manifold. Disconnect the hose from the fuel pressure regulator at the same time.
5. Remove the plug plate from the fuel injectors and unscrew the clamp.
6. Remove the injection pipe with the injectors attached. Lift off the retainer and remove the fuel injector.
7. Check the O-ring and replace, if necessary. Install in the reverse order of the removal. Start the engine and check for leaks.

EMISSION CONTROLS

For further information, please refer to "Professional Emission Component Application Guide".

Emission Warning Lamps

Resetting

SERVICE INTERVAL REMINDER LIGHTS

The on board computer is used to evaluate mileage, average engine speed and engine and coolant temperatures as well as other computer input factors that determine maintenance intervals. There are 5 green, a yellow and a red **LED** used to remind the driver of oil changes and other maintenance services.

The green LEDS will be illuminated when the ignition is in the **ON** position and the engine OFF. There will not be as many green LEDS illuminated when as the maintenance time get clos-er. A yellow LED that is illuminated when the engine is running, will indicate maintenance is now due. The red LED will be illuminated when the service interval has been exceeded by approximately 1000 miles. This is the computers way of saying this is your last warning.

There is a service interval reset tool manufactured by the Assenmacher Tool Company tool 62-1-100. This tool is used to reset BMW 6 cylinder vehicles and the 4 cylinder vehicles. With the aid of an additional adapter tool can also be used on 1988–91 vehicles.

1. Locate the diagnostic connector near the thermostat housing.
2. Plug the special reset tool into the diagnostic connector and place the ignition switch in the **ON** position.
3. Depress the reset button on the tool until all 5 green LEDS are illuminated, showing that the reset has completed.

ENGINE MECHANICAL

NOTE: Disconnecting the negative battery cable on some vehicles may interfere with the functions of the on board computer systems and may require the computer to undergo a relearning process, once the negative battery cable is reconnected.

Engine Assembly

Removal and Installation

1987 325, 325i AND 325iS

1. Disconnect the negative battery cable. Remove the transmission.
2. Without disconnecting hoses, loosen and remove the power steering pump bolts and remove the pump and belts and support the pump out of the way.

3. Remove the drain plug and remove the coolant from the radiator. Then, remove the radiator (see the appropriate procedure).
4. Without disconnecting hoses, remove the mounting bolts and remove the air conditioner compressor and drive belt and support the compressor out of the way.
5. Remove the through-bolts to disconnect the engine hood supports and then open the hood and support it securely.

NOTE: The hood must be propped in a secure manner. If it falls during work serious injury could result.

6. Remove the trim panel inside the glove box.
a. On 325i and 325iS models:
    a. Pull the main, multi-prong plug off the control unit. Also

unplug one plug in a wire coming into the unit, located below the unit and to the left.

b. If equipped with an automatic transmission, disconnect the plug for the main wiring harness.

7. Lift out and disconnect the plug for the oxygen sensor and the additional wires. Pull off the temperature sensor plug. Disconnect the other connections for this harness, which are nearby. Then, loosen the straps and pull this harness into the engine compartment.

8. Remove the coolant expansion tank. Pull off the ignition coil high tension and low tension wires. Disconnect the wiring harness.

9. On 325i and 325iS:

a. Near the air cleaner, next to the strut mount in the wheel well, there is an L-shaped relay box. Unplug it and remove it.

b. Loosen the clamp on the air intake hose.

c. Disconnect the multi-prong connector from the airflow sensor (integral with the air cleaner). Then, open all the fasteners associated with this wiring harness so it will not interfere with engine removal.

d. Disconnect the mounting nuts and remove the air cleaner/airflow sensor unit.

e. Disconnect the large, multi-prong plug at the rear of the engine, near the firewall. Then, open all the fasteners associated with this wiring harness as well. Also, disconnect the 2 vacuum hoses.

f. Disconnect the accelerator cable. If the vehicle has cruise control, disconnect the cruise control cable as well. Also disconnect the large vacuum line supplying the cruise control servo on these vehicles.

10. Lift out and unscrew the large, multi-prong plug at the firewall and then open up the fasteners associated with its harness.

11. Unscrew the fuel lines, pull off the hose and disconnect the fuel filter.

12. Disconnect both heater hoses. Disconnect the engine ground strap. Unbolt the engine mounts.

13. Lift out the engine with a suitable hoist, using hooks at front and rear.

To install:

14. Reverse the procedures used for removal and lower the engine into the engine compartment. When the engine is positioned, the guide pin must fit in the bore of the axle carrier.

a. Torque the mounting bolts on the front axle carrier (small bolt) to 18–20 ft. lbs.; the larger bolt to 31–35 ft. lbs.

b. Torque the mount-to-bracket bolts to 31–35 ft. lbs.

c. Torque the engine-to-bracket mounts to (small bolt) 16–17 ft. lbs., (large bolt) 31–35 ft. lbs.

15. Connect the fuel lines, use new hose clamps to connect the fuel lines to the fuel filter. Connect all of the multi-prong plugs and all vacuum hoses.

16. Connect the accelerator cable and cruise control cable to the throttle body and adjust the accelerator cable and cruise control cable.

17. Install the coolant recovery tank, use a new hose clamp on the coolant expansion tank.

18. Install the air cleaner and reconnect all electrical plugs. Connect and install the "L" shaped relay box on the wheel well.

19. Reconnect the wiring to the main control unit and install the idle control unit.

20. Install the air conditioning compressor and power steering pump, properly route the accessory drive belt. Adjust the belt tension.

21. Install the radiator and connect the hoses.

22. Install the transmission.

23. Install the hood support and lower the hood.

24. Make sure all fluid levels are correct before starting the engine. Bleed air from the cooling system.

1988–91 325, 325i AND 325iS

1. Disconnect the negative battery cable. Remove the transmission.

2. Without disconnecting hoses, loosen and remove the power steering pump bolts and remove the pump and belts and support the pump out of the way.

3. Remove the drain plug and remove the coolant from the radiator. Then, remove the radiator. Unbolt and remove the fan from the engine. Store it in an upright position.

4. Without disconnecting hoses, remove the mounting bolts that run through the compressor body and remove the air conditioner compressor and drive belt and support the compressor out of the way.

5. Remove the through-bolts to disconnect the engine hood supports and then open the hood and support it securely.

NOTE: The hood must be propped in a secure manner. If it falls during work serious injury could result.

6. Disconnect the accelerator cable. If the vehicle has cruise control, disconnect the cruise control cable. If the vehicle has an automatic transmission, disconnect the throttle cable leading to the transmission.

7. Pull the large, multi-prong plug off the airflow sensor (an integral part of the air cleaner). Loosen the clamp and disconnect the air intake hose at the airflow sensor. Remove the mounting nuts and remove the air cleaner/airflow sensor unit.

8. Disconnect the coolant expansion tank hose. Disconnect the large, multi-prong connector near the air intake hose.

9. The diagnosis plug is a large, screw-on connector located near the thermostat and associated hoses. Unscrew and disconnect this connector.

10. Disconnect the large coolant hoses connecting to the thermostat.

11. Make sure the engine is cold. Place a metal container under the connection to collect fuel; then, disconnect the fuel line at the connection right near the thermostat housing by unscrewing it. Unfasten the fuel line clip about a foot away from this connection.

12. Disconnect the electrical plugs near the diagnosis plug connector. Disconnect the bracket for the dipstick guide tube.

13. Remove the bolts which attach the water pipes going to the engine to mounting brackets.

14. Disconnect the heater hoses at the heater core (near the firewall). Remove the coolant hose running to the top of the block.

15. Place a metal container under the connection to collect fuel; then, disconnect the remaining fuel hose supplying the engine injectors. Disconnect the electrical connectors.

16. Remove the bolt from the mounting brace connecting with the cylinder head.

17. Mark and then disconnect the electrical leads from the starter. Unbolt the starter and lift it out from above.

18. Place a metal container under the connection to collect fuel; then, disconnect the fuel pipe that runs right near the starter.

19. Label electrical connectors on the alternator. Then, pull off the rubber caps for the connectors which are attached with nuts and remove the nuts and any washers. Disconnect the plug-on connector.

20. Disconnect the electrical leads for the coil. Loosen the clips attaching the leads under the distributor and pull the harness away to the left. Disconnect the oil pressure sending unit.

21. Place a drain pan underneath the connections and then disconnect the oil cooler pipes at the crankcase by unscrewing the flare nut fittings.

22. Take the cover off the relay box. Then, lift out the relays and their mounting sockets. Place the relays and associated wiring on top of the engine so they will come out with it.

23. Loosen its mounting clamp and then remove the carbon canister. There is a plate to which a number of electrical leads

are connected. Remove the mounting screws and move the plate aside so it will clear the dipstick guide tube when the engine is removed.

24. Remove the 2 bolts that fasten the wiring harness to the firewall. Then, disconnect the engine ground strap.

25. Remove both engine mount through-bolts. Lift out the engine with a suitable hoist, using hooks at front and rear.

To install:

26. Reverse the procedures used for removal and lower the engine into the engine compartment. When the engine is positioned, the guide pin must fit in the bore of the axle carrier. Torque the mounting bolts on the front axle carrier (small bolt) to 18–20 ft. lbs.; the larger bolt to 31–35 ft. lbs. The mount-to-bracket bolts are torqued to 31–35 ft. lbs. Engine-to-bracket mounts are torqued to (small bolt) 16–17 ft. lbs., (large bolt) 31–35 ft. lbs.

27. Connect the fuel lines, use new hose clamps to connect the fuel lines to the fuel filter. Connect all of the multi-prong plugs and all vacuum hoses.

28. Connect the accelerator cable and cruise control cable to the throttle body and adjust the accelerator cable and cruise control cable.

29. Install the coolant recovery tank, use a new hose clamp on the coolant expansion tank.

30. Install the air cleaner and reconnect all electrical plugs. Connect and install the relays in the relay box.

31. Reconnect the wiring to the main control unit and install the idle control unit.

32. Install the air conditioning compressor and power steering pump, properly route the accessory drive belt. Adjust the belt tension.

33. Install the radiator and connect the hoses.

34. Install the transmission.

35. Install the hood support and lower the hood.

36. Make sure all fluid levels are correct before starting the engine. Bleed air from the cooling system.

M3

1. Disconnect the negative battery cable. Remove the transmission.

2. Remove the splash guard from underneath the engine. Put a drain pan underneath and then drain coolant from both the radiator and block.

3. Loosen the hose clamps at either end of the air intake hose leading to the air intake sensor. Pull off the hose. Then, pull both electrical connectors off the air cleaner/airflow sensor unit. Remove both mounting nuts and remove the unit.

4. Disconnect the accelerator and cruise control cables. Unscrew the nuts mounting the cable housing mounting bracket and set the housings and bracket aside.

5. Loosen the clamp and disconnect the brake booster vacuum hose.

6. Loosen the clamp and disconnect the other end of the booster vacuum hose at the manifold. Remove the nut from the intake manifold brace.

7. Loosen the hose clamp and disconnect the air intake hose at the manifold. Then, remove all the nuts attaching the manifold assembly to the outer ends of the intake throttle necks and remove the assembly.

8. Put a drain pan underneath and then loosen the hose clamps and disconnect the coolant expansion tank hoses. Disconnect the engine ground strap.

9. Disconnect the ignition coil high tension lead. Then, label and disconnect the plugs on the front of the block. Remove the nut fastening another lead farther forward of the plugs and move the lead aside so it will not interfere with engine removal.

10. Label and disconnect the plugs from the rear of the alternator. Label the additional leads and then remove the nuts and disconnect those leads. It's best to reinstall nuts once the leads are removed to keep them from being mixed up.

11. Remove the cover for the electrical connectors from the starter. Label the leads and then remove the attaching nuts and disconnect them. Reinstall the nuts.

12. There is a wire running to a connector on the oil pan to warn of low oil level. Pull off the connector, unscrew the carrier for the lead, and then pull the lead out from above. Pull off the connectors near where the lead for the low oil warning system ran and unclip the wires from the carrier.

13. Find the vacuum hose leading to the fuel pressure regulator. Pull it off. Label and then disconnect the plugs. Unscrew the mounting screw for the electrical lead connecting with the top of the block and remove the lead and its carrier.

14. There is a vacuum hose connecting with one of the throttle necks. Disconnect it and pull it out of the intake manifold bracket. Pull off the electrical connector. Pull out the rubber retainer, and then pull the idle speed control out and put it aside. The engine wiring harness is located nearby. Take it out of its carriers.

15. All the fuel injectors are plugged into a common plate. Carefully and evenly pull the plate off the injectors, pull it out past the pressure regulator, and lay it aside.

16. Loosen the clamp and then disconnect the PCV hose. Label and then disconnect the fuel lines connecting the injector circuit. Put a drain pan underneath and then disconnect the heater hose from the cylinder head.

17. Loosen the clamp near the throttle necks and then pull the engine wiring harness out and put it aside. Put a drain pan underneath and then disconnect the heater hose that connects to the block.

18. Loosen the mounting clamp for the carbon canister, slide it out of the clamp, and place it aside with the hoses still connected.

19. Note the routing of the oil cooler lines where they connect at the base of the oil filter. Label them if necessary. Put a drain pan underneath and then unscrew the flared connectors for the lines.

20. Unbolt and remove the fan. Store it in an upright position. Remove the radiator.

21. Support the power steering pump. Remove the adjusting bolt and disconnect and remove the belt. Then, remove the nuts and bolts on which the unit hinges. Pull the unit aside and hang it so there will not be strain on the hoses.

22. Remove the adjusting bolt for the air conditioning compressor and disconnect and remove the belt. Then, remove the nut at one end of the hinge bolt and pull the bolt out, suspending the compressor.

23. Remove the through-bolts to disconnect the engine hood supports and then open the hood and support it securely.

24. Suspend the engine with a suitable lifting device. Then, remove the nuts for the engine mounting bolts. The mounts are on the axle carrier and the nut is at the top on the left and on the bottom on the right. Then, carefully lift the engine out of the compartment, avoiding contact between it and the components remaining in the vehicle.

To install:

25. Keep these points in mind during installation:

    a. Torque the engine mounting bolts to 32.5 ft. lbs.

    b. Adjust the belt tension for the air conditioning compressor and power steering pump drive belts to give 1/2–3/4 in. deflection.

    c. Torque the oil cooler line flare nuts to 25 ft. lbs.

    d. When reconnecting the intake manifold to the throttle necks, inspect and, if necessary, replace the O-rings. Torque the mounting nuts to 6.5 ft. lbs.

26. Reverse the procedures used for removal and lower the engine into the engine compartment. When the engine is positioned, the guide pin must fit in the bore of the axle carrier. Torque the mounting bolts on the front axle carrier (small bolt) to 18–20 ft. lbs.; the larger bolt to 31–35 ft. lbs. The mount-to-bracket bolts are torqued to 31–35 ft. lbs.

27. Install the intake manifold assembly and connect the fuel lines, use new hose clamps to connect the fuel lines to the fuel

filter. Connect all of the multi-prong plugs and all vacuum hoses.

28. Connect the accelerator cable and cruise control cable to the throttle body and adjust the accelerator cable and cruise control cable.

29. Install the coolant recovery tank, use a new hose clamp on the coolant expansion tank.

30. Install the air cleaner and reconnect all electrical plugs. Connect and install the relays in the relay box.

31. Reconnect the wiring to the main control unit and install the idle control unit.

32. Install the air conditioning compressor and power steering pump, properly route the accessory drive belt. Adjust the belt tension.

33. Install the radiator and connect the hoses.

34. Install the transmission.

35. Install the hood support and lower the hood.

36. Make sure all fluid levels are correct before starting the engine. Bleed air from the cooling system.

528e

1. Disconnect the negative battery cable. Remove the transmission. Disconnect the exhaust pipe from the exhaust manifold.

2. Remove the splash guard.

3. With the hoses still attached, remove the power steering pump and position it out of the way.

4. Unscrew the drain plug on the engine block, remove the upper and lower radiator hoses and drain the cooling system. After draining, remove the radiator.

5. With the refrigerant hoses still connected, remove the air conditioning compressor and position it out of the way.

6. Disconnect the gas pressure springs, scribe around the hinges and then remove the hood.

7. Disconnect the battery cables, negative cable first and remove the battery.

8. Disconnect the accelerator and cruise control cables. Disconnect and tag all hoses from the throttle housing. Disconnect the air duct.

9. Remove the air filter housing along with the air flow sensor.

10. Tag and disconnect all remaining lines, hoses and wires which may interfere with engine removal.

11. Tag and disconnect all plugs and wires attached to the control unit in the glove box. Unscrew the straps on the firewall and pull the wire harness through to the engine compartment.

12. Disconnect the engine ground strap and then loosen both engine mounts.

13. Attach an engine lifting hoist to the front and rear of the engine, remove the engine mount bolts and then lift out the engine.

To install:

14. Reverse the procedures used for removal and lower the engine into the engine compartment. When the engine is positioned, the guide pin must fit in the bore of the axle carrier. Torque the mounting bolts on the front axle carrier (small bolt) to 18–20 ft. lbs.; the larger bolt to 31–35 ft. lbs. The mount-to-bracket bolts are torqued to 31–35 ft. lbs.

15. Connect all of the electrical wiring and all vacuum hoses.

16. Connect the accelerator cable and cruise control cable to the throttle body and adjust the accelerator cable and cruise control cable.

17. Install the air cleaner and reconnect all electrical plugs.

18. Reconnect the wiring to the main control unit.

19. Install the air conditioning compressor and power steering pump, properly route the accessory drive belt. Adjust the belt tension.

20. Install the radiator and connect the hoses.

21. Install the transmission.

22. Install the hood support and lower the hood.

23. Make sure all fluid levels are correct before starting the engine. Bleed the air from the cooling system.

525i, 535i, AND 635CSi

1. Disconnect both battery cables, negative first. There is a lead coming from the engine to the positive battery terminal. Disconnect it at the battery. On the 6 Series vehicles, disconnect the ground strap.

2. Unscrew the ground strap for the hood. Support the hood securely and then disconnect the gas props. Then, raise the hood until it is vertical and securely fasten it in place.

3. Remove the transmission. With the engine cool, place a clean container under the coolant drain plug in the side of the block. Remove the plug and drain all coolant from the block. Remove the fan and radiator.

4. Support the power steering pump. Remove the mounting bolts and then hang the pump out of the way in a position that will not put stress on the hoses.

5. Support the air conditioning compressor. Remove the mounting bolts and then hang the compressor out of the way in a position that will not put stress on the hoses.

6. Pull the wire leading to the oxygen sensor out of the clips under the floor. Disconnect the sensor at the exhaust pipe.

7. Pull off the plug at the airflow sensor and remove associated wiring. Remove the hoses and pipes connected to the air cleaner and airflow sensor. Remove the nuts and remove the airflow sensor and air cleaner as an assembly.

8. Pull the large, multi-prong plug off the DME box in the glove compartment. Disconnect the smaller plug that's connected to the same harness and plugged in. Then, run the entire harness back into the engine compartment.

9. Disconnect the engine ground wire located at the rear of the block. Unclip the harness for the DME from the firewall.

10. Disconnect both the low tension and the high tension wire from the coil. Disconnect the wires from the solenoid. Pull the wiring harness out of the holders.

11. Pull off the fuse box cover and the cap. Remove the relays (they have metal covers) on one side of the fuse box. Then, disconnect the wiring harness that leads into the fuse box. On the 635CSi, unclamp the harness where it is clamped to the fender well and remove the diagnosis socket, located right near the fusebox.

12. Disconnect the accelerator and cruise control cables.

13. Unclamp and remove the coolant hose that leads to the expansion tank. Disconnect the fuel return line, collecting any fuel in a metal container for safe disposal. Unclip the wiring harness clips on the wires that run through this area of the engine compartment.

14. Disconnect the fuel supply line, collecting any fuel in a metal container for safe disposal. Disconnect the heater hoses at connections.

15. Pull the main vacuum supply hose off at the intake manifold.

16. Disconnect the remaining main coolant hose and plug it.

17. Install a lifting sling to the hooks on top of the engine. Unbolt the left side engine mount. Remove the main engine ground strap. Unbolt the right side engine mount. Carefully pull the engine out of the compartment.

To install:

18. Reverse the procedures used for removal and lower the engine into the engine compartment. When the engine is positioned, the guide pin must fit in the bore of the axle carrier. Torque the mounting bolts on the front axle carrier (small bolt) to 18–20 ft. lbs.; the larger bolt to 31–35 ft. lbs. The mount-to-bracket bolts are torqued to 31–35 ft. lbs.

19. Install the intake manifold assembly and connect the fuel lines, use new hose clamps to connect the fuel lines to the fuel filter. Connect all of the multi-prong plugs and all vacuum hoses.

20. Connect the accelerator cable and cruise control cable to the throttle body and adjust the accelerator cable and cruise control cable.

21. Install the coolant recovery tank, use a new hose clamp on the coolant expansion tank.

22. Install the air cleaner and reconnect all electrical plugs. Connect and install the relays in the relay box.

23. Reconnect the wiring to the main control unit and install the idle control unit.

24. Install the air conditioning compressor and power steering pump, properly route the accessory drive belt. Adjust the belt tension.

25. Install the radiator and connect the hoses.

26. Install the transmission.

27. Install the hood support and lower the hood.

28. Make sure all fluid levels are correct before starting the engine. Bleed air from the cooling system.

M5 AND M6

1. Disconnect the battery negative cable. Then, disconnect the positive cable. Scribe matchmarks and then remove the hood.

2. Remove the fan. Remove the drain plugs in the block and radiator. Disconnect the hoses and remove the radiator.

3. Support the power steering pump. Remove the mounting bolts and then hang the pump out of the way in a position that will not put stress on the hoses.

4. Support the air conditioning compressor. Remove the mounting bolts and then hang the compressor out of the way in a position that will not put stress on the hoses.

5. Remove the transmission.

6. Remove the attaching bolt and, with an appropriate puller, remove the vibration damper from the front of the engine.

7. Remove the bolts at either end and remove the cross brace that runs under the engine. Remove the heat shield.

8. Disconnect the electrical connector going to the airflow sensor. Pull the electrical leads out of the wiring holders. Loosen the hose clamp for the air intake hose. Remove the mounting nut for the air cleaner. Then, remove the air cleaner and airflow sensor as an assembly.

9. Disconnect the large vacuum hose at the bottom of the intake manifold.

10. Disconnect the PCV hoses where they connect to the top of the manifold. Disconnect the throttle cable that runs across the top of the manifold, and the hose running near the front. Remove the bolts fastening the manifold to the outer ends of the intake tubes and remove it.

11. Working inside the glove compartment, disconnect the plug that connects to the DME control. Then, guide the leads through and into the engine compartment. Disconnect the high tension lead and the low tension leads at the coil. Then, unfasten the wiring harness holders for the harness running to the coil where the harness runs along the fender well.

12. Disconnect the fuel hose connection at the rear of the fuel manifold on top of the engine. Disconnect the vacuum hose that runs along the firewall.

13. Disconnect the plugs for the reference mark and speed sensors. Disconnect the hoses on the coolant expansion tank.

14. Working on the fuse box, pull off the large electrical connector. Pull off the diagnosis socket. Disconnect the remaining leads.

15. Disconnect the heater hoses near the firewall. Using a backup wrench, disconnect the lines at the oil cooler. Disconnect the low pressure fuel line at the pressure regulator.

16. Disconnect the starter leads. Cut the straps and remove the solenoid heat shield.

17. Attach a lifting sling to the engine and support the assembly. Disconnect the ground lead. Then, disconnect the left side engine mount, removing the nut from underneath and then unscrewing the bolt out the top. Do the same for the right mount.

Carefully lift the engine out of the compartment, tilting the front of the engine upward for clearance.

To install:

18. Keep these points in mind during installation:
   a. Torque the engine mounting bolts to 32.5 ft. lbs.
   b. Adjust the belt tension for the air conditioning compressor and power steering pump drive belts to give ½–¾ in. deflection.
   c. Torque the oil cooler line flare nuts to 25 ft. lbs.
   d. When reconnecting the intake manifold to the throttle necks, inspect and, if necessary, replace the O-rings. Torque the mounting nuts to 6.5 ft. lbs.

19. Reverse the procedures used for removal and lower the engine into the engine compartment. When the engine is positioned, the guide pin must fit in the bore of the axle carrier. Torque the mounting bolts on the front axle carrier (small bolt) to 18–20 ft. lbs.; the larger bolt to 31–35 ft. lbs. The mount-to-bracket bolts are torqued to 31–35 ft. lbs.

20. Install the intake manifold assembly and connect the fuel lines, use new hose clamps to connect the fuel lines to the fuel filter. Connect all of the multi-prong plugs and all vacuum hoses.

21. Connect the accelerator cable and cruise control cable to the throttle body and adjust the accelerator cable and cruise control cable.

22. Install the coolant recovery tank, use a new hose clamp on the coolant expansion tank.

23. Install the air cleaner and reconnect all electrical plugs. Connect and install the relays in the relay box.

24. Reconnect the wiring to the main control unit and install the idle control unit.

25. Install the air conditioning compressor and power steering pump, properly route the accessory drive belt. Adjust the belt tension.

26. Install the radiator and connect the hoses.

27. Install the transmission.

28. Install the hood support and lower the hood.

29. Make sure all fluid levels are correct before starting the engine. Bleed air from the cooling system.

735i, 735iL AND 750iL

1. Disconnect the negative battery cable and then the positive. Remove the transmission as described. Scribe hinge locations and remove the hood, or remove support struts and prop it securely all the way up.

2. Remove the splash guard from underneath the engine. Then, with the engine cool, remove the drain plugs in the radiator and block and drain the engine coolant.

3. Loosen the power steering pump bolts from underneath. Turn the adjusting pinion to loosen the belt and remove the belt. Then, remove the mounting bolts and remove the power steering pump without disconnecting the hoses. Support the pump out of the way so as to avoid stressing the hoses.

4. Do the same with the air conditioner compressor, this unit does not have the belt adjusting pinion—it is necessary only to loosen all the bolts and push the compressor toward the engine to remove the belt.

5. Loosen the air intake hose clamp and disconnect the hose. Remove the mounting nut and then remove the air cleaner(s).

6 Unscrew the oil filter cover bolt and disconnect the oil cooler lines and the plug from the oil pressure switch on 750iL.

7. The unit on the opposite side of the intake hose from the air cleaner contains the idle speed control valve, which must be removed next. Loosen the hose clamps and pull off the hoses. Disconnect the electrical connector. Remove the mounting nut and then pull the idle speed control out of the air intake hose.

8. Pull off the retainers for the airflow sensor, and then pull the unit off its mountings, disconnecting the vacuum hose from the PCV system at the same time.

9. Working on the coolant expansion tank, disconnect the electrical connector. Remove the nuts on both sides. Loosen

their clamps and then disconnect the hoses and remove the tank.

10. Disconnect the heater hoses at both the control valve and at the heater core.

11. Disconnect the throttle and cruise control cables at the throttle lever. Unbolt the cable housing retainer and remove the housing and cables.

12. Pull off the low amperage starter connectors and disconnect the high amperage connector coming from the battery.

13. Loosen its clamp and then disconnect the coolant hose that runs to the alternator.

14. Disconnect the connecting plug for the oxygen sensor, as well as the other plugs.

15. Loosen the clamps and then disconnect the fuel supply and return pipes.

16. Disconnect the fuel pipe at the injector supply manifold. Disconnect the plug: Disconnect the electrical connector at the throttle body. Lift off the protective caps and then remove the attaching nuts for the protective cover for the wiring harness for the injectors and remove it.

17. Disconnect the ground strap at the block. Remove the engine mount nut from the top on both sides.

18. Attach a lifting sling to the engine and support the assembly. Disconnect the ground lead. Carefully lift the engine out of the compartment, tilting the front of the engine upward for clearance.

To install:

19. Keep these points in mind during installation:
    a. Torque the engine mounting bolts to 32.5 ft. lbs.
    b. Adjust the belt tension for the air conditioning compressor and power steering pump drive belts to give ½–¾ in. deflection.
    c. Torque the oil cooler line flare nuts to 25 ft. lbs.
    d. When reconnecting the intake manifold to the throttle necks, inspect and, if necessary, replace the O-rings. Torque the mounting nuts to 6.5 ft. lbs.

20. Reverse the procedures used for removal and lower the engine into the engine compartment. When the engine is positioned, the guide pin must fit in the bore of the axle carrier. Torque the mounting bolts on the front axle carrier (small bolt) to 18–20 ft. lbs.; the larger bolt to 31–35 ft. lbs. The mount-to-bracket bolts are torqued to 31–35 ft. lbs.

21. Connect the fuel lines, use new hose clamps to connect the fuel lines to the fuel filter. Connect all of the multi-prong plugs and all vacuum hoses.

22. Connect the accelerator cable and cruise control cable to the throttle body and adjust the accelerator cable and cruise control cable.

23. Install the coolant recovery tank, use a new hose clamp on the coolant expansion tank.

23. Install the air cleaner(s) and reconnect all electrical plugs. Connect and install the relays in the relay box.

24. Install the oil filter cover bolt and connect the oil cooler lines and the plug to the oil pressure switch on the 750iL.

25. Reconnect the wiring to the main control unit and install the idle control unit.

26. Install the air conditioning compressor and power steering pump, properly route the accessory drive belt. Adjust the belt tension.

27. Install the radiator and connect the hoses.

28. Install the transmission.

29. Install the hood support and lower the hood.

30. Make sure all fluid levels are correct before starting the engine. Bleed air from the cooling system.

Engine Mounts

Removal and Installation

1. Raise and safely support the vehicle.

2. Support the engine using a suitable jacking device. Disconnect the mounting bolts.

3. Remove the ground strap, if equipped. Remove the engine mounts.

4. Install the mount onto the mounting bracket and replace the bolts.

5. Replace the ground strap, if equipped. Remove the jacking device.

6. Lower the vehicle.

Cylinder Head

Removal and Installation

1987 325, 325i, 325iS, 325iX AND 528e

1. Disconnect the negative battery cable. Make sure the engine is cool. Disconnect the exhaust pipes at the manifold and at the transmission clamp. Remove the drain plug at the bottom of the radiator and drain the coolant. Drain the engine oil.

2. Disconnect the accelerator and cruise control cables. If the vehicle has automatic transmission, disconnect the throttle cable that goes to the transmission.

3. Working at the front of the block, disconnect the upper radiator hose, the bypass water hose, and several smaller water hoses. Remove the diagnosis plug located at the front corner of the manifold. Remove the bracket located just underneath. Disconnect the fuel line and drain the contents into a metal container for safe disposal.

4. On the 325, 325i, 325iS and 325iX:
    a. Working on the air cleaner/airflow sensor, disconnect the vacuum hoses, labeling them if necessary. Disconnect all electrical connectors and unclip and remove the wiring harness. There is a relay located in an L-shaped box near the strut tower. Disconnect and remove it. Unclamp and remove the air hose. Remove the mounting nuts and remove the assembly.
    b. Disconnect the hose at the coolant overflow tank. Disconnect the idle speed positioner vacuum hose and then remove the positioner from the manifold.
    c. If equipped with 4 wheel drive, disconnect the vacuum hose from the servo mounted on the manifold.
    d. Place a drain pan underneath and then disconnect the water connections at the front of the intake manifold. Disconnect the electrical connector.

5. On the 528e, perform the following procedures:
    a. Working near the air cleaner/air flow sensor unit, disconnect the vacuum hoses at the intake manifold and at the air intake hose.
    b. Disconnect the electrical connectors and then remove the wiring harness.
    c. Pull off the large hose leading into the unit and loosen the clamp where the air intake hose connects at the intake manifold.
    d. Remove the mounting nuts and remove the air cleaner/airflow sensor.
    e. Disconnect the water hoses at the throttle body.
    f. Disconnect the electrical connector under the throttle body.
    g. Disconnect the bracket under the intake manifold tube.

6. Disconnect the heater water hoses. Press down, in the arrowed direction, on the vent tube collar and install the special tool or a similar device to retain the collar in the unlocked position. Disconnect the vent tube and inspect its O-ring seal, replacing it, if necessary.

7. Unbolt the dipstick tube at the manifold. Remove the fuel hose bracket at the cylinder head. Make sure the engine is cold. Then, place a metal container under the connection and disconnect the fuel hose at the connection.

8. Disconnect the high tension lead from the coil. Disconnect and remove the coolant expansion tank.

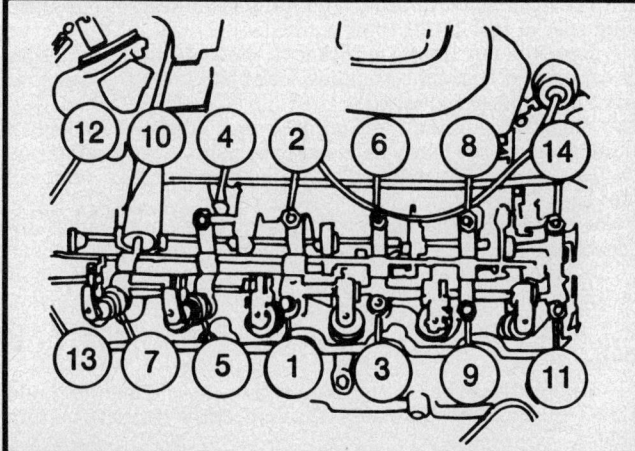

Cylinder head torque sequence—M20B27 and M20B25 engines

Alignment of dowel pin (1) with the sprocket and upper bolt hole and cylinder head cast tab—6 cylinder engines

9. On the 325, 325i, 325iS and 325iX:

a. If equipped with 4 wheel drive, disconnect the intake manifold vacuum hose leading the the servo that engages 4 wheel drive.

b. Disconnect the fuel injector connectors at all 6 injectors, as well as the 2 additional electrical connectors to sensors on the head. Disconnect the oil pressure sending unit connector. Then, unfasten the carriers and remove this wiring harness toward the left side of the vehicle.

10. On the 528e, perform the following procedures:

a. There is a bracket with various vacuum and electrical fittings that runs from the cam cover over toward the intake manifold. Disconnect the electrical connector connected on this bracket and the plug to its left. Remove the nuts fastening the bracket to the cam cover and the gasketed flange on the opposite end and remove the bracket. Inspect the gasket and supply a new one for use in installation, if necessary. Unplug the fuel injectors.

b. Disconnect the DME plugs. Disconnect the plugs located near the front 3 fuel injectors and any remaining injector connectors. Unplug the oil pressure sending unit connector. Then, unfasten the mounting clips and pull the wiring harness out toward the left.

11. Disconnect the coil high tension wire and disconnect the high tension wires at the plugs. Then, disconnect the tube in which the wires run at the cam cover. Disconnect the PCV hose. Then, remove the retaining nuts and remove the cam cover.

12. Turn the crankshaft so the TDC line is aligned with the indicator and the valves of No. 6 cylinder are in overlapping, slightly open position.

13. Remove the distributor cap. Then, unscrew and remove the rotor. Unscrew and remove the adapter just underneath the rotor. Remove the cover underneath the adapter. Check its O-ring and replace it, if necessary.

14. Remove the distributor mounting bolts and the protective cover.

15. These engines are equipped with a rubber drive and timing belt. Remove the belt covers. To loosen belt tension, loosen the tension roller bracket pivot bolt and adjusting slot bolt. Push the roller and bracket away from the belt to release the tension, hold the bracket in this position, and retighten the adjusting slot bolt to retain the bracket it this position.

16. Remove the timing belt.

NOTE: Make sure to avoid rotating both the engine and camshaft from this point onward.

17. Remove the cylinder head mounting bolts in exact reverse order of the proper tightening sequence. Then, remove the cylinder head.

To install:

18. Install the head with a new gasket. Check that all passages line up with the gasket holes. Clean the threads on the head bolts and coat with a light coating of oil. Keep oil out of the bolt cavities in the head or the head could be cracked or proper torquing affected.

19. Install the bolts and torque in stages, to the correct specifications. Then, adjust the valves.

20. Clean both cylinder head and block sealing surfaces thoroughly with a hardwood scraper. Inspect the surfaces for flatness. Note that the M20B25 engine gasket is coded 2.5 and the M20B27 engine gasket is coded 2.7.

21. Complete the installation by reversing all removal procedures. Make sure to refill the engine oil pan and cooling system with proper fluids and to bleed the cooling system.

22. Replace the gaskets for the exhaust system connections, if necessary. Coat the studs with the proper sealant. Note that the plugs for the DME reference mark and speed signals should be connected so the gray plug goes to the socket with a ring underneath.

NOTE: Align the timing marks when installing the timing belt. The crankshaft sprocket mark must point at the notch in the flange of the front engine cover. The camshaft sprocket arrow must point at the alignment mark on the cylinder head. Also, the No. 1 piston must be at TDC of the compression stroke. BMW recommends that the timing belt be replaced every time the cylinder head is removed and the belt is disturbed as a consequence. Tension the belt.

23. Start the engine and run it until it is hot. Stop the engine and again remove the cam cover. Using an angle gauge, tighten the head bolts 25 degrees farther in numbered order. Reinstall the cam cover.

318iS

1. Disconnect the negative battery cable.

2. Remove the ignition coil cover and pull off the spark plug connectors.

3. Remove the complete ignition tackle. Remove the cylinder head cover.

4. Disconnect the coolant hoses and unscrew the temperature sensor.

5. Remove the thermostat housing and thermostat. Unscrew the upper timing case cover.

6. Rotate the engine in the direction of the rotation until the

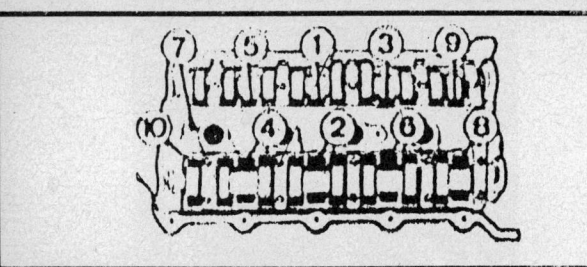

Cylinder head tightening sequence—318iS

cam peaks of the intake and exhaust cams for cylinder no.1 face each other. The arrows on the sprocket face up.

7. Remove the chain tensioner. Remove the upper chain guide, chain guide bolt on the right side and the sprockets.

8. Remove the cylinder head bolts from the outside to the inside in several steps using the proper tool.

9. Remove the cylinder head. Clean the sealing surfaces on the cylinder head and the crankcase.

10. The installation is the reverse of the removal procedure

535i (M30 B34 ENGINES)

1. Unbolt the exhaust pipes at the exhaust manifold. Unclamp the exhaust pipe at the transmission.

2. Disconnect the battery negative and positive cables and drain the coolant by removing the plugs from the radiator and block.

3. Disconnect the throttle, accelerator, and cruise control cables at the throttle body.

4. Disconnect all wiring that goes to the cylinder head or would obstruct its removal. This includes: wiring to the airflow sensor; ignition wiring and, where used, the ignition wiring tube; wires to the fuel injectors. It may be necessary to disconnect the alternator wiring and the main harness to the fuse box. Disconnect the starter wiring.

5. Disconnect fuel lines, vacuum lines, and heater and coolant hoses that are in the way. Disconnect DME plugs. Note that the gray plug connects to the plug with a ring underneath, for proper installation.

6. Remove the air cleaner and the windshield washer tank.

7. Remove the rocker cover. Disconnect the injector electrical connections, cold start valve and idle positioner. Disconnect the ground lead on all engines. Then, complete disconnecting the engine wiring harness by disconnecting the oil pressure sending unit and set the harness aside.

8. See the procedures below for removal of the front cover and timing chain and tensioner. Remove the upper timing case cover, tensioner piston, open the lock plates and remove the timing chain upper sprocket. Suspend the sprocket to retain the timing chain position.

9. Loosen the cylinder head bolts in reverse order of the tightening sequence. Then, install 4 special pins part No. 11 1 063 or equivalent. This is necessary to keep the rocker arm shafts from moving. Then, lift off the head.

To install:

10. Make checks of the lower cylinder head and block deck surface to make sure they are true. Install a new head gasket, making sure all bolt, oil, and coolant holes line up.

11. Apply a very light coating of oil to the head bolts. Don't let oil get into the bolt holes or apply excessive amounts of oil, or torque could be incorrect and the block could crack. Use the newer type of bolt without a collar. Install the bolts, finger tight.

12. Torque bolts 1–6 in the correct sequence to 42–44 ft. lbs. Remove the pins holding the rocker shafts in place. Now, complete the first stage of torquing by torquing bolts 7–14 in the correct sequence, to the proper specifications. Follow the remaining torquing procedures. Wait between steps as mentioned. Adjust the valves. Then, reassemble the engine as described below and run it until hot. Then, again remove the valve cover and

turn the head bolts, in order, the number of degrees specified, using special tool 11 2 110 or equivalent.

13. Reinstall the timing sprocket to the camshaft. Make sure the cam is in proper time, that new lock plates are used, and that nuts are properly tightened.

14. When reinstalling the timing cover, make sure to apply a liquid sealer to the joints between upper and lower timing covers. The remainder of installation is the reverse of removal. Note these points.

    a. Adjust throttle, speed control, and accelerator cables. Inspect and if necessary replace the exhaust manifold gasket.

    b. When reinstalling the cylinder block coolant plug, coat it with sealer. Make sure to refill the cooling system and bleed it.

525i, 535i, 635CSi, 735i, 735iL (M30 B35 ENGINE) AND 750iL

1. Unbolt the exhaust pipe connections at the manifold and at the transmission pipe clamp. Disconnect the negative battery cable.

2. Remove the splash shield from under the engine. With the engine cool, remove the drain plugs from the bottom of the radiator and block. Drain the engine oil.

3. Remove the fan. Lift out the expansion rivets on either side and remove the fan shroud.

4. Loosen the hose clamp and disconnect the air inlet hose. Remove the mounting nut and remove the air cleaner.

5. The unit on the opposite side of the intake hose from the air cleaner contains the idle speed control valve, which must be removed next. Loosen the hose clamps and pull off the hoses. Disconnect the electrical connector. Remove the mounting nut and then pull the idle speed control out of the air intake hose.

6. Pull off the retainers for the airflow sensor, and then pull the unit off its mountings, disconnecting the vacuum hose from the PCV system at the same time.

7. Working on the coolant expansion tank, disconnect the electrical connector. Remove the nuts on both sides. Loosen their clamps and then disconnect all hoses and remove the tank.

8. Disconnect the heater hoses at both the control valve and at the heater core. Remove the valve, if needed.

9. Disconnect the throttle and cruise control cables at the throttle lever. Unbolt the cable housing retainer and remove the housing and cables.

10. Disconnect the plugs near the thermostat housing. Loosen the hose clamps and pull off the coolant hoses.

11. Disconnect the plug in the line leading to the oxygen sensor. Disconnect the other plugs.

12. Disconnect the fuel supply and return lines, collecting fuel in a metal container for safe disposal.

13. Disconnect the fuel pipe running along the cylinder head, near the manifold. Pull off the electrical connector at the throttle body. Remove the caps, then remove the attaching bolts and remove the wiring harness carrier and harness for the fuel injectors.

14. Disconnect the coil high tension lead. Disconnect the high tension wires at the plugs. Then, remove the mounting nuts and remove the carrier for the high tension wires from the head.

15. Remove the attaching nuts for the cam cover and remove it.

16. Turn the engine until the timing marks are at TDC and the No. 6 valves are at overlap, both slightly open, position.

17. Remove the upper timing case cover. Remove the timing chain tensioner piston.

18. Remove the upper timing chain sprocket bolts and pull the sprocket off, holding it upward and then supporting it securely so the relationship between the chain and sprockets top and bottom will not be lost.

19. Disconnect the upper radiator hose at the thermostat housing. Remove the bolts and remove the support for the intake manifold.

20. Remove the cylinder head bolts in the opposite of numbered order. Then, install 4 special pins part No. 11 1 063 or

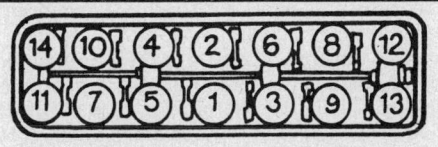

Cylinder head torque sequence—S38Z engine used with M5 and M6

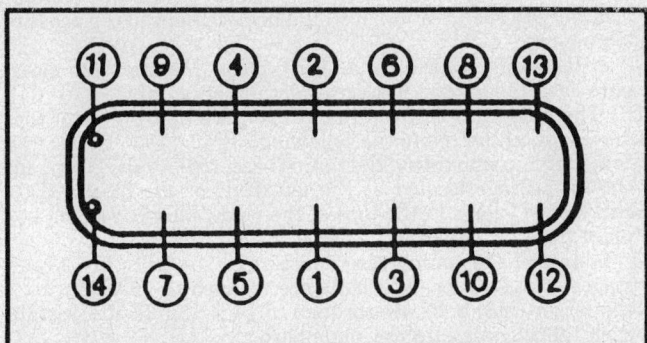

Cylinder head tightening sequence—M30B35 engine

equivalent. This is necessary to keep the rocker arm shafts from moving. Then, lift off the head.

21. Make checks of the lower cylinder head and block deck surface to make sure they are true. Install a new head gasket, making sure all bolt, oil, and coolant holes line up. Use a gasket marked M30 B35. Use a 0.3mm thicker gasket, if the head has been machined.

To install:

22. Apply a very light coating of oil to the head bolts. Don't let oil get into the bolt holes or apply excessive amounts of oil, or torque could be incorrect and the block could crack. Use the type of bolt without a collar. Install the bolts, finger tight.

23. Torque bolts 1–6 in the correct order to 42–44 ft. lbs. Remove the pins holding the rocker shafts in place. Now, complete the first stage of torquing by torquing bolts 7–14 in the correct order, to the same specification. Adjust the valves after a 15 minute wait. Tighten the bolts, in the correct order, with a torque angle gauge 30–36 degrees, using special tool 11 2 110 or equivalent. Then, reassemble the engine as described below and run it until hot (25 minutes). Then, again remove the valve cover and turn the head bolts, in the correct order, 30–40 degrees.

24. Reinstall the timing sprocket to the camshaft. Make sure the cam is in proper time, that new lock plates are used, and that nuts are properly torqued.

25. When reinstalling the timing cover, make sure to apply a liquid sealer to the joints between upper and lower timing covers. The remainder of installation is the reverse of removal. Note these points:

   a. Adjust throttle, speed control, and accelerator cables. Inspect and if necessary replace the exhaust manifold gasket.

   b. When reinstalling the cylinder block coolant plug, coat it with sealer. Make sure to refill the cooling system and bleed it. Make sure to refill the oil pan with the correct amount of oil.

   c. Install the timing chain so the down pin on the camshaft sprocket is at the 8 o'clock when its tapped bores are at right angles to the engine. Torque the sprocket bolts to 6.5–7.5 ft. lbs.

   d. Check the cam cover gasket, replacing, as necessary. Retighten cam cover bolts in the order shown. Torque the bolts to 6.5–7.5 ft. lbs.

   e. When reinstalling the fan shroud, make sure all guides are located properly.

   f. Coat the tapered portion of the exhaust pipe connection flange with the proper sealant. Torque the attaching nuts to 4.5 ft. lbs. and loosen 1½ turns.

M3

1. Disconnect the negative battery cable. Remove the splash guard from under the engine. Put drain pans underneath and remove the drain plugs from both the radiator and block to drain all coolant.

2. Loosen the hose clamps for the air intake hose located next to the radiator and then remove the hose. Disconnect the electrical connectors for the airflow sensor. Then, remove the attaching nuts and remove the air cleaner/ airflow sensor unit.

3. Disconnect the accelerator and cruise control cables. Unbolt the cable mounting bracket and move the cables and bracket aside.

4. Remove the attaching nut, pull off the clamp, and then detach the vacuum hose from the brake booster.

5. Loosen the hose clamp and remove the air intake hose from the intake manifold. Remove the nut from the manifold brace.

6. Loosen the clamp and disconnect the other end of the booster vacuum hose at the manifold. Remove the nut from the intake manifold brace.

7. Loosen the hose clamp and disconnect the air intake hose at the manifold. Then, remove the nuts attaching the manifold assembly to the outer ends of the intake throttle necks and remove the assembly.

8. Put a drain pan underneath and loosen the hose clamps and disconnect the coolant expansion tank hoses. Disconnect the engine ground strap.

9. Disconnect the ignition coil high tension lead. Label and then disconnect the plugs on the front of the block. Remove the nut fastening the lead farther forward of the plugs and move the lead aside so it will not interfere with cylinder head removal.

10. Find the vacuum hose leading to the fuel pressure regulator. Pull it off. Label and then disconnect the 2 plugs. Unscrew the mounting screw for the electrical lead connecting with the top of the block and remove the lead and its carrier.

11. There is a vacuum hose connecting with one of the throttle necks. Disconnect it and pull it out of the intake manifold bracket. Pull off the electrical connector. Pull out the rubber retainer, and then pull the idle speed control out and put it aside. The engine wiring harness is located nearby. Take it out of its carriers.

12. All the fuel injectors are plugged into a common plate. Carefully and evenly pull the plate off the injectors, pull it out past the pressure regulator, and lay it aside.

13. Loosen the clamp and then disconnect the PCV hose. Label and then disconnect the fuel lines connecting with the injector circuit. Put a drain pan underneath and then disconnect the heater hose from the cylinder head.

14. Loosen the clamp near the throttle necks and then pull the engine wiring harness out and put it aside. Put a drain pan underneath and then disconnect the heater hose that connects to the block.

15. Remove the bolts from the flanges connecting the exhaust pipes to the exhaust manifold. Provide new gaskets and self-locking nuts. Disconnect the oxygen sensor plug.

16. Put a drain pan underneath and then disconnect the radiator hoses from the pipe at the front of the block.

17. It is not necessary to remove the timing chain completely, but it is necessary to remove the cam cover, front covers for the camshaft drive sprockets, the upper guide rail for the timing chain and then turn the engine to TDC firing position for No. 1. Remove the timing chain tensioner. Note the relationship between the chain and both the crankshaft and camshaft sprockets, and then remove both camshaft drive sprockets. Leave the chain in a position that will not interfere with removal of the head and which will minimize disturbing its routing through the areas on the front of the block.

18. Remove the camshafts.

19. Remove the cam followers one at a time, keeping them in exact order for installation in the same positions.

20. Pull off the spark plug connectors. Remove the nuts from the cam cover, located just to one side of the row of spark plugs. Remove the ignition lead tube. Remove the remaining nuts and remove the cam cover. Provide new gaskets.

21. Remove the bolts, some are accessible from below, that retain the timing case to the head at the front, the timing case houses the lifters and the camshaft lower bearing saddles. Note that one bolt, on the right side of the vehicle, is longer and retains the shaft for the upper timing chain tensioning rail.

22. Remove the coolant pipe that runs along the left/rear of the block. Remove one bolt at the left/front of the block that is located outside the cam cover. Then, go along in the area under the cam cover and remove all the remaining bolts for the timing case. Remove the timing case.

23. Remove the hex bolts fastening the head to the block at the front. These are located outside the cam cover and just behind the water pump drive belt. Then, remove the head bolts located under the cam cover in reverse order of the cylinder head torque sequence.

To install:

24. Make checks of the lower cylinder head and block deck surface to make sure they are true. Clean both cylinder head and block sealing surfaces thoroughly. Lubricate the head bolts with a light coating of engine oil. Make sure there is no oil or dirt in the bolt holes in the block. Install a new head gasket, making sure all bolt, oil, and coolant holes line up. Install the bolts as follows:

   a. Torque them in the correct order to 35–37 ft. lbs.
   b. Then, torque them, in order, to 57–59 ft. lbs.
   c. Wait 15 minutes.
   d. Torque them, in order, to 71–73 ft. lbs.
   e. Remember to reinstall the bolts that go outside the cylinder head cover and fasten the front of the head to the block at front and rear.

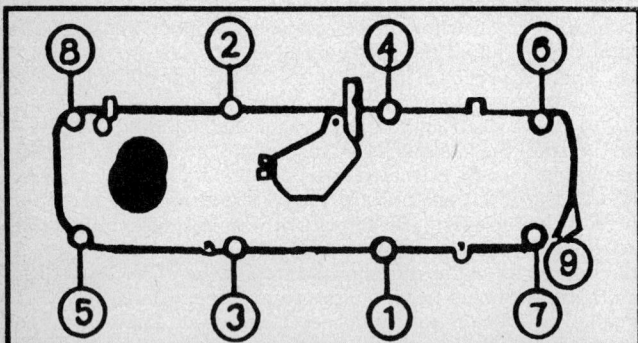

Torque the cam cover bolts—M30 B34 and B35 engines, in the order shown

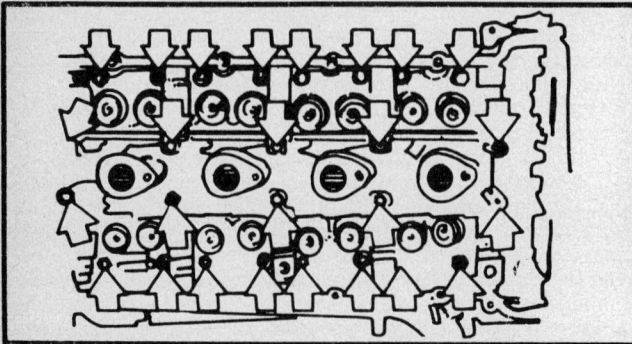

Removing the timing case for the M3. Remove all arrowed bolts

25. BMW recommends checking the fit of each tappet in the timing case, by performing the following procedure:

   a. Measure a tappet's outside diameter with a micrometer. Then, zero an inside micrometer at this exact dimension.

   b. Then, use the inside micrometer to measure the tappet bore that corresponds to this particular tappet. If the resulting measurement is 0.0001–0.0026 in. the tappet may be reused. If it is worn past this dimension, replace it with a new one. If the tappet is being replaced, repeat steps a and b to make sure it will now meet specifications. If the bore were to be worn so much that even a new tappet would not restore clearance to specification, it would be necessary to replace the timing case.

   c. Repeat for all the remaining tappets. Make sure to measure each tappet and its corresponding bore only.

26. The remaining steps of installation are the reverse of the removal procedure. Note the following:

   a. Before remounting the timing case, replace the O-ring in the oil passage located at the left/front of the block. Also, check the O-rings in the tops of the spark plug bores and replace these as necessary.

   b. Install the timing case and torque the bolts in several stages. The smaller (M7) bolts are torqued to 10–12 ft. lbs.; the larger (M8) bolts are torqued to 14.5–15.5 ft. lbs. Install each tappet back into the same bore.

   c. When bolting the exhaust pipes to the flange at the manifold, use new gaskets and self-locking nuts and torque the nuts to 36 ft. lbs.

   d. When reinstalling the intake manifold, check and, if necessary, replace the O-rings where the manifold tubes connect to the throttle necks. Torque the nuts to 6.5 ft. lbs.

   d. Make sure to refill the radiator and bleed the cooling system.

M5 AND M6

1. Disconnect the negative battery cable. Scribe matchmarks where the hood hinges attach to the hood. Then, disconnect the support struts, unbolt the hood at the hinges and remove it.

2. Disconnect the electrical connector at the airflow sensor. Loosen the hose clamp at the air intake hose going to the air cleaner, remove the air cleaner attaching nut and remove the air cleaner and airflow sensor.

3. Disconnect the large vacuum hose that connects to the bottom of the intake manifold. Disconnect the PCV hoses where they connect to the top of the manifold. Disconnect the throttle cable that runs across the top of the manifold, and the hose running near the front. Remove the bolts fastening the manifold to the outer ends of the intake tubes and remove it.

4. With the engine cool, drain the coolant from the block. Disconnect the exhaust pipe at the manifold.

5. Working underneath, remove the heat shields. Remove the cross brace and stabilizer bar where they connect to the engine carrier. Remove the exhaust manifold.

6. Disconnect the upper radiator hose. Pull the plugs off the water manifold that connects with the upper radiator hose. Pull off the plug coming from the same harness and connecting to the top of the engine. Then, unclip this harness and pull it out of the way.

7. Loosen the retaining straps and disconnect the electrical connector that runs directly across the front of the block. Disconnect the fuel pipe on the driver's side of the block, collecting fuel in a metal container for safe disposal.

8. Pull the electrical connector off the throttle bypass valve. Disconnect the water hose and remove the bypass valve. Disconnect the large hose just to the right of the throttle bypass valve. Remove the wiring harness clips just to the right.

9. At the rear of the engine, disconnect the fuel return line and collect fuel in a metal container for safe disposal. Disconnect both heater hoses. Remove the conduit for the injector wiring harness from the head. Remove the bolts in the front of the head which run down into the timing cover.

10. It is not necessary to remove the timing chain completely, but it will be necessary to remove the cam cover, front covers for the camshaft drive sprockets and the upper guide rail for the timing chain, and then turn the engine to TDC firing position for No. 1. Then, it will be necessary to remove the timing chain tensioner. Note the relationship between the chain and both the crankshaft and camshaft sprockets, and then remove both camshaft drive sprockets. Leave the chain in a position that will not interfere with removal of the head and which will minimize disturbing its routing through the areas on the front of the block.

11. Remove the camshafts as described below.

12. Remove the cam followers one at a time, keeping them in exact order for installation in the same positions.

13. Remove the coolant pipe that runs across the front of the block. Remove the bolts (some are accessible from below) that retain the timing case to the head at the front, the timing case houses the lifters and the camshaft lower bearing saddles. Then, go along in the area under the cam cover and remove all the remaining bolts for the timing case. Remove the timing case.

14. Loosen the head bolts in reverse of the tightening sequence. Remove the cylinder head.

To install:

15. Make checks of the lower cylinder head and block deck surface to make sure they are true. Lubricate the head bolts with a light coating of engine oil. Make sure there is no oil or dirt in the bolt holes in the block. Install a new head gasket, making sure all bolt, oil, and coolant holes
line up. Use a gasket type M6 marked 3.5M 88.3.

16. Replace the O-ring in the head at the right/rear where the coolant pipe comes up from the block. Coat the pipe with a suitable sealer.

17. Install the head onto the block. Install the head bolts and tighten in the correct sequence.

18. When installing the timing case, replace the O-rings in the small oil passages in the ends of the head. Inspect the O-rings in the center of the block and replace them if necessary. Coat all sealing surfaces with a sealer. Tighten the bolts evenly, torquing the smaller (M7) bolts to 10–12 ft. lbs. and the larger (M8) bolts to 14.5–15.5 ft. lbs. Install all lifters back into the same bores.

19. Install the camshafts.

20. Reroute the timing chain, as necessary, and remount the drive sprockets for the camshaft. Install the tensioning rail that goes at the top of the timing chain.

21. Install the front cover.

22. Continue to reverse the removal procedure. Note these points:

    a. When reinstalling the intake manifold, inspect the O-rings and replace, as necessary.

    b. Refill the cooling system with an appropriate antifreeze/water mix and bleed the cooling system.

Valve Lash

Adjustment

EXCEPT M3, M5 AND M6

All engines except the M series, dual overhead designs, are equipped with an overhead camshaft operating the intake and exhaust valves through rocker arm linkage.

NOTE: The valves must be adjusted cold.

1. Disconnect the negative battery cable. Remove the rocker cover.

2. Rotate the engine until the No. 1 cylinder is at TDC on the compression stroke.

NOTE: Locate No. 1 cylinder firing position by the distributor rotor-to-cap position, or by observing the valve action in the opposite cylinder.

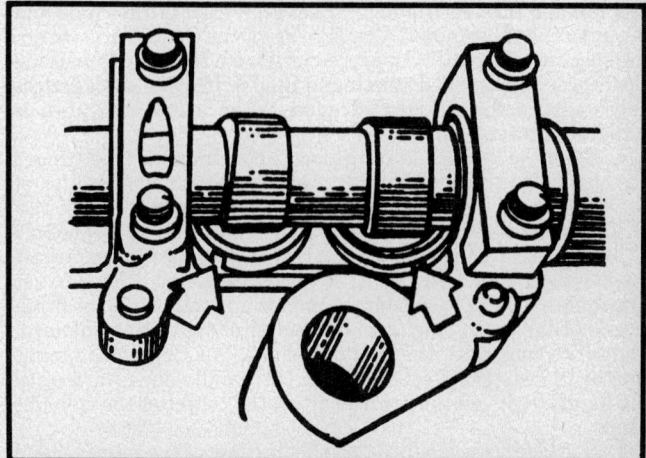

On M5 and M6 DOHC engines, rotate the valve tappets so the grooves machined in the tops are facing as shown before attempting to measure valve clearance

Adjusting of engine valve clearance with bent rod after loosening the locknut (1)

3. Measure the valve clearance between the valve stem end and the rocker arm on the No. 1 cylinder.

4. Adjust the clearance by loosening the locknut on the rocker arm and turning the eccentric with a bent rod inserted through a hole provided on the surface of the eccentric.

5. When the proper clearance is obtained, tighten the locknut and recheck the valve clearance. Complete the adjustment on both valves.

6. Rotate the engine crankshaft to the next cylinder in the firing order, adjust the valves and repeat the procedures until all the valves are adjusted.

7. Replace the rocker cover, using a new gasket.

M3, M5 AND M6

NOTE: To perform this procedure, a special tool is needed to depress the valves against spring pressure to gain access to the valve adjusting discs. Use tool 11 3 170 or equivalent. Also needed are: compressed air to lift valve adjusting discs that must be replaced out of the valve tappet; an assortment of adjusting discs of various thicknesses and a precise outside micrometer.

1. Make sure the engine is overnight cold. Disconnect the negative battery cable. Remove the rocker cover.

2. Turn the engine until the No. 1 cylinder intake valve cams, the intake cam is labeled **A** on the head, are both straight up.

3. Slide a flat feeler gauge in between each of the cams and the adjacent valve tappet. Check to see if the clearance is within the specified range. If it is, proceed with checking the remaining clearances as described starting in Step 8. If not, switch gauges and measure the actual clearance. When actual clearance is achieved, proceed with Steps 4–7.

4. Turn the tappets so the grooves machined into their edges are aligned as shown. Looking at the valves from the center of the engine, the right hand tappet's groove should be at about 5 o'clock and the left hand tappet's groove should be at about 7 o'clock. Use the end of the special tool required for the camshaft involved—in this case the **A** or intake camshaft, the exhaust camshaft end is labeled **E** on the engine and tool. Slide the proper end of the tool, going from the center of the engine outward, under the cam, with the heel of the tool pivoting on the inner side of the camshaft valley. Force the handle downward until the handle rests on the protrusion on the center of the cylinder head.

5. Use compressed air to pop the disc out of the tappet. Read the thickness dimension on the disc.

6. Determine the thickness required as follows:

   a. If the valve clearance is too tight, try the next thinner disc.

   b. If the valve clearance is too loose, try the next thicker disc.

7. Slip the thinner or thicker disc into the tappet with the letter facing downward. Rock the valve spring depressing tool out and remove it. Then, recheck the clearance. Change the disc again, if necessary, until the clearance falls within the specified range.

8. Turn the engine in firing order sequence, turning the crankshaft forward ⅓ of a turn each time to get the intake cams to the upward position for each cylinder. Measure the clearance as in Step 3 and, if it is outside the specified range, follow Steps 4–7 to adjust either or both valves. Repeat this for all the intakes, and then turn the engine until No. 1 cylinder exhaust valves are upward.

9. Follow the same sequence for all the exhaust valves, going through the firing order, checking clearance as described in Step 3 and adjusting the valves as in Steps 4–7. Note that it is necessary, however, to use the opposite end of the special tool, the end marked **E** to depress the exhaust valves.

10. When all the clearances are in the specified range, replace the cam cover, start the engine, and check for leaks.

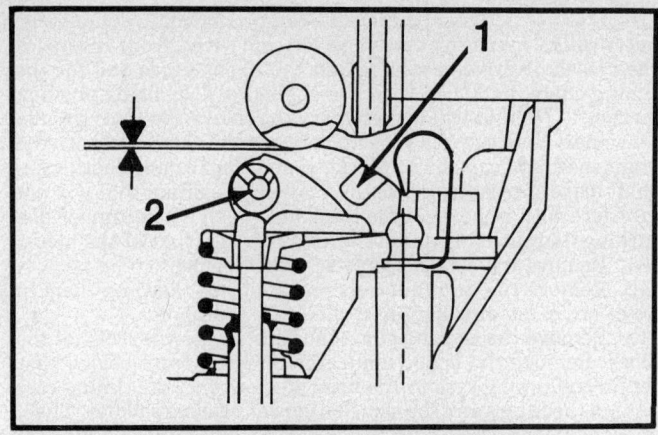

A back-up wrench should be used at (1) when adjusting valves. The locknut that holds the adjusting eccentric is at (2). "V" shows the valve clearance

3. Spring
4. Washer
5. Rocker arm
6. Thrust ring

Installed position of rocker arm components

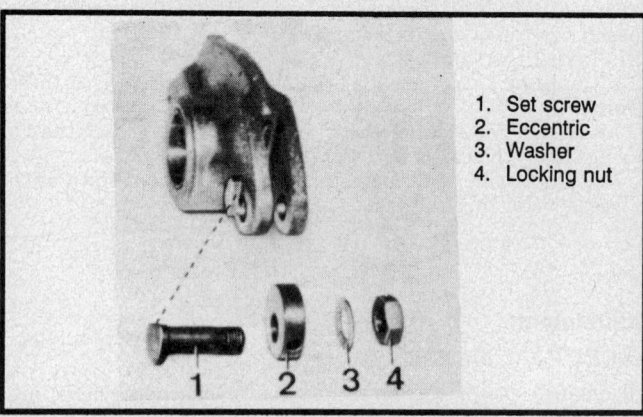

1. Set screw
2. Eccentric
3. Washer
4. Locking nut

Rocker arm valve adjusting mechanism

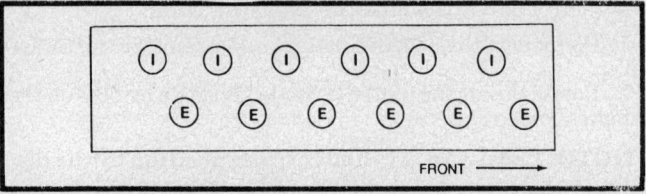

6 cylinder valve location

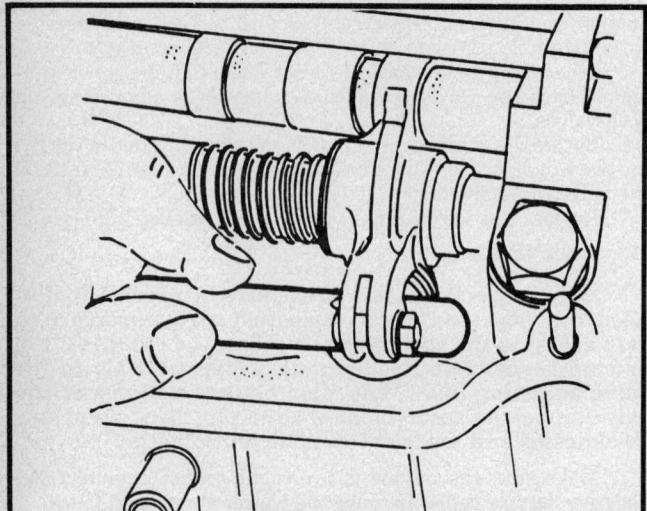

Checking the valve clearance with a flat feeler gauge

Rocker Arms/Shafts

Removal and Installation

EXCEPT 325, 325i, 325iS, 325iX AND 528e

1. Disconnect the negative battery cable. Remove the cylinder head.

2. Remove the camshaft.

3. On 6 cylinder engines, remove the retaining bolts and remove the end cover from the rear of the cylinder head. Slide the thrust rings and rocker arms rearward and remove the circlips from the rocker arm shafts.

4. On 4 cylinder engines:

a. Remove the distributor flange from the rear of the cylinder head.

b. Using a long punch, drive the rocker arm shaft from the rear to the front of the cylinder head.

NOTE: Be sure all circlips are off the shaft before attempting to drive the shaft from the cylinder head.

c. The intake rocker shaft is not plugged at the rear, while the exhaust rocker shaft must be plugged. Replace the plug if necessary, during the installation.

5. On 6 cylinder engines:

a. Install dowel pins part No. 11 1 063 or equivalent to keep the rocker shafts from turning. Then, remove the rocker shaft retaining plugs from the front of the cylinder head. These require a hex head wrench. Then, push back the rocker arms against spring pressure and remove the circlips retaining the shafts. Remove the dowel pins. If the rocker shafts have welded plugs, the shafts will have to be pressed out of the head with a tool such as 11 3 050 or equivalent.

NOTE: There is considerable force on the springs positioning the rockers. They may pop out. Be cautious and wear safety glasses.

b. Install a threaded slide hammer into the ends of the rear rocker shafts and remove.

To install:

6. The rocker arms, springs, washers, thrust rings and shafts should be examined and worn parts replaced. Special attention should be given to the rocker arm cam followers. If these are loose, replace the arm assembly. The valves can be removed, repaired or replaced, as necessary, while the shafts and rocker arms are out of the cylinder head.

7. Install the rocker arms in position, noting the following procedures:

a. Design changes of the rocker arms and shafts have occurred with the installation of a bushing in the rocker arm and the use of 2 horizontal oil flow holes drilled into the rocker shaft for improved oil supply. Do not mix the previously designed parts with the later design.

b. When installing the rocker arms and components to the rocker shafts, install locating pins in the cylinder head bolt bores to properly align the rocker arm shafts. Note that on 6 cylinder engines, the longer rocker shafts go on the chain end of the engine; the openings face the bores for the cylinder head bolts; and the plug threads face outward. The order of installation is: spring, washer, rocker arm, thrust washer, circlip. Note also that newer, short springs may be used with the older design.

c. Install sealer on the rocker arm shaft retaining plugs and rear cover.

d. On the 4 cylinder engines, position the rocker shafts so the camshaft retaining plate ends can be engaged in the slots of shafts during camshaft installation.

e. Adjust the valve clearance.

325, 325i, 325iS, 325iX AND 528e

The cylinder head must be removed before the rocker arm shafts can be removed.

1. Disconnect the negative battery cable. Remove the cylinder head.

2. Mount the head on a suitable holding fixture.

3. Remove the camshaft sprocket bolt and remove the camshaft distributor adapter and sprocket. Reinstall the adapter on the camshaft.

4. Adjust the valve clearance to the maximum allowable on all valves.

5. Remove the front and rear rocker shaft plugs and lift out the thrust plate.

6. Remove the spring-clips from the rocker arms by lifting them off.

7. Remove the exhaust side rocker arm shaft:

a. Set the No. 6 cylinder rocker arms at the valve overlap position (rocker arms parallel), by rotating the camshaft through the firing order.

b. Push in on the front cylinder rocker arm and then turn the camshaft in the direction of the intake rocker shaft, using a ½ in. drive breaker bar and a deep well socket to fit over the camshaft adapter. Slide each rocker arm to one side as it develops sufficient clearance away from its actuating cam and the valve it actuates. Rotate the camshaft until all of the rocker arms are relaxed.

c. Remove the rocker arm shaft.

8. Remove the intake side rocker arm shaft:

a. Turn the camshaft in the direction of the exhaust rocker arm.

b. Use a deep well socket and ½ in. drive breaker bar on the camshaft adapter to turn the camshaft. Slide each rocker arm to one side as it develops sufficient clearance away from its actuating cam and the valve it actuates. Rotate the camshaft until all of the rocker arms are relaxed.

c. Remove the rocker arm shaft.

9. Install the rocker arm shafts by reversing the removal procedure. Keep the following points in mind:

a. The large oil bores in the rocker shafts must be installed downward, toward the valve guides and the small oil bores and grooves for the guide plate face inward toward the center of the head.

b. The straight sections of the spring clamps must fit into the grooves in the rocker arm shafts.

c. The guide plate must fit into the grooves in the rocker arm shafts.

d. Adjust the valve clearance.

Intake Manifold

Removal and Installation

M3

NOTE: A Torx® nut driver is needed to perform this operation.

1. Disconnect the negative battery cable. Remove the cap nuts at the outer ends of the 4 throttle necks. Then remove the mounting nuts underneath.

2. Make sure the engine has cooled off. Loosen the hose clamps for the air intake lines and for the fuel lines where they connect with the injection pipe. Collect fuel in a metal container.

3. Disconnect the throttle cable.

4. Pull off the intake manifold. Cut off the crankcase ventilation hose running to it from the crankcase. Then, remove the manifold and place it aside. Supply a new crankcase ventilation hose.

5. Pull off the throttle valve switch plug. Carefully pull the injector plug plate evenly off all 4 injectors.

6. Pull the fuel pressure regulator vacuum hose off the pressure regulator.

7. Remove the 2 mounting bolts for the injector pipe. Then, carefully lift off the pipe and injectors.

8. Unscrew the nut attaching the ball joint at the end of the throttle actuating rod to the throttle linkage. Supply a new self-locking nut.

9. Remove the nuts attaching the throttle necks to the cylinder head. Then, remove the 4 throttle necks as an assembly.

10. Separate the throttle neck assemblies by pulling them apart at the connecting pipe.

11. Inspect the O-rings in the connecting pipe and at the outer ends of the throttle necks. Replace as necessary.

12. Reverse the removal procedure to install. Use the new throttle linkage self-locking nut and the new crankcase ventilation hose.

13. Torque the nuts attaching the throttle necks to the head and the intake manifold to the throttle necks to 6.5–7.0 ft. lbs. Adjust the throttle cable.

6 CYLINDER VEHICLES EXCEPT M5 AND M6

1. Disconnect the negative battery cable and drain the cooling system.

2. Disconnect the wire harness at the air flow sensor. Remove the air cleaner and sensor as an assembly. Disconnect the air intake hose running from the air cleaner to the manifold.

3. Remove and tag the vacuum hoses and electrical plugs. Disconnect the accelerator linkage and cruise control linkage, if equipped from the throttle housing.

4. Disconnect the coolant hoses from the throttle housing.

5. Working from the rear of the collector housing, disconnect the vacuum lines, and starting valve connector, fuel line and air line. Tag the hoses and lines for ease of assembly.

6. Remove the EGR valve and line.

7. Remove all intake pipes.

8. Remove the air collector housing from the engine. On vehicles with a single intake manifold casting, remove the nuts and remove the throttle valve body.

9. Disconnect the plugs at the injector valves and remove the valves.

10. Disconnect the wire plugs at the coolant temperature sensor, the temperature time switch and the temperature switch.

11. Pull the wire loom upward through the opening in the intake manifold neck.

12. Remove the coolant hoses from the intake neck.

NOTE: Mark the heater hoses for proper reinstallation.

13. Remove the retaining bolts or nuts and remove either front, rear or both intake manifold necks. On some vehicles, remove the entire assembly.

To install:

14. To install the manifold, use new gaskets and install the manifold to the engine.

15. Install the air intake tubes and the injector valves. Install the collector and bracket.

16. Connect the vacuum line and electrical connections to the timing valve. Install the cold start valve.

17. Connect the line at the EGR valve and the electrical connections at the temperature timing switch.

18. Connect all vacuum, cooling and fuel lines at the throttle housing. Install the accelerator cable and vacuum hoses to the air collector.

19. Install the air cleaner and fill the cooling system. Check all hose connections and fluid levels before operating the engine.

M5 AND M6

The M5 and M6 employ a manifold chamber in combination with 6 throttle necks (one for each cylinder), each of which contains its own throttle. The throttle necks are divided into 3 assemblies each containing the necks for 2 adjacent cylinders.

Intake manifold mounting bolts—318iS

1. Disconnect the negative battery cable. Remove the nuts at the outer ends of the throttle necks, these attach the manifold to the outer ends of the necks. Loosen the hose clamps for the crankcase ventilation hoses and for the air intake hose. Disconnect the accelerator cable.

2. Pull the intake manifold off the throttle necks. Check O-rings and replace any that are hard or cracked.

3. Disconnect the electrical connectors to the cold start valve, throttle bypass valve, and throttle valve switch. Disconnect all the electrical connections going to the fuel injectors and remove the conduit for the injector wires from the throttle necks.

4. Disconnect the vacuum hoses for the fuel pressure regulator and the heater temperature sensor. Disconnect the fuel return pipe, and collect the fuel in a metal container for safe disposal.

5. Remove the attaching nuts and bolts, and remove the injection pipe and injectors.

NOTE: Clean the throttle shaft thoroughly and be sure not to use pliers on the shaft surface. Otherwise, needle bearings on which the shaft rides may be damaged.

6. Using a center punch, drive out the 4 pins locking the throttle shaft in place. Slide the shaft out of the bearings.

7. Unscrew its mounting nuts and remove the throttle bypass valve. Disconnect the air hoses from this valve.

8. Remove the nuts attaching the throttle valve necks to the head and remove them.

9. Remove the connecting pipes that run between the valve neck units. Replace O-rings, if necessary. Replace all gaskets and make sure gasket surfaces on the head and inner ends of valve necks are clean.

10. Install in reverse order, providing new pins for the throttle shaft and coating its bearing surfaces with a proper lubricant before assembly.

11. Replace the sleeves in the intake manifold, if necessary. Replace the crankcase ventilation hose connecting the intake manifold and crankcase.

318iS

1. Disconnect the negative battery cable. Unscrew the upper manifold section.

2. Disconnect the rear mounting bracket and remove the coolant hose.

3. Loosen the front mounting bracket and disconnect the holder for the preheater.

4. Remove the mounting bolts and lift off the upper manifold section. Pull the hose off the fuel pressure regulator at the same time.

5. Pull the plug plate off the fuel injectors and remove the wire holding clamp.

6. Remove the injection pipe with the fuel injectors attached and remove the lower manifold section.

7. The installation is the reverse of the removal procedure.

750iL

1. Disconnect the negative battery cable. Loosen the clamps for the fuel lines.

2. Pull off the vacuum hoses for the pressure regulators. Lift out the injection pipes with the injectors attached.

3. Remove the distributor caps and the throttle valve necks on the manifolds.

4. Disconnect the spark plug wires and remove the ignition lead pipes.

5. Disconnect the crankcase breather hose and loosen the manifold support nuts.

6. Disconnect the nose guard and remove the intake manifold, using the proper tool.

7. The installation is the reverse of the removal procedure. Tighten the intake manifold mounting bolts to 14–17 ft. lbs.

Exhaust Manifold

Removal and Installation

EXCEPT M3, M5 AND M6

The 4 cylinder manifold is a one piece, one outlet unit, while the 6 cylinder manifold assembly consists of a 2 piece, double outlet to the exhaust pipe. One piece can be replaced independently of the other.

1. Disconnect the negative battery cable. Remove the air volume control and if necessary, air cleaner.

2. Disconnect the exhaust pipe at the reactor outlet(s).

3. Remove the guard plate from the reactor(s).

4. Disconnect the air injection pipe fitting, the EGR counterpressure line, EGR pressure line and any supports.

NOTE: An exhaust filter is used between the reactor and the EGR valve and must be disconnected. Replace the filter if found to be defective.

5. Remove the retaining bolts or nuts at the reactor and remove it from the cylinder head.

6. Install the manifold, using new gaskets. Install the air injection fittings.

7. Connect the exhaust pipe at the reactor. Install the air cleaner.

M3

1. Disconnect the negative battery cable. With the engine cool, remove the drain plug from the block. Remove the 3 electrical connectors from the front of the coolant manifold that runs along the left side of the engine. Disconnect the radiator hose from the front of this pipe. Then, remove all the mounting bolts for this pipe and remove it. Inspect the O-rings and replace any that are worn or damaged.

2. Disconnect the exhaust pipe at the manifold flange. Remove the heat shields from under the engine.

3. Remove the mounting nuts at the cylinder head and remove the manifold.

4. Clean all gasket material from the surfaces of the manifold and head and replace the gaskets.

5. To install, position the manifold on the head, torquing the manifold bolts to 6.5–7.0 ft. lbs. and the coolant pipe mounting bolts to 7.5–8.5 ft. lbs. Torque the bolts at the flange attaching manifold and exhaust pipe first to 22–25 ft. lbs. and then to 36–40 ft. lbs. Make sure to refill the cooling system with fresh anti-freeze/water mix and bleed the cooling system.

M5 AND M6

1. Disconnect the negative battery cable. With the engine cool, remove the drain plug from the block. Remove the 3 electrical connectors from the front of the coolant manifold that runs along the left side of the engine. Disconnect the radiator hose from the front of this pipe. Then, remove all the mounting bolts for this pipe and remove it. Inspect the O-rings (one for each cylinder, located in the block), and replace any that are worn or damaged.

2. Disconnect the exhaust pipe at the manifold. Remove the heat shields from under the engine.

3. Remove the crossbrace that runs under the engine by removing the 2 bolts from either end and then removing it.

4. Disconnect the stabilizer bar near both ends where it is bushed to the engine carrier.

5. Attach a lifting sling to the engine. Remove the nut from the right side engine mount and lift the engine slightly for clearance.

6. Remove the mounting bolts and remove the manifold.

7. Clean all gasket material from the surfaces of the manifold and head and replace the gaskets.

8. To install, position the manifold, torquing the manifold bolts to 36–40 ft. lbs. and the coolant pipe mounting bolts to 7.5–8.5 ft. lbs. Make sure to refill the cooling system with fresh anti-freeze/water mix and bleed the cooling system.

Timing Chain Front Cover

Removal and Installation

318iS

1. Disconnect the negative battery cable. Drain the cooling system and remove the radiator and fan assembly.

2. Remove the drive belts. Remove the engine splash shield, if necessary.

3. Remove the vibration damper using the proper tool. Unscrew the central bolt and remove the vibration damper hub.

4. Remove the timing case cover bolts and remove the timing cover.

NOTE: The timing case cover can be removed without removing the water pump.

5. Reverse the removal procedure to install. Tighten the central hub bolt to 224 ft. lbs. and the vibration damper bolts to 17 ft. lbs.

M3

1. Disconnect the negative battery cable. Drain the cooling system through the bottom of the radiator. Remove the radiator and fan.

2. Disconnect all electrical plugs, remove the attaching nuts, and remove the air cleaner and airflow sensor.

3. Note and, if necessary, mark the wiring connections. Then, disconnect all alternator wiring. Unbolt the alternator and remove it and the drive belt.

4. Unbolt the power steering pump. Remove the belt and then move the pump aside, supporting it out of the way but in a position where the hoses will not be stressed.

5. Remove the 3 bolts from the bottom of the bell housing and the 2 bolts below it which fasten the reinforcement plate in place.

6. Remove the drain plug and drain the oil from the lower oil pan. Then, remove the lower oil pan bolts and remove the lower pan.

7. Remove the 3 bolts fastening the bottom of the front cover to the front of the oil pan. Loosen all the remaining oil pan bolts so the pan may be shifted downward just slightly to separate the gasket surfaces.

8. Remove the water pump. Remove the center bolt and use a puller to remove the crankshaft pulley.

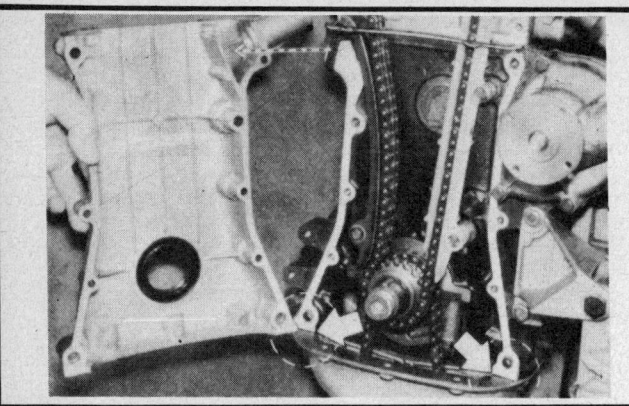

Installation of the timing cover housing showing special sealing locations

9. Remove the piston for the timing chain tensioner.

10. Remove the bolts attaching the top of the front cover to the cylinder head. Then, remove all the bolts fastening the cover to the block.

11. Run a sharp bladed tool carefully between the upper surface of the oil pan gasket and the lower surface of the front cover to separate them without tearing the gasket. If the gasket is damaged, remove the oil pan and replace it.

To install:

12. Before reinstalling the cover, use a file to break or file off flashing at the top/rear of the casting on either side so the corner is smooth. Replace all gaskets, coating them with silicone sealer. Where gasket ends extend too far, trim them off. Apply sealer to the area where the oil pan gasket passes the front of the block.

13. Slide the cover straight on to avoid damaging the seal. Install all bolts in their proper positions. Coat the 3 bolts fastening the front cover to the upper oil pan with the proper sealant.

14. Tighten the bolts at the top, fastening the lower cover to the upper cover first. Then, tighten the remaining front cover bolts and, finally, the oil pan bolts to 7 ft. lbs. Inspect the sealing O-rings and replace, as necessary. If it uses the DME distributor with the screw-off type rotor, make sure the bolt at the center of the rotor has its seal in place and that it is installed with a sealer designed to prevent the bolt from backing out.

15. Reverse the remaining portions of the removal procedures, making sure to fill and bleed the cooling system and to refill the oil pan with the correct oil.

16. Torque the oil drain plug to 24 ft. lbs. and both upper and lower oil pan bolts to 7 ft. lbs.

525i, 535i, 635CSi AND 735 SERIES

NOTE: On 535 Series, and 735 Series engines, this procedure requires the use of a special gauge.

1. Disconnect the negative battery cable. Remove the cylinder head cover. Remove the distributor.

2. Drain the coolant to below the level of the thermostat and remove the thermostat housing cover.

3. Remove the mounting bolts and remove the upper timing case cover.

4. Remove the piston which tensions the timing chain, working carefully because of very high spring pressure.

5. Remove the cooling fan and all drive belts. On 6 Series vehicles, the alternator must be swung aside by loosing the front bolt and removing the 2 side bolts. On all vehicles with the M30B35MZ engine, remove its attaching bolts and then remove the drive pulley from the water pump. The power steering pump must be removed, leaving the pump hoses connected and supporting the pump out of the way but so the hoses are not stressed.

6. Remove the flywheel housing cover and lock the flywheel in position with an appropriate tool.

7. Unscrew the nut from the center of the pulley and pull the pulley/vibration damper off the crankshaft.

8. Detach the TDC position transmitter on 635CSi and 7 Series.

9. Loosen all the oil pan bolts, and then unscrew all the bolts from the lower timing case cover, noting their lengths for reinstallation in the same positions. Carefully, use a sharp bladed tool to separate the gasket at the base of the lower timing cover. Then, remove the cover.

To install:

10. To install the lower cover, first coat the surfaces of the oil pan and block with sealer. Put it into position on the block, making sure the tensioning piston holding web (cast into the block) is in the oil pocket. Install all bolts; then tighten the lower front cover bolts evenly; finally, tighten the oil pan bolts evenly.

11. Inspect the hub of the vibration damper. If the hub is scored, install the radial seal so the sealing lip is in front of or to the rear of the scored area. Pack the seal with grease and install it with a sealer installer.

12. Install the pulley/damper and torque the bolt to specifications. When installing, make sure the key and keyway are properly aligned.

13. Remove the flywheel locking tool and reinstall the cover. Reinstall and tension all belts.

14. Before installing the upper cover, use sealer to seal the joint between the back of the lower timing cover and block at the top. On some vehicles, there are sealer wells which are to be filled with sealer. If these are present, fill them carefully. Check the cork seal at the distributor drive coupling and replace it, if necessary.

15. On all but M30B35MZ engines, tighten bolts 1 and 2 on 4 cylinder engines, the lower bolts, slightly. Then, tighten bolts 3–8. Finally, fully tighten the lower bolts.

16. On M30B35MZ engines, note that the top bolt on the driver's side and the bottom bolt on the passenger's side are longer. Tighten the 2 bolts that run down into the lower timing cover first; then tighten the remaining 6 bolts.

17. On the M30B35MZ engine, install the TDC transmitter and its mounting bracket. On remaining engines, install the TDC position transmitter loosely, if so equipped. With the engine at exactly 0 degrees Top Center, as shown by the marker on the front cover, adjust the position of the transmitter, it must fit the curve on the outside of the balancer, and incorporate a notch (for the pin on the balancer) and a ridge against which the transmitter must rest. The straight line distance between the center of the notch and bottom of the ridge must be exactly 37.5mm. Then, tighten the transmitter mounting screw.

18. Just before installing the upper timing case cover, check the condition of that area of the head gasket. It will usually be in good condition. If it should show damage, it must be replaced.

19. Inspect the sealing O-rings and replace, as necessary. Make sure the bolt at the center of the rotor has its seal in place and that it is installed with a sealer designed to prevent the bolt from backing out.

20. Complete the installation, making sure to bleed the cooling system.

M5 AND M6

1. Disconnect the negative battery cable. Pull out the plug and remove the wiring leading to the airflow sensor. Loosen the hose clamp and disconnect the air intake hose. Remove the mounting nut and remove the air cleaner and airflow sensor as an assembly.

2. Remove the radiator and fan. Remove the flywheel housing cover and install a lock, to lock the position of the flywheel. Remove the mounting nut for the vibration damper with a deepwell socket. Pull the damper off with a puller.

3. Remove the pipe that runs across in front of the front cov-

er. Remove the mounting bolts and remove the water pump pulley.

4. Loosen the top/front mounting bolt for the alternator. Remove the lower/front bolt. Loosen the 2 side bolts. Swing the alternator aside.

5. Remove the power steering pump mounting bolts. Make sure to retain the spacer that goes between the pump and oil pan. Swing the pump aside and support it so the hoses will not be under stress.

6. Remove the flywheel housing cover and lock the flywheel in position with an appropriate tool.

7. Unscrew the nut from the center of the pulley and pull the pulley/vibration damper off the crankshaft.

8. Remove the bolts at the top, fastening the lower front cover to the upper front cover. Remove the bolts at the bottom, fastening the lower cover to the oil pan. Loosen the remaining oil pan mounting bolts.

9. Run a sharp bladed tool carefully between the upper surface of the oil pan gasket and the lower surface of the front cover to separate them without tearing the gasket.

10. Loosen and remove the remaining front cover mounting bolts, noting the locations of the TDC sending unit on the upper/right side of the engine and the suspension position sending unit on the upper left. Also, keep track of the bolts that mount these accessories, as their lengths are slightly different. Remove the timing cover, pulling it off squarely.

To install:

11. Before reinstalling the cover, use a file to break or file off flashing at the top/rear of the casting on either side so the corner is smooth. Replace all gaskets, coating them with silicone sealer. Where gasket ends extend too far, trim them off. Apply sealer to the area where the oil pan gasket passes the front of the block.

12. Slide the cover straight on to avoid damaging the seal. Install all bolts in their proper positions. Tighten the bolts at the top, fastening the lower cover to the upper cover first. Then, tighten the remaining front cover bolts and, finally, the oil pan bolts. Inspect the sealing O-rings and replace as necessary. If it uses the DME distributor with the screw-off type rotor, make sure the bolt at the center of the rotor has its seal in place and that it is installed with a sealer designed to prevent the bolt from backing out.

13. Complete the installation procedure, making sure to refill and bleed the cooling system.

750iL

1. Disconnect the negative battery cable. Drain the cooling system and remove the fan assembly.

2. Remove both intake manifolds and distributor housings.

3. Disconnect the round rubber mounts, bolts and nuts. Remove both cylinder head covers.

4. Remove the mounting bolts and lift out the timing cover.

5. To install, reverse the removal procedure.

Lower

1. Disconnect the negative battery cable. Drain the cooling system and remove the fan assembly.

2. Remove the drive belts and the engine splash shield. Remove the tensioning bolt.

3. Unscrew the bolts but do not remove the vibration damper. Remove the central hub bolt with the proper tool.

4. Remove the vibration damper using the proper tool to pull the vibration damper hub from the crankshaft.

5. Drain the engine oil and remove the lower section of the oil pan. Remove the bottom mounting screws from the timing case cover and loosen the adjacent oil pan bolts on both sides.

6. Remove the timing belt tensioner and reference mark sender.

7. Remove the mounting screws and take off the timing case cover.

8. To install, reverse the removal procedure. Tighten the central hub bolt to 318 ft. lbs. and the vibration damper mounting bolts to 17 ft. lbs.

Front Cover Oil Seal

Replacement

525i, 535i, 635CSi AND 735 SERIES

1. Disconnect the negative battery cable. Position the No. 1 piston at TDC on the beginning of its compression stroke.

2. Remove the flywheel guard and lock the flywheel with a locking tool.

3. Remove the drive belts and the fan.

4. Remove the retaining nut and remove the vibration damper from the crankshaft.

NOTE: The Woodruff® key should be at the 12 o'clock position on the crankshaft.

5. Remove the seal from the timing housing cover with a small pry bar.

6. Using a special seal installer or equivalent, lubricate and install the seal in the cover. This tool is used to press the seal into the bore with even pressure around the entire perimeter.

NOTE: If the balancer hub has serious scoring on the sealing surface, position the seal in the cover so the sealing lip is in front of or behind the scored groove.

7. Lubricate the balancer hub and install it on the crankshaft, being careful not to damage the seal.

8. Complete the assembly, using the reverse of the removal procedure. Be sure to remove the flywheel locking tool before attempting to start the engine.

318iS AND 750iL

1. Disconnect the negative battery cable.

2. Remove the vibration damper and hub assembly.

3. Press out the radial oil seal, using the proper tool.

4. Install the new seal flush in conjunction with the central bolt and washer, using the proper seal installer.

5. The remainder of the installation is the reverse of the removal procedure.

Timing Chain and Sprockets

Removal and Installation

318iS

1. Disconnect the negative battery cable. Remove the vibration damper and hub assembly.

2. Remove the lower timing case cover. Remove the timing chain tensioner.

3. Unscrew the upper chain guide and top bolt on the right chain guide.

4. Remove the timing chain sprockets and the lift out the chain. Remove the timing chain guide.

5. Remove the tensioning rail, if necessary. Remove the crankshaft sprocket with the proper tool and lift out the Woodruff® key.

6. Remove the reversing roller, if needed.

NOTE: The reversing roller can only be replaced complete with bearings.

7. The installation is the reverse of the removal procedure.

M3

1. Disconnect the negative battery cable. Remove the timing case cover.

2. Remove the camshafts and sprockets. It is not necessary to remove the cover from the rear of the head.

3. Make sure to catch the washer and lock washers which will be released at the front. Remove the 2 mounting bolts for the guide rail, which is located on the left (driver's) side of the engine. These are accessible from the rear.

4. Pull the guide rail forward and then turn it clockwise on its axis, looking at it from above, to free it from the chain.

5. Note the relationships between timing chain and sprocket marks. Remove the chain by separating it from the sprockets at top and bottom.

To install:

6. Engage the timing chain with the crankshaft sprocket so marks line up. Route the chain up through where the guide rail will go. Install the guide rail in reverse of the removal procedure.

7. Then engage the chain with the driver's side (E) sprocket with the marks aligned. Bolt this sprocket and the lock plate onto the front end of the intake camshaft. Use the adapter to keep the sprocket from turning, and torque the bolts to 6–7 ft. lbs. Turn this camshaft in the direction opposite to normal rotation to tension the timing chain on that side.

8. Engage the timing marks with the mark on the passenger's side (A) sprocket and install the sprocket and lock plate onto the front end of the exhaust camshaft. Again, use the adapter to keep the sprocket from turning, and torque the bolts to 6–7 ft. lbs. Make sure the timing chain has stayed in time.

9. Slide the chain tensioner piston into its cylinder. Install a new seal. Now install the spring with the conical end out. Install the cap which retains the spring and torque it to 29 ft. lbs.

10. Turn the engine one revolution in the normal direction of rotation. Recheck the timing. With the crankshaft at TDC, one groove on each camshaft faces inward and another on each faces the cast boss on the bearing cap.

11. Install the camshaft and timing chain guides.

12. Install the timing case cover.

M5 AND M6

1. Disconnect the negative battery cable. Remove the fan shroud and the fan. Remove the cylinder head cover. Remove the timing cover.

2. Remove the camshaft. Remove the cover from the rear of the head.

3. Remove the water pump.

4. Remove the 2 mounting bolts for the guide rail, which is located on the left (driver's) side of the engine. These are accessible from the rear. Turn the guide rail counterclockwise on it's axis
looking at it from above to clear the chain and block and remove it. Be careful to retain all washers.

5. Note the relationships between timing chain and sprocket marks. Remove the timing chain.

To install:

6. Install the timing chain with the marks on all 3 sprockets aligned with marked links on the chain. Make sure the chain runs on the inside of the guide sprocket on the left side of the engine and along the groove in the lower tensioning rail. Install the chain onto the camshaft drive sprockets and then install the sprockets onto the camshafts (note that the exhaust side sprocket is marked **A** and the intake sprocket is marked **E**. Then, install the guide rail with all washers and lock washers by rotating it into position in reverse of the removal procedure.

7. Tighten the camshaft drive sprockets, install the chain tensioner, and install the upper guide rail as described in the camshaft removal and installation procedure. Reverse the remaining removal steps to complete the procedure. Make sure to refill the cooling system with an appropriate anti-freeze/water mix and to bleed the cooling system.

535i, 635CSi AND 735 SERIES

1. Disconnect the negative battery cable. Rotate the crankshaft to set the No. 1 piston at TDC, at the beginning of its compression stroke.

2. Remove the distributor.

3. Remove the cylinder head cover, air injection pipe and guard plate.

4. Drain the cooling system and remove the thermostat housing.

5. Remove the upper timing housing cover.

6. Remove the timing chain tensioner piston by unscrewing the cap.

NOTE: The piston is under heavy spring tension.

7. Remove the drive belts and fan.

8. Remove the flywheel guard and lock the flywheel with a locking tool.

9. Remove the vibration damper assembly.

NOTE: The crankshaft Woodruff® key should be in the 12 o'clock position.

10. Remove upper and lower timing covers.

11. Turn the crankshaft so the No. 1 cylinder is at firing position. Open the camshaft lock plates, if equipped, remove the bolts and remove the camshaft sprocket.

12. Remove the chain from the lower sprocket, swing the chain to the right front and out of the guide rail and remove the chain from the engine.

To install:

13. Install the chain in position.

14. Be sure No. 1 piston remains at the top of its firing stroke and the key on the crankshaft is in the 12 o'clock position.

15. Position the camshaft flange so the dowel pin bore is at the 7–8 o'clock position and the upper flange bolt hole is aligned with the cast tab on the cylinder head.

16. Position the chain on the guide rail and swing the chain inward and to the left.

17. Engage the chain on the crankshaft gear and install the camshaft sprocket into the chain.

18. Align the gear dowel pin to the camshaft flange and bolt and sprocket into place. Torque the sprocket bolts to 5 ft. lbs. (6.5–7.5 on the M30B35 engine).

19. Install the chain tensioner piston, spring and cap plug, but do not tighten.

20. To bleed the chain tensioner, fill the oil pocket, located on the upper timing housing cover, with engine oil and move the tensioner back and forth with a screwdriver until oil is expelled at the cap plug. Tighten the cap plug securely.

21. Complete the assembly in the reverse order of removal. Check the ignition timing and the idle speed. Be sure the flywheel holder is removed before any attempt is made to start the engine.

Timing Belt Front Cover

Removal and Installation

325, 325i, 325iS, 325iX 525i AND 528e

The 325 and 528e are equipped with a rubber drive and timing belt and the distributor guard plate is actually the upper timing belt cover.

1. Disconnect the negative battery cable. Remove the distributor cap and rotor. Remove the inner distributor cover and seal.

2. Remove the 2 distributor guard plate attaching bolts and one nut. Remove the rubber guard and take out the guard plate (upper timing belt cover).

3. Rotate the crankshaft to set No. 1 piston at TDC of its compression stroke.

NOTE: At TDC of No. 1 piston compression stroke, the camshaft sprocket arrow should align directly with the mark on the cylinder head.

4. Remove the radiator.

5. Remove the lower splash guard and take off the alternator, power steering and air conditioning belts.
6. Remove the crankshaft pulley and vibration damper.
7. Hold the crankshaft hub from rotating with the proper tool. Remove the crankshaft hub bolt.
8. Install the hub bolt into the crankshaft about 3 turns and use the proper gear puller, to remove the crankshaft hub.
9. Remove the bolt from the engine end of the alternator bracket. Loosen the alternator adjusting bolt and swing the bracket out of the way.
10. Lift out the TDC transmitter and set it aside.
11. Remove the remaining bolt and lift off the lower timing belt cover.
11. The installation is the reverse of the removal procedure.

Oil Seal Replacement

1. Disconnect the negative battery cable. Remove the front engine cover.
2. Press the 2 radial oil seals out of the front engine cover.
3. Install the oil seals flush with the front engine cover using the proper tools.
4. Install the front engine cover. Connect the negative battery cable.

Timing Belt and Tensioner

Adjustment

1. Disconnect the negative battery cable.
2. Remove the front engine cover.
3. Loosen the tensioner bolt. The spring force should be capable of moving the tensioner roller.
4. Rotate the crankshaft in the direction of the rotation to TDC mark. The mark on the camshaft sprocket with the mark on the cylinder head with the crankshaft at TDC mark.
5. Tighten the tensioner bolt and install the front engine cover.
6. Connect the negative battery cable.

Removal and Installation

1. Disconnect the negative battery cable. Remove the distributor cap and rotor. Remove the inner distributor cover and seal.
2. Remove the 2 distributor guard plate attaching bolts and one nut. Remove the rubber guard and take out the guard plate, upper timing belt cover.
3. Rotate the crankshaft to set No. 1 piston at TDC of its compression stroke.

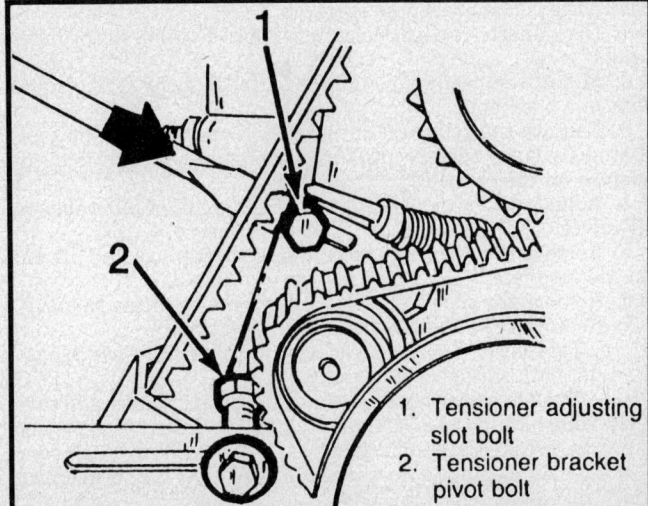

1. Tensioner adjusting slot bolt
2. Tensioner bracket pivot bolt

Releasing the tension on timing belt—528e

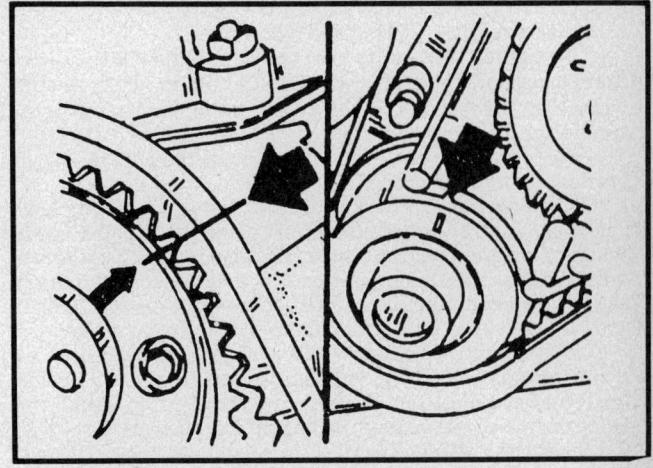

Crankshaft sprocket timing marks aligned for installation of the timing belt—528e

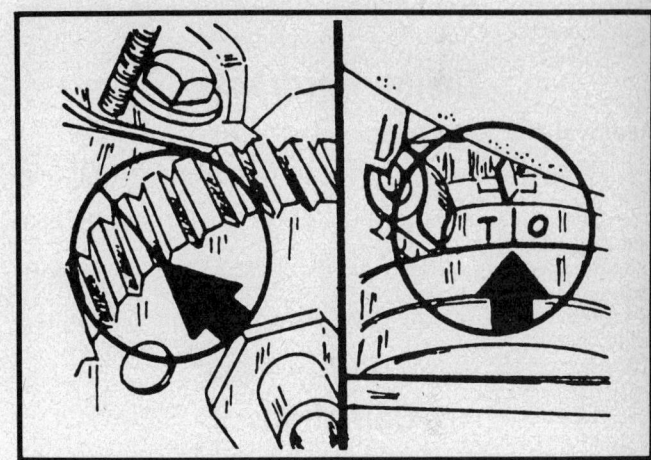

Aligning the marks for timing belt installation—528e

NOTE: At TDC of No. 1 piston compression stroke, the camshaft sprocket arrow should align directly with the mark on the cylinder head.

4. Remove the radiator.
5. Remove the lower splash guard and take off the alternator, power steering and air conditioning belts.
6. Remove the crankshaft pulley and vibration damper.
7. Hold the crankshaft hub from rotating with tool 11 2 150 or equivalent. Remove the crankshaft hub bolt.
8. Install the hub bolt into the crankshaft about 3 turns and use the proper gear puller, to remove the crankshaft hub.
9. Remove the bolt from the engine end of the alternator bracket. Loosen the alternator adjusting bolt and swing the bracket out of the way.
10. Lift out the TDC transmitter and set it out of the way.
11. Remove the remaining bolt and lift off the lower timing belt cover.
12. Loosen the 2 tensioner pulley bolts and release the tension on the belt by pushing on the tensioner pulley bracket.
13. Mark the running direction of the timing belt and remove the belt.
14. Remove the 3 bolts across the front of the oil pan and loosen the remaining oil pan bolts. Try not to damage the oil pan gasket. Remove the 6 front engine cover bolts and remove the front engine cover.

To install:

15. Install the cover, noting the following:

a. To tighten the timing belt, turn the engine in the direction of normal engine operation, with a ½ in. drive ratchet wrench on the crankshaft bolt. When the timing belt is tight, torque the 2 tensioner bolts.

b. Align the hub centering pin through the hole in the vibration damper for proper installation.

c. Align the timing marks when installing the timing belt. The crankshaft sprocket mark must point at the notch in the flange of the front engine cover. The camshaft sprocket arrow must point at the alignment mark on the cylinder head. Also, the No. 1 piston must be at TDC of the compression stroke.

d. If the oil pan gasket is damaged, it must be replaced.

e. Check and replace front cover oil seals, if needed.

f. Use tools 11 2 211 (crankshaft seal aligner) and 11 2 212 (intermediate shaft seal aligner) or equivalent, to install the front engine cover without damaging the oil seals.

16. Check the engine oil level.

17. Install engine coolant and bleed the cooling system. Bring the engine up to operating temperature and loosen the bleed screw on top of the thermostat housing. Continue to bleed until escaping coolant is free of bubbles. Add coolant to the expansion tank if needed.

Timing Sprockets

Removal and Installation

1. Disconnect the negative battery cable. Remove the timing belt.

2. Hold the sprocket with the proper tool. Remove the bolt and take off the collar.

3. Remove the sprocket from the crankshaft with the proper tool.

4. Remove the sprocket from the intermediate shaft in the same way.

5. Reverse the removal procedure to install.

Camshaft

Removal and Installation

535i, 635CSi AND 735 SERIES

1. Disconnect the negative battery cable. Remove the oil line from the top of the cylinder head.

NOTE: Observe the location of the seals when removing the hollow oil line studs. Install new seals in the same position.

2. Remove the cylinder head. Support the head in such a way that the valves can be opened during camshaft removal.

3. Adjust the valve clearance to the maximum clearance on all rocker arms.

4. Remove the fuel pump and pushrod on carbureted engines.

Removing camshaft thrust bearing cover—525i and 528e

Pulling out the camshaft—525i and 528e

5. A tool set 11 1 060 and 00 1 490 or its equivalent, is used to hold the rocker arms away from the camshaft lobes. When installing the tool, move the intake rocker arms of No. 2 and 4 cylinders forward approximately ¼ in. and tighten the intake side nuts to avoid contact between the valve heads. Turn the camshaft 15 degrees clockwise to install the tool. On these engines, to avoid contact between the valve heads, first tighten the tool mounting nuts on the exhaust side to the stop and then tighten the intake side nuts slightly. Reverse this exactly during removal.

6. Remove the camshaft by rotating the camshaft so the 2 cutout areas of the camshaft flange are horizontal and remove the retaining plate bolts.

7. Carefully, remove the camshaft from the cylinder head.

8. The flange and guide plate can be removed from the camshaft by removing the lock plate and nut from the camshaft end.

To install:

9. Install the camshaft and associated components in the reverse order of removal, but observe the following:

10. After installing the camshaft guide plate, the camshaft should turn easily. Measure and correct the camshaft end play.

11. The camshaft flange must be properly aligned with the cylinder head before the sprocket is installed.

12. Install the oil tube hollow stud washer seals properly, one above and one below the oil pipe. The arrow on the oil line must face forward.

13. Install the cylinder head. Adjust the valves.

325, 325i, 325iS, 325iX, 525i AND 528e

The cylinder head and the rocker arm shafts must be removed before the camshaft can be removed.

1. Disconnect the negative battery cable. Remove the cylinder head.

2. Mount the head on a stand. Secure the head to the stand with one head bolt.

3. Remove the camshaft sprocket bolt and remove the camshaft distributor adapter and sprocket. Reinstall the distributor adapter on the camshaft.

4. Adjust the valve clearance to the maximum allowable on all valves.

5. Remove the front and rear rocker shaft plugs and lift out the thrust plate.

6. Remove the clips from the rocker arms by lifting them off.

7. Remove the exhaust side rocker arm shaft:

a. Set the No. 6 cylinder rocker arm to the valve overlap position, both rocker arms parallel.

b. Push in on the rocker arm on the front cylinder and turn the camshaft in the direction of the intake rocker shaft, using a ½ in. breaker bar and a deep well socket to fit over the camshaft adapter. Rotate the camshaft until all of the rocker arms are relaxed.

c. Remove the rocker arm shaft.

8. Remove the intake side rocker arm shaft:

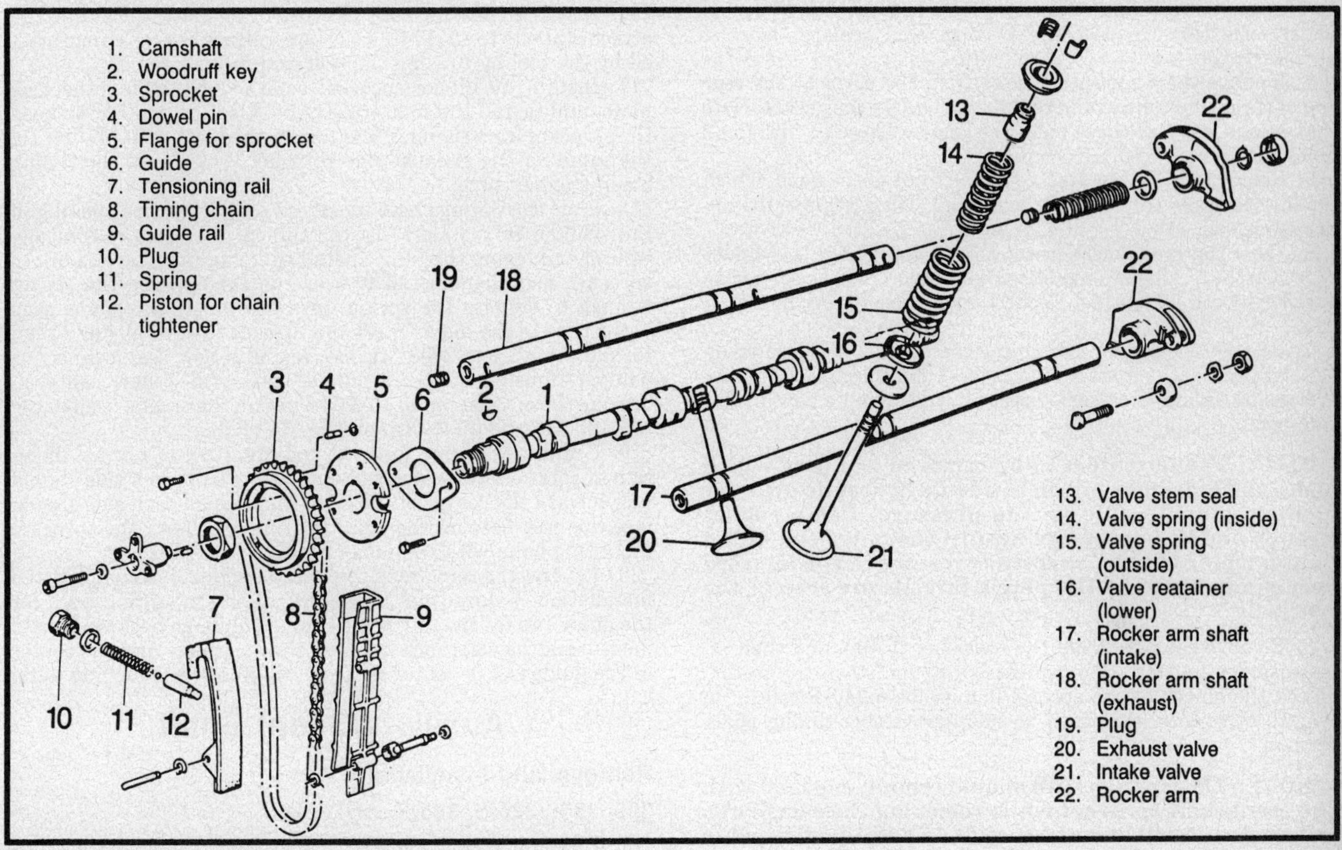

1. Camshaft
2. Woodruff key
3. Sprocket
4. Dowel pin
5. Flange for sprocket
6. Guide
7. Tensioning rail
8. Timing chain
9. Guide rail
10. Plug
11. Spring
12. Piston for chain tightener

13. Valve stem seal
14. Valve spring (inside)
15. Valve spring (outside)
16. Valve reatainer (lower)
17. Rocker arm shaft (intake)
18. Rocker arm shaft (exhaust)
19. Plug
20. Exhaust valve
21. Intake valve
22. Rocker arm

Exploded view of the camshaft assembly—535i

a. Turn the camshaft in the direction of the exhaust valves.

b. Use a deep well socket and ½ in. drive breaker bar on the camshaft adapter to turn the camshaft until all of the rocker arms are relaxed.

c. Pull out the rocker arm shaft.

9. Remove the camshaft thrust bearing cover. Check the radial oil seal and round cord seal and replace them if needed.

10. Pull out the camshaft.

To install:

11. Install the camshaft, noting the following:

a. Place the proper tool over the end of the camshaft during installation of the thrust bearing cover; this will protect the oil seals and guide the cover on.

b. The rocker arm thrust plate must be fit into the grooves in the rocker shafts.

c. The straight side of the spring clip must be installed in the groove of the rocker arm shafts.

d. The large oil bores in the rocker shafts must be installed down to the valve guides and the small oil bores must face inward toward the center of the head.

e. Adjust the valve clearance.

12. To complete the installation, reverse the removal procedures.

M3, M5 AND M6

NOTE: To perform this operation it is necessary to have a special tool 11 3 010 or equivalent. This is necessary to permit safe removal of the camshaft bearing caps and then safe release of the tension the valve springs put on the camshafts. The job also requires an adapter to keep the camshaft sprockets from turning while loosening and tightening their mounting bolts.

1. Disconnect the negative battery cable. Remove the cylinder head cover. Remove the fan cowl and the fan.

2. Remove the mounting bolts and remove the distributor cap. Remove the mounting screws and remove the rotor. Unscrew the distributor adapter and the protective cover underneath. Inspect the O-ring that runs around the protective cover and replace it, if necessary.

3. Remove the 2 bolts and remove the protective cover from in front of the right side (intake) camshaft. Remove the bolts

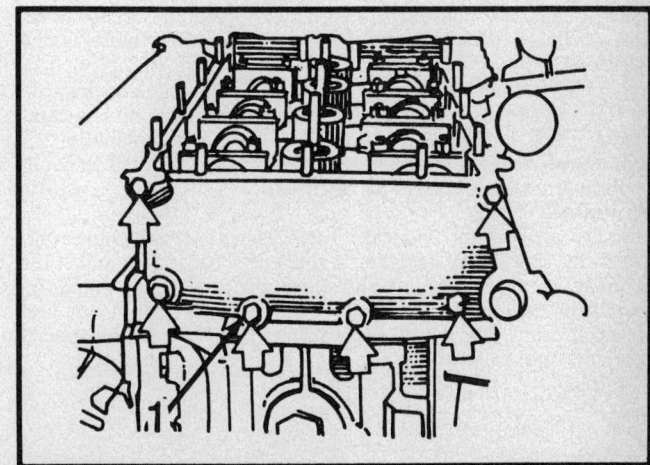

On the rear cover of the M3, install the longer bolts into the two holes marked "1"

and remove the distributor housing from in front of the left (exhaust) side cam. Inspect the O-rings, and replace them, if necessary.

4. Remove the 6 mounting bolts from the cover at the rear end of the cylinder head and remove it. Replace the gasket. Note that on the M3, 2 of these bolts are longer. These fit into the 2 holes that are sleeved.

5. Remove the 2 nuts, located at the front of the head, which mount the upper timing chain guide rail. Then, remove the upper guide rail.

6. Turn the crankshaft to set the engine at No. 1 cylinder TDC. On the 6 cylinder engine, valves for No. 6 will be at overlap position—both valves just slightly open with timing marks at TDC.

7. Remove the cap for the timing chain tensioner, located on the right side of the front timing cover. Then, slide off the damper housing. Remove the seal, discard it, and supply a new one for re-assembly.

NOTE: The next item to be removed is a plug which keeps the tensioner piston inside its hydraulic cylinder against considerable spring pressure. Use a socket wrench and keep pressure against the outer end of the plug, pushing inward, so spring pressure can be released very gradually once the plug's threads are free of the block.

8. Remove the plug from the tensioner piston, and then release spring tension. Remove the spring and then the piston. Check the length of the spring. It must be 6.240–6.280 in. in length; otherwise, replace it to maintain stable timing chain tension.

NOTE: The timing chain should remain engaged with the crankshaft sprocket while removing the camshafts. Otherwise, it will be necessary to do additional work to restore proper timing. Keep the timing chain under slight tension by supporting it at the top while removing the camshaft sprockets.

9. Pry open the lock plates for the camshaft sprocket mounting bolts. Install an adapter to hold the sprockets still and remove the mounting bolts.

10. Using an adapter to keep the sprockets from turning and putting tension on the timing chain, loosen and remove the sprocket mounting bolts, keeping the chain supported.

11. Mount the special tool on the timing case, which mounts to the top of the head. Then, tighten the tool's shaft to the stop. This will hold both camshafts down against their lower bearings. Also, mark the camshafts as to which end faces forward.

12. Remove the mounting bolts and remove the camshaft bearing caps. It is possible to save time by keeping the caps in order, although they are marked for installation in the same positions.

13. Once all bearing caps are removed, slowly crank backwards on the tool's shaft to gradually release the tension on the camshafts. Once all tension is released, remove the camshafts.

14. Carefully, remove the camshafts in such a way as to avoid nicking any bearing surfaces or cams.
To install:
15. Oil all bearing and cam surfaces with clean engine oil. Carefully, install the camshafts, marked E for intake and A for exhaust, to avoid nicking any wear surfaces. The camshafts should be turned so the groove between the front cam and sprocket mounting flange faces straight up. Install the special tool and tighten down on the shaft to seat the camshafts.

16. Install all bearing caps in order or as marked. Torque the attaching bolts to 15–17 ft. lbs. Then, release the tension provided by the tool by turning the bolt and remove the tool.

17. Install the intake sprocket (marked E), install the lock plate, and install the mounting bolts. Use the adapter to keep the sprocket from turning, and torque the bolts to 6–7 ft. lbs. Do the same for the exhaust side sprocket. Make sure the timing chain stays in time.

18. Slide the timing chain tensioner piston into the opening in the cylinder in the block. Install the spring with the conically wound end facing the plug. Install the plug into the end of the sprocket and then install it over the spring. Use the socket wrench to depress the spring until the plug's threads engage with those in the block. Start the threads in carefully and then torque the plug to 27–31 ft. lbs. Install a new seal, connector, damper housing, and the outside cap with a new cap seal. Torque the outside cap to 16–20 ft. lbs. on the engine used in the M5 and M6 and 29 ft. lbs. on the M3 engine.

19. Crank the engine forward just one turn in normal direction of rotation. Now, one camshaft groove on each side should face toward the center of the head and one on each side should face the case boss on the front bearing cap. Lock the sprocket mounting bolts with the tabs on the lockplates.

20. Reverse the remaining removal procedures to complete the installation. Before final tightening of the mounting nuts for the guide rail for the top of the timing chain, go back and forth, measuring the clearance between the sprockets and the center of the guide rail to center it. Then, tighten the mounting nuts.

Auxiliary/Silent Shaft

Removal and Installation
325, 325i, 325iS, 325iX, AND 528e

1. Disconnect the negative battery cable. Remove the front cover.
2. Remove the intermediate shaft sprocket.
3. Loosen and remove the 2 retaining screws and then remove the intermediate shaft guide plate.
4. Carefully, slide the intermediate shaft out of the block. Turn the crankshaft, if necessary, to remove it. Inspect the gear on the intermediate shaft, replacing it, if necessary.
5. Install the intermediate shaft to the block. Install the guide plate.
6. Install the front cover.

Piston and Connecting Rod

Positioning

Location of piston in the cylinder bore with ring gaps located 180 degrees apart

ENGINE LUBRICATION

Oil Pan

Removal and Installation

318iS

1. Disconnect the negative battery cable. Raise and safely support the vehicle.
2. Drain the engine oil.
3. Disconnect the exhaust pipe, if necessary.
4. Remove the oil pan mounting bolts and take off the oil pan.
5. Clean the mounting surfaces and install a new gasket.
6. The installation is the reverse of the removal procedure. Tighten the mounting bolts to 6.5 ft. lbs.

325, 325i, 325iS, 325iX AND 528e

1. Disconnect the negative battery cable. Raise the vehicle and support it. Drain the engine oil.
2. Remove the front lower splash guard, if necessary.
3. Disconnect the electrical terminal from the oil sending unit.
4. Remove the power steering gear from the front axle carrier, if necessary.
5. Remove the flywheel cover.
6. Remove the oil pan bolts and lower the oil pan. Remove the oil pump bolts and take out the oil pump and oil pan.
7. Install the oil pan, paying attention to the following points:
   a. Clean the gasket surfaces and use a new gasket on the oil pan.
   b. Coat the joints on the ends of the front engine cover with a universal sealing compound.
   c. Install the sending unit wire and the engine oil. If the power steering gear was removed, make sure to refill and bleed this system.

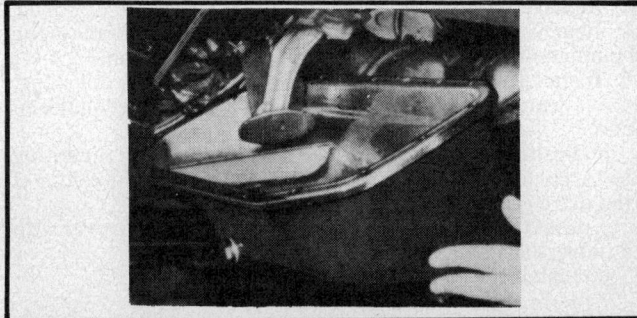

Removal of engine oil pan—typical

Rear main bearing oil seal and end cover housing showing special sealing locations

M3

1. Remove the dipstick. Remove the splash guard from underneath the engine. Raise and safely support the vehicle.
2. Remove the drain plug and drain the oil. Unscrew all the bolts for the lower oil pan and remove it.
3. Remove the oil pump.
4. Remove the lower flywheel housing cover by removing the 3 bolts at the bottom of the flywheel housing and the 2 bolts in the cover just ahead of the flywheel housing.
5. Disconnect the oil pressure sending unit plug. Unbolt the oil pan bracket. Disconnect the ground lead. Loosen its clamp and disconnect the crankcase ventilation hose.
6. Remove the oil pan bolts and remove the upper oil pan. Clean all sealing surfaces. Supply a new gasket and the coat the joints where the timing case cover and block meet with a brush-on sealant. Install the pan and torque the bolts evenly to 7 ft. lbs.
7. Reverse the remaining removal procedures to install, cleaning all sealing surfaces and using a new gasket on the lower pan, also. Torque the lower pan bolts, also, to 7 ft. lbs.
8. Install the oil pan drain plug, torquing to 24 ft. lbs. Refill the oil pan with the required amount of approved oil. Start the engine and check for leaks.

525i, 535i, 635CSi, M5 AND M6

1. Disconnect the negative battery cable. Disconnect the electrical connector and separate the leads from the air cleaner/air flow sensor. Loosen the hose clamp and disconnect the air intake hose. Remove the mounting nut and remove the air cleaner and the airflow sensor as a unit. Remove the fan shroud.
2. Raise and safely support the vehicle. Drain the engine oil. Lower the vehicle.
3. Loosen the belt tension and remove the alternator drive belt. Loosen the upper/front mounting bolt for the alternator and the 2 bolts on the side of the block that mount it at the rear. Remove the lower/front mounting bolt. Then, swing the alternator to the side.
4. Loosen the power steering pump mounts and remove the drive belt. Then, remove the mounting bolts and remove the pump and pump mounting bracket. Make sure to retain spacers. Remove the nuts and bolts that fasten the compressor to the hinge type mounting bracket. Make sure the compressor is suspended so there is no tension on the hoses. Unbolt the hinge type mounting bracket and remove it.
5. Remove the brace plate located under the oil pan. Remove those oil pan bolts that can be reached.
6. Remove the engine ground strap. Remove the engine mount through bolts. Attach a lifting sling to the hooks on top of the engine. Lift the engine slightly for clearance.
7. Shift the power steering pump out of the way and support it so no tension will be placed on the hoses.
8. Remove the remaining oil pan mounting bolts. Turn the crankshaft so the rods for cylinders 5 and 6 are as high as possible. Then, remove the pan.

To install:

9. Clean all sealing surfaces and supply a new gasket. Apply a liquid sealer to the joints between the block and the timing cover on the front and the rear main seal cover at the rear.
10. Install the oil pan in reverse order. Torque the pan bolts to 6.5–7.5 ft. lbs. Make sure to refill the pan with the required amount of the correct oil. Mount all accessories securely and adjust the drive belts.

735i AND 735iL

1. Disconnect the negative battery cable. Loosen the hose clamp for the air intake hose. Remove the mounting nut for the air cleaner, and remove the air cleaner. Remove the fan and shroud.

2. Disconnect the electrical plug and overflow hose from the coolant expansion tank. Be careful not to kink the hose. Remove the mounting nuts and remove the tank.

3. Remove the splash guard for the power steering pump. Loosen the locknut for the pump adjustment and remove the through bolt that mounts the pump lower bracket (which contains the adjustment mechanism) to the block. Swing the bracket aside. Unscrew the bolt attaching the power steering pump lines to the block and shift them aside too.

4. Disconnect the electrical plug for the suspension leveling switch on the left side engine mounting bracket. Raise and safely support the vehicle.
Remove the oil pan drain plug and drain the oil.

5. Remove the bracket for the exhaust pipes located near the oil pan.

6. Disconnect the ground strap from the engine. Remove the nuts and washers attaching the engine to the mounts on both sides.

7. Attach an engine lifting sling to the hooks at either end of the cylinder head. Lift the engine as necessary for clearance.

8. Remove all oil pan mounting bolts and remove the pan.

9. Clean both sealing surfaces and supply a new gasket. Coat the 4 joints, between the block and timing case cover at the front and the block and rear main seal housing cover at the rear, with a proper sealer. Install the oil pan bolts and torque them to 6.5-7.5 ft. lbs.

10. Reverse the remaining procedures to install the oil pan. Torque the engine mount nuts to 31-34 ft. lbs. Refill the oil pan with the required amount and type of oil.

750iL

1. Disconnect the negative battery cable. Raise and safely support the vehicle.

2. Remove the transmission and the oil pump assembly. Lower the vehicle.

3. Disconnect and remove the windshield washer tank and the coolant expansion tank.

4. Remove the guide tube for the oil dipstick. Disconnect the oil pipe on the tandem pump. Remove the mounting bracket.

5. Unscrew the belt tensioner and remove the oil drain hose.

6. Crank the engine to TDC and unscrew the flywheel using the proper tool.

7. Disconnect the left and right engine mounts at the bottom. Pull off the pipe adapter for oil extraction.

NOTE: Heat the oil pan with a hot air blower to make removing and installing easier.

8. Remove the oil pump consoles. Unscrew the oil pan bolts and remove the oil pan.

To install

9. Clean the mounting surfaces and install a new gasket.

10. Install the oil pan and tighten the mounting bolts to 7 ft. lbs.

11. Connect the left and right engine mounts at the bottom and tighten to 32.5 ft. lbs.

12. Replace the oil consoles and tighten to 25 ft. lbs.

13. Install the flywheel and tighten the bolts to 72 ft. lbs.

14. The remainder of the installation is the reverse of the removal procedure.

Oil Pump

Removal and Installation
EXCEPT 318iS, 325, 325i, 325iS, 325iX, M3 AND 528e

1. Disconnect the negative battery cable and remove the oil pan.

2. Remove the bolts retaining the sprocket to the oil pump shaft and remove the sprocket.

3. Remove the oil pump retaining bolts and lower the oil pump from the engine block. On 6 cyl. engines other than the M30B35, there are 3 bolts at the front and 2 bolts attaching the rear of the oil pickup to the lower end of a support bracket. It is necessary to remove all 5 bolts. On the M30B35, there are only 3 bolts.

4. Do not loosen the chain adjusting shims from the 2 mounting locations.

5. Add or subtract shims between the oil pump body and the engine block to obtain a slight movement of the chain under light thumb pressure.

6. Install the oil pump in position.

NOTE: When used, the 2 shim thicknesses must be the same. Tighten the pump holder at the pick-up end after shimming is completed to avoid stress on the pump.

7. On 6 cylinder engines, other than the M30B35, after the main pump mounting bolts are torqued, loosen the bolts at the bracket on the rear of the pick-up, allowing the pick-up to assume its most natural position. This will relieve tension on the bracket. Tighten the bolts. On the M30B35, torque the oil pump mounting bolts to 16 ft. lbs. and the sprocket bolts to 19 ft. lbs.

318iS

1. Disconnect the negative battery cable.

2. Raise and safely support the vehicle. Drain the engine oil.

3. Remove the timing case cover.

4. Disconnect the oil pump mounting bolts and remove the oil pump assembly.

5. Reverse the removal procedure for installation.

325, 325i, 325iS, 325iX, M3 AND 528e

1. Raise an safely support the vehicle. Drain the engine oil.

2. Remove the front lower splash guard.

3. Disconnect the electrical terminal from the oil sending unit.

4. Remove the flywheel cover.

5. Remove the oil pan bolts and lower the oil pan. Remove the oil pump bolts and take out the oil pump and oil pan.

6. Installation is the reverse of removal. Note the following:
   a. Clean the gasket surfaces and use a new gasket on the oil pan.
   b. Positioning the pump for installation of its mounting bolts, guide the pump driveshaft into the hole in the center of the drive gear.
   c. Coat the joints on the ends of the front engine cover with a universal sealing compound.
   d. Install the sending unit wire and the engine oil.

Checking
318iS

1. Disconnect the negative battery cable.

2. Remove the timing case cover.

3. Measure the play between the pump body and the outer rotor; outer rotor and inner rotor. The distance should be 0.12-0.20 mm (0.005-0.008 in.).

4. Replace the timing cover assembly and connect the negative battery cable.

Rear Main Bearing Oil Seal

Removal and Installation

The rear main bearing oil seal can be replaced after the transmission, and clutch/flywheel or the converter/flywheel has been removed from the engine.

Removal and installation, after the seal is exposed, is as follows.

1. Raise and safely support the vehicle. Drain the engine oil and loosen the oil pan bolts. Carefully use a sharp bladed tool to

separate the oil pan gasket from the lower surface of the end cover housing.

2. Remove the 2 rear oil pan bolts.

3. Remove the bolts around the outside of the cover housing and remove the end cover housing from the engine block. Remove the gasket from the block surface.

4. Remove the seal from the housing. Coat the sealing lips of the new seal with oil. Install a new seal into the end cover housing with a special seal installer tool. On the 6 cylinder engines, press the seal in until it is about 0.039–0.079 in. deeper than the standard seal, which was installed flush.

5. While the cover is off, check the plug in the rear end of the main oil gallery. If the plug shows signs of leakage, replace it with another, coating it with the proper sealant to keep it in place.

NOTE: Fill the cavity between the sealing lips of the seal with grease before installing.

6. Coat the mating surface between the oil pan and end cover with sealer. Using a new gasket, install the end cover on the engine block and bolt it into place.

7. Complete the installation. If the oil pan gasket has been damaged, replace it. Install the transmission.

MANUAL TRANSMISSION

For further information, please refer to "Professional Transmission Repair Manual" for additional coverage.

Transmission Assembly

Removal and Installation

318iS, 325, 325i, 325iS, 325iX, AND M3

1. Disconnect the negative battery cable. Raise and safely support the vehicle. Remove the exhaust system. Remove the cross brace and heat shield. On the 325iX, remove the transfer case.

2. Hold the nuts on the front with one wrench, and remove bolts from the rear with another to disconnect the flexible coupling at the front of the driveshaft. Some vehicles have a vibration damper at this point in the drivetrain. This damper is mounted on the transmission output flange with bolts that are pressed into the damper. On these vehicles, unscrew and remove the nuts located behind the damper.

3. Loosen the threaded sleeve on the driveshaft. Get a special tool to hold the splined portion of the shaft while turning the sleeve.

4. Remove its mounting bolts and remove the center driveshaft mount. Then, bend the driveshaft down at the center and pull it off the transmission output flange. Keep the sections of the driveshaft from pulling apart and suspend it from the vehicle with wire.

5. Remove the retainer and washer, and pull out the shift selector rod.

6. Use a hex-head wrench to remove the self-locking bolts that retain the shift rod bracket at the rear of the transmission and then remove the bracket. If the vehicle has a shift arm, use a screwdriver to pry the spring clip up off the boss on the transmission case and swing it upward. Then, pull out the shift shaft pin.

7. Unscrew and remove the clutch slave cylinder and support it so the hydraulic line can remain connected.

8. The transmission incorporates sending units for flywheel rotating speed and position. Remove the heat shield that protects these from exhaust heat and then remove the retaining bolt for each sending unit. Note that the speed sending unit, which has no identifying ring goes in the bore on the right, and that the reference mark sending unit, which has a marking ring, goes in the bore on the left. If the sending units are installed in reverse positions, the engine will not run at all. Pull these units out of the flywheel housing.

9. Disconnect the wiring connector going to the backup light switch and pull the wires out of the harness.

10. Support the transmission from underneath in a secure manner. Remove mounting bolts and remove the crossmember holding the rear of the transmission to the body. Then, lower the transmission onto the front axle carrier.

11. Using the proper tool, remove the bolts holding the transmission flywheel housing to the engine at the front. Make sure to retain the washers with the bolts. Pull the transmission rearward to slide the input shaft out of the clutch disc and then lower the transmission and remove from the vehicle.

To install:

12. Install the transmission in position under the vehicle. Align the input shaft and install the transmission, note the following points in:

a. Coat the input shaft splines and flywheel housing guide pins with a light coating of suitable grease.

b. Make sure the front mounting bolts are installed with their washers. Torque them to 46–58 ft. lbs.

c. Before reinstalling the sending units for flywheel position and speed, make sure their faces are free of either grease or dirt and then coat them with a light coating of a suitable lubricant. Inspect the O-rings and replace them if they are cut, cracked, crushed, or stretched.

d. When installing the shift rod bracket at the rear of the transmission, use new self-locking bolts and make sure the bracket is level before tightening them. Torque the shift rod bracket bolts to 16.5 ft. lbs. except on the M3, which uses an aluminum bracket. On the M3, torque these bolts to 8 ft. lbs.

e. Install the clutch slave cylinder with the bleed screw downward.

f. When installing the driveshaft center bearing, preload it forward 0.157–0.236 in. Check the driveshaft alignment with an appropriate tool such. Replace the nuts and then torque the center mount bolts to 16–17 ft. lbs.

g. Torque the flexible coupling bolts to 83–94 ft. lbs.

525i, 535i, 635CSi, M5 AND M6

1. Disconnect the negative battery cable. Raise and safely support the vehicle. Disconnect and lower the exhaust system to provide clearance for transmission removal. Remove the heat shield brace and transmission heat shield.

2. Support the driveshaft and then unscrew the driveshaft coupling at the rear of the transmission. Use a wrench on both the nut and the bolt.

3. Working at the front of the driveshaft center bearing, unscrew the screw-on type ring type connector which attaches the driveshaft to the center bearing. Then, unbolt the center bearing mount. Bend the driveshaft down and pull it off the centering pin. If the vehicle has a vibration damper, turn it and pull it back over the output flange before pulling the driveshaft off the guide pin. Suspend it from the vehicle.

4. Pull off the wires for the backup light switch. Unscrew the passenger compartment console to disconnect it from the top of

the transmission by removing the self-locking bolts. Discard and replace.

5. Pull out the locking clip, and disconnect the shift rod at the rear of the transmission. Take care to keep all the washers.

6. If the transmission is linked to the shift lever with an arm, use a small prybar to lift the spring out of the holder on the bracket and then raise the arm. Pull out the shift shaft bolt.

7. If the vehicle has a flywheel housing cover (semi-circular in shape), remove the mounting bolts and remove the cover.

8. The speed sensor and reference mark sensor on the flywheel housing must be disconnected. Note their locations. The speed sensor goes in the upper bore, marked D. The reference mark sensor, which has a ring, goes in the lower bore, marked B. Check the O-rings for the sensors and install new ones if they are damaged.

9. Support the transmission securely. Then, unbolt and remove the rear transmission crossmember.

10. Remove the upper and lower attaching nuts and remove the clutch slave cylinder, supporting it so the hydraulic line need not be disconnected. Disconnect the reverse gear backup light switch and pull the wires out of the holders.

11. Unscrew the bolts fastening the transmission to the bell housing, using the proper tool. On some vehicles there are Torx® bolts used ; use a Torx® wrench for these. Pull the transmission rearward until the input shaft has disengaged from the clutch disc and then lower and remove it.

To install:

12. Place the transmission in gear. Insert the guide sleeve of the input shaft into the clutch pilot bearing carefully. Turn the output shaft to rotate the front of the input shaft until the splines line up and it engages the clutch disc.

13. Perform the remaining portions of the procedure in reverse of removal, observing the following points:

   a. Make sure the arrows on the rear crossmember point forward.

   b. Preload the center bearing mount forward of its most natural position 0.079–0.157 in. On 7 Series vehicles with the M30 B35 engine only, and 6 Series vehicles with the 265/6 transmission (no integral clutch housing), preload the bearing 0.157–0.236 in.

   c. In tightening the driveshaft screw on ring, use tool 26 1 040 or equivalent.

   d. When reconnecting the nuts and bolt at the transmission coupling, replace the nuts with new ones and turn only the nut, holding the bolts stationary.

   e. Make sure DME sensor faces are clean. Coat the sensor outside diameters with the proper lubricant.

   f. If equipped with a shift arm, lubricate the bolt with a light layer of a suitable lubricant.

   g. Observe these torque figures in ft. lbs:
   Transmission to bell housing—52–58 ft. lbs.
   Rear/top transmission Torx® bolts—46–58 ft. lbs.

Center mount to body—16–17 ft. lbs.
Front joint-to-transmission—83–94 ft. lbs.

735i AND 735iL

1. Disconnect the negative battery cable. Raise and safely support the vehicle. Remove the exhaust system. Remove the attaching bolts and remove the heat shield mounted just to the rear of the transmission on the floorpan.

2. Support the transmission securely from underneath. Then, remove the crossmember that supports it at the rear from the body by removing the mounting bolts on both sides.

3. Using wrenches on both the bolt heads and on the nuts, remove the bolts passing through the vibration damper and front universal joint at the front of the driveshaft.

4. Remove its mounting bolts and remove the center driveshaft mount. Then, bend the driveshaft down at the center and pull it off the transmission output flange. Keep the sections of the driveshaft from pulling apart and suspend it from the vehicle with wire.

5. Pull out the circlip, slide off the washer, and then pull the shift selector rod off the transmission shift shaft. Disconnect the backup light switch.

6. Lower the transmission slightly for access. Then, use a small prybar to lift the spring out of the holder on the bracket and then raise the arm. Pull out the shift shaft bolt.

7. Remove the upper and lower attaching nuts and remove the clutch slave cylinder, supporting it so the hydraulic line need not be disconnected.

8. Unscrew the bolts fastening the transmission to the bell housing. Use a Torx® wrench to remove the bolts. Make sure to retain the washer with each bolt to ensure that they can be readily removed later, if necessary. Pull the transmission rearward until the input shaft has disengaged from the clutch disc and then lower and remove the transmission.

To install:

9. Install the transmission in position under the vehicle. Align the input shaft and install the transmission. Follow these procedures:

   a. Preload the center bearing mount forward of its most natural position 0.157–0.236 in.

   b. When reconnecting the nuts and bolt at the transmission coupling, replace the nuts with new ones and turn only the nut, holding the bolts stationary.

   c. When reconnecting the shift arm, if equipped, lubricate the bolt with a light layer of a suitable lubricant and check the O-ring for crushing, cracks or cuts, replacing it, if damaged.

   d. When installing the clutch slave cylinder, make sure the bleeder screw faces downward.

   e. Observe these torque figures:
   Center mount to body—16–17 ft. lbs.
   Front joint-to-transmission—58.5 ft. lbs.

CLUTCH

Clutch Assembly

Removal and Installation

1. Disconnect the negative battery cable. Remove the heat shield and then the mounting bolts. Disconnect the speed and reference mark sensors at the flywheel housing. Mark the plugs for reinstallation.

2. Remove the transmission and clutch housing.

3. On vehicles with 6 cylinder engines, a Torx® socket is required. If equipped with a 265/6 transmission (without an inte-

gral clutch housing), remove the clutch housing.

4. Prevent the flywheel from turning, using a locking tool.

5. Loosen the mounting bolts one after another gradually, 1–1½ turns at a time, to relieve tension from the clutch.

6. Remove the mounting bolts, clutch, and drive plate. Coat the splines of the transmission input shaft with Molykote® Longterm 2, Microlube® GL 2611 or equivalent. Make sure the clutch pilot bearing, located in the center of the crankshaft, turns easily.

7. Check the clutch driven disc for excess wear or cracks.

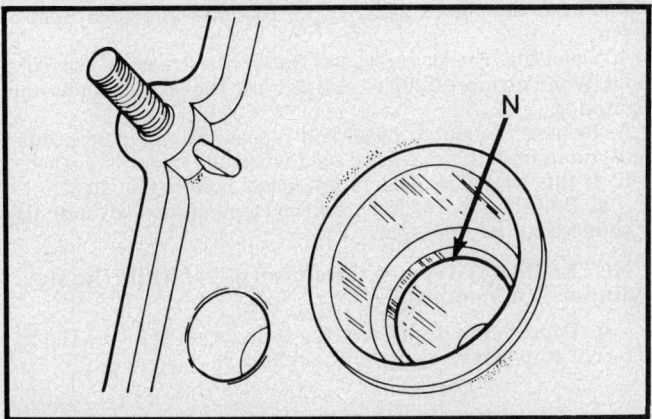

Pack the groove "N" with the proper grease before installing the transmission—M6, 635CSi and the 735i models

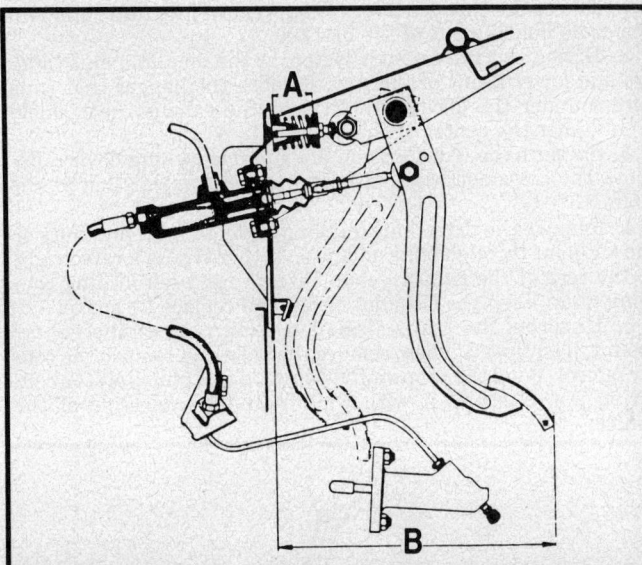

Adjusting the pedal height and overcenter spring—6 cylinder vehicles

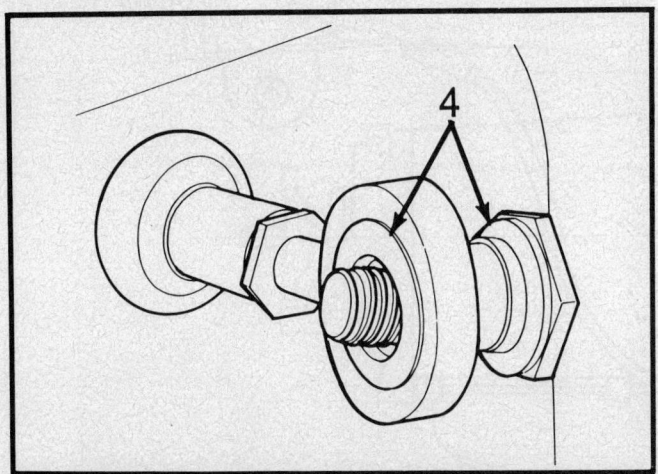

On the 7 series vehicles, make sure the bushing (4) on the clutch master cylinder are still in position

Check the integral torsional damping springs, used with lighter flywheels only, for tight fit. Inspect the rivets to make sure they are all tight. Check the flywheel to make sure it is not scored, cracked, or burned, even at a small spot. Use a straight edge to make sure the contact surface is true. Replace any defective parts.

To install:

8. To install, fit the new clutch plate and disc in place and install the mounting bolts.

9. When installing the clutch retaining bolts turn them in gradually to evenly tighten the clutch disc and to prevent warpage.

10. Install the transmission and the clutch housing.

11. If equipped, install the speed and reference mark sensors. Install the heat shield.

12. Note that on vehicles with 6 cylinder engines, the clutch pressure plate must fit over dowel pins. Torque the clutch mounting bolts to 16–19 ft. lbs.

Pedal Height/Free-Play Adjustment

EXCEPT 4 CYLINDER VEHICLES AND 325, 325i, 325iS, 325iX AND 750iL

Measure the length of the over-center spring (Dimension "A") and, if necessary, loosen the locknut and rotate the shafts as necessary to get the proper clearance. Measure the distance (Dimension "B") from the firewall to the tip of the clutch pedal and move the pedal in or out, if necessary, by loosening the locknut and rotating the shaft.

4 CYLINDER VEHICLES AND 325, 325i, 325iS, 325iX AND 750iL

3 Series vehicles and M3 do not require clutch pedal adjustment. If out of specification, loosen the locknut and rotate the piston rod to correct it.

Clutch Master Cylinder

Removal and Installation

1. Remove the necessary trim panel or carpet.

2. Disconnect the pushrod at the clutch pedal.

3. Remove the cap on the reservoir tank. On some vehicles, there is a clutch master cylinder reservoir, while on others there is a common reservoir shared with the brake master cylinder. Remove the float container, if equipped. Remove the screen and remove enough brake fluid from the tank until the level drops below the refill line or the connection for the filler pipe, if there is one.

4. Disconnect the coolant expansion tank without removing the hoses on the 735i and 735iL (vehicles with the M30 B35 engine do not require this).

5. Remove the lower/left instrument panel trim. Then, remove the retaining nut from the end of the master cylinder actuating rod where the bolt passes through the pedal mechanism.

6. Disconnect the line to the slave cylinder and the fluid fill line going to the top of the master cylinder. Remove the retaining bolts and remove the master cylinder from the firewall.

7. Install the clutch master cylinder in position. The piston rod bolt should be coated with the proper lubricant. Make sure all bushings remain in position. Bleed the system and adjust the pedal travel with the pushrod to 6 in.

Clutch Slave Cylinder

Removal and Installation

1. Remove enough brake fluid from the reservoir until the level drops below the refill line connection.

2. Remove the circlip or retaining bolts and pull the unit down.

3. Disconnect the line and remove the slave cylinder.

4. Install the slave cylinder on the transmission. On the 3 Series and M3, if the engine uses the 2-section flywheel, make sure a larger cylinder with a diameter of 0.874 in. is used instead of the usual cylinder (diameter 0.809 in.). Make sure to install the cylinder with the bleed screw facing downward. When installing the front pushrod, coat it with the proper anti-seize compound. Bleed the system.

Hydraulic Clutch System Bleeding

1. Fill the reservoir.

2. Connect a bleeder hose from the bleeder screw to a container filled with brake fluid so air cannot be drawn in during bleeding procedures.

3. Pump the clutch pedal about 10 times and then hold it down.

4. Open the bleeder screw and watch the stream of escaping fluid. When no more bubbles escape, close the bleeder screw and tighten it.

5. Release the clutch pedal and repeat the above procedure until no more bubbles can be seen when the screw is opened.

6. If this procedure fails to produce a bubble-free stream:

a. Pull the slave cylinder off the transmission without disconnecting the fluid line.

NOTE: Do not depress the clutch pedal while the slave cylinder is dismounted.

b. Depress the pushrod in the cylinder until it hits the internal stop. Then, reinstall the cylinder.

AUTOMATIC TRANSMISSION

For further information, please refer to "Professional Transmission Repair Manual" for additional coverage.

Transmission Assembly

Removal and Installation
EXCEPT 325i AND 325iX

NOTE: To perform this operation, a support for the transmission, tool 24 0 120 and 00 2 020 or equivalent and a tool for tightening the driveshaft locking ring, tool 26 1 040 or equivalent are required. If the vehicle has the M30 B35 type engine, a special socket, tool 24 1 110 or equivalent will be needed.

1. Disconnect the battery ground cable. Loosen the throttle cable adjusting nuts, release the cable tension, and disconnect the cable at the throttle lever. Then, remove the nuts, and pull the cable housing out of the bracket.

2. Disconnect the exhaust system at the manifold and hangers and lower it out of the way. Remove the hanger that runs across under the driveshaft. Remove the exhaust heat shield from under the center of the vehicle.

3. Support the transmission a a suitable jacking device. Remove the crossmember that supports the transmission at the rear.

4. Remove the driveshaft coupling through bolts and nuts or the CV-joint through bolts and nuts. Either type is located right at the rear of the transmission. Discard used self-locking coupling nuts. Keep the CV-joint clean, and replace its gasket.

5. Unscrew the transmission locking ring at the center mount, if equipped. Then, remove the bolts and remove the center mount. Bend the propshaft downward and pull it off the centering pin. Suspend it with wire from the underside of the vehicle.

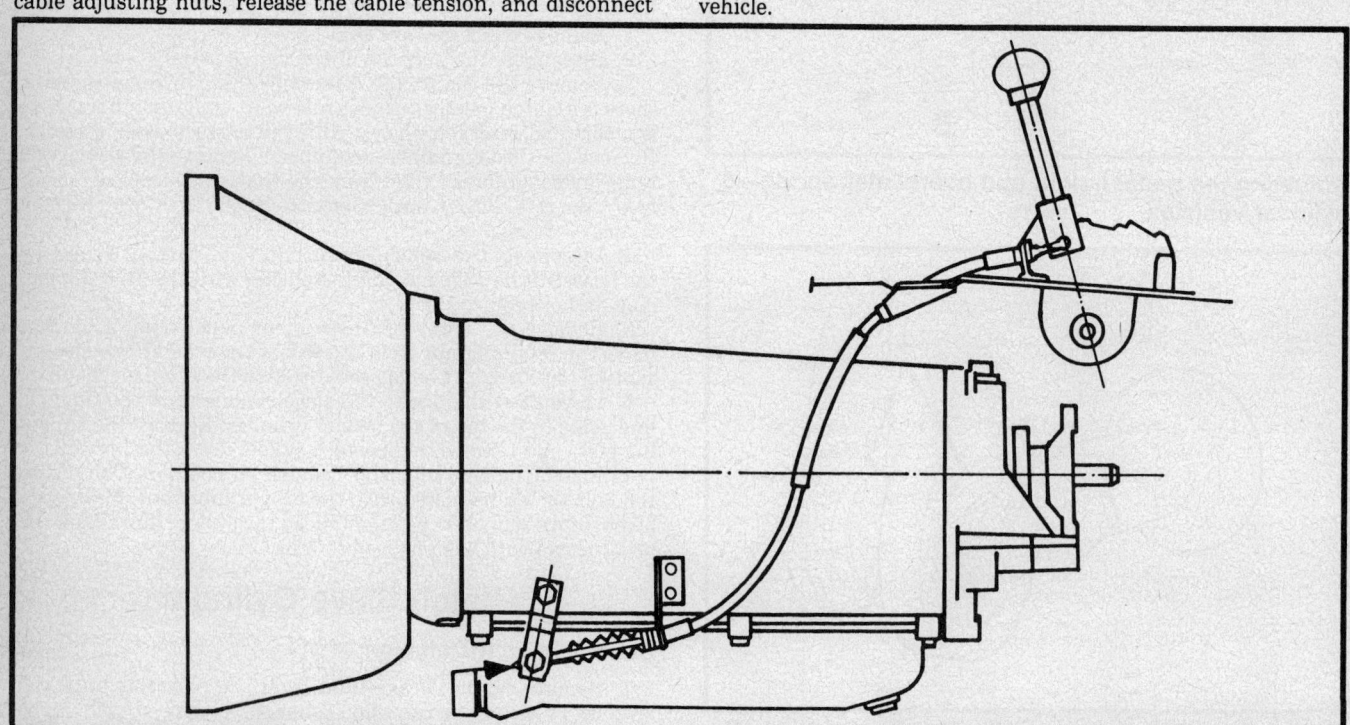

Adjusting the automatic transmission selector lever— 735I and 735II

Remove the 4 torque convertor retaining bolts

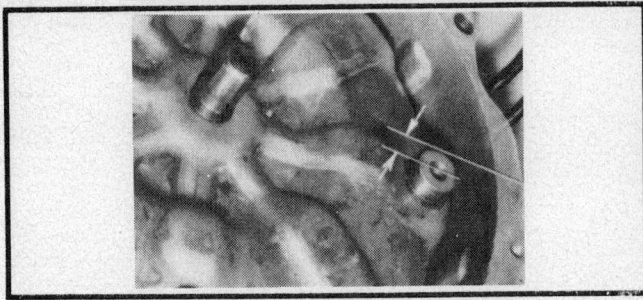

The torque converter is installed correctly if the drive shell mounting parts are located under the converter housing

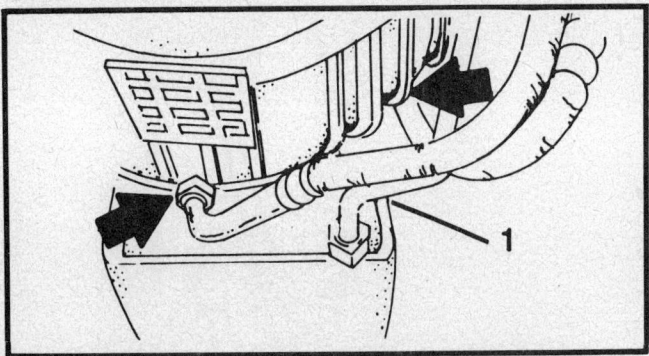

Remove the oil filler neck (1) and disconnect the arrowed hoses to drain fluid from the 4HP-22 transmission

6. Drain the transmission oil and discard it. Remove the oil filler neck. Disconnect the oil cooler lines at the transmission by unscrewing the flare nuts and plug the open connections.

7. If equipped, remove the converter cover by removing the Torx® bolts from behind and the regular bolts from underneath. If equipped with a M30 B35 type engine pull the cover out of the bottom of the transmission housing, just behind the oil pan.

8. Remove the bolts fastening the torque converter to the drive plate, turning the flywheel as necessary to gain access from below. Use a proper socket on vehicles with the M30 B35 type engine.

9. If equipped, remove the guard for the speed and reference mark sensors. Remove the attaching bolt for each and remove each sensor. Keep the sensors clean.

10. Disconnect the shift cable by loosening the locknut fasten-

ing it to the shift lever and disconnecting the cable at the cable housing bracket.

11. If the transmission has an electrical connection, turn the bayonet fastener to the left to release the connection, disconnect it, and pull the wire out of the ties.

12. Lower the transmission as far as possible. Then, remove all the Torx® or standard type bolts attaching the transmission to the engine.

13. Remove the small grill from the bottom of the transmission. Then press the converter off with a large prybar through this opening while sliding the transmission out.

To install:

14. Install the transmission under the vehicle and raise it into position. Observe the following points:

a. Make sure the converter is fully installed onto the transmission — so the ring on the front is inside the edge of the case.

b. When reinstalling the driveshaft, tighten the lockring with a special tool.

c. If the driveshaft has a simple coupling, rather than a CV-joint, make sure to replace the self-locking nuts and to hold the bolts still while tightening the nuts to keep from distorting the coupling.

d. When installing the center mount, preload it forward from its most natural position 0.157–0.236 in.

e. Adjust the throttle cables.

325i AND 325iX

NOTE: To perform this operation, a support for the transmission, BMW tool 24 0 120 and 00 2 020 or equivalent and a tool for tightening the driveshaft locking ring, BMW tool 26 1 040 or equivalent, are required. If the vehicle the M30 B35 type engine, a special socket, that retains bolts, will also be needed.

1. Disconnect the battery ground cable. Loosen the throttle cable adjusting nuts, release the cable tension, and disconnect the cable at the throttle lever. Then, remove (and retain) the nuts, and pull the cable housing out of the bracket.

2. Disconnect the exhaust system at the manifold and hangers and lower it aside. Remove the hanger that runs across under the driveshaft. Remove the exhaust heat shield from under the center of the vehicle.

3. On the 325iX, remove the transfer case from the rear of the transmission.

4. Drain the transmission oil and discard it. Remove the oil filler neck. Disconnect the oil cooler lines at the transmission by unscrewing the flare nuts and plug the open connections.

5. Support the transmission with the proper tools. Separate the torque converter housing from the transmission by removing the Torx® bolts with the proper tool from behind and the regular bolts from underneath. Retain the washers used with the Torx® bolts.

6. On the 325iX, disconnect the front driveshaft.

7. Remove bolts attaching the torque converter housing to the engine, making sure to retain the spacer used behind one of the bolts. Then, loosen the mounting bolts for the oil level switch just enough so the plate can be removed while pushing the switch mounting bracket to one side.

8. Remove the bolts attaching the torque converter to the drive plate. Turn the flywheel as necessary to gain access to each of the bolts, which are spaced at equal intervals around it. Make sure to re-use the same bolts and retain the washers.

9. To remove the speed and reference mark sensors, remove the attaching bolt for each and remove each sensor. Keep the sensors clean.

10. Turn the bayonet type electrical connector counterclockwise and then pull the plug out of the socket. Then, lift the wiring harness out of the harness bails.

11. Support the transmission using the proper jack. Then, remove the crossmember that supports the transmission at the rear.

12. Disconnect the transmission shift rod. Then, remove the nuts and then the through bolts from the damper-type U-joint at the front of the transmission.

13. Unscrew the transmission locking ring at the center mount, if equipped, using the special tool designed for this purpose. Then, remove the bolts and remove the center mount. Bend the driveshaft downward and pull it off the centering pin. Suspend it with wire from the underside of the vehicle.

14. Lower the transmission as far as possible. Then, remove all the Torx® or standard type bolts attaching the transmission to the engine.

15. Remove the small grill from the bottom of the transmission. Then press the converter off with a large prybar passing through this opening while sliding the transmission out.

To install:

16. Install the transmission in position under the vehicle and raise it into position. Observe the following points:

a. Make sure the converter is fully installed onto the transmission—so the ring on the front is inside the edge of the case.

b. When reinstalling the driveshaft, tighten the lockring with the proper tool.

c. Make sure to replace the self-locking nuts on the driveshaft flexible joint and to hold the bolts still while tightening the nuts to keep from distorting it.

d. When installing the center mount, preload it forward from its most natural position 0.157–0.236 in.

e. When reconnecting the bayonet type electrical connector, make sure the alignment marks are aligned after the plug it twisted into its final position.

f. When reinstalling the speed and reference mark sensors, inspect the O-rings used on the sensors and install new ones, if necessary. Make sure to install the speed sensor into the bore marked D and the reference mark sensor, which is marked with a ring, into the bore marked B.

g. Torque the crossmember mounting bolts to 16–17 ft. lbs.

h. If O-rings are used with the transmission oil cooler connections, replace them.

i. Adjust the throttle cables.

Shift Linkage Adjustment

1. Move the selector lever to **P** position. Loosen the nut until the cable is free.

2. Push the transmission lever to the **D** or **P** position. Then push the cable rod in the opposite direction.

3. Clamp down the cable rod without tension.

4. Tighten the nut to 7.0–8.5 ft. lbs.

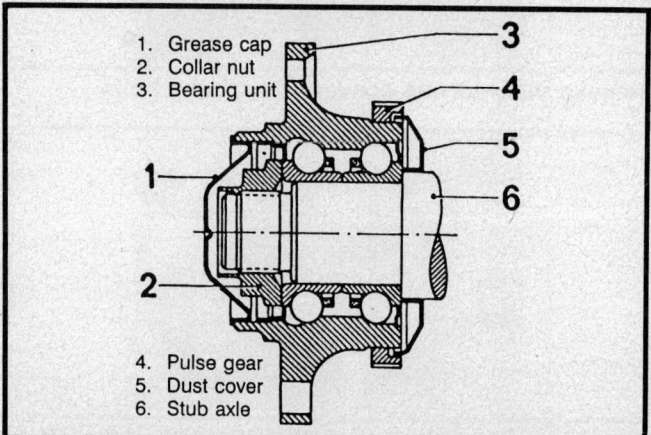

1. Grease cap
2. Collar nut
3. Bearing unit
4. Pulse gear
5. Dust cover
6. Stub axle

Front wheel bearing assembly—5 and 7 Series vehicles

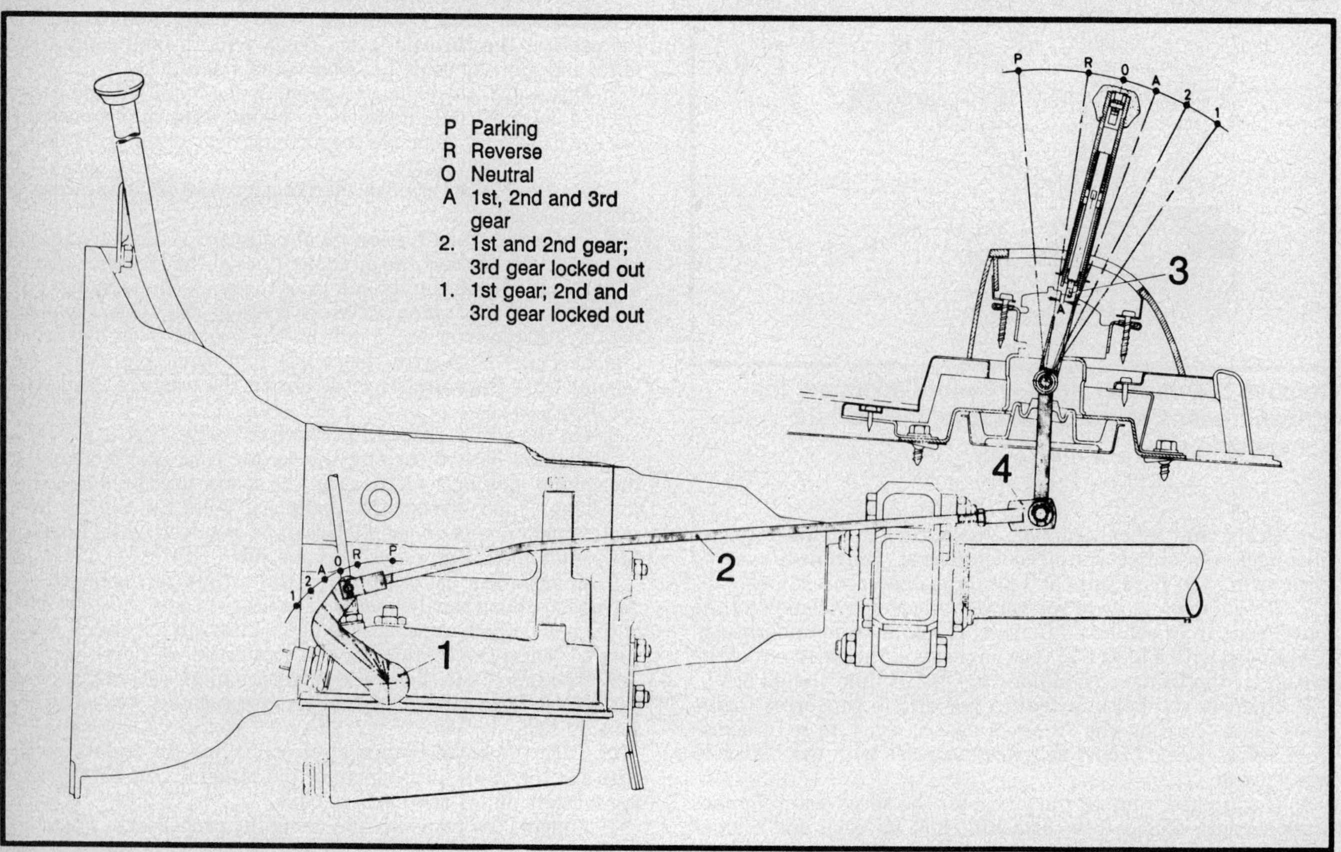

P Parking
R Reverse
O Neutral
A 1st, 2nd and 3rd gear
2. 1st and 2nd gear; 3rd gear locked out
1. 1st gear; 2nd and 3rd gear locked out

Selector lever adjustment—typical all models

NOTE: Do not bend the cable.

Throttle Linkage Adjustment

1. On the injection system throttle body, loosen the 2 locknuts at the end of the throttle cable and adjust the cable until there is a play of 0.010–0.030 in.

2. Loosen the locknut and lower the kickdown stop under the accelerator pedal. Have someone depress the accelerator pedal until the transmission detent can be felt. Then, back the kickdown stop back out until it just touches the pedal.

3. Check that the distance from the seal at the throttle body end of the cable housing is at least 1.732 in. from the rear end of the threaded sleeve. If this dimension checks out, tighten all the locknuts.

TRANSFER CASE

Transfer Case Assembly

Removal and Installation

WITH MANUAL TRANSMISSION

NOTE: To perform this procedure, a special, large wrench that locks onto flats on alternate sides of a section of the rear driveshaft is required. Use tool 26 1 060 or an equivalent.

1. Disconnect the negative battery cable. Raise and safely support the vehicle. Remove the exhaust system. Unbolt and remove the exhaust system heat shields located behind and below the transfer case.

2. Unscrew the rear section of the driveshaft at the sliding joint located behind the output flange of the transfer case.

3. Hold the through-bolts stationary and remove the self-locking nuts from in front of the flexible coupling at the transfer case output flange. Discard all the self-locking nuts and replace them.

NOTE: During the next step, be careful not to let the driveshaft rest on the metal fuel line that crosses under it or the line could be damaged.

4. Slide the sections of the driveshaft together at the sliding joint and then pull the front of the driveshaft off the centering pin at the transmission output shaft.

5. Remove the nuts and through bolts from the flexible coupling linking the transmission output flange with the short driveshaft linking the transmission and the transfer case.

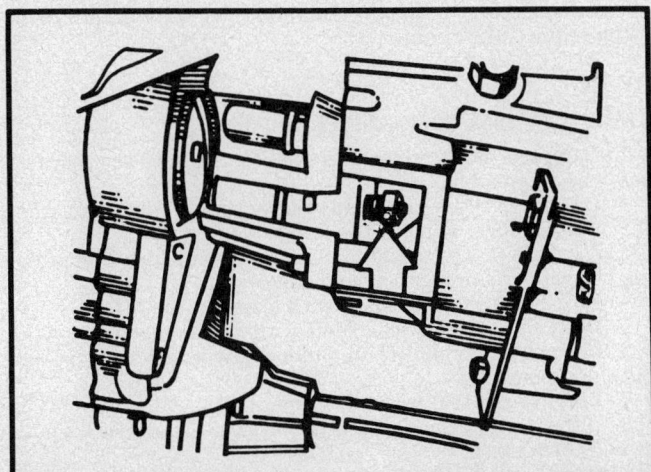

The arrow shows the location of the flexible coupling linking the transmission output flange with the input flange of the transfer case

6. Support the transmission from underneath in a secure manner. Then, mark each of the 4 bolts fastening the crossmember that supports the transmission at the rear to the body, bolts are of different lengths. Remove the crossmember.

7. Lower the transmission/transfer case unit just enough to gain access to the bolts linking the 2 boxes together. Remove the 2 lower and 2 upper bolts. It is possible to gain access to the upper bolts using a socket wrench with a U-joint and extension.

8. There is a protective cap on the forward driveshaft where it links up with the transfer case. The cap is made of a brittle material, so it must be handled carefully. Gently slide the cap forward until is free of the transfer case.

9. Slide the transfer case to the rear so it can be separated from both the transmission and the forward driveshaft. When it is free, remove it.

To install:

10. Install the transfer case under the vehicle and raise it into position, bearing the following points in mind:

   a. Inspect the dowel holes locating the transfer case with the transmission and the guide hole for the output shaft where it slides into the transfer case to make sure these parts will be properly located. Lubricate the guide pin and the splines of the front driveshaft section with grease.

   b. When fitting the transfer case onto the transmission, check to make sure the output flange of the transmission is properly aligned with the flexible coupling. Put the through-bolts through the flexible coupling and then install and torque the nuts to 65 ft. lbs. while holding the bolts stationary, rather than turning them.

   c. When reconnecting the transfer case to the gearbox, torque the bolts to 30 ft. lbs.

   d. Before fitting the driveshaft back onto the rear of the transmission, retain the seal in the protective cap by applying grease to it.

   e. Torque the transmission crossmember bolts to 17 ft. lbs.

   f. Check the fluid level and fill with the recommended lubricant.

WITH AUTOMATIC TRANSMISSION

NOTE: To perform this procedure, a special, large wrench that locks onto flats on alternate sides of a section of the rear driveshaft is required. Use tool 26 1 060 or an equivalent.

1. Disconnect the negative battery cable. Raise and safely support the vehicle. Remove the exhaust system. Unbolt and remove the exhaust system heat shields located behind and below the transfer case.

2. Unscrew the rear section of the driveshaft at the sliding joint located behind the output flange of the transfer case.

3. Hold the through-bolts stationary and remove the self-locking nuts from in front of the flexible coupling at the transfer case output flange. Discard all the self-locking nuts and replace them.

NOTE: During the next step, be careful not to let the driveshaft rest on the metal fuel line that crosses under it or the line could be damaged.

4. Slide the sections of the driveshaft together at the sliding joint and then pull the front of the driveshaft off the centering pin at the transmission output shaft.

5. Remove the nuts and through bolts from the flexible coupling linking the transmission output flange with the short driveshaft linking the transmission and the transfer case.

6. Note the locations of all the washers and then loosen the retaining nut and disconnect the range selector lever cable at the transmission by pulling out the pin. Be careful not to bend the cable in doing this. Then, loosen the nuts that position the cable housing onto the transmission and slide the cable housing backward so it can be separated from the bracket on the transmission housing.

7. There is a protective cap on the forward driveshaft where it links up with the transfer case. The cap is made of a brittle material, so it must be handled carefully. Gently slide the cap forward until is free of the transfer case.

8. Remove the drain plug in the bottom of the pan and drain the transmission fluid.

9. Support the transmission from underneath in a secure manner. Then, mark each of the 4 bolts fastening the crossmember that supports the transmission at the rear to the body, bolts are of different lengths. Remove the crossmember.

10. Remove the 9 nuts fastening the transfer case to the transmission housing. Note the location of the wiring holder so it will be possible to reinstall it on the same bolt.

11. Slide the transfer case to the rear and off the transmission.

To install:

12. Install the transfer case under the vehicle and raise it into position, bearing the following points in mind:

   a. Inspect the sealing surfaces as well as the dowel holes in the transfer case to make sure they will seal and locate properly. Clean the sealing surfaces and replace the gasket.

   b. When sliding the transfer case back onto the transmission, turn the front driveshaft section slightly to help make the splines mesh.

   c. When reconnecting the shift cable, inspect the rubber mounts and replace any that are cut, crushed, or cracked. Adjust the shift cable.

   d. Before fitting the driveshaft back onto the rear of the transmission, retain the seal in the protective cap by applying grease to it.

   e. When fitting the transfer case onto the transmission, check to make sure the output flange of the transmission is properly aligned with the flexible coupling. Put the through-bolts through the flexible coupling and then install and torque the nuts to 65 ft. lbs. while holding the bolts stationary, rather than turning them.

   f. Torque the bolts holding the transfer case to the transmission to 65 ft. lbs.

   g. Torque the transmission crossmember bolts to 17 ft. lbs.

   h. Check the fluid level and fill with the recommended lubricant.

DRIVE AXLE

Halfshaft

Removal and Installation

FRONT

325iX

1. Raise and safely support the vehicle. Remove the front wheels. Remove the drain plug and drain the lube oil from the front axle.

2. Lift out the lock plate in the center of the brake disc with a small prybar. Then, unscrew the collar nut.

3. Remove the attaching nut from each tie rod and then press the rod off the steering knuckle with the proper tool.

4. Remove the retaining nut and then press the control arm off the steering knuckle on either side.

5. Mount the proper tool to the brake disc with 2 wheel bolts. Press the output shaft out of the center of the steering knuckle on that side. Repeat on the other side.

6. To remove the drive axle from the differential on the left side: Install special tool by bolting it together around the axle so the ring on its inner diameter fits into the groove on the shaft. Install the tool onto the shaft so it will rest against the housing and the bolt heads of the tool will rest against it. Screw the 2 bolts in alternately in small increments to get even pressure on the shaft, pulling it out of the differential.

7. To remove the drive axle on the right side: Install the proper tool on the diameter of the shaft directly against the housing. Install the tool by bolting it together around the axle so the ring on its inner diameter fits into the groove on the shaft. Screw the 2 bolts in alternately in small increments to get even pressure on the shaft, pulling it out of the differential.

To install:

8. Install the halfshafts, bearing the following points in mind:

   a. Install the shafts into the housing until the circlip inside engages in the groove of the shaft. It may be necessary to install the removal tool and tap against it with a plastic-headed hammer to drive the shaft far enough into the housing.

   b. Before installing the shafts into the steering knuckle, coat the spline with light oil.

   c. When installing the control arms onto the steering knuckle, torque the nut to 61.5 ft. lbs. and use a new cotter pin. When installing the tie rod onto the steering knuckle, torque to 61.5 ft. lbs. and use a new self-locking nut.

   d. Drive a new lock plate into the brake disc with the proper tool. Torque the nut to 181 ft. lbs.

   e. Replace the drain plug and refill the final drive unit with the required lubricant.

REAR

318iS, 325, 325i, 325iS, 325iX and M3

1. Raise and safely support the vehicle. Remove the rear tire and wheel assembly.

2. Lift out the lock plate and remove the retaining nut from the output flange. Remove the flange.

3. Disconnect the output shaft from the final drive by pressing out with the proper tool and suspend it.

4. Pull out the output shaft with a special tool.

5. Drive out the rear axle shaft with the proper tool.

6. Lift out the circlip. Then, pull out the wheel bearings, using the proper tool.

7. Pull out the seal with the proper tool.

8. If the inner bearing shell is damaged, pull it off with a puller and thrust pad.

To install:

9. To install, pull in the wheel bearing assembly, pull in the seal, insert the circlip and then pull in the rear axle shaft, all in reverse of the removal procedure. Install the axle shaft seal.

10. To install the output shaft, screw the threaded spindle into

the shaft all the way, and then use the nut and washer against the outside of the bridge.

10. Reconnect the output shaft to the final drive.

11. Lubricate the bearing surface of the outer nut with oil. Then install and torque the nut.

12. Using the proper installers or equivalent, knock in the lock plate. Use the following torque figures:
Output shaft to drive flange, 42–46 ft. lbs.
Drive flange hub to output shaft,140–152 ft. lbs.

525i, 525iS, 535i, M5, 635CSi, M6, 735i, 735iL and 750iL

1. Raise and safely support the vehicle.

2. Unscrew the output shaft on the rear drive assembly and the axle shaft end.

3. Remove the output shaft.

4. Install new washers on the rear drive assembly and the axle shaft end.

5. Install the output shaft and tighten to 42–46 ft. lbs.

CV-Boot

Removal and Installation

FRONT

325iX

1. Raise and safely support the vehicle. Remove the front wheel assembly.

2. Drain the gear lube and unscrew the collar nut.

3. Disconnect the tie rod ends and the control arm with the proper tool.

4. Remove the output shaft using the proper tool.

5. Loosen both clamps and pull the dust boot off the joint. Clean and remove grease from the joint. Add the required amount of the proper grease and install the boot and tighten the clamps.

6. The remainder of the installation is the reverse of the removal procedure.

REAR

1. Raise and safely support the vehicle.

2. Remove the output shaft and the circlip. Press off the cap and the dust cover.

3. Press the output shaft out of the CV-joint. Clean and remove the grease from the splines of the joint.

4. Install the dust cover with the inside cover on the output shaft.

5. Press on the joint with the cap and install the circlip. Pack the joint and dust cover with the proper grease.

6. Mount he dust cover and install new clamps.

7. Install the output shaft and lower the vehicle.

Driveshaft and U-Joints

Removal and Installation

318iS, 325, 325i, 325iS AND M3

1. Raise and safely support the vehicle. Remove the mufflers. Unscrew and remove the exhaust system heat shield near the fuel tank.

2. Unbolt and remove the cross brace that runs under the driveshaft.

3. Support the transmission. The automatic transmission must be supported by the case and not the pan. Loosen all transmission support bolts and remove. Remove the transmission rear support crossmember.

4. Lower the manual transmission for clearance. Remove the driveshaft bolts from the front coupling.

NOTE: Make sure the drive axle does not rest on the fuel line that runs across under it.

5. Unscrew and remove bolts at the coupling near the final drive.

6. Loosen the threaded sleeve on the driveshaft with a tool such as tool 26 1 040 or equivalent. Unbolt and remove the center mount.

7. Bend the driveshaft downward and remove it, being careful not to allow it to rest on the connecting line on the fuel tank.

To install:

8. Upon installation:
   a. Mount the holder for the oxygen sensor plug.
   b. Make sure the heat shield clears the fuel tank.
   c. Wherever self-locking nuts are used, replace them. On the transmission-end flange, tighten the nuts/bolts only on the flange side, holding the other end stationary.
   d. Preload the center mount to 0.157–0.236 in. before tightening the bolts. Torque the mounting bolts to 16 ft. lbs.
   e. Lubricate the center bearing with the proper lubricant.
   f. Make sure to reinstall the bracket for the oxygen sensor plug.
   g. Make sure there is sufficient clearance between the rear heat shield and fuel tank.

325iX

NOTE: Never drive the vehicle with either driveshaft disconnected. This could damage the lockup mechanism in the transfer case.

1. Raise and safely support the vehicle. Remove the exhaust system. Remove both exhaust system heat shields.

2. Loosen the threaded sleeve near the front of the driveshaft with the proper tool. Turn the sleeve several turns outward, but do not disconnect it entirely.

3. Disconnect the driveshaft at the output flange of the transfer case by removing the nuts and the through bolts.

4. Disconnect the driveshaft at the final drive by removing the nuts and the through bolts.

NOTE: Make sure the drive axle does not rest on the fuel line that runs across under it.

5. Slide the sections of the driveshaft together and slide it out of the centering pin on the output flange of the transfer case. Remove it from the vehicle.

To install:

6. Install the driveshaft in reverse order, keeping these points in mind:
   a. Whenever self-locking nuts are used, replace them.
   b. Hold the nut or bolt in place where it runs through a U-joint and tighten at the opposite end, where the driveshaft flange is located.
   c. Check the center bearing for lubrication and if it's dry, lubricate with the proper lubricant.

528e, 525i AND 535i

1. Raise and safely support the vehicle.

2. Support the transmission from underneath with the special tools and a floorjack. Remove the nuts and washers from the transmission mounts on top of the rear transmission mounting crossmember. Loosen but do not remove the nuts located underneath which fasten the crossmember to the body. Then, slide this crossmember as far to the rear as it will go.

3. Unscrew the fastening nuts on the forward end of the CV-joint and then discard them.

4. Using a prybar to keep the driveshaft from turning, remove the self locking nuts and bolts fastening the rear of the driveshaft to the final drive.

5. Remove the bolts fastening the center mount to the body. Bend the propshaft down and pull the CV-joint off the transmission flange. Cover the joint to keep it clean.

To install:

6. Replace the gasket that fits between the joint bolts. Install in reverse order, keeping these points in mind:

a. Replace the self-locking nuts used at either end of the shaft.

b. Preload the center mount forward by forcing the bracket 0.157–0.197 in. forward from the neutral position.

635CSi

1. Raise and safely support the vehicle. Remove the exhaust system.

3. Remove the heat shield near the fuel tank, if so equipped.

4. Disconnect the driveshaft at the transmission by removing the nuts and bolts from the flexible coupling. If the vehicle has a vibration damper where the shaft connects to the transmission, turn the damper 60 degrees counterclockwise and remove it with the rubber coupling.

5. Loosen the center bearing bolts and remove them.

6. Disconnect the driveshaft at the final drive.

7. Bend the driveshaft down and pull out.

To install:

8. Installation is the reverse of removal.

9. The driveshaft is balanced as an assembly and must only be renewed as a complete assembly.

10. Preload the center bearing in the forward direction to 0.157–0.236 in.

11. Wherever self-locking nuts are used, replace them. Hold the nut or bolt in place where it runs through a U-joint, and torque at the opposite end—where the driveshaft flange is located. Check the center bearing for lubrication and if it's dry, lubricate with the proper lubricant.

735i, 735iL AND 750iL

NOTE: If the vehicle has a front universal joint, use tools 24 0 120 and 00 2 020 to support the transmission during this operation.

1. Raise and safely support the vehicle. Remove the exhaust system. Remove the heat shield from the floorpan. Remove the nuts and bolts fastening the driveshaft to the transmission at the flexible coupling. Replace the self-locking nuts.

2. If equipped with a front U-joint, support the transmission from underneath with the proper tools. When the transmission is securely supported, remove the 6 bolts and remove the rear transmission mounting crossmember.

3. Remove the self-locking nuts and then the bolts fastening the driveshaft to the final drive. Replace the self-locking nuts.

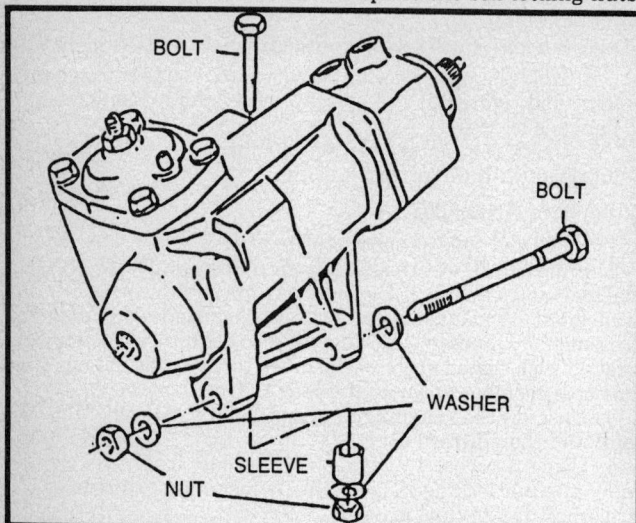

Power steering gear assembly—5 and 7 Series vehicles

Remove the driveshaft, taking care to keep it protected from dirt.

4. Remove the bolts from the crossbrace and remove the center driveshaft mount. Then, bend the shaft at the middle and remove it from the vehicle by pulling it off the centering pin on the forward end.

To install:

5. Install in reverse order, keeping the following points in mind:

a. Repack the CV-joint with approved grease and replace the gasket, if necessary.

b. Check the center bearing for lubrication and if it's dry, lubricate with the proper lubricant.

c. If the vibration damper at the forward end of the driveshaft must be replaced, turn it 60 degrees to remove it.

d. When remounting the center mount, preload it forward from its most natural position 0.157–0.236 in.

e. Torque U-joint bolts to 52 ft. lbs. and CV-joint bolts to 51 ft. lbs.

Front Wheel Hub, Knuckle and Bearings

Removal and Installation

EXCEPT 735i, 735iL AND 750iL

1. Raise and safely support the vehicle. Remove the front tire and wheel assembly.

2. Disconnect and suspend the brake caliper from the body without disconnecting the brake line.

2. Remove the setscrew with an Allen® wrench. Pull off the brake disc and pry off the dust cover with a small prybar.

3. Using a chisel, knock the tab on the collar nut away from the shaft. Unscrew and discard the nut.

4. Pull off the bearing with the proper puller set and discard it. On the M3, use a puller set such as 31 2 102/105/106. On the M3, install the main bracket of the puller with wheel bolts.

5. If the inside bearing inner race remains on the stub axle, unbolt and remove the dust guard. Bend back the inner dust guard and pull the inner race off with a special tool capable of getting under the race. Reinstall the dust guard.

NOTE: Do not reuse the bearing unit if removed.

6. If the dust guard has been removed, install a new one. Install a special tool on M3, over the stub axle and screw it in for the entire length of the guide sleeve's threads. Press the bearing on.

7. Reverse the remaining removal procedures to install the disc and caliper. Torque the wheel hub collar nut to 188 ft. lbs. Lock the collar nut by bending over the tab.

735i, 735iL AND 750iL

1. Raise and safely support the vehicle. Remove the front tire and wheel assemblies. Remove the attaching bolts and remove and suspend the brake caliper, hanging it from the body so as to avoid putting stress on the brake line.

2. Remove the setscrew with an Allen® wrench. Pull off the brake disc and pry off the dust cover with a small prybar.

3. Using a chisel, knock the tab on the collar nut away from the shaft. Unscrew and discard the nut.

4. Install a puller collar such as 31 2 105 to the bearing housing with 3 bolts. Install a puller such as 31 2 102 and 312 2 106 and pull off the bearing and discard it.

5. If the inside bearing inner race remains on the stub axle, unscrew and remove the dust guard, using a socket extension. Bend back the inner dust guard and pull the inner race off with a special tool capable of getting under the race. Reinstall the dust guard and install a new dust cover.

6. Then install a special tool over the stub axle and screw it in for the entire length of the guide sleeve's threads. Slide the

bearing on and follow it with 31 2 100 or equivalent, and use this tool to press the bearing on.

7. Reverse the remaining removal procedures to install the disc and caliper. Torque the wheel hub collar nut to 210 ft. lbs. Lock the collar nut by bending over the tab.

8. Install a new grease cap coated with the proper lubricant.

Rear Axle Shaft, Bearing and Seal

Removal and Installation

318iS, 325, 325i, 325iS, 325iX AND M3

1. Raise and safely support the vehicle. Remove the rear tire and wheel assembly.

2. Lift out the lock plate and remove the retaining nut from the output flange. Remove the flange.

3. Disconnect the output shaft from the final drive by pressing out with the proper tool and suspend it.

4. Pull out the output shaft with a special tool.

5. Drive out the rear axle shaft with the proper tool.

6. Lift out the circlip. Then, pull out the wheel bearings, using the proper tool.

7. Pull out the seal with a tool such as 33 4 045.

8. If the inner bearing shell is damaged, pull it off with a puller and thrust pad.

To install:

9. Using the an appropriate bearing installer, pull in the wheel bearing assembly, pull in the seal, insert the circlip and then pull in the rear axle shaft, all in reverse of the removal procedure. Install the axle shaft seal.

10. To install the output shaft, screw the threaded spindle into the shaft all the way, and then use the nut and washer against the outside of the bridge.

10. Reconnect the output shaft to the final drive.

11. Lubricate the bearing surface of the outer nut with oil. Then install and torque the nut.

12. Using the proper installers or equivalent, knock in the lock plate. Use the following torque figures:

Output shaft to drive flange, 42–46 ft. lbs.

Drive flange hub to output shaft, 140–152 ft. lbs.

318iS, 325, 325i, 325iS, 325iX AND M3

1. Raise and safely support the vehicle. Remove the rear tire and wheel assembly.

2. Disconnect the output shaft at the outer flange and suspend it with wire.

3. Unbolt the caliper and suspend it with the brake line connected. Unbolt and remove the rear disc.

4. Remove the large nut and remove the lock plate. If equipped with ABS, disconnect and then remove the ABS speed sensor by unscrewing it.

5. Unscrew the collar nut. Then, pull off the drive flange with the proper tool(s).

6. Screw on the collar nut until it is just flush with the end of the shaft and use a suitable hammer to knock out the shaft.

7. Remove the circlip. Pull out the wheel bearings, using the proper tool.

8. Pull the inner bearing race off the axle shaft with tool 00 7 500 or equivalent.

To install:

9. Install the new bearing assembly using the proper tools. Then, reinstall the circlip.

10. Install the rear axle shaft with special tools 23 1 300, 33 4 080 and 33 4 020 or equivalent.

11. Install the collar nut and drive in the lock plate with the proper tool(s).

12. Reconnect the output shaft. Remount the brake disc and caliper.

13. Lower the vehicle.

Axle Housing

Removal and Installation

1. Disconnect the negative battery cable.

2. Raise and safely support the vehicle. Disconnect and remove the rear exhaust.

3. Remove the heat shield, if equipped. Remove the driveshaft and disconnect the center support mount, if necessary.

4. Disconnect the parking brake lever cables. Disconnect and plug the rear brake lines.

5. Support the rear axle housing with a suitable jack device. Disconnect the thrust struts on both sides, if necessary.

6. Disconnect and plug the pulse senders and remove the rear seat cushion, if needed.

7. Remove the rear side trim panel on 3 series convertible.

8. Disconnect the wires at the speedometer pulse sender. Unscrew the rear rubber mounting bolt.

9. Unplug the rear brake pad indicator and disconnect the wire connection.

10. Disconnect the switching valve for the ride control height and the plug on the camber warning sender on the 750iL.

11. Disconnect both rear shock absorbers at the trailing arms and move the brake cables out of the way.

12. Lower the rear axle assembly, using a suitable lifting device.

To install:

13. Install the rear axle assembly, lifting into position with a suitable lifting device.

14. Connect the shock absorbers to the trailing arms. Tighten the bolts when the vehicle is in the normal position to 52–63 ft. lbs. on 3 Series or 90–144 ft. lbs. except 3 Series.

15. Connect the switching valve for the ride control height and the plug on the camber warning sender on the 750iL.

16. Connect the rear brake pad indicator plug and the wire connection.

17. Connect the wires at the speedometer pulse sender. Replace the rear rubber mounting bolt and tighten to 31–35 ft. lbs. except on the 7 series and 36–38 ft. lbs. on the 7 series.

18. Replace the rear side trim panel on 3 series convertible.

19. Connect and plug the pulse senders and replace the rear seat cushion, if needed.

20. Connect the thrust struts on both sides, if needed. Remove the jacking device from under the rear axle assembly.

21. Connect the parking brake cables and the brake lines.

22. Replace the heat shield, if equipped. Replace the driveshaft and connect the center support mount, if necessary.

23. Replace the rear exhaust. Lower the vehicle.

24. Connect the negative battery cable.

STEERING

Steering Wheel

――――― CAUTION ―――――

On vehicles equipped with an air bag, the negative battery cable must be disconnected, before working on the system. Failure to do so may result in deployment of the air bag and possible personal injury.

Removal and Installation

1. Disconnect the negative battery cable. Remove steering wheel pad or BMW emblem. Mark the relationship between the steering wheel and shaft for installation in the same position. Unlock the steering wheel lock with the key. Otherwise, the wheel cannot be removed.
2. Unscrew retaining nut and remove the wheel.

NOTE: Be careful not to damage the direction signal cancelling cam, which is right under the steering wheel, in performing this operation. On vehicles equipped with an air bag, it is important to avoid banging on the wheel in any way.

3. Installation is the reverse of removal. Lubricate the direction signal cancelling cam. Replace the self-locking nut on all models, and torque it to 58 ft. lbs.

Steering Column

――――― CAUTION ―――――

On vehicles equipped with an air bag, the negative battery cable must be disconnected, before working on the system. Failure to do so may result in deployment of the air bag and possible personal injury.

Removal and Installation

1. Disconnect the negative battery cable. Remove the steering wheel.
2. Remove the lower instrument trim panel. Disconnect the steering column casing.
3. Disconnect the electrical connections. Press down on the steering spindle, remove the bolt and the spindle.
4. Remove the shear-off bolts with a proper chisel. Remove the mounting nuts/bolts.
5. Press down and remove the steering column.
6. The installation is the reverse of the removal procedure. Install new bolts.

Power Steering Rack

Removal and Installation

318iS, 325 SERIES AND M3

1. Raise and safely support the vehicle and remove front wheels. Remove the pinch bolt and loosen bolt. Press the spindle off the steering gear.
2. Use a syringe to empty the power steering fluid reservoir. Loosen the clamp and pull off the hydraulic fluid return line from the power steering unit. Discard drained fluid.
3. Disconnect and plug the pressure line.
4. Unscrew left and right side nuts, and press off the tie rods where they connect to the spring struts.
5. Remove the bolts attaching the steering unit to the front axle carrier and remove it.
To install:
6. Install in reverse order, keeping the following points in mind:

   a. The steering unit bolts to the rear holes of the axle carrier. Use new self-locking nuts and torque them to 29–34 ft. lbs.

   b. When reconnecting tie rods to the spring struts, make sure tie rod pins and strut bores are clean. Replace self-locking nut and torque to 40–48 ft. lbs.

   c. Replace the seals on the power steering pump connection, and torque the bolt to 29–32 ft. lbs.
7. Refill the fluid reservoir with specified fluid. Idle the engine and turn the steering wheel back and forth until it has reached right and left lock 2 times each. Then, turn off the engine and refill the reservoir.

325iX

NOTE: To remove the steering gear on 4WD vehicles, use a special tool to support the engine via the body. It is also advisable to use a special tool to support the front axle carrier without damaging it. It is necessary to remove the entire front axle carrier to gain access to the mounting bolts for the steering gear on this vehicle.

1. Raise the vehicle and support it securely. Remove the splash guard. Remove the front wheels.
2. Remove the air cleaner. Use a clean syringe to remove the power steering fluid from the pump reservoir.
3. Attach the support tool and connect it to the engine hooks to be sure the engine is securely supported.
4. Remove the through bolts from the right and left engine mounts.
5. Disconnect both the hydraulic lines running from the power steering pump to the steering gear, and then plug the openings.
6. Loosen both the retaining bolts and then disconnect the steering column spindle off the steering gear.
7. Remove the retaining nuts on both sides and then press the tie rod ends off the steering knuckles with the proper tools. Be careful to keep grease out of the bores and off the tie rod ball studs.
8. Remove the cotter pins, remove the retaining nuts on both sides and then use the proper tool to press the control arm ball joint studs out of the steering knuckles. Be careful to keep grease out of the bores and off the control arm ball studs.
9. Remove the bolts on either side attaching the control arm brackets to the body.
10. Remove the bolts and remove the stabilizer bar mounting brackets from the front axle carrier on both sides.
11. Support the front axle carrier with a suitable jacking device. Then, remove the mounting bolts on either side and remove the axle carrier. Remove the mounting bolts and remove the steering gear from the axle carrier.
To install:
12. Install in reverse order, noting these points:

    a. Clean the bores into which the axle carrier bolts are mounted. Use some sort of locking sealer and torque the bolts to 30 ft. lbs.

    b. Torque the mounting bolts holding the steering gear to front axle carrier to 30 ft. lbs.

    c. Install new cotter pins on the retaining nuts for the control arm ball studs. Torque to 61.5 ft. lbs.

    d. Replace the self-locking nuts on the tie rod end ball studs and connecting the steering column spindle to the steering box. Torque tie rod ball stud nuts to 24–29 ft. lbs.

    e. Replace the gaskets on power steering hydraulic lines. Refill the fluid reservoir with specified fluid. Idle the engine and turn the steering wheel back and forth until it has reached right and left lock 2 times each. Then, turn off the engine and refill the reservoir.

Power Steering Gear

Adjustment

525i, 535iS, 528e, 535i, M5, M6, 635CSi, 735i, 735iL AND 750iL

1. Remove the steering wheel center.
2. With the front wheels in the straight ahead position, remove the cotter pin and loosen the castle nut.
3. Press the center tie rod off the steering drop arm.
4. Turn the steering wheel to the left about one turn. Install a friction gauge and turn the wheel to the right, past the point of pressure and the gauge should read 0.72–0.87 ft. lbs.
5. To adjust, turn the steering wheel about one turn to the left. Loosen the counter nut and turn the adjusting screw until the specified friction is reached when passing over the point of pressure.

Removal and Installation

525i, 535iS, 528e, 535i, M5, M6, 635CSi, 735i, 735iL AND 750iL

1. Disconnnect the negative battery cable.
2. Remove the steering wheel, if equipped with an airbag (SRS).
3. Discharge the pressure reservoir by pushing in on the brake pedal about 10 times. Draw off hydraulic fluid in the supply tank.
4. Unscrew the bolt and press the tie rod off the steering drop arm with the proper tool.
5. Remove the heat shield on the steering gear and disconnect the ride level height control pipes on the 750iL.
6. Remove the bolt and push the U-joint from the steering gear. Disconnect and plug the hydraulic lines.
7. Unscrew the steering gear mounting bolts and remove the steering gear.

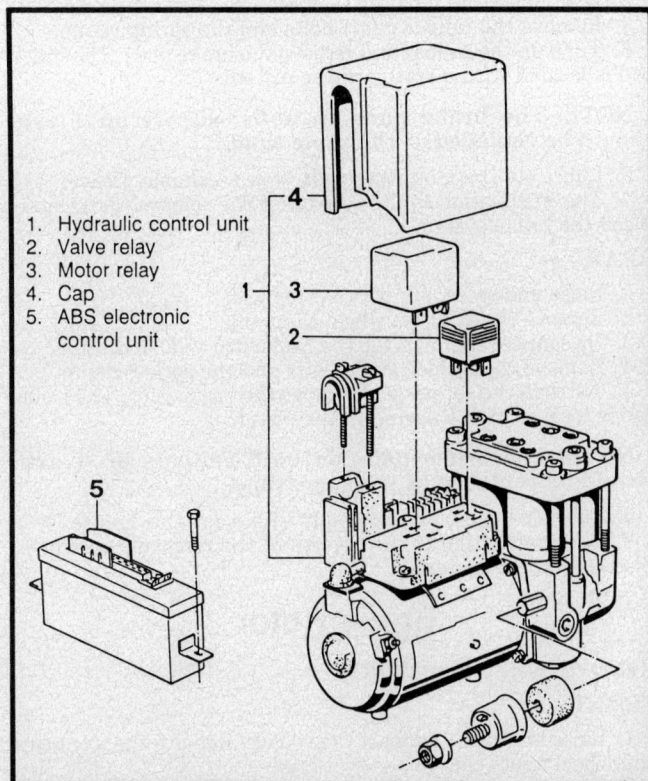

1. Hydraulic control unit
2. Valve relay
3. Motor relay
4. Cap
5. ABS electronic control unit

ABS components

NOTE: If necessary, move the steering drop arm by turning the steering stub to enable the removal of the gear assembly.

To install:

8. Install the steering gear and tighten the mounting bolts.
9. Connect the hydraulic lines, using new seals.
10. Turn the steering wheel counterclockwise or clockwise against the stop and then it back about 1.7 turns until the marks are aligned.
11. Connect the U-joint to the steering gear making sure the bolt is in the locking groove of the steering stub.
12. Install the tie rod to the steering drop arm and replace the self locking nut.
13. Replace the heat shield on the steering gear and connect the ride level height control pipes on the 750iL.
14. Refill the hydraulic fluid and replace the steering wheel, if equipped with an airbag (SRS).
15. Connect the negative battery cable.

Power Steering Pump

Removal and Installation

1. Disconnect the negative battery cable. Release the pressure from the reservoir.
2. Draw the hydraulic fluid from the pump reservoir. Disconnect and plug the hydraulic lines.
3. Disconnect and plug the hydraulic lines. Remove the bolts and loosen the nuts to turn the adjusting pinion.
4. Remove the drive belt.
5. Remove the bolts from the brackets holding the pump and remove the pump assembly.
6. Reverse the removal procedure for installation. Tighten the adjusting pinion to 6 ft. lbs.
7. If equipped with a tandem pump the removal and installation procedure is the same.

Belt Adjustment

Tighten the drive belt so when pressure is applied to the belt, the distance between both belt pulleys is 5–10mm of deflection.

1. Disconnect the negative battery cable. Loosen the nuts on the adjusting pinion.
2. Tighten the belt to the recommended specification and tighten the adjusting pinion nuts.
3. Connect the negative battery cable.

System Bleeding

1. Fill the reservoir to the **MAX** mark on the oil stick.
2. Rotate the steering in both directions fully, to each stop, until all the air is removed from the fluid.
3. Check the oil level and fill to the specified mark, if necessary.

Tie Rod Ends

Removal and Installation

1. Raise and safely support the vehicle. Loosen the clamping bolt that retains the toe-in adjustment by keeping the tie rod end from turning in relation to the tie rod.
2. Remove the cotter pin and castellated or self-locking nut from the bottom of the tie rod end. Then, press the tie rod end out of the steering knuckle with the proper tool. Then, unscrew the tie rod end from the tie rod and remove it, counting the number of turns required.
3. Install in reverse order, using a new cotter pin or castellated nut. Recheck the front alignment and reset the toe-in if necessary. Torque the castellated or self-locking nut to 26.5 ft. lbs. and the clamping screw to 10 ft. lbs. Final torque the clamping bolt with the vehicle resting on its wheels.

BRAKES

Master Cylinder

Removal and Installation

1. Disconnect the negative battery cable. Draw off the brake fluid from the reservoir.
2. Remove the plug and disconnect the hydraulic lines. Remove the hose for the hydraulic clutch, if needed.
3. Remove the reservoir. Remove the mounting bolts and lift out the master cylinder.
4. Install the master cylinder, making sure the rubber ring is making a good seal.
5. The remainder of the installation is the reverse of the removal procedure. Bleed the brake system and connect the negative battery cable.

Proportioning Valve

Removal and Installation

318iS, 325, 325i, 325iS, 325iX AND M3

1. Disconnect the negative battery cable. Draw off hydraulic fluid from the master cylinder with a syringe or hose used only with clean brake fluid.
2. Disconnect the brake lines at the top and bottom of the proportioning valve.
3. Remove the clamp from the valve and disconnect the pressure connection at the union.
4. Check day/year codes, reduction factor, and switch-over pressure to make sure the new valve is identical.
5. Install in reverse order. Bleed the system.

Power Brake Booster

Removal and Installation

1. Disconnect the negative battery cable. Draw off brake fluid in the reservoir and discard.
2. Remove the reservoir and disconnect the clutch hydraulic hose.
3. Disconnect all brake lines from the master cylinder.
4. Remove the instrument panel trim from the bottom/left inside the passenger compartment.
5. Remove the return spring from the brake pedal. Press off the clip and remove the pin which connects the booster rod to the brake pedal.
6. Remove the 4 nuts and pull the booster and master cylinder off in the engine compartment.
7. If the filter in the brake booster is clogged, it will have to be cleaned. To do this, remove the dust boot, retainer, damper, and filter, and clean the damper and filter. Make sure when reinstalling that the slots in the damper and filter are offset 180 degrees.
8. Install in reverse order. Adjust the stoplight switch for a clearance of 0.197–0.236 in.
9. Inspect the rubber seal between the master cylinder and booster and replace it, if necessary.

Brake Caliper

Removal and Installation
FRONT

1. Disconnect the negative battery cable. Draw off brake fluid with a suitable syringe.

2. Disconnect the hydraulic brake lines.
3. Raise and safely support the vehicle. Remove the front tire and wheel assembly.
4. Remove the caliper mounting bolts and disconnect the brake pad wear indicator plug.
5. Remove the caliper assembly.
6. The installation is the reverse of the removal procedure. Bleed the brake system. Tighten the caliper mounting bolts to 63–79 ft. lbs. on the 3 Series and 80–89 ft. lbs. except on the 3 Series. Tighten the guide bolts to 22–25 ft. lbs.

NOTE: Make sure the brake wear indicator wire is held in the correct position by the tab of the dust cap.

REAR

1. Disconnect the negative battery cable. Draw off brake fluid with a suitable syringe.
2. Disconnect the hydraulic brake lines.
3. Raise and safely support the vehicle. Remove the rear tire and wheel assembly.
4. Remove the caliper mounting bolts and disconnect the brake pad wear indicator plug.
5. Remove the caliper assembly by pulling to the rear.
6. The installation is the reverse of the removal procedure. Bleed the brake system. Tighten the mounting bolts to 42–48 ft. lbs. and the guide bolts to 22–25 ft. lbs.

Disc Brake Pads

Removal and Installation
FRONT

1. Raise and safely support the vehicle.
2. Remove the tire and wheel assembly.
3. Disconnect the plug for the brake pad wear indicator
4. Remove the caliper guide bolts and the spring clamp.
5. Turn up the caliper and remove the brake pads. The inner pad is located with a spring in the piston.

NOTE: The brake pads on both calipers on 1 axle should be replaced at the same time.

6. Lubricate the mounting pads with a suitable grease.
7. The installation is the reverse of the removal procedure. Bleed the brake system.

REAR

1. Raise and safely support the vehicle.
2. Remove the tire and wheel assembly.
3. Disconnect the plug for the brake pad wear indicator
4. Remove the caliper guide bolts and the spring clamp.
5. Turn up the caliper and remove the brake pads. The inner pad is located with a spring in the piston.

NOTE: The brake pads on both calipers on 1 axle should be replaced at the same time.

6. Lubricate the mounting pads with a suitable grease.
7. The installation is the reverse of the removal procedure. Bleed the brake system.

Brake Rotor

Removal and Installation
FRONT

1. Raise and safely support the vehicle. Remove the front tire and wheel assembly.
2. Disconnect the rubber grommet from the bracket, if equipped.

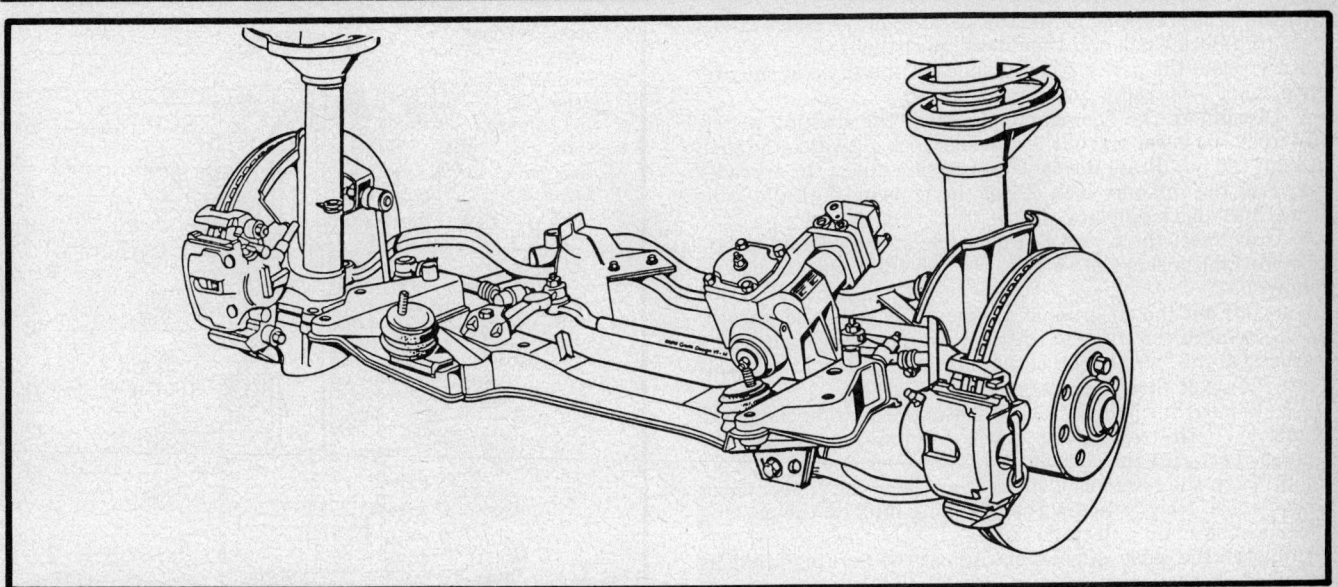

View of the front suspension—5 and 7 Series vehicles

3. Disconnect the plug for the brake pad indicator, if necessary.

4. Disconnect and support the caliper, using a piece of wire.

5. Remove the mounting bolts and remove the brake rotor with the proper tool.

NOTE: The inboard vented discs are balanced. Never remove or reposition the balance clamps.

6. The installation is the reverse of the removal procedure.

REAR

1. Raise and safely support the vehicle. Remove the tire and wheel assembly.

2. Disconnect and support the caliper, using a piece of wire.

3. Remove the mounting bolts and remove the brake rotor with the proper tool.

4. Always replace both discs of 1 axle.

5. The installation is the reverse of the removal procedure. Adjust the parking brake.

6. The parking brake must be broken in after replacing the rear brake discs. This is done in the following steps:
   a. Step 1—5 complete stops from 30 mph
   b. Step 2—Allow the brakes to cool off
   c. Step 3—5 complete stops from 30 mph

Parking Brake Cable

Adjustment

1. The parking brake should be adjusted when the lever can be pulled up more than 8 notches. First, remove the cover pate on the console, the handbrake lever protrudes through this plate. Then, loosen the locknuts and loosen the adjusting nuts for the cables until they are nearly at the ends of the threads.

2. Support the vehicle securely off the rear wheels. Remove one wheel bolt from each rear wheel. Then, rotate one wheel until the hole left by removing the bolt is about 45 degrees counterclockwise from the 6 o'clock position. This will line the hole in the wheel with the star wheel which adjusts the rear brake shoes which is used for parking only. If it is difficult to turn the star wheel it will help to remove the rear wheel and, if necessary, the brake disc.

3. Turn the adjusting star wheel with a screwdriver until the rear wheel or brake disc can no longer be turned. Then, back it off 4–6 threads.

4. In the passenger compartment, pull the handbrake up 4 notches. Then, turn the cable adjusting nuts in the tightening direction until the rear wheels can just barely be turned. Make sure the adjustment is uniform. Lock the adjusting nuts in position.

5. Release the handbrake and make sure the wheels can now be turned easily, repeating Step 4 to correct a failure to release if necessary.

Removal and Installation

1. Raise and safely support the vehicle. Remove the rear tire and wheel assembly.

2. Remove the rear brake discs.

2. Using brake spring pliers, disconnect the upper return spring for the parking brake shoes. Then, using the proper tool,

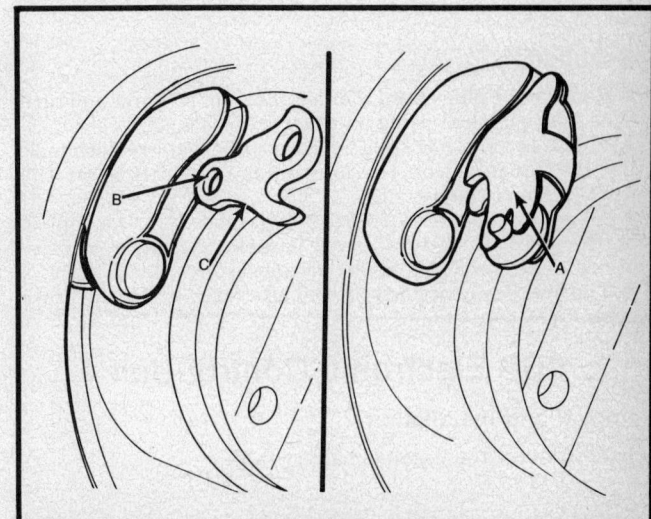

To disconnect the rear brake cable on the 735i, pull the spreader lock assembly (A) out of the housing and remove the pin at the lower end. Disconnect the cable at (B); pull the inner portion of the spreader lock (C) out of the housing

turn the retaining springs for the parking brake shoes 90 degrees to unlock them and then disconnect them.

3. Separate the parking brake shoes at the top and then remove them from below.

4. Disconnect the spreader locks from the backing plates: first, rock the lower end of the spreader lock outward, and then pull out the pin. Press the cable connection out of the spreader lock. Pull the spreader lock out of the housing. Pull the cable through the backing plate.

5. Disconnect the parking brake cable at the trailing arm.

6. Working inside the vehicle, remove the console cover as follows:

  a. Lift out the air grille and remove the nuts underneath.

  b. Remove the cap and unscrew the mounting bolt that's located at the forward end of the console on the right side. Lift out the cover that the bolt retains.

  c. Remove the bolt on the left side of the forward end of the console. If the vehicle has power windows, disconnect the plugs. Then, lift the console and remove air ducts.

  d. Turn the retainer 90 degrees and peel the rubber cover downward. Now, unscrew the adjusting nuts on the parking brake cables and pull them out.

7. Install the cable in position. Adjust the parking brake as described above.

Brake System Bleeding

1. Fill the master cylinder to the maximum level with the proper brake fluid.

2. Raise and safely support the vehicle. Remove the protective caps from the bleeder screws.

3. The proper bleeding sequence always start with the brake unit farthest from the master cylinder. The proper bleeding sequence is: right rear, left rear, right front and lrft front.

4. Insert a tight fitting plastic tube over the bleeder screw on the caliper and the other end of the tube in a transparent container partially filled with clean brake fluid.

5. Loosen the bleeder screw and release the brake fluid. Tighten the bleeder screw when the escaping brake fluid is free of air bubbles.

6. Repeat this step on all 4 wheels. Lower the vehicle.

Anti-Lock Brake System Service

Precautions

- Remove the plugs from the electronic control unit and turn off the ignition when using an electric welder.
- If the battery has been removed, the battery terminals must be tightened on the end poles perfectly after the reinstallation of the battery.
- After the replacement of the hydraulic unit, the control unit, the speed sensors or the wire harness, the entire ABS system has to be checked with the proper tester.
- The brake system must be bled after each job on the brake system.

ABS Electronic Control Unit

Removal and Installation

1. Disconnect the negative battery cable.

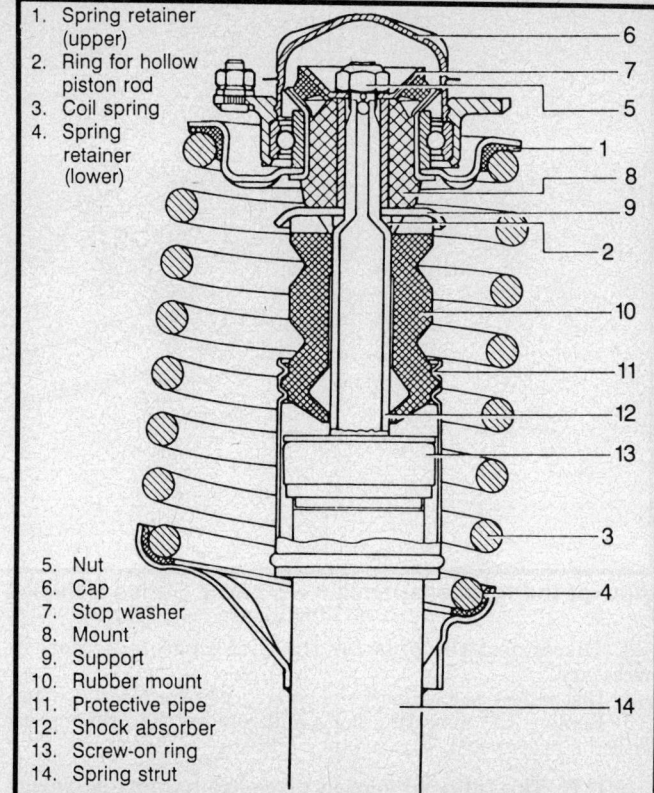

1. Spring retainer (upper)
2. Ring for hollow piston rod
3. Coil spring
4. Spring retainer (lower)
5. Nut
6. Cap
7. Stop washer
8. Mount
9. Support
10. Rubber mount
11. Protective pipe
12. Shock absorber
13. Screw-on ring
14. Spring strut

Exploded view of the spring strut assembly

2. Remove the cover in the engine compartment on the right side.

3. Push back the clamp. Pull off the right side then disengage the left side of the multiple plug.

4. Remove the mounting bolts and lift out the control unit.

5. The installation is the reverse of the removal procedure.

Hydraulic Unit

Removal and Installation

1. Disconnect the negative battery cable.

2. Disconnect and plug the hydraulic brake lines at the unit. Do not mix up the brake lines. The lines are marked as follows:

  a. VL–LF Brake Caliper
  b. VR–RF Brake Caliper
  c. HL–LR Brake Caliper
  d. HR–RR Brake Caliper

3. Remove the cover mounting bolts and lift off the cover.

4. Disconnect the electrical connections and plugs.

5. Loosen the mounting nuts, pull up and remove the hydraulic control unit.

6. The installation is the reverse of the removal procedure. Bleed the brake system.

FRONT SUSPENSION

MacPherson Strut

Removal and Installation

318iS, 325, 325i, 325iS AND M3

1. Disconnect the negative battery cable.
2. Raise and safely support the vehicle. Remove the tire and wheel assembly.
3. Disconnect the brake pad wear indicator plug and ground wire. Pull the wires out of the holder on the strut. Remove the ABS pulse sender, if equipped.
4. Unbolt the caliper and pull it away from the strut, suspending it with a piece of wire from the body. Do not disconnect the brake line.
5. Remove the attaching nut and then detach the push rod on the stabilizer bar at the strut.
6. Unscrew the attaching nut and press off the guide joint with the proper tool.
7. Unscrew the nut and press off the tie rod joint.
8. Press the bottom of the strut outward and push it over the guide joint pin, using the proper tool. Support the bottom of the strut.

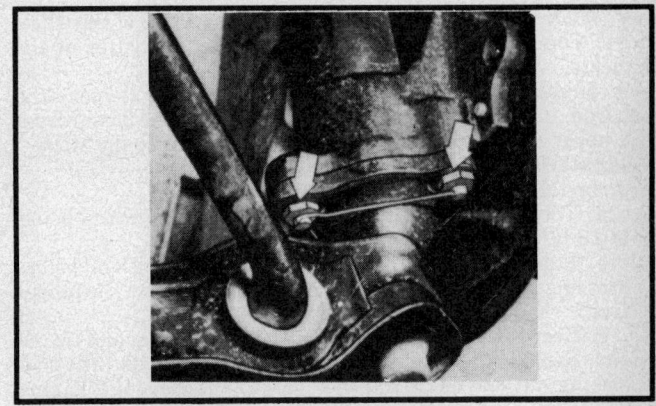

Lock wire location at strut assembly

9. Unscrew the nuts at the top of the strut, from inside the engine
compartment, then remove the strut.

To install:

10. Install in reverse order, observing the following points:
    a. Replace the self-locking nuts that fasten the top of the strut.
    b. Tie rod and guide joints must have both pins and both bores clean for reassembly. Replace both self-locking nuts.
    c. Torque the control arm to spring strut attaching nut to 43–51 ft. lbs. Torque the spring strut to wheel well nuts to 16–17 ft. lbs.

325iX

1. Disconnect the negative battery cable.
2. Raise and safely support the vehicle. Remove the front tire and wheel assembly. Unplug the ABS pulse transmitter.
3. Lift out the lock plate at the center of the brake disc with a screwdriver. Unscrew the collar nut.
4. Disconnect the brake pad wear indicator plug and the ground wire. Pull the wires and brake hose out of the clip on the spring strut. Then, disconnect the small rod at the strut.
5. Remove the brake caliper mounting bolts and support the assembly with a piece of wire, keeping stress off the brake hose.

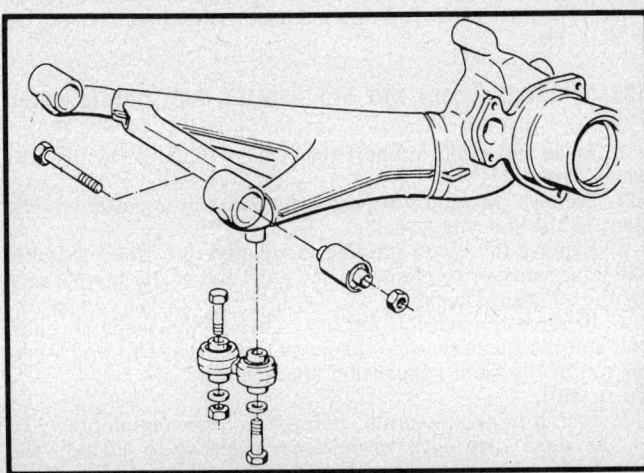

View of the trailing arm assembly—5 and 7 series

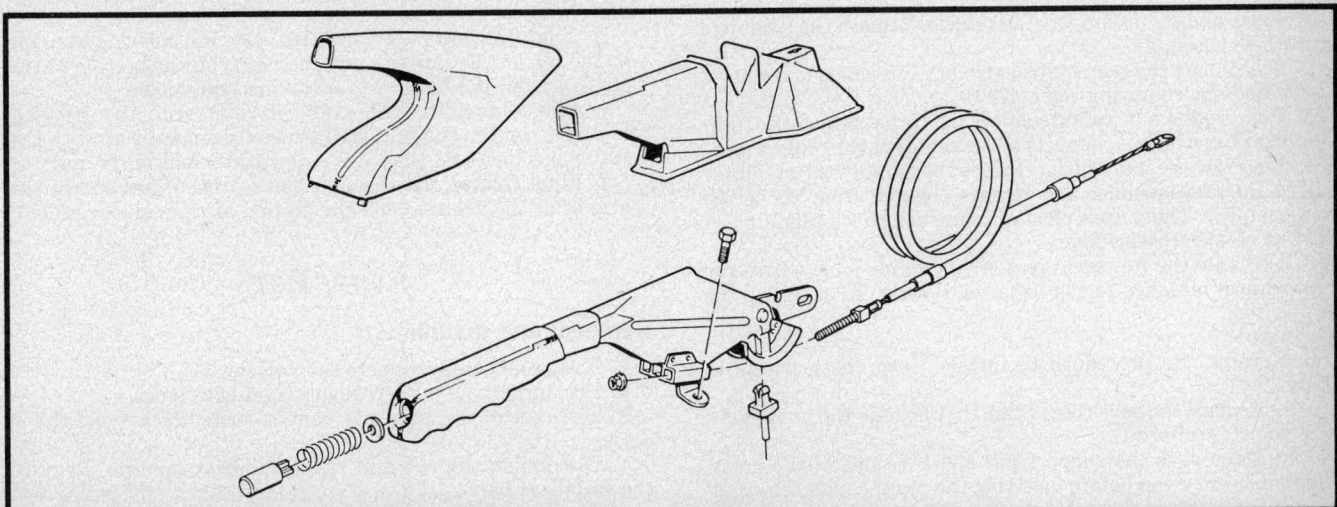

Exploded view of the parking brake lever assembly

6. Remove the attaching nut from the tie rod end. Then press the stud off the knuckle with the proper tool.

7. Remove the attaching nut for the control arm and then press the stud off the knuckle with an appropriate tool.

8. Mount the proper tool to the brake disc with 2 of the wheel bolts. Then, press the output shaft out of the center of the knuckle.

9. Support the spring strut from underneath. Remove the cap from the center of the wheel house. Remove the 3 bolts from the upper mount near the wheel housing. Remove the strut.

To install:

10. Install the strut, observing these points:

a. Torque the nuts attaching the strut to the wheel house to 16 ft. lbs.

b. Lubricate the splines of the output shaft with oil before pressing it back into the center of the knuckle with the proper tool.

c. Keep grease off the studs for the control arm and tie rod end. Replace the cotter pin on the control arm and the self-locking nut on the tie rod end. Torque the control arm stud nut to 61.5 ft. lbs. Torque the tie rod nut to 61.5 ft. lbs. and then tighten it further to install the cotter pin, if necessary.

d. Replace the lock plate in the center of the disc with the proper tool.

e. Torque the bolts attaching the caliper to the steering knuckle to 63–79 ft. lbs. Lower the vehicle.

f. Connect the negative battery cable.

525, 525i, 528e, 535i, M5, M6, 635CSi, 735i, 735iL AND 750iL

1. Disconnect the negative battery cable.

2. Raise and safely support the vehicle. Remove the tire and wheel assembly.

3. Disconnect the brake pad wear indicator plug and ground wire. Pull the wires out of the holder on the strut. Remove the ABS pulse sender, if equipped.

4. Disconnect the stabilizer pushrod with the proper tool.

5. Disconnect the lower strut bolts at the control arm.

6. Support the bottom of the strut and unscrew the nuts at the top of the strut, from inside the engine compartment. Remove the strut.

7. The installation is the reverse of the removal procedure.

Lower Control Arms

Removal and Installation

318iS, 325, 325i 325iS AND M3

1. Raise and safely support the vehicle. Remove the front tire and wheel assembly.

2. Disconnect the rear control arm bracket where it connects to the body by removing the bolts.

3. Remove the nut and disconnect the thrust rod on the front stabilizer bar where it connects to the center of the control arm.

4. Unscrew the nut which attaches the front of the stabilizer bar to the crossmember and remove the nut from above the crossmember. Then, use a plastic hammer to knock this support pin out of the crossmember.

5. Unscrew the nut and press off the guide joint where the control arm attaches to the lower end of the strut, using the proper tool.

To install:

6. Reverse the procedure to install. Keep these points in mind:

a. Replace the self-locking nut that fastens the guide joint to the control arm.

b. Make sure the support pin and the bore in the crossmember are clean before inserting the pin through the crossmember. Replace the original nut with a replacement nut and washer.

c. Torque the control arm-to-spring strut nut to 43–51 ft. lbs. Torque the control arm support to crossmember nut to 29–34 ft. lbs. Torque the push rod on the stabilizer bar to 29–34 ft. lbs.

325iX

1. Raise and safely support the vehicle. Remove the tire and wheel assembly.

2. Disconnect the rear control arm bracket where it connects to the body by removing the bolts.

2. Remove the nut from the top of the stud that attaches to one corner of the control arm and runs through the crossmember.

3. Remove the cotter pin and then remove the nut from the ball joint stud where it passes through the steering knuckle. Then, press the ball joint stud out of the knuckle with the proper tool. Make sure to keep the stud and bore free of grease.

4. Reverse the procedure to install. Keep these points in mind:

a. Make sure the support pin and the bore in the crossmember are clean before inserting the pin through the crossmember. Replace the original nut with a replacement nut and washer equivalent to those shown in the illustration.

b. Torque the control arm-to-spring strut nut to 61.5 ft. lbs. Turn the nut farther, as necessary to align the castellations with the cotter pin hole and install a new cotter pin. Torque the control arm support to crossmember nut to 30 ft. lbs.

525, 525i, 528e, 535i, M5, M6, 635CSi, 735i, 735iL AND 750iL

1. Raise and safely support the vehicle. Remove the tire and wheel assembly.

2. Remove the mounting bolts that fasten the bottom of the strut to the steering knuckle.

3. Remove the cotter pin and castellated nut. Use a suitable ball joint remover to press the ball joint end of the control arm off the steering knuckle.

4. Remove the self-locking nut. Then, remove the through bolt and the washers, slide the inner end of the strut and bushing out of the front suspension crossmember.

To install:

5. Install in reverse order, noting the following points:

a. Make sure both washers are replaced to cushion the bushing where it contacts the suspension crossmember.

b. Replace the bushing if it is worn or cracked.

c. Use a new self-locking nut on the bolt fastening the inner end of the strut.

d. Align the bottom of the strut with the steering knuckle so the tab on the arm fits into the notch on the bottom of the strut. Install the bolts with a locking type sealer.

e. When installing the arm ball joint onto the steering knuckle, tighten the nut until a castellation lines up with the cotter pin hole and then use a new cotter pin in the nut.

f. Final tighten the through bolt for the inner end of the arm after the vehicle is on the ground at normal ride height.

Sway Bar

Removal and Installation

1. Raise and safely support the vehicle.

2. Disconnect the push/thrust rod on both sides.

3. Disconnect the left side control arm bracket on the 3 Series.

4. Disconnect the left and right stabilizer mounts. Remove the stabilizer bar.

5. The installation is the reverse of the removal procedure. Tighten the stabilizer mount bolts to 16 ft. lbs.

Front Wheel Bearings

Removal and Installation

318iS, 325, 325i, 325iS AND M3

1. Raise and safely support the vehicle. Remove the tire and wheel assembly.

2. Remove the attaching bolts and remove and suspend the brake caliper, hanging it from the body so as to avoid putting stress on the brake line.

3. Remove the setscrew with an Allen® wrench. Pull off the brake disc and pry off the dust cover with a small prybar.

4. Using a chisel, knock the tab on the collar nut away from the shaft. Unscrew and discard the nut.

5. Pull off the bearing with a suitable bearing puller and discard it. On the M3, install the main bracket of the puller with 3 wheel bolts.

6. If the inside bearing inner race remains on the stub axle, unbolt and remove the dust guard. Bend back the inner dust guard and pull the inner race off with a special tool capable of getting under the race. Reinstall the dust guard.

7. If the dust guard has been removed, install a new one. Install a special tool over the stub axle and screw it in for the entire length of the guide sleeve's threads. Press the bearing on.

8. Reverse the remaining removal procedures to install the disc and caliper. Torque the wheel hub collar nut to 188 ft. lbs. Lock the collar nut by bending over the tab.

525, 525i, 528e, 535i, M5, M6, 635CSi, 735i, 735iL AND 750iL

1. Raise and safely support the vehicle. Remove the tire and wheel assembly.

2. Remove the attaching bolts and remove and suspend the brake caliper, hanging it from the body so as to avoid putting stress on the brake line.

3. Remove the setscrew with an Allen® wrench. Pull off the brake disc and pry off the dust cover with a small prybar.

4. Using a chisel, knock the tab on the collar nut away from the shaft. Unscrew and discard the nut.

5. Using the proper tool, pull off the bearing and discard it.

6. If the inside bearing inner race remains on the stub axle, unscrew and remove the dust guard, using a socket extension. Bend back the inner dust guard and pull the inner race off with a special tool capable of getting under the race. Reinstall the dust guard and install a new dust cover.

7. Then install a special tool over the stub axle and screw it in for the entire length of the guide sleeve's threads. Slide the bearing on and follow it with the proper tool and use this tool to press the bearing on.

8. Reverse the remaining removal procedures to install the disc and caliper. Torque the wheel hub collar nut to 210 ft. lbs. Lock the collar nut by bending over the tab.

9. Install a new grease cap coated with a suitable sealer.

REAR SUSPENSION

Shock Absorbers

Removal and Installation

318iS, 325, 325i, 325iS, 325iX AND M3

1. Raise and safely support the vehicle. Support the control arms.

2. If equipped with ride level control, perform the following:
   a. Disconnect the negative battery cable.
   b. Remove the rear seat cushion. Disconnect the left or right plug under the insulation sheet and guide the electric wire through the hole in the floor plate.
   c. Remove the rear tire and wheel assembly. Disconnect the electrical connection.

NOTE: The control arm must be securely supported throughout this procedure.

3. Remove the side backrest, seat belts and unscrew the centering shell on the wheel house.

4. Remove the lower shock retaining bolt.

5. Remove trim inside the trunk, if necessary, and disconnect the upper strut retaining nuts at the wheel arch and remove the assembly.

6. Remove the shock absorber.

To install:

7. Install in reverse order, using new gaskets between the shock and the wheel arch, and new self-locking nuts on top of the strut.

8. Torque the shock-to-body nuts to 16–17 ft. lbs.; spring retainer-to-wheel house nuts—6 cyl. to 16–17 ft. lbs.; lower bolt to 52–63 ft. lbs. on 4 cylinder engines or 90–103 ft. lbs. on 6 cylinder engines.

9. Final torquing of the lower strut bolt should be done with the vehicle in the normal riding position.

MacPherson Strut

Removal and Installation

525, 525i, 528e, 535i, M5, M6, 635CSi, 735i, 735iL AND 750iL

1. Disconnect the negative battery cable. Remove the rear seat and back rest.

2. Raise and safely support the vehicle. Support the control arms.

NOTE: The coil spring, shock absorber assembly acts as a strap so the control arm should always be supported.

3. If equipped with automatic ride control perform the following:
   a. Diasconnect the low pressure switch electrical connection and turn on the ignition.
   b. Disconnect the control rod nut, holding the collar with an 8mm wrench against torque. Don't disconnect the rod at the ball joint.
   c. Operate the lever on the control switch in the "discharge" direction for about 20 seconds to discharge fluid from the lines.
   d. Disconnect the hydraulic line on the shock absorber.

4. Remove the lower shock retaining bolt.

5. Remove trim if necessary and disconnect the upper strut retaining nuts at the wheel arch and remove the assembly.

To install:

6. Install in reverse order, using new gaskets between the strut and the wheel arch, and new self-locking nuts on top of the strut. Torque the shock-to-body nuts to 16–17 ft. lbs.; spring retainer-to-wheel house nut to 16–17 ft. lbs. Tighten the lower bolt to 52–63 ft. lbs. on the M3 and 90–103 ft. lbs. except on the M3. Replace the gasket that goes between the top of the strut and the lower surface of the wheel well, if necessary. Final

torquing of the lower strut bolt should be done with the vehicle in the normal riding position.

Coil Springs

Removal and Installation

318iS, 325, 325i, 325iS, 325iX AND M3

1. Raise and safely support the vehicle.
2. Disconnect the rear portion of the exhaust system and hang it from the body.
3. Disconnect the final drive rubber mount, push it down, and hold it down with a wedge.
4. Remove the bolt that connects the rear stabilizer bar to the strut on the side being worked on. Be careful not to damage the brake line.

NOTE: **Support the lower control arm securely with a jack or other device that will permit it to be lowered gradually, while maintaining secure support.**

5. Then, to prevent damage to the output shaft joints, lower the control arm only enough to slip the coil spring off the retainer.
6. Make sure, in replacing the spring, that the same part number, color code, and proper rubber ring are used.
7. Reverse all removal procedures to install, making sure the spring is in proper position, keeping the control arm securely supported until the shock bolt is replaced, and tightening stabilizer bar and lower shock mount bolts with the control arm in the normal ride position.
8. Torque the stabilizer bolt to 22–24 ft. lbs. and the shock bolt to 52–63 ft. lbs.

Trailing Arms

Removal and Installation

318iS, 325, 325i, 325iS, 325iX AND M3

1. Raise and safely support the vehicle. Remove the tire and wheel assembly.
2. Apply the parking brake and disconnect the output shaft at the rear axle shaft, if necessary. Remove the parking brake lever.
3. Remove the brake fluid from the master cylinder reservoir. To do this, it will be necessary to remove the strainer at the top of the reservoir. Disconnect the brake line connection on the rear control arm. Plug the openings.
34. Support the trailing arm securely. Disconnect the shock absorber at the control arm.
4. Remove the nuts and then slide the bolts out of the mounts where the trailing arm is mounted to the axle carrier.
To install:
5. Install in reverse order. Install the bolt that goes into the inner bracket first.
6. Torque the bolts holding the trailing arm to the axle carrier to 48–54 ft. lbs.

1. Spacer ring
2. Washer
3. Wishbone

Detaching the lower arm at front axle beam

7. Make sure the spring is positioned properly top and bottom. Torque the strut bolt to 52–63 ft. lbs.
8. Reinstall the handbrake or reconnect the cable and adjust. Then apply the brake and reconnect the output shaft.
9. Reconnect the brake line, replenish with the proper brake fluid, and bleed the system.

525, 525i, 528e, 535i, M5, M6, 635CSi, 735i, 735iL AND 750iL

1. Raise and safely support the vehicle. Remove the tire and wheel assembly.
2. Apply the parking brake to hold the driveshaft stationary. Disconnect the output shaft at the drive flange. Hang the shaft from the body by a piece of wire.
3. Disconnect the parking brake cable at the lever.
4. Remove the float housing from the brake fluid reservoir and then remove as much fluid as possible from the reservoir.
5. Pull the brake cable housing out of the mounting bracket near the control arm. Disconnect the brake line.
6. Pull down and disconnect the plug for the pulse sender, do not damage the rubber grommet. On the 750iL, remove the rear seat to gain access to the pulse sender.
7. Remove the rear pushrod and disconnect the camber warning sender on the rear axle carrier on the 750iL.
8. Support the trailing arm from underneath in a secure manner.
9. Remove the nuts and then remove the bolts to disconnect the control arm from the rear axle carrier.
10. If the vehicle has a stabilizer bar, remove the bolts and remove the attaching bracket for the stabilizer bar.
11. Disconnect the shock absorber and remove the control arm.
12. Installation is the reverse of removal. When reattaching the control arm, insert the bolt on the inner bracket first.
13. Tighten all mounting bolts with the vehicle resting on its wheels. Torque the bolts attaching the control arm to the axle carrier to 49–54 ft. lbs. Refill and bleed the brake system.

SERIAL NUMBER IDENTIFICATION

Vehicle Identification Plate

The Vehicle Information Code is attached to the bulkhead on the firewall, in the engine compartment. The plate shows model code, engine model, transaxle model and body color code.

Engine Number

The engine number is stamped at the right front side, on the top edge of the cylinder block and contains the engine model number and engine serial number.

Serial number location

Vehicle Identification Number

The vehicle identification plate is mounted on the instrument panel, adjacent to the lower corner of the windshield on the driver's side and is visible through the windshield. A standardized 17 digit Vehicle Identification Number (VIN) is used.

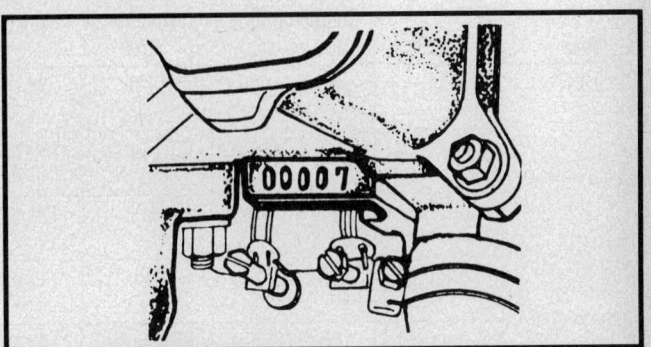

Engine number location

Engine model number

Chassis Number

The chassis number plate is stamped on the top center of the firewall, located in the engine compartment.

SPECIFICATIONS
ENGINE IDENTIFICATION

Year	Model	Engine Displacement cu. in. (cc/liter)	Engine Series Identification	No. of Cylinders	Engine Type
1987	Colt	89.6 (1468/1.5)	G15B	4	SOHC
	Colt	97.5 (1597/1.6)	G32B, 4G32	4	SOHC
	Colt Vista	121.9 (1997/2.0)	G63B	4	SOHC
	Conquest	155.9 (2555/2.6)	G54B	4	SOHC
1988	Colt	89.6 (1468/1.5)	G15B	4	SOHC
	Colt	97.5 (1597/1.6)	G32B	4	SOHC
	Colt Vista	121.9 (1997/2.0)	G63B	4	SOHC
	Conquest	155.9 (2555/2.6)	G54B	4	SOHC
1989	Colt	89.6 (1468/1.5)	4G15	4	SOHC
	Colt	97.3 (1595/1.6)	4G61	4	DOHC
	Colt Wagon	107.1 (1755/1.8)	G37	4	SOHC
	Colt Vista	121.9 (1997/2.0)	G63B	4	SOHC
	Conquest	155.9 (2555/2.6)	G54B	4	SOHC
1990-91	Colt	89.6 (1468/1.5)	4G15	4	SOHC
	Colt	97.3 (1595/1.6)	4G61	4	DOHC
	Colt Wagon	107.1 (1755/1.8)	G37	4	SOHC
	Colt Vista	121.9 (1997/2.0)	G63B	4	SOHC

GENERAL ENGINE SPECIFICATIONS

Year	Model	Engine Displacement cu. in. (cc)	Fuel System Type	Net Horsepower @ rpm	Net Torque @ rpm (ft. lbs.)	Bore × Stroke (in.)	Compression Ratio	Oil Pressure @ rpm
1987	Colt	89.6 (1468)	Carb.	68 @ 5000	84 @ 3000	2.99 × 3.23	9.4:1	50–64 @ 750
	Colt	97.5 (1597)	EFI/Turbo	102 @ 5500	122 @ 3000	3.03 × 3.39	7.6:1	57–71 @ 700
	Colt Vista	121.9 (1997)	MPI	120 @ 5000	108 @ 3500	3.34 × 3.46	8.5:1	57–71 @ 700
	Conquest	155.9 (2555)	EFI	145 @ 5000	185 @ 2500	3.59 × 3.86	7.0:1	50–54 @ 850
	Conquest	155.9 (2555)	EFI/Turbo	170 @ 5000	220 @ 2500	3.59 × 3.86	7.0:1	50–54 @ 850
1988	Colt	89.6 (1468)	Carb.	68 @ 5000	84 @ 3000	2.99 × 3.23	9.4:1	50–64 @ 750
	Colt	97.5 (1597)	ECI	102 @ 5500	122 @ 3000	3.03 × 3.39	7.6:1	57–71 @ 700
	Colt Vista	121.9 (1997)	MPI	120 @ 5000	108 @ 3500	3.34 × 3.46	8.5:1	57–71 @ 700
	Conquest	155.9 (2555)	EFI/Turbo	170 @ 5000	220 @ 5000	3.59 × 3.86	7.0:1	50–54 @ 850
1989	Colt	89.6 (1468)	MPI	68 @ 5500	82 @ 3500	3.00 × 3.23	9.4:1	50–64 @ 750
	Colt	97 (1595)	MPI	102 @ 5500	122 @ 3000	3.24 × 2.95	8.0:1	57–71 @ 700
	Colt Wagon	107.1 (1755)	MPI	87 @ 5000	102 @ 5000	3.17 × 3.39	9.0:1	63 @ 2000
	Colt Vista	121 (1997)	MPI	120 @ 5000	116 @ 4500	3.35 × 3.46	8.5:1	42.7 @ 2000
	Conquest	155.9 (2555)	EFI/Turbo	140 @ 5000	317 @ 2500	3.59 × 3.86	7.0:1	56.5 @ 2000
1990–91	Colt	89.6 (1468)	MPI	68 @ 5500	126 @ 3000	2.99 × 3.23	9.4:1	42 @ 2000
	Colt	97 (1595)	MPI	92 @ 6500	134 @ 5000	3.24 × 2.95	8.0:1	42 @ 2000
	Colt Wagon	107.1 (1755)	MPI	65 @ 5000	138 @ 3000	3.17 × 3.39	9.0:1	42 @ 2000
	Colt Vista	122 (1997)	MPI	72 @ 5000	153 @ 3500	3.35 × 3.46	8.5:1	42.7 @ 2000

GASOLINE ENGINE TUNE-UP SPECIFICATIONS

Year	Model	Engine Displacement cu. in. (cc)	Spark Plugs Type	Spark Plugs Gap (in.)	Ignition Timing (deg.) MT	Ignition Timing (deg.) AT	Compression Pressure (psi)	Fuel Pump (psi)	Idle Speed (rpm) MT	Idle Speed (rpm) AT	Valve Clearance In.	Valve Clearance Ex.
1987	Colt	89.6 (1468)	BPR6ES-11	0.039–0.040	5B	5B	NA	2.7–3.7	700	750	0.006	0.010 ①
	Colt	97.4 (1597)	BPR6ES-11	0.039–0.040	10B	10B	NA	33.6	700	700	0.006	0.010 ①
	Colt Vista	121.9 (1997)	BPR6ES-11	0.039–0.040	5B	5B	NA	36.3	700	700	Hyd. ①	Hyd. ①
	Conquest	155.9 (2555)	BPR6ES-11	0.039–0.040	10B	10B	NA	33.6	850	850	Hyd. ①	Hyd. ①

GASOLINE ENGINE TUNE-UP SPECIFICATIONS

Year	Model	Engine Displacement cu. in. (cc)	Spark Plugs Type	Gap (in.)	Ignition Timing (deg.) MT	AT	Compression Pressure (psi)	Fuel Pump (psi)	Idle Speed (rpm) MT	AT	Valve Clearance In.	Ex.
1988	Colt	89.6 (1468)	BPR6ES-11	0.039–0.040	5B	5B	NA	2.7–3.7	700	750	0.006	0.010 ①
	Colt	97.4 (1597)	BPR6ES-11	0.039–0.040	10B	10B	NA	33.6 ②	700	700	0.006	0.010
	Colt Vista	121.9 (1997)	BPR6ES-11	0.039–0.040	5B	5B	NA	36.3	700	700	Hyd. ①	Hyd. ①
	Conquest	155.9 (2555)	BPR6ES-11	0.039–0.040	10B	10B	NA	33.6	850	850	0.006	Hyd. ①
1989	Colt	86.9 (1468)	BPR6ES-11	0.039–0.043	5B	5B	NA	47.6	700	750	0.006	0.010
	Colt	97 (1595)	BPR6ES-11	0.028–0.031	5B	5B	NA	47.6 ③	700	750	0.006	0.010
	Colt Wagon	107.1 (1755)	BPR6ES-11	0.039–0.043	5B	5B	NA	47.6	700	700	0.006	0.010
	Colt Vista	121.9 (1997)	WZ0EPR-11	0.039–0.043	5B	5B	NA	47.6	700	700	Hyd.	Hyd.
	Conquest	155.9 (2555)	BPR7EA-11	0.039–0.043	10B	10B	NA	33.6	850	850	Hyd. ①	Hyd. ①
1990	Colt	86.9 (1468)	BPR6ES-11	0.039–0.043	5B	5B	NA	47.6	700	750	0.006	0.010
	Colt	97 (1595)	BPR6ES-11	0.039–0.043	5B	5B	NA	47.6	700	750	Hyd.	Hyd.
	Colt Wagon	107.1 (1755)	BPR6ES-11	0.039–0.043	5B	5B	NA	47.6	700	700	0.006	0.010
	Colt Vista	121.9 (1997)	W20EPR-11	0.039–0.043	5B	5B	NA	47.6	700	700	Hyd.	Hyd.
1991	SEE UNDERHOOD SPECIFICATIONS STICKER											

NOTE: The Underhood Specifications sticker often reflects tune-up specification changes in production. Sticker figures must be used if they disagree with those in this chart.   ① Jet valve clearance—0.010 in.   ② MPI 47.6   ③ Engines equipped with Turbocharger—36.3 PSI

FIRING ORDERS
NOTE: To avoid confusion, always replace spark plug wires one at a time.

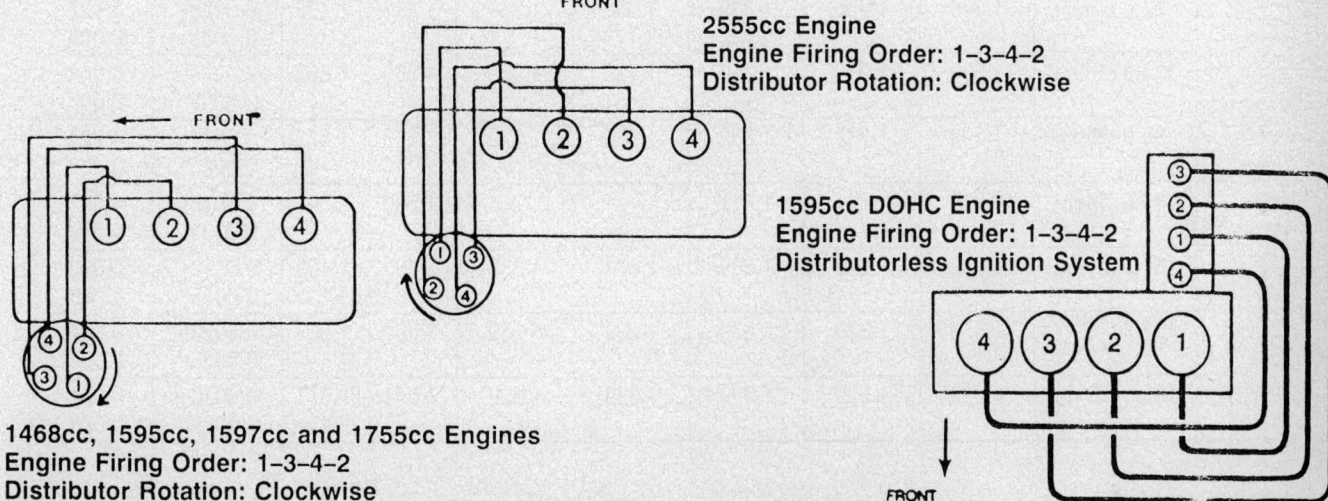

FRONT

2555cc Engine
Engine Firing Order: 1–3–4–2
Distributor Rotation: Clockwise

1595cc DOHC Engine
Engine Firing Order: 1–3–4–2
Distributorless Ignition System

FRONT

1468cc, 1595cc, 1597cc and 1755cc Engines
Engine Firing Order: 1–3–4–2
Distributor Rotation: Clockwise

CAPACITIES

Year	Model	Engine Displacement cu. in. (cc)	Engine Crankcase (qts.) with Filter	Engine Crankcase (qts.) without Filter	Transmission (pts.) 4-Spd	Transmission (pts.) 5-Spd	Transmission (pts.) Auto.	Drive Axle (pts.)	Fuel Tank (gal.)	Cooling System (qts.)
1987	Colt	89.6 (1468)	3.7	3.2	3.6	3.8	12.3	—	11.9	5.3
	Colt	97.5 (1597)	4.5	3.7	—	3.8	12.3	—	11.9	5.3
	Colt Vista	121.9 (1997)	4.2	3.7	—	5.3③	12.3	1.48	13.2②	7.4
	Conquest	155.9 (2555)	5.0①	4.5	—	4.8	14.8	2.7	19.8	9.2
1988	Colt	89.6 (1468)	3.7	3.2	3.6	3.8	13.0	—	13.2	5.3
	Colt	97.5 (1597)	4.5	3.7	—	4.4	12.3	—	11.9	5.3
	Colt Vista	121.9 (1997)	4.2	3.7	—	5.3③	12.3	1.48	13.2②	7.4
	Conquest	155.9 (2555)	5.0①	4.5	—	2.4	7.4	2.7	19.8	9.2
1989	Colt	89.6 (1468)	3.6	3.1	3.6	3.8	13.0	—	13.2	5.3
	Colt	97 (1595)	4.6	4.1	—	4.4	13.0	—	13.2	5.3
	Colt Wagon	107.1 (1755)	3.9	3.4	—	4.7	12.2	1.3	12.4	5.3
	Colt Vista	121 (1997)	4.2	3.7	—	5.3③	12.3	1.48	14.5	7.4
	Conquest	155.9 (2555)	5.0①	4.5	—	4.8	14.8	2.7	19.8	9.5
1990–91	Colt	89.6 (1468)	4.0	3.6	3.6	4.8	12.5	—	13.2	5.3
	Colt	97 (1595)	5.0	4.6	—	4.8	12.5	—	13.2	5.3
	Colt Wagon	107.1 (1755)	4.0	3.5	—	4.7	12.2	1.3	12.4	5.3
	Colt Vista	121.9 (1997)	4.2	3.7	—	5.3③	12.3	1.48	14.5	7.4

① Including oil filter and oil cooler
② 4WD—14.5 gals.
③ 4WD—4.4 pts.

CAMSHAFT SPECIFICATIONS

All measurements given in inches.

Year	Engine Displacement cu. in. (cc)	Journal Diameter 1	Journal Diameter 2	Journal Diameter 3	Journal Diameter 4	Journal Diameter 5	Lobe Lift In.	Lobe Lift Ex.	Bearing Clearance	Camshaft End Play
1987	89.6 (1468)	1.811	1.811	1.811	—	—	1.500	1.541	0.0015–0.0031	0.002–0.008
	97.5 (1597)	1.339	1.339	1.339	1.339	1.339	1.433	1.433	0.0020–0.0035	0.002–0.006
	121.9 (1997)	1.339	1.339	1.339	1.339	1.339	1.660	1.663	0.0020–0.0035	0.004–0.008
	155.9 (2555)	1.339	1.339	1.339	1.339	1.339	1.673	1.673	0.0012–0.0020	0.004–0.008
1988	89.6 (1468)	1.811	1.811	1.811	—	—	1.500	1.541	0.0015–0.0031	0.002–0.008
	97.5 (1597)	1.339	1.339	1.339	1.339	1.339	1.433	1.433	0.0020–0.0035	0.002–0.006
	121.9 (1997)	1.339	1.339	1.339	1.339	1.339	1.660	1.663	0.0020–0.0035	0.004–0.008
	155.9 (2555)	1.339	1.339	1.339	1.339	1.339	1.671	1.671	0.0020–0.0035	0.004–0.008

CAMSHAFT SPECIFICATIONS

All measurements given in inches.

Year	Engine Displacement cu. in. (cc)	Journal Diameter 1	2	3	4	5	Lobe Lift In.	Ex.	Bearing Clearance	Camshaft End Play
1989	89.6 (1468)	1.811	1.811	1.811	—	—	1.532	1.534	0.0015–0.0031	0.002–0.008
	97 (1595)	1.020	1.020	1.020	1.020	1.020	1.386	1.375	0.0020–0.0035	0.004–0.008
	107.1 (1755)	1.337	1.337	1.337	1.337	1.337	1.414	1.414	0.0020–0.0035	0.002–0.006
	121.9 (1997)	1.339	1.339	1.339	1.339	1.339	1.660	1.663	0.0020–0.0045	0.004–0.008
	155.9 (2555)	1.339	1.339	1.339	1.339	1.339	1.673	1.673	0.0020–0.0045	0.004–0.008
1990–91	89.6 (1468)	1.811	1.811	1.811	—	—	1.500	1.532	0.0015–0.0032	0.002–0.008
	97 (1595)	1.020	1.020	1.020	1.020	1.020	1.386	1.374	0.0020–0.0035	0.004–0.008
	107.1 (1755)	1.337	1.337	1.337	1.337	1.337	1.414	1.414	0.0020–0.0035	0.002–0.008
	121.9 (1997)	1.339	1.339	1.339	1.339	1.339	1.660	1.663	0.0020–0.0035	0.004–0.008

CRANKSHAFT AND CONNECTING ROD SPECIFICATIONS

All measurements are given in inches.

Year	Engine Displacement cu. in. (cc)	Crankshaft Main Brg. Journal Dia.	Main Brg. Oil Clearance	Shaft End-play	Thrust on No.	Connecting Rod Journal Diameter	Oil Clearance	Side Clearance
1987	89.6 (1468)	1.8898	0.0008–0.0028	0.002–0.007	3	1.6535	0.0004–0.0024	0.004–0.010
	97.5 (1597)	2.2441	0.0008–0.0028	0.002–0.007	3	1.7717	0.0004–0.0028	0.004–0.010
	121.9 (1997)	2.2441	0.0008–0.0028	0.002–0.007	3	1.7717	0.0008–0.0020	0.004–0.010
	155.9 (2555)	2.5984	0.0008–0.0028	0.002–0.007	3	2.0866	0.0008–0.0028	0.004–0.010
	155.9 (2555) Turbo	2.3622	0.0008–0.0020	0.002–0.007	3	2.0866	0.0008–0.0024	0.004–0.010
1988	89.6 (1468)	1.8898	0.0008–0.0028	0.002–0.007	3	1.6535	0.0004–0.0024	0.004–0.010
	97.5 (1597)	2.2441	0.0008–0.0028	0.002–0.007	3	1.7717	0.0004–0.0028	0.004–0.010
	121.9 (1997)	2.2441	0.0008–0.0028	0.002–0.007	3	1.7717	0.0008–0.0020	0.004–0.010
	155.9 (2555)	2.5984	0.0008–0.0028	0.002–0.007	3	2.0866	0.0008–0.0028	0.004–0.010
	155.9 (2555) Turbo	2.3622	0.0008–0.0020	0.002–0.007	3	2.0866	0.0008–0.0024	0.004–0.010

CRANKSHAFT AND CONNECTING ROD SPECIFICATIONS

Year	Engine Displacement cu. in. (cc)	Crankshaft Main Brg. Journal Dia.	Main Brg. Oil Clearance	Shaft End-play	Thrust on No.	Connecting Rod Journal Diameter	Oil Clearance	Side Clearance
1989	89.6 (1468)	1.8898	0.0008–0.0028	0.002–0.007	3	1.6535	0.0004–0.0024	0.004–0.010
	97 (1595)	2.2441	0.0008–0.0028	0.002–0.007	3	1.7717	0.0004–0.0028	0.004–0.010
	107.1 (1755)	2.2441	0.0008–0.0020	0.002–0.007	3	1.7717	0.0008–0.0020	0.004–0.010
	121.9 (1997)	2.2441	0.0008–0.0028	0.002–0.007	3	1.7717	0.0008–0.0020	0.004–0.010
	155.9 (2555)	2.5984	0.0008–0.0028	0.002–0.007	3	2.0866	0.0008–0.0028	0.004–0.010
	155.9 (2555) Turbo	2.3622	0.0008–0.0020	0.002–0.007	3	2.0866	0.0008–0.0024	0.004–0.010
1990-91	89.6 (1468)	1.8898	0.0008–0.0018	0.002–0.007	3	1.6535	0.0006–0.0017	0.004–0.010
	97 (1595)	2.2441	0.0008–0.0020	0.002–0.007	3	1.7717	0.0008–0.0020	0.004–0.010
	107.1 (1755)	2.2441	0.0008–0.0020	0.002–0.007	3	1.7717	0.0008–0.0020	0.004–0.010
	121.9 (1997)	2.2441	0.0008–0.0020	0.002–0.007	3	1.7717	0.0006–0.0020	0.004–0.010

VALVE SPECIFICATIONS

Year	Engine Displacement cu. in. (cc)	Seat Angle (deg.)	Face Angle (deg.)	Spring Test Pressure (lbs.)	Spring Installed Height (in.)	Stem-to-Guide Clearance (in.) Intake	Exhaust	Stem Diameter (in.) Intake	Exhaust
1987	89.6 (1468)	45	45	69 @ 1.417	1.417	0.0012–0.0024	0.0020–0.0035	0.3147–0.3153	0.3147–0.3153
	97.5 (1597)	45	45	61 @ 1.470	1.470	0.0012–0.0024	0.0020–0.0035	0.3147–0.3153	0.3147–0.3153
	121.9 (1997)	45	45	40 @ 1.591	1.591	0.0012–0.0024	0.0020–0.0035	0.3147–0.3153	0.3147–0.3153
	155.9 (2555)	45	45	61 @ 1.590	1.590	0.0012–0.0024	0.0020–0.0035	0.3147–0.3153	0.3147–0.3153
1988	89.6 (1468)	45	45	69 @ 1.417	1.417	0.0012–0.0024	0.0020–0.0035	0.3147–0.3153	0.3147–0.3153
	97.5 (1597)	45	45	61 @ 1.470	1.470	0.0012–0.0024	0.0020–0.0035	0.3147–0.3153	0.3147–0.3153
	121.9 (1997)	45	45	40 @ 1.591	1.591	0.0012–0.0024	0.0020–0.0035	0.3147–0.3153	0.3147–0.3153
	155.9 (2555)	45	45	61 @ 1.590	1.590	0.0012–0.0024	0.0020–0.0035	0.3147–0.3153	0.3147–0.3153
1989	89.6 (1468)	44	45	53	—	0.0008–0.0020	0.0020–0.0035	0.2600	0.2600
	97 (1595)	44	45	53	—	0.0008–0.0020	0.0020–0.0033	0.2585–0.2586	0.2571–0.2580
	107.1 (1755)	45	45	62	1.470	0.0012–0.0024	0.0020–0.0035	0.3200	0.3200

VALVE SPECIFICATIONS

Year	Engine Displacement cu. in. (cc)	Seat Angle (deg.)	Face Angle (deg.)	Spring Test Pressure (lbs.)	Spring Installed Height (in.)	Stem-to-Guide Clearance (in.) Intake	Exhaust	Stem Diameter (in.) Intake	Exhaust
	121.9 (1997)	45	45	73 @ 1.591	1.591	0.0012–0.0024	0.0020–0.0035	0.3147–0.3153	0.3147–0.3153
	155.9 (2555)	45	45	73 @ 1.591	1.591	0.0012–0.0024	0.0020–0.0035	0.3147–0.3153	0.3147–0.3153
1990–91	89.6 (1468)	44	45	69 @ 1.417	1.417	0.0008–0.0020	0.0020–0.0035	0.2600	0.2600
	97 (1595)	44	45	53	—	0.0008–0.0020	0.0020–0.0033	0.2585–0.2586	0.2571–0.2580
	107.1 (1755)	45	45	62	1.470	0.0012–0.0024	0.0020–0.0035	0.3200	0.3200
	121.9 (1997)	45	45	73 @ 1.591	1.591	0.0012–0.0024	0.0020–0.0035	0.3147–0.3153	0.3147–0.3153

PISTON AND RING SPECIFICATIONS

All measurements are given in inches.

Year	Engine Displacement cu. in. (cc)	Piston Clearance	Ring Gap Top Compression	Bottom Compression	Oil Control	Ring Side Clearance Top Compression	Bottom Compression	Oil Control
1987	89.6 (1468)	0.0008–0.0016	0.0080–0.0160	0.0080–0.0160	0.0080–0.0200	0.0012–0.0028	0.0008–0.0024	0.0010–0.0030
	97.5 (1597)	0.0008–0.0016	0.0100–0.0160	0.0080–0.0140	0.0080–0.0280	0.0012–0.0028	0.0008–0.0024	Snug
	121.9 (1997)	0.0008–0.0016	0.0100–0.0180	0.0080–0.0160	0.0080–0.0028	0.0020–0.0040	0.0010–0.0020	Snug
	155.9 (2555)	0.0008–0.0016	0.0098–0.0177	0.0098–0.0177	0.0078–0.0354	0.0024–0.0039	0.0008–0.0024	0.0008–0.0024
	155.9 (2555) Turbo	0.0008–0.0016	0.0120–0.0200	0.0100–0.0160	0.0120–0.0310	0.0020–0.0040	0.0010–0.0020	Snug
1988	89.6 (1468)	0.0008–0.0016	0.0080–0.0160	0.0080–0.0160	0.0080–0.0200	0.0012–0.0028	0.0008–0.0024	0.0010–0.0030
	97.5 (1597)	0.0008–0.0016	0.0100–0.0160	0.0080–0.0140	0.0080–0.0280	0.0012–0.0028	0.0008–0.0024	Snug
	121.9 (1997)	0.0008–0.0016	0.0100–0.0180	0.0080–0.0160	0.0080–0.0028	0.0020–0.0040	0.0010–0.0020	Snug
	155.9 (2555)	0.0008–0.0016	0.0098–0.0177	0.0098–0.0177	0.0078–0.0354	0.0024–0.0039	0.0008–0.0024	0.0008–0.0024
	155.9 (2555) Turbo	0.0008–0.0016	0.0120–0.0200	0.0100–0.0160	0.0120–0.0310	0.0020–0.0040	0.0010–0.0020	Snug
1989	89.6 (1468)	0.0008–0.0016	0.0080–0.0138	0.0080–0.0138	0.0080–0.0280	0.0012–0.0028	0.0012–0.0028	Snug
	97 (1595)	0.0008–0.0016①	0.0100–0.0160	0.0140–0.0197	0.0080–0.0280	0.0012–0.0028	0.0008–0.0024	Snug
	107.1 (1755)	0.0008–0.0016	0.0118–0.0140	0.0080–0.0140	0.0080–0.0280	0.0018–0.0033	0.0008–0.0024	Snug
	121.9 (1997)	0.0004–0.0012	0.0100–0.0160	0.0080–0.0140	0.0080–0.0028	0.0012–0.0028	0.0008–0.0024	Snug
	155.9 (2555) Turbo	0.0012–0.0020	0.0120–0.0177	0.0098–0.0177	0.0118–0.0315	0.0020–0.0035	0.0008–0.0024	Snug

PISTON AND RING SPECIFICATIONS
All measurements are given in inches.

Year	Engine Displacement cu. in. (cc)	Piston Clearance	Ring Gap			Ring Side Clearance		
			Top Compression	Bottom Compression	Oil Control	Top Compression	Bottom Compression	Oil Control
1990–91	89.6 (1468)	0.0008–0.0016	0.0080–0.0138	0.0080–0.0138	0.0080–0.0280	0.0012–0.0028	0.0008–0.0024	Snug
	97 (1595)	0.0008–0.0016	0.0100–0.0160	0.0140–0.0197	0.0080–0.0280	0.0012–0.0028	0.0012–0.0028	Snug
	107.1 (1755)	0.0008–0.0016	0.0118–0.0177	0.0080–0.0140	0.0080–0.0280	0.0018–0.0033	0.0008–0.0024	Snug
	121.9 (1997)	0.0004–0.0012	0.0100–0.0160	0.0080–0.0140	0.0080–0.0028	0.0012–0.0028	0.0008–0.0024	Snug

① With Turbocharger 0.0012–0.0020

TORQUE SPECIFICATIONS
All readings in ft. lbs.

Year	Engine Displacement cu. in. (cc)	Cylinder Head Bolts	Main Bearing Bolts	Rod Bearing Bolts	Crankshaft Pulley Bolts	Flywheel Bolts	Manifold		Spark Plugs
							Intake	Exhaust	
1987	89.6 (1468)	50–54	37–39	23–25	57–72	94–101	11–14	11–14	15–21
	97.5 (1597)	50–54	36–40	23–25	80–93	94–101①	11–14	11–14	15–21
	121.9 (1997)	65–72	37–39	37–38	80–94	94–101①	11–14	11–14	15–21
	155.9 (2555)	65–72	55–61	33–34	80–94	94–101	11–14	11–14	15–21
1988	89.6 (1468)	50–54	37–39	23–25	57–72	94–101	11–14	11–14	15–21
	97.5 (1597)	50–54	36–40	23–25	80–93	94–101①	11–14	11–14	15–21
	121.9 (1997)	65–72	37–39	37–38	80–94	94–101①	11–14	11–14	15–21
	155.9 (2555)	65–72	55–61	33–34	80–94	94–101	11–14	11–14	15–21
1989	89.6 (1468)	50–54	37–40	23–25	57–72	94–101	11–14	11–14	15–21
	97 (1595)	65–72	47–51	36–38	80–94	94–101①	11–14	11–14	15–21
	107.1 (1755)	51–54	37–39	24–25	11–13	94–101	11–14	11–14	15–21
	121.9 (1997)	65–72	37–39	33–35	15–21	94–101	11–14	11–14	15–21
	155.9 (2555)	65–72	55–61	33–34	80–94	94–101	11–14	11–14	15–21
1990–91	89.6 (1468)	50–54	36–40	14②	51–72	94–101	11–14	11–14	15–21
	97 (1595)	50–54	47–51	36–38	80–94	94–101①	11–14	11–14	15–21
	107.1 (1755)	51–54	37–39	24–25	11–13	94–101	11–14	11–14	15–21
	121.9 (1997)	65–72	37–39	37–38	15–21	94–101①	11–14	11–14	15–21

① With automatic transmission—84–90 ft. lbs.
② Torque nuts to 14 ft. lbs. and back off. Torque nuts again to 14 ft. lbs., then tighten an additional ¼ turn.

BRAKE SPECIFICATIONS
All measurements in inches unless noted.

Year	Model	Lug Nut Torque (ft. lbs.)	Master Cylinder Bore	Brake Disc		Standard Brake Drum Diameter	Minimum Lining Thickness	
				Minimum Thickness	Maximum Runout		Front	Rear
1987	Colt	51–58	0.8125①	0.450④	0.006	7.100	0.040	0.040
	Colt Vista	51–58	0.8750	0.650③	0.006	8.000⑥	0.040	0.040
	Conquest	51–58	0.9400	0.880②	0.006	—	0.040	0.040

BRAKE SPECIFICATIONS

All measurements in inches unless noted.

Year	Model	Lug Nut Torque (ft. lbs.)	Master Cylinder Bore	Brake Disc Minimum Thickness	Brake Disc Maximum Runout	Standard Brake Drum Diameter	Minimum Lining Thickness Front	Minimum Lining Thickness Rear
1988	Colt	51–58	0.8125 ①	0.450 ④	0.006	7.100	0.080	0.040
	Colt Vista	51–58	0.8750	0.650 ③	0.006	8.000 ⑥	0.080	0.040
	Conquest	51–58	0.9400	0.880 ②	0.006	—	0.080	0.040
1989	Colt	51–58	0.8125 ①	0.450 ④	0.006	7.100	0.080	0.040
	Colt Wagon	51–58	0.8700	⑤	0.006	8.000	0.080	0.040
	Colt Vista	51–58	0.8750	0.650 ③	0.006	8.000 ⑥	0.080	0.040
	Conquest	51–58	0.9400	0.880 ②	0.006	—	0.080	0.040
1990–91	Colt	51–58	0.8125 ①	0.450	0.006	7.100	0.080	0.040
	Colt Wagon	51–58	0.8700	⑤	0.006	8.000	0.080	0.040
	Colt Vista	51–58	0.8750	0.650 ③	0.006	8.000	0.080	0.040

① Colt Turbo—0.8750
② Rear—0.650 in.
③ 4WD—0.880 in.
④ Turbo—0.645 in.
⑤ AD54 type—0.650 in.
PF515 type—0.450 in.
⑥ 4WD—9.000 in.

WHEEL ALIGNMENT

Year	Model	Caster Range (deg.)	Caster Preferred Setting (deg.)	Camber Range (deg.)	Camber Preferred Setting (deg.)	Toe-in (in.)	Steering Axis Inclination (deg.)
1987	Colt	$1^3/_{16}$–$2^3/_{16}$ ①	$1^3/_{16}$	$^{11}/_{16}$N–$^1/_2$P	0	0	NA
	Colt Vista	$^5/_{16}$–$1^5/_{16}$	$1^3/_{16}$ ①	$^1/_{16}$N–$^{15}/_{16}$P	$^7/_{16}$ ②	0	NA
	Conquest	—	$5^{13}/_{16}$	—	$-^1/_2$N ③	0	NA
1988	Colt	$^3/_{16}$–$1^3/_{16}$	$^{11}/_{16}$	$^1/_2$N–$^1/_2$P	0	0	NA
	Colt Vista	$^5/_{16}$–$1^5/_{16}$	$1^3/_{16}$ ①	$^1/_{16}$N–$^{15}/_{16}$P	$^7/_{16}$ ②	0	NA
	Conquest	—	$5^{13}/_{16}$	—	0 ③	0	NA
1989	Colt	$^3/_{16}$–$1^3/_{16}$	$^{11}/_{16}$	$^1/_2$N–$^1/_2$P	0	0	NA
	Colt Wagon	$^3/_{16}$–$1^3/_{16}$ ①	$1^3/_{16}$	$^1/_2$N–$^1/_2$P	0 ②	0	NA
	Colt Vista	$^5/_{16}$–$1^5/_{16}$	$1^3/_{16}$ ①	$^1/_{16}$N–$^{15}/_{16}$P	$^7/_{16}$ ②	0	NA
	Conquest	—	$5^5/_{16}$	—	0 ③	0	NA
1990–91	Colt	$^3/_{16}$–$1^3/_{16}$	$^{11}/_{16}$	$^1/_2$N–$^1/_2$P	0	0	NA
	Colt Wagon	$^3/_{16}$–$1^3/_{16}$ ①	$1^3/_{16}$	$^1/_2$N–$^1/_2$P	0 ②	0	NA
	Colt Vista	$^5/_{16}$–$1^5/_{16}$	$1^3/_{16}$ ①	$^1/_{16}$N–$^{15}/_{16}$P	$^7/_{16}$ ②	0	NA

① 4WD Front
$^{13}/_{16}$ degree caster
$^{13}/_{16}$ degree camber
4WD Rear
0 degrees caster
0 degrees toe-in

② Rear
$^5/_8$ degree camber
0 degrees toe-in

③ Rear
0 degree camber
0 in. toe-in
2WD without Power Steering—$^3/_{16}$–$1^3/_{16}$
Preferred setting $^{11}/_{16}$

ENGINE ELECTRICAL

NOTE: Disconnecting the negative battery cable on some vehicles may interfere with the functions of the on board computer systems and may require the computer to undergo a relearning process, once the negative battery cable is reconnected.

Distributor

Removal

Before removing the distributor, position No. 1 cylinder at TDC on the compression stroke and align the timing marks.

1. Disconnect the negative battery cable.

2. Disconnect the spark plug wires from the distributor cap.

3. Disconnect the ignition coil high tension wire from the distributor cap.

4. Remove the vacuum hose from the advance unit.

5. Remove the cap from the distributor.

6. Verify the rotor points to the No. 1 cylinder position and the timing marks on the crankshaft pulley and the timing tab are aligned at TDC.

7. Mark the distributor body to the exact place the rotor points. Matchmark both the distributor mounting flange and the cylinder head.

8. Loosen and remove the retaining nut from the mounting stud. Lift the distributor from the cylinder head. The rotor may turn slightly from the mark on the distributor body. Make note of how far. When the distributor is reinstalled, this is the point to position the rotor.

Installation

TIMING NOT DISTURBED

1. Position the distributor into the engine while aligning the matchmarks made during removal.

2. Verify the rotor points to the No. 1 cylinder position and the timing marks on the crankshaft pulley and the timing tab are aligned at TDC.

3. Install the distributor retaining nut on the mounting stud and tighten.

4. Install the cap on the distributor.

5. Connect the spark plug wires to the distributor cap.

6. Connect the ignition coil high tension wire to the distributor cap.

7. Connect the negative battery cable to the battery.

8. Start the engine and check the ignition timing whenever the distributor has been removed.

TIMING DISTURBED

1. With the distributor removed from the engine, turn the crankshaft so the No. 1 piston is on the compression stroke and the timing marks are aligned.

2. Turn the distributor shaft so the rotor points approximately 15 degrees before the rotor position that was marked on the distributor.

3. Insert the distributor, if resistance is met, slight wiggling of the rotor shaft will help seat the distributor.

4. When the distributor seats against the head, align the matchmarks and install the retaining nut. Do not tighten the retaining nut all the way, as the timing must be checked.

5. Reinstall the rotor, cap, plug wires, coil lead, primary lead or harness and connect the vacuum hoses.

6. Connect the negative battery cable. Start the engine, allow it to reach operating temperature and check the ignition timing.

Ignition Timing

Adjustment

EXCEPT 1595CC DOHC ENGINE

1. Attach the timing light according to the manufacturer's instructions.

2. Locate the timing tab line on the front of the engine and the notch on the crankshaft pulley. Mark them so they are easily recognizable with the timing light.

3. Start the engine and allow it to reach operating temperature.

4. Point the timing light at the crankshaft pulley marks. The marked line should align with the pulley notch.

5. If the marks do not align, loosen the distributor mounting nut and rotate the distributor slowly, in either direction, to align the timing marks.

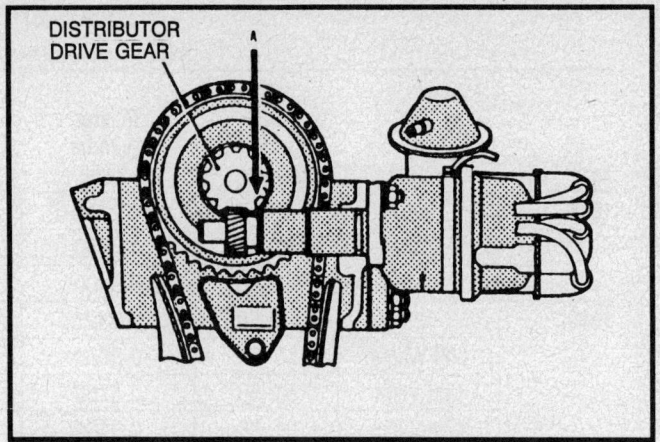

Distributor installation—cylinder head mounted distributors

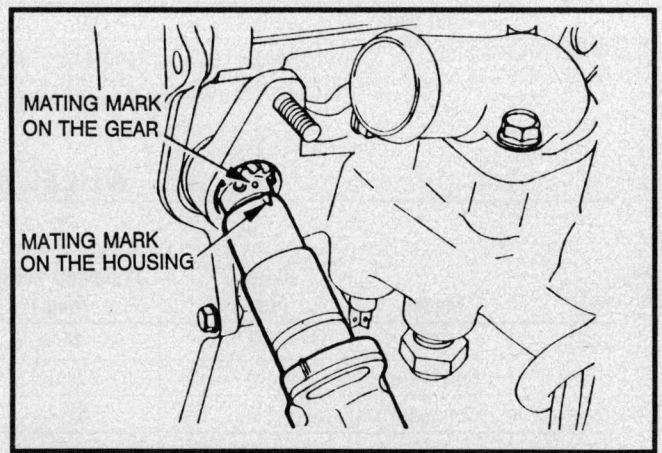

Aligning mating marks for installation of cylinder head mounted distributors

6. Tighten the mounting nut when the ignition timing is correct. Stop the engine and remove the timing light.

1595CC DOHC ENGINE

1. Run the engine until the normal operating temperature is reached. Shut off the engine. Make sure all lights and electrical accessories are off. Make sure the electric cooling fan is not operating when timing. Disconnect the fan harness, if necessary, but take care not to allow the engine to overheat.

2. Connect a timing light, following the light manufacturer's instructions.

3. Insert a paper clip along the terminal surface, of the terminal parallel to the fastener side of the ignition connecter harness, in the engine compartment.

4. Connect a tachometer to the paper clip. Start the engine and check the curb idle speed. The idle speed should be 650–850 rpm.

5. Shut off the engine, connect a lead wire with alligator clips to the terminal for ignition timing adjustment and ground it to a good chassis grounding point.

6. Start the engine and point the timing light at the pulley and timing cover marks. The base timing is 5 degrees before TDC.

7. If timing adjustment is necessary, loosen the crank angle sensor pivot bolt and turn the sensor. Turning the sensor to the right advances the timing, to the left retards it. Tighten the sensor pivot bolt when correct timing is reached. Do not allow the engine to overheat.

SECTION

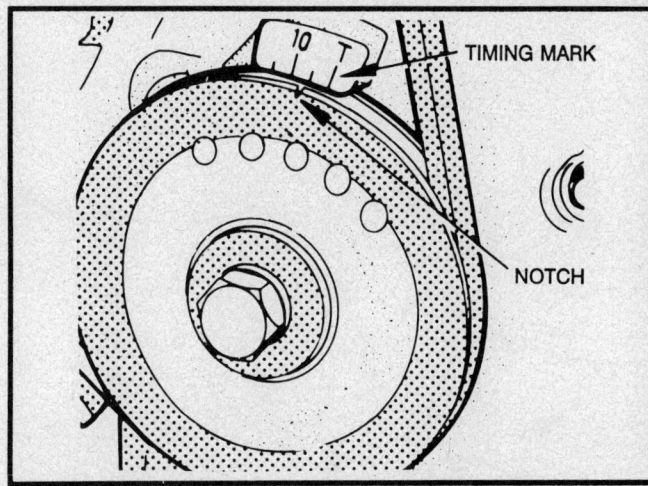

Timing mark positions—1468cc, 1595cc, 1597cc engines

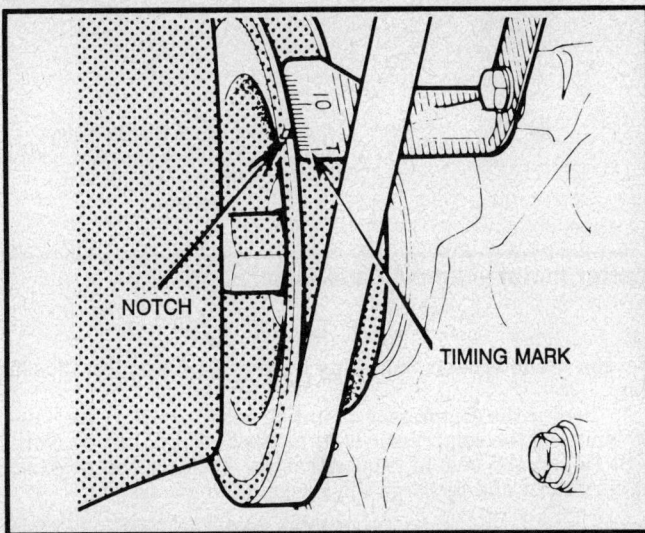

2555cc engine timing marks

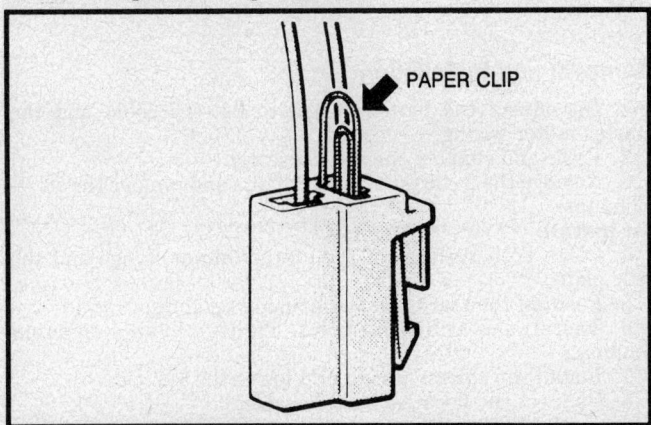

Paper clip installation

8. Stop the engine and disconnect the ground wire. Start the engine and check the curb idle speed. Check the ignition timing, it should now be about 8 degrees before TDC.

9. Timing may vary depending upon the engine control module. If the timing is not about 8 degrees, check the base timing

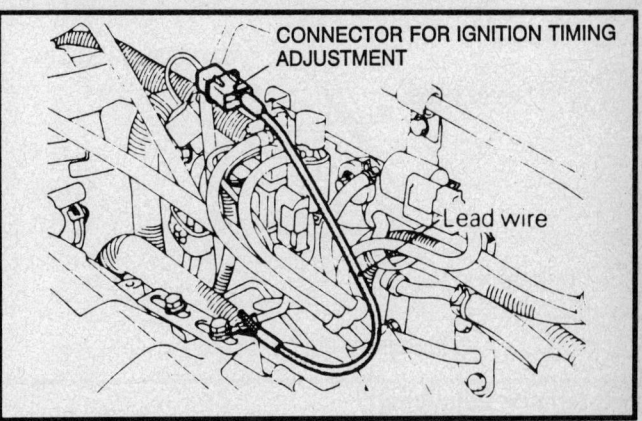

Lead wire connection

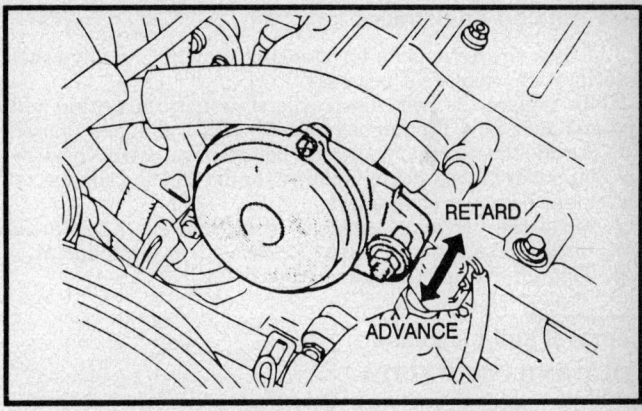

Timing adjustment with crank angle sensor

again. If the base timing is still 5 degrees, the ignition timing is functioning normally.

Alternator

Precautions

Several precautions must be observed with alternator equipped vehicles to avoid damage to the unit.

• If the battery is removed for any reason, make sure it is reconnected with the correct polarity. Reversing the battery connections may result in damage to the one-way rectifiers.

• When utilizing a booster battery as a starting aid, always connect the positive to positive terminals and the negative terminal from the booster battery to a good engine ground on the vehicle being started.

• Never use a fast charger as a booster to start vehicles.

• Disconnect the battery cables when charging the battery with a fast charger.

• Never attempt to polarize the alternator.

• Do not use test lamps of more than 12 volts when checking diode continuity.

• Do not short across or ground any of the alternator terminals.

• The polarity of the battery, alternator and regulator must be matched and considered before making any electrical connections within the system.

• Never separate the alternator on an open circuit. Make sure all connections within the circuit are clean and tight.

• Disconnect the battery ground terminal when performing any service on electrical components.

• Disconnect the battery if arc welding is to be done on the vehicle.

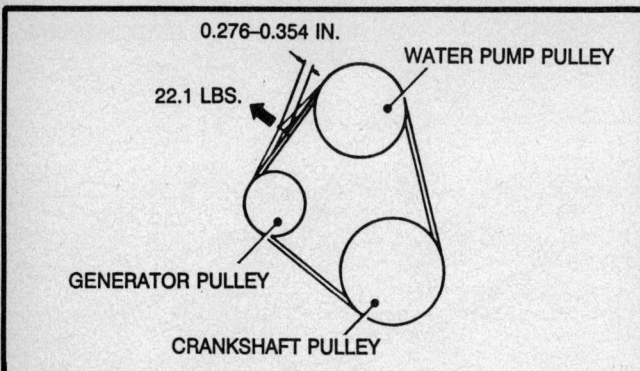

Belt tension adjustment

Belt Tension Adjustment

1. Check the drive belts for cracking, fraying and any other deterioration. Replace if necessary.

2. To replace the belt, loosen the stationary mounting bolt and and pivot bolt. If equipped with an adjustment bolt, loosen it to provide the necessary slack for belt removal. Pivot the driven component in its bracket. Remove the old belt and slip the replacement belt over the pulleys.

3. Move the driven component or tighten the adjustment bolt, until the belt can be deflected $\frac{1}{4}$–$\frac{3}{8}$ in. at its midpoint.

4. Tighten the mounting and pivot bolts.

Removal and Installation

COLT AND COLT VISTA

1. Disconnect the negative battery cable.

2. Remove the condenser fan motor.

3. Remove the power steering pump from the bracket and support it on the oil reservoir using wire.

4. Remove the power steering pump bracket.

5. Disconnect the wiring connectors from the alternator.

6. Remove the lock bolt and the support bolt.

7. Remove the alternator and the adjusting bolt.

To install:

8. Installation is the reverse order of the removal procedure. Torque alternator brace bolts to to 9–11 ft. lbs. (12–15 Nm) and the pivot bolt to 15–18 ft. lbs. (20–25 Nm).

9. Adjust the belt to proper tension. Connect the negative battery cable.

CONQUEST

1. Disconnect the negative battery cable.

2. Disconnect the wire connectors from the alternator.

3. If equipped with air conditioning, discharge the air conditioning system and remove the discharge and suction hose connections from the compressor.

4. Remove the compressor mounting bolts and remove the compressor from the engine.

5. Remove alternator mounting bolts and remove the alternator from the engine.

To install:

6. Installation is the reverse order of the removal procedure.

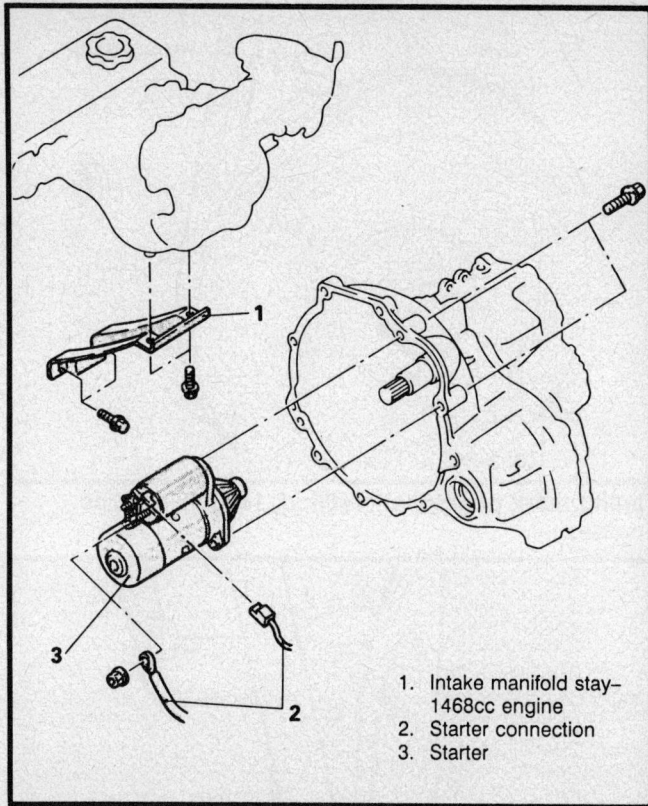

1. Intake manifold stay–1468cc engine
2. Starter connection
3. Starter

Starter motor—removal and installation

Torque the alternator mounting bolts to 14–18 ft. lbs. (20–25 Nm).

7. Torque the compressor mounting bolts to 9–10 ft. lbs. (12–15 Nm) and the compressor lines to 22–26 ft. lbs. (30–34 Nm).

8. Adjust the belt to proper tension. Connect the negative battery cable and recharge the air conditioning system.

Starter

Removal and Installation

1. Disconnect the battery negative battery cable and the starter motor wiring.

2. Raise and support the vehicle safely.

3. Remove the 2 starter attaching bolts and remove the starter motor.

To install:

4. Clean both surfaces of the starter motor flange and the rear plate.

5. Position the starter in the housing opening.

6. Install the attaching bolts. Tighten evenly to avoid binding.

7. Install the starter wiring and lower the vehicle.

8. Connect the negative battery cable.

CHASSIS ELECTRICAL

Heater Blower Motor

Removal and Installation

COLT

1. Disconnect the negative battery cable.
2. Remove the glove box and parcel tray.
3. Disconnect the change over control wire and duct.
4. Disconnect the harness connector at the ECU unit and remove the ECU unit.
5. Remove the blower case assembly from the dash.
6. Unbolt and remove the blower motor from the case.
7. The fan is removable from the motor shaft.

To install:

8. Installation is the reverse of removal.
9. Connect the negative battery cable and test the blower motor operation.

COLT VISTA

1. Disconnect the negative battery cable.
2. Remove the upper and lower glove boxes.
3. Disconnect the wiring from the blower assembly.
4. Remove the blower motor mounting bolts and lift out the motor. If the entire blower case is to be removed, the instrument panel will have to be removed first.

To install:

5. Installation is the reverse order of the removal procedures.
6. Connect the negative battery cable and test the blower motor operation.

CONQUEST

1. Disconnect the negative battery cable.
2. Remove the lower panel cover and the glove box.
3. Disconnect the air change over cable from the blower.
4. Disconnect the duct from the blower.
5. Disconnect the blower wiring.
6. Unbolt and remove the blower motor.

To install:

7. Installation is the reverse order of the removal procedures.
8. Connect the negative battery cable and test the blower motor operation.

Windshield Wiper Motor

Removal and Installation

COLT AND COLT VISTA

1. Disconnect the negative battery cable.
2. Remove the wiper arms.
3. Remove the front cowl trim plate.
4. Remove the pivot shaft mounting nuts and push the pivot shaft toward the inside.
5. Disconnect the linkage from the motor and lift out the linkage.
6. Disconnect the harness connector at the wiper motor.
7. Unbolt and remove the motor.

To install:

8. Installation is the reverse order the of removal procedures.

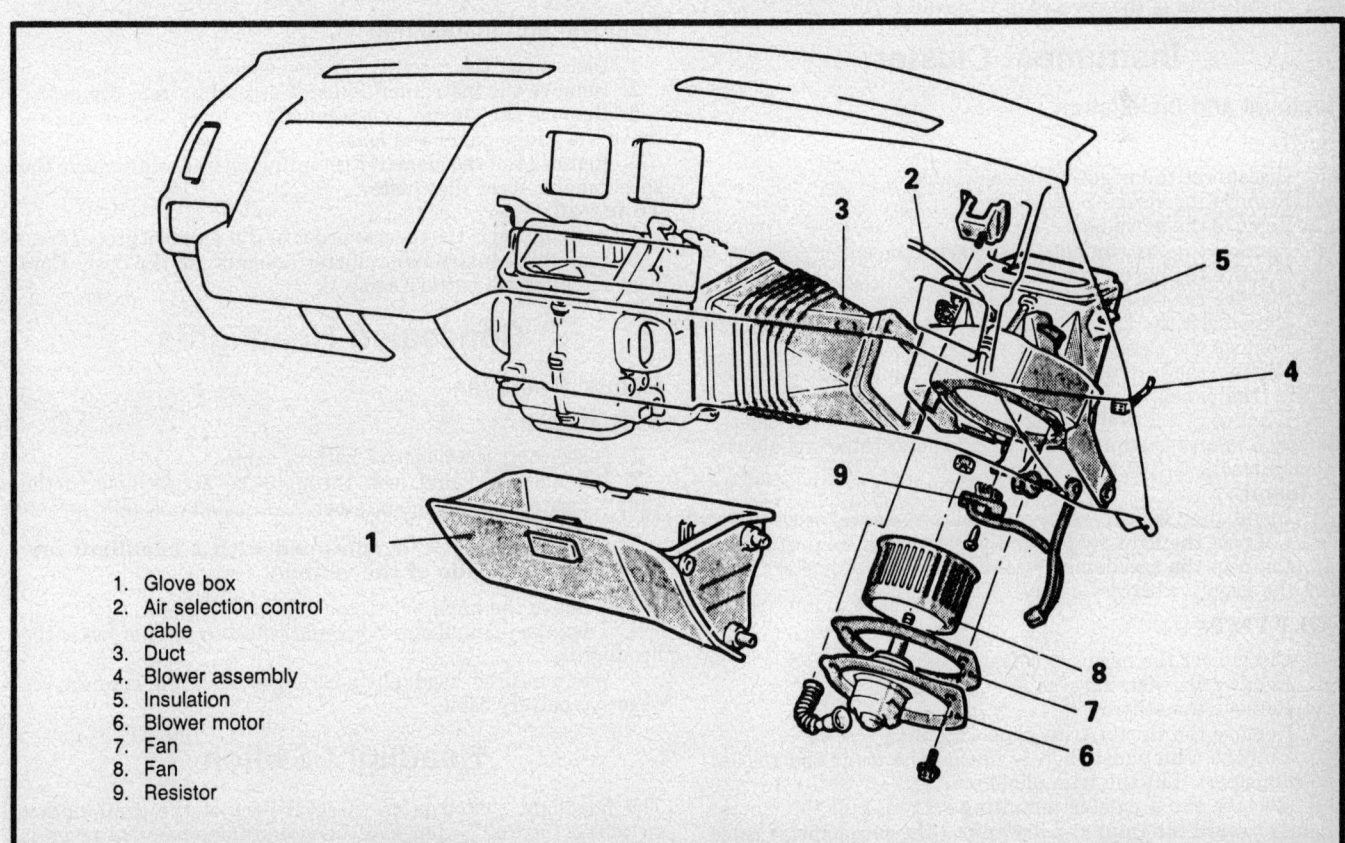

1. Glove box
2. Air selection control cable
3. Duct
4. Blower assembly
5. Insulation
6. Blower motor
7. Fan
8. Fan
9. Resistor

Blower motor—removal and installation

9. Connect the negative battery cable and test the wiper motor operation.

10. When installing the arms, the at-rest position of the blade tips-to-windshield molding should be as follows:

a. Colt passenger's side–20mm, driver's side: 15mm.

b. Colt Vista passenger's side–30mm, driver's side: 25mm.

CONQUEST

1. Disconnect the negative battery cable.

2. Remove the wiper arm and pivot shaft mounting nut, remove the arms and push the pivot shaft toward the inside.

3. Remove the cover from the wiper access hole on the right side of the front deck panel.

4. Loosen the wiper motor mounting bolts, pull the motor out slightly, disconnect the motor from the linkage, then remove the motor and linkage. If the motor's crank arm is to be removed, mark its position first.

To install:

5. Installation is the reverse of order of the removal procedures. Install the wiper arms so the blade tip-to-windshield molding distance, at rest, is ½ in.

6. Connect the negative battery cable and test the wiper motor operation.

Windshield Wiper Switch

Removal and Installation

NOTE: On Colt Vista and Conquest, the wiper switch is integral with the turn signal switch.

1. Remove the steering wheel.

2. Remove the steering column cover.

3. Pull out and remove the switch knob.

4. Remove the 2 mounting screws and pull the switch out.

5. Installation is the reverse of removal.

Instrument Cluster

Removal and Installation

COLT

1. Disconnect the negative battery cable.

2. Remove the steering wheel.

3. Remove the glove box.

4. Remove the instrument panel heater duct.

5. Remove the parcel tray.

6. Remove the steering column lower cover.

7. Disconnect the light switch and wiper switch connectors.

8. Remove the steering column upper cover.

9. Remove the instrument cluster trim panel screws and lift off the trim panel.

10. Remove the cluster mounting screws and pull the cluster slightly forward. Disconnect the speedometer cable and electrical connectors. Lift out the cluster.

To install:

11. Installation is the reverse order of the removal procedures.

12. Connect the light switch and wiper switch connectors.

13. Connect the speedometer cable to the speedometer. Connect the negative battery cable.

COLT VISTA

1. Disconnect the negative battery cable.

2. Remove the steering wheel.

3. Remove the ashtray.

4. Remove the cluster trim panel retaining screws.

5. Pull the trim panel slightly toward the front and release the connectors. Lift the trim panel off.

6. Remove the 4 cluster mounting screws, pull the cluster slightly toward the front and disconnect the speedometer cable and electrical connectors.

7. Lift out the cluster.

To install:

8. Installation is the reverse order of the removal procedures.

9. Connect all electrical connectors. Connect the speedometer cable to the speedometer.

10. Connect the negative battery cable.

CONQUEST

NOTE: The following procedure applies to both the conventional needle type gauge cluster and to the liquid crystal display type. Because the LCD gauges are composed of very delicate components, they must not be subjected to severe shocks. Furthermore, the LCD gauges must not be disassembled.

1. Disconnect the negative battery cable.

2. Remove the cluster hood attaching screws.

3. Pull outward on both bottom side edges of the hood and while holding it in that position, pull it upward and off.

4. Disconnect the wiring from the panel switches.

5. Remove the cluster case attaching screws.

6. Pull both sides of the lower part of the cluster case up and toward the rear of the vehicle.

7. Disconnect the speedometer cable from the back of the case.

8. Disconnect all wiring at the back of the case and lift the case out.

To install:

9. Installation is the reverse order of removal procedure.

10. Connect the electrical wiring at the rear of the instrument cluster.

11. Connect the speedometer cable to the speedometer. Connect the negative battery cable.

Speedometer

Removal and Installation

1. Disconnect the negative battery cable.

2. Remove the instrument cluster assembly from the dash.

3. Remove the cluster gauge panel retaining screws and remove the gauge panel and lense.

4. Remove the speedometer retaining screws and remove the speedometer from the cluster.

To install:

5. Installation is the reverse order of the removal procedures.

6. Install the instrument cluster assembly to the dash. Connect the negative battery cable.

Concealed Headlights

Manual Operation

CONQUEST

1. Disconnect the negative battery cable.

2. Lift the hood and look through the access hole in the shield, located behind the bumper.

NOTE: The vehicle is equipped with 2 headlight motors; 1 on each side of the vehicle.

3. Remove the hand wheel cover boot.

4. Turn the manual override hand wheel to raise or lower the headlights.

5. When desired headlight position is achieved, connect the negative battery cable.

Headlight Switch

The headlight switch is an integral part of the combination switch on the Colt Sedan, Colt Vista and Conquest. However, it is separate on the Colt Wagon and is located on left side of the steering column cover.

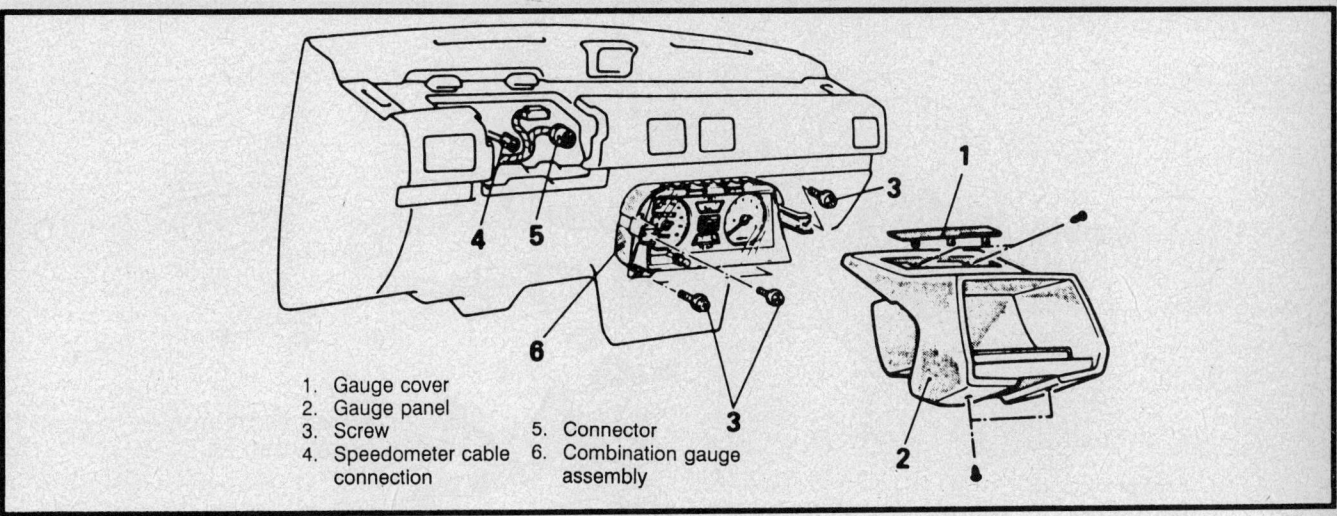

1. Gauge cover
2. Gauge panel
3. Screw
4. Speedometer cable connection
5. Connector
6. Combination gauge assembly

Speedometer—removal and installation

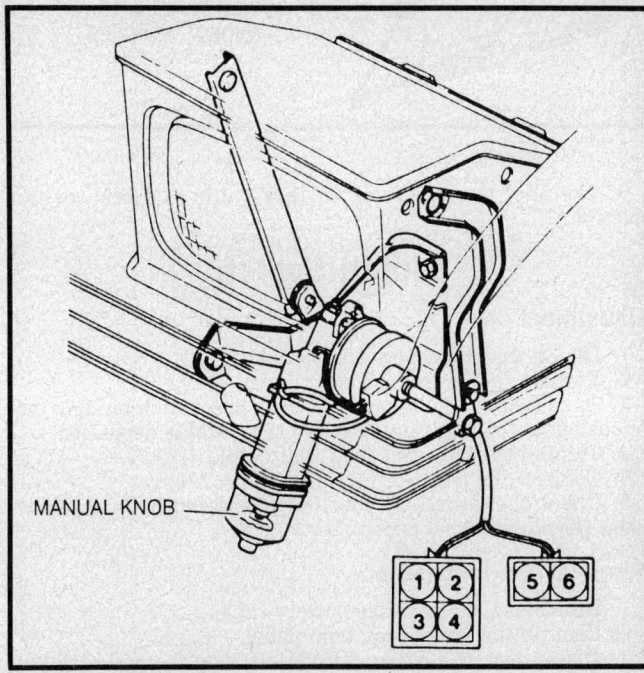

MANUAL KNOB

Concealed headlight motor and related components

Removal and Installation
COLT WAGON

1. Disconnect the negative battery cable.
2. Remove the lower column cover and harness band.
3. Disconnect the electrical connections from the switch.
4. Remove the switch knob retainer screw and knob.
5. Pull the switch out, from behind the upper column cover panel.

To install:

6. Install the switch under and through the upper column cover opening, on the left side of column.
7. Install the knob and retaining screw, securing the switch in place.
8. Connect the electrical connections to the switch. Secure the harness in place with the band.
9. Install the lower column cover and retaining screws. Connect the negative battery cable and test the switch operation.

Combination Switch
Removal and Installation

1. Disconnect the negative battery cable.
2. Remove the steering wheel.
3. Remove heater duct and the lower dash panel assembly.
4. Remove the column covers.
5. Remove the switch retaining screws, disconnect the wiring and remove the switch.

To install:

6. Position the switch to the steering column and secure it in place with the retaining screws. Connect the wiring to the harness connections.
7. Install the heater duct, lower dash panel assembly and the column covers.
8. Install the steering wheel. Connect the negative battery cable.

Ignition Lock/Switch
Removal and Installation

NOTE: When replacing the ignition switch or key reminder switch only, remove the column cover, remove the screw holding the switch and pull out the switch.

1. Disconnect the negative battery cable.
2. Remove the turn signal switch.
3. Cut a notch in the lock bracket bolt head with a hacksaw.
4. Remove the bolt and lock.
5. Remove the column cover and unbolt and remove the ignition switch.

To install:

6. Install both lock and switch in reverse of removal.

NOTE: When installing the lock, use special break off retaining bolts. The special bolt should be tightened until the head of bolt breaks off. When installing the switch, install the switch bolt loosely and insert and work the key a few times to make sure everything checks out before tightening the bolt.

7. Connect the negative battery cable.

Stoplight Switch
Adjustment

1. Disconnect the negative battery cable.

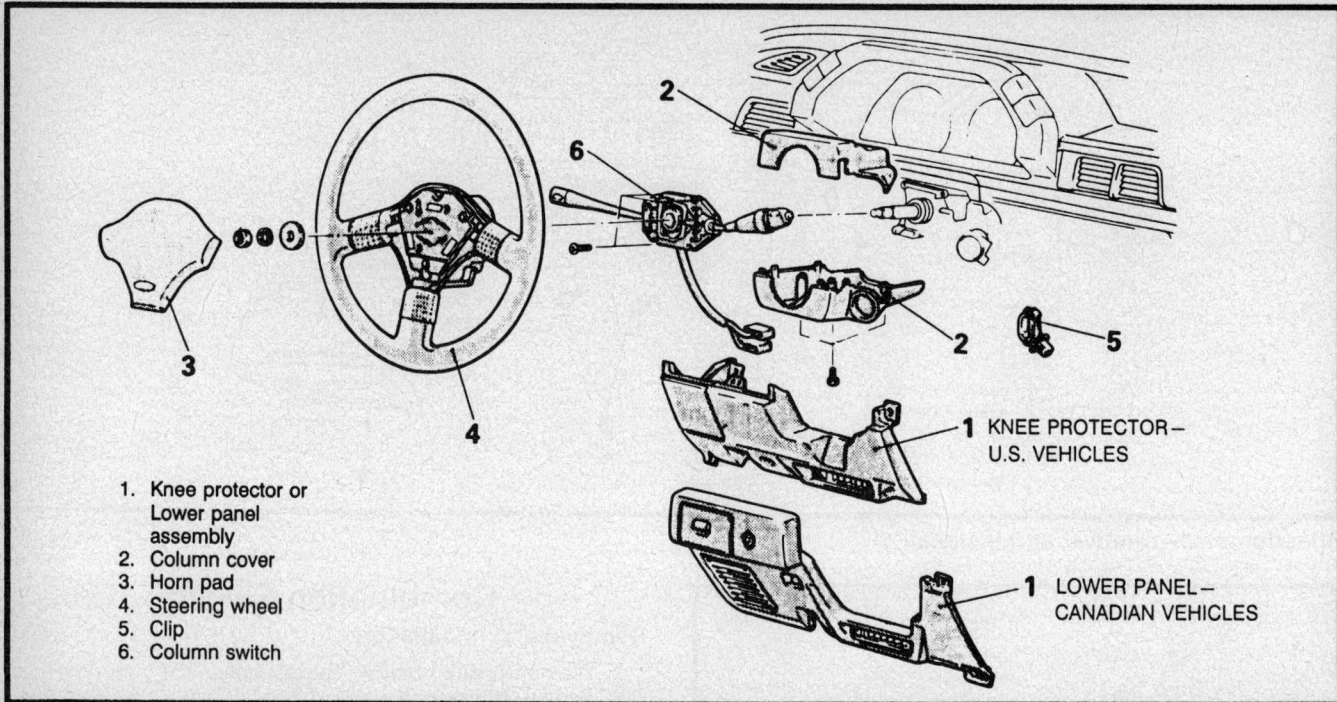

1. Knee protector or Lower panel assembly
2. Column cover
3. Horn pad
4. Steering wheel
5. Clip
6. Column switch

1 KNEE PROTECTOR— U.S. VEHICLES

1 LOWER PANEL— CANADIAN VEHICLES

Combination switch and related components

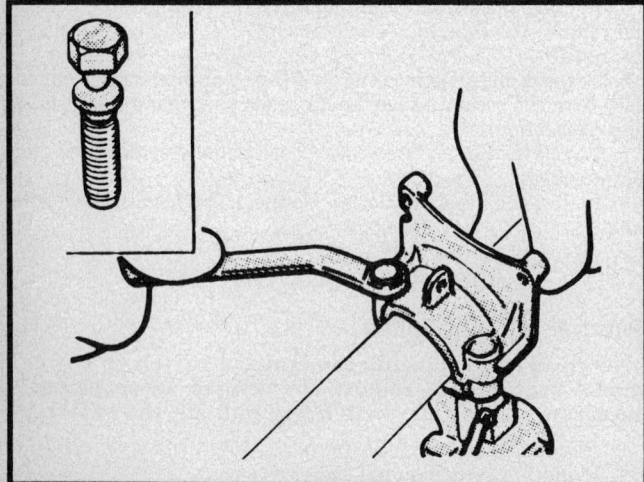

Installation of the ignition lock/switch

2. Remove the lower dash trim panel.
3. Turn switch adjustment nut until the switch plunger can be pushed in 0.16 in. (4mm), when the pedal is depressed.
4. Tighten the adjustment at that point.
5. Connect the negative battery cable and test the switch operation.

Removal and Installation

1. Disconnect the negative battery cable.
2. Remove the lower dash trim panel.
3. Disconnect the electrical connections from the switch assembly.
4. Remove the adjustment nut from the switch and pull the switch from the support.
To install:
5. Installation is the reverse order of the removal procedure. Adjust the switch.

6. Connect the negative battery cable and test switch operation.

Clutch Switch

Adjustment

1. Disconnect the negative battery cable.
2. Remove the lower dash trim panel.
3. Turn switch adjustment nut until the switch plunger can be pushed in 0.16 in. (4mm), when the pedal is depressed.
4. Tighten the adjustment at that point.
5. Connect the negative battery cable.
6. Check the switch for continuity between both terminals when the clutch pedal is depressed.

Removal and Installation

1. Disconnect the negative battery cable.
2. Remove the lower dash trim panel.
3. Disconnect the electrical connections from the switch assembly.
4. Remove the adjustment nut from the switch and pull the switch from the support.
To install:
5. Installation is the reverse order of the removal procedure. Adjust the switch.
6. Connect the negative battery cable and test switch operation.

Neutral Safety Switch

Adjustment

COLT AND COLT VISTA

1. Disconnect the negative battery cable.
2. Place the selector lever in the **N** position.
3. Working under the hood. Place the manual valve in the neutral position.
4. Loosen the switch mounting bolts.

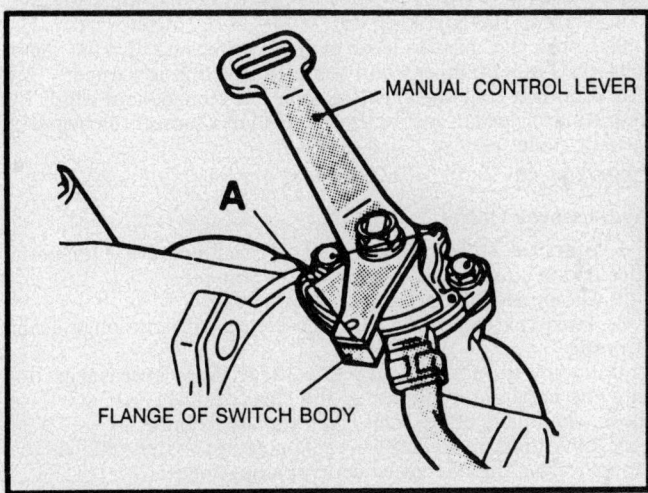

Adjusting the neutral safety switch

5. Turn the switch until the small end of the the manual lever aligns with the alignment flange on the switch.

6. Tighten the mounting bolts, being careful not to allow the switch to move out of position. Torque the mounting bolts to 7–8 ft. lbs. (10–11 Nm).

7. Connect the negative battery cable.

8. Place the selector lever in **P** and apply the foot brake. Check the starter operation in **P** and **N**.

NOTE: The engine should not start in any other gear range. If it does, repeat adjustment procedure or replace the switch as required.

9. With the ignition switch turned to the **ON** position engine off, place the selector lever in **R** and observe the back-up light operation. The back-up lights should be illuminated.

CONQUEST

1. Disconnect the negative battery cable.

2. Place the selector lever in the **N** position.

3. Raise the vehicle and support it safely.

4. Place the manual valve in the neutral position.

5. Remove the small centering screw from the switch and loosen the switch mounting bolts.

6. Using a 0.080 in. (2.0mm) drill or aligning pin, place it in the switch alignment hole.

7. Turn the switch until the pin falls into the hole. Tighten the mounting bolts, being careful not to allow the switch to move out of position.

8. Lower the vehicle. Connect the negative battery cable.

9. Place the selector lever in **P** and apply the foot brake. Check the starter operation in **P** and **N**.

NOTE: The engine should not start in any other gear range. If it does, repeat adjustment procedure or replace the switch as required.

10. With the ignition switch turn to the **ON** position engine off, place the selector lever in **R** and observe the back-up light operation. The back-up lights should be illuminated.

Removal and Installation

COLT AND COLT VISTA

1. Disconnect the negative battery cable.

2. Place the selector lever in the **N** position.

3. Working under the hood. Place the manual valve in the neutral position.

4. Remove the manual lever retaining nut and remove the manual lever.

5. Disconnect the electrical connector from the neutral safety switch.

6. Remove the switch mounting bolts and remove the switch from the transaxle.

To install:

7. Place the neutral safety switch on the transaxle manual shaft and install the mounting bolts. Do not tighten at this time.

8. Install the manual lever and retaining nut. Torque the nut to 9–10 ft. lbs. (12–14 Nm).

9. Adjust the switch as required and tighten the mounting bolts to 4–5 ft. lbs. (5–7 Nm).

10. Connect the electrical connector to the switch.

11. Connect the negative battery cable and test the switch operation.

CONQUEST

1. Disconnect the negative battery cable.

2. Place the selector lever in the **N** position.

3. Raise the vehicle and support it safely.

4. Place the manual valve in the neutral position.

5. Remove the manual lever retaining nut and remove the manual lever.

6. Disconnect the electrical connector from the neutral safety switch.

7. Remove the switch mounting bolts and remove the switch from the transaxle.

To install:

8. Place the neutral safety switch on the transaxle manual shaft and install the mounting bolts. Do not tighten at this time.

9. Install the manual lever and retaining nut. Torque the nut to 9–10 ft. lbs. (12–14 Nm).

10. Adjust the switch as required and tighten the mounting bolts to 4–5 ft. lbs. (5–7 Nm).

11. Connect the electrical connector to the switch.

12. Lower the vehicle and connect the negative battery cable.

13. Test the switch operation.

Fuses and Relays

Location

FUSE BLOCK

The fuse block is located up under the instrument panel on the driver's side of the steering column.

RELAYS

The relays are located in 2 separate relay blocks under the hood.

Relay block A and B contain the alternator, radiator fan, power window or tail light and headlight relays. This relay block is located on the right fender at the rear of the battery.

Relay block C contains the relays for the air conditioning compressor, condenser fan motor and condenser fan motor control. This relay block is located on the left front fender well near the left headlight.

Computers

Location

The Electronic Control Unit (ECU) is located on the passenger's lower kick panel.

Flashers

Location

The turn signal and hazard flashers are located in the fuse block, located under the instrument panel on the driver's side of the steering column.

Cruise Control

For further information, please refer to "Chilton's Chassis Electronics Service Manual" for additional coverage.

Adjustment
COLT AND COLT VISTA

Accelerator Cable

1. Start the engine and allow it to reach operating temperature and is stable at idle. Shut the engine off.
2. Disconnect the negative battery cable. Remove the air cleaner.
3. Adjust the cable at the throttle side.
4. Loosen the adjustment bolts at the air intake plenum side, freeing the inner cable, use the adjustment bolts to secure the plate so the free-play of the inner cable is 0.04–0.08 in. (1–2mm).

NOTE: If the free-play adjustment is incorrect, either an increase of idle speed or lack of speed control in the high speed range will result.

5. Check and make sure the throttle lever touches the idle position switch.
6. Adjust the accelerator cable at the pedal side.
7. Loosen the adjusting bolt. While keeping the intermediate link of the actuator in close contact with the stopper. Adjust the inner cable free-play to the following:
   Manual transalxe – 0–0.04 in. (0–1mm)
   Automatic transaxle – 0.08–0.12 in. (2–3mm).

8. Tighten the adjusting nut.
9. Check the throttle lever at the engine side, it must move 0.04–0.08 in. (1–2mm) when the actuator link is turned.
10. Confirm that the throttle valve fully opens and closes by operating the pedal. Install the air cleaner. Connect the negative battery cable.

CONQUEST

Accelerator Cable

1. Start the engine and allow it to reach operating temperature and is stable at idle. Shut the engine off.
2. Disconnect the negative battery cable.
3. Turn the engine on for 15 seconds with the engine not running.
4. Loosen the adjustment nut so the throttle lever is free. Rotate the accelerator nut until the throttle lever just starts to move, then back off ½ turn. Tighten the locknut.
5. Check and make sure the idle position switch touches the stopper after the idle speed control adjustment.

Control Cable

1. Adjust the accelerator cable.
2. Pull the auto-cruise control cable back until the accelerator pedal just begins to move. Secure the control cable by inserting a clip.
3. Check to ensure that control cable free-play is 0–0.01 in. (0–3mm).

NOTE: If the free-play adjustment is incorrect, either an increase of idle speed or lack of speed control in the high speed range will result.

ENGINE COOLING

Radiator

Removal and Installation

1. Remove the splash panel from the bottom of the vehicle. Drain the radiator by opening the petcock. Remove the shroud, if equipped. On the Conquest, remove the battery.
2. Disconnect the radiator hoses at the engine. On automatic transmission equipped vehicles, disconnect and plug the transmission lines to the bottom of the radiator.
3. Remove the 2 retaining bolts from either side of the radiator. Lift out the radiator. On front wheel drive vehicles, disconnect the electric fan wiring harness. Do not remove the fan motor, blades or bracket – remove as a unit with the radiator.
To install:
4. Installation is the reverse order of the removal procedure.
5. Install the radiator and retaining bolts. Tighten the retaining bolts gradually in a criss-cross pattern.

NOTE: Work around the electric cooling fan when the engine is cold or disconnect the negative battery cable. On some vehicles, the fan will run to cool the engine even when the ignition is off.

Electric Cooling Fan

Testing

1. Disconnect the negative battery cable and the fan motor connector.
2. Connect a 12 volt battery source to the fan connector.

3. If the fan operates, the motor is functioning properly. If the fan does not run replace the motor.

Removal and Installation

1. Disconnect the negative battery cable.
2. Disconnect the electrical connectors from the cooling fan.
3. Remove the fan and shroud-to-radiator bolts. Remove the fan shroud assembly.
To install:
4. Installation is the reverse order of the removal procedures.
5. Connect the negative battery cable. Start the engine and check fan operation.

Heater Core

For further information, please refer to "Chilton's Heating and Air Conditioning Manual" for additional coverage.

Removal and Installation
COLT AND COLT VISTA

1. Disconnect the negative battery cable.
2. Set the heater control lever to warm.
3. Drain the cooling system.
4. Remove the instrument panel.
5. Remove the duct from between the heater unit and the blower case.
6. Disconnect the coolant hoses at the heater case.
7. Unbolt and remove the heater case.

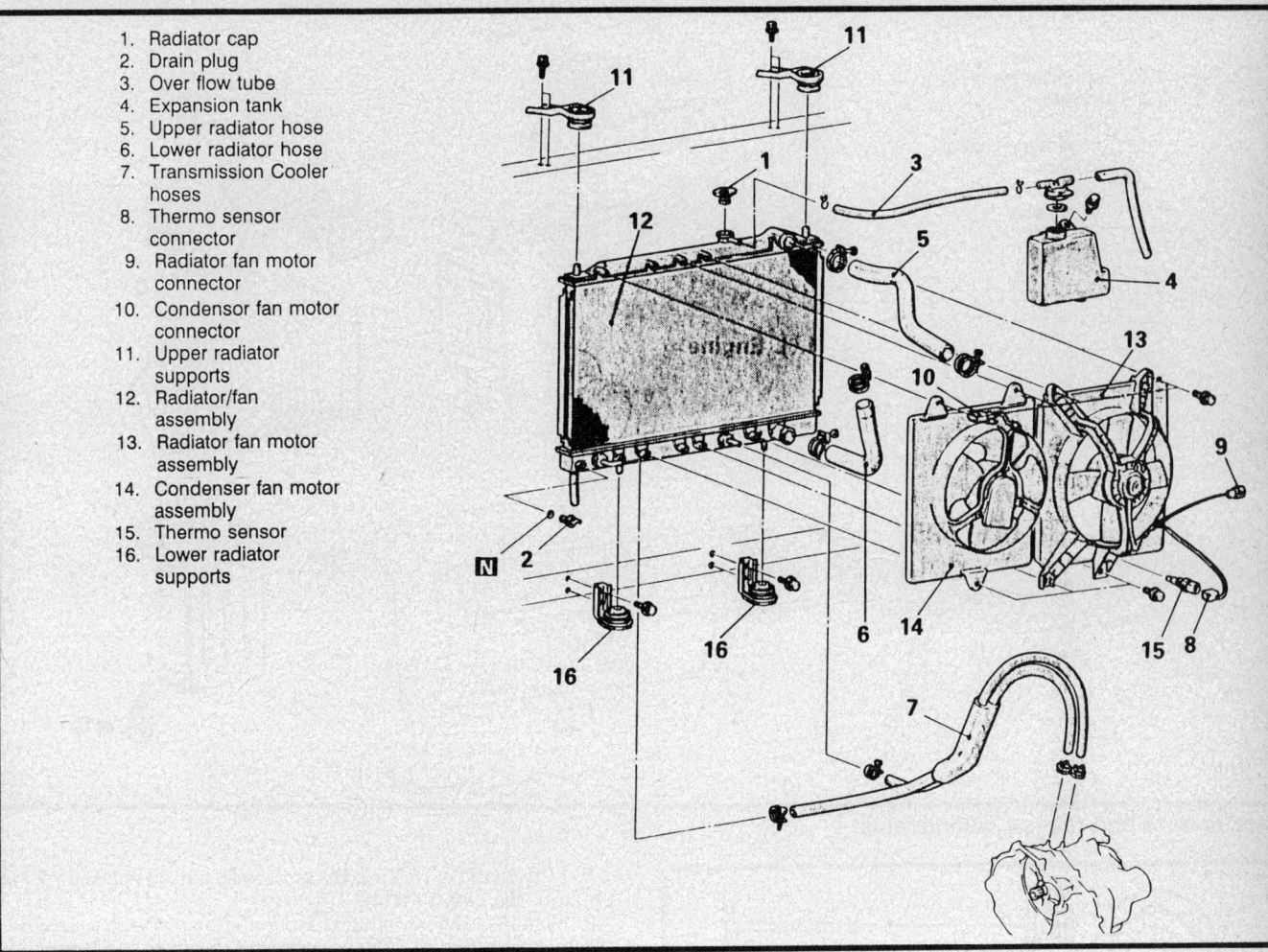

1. Radiator cap
2. Drain plug
3. Over flow tube
4. Expansion tank
5. Upper radiator hose
6. Lower radiator hose
7. Transmission Cooler hoses
8. Thermo sensor connector
9. Radiator fan motor connector
10. Condensor fan motor connector
11. Upper radiator supports
12. Radiator/fan assembly
13. Radiator fan motor assembly
14. Condenser fan motor assembly
15. Thermo sensor
16. Lower radiator supports

Electric cooling fan and related components

8. Remove the hose and pipe clamps. Remove the water valve.
9. Remove the core from the case.

To install:

10. Set the mixing damper to the closed position; with the damper in that position, install the rod so the water valve is fully closed.

11. Place the damper lever in the vent position and adjust the linkage so the foot and defrost damper opens to the defrost side and the vent damper is level with the separator.

12. Install the hoses. They are marked for flow direction.

13. Complete the installation in the the reverse order of the removal procedures.

14. Connect the negative battery cable. Refill the system and check for leaks.

CONQUEST

1. Disconnect the negative battery cable.
2. Move the control lever to warm.
3. Drain the coolant at the radiator.
4. Disconnect the coolant hoses at the heater unit.
5. Remove the instrument panel and floor console.
6. Remove the center ventilation duct, defroster duct and lap heater duct.
7. Remove the center instrument panel brace.
8. Remove the heater control assembly.
9. Remove the 3 screws and lift out the heater case.
10. Check the core for leaks, clogging and bent fins. Replace or repair as necessary.

11. Installation is the reverse order of the removal procedures. Replace any cracked hoses or damaged insulation. Refill the system and check for leaks.

Water Pump

Removal and Installation

COLT AND COLT VISTA

1. Drain the cooling system.
2. Remove the drive belt and water pump pulley.
3. Remove the timing belt covers and timing belt tensioner.
4. Remove the water pump bolts and alternator bracket.
5. Remove the water pump retaining bolts, it is important to observe the location of each bolt, they are different lengths.
6. Remove the water pump.

NOTE: The pump is not rebuildable. If there are signs of damage or leakage from the seals or vent hole, the unit must be replaced.

To install:

7. Discard the O-ring in the front end of the water pipe. Install a new O-ring coated with water.

8. Using a new gasket, mount the water pump and alternator bracket on the engine. Torque the bolts with a head marked "4"

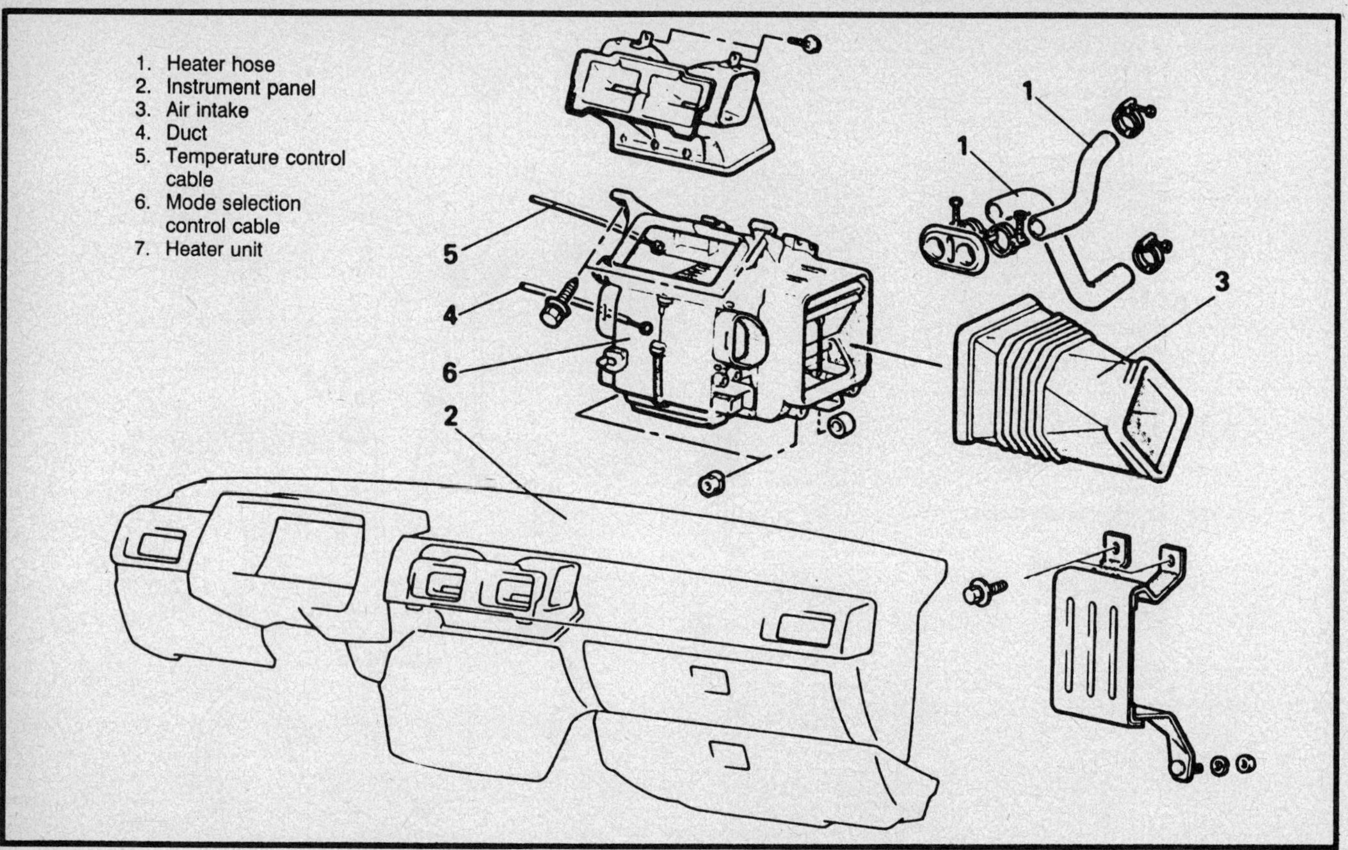

CHRYSLER CORPORATION IMPORTS
COLT • COLT VISTA • CONQUEST

1. Heater hose
2. Instrument panel
3. Air intake
4. Duct
5. Temperature control cable
6. Mode selection control cable
7. Heater unit

Heater core and related components

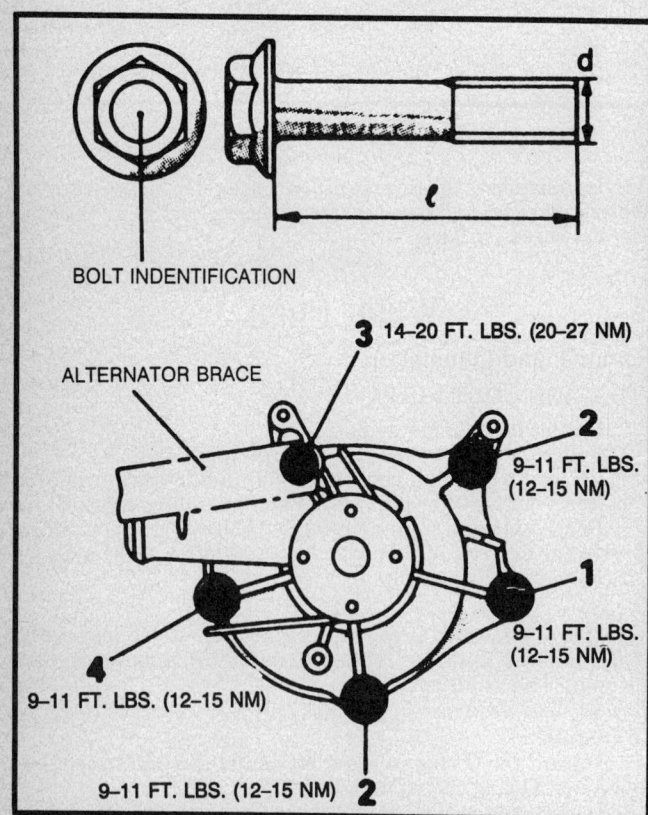

BOLT INDENTIFICATION

ALTERNATOR BRACE

3 14–20 FT. LBS. (20–27 NM)

2 9–11 FT. LBS. (12–15 NM)

1 9–11 FT. LBS. (12–15 NM)

4 9–11 FT. LBS. (12–15 NM)

9–11 FT. LBS. (12–15 NM) **2**

Water pump bolt torque identification

to 9–11 ft. lbs. (12–15 Nm); the bolts with a head marked **"7"** to 14–20 ft. lbs. (20–27 Nm).

9. Complete the remainder of installation in the reverse order of removal procedure. Fill the system with coolant and check for leaks.

CONQUEST

1. Disconnect the negative battery cable.
2. Drain the cooling system.
3. Remove the fan shroud and radiator, if necessary for working room.
4. Remove the alternator belt and accessory belts.
5. Remove the fan blades and/or automatic hub, if equipped.
6. Remove the water pump assembly from the timing chain case or the cylinder block.

To install:

7. Installation is the reverse order of the removal procedures.
8. Fill the radiator with coolant and test for leaks.

Thermostat

Removal and Installation

COLT AND COLT VISTA

1. Disconnect the negative battery cable.
2. Drain the cooling system to a point below the thermostat level.
3. Remove the air cleaner.
4. Disconnect the hose at the thermostat water pipe.
5. Remove the water pipe support bracket nut.

NOTE: This nut is also an intake manifold nut. It is very difficult to get to. A deep offset 12mm box wrench is used to remove or replace it.

6. Unbolt and remove the thermostat housing and pipe.

7. Lift out the thermostat. Discard the gasket.

To install:

8. Clean the mating surfaces of the housing and manifold thoroughly.

9. Install the thermostat with the spring facing downward and position a new gasket. The jiggle valve in the thermostat should be on the manifold side.

10. Install the housing and pipe assembly. Torque the housing bolts to 11 ft. lbs. (14 Nm); the intake manifold nut to 14 ft. lbs. (19 Nm).

11. Refill the system with coolant. Connect the negative battery cable.

12. Start the engine and check for leaks.

CONQUEST

1. Disconnect the negative battery cable.

2. Drain the coolant below the level of the thermostat.

3. Remove the retaining bolts and lift the thermostat housing off the intake manifold with the hose still in position.

4. Raise the small cone shaped cover on the throttle cable to expose the nipple.

NOTE: It is not necessary to remove the upper radiator hose.

5. Lift the thermostat out of the manifold.

To install:

6. Installation is the reverse order of the removal procedures.

Use a new gasket and coat the mating surfaces with sealer.

7. Torque the housing retaining bolts to 13–14 ft. lbs. (17–20 Nm).

Cooling System Bleeding

After working on the cooling system, even to replace the thermostat, the system must bled. Air trapped in the system will prevent proper filling and leave the radiator coolant level low, causing a risk of overheating.

1. To bleed the system, start the system cool, the radiator cap off and the radiator filled to about an inch below the filler neck.

2. Start the engine and run it at slightly above normal idle speed. This will insure adequate circulation. If air bubbles appear and the coolant level drops, fill the system with a mixture of anti-freeze and water to bring the level back to the proper level.

3. Run the engine this way until the thermostat opens. When this happens, the coolant will move abruptly across the top of the radiator and the temperature of the radiator will suddenly rise.

4. At this point, air is often expelled and the level may drop quite a bit. Keep refilling the system until the level is near the top of the radiator and remains constant.

5. If the vehicle has an overflow tank, fill the radiator up to the top of the filler neck.

FUEL SYSTEM

Fuel System Service Precautions

Safety is the most important factor when performing not only fuel system maintenance but any type of maintenance. Failure to conduct maintenance and repairs in a safe manner may result in serious personal injury or death. Maintenance and testing of the vehicle's fuel system components can be accomplished safely and effectively by adhering to the following rules and guidelines.

• To avoid the possibility of fire and personal injury, always disconnect the negative battery cable unless the repair or test procedure requires that battery voltage be applied.

• Always relieve the fuel system pressure prior to disconnecting any fuel system component (injector, fuel rail, pressure regulator, etc.), fitting or fuel line connection. Exercise extreme caution whenever relieving fuel system pressure to avoid exposing skin, face and eyes to fuel spray. Please be advised that fuel under pressure may penetrate the skin or any part of the body that it contacts.

• Always place a shop towel or cloth around the fitting or connection prior to loosening to absorb any excess fuel due to spillage. Ensure that all fuel spillage (should it occur) is quickly removed from engine surfaces. Ensure that all fuel soaked cloths or towels are deposited into a suitable waste container.

• Always keep a dry chemical (Class B) fire extinguisher near the work area.

• Do not allow fuel spray or fuel vapors to come into contact with a spark or open flame.

• Always use a backup wrench when loosening and tightening fuel line connection fittings. This will prevent unnecessary stress and torsion to fuel line piping. Always follow the proper torque specifications.

• Always replace worn fuel fitting O-rings with new. Do not substitute fuel hose or equivalent where fuel pipe is installed.

Relieving Fuel System Pressure

1. Disconnect the fuel pump harness connector at the fuel tank side.

2. Start the engine and allow it to continue running until it stalls.

3. Set the ignition to the **OFF** position.

4. Reconnect the fuel pump harness connector.

Fuel Filter

Removal and Installation

CARBURETED ENGINE

1. Disconnect the negative battery cable.

2. Pull the filter from its bracket and discard it.

To install:

3. Snap the replacement filter into the bracket.

4. Install the lines on the filter and tighten the hose clamps.

5. Start the engine and check for leaks.

FUEL INJECTED ENGINE

1. Relieve the fuel system pressure.

2. Disconnect the negative battery cable. Remove the air cleaner.

3. Using a backup wrench, remove the fuel line fittings from the fuel filter.

NOTE: Some pressure may still remain in the system, cover the filter connections with a rag to prevent splashing.

4. Remove the fuel filter mounting bolts and the filter from the vehicle.

To install:

5. Installation is the reverse order of the removal procedures.

Use a new fuel filter and O-rings. Torque the fuel line-to-filter connectors to 25 ft. lbs. (35 Nm).

Mechanical Fuel Pump

A mechanical fuel pump is used on the 1987–88 1468cc engine.

Pressure Testing

Disconnect the fuel line from the carburetor and attach a pressure tester to the end of the line. Crank the engine. The pressure should be 2.7–3.7 psi.

Removal and Installation

The pump is mounted on the front side of the engine and is driven by an eccentric on the camshaft.

1. Relieve the fuel system pressure. Disconnect the negative battery cable.
2. Disconnect the fuel lines at the fuel pump.
3. Unbolt the pump mounting bolts, remove the pump, insulator and gasket.
4. Coat both sides of a new insulator and gasket with sealer and install the pump in the reverse order of removal.

Electric Fuel Pump

Pressure Testing

1. Install a suitable fuel pressure gauge to the fuel delivery pipe, be sure to tighten the bolt at 18–25 ft. lbs.
2. Apply voltage to the terminal for the fuel pump drive and activate the fuel pump; then, with fuel pressure applied, check that there is no fuel leakage from the pressure gauge or the special tool connection pipe.
3. Disconnect the vacuum hose from the pressure regulator and plug the hose end. Measure the fuel pressure during idling. The standard value is 36–36 psi (245–264 kPa).
4. Measure the fuel pressure when the vacuum hose is connected to the pressure regulator. The standard value is 28 psi (196 kPa).
5. If the fuel pressure readings are not within specifications, determine the probable cause and make the necessary repairs.
6. Remove all test equipment, use a new gasket and tighten the bolt on the delivery pipe to 18–25 ft. lbs. Start the engine and check for fuel leaks.

Removal and Installation

The fuel pump is mounted inside of the fuel tank on Colt and Colt Vista and is mounted externally on top of the fuel tank in the Conquest.

1. Relieve the pressure from the fuel system. Disconnect the negative battery cable.

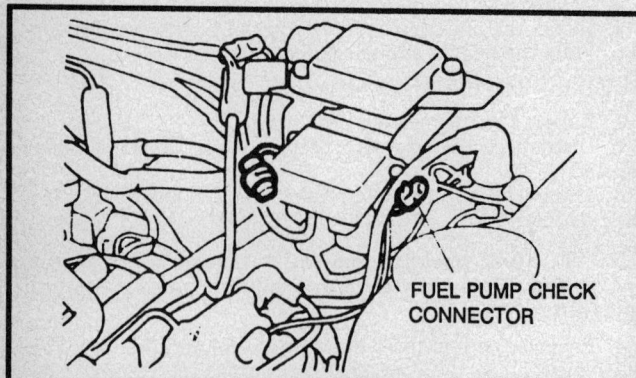

FUEL PUMP CHECK CONNECTOR

Colt Turbo fuel pump test connectors

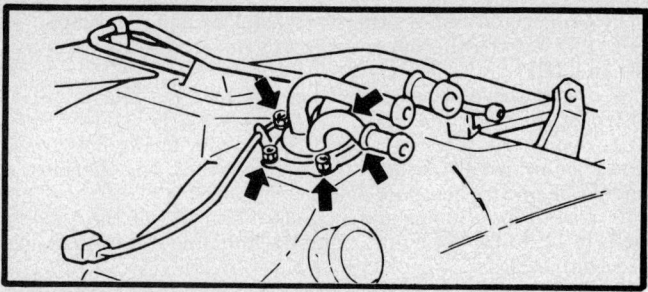

Colt Turbo electric fuel pump location. The arrows indicate the mounting bolts

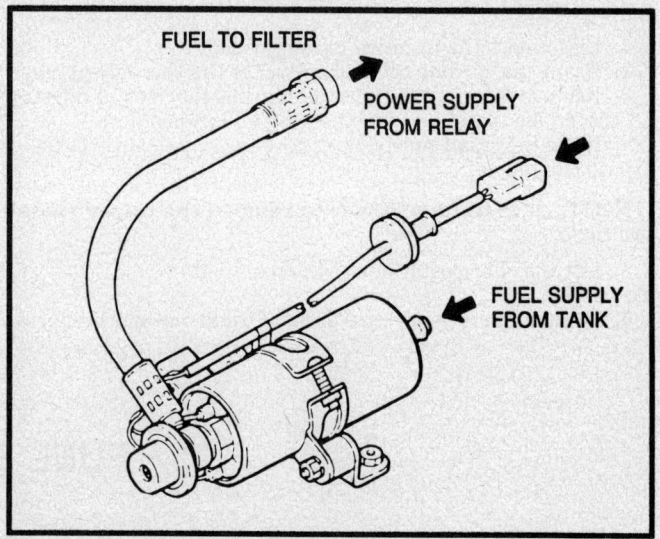

FUEL TO FILTER

POWER SUPPLY FROM RELAY

FUEL SUPPLY FROM TANK

Conquest electric fuel pump

2. If equipped with a drain plug remove it and drain the fuel into a suitable container. Support the vehicle safely. Remove the left rear wheel.
3. Support the fuel tank with a suitable floor jack. Loosen the fuel tank band mounting nuts and lower the tank for access to the pump support. Then, remove the nut and bolt attaching the pump clamp to the support.
4. Disconnect the fuel lines, noting their locations and remove the pump. If the pump is being replaced, switch the mounting clamp to the new pump and install it at the same angle.

To install:

5. Installation is the reverse order of the removal procedure. Make sure fuel line connections are tight and secure. Operate the pump and check for leaks.

Carburetor

Removal and Installation

1. Disconnect the negative battery cable.
2. Remove the solenoid valve wiring.
3. Disconnect the air cleaner breather hose, air duct and vacuum tube.
4. Remove the air cleaner.
5. Remove the air cleaner case.
6. If equipped with automatic transaxle, disconnect the accelerator and shift cables, at the carburetor.
7. Disconnect the purge valve hose. Remove the vacuum compensator and fuel lines.
8. Drain the coolant.

9. Remove the water hose between the carburetor and the cylinder head.

10. Remove the carburetor.

To install:

11. Installation is the reverse order of removal procedures.

12. Clean the manifold and carburetor mounting surfaces.

13. Install the carburetor and mounting bolts. Torque the mounting bolts to 11–14 (15–20 Nm).

Idle Speed Idle and Mixture Adjustment

NOTE: The throttle valve adjusting screw should not be tampered with unless the carburetor has been rebuilt. This screw is preset and determines the relationship between the throttle valve and the free lever and has been accurately set at the factory. If this setting is disturbed, the throttle opener adjustment and or dashpot adjustment cannot be done accurately. Also the improper setting (throttle valve opening) will increase the exhaust gas temperature and deceleration, which in turn will reduce the life of the catalyst greatly and deteriorate the exhaust gas cleaning performance. It will also effect the fuel consumption and the engine braking.

1. Disconnect the negative battery cable.

2. Remove the carburetor from the engine.

3. Place the carburetor in a suitable holding fixture with the idle mixture adjusting screw facing up.

4. Drill a $\frac{5}{64}$ in. (2mm) hole in the casting surrounding the idle mixture adjusting screw, then redrill the hole to $\frac{1}{8}$ in. (3mm).

5. Insert a punch in the hole and drive out plug.

6. Reinstall the carburetor to the engine and connect the negative battery cable.

7. Start the engine and run at fast idle, allow it to reach operating temperature.

8. All lights and accessories must be off.

9. Disconnect the electrical connector from the the coolant fan during idle and mixture adjustments.

10. Place the transaxle in **P** or **N**, if equipped with automatic transaxle and neutral, if equipped with manual transaxle.

11. Connect a timing light or tachometer, check and adjust the basic timing, as required.

12. Disconnect the negative battery cable for 3 seconds, then reconnect it.

13. Disconnect the electrical connector from the oxygen sensor.

14. Run the engine at 2000–3000 rpm for 5–10 seconds and allow it to idle for 2 minutes.

15. Adjust the idle CO and engine speed as follows:

Adjust the idle Speed Adjustment Screw No. 1 (SAS–1) to 800 rpm.

Adjust idle Mixture Adjustment Screw (MAS) to 0.1–0.3 percent CO.

NOTE: The idle Speed Adjustment Screw No. 2 (SAS–2) determines the relationship between the throttle valve and free lever. This adjustment is factory preset and therefore should not be distrubed. If the CO adjustment fails, it is likely there is a loss of vacuum at the secondary air hose. Plug the air hose and try the CO adjustment again.

16. Turn the ignition switch **OFF** and connect the oxygen connector.

17. Install the concealed plug into the hole to seal the idle mixture adjusting screw.

18. Connect the electrical connector to the coolant fan.

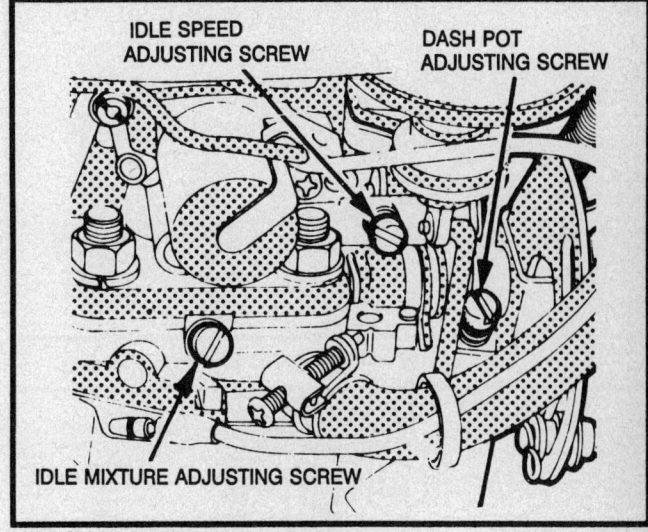

Idle speed adjusting screw

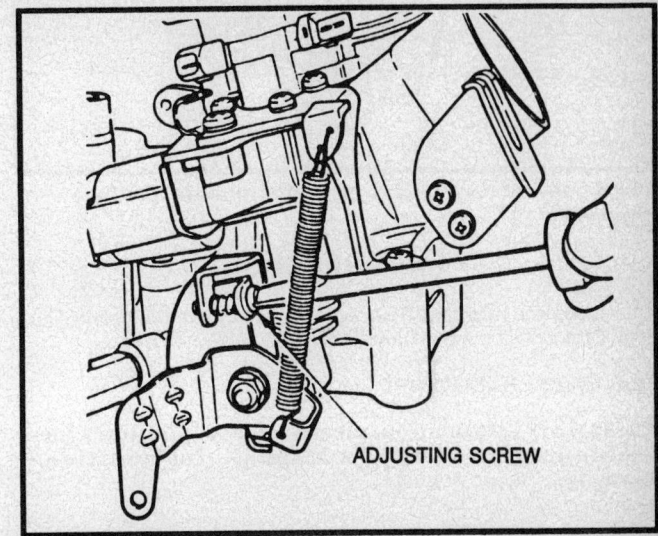

Fuel injection unit idle speed adjusting screw

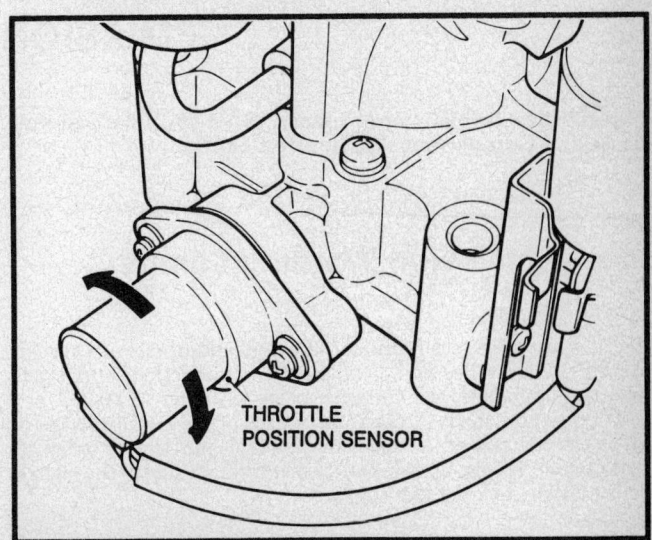

Throttle position sensor adjustment

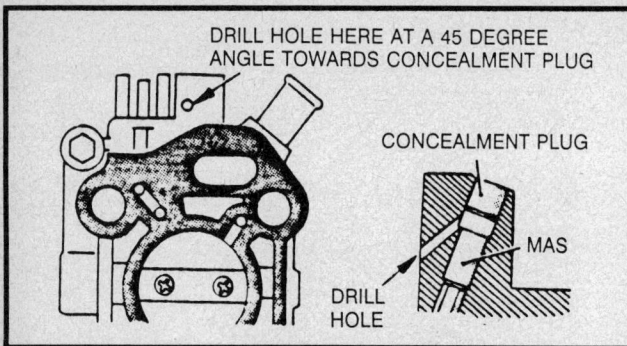

Drilling a hole for the idle mixture screw

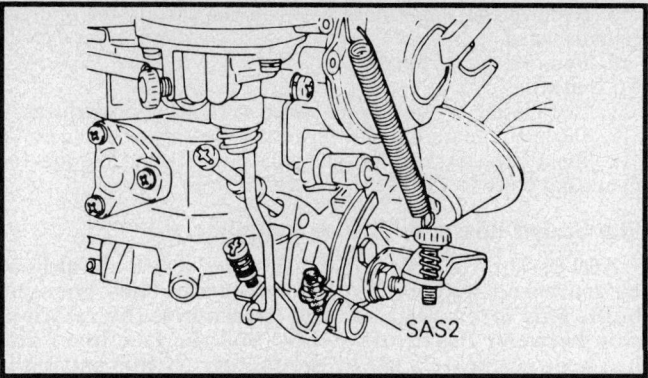

Idle speed adjustment screw SAS-2 — location

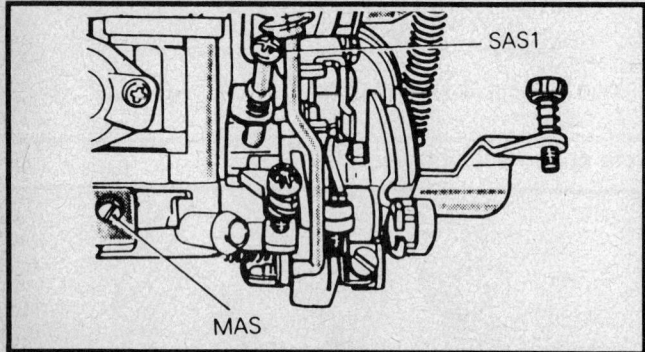

Idle speed screw SAS–1 and idle mixture screw—
locations

Fuel Injection

Idle speed and idle mixture are controlled by the Electronic Control Unit (ECU). Adjustments are therefore not needed.

Idle Speed Adjustment

For further information, please refer to "Chilton's Electronic Engine Control's Manual" for additional coverage.

Fuel Injector

Removal and Installation

1. Relieve the fuel system pressure.
2. Disconnect the negative battery cable.
3. Disconnect the fuel rail assembly, so the fuel injectors are easily accessible.
4. Remove the injector clip from the fuel rail and injector. Pull the injector straight out of the fuel rail receiver cup.
5. Check the injector O-ring for damage. If the O-ring is damaged, replace it. If the injector is being reused, install a protective cap on the injector tip to prevent damage.

To install:
6. Installation is the reverse order of the removal procedures. Before installing the injector, the rubber O-ring must be lubricated with a drop of clean engine oil to aid in installation.
7. Make sure all fuel connections are tight. Connect the negative battery cable.
8. Start the engine and check for leaks.

EMISSION CONTROLS

For further information, please refer to "Professional Emission Component Application Guide".

Emission Warning Lamps

Resetting

An EGR maintenance reminder lamp will illuminate at approximately 50,000 miles and after the EGR inspection/service has been accomplished, the lamp timer switch must be reset.

The reset button is located on the back of the instrument panel, on the left side of the speedometer cable junction or below it. It is only necessary to slide the switch from on side of the switch to the other, to reset the sensor.

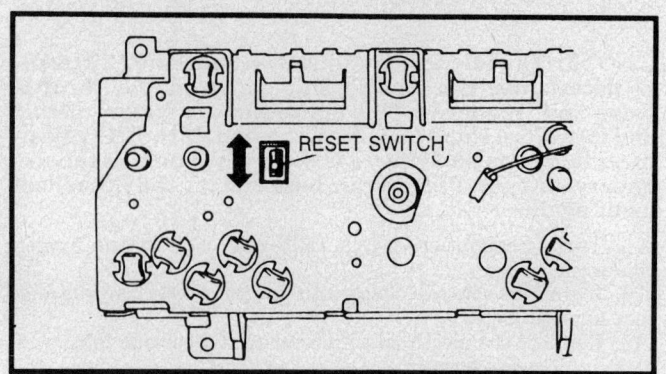

Emission warning Lamp—reset switch location

ENGINE MECHANICAL

NOTE: Disconnecting the negative battery cable on some vehicles may interfere with the functions of the on board computer systems and may require the computer to undergo a relearning process, once the negative battery cable is reconnected.

Engine Assembly

Removal and Installation

1468CC AND 1597CC ENGINES

The factory recommends that the engine and transaxle be removed as a unit.

1. Disconnect the battery cables, negative cable first. Remove the battery and the tray.
2. Remove the air cleaner assembly. Disconnect the purge control valve. Remove the purge control valve mounting bracket. Remove the windshield washer reservoir, radiator tank and carbon canister.
3. Drain the coolant from the radiator. Remove the radiator assembly with the electric cooling fan attached. Be sure to disconnect the fan wiring harness and the transaxle cooler lines, if equipped.
4. Disconnect the following cables, hoses and wires from the engine and transaxle: clutch, accelerator, speedometer, heater hose, fuel lines, PCV vacuum line, high altitude compensator vacuum hose (California vehicles), bowl vent valve purge hose (U.S.A. vehicles), inhibitor switch (automatic transaxle), control cable (automatic transaxle), starter, engine ground cable, alternator, water temperature gauge, ignition coil, temperature sensor, back-up light (manual transaxle), oil pressure wires and the ISC cable on fuel injected vehicles.

NOTE: On fuel injected vehicles, release fuel system pressure before disconnecting any fuel lines.

5. Remove the ignition coil. Be sure all wires and hoses are disconnected.
6. Raise the vehicle and support safely. Remove the splash shield, if equipped.
7. Drain the lubricant out of the transaxle.
8. Remove the right and left halfshafts from the transaxle and support them with wire. Plug the transaxle case holes so dirt cannot enter.

NOTE: The halfshaft retainer ring should be replaced whenever the shaft is removed.

9. Disconnect the assist rod and the control rod from the transaxle. If the vehicle is equipped with a range selector, disconnect the selector cable.
10. Remove the mounting bolts from the front and rear roll control rods.
11. Disconnect the exhaust pipe from the engine and secure it with wire.
12. Loosen the engine and transaxle mounting bracket nuts. On turbocharged engines, disconnect the oil cooler tube.
13. Lower the vehicle.
14. Attach a lifting device to the engine. Apply slight lifting pressure to the engine. Remove the engine and transaxle mounting nuts and bolts.
15. Make sure the rear roll control rod is disconnected. Lift the engine and transaxle from the vehicle.

NOTE: Make sure the transaxle does not hit the battery bracket when the engine and transaxle are lifted.

To install:
16. Lower the engine and transaxle carefully into position and loosely install the mounting bolts.

17. Temporarily tighten the front and rear roll control rod mounting bolts.
18. Lower the full weight of the engine and transaxle onto the mounts, tighten the nuts and bolts.
19. Loosen and retighten the roll control rods.
20. Complete the rest of the installation in the reverse order of the removal procedures.
21. Make sure all cables, hoses and wires are connected.
22. Fill the radiator with coolant, the transaxle with lubricant.
23. Adjust the clutch cable and accelerator cable. Adjust the transaxle control rod.
24. Connnect the negative battery cable. Start the engine and check for leaks.

1595CC DOHC ENGINE

1. Disconnect the battery cables, negative cable first. Remove the battery.
2. Raise the vehicle and support it safely. Relieve the fuel system pressure.
3. Drain the cooling system and the engine oil.
4. Disconnect the exhaust pipe from the turbocharger after removing the heat shields.
5. Remove the radiator. Remove the transaxle.
6. Remove the air cleaner. Disconnect the accelerator cable, the vacuum hose from the brake booster and all vacuum hoses. Label the hoses for correct installation.
7. Disconnect the high pressure fuel line and the fuel return hose. Remove their respective mounting O-rings.
8. Disconnect the heater hoses, the oxygen sensor, the coolant temperature sensor and the connection for the engine coolant temperature gauge unit.
9. Disconnect the engine coolant switch for the air conditioner. Disconnect the fuel injector wiring connection, the ignition coil, the power transistor, vacuum lines and the ISC motor.
10. On California vehicles, disconnect the EGR temperature sensor.
11. Disconnect the detonation sensor, the throttle position sensor, the crankshaft angle sensor and the control wiring harness connectors.
12. Disconnect the oil pressure switch for the power steering. Disconnect the alternator wiring. Remove the wiring harness mounting clamps. Disconnect the engine oil pressure switch.
13. Remove the air conditioning compressor, with lines attached and safely wire the assembly out of the way.
14. Remove the power steering pump, with hoses attached and safely wire it out of the way.
15. Connect a chain hoist to the engine with a suitable lifting bracket. Take up slack on the engine. Check to be sure all cables, hoses, harness connectors and vacuum hoses have been disconnected.
16. Remove the engine mounting bracket. Disconnect the front engine roll stopper and the rear roll stopper. Carefully raise and remove the engine assembly.

To install:
17. Installation is the reverse order of the removal procedure.
18. Make sure all cables, vacuum lines, hose and wire connectors are installed or attached.
19. Fill the radiator with the proper coolant mix. Fill the engine with the proper oil.
20. Adjust the clutch and accelerator cables.
21. Connect the negative battery cable. Start the engine and check for leaks.

1755CC AND 1997CC ENGINES

1. Disconnect the battery cables, negative battery cable first. Remove the battery, battery tray and bracket.
2. Disconnect the engine oil pressure switch and power steering pump connectors.

3. Disconnect the alternator harness.

4. Remove the air cleaner.

5. Remove the high tension cable from the distributor.

6. Disconnect the engine ground wire at the firewall.

7. Remove the windshield washer bottle.

8. Disconnect the brake booster vacuum hose.

9. Disconnect and tag all other vacuum lines connected to the engine.

10. Drain the coolant.

11. Remove the coolant reservoir tank.

12. Remove the radiator.

13. Disconnect the heater hoses at the engine.

14. Disconnect the accelerator cable from the carburetor.

15. Disconnect the speed control cable at the carburetor.

16. Disconnect the speedometer cable at the transaxle.

17. If equipped with air conditioning, the system must be evacuated.

18. Disconnect the hose at the air conditioning compressor and cap all openings immediately.

19. Disconnect the hoses at the power steering pump.

20. Disconnect the fuel return hose, then the fuel inlet hose, at the carburetor.

21. Disconnect the shift control cables at the transaxle.

22. Raise the vehicle and support it safely.

23. Remove the lower cover and skid plate.

24. Drain the transaxle and transfer case.

25. Disconnect the exhaust pipe from the manifold.

26. Remove the clutch slave cylinder.

27. Disconnect the halfshafts at the transaxle.

28. Remove the transfer case extension stopper bracket.

NOTE: The 2 top stopper bracket bolts are easier to get at from the engine compartment, using a T-type box wrench.

29. Lower the vehicle to the ground.

30. Remove the nuts only, from the engine mount-to-body bracket.

31. Remove the range select control valves from the transaxle insulator bracket.

32. Remove the nut only, from the transaxle mounting insulator.

33. Remove the front roll insulator nut.

34. Remove the rear insulator-to-engine nut.

35. Remove the grille and valance panel.

36. Remove the air conditioning condenser.

37. Take up the weight of the engine with a lifting device attached to the lifting eyes.

38. Remove all the mounting bolts.

39. Double check that all wiring, hoses and cables are disconnected from the engine, transaxle and transfer case have been disconnected. Move the assembly forward slightly, to a point at which it will clear the floorpan and lift the whole assembly clear of the vehicle.

To install:

40. Secure the engine to a suitable lifting device.

41. Carefully lower the engine and transaxle into position and loosely install the mounting bolts.

42. Temporarily tighten the front and rear roll control rod mounting bolts.

43. Lower the full weight of the engine and transaxle onto the mounts, tighten the nuts and bolts.

44. Loosen and retighten the roll control rods.

45. Complete the rest of the installation in the reverse order of the removal procedures.

46. Make sure all cables, hoses and wires are connected.

47. Fill the radiator with coolant, the transaxle with lubricant.

48. Adjust the clutch cable and accelerator cable. Adjust the transaxle control rod.

49. Observe the following torques:
   Transaxle stopper—58 ft. lbs. (79 Nm).
   Engine-to-body bracket bolts—47 ft. lbs. (64 Nm).
   Rear insulator—29 ft. lbs. (39 Nm).
   Transaxle mount nuts—58 ft. lbs. (79 Nm).
   Heat shield—7 ft. lbs. (9.5 Nm).
   Front roll bracket nuts—36 ft. lbs. (49 Nm).

50. Connnect the negative battery cable. Start the engine and check for leaks.

2555CC ENGINE

The factory recommends removing the engine and transmission as a unit.

1. Disconnect and remove the battery and tray.

2. Drain the cooling system.

3. Disconnect the coil, throttle positioner solenoid, fuel cut-off solenoid, alternator, starter, transmission switch, backup light switch and temperature and oil pressure gauge sending units.

4. If equipped with air conditioning, the refrigerant must be released from the system. After the system has been drained, disconnect and cap lines at the compressor and condenser.

5. Remove all air cleaners hoses. Remove the wing nut, snap clips and the air cleaner to cover.

6. Remove the 2 retaining nuts and bracket and remove the air cleaner housing.

7. Disconnect the accelerator cable.

8. Remove and plug the radiator hose.

9. Remove the exhaust manifold nuts and drop the pipe down and out of the way.

10. Disconnect and cap the fuel lines at the pump. If equipped with fuel injection, bleed the pressure from the system before disconnecting the lines.

11. Disconnect the vacuum hose from the canister purge valve located on the passenger side firewall. Remove the purge hose which runs from the valve to the intake manifold.

12. Scribe a line around the hood hinges and then remove the hood. Place it away from the work area to avoid it being scratched or dented.

13. Remove the grill, radiator cross panel and the radiator. Disconnect and plug the oil cooler lines, if equipped with automatic transmission. Disconnect and plug the engine oil cooler lines at the engine on turbocharged vehicles. Remove and secure the power steering pump, with hoses connected and place it out of the way.

14. Raise the vehicle and support it safely. Remove the splash shield.

15. Drain the engine oil and the transmission fluid. Remove the driveshaft.

16. Disconnect the speedometer cable and back-up light switch wire. Remove the neutral switch on automatic equipped vehicles.

17. Disconnect the clutch cable from the clutch lever.

18. Remove the control rod and the cross shaft that are located under the transmission.

19. Untie and open the leather shift boot. Pull the rug back. Remove the 4 retaining bolts and remove the shift lever.

20. If equipped with an automatic transmission, disconnect the transmission control rod from the shift linkage.

21. Attach the lifting device to the 2 engine brackets provided by the factory, one near the water neck at the front and the other on the passenger's side at the rear.

22. Raise the engine a slight amount and remove the retaining nuts on the side mounts and the rear crossmember mount.

23. Lift the engine out of the engine compartment.

24. Check the condition of the engine mounts. There are 3: left front, right front and rear. Replace, if required.

To install:

25. Installation is reverse order of the removal procedure.

26. Secure the engine to a suitable lifting device.

27. Carefully lower the engine and transmission into position and loosely install the mounting bolts.

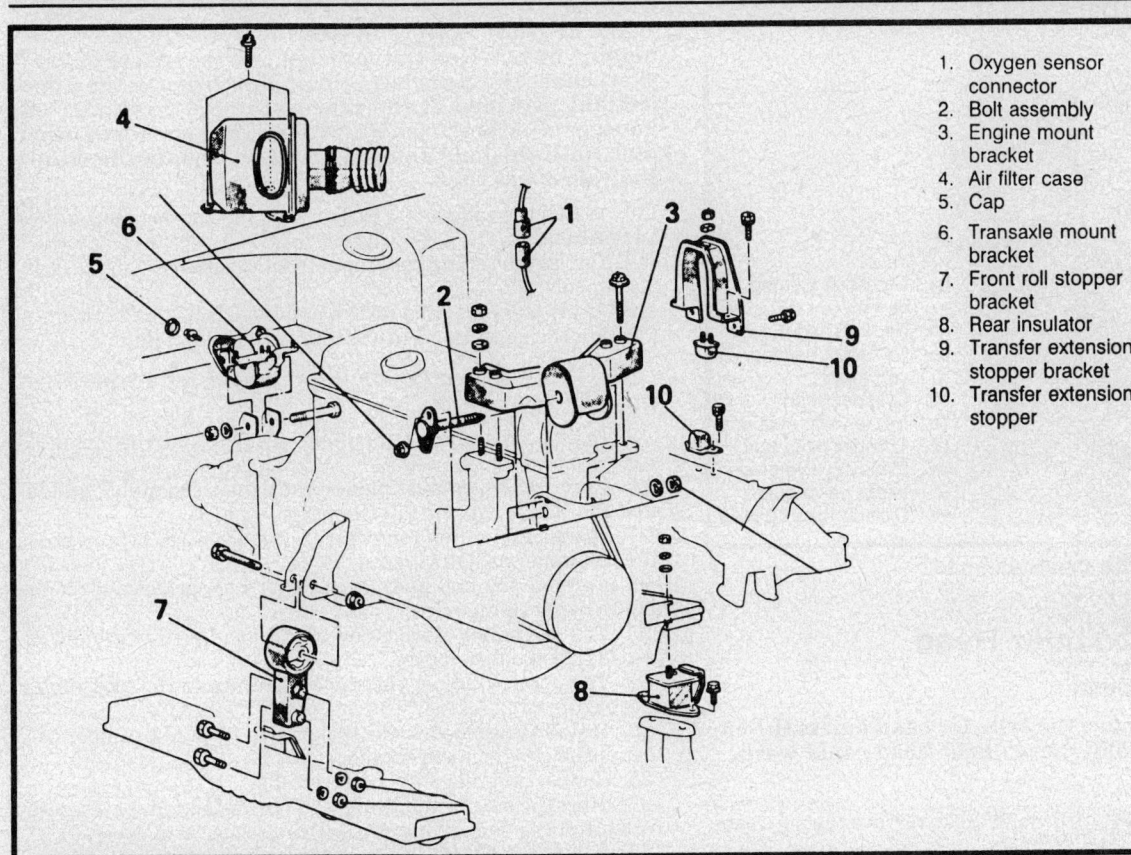

1. Oxygen sensor connector
2. Bolt assembly
3. Engine mount bracket
4. Air filter case
5. Cap
6. Transaxle mount bracket
7. Front roll stopper bracket
8. Rear insulator
9. Transfer extension stopper bracket
10. Transfer extension stopper

Exploded view of the engine mounts

28. Temporarily tighten the front and rear roll control rod mounting bolts.
29. Lower the full weight of the engine and transmission onto the mounts, tighten the nuts and bolts.
30. Loosen and retighten the roll control rods.
31. Make sure all cables, hoses and wires are connected.
32. Fill the radiator with coolant, the transmission with lubricant.
33. Adjust the and accelerator cable. Adjust the transmission control rod.
34. Observe the following torques:
Front mount-to-crossmember—15–17 ft. lbs.
Front mount-to-engine bracket nut—15–17 ft. lbs.
Front engine block-to-bracket bolt—29–36 ft. lbs.
Rear mount-to-support bracket—7–8.5 ft. lbs.
Rear mount-to-frame bolt—15–17 ft. lbs.
Crossmember-to-body bolt—9–11 ft. lbs. for manual transmission or 7–8.5 ft. lbs. for automatic transmission
35. Connnect the negative battery cable. Start the engine and check for leaks.

Engine Mounts

Removal and Installation

COLT AND COLT VISTA

1. Disconnect the negative battery cable.
2. Using an engine support fixture tool, center it on the cowl and attach it to the engine. Raise the engine slightly to take the weight off of the engine mounts.
3. From the front of the engine, remove the engine mount bolts and the mount.

4. Inspect the engine mount for deterioration and replace it, if necessary.
To install:
5. To install, support the engine using a engine support fixture tool.
6. Install the engine mounts and the retaining bolts to the engine.
7. Torque the engine mount-to-bracket bolts to 36–47 ft. lbs. (50–65 Nm) and the mount through bolt to 65–80 ft. lbs. (90–110 Nm).
8. Connect the negative battery cable.

CONQUEST

1. Disconnect the negative battery cable.
2. Raise the vehicle and support it safely.
3. Support the engine and transmission assembly using a suitable jack.
4. Remove the engine mount-to-bracket retaining nuts. Remove the mount-to-frame retaining bolts. Raise the engine slightly, just enough to allow the mount to clear the frame.
5. Remove the mount.
To install:
6. Position the mount between the engine and frame and install the mount-to-bracket retaining nuts.
7. Lower the the engine weight on the engine mounts, but not completely, it may be necessary to move the engine back and forward, order to install the mount-to-frame retaining bolts.
8. Install the mount-to-frame retaining bolts and lower the weight of the engine completely.
9. Torque the mount-to-bracket retaining nuts to 8–12 ft. lbs. (6–9 Nm) and the mount-to-frame retaining bolts to 22–29 ft. lbs. (30–40 Nm).
10. Lower the vehicle. Connect the negative battery cable.

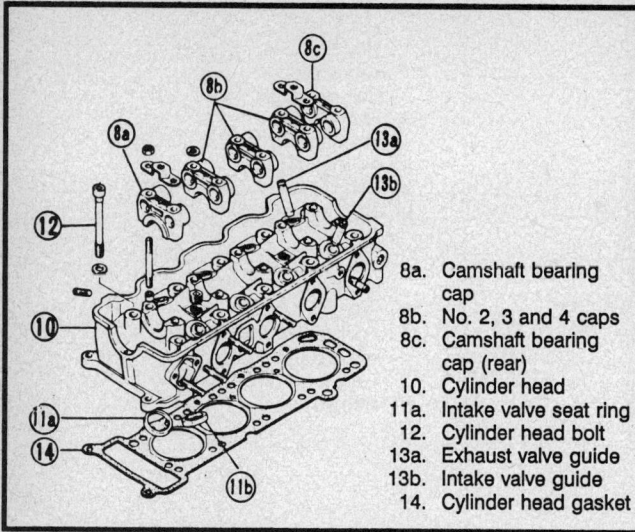

8a. Camshaft bearing cap
8b. No. 2, 3 and 4 caps
8c. Camshaft bearing cap (rear)
10. Cylinder head
11a. Intake valve seat ring
12. Cylinder head bolt
13a. Exhaust valve guide
13b. Intake valve guide
14. Cylinder head gasket

Exploded view of the cylinder head

Cylinder Head

Removal and Installation

NOTE: Never remove the cylinder head unless the engine is absolutely cold; the cylinder head could warp.

1468CC ENGINE

1. Disconnect the battery ground cable, remove the air cleaner assembly and the attached hoses.
2. Drain the coolant, remove the upper radiator hose and the heater hoses.
3. On fuel injected vehicles, release the fuel system pressure. Remove the fuel line, disconnect the accelerator linkage, distributor vacuum lines, purge valve and water temperature gauge wire.
4. Remove the spark plug wires and the fuel pump. Remove the distributor, where necessary.
5. Disconnect the exhaust pipe from the exhaust manifold flange.
6. Remove the exhaust manifold assembly.
7. Remove the intake manifold and carburetor as a unit.
8. Turn the crankshaft to No. 1 piston at TDC on the compression stroke.

NOTE: During the following procedure, do not turn the crankshaft after locating TDC.

9. Remove the timing belt cover. Be sure the knockout pin is at 12 o'clock and the cam sprocket mark and cylinder head pointer are aligned at 3 o'clock. Loosen the timing belt tensioner mounting. Move the tensioner toward the water pump and secure it in that position. Remove the rocker arm cover.

NOTE: The cam pulley need not be removed.

10. Loosen and remove the cylinder head bolts in 2–3 stages to avoid cylinder head warpage.
11. Remove the cylinder head from the engine block.
To install:
12. Clean the cylinder head and block mating surfaces and install a new cylinder head gasket.
13. Position the cylinder head on the engine block, engage the dowel pins front and rear and install the cylinder head bolts.
14. Tighten the head bolts in, 3 stages, to 50–54 ft. lbs. (68–73 Nm).
15. Locate the camshaft in original position. Pull the camshaft sprocket and belt or chain upward and install on the camshaft.

NOTE: If the dowel pin and the dowel pin hole does not line up between the sprocket and the spacer or camshaft, move the camshaft by bumping either of the 2 projections provided at the rear of the No. 2 cylinder exhaust cam of the camshaft, with a light hammer or other tool, until the hole and pin align. Be certain the crankshaft does not turn.

16. Install the camshaft sprocket bolt and the distributor gear and tighten.
17. Install the timing belt upper front cover and spark plug cable support.
18. Apply sealant to the intake manifold gasket on both sides. Position the gasket and install the intake manifold.

NOTE: Be sure no sealant enters the jet air passages when equipped.

19. Install the exhaust manifold gaskets and the manifold assembly.
20. Connect the exhaust pipe to the exhaust manifold and install the fuel pump. Install the purge valve.
21. Install the water temperature gauge wire, heater hoses and the upper radiator hose.
22. Connect the fuel lines, accelerator linkage, vacuum hoses and the spark plug wires.
23. Fill the cooling system and connect the battery ground cable. Install the distributor.
24. Temporarily adjust the valve clearance to the cold engine specifications.
25. Install the gasket on the rocker arm cover and temporarily install the cover on the engine.
26. Connect the negative battery cable.
27. Start the engine and bring it to normal operating temperature. Stop the engine and remove the rocker arm cover.
28. Adjust the valves to hot engine specifications.
29. Install the rocker arm cover and tighten securely.
30. Install the air cleaner, hoses, purge valve hose and any other removed unit.

1595CC DOHC ENGINE

1. Disconnect the negative battery cable.
2. Drain the engine and radiator coolant.
3. Remove the radiator assembly.
4. Disconnect the accelerator cable. Disconnect the air flow sensor wiring connector.
5. Disconnect all of the breather and vacuum hoses to the air intake. Remove the air cleaner assembly.

COLD ENGINE SPECIFICATIONS

	Inch	mm
Jet valve, if equipped	0.003	0.07
Intake valve	0.003	0.07
Exhaust valve	0.007	0.17

HOT ENGINE SPECIFICATIONS

	Inch	mm
Jet valve, if equipped	0.006	0.15
Intake valve	0.006	0.15
Exhaust valve	0.010	0.25

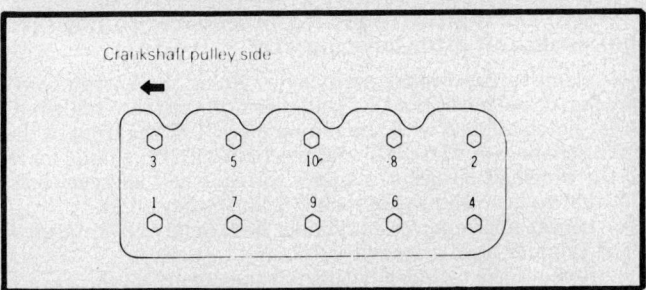

1410cc, 1468cc, 1597cc and 1997cc cylinder head bolt loosening sequence

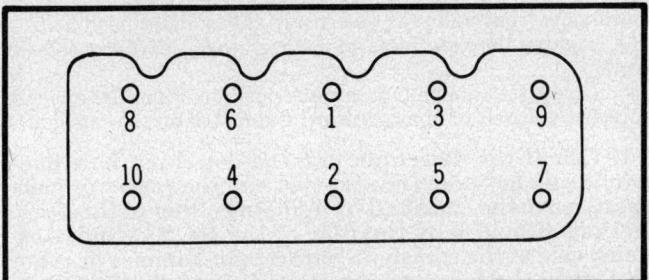

Cylinder head bolt torque sequence—1468cc, 1597cc and 1997cc engines

6. Remove the PCV hose. Disconnect the water bypass hose, the heater hose and vacuum lines from the water inlet connector.

7. Disconnect the vacuum hose to the power brake booster.

8. Release the fuel system pressure and disconnect the high pressure and fuel return lines. Remove the mounting O-rings.

9. Disconnect the oxygen sensor, engine coolant sensor, temperature gauge connection and the air conditioner coolant temperature switch.

10. Disconnect the fuel injector wiring harness, the ignition coil, power transistor, ISC motor and the EGR sensor connector.

11. Disconnect the detonation sensor, throttle position sensor and crankshaft angle sensor wiring connectors.

12. Remove the center cover and the spark plug wires. Disconnect the control wire harness connector.

13. Remove the timing belt.

14. Remove the rocker cover and rear half moon seal.

15. Remove the heat shield, turbocharger water and oil lines.

16. Disconnect the exhaust pipe from the turbocharger.

17. Remove the turbocharger, exhaust manifold and intake manifold assemblies.

18. Remove the head mounting bolts. Start at the outer ends of the head and loosen, in a criss-cross manner, toward the center of the head. Make 2–3 passes to loosen the bolts, a little at a time, in sequence.

19. Remove the cylinder head. Clean all gasket mounting surfaces. Make sure no gasket material gets into the cylinders, coolant passages or oil passages.

To install:

20. Position the cylinder head, with a new gasket, on the engine. Install and tighten the head mounting bolts.

21. Tighten the head bolts from the center outwards. Tighten in, 3 steps, to 65–72 ft. lbs. (88–98 Nm).

22. Install the turbocharger, exhaust manifold and intake manifold assemblies.

23. Connect the exhaust pipe to the turbocharger.

24. Install the heat shield, turbocharger water and oil lines.

25. Install the rocker cover and rear half moon seal.

26. Install the timing belt.

27. Install the center cover and the spark plug wires. Connect the control wire harness connector.

28. Connect the detonation sensor, throttle position sensor and crankshaft angle sensor wiring connectors.

29. Connect the fuel injector wiring harness, the ignition coil, power transistor, ISC motor and the EGR sensor connector.

30. Connect the oxygen sensor, engine coolant sensor, temperature gauge connection and the air conditioner coolant temperature switch.

31. Connect the high pressure and fuel return lines. Install the new O-rings.

32. Connect the vacuum hose to the power brake booster.

33. Install the PCV hose. Connect the water bypass hose, the heater hose and vacuum lines from the water inlet connector.

34. Connect all of the breather and vacuum hoses to the air intake. Install the air cleaner assembly.

35. Connect the accelerator cable. Connect the air flow sensor wiring connector.

36. Install the radiator assembly.

37. Replenish the engine and radiator coolant.

38. Connect the negative battery cable.

1597CC, 1755CC AND 1997CC ENGINES

1. Disconnect the negative battery cable. Remove the air cleaner assembly and the attached hoses.

2. Drain the coolant, remove the upper radiator hose and the heater hoses.

3. On fuel injected vehicles, release the fuel system pressure. Remove the fuel line, disconnect the accelerator linkage, distributor vacuum lines, purge valve and water temperature gauge wire.

4. Remove the spark plug wires and the fuel pump. Remove the distributor, where necessary.

5. Disconnect the exhaust pipe from the exhaust manifold flange.

6. Remove the exhaust manifold assembly.

7. Remove the intake manifold and carburetor as a unit.

8. Turn the crankshaft to No. 1 piston at TDC on the compression stroke.

NOTE: During the following procedure, do not turn the crankshaft after locating TDC.

9. Align the timing mark on the upper under cover of the timing belt with that of the camshaft sprocket. Matchmark the timing belt and the timing mark on the camshaft sprocket with a felt tip pen. Remove the sprocket and insert a 2 in. piece of timing belt or other material between the bottom of the camshaft sprocket and the sprocket holder, on the timing belt lower front cover, to hold the sprocket and belt so the valve timing will not be changed. Remove the timing belt upper under cover and rocker arm cover.

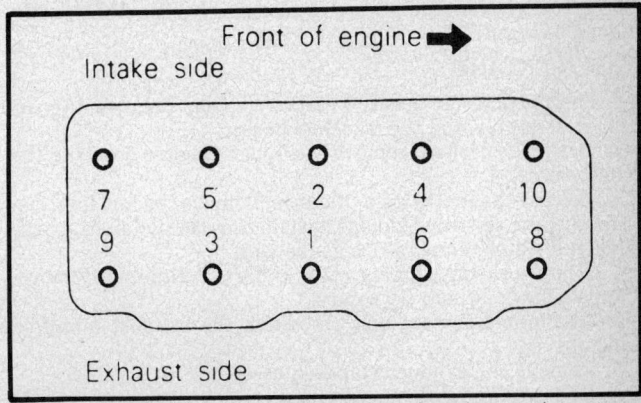

1595cc DOHC engine cylinder head bolt tightening sequence

10. Loosen and remove the cylinder head bolts in 2–3 stages to avoid cylinder head warpage.

11. Remove the cylinder head from the engine block.

To install:

12. Clean the cylinder head and block mating surfaces and install a new cylinder head gasket.

13. Position the cylinder head on the engine block, engage the dowel pins front and rear and install the cylinder head bolts.

14. Tighten the head bolts in 3 stages and then torque to:

1597cc engine—50–54 ft. lbs. (68–73 Nm).

1755cc engine—50–54 ft. lbs. (68–73 Nm).

1997cc engine—65–72 ft. lbs. (88–97).

15. Install the timing belt upper under cover.

16. Locate the camshaft in original position. Pull the camshaft sprocket and belt or chain upward and install on the camshaft.

NOTE: If the dowel pin and the dowel pin hole does not line up between the sprocket and the spacer or camshaft, move the camshaft by bumping either of the 2 projections provided at the rear of the No. 2 cylinder exhaust cam of the camshaft, with a light hammer or other tool, until the hole and pin align. Be certain the crankshaft does not turn.

17. Install the camshaft sprocket bolt and the distributor gear and tighten.

18. Install the timing belt upper front cover and spark plug cable support.

19. Apply sealant to the intake manifold gasket on both sides. Position the gasket and install the intake manifold. Tighten nuts to specifications.

NOTE: Be sure no sealant enters the jet air passages when equipped.

20. Install the exhaust manifold gaskets and the manifold assembly. Tighten the nuts to specifications.

21. Connect the exhaust pipe to the exhaust manifold and install the fuel pump. Install the purge valve.

22. Install the water temperature gauge wire, heater hoses and the upper radiator hose.

23. Connect the fuel lines, accelerator linkage, vacuum hoses and the spark plug wires.

24. Fill the cooling system and connect the battery ground cable. Install the distributor.

25. Temporarily adjust the valve clearance to the cold engine specifications.

26. Install the gasket on the rocker arm cover and temporarily install the cover on the engine.

27. Start the engine and bring it to normal operating temperature. Stop the engine and remove the rocker arm cover.

28. Adjust the valves to hot engine specifications.

29. Install the rocker arm cover and tighten securely.

30. Install the air cleaner, hoses, purge valve hose and any other removed unit.

2555CC ENGINE

1. Disconnect the negative battery cable. Remove the air cleaner assembly and the attached hoses.

2. Drain the coolant, remove the upper radiator hose and the heater hoses.

3. Release the fuel system pressure. Remove the fuel line, disconnect the accelerator linkage, distributor vacuum lines, purge valve and water temperature gauge wire.

4. Remove the spark plug wires and the fuel pump. Remove the distributor, where necessary.

5. Disconnect the exhaust pipe from the exhaust manifold flange.

6. Remove the exhaust manifold assembly.

7. Remove the intake manifold.

8. Turn the crankshaft to No. 1 piston at TDC on the compression stroke.

NOTE: During the following procedure, do not turn the crankshaft after locating TDC.

9. Remove the rocker arm cover. Position the camshaft sprocket dowel pin at the 12 o'clock position with the crankshaft pulley notch aligned with the timing mark **T** at the front of the timing chain case. Match the timing chain with the timing mark on the camshaft sprocket. Remove the camshaft sprocket bolt, distributor, gear and the sprocket from the camshaft.

10. Loosen and remove the cylinder head bolts in 2–3 stages to avoid cylinder head warpage.

11. Remove the cylinder head from the engine block.

To install:

12. Clean the cylinder head and block mating surfaces and install a new cylinder head gasket.

13. Position the cylinder head on the engine block, engage the dowel pins front and rear and install the cylinder head bolts.

14. Tighten the head bolts in, 3 stages, to 65–72 ft. lbs. (88–98 Nm).

15. Locate the camshaft in original position. Pull the camshaft sprocket and belt or chain upward and install on the camshaft.

NOTE: If the dowel pin and the dowel pin hole does not line up between the sprocket and the spacer or camshaft, move the camshaft by bumping either of the 2 projections provided at the rear of the No. 2 cylinder exhaust cam of the camshaft, with a light hammer or other tool, until the hole and pin align. Be certain the crankshaft does not turn.

16. Install the camshaft sprocket bolt and the distributor gear and tighten.

17. Install the timing belt upper front cover and spark plug cable support.

18. Apply sealant to the intake manifold gasket on both sides. Position the gasket and install the intake manifold. Tighten nuts to specifications.

NOTE: Be sure no sealant enters the jet air passages when equipped.

19. Install the exhaust manifold gaskets and the manifold assembly.

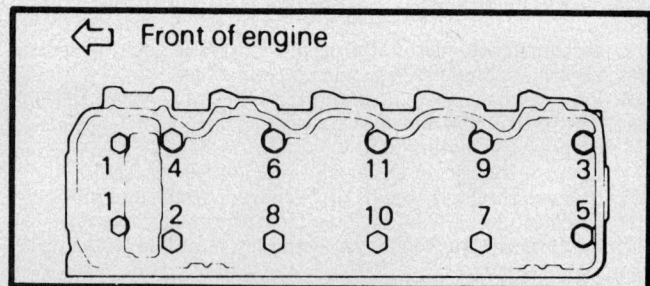

2555cc engine cylinder head bolt loosening sequence

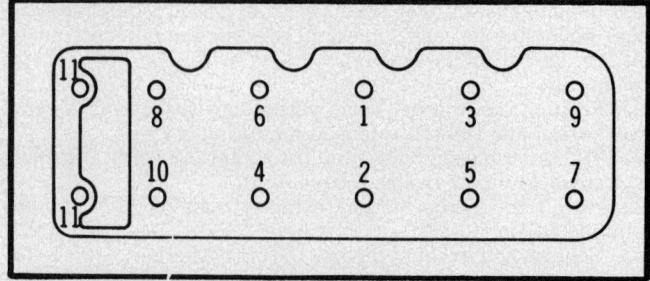

Cylinder head bolt tightening sequence—2555cc engine

20. Connect the exhaust pipe to the exhaust manifold and install the fuel pump. Install the purge valve.

21. Install the water temperature gauge wire, heater hoses and the upper radiator hose.

22. Connect the fuel lines, accelerator linkage, vacuum hoses and the spark plug wires.

23. Fill the cooling system and connect the battery ground cable. Install the distributor.

24. Temporarily adjust the valve clearance to the cold engine specifications.

25. Install the gasket on the rocker arm cover and temporarily install the cover on the engine.

26. Connect the negative battery cable.

27. Start the engine and bring it to normal operating temperature. Stop the engine and remove the rocker arm cover.

28. Adjust the valves to hot engine specifications.

29. Install the rocker arm cover and tighten securely.

30. Install the air cleaner, hoses, purge valve hose and any other removed unit.

Valve Lash

Adjustment

Valve lash must be adjusted on all engines not equipped with automatic lash adjusters. Some engines have a third valve of very small size called a jet valve. The jet valve must be adjusted, whether the engine uses automatic lash adjusters for the normal intake and exhaust valves or not. Thus, on some engines, there are 3 valves per cylinder that must be adjusted.

1. Run the engine until operating temperature is reached.
2. Turn OFF the engine and block the wheels.

Adjusting valve clearance

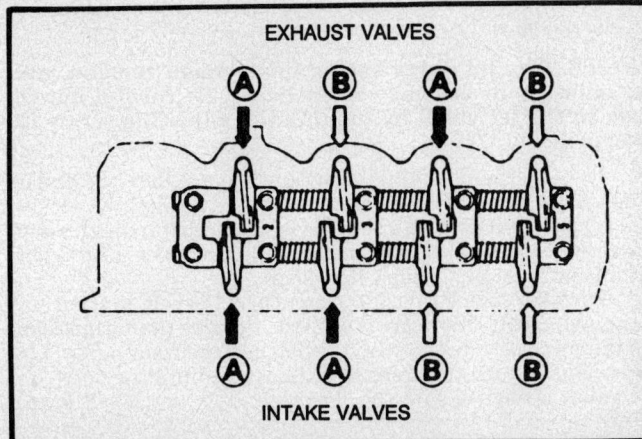

EXHAUST VALVES

INTAKE VALVES

"A" and "B" valve adjusting positions

3. Remove all necessary components in order to gain access to the rocker cover.

4. Remove the spark plugs from the cylinder head for easy operations.

    a. On some engines it may be necessary to remove the air intake pipe and remove the rocker cover.

    b. On some engines it may be necessary to disconnect the oxygen sensor connecting joint. Remove the engine bracket mounting, be sure to place a block of wood on the oil pan and jack it up into to place for the duration of the operation. Remove the upper front timing belt cover, remove the air cleaner assembly on the 1997cc engine and the air intake pipe on the 1755cc engine and remove the rocker cover.

    c. On all other vehicles, remove the air cleaner or air intake pipe assembly and remove the rocker cover.

5. Turn each cylinder head bolt, in sequence, back just until it is loose. Torque the cylinder head bolts in the proper sequence to specification.

6. Position the engine crankshaft at TDC with No. 1 cylinder at the firing position. Turn the engine by using a wrench on the bolt in the front of the crankshaft until the 0 degree timing mark on the timing cover lines up with the notch in the front pulley. On some engines, it may be necessary to turn the crankshaft clockwise unit the notch on the pulley is lined up with the T mark on the timing belt lower cover.

7. Observe the valve rockers for No. 1 cylinder. If both are in identical positions with the valves up, the engine is in the right position. If not, rotate the engine exactly 360 degrees until the 0 degree timing mark is again aligned. Each jet valve is associated with an intake valve that is on the same rocker lever. In this position you'll be able to adjust all the valves marked A, including associated jet valves which are located on the rockers, on the intake side only.

8. To adjust the appropriate jet valves, first loosen the regular (larger) intake valve adjusting stud by loosening the locknut and backing the stud off 2 turns. Note that this particular step is not required on engines that have automatic lash adjusters.

9. Loosen the jet valve (smaller) adjusting stud locknut, back the stud out slightly and insert the feeler gauge between the jet valve and stud. Make sure the gauge lies flat on the top of the jet valve. Be careful not to twist the gauge or otherwise depress the jet valve spring, rotate the jet valve adjusting stud back in until it just touches the gauge. Tighten the locknut. Make sure the gauge still slides very easily between the stud and jet valve and that they both are still just touching the gauge.

NOTE: The clearances must not be too tight.

10. Repeat the entire procedure for the other jet valves associated with rockers labeled A.

11. On engines without automatic lash adjusters, repeat the procedure for the intake valves labeled A.

12. Repeat the basic adjustment procedure for exhaust valves labeled A on engines without automatic lash adjusters.

13. Turn the engine exactly 360 degrees, until the timing marks are again aligned at 0 degrees BTDC.

14. On engines with automatic lash adjusters, after the jet valves and rockers on the intake side and labeled B are adjusted, the valve adjustment procedure is completed. On engines without automatic lash adjusters, adjust the regular intake and exhaust valves labeled B.

15. Reinstall the cam cover. Run the engine to check for oil leaks.

Jet Valve Adjustment

NOTE: An incorrect jet valve clearance would affect the emission levels and could also cause engine troubles, so the jet valve clearance must be correctly adjusted. Adjust the jet valve clearance before adjusting the intake valve clearance. The cylinder head bolts should be retorqued before making this adjustment. The jet valve

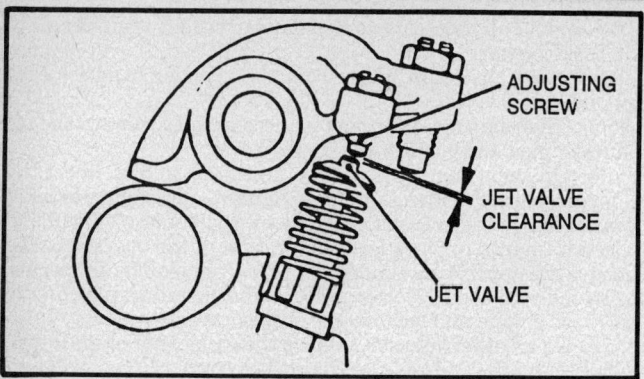

Jet valve adjusting

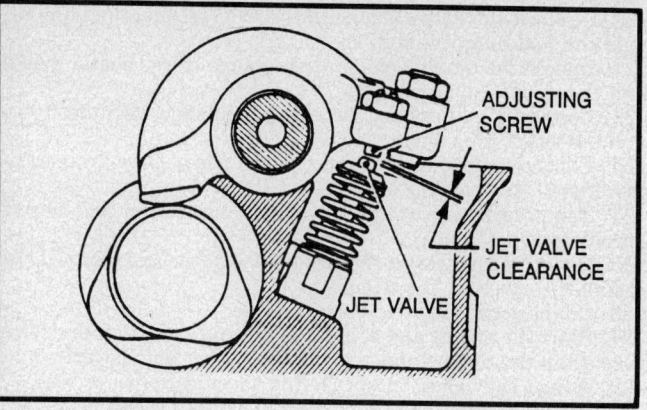

Jet valve clearance

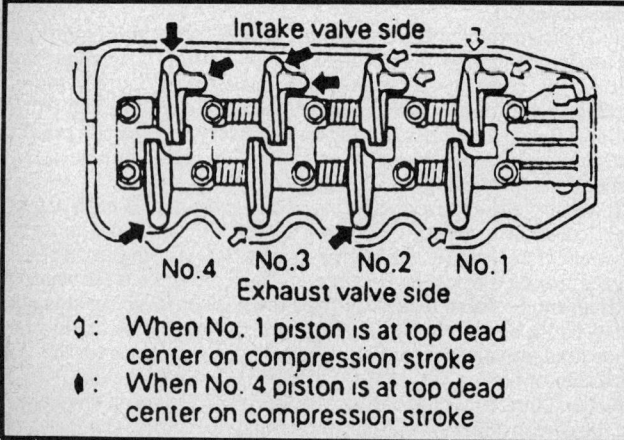

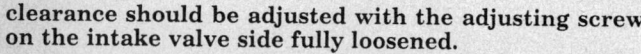

∩ : When No. 1 piston is at top dead center on compression stroke

● : When No. 4 piston is at top dead center on compression stroke

Valve adjustment sequence—typical

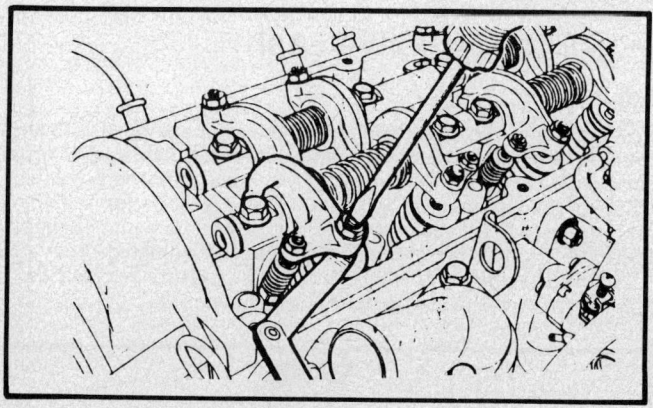

Jet valve clearance adjustment

clearance should be adjusted with the adjusting screw on the intake valve side fully loosened.

1. Start the engine and let it run at idle until it reaches normal operating temperature.
2. Remove all spark plugs from the cylinder head for easy operation.
3. On some vehicles it may be necessary to remove the air intake pipe and remove the rocker cover.
4. It may be necessary to disconnect the oxygen sensor. Remove the engine bracket mounting, be sure to place a block of wood on the oil pan and jack it up into to place for the duration of the operation. Remove the upper front timing belt cover, remove the air cleaner assembly on the 1755cc and 1997cc engine.
5. Remove air intake pipe assembly and remove the rocker cover.
6. Set the engine at TDC with No. 1 cylinder at the firing position. Turn the engine by using a wrench on the bolt in the front of the crankshaft until the 0 degree timing mark on the timing cover lines up with the notch in the front pulley. On some engines, it may be necessary to turn the crankshaft clockwise until the notch on the pulley is lined up with the T mark on the timing belt lower cover. This will bring both No. 1 and No. 4 cylinder pistons up to TDC.

NOTE: Never turn the crankshaft counterclockwise.

7. Move the rocker arms on the No. 1 and No. 4 cylinders up and down by hand to determine if the piston in that cylinder is at TDC center on the compression stroke. If the intake and exhaust rocker arms do not move, the piston in that cylinder is not at TDC on the compression stroke.

8. Measure the jet valve clearance at point A.

NOTE: Measure the valve clearance when the No. 1 cylinder or the No. 4 cylinder pistons are at TDC on the compression stroke. Then give the crankshaft 1 clockwise turn to bring the other cylinder piston to TDC on compression stroke.

9. If the jet valve clearance is not as specified (0.010 in. hot and 0.007 in. cold), loosen the rocker arm locknut of the intake valve and loosen the adjusting screw at least 2 turns or more.
10. Loosen the jet valve locknut and adjust the clearance using a feeler gauge while turning the adjusting screw.

NOTE: The jet valve spring has a small tension and the adjustment is somewhat delicate. Be careful not to push in the jet valve by turning the adjusting screw in too much.

11. Tighten the adjusting screw until it touches the feeler gauge. Turn the locknut to secure it, while holding the rocker arm adjusting screw with a suitable tool to keep it from turning.
12. Check the intake and exhaust valve clearance, if it is not within specifications, adjust the valves.
13. Turn the engine by using a wrench on the bolt, in the front of the crankshaft, 360 degrees until the 0 degree timing mark on the timing cover lines up with the notch in the front pulley. On some vehicles turn the crankshaft clockwise until the notch on the pulley is aligned with the T mark on the timing belt lower cover.
14. Repeat Steps 9 through 13 on the other valves marked B for clearance adjustment.

Rocker Arms/Shafts

Removal and Installation
1468CC, 1597CC AND 1755CC ENGINES

1. Disconnect the negative battery cable. Remove the rocker cover. Matchmark the camshaft/rocker arm bearing caps to their cylinder head location, except 1468cc engine.

2. Loosen the bearing cap bolts or the rocker shaft bolts on 1468cc engine, from the cylinder head but do not remove them from the caps or shafts. Lift the rocker assembly from the cylinder head as a unit.

3. The rocker arm assembly can be disassembled by the removal of the mounting bolts and dowel pins on some vehicles, from the bearing caps and/or shafts.

NOTE: Keep the rocker arms and springs in the same order as disassembly. The left and right springs have different tension ratings and free length. Observe the location of the rocker arms as they are removed. Exhaust and intake, right and left, are different.

1595CC DOHC ENGINE

1. With the cylinder head removed from the vehicle. Remove the crank angle sensor.

2. Remove both camshaft drive sprockets.

3. Remove both rear (opposite end of the drive sprockets) camshaft bearing caps.

4. Remove both front bearing caps and front oil seals.

5. Remove the remaining camshaft bearing caps alternating from the rear of the head to the front.

6. Remove the camshafts.

7. Remove the rocker arms and the lash adjusters. Remove the valve body assembly from the rear of the cylinder head.

8. Clean and inspect all parts. Check the rollers on the end of the rocker arms. If the rollers are warn on do not rotate smoothly, replace, as necessary.

To install:

9. Install the lash adjusters and rocker arms. Lubricate them prior to installation. Install the valve body. Lubricate the camshafts. Place the camshafts in position. The intake side camshaft has a slit in the rear to drive the crank angle sensor. The

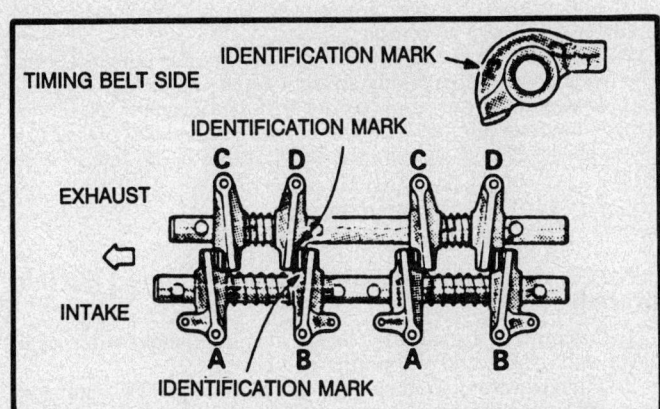

Rocker arm shaft assembly—1468cc and 1597cc engines

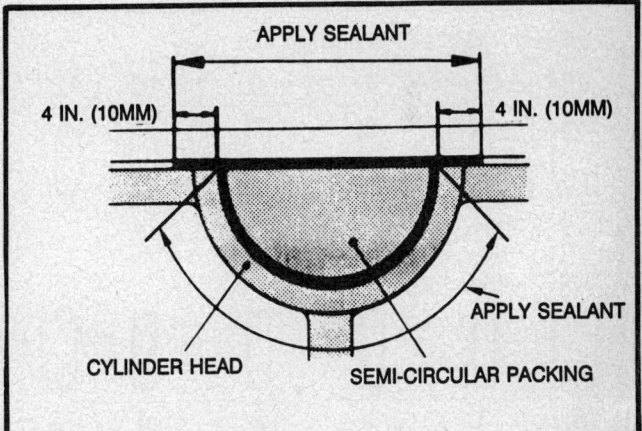

Half moon seal installation

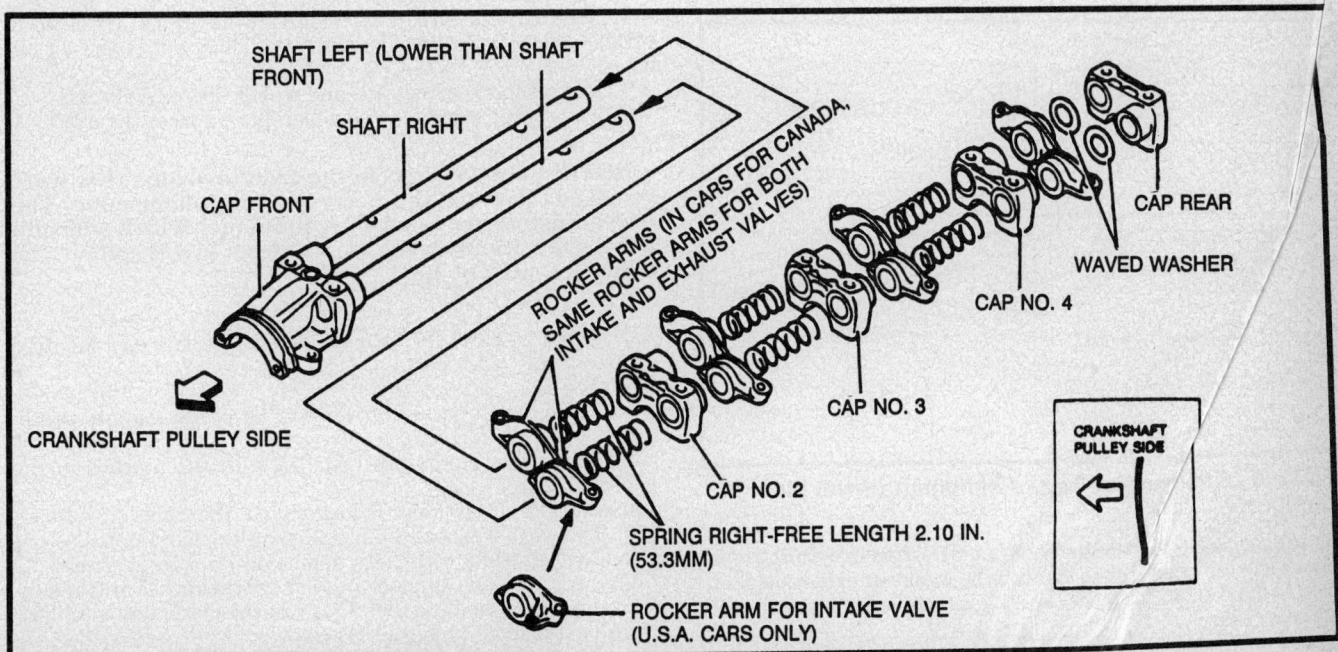

Rocker arm assembly, 1597cc engine

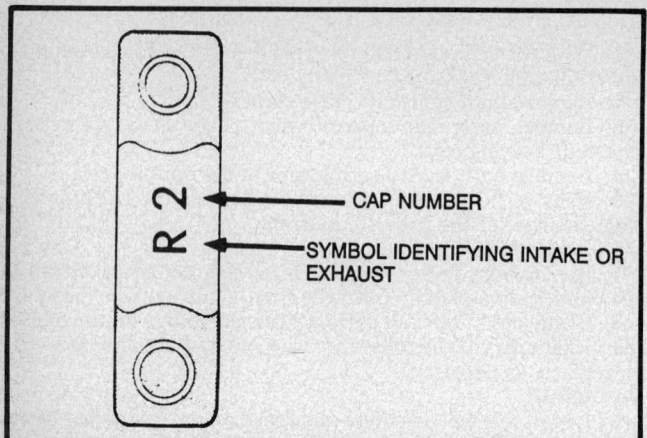

1595cc DOHC engine camshaft bearing cap identification

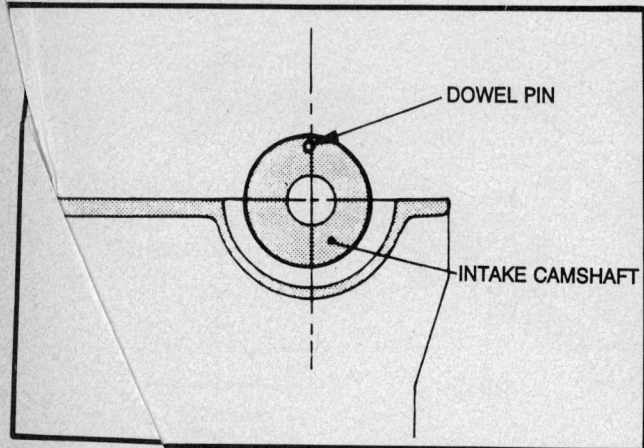

1595cc DOHC engine camshaft bearing cap installation tightening sequence

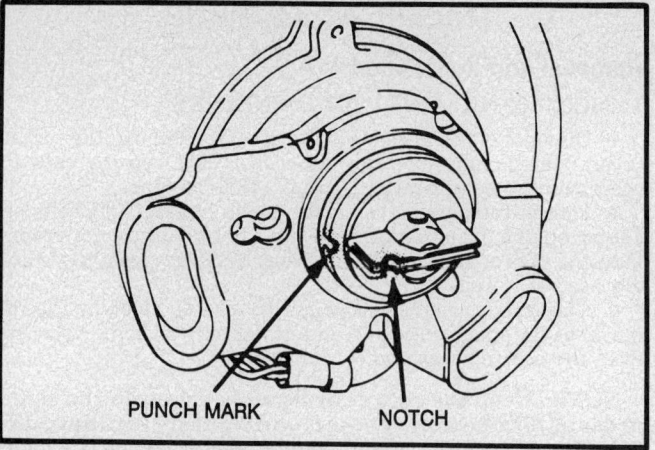

1595cc DOHC engine crank angle sensor installation alignment

11. Make sure the rocker arm is properly mounted on the lash adjuster and valve stem tip.

12. Install the front oil seals. Turn the intake camshaft until the front dowel pin is facing straight up at the 12 o'clock position. Install the crank angle sensor with the punch mark on the sensor housing aligned with the notch in the plate. Install the drive sprocket and tighten the bolts to 58–72 ft. lbs. (79–98 Nm).

1997CC AND 2555CC ENGINES WITH AUTOMATIC LASH ADJUSTERS

NOTE: A special tool, MD998443, is required for this procedure.

1. Disconnect the negative battery cable. Remove the rocker cover and gasket and the timing belt cover.

2. Turn the crankshaft so the No. 1 piston is a TDC compression. At this point, the timing mark on the camshaft sprocket and the timing mark on the head to the left of the sprocket will be aligned.

3. Remove the camshaft bearing cap bolts.

4. Install the automatic lash adjuster retainer tool MD998443, to keep the adjuster from falling out of the rocker arms.

5. Lift off the bearing caps and rocker arm assemblies.

6. The rocker arms may now be removed from the shaft.

NOTE: Keep all parts in the order in which they were removed. None of the parts are interchangeable. The lash adjusters are filled with diesel fuel, which will spill out if they are inverted. If any diesel fuel is spilled, the adjusters must be bled.

7. Check all parts for wear or damage. Replace any damaged or excessively worn parts.

To install:

8. Assemble all parts in reverse order of the removal procedures. Note the following:

9. The rocker shafts are installed with the notches in the ends facing up.

10. The left rocker shaft is longer than the right.

11. The wave washers are installed on the left shaft.

12. Coat all parts with clean engine oil prior to assembly.

13. Insert the lash adjuster from under the rocker arm and install the special holding tool. If any of the diesel fuel is spilled, the adjuster must be bled.

14. Tighten the bearing cap bolts, working from the center towards the ends to 15 ft. lbs. (20 Nm).

1595cc DOHC engine intake camshaft dowel pin position

bearing caps No. 2–5 are the same shape. When installing them, check the top markings to identify the intake or exhaust side. L or R is marked on the front caps, L for the intake side; R for the exhaust side.

10. Tighten the bearing caps, in 2–3 steps, to 14–15 ft. lbs. (20–22 Nm).

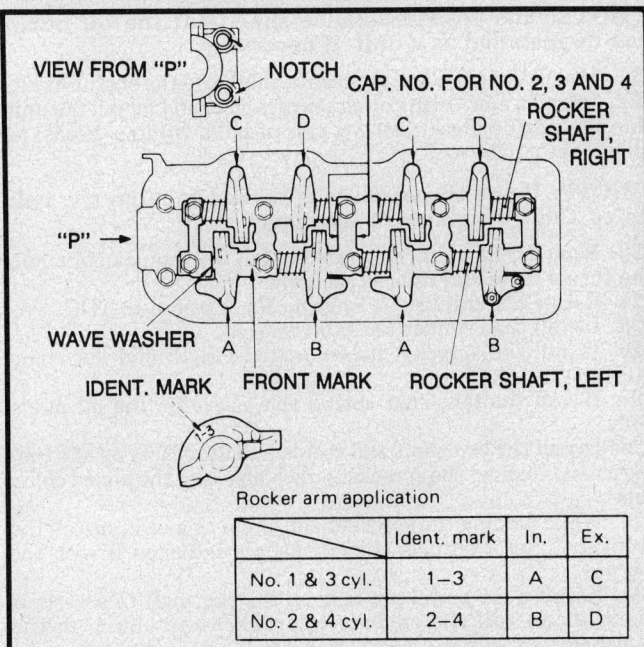

1997cc engine rocker arm shaft assembly

Rocker arm application	Ident. mark	In.	Ex.
No. 1 & 3 cyl.	1–3	A	C
No. 2 & 4 cyl.	2–4	B	D

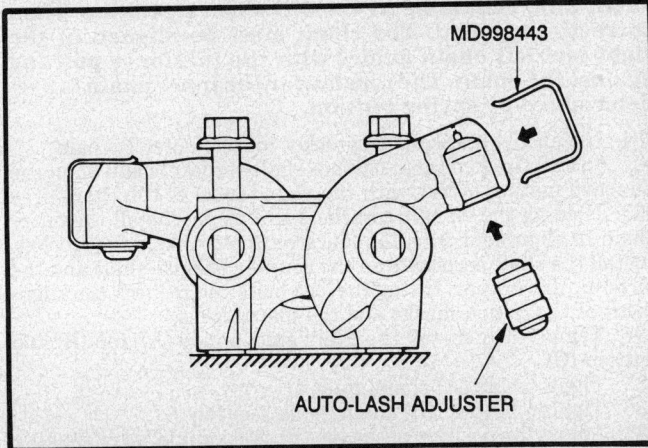

Automatic lash adjuster installation

15. Check the operation of each lash adjuster by positioning the camshaft so the rocker arm bears on the low or round portion of the cam pointed part of the can faces straight down. Insert a thin steel wire, or tool MD998442, in the hole in the top of the rocker arm, over the lash adjuster and depress the check ball at the top of the adjuster. While holding the check ball depressed, move the arm up and down. Looseness should be felt. Full plunger stroke should be 0.0866 in. (2.2mm). If not, remove, clean and bleed the lash adjuster.

Intake Manifold

Removal and Installation
EXCEPT MULTI-POINT FUEL INJECTION

1. Disconnect the negative battery cable. Remove the air cleaner.
2. Disconnect the fuel line and EGR lines, if equipped.

3. Disconnect the throttle positioner solenoid and fuel cut-off solenoid wires.
4. Disconnect the accelerator linkage and, if equipped with an automatic transmission, the shift cables at the carburetor or injection pump.
5. If equipped, remove the injection mixer assembly.
6. On the 1597cc engine, remove the fuel pump and the thermostat housing. Disconnect the choke coolant hose at the manifold. Disconnect the power brake booster vacuum line.
7. Drain the coolant.
8. Remove the water hose from carburetor and cylinder head.
9. Remove the heater and water outlet hoses.
10. Disconnect the water temperature sending unit.
11. Remove the manifold.
12. Clean all mounting surfaces. Before reinstalling the manifold, coat both side with gasket sealer.

NOTE: If the engine is equipped with the jet air system, take care not to get any sealer into the jet air intake passage.

13. Installation is the reverse order of the removal procedure.

MULTI-POINT FUEL INJECTION

1. Disconnect the negative battery cable. Drain the cooling system. Disconnect the air intake hose, accelerator cable and the throttle body stay.
2. Disconnect the water bypass hose and the vacuum hose to the power brake booster.
3. Relieve the fuel system pressure.
4. Disconnect the fuel high pressure and return lines and their mounting O-rings.
5. Disconnect interfering vacuum hose, plug wires and wiring harness connections.
6. Disconnect the oxygen sensor, idle speed control, injector connector, ignition coil and power transistor connectors.
7. Disconnect the crank angle sensor, if so equipped, the throttle position sensor and the control harness connectors.
8. Remove the fuel delivery pipe, fuel injector and pressure regulator as an assembly. Remove the mounting grommets and O-rings.
9. Remove the intake manifold lower support stay shield and the end tension bracket.
10. Remove the intake manifold mounting bolts and the intake manifold assembly.
11. Remove the components from the intake manifold and on 2 piece manifolds, separate the upper and lower halves.
12. Clean all gasket mounting surfaces.
13. Install all components and the intake manifold in reverse order of removal. Torque values follow: manifold to head bolts 11–14 ft. lbs.; upper to lower manifold 11–14 ft. lbs.; fuel delivery manifold 7–9 ft. lbs.; throttle body 11–16 ft. lbs. on DOHC and 1997cc; 7–9 ft. lbs. on 1468cc.

Exhaust Manifold

Removal and Installation

1. Disconnect the negative battery cable. Remove the air cleaner assembly.
2. Remove the manifold heat stove and hose. Disconnect the EGR lines and reed valve, if equipped. On turbocharged vehicles, remove the turbocharger.
3. Disconnect the exhaust pipe bracket from the engine block.
4. Remove the exhaust pipe flange bolts, 1 bolt and nut may have to be removed from under the vehicle.
5. Remove the manifold flange stud nuts and remove the manifold from the cylinder head.
6. Installation is the reverse order of removal procedures. Port liner gaskets may be used along with the exhaust manifold gaskets on some engine models.

Turbocharger

Removal and Installation

NOTE: Make sure the engine and turbocharger are cold, before removing the unit. If replacing the turbocharger, change the engine oil and filter.

1. Drain the cooling system and disconnect the negative battery cable. For clearance on some models, it will be necessary to remove the radiator. Remove the heat shield.
2. Disconnect the air intake hose and vacuum lines. Remove the oxygen sensor from the catalytic converter.
3. Remove the converter-to-turbocharger nuts.
4. Disconnect the hose from the oil return pipe and time chain case.
5. Remove the oil pipe from the turbocharger and oil filter housing.
6. Remove the air intake pipe connecting bolt.
7. Remove the turbocharger mounting nuts and lift the unit off the engine.
8. Installation is the reverse order of removal procedure. Before the oil flare nut is installed at the top of the unit, pour clean engine oil into the turbocharger. Always use new gaskets.

Timing Chain and Sprocket

Removal and Installation

NOTE: The timing chain case is cast aluminum, exercise caution when handling.

2555CC ENGINES WITH SILENT SHAFT

1. Drain the coolant and remove the radiator. Disconnect the battery ground cable.
2. Remove the alternator and accessory belts.
3. Rotate the crankshaft to bring No. 1 piston to TDC, on the compression stroke.
4. Mark and remove the distributor.
5. Remove the crankshaft pulley.
6. Remove the water pump assembly.
8. Raise the vehicle and support it safely.
9. Drain the engine oil and remove the oil pan and screen.
10. Remove the timing case cover.
11. Remove the chain guides. Side (A), top (B), bottom (C), from the outer top (B) chain.
12. Remove the locking bolts from the "B" chain sprockets.
13. Remove the crankshaft sprocket, counter-balance shaft sprocket and the outer chain.
14. Remove the crankshaft and camshaft sprockets and the inner chain.
15. Remove the camshaft sprocket holder and the chain guides, both left and right. Remove the tensioner spring and sleeve from the oil pump.
16. Remove the oil pump by first removing the bolt locking the oil pump driven gear and the right counter-balance shaft and then remove the oil pump mounting bolts. Remove the counter-balance shaft from the engine block.

NOTE: If the bolt locking the oil pump driven gear and the counter-balance shaft is hard to loosen, remove the oil pump and the shaft as a unit.

17. Remove the left counter-balance shaft thrust washer and take the shaft from the engine block.
To install:
18. Install the right counter-balance shaft into the engine block.
19. Install the oil pump assembly. Do not loose the Woodruff® key from the end of the counter-balance shaft. Torque the oil pump mounting bolts to 6–7 ft. lbs.
20. Tighten the counter-balance shaft and the oil pump driven gear mounting bolt.

NOTE: The counterbalance shaft and the oil pump can be installed as a unit, if necessary.

21. Install the left counter-balance shaft into the engine block.
22. Install a new O-ring on the thrust plate and install the unit into the engine block, using a pair of bolts without heads, as alignment guides.

NOTE: If the thrust plate is turned to align the bolt holes, the O-ring may be damaged.

23. Remove the guide bolts and install the regular bolts into the thrust plate and tighten securely.
24. Rotate the crankshaft to bring No. 1 piston to TDC.
25. Install the cylinder head, if removed.
26. Install the sprocket holder and the right and left chain guides.
27. Install the tensioner spring and sleeve on the oil pump body.
28. Install the camshaft and crankshaft sprockets on the timing chain, aligning the sprocket punch marks to the plated chain links.
29. While holding the sprocket and chain as a unit, install the crankshaft sprocket over the crankshaft and align it with the keyway.
30. Keeping the dowel pin hole on the camshaft in a vertical position, install the camshaft sprocket and chain on the camshaft.

NOTE: The sprocket timing mark and the plated chain link, should be at the 2–3 o'clock position when correctly installed. The chain must be aligned in the right and left chain guides with the tensioner pushing against the chain. The tension for the inner chain is predetermined by spring tension.

31. Install the crankshaft sprocket for the outer B chain.
32. Install the 2 counter-balance shaft sprockets and align the punched mating marks with the plated links of the chain.
33. Holding the 2 shaft sprockets and chain, install the outer chain in alignment with the mark on the crankshaft sprocket. Install the shaft sprockets on the counter balance shaft and the oil pump driver gear. Install the lock bolts and recheck the alignment of the punch marks and the plated links.
34. Temporarily install the chain guides, side (A), top (B) and bottom (C).
35. Tighten side (A) chain guide securely.
36. Tighten bottom (B) chain guide securely.
37. Adjust the position of the top (B) chain guide, after shaking the right and left sprockets to collect any chain slack, so when the chain is moved toward the center, the clearance between the chain guide and the chain links will be approximately $\frac{9}{64}$ in. Tighten the Top (B) chain guide bolts.
38. Install the timing chain cover using a new gasket, being careful not to damage the front seal.
39. Install the oil screen and the oil pan, using a new gasket. Torque the bolts to 4.5–5.5 ft. lbs.
40. Install the crankshaft pulley, alternator and accessory belts and the distributor.
41. Install the oil pressure switch, if removed and install the negative battery cable.
42. Install the fan blades, radiator, fill the system with coolant and start the engine.

Timing Belt Front Cover

Removal and Installation

1. Disconnect the negative battery cable. Remove the alternator drive belt.
2. Unbolt and remove the water pump drive pulley. Remove the bolt from the crankshaft pulley. Using a suitable puller, remove the crankshaft pulley.

3. Remove the bolts from the upper and lower covers and remove them. Remove the upper cover first.

4. Installation is the reverse order the removal procedures. Use new gaskets under the cover(s).

Oil Seal Replacement

1. Disconnect the negative battery cable.
2. Remove the air pump and alternator drive belts. Remove the air pump mounting bracket.
3. Raise and safely support the vehicle. Remove the right inner splash shield.
4. Remove the crankshaft pulley bolt and washer and remove the pulley.
5. Install a seal remover tool over crankshaft nose and turn it tightly into the seal.
6. Tighten the thrust screw to remove the seal.

NOTE: If the front cover is removed from the engine, tap the side of the thrust screw to remove the seal.

To install:

7. Using a oil seal installation tool, drive the new seal into the front cover.
8. Install the crankshaft pulley, washer and retaining bolt.
9. Install the right inner splash shield and lower the vehicle.
10. Install the air pump mounting bracket, air pump and alternator drive belts.
11. Connect the negative battery cable.

Timing Belt and Tensioner

Adjustment

1468CC ENGINE

1. Bring the engine to No. 1 piston at TDC timing marks aligned. Disconnect the negative battery cable.
2. Remove the drive belts, water pump pulley, spacer and timing belt cover.
3. Loosen the tensioner from it's temporary position so the spring pressure will allow it to contact the timing belt.
4. Rotate the crankshaft 2 complete turns in the normal rotation direction to remove any belt slack. Turn the crankshaft until the timing marks are lined up. If the timing has slipped, remove the belt and repeat the procedure.
5. Tighten the tensioner mounting bolts, slotted side (right) first, then the spring side.
6. Once again rotate the engine 2 complete revolutions until the timing marks align. Recheck the belt tension.

NOTE: When the tension side of the timing belt and the tensioner are pushed in horizontally with a moderate force, about 11 lbs. and the cogged side of the belt covers about ¼ in. of the tensioner right side mounting bolt head, the across flats, the tension is correct.

7. Reinstall the timing belt cover, the water pump pulley, spacer, fan blades and drive belt.
8. Connect the negative battery cable.

1595CC DOHC ENGINE

1. Bring the engine to No. 1 piston at TDC timing marks aligned. Disconnect the negative battery cable.
2. Raise the vehicle and support it safely. Remove the under engine splash shield.
3. Place a piece of wood on a suitable floor jack and support the engine. Remove the engine mount bracket.
4. Remove the alternator and power steering drive belts. Remove the air conditioner drive belt and tensioner assembly.
5. Remove the water pump pulley and the crankshaft pulley.
6. Remove the upper and lower timing belt covers.
7. Lift up the tensioner pulley against the belt and tighten the center bolt to hold it in position.

8. Make sure the timing marks are aligned. Remove the binder clips. Rotate the crankshaft a ¼ turn counter-clockwise. Then turn the crankshaft clockwise until the timing marks are aligned.
9. Place special tool MD998752 on a torque wrench. Insert the tool into the place provided on the tension pulley. Loosen the center pulley bolt and apply 2.2 ft. lbs. of pressure against the timing belt with the tension pulley. While holding the required torque, tighten the center bolt. Screw in special tool MD998738 through the left engine support bracket until it contacts the tensioner arm bracket. Turn the tool a little more to secure the tensioner and remove the locking wire placed into the automatic adjuster when it was reset.
10. Remove the special tool. Rotate the crankshaft 2 complete turns clockwise and allow it to set, for about 15 minutes. Then measure the protrusion of the automatic adjuster. It should be 0.015–0.018 in. If the proper amount of protrusion is not present, repeat the tensioning process.
11. Install the upper and lower timing belt covers.
12. Install the crankshaft pulley and water pump pulley.
13. Install the alternator and power steering drive belts. Install the air conditioner drive belt and tensioner assembly.
14. Install the engine mount bracket and lower the engine.
15. Install the under engine splash shield.
16. Connect the negative battery cable.

1597CC AND 1755CC ENGINES

1. Bring the engine to No. 1 piston at TDC, aligned. Disconnect the negative battery cable.
2. Remove the drive belts, water pump pulley, spacer and timing belt cover.
3. Ensure that the sprocket timing marks are aligned, before making the adjustment.
4. Loosen the tensioner mounting bolt and nut and allow the spring tension to move the tensioner against the belt.

NOTE: Make sure the belt comes in complete mesh with the sprocket by lightly pushing the tensioner up by hand toward the mounting nut.

5. Tighten the tensioner mounting nut and bolt.

NOTE: Be sure to tighten the nut before tightening the bolt. Too much tension could result from tightening the bolt first.

6. Recheck all sprocket alignments.
7. Turn the crankshaft through a complete rotation in the normal direction. Do not turn in a reverse direction or shake or push the belt.
8. Loosen the tensioner bolt and nut. Retighten the nut and then the bolt.
9. Reinstall the timing belt covers, the water pump pulley, spacer and drive belts. Connect the negative battery cable.

1997CC ENGINE

1. Disconnect the negative battery cable. Remove the water pump drive belt and pulley.
2. Remove the crank adapter and crankshaft pulley.
3. Remove the upper and lower timing belt covers.
4. Check the tensioners for a smooth rate of movement.
5. Replace any tensioner that shows grease leakage through the seal.
6. Install the silent shaft belt and adjust the tension, by moving the tensioner into contact with the belt, tighten enough to remove all slack. Tighten the tensioner bolt to 21 ft. lbs.
7. Tighten the silent shaft sprocket bolt to 28 ft. lbs.
8. Install the upper and lower timing belt covers.
9. Install the crank adapter and crankshaft pulley.
10. Install the water pump drive belt and pulley. Connect the negative battery cable.

Removal and Installation

NOTE: The timing chain case is cast aluminum, so exercise caution when handling this part.

1468CC ENGINE

1. Turn the engine until the No. 1 piston is on TDC with the timing marks aligned.
2. Disconnect the negative battery cable.
3. Remove the fan drive belt, the fan blades, spacer and water pump pulley.
4. Remove the timing belt cover.
5. Loosen the timing belt tensioner mounting bolt and move the tensioner toward the water pump. Temporarily secure the tensioner.
6. Remove the crankshaft pulley and slide the belt off of the camshaft and crankshaft drive sprockets.
7. Inspect the drive sprockets for abnormal wear, cracks or damage and replace, if necessary. Remove and inspect the tensioner. Check for smooth pulley rotation, excessive play or noise. Replace tensioner, if necessary.

To install:

8. Reinstall the tensioner, if removed and temporarily secure it close to the water pump.
9. Make sure the timing mark on the camshaft sprocket is aligned with the pointer on the cylinder head and that the crankshaft sprocket mark is aligned with the mark on the engine case.
10. Install the timing belt on the crankshaft sprocket.
11. Install the belt counterclockwise over the camshaft sprocket making sure there is no play on the tension side of the belt. Adjust the belt fore and aft so it is centered on the sprockets.
12. Loosen the tensioner from it's temporary position so the spring pressure will allow it to contact the timing belt.
13. Rotate the crankshaft 2 complete turns in the normal rotation direction to remove any belt slack. Turn the crankshaft until the timing marks are lined up. If the timing has slipped, remove the belt and repeat the procedure.
14. Tighten the tensioner mounting bolts, slotted side (right) first, then the spring side.
15. Once again rotate the engine 2 complete revolutions until the timing marks line up. Recheck the belt tension.

NOTE: When the tension side of the timing belt and the tensioner are pushed in horizontally with a moderate force, about 11 lbs. and the cogged side of the belt covers about ¼ in. of the tensioner right side mounting bolt head the across flats, the tension is correct.

16. Reinstall the timing belt cover, the water pump pulley, spacer, fan blades and drive belt.
17. Connect the negative battery cable.

1595CC DOHC ENGINE

NOTE: Special tools MD998752 tension pulley torque adapter and MD998738 tension pulley locker or equivalents, are required.

1. Bring the engine to No. 1 piston at TDC (top dead center) timing marks aligned. Disconnect the negative battery cable.
2. Raise the vehicle and support it safely. Remove the under engine splash shield.
3. Place a piece of wood on a suitable floor jack and support the engine. Remove the engine mount bracket.
4. Remove the alternator and power steering drive belts. Remove the air conditioner drive belt and tensioner assembly.
5. Remove the water pump pulley and the crankshaft pulley.
6. Remove the upper and lower timing belt covers.
7. Remove the engine center cover. Remove the breather hose from the rear of the rocker cover. Remove the PCV hose. Disconnect the spark plug cables from the plugs.
8. Remove the rocker cover and rear half-moon seal.

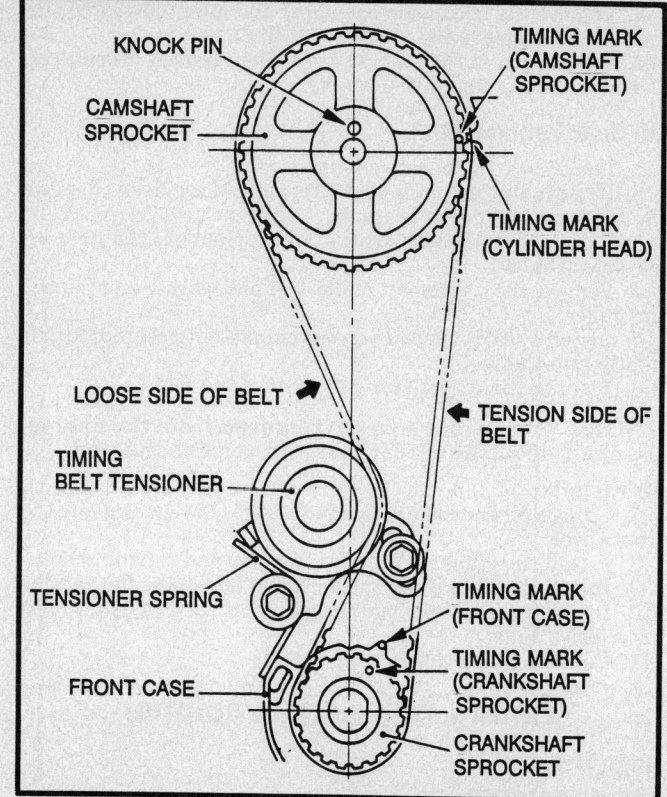

Timing belt Installation—1468cc engine

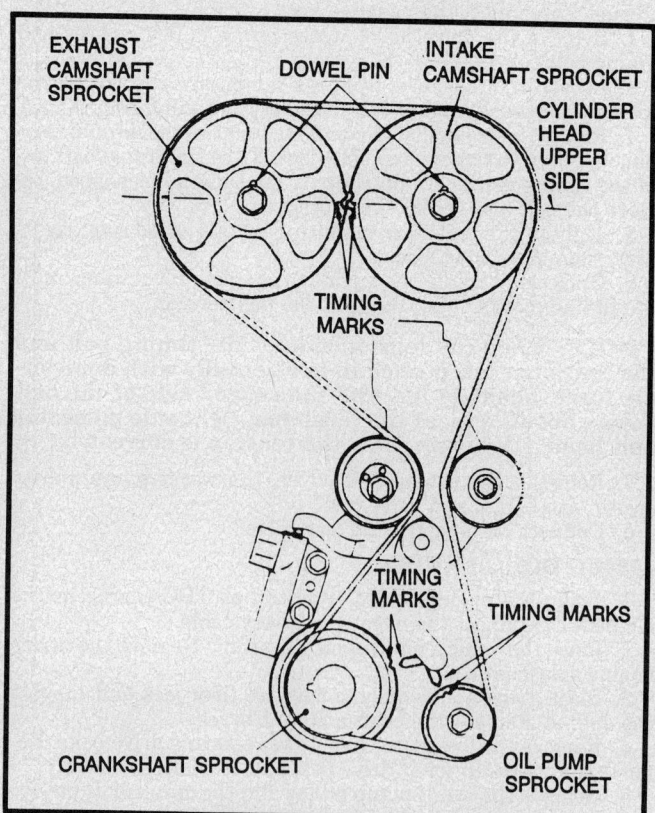

1595cc DOHC engine timing mark alignment for timing belt installation

9. Confirm the engine is still at No. 1 TDC. The timing marks on the camshaft sprocket and the upper surface of the cylinder head should coincide. The dowel pin on the front of the camshafts should be in the 12 o'clock position. Remove the automatic belt tensioner. Loosen the tensioner pulley center bolt.

10. If the timing belt is to be reused, mark an arrow, on the belt, in the direction of rotation, for installation reference. Remove the timing belt.

To install:

11. Install the automatic tensioner, after reset.

NOTE: **To reset the tensioner: Keep the adjuster level and clamp it in a soft jawed vise. Clamp with the extended adjuster on one side and the end mounting a plug on the other side. If the plug extends out of the adjuster body, place a suitable hole sized washer over the plug so the vise jaw pushes on the washer, not the plug. Close the vise slowly, forcing the adjuster back into the body. When the hole in the adjuster boss aligns with the adjuster rod, insert a snug fitting pin or wire into the holes to keep the rod in the compressed position. With the locking pin or wire in place, install the tensioner.**

12. Align the timing marks on the camshaft sprockets. Align the crankshaft timing marks. Align the oil pump timing marks. Place the timing belt around the intake camshaft and secure it to the sprocket with a stationary binder spring clip. Install the timing belt around the exhaust camshaft sprocket, check sprocket marks for alignment and secure the belt with a second binder clip on the exhaust sprocket.

13. Install the timing belt around the idler pulley, oil pump sprocket, crankshaft sprocket and the tensioner pulley.

14. Lift up the tensioner pulley against the belt and tighten the center bolt to hold it in position.

15. Check to see that all of the timing marks are aligned. Remove the binder clips. Rotate the crankshaft a quarter turn counter clockwise. Then turn the crankshaft clockwise until the timing marks are aligned.

16. Place special tool MD998752 on a torque wrench. Insert the tool into the place provided on the tension pulley. Loosen the center pulley bolt and apply 2.2 ft. lbs. of pressure against the timing belt with the tension pulley. While holding the required torque, tighten the center bolt. Screw in special tool MD998738 through the left engine support bracket until it contacts the tensioner arm bracket. Turn the tool a little more to secure the tensioner and remove the locking wire place into the automatic adjuster when it was reset.

17. Remove the special tool. Rotate the crankshaft 2 complete turns clockwise and allow it to sit for about 15 minutes. Then measure the protrusion of the automatic adjuster. It should be 0.015–0.018 in. If the proper amount of protrusion is not present, repeat the tensioning process.

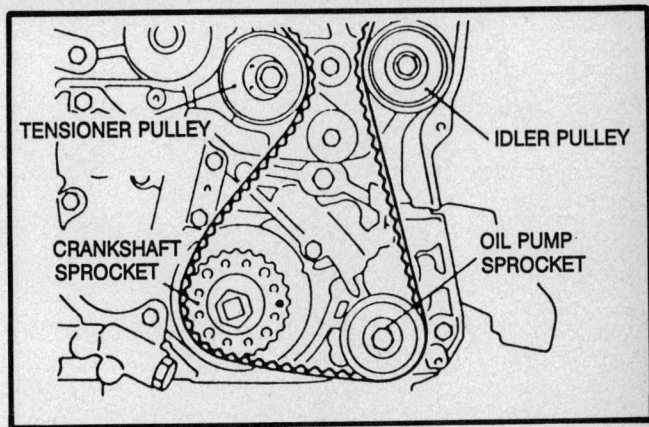

Installing the timing belt around the idler pulley, oil pump sprocket, crankshaft sprocket and tensioner

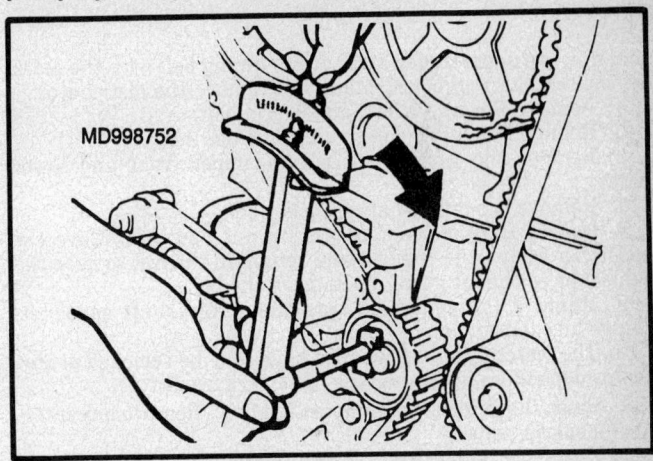

Using special tool MD998752 — 1595cc DOHC engine

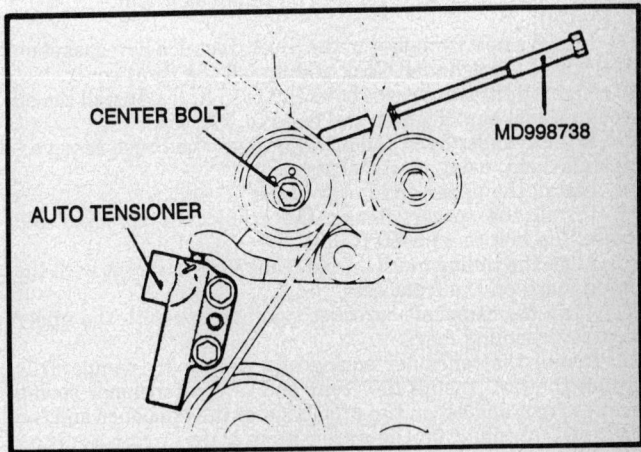

Using special tool MD998738 — 1595cc DOHC engine

1597CC AND 1755CC ENGINES

1. Drain the coolant and remove the radiator on rear wheel drive vehicles only. Disconnect the negative battery cable.

2. Remove the alternator and accessory belts. Remove the belt cover.

3. Rotate the crankshaft to bring No. 1 piston to TDC on the compression stroke. Align the notch on the crankshaft pulley with the T mark on the timing indicator scale and the timing

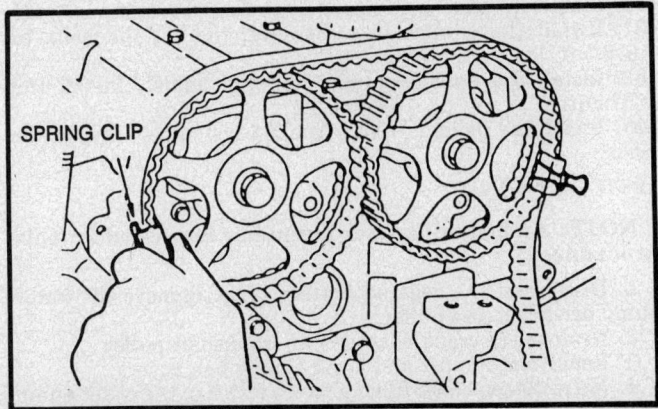

Using binder clips to secure the timing belt

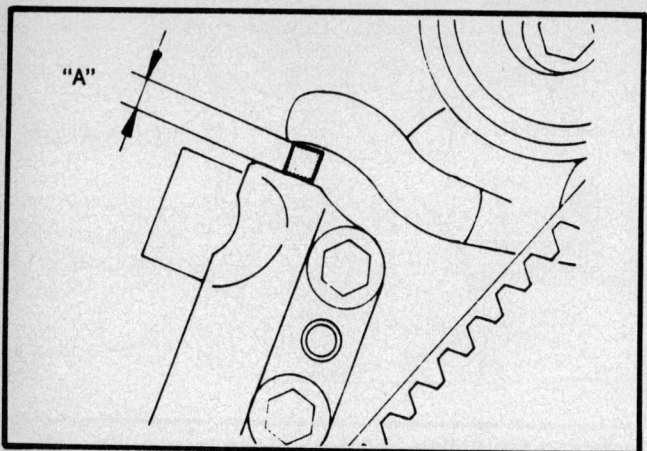

1595cc DOHC engine automatic tensioner extension measurement

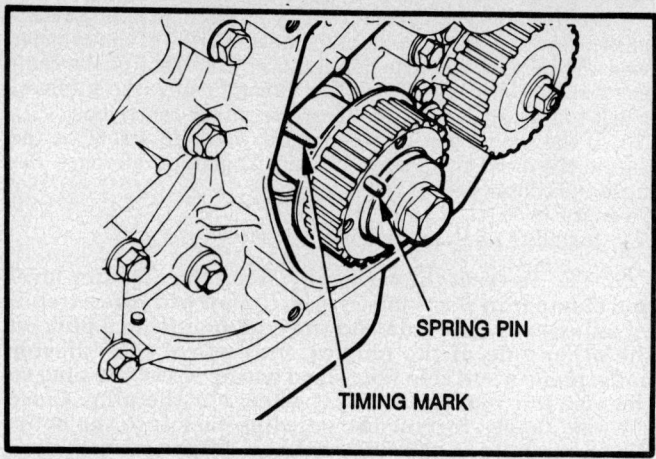

Crankshaft sprocket timing mark alignment—1597cc and 1755cc engines

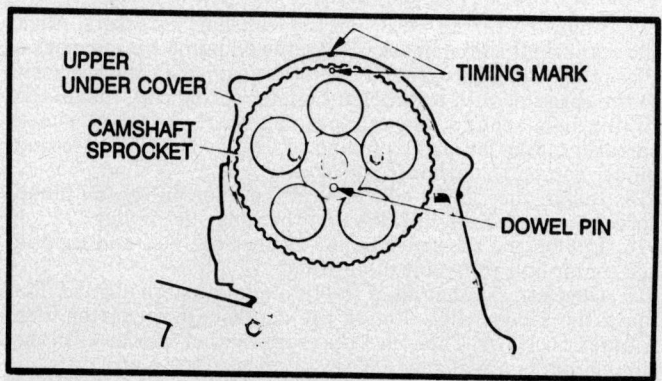

Camshaft sprocket installation alignment—1595cc and 1755cc engines

mark on the upper under cover of the timing belt with the mark on the camshaft sprocket. Mark and remove the distributor.

4. Remove the crankshaft pulley and bolt.

5. Remove the lower splash shield, if necessary.

6. Remove the timing belt covers, upper front and lower front.

7. Remove the crankshaft sprocket bolt.

8. Loosen the tensioner mounting nut and bolt. Move the tensioner away from the belt and retighten the nut to keep the tensioner in the off position. Remove the belt.

9. Remove the camshaft sprocket, crankshaft sprocket, flange and tensioner.

10. The water pump or cylinder head may be removed at this point, depending upon the type of repairs needed.

11. Raise the vehicle and support it safely. Remove any interfering splash pans.

12. Drain the oil pan and remove the pan from the block.

13. Remove the oil pump sprocket and cover.

14. Remove the front cover and oil pump as a unit.

To install:

15. Install a new front seal in the cover. Install a new gasket on the front of the cylinder block and install the front cover.

16. Tighten the front cover bolts to 11–13 ft. lbs. Install the oil screen and oil pan. Tighten the bolts to 5 ft. lbs.

17. If the cylinder head and/or water pump had been removed, reinstall them, using new gaskets.

18. Install the upper and lower under covers.

19. Install the spacer, flange and crankshaft sprocket and tighten the bolt to 43.5–50 ft. lbs.

20. Align the timing mark on the crankshaft sprocket with the timing mark on the front case.

21. Align the camshaft sprocket timing mark with the upper undercover timing mark.

22. Install the tensioner spring and tensioner. Temporarily tighten the nut. Install the front end of the tensioner spring (bent at right angles) on the projection of the tensioner and the other end (straight) on the water pump body.

23. Loosen the nut and move the tensioner in the direction of the water pump. Lock it by tightening the nut.

24. Ensure that the sprocket timing marks are aligned and install the timing belt. The belt should be installed on the crankshaft sprocket, the oil pump sprocket and then the camshaft sprocket, in that order, while keeping the belt tight.

25. Loosen the tensioner mounting bolt and nut and allow the spring tension to move the tensioner against the belt.

NOTE: Make sure the belt comes in complete mesh with the sprocket by lightly pushing the tensioner up by hand toward the mounting nut.

26. Tighten the tensioner mounting nut and bolt.

NOTE: Be sure to tighten the nut before tightening the bolt. Too much tension could result from tightening the bolt first.

27. Recheck all sprocket alignments.

28. Turn the crankshaft through a complete rotation in the normal direction. Do not turn in a reverse direction or shake or push the belt.

29. Loosen the tensioner bolt and nut. Retighten the nut and then the bolt.

30. Install the lower and upper front outer covers.

31. Install the crankshaft pulley and tighten the bolts to 7.5–8.5 ft. lbs.

32. Install the alternator and belt and adjust. Install the distributor.

33. Install the radiator, fill the cooling system and inspect for leaks.

1997CC ENGINE

NOTE: An 8mm diameter metal bar is needed for this procedure.

1. Disconnect the negative battery cable. Remove the water pump drive belt and pulley.

2. Remove the crank adapter and crankshaft pulley.

3. Remove the upper and lower timing belt covers.

4. Move the tensioner fully in the direction of the water pump and temporarily secure it there.

5. If the timing belt is to be reused, make a paint mark on the

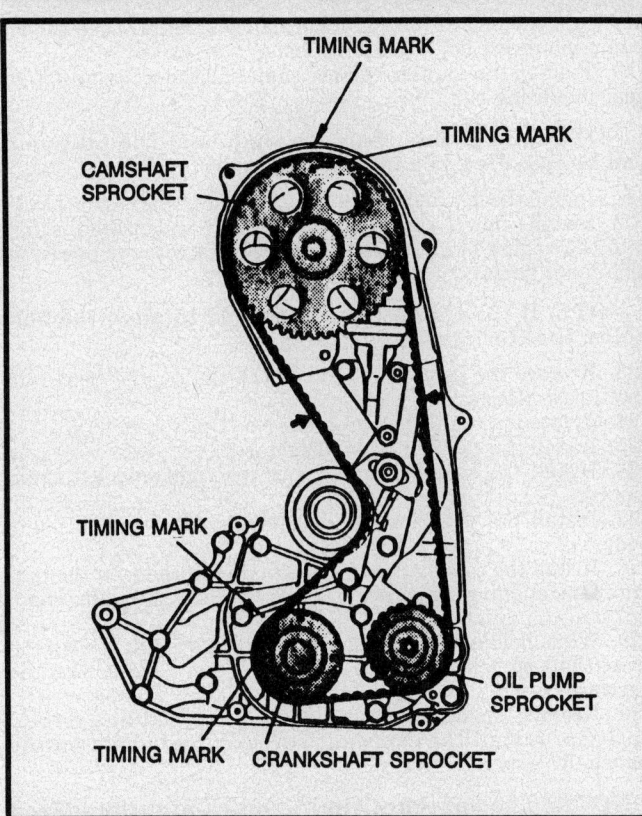

Timing belt installation—1595cc and 1755cc engines

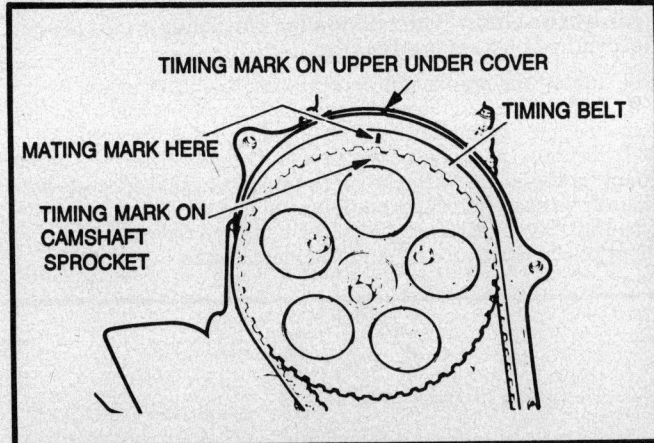

Camshaft timing mark alignment—1595cc and 1755cc engines

belt to indicate the direction of rotation. Slip the belt from the sprockets.

6. Remove the camshaft sprocket bolt and pull the sprocket from the camshaft.

7. Remove the crankshaft sprocket bolt and pull the crankshaft sprocket and flange from the crankshaft.

8. Remove the plug on the left side of the block and insert an 8mm diameter metal bar in the opening to keep the silent shaft in position.

9. Remove the oil pump sprocket retaining nut and remove the oil pump sprocket.

10. Loosen the right silent shaft sprocket mounting bolt until it can be turned by hand.

11. Remove the belt tensioner and remove the timing belt.

NOTE: Do not attempt to turn the silent shaft sprocket or loosen its bolt while the belt is off.

12. Remove the silent shaft belt sprocket from the crankshaft.

13. Check the belt for wear, damage or glossing. Replace it if any cracks, damage, brittleness or excessive wear are found.

14. Check the tensioners for a smooth rate of movement.

15. Replace any tensioner that shows grease leakage through the seal.

To install:

16. Install the silent shaft belt sprocket on the crankshaft, with the flat face toward the engine.

17. Apply light engine oil on the outer face of the spacer and install the spacer on the right silent shaft. The side with the rounded shoulder faces the engine.

18. Install the sprocket on the right silent shaft and install the bolt but do not tighten completely at this time.

19. Install the silent shaft belt and adjust the tension, by moving the tensioner into contact with the belt, tight enough to remove all slack. Tighten the tensioner bolt to 21 ft. lbs.

20. Tighten the silent shaft sprocket bolt to 28 ft. lbs.

21. Install the flange and crankshaft sprocket on the crankshaft. The flange conforms to the front of the silent shaft sprocket and the timing belt sprocket is installed with the flat face toward the engine.

NOTE: The flange must be installed correctly or a broken belt will result.

22. Install the washer and bolt in the crankshaft and torque it to 94 ft. lbs.

23. Install the camshaft sprocket and bolt and torque the bolt to 72 ft. lbs.

24. Install the timing belt tensioner, spacer and spring.

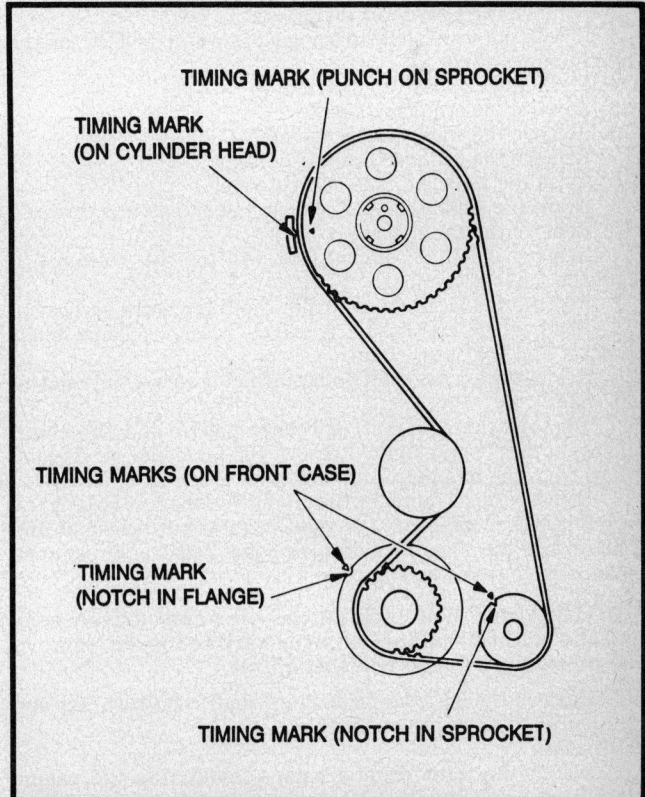

1997cc engine timing mark alignment

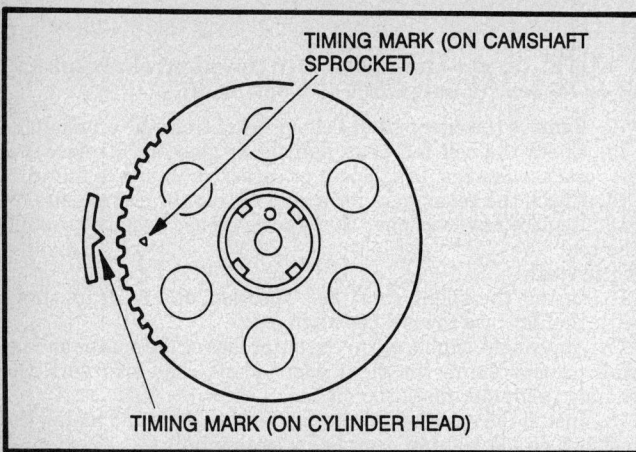

TIMING MARK (ON CAMSHAFT SPROCKET)

TIMING MARK (ON CYLINDER HEAD)

Camshaft timing mark alignment for No. 1 TDC, on the 1997cc engine

25. Align the timing mark on each sprocket with the corresponding mark on the front case.
26. Install the timing belt on the sprockets and move the tensioner against the belt with sufficient force to allow a deflection of 5–7mm along its longest straight run.
27. Tighten the tensioner bolt to 21 ft. lbs.
28. Install the upper and lower covers, the crankshaft pulley and the crank adapter. Tighten the bolts to 21 ft. lbs.
29. Remove the 8mm bar and install the plug. Connect the negative battery cable.

2555CC ENGINE WITH SILENT SHAFT

1. Drain the coolant and remove the radiator. Disconnect the negative battery cable.
2. Remove the alternator and accessory belts.
3. Rotate the crankshaft to bring No. 1 piston to TDC, on the compression stroke.
4. Mark and remove the distributor.
5. Remove the crankshaft pulley.
6. Remove the water pump assembly.
7. Remove the cylinder head, if necessary.
8. Raise the vehicle and support it safely.
9. Drain the engine oil and remove the oil pan and screen.
10. Remove the timing case cover.
11. Remove the chain guides. Side (A), top (B), bottom (C), from the outer B chain.
12. Remove the locking bolts from the B top chain sprockets.
13. Remove the crankshaft sprocket, counter-balance shaft sprocket and the outer chain.
14. Remove the crankshaft and camshaft sprockets and the inner chain.
15. Remove the camshaft sprocket holder and the chain guides, both left and right. Remove the tensioner spring and sleeve from the oil pump.
16. Remove the oil pump by first removing the bolt locking the oil pump driven gear and the right counter-balance shaft and then remove the oil pump mounting bolts. Remove the counter-balance shaft from the engine block.

NOTE: If the bolt locking the oil pump driven gear and the counter-balance shaft is hard to loosen, remove the oil pump and the shaft as a unit.

17. Remove the left counter-balance shaft thrust washer and take the shaft from the engine block.
To install:
18. Install the right counter-balance shaft into the engine block.
19. Install the oil pump assembly. Do not loose the Woodruff®

key from the end of the counter-balance shaft. Torque the oil pump mounting bolts to 6–7 ft. lbs.
20. Tighten the counter-balance shaft and the oil pump driven gear mounting bolt.

NOTE: The counter-balance shaft and the oil pump can be installed as a unit, if necessary.

21. Install the left counter-balance shaft into the engine block.
22. Install a new O-ring on the thrust plate and install the unit into the engine block, using a pair of bolts without heads, as alignment guides.

NOTE: If the thrust plate is turned to align the bolt holes, the O-ring may be damaged.

23. Remove the guide bolts and install the regular bolts into the thrust plate and tighten securely.
24. Rotate the crankshaft to bring No. 1 piston to TDC.
25. Install the cylinder head, if removed.
26. Install the sprocket holder and the right and left chain guides.
27. Install the tensioner spring and sleeve on the oil pump body.
28. Install the camshaft and crankshaft sprockets on the timing chain, aligning the sprocket punch marks to the plated chain links.
29. While holding the sprocket and chain as a unit, install the crankshaft sprocket over the crankshaft and align it with the keyway.
30. Keeping the dowel pin hole on the camshaft in a vertical position, install the camshaft sprocket and chain on the camshaft.

NOTE: The sprocket timing mark and the plated chain link should be at the 2–3 o'clock position when correctly installed. The chain must be aligned in the right and left chain guides with the tensioner pushing against the chain. The tension for the inner chain is predetermined by spring tension.

31. Install the crankshaft sprocket for the outer chain.
32. Install the 2 counter-balance shaft sprockets and align the punched mating marks with the plated links of the chain.
33. Holding the 2 shaft sprockets and chain, install the outer chain in alignment with the mark on the crankshaft sprocket. Install the shaft sprockets on the counter balance shaft and the oil pump driver gear. Install the lock bolts and recheck the alignment of the punch marks and the plated links.

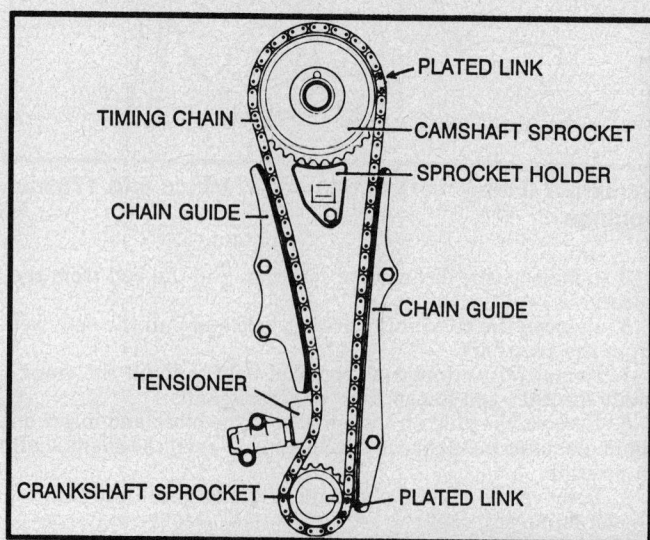

PLATED LINK
TIMING CHAIN
CAMSHAFT SPROCKET
SPROCKET HOLDER
CHAIN GUIDE
CHAIN GUIDE
TENSIONER
CRANKSHAFT SPROCKET
PLATED LINK

2555cc engine timing chain and tensioner installation

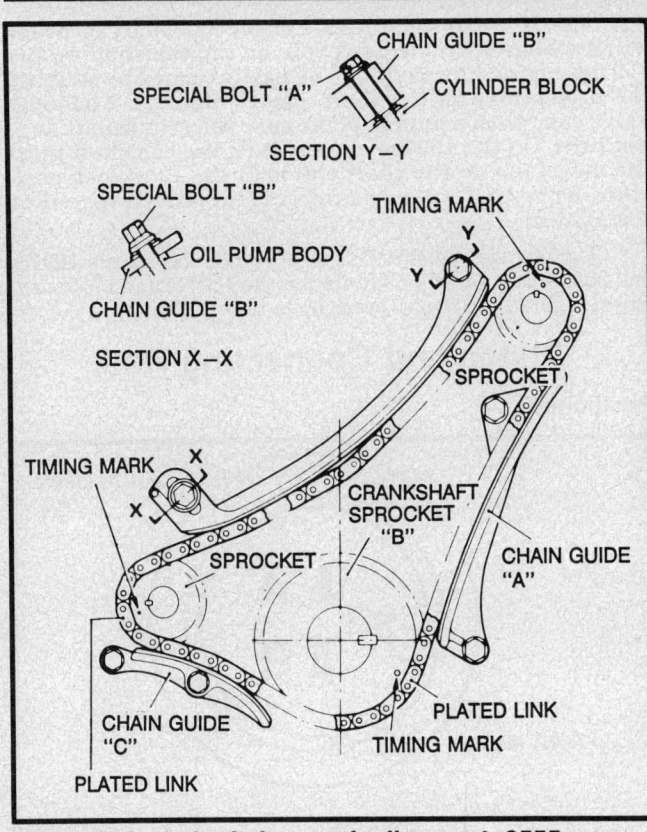

Silent shaft chain timing mark alignment, 2555cc engine

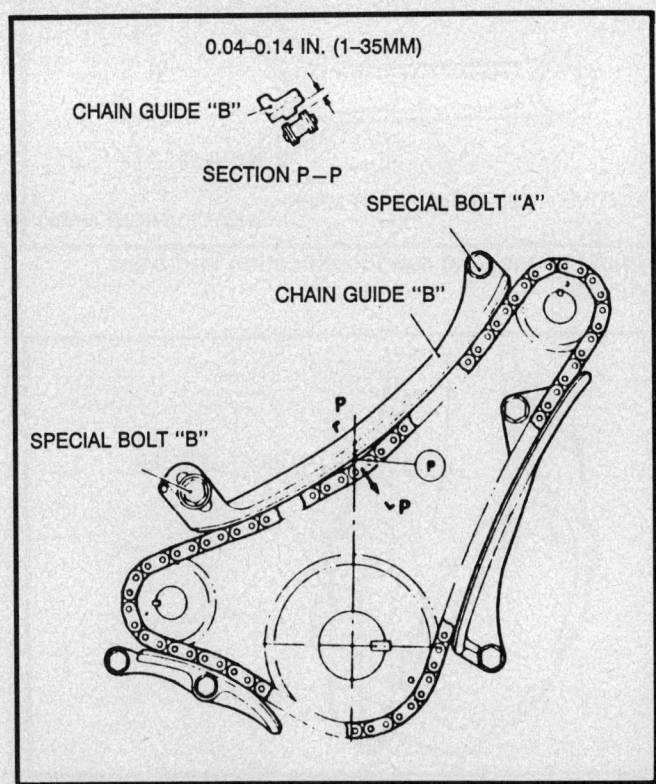

Location of special bolts for chain guide "B," 2555cc engine

34. Temporarily install the chain guides, side (A), top (B) and bottom (C).

35. Tighten side (A) chain guide securely.

36. Tighten bottom (B) chain guide securely.

37. Adjust the position of the top (B) chain guide, after shaking the right and left sprockets to collect any chain slack, so when the chain is moved toward the center, the clearance between the chain guide and the chain links will be approximately $^9/_{64}$ in. Tighten the Top (B) chain guide bolts.

38. Install the timing chain cover using a new gasket, being careful not to damage the front seal.

39. Install the oil screen and the oil pan, using a new gasket. Torque the bolts to 4.5–5.5 ft. lbs.

40. Install the crankshaft pulley, alternator and accessory belts and the distributor.

41. Install the oil pressure switch, if removed. Connnect the battery negative cable.

42. Install the fan blades, radiator, fill the system with coolant and start the engine.

Camshaft

Removal and Installation

1468CC ENGINE

1. Disconnect the negative battery cable.

2. Remove the cylinder head. Remove the cylinder head rear cover.

3. Remove the camshaft thrust case tightening bolt, located on top of the rear mounting boss.

4. Carefully slide the camshaft and thrust case, attached to the rear of the cam out the rear of the cylinder head.

To install:

5. Carefully slide the camshaft and thrust case into the cylinder head from the front.

6. Install a new cylinder head gasket and install the cylinder head and bolts. Torque the cylinder head bolts to 50–54 ft. lbs. (68–73 Nm).

7. Install the cylinder head rear cover.

8. Reinstall the timing belt cover, the water pump pulley, spacer, fan blades and drive belt.

9. Connect the negative battery cable. Start the engine and test engine performance and check for leaks.

1595CC DOHC ENGINE

1. Disconnect the negative battery cable. Remove the cylinder head.

2. Remove the crank angle sensor. Remove both camshaft drive sprockets.

3. Remove both rear (opposite end of the drive sprockets) camshaft bearing caps.

4. Remove both front bearing caps and front oil seals.

5. Remove the remaining camshaft bearing caps alternating from the rear of the head to the front.

6. Remove the camshafts.

7. Clean and inspect all parts. Check the rollers on the end of the rocker arms. If the rollers are warn on do not rotate smoothly, replace as necessary.

To install:

8. Lubricate the camshafts. Place the camshafts in position. The intake side camshaft has a slit in the rear to drive the crank angle sensor. The bearing caps No. 2–5 are the same shape. When installing them, check the top markings to identify the intake or exhaust side. Left or Right is marked on the front caps, L for the intake side; R for the exhaust side.

9. Tighten the bearing caps, in 2 or 3 steps, to 14–15 ft. lbs. (20–22 Nm).

10. Make sure the rocker arm is properly mounted on the lash adjuster and valve stem tip.

11. Install the front oil seals. Turn the intake camshaft until the front dowel pin is facing straight up at the 12 o'clock posi-

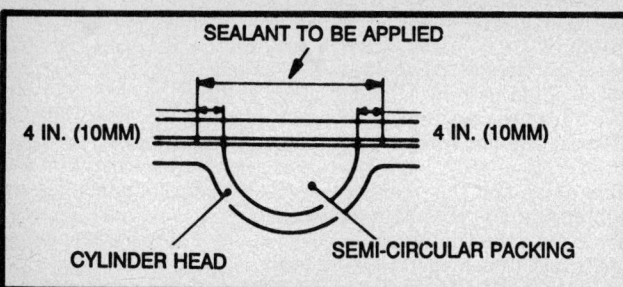

Sealant application on the rocker cover rear seal projections used for turning the shaft in hard-to-turn installations

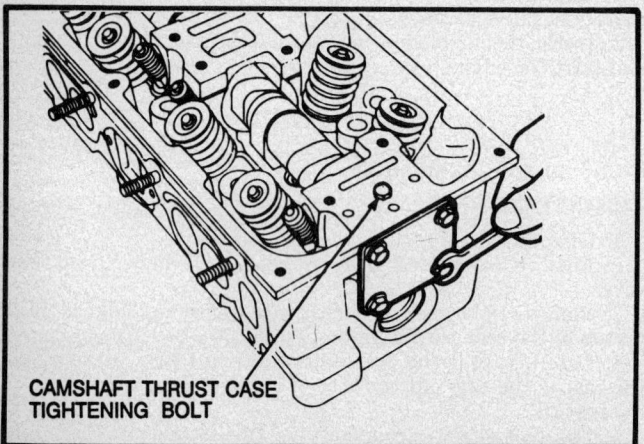

Removing the rear camshaft cover—1468cc engine

tion. Install the crank angle sensor with the punch mark on the sensor housing aligned with the notch in the plate. Install the drive sprocket and tighten the bolts to 58–72 ft. lbs. (79–98 Nm).

1597CC, 1755CC, 1997CC AND 2555CC ENGINES

1. Disconnect the negative battery cable.
2. Remove the rocker cover. Matchmark the rocker arm bearing caps to the cylinder head.
3. Remove the bearing cap bolts from the cylinder head, but do not remove them from the bearing caps and shafts. Lift the rocker arm assembly from the cylinder head.
4. Make sure the timing marks on the camshaft sprocket and head are properly aligned, so No. 1 piston is at TDC of the compression stroke. If the camshaft sprocket is to be removed, do so before removing the camshaft from the head. If not, it will be difficult to remove the sprocket bolt. Prior to removing the bearing caps or belt, remove the camshaft sprocket bolt and lift off the sprocket and belt. Discard the camshaft oil seal.
5. Remove the camshaft from the bearing saddles.

NOTE: On some engines, a distributor drive gear and spacer are used on the front of the camshaft.

6. The valves, valve springs and valve guide seals can now be removed from the cylinder head.
7. Installation is the reverse of removal. Coat all parts with clean engine oil prior to installation. Use a seal driver to install the new oil seal after the camshaft is in place.

NOTE: If the dowel pin hole of the camshaft sprocket will not align with the dowel pin on the camshaft on the 1597cc engine, the shaft can be easily turned by striking the projections on the shaft, just behind No. 2 exhaust valve cam, with a punch. Make sure the crankshaft does not turn. On the 1997cc engine, turn the camshaft until the dowel pin on the shaft end is in the 12 o'clock position. This will ensure correct camshaft sprocket installation.

8. Tighten the sprocket bolt to 50–60 ft. lbs. on the 1997cc and 2555cc engines; 44–55 ft. lbs. on the 1597cc and 1755cc engines. Tighten the rocker cover bolts to 5 ft. lbs.

Piston and Connecting Rod

Positioning

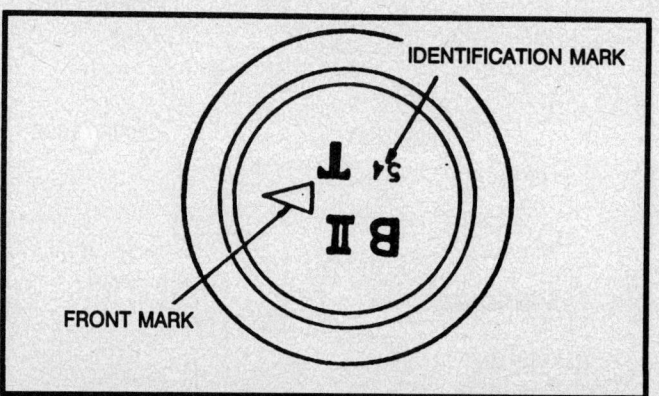

Typical piston identification and direction indicator

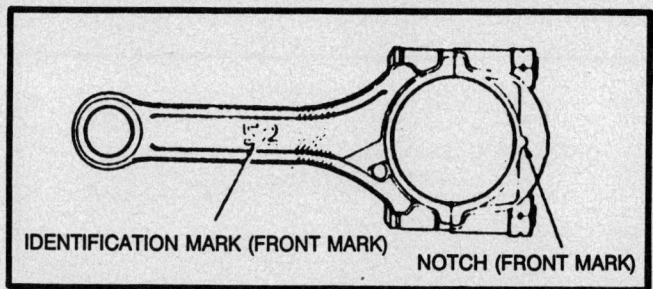

Typical connecting rod identification and front indicator

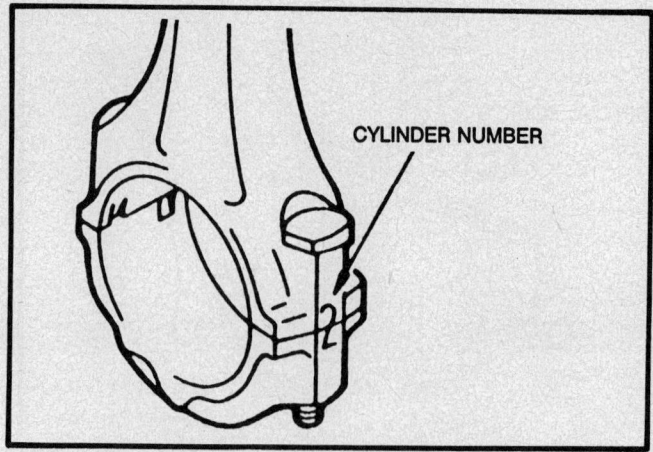

Location of cylinder number on connecting rod

ENGINE LUBRICATION

Oil Pan

Removal and Installation

The engine may have be raised off its mount for the pan to clear the suspension crossmember. However, on most front wheel drive vehicles, there is usually enough clearance without raising the engine.

1. Raise the vehicle and support it safely. Remove the underbody splash shield.
2. Unbolt the left and right engine mounts, except front wheel drive.
3. On rear wheel drive vehicles, place a jack under the bell housing and raise the engine.
4. Remove the oil pan retaining bolts and remove the oil pan.

To install:

5. Installation is the reverse order of removal procedure.
6. Use a new pan gasket. Torque the oil pan retaining bolts to 4–6 ft. lbs. (6–8 Nm).

Oil Pump

Removal and Installation

1468CC ENGINE

1. Remove the timing belt.
2. Remove the oil pan.
3. Remove the oil screen.
4. Unbolt and remove the front case assembly.
5. Remove the oil pump cover.
6. Remove the inner and outer gears from the front case.

NOTE: The outer gear has no identifying marks to indicate direction of rotation. Clean the gear and mark it with an indelible marker.

7. Remove the plug, relief valve spring and relief valve from the case.
8. Check the front case for damage or cracks. Replace the front seal. Replace the oil screen O-ring. Clean all parts thoroughly with a safe solvent.
9. Check the pump gears for wear or damage. Clean the gears thoroughly and place them in position in the case to check the clearances. There is a crescent shaped piece between the 2 gears. This piece is the reference point for 2 measurements. Use the following clearances for determining gear wear:
Outer gear face-to-case—0.0039–0.0079 in.

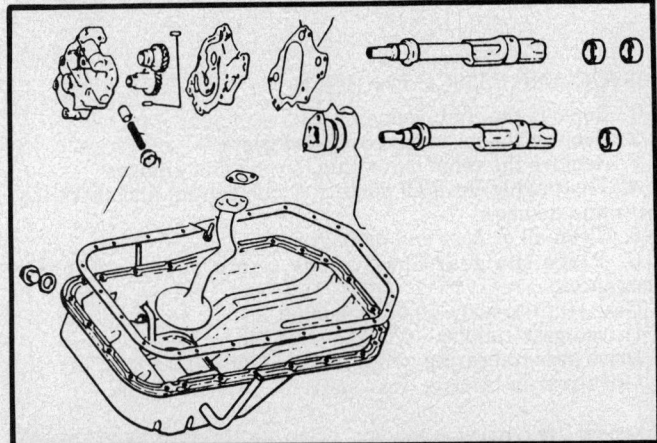

Exploded view of oil pump, oil pan and silent shafts, 2555cc engine

Outer gear teeth-to-crescent—0.0087–0.0134 in.
Outer gear endplay—0.0016–0.0039 in.
Inner gear teeth-to-crescent—0.0083–0.0126 in.
Inner gear endplay—0.0016–0.0039 in.

10. Check that the relief valve can slide freely in the case.
11. Check the relief valve spring for damage. The relief valve free length should be 1.850 in. Load/length should be 9.5 lbs. at 1.575 in.
12. Thoroughly coat both oil pump gears with clean engine oil and install them in the correct direction of rotation.
13. Install the pump cover and torque the bolts to 7 ft. lbs.
14. Coat the relief valve and spring with clean engine oil, install them and tighten the plug to 30–36 ft. lbs.
15. Position a new front case gasket, coated with sealer, on the engine and install the front case. Torque the bolts to 10 ft. lbs. Note that the bolts have different shank lengths.
16. Coat the lips of a new seal with clean engine oil and slide it along the crankshaft until it touches the front case. Drive it into place with a seal driver.
17. Install the sprocket, timing belt and pulley.
18. Install the oil screen.
19. Thoroughly clean both the oil pan and engine mating surfaces. Apply a 4mm wide bead of RTV sealer in the groove of the oil pan mating surface.

NOTE: The sealer will set in approximately 15 minutes.

20. Tighten the oil pan bolts to 5–6 ft. lbs.

1595CC DOHC, 1597CC AND 1755CC ENGINES

1. Remove the timing belt.
2. Drain the oil.
3. Remove the oil filter, on 1595cc DOHC engines. Remove the oil pan and screen.
4. Remove the oil filter bracket, on 1595cc DOHC engines. Unbolt and remove the front case assembly.

NOTE: On 1597cc and 1755cc engines, if the front case assembly is difficult to remove from the block, there is a groove around the case into which a prybar may be inserted, to aid in removal. Pry slowly and evenly. Don't hammer.

5. On 1597cc and 1755cc engines, remove the oil pressure relief plug, spring and plunger.
6. On 1597cc, remove the nut and pull off the oil pump sprocket.
7. On 1597cc and 1755cc engines, remove the oil pump cover.
8. On 1597cc and 1755cc engines, remove the pump rotor.
9. Check the case for cracks and damage.
10. Check the oil screen for damage.
11. Replace the oil screen O-ring.
12. Thoroughly clean all parts in a safe solvent.
13. On 1597cc engines, place the rotor back in the case to check clearances.
Side clearance—0.0024–0.0047 in.
Tip clearance—0.0016–0.0047 in.
Body clearance—0.0039–0.0063 in.
Shaft-to-cover clearance—0.0008–0.0020 in.
14. On 1597cc and 1755cc engines, check that the relief valve plunger slides smoothly in its bore.
15. On 1597cc and 1755cc engines: Check the relief valve spring. The free length should be 1.850 in.; the load length should be 9.5 lbs. at 1.575 in.
16. On 1597cc and 1755cc engines, install a new oil seal, coated with clean engine oil, into the oil pump cover. Drive it into place using a hammer and flat block.

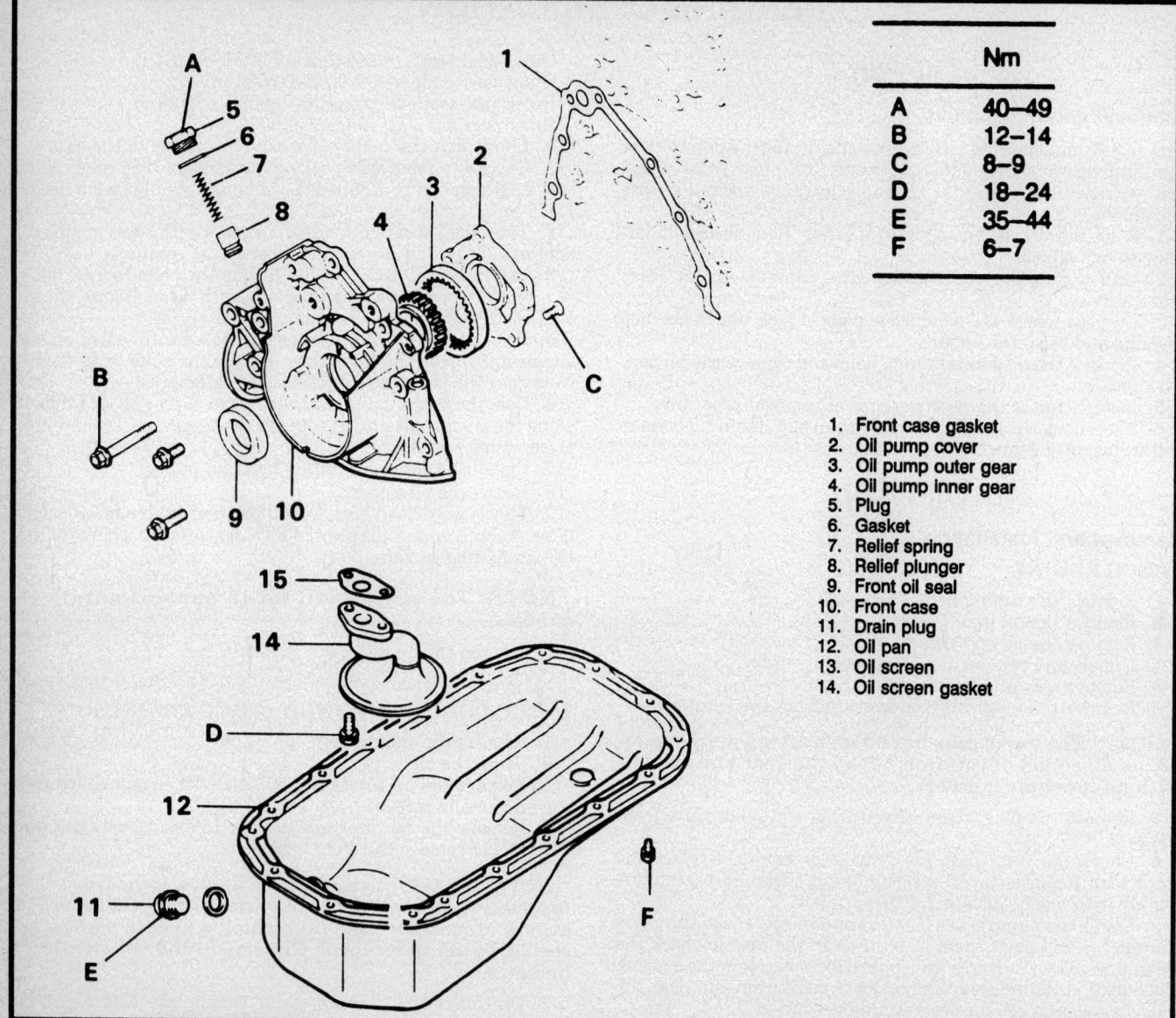

	Nm
A	40–49
B	12–14
C	8–9
D	18–24
E	35–44
F	6–7

1. Front case gasket
2. Oil pump cover
3. Oil pump outer gear
4. Oil pump inner gear
5. Plug
6. Gasket
7. Relief spring
8. Relief plunger
9. Front oil seal
10. Front case
11. Drain plug
12. Oil pan
13. Oil screen
14. Oil screen gasket

View of the oil pump, front case and oil pan—1468cc engine

17. On 1597cc and 1755cc, install a new cover gasket in the groove in the case.
18. On 1597cc and 1755cc, coat the rotor with clean engine oil and install it in the cover.
19. On 1597cc and 1755cc, install the cover and tighten the bolts.
20. On 1597cc and 1755cc, install the sprocket and tighten the nut to 28 ft. lbs.
21. On 1597cc and 1755cc, coat the oil relief valve plunger with clean engine oil and install it, along with the spring and plug.
22. Install a new case gasket, coated with sealer, on the block and install the case. Torque the case bolts, on 1597cc engines, 13 ft. lbs. on 1595cc DOHC engines, 20–25 ft. lbs.

NOTE: There are 2 lengths of case bolts.

23. Install the screen. Tighten the bolts, on 1597cc and 1755cc engines, 18 ft. lbs. On 1595cc DOHC engines, 11–16 ft. lbs.
24. Install the oil pan.

1997CC AND 2555CC ENGINES

1. Remove the timing chain.
2. Remove the oil pump cover and gears.
3. Remove the relief valve plug, spring and plunger.
4. Thoroughly clean all parts in a safe solvent and check for wear and damage.
5. Clean all orifices and passages.
6. Place the gear back in the pump body and check clearances:
Gear teeth-to-body—0.0041–0.0059 in.
Driven gear endplay—0.0024–0.0047 in.
Drive gear-to-bearing (front end)—0.0008–0.0018 in.
Drive gear-to-bearing (rear end)—0.0017–0.0026 in.

NOTE: If gear replacement is necessary, the entire pump body must be replaced.

7. Check the relief valve spring for wear or damage. Free

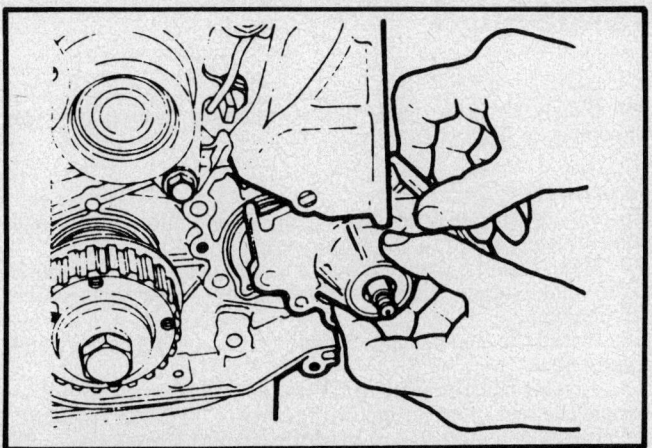

Removing the oil pump cover from 1597cc engine

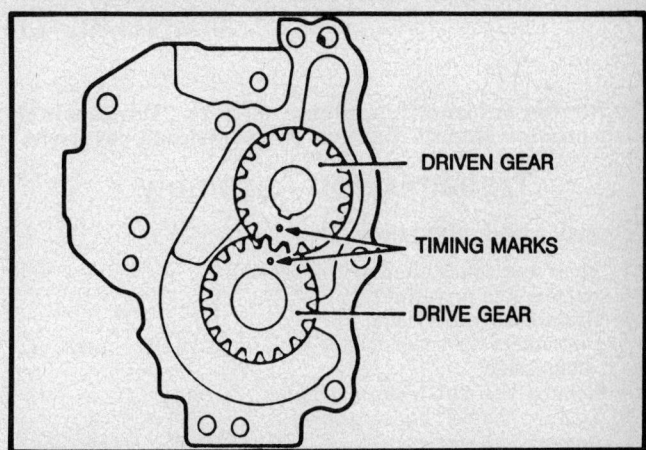

Installation of oil pump drive and driven gears and matching of timing marks, 2555cc engine

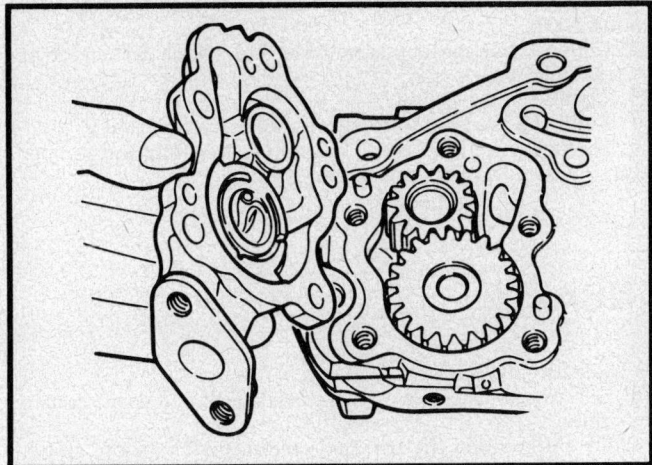

Oil pump cover removal from the 1997cc engine

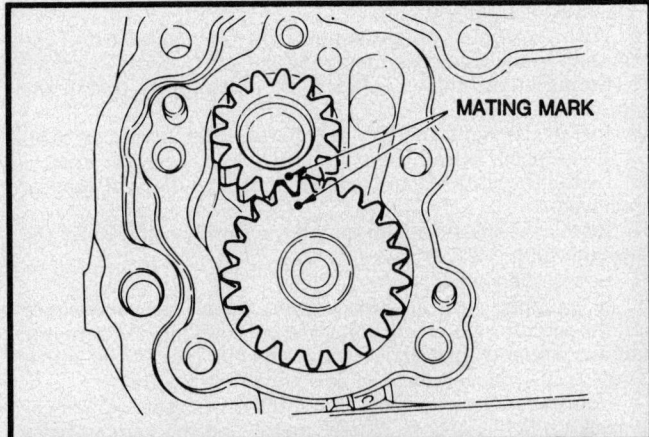

Oil pump gear mating marks on the 1997cc engine

Checking

1. If foreign matter is present, determine it's source.
2. Check the pump cover and housing for cracks, scoring and/or damage; if necessary, replace the housings.
3. Inspect the idler gear shaft for looseness in the housing; if necessary, replace the pump or timing chain, depending on the model.
4. Inspect the pressure regulator valve for scoring or sticking; if burrs are present, remove them with an oil stone.
5. Inspect the pressure regulator valve spring for loss of tension or distortion, if necessary, replace it.
6. Inspect the suction pipe for looseness, if pressed into the housing and the screen for broken wire mesh; if necessary, replace them.
7. Inspect the gears for chipping, galling and/or wear, if necessary, replace them.
8. Inspect the driveshaft and driveshaft extension for looseness and/or wear; if necessary, replace them.

Rear Main Bearing Oil Seal

Removal and Installation

The rear main oil seal is located in a housing on the rear of the block.
1. Raise the vehicle and support it safely.
2. Remove the transmission/transaxle.
3. Remove the oil seal housing from the block.
4. Remove the separator from the housing.
5. Pry out the oil seal.
To install:
6. Lightly oil the replacement seal. The oil seal should be installed so the seal plate fits into the inner contact surface of the seal case.
7. Install the separator with the oil holes facing down and install the oil housing.
8. Install the transmission/transaxle.
9. Lower the vehicle. Refill the the engine with oil.
10. Connect the negative battery cable. Start the engine and check for leaks.

length should be 1.850 in.; load length should be 9.5 lbs. at 1.575 in.
8. Assembly is the reverse of disassembly. Make sure the gears are installed with the mating marks aligned.

MANUAL TRANSMISSION

For further information, please refer to "Professional Transmission Repair Manual" for additional coverage.

Transmission Assembly

Removal and Installation

1. Raise and safely support the vehicle.
2. Remove the driveshaft.
3. Drain the transmission.
4. Disconnect the speedometer cable and switch connector at the transmission.
5. Remove the clutch slave cylinder.
6. Remove the bell housing cover.
7. Remove the starter.
8. Remove the 2 upper transmission mounting bolts.
9. Support the transmission with a suitable floor jack.
10. Remove the remaining transmission mounting bolts.
11. Remove the engine support bracket, insulator assembly and ground strap.
12. Place the shift lever in the neutral position. Remove the trim plate and unbolt the shifter assembly, removing it and the stopper plate underneath it.
13. Cover the rear of the cylinder head with a heavy cloth to prevent damage from contact with the firewall.
14. Slowly lower the jack, pull it rearward to disengage the transmission from the clutch.

To install:
15. Secure the the transmission on a transmission jack and raise it into position to the clutch assembly.
16. Make sure the transmission is seated properly and is flush to the engine flange. Install 2 mounting bolts on each side of the bell housing.
17. Install the engine support bracket, insulator assembly and ground strap.
18. Install the remaining transmission mounting bolts. Torque the transmission mounting bolts to 35 ft. lbs. (47 Nm).
19. Install the starter and mounting bolts. Torque the bolts 20–25 ft. lbs. (27–34 Nm).
20. Install the clutch slave cylinder and the clutch cover plate.
21. Install the engine support bracket, insulator assembly and ground strap.
22. Connect the speedometer cable and switch connector at the transmission.
23. Install the driveshaft.
24. Refill the transmission with an approved gear oil.
25. Lower the vehicle. Install the shifter assembly and stopper plate. Connect the negative battery cable.

MANUAL TRANSAXLE

For further information, please refer to "Professional Transmission Repair Manual" for additional coverage.

Transaxle Assembly

Removal and Installation
COLT

1. Disconnect the negative battery cable.
2. Disconnect from the transaxle: the clutch cable, speedometer cable, back-up light harness, starter motor and the 4 upper bolts connecting the engine to the transaxle.
3. If with a turbocharger, remove the air cleaner case, the actuator mounting bolts, the pin coupling, the actuator and shaft and remove the actuator. Discard the collar used with the pin and replace it with a new collar. If equipped with a 5 speed transaxle, disconnect the selector control valve.
4. Raise and support the vehicle safely.
5. Remove the front wheels. Remove the splash shield. Drain the transaxle fluid.
6. Remove the shift rod and extension. It may be necessary to remove any heat shields that interfere.
7. If equipped, remove the stabilizer bar from the lower arm and disconnect the lower arm from the body side.
8. Remove the right and left halfshafts from the transaxle case.
9. Disconnect the range selector cable, if equipped. Remove the engine rear cover.
10. Support the weight of the engine from above. Support the transaxle and remove the remaining lower mounting bolts.
11. Remove the transaxle mount insulator bolt.
12. Remove the engine and lower the transaxle.

To install:
13. Secure the transaxle on a transaxle jack and position it to the engine.
14. Carefully guide the transaxle input shaft into the clutch assembly. Make sure the transaxle is seated properly and is flush to the engine flange. Install 2 transaxle-to-engine bolts.
15. Install the transaxle mount insulator bolt. Torque the bolt to 29–36 ft. lbs. (40–50 Nm).
16. With the engine weight supported from above. Install the remaining lower transaxle mounting bolts.
17. Connect the range selector cable, if equipped. Install the engine rear cover.
18. Install the right and left halfshafts to the transaxle case.
19. If equipped, install the stabilizer bar to the lower arm.
20. Install the shift rod and extension. Install the heat shields, if removed.
21. Install the splash shield. Install the front wheels. Refill the transaxle fluid.
22. Lower the vehicle.
23. If equipped with a turbocharger, install the air cleaner case, the actuator mounting bolts, the pin coupling, the actuator shaft and actuator. Install new collar and pin. If equipped with a 5 speed transaxle, connect the selector control valve.
24. Connect to the transaxle: the clutch cable, speedometer cable, back-up light harness, starter motor and the 4 upper bolts connecting the engine to the transaxle.
25. Connect the negative battery cable.

2WD COLT VISTA

1. Disconnect the battery cables, negative cable first. Remove the battery and tray.
2. Remove the coolant reservoir.
3. Remove the air cleaner.
4. Disconnect the clutch cable, speedometer cable and backup light wiring from the transaxle.

5. Remove the upper engine-to-transaxle bolts.

6. Disconnect the select control lever and switch harness.

7. Remove the starter.

8. Disconnect and tag all wiring from the transaxle.

9. Raise and support the vehicle safely.

10. Remove the front wheels.

11. Drain the transaxle fluid.

12. Remove the extension and shift rod from the engine compartment.

13. Remove the stabilizer and strut bar from the lower control arm.

14. Remove the left and right halfshafts.

15. Support the transaxle with a suitable floor jack, taking care to avoid damaging the pan.

16. Remove the bell housing cover.

17. Remove the remaining transaxle-to-engine bolts.

18. Remove the transaxle mounting bolt.

19. Lower the jack and slide the transaxle from under the car.

To install:

20. Secure the transaxle on a transaxle jack and position it to the engine.

21. Carefully guide the transaxle input shaft into the clutch assembly. Make sure the transaxle is seated properly and is flush to the engine flange. Install 2 transaxle-to-engine bolts.

22. Install the transaxle mounting bolt. Torque the bolt to 29–36 ft. lbs. (40–50 Nm).

23. Install the lower transaxle-to-engine bolts. Torque the bolts to 32–39 ft. lbs. (43–53 Nm).

24. Remove the floor jack from the transaxle.

25. Install the left and right halfshafts.

26. Install the stabilizer and strut bar to the lower control arm.

27. Install the extension and shift rod.

28. Refill the transaxle with an approved gear oil.

29. Install the front wheels and lower the vehicle.

30. Connect all wiring to the transaxle.

31. Install the starter and mounting bolts. Torque the mounting bolts to 20–24 ft. lbs. (27–34 Nm).

32. Connect the select control lever and switch harness.

33. Install the upper engine-to-transaxle bolts. Torque the bolts to 32–39 ft. lbs. (43–53 Nm).

34. Connect the clutch cable, speedometer cable and backup light wiring to the transaxle.

35. Install the air cleaner.

36. Install the coolant reservoir and refill with coolant.

37. Install the battery tray and battery. Connect the battery cables, positive cable first.

4WD COLT VISTA

1. Disconnect the battery cables, negative cable first. Remove the battery.

2. Remove the coolant reserve tank.

3. Disconnect the speedometer cable, shift control cable and back-up light harness at the transaxle.

4. Remove the range select control valves and connectors.

5. Tag and disconnect all other wiring attached to the transaxle.

6. Remove the clutch slave cylinder.

7. Remove the vacuum reservoir tank.

8. Disconnect the starter wiring.

9. Remove the upper engine-to-transaxle bolts.

10. Raise and support the vehicle safely.

11. Remove the front wheels, lower engine cover and skid plate.

12. Drain the transaxle and transfer case.

13. Remove the driveshaft.

14. Remove the transfer case extension housing.

15. Remove the left and right halfshafts.

16. Disconnect the right strut from the lower arm.

17. Remove the right fender liner.

18. Take up the weight of the transaxle with a suitable floor jack.

19. Remove the bell housing cover bolts and remove the cover.

20. Remove the remaining engine-to-transaxle bolts.

21. Remove the transaxle mount insulator bolt.

22. Remove the transaxle mounting bracket attaching bolts.

23. Move the transaxle/transfer case assembly to the right. Tilt the right side of the transaxle down, until the transfer case is about level with the upper part of the steering rack tube, then turn it to the left and lower the assembly.

To install:

24. Secure the transaxle/transfer case assembly to a transaxle jack.

25. Raise the assembly in position to the engine. It may be necessary to tilt or angle the assembly in and around the steering rack tube.

26. Once the transaxle/transfer assembly is positioned to the engine, carefully guide the input shaft into the clutch assembly.

27. Install the transaxle mounting bracket attaching bolts. Torque the bolts to 40–43 ft. lbs. (55–60 Nm).

28. Install the transaxle mount insulator bolt. Torque to 40–43 ft. lbs. (55–60 Nm).

29. Install the lower engine-to-transaxle bolts. Torque to 31–40 ft. lbs. (43–55 Nm).

30. Install the bell housing cover bolts and install the cover.

31. Remove the the floor jack from the transaxle.

32. Install the right fender liner.

33. Connect the right strut to the lower arm.

34. Install the left and right halfshafts.

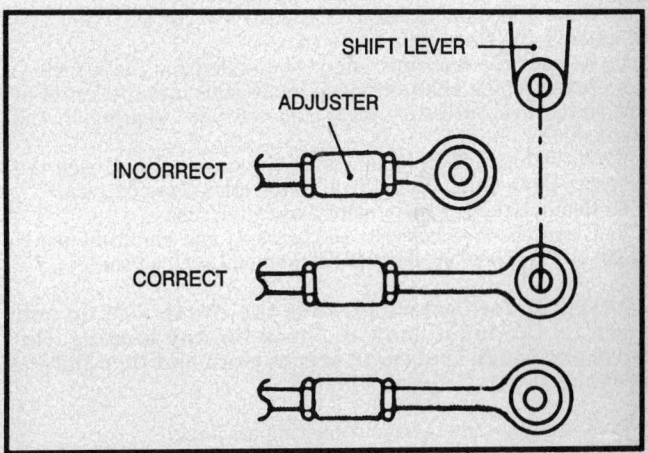

Shift cable position in neutral

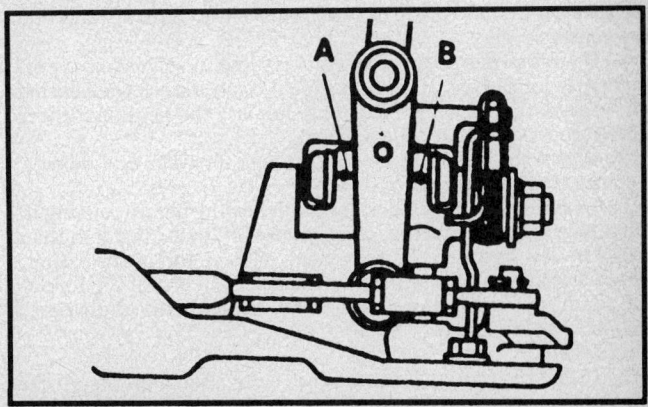

Adjusting the shift cable to make the shift selector's dimension A and B equal

35. Install the transfer case extension housing and the driveshaft.
36. Refill the transaxle and transfer case with an approved gear oil.
37. Install the front wheels, lower engine cover and skid plate.
38. Lower the vehicle.
39. Install the upper engine-to-transaxle bolts. Torque the bolts to 40–43 ft. lbs. (55–60 Nm).
40. Install the starter motor and mounting bolts. Torque the bolts to 22–25 ft. lbs. (30–35 Nm). Connect the starter wiring.
41. Install the vacuum reservoir tank.
42. Install the clutch slave cylinder.
43. Connect all other wiring to the transaxle, as tagged.
44. Install the range select control valves and connectors.
45. Connect the speedometer cable, shift control cable and back-up light harness at the transaxle.
46. Remove the coolant reserve tank.
47. Install the battery. Connect the battery cables, positive cable first.

Linkage Adjustment

1. Disconnect the negative battery cable.
2. Remove the console assembly from the vehicle.
3. At the shift selector assembly, remove the shift cable-to-shift selector cotter pins and disconnect the shift cables from the shift selector assembly.
4. Move the transaxle shift selector and shift selector into the **N** positions.
5. If necessary, turn the shift cable adjuster to adjust the cables length to align with shift lever in the **N** position. Connect the shift cable, flange side of the resin bushing should face cotter pin side of the shift lever, with lever Band install a new cotter pin.
6. At the shift selector, make sure dimensions A and B are equal; if they are not, turn the cable adjuster to make the necessary adjustment.
7. Adjust the other cable in the same fashion.
8. Move the shift selector into each position to make sure it is shifting smoothly.

CLUTCH

Clutch Assembly

Removal and Installation

1. Disconnect the negative battery cable.
2. Raise and support the vehicle safely. On the 4WD Colt Vista, remove the slave cylinder.
3. Remove the transmission or transaxle from the vehicle.
4. Insert a pilot shaft or an old input shaft into the center of the clutch disc, pressure plate and the pilot bearing in the crankshaft.
5. With the pilot tool supporting the clutch disc, loosen the pressure plate bolts gradually and in a criss-cross pattern.
6. Remove the pressure plate and clutch disc.
7. Clean the transmission or transaxle and clutch housing. Clean the flywheel surface with a non-oil based solvent.

NOTE: Before assembly, slide the clutch disc up and down on the input shaft to check for any binding. Remove any rough spots with crocus cloth and then lightly coat the shaft with Lubriplate®.

8. To remove the throwout bearing assembly
9. Remove the return clip and take out the throwout bearing carrier and the bearing.
10. To replace the throwout arm use a $^3/_{16}$ in. punch, knock out the throwout shaft spring pin and remove the shaft, springs and the center lever.
11. Do not immerse the throwout bearing in solvent; it is permanently lubricated. Blow and wipe it clean. Check the bearing for wear, deterioration, or burning. Replace the bearing if there is any question about its condition.
12. Check the shafts, lever and springs for wear and defects. Replace them if necessary.
13. Examine the clutch disc for the following before reusing it: loose rivets, burned facing, oil or grease on the facing, less than 0.012 in. left between the rivet head and the top of the facing.
14. Check the pressure plate and replace it if any of the following conditions exist: scored or excessive wear, bent or distorted diaphragm, loose rivets.
To install:
15. Insert the control lever into the clutch housing. Install the 2 return springs and the throwout shaft.
16. Lock the shift lever to the shaft with the spring pin.
17. Fill the shaft oil seal with multi-purpose grease.

18. Install the throwout bearing carrier and the bearing. Install the return clip.
19. Grease the carrier groove and inner surface.
20. Lightly grease the clutch disc splines.

NOTE: The clutch is installed with the larger boss facing the transmission or transaxle.

21. Support the clutch disc and pressure plate with the pilot tool.
22. Turn the pressure plate so its balance mark aligns with the notch in the flywheel.
23. Install the pressure plate-to-flywheel bolts hand tight. Using a torque wrench and, working in a criss-cross pattern, tighten the bolts to 11–15 ft. lbs. (15–20 Nm).
24. Install the transmission or transaxle.
25. Adjust the clutch free-play.
26. Lower the vehicle and connect the negative battery cable.

Pedal Height/Free-Play Adjustment

1. Measure the distance between the floor and the top of the clutch pedal.
2. The measurement should be as follows:
Colt and 2WD Colt Vista—6.20–6.40 in.
4WD Colt Vista—7.10–1.30 in.
Conquest—7.4–7.6 in.
3. If the measurement is not correct, loosen the clutch switch locknut and move the switch in or out as necessary to obtain proper height.

Clutch Cable

Adjustment

1. Slightly pull the cable out from the firewall.
2. Turn the adjusting wheel on the cable until the play between the wheel and the cable is within the correct dimension.
3. Check the clutch free-play.
   a. Raise and and support the vehicle safely.
   b. Remove the rubber cover from the clutch housing.
   c. Using a 0.030 in. feeler gauge, check the clearance between the pressure plate diaphragm spring and the throwout bearing.
4. If the free travel is not correct, make further adjustments at the cable adjusting wheel.

NOTE: Each turn of the adjusting wheel equals 0.060 in. of adjustment to the wheel and retainer clearance.

5. Lower the vehicle and check the clutch operation.

Removal and Installation

1. Loosen the cable adjusting wheel inside the engine compartment.
2. Loosen the clutch pedal adjusting bolt locknut and loosen the adjusting bolt.
3. Remove the cable end from the clutch throwout lever.
4. Remove the cable end from the clutch pedal.
To install:
5. Installation is the reverse order of removal procedures.

NOTE: Lubricate the cable with engine oil and after installation, install pads isolating the cable from the intake manifold and from the rear side of the engine mount insulator.

Clutch Master Cylinder

Removal and Installation

1. Loosen the bleeder screw on the slave cylinder and drain the system.
2. Disconnect the pushrod from the clutch pedal.
3. Disconnect the clutch pedal from the pedal bracket.
4. Disconnect the fluid line from the master cylinder.
5. Unbolt and remove the master cylinder and remove.
6. Installation is the reverse order of removal procedures.
7. Install the master cylinder and bleed the system.

NOTE: On the 4WD Colt Vista, the lower master cylinder mounting nut is accessed from inside the vehicle.

Clutch Slave Cylinder

Removal and Installation

1. Raise and support the vehicle safely.
2. Disconnect the clutch hose from the slave cylinder.
3. Unbolt and remove the cylinder from the clutch housing.
To install:
4. Installation is the reverse order of removal procedures. Bleed the system.

Hydraulic Clutch System Bleeding

NOTE: An assistant is needed for the bleeding operation.

1. Raise and support the vehicle safely.
2. Loosen the bleeder screw at the slave cylinder.
3. Make sure the master cylinder is full.
4. Attach a length of rubber hose to the bleeder screw nipple and place the other end in a glass jar half full of clean brake fluid.
5. Have the assistant push the clutch pedal down slowly to the floor. If air is in the system, bubbles will appear in the jar as the pedal is being depressed.
6. When the pedal is at the floor, tighten the bleeder screw.
7. Repeat Steps 5 and 6 until no bubbles are found. Check the master cylinder level frequently to make sure of fluid level.

AUTOMATIC TRANSMISSION

For further information, please refer to "Professional Transmission Repair Manual" for additional coverage.

Transmission Assembly

Removal and Installation

1. Disconnect the negative battery cable.
2. Raise the vehicle and support it safely.
3. Drain the fluid.
4. Remove the dipstick and unbolt the filler tube.
5. Remove the 2 upper transmission-to-engine bolts.
6. Disconnect the starter wiring. Remove the starter.
7. Disconnect the oil cooler lines and cap them to avoid spillage.
8. Remove the bell housing cover.
9. Turn the crankshaft so the torque converter bolts appear and remove them, turning the crankshaft for each bolt in turn.
10. Disconnect the speedometer cable at the transmission.
11. Disconnect the linkage and cross shaft.
12. Disconnect the ground strap.
13. Matchmark the flanges and remove the driveshaft.
14. Support the transmission with a transmission jack and the engine with a suitable floor jack.
15. Remove the rear engine support bracket.
16. Remove the remaining engine-to-transmission bolts.
17. Slowly lower the transmission while pulling it rearward to disengage it from the engine. Be careful to avoid dropping the torque converter.
To install:
18. Secure the transmission to a transmission jack.
19. Install the torque converter onto the transmission input shaft. Make sure the converter is fully seated in to the front pump before bolting the transmission to the engine.
20. Raise the transmission and position it to the engine. Install the lower transmission-to-engine bolts. Torque the bolts to 31–39 ft. lbs. (43–54 Nm).
21. Install the rear engine support bracket and bolt. Torque the bolt to 14–18 ft. lbs. (20–25 Nm).
22. Remove the transmisssion jack from the transmission.
23. Install the driveshaft.
24. Connect the ground strap.
25. Connect the linkage and cross shaft.

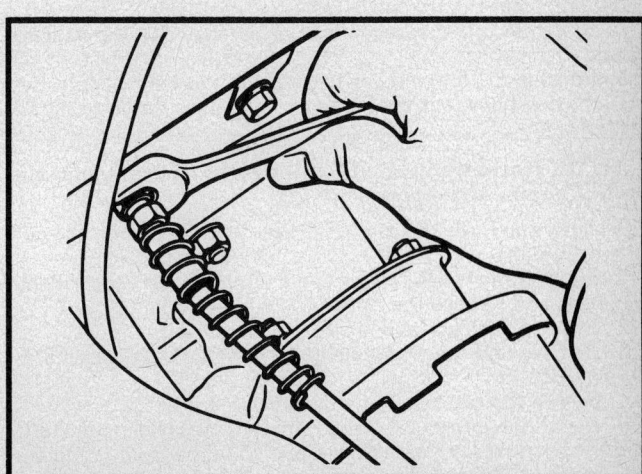

Throttle linkage adjustment—typical

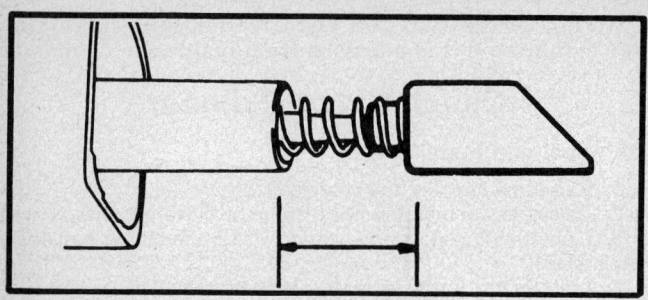

JM600 throttle rod adjustment point

26. Connect the speedometer cable to the transmission.
27. Turn the crankshaft so the flexplate bolt holes, align with the torque converter bolt holes and install the bolts. Torque the flexplate-to-converter bolts to 42–46 ft. lbs. (56–62 Nm).
28. Install the bell housing cover.
29. Connect the oil cooler lines to the the transmission.
30. Install the starter. Connect the starter wiring.
31. Lower the vehicle and install the 2 upper transmission-to-engine bolts.
32. Bolt the filler tube in place and install the dipstick.
33. Adjust the linkage, fill the unit and road test the vehicle.
34. Connect the negative battery cable.

Throttle Linkage Adjustment

1. Apply chassis lube to all sliding parts.
2. Place the selector in the **N** position.
3. Turn the adjusting cam until the distance between the adjusting cam and the selector lever end is 15–16mm.

AUTOMATIC TRANSAXLE

For further information, please refer to "Professional Transmission Repair Manual" for additional coverage.

Transaxle Assembly

Removal and Installation

NOTE: **The transaxle and converter must be removed and installed as an assembly.**

1. Disconnect the battery cables, negative first. Remove the battery and tray. If equipped with a turbocharger, remove the air cleaner case.
2. Disconnect the throttle control cable at the carburetor. If equipped with fuel injection, disconnect the cable at the throttle body. Disconnect the manual control cable at the transaxle.
3. Disconnect from the transaxle: the inhibitor switch (neutral safety) connecter, fluid cooler hoses and the 4 upper bolts connecting the engine to the transaxle.

NOTE: **Cap oil cooler hoses to prevent fluid loss.**

4. Raise and support the vehicle safely.
5. Remove the front wheels. Remove the engine splash shield.
6. Drain the transaxle fluid.
7. Disconnect the stabilizer bar at the lower arms and disconnect the control arms from the body. Remove the right and left halfshafts from the transaxle case.
8. Disconnect the speedometer cable. Remove the starter motor.
9. Remove the lower cover from the converter housing. Remove the 3 bolts connecting the converter to the engine driveplate.

NOTE: **Never support the full weight of the transaxle on the engine driveplate.**

10. Turn and force the converter back and away from the engine driveplate.
11. Support the weight of the engine from above. Support the transaxle and remove the remaining mounting bolts.
12. Remove the transaxle mount insulator bolt.
13. Remove and the transaxle and converter as an assembly.
To install:
14. Secure the transaxle to a transmission jack.
15. Install the torque converter onto the transaxle input shaft. Make sure the converter is fully seated in to the front pump before bolting the transaxle to the engine.
16. Raise the transaxle and position it to the engine. Install the lower transmission-to-engine bolts. Torque the bolts to 31–39 ft. lbs. (43–54 Nm).
17. Install the transaxle mount insulator bolt. Torque the bolts to 31–40 ft. lbs. (43–54 Nm).
18. Install the remaining transaxle-to-engine bolts. Torque the bolts to 31–39 ft. lbs. (43–54 Nm).
19. From the converter housing, install the 3 bolts connecting the converter to the engine driveplate. Torque the bolts to 34–38 ft. lbs. (46–54 Nm).
20. Connect the speedometer cable.
21. Install the starter motor and connect the wiring to it.
22. Connect the stabilizer bar to the lower arms and connect the control arms to the body. Install the right and left halfshafts to the transaxle case.
23. Refill the transaxle fluid.
24. Install the engine splash shield. Install the front wheels.
25. Lower the vehicle.
26. Connect to the transaxle: the inhibitor switch (neutral safety) connecter and the fluid cooler hoses.
27. Connect the throttle control cable to the transaxle.
28. Install the battery and tray. Connect the battery cables, positive first. If equipped with a turbocharger, install the air cleaner case.

Shift Linkage Adjustment

NOTE: **When it is necessary to disconnect the linkage cable from the lever, which uses plastic grommets as retainers, the grommets should be replaced.**

1. Set the parking brake.
2. Move the shift lever into **P**.
3. Loosen the clamp bolt on the gear shift cable bracket.
4. Make sure the preload adjustment spring engages the fork on the transaxle bracket.
5. Pull the shift lever all the way to the front detent position **P** and torque the lock screw to 100 inch lbs. (11 Nm).
6. Check the following conditions:
   a. The detent positions for **N** and **D** should be within limits of hand lever gate stops.
   b. Key start must occur only when the shift lever is in **P** or **N** positions.

Throttle Linkage Adjustment

1. Run the engine to normal operating temperature. Shut it off and make sure the throttle plate is closed (curb idle position).

2. Raise the small cone shaped cover on the throttle cable to expose the nipple.

3. Loosen the lower cable bracket bolt.

4. Move the lower cable bracket until the distance between the nipple and the lower cover directly under it is 0.02–0.06 in.

5. Tighten the bracket bolt to 9–11 ft. lbs.

TRANSFER CASE

Transfer Case Assembly

Removal and Installation

4WD COLT VISTA

1. Raise the vehicle and support it safely. Remove the transaxle.

2. Unbolt the transfer case from the transaxle and using a small prybar, separate the 2.

To install:

3. Installation is the reverse order of the removal procedure. Torque the attaching bolts to 40–43 ft. lbs. (54–58 Nm).

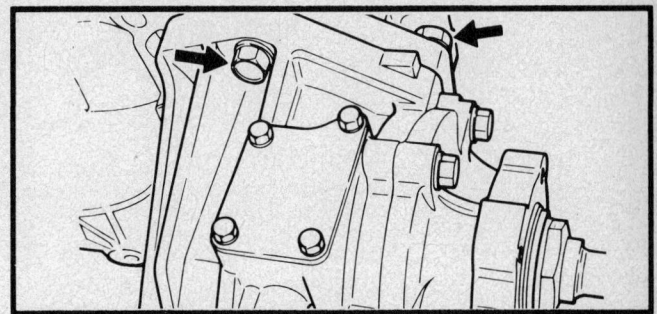

Transfer case attaching bolts

DRIVE AXLE

Halfshaft

Removal and Installation

EXCEPT 4WD COLT VISTA

1. Remove the hub center cap and loosen the halfshaft axle nut. Loosen the wheel lug nuts.

2. Raise the vehicle and support it safely. Remove the front wheels. Remove the engine splash shield.

3. Remove the lower ball joint and strut bar from the lower control arm.

4. Drain the transaxle fluid.

NOTE: If equipped with a turbocharger, remove the snapring which secures the center bearing.

5. Insert a prybar between the transaxle case, on the raised rib and the halfshaft double offset joint case; do not insert the prybar too deeply or the oil seal will be damaged. Move the bar to the right to withdraw the left driveshaft; to the left to remove the right halfshaft.

NOTE: In the case of the tripod joint driveshaft be sure to hold the tripod joint case and pull out the shaft straight. Simply pulling the shaft out of position could cause damage to the tripod joint boot or the spider assembly slipping from the case.

6. Plug the transaxle case with a clean rag to prevent dirt from entering the case.

7. Use a special puller driver tool mounted on the wheel studs to push the halfshaft from the front hub. Take care to prevent the spacer from falling out of place.

NOTE: If equipped with a center bearing, after forcing out the halfshaft, remove it by lightly tapping the double offset joint outer race, with a plastic hammer.

To install:

8. Assembly is the reverse of removal. Insert the halfshaft into the hub first, then install the transaxle end. Torque the shaft nut to 180 ft. lbs.

NOTE: Always use a new retaining ring every time the halfshaft is removed.

9. When installing the kit, use the grease supplied with the kit and apply an amount to the inner race and cage.

10. Install the inner race and cock slightly.

11. Apply grease to the balls and install them in the cage.

12. Place the inner race on the halfshaft and install the snapring.

13. Apply grease to the outer race and install.

14. Install the boots and bands.

15. Install the halfshaft using a new retainer ring.

16. Lower the vehicle.

4WD COLT VISTA

1. Remove the hub cap and halfshaft nut.

2. Raise and support the vehicle safely.

3. Remove the front wheels.

4. Drain the transaxle fluid.

5. Disconnect the lower ball joint from the knuckle.

6. Remove the strut and stabilizer bar from the lower arm.

7. Remove the center bearing snapring from the bearing bracket.

8. Lightly tap the double offset joint outer race with a wood mallet and disconnect the halfshaft from the Cardan joint.

9. Disconnect the halfshaft from the bearing bracket.

10. Using a 2-jawed puller secured to the hub lugs, press the halfshaft from the hub.

11. Unbolt and remove the bearing bracket.

12. Using a wood mallet, lightly tap the Cardan joint yoke and remove it from the transaxle. Never pry the Cardan joint from the transaxle. Prying will damage the Cardan joint dust cover.

To install:

13. Install the Cardan joint.

14. Apply a coating of chassis lube on the center bearing.

15. Attach a new O-ring to the oil seal retainer.

16. Install the bearing bracket. Torque the bolts to 40 ft. lbs. (54 Nm).

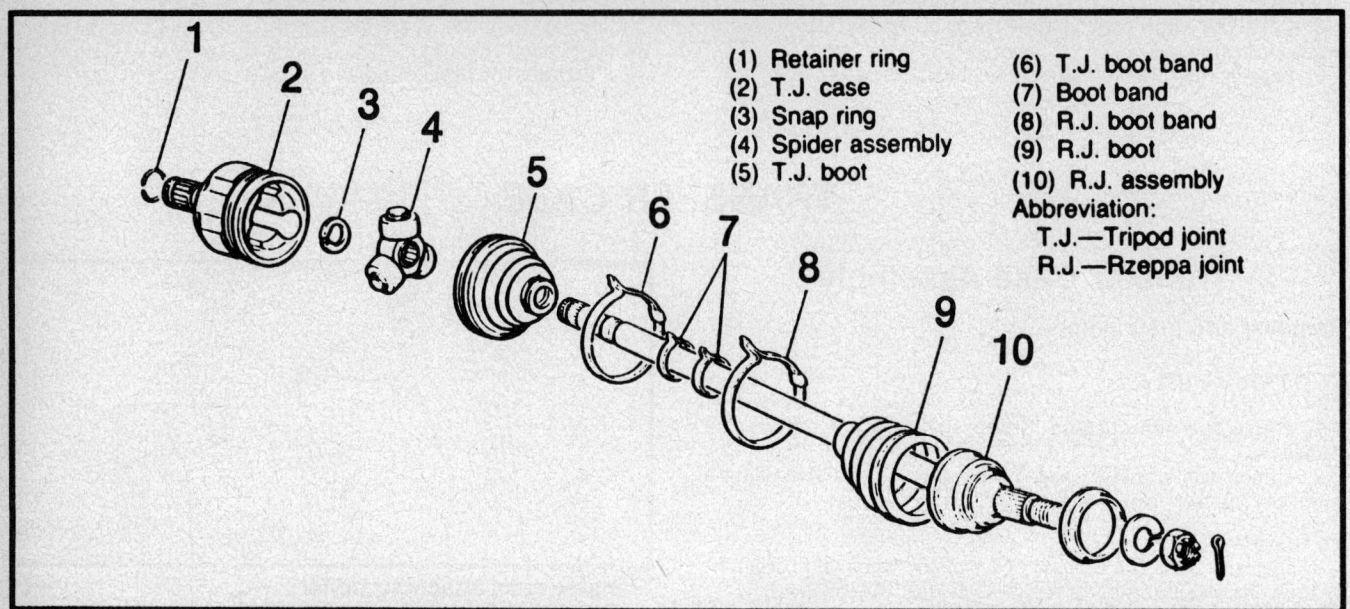

(1) Retainer ring
(2) T.J. case
(3) Snap ring
(4) Spider assembly
(5) T.J. boot
(6) T.J. boot band
(7) Boot band
(8) R.J. boot band
(9) R.J. boot
(10) R.J. assembly
Abbreviation:
  T.J.—Tripod joint
  R.J.—Rzeppa joint

Exploded view of front driveshaft—type T.J. and R.J.

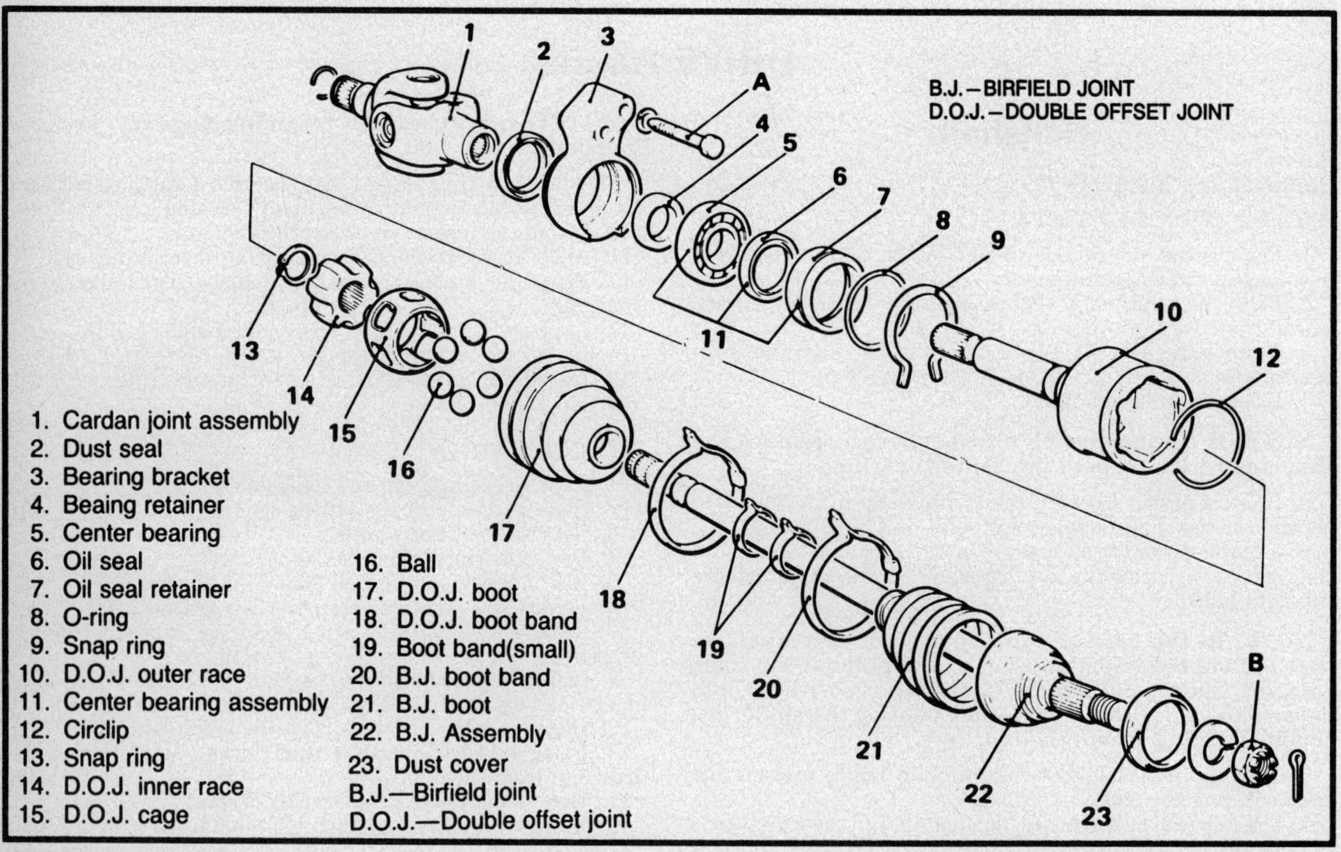

B.J.—BIRFIELD JOINT
D.O.J.—DOUBLE OFFSET JOINT

1. Cardan joint assembly
2. Dust seal
3. Bearing bracket
4. Beaing retainer
5. Center bearing
6. Oil seal
7. Oil seal retainer
8. O-ring
9. Snap ring
10. D.O.J. outer race
11. Center bearing assembly
12. Circlip
13. Snap ring
14. D.O.J. inner race
15. D.O.J. cage
16. Ball
17. D.O.J. boot
18. D.O.J. boot band
19. Boot band(small)
20. B.J. boot band
21. B.J. boot
22. B.J. Assembly
23. Dust cover
B.J.—Birfield joint
D.O.J.—Double offset joint

4WD Vista halfshaft

17. Insert the center bearing in the bearing bracket, making sure it is fully seated, then secure it with the snapring.
18. Coat the halfshaft splines with chassis lube and slide it into the Cardan joint.
19. Slide the halfshaft into the hub and install the nut. Torque the nut to 188 ft. lbs.

CV-Boot
Removal and Installation
INNER BOOT
1. Raise the vehicle and support it safely. Remove the wheel assembly.

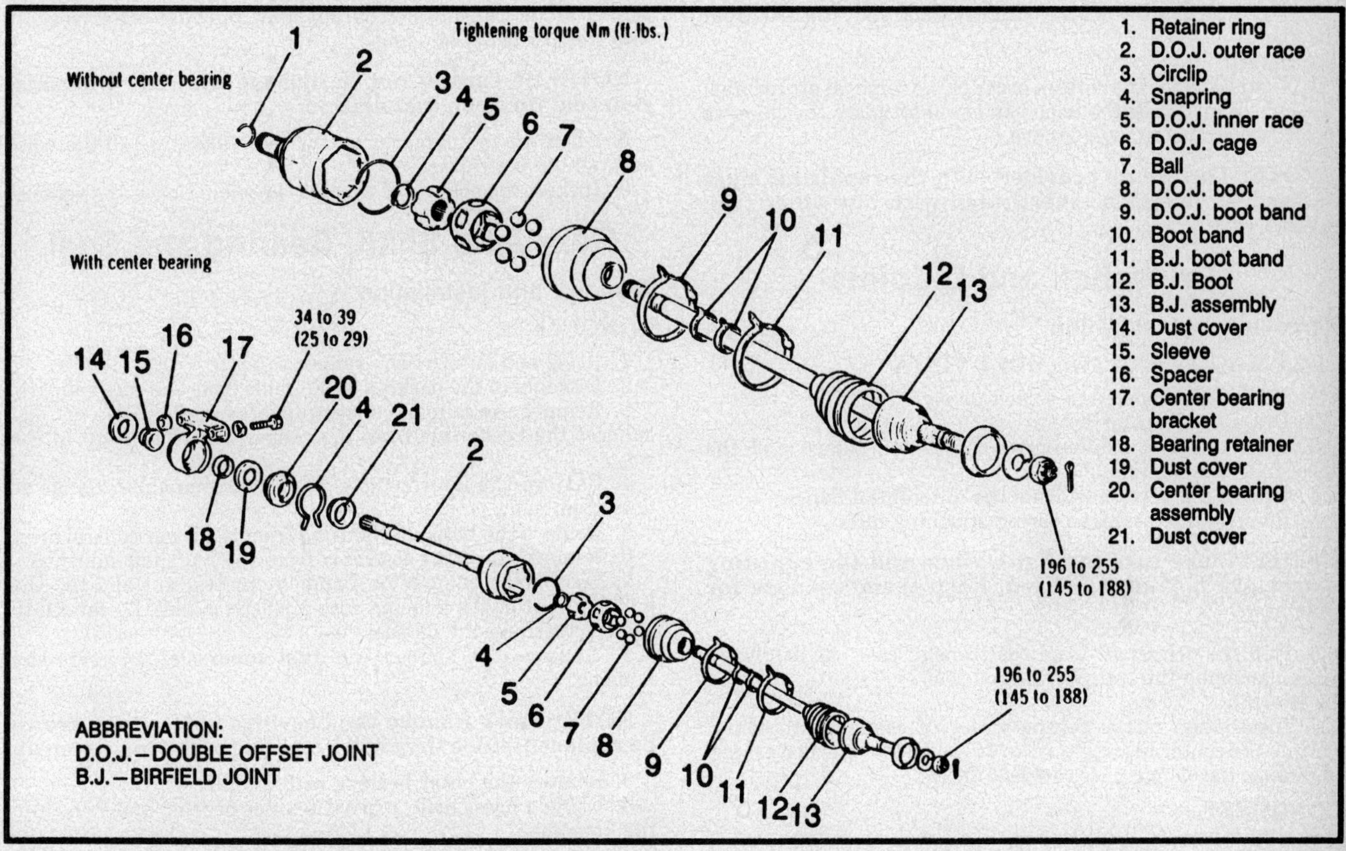

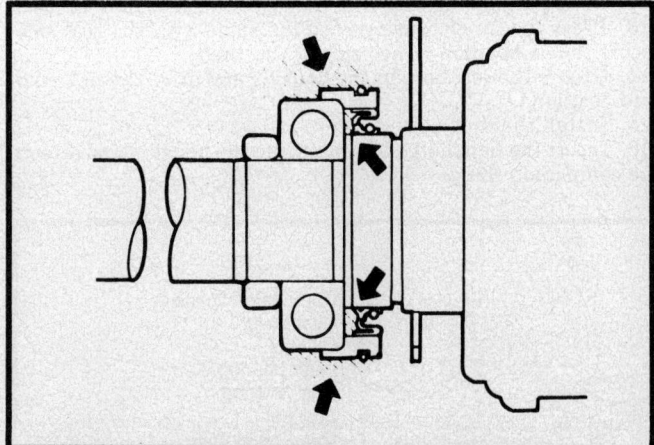

Tightening torque Nm (ft-lbs.)

Without center bearing

With center bearing

34 to 39
(25 to 29)

1. Retainer ring
2. D.O.J. outer race
3. Circlip
4. Snapring
5. D.O.J. inner race
6. D.O.J. cage
7. Ball
8. D.O.J. boot
9. D.O.J. boot band
10. Boot band
11. B.J. boot band
12. B.J. Boot
13. B.J. assembly
14. Dust cover
15. Sleeve
16. Spacer
17. Center bearing bracket
18. Bearing retainer
19. Dust cover
20. Center bearing assembly
21. Dust cover

196 to 255
(145 to 188)

196 to 255
(145 to 188)

ABBREVIATION:
D.O.J.—DOUBLE OFFSET JOINT
B.J.—BIRFIELD JOINT

Exploded view of front driveshaft—type D.O.J. and B.J.

Lubricant application points

2. Remove the halfshaft assembly from the vehicle.

3. Place the assembly in vise. Care must be taken not to crush the tubular shafts.

4. If inner joint needs replacement, cut the small rubber clamp, large metal clamp and remove the rubber boot. These items must be discarded.

5. Inspect for internal wear and/or damage.

6. Clean the grease by hand from inside the joint housing and around the ball trunnion assembly to inspect it.

7. Mark the tripod and housing for proper reassembly, if it is to be reinstalled.

8. To replace the boot, CV-joint or both, remove the snapring from the groove and tap the trunnion lightly with a brass drift pin. Leave the tripod bearings on the trunnion. Care must be taken to support the bearings as they may fall off.

To install:

9. Installation is the reverse order of the removal procedures.

10. When installing the tripod on the shaft place the chamfer face towards the retainer groove.

NOTE: The grease provided with the repair kit must be used. It cannot be substituted with any other type grease.

OUTER BOOT

1. Raise the vehicle and support it safely. Remove the wheel assembly.

2. Remove the halfshaft assembly from the vehicle.

3. Place the assembly in vise. Care must be taken not to crush the tubular shafts.

4. At the inner joint, cut the small rubber clamp, large metal clamp and remove the rubber boot. These items must be discarded.

5. Inspect for internal wear and/or damage.

6. Clean the grease by hand from inside the joint housing and around the ball trunnion assembly to inspect it.

7. Mark the tripod and housing for proper reassembly, if it is to be reinstalled.

8. To replace the boot, CV-joint or both, remove the snapring from the groove and tap the trunnion lightly with a brass drift pin. Leave the tripod bearings on the trunnion. Care must be taken to support the bearings as they may fall off.

9. If equipped with a dynamic damper, remove the band and slide the damper from the shaft.

10. Cut both bands from the outer boot and slide the boot from the shaft.

To install:

11. Installation is the reverse order of the removal procedures.

12. When installing the tripod on the shaft place the chamfer face towards the retainer groove.

NOTE: The grease provided with the repair kit must be used. It cannot be substituted with any other type grease.

Driveshaft and U-Joints

Removal and Installation

COLT WAGON AND 4WD COLT VISTA

1. Raise and support the vehicle safely.
2. Drain the transfer case.
3. Matchmark the differential companion flange and the driveshaft flange yoke.
4. Unbolt the driveshaft from the differential flange.
5. Remove the 2 center bearing attaching nuts.

NOTE: Make sure the flat washer and the adjusting spacer are not interchanged. Keep them separate for assembly.

6. Pull the driveshaft from the transfer case. Be careful to avoid damaging the transfer case oil seal.

To install:

7. Installation is the reverse order of removal procedure. Torque the center bearing nuts to 25–30 ft. lbs.; the driveshaft-to-differential flange nuts to 20–25 ft. lbs.

CONQUEST

1. Raise the vehicle and support it safely.
2. Matchmark the rear flange yoke and the differential pinion flange.
3. Remove the driveshaft-to-pinion shaft flange bolts. Remove the driveshaft by pulling it from the rear of the transmission extension housing.

NOTE: Place a container under the transmission extension housing to collect any oil leakage when the driveshaft is removed.

4. To install the shaft, align the front sleeve yoke with the splines of the transmission output shaft and push the driveshaft into the extension housing.

NOTE: Be careful not to damage the rear transmission seal lip upon installation.

5. Align the matchmarks on the rear yokes, install the bolts and tighten securely.
6. Inspect the oil level of the transmission. Lower the vehicle.

Rear Axle Shaft, Bearing and Seal

Removal and Installation

CONQUEST

1. Raise and support the vehicle safely.
2. Disconnect the parking brake cable from the rear calipers.
3. Remove the caliper, caliper support and rotor. Do not disconnect the brake line from the caliper, suspend it out of the way.
4. Remove the intermediate shaft and companion flange as described below.
5. Remove the halfshaft housing from the lower control arm.
6. Remove the strut assembly from the halfshaft housing.
7. Loosen the companion flange mounting nut and tap the halfshaft out of the housing with a plastic mallet. Be careful to avoid scratching the oil seal.
8. Remove the spacer and dust covers from inside the housing.

NOTE: Don't remove the bearings unless they are to be replaced, since they will be damaged during removal.

9. Remove the outer bearing with a puller.
10. Using a brass drift, drive the inner bearing and seal from the housing.

To install:

11. Press the new outer bearing onto the shaft with the seal side facing the flange side of the shaft.
12. Pack the housing with lithium based wheel bearing grease.
13. Press the inner bearing onto the shaft with the seal side facing the companion flange side of the shaft.
14. Grease the seal bore in the housing and drive the new seal into position.
15. Install the dust covers.
16. Insert the halfshaft and spacer into the housing and attach the companion flange.

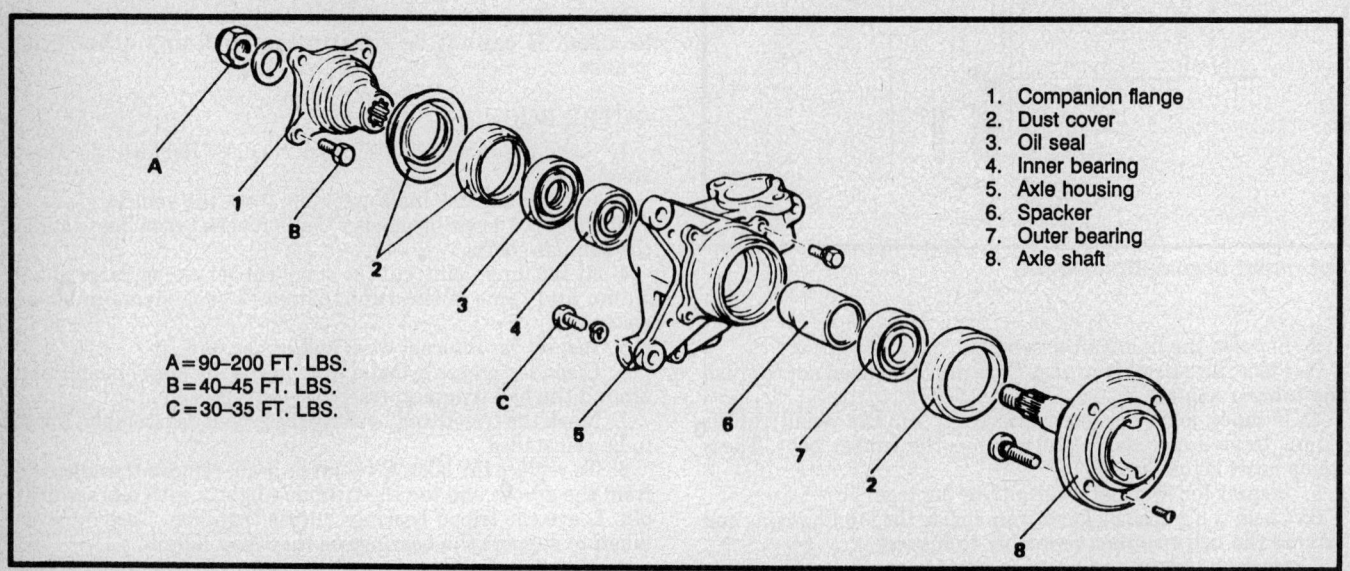

1. Companion flange
2. Dust cover
3. Oil seal
4. Inner bearing
5. Axle housing
6. Spacker
7. Outer bearing
8. Axle shaft

A=90–200 FT. LBS.
B=40–45 FT. LBS.
C=30–35 FT. LBS.

Conquest rear axle axle shaft and housing assembly

17. Place the housing in a vise and install and tighten the companion flange nut to 200–220 ft. lbs.

18. Install all other parts in reverse order of removal. Check halfshaft endplay with a dial indicator. Endplay should be 0.031 in. If endplay exceeds the limit, either the bearing needs replacing or the shaft bearings are not assembled properly.

4WD COLT VISTA

1. Raise and support the vehicle safely.
2. Remove the rear wheels.
3. Remove the brake drums.
4. Remove the 3 bolts securing the halfshaft flange to the intermediate shaft flange.
5. Using a special tool, remove the halfshaft flange nut.
6. Using a slide hammer connected to a 2–jawed adapter secured under 2 lug nuts, pull the halfshaft from the housing.
7. Remove the lower arm.
8. Using a special tool, remove the dust cover and the outer wheel bearing and seal from the halfshaft at the same time. Discard the seal.
9. Using special driver tool and adapter, drive the inner bearing and seal from the housing. The new bearing should be thoroughly packed with chassis lube and driven into place with the same tools.

To install:

10. Install a new inner bearing seal with a seal driver.
11. Using a special driver tool, tape a new dust cover into place. Tap evenly around the tool to seat the cover.
12. Coat the lip of a new seal with chassis lube and pack the new outer bearing thoroughly with chassis lube.
13. Using a press, install the bearing and seal.
14. Mount the inner arm in a vise and, using a press, install the halfshaft.
15. Install the halfshaft and inner arm assembly.
16. Torque the halfshaft nut to 160 ft. lbs.
17. Connect the halfshaft and intermediate shaft flanges and torque the bolts to 43 ft. lbs.

Front Wheel Hub, Knuckle and Bearings

Removal and Installation
COLT AND 2WD COLT VISTA

NOTE: The following procedure requires the use of several special tools.

1. Remove the halfshaft nut.
2. Raise and support the the vehicle safely. Allow the front suspension to hang freely.
3. Remove the wheels.
4. Remove the caliper and suspend it out of the way, without disconnecting the brake hose.
5. Disconnect the lower ball joint from the knuckle.
6. Disconnect the tie rod end from the knuckle.
7. Using a 2–jawed puller, press the halfshaft from the hub.
8. Unbolt the strut from the knuckle. Remove the hub and knuckle assembly from the vehicle.
9. Install first the arm, then the body of special tool MB991056 (Colt) or MB991001 (Colt Vista) on the knuckle and tighten the nut.
10. Using special tool MB990998 or MB990781, separate the hub from the knuckle.

NOTE: Prying or hammering will damage the bearing. Use these special tools or their equivalents, to separate the hub and knuckle.

11. Place the knuckle in a vise and separate the rotor from the hub.
12. Using special tools C–293–PA, SP–3183 and MB990781, remove the outer bearing inner race.
13. Drive the oil seal and inner bearing inner race from the knuckle with a brass drift.
14. Drive out both outer races in a similar fashion.

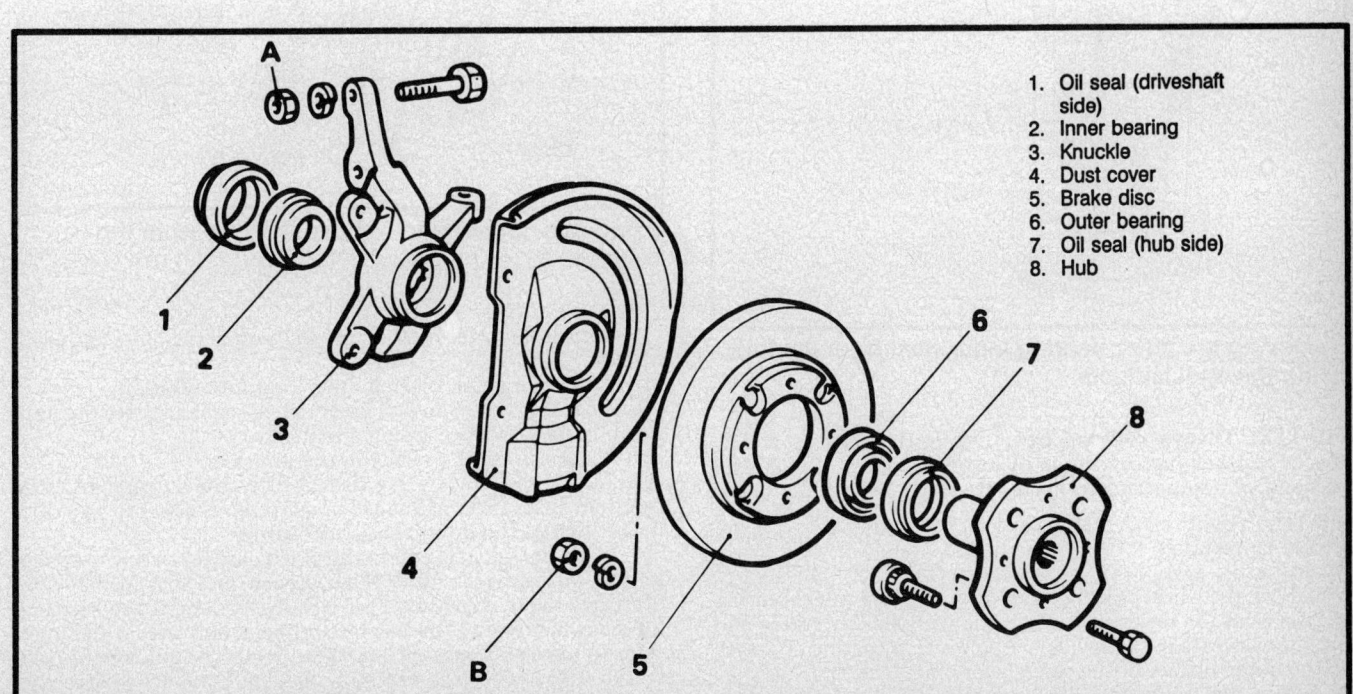

1. Oil seal (driveshaft side)
2. Inner bearing
3. Knuckle
4. Dust cover
5. Brake disc
6. Outer bearing
7. Oil seal (hub side)
8. Hub

Exploded view of the hub and knuckle—Colt

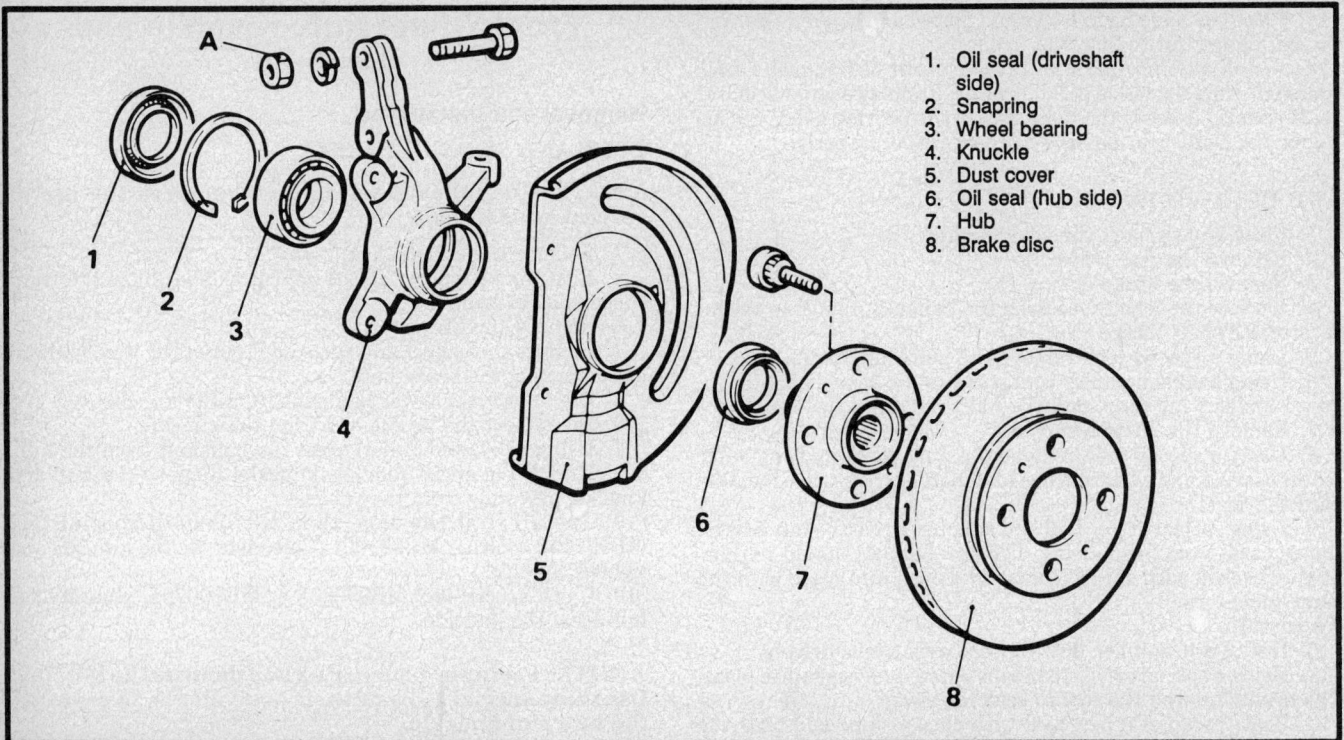

1. Oil seal (driveshaft side)
2. Snapring
3. Wheel bearing
4. Knuckle
5. Dust cover
6. Oil seal (hub side)
7. Hub
8. Brake disc

4WD Vista front hub, knuckle and bearing

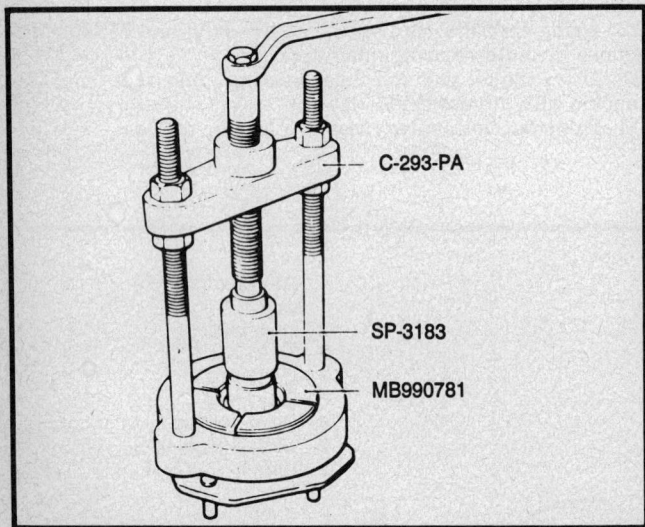

Removing the outer bearing inner race from the hub, using the special tools

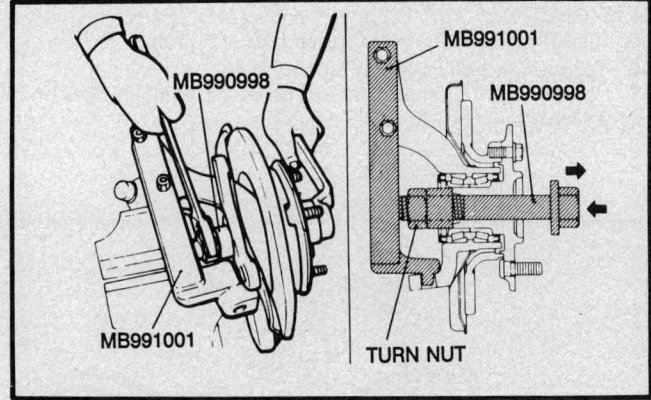

Using special tools to remove the hub from the knuckle

NOTE: **Always replace bearings and races as a set. Never replace just an inner or outer bearing. If either is in need of replacement, both sets must be replaced.**

15. Thoroughly clean and inspect all parts. Any suspect part should be replaced.

To install:

16. Pack the wheel bearings with lithium based wheel bearing grease. Coat the inside of the knuckle with similar grease and pack the cavities in the knuckle. Apply a thin coating of grease to the outer surface of the races before installation.

17. Using special tools C–3893 and MB990776, install the outer races.

18. Install the rotor on the hub and torque the bolts to 36–43 ft. lbs.

19. Drive the outer bearing inner race into position.

20. Coat the outer rim and lip of the oil seal and drive the hub side oil seal into place, using a seal driver.

21. Place the inner bearing in the knuckle.

22. Mount the knuckle in a vise. Position the hub and knuckle together. Install tool MB99098 and tighten the tool to 147–192 ft. lbs. Rotate the hub to seat the bearing.

23. With the knuckle still in the vise measure the hub starting torque with an inch lb. torque wrench and tool MB990998. Starting torque should be 11.5 inch lbs. or less. If the starting torque is 0, measure the hub bearing axial play with a dial indicator. If axial play exceeds 0.0078 in., while the nut is tightened to 145–192 ft. lbs., the assembly has not been done correctly. Disassemble the knuckle and hub, and start again.

24. Remove the special tool.

25. Place the outer bearing in the hub and drive the seal into place.

26. The remainder of installation is the reverse of removal.

4WD COLT VISTA

NOTE: The following procedure requires the use of several special tools.

1. Remove the hub cap and halfshaft nut.
2. Raise the vehicle and support it safely.
3. Remove the front wheels.
4. Drain the transaxle fluid.
5. Disconnect the lower ball joint from the knuckle.
6. Remove the strut and stabilizer bar from the lower arm.
7. Remove the center bearing snapring from the bearing bracket.
8. Lightly tap the double off-set joint outer race with a wood mallet and disconnect the halfshaft from the Cardan joint.
9. Disconnect the halfshaft from the bearing jacket.
10. Using a 2-jawed puller secured to the hub lugs, press the halfshaft from the hub.
11. Unbolt the strut from the hub. Remove the hub and knuckle assembly from the vehicle.
12. Install first the arm, then the body of special tool MB991001 on the knuckle and tighten the nut.
13. Using special tool MB9900998, separate the hub from the knuckle and tighten the nut.

NOTE: Prying or hammering will damage the bearing. Use these special tools or equivalent, to separate the hub and knuckle.

14. Matchmark the hub and rotor. The rotor should slide from the hub. If not, insert M8 × 1.25 bolts in the holes between the lugs and tighten them alternately to press the hub from the rotor. Never hammer the rotor to remove it.
15. Using a 2-jawed puller, remove the outer bearing inner race.
16. Remove and discard the outer oil seal.

17. Remove and discard the inner oil seal.
18. Remove the bearing snapring from the knuckle.
19. Using special tools C-4628 and MB991056 or MB991001, remove the bearing from the knuckle. Using a driver, drive the bearing from the knuckle.

NOTE: Always replace bearings and races as a set. Never replace just an inner or outer bearing. If either is in need of replacement, both sets must be replaced.

20. Thoroughly clean and inspect all parts. Any suspect part should be replaced.
21. Pack the wheel bearings with lithium based wheel bearing grease. Coat the inside of the knuckle with similar grease and pack the cavities in the knuckle. Apply a thin coating of grease to the outer surface of the races before installation.

To install:

22. Using special tools C-4171 and MB990985, press the bearing into place in the knuckle. Install the snapring.
23. Coat the lips of a new hub side seal with lithium grease. Using a seal driver, install the seal. Make sure it is flush.
24. Install the rotor on the hub.
25. Using special tool MB990998, join the hub and knuckle. Torque the special tool nut to 188 ft. lbs.
26. Rotate the hub several times to seat the bearing.
27. Mount the knuckle in a vise. Using MB990998 and an inch lb. torque wrench, measure the turning torque. Turning torque should be 15.6 inch lbs. or less. Next, measure the axial play using a dial indicator. Axial play should be 0.008 in. If either the axial play or the turning torque are not within the specified values, the hub and knuckle have not been properly assembled. Repeat the procedure. If everything checks out okay, go on to the next step.
28. Remove all the special tools.
29. Using a seal driver, drive a new seal coated with lithium grease, into place on the halfshaft side, until it contacts the snapring.
30. The remainder of installation is the reverse order of removal procedures.

STEERING

Steering Wheel

Removal and Installation

1. Pry off the steering wheel center foam pad.
2. Remove the steering wheel retaining nut.
3. Using a steering wheel puller, remove the wheel.
4. Be sure the front wheels are in a straight ahead position.

To install:

5. Installation is the reverse order of removal procedure. Tighten the nut to 30 ft. lbs.

Steering Column

Removal and Installation

1. Disconnect the negative battery cable. Remove the steering wheel.
2. Remove the lower column trim cover and the upper column trim cover.
3. Remove the light switch, wiper and washer washer switch. Disconnect the harness connectors.
4. Remove shaft-to-gear retaining bolts and disconnect the shaft at the steering gear.
5. Remove both upper and lower steering column mounting bolts and remove the steering column from the vehicle.

To install:

6. Lower the steering column through the firewall and connect the steering column to the steering gear. Install the retaining bolt. Do not tighten at this time.
7. Install both upper and lower steering column mounting bolts. Torque the mounting bolts to 7-10 ft. lbs. (9-14 Nm).
8. Install the light switch and wiper and washer washer switch. Connect the harness connectors.
9. Install the upper column trim cover and the lower column trim cover.
10. Install the steering wheel. Connect the negative battery cable.

Manual Steering Rack

Removal and Installation

COLT

1. Loosen the lug nuts.
2. Raise and support the vehicle safely.
3. Remove the wheels.
4. Remove the steering shaft-to-pinion coupling bolt.
5. Disconnect the tie rod ends with a separator.
6. Remove the clamps or clamp and bolts securing the rack to the crossmember and remove the unit from the vehicle.

To install:

7. Install the rubber mount for the gear box with the slit on the downside.

8. The remainder of installation is the reverse order of the removal procedures. Torque as follows:
   Rack-to-crossmember — 45–60 ft. lbs.
   Coupling bolt — 22–25 ft. lbs.
   Tie-rod nuts — 11–25 ft. lbs.

9. Fill the system and road test the vehicle.

2WD COLT VISTA

1. Loosen the lug nuts.
2. Raise and support the vehicle safely.
3. Remove the wheels.
4. Remove the steering shaft-to-pinion coupling bolt.
5. Disconnect the tie rod ends with a separator.
6. Remove the crossmember support bracket from the crossmember on the right side of the vehicle.
7. Remove the rear roll stopper-to-center member bolt and move the rear roll stopper forward.
8. Unbolt the rack from the crossmember.

NOTE: The rack is most easily removed using a ratchet and long extension, working from the engine compartment side.

9. Pull the rack out the right side of the vehicle. Pull it slowly to avoid damage.

To install:

10. Installation is the reverse order of the removal procedures. Torque the rack clamp bolts to 43–58 ft. lbs., the tie rod nuts to 17–25 ft. lbs. and the coupling bolt to 22–25 ft. lbs. Fill the system and road test the vehicle.

4WD COLT VISTA

1. Remove the steering column.
2. Raise and support the vehicle safely.
3. Remove the front wheels.
4. Using a separator, disconnect the tie rod from the knuckle.
5. Disconnect the steering shaft joint at the rack.
6. Remove the air cleaner.
7. Remove the rack attaching bolts from the rear of the No. 2 crossmember. The bolts are most easily accessed using a long extension and working from the top of the engine compartment.
8. Remove the rear roll stopper-to-center member bolt and move the rear roll stopper forward.
9. From under the vehicle, remove the gear box mounting bolts from the front of the No. 2 crossmember and pull out and to the left on the rack.
10. Lower the rack until the left edge of the left feed tube contacts the lower part of the left fender shield. At this point, remove the left and right feed tubes.
11. Remove the rack from the vehicle.

To install:

12. Position the rack to the No. 2 crossmember and connect the left and right feed tubes.
13. Install the rack, mounting brackets, bushing and retaining bolts. Torque the bolts to 43–58 ft. lbs. (60–80 Nm).
14. Connect the tie rods to the steering knuckle and install the retaining nuts. Torque the tie rod end retaining nuts to 17–25 ft. lbs. (24–34 Nm).
15. Install the wheel assemblies.
16. Install the steering column and connect the steering shaft joint to the rack shaft. Torque the steering shaft-to-rack bolts to 22–25 ft. lbs. (30–35 Nm).
17. Lower the vehicle. Install the air cleaner.
18. Replenish the powering fluid. Start the engine and check for leaks.

Power Steering Gear

Adjustment

CONQUEST

NOTE: The steering gear must be disconnected from the steering shaft.

1. Measure the mainshaft preload with an inch lbs. torque wrench. The preload should be 3.5–6.9 inch lbs., with the cross-shaft adjusting bolt backed off.
2. Adjust the valve housing top cover to obtain the proper preload. When correct, lock the top cover with the locking nut.
3. Tighten the cross-shaft adjusting bolt until zero lash is present. Check the total starting torque to rotate the main shaft. The torque should be 5.2–8.7 inch lbs.
4. Adjust the cross-shaft until the required starting torque is obtained and lock the adjusting bolt nut securely.

Removal and Installation

1. Matchmark and disconnect the steering shaft from the gearbox main shaft.
2. Disconnect the tie rod end and pitman arm from the relay rod.
3. Remove the air cleaner and disconnect the pressure and return lines from the steering gear assembly.
4. Raise the vehicle and support it safely. Remove any interfering splash pans from under the vehicle.
5. If necessary, remove the kickdown linkage splash pan shield and bolts. Move the fuel line aside to avoid damage during removal.
6. Remove the frame bolts from the gearbox and lower the unit from the vehicle.
7. Installation is the reverse of removal. Make sure all matchmarks align. After tightening the pitman arm nut make sure the distance between the centerline of the lowest steering gear mounting bolt and the top of the pitman arm is 19.5mm. Observe the following torques:
   Pitman arm nut — 94–109 ft. lbs.
   Steering gear mounting bolts — 40–47 ft. lbs.
   Tie rod socket and relay rod — 25–33 ft. lbs.
   High pressure hose — 22–29 ft. lbs.
   Return hose — 29–36 ft. lbs.

Power Steering Rack

Removal and Installation

COLT

1. Loosen the lug nuts.
2. Raise the vehicle and support it safely.
3. Remove the wheels.
4. Remove the steering shaft-to-pinion coupling bolt.
5. Disconnect the tie rod ends with a separator.
6. Drain the fluid.
7. Disconnect the hoses from the rack.
8. Remove the band from the steering joint cover.
9. Unbolt and remove the stabilizer bar.
10. Remove the rack unit mounting clamp bolts and take the unit out the left side of the vehicle.

To install:

11. Installation is the reverse order of the removal procedures. Make sure the rubber isolators have their nubs aligned with the holes in the clamps. Apply rubber cement to the slits in the gear mounting grommet. Tighten the clamp bolt to 43–58 ft. lbs., the tie rod nuts to 11–25 ft. lbs. and the coupling bolt to 22–25 ft. lbs.
12. Fill the system and road test the car.

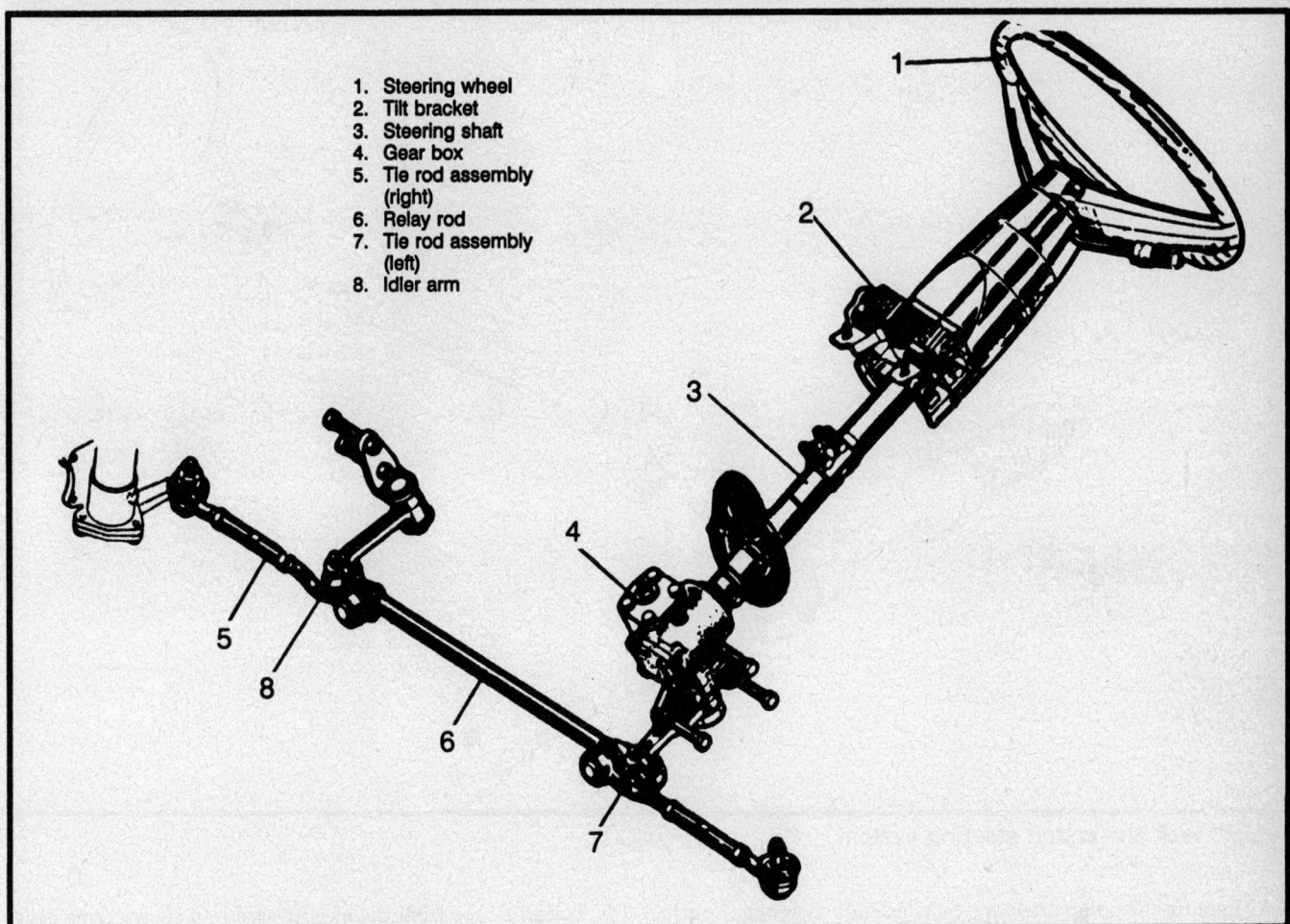

1. Steering wheel
2. Tilt bracket
3. Steering shaft
4. Gear box
5. Tie rod assembly (right)
6. Relay rod
7. Tie rod assembly (left)
8. Idler arm

View of the steering system—Conquest

2WD COLT VISTA

1. Loosen the lug nuts.
2. Raise and support the vehicle safely.
3. Remove the wheels.
4. Remove the steering shaft-to-pinion coupling bolt.
5. Disconnect the tie rod ends with a separator.
6. Disconnect the hoses at the rack.
7. Remove the crossmember support bracket from the crossmember on the right side of the vehicle.
8. Unbolt the rack from the crossmember.

NOTE: The rack is most easily removed using a ratchet and long extension, working from the engine compartment side.

9. Pull the rack out the right side of the vehicle. Pull it slowly to avoid damage.

To install:

10. Installation is the reverse order of the removal procedures. Torque the rack clamp bolts to 43–58 ft. lbs., the tie rod nuts to 17–25 ft. lbs. and the coupling bolt to 22–25 ft. lbs. Fill the system and road test the vehicle.

4WD COLT VISTA

1. Remove the steering column.
2. Raise and support the vehicle safely.
3. Remove the front wheels.
4. Using a separator, disconnect the tie rod from the knuckle.
5. Disconnect the steering shaft joint at the rack.
6. Disconnect the fluid lines at the gear box.
7. Remove the air cleaner.
8. Remove the rack attaching bolts from the rear of the No. 2 crossmember. The bolts are most easily accessed using a long extension and working from the top of the engine compartment.
9. From under the vehicle, remove the rack mounting bolts from the front of the No. 2 crossmember and pull out and to the left on the rack.
10. Lower the gear box until the left edge of the left feed tube contacts the lower part of the left fender shield. At this point, remove the left and right feed tubes.
11. Remove the rack from the vehicle.

To install:

12. Installation is the reverse order of the removal procedures. When installing the clamps, make sure the rubber projections are aligned with the holes in the clamps. Install the tie rods so 191–193mm shows between the tie rod end locknut and the beginning of the boot. Torque the gear box mounting bolts to 55–60 ft. lbs.; the tie rod-to-knuckle nut to 20–25 ft. lbs.

Power Steering Pump

Removal and Installation

1. Remove the drive belt. If the pulley is to be removed, do so now.
2. Disconnect the pressure and return lines. Catch any leaking fluid.

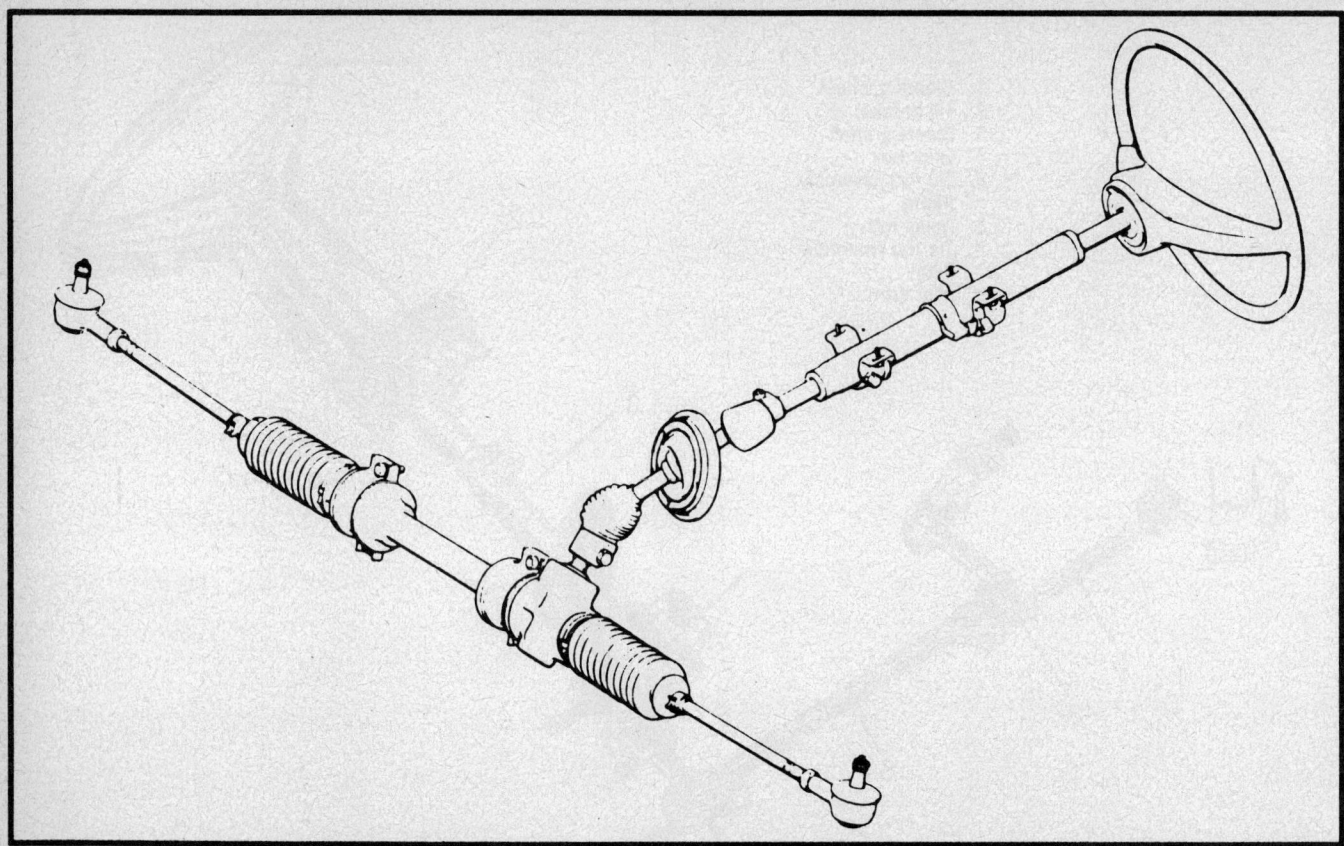

Typical rack and piston steering system

3. Remove the pump attaching bolts and lift the pump from the brackets.

To install:

4. Make sure the bracket bolts are tight and install the pump to the brackets.

5. If the pulley has been removed, install it and tighten the nut securely. Bend the lock tab over the nut.

6. Install the drive belt and adjust to a tension of 22 lbs. at a deflection of 0.28–0.39 in. at the top center of the belt. Tighten the pump bolts securely to hold the tension.

7. Connect the pressure and return lines and fill the reservoir with Dexron® II fluid.

8. Bleed the system.

Belt Adjustment

1. Press the V-belt by applying pressure of 22 lbs. (100 N) at the center of the belt.

2. Measure the deflection to confirm that it is within the standard range.

   a. Colt, standard value—0.2–0.4 in. (6–9mm).
   b. Colt Vista, standard value—0.3–0.4 in. (7–10mm).
   c. Conquest, standard value—0.35–0.47 in. (9–12mm).

3. To adjust the tension of the belt, loosen the oil pump mounting bolts, move the oil pump and then retighten the bolts.

System Bleeding

1. The reservoir should be full of Dexron® II fluid.

2. Raise the vehicle and support it safely.

3. Turn the steering wheel fully to the right and left until no air bubbles appear in the fluid. Maintain the reservoir level.

4. Lower the vehicle and with the engine idling, turn the wheels fully to the right and left. Stop the engine.

5. Install a tube from the bleeder screw on the steering gear box or rack, to the reservoir.

6. Start the engine, turn the steering wheel fully to the left and loosen the bleeder screw.

7. Repeat the procedure until no air bubbles pass through the tube.

8. Tighten the bleeder screw and remove the tube. Refill the reservoir as needed and check that no further bubbles are present in the fluid. An abrupt rise in the fluid level after stopping the engine is a sign of incomplete bleeding. This will cause noise from the pump or control valve.

Tie Rod Ends

Removal and Installation

NOTE: The following applies to rear wheel drive vehicles. On front wheel drive vehicles, the tie rods are serviced with the steering rack.

1. Raise the vehicle and support it safely.

2. Using a puller, disconnect the tie rod ends from the steering knuckle.

3. Loosen the jam nut and remove the tie rod ends from the tie rod. The outer end is left hand threaded and the inner is right hand threaded.

4. Grease the tie rod threads and install the ends. Turn each end in an equal amount.

5. Install the tie rod assembly on the steering knuckle and relay rod. Tighten the castellated nuts to 29–36 ft. lbs. Use new cotter pins.

6. Adjust the toe-in.

Relay Rod

Removal and Installation

1. Raise the vehicle and support it safely.
2. Disconnect the tie rod ends from the steering knuckles with a puller.
3. Again using the puller, disconnect the relay rod from the idler arm and the pitman arm.
4. Remove the relay arm.
5. Install the rod in the reverse order of removal. Tighten the tie rod end nuts to 29–36 ft. lbs. Tighten the relay rod-to-pitman arm nut and relay rod-to-idler arm nut to 29–43 ft. lbs. Always use new cotter pins.

Idler Arm

Removal and Installation

1. Raise the vehicle and support it safely.
2. Disconnect the idler arm from the relay rod using a puller.
3. Remove the retaining bolts and remove the idler arm.
4. Mount the idler arm on the frame and tighten the bolts to 25–29 ft. lbs.
5. Attach the relay rod to the idler arm and tighten the stud nut to 29–43 ft. lbs. Use a new cotter pin.

BRAKES

Master Cylinder

Removal and Installation
REAR WHEEL DRIVE

NOTE: Be careful not to spill brake fluid on the painted surfaces of the vehicle. The brake fluid will cause damage to the paint.

1. Disconnect all hydraulic lines from the master cylinder. If equipped with a remote reservoir, remove and plug the hoses from the master cylinder caps. If the master cylinder has a fluid level warning device, disconnect the wiring harness.
2. Remove the master cylinder mounting nuts from the power brake booster. Remove the master cylinder.

NOTE: Before installing the master cylinder, make sure there is clearance between the pushrod and master cylinder piston. It should be 0.028–0.043 in.

3. Mount the master cylinder to the power brake booster.
4. Connect all brake lines and wiring harnesses and fill the master cylinder reservoirs with clean fluid.
5. Bleed the brake system.

FRONT WHEEL DRIVE

1. Disconnect the fluid level sensor.
2. Disconnect the brake tubes from the master cylinder and cap them immediately.
3. If equipped with a turbocharger, remove the reservoir from the reservoir holder.
4. Unbolt and remove the master cylinder from the booster.
To install:
5. Installation is the reverse order of the removal procedures. Measure the master cylinder pushrod clearance; it should be 0.016–0.31 in. Torque the mounting bolts to 6–9 ft. lbs. (72–108 inch lbs.).

Proportioning Valve

Removal and Installation

1. Disconnect the brake lines at the valve.

NOTE: Use a flare wrench, if possible, to avoid damage to the flare nuts and brake lines.

2. Remove the mounting bolts and the valve.
3. Install in the reverse order of the removal procedures. Refill the master cylinder and bleed the brake system.

Power Brake Booster

Removal and Installation

1. Remove the master cylinder.
2. Disconnect the vacuum line from the booster.
3. Remove the pin connecting the power brake operating rod and the brake lever.
4. Unbolt and remove the booster.
5. Replace the packing on both sides of the booster-to-firewall spacer with new packing.
6. If the check valve was removed, make sure the direction of installation marking on the valve is followed.

To install:
7. Installation is the reverse order of the removal procedures. Torque the booster-to-firewall nuts to 6–9 ft. lbs. (54–108 inch lbs.). Torque the master cylinder-to-booster nuts to 6–9 ft. lbs.
8. Adjust the brake pedal and master cylinder pushrod as explained earlier.

Brake Caliper

Removal and Installation
COLT AND COLT VISTA

1. Raise and support the vehicle safely and remove the wheel assembly.

NOTE: On late vehicles equipped with the PFS15 type front disc brakes, the caliper and pads are retained to the adapter by 2 sleeve pin bolts. Remove the pin bolts and service the assembly as required. Sleeve bolt torque is 16–23 ft. lbs.

2. Disconnect the brake hose from the caliper and plug.
3. Remove the upper and lower pin bolts and remove the caliper and brake pads as an assembly.
4. Remove the inner shim, the anti-squeal shim and the pads from the caliper support assembly.
To install:
5. Installation is the reverse order of the removal procedures. When installing the spacers, apply a coating of an approved grease on the spacers.
6. Torque the caliper retaining bolts to 16–23 ft. lbs. (22–32 Nm). Torque the brake hose fitting to 9–12 ft. lbs. (13–17 Nm).

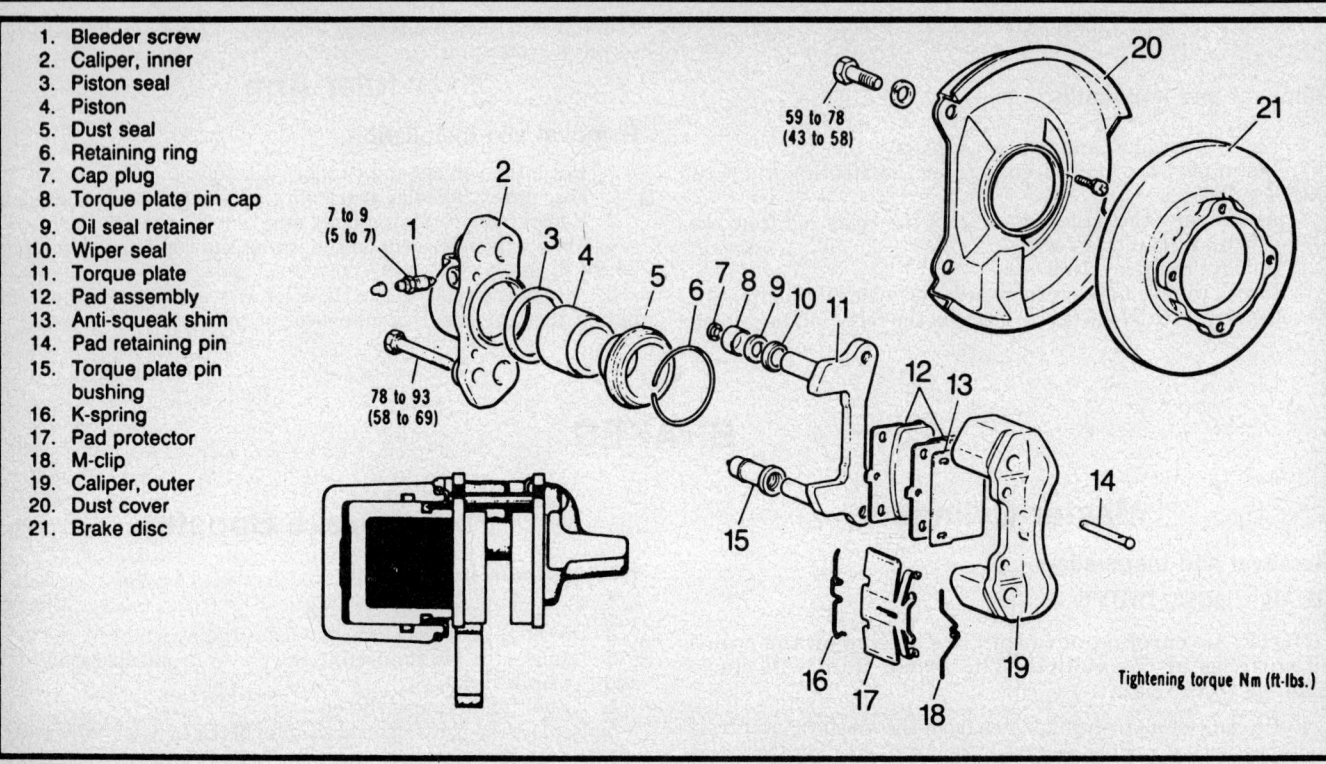

1. Bleeder screw
2. Caliper, inner
3. Piston seal
4. Piston
5. Dust seal
6. Retaining ring
7. Cap plug
8. Torque plate pin cap
9. Oil seal retainer
10. Wiper seal
11. Torque plate
12. Pad assembly
13. Anti-squeak shim
14. Pad retaining pin
15. Torque plate pin bushing
16. K-spring
17. Pad protector
18. M-clip
19. Caliper, outer
20. Dust cover
21. Brake disc

59 to 78 (43 to 58)

7 to 9 (5 to 7)

78 to 93 (58 to 69)

Tightening torque Nm (ft-lbs.)

Typical pin type caliper

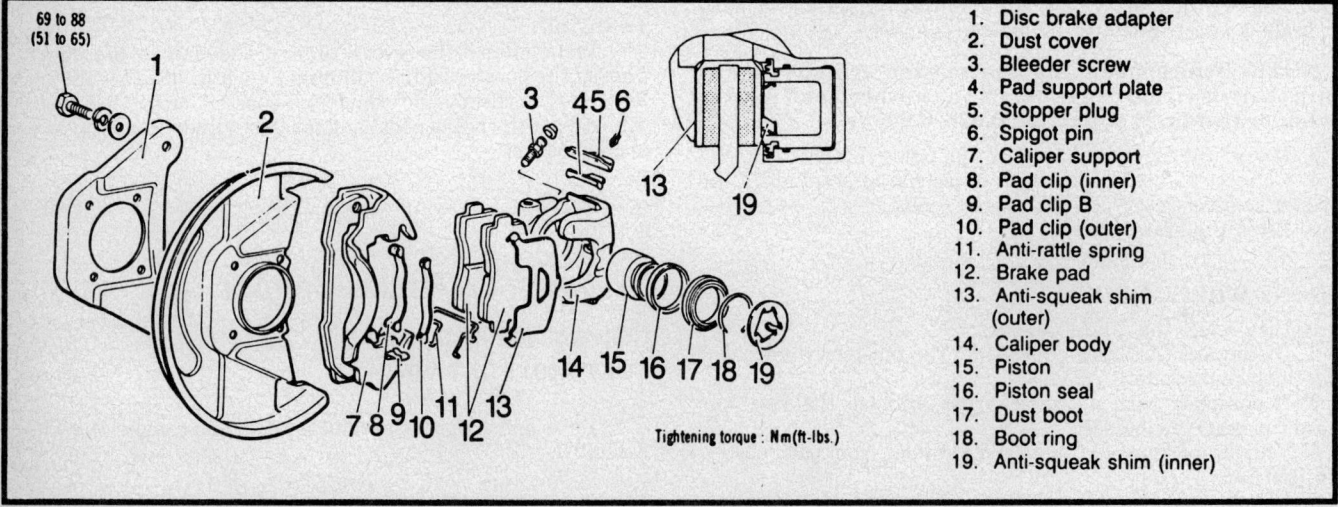

69 to 88 (51 to 65)

1. Disc brake adapter
2. Dust cover
3. Bleeder screw
4. Pad support plate
5. Stopper plug
6. Spigot pin
7. Caliper support
8. Pad clip (inner)
9. Pad clip B
10. Pad clip (outer)
11. Anti-rattle spring
12. Brake pad
13. Anti-squeak shim (outer)
14. Caliper body
15. Piston
16. Piston seal
17. Dust boot
18. Boot ring
19. Anti-squeak shim (inner)

Tightening torque : Nm(ft-lbs.)

Exploded view of a typical sliding type caliper

Disc Brake Pads

Removal and Installation
FRONT

Colt

1. Raise the vehicle and support it safely. Remove the wheels.

NOTE: On late vehicles equipped with the PFS15 type front disc brakes; the caliper and pads are retained to the adapter by 2 sleeve pin bolts. Remove the pin bolts and service the assembly as required. Sleeve pin torque is 16–23 ft. lbs.

2. Remove the lower sleeve bolt from the caliper and rotate the caliper upward.

NOTE: There is a grease coating on the bolt. Make sure it is not removed or contaminated.

3. Support the caliper by suspending it with wire or string from a nearby suspension member.
4. Remove the inner, then outer shims from the caliper.
5. Lift out the brake pads.
6. Remove the pad liners.
To install:
7. Clean all parts in solvent made for brake parts.
8. Inspect the dust boot on the caliper piston. If it is torn or brittle, replace it. and consider rebuilding the caliper.

9. Inspect the shims and liners and replace them if damaged.

10. Remove the cap from the master cylinder reservoir and siphon off about ¼ in. of fluid.

11. Using a C-clamp, force the piston back into the caliper as far as it will go. Remove the clamp.

12. Install the liners, pads and inner, then outer shims.

NOTE: Never replace just one set of pads, pads should be replaced on both front wheels at the same time.

13. Lower the caliper and install the lower sleeve bolt. Torque the bolt to 16–23 ft. lbs.

14. Start the engine and depress the brake pedal several times. Hold it depressed for about 5 seconds. Turn the engine off.

15. Rotate the brake rotor a few times. Using a spring scale hooked to 1 of the lugs, measure the brake drag. Remove the pads and perform the spring scale test again. The difference between the drag test with and without the pads should not exceed 15 lbs. If the difference does exceed 15 lbs., the caliper will have to be rebuilt or replaced. When servicing is complete, pump the brakes several times. Do not move the vehicle until a firm brake pedal is present.

Colt and Colt Vista

1. Raise the vehicle and support it safely. Remove the front wheels.

NOTE: On late vehicles equipped with the PFS15 type front disc brakes, the caliper and pads are retained to the adapter by 2 sleeve pin bolts. Remove the pin bolts and service the assembly as required. Sleeve bolt torque is 16–23 ft. lbs.

2. Remove the lower pin bolt and rotate the caliper upwards. Support the caliper with wire or string from a nearby suspension member.

3. Remove the inner shim, the anti-squeal shim and the pads from the caliper support assembly.

4. Remove the clips from the pads.

To install:

5. Clean all parts in solvent made for brake parts.

6. Inspect the dust boot on the caliper piston. If it is torn or brittle, replace it and consider rebuilding the caliper.

7. Inspect the shims and liners and replace them if damaged.

8. Remove the cap from the master cylinder reservoir and siphon off about ¼ in. of fluid.

9. Using a special tool, force the piston back into the caliper as far as it will go. Remove the clamp.

10. Install the pads with clips attached and the proper shims, in position, on the support.

NOTE: Never replace just one set of pads. Pads should be replaced on both front wheels at the same time.

11. Lower the caliper and install the lower pin bolt. Torque the bolt to 16–23 ft. lbs.

12. Start the engine and depress the brake pedal. Hold it depressed for about 5 seconds. Turn the engine off.

13. Rotate the brake rotor a few times. Using a spring scale hooked to 1 of the lugs, measure the brake drag. Remove the pads and perform the spring scale test again. The difference between the drag test with and without the pads should not exceed 15 lbs. If the difference does exceed 15 lbs., the caliper will have to be rebuilt or replaced.

14. When servicing is complete, pump the brakes several times, do not operate the vehicle until a firm brake pedal is present. Bleed the brakes if necessary.

Conquest

1. Raise the vehicle and support it safely.
2. Remove the front wheels.
3. Remove the caliper lower slide pin.

NOTE: There is a grease coating on the bolt. Make sure it is not removed or contaminated.

4. Rotate the caliper upward and suspend it with string from a nearby suspension member.

5. Remove the brake pads and shims.

6. Remove the clips from the pads.

To install:

7. Clean all parts in solvent made for brake parts.

	Nm	ft. lbs.
A	7–9	5–7
B	22–32	16–23
C	80–100	58–72
D	50–60	36–43

1. Lid
2. Lock pin
3. Sleeve
4. Caliper body
5. Guide pin boot
6. Piston
7. Lock pin boot
8. Piston seal
9. Piston boot
10. Boot ring
11. Inner shim
12. Pad assembly
13. Pad clip B
14. Pad clip C
15. Anti-squeak shim
16. Guide pin
17. Sleeve
18. Support mounting
19. Brake disc
20. Hub

Exploded view of the typical caliper—Vista and Turbo Colt

8. Inspect the dust boot on the caliper piston. If it is torn or brittle, replace it and consider rebuilding the caliper.

9. Inspect the shims and liners and replace them if damaged.

10. Remove the cap from the master cylinder reservoir and siphon off about ¼ in. of fluid.

11. Using a special tool, force the piston back into the caliper as far as it will go. Remove the clamp.

12. Install the pads with clips attached and the proper shims, in position, on the support.

NOTE: Never replace just one set of pads, pads should be replaced on both front wheels at the same time.

13. Rotate the caliper back into position and install the lower slider pin. Torque the pin to 70 ft. lbs.

14. Start the engine and depress the brake pedal. Hold it depressed for about 5 seconds. Turn the engine off.

15. Rotate the brake rotor a few times. Using a spring scale hooked to 1 of the lugs, measure the brake drag. Remove the pads and perform the spring scale test again. The difference between the drag test with and without the pads should not exceed 15 lbs. If the difference does exceed 15 lbs., the caliper will have to be rebuilt or replaced.

16. When servicing is complete, pump the brakes several times, do not operate the vehicle until a firm brake pedal is present. Bleed the brakes if necessary.

REAR

Except Conquest

1. Raise the vehicle and support it safely. Remove the rear wheel and the caliper dust cover.

2. Disconnect the parking brake cable

3. Remove the spring pin and stopper plug.

4. Move the caliper back and forth to loosen, then remove the caliper from the support.

NOTE: The brake hose need not be disconnected; however, do not suspend the weight of the caliper from the hose.

5. Take time to examine the location of the various clips and springs. Remove the pads from the support. Do not mix up the inner and outer clips, they must be installed in the same location.

6. Seat the caliper piston by pushing in while turning clockwise. When fully seated, 1 of the grooves on the piston must be located vertically at 12 o'clock to accommodate a projection of the brake pad. Install new pads into the support and install the caliper.

Conquest

1. Raise the vehicle and support it safely.

2. Remove the wheels.

3. Disconnect the parking brake cable.

4. Remove the lower caliper lockpin and the upper guide pin.

NOTE: There is a grease coating on the bolt. Make sure it is not removed or contaminated.

5. Rotate the caliper upward, if upper guide pin removal is not required. Suspend the caliper with a string from a nearby suspension member.

6. Remove the brake pads and shims.

7. Remove the clips from the pads.

8. Clean all parts in solvent made for brake parts.

9. Inspect the dust boot on the caliper piston. If it is torn or brittle, replace.

10. Inspect the shims and liners and replace them if damaged.

11. Remove the cap from the master cylinder reservoir and siphon off about ¼ in. of fluid.

12. Align the grooves in the caliper and piston and force the piston back into the caliper as far as it will go. Remove the clamp.

To install:

13. Install the pads and shims after attaching the clips in reverse order of removal.

NOTE: Never replace just one set of pads, pads should be replaced on both front wheels at the same time.

14. Rotate the caliper back into position and install the lower slider pin. Torque the pin to 45 ft. lbs.

15. Start the engine and depress the brake pedal. Hold it depressed for about 5 seconds. Turn the engine off.

16. Rotate the brake rotor a few times. Using a spring scale hooked to 1 of the lugs, measure the brake drag. Remove the pads and perform the spring scale test again. The difference between the drag test with and without the pads should not exceed 15 lbs., If the difference does exceed 15 lbs., the caliper will have to be rebuilt or replaced.

Brake Rotor

Removal and Installation
FRONT
Except Conquest

1. Raise the vehicle and support it safely.

2. Remove the wheel assembly. Remove the cotter pin and axle nut.

3. Support the caliper by suspending it with wire from a nearby suspension member.

4. Using halfshaft separator tool, separate the halfshaft from the hub assembly.

5. Matchmark the steering knuckle-to-strut bolts and remove the retaining bolts.

6. Remove the lower ball joint retaining nut. Using a ball joint separator tool, separate the ball joint from the knuckle assembly.

7. Remove the knuckle assembly from the vehicle.

8. Secure the knuckle and rotor assembly in a vise. Remove the rotor-to-hub retaining bolts and separate the rotor from the hub.

To install:

9. Installation is the reverse order of the removal procedures. Torque the rotor-hub-bolts to 56–72 ft. lbs. (80–100 Nm). Torque the steering knuckle-to-strut bolts to 54–65 ft. lbs. (75–90 Nm). Torque lower ball joint retaining nut to 43–52 ft. lbs. (60–72 Nm).

Conquest

1. Raise the vehicle and support it safely.

2. Remove the wheel assembly and remove the caliper assembly.

3. Support the caliper by suspending it with wire from a nearby suspension member.

4. Remove the axle dust cap, cotter pin and outer wheel bearing.

5. Slide the rotor from the axle.

To install:

6. Installation is the reverse of the removal procedures.

7. Clean all parts and inspect, replace the bearings if showing signs of pitting or overheating. Always install new seals.

8. Adjust the bearings.

REAR
All Vehicles

1. Raise the vehicle and support it safely. Remove the wheel assembly.

2. Remove the caliper. Support the caliper by suspending it with wire from a nearby suspension member.

3. Remove the caliper support retaining bolts and remove the support.

4. Remove the rotor-to-hub retaining screws and slide the rotor from the hub. If equipped with retaining rings, remove the rings from the wheel lugs.

To install:

5. Slide the rotor on the hub and install the rotor-to-hub retaining screws. If equipped with retaining rings, install new rings on the wheel lugs.

6. Install the caliper support and retaining bolts. Torque the bolts to 29–36 ft. lbs. (40–50 Nm).

7. Install the caliper, brake pads and caliper retaining bolts. Torque the bolts to 16–23 ft. lbs. (22–32 Nm).

8. Install the wheel assembly and lower the vehicle.

9. When servicing is complete, pump the brakes several times, do not operate the vehicle until a firm brake pedal is present. Bleed the brakes if necessary.

Brake Shoes

Removal and Installation
COLT

1. Raise the vehicle and support it safely. Remove rear wheel and brake drum.

2. Remove the lower pressed metal spring clip, the shoe return spring (the large one piece spring between the 2 shoes) and the 2 shoe hold-down springs.

3. Remove the shoes and adjuster as an assembly. Disconnect the parking brake cable from the lever, remove the spring between the shoes and the lever from the rear (trailing) shoe. Disconnect the adjuster retaining spring and remove the adjuster, turn the star wheel in to the adjuster body after cleaning and lubricating the threads.

4. The wheel cylinder may be removed for service or replacement, if necessary.

To install:

5. Clean the backing plate. Install the wheel cylinder if it was removed. Lubricate all contact points on the backing plate, anchor plate, wheel cylinder to shoe contact and parking brake strut joints and contacts. Install the brake shoes after attaching the parking brake, lever and adjuster assemblies. Install the hold-down and return springs.

6. Pre-adjustment of the brake shoe can be made by turning the adjuster star wheel out until the drum will just slide on over the brake shoes. Before installing the drum make sure the parking brake is not adjusted too tightly, if it is, loosen or the adjustment of the rear brakes will not be correct.

7. If the wheel cylinders were serviced, bleed the brake system. The brake shoes are then adjusted by pumping the brake pedal and applying and releasing the parking brake, Adjust the parking brake stroke. Road test the vehicle.

COLT VISTA

1. Raise the vehicle and support it safely.
2. Remove the wheels.
3. Remove the brake drums.
4. Remove the shoe-to-strut spring.
5. Remove the shoe-to-shoe spring.
6. Remove the shoe hold-down spring.
7. Remove the shoe retainer clip.
8. Remove the leading shoe.
9. Remove the brake cable from the lever.
10. Remove the trailing shoe.
11. Remove the brake cable snapring and remove the cable.
12. Inspect all parts for wear or damage.

NOTE: Never replace shoes on one side only. Replace both sets of shoes at the same time.

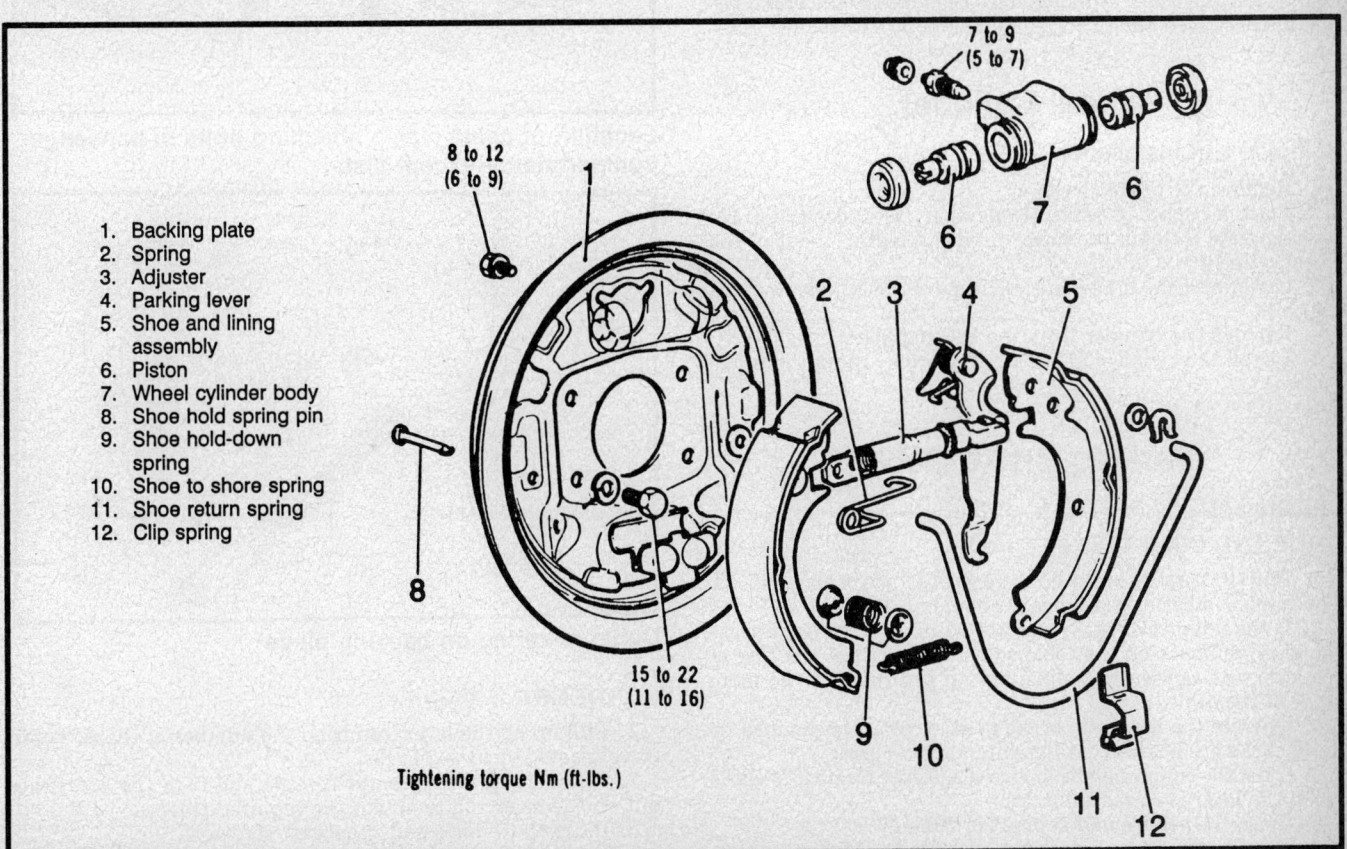

1. Backing plate
2. Spring
3. Adjuster
4. Parking lever
5. Shoe and lining assembly
6. Piston
7. Wheel cylinder body
8. Shoe hold spring pin
9. Shoe hold-down spring
10. Shoe to shore spring
11. Shoe return spring
12. Clip spring

Tightening torque Nm (ft-lbs.)

Typical rear drum brake system used on FWD— except Vista

To install:

13. Assemble the parking brake and adjuster assemblies on the brake shoes.

14. Install the brake shoes and hold-downs. Connect the return springs.

15. Apply a small amount of lithium based grease to the contact pads of the backing plate before installing the shoes.

16. When installing the shoe-to-shoe spring and shoe-to-strut spring, set the adjuster lever all the way back against the shoe.

17. When everything is assembled, pump the pedal several times and adjust the brakes.

CONQUEST

1. Raise the vehicle and support it safely.

2. Remove the wheel. Make sure the front wheels are blocked securely, release the parking brake and remove the brake drum.

NOTE: The brake drum is retained by 2 small bolts.

3. Disconnect the shoe-to-shoe spring and the strut-to-shoe spring. Disconnect the shoe return spring and remove the brake hold-down assemblies.

4. Disconnect the parking brake cable from the parking brake lever and remove the rear brake shoe.

5. Remove the front brake shoe. Transfer levers and adjusters to the new brake shoes using new U-shaped locks.

To install:

6. Prior to assembly, apply No. 2 brake grease to the contact area of the strut and parking brake lever and strut and adjusting lever. After cleaning the backing plate apply grease to the brake shoe contact points.

7. Connect the parking brake and install the brake shoes with the adjusters and hold-down assemblies. Install the return springs. The lining to drum clearance is automatically adjusted by applying the brakes several times after the drums have been installed. If the wheel cylinders have been rebuilt the brake system must be bled before correct adjustment is possible.

Wheel Cylinder

Removal and Installation

1. Remove the brake shoes.

2. Place a bucket or some old newspapers under the brake backing plate to catch the brake fluid that will run out of the wheel cylinder.

3. Disconnect the brake line and remove the cylinder mounting bolts.

4. Remove the cylinder from the backing plate.

5. Install the cylinder in the reverse order. Bleed the brake system.

Parking Brake Cable

Adjustment

COLT AND COLT VISTA

1. Pull the parking brake lever up with a force of about 45 lbs. The total number of clicks heard should be 5–7.

2. If the number of clicks was not within that range, release the lever and back off the cable adjuster locknut at the base of the lever and tighten the adjusting nut until there is no more slack in the cable.

3. Operate the lever and brake pedal several times, until no more clicks are heard from the automatic adjuster.

4. Turn the adjusting nut to give the proper number of clicks when the lever is raised full travel.

5. Raise the vehicle and support it safely.

6. Release the brake lever and make sure the rear wheels turn freely. If not, back off on the adjusting nut until they do.

Colt parking brake cable adjustment

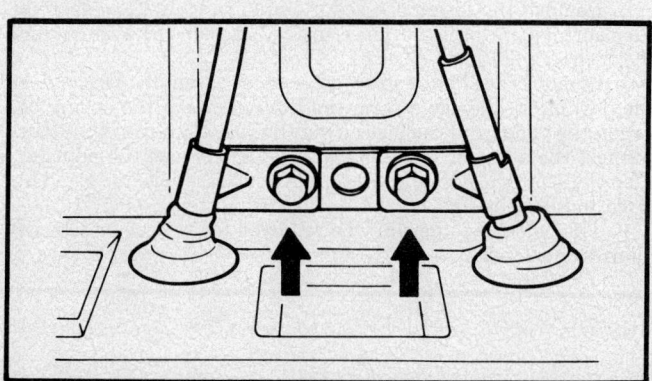
Location of cable clamp attaching bolts in passenger compartment—except Vista

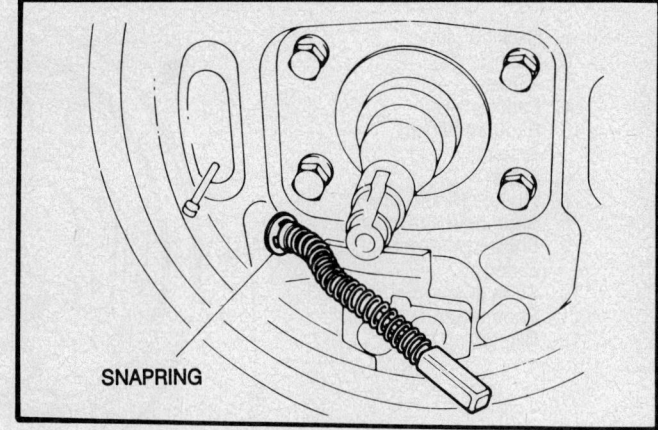
SNAPRING
Cable snapring on backing place

CONQUEST

1. Pull up on the lever, counting the number of clicks. Total travel should yield 4–5 clicks.

2. If not, remove the center console and turn the adjusting nut on the lever rod to obtain the required travel.

3. Raise the vehicle and support it safely.

4. With the parking brake released, make sure the rear wheels turn freely.

Removal and Installation
COLT AND COLT VISTA

1. Raise the vehicle and support it safely.
2. Disconnect the brake cable at the parking brake lever. Remove the cable clamps inside the driver's compartment. Disconnect the clamps on the rear suspension arm.
3. Remove the rear brake drums and the brake shoes assemblies. Disconnect the parking brake cable from the lever on the rear brake shoe. Remove the brake cables.
4. Install the cable and adjust.

CONQUEST

1. Raise the vehicle and support it safely.
2. Release the parking brake. Pull off the clevis pins from both sides of the rear brake. Disconnect the cable from the extension lever.
3. Remove the front cable after disconnecting the parking brake lever. On rear disc brake equipped vehicles, remove the rubber hanger from the center of the axle housing. Remove the parking brake lever and clevis pin linking the lever and cable. Remove the clips under the floor and remove the cable.
4. Install the cable. When installing, make sure the cable clips do not interfere with a rotating part. Adjust the extension lever to stop first. Then adjust the left cable and then the right.

Brake System Bleeding

1. Carefully clean all dirt from around the master cylinder filler cap.
2. If a bleeder tank is used, follow the manufacturer's instructions.
3. Remove the filler cap and refill the master cylinder to the lower edge of the filler neck.
4. Clean off the bleeder connections at all of the wheel cylinders or disc brake calipers. Attach the bleeder hose and fixture to the right rear wheel cylinder bleeder screw and place the end of the tube in a glass jar, submerged in brake fluid.
5. Open the bleeder valve ½–¾ turn. Have an assistant depress the brake pedal and allow it to return slowly. Continue this pumping action to force any air out of the system.
6. When bubbles cease to appear at the end of the bleeder hose, close the bleeder valve and remove the hose. Check the level of the brake fluid in the master cylinder and add fluid, if necessary.

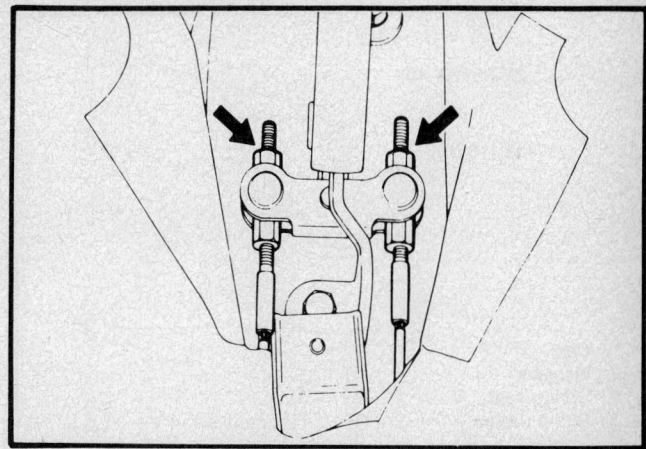

Cable adjusting nuts—FWD models except Vista

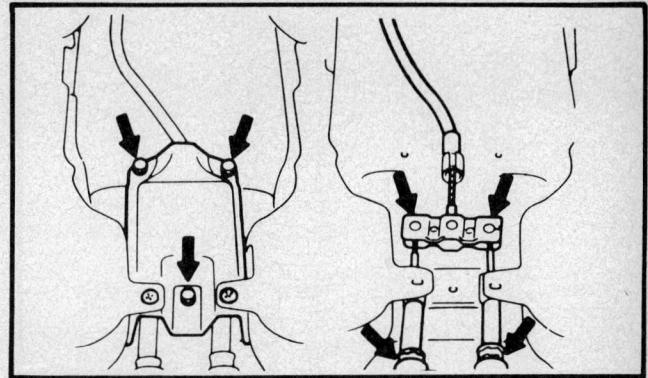

Parking brake equalizer cover bolts and cable coupler—Colt Vista

7. After the bleeding operation at each caliper or wheel cylinder has been completed, refill the master cylinder reservoir and replace the filler plug.

NOTE: Never reuse brake fluid which has been removed from the lines through the bleeding process because it contains air bubbles and dirt.

FRONT SUSPENSION

MacPherson Strut

Removal and Installation
COLT AND COLT VISTA

1. Raise the vehicle and support it safely, with the wheels hanging.
2. Remove the front wheels.
3. Detach the brake hose from the mounting clip on the strut.
4. Remove the nuts securing the strut to the fender housing.
5. Unbolt the strut from the knuckle.
6. Remove the strut from the vehicle.

To install:

7. Installation is the reverse order of the removal procedures. Torque the strut-to-knuckle bolts to 80–94 ft. lbs. (110–130 Nm) on Colt. Torque the strut-to-fender housing nuts to 25–33 ft. lbs. (35–45) on Colt and 18–25 ft. lbs. (24–34 Nm) on Colt Vista.

CONQUEST

1. Raise the vehicle and support it safely. Let the wheels hang.
2. Remove the caliper and suspend it out of the way.
3. Remove the hub and rotor assembly.
4. Remove the brake dust cover.
5. Unbolt the strut from the knuckle.
6. Remove the strut-to-fender mounting nuts and remove the strut.

To install:

7. Installation is the reverse order of the removal procedures. Torque the strut-to-fender nuts; 18–25 ft. lbs.; the strut-to-knuckle arm bolts to 58–72 ft. lbs.

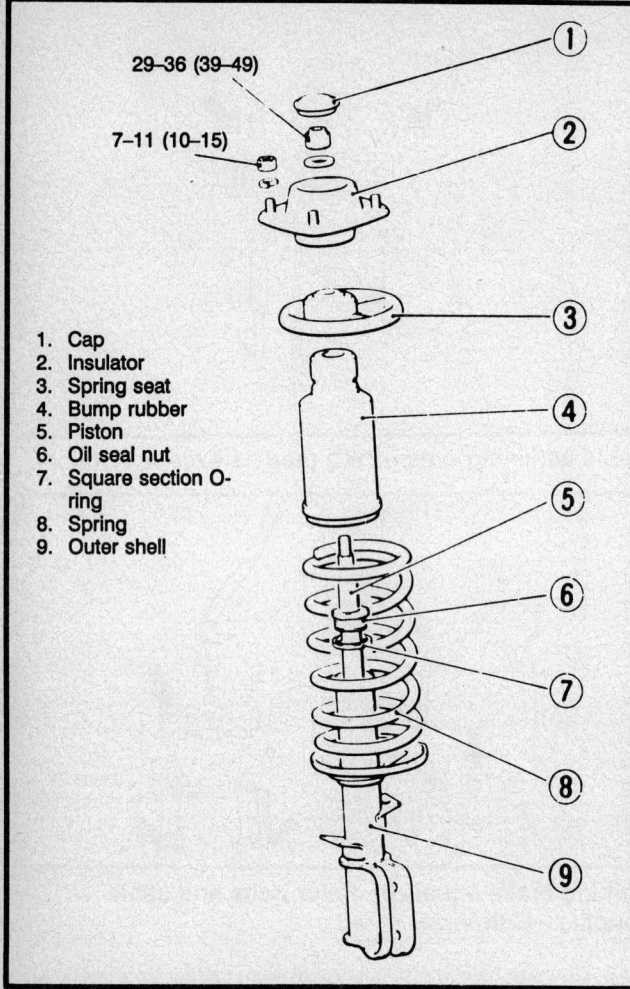

29–36 (39–49)

7–11 (10–15)

1. Cap
2. Insulator
3. Spring seat
4. Bump rubber
5. Piston
6. Oil seal nut
7. Square section O-ring
8. Spring
9. Outer shell

Colt FWD front strut assembly

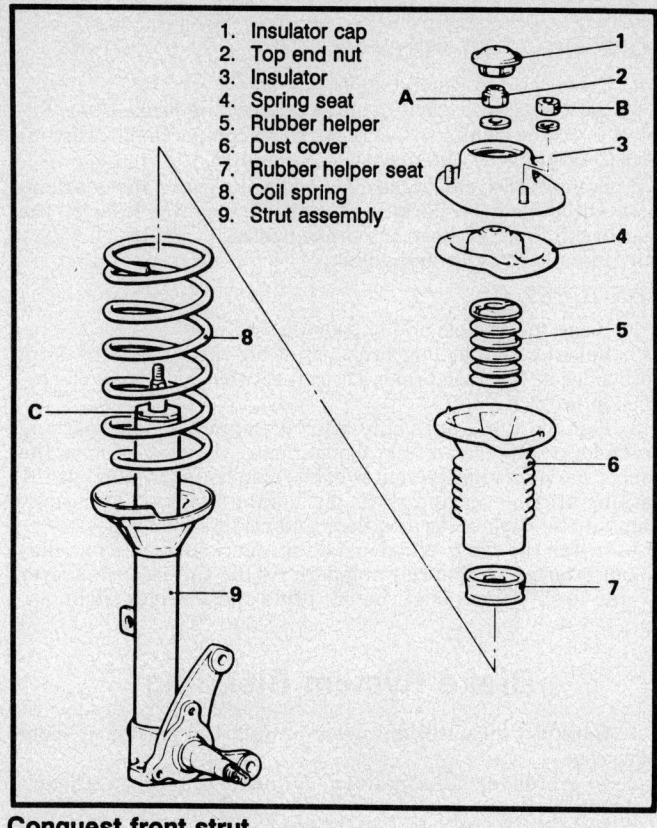

1. Insulator cap
2. Top end nut
3. Insulator
4. Spring seat
5. Rubber helper
6. Dust cover
7. Rubber helper seat
8. Coil spring
9. Strut assembly

Conquest front strut

4. Using snapring pliers, remove the snapring from the ball joint.
5. Using an adapter plate and driver, press the ball joint from the arm.

To install:
6. Installation is the reverse order of removal procedures. Invert the tool in the press for installation. Coat the lip and interior of the dust cover with lithium based chassis lube.

Lower Ball Joints

Inspection

1. Raise and safely support the vehicle.
2. With the ball joint installed to the steering knuckle, Grasp the top and bottom of the wheel, then, move the wheel using an in and out shaking motion.
3. Observe any movement between the steering knuckle and the control arm. If movement exists, replace the ball joint.

Removal and Installation

COLT

The ball joint is not replaceable. The ball joint and lower control arm must be replaced as an assembly.

COLT VISTA

1. Raise the vehicle and support it safely.
2. Remove the ball joint retaining bolt. Using a special tool, separate the ball joint from the steering knuckle. Remove the control arm from the vehicle.
3. Remove the ball joint dust cover.

CONQUEST

1. Raise the vehicle and support it safely. Remove the tire and wheel assembly.
2. Remove the brake caliper and support from the mounting adapter.
3. Anchor assembly out of the way with wire to the strut spring.
4. Remove the tie rod end nut and separate the tie rod end from the steering knuckle using a removing tool.
5. Remove the bolts securing the strut assembly to the steering knuckle.
6. Tap the connection with a plastic hammer to separate.
7. Remove the ball joint to control arm mounting bolts and remove the ball joint with the knuckle arm attached.
8. Remove the ball joint stud nut and separate the ball joint and knuckle arm.

To install:
9. Installation is the reverse order of the removal procedures. Torque specifications are:
Ball joint stud nut – 43–52 ft. lbs.
Strut-to-knuckle bolts – 58–78 ft. lbs.
Ball joint to control arm bolts – 43–51 ft. lbs.

NOTE: When self locking nuts are removed, always replace with new self locking nuts.

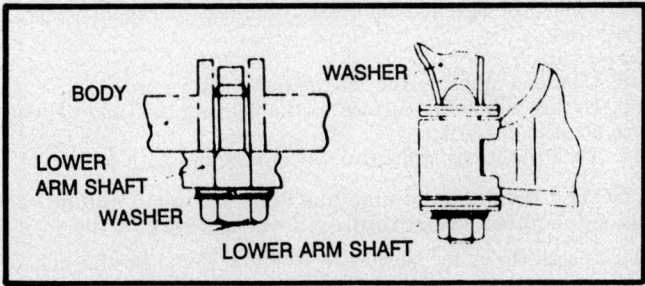

Installation of washer on lower shaft

Lower Control Arms

Removal and Installation

COLT

1. Raise the vehicle and support it safely. Remove the wheels. Remove the splash shield. If equipped, remove the center crossmember.
2. Disconnect the stabilizer bar from the lower arm.
3. Using a ball joint separator, disconnect the ball joint from the knuckle.
4. Unbolt the lower arm from the body and remove it from the vehicle.

NOTE: The ball joint cannot be separated from the control arm, but must be replaced as an assembly.

5. If the stabilizer bar is to be removed, disconnect the tie rod from the knuckle and unbolt and remove the stabilizer.
6. Check all parts for wear and damage and replace any suspect part.
7. Using an inch lb. torque wrench, check the ball joint starting torque. Nominal starting effort should be 22–87 inch lbs. Replace if otherwise.
To install:
8. Installation is the reverse order of the removal procedures. Use a new dust cover, the lip and inside of which is coated with lithium based chassis lube. The dust cover should be hammered into place with a driver tool.
9. Install the stabilizer bar so the serrations on the horizontal part protrude 6mm to the inside of the clamp and 23mm of threaded stud appear below the nut at the control arm.
10. The washer on the lower arm shaft should be installed. The left side lower arm shaft has left handed threads. The lower arm shaft nut must be torqued with the wheels hanging freely. Observe the following torques:
Knuckle-to-strut—54–65 ft. lbs. 1989–90; 80–94 ft. lbs.
Lower arm shaft-to-body—69–87 ft. lbs.
Stabilizer bar-to-body—12–20 ft. lbs.
Ball joint-to-knuckle—44–53 ft. lbs.
Lower arm-to-shaft—70–88 ft. lbs.
Rear shaft bushing bracket-to-body—43–58 ft. lbs.

COLT VISTA

1. Raise the vehicle and support it safely.
2. Remove the wheels.
3. Disconnect the stabilizer bar and strut bar from the lower arm.
4. Remove the nut and disconnect the ball joint from the knuckle with a separator.
5. Unbolt the lower arm from the crossmember.
6. Check all parts for wear or damage and replace any suspect part.
7. Using an inch lb. torque wrench, check the ball joint starting torque. Starting torque should be 20–86 inch lbs. If it is not within that range, replace the ball joint.

To install:
8. Installation is the reverse order of the removal procedures. Tighten all fasteners with the wheels hanging freely. Observe the following torques:
Ball joint-to-knuckle—44–53 ft. lbs.
Arm-to-crossmember-2WD to 90–111 ft. lbs.; 4WD to 58–68 ft. lbs.
Stabilizer bar hanger brackets—7–9 ft. lbs.
9. When installing the stabilizer bar, the nut on the bar-to-crossmember bolts and the bar-to-lower arm bolts, are not torqued, but turned on until a certain length of thread is exposed above the nut:
2WD stabilizer bar-to-crossmember—0.31–0.39 in.
2WD stabilizer bar-to-lower control arm—0.31–0.39 in.
4WD stabilizer bar-to-crossmember—0.31–0.39 in.
4WD stabilizer bar-to-lower arm—0.51–0.59 in..

CONQUEST

1. Raise the vehicle and support it safely.
2. Remove the front wheels.
3. Remove the caliper and suspend it out of the way.
4. Remove the hub and rotor assembly.
5. Disconnect the stabilizer bar and strut bar from the lower arm.
6. Using a separator, remove the attaching nut and disconnect the tie rod from the knuckle arm.
7. Unbolt the strut from the knuckle arm.
8. Unbolt the lower control arm and knuckle arm assembly from the crossmember.
9. Using a special tool, separate the knuckle arm from the lower control arm.
To install:
10. Installation is the reverse order of the removal procedures. Apply sealant to the flange of the knuckle arm where it mates with the strut. Torque the lower control arm shaft bolt to 60–70 ft. lbs.; the ball joint-to-knuckle arm nut to 45–55 ft. lbs.

Sway Bar

Removal and Installation

1. Raise and safely support the vehicle; allow the suspension to hang free. Remove the left front wheel assembly.
2. Disconnect the stabilizer link bolts and nuts from the control arms. Disconnect the stabilizer shaft from the support assemblies.
3. Loosen the front bolts and remove the bolts from the rear and center of the support assemblies, allowing the supports to be lowered enough to remove the stabilizer bar assembly. Remove the assembly from the vehicle.
To install:
4. Installation is the reverse order of the removal procedures. Loosely assemble all components while insuring that the stabilizer bar is centered, side-to-side. Torque the stabilizer bar support assemblies to 9 ft. lbs. (13 Nm).
5. Lower the vehicle.

Front Wheel Bearings

NOTE: Please refer to the "Drive Axle" Section for FWD and 4WD vehicles.

Adjustment

1. Raise the vehicle and support it safely. Remove the wheel and dust cover. Remove the cotter pin and lock cap from the nut.
2. Torque the wheel bearing nut to 14.5 ft. lbs. (19.6 Nm) and then loosen the nut. Retorque the nut to 3.6 ft. lbs. (4.9 Nm) and install the lock cap and cotter pin.
3. Install the dust cover and the wheel.

Removal and Installation

1. Remove the caliper (pin type) or the caliper and support (sliding type).

NOTE: On sliding type calipers, remove the caliper and support as a unit by unfastening the bolts holding it to the adapter. Support the caliper with wire, do not allow the weight to be supported by the brake hose.

2. Pry off the dust cap. Tap out and discard the cotter pin. Remove the locknut.
3. Being careful not to drop the outer bearing, pull off the brake disc and wheel hub.
4. Remove the grease inside the wheel hub.
5. Using a brass drift, carefully drive the outer bearing race out of the hub.
6. Remove the inner bearing seal and bearing.

7. Check the bearings for wear or damage and replace them, if necessary.
To install:
8. Coat the inner surface of the hub with grease.
9. Grease the outer surface of the bearing race and drift it into place in the hub.
10. Pack the inner and outer wheel bearings with grease.

NOTE: If the brake disc has been removed and/or replaced; tighten the retaining bolts to 25–29 ft. lbs.

11. Install the inner bearing in the hub. Being careful not to distort it, install the oil seal with its lip facing the bearing. Drive the seal on until its outer edge is even with the edge of the hub.
12. Install the hub/disc assembly on the spindle, being careful not to damage the oil seal.
13. Install the outer bearing, washer and spindle nut. Adjust the wheel bearing.

REAR SUSPENSION

Shock Absorbers

Removal and Installation
EXCEPT 4WD COLT VISTA

1. Raise the vehicle and support it safely.

NOTE: The body sill is marked with 2 dimples to locate the support position. Never place a stand anywhere but between these marks or the body can be damaged.

2. Remove the wheel. Remove the upper mounting bolt and nut.
3. While holding the bottom stud mount nut with one wrench, remove the locknut with another wrench.
4. Remove the shock absorber.
5. Check the shock for:
   a. Excessive oil leakage; some minor weeping is permissible.
   b. Bent center rod, damaged outer case, or other defects.

c. Pump the shock absorber several times, if it offers even resistance on full strokes it may be considered serviceable.

To install:
6. Install the upper shock mounting nut and bolt. Hand tighten the nut.
7. Install the bottom eye of the shock over the spring stud. Tighten the lower nut to 12–15 ft. lbs. on rear wheel drive vehicles; 47–58 ft. lbs. on front wheel drive vehicles.
8. Finally, tighten the upper nut to 47–58 ft. lbs. on all models except station wagons, which are tightened to 12–15 ft. lbs.

4WD COLT VISTA

1. Raise the vehicle and support it safely.
2. Remove the rear wheels.
3. Using a suitable floor jack, raise the inner control arm slightly.
4. Unbolt the top, then the bottom of the shock absorber. Remove it from the vehicle.

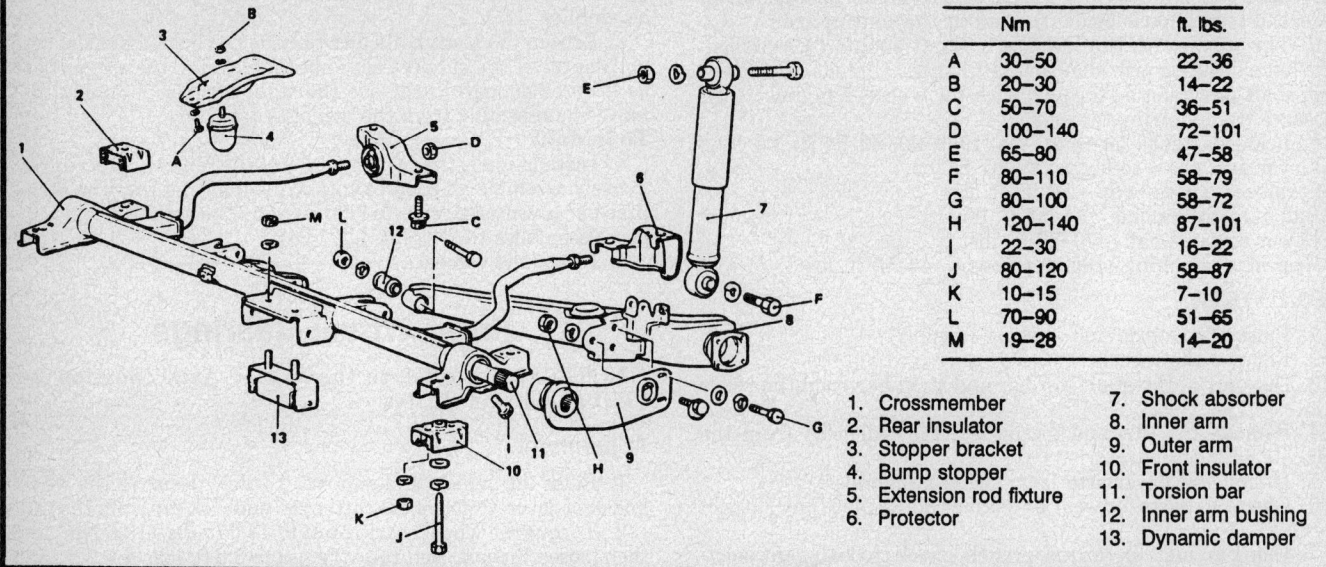

	Nm	ft. lbs.
A	30–50	22–36
B	20–30	14–22
C	50–70	36–51
D	100–140	72–101
E	65–80	47–58
F	80–110	58–79
G	80–100	58–72
H	120–140	87–101
I	22–30	16–22
J	80–120	58–87
K	10–15	7–10
L	70–90	51–65
M	19–28	14–20

1. Crossmember
2. Rear insulator
3. Stopper bracket
4. Bump stopper
5. Extension rod fixture
6. Protector
7. Shock absorber
8. Inner arm
9. Outer arm
10. Front insulator
11. Torsion bar
12. Inner arm bushing
13. Dynamic damper

4WD Vista rear suspension

MacPherson Strut

Removal and Installation

COLT

1. Raise the vehicle and support it safely. Allow the lower arms and suspension to hang. Remove the wheels.
2. Raise the axle slightly to relax the strut and to support the axle when the strut is removed. Position an additional support under the axle.
3. Take care in jacking that no contact is made on the lateral rod.
4. On hatchback, remove the trunk side trim.
5. Remove the upper dust cover cap.
6. Remove the upper mounting nuts. Remove the lower mounting bolt and nut.
7. Remove the strut.

To install:

8. Installation is the reverse order of the removal procedures. Torque the lower mounting bolt and nut to 58–72 ft. lbs.; the upper mounting nuts to 18–25 ft. lbs.

CONQUEST

1. Raise the vehicle and support it safely.
2. Remove the rear wheels.
3. Unclip the brake hose at the strut.
4. Unbolt the intermediate shaft from the companion flange.
5. Unbolt the strut assembly from the halfshaft housing. Remove the housing coupling bolts. Separate the strut from the housing by pushing the housing downward while prying open the coupling on the housing.
6. Remove the strut upper end attaching nuts, found under the side trim in the cargo area.
7. Lift out the strut.

To install:

8. Installation is the reverse order of the removal procedures. Torque the upper end nuts to 20–25 ft. lbs.; the strut-to-housing bolts to 50 ft. lbs.; the coupling bolt to 50 ft. lbs.

Coil Springs

Removal and Installation

EXCEPT 4WD COLT VISTA

1. Raise the vehicle and support it safely. Allow the rear wheels to hang.
2. Place a suitable jack under the rear axle and remove the bottom bolts or nuts of the shock absorbers.
3. Lower the rear axle and remove the left and right coil springs.

To install:

4. Installation is the reverse order of the removal procedure.

NOTE: When installing the spring, pay attention to the difference in shape between the upper and lower spring seats.

Torsion Bar and Control Arms

Instead of springs, the 4WD Colt Vista uses transversely mounted torsion bars housed inside the rear crossmember, attached to which are inner and outer control arms. The conventional style shock absorbers are mounted on the inner arms.

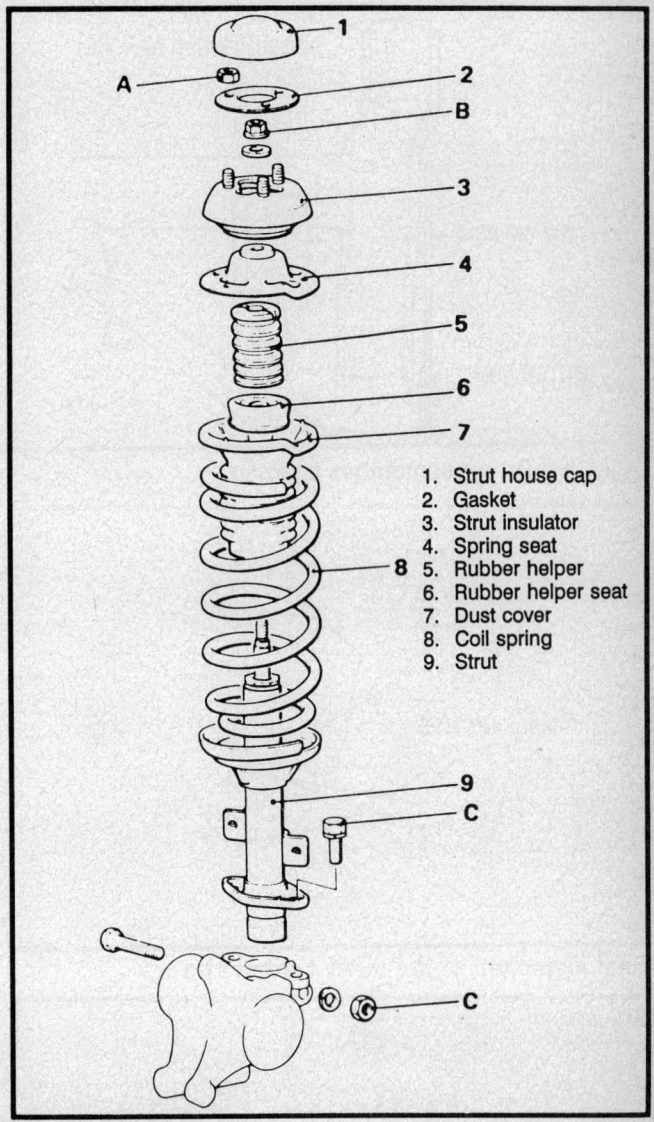

1. Strut house cap
2. Gasket
3. Strut insulator
4. Spring seat
5. Rubber helper
6. Rubber helper seat
7. Dust cover
8. Coil spring
9. Strut

Conquest rear strut

4WD COLT VISTA

1. Raise the vehicle and support it safely.
2. Remove the differential.
3. Remove the intermediate shafts and halfshafts.

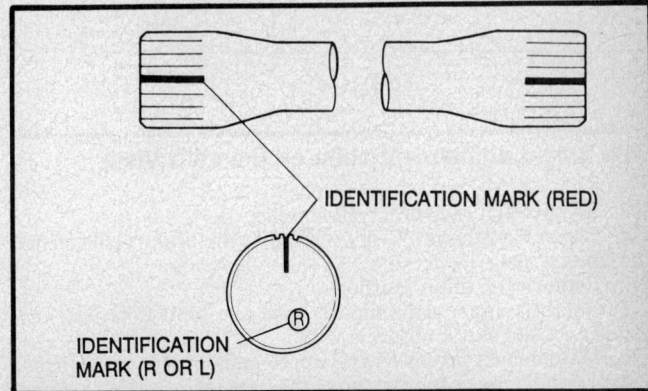

IDENTIFICATION MARK (RED)

IDENTIFICATION MARK (R OR L)

Torsion bar suspension identifying marks

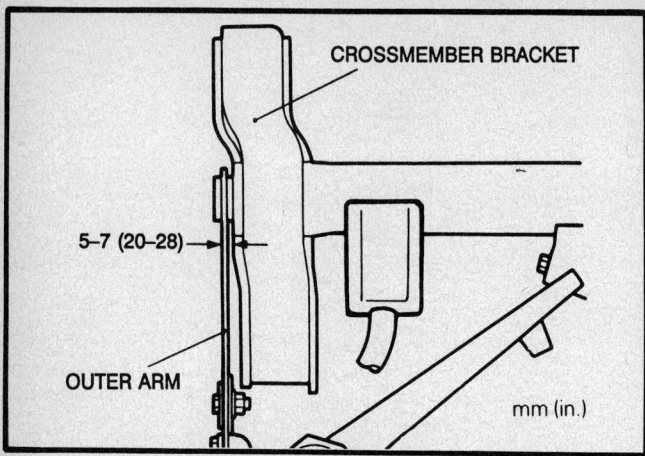

Outer arm-to-crossmember spacing

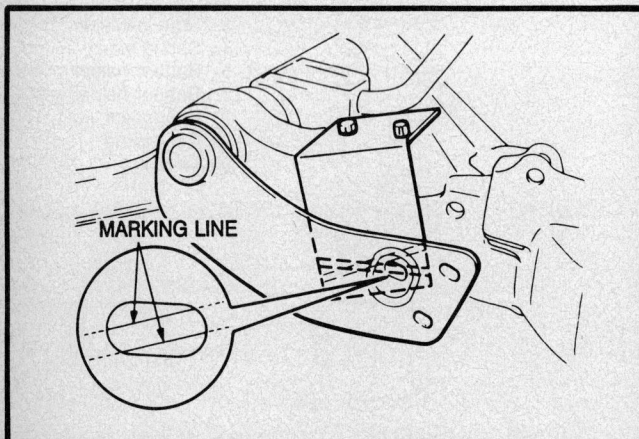

Final alignment of the outer control arm

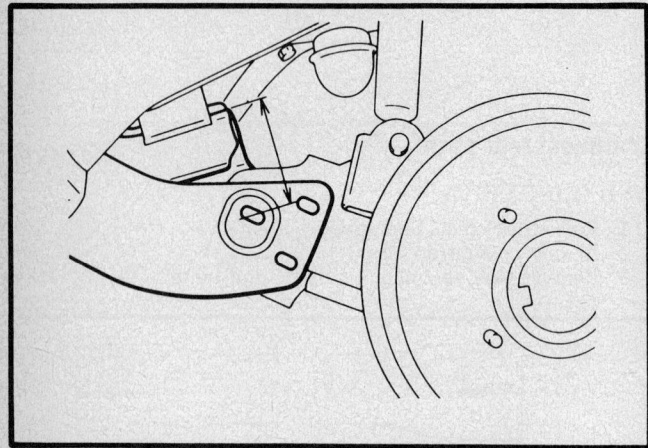

Ride height adjustment point on the 4WD Vista

4. Remove the rear brake assemblies.
5. Disconnect the brake lines and parking brake cables from the inner arms.
6. Remove the main muffler.
7. Raise the inner arms slightly with a suitable floor jack and disconnect the shock absorbers.
8. Matchmark, precisely, the upper ends of the outer arms, the torsion bar ends and the top of the crossmember bracket and remove the inner and outer arm attaching bolts.

9. Remove the extension rods fixture attaching bolts.
10. Remove the crossmember attaching bolts and remove the rear suspension assembly from the vehicle.
11. Unbolt and remove the shock from the crossmember.
12. Remove the front and rear insulators from both ends of the crossmember.
13. Loosen but do not remove, the lock bolts securing the outer arm bushings at both ends of the crossmember.
14. Pull the outer arm from the crossmember. The torsion bar will slide out of the crossmember with the outer arm.
15. Remove the torsion bar from either the crossmember or outer arm.
16. Inspect all parts for wear or damage. Inspect the crossmember for bending or deformation.
17. Inner arm bushings may be replaced at this time using a press. The thicker end of the bushing goes on the inner side.

To install:
18. Prior to installation note that the torsion bars are marked with an L or R on the outer end and are not interchangeable.
19. If the original torsion bars are being installed, align the identification marks on the torsion bar end, crossmember and outer arm, install the torsion bar and arm and tighten the lock bolts. Skip Step 20. If new torsion bars are being installed, proceed to Step 20.
20. A special alignment jig must be fabricated. The jig is bolted to the rear insulator hole on the crossmember bracket. Insert the torsion bar into the outer arm, aligning the red identification mark on the torsion bar end with the matchmark made on the outer arm top side. Install the torsion bar and arm so the center of the flanged bolt hole on the arm is 32mm below the lower marking line on the jig. Then, pull the outer arm off of the torsion bar, leaving the bar undisturbed in the crossmember. Reposition the arm on the torsion bar, 1 serration counterclockwise from its former position. This will make the previously measured dimension, 33mm above the lower line. When the outer arm and torsion bar are properly positioned, the marking lines on the jig will run diagonally across the center of the toe-in adjustment hole. When the adjustment is complete, tighten the lock bolts. The clearance between the outer arm and the crossmember bracket, at the torsion bar, should be 5.0–7.0mm.
21. The remainder of installation is the reverse order of the removal procedure. Observe the following torques:
    Extension rod fixture bolts – 45–50 ft. lbs.
    Extension rod-to-fixture nut – 95–100 ft. lbs.
    Shock absorber lower bolt – 75–80 ft. lbs.
    Outer arm attaching bolts – 65–70 ft. lbs.
    Toe-in bolt – 95–100 ft. lbs.
    Lock bolts – 20–22 ft. lbs.
    Crossmember attaching bolts – 80–85 ft. lbs.
    Front insulator nuts – 7–10 ft. lbs.
    Inner arm-to-crossmember bolts – 60–65 ft. lbs.
    Damper-to-crossmember nuts – 15–20 ft. lbs.
22. Lower the vehicle to the ground and check the ride height. The ride height is checked on both sides and is determined by measuring the distance between the center line of the toe-in bolt hole on the outer arm and the lower edge of the rebound bumper. The distance on each side should be 4.00–4.11 in. If not or if there is a significant difference between sides, the torsion bars positioning is wrong.

Rear Control Arms

Removal and Installation
CONQUEST

1. Raise the vehicle and support it safely. Allow the wheels to hang freely.
2. Remove the rear wheels.
3. Disconnect the parking brake cable from the lower arm.
4. Disconnect the stabilizer bar.
5. Unbolt the lower control arm from the halfshaft housing.

Rear lower control arm identifying marks—RWD except Conquest

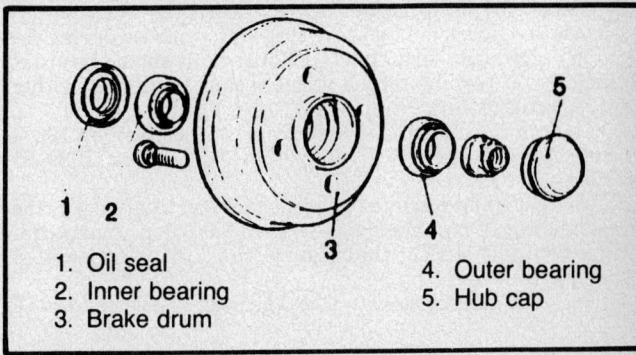

1. Oil seal
2. Inner bearing
3. Brake drum
4. Outer bearing
5. Hub cap

View of the rear brake drum and bearing—Colt

6. Unbolt the lower control arm from the front support.

7. Unbolt the lower control arm from the crossmember and remove it.

8. Installation is the reverse of removal. Apply a thin coating of chassis lube to the cutout portion of the lower arm-to-halfshaft housing shaft. Do not allow the grease to touch the bushings. Insert the shaft with the mark on its head facing downward. When positioning the lower control arm on the crossmember, align the mark on the crossmember with the line on the plate. Use the following torques:

Lower control arm-to-front support bolts—108 ft. lbs.
Arm-to-crossmember bolts—108 ft. lbs.
Arm to halfshaft housing bolts—60 ft. lbs.
Arm locking pin—15 ft. lbs.

9. Have the rear wheel alignment checked.

Rear Wheel Bearings

NOTE: For all RWD vehicles, please refer to the "Drive Axle" section.

Removal and Installation

COLT

1. Loosen the lug nuts. Raise the vehicle and support it safely.

2. Remove the wheel and tire assemblies.

3. Remove the grease cap.

4. Remove the nut.

5. Pull the drum off. The outer bearing will fall out while the drum is coming off. Do not drop it. If equipped with disc brakes; Remove the caliper assembly. Remove the disc rotor. Remove the hub assembly.

6. Pry out the oil seal. Discard it.

7. Remove the inner bearing.

8. Check the bearing races. If any scoring, heat checking or damage is noted, they should be replaced.

NOTE: When bearing or races need replacement, replace them as a set.

9. Inspect the bearings. If wear or looseness or heat checking is found, replace them.

10. If the bearings and races are to be replaced, drive out the race with a brass drift.

To install:

11. Before installing new races, coat them with lithium based wheel bearing grease. Drive into place with a brass drift. Make sure they are fully seated.

12. Thoroughly pack the bearings with lithium based wheel bearing grease. Pack the hub with grease.

13. Install the inner bearing and coat the lip and rim of the grease seal with grease. Drive the seal into place with a seal driver.

14. If equipped with drum brakes, place the drum on the hub and install the outer bearing. Do not install the nut at this time.

15. If equipped with drum brakes, use a pull scale attached to one of the lugs to measure the starting force necessary to get the drum to turn. Starting force should be 5 lbs. If the starting torque is greater than specific, replace the bearings.

16. If equipped with drum brakes, install the nut on the halfshaft. Thread the nut on, to a point at which the back face of the nut is 2–3mm from the shoulder of the shaft, where the threads end.

17. Adjust the wheel bearing. Install the wheel and lower the vehicle.

2WD COLT VISTA

1. Loosen the lug nuts. Raise the vehicle and support it safely. Remove the wheel.

2. Remove the grease cap, cotter pin, nut and washer.

3. Remove the brake drum. While pulling the drum, the outer bearing will fall out. Do not drop it.

4. Pry out the grease seal and discard it.

5. Remove the inner bearing.

6. Check the bearing races. If any scoring, heat checking or damage is noted, they should be replaced.

NOTE: When bearing or races need replacement, replace them as a set.

7. Inspect the bearings. If wear or looseness or heat checking is found replace them.

8. If the bearings and races are to be replaced, drive out the races with a brass drift.

To install:

9. Before installing new races, coat them with lithium based wheel bearing grease. Drive into place with a brass drift. Make sure they are fully seated.

10. Thoroughly pack the bearings with lithium based wheel bearing grease. Pack the hub with grease.

11. Install the inner bearing and coat the lip and rim of the grease seal with grease. Drive the seal into place with a seal driver.

12. Mount the drum onto the hub, slide the outer bearing into place, install the washer and thread the nut into place. Do not tighten.

13. Adjust the wheel bearing, install the wheel and lower the vehicle.

Adjustment

COLT

Drum Brakes

1. Raise the vehicle and support it safely. Remove the rear wheel and wheel bearing cap.

2. Using an inch lb. torque wrench, turn the nut counterclockwise 2–3 turns, noting the average force needed during the turning procedure. Turning torque for the nut should be about 48 inch lbs. If turning torque is not within 5 inch lbs., either way, replace the nut.

3. Tighten the nut to 72–108 ft. lbs. (100–150 Nm) on 1987–88 vehicles and 108–145 ft. lbs. (150–200 Nm) on 1989–91 vehicles.

4. Using a stand mounted gauge, check the axial play of the wheel bearings. Play should be less than 0.0079 in. If play cannot be brought within that figure, the unit is assembled incorrectly.

5. Pack the grease cap with wheel bearing grease and install it.

Disc Brakes

Install the hub and bearing assembly. Tighten the nut to 108–145 ft. lbs. Install the rotor and caliper assembly.

2WD COLT VISTA

1. Raise the vehicle and support it safely. Remove the rear wheel, wheel bearing cap and cotter pin.

2. Install a torque wrench on the nut. While turning the drum by hand, tighten the nut to 15 ft. lbs. Back off the nut until it is loose, then tighten it to 7 ft. lbs.

3. Install the lock cap and insert a new cotter pin. If the lock cap and hole don't align and repositioning the cap can't accomplish alignment, back off the nut no more than 15 degrees. If that won't align the holes either, try the adjustment procedure over again.

Rear Axle Assembly

Removal and Installation

COLT

1. Raise and safely support the vehicle. Remove the wheel and tire assemblies.

2. Remove brake fittings and retaining clips holding flexible brake line.

3. Remove parking brake cable adjusting connection nut.

4. Release both parking brake cables from brackets by slipping ball end of cables through brake connectors. Pull parking brake cable through bracket.

5. Pry off grease cap.

6. Remove cotter pin and castle lock.

7. Remove adjusting nut and brake drum.

8. Remove brake assembly and spindle bolts.

9. Set spindle aside and using a piece of wire, hang brake assembly aside.

10. Place supports under rear crossmember to support the rear suspension.

11. Remove shock absorber brackets.

12. Remove trailing arm-to-hanger bracket bolts.

13. Lower jack and remove axle assembly.

To Install:

14. Using a suitable jack, position the rear axle assembly under vehicle.

15. Install trailing arm-to-hanger mounting bracket, finger tighten bolts only.

16. Install shock absorber bolts loosely.

17. Place spindle and brake assembly in position; install bolts, do not tighten at this time.

18. Torque the bolts to 45 ft. lbs. (60 Nm).

19. Install brake drum. Install washer and nut. Adjust wheel bearing. Install the dust cap.

20. Put parking brake cable through the bracket.

21. Slip ball end of parking brake cables through brake connectors on parking brake bracket.

22. Install both retaining clips.

23. Install parking brake cable adjusting connection nut. Tighten until all slack is removed from cables.

24. Install retaining clips and brake tube fittings. Torque fitting to 9 ft. lbs. (12 Nm).

25. Bleed rear brake system and readjust brakes.

26. Install wheel and tire assembly.

27. With vehicle on ground, torque trailing arm-to-hanger bracket mounting bolts to 58–72 ft. lbs. (80–100 Nm).

28. Torque shock absorber mounting bolts to 58–72 ft. lbs. (80–100 Nm).

COLT VISTA

1. Raise and safely support the vehicle. Remove the wheel assemblies.

2. Separate the parking brake cable at the connector and cable housing at the floor pan bracket.

3. Separate the brake line at backing plate.

4. Remove the muffler-to-middle exhaust pipe retaining bolts, remove the O-ring hangers and remove the exhaust system.

5. Remove the lower shock absorber through bolts and disconnect the shock at the axle end.

6. Lower the axle until the spring and isolator assemblies can be removed.

7. Remove the axle assembly from the vehicle.

To Install:

8. Using a suitable jack, position the rear axle assembly under vehicle.

9. Install the springs and isolators and carefully raise the axle assembly.

10. Install the shock absorber and through bolts; do not tighten.

11. Position brake support to the axle while routing the parking brake cable through the support. Lock it into place.

12. Connect the brake line fitting to the backing wheel cylinder. Torque to 9–12 ft. lbs. (13–17 Nm).

13. Install the hub and drum, if removed.

14. Route the parking brake cable through the fingers in the bracket and lock housing end into the floor pan bracket. Install the cable end into the intermediate connector.

15. Install the exhaust system and hangers. Torque the muffler-to-middle exhaust pipe retaining bolts to 22–29 ft. lbs. (30–40 Nm).

16. Install wheel assemblies and lower vehicle to floor. Torque the lower shock absorber bolts to 58–80 ft. lbs. (80–110 Nm). Torque the axle assembly-to-body mounting bolts to 87–108 ft. lbs. (120–150 Nm).

SPECIFICATIONS

VEHICLE IDENTIFICATION CHART

It is important for servicing and ordering parts to be certain of the vehicle and engine identification. The VIN (vehicle identification number) is a 17 digit number visible through the windshield on the driver's side of the dash and contains the vehicle and engine identification codes. The tenth digit indicates model year, and the eighth digit indicates engine code. It can be interpreted as follows:

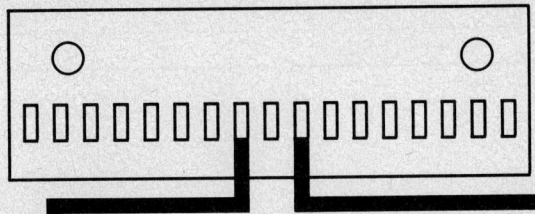

Engine Code

Code	Cu. In.	Liters	Cyl.	Fuel Sys.	Eng. Mfg.
4	97	1.6	4	2 bbl	Toyota
5 ① ②	97	1.6	4	EFI	Toyota
6 ① ②	97	1.6	4	EFI	Toyota
7	90	1.5	4	2 bbl	Isuzu
9	90	1.5	4	Turbo	Isuzu
5 ④	61	1.0	3	2 bbl	Suzuki
2	61	1.0	3	Turbo	Suzuki
6 ④	61	1.0	3	TBI	Suzuki
5 ① ③	97	1.6	4	MFI	Isuzu
6 ③	97	1.6	4	MFI	Isuzu

① Twincam
② Prizm
③ Storm
④ Metro

Model Year

Code	Year
H	1987
J	1988
K	1989
L	1990
M	1991

ENGINE IDENTIFICATION

Year	Model	Engine Displacement cu. in. (liter)	Engine Series Identification (VIN)	No. of Cylinders	Engine Type
1987	Sprint	3-61 (1.0)	5	3	SOHC
	Sprint	3.61 (1.0)	2	3	SOHC
	Spectrum	4-90 (1.5)	7	4	SOHC
	Spectrum	4-90 (1.5)	9	4	SOHC
	Nova	4-97 (1.6)	4	4	SOHC
1988	Sprint	3-61 (1.0)	5	3	SOHC
	Sprint	3.61 (1.0)	2	3	SOHC
	Spectrum	4-90 (1.5)	7	4	SOHC
	Spectrum	4-90 (1.5)	9	4	SOHC
	Nova	4-97 (1.6)	4	4	SOHC
	Nova	4-97 (1.6)	5	4	DOHC
1989	Metro	3-61 (1.0)	6	3	SOHC
	Spectrum	4-90 (1.5)	7	4	SOHC
	Prizm	4-97 (1.6)	6	4	SOHC

ENGINE IDENTIFICATION

Year	Model	Engine Displacement cu. in. (liter)	Engine Series Identification (VIN)	No. of Cylinders	Engine Type
1990–91	Metro	3-61 (1.0)	6	3	SOHC
	Prizm	4-97 (1.6)	6	4	SOHC
	Prizm	4-97 (1.6)	5	4	DOHC
	Storm	4-97 (1.6)	6	4	SOHC
	Storm	4-97 (1.6)	5	4	DOHC

SOHC Single overhead cam engine
DOHC Dual overhead cam engine

GENERAL ENGINE SPECIFICATIONS

Year	VIN	No. Cylinder Displacement cu. in. (liter)	Fuel System Type	Net Horsepower @ rpm	Net Torque @ rpm (ft. lbs.)	Bore × Stroke (in.)	Compression Ratio	Oil Pressure @ rpm
1987	5	3-61 (1.0)	2 bbl	48 @ 5100	77 @ 3200	2.91 × 3.03	9.5:1	48
	5①	3-61 (1.0)	2 bbl	46 @ 4700	78 @ 3200	2.91 × 3.03	9.8:1	48
	2	3-61 (1.0)	EFI	70 @ 5500	107 @ 3500	2.91 × 3.03	8.3:1	48
	7	4-90 (1.5)	2 bbl	70 @ 5400	87 @ 3400	3.03 × 3.11	8.2:1	49 @ 5200
	9	4-90 (1.5)	Turbo	110 @ 5400	120 @ 3400	3.03 × 3.11	8.0:1	49 @ 5200
	4	4-97 (1.6)	2 bbl	74 @ 5200	85 @ 2800	3.19 × 3.03	9.0:1	34 @ 2000
1988	5	3-61 (1.0)	2 bbl	48 @ 5100	77 @ 3200	2.91 × 3.03	9.5:1	48
	5	3-61 (1.0)	2 bbl	46 @ 4700	78 @ 3200	2.91 × 3.03	9.8:1	48
	2	3-61 (1.0)	EFI	70 @ 5500	107 @ 3500	2.91 × 3.03	8.3:1	48
	7	4-90 (1.5)	2 bbl	70 @ 5400	87 @ 3400	3.03 × 3.11	9.6:1	49 @ 5200
	9	4-90 (1.5)	Turbo	110 @ 5400	120 @ 3400	3.03 × 3.11	8.0:1	49 @ 5200
	4	4-97 (1.6)	2 bbl	74 @ 5200	85 @ 2800	3.19 × 3.03	9.0:1	34 @ 2000
	5	4-97 (1.6)	EFI	110 @ 6600	98 @ 4800	3.19 × 3.03	9.4:1	56 @ 3000
1989	6②	3-61 (1.0)	EFI	55 @ 5700	58 @ 3300	2.91 × 3.03	9.5:1	39 @ 4000
	6	3-61 (1.0)	EFI	49 @ 4700	58 @ 3300	2.91 × 3.03	9.5:1	39 @ 4000
	7	4-90 (1.5)	2 bbl	70 @ 5400	87 @ 3400	3.03 × 3.11	9.6:1	49 @ 5200
	6	4-97 (1.6)	MFI	102 @ 5800	101 @ 4800	3.19 × 3.03	9.5:1	56 @ 3000
1990–91	6	3-61 (1.0)	EFI	55 @ 5700	58 @ 3300	2.91 × 3.03	9.5:1	39 @ 4000
	6	4-97 (1.6)	MFI	102 @ 5800	101 @ 4800	3.15 × 3.11	9.1:1	56 @ 3000
	5③	4-97 (1.6)	MFI	130 @ 7000	102 @ 5800	3.15 × 3.11	9.8:1	56 @ 3000
	5③	4-97 (1.6)	MFI	102 @ 5800	101 @ 4800	3.20 × 3.00	9.5:1	—
	6③	4-97 (1.6)	MFI	130 @ 6800	105 @ 6000	3.20 × 3.00	10.3:1	—

① ER model
② LSI model
③ DOHC

GASOLINE ENGINE TUNE-UP SPECIFICATIONS

Year	Model	Engine Displacement cu. in. (cc)	Spark Plugs Type	Spark Plugs Gap (in.)	Ignition Timing (deg.) MT	Ignition Timing (deg.) AT	Compression Pressure (psi)	Fuel Pump (psi)	Idle Speed (rpm) MT	Idle Speed (rpm) AT	Valve Clearance In.	Valve Clearance Ex.
1987	Sprint	61 (1000)	R43CXLS	0.039–0.043	10	6	199	4.0	750[11]	850	0.006	0.008
	Sprint	61 (1000)[9]	R43CXLS	0.039–0.043	12	—	199	25–33	750	—	0.006	0.008
	Spectrum	90 (1471)	BPR6ES-11	0.040	15[1]	10[3]	128–179	3.8–4.7	700	950	0.006	0.010
	Spectrum	90 (1471)[9]	BPR6ES-11	0.040	15[2]	NA	128–179	28.4[5]	950	NA	0.006	0.010
	Nova	97 (1600)	[6]	0.043	0	0	160	2.5–3.5	650	800	0.008	0.012
1988	Sprint	61 (1000)	R43CXLS	0.039–0.043	10	6	199	4.0	750[11]	850	0.006	0.008
	Sprint	61 (1000)[9]	R43CXLS	0.039–0.043	12	—	199	2.5–3.3	750	—	0.006	0.008
	Spectrum	90 (1471)	BPR6ES-11	0.040	15[1]	10[3]	128–179	3.8–4.7	700	950	0.006	0.010
	Spectrum	90 (1471)[9]	BPR6ES-11	0.040	15[2]	NA	128–179	2.8[4]	950	NA	0.006	0.010
	Nova	97 (1600)	[6]	0.043	0	0	128–178	3.5	650	750	0.008	0.012
	Nova	97 (1600)[10]	BCPR5EP11	0.043		10B[4]	142–179	NA	800	800	[7]	[8]
1989	Metro	61 (1000)	R43CXLS	0.039–0.043	[13]	[13]	199	26	750	850	Hyd.	Hyd.
	Spectrum	90 (1471)	R42XLS	0.040	15[1]	10[3]	128–179	3.8–4.7	750	1000	0.006	0.010
	Prizm	97 (1600)	BCPRSEY	0.031	10B	10B	142–191	[12]	700	700	0.006–0.010	0.008–0.012
1990	Metro	61 (1000)	R43CXLS	0.039–0.043	[13]	[13]	199	26	750	850	Hyd.	Hyd.
	Prizm	97 (1600)	BCPRSEY	0.031	10B	10B	142–191	[12]	700	700	0.006–0.010	0.008–0.012
	Storm	97 (1600)	R42XLS	0.040	[13]	[13]	—	NA	700	700	0.006–0.010	0.008–0.0012
	Storm[10]	97 (1600)	—	—	[13]	[13]	—	NA	700	700	0.004–0.008	0.008–0.0012
1991	SEE UNDERHOOD SPECIFICATIONS STICKER											

NOTE: The underhood specifications sticker often reflects tune-up specification changes made in production. Sticker figures must be used if they disagree with those in this chart.

NA Not available
[1] @ 750 rpm
[2] @ 950 rpm
[3] @ 1000 rpm
[4] Use jumper wire to short circuit both terminals of the check engine connector located near the wiper motor. When the jumper wire is removed and the transaxle is in Neutral, the ignition timing should be more than 16 degrees BTDC (manual) or 12 degrees BTDC (automatic)
[5] @ 900 rpm with pressure regulator connected

[6] USA—BPR5EY11
Calif—BPR4EY11
[7] Cold—0.006–0.010 in.
Hot—0.008–0.012 in.
[8] Cold—0.008–0.012 in.
Hot—0.010–0.014 in.
[9] Turbo engine
[10] Twin Cam engine
[11] ER Model—700 rpm
[12] See "Pressure Testing" in text
[13] See Underhood Sticker

FIRING ORDERS

NOTE: To avoid confusion, always replace spark plug wires one at a time.

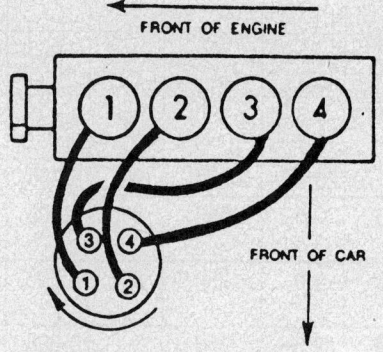

1.6L (Isuzu Twincam) Engine
Engine Code 6
Engine Firing Order: 1–3–4–2
Distributor Rotation: Clockwise

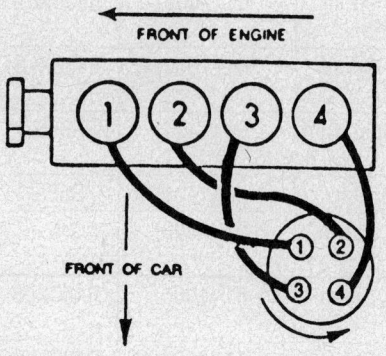

1.6L (Toyota Twincam) Engine
Engine Codes 5 and 6
Engine Firing Order: 1–3–4–2
Distributor Rotation: Counterclockwise

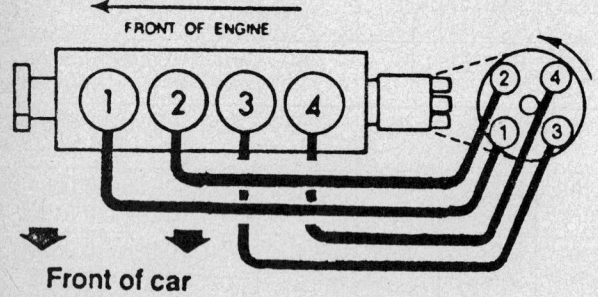

1.5L Engine
Engine Firing Order: 1–3–4–2
Distributor Rotation: Counterclockwise

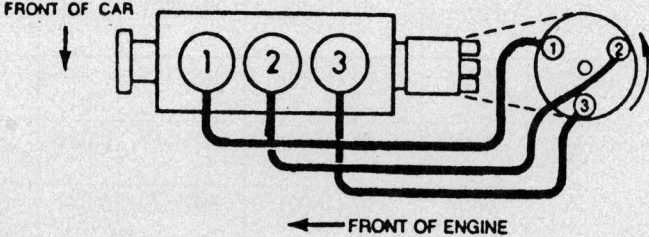

1.0L (Suzuki) Engine
Engine Firing Order: 1–3–2
Distributor Rotation: Counterclockwise

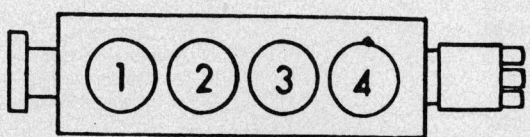

1.6L (Isuzu) Engine
Engine Code 5
Engine Firing Order: 1–3–4–2
Distributor Rotation: Clockwise

CAPACITIES

Year	Model	VIN	No. Cylinder Displacement cu. in. (liter)	Engine Crankcase (qts.) with Filter	Engine Crankcase (qts.) without Filter	Transmission (pts.) 4-Spd	Transmission (pts.) 5-Spd	Transmission (pts.) Auto.	Drive Axle (pts.)	Fuel Tank (gals.)	Cooling System (qts.)
1987	Sprint	5	3-61 (1.0)	3.5	3.5	—	4.8	9.5	—	8.3	4.5
	Sprint	2	3-61 (1.0)	3.5	3.5	—	4.8	9.5	—	8.3	4.5
	Spectrum	7	4-90 (1.5)	3.4	3.0	—	5.8	12.2	—	11.0	7.5
	Spectrum	9	4-90 (1.5)	3.4	3.0	—	5.8	12.2	—	11.0	7.5
	Nova	4	4-97 (1.6)	3.5	3.2	—	5.4	11.6	—	13.2	6.3
1988	Sprint	5	3-61 (1.0)	3.5	3.5	—	4.8	9.5	—	8.3	4.5
	Sprint	2	3-61 (1.0)	3.5	3.5	—	4.8	9.5	—	8.3	4.5
	Spectrum	7	4-90 (1.5)	3.4	3.0	—	5.8	12.2	—	11.0	7.5
	Spectrum	9	4-90 (1.5)	3.4	3.0	—	5.8	12.2	—	11.0	7.5
	Nova	4	4-97 (1.6)	3.5	3.2	—	5.4	11.6	—	13.2	6.4
	Nova	5	4-97 (1.6)	3.9	3.6	—	5.4	16.6	—	13.2	6.3
1989	Metro	6	3-61 (1.0)	3.7	3.7	—	4.8	9.6	—	8.7	4.5
	Spectrum	7	4-90 (1.5)	3.4	3.0	—	4.0	13.8	—	11.0	6.8
	Prizm	6	4-97 (1.6)	3.4	3.2	—	5.8	11.6	—	13.0	6.3
1990-91	Metro	6	3-61 (1.0)	3.7	3.7	—	5.0	10.4	—	10.0	①
	Prizm	6	4-97 (1.6)	3.4	3.2	—	12.0	②	3.0⑦	13.2	③
	Prizm	5	4-97 (1.6)	3.9	3.6	—	12.0	②	3.0⑦	13.2	③
	Storm	6	4-97 (1.6)	3.5	3.1	—	4.0	13.6	3.0	12.4	④
	Storm	5	4-97 (1.6)	4.2	3.8	—	5.4	⑥	3.0	12.4	⑤

① 4.1 qts Manual Transaxle
  4.2 qts Automatic Transaxle
② 11.6 pts 3 speed Automatic
  12.2 pts 4 speed Automatic
③ 6.0 qts Manual Transaxle
  5.8 qts Automatic Transaxle
④ 7.1 qts Manual Transaxle
  7.6 qts Automatic Transaxle

⑤ 7.3 qts Manual Transaxle
  7.8 qts Automatic Transaxle
⑥ 11.6 pts 3 speed Automatic
  15.2 pts 4 speed Automatic
⑦ 3 Speed Automatic Transaxle only

CAMSHAFT SPECIFICATIONS

All measurements given in inches.

Year	VIN	No. Cylinder Displacement cu. in. (liter)	Journal Diameter 1	Journal Diameter 2	Journal Diameter 3	Journal Diameter 4	Journal Diameter 5	Lobe Lift In.	Lobe Lift Ex.	Bearing Clearance	Camshaft End Play
1987	2	3-61 (1.0)	1.7372–1.7381	1.7451–1.7460	1.7530–1.7539	1.7609–1.7618	—	1.512	1.512	0.0029	—
	5	3-61 (1.0)	1.7372–1.7381	1.7451–1.7460	1.7530–1.7539	1.7609–1.7618	—	1.512	1.512	0.0029	—
	7	4-90 (1.5)	1.0210–1.0220	1.0210–1.0220	1.0210–1.0220	1.0210–1.0220	1.021–1.022	1.426	1.426	0.0024–0.0044	0.0039–0.0071
	9	4-90 (1.5)	1.0210–1.0220	1.0210–1.0220	1.0210–1.0220	1.0210–1.0220	1.021–1.022	1.426	1.426	0.0024–0.0044	0.0039–0.0071
	4	4-97 (1.6)	1.1015–0.1022	1.1015–0.1022	1.1015–0.1022	1.1015–0.1022	—	1.541 ①	1.541 ①	0.0015–0.0029	0.0031–0.0071

CAMSHAFT SPECIFICATIONS

All measurements given in inches.

Year	VIN	No. Cylinder Displacement cu. in. (liter)	Journal Diameter					Lobe Lift		Bearing Clearance	Camshaft End Play
			1	2	3	4	5	In.	Ex.		
1988	2	3-61 (1.0)	1.7372–1.7381	1.7451–1.7460	1.7530–1.7539	1.7609–1.7618	—	1.512	1.512	0.0029	—
	5	3-61 (1.0)	1.7372–1.7381	1.7451–1.7460	1.7530–1.7539	1.7609–1.7618	—	1.512	1.512	0.0029	—
	7	4-90 (1.5)	1.0210–1.0220	1.0210–1.0220	1.0210–1.0220	1.0210–1.0220	1.021–1.022	1.426	1.426	0.0024–0.0044	0.0039–0.0071
	9	4-90 (1.5)	1.0210–1.0220	1.0210–1.0220	1.0210–1.0220	1.0210–1.0220	1.021–1.022	1.426	1.426	0.0024–0.0044	0.0039–0.0071
	4	4-97 (1.6)	1.1015–0.1022	1.1015–0.1022	1.1015–0.1022	1.1015–0.1022	—	1.541 ①	1.541 ①	0.0015–0.0029	0.0031–0.0071
	5	4-97 (1.6)	1.0610–0.0616	1.0610–0.0616	1.0610–0.0616	1.0610–0.0616	1.061–1.062	1.399–1.400	1.399–1.400	0.0014–0.0028	0.0031–0.0075
1989	6	3-61 (1.0)	1.0220–1.0228	1.1795–1.1803	1.1795–1.1803	—	—	1.560 2.566	1.560 2.566	0.0008–0.0024	—
	7	4-90 (1.5)	1.0210–1.0220	1.0210–1.0220	1.0210–1.0220	1.0210–1.0220	1.021–1.022	1.426	1.426	0.0024–0.0044	0.00394–0.0071
	6	4-97 (1.6)	0.9822	0.9035	0.9035	0.9035	—	1.370	1.359	0.0014–0.0028	0.0043
1990–91	6	3-61 (1.0)	1.0220–1.0228	1.1795–1.1803	1.1795–1.1803	—	—	1.560 2.566	1.560 2.566	0.0008–0.0024	—
	5 ②	4-97 (1.6)	0.9822	0.9035	0.9035	0.9035	—	1.370	1.359	0.0014–0.0028	0.0043
	6 ②	4-97 (1.6)	1.0610–1.0616	1.0610–1.0616	1.0610–1.0616	1.0610–1.0616	—	1.394–1.398	1.394–1.398	0.0014–0.0028	0.0031–0.0075
	5 ③	4-97 (1.6)	1.0157	1.0157	1.0157	1.0157	—	1.503	1.503	0.0059	0.008
	6 ③	4-97 (1.6)	1.0157	1.0157	1.0157	1.0157	—	1.426	1.426	0.0059	0.008

① Minimum lobe height
② Prizm
③ Storm

CRANKSHAFT AND CONNECTING ROD SPECIFICATIONS

All measurements are given in inches.

Year	VIN	No. Cylinder Displacement cu. in. (liter)	Crankshaft				Connecting Rod		
			Main Brg. Journal Dia.	Main Brg. Oil Clearance	Shaft End-play	Thrust on No.	Journal Diameter	Oil Clearance	Side Clearance
1987	2	3-61 (1.0)	①	0.0012	0.0044–0.0122	3	1.6532	0.0012–0.0190	NA
	5	3-61 (1.0)	①	0.0012	0.0044–0.0122	3	1.6532	0.0012–0.0190	NA
	7	4-90 (1.5)	1.8865–1.8873	0.0008–0.0020	0.0024–0.0095	2	1.5720–1.5726	0.0010–0.0023	0.0079–0.0138
	9	4-90 (1.5)	1.8865–1.8873	0.0008–0.0020	0.0024–0.0095	2	1.5720–1.5726	0.0010–0.0023	0.0079–0.0138
	4	4-97 (1.6)	1.8892–1.8898	0.0006–0.0019 ②	0.0008–0.0073	3	1.5742–1.5748	0.0008–0.0020	0.0059–0.0089

CRANKSHAFT AND CONNECTING ROD SPECIFICATIONS

All measurements are given in inches.

Year	VIN	No. Cylinder Displacement cu. in. (liter)	Crankshaft				Connecting Rod		
			Main Brg. Journal Dia.	Main Brg. Oil Clearance	Shaft End-play	Thrust on No.	Journal Diameter	Oil Clearance	Side Clearance
1988	2	3-61 (1.0)	①	0.0012	0.0044–0.0122	3	1.6532	0.0012–0.0190	NA
	5	3-61 (1.0)	①	0.0012	0.0044–0.0122	3	1.6532	0.0012–0.0190	0.0039–0.780
	7	4-90 (1.5)	1.8865–1.8873	0.0008–0.0020	0.0024–0.0095	2	1.5720–1.5726	0.0010–0.0023	0.0079–0.0138
	9	4-90 (1.5)	1.8865–1.8873	0.0008–0.0020	0.0024–0.0095	2	1.5720–1.5726	0.0010–0.0023	0.0079–0.0138
1989	6	3-61 (1.0)	①	0.0012	0.0044–0.0122	3	1.6529–1.6535	0.0012–0.019	NA
	7	4-90 (1.5)	1.8865–1.8873	0.0008–0.0020	0.0024–0.0095	2	1.5526	0.0009–0.0229	0.0079–0.0138
	6	4-97 (1.6)	1.8865–1.8873	0.0006–0.0013	0.0008–0.0073	3	1.5420–1.5748	0.0008–0.0020	0.0059–0.0098
1990–91	6	3-61 (1.0)	①	0.0012	0.0044–0.0122	3	1.6529–1.6535	0.0012–0.019	NA
	6④	4-97 (1.6)	1.8891–1.8898	0.0006–0.0013	0.0008–0.0073	3	1.6529–1.6535	0.0006–0.0013	0.0059–0.0098
	5④	4.97 (1.6)	1.8891–1.8898	0.0006–0.0013	0.0008–0.0073	3	1.5742–1.5748	0.0006–0.0013	0.0059–0.0098
	5③	4-97 (1.6)	2.0440–2.0448	0.00079–0.00199	0.0024–0.0095	2	1.5722–1.5728	0.00098–0.00229	0.0059–0.0078
	6③	4-97 (1.6)	2.0440–2.0448	0.00079–0.00189	0.0024–0.0095	2	1.5724–1.5728	0.00074–0.00185	0.0079–0.0138

NA Not available
① Bearing cap stamped
  No. 1—1.7710–1.7712
  No. 3—1.7712–1.7714
  No. 2—1.7714–1.7716
  No. 4—1.7710–1.7712
② Maximum clearance—0.0039
③ Storm
④ Prizm

VALVE SPECIFICATIONS

Year	VIN	No. Cylinder Displacement cu. in. (liter)	Seat Angle (deg.)	Face Angle (deg.)	Spring Test Pressure (lbs.)	Spring Installed Height (in.)	Stem-to-Guide Clearance (in.)		Stem Diameter (in.)	
							Intake	Exhaust	Intake	Exhaust
1987	2	3-61 (1.0)	45	45	60	1.63	0.0014	0.0020	0.2745	0.2740
	5	3-61 (1.0)	45	45	60	1.63	0.0014	0.0020	0.2745	0.2740
	7	4-90 (1.5)	45	45	47 @ 1.57	1.57	0.0009–0.0022	0.0012–0.0025	0.2740–0.2750	0.2740–0.2744
	9	4-90 (1.5)	45	45	47 @ 1.57	1.57	0.0009–0.0022	0.0012–0.0025	0.2740–0.2750	0.2740–0.2744
	4	4-97 (1.6)	45	44.5	46.3	1.52	0.0010–0.0024	0.0012–0.0026	0.2744–0.2750	0.2742–0.2748

VALVE SPECIFICATIONS

Year	VIN	No. Cylinder Displacement cu. in. (liter)	Seat Angle (deg.)	Face Angle (deg.)	Spring Test Pressure (lbs.)	Spring Installed Height (in.)	Stem-to-Guide Clearance (in.)		Stem Diameter (in.)	
							Intake	Exhaust	Intake	Exhaust
1988	2	3-61 (1.0)	45	45	60	1.63	0.0014	0.0020	0.2745	0.2740
	5	3-61 (1.0)	45	45	60	1.63	0.0014	0.0020	0.2745	0.2740
	7	4-90 (1.5)	45	45	47 @ 1.57	1.57	0.0009–0.0022	0.0012–0.0025	0.2745–0.2750	0.2740–0.2744
	9	4-90 (1.5)	45	45	47 @ 1.57	1.57	0.0009–0.0022	0.0012–0.0025	0.2745–0.2750	0.2740–0.2744
	5	4-97 (1.6)	45	44.5	32.2	1.366	0.0010–0.0024	0.0012–0.0026	0.2350–0.2356	0.2348–0.2354
	4	4-97 (1.6)	45	44.5	46.3	1.52	0.0010–0.0024	0.0012–0.0026	0.2744–0.2750	0.2742–0.2748
1989	6	3-61 (1.0)	45	45	44 @ 1.28	—	0.0008–0.0021	0.0014–0.0024	0.2148–0.2151	0.2146–0.2151
	7	4-90 (1.5)	45	45	47 @ 1.57	1.57	0.0009–0.0022	0.0118–0.0025	0.2740–0.2750	0.2740–0.2744
	6	4-97 (1.6)	45	45.5	32.2	1.36	0.0031	0.0039	0.2350–0.2356	0.2348–0.2354
1990–91	6	3-61 (1.0)	45	45	44 @ 1.28	—	0.0008–0.0021	0.0014–0.0024	0.2148–0.2151	0.2146–0.2151
	5①	4-97 (1.6)	45	45.5	32.2	1.36	0.0031	0.0039	0.2350–0.2356	0.2348–0.2354
	6①	4-97 (1.6)	45	45.5	—	—	0.0010–0.0024	0.0012–0.0026	0.2350–0.2356	0.2348–0.2354
	6②	4-97 (1.6)	45	45.5	—	—	0.0009	0.0018	0.2335	0.2335
	5②	4-97 (1.6)	45	45	—	—	0.0009	0.0018	0.2335	0.2335

① Prizm
② Storm

PISTON AND RING SPECIFICATIONS

All measurements are given in inches.

Year	VIN	No. Cylinder Displacement cu. in. (liter)	Piston Clearance	Ring Gap			Ring Side Clearance		
				Top Compression	Bottom Compression	Oil Control	Top Compression	Bottom Compression	Oil Control
1987	5	3-61 (1.0)	0.0008–0.0015	0.0079–0.0129	0.0079–0.0137	0.0079–0.0275	0.0012–0.0027	0.0008–0.0023	—
	2	3-61 (1.0)①	0.0008–0.0015	0.0079–0.0119	0.0079–0.0119	0.0079–0.0237	0.0012–0.0030	0.0008–0.0023	—
	5	3-61 (1.0)	0.0008–0.0015	0.0079–0.0157	②	0.0079–0.0275	0.0012–0.0027	—	—
	7	4-90 (1.5)	0.0011–0.0019	0.0098–0.0138	②	0.0039–0.0236	0.0010–0.0026	—	—
	9	4-90 (1.5)	0.0011–0.0019	0.0106–0.0153	0.0098–0.0145	0.0039–0.0236	0.0010–0.0026	0.0008–0.0024	Snug
	4	4-97 (1.6)	0.0035–0.0043	0.0098–0.0185	0.0059–0.0165	0.1180–0.4020	0.0160–0.0031	0.0012–0.0028	

PISTON AND RING SPECIFICATIONS
All measurements are given in inches.

| Year | VIN | No. Cylinder Displacement cu. in. (liter) | Piston Clearance | Ring Gap | | | Ring Side Clearance | | |
				Top Compression	Bottom Compression	Oil Control	Top Compression	Bottom Compression	Oil Control
1988	5	3-61 (1.0)	0.0008–0.0015	0.0079–0.0129	0.0079–0.0137	0.0079–0.0275	0.0012–0.0027	0.0008–0.0023	—
	2	3-61 (1.0)	0.0008–0.0015	0.0079–0.0119	0.0079–0.0119	0.0079–0.0237	0.0012–0.0030	0.0008–0.0023	—
	5	3-61 (1.0) ①	0.0008–0.0015	0.0079–0.0157	②	0.0079–0.0275	0.0012–0.0027	—	—
	7	4-90 (1.5)	0.0011–0.0019	0.0098–0.0138	②	0.0039–0.0236	0.0010–0.0026	—	—
	9	4-90 (1.5)	0.0011–0.0019	0.0106–0.0153	0.0098–0.0145	0.0039–0.0236	0.0010–0.0026	0.0008–0.0024	—
	4	4-97 (1.6)	0.0035–0.0043	0.0098–0.0185	0.0059–0.0165	0.1180–0.4020	0.0160–0.0031	0.0012–0.0028	Snug
	5	4-97 (1.6)	0.0039–0.0047	0.0098–0.0138	0.0078–0.0118	0.0059–0.0031	0.0016–0.0031	0.0012–0.0028	Snug
1989	6	3-61 (1.0)	0.0008–0.0015	0.0079–0.0129	0.0079–0.0137	0.0079–0.0275	0.0012–0.0027	0.0008–0.0023	—
	7	4-90 (1.5)	0.0011–0.3500	0.2500–0.3500	—	—	0.0009–0.0026	—	—
	6	4-97 (1.6)	0.0024–0.0031	0.0098–0.0138	0.0059–0.0118	0.0039–0.0236	0.0016–0.0031	0.0012–0.0028	—
1990–91	6	3-61 (1.0)	0.0008–0.0015	0.0079–0.0129	0.0079–0.0137	0.0079–0.0275	0.0012–0.0027	0.0008–0.0023	—
	6④	4-97 (1.6)	0.0011–0.0019	0.0110–0.0157	0.0177–0.0236	0.0039–0.0236	0.00117–0.00315	0.00078–0.00236	—
	5④	4-97 (1.6)	0.0024–0.0031	0.0110–0.0157	0.0177–0.0236	0.0039–0.0236	0.0012–0.0032	0.0008–0.0024	—
	6③	4-97 (1.6)	0.0039–0.0047	0.0098–0.0185	0.0079–0.0165	0.0059–0.0205	0.0012–0.0028	0.0012–0.0028	0.0039–0.0236
	5③	4-97 (1.6)	0.0024–0.0031	0.0098–0.0138	0.0059–0.0118	0.0039–0.0236	0.0016–0.0031	0.0012–0.0028	—

① ER model
② ER model has only one compression ring
③ Prizm
④ Storm

TORQUE SPECIFICATIONS
All readings in ft. lbs.

| Year | VIN | No. Cylinder Displacement cu. in. (liter) | Cylinder Head Bolts | Main Bearing Bolts | Rod Bearing Bolts | Crankshaft Pulley Bolts | Flywheel Bolts | Manifold | | Spark Plugs |
								Intake	Exhaust	
1987	2	3-61 (1.9)	48	38	25	50	44	17	17	20
	5	3-61 (1.0)	48	38	25	50	44	17	17	20
	7	4-90 (1.5)	②	65	25	108	22 ①	17	17	18
	9	4-90 (1.5)	②	65	25	108	22 ①	17	17	18
	4	4-97 (1.6)	43	43	29	80–94	55–61	15–21	15–21	20

TORQUE SPECIFICATIONS
All readings in ft. lbs.

Year	VIN	No. Cylinder Displacement cu. in. (liter)	Cylinder Head Bolts	Main Bearing Bolts	Rod Bearing Bolts	Crankshaft Pulley Bolts	Flywheel Bolts	Manifold Intake	Manifold Exhaust	Spark Plugs
1988	2	3-61 (1.9)	48	38	25	50	44	17	17	20
	5	3-61 (1.0)	48	38	25	50	44	17	17	20
	7	4-90 (1.5)	②	65	25	108	22①	17	17	18
	9	4-90 (1.5)	②	65	25	108	22①	17	17	18
	4	4-97 (1.6)	43	43	29	87	58	20	18	13
	5	4-97 (1.6)	③	44	36	101	58	20	18	13
1989	6	3-61 (1.0)	54	40	26	8	45	17	17	18
	7	4-90 (1.5)	②	65	25	108	22①	17	17	18
	6	4-97 (1.6)	44	44	36	87	58④	14	18	20
1990-91	6	3-61 (1.0)	54	40	26	8	45	17	17	18
	6	4-97 (1.6)⑤	44	44	36	87	58④	20	18	13
	5⑤	4-97 (1.6)	44	44	36	87	58④	14	18	20
	6⑥	4-97 (1.6)	58	44	11⑦	87	22⑦	17	30	—
	5	4-97 (1.6)⑥	58	44	11⑦	87	22⑦	17	30	—

① Tighten an additional 45 degrees after torquing
② 1st step—29 ft. lbs.; 2nd step—58 ft. lbs.
③ 1st—Torque in sequence to 22 ft. lbs.
   2nd—Torque in sequence another 1/4 turn
   3rd—Torque in sequence another 1/4 turn
④ With automatic transaxle, 47 ft. lbs.
⑤ Prizm
⑥ Storm
⑦ Plus 45–60 Degree turn

BRAKE SPECIFICATIONS
All measurements in inches unless noted.

Year	Model	Lug Nut Torque (ft. lbs.)	Master Cylinder Bore	Brake Disc Minimum Thickness	Brake Disc Maximum Runout	Standard Brake Drum Diameter	Minimum Lining Thickness Front	Minimum Lining Thickness Rear
1987	Sprint	29–50	0.825	0.315	0.0028	7.09	0.315①	0.110①
	Spectrum	65	0.810	0.378	0.0059	7.09	0.039	0.039
	Nova	76	NA	0.492	0.0059	7.87	0.039	0.039
1988	Sprint	29–50	0.825	0.315	0.0028	7.09	0.315①	0.110①
	Spectrum	65	0.810	0.378	0.0059	7.09	0.039	0.039
	Nova	76	NA	0.492	0.0059	7.87	0.039	0.039
1989	Metro	41	0.825	0.315	0.0040	7.09	0.315	0.110①
	Spectrum	65	0.810	0.378	0.0059	7.09	0.039	0.039
	Prizm	76	NA	0.669	0.0035	7.87	0.030	0.039
1990-91	Metro	41	0.825	0.315	0.0040	7.09	0.315	0.110①
	Prizm	76	NA	0.669	0.0035	7.87	0.030	0.039
	Storm	87	NA	0.669	0.0035	7.87	0.030	0.039

NA Not available
① Lining plus shoe rim

WHEEL ALIGNMENT

Year	Model	Caster Range (deg.)	Caster Preferred Setting (deg.)	Camber Range (deg.)	Camber Preferred Setting (deg.)	Toe-in (in.)	Steering Axis Inclination (deg.)
1987	Sprint	—	$3^3/_{16}$	—	$1/_4$	0	$12^3/_{16}$
	Spectrum	$1^3/_4$P–$2^3/_4$P	$2^1/_4$P	$7/_{16}$N–$1^1/_{16}$P	$11/_{32}$P	$0+^1/_{16}$	① ②
	Nova	$1/_8$–$1^1/_2$P	$7/_8$	$1/_4$N–$3/_4$P	$1/_2$N	0.04–0.08	—
1988	Sprint	—	$3^3/_{16}$	—	$1/_4$	0	$12^3/_{16}$
	Spectrum	$1^3/_4$P–$2^3/_4$P	$2^1/_4$P	$7/_{16}$N–$1^1/_{16}$P	$11/_{32}$P	$0+^1/_{16}$	① ②
	Nova	$1/_8$–$1^2/_3$P	$9/_{10}$P	$3/_4$N–$1/_4$P	$1/_4$N	0–0.078	—
	Nova Twincam	1N–$1^1/_2$P	$1/_4$P	$3/_4$N–$1/_4$P	$1/_4$N	0–0.078	—
1989	Metro	1P–5P	3P	1N–1P	0	0	$25^{11}/_{16}$
	Spectrum	$1^3/_4$P–$2^3/_4$P	$2^1/_4$P	$11/_{16}$N–$1^5/_{16}$P	$5/_{16}$	0	16
	Prizm	$11/_{16}$P–$2^3/_{16}$P ③	$1^7/_{16}$P	$9/_6$N–$1^5/_{16}$P	$3/_{16}$	$3/_{64}$	NA
	Prizm	$9/_{16}$P–$2^1/_8$P ④	$1^5/_{16}$P	$1/_2$N–1P	$1/_4$	$3/_{64}$	NA
1990–91	Metro	1P–5P	3P	1N–1P	0	0	$25^{11}/_{16}$
	Prizm	$11/_{16}$P–$2^3/_{16}$P ③	$1^7/_{16}$P	$9/_6$N–$1^5/_{16}$P	$3/_{16}$	$3/_{64}$	NA
	Prizm	$9/_{16}$P–$2^1/_8$P ④	$1^5/_{16}$	$1/_2$N–1P	$1/_4$	$3/_{64}$	NA
	Storm	2P–4P	3P	1N–$1/_4$P	$3/_8$N	0	$10^3/_{16}$

① Inside—37°40' full lock
② Outside—32°30' full lock
③ Manual transaxle
④ Automatic transaxle

ENGINE ELECTRICAL

NOTE: Disconnecting the negative battery cable on some vehicles may interfere with the functions of the on board computer systems and may require the computer to undergo a relearning process, once the negative battery cable is reconnected.

Distributor

Removal

NOVA, PRIZM AND STORM

Except Twincam Engine

The distributor uses vacuum and centrifugal advances for spark timing control. The voltage introduced into the pickup coil turns the ignition module on and off. The ignition module turns the ignition coil on and off creating high voltage for the spark plugs.

1. Disconnect the negative terminal from the battery.
2. Remove the No. 1 spark plug. Place your finger in the spark plug hole and rotate the crankshaft (clockwise) until air is being forced from the cylinder; this is the TDC of the No. 1 cylinder compression stroke. Align the crankshaft pulley notch with the **0** degrees mark on the timing plate.
3. Disconnect the distributor wire from the connector.
4. Disconnect the hoses and the vacuum advance unit.
5. Disconnect the distributor cap and move it aside.
6. Using a piece of chalk, make alignment marks of the distributor housing-to-engine block and the rotor-to-distributor housing.
7. Remove the distributor hold-down bolt(s) and the distributor from the engine; the rotor must be rotated slightly to remove the distributor.

Twincam Engine

The distributor uses an electronic spark advance ESA system. The voltage introduced into the pick-up coils is monitored by the electronic control module ECM. The program within the ECM decides when to, using the collected data from the various sensors, turns the igniter module on and off at precisely the right moment.

1. Disconnect the negative terminal from the battery. Disconnect the spark plug wires from the spark plugs and the ignition coil.
2. Disconnect the distributor wire from the connector.
3. Scribe alignment marks on the distributor housing-to-engine block and the rotor-to-distributor housing.
4. Remove the distributor-to-engine hold-down bolts.
5. Remove the distributor from the engine and the O-ring from the distributor; discard the O-ring.

SPECTRUM

1. Disconnect the negative battery terminal from the battery.

2. Remove the distributor cap.
3. Mark and remove all electrical leads and vacuum lines connected to the distributor assembly.
4. Mark the relationship of the rotor to the distributor housing and the distributor housing to the engine.
5. Remove the hold-down bolt, clamp and distributor.

SPRINT AND METRO

1. Disconnect the negative battery cable.
2. Disconnect the wiring harness at the distributor and the vacuum line at the distributor vacuum unit.
3. Remove the distributor cap.

NOTE: Mark the distributor body in reference to where the rotor is pointing. Mark the distributor hold-down bracket and cylinder head for a reinstallation location point.

4. Remove the hold-down bolt and the distributor from the cylinder head. Do not rotate the engine after the distributor has been removed.

Installation

TIMING NOT DISTURBED

Nova, Prizm and Storm – Except Twincam Engine

1. Use a new O-ring on the distributor housing, lubricate the drive gear teeth with engine oil, align the protrusion at the bottom of the distributor housing with the pin on the side of the distributor drive gear, mesh the gears and install the distributor.

NOTE: Ensure that alignment marks on the distributor housing-to-engine and the rotor-to-distributor housing align before installing distributor.

2. Install the distributor cap.
3. Connect all vacuum hoses and electrical connectors.
4. Connect the battery negative cable.
5. Check and/or adjust the ignition timing.

Nova, Prizm and Storm – Twincam Engine

1. Turn the distributor to align the driveshaft drilled mark with housing cavity.
2. Align the center of the distributor flange with the center of the cylinder head bolt hole, then, install the distributor.
3. Install the hold-down bolt and torque it to 14 ft. lbs.
4. Connect the spark plug wires and ignition coil wire.
5. Connect the distributor electrical connector.
6. Connect the battery negative cable. Check and/or adjust the ignition timing.

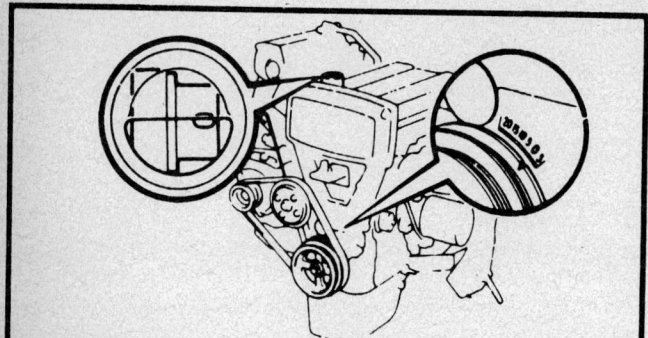

Aligning the crankshaft pulley and the camshaft cavity, twincam engine – Nova and Prizm

Aligning the distributor driveshaft with the housing twincam engine – Nova and Prizm

Spectrum

1. Align the marks on the distributor housing and the distributor housing-to-the engine, then install the distributor.
2. Connect all vacuum hoses and electrical connectors.
3. Install the distributor cap and spark plug wires.
4. Connect the battery negative cable. Check and/or adjust ignition timing.

Sprint and Metro

1. Align the reference marks on the distributor housing to the distributor hold-down bracket.
2. Install the distributor into the offset slot in the camshaft, then the hold-down bolt.
3. Connect vacuum hoses and electrical connectors to the distributor.
4. Install the distributor cap, then connect the battery negative cable. Check and/or adjust the ignition timing.

TIMING DISTURBED

Nova, Prizm and Storm—Except Twincam Engine

If the engine was cranked while the distributor was removed, will have to place the engine on TDC of the compression stroke to obtain the proper ignition timing.

1. Remove the No. 1 spark plug.
2. Place finger over the spark plug hole. Crank the engine slowly until compression is felt. It would be easier to have someone rotate the engine by hand, using a wrench on the crankshaft pulley.
3. Align the timing mark on the crankshaft pulley with the 0 degrees mark on the timing scale attached to the front of the engine. This places the engine at TDC of the compression stroke.
4. Turn the distributor shaft until the rotor points to the No. 1 spark plug tower on the cap.
5. Install the distributor into the engine. Be sure to align the distributor-to-engine block mark made earlier.
6. To complete the installation, reverse the removal procedures and check the timing.

Nova, Prizm and Stform—Twincam Engine

If the engine was cranked while the distributor was removed, you will have to place the engine on TDC of the compression stroke to obtain the proper ignition timing.

1. Remove the No. 1 spark plug.
2. Place thumb over the spark plug hole. Crank the engine slowly until compression is felt. It will be easier to have someone rotate the engine by hand, using a wrench on the crankshaft pulley.
3. Align the timing mark on the crankshaft pulley with the 0 degrees mark on the timing scale attached to the front of the engine. This places the engine at TDC of the compression stroke.
4. Turn the distributor shaft until the rotor points to the No. 1 spark plug tower on the cap.
5. Install the distributor into the engine. Be sure to align the distributor-to-engine block mark made earlier.
6. Install spark plug and wire.
7. Connect battery negative cable. Check and/or adjust ignition timing.

Spectrum

If the engine was cranked while the distributor was removed, you will have to place the engine on TDC of the compression stroke to obtain the proper ignition timing.

1. Remove the No. 1 spark plug.
2. Place thumb over the spark plug hole. Crank the engine slowly until compression is felt. It will be easier to have someone rotate the engine by hand, using a wrench on the crankshaft pulley.
3. Align the timing mark on the crankshaft pulley with the 0 degrees mark on the timing scale attached to the front of the en-

gine. This places the engine at TDC of the compression stroke.
4. Turn the distributor shaft until the rotor points to the No. 1 spark plug tower on the cap.
5. Install the distributor into the engine. Be sure to align the distributor-to-engine block mark made earlier.
6. Install the No. 1 spark plug and connect all vacuum hoses and electrical connectors.

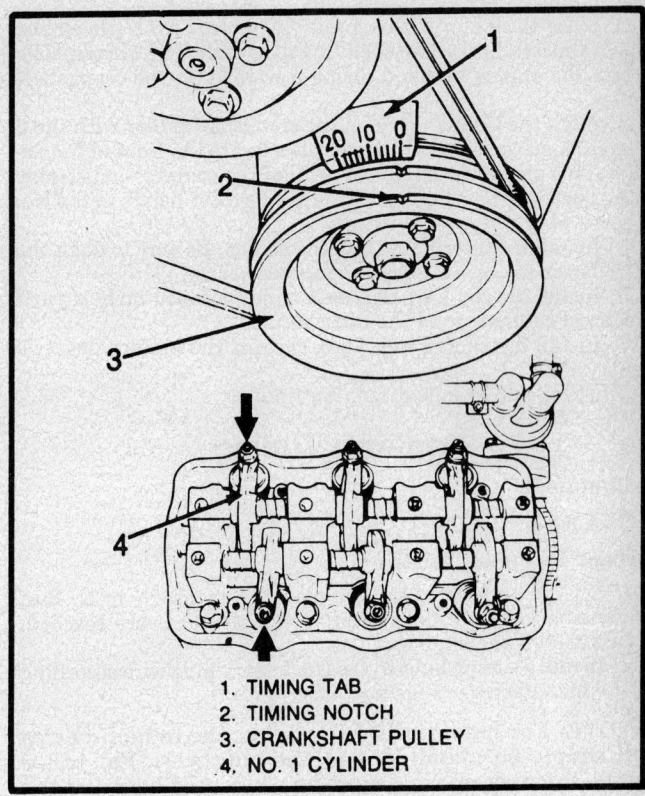

1. TIMING TAB
2. TIMING NOTCH
3. CRANKSHAFT PULLEY
4. NO. 1 CYLINDER

Timing mark and zero mark—Sprint and Metro

TIMING MARK

View of the timing marks—Spectrum

7. Install distributor cap, then connect the battery negative cable.

Check and/or adjust the ignition timing.

Sprint and Metro

If the engine was cranked while the distributor was removed, you will have to place the engine on TDC of the compression stroke to obtain the proper ignition timing.

1. Remove the No. 1 spark plug.

2. Place thumb over the spark plug hole. Crank the engine slowly until compression is felt. It will be easier to have someone rotate the engine by hand, using a wrench on the crankshaft pulley.

3. Align the timing mark on the crankshaft pulley with the **0** degrees mark on the timing scale attached to the front of the engine. This places the engine at TDC of the compression stroke.

4. Turn the distributor shaft until the rotor points to the No. 1 spark plug tower on the cap.

5. Install the distributor into the engine. Be sure to align the distributor-to-engine block mark made earlier.

6. Install the No. 1 spark plug. Connect all vacuum hoses and electrical connectors to the distributor.

7. Install distributor cap, then connect the battery negative cable.

8. Check and/or adjust ignition timing.

Ignition Timing

Adjustment
NOVA AND PRIZM

Except Twincam Engine

1. Set the parking brake and place the transaxle in **N**. Run the engine until normal operating temperatures are reached, then, turn off the engine.

2. Install a timing light to the No. 1 spark plug wire according to the manufacturer's instructions.

NOTE: For inductive timing lights, the induction clip can simply be installed over the plug wire. For other lights, the pick-up wire must be connected between the spark plug boot and the spark plug. Connect a tachometer according to the manufacturer's instructions.

3. Disconnect and plug the distributor-to-intake manifold vacuum hoses.

4. Loosen the distributor flange hold-down bolt to finger tight.

5. Start the engine, then, check and/or adjust the engine rpm; it should be 750 or less.

6. Aim the timing light at the scale on the timing cover near the front pulley; the timing should be 0 degrees BTDC. If the timing is not correct, turn the distributor slightly to correct it. Once the reading is correct, tighten the hold-down bolt and recheck the timing.

7. Stop the engine, remove the timing light, then, unplug and reconnect the distributor vacuum hoses.

NOVA

Twincam Engine

1. Firmly apply the parking brake and place the transaxle in the **N** detent.

2. Run the engine until normal operating temperatures are reached, then, stop the engine.

3. Using a jumper wire, connect it to the check engine connector located near the wiper motor.

4. Using a timing light, connect it to the No. 1 spark plug wire. Loosen the distributor hold-down bolt until it is finger tight.

5. Start the engine, then check and/or adjust the idle speed; it should be 800 rpm.

6. Aim the timing light at the timing cover plate near the crankshaft pulley; the notch on the crankshaft pulley should align the 10 degrees BTDC timing mark on the timing plate.

7. To adjust the engine timing, turn the distributor slightly to align the marks, then, tighten the hold-down bolt and recheck the timing.

8. When the adjustment is correct, remove the jumper wire from the check engine connector and recheck the timing marks. The timing should now be more than 16 degrees BTDC for manual transaxle or more than 12 degrees BTDC for automatic transaxle.

PRIZM

1. Firmly apply the parking brake and place the transaxle in the **N** detent.

2. Connect a tachometer to the battery and the diagnostic connector. Do not ground the tachometer terminal.

3. Run the engine until normal operating temperatures are reached, then stop the engine.

4. Remove the diagnostic connector cap and insert a jumper wire between terminals **E1** and **T**.

5. Using a timing light, connect it to the No. 1 spark plug wire. Loosen the distributor hold-down bolt until it is finger tight.

6. Start the engine, then, check and/or adjust the idle speed; it should be 700 rpm.

7. Aim the timing light at the timing cover plate near the crankshaft pulley; the notch on the crankshaft pulley should align with the specified timing mark on the timing plate. Use the timing specification noted on the underhood sticker.

8. To adjust the engine timing, turn the distributor slightly to align the marks, then, tighten the hold-down bolt and recheck the timing.

9. When the adjustment is correct, remove the jumper wire from diagnostic connector and install the cap.

10. Disconnect the ACV connector.

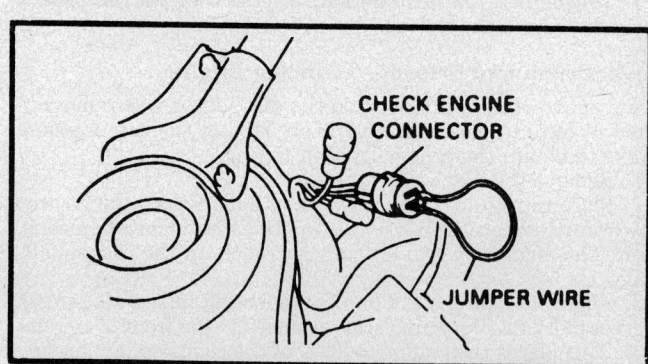

Using a jumper wire to short the check engine connector—Twincam engine—Nova and Prizm

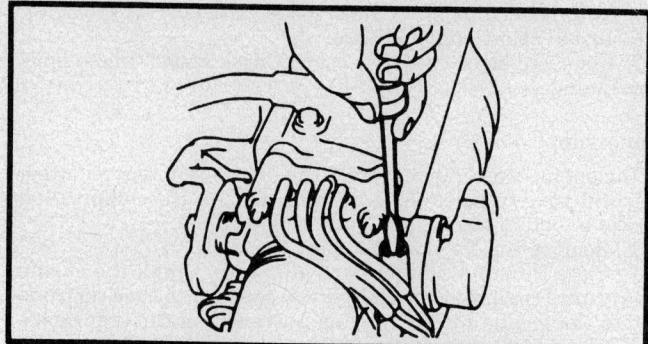

Adjusting the idle speed screw—twincam engine—Nova and Prizm

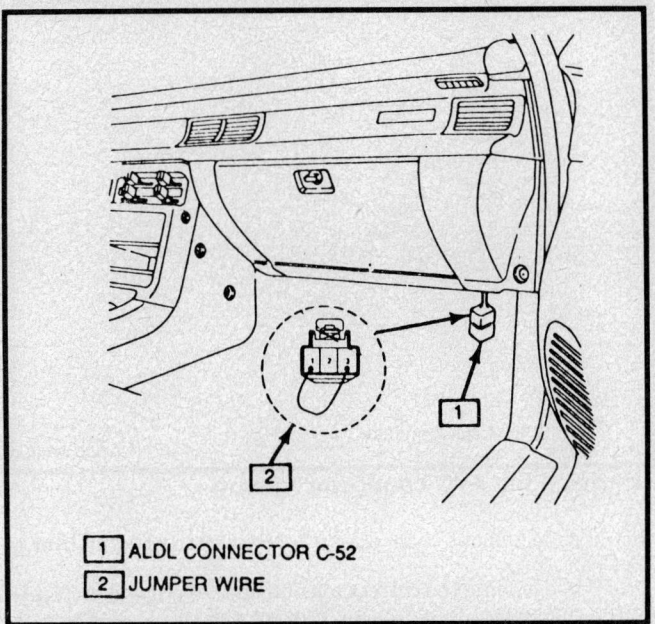

1 ALDL CONNECTOR C-52
2 JUMPER WIRE

ALDL connector location – Storm

11. Recheck the timing marks. The timing should now be 10 degrees BTDC.
12. Reconnect the ACV connector.
13. Disconnect the timing light.

STORM

1. Apply the parking brake and place the transaxle in the **N** detent.
2. Connect a tachometer to the battery and the diagnostic connector. Do not ground the tachometer terminal.
3. Run the engine until normal operating temperatures are reached, then stop the engine.
4. Connect a jumper wire between terminals 1 and 3 on the ALDL connector (located under the right hand instrument panel).
5. Using a timing light, connect it to the No. 1 spark plug wire. Loosen the distributor hold-down bolt until it is finger tight.
6. Start the engine, then, check and/or adjust the idle speed; it should be 700 rpm.
7. Aim the timing light at the timing cover plate near the crankshaft pulley; the notch on the crankshaft pulley should align with the specified timing mark on the timing plate. Use the timing specification noted on the underhood sticker.
8. To adjust the engine timing, turn the distributor slightly to align the marks, then, tighten the hold-down bolt and recheck the timing.
9. When the adjustment is correct, remove the jumper wire from the ALDL connector.
10. Disconnect the timing light.

SPECTRUM

1. Set the parking brake and block the wheels.
2. Place the manual transaxle in **N** or the automatic transaxle in the **P** detent.
3. Allow the engine to reach normal operating temperature. Make sure the choke valve is open. Turn off all of the accessories.
4. If equipped with power steering, place the front wheels in a straight line.
5. Disconnect and plug the distributor vacuum line, the canister purge line, the EGR vacuum line and the ITC valve vacuum line at the intake manifold.

6. Connect a timing light to the No. 1 spark plug wire and a tachometer to the tachometer filter connector on the coil, tachometer filter is mounted near distributor hold-down bolt.

NOTE: Check the idle speed and adjust as needed.

7. Loosen the distributor flange bolt.
8. Using the timing light, align the notch on the crankshaft pulley with the mark on the timing cover by turning the distributor.

NOTE: Adjust the timing to 15 degrees BTDC at 750 rpm for manual transaxle or 10 degrees BTDC at 1000 rpm forautomatic transaxle.

9. After the timing marks have been aligned, tighten the distributor flange bolt, then reinstall all vacuum lines.

SPRINT AND METRO

Before setting timing , make sure the headlights, heater fan, engine cooling fan and any other electrical equipment is turned off. If any current drawing systems are operating, the idle up system will operate and cause the idle speed to be higher than normal.

1. Connect a tachometer to the negative terminal of the ignition coil. Connect a timing light to the No. 1 spark plug wire. Refer to the underhood sticker.
2. Start and run the engine until it reaches normal operating temperature.
3. Check and/or adjust the idle speed. Correct speed should be 750 rpm for engines with manual transaxle and 850 rpm on engines with automatic transaxles.

NOTE: To adjust the idle speed, turn the throttle adjustment screw on the carburetor.

4. With the engine at the proper idle speed, aim the timing light at the crankshaft pulley and timing marks. The **V** timing mark on the pulley should be at the 10 degrees BTDC mark on the timing plate.

NOTE: To adjust the ignition timing, loosen the distributor hold-down bolt and rotate the distributor. When the V mark and the 10 degree mark are aligned, tighten the distributor hold-down bolt and recheck the timing.

5. With the timing adjusted, stop the engine and remove the testing equipment.

Alternator

Precautions

Several precautions must be observed with alternator equipped vehicles to avoid damage to the unit.
• If the battery is removed for any reason, make sure it is reconnected with the correct polarity. Reversing the battery connections may result in damage to the one-way rectifiers.
• When utilizing a booster battery as a starting aid, always connect the positive to positive terminals and the negative terminal from the booster battery to a good engine ground on the vehicle being started.
• Never use a fast charger as a booster to start vehicles.
• Disconnect the battery cables when charging the battery with a fast charger.
• Never attempt to polarize the alternator.
• Do not use test lamps of more than 12 volts when checking diode continuity.
• Do not short across or ground any of the alternator terminals.

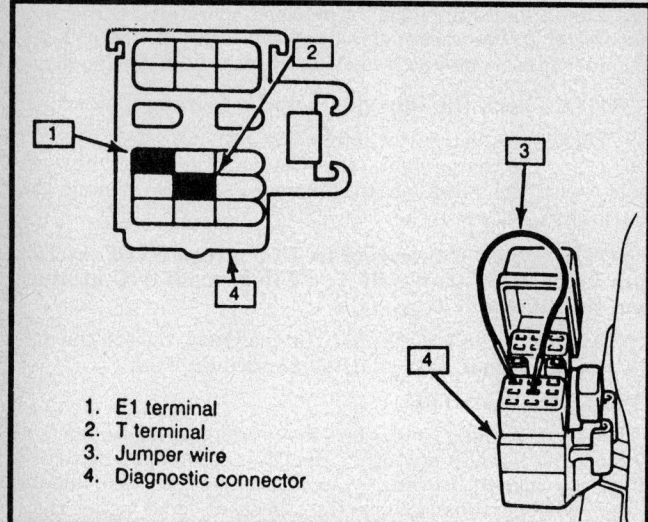

1. E1 terminal
2. T terminal
3. Jumper wire
4. Diagnostic connector

Diagnostic connector with jumper wire—Prizm

- The polarity of the battery, alternator and regulator must be matched and considered before making any electrical connections within the system.
- Never separate the alternator on an open circuit. Make sure all connections within the circuit are clean and tight.
- Disconnect the battery ground terminal when performing any service on electrical components.
- Disconnect the battery if arc welding is to be done on the vehicle.

Belt Tension Adjustment

NOVA

The belt tension on most components is adjusted by moving the components, alternator, within the range of the slotted bracket. Check the belt tension every 12 months or 10,000 miles. Push in on the drive belt about midway between the crankshaft pulley and the driven component. If the belt deflects more than $^9/_{16}$ in., adjustment is required.

1. Loosen the adjustment nut and bolt in the slotted bracket. Slightly loosen the pivot bolt.
2. Pull the component outward to increase tension. Push inward to reduce tension. Tighten the adjusting nut/bolt and the pivot bolt.
3. Recheck the drive belt tension and readjust, if necessary.

SPECTRUM

NOTE: The following procedure requires the use of GM belt tensuion gauge tool BT–33–95–ACBN, regular V-belts, or BT–33–97M, poly V-belts.

1. If the belt is cold, operate the engine, at idle speed, for 15 minutes; the belt will seat itself in the pulleys allowing the belt fibers to relax or stretch. If the belt is hot, allow it to cool, until it is warm to touch.

NOTE: A used belt is one that has been rotated at least 1 complete revolution on the pulleys. This begins the belt seating process and it must never be tensioned to the new belt specifications.

2. Loosen the component-to-mounting bracket bolts.
3. Using a GM belt tension gauge, place the gauge at the center of the belt between the longest span.
4. Applying belt tension pressure on the component, adjust the drive belt tension to the correct specification. Belt tension

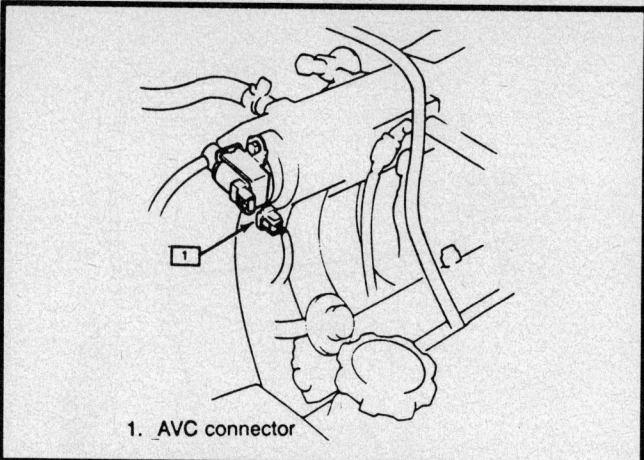

1. AVC connector

Removing the AVC connector—Prizm

should deflect about ¼ in. over a 7–10 in. span or ½ in. over a 13–16 in. span.

5. While holding the correct tension on the component, tighten the component-to-mounting bracket bolt.
6. When the belt tension is correct, 70–110 inch lbs., remove the tension gauge.

PRISM AND STORM

1. Disconnect the battery negative cable.
2. Place a suitable belt tension gauge on the belt.
3. Belt tension should be 110–150 inch lbs. on a old belt and 140–180 inch lbs. on a new belt.
4. If specifications are not as indicated, loosen the upper and lower alternator belt and adjust as necessary.
5. Connect the battery negative cable.

SPRINT AND METRO

1. Disconnect the negative battery cable.
2. Place a suitable belt tension gauge on the belt.
3. Adjust the drive belt to have $^1/_4$–$^3/_8$ in. play on the longest run of the drive belt.

Removal and Installation

NOVA AND PRIZM

1. Disconnect the negative terminal from the battery.
2. Label and disconnect each alternator wiring connector.
3. Loosen the alternator adjusting lockbolt, located in the slotted bar at the bottom of the unit, and the hinge nut/bolt, located at the top of the unit. Turn the adjusting bolt to shift the alternator toward the block ansd remove the drive belt.
4. Remove the adjusting bolt, the hinge nut/bolt and the alternator.
5. To install, reverse the removal procedures.

NOTE: The drive belt serrations run along the length of the belt. Make sure serrations align with indentations on the pulleys; all serrations must ride inside the pulley surface.

SPECTRUM

1. Disconnect the negative battery terminal from the battery.

NOTE: Failure to disconnect the negative cable may result in injury from the positive battery lead at the alternator and may short the alternator and regulator during the removal process.

2. Disconnect and label the 2 terminal plug and the battery leads from the rear of the alternator.

3. Loosen the mounting bolts. Push the alternator inwards and slip the drive belt off the pulley.

4. Remove the mounting bolts and remove the alternator.

To install:

5. Place the alternator in its brackets and install the mounting bolts. Do not tighten them yet.

6. Slip the belt back over the pulley. Pull outwards on the unit and adjust the belt tension. Tighten the mounting and adjusting bolts.

7. Install the electrical leads and the negative battery cable.

STORM

1. Disconnect the battery negative cable and remove the belt adjusting bolt from the alternator.

2. Raise and support vehicle and remove the right undercover.

3. Remove the alternator belt, then tag and disconnect electrical leads from the alternator.

4. Remove alternator mounting bracket-to-engine block attaching bolts, then the alternator and bracket from the vehicle.

SPRINT AND METRO

1. Disconnect the negative battery cable.

2. Disconnect the wiring connectors from the back of the alternator.

3. Remove the adjusting arm mounting bolt, the lower pivot bolt and the drive belt.

4. Remove the alternator.

5. To install, reverse the removal procedures. Adjust the drive belt to have $\frac{1}{4}$–$\frac{3}{8}$ in. play on the longest run of the drive belt.

Starter

Removal and Installation
NOVA, PRIZM AND STORM

1. Disconnect the negative terminal from the battery.

2. Disconnect the electrical connectors from the starter terminals.

3. Remove the transaxle cable and bracket from the transaxle.

4. Remove the starter-to-engine bolts and the starter from the vehicle.

5. To install, reverse the removal procedures. Torque the starter-to-engine bolts to 29 ft. lbs.

SPECTRUM

1. Disconnect the negative battery terminal from the battery.

2. Disconnect the ignition switch lead wire and the battery cable from the starter motor terminal.

3. Remove the 2 mounting bolts from the starter and remove the starter.

4. To install, reverse the removal procedures.

SPRINT AND METRO

1. Disconnect the negative battery cable.

2. Disconnect the ignition switch wire and the battery cable from the starter.

3. Remove the 2 engine-to-starter mounting bolts and remove the starter.

4. To install, reverse the removal procedures.

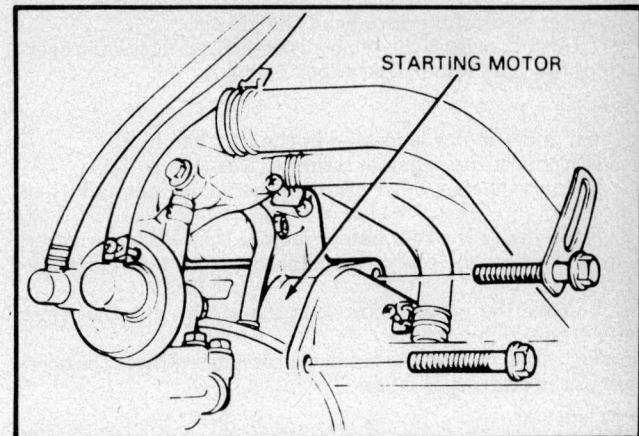

Starter motor mounting—Sprint and Metro

CHASSIS ELECTRICAL

--- **CAUTION** ---
On vehicles equipped with an air bag, the negative battery cable must be disconnected, before working on the system. Failure to do so may result in deployment of the air bag and possible personal injury.

Heater Blower Motor

Removal and Installation
NOVA

The heater blower motor is located inside the vehicle, behind the glove box.

1. Disconnect the negative battery cable. Remove the 3 heater assembly retainer-to-chassis screws.

2. Remove the glove box-to-chassis screws and the glove box.

3. Remove the duct-to-blower/heater assemblies screws and the duct; the duct is located between the blower and heater assemblies.

4. Disconnect the blower motor wiring connector and the air source selector control cable from the blower assembly case.

5. Remove the blower assembly-to-heater case nuts/bolt and blower assembly.

6. Separate the blower motor from the blower assembly.

7. To install, reverse the removal procedures and test the motor.

PRIZM AND STORM

The blower motor is located under the instrument panel at the far right side of the vehicle. It is accessible from below the instrument panel.

1. Disconnect the negative battery cable.

2. Disconnect the rubber air duct between the motor and the heater assembly.

3. Disconnect the electrical connector from the motor.

4. Remove the 3 screws retaining the motor and remove the motor.

5. Installation is the reverse of removal.

SPECTRUM

1. Disconnect the negative battery cable. Disconnect the blower motor electrical connector at the motor case.

2. If equipped with air conditioning, remove the rubber hose from the blower case.

3. Rotate the blower motor case counterclockwise and remove the blower motor assembly.

4. To install, reverse the removal procedures.

SPRINT AND METRO

1. Disconnect the negative battery cable.
2. Disconnect the defroster hose on the steering column side.
3. Disconnect the blower motor electrical connector.
4. Remove the 3 mounting screws and the blower motor.
5. To install, reverse the removal procedures.

Windshield Wiper Motor

Removal and Installation

NOVA, PRIZM AND STORM

Front

1. Disconnect the negative terminal from the battery.
2. From the engine compartment, disconnect the electrical connector from the windshield wiper motor.
3. Remove the wiper motor-to-chassis screws.
4. Disconnect the wiper motor from the windshield wiper crank arm; be careful not to bend the linkage.
5. To install, reverse the removal procedures. Check the operation of the front windshield wiper motor.

Rear

The rear wiper motor is located in the rear hatch.
1. Disconnect the negative terminal from the battery.
2. Remove the rear wiper arm-to-wiper motor nut and wiper arm.
3. From inside the rear hatch, remove the rear wiper cover, then, disconnect the electrical connector from the rear wiper motor.
4. Remove the wiper motor-to-hatch screws and the wiper motor from the hatch.
5. To install, reverse the removal procedures. Check the operation of the rear wiper motor.

SPECTRUM

Front

1. Disconnect the negative battery terminal from the battery.
2. Remove the locknuts retaining the wiper arms and the wiper arms.
3. Remove the cowl cover, wiper motor cover and the electrical connector.
4. Disconnect the drive arm from the wiper link.
5. Remove the mounting bolts and the wiper motor.
6. To install, reverse the removal procedures.

Rear

1. Disconnect the negative battery terminal from the battery.
2. Remove the trim pad and the wiper arm assemblies.
3. Remove the mounting bolts and the motor assembly.
4. Disconnect the electrical connector.
5. To install, reverse the removal procedures.

SPRINT AND METRO

Front

1. Disconnect the negative battery cable.
2. Disconnect the crank arm from the wiper motor.
3. Disconnect the electrical connector from the wiper motor.
4. Remove the wiper motor from the vehicle.
5. To install, reverse the removal procedures.

Rear

1. Disconnect the negative battery cable.
2. Remove the electrical connector from the rear wiper motor.

3. Remove the rear motor mounting bracket.
4. Disconnect the motor from the wiper linkage.
5. Remove the motor from the vehicle.
6. To install, reverse the removal procedures.

Windshield Wiper Switch

Removal and Installation

NOVA, PRIZM AND STORM

Front

The front wiper switch is located on the right-side of the combination switch attached to the steering column.
1. Disconnect the negative battery cable. Remove the wiper/cruise control assembly switch-to-combination switch screws and the switch assembly.
2. Trace the wiper/cruise control assembly switch wiring harness to the multi-connector. Using a scratch awl, push in the multi-connector lock levers and pull wires from the connector.
3. To install, reverse the removal procedures. Check the operation of the windshield wiper switch and the cruise control system.

Rear

1. Disconnect the negative terminal from the battery.
2. On the Nova, use a small prybar and pry the rear wiper switch from the front of the instrument panel.
3. On the Prizm and Storm, remove the trim bezel.
4. Disconnect the electrical connector from the rear wiper switch.
5. To install, reverse the removal procedures. Check the operation of the rear wiper switch.

SPECTRUM

Front

1. Disconnect the negative battery cable. Remove the the instrument cluster bezel.
2. Remove the wiper switch electrical connector, attaching nuts and bracket.
3. Remove the wiper switch.
4. To install, reverse the removal procedures.

Rear

1. Disconnect the negative battery cable. Using a small tool, pry the switch panel from the dash.
2. Pull the switch out and disconnect the electrical connector.
3. To install, reverse the removal procedures.

SPRINT AND METRO

1. Disconnect the negative battery cable.
2. Remove the steering column trim panel.
3. Lower the steering column.
4. Remove the cluster bezel and the bezel.
5. Disconnect the wiper switch connector.
6. Remove the wiper switch.
7. To install, reverse the removal procedures.

Instrument Cluster

Removal and Installation

NOVA

1. Disconnect the negative terminal from the battery.
2. If equipped with air conditioning, remove the air conditioning vents from each side of the instrument panel. Remove the meter hood-to-instrument panel screws and the hood.

NOTE: The meter hood is located above the instrument cluster.

3. Remove the instrument cluster-to-dash screws. Pull the

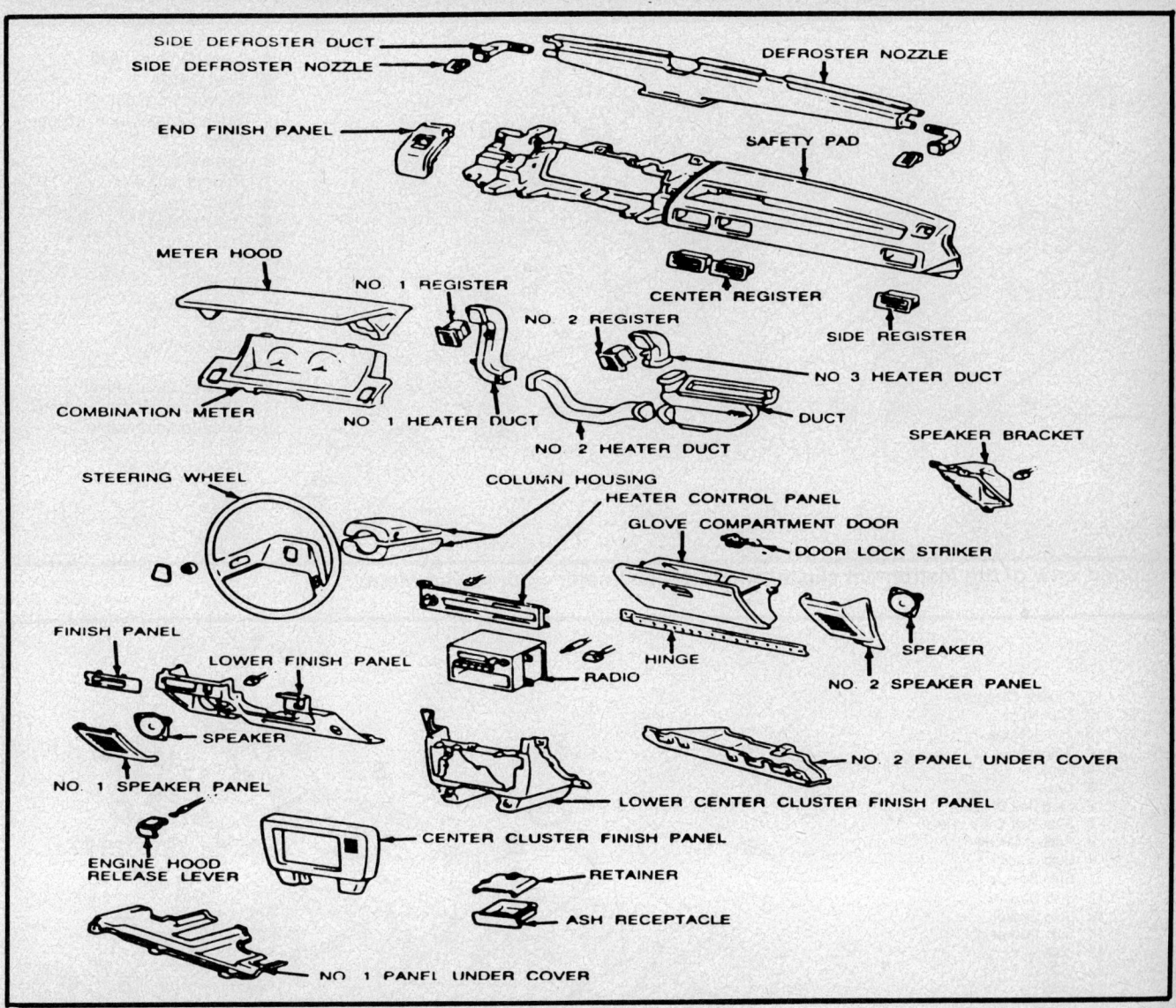

Exploded view of the instrument panel—Nova

instrument cluster forward, then, disconnect the speedometer cable and electrical connectors from the rear of the cluster. Remove the instrument cluster from the vehicle.

4. To install, reverse the removal procedures.

PRIZM

1. Disconnect the negative battery cable.

2. Remove the 2 attaching screws from the hood release lever and remove the lever.

3. Remove the lower left dash trim by removing the 4 attaching screws.

4. Disconnect the speaker wire.

5. Remove the air conditioning duct from the lower air conditioning regester.

6. Remove the left lower dash trim.

7. Remove the steering column covers by removing the 7 retaining screws.

8. Pull out the trim bezel after removing the 2 attaching screws.

9. Disconnect the cruise control/defogger switch from the electrical connector.

10. Disconnect any electrical connections from the trim bezel and remove the trim bezel.

11. Remove the 4 attaching screws from the cluster bezel.

12. Disconnect the electrical connectors from the hazard flasher and dimmer switches.

13. Remove the cluster bezel.

14. Remove the 4 attaching screws from the cluster.

15. Disconnect the speedometer cable and electrical connections from the cluster.

16. Remove the cluster from the vehicle.

17. Installation is the reverse of removal.

STORM

1. Disconnect battery negative cable and position ignition switch in the lock position.

2. Remove the 2 access covers on the meter hood and then the meter hood attaching screws.

3. Disconnect electrical connectors and remove the meter hood.

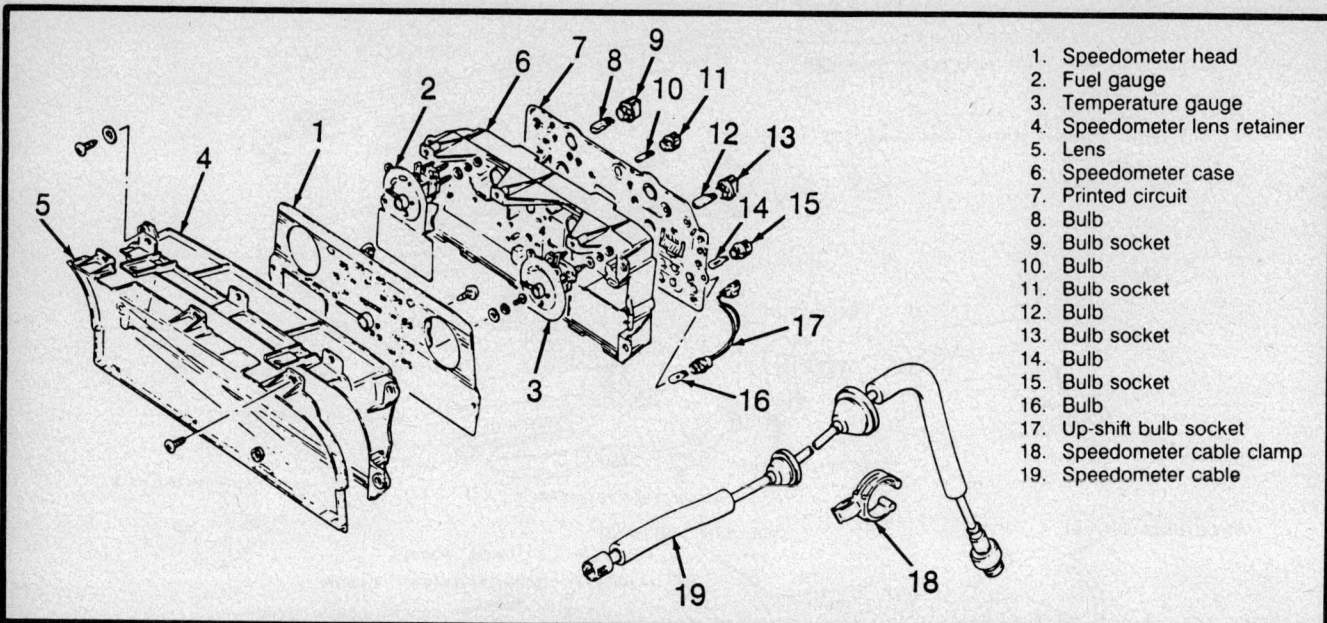

1. Speedometer head
2. Fuel gauge
3. Temperature gauge
4. Speedometer lens retainer
5. Lens
6. Speedometer case
7. Printed circuit
8. Bulb
9. Bulb socket
10. Bulb
11. Bulb socket
12. Bulb
13. Bulb socket
14. Bulb
15. Bulb socket
16. Bulb
17. Up-shift bulb socket
18. Speedometer cable clamp
19. Speedometer cable

Exploded view of the instrument cluster without tachometer—Sprint and Metro

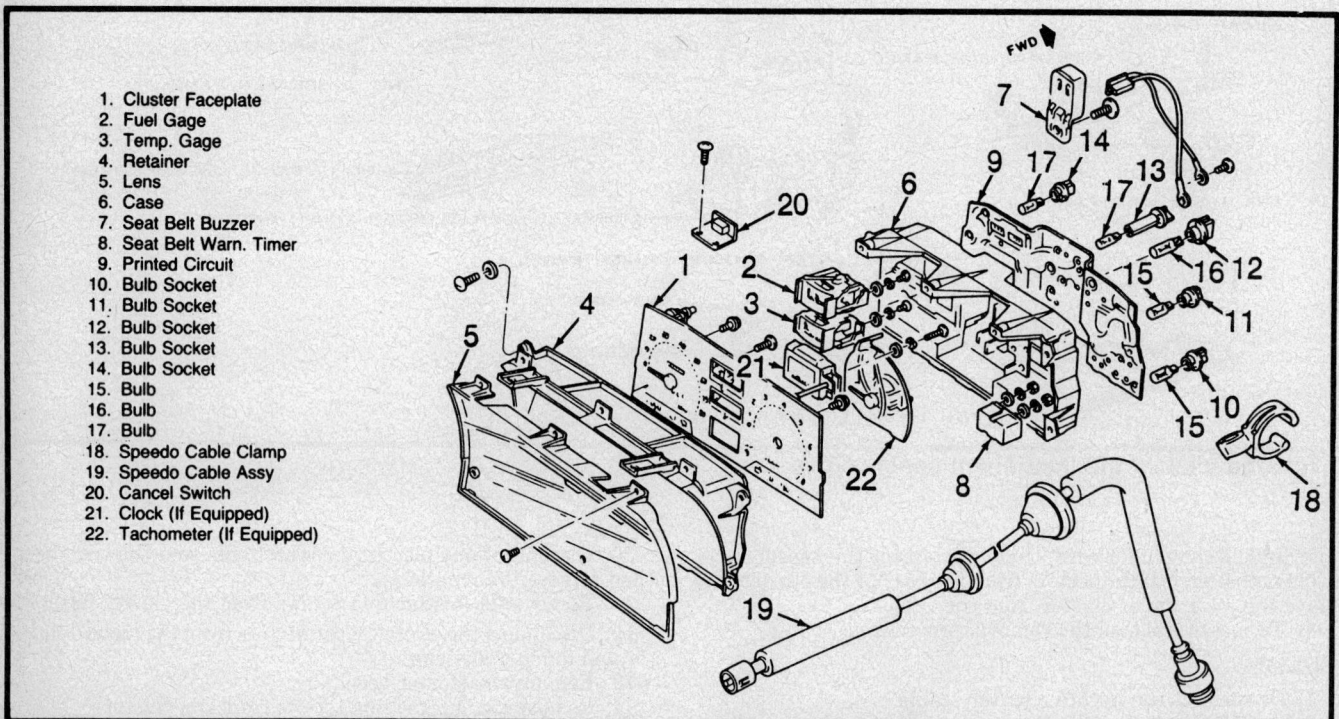

1. Cluster Faceplate
2. Fuel Gage
3. Temp. Gage
4. Retainer
5. Lens
6. Case
7. Seat Belt Buzzer
8. Seat Belt Warn. Timer
9. Printed Circuit
10. Bulb Socket
11. Bulb Socket
12. Bulb Socket
13. Bulb Socket
14. Bulb Socket
15. Bulb
16. Bulb
17. Bulb
18. Speedo Cable Clamp
19. Speedo Cable Assy
20. Cancel Switch
21. Clock (If Equipped)
22. Tachometer (If Equipped)

Exploded view of the instrument cluster with tachometer—Sprint and Metro

4. Remove the screws attaching the cluster and disconnect the electrical connectors.
5. Remove the cluster assembly.
6. Reverse procedure to install. Connect battery negative cable.

SPECTRUM
1. Disconnect the negative battery terminal from the battery.
2. Remove the instrument cluster bezel retaining screws and bezel.

3. Disconnect the windshield wiper and lighting switch connectors.
4. Remove the instrument cluster retaining screws and pull out the assembly.
5. Remove the trip reset knob and the assembly glass.
6. Remove the buzzer, sockets and bulbs.
7. Remove the speedometer assembly, fuel and temperature gauge.
8. Remove the tachometer, if equipped.

9. To install, reverse the removal procedures.

SPRINT AND METRO

1. Disconnect the negative battery cable.
2. Remove the steering column trim panel.
3. Lower the steering column.
4. Remove the cluster lens and the cluster mounting screws.
5. Disconnect the speedometer cable at the transaxle and at the instrument cluster.
6. Disconnect and mark the electrical connectors at the instrument cluster.
7. Remove the instrument cluster from the vehicle.
8. To install, reverse the removal procedures.

Headlight Switch

Removal and Installation

STORM

The headlight control switch is located at the left hand side of the instrument panel on the meter hood.

1. Disconnect the battery negative cable.
2. Remove the meter hood.
3. Remove the instrument cluster from the meter hood.
4. Remove the 2 clips attaching headlight control harness.
5. Remove the 4 screws attaching the headlight switch to the meter hood.
6. Disconnect electrical connectors from the switch and remove the switch.
7. Reverse procedure to install. Connect battery negative cable.

SPECTRUM

The headlight control switch is a 3 position, push type switch which is located at the left side of the instrument panel.

1. Disconnect the negative battery cable. Remove the instrument cluster bezel retaining screw and the bezel.
2. Disconnect the electrical connectors.
3. Place the bezel on a bench and remove the 2 nuts securing the headlight control switch.
4. Remove the headlight control switch.
5. To install, reverse the removal procedures.

SPRINT AND METRO

1. Disconnect the negative battery cable.
2. Remove the steering column trim panel.
3. Lower the steering column.
4. Remove the cluster bezel and the bezel.
5. Disconnect the headlight switch connector.
6. Remove the headlight switch.
7. To install, reverse the removal procedures.

Combination Switch

Removal and Installation

NOVA AND PRIZM

1. Disconnect the negative battery cable. Remove the steering wheel.
2. Remove the lower instrument finish panel, air duct and column lower cover.
3. From the base of the steering column shroud, disconnect the ignition switch and turn signal electrical connector.
4. Remove the combination switch-to-steering column screws and the combination switch with the upper column cover.
5. To install, reverse the removal procedures.

SPECTRUM

1. Disconnect the negative battery terminal from the battery.
2. Remove the horn shroud, steering wheel nut/washer and steering wheel assembly.

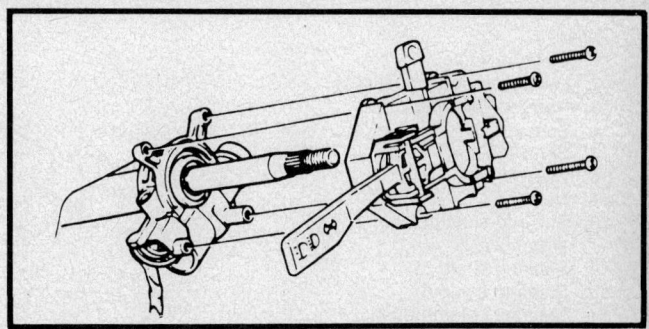

Turn signal/dimmer switch mounting – Sprint and Metro

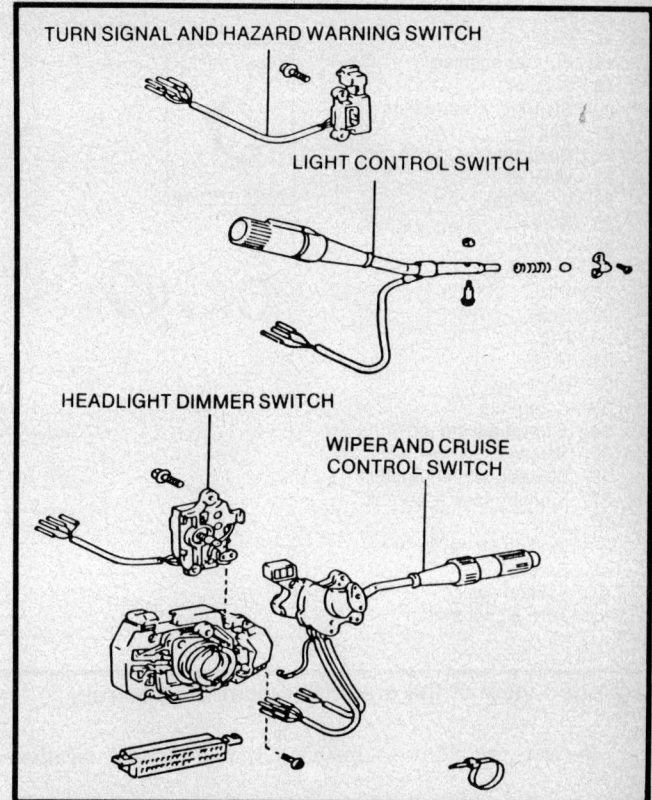

TURN SIGNAL AND HAZARD WARNING SWITCH

LIGHT CONTROL SWITCH

HEADLIGHT DIMMER SWITCH

WIPER AND CRUISE CONTROL SWITCH

Exploded view of the combination switch – Nova and Prizm

3. Remove the steering cowl attaching screw and steering cowl.
4. Disconnect the combination/starter switch connector.
5. Remove the turn signal/dimmer switch attaching screw and switch.
6. To install, reverse the removal procedures.

STORM

1. Disconnect the battery negative cable.
2. Remove the 4 bolts attaching the inflator module to the steering wheel. Disconnect the inflator module electrical connector.
3. Disconnect the electrical connector from the horn.
4. Remove the steering wheel nut and the steering wheel.
5. Remove the steering wheel cowl assembly and harness.
6. Remove the combination switch attaching screws, disconnect electrical connectors and the combination switch from the vehicle.

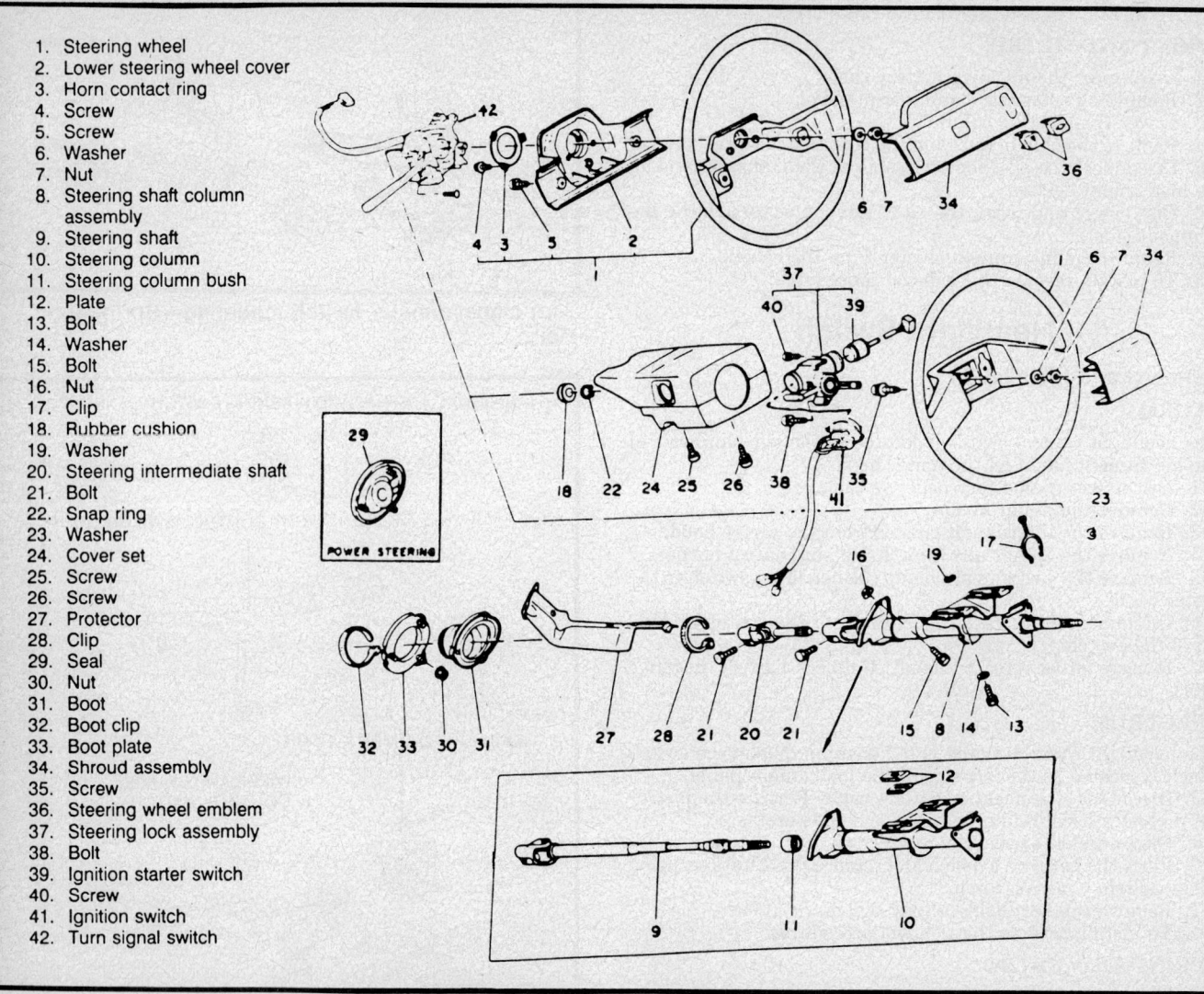

1. Steering wheel
2. Lower steering wheel cover
3. Horn contact ring
4. Screw
5. Screw
6. Washer
7. Nut
8. Steering shaft column assembly
9. Steering shaft
10. Steering column
11. Steering column bush
12. Plate
13. Bolt
14. Washer
15. Bolt
16. Nut
17. Clip
18. Rubber cushion
19. Washer
20. Steering intermediate shaft
21. Bolt
22. Snap ring
23. Washer
24. Cover set
25. Screw
26. Screw
27. Protector
28. Clip
29. Seal
30. Nut
31. Boot
32. Boot clip
33. Boot plate
34. Shroud assembly
35. Screw
36. Steering wheel emblem
37. Steering lock assembly
38. Bolt
39. Ignition starter switch
40. Screw
41. Ignition switch
42. Turn signal switch

Exploded view of the steering column—Spectrum

7. Reverse procedure to install. Connect battery negative cable.

SPRINT AND METRO

1. Disconnect the negative battery cable. Remove the steering wheel.
2. Remove the upper and lower steering column covers.
3. Disconnect electrical connectors.
4. Remove the screws and the turn signal/dimmer switch assembly from the steering column.
5. To install, reverse the removal procedures.

NOTE: **When installing, be careful that the lead wires do not get caught by the lower cover.**

Ignition Lock/Switch

Removal and Installation

NOVA AND PRIZM

1. Disconnect the negative battery cable. Remove the combination switch.
2. If equipped with a tilt steering column, perform the following procedures:

a. Remove the tension springs and grommets, the tilt lever (the bolt has left-hand threads), the adjusting nut/washer.
b. Pull out the lock bolt, then, remove the upper and lower column supports.
3. From the lower steering column, disconnect the ignition switch electrical connector.
4. Remove the retainer-to-upper bracket screws and the retainer from the upper bracket.
5. Using snapring pliers, remove the snapring from the upper bracket.
6. Insert the key into the ignition switch and release the steering lock.
7. Using a hammer and a pin punch, drive the tapered bolt from the upper bracket.
8. Remove the upper bracket-to-steering column tube bolts and the upper bracket.

To install:

9. Release the steering lock and install the upper bracket-to-steering column bolts, tighten the bolts finger tight. Torque the upper bracket-to-steering column bolts to 14 ft. lbs.
10. If installing the tilt steering mechanism, perform the following procedures:

a. Apply grease to the bushings and the O-rings, then, install the lower support-to-tube.

b. Using multi-purpose grease, apply it to the tilt bracket-to-steering column mating surfaces, then, install the upper support and lock bolt.

NOTE: If there is any play in the adjusting support, snug-up the adjusting nut.

c. Install the tilt lever. Move the lever to loosen the bracket-to-column bolt, adjust the column height and move the lever to lock the column position; if the lever is out of position, reposition the adjusting nut.

d. Install the tilt lever retaining screw (left-hand thread) and torque it. Install the tension springs and grommets.

11. To complete the installation, reverse the removal procedures.

SPECTRUM

1. Disconnect the negative battery cable. Remove the combination switch.

2. Insert the key into the ignition and place the key in the **ON** position, the lock bar must be pulled all the way in.

3. Remove the snapring and rubber cushion from the steering shaft.

4. Disconnect the switch wires at the connectors.

5. Remove the 2 screws retaining the ignition/starter switch and remove the switch.

6. To install, reverse the removal procedures.

STORM

1. Disconnect battery negative cable, place wheels in a straight ahead position and set ignition switch in the lock position.

2. Remove the 4 bolts attaching the inflator module to the steering wheel, disconnect the electrical connector and remove the inflator module.

3. Disconnect the horn electrical connector and remove the steering wheel nut.

4. Remove the steering wheel and the steering wheel cowl assembly.

5. Remove the steering wheel harness and the combination switch with coil assembly.

6. Remove the ignition switch snapring and rubber seal, then the ignition switch from the vehicle.

7. Reverse procedure to install. Connect battery negative cable.

SPRINT AND METRO

1. Disconnect the negative battery cable. Remove the steering column.

2. Place the column on a bench.

3. Using a sharp point center punch and a hammer, remove the steering lock mounting bolts.

4. Turn the ignition key to **ACC** or **ON** positions and remove the lock assembly from the steering column.

5. To install, reverse the removal procedures. After installing the lock, turn the key to **LOCK** position and pull out the key. Turn the steering shaft to make sure the shaft is locked. Install new mounting bolts to the lock housing, tighten until the bolt heads break off. Torque the lower bracket bolts to 8–12 ft. lbs.; the upper bracket bolts to 10 ft. lbs. and the steering shaft bolt to 15–22 ft. lbs.

Stoplight Switch

Removal and Installation

NOVA AND PRIZM

1. Disconnect the negative battery cable. Remove the lower instrument panel cover.

2. Disconnect the electrical connector from the stoplight switch.

3. Remove the stoplight switch-to-bracket nut and the switch.

4. To install, reverse the removal procedures. Adjust the switch so the stoplights turn with slight movement of the brake pedal.

SPECTRUM AND STORM

1. Disconnect the negative battery cable. Remove stoplight switch locknut.

2. Remove switch by pulling straight out of pedal assembly.

3. To install push switch straight in, push the brake pedal by

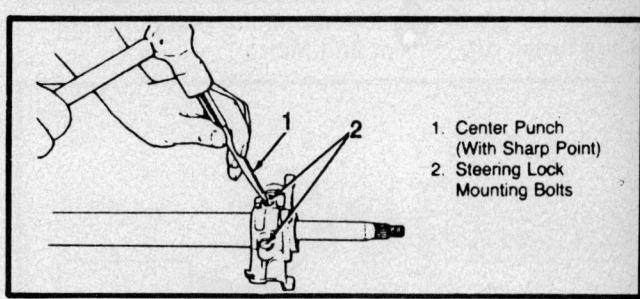

1. Center Punch (With Sharp Point)
2. Steering Lock Mounting Bolts

Removing the ignition switch/key lock assembly— Sprint and Metro

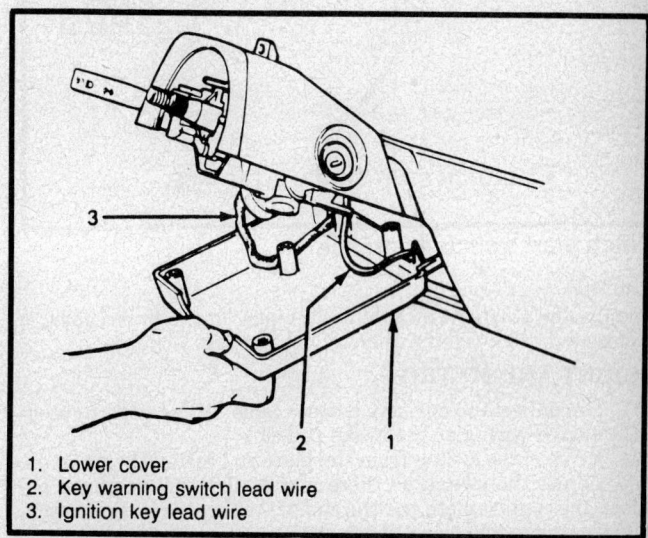

1. Lower cover
2. Key warning switch lead wire
3. Ignition key lead wire

Lower steering column cover—Sprint and Metro

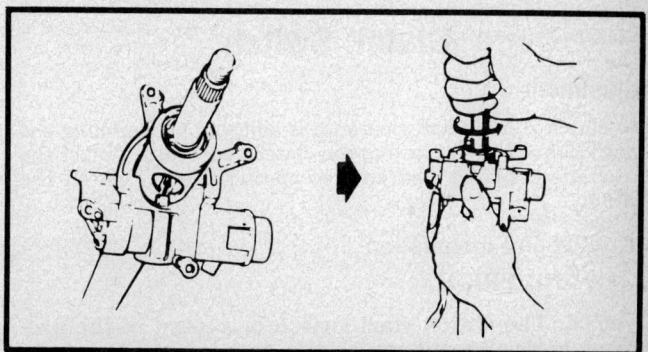

Align the slot in the steering shaft with the tab on the switch to install—Sprint and Metro

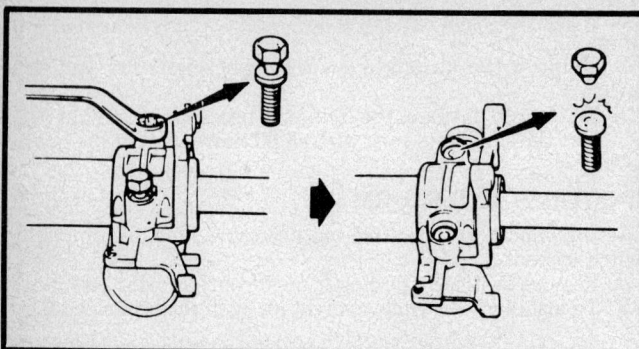

Tighten the ignition switch mounting bolts until the heads break off—Sprint and Metro

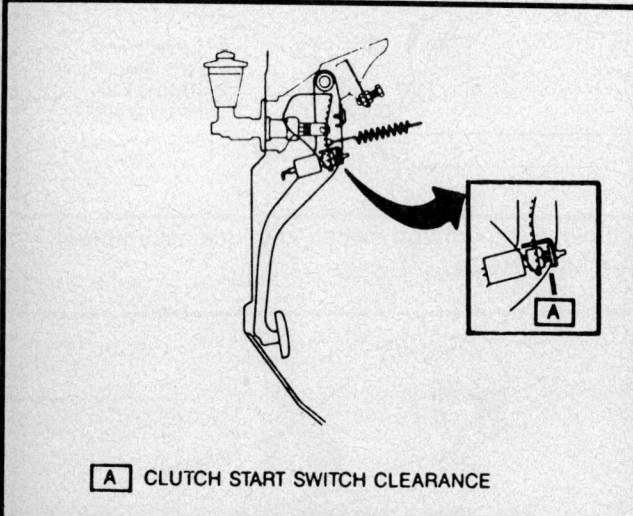

A CLUTCH START SWITCH CLEARANCE

Clutch start switch clearance

turning the stoplight switch, so free-play in the brake pedal is eliminated, then tighten the stoplight switch locknut.

SPRINT AND METRO

1. Disconnect the negative battery cable. Disconnect the stoplight switch wiring at the brake pedal.
2. Remove the switch from the plate and install the new one.
3. Adjust the switch so there is 0.02–0.04 in. clearance between the contact plate and the end of the threads on the switch. Tighten the locknut and check the clearance again.
4. Connect the battery cable and check that the stoplights are not on with the pedal in the resting position.

Clutch Switch

Adjustment

The clutch start switch clearance is adjusted by loosening the front locknut and depressing the clutch pedal fully. Adjust the clutch start switch clearance to specification. Tighten the locknut.

Removal and Installation
NOVA AND PRIZM

NOTE: The clutch start switch is located in the passenger compartment under the dash assembly on the drivers side of the vehicle. The clutch switch has no adjustment and must be replaced if found to be defective.

1. Disconnect the negative terminal from the battery.
2. Remove the necessary trim panels in order to gain access to the clutch switch retaining screws.
3. Remove the clutch switch retaining screws.
4. Pull the switch down from its retainer and disconnect the electrical connections.
5. To install, reverse the removal procedures.

SPECTRUM

1. Disconnect the negative battery terminal from the battery.
2. Disconnect the electrical connector from the switch.
3. Remove the clutch start switch-to-brake pedal stop bracket screw and the switch from the clutch pedal.
4. To install, reverse the removal procedures

SPRINT, METRO AND STORM

1. Disconnect the negative battery terminal from the battery.
2. Disconnect the electrical connector from the switch.
3. Loosen the locknut then unscrew the clutch start switch from the clutch pedal.
4. To install, reverse the removal procedures

Neutral Safety Switch

Adjustment
NOVA AND PRIZM

1. Loosen the neutral start switch bolts and set the shifter lever in the N position.
2. Disconnect the neutral start switch electrical connector.
3. Connect an ohmmeter between the terminals on the switch.
4. Adjust the switch to the point where there is continuity between the terminals.
5. Connect the neutral switch electrical connector. Torque switch bolts to 48 inch lbs. (5.4 Nm). Check switch operation.

STORM

1. Remove the intake air duct and air breather tube from the air cleaner assembly.
2. Loosen the neutral safety switch attaching screws.
3. Place selector lever in the N position.
4. Install a pin into the adjustment holes in both the neutral safety switch and the switch lever.
5. Torque the retaining screws to 26 inch lbs. (3 Nm).
6. Install the air breather tube and intake air duct onto the air cleaner assembly.

Removal and Installation
NOVA, PRIZM AND STORM

1. Disconnect the negative battery cable.
2. On Storm equipped with 4-speed transaxle, proceed as follows:
   a. Remove the intake air duct and breather tube from the air cleaner assembly.
   b. Disconnect the shift control cable from the selector cable.
   c. Remove the neutral safety switch attaching screws and disconnect electrical connectors.
   d. Remove the neutral safety switch. Reverse procedure to install. Adjust neutral safety switch, if necessary.
3. Disconnect the electrical connector at the switch.
4. Raise the vehicle and support it safely.
5. Remove the switch retaining bolts and remove the switch.
6. Installation is the reverse of removal. Align the groove and neutral basic line. Hold the switch in position and tighten the bolts to 48 inch lbs.
7. Check and make sure the engine starts in only the P and N detents.

SPECTRUM

1. Disconnect the negative battery cable.
2. Disconnect the electrical connector for the switch at the left fender.
3. Raise the vehicle and support it safely.
4. Remove the switch retaining bolts and remove the switch.
5. Installation is the reverse of removal. Add transaxle fluid as necessary.
6. Check and make sure the engine starts in only the **P** and **N** detents.

SPRINT AND METRO

These vehicles use a back drive system (solenoid) to keep the selector lever always in the **P** detent position when starting the engine with the ignition key.

1. Disconnect the negative battery cable.
2. Remove the solenoid to housing attaching screws.
3. Disconnect the solenoid wire and remove the solenoid.

To install:

4. Shift the selector lever to the **P** range.
5. Apply grease to the upper and lower edges of the lock plate before installing the back drive solenoid.
6. Position the solenoid to the housing and install the retaining screws hand tight.
7. Connect the solenoid wire.
8. Adjust the solenoid position so there is no clearance between the lock plate and the guide plate and tighten the retaining screws.

Fuses, Circuit Breakers and Relays

Location

FUSIBLE LINKS

Fusible links are located in the engine harness at the starter solenoid and the left hand front of the dash at the battery junction block.

CIRCUIT BREAKERS

The circuit breakers are located either in the switch or mounted on or near the lower lip of the instrument panel, to the right or left of the steering column.

FUSE PANEL

Nova and Prizm

The fuel panel is located on the left side of the vehicle behind the driver side kick panel.

Spectrum and Storm

The fuse panel is located at the lower left hand side of the instrument panel, concealed by a cover.

Sprint and Metro

The fuse panel is located on the underside of the steering column.

VARIOUS RELAYS

Nova and Prizm

Starter Relay—located at the front left side of the engine compartment.
Air Conditioning Relay—located at the front left side of the engine compartment.
Cooling Fan Relay—located at the front left side of the engine compartment.
Main Engine Relays—located at the front left side of the engine compartment.
Defogger Relay—located on the passenger side of the vehicle under the dash assembly.
Heater Relay—located on the passenger side of the vehicle under the dash assembly.

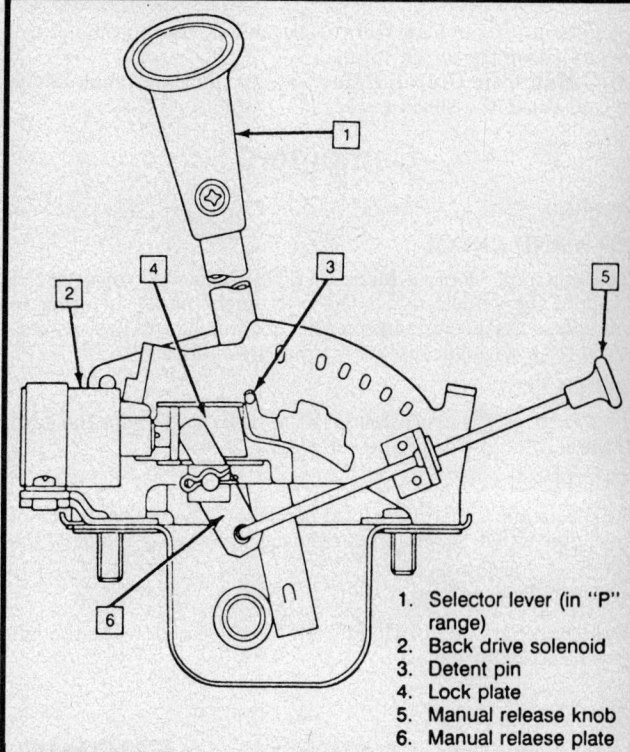

1. Selector lever (in "P" range)
2. Back drive solenoid
3. Detent pin
4. Lock plate
5. Manual release knob
6. Manual relaese plate

Back drive solenoid location—Sprint and Metro

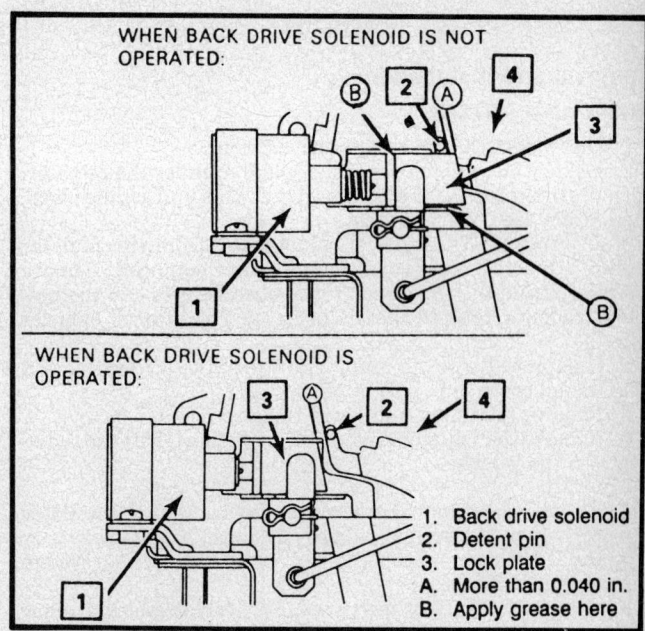

WHEN BACK DRIVE SOLENOID IS NOT OPERATED:

WHEN BACK DRIVE SOLENOID IS OPERATED:

1. Back drive solenoid
2. Detent pin
3. Lock plate
A. More than 0.040 in.
B. Apply grease here

Lock plate position–Sprint and Metro

Charge Light Relay—located on the passenger side of the vehicle under the dash assembly.
Seat Belt Relay—located on the passenger side of the vehicle under the dash assembly.
Tailight Relay—located behind the driver's side kick panel.

Spectrum and Storm

Various relays are attached to the brackets under the left-side of the dash. All units are easily replaced with plug-in modules.

Sprint and Metro

A/C Condenser Fan Relay—located on the left side of the firewall above the shock tower.

A/C Magnetic Clutch Relay—located on the left side of the firewall above the shock tower.

Computers

Location
NOVA AND PRIZM

The Electronic Control Module (ECM) is located towards the center of the vehicle under the instrument panel. In order to gain access to the electronic control module, it will first be necessary to remove various trim panel assemblies.

STORM

The Electronic Control Module (ECM) is located under the dash on the left hand side of the vehicle.

SPECTRUM

The Electronic Control Module (ECM) controls the operation of the engine and is located under the dash on the right side of the vehicle.

SPRINT AND METRO

The Electronic Control Module (ECM) is located inside the left hand instrument panel.

Flashers

Location
NOVA AND PRIZM

The turn signal flasher is located on the driver's-side kick panel. In order to gain access to the unit, it will be necessary to first remove certain under dash padding.

STORM

The turn signal and hazard flasher are located above the fuse box, under the left hand dash panel.

SPECTRUM

The turn signal flasher is located behind the instrument panel, on the left-hand side of the steering column. Replacement is accomplished by unplugging the old flasher and inserting a new one.

The hazard flasher is located behind the instrument panel, on the left-hand side of the steering column. Replacement is accomplished by unplugging the old flasher and inserting a new one.

SPRINT AND METRO

The flasher is located near the junction/fuse block, under the left hand side of the instrument panel.

ENGINE COOLING

Radiator

Removal and Installation
NOVA AND PRIZM

1. Disconnect the battery negative cable.
2. Using a clean catch container, place it under the radiator, open the drain cock in the lower radiator tank and engine block, then, drain the cooling system.
3. Disconnect the electrical connector(s) from the radiator cooling fan and the air conditioning fan, if equipped. Remove the fan shroud, the top 4 radiator-to-chassis bolts and the bottom 2 radiator tank-to-chassis bolts, air conditioned vehicles only.
4. If equipped with an automatic transaxle, disconnect and plug the oil cooler hoses from the radiator.
5. Remove the upper and lower radiator hoses.
6. Remove the radiator hold-down brackets and lift the radiator from the vehicle.
To install:
7. Reverse the removal procedure. Ensure that the radiator fits properly in the bottom rubber cushions.
8. Refill both the automatic transaxle and cooling system with approved fluids.
9. Connect the battery negative cable. Start engine and allow to reach normal operating temperature and check for leaks.

SPECTRUM

1. Disconnect the battery negative cable.
2. Drain the cooling system.
3. Remove the air intake duct.
4. Remove the fan motor cable from the fan motor socketand disconnect the thermo-switch cable.
5. Remove the fan motor assembly.
6. Remove the radiator hoses at the radiator, the coolant recovery hose at the filler neck and the oil cooler lines, if equipped with automatic transaxle.

7. Remove the radiator attaching bolts and the radiator.
8. Reverse procedure to install. Connect the battery negative cable.

STORM

1. Disconnect the battery negative cable.
2. Drain cooling system.
3. If equipped with automatic transaxle, disconnect the oil cooler lines from the radiator.
4. Remove the upper and lower radiator hoses.
5. Disconnect the fan motor cable from the rear of the fan motor socket.
6. Remove the coolant recovery hose from the radiator filler neck.
7. Remove the radiator attaching bolts and the radiator with fan and motor assembly from the vehicle.
8. Reverse procedure to install. Connect the battery negative cable and refill system. start engine and check for leaks.

SPRINT AND METRO

1. Disconnect the battery negative cable.
2. Drain the cooling system.
3. Disconnect the cooling fan motor electrical connector and the air inlet hose.
4. Remove the inlet, outlet and the reservoir tank hoses from the radiator.
5. Remove the mounting bolts, cooling fan motor, shroud and the radiator from the vehicle.
6. Reverse procedure to install. Connect the battery negative cable and refill system.

Electric Cooling Fan

Testing
NOVA, PRIZM AND STORM

1. Disconnect the electrical connector from the cooling fan.

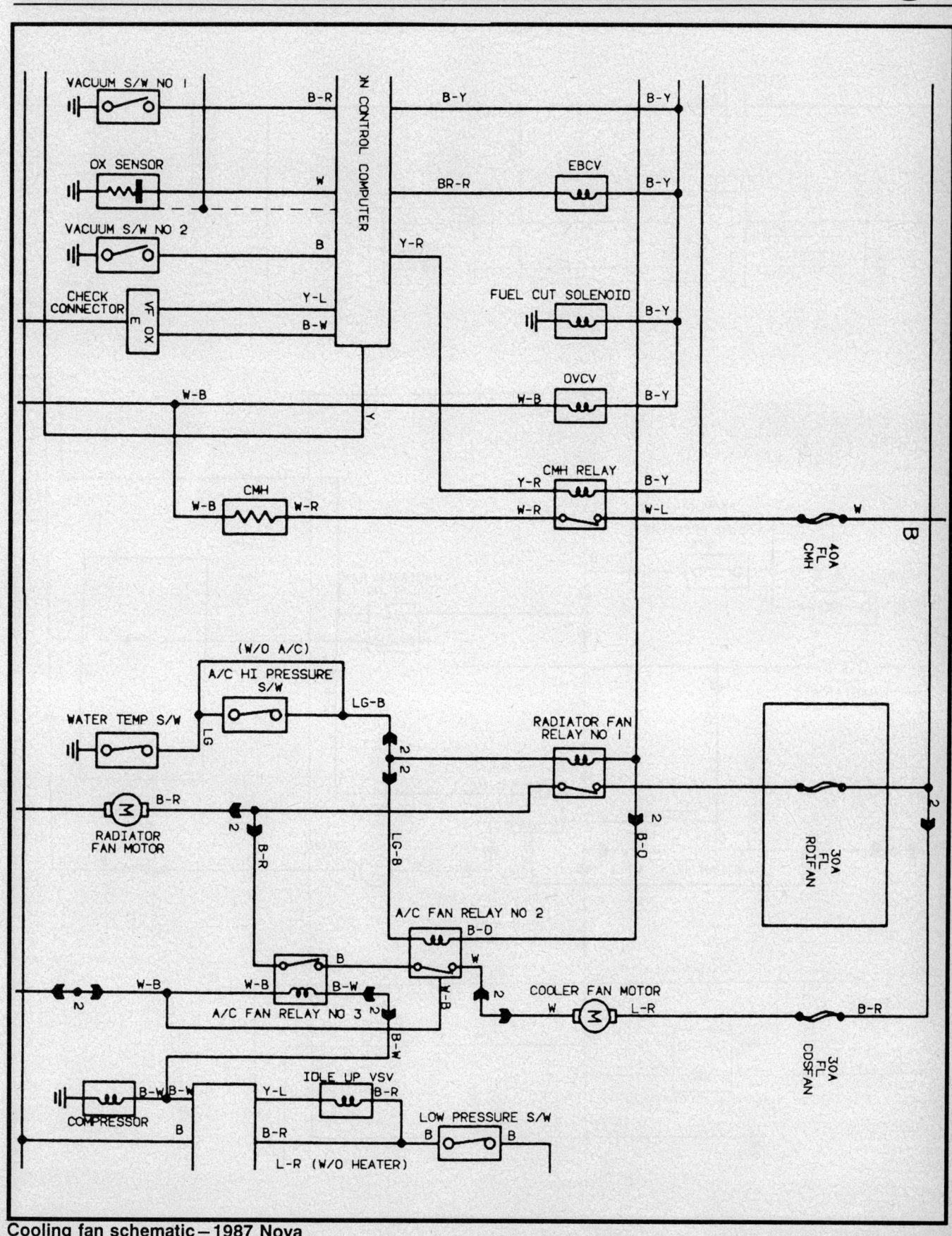

Cooling fan schematic—1987 Nova

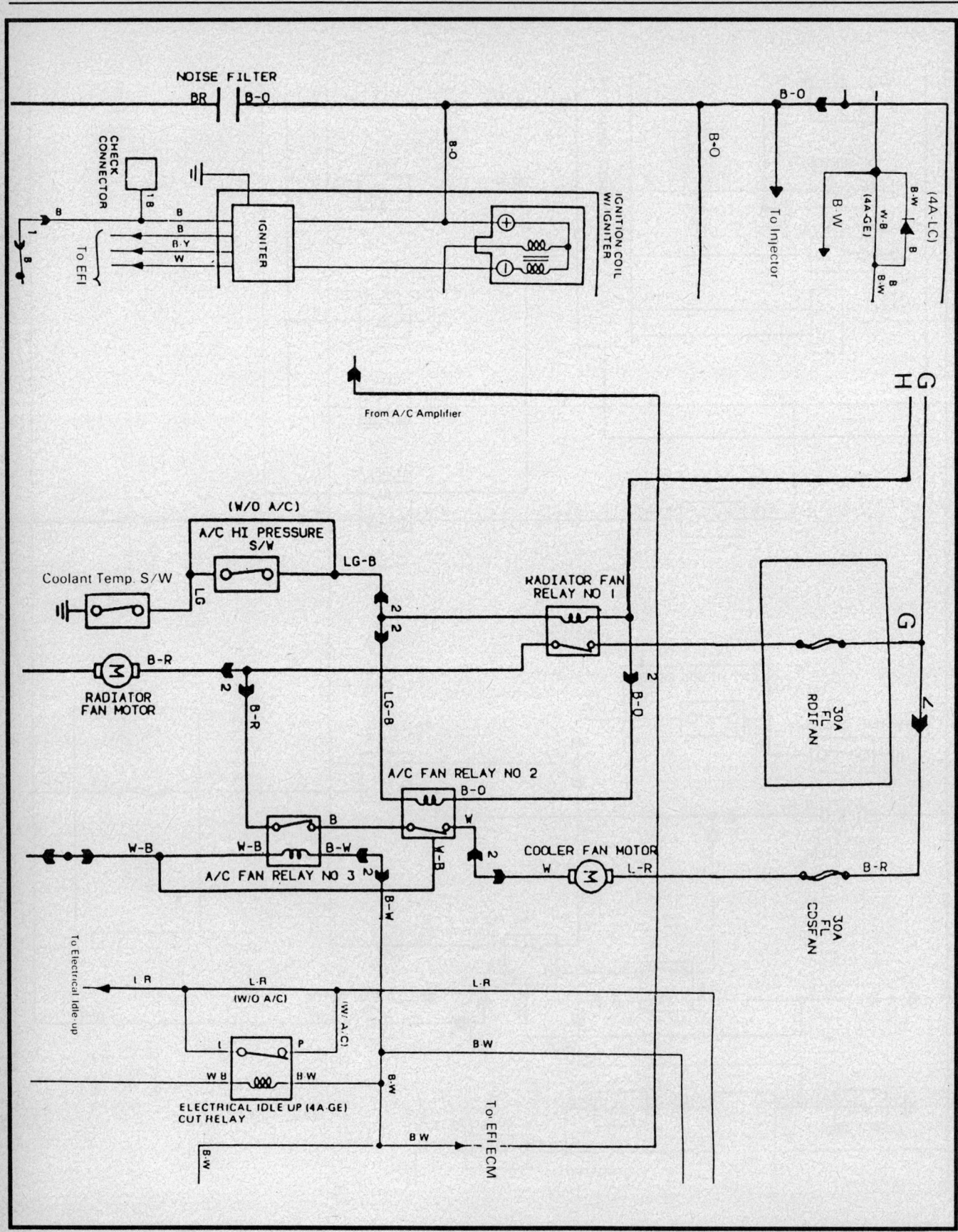

Cooling fan schematic—Nova, except 1987

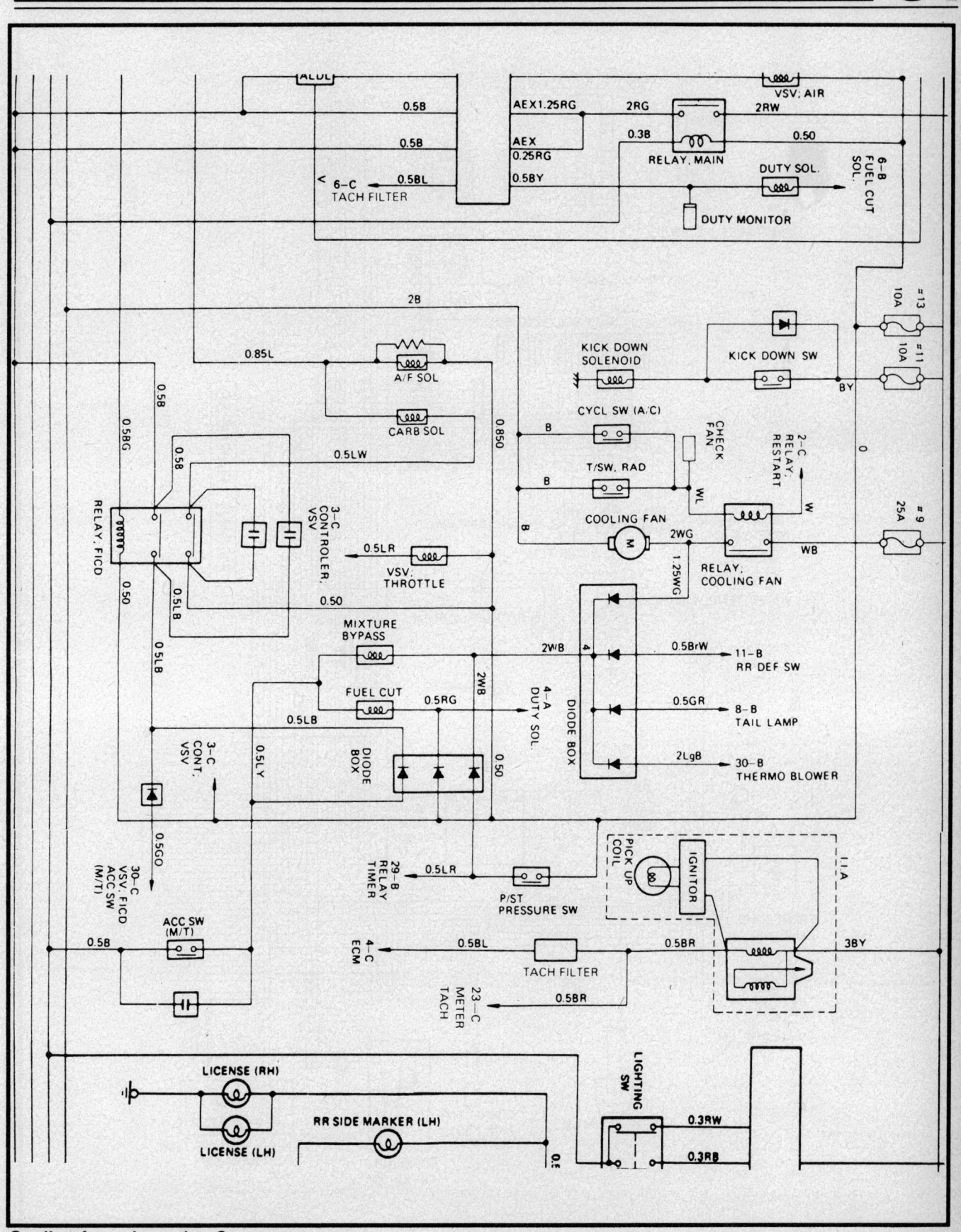

Cooling fan schematic—Spectrum

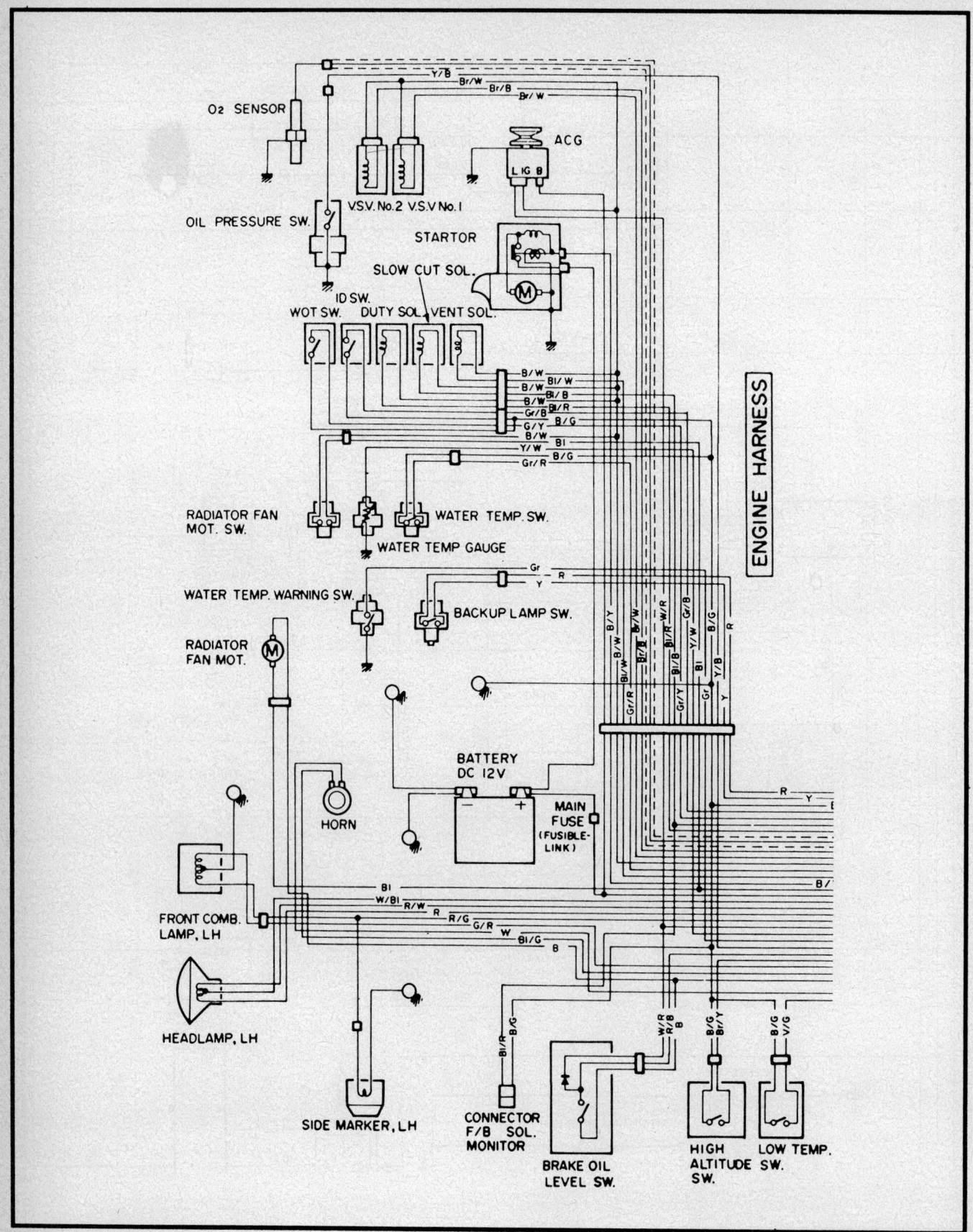

Cooling fan schematic—Sprint

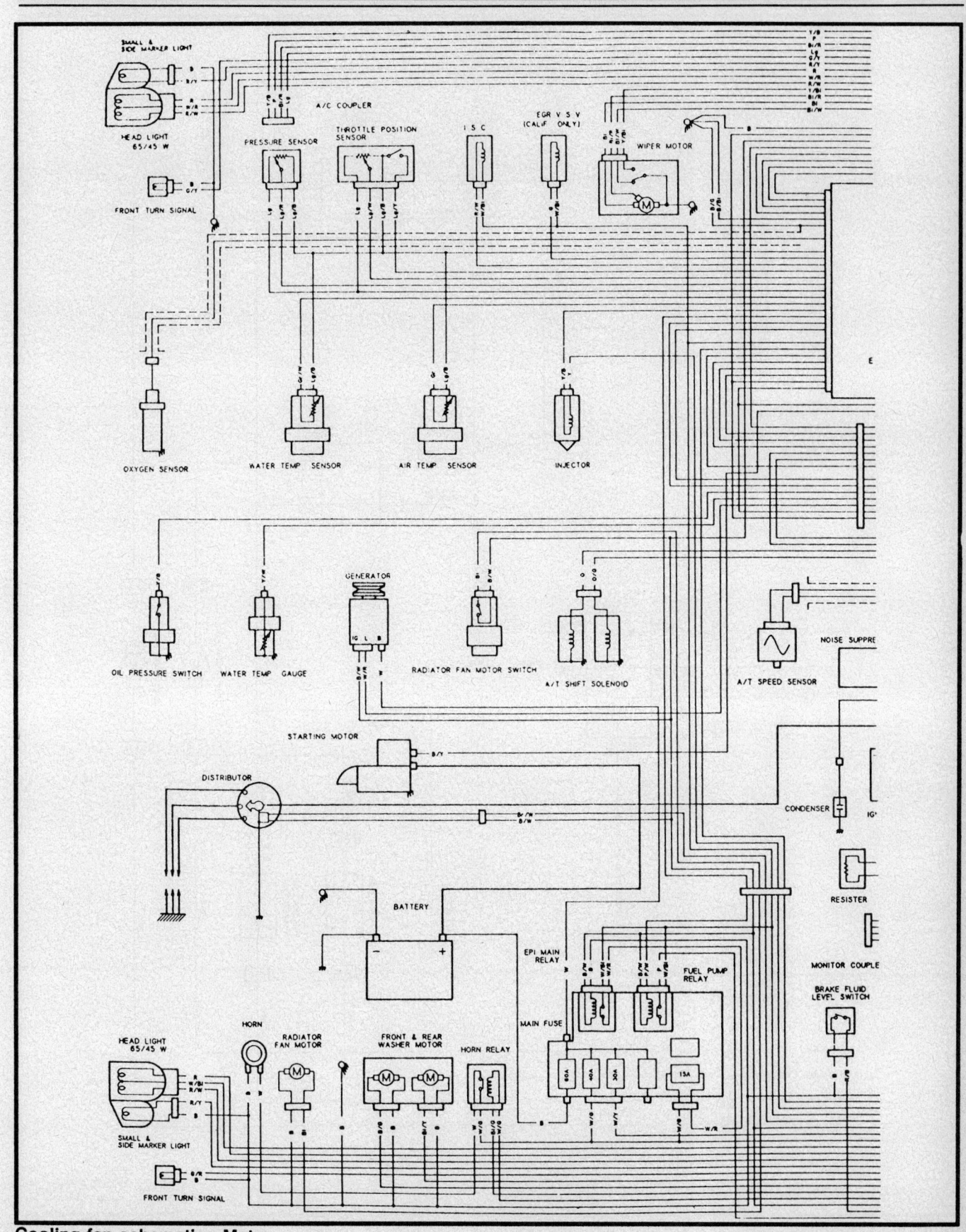

Cooling fan schematic—Metro

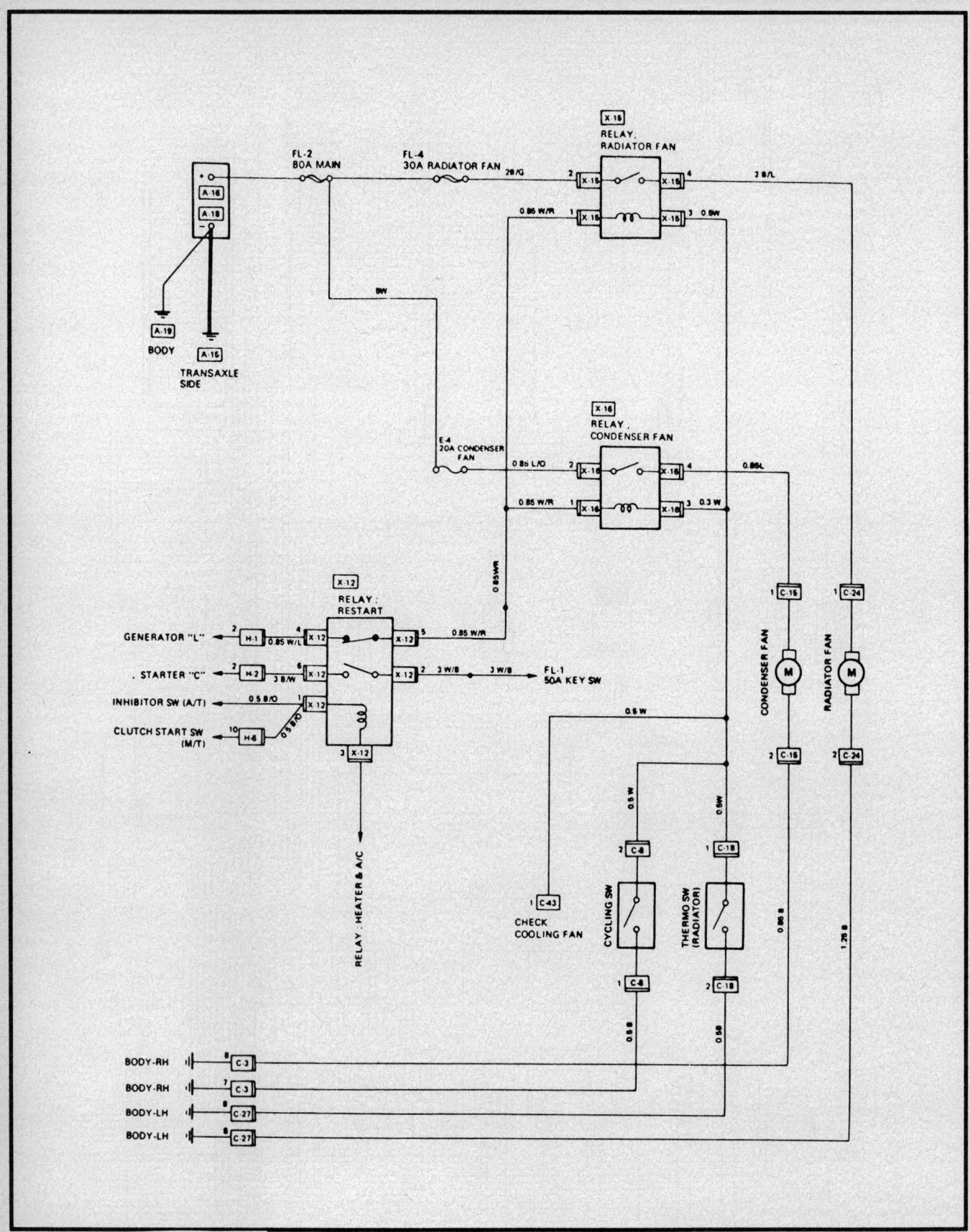

Cooling fan schematic—Storm

2. Using an ammeter and jumper wires, connect the fan motor in series with the battery and ammeter. With the fan running, check the ammeter reading, it should be 3.4–5.0A on all vehicles except Storm and 5.8–7.4A on Storm; if not, replace the motor.

3. Reconnect the fan's electrical connector. Start the engine, allow it to reach temperatures above 194°F and confirm that the fan runs. If the fan doesn't run, replace the temperature switch.

SPECTRUM, SPRINT AND METRO

1. Disconnect the electrical wiring connector from the electric cooling fan.

2. Using a 14 gauge wire, connect it between the fan and the positive terminal; the fan should run.

NOTE: If the fan does not run while connected to the electrical wiring connector, inspect for a defective coolant temperature switch or air conditioning relay, if equipped.

3. If the fan does not run when connected to the jumper wire, replace the fan assembly.

Removal and Installation
ALL VEHICLES

1. Disconnect the negative terminal from the battery.
2. Label and disconnect the electrical connector from the cooling fan motor.
3. Remove the fan shroud-to-radiator frame bolts and the fan/shroud assembly from the vehicle.
4. Remove the fan blade-to-motor nut, fan blade and washer.
5. Remove the fan-to-shroud bolts and the fan motor from the shroud.
6. Test the fan motor and replace it, if necessary.
7. To install, reverse the removal procedures and check the fan operation.

Heater Core

For further information, please refer to "Chilton's Auto Heating and Air Conditioning Manual" for additional coverage.

Removal and Installation
NOVA

1. Disconnect the negative battery cable. Drain the cooling system.
2. In the engine compartment, disconnect the heater hoses from the heater unit.
3. From inside the vehicle (under the dash), remove the lower heater unit case-to-heater case clips and remove the lower case.
4. Using a medium prybar, separate and remove the lower portion of the case from the heater case.
5. Remove the heater core from the heater case.
6. Inspect the heater hoses for cracking and deterioration, then, the heater core for leakage and corrosion; replace the items, if necessary.
7. To install, reverse the removal procedures. Refill the cooling system. Start the engine, allow it to reach normal operating temperatures and check for leaks. Turn the heater controls to max heat and check the heater operation.

PRIZM

The heater case and core are located directly behind the center console. The access the case and core, the entire console must be removed as well as most of the instrument panel assembly.

1. Disconnect the negative battery cable. Remove the steering wheel.
2. Remove the trim bezel from the instrument panel.
3. Remove the cup holder from the console.

4. Remove the radio.
5. Remove the instrument panel assembly, cluster assembly, center console and all console trim, lower dash trim, side window air deflectors, and all instrument panel wiring harnesses.
6. Drain the coolant from the cooling system.
7. Disconnect all cables and ducts from the heater case.
8. Disconnect the blower switch harness and the heater control assembly.
9. Disconnect the 2 center console support braces.
10. Remove all mounting bolts, nuts and clips from the heater and air distribution cases.
11. Remove the heater and air distribution cases.
12. Remove the screws and clips from the case, separate the case halves, and remove the core from the case.
13. Installation is the reverse of removal. Fill the cooling system.

SPECTRUM

1. Disconnect the negative battery cable. Disconnect the heater hoses in the engine compartment.
2. At the lower part of the heater unit case, remove the 6 retaining clips.
3. Using a small prybar, pry open the lower part of the case and remove it.
4. Remove the core assembly insulator and the core assembly.
5. To install, reverse the removal procedures.

STORM

1. Disconnect the battery negative cable.
2. Disconnect heater hoses from inside the engine compartment.
3. Remove the instrument panel assembly.
4. If equipped with air conditioning, remove the evaporator assembly.
5. Remove the duct between the blower motor and the heater unit.
6. Remove the center ventilation duct.
7. Remove the 4 nuts attaching the heater unit and remove the heater unit from the vehicle.
8. Remove the 5 screws attaching the mode control case to the heater core case, then the mode control case.
9. Remove 5 screws to separate the 2 halves of the heater core case and remove the heater core from the case.
10. Reverse procedure to install. Connect the battery negative cable.

SPRINT AND METRO

1. Disconnect the negative battery cable. Drain the cooling system.
2. Disconnect the 2 water hoses from the radiator at the heater unit.
3. Remove the glove box from the upper instrument panel.
4. Remove the defroster hoses from the heater case.
5. Disconnect the electrical connectors from the blower motor and the heater resistor.
6. Disconnect the 3 control cables from the heater case side levers.
7. Pull out the center vent louver.
8. Disconnect both side vent ducts from the center duct vent.
9. Remove the center duct vent and the ashtray's upper plate.
10. Remove the instrument member stay and the heater assembly mounting nuts.
11. Loosen the three heater case top mounting bolts through the glove box opening.
12. Raise the dash panel and remove the heater control assembly.
13. Separate the heater case into 2 sections by removing the clips.
14. Pull the heater core from the heater unit.
15. To install, reverse the removal procedures. Refill the cool-

ing system. Start the engine, bring it to normal operating temperature and check for leaks.

Water Pump

Removal and Installation

NOVA AND PRIZM

1. Disconnect the negative battery cable.
2. Drain the cooling system.
3. Loosen the water pump pulley-to-water pump bolts. If equipped with power steering, remove the power steering pump drive belt.
4. Loosen the alternator adjusting and mounting bolts, move the alternator to relieve the belt tension, then remove the alternator/water pump drive belt.
5. Remove the water pump pulley-to-water pump bolts and the pulley.
6. Remove the water pump inlet-to-engine bolts (from the side of the block), the inlet pipe-to-water pump nuts and the inlet pipe, discard the O-ring.
7. Remove the dipstick tube bracket bolt and the dipstick tube; be sure to plug the hole in the block with a clean rag.

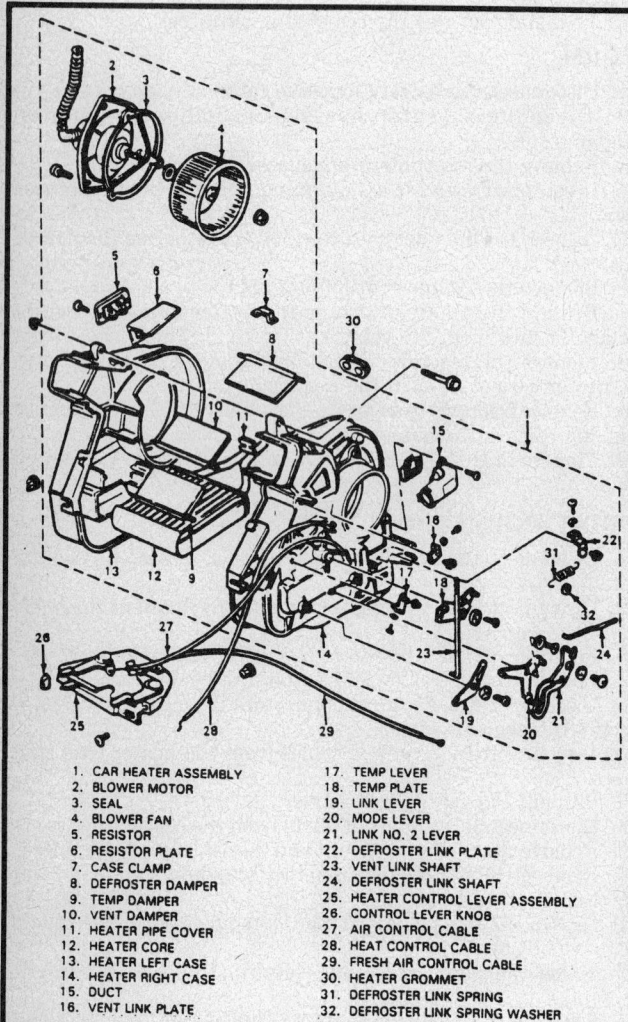

1. CAR HEATER ASSEMBLY
2. BLOWER MOTOR
3. SEAL
4. BLOWER FAN
5. RESISTOR
6. RESISTOR PLATE
7. CASE CLAMP
8. DEFROSTER DAMPER
9. TEMP DAMPER
10. VENT DAMPER
11. HEATER PIPE COVER
12. HEATER CORE
13. HEATER LEFT CASE
14. HEATER RIGHT CASE
15. DUCT
16. VENT LINK PLATE
17. TEMP LEVER
18. TEMP PLATE
19. LINK LEVER
20. MODE LEVER
21. LINK NO. 2 LEVER
22. DEFROSTER LINK PLATE
23. VENT LINK SHAFT
24. DEFROSTER LINK SHAFT
25. HEATER CONTROL LEVER ASSEMBLY
26. CONTROL LEVER KNOB
27. AIR CONTROL CABLE
28. HEAT CONTROL CABLE
29. FRESH AIR CONTROL CABLE
30. HEATER GROMMET
31. DEFROSTER LINK SPRING
32. DEFROSTER LINK SPRING WASHER

Exploded view of the heater assembly—Sprint and Metro

8. For the non-twincam engine, remove the upper timing belt front cover. For the twincam engine, remove the upper and middle timing belt front covers.
9. Remove the water pump-to-engine bolts and the water pump from the engine; discard the water pump-to-engine O-ring.

To install:

10. Using the proper tool, clean the gasket mounting surfaces.
11. To install the water pump, use a new O-ring and reverse the removal procedures. Torque the water pump-to-engine bolts to 11 ft. lbs.
12. When installing the oil dipstick tube, use a new O-ring and coat it with engine oil.
13. To complete the installation, use a new O-ring and reverse the removal procedures. Refill the cooling system. Start the engine, allow it to reach normal operating temperatures and check for leaks.

STORM

Except Twincam Engine

1. Disconnect the battery negative cable and drain cooling system.
2. Remove the power steering pump belt and the timing belt.
3. Remove the belt tension pulley.
4. Remove the water pump-to-block attaching bolts and the water pump from the vehicle.
5. Reverse procedure to install. Clean mating surfaces of all gasket material. Torque water pump bolts to 17.4 ft. lbs. (23.5 Nm). Connect battery negative cable and refill colling system.

Twincam Engine

1. Disconnect the battery negative cable and drain cooling system.
2. Support the engine using a suitable floor jack and remove the right front engine mount.
3. Remove the engine mount bridge and the upper timing belt cover.
4. Remove the power steering belt and the lower timing belt cover.
5. Loosen the timing belt tension pulley and remove the timing belt.
6. Remove the power steering pump and bracket.
7. Remove the water pump attaching bolts, then the water pump from the vehicle.
8. Reverse procedure to install. Connect the battery negative cable and refill cooling system. Start engine and check for leaks.

SPECTRUM

1. Disconnect the negative battery cable and drain the cooling system.
2. Loosen the power steering pump adjustment bolts and remove the belt.
3. Remove the timing belt.
4. Remove the tension pulley and spring.
5. Remove the water pump mounting bolts, the water pump and gasket. Clean the mounting surfaces of all gasket material.
6. To install, reverse the removal procedures. Torque the water pump to 17 ft. lbs. and the tension pulley to 30 ft. lbs.

SPRINT AND METRO

1. Disconnect the negative battery cable.
2. Drain the cooling system.
3. Remove the water pump belt and pulley.
4. Remove the crankshaft pulley, the timing belt outside cover, the timing belt and the tensioner.
5. Remove the mounting bolts and the water pump.
6. Clean the gasket mating surfaces.
7. To install, use a new gasket/sealer and reverse the removal procedures. Torque the water pump bolts to 7.5–9 ft. lbs. Adjust the water pump belt deflection to ¼–⅜ in. between the water pump and the crankshaft pulleys.

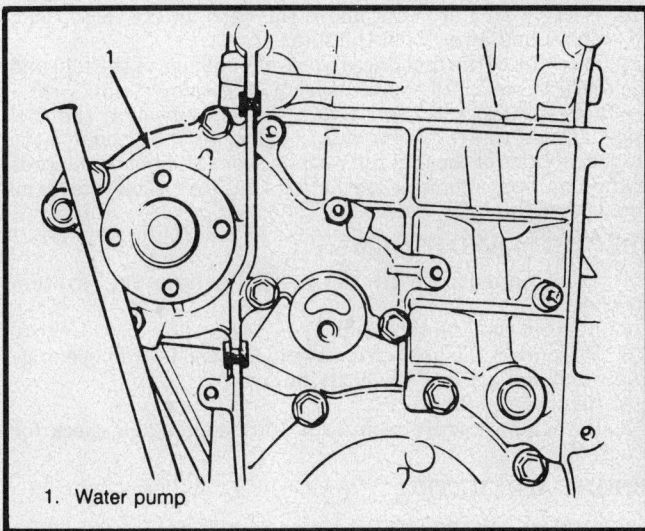

1. Water pump

Water pump mounting — Sprint and Metro

Thermostat

Removal and Installation

NOVA AND PRIZM

1. Disconnect the battery negative cable.
2. Drain cooling system.
3. Loosen the water inlet hose clamps, then disconnect the hoses from the thermostat housing. Remove the water inlet-to-thermostat housing bolts and pull the water inlet housing from the thermostat housing. Remove thermostat and discard O-ring.
4. Position the bellows side of the thermostat facing inward. Ensure that the thermostat fits squarely in the indented portion of the housing.
5. Use a new O-ring and reverse procedure to install. Refill cooling system. Start engine and check for leaks.

SPECTRUM AND STORM

1. Disconnect the battery negative cable. Drain cooling system.
2. Remove the top radiator hose from from the outlet pipe.
3. Remove the oulet pipe bolts, outlet pipe, gasket and thermostat from the thermostat housing.
4. Reverse procedure to install. Refill cooling system. Connect battery negative cable. Start engine and check for leaks.

SPRINT AND METRO

1. Disconnect the battery negative cable.
2. Drain cooling system to a level below the thermostat.
3. Remove the air cleaner.
4. Disconnect the electrical connectors at the thermostat cap.
5. Remove the inlet hose, cap mounting bolts and the thermostat from the themostat housing.
6. Clean the gasket mounting surfaces. Ensure that the thermostat air bleed hose is clear.
7. Reverse procedure to install. Install thermostat into housing with the spring side down. Fill cooling system and connect the battery negative cable. Start engine and check for leaks.

Cooling System Bleeding

After performing any repairs on the cooling system, it must be bled. Air trapped in the system will prevent proper filling and leave the radiator coolant level low, causing a risk of overheating.

1. To bleed the system, start with the system cool, radiator cap off and the radiator filled to about an inch below the filler neck.
2. Start the engine and run it at slightly above normal idle speed. This will ensure adequate circulation. If air bubbles appear and the coolant level drops, fill the cooling system to bring the level back to the proper level.
3. Run the engine until the thermostat opens. When this happens, coolant will will move abruptly across the top of the radiator and the temperature of the radiator will suddenly rise.
4. At this point, air is often expelled and the level may drop quite a bit. Keep refilling the system until the level is near the top of the radiator and remains constant.
5. If the vehicle has an overflow tank, fill the radiator right up to the filler neck. Replace the radiator filler cap.

FUEL SYSTEM

Fuel System Service Precautions

Safety is the most important factor when performing not only fuel system maintenance but any type of maintenance. Failure to conduct maintenance and repairs in a safe manner may result in serious personal injury or death. Maintenance and testing of the vehicle's fuel system components can be accomplished safely and effectively by adhering to the following rules and guidelines.

• To avoid the possibility of fire and personal injury, always disconnect the negative battery cable unless the repair or test procedure requires that battery voltage be applied.
• Always relieve the fuel system pressure prior to disconnecting any fuel system component (injector, fuel rail, pressure regulator, etc.), fitting or fuel line connection. Exercise extreme caution whenever relieving fuel system pressure to avoid exposing skin, face and eyes to fuel spray. Please be advised that fuel under pressure may penetrate the skin or any part of the body that it contacts.
• Always place a shop towel or cloth around the fitting or connection prior to loosening to absorb any excess fuel due to spillage. Ensure that all fuel spillage (should it occur) is quickly removed from engine surfaces. Ensure that all fuel soaked cloths or towels are deposited into a suitable waste container.
• Always keep a dry chemical (Class B) fire extinguisher near the work area.
• Do not allow fuel spray or fuel vapors to come into contact with a spark or open flame.
• Always use a backup wrench when loosening and tightening fuel line connection fittings. This will prevent unnecessary stress and torsion to fuel line piping. Always follow the proper torque specifications.
• Always replace worn fuel fitting O-rings with new. Do not substitute fuel hose or equivalent where fuel pipe is installed.

Relieving Fuel System Pressure
NOVA AND PRIZM

NOTE: Make sure the engine is cold before disconnecting any portion of the fuel system.

1. Disconnect the negative battery cable.
2. Loosen the fuel filler cap to relieve tank vapor pressure.

3. Using a shop rag, wrap it around the fuel line fitting.

4. Open the fuel line and absorb any excess fuel remaining in the line.

5. When replacing the be sure to install a new O-ring.

SPECTRUM AND STORM

1. Remove the fuel pump fuse from the fuse block or disconnect the harness connector at the tank.

2. Start the engine. It should run and then stall when the fuel in the lines is exhausted. When the engine stops, crank the starter for about 3 seconds to make sure all pressure in the fuel lines is released.

3. Disconnect the negative battery cable.

4. Install the fuel pump fuse after repair is made and reconnect the battery cable.

SPRINT AND METRO

1. Release the fuel vapor pressure in the fuel tank by removing the fuel tank cap then reinstalling it.

2. With the engine running, remove the connector of the fuel pump relay and wait until the engine stops itself.

NOTE: The main relay and fuel pump relay are identical. Which one to connect to the fuel lead wire is not specified. Identify the fuel pump relay by the color of the lead wire. The fuel pump relay lead wire is pink, pink/white, white/blue, white/blue.

3. Once the engine is stopped, crank it a few times with the starter for about 3 seconds each time, with the relay connector disconnected.

4. If the fuel pressure can't be released in the above manner because the engine failed to run in Step 2, disconnect the negative battery cable, cover the union bolt of the high fuel pressure line with an appropriate rag and loosen the union bolt slowly to release the fuel pressure gradually.

Fuel Filter

Removal and Installation
NOVA AND PRIZM

1. Disconnect the battery negative cable.
2. Remove the fuel filler cap.

NOTE: Note the routing of the inlet/outlet lines and the direction of flow as marked on the filter; the arrow points toward the carburetor, if equipped.

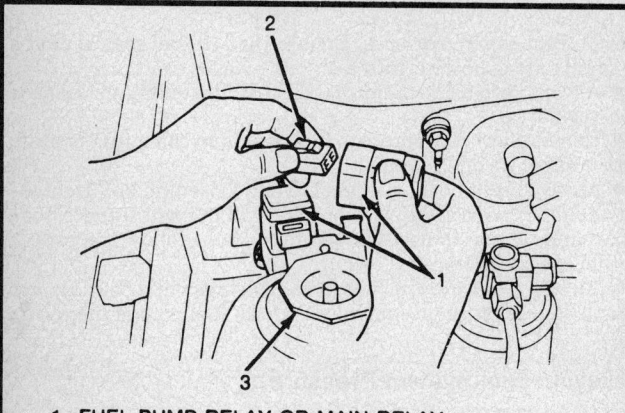

1. FUEL PUMP RELAY OR MAIN RELAY
2. FUEL PUMP RELAY LEAD WIRE
   (PINK, PINK/WHITE, WHITE/BLUE, WHITE/BLUE)
3. RIGHT FRONT SUSPENSION STRUT

Fuel pump relay wire identification—Sprint and Metro

3. Using a pair of pliers, move the clips on the inlet/outlet hoses back and away from the filter.

4. Disconnect the fuel lines to prevent spillage of the fuel and the entry of dirt. Pull the filter from its retaining clip.

5. Reverse procedure to install. When connecting the fuel lines, ensure that the clips are installed to the inside of the bulged sections of the fuel filter connections and not at the ends of the fuel lines. Connect the battery negative cable, start the engine and check for leaks.

SPECTRUM AND STORM

1. If equipped with fuel injection, relieve fuel system pressure.

2. Remove the fuel tank cap.

3. Disconnect the hoses from the fuel filter. Cap all openings to prevent spillage and the entry of dirt.

4. Remove the fuel filter.

5. Reverse procedure to install. Start engine and check for leaks.

SPRINT AND METRO
Carbureted Engine

1. Remove and replace the fuel tank cap. This releases the fuel pressure within the fuel system.

2. Disconnect the battery negative cable.

3. Remove the clamps from the inlet and outlet hoses and remove the hoses from the fuel filter.

4. Remove the fuel filter from the bracket.

5. Reverse procedure to install. Start engine and check for leaks.

Fuel Injected Engine

1. Relieve the fuel system pressure.

2. Place an appropriate container under the fuel filter.

3. Use a 17mm and a 19mm wrench to loosen the inlet and outlet pipes, then remove the fuel filter.

4. Reverse procedure to install. Use new gaskets and ensure that end marked OUT on the filter is placed up. Torque inlet and outlet pipe bolts to 22–28 ft. lbs. Start engine and check for leaks.

Mechanical Fuel Pump

Pressure Testing
NOVA

1. Using a fuel pressure gauge, connect it between the fuel pump and the carburetor; using a pair of vise grips or equivalent, squeeze off the return hose.

2. Operate the engine at idle and note the reading on the gauge.

3. Fuel pump pressure should be 7.6 psi. If specification obtained is not as specified, the fuel pump should be replaced.

4. Remove the gauge, reconnect the fuel lines. Start the engine and check for leaks.

SPECTRUM

1. Disconnect the fuel line from the carburetor. Install a rubber hose about 10 inches long. Attach a low reading pressure gauge.

2. Hold the gauge at least 16 inches above the fuel pump. If equipped, pinch the fuel return line.

3. Start the engine and run it at slow idle, using the fuel that is left in the carburetor.

4. Fuel pump pressure should be 3.8–4.7 psi. If specification obtained is not as indicated, replace the fuel pump.

Removal and Installation
NOVA AND PRIZM

1. Note the routing of the fuel lines and label, if necessary.

2. Remove the fuel line clips, then disconnect the fuel lines.

3. Remove the fuel pump-to-cylinder head bolts, then the pump, gasket and heat shield. Note position of the heat shield.

4. Clean the gasket mounting surface. Ensure not to scratch the aluminum surface of the cylinder head.

5. Reverse procedure to install. Use a new gasket. When reconnecting the fuel lines, ensure that the clips are installed to the inside of the bulged sections of the fuel pump connections. Start the engine and check for leaks.

SPECTRUM

1. Disconnect the fuel and return hoses from the fuel pump.

2. Remove the bolts, fuel pump and heat insulator assembly.

3. After removing the fuel pump, cover the mounting face of the cylinder head to prevent oil discharge.

4. Reverse procedure to install. Replace the heat insulator assembly.

SPRINT AND METRO

1. Remove and replace the fuel tank cap, this procedure releases the pressure within the fuel system.

2. Disconnect the battery negative cable.

3. Remove the air cleaner from the carburetor.

4. Remove the fuel inlet, outlet and return hoses from the fuel pump.

5. Remove the fuel pump mounting bolts, the pump and the pump rod from the cylinder head.

6. Reverse procedure to install. Use a new gasket and lubricate the pump rod.

Electric Fuel Pump

Pressure Testing

NOVA

1. Disconnect the battery negative cable and the electrical connector from the cold start injector.

2. Using a shop cloth, wrap it around the cold start injector pipe, then slowly loosen the union bolt and remove. Discard the gaskets.

3. Install pressure gauge tools J–347301-1 and J–37144 or equivalent onto the fuel delivery pipe.

4. Reconnect the battery negative cable.

5. Using a jumper wire, short the terminals to the fuel pump chcek connector; the connector is located near the wiper motor.

6. Turn the ignition switch **ON** and check the fuel pressure. Fuel pressure should be 38–44 psi. If pressure is too high, replace the pressure regulator. If the pressure is low, check the fuel pump, fuel filter, pressure regulator, hoses and connections.

7. Remove the service wire from the check connector. Start the engine.

8. Disconnect the vacuum sensing hose from the pressure regulator and pinch it off.

9. The fuel pressure at idle should be 38–44 psi.

10. Reconnect the vacuum sensing hose to the pessure regulator and allow the engine to idle for $1\frac{1}{2}$ min. Recheck the fuel pressure. Fuel pressure should be 30–33 psi; if no pressure, check the vacuum sensing hose and the pressure regulator.

11. Stop the engine and inspect the fuel pressure for 5 min.; it should remain above 21 psi. If the pressure does not remain high, check the fuel pump, pressure regulator and/or the injectors.

12. After checking the fuel pressure, disconnect the battery negative cable and remove the fuel pressure gauge.

13. Using new gaskets, reconnect the cold start injector hose to the delivery pipe and the battery negative cable. Start the engine and check for leaks.

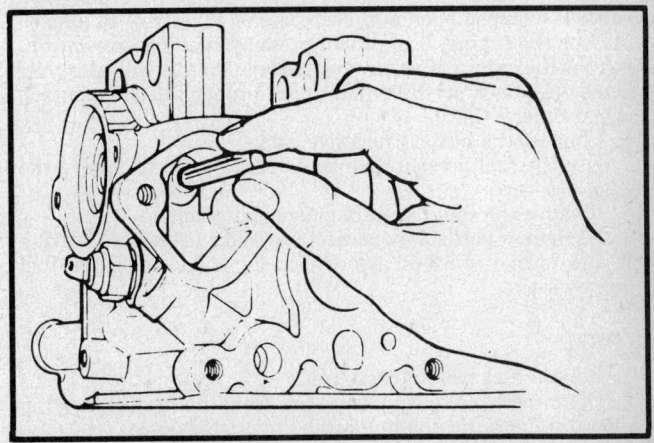

Install the fuel pump push rod in the cylinder head—Sprint and Metro

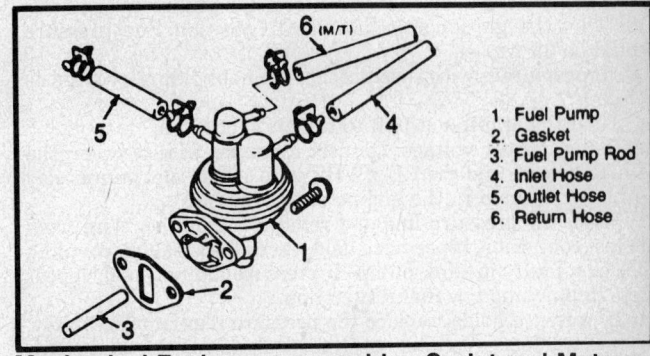

1. Fuel Pump
2. Gasket
3. Fuel Pump Rod
4. Inlet Hose
5. Outlet Hose
6. Return Hose

Mechanical Fuel pump assembly—Sprint and Metro

PRIZM

1. Disconnect the battery negative cable.

2. Using a shop cloth, wrap it around the cold start injector pipe and slowly loosen the union bolt and remove. Discard the gaskets.

3. Remove the delivery pipe to cold start injector banjo fitting bolt and the 2 gaskets. Discard the gaskets.

4. Install pressure gauge tools J–34370-1 and J–38347 onto the fuel delivery pipe. Close the gauge valve.

5. Reconnect the battery negative cable.

6. Open the gauge valve and turn the ignition switch to the **RUN** position.

7. Install a jumper wire between the **+B** and **FP** terminals of the fuel pump check connector. The fuel pump connector is located near the wiper motor.

8. Open the gauge air bleed valve and purge the air from the gauge. Use a suitable container to catch the fuel from the gauge air bleed valve.

9. The gauge reading should be 38–44 psi. If the pressure is too high, replace the pressure regulator or a restricted fuel return line. If the pressure is low, check the fuel pump, fuel filter, pressure regulator, the hoses and connections.

10. Pinch the fuel presssure regulator return hose. The pressure should be 57 psi.

11. Remove the fuel pump jumper wire and observe the pressure gauge. A very slow drop in pressure is normal.

12. The fuel pressure at idle should be 30–33 psi.

13. Remove the fuel pressure regulator sensing hose and plug the hose end. The fuel pressure gauge should read 38–44 psi.

14. Connect the vacuum sensing hose and quickly open and close the throttle valve for the air induction system. The fuel pressure gauge should show quick increases in pressure as the

throttle is snapped open and decreases as it returns to idle.

15. Stop the engine. If improper pressure readings are shown, check the fuel pump, pressure regulator and/or the injectors, restricted fuel lines or filter and for improper injector control, thermal timer/ECM.

16. Connect the battery negative cable.

17. Use the fuel pressure gauge air bleed valve to relieve the system pressure.

18. Remove the fuel pressure gauge and adapter.

19. Using new gaskets, reconnect the cold start injector fitting bolt and torque to 13 ft. lbs. Check for leaks using the fuel jumper wire.

STORM

1. Relieve fuel system pressure.

2. Disconnect the fuel pressure line from the fuel filter. Wrap a shop towel around the line catch any fuel leakage.

3. Install fuel gauge adapter J–35957-10 between the fuel pressure line and the fuel filter, located on the fuel rail.

4. Install fuel gauge J–34730-1 to the adapter.

5. Disconnect the vacuum hose from the pressure regulator.

6. Turn the ignition switch to the **ON** position. Fuel pressure should be 35–42 psi.

7. If pressure is with specification but not holding, proceed as follows:

a. Turn the ignition switch to the **OFF** position.

b. Using battery voltage, connect a jumper wire between the BLK/RED wire and the RED/WHT wire on the fuel pump relay connector, located in the engine compartment.

c. Pinch the pressure line and remove the jumper wire from the test connector. If pressure held, check for a leaking coupling hose or a faulty in-tank pump. If pressure did not hold, repeat Step 7b pinching the fuel return line.

d. If pressure holds, replace the pressure regulator assembly. If pressure does not hold, check for leaking injector and spark plugs.

8. If pressure obtained is below specification, proceed as follows:

a. Check for a restricted in-line fuel filter; replace, if necessary.

b. Turn the ignition switch to the **OFF** position.

c. Apply battery voltage to the fuel pump relay connector with the fuel pump removed.

d. Pinch the fuel return line and note pressure. Pressure should be above 65 psi.

e. If not, check for a faulty in-tank pump. If pressure is above 65 psi, replace the pressure regulator.

9. If pressure obtained is above specification, proceed as follows:

a. Disconnect the vacuum line to the pressure regulator and the fuel return line hose.

b. Install a 5/16 inch hose to the pressure regulator side of the return line and insert the other end into a suitable container.

c. Turn the ignition switch to the **ON** position and check the fuel pressure. Fuel pressure should be 35–42 psi. If not, replace the pressure regulator.

d. If fuel pressure is 35–42 psi, check for a restriction in the fuel return line.

10. If no pressure was obtained on the pressure gauge, proceed as follows:

a. Remove the gas cap and turn the ignition switch to the **ON** position. Fuel pump should operate for approximately 2 seconds.

b. If fuel pump operates, check for faulty wiring and connectors.

c. If fuel pump does not operate, remove the fuel pump relay from the relay center. Using a suitable test light, check RED/WHT wire on the fuel pump relay connector for power.

d. If test light does not light, check for an open circuit in the RED/WHT wire. If test light illuminates, install a jumper wire between the RED/WHT and BLK/RED wire on the fuel pump relay connector. Fuel pump should operate.

e. If fuel pump does not operate, check the fuel pump connector at the fuel tank using the test light. Test light should illuminate. If not, check the BLK/RED wire for an open circuit. If Test light illuminates, check for an open circuit in the fuel ground and/or a faulty fuel pump.

f. If the fuel pump operates, turn the ignition switch OFF for approximately 10 seconds. Connect a test light between the BLK wire and the PNK/WHT wire on the fuel pump relay connector. Turn the ignition switch ON, test light should light for approximately 2 seconds.

g. If test light illuminates, check for a faults fuel pump relay. If test light does not illuminate, turn the ignition switch OFF for approximately 10 seconds. Using the test light check the A1 terminal of the ECM. Turn the ignition switch ON. Test light should light for approximately 2 seconds. If not, replace the ECM. If test light illuminates, check for an open circuit in the PNK/WHT wire and/or the BLK wire.

SPECTRUM

1. Relieve the fuel system pressure.

2. Disconnect the fuel hoses between the pressure regulator and the fuel distributor pipe.

3. Connect fuel pressure gauge J–33945 between the pressure regulator and the fuel distributor pipe.

4. Start the engine and check the fuel pressure under the 2 different condtions:

a. Vacuum hose of the pressure regulator disconnected, intake manifold side end of hose must be plugged. The pressure should read 35.6 psi.

b. Vacuum hose of the pressure regulator connected, at engine speed of 900 rpm. The pressure should read 28.4 psi.

5. After on-vehicle inspection is made, remove the fuel pressure gauge, reconnect fuel line and check for leaks.

SPRINT AND METRO

1. Relieve fuel system pressure.

2. Disconnect the fuel inlet line at the fuel filter and install a suitable pressure gauge on the line.

3. Jump the fuel pump relay, using a suitable jumper wire, and check the system pressure on the gauge.

4. Fuel pressure should be 25–33 lbs.

5. As the pressure reaches 33 lbs., the relief valve in the pump should pulsate the pressure so it is always within specification.

6. If the pressure is not within specification, check for restrictions in the fuel lines or replace the in-tank fuel pump.

7. Before removing the pressure gauge, relieve the fuel pressure again.

8. Reconnect the fuel line. Start the engine and check for leaks.

Removal and Installation

NOVA AND PRIZM

1. Release the fuel system pressure.

2. Disconnect the negative terminal from the battery.

3. Raise and support the vehicle safely. Drain the fuel from the fuel tank. Remove the fuel tank-to-chassis straps and lower the tank slightly. Disconnect the electrical connector and the fuel line from the fuel tube.

4. Remove the fuel pump bracket-to-fuel tank bolts and the bracket.

5. Remove the electrical connectors from the fuel pump, the fuel pump from the bracket and the fuel hose.

6. From the bottom of the fuel pump, remove the rubber cushion, the clip and pull out the filter.

7. To install, use a new bracket-to-fuel tank gasket and reverse the removal procedures. Refill the fuel tank.

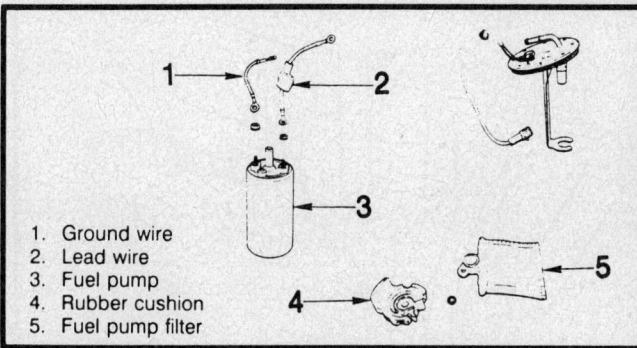

1. Ground wire
2. Lead wire
3. Fuel pump
4. Rubber cushion
5. Fuel pump filter

Electric fuel pump connections—Spectrum

STORM

1. Relieve the fuel system pressure, then disconnect the battery negative cable.
2. Drain the fuel from the fuel tank, then remove the fuel tank attaching bolts and lower the fuel tank.
3. Remove 8 fuel pump attaching screws, then the fuel pump/bracket from the fuel tank.
4. Remove the fuel pump supply hose extension from the bracket.
5. Remove the gasket from the fuel pump bracket and/or tank.
6. Remove the filter from the pump pickup tube.
7. Disconnect the electrical connectors from the the fuel pump, outlet hose from pump and remove the pump from the bracket.
8. Reverse procedure to install. Connect battery negative cable. Start engine and check for leaks.

SPECTRUM

1. Relieve fuel pressure then disconnect negative battery cable.
2. Raise and support the vehicle safely. Drain fuel tank.
3. Remove all gas line hose connections and fuel pump ground wire.
4. Remove filler neck hose and clamp.
5. Remove breather hose and clamp.
6. Disconnect fuel tank hose to evaporator pipe.
7. Remove fuel tank mounting bolts and lower tank from vehicle. At this point remove hose from pump to fuel fiter.
8. Remove fuel pump bracket plate and fuel pump as an assembly.
9. Remove pump bracket, rubber cushion and fuel pump filter.
10. To install, reverse the removal procedures. Be careful, to push the lower side of the fuel pump, together with the rubber cushion, into the fuel pump bracket.

SPRINT AND METRO

NOTE: The fuel tank must be lowered to gain access to the fuel pump which is located in the fuel tank.

1. Relieve the fuel system pressure.
2. Disconnect the negative battery cable.
3. Remove the rear seat cushion and disconnect the fuel gauge and fuel pump lead wires.
4. Raise and support the vehicle safely.
5. Drain the fuel tank by pumping or siphoning the fuel out through the fuel feed line (tank to fuel filter line).
6. Remove the tank from the vehicle.
7. Remove the fuel pump and fuel level gauge bracket from the fuel tank.
8. Remove the fuel pump from the fuel tank.
9. Installation is the reverse of removal. Clean the fuel filter in the tank.

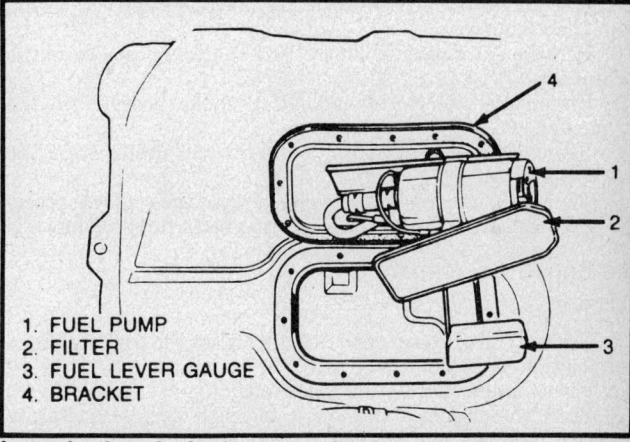

1. FUEL PUMP
2. FILTER
3. FUEL LEVER GAUGE
4. BRACKET

In-tank electric fuel pump—Sprint and Metro

Carburetor

Removal and Installation

NOVA

1. Disconnect the negative battery cable. To remove the air cleaner, perform the following procedures:
   a. Disconnect the air intake hose.
   b. Label and disconnect the emission control hoses from the air cleaner.
   c. Remove the wing nut, mounting bolts and the air cleaner from the carburetor.
2. Disconnect the accelerator cable from the carburetor. If equipped with an automatic transaxle, disconnect the transaxle throttle linkage from the carburetor.
3. Disconnect the wiring connector form the carburetor solenoid valve(s).
4. Label and disconnect the emission control hoses from the carburetor. Disconnect and drain the fuel inlet hose. Disconnect the evaporative emissions canister hose.
5. Remove the cold mixture heater wire clamp and the EGR vacuum control bracket.
6. Remove the carburetor-to-intake manifold nuts, the carburetor and gasket from the intake manifold. Using a clean shop rag, seal off the intake manifold opening.
7. Using the proper tool, clean the gasket mounting surfaces of the carburetor and manifold.
8. To install, use a new gasket and reverse the removal procedures. Install and adjust the throttle and transaxle linkages to the carburetor. Start the engine and check for fuel leaks.

SPECTRUM

1. Disconnect the negative battery terminal from the battery.
2. Remove the air cleaner.
3. Disconnect the harness connector and hoses.
4. Remove the accelerator cable from the carburetor.
5. Remove the bolts securing the carburetor to the intake manifold. Remove the carburetor and place a cover over the intake manifold.
6. To install, reverse the removal procedures and torque carburetor fixing bolts to 7.2 ft. lbs. then start the engine and check for leaks.

SPRINT

1. Remove and replace the fuel tank cap; this procedure releases the pressure within the fuel system.
2. Disconnect the negative battery cable.
3. Disconnect the warm air, the cold air, the second air, the vacuum and the EGR modulator hoses from the air cleaner case.
4. Remove the air cleaner case from the carburetor.

5. Disconnect the accelerator cable and the electrical wiring from the carburetor.

6. Remove the emission control and the fuel hoses from the carburetor.

7. Disconnect the No. 1 and No. 2 choke hoses from the carburetor.

8. Remove the mounting bolts and the carburetor from the intake manifold.

9. To install, use new gaskets and reverse the removal procedures. Torque the carburetor mounting bolts to 18 ft. lbs.

Idle Speed Adjustment

NOVA

1. Turn off all of the accessories, firmly set the parking brake and position the transaxle in **N**.

2. Check and/or adjust the ignition timing.

3. Start the engine and allow it to reach normal operating temperatures; make sure the choke is in the wide open position.

4. Inspect the fuel level sight glass on the carburetor to make sure the fuel is at the correct level.

5. At the distributor, locate the service engine connector, remove the rubber cap from it. Using a tachometer, connect the positive terminal to the service connector.

NOTE: When using a tachometer, consult the manufacturer's information to be sure it is compatible with the system.

6. Adjust the idle speed screw to 650 rpm for manual transaxles and 750 rpm for automatic transaxles.

SPECTRUM

1. Set the parking brake and block the wheels.

2. Place the manual transaxle in **N** or the automatic transaxle in **P**. Check the float level. Establish a normal operating temperature and make sure the choke plate is open.

3. Turn off all of the accessories and wait until the cooling fan is not operating.

4. If equipped with power steering, place the wheels in the straight forward position. Remove the air filter.

5. Disconnect and plug the distributor vacuum line, canister purge line, EGR vacuum line and ITC valve vacuum line.

6. Connect a tachometer to the coil tachometer connector and a timing light to the No. 1 spark plug wire. Check the timing and idle speed.

7. If the idle speed needs adjusting, turn the idle speed adjusting screw.

8. If equipped with air conditioning, adjust the system to MAX/COLD and place the blower on HIGH position. Set the fast idle speed by turning the adjust bolt of the fast idle control diaphragm to 850 rpm on automatic transaxle or 980 rpm on manual transaxle.

9. When adjustment is completed, turn the engine off, remove the test equipment, install the air filter and vacuum lines.

SPRINT AND METRO

Check and/or adjust the accelerator cable free-play, ignition timing, valve lash and the emission control wiring and hoses. Make sure the headlights, heater fan, engine cooling fan and any other electrical equipment is turned OFF. If any current drawing system is operating, the idle up system will operate and cause the idle speed to be higher than normal.

1. Connect a tachometer to the primary negative terminal of the ignition coil and refer to the underhood sticker.

2. Place the transaxle in **N**, set the parking brake and block the wheels.

3. Start and run the engine until it reaches normal operating temperature.

4. Check and/or adjust the idle speed, it should be 700–800 rpm with manual transaxles, 800–900 rpm with automatic transaxles.

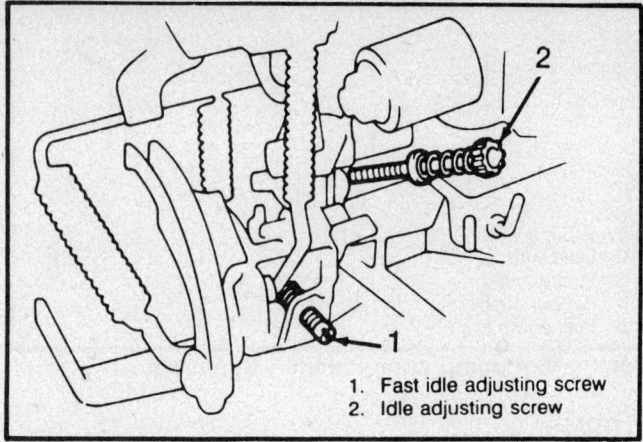

1. Fast idle adjusting screw
2. Idle adjusting screw

View of the carbuuretor's idle and fast idle adjusting screws—Nova

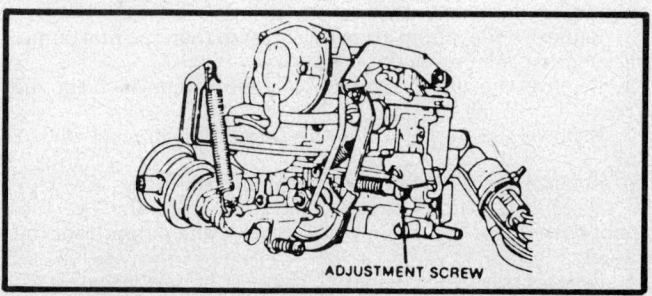

ADJUSTMENT SCREW

Idle speed adjustment screw location—Spectrum

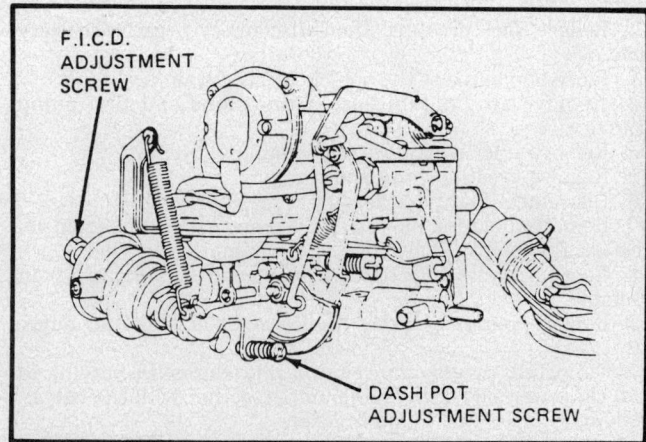

F.I.C.D. ADJUSTMENT SCREW

DASH POT ADJUSTMENT SCREW

Fast idle control device adjustment screw location—Spectrum

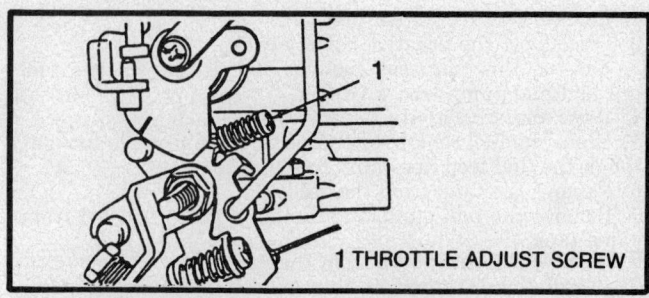

1 THROTTLE ADJUST SCREW

Idle speed adjustment screw—Sprint

NOTE: To adjust the idle speed, turn the throttle adjustment screw on the carburetor.

5. With the engine at the proper idle speed, check and/or adjust the idle up speed.

6. Stop the engine and remove the tachometer.

Idle Mixture Adjustment

NOVA

NOTE: Idle mixture does not require adjustment as a matter of routine maintenance. Only if the engine will not idle properly and all vacuum leaks, tune-up and mechanical problems have been eliminated as possible causes of the rough idle or stalling should the mixture adjustment be performed. Performing this procedure requires drills of 0.256 and 0.295 in. diameter. Be sure to have a source of compressed air to remove metal drillings.

1. Remove the carburetor.

2. To remove the mixture adjusting plug, perform the following procedures:

a. Plug all the carburetor vacuum ports so drillings will not be able to enter them.

b. Using a center punch, mark the center of the mixture adjusting plug. Using a 0.256 in. drill, carefully drill a hole in the center of the plug.

NOTE: Stop drilling as soon as the plug has been drilled through; there is only about 0.04 in. (1mm) clearance between the plug and the top of the mixture screw.

c. Using a suitable tool, reach through the drilled hole and gently turn the mixture adjusting screw inward, until it just touches bottom.

NOTE: If the screw is turned too tight, the tapered tip will become grooved, necessitating replacement.

d. Using a 0.295 in. drill, force the plug from its seat.

3. Using compressed air, remove any metal filings. Remove the mixture screw by screwing it out all the way.

4. Install the mixture adjusting screw, by turning it in slowly and gently until it touches bottom, then, back it out (counting the number of turns) 3¼ turns.

5. Reinstall the carburetor, then, reconnect the vacuum hoses and air cleaner.

6. Start the engine and allow it to reach normal operating temperatures.

7. Adjust the idle speed.

8. Adjust the idle mixture screw until the highest rpm is reached, then, readjust the idle speed screw to 700 rpm. Keep adjusting both screws until the maximum speed will not rise any higher, no matter how much the idle mixture screw is adjusted.

9. Adjust the idle mixture screw until the engine speed is 650 rpm.

10. Adjust the idle speed screw to 650 rpm on manual transaxles or 750 rpm on automatic transaxles.

11. Remove the air cleaner and EGR mounting bracket. Using a hammer and drift, tap a new idle mixture adjusting plug in place with the tapered end inward. Reinstall the air cleaner and EGR vacuum modulator bracket.

SPECTRUM

NOTE: The idle mixture screw is adjusted and sealed at the factory and no service adjustment is required. However, if the necessity of adjustment arises for some reason, adjustment of the idle mixture screw is a possible by removing the plug but it must be replugged again after adjustment is completed.

1. Remove the carburetor from the engine.

2. Using a center punch, make a punch mark on the idle mixture sealing plug. Drill a hole through the plug, insert a threaded screw and pull the plug from the throttle body. The width of the plug is about 0.39 in. (10mm).

NOTE: If the idle mixture screw is damaged from the drilling process, replace the screw.

3. Lightly seat the idle mixture screw, then back out 3 turns on manual transaxle or 2 turns on automatic transaxle. Do not overtighten the idle mixture screw.

4. Reinstall the carburetor and the air cleaner.

5. Adjust the idle speed.

6. Using a dwell meter, connect the positive lead to the duty monitor and the negative lead to ground. Place the meter dial on the 4 cylinder scale. Turn the idle mixture screw until the dwell meter reads 45 degrees (4 cylinder scale).

7. Turn air conditioning on MAX/COLD and blower on HIGH then adjust the bolt on the FICD and set the fast idle to 850 rpm on manual transaxle or 980 on automatic transaxle, if equipped then stop the engine and remove the test equipment.

8. Drive a new idle mixture plug into the throttle body, flush with the throttle body apply Locktite No.262 or equivalent, to the plug.

9. Recheck all adjustments and road test.

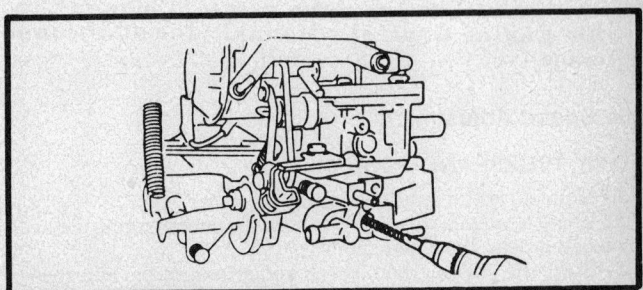

Drilling the mixture adjusting screw plug from the carburetor base—Spectrum

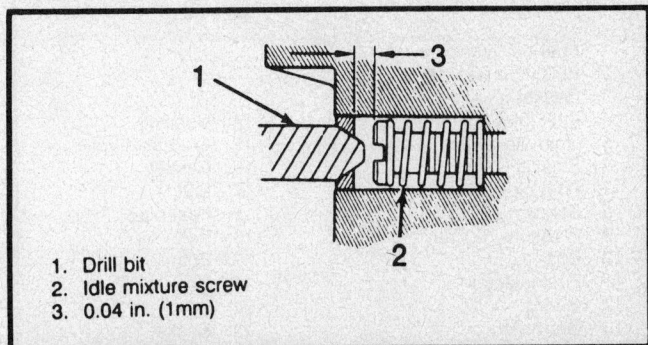

1. Drill bit
2. Idle mixture screw
3. 0.04 in. (1mm)

Drilling the mixture adjusting screw plug from the carburetor base—Nova

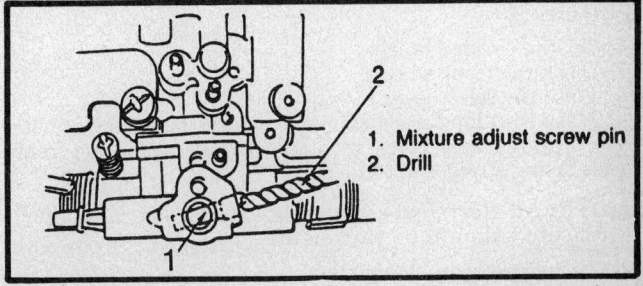

1. Mixture adjust screw pin
2. Drill

Removing the carburetor idle mixture pin—Sprint

SPRINT

The carburetor is adjusted at the factory and no further adjustment should be necessary. However, if the engine performance is poor, the emission test fails, or the carburetor has been replaced or overhauled, an idle mixture adjustment is necessary. Before adjusting the idle mixture, check the timing/idle speed and the valve lash. Make sure all electrical accessories are turned OFF.

1. Remove the carburetor from the intake manifold.
2. Using an $^{11}/_{64}$ in. bit, drill through the idle mixture screw housing, in line with the retaining pin. Use a punch to drive the pin from the housing.
3. Install the carburetor to the intake manifold by reversing the removal procedures.
4. Place the transaxle in **N**, set the parking brake and block the wheels.
5. Start the engine and bring it to normal operating temperatures.
6. Disconnect the duty cycle check connector, located near the water reservoir tank. Connect the positive terminal of a dwell meter to the blue/red wire and the negative terminal to the black/green wire.
7. Set the dwell meter to the 6 cylinder position, make sure the indicator moves.
8. Check and/or adjust the idle speed.
9. Operate the engine at idle speed and adjust the idle mixture screw, allow the engine to stabilize between adjustments. Adjust the dwell to 21–27 degrees; recheck the idle speed and adjust, if necessary.
10. After completing the adjustment, stop the engine, disconnect the dwell meter and connect the duty cycle check connector to the coupler.
11. Install a new idle mixture adjust screw pin in the throttle housing, drive into place.

Fuel Injection

For further information, please refer to "Chilton's Electronic Engine Control's Manual" for additional coverage.

Idle Speed Adjustment

NOVA, PRIZM AND STORM

1. Make sure the ignition timing is correct.
2. Using a jumper wire, connect it to the check engine connector located near the wiper motor.
3. Start the engine, then, check and/or adjust the idle speed; it should be 800 rpm on Nova and 700 rpm on Prizm and Storm.
4. When the adjustment is correct, remove the jumper wire from the check engine connector and recheck the timing marks.

SPECTRUM

1. Set the parking brake.
2. Block the front wheels.
3. Place the select lever in **N**.
4. Make the idling speed adjustment with the engine at normal operating temperature, with air conditioning off and front wheels facing straight ahead.

NOTE: All electrical equipment (lights, rear defogger, heater, etc.) should be turned off.

5. Make sure check engine light is not on.
6. Ground test terminal (ALDL connector).

7. Increase engine speed over 2000 rpm to reset the position of idle air control valve.
8. Set idle adjust screw to 950 rpm.
9. Remove test terminal ground and clear ECM trouble code.

SPRINT AND METRO

1. With a tachometer attached, run the engine until it reaches normal operating temperature.
2. Turn off all electrical loads such as lights, A/C etc.
3. Turn the idle speed adjusting screw until the idle speed is

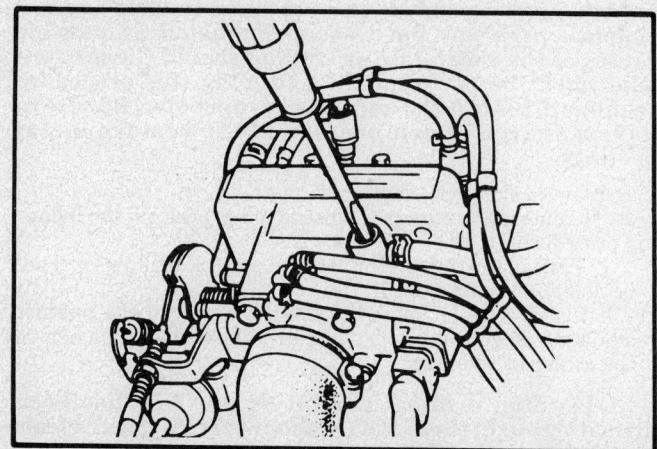

Idle speed adjustment screw—Sprint

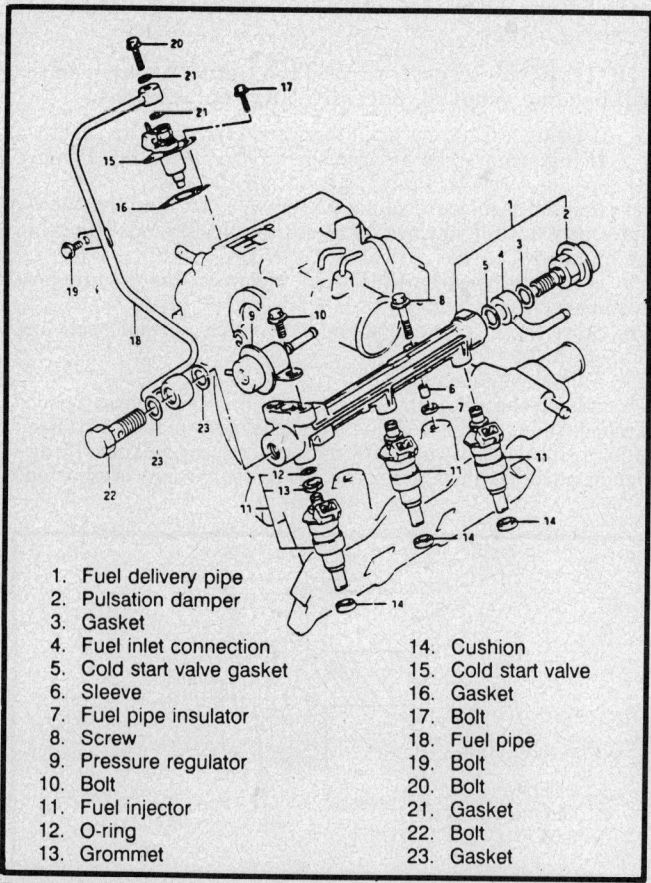

1. Fuel delivery pipe
2. Pulsation damper
3. Gasket
4. Fuel inlet connection
5. Cold start valve gasket
6. Sleeve
7. Fuel pipe insulator
8. Screw
9. Pressure regulator
10. Bolt
11. Fuel injector
12. O-ring
13. Grommet
14. Cushion
15. Cold start valve
16. Gasket
17. Bolt
18. Fuel pipe
19. Bolt
20. Bolt
21. Gasket
22. Bolt
23. Gasket

Fuel rail and injector mounting, turbocharged engine—Sprint

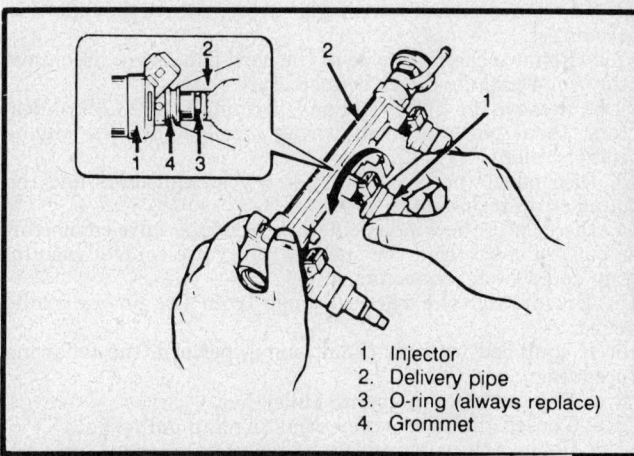

1. Injector
2. Delivery pipe
3. O-ring (always replace)
4. Grommet

Injector must rotate freely in the fuel rail, turbocharged engine—Sprint

at 700–800 rpm on Sprint and Metro equipped with manual transaxle or 800–900 rpm on Metro equipped with automatic transaxle.

Fuel Injector

Removal and Installation
NOVA AND PRIZM

1. Disconnect the negative terminal from the battery. Relieve the pressure in the fuel system.
2. Disconnect the electrical connectors from the fuel injectors.
3. Remove the fuel injector-to-engine bolts and pull the fuel injector assembly from the block.
4. Separate the fuel injector from the fuel line and discard the O-rings.
5. To install, use new O-rings, lubricate the O-rings with engine oil or gasoline and reverse the removal procedures.
6. Turn the ignition switch **ON** and check for fuel leaks. Start the engine and check the operation.

SPRINT
1. Relieve the fuel system pressure.
2. Disconnect the negative battery cable.

3. Remove the intake air hose between the throttle body and intercooler.
4. Disconnect the accelerator cable.
5. Disconnect the PCV and fuel return hoses from the delivery pipe.
6. Disconnect the throttle position sensor wiring coupler.
7. Disconnect the fuel injector wiring harness.
8. Remove the cold start valve from the delivery pipe.
9. Disconnect the fuel pressure regulator vacuum hose.
10. Disconnect the fuel feed hose from the delivery pipe.
11. Remove the fuel pressure regulator from the delivery pipe.
12. Remove the delivery pipe from the engine with the fuel injectors attached.
13. Remove the fuel injector(s) from the delivery pipe.
To install:
14. Replace the O-ring on any injector removed from the delivery pipe.
15. Lightly coat the new O-ring with engine oil when installing.

NOTE: After the injectors are installed in the fuel delivery pipe, make sure they rotate freely in the pipe before installation.

16. Check the insulator in the engine and replace, if necessary.
17. Install the delivery pipe and injector assembly in the engine.
18. Continue the installation in the reverse of the removal procedure.
19. When finished, run the engine and check for fuel leaks.

METRO
1. Relieve the fuel system pressure.
2. Disconnect the negative battery cable.
3. Remove the air cleaner assembly.
4. Remove the injector cover and upper insulator.
5. Disconnect the electrical connector and remove the injector.
To install:
6. Apply a thin coat of transaxle fluid or gasoline to the new upper and lower O-rings and install them on the injectors.
7. Install a new lower injector insulator into the injector cavity.
8. Push the injector straight into the fuel injection cavity. Do not twist.
9. Install a new upper insulator and the injection cover.
10. Install the injector cover screws to 31 inch lbs.
11. Connect the electrical connector to the injector, facing it lug side upward on clamp subwire securely.
12. Connect the negative battery cable.

ENGINE MECHANICAL

NOTE: Disconnecting the negative battery cable on some vehicles may interfere with the functions of the on board computer systems and may require the computer to undergo a relearning process, once the negative battery cable is reconnected.

Engine Assembly

Removal and Installation
NOVA

Except Twincam Engine

1. Disconnect the negative terminal from the battery. Drain the cooling system.
2. Properly discharge the air conditioning system.
3. Using a scratch awl, scribe the hood hinge-to-hood outline, then, using an assistant remove the hood.

4. Remove the air cleaner assembly and associated ducts.
5. From the radiator, remove the upper coolant hose and the overflow hose. Disconnect the coolant hose from the coolant pipe at the rear of the cylinder head and the coolant hose from the thermostat housing.
6. Disconnect the fuel hoses from the fuel pump.
7. Remove the drive belt from the alternator, the power steering pump, if equipped, and the air conditioning compressor, if equipped. If equipped with power steering, remove the power steering pump-to-engine bolts and move the pump aside, do not disconnect the pressure hoses. If equipped with air conditioning, remove the compressor-to-engine bolts and move it aside; do not disconnect the pressure hoses.
8. Label and disconnect the electrical connectors that will interfere with the engine removal.
9. Label and disconnect the vacuum hoses running between the engine and firewall or fender well mounted accessories.

10. Label and disconnect the electrical connectors from the transaxle.

11. Disconnect the speedometer cable from the transaxle.

12. Raise and support the vehicle safely. Drain the engine oil and the transaxle fluid.

13. Disconnect the exhaust pipe-to-exhaust manifold bolts and separate the exhaust pipe from the manifold.

14. Disconnect the air hose from the catalytic converter, if equipped.

15. If equipped with an automatic transaxle, disconnect and plug the oil cooler tubes from the radiator.

16. Remove the undercovers from both sides of the vehicle.

17. Disconnect the cable and the bracket from the transaxle.

18. Disconnect the steering knuckles from the lower control arms.

19. Disconnect the halfshafts from the transaxle.

20. Remove the flywheel cover. If equipped with an automatic transaxle, mark the torque converter-to-flexplate, then, remove the torque converter-to-flexplate bolts and move the torque converter back into the transaxle.

21. Disconnect the front and rear engine mounts from the center member.

22. Lower the vehicle.

23. Remove the radiator-to-chassis bolts and the radiator (with the fans) from the vehicle.

24. Using a overhead lift, attach it to and support the engine.

25. Remove the through bolt from right-side engine mount, then, the left-side transaxle mount bolt and the mount.

26. Remove the engine/transaxle assembly from the vehicle. Remove the transaxle-to-engine bolts and separate the transaxle from the engine, then, secure the engine to a workstand.

To install:

27. Reverse the procedure to install. Refill the cooling system, the transaxle and the engine with clean fluid.

28. Connect the battery negative cable. Start the engine, allow it to reach normal operating temperatures and check for leaks.

29. If equipped with an automatic transaxle, torque the torque converter-to-flexplate bolts to 58 ft. lbs.

30. Torque the halfshaft-to-transaxle bolts to 27 ft. lbs.

31. Torque the engine-to-crossmember mount bolts to 29 ft. lbs.

32. Torque the exhaust pipe-to-exhaust manifold to 46 ft. lbs.

33. Torque the power steering pump-to-bracket bolt to 29 ft. lbs.

34. Torque the power steering adjusting bolt to 32 ft. lbs.

Twincam Engine

1. Disconnect the negative terminal from the battery.

2. Properly relieve the fuel system pressure.

3. Drain the cooling system.

4. Using a scratch awl, scribe the hood hinge-to-hood outline, then, using an assistant remove the hood.

5. Remove the air cleaner assembly, the coolant tank reservoir and the PVC hose.

6. Disconnect the heater hoses from the water inlet housing and the fuel hose from the fuel filter.

7. If equipped with a manual transaxle, remove the clutch slave cylinder-to-transaxle bolts and the slave cylinder, then, move the cylinder aside.

8. Disconnect the vacuum hose from the charcoal canister.

9. Disconnect the speedometer cable from the transaxle and the accelerator cable from the throttle body.

10. If equipped with cruise control, perform the following procedures:

   a. Remove the cables from the throttle body.

   b. Disconnect the vacuum hose from the actuator.

   c. Remove the actuator cover bolts and the cover.

   d. Disconnect the actuator connector, then, remove the actuator.

11. Remove the ignition coil.

12. To remove the main wiring harness, perform the following procedures:

   a. Remove the right side of the cowl panel and disconnect the No. 4 junction block connectors.

   b. Remove the ECM cover and disconnect the ECM connectors, then, pull the main wiring harness into the engine compartment.

13. Disconnect the No. 2 junction block connectors and the ground strap terminals.

14. Disconnect the windshield washer change valve connector, the battery cable from the starter, the cruise control vacuum pump and switch connectors.

15. Disconnect the vacuum hose from the power brake booster.

16. If equipped with air conditioning, perform the following procedures:

   a. Remove the vane pump pulley nut.

   b. Loosen the idler pulley adjusting and pulley nuts.

   c. Remove the compressor-to-bracket bolts, then, move the compressor aside and secure it.

   d. Disconnect the oil pressure connector.

   e. Remove the compressor bracket bolts, the vane pump bolts, then, move the vane pump and bracket aside and suspend it.

17. Raise and support the vehicle safely. Drain the engine crankcase and transaxle fluid.

18. Remove the splash shields.

19. If equipped with an automatic transaxle, disconnect and plug the oil cooler from the radiator.

20. Remove the exhaust pipe-to-exhaust manifold bolts and separate the pipe from the manifold. Disconnect the oxygen sensor connector.

21. Remove the flywheel housing cover.

22. Remove the front and rear engine mounts from the center member, then, the center member.

23. Disconnect the right-side control arm from the steering knuckle and halfshafts from the transaxle.

24. Lower the vehicle.

25. Using a vertical hoist, secure the engine to it and support the engine; secure the engine wiring and hoses to the lift chain.

26. Remove the right-side engine mount, then, the left-side engine mount from the transaxle bracket.

NOTE: When lifting the engine be careful not to damage the throttle position sensor or the power steering gear housing.

27. Lift the engine/transaxle assembly from the vehicle.

28. To separate the transaxle from the engine, perform the following procedures:

   a. Remove the radiator fan temperature switch connector and the start injector time switch connector.

   b. Disconnect the vacuum hoses from the BVSV's.

   c. Remove the No. 1 and 2 hoses from the water bypass pipes.

   d. Disconnect the electrical connector from the back-up switch, the water temperature sensor and the water temperature switch.

   e. If equipped with an automatic transaxle, disconnect the neutral start switch connector and the transaxle solenoid connector, then, remove the torque converter-to-flexplate bolts; be sure to push the torque converter back into the transaxle.

   f. Remove the starter, the transaxle-to-engine bolts and the transaxle.

To install:

29. Reverse the removal procedures to install. Refill the cooling system, the engine crankcase and transaxle.

30. Start the engine, allow it to reach normal operating temperatures and check for leaks.

31. Torque the torque converter-to-flexplate bolts to 20 ft. lbs.

32. Torque the starter-to-engine bolts to 29 ft. lbs.

33. Torque the halfshaft-to-transaxle nuts to 27 ft. lbs.
34. Torque the right-side control arm-to-steering knuckle nuts/bolts to 47 ft. lbs.
35. Torque the crossmember-to-chassis bolts to 29 ft. lbs.
36. Torque the engine mounts-to-cross member bolts to 35 ft. lbs.
37. Torque the exhaust pipe to-exhaust manifold nuts to 46 ft. lbs.

PRIZM

1. Scribe matchmarks around the hood hinges and then remove the hood. Remove the engine undercovers.
2. Properly relieve the fuel system pressure.
3. Remove the air cleaner along with its hose.
4. Remove the coolant reservoir tank. Remove the radiator and cooling fan.
5. Disconnect the accelerator and throttle cables at the carburetor on models with automatic transaxle.
6. Disconnect the No. 2 junction block, the graound strap connector and the ground strap. Disconnect the vacuum hoses at the brake booster, power steering pump, A/C compressor and EBCV.
7. Disconnect the fuel lines at the fuel pump. Disconnect the heater hoses at the water inlet housing.
8. Disconnect the power steering pump and lay it aside with the hydraulic lines still attached. Do the same with the air conditioningcompressor.
9. Disconnect the speedometer cable. On vehicles with a manual transaxle, remove the clutch release cylinder and position it out of the way with the hydraulic lines still attached.
10. Disconnect the shift control cables and then raise and support the vehicle safely. Drain the engine coolant and oil. Drain the gear oil from the transaxle.
11. Remove the 2 nuts from the flange and then disconnect the exhaust pipe at the manifold. Disconnect the halfshafts at the transaxle.
12. Remove the 2 hole covers and then remove the front, center and rear engine mounts from the center member. Remove the 5 bolts, insulators and the center member.
13. Attach an engine hoist chain to the lifting brackets on the engine and then remove the 3 bolts and mounting stay. Remove the bolt, 2 nuts and the through bolt and pull out the right side engine mount. Remove the 2 bolts and the left mounting stay. Remove the 3 bolts and disconnect the left engine mount bracket from the transaxle. Lift the engine/transaxle assembly out of the vehicle.
To install:
14. Installation is in the reverse order of removal.
15. Tighten the right engine mount insulator bolt to 47 ft. lbs. (64 Nm); tighten the nut to 38 ft. lbs. (52 Nm). Align the insulator with the bracket on the body and tighten the bolt to 64 ft. lbs. (87 Nm).
16. Align the left engine mount insulator bracket with the transaxle bracket and tighten the bolt to 35 ft. lbs. (48 Nm).
17. Install the right mounting stay and tighten the 3 bolts to 31 ft. lbs. (42 Nm). Install the left stay and tighten the 2 bolts to 15 ft. lbs. (21 Nm).
18. Install the engine center member and tighten the 5 bolts to 45 ft. lbs. (61 Nm).
19. Install the front and rear engine mounts and bolts. Align the bolts holes in the brackets with the center member and tighten the front mount bolts to 35 ft. lbs. (48 Nm); tighten the center and rear mounts to 38 ft. lbs. (52 Nm). Install the 2 hole covers and tighten the rear mounting bolt to 58 ft. lbs. (78 Nm).

STORM

1. Disconnect the battery negative cable, then remove battery and battery tray from vehicle.
2. Scribe match marks on the hood hinge-to-hood, then remove the hood.

3. Discharge air conditioning system.
4. Drain cooling system, then disconnect the accelerator cabloe from the throttle valve.
5. Disconnect the breather hose from the intake air duct, then remove thge intake air duct from the throttle valve.
6. Remove the air cleaner cover, filter and the body from the vehicle.
7. Remove the MAP sensor hose from the MAP sensor, then the brake booster vacuum hose.
8. Disconnect the 2 canister hoses from the pipes on the intake manifold (common chamber). If equipped with twincam engine, remove the canister pipe supoport bracket.
9. Disconnect the 2 cable harness connectors, located near the left shock tower.
10. Disconnect the ignition coil ground cable from the terminal on the thermostat housing flange.
11. Disconnect the ignition coil-to-distributor wire, the 2 primary wires from the ignition coil, then remove the ignition coil and bracket from the vehicle.
12. Disconnect the engine harness ground cable from the left inner fender.
13. Disconnect the harness terminal from the relay and fuse box.
14. Disconnect the cooling fan electrical connector and the 2 battery cable connectors.
15. Disconnect the oxygen sensor electrical connector, then the ground cable terminal from the rear of the cylinder head cover.
16. If equipped with automatic transaxle, disconnect the electrical connectors from transaxle.
17. If equipped with manual transaxle, loosen the tow adjusting nuts and disconnect the clutch cable. Disconnect the 2 transaxle shaft cables by removing the cotter pin and clip from the shaft cable bracket.
18. If equipped with automatic transaxle, Disconnect the shift cable by removing the cotter pin from the shaft cable lever.
19. On all vehicles, remove the 2 heater hoses from the engine.
20. Disconnect the speedometer from the transaxle, then the upper radiator hose from the radiator.
21. Disconnect the fuel feed line and fuel return hose, near the filter, then the coolant recovery tank with bracket.
22. Remove the power steering belt, power steering pump and bracket from the vehicle.
23. Remove the cooling fan and shroud, then raise and support the vehicle safely.
24. Remove the right and left under covers and the lower radiator hose from the engine.
25. If equipped with automatic transaxle, disconnect the oil cooler, lines from the transaxle.
26. Remove the air conditioning compressor bracket bolts and position compressor aside.
27. Remove the front tire and wheel assemblies, then the halfshafts.
28. Remove the front exhaust pipe from the exhaust manifold.
29. Lower the vehicle and install a suitable engine hoist onto the lifting brackets on the engine.
30. Remove the engine mounts and transaxle mounts, then lift the engine and transaxle assembly out from the vehicle. Separate the transaxle from the engine.

To install:
31. Install the transaxle to the engine, then a suitable hoist onto the engine lifting brackets.
32. Install engine and transaxle into vehicle, then the transaxle mounts and engine mounts.
33. Remove the engine hoist from the vehicle, then raise and support vehicle safely.
34. Install the front exhaust pipe to the exhaust manifold, then the halfshafts.
35. Install the tire and wheel assemblies, then the 2 air conditioning bracket mounting bolts.

36. If equipped with automatic transaxle, connect the 2 cooler lines to the transaxle.

37. Install the lower radiator hose, then the right and left undercovers. Lower the vehicle.

38. Install the cooling fan and shroud, then the power steering pump and belt onto the engine.

39. Install the coolant recovery tank with bracket, then connect the fuel feed line and fuel return hose.

40. Install the upper radiator hose, then connect the speedometer cable to the transaxle.

41. Connect the 2 heater hoses to the engine, then the transaxle shift cables, if equipped.

42. If equipped with manual transaxle, connect the clutch cable and adjust.

43. If equipped with automatic transaxle, connect the electrical connectors to the transaxle.

44. Connect the ground cable terminal to the rear of the cylinder head cover.

45. Connect the 2 ground terminals to the right side of the intake manifold (common chamber). If equipped with twincamengine, install the canister pipe support bracket.

46. Connect the oxygen sensor electrical connector and the 2 battery cable harness connectors.

47. Connect the cooling fan harness connector, then the chassis harness terminal connector to the relay and fuse box.

48. Connect the engine ground cable to the left inner fender, then install tyhe ignition coil and bracket.

49. Connect the 2 primary wires to the ignition coil and the ignition coil-to-distributor wire.

50. Connect the ignition coil ground wire to the terminal at the thermostat housing.

51. Connect the 2 cable harness connectors, located near the left shock tower.

52. Connect the 2 canister hoses to the intake manifold (common chamber).

53. Connect the brake booster vacuum hose, then the MAP sensor hose to the MAP sensor.

54. Install the air cleaner body, air cleaner filter and the cover.

55. Connect the air intake duct to the throttle body and the breather hose to the air intake duct.

56. Connect the accelerator cable to the throttle valve.

57. Fill the cooling system, engine oil and transaxle with suitable fluids. Install the battery tray and battery.

58. Align match marks on the hood hinge during removal and install the hood. Connect the battery negative cable. Start the engine and check for leaks.

SPECTRUM

1. Remove the hood, relieve the fuel system pressure and disconnect the negative battery cable.

2. Drain the cooling system.

3. If equipped with carburetor, remove the air cleaner and the throttle cable at the carburetor.

4. Disconnect the heater hoses at the intake manifold, the coolant hose at the thermostat housing and the thermostat housing at the cylinder head.

5. On turbocharged models, remove the throttle cable, fuel lines and connectors, and also remove turbocharger vacuum, oil and water lines.

6. Remove the distributor from the cylinder head.

7. Disconnect the oxygen sensor electrical connector.

8. Support the engine using a vertical lift and remove the right motor mount.

9. Disconnect the necessary electrical connectors and vacuum hoses.

10. Disconnect the flex hose at the exhaust manifold and the lower radiator hose at the block.

11. Remove the upper air conditioning compressor bolt and remove the belt.

12. Disconnect the power steering bracket at the block and remove the belt.

13. Disconnect the fuel lines from the fuel pump and the electrical connectors from under the carburetor, if equipped.

14. Remove the upper starter bolt. Raise and support the vehicle safely.

15. Drain the oil from the crankcase and remove the oil filter.

16. Disconnect the oil temperature switch connector.

17. Disconnect the exhaust pipe bracket at the block and the exhaust pipe at the manifold.

18. Remove the air conditioning compressor and move to one side. Do not disconnect the air conditioning refrigerant lines. Remove the alternator wires.

19. Remove the flywheel cover and the converter bolts, then install a flywheel holding tool J–35271 or equivalent.

20. Disconnect the starter wires and remove the starter.

21. Remove the front right wheel and inner splash shield.

22. Lower the engine by lowering the crossmember enough to gain access to the crankshaft pulley bolts, then remove the pulley.

23. Raise the engine and crossmember. Remove the engine support.

24. Lower the vehicle and support the transaxle.

25. Remove the transaxle to engine bolts. Remove the engine.

To install:

26. Reverse the procedure to install.

27. Adjust the drive belts and refill the fluids.

28. Connect all electrical connectors and vacuum lines.

29. Connect the battery negative cable. Start engine and check for leaks.

SPRINT AND METRO

1. Properly relieve the fuel system pressure. Remove the battery cables.

2. Remove the hood, battery, battery tray, air cleaner and the outside air duct.

3. Drain the cooling system.

4. Disconnect and tag the radiator, heater and vacuum hoses from the engine.

5. Disconnect the cooling fan wiring.

6. Remove the cooling fan, shroud and radiator as an assembly.

7. Remove the fuel hoses from the fuel pump.

8. Remove the brake booster hose from the intake manifold, accelerator cable from the carburetor and speed control cable from the transaxle.

9. Remove the clutch cable and bracket from the transaxle.

10. Disconnect and tag the necessary wiring from the engine and transaxle.

11. Remove the air conditioning compressor adjusting bolt and drive belt splash shield.

12. Raise and support the vehicle safely. Drain the engine oil and the transaxle fluid.

13. Disconnect the exhaust pipe from the exhaust manifold.

14. Remove the air conditioning pivot bolt, the drive belt and the mounting bracket.

15. Disconnect the gear shift control shaft and extension rod at the transaxle.

16. Disconnect the ball joints.

17. Remove the axle shafts from the transaxle.

18. Remove the engine torque rods and the transaxle mount nut.

19. Lower the vehicle.

20. Remove the engine side mount and the mount nuts.

21. Connect a vertical hoist to the engine, then lift the engine and transaxle assembly from the vehicle.

To install:

22. Reverse the procedure to install.

23. Connect all electrical connectors and vacuum hoses.

24. Refill the engine, the transaxle and the cooling system.

24. Connect the battery negative cable. Start the engine and check for leaks.

Engine Mounts

Removal and Installation
NOVA AND PRIZM

1. Disconnect the negative terminal from the battery.
2. Raise and support the vehicle safely.
3. Using an engine support fixture tool No. J-28467 or equivalent, attach it to the engine and support it.
4. Remove the center member hole covers, loosen the engine center mount and lower the vehicle.
5. Remove the two bolts/nuts from the front, rear and right-side engine mounts.
6. Lower the vehicle.
7. From the left-side engine mount, remove the 2 bolts on manual transaxle or 3 bolts on automatic transaxle.
8. Remove the through bolts from the engine mounts. Raise the engine in order to relieve engine weight from the mount. Remove the mounts from the vehicle.
9. To install, reverse the removal procedures. Torque the engine-to-cross member bolts to 35 ft. lbs. and the engine mount through bolts to 58 ft. lbs.

STORM
Right

1. Disconnect the battery negative cable.
2. Support the engine using support support tool J–28467-Aor equivalent.
3. Raise and support vehicle safely, then remove the nut and bolt from the mounting bracket.
4. Remove the through bolt from the engine mount, then the engine mount from the vehicle.
5. Reverse procedure to install. Torque bridge bracket bolt to 29 ft. lbs. (40 Nm) and the right mount through bolt to 50 ft. lbs. (68 Nm).

Left

1. Disconnect the battery negative and positive cables, then remove the battery.
2. Remove the cover plate.
3. Remove the left engine mount bolts from the transaxle case.
4. Remove the left engine mount center bolt, then the left engine mount from the vehicle.
5. Reverse procedure to install. Torque left engine mount center bolt to 50 ft. lbs (68 Nm) and the engine mount-to-transaxle case bolts to 35 ft. lbs. (48 Nm).

Rear

1. Disconnect the battery negative cable.
2. Support the engine using engine support tool J–28467–A or equivalent.
3. Raise and support vehicle safely.
4. Remove the dampener weight from the engine mounting, then the bolt from the transaxle case.
5. Remove the center bolts from the center beam and the rear engine mount from the vehicle.
6. Reverse procedure to install. Torque rear mount center bolts to 76 ft. lbs. (102 Nm) and the rear mount transaxle case bolt to 37 ft. lbs. (50 Nm).

SPECTRUM

1. Disconnect the negative battery terminal from the battery.
2. Raise and support the vehicle safely.
3. Support the engine.
4. Remove the through nuts and bolts from engine mounts.
5. Remove the 4 bolts attaching the beam and remove beam.

6. Remove the front and or rear engine mounting rubbers.

NOTE:Install new bolts for mounts and torque engine mounting nut and bolts to 60 ft. lbs.

7. To install, reverse the removal procedures.

SPRINT AND METRO
Front

1. Disconnect the negative battery cable.
2. Remove the motor mount nut.
3. Raise the and support the vehicle safely. Support the engine.
4. Remove the mount and frame bracket. Separate and remove the mount from the bracket.
5. Installation is the reverse of the removal procedure.

Rear

1. Disconnect the negative battery cable.
2. Raise and support the vehicle safely.
3. Remove the motor mount to body bracket nut.
4. Support the engine.
5. Remove the mount and frame bracket. Separate and remove the mount from the bracket.
6. Installation is the reverse of the removal procedure.

Cylinder Head

Removal and Installation
NOVA
Except Twincam Engine

1. Disconnect the negative terminal from the battery.
2. Drain the engine coolant into a clean container, opening both the radiator and cylinder block drain cocks.
3. Remove the air cleaner. Label and disconnect all vacuum hoses.
4. Raise and support the vehicle safely. Drain the engine oil. Remove the exhaust pipe-to-exhaust manifold nuts and separate the exhaust pipe from the manifold. Remove the exhaust pipe bracket from the engine. Remove the hose from the catalytic converter pipe.
5. If equipped with power steering, loosen the power steering pump pivot bolt. Lower the vehicle.
6. Disconnect the accelerator and throttle cables from the carburetor and cable bracket.
7. Disconnect electrical harness from the cowl, the oxygen sensor and the distributor.
8. Disconnect the fuel hoses from the fuel pump.
9. Disconnect the upper radiator hose from the water outlet, then, remove the water outlet from the cylinder head. Remove the heater hose.
10. If equipped with power steering, remove the adjusting bracket from the engine.
11. Remove the PCV valve and the wiring harness that passes over the valve cover.
12. Label and disconnect the spark plug wires, the electrical connector and the vacuum hoses from the distributor.
13. Remove the upper timing belt cover-to-cylinder head bolts and the cover.
14. Remove the cylinder head cover-to-cylinder head bolts, the cover and the gasket.
15. Remove the alternator drive belt. Remove the water pump pulley-to-water pump bolts and the pulley.
16. Using socket wrench on the crankshaft pulley bolt, rotate the crankshaft to position the No. 1 cylinder on the TDC of its compression stroke; the crankshaft pulley notch is aligned with the **0** degrees mark on the timing plate and the No. 1 cylinder rocker arms are loose.
17. Remove the distributor-to-cylinder head hold-down bolts and the distributor.

18. Matchmark the timing belt and sprocket for reassembly in the same position; mark an arrow on the timing belt for rotation direction.

19. Loosen the idler pulley bolt. Move it so as to release the timing belt tension and snug the idler pulley bolt. Remove the timing belt; avoid twisting or bending it.

20. Loosen the head bolts, in sequence, in 3 stages, then, remove them. Lift the head directly off the block. If it is necessary to pry the head off the block, use a bar between the head and the projection provided on top of the block.

NOTE: **Do not pry except at the projection provided. Be careful not to damage the block or cylinder head sealing surface.**

To install:

21. Using the proper tool, clean the gasket mounting surfaces. Using wire brush, clean the cylinder head chambers.

22. Use new gaskets, sealant, if necessary, and reverse the removal procedures.

NOTE: **When installing the cylinder head gasket, position the side with the sealer facing upwards.**

23. Torque the cylinder head-to-engine bolts, in sequence, using 3 passes, to 43 ft. lbs., the camshaft sprocket-to-camshaft bolt to 34 ft. lbs. and the timing belt idler bolt to 27 ft. lbs.

24. Rotate the crankshaft through 2 complete revolutions and check the timing belt tension; the tension should be 0.024–0.28 in.

25. Adjust the valves with the engine **COLD**. Operate the engine until normal operating temperatures are reached and check for leaks. Readjust the valves with the engine **HOT**. Set the ignition timing.

Twincam Engine

1. Disconnect the negative terminal from the battery. Relieve the fuel system pressure.

2. Drain the engine coolant. Remove the air cleaner assembly.

3. Disconnect the throttle cable and the cruise control cable from the throttle linkage. Remove the ignition coil.

4. From the rear of the cylinder head, remove the heater hose. Remove the vacuum hoses from the throttle body. Remove the water outlet hose from cylinder head and the radiator.

5. If equipped with cruise control, remove the actuator and the bracket assembly.

6. Remove the hoses from the PCV valve and the power brake booster.

7. Remove the pressure regulator, the EGR valve (with lines) and the cold start injector hose.

8. Disconnect and remove the No. 1 fuel line.

9. From the auxiliary air valve, remove the No. 1 and No. 2 water bypass hoses.

10. Remove the vacuum pipe and the cylinder head rear cover.

11. Label and disconnect the electrical harness connectors. Remove the distributor-to-cylinder hold-down bolt and the distributor.

12. Remove the exhaust manifold-to-cylinder head bolts and separate the exhaust manifold from the cylinder head.

13. Remove the fuel delivery pipe-to-engine bolts and the delivery pipe with the injectors; do not drop the fuel injectors.

14. Remove the intake manifold bracket, the intake manifold-to-cylinder head bolts (in sequence), the intake manifold and the intake air control valve.

15. If equipped with power steering, remove the drive belt. Remove the alternator drive belt and the cylinder head covers.

16. Remove the water outlet with the No. 1 bypass pipe and drive belt adjusting bar assembly.

17. To position the No. 1 cylinder on the TDC of its compression stroke, perform the following procedures:
  a. Remove the spark plugs.

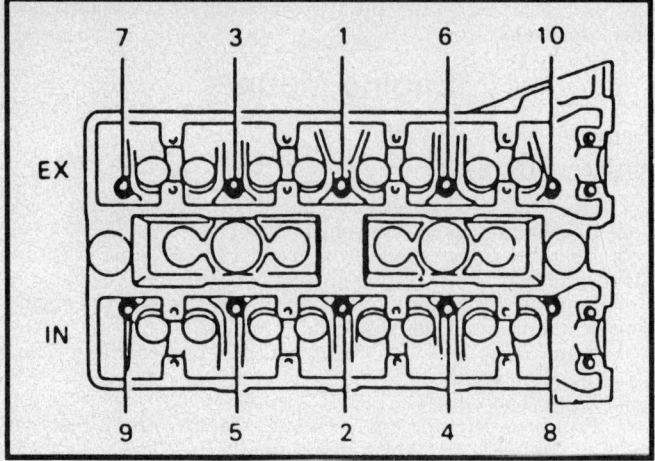

Cylinder head bolt torquing sequence, twincam engine—Nova

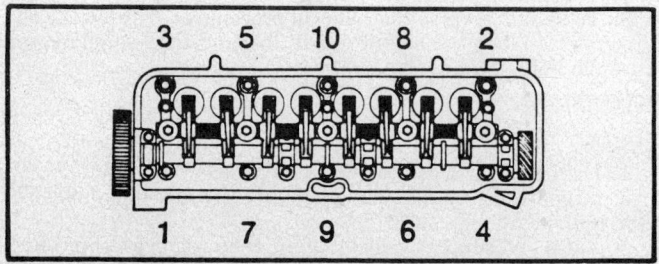

Cylinder head bolt loosening sequence except twincam engine—Nova

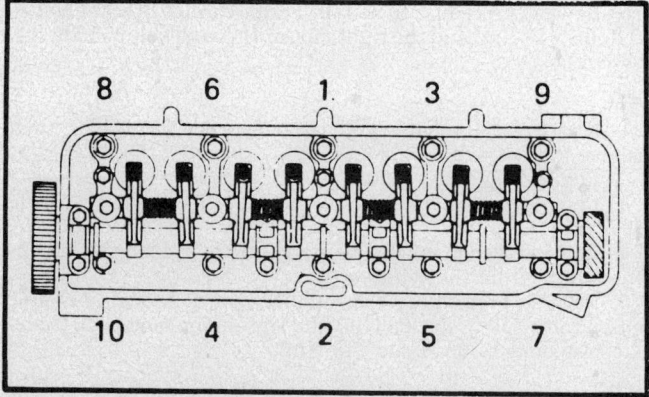

Cylinder head bolt torquing sequence except twincam engine—Nova

  b. Using a socket wrench on the crankshaft pulley, rotate the crankshaft to align the notch in the crankshaft pulley with the idler pulley bolt.

  c. The valve lifters of the No. 1 cylinder should be loose; if not, rotate the crankshaft 1 complete revolution.

18. Remove the right side engine mount, the right-side engine mount bracket, then, the upper and middle timing belt covers.

19. Using chalk or paint, place matchmarks on the timing belt and the timing belt pulleys, then, remove the timing belt from the timing belt pulleys.

NOTE: **When removing the timing belt, be sure to support it so the meshing with the timing belt pulleys does not change. Do not allow it to come in contact with oil or water.**

20. While securing the camshafts, remove each camshaft pulley-to-camshaft bolt, washer and pulley. Remove the inner timing belt cover.

21. Remove the camshaft bearing cap-to-cylinder head bolts, the caps (keep them in order) and the camshafts (keep them in order).

22. Using the cylinder head bolt removal sequence, remove the cylinder head bolts and lift the cylinder head from the engine.

23. Using the proper tool, clean the gasket mounting surfaces. Using a wire brush, clean the carbon from the cylinder head cavities. Inspect the cylinder head for damage and/or warpage.

NOTE: When cleaning the cylinder head, be careful, the cylinder head is made of aluminum which is a soft material:

To install:

24. To install the cylinder head, use a new gasket, make sure it is installed in the correct direction, lubricate the bolt threads in engine oil and reverse the removal procedures.

NOTE: The intake-side bolts are 3.45 in. long and the exhaust-side bolts are 4.25 in. long.

25. To torque the cylinder head-to-engine bolts, perform the following procedures:

a. Torque the cylinder head-to-engine bolts, in sequence, to 22 ft. lbs.

b. Using paint, place a paint mark on the cylinder head bolts.

c. Torque the bolts, in sequence, ¼ turn (90 degrees).

d. Retorque the bolts, in sequence, another ¼ turn (90 degrees).

26. To install the camshafts, apply RTV sealant to the camshaft oil seal bearing cap-to-cylinder head surfaces, lightly coat the seal lip with multi-purpose grease, then, install the new oil seals and camshafts. Torque the camshaft bearing cap-to-cylinder head bolts to 9 ft. lbs.

27. Install the camshaft pulleys-to-camshaft bolts to 34 ft. lbs. Align the timing belt marks with the camshaft pulley marks and install the timing belt onto the camshaft pulleys.

28. Using a wrench on the timing belt pulley, rotate the crankshaft 2 complete revolutions and check the timing belt alignment points.

29. To complete the installation, use new O-rings, new gaskets, sealant, if necessary, and reverse the removal procedures. Torque the intake manifold-to-cylinder head bolts to 20 ft. lbs., the exhaust manifold-to-cylinder head bolts to 18 ft. lbs. Refill the cooling system. Start the engine, allow it to reach normal operating temperatures and check for leaks. Check and/or adjust the ignition timing.

PRIZM

1. Disconnect the negative battery cable. Relieve the fuel system pressure. Drain the coolant.

2. Raise and support the vehicle safely. Remove the right lower stone shield.

3. Remove the 2 mount nut and stud protectors. Remove the 2 rear transaxle mount to main crossmember mount nuts.

4. Remove the 2 center mount to center crossmember nuts. Lower the vehicle.

5. Remove the air cleaner assembly, disconnect the throttle cable and the cruise control actuator cable.

6. Disconnect the transaxle kickdown cable. Disconnect all necessary electrical connections and vacuum lines.

7. Disconnect the fuel inlet line. Disconnect the cold start injector pipe. Remove the fuel rail. Disconnect the coolant and heater hoses.

8. Remove the water outlet and inlet housings. Disconnect the spark plug wires and remove the PCV valve.

9. Remove the cylinder head cover. Loosen the air condi-

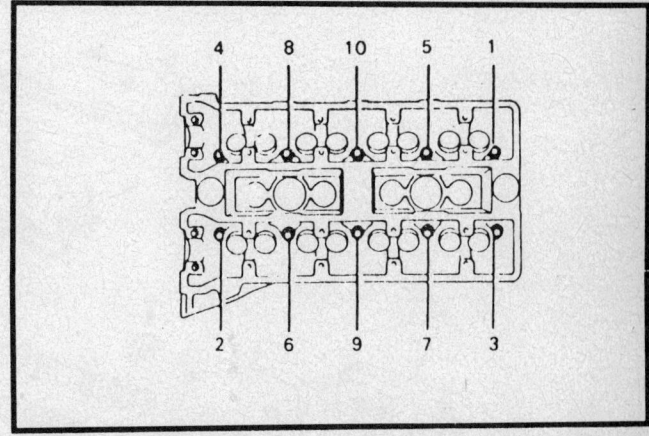

Cylinder head bolt loosening sequence, twincam engine—Nova

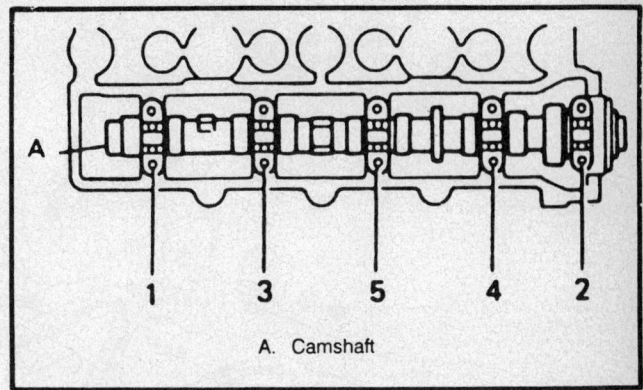

A. Camshaft

Camshaft bearing cap removal sequence, twincam engine—Nova

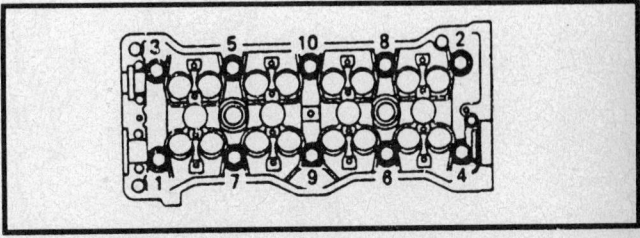

Cylinder head bolt loosening sequence—Prizm

tioning compressor, power steering pump and generator brackets as applicable.

10. Remove the accessory drive belts. Remove the air conditioning idler pulley. Disconnect the electrical connections at cruise control actuator and remove the cruise control actuator and bracket.

11. Remove windshield washer reservoir. Support the engine with a J–28467–A support fixture or its equivalent.

12. Remove the right engine mount through bolt. Raise the engine and properly support it.

13. Remove the water pump pulley. Lower the engine. Disconnect the engine wiring harness from upper timing belt cover.

14. Raise and suitably support the vehicle. Remove the cylinder head-to-cylinder block bracket.

15. Remove the exhaust manifold support bracket. Disconnect the exhaust pipe from exhaust manifold.

16. Remove the upper and center timing belt cover. Remove the right engine mount bracket. Remove the distributor.

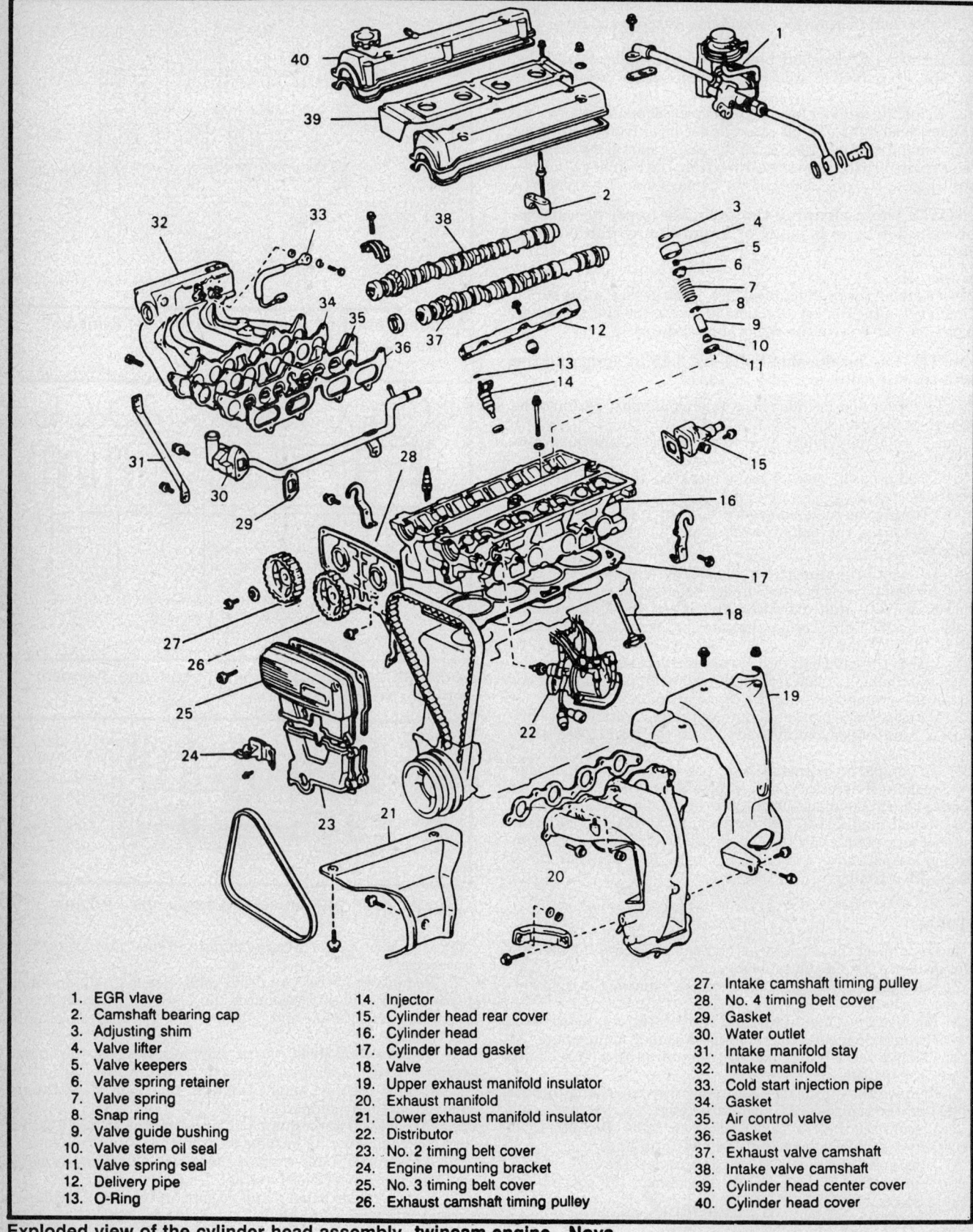

1. EGR vlave
2. Camshaft bearing cap
3. Adjusting shim
4. Valve lifter
5. Valve keepers
6. Valve spring retainer
7. Valve spring
8. Snap ring
9. Valve guide bushing
10. Valve stem oil seal
11. Valve spring seal
12. Delivery pipe
13. O-Ring
14. Injector
15. Cylinder head rear cover
16. Cylinder head
17. Cylinder head gasket
18. Valve
19. Upper exhaust manifold insulator
20. Exhaust manifold
21. Lower exhaust manifold insulator
22. Distributor
23. No. 2 timing belt cover
24. Engine mounting bracket
25. No. 3 timing belt cover
26. Exhaust camshaft timing pulley
27. Intake camshaft timing pulley
28. No. 4 timing belt cover
29. Gasket
30. Water outlet
31. Intake manifold stay
32. Intake manifold
33. Cold start injection pipe
34. Gasket
35. Air control valve
36. Gasket
37. Exhaust valve camshaft
38. Intake valve camshaft
39. Cylinder head center cover
40. Cylinder head cover

Exploded view of the cylinder head assembly, twincam engine—Nova

17. Set the No. 1 cylinder at TDC on its compression stroke. Turn the crankshaft pulley and align its groove with the **0** mark of the timing belt cover.

18. Check that the camshaft gear hole is aligned with the exhaust camshaft cap mark. Remove the plug from the lower timing belt cover.

19. Place alignment marks on the camshaft timing gear and belt.

20. Loosen the idler pulley mount bolt and push the idler pulley toward the left as far as it will go, then tighten temporarily.

21. Remove the timing belt from the camshaft timing gear after marking its position in relation to the camshaft timing gear.

22. Hold the timing belt with a cloth.

NOTE: Support the belt so the meshing of the crankshaft timing gear and timing belt does not shift. Be careful not to drop anything inside the timing belt cover. Do not allow the belt to come in contact with oil, water or dust.

23. Remove the cylinder head bolts, in sequence, using a 10mm, 12 point deep well socket.

NOTE: Head warping or cracking could result from incorrect removal.

24. Remove the cylinder head with intake and exhaust manifolds. If the head is difficult to lift off, carefully pry with a bar between the cylinder head and a cylinder block projection.

NOTE: Be careful not to damage the cylinder head and block mating surface. Lift the cylinder head from the dowels on the cylinder block and place it on wooden blocks on a bench.

25. Remove the intake and exhaust manifolds.

26. Remove as necessary the camshafts, the valve lifters and shims, the spark plug tubes, the valves using a J–8062 spring compressor and a J–37979–A adapter, the valve stem oil seals and the half circle plug.

To install:

27. Install the half circle plug to the cylinder head. Apply GM No. 1052751 or equivalent, sealant to the plug.

28. Install the valves. Install the new oil seals on the valves using a J–38232 seal installer.

NOTE: The intake valve oil seal is brown and the exhaust valve oil seal is black.

29. Install the spring seat, spring, and spring retainer on the cylinder head. Using a J–8062 spring compressor and a J–37979–A adapter, compress the valve springs and place the 2 keepers around valve stem. Remove the J 8062 spring compressor and the J–37979–A adapter.

30. Apply GM No. 1052751 sealant to the spark plug tube hole of the cylinder head and using a press, install a new spark plug tube to a protrusion height of 1.835 – 1.866 in. (46.6 – 47.4mm).

31. Install the engine hangers to the cylinder head. Install the valve lifters and shims. Install the camshafts. Install the intake manifold.

32. Carefully install the cylinder head in position on the cylinder head gasket.

NOTE: Apply a light coating of engine oil on the bolt threads and under the bolt head before installation.

33. Install the 10 cylinder head bolts, in several passes and in sequence. Tighten the cylinder head bolts to 44 ft. lbs. (60 Nm).

34. Install the timing belt. Install the distributor. Install the engine mount bracket. Install the air conditioning idler pulley.

35. Install the center and upper timing belt covers. Raise and suitably support the vehicle. Install the exhaust manifold to exhaust pipe with a new gasket.

36. Install the 2 new exhaust pipe bolts. Tighten the exhaust

pipe bolts to 18 ft. lbs. (25 Nm). Install the exhaust manifold support bracket.

37. Install the cylinder head-to-cylinder block bracket. Lower the vehicle.

38. Connect the engine harness to upper timing belt cover. Raise and properly support the engine.

39. Install the water pump pulley. Lower engine. Install the right engine mount through bolt. Tighten to 64 ft. lbs. (87 Nm).

40. Remove the J–28467–A support fixture. Install the windshield washer reservoir.

41. Install the cruise control actuator and bracket and connect the electrical connector.

42. Install the accessory drive belts and adjust to the proper tensions, as applicable.

43. Install the cylinder head cover. Install the PCV valve and spark plug wires. Install the water inlet and outlet housings.

44. Install the heater hoses and all coolant hoses. Install the fuel rail. Install the cold-start injector pipe.

45. Install the fuel inlet line. Connect all necessary electrical connections and vacuum lines.

46. Install the transaxle kickdown cable, connect the cruise control actuator cable and the throttle cable. Install the air cleaner assembly.

47. Raise and safely support the vehicle. Install the 2 rear mount-to-main crossmember nuts. Install the 2 center transaxle mount-to-center crossmember nuts.

48. Tighten the rear transaxle mount-to-main crossmember nuts to 45 ft. lbs. (61 Nm). Tighten the center transaxle mount-to-center crossmember nuts to 45 ft. lbs. (61 Nm).

49. Install both mount nut and stud protectors. Install the right lower stone shield.

51. Lower the vehicle. Refill coolant and install the battery negative cable.

STORM

1. Disconnect the battery negative cable.

2. Drain cooling system.

3. Disconnect the accelerator cable from the throttle valve, then the breather hose from the intake air duct.

4. Disconnect the intake air duct from the throttle valve, then the MAP sensor hose from the MAP sensor.

5. Disconnect the brake booster hose, then the 2 canister hoses from the pipes on the intake manifold (common chamber).

6. Disconnect the EGR vacuum hoses, then the oxygen sensor harness electrical connector.

7. Disconnect the ignition coil ground cable from the thermostat housing flange.

8. Disconnect the coolant temperature sensor and thermo unit harness connector from the thermostat housing.

9. Remove the cable harness clip from the coolant outlet pipe bracket.

10. Disconnect the 2 cable harness electrical connectors, located near the left strut tower.

11. Disconnect the engine heater hoses, then the upper radiator hose from the radiator.

12. Disconnect the fuel feed and return hoses, then raise and support vehicle safely.

13. Remove the right undercover, then the front exhaust pipe from the exhaust manifold. Lower the vehicle.

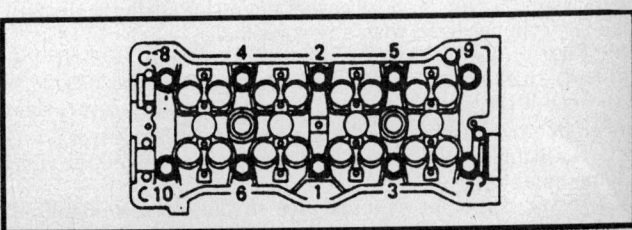

Cylinder head bolt tightening sequence–Prizm

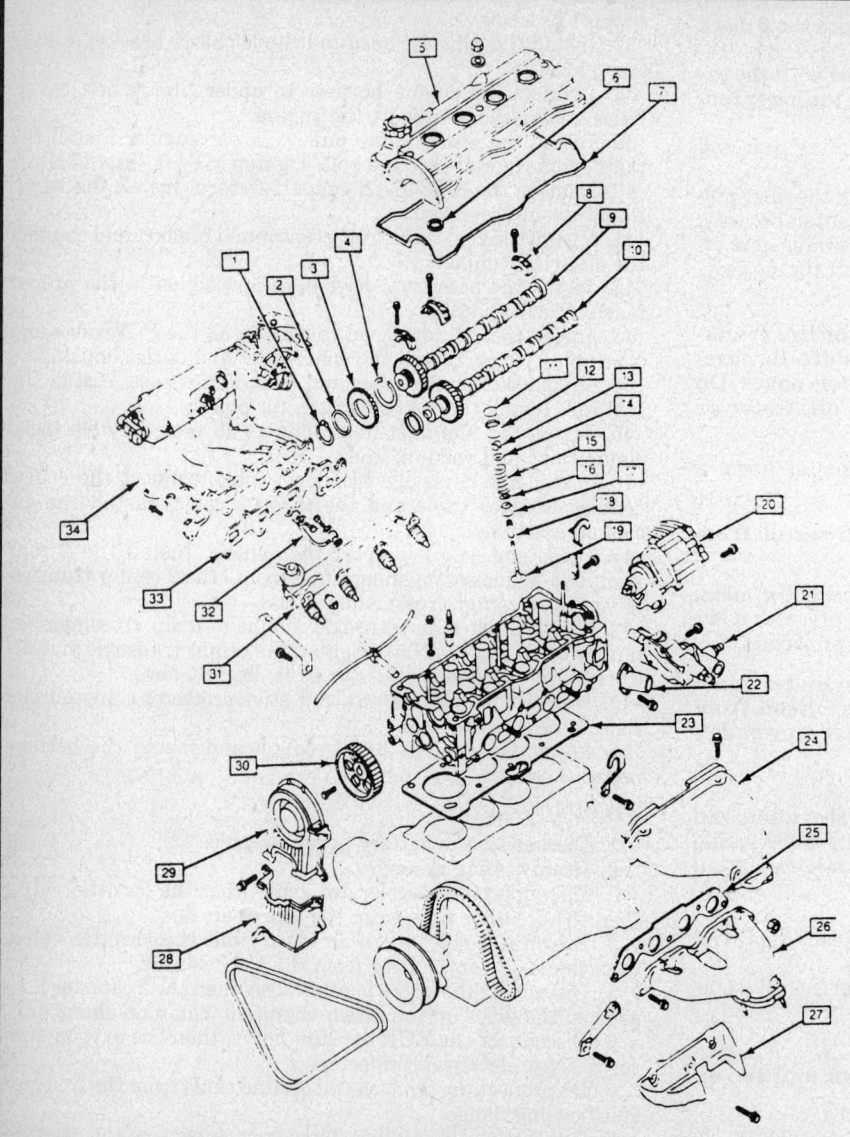

1. Camshaft snap ring
2. Wave washer
3. Camshaft sub gear
4. Camshaft gear spring
5. Cylinder head cover
6. Spark plug tube gasket
7. Cylinder head cover gasket
8. Camshaft bearing cap
9. Camshaft (intake)
10. Camshaft (exhaust)
11. Adjusting shim
12. Valve lifter
13. Valve keepers
14. Valve spring retainer
15. Valve spring
16. Valve spring seat
17. Valve stem oil seal
18. Valve guide bushing
19. Valve
20. Distributor
21. Water inlet housing
22. Water outlet housing
23. Head gasket
24. Exhaust manifold upper insulator
25. Exhaust manifold gasket
26. Exhaust manifold
27. Exhaust manifold lower insulator
28. Center timimg belt cover
29. Upper timing belt cover
30. Camshaft timimn gear
31. Fuel rail
32. Cold start injector pipe
33. Intake manifold gasket
34. Intake manifold

Exploded view of the cylinder head assembly — Prizm

14. Remove the right engine mount, then the alternator drive belt.

15. Remove the power steering belt.

16. Remove the engine mounting bracket from the timing case cover, then remove the timing belt.

17. Remove the cylinder head center cover, cylinder head bolts, then the cylinder head.

To install:

18. Clean the cylinder head gasket mounting surfaces, then install the cylinder head with a new gasket.

19. First torque cylinder head bolts in sequence to 29 ft. lbs. (40 Nm), then a final torque in sequence of 58 ft. lbs. (79 Nm).

20. Install the timing belt and the cylinder head cover, then the engine mounting bracket onto the timing case cover.

21. Raise and safely support the vehicle, then install the right engine mount.

22. Install the front exhaust pipe to the exhaust manifold, then right side under cover. Lower the vehicle.

23. Connect the fuel feed line and fuel return hose.

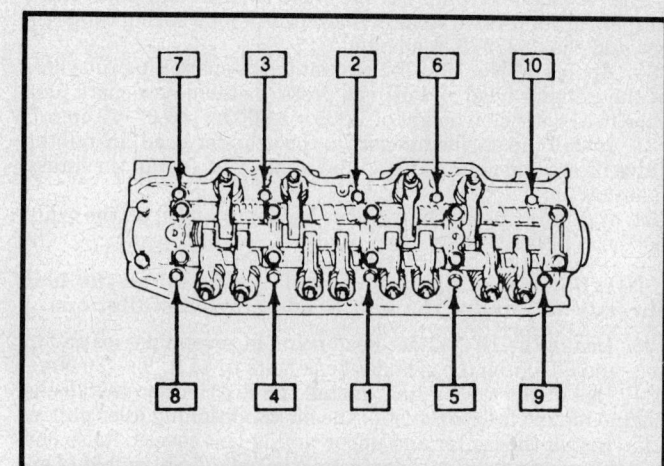

Cylinder head bolt tightening sequence — Storm without twincam engine

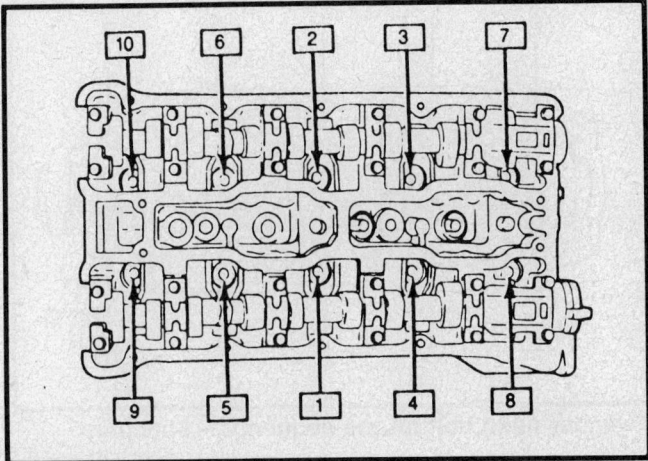

10
6
2
3
7
9
5
1
4
8

Cylinder head bolt tightening sequence—Storm with twincam engine

2
6
10
7
3
1
5
9
8
4

Cylinder head bolt removal sequence—Storm with twincam engine

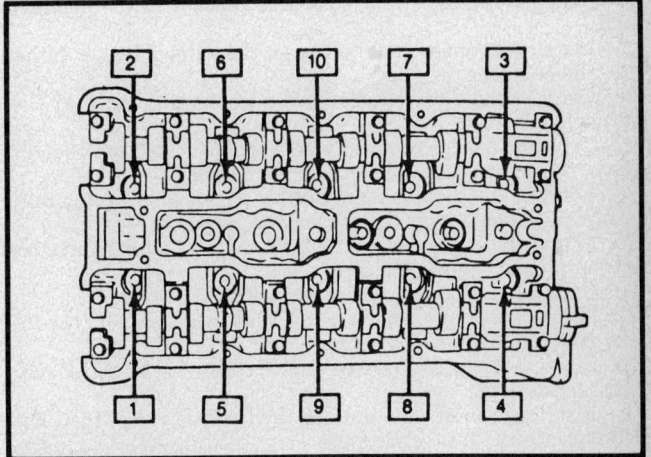

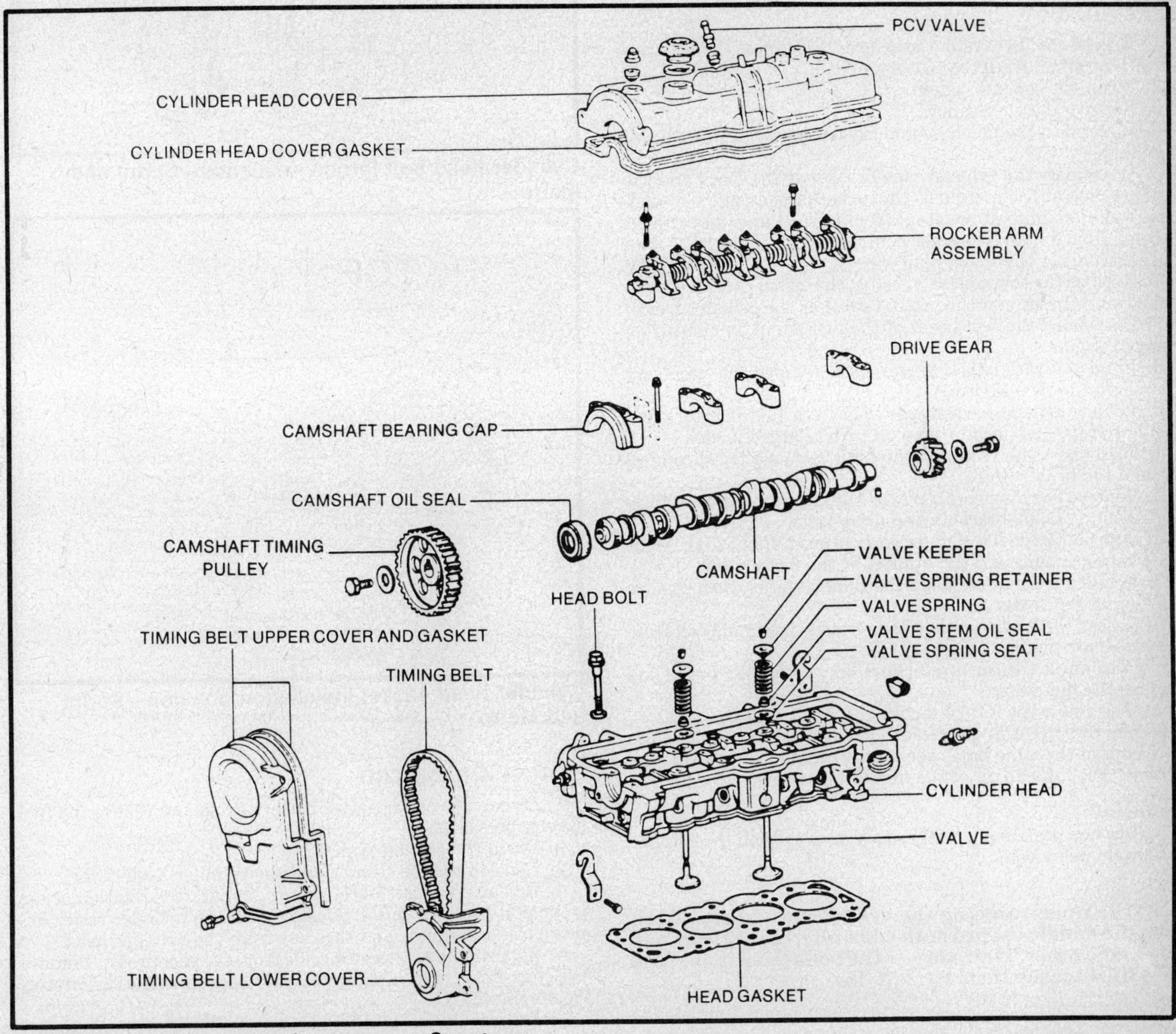

PCV VALVE
CYLINDER HEAD COVER
CYLINDER HEAD COVER GASKET
ROCKER ARM ASSEMBLY
DRIVE GEAR
CAMSHAFT BEARING CAP
CAMSHAFT OIL SEAL
CAMSHAFT TIMING PULLEY
CAMSHAFT
VALVE KEEPER
VALVE SPRING RETAINER
VALVE SPRING
VALVE STEM OIL SEAL
VALVE SPRING SEAT
HEAD BOLT
TIMING BELT UPPER COVER AND GASKET
TIMING BELT
CYLINDER HEAD
VALVE
TIMING BELT LOWER COVER
HEAD GASKET

Cylinder head bolt removal sequence—Spectrum

24. Connect the coolant bypass pipe bracket to the cylinder head.

25. Install the upper radiator hose, then the 2 heater hoses onto the engine.

26. Connect the 2 cable harness connectors, located near the left strut tower.

27. Connect the 2 ground cable terminals, located to the right side of the intake manifold (common chamber).

28. Connect the coolant temperature sensor and thermo unit electrical connectors on the thermostat housing.

29. Connect the ignition coil ground cable to the terminal on the thermostat housing flange.

30. Connect the oxygen sensor electrical connector.

31. Connect the canister hoses to the canister pipes on the intake manifold (common chamber).

32. Connect the brake booster vacuum hose and the MAP sensor vacuum hose.

33. Install the intake air duct to the throttle valve, then the PCV hose to the intake air duct.

34. Connect the accelerator cable to the throttle valve.

35. Connect the battery negative cable and fill cooling system. Start engine and check for leaks.

SPECTRUM

1. Relieve the fuel system pressure. Disconnect the negative battery terminal from the battery.

2. Drain the cooling system.

3. Remove the air cleaner.

4. Disconnect the flex hose and oxygen sensor at the exhaust manifold.

5. Disconnect the exhaust pipe bracket at the block and the exhaust pipe at the manifold. On turbocharged engine disconnect exhaust pipe at wastegate manifold and disconnect vacumm line for turbocharger control.

6. Disconnect the spark plug wires.

7. Remove the thermostat housing, the distributor, the vacuum advance hoses and the ground cable at the cylinder head.

8. Disconnect the fuel hoses at the fuel pump on non-turbocharged engine.

9. From the carburetor, if equipped, remove the necessary hoses and the throttle cable.

10. Remove engine harness asembly from fuel injectors and fuel line from fuel injector pipe on turbocharged model.

11. Disconnect the vacuum switching valve electrical connector and the heater hoses.

12. Remove the alternator, power steering and air conditioning adjusting bolts, brackets and drive belts.

13. Support the engine using a vertical hoist. Remove the right hand motor mount and the bracket at the front cover.

14. Rotate the engine to align the timing marks, then remove the timing gear cover.

15. Loosen the tension pulley and remove the timing belt from the camshaft timing pulley.

16. Disconnect the carburetor fuel line at the fuel pump and remove the fuel pump.

17. Disconnect the intake manifold coolant hoses.

18. Remove the cylinder head bolts (remove the bolts from both ends at the same time, working toward the middle) and the cylinder head. Clean all of the mounting surfaces.

To install:

20. Use new seals and gaskets, apply oil to the bolt threads and torque the head bolts.

NOTE: When torquing the cylinder head bolts, work from the middle toward both ends, alternating from one side to the other. First, torque the bolts to 29 ft. lbs. and then final torque them to 58 ft. lbs.

21. After torquing, adjust the valve clearance and complete the installation procedures, by reversing the removal procedures.

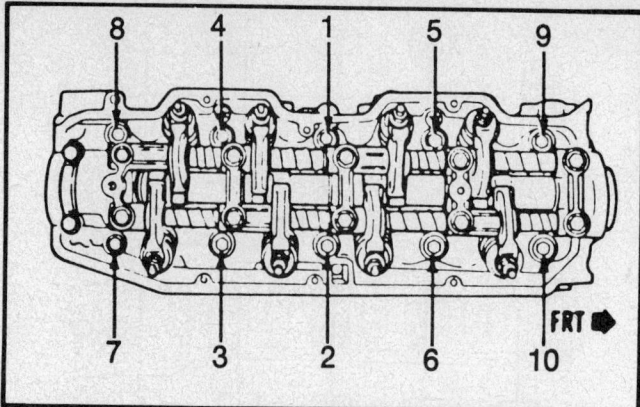

Cylinder head bolt torque sequence—Spectrum

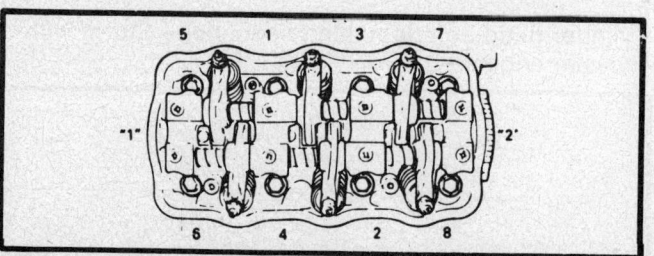

Cylinder head bolt torque sequence—Sprint and Metro

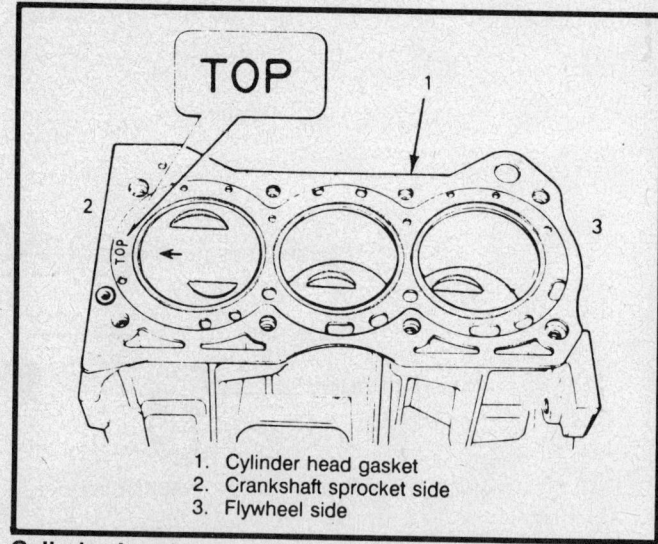

1. Cylinder head gasket
2. Crankshaft sprocket side
3. Flywheel side

Cylinder head gasket installation position—Sprint and Metro

SPRINT AND METRO

1. Disconnect the negative battery cable and relieve the fuel system pressure.

2. Drain the cooling system.

3. Remove the air cleaner and the cylinder head cover.

4. Remove the distributor cap, then mark the position of the rotor and the distributor housing with the cylinder head. Remove the distributor and the case from the cylinder head.

5. Remove the accelerator cable from the carburetor. Remove the emission control and the coolant hoses from the carburetor/intake manifold.

6. Remove the electrical lead connectors from the carburetor/intake manifold and the lead wire from the oxygen sensor.

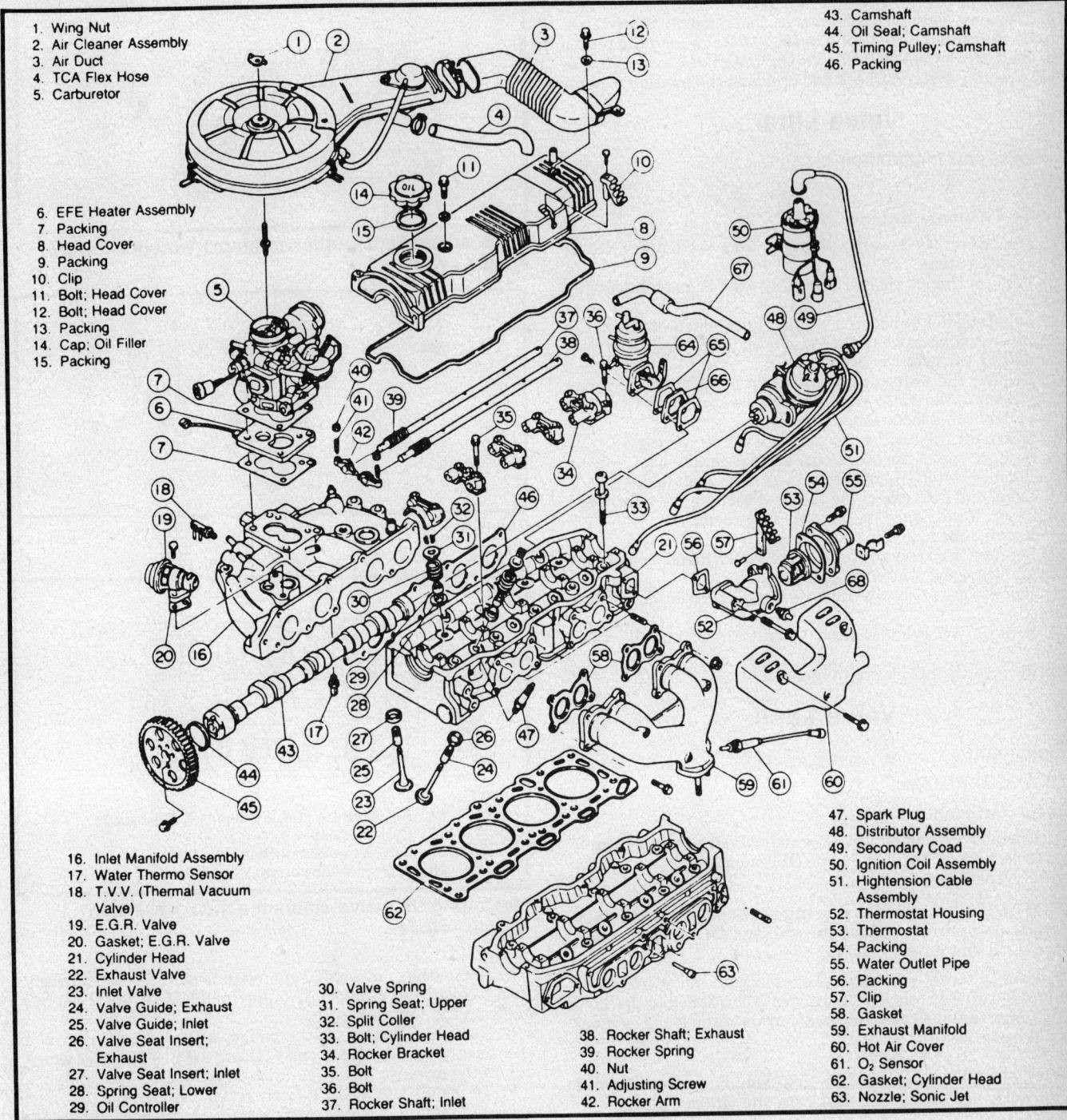

1. Wing Nut
2. Air Cleaner Assembly
3. Air Duct
4. TCA Flex Hose
5. Carburetor
6. EFE Heater Assembly
7. Packing
8. Head Cover
9. Packing
10. Clip
11. Bolt; Head Cover
12. Bolt; Head Cover
13. Packing
14. Cap; Oil Filler
15. Packing
16. Inlet Manifold Assembly
17. Water Thermo Sensor
18. T.V.V. (Thermal Vacuum Valve)
19. E.G.R. Valve
20. Gasket; E.G.R. Valve
21. Cylinder Head
22. Exhaust Valve
23. Inlet Valve
24. Valve Guide; Exhaust
25. Valve Guide; Inlet
26. Valve Seat Insert; Exhaust
27. Valve Seat Insert; Inlet
28. Spring Seat; Lower
29. Oil Controller
30. Valve Spring
31. Spring Seat; Upper
32. Split Coller
33. Bolt; Cylinder Head
34. Rocker Bracket
35. Bolt
36. Bolt
37. Rocker Shaft; Inlet
38. Rocker Shaft; Exhaust
39. Rocker Spring
40. Nut
41. Adjusting Screw
42. Rocker Arm
43. Camshaft
44. Oil Seal; Camshaft
45. Timing Pulley; Camshaft
46. Packing
47. Spark Plug
48. Distributor Assembly
49. Secondary Coad
50. Ignition Coil Assembly
51. Hightension Cable Assembly
52. Thermostat Housing
53. Thermostat
54. Packing
55. Water Outlet Pipe
56. Packing
57. Clip
58. Gasket
59. Exhaust Manifold
60. Hot Air Cover
61. O_2 Sensor
62. Gasket; Cylinder Head
63. Nozzle; Sonic Jet

Exploded view of the top of the engine—Spectrum

7. Remove the fuel hoses from the fuel pump and the pump from the cylinder head.

8. Remove the brake vacuum hose from the intake manifold.

9. Remove the crankshaft pulley, the outside cover, the timing belt and the tensioner from the front of the engine.

10. Remove the exhaust and the 2nd air pipes from the exhaust manifold.

11. Remove the exhaust/intake manifolds and the engine side mount from the cylinder head.

12. Loosen the rocker arm valve adjusters, turn back the ad-justing screws so the rocker arms move freely. Remove the rocker arm shaft retaining screws and pull out the shafts. Remove the rocker arms and springs from the cylinder head.

NOTE: Make a note of the differences between the rocker arm shafts. The intake shaft's stepped end is 0.55 in., which faces the camshaft pulley; the exhaust shaft's stepped end is 0.59 in., which faces the distributor.

13. Remove the mounting bolts and the cylinder head from the engine.

To install:

14. Use new gaskets and reverse the removal procedures. Torque the cylinder head bolts to 46–50.5 ft. lbs. and the rocker arm shaft screws to 7–9 ft. lbs. Adjust the valve clearances. Refill the cooling system. Check and/or adjust the ignition timing.

Valve Lifters

Removal and Installation

NOVA

Except Twincam Engine

1. Disconnect the negative terminal from the battery. Drain the cooling system.
2. Remove the air cleaner assembly with the accompanying hoses.
3. Label and disconnect the vacuum lines which run from the vacuum switching valve to the various emission control devices mounted on the cylinder head.
4. Remove the water hose clamps and hoses from the water pump. Remove the water valve. Disconnect the heater temperature control cable from the water valve.
5. Disconnect the water temperature sender wiring.
6. Remove the choke stove pipe and the intake pipe.
7. Remove the PCV hose from the intake manifold.
8. Label and disconnect the fuel and vacuum lines from the carburetor, if necessary, to gain working room.
9. Remove the cylinder head cover.
10. Remove the valve rocker assembly-to-cylinder head bolts/nuts and the valve rocker assembly.
11. Remove the pushrods. Remove the cylinder head retaining bolts.
12. Remove the cylinder head assembly. Lift out the valve lifters.
13. Reverse the procedure to install.

Valve Lash

Adjustment

NOVA AND PRIZM

Except Twincam Engine

1. Operate the engine until normal operating temperatures are reached, then, turn the engine OFF. Remove the air cleaner and the valve cover.

NOTE: If clearances are being set because parts have been disassembled, adjust the valves COLD, then, reset them with the engine HOT.

2. Using a socket wrench on the crankshaft pulley bolt, turn the crankshaft until the No. 1 cylinder is positioned to the TDC of its compression stroke; the rocker arms of the No. 1 cylinder should be loose.

NOTE: The notch on the crankshaft pulley should align with the 0 degrees mark on the timing plate.

3. Using a 0.008 in. feeler gauge, adjust the intake valve clearance of cylinder No. 1 and 2. Using a 0.012 in. feeler gauge, adjust the exhaust valve clearance of cylinders No. 1 and 3.
4. To adjust each valve, perform the following procedures:
   a. Loosen the rocker arm adjusting nut; it may be necessary to back-off the adjusting screw.
   b. Slide the feeler gauge between the rocker arm and valve tip. The surfaces will just touch, giving a very slight pull on the gauge.
   c. Using a adjusting tool and a wrench, to hold the rocker arm locknut, adjust the valve clearance, then, tighten the rocker arm locknut.
   d. Recheck the clearance and readjust, if necessary.

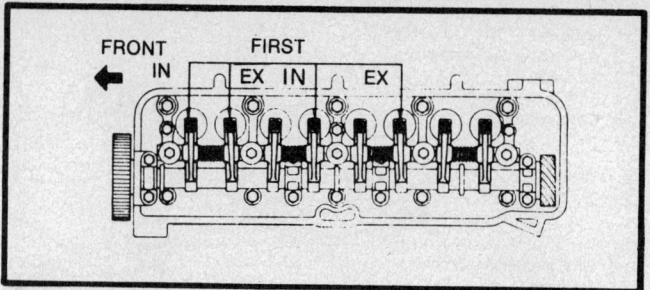

Valve adjustment sequence-step 1 except twincam engine—Nova

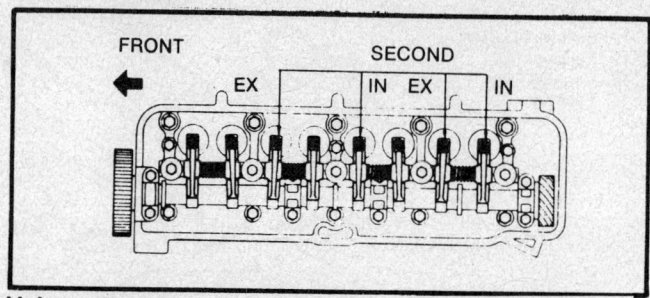

Valve adjustment sequence-step 2 except twincam engine—Nova

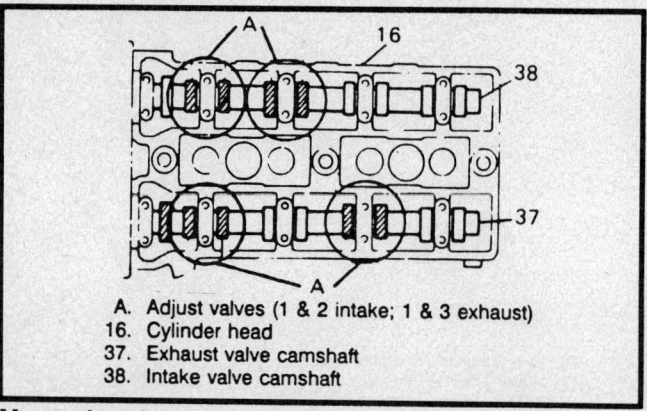

A. Adjust valves (1 & 2 intake; 1 & 3 exhaust)
16. Cylinder head
37. Exhaust valve camshaft
38. Intake valve camshaft

Measuring the valve clearance step 1-twincam engine—Nova

5. Rotate the crankshaft 1 complete revolution (360 degrees), then, realign the crankshaft pulley notch with the 0 degrees mark on the timing plate.
6. Using a 0.008 in. feeler gauge, adjust the intake valve clearance of cylinder No. 3 and 4. Using a 0.012 in. feeler gauge, adjust the exhaust valve clearance of cylinders No. 2 and 4.
7. To install, use a new gasket, sealant, if necessary, and reverse the removal procedures. Install the air cleaner. Adjust the engine timing and idle speed.

Twincam Engine

1. With the engine COLD, remove the valve covers.
2. To inspect the valve clearances, perform the following procedures:
   a. Using a socket wrench on the crankshaft pulley, rotate the crankshaft until the No. 1 cylinder is positioned to the TDC of its compression stroke; the valve lifters of the No. 1 cylinder should be loose.

NOTE: The crankshaft pulley notch will align with the 0 degrees mark on the timing plate.

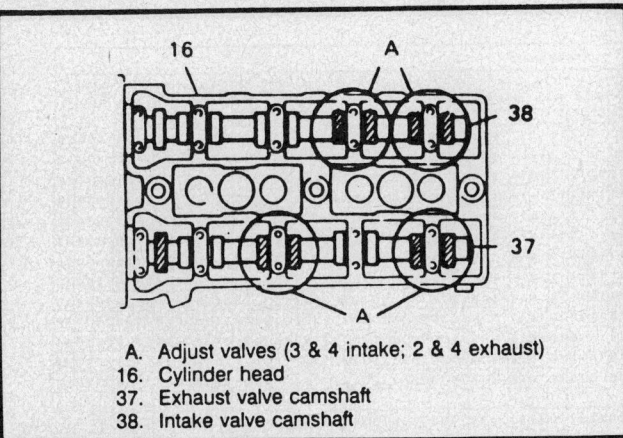

A. Adjust valves (3 & 4 intake; 2 & 4 exhaust)
16. Cylinder head
37. Exhaust valve camshaft
38. Intake valve camshaft

Measuring the valve clearance-step 2-twincam engine—Nova

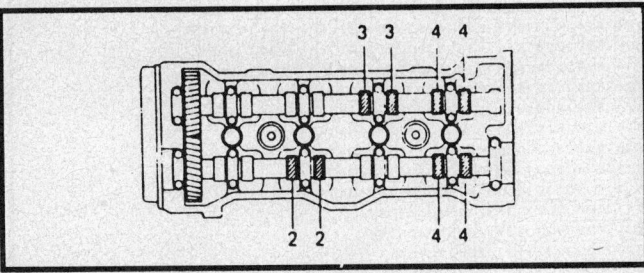

Adjust these valves first—Prizm

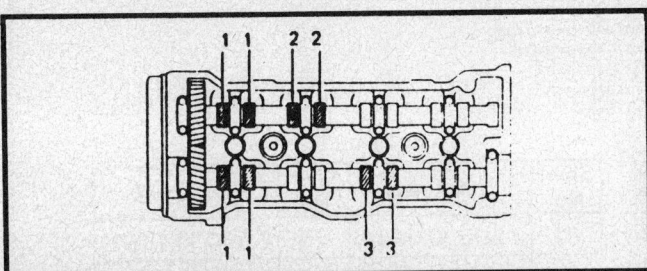

Adjust these valves second—Prizm

b. Using a feeler gauge, measure and record (valves not within specifications) the intake valve-to-lifter clearances of cylinders No. 1 and 2; the exhaust valve-to-lifter clearances of cylinders No. 1 and 3.

c. Rotate the crankshaft 1 complete revolution (360 degrees) and realign the crankshaft pulley notch with the **0** degrees mark on the timing plate; the valve lifters of the No. 4 cylinder should be loose.

d. Using a feeler gauge, measure and record (valves not within specifications) the intake valve-to-lifter clearances of cylinders No. 3 and 4; the exhaust valve-to-lifter clearances of cylinders No. 2 and 4.

3. Rotate the crankshaft pulley until the cam lobe, valve being worked on, is positioned in the upward direction.

4. Using the valve clearance adjustment tool set No. J-37141 or equivalent, press the valve lifter downward, then, secure it in downward position (using another tool) and remove the first tool.

5. Using a prybar or a magnetic finger, remove the adjusting shim.

6. To select the correct valve shim(s), perform the following procedures:

a. Using a micrometer, measure the thickness of the old shim.

b. Using the valve clearance measurement (already acquired), subtract 0.008 in. (intake valve) or 0.010 in. (exhaust valve) from it; the new calculation is the difference between the old shim and the new shim.

c. Using the difference (just calculated), add it to the old shim thickness, then, select (from the chart) a new shim with the thickness closest to the new calculation.

7. Install the new shim and remove the hold-down tool.

8. After all valves have met specifications, use new gaskets, sealant (if necessary) and reverse the removal procedures. Adjust the engine timing and idle speed.

SPECTRUM AND STORM

Except Twincam Engine

1. Remove the cylinder head cover.

2. Rotate the engine until the notched line on the crankshaft pulley aligns with the **0** degree mark on the timing gear case. The position of the No. 1 piston should be at TDC of the compression stroke.

3. Set the intake valve to 0.006 in. (cold) for No. 1 and 2 cylinders; exhaust valves to 0.010 in. (cold) for No. 1 and 3 cylinders.

4. When piston in No. 4 cylinder is at TDC on compression stroke set the intake valves to 0.006 in. (cold) for No. 3 and 4 cylinders; exhaust valves to 0.010 in. (cold) for No. 2 and 4 cylinders.

5. After the adjustment has been completed, replace the head cover.

STORM

Twincam Engine

1. Disconnect the battery negative cable.

2. Remove the cylinder head cover.

3. Position the No. 1 cylinder at TDC on its compression stroke.

NOTE: The crankshaft pulley notch will align with the 0 degrees mark on the timing plate.

4. Check that the No. 1 cylinder valves have play and the No. 4 cylinder valves do not. If not, rotate the crankshaft 360 degrees and check the valves again.

5. Using a feeler gauge, measure the clearance between the cam lobe and the selective shim on the intake and exhaust valves on the No. 1 cylinder, then the intake valves on the No. 2 cylinder and the exhaust valves on the No. 3 cylinder. Note readings.

6. Rotate the crankshaft 360 degrees. Using a feeler gauge, measure the clearance between the cam lobe and the selective shim on the intake and exhaust valves on the No. 4 cylinder, then the intake valves on the No. 3 cylinder and the exhaust valves on the No. 2 cylinder. Note readings.

7. The valve clearance obtained on the exhaust valves should be between 0.008–0.012 in. (0.20–0.30mm). If not, replace the selective shim by turning the camshaft lobe downward and installing tool J–38413–2 or J–38413–3 between the camshaft journal and the cam lobe next to the selective shim. Turn cam lobe upward and remove the selective shim. Install new shim using the slective shim chart.

8. The valve clearance obtained on the intake valves should be between 0.004–0.008 in. (0.10–0.20mm). If not, replace the selective shim by turning the camshaft lobe downward and installing tool J–38413–2 or J–38413–3 between the camshaft journal and the cam lobe next to the selective shim. Turn cam lobe upward and remove the selective shim. Install new shim using the slective shim chart.

9. Install the cylinder head covers and connect the battery negative cable. Start the engine and check for leaks.

GEO
METRO • NOVA • PRIZM • SPECTRUM • SPRINT • STORM

Installed Shim Thickness (mm)

Column headers (Installed Shim Thickness, mm):
2.500, 2.525, 2.550, 2.575, 2.600, 2.620, 2.625, 2.640, 2.650, 2.660, 2.675, 2.680, 2.700, 2.720, 2.725, 2.740, 2.750, 2.775, 2.780, 2.800, 2.820, 2.825, 2.850, 2.860, 2.875, 2.880, 2.900, 2.920, 2.925, 2.940, 2.950, 2.960, 2.975, 2.980, 3.000, 3.020, 3.025, 3.040, 3.050, 3.060, 3.075, 3.080, 3.100, 3.120, 3.125, 3.140, 3.150, 3.160, 3.175, 3.180, 3.200, 3.225, 3.250, 3.275, 3.300

Row labels (Measured Clearance, mm):

Measured Clearance (mm)
0.000 – 0.009
0.010 – 0.025
0.026 – 0.029
0.030 – 0.040
0.041 – 0.050
0.051 – 0.070
0.071 – 0.075
0.076 – 0.090
0.091 – 0.100
0.101 – 0.120
0.121 – 0.125
0.126 – 0.140
0.141 – 0.149
0.150 – 0.250
0.251 – 0.270
0.271 – 0.275
0.276 – 0.290
0.291 – 0.300
0.301 – 0.320
0.321 – 0.325
0.326 – 0.340
0.341 – 0.350
0.351 – 0.370
0.371 – 0.375
0.376 – 0.390
0.391 – 0.400
0.401 – 0.420
0.421 – 0.425
0.426 – 0.440
0.441 – 0.450
0.451 – 0.470
0.471 – 0.475
0.476 – 0.490
0.491 – 0.500
0.501 – 0.520
0.521 – 0.525
0.526 – 0.540
0.541 – 0.550
0.551 – 0.570
0.571 – 0.575
0.576 – 0.590
0.591 – 0.600
0.601 – 0.620
0.621 – 0.625
0.626 – 0.640
0.641 – 0.650
0.651 – 0.670
0.671 – 0.675
0.676 – 0.690
0.691 – 0.700
0.701 – 0.720
0.721 – 0.725
0.726 – 0.740
0.741 – 0.750
0.751 – 0.770
0.771 – 0.775
0.776 – 0.790
0.791 – 0.800
0.801 – 0.820
0.821 – 0.825
0.826 – 0.840
0.841 – 0.850
0.851 – 0.870
0.871 – 0.875
0.876 – 0.890
0.891 – 0.900
0.901 – 0.925
0.926 – 0.950
0.951 – 0.975
0.976 – 1.000
1.001 – 1.025

AVAILABLE SHIMS

Shim No.	Thickness	Shim No.	Thickness
02	2.500 (0.0984)	20	2.950 (0.1161)
04	2.550 (0.1004)	22	3.000 (0.1181)
06	2.600 (0.1024)	24	3.050 (0.1201)
08	2.650 (0.1043)	26	3.100 (0.1220)
10	2.700 (0.1063)	28	3.150 (0.1240)
12	2.750 (0.1083)	30	3.200 (0.1260)
14	2.800 (0.1102)	32	3.250 (0.1280)
16	2.850 (0.1122)	34	3.300 (0.1299)
18	2.900 (0.1142)		

Intake valve clearance (cold):
0.15 – 0.25 mm (0.006 – 0.010 in.)

Example: A 2.800 mm shim is installed and the measured clearance is 0.450 mm. Replace the 2.800 mm shim with shim No. 24 (3.050 mm).

Intake valve shim size chart—Nova twincam engine and Prizm

Exhaust valve shim size chart, twincam engine — Nova and Prizm

Measured Clearance (mm) rows / Installed Shim Thickness (mm) columns lookup chart.

Installed Shim Thickness (mm) column headers: 2.500, 2.525, 2.550, 2.575, 2.600, 2.620, 2.625, 2.640, 2.650, 2.660, 2.675, 2.680, 2.700, 2.720, 2.725, 2.740, 2.750, 2.760, 2.775, 2.780, 2.800, 2.820, 2.825, 2.840, 2.850, 2.860, 2.875, 2.880, 2.900, 2.920, 2.925, 2.940, 2.950, 2.960, 2.975, 2.980, 3.000, 3.020, 3.025, 3.040, 3.050, 3.060, 3.075, 3.080, 3.120, 3.125, 3.140, 3.150, 3.175, 3.180, 3.200, 3.225, 3.250, 3.275, 3.300

Measured Clearance (mm) row labels:
0.000–0.009, 0.010–0.025, 0.026–0.040, 0.041–0.050, 0.051–0.070, 0.071–0.090, 0.091–0.100, 0.101–0.120, 0.121–0.140, 0.141–0.150, 0.151–0.170, 0.171–0.190, 0.191–0.199, 0.200–0.300, 0.301–0.320, 0.321–0.325, 0.326–0.340, 0.341–0.350, 0.351–0.370, 0.371–0.375, 0.376–0.390, 0.391–0.400, 0.401–0.420, 0.421–0.425, 0.426–0.440, 0.441–0.450, 0.451–0.470, 0.471–0.475, 0.476–0.490, 0.491–0.500, 0.501–0.520, 0.521–0.525, 0.526–0.540, 0.541–0.550, 0.551–0.570, 0.571–0.575, 0.576–0.590, 0.591–0.600, 0.601–0.620, 0.621–0.625, 0.626–0.640, 0.641–0.650, 0.651–0.670, 0.671–0.675, 0.676–0.690, 0.691–0.700, 0.701–0.720, 0.721–0.725, 0.726–0.740, 0.741–0.750, 0.751–0.770, 0.771–0.775, 0.776–0.790, 0.791–0.800, 0.801–0.820, 0.821–0.825, 0.826–0.840, 0.841–0.850, 0.851–0.870, 0.871–0.875, 0.876–0.890, 0.891–0.900, 0.901–0.925, 0.926–0.950, 0.951–0.975, 0.976–1.000, 1.001–1.025, 1.026–1.050, 1.051–1.075

AVAILABLE SHIMS   mm (in.)

Shim No.	Thickness	Shim No.	Thickness
02	2.500 (0.0984)	20	2.950 (0.1161)
04	2.550 (0.1004)	22	3.000 (0.1181)
06	2.600 (0.1024)	24	3.050 (0.1201)
08	2.650 (0.1043)	26	3.100 (0.1220)
10	2.700 (0.1063)	28	3.150 (0.1240)
12	2.750 (0.1083)	30	3.200 (0.1260)
14	2.800 (0.1102)	32	3.250 (0.1280)
16	2.850 (0.1122)	34	3.300 (0.1299)
18	2.900 (0.1142)		

Exhaust valve clearance (cold): 0.20 – 0.30 mm (0.008 – 0.012 in.)

Example: A 2.800 mm shim is installed and the measured clearance is 0.450 mm. Replace the 2.800 mm shim with shim No. 22 (3.000 mm).

Intake valve selective shim chart — Storm with twincam engine

Original Adjuster (Shim) Thickness (mm)

Measured clearance (mm)	(inch)	2.52	2.54	2.56	2.58	2.60	2.62	2.64	2.66	2.68	2.70	2.72	2.74	2.76	2.78	2.80	2.82	2.84	2.86	2.88	2.90	2.92	2.94	2.96	2.98	3.00	3.02	3.04	3.06	3.08	3.10	3.12	3.14	3.16	3.18	3.20	3.22	3.24	3.26	3.28	3.30	3.32	3.34	3.36	3.38	3.40	3.42	3.44	3.46	3.48
0.000-0.025	0.000-0.001									1	1	2	2	2	3	3	4	4	4	5	5	6	6	6	7	7	8	8	8	9	9	10	10	10	11	11	12	12	12	13	13	14	14	14	15	15	16	16	16	17
0.026-0.050	0.001-0.002							1	1	1	2	2	3	3	3	4	4	5	5	5	6	6	7	7	7	8	8	9	9	9	10	10	11	11	11	12	12	13	13	13	14	14	15	15	15	16	16	17	17	17
0.051-0.075	0.002-0.003						1	1	1	2	2	3	3	3	4	4	5	5	5	6	6	7	7	7	8	8	9	9	9	10	10	11	11	11	12	12	13	13	13	14	14	15	15	15	16	16	17	17	17	18
0.076-0.100	0.003-0.004					1	1	2	2	2	3	3	4	4	4	5	5	6	6	6	7	7	8	8	8	9	9	10	10	10	11	11	12	12	12	13	13	14	14	14	15	15	16	16	16	17	17	18	18	18
0.101-0.200	0.004-0.008	Replacement not to be required																																																
0.201-0.225	0.008-0.009	2	2	2	3	3	4	4	4	5	5	6	6	6	7	7	8	8	8	9	9	10	10	10	11	11	12	12	12	13	13	14	14	14	15	15	16	16	16	17	17	18	18	18	19	19				
0.226-0.250	0.009-0.010	2	3	3	3	4	4	5	5	5	6	6	7	7	7	8	8	9	9	9	10	10	11	11	11	12	12	13	13	13	14	14	15	15	15	16	16	17	17	17	18	18	19	19	19					
0.251-0.275	0.010-0.011	3	3	3	4	4	5	5	5	6	6	7	7	7	8	8	9	9	9	10	10	11	11	11	12	12	13	13	13	14	14	15	15	15	16	16	17	17	17	18	18	19	19	19						
0.276-0.300	0.011-0.012	3	4	4	4	5	5	6	6	6	7	7	8	8	8	9	9	10	10	10	11	11	12	12	12	13	13	14	14	14	15	15	16	16	16	17	17	18	18	18	19	19								
0.301-0.325	0.012-0.013	4	4	4	5	5	6	6	6	7	7	8	8	8	9	9	10	10	10	11	11	12	12	12	13	13	14	14	14	15	15	16	16	16	17	17	18	18	18	19	19									
0.326-0.350	0.013-0.014	4	5	5	5	6	6	7	7	7	8	8	9	9	9	10	10	11	11	11	12	12	13	13	13	14	14	15	15	15	16	16	17	17	17	18	18	19	19	19										
0.351-0.375	0.014-0.015	5	5	5	6	6	7	7	7	8	8	9	9	9	10	10	11	11	11	12	12	13	13	13	14	14	15	15	15	16	16	17	17	17	18	18	19	19	19											
0.376-0.400	0.015-0.016	5	6	6	6	7	7	8	8	8	9	9	10	10	10	11	11	12	12	12	13	13	14	14	14	15	15	16	16	16	17	17	18	18	18	19	19													
0.401-0.425	0.016-0.017	6	6	6	7	7	8	8	8	9	9	10	10	10	11	11	12	12	12	13	13	14	14	14	15	15	16	16	16	17	17	18	18	18	19	19														
0.426-0.450	0.017-0.018	6	7	7	7	8	8	9	9	9	10	10	11	11	11	12	12	13	13	13	14	14	15	15	15	16	16	17	17	17	18	18	19	19	19															
0.451-0.475	0.018-0.019	7	7	7	8	8	9	9	9	10	10	11	11	11	12	12	13	13	13	14	14	15	15	15	16	16	17	17	17	18	18	19	19	19																
0.476-0.500	0.019-0.020	7	8	8	8	9	9	10	10	10	11	11	12	12	12	13	13	14	14	14	15	15	16	16	16	17	17	18	18	18	19	19																		
0.501-0.525	0.020-0.021	8	8	8	9	9	10	10	10	11	11	12	12	12	13	13	14	14	14	15	15	16	16	16	17	17	18	18	18	19	19																			
0.526-0.550	0.021-0.022	8	9	9	9	10	10	11	11	11	12	12	13	13	13	14	14	15	15	15	16	16	17	17	17	18	18	19	19	19																				
0.551-0.575	0.022-0.023	9	9	9	10	10	11	11	11	12	12	13	13	13	14	14	15	15	15	16	16	17	17	17	18	18	19	19	19																					
0.576-0.600	0.023-0.024	9	10	10	10	11	11	12	12	12	13	13	14	14	14	15	15	16	16	16	17	17	18	18	18	19	19																							
0.601-0.625	0.024-0.025	10	10	10	11	11	12	12	12	13	13	14	14	14	15	15	16	16	16	17	17	18	18	18	19	19																								
0.626-0.650	0.025-0.026	10	11	11	11	12	12	13	13	13	14	14	15	15	15	16	16	17	17	17	18	18	19	19	19																									
0.651-0.675	0.026-0.027	11	11	11	12	12	13	13	13	14	14	15	15	15	16	16	17	17	17	18	18	19	19	19																										
0.676-0.700	0.027-0.028	11	12	12	12	13	13	14	14	14	15	15	16	16	16	17	17	18	18	18	19	19																												
0.701-0.725	0.028-0.029	12	12	12	13	13	14	14	14	15	15	16	16	16	17	17	18	18	18	19	19																													
0.726-0.750	0.029-0.030	12	13	13	13	14	14	15	15	15	16	16	17	17	17	18	18	19	19	19																														
0.751-0.775	0.030-0.031	13	13	13	14	14	15	15	15	16	16	17	17	17	18	18	19	19	19																															
0.776-0.800	0.031-0.032	13	14	14	14	15	15	16	16	16	17	17	18	18	18	19	19																																	
0.801-0.825	0.032-0.033	14	14	14	15	15	16	16	16	17	17	18	18	18	19	19																																		
0.826-0.850	0.033-0.034	14	15	15	15	16	16	17	17	17	18	18	19	19	19																																			
0.851-0.875	0.034-0.035	15	15	15	16	16	17	17	17	18	18	19	19	19																																				
0.876-0.900	0.035-0.036	15	16	16	16	17	17	18	18	18	19	19																																						
0.901-0.925	0.036-0.037	16	16	16	17	17	18	18	18	19	19																																							
0.925-0.950	0.0365-0.0374	16	17	17	17	18	18	19	19	19																																								
0.951-0.975	0.037-0.038	17	17	17	18	18	19	19	19																																									
0.976-1.000	0.038-0.039	17	18	18	18	19	19																																											
1.001-1.025	0.039-0.040	18	18	18	19	19																																												
1.026-1.050	0.040-0.041	18	19	19	19																																													
1.051-1.075	0.041-0.042	19	19	19																																														
1.076-1.100	0.042-0.043	19																																																

Thickness of available adjuster (Shim)

NO in Chart	Thickness (mm)	NO in Chart	Thickness (mm)
1	2.55	11	3.05
2	2.60	12	3.10
3	2.65	13	3.15
4	2.70	14	3.20
5	2.75	15	3.25
6	2.80	16	3.30
7	2.85	17	3.35
8	2.90	18	3.40
9	2.95	19	3.45
10	3.00		

How to use the chart

[Example]
Measured clearance; 0.550mm
Original adjuster thickness; 2.96mm
(Thickness mark (2.96) is printed on the adjuster surface)

1. Draw straight lines as shown in the chart.
2. Select No.17 available adjuster to be replaced by finding cross point of straight lines.
3. Replace the 2.96mm adjuster with No.17 (3.35mm) adjuster.

Measured clearance		Original Adjuster (Shim) Thickness (mm)
mm	inch	2.96
0.526-0.550		→17

Exhaust valve selective shim chart — Storm with twincam engine

Measured clearance mm	inch	2.52	2.54	2.56	2.58	2.60	2.62	2.64	2.66	2.68	2.70	2.72	2.74	2.76	2.78	2.80	2.82	2.84	2.86	2.88	2.90	2.92	2.94	2.96	2.98	3.00	3.02	3.04	3.06	3.08	3.10	3.12	3.14	3.16	3.18	3.20	3.22	3.24	3.26	3.28	3.30	3.32	3.34	3.36	3.38	3.40	3.42	3.44	3.46	3.48
0.000–0.025	0.000–0.001														1	1	2	2	2	3	3	4	4	4	5	5	6	6	6	7	7	8	8	8	9	9	10	10	10	11	11	12	12	12	13	13	14	14	14	15
0.026–0.050	0.001–0.002												1	1	1	2	2	3	3	3	4	4	5	5	5	6	6	7	7	7	8	8	9	9	9	10	10	11	11	11	12	12	13	13	13	14	14	15	15	15
0.051–0.075	0.002–0.003											1	1	1	2	2	3	3	3	4	4	5	5	5	6	6	7	7	7	8	8	9	9	9	10	10	11	11	11	12	12	13	13	13	14	14	15	15	15	16
0.076–0.100	0.003–0.004										1	1	2	2	2	3	3	4	4	4	5	5	6	6	6	7	7	8	8	8	9	9	10	10	10	11	11	12	12	12	13	13	14	14	14	15	15	16	16	16
0.101–0.125	0.004–0.005									1	1	2	2	2	3	3	4	4	4	5	5	6	6	6	7	7	8	8	8	9	9	10	10	10	11	11	12	12	12	13	13	14	14	14	15	15	16	16	16	17
0.126–0.150	0.005–0.006							1	1	1	2	2	3	3	3	4	4	5	5	5	6	6	7	7	7	8	8	9	9	9	10	10	11	11	11	12	12	13	13	13	14	14	15	15	15	16	16	17	17	17
0.151–0.175	0.006–0.007						1	1	1	2	2	3	3	3	4	4	5	5	5	6	6	7	7	7	8	8	9	9	9	10	10	11	11	11	12	12	13	13	13	14	14	15	15	15	16	16	17	17	17	18
0.176–0.200	0.007–0.008					1	1	2	2	2	3	3	4	4	4	5	5	6	6	6	7	7	8	8	8	9	9	10	10	10	11	11	12	12	12	13	13	14	14	14	15	15	16	16	16	17	17	18	18	18
0.201–0.300	0.008–0.012	Replacement not to be required																																																
0.301–0.325	0.012–0.013	2	2	2	3	3	4	4	4	5	5	6	6	6	7	7	8	8	8	9	9	10	10	10	11	11	12	12	12	13	13	14	14	14	15	15	16	16	16	17	17	18	18	18	19	19				
0.326–0.350	0.013–0.014	2	3	3	3	4	4	5	5	5	6	6	7	7	7	8	8	9	9	9	10	10	11	11	11	12	12	13	13	13	14	14	15	15	15	16	16	17	17	17	18	18	19	19	19					
0.351–0.375	0.014–0.015	3	3	3	4	4	5	5	5	6	6	7	7	7	8	8	9	9	9	10	10	11	11	11	12	12	13	13	13	14	14	15	15	15	16	16	17	17	17	18	18	19	19	19						
0.376–0.400	0.015–0.016	3	4	4	4	5	5	6	6	6	7	7	8	8	8	9	9	10	10	10	11	11	12	12	12	13	13	14	14	14	15	15	16	16	16	17	17	18	18	18	19	19								
0.401–0.425	0.016–0.017	4	4	4	5	5	6	6	6	7	7	8	8	8	9	9	10	10	10	11	11	12	12	12	13	13	14	14	14	15	15	16	16	16	17	17	18	18	18	19	19									
0.426–0.450	0.017–0.018	4	5	5	5	6	6	7	7	7	8	8	9	9	9	10	10	11	11	11	12	12	13	13	13	14	14	15	15	15	16	16	17	17	17	18	18	19	19	19										
0.451–0.475	0.018–0.019	5	5	5	6	6	7	7	7	8	8	9	9	9	10	10	11	11	11	12	12	13	13	13	14	14	15	15	15	16	16	17	17	17	18	18	19	19	19											
0.476–0.500	0.019–0.020	5	6	6	6	7	7	8	8	8	9	9	10	10	10	11	11	12	12	12	13	13	14	14	14	15	15	16	16	16	17	17	18	18	18	19	19													
0.501–0.525	0.020–0.021	6	6	6	7	7	8	8	8	9	9	10	10	10	11	11	12	12	12	13	13	14	14	14	15	15	16	16	16	17	17	18	18	18	19	19														
0.526–0.550	0.021–0.022	6	7	7	7	8	8	9	9	9	10	10	11	11	11	12	12	13	13	13	14	14	15	15	15	16	16	17	17	17	18	18	19	19	19															
0.551–0.575	0.022–0.023	7	7	7	8	8	9	9	9	10	10	11	11	11	12	12	13	13	13	14	14	15	15	15	16	16	17	17	17	18	18	19	19	19																
0.576–0.600	0.023–0.024	7	8	8	8	9	9	10	10	10	11	11	12	12	12	13	13	14	14	14	15	15	16	16	16	17	17	18	18	18	19	19																		
0.601–0.625	0.024–0.025	8	8	8	9	9	10	10	10	11	11	12	12	12	13	13	14	14	14	15	15	16	16	16	17	17	18	18	18	19	19																			
0.626–0.650	0.025–0.026	8	9	9	9	10	10	11	11	11	12	12	13	13	13	14	14	15	15	15	16	16	17	17	17	18	18	19	19	19																				
0.651–0.675	0.026–0.027	9	9	9	10	10	11	11	11	12	12	13	13	13	14	14	15	15	15	16	16	17	17	17	18	18	19	19	19																					
0.676–0.700	0.027–0.028	9	10	10	10	11	11	12	12	12	13	13	14	14	14	15	15	16	16	16	17	17	18	18	18	19	19																							
0.701–0.725	0.028–0.029	10	10	10	11	11	12	12	12	13	13	14	14	14	15	15	16	16	16	17	17	18	18	18	19	19																								
0.726–0.750	0.029–0.030	10	11	11	11	12	12	13	13	13	14	14	15	15	15	16	16	17	17	17	18	18	19	19	19																									
0.751–0.775	0.030–0.031	11	11	11	12	12	13	13	13	14	14	15	15	15	16	16	17	17	17	18	18	19	19	19																										
0.776–0.800	0.031–0.032	11	12	12	12	13	13	14	14	14	15	15	16	16	16	17	17	18	18	18	19	19																												
0.801–0.825	0.032–0.033	12	12	12	13	13	14	14	14	15	15	16	16	16	17	17	18	18	18	19	19																													
0.826–0.850	0.033–0.034	12	13	13	13	14	14	15	15	15	16	16	17	17	17	18	18	19	19	19																														
0.851–0.875	0.034–0.035	13	13	13	14	14	15	15	15	16	16	17	17	17	18	18	19	19	19																															
0.876–0.900	0.035–0.036	13	14	14	14	15	15	16	16	16	17	17	18	18	18	19	19																																	
0.901–0.925	0.036–0.037	14	14	14	15	15	16	16	16	17	17	18	18	18	19	19																																		
0.926–0.950	0.0365–0.0374	14	15	15	15	16	16	17	17	17	18	18	19	19	19																																			
0.951–0.975	0.037–0.038	15	15	15	16	16	17	17	17	18	18	19	19	19																																				
0.976–1.000	0.038–0.039	15	16	16	16	17	17	18	18	18	19	19																																						
1.001–1.025	0.039–0.040	16	16	16	17	17	18	18	18	19	19																																							
1.026–1.050	0.040–0.041	16	17	17	17	18	18	19	19	19																																								
1.051–1.075	0.041–0.042	17	17	17	18	18	19	19	19																																									
1.076–1.100	0.042–0.043	17	18	18	18	19	19																																											
1.101–1.125	0.043–0.044	18	18	18	19	19																																												
1.126–1.150	0.044–0.045	18	19	19	19																																													
1.151–1.175	0.045–0.046	19	19	19																																														
1.176–1.200	0.046–0.047	19																																																

Header spanning all thickness columns: **Original Adjuster (Shim) Thickness (mm)**

Thickness of available adjuster (Shim)

NO in Chart	Thickness (mm)	NO in Chart	Thickness (mm)
1	2.55	11	3.05
2	2.60	12	3.10
3	2.65	13	3.15
4	2.70	14	3.20
5	2.75	15	3.25
6	2.80	16	3.30
7	2.85	17	3.35
8	2.90	18	3.40
9	2.95	19	3.45
10	3.00		

Note: Thickness mark is printed on the surface to be contacted with tappet.

How to use the chart

[Example]
Measured clearance; 0.550mm
Original adjuster thickness; 2.96mm
(Thickness mark (2.96) is printed on the adjuster surface)

1. Draw straight lines as shown in the chart.
2. Select No.15 available adjuster to be replaced by finding cross point of straight lines.
3. Replace the 2.96mm adjuster with No.15 (3.25mm) adjuster.

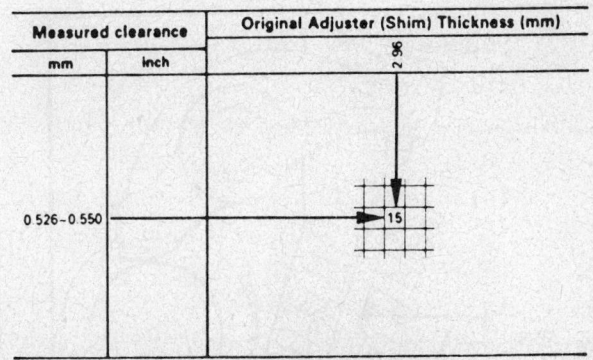

Measured clearance mm	inch	Original Adjuster (Shim) Thickness (mm) — 2.96
0.526–0.550		15

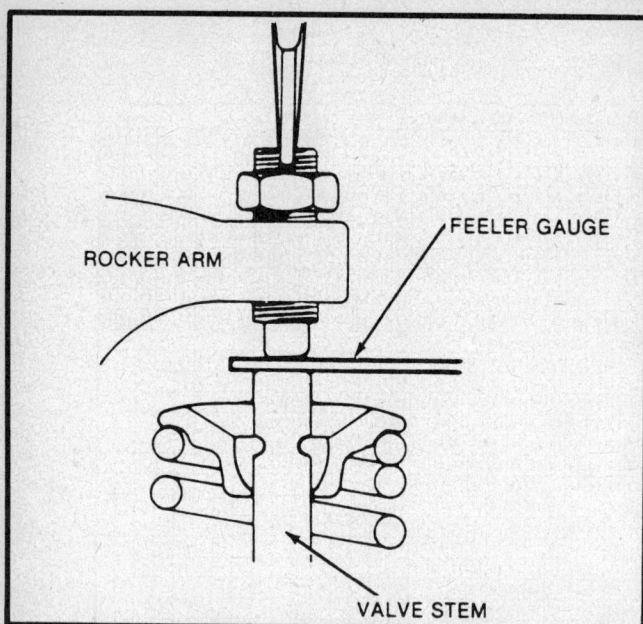

Valve lash adjustment—Spectrum

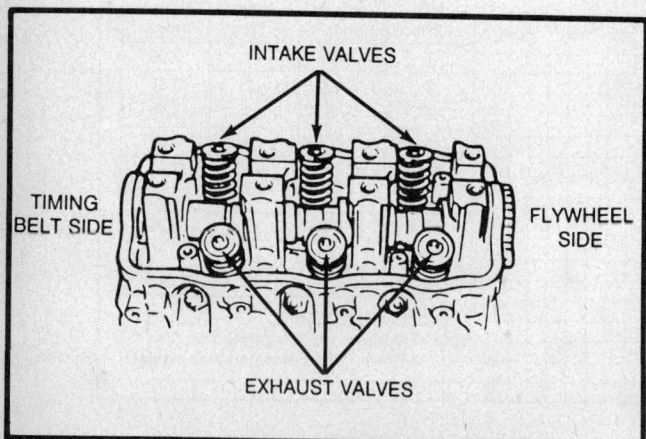

Valve identification in cylinder head—Sprint and Metro

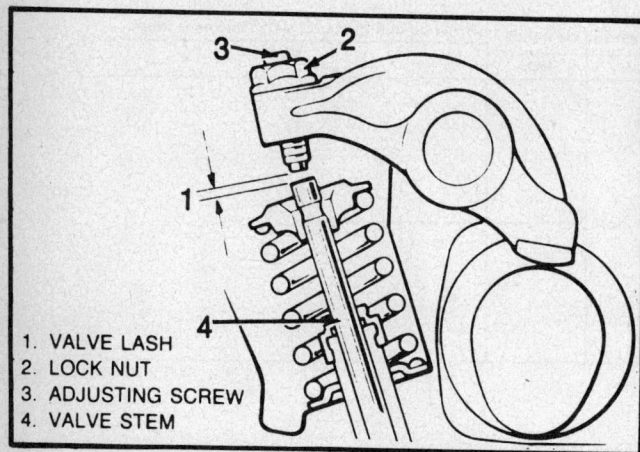

1. VALVE LASH
2. LOCK NUT
3. ADJUSTING SCREW
4. VALVE STEM

Valve lash adjusting screw—Sprint and Metro

SPRINT AND METRO

1. Remove the air cleaner on carbureted engine. Remove the rocker cover.

2. Rotate the crankshaft clockwise and align the **V** mark on the crankshaft pulley with the **0** mark on the timing tab.

3. Remove the distributor cap and make sure the rotor is facing the fuel pump. If not, rotate the crankshaft 360 degrees.

4. Check and/or adjust the valves of the No. 1 cylinder.

NOTE: On a COLD engine, adjust the valves to 0.006 in. (intake) and 0.008 in. (exhaust). On a HOT engine, adjust the valves to 0.010 in. (intake) and 0.012 in. (exhaust).

5. After adjusting the valves of the No. 1 cylinder, rotate the crankshaft pulley 240 degrees, the **V** mark should align with the lower left oil pump mounting bolt, when facing the crankshaft pulley, then adjust the valves of the No. 3 cylinder.

6. After adjusting the valves of the No. 3 cylinder, rotate the crankshaft pulley 240 degrees, the **V** mark should align with the lower right oil pump mounting bolt, when facing the crankshaft pulley, then adjust the valves of the No. 2 cylinder.

7. After the valves have been adjusted, install the removed items by reversing the removal procedures. Torque the valve adjustment locknuts to 11–13 ft. lbs.

Rocker Arms/Shafts

Removal and Installation

NOVA AND PRIZM

Except Twincam Engine

1. Disconnect the negative battery cable. Remove the air cleaner and valve cover.

2. Remove the 5 rocker shaft assembly retaining bolts in several stages—note that they must be loosened in the correct sequence: Front bolt 1st, rear bolt 2nd, forward—center bolt 3rd, rearward-center bolt 4th and the center bolt 5th.

3. Remove the rocker arm/shaft assembly.

4. Inspect for wear by attempting to rock the rocker levers on the shaft. If negligible motion is felt, wear is acceptable. If there is noticeable wear, note the order of assembly and the fact that there are 2 types of rockers. Remove the bolts and slide the rockers, springs and pedestals from the shaft.

5. Using an internal dial indicator, measure the inside diameter of each rocker lever; using a micrometer, measure the shaft diameter at the rocker wear areas. Subtract the shaft shaft diameter from the rocker arm inside diameter; the difference must not exceed 0.0024 in. If necessary, replace the rockers and/or the shaft to correct the clearance problems.

6. Assemble the pedestals, rockers, springs and bolts in reverse order of disassembly. Using clean engine oil, lubricate wear surfaces thoroughly. Install the rocker arm shaft with the oil holes facing downward.

7. Loosen the valve adjusting screw locknuts. Install the rocker arm assembly onto the cylinder head and start the bolts, tightening them finger tight. Torque the rocker arm assembly-to-cylinder head bolts (in sequence) using 3 passes to 18 ft. lbs.:

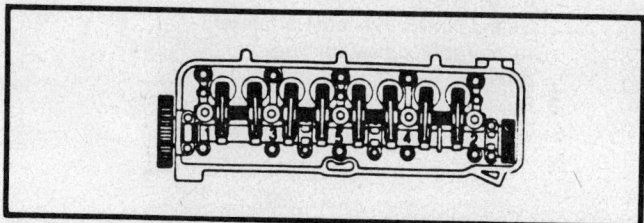

Rocker arm support loosening sequence, except twincam engine—Nova center bolt—first, center/rearward bolt—second, center/forward bolt—third, rear bolt—fourth and front bolt—last. Perform the valve adjustment.

8. To complete the installation, use new gasket(s), sealant, if necessary, and reverse the removal procedures.

STORM

1. Disconnect the battery negative cable.
2. Remove the cylinder head valve cover.
3. Remove the rocker arm bracket bolts as specified.
4. Remove the rocker shaft/arm assembly from the vehicle.
5. Remove the rocker arms from the rocker shaft.
6. Reverse procedure to install. Adjust valves and connect the battery negative cable.

SPECTRUM

1. Disconnect the negative battery terminal from the battery. Remove the PCV hoses.
2. Remove the spark plug wires from the mounting clip.
3. Remove the ground wire from the right rear side of the head cover.
4. Support the engine and remove the right side engine mounting rubber, bolts and plate.
5. Remove the mounting bracket on the timing cover.
6. Remove the 4 bolts holding the timing cover and the 2 bolts holding the cylinder head cover.
7. Loosen the timing cover and remove the cylinder head cover.

NOTE: If the cylinder head cover sticks, strike the end of the cover with a rubber mallet.

8. Remove the rocker arm bracket bolts in sequence, work from both ends equally, toward the middle.
9. Remove the rocker arm shafts and then the rocker arms from the shafts.

10. Using the proper tool, clean the sealing surfaces of the cover and the cylinder head.
To install:
11. To install, apply sealer to the sealing surfaces and reverse the removal procedures.

NOTE: The rocker arm shafts are different from each other, make sure they are installed in the same position that they were removed. Install the rocker arms with the identification marks toward the front of the engine. Apply sealant to the bracket and cylinder head mating surfaces of the front and rear rocker brackets.

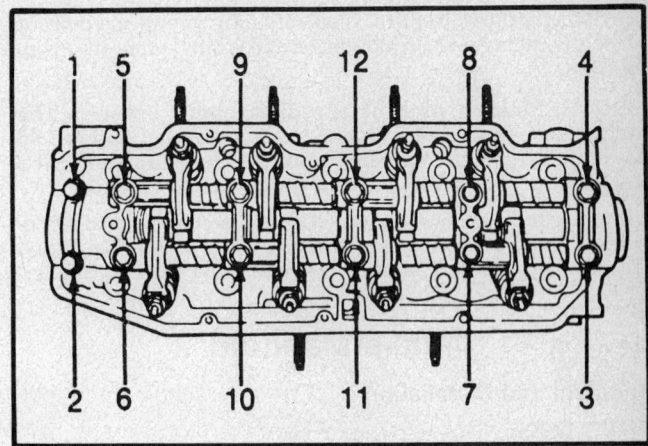

Rocker arm/shaft removal sequence—Spectrum

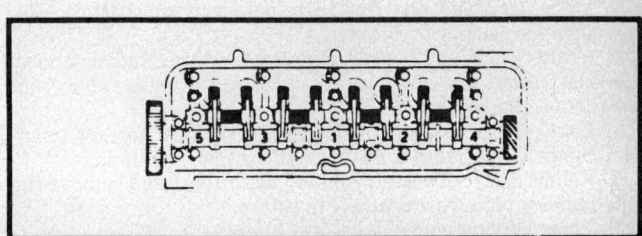

Rocker arm support torquing sequence except twincam engine—Nova

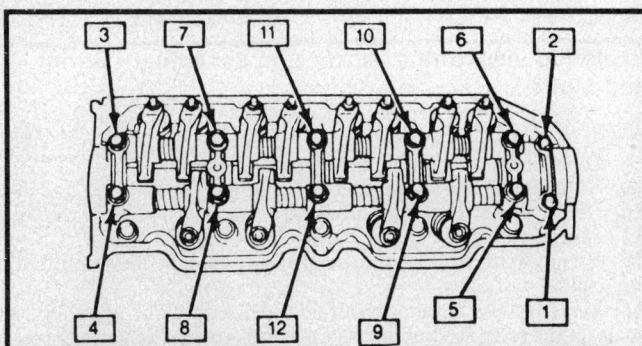

Rocker arm shaft bolt removal sequence—Storm without twincam engine

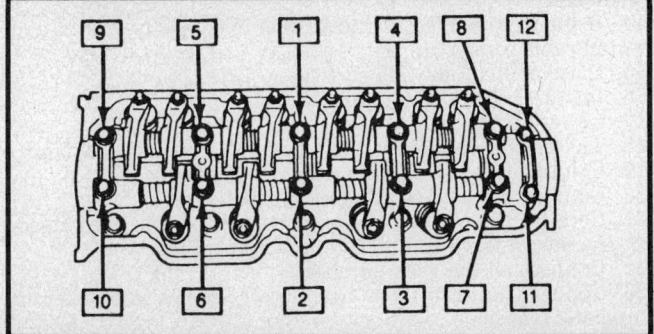

Rocker arm shaft bolt tightening sequence—Storm without twincam engine

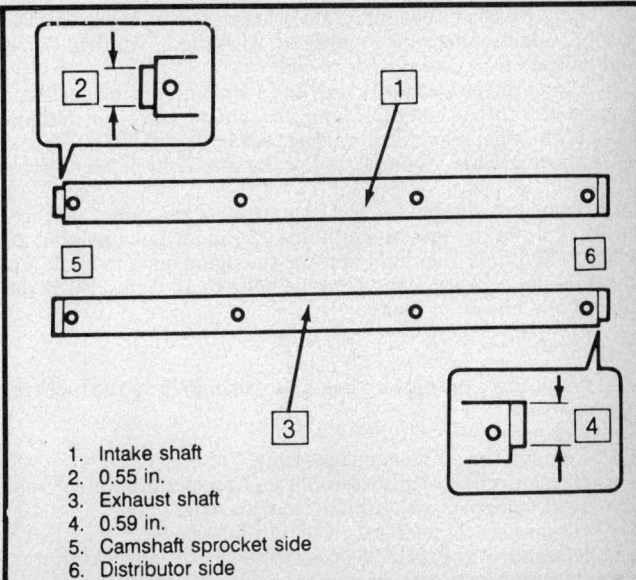

1. Intake shaft
2. 0.55 in.
3. Exhaust shaft
4. 0.59 in.
5. Camshaft sprocket side
6. Distributor side

Identifying rocker arm shafts—Sprint and Metro

12. To complete the installation, mount the rocker assemblies securely to the dowel pins on the cylinder head. Torque the rocker arm bolts to 16 ft. lbs. Start the engine and check for leaks.

SPRINT AND METRO

1. Disconnect the negative battery cable.
2. Remove the air cleaner and the cylinder head cover.
3. Remove the distributor cap, then mark the position of the rotor and the distributor housing with the cylinder head. Remove the distributor and the case from the cylinder head.
4. Loosen the rocker arm valve adjusters, turn back the adjusting screws so the rocker arms move freely.
5. Remove the rocker arm shaft retaining screws and pull out the shafts. Remove the rocker arms and springs from the cylinder head.

NOTE: Make a note of the differences between the rocker arm shafts. The intake shaft's stepped end is 0.55 in., which faces the camshaft pulley; the exhaust shaft's stepped end is 0.59 in., which faces the distributor.

6. To install, use new gaskets and reverse the removal procedures. Torque the rocker arm shaft screws to 7–9 ft. lbs. Adjust the valve clearances. Check and/or adjust the ignition timing.

Intake Manifold

Removal and Installation

NOVA

Twincam Engine

1. Disconnect the negative terminal from the battery. Remove the air cleaner assembly.
2. Drain the cooling system. Remove the upper radiator hose.
3. Disconnect the accelerator and throttle valve cable from the throttle body.
4. Label and disconnect the necessary vacuum hoses. Disconnect the brake vacuum hose from the intake manifold.
5. Relieve the fuel pressure, then, disconnect and remove the fuel delivery pipe with the fuel injectors.
6. Raise and support the vehicle safely.
7. Disconnect the temperature sensor connector from the water outlet housing. Remove the water outlet housing-to-engine bolts with the No. 1 bypass pipe.
8. Remove the intake manifold bracket, the intake manifold-to-engine bolts, the intake manifold, with the air control valve, and gaskets from the cylinder head.
9. Using the proper tool, clean the gasket mounting surfaces. Inspect the intake manifold and air control valve for damage and/or warpage; maximum warpage for both is 0.002 in., if the warpage is greater, replace the intake manifold or air control valve.
10. To install, use new gaskets and reverse the removal procedures. Torque the intake manifold-to-cylinder head bolts to 20 ft. lbs., the intake manifold bracket-to-engine bolts to 20 ft. lbs. and the fuel delivery pipe-to-engine bolts to 13 ft. lbs. Start the engine and check for leaks.

PRIZM

1. Disconnect the battery negative cable. Relieve the fuel system pressure.
2. Drain coolant.
3. Remove the air cleaner assembly.
4. Disconnect the throttle cable and accelerator cable from bracket if equipped with automatic transaxle.
5. Disconnect all necessary vacuum hoses.
6. Disconnect the throttle position sensor, cold start injector, injector connectors, the air control valve and vacuum sensor.
7. Disconnect the cold start injector pipe.

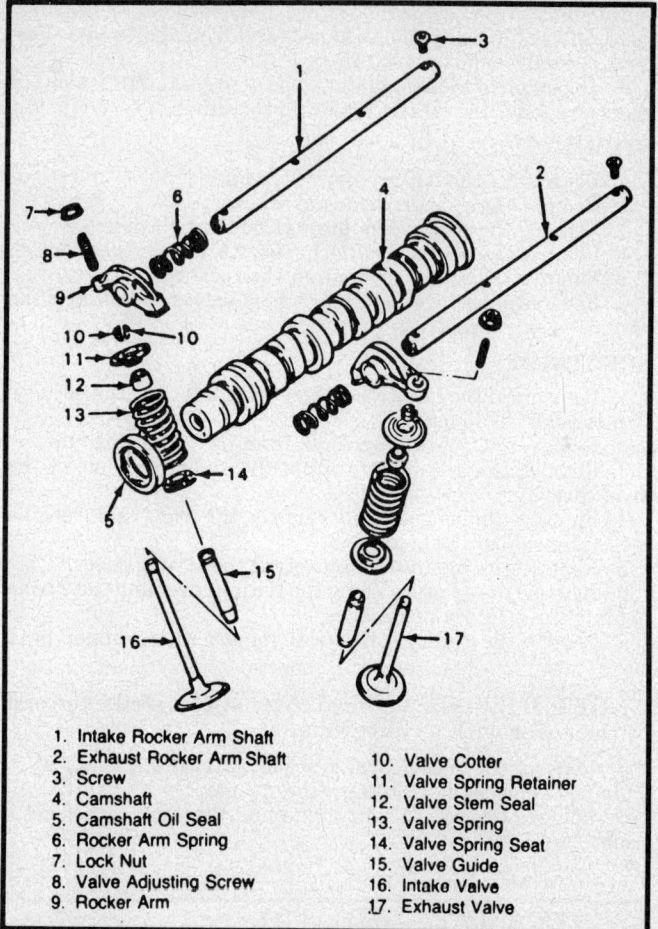

1. Intake Rocker Arm Shaft
2. Exhaust Rocker Arm Shaft
3. Screw
4. Camshaft
5. Camshaft Oil Seal
6. Rocker Arm Spring
7. Lock Nut
8. Valve Adjusting Screw
9. Rocker Arm
10. Valve Cotter
11. Valve Spring Retainer
12. Valve Stem Seal
13. Valve Spring
14. Valve Spring Seat
15. Valve Guide
16. Intake Valve
17. Exhaust Valve

Exploded view of the rocker arm assembly—Sprint and Metro

8. Disconnect the water hose from air valve.
9. Raise and safely support the vehicle.
10. Remove the intake manifold bracket.
11. Lower vehicle.
12. Remove the 7 bolts, 2 nuts, ground cable, intake manifold, and gasket.
13. Measure the intake manifold with a straight edge and a feeler gauge at the cylinder head mating surface. If warpage exceeds 0.008 in. (0.2mm), replace the intake manifold.

To install:
14. Install the new gasket, intake manifold, 7 bolts, 2 nuts, and ground cable connector.
15. Raise and suitably support the vehicle.
16. Install the intake manifold bracket.
17. Lower vehicle.
18. Tighten the intake manifold bolts to 14 ft. lbs. (19 Nm).
19. Connect the water hose to the air valve.
20. Connect the cold-start injector pipe.
21. Connect the throttle position sensor, the cold start injector, the air control valve and the vacuum sensor.
22. Connect all the vacuum hoses.
23. Connect the throttle and accelerator cables to bracket on automatic transaxle.
24. Refill coolant.
25. Install the air cleaner assembly.
26. Connect the battery negative cable.

STORM

Except Twincam Engine

1. Disconnect the battery negative cable and the ignition coil wire.
2. Disconnect the accelerator cable from the throttle valve and the intake manifold (common chamber).
3. Disconnect the 2 cable harness connectors, located near the left shock tower.
4. Disconnect the cable harness from from the MAT sensor, then the TPS sensor and the intake air control valve.
5. Remove the intake air duct from the throttle valve, then the PCV hose from the cylinder head cover.
6. Disconnect the EGR valve and canister vacuum hoses from the throttle valve.
7. Disconnect the EGR pipe from the EGR valve and the exhuast manifold.
8. Remove the intake manifold (common chamber) bracket bolt, then the throttle vale assembly bolts and the throttle valve.
9. Remove the coolant bypass pipe clip bolt, then disconnect the MAP sensor from the intake manifold (common chamber).
10. Disconnect the brake booster vacuum hose, then the canister vacuum hose from the intake manifold (common chamber) and the throttle valve.
11. Disconnect the pressure regulator vacuum hose from the common chamber, then the EGR vacuum hose.
12. Remove the engine hanger bolt, then the intake manifold (common chamber) attaching nuts and bolts. Remove the intake manifold (common chamber) from the vehicle.

To install:

13. Install the intake manifold (common chamber) and a new gasket onto the induction port. Torque nuts and bolts to 17 ft. lbs. (23 Nm).
14. Install the coolant bypass pipe clip bolts.
15. Install the throttle valve with a new gasket. Torque throttle valve bolts to 17 ft. lbs. (23 Nm).
16. Connect the EGR pipe flange to the exhaust manifold. Torque flange bolts to 17 ft. lbs. (23 Nm).
17. Connect the EGR vacuum hose, then the pressure regulator vacuum hose to the inake manifold (common chamber).
18. Connect the canister vacuum hose to the common chamber and the throttle valve, then the breather hose to the intake air duct.
19. Connect the cable harness to the MAT sensor, TPS and the intake air control valve.
20. Connect the 2 cable harness connectors, located near the left shock tower.
21. Connect the accelerator cable to the throttle valve and to the intake manifold (common chamber).
22. Connect the ignition coil wire. Connect the battery negative cable and fill cooling system. Start engine and check for leaks.

Twincam Engine

1. Disconnect the battery negative cable.
2. Disconnect the accelerator cable clip and the PCV hose from the intake air duct.
3. Disconnect the accelerator cable from the throttle valve.
4. Disconnect the MAP sensor hose from the MAP sensor, then the vacuum hose form the brake vacuum booster.
5. Disconnect the 2 canister hoses from intake manifold (common chamber).
6. Remove the canister pipe bracket from the intake manifold (common chamber).
7. Disconnect the vacuum hose from the fuel pressure regulator, then the vacuum hose from the induction port.
8. Remove the throttle valve from the intake manifold (common chmaber).
9. Remove the alternator harness clip, then the 3 fuel injector harness cable clips.

10. Loosen the EGR pipe bracket on the exhaust manifold, then loosen the from the thermostat housing.
11. Remove the 2 intake manifold (common chamber) bracket attaching bolts, located on the left side of the engine and the engine hanger bolt, located on the right side of the intake manifold (common chamber).
12. Remove the intake manifold (common chamber) attaching nuts and bolts, then remove the intake manifold (common chamber) from the induction port assembly.

To install:

13. Install the intake manifold (common chamber) with a new gasket onto the induction port assembly. Torque nuts and bolts to 17 ft. lbs. (23 Nm).
14. Install the intake manifold (common chamber) bracket bolts, located on the left side of engine and the hanger bolt, located on the right side of the engine.
15. Install the EGR pipe braket bolts on the exhaust manifold and the EGR clip on the thermostat housing. Torque EGR bracket bolts to 32 ft. lbs. (44 Nm).
16. Install the alternator harness cable clip, then the 3 fuel injector harness cable clips.
17. Install the throttle valve onto the intake manifold (common chamber), then connect the induction control valve vacuum hose.
18. Connect the fuel pressure regulator vacuum hose to the intake manifold (common chamber).
19. Connect the canister pipe bracket onto the intake manifold (common chamber).
20. Connect the brake booster vacuum hose, then the MAP sensor hose to the MAP sensor.
21. Connect the accelerator cable clip to the intake air duct.
22. Connect the battery negative cable and fill cooling system. Start engine and check for leaks.

SPECTRUM

Non-Turbocharged Engine

1. Disconnect the negative battery terminal from the battery. Drain the cooling system.
2. Remove the bolt securing the alternator adjusting plate to the engine.
3. Disconnect and label all of the hoses attached to the air cleaner and remove the air cleaner.
4. Disconnect the air inlet temperature switch wiring connector.
5. Disconnect and label the hoses, electrical connectors and control cable attached to the carburetor.
6. If equipped with air conditioning, disconnect the FIDC vacuum hose, the pressure tank control valve hose, the distributor 3-way connector hose and the VSV wiring connector.
7. Remove the carburetor attaching bolts, located beneath the intake manifold, then remove the carburetor and the EFE heater.
8. At the intake manifold, remove the PCV hose, the water bypass hose, the heater hoses, the EGR valve/canister hose, the distributor vacuum advance hose and the ground wires.
9. Disconnect the thermometer unit switch wiring connector.
10. Remove the intake manifold attaching nuts/bolts and the intake manifold.
11. Clean the sealing surfaces of the intake manifold and cylinder head.

To install:

12. Use new gaskets and reverse the removal procedures.
13. Torque the intake manifold to 17 ft. lbs.; then adjust the engine control cable and the alternator belt tension. Refill the engine with coolant and check for leaks.

Turbocharged Engine

1. Relieve the fuel system pressure. Disconnect the negative battery terminal from the battery.
2. Remove pressure regulator and oil separator.

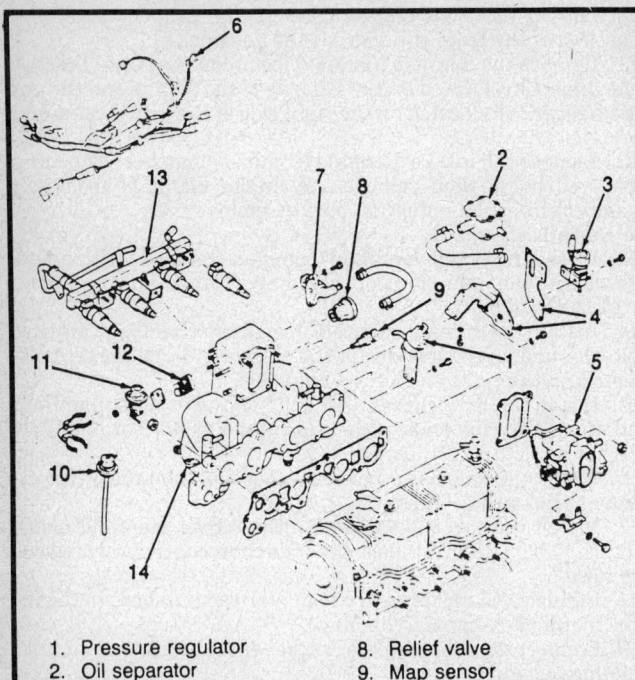

1. Pressure regulator
2. Oil separator
3. VSV
4. Bracket and hanger
5. Throttle valve assembly
6. Engine harness assembly
7. Idle air control valve
8. Relief valve
9. Map sensor
10. Back pressure transducer
11. EGR valve
12. Adaptor
13. Fuel injector with pipe
14. Intake manifold

Intake manifold turbocharged model—Spectrum

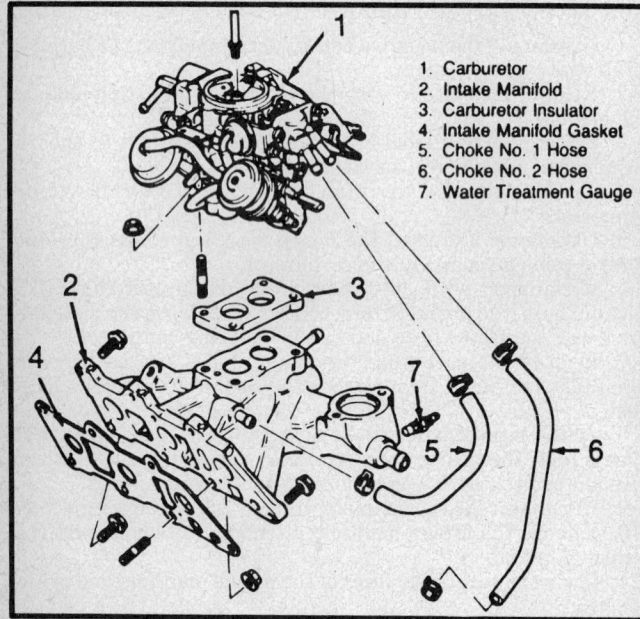

1. Carburetor
2. Intake Manifold
3. Carburetor Insulator
4. Intake Manifold Gasket
5. Choke No. 1 Hose
6. Choke No. 2 Hose
7. Water Treatment Gauge

Exploded view of the intake manifold and carburetor assembly—Sprint

3. Disconnect vacuum line from VSV and remove vacuum switching valve from bracket.
4. Remove oil seperator/VSV bracket and hanger as an assembly.
5. Remove throttle valve assembly and engine harness assembly (mark or tag harness connections if necessary).
6. Remove idle air control valve, relief valve and MAP sensor.

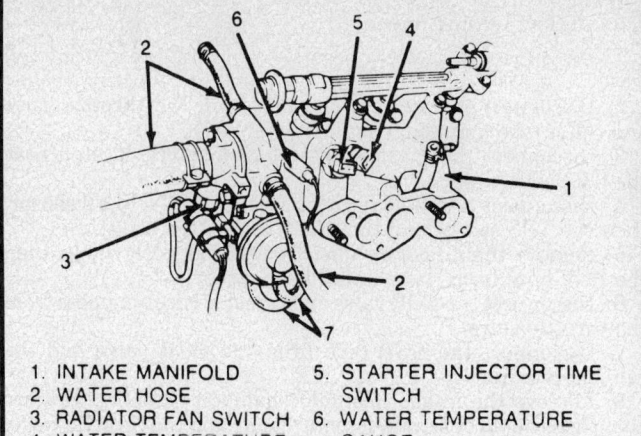

1. INTAKE MANIFOLD
2. WATER HOSE
3. RADIATOR FAN SWITCH
4. WATER TEMPERATURE SENSOR
5. STARTER INJECTOR TIME SWITCH
6. WATER TEMPERATURE GAUGE
7. EGR VALVE VACUUM HOSE

Instake manifold assembly—Sprint with turbocharged engine

7. Disconnect vacuum line from back pressure transducer and unclip transducer from hold-down bracket.
8. Remove EGR valve and adaptor plate.
9. Remove fuel injectors and fuel pipe connected to rail as one unit and position out of way then remove intake manifold with common chamber
10. To install, use new gaskets and reverse the removal procedures. Torque the intake manifold to 17 ft. lbs. Start and run engine check for leaks.

SPRINT

Non-Turbocharged Engine

1. Relieve the fuel system pressure. Disconnect the negative battery cable.
2. Drain the cooling system.
3. Disconnect the air cleaner element, the EGR modulator, the warm air, the cool air, the 2nd air and the vacuum hoses from the air cleaner case.
4. Remove the air cleaner case, the electrical lead wires and the accelerator cable from the carburetor.
5. Disconnect the emission control and the fuel hoses from the carburetor.
6. Remove the water hoses from the choke housing.
7. Remove the electrical lead wires, the emission control, the coolant and the brake vacuum hoses from the intake manifold.
8. Remove the intake manifold from the cylinder head.
9. Clean the mating gasket surfaces.
10. To install, use new gaskets and reverse the removal procedures. Torque the intake manifold-to-cylinder head bolts to 14–20 ft. lbs. Refill the cooling system.

Turbocharged Engine

1. Disconnect the negative battery cable.
2. Drain the cooling system when the engine is cool.

NOTE: The fuel delivery pipe is under high pressure even after the engine is stopped, direct removal of the fuel line may result in dangerous fuel spray. Make sure to release the fuel pressure according to the procedure outlined under Fuel System in this section.

3. Remove the surge tank together with the throttle body.
4. Disconnect the fuel injector couplers.
5. Disconnect the fuel hoses from the delivery pipe.
6. Remove the delivery pipe together with the injectors.

7. Disconnect the water temperature gauge wire (yellow/white).

8. Disconnect the starter injector time switch coupler (brown).

9. Disconnect the water temperature sensor coupler (green).

10. Disconnect the radiator fan switch coupler.

11. Disconnect the water hoses and the EGR vacuum hoses.

12. Remove the intake manifold retaining bolts then remove the manifold fropm the vehicle.

13. Installation is the reverse of removal, with the following precautions:

    a. Use a new intake manifold gasket.

    b. If an injector was removed from the delivery pipe a new O-ring should be used.

    c. Torque the intake manifold retaining bolts to 17 ft. lbs.

    d. After the ignition is turned on check for fuel leaks.

METRO

1. Relieve the fuel system pressure.

2. Disconnect the negative battery cable.

3. Drain the cooling system.

4. Remove the air cleaner assembly.

5. Disconnect the following wires:

    a. Vacuum switching valve for EGR valve

    b. Water temperature sensor

    c. Idle speed control solenoid valve

    d. Ground wires from the intake manifold

    e. Fuel injector

    f. Throttle switch or throttle position sensor

    g. Water temperature gauge

6. Disconnect the fuel return and feed hoses from the throttle body.

7. Disconnect the water hoses from the throttle body and the intake manifold.

8. Disconnect the following hoses:

    a. Canister purge hose from the intake manifold

    b. Canister hose from its pipe

    c. Pressure sensor hose from the intake manifold

    d. Brake booster hose from the intake manifold

9. Disconnect the PCV hose from the cylinder head cover.

10. Disconnect the accelerator cable from the throttle body.

11. Disconnect any other lines and cables, as necessary.

12. Remove the intake manifold with the throttle body from the cylinder head.

To install:

13. Install the intake manifold to the cylinder head, using a new gasket, install the clamps and tighten the intake manifold retaining bolts to 17 ft. lbs.

14. Reinstall all vacuum and water hoses.

15. Install the fuel feed and return hoses.

16. Install all electrical lead wires.

17. Install the accelerator cable to the throttle body.

18. Install the air cleaner assembly.

19. Fill the cooling system and reconnect the negative battery cable.

Exhaust Manifold

Removal and Installation

NOVA AND PRIZM

Twincam Engine

1. Disconnect the negative terminal from the battery.

2. Remove the exhaust manifold heat shield.

3. Raise and support the vehicle safely.

4. Remove the exhaust pipe-to-exhaust manifold nuts and separate the pipe from the manifold. Remove the exhaust manifold bracket from the exhaust manifold, the exhaust manifold-to-engine bolts, the exhaust manifold and gasket (discard the gasket) from the cylinder head.

5. Using the proper tool, clean the gasket mounting surfaces. Inspect the exhaust manifold for damage and/or warpage; maximum warpage is 0.012 in., if the warpage is greater, replace the exhaust manifold.

6. To install, use a new gasket and reverse the removal procedures. Torque the exhaust manifold-to-cylinder head bolts to 18 ft. lbs. Start the engine and check for leaks.

STORM

1. Disconnect the battery negative cable.

2. Remove the heat protector, then disconnect the oxygen sensor electrical connector.

3. If equipped with twincam engine, Disconnect the EGR pipe clip from the thermostat housing.

4. Disconect the EGR pipe from the exhaust manifold and the EGR valve.

5. Remove the front exhaust pipe from the exhaust manifold.

6. Remove the exhaust manifold attaching nuts and bolts, then remove the exhaust manifold from the engine.

7. Reverse procedure to install. Using the proper tool, clean the gasket mounting surfaces. Inspect the exhaust manifold for damage and/or warpage; maximum warpage is 0.0157 in. (0.4mm), if the warpage is greater, replace the exhaust manifold.

8. Torque exhaust manifold attaching nuts and bolts to 30 ft. lbs. (39 Nm) and the EGR pipe bolts to 32 ft. lbs. (44 Nm).

SPECTRUM

1. Disconnect the negative battery terminal from the battery and the oxygen sensor wiring connector.

2. Disconnect the Thermostatic Air Cleaner (TAC) flex hose. Disconnect the vacuum and oil lines on turbocharged engines.

3. Remove the hot air cover and raise the vehicle.

4. Disconnect the vacuum and oil lines on turbocharged engines.

5. Disconnect the exhaust pipe from the exhaust manifold and lower the vehicle.

6. Remove the nuts and bolts securing the exhaust manifold to the cylinder head. Clean the gasket mounting surfaces.

7. To install, use new gaskets and reverse the removal procedures. Torque the exhaust manifold to 17 ft. lbs. or 21 ft. lbs. turbocharged model then start the engine and check for leaks.

SPRINT AND METRO

Non-Turbocharged Engine

1. Disconnect the negative battery cable.

2. Raise and support the vehicle safely.

3. Remove the exhaust pipe at the exhaust manifold.

4. Remove the lower heat shield bolt and the 2nd air pipe at the exhaust manifold.

5. If equipped, remove the air conditioning drive belt and the lower adjusting bracket.

6. Lower the vehicle.

7. Remove the spark plug and the oxygen sensor wires.

8. Remove the hot air shroud from the exhaust manifold.

9. Remove the 2nd air valve hoses, the valve and the pipe from the exhaust manifold.

10. Remove the mounting bolts and the exhaust manifold.

11. Clean the gasket mating surfaces.

12. To install, use a new gasket and reverse the removal procedures. Torque the exhaust manifold fasteners to 14–20 ft. lbs. and the exhaust pipe to 30–43 ft. lbs.

Turbocharged Engine

1. Remove the turbocharger assembly.

2. Remove the exhaust manifold.

3. Installation is the reverse of removal. Install a new gasket.

Combination Manifold

Removal and Installation

NOVA AND PRIZM

Except Twincam Engine

1. Disconnecrt the battery negative cable.
2. Remove the air cleaner assembly. Label and disconnect the vacuum hoses.
3. Disconnect the throttle valve and the accelerator cables from the carburetor. Label and disconnect the electrical connectors from the carburetor.
4. Disconnect the fuel line from the fuel pump and drain the excess fuel into a metal container.
5. Disconnect or remove any emission control hardware that may be in the way. Remove the carburetor-to-combination manifold nuts and the carburetor from the combination manifold; discard the gasket.
6. Remove the Early Fuel Evaporation (EFE) gasket. Remove the vacuum line, the dashpot bracket and the carburetor heat shield.
7. Raise and safely support the vehicle. Remove the exhaust pipe-to-combination manifold bolts, the exhaust bracket from the engine and the air hose from the catalytic converter pipe.
8. Lower the vehicle.
9. Disconnect the brake vacuum hose from the combination manifold. Remove the accelerator and throttle cable brackets.
10. Working from the center outward, remove the combination manifold-to-cylinder head nuts in several stages so tension is gradually released.
11. Remove the combination manifold from the cylinder head.

To install:
12. Using the proper tool, clean the gasket mounting surfaces.
13. Inspect the manifold for damage and/or warpage.
14. Use new gaskets and reverse the removal procedure. Torqure the combination manifold-to-cylinder head bolts to 18 ft. lbs.
15. Connect the battery negative cable. Start the engine and check for leaks.

Turbocharger

Removal and Installation

SPECTRUM

1. Disconnect the battery negative cable.

2. Remove the upper and lower heat protector shields from the turbocharger assembly.
3. Remove the manifold heat protector, then disconnect the oxygen sensor electrical connector.
4. Disconnect the vacuum pipe wastegate and position aside.
5. Disconnect the water lines, then disconnect the return and delivery oil lines.
6. Disconect the exhaust pipe from the wastegate manifold.

NOTE: The exhaust manifold studs should be soaked with CRC or equivalent to prevent studs from breaking before removal.

7. Remove the turbocharger and wastegate from the vehicle as an assembly.
8. To install, use a new gasket on the exhaust manifold-to-turbocharger housing and reverse the removal procedure. Connect the battery negative cable and refill all fluids. Start the engine and check for leaks.

SPRINT

1. Disconnect the battery negative cable and drain the cooling system.
2. Remove the hood.
3. Remove the front grille attaching screws, then the front grille from the vehicle.
4. Remove the intercooler, then thwe radiator hoses.
5. Disconnect the radiator fan motor electrical connector, then remove the front upper member.
6. If equipped with air conditioning, discharge the air conditioning system, then remove the air conditioning condensor.
7. Remove the radiator from the vehicle.
8. Disconnect the front bumper from the damper flange. Place a stand under the front bumper to prevent it from dropping, then remove the coupler clamps and bolts and pull the bumper outward.
9. Remove the exhaust pipe bolts.
10. If equipped with air conditioning, remove the air conditioning compressor.
11. Remove the turbocharger cover, then disconnect the oxygen sensor electrical connector.
12. Remove the turbocharger side cover, then the lower exhaust pipe support bracket bolt.
13. Remove the upper exhaust pipe, along the lower exhaust pipe.

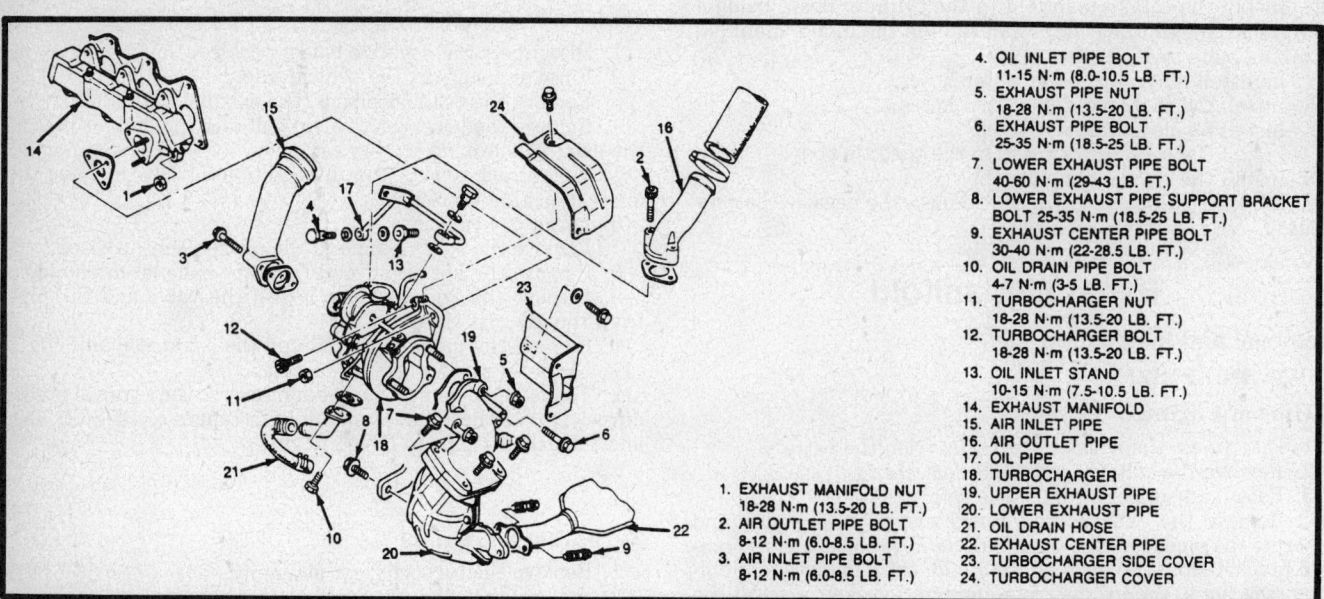

4. OIL INLET PIPE BOLT
   11-15 N·m (8.0-10.5 LB. FT.)
5. EXHAUST PIPE NUT
   18-28 N·m (13.5-20 LB. FT.)
6. EXHAUST PIPE BOLT
   25-35 N·m (18.5-25 LB. FT.)
7. LOWER EXHAUST PIPE BOLT
   40-60 N·m (29-43 LB. FT.)
8. LOWER EXHAUST PIPE SUPPORT BRACKET
   BOLT 25-35 N·m (18.5-25 LB. FT.)
9. EXHAUST CENTER PIPE BOLT
   30-40 N·m (22-28.5 LB. FT.)
10. OIL DRAIN PIPE BOLT
   4-7 N·m (3-5 LB. FT.)
11. TURBOCHARGER NUT
   18-28 N·m (13.5-20 LB. FT.)
12. TURBOCHARGER BOLT
   18-28 N·m (13.5-20 LB. FT.)
13. OIL INLET STAND
   10-15 N·m (7.5-10.5 LB. FT.)
14. EXHAUST MANIFOLD
15. AIR INLET PIPE
16. AIR OUTLET PIPE
17. OIL PIPE
18. TURBOCHARGER
19. UPPER EXHAUST PIPE
20. LOWER EXHAUST PIPE
21. OIL DRAIN HOSE
22. EXHAUST CENTER PIPE
23. TURBOCHARGER SIDE COVER
24. TURBOCHARGER COVER

1. EXHAUST MANIFOLD NUT
   18-28 N·m (13.5-20 LB. FT.)
2. AIR OUTLET PIPE BOLT
   8-12 N·m (6.0-8.5 LB. FT.)
3. AIR INLET PIPE BOLT
   8-12 N·m (6.0-8.5 LB. FT.)

Turbocharger assembly—Sprint

14. Disconnect the air outlet pipe, then the air inlet hose clamp bolt on the cylinder head.

15. Remove the air inlet pipe, then disconnect the oil drain pipe.

16. Disconnect the water pipe cylinder head clamp bolt, then the water hoses.

17. Remove the turbocharger attaching bolts, then the turbocharger from the vehicle.

18. Reverse procedure to install. Connect the battery negative cable and recharge air conditioning system. Check and refill fluids as necessary. Start engine and check for leaks.

Timing Belt Front Cover

Removal and Installation

NOVA – EXCEPT TWINCAM ENGINE

This engine uses a 3 piece timing belt cover assembly; any individual cover can be removed by performing one of the following procedures.

Upper

1. Disconnect the negative terminal from the battery.
2. Loosen the water pump pulley bolts and remove the alternator/water pump drive belt. If equipped with power steering, remove the power steering pump drive belt.
3. Remove the water pump pulley bolts and pulley. Drain the cooling system.
4. Disconnect the upper radiator hose from the water pump outlet. Label and disconnect all vacuum hoses that may be in the way.
5. Remove the upper timing belt front cover-to-engine bolts.

NOTE: To remove the lower timing belt cover-to-engine bolts, it may be necessary to raise and support the vehicle, then, remove them from underneath.

6. Remove the upper timing belt front cover and gasket.
7. Using the proper tool, clean the gasket mounting surfaces.
8. To install, use a new gasket, sealant, if necessary, and reverse the removal procedures. Adjust the drive belts. Refill the cooling system. Start the engine, allow it to reach normal operating temperatures and check for leaks.

Middle

1. Remove the upper timing belt front cover.
2. If equipped with air conditioning, loosen the idler pulley

mounting bolt. Loosen the adjusting nut, then, remove the air conditioning drive belt, the idler pulley, with adjusting bolt.

3. Remove the alternator bolts and move it aside.
4. Remove the middle timing belt front cover-to-engine bolts, the cover and gasket.
5. Using the proper tool, clean the gasket mounting surfaces.
6. To install, use a new gasket, sealant, if necessary, and reverse the removal procedures. Adjust the drive bolts. Refill the cooling system. Start the engine, allow it to reach normal operating temperatures and check for leaks.

Lower

1. Disconnect the negative terminal from the battery.
2. Loosen the alternator adjusting bolts and remove the drive belt.
3. If equipped with air conditioning, remove the drive belt.

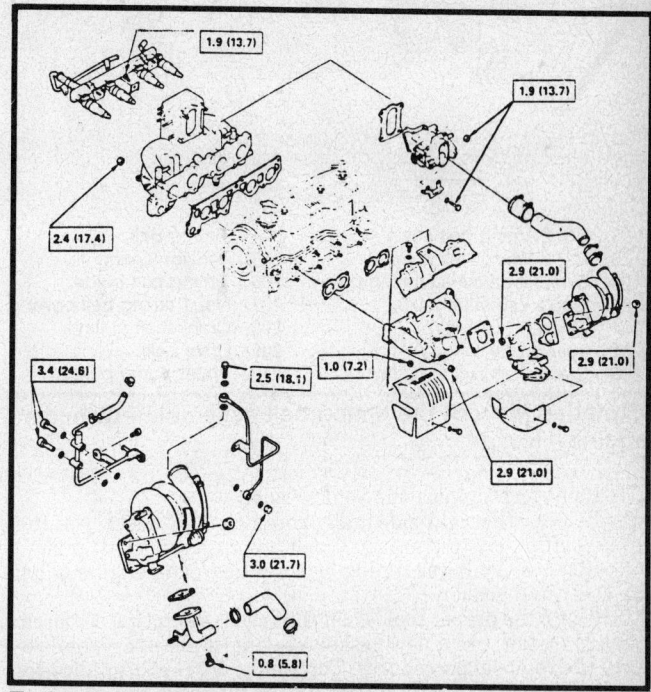

Turbocharger assembly – Spectrum

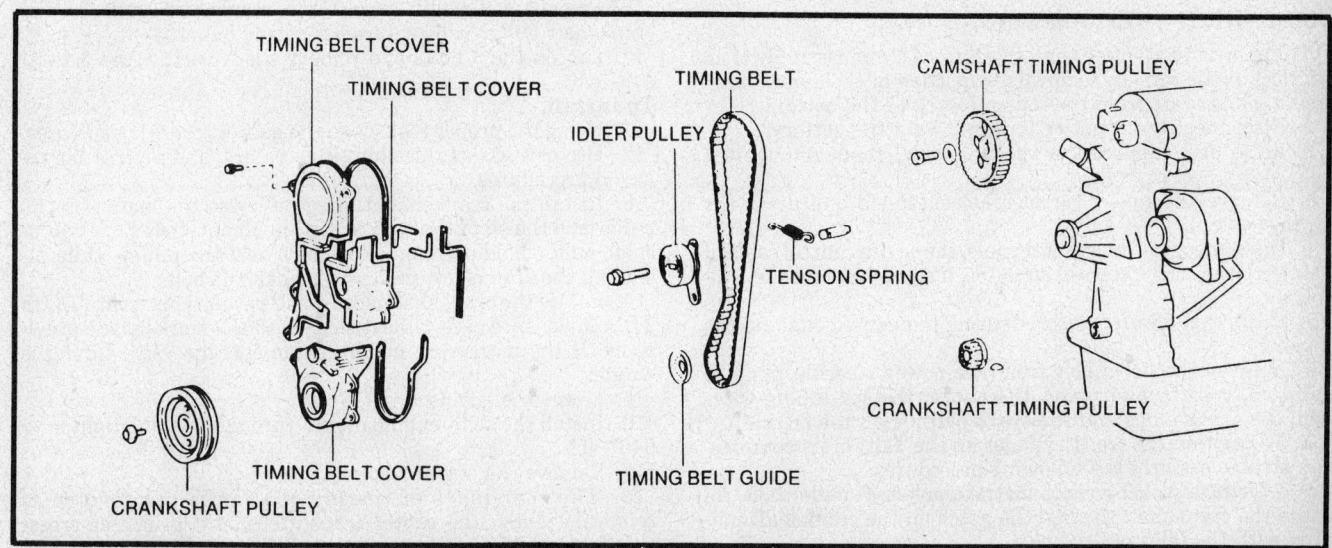

Exploded view of the timing belt assembly – except twincam engine – Nova

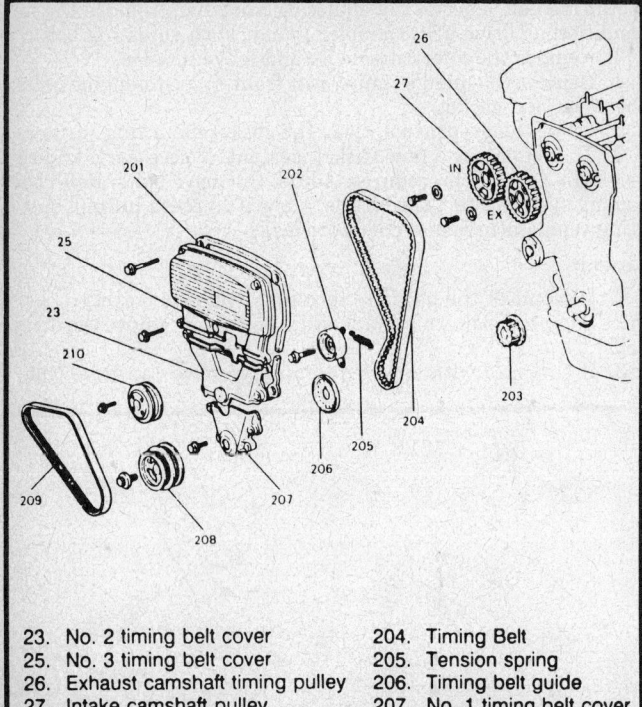

23. No. 2 timing belt cover	204. Timing Belt
25. No. 3 timing belt cover	205. Tension spring
26. Exhaust camshaft timing pulley	206. Timing belt guide
27. Intake camshaft pulley	207. No. 1 timing belt cover
201. Gasket	208. Crankshaft pulley
202. Idler pulley	209. Drive belt
203. Crankshaft timing pulley	210. Water pump pulley

Exploded view of the timing belt assembly—twincam engine—Nova

4. Raise and support the vehicle safely.

5. Remove the right-side under cover, the flywheel cover, the crankshaft pulley-to-crankshaft bolt and the crankshaft pulley.

6. Remove the lower timing belt front cover-to-engine bolts, the cover and gasket.

7. Using the proper tool, clean the gasket mounting surfaces.

8. To install, use a new gasket, sealant, if necessary, and reverse the removal procedures. Torque the crankshaft pulley-to-crankshaft bolt to 80–94 ft. lbs. Adjust the drive belt(s).

NOVA—WITH TWINCAM ENGINE

This engine uses a 3 piece timing belt front cover assembly of an interlocking design. To removal any portion of the cover, disassembly must start from the top and work to the bottom.

1. Disconnect the negative terminal from the battery.

2. Raise and support the vehicle safely, then, remove the right side wheel assembly.

3. Remove the under carriage splash shield and drain the cooling system.

4. Disconnect the accelerator cable, the cruise control cable, if equipped, the cruise control actuator, if equipped, and the ignition coil.

5. Remove the water outlet housing-to-engine bolts and the housing.

6. Remove the drive belt from the power steering pimp, if equipped, and the alternator. Disconnect the spark plug wires from the spark plugs and the spark plugs from the engine.

7. To position the No. 1 cylinder on the TDC of its compression stroke, perform the following procedures:

a. Using a socket wrench on the crankshaft pulley bolt, rotate the crankshaft to align the notch on the crankshaft pulley with the idler pulley bolt.

b. Remove the oil filler cap and look for the hole in the cam-

shaft; if it cannot be seen, rotate the crankshaft 1 complete revolution and check for it again.

8. Remove the right-side engine mount, the water pump pulley bolts and the pulley.

9. To remove the crankshaft pulley, perform the following procedures:

a. Using a crankshaft pulley holding tool, secure and hold the pulley while removing the crankshaft pulley-to-crankshaft bolt.

b. Using the crankshaft pulley puller tool, press the crankshaft pulley from the crankshaft.

10. Remove the timing belt front covers-to-engine bolts, the covers and the gaskets.

11. Using the proper tool, clean the gasket mounting surfaces.

12. To install, use new gaskets, sealant (if necessary) and reverse the removal procedures.

13. Using the crankshaft pulley holding tool, secure and hold the pulley while installing the crankshaft pulley-to-crankshaft bolt.

14. To complete the installation, reverse the removal procedures. Adjust the drive belts. Refill the cooling system. Start the engine, allow it to reach normal operating temperatures and check for leaks.

PRIZM

1. Disconnect the negative battery cable. Raise the vehicle and support it safely. Remove the right wheel and undercover. Remove the air cleaner.

2. Remove the 2 mount nut and stud protectors.

3. Remove the 2 rear transaxle mount to main crossmember nuts.

4. Remove the 2 center transaxle mount to center crossmember nuts.

5. Lower the vehicle.

6. Remove the drive belts. Remove the power steering pump and the air conditioning compressor (and their brackets!) and position them out of the way. Leave the hydraulic and refrigerant lines connected.

7. Remove the spark plugs and the cylinder head cover. Be sure to scrape off any left-over gasket material. Rotate the crankshaft pulley so the **0** mark is in alignment with the groove in the No. 1 front cover. Check that the lifters on the No. 1 cylinder are loose; if not, turn the crankshaft 1 complete revolution (360 degrees).

8. Position a floor jack under the engine and remove the right side engine mounting insulator.

9. Remove the water pump and crankshaft pulleys. The crankshaft pulley will require a 2-armed puller.

10. Loosen the 9 bolts and remove the Nos. 1, 2 and 3 front covers.

To install:

11. Using the proper tool, clean the gasket mounting surfaces.

12. Use new gaskets, sealant, if necessary, and reverse the removal procedures.

13. Install the crankshaft timing pulley so the marks on the pulley and the oil pump body are in alignment. Using the crankshaft pulley holding tool, secure and hold the pulley while installing the crankshaft pulley-to-crankshaft bolt.

14. Rotate the crankshaft clockwise 2 revolutions from TDC to TDC. Make sure each pulley aligns with the marks made previously. If the marks are not in alignment, the valve timing is wrong.

15. Lower the engine.

16. Install the right engine mount through bolt and tighten to 64 ft. lbs.

17. Remove the engine support.

18. The remainder of the installation is the reverse of removal. Tighten the center transaxle mount to center crossmember nuts to 45 ft. lbs. and the rear transaxle mount to main crossmember nuts to 45 ft. lbs.

STORM

Except Twincam Engine

1. Disconnect the battery negative cable.
2. Remove the alternator belt, then the power steering belt.
3. Using tool J–28467–A or equivalent, support the engine.
4. Remove the right engine mount.
5. Remove the timing belt cover attaching screws, then the timing belt cover from the vehicle.
6. Reverse procedure to install. Connect the battery negative cable.

Twincam Engine

1. Disconnect the battery negative cable.
2. Using tool J–28467-A or equivalent, support the engine.
3. Remove the right engine mount.
4. Remove the alternator and power steering belts.
5. Remove the upper timing belt cover attaching screws, then the upper timing belt cover from the vehicle.
6. Raise and support the vehicle safely.
7. Remove the crankshaft pulley bolt, then the crankshaft pulley.
8. Lower the vehicle, then remove the lower timing belt cover.
9. Reverse procedure to install. Connect the battery negative cable.

SPRINT AND METRO

1. Disconnect the negative battery cable.
2. Loosen the water pump pulley bolts and the alternator adjusting bolt.
3. If equipped, remove the air conditioning compressor adjusting bolt.
4. Raise and support the vehicle safely.
5. Remove the drive belt splash shield, the right fender plug and the drive belts.
6. Remove the crankshaft and the water pump pulleys.
7. Remove the bolts from the bottom of the belt cover.
8. Lower the vehicle.
9. Remove the bolts from the top of the belt cover, then the cover from the vehicle.
10. Reverse procedure to install. Connect the battery negative cable.

SPECTRUM

1. Disconnect negative battery cable.
2. Support the engine.
3. Remove the front mount bracket attached to the front cover.
4. Remove front cover.
5. To install, reverse the removal procedures.

Timing Belt and Tensioner

Adjustment

NOVA AND PRIZM

1. Remove the front cover assembly.
2. Using finger pressure on the longest span between pulleys (except twincam) or between the camshaft pulleys (twincam), measure the timing belt deflection; 4.4 lbs. at 0.24–0.28 in. (except twincam) or 0.16 in. (twincam).
3. If adjustment is not correct, loosen the idler pulley bolt and correct the belt tension.
4. To install, the front covers, reverse the removal procedures.

SPECTRUM AND STORM

1. Remove the front cover.
2. Loosen the timing belt tension pulley bolt.

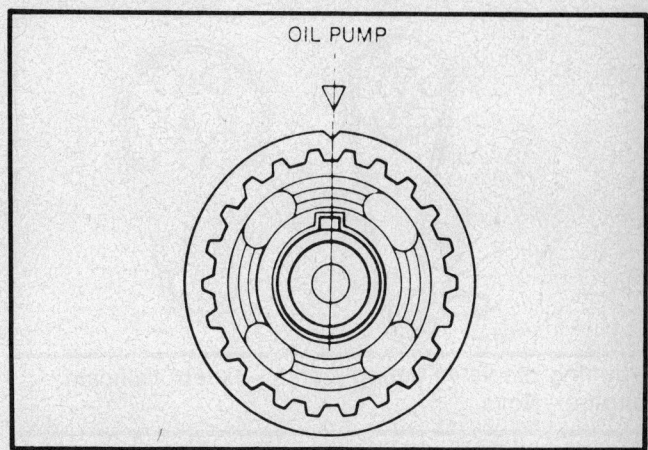

Aligning the crankshaft sprocket timing notch with the oil pump mark—Spectrum

NOTE: If the belt has been removed or replaced with a new one, perform the following procedures to stretch the belt.

3. Using an Allen wrench, insert it into the hexagonal hole of the tension pulley. Hold the pulley stationary and temporarily tighten the tension pulley-to-engine bolt.
4. Rotate the crankshaft two complete revolutions and align the crankshaft timing pulley groove with the mark on the oil pump.
5. Loosen the tension pulley-to-engine bolt.
6. Using the Allen wrench and a timing belt tension gauge, apply 38 ft. lbs. of tension to the timing belt on Spectrum and 31 ft. lbs on tension on the timing belt on Storm. Hold the pulley stationary and torque the tension pulley-to-engine bolt to 37 ft. lbs. on Spectrum and 31 ft. lbs. on Storm.
7. To complete the adjustment, install the front cover.

SPTINT AND METRO

1. Disconnect the battery negative cable.
2. Remove the front cover.
3. Turn the camshaft pulley clockwise and align the mark on the pulley with the **V** mark on the inside cover.
4. Using a 17mm wrench, turn the crankshaft clockwise and align the punch mark on the crankshaft pulley with the arrow mark on the oil pump.
5. With the timing marks aligned, install the timing belt so there is no belt slack on the right side (facing the engine) of the engine, apply belt tension with the tensioner pulley.
6. Turn the crankshaft 1 rotation clockwise to remove the belt slack. Torque the tensioner stud, first, and then the tensioner bolt to 17–21 ft. lbs.

Removal and Installation

NOVA

1. Remove the front covers.
2. Remove the No. 1 spark plug. Using a socket wrench on the crankshaft pulley bolt, rotate the engine (clockwise) to position the No. 1 cylinder on the TDC of its compression stroke.

NOTE: The TDC of the No. 1 cylinder is located when air is expelled from the cylinder.

3. If reusing the timing belt, mark an arrow showing direction of rotation and matchmark the belt to both pulleys.
4. Loosen the idler pulley mounting bolt and push the idler pulley relieve the belt tension, then, retighten the mounting bolt.
5. Remove the timing belt.

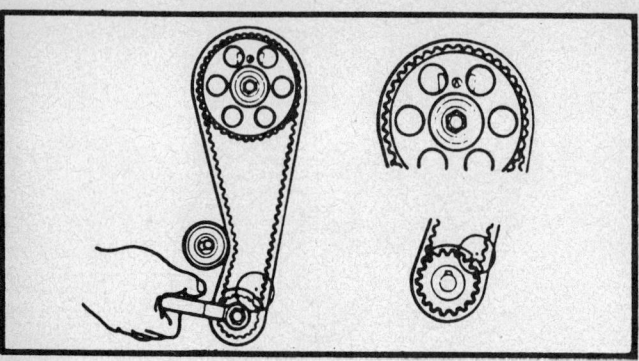

Aligning the valve timing marks—except twincam engine—Nova

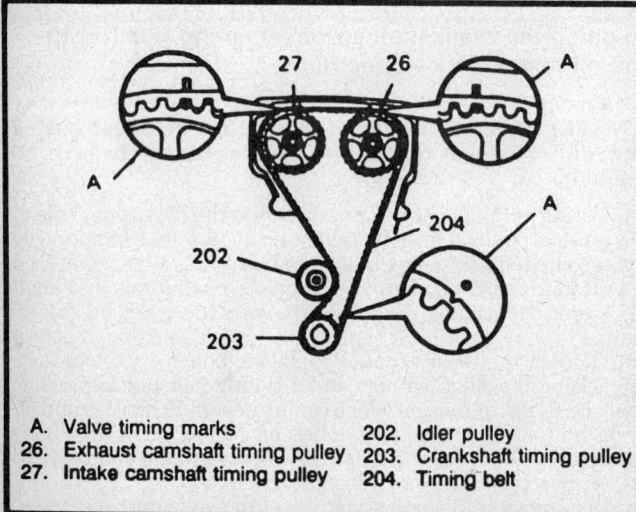

A.   Valve timing marks
26. Exhaust camshaft timing pulley
27. Intake camshaft timing pulley
202. Idler pulley
203. Crankshaft timing pulley
204. Timing belt

Aligning the valve timing marks—twincam engine—Nova

NOTE: Be careful not to bend, twist or turn the belt inside out. Keep grease or water from contacting it. Inspect the belt for cracks, missing teeth or general wear, replace it, if necessary.

6. Install the timing belt by realigning the matchmarks, the belts directional arrow facing clockwise and adjust the timing belt tension. Rotate the crankshaft 2 complete revolutions and recheck the alignment.

7. To complete the installation, reverse the removal procedures. Torque the idler pulley mounting bolt to 27 ft. lbs. Adjust the timing belt tension. Check and/or adjust the timing.

PRIZM

1. Disconnect the negative battery cable. Raise the vehicle and support it safely. Remove the right wheel and undercover. Remove the air cleaner.

2. Remove the 2 mount nut and stud protectors.

3. Remove the 2 rear transaxle mount to main crossmember nuts.

4. Remove the 2 center transaxle mount to center crossmember nuts.

5. Lower the vehicle.

6. Remove the drive belts. Remove the power steering pump and the air conditioning compressor and their brackets and position them out of the way. Leave the hydraulic and refrigerant lines connected.

7. Remove the spark plugs and the cylinder head cover. Be

Aligning the camshaft pulley-except twincam engine—Nova

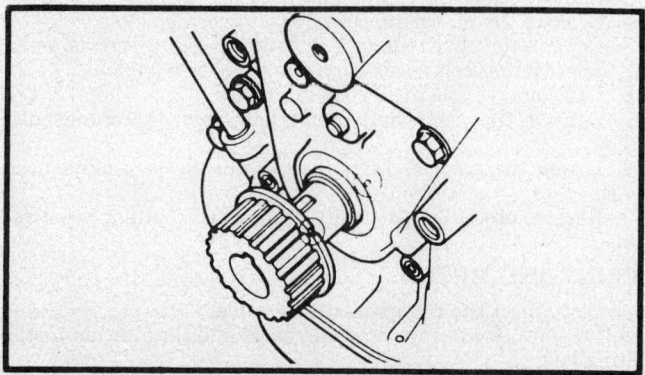

Crankshaft timing pulley alignment—Nova

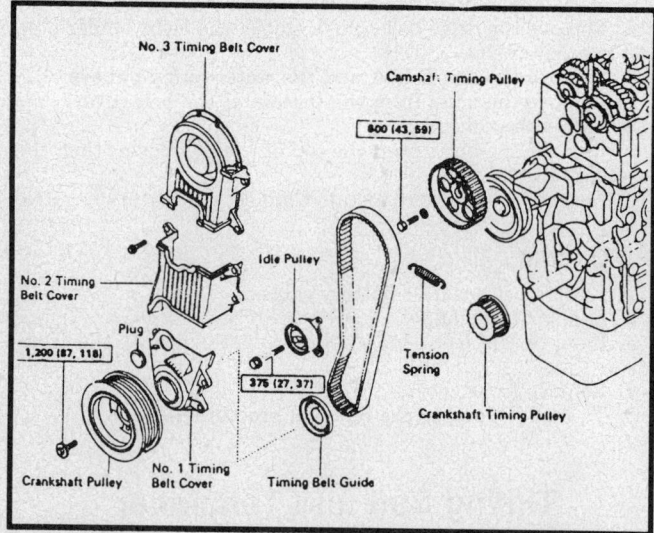

Exploded view of the timing belt assembly—Prizm

sure to scrape off any left-over gasket material. Rotate the crankshaft pulley so the **0** mark is in alignment with the groove in the No. 1 front cover. Check that the lifters on the No. 1 cylinder are loose; if not, turn the crankshaft 1 complete revolution (360 degrees).

8. Position a floor jack under the engine and remove the right side engine mounting insulator.

9. Remove the water pump and crankshaft pulleys.

10. Loosen the 9 bolts and remove the Nos. 1, 2 and 3 front covers. Remove the timing belt guide.

11. Loosen the bolt on the idler pulley, push it to the left as far as it will go and then retighten it. If reusing the timing belt, draw an arrow on it in the direction of engine revolution (clock-

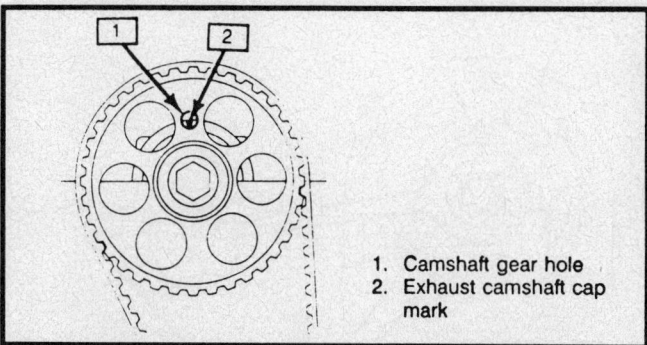

1. Camshaft gear hole
2. Exhaust camshaft cap mark

Aligning the camshaft gear hole and the exhaust camshaft cap mark—Prizm

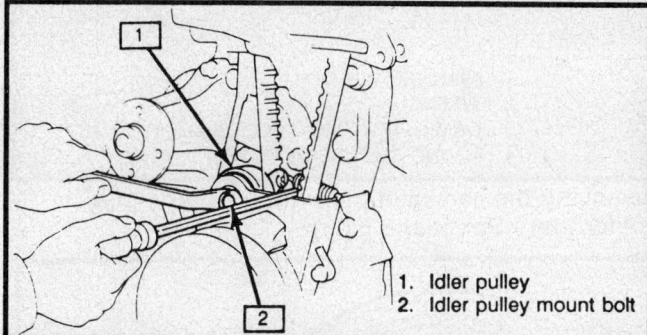

1. Idler pulley
2. Idler pulley mount bolt

Moving the idler pulley to the left—Prizm

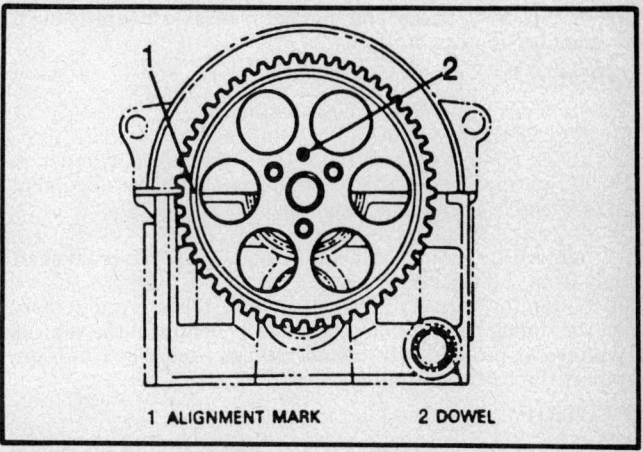

1 ALIGNMENT MARK   2 DOWEL

Aligning the camshaft pulley—Spectrum and Storm

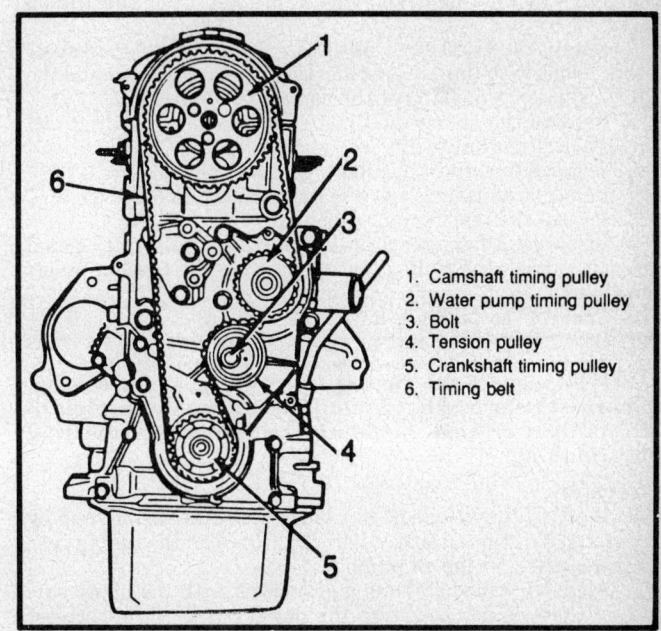

1. Camshaft timing pulley
2. Water pump timing pulley
3. Bolt
4. Tension pulley
5. Crankshaft timing pulley
6. Timing belt

View of the timing belt assembly—Spectrum and Storm

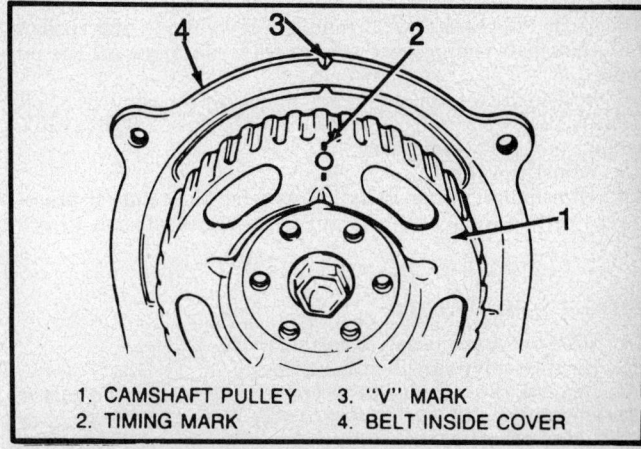

1. CAMSHAFT PULLEY   3. "V" MARK
2. TIMING MARK   4. BELT INSIDE COVER

Camshaft sprocket and inner belt cover timing mark alignment—Sprint and Metro

wise) and then matchmark the belt to the pulleys as indicated.

12. Remove the timing belt. Remove the idler pulley bolt, the pulley and the tension spring.

13. Remove the crankshaft timing pulley.

14. Lock the camshaft and remove the camshaft timing pulleys.

To install:

15. Install the camshaft timing pulley so it aligns with the knockpin on the exhaust camshaft. Tighten the pulley to 34 ft. lbs. (47 Nm). Align the mark on the No. 1 camshaft bearing cap with the center of the small hole in the pulley.

16. Install the crankshaft timing pulley so the marks on the pulley and the oil pump body are in alignment.

17. Install the idler pulley and its tension spring, move it to the left as far as it will go and tighten it temporarily.

18. Align the matchmarks made during removal and then install the timing belt on the camshaft pulley. Loosen the idler pulley set bolt. Make sure the timing belt meshing at the crankshaft pulley does not shift.

19. Rotate the crankshaft clockwise 2 revolutions from TDC to TDC. Make sure each pulley aligns with the marks made previously. If the marks are not in alignment, the valve timing is wrong. Shift the timing belt meshing slightly and then repeat Steps 14–15.

20. Tighten the set bolt on the timing belt idler pulley to 27 ft. lbs. (37 Nm). Measure the timing belt deflection at the top span between the 2 camshaft pulleys. It should deflect no more than 0.16 in. at 4.4 lbs. of pressure. If deflection is greater, readjust by using the idler pulley.

21. Raise the engine and install the water pump pulley.

22. Lower the engine.

23. Install the right engine mount through bolt and tighten to 64 ft. lbs.

24. Remove the engine support.

25. The remainder of the installation is the reverse of removal. Tighten the center transaxle mount to center cross-

member nuts to 45 ft. lbs. and the rear transaxle mount to main crossmember nuts to 45 ft. lbs.

STORM

1. Disconnect the battery negative cable.
2. Remove the front cover(s).
3. Rotate the crankshaft to position the No. 1 cylinder at TDC on its compression stroke. Camshaft sprocket alignment marks should align with the cylinder head cover.
4. Raise and support the vehicle safely.
5. Remove the crankshaft pulley bolt, then the crankshaft pulley from the vehicle.
6. Lower the vehicle. Remove the belt tension pulley bolt, then the timing belt tensioner and timing belt from the vehicle.
7. Reverse procedure to install. Adjust timing belt tension. Connect the battery negative cable.

SPECTRUM

1. Remove the engine and mount the engine to an engine stand.
2. Remove the accessory drive belts.
3. Remove the engine mounting bracket from the timing cover.
4. Rotate the crankshaft until the notch on the crankshaft pulley aligns with the **0** degree mark on the timing cover and the No. 4 cylinder is on TDC of the compression stroke.
5. Remove the starter and install the flywheel holding tool No. J–35271 or equivalent.
6. Remove the crankshaft bolt, boss and pulley.
7. Remove the timing cover bolts and the timing cover.
8. Loosen the tension pulley bolt.
9. Insert an Allen wrench into the tension pulley hexagonal hole and loosen the timing belt by turning the tension pulley clockwise.
10. Remove the timing belt.
11. Remove the head cover.

NOTE: Inspect the timing belt for signs of cracking, abnormal wear and hardening. Never expose the belt to oil, sunlight or heat. Avoid excessive bending, twisting or stretching.

To install:

12. Position the Woodruff key on the crankshaft followed by the crankshaft timing gear. Align the groove on the timing gear with the mark on the oil pump.
13. Align the camshaft timing gear mark with the upper surface of the cylinder head and the dowel pin in its uppermost position.
14. Place the timing belt arrow in the direction of the engine rotation and install the timing belt. Tighten the tension pulley bolt.
15. Turn the crankshaft 2 complete revolutions and realign the crankshaft timing gear groove with the mark on the oil pump.
16. Loosen the tension pulley bolt and apply tension to the belt with an Allen wrench. Torque the pulley bolt to 37 ft. lbs. while holding the pulley stationary.
17. Adjust the valve clearances.
18. To complete the installation, reverse the removal procedures. Torque the crankshaft pulley-to-crankshaft bolt to 109 ft. lbs.

SPRINT AND METRO

1. Disconnect the negative battery cable.
2. Remove the timing belt front cover.
3. Remove the cylinder head cover, then loosen the rocker arm adjusting bolts.
4. Loosen the tensioner pulley and adjusting stud bolt.
5. Remove the timing belt, the tensioner, the tensioner plate and spring.

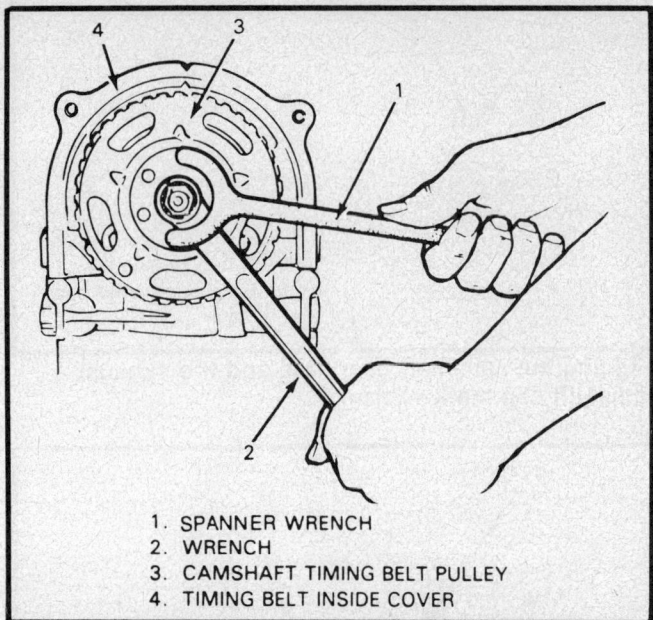

1. SPANNER WRENCH
2. WRENCH
3. CAMSHAFT TIMING BELT PULLEY
4. TIMING BELT INSIDE COVER

Removing the camshaft pulley bolt using a lock holder tool—Sprint and Metro

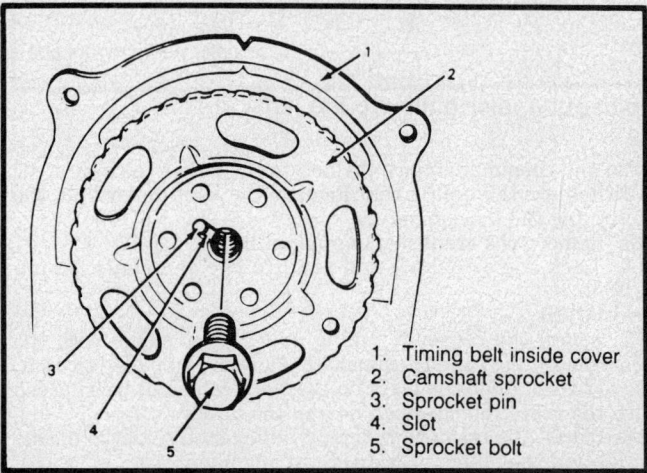

1. Timing belt inside cover
2. Camshaft sprocket
3. Sprocket pin
4. Slot
5. Sprocket bolt

Installing the camshaft sprocket pin and retaining bolt—Sprint and Metro

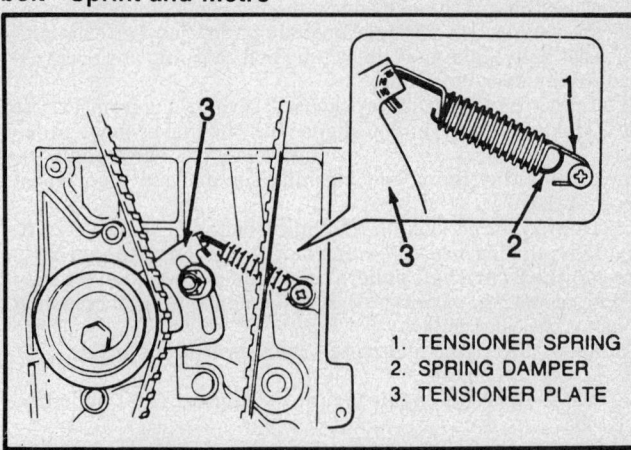

1. TENSIONER SPRING
2. SPRING DAMPER
3. TENSIONER PLATE

Installing tensioner spring and dampener—Sprint and Metro

6. Reverse procedure to install. Torque the crankshaft pulley to 7–9 ft. lbs. Adjust the valve clearances.

Timing Sprockets

Removal and Installation

NOVA AND PRIZM

Except Twincam Engine

1. Disconnect the negative battery cable.
2. Remove the timing belt.
3. To remove the crankshaft timing belt pulley, simply pull it and the key from the crankshaft.
4. To remove the camshaft pulley, perform the following procedures:
   a. Remove the valve cover.
   b. Using an open end wrench, place it on the camshaft flats to secure it.
   c. Using a socket wrench on the camshaft pulley bolt, remove the camshaft pulley bolt and the camshaft pulley.

To install:

5. Reverse the removal procedures. Torque the camshaft pulley-to-camshaft bolt to 34 ft. lbs.
6. After installing the crankshaft pulley bolt, rotate the crankshaft 2 complete revolutions and recheck the alignment. Check and/or adjust the timing belt tension. Torque the idler pulley mounting bolt to 27 ft. lbs.

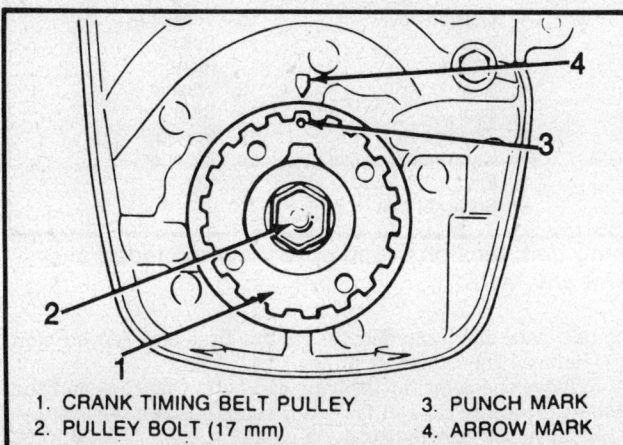

1. CRANK TIMING BELT PULLEY   3. PUNCH MARK
2. PULLEY BOLT (17 mm)   4. ARROW MARK

Crankshaft sprocket and oil pump timing mark alignment—Sprint and Metro

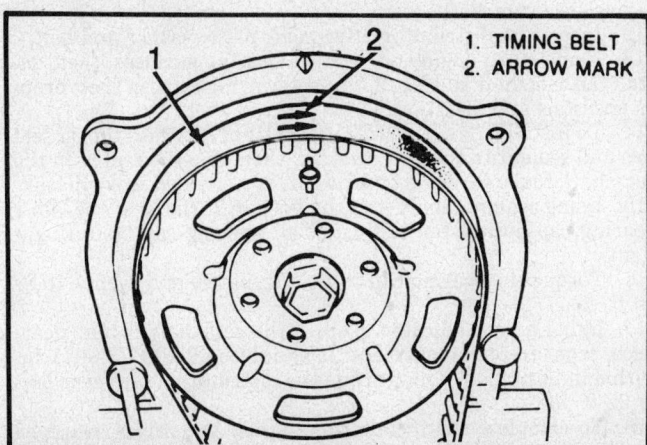

1. TIMING BELT
2. ARROW MARK

Arrow marks on the timing belt show direction of rotation—Sprint and Metro

7. To complete the installation, reverse the removal procedures.

Twincam Engine

1. Disconnect the negative battery cable.
2. Remove the timing belt.
3. To remove the crankshaft timing belt pulley, simply pull it and the key from the crankshaft.
4. To remove the camshaft pulleys, perform the following procedures:
   a. Remove both valve covers.
   b. Secure each camshaft, then, using a socket wrench on the camshaft pulley bolt, remove the camshaft pulley bolt.
   c. Using the pulley remover tool No. J–1859–03 or equivalent, press each camshaft pulley from the camshafts.

To install:

5. To install the camshaft pulleys, align each with the knock pin and reverse the removal procedures. Torque the camshaft pulley-to-camshaft bolt to 34 ft. lbs.
6. To install the crankshaft timing pulley, simply align it with the keyway and slide it onto the crankshaft.
7. Align the timing belt marks with the pulley marks and install the timing belt.
8. After installing the crankshaft pulley bolt, rotate the crankshaft two complete revolutions and recheck the alignment. Check and/or adjust the timing belt tension. Torque the idler pulley mounting bolt to 27 ft. lbs.
9. To complete the installation, reverse the removal procedures.

SPECTRUM AND STORM

Except Twincam engine

1. Disconnect the negative battery terminal from the battery.
2. On Spectrum, rotate the crankshaft to place the No. 4 cylinder on the TDC of compression stroke.
3. On Storm, rotate the crankshaft to place the No. 1 cylinder on TDC of its compression stroke.
4. Remove the front cover-to-mount bracket bolt and the bracket from the vehicle.
5. Remove the front cover-to-engine bolts and the front cover from the engine.

NOTE: Make sure the camshaft dowel pin is positioned at the top and the mark on the cam sprocket is aligned with the upper cylinder head surface.

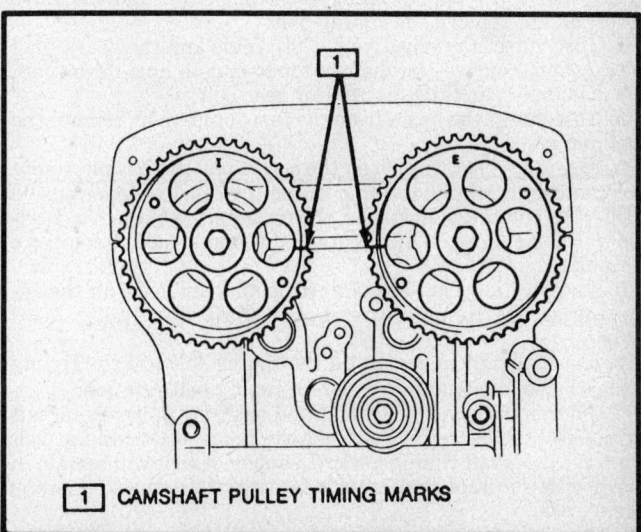

1 CAMSHAFT PULLEY TIMING MARKS

Camshaft pulley timing marks—Storm

6. Loosen the timing belt tension pulley-to-engine bolt, then remove the timing belt.

7. Remove the camshaft sprocket-to-camshaft bolts, the camshaft sprocket; allow the timing belt to hang.

8. If the engine has not been disturbed, reverse the removal procedures. On Spectrum, torque the camshaft sprocket-to-camshaft bolt to 7.2 ft. lbs. and 43 ft. lbs. on Storm. Adjust the timing belt.

9. To complete the installation, reverse the removal procedures.

Twincam Engine

1. Disconnect the battery negative cable.
2. Remove the cylinder head cover.
3. Rotate the crankshaft to bring the number 1 cylinder to TDC on its compression stroke. The camshaft pulley's timing marks should align.
4. Loosen the timing belt tension pulley and remove the timing belt from the camshaft pulleys.
5. Remove the camshaft attaching bolts and the camshafts from the vehicle.
6. Reverse procedure to install. Torque the camshaft attaching bolts to 43 ft. lbs. (59 Nm).

SPRINT AND METRO

1. Disconnect the battery negative cable.
2. Remove the front cover and the timing bellt.
3. Using tool J–34836 or equivalent, hold the camshaft sprocket and remove the retaining bolt, camshaft sprocket, alignment pin and cover.
4. Using a suitable spanner wrench, remove the crankshaft pulley bolt and the crankshaft pulley.
5. Reverse procedure to install. Align the "V" mark on the timing belt cover with the timing mark on the camshaft sprocket and the arrow mark on the engine block with the punch mark on the crankshaft timing sprocket. Torque the camshaft bolt to 41–46 ft. lb. (55–64 Nm) and the crankshaft bolt to 7–9 ft. lbs. 10–13 ft. lbs.

Camshaft

Removal and Installation

NOVA

Except Twincam Engine

1. Remove the upper timing belt front cover and the valve cover; do not remove the timing belt.

2. Disconnect the negative battery cable and the spark plug wires, then, remove the distributor-to-engine hold-down bolt, the distributor and the distributor gear bolt.

3. Disconnect the hoses from the fuel pump, then, remove the fuel pump.

4. Using a socket wrench on the crankshaft pulley bolt, rotate the crankshaft (clockwise) to position the No. 1 cylinder on the TDC of its compression stroke; the rocker arms of the No. 1 cylinder will be loose, if not, rotate the crankshaft 1 complete revolution.

5. Loosen the rocker arm adjusting nuts and back off the adjusting screw. Remove the rocker shaft-to-cylinder head assembly.

6. Place alignment marks on the timing belt and the timing pulleys; also, mark the direction of timing belt rotation.

7. Loosen the idler pulley bolt and push the pulley as far left as possible, then, retighten the bolt. Remove the timing belt from the camshaft timing pulleys, support it so it will remain in mesh with the crankshaft pulley; be careful not to get oil on the timing belt.

8. Use a large open-end wrench, secure the camshaft (on the flats), then remove the camshaft pulley-to-camshaft bolt; the

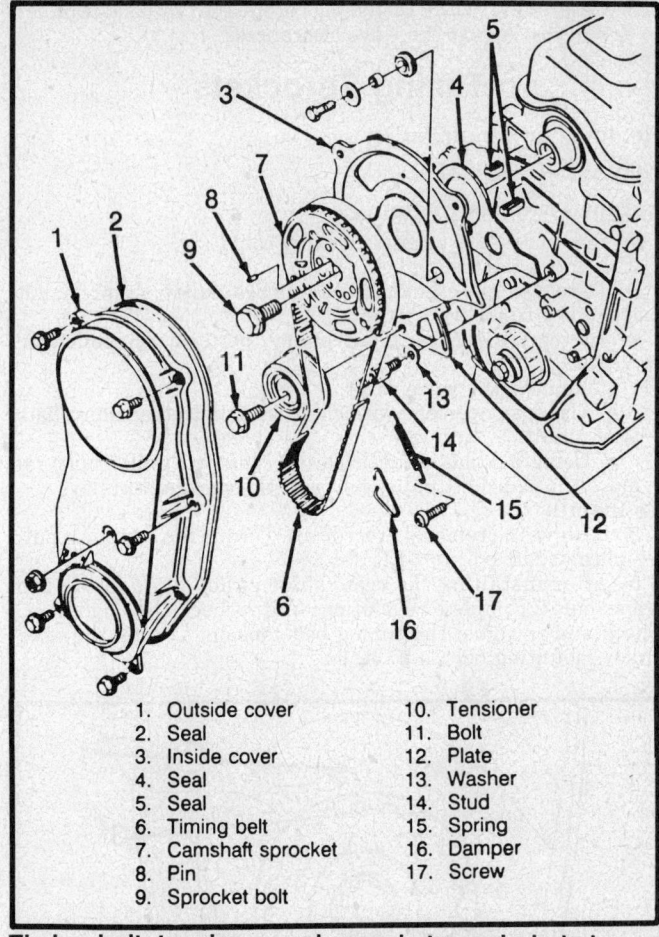

1. Outside cover	10. Tensioner
2. Seal	11. Bolt
3. Inside cover	12. Plate
4. Seal	13. Washer
5. Seal	14. Stud
6. Timing belt	15. Spring
7. Camshaft sprocket	16. Damper
8. Pin	17. Screw
9. Sprocket bolt	

Timing belt, tensioner and sprockets-exploded view— Sprint and Metro

camshaft flats are located between the first and second cam lobes. Remove the camshaft pulley.

9. Remove the camshaft bearing cap bolts, the caps and the camshaft; keep the caps in order for reinstallation purposes.

10. Remove the distributor drive gear.

To install:

11. Inspect the camshaft for damage and/or wear; if necessary, replace the camshaft.

12. Insert the distributor drive gear, plate washer and bolt.

13. Using clean engine oil, coat all bearing surfaces, then, install the camshaft and No. 2, 3 and 4 bearing caps, in their proper positions and direction.

14. To install a new camshaft oil seal, apply grease the oil seal lips and sealant to the outside edge, then, slip the seal onto the camshaft; make sure it is on straight, as a crooked seal will leak.

15. Using sealant, apply it to the bottom surfaces of the No. 1 bearing cap and install it. Install all bearing cap bolts finger tight.

16. Torque the bearing cap bolts, alternately and evenly, to 8–10 ft. lbs.

17. Using a dial indicator, inspect the camshaft thrust clearance, front-to-rear movement; it should be 0.0031–0.0071 in. with a limit of 0.0098 in. Torque the distributor drive gear bolt to 22 ft. lbs.

18. To complete the installation, adjust the valves, use new gaskets, sealant, if necessary, and reverse the removal procedures. Start the engine, allow it to reach normal operating temperatures and check for leaks.

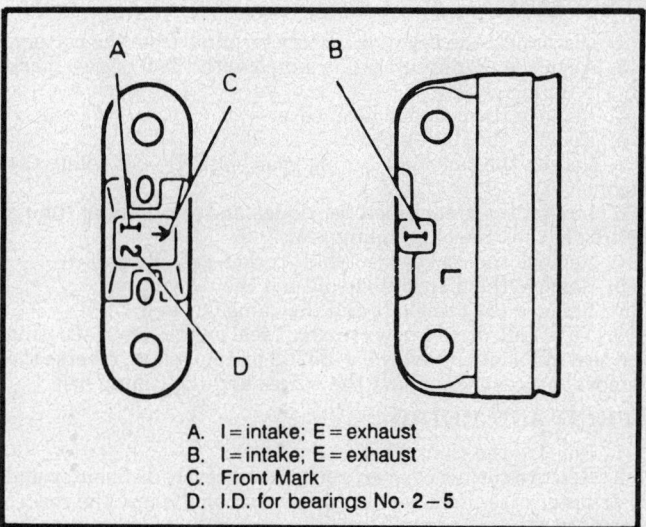

A. I = intake; E = exhaust
B. I = intake; E = exhaust
C. Front Mark
D. I.D. for bearings No. 2 – 5

View of the camshaft bearing caps, twincam engine—Nova

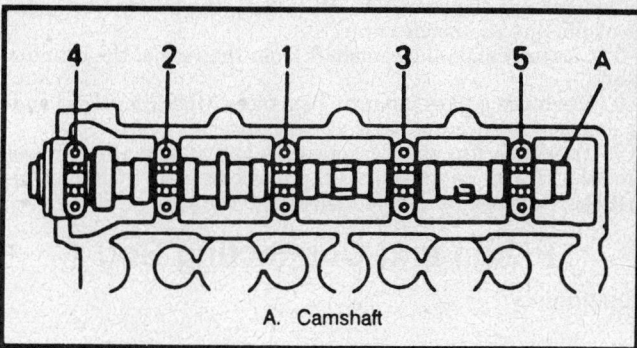

A. Camshaft

Camshaft bearing cap torque sequence, twincam engine—Nova

Twincam Engine

1. Disconnect the negative battery cable.
2. Remove the cylinder head covers and the camshaft pulleys.
3. Loosen and remove the camshaft bearing caps-to-cylinder head bolts in sequence. Remove the camshaft bearing caps and camshafts; be sure to keep the parts in order for reinstallation purposes.
4. Using the proper tool, clean the gasket mounting surfaces. Inspect the camshaft for wear and/or damage, if necessary, replace the camshaft.

To install:

5. Using clean engine oil, coat all bearing surfaces, then, install the camshaft and No. 2, 3 and 4 bearing caps, in their proper positions and direction.
6. To install a new camshaft oil seal, apply grease the oil seal lips and sealant to the outside edge, then, slip the seal onto the camshaft; make sure it is on straight, as a crooked seal will leak.
7. Using sealant, apply it to the bottom surfaces of the No. 1 bearing cap and install it. Install all bearing cap bolts finger tight.
8. Torque the bearing cap bolts, alternately and evenly, to 8–10 ft. lbs.
9. Using a dial indicator, inspect the camshaft thrust clearance, front-to-rear movement; it should be 0.0031–0.0075 in. with a limit of 0.0118 in. Torque the distributor drive gear bolt to 22 ft. lbs.

10. To complete the installation, adjust the valves, use new gaskets and sealant, if necessary, and reverse the removal procedures. Start the engine, allow it to reach normal operating temperatures and check for leaks.

PRIZM

1. Disconnect the negative battery cable at the battery. Drain the engine coolant.
2. Remove the spark plugs and the cylinder head cover.
3. Remove the No. 3 and No. 2 front covers. Turn the crankshaft pulley and align its groove with the **0** mark on the No. 1 front cover. Check that the camshaft pulley hole aligns with the mark on the No. 1 camshaft bearing cap (exhaust side).
4. Remove the plug from the No. 1 front cover and matchmark the timing belt to the camshaft pulley. Loosen the idler pulley mounting bolt and push the pulley to the left as far as it will go; tighten the bolt. Slide the timing belt off the camshaft pulley and support it so it won't fall into the case.
5. Remove the camshaft pulley and check the camshaft thrust clearance. Remove the camshafts.

NOTE: Due to the relatively small amount of camshaft thrust clearance, the camshaft must be held level during removal. If the camshaft is not level on removal, the portion of the head receiving the thrust may crack or be damaged.

6. Set the service bolt hole on the intake camshaft gear, the one not attached to the timing pulley, at the 12 o'clock position so the No. 1 and 3 cylinder camshaft lobes can push their lifters evenly. Loosen the No. 1 bearing caps on each camshaft a little at a time and remove them.
7. Secure the intake camshaft sub-gear to the main gear with a service bolt to eliminate any torsional spring force. Loosen the remaining bearing caps, a little at a time, in the proper sequence, and remove the intake camshaft. If the camshaft cannot be lifted out straight and level, retighten the bolts in the No. 3 bearing cap and loosen them, a little at a time, with the gear pulled up.
8. Turn the exhaust camshaft approximately 105 degrees so the knock pin is about 5 minutes before the 6:30 o'clock position. Loosen the remaining bearing caps a little at a time, in the proper sequence, and remove the exhaust camshaft. If the camshaft cannot be lifted out straight and level, retighten the bolts in the No. 3 bearing cap and loosen them, a little at a time, with the gear pulled up.

To install:

9. Position the exhaust camshaft into the cylinder head as it was removed. Position the bearing caps over each journal so the arrows point forward and tighten the bolts gradually, in the proper sequence to 9 ft. lbs. (13 Nm).
10. Coat the lip of a new oil seal with MP grease and drive it into the camshaft.
11. Set the knock pin on the exhaust camshaft so it is just above the edge of the cylinder head and engage the intake camshaft gear to the exhaust gear so the mark on each gear is in alignment. Roll the intake camshaft down onto the bearing journals while engaging the gears with each other.
12. Position the bearing caps over each journal on the intake camshaft so the arrows point forward and tighten the bolts gradually, in the proper sequence, to 9 ft. lbs. (13 Nm).
13. Remove the service bolt and install the No. 1 intake bearing cap. If it does not fit properly, pry the camshaft gear backwards until it does. Tighten the bolts to 9 ft. lbs. (13 Nm).
14. Rotate the camshafts 1 revolution (360 degrees) from TDC to TDC and check that the marks on the 2 gears are still aligned.
15. Install the camshaft timing pulley making sure the camshaft knock pins and the matchmarks are in alignment. Lock each camshaft and tighten the pulley bolts to 43 ft. lbs. (59 Nm).
16. Align the matchmarks made during removal and then install the timing belt on the camshaft pulley. Loosen the idler

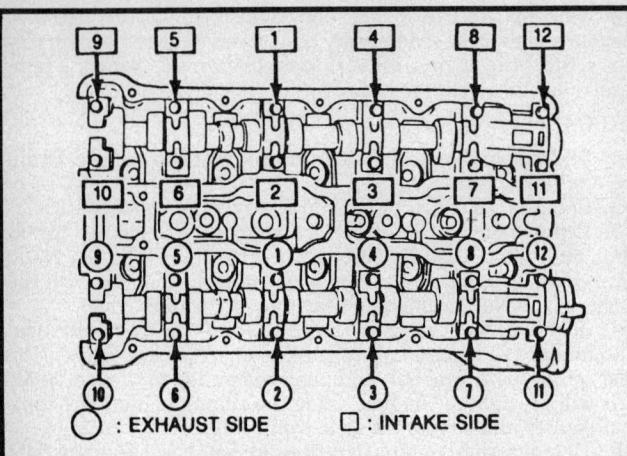

Camshaft bearing cap tightening sequence—Storm with twincam engine

Positioning the No. 1 cylinder on TDC—Spectrum

pulley set bolt. Make sure the timing belt meshing at the crankshaft pulley does not shift.

17. Rotate the crankshaft clockwise 2 revolutions from TDC to TDC. Make sure each pulley aligns with the marks made previously.

18. Tighten the set bolt on the timing belt idler pulley to 27 ft. lbs. (37 Nm). Measure the timing belt deflection at the top span between the 2 camshaft pulleys. It should deflect no more than 0.16 in. at 4.4 lbs. of pressure. If deflection is greater, readjust by using the idler pulley.

19. Installation of the remaining components is in the reverse order of removal.

STORM

1. Disconnect the battery negative cable.
2. Remove the cylinder head cover.
3. Rotate the crankshaft to position No. 1 at TDC on its compression stroke by aligning the camshaft(s) pulley timing mark with the cylinder head cover.
4. Loosen the timing belt tensioner.
5. Remove the timing belt pulley(s) from the camshaft(s).
6. Remove the distributor.
7. Remove the camshaft(s) bearing cap bolts, then remove the camshaft and seal from the vehicle. Discard seal.
8. Reverse procedure to install. Torque camshaft bearing cap bolts to 89 inch lbs. (10 Nm). Connect the battery negative cable. Start the engine and check for leaks.

SPECTRUM

1. Disconnect the negative battery terminal from the battery.
2. Align the crankshaft pulley notch with the **0** degree mark on the timing cover.
3. Remove the cylinder head cover.
4. Remove the timing cover.
5. Loosen the camshaft timing gear bolts; Do not rotate the engine.
6. Loosen the timing belt tensioner and remove the timing belt from the camshaft timing gear.
7. Remove the rocker arm shaft/rocker arm assembly.
8. Remove the distributor bolt and the distributor.
9. Remove the camshaft and the camshaft seal.
10. To install, drive a new camshaft seal on the camshaft using the seal installation tool No. J–35268 or equivalent, reverse the removal procedures, adjust the valves and the timing belt.

SPRINT AND METRO

1. Remove the timing belt.
2. Remove the air cleaner, rocker arm cover, distributor and distributor case. Remove the rocker arm shafts and the rocker arms.
3. Remove the fuel pump and fuel pump pushrod from the cylinder head.
4. Using a spanner wrench tool J–34836 to hold the camshaft pulley, remove the camshaft pulley bolt, the pulley, the alignment pin and the inside cover.
5. Carefully slide the camshaft from the rear of the cylinder head.
6. Clean the gasket mounting surfaces. Check for wear and/or damage, replace the parts as necessary.
7. To install, use new gaskets/seals and reverse the removal procedures. Torque the camshaft pulley bolt to 41–46 ft. lbs. Adjust the valve clearances and check the timing.

Piston and Connecting Rod

Positioning

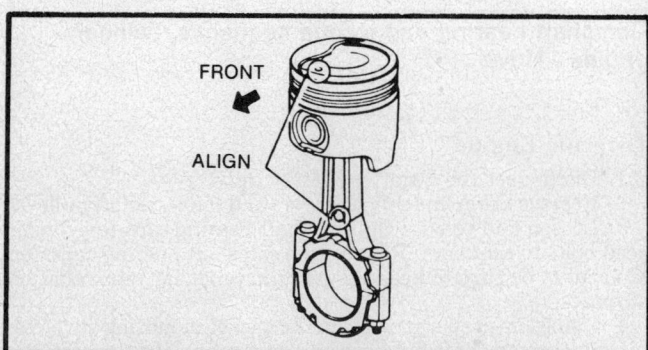

Piston alignment marks—Nova, Prizm and Storm

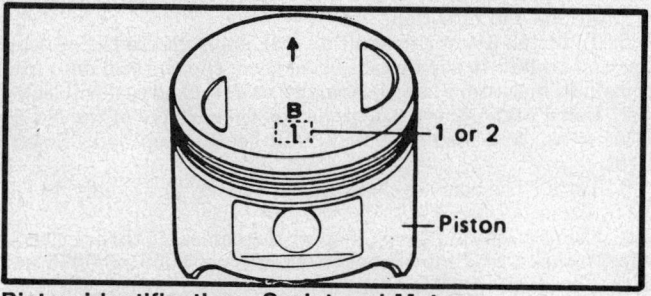

Piston identification—Sprint and Metro

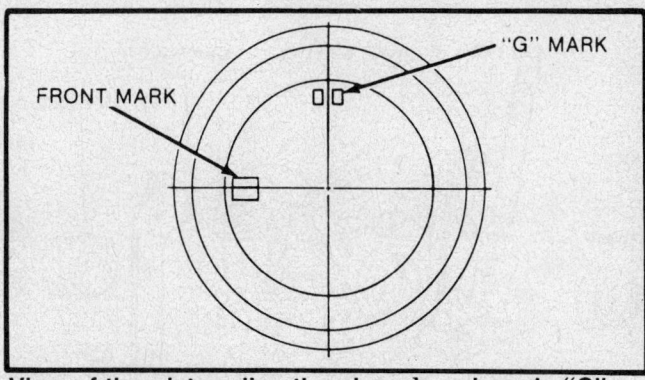

View of the piston directional mark and grade "G" mark—Spectrum

ENGINE LUBRICATION

Oil Pan

Removal and Installation

NOVA

1. Disconnect the negative terminal from the battery. Raise and support the vehicle safely.
2. Drain the crankcase.
3. Remove the right-side undercover.
4. Remove the oil pan-to-engine bolts and the oil pan.

NOTE: When removing the oil pan, be careful not to damage the oil pan flange.

5. Using the proper tool, clean the gasket mounting surfaces.
6. To install, use a new gasket and sealant, if necessary, and reverse the removal procedures. Torque the oil pan-to-engine bolts to 4 ft. lbs. Start the engine and check for leaks.

PRIZM

1. Remove the battery negative cable.
2. Raise and safely support the vehicle.
3. Remove the right and left lower stone shields.
4. Drain the oil.
5. Disconnect the oxygen sensor connector.
6. Disconnect the exhaust pipe from catalytic converter.
7. Disconnect the exhaust pipe from exhaust manifold.
8. Remove the 2 nuts and 19 bolts from the oil pan.
9. Remove the oil pan.

NOTE: Use caution when removing the oil pan on the oil pump body side since damage to the pump body may occur. Also be careful not to damage the oil pan flange.

10. Remove the 2 bolts, 2 nuts and the oil strainer/pickup assembly.
11. Remove the oil strainer/pickup assembly gasket.
12. Clean the mating surfaces of the oil pan and cylinder block of all oil residue. Clean both surfaces with a solvent that will not affect the painted surfaces.
To install:
13. Install the oil strainer/pickup assembly and a new gasket with 2 bolts and 2 nuts.
14. Tighten the oil strainer/pickup assembly bolts and nuts to 89 inch lbs. (10 Nm).
15. Apply a continuous bead of GM 1050026 sealant to both sides of a new oil pan gasket.
16. Install the oil pan to the cylinder block with 19 bolts and 2 nuts.
17. Tighten the oil pan bolts and nuts to 44 inch lbs. (5 Nm).

18. Install the exhaust pipe to exhaust manifold.
19. Install the exhaust pipe to catalytic convertor.
20. Connect the oxygen sensor connector.
21. Install the right and left lower stone shields.
22. Lower the vehicle.
23. Refill the engine oil.
24. Install the battery negative cable.
25. Start the engine and check for leaks.

STORM

1. Disconnect the battery negative cable.
2. Raise and support the vehicle safely, then drain engine oil.
3. Remove the right undercover.
4. Remove the front exhaust pipe from the exhaust manifold, then remove the torque rod.
5. Remove the flywheel dust cover.
6. Remove the oil pan attaching bolts, then remove the oil pan.
7. Reverse procedure to install. Apply suitable sealant to the oil pan gasket. Torque bolts to 89 inch lbs (10 Nm). Connect battery negative cable. Start engine and check for leaks.

SPECTRUM

1. Disconnect the negative battery terminal from the battery.
2. Raise and support the vehicle safely, then drain the crankcase.
3. Disconnect the exhaust pipe bracket from the block and the exhaust pipe at the manifold.
4. Disconnect the right hand tension rod located under the front bumper.
5. Remove the oil pan bolts and oil pan, then clean the sealing surfaces.
6. To install, use a new gasket, apply sealant to the oil pump housing and the rear retainer housing, reverse the removal procedures.

SPRINT AND METRO

1. Remove the negative battery cable.
2. Raise and support the vehicle safely.
3. Drain the engine oil.
4. Remove the flywheel dust cover.
5. Remove the exhaust pipe at the exhaust manifold.
6. Remove the oil pan bolts, the pan and the oil pump strainer.
7. Clean the gasket mating surfaces.
8. To install, use new gaskets and reverse the removal procedures. Torque the oil pan bolts to 9–12 ft. lbs. Refill the engine oil.

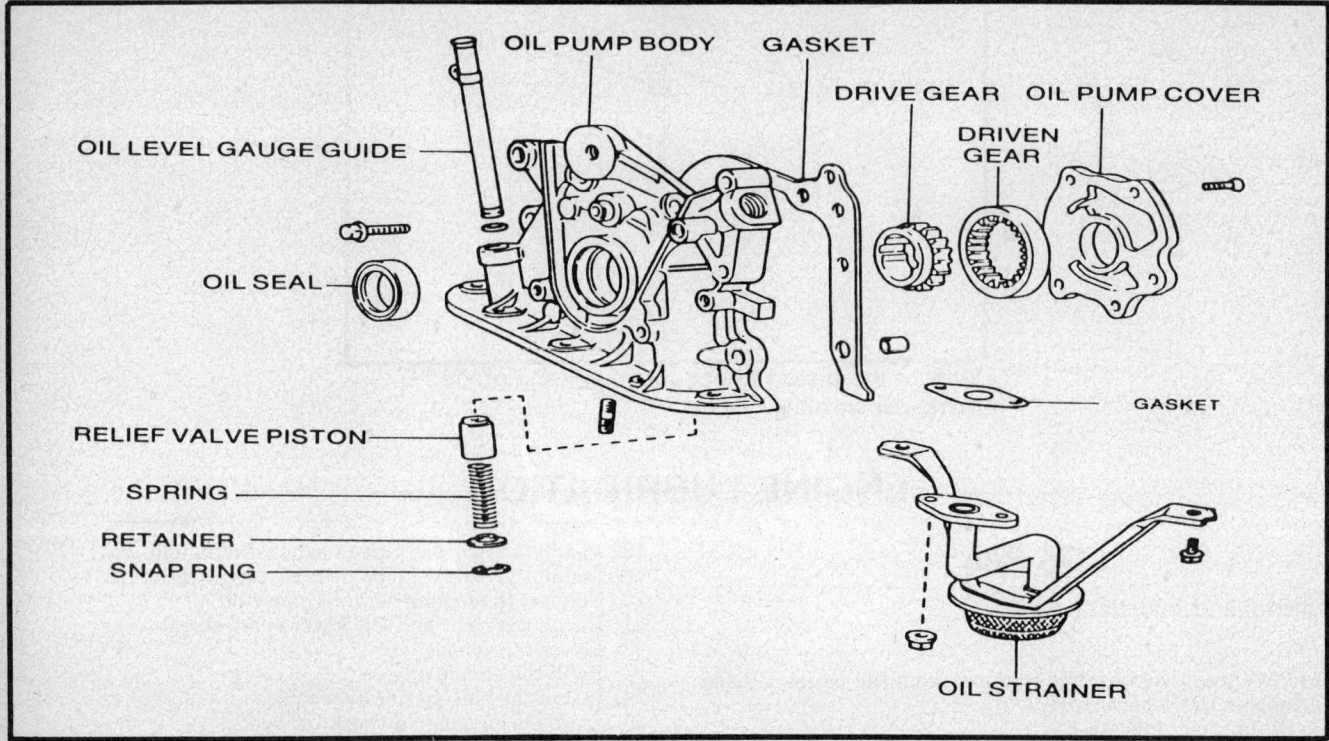

Exploded view of the oil pump—Nova and Prizm

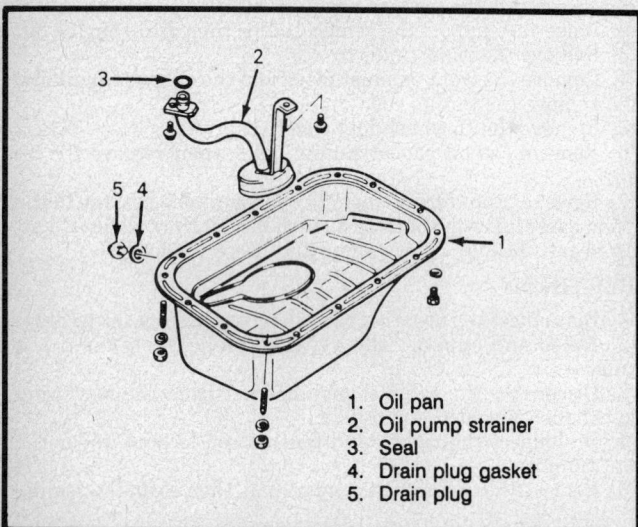

1. Oil pan
2. Oil pump strainer
3. Seal
4. Drain plug gasket
5. Drain plug

Oil pan and strainer mounting —Sprint and Metro

Oil Pump

Removal and Installation

NOVA AND PRIZM

1. Raise and support the vehicle safely. Drain the engine oil and remove the oil pan. Remove the timing belt cover assembly.
2. Remove the oil pickup-to-engine brace bolts and the oil pickup.
3. Attach a lifting sling to the engine lift points and securely suspend the engine.
4. Mark the timing belt alignment between the camshaft and the crankshaft pulleys; also, mark the timing belt's direction of rotation. Loosen the idler pulley bolt, relieve the timing belt ten-

sion and remove the timing belt from the crankshaft sprocket; keep it engaged with the upper pulley.
5. Remove the crankshaft timing belt pulley and the timing belt idler pulley.
6. Remove the dipstick and dipstick tube.
7. Remove the oil pump-to-engine bolts and the oil pump; it may be necessary to tap lightly on the lower rear surface of the oil pump to loosen it.

To install:

8. Using the proper tool, clean the gasket mounting surfaces.
9. To replace the oil pump seal, perform the following procedures:
   a. Using a small prybar, pry the oil seal from the front of the oil pump; be careful not to damage the seal mounting surface.
   b. Clean the oil seal surface.
   c. Using multi-purpose grease, lubricate the lips of the new oil seal.
   d. Using the oil seal driver tool J–35403 or equivalent, drive the new oil seal into the oil pump until it seats against the seat.
10. Inspect the oil pump for wear and/or damage; if necessary, replace or repair the oil pump.
11. Using petroleum jelly, pack the inside of the oil pump.
12. To install, use new gaskets and sealant, if necessary, and reverse the removal procedures. Engage the oil pump drive (smaller) gear with the crankshaft gear; there are both small and large spline teeth, make sure the teeth correspond properly. Torque the oil pick-up-to-engine bolts to 82 inch lbs. and the oil pump-to-engine bolts to 15 ft. lbs.
13. To complete the installation, reverse the removal procedures. Adjust the valve timing and the drive belt tensions. Refill the crankcase and the cooling system. Start the engine, allow it to reach normal operating temperatures and check for leaks.

STORM

1. Disconnect the battery negative cable.
2. Remove the timing belt.

3. Remove the power steering and alternator belts.
4. Raise and support the vehicle safely.
5. Remove the crankshaft pulley.

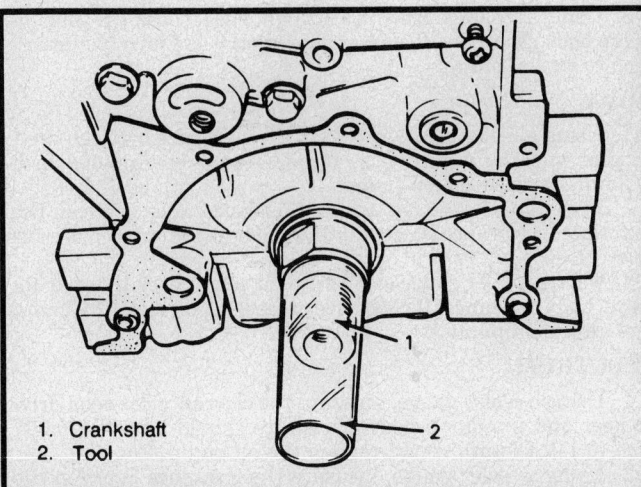

1. Crankshaft
2. Tool

Front seal protector installed on front crankshaft journal—Sprint and Metro

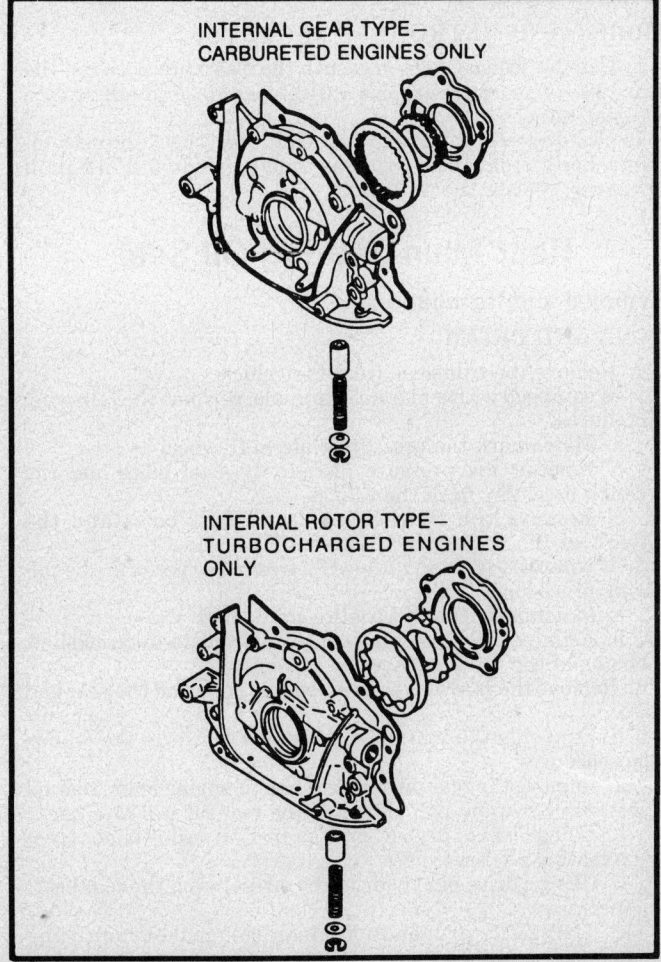

Difference in oil pump design for turbo and non-turbo engine—Sprint and Metro

6. Remove the oil pump attaching bolts, then the oil pump from the vehicle.
7. Reverse procedure to install. Apply suitable sealant to the oil pump gasket. Install bolts and torque to 89 inch lbs. (10 Nm). Connect the battery negative cable. Start engine and check for leaks.

SPECTRUM

1. Remove the engine from the vehicle.
2. Remove the alternator belt and the starter.
3. Install the flywheel holding tool J–35271 or equivalent, to secure the flywheel.
4. Remove the crankshaft pulley and boss.
5. Remove the timing cover bolts and the timing cover.
6. Loosen the tension pulley and remove the timing belt.
7. Remove the crankshaft timing gear and the tension pulley.
8. Remove the oil pan bolts, oil pan, oil strainer fixing bolt and the oil strainer assembly.
9. Remove the oil pump bolts and the oil pump assembly.
10. Remove the sealing material from the oil pump and engine block sealing surfaces.
11. To install, lubricate the oil pump, use new gaskets, apply sealant to the sealing surfaces and reverse the removal procedures.

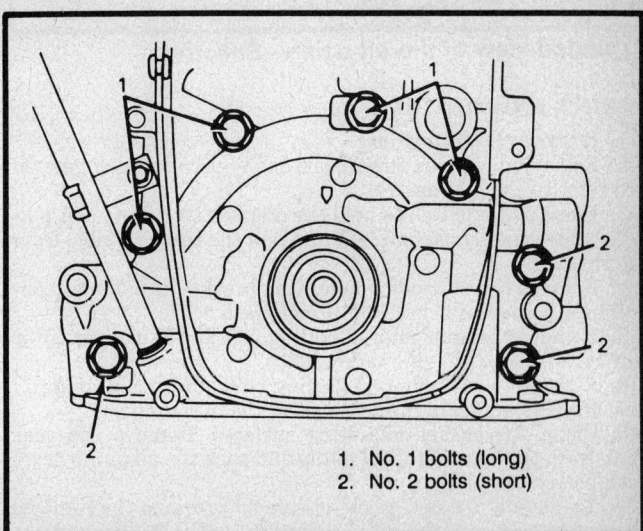

1. No. 1 bolts (long)
2. No. 2 bolts (short)

Oil pump mounting—Sprint and Metro

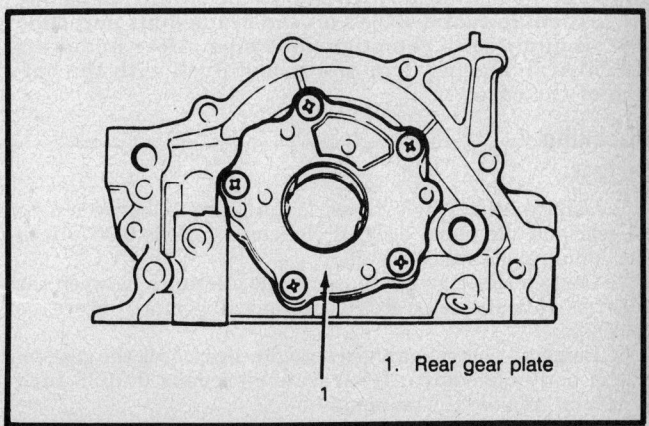

1. Rear gear plate

Remove the rear oil pump gear plate and fill the cavity with petroleum jelly before pump installtion—Sprint and Metro

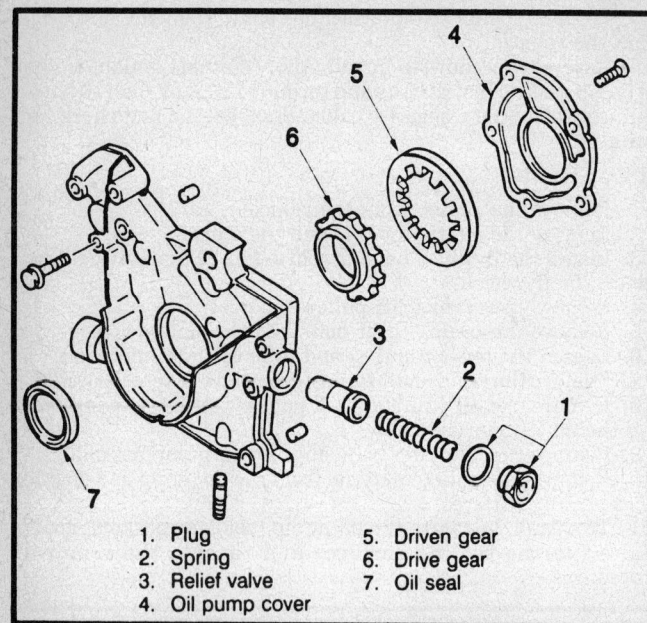

1. Plug
2. Spring
3. Relief valve
4. Oil pump cover
5. Driven gear
6. Drive gear
7. Oil seal

Exploded view of the oil pump – Spectrum

SPRINT AND METRO

1. Remove the timing belt.
2. Raise and support the vehicle safely. Drain the engine oil and remove the oil pan.
3. Use a suitable tool to hold the crankshaft timing belt pulley, remove the crankshaft bolt and pull the timing pulley from the shaft.
4. Remove the alternator mounting bracket and the air conditioning compressor bracket, if equipped.
5. Remove the alternator adjusting bolt and the upper cover bolt.
6. Remove the oil pump mounting bolts and the oil pump.
7. Pry the crankshaft oil seal from the oil pump.
8. Clean the gasket mounting surfaces. Remove the gear plate from the back of the oil pump and pack the oil pump gears with petroleum jelley.
9. To install, use new gaskets/seals and reverse the removal procedures. Torque the oil pump bolts to 7–9 ft. lbs. and the crankshaft timing pulley bolt to 47–54 ft. lbs. Adjust the valve clearances and check the timing.

NOTE: To install the oil pump to the engine, place the oil seal guide tool J–34853 on the crankshaft and slide the oil pump onto the alignment pins. After installing the oil seal housing, trim the gasket flush with the bottom of the case.

Checking
PRIZM

1. Using a feeler gauge, measure the clearance between driven gear and the pump body. If clreaance exceeds 0.0079 inch (0.20mm), replace the oil pump.
2. Using a feeler gauge, measure the clearance between the gear tips. If clearance exceeds 0.0138 inch (0.35mm), replace the gear set.
3. Using a feeler gauge and a straight edge, check the gear-to-pump body clearance. If clearance exceeds 0.0039 inch (0.10mm), replace the oil pump.

STORM

1. Using a feeler gauge, measure the clearance between driv-

en gear and the pump body. If clreaance exceeds 0.0078 inch (0.20mm), replace the oil pump.
2. Using a feeler gauge, measure the clearance between the gear tips. If clearance exceeds 0.012 inch (0.30mm), replace the gear set.
3. Using a feeler gauge and a straight edge, check the gear-to-pump body clearance. If clearance exceeds 0.004 inch (0.10mm), replace the oil pump.

NOVA

1. Using a feeler gauge, measure the clearance between driven gear and the pump body. If clreaance exceeds 0.008 inch (0.2mm), replace the oil pump.
2. Using a feeler gauge, measure the clearance between the gear tips. If clearance exceeds 0.0138 inch (0.35mm), replace the gear set.
3. Using a feeler gauge and a straight edge, check the gear-to-pump body clearance. If clearance exceeds 0.004 inch (0.10mm), replace the oil pump.

SPECTRUM

1. Using a feeler gauge, measure the clearance between driven gear and the pump body. Clearance should be 0.004–0.007 inch (0.1–0.18mm), if not, replace the oil pump.
2. Using a feeler gauge, measure the clearance between the gear tips. If clearance exceeds 0.0138 inch (0.35mm), replace the gear set.
3. Using a feeler gauge and a straight edge, check the gear-to-pump body clearance. If clearance exceeds 0.0038 inch (0.10mm), replace the oil pump.

SPRINT AND METRO

1. Using a feeler gauge, measure the clearance between the gear tips. If clearance exceeds 0.0122 inch (0.310mm), replace the gear set.
2. Using a feeler gauge and a straight edge, check the gear-to-pump body clearance. If clearance exceeds 0.0059 inch (0.15mm), replace the oil pump.

Rear Main Bearing Oil Seal

Removal and Installation
NOVA AND PRIZM

1. Remove the transaxle from the vehicle.
2. If equipped with a manual transaxle, perform the following procedures:
   a. Matchmark the pressure plate-to-flywheel.
   b. Remove the pressure plate-to-flywheel bolts and the clutch assembly from the vehicle.
   c. Remove the flywheel-to-crankshaft bolts and the flywheel.
3. If equipped with an automatic transaxle, perform the following procedures:
   a. Matchmark the flywheel-to-crankshaft.
   b. Remove the torque converter driveplate-to-crankshaft bolts and the torque converter driveplate.
4. Remove the rear end plate-to-engine bolts and the rear end plate.
5. If removing the rear oil seal retainer, perform the following procedures:
   a. Remove the rear oil seal retainer-to-engine bolts, rear oil seal retainer to oil pan bolts and the rear oil seal retainer.
   b. Using a small prybar, pry the rear oil seal retainer from the mating surfaces.
   c. Using a drive punch, drive the oil seal from the rear bearing retainer.
   d. Using the proper tool, clean the gasket mounting surfaces.
6. To remove the rear oil seal, with the rear oil seal retainer installed, use a small prybar and pry the seal from the rear oil

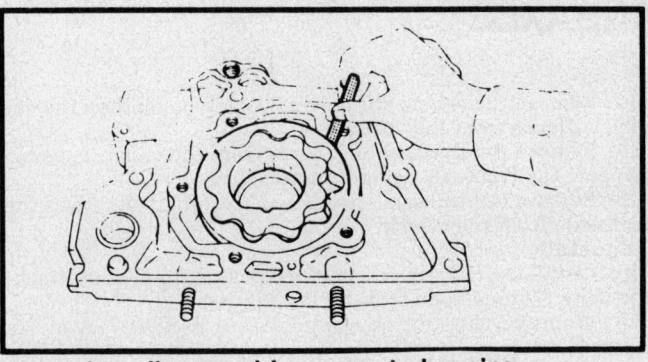

Measuring oil pump driven gear-to-housing clearance—Typical

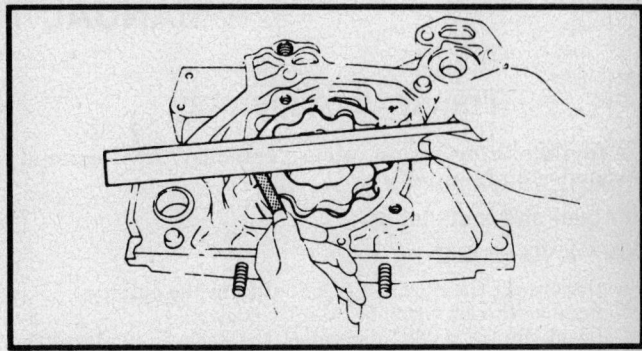

Measuring oil pump body-to-gear clearance—Typical

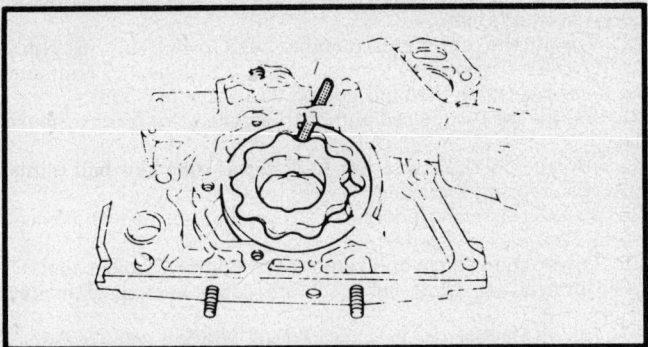

Measuring oil pump drive gear-to-driven gear clearance—Typical

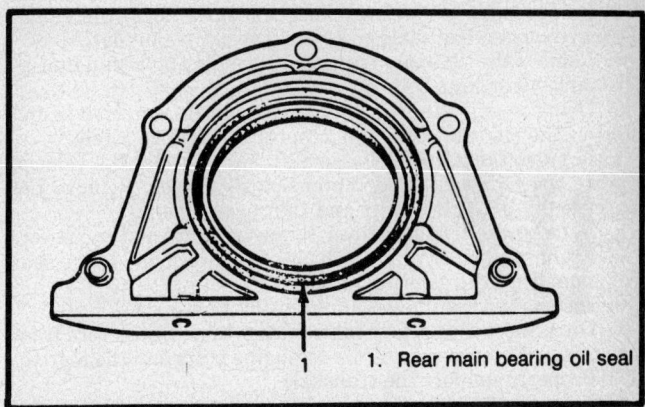

1. Rear main bearing oil seal

Rear main oil seal housing—Sprint and Metro

seal retainer.

NOTE: When removing the rear oil seal, be careful not to damage the seal mounting surface.

To install:
7. Clean the oil seal mounting surface.
8. Using multi-purpose grease, lubricate the new seal lips.
9. Using an rear oil seal installation tool J–35388 or equivalent, tap the seal straight into the bore of the retainer.
10. If the rear oil seal retainer was removed from the vehicle, use a new gasket and sealant, if necessary, and reverse the removal procedures; be careful when installing the oil seal over the crankshaft.
11. To complete the installation, reverse the removal procedures. Torque the flywheel-to-crankshaft bolts to 58 ft. lbs. and the torque converter drive plate-to-crankshaft bolts to 61 ft. lbs.

SPECTRUM AND STORM
1. Remove the transaxle.
2. Remove the oil pan. On Storm, remove the right and left undercovers.
3. Remove the pressure plate and clutch on manual transaxle

or the torque converter on automatic transaxle, the flywheel bolts and the flywheel from the crankshaft.
4. Remove the rear oil seal retainer and remove the oil seal from the retainer. Clean the sealing surfaces.
5. Using a new oil seal, install the new seal in the oil seal retainer.
6. To install, use new gaskets, apply sealer to the mounting surfaces, apply oil to the seal lips, align the dowel pins of the retainer with the engine block and reverse the removal procedures.

SPRINT AND METRO
1. Remove the transaxle.
2. Raise and support the vehicle safely. Drain the oil and remove the oil pan.
3. Remove the pressure plate, the clutch plate and the flywheel.
4. Remove the mounting bolts and the rear seal housing.
5. Pry the oil seal from the oil seal housing.
6. To install, use new gaskets/seals and reverse the removal procedures. Torque the oil seal housing to 7–9 ft. lbs. and the flywheel to 57–65 ft. lbs.

NOTE: After installing the oil seal housing, trim the gasket flush with the bottom of the case.

MANUAL TRANSAXLE

Transaxle Assembly

For further information, please refer to "Professional Transmission Manual".

Removal and Installation

NOVA AND PRIZM

1. Disconnect the negative terminal from the battery.
2. Remove the air cleaner and inlet duct.
3. From the transaxle, disconnect the back-up light switch connector, the speedometer cable, the thermostat housing and the ground wire.
4. Remove the 4 clutch cable-to-transaxle clips, the clutch slave cylinder-to-transaxle bolts and the slave cylinder.
5. Remove the (2) upper transaxle-to-engine bolts and the upper transaxle mount bolt.
6. Using an engine support tool or equivalent, attach it to and support the engine. Raise and support the vehicle safely.
7. Remove the left wheel assembly. From under the vehicle, remove the left, right and center splash shields. Remove the center beam-to-chassis bolts and the center beam.
8. Remove the flywheel cover-to-engine bolts and the cover.
9. From both sides of the vehicle, disconnect the lower control arms from the steering knuckles.
10. Disconnect both halfshaft from the transaxle.
11. Disconnect the battery cable and ignition switch wire from the starter. Remove the starter-to-engine bolts and the starter.
12. Properly support the transaxle.
13. Remove the transaxle-to-engine bolts and the lower the transaxle from the vehicle.
14. Using the proper tool, clean the gasket mounting surfaces.
To install:
15. Make sure the input shaft splines align with the clutch disc splines and reverse the removal procedures.
16. Torque the transaxle-to-engine bolts to 47 ft. lbs. (12mm) and to 34 ft. lbs. (10mm).
17. Torque the halfshaft-to-transaxle nuts to 27 ft. lbs., the crossmember-to-chassis nuts/bolts to 29 ft. lbs.
18. Torque the left side engine mount bolts to 38 ft. lbs. Check and/or refill the transaxle with fluid.

STORM

1. Disconnect the battery cables, then remove the battery and tray from the vehicle.
2. Drain the transaxle fluid.
3. Remove the air cleaner assembly.
4. Disconnect the the electrical connectors from the transaxle.
5. Disconnect the ground cable and engine wiring harness clamp from the transaxle.
6. Disconnect the ignition coil ground cable from the engine, then the ground cable at the ignition coil.
7. Disconnect the speedometer cable, clutch cable and shifter cables.
8. Support the engine using engine support tool J–28467–A or equivalent.
9. Raise and support the vehicle safely, then remove the tire and wheel assemblies.
10. Remove the front undercovers, then the ball joints from the steering knuckles.
11. Remove the left and right halfshaft, then the front exhaust pipe.
12. Remove the torque rod and bracket, then the left transaxle mount.
13. Remove the front transaxle through bolt, then the center beam with the rear transaxle mount.

14. Remove the engine stiffener attaching bolts, then the engine stiffener from the vehicle.
15. Remove the flywheel dust cover from the clutch housing. Support the transaxle using a suitable jack.
16. Remove the transaxle-to-engine attaching bolts, then the transaxle from the vehicle.
To install:
17. Install the transaxle, then the transaxle-to-engine attaching bolts. Torque bolts to 55 ft. lbs. (75 Nm).
18. Remove the engine support tool J–28467–A or its equivalent..
19. Install the flywheel dust cover, engine stiffener and center beam with the rear transaxle mount.
20. Install the left transaxle mount, then the front transaxle mount through bolt.
21. Torque the center crossmember bolts to 45 ft. lbs. (61 Nm). Torque the left transaxle mount bolts to 29 ft. lbs. (39 Nm) and the front transaxle through bolt to 64 ft. lbs. (87 Nm).
22. Install the torque rod and bracket, then the front exhaust pipe.
23. Install the right and left halfshafts, then the ball joints onto the steering knuckles.
24. Install the front undercovers, then the front tire and wheel assemblies.
25. Lower the vehicle and remove the engine support tool.
26. Connect the shift cable, clutch cable and speedometer cable.
27. Install the battery bracket and the ignition coil assembly.
28. Install the ignition coil ground cable onto the engine.
29. Install the engine harness wiring clamp, then the ground cable.
30. Connect all electrical connectors to the transaxle. Install the battery and battery tray.
31. Connect the battery cables. Adjust the shift cables, if necessary. Start engine and check for leaks.

SPECTRUM

1. Disconnect the negative battery terminal from the battery and the transaxle.
2. Disconnect the wiring connectors, speedometer cable, clutch cable and shift cables from the transaxle.
3. Remove the air cleaner heat tube.
4. Remove the upper transaxle-to-engine bolts.
6. Raise and support the vehicle safely. Drain the oil from the transaxle.
7. Remove the left front wheel assembly and splash shield.
8. Disconnect the left tie rod at the steering knuckle and the left tension rod.
9. Disconnect the halfshafts and remove the shafts by pulling them straight out from the transaxle, avoid damaging the oil seals.
10. Remove the dust cover at the clutch housing.
11. Using a floor jack, support the transaxle, then remove the transaxle-to-engine retaining bolts.
12. While sliding the transaxle away from the engine, carefully lower the jack, guiding the right axle shaft out of the transaxle.

NOTE: The right axle shaft must be installed into the transaxle when the transaxle is being mated to the engine.

To install:
12. When installing the transaxle, guide the right haklfshaft into the shaft bore as the transaxle is being raised.
13. Installlk the transaxle-to-engine mounting bolts. Torque bolts to 55 ft. lbs. (75 Nm).
14. Install the left halfshaft into its bore on the transaxle.

15. Install the left tension rtod and torque bolts to 80 ft. lbs. (108 Nm).
16. Install the tie rod to the steering knuckle.
17. Install the clutch housing dust cover bolts and the splash shield.
18. Install the tire and wheel assembly and lower the vehicle.
19. Install the remaining transaxle-to-engine attaching bolts. Torque bolts to 55 ft. lbs. (75 Nm).
20. Connect the ground cable at transaxle, clutch cable, speedometer cable and the battery negative cable.
21. Start engine and check for leaks.

SPRINT AND METRO

1. Disconnect the negative battery cable and the ground strap at the transaxle.
2. Remove the air cleaner and air pipe.
3. Remove the clutch cable from the clutch release lever.
4. Remove the starter and speedometer cable. Disconnect and tag the electrical wires and wiring harness from the transaxle.
5. Remove the front and rear torque rod bolts at the transaxle.
6. Raise and support the vehicle safely.
7. Drain the transaxle fluid.
8. Remove the exhaust pipe at the exhaust manifold and at the 1st exhaust hanger.
9. Remove the clutch housing lower plate.
10. Disconnect the gear shift control shaft and the extension rod at the transaxle.
11. Remove the left front wheel.
12. Using a prybar, pry on the inboard joints of the right and left hand halfshafts. This will detach the halfshafts from the snaprings of the differential side gears.
13. On the left side, remove the stabilizer bar mounting bolts and ball joint stud bolt. Push down on the stabilizer bar and remove the ball joint stud from the steering knuckle.
14. Pull the left halfshaft out of the transaxle.
15. Remove the front torque rod.
16. Secure and support the transaxle case with a jack.
17. Remove the transaxle-to-body mounting bolts and the mounts.
18. Remove the transaxle-to-engine mounting bolts.
19. Disconnect the transaxle from the engine by sliding it to the left side and lower the jack.

NOTE: When removing the transaxle, support the right halfshaft, so it does not become damaged.

To install:
20. Guide the right axle shaft into the transaxle and reverse the removal procedures. Torque the transaxle-to-engine bolts to 35 ft. lbs.
21. Torque the transaxle-to-mount bolts to 34 ft. lbs. Torque the mounting member bolts to 40 ft. lbs.
22. Torque the stabilizer bar bolts to 30 ft. lbs. Torque the ball joint stud bolt to 44 ft. lbs. Adjust the clutch cable and refill the transaxle.
23. Install the clutch housing lower plate.
24. Install the exhaust pipe to the exhaust manifold and the hanger.
25. Connect the gear shift control shaft and the extension rod on the transaxle.
26. Connect the speedometer cable and connect all electrical connectors to the transaxle.
27. Install the air cleaner and air pipe. Connect the battery negative cable.

Linkage Adjustment
NOVA AND PRIZM

Adjustment of shift lever free-play is accomplished through the use of a selective shim installed in the bottom of the lower shift lever seat.

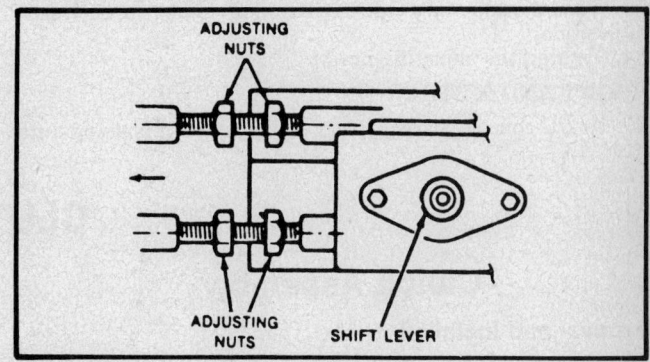

Adjusting the shift linkage of the transaxle—Spectrum

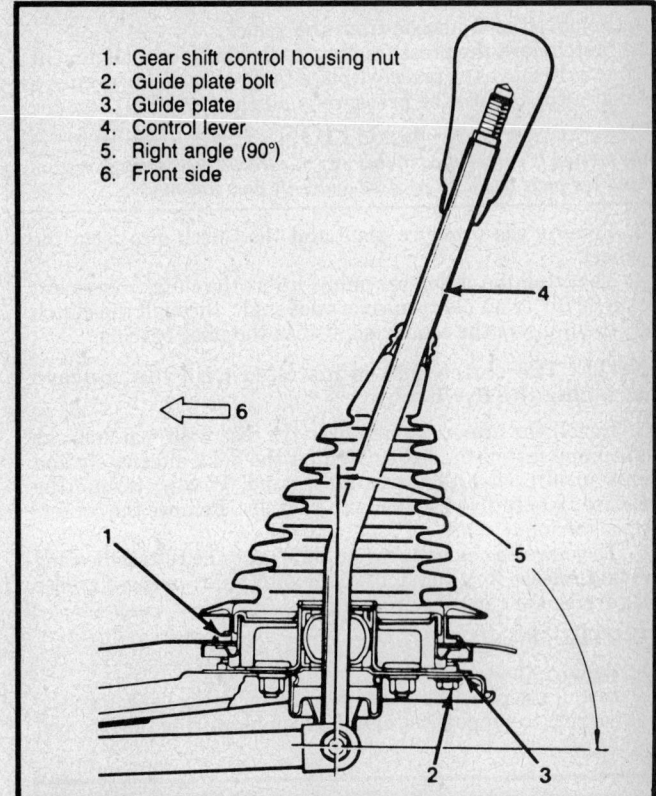

1. Gear shift control housing nut
2. Guide plate bolt
3. Guide plate
4. Control lever
5. Right angle (90°)
6. Front side

Manual transaxle gearshift lever adjustment—Sprint and Metro

Select a shim of a thickness that allows a preload of 0.1–0.2 lbs. at the top of the lever and install it in the shift lever seat.
To install the shim, perform the following procedures:
1. Disconnect the negative terminal from the battery.
2. Remove the console and the shifter boot.
3. Remove the shifter cover, shift support and cap.
4. Remove the shifter spacer, shifter seat and the shim.
5. Install the new shim and reassemble the shifter.
6. Check the shifter freeplay, using a pull scale, for the proper preload.
7. Repeat the procedure, if necessary.

SPECTRUM AND STORM

1. Loosen the adjusting nuts.
2. Place the transaxle and the shift lever in the **N** position.

3. Turn the adjusting nuts until the shift lever is in the vertical position.

4. Tighten the adjusting nuts.

SPRINT AND METRO

1. At the console, loosen the gear shift control housing nuts and the guide plate bolts.

2. Adjust the guide plate, so the shift lever is centered and at a right angle to the plate.

3. When the guide plate is positioned correctly, torque the guide plate bolts to 7 ft. lbs. and the housing nuts to 4 ft. lbs.

CLUTCH

Clutch Assembly

Removal and Installation
NOVA AND PRIZM

NOTE: Do not allow grease or oil to contaminate any of the disc, pressure plate or flywheel friction surfaces.

1. Remove the transaxle from the vehicle.

2. Matchmark the pressure plate to flywheel for realignment purposes. Remove the pressure plate-to-flywheel bolts, evenly, a little at a time, until the pressure is off the springs.

— CAUTION —

If the tension is not released in this way, the tremendous spring pressure behind the plate could be released suddenly and violently!

3. Remove the pressure plate and the clutch disc from the flywheel.

4. To install the clutch assembly, insert the clutch alignment tool J–35757 or an old transaxle pilot shaft, through the clutch disc, then, insert the tool or shaft into the pilot bearing.

NOTE: The clutch disc is installed with the concave side facing the flywheel.

5. Install the pressure plate over the disc with matchmarks aligned and install the bolts. Tighten the bolts alternately and evenly until even pressure is all around. Finally, torque the pressure plate-to-flywheel bolts to 14 ft. lbs. Remove the centering tool or input shaft.

6. To complete the installation, lubricate the release bearing hub and release fork contact points with multi-purpose grease and reverse the removal procedures.

SPECTRUM AND STORM

1. Remove the transaxle.

2. Install the pilot shaft tool J–35282 or equivalent, into the pilot bearing to support the clutch assembly during the removal procedures.

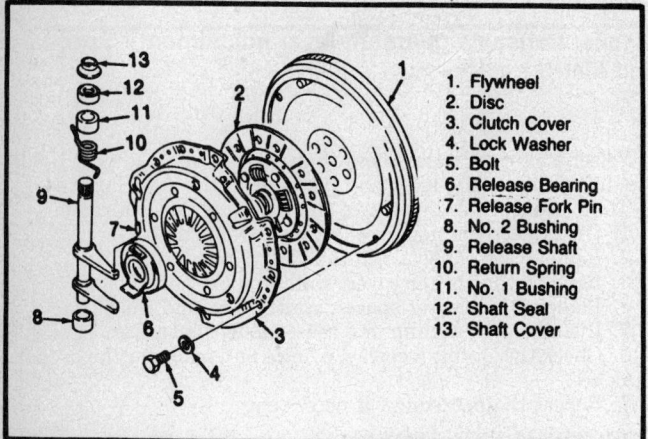

1. Flywheel
2. Disc
3. Clutch Cover
4. Lock Washer
5. Bolt
6. Release Bearing
7. Release Fork Pin
8. No. 2 Bushing
9. Release Shaft
10. Return Spring
11. No. 1 Bushing
12. Shaft Seal
13. Shaft Cover

Exploded view of the clutch assembly – Sprint and Metro

NOTE: Observe the alignment marks on the clutch and the clutch cover and pressure plate assembly. If the markings are not present, be sure to add them.

3. Loosen the clutch cover and pressure plate assembly retaining bolts evenly, one at a time, until the spring pressure is released.

4. Remove the clutch cover and pressure plate assembly and clutch plate.

NOTE: Check the clutch disc, flywheel and pressure plate for wear, damage or heat cracks. Replace all damaged parts.

5. Before installation, lightly lubricate the pilot shaft splines, pilot bearing and pilot release bearing surface with grease.

6. To install, reverse the removal procedures. Torque the clutch cover/pressure plate-to-flywheel bolts evenly to 13 ft. lbs., to avoid distortion.

SPRINT AND METRO

1. Remove the transaxle.

2. Install tool J–34860 into the pilot bearing to support the clutch assembly.

NOTE: Look for the X mark or white painted number on the clutch cover and the X mark on the flywheel. If there are no markings, mark the clutch cover and the flywheel for reassembly purposes.

3. Loosen the clutch cover-to-flywheel bolts, one turn at a time (evenly) until the spring pressure is released.

4. Remove the clutch cover and clutch plate.

5. Inspect the parts for wear, if necessary, replace the parts.

6. To install, reverse the removal procedures. Torque the clutch cover bolts to 14–20 ft. lbs.

Pedal Height/Free-Play Adjustment
NOVA AND PRIZM

1. Check pedal height as measured from the insulating sheet on the floor to the front-center of the pedal; it should be 5.65–6.043 in. If the height is not correct, perform the following procedures:

    a. Remove the lower instrument finish panel and air duct.

    b. Loosen the locknut on the pedal stopper bolt, located at the top of the pedal.

    c. Turn the stopper bolt inward (to decrease) or outward (to increase) until it is within specifications.

    d. Tighten the locknut, recheck and readjust, if necessary.

2. To check and/or adjust the clutch pedal free-play, perform the following procedures:

    a. Measure the clutch pedal height.

    b. Push the pedal until you feel increased resistance as the clutch pressure plate springs begin to be compressed. Measure the pedal at this point, then, subtract the smaller figure from the larger one; this is the free-play dimension.

NOTE: The free-play dimension should be 0.20–0.59 in.

    c. If necessary to adjust the free-play, loosen the pushrod

locknut, located between the pedal and the clutch master cylinder. Turn the pushrod, clockwise to decrease or counterclockwise to increase, until the dimension is within specifications.

   d. Tighten the locknut, recheck and readjust, if necessary.

SPECTRUM AND STORM

   1. Disconnect the negative battery terminal from the battery.
   2. Loosen the adjusting nut and pull the cable to the rear until it turns freely.
   3. Adjust the cable length by turning the adjusting nut.
   4. When the clutch pedal freeplay travel reaches 0.39–0.79 in. release the cable.
   5. When the adjustment has been completed, tighten the locknut.

SPRINT AND METRO

   1. At the transaxle, move the clutch release arm to check the freeplay, it should be 0.08–0.16 in.
   2. If necessary, turn the clutch cable joint nut to adjust the cable length.

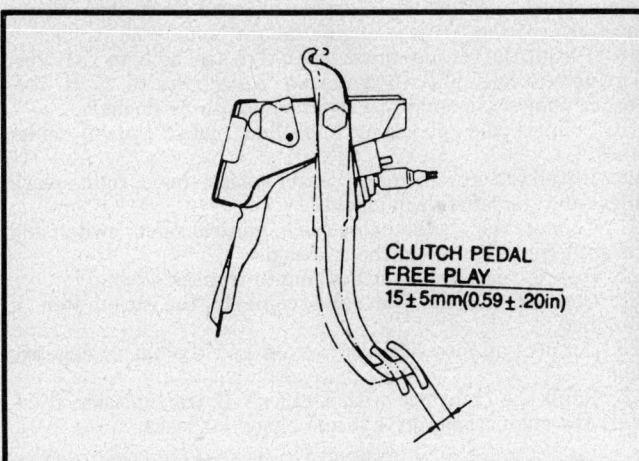

Clutch pedal freeplay adjustment – Spectrum and Storm

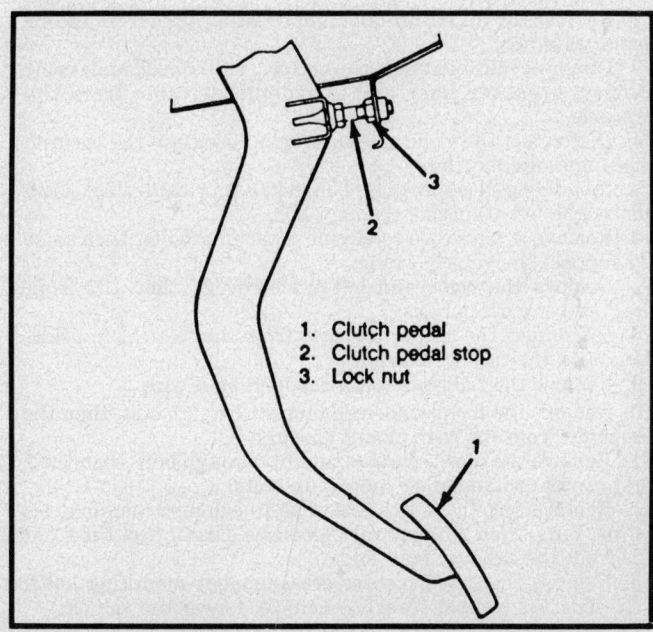

Clutch pedal height adjustment – Sprint and Metro

NOTE: The clutch pedal height should be adjusted so the clutch pedal is the exact same height as the brake pedal. The pedal is adjusted at the stop bolt on the upper end of the pedal pivot.

Clutch Cable

Removal and Installation
SPECTRUM AND STORM

   1. Disconnect the negative battery terminal from the battery.
   2. Loosen the clutch cable adjusting nuts. Disconnect the cable from the release arm and cable bracket.
   3. At the clutch pedal, remove the cable retaining bolt.
   4. Disconnect the cable from the front of the dash.
   5. Remove the clutch cable from the vehicle.
   6. To install, grease the clutch cable pin and reverse the removal procedures.
   7. Adjust the pedal freeplay.

SPRINT AND METRO

   1. Disconnect the negative battery cable.
   2. Remove the clutch cable joint nut and disconnect the cable from the release arm.
   3. Remove the clutch cable bracket mounting nuts and remove the bracket from the cable.
   4. Remove the cable retaining bolts at the clutch pedal.
   5. Remove the cable from the vehicle.
To install:
   6. Before installation, apply grease to the hook and pin end of the cable.
   7. Connect the cable to the clutch pedal and install the retaining bolts.
   8. Install the clutch cable bracket on the cable.
   9. Position the bracket on the transaxle and install the mounting bolts.
   10. Connect the cable to the release lever and install the joint nut on the cable.
   11. Adjust the pedal free-play as previously outlined and connect the negative battery cable.

Clutch Master Cylinder

Removal and Installation
NOVA AND PRIZM

   1. Disconnect the negative battery cable.
   2. Drain or siphon the fluid from the master cylinder.
   3. Remove the lower instrument finish panel and air duct.
   4. Remove the pedal return spring, clevis pin and clip.
   5. Disconnect the hydraulic line the clutch master cylinder.

NOTE: Do not spill brake fluid on the painted surface of the vehicle.

   6. Remove the master cylinder-to-firewall nuts and withdraw the assembly.
   7. To install, reverse the removal procedures. Refill the master cylinder reservoir with brake fluid. Bleed the clutch hydraulic system.
   8. Operate the clutch pedal and check the system for leaks.
   9. Check and/or adjust the clutch pedal height and free-play.

Clutch Slave Cylinder

Removal and Installion
NOVA AND PRIZM

NOTE: Do not spill brake fluid on the painted surface of the vehicle.

1. Disconnect the negative battery cable.
2. Disconnect the hydraulic line from the clutch slave cylinder.
3. Remove the slave cylinder-to-engine bolts and the cylinder.
4. To install, reverse the removal procedures. Refill the clutch master cylinder reservoir with clean brake fluid. Bleed the clutch hydraulic system. Operate the clutch pedal and check for leaks.

Hydraulic Clutch System Bleeding

NOVA AND PRIZM

1. Fill the clutch master cylinder reservoir with brake fluid.

NOTE: Do not spill brake fluid on the painted surface of the vehicle.

2. Fit a vinyl bleeder tube over the bleeder screw at the front of the slave cylinder and place the other end in a clean jar half filled with brake fluid.
3. Have an assistant depress the clutch pedal several times. Loosen the bleeder screw and allow the fluid to flow into the jar.
4. Tighten the screw and have the assistant release the clutch pedal.
5. Repeat bleeding procedure until no air bubbles are present in the fluid.
6. Refill the master cylinder to the specified level, check the system for leaks, then, adjust the clutch pedal height and free-play.

AUTOMATIC TRANSAXLE

Transaxle Assembly

For further information, please refer to "Professional Transmission Manual".

Removal and Installation

NOVA AND PRIZM

1. Disconnect the negative terminal from the battery and the ground cable from the transaxle. Label and disconnect the necessary electrical connectors. Drain the transaxle.
2. Remove the air intake duct. Disconnect the Throttle Valve (TV) cable from the carburetor, if equipped.
3. Disconnect the neutral safety switch, the speedometer cable and the shift control cable from the transaxle. Remove the shift cable bracket from the transaxle.
4. From the top of the transaxle, disconnect the thermostat housing-to-transaxle bolts.
5. Remove the single upper mount-to-bracket bolt. Remove the 2 upper bellhousing bolts.
6. Remove the upper 2 bell housing bolts.
7. Using a engine supporting tool, connect it to and support the engine. Raise and support the vehicle safely.
8. Remove the left wheel assembly, the left splash shield, the right splash shield and the center splash shield. Remove the crossmember-to-chassis bolts and the crossmember.
9. Remove the oil line cooler bracket. Disconnect and plug the oil cooler lines from the transaxle.
10. Remove the flywheel cover. Matchmark the torque converter-to-flywheel, then, remove the torque converter-to-flywheel bolts and separate the torque converter from the flywheel.

NOTE: The crankshaft must be rotated to gain access to the other bolts.

11. Remove both control arm-to-ball joint nuts/bolts and separate the lower control arms from the ball joints.
12. Remove both halfshaft-to-transaxle flange nuts and separate the halfshaft from the transaxle; support the halfshaft on a wire.
13. Disconnect the battery cable and ignition wire from the starter. Remove the starter-to-engine bolts and the starter.
14. Remove the lower transaxle-to-engine bolts.
15. Using a wooden block atop a floor jack, support the transaxle.
16. Remove the remaining transaxle-to-engine bolts. Separate the transaxle from the engine and lower it from the vehicle.
To install:
17. Align the torque converter-to-flywheel alignment marks and reverse the removal procedures. Torque the transaxle-to-engine bolts to 47 ft. lbs. (12mm bolt) and 34 ft. lbs. (10mm bolt). Torque the left-side engine mount bolts to 38 ft. lbs.
18. Torque the torque converter-to-flywheel bolts to 13 ft. lbs. Torque the halfshaft-to-transaxle nuts/bolts to 27 ft. lbs. Torque the crossmember-to-chassis bolts to 29 ft. lbs.
19. Connect the oil cooler lines and install the oil cooler bracket.
20. Install the crossmember, center splash shield, right splash shield and the left splash shield.
21. Connect the speedomater cable, neutral safety switch and the shift control cable to the transaxle.
22. Install the thermostat housing-to-transaxle bolts.
23. Connect the throttle valve cable to the carburetor, if equipped.
24. Connect all electrical connectors and the batter negative cable.
25. Refill the transaxle with Dexron® II transmission fluid. Start the engine, test drive it and check for leaks.

STORM

1. Disconnect the battery cables, then remove the battery and tray from the vehicle.
2. Remove the intake air duct and breather tube from the air cleaner assembly.
3. Disconnet the electrical connectors, shift cable, shift cable bracket, breather hose and speedometer cable from the transaxle.
4. Disconnect the vacuum diaphragm hose from the vacuum diaphragm, if equipped.
5. Install engine support tool J–28467–A or equivalent, then remove the left transaxle through bolt.
6. Remove 4 transaxle-to-engine attaching bolts, then raise and support the vehicle safely.
7. Remove the right and left undercovers, then the front wheel and tire assemblies.
8. Disconnect the left control arm from the steering knuckle, then drain the transaxle fluid.
9. Remove the halfshafts and suspend on a wire.
10. Remove the front transaxle mount through bolt, then the dampener from the rear mount through bolt.
11. Remove the rear transaxle mount through bolt, then the 2 front center crossmember mounting bolts.
12. Remove the front exhaust pipe-to-exhaust manifold attaching nuts, then 2 rear front pipe bolts. Disconnect the front pipe from the exhaust manifold.
13. Remove the 2 rear center crossmember mounting bolts, then the crossmember from the vehicle. Lower the vehicle.
14. Lower the engine using engine support tool J–28467 or equivalent.

15. Raise and safely support the vehicle, then position a suitable jack under the transaxle.

16. Remove the rear mount to transaxle case bolt, the the front mount attaching bolt.

17. Remove the front mounting bracket attaching bolts, then the front mounting bracket from the engine.

18. Remove the flywheel cover, then the flywheel-to-torque converter attaching bolts.

19. Disconnect the oil cooler lines from the transaxle, then remove the 2 rear transaxle mount bolts. Lower the transxale from the vehicle.

To install:

20. Raise the transaxle into position, then install the 2 rear transaxle mounting bolts. Remove transaxle jack.

21. Lower the vehicle, then install the 4 transaxle-to-engine mounting bolts.

22. Using engine support tool J–28467–A or equivalent, raise the engine slightly.

23. Install the through bolt on the left transaxle mount. Torque through bolt to 64 ft. lbs. (87 Nm).

24. Raise and safely support the vehicle, then install the flywheel-to-torque converter attaching bolts. Torque converter bolts to 31 ft. lbs. (42 Nm).

25. Install the flywheel cover, then connect the oil cooler lines to the transaxle. Torque oil cooler line trunion bolts tov 10 ft. lbs. (15 Nm).

26. Install the front transaxle mount nut and bolt. Torque bolt to 45 ft. lbs. (61 Nm).

27. Install the rear mount through bolt. Torque rear transaxle mount attaching bolts to 29 ft. lbs. (39 Nm) and the rear mount through bolt to 64 ft. lbs. (87 Nm).

28. Install the center crossmember. Torque crossmember bolts to 45 ft. lbs. (61 Nm).

29. Install the front mount through bolt. Torque bolt to 64 ft. lbs. (87 Nm).

30. Install the dampener on the rear mount through bolt.

31. Install the front pipe to the exhaust manifold, the 2 rear front pipe attaching bolts.

32. Install the halfshafts.

33. Install the left control arm onto the steering knuckle, then the right and left under covers.

34. Install the tire and wheel assemblies, then lower the vehicle. Torque the engine-to-transaxle attaching bots to 31 ft. lbs. (42 Nm).

35. Remove the engine support tool, then install the speedometer to the transaxle.

36. Install the breather hose, shaft cable bracket and shift cable to the transaxle.

37. Install the vacuum hose to the vacuum diaphragm, if equipped.

38. Connect the electrical connectors to the transaxle.

39. Install the air breather tube and the air intake duct onto the air cleaner assembly.

40. Install the batterty and battery tray. Connect the battery cables and check transaxle fluid. Start engine and check for leaks.

SPECTRUM

1. Disconnect the negative battery terminal from the battery.

2. Remove the air duct tube from the air cleaner.

3. From the transaxle, disconnect the shift cable, speedometer cable, vacuum diaphragm hose, engine wiring harness clamp and the ground cable.

4. At the left-fender, disconnect the inhibitor switch and the kickdown solenoid wiring connectors.

5. Disconnect the oil cooler lines from the transaxle.

6. Remove the three upper transaxle-to-engine mounting bolts. Raise and support the vehicle safely.

7. Remove both front-wheels and the left-front fender splash shield.

8. Disconnect both tie rod ends at the steering knuckles.

9. Remove both front tension rod brackets and disconnect the rods from the control arms.

10. Disengage the halfshafts from the transaxle.

11. Remove the flywheel dust cover and the converter-to-flywheel attaching bolts.

12. Remove the transaxle rear mount through bolt.

13. Disconnect the starter wiring and the starter. Support the transaxle.

14. Remove the lower transaxle-to-engine mounting bolts and remove the transaxle.

To install:

15. Install transaxle onto engine and converter to the flywheel. Torque the converter-to-flywheel at 30 ft. lbs., the transaxle-to-engine at 56 ft. lbs.

16. Install the flywheel dust cover.

17. Install both halfshafts into the transaxle.

18. Install the tension rod brackets and both tie rod ends to the steering knuckle.

19. Instal;l the splash shield to the left front fender and the tire and wheel assemblies.

20. Connect the transaxle cooler lines.

21. Connect all electcrical connectors and hoses that were disconnected during the removal.

22. Connect the speedometer cable and shift cable to the transaxle.

23. Connect the battery negative cable, adjust the shift linkage and fill the transaxle with Dexron®II automatic transmission fluid. Start engine and check for leaks.

SPRINT AND METRO

1. Disconnect the air suction guide from the air cleaner.

2. Disconnect the negative and the positive battery cables.

3. Remove the battery and the battery bracket tray.

4. Remove the negative cable from the transaxle.

5. Disconnect the solenoid wire coupler and the shift lever switch wire couplers.

6. Remove the wiring harness from the transaxle.

7. Remove the speedometer cable from the transaxle.

8. Disconnect the oil pressure control cable from the accelerator cable and the accelerator cable from the transaxle.

9. Remove the select cable from the transaxle.

10. Remove the starter motor.

11. Drain the transaxle fluid.

12. Disconnect the oil outlet and inlet hoses from the oil pipes. After disconnecting, plug the 2 oil hoses to prevent fluid in the hoses and oil cooler from draining.

13. Raise the vehicle and support it safely.

14. Remove the exhaust No. 1 pipe.

15. Remove the clutch housing lower plate.

16. Remove the 6 driveplate bolts. To lock the driveplate, engage a prybar with the driveplate gear through the notch provided at the under side of the transaxle case.

17. Remove the left hand front halfshaft.

18. Detach the inboard joint of the right hand halfshaft from the differential.

19. Disconnect the transaxle mounting member.

20. Securely support the transaxle with a suitable jack for removal.

21. Remove the transaxle left mounting.

22. Remove the bolts fastening the engine and the transaxle.

23. Disconnect the transaxle from the engine by sliding towards the left side and carefully lower the jack.

NOTE: When removing the transaxle assembly from the engine, move it in parallel with the crankshaft and use care so as not to apply excessive force to the driveplate and torque converter. After removing the transaxle assembly, be'sure to keep it so the oil pan is at the bottom. If the transaxle is tilted, fluid in it may flow out.

To install:

24. Reverse the removal procedure noting the following important steps.

25. Before installing the transaxle assembly apply grease around the cup at the center of the torque converter. Then measure the distance between the torque converter flange nut and the transaxle case housing. The distance should be more than 0.85 in. (21.4mm). If the distance is less than 0.85 in. (21.4mm), the torque converter has been installed incorrectly and must be removed and reinstalled correctly.

26. When installing the transaxle, guide the right halfshaft into the differential side gear as the transaxle is being raised.

27. After inserting the inboard joints of the right hand and left hand halfshafts into the differential side gears, push the inboard joints into the side gears until the snaprings on the halfshafts engage the side gears.

28. After connecting the oil pressure control cable to the accelerator cable, check the oil pressure control cable play and adjust if necessary.

29. Install the select cable.

30. Refill the transaxle and check the fluid level.

31. Tighten the following bolts and nuts to specifications.
   a. Drive plate bolts—14 ft. lbs. (19 Nm).
   b. Mounting member bolts—40 ft. lbs. (55 Nm).
   c. Transaxle mounting nuts—33 ft. lbs. (45 Nm).
   d. Transaxle mounting bolts (8mm)—40 ft. lbs. (55 Nm).
   e. Transaxle mounting nuts (8mm)—40 ft. lbs. (55 Nm).
   f. Stabilizer shaft mounting bolts—31 ft. lbs. (42 Nm).
   g. Ball stud bolt—44 ft. lbs. (60 Nm).
   h. Wheel nuts—40 ft. lbs. (55 Nm).

Shift Linkage Adjustment
NOVA AND PRIZM

1. Loosen the swivel nut on the lever.
2. Push the manual lever fully towards the right side of the vehicle.
3. Return the lever 2 notches to the **N** position.
4. Set the shift lever in the **N** position.
5. While holding the lever lightly towards the **R** position, tighten the swivel nut.

SPECTRUM

1. Loosen the 2 adjusting nuts at the control rod link and connect the shift cable to the link on the transaxle.
2. Shift the transaxle into the **N** detent.
3. Place the shifter lever into the **N** position.
4. Rotate the link assembly clockwise to remove slack in the cable.
5. Tighten the rear adjusting nut until it makes contact with the link. Tighten the front adjusting nut until it makes contact with the link and tighten the adjusting nuts.

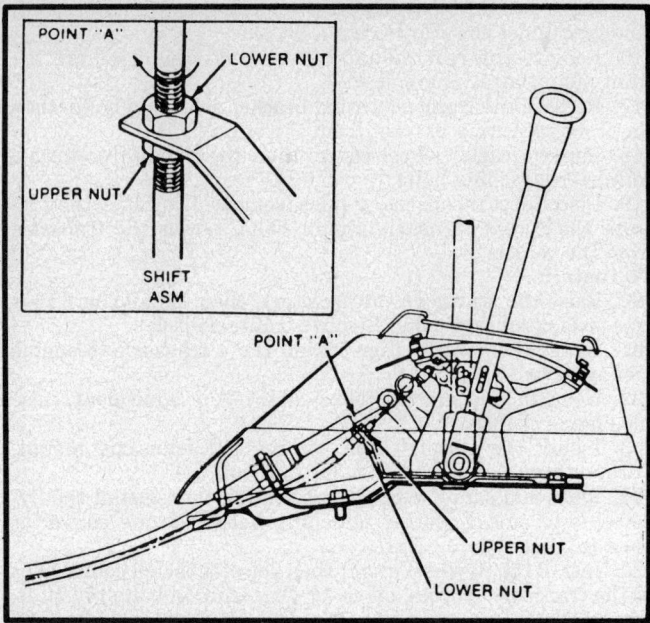

Adjusting the parking lock—Spectrum

Throttle Linkage Adjustment
NOVA AND PRIZM

1. Depress the accelerator pedal completely and check that the throttle valve opens fully. If the throttle valve does not open fully, adjust the accelerator link
2. Fully depress the accelerator
3. Loosen the adjustment nuts.
4. Adjust the throttle cable housing so the distance between the end of the boot and the stopper on the cable is correct. The distance must be 0.04 in. (0.1mm).
5. Tighten the adjusting nuts and recheck the adjustment.

STORM

1. Position the ignition switch/key in the **LOCK** position.
2. Place the selector lever in the **P** position.
3. Loosen the adjuster nuts on the transaxle. Ensure that the shift lever on the transaxle is in the **P** position.
4. Pull the cable forward, then tighten the forward adjuster nut until it contacts the shift lever. Tighten the rear nut until it contacts the shift lever.
5. Tighten both adjuster nuts.

DRIVE AXLE

Halfshaft

Removal and Installation
NOVA AND PRIZM

1. From the front wheel assemblies, remove the grease cup, then, loosen the wheel lug nuts and the halfshaft hub nut.
2. Raise and support the vehicle safely, then, remove the wheel/tire assemblies, the cotter pin, the locknut cap, hub nut and washer.
3. Loosen and remove the (6) halfshaft flange-to-transaxle flange nuts

NOTE: When removing the halfshaft-to-transaxle

nuts, have an assistant depress the brake pedal to keep the shaft from turning.

4. Remove the lower control arm-to-ball joint nuts/bolts and separate the lower control arm from the steering knuckle from lower control arm.

NOTE: If the vehicle is equipped with a twincam engine, it may be necessary to remove the stabilizer bar from the lower control arm.

5. Turn the steering knuckle to separate the halfshaft from the transaxle.
6. Cover the outboard CV-joint rubber boot with a cloth to prevent damage. Using the wheel puller tool J–25287 or equiva-

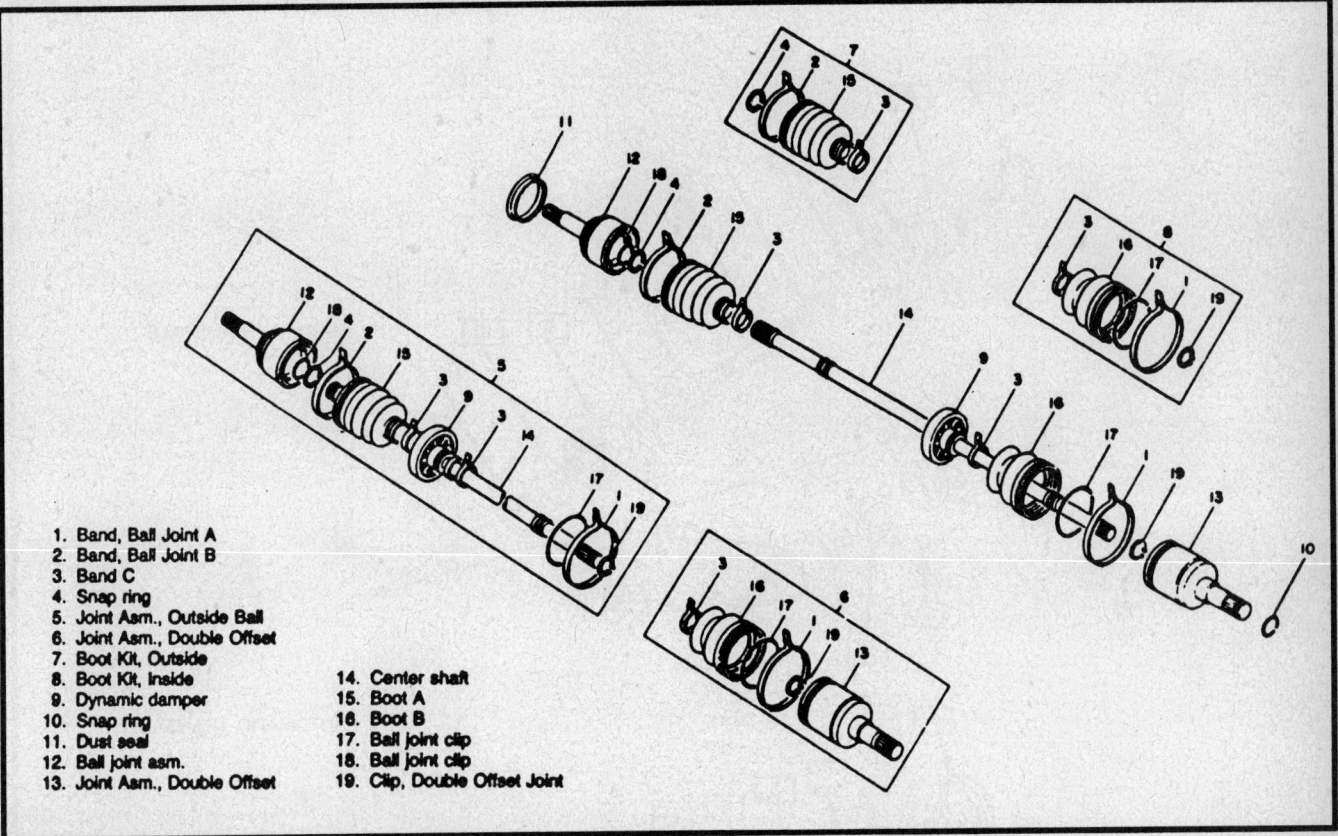

1. Band, Ball Joint A
2. Band, Ball Joint B
3. Band C
4. Snap ring
5. Joint Asm., Outside Ball
6. Joint Asm., Double Offset
7. Boot Kit, Outside
8. Boot Kit, Inside
9. Dynamic damper
10. Snap ring
11. Dust seal
12. Ball joint asm.
13. Joint Asm., Double Offset
14. Center shaft
15. Boot A
16. Boot B
17. Ball joint clip
18. Ball joint clip
19. Clip, Double Offset Joint

Exploded view of the halfshafts — Spectrum

lent, press the halfshaft from the steering knuckle and remove the halfshaft.

To install:

7. Lubricate the splines with multi-puprose grease, insert the it into the steering knuckle hub, install the washer and the hub nut, then, tighten the hub nut to draw the halfshaft into the steering knuckle hub until it seats.

NOTE: When torquing the hub nut, have an assistant depress the brake pedal; it may be necessary final torque the hub nut with the vehicle resting on the ground.

8. To complete the installation, reverse the removal procedures. Torque the lower control arm-to-ball joint nuts/bolts to 59 ft. lbs., the halfshaft-to-transaxle flange nuts to 27 ft. lbs. and the halfshaft-to-steering knuckle hub nut to 137 ft. lbs. Install a new cotter pin.

SPECTRUM AND STORM

1. Raise and support the vehicle safely, allowing the wheels to hang.
2. Remove the front wheel assemblies, the hub grease caps, the hub nuts and the cotter pins.
3. Install the halfshaft boot seal protector tool J–28712 or equivalent, on the outer CV-joints and the halfshaft boot seal protector tool J–34754 or equivalent, on the inner Tri-Pot joints.

NOTE: Clean the halfshaft threads and lubricate them with a thread lubricant.

4. Have an assistant depress the brake pedal, then remove the hub nut and washer.

5. Remove the caliper-to-steering knuckle bolts and support the caliper, on a wire, out of the way.
6. Remove the rotor. Remove the drain plug and drain the oil from the transaxle.
7. Using a slide hammer puller and the puller attachment tool J–34866 or equivalent, pull the hub from the halfshaft.
8. Remove the tie rod-to-steering knuckle cotter pin and the nut. Using the ball joint separator tool J–21687–02 or equivalent, press the tie rod ball joint from the steering knuckle.
9. Remove the lower ball joint-to-control arm nuts/bolts.
10. Swing the steering knuckle assembly outward and slide the halfshaft from the steering knuckle.
11. Place a large prybar between the differential case and the inboard constant velocity joint. Pry the axle shaft from the differential case.
12. Remove the halfshaft assembly.

NOTE: When installing the halfshaft, press it into the differential case until it locks with with snapring.

To install:

13. Use new cotter pins and reverse the removal procedures.
14. On Spectrum, torque the ball joint-to-control arm nuts/bolts to 80 ft. lbs. (108 Nm), the caliper-to-steering knuckle bolts to 41 ft. lbs. (55 Nm) and the halfshaft-to-hub nut to 137 ft. lbs. (186 Nm).
15. On Storm, torque lower control arm nuts and bolts to 105 ft. lbs. (142 Nm), tie rod-to-steering knuckle nut to 36 ft. lbs. (49 Nm) and the hub nut to 137 ft. lbs. (186 Nm).
16. Check and/or adjust the front alignment.

SPRINT AND METRO

1. Remove the grease cap, the cotter pin and the halfshaft nut from both front wheels.

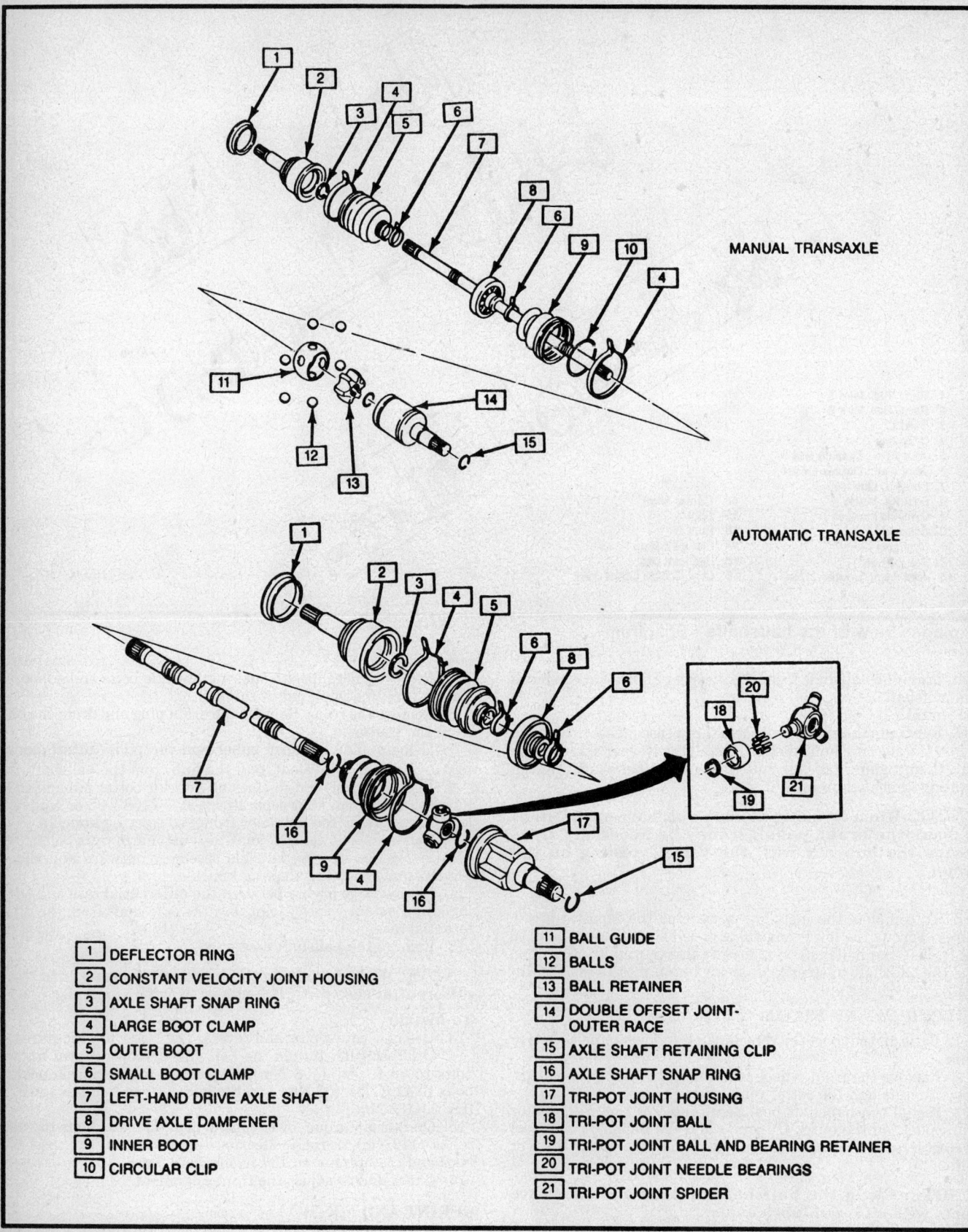

MANUAL TRANSAXLE

AUTOMATIC TRANSAXLE

1	DEFLECTOR RING	11	BALL GUIDE
2	CONSTANT VELOCITY JOINT HOUSING	12	BALLS
3	AXLE SHAFT SNAP RING	13	BALL RETAINER
4	LARGE BOOT CLAMP	14	DOUBLE OFFSET JOINT-OUTER RACE
5	OUTER BOOT	15	AXLE SHAFT RETAINING CLIP
6	SMALL BOOT CLAMP	16	AXLE SHAFT SNAP RING
7	LEFT-HAND DRIVE AXLE SHAFT	17	TRI-POT JOINT HOUSING
8	DRIVE AXLE DAMPENER	18	TRI-POT JOINT BALL
9	INNER BOOT	19	TRI-POT JOINT BALL AND BEARING RETAINER
10	CIRCULAR CLIP	20	TRI-POT JOINT NEEDLE BEARINGS
		21	TRI-POT JOINT SPIDER

Exploded view of the halfshafts—Storm

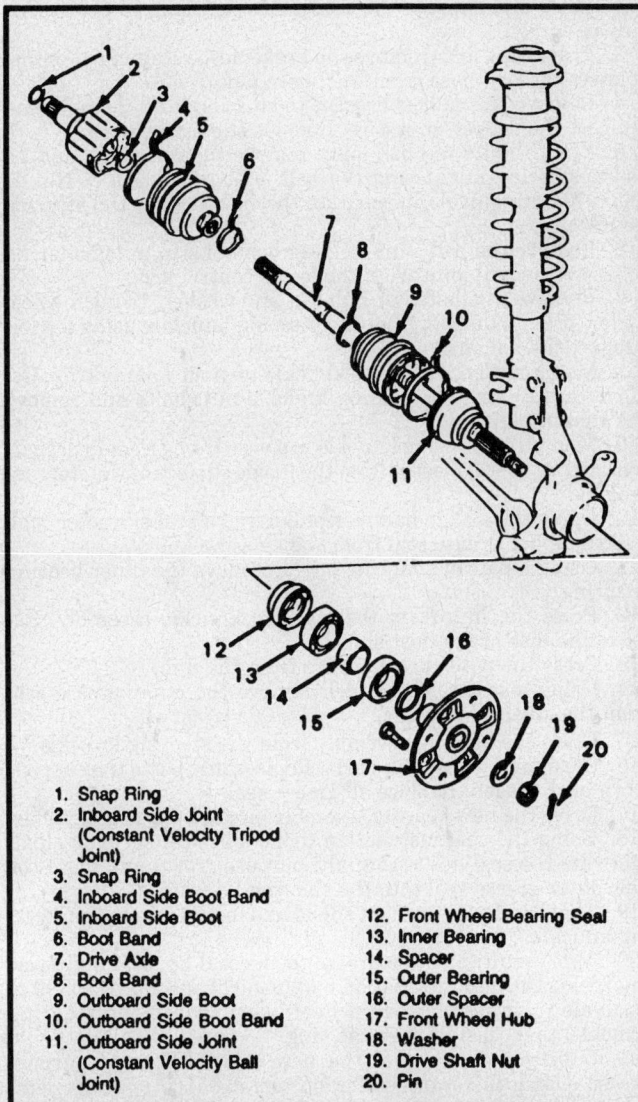

1. Snap Ring
2. Inboard Side Joint
   (Constant Velocity Tripod
   Joint)
3. Snap Ring
4. Inboard Side Boot Band
5. Inboard Side Boot
6. Boot Band
7. Drive Axle
8. Boot Band
9. Outboard Side Boot
10. Outboard Side Boot Band
11. Outboard Side Joint
    (Constant Velocity Ball
    Joint)
12. Front Wheel Bearing Seal
13. Inner Bearing
14. Spacer
15. Outer Bearing
16. Outer Spacer
17. Front Wheel Hub
18. Washer
19. Drive Shaft Nut
20. Pin

Exploded view of the halfshaft—Sprint and Metro

2. Loosen the wheel nuts.
3. Raise and support the vehicle safely.
4. Remove the front wheels.
5. Drain the transaxle fluid.
6. Using a prybar, pry on the inboard joints of the right and left hand axle shafts to detach the axle shafts from the snaprings of the differential side gears.
7. Remove the stabilizer bar mounting bolts and the ball joint stud bolt. Pull down on the stabilizer bar and remove the ball joint stud from the steering knuckle.
8. Pull the axle shafts out of the transaxle's side gear, first, and then from the steering knuckles.

NOTE: To prevent the axle shaft boots from becoming damaged, be careful not to bring them into contact with any parts. If any malfunction is found in the either of the joints, replace the joints as an assembly.

9. To install, snap the axle shaft into the transaxle, first, and then into the steering knuckle.
10. To complete the installation, reverse the removal procedures. Torque the stabilizer bar mounting bolts to 30 ft. lbs.; the

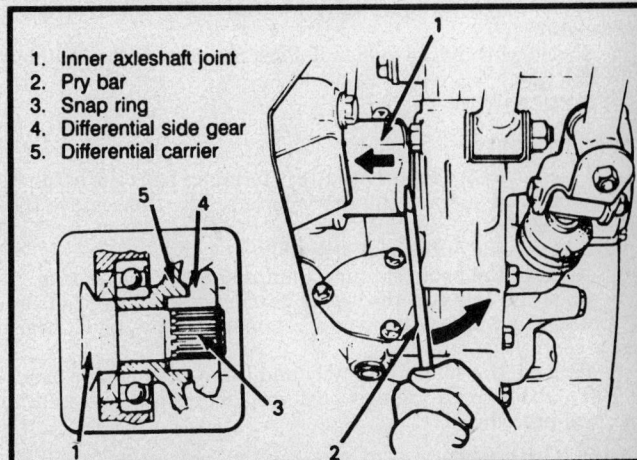

1. Inner axleshaft joint
2. Pry bar
3. Snap ring
4. Differential side gear
5. Differential carrier

Disengaging the halfshaft from the differential side gear snapring—Sprint and Metro

ball joint stud bolt to 44 ft. lbs. and the axle shaft nut to 144 ft. lbs.

CV-Boot

Removal and Installation

NOVA AND PRIZM

1. Raise and safely support the vehicle and remove the tire and wheel assembly.
2. Remove the halfshaft.
3. Remove the boot retaining clamps.
4. Remove the inboard joint tulip.
5. Remove the tripod joint snapring and the tripod joint from the halfshaft.
6. Remove the inboard and outboard joint boots.
7. To install, reverse the removal procedures; the inboard joint and clamp is larger than the outboard clamp. Face the beveled side of the tripod axial spline towards the outboard joint.

STORM

Outer (Outboard)

1. Raise and safely support the vehicle and remove the tir and wheel assembly.
2. Remove the halfshaft.
3. Place halfshaft into a suitable vise.
4. Using a suitable prybar, remove the circlip.
5. Remove the case housing from the shaft.
6. Remove the 6 balls from the ball guide, then move ball guide towards center of shaft.
7. Remove the snapring from the shaft, then the ball guide and ball retainer from the shaft.
8. Remove boot from shaft. Reverse procedure to install. Pack new boot with suitable grease.

Inner (Inboard)

1. Raise and safely support the vehicle and remove the tire and wheel assembly.
2. Remove halfshaft.
3. Place halfshaft into a suitable vise and remove the large boot clamp.
4. Remove the tri-pot housing from the drive axle shaft.
5. Using a suitable brass drift and hammer, remove the spider assembly from the axle shaft.
6. Remove the small boot clamp, then the boot from the shaft. Note the alignment marks on the spider assembly and the halfshaft and on the drive axle shaft and the tri-pot housing. If

no marks are present, make alignment marks for easy installation.

7. Reverse procedure to install. Pack new boot with a suitable grease.

SPECTRUM

Inner (Inboard)

1. Disconnect the negative battery terminal from the battery.
2. Raise and support the the vehicle safely, the remove the front wheels.
3. Remove the outer boot assembly.
4. Remove the boot retaining clamps and the spacer ring.
5. Slide the axle and the spider bearing assembly out of the tri-pot housing. Install the spider retainer onto the spider bearing assembly.
6. Remove the spider assembly and the boot from the axle.
7. To install, pack the new boot with grease and reverse the removal procedures.

Outer (Outboard)

1. Disconnect the negative battery terminal from the battery.
2. Raise and support the vehicle safely, then remove the front wheels.
3. Remove the brake caliper and support on a wire, then remove the rotor.
4. Slide the outer CV-joint assembly off the axle shaft.
5. Remove the bearing retaining ring, the boot retainer, the clamp and the outer boot.
6. To install, pack the new boot with grease and reverse the removal procedures.

SPRINT AMD METRO

NOTE: **Do not disassemble the wheel side joint (outboard). Replace if found to be defective. Do not disassemble the spider of the differential side joint. If the spider is found to be defective, replace the differential side joint assembly.**

1. With the axleshaft removed from the vehicle, remove the boot band from the differential side joint.
2. Remove the housing from the differential side joint.
3. Remove the snapring and spider from the shaft.
4. Remove the inside and outside boots from the shaft.

To install:

5. Liberally apply the joint grease to the wheel side joint. Use the black joint grease in the tube included in the wheel side boot set or wheel side joint assembly.
6. Fit the wheel side boot on the shaft. Fill the inside of the boot with the joint grease, approximately 80 grams and fix the boot bands.
7. Fit the differential side boot on the shaft.
8. Liberally apply the joint grease to the differential side joint on the shaft. Use the yellow grease in the tube included in the differential side boot set or differential side joint assembly.
9. Install the spider of the differential side joint on the shaft, facing its chamfered side to the wheel side joint.
10. After installing the spider, fit the snapring in the groove on the shaft.
11. Fill the inside of the differential side boot with the joint grease, aproximately 130 gram and install the housing. Fix the boot to the housing with a boot band.
12. Correct any distortions or bends in the boots.
13. Install the halfshaft in the vehicle.

Front Wheel Hub, Knuckle and Bearings

Removal and Installation

NOVA AND PRIZM

1. Loosen the wheel nuts and hub nut.

2. Raise and support the vehicle safely. Remove the wheel/tire assembly.
3. From the strut, remove the brake hose retaining clip. Disconnect the flex hose from the brake pipe.
4. Remove the caliper bracket-to-steering knuckle bolts and support the caliper on a wire. Remove the brake disc.
5. From the tie rod ball joint, remove the cotter pin and tie rod-to-steering nut. Using the ball joint removal tool No. J–24319–01 or equivalent, separate the tie rod from the steering knuckle.
6. Remove the ball joint-to-lower control arm nuts/bolts and separate the ball joint from the lower control arm.
7. Remove the halfshaft hub nut and washer. Using a wheel puller, press halfshaft from the steering knuckle; using a wire, support the halfshaft.
8. Matchmark the steering knuckle-to-strut relationship. Remove the (2) strut-to-steering knuckle nuts/bolts and remove the steering knuckle.
9. Mount the steering knuckle in a vise. Using a small prybar, remove the dust deflector from the inside surface of the steering knuckle.
10. Using the a slide hammer puller and a seal extractor tool, pull the inner grease seal from the steering knuckle.
11. Using a pair of snapring pliers, remove the inner bearing snapring.
12. Press the hub from the steering knuckle assembly. Remove the disc brake dust shield.
13. Press the outer bearing race from the hub.
14. Using a seal removal tool, remove the outer grease seal from the steering knuckle.
15. Drive the bearing assembly from the steering knuckle.
16. Clean and inspect all parts. Replace any parts that appear worn or damaged. Replace all grease seals.
17. Drive the new bearing assembly into the steering knuckle.
18. Using the seal installation tool J–35737–1 or equivalent, lubricate the seal lips with multi-purpose grease and drive the new outer grease seal into the steering knuckle.
19. Apply sealer to the dust shield and install it onto the steering knuckle.
20. Apply multi-purpose grease to the seal lip, seal and bearing. Using the hub installation tools J–8092 and No. J–35399 or equivalent, press the new wheel bearing into the steering knuckle, then, install the snap ring.
21. Lubricate the lips of the new seal with multi-purpose grease. Using the seal installation tool J–35737 or equivalent, drive the new inner grease seal into the steering knuckle.
22. Using tool J–35379 or equivalent (open end down), install the dust deflector ring onto the steering knuckle.
23. Install the lower ball joint-to-control arm nuts/bolts, then, torque to 59 ft. lbs.

NOTE: **If installing the ball joint-to-steering knuckle, torque the nut to 14 ft. lbs. (to seat the ball joint) and remove it. Using a new ball joint nut, torque it to 82 ft. lbs.**

24. Install the camber adjusting cam to steering knuckle, the steering steering knuckle to strut. Insert the steering knuckle-to-strut bolts (from rear to front) and align the camber adjusting marks. Torque the steering knuckle-to-strut nuts/bolts to 105 ft. lbs. (except twincam engine) or 166 ft. lbs. (twincam engine).
25. Install the tie rod-to-steering knuckle nut and torque it to 36 ft. lbs.; be sure to install a new cotter pin.
26. To complete the installation, reverse the removal procedures. Torque the brake caliper-to-steering knuckle bolts to 65 ft. lbs.
27. Lower the vehicle so the wheels are resting on the ground. Torque the wheel nuts to 76 ft. lbs., the halfshaft hub 137 ft. lbs.; be sure to install a new cotter pin. Bleed the brake system.
28. Check the wheel alignment; it may be necessary to have

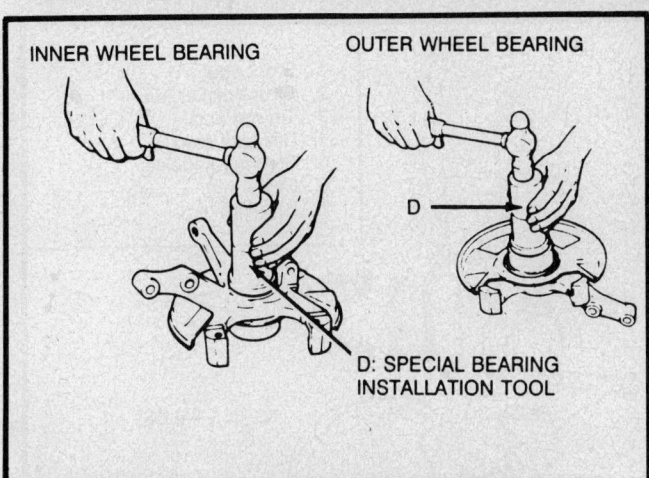

INNER WHEEL BEARING   OUTER WHEEL BEARING

D

D: SPECIAL BEARING
INSTALLATION TOOL

Installing inner and outer wheel bearings in the steering knuckle—Sprint and Metro

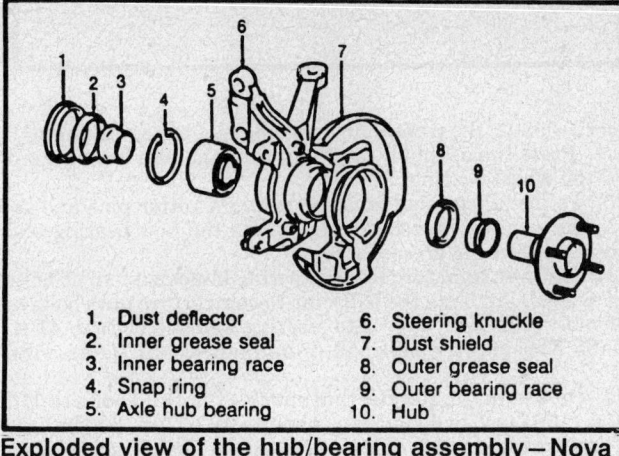

1. Dust deflector
2. Inner grease seal
3. Inner bearing race
4. Snap ring
5. Axle hub bearing
6. Steering knuckle
7. Dust shield
8. Outer grease seal
9. Outer bearing race
10. Hub

Exploded view of the hub/bearing assembly—Nova and Prizm

the wheels aligned when the strut or the knuckle has been replaced with a new part.

NOTE: Never reinstall used grease seals, self locking nuts or cotter pins; always replace these parts with new ones once they have been removed.

29. If the cotter pin holes are not aligned, bend the tangs on the cap, slightly to align the holes; Never back off the nut.

SPECTRUM AND STORM

1. Raise and support the vehicle safely, allowing the wheels to hang.
2. Remove the front wheel assemblies, the hub grease caps and the cotter pins.
3. Install the halfshaft boot seal protector tool No. J–28712 or equivalent, on the outer CV-joints and the halfshaft boot seal protector tool No. J–34754 or equivalent, on the inner Tri-Pot joints.

NOTE: Clean the halfshaft threads and lubricate them with a thread lubricant.

4. Remove the hub nut and washer.
5. Remove the caliper-to-steering knuckle bolts and support the caliper, on a wire, out of the way.
6. Remove the rotor.
7. Using a slide hammer puller and the puller attachment tool J–34866 or equivalent, pull the hub from the halfshaft.

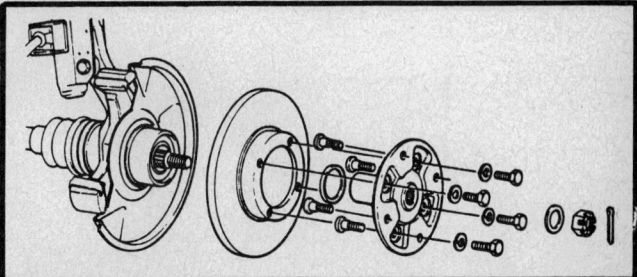

Exploded view of the front wheel hub assembly— Sprint and Metro

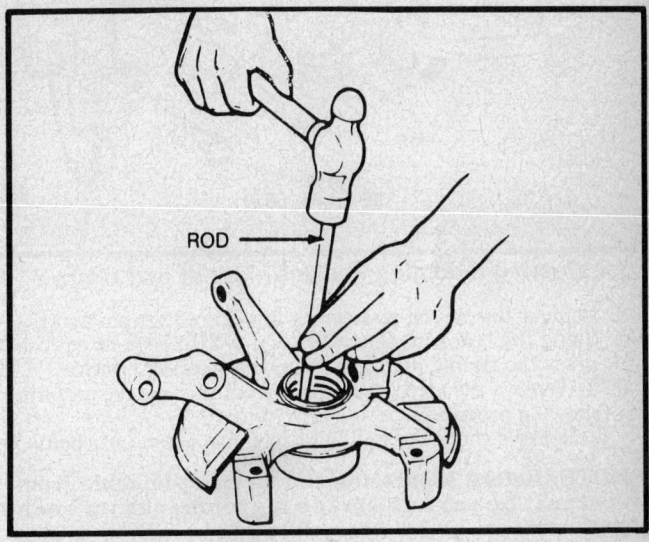

ROD

Removing the outer wheel bearing from the steering knuckle—Sprint and Metro

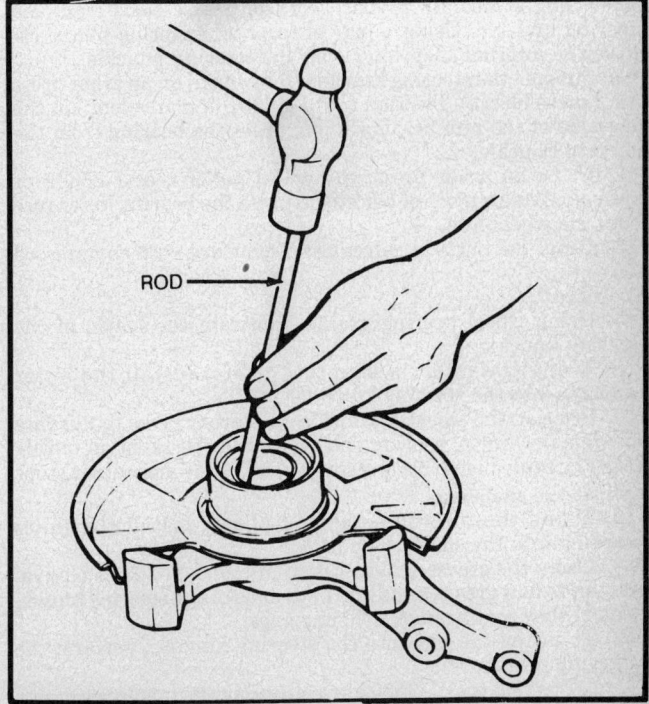

ROD

Remove inner wheel bearing from the steering knuckle—Sprint and Metro

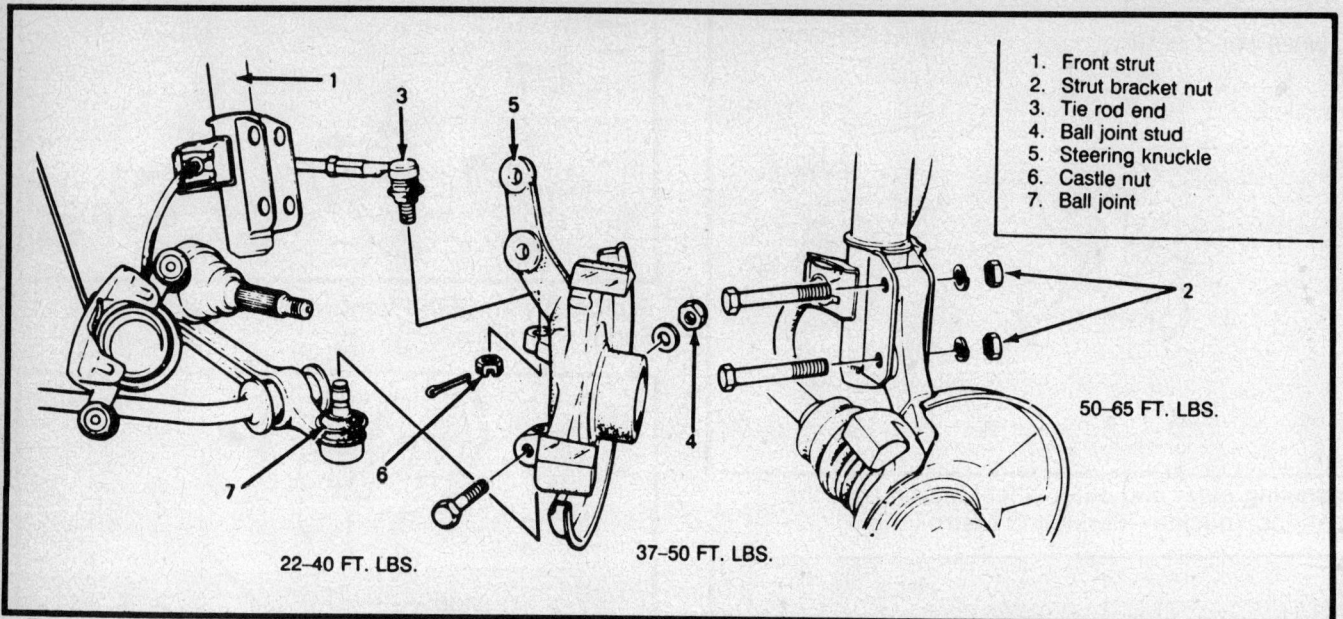

1. Front strut
2. Strut bracket nut
3. Tie rod end
4. Ball joint stud
5. Steering knuckle
6. Castle nut
7. Ball joint

50–65 FT. LBS.

22–40 FT. LBS.

37–50 FT. LBS.

Front steering mounting knuckle—Sprint and Metro

8. Remove the tie rod-to-steering knuckle cotter pin and the nut. Using the ball joint separator tool J–21687–02 or equivalent, press the tie rod ball joint from the steering knuckle.
9. To remove the steering knuckle from the vehicle, perform the following procedures:
   a. Remove the lower ball joint-to-control arm nuts/bolts.

NOTE: Before separating the steering knuckle from the strut, be sure to scribe matchmarks on each component.

   b. Remove the steering knuckle-to-strut nuts/bolts and the steering knuckle from the vehicle.
10. Using a medium prybar, pry the grease seals from the steering knuckle. Using a pair of internal snapring pliers, remove the internal snaprings from the steering knuckle.
11. Support the steering knuckle (face down) on an arbor press (on 2 press blocks). Position tool J–35301 or equivalent, on the rear-side of the hub bearing, then, press the bearing from the steering knuckle.
12. Using an arbor press, the wheel puller tool J–35893 or equivalent and a piece of bar stock, press the bearing inner race from the wheel hub.
13. Clean the parts in solvent and blow dry with compressed air.
To Install:
14. Using wheel bearing grease, lubricate the inside of the steering knuckle.
15. Using the internal snapring pliers, install the outer snapring into the steering knuckle.
16. Position the steering knuckle on a arbor press (outer face down), a new wheel bearing and the bearing installation tool J–35301 or equivalent, then press the bearing inward until it stops against the snapring.
17. Using the internal snapring pliers, install the inner snapring into the steering knuckle.
18. Using the grease seal installation tool J–35303 or equivalent, drive new grease seals into both ends of the steering knuckle until they seat against the snaprings.
19. To install the hub into the steering knuckle, perform the following procedure:
   a. Position tool J–35302 or equivalent, facing upward on a arbor press.
   b. Position the steering knuckle (facing upward) on the

tool J–35302, the wheel hub and a piece of bar stock (on top).
   c. Press the assembly together until the hub bottoms out on the wheel bearing.
20. To install steering knuckle, use new cotter pins and reverse the removal procedures. Lubricate the new bearing seal with wheel bearing grease.
21. On Spectrum, torque the steering knuckle-to-strut bolts to 87 ft. lbs. (118 Nm), the ball joint-to-control arm nuts/bolts to 80 ft. lbs. (108 Nm), caliper-to-steering knuckle bolts to 41 ft. lbs. (55 Nm) and the halfshaft-to-hub nut to 137 ft. lbs. (186 Nm).
22. On Storm, torque steering knuckle nuts and bolts to 115 ft. lbs. (156 Nm), ball joint pinch bolt to 48 ft. lbs. (66 Nm), tie rod-to-steering knuckle nut to 40 ft. lbs. (54 Nm), brake caliper-to-steering knuckle bolts to 72 ft. lbs. (98 Nm) and hub nut to 137 ft. lbs. (186 Nm).
23. Check and/or adjust the front end alignment.

SPRINT AND METRO

1. Raise and support the vehicle safely. Remove the front wheel assembly. Remove the hub from the steering knuckle.
2. Remove the tie rod end cotter pin and nut.
3. Using the ball joint removal tool J–21687–02, remove the ball joint from the steering knuckle.
4. Remove the ball stud bolt from the steering knuckle.
5. Remove the strut-to-steering knuckle bolts.
6. Remove the steering knuckle and support the axleshaft.
7. Using a brass drift, drive the inner and outer wheel bearings from the steering knuckle.
8. Remove the spacer and clean the steering knuckle cavity.
To install:
9. Lubricate the new bearings and the steering knuckle cavity.
10. Using the installation tool J–34856, drive the new bearings, with the internal seals facing outward, into the steering knuckle.
11. Using the seal installation tool J–34881, drive the new seal into the steering knuckle, grease the seal lip.
12. To complete the installation, reverse the removal procedures.
13. Torque the strut-to-steering knuckle bolts to 50–65 ft. lbs. Torque the ball joints-to-steering knuckle nuts to 22–40 ft. lbs.
14. Torque the axleshaft castle nut to 108–195 ft. lbs.

STEERING

Steering Wheel

— CAUTION —

On vehicles equipped with an air bag, the negative battery cable must be disconnected, before working on the system. Failure to do so may result in deployment of the air bag and possible personal injury.

Removal and Installation

NOVA AND PRIZM

1. Disconnect the negative terminal from the battery.
2. Remove the screw from the bottom of the steering wheel pad and pull the pad upward and off the steering wheel.
3. Remove the steering wheel-to-steering column nut. Matchmark the steering wheel-to-steering column relationship.
4. Using a steering wheel puller tool, screw the bolts into both sides of the steering column, turn the puller center bolt to press the steering wheel from the steering shaft.

NOTE: When working on the steering column, be careful not to strike the column in any way, for it is constructed of a collapsible design and will not withstand major shock.

5. To install, align the matchmarks and reverse the removal procedures. Torque the steering wheel-to-steering column nut to 25 ft. lbs.

STORM

1. Disconnect the battery negative cable.
2. Remove the air bag module attaching screws, then the air bag assembly from the vehicle.
3. Remove the steering wheel attaching nut, then using a suitable puller, remove the steering wheel.
4. Disconnect the electrical connectors from the steering wheel, then the rear steering wheel cover.
5. Reverse procedure to install. Torque steering nut to 25 ft. lbs. (34 Nm) and the air bag module attaching screws to 44 inch lbs. (5 Nm).

SPECTRUM

1. Disconnect the negative battery terminal from the battery.
2. Using a suitable tool, remove the shroud screws from the rear-side of the steering wheel (Type 1) or pry the shroud from the steering wheel (Type 2).
3. Disconnect the horn connector and remove the shroud.
4. Remove the nut/washer retaining the steering wheel to the steering shaft.
5. Using a steering wheel puller, remove the steering wheel.
6. To install, reverse the removal procedures.

SPRINT AND METRO

1. Disconnect the negative battery cable.
2. Loosen the pad screws and remove the the pad.
3. Remove the steering wheel nut.
4. Scribe a matchmark line on the steering wheel and the shaft.

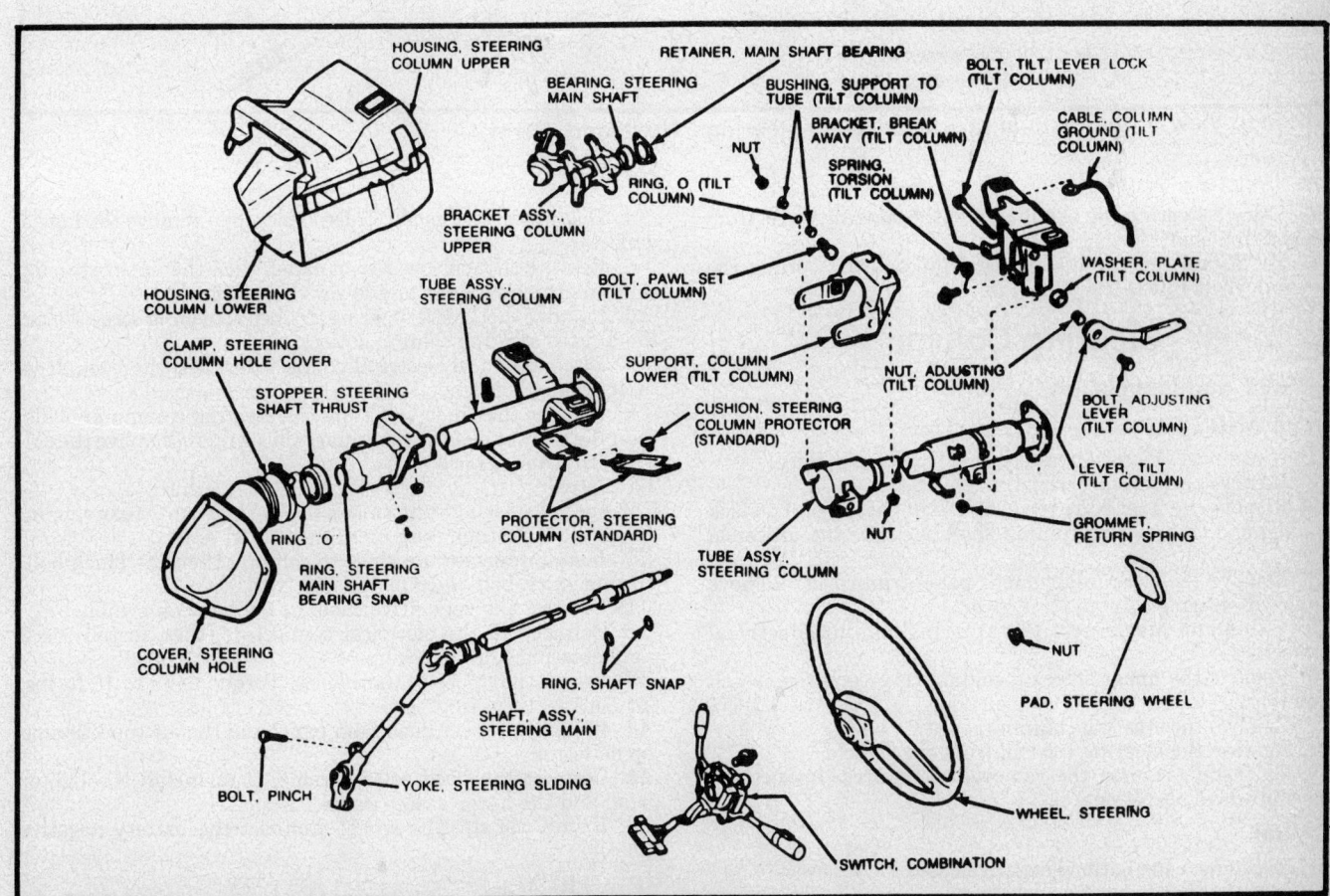

Exploded view of the steering column—Nova and Prizm

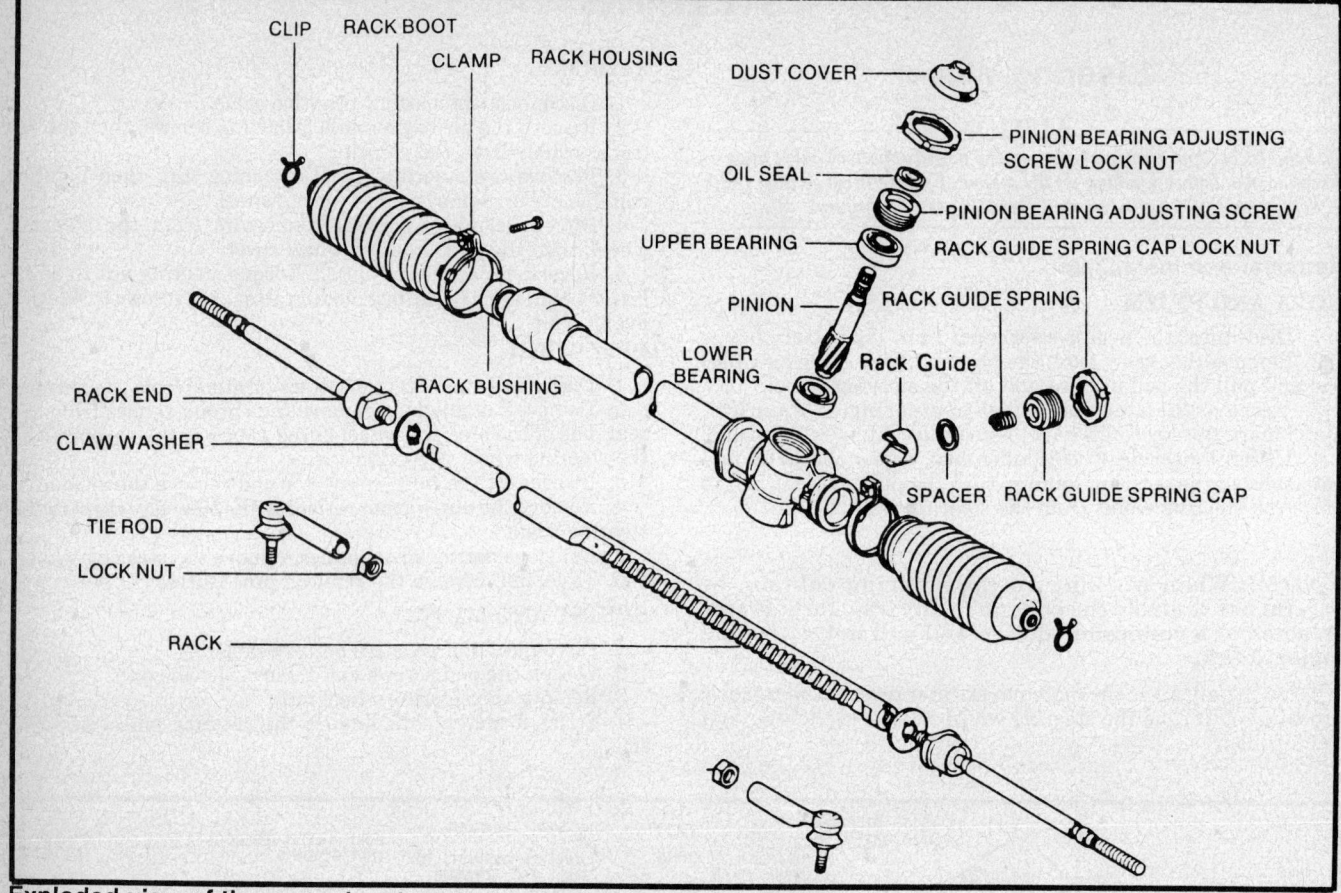

Exploded view of the manual rack and pinion steering—Nova and Prizm

5. Using a steering wheel puller, pull the steering wheel from the steering shaft.

6. To install, reverse the removal procedures. Torque the steering wheel nut to 19–29 ft. lbs.

Steering Column

Removal and Installation

NOVA AND PRIZM

1. Disconnect the negative terminal from the battery.
2. Remove the steering wheel.
3. Remove the 2 set bolts securing the universal joint-to-jack housing and the steering column shaft. Remove the universal joint.
4. Remove the lower instrument panel trim cover. Remove the lower steering column trim cover.
5. Label and disconnect the steering column electrical connectors.
6. Remove the upper steering column cover and the switch assembly.
7. Remove the steering column mounting bolts.
8. Remove the steering column from the vehicle.
9. To install, reverse the removal procedures. Inspect the steering wheel operations.

STORM

1. Disconnect the battery negative cable.
2. Remove the steering wheel.
3. Remove the lower switch panel and the dash lighter panel.

4. Disconnect the hood release cable, then remove the lap air deflector.
5. Remove the left lower trim panel, then the upper steering column attaching bolts and lower the column.
6. Remove the 2 piece steering column attaching screws, then the 2 piece steering column cover.
7. Disconnect the electrical connectors, then the back drive cable from the ignition switch.
8. Remove the pinch bolt from the steering column knuckle, then the 2 lower column mount attaching nuts. Remove the column from the vehicle.

To install:

9. Install steering column assembly, then the 2 rear column mount nuts. Torque nuts to 18 ft. lbs. (24 Nm).
10. Install intermediate shaft to column, then the pinch bolt. Torque pinch bolt to 30 ft. lbs. (40 Nm).
11. Connect the back drive cable to the ignition switch.
12. Connect all the electrical connectors, then install the 2 piece steering column cover.
13. Install the upper column bolts. Torque bolts to 18 ft. lbs. (24 Nm).
14. Install the lower dash trim panel and the air conditioning lap deflector.
15. Connect the hood release cable, then install the lighter panel and the lower switch panel.
16. Install the steering wheel. Connect the battery negative cable.

SPECTRUM

1. Disconnect the negative battery cable.

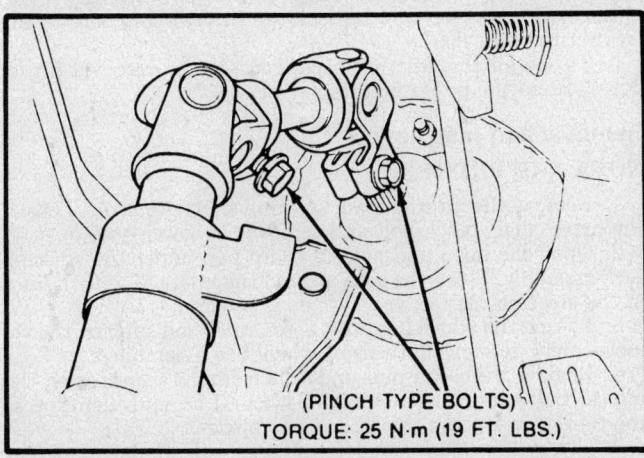

View of the steering column pinch bolts—Spectrum

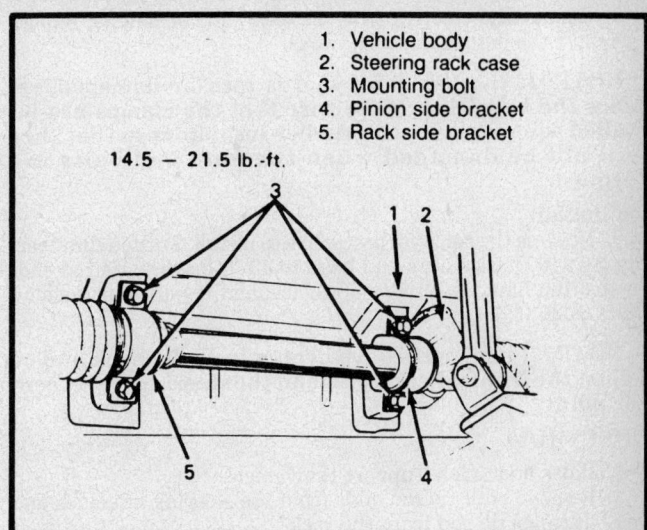

1. Vehicle body
2. Steering rack case
3. Mounting bolt
4. Pinion side bracket
5. Rack side bracket

14.5 — 21.5 lb.-ft.

Rack and pinion steering mounting—Sprint and Metro

2. From under the dash, remove the steering column protector nut, clip and protector.

3. Remove the pinch bolt between the intermediate shaft and the steering shaft.

4. Remove the mounting bracket bolts from the lower column.

5. Remove the steering column-to-instrument panel mounting bolts.

6. Remove the electrical connectors and park lock cable at the ignition switch.

NOTE: If equipped with an automatic transaxle, remove the park lock cable bracket.

7. Remove the steering column assembly.

8. To install, reverse the removal procedures. Torque the steering shaft pinch bolts to 19 ft. lbs.

SPRINT AND METRO

1. Disconnect the negative battery cable. Remove the steering wheel and combination switch.

2. Remove the lower pinch bolt and separate the lower steering column shaft from the steering column. Disconnect and tag the electrical connectors from the steering column.

3. Remove the upper steering column mounting bolts and the column from the dash.

4. To install, reverse the removal procedure. Torque the lower bracket bolts to 8–12 ft. lbs., the upper bracket bolts to 10 ft. lbs. and the steering shaft bolt to 15–22 ft. lbs.

Manual Steering Rack And Pinion

Adjustment

NOVA AND PRIZM

NOTE: To perform the adjustment procedure, the steering rack and pinion assembly should be removed from the vehicle.

1. Remove the steering rack and pinion and place it in a vise.

2. To adjust the pinion bearing turning torque, perform the following procedures:

a. Using the pinion bearing locknut wrench tool No. J–35415 or equivalent, loosen the pinion bearing locknut.

b. Using a torque wrench, pinion spanner wrench tool No. J–35416 or equivalent, and socket tool No. J–35422 or equivalent, adjust the pinion bearing screw torque to 3.2 inch lbs.

c. Loosen the adjusting screw until the turning torque is 2–2.9 inch lbs.

d. Using sealant, coat the pinion locknut threads, then, torque the nut to 83 ft. lbs.

e. Recheck the turning torque, if it is incorrect, repeat this procedure.

3. To adjust the rack guide screw, perform the following procedure:

a. At the rear of the steering rack, loosen the rack guide spring cap locknut.

b. Remove the rack guide adjusting plug.

c. Install the rack guide adjusting plug and count the number of rotations, then, back-off the plug ½ the number of turns.

d. Using a socket wrench and socket tool J–35423 or equivalent, hold the rack guide adjusting plug. Using a torque wrench with a locknut wrench adapter tool J–35692 or equivalent, torque the rack guide locknut to 18 ft. lbs., then, back-off the nut 25 degrees (use a compass to measure the position in degrees).

e. Using a torque wrench and socket tool J–35422 or equivalent, check the pinion shaft preload; it should be 6.9–11.3 inch lbs.

NOTE: If the preload is insufficient, retorque the locknut and back it off 12 degrees, then, recheck the preload.

4. Using sealant, coat the locknut threads and torque the locknut to 51 ft. lbs.

5. To install the steering gear, reverse the removal procedures.

Removal and Installation

NOVA AND PRIZM

1. Disconnect the battery negative cable.

2. Remove the intermediate shaft cover.

3. From the steering gear pinion shaft, loosen the upper pinch bolt, then remove the lower pinch bolt.

4. Loosen the tire and wheel assembly lug nuts.

5. Raise and safely support the vehicle.

6. Remove the tie rod ends, cotter pin and nuts. Using the ball joint remover tool J–24319–01 or equivalent, press the ball joint from the steering knuckle.

7. Remove the steering gear-to-chassis nuts/bolts and brackets, then separate the universal joint from the steering gear and slide the steering gear through the access hole.

8. Inspect the steering gear for wear, and/or damge; replace or repair the damaged parts.

NOTE: If the ball joint seal is torn or damaged, replace the ball joint. Make sure that the clamps are installed squarely over the rubber insulators so that they will not be damaged when the nuts and bolts are torqued.

To install:

9. Reverse the removal procedure to install. Torque the steering gear-to-chassis nuts and bolts to 43 ft. lbs., the tie rod end-to-steering knuckle nuts to 36 ft. lbs. and U-joint pinch clamp bolts to 26 ft. lbs.

NOTE: If new parts have been installed, check and/or adjust the front wheel toe-in and the steering wheel center point.

SPECTRUM

1. Raise and safely support the vehicle.
2. Remove both tie rod ends from the steering knuckles and the left inner tie rod from the rack.
3. Remove tyhe intermediate shaft cover.
4. Loosen the upper pinch bolt and remove the lower pinch bolt at the pinion shaft.
5. Remove the steering gear-to-body attaching nuts and the rack and pinion assembly from the vehicle.
6. Reverse the removal procedure to install.

SPRINT AND SPECTRUM

1. Remove the tie rod ends from the steering knuckles.
2. From under the dash, remove the steering joint cover.
3. Remove the lower steering shaft-to-steering gear clinch bolt and separate the steering shaft from the steering gear.
4. Remove the steering gear mounting bolts, the brackets and the steering gear case from the vehicle.
5. Reverse procedure to intsall. Torque the steering geasr case bolts to 14–22 ft. lbs.; the steering gear-to-steering shaft bolt to 14–22 ft. lbs. and the tie rod end-to-steering knuckle nut to 22–40 ft. lbs.

Power Steering Rack And Pinion

Adjustment

NOVA AND PRIZM

NOTE: To perform the adjustment procedure, the steering rack and pinion assembly should be removed from the vehicle.

1. Remove the steering rack and place it in a vise.
2. To adjust the pinion bearing turning torque, perform the following procedures:
   a. Using the socket wrench and socket tool No. J-35428 or equivalent, loosen the pinion bearing locknut.
   b. Using a socket wrench and socket tool No. J-35428 or equivalent, hold the pinion from turning. Using a torque wrench and socket, torque the lower pinion locknut to 48 ft. lbs.
3. To adjust the rack guide cap, perform the following procedure:
   a. At the rear of the steering gear, loosen the rack guide spring cap locknut.
   b. Using a socket wrench and socket tool No. J-35423 or equivalent, torque the rack guide locknut to 18 ft. lbs., then, back-off the nut 12 degrees, use a compass to measure the position in degrees.
   c. Using a torque wrench and socket tool No. J-35428 or equivalent, check the pinion shaft preload; it should be 7–11 inch lbs.

4. Using sealant, coat the locknut threads and torque the locknut to 33 ft. lbs.
5. To install the steering rack, reverse the removal procedures. Bleed the power steering system.

Removal and Installation

NOVA AND PRIZM

1. Remove the intermediate steering shaft protector. Loosen the upper shaft pinch bolt and remove the lower one.
2. Open the hood and place a drain pan under the steering rack assembly. Clean the area around the inlet and return lines at the steering rack valve.
3. Loosen the wheel lug nuts, then, raise and support the vehicle safely. Remove both front wheel/tire assemblies.
4. Remove the cotter pins and nuts from the tie rod ends. Using the ball joint removal tool J-24319-01 or equivalent, press the tie rod ends from the steering knuckles.
5. Using a floor jack, support the transaxle. Remove the rear center engine mounting member-to-chassis mounting bolts.
6. Remove the rear engine mount-to-mount bracket nut and bolt.
7. Disconnect the pressure and return lines from the steering rack. Remove the steering rack-to-chassis nuts and bolts; raise and lower the rear of the transaxle, as necessary, to gain access to the steering rack-to-chassis nuts and bolts.
8. Remove the steering rack through the access hole.
9. To install, reverse the removal procedures. Torque the steering gear-to-chassis nuts/bolts to 43 ft. lbs., the tie rod end-to-steering knuckle nuts to 36 ft. lbs. and the U-joint pinch clamp bolts to 26 ft. lbs. Add fluid to the pump reservoir and bleed the system.

NOTE: If new parts have been installed, check and/or adjust the front wheel toe-in and the steering wheel center point.

SPECTRUM AND STORM

1. Raise and support the vehicle safely.
2. Remove both tie rod ends from the steering knuckles and the right inner tie rod from the rack.
3. Place a drain pan under the rack assembly and clean around the pressure lines at the rack valve.
4. Cut the plastic retaining straps at the power steering lines and hose.
5. Remove the power steering pump lines, the rack valve and drain the fluid into the pan.
6. Remove the rack and pinion.
7. To install, reverse the removal procedures, add fluid, bleed the system and check the toe-in.

Power Steering Pump

Removal and Installation

NOVA AND PRIZM

Except Twincam Engine

1. Disconnect the negative battery cable.
2. Place a catch pan under the power steering pump. Remove the air cleaner.
3. Remove the return hose clamp, then, disconnect the pressure and return hoses from the pump; drain the power steering fluid into the pan.
4. While pushing downward on the drive belt, to keep the belt from turning, loosen the pump pulley center nut. Remove the pump pulley and Woodruff key; be sure not to loose the key.
5. Remove the pump pivot and adjusting bolts, then, move the pump to reduce the belt tension and remove the drive belt.
6. Remove the pump assembly and bracket.
7. To install, reverse the removal procedures. Torque the

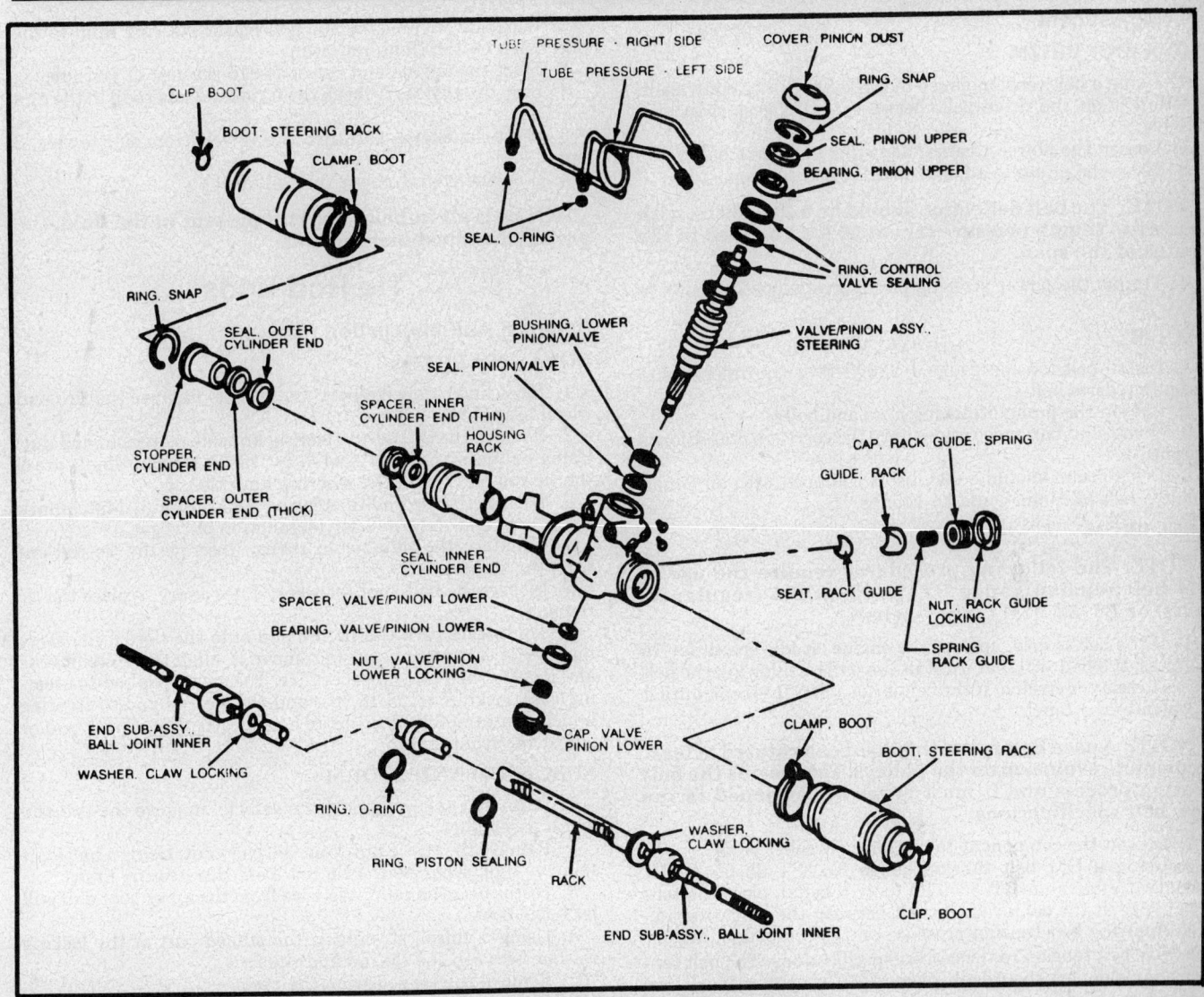

Exploded view of the power rack and pinion steering—Nova and Prizm

pressure hose-to-pump hose to 34 ft. lbs. and the power steering pump adjusting/pivot bolts to 29 ft. lbs. Refill the power steering reservoir with Dexron® II automatic transmission fluid. Bleed the power steering system. Operate the engine, then, check and/or repair the leaks.

NOTE: If replacing the pump, switch the pulley and the mounting nut to the new pump.

Twincam Engine

1. Disconnect the negative battery cable. Remove the air cleaner.
2. Place a catch pan under the power steering pump.
3. From the power steering pump, disconnect the pressure and return hoses.
4. Remove the engine under cover.
5. Push downward of the drive belt to keep the pulley from turning, then, remove the pump pulley set nut. Remove the drive belt.
6. Remove the pump pulley and the Woodruff key; be careful not to loose the key.
7. Remove the upper, lower and pivot bolts.
8. Disconnect the oil pressure switch connector.

9. Remove the power steering pulley, pump-to-bracket bolts and the pump.
10. To install, reverse the removal procedures. Torque the pressure hose-to-pump hose to 33 ft. lbs. and the power steering pump adjusting/pivot bolts to 29 ft. lbs. Refill the power steering reservoir with Dexron® II automatic transmission fluid. Bleed the power steering system. Operate the engine, then, check and/or repair the leaks.

SPECTRUM AND STORM

1. Disconnect the negative battery cable.
2. Place a drain pan below the pump.
3. Remove the pressure hose clamp, pressure hose and return hose. Drain the fluid from the pump and reservoir.
4. Remove the adjusting bolt, pivot bolt and drive belt.
5. Remove the pump assembly.
6. To install, reverse the removal procedures, tighten the pressure hose to 20 ft. lbs. (27 Nm), and the pivot bolt to 15 ft. lbs. (20 Nm), adjust the drive belt, fill the reservoir and bleed the system.

Belt Adjustment
NOVA AND PRIZM

1. Using a belt tension gauge tool BT–33–73F or equivalent, position it on the drive belt, between the longest span of 2 pulleys.
2. Loosen the power steering adjusting and pivot bolts.
3. Move the pump to adjust the drive belt tension.

NOTE: The belt deflection should be 0.31–0.39 in. with moderate thumb pressure (about 20 lbs.) applied in the center of the span.

4. Torque the power steering pump pivot/adjusting bolts to 29 ft. lbs.

STORM

1. Install belt tension gauge J–23600–B or equivalent, onto the pump drive belt.
2. Loosen the pump attaching nuts and bolts.
3. Using a prybar, move pump until the correct belt tension is obtaned.
4. Belt tension should be 90 lbs. If equipped with air conditioning, belt tension should be 145 lbs.

SPECTRUM

NOTE: The following procedures require the use of GM belt tension gauge BT–33–95–ACBN (regular V-belts) or BT–33–97M (poly V-belts).

1. If the belt is cold, operate the engine, at idle speed, for 15 minutes; the belt will seat itself in the pulleys allowing the belt fibers to relax or stretch. If the belt is hot, allow it to cool, until it is warm to the touch.

NOTE: A used belt is one that has been rotated at least 1 complete evolution on the pulleys. This begins the belt seating process and it must never be tensioned to the new belt specifications.

2. Loosen the component-to-mounting bracket bolts.
3. Using a GM belt tension gauge No. BT–33–95–ACBN (standard V-belts) or BT–33–97M (poly V-belts), place the tension gauge at the center of the belt between the longest span.
4. Applying belt tension pressure on the component, adjust the drive belt tension to the correct specifications. The belt tension should deflect about ¼ in. over a 7–10 in. span or ½ in. over a 13–16 in. span.
5. While holding the correct tension on the component, tighten the component-to-mounting bracket bolt.
6. When the belt tension is correct (70–110 inch lbs.), remove the tension gauge.

System Bleeding
NOVA AND PRIZM

1. Raise and support the vehicle safely.
2. The engine must be turned off and the wheels turned all the way to the left. Fill the power steering pump reservoir with Dexron®II to the cold mark.
3. Start the engine and allow it to run at fast idle for 30 seconds. Turn the engine off and recheck the power steering reservoir; if necessary, refill the reservoir to the cold mark.
4. Start the engine and turn the steering wheel from lock-to-lock several times.
5. Repeat the bleeding procedure until all the air is bled from the steering system.
6. After bleeding the system, road test the vehicle to make sure the steering is functioning properly and is free of noise.

SPECTRUM AND STORM

1. Turn the wheels to the extreme left.

2. With the engine stopped, add power steering fluid to the min mark on the fluid indicator.
3. Start the engine and run it for 15 seconds at fast idle.
4. Stop the engine, recheck the fluid level and refill to the min mark.
5. Start the engine and turn the wheels from side to side, 3 times.
6. Stop the engine check the fluid level.

NOTE: If air bubbles are still present in the fluid, the procedures must be repeated.

Tie Rod Ends

Removal And Installation
NOVA AND PRIZM

1. Raise and safely support the vehicle. Remove the tire and wheel assembly.
2. Remove the tie rod-to-steering knuckle cotter pin and nut. Using ball joint remover tool J–24319–01 or equivalent, press the tie rod ends from the steering knuckle.
3. Loosen the tie rod-to-steering rack locknut. Matchmark the tie rod end-to-tie rod for installation purposes.
4. Counting the number of turns, unscrew the tie rod enf from the tie rod.
5. Inspect the ball joint for wear; if necessary, replace the tir rod end.
6. Toi install, turn the tie rod end onto the tierod, the same number of turns necessary to remove it, align the matchmarks and reverse the removal procedure. Torque the tie rod-to-steering rack locknut to 35 ft. lbs. and the tie rod end-to-steering knuckle nut to 36 ft. lbs. Install a new cotter pin. Check and/or adjust the front end toe.

SPECTRUM AND STORM

1. Raise and safely support the vehicle. Remove the tire and wheel assemblies.
2. Remove the castle nut from the ball joint. Using a ball joint removal tool, separate the tie rod from the steering knuckle.
3. Disconnect the retaining wire from the inner boot and pull back the boot.
4. Using a chisel, straighten the staked part of the locking washer between the tie rod and the rack.
5. Remove the tie rod from the rack.
6. Reverse procedure to install.

SPRINT AND METRO

1. Raise and safely support the front of the vehicle on jackstands. Remove the front wheel assembly.
2. Remove the cotter pin and the castle nut from the tie rod end.
3. Using the ball joint removal tool J–21687–02, remove the tie rod end ball joint from the steering knuckle.
4. Loosen the locknut on the tie rod end.
5. Unscrew the tie rod end from the tie rod, count the number of revolutions necessary to remove the tie rod end, for installation purposes.
6. At the steeering gear, remove the boot clamps and pull the boot back over the tie rod.
7. Using a pair of pliers, bend the lockwasher back from the tie rod joint.
8. Using 2 wrenches, hold the steering rack and unscrew the tie rod end. Remove the tie rod and slide the boot from the tie rod.
9. To install, reverse the removal procedure. Torque the tie rod-to-steering rack to 51–72 ft. lbs.; the tie rod end locknut to 26–44 ft. lbs. and the tie rod end to steering knuckle to 22–40 ft. lbs. With the tie rod secured tov the steering gear, bend the lockwasher over the flat spot on the tie rod ball end.

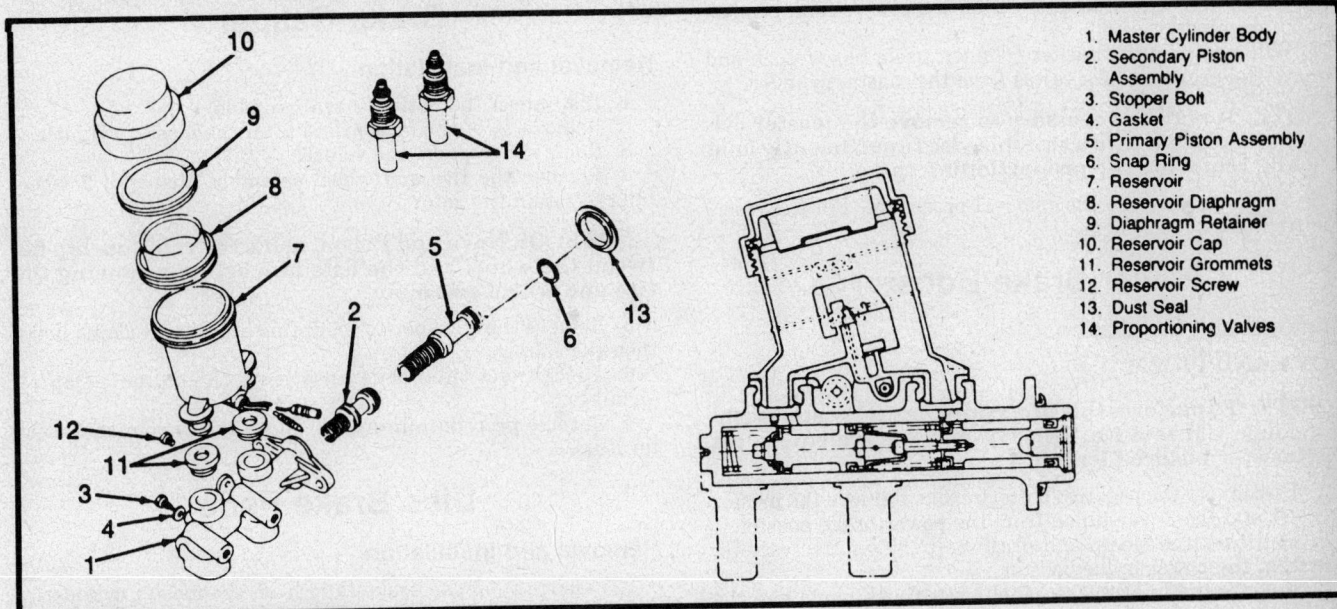

1. Master Cylinder Body
2. Secondary Piston Assembly
3. Stopper Bolt
4. Gasket
5. Primary Piston Assembly
6. Snap Ring
7. Reservoir
8. Reservoir Diaphragm
9. Diaphragm Retainer
10. Reservoir Cap
11. Reservoir Grommets
12. Reservoir Screw
13. Dust Seal
14. Proportioning Valves

Exploded view of the master cylinder assembly—Spectrum

BRAKES

Master Cylinder

Removal and Installation

NOTE: Be careful not to spill brake fluid on the painted surfaces of the vehicle; it will damage the finish.

NOVA AND PRIZM

1. Disconnect the negative battery cable. Using a syringe, remove the brake fluid from the master cylinder.
2. Disconnect the fluid level warning switch connector from the master cylinder.

NOTE: If planning to disassemble the master cylinder, loosen the master cylinder reservoir mounting (or set) bolts.

3. Disconnect the hydraulic lines from the master cylinder and plug the openings.
4. Remove the master cylinder-to-power brake booster nuts and the master cylinder; discard the gasket.
5. To install the master cylinder, use a new gasket, clean out the groove on the lower installation surface, confirm that the UP mark on the master cylinder boot is in the correct position (at the top), adjust the pushrod and reverse the removal procedures.
6. Torque the master cylinder-to-power brake booster nuts to 9 ft. lbs. and the brake lines to 11 ft. lbs.
7. Connect the level warning switch connector. Refill the fluid reservoir and bleed the brake system.
8. Check for fluid leakage and tighten or replace fittings, as necessary.
9. Adjust the pedal height and free-play.

SPECTRUM AND STORM

1. Disconnect the negative battery cable. Remove some brake fluid from the master cylinder with a syringe.

2. On Storm, remove the top of the air cleaner and the air duct.
3. Disconnect and cap or tape the openings of the brake tube.
4. Disconnect the brake fluid level warning switch connector.
5. Remove the 2 nuts securing the master cylinder to the power brake booster.
6. Remove the master cylinder from the power brake booster.
7. To install, reverse the removal procedures, add fluid to the reservoir and bleed the brake system.

SPRINT AND METRO

1. Disconnect the negative battery cable. Clean around the reservoir cap and take some of the fluid out with a syringe.
2. Disconnect and plug the brake tubes from the master cylinder.
3. Remove the mounting nuts and washers.
4. Remove the master cylinder.
5. To install, reverse the removal procedures. Torque the mounting bolts to 8–12 ft. lbs. Bleed the brake system.

Proportioning Valve

Removal and Installation

NOVA AND PRIZM

1. Disconnect and plug the brake lines from the proportioning valve unions.
2. Remove the proportioning valve-to-bulkhead bolts, then the valves.

NOTE: If the proportioning valve is defective, it must be replaced as an assembly; it cannot be rebuilt.

3. To install, reverse the removal procedure. Bleed the brake system and check for leaks.

SPECTRUM AND STORM

1. Clean the area around the reservoir and the brake pipe connections.
2. Remove the brake fluid from the master cylinder reservoir using a syringe.

3. Disconnect the brake pipes from the proportioning valve. Cap all openings.

4. While holding the master cylinder, use a box wrench and remove the proportioning valves from the master cylinder.

NOTE: It may be necessary to remove the master cylinder and place it into a suitable vise to sufficiently hold it while removing the proportioning valves.

5. To install, reverse the removal procedure. Fill the reservoir and bleed the system.

Power Brake Booster

Removal and Installation
NOVA AND PRIZM

NOTE: To perform this procedure, use a booster pushrod gauge GM tool No. J–34873–A or equivalent, to set the booster pushrod length.

1. Disconnect the negative battery cable. Remove the master cylinder and the 3-way union from the power brake booster.
2. Pull back the clamp and disconnect the booster vacuum line from the power brake booster.
3. Remove the instrument panel lower finish panel and the air duct.
4. Remove the brake pedal return spring.
5. Locate the clevis rod at the brake pedal (under the dash), then, pull out the clip and remove the clevis pin.
6. Remove the brake booster-to-cowl, the the booster, bracket and gasket.
7. To adjust the power brake booster pushrod, perform the following procedures:
   a. Using the push rod gauge tool J–34873–A or equivalent, set the short-side on the booster.

NOTE: The head of the pin sits near the end of the booster pushrod.

   b. Check the gap between the head of the tool's pin and the pushrod; it should be 0. If necessary, adjust the pushrod by turning it until the pushrod just touches the pin.
8. To install, reverse the removal procedures. Torque the power brake booster-to-chassis nuts to 9 ft. lbs. Bleed the brake system and check for leaks in the system. Adjust the pedal height and free-play.

SPECTRUM AND STORM

1. Disconnect the negative battery cable.
2. On Storm, remove the top of the air cleaner and the air cleaner duct.
3. Remove the master cylinder.
4. Remove the vacuum hose from the vacuum servo.
5. Remove the clevis pin from the brake pedal.
6. Remove the 4 nuts from the brake assembly under the dash and remove the power booster from the engine compartment.
7. To install, reverse the removal procedures.

SPRINT AND METRO

1. Disconnect the negative battery cable.
2. Remove the master cylinder.
3. Disconnect the pushrod clevis pin from the brake pedal arm.
4. Disconnect the vacuum hose from the brake booster.
5. Remove the mounting nuts from under the dash and the booster.
6. To install, reverse the removal procedures. Torque the booster-to-cowl nuts to 14–20 ft. lbs. Bleed the brake system, if necessary.

Brake Caliper

Removal and Installation

1. Disconnect the battery negative cable.
2. Remove ⅔ of the brake fluid from the master cylinder.
3. Raise and support the vehicle.
4. Remove the tire and wheel assembly. Reinstall 2 wheel nuts to retain the rotor.

NOTE: On Nova and Prizm, mark the relationship between the wheel and the axle hub before removing the tire and wheel assembly.

5. Remove the 2 caliper-to-mounting bracket attaching bolts, then the caliper.
6. Disconnect the brake hose from the caliper. Cap all openings.
7. Reverse procedure to install. Bleed the system and check for leaks.

Disc Brake Pads

Removal and Installation

1. Remove ⅔ of the brake fluid from the master cylinder.
2. Raise and support the vehicle.
3. Mark the relationship between the wheel and the axle hub, then remove the tire and wheel assembly. Reinstall 2 wheel nuts to retain the rotor.
4. Remove the caliper-to-mounting bracket pins and/or bolts. Support the caliper with wire so there is no strain on the brake hose.
5. Using a C-clamp or equivalent, force the piston back into its bore, being careful not to scratch piston and/or bore.
6. Remove the pads from the caliper. If equipped, remove the wear indicators, anti-squeal shims and support plates.
7. Reverse procedure to install.

Brake Rotor

Removal and Installation

1. Remove ⅔ of the brake fluid from the master cylinder.
2. Raise and support the vehicle.
3. Mark the relationship between the wheel and the axle hub, then remove the tire and wheel assembly. Reinstall 2 wheel nuts to retain the rotor.
4. Remove the caliper-to-mounting bracket pins and/or bolts. Support the caliper with wire so there is no strain on the brake hose.
5. Remove the 2 wheel nuts and the rotor.
6. Reverse procedure to install.

Brake Drums

Removal and Installation
NOVA, PRIZM AND STORM

1. Raise and support the vehicle safely.
2. Remove the tire and wheel assembly.
3. Insert a suitable tool through the hole in the backing plate and hold the automatic adjusting lever away from the adjusting bolt.
4. Using another suitable tool, turn the adjusting bolt to reduce the brake shoe adjustment.
5. Remove the brake drum.
6. Reverse procedure to install. Adjust brakes.

SPECTRUM

1. Raise and support the vehicle safely.
2. Remove the tire and wheel assembly.

3. Remove the cotter pin, nut and washer, then the hub and drum.

4. Reverse procedure to install.

SPRINT AND METRO

1. Raise and support the vehicle safely.
2. Remove the tire and wheel assembly.
3. Remove the spindle cap without damaging the sealing portion of the cap.
4. Unfasten the staked portion of the nut using a suitable chisel.
5. Remove the castle nut and washer.
6. Slacken the parking brake cable by loosening its adjusting nuts.
7. Remove the backing plate plug, located on the back side on the backing plate.
8. Insert a suitable tool into the plug until its tip contacts the shoe hold-down and push the spring in the direction of the leading shoe. The allows a greater clearance between the shoes and the drum.
9. Using slide hammer J–2619-01 and drum remover J–34866 or equivalent, remove the drum.
10. Reverse procedure to install.

Brake Shoes

Removal and Installation
NOVA, PRIZM AND STORM

1. Disconnect the battery negative cable.
2. Raise and support the vehicle safely.
3. Remove the brake drums.
4. Remove the return spring, retainers, hold-down springs and pins.
5. Remove the anchor spring, then disconnect the parking brake cable from the parking brake lever.
6. Remove the adjuster spring, then the shoes and adjuster.
7. Reverse procedure to install. Adjust brakes.

SPECTRUM

1. Raise and support the vehicle safely.
2. Remove the brake drums.
3. Remove the return spring and the automatic adjuster spring.
4. Remove the leading shoe holding pin, then the shoe and adjuster.
5. Remove the trailing shoe holding pin, then disconnect the parking brake cable from the lever and remove the trailing shoe. Remove the lever from the shoe.
6. Reverse procedure to install. Adjust brakes.

SPRINT AND METRO

1. Disconnect the battery negative cable.
2. Raise and support the vehicle safely.
3. Remove the brake drum.
4. Remove the brake shoe hold-down spring, then disconnect the parking brake shoe lever and remove the parking brake shoes.
5. Disconnect the bottom return spring, then remove the strut and upper return spring from the shoe.
6. Remove the parking brake shoe lever from the shoe.
7. Reverse procedure to install. Adjust brakes.

Wheel Cylinder

Removal and Installation
NOVA, PRIZM AND STORM

1. Raise and safely support the rear of the vehicle.
2. Remove the rear tire and wheel assembly.

3. Disconnect and plug the brake line at the wheel cylinder to prevent hydraulic fluid from leaking.
4. Remove the brake drums and shoes.
5. Remove the wheel cylinder-to-backing plate attaching bolts, then the wheel cylinder from the vehicle.
6. Reverse procedure to install. Torque the wheel cylinder-to-backing plate bolts to 7 ft. lbs. (10 Nm). Bleed system and adjust brakes.

SPECTRUM

1. Disconnect the battery negative cable.
2. Raise and support the vehicle safely.
3. Remove the brake drums and shoes.
4. Clean the area around the brake pipe, then disconnect the brake pipe from the wheel cylinder. Cap all openings.
5. Remove the 2 wheel cylinder attaching bolts, then the wheel cylinder from the vehicle.
6. Reverse procedure to install. Torque the wheel cylinder attaching bolts to 7 ft. lbs. (10 Nm). Bleed system and adjust brakes.

SPRINT AND METRO

1. Disconnect the battery negative cable.
2. Raise and support the vehicle safely, then remove the tire and wheel assembly.
3. Remove the brake drum and shoes.
4. Remove the bleeder screw from the wheel cylinder.
5. Loosen the brake pipe flare nut, then remove the wheel cylinder attaching bolts. Disconnect the brake pipe from the wheel cylinder. Cap all openings.
6. Reverse procedure to install. Fill the master cylinder with brake fluid and bleed the system.

Parking Brake Cable

Adjustment
NOVA AND PRIZM

1. Release the parking brake (all the way). Using 44 lbs. of pulling pressure, slowly pull the lever upward and count the number of clicks; 4–7 clicks (except twincam engine) or 5–8 (twincam engine).
2. If the number of clicks is incorrect, adjust the parking brake cable by performing the following procedures:
   a. Remove the console box.
   b. At the rear of the parking brake handle, loosen the cable nut, then, turn the adjusting nut.
3. Secure the adjusting nut position when tighten the locknut. Check the adjustment and repeat Steps 2 and 3, if necessary. Tighten the adjusting nut securely and ensure that the adjustment is correct.

SPECTRUM AND STORM

The parking brake adjustment is normal when the lever moves 7–9 notches at 66 lbs. of force on Spectrum and 4–7 notches on Storm. If it is not within limits, adjust the rear brakes. If this adjustment does not affect the specifications, adjust the parking brake turn buckle.

SPRINT AND METRO

1. Remove both door seal plates and the seat belt buckle bolts at the floor.
2. Disconnect the shoulder harness bolts at the floor and the interior, bottom trim panels.
3. Raise the rear seat cushion.
4. Pull up the carpet to gain access to the parking brake lever.
5. Loosen the parking brake cable adjusting nuts.
6. Adjust the parking brake cables, so they work evenly.
7. Adjust the cable, so when the parking brake handle is pulled, its travel is between 5–8 notches, with 44 lbs. of force.
8. After adjustment, reverse the removal procedures.

Removal and Installation

NOVA AND PRIZM

Front Cable

1. Raise and safely support the rear of the vehicle.
2. Fully release the parking brake lever, then remove the front parking cable-to-lever lock and adjusting nuts.
3. Disconnet the front parking brake cable from the equalizer.
4. Reverse procedure to install. Lubricate the cable with suitable grease. Adjust parking brake cable.

Rear Cable(s)

1. Raise and support the rear of the vehicle.
2. Remove the rear tire and wheel assembly.
3. Fully release the parking brake cable. Back-off the front parking brake cable adjusting nut to provide slack on the rear cable(s).
4. Remove the rear brake cable(s)-to-chassis clamp bolts, then disconnect the rear parking brake cable(s) from the equalizer.
5. If equipped with drum brakes, disassemble the rear brake assembly, then disconnect the parking brake cable from the parking brake lever. If equipped with rear disc brakes, disconnect the brake cable from the parking brake crank.

NOTE: If the brake disc sticks, preventing removal, it will be necessary to back-off the self adjusters. This is accomplished through the access hole in the brake disc.

6. Reverse procedure to install. Lubricate the brake cable with a suitable grease. Adjust the parking brake.

SPECTRUM AND STORM

1. Remove the parking brake lever assembly as follows:
    a. Remove the console box.
    b. Disconnet the parking brake switch electrical connector.
    c. Remove the lever-to-chassis bolts, then the lever.
    d. Remove the parking brake lever and switch from the lever.
2. Raise and safely support the vehicle.
3. Remove the parking brake cable as follows:
    a. Separate the front cable from the rear cable.

b. Remove the tension spring from the rear axle housing assembly.
    c. Remove the rear wheel assembly, hub and drum.
    d. Disconnect the parking brake cable from the rear brake lever.
    e. Remove the parking brake cable-to-chassis bolt, then the cable(s) from the vehicle.
4. Reverse procedure to install. Lubricate the cable(s) with a suitable grease. Torque the backplate-to-chassis bolt to 30 ft. lbs. and the lever-to-chassis bolts to 10 ft. lbs. Adjust the parking brake.

SPRINT AND METRO

1. Raise and support the vehicle safely, then remove the tire and wheel assembly.
2. Remove the brake drum.
3. Disconnect the parking cable from the brake shoe lever and the backing plate.
4. Remove the cable(s) from the chassis mounts, then the cable from the vehicle.
5. Reverse procedure to install.

Brake System Bleeding

1. Clean the bleeder screw at each wheel.
2. Start with the wheel farthest from the master cylinder (right rear).
3. Attach a rubber hose to the bleeder screw and place the end in a clear container of brake fluid.
4. Fill the master cylinder with brake fluid. Have an assistant slowly pump up the brake pedal and hold the pressure.
5. Open the bleed screw about $\frac{1}{4}$ turn, press the brake pedal to the floor, close the bleed screw and slowly release the pedal. Continue until no more air bubbles are forced from the cylinder on application of the brake pedal.
6. Repeat procedure on remaining wheel cylinders and calipers, still working from the cylinder/caliper farthest from the master cylinder.

NOTE: Master cylinders equipped with bleed screws may be bled independently. When bleeding the master cylinder, it is necessary to cap 1 reservoir section while bleeding the other to prevent pressure loss through the cap vent hole.

FRONT SUSPENSION

MacPherson Strut

Removal and Installation

NOVA AND PRIZM

1. From inside the engine compartment, remove the strut-to-body nuts.
2. Loosen the tire/wheel assembly lug nuts. Raise and support the front of the vehicle so the jack stands are not under the lower control arms, then remove the tire/wheel assembly.
3. Detach the flexible brake line from the strut clip. Disconnect the brake hose-to-brake pipe connection from the body mount. Using a catch pan, drain the excess brake fluid. Pull the brake hose back through the opening in the strut bracket; cap both open ends of the hydraulic system.
4. Remove the brake caliper-to-steering knuckle bolts. Using a wire, support the caliper out of the way; do not disconnect the brake hose from the caliper.
5. Mark the adjusting cam so the camber adjustment can be restored when the strut is reassembled. Remove the steering knuckle-to-strut bolts, then the strut assemble and the camber adjusting cam from the steering knuckle.

6. Using a cloth, cover the halfshaft boot, to protect it while the strut is removed.
7. Check the strut for cracks, wear, distortion and/or damage; replace the strut, if necessary.
To install:
8. Lubricate the upper strut bearing with multi-purpose grease and reverse the removal procedure to install. Align the strut-to-steering knuckle marks. Torque the steering knuckle-tp-strut bolts to 105 ft. lbs., except twincam engine and 166 ft. lbs., twincam engine, strut-to-body bolts.
9. Lower the vehicle so the strut can be aligned with the body mounting holes.
10. Install and torque the strut-to-body nuts to 23 ft. lbs., except twincam engine and 29 ft. lbs., twincam engine. Lower the vehicle to the ground and torque the lugnuts to 76 ft. lbs.

SPECTRUM AND STORM

1. From in the engine compartment, remove the nuts attaching the strut to the body.
2. Loosen the wheel nuts. Raise and support the vehicle safely.
3. Remove the wheel and tire assembly.

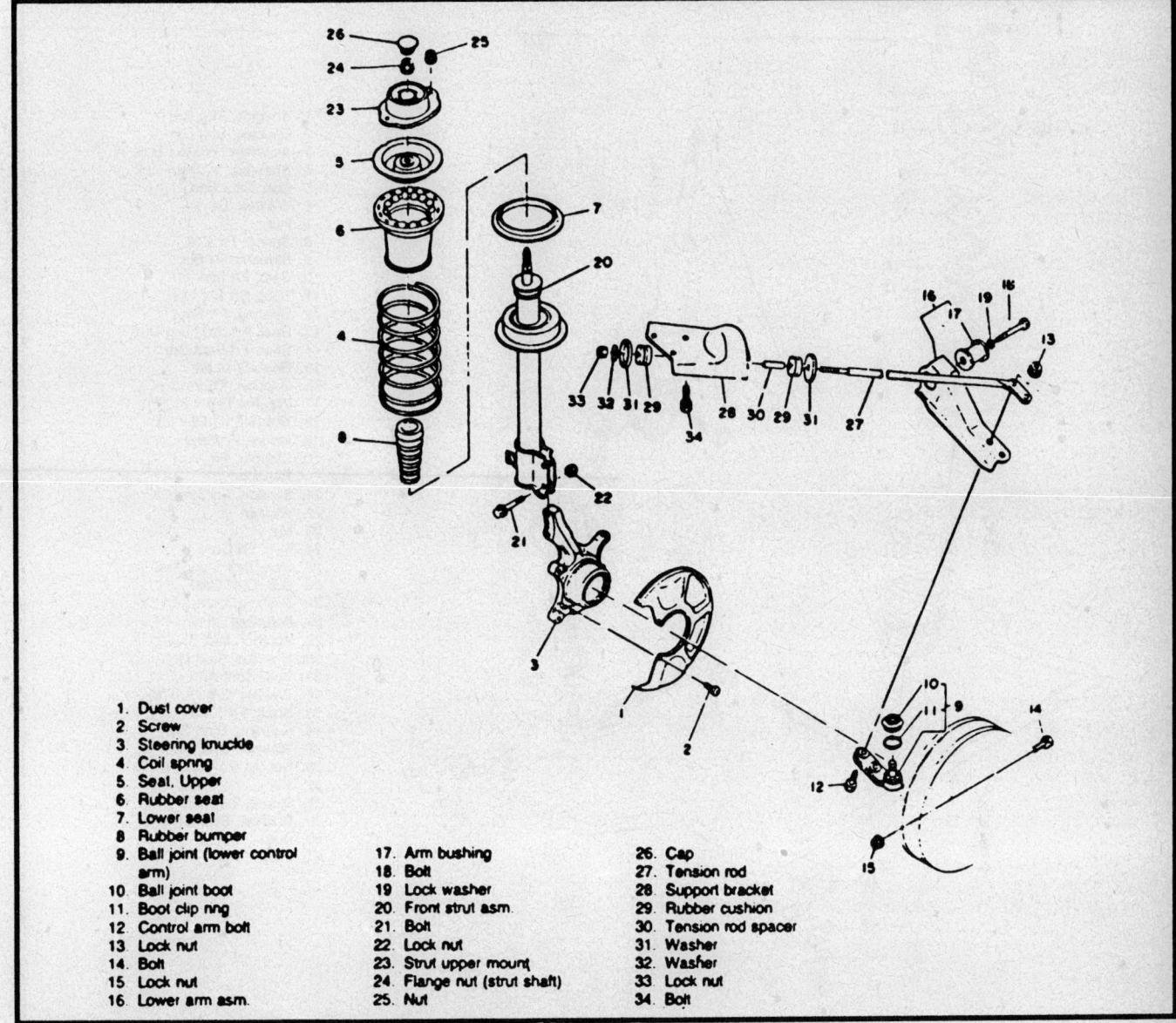

1. Dust cover
2. Screw
3. Steering knuckle
4. Coil spring
5. Seal, Upper
6. Rubber seat
7. Lower seal
8. Rubber bumper
9. Ball joint (lower control arm)
10. Ball joint boot
11. Boot clip ring
12. Control arm bolt
13. Lock nut
14. Bolt
15. Lock nut
16. Lower arm asm.

17. Arm bushing
18. Bolt
19. Lock washer
20. Front strut asm.
21. Bolt
22. Lock nut
23. Strut upper mount
24. Flange nut (strut shaft)
25. Nut

26. Cap
27. Tension rod
28. Support bracket
29. Rubber cushion
30. Tension rod spacer
31. Washer
32. Washer
33. Lock nut
34. Bolt

Exploded view of the front suspension assembly— Spectrum

4. Remove the brake hose clip at the strut bracket.
5. Disconnect the brake hose at the brake caliper. Cap all openings.
6. Pull the brake hose through the opening in the strut bracket.
7. Remove the nuts attaching the strut to the steering knuckle, then the strut assembly from the vehicle.
8. Reverse procedure to install. Torque the strut-to-body nuts to 50 ft. lbs. (69 Nm) and the steering knuckle-to-strut nuts to 116 ft. lbs. (157 Nm).

SPRINT AND METRO

1. Raise and support the vehicle safely.
2. Remove the tire and wheel assembly.
3. Remove the brake hose clip, then the hose from the strut.
4. Remove the upper strut support nuts from the engine compartment.
5. Remove the strut-to-steering knuckle bolts, then the strut assembly from the vehicle.
6. Reverse procedure to install. Torque upper mounting nuts

to 13–20 ft. lbs. and the strut-to-steering knuckle bolts to 50–60 ft. lbs.

Torsion Bars

Removal and Installation

SPECTRUM

1. Raise and support the vehicle safely.
2. If equipped with a stabilizer bar, remove the nuts, bolts and insulators attaching it to the tension rod.
3. Remove the nut and washer attaching the tension rod to the body.
4. Remove the nuts and bolts attaching the tension rod to the control arm, then the tension rod from the vehicle.
5. Reverse procedure to install. Torque tension rod-to-body nuts to 72 ft. lbs. (98 Nm) and the tension rod-to-control arm nuts to 80 ft. lbs. (108 Nm).

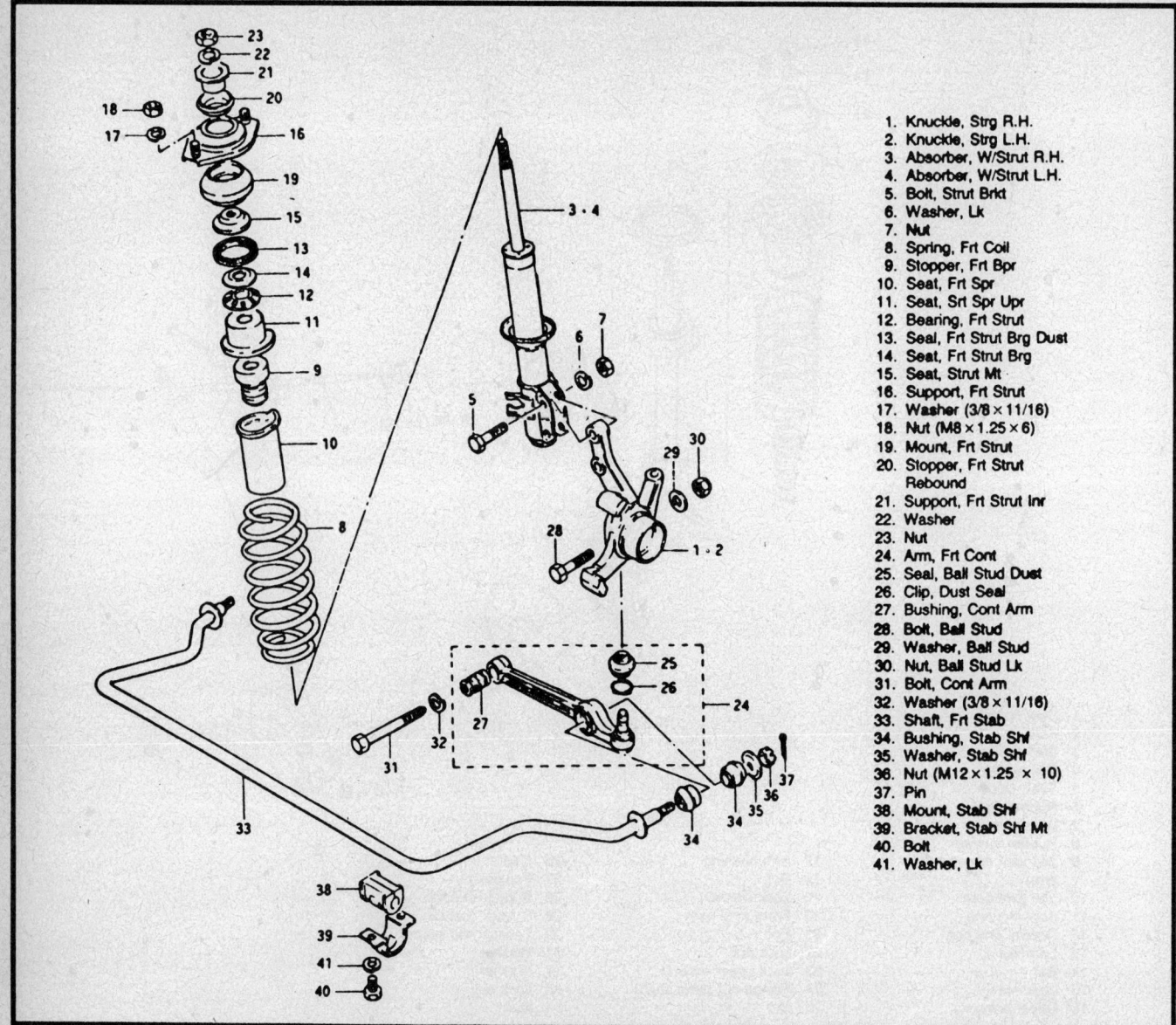

1. Knuckle, Strg R.H.
2. Knuckle, Strg L.H.
3. Absorber, W/Strut R.H.
4. Absorber, W/Strut L.H.
5. Bolt, Strut Brkt
6. Washer, Lk
7. Nut
8. Spring, Frt Coil
9. Stopper, Frt Bpr
10. Seat, Frt Spr
11. Seat, Srt Spr Upr
12. Bearing, Frt Strut
13. Seal, Frt Strut Brg Dust
14. Seat, Frt Strut Brg
15. Seat, Strut Mt
16. Support, Frt Strut
17. Washer (3/8 × 11/16)
18. Nut (M8 × 1.25 × 6)
19. Mount, Frt Strut
20. Stopper, Frt Strut Rebound
21. Support, Frt Strut Inr
22. Washer
23. Nut
24. Arm, Frt Cont
25. Seal, Ball Stud Dust
26. Clip, Dust Seal
27. Bushing, Cont Arm
28. Bolt, Ball Stud
29. Washer, Ball Stud
30. Nut, Ball Stud Lk
31. Bolt, Cont Arm
32. Washer (3/8 × 11/16)
33. Shaft, Frt Stab
34. Bushing, Stab Shf
35. Washer, Stab Shf
36. Nut (M12 × 1.25 × 10)
37. Pin
38. Mount, Stab Shf
39. Bracket, Stab Shf Mt
40. Bolt
41. Washer, Lk

Front suspension—Sprint and Metro

Lower Ball Joints

Inspection

NOVA AND PRIZM

1. Turn the front wheels so they are in a straight ahead position, then chock the rear wheels.

2. Raise and support the front of the vehicle, then place a wooden block approximately 7–8 in. under it. Lower the vehicle onto the block until the spring is compressed to only about half its compression when the vehicle is resting on it.

3. Attempt to move the lower arm up and down. There should be no noticeable play.

4. If the ball joint is removed from the vehicle, check the required rotating torque with an inch lb. torque wrench. Flip the ball joint back and forth several times. Install the nut and turn the stud with a torque wrench at a rate of about 1 turn in 3 seconds. At the fifth turn, measure the required torque; it should

be 9–30 inch lbs. If specifications are not as indicated, replace the ball joint.

SPECTRUM AND STORM

Before removing the ball joint for replacement, check it and the boot for excessive wear or damage.

SPRINT AND METRO

The lower ball is part of the lower control arm. Therefor, if ball joint replacement is necessary, it must be replace as an assembly.

Removal and Installation

NOVA AND PRIZM

1. Loosen the wheel lug nuts, then raise and support the front of the vehicle safely. Remove the tire and wheel assembly.

2. Remove the ball joint-to-lower control arm nuts and bolts.

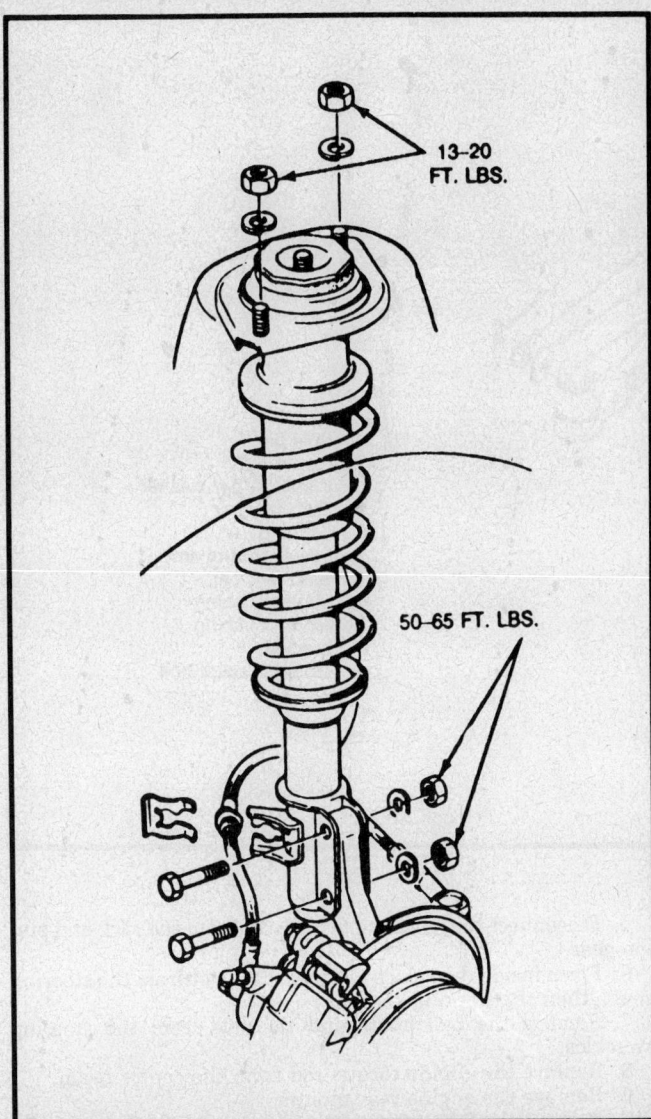

13–20 FT. LBS.

50–65 FT. LBS.

Front suspension strut mounting—Sprint and Metro

3. Remove the ball joint-to-steering knuckle cotter pin and nut.

4. Using ball joint removal tool J–35413 or equivalent, remove the ball joint from the steering knuckle.

5. Reverse procedure to install. Torque ball joint-to-steering knuckle nut to 82 ft. lbs. on Nova and 94 ft. lbs. on Prizm. Torque ball joint-to-lower control arm to nuts and bolts to 57 ft. lbs. on Nova and 105 ft. lbs. on Prizm.

SPECTRUM AND STORM

1. Loosen the wheel nuts.
2. Raise and support the vehicle safely.
3. Remove the tire and wheel assembly.
4. Remove the 2 nuts attaching the ball joint to the tension rod and the control arm assembly.
5. Remove the pinch bolt attaching the ball joint to the steering knuckle, then the ball joint from the vehicle.
6. Reverse procedure to install. On Spectrum, torque the knuckle-to-ball joint nut to 51 ft. lbs. (69 Nm) and the tension rod-to-control arm nuts to 72 ft. lbs. (98 Nm). On Storm, torque the ball joint-to-control arm bolts to 115 ft. lbs. (156 Nm).

Lower Control Arms

Removal and Installation

NOVA

1. Raise and safely support the front of the vehicle.
2. Remove the ball joint-to-lower control arm nuts and bolts.

NOTE: If equipped with a twincam engine, remove the stabilizer bar-to-lower control arm nut, then disconnect the stabilizer bar.

3. Remove the control arm-to-chassis nuts and bolts, then the control arm.

4. Check the control arm for cracks or distortion. Check bushing, replace if necessary.

5. If replacing the lower control arm bushing, remove the nut, retainer and then the bushing.

6. Reverse procedure to install. Torque the control arm bushing nut to 76 ft. lbs., the control arm-to-chassis bolts to 105 ft. lbs. (front) or 72 ft. lbs (rear), then stabilizer bar-to-lower control arm nut to 13 ft. lbs. and the ball joint to lower control arm nuts and bolts to 57 ft. lbs.

PRIZM

1. Raise and support the vehicle safely.
2. Disconnect the right and left lower control arms from the steering knuckles
3. Remove the left and right lower arm rear brackets.
4. Remove the control arm rear bracket-to-crossmember nut and bolt.
5. Remove the crossmember attaching nuts and bolts, then the crossmember with the lower arms.
6. Reverse procedure to install. Torque lower arm bolt to 152 ft. lbs. and the rear bracket-to-crossmember nut to 14 ft. lbs. Check the front end alignment.

STORM

1. Raise and support the vehicle safely.
2. Remove the tire and wheel assembly.
3. Remove the stabilizer bar from the control arm.
4. Remove the ball stud from the steering knuckle.
5. Remove the front bushing-to-body attaching bolt, then the rear bushing-to-crossmember attachijng bolts.
6. Remove the control arm from the vehicle.
7. Reverse procedure to install. Torque the rear bushing-to-crossmember bolt to 51 ft. lbs. (69 Nm); front bushing-to-body attaching bolt to 95 ft. lbs. (129 Nm) and the ball stud-to-knuckle pinch bolt to 46 ft. lbs.

SPECTRUM

1. Raise and safely support the vehicle.
2. Remove the tire and wheel assembly.
3. Remove the control arm-to-tension arm attaching nuts and bolts.
4. Remove the nut and bolt attaching the control arm to the body, then the control arm from the vehicle.
5. Reverse procedure to install.

NOTE: Raise the control arm to a distance of 15 inches from the top of the wheel well to the center of the hub. Rorque the control arm-to-body bolts to 41 ft. lbs. and the control arm-to-tension rod bolts to 80 ft. lbs. This procedure aligns the bushing arm to the body.

SPRINT AND METRO

1. Raise and support the front of the vehicle safely.
2. Remove the front tire and wheel assembly.
3. Remove the cotter pin, castle nut, washer and the bushing from the stabilizer bar.
4. Remove the stabilizer bar-to-body mounting bracket bolts.

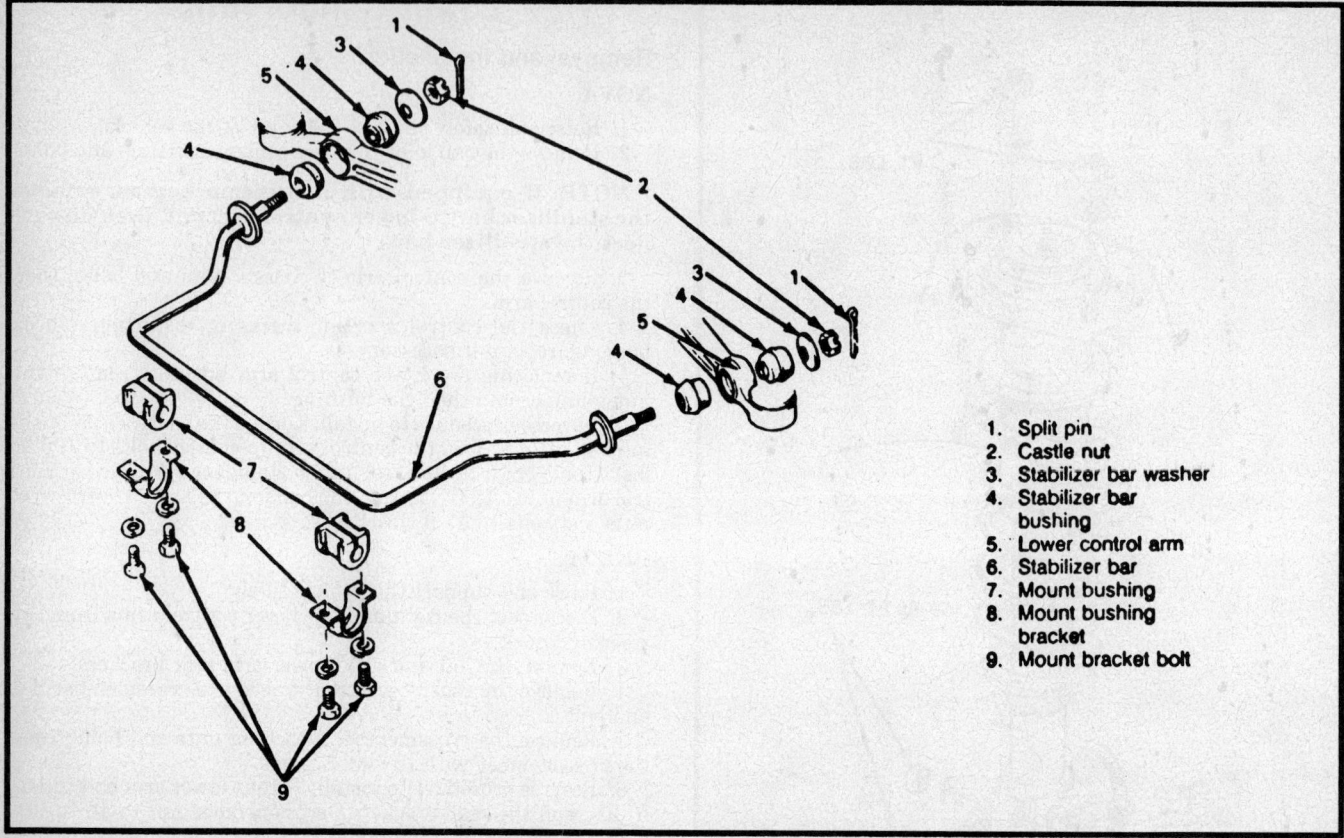

1. Split pin
2. Castle nut
3. Stabilizer bar washer
4. Stabilizer bar bushing
5. Lower control arm
6. Stabilizer bar
7. Mount bushing
8. Mount bushing bracket
9. Mount bracket bolt

Front stabilizer bar mounting—Sprint and Metro

5. Remove the ball studs and the control arm bolts, then the control arm from the vehicle.

6. Reverse procedure to install. Torque the control arm-to-body bolt to 36–50 ft. lbs; ball stud-to-steering knuckle to 36–50 ft. lbs.; stabilizer bar-to-control arm nut to 29–65 ft. lbs. and the stabilizer bar-to-body nuts to 22–39 ft. lbs.

Stabilizer Bar

Removal and Installation

NOVA AND PRIZM

1. Raise and safely support the vehicle.
2. Disconnect the stabilizer-to-lower control arm bolts.
3. Remove the stabilizer bar-to-chassis brackets.
4. Disconnect the exhaust pipe from the exhaust manifold.
5. Remove the stabilizer bar from the vehicle.

NOTE: Never reuse a self locking nut, always use a new one.

6. Reverse procedure to install. Torque the exhaust pipe-to-exhaust manifold bolts to 46 ft. lbs., the stabilizer bar-to-body bolts to 14 ft. lbs. and the stabilizer bar-to-lower control arm bolts to 13 ft. lbs.

STORM

1. Install engine support tool J–28467–A onto the engine.

2. Raise the vehicle, then position suitable jackstands under the suspension supports. Lower the vehicle onto the jackstands, not the control arms.

3. Remove the tire and wheel assemblies.

4. Disconnect the front exhaust pipe from the exhaust manifold.

5. Dsiconnect the power steering lines from the rack and pinion gear.

6. From inside the vehicle, remove the boot from the steering shaft, then the steering shaft.

7. Remove the ball joints and tie rods from the steering knuckles.

8. Remove the engine torque rod from the center beam.

9. Remove the engine rear mount.

10. Remove the 2 bolts from the center beam and the 4 bolts from the crossmember, then the center beam and crossmember assembly with the rack and pinion gear and stabilizer bar.

11. Remove the rack and pinion assembly from the crossmember, then the stabilizer bar from the crossmember.

To install:

12. Install the stabilizer bar and rack and pinion assembly to the crossmember.

13. Install the center beam and crossmember assembly with the rack and pinion gear and stabilizer bar.

14. Install the 2 bolts at the center beam and the 4 bolts at the crossmember.

15. Install the rear engine mount.

16. Install the engine torque rod at the center beam, then the tie rods to the steering knuckle.

17. From inside the vehicle, install the steering shaft and boot.

18. Install the front exhaust pipe, then the tire and wheels.

19. Torque ball joint bolt to 48 ft. lbs. (66 Nm); tie rod-to-knuckle bolt 40 ft. lbs. (54 Nm); rack and pinion-to-crossmember nuts 65 ft. lbs.; stabilizer bar-to-control arm bolts 19 ft. lbs. (26 Nm); stabilizer bar-to-crossmember bolts to 12 ft. lbs. (16 Nm) and the crossmember-to-body bolts to 137 ft. lbs.

20. Lower the vehicle and remove the engine support tool.

SPRINT AND METRO

1. Raise and safely support the vehicle.

2. Remove the tire and wheel assemblies.
3. Remove the stabilizer bar-to-body attaching bolts.
4. Remove the cotter pin, castle nut, washer and bushing, then the stabilizer bar from the lower control arms.

REAR SUSPENSION

Shock Absorbers

Removal and Installation

SPECTRUM

1. Open the trunk and lift off the trim cover, hatch back vehicles only. Remove the upper shock absorber nut and raise and safely support the vehicle.
2. Remove the shock absorber lower attaching bolt.
3. Remove the shock absorber from the vehicle.
4. Reverse procedure to install.

NOTE: When replacing the shock absorber, never reuse the old lower bolt, always use a new one.

SPRINT AND METRO

1. Raise and safely support the vehicle on jackstands.
2. Remove the lower mounting nut, lock washer and the outer washer.
3. Remove the upper mounting bolt, lock washer and nut.
4. Remove the shock absorber from the vehicle.
5. Reverse procedure to install. Torque upper mounting bolt to 33–50 ft. lbs. and the lower mounting nut to 8–12 ft. lbs.

MacPherson Strut

Removal and Installation

NOVA

1. Working inside the rear of the vehicle, remove the rear quarter window garnish molding, back window panel and the speaker grille, if necessary.
2. Raise and safely support the vehicle by placing jackstands under the rear of the vehicle. Remove the tire and wheel assembly.
3. Disconnect the flexible brake hose from the strut. Remove the flexible hose and clip from the mounting point on the strut, then reconnect thew brake line to the flex hose to prevent an excessive amount of brake fluid from draining.

NOTE: Before removing the strut from the hub carrier, be sure to mark the location of the strut to the hub carrier for reinstallation purposes.

4. Remove the strut to hub attaching nuts and bolts, then separate the strut from the hub carrier.
5. Remove the strut-to-chassis nuts, then carefully remove the strut assembly from the vehicle.
6. Reverse procedure to install. Torque the strut-to-chassis nuts to 17 ft. lbs. and the strut to hub carrier nuts and bolts to 105 ft. lbs. Bleed the brake system.

PRIZM

1. On Sedans, remove the seat back side cushion. On Hatchbacks, remove the rear sill side panel.
2. Raise and safely support the vehicle, then place jackstands under the suspension support.
3. Lower the vehicle slightly so the weight rest on the jackstands and not the suspension arms.
4. Remove the tire and wheel assembly.
5. Disconnect the brake line hose and backing plate, then the brake hose from the brake hose bracket.
6. Disconnect the stabilizer bar link from the strut assembly, then the strut assembly mounting nuts and bolts.

5. Reverse procedure to install. Torque stabilizer bar-to-control arm nuts to 29–60 ft. lbs. and the stabilizer bar-to-body bolts to 22–39 ft. lbs.

7. Remove the strut assembly mounting nuts holding the top of the strut support, then the strut assembly from the vehicle.
8. Reverse procedure to install. Torque the strut to body nuts to 29 ft. lbs.; strut assembly to knuckle mounting bolts to 105 ft. lbs. and the stabilizer bar link to the strut assembly to 26 ft. lbs. Bleed the brake system.

STORM

1. Raise and safely support the rear of the vehicle, then place jackstands under the suspension support. Remove the tire and wheel assembly.
2. Lower the vehicle slightly so the weight rest on the jackstands and not the suspension arms.
3. Remove the flexible bake hose clip at the strut and the brake hose from the brake pipe.
4. Disconnect the stabilizer bar link from the strut assembly, then the strut assembly mounting nuts and bolts.

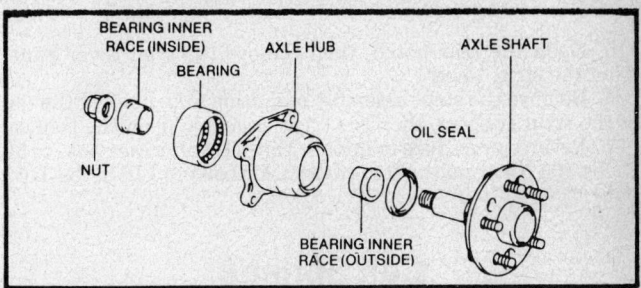

Bearing and oil seal assembly—Nova and Prizm

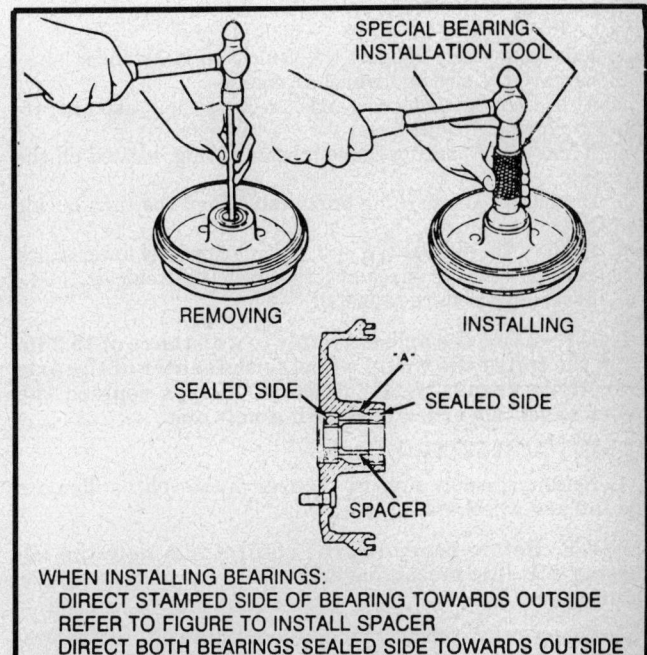

Removing and installing rear wheel bearings indrum—Sprint and Metro

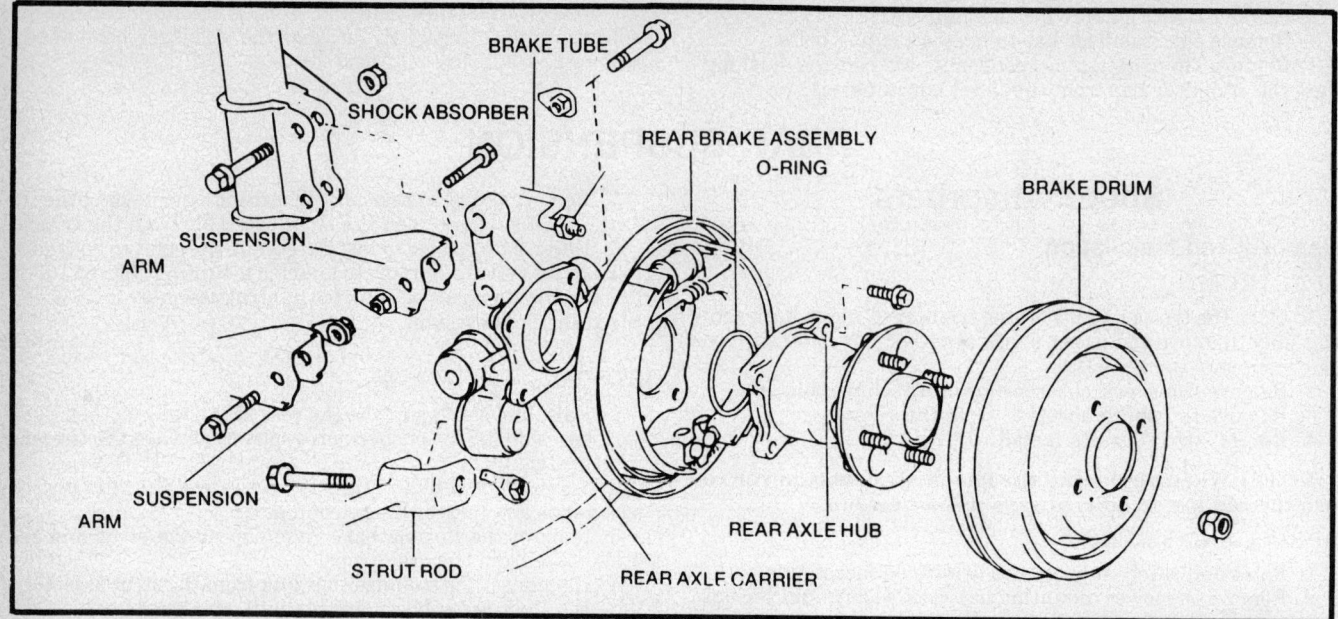

Exploded view of the rear axle hub assembly—Nova and Prizm

5. Open the rear hatch, then remove the trim cover panel from the strut tower.

6. Remove the strut assembly mounting nuts holding the top of the strut support, then the strut assembly from the vehicle.

7. Reverse procedure to install. Torque strut tower nuts to 50 ft. lbs. (68 Nm) and the strut to knuckle bolts to 116 ft. lbs. (157 Nm).

Coil Springs

Removal and Installation

SPECTRUM

1. Raise and safely support the vehicle on jackstands.
2. Remove the tire and wheel assembly.
3. At the center of the rear axle , remove the brake line, retaining clip and flexible hose.
4. Remove the parking brake tension spring, located on the rear axle.
5. Disconnect the parking brake cable from the turn buckle and the cable joint.
6. Support the axle with a jack, then remove the lower shock absorber bolt and the shock absorber from the vehicle.
7. Reverse procedure to install.

NOTE: Raise the axle assembly to a distance of 15.2 in. from the top of the wheel wheel to the center of the axle hub, then torque thew fasteners. Always replace the lower shock absorber bolt with a new one.

SPRINT AND METRO

1. Raise and safely support the rear of the vehicle. Remove the tire and wheel assembly.

NOTE: Before removing the control rod, note the adjusting bolt line matchmarked with A for easy readjustment of the toe.

2. Remove the control rod-to-knuckle nut/bolt, the control rod-to-chassis nut/bolt, then the control rod from the vehicle.
3. Loosen both suspension arm-to-chassis mount nuts and the ssuspension arm-to-knuckle nut. Using a floor jack, position it under the suspension arm to prevent it from lowering.

4. Remove the suspension arm-to-knuckle nut and raise the jack slightly to allow removal of the bolt.
5. Pull the brake drum/backing plate assembly outward to disengage knuckle's lower mount from the suspension arm.
6. Lower the jack and remove the coil spring.
7. Reverse procedure to install. Torque the front suspension arm-to-chasissis nut to 44 ft. lbs. (60 Nm). and the rear to 37 ft. lbs. (50 Nm).
8. Check and/or adjust the toe.

Rear Control Arms

Removal and Installation

NOVA

Front

1. Raise and support the vehicle by placing jackstands under the frame, then remove the rear wheel.
2. If equipped with a twincam engine, remove the rear suspension arm-to-stabilizer bar nut, retainer and cushion.
3. Remove the front suspension arm-to-hub carrier nut/bolt.
4. Remove the front suspension arm to chassis nut/bolt, then the suspension arm from the vehicle.
5. Reverse procedure to install. On twincam, torque the stabilizer bar-to-front suspension arm nut/bolt to 11 ft. lbs.
6. Lower the vehicle, then bounce the vehicle to stabilize the suspension. Torque the front suspension arm bolts to 64 ft. lbs.

Rear

1. Raise and support the vehicle by placing jack stands under the frame, then remove the rear tire and wheel assembly.
2. Remove the rear suspension arm-to-hub carrier nut and bolt.

NOTE: Before removing the rear cam bolt, mark the alignment of the cam bolt for reinstallation purposes.

3. Remove the rear suspension arm-to-chassis cam bolt, then the suspension arm.
4. Reverse procedure to install. Torque rear suspension arm-to-chassis cam bolt to 64 ft. lbs.

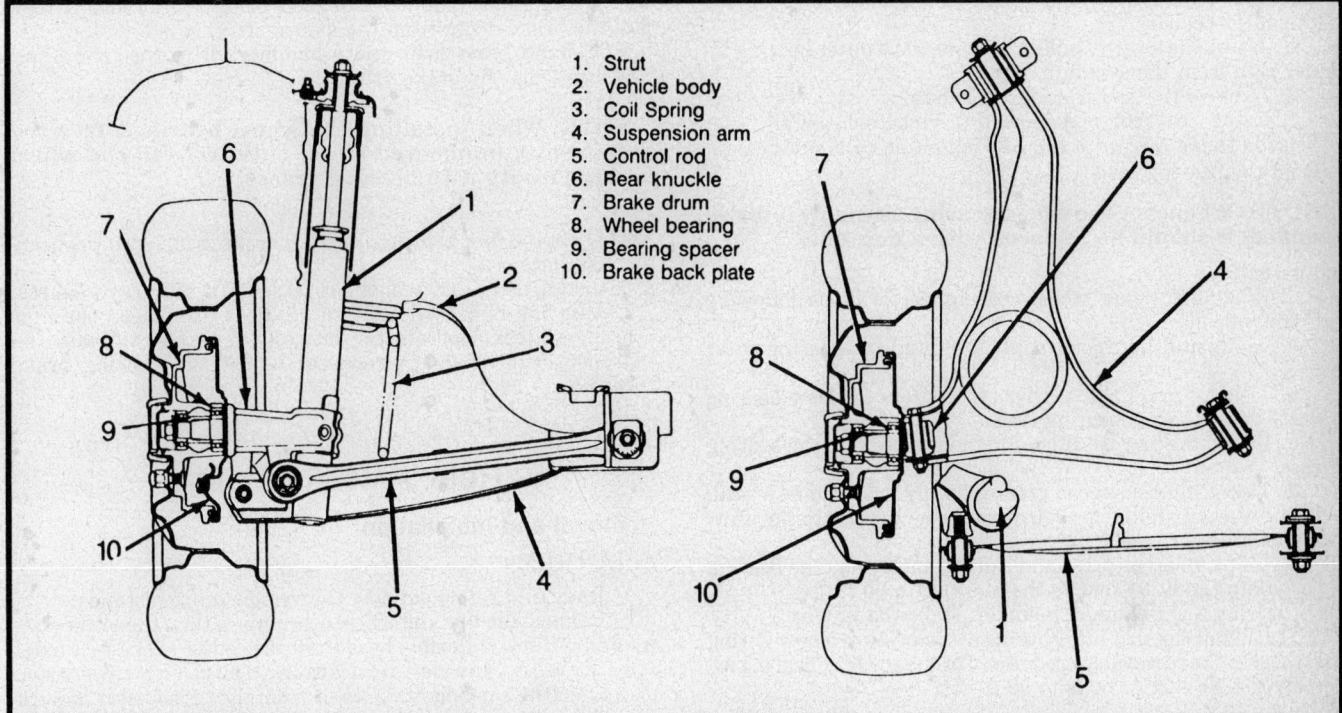

1. Strut
2. Vehicle body
3. Coil Spring
4. Suspension arm
5. Control rod
6. Rear knuckle
7. Brake drum
8. Wheel bearing
9. Bearing spacer
10. Brake back plate

Rear suspension cross section – Metro

PRIZM

1. Raise and safely support the vehicle.
2. Remove the rear suspension arm to body attaching nut, then suspension knuckle bolt.
3. Remove the rear suspension arm to rear knuckle mounting bolts.
4. Remove the rear suspension arm from the vehicle.
5. Reverse procedure to install. Torque suspension arm mounting bolts to 87 ft. lbs.

STORM

1. Raise and safely support the vehicle.
2. Remove the tire and wheel assembly.
3. Remove trailing control arm nuts, then the trailing control arm from the vehicle.
4. Remove the right and left lateral control arms as follows:
   a. Remove the right lateral control arm attaching bolts from the rear crossmember and the rear suspension knuckle, then the right lateral control arm from the vehicle.
   b. Remove the left lateral control arms by loosening the 2 rear crossmember-to-body attaching bolts/nuts, then push crossmember down as far as possible and support with a jack. Remove the bolt from the rear crossmember and rear suspension knuckle, then the left lateral control arms from the vehicle.
5. Reverse procedure to install. Torque all nuts and bolts to 94 ft. lbs. (128 Nm).

SPRINT AND METRO

1. Raise and safely support the rear of the vehicle. Remove the tire and wheel assembly.

NOTE: Before removing the control rod, note the adjusting bolt line matchmarked with A for easy readjustment of the toe.

2. Remove the control rod-to-knuckle nut/bolt, the control rod-to-chassis nut/bolt, then the control rod from the vehicle.
3. Loosen both suspension arm-to-chassis mount nuts and the suspension arm-to-knuckle nut. Using a floor jack, position it under the suspension arm to prevent it from lowering.
4. Remove the suspension arm-to-knuckle nut and raise the jack slightly to allow removal of the bolt.
5. Pull the brake drum/backing plate assembly outward to disengage knuckle's lower mount from the suspension arm.
6. Lower the jack and remove the coil spring.
7. Remove the suspension arm-to-chassis nuts and bolts, then the suspension arm.
8. Reverse procedure to install. Torque the suspension arm to knuckle nut/bolt to 37 ft. lbs. (50 Nm); front suspension arm-to-chassis nut to 44 ft. lbs. (60 Nm) and the rear to 37 ft. lbs. (50 Nm).
9. Check and/or adjust the toe.

Rear Wheel bearings

Removal and Installation

NOVA AND PRIZM

1. Raise and support the vehicle safely.
2. Remove the rear wheel/tire assembly. Remove the brake drum (except twincam engine) or caliper, caliper support and disc (twincam engine).
3. If equipped with a drum brake, disconnect and plug the brake line from the wheel cylinder.
4. Remove the 4 axle hub/bearing assembly-to-carrier bolts and the hub/bearing assembly and drum brake assembly (except twincam engine) or dust cover (twincam). Remove and discard the O-ring.
5. To disassemble the hub/bearing assembly, perform the following procedures:
   a. Using copper or aluminum, cover the vise jaws, then, insert the hub/bearing assembly into the vise.
   b. Using a socket wrench, remove the hub nut from the hub/bearing assembly.
   c. Using a wheel puller tool, press the bearing case from the

axle hub, then, remove the inner race, the inner bearing and the outer bearing.

    d. Using the a wheel puller tool, press the outer bearing inner race from the axle hub.

    e. Remove the seal from the axle hub.

    f. Using an arbor press and a driving tool, install outer bearing inner race onto the bearing outer race and press it from the bearing case.

NOTE: Whenever the wheel bearing assembly is disassembled, it should be replaced with a new one.

To install:

  6. To install the new wheel bearing, perform the following procedures:

    a. Using multi-purpose, apply it around the bearing outer race.

    b. Using a press and a driver tool, press the new bearing outer race into the bearing case.

    c. Install the new bearings and inner races into the bearing case.

    d. Using multi-purpose grease, lightly coat the new seal. Using a seal installation tool, drive the new seal into the bearing case until it seats.

    e. Using an arbor press and a driver tool, press the bearing case onto the hub. Torque the hub nut to 90 ft. lbs.

    f. Using a chisel and a hammer, stake the hub nut.

  7. To install the rear hub/bearing assembly, use a new O-ring and reverse the removal procedures. Torque the hub/bearing assembly-to-axle carrier bolts to 59 ft. lbs.

NOTE: If equipped with drum brakes, reconnect the brake line to the wheel cylinder. Refill the brake master cylinder and bleed the brake system.

SPECTRUM AND STORM

  1. Raise and support the vehicle safely.

  2. Remove the rear wheel assemblies.

  3. Rcmove the hub cap, cotter pin, hub nut, washer and outer bearing.

  4. Remove the hub.

  5. Using a slide hammer puller and attachment, pull the oil seal from the hub. Remove the inner bearing.

  6. Using a brass drift and a hammer, drive both bearing races from the hub.

  7. Clean, inspect and/or replace all parts.

  8. To install, pack the bearings with grease, coat the oil seal lips with grease and reverse the removal procedures. Torque hub nut to 22 ft. lbs.

NOTE: If the cotter pin holes are out of alignment upon reassembly, use a wrench to tighten the nut until the hole in the shaft and a slot of the nut align.

SPRINT AND METRO

  1. Raise and support the vehicle safely.

  2. Remove the wheel assembly.

  3. Remove the dust cap, the cotter pin, the castle nut and the washer.

  4. Loosen the adjusting nuts of the parking brake cable.

  5. Remove the plug from the rear of the backing plate. Insert a suitable tool through the hole, making contact with the shoe hold-down spring, then push the spring to release the parking brake shoe lever.

  6. Using a slide hammer tool and a brake drum remover tool, pull the brake drum from the axle shaft.

  7. Using a brass drift and a hammer, drive the rear wheel bearings from the brake drum.

NOTE: When installing the wheel bearings, face the sealed sides (numbered sides) outward. Fill the wheel bearing cavity with bearing grease.

  8. Drive the new bearings into the brake drum with the bearing installation tool.

  9.To install, use a new seal and reverse the removal procedures. Torque the hub castle nut to 58–86 ft. lbs. Bleed the rear brake system. Operate the brakes 3–5 times to obtain the proper drum-to-shoe clearance. Adjust the parking brake cable.

Rear Axle Assembly

Removal and Installation

SPECTRUM

  1. Raise and safely support the vehicle on jack stands.

  2. Remove the tire and wheel assemblies, then the brake line, retaining clip and flexible hose from the center of the rear axle.

  3. Remove the tension spring from the rear axle, disconnect the parking brake cable from the turn buckle and the cable joint.

  4. Using a suitable jack, support the lower side of the rear axle and remove the lower shock absorber bolt, then the shock absorber from the vehicle.

  5. Carefully lower the jack and remove the coil spring.

  6. Remove the bolts attaching the rear axle to the body, then the rear axle assembly from the vehicle.

  7. Reverse procedure to install. Set rear trim height.

SPRINT AND METRO

  1. Raise and safely support the rear of the vehicle.

  2. Remove the brake drum, then the bake cable clip from the trailing arm bracket.

  3. Disconnect the brake line from the wheel cylinder, then remove the brake line from the bracket on the trailing arm.

  4. Remove the shoe hold-down spring, then disconnect the parking brake cable from the shoe.

  5. Remove the brake shoes.

  6. Remove the parking brake cable attaching clip, then the parking brake cable from the backing plate and trailing arm hole.

  7. Remnove brake backing plate attaching bolts, then the brake backing plate.

  8. Support the axle using a suitable jack, then remove the lateral arm attaching bolts and the lower shock absorber nut.

  9. Lower the rear axle slowly and remove the coil spring.

  10. Remove the trailing arm bolts, then remove the rear axle assembly from the vehicle.

  11. Reverse procedure to install. Torque baking plate bolts to 13.5–20 ft. lbs. (18–28 Nm), trailing arm bolts to 50.5–65 ft. lbs. (70–90 Nm), lateral rod bolts to 32–50 ft. lbs. (45–70 Nm) and shock absorber bolt to 32–50 ft. lbs.

SERIAL NUMBER IDENTIFICATION

Vehicle Identification Plate

There are 2 vehicle identification plates. One is located on the left top of the instrument panel, visible from outside the vehicle. The other is located on the front cowl of the engine compartment.

Engine Number

CB ENGINE

The engine serial number is stamped on the front side of the cylinder head.

HC ENGINE

The engine serial number is stamped on the side wall of the cylinder block at the transaxle side.

Vehicle Identification Number

The Vehicle Identification Number (VIN) can be found on the vehicle identification plates. The VIN is a 17 digit code which identifies the carline, model, year, body type and engine among other things. Character number 8, counting from the left, identifies the type of engine the vehicle is equipped with. A "0" indicates the vehicle is equipped with the the CB EFI, 1.0L 3 cylinder engine. A "2" indicates the vehicle is equipped with the HC EFI, 1.3L 4 cylinder engine.

Chassis Number

The chasis number can be found on the manufacturer's plate which is affixed to the cowl panel inside the engine compartment.

SPECIFICATIONS
ENGINE IDENTIFICATION

Year	Model	Engine Displacement cu. in. (cc/liter)	Engine Series Identification	No. of Cylinders	Engine Type
1988	G100LS	60.6 (993/1.0)	CB-90	3	OHC
1989	G100LS	60.6 (993/1.0)	CB-90	3	OHC
1990–91	G100LS	60.6 (993/1.0)	CB-90	3	OHC
	G102LS	79 (1295/1.3)	HC-E	4	OHC 16V

GENERAL ENGINE SPECIFICATIONS

Year	Model	Engine Displacement cu. in. (cc)	Fuel System Type	Net Horsepower @ rpm	Net Torque @ rpm (ft. lbs.)	Bore × Stroke (in.)	Compression Ratio	Oil Pressure @ 3,000 rpm
1988	G100LS	60.6 (993)	MPFI	53 @ 5200	58 @ 3600	2.99 × 2.87	9.5:1	36–71
1989	G100LS	60.6 (993)	MPFI	53 @ 5200	58 @ 3600	2.99 × 2.87	9.5:1	36–71
1990–91	G100LS	60.6 (993)	MPFI	53 @ 5200	58 @ 3600	2.99 × 2.87	9.5:1	36–71
	G102LS	79 (1295)	MPFI	80 @ 6000	75 @ 4400	2.99 × 2.81	9.5:1	36–71

MPFI—Multi point fuel injection

GASOLINE ENGINE TUNE-UP SPECIFICATIONS

Year	Model	Engine Displacement cu. in. (cc)	Spark Plugs Type	Spark Plugs Gap (in.)	Ignition Timing (deg.) MT	Ignition Timing (deg.) AT	Compression Pressure (psi)	Fuel Pump (psi)	Idle Speed (rpm) MT	Idle Speed (rpm) AT	Valve Clearance In.	Valve Clearance Ex.
1988	G100LS	60.6 (993)	①	0.039–0.043	5③	—	178	37–46	800	—	0.006–0.010⑤	0.006–0.010⑤
1989	G100LS	60.6 (993)	①	0.039–0.043	5③	—	178	37–46	800	—	0.006–0.010⑤	0.006–0.010⑤
1990–91	G100LS	60.6 (993)	①	0.039–0.043	5③	—	178	37–46	800	—	0.006–0.010⑤	0.006–0.010⑤
	G102LS	79 (1295)	②	0.039–0.043	0④	0④	199	37–46	800	850	0.007–0.013⑤	0.010–0.016⑤

① Champion—RN11YC4
Nippondenso—W16EXR-U11
NGK—BPR5EY-11

② Champion—RC9YC4
Nippondenso—K20PR-U11
NGK—BKR6E-11

③ BTDC with T-E, shorted
④ BTDC with sub advance disconnected
⑤ Hot

FIRING ORDERS

NOTE: To avoid confusion, always replace spark plug wires one at a time.

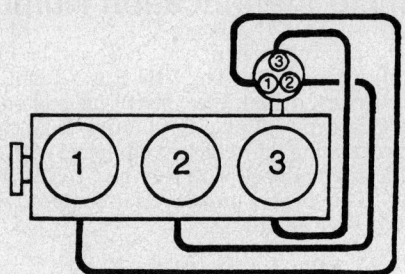

993cc Engine
Engine Firing Order: 1–2–3
Distributor Rotation: Counterclockwise

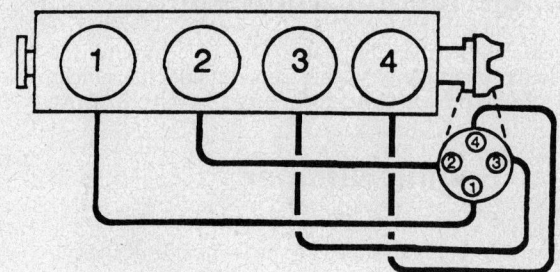

1295cc Engine
Engine Firing Order: 1–3–4–2
Distributor Rotation: Counterclockwise

CAPACITIES

Year	Model	Engine Displacement cu. in. (cc)	Engine Crankcase (qts.) with Filter	without Filter	Transmission (pts.) 4-Spd	5-Spd	Auto.	Drive Axle (pts.)	Fuel Tank (gal.)	Cooling System (qts.)
1988	G100LS	60.6 (993)	3.2	2.8	—	2.9	—	—	10.6	4.1①
1989	G100LS	60.6 (993)	3.2	2.8	—	2.9	—	—	10.6	4.1①
1990–91	G100LS	60.6 (993)	3.2	2.8	—	2.9	—	—	10.6	4.1①
	G102LS	79 (1295)	3.7	3.5	—	2.9	5.3	—	10.6	5.8①

① Including 0.6 for reserve tank

CAMSHAFT SPECIFICATIONS

Year	Engine Displacement cu. in. (cc)	Journal Diameter 1	2	3	4	5	Lobe Lift In.	Ex.	Bearing Clearance	Camshaft End Play
1988	60.6 (993)	1.258–1.259	1.866–1.867	1.906–1.907	—	—	1.574–1.582	1.574–1.582	①	NA
1989	60.6 (993)	1.258–1.259	1.866–1.867	1.906–1.907	—	—	1.574–1.582	1.574–1.582	①	NA
1990–91	60.6 (993)	1.258–1.259	1.866–1.867	1.906–1.907	—	—	1.574–1.582	1.574–1.582	①	NA
	79 (1295)	NA	NA	NA	—	—	1.314–1.322	1.290–1.298	0.0014–0.0029	0.0040–0.0098

NA—Not available
① Front: 0.0016–0.0055
  Center: 0.0035–0.0075
  Rear: 0.0024–0.0063

CRANKSHAFT AND CONNECTING ROD SPECIFICATIONS

All measurements are given in inches.

Year	Engine Displacement cu. in. (cc)	Crankshaft Main Brg. Journal Dia.	Main Brg. Oil Clearance	Shaft End-play	Thrust on No.	Connecting Rod Journal Diameter	Oil Clearance	Side Clearance
1988	60.6 (993)	1.652–1.653	0.0008–0.0017	0.0008–0.0087	3①	1.573–1.576	0.0008–0.0017	0.0059–0.0098
1989	60.6 (993)	1.652–1.653	0.0008–0.0017	0.0008–0.0087	3①	1.573–1.576	0.0008–0.0017	0.0059–0.0098
1990–91	60.6 (993)	1.652–1.653	0.0008–0.0017	0.0008–0.0087	3①	1.573–1.576	0.0008–0.0017	0.0059–0.0098
	79 (1295)	1.968–1.969	0.0010–0.0016	0.0008–0.0086	4①	1.7707–1.7716	0.0008–0.0017	0.006–0.015

① Thrust washers fitted in cylinder block

VALVE SPECIFICATIONS

Year	Engine Displacement cu. in. (cc)	Seat Angle (deg.)	Face Angle (deg.)	Spring Test Pressure (lbs.)	Spring Installed Height (in.)⑤	Stem-to-Guide Clearance (in.) Intake	Exhaust	Stem Diameter (in.) Intake	Exhaust
1988	60.6 (993)	45①	45.5	56.7③	1.705 in.	0.0016–0.0028	0.0018–0.0030	NA	NA
1989	60.6 (993)	45①	45.5	56.7③	1.705 in.	0.0016–0.0028	0.0018–0.0030	NA	NA
1990–91	60.6 (993)	45①	45.5	56.7③	1.705 in.	0.0016–0.0028	0.0018–0.0030	NA	NA
	79 (1295)	45②	45.5	58.2④	1.78–1.81 in.	0.0008–0.0023	0.0010–0.0025	NA	NA

NA—Not available
① Valve contacting angle—45°
 Refacing angle—intake: 20° 45° 60°
 exhaust: 30° 45° 70°
② Valve contacting angle—45°
 Refacing angle—intake: 30° 45° 70°
 exhaust: 20° 45° 70°
③ Installed tension at 1.374 in.
④ Installed tension at 1.50 in.
⑤ Spring free length

PISTON AND RING SPECIFICATIONS

All measurements are given in inches.

Year	Engine Displacement cu. in. (cc)	Piston Clearance	Ring Gap Top Compression	Bottom Compression	Oil Control	Ring Side Clearance Top Compression	Bottom Compression	Oil Control
1988	60.6 (993)	0.0014–0.0022	0.0079–0.0157	0.0079–0.0138	0.0079–0.0315	0.0012–0.0028	0.0008–0.0024	0.0004–0.0012
1989	60.6 (993)	0.0014–0.0022	0.0079–0.0157	0.0079–0.0138	0.0079–0.0315	0.0012–0.0028	0.0008–0.0024	0.0004–0.0012
1990–91	60.6 (993)	0.0014–0.0022	0.0079–0.0157	0.0079–0.0138	0.0079–0.0315	0.0012–0.0028	0.0008–0.0024	0.0004–0.0012
	79 (1295)	0.0018–0.0026	0.011–0.016	0.014–0.020	0.008–0.027	0.0012–0.0027	0.0008–0.0023	NA NA

Not available

TORQUE SPECIFICATIONS

All readings in ft. lbs.

Year	Engine Displacement cu. in. (cc)	Cylinder Head Bolts	Main Bearing Bolts	Rod Bearing Bolts	Crankshaft Pulley Bolts ①	Flywheel Bolts	Manifold Intake	Manifold Exhaust	Spark Plugs
1988	60.6 (993)	39.8–47.0	39.1–47.7	17.4–22.4	65.1–72.0	28.9–36.2	10.8–15.9	121.7–32.5	10.8–15.9
1989	60.6 (993)	39.8–47.0	39.1–47.7	17.4–22.4	65.1–72.0	28.9–36.2	10.8–15.9	121.7–32.5	10.8–15.9
1990–91	60.6 (993)	39.8–47.0	39.1–47.7	17.4–22.4	65.1–72.0	28.9–36.2	10.8–15.9	121.7–32.5	10.8–15.9
	79 (1295)	43.4–49.2	32.5–39.8	25.3–32.5	65.1–72.0	57.9–72.0	10.8–15.9	21.7–32.5	10.8–15.9

① Crankshaft timing belt attaching bolt

BRAKE SPECIFICATIONS

All measurements in inches unless noted.

Year	Model	Lug Nut Torque (ft. lbs.)	Master Cylinder Bore	Brake Disc Minimum Thickness	Brake Disc Maximum Runout	Standard Brake Drum Diameter	Minimum Lining Thickness Front	Minimum Lining Thickness Rear
1988	G100LS	NA	0.81	0.39	0.04	7.126	0.12	0.04
1989	G100LS	NA	0.81	0.39	0.04	7.126	0.12	0.04
1990–91	G100LS	NA	0.81	0.39	0.04	7.126	0.12	0.04
	G102LS	NA	0.81	0.67	0.04	7.913	0.12	0.04

WHEEL ALIGNMENT

Year	Model		Caster Range (deg.)	Caster Preferred Setting (deg.)	Camber Range (deg.)	Camber Preferred Setting (deg.)	Toe-in (in.)	Steering Axis Inclination (deg.)
1988	G100LS	Front	$2^7/_{16}$–$3^7/_{16}$	$2^{15}/_{16}$	0–1	$^{11}/_{32}$	0	12
		Rear			$1^9/_{32}$N–$^3/_{32}$N	$^{11}/_{16}$N	$^1/_4$	
1989	G100LS	Front	$2^7/_{16}$–$3^7/_{16}$	$2^{15}/_{16}$	0–1	$^{11}/_{32}$	0	12
		Rear			$1^9/_{32}$N–$^3/_{32}$N	$^{11}/_{16}$N	$^1/_4$	
1990–91	G100LS	Front	$2^7/_{16}$–$3^7/_{16}$	$2^{15}/_{16}$	0–1	$^{11}/_{32}$	0	12
		Rear			$1^9/_{32}$N–$^3/_{32}$N	$^{11}/_{16}$N	$^1/_4$	
	G102LS	Front	$2^7/_{16}$–$3^7/_{16}$	$2^{15}/_{16}$	0–1	$^{11}/_{32}$	0	12
		Rear			$1^9/_{32}$N–$^3/_{32}$N	$^{11}/_{16}$N	$^1/_4$	

ENGINE ELECTRICAL

NOTE: Disconnecting the negative battery cable on some vehicles may interfere with the functions of the on board computer systems and may require the computer to undergo a relearning process, once the negative battery cable is reconnected.

Distributor

Removal

1.0L ENGINE

1. Disconnect the negative battery cable.
2. Disconnect the spark plug and coil wires from the distributor cap.
3. Disconnect the distributor connector.
4. Remove the distributor set bolt.
5. Pull out the distributor from the distributor housing.
6. Remove the O-ring from the distributor housing and discard.

1.3L ENGINE

1. Disconnect the negative battery cable.
2. Disconnect the spark plug wire from the distributor cap.
3. Disconnect the distributor connector.

4. Disconnect the vacuum advance hoses.

NOTE: Tag the hoses prior to disconnecting so they can be reinstalled in their original positions.

5. Remove the distributor set bolt.
6. Pull out the distributor from the cylinder head.

NOTE: Insert a suitable cloth under the distributor opening to catch the oil.

7. Remove O-ring from the distributor housing and discard.

Installation
TIMING NOT DISTURBED

1.0L Engine

1. Install a new O-ring to the distributor.
2. Remove the distributor cap.
3. Position the distributor shaft so the drilled mark at the forward end of the distributor drive gear is aligned with the drilled mark on the distributor body.
4. Insert the distributor assembly into the distributor housing so the split line of the distributor body is aligned with the embossed line of the distributor housing.
5. Temporarily tighten the distributor attaching bolt.
6. Install the distributor cap.
7. Connect distributor connector.
8. Connect spark plug wires.
9. Connect negative battery cable.
10. Start engine and allow to come to normal operating temperature. Check timing.
11. Check idle speed. Tighten distributor attaching bolt.

1.3L Engine

1. Align the cut-out section of the distributor housing with the cut-out section of the coupling.
2. Install the distributor. Ensure that the distributor attaching bolt holes in the cylinder head are in the center of the elongated holes in the base of the distributor housing.
3. Tighten the distributor attaching bolts temporarily.
4. Connect the vacuum advance hoses.
5. Connect the distributor connector and install it to the clamp.
6. Connect the spark plug wires.
7. Install the clamp to spark plug wire.
8. Connect negative battery cable.
9. Start engine and allow to come to normal operating temperature. Check timing.

TIMING DISTURBED

1.0L Engine

1. Remove the oil filler cap.
2. Observe the cam lobes of No. 1 cylinder through the oil fill hole while rotating the engine in the direction of normal rotation until the lobes are on their base circles (valves closed) indicating that cylinder No. 1 is on its compression stroke. Confirm that No. 1 cylinder is on its compression stroke by feeling for play in rocker arms with fingers.
3. Continue rotating engine in direction of normal rotation until timing marks are aligned.
4. Install a new O-ring to the distributor.
5. Remove the distributor cap.
6. Position the distributor shaft so the drilled mark at the forward end of the distributor drive gear is aligned with the drilled mark on the distributor body.
7. Insert the distributor assembly into the distributor housing so the split line of the distributor body is aligned with the embossed line of the distributor housing.
8. Temporarily tighten the distributor attaching bolt.
9. Install the distributor cap.

10. Connect distributor connector.
11. Connect spark plug wires.
12 Connect negative battery cable.
13. Start engine and allow to come to normal operating temperature. Check timing.
14. Check idle speed. Tighten distributor attaching bolt.

1.3L Engine

1. Remove the oil filler cap.
2. Observe the cam lobes of No. 1 cylinder through the oil fill hole while rotating the engine in the direction of normal rotation until the lobes are on their base circles (valves closed) indicating that cylinder No. 1 is on its compression stroke. Confirm that No. 1 cylinder is on its compression stroke by feeling for play in rocker arms with fingers. Reinstall oil filler cap.
3. Continue rotating engine in direction of normal rotation until timing marks are aligned.
4. Align the cut-out section of the distributor housing with the cut-out section of the coupling.
5. Install the distributor. Ensure that the distributor attaching bolt holes in the cylinder head are centered in the elongated holes in the base of the distributor housing.
6. Tighten the distributor attaching bolts temporarily.
7. Connect the vacuum advance hoses.
8. Connect the distributor connector and install it to the clamp.
9. Connect the spark plug wires.
10. Install the clamp to spark plug wire.
11. Connect negative battery cable.
12. Start engine and allow to come to normal operating temperature. Check timing.

Ignition Timing

Adjustment
1.0L ENGINE

1. Connect positive lead of timing light to positive battery terminal and negative lead of timing light to a solid engine ground. Clamp timing light inductive pick-up to No. 1 spark plug wire (at timing belt end of engine).
2. Connect tachometer positive lead to negative terminal on ignition coil and tachometer negative lead to a solid engine ground.

NOTE: If the tachometer does not have a 3 cylinder setting, set the tachometer to the 6 cylinder range and multiply the reading by 2.

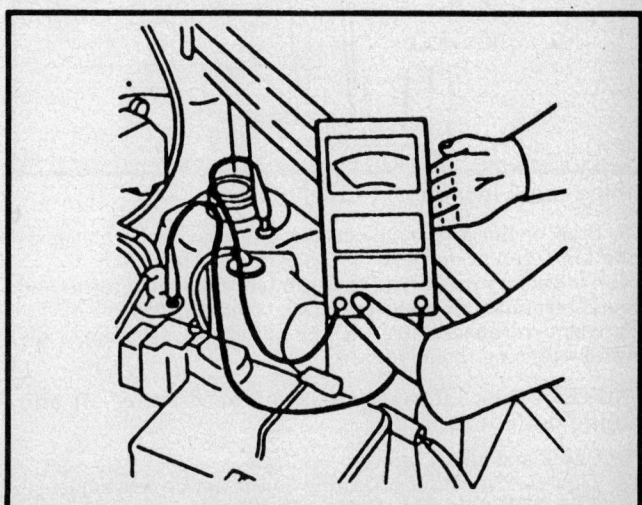

Tachometer lead connection – 1.0L engine

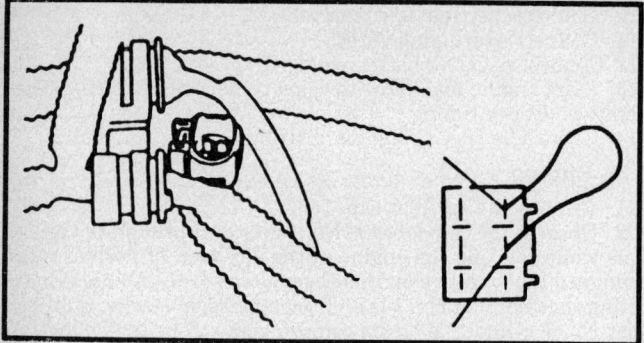

Connect jumper lead to check connector—1.0L engine

Idle speed setting—1.0L engine

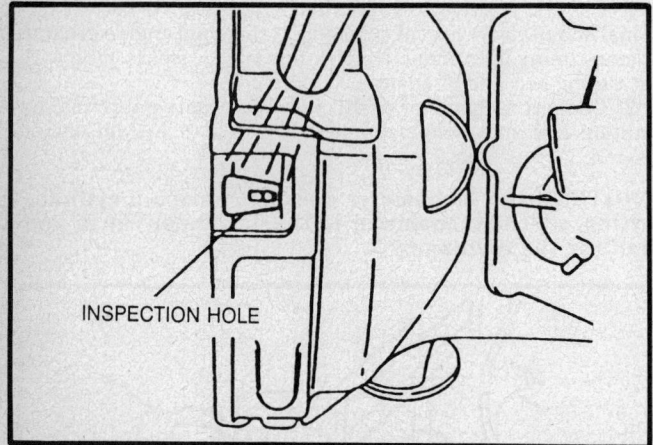

INSPECTION HOLE

Timing mark location—1.0L engine

3. Start engine and let idle until engine reaches normal operating temperature and cooling fan cycles on and off.

4. Connect a jumper wire between terminals 11 (brown) and ground terminal (black) of the check connector.

5. Remove rubber cap from the throttle body. Adjust idle speed by turning the idle screw.

NOTE: Check idle speed with all accessories off and cooling fan not running.

6. Check and adjust ignition timing.
7. Tighten distributor attaching bolt if timing was adjusted.
8. Recheck timing after tightening bolt.
9. Remove jumper wire from the check connector.

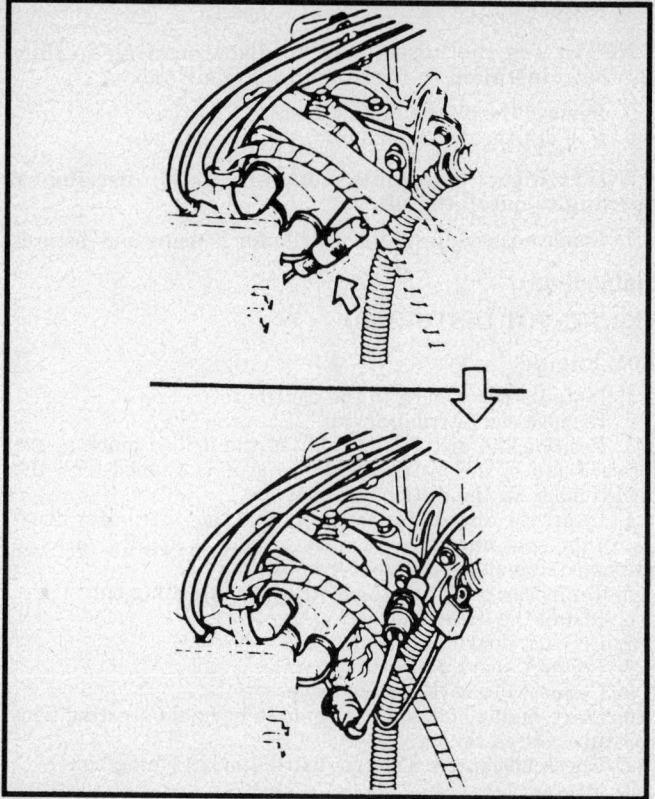

Distributor connector adapter installation—1.3L engine

10. Install cap to the check connector.
11. Check and readjust engine idle speed.
12. Install the rubber cap to the throttle body.
13. Disconnect timing light and tachometer.

1.3L ENGINE

1. Connect positive lead of timing light to positive battery terminal and negative lead of timing light to a solid engine ground. Clamp timing light inductive pick-up to No. 1 spark plug wire (at timing belt end of engine).

2. Connect adapter wire to distributor connector. Connect tachometer positive lead to distributor connector adapter and tachometer negative lead to a solid engine ground.

3. Disconnect and plug the vacuum advance hose.
4. Ensure engine idle speed is under 1000 rpm.
5. Check and adjust ignition timing.
6. Reconnect the vacuum hose to the distributor.
7. Check and readjust engine idle speed.
8. Disconnect timing light and tachometer. Remove distributor connector adapter and connect distributor connector.

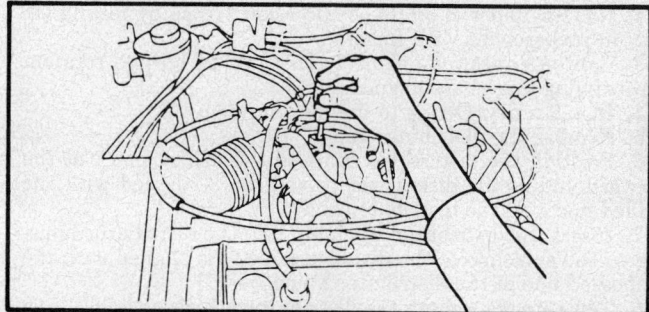

Idle speed setting—1.3L engine

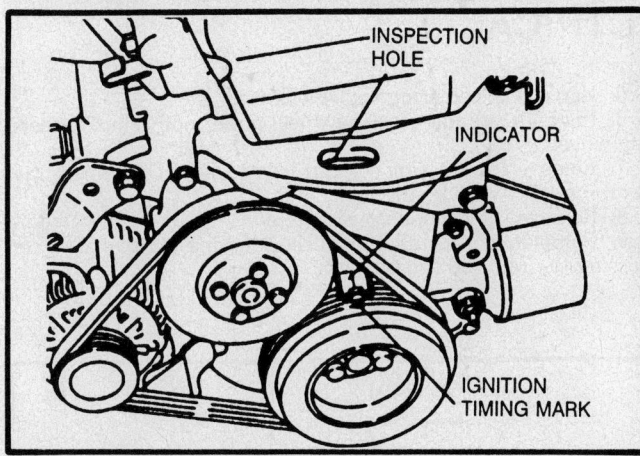

INSPECTION HOLE

INDICATOR

IGNITION TIMING MARK

Timing mark location — 1.3L engine

Alternator

Precautions

Several precautions must be observed with alternator equipped vehicles to avoid damage to the unit.
• If the battery is removed for any reason, make sure it is reconnected with the correct polarity. Reversing the battery connections may result in damage to the one-way rectifiers.
• When utilizing a booster battery as a starting aid, always connect the positive to positive terminals and the negative terminal from the booster battery to a good engine ground on the vehicle being started.
• Never use a fast charger as a booster to start vehicles.
• Disconnect the battery cables when charging the battery with a fast charger.
• Never attempt to polarize the alternator.
• Do not use test lamps of more than 12 volts when checking diode continuity.
• Do not short across or ground any of the alternator terminals.
• The polarity of the battery, alternator and regulator must be matched and considered before making any electrical connections within the system.
• Never separate the alternator on an open circuit. Make sure all connections within the circuit are clean and tight.
• Disconnect the battery ground terminal when performing any service on electrical components.
• Disconnect the battery if arc welding is to be done on the vehicle.

Belt Tension Adjustment

1. Disconnect the negative battery cable.
2. Check tension of the alternator belt by applying 22 lbs. (10 kg) of pressure to the belt at the midpoint between the alterna-

tor and water pump pulleys. Deflection should not exceed 0.163–0.204 in. (4.0–5.0mm) for a new belt and 0.204–0.245 in. (5.0–6.0mm) for a used belt.
3. To adjust, loosen alternator mounting bolts and adjuster locknut.
4. Adjust belt tension, as necessary.
5. Tighten adjuster locknut and mounting bolts.
6. Connect negative battery cable.

Removal and Installation
1.0L ENGINE

1. Disconnect the negative battery cable.
2. Remove alternator connector cover plate and disconnect the connector.
3. Remove the nut and wires from the alternator.
4. Remove alternator drive belt.
5. Remove right rear engine undercover.
6. Remove alternator mounting and lock bolts and remove alternator from the underside of the vehicle.
7. Complete the installation of the alternator by reversing the removal procedure.

1.3L ENGINE

1. Disconnect the negative battery cable.
2. Disconnect the alternator wire from terminal B. Disconnect the alternator connector.
3. Remove the accessory drive belts.
4. Remove the alternator locking plate. Loosen the attaching and adjusting bolts. Remove the alternator.
5. Remove the engine under rear cover. Remove the alternaor attaching bolts. Remove the alternator from the engine compartment.
6. Complete the installation of the alternator by reversing the removal procedure.

Starter

Removal and Installation
1.0L ENGINE

1. Disconnect the negative battery cable.
2. Disconnect the wires from the starter.
3. Remove the 2 starter retaining bolts and remove the starter.
4. Complete the installation of the starter by reversing the removal procedure.

1.3L ENGINE

1. Disconnect the negative battery cable.
2. Raise and safely support the vehicle.
3. Remove the crossmember.
4. Disconnect the wires from the starter.
5. Remove the starter motor attaching bolts.
6. Remove the starter from the vehicle.
7. Complete the installation of the starter by reversing the removal procedure.

CHASSIS ELECTRICAL

Heater Blower Motor

Removal and Installation

1. Disconnect the negative battery cable.
2. Remove the glove box door assembly.
3. Remove glove box/instrument panel reinforcement.
4. Remove glove box trim piece.
5. Remove blower motor connector and 3 blower motor retaining screws.
6. Remove blower motor.
7. Complete the installation of the blower motor by reversing the removal procedure.

Windshield Wiper Motor

Removal and Installation
FRONT MOTOR

1. Disconnect the negative battery cable.
2. Remove the front wiper arm covers and wiper arm retaining nuts. Remove wiper arm and blade assemblies.
3. Remove the cowl top ventilator louver.
4. Remove the hood-to-cowl top seal.
5. Disconnect the wiper motor connector.
6. Remove the set bolt.
7. Disconnect the motor from the link. Remove the motor.
8. Complete the installation of the front wiper motor by reversing the removal procedure.

REAR MOTOR

1. Disconnect the negative battery cable.
2. Remove the wiper arm cover.
3. Remove the wiper arm and blade by removing the nut.
4. Remove the wiper link cap.
5. Remove the washer and wiper link packing by removing the hexagonal nut.
6. Open the back door. Remove back door trim board by pushing the center section of the clip and detaching.
7. Disconnect the connector. Remove the rear wiper motor assembly.
8. Complete the installation of the rear wiper motor by reversing the removal procedure.

Instrument Cluster

Removal and Installation

1. Disconnect the negative battery cable.
2. Remove the finish panel sub-assembly from the instrument panel.
3. Disconnect the speedometer cable.
4. Disconnect electrical connectors from the instrument panel.
5. Remove the combination meter assembly from the instrument panel.
6. Remove speedometer assembly from instrument panel.
7. Complete the installation of the speedometer and instrument panel by reversing the removal procedure.

Combination Switch

Removal and Installation

1. Disconnect the negative battery cable.
2. Remove 2 screws retaining the steering wheel pad.
3. Remove the steering wheel pad by pushing it upward.
4. Disconnect the horn switch connector.

5. Remove the steering wheel locknut.
6. Install a suitable steering wheel puller and remove steering wheel.
7. Remove the steering column lower cover. Disconnect the combination switch connector.
8. Remove the combination switch.
9. Complete the installation of the combination switch by reversing the removal procedure.

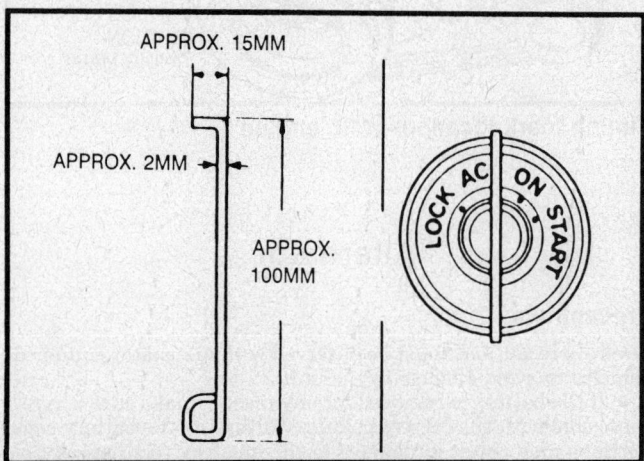

Special tool for removing ignition key cylinder

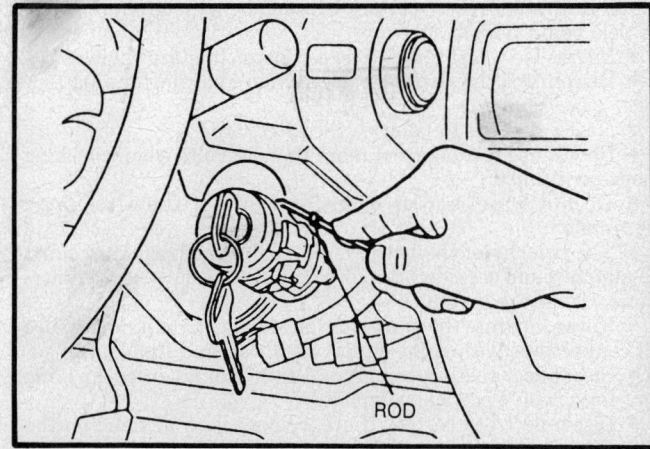

Removal of ignition key cylinder

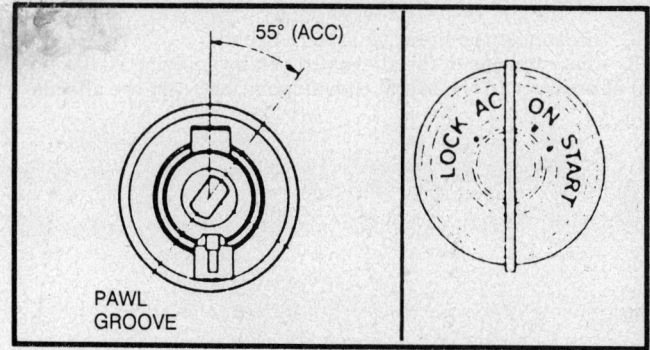

Key position to remove ignition key cylinder

Ignition Lock Cylinder

Removal and Installation

1. Disconnect the negative battery cable.
2. Remove the steering column lower cover.
3. Fabricate a rod of approximately 0.078 in. (2mm) in diameter and 4 in. (100mm) in length with a 90 degree turn of 0.591 in. (15mm).
4. Set the ignition key to the **ACC** position.
5. Push down on the stop pin with the rod and draw out the cylinder.
6. Complete the installation of the ignition key cylinder by reversing the removal procedure.

Stoplight Switch

Adjustment

Loosen the locknut and turn the switch until the pedal cushion comes in contact with the edge of the threaded portion of the stoplight switch. Tighten the locknut.

Removal and Installation

1. Disconnect the negative battery cable.
2. Disconnect the stoplight switch electrical connector.
3. Loosen the locknut and remove the switch.
To install:
4. Install new switch and turn until the pedal cushion comes in contact with the edge of the threaded portion of the stoplight switch. Tighten the locknut.
5. Connect the electrical connector.
6. Connect negative battery cable.

Neutral Safety Switch

Adjustment

1. Disconnect neutral safety switch connector.
2. Set the control shaft lever to the **N** position. Check continuity between terminals N (neutral) and E (ground) to determine proper installation angle of neutral safety switch.
3. Secure the neutral safety switch at the center position of the range where continuity exists between terminals N and E.
4. Connect neutral safety switch connector.

Removal and Installation

1. Disconnect the negative battery cable.
2. Disconnect neutral safety switch connector.
3. Remove the shift shaft lever.
4. Remove the neutral safety switch retaining bolt and the neutral safety switch connector clamp.
5. Remove the neutral safety switch.
To install:
6. Install neutral safety switch and loosely install retaining bolt and connector clamp.
7. Install the shift shaft lever.
8. Set the control shaft lever to the **N** position. Check continuity between terminals N (neutral) and E (ground) to determine proper installation angle of neutral safety switch.
9. Secure the neutral start switch at the center position of the range where continuity exists between terminals N and E.
10. Tighten the neutral safety switch retaining bolt to 31 ft. lbs. (22.6 Nm).
11. Connect neutral safety switch connector.
12. Connect negative battery cable.

Fuses, Circuit Breakers and Relays

Location
FUSES

The fuse panels are located under the instrument panel near the steering column and in the engine compartment, next to the battery. When replacing a blown fuse, ensure that the fuse is of the proper value for that circuit. Never substitute a fuse of higher value. A fuse that blows repeatedly, is evidence of a grounded or shorted circuit.

CIRCUIT BREAKERS

The circuit breakers are located on the sub-fuse block near the main fuse block. When testing a circuit breaker, ensure that there is continuity between the terminals.

RELAYS

The relays are found in various locations near the circuits they control and in a relay box in the engine compartment, next to the battery. Relays are remote switches that control high amperage circuits. Problems in a relay-controlled circuit can result from the control circuit, the load circuit, the electrical consumer or the relay itself.

Computers

Location
ELECTRONIC FUEL INJECTION (EFI) ELECTRONIC CONTROL UNIT (ECU)

The ECU is located behind the glove box. The ECU monitors and controls engine functions. Check EFI circuit wiring by measuring voltage and resistance at the ECU connector terminals. Measurements should be taken while all connectors are connected. Ensure that battery voltage is 11 volts or more.

AUTOMATIC TRANSAXLE ECU

The automatic transaxle ECU is located behind and to the left of the instrument cluster.

CRUISE CONTROL ECU

The cruise control ECU is located to the driver's side of the center console, adjacent to the radio.

BELT CONTROL ECU

The belt control ECU is located behind the left front kick panel, below the instrument panel.

Flashers

Location
The turn signal/hazard flasher is located on the main fuse block.

ENGINE COOLING

Radiator

Removal and Installation

1.0L ENGINE

1. Disconnect the negative battery cable.
2. Drain the cooling system into a clean container for reuse.
3. Disconnect the coolant reservoir hose.
4. Disconnect the upper and lower radiator hoses.
5. Disconnect the fan motor connector.
6. Remove the 2 radiator retaining bolts. Note position of ground cable on right side bolt and set aside.
7. Remove the radiator with fan shroud and fan motor assembly attached from the vehicle.

To install:

8. Install fan shroud and fan motor assembly to the radiator.
9. Install radiator in vehicle and install 2 retaining bolts.

NOTE: Ensure that ground cable is reconnected with right side retaining bolt.

10. Connect fan motor connector.
11. Connect upper and lower radiator hoses.
12. Connect coolant reservoir hose.
13. Fill cooling system.
14. Connect negative battery cable.
15. Start engine and check for leaks. Allow engine to come to normal operating temperature and recheck for leaks. Allow engine to warm up sufficiently to confirm operation of cooling fan.

1.3L ENGINE

1. Disconnect the negative battery cable.
2. Remove the engine under cover.
3. Drain the cooling into a clean container for reuse.
4. If equipped with automatic transaxle, disconnect the 2 oil cooler hoses for the automatic transaxle.

NOTE: Plug oil lines to prevent excessive loss of transaxle fluid.

5. Disconnect the coolant reservoir hose and radiator upper and lower hoses.
6. If equipped with manual transaxle, disconnect the oil cooler hose from the radiator lower tank.
7. Disconnect the fan motor connector.
8. Disconnect the upper radiator hose from the clamp.
9. Remove the radiator upper bracket.
10. Remove the radiator together with the fan shroud from the vehicle.
11. Remove the fan shroud from the radiator.

To install:

12. If equipped with automatic transaxle, replace the automatic transaxle oil hoses and hose bands with new ones.
13. Install the fan shroud together with the fan motor on the radiator.
14. Inspect the rubber mounting grommet and replace if cracked or damaged.
15. Ensure that the radiator is positioned on the grommet when installing.
16. Install the radiator bracket.

NOTE: If equipped with radio, ensure that the ground cable is installed together with bracket on the air cleaner side.

17. Install the radiator hose to the fan shroud clamp.
18. Connect the fan motor connector.
19. Connect the oil cooler hose to radiator. Install new hose bands.
20. Connect the radiator upper and lower hoses to the radiator. Install new hose bands.
21. Connect the coolant reservoir hose. Install new hose bands.
22. If equipped with automatic transaxle, connect the oil cooler hoses.

NOTE: Never reuse oil cooler hoses and hose bands.

23. Install the engine under cover.
24. Connect negative battery cable.
25. If equipped with automatic transaxle, add automatic transaxle fluid.
26. Fill cooling system.
27. Start engine and check for leaks. Allow engine to come to normal operating temperature and recheck for leaks. Allow engine to warm up sufficiently to confirm operation of the cooling fan.

Electric Cooling Fan

Testing

1. Check fuse or circuit breaker for power to cooling fan motor.
2. Remove connector(s) at cooling fan motor(s). Connect jumper wire and apply battery voltage to the positive terminal of the cooling fan motor.
3. Using and ohmmeter, check for continuity in cooling fan motor.
4. Ensure proper continuity of cooling fan motor ground circuit at chassis ground connector.

Removal and Installation

1.0L ENGINE

1. Disconnect the negative battery cable.
2. Drain cooling system enough to permit removal of the upper radiator hose. Save coolant for reuse.
3. Disconnect the radiator upper hose.
4. Disconnect the radiator fan motor connector.
5. Remove the fan shroud subassembly together with the fan motor from the radiator.
6. Remove the fan from the fan motor.
7. Remove the fan motor from the fan shroud.

To install:

8. Install new fan motor to fan shroud.
9. Install the fan to the fan motor.
10. Install the fan shroud subassembly to the radiator.
11. Connect the radiator fan motor connector.
12. Connect negative battery cable.
13. Refill the radiator with coolant and check for leaks. Start engine and allow to come normal operating temperature and recheck for leaks. Allow engine to warm up sufficiently to confirm operation of the cooling fan.

1.3L ENGINE

1. Disconnect the negative battery cable.
2. Remove the engine under cover.
3. Drain cooling system into a clean container for reuse.
4. Disconnect the radiator upper hose.
5. Disconnect the radiator fan motor connector.
6. Disconnect the radiator lower hose from the clamp.
7. Remove the radiator fan shroud with fan motor from the radiator.
8. Remove the fan from fan motor.
9. Remove the fan motor from the fan shroud.

To install:

10. Install the radiator fan motor to the fan shroud.

NOTE: Ensure that fan motor is mounted on shroud so drainage hose will point down when installed in vehicle.

11. Install the radiator fan shroud to the radiator.
12. Connect the radiator lower hose to the clamp.
13. Connect the radiator fan motor connector.
14. Connect the radiator upper hose. Install new hose bands.
15. Connect negative battery cable.
16. Fill cooling system and check for leaks. Start engine and allow to come to normal operating temperature and recheck for leaks. Allow engine to warm up sufficently to confirm operation of cooling fan.

Heater Core

For further information, please refer to "Chilton's Heating and Air Conditioning Manual" for additional coverage.

Removal and Installation

1. Disconnect the negative battery cable.
2. Drain the cooling system into a clean container for reuse.

NOTE: The instrument panel must be removed to gain access to heater assembly containing the heater core.

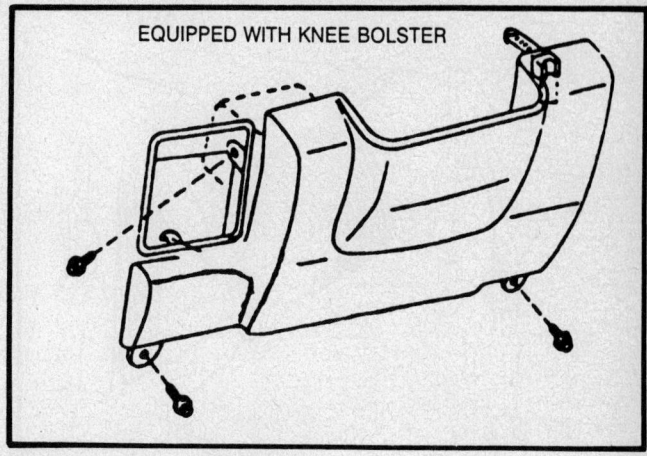

EQUIPPED WITH KNEE BOLSTER

Removal of knee bolster

3. Remove the 4 screws retaining the instrument cluster finish panel subassembly.
4. Pull subassembly out slightly to allow room to disconnect the rear window defogger switch and rear wiper switch couplers.
5. Remove instrument cluster finish panel subassembly.
6. Remove 4 instrument cluster assembly retaining screws.

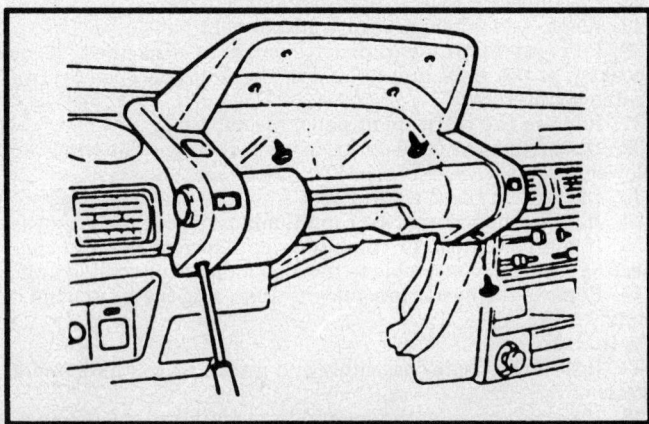

Removal of instrument cluster finish panel

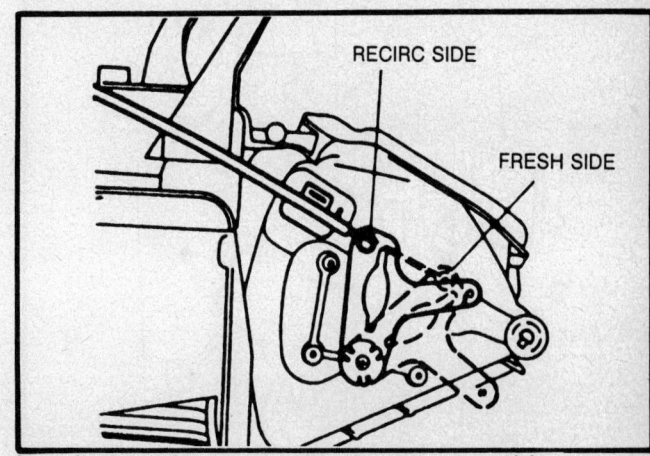

RECIRC SIDE

FRESH SIDE

Installation of control cable–heater assembly

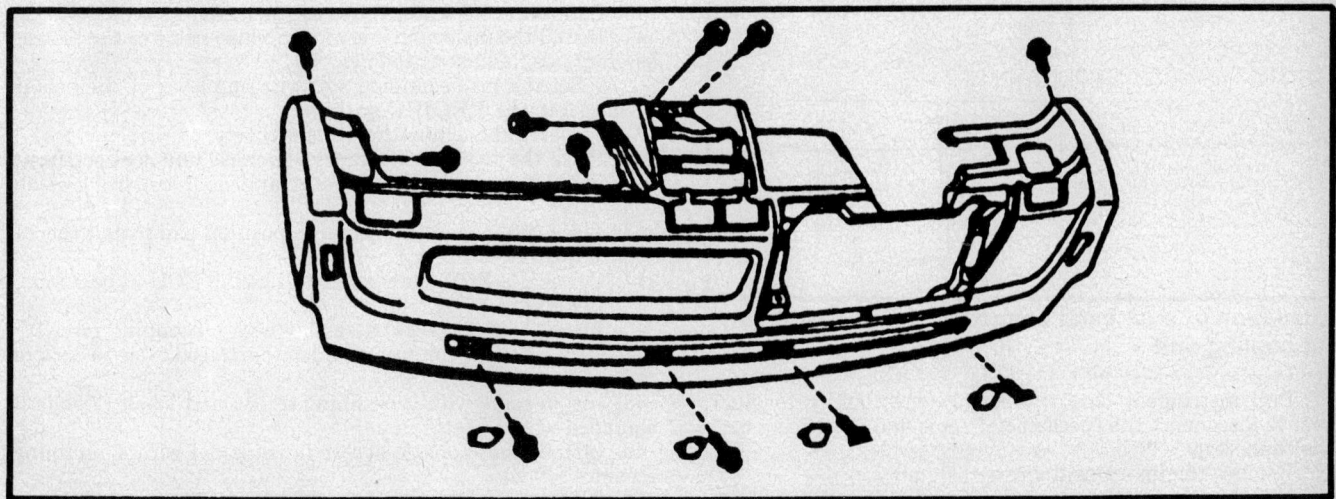

Removal of instrument panel

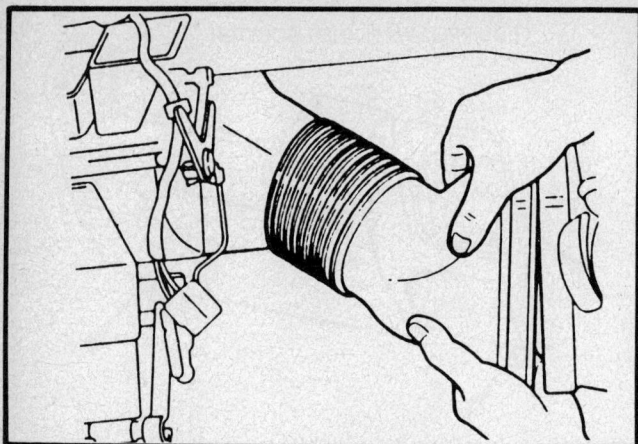

Removal of air duct

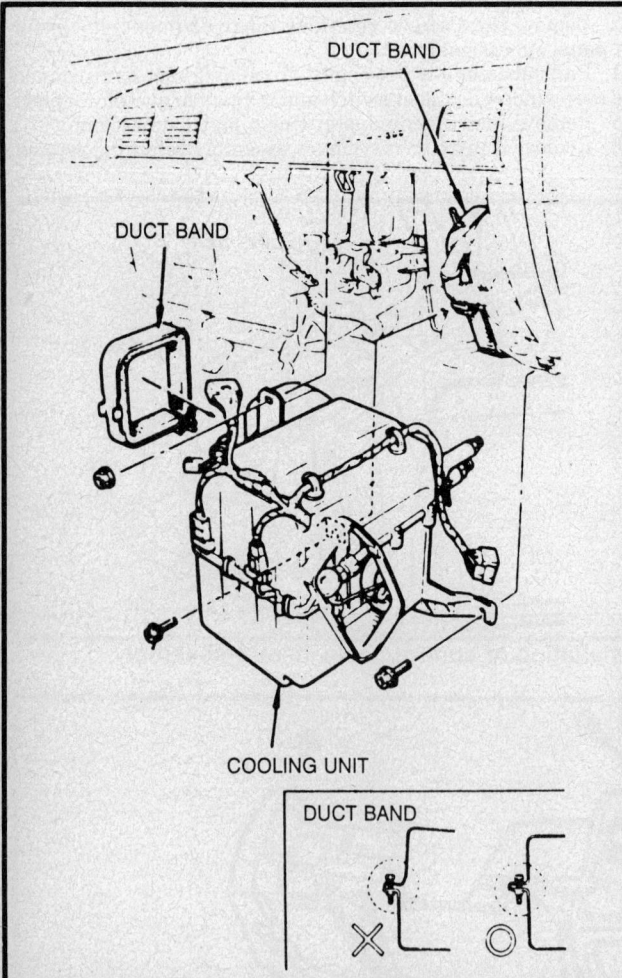

Installation of duct band connecting heater assembly and cooling unit

7. Pull instrument cluster assembly out slightly to allow room to disconnect the speedometer cable and the wiring harness connector.

8. Remove the instrument cluster assembly.

9. Remove the switch base plate from the driver's side knee bolster by pushing it out from behind.

10. Remove the 3 bolts retaining the knee bolster.

11. Detach the clip located at the right side of the knee bolster by reaching through opening in instrument panel for instrument cluster.

12. Remove the knee bolster.

13. Remove the 4 instrument panel lower reinforcement retaining bolts.

14. Disconnect the steering column wiring harness connector.

15. Remove the steering shaft universal joint connector bolts.

16. Remove the 2 steering column attaching bolts and 3 nuts and remove the steering column.

17. Remove the 2 screws retaining the glove box door subassembly and remove the subassembly.

18. Remove the shift knob and shift lever boot.

19. Remove the 6 screws retaining the console box assembly and remove assembly.

20. Remove the 6 bolts retaining the front console assembly.

21. Pull front console assembly out to disconnect the clock connector.

22. Remove the 4 screws retaining the front console center finish panel and remove panel.

23. Disconnect cigar lighter and ashtry illumination lamp connectors and remove ashtray.

24. Remove 2 retaining screws and 1 bolt (2 bolts if equipped with cassette/radio).

25. Pull radio out enough to disconnect connector and antenna feed cable and remove radio.

26. Detach heater control assembly by removing the 3 screws.

27. Remove glove box trim at back of glove box.

28. Disconnect 2 ECU connectors and remove.

29. Remove 11 screw retaining instrument panel.

30. Pull out instrument panel enough to disconnect front speakers at the right and left sides, rheostat and door control switch connectors.

31. Remove the instrument panel assembly.

32. Disconnect the inside/outside air switching cable from the blower assembly.

33. Disconnect the 2 water hoses from the heater assembly.

34. If not equipped with air conditioning, remove the air duct.

35. If equipped with air conditioning, remove duct band connecting the heater assembly to the air conditioning cooling unit.

36. Remove the heater assembly by removing the 2 nuts and 2 bolts.

To install:

37. Install the heater assembly and attach with 2 nuts and 2 bolts.

38. If not equipped with air conditioning, install the air duct.

39. If equipped with air conditioning, install the duct band connecting the heater assembly to the cooling unit.

40. Connect the 2 water hoses to the heater assembly.

41. Install the inside/outside air switching cable to the blower assembly and adjust as follows:

   a. Set the inside/outside air switching lever of the heater control to the **RECIRC** position.

   b. Insert and clamp the cable securely.

42. Place the instrument panel in vehicle and connect front left and right speakers, rheostat and door control switch connectors.

43. Place the instrument panel in position and install the 11 retaining screws.

44. Connect 2 ECU connectors and install ECU in position.

45. Install glove box trim.

46. Install heater control assembly with 3 retaining screws.

47. Connect radio connector and antenna feed cable to back of radio.

48. Install radio with 2 retaining screws and 1 bolt (2 bolts if equipped with cassette/radio).

49. Install front console center finish panel with 4 retaining screws.

50. Connect clock connector to front console assembly.

51. Install front console assembly with 6 bolts.

52. Install console box assembly with 6 retaining screws.
53. Install the shift lever boot and shift knob.
54. Install glove box subassembly with 2 screw.
55. Install the steering shaft universal joint connecting bolts.
56. Install steering column with 2 attaching bolts and 3 nuts.
57. Install the 4 instrument panel lower reinforcement retaining bolts.
58. Install the knee bolster with 3 bolts, making sure right side clip is in place.
59. Install the switch base plate in knee bolster.
60. Install instrument cluster enough to connect wiring harness connector and speedometer cable and attach with 4 screws.
61. Install instrument cluster finish panel enough to connect rear window defogger switch and rear wiper switch connectors.
62. Install instrument cluster finish panel with 4 screws.
63. Connect negative battery cable.
64. Fill cooling system and check for leaks. Start engine and allow engine to come to normal operating temperature. Recheck for coolant leaks. Allow engine to warm up sufficently to confirm operation of cooling fan.
65. Operate heating system to insure proper installation and function of system.

Water Pump

Removal and Installation

1.0L ENGINE

1. Disconnect the negative battery cable.
2. Drain coolant into a clean container for reuse.
3. Remove the timing belt.
4. Remove the water inlet.
5. Remove the throttle body hose from water pump.
6. Remove the water pump by removing the 3 bolts.

To install:
7. Replace the O-ring for the water inlet pipe.
8. Install the water pump to the cylinder block with new gasket. Tighten water pump to 11–16 ft. lbs. (15–22 Nm).
9. Install the water inlet to the cylinder block with an new gasket. Insert the water inlet pipe into the water inlet at the same time.
10. Connect the throttle body hose to the water pump.
11. Install the timing belt.
12. Install the timing belt cover.
13. Install the water pump pulley.
14. Connect negative battery cable.
15. Fill cooling system and check for leaks. Start engine and allow engine to come to normal operating temperature. Recheck for coolant leaks. Allow engine to warm up sufficently to confirm operation of cooling fan.

1.3L ENGINE

1. Disconnect the negative battery cable.
2. Drain coolant into a clean container for reuse.
3. Remove the timing belt.
4. Remove the water pump by removing the attaching bolts and nuts of the water pump.

To install:
5. Remove the gasket material from the water pump installing surface of the cylinder block.
6. Install the water pump to the cylinder block with new gasket. Tighten water pump to 11–16 ft. lbs. (15–22 Nm).
7. Install the timing belt.
8. Install the timing belt cover.
9. Install the water pump pulley.
10. Connect negative battery cable.
11. Fill cooling system and check for leaks. Start engine and allow engine to come to normal operating temperature. Recheck for coolant leaks. Allow engine to warm up sufficently to confirm operation of cooling fan.

Thermostat

Removal and Installation

1.0L ENGINE

1. Disconnect the negative battery cable.
2. Drain the coolant into a clean container for reuse.
3. Remove the water outlet hose.
4. Remove the water outlet.
5. Remove the thermostat.

To install:
6. Install the thermostat to the intake manifold.
7. Install the water inlet with the 2 nuts, using a new gasket.
8. Connect the water outlet pipe.
9. Connect negative battery cable.
10. Fill cooling system and check for leaks. Start engine and allow engine to come to normal operating temperature. Recheck for coolant leaks. Allow engine to warm up sufficently to confirm operation of cooling fan.

1.3L ENGINE

1. Disconnect the negative battery cable.
2. Drain the coolant into a clean container for reuse.
3. Disconnect the radiator thermo control switch connector.
4. Remove the water inlet and thermostat.

To install:
5. Install the thermostat so the jiggle pin faces up.
6. Install the water inlet. Tighten to 4–7 ft. lbs. (6–9 Nm).
7. Connect the radiator thermo control switch connector.
8. Connect negative battery cable.
9. Fill cooling system and check for leaks. Start engine and allow engine to come to normal operating temperature. Recheck for coolant leaks. Allow engine to warm up sufficently to confirm operation of cooling fan.

Cooling System Bleeding

The cooling system is self-bleeding due to a jiggle pin bleeder valve designed into the thermostat. The jiggle pin allows air bubbles to pass through the thermostat and out of the system. It is essential that the thermostat be installed with the jiggle pin facing up in order for the self-bleeding capability to function properly. Failure to due so could lead to air being trapped in the cooling system resulting in a dangerous overheating condition.

FUEL SYSTEM

Fuel System Service Precautions

Safety is the most important factor when performing not only fuel system maintenance but any type of maintenance. Failure to conduct maintenance and repairs in a safe manner may result in serious personal injury or death. Maintenance and testing of the vehicle's fuel system components can be accomplished safely and effectively by adhering to the following rules and guidelines.
• To avoid the possibility of fire and personal injury, always disconnect the negative battery cable unless the repair or test procedure requires that battery voltage be applied.

• Always relieve the fuel system pressure prior to disconnecting any fuel system component (injector, fuel rail, pressure regulator, etc.), fitting or fuel line connection. Exercise extreme caution whenever relieving fuel system pressure to avoid exposing skin, face and eyes to fuel spray. Please be advised that fuel under pressure may penetrate the skin or any part of the body that it contacts.

• Always place a shop towel or cloth around the fitting or connection prior to loosening to absorb any excess fuel due to spillage. Ensure that all fuel spillage (should it occur) is quickly removed from engine surfaces. Ensure that all fuel soaked cloths or towels are deposited into a suitable waste container.

• Always keep a dry chemical (Class B) fire extinguisher near the work area.

• Do not allow fuel spray or fuel vapors to come into contact with a spark or open flame.

• Always use a backup wrench when loosening and tightening fuel line connection fittings. This will prevent unnecessary stress and torsion to fuel line piping. Always follow the proper torque specifications.

• Always replace worn fuel fitting O-rings with new. Do not substitute fuel hose or equivalent where fuel pipe is installed.

Relieving Fuel System Pressure

1. Disconnect the negative battery cable.
2. Place a suitable container near the fuel filter fitting.
3. Put a wrench on the fitting and a backup wrench on the filter fitting boss and wrap a shop towel around the connection.
4. Slowly, loosen the connection allowing the shop towel to absorb as much of the fuel as possible.
5. After repairs have been completed, tighten the fitting using the backup wrench.
6. Connect negative battery cable.
7. Start the engine and check for fuel leaks.

Fuel Filter

Removal and Installation

1. Disconnect the negative battery cable.
2. Relieve fuel system pressure.
3. Remove fuel line connectors.
4. Remove the fuel filter mounting screw.
5. Remove fuel filter.

To install:
6. Install new fuel filter and mounting screw.
7. Replace fuel line gaskets and coat with a thin film of oil. Connect fuel lines to fuel filter finger tight.
8. Using a backup wrench to hold fuel filter, tighten fuel line nut to 26–32 ft. lbs. (34–43 Nm).
9. Connect negative battery cable.
10. Start engine and check for fuel leaks.

Electric Fuel Pump

Pressure Testing

1. Ensure that the battery voltage is 12 volts or more.
2. Disconnect the negative battery cable.
3. Relieve the fuel system pressure.
4. Disconnect fuel line from fuel filter.
5. Install a suitable fuel pressure gauge between the fuel line and the fuel filter using a new gasket.
6. Connect negative battery cable.
7. Remove the cap on the check terminal.
8. Connect a jumper wire between fuel pump terminal F (white/black) and the ground terminal (black).
9. Turn the ignition switch to the **ON** position.
10. Check fuel pressure. Specified fuel pressure: 37–46 psi. (2.6–3.2 kg/cm^2).

11. Turn ignition switch to the **OFF** position. Let stand for 3 minutes.
12. Check residual pressure. Specified fuel pressure: 35.5 psi. (2.5 kg/cm^2) or more.
13. Disconnect the negative battery cable.
14. Relieve fuel system pressure.
15. Remove fuel pressure gauge from the system and reconnect fuel line to fuel filter replacing old gaskets. Coat new gaskets with a thin film of oil and install finger tight. Using a backup wrench to hold fuel filter, tighten fuel line nut to 26–32 ft. lbs. (34–43 Nm).
16. Remove jumper wire and install cap on check terminal.
17. Connect negative battery cable.
18. Start engine and check for fuel leaks.

Removal and Installation

1.0L ENGINE

1. Disconnect the negative battery cable.
2. Drain fuel from the fuel tank.
3. Remove the tank from the vehicle.
4. Remove the fuel main hose and fuel return pipe from the fuel pump bracket.
5. Disconnect the wire from the fuel pump bracket.
6. Remove the fuel pump bracket attaching bolts.
7. Remove the fuel pump bracket from the fuel tank.
8. Remove the nut retaining the fuel pump to the fuel pump bracket.
9. Disconnect the 2 lines from the fuel pump bracket.
10. Detach the fuel hose clip from the fuel hose.
11. Remove the ground cable attaching screw. Remove the ground wire.
12. Remove the fuel pump from the fuel pump bracket.
13. Remove the 2 nuts and disconnect the wires.
14. Remove the fuel hose from the fuel pump.

To install:
15. Connect the fuel hose to the fuel pump. Attach the hose clip.
16. Connect the 2 wires to the fuel pump. Ensure that the blue cable is on the positive terminal.
17. Install the rubber cushion on the fuel pump and install fuel pump to the fuel pump bracket.
18. Install the rubber cushion to the fuel pump bracket. Connect the ground cable. Secure the fuel pump by tightening the attaching bolts.
19. Attach the fuel hose clip to the fuel hose.
20. Install the positive wire of the fuel pump to the fuel pump bracket.
21. Install the fuel pump bracket with a new gasket to the fuel tank. Tighten the bolts in stages to 2–4 ft. lbs. (1.5–4.9 Nm).
22. Connect the wire to the fuel pump bracket.
23. Connect the hose and pipe to the fuel pump bracket. Coat a new gasket with a thin film of oil and install flare nut finger tight. Tighten to 25–32 ft. lbs. (34.3–43.1 Nm).
24. Install the fuel tank.
25. Fill fuel tank with fuel.
26. Connect negative battery cable.
27. Start engine and check for leaks.

Fuel Injection

For further information, please refer to "Chilton's Electronic Engine Control's Manual" for additional coverage.

Idle Speed Adjustment

1. Ensure that engine is at normal operating temperature.
2. Connect a timing light to verify proper ignition timing. Adjust, as necessary.

3. Connect a tachometer and adjust engine idle speed to specification.

4. Disconnect tachometer and timing light.

5. Test drive vehicle.

Idle Mixture Adjustment

The idle mixture is controlled automatically by the Electronic Control Unit (ECU).

Fuel Injector

Removal and Installation

1. Disconnect the negative battery cable.

2. Relieve fuel system pressure.

3. Remove the pressure regulator.

4. Remove the injector.

To install:

5. Check the insulator and grommet of each injector for damage.

6. Install the insulator on the manifold section.

7. Install the grommet on the injector.

8. Replace the injector O-ring.

9. Insert the injector into the insulator.

10. Install the delivery pipe.

11. Connect negative battery cable.

12. Start the engine and check for fuel leaks.

EMISSION CONTROLS

For further information, please refer to "Professional Emission Component Application Guide".

ENGINE MECHANICAL

NOTE: Disconnecting the negative battery cable on some vehicles may interfere with the functions of the on board computer systems and may require the computer to undergo a relearning process, once the negative battery cable is reconnected.

Engine Assembly

Removal and Installation

1.0L ENGINE

1. Disconnect the positive and negative battery cables and remove the battery.

2. Disconnect the windshield washer hose and remove the hood.

3. Drain the engine coolant by removing the plug from the bottom of the radiator.

4. Drain the engine oil.

5. Drain the transaxle oil.

6. Remove the 2 wiring clamps from the battery tray.

7. Remove the 4 bolts retaining the battery tray and remove the tray.

8. Disconnect the accelerator cable from the throttle body. Remove the accelerator cable from the clamp. Position the cable aside.

9. Label and disconnect the hoses attached to the air cleaner assembly.

10. Disconnect the air cleaner hose at the air cleaner side.

11. Remove the air cleaner by removing the 4 bolts.

12. Remove the PCV hose.

13. Remove the air cleaner hose from the throttle body.

14. Label and disconnect the brake booster, air conditioning fast idle VSV (air conditioning equipped vehicles only) and barometric pressure VSV vacuum hoses.

15. Disconnect the spark plug wires.

16. Disconnect the engine-to-fuse block wiring harness connector.

17. Disconnect the transaxle ground cable at the transaxle side.

18. Disconnect the engine wire clamp at the lower side of the ignitor.

19. Disconnect the ignitor connector.

20. Disconnect the engine wire and cowl wire.

21. Remove the clutch cable weight. Disconnect the clutch cable.

22. Disconnect the speedometer cable from the transaxle.

23. Disconnect the ground cable between the engine and the radiator.

24. Disconnect the ground cable to the alternator.

25. If equipped with air conditioning, disconnect the compressor clutch wire.

26. Relieve the fuel system pressure. Disconnect the fuel hose at the upper side of the fuel filter.

27. Remove the engine harness clamp bolt at the lower side of the pressure sensor. Disconnect the pressure sensor connector.

28. Remove the upper and lower radiator hoses.

29. Remove the heater inlet pipe hose.

30. Remove the heater hose from the air plenum.

31. Remove the vacuum hose between the BVSV and the charcoal canister.

32. Disconnect the radiator fan motor connector.

33. Remove the radiator.

34. Remove the compressor drive belt. Remove the 4 compressor retaining bolts from the bracket. Remove the compressor from the bracket and set aside supporting compressor with a length of mechanics wire.

35. Remove the glove box door subassembly.

36. Disconnect the ECU connector from the engine wiring harness.

37. Remove the 2 engine harness clamps. Draw the engine harness toward the engine compartment.

38. Raise and safely support the vehicle.

39. Remove the right and left engine under covers.

40. Disconnect the exhaust pipe frm the exhaust manifold by removing the 3 nuts.

41. Remove the exhaust pipe support No. 1.

42. Remove the stabilizer bar. Remove the lower arm from the lower arm bracket.

43. Disconnect the control rod.

44. Remove the halfshaft.

45. Disconnect the oengine mounting front stopper and engine mounting rear bracket from the engine lower member.

46. Remove the damper weight.

47. Install a suitable engine lifting device and support the engine.

48. Remove the engine mounting upper right insulator and front mounting bracket attaching nuts.

49. Disconnect the engine mounting lower left insulator and rear mounting attaching bolts.

50. Remove the engine front mounting bracket from the cylinder head.

51. Remove the engine from the vehicle.

To install:

52. Lower engine into vehicle and install the engine front mounting bracket to the cylinder head.

53. Tighten the engine mounting lower left bracket to transaxle. Tighten to 22–33 ft. lbs. (30–44 Nm).

54. Fit the front mounting bracket to the engine mounting upper right insulator. Secure the front mounting bracket. Tighten to 29–40 ft. lbs. (39–54 Nm).

55. Remove the lifting device.

56. Install the engine mounting front stopper and engine mounting rear bracket to the engine lower mounting member. Tighten the front stopper to 54–76 ft. lbs. (74–103 Nm). Tighten the rear bracket to 54–76 ft. lbs. (74–103 Nm).

NOTE: The front stopper should be mounted at the center of the lower engine mounting stopper.

57. Install the damper weight to the engine mounting rear bracket.

58. Install the halfshaft using a new snapring at the end of the halfshaft.

59. Install the transaxle control rod. Tighten to 12–22 ft. lbs. (17–30 Nm).

60. Install the lower arm to the lower arm bracket. Tighten to 58–76 ft. lbs. (79–103 Nm).

61. Install the stabilizer bar. Tighten stabilizer bracket to 29–43 ft. lbs. (39–58 Nm). Tighten stabilizer nut, using a new nut, to 54–80 ft. lbs. (74–108 Nm).

62. Install the exhaust pipe using a new gasket. Tighten 3 nuts to 36–55 ft. lbs. (49–75 Nm).

63. Install the exhaust pipe support. Tighten to 25–36 ft. lbs. (34–49 Nm).

64. Install the right and left engine undercovers.

65. Lower the vehicle.

66. Connect the ECU wiring harness connector. Fit the rubber grommet into the dash panel.

67. Install the 2 clamps retaining the engine wiring harness.

68. Connect the ECU connector to the engine harness.

69. Install the glove box door subassembly.

70. Install the air conditioning compressor. Tighten the 4 bolts to 18 ft. lbs. (25 Nm).

71. Install the compressor drive belt and adjust tension.

72. Connect the alternator ground cable.

73. Connect the compressor clutch wiring connector.

74. Install the radiator. Ensure that the ground cable is connected to the right side bolt.

75. Connect the radiator cooling fan motor connector.

76. Connect the heater hose to the air plenum.

77. Install the heater hose to the inlet pipe.

78. Install the upper and lower radiator hoses.

79. Connect the pressure sensor connector and install the wiring harness clamp and retaining bolt.

80. Connect the fuel line hose to the fuel filter, using the union bolt and a new gasket. Tighten to 25–33 ft. lbs. (34–44 Nm).

81. Connect the ground cable connecting the exhaust manifold with the radiator attaching bolt.

82. Connect the speedometer cable.

83. Connect the clutch cable. Install the clutch cable weight.

84. Connect the engine-to-cowl wiring harness connector.

85. Connect the ignitor connector.

86. Install the engine wire clamp under the ignitor.

87. Connect the transaxle ground cable.

88. Connect the engine-to-fuse block connector.

89. Connect the spark plug wires.

90. Connect the vacuum hoses for the brake booster, air conditioning VSV, if equipped with air conditioning, and the barometric pressure VSV.

91. Install the air cleaner hose to the throttle body.

92. Install the PCV hose to the cylinder head cover.

93. install the air cleaner assembly.

94. Connect the air cleaner hose. Connect the air cleaner rubber hoses.

95. Connect the vacuum hose between the charcoal canister and the BVSV.

96. Connect the accelerator cable to the throttle body.

NOTE: Adjust play in accelerator cable to 0.118–0.315 in. (3.0–8.0mm).

97. Install battery tray with the 4 mounting bolts. Install wire harness clamps.

98. Fill the engine and transaxle with oil.

99. Fill cooling system.

100. Install the battery.

101. Connect the alternator wire and terminal of the relay block assembly to the positive battery terminal.

102. Connect negative battery cable.

103. Install the hood.

104. Start the engine and check for coolant, fuel and oil leaks. Stop engine and check oil level. Add, as necessary.

1.3L ENGINE

1. Disconnect the positive and negative battery cables and remove the battery.

2. Disconnect the windshield washer hose and remove the hood.

3. Drain the engine coolant by removing the plug from the bottom of the radiator.

4. Drain the engine oil. Remove the oil filter.

5. Drain the transaxle oil.

6. Remove the wiring clamp and washer hose clamp from the battery tray.

7. Remove the 4 bolts retaining the battery tray and remove the tray.

8. Disconnect the accelerator cable from the throttle body. Remove the accelerator cable from the clamp. Position the cable aside.

9. Remove the power steering pump drive belt. Remove the power steering pump and set aside, supporting with a length of mechanics wire.

10. Remove th air conditioning belt. Remove the belt tensioner assembly.

11. If equipped with air conditioning, disconnect the compressor clutch wire.

12. Remove the compressor drive belt. Remove the 4 compressor retaining bolts from the bracket. Remove the compressor from the bracket and set aside supporting compressor with a length of mechanics wire.

13. Remove the glove box door sub-assembly.

14. Disconnect the ECU connector from the engine wiring harness.

15. Remove the air cleaner by removing the 4 bolts.

16. Remove the PCV hose.

17. Remove the air cleaner hose from the throttle body.

18. Label and disconnect the brake booster, air conditioning fast idle VSV, if equipped with air conditioning, and barometric pressure VSV vacuum hoses.

19. Disconnect the spark plug wires.

20. Disconnect the engine-to-fuse block wiring harness connector.

21. Disconnect the transaxle ground cable at the transaxle side.

22. Disconnect the engine wire clamp at the lower side of the ignitor.

23. Disconnect the engine-to-cowl wiring harness connector.

24. Remove the clutch cable weight. Disconnect the clutch cable.
25. Disconnect the speedometer cable from the transaxle.
26. Disconnect the ground cable between the engine and the radiator.
27. Disconnect the ground cable to the alternator.
28. Relieve the fuel system pressure. Disconnect the fuel hose at the upper side of the fuel filter.
29. Remove the engine harness clamp bolt at the lower side of the pressure sensor. Disconnect the barometric pressure sensor connector.
30. Remove the upper and lower radiator hoses.
31. Remove the heater hoses.
32. Remove the vacuum hose between the BVSV and the charcoal canister.
33. Disconnect the radiator fan motor connector.
34. Remove the radiator.
35. Remove the 2 engine harness clamps. Draw the engine harness toward the engine compartment.
36. Raise and safely support the vehicle.
37. Remove the engine under cover.
38. Disconnect the exhaust pipe from the exhaust manifold by removing the 3 nuts.
39. Remove the exhaust pipe support No. 1.
40. Remove the stabilizer bar. Remove the lower arm from the lower arm bracket.
41. Disconnect the control rod.
42. Remove the halfshafts at the transaxle end.
43. Remove the attaching bolt at the exhaust manifold side of the exhaust pipe.
44. Remove the attaching bolt of the exhaust pipe support bracket clamp to the exhaust front pipe.
45. Install a suitable engine lifting device and support the engine.
46. Remove the bolts connecting the engine mounting rear brackets.
47. Remove the engine mounting left support attaching bolts from the engine mounting lower left insulator and the engine mounting front left bracket. Remove support.
48. Remove the bolt and nut connecting the engine mounting front left bracket to the insulator.
49. Lower the engine slightly. Remove the engine mounting bracket from the vehicle.
50. Remove the engine from the vehicle.

To install:

51. Lower engine into vehicle and install the engine front mounting bracket to the cylinder head.
52. Tighten the engine mounting front insulator attaching bolts. Tighten bolt to 29–40 ft. lbs. (39–54 Nm). Tighten nut to 11–17 ft. lbs. (15–23 Nm).
53. Connect the left front mounting bracket to the body. Tighten to 29–40 ft. lbs. (39–54 Nm).
54. Install engine mounting lower left insulator to the engine mounting lower left bracket. Tighten to 29–40 ft. lbs. (39–54 Nm).
55. Install the engine mounting left support. Tighten to 29–40 ft. lbs. (39–54 Nm).
56. Adjust engine height so the engine rear bracket is aligned with the engine mounting bracket.
57. Connect the engine mounting rear bracket to the engine mounting bracket. Tighten to 40–51 ft. lbs. (54–69 Nn).
58. Remove the lifting device.
59. Install the transaxle control rod. Tighten to 12–22 ft. lbs. (17–30 Nm).
60. Install the stabilizer bar. Tighten stabilizer bracket to 29–43 ft. lbs. (39–58 Nm). Tighten stabilizer nut, using a new nut, to 54–80 ft. lbs. (74–108 Nm).
61. Install the engine undercover.
62. Install the exhaust pipe using a new gasket. Tighten 3 nuts to 36–55 ft. lbs. (49–75 Nm).

63. Install the exhaust pipe support. Tighten to 25–36 ft. lbs. (34–49 Nm).
64. Lower the vehicle.
65. Connect the ECU wiring harness connector. Fit the rubber grommet into the dash panel.
66. Install the 2 clamps retaining the engine wiring harness.
67. Connect the ECU connector to the engine harness.
68. Install the glove box door subassembly.
69. Install the air conditioning compressor. Tighten the 4 bolts to 18 ft. lbs. (25 Nm).
70. Install the compressor drive belt and adjust tension.
71. Connect the compressor clutch wiring connector.
72. Install the vane pump. Install power steering pump belt and adjust.
73. Connect the alternator ground cable.
74. Install the radiator. Ensure that the radiator is properly seated in the mounting grommets.
75. Connect the radiator cooling fan motor connector.
76. Connect the heater hoses.
77. Install the upper and lower radiator hoses.
78. Connect the barometric pressure sensor connector and install the wiring harness clamp and retaining bolt.
79. Install the fuel line hose to the fuel filter, using the union bolt and a new gasket. Tighten to 25–33 ft. lbs. (34–44 Nm).
80. Connect the ground cable connecting the exhaust manifold with the radiator attaching bolt.
81. Connect the speedometer cable.
82. Connect the clutch cable. Install the clutch cable weight.
83. Connect the engine-to-cowl wiring harness connector.
84. Connect the transaxle ground cable.
85. Connect the engine-to-fuse block connector.
86. Connect the spark plug wires.
87. Connect the vacuum hoses for the brake booster, air conditioning VSV, if equipped with air conditioning, and the barometric pressure VSV.
88. Install the air cleaner hose to the throttle body.
89. Install the PCV hose to the cylinder head cover.
90. install the air cleaner assembly.
91. Connect the air cleaner hose. Connect the air cleaner rubber hoses.
92. Connect the vacuum hose between the charcoal canister and the BVSV.
93. Connect the accelerator cable to the throttle body.

   NOTE: Adjust play in accelerator cable to 0.118–0.315 in. (3.0–8.0mm).

94. Install battery tray with the 4 mounting bolts. Install wire harness clamps.
95. Fill the engine and transaxle with oil.
96. Fill cooling system.
97. Install the battery.
98. Connect the alternator wire and terminal of the relay block assembly to the positive battery terminal.
99. Connect negative battery cable.
100. Install the hood.
101. Start the engine and check for coolant, fuel and oil leaks. Stop engine and check oil level. Add, as necessary.

Engine Mounts

Removal and Installation

1. Support the engine.
2. Remove the bolts attaching the mount bracket to the engine and body.
3. Remove insulator attaching bolts.
4. Remove insulator.

To install:

5. Install insulator attaching bolts.
6. Install mount bracket and attach bracket-to-body bolts.
7. Remove engine support.

Cylinder Head

Removal and Installation

1.0L ENGINE

1. Disconnect the negative battery cable.
2. Drain the coolant.
3. Drain the engine oil.
4. Remove the timing belt.
5. Label and disconnect all vacuum hoses necessary to remove cylinder head.
6. Disconnect the fuel hose at the upper side of the fuel filter.
7. Disconnect the radiator lower hose from the inlet pipe.
8. Remove the heater hose from the inlet pipe.
9. Disconnect the radiator upper hose at the cylinder head.
10. Disconnect the heater hose from the intake manifold.
11. Remove the EGR pipe.
12. Label and disconnect all electrical connectors necessary to remove cylinder head.
13. Disconnect the fuel hose between the cold start injector and the fuel delivery pipe.
14. Remove the air plenum support. Disconnect the fuel hose clamp at the back of the air plenum. Remove the air plenum retaining bolts and nuts and remove the air plenum.
15. Remove the fuel return hose from the presssure regulator. Remove the fuel hose from the delivery pipe. Remove the fuel delivery pipe from the intake manifold.
16. Remove the 3 fuel delivery pipe insulators from the intake manifold. Remove the fuel injectors.

NOTE: Label injectors so they may be reinstalled in their original positions.

17. Disconnect the radiator fan motor connector.
18. Remove the engine wire harness clamp under the cold start injector time switch.
19. Remove the engine wire harness from the water outlet pipe bracket clamp.
20. Disconnect the oil cooler hose from the intake manifold.
21. Remove the intake manifold retaining bolts and nuts and remove the intake manifold. Remove the intake manifold gasket and discard.
22. Label and remove the spark plug wires. Remove the spark plugs.
23. Remove the exhaust pipe-to-exhaust manifold retaining nuts. Remove the exhaust pipe clamp. Disconnect the exhaust pipe from the exhaust manifold. Remove the exhaust manifold cover. Remove the exhaust manifold support attaching bolts. Remove the oxygen sensor. Remove the exhaust manifold attaching bolts and nuts and remove the exhaust manifold.

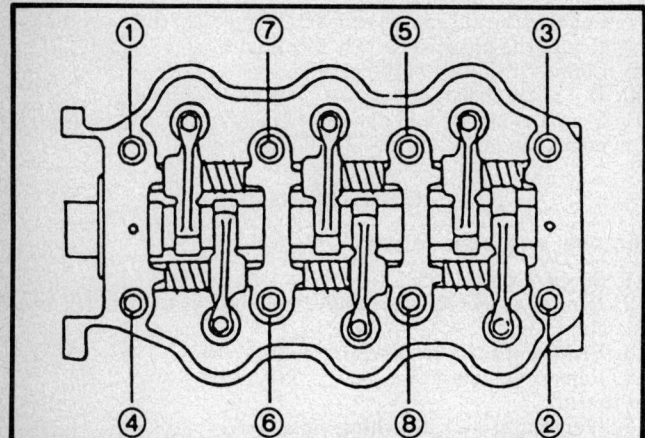

Cylinder head bolt removal sequence – 1.0L engine

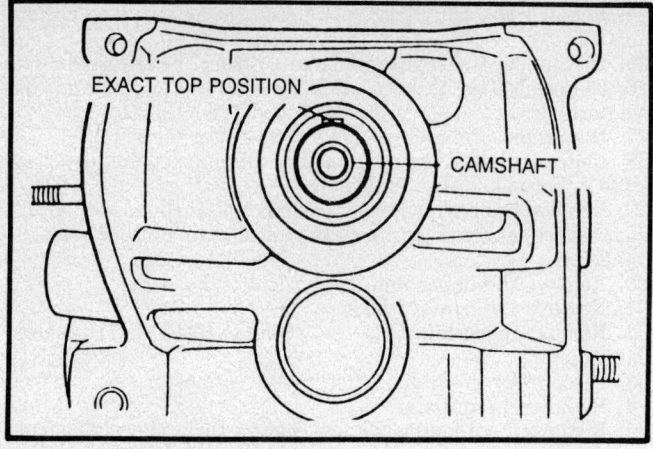

Proper camshaft position prior to cylinder head installation – 1.0L engine

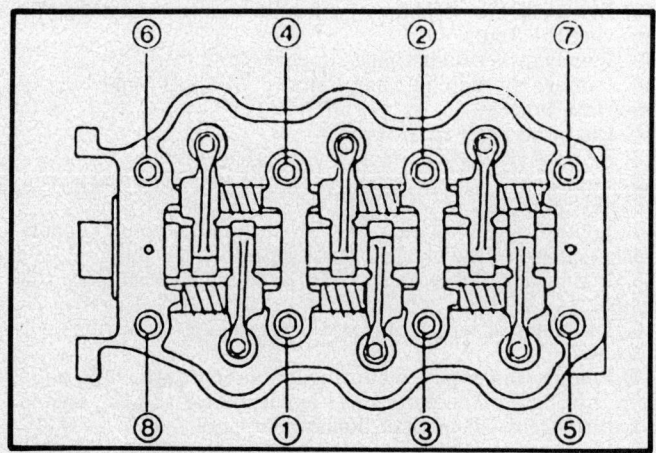

Cylinder head bolt installation sequence – 1.0L engine

24. Remove distributor attaching bolt and remove distributor.
25. Remove the alternator bracket attaching bolt from the head.
26. Remove the cylinder head cover.
27. Loosen the cylinder head bolts over 2–3 stages, in sequence. Remove the cylinder head.

To install:

NOTE: Before installing the cylinder head, ensure that the cylinder head bolt holes are free of oil or coolant.

28. Install a new cylinder head gasket on the engine block.
29. Rotate the camshaft until the key groove is at the top position.
30. Place the cylinder head on the engine block.
31. Ensure that the threads of the cylinder head bolts are dry and install them into the engine block.
32. Tighten the clinder head bolts, in sequence, over 2–3 stages. Tighten to 40–47 ft. lbs. (54–64 Nm).
33. Fill the camshaft chamber of each cylinder with approximately 1.84 cu. in. (30cc) of oil.
34. Fill the distributor drive gear chamber with approximately 1.84 cu. in. (30cc) of oil.
35. Replace the O-ring on the distributor body. Remove the distributor cap. Set the distributor shaft so drilled mark at the end of the distributor drive gear is aligned with the drilled mark on the distributor body. Insert the distributor assembly into the

distributor housing so the split line of the distributor body is aligned with the embossed line of the distributor housing.

36. Tighten the distributor attaching bolts. Install the distributor cap on the distributor.

37. Install a new exhaust manifold gasket and install the exhaust manifold. Tighten bolts to 11–16 ft. lbs. (15–22 Nm) starting in the center and working toward the outside.

38. Install the exhaust manifold support. Tighten to 22–33 ft. lbs. (29–44 Nm).

39. Install the oxygen sensor using a new gasket. Tighten to 22–29 ft. lbs. (30–39 Nm).

40. Install the exhaust manifold cover. Tighten to 4–7 ft. lbs. (6–9 Nm).

41. Install the exhaust pipe using an new gasket. Tighten to 36–55 ft. lbs. (49–75 Nm). Install the exhaust pipe clamp. Tighten to 25–36 ft. lbs. (34–49 Nm).

42. Install the spark plugs. Connect the spark plug wires.

43. Install the intake manifold using a new gasket. Connect the engine wiring harness to the 2 stud bolts on the cylinder head. Tighten the bolts to 11–16 ft. lbs. (15–22 Nm) starting in the center and working toward the outside.

44. Connect the oil cooler hose.

45. Connect the radiator fan motor connector.

46. Install the 3 injector insulators to the intake manifold.

47. Install a new O-ring on the injectors.

48. Install the injectors into the insulators.

49. Install the fuel delivery pipe heat insulator to the intake manifold. Apply a small amount of silicone or gasoline to the O-ring of the injector. Install the fuel delivery pipe to the intake manifold. Secure the fuel delivery pipe using the retaining nuts. Tighten to 7–12 ft. lbs. (10–16 Nm).

50. Connect the fuel return hose to the pressure regulator.

51. Connect the fuel hose union bolt using a new gasket. Tighten to 25–33 ft. lbs. (34–44 Nm).

52. Connect the injector connector.

53. Install the air plenum using a new gasket. Tighten to 11–16 ft. lbs. (15–22 Nm).

54. Install the fuel hose clamp to the back of the air plenum.

55. Connect the fuel hose to the cold start injector and fuel delivery pipe using a new gasket. Tighten the union bolt to 8–13 ft. lbs. (12–18 Nm).

56. Install the engine wiring harness to the bolt at the back of the air plenum.

57. Install install the EGR pipe.

58. Connect all wiring connectors that were disconnected for cylinder head removal.

59. Connect all vacuum lines that were disconnected for cylinder head removal.

60. Install the heater hose to the intake manifold.

61. Install the radiator upper hose to the cylinder head.

62. Connect the heater hose to the water inlet pipe.

63. Install the radiator lower hose to the inlet pipe.

64. Connect the fuel hose to the fuel filter using a new gasket. Tighten to 25–33 ft. lbs. (34–44 Nm).

65. Connect the pressure sensor connector.

66. Install the alternator bracket to the cylinder head.

67. Install the timing belt.

68. Adjust the valve clearance.

69. Install the cylinder head cover. Tighten to 6–9 ft. lbs. (8–12 Nm).

70. Connect the accelerator cable to the throttle body. Adjust the accelerator cable freeplay to 3.0–8.0mm. Secure it to the throttle body with the locknut. Tighten to 7–12 ft. lbs. (10-16 Nm). Secure the accelerator cable wire to the clamp.

71. Install the air plenum support.

72. Fill the engine with oil.

73. Connect negative battery cable.

74. Fill the cooling system and check for leaks. Start engine and allow engine to come to normal operating temperature. Recheck for coolant leaks. Allow engine to warm up sufficiently to confirm operation of cooling fan.

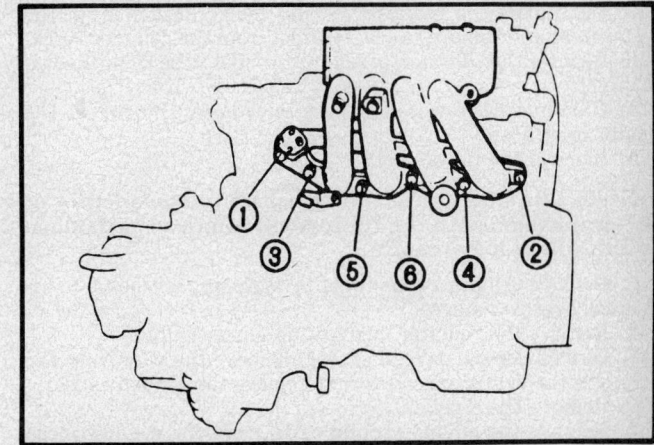

Air plenum removal sequence – 1.3L engine

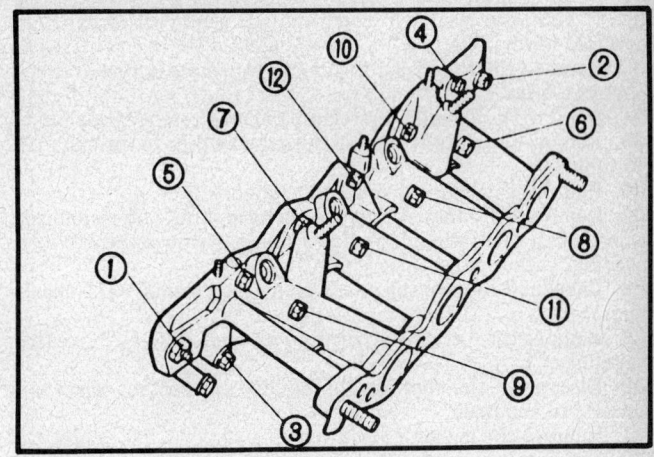

Intake manifold removal sequence – 1.3L engine

75. Check engine timing.

1.3L ENGINE

1. Disconnect the negative battery cable.

2. Drain the coolant into a clean container for reuse.

3. Relieve fuel system pressure.

4. Remove the air cleaner. Disconnect the PCV.

5. Remove the accelerator cable.

6. If equipped with automatic transaxle, remove the throttle valve (TV) cable.

7. Label and remove the rubber hoses from the air plenum.

8. Remove the modulator.

9. Remove the EGR valve assembly.

10. Label and disconnect electrical connectors required for removal of the head.

11. Label and disconnect injector connectors.

12. Remove the engine wire clamp and clamp bolt.

13. Disconnect the throttle body coolant circulating hose.

14. Remove the throttle body attaching nuts and bolts and the air plenum support. Remove the throttle body.

15. Remove the vacuum pipe assembly.

16. Remove the air plenum supports.

17. Remove the air plenum attaching nuts and bolts, loosening evenly, in 2–3 steps, in sequence. Remove the air plenum.

18. Disconnect the fuel supply and return hoses from the fuel rail.

19. Remove the fuel rail.

20. Label and remove the fuel injectors.

21. Remove the injector vibration and fuel rail insulators.

22. Disconnect the radiator thermo control switch from the water inlet and remove the water inlet from the cylinder block.
23. Remove the thermostat and water inlet hose from the water inlet.
24. Disconnect the water by-pass inlet hose. Disconnect the heater inlet hose.
25. Remove the timing belt.

NOTE: Do not rotate the camshaft independently of the crankshaft with the timing belt removed as damage to the valves may result.

26. Remove the intake manifold by loosening the bolts, in sequence, over 2-3 stages.
27. Remove the radiator and cooling fan assembly.
28. Disconnect the oxygen sensor. Remove the wire from the clamp in the cylinder head cover. Remove the oxygen sensor.
29. Remove the dipstick.
30. Remove the engine ground cable from the cylinder head cover.
31. Remove the exhaust manifold top and side covers.
32. If equipped with air conditioning, remove the exhaust manifold lower cover.
33. Remove the dipstick tube clamp attaching screw and remove the tube.
34. Remove the exhaust pipe clamp bolt and remove the clamp.
35. Remove the nuts attaching the exhaust pipe to the exhaust manifold.
36. Remove the exhaust manifold support.
37. Remove the exhaust manifold bolts and nuts, in sequence, by loosening them evenly, over 2-3 stages. Remove the exhaust manifold gasket and discard.
38. Label and remove the spark plug wires. Remove the spark plugs.
39. Remove the distributor vacuum advance hose. Remove the distributor.
40. Disconnect the appropriate radiator and coolant hoses for removal of the head.
41. Remove the cylinder head cover.
42. Remove the camshaft pulley attaching bolt from the camshaft and remove the pulley.

NOTE: Do not allow the camshaft to turn during removal.

43. Loosen the 10 bolts retaining the rocker arm shaft, in sequence, over 2-3 stages. Remove the valve rocker shaft together with the rocker arms from the cylinder head.

NOTE: Remove the rocker arm spacers and wave washers from the shaft. Arrange the spacers and washers in order so they may be reinstalled in their original positions.

44. Remove the 2 attaching bolts from camshaft cap No. 5. Remove the remaining camshaft bearing cap bolts and caps.
45. Remove the camshaft from the cylinder head.

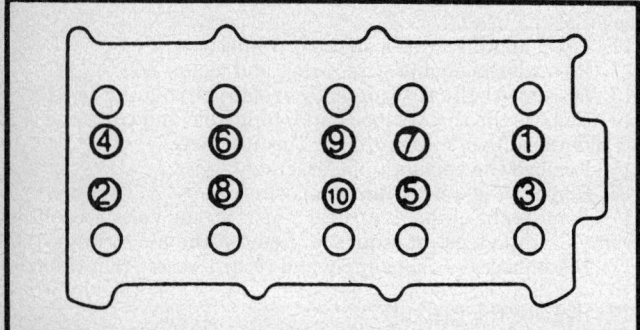

Cylinder head bolt removal sequence—1.3L engine

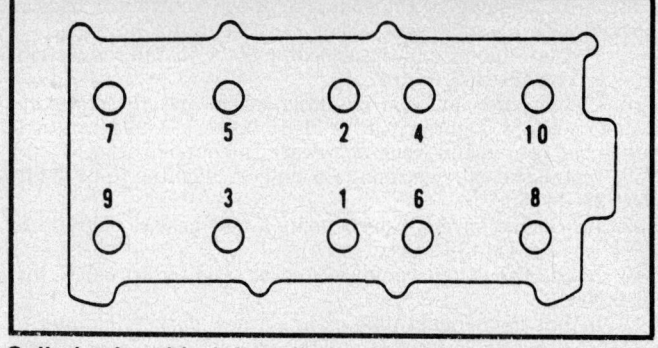

Cylinder head bolt installation torque sequence—1.3L engine

46. Loosen the cylinder head bolts, in sequence, over 2-3 stages.

NOTE: Head bolts 1 and 3 are shorter than the other bolts. Bolts 1 and 3 are 4.41 in. (112mm) and the other bolts are 6.10 in. (155mm).

47. Remove the cylinder head.
To install:
48. Clean the cylinder bolt holes.
49. Clean the cylinder block upper gasket surface. Install the cylinder head gasket using the aligning pins for reference.
50. Turn the crankshaft so the crankshaft key groove is at the top position.
51. Install the cylinder head on the engine block.
52. Coat each cylinder head bolt with a thin film of engine oil and install in the engine block. Tighten the cylinder head bolts, in sequence, over 2-3 stages. Tighten to 43.4–49.2 ft. lbs. (58.8–66.7 Nm).
53. Clean camshaft and rocker arm bolts holes.
54. Apply engine oil to the camshaft journals and thrust bearing sections.
55. Install the camshaft in the cylinder head so the locating pin for the camshaft timing belt pulley is at the top position.
56. Apply Three Bond 1104 or equivalent, to No. 1 camshaft bearing cap attaching section. Wipe off any excess bond that oozes from No. 1 cap. Install the camshaft bearing caps in sequence embossed on the caps.
57. Assemble the rocker arms and wave washers onto the valve rocker shafts in the same order as when disassembled.
58. Install the rocker shaft on the camshaft caps.
59. Ensure that the rocker shaft retaining bolts are clean and install in the cylinder head. Tighten evenly, over 2-3 stages, to 26.7 ft. lbs. (36.2 Nm) for M10 bolts and 12.29 ft. lbs. (16.6 Nm) for M8 bolts.
60. Install the spacers on the rocker shaft between the intake valve rocker arms.
61. Apply sealant tape to the threads and install the coolant temperature sensor. Tighten to 18.1–25.3 ft. lbs. (24.5–34.3 Nm).
62. Connect the bypass hoses and bypass pipe to the water outlet. Install the water outlet using a new gasket.
63. Apply sealant tape to the threads and install the Bi-metal Vacuum Switching Valve (BVSV). Tighten to 18.1–25.3 ft. lbs. (24.5–34.3 Nm).
64. Apply sealant tape to the threads and install the air conditioning water temperature switch. Tighten to 18.1–25.3 ft. lbs. (24.5–34.3 Nm).
65. Apply engine oil to the bore of the T-type camshaft seal and install using a suitable seal installer.
66. Install the camshaft timing belt pulley aligning the pulley with the locating pin on the camshaft and the **F** mark faces out. Install the retaining bolts and tighten to 10.9–15.9 ft. lbs. (14.7–21.5 Nm).

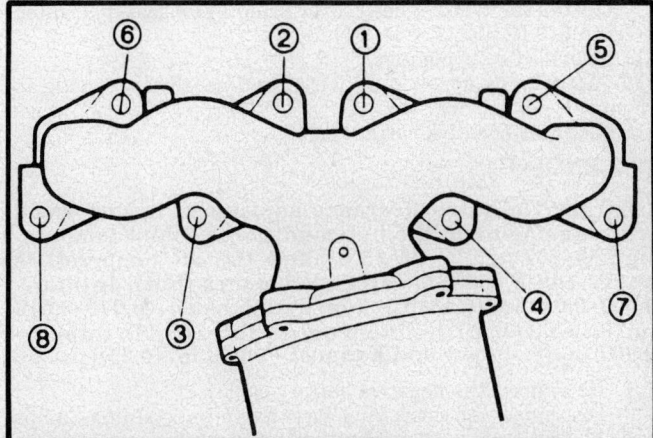

Exhaust manifold bolt installation torque sequence—
1.3L engine

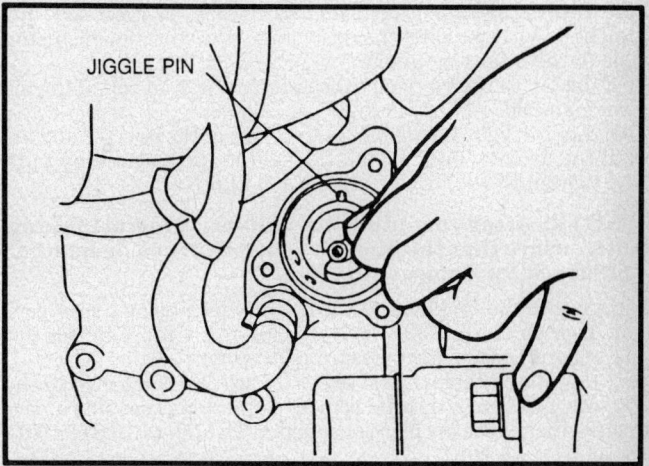

Thermostat installation—1.3L engine

NOTE: Prevent the camshaft from turning while torquing the camshaft timing belt pulley.

67. Replace the O-ring on the distributor body. Align the cut-out section of the distributor body with the cut-out groove of the cup ring. Apply a few drops of engine oil to the O-ring and install the distributor in the cylinder head with the cut-out sections facing the top of the engine.

68. Center the distributor mounting bolt holes in the elongated holes in the distributor mounting flange and install the mounting bolts. Tighten to 10.9–15.9 ft. lbs. (14.7–21.5 Nm).

69. Connect the distributor connector, the water temperature sender gauge, the water temperature sensor and the air conditioning water temperature switch connectors.

70. Fill the oil well of each cylinder with 30cc of engine oil.

71. Install the exhaust manifold gasket on the cylinder head. Ensure that the side of the gasket where the grommet bulges out faces the exhaust manifold.

72. Connect exhaust manifold intermediate pipe to exhaust manifold using a new gasket. Tighten to 14.5–21.6 ft. lbs. (19.6–29.4 Nm).

73. Install exhaust manifold to cylinder head. Tighten, in sequence, over 2–3 stages, to 21.7–32.5 ft. lbs. (29.4–44.1 Nm).

74. Install exhaust manifold support to the cylinder block. Tighten 21.7–32.5 ft. lbs. (29.4–44.1 Nm).

75. Connect the exhaust pipe to the exhaust manifold intermediate pipe using a new gasket. Tighten to 36.2–55.0 ft. lbs. (49.0–74.5 Nm).

76. Install the exhaust pipe clamp. Tighten to 25.3–36.2 ft. lbs. (34.3–49.0 Nm).

77. Replace the O-ring on the dipstick tube and install dipstick tube in cylinder block. Install the dipstick.

78. Install the exhaust manifold covers.

79. Connect the water outlet hose to the water outlet.

80. Install the intake manifold using a new gasket. Install nuts hand tight.

81. Connect the heater inlet hose to the cylinder head.

82. Install the water bypass pipe to the adjacent intake manifold stud bolt.

83. Tighten intake manifold bolts in sequence to 10.9–15.9 ft. lbs. (14.7–21.5 Nm).

84. Connect the water bypass inlet hose.

85. Install the thermostat so the jiggle pin faces up. Install the water inlet. Tighten to 4.4–6.5 ft. lbs. (5.9–8.8 Nm).

86. Connect the thermo control switch connector.

87. Install the air plenum. Tighten, in sequence, over 2–3 stages, to 21.7–32.5 ft. lbs. (29.4–44.1 Nm).

88. Install the engine hanger and air plenum support to the stud bolt on the cylinder head. Tighten the nut and bolt to 13.8–22.4 ft. lbs. (18.6–30.3 Nm).

89. Install the air plenum support. Tighten to 10.9–15.9 ft. lbs. (14.7–21.5 Nm).

90. If removed, install the intake air temperature sensor to the surge tank using a new washer. Tighten to 21.7–28.9 ft. lbs. (29.4–39.2 Nm).

91. If removed, apply sealant tape to the threads and install the fuel filter. Tighten to 8.7–14.4 ft. lbs. (11.8–19.6 Nm).

92. Install the injector vibration insulator to the intake manifold.

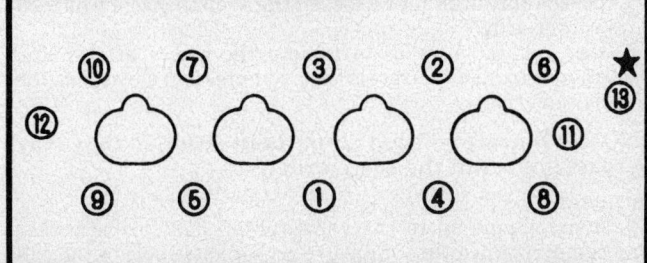

Intake manifold bolt installation torque sequence—
1.3L engine

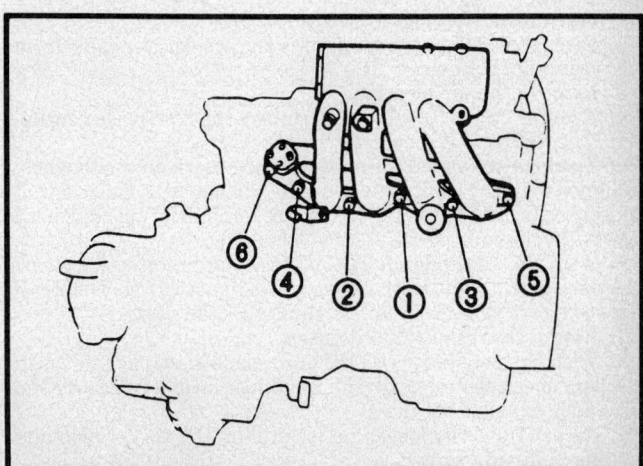

Air plenum bolt installation torque sequence—1.3L engine

93. Inspect injector grommets and replace, as necessary. Install new O-rings. Insert the injector into the vibration insulator hole of the intake manifold.

94. Install the delivery pipe insulator to the stud bolt of the intake manifold.

95. Apply a light film of oil to the O-ring of the injector and install the delivery pipe. Install the delivery pipe attaching nuts and tighten to 10.8–15.9 ft. lbs. (14.7–21.6 Nm).

NOTE: After torquing the delivery pipe attaching nuts, ensure that the injectors can be turned by hand. If not, check for damaged O-rings.

96. Install the fuel hose to the delivery pipe using a new gasket. Tighten to 25.4–32.5 ft. lbs. (23.2–44.1 Nm). Connect the fuel return hose to the pressure regulator.

97. Apply a suitable thread sealer to each throttle body attaching bolt. Install the throttle body to the air plenum using a new gasket. Install the air plenum support. Tighten to 10.9–15.9 ft. lbs. (14.7–21.5 Nm).

98. Install the vacuum pipe assembly to the air plenum.

99. Connect the coolant hoses to the throttle body.

100. Install and connect wiring harness connectors.

101. Install the EGR valve to the intake manifold using a new gasket.

102. Install the modulator.

103. Connect vacuum hoses removed for disassembly.

104. If equipped with automatic transaxle, install the TV cable.

105. Install the accelerator cable.

106. Connect the PCV valve. Install the air cleaner.

107. Connect negative battery cable.

108. Fill cooling system and check for leaks. Start engine and allow engine to come to normal operating temperature. Recheck for coolant leaks. Allow engine to warm up sufficently to confirm operation of cooling fan.

Valve Lash

Adjustment
1.0L ENGINE

NOTE: The valve clearance adjustment is performed with the engine in the hot condition: coolant temperature above 176°F (80°C) and the oil temperature above 140°F (60°C). Valve clearances (hot): Intake and Exhaust—0.006–0.010 in. (0.15–0.25mm). Reference clearances (cold): Intake and Exhaust—0.004–0.008 in. (0.10–0.020mm).

1. Disconnect the negative battery cable.

2. Disconnect the spark plug wires and accelerator cable from the retaining clamps.

3. Remove the air plenum.

4. Remove the oil filler cap. Disconnect the crankcase ventilation hose. Remove the cylinder head cover.

5. Turn the crankshaft until the timing mark on the flywheel is aligned with the timing mark on the bell housing. Ensure that the rocker arms for No.1 cylinder are up, indicating that both valves are closed.

6. With No. 1 cylinder at TDC of its compression stoke, check clearance of: No. 1 cylinder intake and exhaust valves; No. 2 cylinder exhaust valve and No. 3 cylinder intake valve.

7. Rotate crankshaft 360 degrees.

8. With No. 1 cylinder at TDC of its exhaust stroke (valves in overlap), check clearance of: No. 2 cylinder intake valve and No. 3 cylinder exhaust valve.

9. Adjust valves by loosening locknut on the rocker arm and turning adjusting screw.

NOTE: A stubby prybar of no more than 2 in. in length is required to adjust the intake valves.

10. Install the cylinder head cover using a new gasket. Tighten bolts to 6–9 ft. lbs. (7.8–11.8 Nm).

11. Install the air plenum.

12. Attach the spark plug wires and accelerator cable to clamps.

13. Connect negative battery cable.

1.3L ENGINE

NOTE: The valve clearance adjustment is performed with the engine in the hot condition: coolant temperature is 167–185°F (75–85°C) and the oil temperature above 149°F (65°C). Valve clearances (hot): Intake—0.007–0.013 in. (0.18–0.32mm) and Exhaust—0.010–0.016 in. (0.26–0.40mm). Reference clearances (cold): Intake—0.007 in. (0.18mm) and Exhaust—0.010 in. (0.25mm).

1. Disconnect the negative battery cable.

2. Disconnect the spark plug wires from the retaining clamps and the accelerator cable from the throttle body.

3. Disconnect the crankcase ventilation hose. Detach the oxygen sensor harness from the clamp. Detach the engine ground wire from the cylinder head cover. Detach the accelerator cable from the clamps.

4. Remove the cylinder head cover.

5. Turn the crankshaft until the recessed mark on the crankshaft pulley is aligned with the timing mark timing belt cover. Ensure that the rocker arms of No. 1 cylinder are up, indicating that both valves are closed.

6. With No. 1 cylinder at TDC of its compression stoke, check clearance of: No. 1 cylinder intake and exhaust valves; No. 2 cylinder intake valve and No. 3 cylinder exhaust valve.

7. Rotate crankshaft 360 degrees.

8. With No. 4 cylinder at TDC of its compression stroke, check clearance of: No. 2 cylinder exhaust valve; No. 3 cylinder intake valve and No. 4 intake and exhaust valves.

9. Adjust valves by loosening locknut on the rocker arm and turning adjusting screw.

10. Install the cylinder head cover using a new gasket. Inspect spark plug rubber grommets for wear. Replace, as required. Ensure that the grommets are seated properly.

11. Tighten the cylinder head cover bolts, over 2–3 stages, in sequence, to 2–4 ft. lbs. (3–5 Nm).

12. Attach the accelerator cable to clamp. Install the oxygen sensor harness. Install the engine ground wire to the cylinder head. Connect the PCV hoses to the cylinder head cover. Install the spark plug wires and position wires in retainers.

13. Connect negative battery cable.

Rocker Arms/Shafts

Removal and Installation
1.0L ENGINE

1. Disconnect the negative battery cable.

2. Drain the cooling system.

3. Remove the cylinder head and place in a suitable holding fixture.

4. Loosen the locknut and loosen the adjusting screw of each valve rocker arm.

5. Use a suitable puller to remove the rocker arm shafts, making sure to hold the rocker arm compression springs as the shaft is removed.

NOTE: Be sure to keep all parts in order so they may be reassembled in the same order.

To install:

6. Apply engine oil to the valve rocker shaft, valve rocker arm, compression spring and valve rocker shaft hole of the cylinder block.

7. Fit the rocker arms and compression springs onto the shaft while inserting into position.

NOTE: The valve rocker shafts differ in length between the intake and exhaust sides. The intake rocker shaft is 11.004 in. (279.5mm) in length. The exhaust rocker shaft is 11.201 in. (284.5mm) in length.

8. Install the cylinder head on the engine block.
9. Adjust the valve clearances to cold specifications.
10. Connect negative battery cable.
11. Fill cooling system and check for leaks. Start engine and allow engine to come to normal operating temperature. Recheck for coolant leaks. Allow engine to warm up sufficiently to confirm operation of cooling fan.
12. Readjust valve clearances to hot specifications.

1.3L ENGINE

1. Disconnect the negative battery cable.
2. Drain the cooling system.
3. Remove the cylinder head cover and timing belt.
4. Loosen the 10 rocker arm retaining bolts evenly, over 2–3 stages, and remove.
5. Remove the rocker arm shaft together with the rocker arms from the cylinder head.

NOTE: When disassembling the rocker arms, spacers and wave washers from the rocker arm shaft, keep all disassembled parts in order so they can be reassembled in the same position.

To install:

6. Assemble the valve rocker arms and wave washers onto the valve rocker shaft. The intake rocker shaft is identified by recessed sections along the shaft.
7. Install the valve rocker shaft on the camshaft caps. For ease of installation, insert the rocker arm onto the camshaft side first.
8. Install the 10 rocker arm retaining bolts and tighten, evenly, over 2–3 stages. Tighten the M10 bolts to 27 ft. lbs. (36 Nm). Tighten the M8 bolts to 13 ft. lbs. (17 Nm).
9. Install the spacers between the rocker arms on the intake valve rocker arm shaft.
10. Install the timing belt.
11. Adjust the valve clearances to the cold specification.
12. Connect negative battery cable.
13. Fill cooling system and check for leaks. Start engine and allow engine to come to normal operating temperature. Recheck for coolant leaks. Allow engine to warm up sufficiently to confirm operation of cooling fan.
14. Readjust the valves to the hot specifications.

Intake Manifold

Removal and Installation

1.0L ENGINE

1. Disconnect the negative battery cable.
2. Drain the cooling system to a point where the heater hose to the intake manifold can be removed.
3. Remove the heater hose from the intake manifold.
4. Remove the EGR pipe.
5. Disconnect the idle-up Vacuum Switching Valve (VSV) connector.
6. Disconnect the EGR VSV connector.
7. Disconnect the intake air temperature sensor connector.
8. Disconnect the wire clamp attached to the back of the air plenum.
9. Disconnect the fuel line to the cold start injector.
10. Disconnect the throttle body and cold start injector connectors.
11. Remove the air plenum support.
12. Disconnect the vacuum hose connecting the air plenum and oil filler cap.

13. Disconnect the fuel hose clamp at the back of the air plenum.
14. Remove the bolts and nuts attaching the air plenum and remove the air plenum and gasket.
15. Disconnect the injector connectors.
16. Remove the fuel return hose from the pressure regulator.
17. Remove the fuel hose from the delivery pipe.
18. Remove the fuel delivery pipe from the intake manifold.
19. Remove the 3 fuel delivery pipe insulators from the intake manifold. Remove the fuel injectors.
20. Disconnect the engine ground terminal at the intake manifold.
21. Disconnect the water temperature switch, water temperature sender, cold start injector time switch and radiator fan motor switch connectors, as required.
22. Remove th engine wire clamp under the cold start injector time switch.
23. Remove the clamp from the water outlet pipe bracket.
24. Disconnect the oil cooler hose from the intake manifold.
25. Remove the bolts and nuts attaching the intake manifold.
26. Remove the vacuum hose between the Bimetal Vacuum Switching Valve (BVSV) and the charcoal cannister.
27. Remove the intake manifold and gasket.

To install:

28. Ensure that the gasket mounting surfaces are free of gasket material and install a new intake manifold gasket.
29. Position the intake manifold in place and loosely install the attaching bolts and nuts.
30. Position the engine wiring harness clamps onto the intake manifold studs.
31. Tighten the nuts to 11–16 ft. lbs. (15–22 Nm).
32. Connect the vacuum hose between the BVSV and the charcoal cannister.
33. Connect the oil cooler hose to the intake manifold.
34. Install the wire clamp for the intake manifold water temperature sensor.
35. Connect the engine ground terminal to the intake manifold.
36. Connect the water temperature switch, water temperature sender, cold start injector time switch and radiator fan motor switch connectors, if removed.
37. Install the clamp to the water outlet pipe bracket.
38. Install the engine wire clamp to the cold start injector time switch.
39. Install the 3 fuel delivery pipe insulators to the intake manifold. Install the injectors.
40. Connect the fuel delivery pipe to the intake manifold.
41. Connect the fuel hose to the fuel delivery pipe.
42. Connect the fuel return hose to the pressure regulator.
43. Connect the fuel injector connectors.
44. Install a new air plenum gasket and position the air plenum on the intake manifold and install the attaching nuts and bolts.
45. Connect the fuel hose clamp at the back of the air plenum.
46. Connect the air plenum support.
47. Connect the throttle body and cold start injector connectors.
48. Connect the fuel line to the cold start injector.
49. Connect the wire clamp to the back of the air plenum.
50. Connect the intake air temperature sensor connector.
51. Connect the EGR VSV connector.
52. Connect the idle-up VSV connector.
53. Connect the heater hose to the intake manifold.
54. Connect negative battery cable.
55. Fill cooling system and check for leaks. Start engine and allow engine to come to normal operating temperature. Recheck for coolant leaks. Check for vacuum leaks. Allow engine to warm up sufficiently to confirm operation of cooling fan.

1.3L ENGINE

1. Disconnect the negative battery cable.

2. Remove the air cleaner.

3. Disconnect the coolant circulating hose from the throttle body. Disconnect the accelerator cable from the throttle body.

4. Remove the nuts and bolts retaining the air plenum supports and remove the supports.

5. Remove the air plenum attaching nuts and bolts, evenly, over 2–3 stages, and remove the air plenum.

6. Remove the intake manifold attaching nuts and bolts, evenly, over 2–3 stages, and remove the intake manifold.

To install:

7. Position the intake manifold in place using a new gasket and install the attaching nuts and bolts, in sequence, evenly over 2–3 stages. Tighten to 11–16 ft. lbs. (15–22 Nm).

8. Position the air plenum in place and install the attaching nuts and bolts. Tighten evenly, over 2–3 stages, in sequence, to 22–33 ft. lbs. (29–44 Nm).

9. Install the air plenum supports.

10. Connect the coolant circulating hose and the accelerator cable to the throttle body.

11. Install the air cleaner.

12. Connect negative battery cable.

Exhaust Manifold

Removal and Installation

1.0L ENGINE

1. Disconnect the negative battery cable.

2. Disconnect the oxygen sensor connector.

3. Disconnect the distributor connector.

4. Raise and safely support the vehicle.

5. Remove the nuts attaching the exhaust pipe to the exhaust manifold.

6. Remove the exhaust pipe clamp.

7. Disconnect the exhaust pipe from the exhaust manifold.

8. Lower vehicle.

9. Remove the exhaust manifold cover.

10. Remove the exhaust manifold support attaching bolts.

11. Remove the exhaust manifold.

To install:

12. Install a new exhaust manifold gasket and position the exhaust manifold in place. Install the attaching bolts and tighten to 11–16 ft. lbs. (15–22 Nm).

13. Install the exhaust manifold support and tighten to 22–33 ft. lbs. (30–44 Nm).

14. Install the oxygen sensor, if removed, using a new gasket. Tighten to 22–29 ft. lbs. (29–39 Nm).

15. Install the exhaust manifold cover. Be sure to connect the engine ground cable with the proper attaching bolt. Tighten to 4–7 ft. lbs. (6–9 Nm).

16. Raise and safely support the vehicle.

17. Connect the exhaust pipe to the exhaust manifold using a new gasket. Tighten bolts to 36–55 ft. lbs. (49–75 Nm).

18. Install the exhaust pipe clamp. Tighten to 25–36 ft. lbs. (34–49 Nm).

19. Lower vehicle.

20. Install the distributor connector.

21. Install the oxygen sensor connector.

22. Connect negative battery cable.

1.3L ENGINE

1. Disconnect the negative battery cable.

2. Drain the cooling system.

3. Remove the radiator and cooling fan assembly.

4. Disconnect the oxygen sensor wire. Remove the wire from the clamp on the cylinder head cover. Remove the oxygen sensor.

5. Remove the oil dipstick.

6. If equipped with radio, disconnect the engine ground cable from the cylinder head.

7. Remove the exhaust manifold top and side covers. If equipped with air conditioning, remove the exhaust manifold lower covers.

8. Remove the dipstick tube.

9. Raise and safely support the vehicle.

10. Remove the exhaust pipe clamp.

11. Disconnect the exhaust pipe from the exhaust manifold.

12. Remove the exhaust manifold support.

13. Lower vehicle.

14. Remove the exhaust manifold attaching bolts, evenly, over 2–3 stages, and remove the exhaust manifold and gasket.

To install:

15. If separated, connect the 2 sections of the exhaust manifold using a new gasket. Tighten bolts to 15–22 ft. lbs. (20–29 Nm).

16. Install a new exhaust manifold gasket, making sure gasket mating surfaces are free of gasket material.

17. Position the exhaust manifold and install the attaching bolts. Tighten, in sequence, evenly, over 2–3 stages, to 22–33 ft. lbs. (29–44 Nm).

18. Raise and safely support the vehicle.

19. Install the exhaust manifold support and tighten to 22–33 ft. lbs. (29–44 Nm).

20. Connect the exhaust pipe to the exhaust manifold using a new gasket. Tighten to 36–55 ft. lbs. (49–75 Nm).

21. Install the exhaust pipe clamp. Tighten to 25–36 ft. lbs. (34–49 Nm).

22. Lower vehicle.

23. Insert the dipstick tube using a new O-ring. Install the dipstick tube attaching bolt and tighten a few turns. Do not tighten completely at this time.

24. Install the exhaust manifold top cover.

25. Tighten the dipstick tube. Install the dipstick.

26. Install the exhaust manifold side cover and, if equipped with air conditioning, install the exhaust manifold lower cover.

27. Install the oxygen sensor using a new gasket. Connect the oxygen sensor wire connector. Install the wire from the clamp to the cylinder head cover.

28. Install the radiator and cooling fan assembly.

29. Connect negative battery cable.

30. Fill cooling system and check for leaks. Start engine and allow engine to come to normal operating temperature. Recheck for coolant leaks. Allow engine to warm up sufficiently to confirm operation of cooling fan.

Timing Belt Front Cover

Removal and Installation

1.0L ENGINE

1. Disconnect the negative battery cable.

2. Loosen the accelerator cable locknut from the throttle body support. Remove the accelerator cable from the throttle lever. Remove the accelerator cable from the clamp.

3. Remove the PCV hose.

4. Label and remove the air cleaner hoses. Remove the air cleaner assembly.

5. Disconnect the alternator ground cable.

6. If equipped with air conditioning, perform the following:

   a. Loosen the idler pulley mount nut.

   b. Loosen the adjusting bolt.

   c. Remove the drive belt.

7. Loosen the alternator lock bolts, relieve the tension and remove the alternator drive belt.

8. Remove the right front engine under cover.

9. Using a supporting pad under the oil pan, slightly raise the engine to release the tension on the engine mount.

10. Remove the nuts attaching the front engine mount bracket.

11. Remove the 3 bolt attaching the front engine mount to the cylinder head.

12. Lower the lifting device slightly and remove the front engine mount bracket.

13. Remove the water pump pulley.

14. Set the engine to TDC of No. 1 cylinder on the compression stroke.

15. Prevent the crankshaft from turning by inserting a suitable tool into the ring gear.

16. Remove the crankshaft pulley.

17. Remove the timing belt upper and lower covers.

To install:

18. Install the timing belt upper and lower covers. Tighten to 1.4–2.9 ft. lbs. (2.0–3.9 Nm).

19. Remove the crankshaft pulley bolt. Insert the crankshaft pulley with the key groove on the crankshaft pulley aligned with the crankshaft key. Install the crankshaft pulley bolt and tighten to 65–72 ft. lbs. (88–98 Nm).

20. Install the water pump pulley. Tighten to 4–7 ft. lbs. (6–9 Nm).

21. Install the front engine mount bracket to the cylinder head. Tighten M12 bolt to 36–51 ft. lbs. (49–67 Nm). Tighten M10 bolt to 22–33 ft. lbs. (29–44 Nm).

22. Tighten the front engine mount bracket to 29–40 ft. lbs. (39–54 Nm).

23. Install the front right engine under cover.

24. Remove the lifting device.

25. Install the alternator drive belt. Adjust the alternator drive belt tension to 22 lbs. (10 kg) with 0.197–0.276 in. (5–7mm) deflection applied at the midpoint between the alternator and water pump pulleys.

26. If equipped with air conditioning, install the air conditioning drive belt. Adjust the air conditioning compressor drive belt tension to 22 lbs. (10 kg) with 0.16–0.24 in. (4.0–6.0mm) deflection at the midpoint between the crankshaft and compressor pulleys.

27. Tighten the idler pulley mounting nut. Tighten to 23–35 ft. lbs. (31–47 Nm).

28. Connect the alternator ground cable.

29. Install the air cleaner assembly. Tighten bolts to 7.2–11.6 ft. lbs. (9.8–15.7 Nm). Install the rubber hoses to the air cleaner.

30. Install the PCV hose.

31. Install the accelerator cable to the throttle lever.

32. Tighten the locknut to the throttle body support. Tighten to 7.2–11.6 ft. lbs. (9.8–15.7 Nm).

33. Connect negative battery cable.

1.3L ENGINE

1. Disconnect the negative battery cable.

2. If equipped with air conditioning, perform the following:
   a. Drain the cooling system into a clean container for reuse.
   b. Remove the radiator and cooling fan assembly.
   c. Remove the air conditioning belt by loosening the locknut and tensioner bolt on the air conditioning idler pulley.
   d. Remove the idler pulley assembly.
   e. Remove the air conditioning compressor and set aside. Support the compressor using a length of mechanics wire.

3. If equipped with power steering, perform the following:
   a. Loosen the power steering belt tensioner locknut and tensioner bolt. Remove the power steering belt.
   b. Remove the power steering pump and set aside. Support the power steering pump using a length of mechanics wire.

4. Remove the hoses from the air cleaner case. Remove the attaching bolts and hose bands and remove the air cleaner case.

5. Disconnect the oil pressure switch connector.

6. Remove the bolts attaching the oil pressure switch wire. Pull wire through the hole in the engine mount and set wire aside.

7. Using the alternator belt tension, loosen the bolts on the water pump pulley.

8. Loosen the adjusting bolt and 2 alternator mounting bolts to slacken tension on the alternator belt and remove the water pump pulley and alternator belt.

9. Using a supporting pad under the oil pan, slightly raise the engine to release the tension on the engine mount.

10. Remove the 3 attaching bolts and 1 nut for the right engine mount.

11. Remove the 3 attaching bolts for the engine mount front insulator.

12. Remove the right front engine mount bracket.

13. Remove the service hole cover in the fender well, just forward of the right front wheel.

14. Remove the crankshaft pulley, accessing the 4 bolts through service hole in the fender well.

15. Remove the timing belt upper and lower covers.

To install:

16. Install the timing belt upper and lower covers. Tighten to 1.4–3.9 ft. lbs. (2–4 Nm).

17. Install the crankshaft timing belt pulley. Tighten bolts to 15–22 ft. lbs. (20–29 Nm). Install the service hole cover.

18. Install the right front engine mount bracket. Tighten bolt to 29–40 ft. lbs. (39–54 Nm).

19. Install the right side engine mount bracket and front engine mount insulator. Tighten bolt to 29–40 ft. lbs. (39–54 Nm). Tighten nut to 11–17 ft. lbs. (15–23 Nm).

20. Remove lifting device from under oil pan.

21. Temporarily attach the water pump pulley.

22. Install the alternator belt and adjust tension using the alternator adjuster. Tighten alternator locknut .

23. Tighten the water pump pulley attaching belts, using the belt tension. Tighten to 4–7 ft. lbs. (4–9 Nm).

24. Check belt tension at the midpoint of the belt between the alternator and water pump pulleys.

25. Route the oil pressure switch wire through the hole in the engine mount. Install the clamp bolt for the oil pressure switch wire. Ensure that there is no slack in the wire between the clamps. Connect the oil pressure switch connector.

26. If equipped with air conditioning, perform the following:
   a. Install the air conditioning compressor to the engine block.
   b. Install the air conditioning belt tensioner pulley assembly to the cylinder block. Install the air conditioner belt and adjust tension.
   c. Install the radiator and cooling fan assembly.

27. If equipped with power steering, perform the following:
   a. Install the power steering pump to the cylinder head.
   b. Install the power steering belt and adjust tension.

28. Connect negative battery cable.

29. Fill cooling system and check for leaks. Start engine and allow engine to come to normal operating temperature. Recheck for coolant leaks. Allow engine to warm up sufficiently to confirm operation of cooling fan.

Oil Seal Replacement

1. Disconnect the negative battery cable.
2. Remove the timing belt.
3. Remove the idler pulley and return spring.
4. Remove the crankshaft timing belt sprocket.
5. Remove the crankshaft timing belt sprocket flange.
6. Remove the front oil seal.

To install:

7. Install a new front oil seal.
8. Install the crankshaft timing belt sprocket flange.
9. Install the crankshaft timing belt sprocket.
10. Install the idler pulley and return spring.
11. Install the timing belt.
12. Connect negative battery cable.

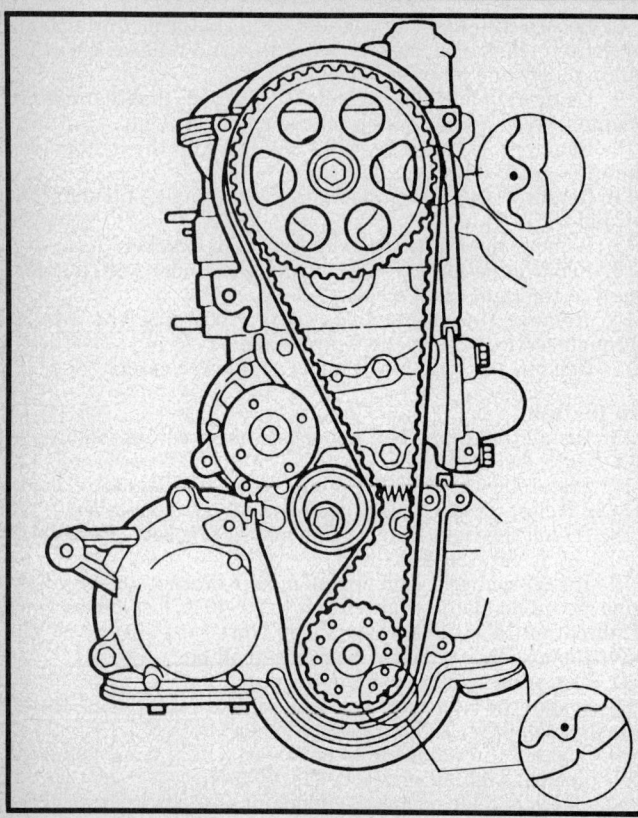

Timing mark locations—1.0L engine

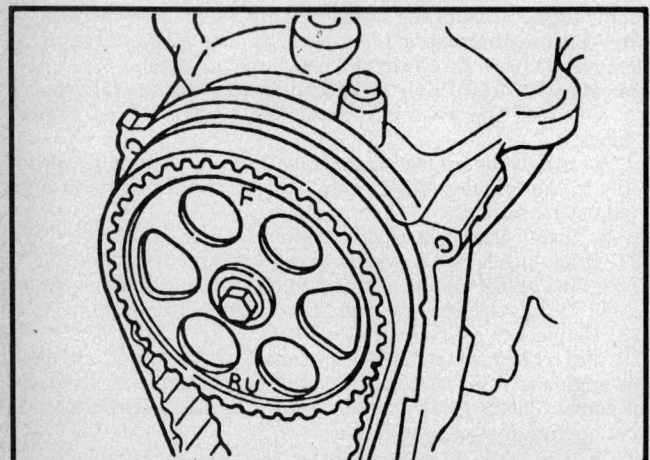

"F" mark position on camshaft timing belt sprocket—
1.0L engine

Timing Belt and Tensioner

Adjustment

1.0L ENGINE

1. Disconnect the negative battery cable.
2. Remove the timing belt upper and lower covers.
3. Rotate the engine so the **F** mark on the camshaft is at the top position.
4. Loosen the idler pulley locknut. Apply tension to the timing belt exceeding the tension exerted by the tension spring. Temporarily tighten the attaching bolt.

5. Turn the crankshaft approximately 2 turns in the direction of normal rotation until No. 1 piston is at TDC on its compression stroke. The **F** mark on the camshaft should be at the top position.
6. Loosen the idler pulley locknut.
7. Tighten the timing belt tensioner locknut to 25–33 ft. lbs. (33–44 Nm).
8. Ensure that the timing marks on the camshaft and crankshaft timing belt sprockets are aligned with the corresponding marks on the timing belt.
9. Install the timing belt upper and lower covers.
10. Connect negative battery cable.

1.3L ENGINE

1. Disconnect the negative battery cable.
2. Remove the timing belt upper and lower covers.
3. Rotate the engine so the **F** mark on the camshaft is at the top position. Ensure that the drilled timing mark on the crankshaft timing belt sprocket is aligned with the mark on the engine block.
4. Loosen the idler pulley locknut. Apply tension to the timing belt exceeding the tension exerted by the tension spring. Temporarily tighten the attaching bolt.
5. Turn the crankshaft approximately 2 turns in the direction of normal rotation until No. 1 piston is approaching TDC on its compression stroke. The **F** mark on the camshaft should be at the 11 o'clock position or 3 camshaft sprocket teeth before the reference mark on the valve cover.
6. Loosen the idler pulley locknut.

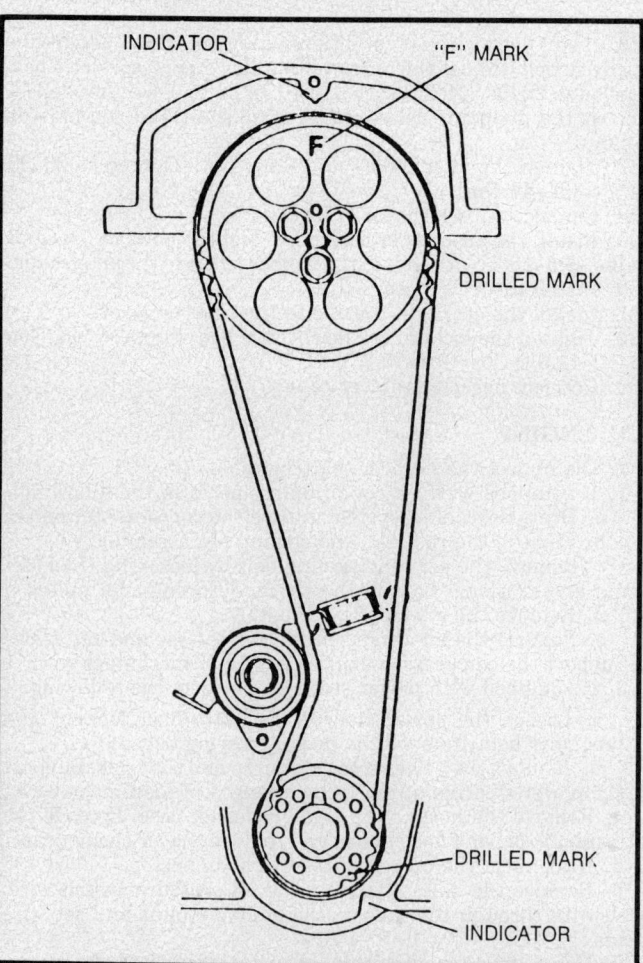

Timing mark locations—1.3L engine

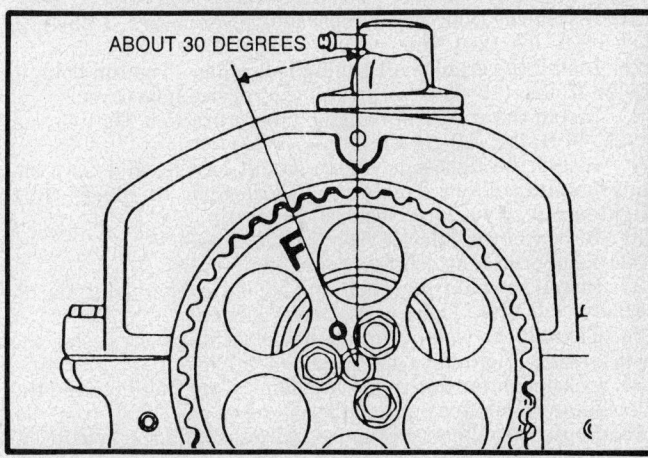

ABOUT 30 DEGREES

"F" mark position on camshaft timing belt sprocket for adjusting timing belt tension—1.3L engine

7. Turn the crankshaft in the direction of rotation until the **F** mark is at the 12 o'clock position and aligned with the reference mark on the valve cover.

8. Tighten the timing belt tensioner locknut to 22–33 ft. lbs. (29–44 Nm).

9. Ensure that the timing marks on the camshaft and crankshaft timing belt sprockets are aligned with the corresponding marks on the timing belt.

10. Install the timing belt upper and lower covers.

11. Connect negative battery cable.

Removal and Installation

1.0L ENGINE

1. Disconnect the negative battery cable.

2. Loosen the accelerator cable locknut from the throttle body support. Remove the accelerator cable from the throttle lever. Remove the accelerator cable from the clamp.

3. Remove the PCV hose.

4. Label and remove the air cleaner hoses. Remove the air cleaner assembly.

5. Disconnect the alternator ground cable.

6. If equipped with air conditioning, perform the following:
   a. Loosen the idler pulley mount nut.
   b. Loosen the adjusting bolt.
   c. Remove the drive belt.

7. Loosen the alternator lock bolts, relieve the tension and remove the alternator drive belt.

8. Remove the right front engine under cover.

9. Using a supporting pad under the oil pan, slightly raise the engine to release the tension on the engine mount.

10. Remove the nuts attaching the front engine mount bracket.

11. Remove the 3 bolts attaching the front engine mount to the cylinder head.

12. Lower the lifting device slightly and remove the front engine mount bracket.

13. Remove the water pump pulley.

14. Set the engine to TDC of No. 1 cylinder on the compression stroke.

15. Prevent the crankshaft from turning by inserting a suitable tool into the ring gear.

16. Remove the crankshaft pulley.

17. Remove the timing belt upper and lower covers.

18. Remove the crankshaft timing belt pulley flange.

NOTE: If the timing belt is to be reinstalled, use chalk or a suitable marker to indicate the direction of normal rotation prior to removing the belt.

19. Loosen the tensioner pulley bolt. Push the bolt to the left as far as it will go and tighten it temporarily.

NOTE: Do not rotate the crankshaft or camshaft with the timing belt removed as internal engine damage will result.

20. Remove the timing belt.

To install:

21. Ensure that the timing marks on the camshaft and crankshaft are aligned with corresponding marks on the engine.

22. Install the timing belt on the camshaft and crankshaft timing sprockets.

NOTE: When installing a new belt, align the mark on the back side of the belt with the corresponding mark on each pulley.

23. Loosen the tensioner pulley locknut. Apply tension to the timing belt exceeding the tension exerted by the tension spring. Temporarily tighten the attaching bolt.

24. Turn the crankshaft approximately 2 turns in the direction of normal rotation until No. 1 piston is at TDC on its compression stroke. The **F** mark on the camshaft should be at the top position.

25. Loosen the tensioner pulley locknut.

26. Tighten the timing belt tensioner locknut to 25–33 ft. lbs. (33–44 Nm).

27. Ensure that the timing marks on the camshaft and crankshaft timing belt sprockets are aligned with the corresponding marks on the timing belt.

28. Install the crankshaft timing belt pulley flange. Ensure that the crankshaft timing belt pulley flange with the protruding side faces toward the crankshaft timing belt sprocket.

29. Install the timing belt upper and lower covers. Tighten to 1.4–2.9 ft. lbs. (2.0–3.9 Nm).

30. Remove the crankshaft pulley bolt. Insert the crankshaft pulley with the key groove on the crankshaft pulley aligned with the crankshaft key. Install the crankshaft pulley bolt and tighten to 65–72 ft. lbs. (88–98 Nm).

31. Install the water pump pulley. Tighten to 4–7 ft. lbs. (6–9 Nm).

32. Install the front engine mount bracket to the cylinder head. Tighten M12 bolt to 36–51 ft. lbs. (49–67 Nm). Tighten M10 bolt to 22–33 ft. lbs. (29–44 Nm).

33. Tighten the front engine mount bracket to 29–40 ft. lbs. (39–54 Nm).

34. Install the front right engine under cover.

35. Remove the lifting device.

36. Install the alternator drive belt. Adjust the alternator drive belt tension to 22 lbs. (10 kg) with 0.197–0.276 in. (5–7mm) deflection applied at the midpoint between the alternator and water pump pulleys.

37. If equipped with air conditioning, install the air conditioning drive belt. Adjust the air conditioning compressor drive belt tension to 22 lbs. (10 kg) with 0.16–0.24 in. (4.0–6.0mm) deflection at the midpoint between the crankshaft and compressor pulleys.

38. Tighten the idler pulley mounting nut. Tighten to 23–35 ft. lbs. (31–47 Nm).

39. Connect the alternator ground cable.

40. Install the air cleaner assembly. Tighten bolts to 7.2–11.6 ft. lbs. (9.8–15.7 Nm). Install the rubber hoses to the air cleaner.

41. Install the PCV hose.

42. Install the accelerator cable to the throttle lever.

43. Tighten the locknut to the throttle body support. Tighten to 7.2–11.6 ft. lbs. (9.8–15.7 Nm).

44. Connect negative battery cable.

1.3L ENGINE

1. Disconnect the negative battery cable.

2. If equipped with air conditioning, perform the following:

a. Drain the cooling system into a clean container for reuse.

b. Remove the radiator and cooling fan assembly.

c. Remove the air conditioning belt by loosening the lock-nut and tensioner bolt on the air conditioning idler pulley.

d. Remove the idler pulley assembly.

e. Remove the air conditioning compressor and set aside. Support the compressor using a length of mechanics wire.

3. If equipped with power steering, perform the following:

a. Loosen the power steering belt tensioner locknut and tensioner bolt. Remove the power steering belt.

b. Remove the power steering pump and set aside. Support the power steering pump using a length of mechanics wire.

4. Remove the hoses from the air cleaner case. Remove the attaching bolts and hose bands and remove the air cleaner case.

5. Disconnect the oil pressure switch connector.

6. Remove the bolts attaching the oil pressure switch wire. Pull wire through the hole in the engine mount and set wire aside.

7. Using the alternator belt tension, loosen the bolts on the water pump pulley.

8. Loosen the adjusting bolt and 2 alternator mounting bolts to slacken tension on the alternator belt and remove the water pump pulley and alternator belt.

9. Using a supporting pad under the oil pan, slightly raise the engine to release the tension on the engine mount.

10. Remove the 3 attaching bolts and 1 nut for the right engine mount.

11. Remove the 3 attaching bolts for the engine mount front insulator.

12. Remove the right front engine mount bracket.

13. Remove the service hole cover in the fender well, just forward of the right front wheel.

14. Remove the crankshaft pulley, accessing the 4 bolts through service hole in the fender well.

15. Remove the timing belt upper and lower covers.

NOTE: If the timing belt is to be reinstalled, use chalk or a suitable marker to indicate the direction of normal rotation prior to removing the belt.

16. Rotate the crankshaft until the **F** mark on the camshaft timing belt pulley is aligned with the indicator or the cylinder head cover.

17. Loosen the timing belt tensioner locknut. Move the tensioner as far left as it will go and tighten it temporarily.

18. Remove the timing belt.

NOTE: Do not rotate the crankshaft or camshaft with the timing belt removed as internal engine damage will result.

To install:

19. Check alignment of timing marks of the crankshaft and camshaft sprockets with their corresponding timing marks.

20. Install the timing belt.

21. Loosen the tensioner locknut and apply tension to the timing belt. Temporarily tighten the locknut.

22. Turn the crankshaft approximately 2 turns in the direction of normal rotation until No. 1 piston is approaching TDC on its compression stroke. The **F** mark on the camshaft should be at the 11 o'clock position or 3 camshaft sprocket teeth before the reference mark on the valve cover.

23. Loosen the idler pulley locknut.

24. Turn the crankshaft in the direction of rotation until the **F** mark is at the 12 o'clock position and aligned with the reference mark on the valve cover.

25. Tighten the timing belt tensioner locknut to 22–33 ft. lbs. (29–44 Nm).

26. Ensure that the timing marks on the camshaft and crankshaft timing belt sprockets are aligned with the corresponding marks on the timing belt.

27. Install the timing belt upper and lower covers. Tighten to 1.4–3.9 ft. lbs. (2–4 Nm).

28. Install the crankshaft timing belt pulley. Tighten bolts to 15–22 ft. lbs. (20–29 Nm). Install the service hole cover.

29. Install the right front engine mount bracket. Tighten bolt to 29–40 ft. lbs. (39–54 Nm).

30. Install the right side engine mount bracket and front engine mount insulator. Tighten bolt to 29–40 ft. lbs. (39–54 Nm). Tighten nut to 11–17 ft. lbs. (15–23 Nm).

31. Remove lifting device from under oil pan.

32. Temporarily attach the water pump pulley.

33. Install the alternator belt and adjust tension using the alternator adjuster. Tighten alternator locknut .

34. Tighten the water pump pulley attaching belts, using the belt tension. Tighten to 4–7 ft. lbs. (4–9 Nm).

35. Check belt tension at the midpoint of the belt between the alternator and water pump pulleys.

36. Route the oil pressure switch wire through the hole in the engine mount. Install the clamp bolt for the oil pressure switch wire. Ensure that there is no slack in the wire between clamps. Connect the oil pressure switch connector.

37. If equipped with air conditioning, perform the following:

a. Install the air conditioning compressor to the engine block.

b. Install the air conditioning belt tensioner pulley assembly to the cylinder block. Install the air conditioner belt and adjust tension.

c. Install the radiator and cooling fan assembly.

38. If equipped with power steering, perform the following:

a. Install the power steering pump to the cylinder head.

b. Install the power steering belt and adjust tension.

39. Connect negative battery cable.

40. Fill cooling system and check for leaks. Start engine and allow engine to come to normal operating temperature. Recheck for coolant leaks. Allow engine to warm up sufficiently to confirm operation of cooling fan.

Timing Sprockets

Removal and Installation

1.0L ENGINE

1. Disconnect the negative battery cable.
2. Remove the timing belt.
3. Remove the timing belt tensioner pulley and return spring.
4. Remove the crankshaft timing belt sprocket.
5. If required, remove the crankshaft timing belt sprocket flange.

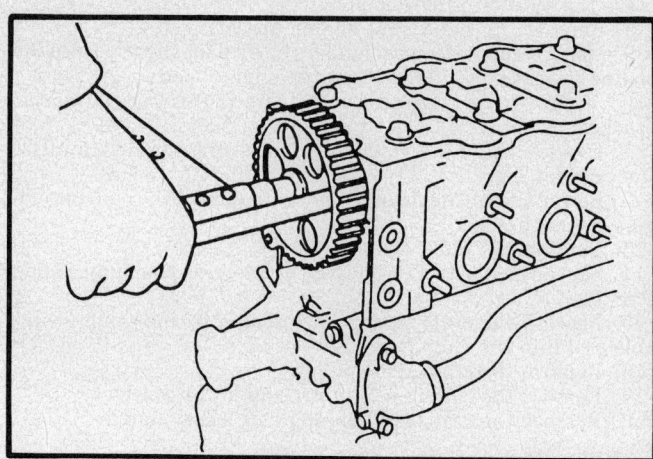

Removal of camshaft timing belt sprocket—1.0L engine

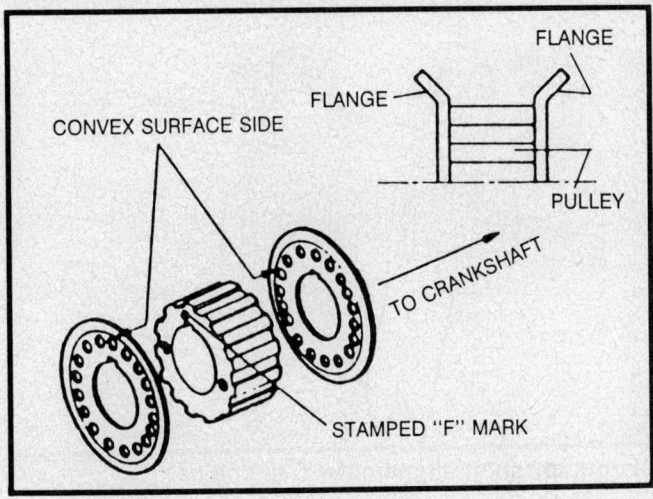

Crankshaft pulley and flange position—1.0L engine

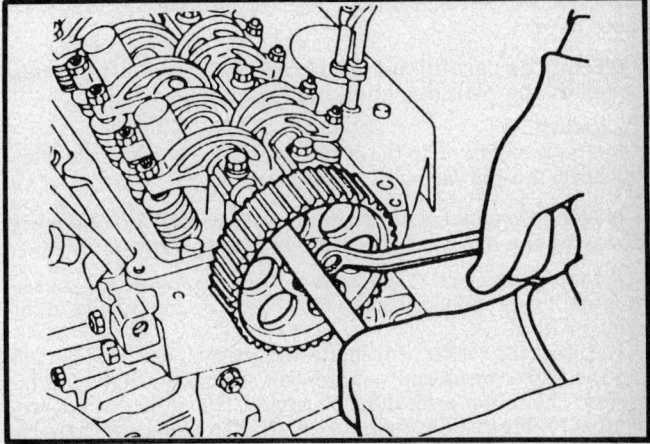

Removal of camshaft timing belt sprocket—1.3L engine

6. Prevent the camshaft from turning by inserting a rod through a hole in the sprocket into the rib in the cylinder head and remove the set bolt.

7. Remove the camshaft timing belt sprocket using a suitable puller.

To install:

8. Align the groove in the camshaft timing belt sprocket with the key in the camshaft and push the sprocket onto the camshaft.

9. Prevent the camshaft from turning and tighten the set bolt to 22–33 ft. lbs. (29–44 Nm).

10. If removed, install the crankshaft timing belt sprocket flange with its recessed side facing the sprocket.

11. Align the groove in the crankshaft timing belt sprocket with the key in the crankshaft and push the sprocket onto the crankshaft.

12. Install the timing belt tensioner pulley and spring. Push the pulley assembly to the left and temporarily tighten the locknut.

13. Install the timing belt.

14. Connect negative battery cable.

1.3L ENGINE

1. Disconnect the negative battery cable.

2. If equipped with air conditioning, remove the radiator and cooling fan assembly. Remove the air conditioning compressor.

3. If equipped with power steering, remove the power steering pump.

NOTE: Do not rotate the crankshaft or camshaft with the timing belt removed as internal engine damage will result.

4. Remove the timing belt.

5. Remove the oxygen sensor wire from its clamp.

6. Label and disconnect the spark plug wires from the spark plugs.

7. Disconnect the PCV hoses.

8. Disconnect the accelerator cable from its clamp.

9. If equipped with a radio, remove the engine ground wire from the cylinder head cover.

10. Remove the cylinder head cover loosening the 8 attaching bolts, evenly, in 2–3 stages.

11. Prevent the camshaft timing belt sprocket from turning by inserting a rod through one of the holes in the sprocket.

NOTE: Be careful not to allow the rod to rest on the gasket surface while holding the camshaft timing sprocket.

12. Remove the bolts attaching the camshaft timing sprocket and remove the sprocket.

13. Prevent the crankshaft from turning.

14. Remove the crankshaft timing belt sprocket set bolt.

15. Remove the crankshaft timing belt sprocket. If any difficulty is encountered in removing the sprocket reinstall the set bolt a few turns and use a suitable gear puller to remove the sprocket.

To install:

16. Install the crankshaft timing belt sprocket flange with its recessed side facing the oil pump.

17. Install the crankshaft timing belt sprocket, aligning it with the key groove.

18. Install the crankshaft timing belt sprocket set bolt. Prevent the crankshaft from turning and tighten the set bolt to 65–72 ft. lbs. (88–98 Nm).

19. Install the camshaft timing belt sprocket on the camshaft so the **F** mark faces away from the cylinder head and the locating pin hole is aligned with the pin.

20. Install the camshaft timing belt sprocket attaching bolts. Prevent the camshaft from turning and tighten the bolts to 11–16 ft. lbs. (15–22 Nm).

21. Install the cylinder head cover and tighten the attaching bolts, evenly, over 2–3 stages, to 2.2–3.6 ft. lbs. (3.0–4.9 Nm).

22. If equipped with a radio, install the engine ground wire to the cylinder head cover.

23. Connect the accelerator cable to its clamp.

24. Connect the PCV hoses.

25. Connect the spark plug wires.

26. Connect the oxygen sensor wire to its clamp.

27. Install the timing belt.

28. If equipped with power steering, install the power steering pump and drive belt.

29. If equipped with air conditioning, install the air conditioning compressor and drive belt.

30. Connect negative battery cable.

Camshaft

Removal and Installation

1.0L ENGINE

1. Disconnect the negative battery cable.

2. Drain the cooling system into a clean container for reuse.

3. Remove the cylinder head and place in a suitable fixture.

4. Remove the distributor housing.

5. Remove the wave washer.

6. Loosen each valve rocker arm adjusting screw.

7. Remove the valve rocker arm shafts using a suitable puller.

8. Remove the camshaft, pulling it toward the rear of the cylinder head.

NOTE: Be careful not to damage the camshaft bearing bores in the cylinder head during removal.

To install:

9. Apply engine oil to the camshaft bearing bores in the cylinder head and the camshaft bearing journals.

NOTE: Be careful not to damage the camshaft bearing bores in the cylinder head during installation.

10. Apply engine oil to the valve rocker arm shafts, valve rocker arms, compression springs and valve rocker shaft holes in the cylinder head.
11. Insert the rocker arm shafts into the cylinder head installing the rocker arms and compression springs as shafts are inserted. The rocker arms differ in length. The intake rocker arm shaft is 11.004 in. (279.5mm) in length. The exhaust rocker arm shaft is 11.201 in. (284.5mm) in length.
12. Apply engine oil and install the wave washer into the cylinder head.
13. Install a new O-ring in the distributor housing and install the housing on the cylinder head. Tighten bolts to 3–5 ft. lbs. (4–7 Nm).
14. Install the cylinder head on the engine block.
15. Connect negative battery cable.
16. Fill cooling system and check for leaks. Start engine and allow engine to come to normal operating temperature. Recheck for coolant leaks. Allow engine to warm up sufficiently to confirm operation of cooling fan.

1.3L ENGINE

1. Disconnect the negative battery cable.
2. Drain the cooling system into a clean container for reuse.
3. Remove the timing belt.
4. Remove the camshaft timing belt sprocket.
5. Remove the distributor.
6. Remove the cylinder head cover. Loosen the 10 hexagonal head bolts attaching the rocker arm shafts, evenly, over 2–3 stages. Remove the valve rocker shafts together with the rocker arms from the cylinder head.
7. Remove the 2 bolts attaching camshaft bearing cap No.5.
8. Remove the remaining camshaft bearing caps.
9. Remove the camshaft from the cylinder head.

To install:

10. Apply engine oil to the camshaft bearing saddles in the cylinder head and the thrust surfaces. Apply engine oil to the bearing journals and lobes on the camshaft. Set the camshaft on the cylinder head so the locating pin for the camshaft timing belt pulley is at the top position.
11. Install the camshaft bearing caps in the sequence embossed on the bearing caps.
12. Assemble the valve rocker arms and wave washers onto the valve rocker arm shafts. Apply engine oil while assembling the rocker arms and wave washers.
13. Install the valve rocker arm shafts on the camshaft bearing caps.
14. Ensure that the attaching bolts and the mounting holes in the cylinder head are clean and free of oil and dirt.
15. Tighten the bolts, evenly, in 2–3 stages. Tighten the M10 bolts to 27 ft. lbs. (36 Nm). Tighten the M8 Bolts to 12 ft. lbs. (17 Nm).
16. Install the spacers between the intake valve rocker arms on the rocker shaft.

NOTE: Do not allow the camshaft to turn independently of the crankshaft with the timing belt removed as internal engine damage will result.

17. Install the camshaft timing belt sprocket to the end of the

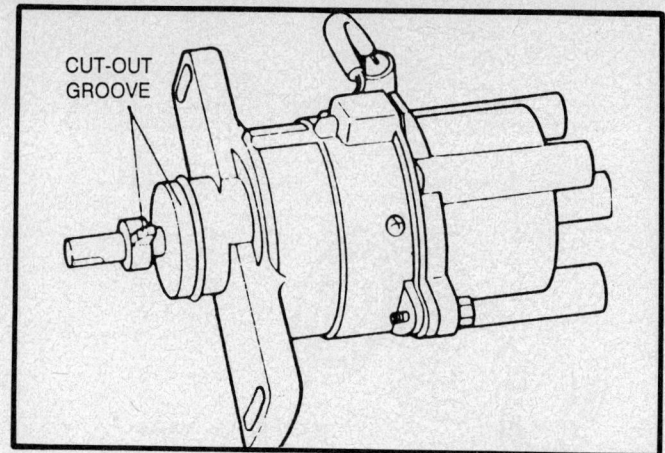

Distributor shaft alignment—1.3L engine

camshaft. Prevent the camshaft from turning and tighten the bolts to 11–16 ft. lbs. (15–21 Nm).
18. Replace the O-ring at the base of the distributor. Align the cut-out section of the distributor proper with the cut-out groove of the cup ring. Install the distributor in the cylinder head, aligning the protrusion of the distributor with the camshaft groove. The aligned cut-out sections must be at the top position on the engine.
19. Center the threaded holes in the cylinder in the elongated holes on the distributor flange and install the attaching bolts. Tighten to 11–16 ft. lbs. (15–22 Nm).
20. Install the cylinder head cover.
21. Install the timing belt.
22. Connect negative battery cable.
23. Fill cooling system and check for leaks. Start engine and allow engine to come to normal operating temperature. Recheck for coolant leaks. Allow engine to warm up sufficiently to confirm operation of cooling fan.
24. Check ignition timing.

Balance Shaft

Removal and Installation

1.0L ENGINE

1. Disconnect the negative battery cable.
2. Drain the cooling system into a clean container for reuse.
3. Drain the engine oil.
4. Remove the engine assembly from the vehicle and place in a suitable holding fixture.

NOTE: Do not allow the camshaft to turn independently of the crankshaft with the timing belt removed as internal engine damage will result.

5. Remove the timing belt.
6. Remove the crankshaft timing belt sprocket.
7. Remove the oil pan and gasket.
8. Remove the balance shaft gear cover and gasket.
9. Remove the oil pump driven sprocket and drive chain.
10. Remove the oil pump and oil pump outlet pipe.
11. Remove the balance weight.
12. Remove the oil pump sprocket and drive chain.
13. Align the stamped mark on the crankshaft gear with the stamped mark on the balance shaft gear.
14. Remove the hexagonal socket head cap bolt, using a hexagonal wrench key (5mm).
15. Pull the balance shaft toward the front of the cylinder block.

To install:

16. Apply engine oil to the bearing bores in the engine block and the bearing journals on the balance shaft.

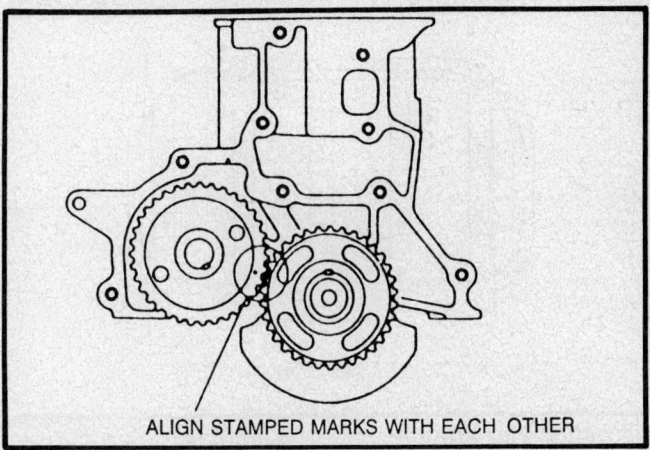

Balance shaft gear alignment marks—1.0L engine

17. Slide the balance shaft into its bore making sure the alignment marks on the balance shaft and crankshaft gears line up.

18. Secure the thrust plate of the balance shaft by tightening the hexagonal bolt to 7–11 ft. lbs. (10–15 Nm).

19. Install the oil pump drive sprocket to the balance shaft.

20. Install the balance weight to the balance shaft with the key groove aligned. Insert the washer. Tighten the bolt to 22–33 ft. lbs. (29–44 Nm).

21. Replace the O-ring on the oil pump outlet. Connect the outlet pipe and tighten the bolts temporarily.

22. Install the oil pump and outlet pipe to the cylinder block.

23. Install the oil pump drive chain to the oil pump sprocket on the balance shaft.

24. Install the oil pump drive sprocket to the oil pump with the drive chain installed. Ensure that the stamped marks "CB OUTSIDE" face the front of the engine. Tighten the attaching bolt.

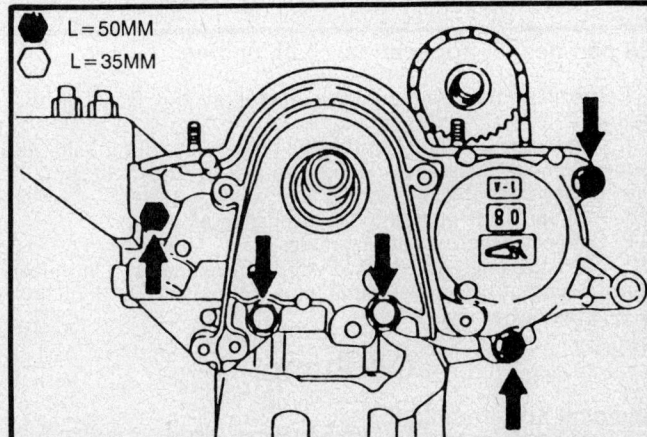

Balance shaft gear cover bolt pattern—1.0L engine

25. Apply engine oil to the balance shaft gear cover oil seal.

26. Install the balance shaft gear cover using a new gasket. Tighten to 7–12 ft. lbs. (10–16 Nm).

27. Install the oil pan using a new gasket.

28. Install the crankshaft timing belt sprocket.

29. Install the engine assembly in the vehicle.

30. Install the timing belt.

31. Add oil to the crankcase.

32. Connect negative battery cable.

33. Fill cooling system and check for leaks. Start engine and allow engine to come to normal operating temperature. Recheck for coolant leaks. Allow engine to warm up sufficiently to confirm operation of cooling fan.

Piston and Connecting Rod

Positioning

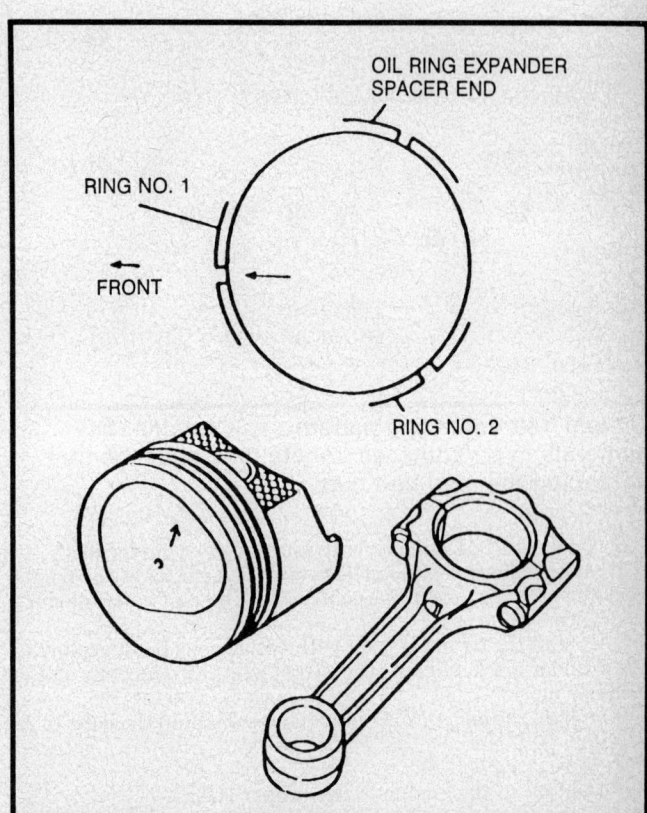

Piston and connecting rod for 1.0L and 1.3L engines

ENGINE LUBRICATION

Oil Pan

Removal and Installation

1.0L ENGINE

1. Disconnect the negative battery cable.

2. Drain the engine oil.

3. Raise and safely support the vehicle.

4. Remove the 26 bolts attaching the oil pan to the engine block. Remove the oil pan and gasket.

To install:

5. Clean the gasket sealing surfaces on the oil pan and engine block.

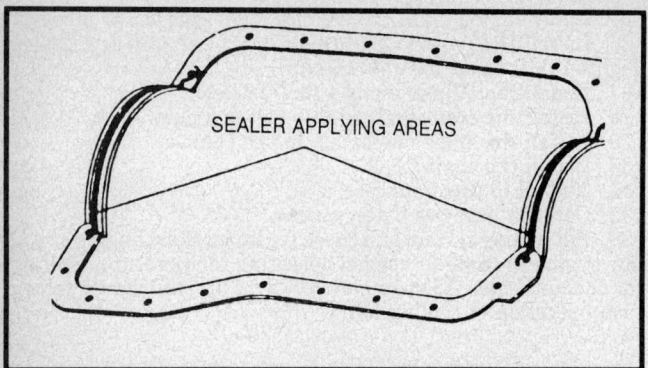

Sealer application on oil pan gasket—1.0L engine

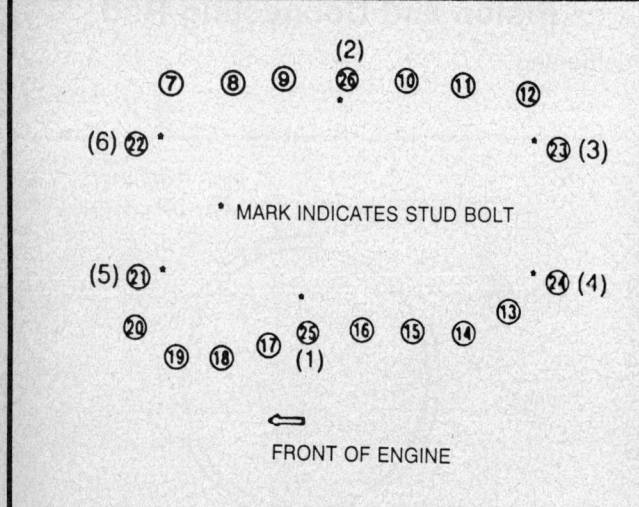

Oil pan bolt tightening pattern—1.0L engine. The numerals in parentheses denote the sequence for tightening the stud bolt nuts.

6. Apply silicone bond to both ends of the cylinder block.

7. Apply silicone bond to the new oil pan gasket at the points near the indentations in the center of the oil pan for crankshaft clearance.

8. Install the oil pan gasket with the silicone bond applied to the cylinder block, aligning the gasket with the stud bolts on the cylinder block.

9. Install the oil pan bolts in sequence. Tighten the bolts to 3–5 ft. lbs. (4–7 Nm).

10. Lower the vehicle.

11. Add oil to the engine to the proper level.

12. Connect negative battery cable.

13. Start the engine and let idle for approximately 1 minute. Shut the engine off and let stand for 3–5 minutes. Check oil level. Add, as necessary.

1.3L ENGINE

1. Disconnect the negative battery cable.

2. Drain the engine oil.

3. Raise and safely support the vehicle.

4. Remove the 14 bolts attaching the oil pan to the engine block. Remove the oil pan and gasket.

To install:

5. Clean the gasket sealing surfaces on the oil pan and engine block.

6. Apply silicone bond to the gasket sealing surface on the cylinder block.

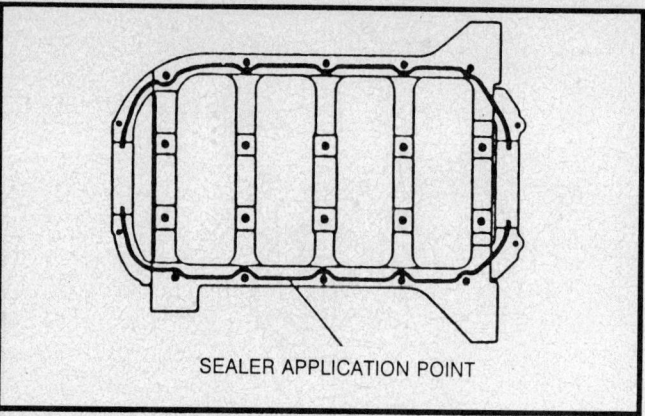

Oil pan sealer application—1.3L engine

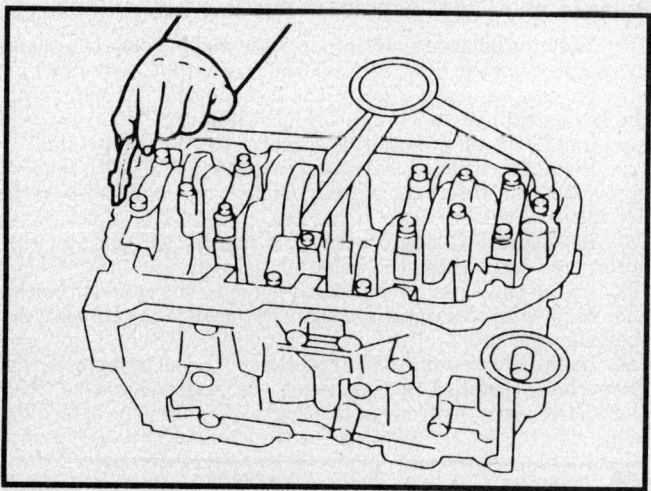

Oil pan gasket application—1.3L engine

7. Install a new semi-circular gasket at the front of the engine.

8. Install the oil pan. Tighten the oil pan attaching bolts, in sequence, over 2–3 stages. Tighten to 5–9 ft. lbs. (7–11 Nm).

9. Lower the vehicle.

10. Add oil to the engine to the proper level.

11. Connect negative battery cable.

12. Start the engine and let idle for approximately 1 minute. Shut the engine off and let stand for 3–5 minutes. Check oil level. Add, as necessary.

Oil Pump

Removal and Installation

1.0L ENGINE

1. Disconnect the negative battery cable.

2. Drain the engine oil.

3. Raise and safely support the vehicle.

4. Remove the 26 bolts attaching the oil pan to the engine block. Remove the oil pan and gasket.

5. Remove the oil pump driven sprocket and drive chain.

6. Remove the oil pump and oil pump outlet pipe.

To install:

7. Replace the oil pump outlet pipe O-ring. Apply engine oil to the new O-ring.

8. Connect the outlet pipe to the oil pump tightening the bolts temporarily.

9. Install the oil pump with the outlet pipe to the cylinder block Tighten the attaching bolts.

10. Install the oil pump drive chain to the balance shaft oil pump sprocket.

11. Install the oil pump drive sprocket to the oil pump with the drive chain installed. Ensure that the stamped marks "CB OUTSIDE" face the front of the engine. Tighten the attaching bolt.

12. Clean the gasket sealing surfaces on the oil pan and engine block.

13. Apply silicone bond to both ends of the cylinder block.

14. Apply silicone bond to the new oil pan gasket at the points near the indentations in the center of the oil pan for crankshaft clearance.

15. Install the oil pan gasket with the silicone bond applied to the cylinder block, aligning the gasket with the stud bolts on the cylinder block.

16. Install the oil pan bolts in sequence. Tighten the bolts to 3–5 ft. lbs. (4–7 Nm).

17. Lower the vehicle.

18. Add oil to the engine to the proper level.

19. Connect negative battery cable.

20. Start the engine and let idle for approximately 1 minute. Shut the engine off and let stand for 3–5 minutes. Check oil level. Add, as necessary.

1.3L ENGINE

1. Disconnect the negative battery cable.
2. Remove the timing belt.
3. Remove the crankshaft timing belt sprocket and flange.
4. Remove the timing belt tensioner and tension spring.
5. Drain the engine oil.
6. Raise and safely support the vehicle.
7. Remove the 14 bolts attaching the oil pan to the engine block. Remove the oil pan and gasket.
8. Remove the oil pump strainer.
9. Lower the vehicle.
10. Remove the oil pump.

To install:

11. Apply a suitable sealer to the oil pump installation surface on the cylinder block.
12. Replace the oil pump O-ring.
13. Apply engine oil to the inner surface of the oil seal. Install the oil pump to the cylinder block. Tighten the oil pump bolts attaching bolts to 4–7 ft. lbs. (6–9 Nm).
14. Raise and safely support the vehicle.
15. Install the oil strainer using a new gasket.
16. Clean the gasket sealing surfaces on the oil pan and engine block.
17. Apply silicone bond to the gasket sealing surface on the cylinder block.
18. Install a new semi-circular gasket at the front of the engine.
19. Install the oil pan. Tighten the oil pan attaching bolts, in sequence, over 2–3 stages. Tighten to 5–9 ft. lbs. (7–11 Nm).
20. Lower the vehicle.
21. Add oil to the engine to the proper level.
22. Connect negative battery cable.
23. Start the engine and let idle for approximately 1 minute. Shut the engine off and let stand for 3–5 minutes. Check oil level. Add, as necessary.

Checking
1.0L ENGINE

With the oil pump removed from the engine, make the following checks.

1. Body clearance: Standard—0.0039–0.0063 in. (0.10–0.16mm); Maximum—0.0118 in. (0.30mm).
2. Tip clearance: Standard—0.0059 in. (0.15mm) or less; Maximum—0.0098 in. (0.25mm).
3. Side clearance: Standard—0.0012–0.0035in. (0.03–0.09mm); Maximum—0.0079 in. (0.20mm).
4. Shaft clearance: Standard—0.0018–0.0033 in. (0.045–0.085mm); Maximum—0.0039 in. (0.10mm).

With the oil pump installed in the engine and the oil pan removed, check the deflection of the oil pump drive chain at the midpoint between the 2 drive sprockets. If the deflection exceeds 0.276 in. (7mm), replace the drive chain and sprockets.

1.3L ENGINE

With the oil pump removed from the engine, make the following checks.

1. Compression spring free length: 2.24 in. (57mm).
2. Body clearance: 0.0079–0.011 in. (0.020–0.28mm).
3. Tip clearance: 0.0063–0.0094 in. (0.16–0.24mm).
4. Side clearance: 0.0014–0.0033 in. (0.035–0.085mm).

Rear Main Bearing Oil Seal

Removal and Installation
1.0L ENGINE

1. Disconnect the negative battery cable.
2. Remove the transaxle assembly from the vehicle.
3. If equipped with manual transaxle, remove the clutch assembly from the flywheel.
4. Prevent the crankshaft from turning. Remove the flywheel or drive plate.
5. Remove the rear main oil seal retainer.
6. Remove the oil seal from the retainer.

To install:

7. Install a new rear main oil seal using a suitable installer.
8. Apply engine oil to the oil seal. Install the retainer assembly on the engine block.
9. Install the flywheel with locating pins aligned or the drive plate.
10. Prevent the crankshaft from turning. Tighten the bolts evenly, over 2–3 stages, in a star pattern. On the 1.0L engine, tighten the bolts to 29–36 ft. lbs. (39–49 Nm). On the 1.3L engine, tighten the bolts to 33–47 ft. lbs. (44–64 Nm).
11. If equipped with manual transaxle, install the clutch assembly.
12. Install the transaxle assembly.
13. Connect the negative battery cable.

MANUAL TRANSAXLE

For further information, please refer to "Professional Transmission Repair Manual" for additional coverage.

Transaxle Assembly

Removal and Installation

1.0 ENGINE

1. Disconnect the negative and positive battery cables.
2. Remove the battery hold-down clamp.
3. Disconnect the harness clamp and washer hose.
4. Remove the battery tray.
5. Remove the clutch cable weight. Loosen the adjusting nut. Disconnect the clutch cable from the clutch release lever. Remove the clutch cable through the bracket hole.
6. Disconnect the starter harness.
7. Remove the 2 starter attaching bolts.
8. Disconnect the speedometer cable.
9. Disconnect the check engine terminal, cowl harness clamp, backup lamp connector and transaxle ground cable.
10. Detach the 3 transaxle wiring harness clamps.
11. Remove the transaxle attaching bolts except for 1 bolt in the front center.
12. Raise and safely support the vehicle.
13. Remove the engine undercovers.
14. Disconnect the front exhaust pipe from the manifold and the front bracket.
15. Remove the stiffener attaching bolt and exhaust pipe bracket support attaching bolts.
16. Disconnect the shift and select shaft and extension rod connectors.
17. Remove the stabilizer bar.
18. Remove the lower control arm installing nut from the bracket and remove the lower arm.
19. Remove the tie rod cotter pin and castellated nut.
21 Separate the tie rod end from the steering knuckle. Remove the halfshafts.
22. Remove the 2 attaching bolts and detach the left hand steering rack cover.
23. Support the lower part of the transaxle. Remove the lower left engine mount bracket attaching bolts.
24. Remove the 2 remaining transaxle attaching bolt at the front center of the housing. Slowly lower the transaxle and remove from under the vehicle.

To install:

25. Ensure that the clutch disc is centered.
26. Raise the transaxle and position it to the engine, making sure the locating pins are properly aligned.
27. Install and temporarily tighten the attaching bolts, making sure not to cause the clutch disc to slip.
28. Attach the clutch housing undercover. Tighten the undercover together with the exhaust pipe bracket support to 11–16 ft. lbs. (15–22 Nm).
29. Tighten the transaxle assembly attaching bolts to 36–51 ft. lbs. (49–67 Nm).
30. Tighten the lower left engine mount bolts to 22–33 ft. lbs. (29–44 Nm).
31. Install the halfshafts.
32. Attach the lower control arm bracket and temporarily tighten the installing nut.
33. Temporarily tighten the stabilizer bar end nut. Tighten the cushion and stabilizer bar bracket. Tighten to 29–43 ft. lbs. (39–59 Nm).
34. Attach the tie rod end to the steering knuckle and tighten the castellated nut to 22–32 ft. lbs. (29–44 Nm). Install a new cotter pin.

35. Connect the shift and select shaft connectors. Tighten to 12–22 ft. lbs. (17–30 Nm).
36. Connect the extension rod connector. Tighten to 12–22 ft. lbs. (17–30 Nm).
37. Install the left hand steering rack cover.
38. Install the front exhaust pipe to the exhaust manifold and tighten to 36–51 ft. lbs. (49–69 Nm). Install the front support bracket and tighten to 25–36 ft. lbs. (34–49 Nm).
39. Install the engine under covers.
40. Lower the vehicle.
41. Rock the vehicle to settle the suspension.
42. Tighten the stabilizer bar installing nut to 54–80 ft. lbs. (74–108 Nm).
43. Tighten the lower control arm bolt at the bracket to 51–72 ft. lbs. (69–98 Nm).
44. Fill the transaxle with the 2.4 qts. (2.24L) of transaxle oil. Install the filler plug.
45. Attach the 3 wiring harness clamps to the transaxle.
46. Connect the speedometer transaxle ground cables.
47. Connect the cowl harness clamp and check engine terminal to the bracket.
48. Install the starter and tighten the 2 bolts to 29–40 ft. lbs. (39–54 Nm). Install the starter harness. Connect the backup lamp connector.
49. Connect the clutch cable to the clutch release lever through the bracket hoe. Adjust clutch cable free-play. Attach the clutch cable weight.
50. Install the battery tray and battery. Secure the hold-down clamp. Connect the positive and negative battery cables.

1.3L ENGINE

1. Disconnect the negative and positive battery cables. Remove the battery and battery tray. Disconnect the wire harness clamp with the EFI check terminal from the upper part of the transaxle. Disconnect the backup lamp switch.
2. Drain the cooling system into a clean container for reuse.
3. Drain the transaxle oil if the transaxle is to be disassembled.
4. Raise and safely support the vehicle.
5. Remove the engine undercover.
6. Remove the lower suspension brace from the lower control arm brackets.
7. Remove the extension rod and shift and select shaft from the transaxle case.
8. Remove the exhaust pipe.

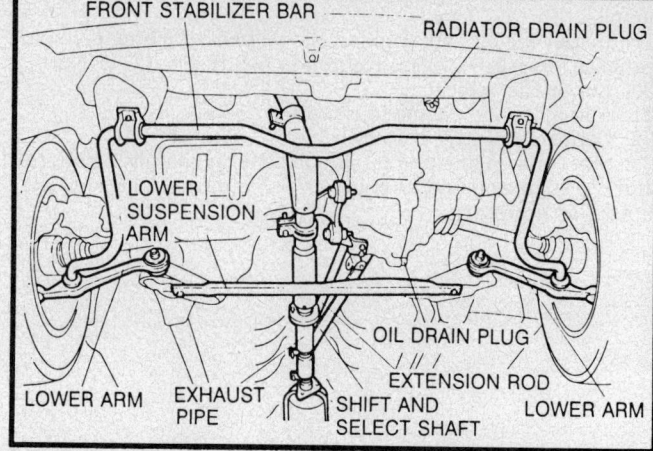

Under-vehicle parts to be removed prior to manual transaxle removal – 1.3L engine

9. Remove the front stabilizer bar.

10. Disconnect the lower control arms from the bracket ends.

11. Remove the exhaust support bracket from the engine stiffener.

12. Remove the halfshafts on the right and left sides.

13. Remove the speedometer cable and transaxle ground cable.

14. Disconnect the clutch cable from the clutch release fork lever and clutch cable bracket.

15. Disconnect the coolant inlet hose from the radiator.

16. Remove the engine compartment stiffener from the engine and clutch housing.

17. Remove the starter.

18. Support the engine and transalxe.

19. Remove 3 of the 4 bolts connecting the transaxle to the engine. Leave 1 in the front loose.

20. Remove the engine mount bolts. from the rear engine mount bracket and the lower left transaxle mount. Remove the support bolt from the upper side of the transaxle case.

21. Remove the remaining transaxle-to-engine bolt.

22. Slowly lower the transaxle and remove from under the vehicle.

To install:

23. Ensure that the clutch disc is centered.

24. Attach the transaxle to the engine block. Tighten 2 bolts at the front , 1 bolt at the rear and 2 upper bolts to 36–51 ft. lbs. (49–69 Nm).

NOTE: Installing the transaxle may require lowering the engine slightly.

25. Install the lower left engine mount-to-transaxle case bracket bolts. Install the upper transaxle case support bolt. Tighten to 36–51 ft. lbs. (49–69 Nm).

26. Install the rear engine mount insulator bolts to the transaxle case bracket. Tighten to 29–40 ft. lbs. (39–54 Nm).

27. Remove the engine and transmission lifting devices.

28. Install the starter motor assembly to the engine.

29. Connect the electrical connectors. Tighten to 29–40 ft. lbs. (39–54 Nm).

30. Install the clutch housing undercover. Install the engine compartment stiffener to the clutch housing. Tighten to 22–33 ft. lbs. (29–44 Nm).

31. Connect the coolant inlet hose to the radiator.

32. Install the clutch cable to the clutch cable bracket. Connect the clutch cable to the clutch release fork lever. Adjust the clutch pedal free-play.

33. Attach the clutch weight.

34. Connect the speedometer cable and ground cable to the transaxle.

35. Install the wire harness clamp with the EFI check terminal to the upper transaxle. Connect the backup lamp connector.

36. Install the battery tray. Install the wire harness clamp with the battery tray. Install the battery hold-down.

37. Connect the fusible link to the battery.

38. Connect the halfshafts.

39. Install the exhaust support bracket to the engine stiffener. Tighten to 22–33 ft. lbs. (29–44 Nm).

40. Install the lower control arms to the brackets. Tighten to 51–72 ft. lbs. (69–98 Nm).

41. Install the front stabilizer bar to the lower control arm and stabilizer bracket. Tighten lower control arm to 54–80 ft. lbs. (84–108 Nm). Tighten stabilizer bracket to 29–43 ft. lbs. (39–59 Nm).

42. Connect the exhaust pipe.

43. Install the extension rod and shift and select shaft to the transaxle case using new attaching bolts. Tighten extension rod to 12–22 ft. lbs. (17–30 Nm). Tighten shift and select shaft to 12–22 ft. lbs. (17–30 Nm).

44. Install the lower suspension brace to the lower arm brackets. Tighten to 29–40 ft. lbs. (39–54 Nm).

45. Lower the vehicle.

46. If drained, fill the transaxle with 2.4 qts. (2.25L of oil).

47. Fill the radiator with coolant and check for leaks.

48. Install the engine undercover.

49. Connect the positive and negative battery cables.

50. Start engine and allow engine to come to normal operating temperature. Recheck for coolant leaks. Allow engine to warm up sufficiently to confirm operation of cooling fan.

CLUTCH

Clutch Assembly

Removal and Installation

1. Disconnect the negative battery cable.

2. Raise and safely support the vehicle.

3. Remove the transaxle assembly from the vehicle.

4. Remove the lock plate.

5. Remove the clutch release fork lever. Remove the bushing, release lever yoke, spring, release bearing clip and release bearing hub.

6. Remove the clutch cover and clutch disc from the flywheel.

To install:

7. Install the clutch disc and clutch cover using an appropriate pilot to center the clutch disc and clutch cover. Tighten bolts evenly, starting with bolts near the locating pin.

NOTE: Ensure that clutch disc is installed in the proper direction. Apply a long-life grease to the clutch disc splines.

8. Assemble the release bearing and clip to the clutch release lever yoke by placing clip on the release bearing. Place the cutout section of the release lever yoke face down on the clip. Pivot the release lever yoke 180 degrees over the clip to connect the yoke to the clip.

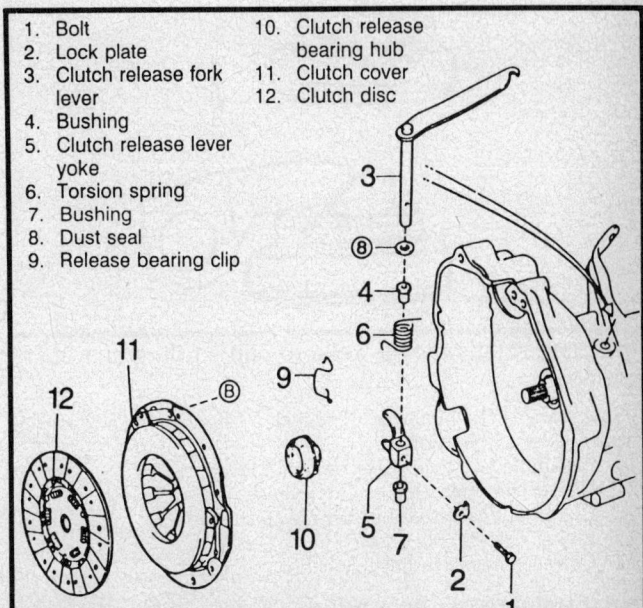

1. Bolt
2. Lock plate
3. Clutch release fork lever
4. Bushing
5. Clutch release lever yoke
6. Torsion spring
7. Bushing
8. Dust seal
9. Release bearing clip
10. Clutch release bearing hub
11. Clutch cover
12. Clutch disc

Clutch assembly—1.0L and 1.3L engines

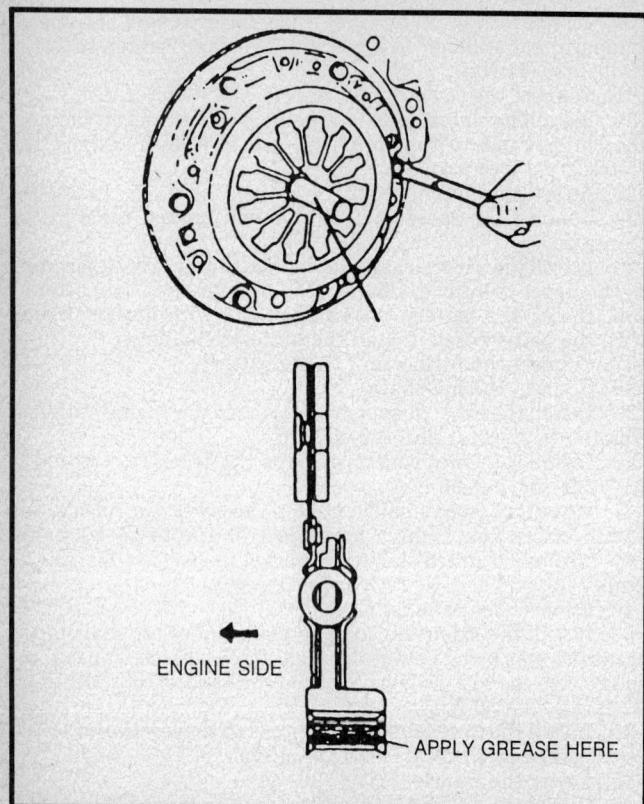

Proper clutch disc installation—1.0L and 1.3L engines

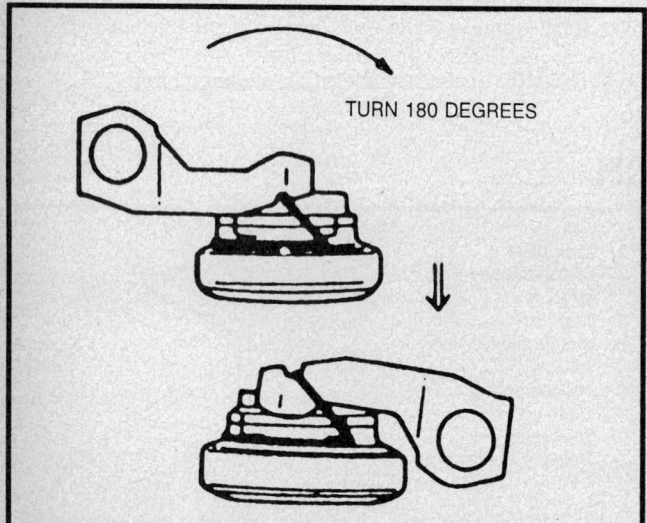

Attaching release lever yoke to clip—1.0L and 1.3L engines

9. Assemble the bushing, dust seal, torsion spring and clutch release lever in position.
10. Assemble the lock plate bolt and lever.
11. Check the operation of the release hub and yoke.
12. Install the transaxle assembly to the vehicle.
13. Lower the vehicle.
14. Connect negative battery cable.

Pedal Height/Free-Play Adjustment

1. Slacken the locknut. Turn the stopper bolt until the instal-

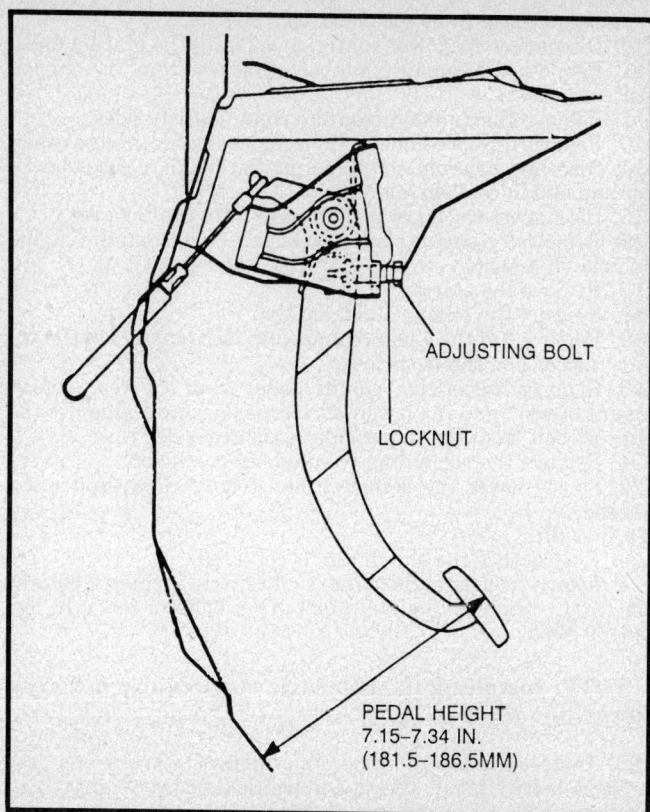

Clutch pedal height adjustment

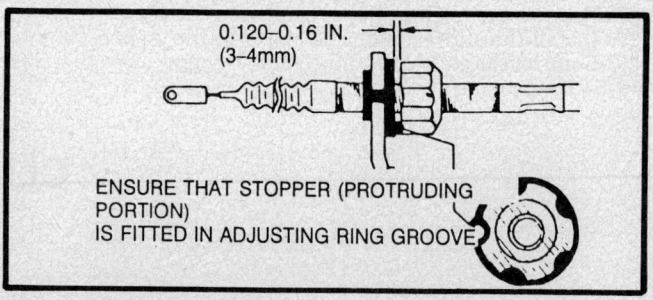

Clutch cable adjustment

lation height conforms to specification. Clutch pedal free travel should be: 0.59–1.18 in. (15–30mm).
2. Tighten the locknut.

Clutch Cable

Adjustment

1. Pull the outer cable lightly until resistance from the clutch is felt.
2. Turn the adjusting ring until it lightly touches the protruding portion of the rubber grommet. Clutch cable endplay should be: 0.120–0.160 in. (3–4mm).

NOTE: Ensure that the stopper (protruding portion) is fitted securely in the adjusting groove. If the stopper is not aligned in the adjusting groove, turn the adjusting ring counterclockwise to fit the stopper.

Removal and Installation

1. Remove the brake pedal.

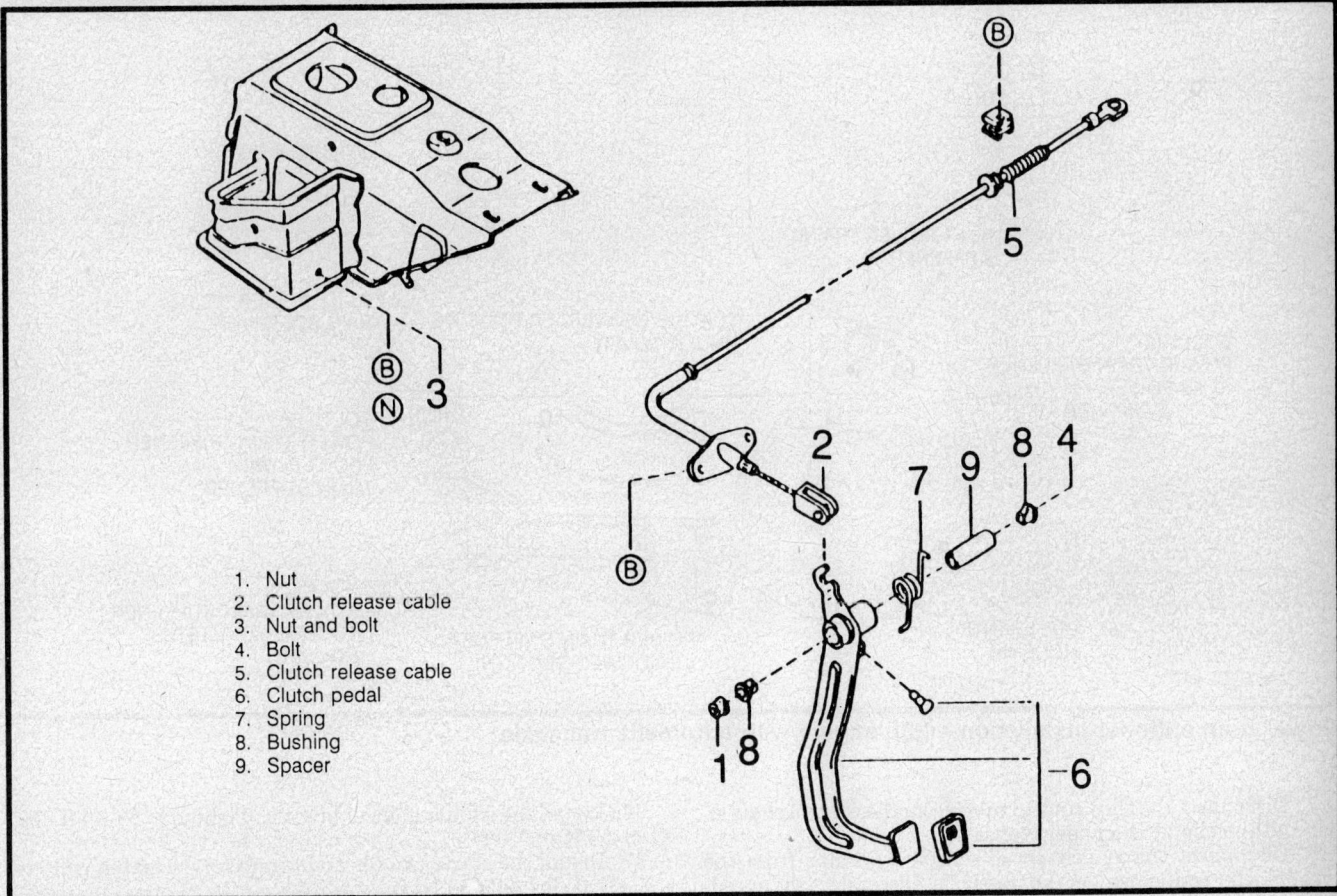

1. Nut
2. Clutch release cable
3. Nut and bolt
4. Bolt
5. Clutch release cable
6. Clutch pedal
7. Spring
8. Bushing
9. Spacer

Clutch pedal and cable installation

2. Remove the clutch pedal mounting nut and remove the clutch pedal.

3. Remove the adjusting bolt.

4. Remove the bolt and washer.

5. Remove the cable bracket attaching bolts. Remove the clutch cable at both ends and remove from firewall and transaxle mounts.

To install:

6. Feed new cable through firewall and transaxle mount grommets.

7. Connect cable at both ends.

8. Install adjusting bolt.

9. Install the clutch pedal and mounting bolt.

10. Install the brake pedal.

11. Adjust clutch cable and clutch pedal free-play.

AUTOMATIC TRANSAXLE

For further information, please refer to "Professional Transmission Repair Manual" for additional coverage.

Transaxle Assembly

Removal and Installation

1. Disconnect the negative battery cable.
2. Raise and safely support the vehicle.
3. Remove the engine undercover.
4. Drain the cooling system into a clean container for reuse.
5. Drain the automatic transaxle fluid.
6. Disconnect the fusible link from the positive battery terminal. Remove the battery from the vehicle.
7. Remove the wire harness clamp and windshield washer hose from the battery tray. Remove the battery tray from the vehicle.

8. Remove the clamp bolt for the engine and alternator wire harness from the upper part of the transaxle. Remove the check terminal from the transaxle.

9. Disconnect the automatic transaxle solenoid valve connector. Disconnect the neutral start switch. Remove the connector clamp.

10. Disconnect the transaxle ground cable.

11. Remove the front stabilizer bar.

12. Remove the lower suspension brace from the lower control arm brackets.

13. Remove the halfshafts.

14. Remove the bolts which connect the power train stiffener with the front and rear power train stiffeners.

15. Remove the power train stiffener with the clutch housing undercover from the clutch housing.

16. Remove the throttle cable from the throttle lever and clamps.

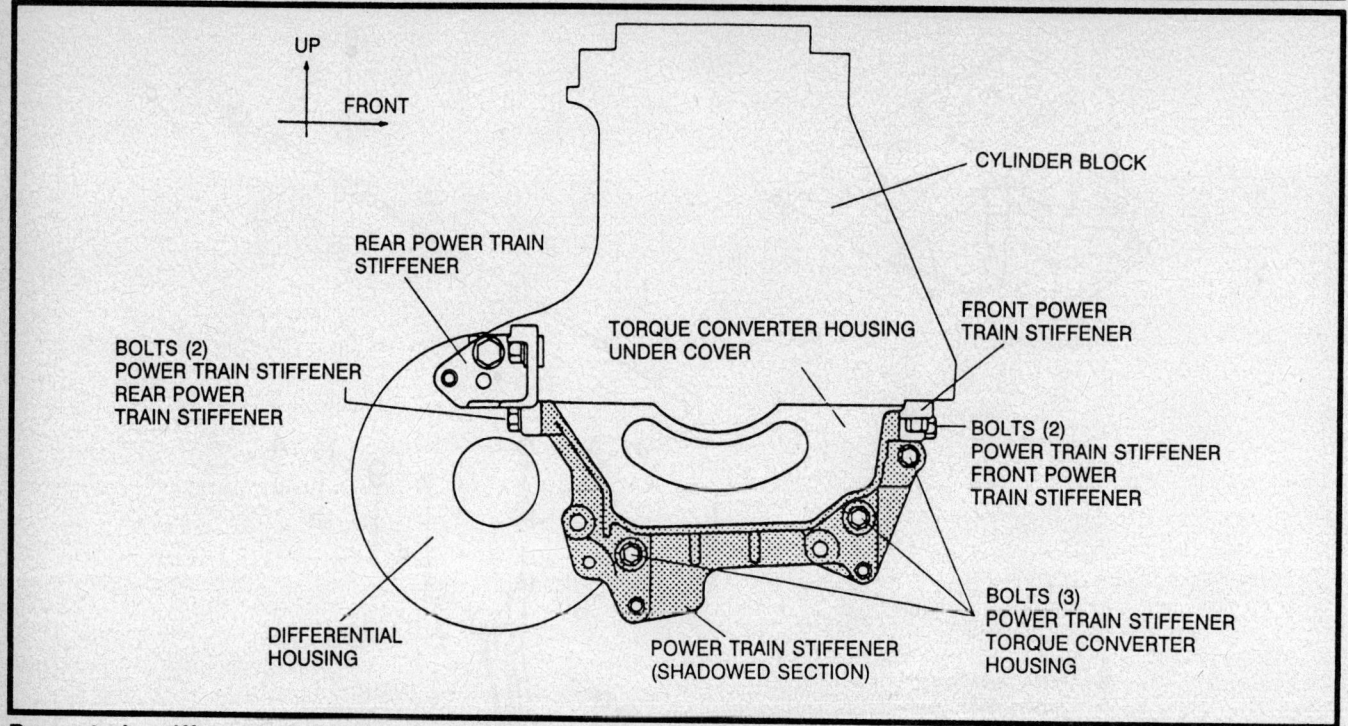

UP

FRONT

CYLINDER BLOCK

REAR POWER TRAIN STIFFENER

BOLTS (2)
POWER TRAIN STIFFENER
REAR POWER TRAIN STIFFENER

TORQUE CONVERTER HOUSING UNDER COVER

FRONT POWER TRAIN STIFFENER

BOLTS (2)
POWER TRAIN STIFFENER
FRONT POWER TRAIN STIFFENER

BOLTS (3)
POWER TRAIN STIFFENER
TORQUE CONVERTER HOUSING

DIFFERENTIAL HOUSING

POWER TRAIN STIFFENER (SHADOWED SECTION)

Power train stiffener installation—1.3L engine with automatic transaxle

17. Disconnect the shift control cable from the control shaft lever and the clip at the upper transaxle.

18. Disconnect the vehicle speed sensor connector from the speedometer connection on the transaxle. Disconnect the speedometer cable.

19. Disconnect the radiator fan motor. Disconnect the upper and lower radiator hoses. Remove the radiator assembly with the fan shroud from the vehicle.

20. Remove the oil cooler hoses.

21. Prevent the ring gear from turning and remove the 6 bolts connecting the drive plate to the torque converter.

22. Remove the shift control cable clamp from the rear engine mount bracket.

23. Remove the electrical connectors and 2 mounting bolts and remove starter.

24. Detach the front left stabilizer bracket.

25. Support the engine and transaxle separately.

26. Remove 3 of the 4 transaxle-to-engine block mounting bolts.

27. Remove the rear engine mount insulator bracket bolts from the transaxle case.

28. Remove the lower left engine mount bolts from the transaxle case.

29. Remove the remaining transaxle-to-engine block bolt.

30. Lower the transaxle and remove from the vehicle.

To install:

31. Ensure that the torque converter is fitted positively with the automatic transaxle. Apply grease to the crankshaft fitting on the torque converter.

32. Install the automatic transaxle in the vehicle, making sure not to pry on the torque converter or drive plate during installation. Install the 4 attaching bolts. Tighten to 36–51 ft. lbs. (49–68 Nm).

33. Install the lower left engine mount bolts to the transaxle bracket. Tighten to 21–32 ft. lbs. (29–44 Nm).

34. Install the rear engine mount insulator bracket bolts to the transaxle. Tighten to 40–51 (54–69 Nm).

35. Remove the engine and transaxle support devices.

36. Install the front stabilizer bracket. Tighten to 29–44 ft. lbs. (39–59 Nm).

37. Install the starter motor and connectors. Tighten bolts to 36–51 ft. lbs. (49–69 Nm).

38. Install the shift control cable clamp to the rear engine mount bracket. Tighten to 10–18 ft. lbs. (13–24 Nm).

39. Prevent the ring gear from turning and install the 6 drive plate-to-converter bolts. Tighten to 17–23 ft. lbs. (23–32 Nm).

40. Install the oil cooler lines using new line.

41. Install the radiator fan motor and shroud to the radiator. Connect the upper and lower radiator hoses. Connect the radiator fan motor.

42. Connect the speedometer cable. Connect the vehicle speed sensor.

43. Attach the clip for the shift control cable to the upper part of the transaxle.

44. Position the shift control shaft to the **N** position. Tighten the adjusting bolt while the shift lever is being pulled slightly from the **N** position to the **R** position with the shift control cable at the transaxle.

45. Ensure that the shift lever can be moved to each of the drive ranges with the proper amount of detent resistance. Tighten the adjusting bolt to 12–18 ft. lbs. (16–24 Nm).

46. Connect the throttle cable from the transaxle to the throttle lever. Secure the cable clamps.

47. Install the power train stiffener to the torque converter housing undercover temporarily.

48. Install the bolts connecting the power train stiffener to the front and rear stiffeners, tightening the power train stiffener-to-torque converter housing bolts first. Tighten bolts to 21–32 ft. lbs. (29–44 Nm).

49. Install the halfshafts.

50. Install the lower control arms to the brackets. Tighten to 55–76 ft. lbs. (74–103 Nm).

51. Install the front stabilizer bar. Tighten to 29–44 ft. lbs. (39–59 Nm).

52. Connect the exhaust pipe.

53. Install the lower suspension brace to the lower control arm

brackets. Tighten bolts to 29–44 ft. lbs. (39–54 Nm).

54. Install the transaxle ground cable. Install the neutral start switch connector. Connect the solenoid valve connector.

55. Install the engine and alternator wire harness clamp bolt to the upper side of the transaxle.

56. Install the battery tray. Attach the windshield washer hose and wire harness clamp to the battery tray. Install the battery and the battery hold-down clamp. Connect the fusible link and positive battery cable.

57. Fill the automatic transaxle with fluid.

58. Fill the radiator with coolant.

59. Install the engine undercover.

60. Lower the vehicle. Tighten lower control arm-to-bracket bolts to 51–72 ft. lbs. (69–98 Nm). Tighten stabilizer bar-to-lower control arm bolts to 55–80 ft. lbs. (74–108 Nm).

61. Connect negative battery cable.

62. Start engine and allow engine to come to normal operating temperature. Recheck for coolant leaks. Allow engine to warm up sufficiently to confirm operation of cooling fan.

63. Check automatic transaxle fluid level.

Shift Linkage Adjustment

1. Disconnect the control cable from the transaxle control shaft lever.

2. Ensure that the shift lever can be moved smoothly while operating the shift lever button. If shift lever action is difficult, replace the shift lever assembly.

3. Align the control shaft lever with the **N** range. With the shift lever in the **N** and pulled lightly toward the **R** at the transaxle, install the control cable on the control shaft lever. Tighten the adjusting bolt.

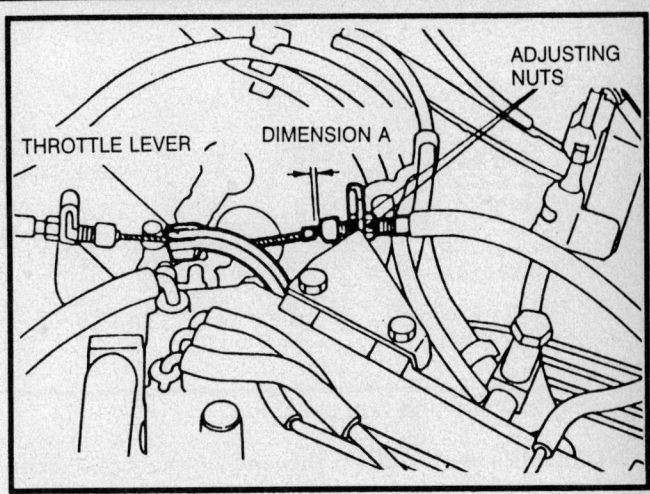

Throttle cable adjustment

4. Ensure that the shift lever can be moved smoothly.

Throttle Linkage Adjustment

1. Ensure that the throttle valve cable can be moved smoothly when operated independently.

2. Connect the cable to the throttle lever. Turn the adjusting nut so the gap between the cable and the adjusting nut (dimension A) is 0.0–0.020 in. (0.0–0.5mm).

DRIVE AXLE

Halfshaft

Removal and Installation

1. Disconnect the negative battery cable.
2. Raise and safely support the vehicle.
3. Remove the front wheels.
4. Drain the transaxle oil.
5. Remove the cotter pin and front wheel adjusting lock cap.
6. Remove the stub shaft nut.
7. Disconnect the outer tie rod from the steering knuckle.
8. Remove the engine undercovers.
9. Remove the stabilizer bar.
10. Remove the lower control arm from the bracket.
11. Separate the extension rod subassembly and shift and selector subassembly from the transaxle.
12. Remove the outer stub shaft from the steering knuckle.
13. Remove the inner stub shaft from the differential fitting.

NOTE: Be careful not to damage oil seals during removal.

To install:

14. Inspect the differential oil seal prior to installation of the halfshaft. Replace as needed.

15. Apply grease to the serrated section of the outboard joint stub shaft. Insert the outboard joint section into the knuckle. Temporarily, install the plate washer and nut.

16. Apply grease to the lip of the oil seal. Insert the inboard joint stub shaft into the differential.

17. Install the shift and selector shaft and extension rod. Tighten to 12–22 ft. lbs. (9–16 Nm).

18. Install the lower control arm to the bracket. Tighten to 54–76 ft. lbs. (40–56 Nm).

19. Install the stabilizer bar to the lower control arm assembly. Tighten to 54–76 ft. lbs. (40–56 Nm).

20. Install the stabilizer lower bracket to the body. Tighten to 43–61 ft. lbs. (32–45 Nm).

21. Install the engine undercovers.

22. Attach the tie rod end to the steering knuckle and tighten the castellated nut to 22–33 ft. lbs. (16–24 Nm). Install a new cotter pin.

23. Install the stub shaft nut and tighten to 130–166 ft. lbs. (96–123 Nm). Install the front wheel adjusting lock cap to the nut. Install a new cotter pin.

24. Install the front wheels.

25. Connect negative battery cable.

CV-Boot

Removal and Installation

1. Disconnect the negative battery cable.
2. Raise and safely support the vehicle.
3. Remove the halfshaft assembly from the vehicle and place in a vise.
4. Pry up the boot band clip and detach the boot.
5. Paint a match mark on the inboard joint and shaft prior to disassembly to ensure reassembly in the same position. Do not use a punch to make match marks on the joint or shaft. Remove the front axle inboard joint subassembly.
6. Remove the snapring retaining the inboard tripod joint.
7. Punch a match mark on the tip of the tripod joint and shaft.
8. Use a brass drift to remove the tripod joint from the shaft.

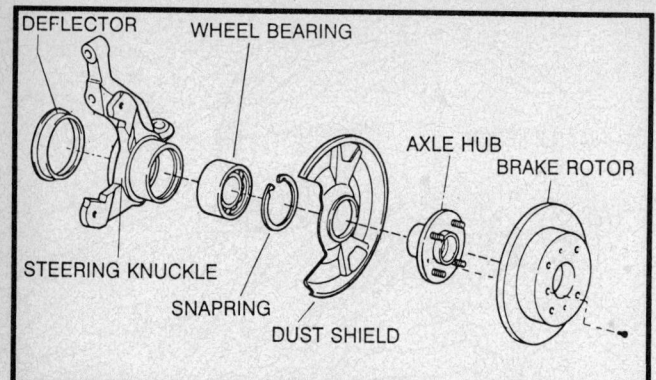

Steering knuckle and hub assembly

NOTE: Be sure to place the end of the brass drift against the boss section of the joint, not the roller section.

9. Pry up the inner boot band. Remove the front halfshaft joint inboard boot.
10. Pry up the outboard boot band.
11. Remove the front halfshaft joint outboard boot.

To install:
12. Wind vinyl tape or equivalent around the splined tip of the shaft so boot will not be damaged during installation.
13. Fit the boot and a new boot band (smaller diameter) on the outboard joint.
14. Pack the outboard joint with grease.
15. Fit a new band (large diameter) in place.
16. Temporarily install the outboard joint boot onto the halfshaft.
17. Remove the vinyl tape that was wound around the splined portion.
18. Face the non-splined side of the inboard tripod joint toward the outboard joint.
19. Align the match marks.
20. Drive the tripod assembly onto the shaft lightly using the brass drift.
21. Attach the snapring onto the shaft.
22. Pack the inboard joint with grease.
23. Install the inboard join, aligning the match marks.
24. Fit new boot bands in place.
25. Install the halfshaft assembly in the vehicle.
26. Lower the vehicle.
27. Connect the negative battery cable.

Front Wheel Hub, Spindle and Bearings

Removal and Installation

1. Disconnect the negative battery cable.

2. Raise and safely support the vehicle.
3. Remove the front wheel.
4. Disconnect the disc brake caliper from the steering knuckle and support using a length of mechanics wire.
5. Remove the front disc attaching screws and remove the disc from the front axle hub.
6. Remove the cotter pin and front wheel adjusting lock cap. Remove the nut, using a 30mm socket and a suitable tool to prevent the axle from turning.
7. Use a slide hammer or equivalent to remove the axle hub.
8. Separate the outer tie rod from the steering knuckle.
9. Remove the lower ball joint attaching bolt and nut.
10. Remove the steering knuckle attaching nuts. Leave the bolts in place at this time.
11. Support the steering knuckle and draw out the attaching bolts for the strut lower bracket.

NOTE: Protect the outer CV-joint boot during removal. Be careful not to distort the disc brake outer cover during hub removal.

12. Place the hub in a vise and remove the dust seal from the axle hub.
13. Remove the bearing inner race from the axle hub.
14. Detach the hole snapring.
15. Press the bearing out of the hub.

To install:
16. Press the new bearing into the hub.
17. Install a new hole snapring.
18. Press the front axle hub into position.

NOTE: Be sure to press only on the inner race.

19. Insert the steering knuckle into the halfshaft.
20. Connect the steering knuckle to the ball joint. Connect the steering knuckle to the strut lower bracket. Tighten to 65–94 ft. lbs. (48–69 Nm).
21. Install the lower ball joint. Tighten to 58–76 ft. lbs. (43–56 Nm).
23. Install the plate washer in the proper direction. Install the nut temporarily.
24. Install the front disc.
25. Attach the tie rod end to the steering knuckle and tighten the castellated nut to 22–33 ft. lbs. (16–24 Nm). Install a new cotter pin.
26. Install the disc pad guide plates to the steering knuckle. Tighten the caliper attaching bolts to 23–30 ft. lbs. (17–22 Nm).
27. Prevent the halfshaft from turning and tighten the axle nut to 130–166 ft. lbs. (96–121 Nm).
28. Install the front wheel adjusting lock cap to the nut. Install a new cotter pin.
30. Install the front wheel.
31. Connect negative battery cable.
32. Check front wheel alignment.

STEERING

Steering Wheel

Removal and Installation

1. Disconnect the negative battery cable.
2. Remove the 2 screws retaining the steering wheel pad.
3. Remove the steering wheel pad by pushing it upward.

4. Disconnect the horn pad connector.
5. Remove the steering wheel locknut.
6. Remove the steering wheel using a suitable puller.
To install:
7. Fit the steering wheel and tighten the locknut to 24–40 ft. lbs. (34–54 Nm).
8. Connect the horn pad connector.

9. Slide the steering wheel pad into position.
10. Install the 2 steering wheel pad retaining screws.
11. Connect negative battery cable.

Steering Column

Removal and Installation

1. Disconnect the negative battery cable.
2. Remove the steering wheel.
3. Remove the lower instrument finish panel and lower steering column covers. Except for vehicles equipped with automatic seat belts.
4. If equipped with automatic seat belts, perform the following:
    a. Remove the switch base by pushing it out from the back.
    b. Straighten the forward end of the hooked section of the iron plate insert for the switch base.
    c. Remove the 3 bolts retaining the knee bolster.
    d. Remove the 4 screws retaining the instrument cluster.
    e. Remove the 4 screws retaining the instrument cluster and remove the cluster.
    f. Detach the clip on the right side of the knee bolster by inserting finger through the aperture left by the removed cluster.
    g. Remove the lower steering column cover.
5. Remove the lower instrument panel reinforcement.
6. Disconnect the multi-use lever switch, ignition switch and key reminder buzzer connectors.
7. Remove the universal joint bolt.
8. Remove the 3 bolts and 2 nuts attaching the steering column.
9. Remove the steering column assembly from the vehicle.

To install:
10. Install the upper steering column cover to the steering column.
11. Install the universal joint attaching bolt. Tighten to 18–25 ft. lbs. (25–34 Nm).

NOTE: Install the bolt so the side having the resin injection faces the main steering shaft.

12. Install the 3 bolts and 2 nuts attaching the steering column. Tighten the bolts to 11–16 ft. lbs. (15–22 Nm). Tighten the nuts to 18–25 ft. lbs. (25–34 Nm).
13. Connect the multi-use lever switch, ignition switch and key reminder buzzer connectors.
14. Install the lower instrument panel reinforcement.
15. Install the lower instrument finish panel and lower steering column cover. Except for vehicles equipped with automatic seat belts.
16. If equipped with automatic seat belts, perform the following:
    a. Install the lower steering column cover screws.
    b. Insert the clip for the knee bolster to the instrument panel.
    c. Bend the forward end of the hook section of the iron plate.
    d. Tighten the 3 bolts attaching the knee bolster.
    e. Install the switch base by pushing it in from the front.
17. Install the steering wheel.
18. Connect negative battery cable.

Manual Steering Rack

Adjustment

With the steering rack removed from the vehicle and installed in a vise, measure the rack preload and the steering pinion preload.

NOTE: Steps 1 and 2 below should be carried out with the steering rack in the neutral position (equivalent to the wheel straight ahead).

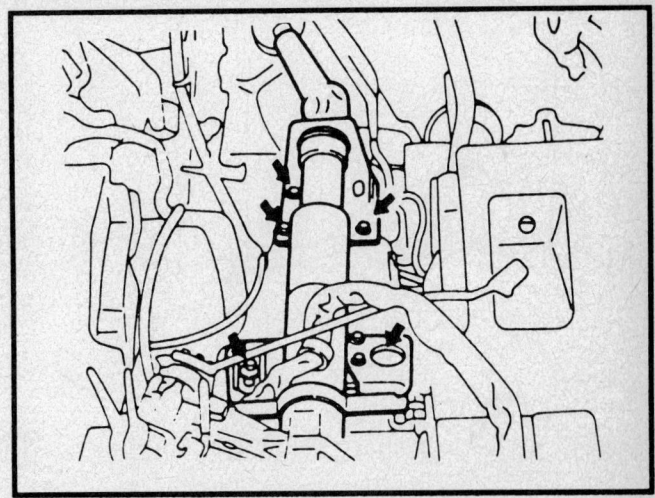

Steering column mounting bolts

1. Tighten the rack guide spring cap. Tighten to 5 ft. lbs. (7 Nm).
2. Move the steering rack back and for the about 15 times so as to settle the rack. Tighten the rack guide spring cap again to 9 ft. lbs. (12 Nm).
3. Back off the rack guide spring cap 35–55 degrees.
4. Using an inch pound torque wrench, measure the steering pinion preload. Specified value (starting torque) should be: 4.8–5.9 inch lbs. (0.6–1.1 Nm).
5. Measure the starting force of the steering rack, using a spring scale with a rope attached to the end of the steering rack. Specified value: not to exceed 14 kg.
6. If the preload does not fall within specification, repeat Steps 1 through 5.

Removal and Installation

1. Disconnect the negative battery cable.
2. Raise and safely support the vehicle.
3. Remove the front wheels.
4. Remove the rear engine undercovers.
5. Remove the bolt from the universal joint at the manual rack input shaft. Disconnect the universal joint.
6. Remove the cotter pins and castellated nuts from the outer tie rods. Disconnect the tie rod ends from the steering knuckles.
7. Remove the 2 bolts attaching the damper weights.
8. Remove the 4 steering rack housing bracket set bolts.
9. Remove the steering gear assembly from the vehicle.

To install:
10. Install the grommets to the steering rack assembly. Insert the rack unit into the vehicle.
11. Install the steering rack universal joint to the pinion. Install the bolt and tighten temporarily.
12. Connect the steering rack to the body. Tighten the bolts to 29–40 ft. lbs. (39–54 Nm.).

NOTE: Install the steering rack housing brackets so the end with the elongated hole faces up.

13. Tighten the universal joint attaching bolt to 18–25 ft. lbs. (25–34 Nm).

NOTE: When tightening the bolt, be sure to limit the length of exposed splines on the pinion shaft to 0.200 in. (5mm) or less.

14. Install the damper weight.
15. Install the rear undercover.
16. Connect the tie rod end to the steering knuckle. Tighten

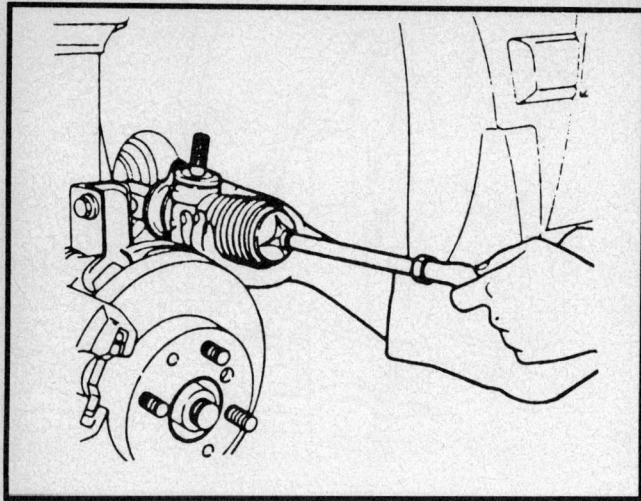

Installation of steering gear

the castellated nut to 21–32 ft. lbs. (29–44 Nm). Install a new cotter pin.

17. Install the wheels.
18. Lower the vehicle.
19. Connect negative battery cable.
20. Check alignment.

Power Steering Rack

Adjustment

The procedure for checking the rack preload and steering pinion preload is the same as manual steering gear.

Removal and Installation

1. Disconnect the negative battery cable.
2. Raise and safely support the vehicle.
3. Remove the front wheels.
4. Remove the rear engine undercovers. Disconnect the fluid lines from the rack and drain the fluid.
5. Remove the bolt from the universal joint at the rack input shaft. Disconnect the universal joint.
6. Remove the cotter pins and castellated nuts from the outer tie rods. Disconnect the tie rod ends from the steering knuckles.
7. Remove the 2 bolts attaching the damper weights.
8. Remove the 4 steering rack housing bracket set bolts.
9. Remove the steering gear assembly from the vehicle.

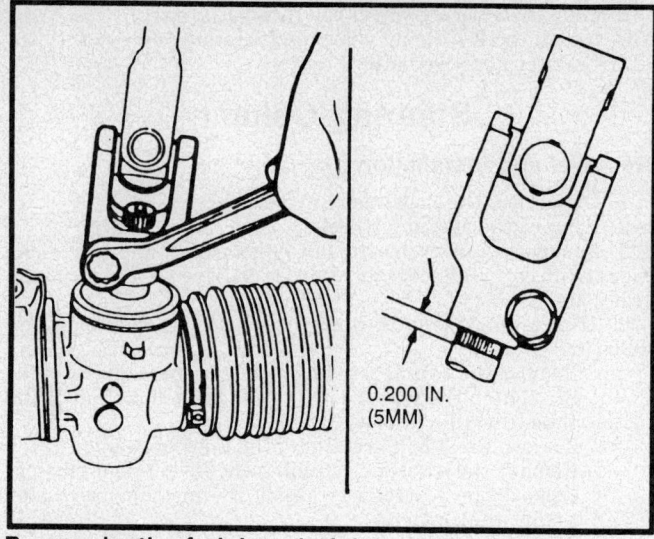

Proper depth of pinion shaft into universal joint

To install:

10. Install the grommets to the steering rack assembly. Insert the rack unit into the vehicle.
11. Install the steering rack universal joint to the pinion. Install the bolt and tighten temporarily.
12. Connect the steering rack to the body. Tighten the bolts to 29–40 ft. lbs. (39–54 Nm.).

NOTE: Install the steering rack housing brackets so the end with the elongated hole faces up.

13. Connect the fluid lines. Tighten the universal joint attaching bolt to 18–25 ft. lbs. (25–34 Nm).

NOTE: When tightening the bolt, be sure to limit the length of exposed splines on the pinion shaft to 0.200 in. (5mm) or less.

14. Install the damper weight.
15. Install the rear undercover.
16. Connect the tie rod end to the steering knuckle. Tighten the castellated nut to 21–32 ft. lbs. (29–44 Nm). Install a new cotter pin.
17. Install the wheels.
18. Lower the vehicle.
19. Connect negative battery cable.
20. Fill the steering system with fluid and bleed. Check alignment.

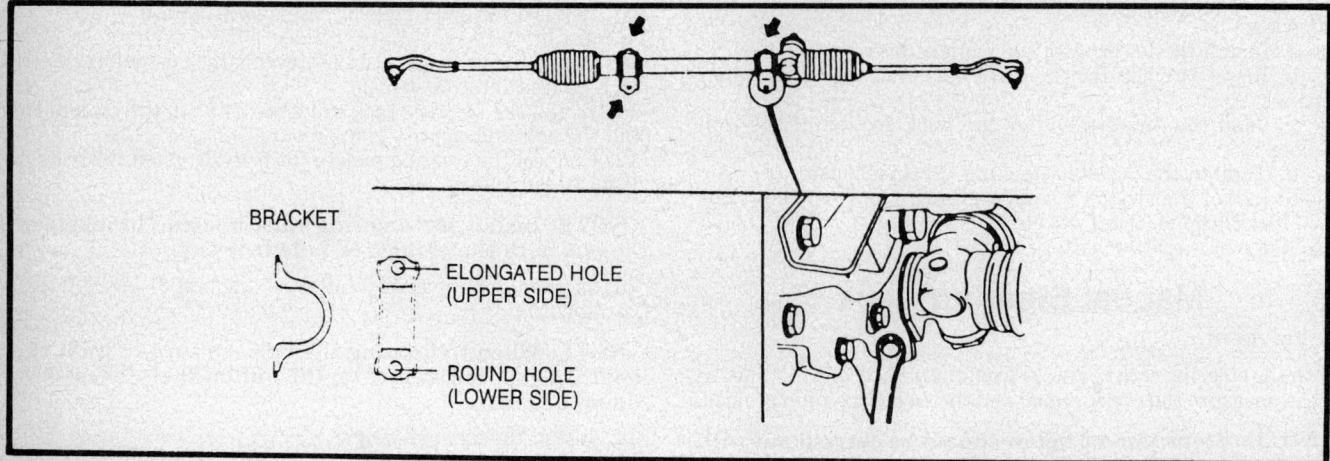

BRACKET

ELONGATED HOLE (UPPER SIDE)

ROUND HOLE (LOWER SIDE)

Positioning of steering gear brackets

Power Steering Pump

Removal and Installation

1. Disconnect the negative battery cable.
2. Remove the air cleaner.
3. Remove hoses leading to the power steering rack assembly and reservoir tank from the power steering pump.
4. Remove the power steering drive belt.
5. Remove the vane pump assembly.

To install:

6. Install the power steering pump temporarily with attaching bolts.
7. Install the power steering pump drive belt. Adjust the belt tension.
8. Tighten the attaching bolts to the proper torque specifications.
9. Install the hoses from the power steering gear and the reservoir tank. Tighten the union bolt to 36–44 ft. lbs. (49–59 Nm).
10. Fill the system with fluid. Bleed the air from the system.
11. Connect negative battery cable.
12. Start the engine and operate the power steering system checking for abnormal sounds from the pump or drive belt.
13. Install the air cleaner.

Belt Adjustment

1. Loosen the attaching and adjusting bolts.
2. Check the belt tension at midpoint between the pulleys. For a new belt: tension should be 55–88 lbs. (25–40 kg) at 0.315–0.394 in. (8–10mm) deflection. For a used belt: tension should be 33–55 lbs. (15–25 kg) at 0.394–0.551 in. (10–14mm).
3. Tighten the attaching and adjusting bolts.

System Bleeding

1. Check the fluid level in the reservoir tank, add as necessary.
2. With the engine running at idle speed, turn the steering wheel to either lock position. Hold there for 2–3 seconds. Turn the steering wheel to the opposite lock position and hold for 2–3 seconds. Repeat sequence 2–3 times.
3. Check the fluid level.

Tie Rod Ends

Removal and Installation

1. Disconnect the negative battery cable.
2. Raise and safely support the vehicle.
3. Remove the front wheel.
4. Mark the position of the tie rod end on the rack end.
5. Loosen the locknut.
6. Remove the cotter pin and castellated nut attaching tie rod to the steering knuckle.
7. Remove the tie rod end.

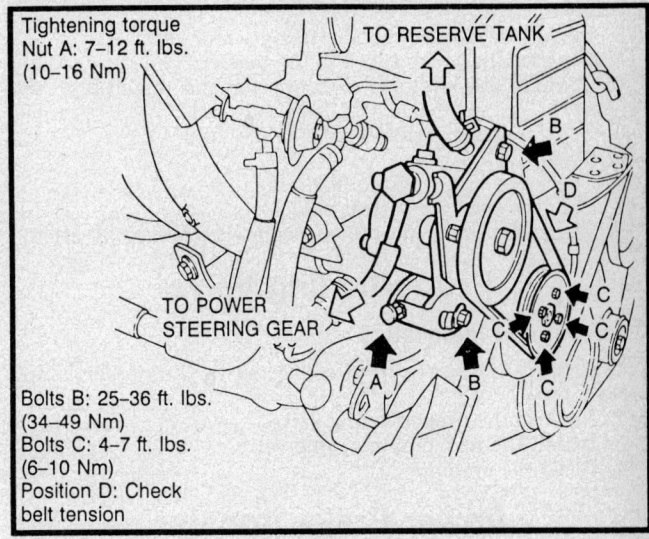

Tightening torque
Nut A: 7–12 ft. lbs. (10–16 Nm)

TO RESERVE TANK

TO POWER STEERING GEAR

Bolts B: 25–36 ft. lbs. (34–49 Nm)
Bolts C: 4–7 ft. lbs. (6–10 Nm)
Position D: Check belt tension

Power steering pump installation

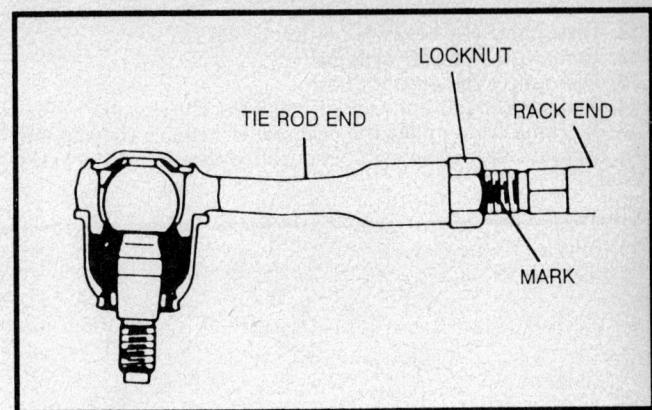

LOCKNUT
TIE ROD END
RACK END
MARK

Tie rod end installation

To install:

8. Install the new tie rod end on the rack end. Thread the tie rod end up to the mark made on rack end before removal of the old tie rod end.
9. Connect new tie rod end to the steering knuckle.
10. Install castellated nut and tighten to 22–33 ft. lbs. (29–44 Nm). Install a new cotter pin.
11. Install the front wheel.
12. Lower the vehicle.
13. Connect negative battery cable.
14. Check alignment.

BRAKES

Master Cylinder

Removal and Installation

1. Disconnect the negative battery cable.
2. Disconnect the level switch connector.
3. Disconnect the brake lines from the master cylinder.

NOTE: Do not allow brake fluid to touch painted surfaces. If a spill occurs, wipe up immediately.

4. Remove the 2 attaching nuts and remove the master cylinder and gasket from the brake booster.
5. Remove the level switch connector from the bracket.

To install:

6. Install the master cylinder using a new gasket.
7. Connect the brake tubes to the master cylinder.
8. Connect the level switch connector and install it to the bracket.
9. Fill the master cylinder with brake fluid.
10. Bleed the system.
11. Check the brake system for leaks.
12. Connect negative battery cable.
13. Test drive the vehicle to ensure proper brake operation.

Proportioning Valve

Removal and Installation

1. Remove the brake lines connected to the proportioning valve.
2. Remove the proportioning valve.
3. Install the new proportioning valve.
4. Bleed the system.

Power Brake Booster

Removal and Installation

1. Disconnect the negative battery cable.
2. Remove the master cylinder.
3. Disconnect the vacuum hose.
4. Remove the ignition coil wire and the clutch cable.
5. Working from under the dash panel, remove the clip and pin. Separate the master cylinder push rod clevis from the brake pedal.

6. Remove the brake booster assmbly and gasket from the vehicle.

To install:

7. Install the brake booster assembly using a new gasket.
8. Attach the master cylinder push rod clevis to the brake pedal using the pin and clip.
9. Attach the vacuum hose.
10. Install the clutch cable.
11. Install the master cylinder.
12. Install the ignition coil wire.
13. Connect negative battery cable.

Brake Caliper

Removal and Installation

1. Disconnect the negative battery cable.
2. Raise and safely support the vehicle.
3. Remove the front wheel.
4. Separate the flexible hose from the brake tube.
5. Detach the clip from the strut.
6. Disconnect the flexible hose from the strut bracket.
7. Disconnect the flexible hose from the disc brake caliper.
8. Remove the attaching bolts and remove the caliper from the vehicle.
9. Remove the disc brake pad with the anti-squeal shims from the caliper.

To install:

10. Install the disc brake pad guide plate on the knuckle.
11. Install the brake pad in the caliper, with the anti-squeal shims.

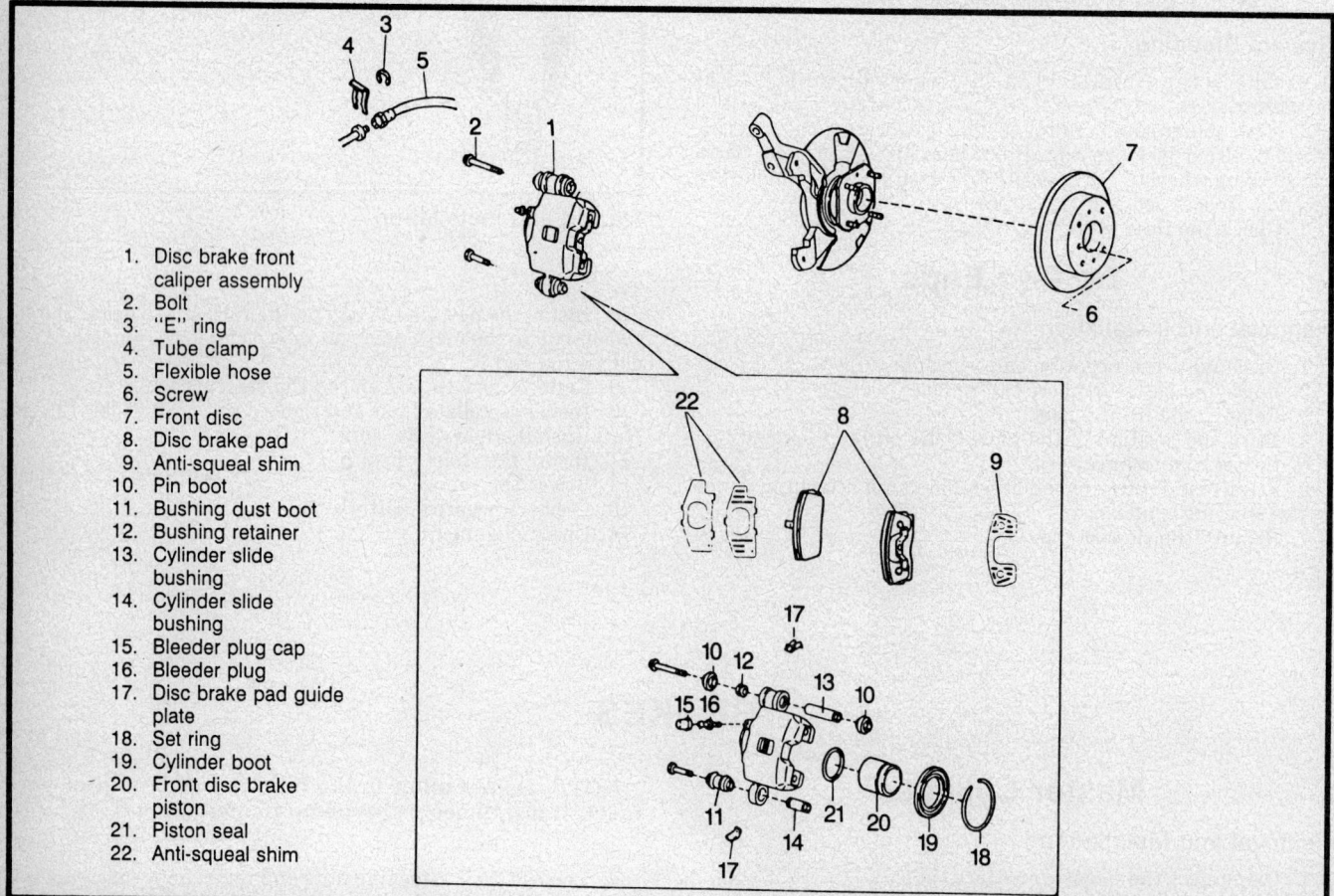

1. Disc brake front caliper assembly
2. Bolt
3. "E" ring
4. Tube clamp
5. Flexible hose
6. Screw
7. Front disc
8. Disc brake pad
9. Anti-squeal shim
10. Pin boot
11. Bushing dust boot
12. Bushing retainer
13. Cylinder slide bushing
14. Cylinder slide bushing
15. Bleeder plug cap
16. Bleeder plug
17. Disc brake pad guide plate
18. Set ring
19. Cylinder boot
20. Front disc brake piston
21. Piston seal
22. Anti-squeal shim

Front disc brake installation

12. Install the disc brake front caliper assembly on the steering knuckle. Tighten to 23–33 ft. lbs. (31–41 Nm).
13. Attach the flexible hose to the front disc brake caliper.
14. Attach the flexible hose to the bracket on the strut using the clip.
15. Temporarily install the flexible hose and brake tube by hand.
16. Tighten the flexible hose and brake tube.
17. Attach the clip at the bracket on the body.

NOTE: After installation of the flexible brake hose, turn the wheel from lock to lock to ensure free and unobstructed movement of the brake hose.

18. Bleed the air from the system.
19. Install the front wheel.
20. Lower the vehicle.
21. Test drive the vehicle to ensure proper brake operation.

Disc Brake Pads

Removal and Installation

1. Disconnect the negative battery cable.
2. Raise and safely support the vehicle.
3. Remove the front wheel.
4. Remove the caliper attaching bolts and remove the caliper from the brake disc.
5. Remove the disc brake pad with anti-squeal shims.
6. Support the caliper using a length of mechanics wire. Do not allow the caliper to hang by the flexible brake hose unsupported.
7. Detach the disc brake pad guide plate.
To install:
8. Drain a small amount of brake fluid from the master cylinder. Use a clamp to press the caliper piston into the bore.

NOTE: Remove only 1 caliper at a time. If both calipers are removed at the same time, the hydraulic pressure created by pressing one piston into its bore may force the piston of the other caliper out of its bore.

9. Install a new disc brake pad guide plate on the knuckle.
10. Install the new brake pad in the caliper, with anti-sqeal shims.
11. Install the front disc brake caliper assembly on the knuckle. Tighten to 23–30 ft. lbs. (31–41 Nm).
12. Install the front wheel.
13. Lower the vehicle.
14. Connect negative battery cable.
15. Check the brake fluid level in the master cylinder reservoir and add, as necessary.
16. Before starting the engine, slowly press the brake pedal until the pedal rises to the normal position and a steady pedal is felt.
17. Recheck the brake fluid level in the master cylinder reservoir.
18. Start the engine and test drive to ensure proper brake operation.

Brake Rotor

Removal and Installation

1. Disconnect the negative battery cable.
2. Raise and safely support the vehicle.
3. Remove the front wheel.
4. Remove the bolts attaching the brake caliper and remove the caliper from the brake rotor and support the caliper using a length of mechanics wire. Do not allow the caliper to hang by the flexible brake hose unsupported.
5. Remove the screw attaching the brake rotor to the wheel hub. Remove the rotor.

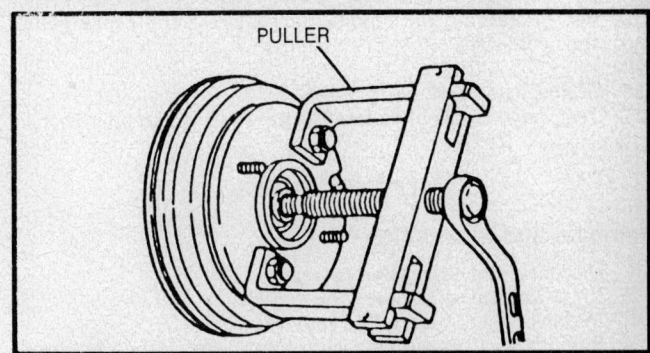

Removal of brake drum using puller

To install:
6. Install the rotor on the wheel hub and attach with screw.
7. Install the brake caliper on the steering knuckle and tighten to 23–30 ft. lbs. (31–41 Nm).

NOTE: If installing a new rotor, it may be necessary to press the caliper piston into its bore a small amount to allow for the additional thickness of the new rotor.

8. Install the front wheel.
9. Lower the vehicle.
10. Connect negative battery cable.
11. Before starting the engine, slowly press the brake pedal until the pedal rises to the normal position and a steady pedal is felt.
12. Test drive the vehicle to ensure proper brake operation.

Brake Drums

Removal and Installation

1. Disconnect the negative battery cable.
2. Raise and safely support the vehicle.
3. Remove wheel covers and rear wheels.
4. Remove the grease cap, cotter pin, castellated nut and plate washer.
5. Remove the brake drum using an appropriate puller.
To install:
6. Install the brake drum and install the plate washer and castellated nut. Tighten the nut to 43–72 ft. lbs. (49–98 Nm).
7. Install a new cotter pin. Install the grease cap.
8. Install the rear wheels and wheel covers.
9. Lower the vehicle.

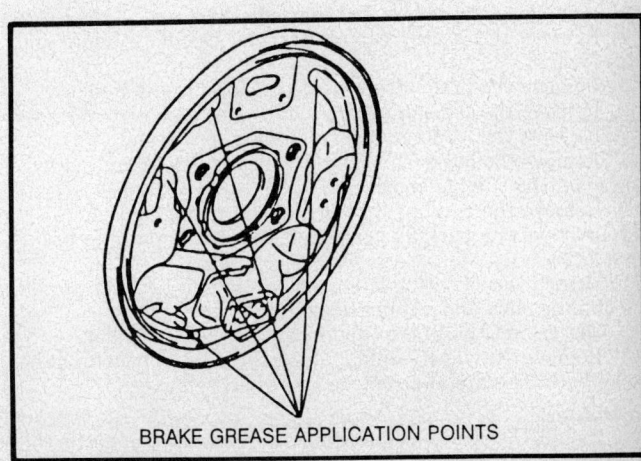

BRAKE GREASE APPLICATION POINTS

Grease points on backing plate

10. Before starting the engine, slowly press the brake pedal until the pedal rises to the normal position and a steady pedal is felt.
11. Connect negative battery cable.
12. Test drive the vehicle to ensure proper brake operation.

Brake Shoes

Removal and Installation

1. Disconnect the negative battery cable.
2. Raise and safely support the vehicle.
3. Remove wheel covers and rear wheels.
4. Remove the grease cap, cotter pin, castellated nut and plate washer.
5. Remove the brake drum using an appropriate puller.
6. Remove the tension spring.
7. Remove the leading shoe hold-down spring and pin.
8. Remove the brake shoe, parking brake shoe strut and tension from the leading shoe.
9. Remove the trailing shoe hold-down spring and pin.
10. Remove the parking brake cable from the parking brake shoe lever.
11. Detach the "C" ring from the parking brake lever pin on the trailing shoe and automatic adjusting lever parts.
To install:
12. Install the parking brake shoe lever and automatic adjusting lever parts to the trailing brake shoe.
13. Apply grease to the brake shoe contact points on the backing plate.
14. Connect the parking brake cable to the parking brake shoe lever.
15. Connect the brake shoe to the backing plate. Install the shoe hold-down spring and pin.
16. Connect the leading brake shoe to the rear brake backing plate. Install the shoe hold-down spring and pin.
17. Install the tension spring.
18. Install the brake drum.
19. Adjust the brake shoes.
20. Install the rear wheel and wheel cover.
21. Bleed the brake system.
22. Connect negative battery cable.
23. Test drive the vehicle to ensure proper brake operation.

Wheel Cylinder

Removal and Installation

1. Disconnect the negative battery cable.
2. Raise and safely support the vehicle.
3. Remove wheel covers and rear wheels.
4. Remove the grease cap, cotter pin, castellated nut and plate washer.
5. Remove the brake drum using an appropriate puller.
6. Remove the tension spring.
7. Remove the leading shoe hold-down spring and pin.
8. Remove the brake shoe, parking brake shoe strut and tension from the leading shoe.
9. Remove the trailing shoe hold-down spring and pin.
10. Remove the parking brake cable from the parking brake shoe lever.
11. Detach the "C" ring from the parking brake lever pin on the trailing shoe and automatic adjusting lever parts.
12. Disconnect the brake tube from the wheel cylinder.
13. Remove the wheel cylinder attaching bolts from behind the brake backing plate and remove the wheel cylinder.
To install:
14. Install the wheel cylinder on the backing plate. On the G102 vehicles, tighten the 2 bolts to 7–9 ft. lbs. (10–13 Nm). On the G100 vehicles, tighten the 2 bolts to 6–9 ft. lbs. (8–12 Nm).

15. Connect the brake tube to the wheel cylinder. Tighten nut to 9–13 ft. lbs. (13–18 Nm).
16. Install the parking brake shoe lever and automatic adjusting lever parts to the trailing brake shoe.
17. Apply grease to the brake shoe contact points of the backing plate.
18. Connect the parking brake cable to the parking brake shoe lever.
19. Connect the brake shoe to the rear brake backing plate. Install the shoe hold-down spring and pin.
20. Connect the leading brake shoe to the rear brake backing plate. Instll the shoe hold-down spring and pin.
21. Install the tension spring.
22. Install the brake drum.
23. Adjust the brake shoes.
24. Install the rear wheel and wheel cover.
25. Bleed the brake system.
26. Connect negative battery cable.
27. Test drive the vehicle to ensure proper brake operation.

Parking Brake Cable

Adjustment

1. Ensure that the rear drum service brakes are in proper adjustment.
2. If equipped with automatic seat belts, remove the front seats.
3. Remove the coin box and console box from the vehicle.
4. Loosen parking brake cable adjusting nut.
5. Turn adjusting nut until the handle moves 4–7 notches when pulled by a force of 44 lbs. (20 kg).
6. Confirm operation of the parking brake indicator lamp.
7. Install the console box and coin box.
8. If equipped with automatic seat belts, install the front seats.

Removal and Installation

1. If equipped with automatic seat belts, remove the front seats.
2. Remove the coin box and console box from the vehicle.
3. Remove the parking brake cable adjusting nut and connector.
4. Remove the parking brake handle.
5. Remove the parking brake tube protector.
6. Remove the parking brake cable from the parking brake pull rod.
7. Raise and safely support the vehicle.
8. Remove the exhaust pipe.
9. Remove the brake shoe.
10. Remove the parking brake cable from the rear brake backing plate.
To install:
11. Install the parking brake cable to the rear brake backing plate.
12. Install the brake shoe-releated parts.
13. Install the under-body parking brake cable clamps.
14. Install the exhaust pipe.
15. Lower the vehicle.
16. Attach the parking brake cable to the parking brake pull rod.
17. Temporarily install the adjusting nut.
18. Install the parking brake tube protector.
19. Depress the brake pedal 4–5 times to adjust the rear brake clearance.
20. Turn adjusting nut until the handle moves 4–7 notches when pulled by a force of 44 lbs. (20 kg).
21. Confirm operation of the parking brake indicator lamp.
22. Install the console box and coin box.
23. If equipped with automatic seat belts, install the front seats.

Brake System Bleeding

1. Fill the brake master cylinder reservoir with brake fluid.
2. Raise and safely support the vehicle.
3. Connect a length of vinyl hose to the bleeder plug of the right rear wheel cylinder.
4. Submerge one end of the vinyl hose in a container filled with brake fluid. Connect the other end of the vinyl hose to the wheel cylinder bleeder plug.
5. Have an assistant slowly depress the brake pedal and hold it.
6. Open the bleeder plug of the right rear wheel cylinder $\frac{1}{3}$–$\frac{1}{2}$ turn until the bubbles stop coming out of the tube. Close the bleeder plug.

7. Have the assistant release the brake pedal.

NOTE: The assistant must keep the brake pedal depressed until the bleeder plug is closed.

8. Continue the above procedure until air bubbles are no longer observed in the brake fluid.
9. Remove the vinyl tube and replace the bleeder plug cap.
10. Repeat the procedure for the remaining wheels in the following order:
   Left front
   Left rear
   Right front
11. Check the brake fluid level in the master cylinder reservoir frequently during the bleeding operation.

FRONT SUSPENSION

MacPherson Strut

Removal and Installation

1. Disconnect the negative battery cable.
2. Raise and safely support the vehicle.
3. Remove the front wheel.
4. Remove the clip retaining the flexible brake hose to the strut housing. Disconnect the hose from the strut housing.
5. Remove the nuts attaching the strut to the steering knuckle.

NOTE: Before removing the left strut, remove the disc brake caliper attaching bolt from the upper side.

6. Working in the engine compartment, remove the 2 nuts attaching the suspension support.
7. Remove the bolts attaching the strut to the steering knuckle.
8. Remove the strut from the vehicle.
To install:
9. Working in the engine compartment, install the suspension support on the fender apron using new nuts. Tighten to 15–22 ft. lbs. (20–30 Nm).
10. Mount the lower strut bracket on the steering knuckle using new nuts and bolts. Tighten to 80–116 ft. lbs. (108–158 Nm).

NOTE: If the left strut was removed, install the disc brake caliper upper attaching bolt to the knuckle and tighten to 23–30 ft. lbs. (31–41 Nm).

11. Install the flexible hose to the strut bracket.
12. Install the flexible hose clip.
13. Install the wheels.
14. Lower the vehicle.
15. Check the front end alignment.

Lower Ball Joints

Inspection

With the lower ball joint separated from the steering knuckle, check for looseness and excessive play in the ball joint.

Removal and Installation

The lower ball joint is integral to the lower control arm. If the lower ball joint is determined to be defective, replace the lower control arm.

Lower Control Arms

Removal and Installation

1. Disconnect the negative battery cable.
2. Raise and safely support the vehicle.
3. Remove the front wheel.
4. Remove the end nut from the stabilizer bar.
5. Remove the ball joint nut and bolt.
6. Remove the nut attaching the lower control arm to the body.
7. On G102 vehicles, remove the lower suspension brace attaching bolts.
8. Remove the engine undercovers.
9. Remove the lower control arm bracket.
10. Remove the lower control arm.
To install:
11. Install and temporarily tighten the lower control arm ball joint and stabilizer bar end nut.
12. Install the ball joint nut and bolt. Tighten to 58–76 ft. lbs. (79–103 Nm).
13. Install the lower control arm bracket. Tighten to 54–76 ft. lbs. (73–103 Nm).
14. Tighten the lower control arm attaching nut temporarily.
15. Install the engine undercovers.
16. On G102 vehicles, install the lower suspension brace. Tighten to 29–40 ft. lbs. (39–54 Nm).
17. Install the front wheel.
18. Lower the vehicle.
19. Rock the front suspension several times to settle the suspension. Tighten the stabilizer bar and lower control arm bolts and nuts to 54–76 ft. lbs. (73–103 Nm).

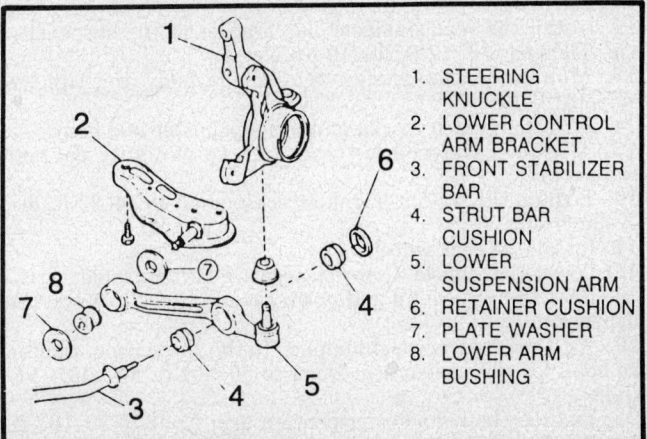

1. STEERING KNUCKLE
2. LOWER CONTROL ARM BRACKET
3. FRONT STABILIZER BAR
4. STRUT BAR CUSHION
5. LOWER SUSPENSION ARM
6. RETAINER CUSHION
7. PLATE WASHER
8. LOWER ARM BUSHING

Lower control arm installation

20. Check front end alignment.

Stabilizer Bar

Removal and Installation

1. Disconnect the negative battery cable.
2. Raise and safely support the vehicle.
3. Remove the engine undercovers.
4. Remove the bolts attaching the stabilizer bar bracket to the body.

5. Remove the nuts attaching the stabilizer bar to the lower control arm.
6. Remove the stabilizer bar from the vehicle.

To install:

7. Install the stabilizer bar in the lower control arm. Tighten the bolts to 54–76 ft. lbs. (40–56 Nm).
8. Install the stabilizer bar brackets to the body. Tighten to 43–61 ft. lbs. (32–45 Nm).
9. Install the engine undercovers.
10. Lower the vehicle.
11. Connect negative battery cable.

REAR SUSPENSION

MacPherson Strut

Removal and Installation

1. Disconnect the negative battery cable.
2. Raise and safely support the vehicle.
3. Remove the rear wheel.
4. Remove the brake tube from the bracket.
5. Detach the clip and disconnect the flexible hose from the shock absorber.
6. Remove the clamp retaining the brake tube located at the back of the strut housing.
7. Remove the nuts attaching the strut to the axle carrier. Do not remove the bolts at this time.
8. On G100 and G102 Hatchback, working inside the vehicle, perform the following:
   a. Remove the package tray.
   b. Tilt the seat back.
   c. Remove the package tray side trim.
   d. Disconnect the speaker.
   e. Loosen, but do not remove, the nut attaching the strut to the suspension support.
   f. Remove the nuts attaching the suspension support to the body.
9. On G102 Sedan, working inside the vehicle, perform the following:
   a. Remove the rear seat back hinge bolts.
   b. Remove the screw attaching the rear wheel quarter trim.
   c. Remove the rear quarter trim.
10. Remove the bolts attaching the axle carrier to the strut. Remove the strut from the body.

To install:

11. Install the suspension support to the body. Tighten to 7–12 ft. lbs. (9–16 Nm).
12. Mount the strut to the axle carrier and install new nuts and bolts. Push the axle carrier to the lower (positive) side and tighten to 80–116 ft. lbs. (108–158 Nm).
13. Install the flexible hose to the strut housing. Secure the clip.
14. Install the brake tube to the fitting.
15. Install the brake tube retaining clamp located at the back of the strut housing.
16. On G100 and G102 Hatchback, working inside the vehicle, perform the following:
   a. Tighten the strut-to-suspension support attaching nut to 25–40 ft. lbs. (34–54 Nm).
   b. Connect the speaker.
   c. Install the package tray side trim.
   d. Raise the seatback.
   e. Install the package tray.
17. On G102 Sedan, working inside the vehicle, perform the following:
   a. Install the rear wheel quarter trim.

   b. Install the rear seat back hinge.
18. Bleed the rear brakes.
19. Install the rear wheel.
20. Lower the vehicle.
21. Connect negative battery cable.
22. Check the rear wheel alignment.

Rear Control Arms

Removal and Installation

1. Disconnect the negative battery cable.
2. Raise and safely support the vehicle.
3. Remove the wheel.
4. Remove the bolt and nut attaching the stabilizer link to suspension arm No. 1.
5. Remove the bolt and nut attaching the suspension arm to the axle carrier.
6. Put a match mark on the body bracket and toe adjusting cam as a guide during reinstallation. Remove the bolt attaching the suspension arm to the adjusting cam on the body. Remove suspension arm No. 1.
7. Remove the rear stabilizer bar bracket from the suspension arm.
8. Remove the bolt and nut attaching suspension arm No. 2 to the axle carrier.
9. Remove the bolt and nut attaching suspension arm No. 2 to the body. Remove the suspension arm.

To install:

10. Install suspension arm No. 1 to the body temporarily.
11. Install suspension arm No. 1 to the axle carrier temporarily.
12. Install the rear stabilizer bar bracket to the suspension arm. Tighten to 7–12 ft. lbs. (9–16 Nm).
13. Mount the suspension arm to the body and tighten temporarily.
14. Align the match marks on the toe adjuster and body.
15. Tighten the suspension arm to the axle carrier temporarily.
16. Tighten the stabilizer link attaching bolt to 14–22 ft. lbs. (19–30 Nm).
17. Install the rear wheel.
18. Lower the vehicle. Connect negative battery cable.
19. Rock the vehicle up and down several times to settle the suspension.
20. With the vehicle weight applied to the suspension, tighten the bolts for suspension arm No. 1 to 80–101 ft. lbs. (108–137 Nm).
21. Tighten the bolts for suspension arm No. 2 to 80–101 ft. lbs. (108–137 Nm) for the bolts to the axle carrier and 51–64 ft. lbs. (69–87 Nm) for the bolts to the body.

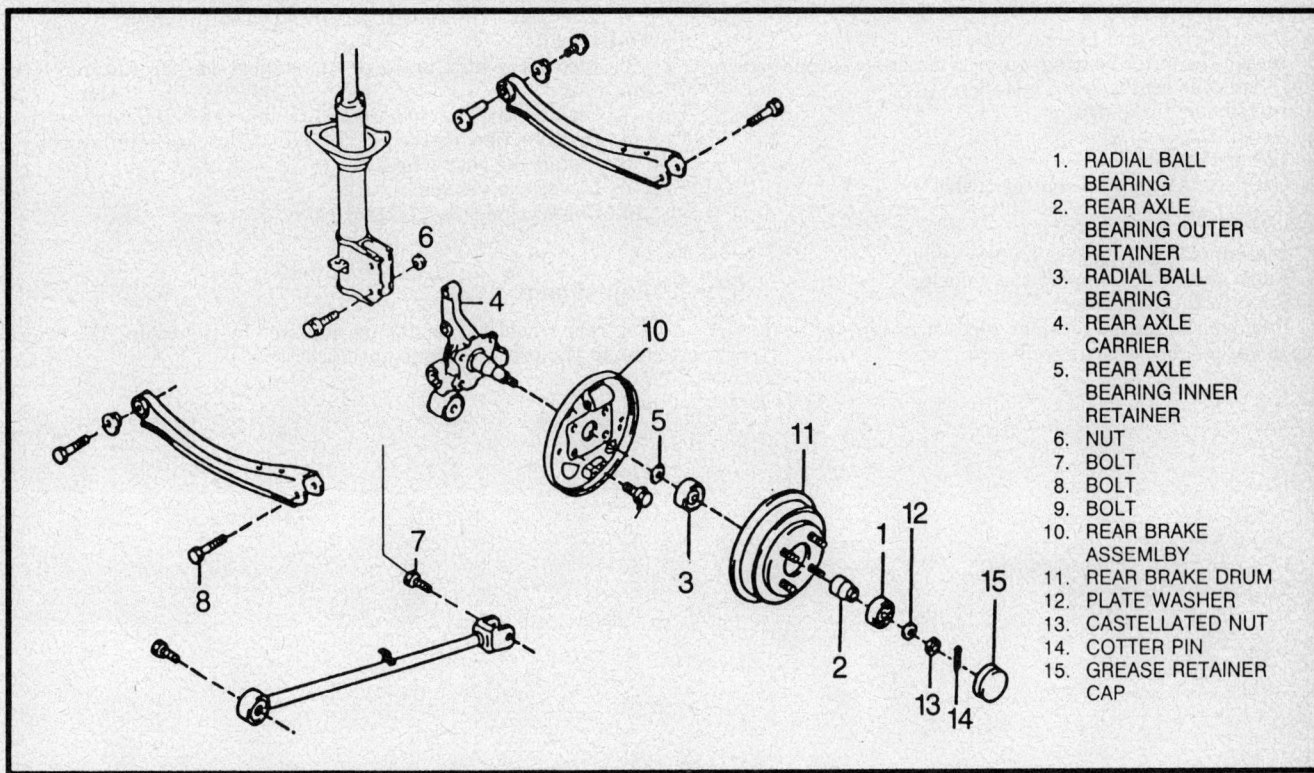

1. RADIAL BALL BEARING
2. REAR AXLE BEARING OUTER RETAINER
3. RADIAL BALL BEARING
4. REAR AXLE CARRIER
5. REAR AXLE BEARING INNER RETAINER
6. NUT
7. BOLT
8. BOLT
9. BOLT
10. REAR BRAKE ASSEMLBY
11. REAR BRAKE DRUM
12. PLATE WASHER
13. CASTELLATED NUT
14. COTTER PIN
15. GREASE RETAINER CAP

Rear suspension components—G100 and G102 Hatchback

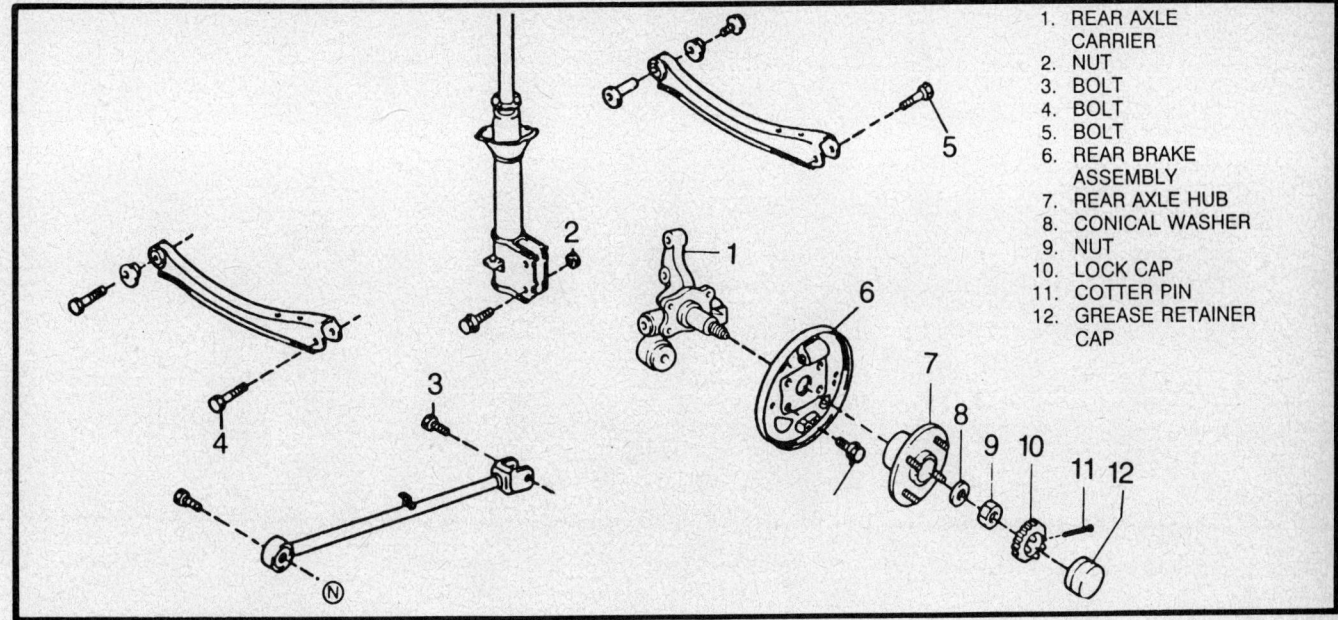

1. REAR AXLE CARRIER
2. NUT
3. BOLT
4. BOLT
5. BOLT
6. REAR BRAKE ASSEMBLY
7. REAR AXLE HUB
8. CONICAL WASHER
9. NUT
10. LOCK CAP
11. COTTER PIN
12. GREASE RETAINER CAP

Rear suspension components—G102 Sedan

Rear Wheel Bearings

Removal and Installation

G100 AND G102 HATCHBACK

1. Disconnect the negative battery cable.
2. Raise and safely support the vehicle.
3. Remove the rear wheel.

4. Remove the grease cap. Remove the cotter pin and castellated nut and plate washer.

5. Remove the brake drum using a suitable puller.

6. Place the brake drum on the work bench. Using a brass drift, drive out the inner bearing. With the drum in this position, drive out the outer bearing retainer.

7. Invert the brake drum and drive out the outer bearing.

To install:

8. Pack the hub and bearing with grease.

9. Install the outer bearing, outer retainer and inner bearing using a suitable seal/bearing installer.

10. Install the brake drum.

11. Install the rear wheel.

12. Lower the vehicle.

13. Connect the negative battery cable.

G102 SEDAN

1. Disconnect the negative battery cable.

2. Raise and safely support the vehicle.

3. Remove the rear wheel.

4. Remove the grease retainer cap, cotter pin, lock cap, nut, conical washer, brake drum and hub.

5. The unit wheel bearing is integral to the hub.

To install:

6. Install the hub, brake drum, conical washer, nut and lock cap.

7. Tighten the nut to 123–166 ft. lbs. (167–225 Nm).

8. Install a new cotter pin. Install the grease retainer cap.

9. Install the rear wheel.

10. Lower the vehicle.

11. Connect negative battery cable.

Adjustment

The rear wheel bearing(s) are adjusted by tightening the wheel nut to the proper torque specification.

SERIAL NUMBER IDENTIFICATION

Vehicle Identification Plate

The vehicle identification plate is mounted on the top edge of the instrument panel and is visible from the outside of the vehicle.

Engine Number

The engine number is stamped into the side of the cylinder block, near the transaxle. The first 5 digits indicate engine model identification. The remaining numbers refer to emission equipment and production sequence.

Vehicle Identification Number

The vehicle identification number is located on the vehicle identification plate and on the engine cowl under the hood. The vehicle identification number is also located on the driver's side door jam, near the lock striker plate.

Transaxle Number

The transaxle serial number is stamped on the top of the transaxle/clutch case.

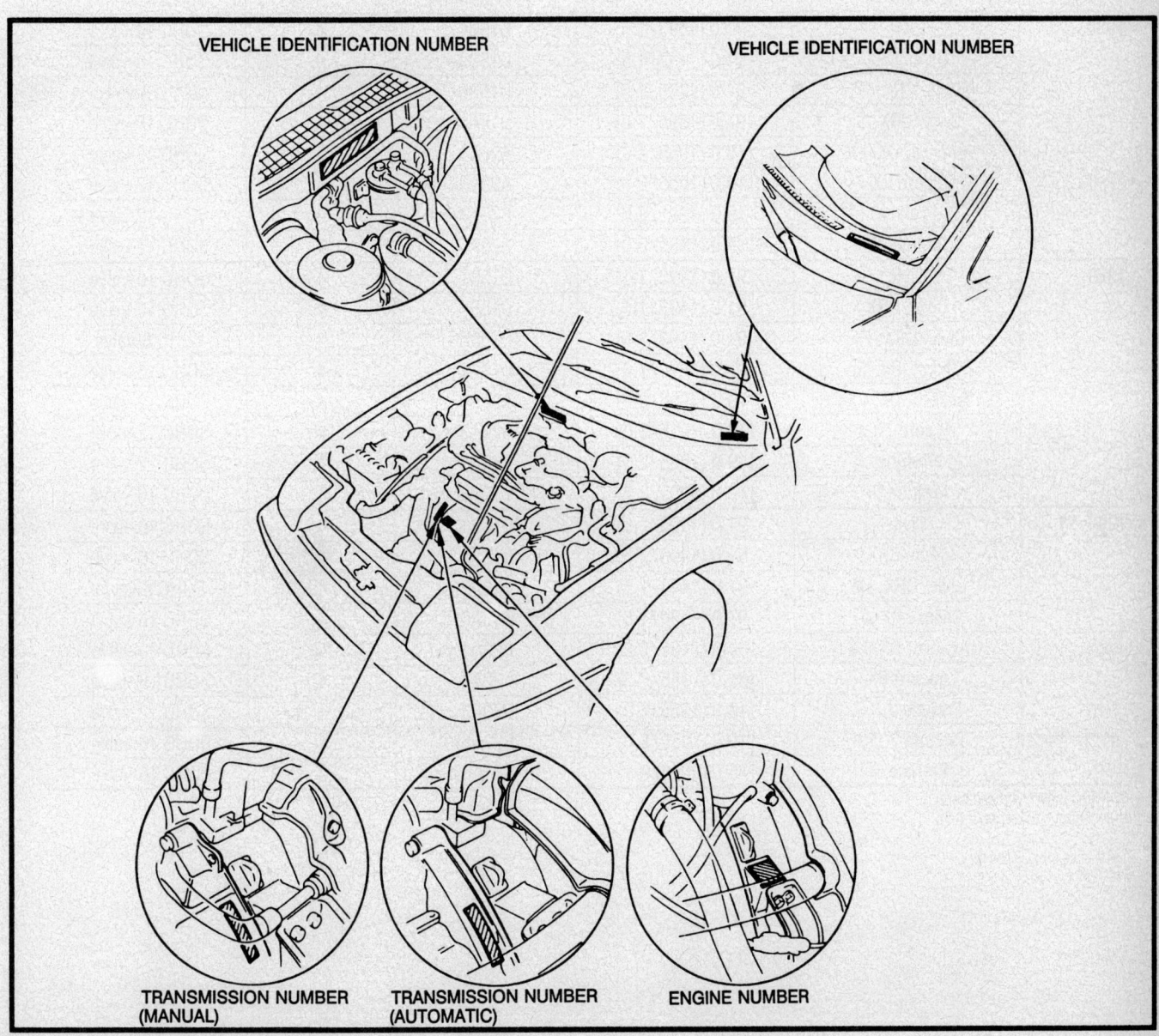

VEHICLE IDENTIFICATION NUMBER

VEHICLE IDENTIFICATION NUMBER

TRANSMISSION NUMBER (MANUAL)

TRANSMISSION NUMBER (AUTOMATIC)

ENGINE NUMBER

Honda identification numbers

SPECIFICATIONS

ENGINE IDENTIFICATION

Year	Model	Engine Displacement cu. in. (cc/liter)	Engine Series Identification	No. of Cylinders	Engine Type
1987	Civic/CRX, 1.3	81.9 (1342/1.3)	D15A2	4	SOHC 8-valve
	Civic/CRX, HF, 1.5	90.8 (1488/1.5)	D13A2	4	SOHC 12-valve
	Civic/CRX, Si	90.8 (1488/1.5)	D15A3	4	SOHC 12-valve
	Accord	119.0 (1955/2.0)	A20A1	4	SOHC 12-valve
	Accord LX-i	119.0 (1955/2.0)	A20A3	4	SOHC 12-valve
	Prelude	111.6 (1829/1.8)	A18AI	4	SOHC 12-valve
	Prelude Si	119.0 (1955/2.0)	A20A3	4	SOHC 12-valve
1988	Civic	91.0 (1493/1.5)	D15B1	4	SOHC 16-valve
	Civic/CRX	91.0 (1493/1.5)	D15B2	4	SOHC 16-valve
	Civic/CRX, HF	91.0 (1493/1.5)	D15B6	4	SOHC 8-valve
	Civic/CRX, Si	97.0 (1590/1.6)	D16A6	4	SOHC 16-valve
	Accord, DX/LX	119.0 (1955/2.0)	A20A1	4	SOHC 12-valve
	Accord LX-i	119.0 (1955/2.0)	A20A3	4	SOHC 12-valve
	Prelude	119.0 (1955/2.0)	B20A3	4	SOHC 12-valve
	Prelude Si	119.0 (1955/2.0)	B20A5	4	SOHC 12-valve
1989	Civic	91.0 (1493/1.5)	D15B1	4	SOHC 16-valve
	Civic/CRX	91.0 (1493/1.5)	D15B2	4	SOHC 16-valve
	Civic/CRX, HF	91.0 (1493/1.5)	D15B6	4	SOHC 8-valve
	Civic/CRX, Si	97.0 (1590/1.6)	D16A6	4	SOHC 16-valve
	Accord, DX/LX	119.0 (1955/2.0)	A20A1	4	SOHC 12-valve
	Accord LX-i	119.0 (1955/2.0)	A20A3	4	SOHC 12-valve
	Prelude	119.0 (1955/2.0)	B20A3	4	SOHC 12-valve
	Prelude Si	119.0 (1955/2.0)	B20A5	4	DOHC 16-valve
1990-91	Civic	91.0 (1493/1.5)	D15B1	4	SOHC 16-valve
	Civic/CRX	91.0 (1493/1.5)	D15B2	4	SOHC 16-valve
	Civic/CRX, HF	91.0 (1493/1.5)	D15B6	4	SOHC 8-valve
	Civic/CRX, Si	97.0 (1590/1.6)	D16A6	4	SOHC 16-valve
	Accord, DX/LX	132.0 (2156/2.2)	F22A1	4	SOHC 16-valve
	Accord EX	132.0 (2156/2.2)	F22A4	4	SOHC 16-valve
	Prelude 2.0 S	119.0 (1955/2.0)	B20A3	4	SOHC 12-valve
	Prelude 2.0 Si	119.0 (1955/2.0)	B20A5	4	DOHC 16-valve
	Prelude Si	125.0 (2056/2.1)	B21A1	4	DOHC 16-valve

SOHC—Single Overhead Cam
DOHC—Double Overhead Cam

GENERAL ENGINE SPECIFICATIONS

Year	Model	Engine Displacement cu. in. (cc)	Fuel System Type	Net Horsepower @ rpm	Net Torque @ rpm (ft. lbs.)	Bore × Stroke (in.)	Compression Ratio	Oil Pressure @ rpm
1987	Civic/CRX, 1.3	81.9 (1392)	3 bbl	60 @ 5500	73 @ 3500	2.91 × 3.07	10.0:1	50 @ 2000
	Civic/CRX, 1.5	90.8 (1488)	3 bbl	76 @ 6000	84 @ 3500	2.91 × 3.41	9.2:1	50 @ 2000
	Civic/CRX, HF	90.8 (1488)	3 bbl	58 @ 4500	80 @ 2500	2.91 × 3.41	9.6:1	50 @ 2000
	Civic/CRX, Si	90.8 (1488)	EFI	91 @ 5500	93 @ 4500	2.91 × 3.41	8.7:1	50 @ 2000
	Accord	119.0 (1955)	2 bbl	98 @ 5500	109 @ 3500	3.25 × 3.58	9.1:1	55 @ 2000
	Accord LX-i	119.0 (1955)	EFI	110 @ 5500	114 @ 4500	3.25 × 3.58	8.8:1	55 @ 2000
	Prelude	111.6 (1829)	Dual Sidedraft	100 @ 5500	107 @ 4000	3.15 × 3.58	9.1:1	50 @ 2000
	Prelude Si	119.0 (1955)	EFI	110 @ 5500	114 @ 4500	3.25 × 3.58	8.8:1	50 @ 2000
1988	Civic	91.0 (1493)	DP-FI	70 @ 5500	83 @ 3000	2.95 × 3.33	9.6:1	50 @ 2000
	Civic/CRX	91.0 (1493)	DP-FI	92 @ 6000	89 @ 4500	2.95 × 3.33	9.2:1	50 @ 2000
	Civic/CRX, HF	91.0 (1493)	MP-FI	62 @ 4500	90 @ 2000	2.95 × 3.33	9.6:1	50 @ 2000
	Civic/CRX, Si	97.0 (1590)	MP-FE	105 @ 6000	98 @ 5000	2.95 × 3.54	9.1:1	50 @ 2000
	Accord DX/LX	119.0 (1955)	2 bbl	98 @ 5500	109 @ 3500	3.25 × 3.58	9.1:1	55 @ 2000
	Accord LX-i	119.0 (1955)	MP-PFI	110 @ 5500	114 @ 4500	3.25 × 3.58	9.3:1	55 @ 2000
	Prelude	119.0 (1955)	Dual Sidedraft	100 @ 5500	107 @ 4000	3.19 × 3.74	9.1:1	50 @ 2000
	Prelude Si	119.0 (1955)	FI	110 @ 5500	114 @ 4500	3.18 × 3.74	9.0:1	50 @ 2000
1989	Civic	91.0 (1493)	DP-FI	70 @ 5500	83 @ 3000	2.95 × 3.33	9.2:1	74 @ 3000
	Civic/CRX	91.0 (1493)	DP-FI	92 @ 6000	89 @ 4500	2.95 × 3.33	9.2:1	74 @ 3000
	Civic/CRX, HF	91.0 (1493)	MP-FE	62 @ 4500	90 @ 2000	2.95 × 3.33	9.2:1	74 @ 3000
	Civic/CRX, Si	97.0 (1590)	MP-FE	108 @ 6000	100 @ 5000	2.95 × 3.54	9.1:1	74 @ 3000
	Accord DX/LX	119.0 (1955)	2 bbl	98 @ 5500	109 @ 3500	3.26 × 3.58	9.1:1	55–65 @ 3000
	Accord LX-i/SE-i	119.0 (1955)	MP-PFI	120 @ 5800	122 @ 4000	3.26 × 3.58	9.3:1	55–65 @ 3000
	Prelude	119.0 (1955)	Dual Sidedraft	①	111 @ 4800	3.19 × 3.74	9.1:1	75–87 @ 3000
	Prelude Si	110.3 (1955)	MP-PFI	135 @ 6200	127 @ 4500	3.19 × 3.74	9.0:1	75–87 @ 3000
1990–91	Civic	91.0 (1493)	DP-FI	70 @ 5500	83 @ 3000	2.95 × 3.33	9.2:1	50 @ 3000
	Civic/CRX	91.0 (1493)	DP-FI	92 @ 6000	89 @ 4500	2.95 × 3.33	9.2:1	50 @ 3000
	Civic/CRX, HF	91.0 (1493)	MP-FI	62 @ 4500	90 @ 2000	2.95 × 3.33	9.6:1	50 @ 3000
	Civic/CRX, Si	97.0 (1590)	MP-FI	108 @ 6000	100 @ 5000	2.95 × 3.54	9.1:1	50 @ 3000
	Accord DX/LX	132.0 (2156)	MP-FI	125 @ 5200	137 @ 4000	3.35 × 3.74	8.8:1	50 @ 3000
	Accord EX	132.0 (2156)	MP-FI	130 @ 5200	142 @ 4000	3.35 × 3.74	8.8:1	50 @ 3000
	Prelude 2.0 S	119.0 (1955)	Dual Sidedraft	①	111 @ 4000	3.19 × 3.74	9.1:1	50 @ 3000
	Prelude 2.0 Si	119.0 (1955)	MP-FI	135 @ 6200	127 @ 4000	3.19 × 3.74	9.0:1	50 @ 3000
	Prelude Si	125.0 (2056)	MP-FI	140 @ 5800	135 @ 5000	3.27 × 3.74	9.4:1	50 @ 3000

DP-FI   Duel Point Fuel Injected
MP-FI   Multipoint Fuel Injected
MP-PFI   Multipoint Port Fuel Injected
① Manual transaxle—104 @ 5800
   Automatic transaxle—105 @ 5800

GASOLINE ENGINE TUNE-UP SPECIFICATIONS

Year	Model	Engine Displacement cu. in. (cc)	Spark Plugs Type	Gap (in.)	Ignition Timing (deg.) MT	AT	Compression Pressure (psi)	Fuel Pump (psi)	Idle Speed (rpm) MT	AT	Valve Clearance ⑦ In.	Ex.
1987	Civic/CRX 1.3	81.9 (1342)	BUR4EB-11	0.042	21B ③ ⑤	—	225	3.0	650–750	—	0.007–0.009	0.009–0.011
	Civic/CRX 1.5	90.8 (1488)	BUR4EB-11	0.042	20B ⑪	15B ④ ⑤	200	3.0	650–750	650–750	0.007–0.009	0.009–0.011
	Civic/CRX HF	90.8 (1488)	BUR4EB-11	0.042	26B ③ ⑤	—	164	3.0	650–750	650–750	0.007–0.009	0.009–0.011
	Civic/CRX Si	90.8 (1488)	BPR6EY-11	0.042	16B ② ⑤	—	156	35	700–800	—	0.007–0.009	0.009–0.011
	Accord	119.0 (1955)	BPR5EY-11	0.042	24B ① ⑥	15B ①	171	3.0	700–800	650–750	0.005–0.007	0.010–0.012
	Accord LX-i	119.0 (1955)	BPR5EY-11	0.042	15B ①	15B ①	178	35	700–800	700–800	0.005–0.007	0.010–0.012
	Prelude	111.6 (1829)	BPR6EY-11	0.042	20B ①	12B ①	156	2.5	750–850	750–850	0.005–0.007	0.010–0.012
	Prelude Si	119.0 (1955)	BPR5EY-11	0.042	15B ①	15B ①	178	35	700–800	700–800	0.005–0.007	0.010–0.012
1988	Civic/CRX HF, 1.5	91.0 (1493)	BCPR6E-11	0.042	14B	14B	185	35	600–700	700–800	0.005–0.007	0.007–0.009
	Civic/CRX Std., 1.5	91.0 (1493)	BCPR6E-11	0.042	18B	18B	185	35	600–700	700–800	0.007–0.009	0.009–0.011
	Civic/CRX Si, 1.6	97.0 (1590)	BCPR6E-11	0.042	18B	18B	185	35	700–800	700–800	0.007–0.009	0.009–0.011
	Accord DX/LX	119.0 (1955)	BPR5EY-11	0.042	24B ⑥	15B ①	171	3.0	800–850	700–800	0.005–0.007	0.010–0.012
	Accord LX-i	119.0 (1955)	BPR5EY-11	0.042	15B ①	15B ①	178	35	750–800	750–800	0.005–0.007	0.010–0.012
	Prelude	119.0 (1955)	BCPR5E-11	0.042	20B	12B	156	2.5	800–850	750–800	0.005–0.007	0.0010–0.0012
	Prelude Si	119.0 (1955)	BCPR6E-11	0.042	15B	15B	178	35	750–800	750–800	0.003–0.005	0.006–0.008
1989	Civic/CRX	91.0 (1493)	BCPR6E-11	0.042	18B	18B	185	36	700–800	700–800	0.007–0.009	0.009–0.011
	Civic HF	91.0 (1493)	BCPR6E-11	0.042	18B	18B	185	36	600–650	600–650	0.005–0.007	0.007–0.009
	Civic/CRX Si	97.0 (1590)	BCPR6E-11	0.042	18B	18B	185	36	700–800	700–800	0.007–0.009	0.009–0.011
	Accord DX/LX	119.0 (1955)	BPR5EY-11	0.042	24B ⑩	15B	171	2.6–3.3	750–850	680–790	0.005–0.007	0.010–0.012
	Accord LX-i	119.0 (1955)	BPR5EY-11	0.042	15B	15B	178	33–39	700–800	700–800	0.005–0.007	0.010–0.012
	Prelude	119.0 (1955)	BCPR5E-11	0.042	20B ⑧	15B ⑨	171	1.3–2.1	750–850	700–800	0.005–0.007	0.010–0.012
	Prelude Si	119.0 (1955)	BCPR6E-11	0.042	15B	15B	178	36	700–800	700–800	0.003–0.005	0.006–0.008

GASOLINE ENGINE TUNE-UP SPECIFICATIONS

Year	Model	Engine Displacement cu. in. (cc)	Spark Plugs Type	Gap (in.)	Ignition Timing (deg.) MT	AT	Compression Pressure (psi)	Fuel Pump (psi)	Idle Speed (rpm) MT	AT	Valve Clearance ⑦ In.	Ex.
1990	Civic	91.0 (1493)	BCPR6E-11	0.042	18B	18B	185	36	700–800	700–800	0.007–0.009	0.009–0.011
	Civic/CRX	91.0 (1493)	BCPR6E-11	0.042	18B	18B	185	36	700–800	700–800	0.007–0.009	0.009–0.011
	Civic/CRX, HF	91.0 (1493)	BCPR5E-11	0.042	14B	14B	185	36	600–700 ⑪	700–800	0.005–0.007	0.007–0.009
	Civic/CRX, Si	97.0 (1590)	BCPR6E-11	0.042	18B	18B	185	36	700–800	700–800	0.007–0.009	0.009–0.011
	Accord DX/LX	132.0 (2156)	ZFR5F-11	0.042	15B	15B	178	36	650–750	650–750	0.0094–0.011	0.0110–0.0126
	Accord EX	132.0 (2156)	ZFR5F-11	0.042	15B	15B	178	36	650–750	650–750	0.0094–0.011	0.0110–0.0126
	Prelude 2.0 S	119.0 (1955)	BCPR5E-11	0.042	20B ⑧	15B ⑨	178	1.3–2.1	750–850	700–800	0.005–0.007	0.010–0.012
	Prelude 2.0 Si	119.0 (1955)	ZFR5F-11	0.042	15B	15B	178	36	700–800	700–800	0.003–0.005	0.006–0.008
	Prelude Si	125.0 (2056)	ZFR5F-11	0.042	15B	15B	178	36	700–800	700–800	0.003–0.005	0.006–0.008
1991	All				SEE UNDERHOOD SPECIFICATIONS STICKER							

NOTE: The underhood specifications sticker often reflects tune-up changes made in production. Sticker figures must be used if they disagree with those in this chart.

B   Before top dead center
A   After top dead center
—Not applicable
① Aim timing light at red mark on flywheel or torque converter drive plate with the distributor vacuum hose connected at the specified idle speed.

② California—12B
③ Std., California—16B
     MT—20B, AT—15B
④ Models with power steering—17B
⑤ Aim timing light at red mark on crankshaft pulley
⑥ California—20B

⑦ Jet valve adjustment
     Except 1342cc and 1488cc—0.005– 0.007
     1342cc and 1488cc—0.007– 0.009
⑧ California—15B
⑨ California—10B
⑩ California—20B
⑪ California—550–650

FIRING ORDERS

NOTE: To avoid confusion, always replace spark plug wires one at a time.

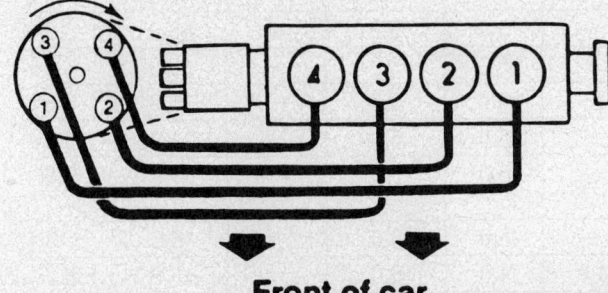

Front of car

1342cc and 1488cc 1987 Civic
Engine Firing Order: 1–3–4–2
Disributor Rotation: Clockwise

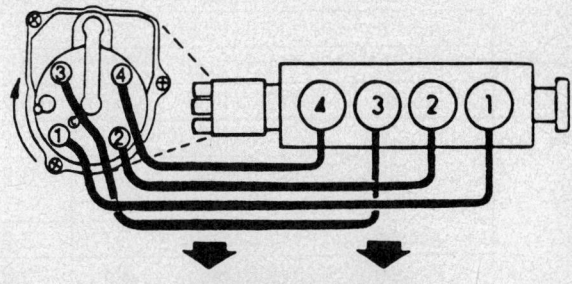

Front of car

1493cc and 1590cc 1988–91 Civic
Engine Firing Order: 1–3–4–2
Distributor Rotation: Clockwise

FIRING ORDERS

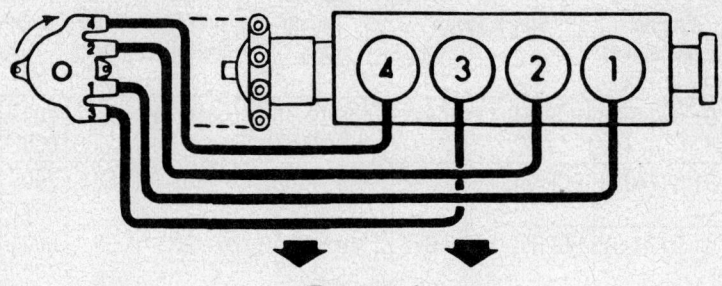

Front of car

1955cc 1987–89 Accord, 1987 Prelude (all) and 1988–
91 Prelude (carbureted)
Engine Firing Order: 1–3–4–2
Distributor Rotation: Clockwise

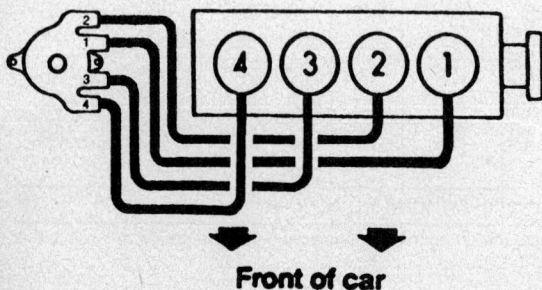

Front of car

1955cc and 2056cc 1988–91 Prelude (fuel injected)
Engine Firing Order: 1–3–4–2
Distributor Rotation: Clockwise

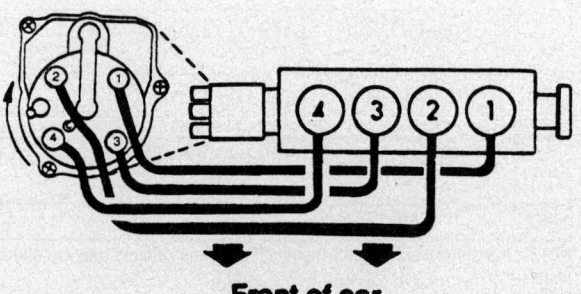

Front of car

2156cc 1990–91 Accord
Engine Firing Order: 1–3–4–2
Distributor Rotation: Clockwise

CAPACITIES

Year	Model	Engine Displacement cu. in. (cc)	Engine Crankcase (qts.) with Filter	without Filter	Transmission (pts.) 4-Spd	5-Spd	Auto. ①	Drive Axle (pts.)	Fuel Tank (gal.)	Cooling System (qts.)
1987	Civic/CRX	81.9 (1342)	3.7	3.2	5.0	5.0	5.0⑤	⑦	11.9②	4.8③
	Civic/CRX	90.8 (1488)	3.7	3.2	5.0	5.0	5.0⑤	⑦	11.9②	4.8③
	Accord	119.0 (1955)	3.7	3.2	—	5.0	5.2	—	15.9	5.2⑥
	Prelude	111.6 (1829)	3.7	3.2	—	5.0	5.8	—	15.9	6.3④
	Prelude	119.0 (1955)	3.7	3.2	—	5.0	5.8	—	15.9	6.3④
1988	Civic/CRX	91.0 (1493)	3.7	3.2	—	5.0	5.0	—	11.9	5.8
	Civic/CRX Si	97.0 (1590)	3.7	3.2	—	5.0	5.0	—	11.9⑧	5.8
	Accord	119.0 (1955)	3.7	3.2	—	5.0	6.0	—	15.9	5.8
	Prelude	119.0 (1955)	4.1	3.6	4.0	4.0	6.0	—	15.9	8.2
1989	Civic/CRX	91.0 (1493)	3.7	3.2	—	4.0⑨	5.0⑩	—	11.9⑪	⑫
	Civic/CRX	91.0 (1590)	3.7	3.2	—	4.0⑨	5.0⑩	—	11.9⑪	⑫
	Accord	119.0 (1955)	3.7	3.2	—	4.8	6.4	—	15.9	⑭
	Prelude	119.0 (1955)	4.1	3.6	4.0	4.0	6.0	—	15.9	⑬

CAPACITIES

Year	Model	Engine Displacement cu. in. (cc)	Engine Crankcase (qts.) with Filter	Engine Crankcase (qts.) without Filter	Transmission (pts.) 4-Spd	Transmission (pts.) 5-Spd	Transmission (pts.) Auto. ①	Drive Axle (pts.)	Fuel Tank (gal.)	Cooling System (qts.)
1990-91	Civic/CRX	91.0 (1493)	3.7	3.2	—	4.0 ⑨	5.0 ⑩	—	11.9 ⑪	⑫
	Civic/CRX	91.0 (1590)	3.7	3.2	—	4.0 ⑨	5.0 ⑩	—	11.9 ⑪	⑫
	Accord	132.0 (2156)	4.0	3.7	—	4.0	5.0	—	17.0	⑮
	Prelude	119.0 (1955)	4.0	3.6	—	4.4	6.0	—	15.9	⑯
	Prelude	125.0 (2056)	4.0	3.6	—	4.4	6.0	—	15.9	8.2

① Does not include torque converter
② 4 door—12.1
　CRX—10.8
　CRX HF—10.0
　CRX Si—11.9
③ 1342cc—3.6
④ Automatic transaxle—7.1
⑤ CRX—6.0
⑥ Automatic transaxle—5.8
⑦ 4WD—2.5

⑧ All others—10.6
⑨ 4WD—5.0
⑩ 4WD—6.0
⑪ HF—10.6
⑫ Automatic transaxle—5.7
　Manual transaxle—5.8
⑬ Fuel injection—8.2
　Carbureted with manual transaxle—7.2
　Carbureted with automatic transaxle—7.9

⑭ Manual transaxle—6.9
　Automatic transaxle—7.2
⑮ Manual transaxle—7.0
　Automatic Transaxle—7.5
⑯ Prelude 2.06—Manual transaxle—7.2
　Automatic transaxle—7.9

CRANKSHAFT AND CONNECTING ROD SPECIFICATIONS

All measurements are given in inches.

Year	Engine Displacement cu. in. (cc)	Crankshaft Main Brg. Journal Dia.	Crankshaft Main Brg. Oil Clearance	Crankshaft Shaft End-play	Crankshaft Thrust on No.	Connecting Rod Journal Diameter	Connecting Rod Oil Clearance	Connecting Rod Side Clearance
1987	81.9 (1342)	1.7707–1.7717	0.0009–0.0017	0.004–0.014	4	1.4951–1.4961	0.0008–0.0015	0.006–0.012
	90.8 (1488)	1.9676–1.9685	0.0009–0.0017	0.004–0.014	4	1.6526–1.6535	0.0008–0.0015	0.006–0.012
	111.6 (1829) 119.0 (1955)	1.9673–1.9683 ②	0.0010–0.0022 ①	0.004–0.014	3	1.7707–1.7717	0.0006–0.0015	0.006–0.012
1988	91.0 (1493)	1.7707–1.7718	0.0010–0.0017	0.004–0.014	4	③	0.0008–0.0015	0.006–0.012
	97.0 (1590)	2.1644–2.1654	0.0010–0.0017	0.004–0.014	4	1.7707–1.7717	0.0008–0.0015	0.006–0.012
	119.0 (1955) Accord	②	0.0010–0.0022 ①	0.004–0.014	3	1.7707–1.7717	0.0008–0.0015	0.006–0.012
	119.0 (1955) Prelude	2.1644–2.1654	0.0010–0.0017 ④	0.004–0.014	3	1.7707–1.7717 ⑤	0.0010–0.0017	0.006–0.012
1989	91.0 (1493)	1.7707–1.7718	⑥	0.004–0.014	4	1.6526–1.6535	0.0008–0.0015	0.006–0.012
	97.0 (1590)	2.1644–2.1654	⑦	0.004–0.014	4	1.7707–1.7717	0.0008–0.0015	0.006–0.012
	119.0 (1955) Accord	②	0.0010–0.0022 ①	0.004–0.014	3	1.7707–1.7717	0.0008–0.0015	0.006–0.012
	119.0 (1955) Prelude	2.1644–2.1654	0.0010–0.0017 ④	0.004–0.014	3	1.7707–1.7717 ⑤	0.0010–0.0017 ⑧	0.006–0.012
	119.0 (1955) Prelude Si	2.1644–2.1654	0.0010–0.0017 ④	0.004–0.014	3	1.8888–1.8900 ⑤	0.0010–0.0017	0.006–0.012

CRANKSHAFT AND CONNECTING ROD SPECIFICATIONS

All measurements are given in inches.

| Year | Engine Displacement cu. in. (cc) | Crankshaft | | | | Connecting Rod | | |
		Main Brg. Journal Dia.	Main Brg. Oil Clearance	Shaft End-play	Thrust on No.	Journal Diameter	Oil Clearance	Side Clearance
1990–91	91.0 (1493)	1.7707–1.7718	⑥	0.004–0.014	4	1.6526–1.6535	0.0008–0.0015	0.006–0.012
	97.0 (1590)	2.1644–2.1654	⑦	0.004–0.014	4	1.7707–1.7717	0.0008–0.0015	0.006–0.012
	132.0 (2156)	⑨	⑩	0.004–0.014	4	1.7710–1.7717	0.0008–0.0017	0.006–0.012
	119.0 (1955)	2.1644–2.1654 ⑫	⑦	0.004–0.014	3	1.7707–1.7717	⑪	0.006–0.012
	125.0 (2056)	2.1644–2.1654 ⑫	⑦	0.004–0.014	3	1.8888–1.8900	0.0010–0.0017	0.006–0.012

① No. 3—0.0013–0.0024
② Accord:
   No. 1—1.9676–1.9685
   No. 3—1.9671–1.9680
   No. 2, 4, 5:1.9673–1.9683
③ HF—1.4951–1.4961
   Std.—1.5739–1.5748
④ No. 3—0.0012–0.0019
⑤ Prelude Si—1.8888–1.8900
⑥ No. 2, 3, 4—0.0010–0.0017
   No. 1, 5—0.0007–0.0014

⑦ No. 1, 5—0.0007–0.0014
   No. 2, 4—0.0010–0.0017
   No. 3—0.0012–0.0019
⑧ Prelude with fuel injection—0.0010–0.0017
⑨ No. 1, 2—1.9676–1.9685
   No. 3—1.9674–1.9683
   No. 4, 5—1.9655–1.9688

⑩ No. 1, 2—0.0009–0.0018
   No. 3—0.0014–0.0017
   No. 4, 5—0.0005–0.0015
⑪ Prelude 2.0S—0.0008–0.0015
   Prelude 2.0Si—0.0010–0.0017
⑫ No. 3—2.1642–2.1651

VALVE SPECIFICATIONS

| Year | Engine Displacement cu. in. (cc) | Seat Angle (deg.) | Face Angle (deg.) | Spring Test Pressure (lbs.) | Spring Installed Height (in.) | Stem-to-Guide Clearance (in.) ① | | Stem Diameter (in.) ① | |
						Intake	Exhaust	Intake	Exhaust
1987	81.9 (1342)	45	45	NA	②	0.001–0.002	0.002–0.003	0.2591–0.2594	0.2579–0.2583
	90.8 (1488)	45	45	NA	②	0.001–0.002	0.002–0.003	0.2591–0.2594	0.2579–0.2583
	111.6 (1829)	45	45	NA	③	0.001–0.002	0.002–0.004	0.2591–0.2594	0.2732–0.2736
	119.0 (1955)	45	45	NA	③	0.001–0.002	0.002–0.004	0.2591–0.2594	0.2732–0.2736
1988	91.0 (1493)	45	45	NA	④	0.001–0.002	0.002–0.003	0.2157–0.2161	0.2147–0.2150
	97.0 (1590)	45	45	NA	④	0.001–0.002	0.002–0.003	0.2157–0.2161	0.2147–0.2150
	119.0 (1955) Accord Prelude	45	45	NA	③	0.001–0.002	0.002–0.004	0.2591–0.2594	0.2732–0.2736
	119.0 (1955) Prelude Si	45	45	NA	1.683	0.001–0.002	0.002–0.003	0.2591–0.2594	0.2579–0.2583
1989	91.0 (1493)	45	45	NA	⑤	0.001–0.002	0.002–0.003	0.2157–0.2161	0.2147–0.2150
	97.0 (1590)	45	45	NA	⑤	0.001–0.002	0.002–0.003	0.2157–0.2161	0.2147–0.2150

VALVE SPECIFICATIONS

Year	Engine Displacement cu. in. (cc)	Seat Angle (deg.)	Face Angle (deg.)	Spring Test Pressure (lbs.)	Spring Installed Height (in.)	Stem-to-Guide Clearance (in.) [1]		Stem Diameter (in.) [1]	
						Intake	Exhaust	Intake	Exhaust
1989	119.0 (1955) Accord Prelude	45	45	NA	[3]	0.001–0.002	0.002–0.004	0.2591–0.2594	0.2732–0.2736
	119.0 (1955) Prelude Si	45	45	NA	1.683	0.001–0.002	0.002–0.003	0.2591–0.2594	0.2579–0.2583
1990-91	91.0 (1493)	45	45	NA	NA	0.001–0.002	0.002–0.003	0.2157–0.2161	0.2147–0.2150
	97.0 (1590)	45	45	NA	NA	0.001–0.002	0.002–0.003	0.2157–0.2161	0.2147–0.2150
	132.0 (2156)	45	45	NA	NA	0.0009–0.0019	0.002–0.003	0.2157–0.2161	0.2146–0.2150
	119.0 (1955)	45	45	NA	NA	0.001–0.002	[6]	0.2591–0.2594	[7]
	125.0 (2056)	45	45	NA	NA	0.001–0.002	0.002–0.003	0.2591–0.2594	0.2579–0.2583

NA Not Available
[1] Jet Valve—0.0009–0.0023
[2] 1342cc, 1488cc:
  Intake: 1.660
  Exhaust—1.690
  Auxiliary—0.980 (carbureted)
[3] Intake—1.913
  Exhaust—1.876

[4] 1493cc:
  Intake—1.8498–1.8880
  Exhaust—1.9278–1.9463
1590cc:
  Intake—1.8498–1.8683
  Exhaust—1.9278–1.9263
[5] Intake—1.8498–1.8683
  Exhaust—1.9278–1.9263

[6] Prelude 2.0S—0.002–0.004
  Prelude 2.0Si—0.002–0.003
[7] Prelude 2.0S—0.2732–0.2736
  Prelude 2.0Si—0.2579–0.2583

PISTON AND RING SPECIFICATIONS

All measurements are given in inches

Year	Engine Displacement cu. in. (cc)	Piston Clearance	Ring Gap			Ring Side Clearance		
			Top Compression	Bottom Compression	Oil Control	Top Compression	Bottom Compression	Oil Control
1987	81.9 (1342)	0.0004–0.0020	0.006–0.014	0.006–0.014	0.008–0.024	0.0012–0.0024	0.0012–0.0022	Snug
	90.8 (1488)	0.0004–0.0020	0.006–0.014	0.006–0.014	0.008–0.024	0.0012–0.0024	0.0012–0.0022	Snug
	111.6 (1829)	0.0008–0.0016	0.008–0.014	0.008–0.014	0.008–0.035	0.0008–0.0018	0.0008–0.0018	Snug
	119.0 (1955)	0.0008–0.0016	0.008–0.014	0.008–0.014	0.008–0.020	0.0012–0.0024	0.0012–0.0024	Snug
1988	91.0 (1493)	0.0004–0.0016	0.006–0.014	0.006–0.014	0.008–0.024	0.0012–0.0024	0.0012–0.0022	Snug
	97.0 (1590)	0.0004–0.0016	0.006–0.014	0.006–0.014	0.008–0.024	0.0012–0.0024	0.0012–0.0022	Snug
	119.0 (1955)	0.0008–0.0016	0.008–0.014	0.016–0.022	0.008–0.028 [1]	0.0012–0.0024 [2]	0.0012–0.0024 [2]	Snug
1989	91.0 (1493)	0.0004–0.0016	0.006–0.012	0.012–0.018	0.008–0.024	0.0012–0.0024	0.0012–0.0022	Snug
	97.0 (1590)	0.0004–0.0016	0.006–0.012	0.012–0.018	0.008–0.024	0.0012–0.0024	0.0012–0.0022	Snug
	119.0 (1955)	0.0008–0.0016	0.008–0.014	0.016–0.022 [3]	0.008–0.028 [1]	0.0012–0.0024 [2]	0.0012–0.0024	Snug

PISTON AND RING SPECIFICATIONS

All measurements are given in inches

Year	Engine Displacement cu. in. (cc)	Piston Clearance	Ring Gap			Ring Side Clearance		
			Top Compression	Bottom Compression	Oil Control	Top Compression	Bottom Compression	Oil Control
1990–91	91.0 (1493)	0.0004–0.0016	0.006–0.012	0.012–0.018	0.008–0.031	0.0012–0.0024	0.0012–0.0022	Snug
	97.0 (1590)	0.0004–0.0016	0.006–0.012	0.012–0.018	0.008–0.031	0.0012–0.0024	0.0012–0.0022	Snug
	132.0 (2156)	0.0008–0.0016	0.008–0.014	0.016–0.022	0.0079–0.0276	0.0014–0.0024	0.0011–0.0022	Snug
	119.0 (1955)	0.0008–0.0016	0.008–0.014	0.016–0.022	0.008–0.020	0.0012–0.0022	0.0012–0.0022	Snug
	125.0 (2056)	0.0004–0.0013	0.010–0.014	0.018–0.022	0.008–0.020	0.0014–0.0026	0.0012–0.0024	Snug

① Prelude equipped with carburetor—0.008–0.020
② Prelude—0.0012–0.0022
③ Prelude—0.016–0.022

TORQUE SPECIFICATIONS

All readings in ft. lbs.

Year	Engine Displacement cu. in. (cc)	Cylinder Head Bolts	Main Bearing Bolts	Rod Bearing Bolts	Crankshaft Pulley Bolts	Flywheel Bolts	Manifold		Spark Plugs
							Intake	Exhaust	
1987	81.9 (1342)	43	33	20	83	76②	16	23	13
	90.8 (1488)	43	33	20	83	76②	16	23	13
	111.6 (1829)	49	48③	23	83	76②	16	22	13
	119.0 (1955)	49	48③	23	83	76②	16	22	13
1988	91.0 (1493)	49	48	23	83	87②	25	25	13
	97.0 (1590)	49	48	23	83	87②	25	25	13
	119.0 (1955)	49	49	23④	83	76②	20⑤	23⑥	13
1989	91.0 (1493)	47	⑦⑨⑩	23	119⑦	87②	16	23	13
	97.0 (1590)	47	⑦⑨⑩	23	119⑦	87②	16	23	13
	119.0 (1955)	49	49⑦	23	108	76②	16	23⑧	13
1990–91	91.0 (1493)	47	33⑦	23	119⑦	87②	16	23	13
	97.0 (1590)	47	47⑦	23	119⑦	87②	16	23	13
	132.0 (2156)	78	52⑦	34	159⑦	76②	16	23	13
	119.0 (1955)	49⑦	49⑦	23⑪	108⑦	76②	16	22	13
	125.0 (2056)	49⑦	49⑦	34	108⑦	76②	16	22	13

① See text for tightening procedure
② Auto Transaxle—54 ft. lbs.
③ Fuel injected engine—49 ft. lbs.
④ Fuel injected engine—33 ft. lbs.
⑤ Prelude—16 ft. lbs.
⑥ Prelude—26 ft. lbs.
⑦ Dip bolts in clean engine oil
⑧ Prelude with fuel injection—26 ft. lbs.
⑨ Civic and CRX except Si—33 ft. lbs.
   Civic and CRX Si—47 ft. lbs.
⑩ Station Wagon 2WD—33 ft. lbs.
   Station Wagon 4WD—47 ft. lbs.
⑪ Fuel injected engine—34 ft. lbs.

BRAKE SPECIFICATIONS

Year	Model	Lug Nut Torque (ft. lbs.)	Master Cylinder Bore	Brake Disc Minimum Thickness	Brake Disc Maximum Runout	Standard Brake Drum Diameter	Minimum Lining Thickness Front	Minimum Lining Thickness Rear
1987	Civic/CRX	80	NA	①	0.004	7.070③	0.120	0.080
	Accord	80	NA	0.67	0.004	7.850	0.120	0.080
	Prelude	80	NA	0.67②	0.004	7.850	0.120	0.060
1988	Civic/CRX	80	NA	④	0.004	7.070③	0.120	0.080
	Accord	80	NA	②⑤	0.006	7.850	0.120	0.080
	Prelude	80	NA	②⑤	0.004	7.850	0.120	0.080
1989	Civic	80	NA	0.67	⑬	7.090	0.120	0.080
	Civic SW	80	NA	0.67	⑬	7.870	⑦	0.080
	CRX	80	NA	⑥	⑬	7.090	0.120	0.080
	Accord	80	NA	⑪	⑬	7.870⑩	0.120	0.031
	Prelude	80	NA	⑧	⑨	⑩	0.120	0.080
1990-91	Civil	80	NA	0.67⑫	0.004	7.090	0.120	0.079
	Civic SW	80	NA	0.67⑬	0.004	7.090	0.120	0.080
	CRX	80	NA	0.67	0.004	7.090	0.120	0.080
	Accord	80	NA	0.83	0.004	8.660	0.063	0.080
	Prelude	80	NA	⑧	⑨	⑩	0.120	0.080

NA Not Available
① Civic 1300—0.390
   Civic 1500—0.590
   CRX St & Std.—0.670
   1987—0.430
② Rear disc—0.310
③ Civic Wagon—7.850
④ Civic/CRX HF—0.590
   All others—0.670

⑤ Accord DX/LX and Prelude—0.670
   Accord LX-i and Prelude Si—0.750
⑥ Std and Si—0.670
   HF—0.590
⑦ 4WD—0.120
   Except 4WD—0.060
⑧ Si—0.750
   S—0.670

⑨ Front—0.004
   Rear—0.006
⑩ Rear disc rotor—0.390
⑪ DX, LX—0.670
   LXi, SEi—0.750
⑫ Civic EX—0.750
⑬ Civic Wagon DX—0.750
⑭ CRX Std—0.750
   CRX HF—0.590

WHEEL ALIGNMENT

Year	Model	Caster Range (deg.)	Caster Preferred Setting (deg.)	Camber Range (deg.)	Camber Preferred Setting (deg.)	Toe-in (in.)	Steering Axis Inclination (deg.)
1987	Civic exc. SW	1¹/₂P–3¹/₂P①	2¹/₂P②	1N–1P	0	0	13
	Civic SW	1P–3P	2P	1N–1P	0	0	12
	Accord	1N–1P	0	1N–1P	0	0	6¹³/₁₆
	Prelude	1N–1P	0	1N–1P	0	0	6¹³/₁₆
1988	Civic exc. SW	2P–4P	3P	1N–1P	0	0	7⁵/₁₆
	Civic SW	1¹⁵/₁₆P–3¹⁵/₁₆P	2¹⁵/₁₆P	¹¹/₁₆N–1⁵/₁₆P	⁵/₁₆P	0	7¹/₄
	Civic 4WD	1¹⁵/₁₆P–3¹⁵/₁₆P	2¹⁵/₁₆P	⁷/₁₆N–1⁹/₁₆P	⁹/₁₆P	0	6¹⁵/₁₆
	Accord	¹/₂N–1¹/₂P	¹/₂P	1N–1P	0	0	6¹³/₁₆
	Prelude	1³/₁₆P–2¹³/₁₆P	2³/₈P	1N–1P	0	0	6¹³/₁₆
1989	Civic exc. SW	2P–4P	3P	1N–1P	0	0	—
	Civic SW	1¹⁵/₁₆P–3¹⁵/₁₆P	2¹⁵/₁₆P	¹¹/₁₆N–1⁵/₁₆P	⁵/₁₆P	0	—
	Civic 4WD	1¹⁵/₁₆P–3¹⁵/₁₆P	2¹⁵/₁₆P	⁷/₁₆N–1⁹/₁₆P	⁹/₁₆P	0	—
	Accord	¹/₂N–1¹/₂P	¹/₂P	1N–1P	0	0	—
	Prelude	1¹³/₁₆P–2¹³/₁₆P	2³/₈P	1N–1P	0	0	—

WHEEL ALIGNMENT

Year	Model	Caster Range (deg.)	Caster Preferred Setting (deg.)	Camber Range (deg.)	Camber Preferred Setting (deg.)	Toe-in (in.)	Steering Axis Inclination (deg.)
1990–91	Civic exc. SW	2P–4P	3P	1N–1P	0	0	—
	Civic SW	$1^{15}/_{16}P$–$3^{15}/_{16}P$	$2^{15}/_{16}P$	$^{11}/_{16}N$–$1^5/_{16}P$	$^5/_{16}P$	0	—
	Civic 4WD	$1^{15}/_{16}P$–$3^{15}/_{16}P$	$2^{15}/_{16}P$	$^7/_{16}N$–$1^9/_{16}P$	$^9/_{16}P$	0	—
	Accord	2P–4P	3P	1N–1P	0	0	—
	Prelude	$1^{13}/_{16}P$–$2^{13}/_{16}P$	$2^3/_8P$	1N–1P	0	0	—

SW Station Wagon
P Positive
N Negative
① With power steering 2P–4P
② With power steering 3P

ENGINE ELECTRICAL

NOTE: Disconnecting the negative battery cable on some vehicles may interfere with the functions of the on board computer systems and may require the computer to undergo a relearning process, once the negative battery cable is reconnected.

Distributor

Removal

1. Disconnect the negative battery cable.
2. Disconnect the spark plug wires and tag for reassembly in the same positions.
3. Disconnect the coil wire and primary lead wire, if equipped.
4. Disconnect the vacuum advance hoses, if equipped.
5. Disconnect the necessary electrical connectors.
6. Remove the distributor cap.
7. Using a suitable marking tool, mark the position of the distributor rotor in relation to the distributor housing and mark the position of the distributor housing in relation to the cylinder head.
8. Remove the distributor hold-down bolts and remove the distributor. Remove and discard the distributor O-ring.

Installation

TIMING NOT DISTURBED

1. Coat a new distributor O-ring with engine oil and install on the distributor. Install the distributor, aligning the distributor housing and distributor rotor with the marks that were made during the removal procedure.

NOTE: The distributor is equipped with locating lugs which mesh with corresponding grooves in the end of the camshaft. The lugs and grooves are both offset to prevent installing the distributor 180 degrees out of time.

2. Install the distributor hold-down bolts and tighten temporarily.
3. Install the distributor cap.
4. Connect the electrical connectors.
5. Connect the vacuum hoses, if equipped.
6. Connect the coil wire and the primary lead wire, if equipped.
7. Connect the spark plug wires in their original positions.
8. Check the ignition timing and tighten the distributor hold-

down bolts to 16 ft. lbs. (22 Nm). Recheck the ignition timing.

TIMING DISTURBED

1. Disconnect the spark plug wire from the No. 1 cylinder spark plug and remove the spark plug.
2. Place a finger over the spark plug hole and turn the engine over slowly, by hand, until compression is felt.
3. On Civic vehicles, align the **RED** timing mark on the crankshaft pulley with the pointer on the timing belt cover. On Accord and Prelude vehicles, remove the rubber cap from the inspection window at the rear of the cylinder block. Align the **RED** timing mark on the driveplate (automatic transaxle) or flywheel (manual transaxle) with the pointer on the cylinder block.
4. Coat a new distributor O-ring with engine oil and install on the distributor. Install the distributor with the distributor rotor pointing to the No. 1 spark plug tower on the distributor cap.

NOTE: The distributor is equipped with locating lugs which mesh with corresponding grooves in the end of the camshaft. The lugs and grooves are both offset to prevent installing the distributor 180 degrees out of time.

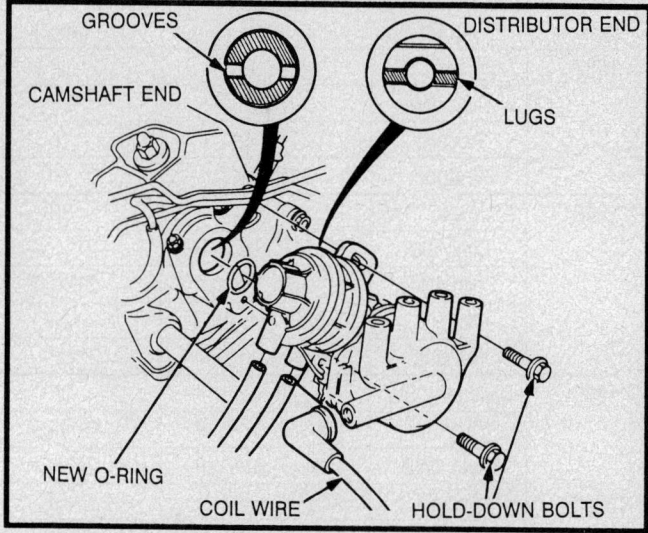

Typical distributor installation

5. Install the distributor hold-down bolts and tighten temporarily.

6. Install the distributor cap.

7. Connect the electrical connectors.

8. Connect the vacuum hoses, if equipped.

9. Connect the coil wire and the primary lead wire, if equipped.

10. Install the No. 1 spark plug and tighten to 13 ft. lbs. (18 Nm). Connect the No. 1 spark plug wire to the spark plug.

11. Connect the spark plug wires to the distributor cap in their original positions.

12. Set the ignition timing and tighten the distributor hold-down bolts to 16 ft. lbs. (22 Nm). Recheck the ignition timing.

Ignition Timing

Adjustment

1987 CIVIC, 1987–89 ACCORD, 1987 PRELUDE AND 1988–91 CARBURETOR EQUIPPED PRELUDE

1. On Accord and Prelude vehicles, remove the rubber cap from the inspection window of the cylinder block.

2. Start the engine and allow it to warm up. The cooling fan must come on at least once.

3. Disconnect the vacuum hoses from the vacuum advance diaphragm and plug them.

4. Connect the pick-up lead from a suitable timing light to the No. 1 spark plug wire. Make the remaining timing light connections according to the manufacturers instructions.

5. With the engine idling, aim the timing light at the pointer on the timing cover and the crankshaft pulley on Civic vehicles. On Accord and Prelude vehicles, aim the timing light at the pointer on the engine block and the driveplate (automatic transaxle) or flywheel (manual transaxle).

6. Adjust the ignition timing according to the specification listed on the underhood emission label. Adjust as necessary by loosening the distributor adjusting bolts and turning the distributor housing counterclockwise to advance the timing, or clockwise to retard the timing.

7. Tighten the adjusting bolts to 16 ft. lbs. (22 Nm) and recheck the timing.

8. Connect the vacuum advance hoses and replace the rubber cap to the inspection window.

1988–91 CIVIC, 1990–91 ACCORD AND 1988–91 PRELUDE WITH FUEL INJECTION

1. On Accord and Prelude vehicles, remove the rubber cap from the inspection window of the cylinder block.

2. Start the engine and allow it to warm up. The engine cooling fan must come on at least once.

3. On 1988–89 Civic vehicles, remove the YELLOW rubber cap from the ignition timing connector located in the left rear of the engine compartment. Connect the BROWN and GREEN/WHITE terminals of the connector with a jumper wire. On 1990–91 Civic vehicles, pull out the BLUE ignition timing adjusting connector located under the right side of the dash and connect the BROWN and GREEN/WHITE connector.

4. On Accord vehicles, connect the ORANGE/RED and GREEN/WHITE terminals of the BLUE service check connector with a jumper wire. The service check connector is located in the far right corner under the dashboard.

5. On Prelude vehicles, remove the YELLOW cap from the ignition timing adjusting connector located behind the ignition coil and connect the BROWN and GREEN/WHITE terminals with a jumper wire.

6. Connect the pick-up lead of a suitable timing light to the No. 1 spark plug wire. Make the other timing light connections according to the manufacturers instructions.

7. With the engine idling, aim the timing light at the pointer on the timing belt cover and the crankshaft pulley on Civic vehi-

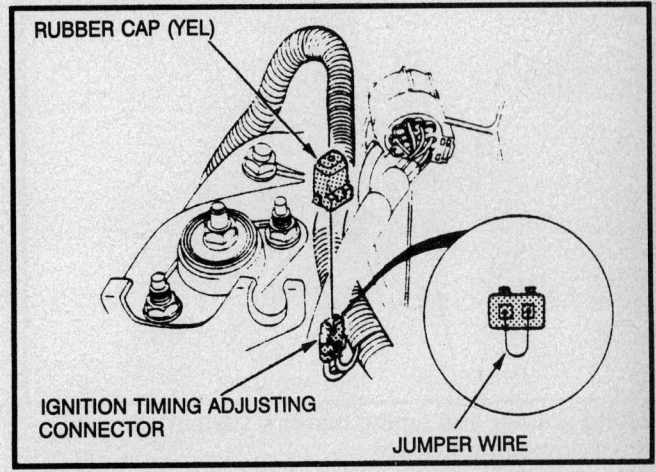

Location of ignition timing adjusting connector — 1988–89 Civic

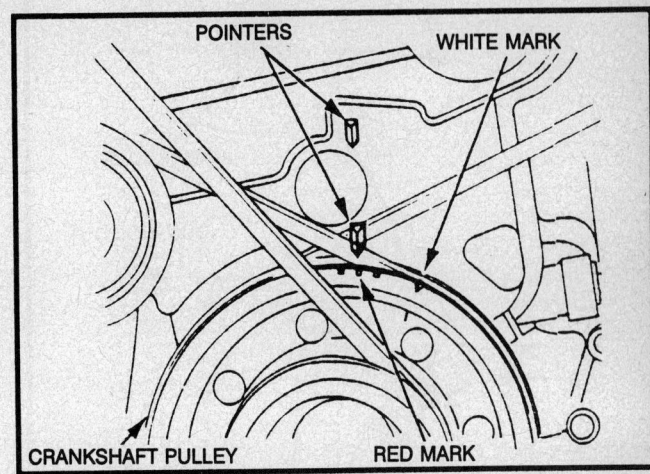

Location of ignition timing marks — 1988–91 Civic

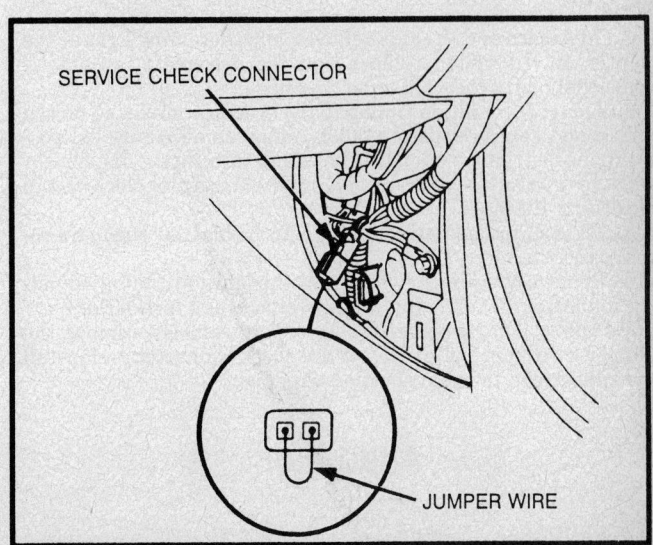

Location of service check connector — 1990–91 Accord

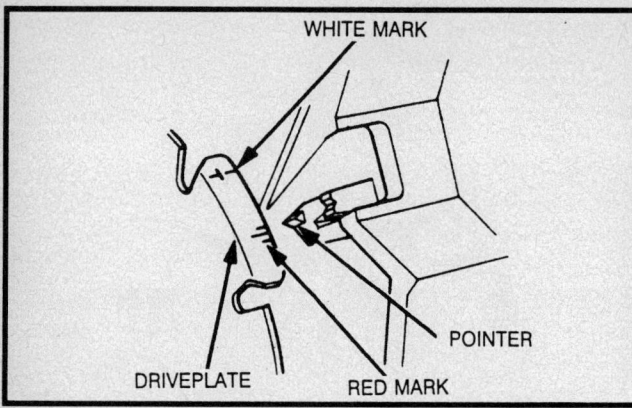

Timing pointer and timing marks—1990-91 Accord with automatic transaxle

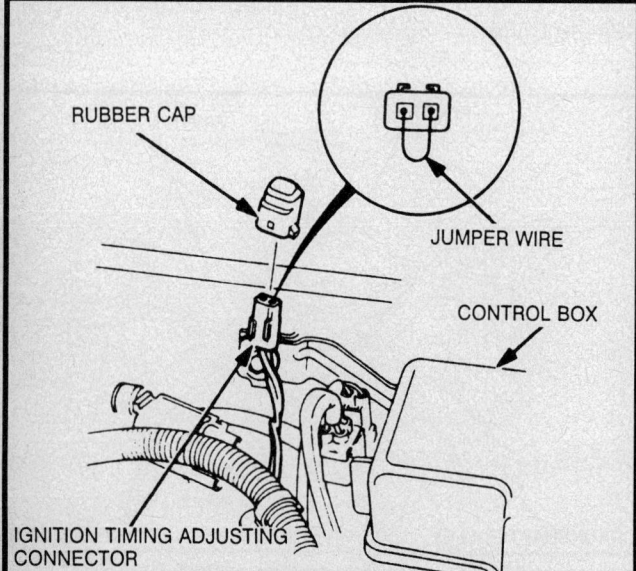

Location of ignition timing adjusting connector—1988-91 Prelude with fuel injection

cles. On Accord and Prelude vehicles, aim the timing light at the pointer on the cylinder block and the driveplate (automatic transaxle) or flywheel (manual transaxle).

8. Adjust the ignition timing to the specification listed on the underhood vehicle emission label. Adjust as necessary by loosening the distributor adjusting bolts and turning the distributor housing counterclockwise to advance the timing, or clockwise to retard the timing.

9. Tighten the adjusting bolts to 16 ft. lbs. (22 Nm) and re-check the timing.

10. Remove the jumper wire from the ignition timing adjusting connector on Civic and Prelude vehicles and install the YELLOW rubber cap, if equipped. On Accord vehicles, remove the jumper wire from the BLUE service check connector and install the rubber cap to the inspection window.

Alternator

Precautions

Several precautions must be observed with alternator equipped vehicles to avoid damage to the unit.

• If the battery is removed for any reason, make sure it is reconnected with the correct polarity. Reversing the battery connections may result in damage to the one-way rectifiers.

• When utilizing a booster battery as a starting aid, always connect the positive to positive terminals and the negative terminal from the booster battery to a good engine ground on the vehicle being started.

• Never use a fast charger as a booster to start vehicles.

• Disconnect the battery cables when charging the battery with a fast charger.

• Never attempt to polarize the alternator.

• Do not use test lamps of more than 12 volts when checking diode continuity.

• Do not short across or ground any of the alternator terminals.

• The polarity of the battery, alternator and regulator must be matched and considered before making any electrical connections within the system.

• Never separate the alternator on an open circuit. Make sure all connections within the circuit are clean and tight.

• Disconnect the battery ground terminal when performing any service on electrical components.

• Disconnect the battery if arc welding is to be done on the vehicle.

Belt Tension Adjustment

1. On all Civic vehicles, 1988-91 Prelude and 1990-91 Accord, apply a force of 22 lbs. and measure the deflection of the alternator belt between the alternator and the crankshaft pulley. On 1987 Prelude and 1987-89 Accord, apply a force of 22 lbs. and measure the deflection of the alternator belt between the alternator and the water pump pulley.

2. On a belt in service, the deflection should be as follows:
1987 Civic: 0.28-0.39 in. (7-10mm)
1988-91 Civic: 0.35-0.43 in. (9-11 mm)
1987-89 Accord: 0.24-0.35 in. (6-9mm)
1990-91 Accord: 0.39-0.47 in. (10-12mm)
1987 Prelude with carbureted engine: 0.28-0.39 in. (7-10mm)
1987 Prelude with fuel injected engine: 0.24-0.35 in. (6-9mm)
1988-91 Prelude: 0.39-0.47 in. (10-12mm)

3. If the belt deflection is not as specified, loosen the alterna-

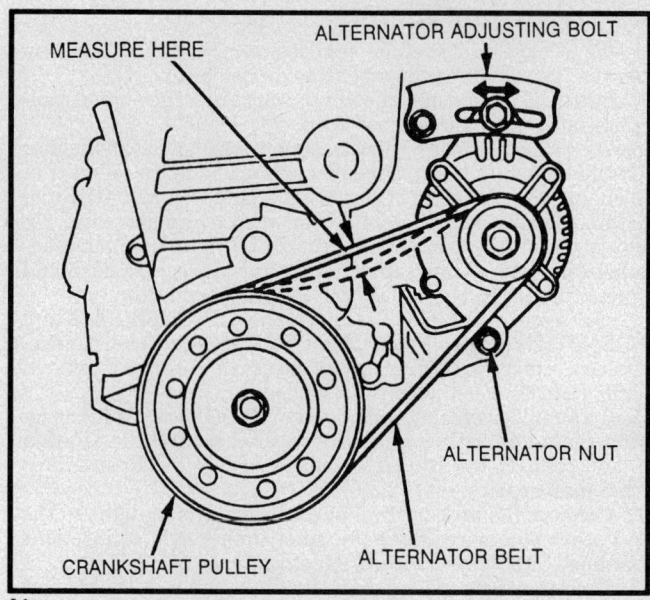

Alternator belt adjustment—Civic

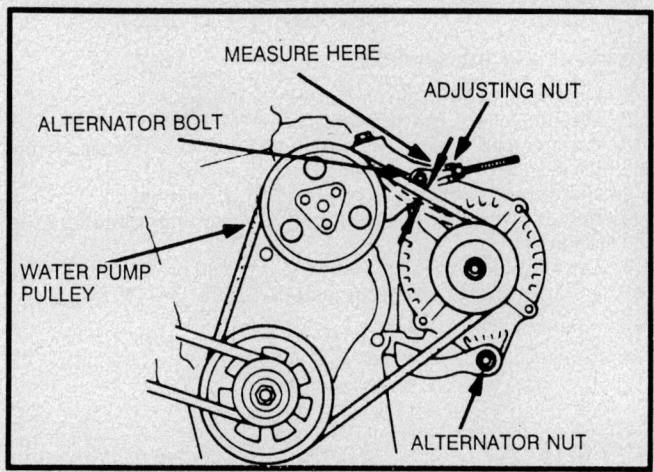

Alternator belt adjustment—1987–89 Accord

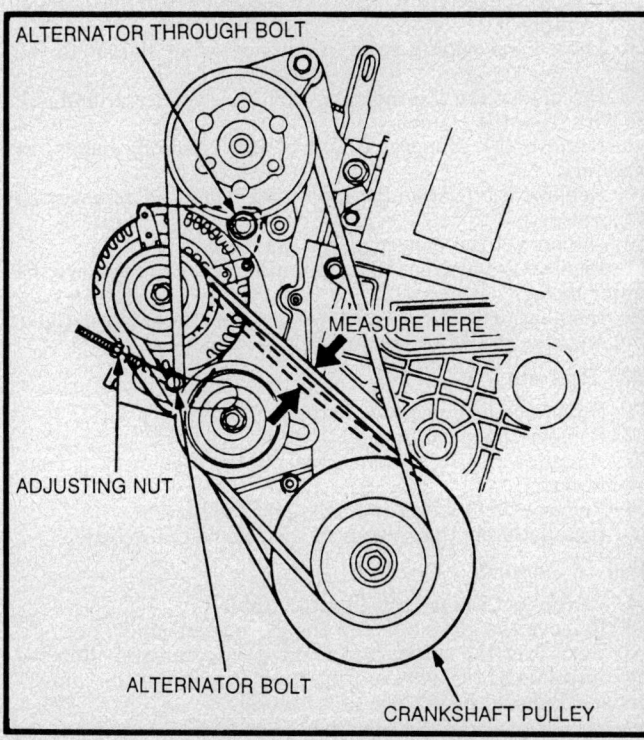

Alternator belt adjustment—1988–91 Prelude

tor pivot bolt. On Civic vehicles, loosen the alternator adjusting bolt and move the alternator using a suitable prybar positioned against the front of the alternator housing. Tighten the adjusting bolt when the proper tension is obtained. On Accord and Prelude vehicles, loosen the alternator nut or bolt and turn the adjusting nut or bolt until the proper tension is obtained. Tighten the alternator nut or bolt and the pivot bolt. Recheck the belt deflection.

4. If a new belt is installed, the deflection should be as follows when first measured:

1987 Civic: 0.16–0.26 in. (4–6.5mm)
1988–91 Civic: 0.25–0.35 in. (7–9mm)
1987–89 Accord: 0.16–0.24 in. (4–6mm)
1990–91 Accord without air conditioning: 0.33–0.43 in. (8.5–11mm)
1990–91 Accord with air conditioning: 0.18–0.28 in. (4.5–7mm)

1987 Prelude with carbureted engine: 0.24 in. (6mm)
1987 Prelude with fuel injected engine: 0.16–0.24 in. (4–6mm)
1988–91 Prelude: 0.31–0.39 in. (8–10mm)

Removal and Installation

EXCEPT 1990–91 ACCORD

1. Disconnect the negative battery cable.
2. Remove the air cleaner assembly on 1987 Prelude.
3. Disconnect the left driveshaft from the steering knuckle on 1987–89 Accord.
4. Disconnect the electrical connectors from the alternator.
5. Loosen the alternator adjusting bolt or nut and through bolt and remove the alternator belt.
6. Remove the alternator adjusting bolt or nut and through bolt and remove the alternator. If necessary, remove the mount bracket bolts and the upper and lower mount brackets.
7. Installation is the reverse of the removal procedure. Tighten the alternator through bolt or through bolt nut to 33 ft. lbs. (45 Nm). Tighten the alternator adjusting bolt on Civic vehicles and the alternator bolt on Prelude and Accord vehicles to 17 ft. lbs. (24 Nm).

1990–91 ACCORD

1. Disconnect the negative battery cable.
2. Remove the power steering pump and the cruise control actuator. Do not disconnect the actuator cable.
3. Disconnect the electrical connectors from the alternator.
4. Loosen the adjusting bolt, then remove the alternator nut. Remove the alternator belt from the alternator pulley.
5. Remove the adjusting bolt, the lower through bolt and the stay.
6. Remove the upper through bolt and the alternator. If necessary, remove the 4 mount bracket bolts, the mount bracket and the heat insulator.
7. Installation is the reverse of the removal procedure. Tighten the upper through bolt to 33 ft. lbs. (45 Nm) and the alternator nut to 18 ft. lbs. (26 Nm). If the mount bracket was removed, apply liquid gasket to the mount bracket bolt threads and tighten to 36 ft. lbs. (50 Nm).

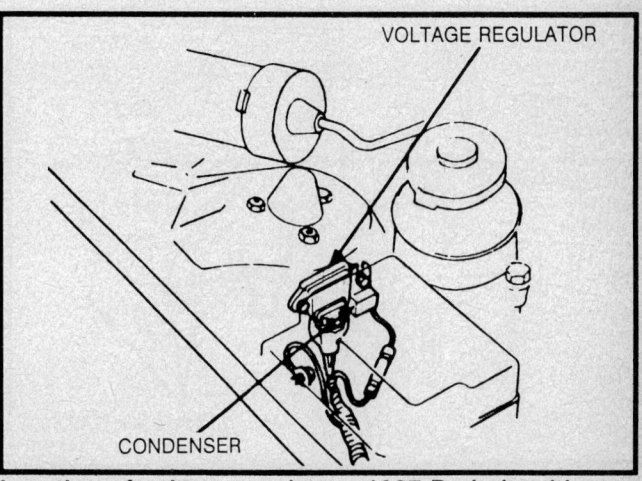

Location of voltage regulator—1987 Prelude with carbureted engine

Removal and Installation

1987 PRELUDE WITH CARBURETED ENGINE

1. Disconnect the negative battery cable.
2. Disconnect the electrical connector from the voltage regulator.
3. Remove the regulator retaining screws and remove the voltage regulator.
4. Installation is the reverse of the removal procedure.

Starter

Removal and Installation

1. Disconnect the negative battery cable.
2. Disconnect the starter cable from the starter motor.
3. Remove the engine compartment sub wire harness from the harness clip on the starter motor, if equipped.
4. Disconnect the wire from the starter solenoid.
5. Remove the 2 bolts retaining the starter motor and remove the starter motor.
6. Installation is the reverse of the removal procedure. Tighten the starter motor retaining bolts to 32 ft. lbs. (45 Nm).

CHASSIS ELECTRICAL

Heater Blower Motor

Removal and Installation

WITHOUT AIR CONDITIONING

1. Disconnect the negative battery cable.
2. Remove the glove box and glove box frame or passenger's tray on 1987 Civic station wagon.
3. Remove the heater duct.
4. Disconnect the electrical connectors from the blower motor.
5. Disconnect the vacuum hose on 1987 Prelude.
6. Remove the blower motor mounting bolts and the blower motor.
7. Installation is the reverse of the removal procedure.

WITH AIR CONDITIONING

Except 1987 Prelude and 1990–91 Accord

1. Disconnect the negative battery cable.
2. Properly discharge the air conditioning system.
3. Disconnect the receiver line and suction hose from the evaporator.

NOTE: Cap the open fittings immediately to keep moisture out of the system.

4. Remove the glove box and glove box frame or passenger's tray on 1987 Civic.

5. Disconnect the drain hose from the evaporator lower housing, if equipped.
6. Loosen the sealing band, if equipped, and slide it to the right.
7. Disconnect the thermostat switch wire connector and pull the wire from the clamps.
8. Remove the evaporator and blower retaining bands, as necessary.
9. Remove the evaporator mounting bolts and remove the evaporator.
10. Disconnect the blower motor electrical connectors.
11. Remove the blower motor mounting bolts and remove the blower motor.
12. Installation is the reverse of the removal procedure. Evacuate and charge the air conditioning system.

1987 Prelude

1. Disconnect the negative battery cable.
2. Remove the glove box.
3. Disconnect the wire connector and the vacuum hose from the blower.
4. Remove the 3 mounting bolts and the blower.
5. Installation is the reverse of the removal procedure.

1990–91 Accord

1. Disconnect the negative battery cable.
2. Remove the glove box and the glove box frame.
3. Turn over the carpet and remove the side cover. Remove the control unit bracket mounting nuts. Disconnect the connectors and remove the control unit bracket.

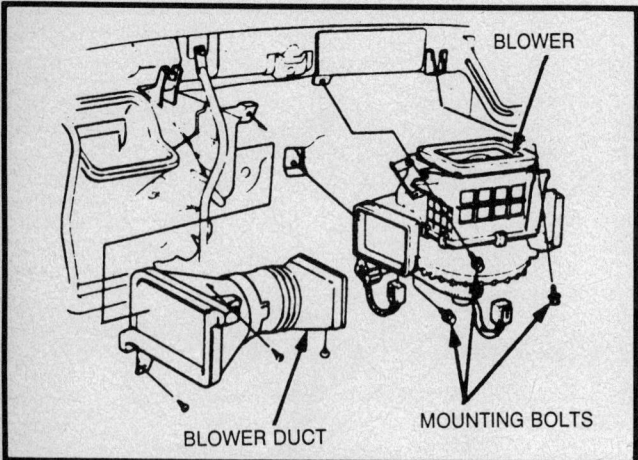

Heater blower motor installation—1987–89 Accord without air conditioning

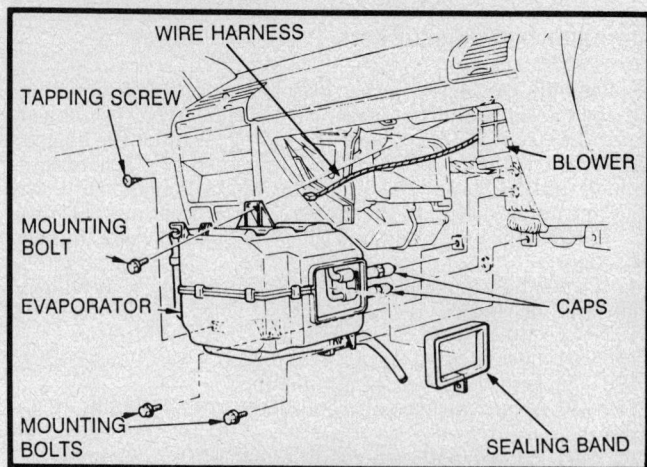

Evaporator installation—1987–89 Accord

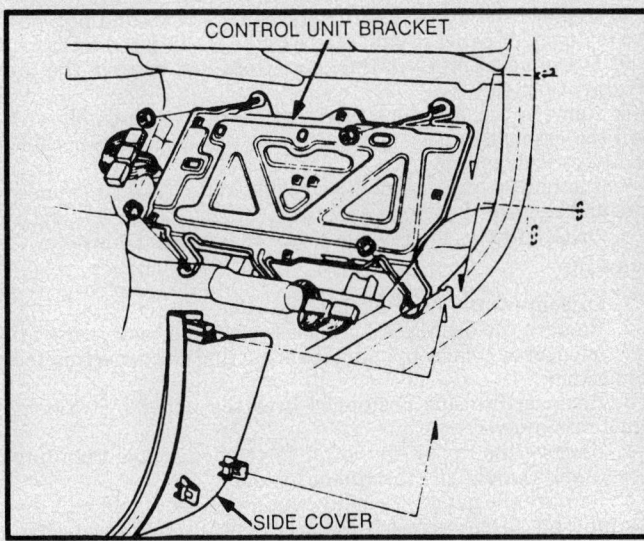

Control unit location – 1990–91 Accord

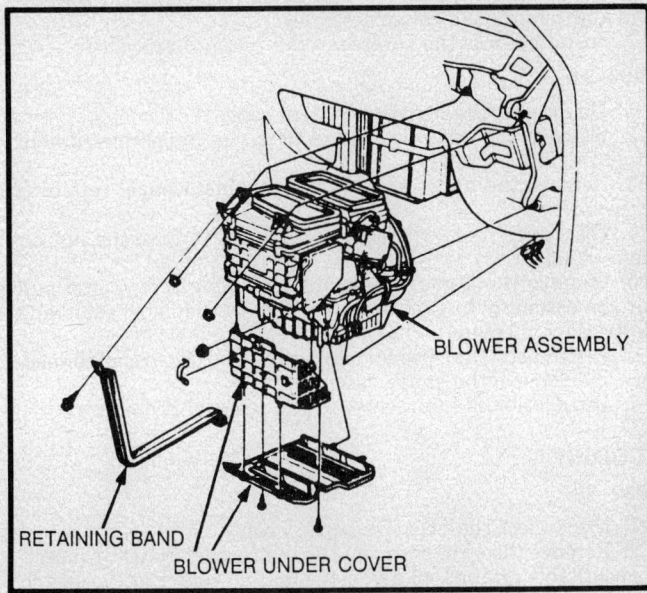

Blower installation – 1990–91 Accord

4. Remove the retaining band and remove the blower undercover.

NOTE: Be careful not to break the tabs while removing the blower undercover.

5. Remove the blower mounting nuts, disconnect the electrical connectors and remove the blower.

6. Installation is the reverse of the removal procedure. When installing the glove box frame, the face which covers the dashboard is installed with double-sided adhesive tape.

Windshield Wiper Motor

Removal and Installation

1. Disconnect the negative battery cable.
2. Remove the wiper arm retaining nuts and remove the wiper arms.
3. Remove the front air scoop, if equipped, and hood seal located over the wiper linkage at the bottom of the windshield.

4. Disconnect the linkage from the wiper motor.
5. Remove the wiper motor water seal cover clamp and remove the cover, if equipped.
6. Disconnect the wiper motor electrical connector, remove the motor mounting bolts and remove the motor.
7. Installation is the reverse of the removal procedure. Coat the linkage joints with grease and make sure the linkage moves smoothly.

Instrument Cluster

Removal and Installation

CIVIC

1987

1. Disconnect the negative battery cable.
2. Remove the upper caps positioned over the upper instrument panel retaining screws.
3. Remove the 2 upper and 2 lower instrument panel retaining screws and remove the instrument panel.
4. Remove the 4 screws retaining the gauge assembly and lift the assembly to gain access to the speedometer cable and electrical connectors.
5. Disconnect the speedometer cable and electrical connectors and remove the gauge assembly.
6. Installation is the reverse of the removal procedure.

1988–89

1. Disconnect the negative battery cable.
2. Remove the dashboard lower panel.
3. Remove the dashlight brightness controller and rear window defogger switch by pushing them out and then disconnecting the connectors.
4. Remove the 4 instrument panel retaining screws and remove the instrument panel from the dashboard.
5. Remove the caps positioned over the 2 screws retaining the gauge visor.
6. Remove the gauge visor retaining screws and remove the gauge visor.
7. Remove the 4 screws retaining the gauge assembly and pull out the assembly to gain access to the speedometer cable and electrical connectors.
8. Disconnect the electrical connectors and the speedometer cable. Remove the gauge assembly.
9. Installation is the reverse of the removal procedure.

1990–91

1. Disconnect the negative battery cable.
2. Remove the caps positioned over the 2 gauge visor retaining screws.
3. Remove the gauge visor retaining screws and remove the gauge visor.
4. Remove the 4 screws retaining the instrument panel to the dashboard, disconnect the switch connectors and remove the instrument panel.
5. Remove the 4 screws retaining the gauge assembly and pull out the assembly to gain access to the speedometer cable and the electrical connectors.
6. Disconnect the speedometer cable and electrical connectors and remove the gauge assembly.
7. Installation is the reverse of the removal procedure.

CIVIC WAGON

1987

1. Disconnect the negative battery cable.
2. Remove the lower dashboard panel retaining screws and remove the dashboard lower panel.
3. Remove the 4 bolts attaching the instrument panel from under the dashboard.

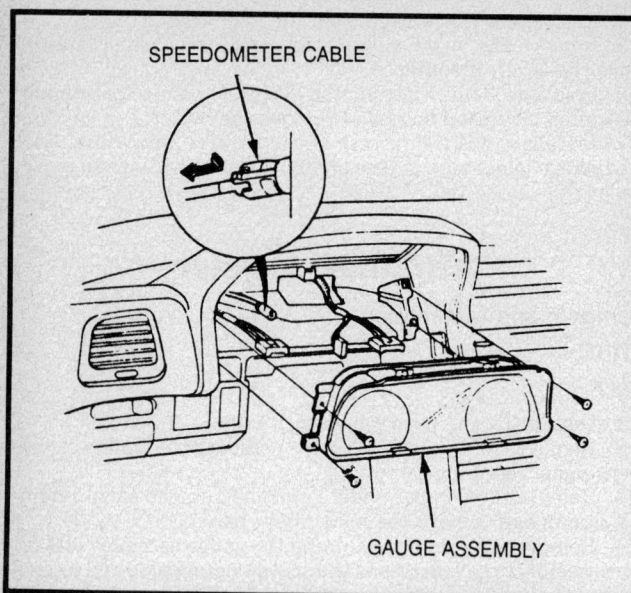

SPEEDOMETER CABLE

GAUGE ASSEMBLY

Instrument cluster installation—1990–91 Civic

4. Disconnect the speedometer cable and the electrical connectors and remove the instrument panel.

5. Separate the gauge assembly from the instrument panel by removing the attaching screws.

6. Installation is the reverse of the removal procedure.

1988–89

1. Disconnect the negative battery cable.

2. Remove the dashlight brightness controller and rear window defogger switch by pushing them out and disconnecting the connectors.

3. Remove the caps positioned over the upper instrument panel retaining screws.

4. Remove the upper and lower instrument panel retaining screws and remove the instrument panel.

5. Remove the gauge assembly retaining screws and pull the assembly out to gain access to the speedometer cable and electrical connectors.

6. Disconnect the speedometer cable and electrical connectors and remove the gauge assembly.

7. Installation is the reverse of the removal procedure.

1990–91

1. Disconnect the negative battery cable.

2. Remove the caps positioned over the upper instrument panel retaining screws.

3. Remove the upper and lower instrument panel retaining screws.

4. Disconnect the switch connectors and remove the instrument panel.

5. Remove the 4 gauge assembly retaining screws and pull out the assembly to gain access to the speedometer cable and electrical connectors.

6. Disconnect the speedometer cable and electrical connectors and remove the gauge assembly.

7. Installation is the reverse of the removal procedure.

CRX

1987

1. Disconnect the negative battery cable.

2. Remove the screws and clips retaining the lower dash panel and remove the lower dash panel.

3. Remove the heater control knob and heater control lower panel. Remove the heater control mount screws.

4. Remove the upper instrument panel screws and pull out the instrument panel to gain access to the electrical connectors.

5. Disconnect the electrical connectors and remove the instrument panel.

6. Remove the 4 screws retaining the gauge assembly and pull the assembly out to gain access to the speedometer cable and electrical connectors.

7. Disconnect the speedometer cable and electrical connectors and remove the gauge assembly.

8. Installation is the reverse of the removal procedure.

1988–89

1. Disconnect the negative battery cable.

2. Remove the dashlight brightness controller and rear window defogger switch by pushing them out and disconnecting the connectors.

3. Remove the caps positioned over the upper instrument panel retaining screws.

4. Remove the upper and lower instrument panel retaining screws and remove the instrument panel.

5. Remove the gauge assembly retaining screws and pull the assembly out to gain access to the speedometer cable and electrical connectors.

6. Disconnect the speedometer cable and electrical connectors and remove the gauge assembly.

7. Installation is the reverse of the removal procedure.

1990–91

1. Disconnect the negative battery cable.

2. Remove the caps positioned over the upper instrument panel retaining screws.

3. Remove the upper and lower instrument panel retaining screws.

4. Disconnect the switch connectors and remove the instrument panel.

5. Remove the 4 gauge assembly retaining screws and pull out the assembly to gain access to the speedometer cable and electrical connectors.

6. Disconnect the speedometer cable and electrical connectors and remove the gauge assembly.

7. Installation is the reverse of the removal procedure.

ACCORD

1987–89

1. Disconnect the negative battery cable.

2. Remove the switches from the instrument panel by inserting a suitable prying tool under the bottom center of the switch and prying it loose. Pull the switch straight back and disconnect the connectors.

3. Use a suitable prying tool to remove the upper lid.

4. Remove the 2 upper and 4 lower instrument panel screws and the instrument panel.

5. Remove the 4 gauge assembly screws and pull the assembly back to gain access to the speedometer cable and electrical connectors.

6. Disconnect the speedometer cable and the electrical connectors and remove the gauge assembly.

7. Installation is the reverse of the removal procedure.

1990–91

1. Disconnect the negative battery cable.

2. Remove the front console mounting screws. On manual transaxle equipped vehicles, remove the shift lever knob.

3. Remove the front console.

4. Remove the ashtray and ashtray holder.

5. Loosen the 2 screws retaining the radio and disconnect the wire harness connector and the antenna lead. Remove the radio.

6. Remove the coin box, cruise control master switch, sunroof switch and panel brightness controller.

7. Remove the side and center air vents.

8. Remove the 12 mounting screws and disconnect the electrical connectors.

9. Remove the instrument panel.

10. Remove the 4 gauge assembly screws and the gauge assembly. Disconnect the electrical connectors from the gauge assembly.

11. Installation is the reverse of the removal procedure.

PRELUDE

1987

1. Disconnect the negative battery cable.

2. Remove the fuse box cover and lower trim panel. Remove the 4 bolts retaining the lower left dash panel and the panel.

3. Lower the steering column.

4. Remove the 4 instrument panel screws. Pull the instrument panel out and disconnect the electrical connectors. Remove the instrument panel.

5. Remove the 2 gauge assembly screws and lift the assembly to gain access to the speedometer cable and electrical connectors.

6. Disconnect the speedometer cable and electrical connectors and remove the gauge assembly.

7. Installation is the reverse of the removal procedure.

1988–91

1. Disconnect the negative battery cable.

2. Remove the dashlight brightness controller and retractor/fog light switch from the instrument panel and disconnect the connectors.

3. Remove the 5 retaining screws and the instrument panel from the gauge visor.

4. Remove the 4 screws and pull out the gauge assembly from the dashboard to gain access to the electrical connectors.

5. Disconnect the electrical connectors and remove the gauge assembly.

6. Installation is the reverse of the removal procedure.

Concealed Headlights

Manual Operation

1. Remove the cover from the engine compartment fuse box and remove the fuse for the headlight motor that does not work.

NOTE: Always remove the fuse before manually operating a headlight motor, otherwise the motor may suddenly activate.

2. Remove the cap from the top of the headlight motor, then turn the knob in the direction of the arrow (clockwise) until the headlight is as far up or down as it will go.

3. Replace the cap and reinstall the fuse.

Combination Switch

Removal and Installation

1. Disconnect the negative battery cable.

2. Remove the steering wheel.

3. Remove the lower cover and driver's knee bolster, if equipped.

4. Remove the upper and lower column covers.

5. Remove the turn signal cancelling sleeve.

6. Remove the cruise control slip ring, if equipped.

7. Disconnect the electrical connectors and remove the combination switch assembly.

8. Installation is the reverse of the removal procedure.

Ignition Switch

Removal and Installation

1. Disconnect the negative battery cable.

2. Remove the steering wheel and steering column covers as necessary, to gain access to the switch.

3. Disconnect the electrical connector.

4. Insert the ignition key and turn it to the **O** position.

5. Remove the 2 screws and remove the base of the switch.

6. Installation is the reverse of the removal procedure.

Ignition Lock

Removal and Installation

1. Disconnect the negative battery cable.

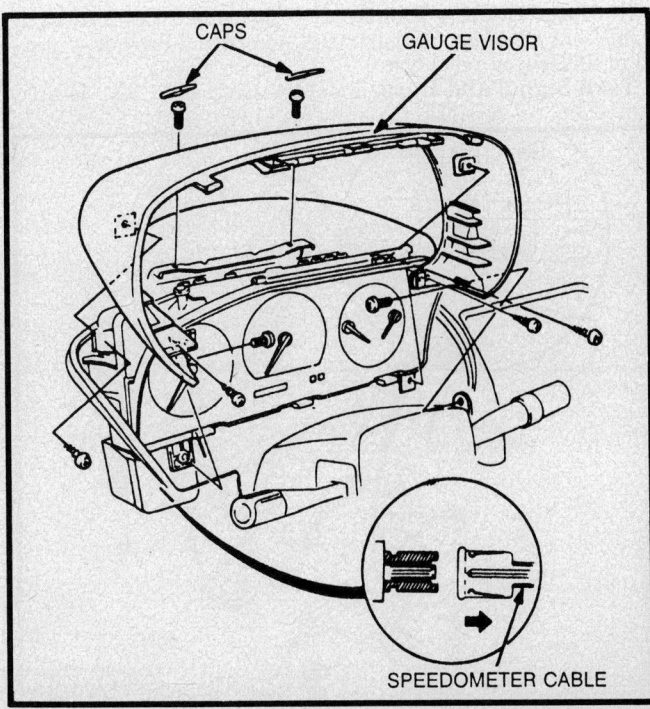

CAPS   GAUGE VISOR

SPEEDOMETER CABLE

Instrument cluster installation – 1988–91 Prelude

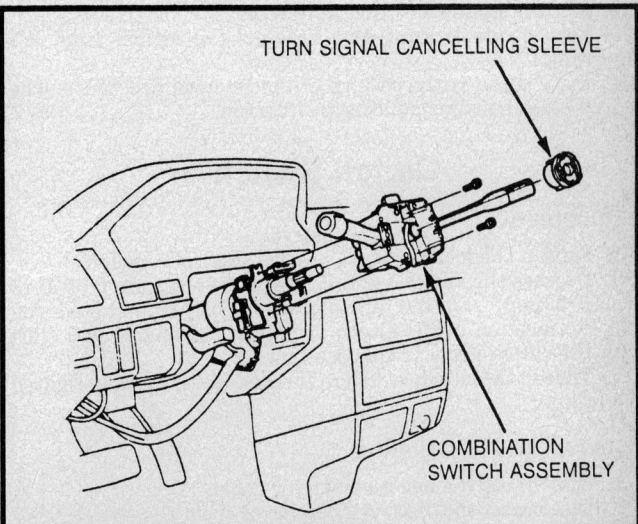

TURN SIGNAL CANCELLING SLEEVE

COMBINATION SWITCH ASSEMBLY

Combination switch installation

2. Remove the steering wheel and the steering column covers.

3. Disconnect the ignition switch connector.

4. Center punch each of the 2 shear bolts and drill their heads off with a suitable drill bit.

NOTE: Do not damage the switch body when removing the shear bolt heads.

5. Remove the shear bolts from the switch body and remove the switch.

To install:

6. Install the new ignition switch without the key inserted.

7. Loosely tighten the new shear bolts.

NOTE: Make sure the projection on the ignition switch is aligned with the hole in the steering column.

8. Insert the ignition key and check for proper operation of the steering wheel lock and that the ignition key turns freely.

9. Tighten the shear bolts until the hex heads twist off.

Stoplight Switch

Adjustment

1. Loosen the stoplight switch locknut and back off the stoplight switch until it is no longer touching the brake pedal.

2. Loosen the brake pushrod locknut and screw the pushrod in or out until the pedal height from the floor is as follows:

1987 Civic (except Wagon) and CRX—6.875 in. (174mm).
1987 Civic Wagon—6.625 in. (168mm).
1988–91 Civic and CRX—6.02 in. (153mm).
1987–89 Accord—8.07 in. (205mm).
1990–91 Accord with manual transaxle—7.48 in. (190mm).
1990–91 Accord with automatic transaxle—7.68 in. (195mm).
1987 Prelude and 1988–91 Prelude with manual transaxle—7.0 in. (176mm).
1988–91 Prelude with automatic transaxle—7.2 in. (183mm).

3. After adjustment, tighten the brake pushrod locknut.

4. Screw in the stoplight switch until it's plunger is fully depressed, threaded end touching the pad on the pedal arm, then back off the switch ½ turn and tighten the locknut.

NOTE: Make sure the brake lights go off when the pedal is released.

Removal and Installation

1. Disconnect the negative battery cable.

2. Disconnect the electrical connector.

3. Loosen the locknut and unscrew the switch from it's mounting.

4. Installation is the reverse of the removal procedure. The switch must be adjusted after installation.

Clutch Switch

Adjustment

1. Loosen the locknut on the clutch interlock switch.

2. Depress the clutch pedal fully and then release 0.59–0.79 in. (15–20mm) from the fully depressed position and hold. Adjust the position of the clutch switch so the engine will start with the clutch pedal in this position.

3. Thread the clutch switch in further ¼–½ turn and tighten the locknut.

Removal and Installation

1. Disconnect the negative battery cable.

2. Disconnect the electrical connector from the switch.

3. Loosen the locknut on the clutch switch and unscrew the switch from it's mounting.

4. Installation is the reverse of the removal procedure. Adjust the switch after installation.

Neutral Safety Switch

Removal and Installation

1. Disconnect the negative battery cable.

2. Remove the console and disconnect the electrical connectors from the neutral safety switch.

3. Remove the 2 neutral safety switch mounting nuts and remove the neutral safety switch.

To install:

4. Position the switch slider to the **N** position.

5. Shift the selector lever to **N**, then slip the neutral safety switch into position.

6. Attach the switch with the 2 nuts.

7. Connect the electrical connectors and the negative battery cable. Make sure the engine starts when the shift lever is in the **N** position in the range of free-play in the switch.

8. Install the console.

Fuses and Relays

Location

FUSES

The fuse panel is located under the left side of the dashboard on all vehicles. 1988–91 Civic and CRX and all Accord and Prelude vehicles also have a fuse box in the right side of the engine compartment.

RELAYS

Air Conditioner Condenser Fan Relay—Civic and CRX—located in right front of engine compartment. Accord—located in left front of engine compartment. Prelude—located in underhood relay box.

Air Conditioner Clutch Relay—Civic, CRX and Prelude—located in right front of engine compartment. Accord—located in left front of engine compartment.

Radiator Cooling Fan Relay—Civic and CRX—located in right front of engine compartment. Accord and Prelude—located in underhood relay box.

Turn Signal and Hazard Relay—Civic and CRX—located

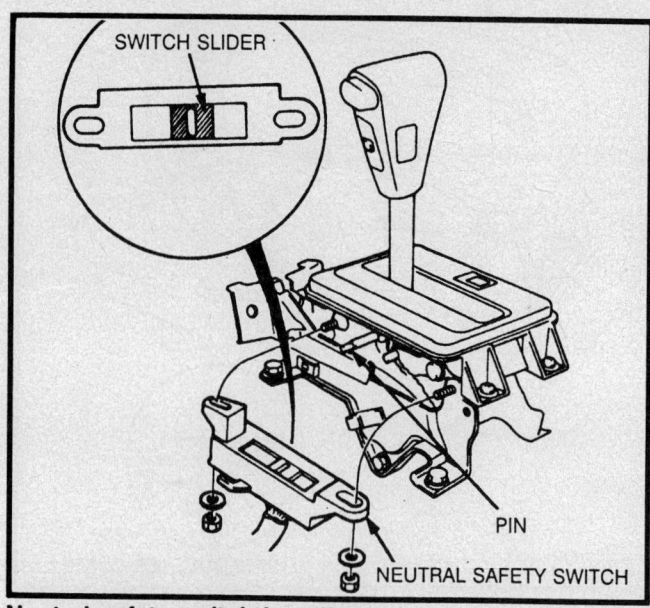

SWITCH SLIDER

PIN

NEUTRAL SAFETY SWITCH

Neutral safety switch installation

on dashboard fuse panel. Accord—located on underdash fuse panel. Prelude—located on underdash relay panel.

Intermittent Windshield Wiper Relay—1987 Civic and CRX—located on dashboard fuse panel. 1987–89 Accord—located on underdash fuse panel. 1990–91 Accord—located under underhood relay box.

Brake Check Relay—1987 Civic and CRX—located under left side of dashboard.

Rear Window Defogger Relay—1987 Civic and CRX—located under left side of dashboard. 1988–91 Civic and CRX—located on dashboard fuse panel. Accord—located on underdash fuse panel. Prelude—located on underdash relay panel.

Power Window Relay—1988–91 Civic—located on dashboard fuse panel. Accord—located in underhood relay box. Prelude—located on underdash relay panel.

ECM Main Relay—1988–91 Civic and CRX—located under left side of dashboard. Accord and Prelude—located under left side of dashboard.

Starter Relay—1989–91 Civic and CRX—located under left side of dashboard. Accord—located under left side of dashboard. Prelude—located on underdash relay box.

Cigarette Lighter Relay—1990–91 Civic and CRX—located under dashboard to the right of steering column. Accord—located under left side of dashboard.

Heater Motor Relay—1990–91 Civic Wagon—located under dashboard to the right of steering column.

Sunroof Relay—1987 CRX—located under left side of dashboard. 1988–91 CRX—located behind underdash fuse panel. 1990–91 Accord—located on underdash fuse panel. Prelude—located on underdash relay panel.

Blower Motor Relay—1990–91 Accord—located on underdash fuse panel.

Headlight Retractor Relays—1987–89 Accord—located in right front of engine compartment. Prelude—right retractor relay located in right front of engine compartment, left retractor relay located in left front of engine compartment.

Dimmer Relay—Prelude and 1990–91 Accord—located in underhood relay box.

Lighting Relay—Prelude and 1990–91 Accord—located in underhood relay box.

Fuel Cut-Off Relay—1987–89 Accord with carbureted engine—located on underdash fuse panel.

Computers

Location

CIVIC AND CRX

The engine Electronic Control Module (ECM) is located under the driver's seat on 1987 Civic and under the passenger's seat on 1987 CRX. On 1988–91 vehicles the ECU is located under a panel on the right front floor. The automatic transaxle control unit on 1989–91 Civic Wagon is located under the driver's seat.

ACCORD

The engine Electronic Control Module (ECM) is located under the driver's seat on 1987–89 Accord. The ECM is located under a panel on the right front floor on 1990–91 Accord. The automatic transaxle control unit on 1990–91 Accord is located next to the engine ECM.

PRELUDE

The engine Electronic Control Module (ECM) is located behind the driver's side trim panel next to the back seat on 1987 Prelude. The ECM is located under a panel on the right front floor on 1988–91 Prelude. The automatic transaxle control unit is located next to the ECM on 1988–89 Prelude and 1990–91 Prelude equipped with the 2.1L engine. The automatic transaxle control unit is located behind the center console on 1990–91 Prelude equipped with the 2.0L engine. The anti-lock brake control unit is located behind the center console.

Flashers

Location

The turn signal/hazard flasher function is contained in the integrated control unit. The integrated control unit is located under the left side of the dashboard on Civic and CRX, under the dash next to the steering column on 1987–89 Accord, under the dash on the left kick panel on 1990–91 Accord and under the center of the dash on Prelude.

Cruise Control

For further information, please refer to "Chilton's Chassis Electronics Service Manual" for additional coverage.

Adjustment

1. Make sure the actuator cable operates smoothly, with no binding or sticking.
2. Start the engine and warm it up to normal operating temperature.
3. Measure the amount of movement of the actuator rod or output linkage on 1990–91 Civic Sedan, until the engine speed starts to increase. At first, the actuator linkage should be located at the full close position. Free-play should be 0.37–0.49 in. (9.5–12.5mm).
4. If free-play is not within specification, loosen the locknut and turn the adjusting nut as required.

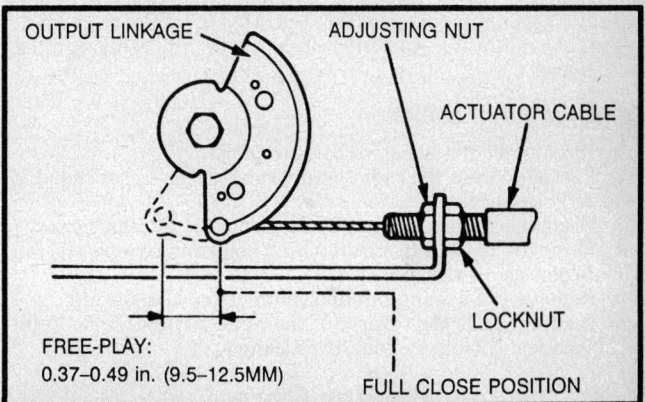

Cruise control actuator cable adjustment—1990–91 Civic Sedan

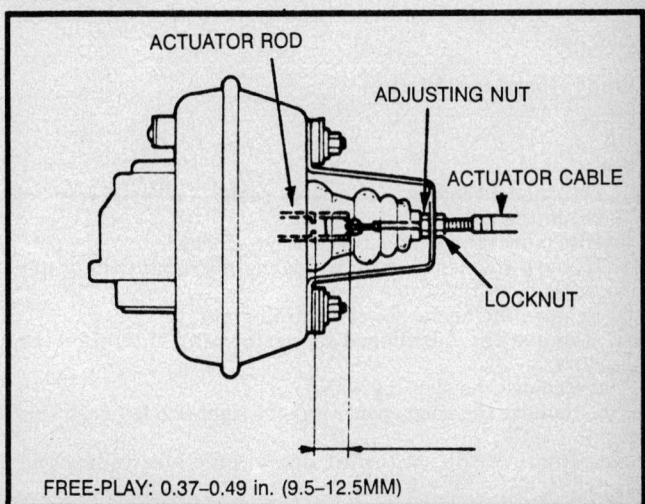

Cruise control actuator cable adjustment—Accord and Prelude

ENGINE COOLING

Radiator

Removal and Installation

1. Disconnect the negative battery cable. Drain the radiator.
2. Disconnect the thermo-switch wire and the fan motor wire.
3. Disconnect the upper coolant hose at the upper radiator tank and the lower hose at the water pump connecting pipe. Disconnect and plug the automatic transaxle cooling lines at the bottom of the radiator, if equipped.
4. Remove the hoses to the coolant reservoir, if equipped.
5. Detach the radiator mounting bolts and remove the radiator with the fan attached.
6. Remove the cooling fan and shroud assembly from the radiator.
7. To install, reverse the removal procedure. Refill and bleed the cooling system.

Electric Cooling Fan

Testing

1. Disconnect the electrical connector from the fan motor.
2. Connect a jumper wire from the positive terminal of the battery to 1 of the terminals of the fan connector.
3. Connect a jumper wire from the other terminal to ground.
4. If the motor fails to run or does not run smoothly, it must be replaced.

Removal and Installation

1. Disconnect the negative battery cable.
2. Partially drain the radiator and remove the upper radiator hose, if necessary.
3. Disconnect the electrical connector from the fan motor.
4. Remove the fan shroud attaching bolts and remove the fan and shroud as an assembly.
5. Remove the cooling fan and motor from the shroud.
6. Installation is the reverse of the removal procedure. Refill and bleed the cooling system, if necessary.

Heater Core

For further information, please refer to "Chilton's Heating and Air Conditioning Manual" for additional coverage.

Removal and Installation

CIVIC

1987

1. Disconnect the negative battery cable.
2. Drain the cooling system.
3. Disconnect the heater hoses at the firewall.
4. Remove the water valve cover and disconnect the water valve cable from the water valve.
5. Remove the heater lower mounting nut.
6. Remove the dashboard by performing the following procedure:
    a. Remove the steering wheel.
    b. Remove the hood opener and the right and left dash side caps.
    c. Remove the center air outlet on Civic Sedan and Hatchback.
    d. Remove the ashtray.
    e. Remove the right and left side defroster garnish and the clock on Civic Wagon.

    f. Remove the dashboard lower panel, then disconnect the ground and speedometer cables from under the dashboard.
    g. Remove the glovebox on Civic Sedan and Hatchback or the underdash tray on Civic Wagon, then disconnect the antenna cable.
    h. Remove the heater control face plate and the 3 screws attaching the heater control panel to the dashboard.
    i. Disconnect the instrument wire harness from the fuse box.
    j. Remove the dashboard mounting bolts.
    k. Lift the dashboard as it is removed so it will slide up and off of the guide pin at the middle. Hold the dash from underneath so it will not fall when it comes off of the pin.
7. Remove the 2 heater mounting bolts, then pull the heater away from the body and remove it.
8. Remove the heater core from the heater assembly.
9. Installation is the reverse of the removal procedure. Fill and bleed the cooling system.

1988–91

1. Disconnect the negative battery cable.
2. Drain the cooling system.
3. Disconnect the heater hoses at the firewall.
4. Disconnect the water valve cable from the water valve.
5. Remove the dashboard by performing the following procedure:
    a. Slide the seats back fully and remove the dashboard center panel on 1988–89 vehicles or the center console on 1990–91 vehicles.
    b. Remove the fuse lid.
    c. Remove the knee bolster on 1990–91 vehicles.
    d. Disconnect the wire harnesses from the connector holder and disconnect the sunroof switch connector, if equipped. Remove the fuse box mounting nuts and lower the fuse box, if necessary.
    e. Disconnect the ground cable at the right of the steering column and the power door mirror switch connector.
    f. Remove the knob, then remove the side air vent face plate.
    g. Remove the 2 screws attaching the side air vent control lever.
    h. Remove the center panel and radio, then remove the 3 screws attaching the heater control panel to the dashboard.
    i. Remove the gauge upper panel or instrument panel, as necessary.
    j. Disconnect the speedometer cable.
    k. Remove the center upper lid from the top of the dashboard.
    l. Remove the side defroster garnishes from both ends of the dashboard.
    m. Lower the steering column.
    n. Remove the dashboard mounting bolts, lift and remove the dashboard.
6. Remove the heater duct.
7. Remove the heater lower mounting nut.
8. Remove the steering column bracket and duct assembly.
9. Remove the 2 heater mounting bolts and the clip, then remove the heater assembly.
10. Remove the tapping screws and heater core cover.
11. Remove the tapping screw and clamp and remove the heater core.
12. Installation is the reverse of the removal procedure. Fill and bleed the cooling system.

CRX

1987

1. Disconnect the negative battery cable.

2. Drain the cooling system.
3. Disconnect the heater hoses at the firewall.
4. Remove the water valve cover and disconnect the water valve cable from the water valve.
5. Remove the heater lower mounting nut.
6. Remove the dashboard by performing the following procedure:
  a. Remove the steering wheel and column lower cover.
  b. Remove the instrument panel and the right and left air vents.
  c. Remove the center dash mount bolt cover and the ashtray.
  d. Disconnect the ground and antenna cables from under the dashboard.
  e. Disconnect the instrument wire harness from the fuse box.
  f. Remove the 7 dashboard mounting bolts.
  g. Lift the dashboard as it is removed so it will slide up and off of the guide pin at the middle. Hold it from underneath so it will not fall when it comes off of the pin.
7. Remove the 2 heater mounting bolts, then pull the heater away from the body and remove it.
8. Remove the heater core from the heater assembly.
9. Installation is the reverse of the removal procedure. Fill and bleed the cooling system.

1988–91

1. Disconnect the negative battery cable.
2. Drain the cooling system.
3. Disconnect the heater hoses at the firewall.
4. Disconnect the water valve cable from the water valve.
5. Remove the dashboard by performing the following procedure:
  a. Slide the seats back fully and remove the front console.
  b. Remove the fuse lid. Disconnect the wire harnesses from the connector holder and disconnect the sunroof switch connector, if equipped. Remove the fuse box mounting nuts and lower the fuse box, if necessary.
  c. Disconnect the ground cable at the right of the steering column.
  d. Remove the coin box.
  e. Remove the knob, then remove the side air vent face plate.
  f. Remove the 2 screws attaching the side air vent control lever.
  g. Remove the 3 screws attaching the heater control panel to the dashboard.
  h. Remove the instrument panel.
  i. Disconnect the speedometer cable.
  j. Remove the center upper lid from the top of the dashboard.
  k. Remove the side defroster garnishes from both ends of the dashboard.
  l. Lower the steering column.
  m. Remove the dashboard mounting bolts, lift and remove the dashboard.
6. Remove the heater duct.
7. Remove the heater lower mounting nut.
8. Remove the steering column bracket and duct assembly.
9. Remove the 2 heater mounting bolts, disconnect the wire harness connector from the function control motor and then remove the heater assembly.
10. Remove the tapping screws and heater core cover.
11. Remove the tapping screw and clamp and remove the heater core.
12. Installation is the reverse of the removal procedure. Fill and bleed the cooling system.

ACCORD
1987–89

1. Disconnect the negative battery cable.

2. Drain the cooling system.
3. Disconnect the heater hoses at the firewall.
4. Disconnect the heater valve cable from the heater valve.
5. Remove the 2 heater lower mounting nuts.
6. Remove the dashboard by performing the following procedure:
  a. Slide the seats back fully and remove the front console.
  b. Remove the dashboard lower panel and lower the steering column.
  c. Remove the hood release handle but do not disconnect the cable.
  d. Disconnect the wire harnesses from the connector holders at the fuse area.
  e. Remove the ashtray, ashtray holder and the radio.
  f. Remove the heater control knobs, the heater control cover, disconnect the heater control connectors and remove the heater control.
  g. Remove the instrument cluster and the clock.
  h. Remove the dashboard mounting bolts. Lift the dashboard as it is removed so it will slide up and off the guide pin at the middle. Support it from underneath so it will not fall when it comes off the pin.
7. Disconnect the cables from the heater assembly.
8. Remove the heater duct.
9. Remove the 4 heater mounting bolts, then pull the heater away from the body.
10. Remove the tapping screws and retaining plates and the heater core from the heater housing.
11. Installation is the reverse of the removal procedure. Fill and bleed the cooling system.

1990–91

1. Disconnect the negative battery cable.
2. Drain the cooling system.
3. Disconnect the heater hoses at the heater.
4. Disconnect the heater valve cable from the heater valve.
5. Remove the dashboard by performing the following procedure:
  a. Slide the seats back fully and remove the console.
  b. Remove the knee bolster, lower panel and steering column.
  c. Disconnect the dashboard wire harness from the connectors and fuse box.
  d. Remove the carpet clips and disconnect the antenna lead.
  e. Disconnect the heater control cable and function control cable.
  f. Remove the caps from both sides of the dash and the clock.
  g. Remove the 7 dashboard mounting bolts, lift and remove the dashboard.
6. Remove the heater duct.
7. Remove the instrument sub-pipe.
8. Remove the 4 heater mounting nuts and the heater assembly.
9. Remove the air mix rod from the clip, the self-tapping screws and heater core cover and the self tapping screw and clamp. Remove the heater core from the heater housing.
10. Installation is the reverse of the removal procedure. Fill and bleed the cooling system.

PRELUDE
1987

NOTE: The heater core can be removed without removing the heater assembly on 1987 Prelude.

1. Disconnect the negative battery cable.
2. Drain the cooling system.
3. Remove the heater pipe cover and heater pipe clamp.
4. Remove the heater core retaining plate.

5. Pull out the cotter pin of the joint hose clamp and separate the heater pipes.

6. Pull out the heater core from the heater housing.

7. Installation is the reverse of the removal procedure.

1988–91

1. Disconnect the negative battery cable.
2. Drain the cooling system.
3. Disconnect the heater hoses at the heater.
4. Disconnect the heater valve cable from the heater.
5. Remove the dashboard by performing the following procedure:

   a. Slide the seats back fully and remove the dashboard lower panel and the front and rear consoles.

   b. Disconnect the wire harnesses from the connector holder and fuse box.

   c. Remove the 6 screws and radio panel, then disconnect the wire connectors and antenna cable.

   d. Remove the radio assembly.

   e. Disconnect the heater control cable and the connector and wire harnesses from the heater control unit.

   f. Remove the clock from the top of the dashboard.

   g. Lower the steering column.

   h. Remove the dashboard mounting bolts. Lift the dashboard as it is removed, so it will slide up and off the guide pin in the middle. Hold the dashboard from underneath so it will not fall when it comes off of the pin.

6. Remove the heater duct.
7. Remove the heater lower mounting nuts.
8. Remove the steering column bracket.
9. Remove the 2 heater mounting bolts, disconnect the wire harness connector from the function control motor and then remove the heater assembly.
10. Remove the integrated control unit and bracket from the heater assembly.
11. Remove the 2 tapping screws, bracket, set plate and heater core cover.
12. Remove the 2 tapping screws, heater core setting plate and clamp.
13. Pull the heater core from the heater housing.
14. Installation is the reverse of the removal procedure. Fill and bleed the cooling system.

Water Pump

Removal and Installation

EXCEPT 1987–89 ACCORD AND 1987 PRELUDE

1. Disconnect the negative battery cable.
2. Drain the cooling system.
3. Remove the accessory drive belts.
4. Remove the timing belt cover and the timing belt.
5. Remove the water pump mounting bolts and the water pump.
6. Installation is the reverse of the removal procedure. Use a new O-ring seal when installing the pump. Tighten the water pump mounting bolts to 9 ft. lbs. (12 Nm).
7. Fill and bleed the cooling system.

1987–89 ACCORD AND 1987 PRELUDE

1. Disconnect the negative battery cable.
2. Drain the cooling system.
3. Remove the accessory drive belts.
4. Remove the timing belt cover.
5. Remove the water pump pulley and the water pump mounting bolts.
6. Remove the water pump and the O-ring seal.
7. Installation is the reverse of the removal procedure. Use a new O-ring seal when installing the pump. Tighten the water pump mounting bolts and the pulley bolts to 9 ft. lbs. (12 Nm).
8. Fill and bleed the cooling system.

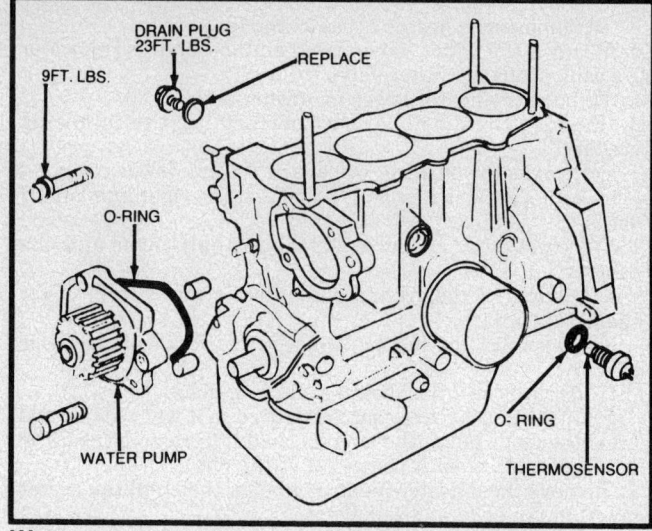

Water pump installation—1987 Civic and CRX

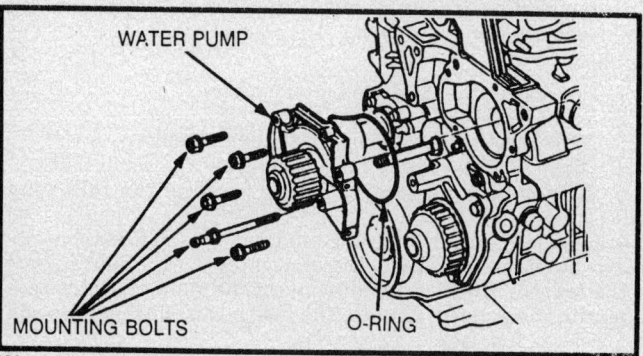

Water pump installation—1990–91 Accord

Thermostat

The thermostat housing is located on the cylinder head with the exception of Civic and CRX and 1990–91 Accord, where it is located at the end of the water pump inlet tube.

Removal and Installation

1. Disconnect the negative battery cable.
2. Drain the cooling system.
3. Disconnect the radiator hose from the thermostat housing outlet.
4. Remove the thermostat housing outlet and remove the thermostat.
5. Installation is the reverse of the removal procedure. Use new gaskets and O-rings. Install the thermostat with the pin towards the thermostat housing outlet. Tighten the thermostat housing outlet bolts to 9 ft. lbs. (12 Nm).
6. Fill and bleed the cooling system.

Cooling System Bleeding

1. Loosen the air bleed bolt in the water outlet and fill the radiator to the bottom of the filler neck with antifreeze/coolant. Tighten the bleed bolt as soon as the coolant starts to run out in a steady stream without any air bubbles in it.
2. With the radiator cap off, start the engine and allow it to warm up (the cooling fan should go on at least twice). Then if necessary add more antifreeze/coolant to bring the level back up to the bottom of the filler neck.
3. Put the radiator cap on, restart the engine and check for any leaks.

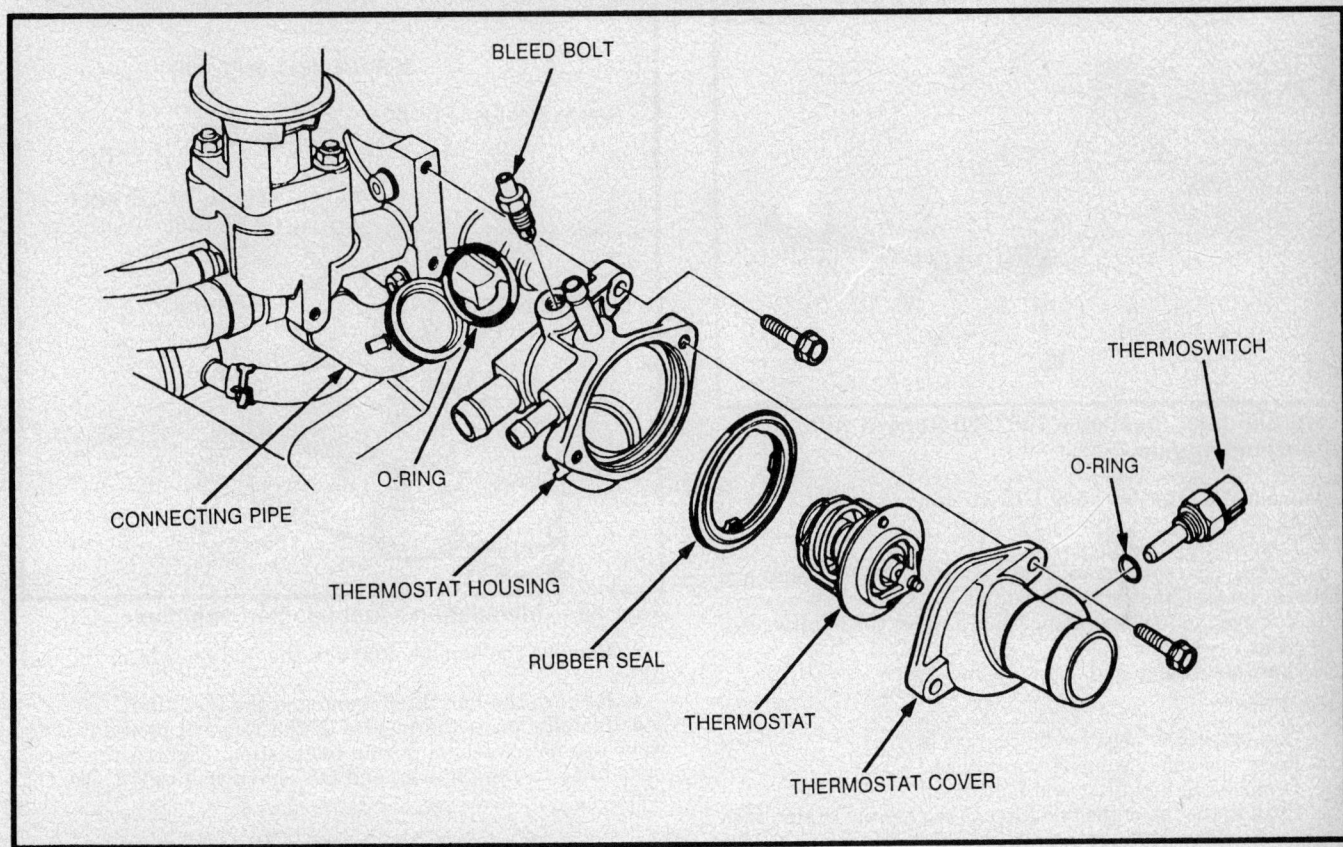

Thermostat housing assembly—1990–91 Accord

FUEL SYSTEM

Fuel System Service Precautions

Safety is the most important factor when performing not only fuel system maintenance but any type of maintenance. Failure to conduct maintenance and repairs in a safe manner may result in serious personal injury or death. Maintenance and testing of the vehicle's fuel system components can be accomplished safely and effectively by adhering to the following rules and guidelines.

• To avoid the possibility of fire and personal injury, always disconnect the negative battery cable unless the repair or test procedure requires that battery voltage be applied.

• Always relieve the fuel system pressure prior to disconnecting any fuel system component (injector, fuel rail, pressure regulator, etc.), fitting or fuel line connection. Exercise extreme caution whenever relieving fuel system pressure to avoid exposing skin, face and eyes to fuel spray. Please be advised that fuel under pressure may penetrate the skin or any part of the body that it contacts.

• Always place a shop towel or cloth around the fitting or connection prior to loosening to absorb any excess fuel due to spillage. Ensure that all fuel spillage (should it occur) is quickly removed from engine surfaces. Ensure that all fuel soaked cloths or towels are deposited into a suitable waste container.

• Always keep a dry chemical (Class B) fire extinguisher near the work area.

• Do not allow fuel spray or fuel vapors to come into contact with a spark or open flame.

• Always use a backup wrench when loosening and tightening fuel line connection fittings. This will prevent unnecessary stress and torsion to fuel line piping. Always follow the proper torque specifications.

• Always replace worn fuel fitting O-rings with new. Do not substitute fuel hose or equivalent where fuel pipe is installed.

Relieving Fuel System Pressure

1. Make sure the engine is cold.
2. Disconnect the negative battery cable.
3. Remove the fuel filler cap.
4. Use a suitable box end wrench on the 6mm service bolt at the top of the fuel filter (fuel pipe on 1990–91 Accord), while holding the special banjo bolt with another wrench.
5. Place a rag or shop towel over the 6mm service bolt.
6. Slowly loosen the 6mm service bolt 1 complete turn.

Fuel Filter

Removal and Installation
CARBURETED VEHICLES
Front Filter

1. Disconnect the negative battery cable.
2. Use suitable fuel line clamps to pinch off the fuel lines and prevent fuel from leaking.
3. Slide the fuel line retaining clamps back. Remove the fuel

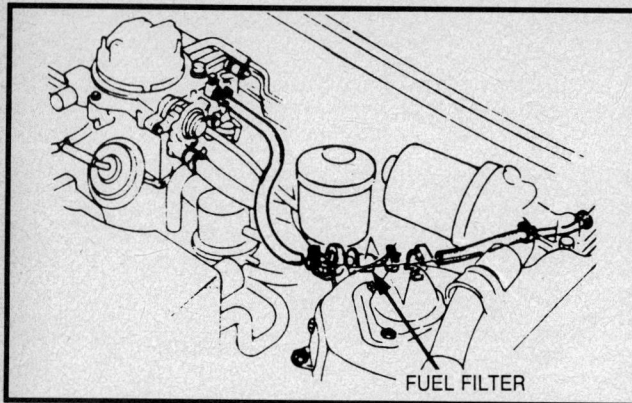

Front fuel filter location—1987–89 Accord with carbureted engine

lines from the filter by using a twisting motion as the line is pulled off.

4. Remove the fuel filter.
5. Install the replacement filter, connect the fuel lines and position the fuel line retaining clamps.
6. Remove the fuel line clamps and connect the negative battery cable.
7. Start the engine and check for fuel leaks.

Rear Filter

1. Disconnect the negative battery cable.
2. Raise and safely support the vehicle.
3. Remove the fuel filter and holder.
4. Push in the tab of the fuel filter to release the holder, then remove the filter from the holder.
5. Attach suitable fuel line clamps to pinch off the fuel lines and prevent fuel from leaking.
6. Slide the fuel line retaining clamps back. Remove the fuel lines from the filter by using a twisting motion as the line is pulled off.
7. Remove the fuel filter.
8. Install the replacement filter, connect the fuel lines and position the fuel line retaining clamps.
9. Remove the fuel line clamps and install the holder on the fuel filter.
10. Install the fuel filter and holder.
11. Lower the vehicle, connect the negative battery cable, start the engine and check for fuel leaks.

FUEL INJECTED VEHICLES

1. Disconnect the negative battery cable.
2. Relieve the fuel system pressure.

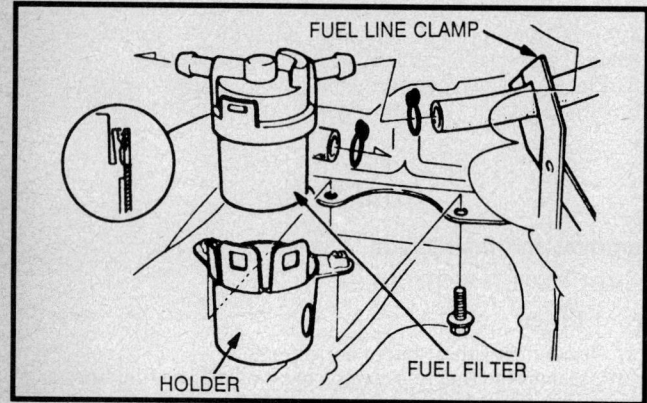

Rear fuel filter—carbureted vehicles

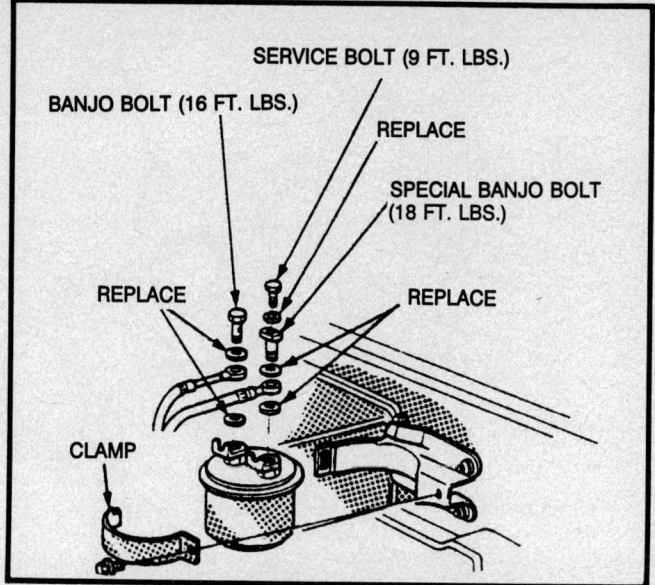

Fuel filter installation—fuel injected vehicles

3. Remove the banjo bolt(s) and the fuel lines from the fuel filter.
4. Remove the fuel filter clamp and the fuel filter.
5. Installation is the reverse of the removal procedure. Always use new washers during installation. Tighten the banjo bolts to 16 ft. lbs. (22 Nm) and the service bolt to 9 ft. lbs. (12 Nm).

Mechanical Fuel Pump

Pressure Testing

1987 CIVIC AND CRX

1. Disconnect the fuel line at the fuel filter in the engine compartment and connect a suitable fuel pressure gauge.
2. Disconnect the fuel return line at the fuel pump and plug the return fitting.
3. Start the engine and allow it to idle until pressure stabilizes, then stop the engine. Fuel pressure should be 2.7–3.8 psi at idle. If the fuel pressure is at least 2.7 psi, go on to Step 4. If the fuel pressure is less than 2.7 psi, replace the pump and retest.
4. Remove the pressure gauge and hold a graduated container under the hose.
5. Start the engine and allow it to idle for 60 seconds, then stop the engine. The fuel volume should be 5.7 oz. (170cc) or more. If the fuel volume is less than specified, replace the fuel pump and retest.

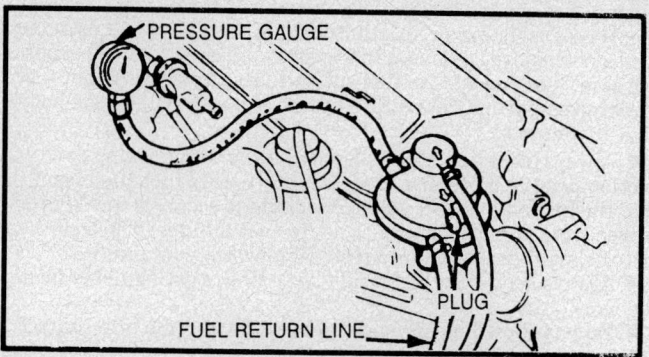

Fuel pressure testing—mechanical fuel pump

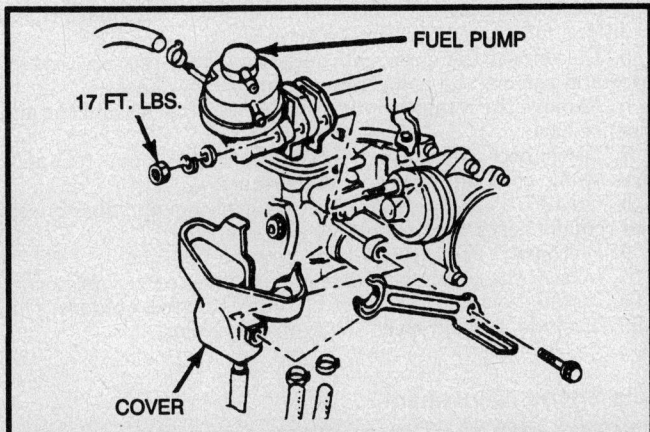

Mechanical fuel pump installation—1987 Civic and CRX with carbureted engine

NOTE: Check for a clogged fuel filter and/or fuel line before replacing the pump.

6. Connect the fuel line at the fuel filter, remove the plug from the fuel pump return fitting and reconnect the return line.

Removal and Installation

1987 CIVIC AND CRX

1. Disconnect the negative battery cable.
2. Attach fuel line clamps to pinch off the fuel lines and prevent fuel from leaking.
3. Slide the fuel line retaining clamps back. Disconnect the fuel lines from the pump by using a twisting motion as they are pulled off.
4. Remove the fuel pump mounting nuts and remove the fuel pump.
5. Installation is the reverse of the removal procedure. Make sure all gasket mating surfaces are clean prior to installation. Use a new gasket and tighten the fuel pump mounting nuts to 17 ft. lbs. (24 Nm).

Electric Fuel Pump

Pressure Testing

CARBURETED VEHICLES

1. Remove the fuel cut-off relay from the underdash fuse panel.
2. Using a jumper wire, connect the No. 1 terminal to the No. 2 terminal located at the fuse box side of the fuel cut-off relay.
3. Disconnect the fuel line at the fuel filter in the engine compartment and connect a suitable fuel pressure gauge.
4. Turn the ignition **ON** until the pressure stabilizes, then turn the key **OFF**. The fuel pressure should be as follows:
1987 Prelude—2–3 psi.
1988 Prelude and 1987–89 Accord—2.6–3.3 psi.
1989–91 Prelude—1.3–2.1 psi.
5. If the fuel pressure is less than specified, replace the fuel pump and retest.
6. If the fuel pressure is correct, remove the pressure gauge and hold a graduated container under the hose.
7. Turn the ignition **ON** for 1 minute, then turn the ignition **OFF** and measure the amount of fuel flow.
8. The fuel flow should be as follows:
1987 Prelude—23 oz. (680cc) or more.
1988 Prelude and 1987–89 Accord—25.7 oz. (760cc) or more.
1989–91 Prelude—20 oz. (600cc) or more.
9. If the fuel flow is as specified, reconnect the fuel cut-off re-

lay and the fuel line. If the fuel flow is less than specified, replace the fuel pump and retest.

NOTE: Check for a clogged fuel filter and/or fuel line before replacing the pump.

FUEL INJECTED VEHICLES

1. Disconnect the negative battery cable.
2. Relieve the fuel system pressure.
3. Attach a suitable fuel pressure gauge to service port of the fuel filter (fuel pipe on 1990–91 Accord).
4. Connect the negative battery cable and disconnect the vacuum hose at the pressure regulator.
5. Start the engine and allow it to idle. The fuel pressure should be 36–41 psi.
6. If the fuel pressure is not as specified, check if there is battery voltage available at the fuel pump. If battery voltage is available, replace the fuel pump. If there is no voltage, check the main relay and wire harness.
7. If the fuel pump is OK, check the following:
   a. If the fuel pressure is higher than specified, inspect for a pinched or clogged fuel return hose or pipe or a faulty pressure regulator.
   b. If the fuel pressure is lower than specified, inspect for a clogged fuel filter, pressure regulator failure or leakage in the fuel line.

Removal and Installation

1987 CIVIC, CRX AND PRELUDE

The fuel pump is located on the underside of the vehicle, in front of the left rear wheel.
1. Disconnect the negative battery cable.
2. Relieve the fuel pressure on fuel injected vehicles.
3. Raise and safely support the vehicle.
4. Remove the left rear wheel.
5. On carbureted vehicles, attach fuel line clamps to pinch the fuel lines and prevent fuel from leaking. On fuel injected vehicles, remove the fuel pump cover.
6. Disconnect the fuel lines and electrical connectors.
7. Remove the fuel pump and pump mount. Separate the fuel pump from the mount. On fuel injected vehicles, remove the fuel line and pulsation damper from the fuel pump.
8. Installation is the reverse of the removal procedure. Tighten the pulsation damper to 20 ft. lbs. (28 Nm). Before starting the engine, turn the ignition switch **ON** and check for fuel leaks.

1987–89 ACCORD AND 1988–91 PRELUDE

The fuel pump is located in the fuel tank.
1. Disconnect the negative battery cable.
2. Relieve the fuel system pressure on fuel injected vehicles.
3. Remove the left maintenance access cover in the trunk.
4. Disconnect the fuel lines.
5. Remove the fuel pump mounting bolts and remove the fuel pump from the fuel tank. If the pump is hard to remove, slightly lower the fuel tank by loosening the fuel tank mounting nuts.
6. Installation is the reverse of the removal procedure. Use a new O-ring when installing the pump. Before installing the maintenance access cover, turn the ignition switch **ON** and check for fuel leaks.

NOTE: When installing the maintenance access cover, make sure the seal is attached to the cover.

1988–91 CIVIC AND CRX AND 1990–91 ACCORD

The fuel pump is located in the fuel tank.
1. Disconnect the negative battery cable.
2. Relieve the fuel system pressure.
3. Raise and safely support the vehicle.
4. Remove the fuel tank drain bolt and drain the fuel into a suitable container.
5. On Civic and Accord, disconnect the fuel pump electrical

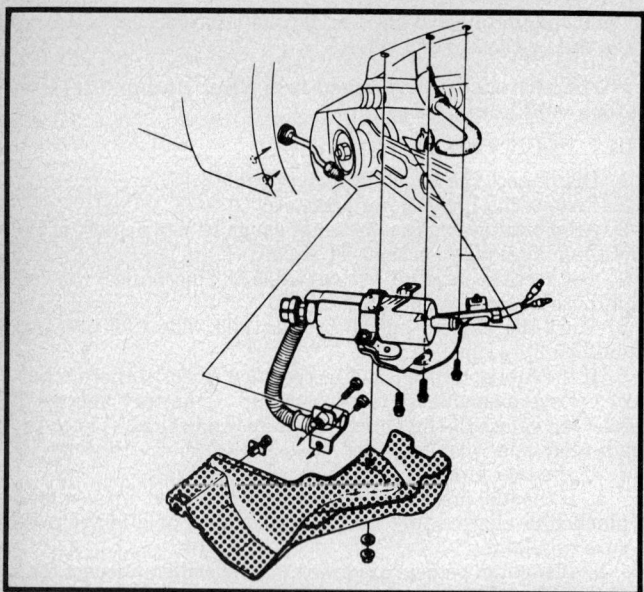

Electric fuel pump mounting—fuel injected models

connector in the trunk. On CRX, remove the storage compartment and disconnect the fuel pump electrical connector. On Civic Wagon, remove the rear seat and disconnect the fuel pump electrical connector.

6. On Civic Wagon with 4WD, remove the driveshaft from the rear differential and the exhaust pipe and muffler.
7. Remove the 2-way valve cover and fuel hose protector.
8. Disconnect the fuel lines.
9. Place a suitable support under the fuel tank.
10. Remove the fuel tank strap nuts and let the straps hang.
11. Remove the fuel tank.
12. Remove the fuel pump mounting nuts and the fuel pump.
13. Installation is the reverse of the removal procedure. Install a new washer on the fuel tank drain bolt.

Carburetor

Removal and Installation
EXCEPT PRELUDE

1. Disconnect the negative battery cable.
2. Remove the air cleaner cover.
3. Disconnect the fresh air and hot air hoses from the air cleaner.
4. Disconnect the vacuum lines from the air cleaner and mark their positions for proper reassembly. Disconnect the breather hose from the valve cover.
5. Remove the air cleaner mounting nuts and the air cleaner.
6. Disconnect the vacuum lines and electrical connectors from the carburetor and mark their positions for proper reassembly.
7. Disconnect the throttle cable.
8. Disconnect and plug the fuel line.
9. Remove the carburetor mounting nuts and the carburetor.
10. Installation is the reverse of the removal procedure. Tighten the carburetor mounting nuts to 17 ft. lbs. (24 Nm).

PRELUDE

1. Disconnect the negative battery cable.
2. Disconnect the fresh air intake duct and hot air intake hose from the air cleaner cover.
3. Disconnect the vacuum hose from the hot air intake control diaphragm and remove the air cleaner cover and element.
4. Disconnect the breather hose from the valve cover. Discon-

nect the vacuum lines from the air cleaner base and mark their positions for proper reassembly.
5. Disconnect the electrical connectors from the air cleaner base and remove the bolts from the air cleaner base.
6. Remove the retaining nuts, air screens, flanges and the air cleaner base.
7. Disconnect all vacuum hoses and electrical connectors and mark their position for proper reassembly.
8. On 1987 Prelude, drain the cooling system and disconnect the coolant hoses at the thermowax valve.
9. Disconnect the throttle cable and the fuel line.
10. Loosen the insulator bands and remove the carburetor.
11. Installation is the reverse of the removal procedure. On 1987 Prelude, fill and bleed the cooling system.

Idle Speed Adjustment
EXCEPT 1987–89 ACCORD WITH AUTOMATIC TRANSAXLE

NOTE: The carburetor must be properly synchronized on Prelude before making idle speed adjustments.

1. Start the engine and warm it up to normal operating temperature. The cooling fan must come on at least once.
2. Disconnect the vacuum hose from the intake air control diaphragm and clamp the hose end.
3. Connect a tachometer according to the manufacturers instructions.
4. On 1988–91 Prelude, make sure the fast idle lever is not seated against the fast idle cam. If it is, replace the left carburetor.
5. On 1987 Civic, make sure the front wheels are in the straight ahead position. If the wheels are turned, the idle boost solenoid will operate and a false idle speed reading will be obtained.
6. Check the idle speed with the headlights, heater blower, rear window defroster, cooling fan and air conditioner **OFF**. Check the underhood emission label for idle speed specification.
7. Adjust the idle speed, if necessary, by turning the throttle stop screw.
8. If the idle speed is excessively high on 1987 Civic and CRX and 1987–89 Accord with manual transaxle, check the dashpot system as follows:
   a. Disconnect the vacuum hose from the throttle controller and check for vacuum. If there is no vacuum, check the vacuum line for leaks or blockage and replace as necessary. If there is vacuum, replace the throttle controller and retest.
   b. With the engine idling, disconnect the vacuum hose from the throttle controller. The engine speed should rise to 1400–2000 rpm.
   c. If the engine speed is not within 1400–2000 rpm, loosen the locknut and adjust by turning the adjusting nut.
   d. If the engine speed does not change, check the throttle controller linkage for free movement. If there is no problem, replace the throttle controller and retest.
9. If the engine speed is excessively high on 1988–91 Prelude, check the throttle control as follows:
   a. Disconnect the vacuum hose from the throttle controller and check the engine speed. The engine speed should be 1700–2700 rpm on manual transaxle equipped vehicles and 1400–2400 rpm on automatic transaxle equipped vehicles.
   b. If the engine speed is excessively high, adjust the engine speed by bending the tab.
   c. If the engine speed does not change, connect a suitable vacuum pump to the throttle control vacuum hose and check the vacuum. There should be vacuum.
   d. If there is no vacuum, check the vacuum hose for proper connection, cracks or a bad check valve and replace as necessary. If there is vacuum, replace the throttle controller and retest.

e. Reconnect the vacuum hose to the throttle controller and check the idle speed.

1987–89 ACCORD WITH AUTOMATIC TRANSAXLE

1. Start the engine and warm it up to normal operating temperature. The cooling fan must come on at least once.

2. Disconnect the vacuum hose from the intake air control diaphragm and clamp the hose end.

3. Connect a tachometer according to the manufacturers instructions.

4. On 1987–88 Accord, remove the air filter from frequency solenoid valve C and plug the opening in the solenoid valve.

5. On 1989 Accord, disconnect the vacuum hose from the 2-way joint between the frequency solenoid valve C and the vacuum hose manifold and plug the vacuum hose. Disconnect the vacuum hose from the 2-way joint between the frequency solenoid valve C and the throttle controller and plug the hose of the frequency solenoid valve side. Connect a vacuum pump to the hose of the throttle controller and apply 20 in. Hg.

6. Turn back the idle control screw until the end is flush with the bracket. With the headlights, heater blower, rear window defogger, cooling fan and air conditioner off and the transaxle in **N** or **P**, lower the idle speed as much as possible by turning the throttle stop screw.

7. Adjust the idle speed by turning the idle control screw to 580–680 rpm.

8. Adjust the idle speed by turning the throttle stop screw to 650–750 rpm.

9. With the transaxle in any gear except **P** or **N**, adjust the

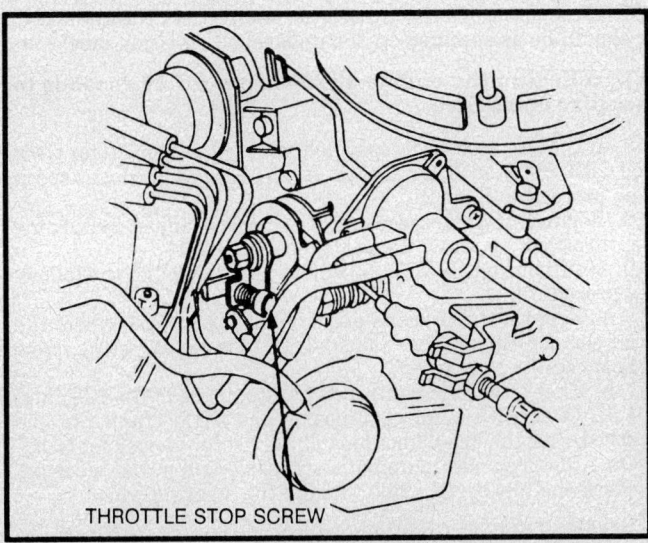

Throttle stop screw location—1987 Civic and CRX

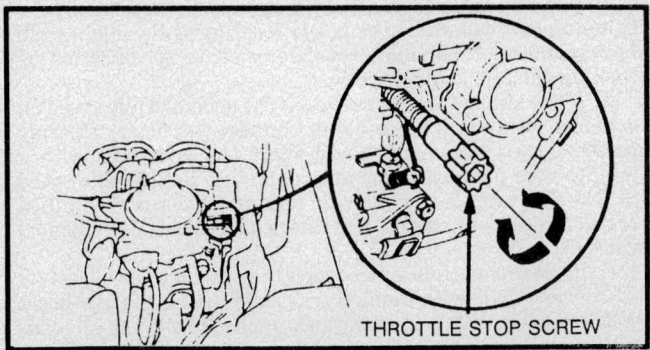

Throttle stop screw location—1987–89 Accord

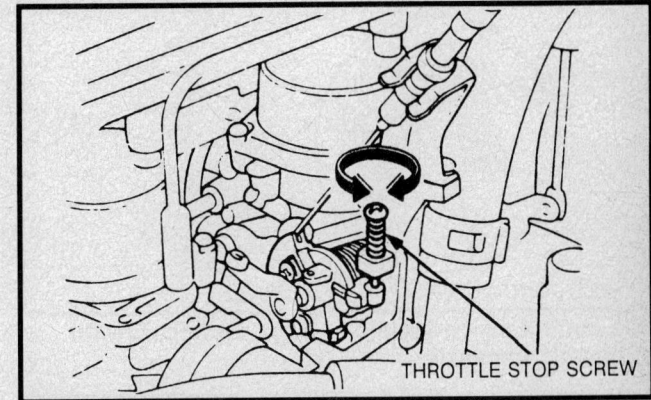

Throttle stop screw location—1988–91 Prelude

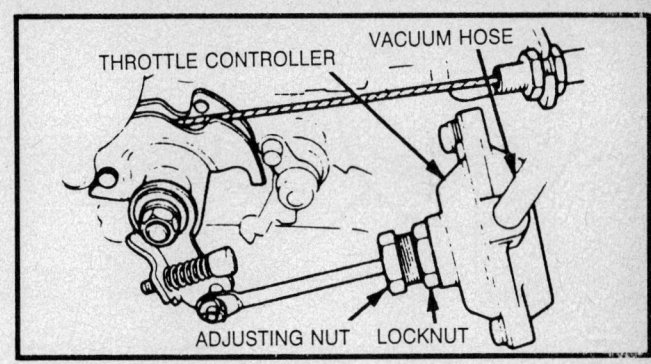

Throttle controller—1987 Civic, CRX and 1987–89 Accord

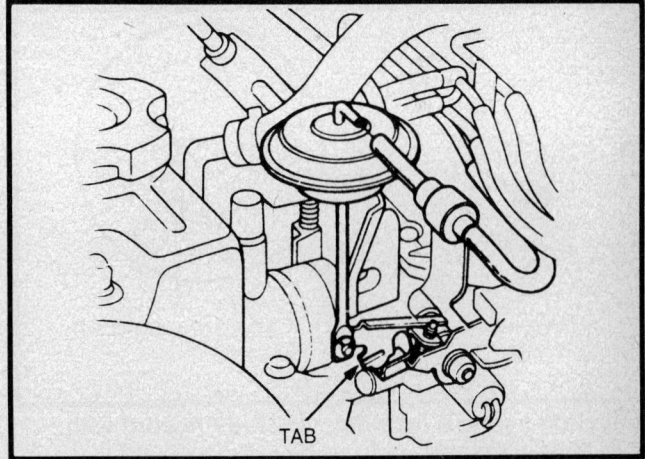

Throttle controller adjusting tab—1988–91 Prelude

idle speed by turning adjusting screw A. The idle speed should be 625–725 rpm at high altitude and 650–750 rpm at low altitude.

10. Shift the transaxle to **N** or **P**.

11. If equipped with air conditioning, adjust the idle speed by turning adjusting screw B to 650–750 rpm with the air conditioning on.

Idle Mixture Adjustment

1987 CIVIC, CRX AND 1987–89 ACCORD WITH MANUAL TRANSAXLE

NOTE: The following procedure requires a propane enrichment kit.

Idle control screw location—1987–89 Accord with automatic transaxle

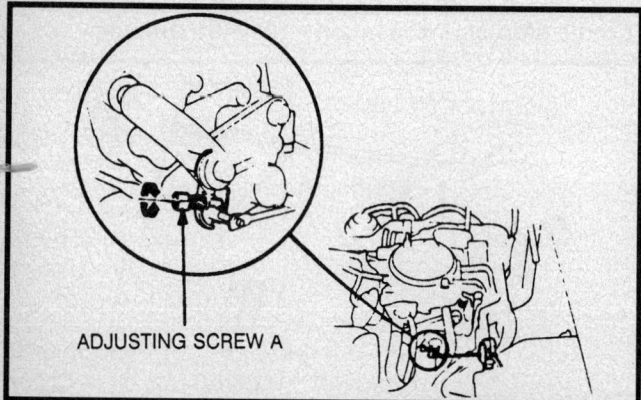

Adjusting screw A location—1987–89 Accord with automatic transaxle

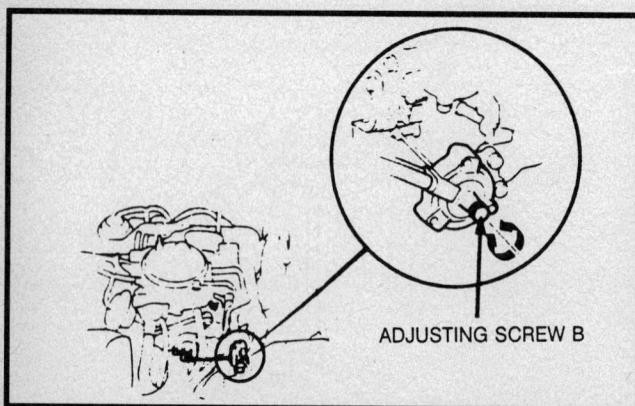

Adjusting screw B location—1987–89 Accord with automatic transaxle

1. Make the initial idle speed adjustment according to the proper procedure.
2. Disconnect the air cleaner tube from the air intake duct.
3. Insert the hose of the propane enrichment kit into the intake tube about 4 inches. Make sure the propane bottle has adequate gas before beginning the test.
4. With the engine idling, depress the button on top of the propane device, then slowly open the propane control valve to obtain maximum engine speed. Engine speed should increase as percentage of propane injected goes up.

NOTE: Open the propane control valve slowly; a sudden burst of propane may stall the engine.

5. The engine speed should increase by 39–70 rpm on Accord, by 100–150 rpm on 1.3L Civic and CRX HF, by 75–125 rpm on 1.5L Civic and CRX standard with manual transaxle and by 30–70 rpm on 1.5L Civic and CRX standard with automatic transaxle. If the engine speed does not increase per specification, the mixture is improperly adjusted. Proceed to Step 6. If the engine speed increases as specified, proceed to Step 17.
6. Close the propane control valve and shut **OFF** the engine.
7. Remove the air cleaner and disconnect the vacuum hoses from the fast idle unloader.
8. Pull the throttle cable out of it's bracket.
9. Remove the carburetor nuts and the bolt securing the steel tubing vacuum manifold.
10. Lift the carburetor clear of it's studs, then tilt it backwards so the idle controller bracket screws can be removed. Remove the idle controller bracket.
11. Remove the mixture adjusting screw hole cap, then reinstall the idle controller bracket.
12. Reinstall the carburetor and reconnect the vacuum hose to the fast idle unloader.
13. Reinstall the air cleaner.
14. Start the engine and warm it up until it reaches normal operating temperature. The cooling fan must come on at least once.
15. Disconnect the vacuum hose from the intake air control diaphragm and clamp the hose end.
16. Reinstall the propane enrichment kit and recheck maximum propane enriched rpm. If the propane enriched speed is too low, the mixture is too rich: turn the mixture screw ¼ turn clockwise and recheck. If the propane enriched speed is too high, the mixture is too lean: turn the mixture screw ¼ turn counterclockwise and recheck.
17. Close the propane control valve and recheck the idle speed. It should be as specified on the underhood emission label.

NOTE: Run the engine at 2500 rpm for 10 seconds to stabilize condition.

18. If the idle speed is as specified, proceed to Step 20 for Civic and CRX and Step 21 for Accord. If the idle speed is not as specified, proceed to Step 19.
19. Recheck the idle speed and if necessary, adjust by turning the throttle stop screw. Repeat Steps 16 and 17.
20. On Civic and CRX, finish adjustments through the following procedure:
   a. Remove the propane enrichment kit and reconnect the air cleaner intake tube. Reinstall the mixture adjusting screw hole cap.
   b. Check the idle controller boosted speed. On 1.3L and 1.5L Civic with manual transaxle and CRX, check the idle speed with the headlights on and the heater blower set to III. On 1.5L Civic with automatic transaxle and power steering, check the idle speed while turning the steering wheel.

NOTE: There is no idle controller on automatic transaxle equipped Civic and CRX without air conditioning and power steering.

   c. The idle controller should maintain the idle speed despite the load caused by the power steering or headlights and blower motor. If the idle drops, adjust it to specification by turning the idle control screw.
   d. If the idle speed does not reach the specified idle speed on vehicles with power steering, disconnect the power steering pressure switch connector and short the terminals with a jumper wire to activate the idle controller. Set the idle speed to 700–800 rpm. If the idle rpm does not reach the specified speed, proceed to Step e and check the idle boost solenoid valve.
   e. If the idle rpm does not reach the specified idle speed on CRX or on Civic with manual transaxle, check the idle boost solenoid valve. Disconnect the vacuum hose from the idle controller and check for vacuum. If there is vacuum, replace the controller. If there is no vacuum, check for voltage at the idle

boost solenoid valve. If there is no voltage, check the wiring and the control unit. If there is voltage, check the vacuum lines for blockage or leaks and replace as necessary. If there is no problem, replace the idle boost solenoid valve.

f. If equipped with air conditioning, make a second check with the air conditioning on. The idle speed should increase approximately 50 rpm. Adjust the speed, if necessary, by turning the adjusting screw on the idle boost diaphragm.

21. On Accord, finish adjustments through the following procedure:

a. The intake air temperature must be above 149°F (65°C).

b. Disconnect the vacuum hose from the air suction valve and plug the hose.

c. On 1987–88 Accord, open the control box lid. Disconnect the lower vacuum hose of the air leak solenoid valve, located between the solenoid valve and the air filter, from the air filter and connect a vacuum gauge to the hose. On 1989 Accord, disconnect the No. 27 vacuum hose from the pipe and plug the pipe. Attach a vacuum pump/gauge to the hose and apply vacuum. The vacuum pump should hold vacuum. If it does, proceed to Step d. If the pump does not hold vacuum, disconnect the control box connector and then apply vacuum. If the pump still does not hold vacuum, replace the solenoid or the No. 27 vacuum hose. If the pump now holds vacuum proceed to Step d.

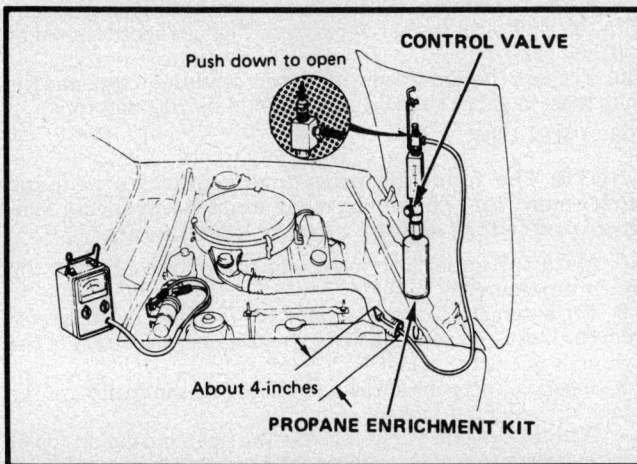

Mixture adjustment using propane enrichment method

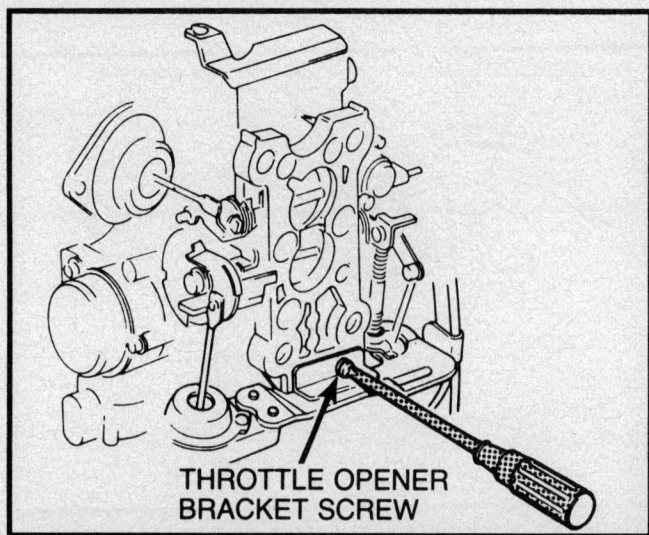

Civic and Accord throttle opener bracket

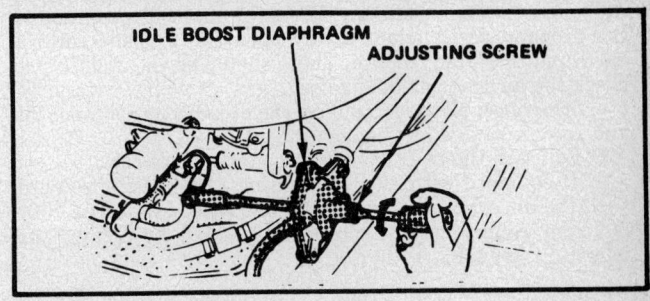

Adjusting idle boost diaphragm

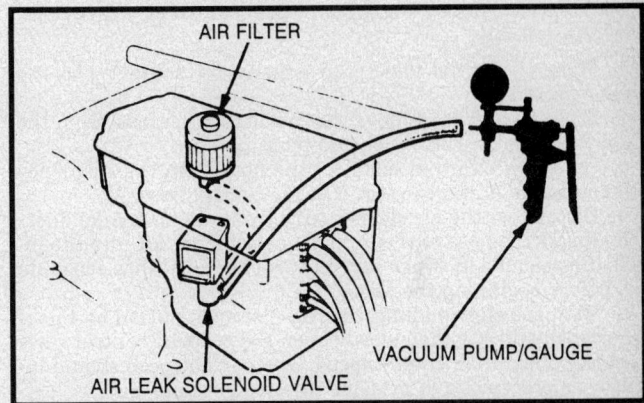

Air leak solenoid valve location—1987–88 Accord

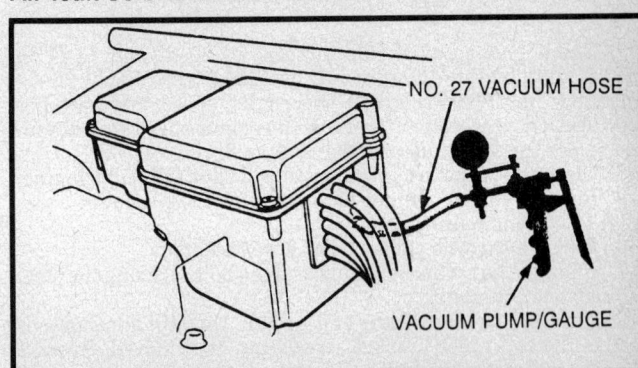

No. 27 vacuum hose location—1989 Accord

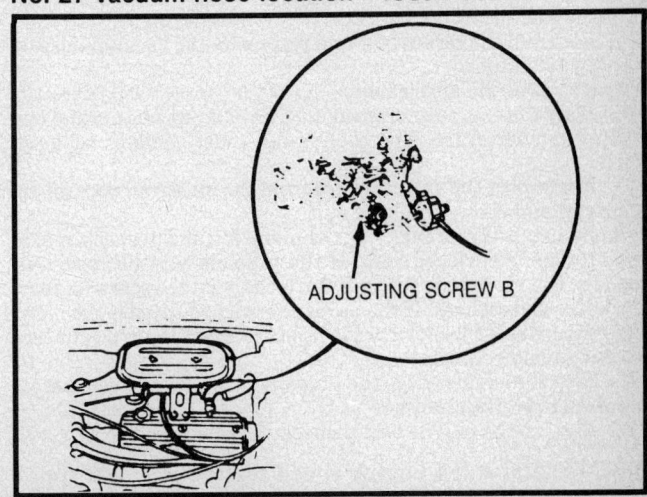

Adjusting screw B location—1987–89 Accord with manual transaxle.

d. With the engine idling, depress the push button on top of the propane device, then slowly open the propane control valve and check for vacuum. There should be vacuum. If not, check the air leak solenoid valve.

e. Reconnect all hoses, remove the propane enrichment kit and reconnect the air cleaner intake tube.

f. Reinstall the mixture adjusting screw hole cap.

g. If equipped with air conditioning, check the idle speed with the air conditioning on. The idle speed should be 700–800 rpm. Adjust the idle speed, if necessary, by turning the adjusting screw B.

1987–89 ACCORD WITH AUTOMATIC TRANSAXLE

NOTE: The following procedure requires a propane enrichment kit.

1. Make the initial idle speed adjustment according to the proper procedure.

2. Stop the engine, remove the inside vacuum hose from the idle boost throttle controller and plug the hose.

3. On 1988 Accord, disconnect the hose from the frequency solenoid valve A and connect it to air control valve A.

4. Disconnect the air cleaner tube from the air intake duct.

5. Insert the hose of the propane enrichment kit into the intake tube about 4 in. Make sure the propane bottle has adequate gas before beginning the test.

6. With the engine idling, depress the push button on top of the propane device, then slowly open the propane control valve to obtain maximum engine speed. The engine speed should increase as percentage of propane injected goes up.

NOTE: Open the propane control valve slowly; a sudden burst of propane may stall the engine.

7. The engine speed should increase by 20–40 rpm in **D** on 1987 Accord, by 110–160 rpm in **D** on 1988 Accord and by 20–40 rpm in **P** on 1989 Accord. If the engine speed increases per specification, proceed to Step 19. If the engine speed does not increase per specification, proceed to Step 8.

8. Close the propane control valve and shut **OFF** the engine.

9. Remove the air cleaner and disconnect the vacuum hoses from the fast idle unloader.

10. Pull the throttle cable out of it's bracket.

11. Remove the carburetor nuts and the bolt securing the steel tubing vacuum manifold.

12. Lift the carburetor clear of it's studs, then tilt it backwards so the idle controller bracket screws can be removed. Remove the idle controller bracket.

13. Remove the mixture adjusting screw hole cap, then reinstall the idle controller bracket.

14. Reinstall the carburetor and reconnect the vacuum hose to the fast idle unloader.

15. Reinstall the air cleaner.

16. Start the engine and warm it up until it reaches normal operating temperature. The cooling fan must come on at least once.

17. Disconnect the vacuum hose from the intake air control diaphragm and clamp the hose end.

18. Reinstall the propane enrichment kit and recheck maximum propane enriched rpm. If the propane enriched speed is too low, the mixture is too rich: turn the mixture screw ¼ turn clockwise and recheck. If the propane enriched speed is too high, the mixture is too lean; turn the mixture screw ¼ turn counterclockwise and recheck.

19. Stop the engine, close the propane control valve, remove all plugs and reconnect all hoses.

20. Restart the engine and recheck the idle speed.

NOTE: Raise the engine speed to 2500 rpm 2–3 times in 10 seconds and then check the idle speed.

21. The idle speed should be 680–780 rpm in **N** or **P**. If the idle speed is as specified, proceed to Step 22. If the idle speed is not as specified, repeat the initial idle setting procedure.

22. The intake air temperature must be above 149°F (65°C).

23. Disconnect the vacuum hose from the air suction valve and plug the hose.

24. On 1987–88 Accord, open the control box lid. Disconnect the lower vacuum hose of the air leak solenoid valve, located between the solenoid valve and the air filter, from the air filter and connect a vacuum gauge to the hose. On 1989 Accord, disconnect the No. 27 vacuum hose from the pipe and plug the pipe. Attach a vacuum pump/gauge to the hose and apply vacuum. The vacuum pump should hold vacuum. If it does, proceed to Step 25. If the pump does not hold vacuum, disconnect the control box connector and then apply vacuum. If the pump still does not hold vacuum, replace the solenoid or the No. 27 vacuum hose. If the pump now holds vacuum proceed to Step 25.

25. With the engine idling, depress the push button on top of the propane device, then slowly open the propane control valve and check for vacuum. There should be vacuum. If not, check the air leak solenoid valve.

26. Reconnect all hoses, remove the propane enrichment kit and reconnect the air cleaner intake tube.

27. Reinstall the mixture adjusting screw hole cap.

28. Recheck the idle speed with the automatic transaxle shift lever in gear. The idle speed should be 680–780 rpm.

29. Recheck the idle speed with the air conditioning on and with the shift lever in **P** or **N** position. The idle speed should be 700–800 rpm.

30. Recheck the idle speed with the air conditioning on and the shift lever in gear. The idle speed should be 700–800 rpm.

1987 PRELUDE

NOTE: The following procedure requires a propane enrichment kit. The carburetor must be properly synchronized before making mixture adjustments.

1. Make the initial idle speed adjustment according to the proper procedure.

2. On automatic transaxle vehicles, remove the connector from the frequency solenoid valve A and connect a battery to the terminals of the connector.

3. Insert the propane enrichment hose into the opening of the intake tube about 4 inches.

4. With the engine idling, depress the push button on top of the propane device, then slowly open the propane control valve to obtain maximum engine speed. The engine speed should increase as the percentage of propane goes up.

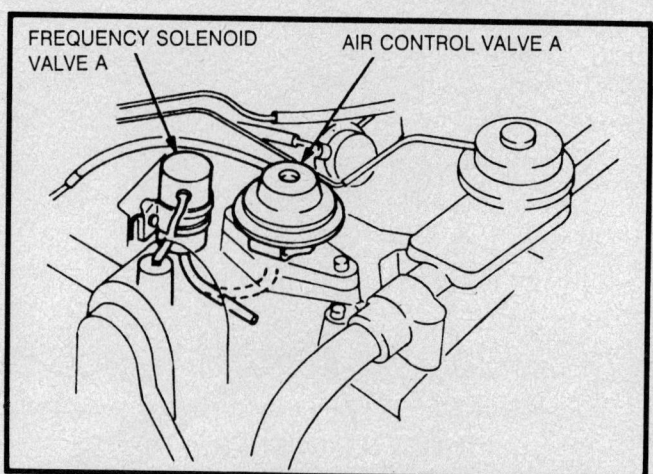

FREQUENCY SOLENOID VALVE A

AIR CONTROL VALVE A

Frequency solenoid valve A and air control valve A location – 1988 Accord

NOTE: Open the propane control valve slowly; a sudden burst of propane may stall the engine.

5. On manual transaxle equipped vehicles, the engine speed should increase by 45–85 rpm. On automatic transaxle equipped vehicles, the engine speed should increase by 105–155 rpm with the transaxle lever in **D3** or **D4**. If the engine speed does not increase per specification, the mixture is improperly adjusted. Proceed to Step 6. If the engine speed increases per specification, proceed to Step 16.

6. Remove the carburetor.

7. Place a drill stop on a ⅛ in. (3mm) drill bit, then drill through the center of each carburetor's mixture screw hole plug.

NOTE: If drilled deeper than this measurement, damage to the mixture adjusting screw may result from the bit.

8. Screw a 5mm sheet metal screw into the hole plug.

9. Grab the screw head with a suitable tool and remove the hole plug.

10. Reinstall the carburetor.

11. Start the engine and warm it up to normal operating temperature. The cooling fan must come on at least once.

12. Recheck the maximum propane enriched rpm. If the propane enriched speed is too low, the mixture is too rich: turn both mixture screws ¼ turn clockwise and recheck. If the propane enriched speed is too high, the mixture is too lean: turn both mixture screws ¼ turn counterclockwise and recheck.

13. Close the propane control valve.

14. Run the engine at 2500 rpm for 10 seconds to stabilize mixture conditions, then recheck the idle speed. If the idle speed is as specified on the underhood emission label, proceed to Step 16. If the idle speed is not as specified, proceed to Step 15.

15. Adjust the idle speed by turning the throttle stop screw, then repeat Steps 12–14.

16. Disconnect the vacuum hose from air suction valve and plug the hose.

17. Disconnect the upper No. 22 vacuum hose from the air leak solenoid valve at air jet controller stay and plug the end of the hose, than connect a vacuum gauge to the solenoid valve.

18. With the engine idling, depress the push button on top of the propane device, then slowly open the propane control valve and check the vacuum. There should be vacuum.

19. If there is no vacuum, inspect air leak solenoid valve.

20. Inspect thermo valve C.

21. Remove the propane enrichment kit and reconnect the connector.

22. Install new plugs into the idle mixture screw holes.

1988–91 PRELUDE

NOTE: The following procedure requires a propane enrichment kit. The carburetor must be properly adjusted before making mixture adjustments.

1. Make the initial idle speed adjustment according to the proper procedure.

2. Disconnect the 2P connector from the EACV and disconnect the hose from the vacuum hose manifold, then cap the hose end.

3. Disconnect the cap from the vacuum hose manifold. If equipped with air conditioning, disconnect the vacuum hose from the vacuum hose manifold. Disconnect the air cleaner intake tube from the air intake duct. Note the engine speed when starting the engine and that the idle speed is stable.

4. Insert the propane enrichment hose into the opening of the intake tube about 4 in.

5. With the engine idling, depress the push button on top of the propane device, then slowly open the propane control valve to obtain maximum engine speed. The engine speed should increase as the percentage of propane goes up.

NOTE: Open the propane control valve slowly; a sudden burst of propane may stall the engine.

6. The idle rpm should increase by 150–190 rpm on vehicles with manual transaxle and 40–60 rpm on automatic transaxle vehicles in **D**. If the engine speed does not increase per specification, the mixture is improperly adjusted. Proceed to Step 7. If the engine speed increases as specified, proceed to Step 8.

7. Remove the mixture adjusting screw hole caps and recheck the maximum propane enriched rpm. If the propane enriched speed is too low, the mixture is too rich; turn both mixture screws ¼ turn clockwise and recheck. If the propane enriched speed is too high, the mixture is too lean; turn both mixture screws ¼ turn counterclockwise and recheck.

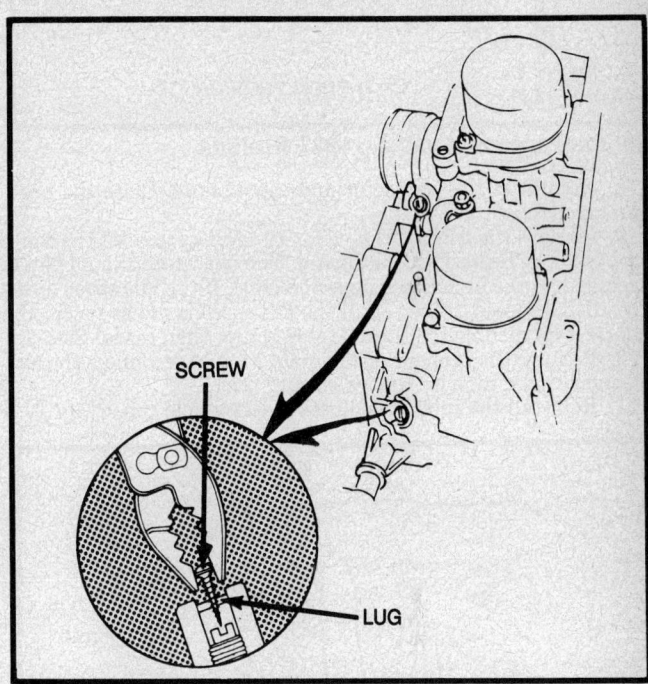

Mixture screw plug removal – 1987 Prelude

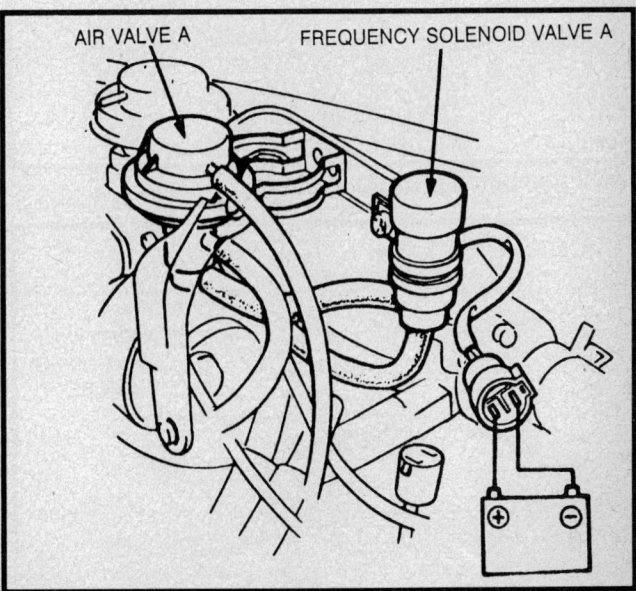

Battery connection to frequency solenoid valve A – 1987 Prelude

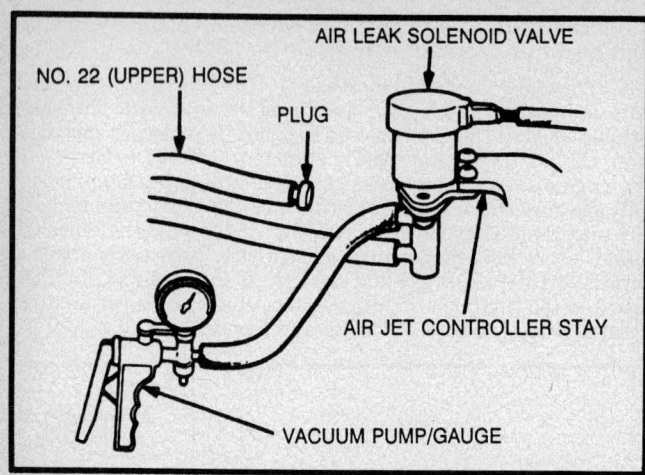

Air leak solenoid valve—1987 Prelude

8. Reconnect the connector and cap or hose. Close the propane control valve.

9. Remove the EFI-ECU fuse for 10 seconds to reset the control unit and recheck the idle speed. The idle speed should be as specified on the underhood emission label. If the idle speed is as specified, proceed to Step 10. If the idle speed is not as specified, adjust it by turning the throttle stop screw, then repeat Step 7.

10. Remove the propane enrichment kit and reconnect the air cleaner intake tube on the air cleaner duct.

11. Reinstall the mixture adjusting screw hole cap.

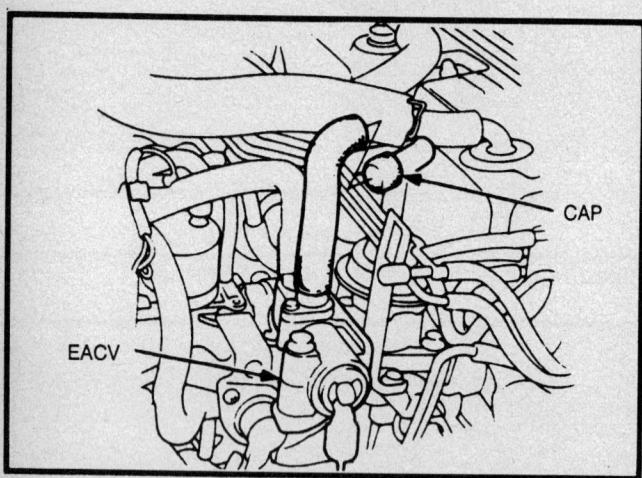

EACV location—1988-91 Prelude

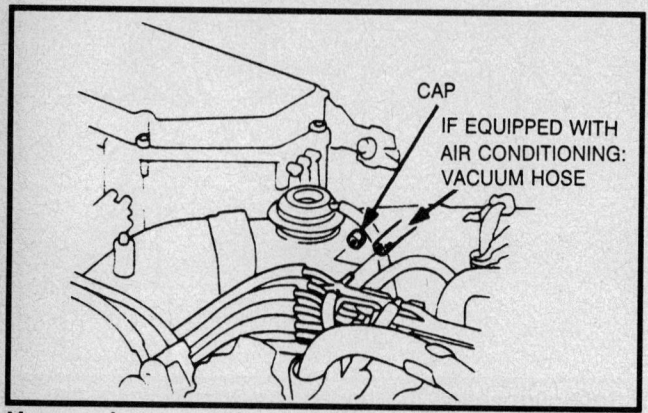

Vacuum hose manifold location—1988-91 Prelude

12. If equipped with air conditioning, check the idle speed with the air conditioning on. The idle speed should be 700-800 rpm for manual transaxle equipped vehicles and automatic transaxle equipped vehicles in **D**. Adjust the idle speed, if necessary, by turning the adjusting screw.

Fuel Injection

For further information, please refer to "Chilton's Electronic Engine Control's Manual" for additional coverage.

Idle Speed Adjustment

EXCEPT 1987 CIVIC, CRX, ACCORD AND PRELUDE

1. Start the engine and warm it up to normal operating temperature. The cooling fan must come on at least once.

2. Connect a tachometer according to the manufacturers instructions.

3. Disconnect the 2P connector from the EACV.

4. Set the front wheels in the straight ahead position and check the idle speed in no-load conditions in which the headlights, blower fan, rear defroster, cooling fan and air conditioner are not operating. Vehicles with automatic transaxle should be checked with the transaxle in **N** or **P**.

5. The idle speed should be as follows:
1988-91 Civic and CRX with 1.5L engine—575-675 rpm.
1988-91 Civic and CRX with 1.6L engine—500-600 rpm.
1988-91 CRX HF—450-550 rpm.
1988-89 Accord and 1988-91 Prelude—600-700 rpm.
1990-91 Accord—550-650 rpm.

6. Adjust the idle speed, if necessary, by turning the adjusting screw. If the idle speed is excessively high on Civic and CRX, check the throttle control system.

7. Turn the ignition switch **OFF**.

8. Reconnect the 2P connector on the EACV.

9. On 1988-91 Civic and CRX, remove the HAZARD fuse in the main fuse box for 10 seconds to reset the ECU. On 1988-89 Accord, remove the No. 11 (10A) fuse in the underhood relay box for 10 seconds to reset the ECU. On 1990-91 Accord, remove the BACK-UP fuse in the underhood relay box for 10 seconds to reset the ECU. On 1988-91 Prelude, remove the CLOCK (10A) fuse from the underhood relay box for 10 seconds to reset the ECU.

10. Set the front wheels in the straight ahead position and restart the engine. Idle the engine with no-load conditions in which the headlights, blower fan, rear window defogger, cooling fan and air conditioner are not operating for 1 minute. Recheck the idle speed. Vehicles with automatic transaxle should be checked with the transaxle in **N** or **P**.

11. The idle speed should be 700-800 rpm for all except CRX HF and 1990-91 Accord. The idle speed on CRX HF should be 550-650 rpm for 49 state vehicles and 600-700 rpm for California vehicles. The idle speed for 1990-91 Accord should be 650-750 rpm.

12. Idle the engine for 1 minute with the headlights on high and the rear window defogger on. On all vehicles with automatic transaxle except 1990-91 Accord, place the transaxle in gear. The idle speed should be as follows:
1988 Civic and CRX standard, 1989-91 1.6L Civic and CRX Si—730-830 rpm.
1989-91 Civic and CRX except HF and Si—750-850 rpm.
1989-91 CRX HF 49 state—600-700 rpm.

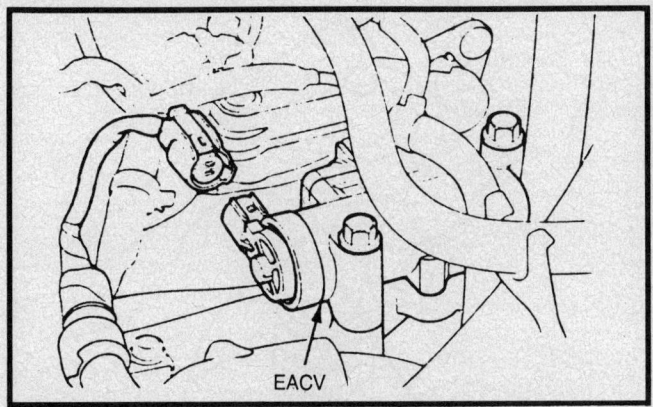

EACV location—Civic and CRX with 1.5L engine

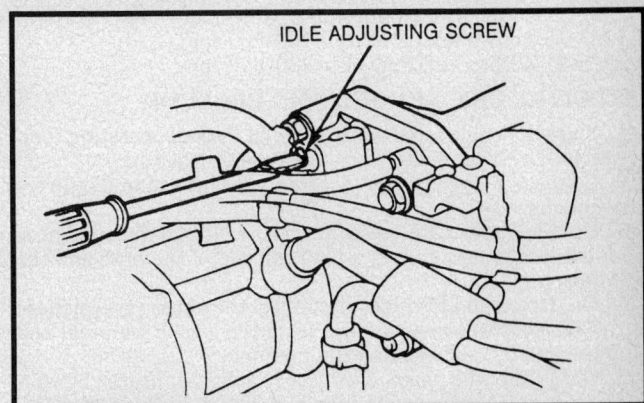

Idle adjusting screw—Civic and CRX with 1.6L fuel injected engine

Idle adjusting screw location—Civic and CRX with 1.5L fuel injected engine

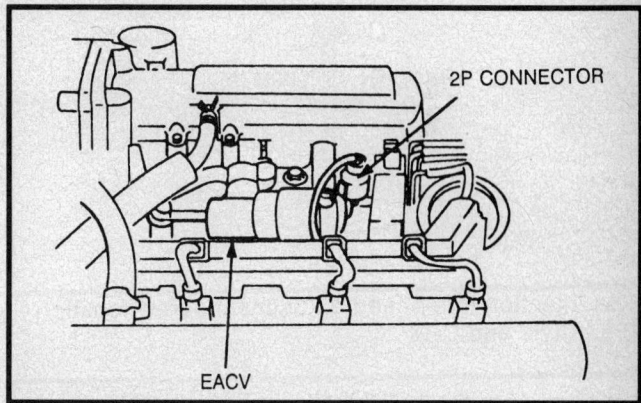

EACV location—1987–89 Accord

EACV location—Civic and CRX with 1.6L engine

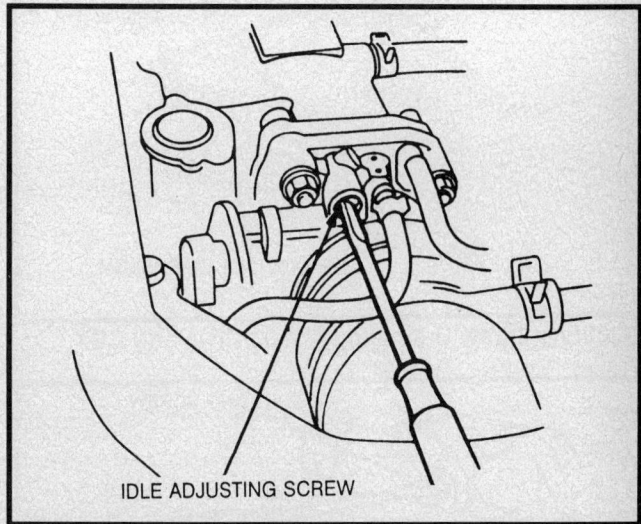

Idle adjusting screw location—1987–89 Accord with fuel injection

1988 CRX HF and 1989–91 CRX HF California—700–800 rpm.

1988–89 Accord and 1988–91 Prelude—700–800 rpm.

1990–91 Accord—720–820 rpm, automatic transaxle in **N** or **P**.

13. Idle the engine for 1 minute with the heater fan switch on high and the air conditioner on, then check the idle speed. Vehicles with automatic transaxle should be checked with the transaxle in **N** or **P**.

14. The idle speed should be as follows:

1988 Civic and CRX except HF—730–830 rpm.

1988–91 CRX HF—700–800 rpm.

1989–91 Civic, CRX except HF, 1.5L Civic Wagon and 1.6L Civic Wagon with manual transaxle—750–850 rpm.

1.6L Civic Wagon with automatic transaxle—770–870 rpm.
1987–89 Accord and Prelude—700–800 rpm.
1990–91 Accord and Prelude—720–820 rpm.

1987 CIVIC, CRX, ACCORD AND PRELUDE

1. Start the engine and warm it up to normal operating temperature. The cooling fan must come on at least once.

2. Connect a tachometer according to the manufacturers instructions.

3. On Civic and CRX, disconnect the No. 10 vacuum hose from the intake manifold and plug the end of the hose and the manifold.

4. On Accord and Prelude, disconnect the upper vacuum hose of the idle control solenoid valve from the intake manifold and plug the end of the hose and the manifold.

5. Check the idle speed with the headlights, heater blower, rear window defogger, cooling fan and air conditioner off. Vehi-

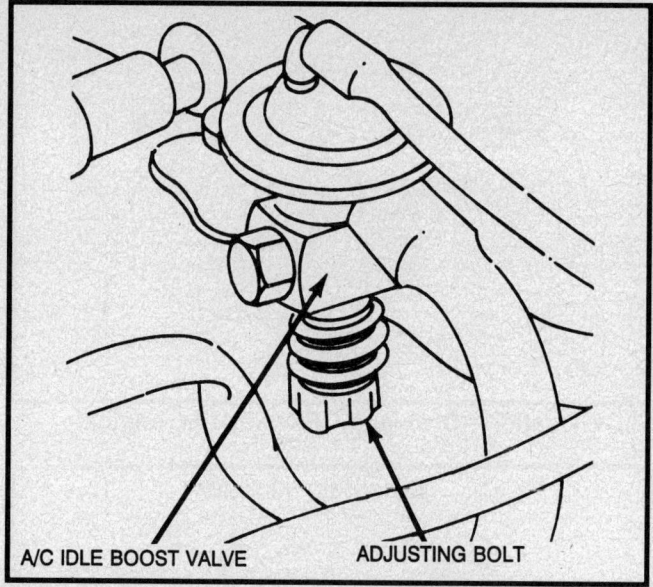

Air conditioner idle boost valve location—1987 Accord and Prelude

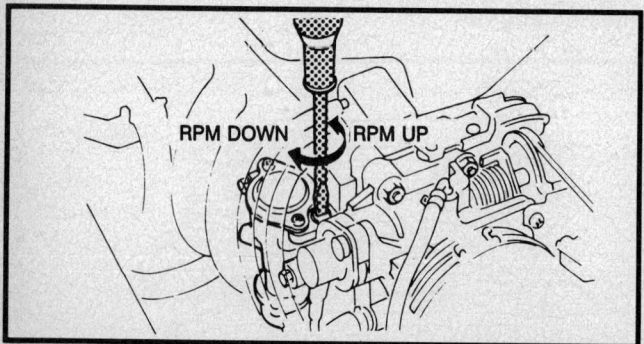

Fuel injection idle speed adjustment screw location—1987 Civic and CRX

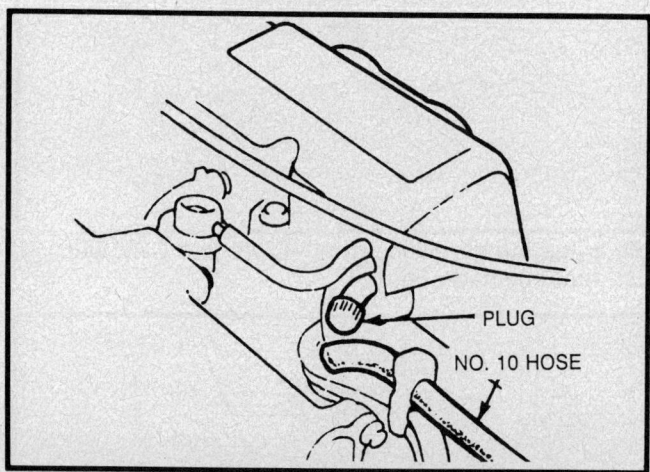

No. 10 vacuum hose location—1987 Civic and CRX

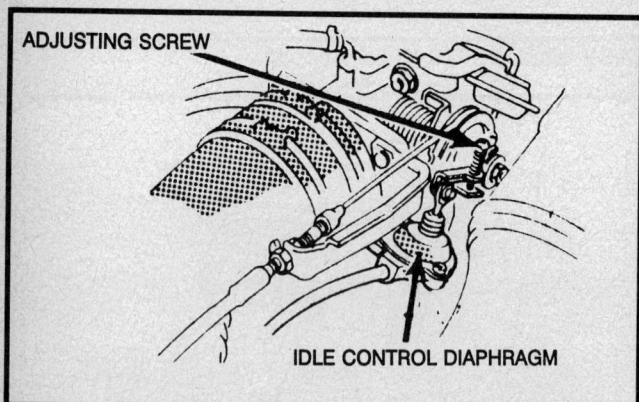

Adjusting screw B location—1987 Civic and CRX

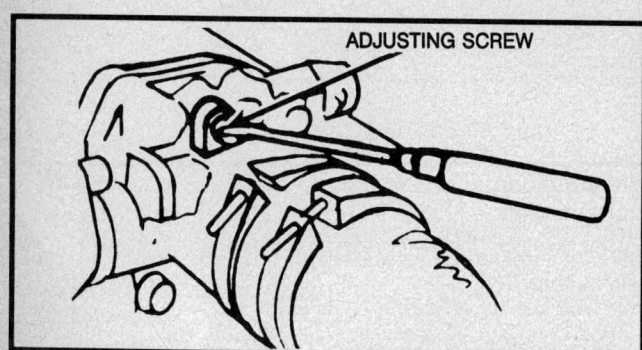

Fuel injection idle speed adjustment screw location—1987 Accord and Prelude

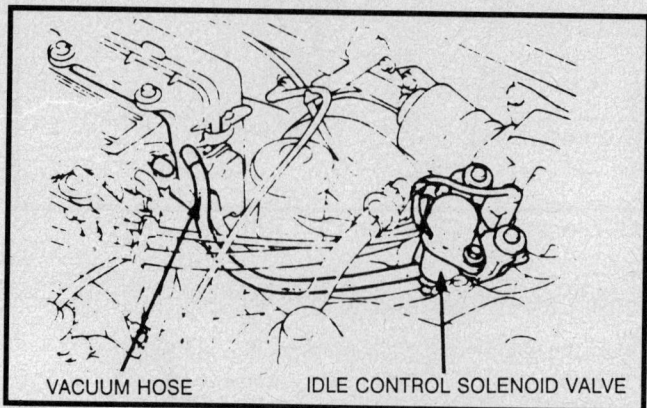

Idle control solenoid valve location—1987 Accord and Prelude

cles with automatic transaxle should be checked with the transaxle in **N** or **P**.

6. The idle speed should be 700–800 rpm. Adjust the idle speed, if necessary, by turning the adjusting screw on the top of the throttle body.

7. Check the idle speed with the heater fan switch on high and the air conditioner on. The idle speed should maintain 700–800 rpm. Adjust the idle speed, if necessary, by turning adjusting screw B on Civic and CRX or by turning the adjusting bolt on the air conditioner idle boost valve on Accord and Prelude.

8. After adjustment, connect the No. 10 vacuum hose on Civic and CRX or connect the idle control solenoid valve vacuum hose on Accord and Prelude.

9. On Accord and Prelude with automatic transaxle, after adjusting the idle speed, check that the idle remains within the specified limit when shifted into **D3** or **D4**. Check the idle speed with the headlights, heater blower, rear window defroster and cooling fan on but the air conditioner off. It should be the same as normal idle speed.

Idle Mixture Adjustment

The idle mixture is electronically controlled and is not adjustable.

Fuel Injector

Removal and Installation

EXCEPT 1.5L ENGINE WITH DUAL POINT FUEL INJECTION

1. Disconnect the negative battery cable.
2. Relieve the fuel pressure.
3. Disconnect the electrical connectors from the fuel injectors.
4. Disconnect the vacuum hose and fuel return hose from the fuel pressure regulator.

NOTE: Place a rag or shop towel over the hose and tube before disconnecting them.

5. Disconnect the fuel line from the fuel pipe.
6. On 1988–91 Prelude, disconnect the EACV from the intake manifold.
7. Remove the fuel pipe retainer nuts and the fuel pipe.
8. Remove the injectors from the intake manifold.
To install:
9. Slide new cushion rings onto the injectors.
10. Coat new O-rings with clean engine oil and install them on the injectors.
11. Insert the injectors into the fuel pipe first.
12. Coat new seal rings with clean engine oil and press them into the intake manifold.
13. Install the injectors and fuel pipe assembly in the intake manifold.

NOTE: To prevent damage to the O-rings, install the injectors in the fuel pipe first, then install them in the intake manifold.

14. Align the center line marking on the fuel injector with the mark on the fuel pipe.
15. Install and tighten the fuel pipe retainer nuts.
16. Connect the fuel line to the fuel pipe and the vacuum hose and fuel return line to the pressure regulator.
17. Connect the electrical connectors to the injectors.
18. Connect the negative battery cable and turn the ignition switch **ON** for 2 seconds, but do not operate the starter. Repeat 2–3 times and check for fuel leaks.

1.5L ENGINE WITH DUAL POINT FUEL INJECTION

1. Disconnect the negative battery cable.
2. Relieve the fuel pressure.

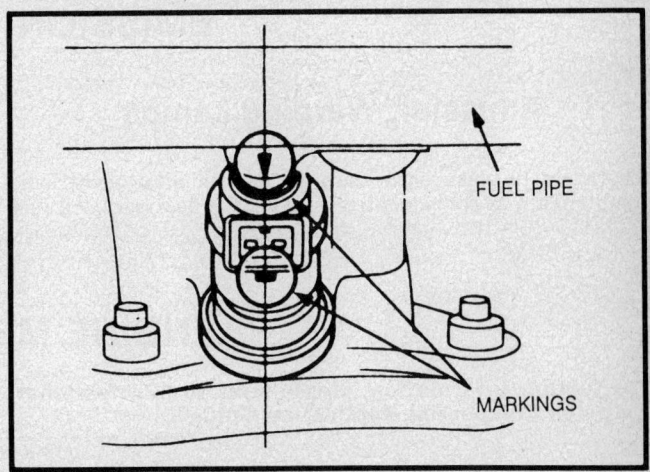

Aligning the fuel injector and fuel pipe marks

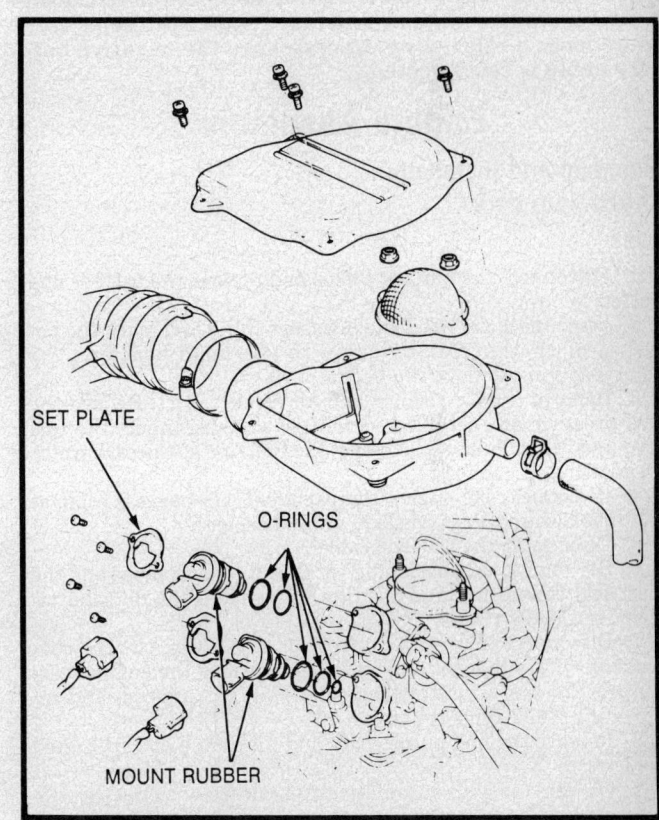

Fuel injector installation—1.5L engine with dual-point fuel injection

3. Remove the air intake chamber.
4. Disconnect the electrical connector from the fuel injector.
5. Loosen the screws and remove the injector from the throttle body. Place a rag or shop towel over the throttle body after removal.
6. Installation is the reverse of the removal procedure. Use new O-rings and coat them with engine oil prior to installation. After the injector is inserted, make sure it turns smoothly approximately 30 degrees.
7. Before installing the air intake chamber, connect the negative battery cable and turn the ignition switch **ON** for approximately 2 seconds. Repeat 2–3 times and check for fuel leaks.

EMISSION CONTROLS

Emission Warning Lamps

There are no dashboard warning lamps indicating periodic maintenance or component replacement is necessary. All fuel injected and some carbureted vehicles are equipped with a CHECK ENGINE light. This light comes on momentarily each time the ignition is turned **ON**. It will also come on and remain on when there is a malfunction in the fuel injection or carburetion system.

ENGINE MECHANICAL

For further information, please refer to "Professional Emission Component Application Guide".

NOTE: Disconnecting the negative battery cable on some vehicles may interfere with the functions of the on board computer systems and may require the computer to undergo a relearning process, once the negative battery cable is reconnected.

Engine Assembly

Removal and Installation

CIVIC AND CRX

1987

1. Disconnect the battery cables and remove the battery and battery mount.
2. Disconnect the windshield washer tubes and mark the position of the hood in relation to the hood brackets for reinstallation. Remove the hood.
3. Remove the air cleaner and air cleaner duct. Relieve the fuel pressure on fuel injected vehicles and disconnect the fuel feed and return lines. Disconnect the fuel line at the carburetor on carbureted vehicles.
4. Disconnect the engine compartment sub-harness cable at the fuse box and the transaxle ground cable.
5. Disconnect the throttle cable.
6. Disconnect the spark plug wires at the spark plugs and the electrical connectors and vacuum hoses from the distributor. Remove the distributor.
7. Disconnect the No. 1 control box connector. Lift the control box off it's bracket and let it hang next to the engine. Disconnect the No. 2 control box connector, if equipped, and remove the No. 2 control box.
8. Remove the fuel pump cover and fuel pump on carbureted vehicles.
9. On vehicles with automatic transaxle, remove the throttle control cable by first removing the cable end, then the locknut and finally the cable.
10. Remove the air jet controller, if equipped.
11. Disconnect the power steering pump from it's bracket, if equipped and lay it aside.
12. If equipped with automatic transaxle, remove the center console, place the shift lever in **R** and remove the lock pin from the end of the shift cable. Remove the shift cable retaining bolts.
13. On manual transaxle equipped vehicles, disconnect the clutch cable.
14. Raise and safely support the vehicle.
15. Remove the wheelwell and engine splash shields.
16. Disconnect the exhaust pipe from the exhaust manifold.
17. Drain the engine oil, coolant and transaxle fluid.
18. On manual transaxle equipped vehicles, disconnect the shift rod by removing the pin retainer and spring pin. Remove the shift lever torque rod.

19. On 4WD vehicles, disconnect the control cables and the driveshaft at the transaxle.
20. Remove the halfshafts as follows:
    a. Loosen the front wheel spindle nut.
    b. Remove the front wheel and the spindle nut.
    c. Use a suitable floor jack to support the lower control arm.
    d. Remove the ball joint cotter pin and nut and, using a suitable tool, separate the ball joint from the knuckle.
    e. Slowly lower the control arm with the jack.
    f. Pull the front hub outward, all the way off the halfshaft.
    g. Using a suitable tool, pry out the inboard CV-joint in order to force the spring clip out of the groove in the differential side gears (the groove is in the intermediate shaft when removing the left side halfshaft on 4WD vehicles).
    h. Pull the driveshaft from the transaxle shaft or intermediate shaft.
21. Disconnect the transaxle cooler lines and radiator and heater hoses.
22. Disconnect the speedometer cable. Do not remove the holder as the speedometer gear may fall into the housing.
23. If equipped with air conditioning, loosen the belt adjusting bolt and idler pulley. Remove the compressor mounting bolts, then lift the compressor out of the bracket with the hoses attached and wire it up to the front beam.
24. Disconnect the alternator belt and wire harness and remove the alternator.
25. Attach a suitable engine lifting device and raise the engine just enough to take the weight of the engine off of the engine mounts.
26. Remove the rear engine mount brackets and the bolts from the front and side engine mounts.
27. Check that the engine/transaxle assembly is completely free of vacuum, fuel and coolant hoses and electrical wires.
28. Slowly raise the engine/transaxle assembly approximately 6 in. and stop. Check again that all wires and hoses have been disconnected.
29. Raise the engine/transaxle assembly all the way and remove it from the vehicle. Separate the engine from the transaxle.

To install:
30. Attach the engine to the transaxle and tighten the transaxle-to-engine bolts to 33 ft. lbs. (45 Nm).
31. Position the engine/transaxle assembly in the vehicle.
32. Install and tighten the engine mounting bolts in the following sequence:
    a. Install the engine side mount bolt and tighten snug only.
    b. Install the rear engine mount bracket and tighten the mounting nuts snug only.
    c. Install the front engine mount bolts and tighten snug only.
    d. Install the rear engine mount bolt and tighten snug only.
    e. Tighten the front engine mount bolt to 33 ft. lbs. (45 Nm).
    f. Tighten the engine side mount bolt to 47 ft. lbs. (65 Nm).

g. Tighten the rear engine mount bolt to 54 ft. lbs. 75 Nm).

h. Tighten the rear engine mount bracket nuts to 31 ft. lbs. (43 Nm).

NOTE: Failure to tighten the engine mount bolts in the proper sequence can cause excessive noise and vibration and reduce bushing life. Make sure the bushings are not twisted or offset.

33. Install the air conditioner compressor and the alternator. Install the accessory drive belts.

34. Connect the transaxle cooler lines and the heater and radiator hoses.

35. Connect the speedometer cable by aligning the tab on the cable end with the slot in the holder. Install the clip so the bent leg is on the groove side. After installing, pull the speedometer cable to make sure it is secure.

36. Install the halfshafts. Make sure the spring clip on the end of each halfshaft clicks into place. Tighten the ball joint nut to 33 ft. lbs. (45 Nm) and install a new cotter pin.

37. On 4WD vehicles, connect the driveshaft and the control cables.

38. On manual transaxle vehicles, connect the shift rod, shift lever torque rod and clutch cable.

39. Connect the exhaust pipe to the exhaust manifold and tighten the nuts to 25 ft. lbs. (34 Nm).

40. Install the wheel well and engine splash shields.

41. Lower the vehicle.

42. On automatic transaxle vehicles, connect the shift cable and replace the console. Connect the throttle control cable.

43. Install the power steering pump and belt.

44. Install the air jet controller, if equipped.

45. Install the distributor and the fuel pump and fuel pump cover. Connect the spark plug wires to the spark plugs and the vacuum hoses and electrical connectors to the distributor.

46. Install the No. 2 control box, if equipped, and connect the control box connector. Lift the No. 1 control box onto it's bracket and connect the control box connector.

47. Connect the throttle cable.

48. Connect the engine compartment sub-harness cable at the fuse box and the transaxle ground cable.

49. Connect the fuel lines and install the air cleaner and air intake duct.

50. Install the hood, aligning the marks that were made during removal.

51. Install the battery mount and battery.

52. Fill the crankcase and transaxle with the proper type of oil to the required level.

53. Adjust the accessory drive belts.

54. Adjust the throttle cable and check the clutch pedal freeplay.

55. Fill and bleed the cooling system with the proper type and quantity of coolant.

56. Connect the battery cables, start the engine and check the timing. Check for leaks.

1988–91

1. Disconnect the negative battery cables. Remove the battery and the battery tray.

2. Apply the parking brake and place blocks behind the rear wheels. Raise the vehicle and support it safely.

3. Scribe a line where the hood brackets meet the inside of the hood.

4. Disconnect the windshield washer fluid tubes. Unbolt and remove the hood.

5. Remove the engine and wheelwell splash shields.

6. Drain the oil from the engine, the coolant from the radiator and the transaxle oil from the transaxle.

7. Remove the air intake duct and the front air intake duct.

8. Relieve the fuel pressure from the fuel system, by slowly loosening the banjo bolt on the fuel filler approximately 1 turn.

NOTE: Keep any and all open flames away from the work area. Before disconnecting any fuel lines, the fuel pressure should be relieved. Place a suitable shop towel over the fuel filler to prevent the pressurized fuel from spraying over the engine.

9. Disconnect and tag the engine compartment harness connectors, battery wires and transaxle ground cable.

10. Remove the throttle cable by loosening the lock nut and the throttle cable adjust nut, then slip the throttle cable end out of the throttle bracket and accelerator linkage. Be sure not to bend the cable when removing it. Do not use pliers to remove the cable from the linkage. Always replace a kinked cable with a new one.

11. Disconnect and tag the engine wire connectors and spark plug wires. Bring the engine up to TDC on the No. 1 cylinder. Mark the position of the distributor rotor in relation to the distributor housing and the distributor in relation to the engine block. Remove the distributor assembly from the cylinder head.

12. Disconnect the radiator hoses and heater hoses. Disconnect the transaxle fluid cooler lines. Remove the speedometer cable.

NOTE: Do not remove the speedometer cable holder, because the speedometer gear may fall into the transaxle housing.

13. If equipped with power steering, remove the mounting bolts and power steering belt, then without disconnecting the hoses, pull the pump away from it's mounting bracket and lay aside.

14. Disconnect and tag the alternator wiring, remove the alternator adjusting bolts, mounting bolts and belt. Remove the alternator from the vehicle.

15. Loosen the air conditioning belt adjust bolt and the idler puller nut. Remove the compressor mounting bolts. Disconnect the air conditioning suction and discharge lines, only if it is necessary. Lift the compressor out of the bracket with the air conditioning hoses attached and wire the compressor to the front beam of the vehicle.

NOTE: If it is necessary to remove the air conditioning suction and discharge lines, discharge the refrigerant from the air conditioning system. Be sure to properly discharge the refrigerant into a suitable container and be sure to wear safety goggles and gloves.

16. If equipped with automatic transaxles, proceed as follows:

a. Remove the header pipe, header pipe bracket, torque converter cover and shift control cable holder.

b. Remove the shift control cable by removing the cotter pin, control pin and control lever roller from the control lever.

17. If equipped with manual transaxles, remove the shift lever torque rod, shift rod and clutch cable. On reassembly, slide the retainer back into place after driving in the spring pin.

18. Remove the wheelwell splash shields and engine splash shields. Remove the right and left halfshafts from the transaxle and cover the shafts with a plastic bag so as to prevent the oil from spilling over the work area. Be sure to coat all precision finished surfaces with clean engine oil or grease.

19. On 4WD vehicles equipped with automatic transaxles, remove the cable clip and the control pin. Loosen the shift control cable nut and then remove the control cable.

20. On 4WD vehicles equipped with manual transaxles, remove the cotter pins and the 3 cable bracket mounting bolts. Remove the cable bracket from the rear of the transaxle mount bracket.

21. Attach a suitable chain hoist to the engine block hoist brackets and raise the hoist just enough to remove the slack from the chain. To attach the rear engine chain, remove the plastic radiator hose bracket and hook the chain to the top of the clutch cable bracket.

22. Remove the rear transaxle mount bracket. Remove the bolts from the front transaxle bolt mount. Remove the bolts from the engine side mount. Remove the bolts from the engine side transaxle mounts.
23. Check that the engine/transaxle assembly are completely free of vacuum, fuel, coolant hoses and electrical wires.
24. Slowly raise the engine approximately 6 inches and stop. Check again that the engine/transaxle assembly are completely free of vacuum, fuel, coolant hoses and electrical wires.
25. Raise the engine/transaxle assembly all the way up and out of the vehicle, once it is clear from the vehicle, lower the assembly into a suitable engine stand.
To install:
26. Installation is the reverse order of the removal procedure. Use the following steps to aid in the installation procedure.
27. Torque the engine mount bolts in the following sequence; be sure to replace the rear transaxle bolt and the front transaxle bolt with new bolts:
    a. Side transaxle mount—40 ft. lbs.
    b. Rear transaxle mount bracket—43 ft. lbs.
    c. Front transaxle mount—43 ft. lbs.
    d. Engine side mount—40 ft. lbs.

NOTE: Failure to tighten the bolts in the proper sequence can cause excessive noise and vibration and reduce bushing life. Be sure to check that the bushings are not twisted or offset.

28. Check that the spring clip on the end of each driveshaft clicks into place. Be sure to use new spring clips on installation.
29. After assembling the fuel line parts, turn the ignition switch (do not operate the starter) to the **ON** position so the fuel pump is operated for approximately 2 seconds so as to pressurize the fuel system. Repeat this procedure 2–3 times and check for a possible fuel leak.
30. Bleed the air from the cooling system at the bleed bolt with the heater valve open.
31. Adjust the throttle cable tension, install the air conditioning compressor and belt and adjust all belt tensions. Adjust the clutch cable free-play and check that the transaxle shifts into gear smoothly.
32. Check the ignition timing.
33. Install the speedometer cable, be sure to align the tab on the cable end with the slot holder. Install the clip so the bent leg is on the groove side. After installing, pull the speedometer cable to make sure it is secure.

1987–89 ACCORD AND 1987–91 PRELUDE

1. Raise the vehicle and support it safely.
2. Disconnect both battery cables from the battery. Remove the battery, and then remove the battery tray from the engine compartment.
3. On Prelude, remove the knob caps covering the headlights' manual retracting knobs, then turn the knobs to bring the headlights to the **ON** position.
4. On Prelude, remove the 5 screws retaining the grille and remove the grille.
5. Remove the splash guard from under the engine. Unbolt and remove the hood.
6. Remove the oil filler cap and drain the engine oil.
7. Remove the radiator cap, then open the radiator drain petcock and drain the coolant from the radiator.
8. Remove the transaxle filler plug, then remove the drain plug and drain the transaxle.
9. On carbureted vehicles:
    a. Label and then remove the wires at the coil and the engine secondary ground cable located on the valve cover.
    b. Remove the air cleaner cover and filter.
    c. Remove the air intake ducts. Remove the 2 nuts and 2 bolts from the air cleaner, remove the air control valve. Remove the air cleaner as required.

d. Loosen the locknut on the throttle cable and loosen the cable adjusting nut, then slip the cable end out of the carburetor linkage.

NOTE: Be careful not to bend or kink the throttle cable. Always replace a damaged cable.

    e. Disconnect the No. 1 control box connector. Remove the control box from its bracket and let it hang next to the engine.
    f. Disconnect the fuel line at the fuel filter and remove the solenoid vacuum hose at the charcoal canister.
    g. On California and high altitude vehicles, remove the air jet controller.
10. On fuel injected vehicles:
    a. Remove the air intake duct. Disconnect the cruise control vacuum tube from the air intake duct and remove the resonator tube.
    b. Remove the secondary ground cable from the top of the engine.
    c. Disconnect the air box connecting tube. Unscrew the tube clamp bolt and disconnect the emission tubes.
    d. Remove the air cleaner case mounting nuts and remove the air cleaner case assembly.
    e. Loosen the locknut on the throttle cable and loosen the cable adjusting nut, then slip the cable end out of the bracket and linkage.

NOTE: Be careful not to bend or kink the throttle cable. Always replace a damaged cable.

    f. Disconnect the following wires, the ground cable at the fuse box. The engine compartment sub-harness connector and clamp. The high tension wire and ignition primary leads at the coil. The radio condenser connector at the coil.
    g. Using the following procedures relieve the fuel system pressure by placing a shop rag over the fuel filter to absorb any gasoline which may be sprayed on the engine while relieving the pressure. Slowly loosen the service bolt approximately 1 full turn. This will relieve any pressure in the system. Using a new sealing washer, retighten the service bolt.
    h. Disconnect the fuel return hose from the pressure regulator. Remove the banjo nut and then remove the fuel hose.
    i. Disconnect the vacuum hose from the brake booster.
11. Disconnect the radiator and heater hoses at the engine. Label the heater hoses so they can be installed correctly.
12. On automatic transaxle equipped vehicles, disconnect the transaxle oil cooler hoses at the transaxle, let the fluid drain from the hoses, then hang the hoses up near the radiator.
13. On manual transaxle equipped vehicles, loosen the clutch cable adjusting nut and remove the clutch cable from the release arm.
14. Disconnect the battery cable at the transaxle and the starter cable at the starter motor terminal.
15. Disconnect both engine harness connectors.
16. Remove the speedometer cable clip, then pull the cable out of the holder.

NOTE: Do not remove the holder as the speedometer gear may drop into the transaxle.

17. If equipped with power steering:
    a. Remove the speed sensor complete with hoses.
    b. Remove the adjusting bolt and the drive belt.
    c. Without disconnecting the hoses, pull the pump away from its mounting bracket and position it out of the way.
    d. Remove the power steering hose bracket from the cylinder head.
18. Remove the center beam beneath the engine. On Accord loosen the radius rod nuts to aid in the removal of the driveshafts.
19. If equipped with air conditioning:
    a. Remove the compressor clutch lead wire.
    b. Loosen the belt adjusting bolt.

NOTE: Do not remove the air conditioner hoses. The air conditioner compressor can be moved without discharging the air conditioner system.

c. Remove the compressor mounting bolts, then lift the compressor out of the bracket with the hoses attached, and hang it on the front bulkhead with a piece of wire.

20. If equipped with manual transaxle, remove the shift rod yoke attaching bolt and disconnect the shift lever torque rod from the clutch housing.

21. If equipped with automatic transaxle:

a. Remove the center console.

b. Place the shift lever in reverse, then remove the lock pin from the end of the shift cable.

c. Unscrew the cable mounting bolts and remove the shift cable holder.

d. Remove the throttle cable from the throttle lever. Loosen the lower locknut, then remove the cable from the bracket.

NOTE: Do not loosen the upper locknut as it will change the transaxle shift points.

22. Disconnect the right and left lower ball joints and the tie rod ends.

23. Remove the halfshafts as follows:

a. Lower the vehicle. Loosen the 32mm spindle nuts with a socket. Raise and support the vehicle safely.

b. Remove the front wheel, and the spindle nut.

c. Remove the damper fork and the damper pinch bolts.

d. Remove the ball joint bolt and separate the ball joint from the front hub (Accord) or lower arm control (Prelude).

e. Disconnect the tie rods from the steering knuckles.

f. On Accord, remove the sway bar bolts.

g. Pull the front hub outward and off the halfshafts.

h. Using a small pry bar, pry out the inboard CV-joint approximately ½ in. in order to release the spring clip from the differential, then pull the halfshaft out of the transaxle case.

NOTE: When installing the halfshaft, insert the shaft until the spring clip clicks into the groove. Always use a new spring clip when installing driveshafts.

24. On fuel injected vehicles, disconnect the sub-engine harness connectors and clamp.

25. Remove the exhaust header pipe.

26. Attach a chain hoist to the engine and raise it just enough to remove the slack.

27. Disconnect the No. 2 control box connector, lift the control box off its bracket, and let it hang next to the engine.

28. If equipped with air conditioning, remove the idle control solenoid valve.

29. Remove the air chamber (if equipped).

30. Remove the 3 engine mount bolts located under the air chamber, then push the engine mount into the engine mount tower.

31. Remove the front engine mount nut, then remove the rear engine mount nut.

32. Loosen and remove the alternator belt. Disconnect the alternator wire harness and remove the alternator.

33. Remove the bolt from the rear torque rod at the engine, then loosen the bolt in the frame mount and swing the rod up and out of the way.

34. Raise the engine carefully from the vehicle, checking that all wires and hoses have been removed from the engine/transaxle. Raise the engine all the way up and remove it from the vehicle.

To install:

35. Installation is the reverse of the removal procedure. Use the following steps to aid in the installation procedure.

36. Tighten the engine mount bolts on 1987–89 Accord in the following sequence:

a. Tighten the side engine mount through bolt snug only.

b. Tighten the side engine mount mounting bolts to 40 ft. lbs. (55 Nm).

c. Tighten the front engine mount nut to 28 ft. lbs. (39 Nm).

d. Tighten the rear engine mount nut to 28 ft. lbs. (39 Nm).

e. Tighten the side engine mount through bolt to 28 ft. lbs. (39 Nm).

f. Tighten the rear torque rod-to-frame mount bolt snug only.

g. Tighten the rear torque rod-to-engine mount bolt to 54 ft. lbs. (75 Nm).

h. Tighten the rear torque rod-to-frame mount bolt to 54 ft. lbs. (75 Nm).

i. Check that the rubber damper on the center beam is centered in it's mount on the transaxle. If not, loosen the bolts for the center beam and insulator and adjust as necessary. Tighten the center beam mounting bolts to 37 ft. lbs. (51 Nm) and the center beam transaxle mount nuts to 40 ft. lbs. (55 Nm).

37. Tighten the engine mount bolts on 1987 Prelude in the following sequence:

a. Tighten the side engine mount through bolt on fuel injected engines or the mount-to-frame bolt on carbureted engines snug only.

b. Tighten the side engine mount mounting bolts on carbureted engines to 40 ft. lbs. (55 Nm) or 33 ft. lbs. (45 Nm) on fuel injected engines.

c. Tighten the front engine mount nut to 14 ft. lbs. (20 Nm).

d. Tighten the rear engine mount nut to 14 ft. lbs. (20 Nm).

e. Tighten the side engine mount through bolt on fuel injected engines or the engine-to-frame bolt on carbureted engines to 28 ft. lbs. (39 Nm).

f. Tighten the rear torque rod-to-frame mount bolt snug only.

g. Tighten the rear torque rod-to-engine mount bolt to 54 ft. lbs. (75 Nm).

h. Tighten the rear torque rod-to-frame mount bolt to 54 ft. lbs. (75 Nm).

i. Check that the rubber damper on the center beam is centered in it's mount on the transaxle. If not, loosen the bolts for the center beam and insulator and adjust, as necessary. Tighten the center beam mounting bolts to 37 ft. lbs. (51 Nm). and the center beam transaxle mount nuts to 40 ft. lbs. (55 Nm).

38. Tighten the engine mount bolts on 1988–91 Prelude in the following sequence:

a. Replace the 3 rear engine mount bolts with new ones and tighten to 40 ft. lbs. (55 Nm).

b. Replace the rear engine mount-to-frame bolt with a new one and tighten temporarily.

c. Replace the front engine mount-to-frame bolt with a new one and tighten temporarily.

d. Tighten the transaxle mount bolts to 28 ft. lbs. (39 Nm) for the vertical bolt and 40 ft. lbs. (55 Nm) for the horizontal bolt. Tighten the transaxle mount-to-frame bolt to 54 ft. lbs. (75 Nm).

e. Tighten the side engine mount bolts to 28 ft. lbs. (39 Nm) and the side engine mount through bolt to 54 ft. lbs. (75 Nm).

f. Tighten the rear engine mount-to-frame bolt to 51 ft. lbs. (70 Nm).

g. Tighten the front engine mount-to-frame bolt to 51 ft. lbs. (70 Nm).

NOTE: Failure to tighten the bolts in the proper sequence can cause excessive noise and vibration and reduce bushing life. Check that the bushings are not twisted or offset.

39. Check that the spring clip on the end of each halfshaft clicks into the differential. Use new clips on installation.

40. After assembling the fuel line parts, turn the ignition switch (do not operate the starter) to the **ON** position, so the fuel pump is operated for approximately 2 seconds so as to pressurize the fuel system. Repeat this procedure 2–3 times and check for a possible fuel leak.

41. Bleed the air from the cooling system at the bleed bolt, with the heater valve open.

42. Adjust the throttle cable tension, install the air conditioning compressor and belt and adjust all belt tensions. Adjust the clutch cable free-play and check that the transaxle shifts into gear smoothly.

43. Check the ignition timing.

1990–91 ACCORD

1. Disconnect the battery cables and remove the battery and battery case.

2. Raise and safely support the vehicle.

3. Place the hood in a vertical position and safely support it in place. Do not remove the hood.

4. Remove the engine splash shield. Drain the engine oil, coolant and transaxle fluid.

5. Remove the air intake duct and the air cleaner case.

6. Relieve the fuel system pressure by slowly loosening the service bolt on the fuel pipe about 1 turn.

7. Remove the fuel feed hose from the fuel pipe and the return hose from the pressure control valve.

8. Disconnect the 2 connectors and remove the control box from the firewall.

NOTE: Do not disconnect the vacuum hoses.

9. Disconnect the vacuum hose from the charcoal canister and the charcoal canister hose from the throttle body.

10. Remove the ground cable from the transaxle.

11. Remove the throttle cable by loosening the locknut, then slip the cable end out of the throttle bracket and accelerator linkage.

NOTE: Be careful not to bend the cable when removing. Do not use pliers to remove the cable from the linkage. Always replace a kinked cable with a new one.

12. Disconnect the connector and the vacuum hose, then remove the cruise control actuator.

13. Remove the brake booster vacuum hose and mount vacuum hose from the intake manifold.

14. Disconnect the 3 engine wire harness connectors from the main wire harness at the right side of the engine compartment and remove the engine wire harness terminal and the starter cable terminal from the underhood relay box and clamps. Then remove the transaxle ground terminal.

15. Disconnect the 2 engine wire harness connectors from the main harness and the resistor at the left side of the engine compartment.

16. Remove the engine ground wire from the cylinder head cover and power steering pump bracket.

17. Remove the mounting bolts and the power steering belt from the power steering pump, then without disconnecting the hoses, pull the pump away from it's mounting bracket. Support the pump out of the way.

18. Remove the mounting bolts and belt from the air conditioning compressor, then without disconnecting the hoses, pull the compressor away from it's mounting bracket. Support the compressor out of the way.

19. Disconnect the heater hoses. Disconnect the radiator hoses, automatic transaxle cooler hoses and the cooling fan motor connectors. Remove the radiator/cooling fan assembly.

20. Remove the speed sensor without disconnecting the hoses or connector.

21. Remove the center beam.

22. Remove the exhaust pipe nuts and bracket mounting bolts.

23. Remove the halfshafts as follows:

   a. Remove the wheel and tire assemblies.

   b. Raise the locking tab on the spindle nut and remove it.

   c. Remove the damper fork nut and damper pinch bolt and remove the damper fork.

   d. Remove the cotter pin and castle nut from the lower ball joint.

   e. Using a suitable puller, separate the lower control arm from the knuckle.

   f. Pull the knuckle outward and remove the halfshaft outboard CV-joint from the knuckle using a suitable plastic hammer.

   g. Using a suitable pry bar, pry the halfshaft out to force the set ring at the end of the halfshaft past the groove.

   h. Pull the inboard CV-joint and remove the halfshaft and CV-joint out of the differential case or intermediate shaft as an assembly.

NOTE: Do not pull on the halfshaft, as the CV-joint may come apart. Tie plastic bags over the halfshaft ends to protect them.

24. On manual transaxle equipped vehicles, remove the clutch release hose from the clutch damper on the transaxle housing. Remove the shift cable and the select cable with the cable bracket from the transaxle.

NOTE: Be careful not to bend the cable when removing. Do not use pliers to remove the cable. Always replace a kinked cable with a new one.

25. On automatic transaxle equipped vehicles, remove the engine stiffener, then remove the torque converter cover. Remove the cable holder, then remove the shift control lever bolt and shift control cable.

NOTE: Be careful not to bend the cable when removing. Do not use pliers to remove the cable. Always replace a kinked cable with a new one.

26. Attach a suitable lifting device to the engine. Raise the engine to unload the engine mounts.

27. Remove the front and rear engine mounting bolts.

28. Remove the engine side mount and mounting bolt and the side transaxle mount and mounting bolt.

29. Make sure the engine/transaxle assembly is completely free of vacuum hoses, fuel and coolant hoses and electrical wires.

30. Slowly raise the engine approximately 6 in. Check again that all hoses and wires have been disconnected from the engine/transaxle assembly.

31. Raise the engine/transaxle assembly all the way and remove it from the vehicle.

To install:

32. Installation is the reverse of the removal procedure. Attention to the following steps will aid installation.

33. Tighten the engine mounting bolts in the following sequence:

   a. Tighten the rear engine mount-to-frame bolts snug only.

   b. Replace the rear engine mount through bolt with a new one and tighten snug only.

   c. Replace the front engine mount through bolt with a new one and tighten snug only.

   d. Tighten the side transaxle mount through bolt snug only.

   e. Tighten the engine side mount through bolt snug only.

   f. Tighten the side transaxle mount-to-block nuts to 28 ft. lbs. (39 Nm).

   g. Tighten the engine side mount-to-block bolt and nut to 40 ft. lbs. (55 Nm).

h. Tighten the rear engine mount through bolt to 47 ft. lbs. (65 Nm).

i. Tighten the rear engine mount-to-frame bolts to 40 ft. lbs. (55 Nm).

j. Tighten the front engine mount through bolt to 47 ft. lbs. (65 Nm).

k. Tighten the side transaxle mount through bolt to 40 ft. lbs. (55 Nm).

l. Tighten the engine side mount through bolt to 40 ft. lbs. (55 Nm).

NOTE: Failure to tighten the bolts in the proper sequence can cause excessive noise and vibration and reduce bushing life. Check that the bushings are not twisted or offset.

34. Make sure the spring clip on the end of each halfshaft clicks into place. Use new clips when installing.

35. Bleed the air from the cooling system at the bleed bolt with the heater valve open.

36. Adjust the throttle cable tension and check the clutch pedal free-play.

37. Check that the transaxle shifts into gear smoothly.

38. Adjust the tension of the accessory drive belts.

39. After assembling the fuel line parts, turn the ignition switch **ON**, but do not operate the starter, so the fuel pump is operated for approximately 2 seconds and the fuel is pressurized. Repeat 2–3 times and check for fuel leakage.

40. Check the ignition timing.

Cylinder Head

Removal and Installation

CIVIC AND CRX

1987

1. Be sure the engine is cold. Disconnect the negative battery cable.

2. Relieve the fuel system pressure and drain the radiator.

3. Remove the air cleaner as follows:

a. Remove the air cleaner cover and filter.

b. Disconnect the hot and cold air intake ducts, and remove the air chamber hose.

c. Remove the 3 bolts holding the air cleaner.

d. Lift up on the air cleaner housing, then remove the remaining hoses and the air temperature sensor wire.

e. Remove the air cleaner.

4. On fuel injected vehicles, relieve the fuel pressure using the following procedure:

a. Slowly loosen the service bolt on the top of the fuel filter about 1 turn.

NOTE: Place a rag under the filter during this procedure to prevent fuel from spilling onto the engine.

b. Disconnect the fuel return hose from the pressure regulator. Remove the special nut and remove the fuel hose.

5. Remove the brake booster vacuum tube from the intake manifold.

6. Remove the engine ground wire from the valve cover and disconnect the wires from the fuel cut-off solenoid valve, automatic choke and thermosensor.

7. Disconnect the fuel lines.

8. Disconnect the spark plug wires from the spark plugs, then remove the distributor assembly.

9. Disconnect the throttle cable from the carburetor or throttle body.

10. Disconnect the hoses from the charcoal canister, and from the No. 1 control box at the tubing manifold.

11. Disconnect the air jet controller on California and high altitude vehicles.

12. Disconnect the idle control solenoid hoses, if the vehicle is equipped with air conditioning.

13. Disconnect the upper radiator heater and bypass hoses.

14. On fuel injected vehicles, disconnect the engine sub-harness connectors and the following couplers from the head and the intake manifold:

a. The 4 injector couplers

b. The TA sensor connector

c. The ground connector

d. The TW sensor connector

e. The throttle sensor connector

f. The crankshaft angle sensor coupler

15. Remove the thermostat housing-to-intake manifold hose.

16. Disconnect the oxygen sensor coupler.

17. Remove the exhaust manifold bracket and manifold bolts, then remove the manifold.

18. Remove the bolts from the intake manifold and bracket.

19. Disconnect the breather chamber to the intake manifold hose.

20. Remove the valve and timing belt covers.

21. Loosen the timing belt tensioner adjustment bolt, then remove the belt.

22. Remove the cylinder head bolts in the reverse order of the head bolt torque sequence.

NOTE: Unscrew the bolts $\frac{1}{3}$ of a turn each time and repeat the sequence to prevent cylinder head warpage.

23. Carefully remove the cylinder head from the engine.

To install:

24. Installation is the reverse of the removal procedure.

25. Always use a new head gasket and make sure the head, engine block, and gasket are clean.

26. Be sure the No. 1 cylinder is at top dead center and the camshaft pulley **UP** mark is on the top before positioning the head in place.

27. The cylinder head dowel pins and oil control jet must be aligned.

28. Tighten the cylinder head bolts in 2 progressive steps and in the proper torque sequence. First tighten them to 22 ft. lbs. (30 Nm) in sequence and then to 43 ft. lbs. (60 Nm) in sequence.

29. On the 1.3L engine torque the valve cover, 2 turns at a time, to 9 ft. lbs.

30. After installation, check to see that all hoses and wires are installed correctly.

1988–91

1. Be sure the engine is cold. Disconnect the negative battery cable. Drain the cooling system.

2. Remove the brake booster vacuum hose from the brake master cylinder power booster. Remove the engine secondary ground cable from the valve cover.

3. Remove the air intake hose and the air chamber. Relieve the fuel pressure. Disconnect the fuel hoses and fuel return hose.

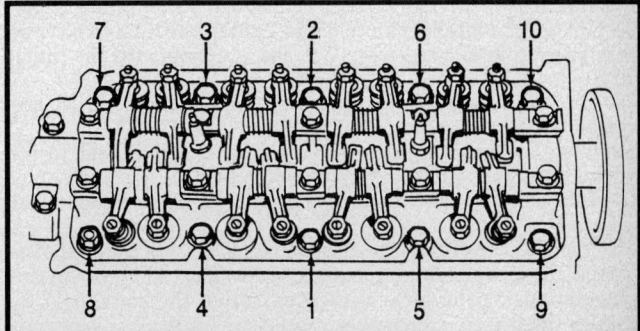

Cylinder head bolt torque sequence—1987 Civic and CRX

4. Remove the air intake hose and resonator hose. Disconnect the throttle cable at the throttle body. On vehicles equipped with automatic transaxles, disconnect the throttle control cable at the throttle body.

5. Disconnect the charcoal canister hose at the throttle valve.

6. Disconnect the following engine wire connectors from the cylinder head and the intake manifold:

    a. 14 prong connector from the main wiring harness

    b. EACV connector

    c. Intake air temperature sensor connector

    d. Throttle angle sensor connector

    e. Injector connectors

    f. Ignition coil from the distributor

    g. Top dead center/crank sensor connector from the distributor.

    h. Coolant temperature gauge sender connector.

    i. Coolant temperature sensor connector.

    j. Oxygen sensor.

7. Disconnect the vacuum hoses and the water bypass hoses from the intake manifold and throttle body.

8. Remove the upper radiator hose and the heater hoses from the cylinder head.

9. Remove the PCV hose, charcoal canister hose and vacuum hose from the intake manifold, and remove the vacuum hose from the brake master cylinder power booster.

10. Loosen the air conditioning idler pulley and remove the air conditioning belt. Remove the alternator belt. If equipped with power steering, remove the power steering belt and pump bracket.

11. Remove the intake manifold bracket. Remove the exhaust manifold bracket, then remove the header pipe.

12. Remove the exhaust manifold shroud, then remove the exhaust manifold.

13. Mark the position of the distributor in relation to the engine block, remove and tag the spark plug wires and remove the distributor assembly.

14. Remove the valve cover. Remove the timing belt cover.

15. Mark the direction of rotation on the timing belt. Loosen the timing belt adjuster bolt, then remove the timing belt from the camshaft pulley.

NOTE: Do not crimp or bend the timing belt more than 90 degrees or less than 1 in. (25mm) in diameter (width).

16. Remove the cylinder head bolts. Once the bolts are all removed, remove the cylinder head along with the intake manifold from the engine. Remove the intake manifold from the cylinder head.

To install:

17. Install the cylinder head in the reverse order of the removal procedure.

18. Always use a new head gasket.

19. Be sure the cylinder head and the engine block surfaces are clean, level and straight.

20. Be sure the **UP** mark on the timing belt pulley is at the top.

21. Install the intake manifold and tighten the nuts in a crisscross pattern in 2-3 steps to 17 ft. lbs. starting with the inner nuts.

22. Be sure the cylinder head dowel pins and control jet are aligned.

23. Install the bolts that secure the intake manifold to its bracket but do not tighten them at this point.

24. Position the cam correctly and install the cylinder head bolts.

25. Tighten the cylinder head bolts in 2 steps. On the first step tighten all the bolts, in sequence, to 22 ft. lbs. (30 Nm). On the final step, using the same sequence, tighten the bolts to 47 ft. lbs. (65 Nm).

26. On the Standard and Si vehicles, install the exhaust manifold and tighten the nuts in a criss-cross pattern in 2 or 3 steps to 25 ft. lbs. (34 Nm) starting with the inner nuts.

27. On the CRX HF vehicles, install the catalytic converter to the exhaust manifold, then install the exhaust manifold assembly and tighten the bolts to 25 ft. lbs. (34 Nm).

28. Install the header pipe onto the exhaust manifold. tighten the bolts to the intake manifold bracket. Install the header pipe on to its bracket.

29. After the installation procedure is complete, check that all tubes, hoses and connectors are installed correctly. Adjust the valve timing.

1987–89 ACCORD AND 1987 PRELUDE

1. Be sure the engine is cold. Disconnect the battery ground cable.

2. Raise and safely support the vehicle. Drain the cooling system.

3. Remove the vacuum hose from the brake booster.

4. Remove the air intake ducts from the air cleaner case.

5. On fuel injected vehicles, relieve the fuel pressure using the following procedure:

    a. Slowly loosen the service bolt on the top of the fuel filter about 1 turn.

NOTE: Place a rag under the filter during this procedure to prevent fuel from spilling onto the engine.

    b. Disconnect the fuel return hose from the pressure regu-

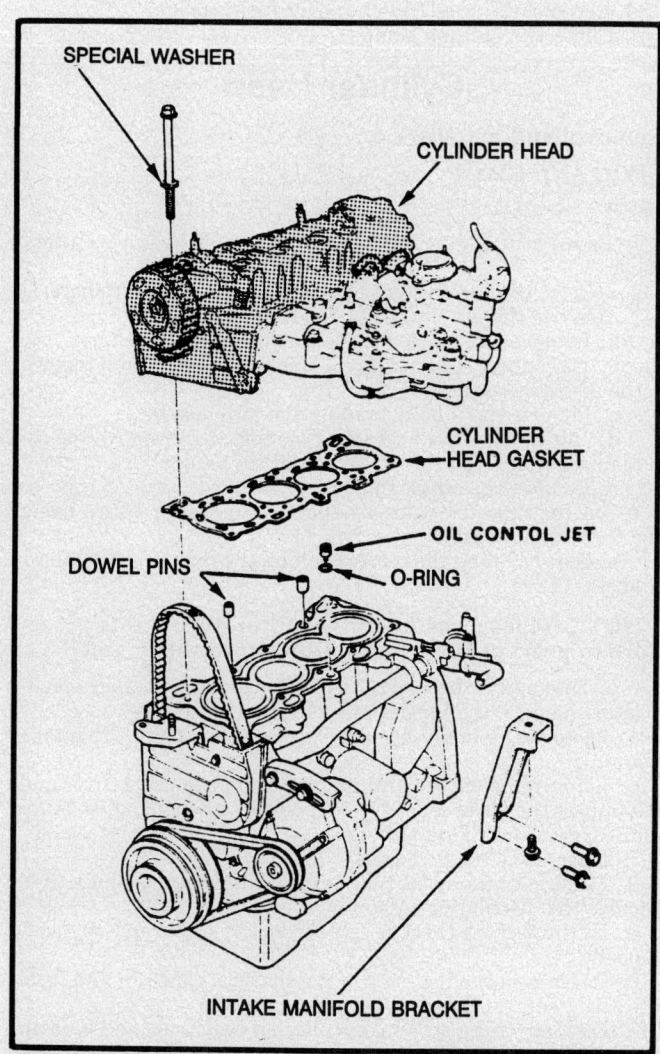

SPECIAL WASHER

CYLINDER HEAD

CYLINDER HEAD GASKET

OIL CONTOL JET

O-RING

DOWEL PINS

INTAKE MANIFOLD BRACKET

Cylinder head installation – 1988–91 Civic and CRX

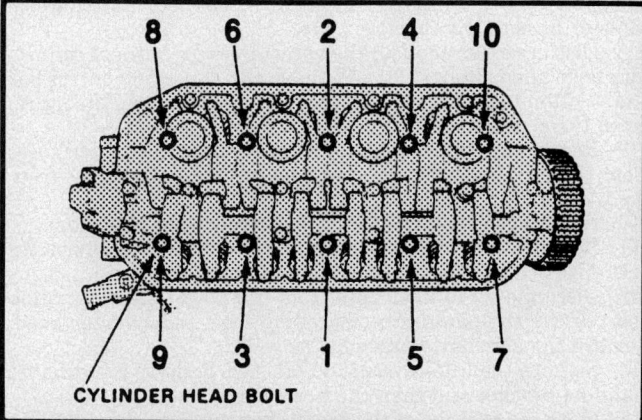

Cylinder head bolt torque sequence—1988–91 Civic and CRX except CRX HF

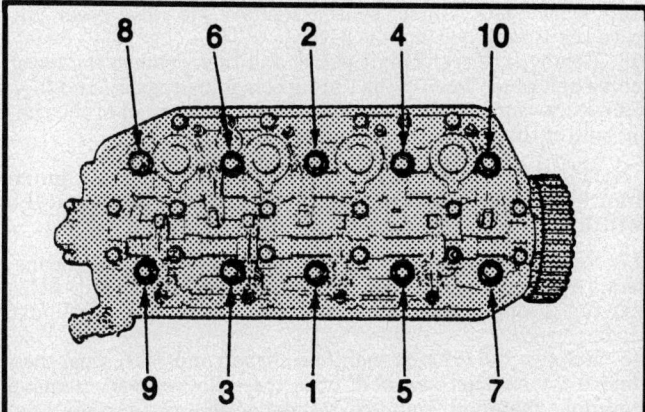

Cylinder head bolt torque sequence—1988–91 CRX HF

lator. Remove the special nut and then remove the fuel hose.

6. Remove the secondary ground cable from the valve cover.

7. Remove the air cleaner, tagging all hoses for installation.

8. Disconnect the wires from the automatic choke and the fuel cut-off solenoid valve.

9. Disconnect the throttle cable and the fuel lines.

10. Disconnect the connector and hoses from the distributor.

11. On fuel injected vehicles, disconnect the engine sub-harness connectors and the following couplers from the head and the intake manifold:

    a. The 4 injector couplers

    b. The TA sensor connector

    c. The ground connector

    d. The TW sensor connector

    e. The throttle sensor connector

    f. The crankshaft angle sensor coupler

    g. EGR valve connector

    h. Four wire harness connectors and clamps

12. Disconnect the No. 1 control box hoses from the tubing manifold.

13. On California and high altitude vehicles, disconnect the air jet controller hoses.

14. Disconnect the oxygen sensor coupler.

15. Disconnect the cooling system hoses at the cylinder head.

16. Remove the power steering pump, if equipped. Do not disconnect the pump hoses. Also, remove the hose clamp bolt on the cylinder head.

17. Remove the power steering pump bracket.

18. Remove the cruise control actuator, if equipped.

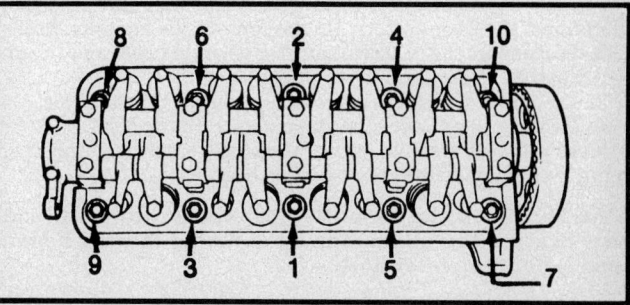

Cylinder head bolt torque sequence—1987–89 Accord and 1987–91 Prelude with SOHC engine

19. If equipped with air conditioning, disconnect the idle boost solenoid hoses.

20. Remove the engine splash guard from under the vehicle, if equipped.

21. Remove the exhaust header pipe and pull it clear of the exhaust manifold.

22. Remove the air cleaner base mount bolts and disconnect the hose from the intake manifold to the breather chamber.

23. Remove the valve cover, upper timing belt cover and then loosen the belt tensioner to remove the belt.

24. Remove the cylinder head bolts and remove the head.

NOTE: Unscrew the cylinder head bolts $\frac{1}{3}$ of a turn in the reverse order of the torque sequence each turn until loose to prevent warpage to the cylinder head.

To install:

25. Installation is the reverse of the removal procedure.

26. Make sure the cylinder head gasket surfaces are clean.

27. Make sure the **UP** mark on the timing belt pulley is at the top.

28. Install the intake and exhaust manifolds and tighten the nuts in a criss-cross pattern in 2–3 steps, beginning with the inner nuts.

29. Make sure the head dowel pins and oil control jet are aligned.

30. Install the bolts that secure the intake manifold to it's bracket, but do not tighten them yet.

31. Position the cam correctly.

32. Tighten the cylinder head bolts in 2 steps. Tighten all bolts in sequence to 22 ft. lbs. (30 Nm) and then to 49 ft. lbs. (68 Nm) in the same sequence.

33. Install the exhaust pipe on the exhaust manifold. Tighten the bolts for the intake manifold bracket.

34. Install the exhaust pipe on it's bracket.

35. After installation, check that the tubes, hoses and connectors are installed correctly.

36. Adjust the valve timing.

1988–91 PRELUDE

SOHC Engine

1. Disconnect the negative battery cable.

2. Bring the No. 1 cylinder to TDC.

3. Drain the cooling system.

4. Remove the brake booster vacuum hose from the tubing manifold.

5. Remove the engine secondary ground cable from the valve cover.

6. Disconnect the radio condenser connector, ignition coil wire and ignition primary connector.

7. Remove the air cleaner cover.

8. Remove the fuel tube from the fuel filter.

9. Disconnect the throttle cable from the carburetor.

10. Disconnect the engine wire harness connectors from the cylinder head.

11. Remove the emission control box and vacuum tank, then disconnect the 2 connectors. Do not remove the emission hoses.

12. Disconnect the charcoal canister vacuum hoses and the upper radiator, heater and bypass hoses.

13. If equipped with cruise control, remove the actuator.

14. Remove the power steering and alternator belts.

15. Disconnect the inlet hose of the power steering pump, then remove the pump from the cylinder head.

NOTE: When the hose is disconnected fluid will run out. Protect the alternator by covering it with a shop towel. Plug the inlet hose.

16. Remove the alternator.

17. Remove the intake manifold bracket.

18. Remove the exhaust manifold bracket and the exhaust pipe.

19. Remove the valve cover and the timing belt upper cover.

20. Remove the crankshaft pulley, then remove the timing belt lower cover.

21. Loosen the timing belt adjust bolt, then remove the timing belt.

22. Remove the cylinder head bolts and remove the cylinder head.

23. Remove the EGR pipe, if equipped, and air suction pipe from the intake and exhaust manifolds.

24. Remove the exhaust manifold shroud, oxygen sensor and exhaust manifold from the cylinder head.

25. Remove the intake manifold from the cylinder head.

To install:

26. Install the cylinder head in the reverse order of removal. Always use a new head gasket and make sure the cylinder head and block surfaces are clean. Check the cylinder head surface for warpage. If warpage is less than 0.002 in. (0.05mm), resurfacing is not required. The maximum resurface limit is 0.008 in. (0.2mm) based on a cylinder head height of 3.54 in. (90.0mm).

27. The **UP** mark on the timing belt pulley should be at the top.

28. Install the intake and exhaust manifolds and tighten the nuts in a criss-cross pattern in 2–3 steps, beginning with the inner nuts.

29. Make sure the head dowel pins and oil control jet are aligned.

30. Install the bolts that secure the intake manifold to it's bracket, but do not tighten.

31. Position the cam correctly.

32. Tighten the cylinder head bolts in 2 steps. Tighten all bolts in sequence to 22 ft. lbs. (30 Nm) and then to 49 ft. lbs. (68 Nm) in the same sequence.

33. Install the exhaust pipe on the exhaust manifold. Tighten the bolts for the intake manifold bracket.

34. Install the exhaust pipe on it's bracket.

35. After installation, check that the tubes, hoses and connectors are installed correctly.

36. Adjust the valve timing.

DOHC Engine

1. Be sure the engine is cold. Disconnect the negative battery cable.

2. Drain the cooling system.

3. Remove the brake booster vacuum hose from the intake manifold.

4. Remove the engine secondary ground cable from the valve cover. Disconnect the radio condenser connector and the ignition coil wire.

5. Remove the air cleaner assembly. Relieve the fuel system pressure.

6. Disconnect the fuel lines. Remove the air intake hose and the resonator hose. Disconnect the throttle cable at the throttle body.

7. Disconnect the throttle control cable at the throttle body, if equipped with automatic transaxle. Disconnect the charcoal canister hose at the throttle valve.

8. Disconnect and tag all the necessary wire harness connectors from the cylinder head. Remove the emission control box and vacuum tank, then disconnect the 2 connectors. Do not remove the emission hoses.

9. Remove the upper radiator hose. Remove the heater hoses from the cylinder head. Remove the water bypass hoses from the water pump inlet pipe.

10. If equipped with cruise control, remove the actuator.

11. Remove the power steering pump belt and the alternator belt. Also remove the air conditioning belt if equipped.

12. Disconnect the inlet hose from the power steering pump and remove the power steering pump from the cylinder head. Remove the alternator assembly as well.

13. Remove the intake manifold bracket. Remove the exhaust manifold bracket and then the header pipe.

14. Mark the position of the distributor rotor in relation to the distributor housing and the distributor housing in relation to the cylinder head. Remove and tag the ignition wires and then remove the distributor assembly.

15. Remove the cylinder sensor. Remove the valve cover. Remove the timing belt middle cover.

16. Remove the crankshaft pulley and then remove the lower timing belt cover. Loosen the timing belt adjusting bolt and then remove the timing belt. Be sure to mark the rotation of the timing belt, if the belt is to be used again.

NOTE: Do not crimp or bend the timing belt more than 90 degrees or less than 1 in. (25mm) in diameter (width).

17. Remove the camshaft holders, camshafts and rocker arms. Remove the cylinder head bolts taking notice of the bolt holes that the 2 longer bolts come out of and remove the cylinder head.

18. Remove the exhaust manifold shroud and EGR pipe, then remove the exhaust manifold from the cylinder head. Remove the intake manifold from the cylinder head.

To install:

19. Installation is the reverse of the removal procedure. Attention to the following steps will aid installation.

20. Thoroughly clean the mating surfaces of the head and block.

21. Always use a new gasket.

22. Make sure the head dowel pins and oil control jet are aligned. Make sure the **UP** marks or cut-out on the timing belt pulleys are at the top. Tighten the cylinder head bolts in 2 equal steps. Apply engine oil to all the cylinder head bolts and the washers. Place the 2 longer bolts in the No. 1 and No. 2 positions in the cylinder head torque sequence. Tighten all bolts to 22 ft. lbs. (30 Nm), in sequence, and then to 49 ft. lbs. (68 Nm) in sequence.

23. Install the intake manifold and tighten the nuts in a criss-cross pattern in 2–3 steps to 16 ft. lbs. (21 Nm).

24. Install the exhaust manifold and bracket and tighten the nuts in a criss-cross pattern in 2–3 steps to 26 ft. lbs. (35 Nm).

25. After the installation procedure is complete, check that all tubes, hoses and connectors are installed correctly. Adjust the valve timing.

1990–91 ACCORD

1. Disconnect the negative battery cable.

2. Bring the No. 1 cylinder to TDC.

3. Drain the cooling system.

4. Relieve the fuel system pressure.

5. Remove the fuel feed and return hose.

6. Remove the vacuum hose, breather hose and air intake duct.

7. Remove the water by pass hose from the cylinder head.

8. Remove the charcoal canister hose from the throttle body.

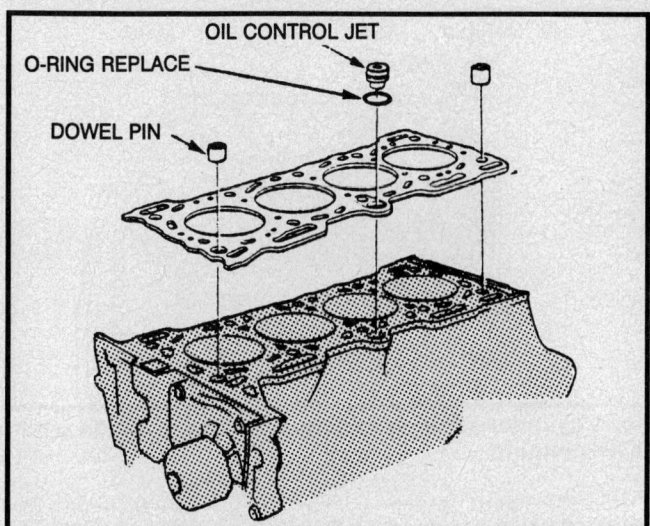

Cylinder head gasket installation—1988–91 Prelude with DOHC engine

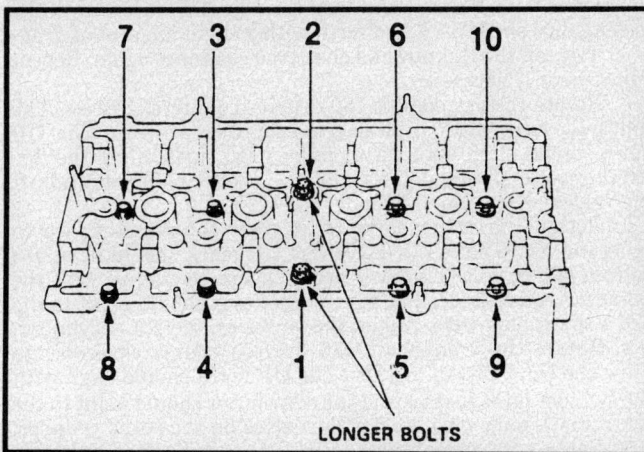

Cylinder head torque sequence—1988–91 Prelude with DOHC engine

9. Remove the brake booster vacuum hose from the intake manifold. On automatic transaxle equipped vehicles, remove the vacuum hose mount.

10. Remove the cruise control vacuum hose.

11. Remove the throttle cable from the throttle body. On automatic transaxle equipped vehicles, remove the throttle control cable at the throttle body.

NOTE: Be careful not to bend the cable when removing. Do not use pliers to remove the cable from the linkage. Always replace a kinked cable with a new one.

12. Disconnect the 2 connectors from the distributor and the spark plug wires from the spark plugs. Mark the position of the distributor and remove it from the cylinder head.

13. Disconnect the 2 connectors from the emission control box and remove the box. Do not disconnect the emission hoses.

14. Remove the connector and the terminal from the alternator, then remove the engine wire harness from the valve cover.

15. Disconnect the engine wire harness connectors, then remove the harness clamps from the cylinder head and the intake manifold.

16. Remove the upper radiator hose and the heater inlet hose from the cylinder head, then remove the heater outlet pipe bracket bolt from the intake manifold.

17. Remove the thermostat assembly from the intake manifold.

18. Disconnect the connector and the vacuum tube, then remove the cruise control actuator.

19. Remove the mounting bolts and drive belt from the power steering pump, then without disconnecting the hoses, pull the pump away from the mounting bracket. Support the pump out of the way.

20. Raise and safely support the vehicle.

21. Remove the front wheel and tire assemblies.

22. Remove the splash shield.

23. Remove the intake manifold bracket bolts.

24. Remove the exhaust manifold and the exhaust manifold heat insulator.

25. Remove the intake manifold.

26. Remove the valve cover and engine ground wire.

27. Remove the side engine mount bracket stay, then remove the timing belt upper cover.

28. Mark the rotation of the timing belt if it is to be used again. Loosen the timing belt adjusting bolt and then release the timing belt.

NOTE: Push the tensioner to release tension from the belt, then retighten the adjusting bolt.

29. Remove the timing belt from the driven pulley.

30. Remove the cylinder head bolts, then remove the cylinder head.

NOTE: To prevent warpage, unscrew the bolts in sequence $\frac{1}{3}$ turn at a time. Repeat the sequence until all bolts are loosened.

To install:

31. Installation is the reverse of the removal procedure. Attention to the following steps will aid installation.

32. Make sure all cylinder head and block gasket surfaces are clean. Check the cylinder head for warpage. If warpage is less than 0.002 in. (0.05mm), cylinder head resurfacing is not required. Maximum resurface limit is 0.008 in. (0.2mm) based on a cylinder head height of 3.935 in. (99.95mm).

33. Always use a new head gasket.

34. The **UP** mark on the camshaft pulley should be at the top.

35. Make sure the No. 1 cylinder is at TDC.

36. The cylinder head dowel pins and oil control jet must be aligned.

37. Install the bolts that secure the intake manifold to it's bracket but do not tighten them.

38. Position the cam correctly.

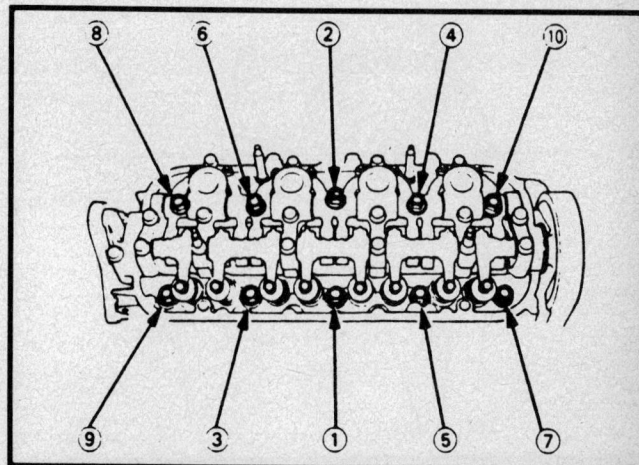

Cylinder head bolt torque sequence—1990–91 Accord

39. Tighten the cylinder head bolts sequentially in 3 steps:
Step 1 — 29 ft. lbs. (40 Nm).
Step 2 — 51 ft. lbs. (70 Nm).
Step 3 — 78 ft. lbs. (108 Nm).
40. Install the intake manifold and tighten the nuts in a criss-cross pattern, in 2–3 steps, beginning with the inner nuts. Final torque should be 16 ft. lbs. (22 Nm). Always use a new intake manifold gasket.
41. Install the heat insulator to the cylinder head and the block.
42. Install the exhaust manifold and tighten the nuts in a criss-cross pattern in 2–3 steps, beginning with the inner nut. Final torque should be 23 ft. lbs. (32 Nm). Always use a new exhaust manifold gasket.
43. Install the exhaust manifold bracket, then install the exhaust pipe, the bracket and upper shroud.
44. Check the ignition timing.

Valve Lash

Adjustment

NOTE: The valves should be adjusted cold. Cylinder head temperature must be less than 100°F (38°C). Adjustment is the same for intake and exhaust valves.

1. Disconnect the negative battery cable and remove the valve cover.
2. Bring the No. 1 piston to TDC. The **UP** mark on the pulley(s) should be at the top and the TDC grooves on the back side of the pulley(s) should align with the cylinder head surface. The distributor rotor must be pointing towards the No. 1 spark plug wire.
3. Adjust the valves on the No. 1 cylinder. Valve clearance is as follows:
Civic and CRX except CRX HF: Intake, and auxiliary, if equipped — 0.007–0.009 in. (0.17–0.22mm). Exhaust — 0.009–0.011 in. (0.22–0.27mm).
1987 CRX HF: Intake and auxiliary — 0.007–0.009 in. (0.17–0.22mm). Exhaust — 0.007–0.009 in. (0.17–0.22mm).
1988–91 CRX HF: Intake — 0.005–0.007 in. (0.12–0.17mm). Exhaust — 0.007–0.009 in. (0.17–0.22mm).
1987–89 Accord and Prelude with SOHC engine: Intake — 0.005–0.007 in. (0.12–0.17mm). Exhaust — 0.010–0.012 in. (0.25–0.30mm).

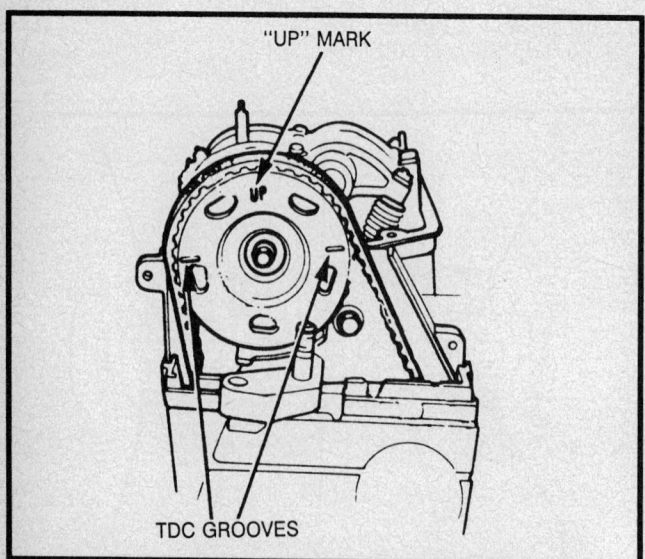

No. 1 cylinder valve adjusting position — Civic and CRX with 1.5L engine

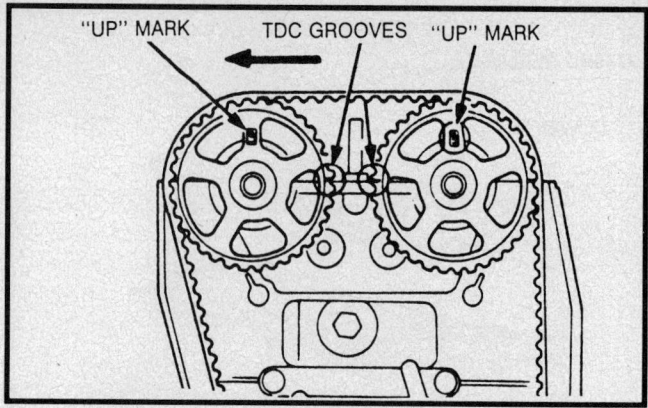

No. 1 cylinder valve adjusting position — Prelude with DOHC engine

1990–91 Accord: Intake — 0.009–0.011 in. (0.24–0.28mm). Exhaust — 0.011–0.013 in. (0.28–0.32mm).
1988–91 Prelude with DOHC engine: Intake — 0.003–0.005 in. (0.08–0.12mm). Exhaust — 0.006–0.008 in. (0.16–0.20mm).
4. Loosen the locknut and turn the adjusting screw until the feeler gauge slides back and forth with a slight amount of drag.
5. Tighten the locknut and check the clearance again. Repeat adjustment if necessary.
6. Rotate the crankshaft 180 degrees counterclockwise. The cam pulley(s) will turn 90 degrees counterclockwise. The **UP** mark should align with the cylinder head surface and the distributor rotor should point to the No. 3 spark plug wire. Adjust the valves on the No. 3 cylinder.
7. Rotate the crankshaft 180 degrees counterclockwise to bring the No. 4 piston to TDC. The **UP** mark should be at the bottom and the TDC grooves should again be aligned with the cylinder head surface. The distributor rotor should point to the No. 4 spark plug wire. Adjust the valves on the No. 4 cylinder.
8. Rotate the crankshaft 180 degrees counterclockwise to bring the No. 2 piston to TDC. The **UP** mark should align with the cylinder head surface and the distributor should point to the No. 2 spark plug wire. Adjust the valves on the No. 2 cylinder.
9. Replace the valve cover.

Rocker Arms/Shafts

Removal and Installation
EXCEPT DOHC ENGINE
1. Disconnect the negative battery cable.
2. Remove the valve cover and bring the No. 1 cylinder to TDC.
3. Remove the rocker arm bolts. Unscrew the bolts 2 turns at a time, in a criss-cross pattern, to prevent damaging the valves or rocker assembly.
4. Remove the rocker arm/shaft assemblies. Leave the rocker arm bolts in place as the shafts are removed to keep the bearing caps, springs and rocker arms in place on the shafts.
5. If the rocker arms or shafts are to be replaced, identify the parts as they are removed from the shafts to ensure reinstallation in the original location.
To install:
6. Lubricate the camshaft journals and lobes.
7. On 1987 Civic and CRX, apply liquid gasket to the mating surfaces of the No. 1 and No. 5 bearing caps and place them in position along with the other bearing caps.
8. Set the rocker arm assembly in place and loosely install the bolts. Tighten each bolt 2 turns at a time in the proper sequence to ensure that the rockers do not bind on the valves. Tighten the rocker arm bolts to 16 ft. lbs. (22 Nm) except on 1990–91 Ac-

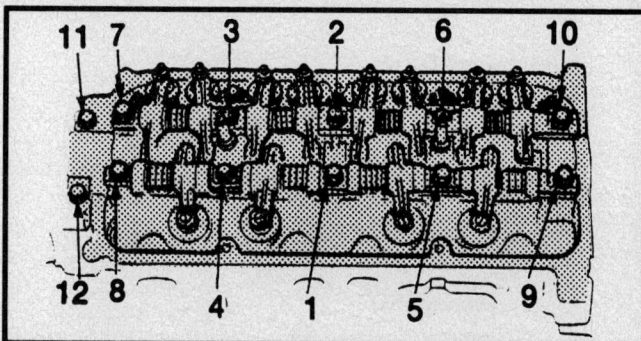

Rocker arm shaft torque sequence—1987 Civic and CRX

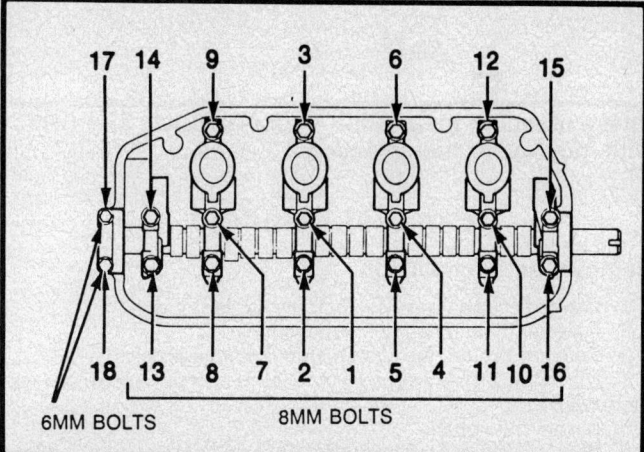

Rocker arm shaft torque sequence—1988–91 Civic and CRX

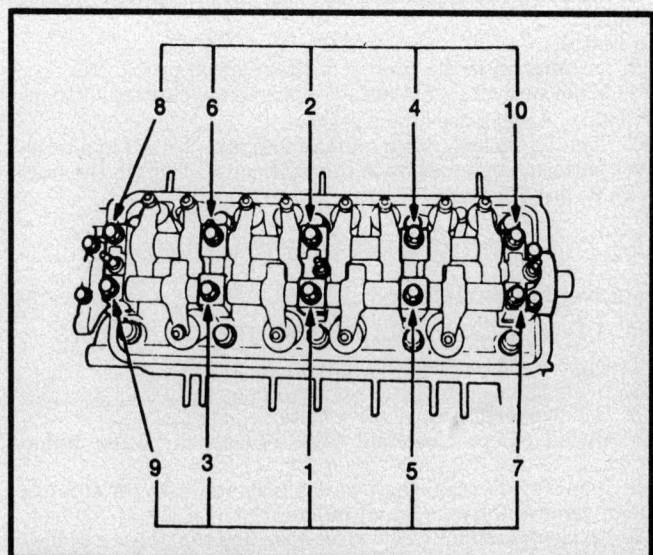

Rocker arm shaft torque sequence—1989 Accord and 1989–91 Prelude with SOHC engine

cord. On 1990–91 Accord tighten the 6mm bolts to 9 ft. lbs. (12 Nm) and the 8mm bolts to 16 ft. lbs. (22 Nm).

9. Replace the valve cover and connect the negative battery cable.

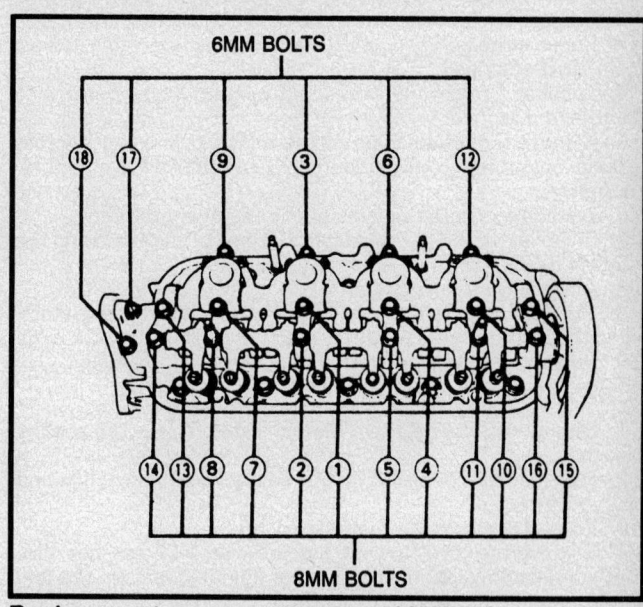

Rocker arm torque sequence—1990–91 Accord

DOHC ENGINE

1. Disconnect the negative battery cable.
2. Remove the valve cover and bring the No. 1 cylinder to TDC.
3. Remove the timing belt cover and the timing belt.
4. Remove the camshaft bearing caps and remove the camshafts.
5. Remove the rocker arms.
6. Installation is the reverse of the removal procedure.
7. Apply liquid gasket to the No. 1 and No. 6 camshaft bearing caps and install them with the rest of the caps. Make sure the caps are installed in their proper positions as indicated by their markings.
8. Tighten each camshaft bearing cap bolt gradually, to prevent binding. Tighten the bolts to 9 ft. lbs. (12 Nm).

Intake Manifold

Removal and Installation

CARBURETED ENGINE

1. Disconnect the negative battery cable. Drain the coolant from the radiator.

Non-hardening sealant application locations—DOHC engine

8–51

2. Remove the air cleaner and case from the carburetor(s).

3. Remove the air valve, EGR valve, air suction valve and air chamber if equipped.

4. Label and remove all wires and vacuum hoses running to the intake manifold.

5. Remove the intake manifold attaching nut in a criss-cross pattern, beginning from the center. Then remove the manifold.

To install:

6. Installation is the reverse of the removal procedure.

7. Clean all the old gasket material from the manifold and the cylinder head.

8. Always use a new gasket.

9. Tighten the nuts in a criss-cross pattern in 2–3 steps, starting with the inner nuts. Tighten the nuts to 16 ft. lbs. (22 Nm).

10. Be sure all hoses and wires are connected properly.

FUEL INJECTED ENGINE

1. Disconnect the negative battery cable. Drain the cooling system.

2. Label and disconnect all required electrical connectors and vacuum lines.

3. Properly relieve the fuel system pressure.

4. Remove the throttle body assembly on 1.5L engines with dual-point fuel injection. On all other engines, remove the fuel injector manifold and fuel injectors.

5. As required, remove the fast idle control valve, the air bleed valve, the EGR valve and all related brackets.

6. Remove the intake manifold retaining bolts. Remove the intake manifold assembly from the vehicle. Discard the gaskets.

NOTE: **1989–91 Accord and 1988–91 Prelude use an upper and lower manifold assembly. Separate the upper manifold from the lower manifold before removing the assembly from the vehicle.**

To install:

7. Installation is the reverse of the removal procedure.

8. Make sure all gasket mating surfaces are clean prior to installation.

9. Always use a new gasket.

10. Tighten the intake manifold nuts in 2–3 steps in a criss-cross pattern starting with the inside nuts. Tighten the nuts to 16 ft. lbs. (22 Nm).

11. Make sure that all hoses and wires are connected properly.

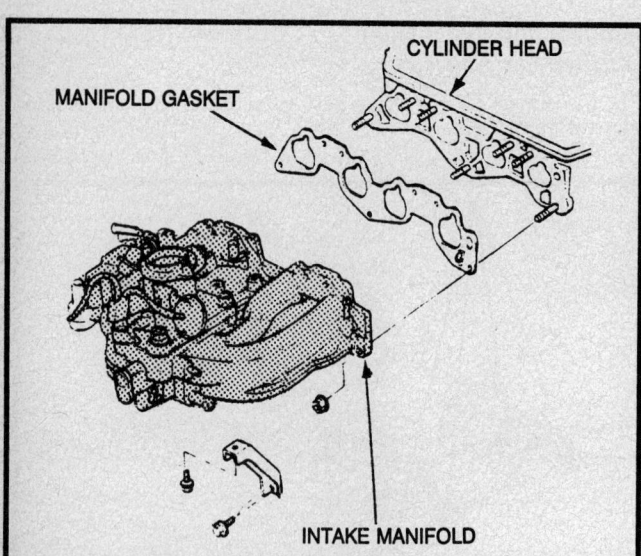

Intake manifold installation – 1988–91 1.5L engine with dual-point fuel injection

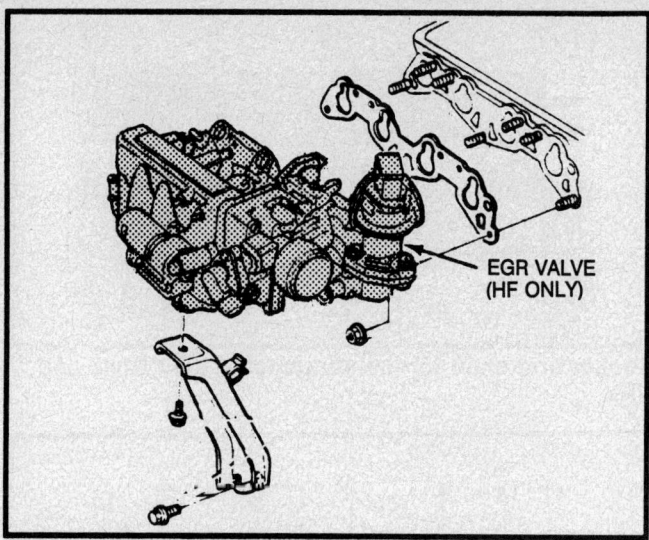

Intake manifold installation – 1988–91 Civic and CRX with multi-point fuel injection

Exhaust Manifold

Removal and Installation

1. Disconnect the negative battery cable.
2. Raise and safely support the vehicle.
3. Remove the engine splash shield, as necessary.
4. Disconnect the exhaust pipe or catalytic converter, as required.
5. Lower the vehicle.
6. Remove the exhaust manifold heat shield.
7. Disconnect the exhaust manifold brackets, EGR tube and oxygen sensor, as required.
8. Remove the exhaust manifold nuts and the exhaust manifold.

To install:

9. Installation is the reverse of the removal procedure.
10. Make sure all gasket mating surfaces are clean prior to installation. Always use a new gasket.
11. Tighten the exhaust manifold nuts in 2–3 steps in a criss-cross pattern, beginning with the inner nuts. Tighten the nuts to 22 ft. lbs. (32 Nm).

Timing Belt Front Cover

Removal and Installation

1987 CIVIC, CRX, PRELUDE AND 1987–89 ACCORD

1. Disconnect the negative battery cable.
2. Bring the piston of the No. 1 cylinder to TDC.
3. Remove all accessory drive belts.
4. On all except Civic and CRX, remove the water pump pulley.
5. Remove the crankshaft pulley bolt and using a suitable puller, remove the crankshaft pulley.
6. Remove the timing belt cover bolts and the upper and lower covers.
7. Installation is the reverse of the removal procedure. Tighten the crankshaft pulley bolt to 83 ft. lbs. (115 Nm) on all but 1989 Accord. Tighten the crankshaft pulley bolt to 108 ft. lbs. (150 Nm) on 1989 Accord.

1988–91 CIVIC AND CRX

1. Disconnect the negative battery cable.
2. Raise and safely support the vehicle.

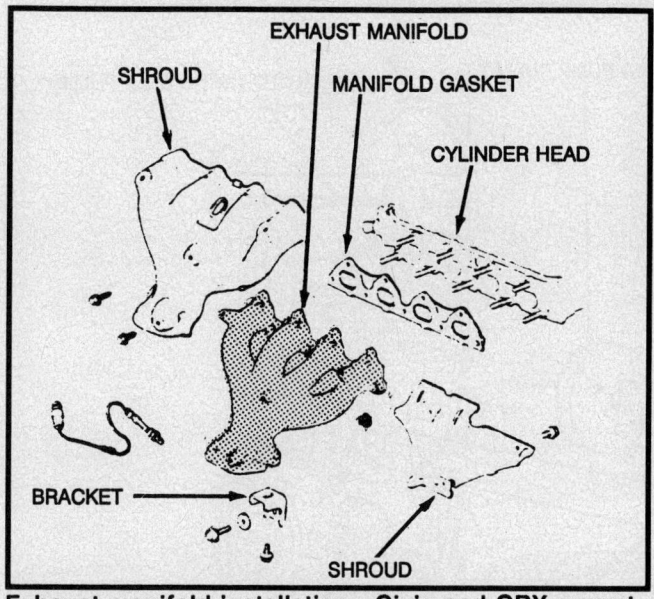

Exhaust manifold installation—Civic and CRX except CRX HF

3. Remove the left front wheel and tire assembly.
4. Remove the left front wheel well splash shield.
5. If equipped, remove the power steering belt and pump.
6. If equipped with air conditioning, remove the adjust pulley with bracket and the belt.
7. Remove the power steering bracket, loosen the alternator adjust bolt and through bolt and remove the alternator belt.

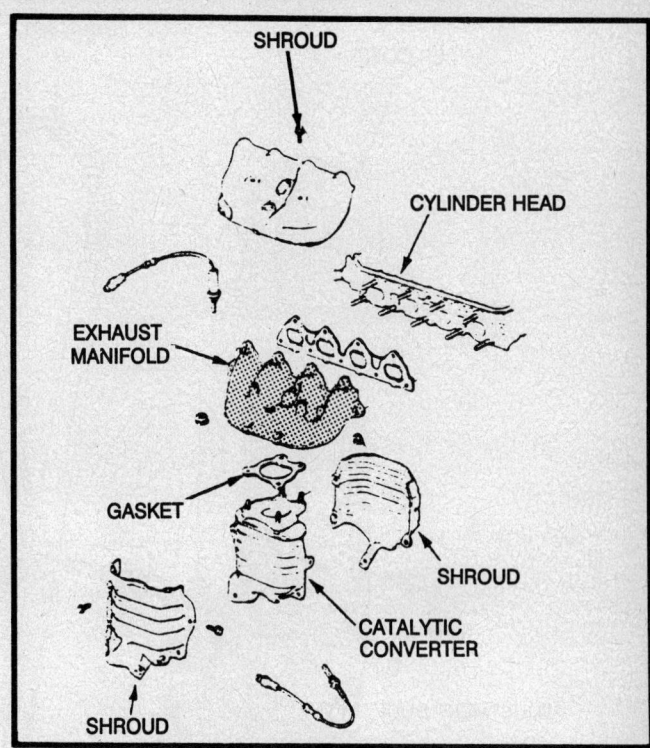

Exhaust manifold installation—CRX HF

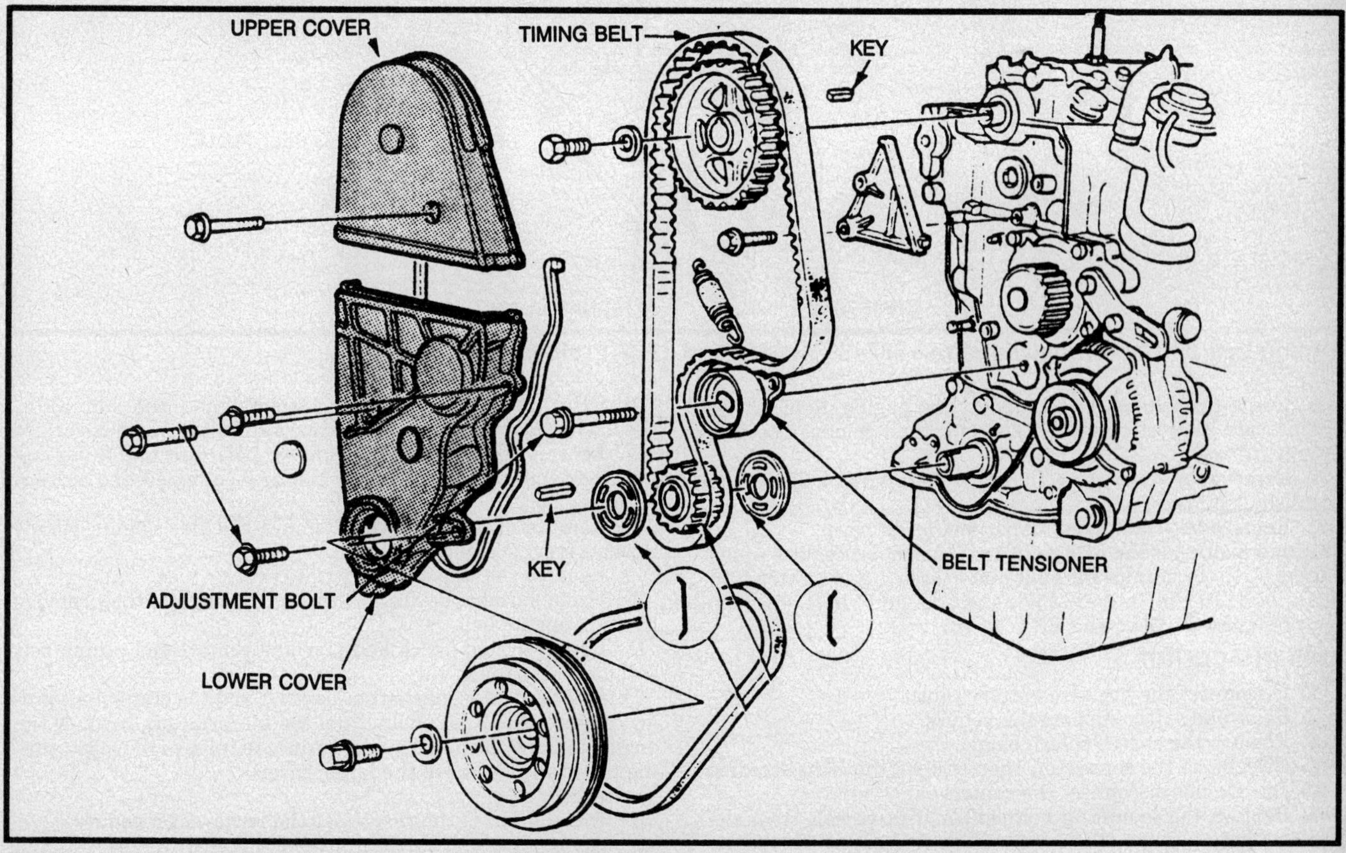

Timing belt and cover installation—1987 Civic and CRX

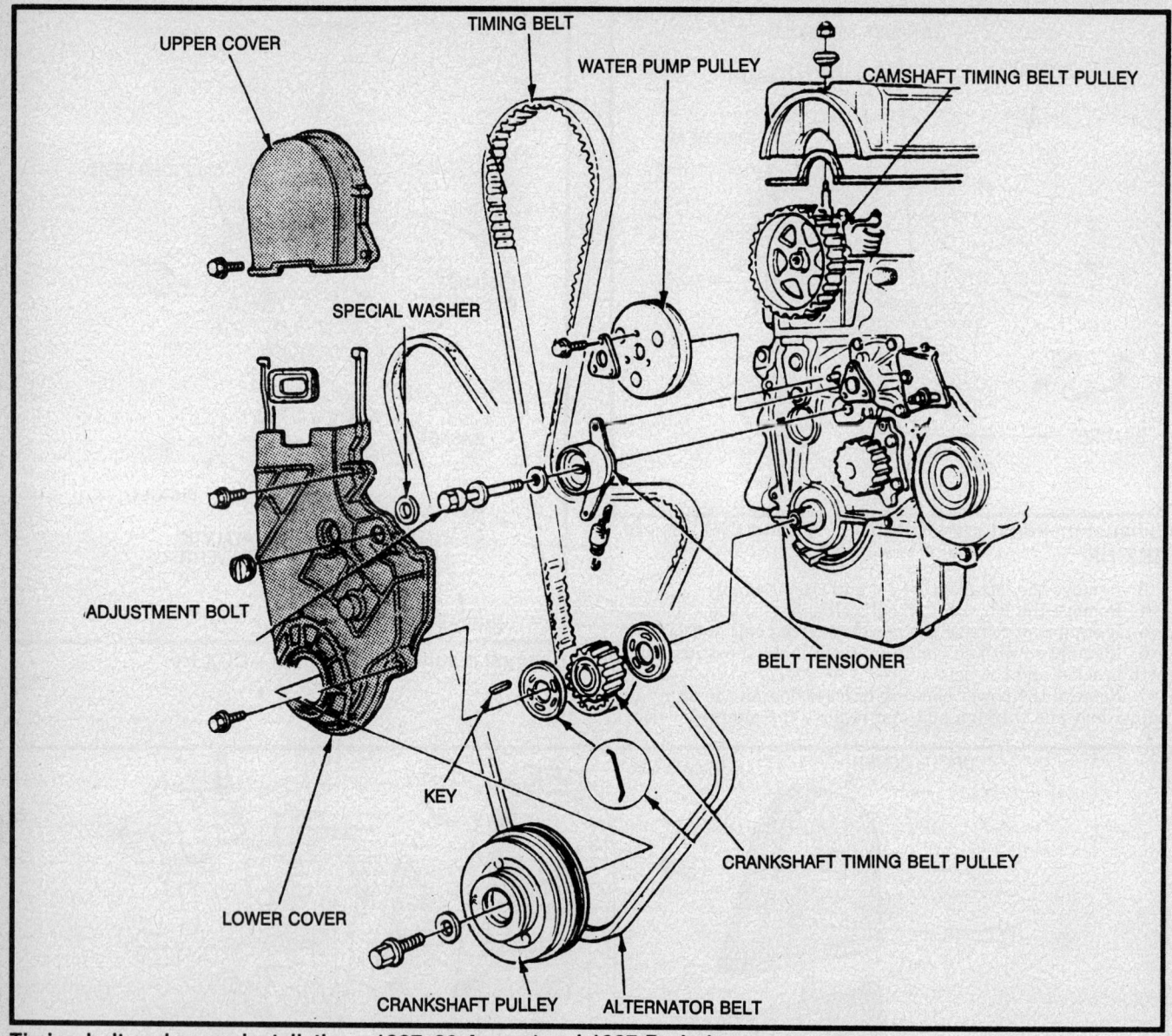

Timing belt and cover installation—1987–89 Accord and 1987 Prelude

8. Use a suitable device to support the engine. Remove the engine side support bolts and nut and then remove the side mount rubber.

9. Remove the valve cover, the crankshaft pulley bolt and the crankshaft pulley.

10. Remove the timing belt upper and lower cover.

11. Installation is the reverse of the removal procedure. Apply engine oil to the crankshaft pulley bolt threads and tighten it to 83 ft. lbs. (115 Nm) on 1988 Civic and CRX and 119 ft. lbs. (165 Nm) on 1989–91 Civic and CRX.

1990–91 ACCORD

1. Disconnect the negative battery cable.
2. Raise and safely support the vehicle.
3. Remove the engine splash shield.
4. Disconnect the connector, then remove the cruise control actuator. Do not disconnect the control cable.
5. Remove the mounting bolt, nut and drive belt from the power steering pump, then without disconnecting the hoses, pull the pump away from the mounting bracket.

6. Disconnect the alternator terminal and the connector, then remove the engine wire harness from the valve cover.

7. Loosen the alternator mounting bolt, nut and adjusting nut, then remove the alternator belt or if equipped, the air conditioning belt.

8. Remove the valve cover. Remove the side engine mount bracket stay, if equipped.

9. Remove the upper timing belt cover.

10. Use a suitable device to support the engine, then remove the side engine belt.

11. Remove the dipstick and pipe and remove the timing belt tensioner adjusting nut.

12. Remove the crankshaft pulley bolt and the crankshaft pulley. Remove the 2 rear bolts from the center beam, to allow the engine to drop down and give clearance to remove the lower timing belt cover. Remove the lower cover.

To install:

13. Installation is the reverse of the removal procedure.

14. Apply oil to the threads of the crankshaft pulley bolt and tighten it to 159 ft. lbs. (220 Nm).

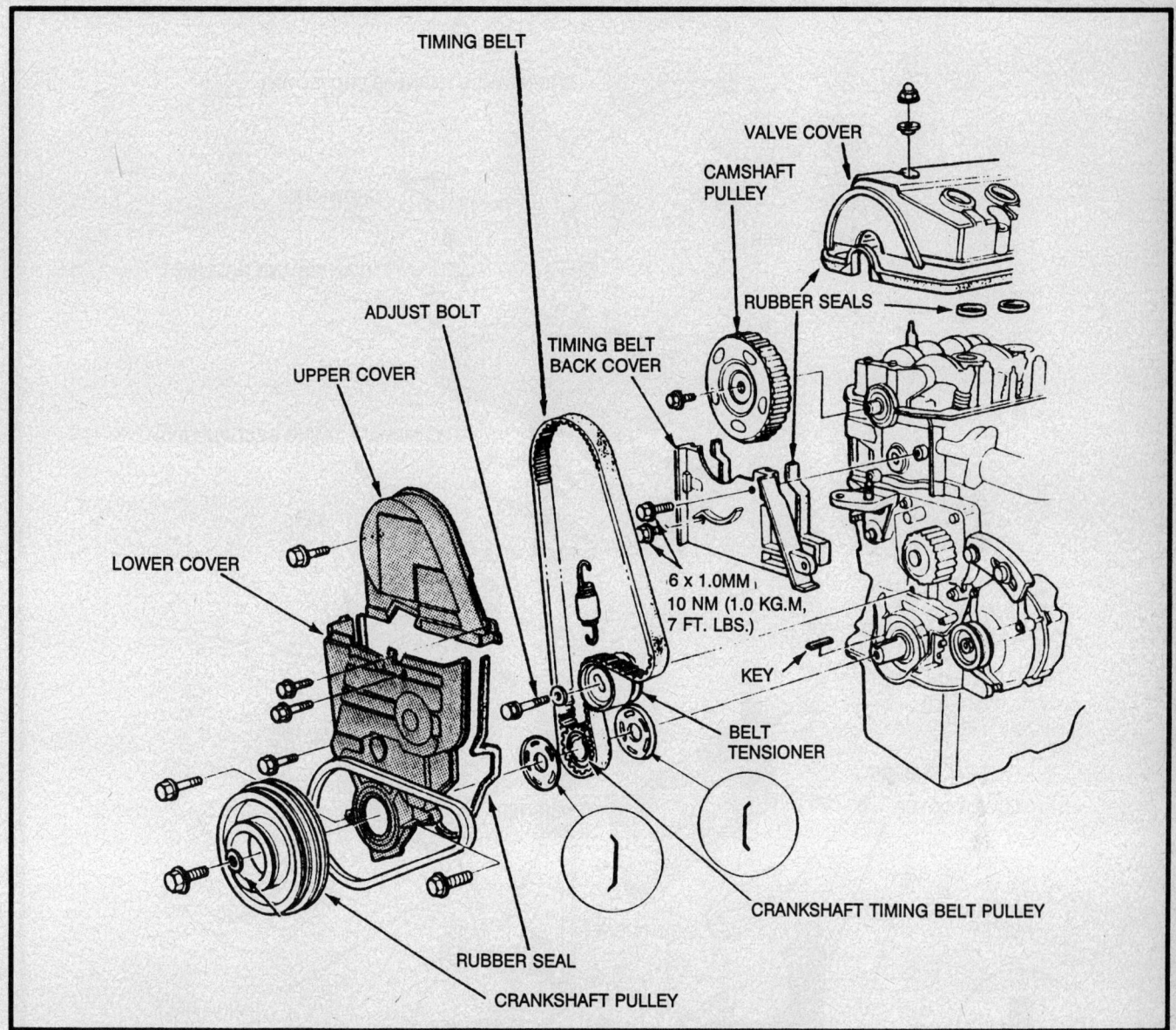

Timing belt and cover installation—1988-91 Civic and CRX

15. After installing the lower cover, the timing belt and balancer belt tension must be adjusted as follows:
   a. Make sure the No. 1 cylinder is at TDC.
   b. Loosely install the adjusting nut.
   c. Rotate the crankshaft counterclockwise 3 teeth on the camshaft pulley to create tension on the timing belt.
   d. Tighten the adjusting nut.
   e. If the crankshaft pulley loosens while turning the crank, retighten it to 159 ft. lbs. (220 Nm).

1988-91 PRELUDE

1. Disconnect the negative battery cable.
2. Raise and safely support the vehicle.
3. Remove the engine splash shield.
4. Use a suitable device to support the engine. Remove the engine support bolts and nuts, then remove the side mount rubber and side mount bracket. Remove the actuator, if equipped with cruise control.

5. Remove the power steering pump adjusting pulley nut and the adjusting bolt, then remove the adjusting pulley, power steering pump and belt.
6. Remove the alternator through bolt, mount bolt and adjust nut, then remove the alternator and belt.
7. If equipped with air conditioning, remove the air conditioning compressor mount bolts, then remove the air conditioning compressor and the belt.
8. Remove the ignition wire and the engine wire harness protector from the valve cover, if necessary.
9. Remove the valve cover.
10. Remove the crankshaft pulley bolt and the crankshaft pulley.
11. Remove the timing belt covers.
12. Installation is the reverse of the removal procedure. Apply engine oil to the threads of the crankshaft pulley bolt and tighten it to 83 ft. lbs. (115 Nm) on 1988 Prelude and 108 ft. lbs. (150 Nm) on 1989-91 Prelude.

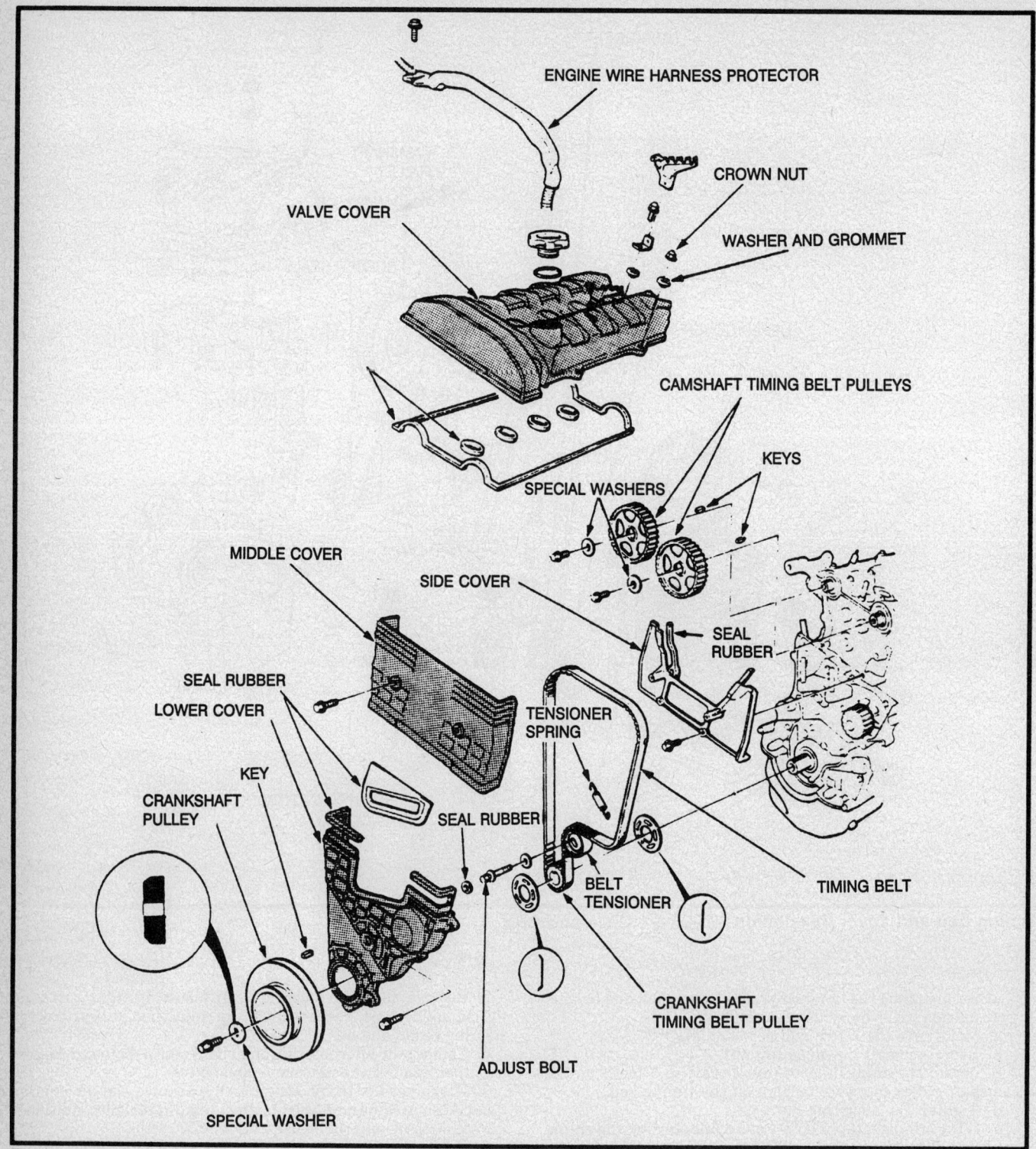

Timing belt and cover installation—1988–91 Prelude with DOHC engine

Oil Seal Replacement

1. Disconnect the negative battery cable.
2. Remove the timing belt cover and the timing belt.
3. Remove the crankshaft timing sprocket.
4. Using a suitable seal removal tool, remove the seal from the front of the engine.

5. Installation is the reverse of the removal procedure. Place a thin coat of oil on the seal lip prior to installation. Use a suitable seal driver to install the seal. Be sure to install the seal with the open (spring) side facing the inside of the engine.

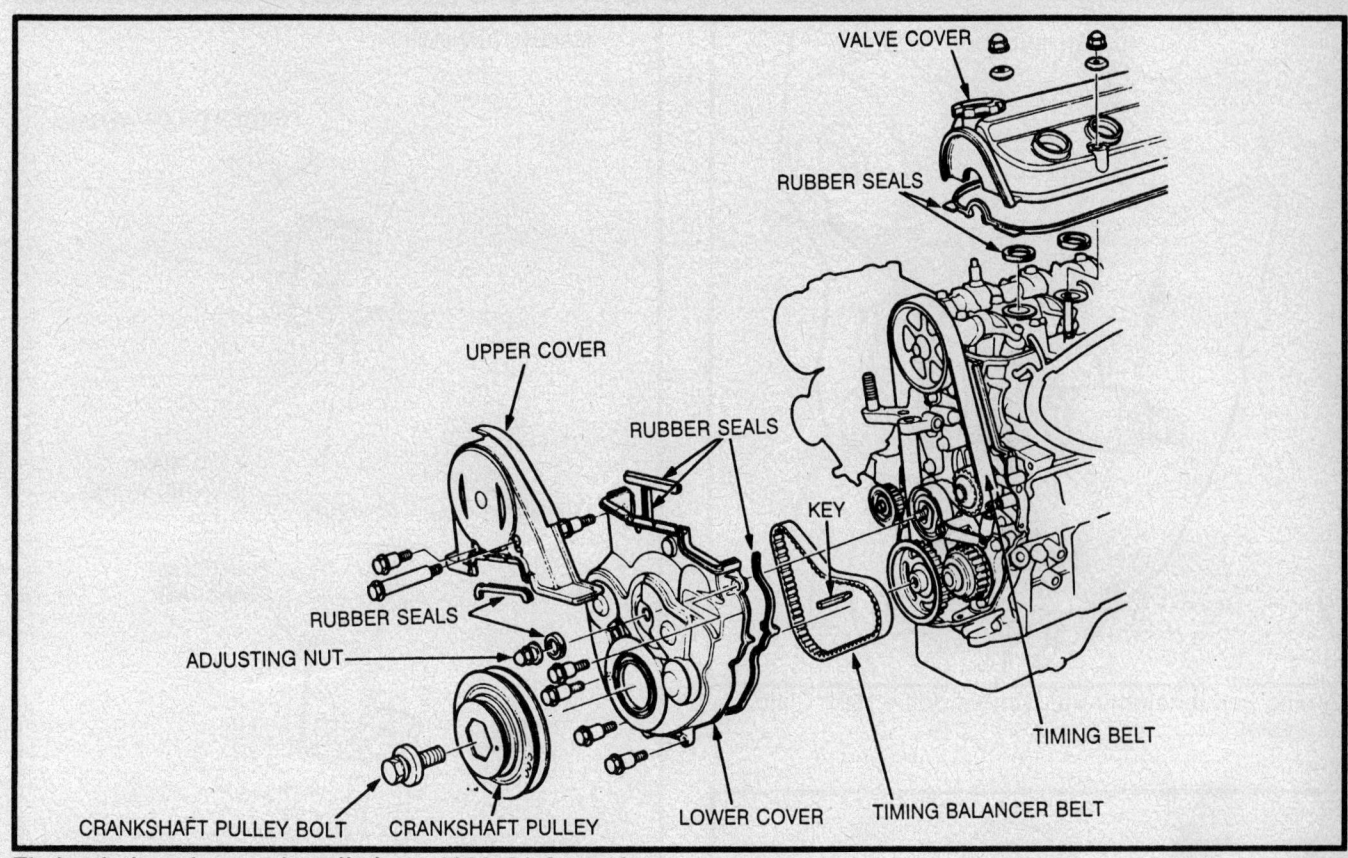

Timing belt and cover installation—1990–91 Accord

Timing Belt and Tensioner

Adjustment

NOTE: The timing belt tensioner is spring loaded, to apply proper tension to the belt automatically, after making the following adjustment.

1. Disconnect the negative battery cable.
2. Remove the valve cover or upper timing belt cover.
3. Set the piston in No. 1 cylinder at TDC.
4. Loosen, but do not remove, the adjusting bolt.
5. Rotate the crankshaft counterclockwise 3 teeth on the camshaft pulley to create tension on the timing belt.
6. Tighten the adjusting bolt.
7. If the crankshaft pulley broke loose while turning the crankshaft, retighten it to specification.
8. Reinstall or connect the remaining components after adjustment is completed.

Removal and Installation

1. Disconnect the negative battery cable.
2. Bring the piston in No. 1 cylinder to TDC on the compression stroke.
3. Remove the valve cover and timing belt front covers.
4. Mark the direction of timing belt rotation. On 1990–91 Accord, mark the direction of timing balancer belt rotation.
5. On all except 1990–91 Accord, loosen the adjusting bolt and remove the timing belt. On 1990–91 Accord, push the timing balancer belt tensioner and the timing belt tensioner to remove tension on the belts, then reinstall and tighten the adjusting nut. Remove the timing balancer belt and the timing belt.

To install:
6. Align the camshaft sprocket(s) and crankshaft sprocket as follows:
   a. Make sure the **UP** mark on the camshaft sprocket(s) is at the top most position. The sprocket timing marks should be aligned with the cylinder head upper surface.
   b. On all except Civic and CRX, remove the timing inspection hole cover at the rear of the engine block. Make sure the TDC mark on the flywheel, indicated by a white painted mark, is aligned with the pointer in the inspection hole.
   c. On Civic and CRX, temporarily reinstall the lower timing belt cover and crankshaft pulley. Make sure the TDC mark on the crankshaft pulley, indicated by a white painted mark, is aligned with the pointer on the timing cover. Remove the lower timing belt cover and crankshaft pulley.
7. Install the timing belt. If the old timing belt is reused, install the belt in the same rotational direction, as indicated by the mark that was made during removal.
8. On 1990–91 Accord, align the timing belt balancer pulleys and install the balancer belt as follows:
   a. The timing belt balancer drive pulley should already be at TDC, if the timing belt is installed correctly.
   b. Align the groove on the front timing balancer belt driven pulley with the pointer on the oil pump body.
   c. Remove the bolt from the maintenance hole on the cylinder block, next to the rear balancer shaft. Align the rear timing balancer belt driven pulley using a 6 × 100mm bolt, or equivalent. Mark a line at the 74mm length of the bolt. Align the pulley by inserting the bolt through the maintenance hole. The bolt must be inserted to a depth where the line is flush with the maintenance hole surface.
   d. Install the timing balancer belt. If the old balancer belt is

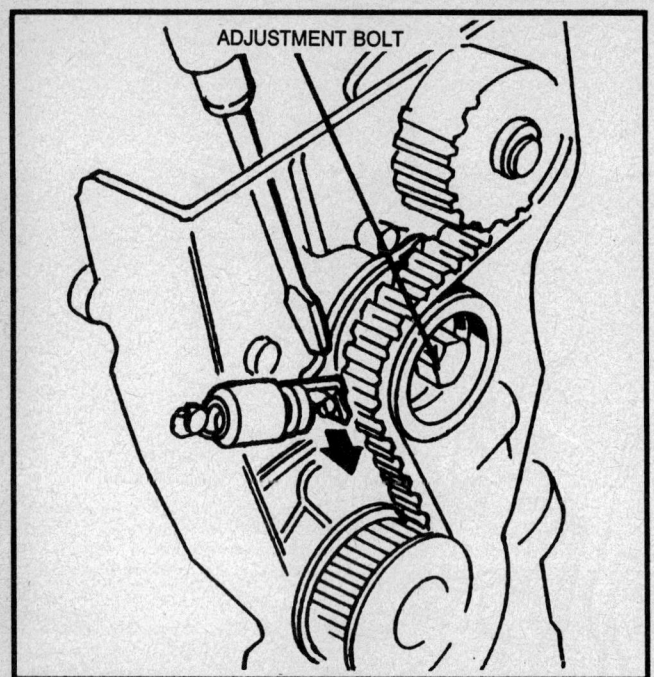

Timing belt tensioner adjustment bolt—1987 Civic and CRX

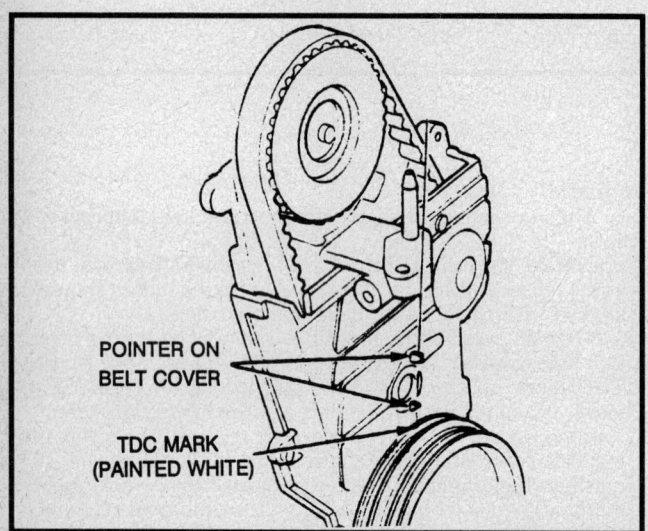

TDC locating marks—1988–91 Civic and CRX

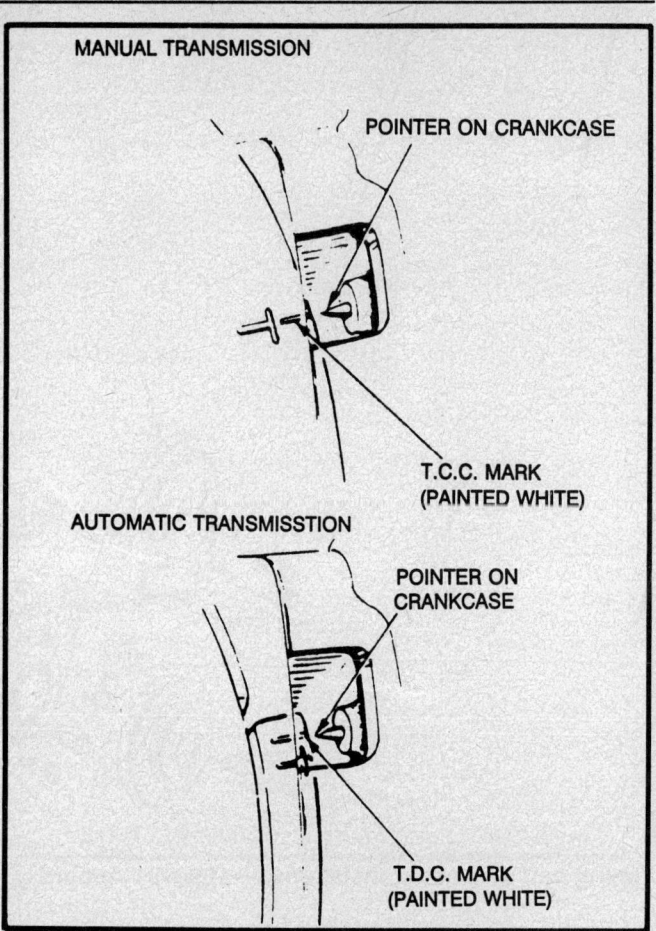

TDC locating marks—except Civic and CRX

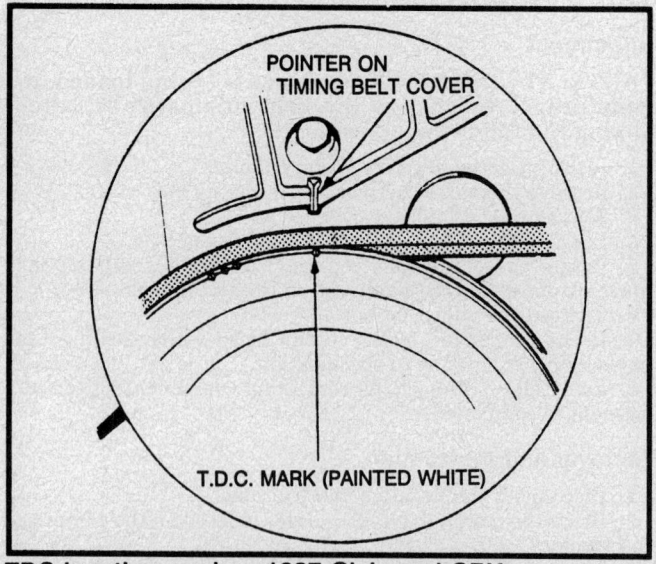

TDC locating marks—1987 Civic and CRX

reused, install the belt in the same rotational direction, as indicated by the mark that was made during removal. After the balancer belt is installed, remove the rear balancer belt driven pulley alignment bolt and reinstall the original bolt in the maintenance hole. Tighten the bolt to 22 ft. lbs. (30 Nm).

9. Installation of the remaining components is the reverse of the removal procedure. Be sure to properly adjust the timing belt tension. On 1990–91 Accord, the balancer belt tension is automatically adjusted when the timing belt tension is adjusted.

10. Tighten the crankshaft pulley bolt to 83 ft. lbs. (115 Nm) on 1987–88 Civic, CRX, Accord and Prelude, 108 ft. lbs. (150 Nm) on 1989 Accord and 1989–91 Prelude, 119 ft. lbs. (165 Nm) on 1989–91 Civic and CRX and 159 ft. lbs. (220 Nm) on 1990–91 Accord.

Timing Sprockets

Removal and Installation

1. Disconnect the negative battery cable.

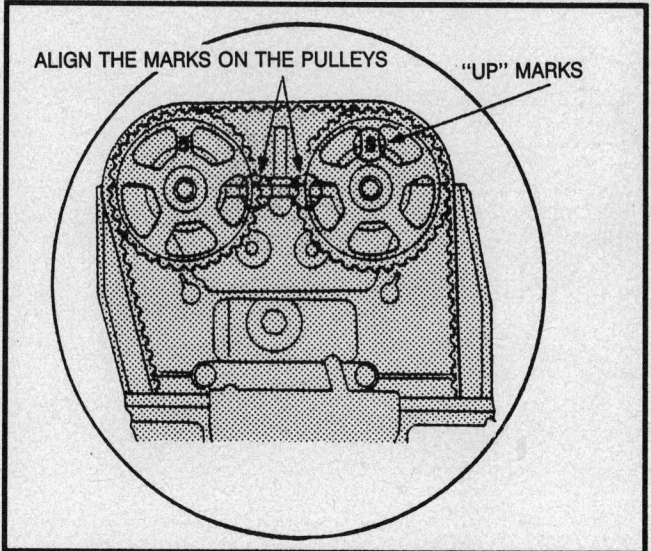

Aligning the timing marks on the camshaft sprockets—Prelude with DOHC engine

2. Remove the valve cover, timing belt covers and the timing belt.
3. Remove the crankshaft and camshaft timing sprockets.
4. Installation is the reverse of the removal procedure. Tighten the camshaft sprocket retaining bolts to 27 ft. lbs. (38 Nm).

Camshaft

Removal and Installation

EXCEPT DOHC ENGINE

1. Disconnect the negative battery cable.
2. Bring the piston in No. 1 cylinder to TDC on the compression stroke.
3. Remove the valve cover, timing belt front covers and the timing belt.
4. Remove the camshaft sprocket.

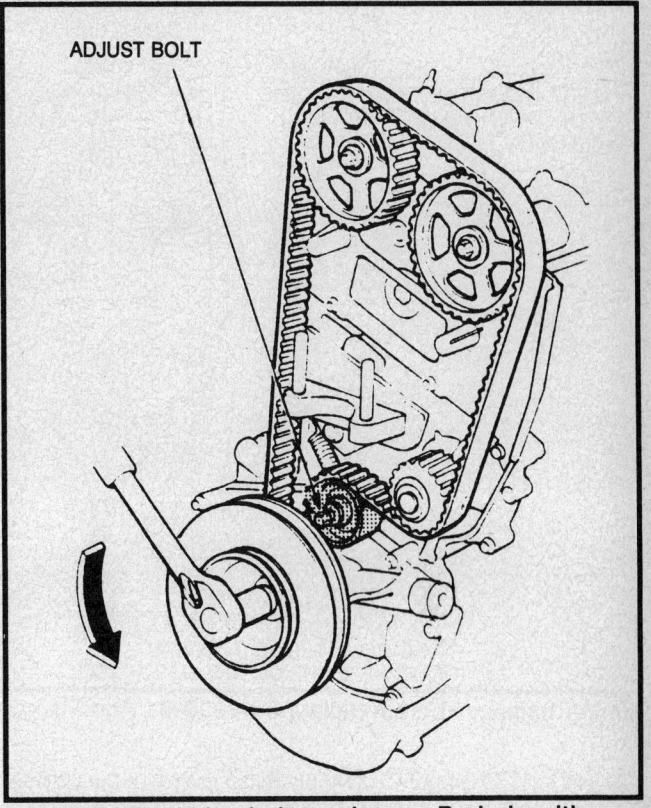

Adjusting the timing belt tensioner—Prelude with DOHC engine

5. Remove the rocker arm/shaft assembly.
6. Remove the camshaft and camshaft seal.

To install:

7. Installation is the reverse of the removal procedure. Lubricate the lobes and journals of the camshaft prior to installation. Install the camshaft with the keyway facing up.

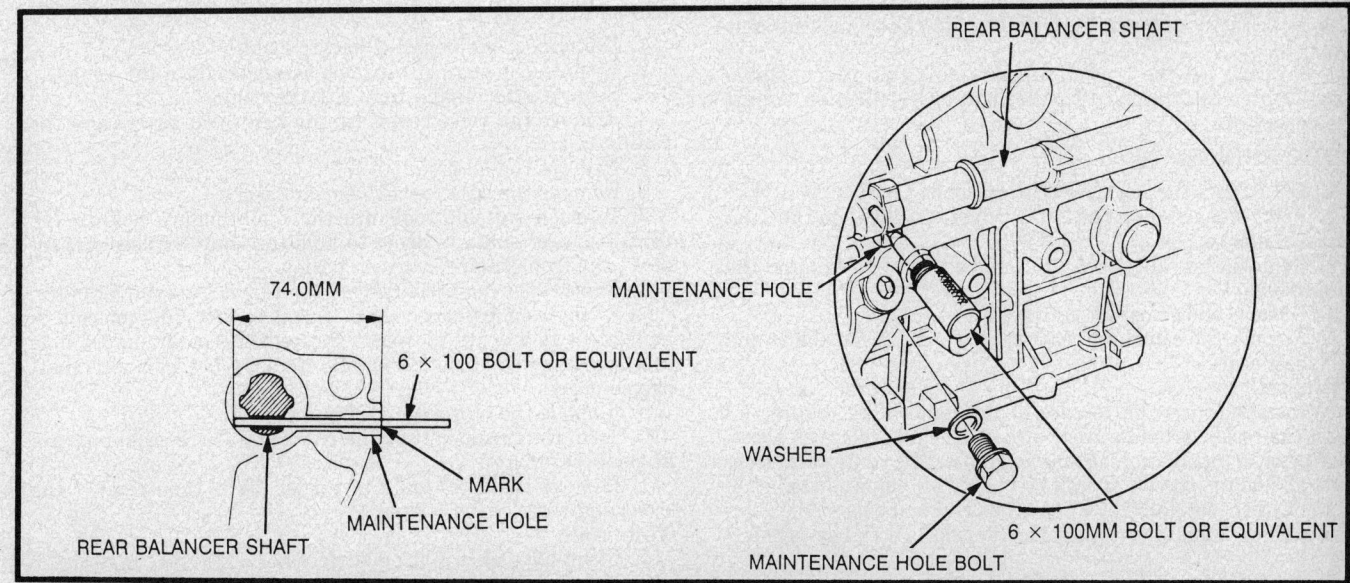

Aligning the rear timing balancer belt driven pulley— 1990–91 Accord

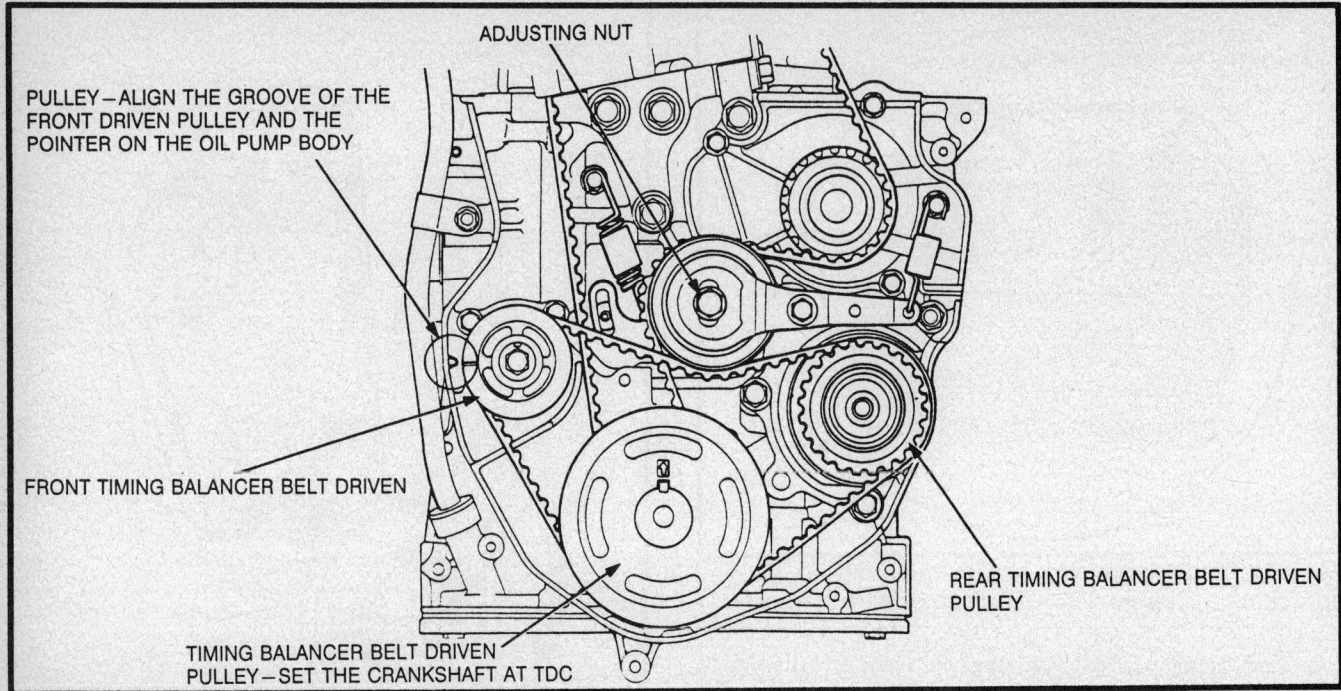

ADJUSTING NUT

PULLEY—ALIGN THE GROOVE OF THE FRONT DRIVEN PULLEY AND THE POINTER ON THE OIL PUMP BODY

FRONT TIMING BALANCER BELT DRIVEN

REAR TIMING BALANCER BELT DRIVEN PULLEY

TIMING BALANCER BELT DRIVEN PULLEY—SET THE CRANKSHAFT AT TDC

Timing balancer belt installation—1990–91 Accord

8. On 1987 Civic and CRX, apply liquid gasket to the mating surfaces of the No. 1 and No. 5 bearing caps and place them in position along with the other bearing caps.

9. Install the rocker arm/shaft assembly as follows:

a. Loosen the rocker arm locknuts and back off the adjust screws.

b. Set the rocker arm/shaft assembly in place and loosely install the bolts. c. Tighten each bolt 2 turns at a time in the proper sequence to ensure that the rockers do not bind on the valves.

d. Tighten the rocker arm bolts to 16 ft. lbs. (22 Nm) except on 1990–91 Accord. On 1990–91 Accord tighten the 6mm bolts to 9 ft. lbs. (12 Nm) and the 8mm bolts to 16 ft. lbs. (22 Nm).

10. Lubricate a new camshaft seal and install using a suitable tool.

11. Properly set the tension of the timing belt after installation. Tighten the crankshaft pulley bolt to specification. Adjust the valve lash.

DOHC ENGINE

1. Disconnect the negative battery cable.

2. Bring the piston in the No. 1 cylinder to TDC on the compression stroke.

3. Remove the valve cover, timing belt front covers and the timing belt.

4. Remove the camshaft sprockets.

5. Remove the camshaft bearing caps and the camshafts and camshaft seals.

To install:

6. Installation is the reverse of the removal procedure. Inspect the rocker arms for wear or damage and replace as necessary prior to installation of the camshafts. The rocker arm locknuts and adjust screws should be backed off before installation of the camshafts. Lubricate the lobes and journals of the camshafts before installing. Install the camshafts with keyways facing UP.

7. Apply liquid gasket to the No. 1 and No. 6 camshaft bearing caps and install them with the rest of the caps. Make sure the caps are installed in their proper positions as indicated by their markings.

8. Tighten each camshaft bearing cap bolt gradually, to prevent binding. Tighten the bolts to 9 ft. lbs. (12 Nm).

9. Lubricate new camshaft seals and install using a suitable tool.

10. Properly tension the timing belt after installation. Tighten the crankshaft pulley to specification. Adjust the valve lash.

Balancer Shafts

Removal and Installation

1990–91 ACCORD

1. Disconnect the negative battery cable.

2. Remove the engine/transaxle assembly from the vehicle.

3. Separate the engine from the transaxle.

4. Remove the valve cover, timing belt front covers and the timing belt.

5. Remove the oil pan.

6. Remove the balancer drive gear case.

7. Insert a suitable tool into the maintenance hole in the front balancer shaft, in order to hold the shaft in place and remove the front balancer driven pulley.

8. Remove the maintenance hole bolt from the cylinder block, next to the rear balancer shaft. Insert a 6 × 100mm bolt or equivalent to a depth of 74mm through the maintenance hole and into the rear balancer shaft. Remove the balancer shaft driven gear.

9. Remove the oil screen and pump.

10. Turn the crankshaft so the No. 2 and No. 3 crankpins are at the bottom.

11. Remove the bolts and the thrust plate, then remove the front and rear balancer shaft.

To install:

12. Clean all gasket mating surfaces of old gasket material.

13. Lubricate the balancer shaft bearings.

14. Insert the balancer shafts into the block, then install the

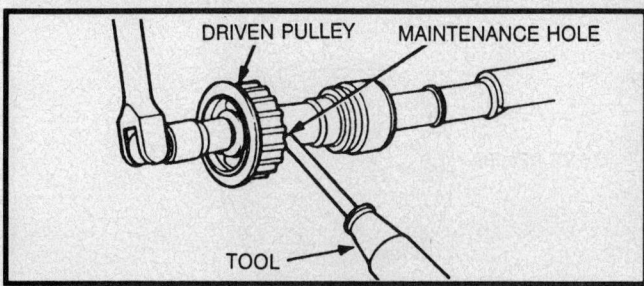

Front balancer shaft driven gear installation—1990–91 Accord

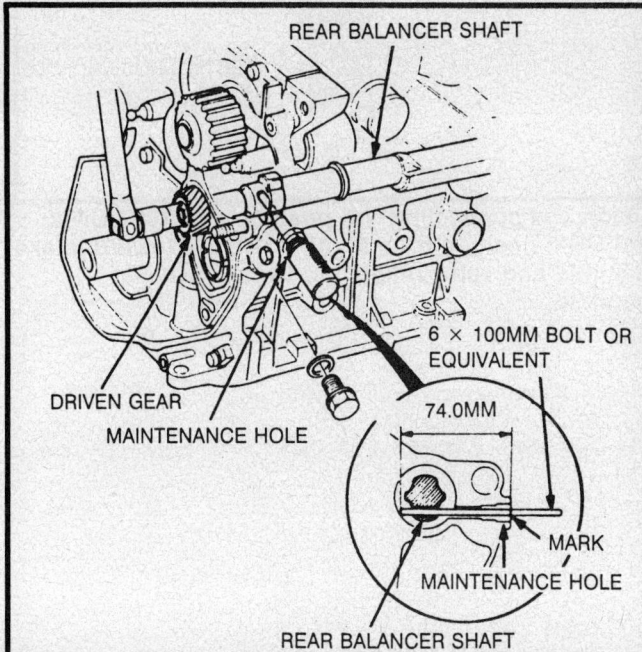

Rear balancer shaft driven gear installation—1990–91 Accord

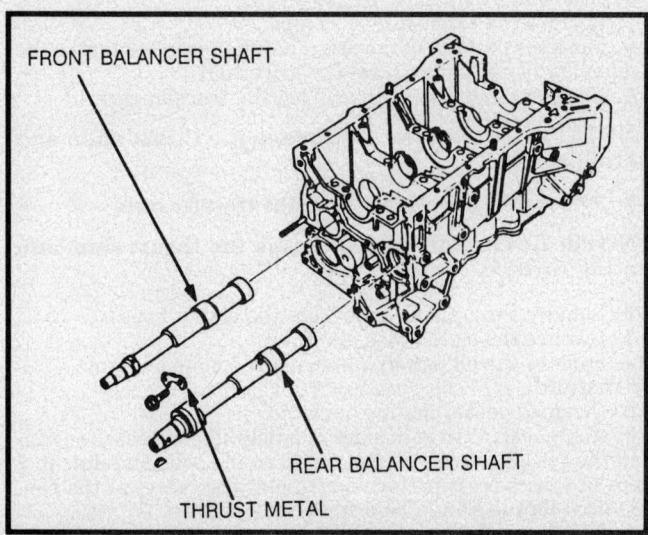

Front and rear balancer shafts—1990–91 Accord

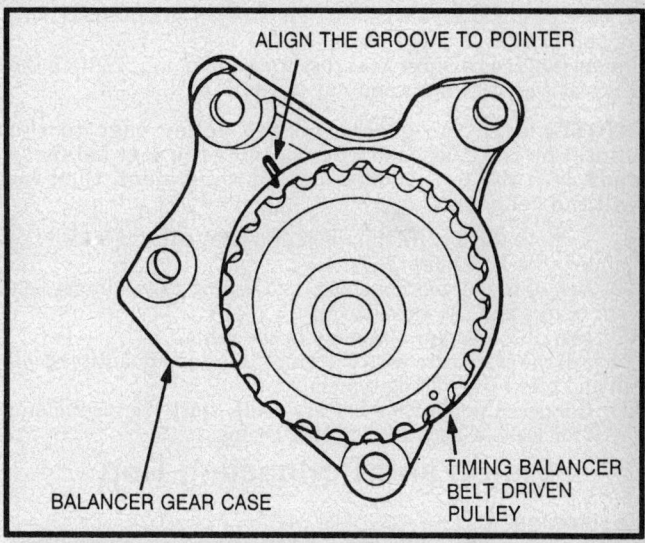

Timing balancer belt driven pulley—1990–91 Accord

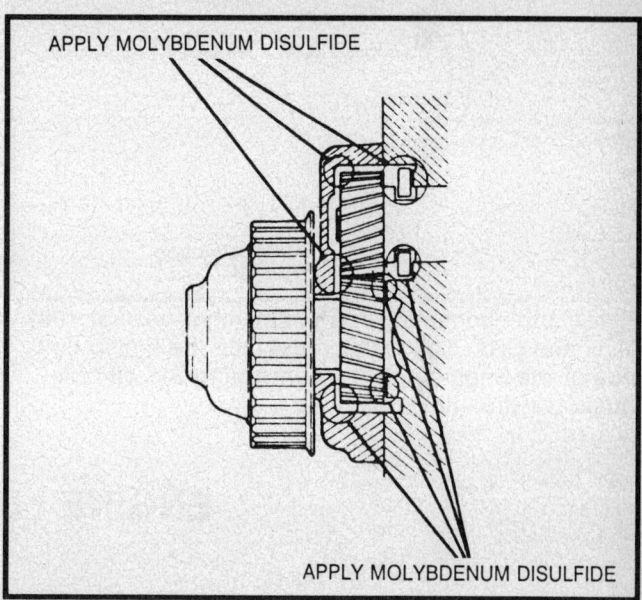

Apply molybdenum disulfide to the thrust surfaces of the balancer gears

thrust plate to the front balancer shaft and the block. Tighten the thrust plate bolts to 9 ft. lbs. (12 Nm).

15. Apply liquid gasket to the block mating surfaces of the oil pump, then install it on the engine block. Apply grease to the lips of the oil pump seal and the balancer seal. Then, install the oil pump onto the inner rotor to the crankshaft. When the pump is in place, clean any excess grease off the crankshaft and the balancer shaft, then check that the oil seal lips are not distorted. Apply liquid gasket to the oil pump retaining bolts and tighten the bolts to 9 ft. lbs. (12 Nm).

16. Install the oil screen.

17. Apply molybdenum disulfide to the thrust surfaces of the balancer gears, before installing the balancer driven gear and the balancer drive gear case.

18. Hold the rear balancer shaft with the 6 × 100mm bolt or equivalent, then install the balancer driven gear and the balancer drive belt pulley. Tighten the retaining bolt to 18 ft. lbs. (25 Nm).

19. Hold the front balancer shaft with a suitable tool, then in-

stall the timing balancer belt driven pulley. Tighten the retaining bolt to 22 ft. lbs. (30 Nm).

20. Install the balancer gear case to the oil pump. Tighten the balancer gear case bolts and nut to 18 ft. lbs. (25 Nm).

NOTE: Align the groove on the pulley edge to the pointer on the gear case when holding the rear balancer shaft with the 6 × 100mm bolt or equivalent, then install the gear case.

21. Remove the 6 × 100mm bolt or equivalent and install the maintenance hole bolt.

22. Install the oil pan, balancer and timing belts, timing belt front covers and the valve cover.

23. Install the engine assembly in the vehicle.

24. Fill the crankcase with the proper type and quantity of oil. Fill and bleed the cooling system.

25. Connect the negative battery cable, start the engine and check for leaks. Check the ignition timing.

Piston and Connecting Rod

Positioning

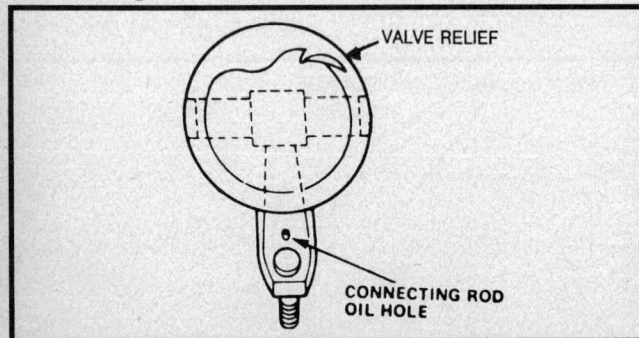

Piston and connecting rod positioning—except 1987 Civic and CRX: The arrow must face the timing belt side of the engine and the connecting rod oil hole must face the intake manifold

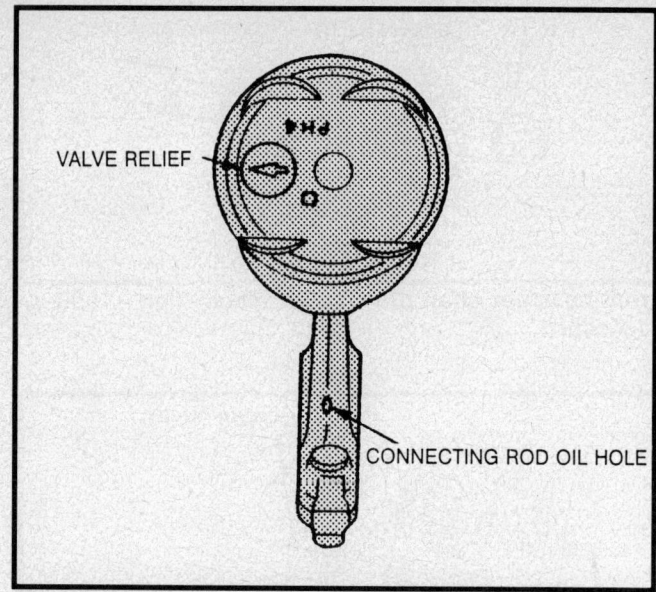

Piston and connecting rod positioning—1987 Civic and CRX: position rods so oil holes are toward intake manifold and valve reliefs are toward exhaust manifold

ENGINE LUBRICATION

Oil Pan

Removal and Installation

EXCEPT 4WD CIVIC WAGON

1. Disconnect the negative battery cable.
2. Raise and safely support the vehicle.
3. Remove the engine splash shield, if equipped.
4. Drain the engine oil.
5. Remove the exhaust header pipe, if necessary.
6. Remove the oil pan bolts and nuts and the oil pan.
7. Installation is the reverse of the removal procedure. Make sure all gasket mating surfaces are clean prior to installation.
8. Apply a coat of sealant to both sides of the oil pan gasket. Tighten the bolts and nuts in 2 steps in a criss-cross pattern beginning at the center of the pan. The final torque should be 9 ft. lbs. (12 Nm). Tighten the oil pan drain plug to 33 ft. lbs. (45 Nm).

4WD CIVIC WAGON

Manual Transaxle

1. Disconnect the negative battery cable.
2. Raise and safely support the vehicle.
3. Remove the engine and transaxle splash shield.
4. Drain the engine and transaxle oil.
5. Remove the exhaust header pipe.
6. Mark the position of the driveshaft flange in relation to the companion flange and remove the driveshaft.
7. Remove the left side cover from the transfer case.

NOTE: Be careful not to damage the thrust shim and mating surface.

8. Remove the driven gear from the transfer case.

NOTE: Be careful not to damage the thrust shim and mating surface.

9. Remove the transfer case from the clutch housing.
10. Remove the clutch case cover.
11. Remove the oil pan by removing the bolts and nuts.

To install:

12. Clean all gasket mating surfaces.
13. Apply sealant to both sides of a new oil pan gasket and install the gasket and the oil pan. Tighten the bolts and nuts in 2 steps in a criss-cross pattern starting at the center of the pan. The final torque should be 9 ft. lbs. (12 Nm).
14. Install and tighten the oil drain plug to 33 ft. lbs. (45 Nm).
15. Apply liquid gasket to the clutch housing mating surface of

the transfer case. Install the transfer case on the clutch housing. Tighten the transfer case bolts to 33 ft. lbs. (45 Nm).

16. Install the drive gear thrust shim on the transfer shaft. Lubricate the drive gear and install it on the transfer shaft. Install the transfer thrust shim and left side cover on the transfer case. Apply liquid gasket to the side cover bolts and tighten them to 33 ft. lbs. (45 Nm).

17. Apply a thin film of sealant at the top and bottom of the transfer case opening and install the driven gear thrust shim and the driven gear. Tighten the mouning bolts to 19 ft. lbs. (26 Nm).

18. Install the driveshaft, aligning the marks that were made during the removal procedure. Tighten the bolts to 24 ft. lbs. (33 Nm).

19. Install the exhaust header pipe and the engine and transaxle splash shields. Install and tighten the transaxle drain plug to 30 ft. lbs. (40 Nm).

20. Fill the transaxle with the proper type of oil, to the required level.

21. Lower the vehicle and fill the crankcase with the proper type of oil, to the required level.

22. Connect the negative battery cable, start the engine and check for leaks.

Automatic Transaxle

1. Disconnect the negative battery cable.
2. Raise and safely support the vehicle.
3. Remove the engine and transaxle splash shield.
4. Drain the engine and transaxle oil.
5. Remove the exhaust header pipe.
6. Mark the position of the driveshaft flange in relation to the companion flange and remove the driveshaft.
7. Remove the driven gear assembly from the transfer case.
8. Remove the left side cover and then the drive gear from the transfer case. Rotate the cover using the bolt closest to the front of the vehicle as the axis. This bolt is not removed from the cover.

NOTE: Be careful not to damage the thrust shim and mating surface.

9. Remove the transfer case from the clutch housing.
10. Remove the clutch case cover.
11. Remove the oil pan by removing the bolts and nuts.
To install:
12. Clean all gasket mating surfaces.
13. Apply sealant to both sides of a new oil pan gasket and install the gasket and the oil pan. Tighten the bolts and nuts in 2 steps in a criss-cross pattern starting at the center of the pan. The final torque should be 9 ft. lbs. (12 Nm).
14. Install and tighten the oil drain plug to 33 ft. lbs. (45 Nm).
15. Apply liquid gasket to the clutch housing mating surface of the transfer case. Attach a new O-ring to the groove in the transfer left side cover.
16. Install the transfer case on the clutch housing. Install the bolt that remained in the left side cover, in the transfer case before installing the case on the clutch housing. Tighten the transfer case bolts to 33 ft. lbs. (45 Nm).
17. Install the drive gear thrust shim on the transfer shaft. Lubricate the drive gear and install it on the transfer shaft. Install the transfer thrust shim and left side cover on the transfer case. Apply liquid gasket to the side cover bolts and tighten them to 33 ft. lbs. (45 Nm).
18. Apply a thin film of sealant at the top and bottom of the transfer case opening and install the driven gear thrust shim and the driven gear. Tighten the mounting bolts to 19 ft. lbs. (26 Nm).
19. Install the driveshaft, aligning the marks that were made during the removal procedure. Tighten the bolts to 24 ft. lbs. (33 Nm).
20. Install the exhaust header pipe and the engine and trans-

axle splash shields. Install and tighten the transaxle drain plug to 29 ft. lbs. (40 Nm).

21. Lower the vehicle and fill the crankcase with the proper type of oil, to the required level. Fill the transaxle with the proper type and quantity of oil.

22. Connect the negative battery cable, start the engine and check for leaks.

Oil Pump

Removal and Installation
EXCEPT 1987–89 ACCORD AND 1987 PRELUDE

1. Disconnect the negative battery cable.
2. Raise and safely support the vehicle.
3. Drain the engine oil.
4. Bring the No. 1 cylinder to TDC. On Civic and CRX, the mark on the crankshaft pulley should align with the index mark on the timing cover. On Accord and Prelude, the mark on the flywheel should align with the pointer in the inspection hole.
5. Remove the necessary accessory drive belts and the crankshaft pulley.
6. Remove the valve cover and the timing belt covers.
7. On 1990–91 Accord, remove the following:
   a. Timing balancer belt
   b. Timing belt
   c. Timing belt tensioner
   d. Timing balancer belt tensioner
   e. Timing belt drive pulley
   f. Timing balancer belt driven pulley. Insert a suitable tool into the maintenance hole in the front balancer shaft in order to hold the shaft in place and remove the front balancer driven pulley.
   g. Balancer drive gear case
   h. Balancer driven gear. Remove the maintenance hole bolt from the cylinder block next to the rear balancer shaft. Insert a 6 × 100mm bolt or equivalent, to a depth of 74mm through the maintenance hole and into the rear balancer shaft. Remove the balancer shaft driven gear.
8. On all other vehicles, remove the following:
   a. Timing belt tensioner
   b. Timing belt
   c. Timing belt drive pulley
9. Remove the oil pan and oil screen.
10. Remove the oil pump mount bolts and the oil pump assembly.
To install:
11. Installation is the reverse of the removal procedure. Make sure all gasket mating surfaces are clean prior to installation.
12. Inspect the crankshaft oil seal and replace as necessary prior to installing the oil pump.
13. Apply liquid gasket to the cylinder block mating surface of the block. Apply a light coat of oil to the crankshaft seal lip. Install a new O-ring on the cylinder block and install the oil pump. Apply liquid gasket to the threads of the oil pump mounting bolts and tighten them to 9 ft. lbs. (12 Nm).
14. Install the oil screen.
15. On 1990–91 Accord, perform the following procedure:
   a. Apply molybdenum disulfide to the thrust surfaces of the balancer gears, before installing the balancer driven gear and the balancer drive gear case.
   b. Hold the rear balancer shaft with the 6 × 100mm bolt or equivalent, then install the balancer driven gear and the balancer drive belt pulley. Tighten the retaining bolt to 18 ft. lbs. (25 Nm).
   c. Hold the front balancer shaft with a suitable tool, then install the timing balancer belt driven pulley. Tighten the retaining bolt to 22 ft. lbs. (30 Nm).
   d. Install the balancer gear case to the oil pump. Align the groove on the pulley edge to the pointer on the gear case when

holding the rear balancer shaft with the 6 × 100mm bolt or equivalent, then install the gear case. Tighten the balancer gear case bolts to 18 ft. lbs. (25 Nm).

   e. Remove the 6 × 100mm bolt or equivalent and install the maintenance hole bolt.

16. Install the oil pan and the remainder of the components. Be sure to properly tension the timing belt after installation. Tighten the crankshaft pulley bolt to specification.

1987–89 ACCORD AND 1987 PRELUDE

1. Disconnect the negative battery cable.
2. Remove the necessary accessory drive belts.
3. Remove the crankshaft pulley, timing belt covers and timing belt.

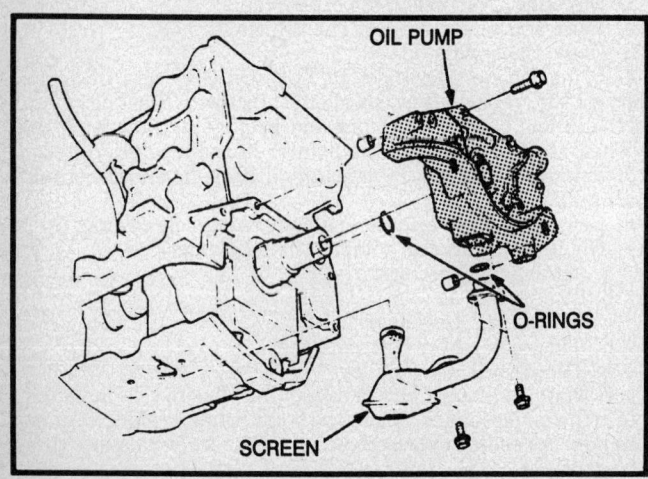

Oil pump installation – 1988–91 Prelude

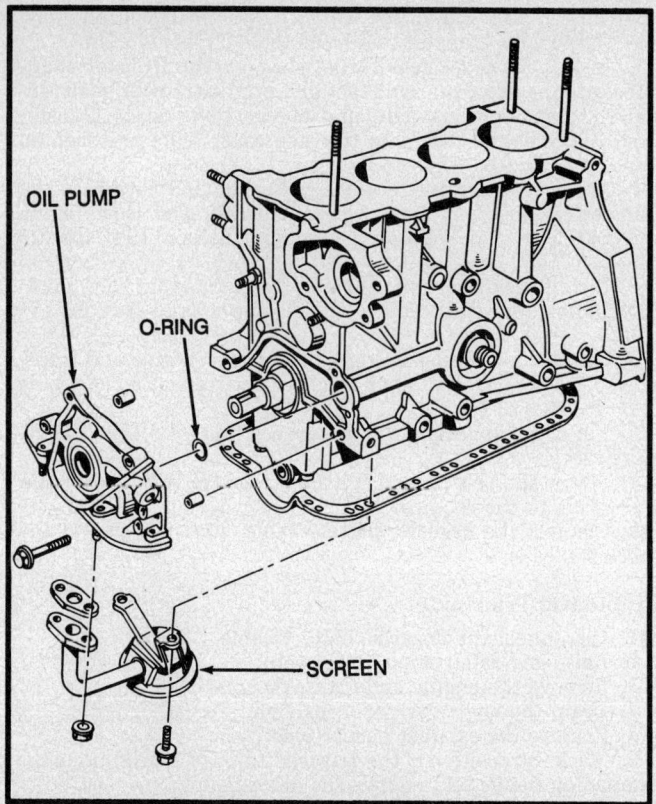

Oil pump installation – 1987 Civic and CRX

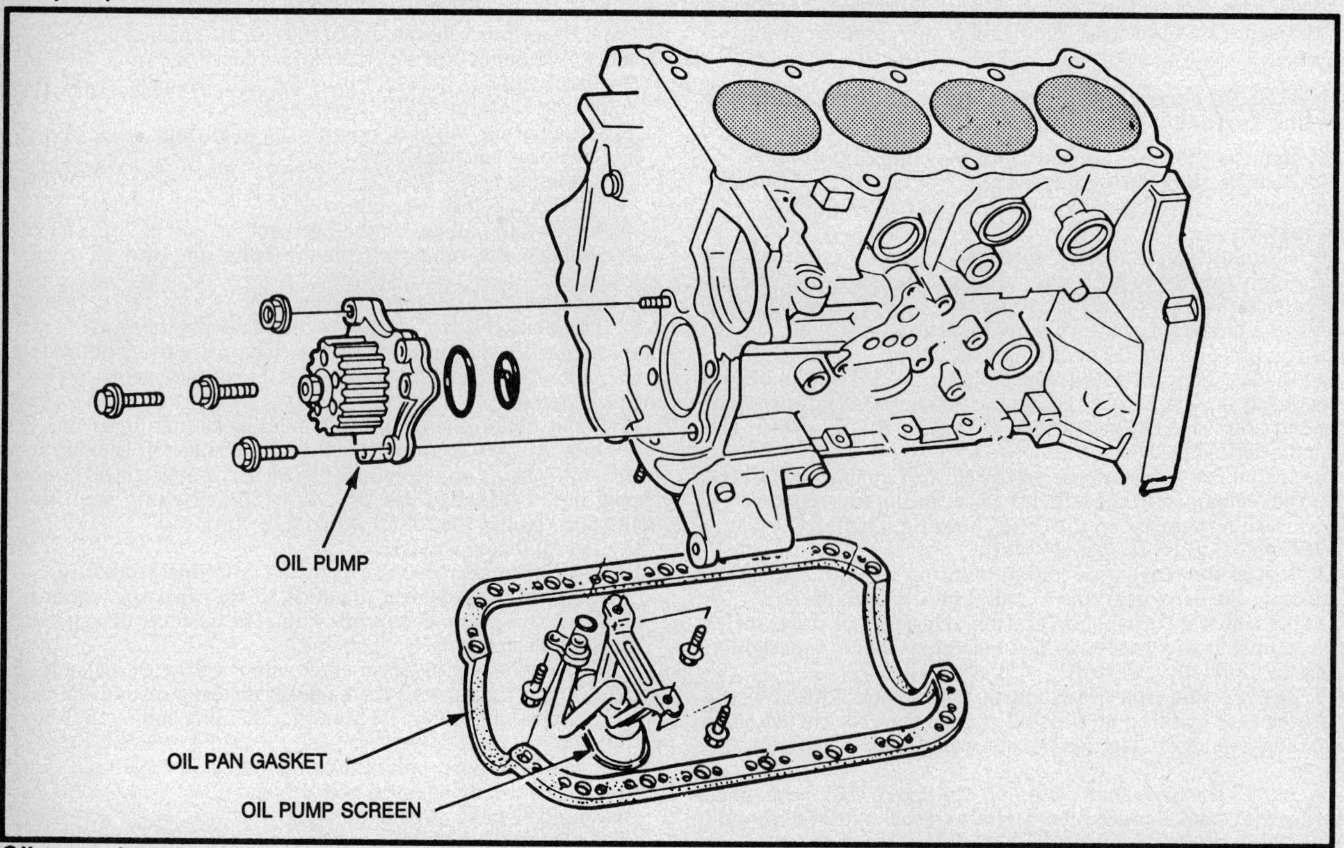

Oil pump installation – 1987–89 Accord and 1987 Prelude

4. Remove the 3 bolts and 1 nut retaining the oil pump to the cylinder block and remove the pump.

5. Installation is the reverse of the removal procedure. Make sure all gasket mating surfaces are clean prior to installation.

6. Apply liquid gasket around the O-ring groove, then install the new O-ring. Install a new gasket to the pump housing and install the pump. Tighten the pump bolts and nut to 9 ft. lbs. (12 Nm).

7. Install the remainder of the components. Be sure to properly tension the timing belt after installation. Tighten the crankshaft pulley bolt to specification.

Checking

1. Remove the oil pump.

2. Check the rotor radial clearance using a feeler gauge. The clearance must be less than 0.008 in. (0.2mm).

3. Check the housing-to-rotor axial clearance using a feeler gauge on 1987–89 Accord and 1987 Prelude, and a feeler gauge and straight-edge on all others. The clearance must be less than 0.005 in. (0.12mm) on 1988–91 Prelude and 1990–91 Accord, and less than 0.006 in. (0.15mm) on all others.

4. Check the housing-to-rotor radial clearance using a feeler gauge. The clearance must be less than 0.008 in. (0.2mm). It is necessary to remove the 2 screws and disassemble the pump housing on 1987–89 Accord and 1987 Prelude to perform this procedure.

5. Inspect both rotors and pump housing for scoring or other damage.

6. Replace components that are not within specification or appear worn.

7. Reassemble the oil pump on 1987–89 Accord and 1987 Prelude, using thread locking fluid on the 2 screws.

8. Install the oil pump.

Rear Main Bearing Oil Seal

Removal and Installation

The rear main seal is installed in the rear main bearing cap on 1987–89 Accord and 1987 Prelude. On all other vehicles, the rear main seal is housed in a separate cover which is mounted on the engine block with 4 bolts.

1. Disconnect the negative battery cable.
2. Raise and safely support the vehicle.
3. Remove the transaxle assembly.
4. On Civic Wagon with 4WD, remove the transfer case.
5. Remove the flywheel.
6. Remove the oil pan.

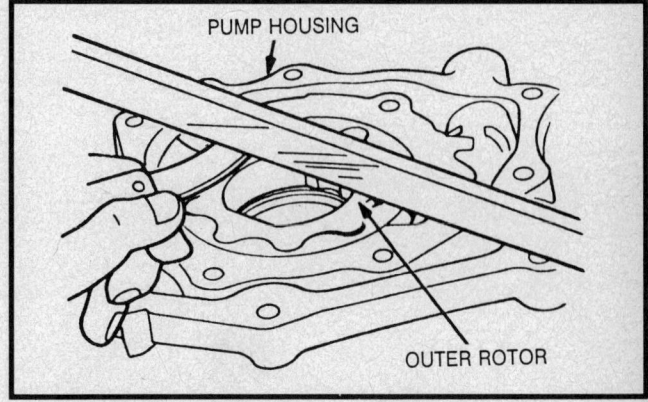

Checking housing-to-rotor axial clearance—except 1987–89 Accord and 1987 Prelude

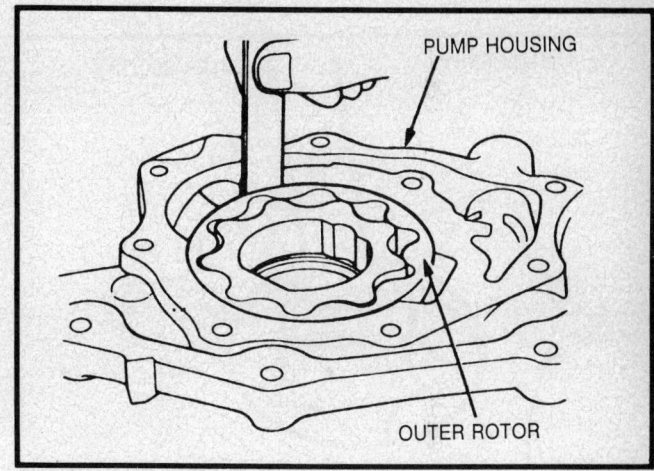

Checking housing-to-rotor radial clearance—except 1987–89 Accord and 1987 Prelude

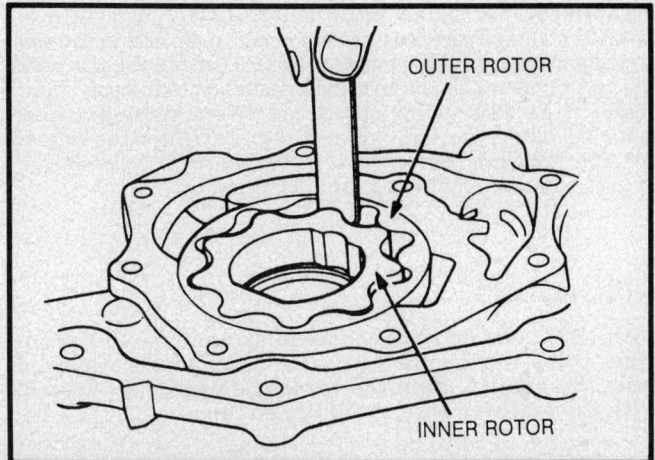

Checking rotor radial clearance—except 1987–89 Accord and 1987 Prelude

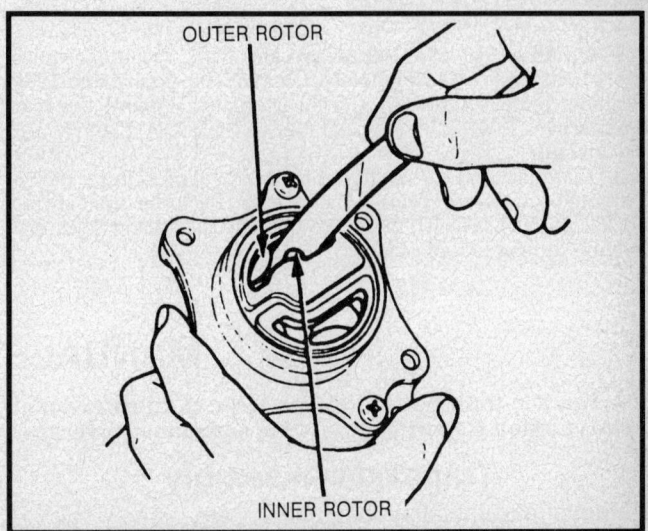

Checking rotor radial clearance—1987–89 Accord and 1987 Prelude

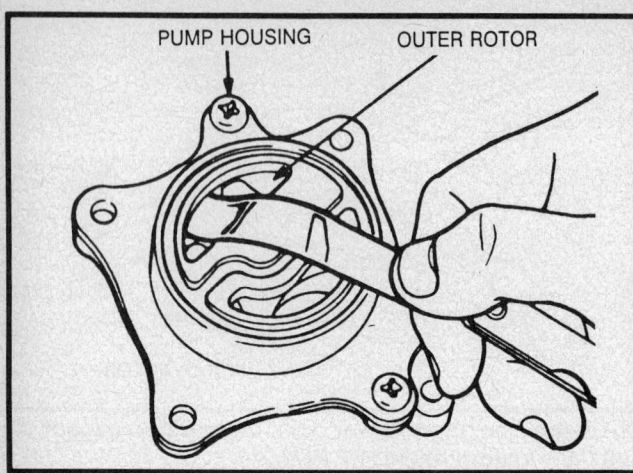

Checking housing-to-rotor axial clearance—1987–89 Accord and 1987 Prelude

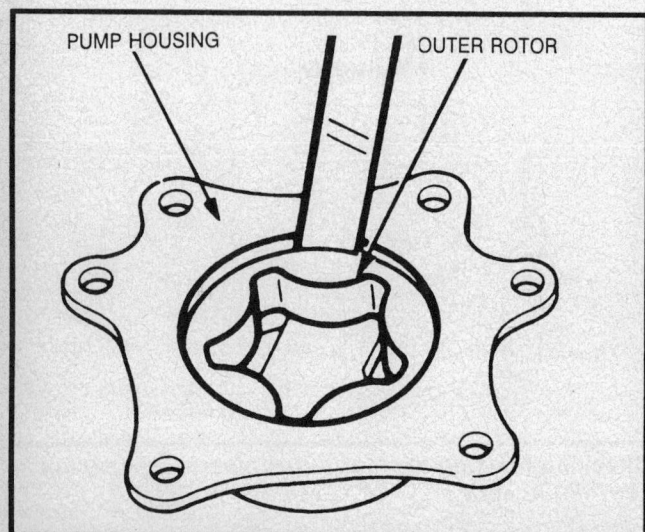

Checking housing-to-rotor radial clearance—1987–89 Accord and 1987 Prelude

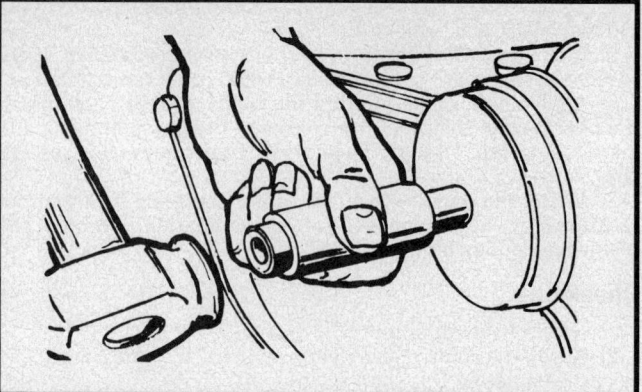

Installing the rear main seal—1987–89 Accord and 1987 Prelude

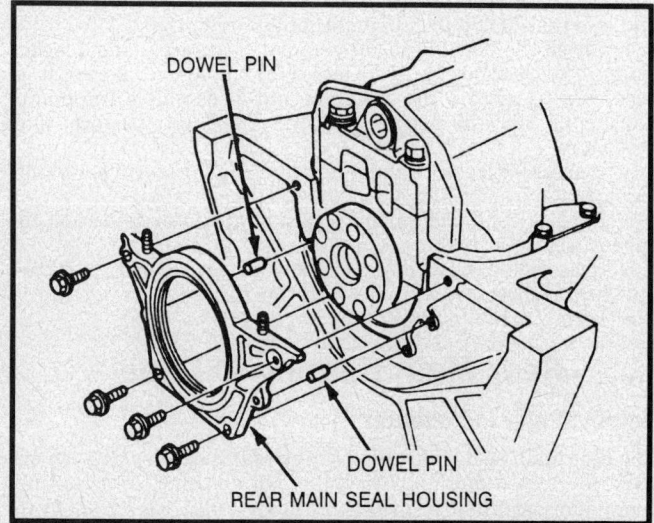

Installing the rear main seal housing—except 1987–89 Accord and 1987 Prelude

7. On all except 1987–89 Accord and 1987 Prelude, remove the 4 bolts and the seal housing. On 1987–89 Accord and 1987 Prelude, remove the rear main bearing cap. Remove the rear main seal.

To install:

8. Installation is the reverse of the removal procedure. Lubricate the lip of the seal prior to installation. Pack the inner spring pocket of the seal with grease to prevent the spring from dislodging during installation.

9. On 1987–89 Accord and 1987 Prelude, install the rear main bearing cap and tighten the bolts to 49 ft. lbs. (68 Nm). Install the rear main seal with the part number side facing out, using a suitable installation tool.

10. On all other vehicles, install the rear main seal in the seal housing using a suitable installation tool. Install the seal with the part number side towards the installation tool. Apply liquid gasket to the block mating surface and the seal housing retainer bolts. Install the seal housing on the block. Tighten the bolts to 9 ft. lbs. (12 Nm).

11. Install the remainder of the components.

MANUAL TRANSAXLE

For further information, please refer to "Professional Transmission Repair Manual" for additional coverage.

Transaxle Assembly

Removal and Installation

1987 CIVIC AND CRX

NOTE: The manual transaxle in 1987 Civic Wagon with 4WD must be removed as an assembly with the engine. Once the engine/transaxle assembly is removed from the vehicle, then the transaxle can be separated, with the transfer case, from the engine.

1. Disconnect the negative battery cable.
2. Unlock the steering and place the transaxle in neutral.

3. Disconnect the following wires in the engine compartment:
   a. battery positive cable
   b. black/white wire from the solenoid
   c. back-up light switch
   d. transaxle ground cable.

4. Unclip and remove the speedometer cable at the transaxle. Do not disassemble the speedometer gear holder.

5. Disconnect the clutch cable at the release arm.

6. Remove the transaxle side starter mounting bolts and the top transaxle bolts. Loosen the front wheel lug nuts.

7. Raise and support the vehicle safely. Remove the front wheel and tire assemblies.

8. Attach a suitable chain hoist to the rear of the engine, then raise the engine slightly to take the weight off of the mounts. Drain the transaxle, then reinstall the drain plug and washer.

9. Remove the splash shields from the underside. Remove the stabilizer bar. Disconnect the left and right lower ball joints and tie end rods, using a ball joint remover.

NOTE: Use caution when removing the ball joints. Place a floor jack under the lower control arm, securely at the ball joint. Otherwise, the lower control arm may jump suddenly away from the steering knuckle as the ball joint is removed.

10. Disconnect the header pipe at the exhaust manifold.

11. Turn the right steering knuckle out as far as it will go. Place a pry bar against the inboard CV-joint, pry the right axle out of the transaxle about ½ in. This will force the spring clip out of the groove inside the differential gear splines. Pull it out the rest of the way. Repeat this procedure on the other side.

12. Disconnect the shift lever torque rod from the clutch housing.

13. Slide the pin retainer back, drive out the spring pin using a pin punch, then disconnect the shift rod.

14. Place a transaxle jack under the transaxle and raise the transaxle jack securely against the transaxle to take up the weight.

15. Remove the bolts from the front transaxle mount. Remove the transaxle housing bolts from the engine torque bracket.

16. Remove the clutch housing bolts from the rear transaxle mount. Remove the 2 remaining transaxle bolts.

17. Pull the transaxle away from the engine until the mainshaft clears the clutch pressure plate, then lower the transaxle clear of the engine and lower the jack.

To install:

18. Clean and grease the release bearing sliding surfaces.

19. Make sure two 14mm dowel pins are installed in the clutch housing.

20. Raise the transaxle and slide it onto the dowels. Slide the transaxle into position aligning the mainshaft splines with the clutch plate.

21. Install the engine-to-transaxle mounting bolts and tighten to 50 ft. lbs. (68 Nm).

22. Install the rear transaxle mount on the transaxle housing and tighten to 47 ft. lbs. (65 Nm).

23. Install the engine torque bracket on the transaxle housing. Tighten the bolts to 33 ft. lbs. (45 Nm).

24. Loosely install the bolts for the front transaxle mount. Tighten the horizontal bolt to 33 ft. lbs. (45 Nm), then tighten the vertical bolts to 18 ft. lbs. (24 Nm) starting with the bolt closest to the transaxle housing.

25. Install the starter mounting bolts and tighten to 33 ft. lbs. (45 Nm).

26. Turn the right steering knuckle out far enough to fit the end of the halfshaft into the transaxle. Use new 26mm spring clips on both axles. Repeat procedure for the other side.

27. Make sure the axles bottom fully so the spring clips can be felt engaging the differential.

28. Install the lower ball joints. Tighten the nuts to 33 ft. lbs. (45 Nm).

29. Install the tie rods. Tighten the nuts to 33 ft. lbs. (45 Nm).

30. Connect the shift linkage.

31. Connect the shift lever torque rod to the clutch housing.

32. Install the stabilizer bar.

33. Install the lower shields.

34. Reconnect the exhaust header pipe.

35. Install the front wheels and tighten the lug nuts to 80 ft. lbs. (110 Nm).

36. Remove the hoist chain and install the top transaxle mounting bolts. Tighten the bolts to 33 ft. lbs. (45 Nm).

37. Install the clutch cable at the release arm.

38. Install the speedometer cable into the gear holder, then secure the cable with the clip and install the boot.

39. Connect all engine compartment wiring.

40. Fill the transaxle with the proper type and quantity of oil.

41. Adjust the clutch pedal free-play.

1988–91 CIVIC AND CRX

1. Disconnect the battery cables from the battery.

2. Remove the 3 mount bolts and loosen the 1 bolt located at the side of the battery base. Remove the intake hose band at the throttle body.

3. Remove the air cleaner case complete with the intake hose. Disconnect the starter and transaxle ground cables.

4. Disconnect the speedometer, but be sure not to disassemble the speedometer gear holder.

5. Disconnect the back-up light switch connector and the clutch cable release arm.

6. Drain the transaxle fluid into a suitable drain pan. Disconnect the connectors and remove the mount bolts.

7. Remove the distributor assembly, as required.

8. Remove the starter mounting bolts and remove the starter assembly. Remove the engine splash shield and the right wheelwell splash shield.

9. Remove the header pipe. Remove the cotter pin and the lower arm ball joint nut, separate the ball joint and lower arm.

10. Remove the bolts and nut, then remove the right radius rod. Remove the right and left halfshafts. Remove the header pipe bracket. Remove the shift lever torque rod and shift rod from the clutch housing.

11. On 4WD vehicles, remove the driveshaft and the intermediate shaft. Remove the cable bracket and the side transaxle mount from the transaxle housing and body.

12. Install a bolt at the cylinder head and attach a suitable chain hoist to the bolt and the other end to the engine hanger plate. Lift the engine slightly to unload the mounts.

13. Place a suitable transaxle jack under the transaxle and raise it just enough to take the weights off of the mounts.

14. Remove the front transaxle mounting bolts. Remove the rear transaxle mounting bolts. Remove the side transaxle mount, remove the 5 remaining transaxle mounting bolts and pull the transaxle assembly far enough away from the engine to clear the 14mm dowel pins.

15. Separate the mainshaft from the clutch pressure plate and remove the transaxle by lowering the jack.

To install:

16. Make sure the two 14mm dowel pins are installed in the clutch housing.

17. Raise the transaxle into position with the transaxle jack. Loosely install the transaxle mount bolts and then tighten to 43 ft. lbs. (60 Nm).

18. Install the engine side mount bolt and tighten to 50 ft. lbs. (68 Nm).

19. Install the transaxle-to-rear transaxle mount bracket. Tighten the bolts to 40 ft. lbs. (55 Nm).

20. Install the transaxle-to-front transaxle mount and tighten the bolts to 29 ft. lbs. (40 Nm).

21. Install the transaxle-to-side transaxle mount and tighten the bolts to 43 ft. lbs. (60 Nm).

22. Install the starter and tighten the starter bolts to 33 ft. lbs. (45 Nm).
23. Remove the transaxle jack and the chain hoist and bolts.
24. Install the shift lever torque rod and shift rod. After reassembly, slide the retainer back into place after driving in the spring pin.
25. Install the header pipe bracket and tighten the bolts to 16 ft. lbs. (22 Nm).
26. On 4WD vehicles, install the cable bracket to the rear transaxle mount bracket. Install the select and shift cables. Install the intermediate shaft and the driveshaft.
27. Install a new set ring on the end of each halfshaft. Install the right and left halfshafts. Turn the right steering knuckle fully outward and slide the axle into the differential, until the spring clip is felt to engage the differential side gear.
28. Install the damper fork and radius rod. Tighten the radius rod nut to 39 ft. lbs. (44 Nm).
29. Install the ball joints to the lower arm. Tighten the stud nuts to 40 ft. lbs. (55 Nm) and install a new cotter pin.
30. Install the splash shields and exhaust header pipe.
31. Install the distributor.
32. Connect the speedometer cable and connect the clutch cable to the release arm.
33. Connect the back-up light switch connector.
34. Install the 3 bolts located at the side of the battery base and retighten the intake hose band of the throttle body.
35. Fill the transaxle with the proper type and quantity of oil.
36. Connect the starter and transaxle ground cable.
37. Install the air cleaner case and intake hose.
38. Connect the battery cables, start the engine and check the ignition timing.

1987-89 ACCORD AND 1987 PRELUDE

1. Disconnect the battery ground cable at the battery and the transaxle case. Unlock the steering column; place the transaxle in neutral.
2. Disconnect the engine compartment wiring as follows:
   a. Positive battery cable from the starter.
   b. Back-up light switch wires.
   c. Black/white wire from the starter solenoid.
3. Release the engine sub wiring harness from the clamp at the clutch housing. Disconnect the clutch cable at the release arm and remove the upper 2 transaxle mounting bolts.
4. Raise the vehicle and support it safely. Drain the transaxle fluid.
5. Remove the front wheels. Place a suitable transaxle jack into position under the transaxle.
6. Disconnect the speedometer cable.

NOTE: When removing the speedometer cable from the transaxle, it is not necessary to remove the entire cable holder. Remove the end boot, gear holder seal, the cable retaining clip and then pull the cable out of the holder.

7. Disconnect the shift lever torque rod from the clutch housing. Remove the bolt from the shift rod clevis.
8. Disconnect the tie rod ball joints and remove them using a suitable ball joint remover tool.
9. Remove the lower arm ball joint bolt from the right side lower control arm, then using a puller disconnect the ball joint from the knuckle. Remove the damper fork bolt.
10. Turn each steering knuckle to its most outboard position. Using a suitable tool, pry the right side CV-joint out approximately ½ in., then pull the sub axle out of the transaxle housing. Repeat this procedure for the opposite side. Remove the right side radius rod.
11. Remove the torque arm bracket bolts from the clutch housing.
12. Remove the damper bracket from the transaxle. Remove the clutch housing bolts from the front transaxle mount.

13. Remove the clutch housing bolts from the rear transaxle mounting bracket. Remove the clutch cover.
14. Remove the starter mounting bolts and remove the starter. Remove the transaxle mounting bolt.
15. Pull the transaxle away from the engine block to clear the two 14mm dowel pins and lower the transaxle jack.
To install:
16. Clean and grease the release bearing sliding surface. Make sure that the two 14mm dowel pins are installed in the clutch housing.
17. Raise the transaxle enough to align the dowel pins with the matching holes in the block.
18. Move the transaxle toward the engine and fit the mainshaft into the clutch disc splines. Push and maneuver the transaxle until it fits flush with the engine flange.
19. Tighten the bolts until the clutch housing is seated against the block.
20. Loosely install the bolts for the front transaxle mount. Tighten the uppermost horizontal bolt to 33 ft. lbs. (45 Nm), then tighten the vertical bolt closest to the transaxle case, to the same torque specification. Tighten the 2 remaining bolts to 33 ft. lbs. (45 Nm), beginning with the remaining horizontal bolt.
21. Install the upper torque arm and it's bracket. Tighten the bracket mounting bolts to 47 ft. lbs. (65 Nm) and the torque arm bolts to 54 ft. lbs. (75 Nm).
22. Remove the transaxle jack.
23. Install the starter and tighten the mounting bolts to 33 ft. lbs. (45 Nm).
24. Install new spring clips on the end of each stub axle. Turn the right steering knuckle/axle assembly outward enough to insert the free end of the axle into the transaxle. Repeat on the opposite side. Slide the axle in until the spring clips are felt engaging the differential.
25. Install the lower ball joints and tie rods. Tighten the tie rod nuts to 32 ft. lbs. (44 Nm) and the ball joint nuts to 40 ft. lbs. (55 Nm). Install new cotter pins. Install the damper fork bolt.
26. Connect the shift linkage.
27. Connect the shift lever torque rod to the clutch housing and tighten the bolt to 16 ft. lbs. (22 Nm).
28. Install the front wheel and tire assemblies. Install transaxle drain plug and tighten to 29 ft. lbs. (40 Nm).
29. Lower the vehicle.
30. Install the clutch cable at the release arm.
31. Coat a new O-ring with oil, put it on the speedometer gear holder, then install the holder in the transaxle housing and secure with the hold-down tab and bolt.
32. Install the engine sub-wire harness in the clamp at the clutch housing.
33. Connect all engine compartment wiring.
34. Fill the transaxle with the proper type and quantity of oil.
35. Connect the negative battery cable.

1990-91 ACCORD

1. Disconnect the battery cables and remove the battery.
2. Raise and safely support the vehicle.
3. Remove the air intake hose and battery base.
4. Disconnect the starter wires and remove the starter.
5. Disconnect the transaxle ground cable and the back-up light switch wire.
6. Remove the cable stay and then disconnect the cables from the top housing of the transaxle. Remove both cables and the stay together.
7. Disconnect the connector and remove the speed sensor, but leave it's hoses connected.
8. Remove the front wheel and tire assemblies.
9. Remove the engine splash shield and drain the transaxle fluid.
10. Remove the mounting bolts and clutch slave cylinder with the clutch pipe and pushrod.
11. Remove the mounting bolt and clutch hose joint with the clutch pipe and clutch hose.

NOTE: Do not operate the clutch pedal once the slave cylinder has been removed. Be careful not to bend the pipe.

12. Remove the center beam and the header pipe.
13. Remove the cotter pins and lower arm ball joint nuts. Separate the ball joints and lower arms using a suitable tool.
14. Remove the damper fork bolt.
15. Use a suitable tool to pry the right and left halfshafts out of the differential and the intermediate shaft. Pull on the inboard joint and remove the right and left halfshafts.
16. Remove the 3 mounting bolts and lower the bearing support.
17. Remove the intermediate shaft from the differential.
18. Remove the right damper pinch bolt, then separate the damper fork and damper. Remove the bolts and nut, then remove the right radius rod.
19. Remove the engine stiffener and the clutch cover.
20. Remove the intake manifold bracket.
21. Remove the rear engine mount bracket stay and remove the 3 rear engine mount bracket mounting bolts.
22. Remove the transaxle housing mounting bolt on the engine side. Swing the right halfshaft to the inner fender.
23. Place a suitable jack under the transaxle and raise the transaxle just enough to take the weight off the mounts.
24. Remove the transaxle mount bolt and loosen the mount bracket nuts.
25. Remove the 3 transaxle housing mounting bolts.
26. Remove the transaxle from the vehicle.

To install:

27. Make sure the 4 dowel pins are installed.
28. Raise the transaxle into position.
29. Install the 3 transaxle mounting bolts and tighten to 47 ft. lbs. (65 Nm).
30. Install the transaxle mount and mount bracket. Install the through bolt and tighten temporarily. Make sure the engine is level and tighten the 3 mount bracket nuts to 40 ft. lbs. (55 Nm). Tighten the through bolt to 47 ft. lbs. (65 Nm).
31. Install the transaxle housing mounting bolts on the engine side and tighten to 47 ft. lbs. (65 Nm).
32. Install the 3 rear engine bracket mounting bolts and tighten to 40 ft. lbs. (55 Nm).
33. Install the rear engine mount bracket stay. Tighten the mounting bolt to 28 ft. lbs. (39 Nm) and then tighten the mounting nut to 15 ft. lbs. (21 Nm).
34. Install the intake manifold bracket and tighten the bolts to 16 ft. lbs. (22 Nm).
35. Install the clutch cover and tighten the bolts to 9 ft. lbs. (12 Nm).
36. Install the engine stiffener and loosely install the mounting bolts. Tighten the stiffener-to-transaxle case mounting bolt to 28 ft. lbs. (39 Nm), then tighten the 2 stiffener-to-cylinder block mounting bolts to 28 ft. lbs. (39 Nm) beginning with the bolt closest to the transaxle.
37. Install the radius rod. Tighten the radius rod mounting bolts to 76 ft. lbs. (105 Nm) and the radius rod nut to 32 ft. lbs. (44 Nm).
38. Install the damper fork. Tighten the damper pinch bolt to 32 ft. lbs. (44 Nm).
39. Install the intermediate shaft.
40. Install a new set ring on the end of each halfshaft. Install the right and left halfshafts. Turn the right and left steering knuckle fully outward and slide the axle into the differential, until the spring clip is felt engaging the differential side gear.
41. Install the damper fork bolt and ball joint nut to the lower arms. Tighten the nut while holding the damper fork bolt to 40 ft. lbs. (55 Nm). Tighten the ball joint nut to 40 ft. lbs. (55 Nm). Install a new cotter pin.
42. Install the header pipe and center beam. Tighten the center beam bolts to 28 ft. lbs. (39 Nm).

43. Install the clutch hose joint and clutch slave cylinder to the transaxle housing. Tighten the slave cylinder mounting bolts to 16 ft. lbs. (22 Nm).
44. Install the speed sensor. Tighten the mounting bolt to 13 ft. lbs. (18 Nm).
45. Install the shift cable and select cable to the shift arm lever and to the select lever respectively. Tighten the cable bracket mounting bolts to 16 ft. lbs. (22 Nm). Install new cotter pins.
46. Connect the back-up light switch coupler.
47. Install the starter. Tighten the 10 × 1.25mm bolt to 32 ft. lbs. (45 Nm) and the 12 × 1.25mm bolt to 54 ft. lbs. (75 Nm). Connect the starter wires.
48. Install the transaxle ground cable.
49. Install the front wheel and tire assemblies.
50. Fill the transaxle with the proper type and quantity of oil.
51. Lower the vehicle.
52. Install the battery and connect the battery cables.
53. Check the clutch pedal free-play.
54. Start the vehicle and check the transaxle for smooth operation.

1988–91 PRELUDE

1. Disconnect the negative battery cable at the battery and the transaxle. Raise and safely support the vehicle.
2. Disconnect the wiring for the starter and the back-up light switch.
3. On fuel injected vehicles, remove the air cleaner case.
4. Remove the power steering speed sensor from the transaxle, without removing the power steering hoses.
5. Remove the shift cable and the select cable from the top cover of the transaxle. Remove the mounting bolt from the cable stay. Remove the cables and the stay together.
6. Remove the upper transaxle mounting bracket.
7. Remove the 4 transaxle-to-block attachment bolts, that must be removed from the engine compartment.
8. Raise and safely support the vehicle.
9. Remove the front wheel and tire assemblies.
10. Remove the engine splash shield.
11. Drain the transaxle oil.
12. Remove the clutch slave cylinder and the center beam.
13. Remove the right radius rod. Remove the right and left halfshafts.
14. Remove the intermediate shaft.
15. Remove the engine stiffener and the clutch cover.
16. Support the transaxle with a suitable jack.
17. Remove the 3 lower bolts from the rear engine mounting bracket. Loosen but do not remove the top bolt. This bolt will support the weight of the engine.
18. Remove the 2 remaining engine-to-transaxle mounting bolts.
19. Pull the transaxle away from the engine and disengage the input shaft from the clutch disc. Lower the transaxle and remove it from the vehicle.

To install:

20. Make sure the 14mm dowel pin is installed in the transaxle.
21. Raise the transaxle into position.
22. Install the engine side transaxle mount bolts and tighten to 47 ft. lbs. (65 Nm). Install the transaxle side transaxle mount bolts and tighten to 47 ft. lbs. (65 Nm).
23. Attach the transaxle mounting bracket. Tighten the transaxle mount bolts to 28 ft. lbs. (39 Nm) and the mount through bolt to 54 ft. lbs. (75 Nm).
24. Install and tighten the rear engine mounting bracket bolts to 54 ft. lbs. (75 Nm).
25. Attach the clutch cover and tighten the bolts to 9 ft. lbs. (12 Nm).
26. Attach the engine stiffener and tighten the mounting bolts to 28 ft. lbs. (39 Nm). The bolts should be tightened in sequence beginning with the top most stiffener-to-transaxle case bolt, fol-

lowed by the remaining stiffener-to-transaxle bolt, then the stiffener-to-cylinder block bolt closest to the transaxle and finally the remaining stiffener-to-cylinder block bolt.

27. Install the intermediate shaft and the left and right halfshaft.

28. Install the center beam and tighten the bolts to 37 ft. lbs. (51 Nm).

29. Install the clutch slave cylinder with the clutch hose and pushrod. Tighten the slave cylinder bolts to 16 ft. lbs. (22 Nm).

30. Attach the transaxle side shift cable and select cable to the shift arm lever and to the select lever respectively. Tighten the bracket mounting bolts to 16 ft. lbs. (22 Nm).

31. Connect the back-up light switch coupler.

32. Attach the right and left front damper forks.

33. Install the speed sensor assembly and the air cleaner case.

34. Connect the starter cable and connect the ground cable to the transaxle.

35. Install the wheel and tire assemblies.

36. Fill the transaxle with the proper type and quantity of oil.

37. Lower the vehicle and connect the negative battery cable. Check the clutch pedal free-play.

Linkage Adjustment

1988–91 Prelude, 1990–91 Accord and Civic Wagon with 4WD, feature cable operated gear shift mechanisms that are adjustable. All other vehicles have non-adjustable, rod operated, gear shift linkage.

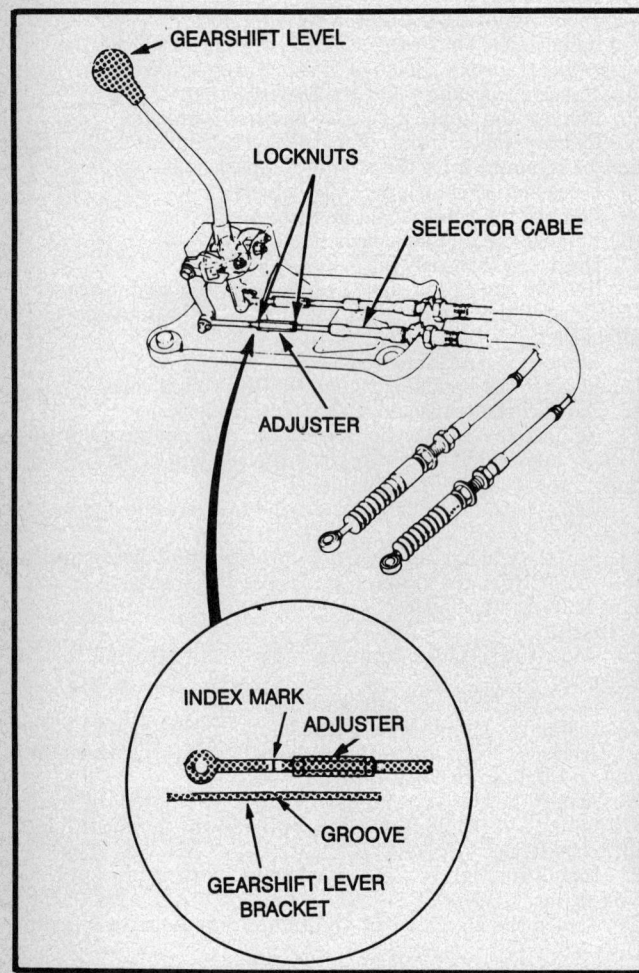

Selector cable adjustment—4WD Civic Wagon and 1988–91 Prelude

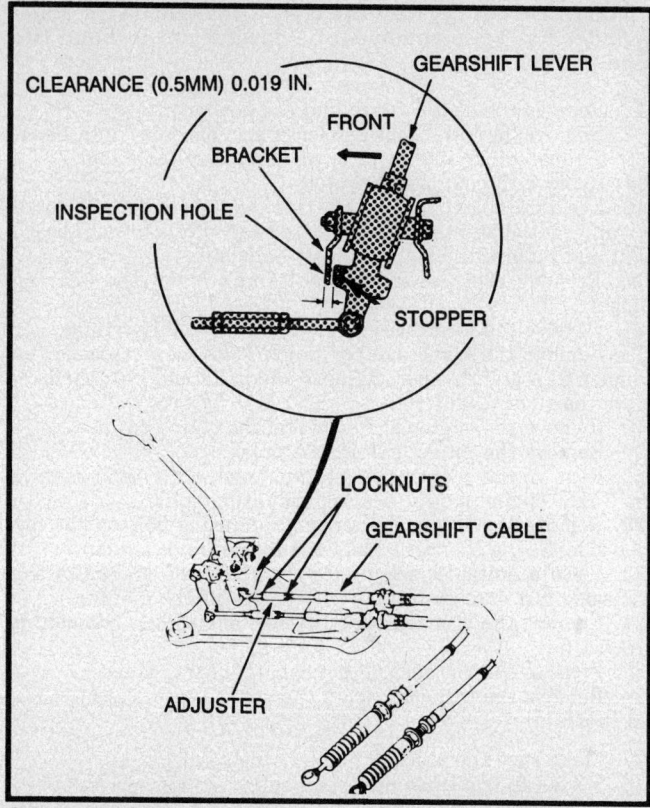

Gear shift cable adjustment—4WD Civic Wagon and 1988–91 Prelude

1988–91 PRELUDE AND 4WD CIVIC WAGON

Select Cable

1. Disconnect the negative battery cable.
2. Remove the console.
3. With the transaxle in neutral, check that the groove in the lever bracket is aligned with the index mark on the selector cable.
4. If the index mark is not aligned with the groove in the cable, loosen the locknuts and turn the adjuster as necessary.

NOTE: After adjustment, check the operation of the gear shift lever. Make sure the threads of the cables do not extend out of the cable adjuster by more than 0.4 in. (10mm).

5. Replace the console and connect the negative battery cable.

Shift Cable

1. Disconnect the negative battery cable.
2. Remove the console.
3. Place the transaxle in 4th gear.
4. Measure the clearance between the gear shift lever bracket and stopper, while pushing the lever forward. The clearance should be 0.15–188 in. (3.8–4.8mm) on 1987 4WD Civic Wagon and 0.24–28 in. (6.0–7.0mm) on 1988–91 4WD Civic Wagon and Prelude.
5. If the clearance is outside specification, loosen the locknuts and turn the adjuster in or out until the correct clearance is obtained.

NOTE: After adjustment, check the operation of the gear shift lever. Make sure the threads of the cables do not extend out of the cable adjuster by more than 0.4 in. (10mm).

6. Replace the console and connect the negative battery cable.

1990–91 ACCORD
Select Cable

1. Disconnect the negative battery cable.
2. Remove the console.
3. Place the shift lever in the neutral position.
4. Measure the clearance between (A) and (B). It should be 8.37–8.40 in. (212.5–213.5mm).
5. If the clearance is incorrect, disconnect the select cable from the linkage, loosen the locknut and turn the adjuster, as necessary.
6. Tighten the locknut and connect the select cable to the linkage. Install a new cotter pin.

NOTE: Make sure the new cotter pin is seated firmly. After adjustment, check the operation of the shift lever.

7. Install the console and connect the negative battery cable.

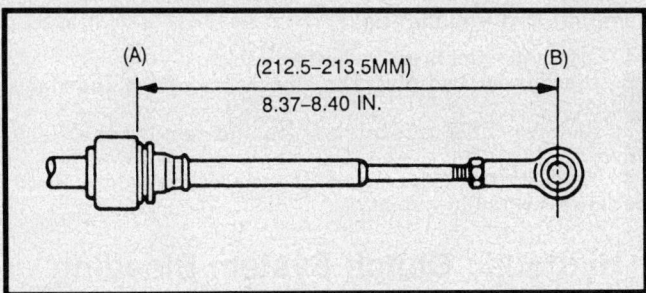

Select cable clearance measurement—1990–91 Accord

Shift Cable

1. Disconnect the negative battery cable.
2. Remove the console.
3. Place the shift lever in the neutral position.
4. Measure the clearance between (A) and (B). The clearance should be 6.86–6.90 in. (174.3–175.3mm).
5. If the clearance is incorrect, disconnect the shift cable from the change lever, loosen the locknut and turn the adjuster, as necessary.
6. Tighten the locknut and connect the shift cable to the change lever. Install a new cotter pin.

NOTE: Make sure the new cotter pin is seated firmly. After adjustment, check the operation of the gear shift lever.

7. Install the console and connect the negative battery cable.

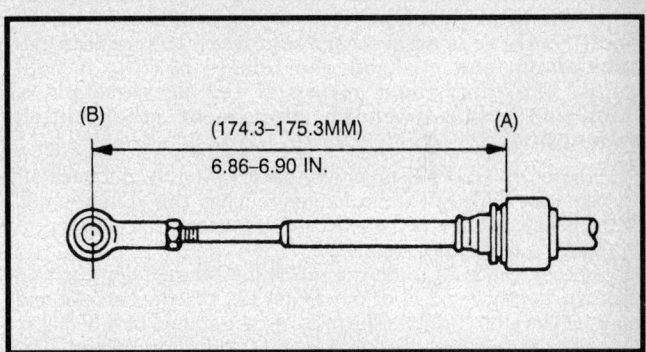

Shift cable clearance measurement—1990–91 Accord

CLUTCH

Clutch Assembly

Removal and Installation

1. Disconnect the negative battery cable. Raise and safely support the vehicle. Remove the transaxle from the vehicle. Matchmark the flywheel and clutch for reassembly.
2. Hold the flywheel ring gear with a tool made for this purpose, remove the retaining bolts and remove the pressure plate and clutch disc. Remove the bolts 2 turns at a time working in a criss-cross pattern, to prevent warping the pressure plate.
3. At this time, inspect the flywheel for wear, cracks or scoring and resurface or replace, as necessary.
4. If the clutch release bearing is to be replaced, perform the following procedure on all except 1988–91 Prelude and 1990–91 Accord:
    a. Remove the 8mm special bolt.
    b. Remove the release shaft and the release bearing assembly.
    c. Separate the release fork from the bearing by removing the release fork spring from the holes in the release bearing.
5. To remove the release bearing on 1988–91 Prelude and 1990–91 Accord, perform the following procedure:
    a. Remove the boot from the clutch housing.
    b. Remove the release fork from the clutch housing by squeezing the release fork set spring with a suitable tool.
    c. Remove the release bearing from the release fork.
6. Check the release bearing for excessive play by spinning it by hand. Replace if there is excessive play.
To install:
7. If the flywheel was removed, make sure the flywheel and crankshaft mating surfaces are clean. Align the hole in the flywheel with the crankshaft dowel pin and install the flywheel bolts finger tight. Install the ring gear holder and tighten the flywheel bolts in a criss-cross pattern. Tighten the flywheel bolts to 76 ft. lbs. (105 Nm) except on 1988–91 Civic and CRX where they are tightened to 87 ft. lbs. (120 Nm).
8. Install the clutch disc and pressure plate by aligning the dowels on the flywheel with the dowel holes in the pressure plate. If the same pressure plate is being installed that was removed, align the marks that were made during the removal procedure. Install the pressure plate bolts finger tight.
9. Insert a suitable clutch disc alignment tool into the splined hole in the clutch disc. Tighten the pressure plate bolts in a criss-cross pattern 2 turns at a time to prevent warping the pressure plate. The final torque should be 19 ft. lbs. (26 Nm).
10. Remove the alignment tool and ring gear holder.
11. If the release bearing was removed, replace it in the reverse order of the removal procedure. Place a light coat of molybdenum disulfide grease on the inside diameter of the bearing prior to installation.
12. Install the transaxle, making sure the mainshaft is properly aligned with the clutch disc splines and the transaxle case is properly aligned with the cylinder block, before tightening the transaxle case bolts.
13. Adjust the clutch pedal free-play and connect the negative battery cable.

Pedal Height/Free-Play Adjustment
EXCEPT 1988–91 PRELUDE AND 1990–91 ACCORD

1. Measure the clutch pedal disengagement height.

2. Measure the clutch pedal free play.

3. Adjust the clutch pedal free-play by turning the clutch cable adjusting nut, found at the end of the clutch cable housing near the release shaft.

4. Turn the adjusting nut until the clutch pedal free-play is as follows:

1987 Civic and CRX—0.63–0.83 in. (16–21mm).
1988–91 Civic and CRX—0.6–0.8 in. (15–20mm).
1987–89 Accord and 1987 Prelude—0.6–1.0 in. (15–25mm).

5. After adjustment, make sure the free-play at the tip of the release arm is as follows:

1987–88 Civic and CRX—0.16–0.20 in. (4.0–5.0mm).
1989–91 Civic and CRX—0.12–0.16 in. (3.0–4.0mm).
1987–89 Accord and 1987 Prelude—0.20–0.25 in. (5.2–6.4mm).

1988–91 PRELUDE AND 1990–91 ACCORD

NOTE: The clutch is self adjusting to compensate for wear. The total clutch pedal free-play is 0.35–0.59 in. (9–15mm). If there is no clearance between the master cylinder piston and pushrod, the release bearing is held against the diaphragm spring of the pressure plate, which can result in clutch slippage or other clutch malfunction.

1. Loosen the locknut on clutch pedal switch A and back off the pedal switch until it no longer touches the clutch pedal. Clutch pedal switch A is the switch that contacts the clutch pedal below the clutch pedal pivot.

2. Loosen the locknut on the clutch master cylinder pushrod and turn the pushrod in or out to get the specified stroke and height at the clutch pedal. The pedal stroke should be 5.3–5.5 in. (135–140mm) on Prelude and 5.6 in. (142mm) on Accord. The pedal height should be 8.1 in. (207mm) on Prelude and 8.27 in. (210mm) on Accord.

3. Tighten the pushrod locknut.

4. Thread in clutch pedal switch A until it contacts the clutch pedal, then turn it in ¼–½ turn further.

5. Tighten the locknut on clutch pedal switch A.

Clutch Cable

Removal and Installation

1. Disconnect the negative battery cable.
2. Disconnect the cable end from the brake pedal.
3. Remove the adjuster nut assembly from its mounting.
4. Raise and support the vehicle safely.

5. Disconnect the cable end from the release arm. Remove the cable from the vehicle.

6. Installation is the reverse of the removal procedure. Adjust the cable to specification.

Clutch Master Cylinder

Removal and Installation

1. Disconnect the negative battery cable. Pry out the cotter pin and pull the pedal pin out of the yoke.

2. Remove the nuts and bolts retaining the clutch master cylinder and remove the cylinder from the engine compartment.

3. Disconnect and plug the hydraulic lines from the master cylinder.

4. Installation is the reverse order of the removal procedure. Bleed the clutch hydraulic system.

Clutch Slave Cylinder

Removal and Installation

1. Disconnect the negative battery cable.
2. Disconnect and plug the clutch hose from the slave cylinder.

3. Remove the 2 retaining bolts and remove the slave cylinder.

4. Installation is the reverse of the removal procedure. Bleed the clutch hydraulic system.

Hydraulic Clutch System Bleeding

The hydraulic system must be bled whenever the system has been leaking or dismantled. The bleed screw is located on the slave cylinder.

1. Remove the bleed screw dust cap.

2. Attach a clear hose to the bleed screw. Immerse the other end of the hose in a clear jar, half filled with brake fluid.

3. Fill the clutch master cylinder with fresh brake fluid.

4. Open the bleed screw slightly and have an assistant slowly depress the clutch pedal. Close the bleed screw when the pedal reaches the end of its travel. Allow the clutch pedal to return slowly.

5. Repeat Steps 3–4 until all air bubbles are expelled from the system.

6. Discard the brake fluid in the jar. Replace the dust cap. Refill the master cylinder.

AUTOMATIC TRANSAXLE

Transaxle Assembly

Removal and Installation

1987 CIVIC AND CRX

1. Disconnect the negative battery cable at the battery and the transaxle.

2. Unlock the steering and place the transaxle in **N**.

3. Disconnect the positive battery cable from the starter and the wire from the solenoid.

4. Disconnect and plug the transaxle cooler hoses.

5. Remove the starter and the top 3 transaxle mounting bolts.

6. Raise and safely support the vehicle.

7. Remove the front wheel and tire assemblies.

8. Drain the transaxle and reinstall the drain plug and washer.

9. Remove the throttle cable by first removing the cable end, then loosen the locknut on the cable end side of the bracket. Remove the cable from the bracket.

10. Remove the cable clip, then pull the speedometer cable out of the holder. Do not remove the holder as the speedometer gear may fall into the transaxle housing.

11. Remove the engine and wheelwell splash shields and remove the exhaust header pipe.

12. Position a suitable jack under the lower control arm and disconnect the right and left lower arm ball joints and tie rod end ball joints, using a suitable ball joint remover.

NOTE: Make sure the floor jack is positioned securely under the lower control arm, at the ball joint. Otherwise, torsion bar tension on the lower control arm may cause the arm to jump suddenly away from the steering knuckle as the ball joint is being removed.

13. Turn the right steering knuckle outward as far as it will go. With a suitable tool against the inboard CV-joint, pry the right axle out of the transaxle housing approximately ½ in., to force the spring clip out of the groove inside the differential side gear splines. Pull the axle out the rest of the way. Repeat the procedure on the opposite side.

14. Attach a suitable hoist to the 8mm bolt near the distributor, then lift the engine slightly to unload the mounts.

15. Position a suitable transaxle jack under the transaxle and raise it into position.

16. Remove the bolts from the front transaxle mount.

17. Remove the transaxle housing bolts from the engine torque bracket.

18. Remove the torque converter housing bolts from the rear transaxle mount.

19. Remove the torque converter cover plate and the bolts from the driveplate.

20. Remove the center console and remove the cotter pin from the shift cable control pin, then pull out the control pin.

21. Remove the cable holder and carefully remove the shift cable. Be careful not to lose the shift cable bushing.

22. Remove the remaining transaxle mounting bolt from the engine side.

23. Pull the tranaxle away from the engine to clear the two 14mm dowel pins, then lower the jack.

To install:

24. Make sure the two 14mm dowel pins are installed in the torque converter housing.

25. Raise the transaxle into position and align the dowel pins with the holes in the block and the torque converter bolt heads with the holes in the driveplate.

26. Install the 12 × 1.25 × 70mm engine side mounting bolt and tighten to 42 ft. lbs. (58 Nm).

27. Attach the torque converter to the driveplate with the 8 mounting bolts. Tighten the bolts in 2 steps, first to 4.5 ft. lbs. (6 Nm) in a criss-cross pattern and finally to 9 ft. lbs. (12 Nm) in the same pattern. Check for free rotation after tightening the last bolt.

28. Install the shift cable.

29. Remove the transaxle jack.

30. Install the torque converter cover plate.

31. Install the rear transaxle bolt. Tighten the mounting bolts to 47 ft. lbs. (65 Nm).

32. Install the engine torque bracket and tighten the bolts to 33 ft. lbs. (45 Nm).

33. Loosely install the front transaxle mount bolts. Tighten the mount-to-transaxle bolt to 33 ft. lbs. (45 Nm), then tighten the 2 mount-to-cylinder block bolts to 18 ft. lbs. (24 Nm) beginning with the bolt closest to the transaxle.

34. Install the starter and tighten the mounting bolts to 33 ft. lbs. (45 Nm).

35. Install a new 26mm spring clip on the end of each axle.

36. Turn the right steering knuckle fully outward and slide the axle into the differential, until the spring clip is felt to engage the differential side gear. Repeat the procedure on the left side.

37. Reconnect the lower arm ball joints and tighten the nuts to 33 ft. lbs. (45 Nm). Install new cotter pins.

38. Reconnect the tie rod end ball joints and tighten to 33 ft. lbs. (45 Nm). Install new cotter pins.

39. Install the splash shields and exhaust header pipe.

40. Install the front wheel and tire assemblies.

41. Lower the vehicle and remove the hoist.

42. Insert the speedometer cable into the gear holder, then secure the cable with the clip and install the boot.

43. Install the top 3 transaxle mounting bolts and tighten them to 42 ft. lbs. (58 Nm).

44. Connect the transaxle cooler hoses and tighten the banjo bolts to 21 ft. lbs. (29 Nm).

45. Attach the shift control cable to the shaft lever with the pin and clip. Check the cable adjustment and reinstall the center console.

46. Connect the positive battery cable to the starter, the wire to the solenoid and the transaxle ground cable.

47. Connect the negative battery cable to the transaxle.

48. Unscrew the dipstick from the top of the transaxle end cover and add 2.5 quarts of Dexron® ATF through the hole. Reinstall the dipstick.

NOTE: If the torque converter was replaced, the ATF fill quantity is 5.7 quarts.

49. Connect the negative battery cable, start the engine, set the parking brake and shift the transaxle through all gears 3 times. Check for proper control cable adjustment.

50. Let the engine reach operating temperature with the transaxle in **N** or **P**, then turn the engine off and check the fluid level.

51. Install the throttle control cable and adjust.

1988–91 CIVIC AND CRX

1. Disconnect the battery cables and remove the battery.

2. Raise and safely support the vehicle.

3. Remove the 3 mount bolts and loosen the 1 bolt located at the side of the battery base and intake hose band of the throttle body.

4. Remove the air cleaner case, complete with the intake hose.

5. Remove the starter and the transaxle ground cable.

6. Disconnect the lock-up control solenoid valve wire connector. On 4WD Civic Wagon, disconnect the lock-up control solenoid valve and shift control solenoid valve wire connectors and disconnect the automatic transaxle speed pulser connector.

7. Disconnect the control cable at the control lever.

8. Drain the transaxle fluid. Remove the filler plug to speed draining. After draining reinstall the drain plug with a new washer.

9. Disconnect and plug the cooler hoses at the joint pipes.

10. Mark the position of the distributor housing in relation to the cylinder head. Disconnect the connectors and remove the mount bolts, then remove the distributor from the cylinder head.

11. Remove the shift cable by removing the cotter pin, control pin, control lever roller and loosening the locknut.

12. Disconnect the speedometer cable. Do not disassemble the speedometer gear holder.

13. On 4WD Civic Wagon, remove the driveshaft.

14. Remove the torque converter cover. Remove the plug, then remove the driveplate bolts 1 at a time while rotating the crankshaft pulley.

15. Remove the engine splash shield and the right wheel well splash shield.

16. Remove the header pipe.

17. Remove the cotter pins and lower arm ball joint nuts and then separate the ball joints using a suitable tool.

18. Remove the bolts and nut, then remove the right radius rod.

19. Remove the right and left halfshafts. On 4WD Civic Wagon, remove the intermediate shaft.

20. On 4WD Civic Wagon, remove the 9 mounting bolts, then remove the transaxle cover.

21. Install bolts in each end of the cylinder head and attach a suitable hoist to the bolts. Lift the engine slightly to unload the mounts.

22. Place a suitable jack under the transaxle and raise the transaxle just enough to take weight off of the mounts.

23. On 4WD Civic Wagon, remove the transaxle mounting bolt on the engine side.

24. Remove the bolts from the front transaxle mount.

25. Remove the rear transaxle mount bracket by removing the 4 mounting bolts.

26. Remove the 4 mounting bolts. Remove the side transaxle mount.

27. Remove the transaxle-to-cylinder block mounting bolts.

28. On 4WD Civic Wagon, loosen the side engine mounting bolt and tilt the engine.

29. Pull the transaxle away from the engine until it clears the 14mm dowel pins, then lower the transaxle jack.

To install:

30. Make sure the two 14mm dowel pins are installed in the torque converter housing.

31. Raise the transaxle into position and loosely install the transaxle-to-cylinder block bolts. Tighten them to 43 ft. lbs. (60 Nm).

32. Install the engine side mounting bolt (12 × 1.25 × 70mm) and tighten to 50 ft. lbs. (68 Nm).

33. Install the transaxle to rear transaxle mount bracket and tighten the bolts to 40 ft. lbs. (55 Nm).

34. Install the transaxle to the front and side transaxle mounts. Tighten the mount retaining bolts to 29 ft. lbs. (40 Nm) and the mount through bolts to 40 ft. lbs. (55 Nm).

35. Remove the transaxle jack. On 4WD Civic Wagon, tighten the side engine mount bolt to 40 ft. lbs. (55 Nm).

36. Remove the hoist chain and bolts from the cylinder head.

37. Attach the torque converter to the driveplate with the eight 12mm bolts. Tighten the bolts in 2 steps, first to 4.5 ft. lbs. (6 Nm) in a criss-cross pattern and finally to 9 ft. lbs. (12 Nm) in the same pattern.

38. Install the shift cable and cable holder.

39. Install the torque converter cover and header pipe bracket.

40. On 4WD Civic Wagon, install the transaxle cover and the intermediate shaft.

41. Install a new set ring on the end of each halfshaft.

42. Turn the right steering knuckle fully outward and slide the axle into the differential, until the spring clip can be felt engaging the differential side gear. Repeat the procedure on the left side.

43. Install the damper fork bolt and radius rod.

44. Install the ball joints to the lower arms and tighten the nuts to 40 ft. lbs. (55 Nm). Install new cotter pins.

45. On 4WD Civic Wagon, install the driveshaft.

46. Install the splash shields and header pipe.

47. Install the distributor.

48. Connect the lock-up control solenoid valve wire connector. On 4WD Civic Wagon, connect the lock-up control solenoid valve and shift control solenoid valve wire connectors and connect the automatic transaxle speed pulser connector.

49. Connect the transaxle cooler hoses to the joint pipes and the control cable to the control lever.

50. Connect the speedometer cable.

51. Install the starter and tighten the bolts to 33 ft. lbs. (45 Nm).

52. Connect the positive battery cable to the starter and connect the ground cable at the transaxle.

53. Install the air intake case and hose.

54. Install the 3 bolts located at the side of the battery base and retighten the intake hose band of the throttle body.

55. Lower the vehicle, install the battery and connect the battery cables.

56. Fill the transaxle with the proper type and quantity of fluid.

57. Start the engine, set the parking brake and shift through all gears 3 times. Check for proper control cable adjustment. Check the ignition timing.

58. Let the engine reach operating temperature with the transaxle in **N** or **P**, then turn the engine off and check the fluid level.

1987-89 ACCORD AND 1987 PRELUDE

1. Disconnect the negative battery cable at the battery and the transaxle.

2. Unlock the steering and place the transaxle in **N**.

3. Disconnect the positive battery cable from the starter and the wire from the starter solenoid.

4. Disconnect and plug the transaxle cooler hoses.

5. Remove the starter and the top transaxle mounting bolt.

6. Raise and safely support the vehicle.

7. Remove the front tire and wheel assemblies.

8. Drain the transaxle and reinstall the drain plug with a new washer.

9. Remove the throttle control cable by removing the cable end from the throttle lever, loosening the locknut on the cable end side of the bracket and removing the cable from the bracket.

10. Remove the power steering speed sensor complete with speedometer cable and hoses.

11. Remove 2 upper transaxle mounting bolts.

12. Place a suitable transaxle jack securely beneath the transaxle. Attach a suitable hoist to the engine and raise the engine to just take the weight of the engine off the mounts.

13. Remove the subframe center beam and splash pan.

14. Remove the ball joint pinch bolt from the right side lower control arm, then use a suitable puller to disconnect the ball joint from the knuckle. Remove the damper fork bolt.

15. Turn the right side steering knuckle to it's most outboard position. Using a suitable tool, pry the CV-joint out approximately ½ inch, then pull the CV-joint out of the transaxle housing.

NOTE: Do not pull on the halfshaft or knuckle since this may cause the inboard CV-joint to separate. Pull on the inboard CV-joint.

16. Remove the transaxle damper bracket located in front of the torque converter cover plate.

17. Remove the torque converter cover plate.

18. Remove the center console and shift indicator.

19. Remove the lock pin from the adjuster and shift cable. Remove both bolts and pull the shift cable out of the housing.

20. Unbolt the torque converter assembly from the driveplate by removing the 8 bolts.

21. Remove the 3 rear engine mounting bolts from the transaxle housing. Remove the rear engine mount.

22. Remove the front transaxle mount's 2 bolts.

23. Remove the lower transaxle mounting bolt.

24. Pull the transaxle away from the engine to clear the two 14mm dowel pins. Pry the left side CV-joint out approximately ½ inch. Pull the transaxle out and lower the transaxle.

To install:

25. Attach the shift cable to the shift arm with the pin, then secure the cable to the edge of the housing with the cable holder and bolt. Tighten the bolt to 9 ft. lbs. (12 Nm).

26. Make sure the two 14mm dowel pins are installed in the transaxle housing.

27. Install new spring clips on the end of each axle.

28. Raise the transaxle into position, aligning the dowel pins with the holes in the block and the torque converter bolt heads with the holes in the driveplate. Fit the left axle into the differential as the transaxle is raised up to the engine.

29. Install the 2 lower transaxle mounting bolts but do not torque at this time.

30. Install the rear engine mounts on the transaxle housing and tighten the bolts to 28 ft. lbs. (39 Nm).

31. Install the front transaxle mount bolts and tighten to 28 ft. lbs. (39 Nm).

32. Attach the torque converter to the driveplate with the eight 12mm bolts. Tighten the bolts in 2 steps, first to 4.5 ft. lbs.

(6 Nm) in a criss-cross pattern and finally to 9 ft. lbs. (12 Nm) in the same pattern.

33. Remove the transaxle jack.

34. Install the torque converter cover plate and tighten the bolts to 9 ft. lbs. (12 Nm).

35. Install the wind stop rubber on the center beam and tighten the nuts to 40 ft. lbs. (55 Nm). Install the wind stop bracket on the transaxle housing and tighten the 3 bolts to 22 ft. lbs. (31 Nm).

36. Remove the hoist.

37. Install the starter and tighten the bolts to 33 ft. lbs. (45 Nm).

38. Install the rear torque rod and brackets. Tighten the bracket mounting bolts to 46 ft. lbs. (65 Nm) and the torque rod bolts to 54 ft. lbs. (75 Nm).

39. Turn the right steering knuckle fully outward and slide the axle into the differential until the spring clip is felt engaging the differential side gear.

40. Reconnect the ball joint to the knuckle, then tighten it's bolt to 40 ft. lbs. (55 Nm). Reinstall the damper fork and tighten it's bolt to 32 ft. lbs. (44 Nm).

41. Install the speedometer cable. Align the tab on the cable end with the slot in the holder. Install the clip so the bent leg is on the groove side.

NOTE: After installing, pull the speedometer cable to see if it is secure.

42. Install the wheel and tire assemblies and lower the vehicle.

43. Install the remaining transaxle mounting bolts. Tighten all the transaxle mounting bolts to 33 ft. lbs. (45 Nm).

44. Connect the transaxle cooler hoses and tighten the banjo bolts to 21 ft. lbs. (29 Nm).

45. Connect the positive battery cable to the starter, the solenoid wire to the solenoid, the wire to the water temperature sending unit and the wires to the ignition timing thermosensor.

46. Connect the negative battery cable to the transaxle.

47. Unscrew the dipstick from the top of the transaxle end cover and add 3.2 quarts of Dexron® ATF through the hole. Reinstall the dipstick.

NOTE: If the transaxle and torque converter have been disassembled, add a total of 6.3 quarts.

48. Install and reconnect the shift cable. Install the console.

49. Connect the negative battery cable, start the engine, set the parking brake and shift the transaxle through all gears 3 times. Check for proper shift cable adjustment.

50. Let the engine reach operating temperature with the transaxle in **N** or **P**, then turn the engine off and check the fluid level.

51. Install the throttle control cable and adjust.

1990–91 ACCORD

1. Disconnect the battery cable and remove the battery.
2. Raise and safely support the vehicle.
3. Remove the air intake hose, air cleaner case and battery base.
4. Disconnect the throttle cable from the throttle control lever.
5. Disconnect the transaxle ground cable and the speed sensor connectors.
6. Disconnect the starter cables and remove the starter.
7. Remove the rear mount bracket stay nut first. Remove the bolt, then remove the rear mount bracket stay.
8. Remove the speed sensor, but leave it's hoses connected.
9. Disconnect the lock-up control solenoid valve and shift control solenoid valve connectors.
10. Drain the transaxle fluid and reinstall the drain plug with a new washer.
11. Disconnect the transaxle cooler hoses from the joint pipes. Plug the hoses.

12. Remove the center beam.
13. Disconnect the oxygen sensor connector.
14. Remove the exhaust header pipe and the splash shield.
15. Remove the cotter pins and lower arm ball joint nuts, then separate the ball joints from the lower arms using a suitable tool.
16. Using a suitable tool, pry the right and left halfshafts out of the differential. Pull on the inboard CV-joints and remove the right and left halfshafts.
17. Remove the right damper pinch bolt, then separate the damper fork and damper.
18. Remove the bolts and nut, then remove the right radius rod.
19. Tie plastic bags over the halfshaft ends.
20. Remove the torque converter cover and control cable holder.
21. Remove the shift control cable by removing the cotter pin, control pin and control lever roller from the control lever.
22. Remove the plug, then remove the driveplate bolts 1 at a time while rotating the crankshaft pulley.
23. Remove the rear, engine side transaxle housing mounting bolts.
24. Remove the mounting bolts from the rear engine mount bracket.
25. Attach a suitable hoist to the transaxle housing hoisting brackets, then lift the engine slightly.
26. Place a suitable jack under the transaxle and raise the jack just enough to take weight off of the mounts.
27. Remove the 4 transaxle housing mounting bolts and 3 mount bracket nuts.
28. Pull the transaxle away from the engine until it clears the 14mm dowel pins, then lower it on the transaxle jack.

To install:

29. Make sure the two 14mm dowel pins are installed in the torque converter housing.
30. Raise the transaxle into position and install the 4 transaxle housing mounting bolts. Tighten the bolts to 47 ft. lbs. (65 Nm).
31. Install the transaxle to transaxle mount bracket and tighten the nuts to 28 ft. lbs. (39 Nm).
32. Remove the transaxle jack.
33. Install the 2 engine side transaxle housing mounting bolts and tighten to 47 ft. lbs. (65 Nm). Install the rear engine mount bracket bolts and tighten to 40 ft. lbs. (55 Nm).
34. Attach the torque converter to the driveplate with 8 bolts. Tighten the bolts in 2 steps, first to 4.5 ft. lbs. (6 Nm) in a criss-cross pattern and finally to 9 ft. lbs. (12 Nm) in the same pattern. Check for free rotation after tightening the last bolt.
35. Install the shift control cable and control cable holder. Tighten the control cable holder bolts to 13 ft. lbs. (18 Nm).
36. Install the torque converter cover and tighten the bolts to 9 ft. lbs. (12 Nm).
37. Remove the hoist.
38. Install the radius rod. Tighten the mounting bolts to 76 ft. lbs. (105 Nm) and the nut to 32 ft. lbs. (44 Nm).
39. Install the damper fork. Tighten the damper pinch bolt to 32 ft. lbs. (44 Nm).
40. Install a new set ring on the end of each halfshaft.
41. Turn the right steering knuckle fully outward and slide the axle into the differential until the spring clip is felt engaging the differential side gear. Repeat the procedure on the left side.
42. Install the damper fork bolts and ball joint nuts to the lower arms. Tighten the nut to 40 ft. lbs. (55 Nm) while holding the damper fork bolt. Tighten the ball joint nut to 40 ft. lbs. (55 Nm) and install a new cotter pin.
43. Install the splash shield, the center beam and the exhaust header pipe. Tighten the center beam bolts to 28 ft. lbs. (39 Nm).
44. Connect the oxygen sensor connector.
45. Install the speed sensor and tighten the bolt to 13 ft. lbs. (18 Nm).
46. Install the rear mount bracket stay. Tighten the mounting

bolt first, to 28 ft. lbs. (39 Nm) and then tighten the nut to 15 ft. lbs. (21 Nm).

47. Install the starter and tighten the bolts to 33 ft. lbs. (45 Nm). Connect the cables to the starter.

48. Connect the lock-up control solenoid valve and shift control solenoid valve connectors.

49. Connect the speed sensor connectors and the transaxle ground cable.

50. Connect the transaxle cooler hoses to the joint pipes.

51. Install the battery base, air cleaner case and air intake hose. Install the battery.

52. Lower the vehicle and connect the battery cables at the battery.

53. Fill the transaxle with the proper type and quantity of fluid.

54. Start the engine, set the parking brake and shift the transaxle through all gears 3 times. Check for proper control cable adjustment.

55. Let the engine reach operating temperature with the transaxle in **N** or **P**, then turn the engine off and check the fluid level.

1988–91 PRELUDE

1. Disconnect the negative battery cable at the battery and the transaxle.

2. Drain the transaxle fluid and replace the drain plug.

3. Disconnect the wiring for the starter, lock-up control solenoids, shift control solenoids and speed pulser.

4. On fuel injected vehicles, remove the air inlet hose and the air cleaner case.

5. Remove the speed sensor from the transaxle without removing the hoses.

6. Disconnect the throttle control cable at the transaxle bracket.

7. Disconnect the transaxle cooler hoses at the joint pipes and cap the joint pipes.

8. Remove the upper transaxle mounting bracket.

9. Remove the transaxle-to-cylinder block attachment bolts that must be removed from the engine compartment.

10. Raise and safely support the vehicle.

11. Remove the front wheel and tire assemblies.

12. Remove the splash shield and the center beam.

13. Remove the right radius rod completely.

14. Remove the right and left halfshafts and the intermediate shaft.

15. Remove the engine stiffener and the torque converter cover.

16. Remove the shift cable from the transaxle.

17. Remove the bolts from the driveplate.

18. Support the transaxle with a suitable jack.

19. Remove the lower bolt from the rear engine mounting bracket. Loosen, but do not remove the top bolt. This bolt will support the weight of the engine.

20. Remove the remaining engine-to-transaxle mounting bolts.

21. Separate the transaxle from the engine block. Disengage the two 14mm dowel pins and lower the transaxle.

To install:

22. Raise the transaxle into position and install the mounting bolts. Tighten the bolts to 47 ft. lbs. (65 Nm).

23. Attach the torque converter to the driveplate with the mounting bolts. Tighten the bolts in 2 steps, first to 4.5 ft. lbs. (6 Nm) in a criss-cross pattern and finally to 9 ft. lbs. (12 Nm) in the same pattern. Check for free rotation after tightening the last bolt.

24. Install the transaxle to the rear engine mount bracket with the mounting bolts. Tighten the bolts to 54 ft. lbs. (75 Nm).

25. Install the shift cable with the control pin and a new cotter pin.

26. Install the torque converter cover and the cable holder.

27. Install the engine stiffener. The engine stiffener bolts must be tightened to 28 ft. lbs. (39 Nm) in their proper order. First tighten the uppermost stiffener-to-transaxle housing bolt followed by the remaining stiffener-to-transaxle housing bolt. Next tighten the stiffener-to-cylinder block bolt closest to the transaxle followed by the remaining stiffener-to-cylinder block bolt.

28. Install the intermediate shaft and the halfshafts.

29. Install the center beam and the right and left front damper fork.

30. Install the radius rod on the transaxle side.

31. Install the transaxle mounting bracket and tighten the bolts to 28 ft. lbs. (39 Nm).

32. Connect the lock-up control solenoid valve connector, the shift control solenoid valve coupler and the connector of the speed pulser.

33. Connect the throttle control cable to the throttle control lever.

34. Install the speed sensor assembly and the air cleaner case.

35. Connect the oil cooler hoses and connect the starter and ground cables.

36. Connect the battery cables to the battery.

37. Start the engine, set the parking brake and shift the transaxle through all gears 3 times. Check for proper control cable adjustment.

38. Let the engine reach operating temperature with the transaxle in **N** or **P**, then turn the engine off and check the fluid level.

Shift Cable Adjustment

1. Start the engine. Shift the transaxle to **R**, to see if the reverse gear engages.

2. Shut the engine off and disconnect the negative battery cable.

3. Remove the console.

4. On 1987–88 Civic, CRX and Accord and 1987 Prelude, place the selector lever in **D**. On 1988 Prelude, place the selector lever in **R**. On 1989 Accord and Prelude and 1989–91 Civic and CRX, place the selector lever in **N** or **R**. On 1990–91 Accord and Prelude, place the selector lever in **N**. Remove the lock pin from the cable adjuster.

5. Check that the hole in the adjuster is perfectly aligned with the hole in the shift cable.

NOTE: There are 2 holes in the end of the shift cable. They are positioned 90 degrees apart to allow cable adjustments in ¼ turn increments.

6. If not perfectly aligned, loosen the locknut on the shift cable and adjust as required.

7. Tighten the locknut and install the lock pin on the adjuster.

NOTE: If the lock pin feels like it is binding when being installed, the cable is still out of adjustment and must be adjusted again.

8. Connect the negative battery cable, start the engine and check the shift lever in all gears. Install the console.

Throttle Linkage Adjustment

CARBURETED ENGINE

Throttle Control Cable Bracket

1. Disconnect the negative battery cable.

2. Disconnect the throttle control cable from the throttle control lever.

3. Bend down the lock tabs of the lock plate and remove the two 6mm bolts to free the bracket.

4. Loosely install a new lock plate.

5. Adjust the position of the bracket by measuring the distance between the cable housing side of the bracket and the

bracket side edge of the throttle control lever. Measure between the same points that the cable would pass through the bracket and lever.

6. Tighten the two 6mm bolts when the measurement is 3.287 in. (83.5mm) on 1987 Civic, CRX and Prelude and 1987–89 Accord. Tighten the two 6mm bolts when the measurement is 6.18 in. (157.0mm) on 1988–91 Prelude. The bolts should be tightened to 9 ft. lbs. (12 Nm).

NOTE: Make sure the control lever does not get pulled toward the bracket side as the bolts are tightened.

7. Bend up the lock plate tabs against the bolt heads, connect the throttle control cable and connect the negative battery cable.

Throttle Control Cable – 1987–88

1. Start the engine and warm it up to normal operating temperature. The cooling fan must come on at least once.
2. Make sure the throttle cable play, idle speed and automatic choke operation are correct.
3. Check the distance between the throttle control lever and the throttle control bracket and adjust as necessary.
4. Turn the engine off and disconnect the negative battery cable.
5. Disconnect the throttle control cable from the control lever.
6. If the vehicle is equipped with a dash pot, disconnect the vacuum hose from the dash pot, connect a vacuum pump and apply vacuum. This simulates a normal operating amount of pull by the dash pot, as if the engine were running.
7. Attach a weight of about 3 lbs. to the accelerator pedal. Raise the pedal, then release it. This will allow the weight to remove the normal free-play from the throttle cable.
8. Secure the throttle cable with clamps.
9. Lay the end of the throttle cable aside on Civic and CRX and on the shock tower on Accord and Prelude.
10. Adjust the distance between the throttle control cable end and the locknut closest to the cable housing to 3.366 in. (85.5mm) on all except 1988 Prelude. The distance on 1988 Prelude should be 6.22 in. (158.0mm).
11. Insert the end of the throttle control cable in the groove of the throttle control lever. Insert the throttle control cable in the bracket and secure with the other locknut.

NOTE: Make sure the cable is not kinked or twisted.

12. Check that the cable moves freely by depressing the accelerator.
13. Remove the weight on the accelerator pedal and push the pedal to make sure there is at least 0.08 in. (2.0mm) play at the throttle control lever.
14. Connect the negative battery cable and the vacuum hose to the dash pot.
15. Start the engine and check the synchronization between the carburetor and the throttle control cable. The throttle control lever should start to move as the engine speed increases.
16. If the throttle control lever starts to move before the engine speed increases, turn the cable locknut closest to the cable housing counterclockwise and retighten the locknut closest to the cable end.
17. If the throttle control lever moves after the engine speed increases, turn the locknut closest to the cable housing clockwise and retighten the locknut closest to the cable end.

Throttle Control Cable – 1989–91

1. Start the engine and bring it to normal operating temperature. The cooling fan must come on at least once.

2. Make sure the throttle cable free-play and idle speed are correct.
3. Check the distance between the throttle control lever and throttle control bracket and adjust, as necessary.
4. On 1990–91 Prelude, disconnect the vacuum hose from the throttle controller and connect a vacuum pump to the controller and apply vacuum.
5. Apply light thumb pressure to the throttle control lever. Have an assistant depress the accelerator. The lever should move just as the engine speed increases above idle. If not, proceed to Step 6.
6. Loosen the nuts on the control cable at the transaxle end and synchronize the control lever to the throttle.

NOTE: The shift/lock-up characteristics can be tailored to the driver's expectations by adjusting the control cable up to 3mm shorter than the synchronized point.

FUEL INJECTED ENGINE
Throttle Control Cable – 1987–88

1. Loosen the locknuts on the throttle control cable.
2. Press down on the throttle control lever until it stops.
3. While pressing down on the throttle control lever, pull on the throttle linkage to check the amount of throttle control cable free-play.
4. Remove all throttle control cable free-play by gradually turning the locknut closest to the cable housing. Keep turning the locknut until no movement can be felt in the throttle link, while continuing to press down on the throttle control lever, pull open the throttle link. The control lever should begin to move at precisely the same time as the link.

NOTE: The adjustment of the throttle control cable is critical for proper operation of the transaxle and lock-up torque converter.

5. Have an assistant depress the accelerator to the floor. While depressed, check that there is at least 0.08 in. (2.0mm) play in the throttle control lever. Check that the cable moves freely by depressing the accelerator.

Throttle Control Cable – 1989–91

1. Start the engine and bring it up to operating temperature. The cooling fan must come on at least once.
2. Make sure the throttle cable free-play and idle speed are correct.
3. On dash pot equipped vehicles, disconnect the vacuum hose from the dash pot, connect a vacuum pump and apply vacuum. This simulates a normal operating amount of pull by the dash pot as if the engine were running.
4. Remove the throttle cable free-play.
5. Apply light thumb pressure to the throttle control lever, then work the throttle linkage. The lever should move just as the engine speed increases above idle. If not, proceed to Step 6.
6. Loosen the nuts on the control cable at the transaxle end and synchronize the control lever to the throttle.

NOTE: The shift/lock-up characteristics can be tailored to the driver's expectations by adjusting the control cable up to 3mm shorter than the synchronized point.

7. Remove the vacuum pump and connect the vacuum hose to the dash pot.

TRANSFER CASE

Transfer Case Assembly

Removal and Installation

MANUAL TRANSAXLE

1. Disconnect the negative battery cable.
2. Raise and safely support the vehicle.
3. Drain the transaxle fluid and replace the drain plug.
4. Remove the exhaust header pipe.
5. Disconnect the driveshaft from the transfer case.
6. Remove the transaxle splash shield.
7. Remove the left side cover from the transfer case.
8. Remove the driven gear from the transfer case.

NOTE: Be careful not to damage the thrust shim and mating surface.

9. Remove the transfer case from the clutch housing.
10. Remove the clutch case cover.

To install:

11. Make sure all mating surfaces are clean prior to installation.
12. Apply liquid gasket to the clutch housing mating surface of the transfer case and install the transfer case on the clutch housing. Tighten the bolts to 33 ft. lbs. (45 Nm).
13. Lubricate the drive gear with oil and install the drive gear thrust shim and the drive gear on the transfer shaft. Install the transfer thrust shim and left side cover on the transfer case. Apply liquid gasket to the threads and tighten the bolts to 33 ft. lbs. (45 Nm).
14. Apply liquid gasket to the mating surface on the top and bottom of the transfer case opening, install a new O-ring and install the driven gear thrust shim and driven gear in the transfer case. Tighten the bolts to 19 ft. lbs. (26 Nm).
15. Installation of the remaining components is the reverse of the removal procedure. Lower the vehicle and fill the transaxle with the proper type and quantity of fluid.
16. Connect the negative battery cable, start the vehicle and check for leaks.

AUTOMATIC TRANSAXLE

1. Disconnect the negative battery cable.
2. Raise and safely support the vehicle.
3. Drain the transaxle fluid and replace the drain plug.
4. Remove the exhaust header pipe.
5. Disconnect the driveshaft from the transfer case.
6. Remove the transaxle splash shield.
7. Remove the driven gear assembly from the transfer case.
8. Remove the drive gear from the transfer case. In this procedure, remove all of the left side cover bolts except the 1 closest to the front of the vehicle. Loosen this bolt and use it as the axis, about which the cover can be rotated to gain access to the drive gear. Leave this bolt in the cover and transfer case.

NOTE: Be careful not to damage the thrust shim and mating surface.

9. Remove the transfer case from the clutch housing.
10. Remove the clutch case cover.

To install:

11. Make sure all mating surfaces are clean prior to installation.
12. Apply liquid gasket to the clutch housing mating surface of the transfer case. Attach a new O-ring to the groove on the left side cover.
13. Install the transfer case with the 1 bolt and left side cover still attached. Tighten the transfer case bolts to 33 ft. lbs. (45 Nm).
14. Lubricate the drive gear with oil and install the drive gear

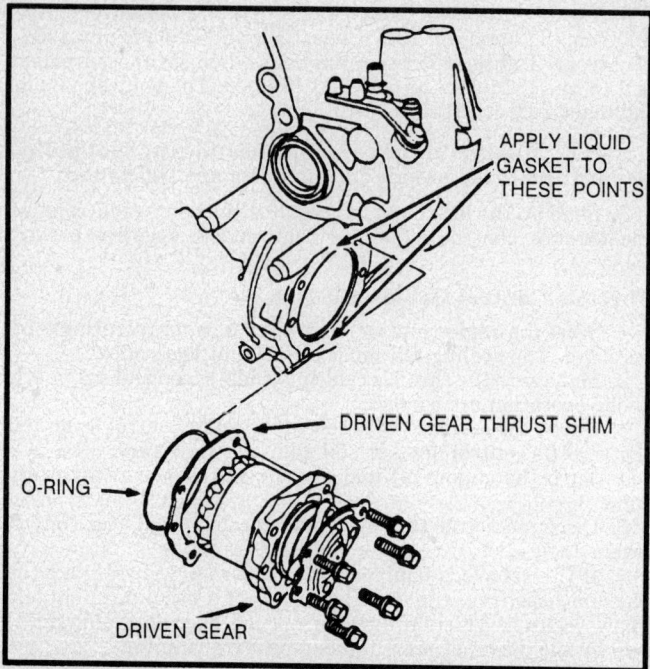

Transfer case driven gear installation—4WD Civic Wagon with

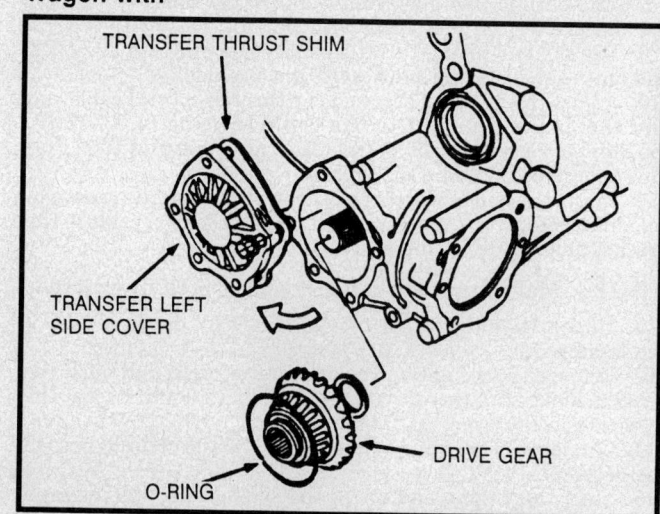

Transfer case drive gear and left side cover installation—4WD Civic Wagon with automatic transaxle

thrust shim and the drive gear on the transfer shaft. Install the transfer thrust shim and left side cover on the transfer case. Apply liquid gasket to the threads and tighten the bolts to 33 ft. lbs. (45 Nm).
15. Apply liquid gasket to the mating surface on the top and bottom of the transfer case opening, install a new O-ring and install the driven gear thrust shim and driven gear in the transfer case. Tighten the bolts to 19 ft. lbs. (26 Nm).
16. Installation of the remaining components is the reverse of the removal procedure. Lower the vehicle and fill the transaxle with the proper type and quantity of fluid.
17. Connect the negative battery cable, start the vehicle and check for leaks.

DRIVE AXLE

Halfshaft

Removal and Installation

EXCEPT 4WD CIVIC WAGON – REAR HALFSHAFTS

1. Raise and safely support the vehicle.
2. Remove the front wheel and tire assemblies.
3. Remove the spindle nut.
4. Drain the transaxle fluid and replace the drain plug.
5. On 1987 Civic and CRX, perform the following procedure:
   a. Position a suitable floor jack under the lower control arm.
   b. Remove the ball joint cotter pin and nut.
   c. Separate the ball joint from the front hub using a suitable tool.

NOTE: Make sure the floor jack is positioned securely under the lower control arm, at the ball joint. Otherwise, torsion bar tension on the lower control arm will cause the arm to jump or spring suddenly away from the hub as the ball joint separator tool is being used.

   d. Slowly lower the floor jack to lower the control arm.
6. On all other vehicles, perform the following procedure:
   a. Remove the damper fork nut and damper pinch bolt.
   b. Remove the damper fork.
   c. Remove the knuckle-to-lower arm cotter pin and castle nut.
   d. Using a suitable puller, separate the lower arm from the knuckle.
7. Pull the knuckle outward and remove the halfshaft outboard joint, from the knuckle, using a plastic hammer.
8. Using a suitable tool, pry on the inner CV-joint in order to force the set ring at the end of the halfshaft assembly out of the groove.
9. Pull on the inboard CV-joint and remove the halfshaft and joint from the differential case or intermediate shaft.

NOTE: Do not pull on the halfshaft as the CV-joint may come apart. Use care when prying out the assembly and pull it straight to avoid damaging the differential oil seal or intermediate shaft dust seal.

10. Installation is the reverse of the removal procedure. Always install new set rings on the ends of the halfshafts.
11. Make sure the set ring locks in the differential side gear groove and the axle bottoms in the differential or intermediate shaft.
12. Tighten the ball joint nut to 32 ft. lbs. (44 Nm) on 1987 Civic and CRX and 40 ft. lbs. (55 Nm) on all others. Always install a new cotter pin.
13. Fill the transaxle with the proper type and quantity of fluid.

4WD CIVIC WAGON – REAR HALFSHAFTS

1. Pry the spindle nut stake away from the spindle. Loosen the nut. Loosen the wheel nuts.
2. Raise and support the vehicle safely. Remove the tire and wheel assemblies.
3. Disconnect the brake hose from the brake pipe.
4. Using a floor jack raise the rear suspension until the weight of the lower arm is relieved.
5. Remove the trailing arm bushing bolts. Disconnect the upper arm and the lower arm from the trailing arm.
6. Pull the trailing arm outward. Remove the rear halfshaft outboard joint from the trailing arm, using the proper tool.
7. Using a suitable tool, pry the halfshaft assembly to force the set ring at the halfshaft end past the groove.

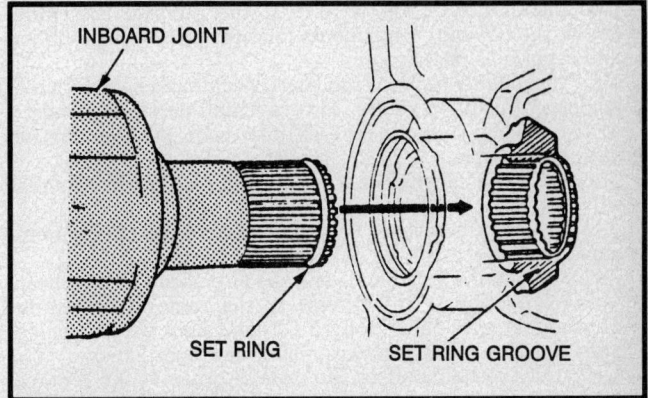

Installing the inboard CV-joint into the differential assembly

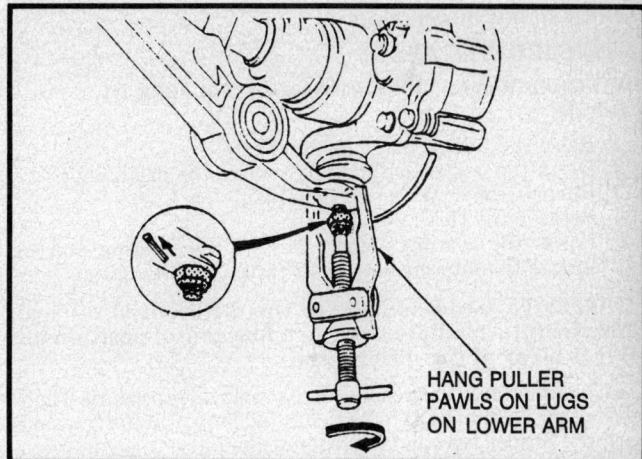

Separating the steering knuckle from the lower arm assembly – except 1987 Civic and CRX

8. Pull the inboard joint and remove the halfshaft and the CV-joint from the differential case as an assembly.
9. Installation is the reverse of the removal procedure. Always install a new set ring on the end of the axle. Make sure the set ring locks in the differential side gear groove and the CV-joint subaxle bottoms in the differential.
10. Tighten the upper and lower arm bushing bolts to 40 ft. lbs. (55 Nm) and the trailing arm bushing bolts to 47 ft. lbs. (65 Nm).

CV-Boot

Removal and Installation

1. Raise and safely support the vehicle.
2. Remove the halfshaft.
3. If replacing the inboard CV-joint boot, perform the following procedure:
   a. Place the halfshaft in a suitable holding fixture where it will remain in position during disassembly.
   b. Remove the boot bands. If the boot bands are the welded type, they must be cut to be removed. After removing the bands, push the CV-joint boot away from the end of the halfshaft to gain access to the CV-joint.
   c. Remove the inboard CV-joint. Mark the components

during disassembly to ensure proper positioning during reassembly.

d. Remove the CV-joint boot.

e. Installation is the reverse of the removal procedure. Check the CV-joint components for wear prior to installation and replace as necessary.

f. Thoroughly pack the inboard CV-joint and boot with molybdenum disulfide grease. Always install new boot bands.

4. If replacing the outboard CV-joint boot, perform the following procedure:

a. Place the halfshaft in a suitable holding fixture where it will remain in position during disassembly.

b. Remove the inboard CV-joint and boot. Do not try to remove or disassemble the outboard CV-joint.

c. Remove the boot bands and the outboard CV-joint boot.

d. Installation is the reverse of the removal procedure. Thoroughly pack the outboard CV-joint boot with molybdenum disulfide grease. Always install new boot bands.

5. Install the halfshaft in the reverse order of the removal procedure.

Driveshaft and U-Joints

Removal and Installation

INTERMEDIATE SHAFT

4WD Civic Wagon, 1990–91 Accord and 1988–91 Prelude

1. Raise the vehicle and support it safely.
2. Drain the transaxle fluid and replace the drain plug.
3. Remove the driver's side halfshaft.
4. Remove the three 10mm bolts.
5. Lower the bearing support close to the steering gearbox and remove the intermediate shaft from the differential.

NOTE: To avoid damage to the differential oil seal, hold the intermediate shaft in a horizontal position until it is clear of the differential.

6. Installation is the reverse of the removal procedure. Tighten the three 10mm bolts to 29 ft. lbs. (40 Nm). Fill the transaxle with the proper type and quantity of fluid.

REAR DRIVESHAFTS

4WD Civic Wagon – 1987

1. Raise the vehicle and support it safely.

2. Mark the position of the driveshafts on both of the flanges for reassembly.

3. Remove the No. 1 driveshaft protector.
4. Remove the No. 3 driveshaft by disconnecting the U-joints.
5. Remove the bolts holding the rear bearing support, then remove the No. 2 driveshaft.
6. Remove the bolts holding the front bearing support, then remove the No. 1 driveshaft by disconnecting the U-joint.
7. To install, reverse the removal procedures.

4WD Civic Wagon – 1988–91

1. Raise the vehicle and support it safely.
2. Mark the position of the driveshafts in relation to the flanges for reassembly.
3. Remove the No. 1 driveshaft protector.
4. Disconnect the No. 1 driveshaft and viscous coupling.
5. Remove the front center bearing support from the body.
6. Remove the No. 1 driveshaft by disconnecting the U-joint.
7. Remove the No. 3 driveshaft protector.
8. Disconnect the No. 3 driveshaft and rear differential.
9. Remove the rear center bearing support from the body, then remove the viscous coupling and No. 3 driveshaft.

To install:

10. Install the rear center bearing support on the frame and tighten the bolts to 29 ft. lbs. (40 Nm).
11. Temporarily connect the No. 3 driveshaft and rear differential using the 12-point bolts and yoke nuts. Tighten the bolts to 24 ft. lbs. (33 Nm).
12. Install the No. 3 driveshaft protector and tighten the bolts to 29 ft. lbs. (40 Nm).
13. Temporarily connect the No. 1 driveshaft and front differential using the 12-point bolts and yoke nuts. Tighten the bolts to 24 ft. lbs. (33 Nm).
14. Install the front center bearing support on the frame and tighten the bolts to 29 ft. lbs. (40 Nm). Temporarily connect the No. 1 driveshaft and viscous coupling using 12-point bolts. Tighten the bolts to 24 ft. lbs. (33 Nm).
15. Install the No. 1 driveshaft protector and tighten the bolts to 29 ft. lbs. (40 Nm).

Rear Axle Shaft, Bearing and Seal

Removal and Installation

1987 4WD CIVIC WAGON

1. Raise and safely support the vehicle.

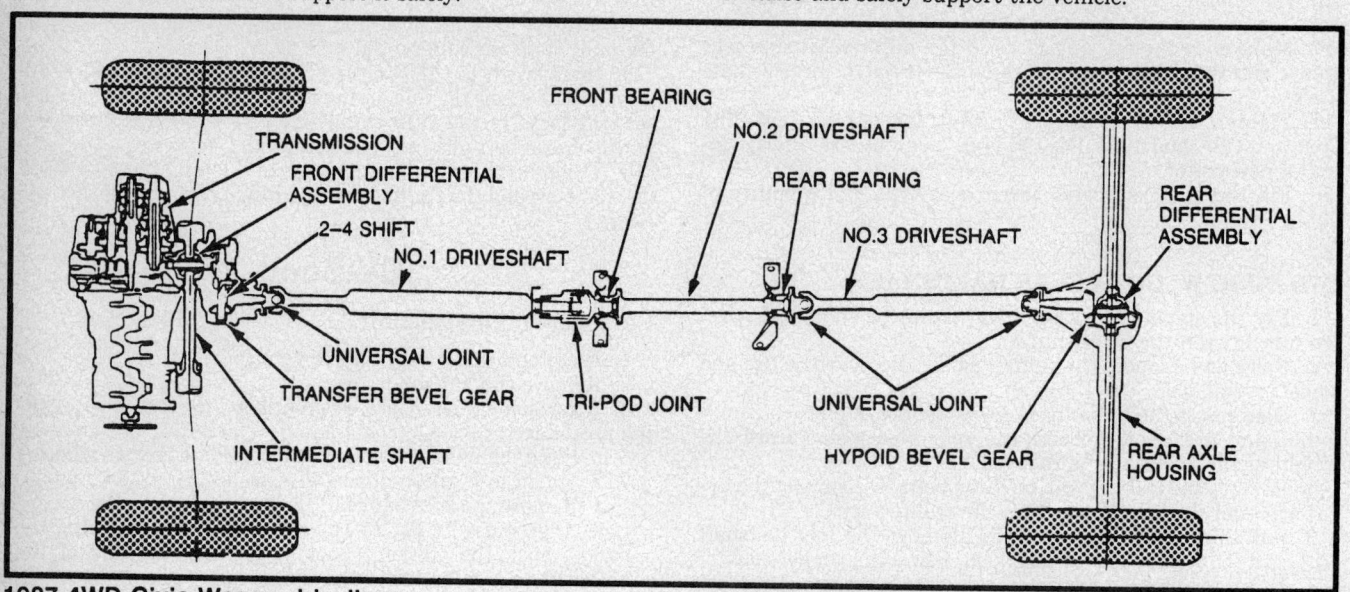

1987 4WD Civic Wagon driveline

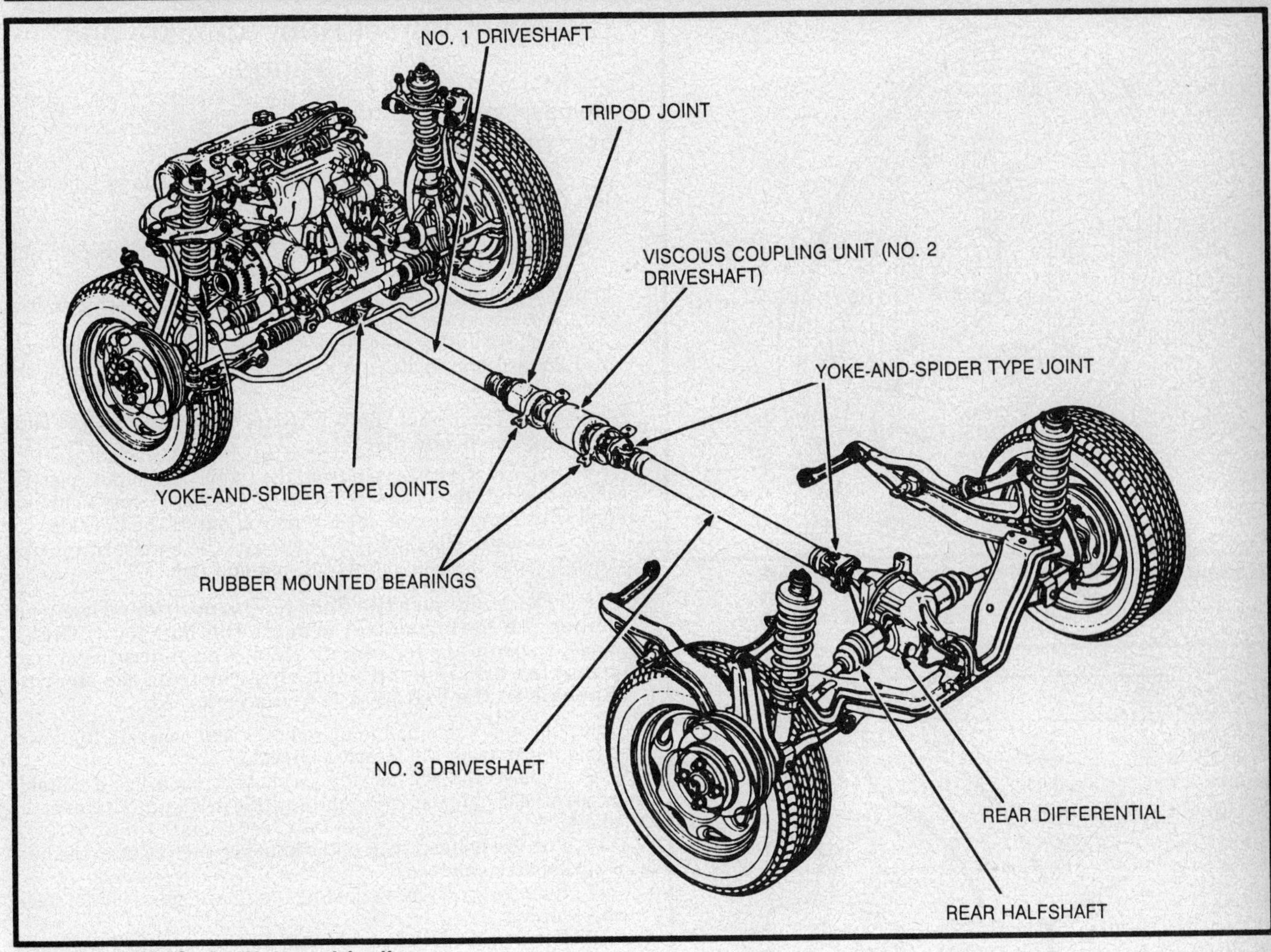

NO. 1 DRIVESHAFT

TRIPOD JOINT

VISCOUS COUPLING UNIT (NO. 2 DRIVESHAFT)

YOKE-AND-SPIDER TYPE JOINT

YOKE-AND-SPIDER TYPE JOINTS

RUBBER MOUNTED BEARINGS

NO. 3 DRIVESHAFT

REAR DIFFERENTIAL

REAR HALFSHAFT

1988–91 4WD Civic Wagon driveline

2. Remove the rear wheel and tire assembly and remove the brake drum.

3. Disconnect the brake line from the wheel cylinder. Plug the line.

4. Remove the brake shoes and parking brake cable.

5. Remove the nuts from the axle shaft retainer studs.

6. Using a suitable slide hammer puller, remove the axle shaft.

7. Remove the brake backing plate and using a suitable removal tool, remove the axle seal.

8. Using a suitable bench grinder, grind part of the axle bearing holder until the thickness is reduced to about 0.02 in. (0.5mm). Be careful not to damage the axle.

9. Place the axle in a suitable vice and break the holder off using a suitable tool. Be careful not to damage the axle.

10. Press off the rear axle bearing using a suitable press.

To install:

11. Use a suitable installation tool to drive a new axle seal into the axle housing. Coat the sealing lip with grease.

12. Thoroughly clean the axle shaft. Install the axle holder, bearing and bearing holder on the axle. The projected end of the bearing race must face toward the axle flange.

NOTE: Do not get oil or grease on the contact surfaces of the axle, bearing or bearing holder.

13. Press the bearing and bearing holder onto the axle.

14. Measure the width "a" of the axle bearing outer race and record the reading. Measure the thickness "b" of the backing plate and record the reading. Measure the depth "c" from the edge of the axle housing to the bearing seating surface and record the reading.

15. The measurements are used to calculate the thickness of the shim needed between the backing plate and the axle shaft

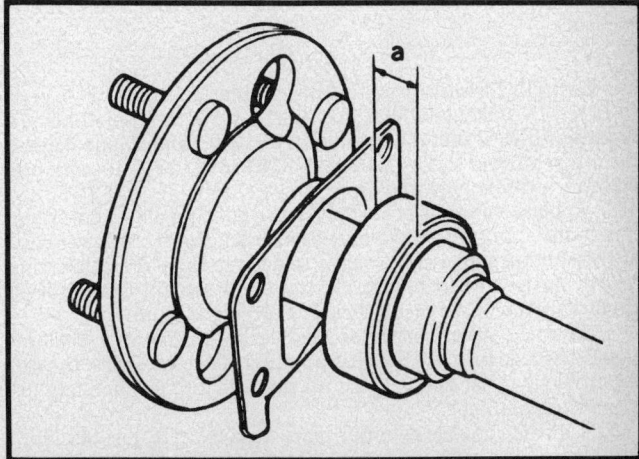

Measuring the bearing outer race thickness

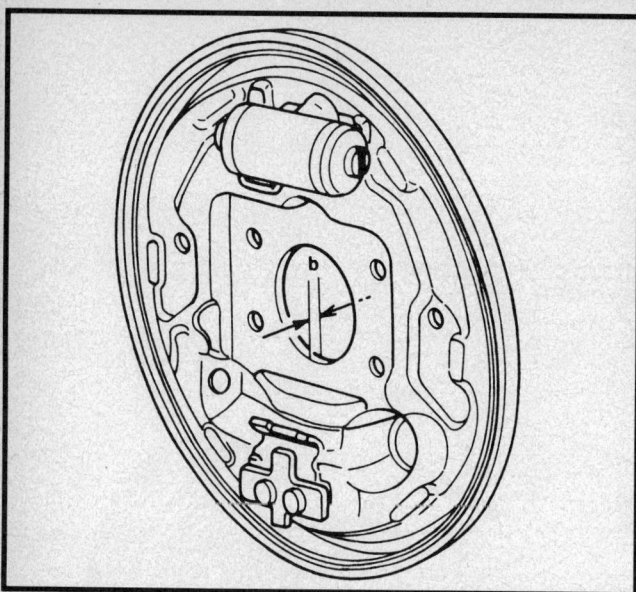

Measuring the brake backing plate thickness

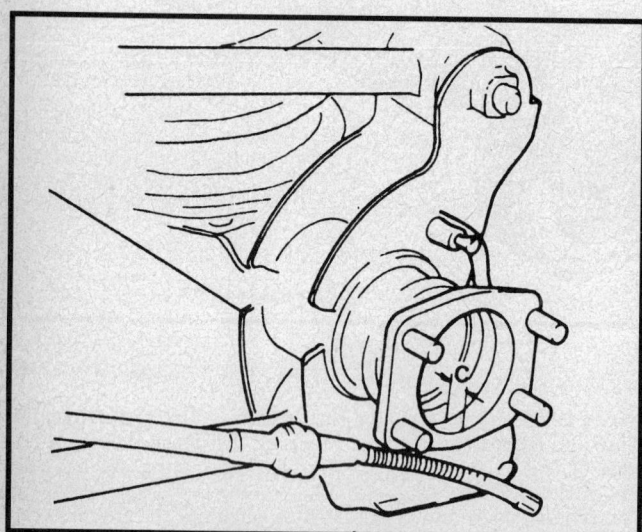

Measuring the axle housing depth

retainer. The formula used for this calculation is: a − (b + c) = X. If X = −0.0063–0.0039 in. (−0.16–0.10mm), no shims are required. If X = 0.0039–0.0098 in. (0.10–0.25mm), one 0.1mm shim is required. If X = 0.0098–0.0157 in. (0.25–0.40mm), one 0.25mm shim is required.

16. Apply a thin coat of sealant to the backing plate contacting face of the shim. Do not cover the lower 2 holes at the lower edge of the shim. Apply a thin coat of sealant to the shim contacting face of the axle shaft holder. Do not apply sealant to the raised surface in the lower right corner. Install the shim.

17. Coat the inner corner of the bearing holder with sealant. Insert the axle into the housing aligning it's splines with the differential side gear splines. Install the axle into the housing using a slide hammer.

18. Tighten the axle retainer plate nuts to 30 ft. lbs. (41 Nm).

19. Install the remainder of the components in the reverse order of their removal. Bleed the brakes.

Front Wheel Hub, Knuckle and Bearings

Removal and Installation

1987 CIVIC AND CRX

1. Pry the spindle nut lock tab away from the spindle, then loosen the nut.
2. Raise and safely support the vehicle.
3. Remove the wheel and tire assembly and the spindle nut.
4. Remove the caliper retaining bolts and the caliper from the knuckle. Support the caliper out of the way with a length of wire. Do not let the caliper hang from the brake hose.
5. Remove the 6mm brake disc retaining screws. Screw two 8 × 1.25 × 12mm bolts into the disc to push it away from the hub.

NOTE: Turn each bolt 2 turns at a time to prevent cocking the brake disc.

6. Remove the cotter pin from the tie rod castle nut, then remove the nut. Break the tie rod ball joint loose using a suitable ball joint remover, then lift the tie rod out of the knuckle.
7. Use a suitable floor jack to support the lower control arm, then remove the ball joint cotter pin and nut.

NOTE: Make sure the floor jack is positioned securely under the lower control arm, at the ball joint. Otherwise, torsion bar tension on the lower control arm may cause the arm to jump suddenly away from the steering knuckle as the ball joint is being removed.

8. Use a suitable ball joint remover and separate the lower control arm from the steering knuckle.
9. Remove the self locking pinch bolt, then use a suitable brass or lead hammer to tap the knuckle down until it clears the shock.
10. Pull the halfshaft out of the knuckle, then remove the hub/knuckle assembly.
11. Remove the 2 screws holding the splash guard on the steering knuckle.
12. Position the hub/knuckle assembly on a suitable hydraulic press. Press out the hub with a suitable driver while supporting the knuckle with a suitable base.

NOTE: Make sure the knuckle is securely mounted on the support tool. Be careful not to distort the splash guard. Support the hub by hand, to prevent it from falling.

13. Remove the circlip.
14. Press the bearing from the steering knuckle using a suitable driver, while supporting the knuckle with a suitable base.
15. Remove the outboard bearing inner race from the hub, using a suitable bearing removal tool.

To install:

16. Clean the knuckle and hub thoroughly.
17. Position the steering knuckle on a hydraulic press. Press the bearing assembly into the knuckle using a suitable driver, while supporting the knuckle with a suitable base.
18. Install the circlip and the splash guard.
19. Press the front hub into the knuckle with a suitable driver, while supporting the hub with a suitable base. The maximum necessary press load should be 2 tons.
20. Install the steering knuckle/hub assembly on the vehicle in the reverse of the removal procedure. Tighten the ball joint nut and tie rod nut to 32 ft. lbs. (44 Nm) and install new cotter pins. Tighten the spindle nut to 134 ft. lbs. (185 Nm).

1988–91 CIVIC AND CRX

1. Pry the spindle nut stake away from the spindle, then loosen the nut.
2. Raise and safely support the vehicle.

3. Remove the wheel and tire assembly and the spindle nut.

4. Remove the caliper mounting bolts and the caliper. Support the caliper out of the way with a length of wire. Do not let the caliper hang from the brake hose.

5. Remove the 6mm brake disc retaining screws. Screw two 8 × 1.25 × 12mm bolts into the disc to push it away from the hub.

NOTE: Turn each bolt 2 turns at a time to prevent cocking the brake disc.

6. Remove the cotter pin from the tie rod castle nut, then remove the nut. Break the tie rod ball joint using a suitable ball joint remover, then lift the tie rod out of the knuckle.

7. Remove the cotter pin and loosen the lower arm ball joint nut half the length of the joint threads.

8. Separate the ball joint and lower arm using a suitable puller with the pawls applied to the lower arm.

NOTE: Avoid damaging the ball joint boot. If necessary, apply penetrating type lubricant to loosen the ball joint.

9. Remove the knuckle protector.

10. Remove the cotter pin and remove the upper ball pin nut.

11. Separate the upper ball joint and knuckle using a suitable tool.

12. Remove the knuckle and hub by sliding them off the halfshaft.

13. Remove the splash guard screws from the knuckle.

14. Position the knuckle/hub assembly on a hydraulic press. Press the hub from the knuckle using a suitable driver while supporting the knuckle with a suitable base.

NOTE: The bearing must be replaced with a new one after removal.

15. Remove the 76mm snapring and knuckle ring from the knuckle.

16. Press the wheel bearing out of the knuckle using a suitable driver while supporting the knuckle with a suitable base.

17. Remove the outboard bearing inner race from the hub using a suitable bearing puller.

To install:

18. Clean the knuckle and hub thoroughly before reassembly.

19. Press a new wheel bearing into the hub using a suitable driver while supporting the knuckle with a suitable base.

20. Install the 76mm snapring securely in the knuckle groove.

21. Install the splash guard and tighten the screws to 7 ft. lbs. (10 Nm).

22. Place the knuckle into position on the hydraulic press and press onto the hub using a suitable driver. The maximum press load should be 2 tons.

23. Install the front knuckle ring on the knuckle.

24. Install the knuckle/hub assembly onto the vehicle in the reverse order of the removal procedure. Tighten the upper ball pin nut and tie rod nut to 32 ft. lbs. (44 Nm) and the lower ball joint castle nut to 40 ft. lbs. (55 Nm). Tighten the spindle nut to 134 ft. lbs. (185 Nm).

1987 PRELUDE

1. Pry the lock tab away from the spindle, then loosen the nut. Slightly loosen the lug nuts.

2. Raise the vehicle and support it safely. Remove the front wheel and spindle nut.

3. Remove the bolts retaining the brake caliper and remove the caliper from the knuckle. Do not let the caliper hang by the brake hose, support it with a length of wire.

4. Remove the disc brake rotor retaining screws, if equipped. Screw two 8 × 1.25 × 12mm bolts into the disc brake removal holes and turn the bolts to push the rotor away from the hub.

NOTE: Turn each bolt 2 turns at a time to prevent cocking the disc excessively.

5. Remove the tie rod from the knuckle using a tie rod end removal tool. Use care not to damage the ball joint seals.

6. Remove the cotter pin from the lower arm ball joint and remove the castle nut.

7. Remove the lower arm from the knuckle using the ball joint remover tool.

8. Remove the cotter pin from the upper arm ball joint and remove the castle nut.

9. Remove the upper arm from the knuckle using the ball joint remover tool.

10. Remove the knuckle and hub by sliding the assembly off of the halfshaft.

11. Remove the 2 back splash guard screws from the knuckle.

12. Remove the hub from the knuckle using suitable tools and a hydraulic press.

13. Remove the splash guard, dust seal and the snapring, then remove the outer bearing race.

14. Turn the knuckle over and remove the inboard dust seal, bearing and inner race and bearing.

15. Press the bearing outer race out of the knuckle using special tools and a hydraulic press.

16. Remove the outboard bearing inner race from the hub using special tools and a bearing puller.

17. Remove the outboard dust seal from the hub.

18. Remove all old grease from the wheel bearings, hub and knuckle and thoroughly dry and wipe clean all components.

To install:

19. Press the bearing outer race into the knuckle using a suitable driver, while supporting the knuckle.

20. Pack both bearings with grease. If a bearing packer is not available, pack the bearings by hand, making sure grease thoroughly penetrates the bearings. Also apply grease to the outer race and both inner races.

21. Install the outboard ball bearing and its inner race in the knuckle.

22. Install the snapring. Pack grease in the groove around the sealing lip of the outboard grease dust seal.

23. Drive the outboard grease seal into the knuckle, using a seal driver and hammer, until it is flush with the knuckle surface.

24. Install the splash guard, then turn the knuckle upside down and install the inboard ball bearing and its inner race.

25. Place the hub in a suitable tool fixture, then set the knuckle in position on a press and apply downward pressure.

26. Pack grease in the groove around the sealing lip of the inboard dust seal.

27. Drive the dust seal into the knuckle using a seal driver.

28. Install the knuckle/hub assembly to the vehicle in the reverse of the removal procedure. Tighten the spindle nut to 134 ft. lbs. (185 Nm).

1987–89 ACCORD AND 1988–91 PRELUDE

1. Pry the spindle nut stake away from the spindle and loosen the nut.

2. Raise and safely support the vehicle.

3. Remove the wheel and tire assembly and the spindle nut.

4. Remove the caliper mounting bolts and the caliper. Support the caliper out of the way with a length of wire. Do not let the caliper hang from the brake hose.

5. Remove the 6mm brake disc retaining screws. Screw two 8 × 1.25 × 12mm bolts into the disc to push it away from the hub.

NOTE: Turn each bolt 2 turns at a time to prevent cocking the brake disc.

6. Remove the cotter pin from the tie rod castle nut, then remove the nut. Break the tie rod ball joint using a suitable ball joint remover, then lift the tie rod out of the knuckle.

7. Remove the cotter pin and loosen the lower arm ball joint nut half the length of the joint threads.

8. Separate the ball joint and lower arm using a suitable puller with the pawls applied to the lower arm.

NOTE: Avoid damaging the ball joint boot. If necessary, apply penetrating type lubricant to loosen the ball joint.

9. Remove the upper ball joint shield, if equipped.
10. Pry off the cotter pin and remove the upper ball joint nut.
11. Separate the upper ball joint and knuckle using a suitable tool.
12. Remove the knuckle and hub by sliding them off the halfshaft.
13. Remove the splash guard screws from the knuckle.
14. Position the knuckle/hub assembly in a hydraulic press. Press the hub from the knuckle using a suitable driver while supporting the knuckle.

NOTE: The bearing must be replaced with a new one after removal.

15. Remove the splash guard and snapring from the knuckle.
16. Press the wheel bearing out of the knuckle using a suitable driver while supporting the knuckle.
17. Remove the outboard bearing inner race from the hub using a suitable bearing puller.

To install:

18. Clean the knuckle and hub thoroughly.
19. Press a new wheel bearing into the knuckle using a suitable driver while supporting the knuckle.
20. Install the snapring.
21. Install the splash shield and tighten the screws to 4 ft. lbs. (5 Nm).
22. Press the knuckle onto the hub using a suitable fixture.
23. Install the front knuckle ring on the knuckle.
24. Install the knuckle/hub assembly on the vehicle in the reverse of the removal procedure. Tighten the upper ball joint nut and tie rod end nut to 32 ft. lbs. (44 Nm). Install new cotter pins. Tighten the lower ball joint nut to 40 ft. lbs. (55 Nm) and install a new cotter pin. Tighten the spindle nut to 134 ft. lbs. (185 Nm) except 1990–91 Prelude, where it is tightened to 180 ft. lbs. (250 Nm).

1990–91 ACCORD

1. Pry the spindle nut stake away from the spindle, then loosen the nut.
2. Raise and safely support the vehicle.
3. Remove the wheel and tire assembly and the spindle nut.
4. Remove the caliper mounting bolts and the caliper. Support the caliper out of the way with a length of wire. Do not let the caliper hang from the brake hose.
5. Remove the cotter pin from the tie rod castle nut, then remove the nut. Break loose the tie rod ball joint using a suitable ball joint remover, then lift the tie rod out of the knuckle.
6. Remove the cotter pin and loosen the lower arm ball joint nut half the length of the joint threads.
7. Separate the ball joint and lower arm using a suitable puller with the pawls applied to the lower arm.

NOTE: Avoid damaging the ball joint boot. If necessary, apply penetrating type lubricant to loosen the ball joint.

8. Pull the knuckle outward and remove the halfshaft outboard joint from the knuckle using a suitable tool.
9. Remove the cotter pin and the upper ball joint nut. Break loose the upper ball joint using a suitable tool.

NOTE: Avoid damaging the ball joint boot. If necessary, apply penetrating type lubricant to loosen the ball joint.

10. Remove the 4 bolts and remove the knuckle from the hub unit.

11. Remove the splash guard screws and the splash guard from the knuckle.
12. Remove the 4 bolts, then separate the hub unit from the brake disc.
13. Position the hub in a suitable hydraulic press. Press the wheel bearing from the hub while adequately supporting the hub.
14. Remove the outboard bearing inner race from the hub using a suitable bearing puller.

NOTE: The wheel bearing must be replaced with a new one after removal.

To install:

15. Clean the knuckle and hub thoroughly.
16. Position the hub in a suitable hydraulic press. Press a new wheel bearing into the hub using a suitable driver.
17. Install the hub on the brake disc and tighten the bolts to 40 ft. lbs. (55 Nm).
18. Install the splash guard and tighten the screws to 7 ft. lbs. (10 Nm).
19. Install the knuckle on the hub and tighten the bolts to 33 ft. lbs. (45 Nm).
20. Installation of the knuckle/hub assembly on the vehicle is the reverse of the removal procedure. Tighten the upper ball joint nut and the tie rod nut to 32 ft. lbs. (44 Nm) and install new cotter pins. Tighten the lower ball joint nut to 40 ft. lbs. (55 Nm) and install a new cotter pin.
21. Replace the spindle nut with a new one and tighten to 180 ft. lbs. (245 Nm). After tightening, use a suitable drift to stake the spindle nut shoulder against the spindle.

Pinion Seal

Removal and Installation

4WD CIVIC WAGON

1. Raise and safely support the vehicle.
2. Remove the rear wheel and tire assemblies and brake drums.
3. On 1988–91 vehicles, keep the rear halfshafts in their normal horizontal position by raising the lower arms to their normal road level position.
4. Mark the position of the driveshaft in relation to the pinion flange, then disconnect the driveshaft from the pinion flange.
5. Using a suitable inch lb. torque wrench, turn the pinion

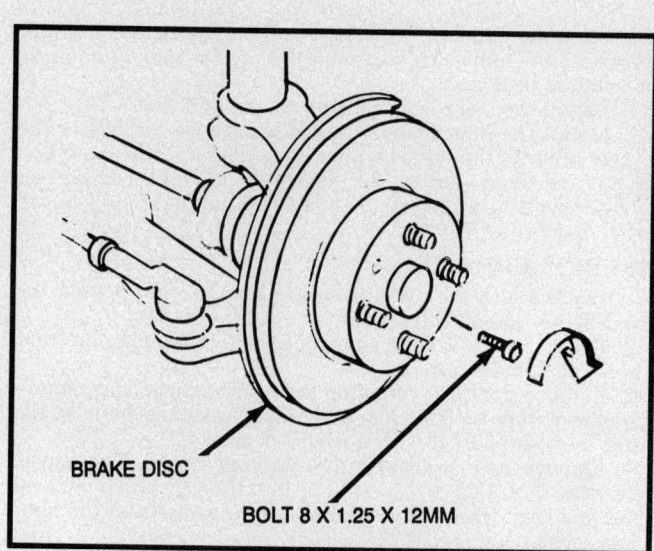

BRAKE DISC

BOLT 8 X 1.25 X 12MM

Disc brake rotor removal—except 1990–91 Accord

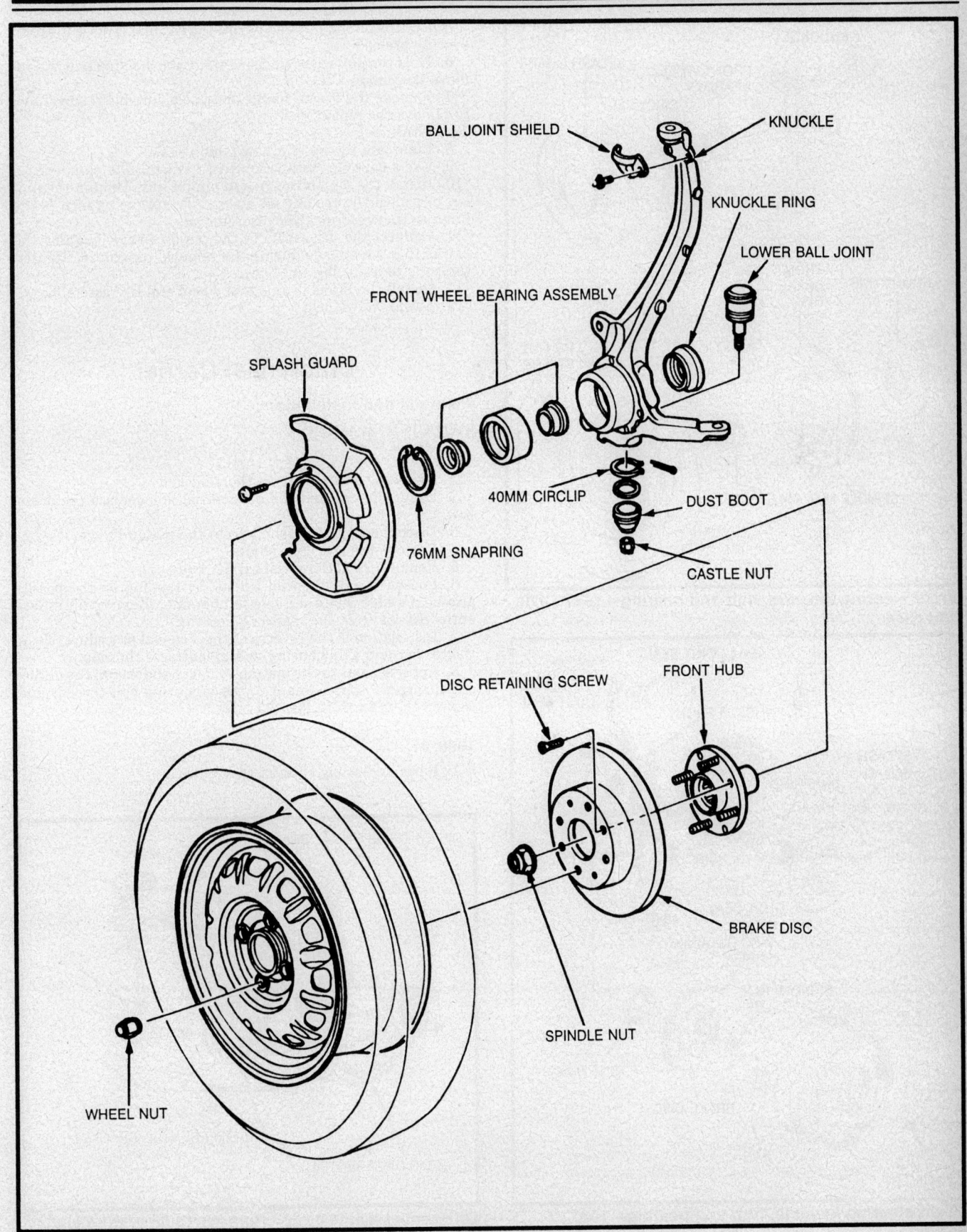

BALL JOINT SHIELD

KNUCKLE

KNUCKLE RING

LOWER BALL JOINT

FRONT WHEEL BEARING ASSEMBLY

SPLASH GUARD

40MM CIRCLIP

DUST BOOT

76MM SNAPRING

CASTLE NUT

DISC RETAINING SCREW

FRONT HUB

BRAKE DISC

SPINDLE NUT

WHEEL NUT

Front steering knuckle, hub and bearing—1987-89 Accord

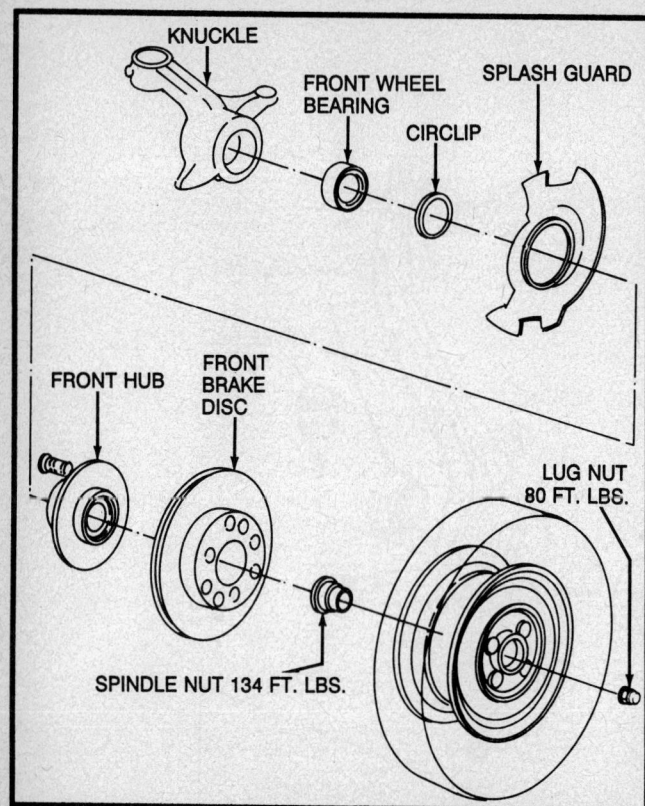

Front steering knuckle, hub and bearing—1987 Civic and CRX

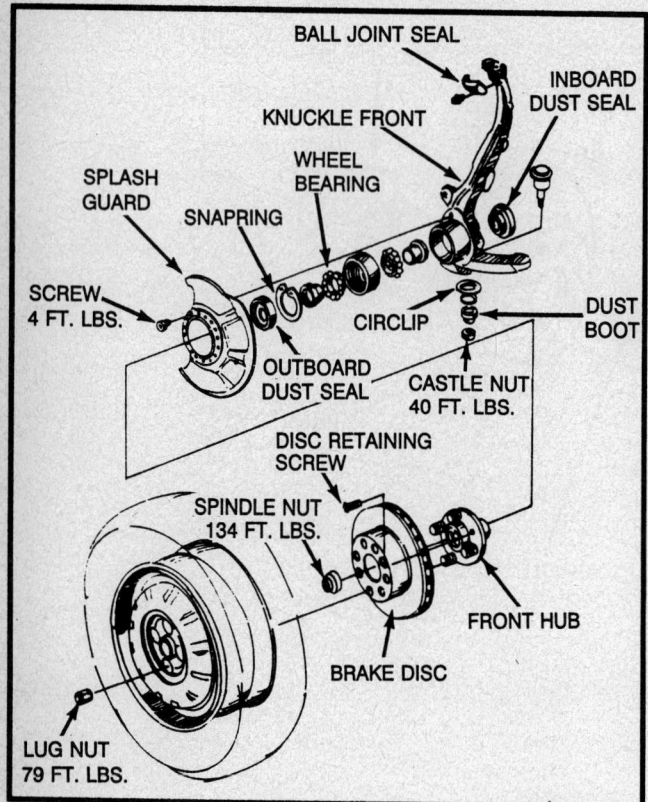

Front steering knuckle, hub and bearing—1987 Prelude

flange by the pinion nut and record the reading. This is the total bearing preload.

6. Hold the pinion flange using a suitable holding tool and remove the pinion nut.

7. Remove the pinion flange and use a suitable removal tool to remove the pinion seal.

To install:

8. Lubricate the lip of a new pinion seal.

9. Use a suitable installation tool to install the pinion seal.

10. Install the pinion flange and pinion nut. Tighten the pinion nut until the reading on an inch lb. torque wrench is the same as that recorded prior to removal.

11. Connect the driveshaft to the pinion flange, aligning the marks that were made during the removal procedure. Tighten the bolts to 24 ft. lbs. (33 Nm).

12. Install the brake drums and wheel and tire assemblies.

13. Lower the vehicle.

Differential Carrier

Removal and Installation

4WD CIVIC WAGON

1987

1. Raise and safely support the vehicle.

2. Drain the oil from the differential and replace the drain bolt.

3. Disconnect the driveshaft from the pinion flange.

4. Remove the rear axle shafts.

5. Remove the differential carrier bolts.

6. Loosen the differential carrier by tapping on the bosses around it's edge with a suitable soft hammer. Remove the differential carrier from the rear axle housing.

7. Installation is the reverse of the removal procedure. clean the carrier and axle housing mating surfaces thoroughly.

8. Apply sealant to the mating surfaces and install the differential carrier. Apply sealant to the mounting bolt threads and tighten them to 16 ft. lbs. (22 Nm).

1988-91

1. Raise and safely support the vehicle.

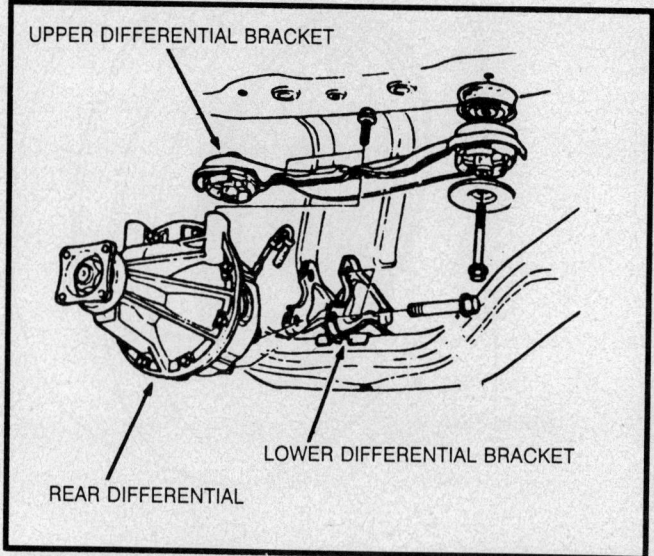

Differential installation—1988-91 Civic Wagon with 4WD

2. Drain the oil from the differential and replace the drain bolt.

3. Remove the driveshaft and the right and left rear halfshafts.

4. Remove the differential mounting bolts from the lower differential mounting bracket.

5. Remove the 2 bolts from the upper differential bracket and remove the differential and bracket as an assembly.

6. Remove the upper differential bracket from the differential and remove the differential carrier from the differential housing.

To install:

7. Clean the mating surfaces of the differential carrier and differential housing.

8. Apply sealant to the mating surfaces and install the carrier to the housing, aligning the dowel pin. Apply sealant to the bolt threads and tighten them to 16 ft. lbs. (22 Nm).

9. Install the differential bracket on the differential and tighten the bolts to 40 ft. lbs. (55 Nm).

10. Install the differential and upper bracket and tighten the upper bracket bolts to 43 ft. lbs. (59 Nm).

11. Install and tighten the lower differential bracket bolts to 40 ft. lbs. (55 Nm).

12. Installation of the remainder of the components is the reverse of the removal procedure.

Axle Housing

Removal and Installation

1987 4WD CIVIC WAGON

1. Raise and safely support the vehicle.
2. Remove the rear wheel and tire assemblies.
3. Disconnect the brake line to the axle housing. Plug the line.
4. Remove the brake drums and disconnect the parking brake cables.
5. Mark the position of the driveshaft in relation to the pinion flange and disconnect the driveshaft from the pinion.
6. Remove the panhard rod.
7. Support the rear axle housing and disconnect the shocks from the axle housing.
8. Lower the axle housing slowly and remove the coil springs.
9. Disconnect the upper and lower control arms from the vehicle.
10. Lower the axle housing from the vehicle.
11. Installation is the reverse of the removal procedure. Tighten the control arm bolts to 60 ft. lbs. (83 Nm). Tighten the shock mounting bolts to 60 ft. lbs. (83 Nm). Tighten the panhard rod-to-body bolt to 40 ft. lbs. (55 Nm) and the panhard rod-to-axle housing bolt to 54 ft. lbs. (75 Nm).
12. Bleed the rear brakes.

STEERING

Steering Wheel

Removal and Installation

1. Disconnect the negative battery cable. Remove the steering wheel pad. Disconnect the necessary electrical connections under the steering wheel pad.

2. Remove the steering wheel retaining nut. Remove the steering wheel by rocking it from side to side, as it is pulled up steadily by hand.

3. Installation is the reverse of the removal procedure. Be sure to tighten the steering wheel nut to 36 ft. lbs. (50 Nm).

Steering Column

Removal and Installation

1. Disconnect the negative battery cable.
2. Remove the steering wheel.
3. Remove the lower cover panel. Remove the driver's knee bolster, if equipped.
4. Remove the upper and lower column covers.
5. Disconnect the wire couplers from the combination switch. Remove the turn signal cancelling sleeve and the combination switch.
6. Remove the steering joint cover and remove the steering joint bolt(s).
7. Disconnect each wire coupler from the fuse box under the left side of the dashboard.
8. Remove the steering column retaining brackets.
9. Remove the nuts attaching the bending plate guide and bending plate and remove the steering column assembly.
10. Installation is the reverse of the removal procedure. Tighten the column bracket bolts and the steering joint bolts to 16 ft. lbs. (22 Nm).

Manual Steering Rack and Pinion

Adjustment

1. Raise and safely support the vehicle.
2. Turn the steering wheel with a suitable spring gauge and check the reading.
3. If the reading exceeds 3.3 lbs., adjust the steering gear as oulined in the following Steps.
4. Place the front wheels in the straight ahead position.
5. Loosen the rack screw locknut.
6. On 1987 Civic, perform the following procedure:
   a. Tighten the adjusting screw to just less than 36 inch lbs. (less than 48 inch lbs. on variable ratio steering).
   b. On all vehicles except 1988–90 Civic, back off the adjusting screw 20–30 degrees (12–18 degrees on variable ratio steering) from the bottomed (torqued) position and hold it there while adjusting the locknut to 18 ft. lbs. (60 ft. lbs. on variable ratio steering).
7. On 1987 CRX, perform the following procedure:
   a. Tighten the rack guide screw to 36 inch lbs. (4 Nm).
   b. Back off the screw approximately $1/10$ of a turn from the bottomed (torqued) position and tighten the locknut to 18 ft. lbs. (25 Nm).
8. On 1988–91 Civic Si, perform the following procedure:
   a. Tighten, loosen and retighten the rack guide screw 2 times, to 3.6 ft. lbs. (5 Nm), then back it off 15 degrees.
   b. Tighten the locknut on the rack guide screw to 49 ft. lbs. (68 Nm).
9. On 1988–91 CRX Si, perform the following procedure:
   a. Retighten the rack guide screw until it compresses the spring and seats against the rack guide.
   b. Back off the rack guide screw 15 degrees and install the locknut on the rack guide screw. Tighten the locknut to 18 ft. lbs. (25 Nm).

10. On all other vehicles, perform the following procedure:

a. Tighten the rack screw until it compresses the spring and seats against the rack guide.

b. Back the rack guide screw off 40–60 degrees and tighten the locknut on the rack guide screw to 18 ft. lbs. (25 Nm).

11. Check for tight or loose steering through the complete turning travel.

12. Recheck the steering effort.

13. Lower the vehicle and with the wheels in the straight ahead position, measure the distance the steering wheel can be turned without moving the front wheels. The play should not exceed 0.4 in. (10mm). If it does, check all steering components.

Removal and Installation

1. Raise the vehicle and support it safely.

2. Remove the cover panel and steering joint cover. Unbolt and separate the steering shaft at the coupling.

3. Remove the front wheels.

4. Remove the cotter pins and unscrew the castle nuts on the tie rod ends. Using a ball joint tool disconnect the tie rod ends. Lift the tie rod ends out of the steering knuckles.

5. If equipped with manual transaxle, disconnect the shift lever torque rod from the clutch housing. Slide the pin retainer out of the way, drive out the spring pin and disconnect the shift rod.

6. If equipped with automatic transaxles, remove the shift cable guide from the floor and pull the shift cable down by hand.

7. Remove the 2 nut connecting the exhaust header pipe to the exhaust pipe and move the exhaust pipe out of the way.

8. Push the rack all the way to the right and remove the brackets or mounting bolts. Slide the tie rod ends all the way to the right.

9. Drop the rack far enough to permit the end of the pinion

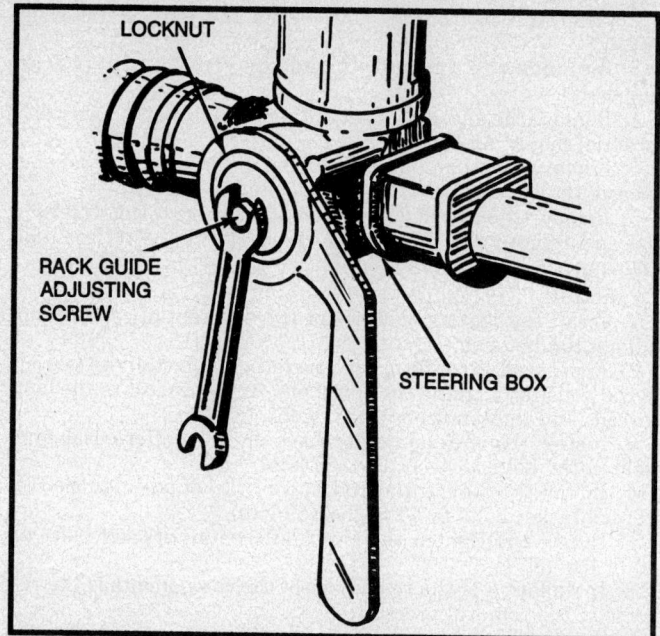

Steering box adjustment

shaft to come out of the hole in the frame channel, then rotate it forward until the shaft is pointing rearward.

10. Slide the rack to the right until the left tie rod clears the exhaust pipe, then drop it down and out of the vehicle to the left.

11. Installation is the reverse of removal. Torque the mount-

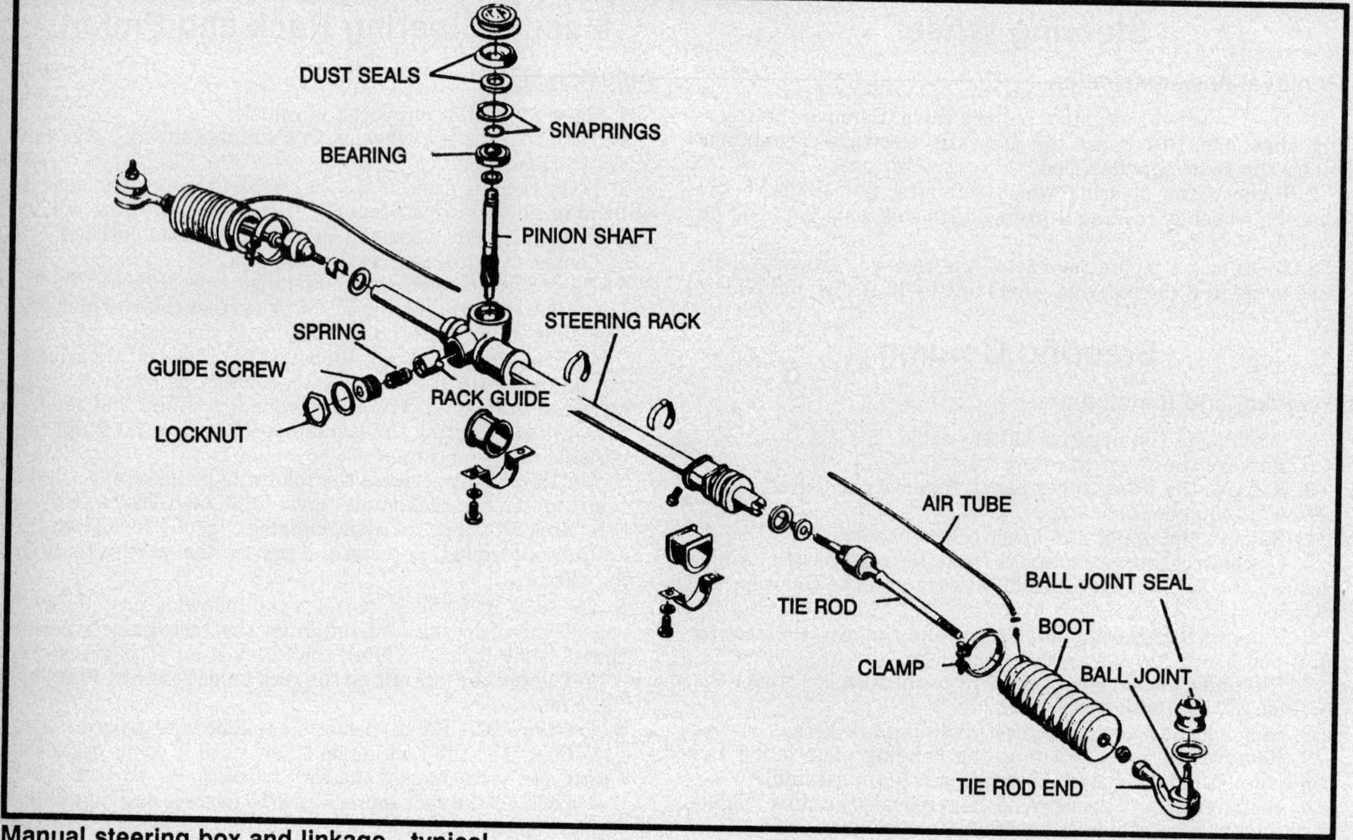

Manual steering box and linkage—typical

ing bracket bolts to 29 ft. lbs. If equipped with manual transaxles, reinstall the pin retainer after driving in the pin and be sure the projection on the pin retainer is in the hole.

Rear Wheel Steering Gear

1988–91 Prelude vehicles may be equipped with 4WS (Four Wheel Steering).

Gearbox Centering Adjustment

NOTE: The following procedure must be used after re-assembling/replacing the steering gearbox components or in preparing to solve complaints of mis-adjusted steering wheel angle.

1. Center the steering and steering wheel by eye.
2. Raise and safely support the vehicle.
3. Remove the gearbox cap bolt using a TORX® T-40 bit.
4. Insert rear steering center lock pin 07HAJ–SF1020A or equivalent, in the gearbox.
5. Turn the steering wheel right or left slightly until the pin of the tool seats fully. The red mark on the pin should not be visible.

NOTE: Do not turn the steering wheel quickly when the tool is seated and do not force past the locking point after the pin is seated or the pin may be damaged.

Removal and Installation

1. Raise and safely support the vehicle.
2. Remove the rear wheel and tire assemblies.
3. Use a suitable tool to separate the tie-rods from the steering knuckles.
4. Slide the rear steering joint guard toward the front.
5. Remove the steering yoke bolt.
6. Remove the cap bolt and install rear steering center lock pin 07HAJ–1020A or equivalent, then remove the 4 rear steering gearbox bolts.
7. Remove the rear steering gearbox assembly.
8. Installation is the reverse of the removal procedure. Tighten the 4 gearbox mounting bolts to 29 ft. lbs. (40 Nm). Tighten the steering yoke bolt to 22 ft. lbs. (30 Nm). Tighten the tie-rod nuts to 32 ft. lbs. (44 Nm) and install new cotter pins.

Power Steering Rack and Pinion

Adjustment
CIVIC AND ACCORD

1. Remove the steering gear splash shield, if equipped.
2. Loosen the rack guide adjusting locknut.
3. Tighten the adjusting screw until it compresses the spring and seats against the guide, then loosen it. Retorque it to 35 inch lbs., then back it off 20 degrees on 1988–91 Civic, 25 degrees on 1987–89 Accord and 35 degrees on 1987 Civic and 1990–91 Accord.
4. Hold it in that position while adjusting the locknut to 18 ft. lbs.
5. Recheck the play, and then move the wheels lock-to-lock, to make sure the rack moves freely.

PRELUDE

1. Make sure the rack is well lubricated.
2. Loosen the rack guide adjusting locknut.
3. Tighten the adjusting screw until it compresses the spring and seats against the guide, then loosen it. Retorque it to 24 inch lbs., then back it off 20–30 degrees (15–25 degrees on 1990–91 vehicles) on 2 wheel steering vehicles. Retorque it to 3 ft. lbs. and 30–40 degrees on 4 wheel steering vehicles).

4. Hold it in that position while adjusting the locknut to 18 ft. lbs.
5. Recheck the play, and then move the wheels lock-to-lock, to make sure the rack moves freely.

Removal and Installation
CIVIC

1. Disconnect the negative battery cable. Raise the vehicle and support it safely.
2. Remove the cover panel and steering joint cover. Unbolt and separate the steering shaft at the coupling.
3. Drain the power steering fluid by disconnecting the return hose at the box and running the engine while turning the steering wheel lock to lock until fluid stops draining. Remove the gearbox shield, if equipped. Remove the front wheels.
4. Remove the cotter pins and unscrew the castle nuts on the tie rod ends. Using a ball joint tool, disconnect the tie rod ends. Lift the tie rod ends out of the steering knuckles.
5. If equipped with manual transaxle, disconnect the shift lever torque rod from the clutch housing. Slide the pin retainer out of the way, drive out the spring pin and disconnect the shift rod.
6. If equipped with automatic transaxle, remove the shift cable guide from the floor and pull the shift cable down by hand.
7. Remove the 2 nuts connecting the exhaust header pipe to the exhaust pipe and remove the exhaust header pipe. Disconnect the 3 hydraulic lines from the control unit.
8. Slide the tie rod ends all the way to the right and remove the steering rack mounting bolts.
9. Drop the gearbox far enough to permit the end of the pinion shaft to come out of the hole in the frame channel, then rotate it forward until the shaft is pointing rearward.
10. Slide the gearbox to the right until the left tie rod clears the beam, then drop it down and out of the vehicle to the left.
11. Installation is the reverse of removal. Torque the mounting bracket bolts to 29 ft. lbs. (40 Nm). If equipped with manual transaxles, reinstall the pin retainer after driving in the pin and be sure the projection on the pin retainer is in the hole.
12. Fill the system with fluid and bleed the air from the system.

ACCORD AND PRELUDE

1. Disconnect the negative battery cable. Raise the vehicle and support it safely.
2. Remove the steering shaft joint cover and disconnect the steering shaft at the coupling.
3. Drain the power steering fluid by disconnecting the return hose at the box and running the engine, while turning the steering wheel lock to lock until fluid stops draining.
4. Remove the gearbox shield.
5. Remove the front wheels.
6. Using a ball joint tool, disconnect the tie rods from the knuckles.
7. If equipped with manual transaxle, remove the shift extension from the transaxle case. Disconnect the gear shift rod from the transaxle case by removing the 8mm bolt.
8. If equipped with automatic transaxle, remove the control cable clamp.
9. Remove the center beam.
10. On the 4 wheel steering vehicles, separate the joint guard cap and the joint guard. Remove the joint bolt from the driven pinion side. Remove the joint bolt from the center steering shaft side, then slide the joint back to disconnect it from the driven pinion.
11. Remove the exhaust header pipe.
12. Disconnect the hydraulic lines at the steering control unit. On 4 wheel steering vehicles, disconnect the driven drain hose.
13. On Prelude, remove the mounting bolts and lower the front sway bar.

14. Shift the tie rods all the way right.

15. Remove the gearbox mounting bolts.

16. Slide the gearbox right so the left tie rod clears the bottom of the rear beam. Remove the gearbox.

17. Installation is the reverse of removal. Tighten the gearbox clamp bolts to 16 ft. lbs. (22 Nm) on 1987-89 Accord and 29 ft. lbs. (40 Nm) on all others.

18. Fill the system with fluid and bleed the air from the system.

Power Steering Pump

Removal and Installation

1. Drain the fluid from the system as follows:

   a. Disconnect the cooler return hose from the reservoir and place the end in a large container.

   b. Start the engine and allow it to run at fast idle. Turn the steering wheel from lock to lock several times, until fluid stops running from the hose. Shut off the engine and discard the fluid.

   c. Reattach the hose on all vehicles with a separate reservoir.

2. Disconnect the inlet and outlet hoses at the pump. Remove the drive belt.

3. Remove the bolts and remove the pump.

4. Installation is the reverse of the removal procedure. Adjust the belt tension, fill the reservoir and bleed the air from the system.

Belt Adjustment

1. Push on the belt mid way between the pulleys with a force of about 22 lbs. The belt deflection should be as follows:

1987 Civic and Prelude—0.75-0.875 in. (18-22mm).

1988-91 Civic—0.35-0.47 in. (9-12mm).

1987-89 Accord—0.55-0.67 in. (14-17mm).

1990-91 Accord—0.50-0.62 in. (12.5-16mm).

1988-91 Prelude—0.43-0.51 in. (11-13mm).

2. If belt deflection is not as specified, adjust as follows:

   a. 1987 Civic—Loosen the 4 adjusting bolts and slide the pump body until the proper tension is obtained. Tighten the bolts to 33 ft. lbs. (45 Nm).

   b. 1990-91 Accord—Loosen the pivot bolt and mounting nut. Turn the adjusting bolt to get the proper tension. Tighten the pivot bolt to 33 ft. lbs. (45 Nm) and the mounting nut to 16 ft. lbs. (22 Nm).

   c. 1988-91 Prelude—Loosen the adjusting pulley bolt and turn the adjusting bolt to get the proper tension. Tighten the pulley bolt to 35 ft. lbs. (49 Nm).

   d. All others—Loosen the pump pivot bolt and the adjusting nut or bolt. Pry the pump away from the engine to get the proper tension. Tighten the pivot bolt to 28 ft. lbs. (39 Nm). Tighten the adjusting nut or bolt to 28 ft. lbs. (39 Nm) except 1987-89 Accord. Tighten the adjusting nut on Accord to 16 ft. lbs. (22 Nm).

System Bleeding

1. Make sure the reservoir is filled to the full mark.

2. Start the engine and allow it to idle.

3. Turn the steering wheel from side to side several times, lightly contacting the stops.

4. Turn the engine off.

5. Check the fluid level in the reservoir and add if necessary.

Tie Rod Ends

Removal and Installation

1. Raise the vehicle and support it safely. Remove the front wheels.

2. Remove the cotter pins and castle nuts from the tie rod ends. Use a ball joint remover to remove the tie rod from the knuckle.

3. Disconnect the air tube at the dust seal joint. Remove the tie rod dust seal bellows clamps and move the rubber bellows on the tie rod rack joints.

4. Straighten the tie rod lock washer tabs at the tie rod-to-rack joint and remove the tie rod by turning it with a wrench.

5. To install, reverse the removal procedure. Always use a new tie rod lock washer during reassembly. Install the locating lugs into the slots on the rack and bend the outer edge of the washer over the flat part of the rod, after the tie rod nut has been properly tightened.

6. Check the toe setting of the front end alignment.

BRAKES

Master Cylinder

Removal and Installation

1. Disconnect the negative battery cable. Disconnect and plug the brake lines at the master cylinder.

2. Remove the master cylinder-to-vacuum booster attaching bolts and remove the master cylinder from the vehicle.

3. To install, reverse the removal procedure. Before operating the vehicle, bleed the brake system.

Proportioning Valve

Removal and Installation

1. Disconnect the negative battery cable.

2. Disconnect and plug the brake lines at the valve.

3. Remove the valve mounting bolts and the valve.

4. Installation is the reverse of the removal procedure. Bleed the brake system.

Power Brake Booster

Removal and Installation

1. Disconnect the negative battery cable. Disconnect the vacuum hose at the booster.

2. It may be possible to remove the master cylinder to brake booster retaining nuts and than position the master cylinder assembly to the side on some vehicles. If not, the master cylinder will have to be removed from the vehicle.

3. Remove the brake pedal-to-booster link pin and the 4 nuts retaining the booster. The pushrod and nuts are located inside the vehicle under the instrument panel.

4. Remove the booster assembly from the vehicle.

5. To install, reverse the removal procedure. If the master cylinder was removed, bleed the brake system.

Brake Caliper

Removal and Installation

FRONT

1. Raise and safely support the vehicle.

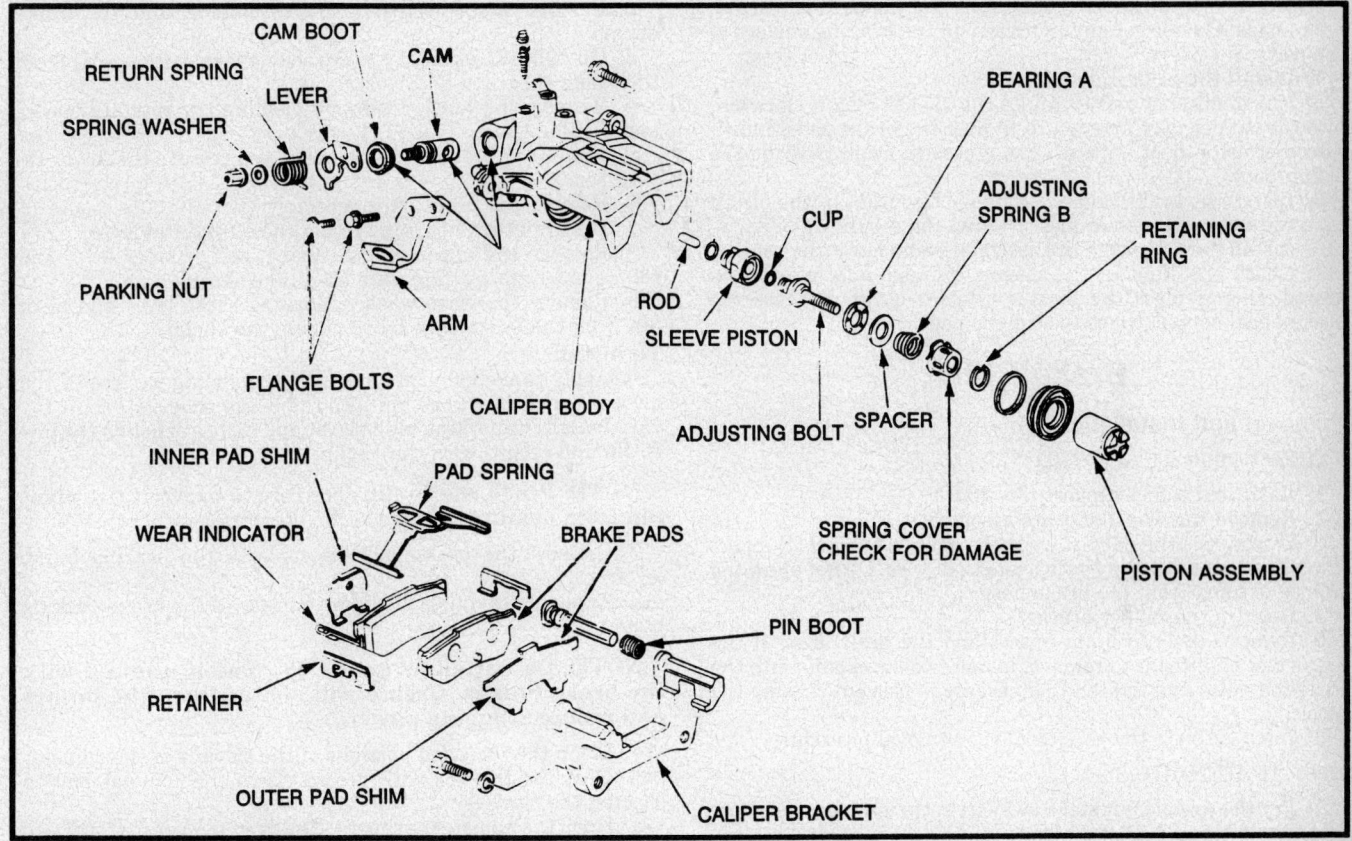

Rear disc brake assembly

2. Remove the front wheel and tire assembly.
3. Remove the banjo bolt and disconnect the brake hose from the caliper. Plug the hose.
4. Remove the mounting bolt(s) and the caliper.
5. Installation is the reverse of the removal procedure. Bleed the front brakes.

REAR

1. Raise and safely support the vehicle.
2. Remove the rear wheel and tire assembly.
3. Remove the caliper shield.
4. Disconnect the parking brake cable from the lever on the caliper by removing the lock pin.
5. Remove the banjo bolt and disconnect the brake hose from the caliper. Plug the hose.
6. Remove the 2 caliper mounting bolts and the caliper from the bracket.
7. Installation is the reverse of the removal procedure. Bleed the rear brakes.

Disc Brake Pads

Removal and Installation

FRONT

1. Remove the master cylinder cover and remove half the quantity of brake fluid in the master cylinder.
2. Raise and support the vehicle safely. Remove the tire and wheel assemblies.
3. As required, separate the brake hose clamp from the knuckle by removing the retaining bolts.
4. Remove the lower caliper retaining bolt and pivot the caliper out of the way.

5. Remove the pad shim and pad retainers. Remove the disc brake pads from the caliper.
To install:
6. Clean the caliper thoroughly; remove any rust. Check the brake rotor for grooves or cracks and machine or replace, as necessary.
7. Install the pad retainers. Apply a suitable disc brake pad lubricant to both surfaces of the shims and the back of the disc brake pads. Do not get any lubricant on the braking surface of the pad.
8. Install the pads and shims.
9. Use a suitable tool to push in the caliper piston so the caliper will fit over the pads.
10. Pivot the caliper down into position and tighten the mounting bolts.
11. Connect the brake hose to the knuckle, if removed. Install the wheel and tire assembly and lower the vehicle.
12. Check the master cylinder and add fluid as required, then replace the master cylinder cover. Depress the brake pedal several times to seat the pads.

REAR

1. Remove the master cylinder cover and remove half the quantity of brake fluid.
2. Raise and safely support the vehicle. Remove the rear wheel and tire assemblies.
3. Remove the 2 caliper mounting bolts and the caliper from the bracket.
4. Remove the pads, shims and pad retainers.
To install:
5. Clean the caliper thoroughly; remove any rust. Check the brake rotor for grooves or cracks and machine or replace, as necessary.
6. Install the pad retainers. Apply a suitable disc brake pad

lubricant to both surfaces of the shims and the back of the disc brake pads. Do not get any lubricant on the braking surface of the pad.

7. Install the pads and shims.

8. Use a suitable tool to rotate the caliper piston clockwise into the caliper bore, enough to fit over the brake pads. Lubricate the piston boot with silicone grease to avoid twisting the piston boot.

9. Install the brake caliper, aligning the cutout in the piston with the tab on the inner pad. Tighten the mounting bolts.

10. Install the wheel and tire assemblies and lower the vehicle.

11. Check the fluid in the master cylinder and add, as required, then replace the master cylinder cover. Depress the brake pedal several times to seat the pads.

Brake Rotor

Removal and Installation

EXCEPT 1990–91 ACCORD

1. Raise and safely support the vehicle.
2. Remove the wheel and tire assembly.
3. Disconnect the caliper from the caliper bracket. Support the caliper out of the way with a length of wire. Do not allow the caliper to hang from the brake hose.
4. Remove the caliper bracket.
5. Remove the two 6mm screws and the brake disc. If the brake disc is difficult to remove, install two 8mm bolts into the threaded holes and tighten them evenly to prevent cocking the rotor.
6. Installation is the reverse of the removal procedure.

1990–91 ACCORD

1. Pry the spindle nut stake away from the spindle, then loosen the nut.
2. Raise and safely support the vehicle.
3. Remove the wheel and tire assembly and the spindle nut.
4. Remove the caliper and support it out of the way with a length of wire. Do not allow the caliper to hang from the brake hose. Remove the caliper bracket.
5. Remove the cotter pin and tie rod ball joint nut. Separate the tie rod from the steering knuckle using a suitable tool.
6. Remove the cotter pin and loosen the lower arm ball joint nut half the length of the joint threads. Separate the ball joint and lower arm using a suitable puller. Remove the lower ball joint nut.
7. Pull the steering knuckle outward and remove the halfshaft outboard CV-joint from the knuckle, using a suitable plastic hammer.
8. Remove the 4 bolts retaining the hub unit to the steering knuckle and remove the hub unit.
9. Remove the 4 bolts, then separate the hub unit from the brake rotor.
10. Installation is the reverse of the removal procedure.

Brake Drums

Removal and Installation

1. Raise and safely support the vehicle.
2. Remove the rear wheel and tire assembly.
3. On 1987 CRX HF, remove the spindle nut and remove the brake drum and hub as a unit. On all others remove the brake drum.
4. Installation is the reverse of the removal procedure. Adjust the brakes if necessary.

Brake Shoes

Removal and Installation

1. Raise and safely support the vehicle.

2. Remove the wheel and tire assemblies and the brake drums.

3. On 1990–91 Accord, remove the upper return spring from the brake shoe.

4. Remove the tension pins by pushing the retainer spring and turning them.

5. Lower the brake shoe assembly and remove the lower return spring.

6. Remove the brake shoe assembly.

7. Disconnect the parking brake cable from the lever.

8. Remove the upper return spring, self-adjuster lever and self-adjuster spring. Separate the brake shoes.

9. Remove the wave washer, parking brake lever and pivot pin from the brake shoe by removing the U-clip.

To install:

10. Apply brake cylinder grease to the sliding surface of the pivot pin and insert the pin into the brake shoe.

11. Install the parking brake lever and wave washer on the pivot pin and secure with the U-clip.

NOTE: Pinch the U-clip securely to prevent the pivot pin from coming out of the brake shoe.

12. Connect the parking brake cable to the parking brake lever.

13. Apply grease on each sliding surface of the brake backing plate.

NOTE: Do not allow grease to come in contact with the brake linings. Grease will contaminate the linings and reduce stopping power.

14. Clean the threaded portions of the clevises of the adjuster bolt. Coat the threads with grease. Turn the adjuster bolt to shorten the clevises.

15. Hook the adjuster spring to the adjuster lever first, then to the brake shoe.

16. Install the adjuster bolt/clevis assembly and the upper return spring.

17. Install the brake shoes to the backing plate.

18. Install the lower return spring, the tension pins and retaining springs.

19. On 1990–91 Accord, connect the upper return spring.

20. Turn the adjuster bolt to force the brake shoes out until the brake drum will not easily go on. Back off the adjuster bolt just enough that the brake drum will go on and turn easily.

21. Install the wheel and tire assemblies and lower the vehicle.

22. Depress the brake pedal several times to set the self adjusting brake. Adjust the parking brake.

Wheel Cylinder

Removal and Installation

1. Raise and support the vehicle safely. Remove the tire and wheel assemblies. Remove the brake drum and shoes.

2. Disconnect the brake line from the wheel cylinder. Plug the line.

3. Remove the 2 wheel cylinder retaining nuts on the inboard side of the backing plate and remove the wheel cylinder.

4. To install, reverse the removal procedure. When assembling, apply a thin coat of grease to the grooves of the wheel cylinder piston and the sliding surfaces of the backing plate. Bleed the brakes.

Parking Brake Cable

Adjustment

1. Raise and safely support the vehicle.

2. On rear disc brake equipped vehicles, make sure the lever of the rear brake caliper contacts the brake caliper pin.

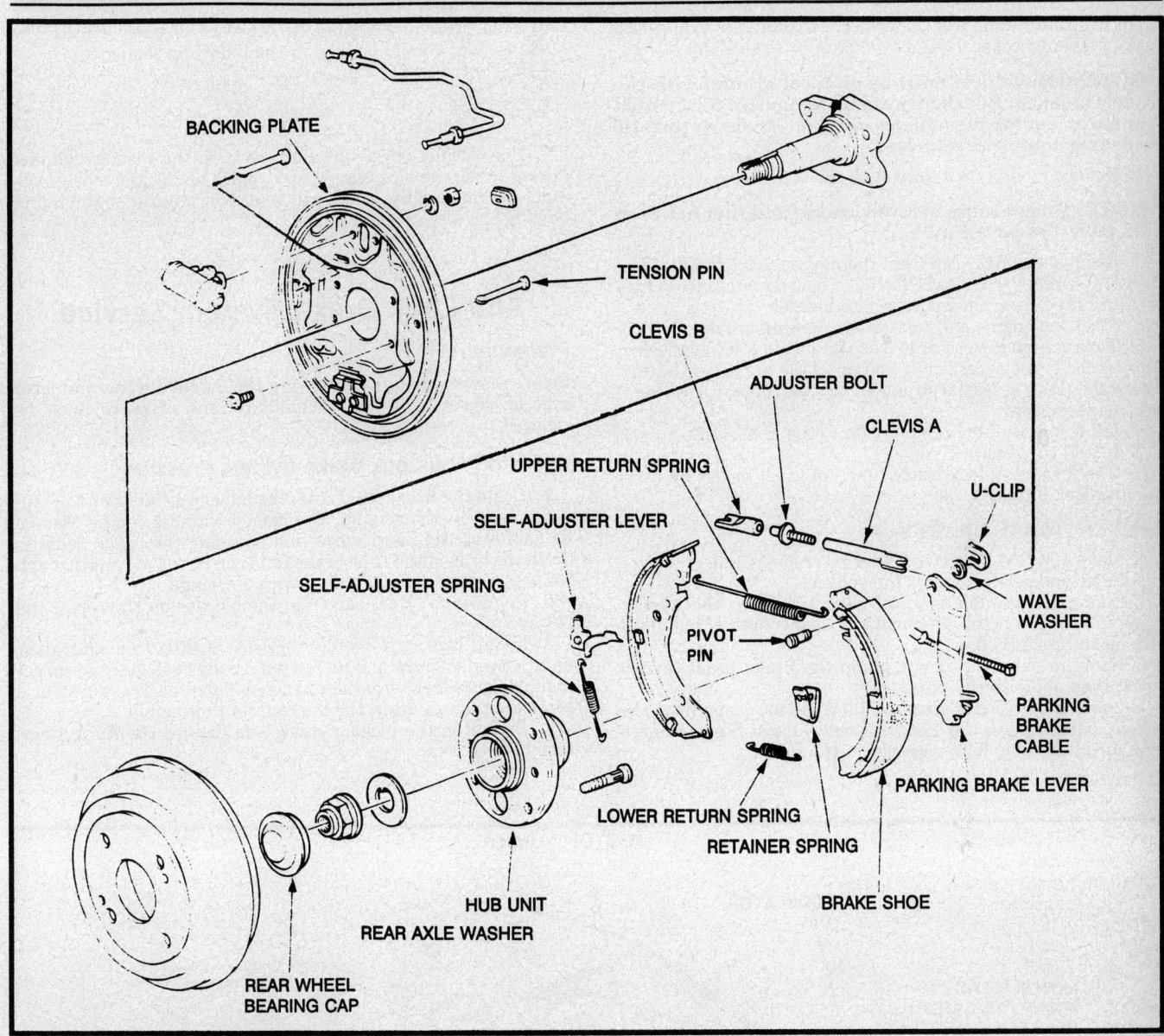

Rear shoe brake assembly

3. On drum brake equipped vehicles, make sure the rear brakes are properly adjusted.

4. Pull the parking brake lever up 1 notch.

5. Remove the access cover at the rear of the console and tighten the adjusting nut until the rear wheels drag slightly when turned.

6. Release the parking brake lever and check that the rear wheels do not drag when turned. Readjust if necessary.

7. With the equalizer properly adjusted, the parking brake should be fully applied when the parking brake lever is pulled up 6–10 clicks on 1988–91 Civic and CRX, 7–11 clicks on 1987–89 Accord and 1988–91 Prelude and 4–8 clicks on all others.

Removal and Installation

1. Remove the access cover at the rear of the console. Loosen the adjusting nut until the cable ends can be disconnected from the equalizer.

2. Raise and safely support the vehicle.

3. Remove the rear wheel and tire assemblies.

4. On disc brake equipped vehicles, pull out the lock pin, remove the clevis pin and remove the clip.

5. On drum brake equipped vehicles, remove the brake drum and brake shoes. Disconnect the cable from the backing plate.

6. Detach the cables from the cable guides and remove the cables from the vehicle.

7. Installation is the reverse of the removal procedure. Adjust the parking brake.

Brake System Bleeding

ANTI-LOCK BRAKES

The following procedure must be used if the modulator, accumulator unit or power unit is removed or disassembled. If a component of the conventional brake system is removed on a vehicle with anti-lock brakes, the conventional brake bleeding procedure is used.

1990–91 Prelude

1. Disconnect the 6 prong connector from the cover in front

of the console and connect the inspection connector to anti-lock brake system checker 07HAJ–SG0010A or equivalent.

NOTE: The vehicle must be on level ground with the wheels blocked. Put the transaxle in neutral for manual transaxle equipped vehicles and in P for automatic transaxle equipped vehicles.

2. Fill the modulator reservoir to the MAX level.

NOTE: Do not reuse aerated brake fluid that has been bled from the power unit.

3. Remove the RED cap from the maintenance bleeder. Use bleeder T-wrench 07HAA–SG00101 or equivalent, to bleed high pressure fluid from the maintenance bleeder.
4. Start the engine and release the parking brake.
5. Turn the mode selector to **6** on the anti-lock brake checker, depress the brake pedal firmly and press the Start Test button. There should be at least 2 strong kickbacks. If not, repeat Steps 2–5, as necessary.
6. Fill the modulator reservoir up to the MAX level.
7. Install the reservoir cap.
8. Check the anti-lock brake function in all modes by using the anti-lock brake checker.

CONVENTIONAL BRAKES
1. Make sure the master cylinder reservoir is full.
2. Raise and safely support the vehicle.
3. Connect a suitable piece of clear tubing to the bleeder screw and submerge the other end in a clear container half filled with clean brake fluid.
4. Have an assistant slowly pump the brake pedal several times, then apply steady pressure.
5. Loosen the bleeder screw to allow air to escape from the system, then tighten the bleeder screw. Repeat Steps 4 and 5 until air bubbles no longer appear in the fluid.

6. This procedure should be repeated at each wheel. The brake system should be bled in the following sequence:
Left front.
Right rear.
Right front.
Left rear.
7. Periodically check the fluid level in the master cylinder during the brake bleeding procedure. Do not let the master cylinder become empty, as air will be drawn into the system, prolonging the bleeding procedure.

Anti-Lock Brake System Service
Precaution
Before disassembling or removing the modulator, accumulator unit or power unit, the accumulator/line pressure must be relieved.

Relieving Anti-Lock Brake System Pressure
1. Drain the brake fluid from the master cylinder and modulator reservoir thoroughly. The master cylinder can be drained by loosening the bleed screw and pumping the brake pedal to drain the brake fluid. The brake fluid can be sucked out through the top of the modulator tank with a syringe.
2. Remove the RED cap from the bleeder on the top of the power unit.
3. Install bleeder T-wrench 07HAA–SG00101 or equivalent on the bleeder screw and turn it out slowly 90 degrees to collect high pressure fluid into the reservoir. Turn the T-wrench out 1 complete turn to drain the brake fluid thoroughly.
4. Retighten the bleeder screw and discard the fluid. Reinstall the RED cap.

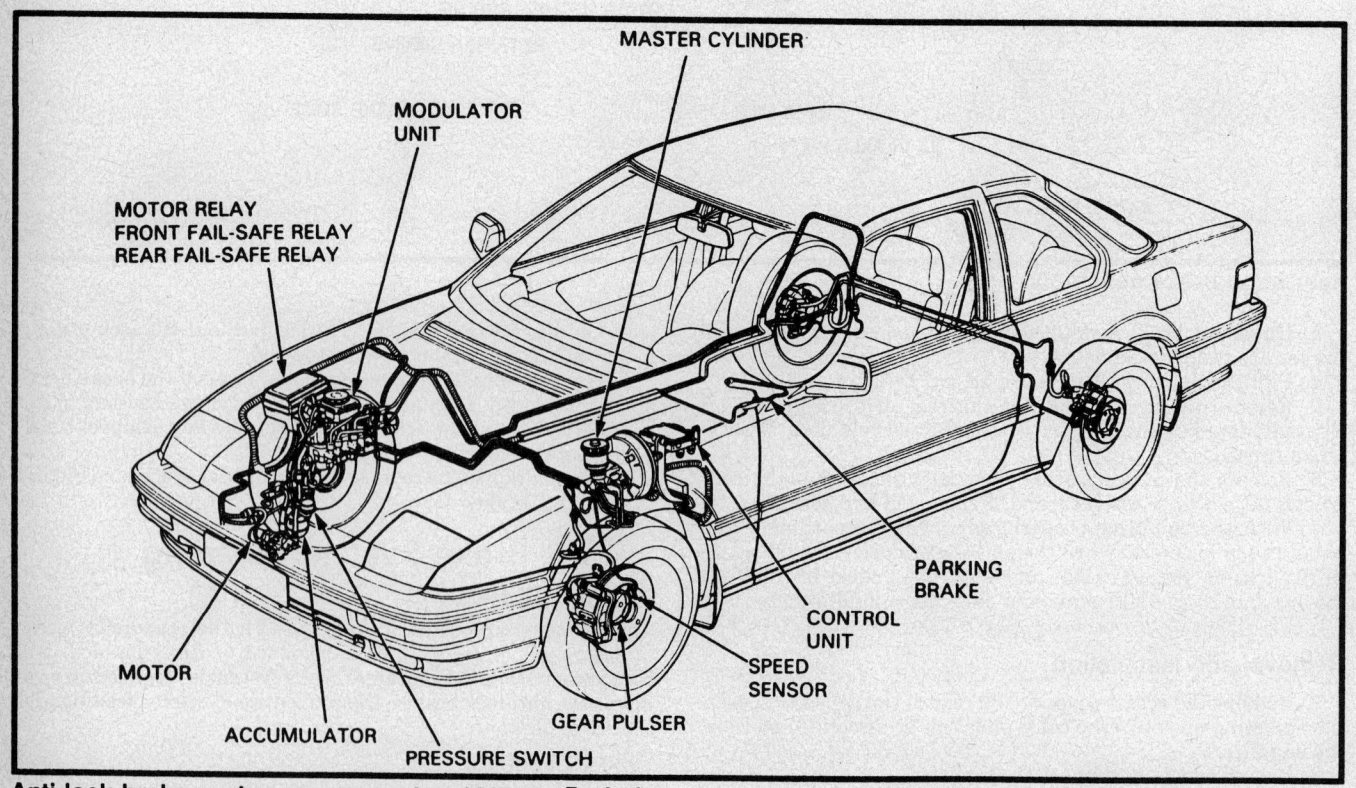

Anti-lock brake system components—1990–91 Prelude

Anti-Lock Brake System Control Unit

Removal and Installation

1. Disconnect the negative battery cable.
2. Remove the cover that is mounted in front of the center console.
3. Remove the control unit mounting bolts, then remove the control unit.
4. Disconnect the electrical connectors and remove the control unit from the vehicle.

NOTE: When the control unit mounting bolts are removed, the control unit's memory is cleared.

5. Installation is the reverse of the removal procedure.

Modulator

Removal and Installation

1. Disconnect the negative battery cable.
2. Relieve the anti-lock brake system pressure.
3. Disconnect the hydraulic lines from the modulator and plug the lines.
4. Disconnect the electrical connectors.
5. Remove the modulator mounting bolts and remove the modulator.
6. Installation is the reverse of the removal procedure. Be sure to bleed the anti-lock brake hydraulic system according to the proper procedure.

Accumulator

Removal and Installation

1. Disconnect the negative battery cable.

2. Relieve the anti-lock brake system pressure.
3. Disconnect the hydraulic lines from the accumulator and plug the lines.
4. Disconnect the electrical connectors.
5. Remove the accumulator mounting bolts and remove the accumulator.
6. Installation is the reverse of the removal procedure. Be sure to bleed the anti-lock brake hydraulic system, according to the proper procedure.

Power Unit

Removal and Installation

1. Disconnect the negative battery cable.
2. Relieve the anti-lock brake system pressure.
3. Disconnect the hoses from the accumulator and plug them.
4. Disconnect the electrical connectors.
5. Remove the power unit mounting bolts and remove the power unit.
6. Installation is the reverse of the removal procedure. Be sure to bleed the anti-lock brake hydraulic system according to the proper procedure.

Speed Sensor

Removal and Installation

1. Raise and safely support the vehicle.
2. Disconnect the sensor electrical connectors.
3. Remove the sensor and wire guide mounting bolts and remove the sensor.
4. Installation is the reverse of the removal procedure.

FRONT SUSPENSION

Shock Absorbers

Removal and Installation

1987 CIVIC AND CRX

1. Raise the vehicle and support it safely. Remove the front wheels.
2. Remove the brake hose clamp bolt.
3. Place a suitable floor jack beneath the lower control arm to support it.
4. Remove the lower shock retaining bolt from the steering knuckle, then slowly lower the jack.

NOTE: Be sure the jack is positioned securely beneath the lower control arm at the ball joint. Otherwise, the tension from the torsion bar may cause the lower control arm to suddenly jump away from the shock absorber as the pinch bolt is removed.

5. Compress the shock absorber by hand, then remove the 2 upper locknuts. Remove the shock absorber from the vehicle. Remove the self locking nut while holding the damper rod. Remove the shock from the shock mount.
6. Installation is the reverse of the removal procedure. Tighten the self locking nut to 33 ft. lbs. (45 Nm) while holding the damper shaft. Tighten the shock mount nuts to 28 ft. lbs. (39 Nm) and the lower shock retaining bolt to 47 ft. lbs. (65 Nm).

MacPherson Strut

Removal and Installation

1. Raise and safely support the vehicle.
2. Remove the front tire and wheel assembly.
3. Remove the damper fork bolts and remove the damper fork.
4. Remove the flange nuts and remove the strut assembly.
5. Installation is the reverse of the removal procedure. Tighten the damper fork nut to 47 ft. lbs. (65 Nm) while holding the damper fork bolt. Tighten the damper fork pinch bolt to 32 ft. lbs. (44 Nm).
6. The flange nuts should not be tightened until the strut is under vehicle load. Tighten them to 28 ft. lbs. (39 Nm).

Torsion Bars

Removal and Installation

1987 CIVIC AND CRX

1. Raise the vehicle and support it safely.
2. Remove the height adjusting nut and the torque tube holder.
3. Remove the 30mm circlip.
4. Remove the torsion bar cap, then remove the torsion bar clip by tapping the bar forward out of the torque tube.

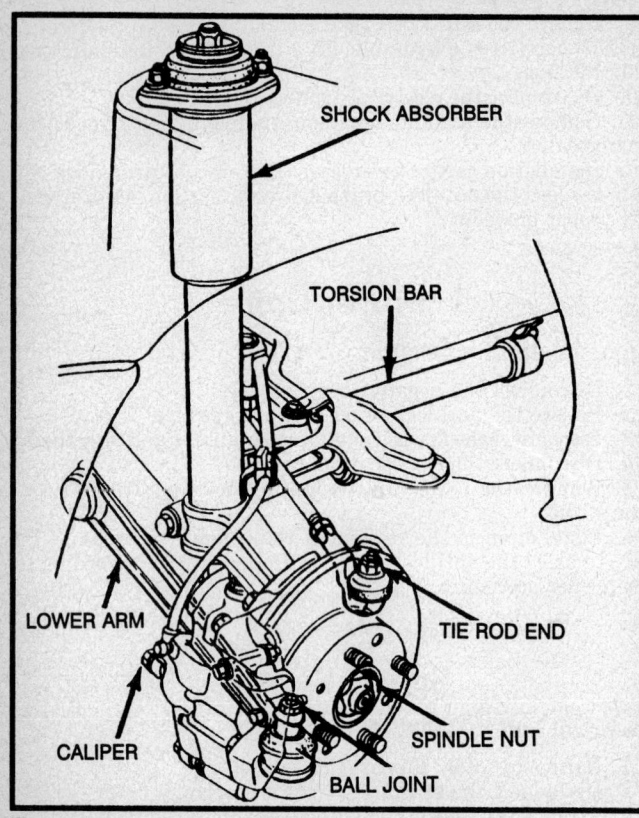

Front suspension—1987 Civic and CRX

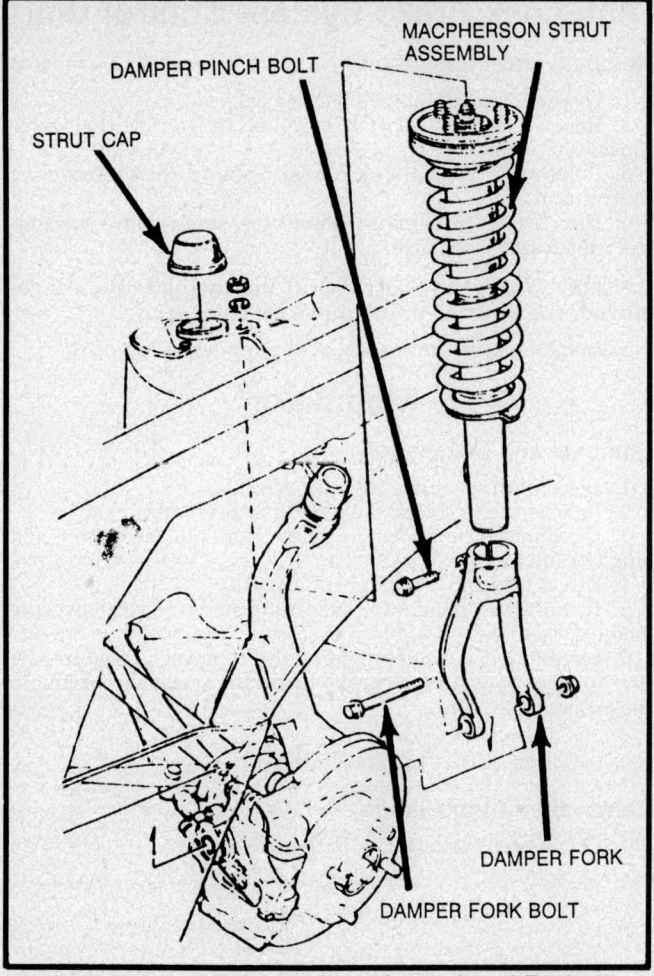

MacPherson strut installation—Accord and Prelude

NOTE: Move the lower arm up and down to make the torsion bar slide easier.

5. Tap the torsion bar backward, out of the torque tube and remove the torque tube.

6. Inspect the torsion bar for cracks or damage and replace, as necessary.

To install:

7. Install a new seal onto the torque tube. Coat the torque tube seal and the torque tube sliding surface with grease, then install the torque tube on the rear beam.

8. Grease the splines at the ends of the torsion bar and insert into the torque tube from the back.

9. Align the projection or punch mark on the torque tube splines with the cutout or paint mark in the torsion bar splines and insert the torsion bar approximately 0.394 in. (10mm).

NOTE: The torsion bar will slide easier if the lower arm is moved up and down. There are 2 types of torsion bars and torque tubes; torque tubes with and without raised lugs and torsion bars with and without lug reliefs. The torque tube with the raised lug will not fit over a torsion bar without a lug relief. But all other combinations of torque tube and torsion bar will fit together and work properly.

10. Install the torsion bar clip and cap, then install the 30mm circlip and the torque tube cap.

NOTE: Push the torsion bar to the front so there is no clearance between the torque tube and the 30mm circlip.

11. Coat the cap bushing with grease and install it on the torque tube. Install the torque tube holder.

12. Temporarily tighten the height adjusting nut.

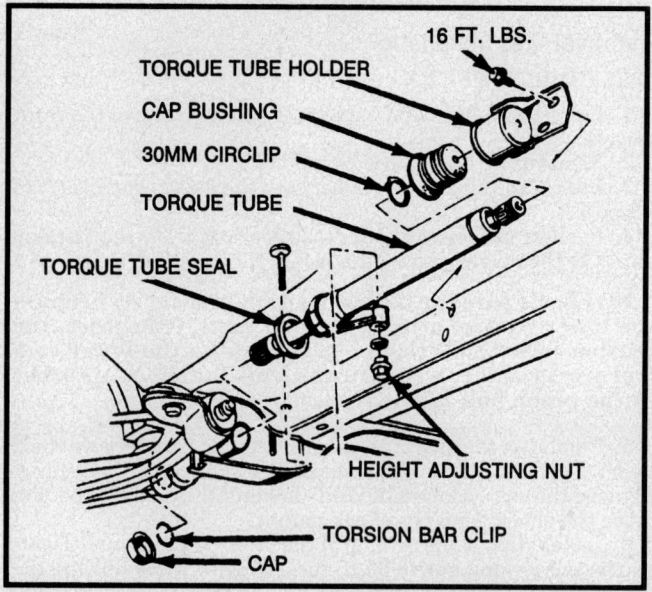

Torsion bar assembly—1987 Civic and CRX

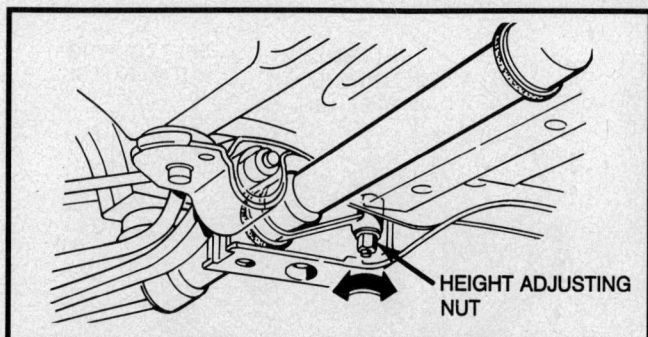

Torsion bar adjustment—1987 Civic and CRX

NOTE: Coat the height adjusting nut and the torque tube sliding surface with grease.

13. Lower the vehicle. Adjust the torsion bar spring height as follows:

    a. Measure the torsion bar spring height between the ground and the wheel arch. The height should be 24.84–26.02 in. (611–661mm) on Civic Hatchback, 25.04–26.22 in. (636–666mm) on Civic Sedan, 24.96–26.14 in. (634–64mm) on Civic Wagon and 24.76–25.94 in. (629–659mm) on CRX.

    b. If the height is not as specified, raise and safely support the vehicle.

    c. If the height needs to be raised, tighten the height adjusting nut. If the height needs to be lowered, loosen the height adjusting nut. The height varies 0.20 in. (5mm) per turn of the adjusting nut.

    d. Lower the vehicle and push it up and down and back and forth several times, then recheck the spring height. Readjust if necessary.

Upper Ball Joints

Inspection

1. Raise and safely support the vehicle.
2. Remove the front wheel and tire assembly.
3. Grasp the steering knuckle and move it back and forth.
4. Replace the upper control arm on all except Prelude if any play is detected. On Prelude, replace the upper ball joint.

Removal and Installation
EXCEPT PRELUDE

The upper ball joint is an integral component of the upper control arm. If the ball joint is defective the entire upper control arm must be replaced.

PRELUDE

1. Raise and safely support the vehicle.
2. Remove the front wheel and tire assembly.
3. Remove the cotter pin and castle nut from the upper ball joint.
4. Using a suitable tool, separate the upper ball joint from the steering knuckle.
5. Remove the 2 retaining nuts and the ball joint.
6. Installation is the reverse of the removal procedure. Tighten the ball joint-to-control arm retaining nuts to 40 ft. lbs. (55 Nm). Tighten the ball joint castle nut to 32 ft. lbs. (44 Nm) and install a new cotter pin.
7. Check the camber adjustment.

Lower Ball Joints

Inspection

1. Raise and safely support the vehicle.

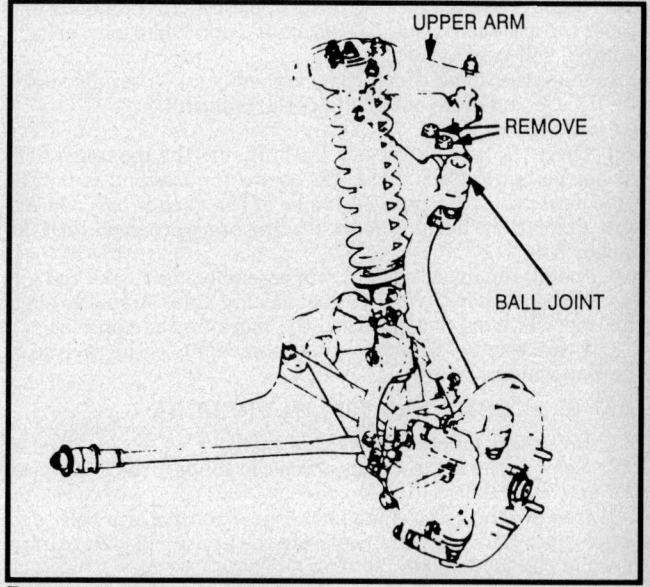

Front suspension—Prelude

2. Remove the wheel and tire assembly.
3. On 1987 Civic and CRX, position a suitable jack under the lower control arm at the ball joint. Raise the jack to bring the suspension to it's normal height.
4. Grasp the steering knuckle close to the lower ball joint and move it back and forth. Replace the ball joint, if any movement is detected, except on 1987 Civic and CRX. On 1987 Civic and CRX, the lower control arm must be replaced.

Removal and Installation
EXCEPT 1987 CIVIC AND CRX

1. Raise and safely support the vehicle.
2. Remove the wheel and tire assembly.
3. Remove the steering knuckle.
4. Pry off the snapring and remove the boot.
5. Remove the circlip.
6. Install a suitable ball joint remover/installer 07965–SB00100 or equivalent, on the ball joint and tighten the ball joint nut.
7. Position ball joint remover base 07JAF–SH20200 or equivalent, over the ball joint and then set the assembly in a suitable vise. Press the ball joint out of the knuckle.

To install:

8. Place the ball joint in position by hand.
9. Install a suitable ball joint remover/installer 07965–SB00100 or equivalent, and ball joint installer base 07965–SB00200 or equivalent, over the ball joint and position in a suitable vise. Press the ball joint in.
10. Installation of the remaining components is the reverse of the removal procedure.

1987 CIVIC AND CRX

The lower ball joint is an integral component of the lower control arm. If the ball joint is defective, the entire lower control arm must be replaced.

Upper Control Arms

Removal and Installation
1988–91 CIVIC AND CRX AND 1990–91 ACCORD

1. Raise and support the vehicle safely.
2. Remove the front wheels. Properly support the lower control arm assemblies.

3. Remove the self locking nuts, upper control arm bolts and upper control anchor bolts. Separate the upper ball joint using a suitable ball joint separator tool.

4. Place the upper control arm assembly into a suitable holding fixture and drive out the upper arm bushing.

To install:

5. Drive the new upper arm bushing into the the upper arm anchor bolts. On Civic and CRX, center the bushing so 0.3543 in. (9mm) protrudes from each side of the anchor bolt. On Accord, drive in the bushing so the leading edges are flush with the anchor bolt.

6. Install the upper control arm assembly and install the upper arm bolts, then tighten the self locking nuts. Be sure to align the upper arm anchor bolt with the mark on the upper arm.

7. Installation of the remaining components is the reverse of the removal procedure.

1987–89 ACCORD AND 1987–91 PRELUDE

1. Raise and support the vehicle safely.

2. Remove the front wheels. Properly support the lower control arm assemblies.

3. Remove the self locking nuts, upper control arm bolts and upper control anchor bolts. Separate the upper ball joint using a suitable ball joint separator tool.

4. Place the upper control arm assembly into a suitable holding fixture and remove the self locking nut, upper arm bolt, upper arm anchor bolts and housing seals.

5. Remove the upper arm collar. Drive out the upper arm bushing, using a suitable drift.

6. Replace the upper control arm bushings, bushing seals and upper control arm collar with new ones. Be sure to coat the ends and the insides of the upper control arm bushings, and the sealing lips of the upper control arm bushing with grease.

7. After Step 6 is completed, apply sealant to the threads and underside of the upper arm bolt heads and self locking nut. Install the upper arm bolt and tighten the self locking nut.

8. Installation of the remaining components is the reverse of the removal procedure.

Lower Control Arms

Removal and Installation

EXCEPT 1987 CIVIC AND CRX

1. Raise the vehicle and support it safely. Remove the front wheels.

2. Properly support the lower control arm assembly. Disconnect the lower arm ball joint. Be careful not to damage the seal.

3. Remove the stabilizer bar retaining brackets, starting with the center brackets.

4. Remove the lower arm pivot bolt.

5. Disconnect the radius rod and remove the lower arm.

6. Installation is the reverse of the removal procedure. Tighten the lower control arm to chassis bolt to 40 ft. lbs. (55 Nm).

1987 CIVIC AND CRX

1. Raise and safely support the vehicle.

2. Remove the front wheel and tire assembly.

3. Position a suitable jack under the lower control arm at the ball joint.

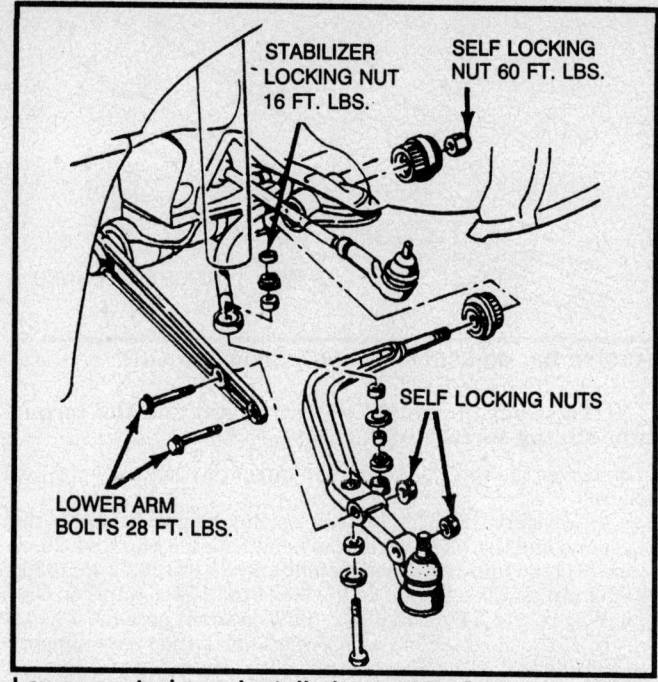

Lower control arm installation—1987 Civic and CRX

NOTE: Make sure the floor jack is positioned securely under the lower control arm at the ball joint. Otherwise, torsion bar tension on the lower control arm may cause the arm to jump suddenly away from the steering knuckle as the ball joint is being removed.

4. Use a suitable tool to separate the lower ball joint from the steering knuckle.

5. Remove the sway bar end links from the lower control arm.

6. Remove the bolts and nuts securing the lower control arm to the torsion bar arm.

7. Remove the nut securing the lower control arm to the vehicle and remove the arm by pulling it down and then forward.

8. Installation is the reverse of the removal procedure. Tighten all bushings and rubber dampered parts only after the vehicle is back on the ground.

9. Tighten the lower control arm-to-torsion bar arm nuts to 28 ft. lbs. (39 Nm) while holding the bolts. Tighten the lower control arm-to-vehicle nut to 60 ft. lbs. (83 Nm).

Sway Bar

Removal and Installation

1. Raise and safely support the vehicle.

2. Remove the front wheel and tire assemblies.

3. Disconnect the sway bar ends from both lower control arms.

4. Remove the bolts retaining the sway bar bushing brackets.

5. Remove the sway bar.

6. Installation is the reverse of the removal procedure.

REAR SUSPENSION

Shock Absorbers

Removal and Installation
1987 CIVIC AND CRX

1. Raise and safely support the vehicle.
2. Remove the rear wheel and tire assemblies.
3. Place a suitable jack under the rear axle.
4. Remove the shock absorber access cover and the upper shock mounting nut.
5. Lower the jack gradually. On all except 4WD Civic Wagon, remove the lower shock mounting bolt and remove the shock absorber with the coil spring and upper spring seat. On 4WD Civic Wagon, remove the lower shock mounting bolt and the shock absorber.
6. Installation is the reverse of the removal procedure. Tighten the lower shock mounting bolt to 40 ft. lbs. (55 Nm) except on 4WD Civic Wagon where it is tightened to 60 ft. lbs. (83 Nm).

MacPherson Strut

Removal and Installation

1. On Civic, CRX and 1987–89 Accord, remove the strut upper cover from inside the vehicle and remove the upper strut retaining nuts.
2. On all other vehicles, remove the strut upper cover from inside the trunk and remove the upper strut retaining nuts.
3. Raise and safely support the vehicle.
4. Remove the rear wheel and tire assembly.
5. On 1987 Prelude, remove the brake hose clamp bolt and disconnect the sway bar from the lower control arm. Loosen the lower arm bolt and loosen the radius rod nut and hub carrier bolt. Remove the strut lock bolt and remove the strut.
6. On all other vehicles, remove the strut mounting bolt, lower the suspension and remove the strut.
7. Installation is the reverse of the removal procedure. Tighten the strut lower mounting bolt to 40 ft. lbs. (55 Nm) with the strut under vehicle load. On 1987 Prelude, align the tab on the strut with the slot in the hub carrier and tighten the strut lock bolt to 40 ft. lbs. (55 Nm).

Coil Springs

Removal and Installation
1987 CIVIC AND CRX

1. Raise and safely support the vehicle.
2. Remove the rear wheel and tire assemblies.
3. Place a suitable jack under the rear axle.
4. Remove the shock absorber access cover and the upper shock mounting nuts.
5. Lower the jack gradually. On all except 4WD Civic Wagon, remove the lower shock mounting bolt and remove the coil spring with the shock absorber and upper spring seat. On 4WD Civic Wagon, remove the coil spring with the upper and lower spring seats.
6. Installation is the reverse of the removal procedure. Tighten the lower shock mounting bolt to 40 ft. lbs. (55 Nm) except on 4WD Civic Wagon where it is tightened to 60 ft. lbs. (83 Nm).

Rear Control Arms

Removal and Installation
TRAILING ARM
Except Accord

1. Raise and safely support the vehicle.

2. Remove the rear wheel and tire assembly.
3. On all except 1988–91 Civic Wagon with 4WD, perform the following procedure:
   a. Remove the brake drum.
   b. Remove the spindle nut and hub unit.
   c. Disconnect the parking brake cable and the brake line from the wheel cylinder. Plug the line.
   d. Remove the brake backing plate.
4. On 1988–91 4WD Civic Wagon, remove the brake drum and spindle nut and disconnect the parking brake cable.
5. Disconnect the brake hose from the brake line. Plug the line.
6. Support the lower control arm or beam axle with a suitable jack.
7. Remove the trailing arm bushing mounting bolts.
8. Disconnect the upper arm and compensator arm from the trailing arm, if equipped.
9. On 1987 Civic and CRX except 4WD Civic Wagon, disconnect the trailing arm from the beam axle.
10. On 1988–91 Civic Wagon with 4WD, remove the rear halfshaft outboard CV-joint from the trailing arm using a suitable puller.
11. Remove the trailing arm from the vehicle.
12. Installation is the reverse of the removal procedure. Tighten all bolts and nuts with the vehicle on the ground. Bleed the brake system.

Accord

1. Raise and safely support the vehicle.
2. Remove the rear wheel and tire assembly.
3. Support the lower control arm using a suitable jack.
4. Remove the bolt from the trailing arm bushing.
5. Remove the mounting nuts from the knuckle and remove the trailing arm.
6. Installation is the reverse of the removal procedure.

UPPER CONTROL ARM

1. Raise and safely support the vehicle.
2. Remove the rear wheel and tire assembly.
3. Support the lower control arm or rear axle, as necessary.
4. On Accord and Prelude, remove the cotter pin and castle nut from the upper ball joint and use a suitable tool to separate the ball joint from the knuckle.
5. Remove the upper control arm mounting bolts and the upper control arm.
6. Installation is the reverse of the removal procedure.

LOWER CONTROL ARM

1. Raise and safely support the vehicle.
2. Remove the rear wheel and tire assembly.
3. Remove the strut and/or radius rod mounting bolts from the lower control arm, if necessary.
4. On Prelude, remove the cotter pin and castle nut from the ball joint and separate the ball joint from the knuckle using a suitable tool.
5. Remove the lower arm mounting bolts and remove the lower control arm.
6. Installation is the reverse of the removal procedure.

Rear Wheel Bearings

Removal and Installation
ACCORD AND CIVIC EXCEPT 1988–91 WAGON WITH 4WD

1. Slightly loosen the rear lug nuts. Raise the vehicle and support it safely.

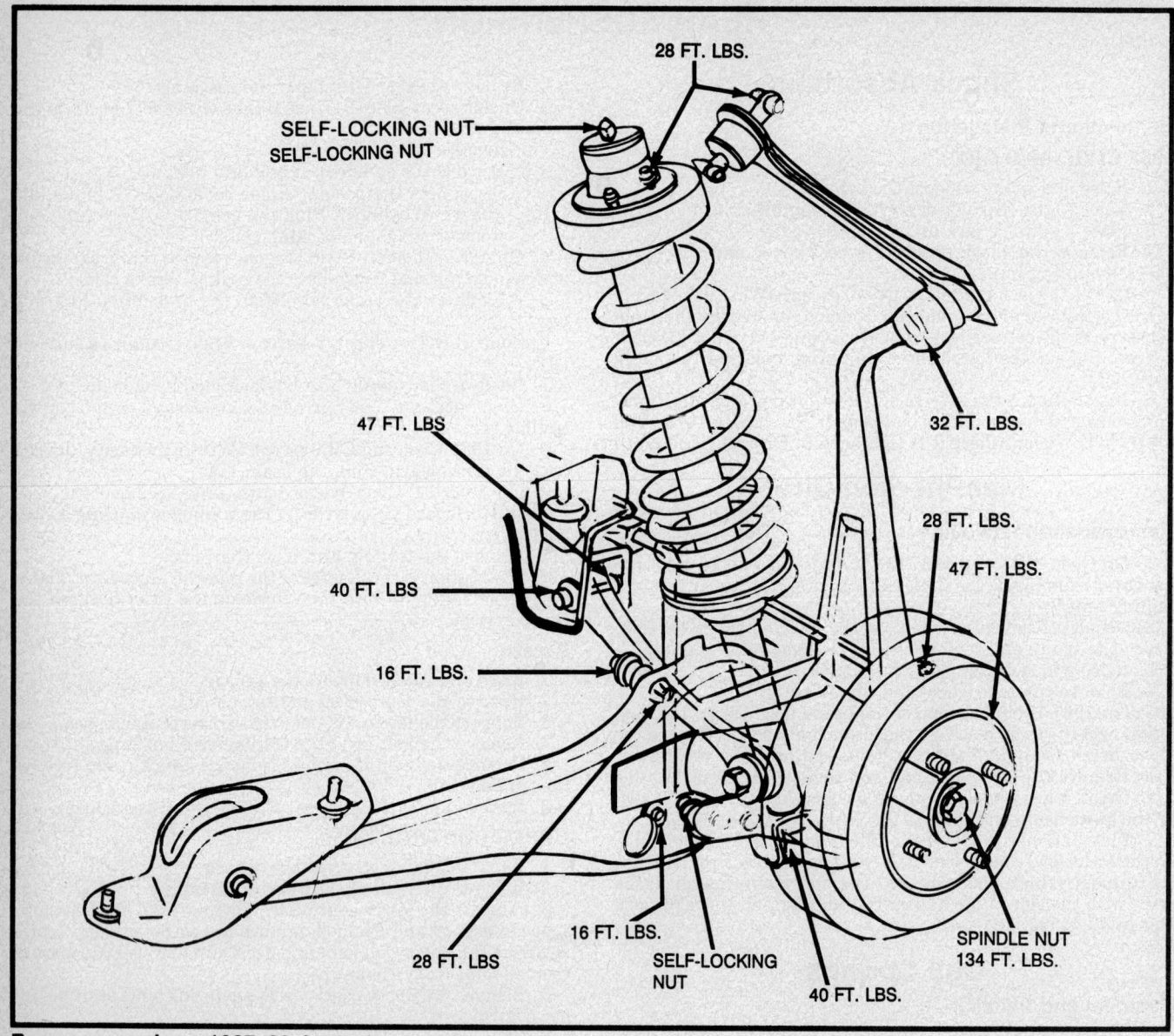

28 FT. LBS.

SELF-LOCKING NUT
SELF-LOCKING NUT

47 FT. LBS

32 FT. LBS.

40 FT. LBS

28 FT. LBS.

47 FT. LBS.

16 FT. LBS.

16 FT. LBS.

28 FT. LBS

SELF-LOCKING NUT

40 FT. LBS.

SPINDLE NUT
134 FT. LBS.

Rear suspension—1987–89 Accord

2. Release the parking brake. Remove the rear wheel and the brake drum.
3. Remove the rear bearing hub cap and nut.
4. Pull the hub unit off of the spindle.
5. Installation is the reverse order of removal. Tighten the new spindle nut to 134 ft. lbs. (185 Nm), then stake the nut.

1988–91 CIVIC WAGON WITH 4WD

1. Raise and safely support the vehicle.
2. Remove the trailing arm from the vehicle.
3. Position the trailing arm in a suitable hydraulic press. Press the hub from the trailing arm using a suitable driver while supporting the trailing arm.

NOTE: Be careful not to distort the brake backing plate. Hold onto the rear hub and trailing arm to keep it from falling when pressed clear.

4. Remove the outboard bearing inner race from the hub using a suitable bearing puller.
5. Remove the 64mm snapring.

6. Remove the bolts and the backing plate.
7. Remove the O-ring from the groove of the bearing holder plate.
8. Press the wheel bearing out of the trailing arm, using a suitable driver, while supporting the trailing arm.
To install:
9. Clean the trailing arm and hub thoroughly.
10. Press a new wheel bearing into the trailing arm, using a suitable driver, while supporting the trailing arm.
11. Install the O-ring on the groove of the bearing holder plate.
12. Install the backing plate and the snapring.
13. Press the trailing arm onto the hub, using a suitable guide and driver, while supporting the hub.
14. Installation of the remaining components is the reverse of the removal procedure.

1987 PRELUDE

1. Slightly loosen the rear lug nuts. Raise the vehicle and support it safely.
2. Release the parking brake. Remove the rear wheels.

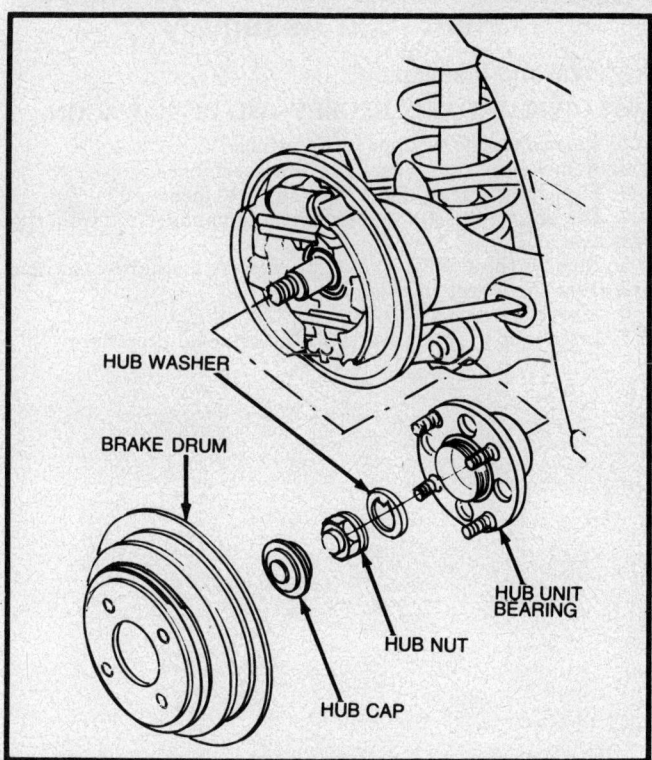

Rear hub and bearing—Accord and Civic except 4WD Wagon

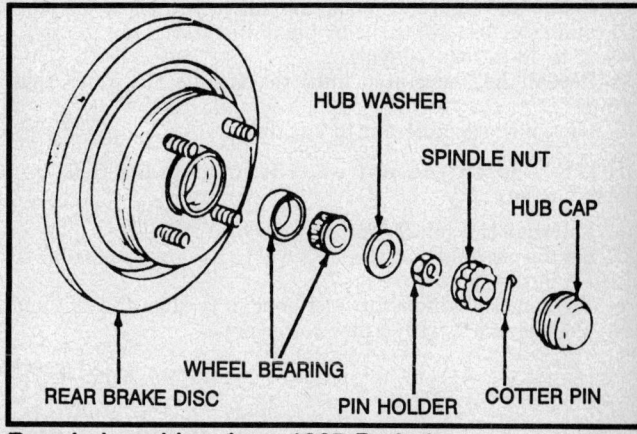

Rear hub and bearing—1987 Prelude

3. Remove the bolts retaining the brake caliper and remove the caliper from the knuckle. Do not let the caliper hang by the brake hose, support it with a length of wire.

4. Remove the rear bearing hub cap, cotter pin and pin holder. Remove the spindle nut, then pull the hub and disc off of the spindle.

5. Drive the outboard and inboard bearing races out of the disc. Punch in a criss-cross pattern to avoid cocking the bearing race in the bore.

To install:

6. Clean the bearing race seats thoroughly.

7. Using a bearing driver, drive the inboard bearing race into the disc.

8. Turn the disc over and drive the outboard bearing race in the same way.

9. Check to see that the bearing races are seated properly.

10. Pack the wheel bearings using a suitable wheel bearing packer. If a wheel bearing packer is not available, the bearings can be packed by hand. Make sure grease is forced past the bearing rollers and onto the inner race.

11. Pack the inside of the hub with a moderate amount of grease. Do not overload the hub with grease.

12. Apply a small amount of grease to the spindle and to the lip of the inner seal before installing.

13. Place the inboard bearing into the hub.

14. Apply grease to the hub seal, and carefully tap into place. Tap in a criss-cross pattern to avoid cocking the seal in the bore.

15. Slip the hub and disc over the spindle, then insert the outboard bearing, hub washer, and spindle nut.

16. Adjust the bearings.

1988–91 PRELUDE

1. Slightly loosen the rear lug nuts. Raise the vehicle and support it safely.

2. Release the parking brake. Remove the rear wheel and tire assemblies.

3. Remove the bolts retaining the brake caliper and remove the caliper from the knuckle. Do not let the caliper hang by the brake hose, support it with a length of wire.

4. Remove the two 6mm screws from the brake disc. Tighten the 8 x 12mm bolts into the holes of the brake disc, then remove the brake disc from the rear hub.

5. Remove the cotter pin of the lower arm B on 2 wheel steering vehicles or the tie rod on 4 wheel steering vehicles and remove the castle nut.

6. Separate the tie rod ball joint using a suitable ball joint removal tool.

7. Remove the cotter pin and loosen the lower arm ball joint nut half the length of the joint threads.

8. Separate the ball joint and lower arm using a suitable puller.

9. Remove the cotter pin and castle nut and separate the upper ball joint, using a ball joint removal tool.

10. Remove the rear hub nut from the rear hub. Remove the splash guard mounting bolts. Using a hydraulic press, separate the hub from the knuckle.

NOTE: Set the rear hub at the hub/disc assembly base firmly, so the knuckle will not tilt the assembly in the press. Take care not to distort the splash guard. Hold onto the hub to keep it from falling after it is pressed out.

11. Remove the splash guard and 68mm circlip from the knuckle.

12. Using a hydraulic press and suitable press tools, press the wheel bearing out of the knuckle.

13. Remove the bearing inner race using a suitable bearing remover.

To install:

14. Place the rear wheel bearing in the tool fixture, then set the knuckle into position and apply downward pressure with a hydraulic press. Fit the 68mm circlip into the groove of the knuckle.

15. Install the splash guard. Place the hub in the tool fixture, then set the knuckle into position and apply downward pressure with a hydraulic press. Install the rear hub nut and tighten it to 180 ft. lbs. (250 Nm).

16. The remaining steps are the reverse of the removal procedure.

Adjustment
1987 PRELUDE

1. Raise and support the vehicle safely. Remove the tire and wheel assembly.

2. Apply grease or oil on the spindle nut and spindle threads.

3. Install and tighten the spindle nut to 18 ft. lbs. (25 Nm) and rotate the disc 2–3 turns by hand, then retighten the spindle nut to 18 ft. lbs. (25 Nm).

4. Repeat the above step until the spindle nut holds that torque.

5. Loosen the spindle nut to 0 ft. lbs.

NOTE: Loosen the nut until it just breaks free but doesn't turn.

6. Retorque the spindle nut to 4 ft. lbs. (5.5 Nm).

7. Set the pin holder so the slots will be as close as possible to the hole in the spindle.

8. Tighten the spindle nut just enough to align the slot and hole, then secure it with a new cotter pin.

Rear Axle Assembly

Removal and Installation

1987 CIVIC AND CRX EXCEPT 4WD CIVIC WAGON

1. Raise and safely support the vehicle.
2. Remove the rear wheel and tire assemblies.
3. Support the rear axle with a suitable jack.
4. Disconnect the shock absorbers and panhard rod from the rear axle.
5. Remove the stabilizer control arms and disconnect the rear axle from the wheel spindles.
6. Lower the axle assembly from the vehicle.
7. Installation is the reverse of the removal procedure.

SERIAL NUMBER IDENTIFICATION

Vehicle Identification Plate

The Vehicle Identification Number (VIN) is located on a plate attached to the left front of the dash panel, so it can be seen through the windshield when standing beside the vehicle, in front of the driver's door.

The letters and numbers in the VIN digits can be interpreted according to their positions in the sequence as follows:

1. Manufacturing country
2. Make
3. Vehicle type
4. Type of seat belt system
5. Vehicle line
6. Trim code/price class
7. Body type
8. Engine displacement
9. Check digit: a special letter or number code is used to verify the serial number. This contains no useful information for the owner.
10. Vehicle year
11. Plant where the vehicle was built
12. Transaxle code

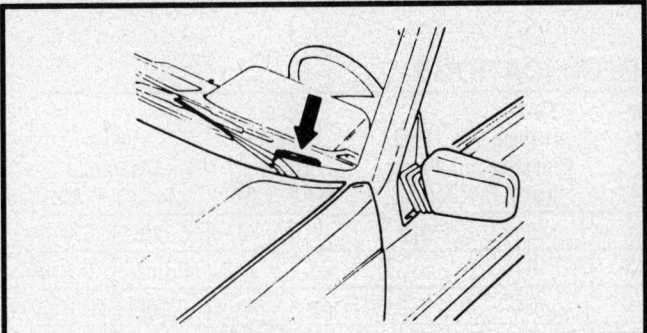

Serial number location

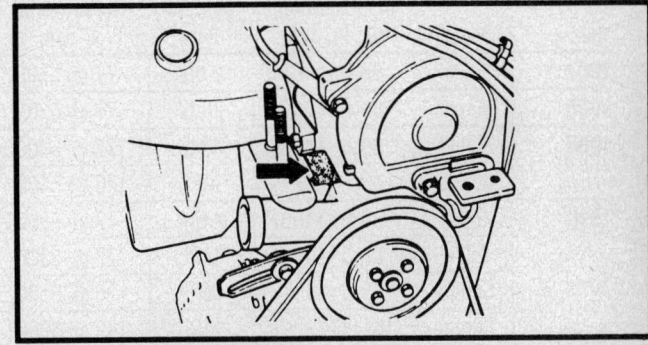

Engine number location

Engine model number

Engine Number

The engine model and serial numbers in all cases are stamped on the top edge of the block near the front of the engine. In most cases, they are located on the right side of the engine.

Vehicle Identification Number

The Vehicle Identification Label (VIN) is located on the top center of the firewall in the engine compartment.

SPECIFICATIONS

ENGINE IDENTIFICATION

Year	Model	Engine Displacement cu. in. (cc/liter)	Engine Series Identification	No. of Cylinders	Engine Type
1987	Excel	89.6 (1468/1.5)	—	4	OHC
1988	Excel	89.6 (1468/1.5)	—	4	OHC
1989	Excel	89.6 (1468/1.5)	—	4	OHC
	Sonata	143.5 (2351/2.4)	—	4	OHC
1990	Excel	89.6 (1468/1.5)	—	4	OHC
	Sonata	143.5 (2351/2.4)	—	4	OHC
	Sonata	181.4 (2972/3.0)	—	6	OHC
1991	Excel	89.6 (1468/1.5)	—	4	OHC
	Sonata	143.5 (2351/2.4)	—	4	OHC
	Sonata	181.4 (2972/3.0)	—	6	OHC
	Scoupe	89.6 (1468/1.5)	—	4	OHC

HYUNDAI
EXCEL • SCOUPE • SONATA

GENERAL ENGINE SPECIFICATIONS

Year	Model	Engine Displacement cu. in. (cc)	Fuel System Type	Net Horsepower @ rpm	Net Torque @ rpm (ft. lbs.)	Bore × Stroke (in.)	Compression Ratio	Oil Pressure @ rpm
1987	Excel	89.6 (1468)	2 bbl	77 @ 5300	84 @ 3000	2.97 × 3.23	9.4:1	45 @ 2000
1988	Excel	89.6 (1468)	2 bbl	77 @ 5300	84 @ 3000	2.97 × 3.23	9.4:1	45 @ 2000
1989	Excel	89.6 (1468)	2 bbl	77 @ 5300	84 @ 3000	2.97 × 3.23	9.4:1	45 @ 2000
	Sonata	143.5 (2351)	MPI	126 @ 5100	180 @ 2600	3.41 × 3.94	8.5:1	45 @ 2000
1990	Excel	89.6 (1468)	2 bbl	77 @ 5300	84 @ 3000	2.97 × 3.23	9.4:1	45 @ 2000
	Excel	89.6 (1468)	MPI	77 @ 5300	84 @ 3000	2.97 × 3.23	9.4:1	45 @ 2000
	Sonata	143.5 (2351)	MPI	126 @ 5100	180 @ 2600	3.41 × 3.94	8.5:1	45 @ 2000
	Sonata	181.4 (2972)	MPI	142 @ 5000	168 @ 2500	3.59 × 2.99	8.9:1	30–80 @ 3000
1991	Excel	89.6 (1468)	2 bbl	77 @ 5300	84 @ 3000	2.97 × 3.23	9.4:1	45 @ 2000
	Excel	89.6 (1468)	MPI	77 @ 5300	84 @ 3000	2.97 × 3.23	9.4:1	45 @ 2000
	Sonata	143.5 (2351)	MPI	126 @ 5100	180 @ 2600	3.41 × 3.94	8.5:1	45 @ 2000
	Sonata	181.4 (2972)	MPI	142 @ 5000	168 @ 2500	3.59 × 2.99	8.9:1	30–80 @ 3000
	Scoupe	89.6 (1468)	MPI	81 @ 5500	91 @ 3000	2.97 × 3.23	9.4:1	11 @ 750

MPI Multi-Port Fuel Injection

ENGINE TUNE-UP SPECIFICATIONS

Year	Model	Engine Displacement cu. in. (cc)	Spark Plugs Type	Gap (in.)	Ignition Timing (deg.) MT	AT	Compression Pressure (psi)	Fuel Pump (psi)	Idle Speed (rpm) MT	AT	Valve Clearance In.	Ex.
1987	Excel	89.6 (1468)	RN9YC4	①	②	②	164	2.5–3.5	③	③	0.006	0.010
1988	Excel	89.6 (1468)	RN9YC4	①	②	②	164	2.8–3.6	③	③	0.006	0.010
1989	Excel	89.6 (1468)	RN9YC4	①	②	②	164	2.8–3.6	③	③	0.006	0.010
	Sonata	143.5 (2351)	RN9YC4	0.039–0.043	5B	5B	160	48.0	750	750	Hyd.	Hyd.
1990	Excel	89.6 (1468)	RN9YC4	①	②	②	164	2.8–3.6	③	③	0.006	0.010
	Excel	89.6 (1468)	RN9YC4	①	②	②	164	2.8–3.6	③	③	0.006	0.010
	Sonata	143.5 (2351)	RN9YC4	0.039–0.043	5B	5B	160	48.0	750	750	Hyd.	Hyd.
	Sonata	181.4 (2972)	PGR5A11	0.039–0.043	12B	12B	178	48.0	750	750	Hyd.	Hyd.
1991	Excel	89.6 (1468)	RN9YC4	①	②	②	164	2.8–3.6	③	③	0.006	0.010
	Excel	89.6 (1468)	RN9YC4	①	②	②	164	2.8–3.6	③	③	0.006	0.010
	Sonata	143.5 (2351)	RN9YC4	0.039–0.043	5B	5B	160	48.0	750	750	Hyd.	Hyd.
	Sonata	181.4 (2972)	PGR5A11	0.039–0.043	12B	12B	178	48.0	750	750	Hyd.	Hyd.
	Scoupe	89.6 (1468)	RN9YC4	0.039–0.043	5B	5B	192	⑤	④	④	0.006	0.010

NOTE: Valve clearance is set with the engine at normal operating temperature. On USA engines, the jet valve must be set before the intake valve. Jet valve clearance is 0.010 in.

① 1987 USA—0.039–0.043;
Canada: 0.027–0.031
1988–89 All models—0.039–0.043
② 49 states—5B
California—3B
Canada—4B

③ 1987 USA MT—700; AT—750
Canada—850
1988–89 USA and Canada—700
(1st 300 miles); 750 (after 300 miles)
④ 700 ± 100 rpm

⑤ 46–49 Fuel pressure regulator vacuum hose disconnected
39 Fuel pressure regulator vacuum hose connected

FIRING ORDERS

NOTE: To avoid confusion, always replace spark plug wires one at a time.

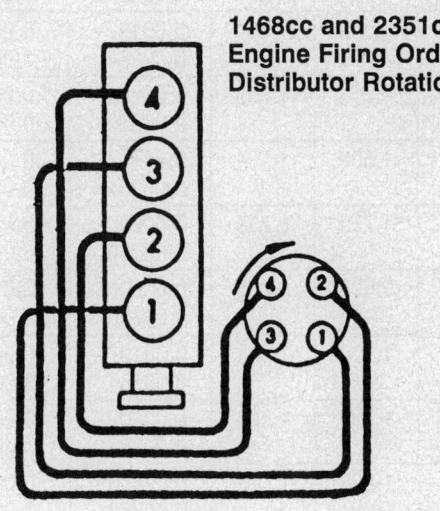

1468cc and 2351cc Engines
Engine Firing Order: 1–3–4–2
Distributor Rotation: Clockwise

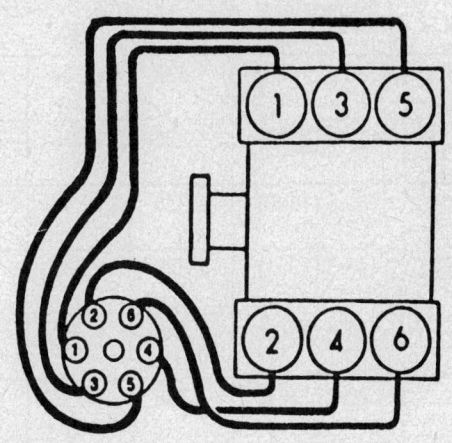

2972cc Engine
Engine Firing Order: 1–2–3–4–5–6
Distributer Rotation: Counterclockwise

CAPACITIES

Year	Model	Engine Displacement cu. in. (cc)	Engine Crankcase with Filter	Engine Crankcase without Filter	Transmission (pts.) 4-Spd	Transmission (pts.) 5-Spd	Transmission (pts.) Auto.	Drive Axle (pts.)	Fuel Tank (gals.)	Cooling System (qts.)
1987	Excel	89.6 (1468)	3.6	—	4.4	4.4	12.2	—	10.6①	5.6
1988	Excel	89.6 (1468)	3.6	—	4.4	4.4	12.2	—	10.6①	5.6
1989	Excel	89.6 (1468)	3.6	—	4.4	4.4	12.2	—	10.6①	5.6
	Sonata	143.5 (2351)	4.0	—	—	5.3	12.3	—	16.0	7.4
1990	Excel	89.6 (1468)	3.6	—	4.4	4.4	12.2	—	10.6①	5.6
	Sonata	143.5 (2351)	4.0	—	—	5.3	12.3	—	16.0	7.4
	Sonata	181.4 (2972)	4.0	—	—	5.3	12.3	—	17.0	7.4
1991	Excel	89.6 (1468)	3.6	—	4.4	4.4	12.2	—	10.6①	5.6
	Sonata	143.5 (2351)	4.0	—	—	5.3	12.3	—	16.0	7.4
	Sonata	181.4 (2972)	4.0	—	—	5.3	12.3	—	17.0	7.4
	Scoupe	89.6 (1468)	3.6	—	3.8	3.8	12.8	—	11.9①	5.6

① Optional 13.2 gal. tank

CAMSHAFT SPECIFICATIONS

All measurements given in inches.

Year	Engine Displacement cu. in. (cc)	Journal Diameter 1	Journal Diameter 2	Journal Diameter 3	Journal Diameter 4	Journal Diameter 5	Lobe Lift In.	Lobe Lift Ex.	Bearing Clearance	Camshaft End Play
1987	89.6 (1468)	1.338	1.338	1.338	—	—	1.500	1.504	0.00197–0.00354	0.002–0.008
1988	89.6 (1468)	1.338	1.338	1.338	—	—	1.500	1.504	0.00197–0.00354	0.002–0.008

HYUNDAI
EXCEL • SCOUPE • SONATA

CAMSHAFT SPECIFICATIONS

All measurements given in inches.

Year	Engine Displacement cu. in. (cc)	Journal Diameter					Lobe Lift		Bearing Clearance	Camshaft End Play
		1	2	3	4	5	In.	Ex.		
1989	89.6 (1468)	1.338	1.338	1.338	—	—	1.500	1.504	0.00197–0.00354	0.002–0.008
	143.5 (2351)	1.336	1.336	1.336	1.336	1.336	1.753	1.758	0.00200–0.00350	0.004–0.008
1990	89.6 (1468)	1.338	1.338	1.336	—	—	1.500	1.504	0.00197–0.00354	0.002–0.008
	143.5 (2351)	1.336	1.336	1.336	1.336	1.336	1.753	1.758	0.00200–0.00350	0.004–0.008
	181.4 (2972)	1.336	1.336	1.336	1.336	1.336	1.628	1.628	0.00200–0.00350	0.004–0.008
1991	89.6 (1468)	1.338	1.338	1.336	—	—	1.500	1.504	0.00197–0.00354	0.004–0.008
	143.5 (2351)	1.336	1.336	1.336	1.336	1.336	1.753	1.758	0.00200–0.00350	0.004–0.008
	181.4 (2972)	1.336	1.336	1.336	1.336	1.336	1.628	1.628	0.00200–0.00350	0.004–0.008

CRANKSHAFT AND CONNECTING ROD SPECIFICATIONS

All measurements are given in inches.

Year	Engine Displacement cu. in. (cc)	Crankshaft				Connecting Rod		
		Main Brg. Journal Dia.	Main Brg. Oil Clearance	Shaft End-play	Thrust on No.	Journal Diameter	Oil Clearance	Side Clearance
1987	89.6 (1468)	1.8898	0.0008–0.0028	0.002–0.007	3	1.6535	0.0004–0.0024	0.004–0.010
1988	89.6 (1468)	1.8898	0.0008–0.0028	0.002–0.007	3	1.6535	0.0004–0.0024	0.004–0.010
1989	89.6 (1468)	1.8898	0.0008–0.0028	0.002–0.007	3	1.6535	0.0004–0.0024	0.004–0.010
	143.5 (2351)	2.2436	0.0008–0.0020	0.0020–0.0071	3	1.7709–1.7715	0.0004–0.0024	0.004–0.010
1990	89.6 (1468)	1.8898	0.0008–0.0028	0.002–0.007	3	1.6535	0.0004–0.0024	0.004–0.010
	143.5 (2351)	2.2436	0.0008–0.0020	0.0020–0.0071	3	1.7709–1.7715	0.0004–0.0024	0.004–0.010
	181.4 (2972)	2.3622	0.0008–0.0020	0.0020–0.0098	3	1.9685	0.0006–0.0018	0.004–0.010
1991	89.6 (1468)	1.8898	0.0008–0.0028	0.002–0.007	3	1.6535	0.0004–0.0024	0.004–0.010
	143.5 (2351)	2.2436	0.0008–0.0020	0.0020–0.0071	3	1.7709–1.7715	0.0004–0.0024	0.004–0.010
	181.4 (2972)	2.3622	0.0008–0.0020	0.0020–0.0098	3	1.9685	0.0006–0.0018	0.004–0.010

VALVE SPECIFICATIONS

Year	Engine Displacement cu. in. (cc)	Seat Angle (deg.)	Face Angle (deg.)	Spring Test Pressure (lbs. @ in.)	Spring Installed Height (in.)	Stem-to-Guide Clearance (in.)		Stem Diameter (in.)	
						Intake	Exhaust	Intake	Exhaust
1987	89.6 (1468)	45	45	53 @ 1.07 ①	1.42 ②	0.0012–0.0024	0.0020–0.0035	0.2598	0.2598
1988	89.6 (1468)	45	45	53 @ 1.07 ①	1.42 ②	0.0012–0.0024	0.0020–0.0035	0.2598	0.2598
1989	89.6 (1468)	45	45	53 @ 1.07 ①	1.42 ②	0.0012–0.0024	0.0020–0.0035	0.2598	0.2598
	143.5 (2351)	45	45	73 @ 1.591 ①	1.591 ②	0.0012–0.0024	0.0020–0.0035	0.3150	0.3150
1990	89.6 (1468)	45	45	53 @ 1.07 ①	1.42 ②	0.0012–0.0024	0.0020–0.0035	0.2598	0.2598
	143.5 (2351)	45	45	73 @ 1.591 ①	1.591 ②	0.0012–0.0024	0.0020–0.0035	0.3150	0.3150
	181.4 (2972)	45	45	74 @ 1.591	1.59	0.0012–0.0024	0.0020–0.0035	0.3150	0.3134
1991	89.6 (1468)	45	45	53 @ 1.07 ①	1.42 ②	0.0012–0.0024	0.0020–0.0035	0.2598	0.2598
	143.5 (2351)	45	45	73 @ 1.591 ①	1.591 ②	0.0012–0.0024	0.0020–0.0035	0.3150	0.3150
	181.4 (2972)	45	45	74 @ 1.591	1.59	0.0012–0.0024	0.0020–0.0035	0.3150	0.3134

① Jet valve—7.7 @ 0.846
② Jet valve—0.846

PISTON AND RING SPECIFICATIONS

All measurements are given in inches.

Year	Engine Displacement cu. in. (cc)	Piston Clearance	Ring Gap			Ring Side Clearance		
			Top Compression	Bottom Compression	Oil Control	Top Compression	Bottom Compression	Oil Control
1987	89.6 (1468)	0.0008–0.0016	0.008–0.014	0.008–0.014	0.008–0.028	0.0012–0.0028	0.0008–0.0024	Snug
1988	89.6 (1468)	0.0008–0.0016	0.008–0.014	0.008–0.014	0.008–0.028	0.0012–0.0028	0.0008–0.0024	Snug
1989	89.6 (1468)	0.0008–0.0016	0.008–0.014	0.008–0.014	0.008–0.028	0.0012–0.0028	0.0008–0.0024	Snug
	143.5 (2351)	0.0004–0.0012	0.0098–0.0157	0.0079–0.0138	0.0079–0.0276	0.0012–0.0028	0.0008–0.0024	Snug
1990	89.6 (1468)	0.0008–0.0016	0.008–0.014	0.008–0.014	0.008–0.028	0.0012–0.0028	0.0008–0.0024	Snug
	143.5 (2351)	0.0004–0.0012	0.0098–0.0157	0.0079–0.0138	0.0079–0.0276	0.0012–0.0028	0.0008–0.0024	Snug
	181.4 (2972)	0.0008–0.0016	0.0120–0.0180	0.010–0.016	0.008–0.028	0.0012–0.0035	0.0008–0.0024	Snug
1991	89.6 (1468)	0.0008–0.0016	0.008–0.014	0.008–0.014	0.008–0.028	0.0012–0.0028	0.0008–0.0024	Snug
	143.5 (2351)	0.0004–0.0012	0.0098–0.0157	0.0079–0.0138	0.0079–0.0276	0.0012–0.0028	0.0008–0.0024	Snug
	181.4 (2972)	0.0008–0.0016	0.0120–0.0180	0.010–0.016	0.008–0.028	0.0012–0.0035	0.0008–0.0024	Snug

HYUNDAI
EXCEL • SCOUPE • SONATA

TORQUE SPECIFICATIONS
All readings in ft. lbs.

Year	Engine Displacement cu. in. (cc)	Cylinder Head Bolts	Main Bearing Bolts	Rod Bearing Bolts	Crankshaft Pulley Bolts	Flywheel Bolts	Manifold Intake	Manifold Exhaust	Spark Plugs
1987	89.6 (1468)	①	36–39	23–25	9–11④	94–101	12–14	12–14	18
1988	89.6 (1468)	①	36–39	23–25	9–11④	94–101	12–14	12–14	18
1989	89.6 (1468)	①	36–39	23–25	9–11④	94–101	12–14	12–14	18
	143.5 (2351)	②	36–40	36–38	14–22③	94–100	11–14	11–14	18
1990	89.6 (1468)	①	36–39	23–25	9–11④	94–101	12–14	12–14	18
	143.5 (2351)	②	36–40	36–38	14–22③	94–100	11–14	11–14	18
	181.4 (2972)	②	55–61	36–38	109–115	65–70	11–14	11–16	18
1991	89.6 (1468)	①	36–39	23–25	9–11④	94–101	12–14	12–14	18
	143.5 (2351)	②	36–40	36–38	14–22③	94–100	11–14	11–14	18
	181.4 (2972)	②	55–61	36–38	109–115	65–70	11–14	11–16	18

① Cold—51–54 ft. lbs.; warm—58–61 ft. lbs.   ③ Sprocket bolt—94
② Cold—65–72; warm—72–80   ④ Sprocket—72

BRAKE SPECIFICATIONS
All measurements in inches unless noted.

Year	Model	Lug Nut Torque (ft. lbs.)	Master Cylinder Bore	Brake Disc Minimum Thickness	Brake Disc Maximum Runout	Standard Brake Drum Diameter	Minimum Lining Thickness Front	Minimum Lining Thickness Rear
1987	Excel	50–58①	0.8125	②	0.006	7.086	0.04	0.04
1988	Excel	50–58①	0.8125	②	0.006	7.086	0.04	0.04
1989	Excel	50–58①	0.8125	②	0.006	7.086	0.04	0.04
	Sonata	50–60	1.0000	0.787	0.006	9.000	0.04	0.04
1990	Excel	50–58①	0.8125	②	0.006	7.086	0.04	0.04
	Sonata	50–60	1.0000	0.866	0.006	9.000	0.04	0.04
1991	Excel	50–58①	0.8125	②	0.006	7.086	0.04	0.04
	Sonata	50–60	1.0000	0.866	0.006	9.000	0.04	0.04
	Scoupe	65–80	0.8750	0.670	0.006	7.165	0.04	0.04

① Aluminum wheels—58–72   ② Sumitomo—0.449 Tokico—0.675

WHEEL ALIGNMENT

Year	Model	Caster Range (deg.)	Caster Preferred Setting (deg.)	Camber Range (deg.)	Camber Preferred Setting (deg.)	Toe-in (in.)	Steering Axis Inclination (deg.)
1987	Excel	1/2P–11/6P	5/6P	0–1P	1/2P	1/16 in–5/64 out	①
1988	Excel	1/2P–11/6P	5/6P	0–1P	1/2P	1/16 in–5/64 out	①
1989	Excel	1/2P–11/6P	5/6P	0–1P	1/2P	1/16 in–5/64 out	①
	Sonata	1/2P–21/2P	2P	0–1P	1/2P	1/8 in–5/64 out	②
1990	Excel	1/2P–11/6P	5/6P	0–1P	1/2P	1/16 in–5/64 out	①
	Sonata	1/2P–21/2P	2P	0–1P	1/2P	1/8 in–5/64 out	②
1991	Excel	1/2P–11/6P	5/6P	0–1P	1/2P	1/16 in–5/64 out	①
	Sonata	1/2P–21/2P	2P	0–1P	1/2P	1/8 in–5/64 out	②
	Scoupe	⑥	③	2/3N–1/3P	1/6N	⑤	④

① Inside wheel—352/3; outside wheel—299/32   ③ Manual steering 11/2P   ④ King pin angle—13°14′
② King pin angle—13°25′   Power steering 1P   ⑤ 0.157 in–0.079 out
⑥ 1/2P–11/2P

ENGINE ELECTRICAL

NOTE: Disconnecting the negative battery cable on some vehicles may interfere with the functions of the on board computer systems and may require the computer to undergo a relearning process, once the negative battery cable is reconnected.

Distributor

Removal

1. Disconnect the battery ground cable. Remove the spark plug wires from the spark plugs and the coil wire from the coil. Then, disconnect the retaining clips or unfasten the 2 screws that hold on the distributor cap and pull the distributor cap and seal off the distributor. Locate the cap and wires away from the distributor. Disconnect the vacuum advance line. Disconnect the distributor wiring connector.
2. Turn the engine until the rotor points to the No. 1 cylinder position and the timing marks on the crankshaft pulley and the timing tab are aligned at **TDC or 0**.
3. Mark the distributor body to the exact place the rotor points. Matchmark both the distributor mounting flange and the cylinder head.
4. Carefully pull the distributor out of the engine, noting the direction and degree to which the rotor turns. Mark the location of the rotor after it has turned.

Installation

TIMING NOT DISTURBED

1. Install the distributor while aligning the matchmarks made during removal.
2. Position the rotor so it is aligned with the matchmark on the distributor body after the distributor was pulled part way out.
3. Carefully work the distributor into the engine until the gears at the bottom engage and then begin turning the rotor. If there is resistance, turn the rotor back and forth slightly so the gears mesh. Once the gears engage and inserting the distributor causes the rotor to turn.
4. Push the distributor in until it seats and the rotor is aligned with the first mark made on the body.
5. Install the distributor hold-down bolt and reconnect the electrical connections.
6. Check and/or adjust the ignition timing.

TIMING DISTURBED

If the engine was cranked with the distributor removed, it will be necessary to position the No. 1 cylinder at TDC on the compression stroke. Follow the procedure listed here. This will enable the proper setting of the ignition timing.

1. Remove the No. 1 spark plug.
2. Place a finger over the spark plug hole. Crank the engine slowly until compression is felt.
3. Align the timing mark on the crankshaft pulley with the **0** degree mark on the timing scale attached to the front of the engine. This places the No. 1 cylinder at the TDC of the compression stroke.
4. Turn the distributor shaft until the rotor points to the No. 1 spark plug tower on the cap.
5. Install the distributor into the engine.
6. Tighten the distributor hold-down bolt and reconnect the electrical connections. Check the timing and adjust, as necessary.

Ignition Timing

Adjustment

1. Locate the timing tab line on the front of the engine and the notch on the crankshaft pulley. Mark them with chalk.
2. Run the engine until it is at normal operating temperature.
3. Leave the engine idling, apply the handbrake and put the transaxle in neutral (manual) or park (automatic). Turn off all accessories.

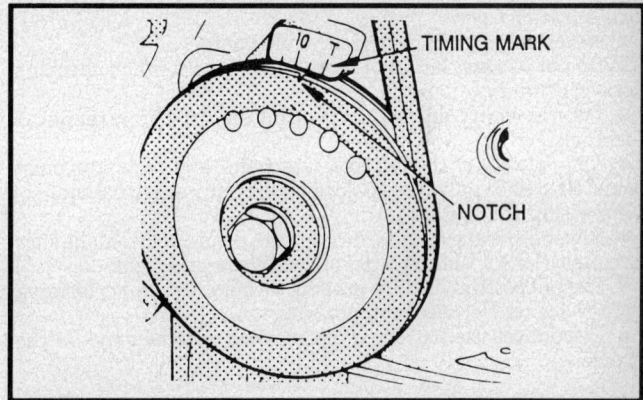

Timing marks

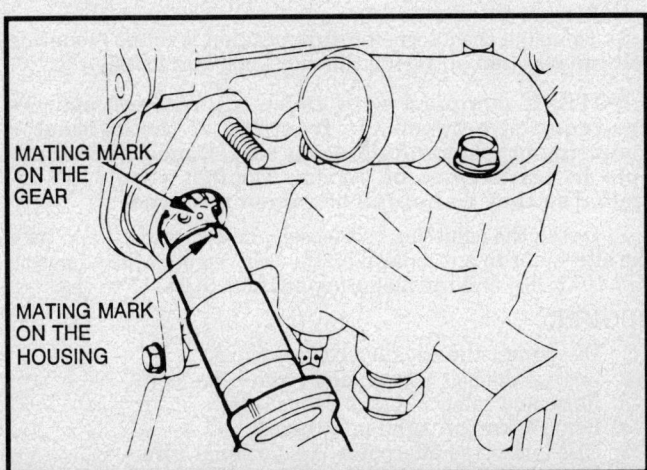

Aligning mating marks for installation of cylinder head mounted distributors

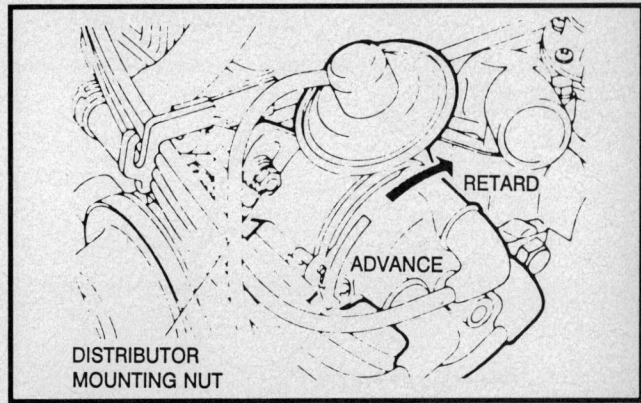

Adjusting ignition timing

NOTE: On high altitude engines equipped with vacuum advance, the distributor vacuum hoses must be disconnected and plugged.

4. Install a tachometer, according to the manufacturer's instructions.

5. Verify that the engine idle speed is correct. If not adjust it, because incorrect idle speed will change the timing.

6. Connect a timing light according to the manufacturer's instructions.

7. Shine the timing light at the crankshaft pulley marks. The marked line should align with the pulley notch.

8. If the marks do not align, loosen the distributor mounting nut and rotate the distributor slowly in either direction to align the timing marks. When the timing is correct, tighten the distributor hold-down bolt. Recheck the timing.

9. Turn the engine off and disconnect the timing light and tachometer.

Alternator

Precautions

Several precautions must be observed with alternator equipped vehicles to avoid damage to the unit.

- If the battery is removed for any reason, make sure it is reconnected with the correct polarity. Reversing the battery connections may result in damage to the one-way rectifiers.
- When utilizing a booster battery as a starting aid, always connect the positive to positive terminals and the negative terminal from the booster battery to a good engine ground on the vehicle being started.
- Never use a fast charger as a booster to start vehicles.
- Disconnect the battery cables when charging the battery with a fast charger.
- Never attempt to polarize the alternator.
- Do not use test lamps of more than 12 volts when checking diode continuity.
- Do not short across or ground any of the alternator terminals.
- The polarity of the battery, alternator and regulator must be matched and considered before making any electrical connections within the system.
- Never separate the alternator on an open circuit. Make sure all connections within the circuit are clean and tight.
- Disconnect the battery ground terminal when performing any service on electrical components.
- Disconnect the battery if arc welding is to be done on the vehicle.

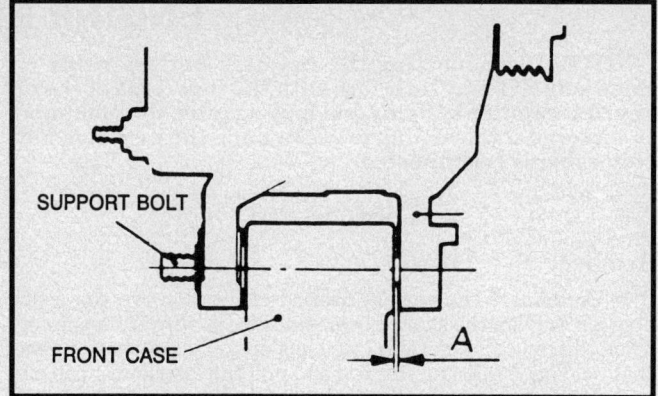

Use shims when installing the Melco alternator

Belt Tension Adjustment

The alternator drive belt is correctly tensioned when the longest span of belt between pulleys can be depressed ⅛–½ in. by moderate thumb pressure. To adjust, loosen the slotted adjusting bracket bolt on the alternator. If the alternator hinge bolts are very tight, it may be necessary to loosen them slightly to move the alternator. Move the alternator in or out by hand to get the correct tension, then tighten the adjusting bolt.

V-belts under 39 in. (100cm) in length should deflect about ⅛ in. (3mm). Belts over 40 in. (101cm) long should deflect about ½ in. (13mm).

NOTE: Be careful not to overtighten the belt, as this may damage the alternator bearings.

Removal and Installation
EXCEPT SCOUPE

1. Turn off the ignition switch and disconnect both battery cables.

2. Loosen the support bolt and adjusting bolt and then shift the alternator toward the engine so belt tension is relieved. Remove the belt.

3. Note the locations of all connectors. Make a drawing, if necessary. Unplug the plug type connectors and unscrew the fastening nuts for terminal type connectors. Clean any dirty connections.

4. Remove the adjusting bolt. Remove the nut from the rear of the mounting bolt.

5. Remove the alternator.

6. To install the alternator, first position it so the mounting bolt can be inserted. Install the mounting bolt loosely.

NOTE: If equipped with Delco alternators, spacers are required between the front leg of the alternator mounting bracket and the front case. Spacers are available in thicknesses of 0.2mm. Enough should be installed so they do not fall out when removed.

7. Install the adjusting bolt loosely. Install the belt and turn the alternator to put tension on the belt. Tighten the adjusting bolt 10 ft. lbs. and the mounting bolt/nut to 15–18 ft. lbs.

SCOUPE

1. Disconnect the negative battery cable.
2. Loosen the belt tension and remove the belt.
3. Raise and safely support the vehicle.
4. Remove the left hand mud guard.
5. Disconnect the alternator B+ terminal wire.
6. Remove the alternator assembly.
7. Install the alternator by reversing the alternator procedure. Adjust drive belt to proper tension.

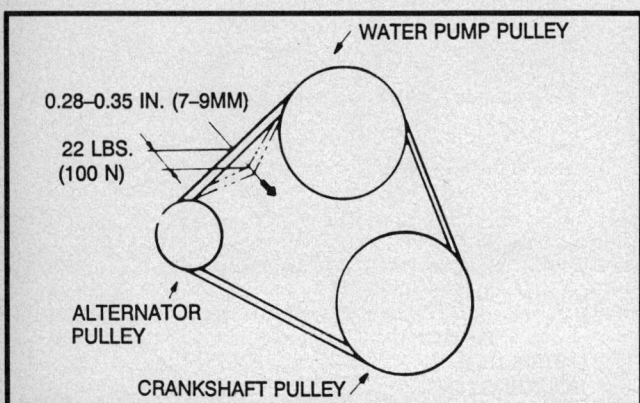

Adjusting the tension on the drive belts

Starter

Removal and Installation

EXCEPT SCOUPE

1. Disconnect the negative battery cable. Then, mark and disconnect all wiring connectors at the starter.

NOTE: It will be helpful to remove the battery and battery tray, as well as the engine underside shield.

2. Raise and support the vehicle safely. Then remove the starter mounting bolts and remove the starter.
3. Clean the surfaces of the starter motor flange and the fly-wheel housing where the starter attaches. Then, install the starter motor. Tighten the bolts to 16–23 ft. lbs.
4. Install the battery and tray, if removed.
5. Reconnect the negative battery cable.

SCOUPE

1. Disconnect the negative battery cable.
2. Remove the EGR valve assembly.
3. Remove the speedometer cable and the heater valve.
4. Disconnect the starter motor connector and terminal.
5. Remove the starter motor assembly.
6. Install the starter motor by reversing the removal procedure.

CHASSIS ELECTRICAL

Heater Blower Motor

Removal and Installation

NOTE: On Excel and Sonata, in order to remove either the blower or core, the heater case must be removed.

EXCEL

1. Disconnect the negative battery cable.
2. Place the control in the **HOT** position.
3. Drain the cooling system.
4. Remove the heater hoses from the core tubes.
5. Remove the lower instrument panel section.
6. Remove the center console and on-board computer.
7. Loosen the heater duct mounting screw. Then, pushing downward and pulling, remove the heater ducts.
8. Disconnect the heater control cable.
9. Disconnect the wiring at the motor.
10. Remove the heater case mounting bolts and remove the heater case from under the dash.
11. Separate the case halves and remove the blower.
12. Installation is the reverse order of the removal procedures. Adjust the control cable and refill the cooling system.

SONATA

─────────── **CAUTION** ───────────

When discharging the refrigerant from the system, extreme care should be observed. Always wear protective eye wear, freon coming in contact with the eyes can cause permanent blindness. Freon coming in contact with the skin can cause frost bit. Always cover fittings with a clean towel and open the fitting slowly.

1. Disconnect the negative battery cable.
2. Place the control in the **HOT** position.
3. Drain the cooling system.
4. Remove the heater hoses from the core tubes.
5. Discharge the air conditioning system.
6. Disconnect the suction and liquid refrigerant lines at the firewall connectors. Always use back-up wrenches. Cap all openings at once.
7. Remove the front and rear center consoles.
8. Remove the heater side covers.
9. Remove the glove box, center crash pad cover, center crash pad and the radio.

10. Remove the lower crash pad.
11. Remove the console mounting bracket and center support.
12. Remove the left and right rear heat duct assemblies and the rear heating joint duct.
13. Remove the control unit.
14. Disconnect the blower speed actuator connector and, in Canada, disconnect the blend door actuator connector.
15. Remove the heater/air conditioning unit.
16. Remove the blower motor from the case.
17. Installation is the reverse order of the removal procedures. Adjust the control cable and refill the cooling system.

SCOUPE

1. Disconnect the negative battery cable.
2. Remove the glove box housing cover assembly.
3. Disconnect the resistor and blower motor connector.
4. Pull out the blower unit and disconnect the fresh/recirc vacuum connector.
5. Install the blower motor by reversing the removal procedure.

Windshield Wiper Motor

Removal and Installation

FRONT

1. Disconnect the negative battery cable. Remove the air inlet and cowl front center trim panels. Remove the 3 pivot shaft mounting nuts and push the pivot shafts into the area under the cowl.
2. Remove the motor mounting bolts. Pull the motor into the best possible position for access and use prybar, to pry the linkage off the motor crank arm. Remove the motor and then the linkage.
3. If the motor is being replaced, matchmark the position of the crank arm of the motor shaft of the new motor and then remove the nut and crank arm, transferring both to the new motor.
4. Installation is the reverse order of the removal procedures.
5. Torque the pivot shaft nuts to 4.3–5.8 ft. lbs.
6. Position the wiper arms so, on the Excel, the blades are about 15mm above the lower windshield molding, on the driver's side and 20mm above it, on the passenger's side.
7. On the Sonata, each blade tip should be about 30mm above the moulding. On Scoupe, the dirvers side blade tip should be

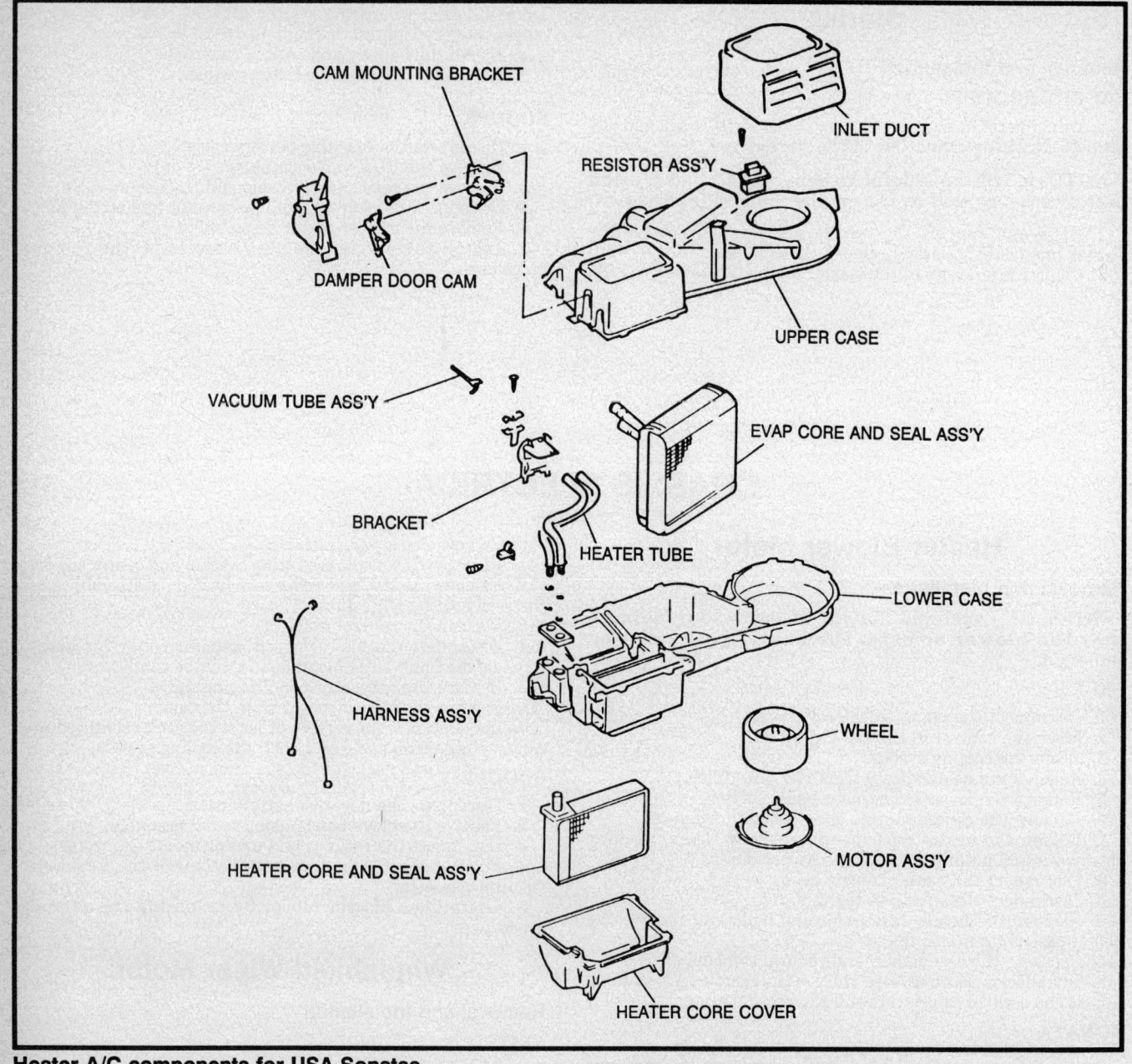

CAM MOUNTING BRACKET

INLET DUCT

RESISTOR ASS'Y

DAMPER DOOR CAM

UPPER CASE

VACUUM TUBE ASS'Y

EVAP CORE AND SEAL ASS'Y

BRACKET

HEATER TUBE

LOWER CASE

HARNESS ASS'Y

WHEEL

MOTOR ASS'Y

HEATER CORE AND SEAL ASS'Y

HEATER CORE COVER

Heater-A/C components for USA Sonatas

about 50mm above the lower windshield moulding and the passenger side blade tip should be about 30mm above the lower windshield moulding. Torque the wiper arm mounting nuts to 7–12 ft. lbs.

8. Make sure the wiper motor is securely grounded. Connect the negative battery cable.

REAR

1. Remove the wiper blade and arm by lifting the wiper blade locknut cover and removing the locknut. Then, pull the arm from the shaft.

2. Remove the lift gate trim panel and disconnect the wiring harness connector.

3. Matchmark the relationship of the crank arm to the motor and remove the crank arm.

4. Remove the inside and outside motor mounting nuts and remove the motor.

5. Installation is the reverse of the removal procedures.

NOTE: When installing the wiper arm, the distance between the tip of the blade and the lower window molding should be 40mm.

Windshield Wiper Switch

Removal and Installation

REAR

1. Pry the switch bezel from the instrument panel.

2. Reach behind the panel and disconnect the wiring from the switch.

3. Depress the 2 retainers and pull the switch from the panel.

4. Installation is the reverse order of the removal procedures.

Instrument Cluster

Removal and Installation

EXCEL

1. Disconnect the negative battery cable. Remove the meter hood attaching screws, located at the bottom and tilt the lower meter hood outward. Pull the hood downward to release the locking tangs at the top and remove it.
2. Remove the meter assembly mounting screws and pull the unit outward. Disconnect the speedometer cable and all connectors. Remove the unit.
3. Installation is the reverse order of the removal procedures.

SONATA

1. Disconnect the negative battery cable. Remove the steering column support bolts and carefully lower the column on the front seat.
2. Remove the cluster trim panel.
3. Remove the cluster mounting screws and slowly pull the cluster outward. Disconnect the wires.
4. Installation is the reverse of removal. Torque the steering column bolts to 20 ft. lbs.

SCOUPE

1. Disconnect the negative battery cable.
2. Remove the ashtray.
3. Remove the lower crash pad center facia panel.
4. Remove the digital clock and remote mirror switch.
5. Remove the 7 screws at the cluster facia panel.
6. Remove the 4 screws retaining the cluster and connectors
7. Install the instrument cluster by reversing the removal procedure.

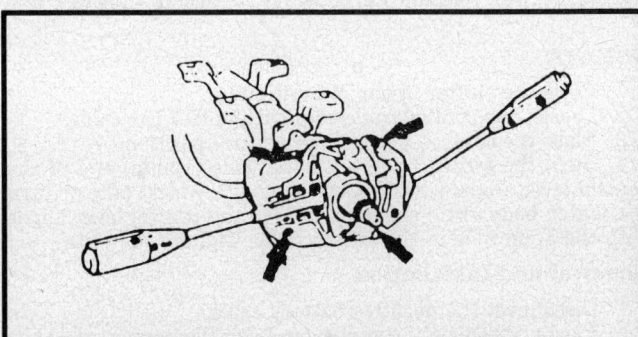

Combination switch removal

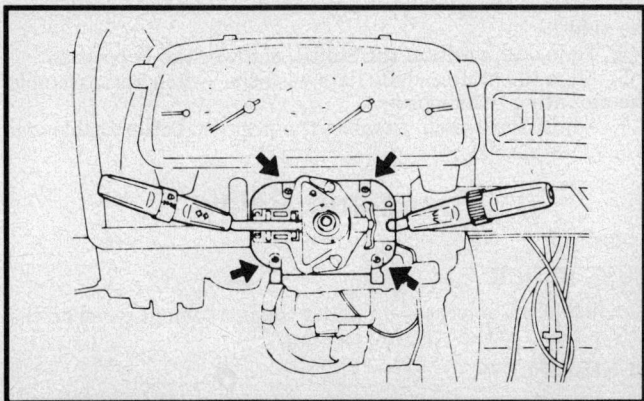

Combination switch removal—Scoupe

Speedometer

Removal and Installation

1. Disconnect the negative battery cable.
2. Remove the instrument cluster from the instrument panel.
4. Place the instrument cluster on clean work area.
5. Remove the speedometer lens retaining screws from the side of the cluster and remove the lens.
6. From the rear side of the cluster, remove the speedometer retaining screws and carefully remove the speedometer from the cluster assembly.

To install:

7 Install the speedometer into the cluster and install the retaining screws.
8. Position the cluster assembly to the dash, while inserting the speedometer cable into the speedometer, push in securely.
9. Install the instrument cluster face plate and lens to the panel.
10. Connect the negative battery cable.

Combination Switch

Removal and Installation

1. Disconnect the negative battery cable. Remove the steering wheel. Remove the steering column cover.
2. Unplug the electrical connectors. If necessary, remove the harness retainer.
3. Remove the retaining screws and slide the switch off the steering column.
4. Installation is the reverse order of the removal procedures.

Ignition Lock/Switch

Removal and Installation

1. Disconnect the negative battery cable. Remove the steering wheel. Remove the steering column cover.
2. Remove the combination switch.
3. Unplug the electrical connector for the ignition lock.
4. Use a hacksaw to cut a slit in the top of each of the fastening bolts. Unscrew the bolts and remove the switch.
5. When installing the new switch, align the halves of the assembly around the steering column, align the assembly with the column boss and then install the special new installation bolts just loosely. Verify that the ignition switch works and then tighten the bolts until their heads break off.

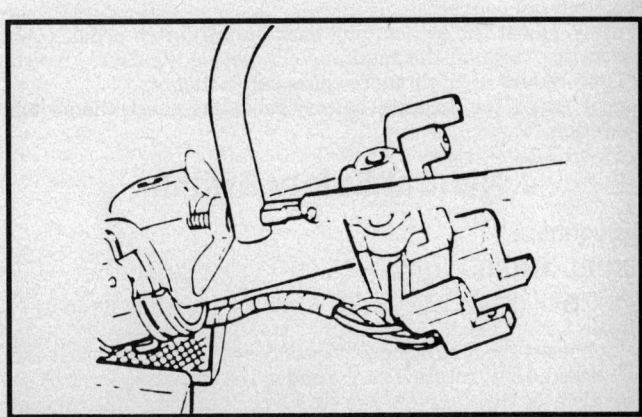

Using a hacksaw to cut screwdriver grooves into the ignition lock mounting bolts

Stoplight Switch

The switch is located on a bracket above the brake pedal arm.

Adjustment

Loosen the locknut and adjust the switch so the distance between the switch outer case and the pedal arm is 0.02–0.04 in. (0.5–1.0mm).

Removal and Installation

1. Disconnect the negative battery cable.
2. Disconnect the electrical connector from the brake light switch, located above the brake pedal.
3. Remove the switch from the tubular clip on the brake pedal mounting bracket.

To install:

4. Insert the switch into the clip until the switch body seats on the clip.
5. Pull the brake pedal rearward against the internal pedal stop. The switch will be moved in the tubular clip providing the proper adjustment.
6. Connect the electrical connector to the switch.
7. Connect the negative battery cable and check the switch operation.

Clutch Switch

Adjustment

1. Disconnect the negative battery cable.
2. Remove the lower, left trim panel and locate the switch on the clutch pedal support.
3. Disconnect the electrical connector from the switch and remove the switch, by twisting it out of the tubular retaining clip.
4. Pull back on the clutch pedal and push the switch through the retaining clip noting the clicks; repeat this procedure until no more clicks can be heard.
5. Connect the electrical connector to the switch.
6. Connect the negative battery cable and check the switch operation.

Removal and Installation

1. Disconnect the negative battery cable.
2. Remove the lower, left trim panel. Locate the switch on the clutch pedal support.
3. Disconnect the electrical connector from the switch and remove the switch, by twisting it out of the tubular retaining clip.

To install:

4. Using a new retaining clip, install the switch and connect the electrical connector.
5. To adjust the switch, pull back on the clutch pedal, push the switch through the retaining clip noting the clicks; repeat this procedure until no more clicks can be heard.
6. Connect the negative battery cable and check the switch operation.

Neutral Safety Switch

Adjustment

EXCEL AND SCOUPE

1. Apply the parking brake. Place the gearshift lever in **N** position.
2. Loosen the mounting screws of the neutral switch so it can be rotated. Now, rotate it so the end of the operating lever (A) is directly over the flange on the switch body and the holes in that flange and the outer end of the lever are aligned.
3. Hold the switch securely in place while torquing the mounting screws to 90–100 inch lbs.

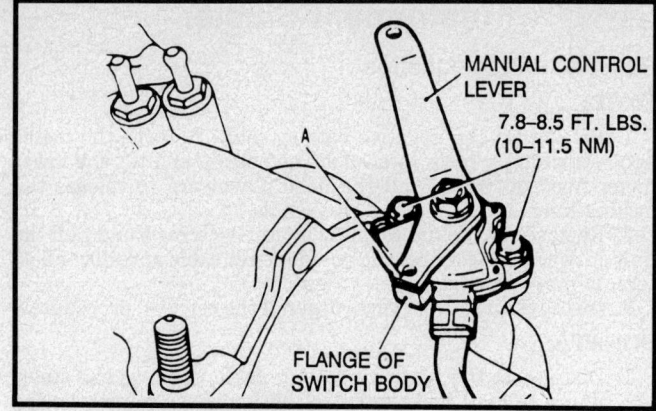

Excel neutral start switch adjustment

Neutral start switch adjustments on the Sonata

4. Recheck the function of the switch by attempting to start the engine in all selector positions. It should start only in **P** and **N**.

SONATA

1. Place the shifter in the **N** position.
2. Loosen the control cable coupler and free the cable.
3. Place the control lever in the neutral position.
4. Turn the switch body until the wide (12mm) end of the control lever aligns with the switch body's widest part or turn the switch body until; the 5mm hole in the control lever aligns with the 5mm hole in the switch body. Tighten the nuts.

Removal and Installation

1. Disconnect the negative battery cable.
2. Raise the vehicle and support it safely. Disconnect the shift linkage from the transaxle.
3. Disconnect the electrical connector from the switch.
4. Remove the switch to transaxle bolts and the switch from the vehicle.
5. To install, position the shifter shaft in the **N** position.
6. Align the shifter shaft flats with the switch and assemble the mounting bolts loosely.
7. Adjust the switch. Connect the negative battery cable and test operation.

Fuses and Relays

Location

FUSE BLOCK

The fuse block is located up under the instrument panel on the driver's side of the steering column.

FUSIBLE LINK

The main fusible link is located under the hood, inline of the positive battery cable.

RELAYS

There are 2 relay boxes located under the hood, on the right front apron. On Scoupe, the relay box is found in the passenger compartment on the firewall below the steering column.

Computers

Location

The Electronic Control Unit (ECU) is located on the passengers lower kick panel. On Scoupe, the ECU is located behind the dash panel on the drivers side, below the air outlet duct.

Flashers

Location

The turn signal and hazard flashers are located in the fuse block, located under the instrument panel on the driver's side of the steering column.

ENGINE COOLING

Radiator

Removal and Installation

1. Disconnect the negative battery cable.
2. On Scoupe, set the warm water flow control knob of the heater control to the hot position.
3. Drain the radiator. Raise the vehicle and support it safely. Remove the splash shield from under the vehicle.
4. Remove the fan shroud and disconnect the fan motor wiring harness.
5. Disconnect the radiator hoses and, if equipped, the automatic transaxle cooler hoses.
6. Disconnect the expansion tank hose.
7. Remove the radiator mounting bolts and lift out the radiator and fan assembly. The fan and motor may be left attached to the radiator and removed with the radiator as one unit.

To install:

8. Install the radiator. Tighten the retaining bolts gradually in a crisscross pattern.
9. Connect the expansion tank hose, the radiator hoses and the automatic transaxle oil cooler lines.
10. Install the fan shroud and connect the fan wiring.
11. Install the splash shield and refill the engine with coolant.
12. Connect negative battery cable.

Electric Cooling Fan

Testing

1. Start the engine and allow it to reach normal operating temperature.
2. When the radiator temperature reaches 230°F, the electric cooling fan should turn on.
3. If the fan fails to operate, perform the following procedures:
   a. Disconnect the electrical connector from the electric cooling fan.
   b. Using a fused jumper wire, connect it from the battery to the cooling fan.
   c. The electric cooling fan should turn on. If not, replace the fan motor.
   d. If the fan still will not operate, inspect the fuse, the fan switch and/or the fan switch relay.
4. If the electrical connector has been disconnected, reconnect it.

Removal and Installation

1. Disconnect the negative battery cable.
2. Remove the upper cooling fan shroud-to-radiator support bolts.
3. Disconnect the electrical leads from the fan motor. Remove the fan and shroud as an assembly.

4. To install, position the fan and shroud as an assembly to the radiator support and install the mounting bolts.
5. Connect the electrical leads to the fan motor.
6. Connect the negative battery cable. Start the engine and check the fan operation.

Heater Core

Removal and Installation

EXCEL

1. Disconnect the negative battery cable.
2. Set the heater control to **HOT** and drain the cooling system.
3. Disconnect the coolant hoses at the heater core tubes, in the engine compartment.
4. Remove the lower instrument panel section.
5. Remove the center console and on-board computer.
6. Loosen the heater duct mounting screw.
7. Pushing downward and pull, remove the heater ducts.
8. Disconnect the heater control cable.
9. Disconnect the wiring at the motor.
10. Remove the heater case mounting bolts and remove the heater case from under the dash.
11. Separate the case halves and remove the blower.
12. Installation is the reverse of removal. Refill the cooling system.

SONATA

1. Disconnect the negative battery cable.
2. Place the control in the HOT position.
3. Drain the cooling system.
4. Remove the heater hoses from the core tubes.
5. Discharge the air conditioning system.
6. Disconnect the suction and liquid refrigerant lines at the firewall connectors. Always use back-up wrenches. Cap all openings at once.
7. Remove the front and rear center consoles.
8. Remove the heater side covers.
9. Remove the glove box, center crash pad cover, center crash pad and the radio.
10. Remove the lower crash pad.
11. Remove the console mounting bracket and center support.
12. Remove the left and right rear heat duct assemblies and the rear heating joint duct.
13. Remove the control unit.
14. Disconnect the blower speed actuator connector and, on Canadian vehicles, disconnect the blend door actuator connector.
15. Remove the heater/air conditioning unit.
16. Remove the blower motor from the case.
17. Separate the case halves and lift out the core.
18. Installation is the reverse of removal. Adjust the control cable and refill the cooling system.

SCOUPE

1. Disconnect the negative battery cable.
2. Set the heater control to **HOT** and drain the cooling system.
3. Disconnect the coolant hoses at the heater core tubes, in the engine compartment.
4. Remove the console assembly, cluster facia panel and lower crash pad center skin.
5. Loosen the heater duct mounting screw.
6. Remove the heater ducts.
7. Disconnect the heater control cable.
8. Disconnect the wiring at the motor.

9. Remove the heater case mounting bolts and remove the heater case from under the dash.
10. Separate the case halves and remove the blower.
11. Installation is the reverse of removal. Refill the cooling system.

Water Pump

Removal and Installation

1468CC ENGINE

1. Disconnect the negative battery cable.

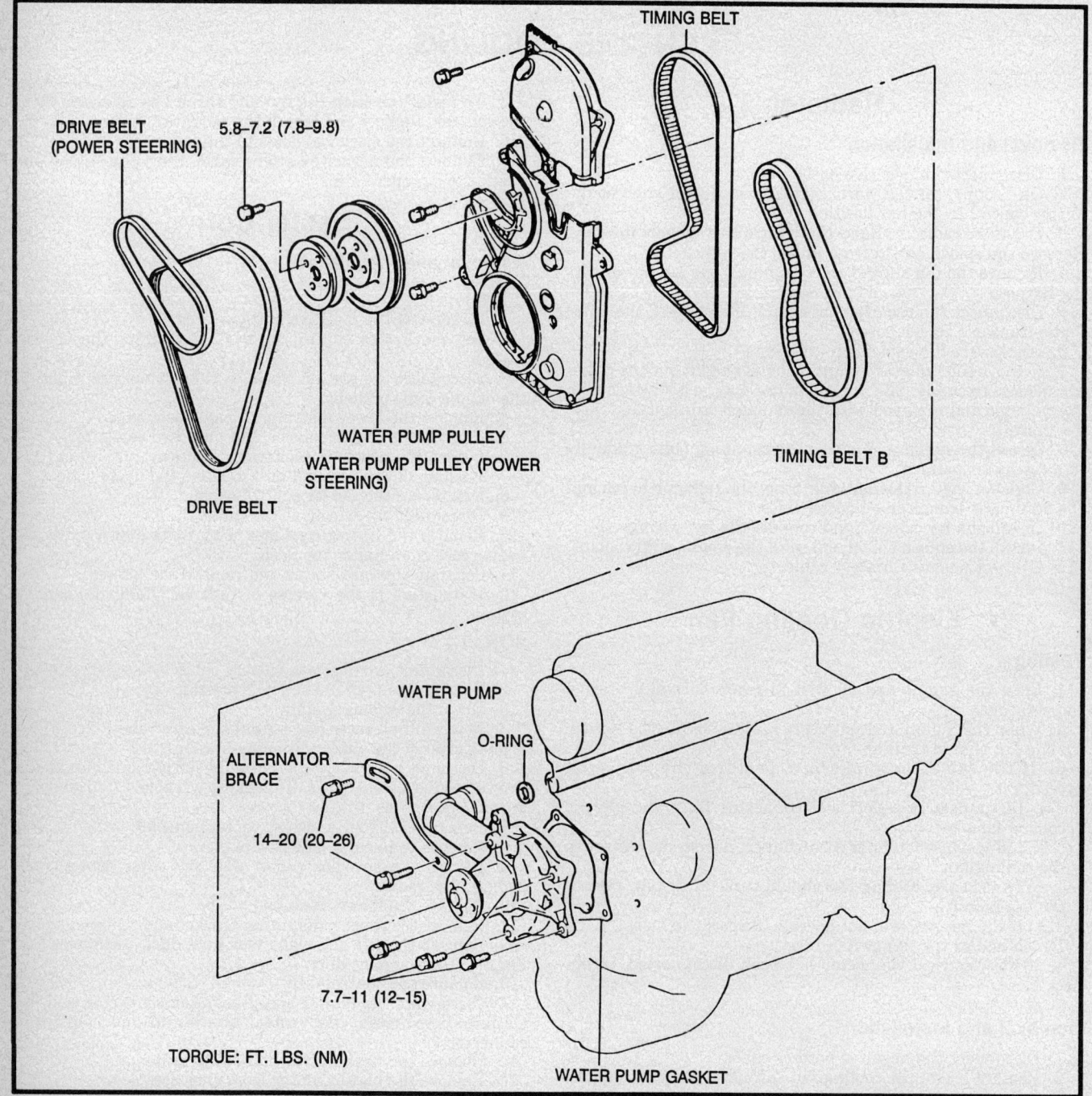

TORQUE: FT. LBS. (NM)

2351cc engine water pump installation

2. Loosen the 4 bolts attaching the water pump pulley to the pulley flange. Loosen the alternator mounting bolts, slide the alternator toward the engine and remove the belt. Remove the radiator cap, open the drain cock at the bottom of the radiator and drain the coolant from the radiator into a clean container.

3. Remove the timing belt covers, timing belt and tensioner.

4. Remove the water pump mounting bolts, noting the 3 different lengths and locations. Remove the pump and gasket, disconnecting the outlet at the water pipe (don't loose the O-ring).

To install:

5. Clean gasket surfaces and coat a new gasket with sealer. Then, position the gasket on the front of the block with all bolt holes aligned. Replace the O-ring for the outlet water pipe.

6. Install the pump connecting the outlet water pipe. Install the bolts with the shortest at the bottom; 2 just slightly longer at the 1 and 4 o'clock positions on the right side of the pump; next-to-longest bolt at the 8 o'clock position, just under the outlet; and the longest bolt at the 11 o'clock position and also attaching the alternator brace. Torque the bolts with a head mark, 4, to 9–11 ft. lbs. (12–15 Nm); those with a head mark 7, to 14–20 ft. lbs. (20–26 Nm).

7. Install the remaining parts in reverse order. Final tightening of the water pump pulley bolts is done after the V-belt has been installed and tensioned. Recheck tension after the pulley bolts are tightened. Close the radiator drain and refill the system. Run the engine until the thermostat opens and then add coolant until the level stabilizes before replacing the radiator cap. Check for leaks. Connect the negative battery cable.

2351CC ENGINE

1. Disconnect the negative battery cable. Drain the cooling system.

2. Remove all drive belts and water pump pulley. It may be necessary to remove an engine mount, the power steering pump and alternator brace to gain necessary clearance, depending the vehicle.

3. Remove the timing belt covers, timing belt tensioner and timing belt.

4. Remove the water pump bolts.

5. Remove the water pump.

NOTE: The pump is not rebuildable. If there are signs of damage or leakage from the seals or vent hole, the unit must be replaced.

6. Discard the O-ring in the front end of the water pipe. Install a new O-ring coated with water.

7. Using a new gasket, mount the water pump. Torque the bolts with a head marked 4, to 10 ft. lbs. or the bolts with a head marked 7, to 20 ft. lbs.

8. Assemble the remaining components, install the timing belt. Fill the system with a 50 percent mix of antifreeze.

2972CC ENGINE

1. Disconnect the negative battery cable.

2. Drain the cooling system.

3. Remove the timing cover. If the same timing belt will be reused, mark the direction of the timing belt's rotation, for installation in the same direction. Make sure the engine is positioned so the No. 1 cylinder is at the TDC of its compression stroke and the sprockets timing marks are aligned with the engine's timing mark indicators.

4. Loosen the timing belt tensioner bolt and remove the belt. Position the tensioner as far away from the center of the engine as possible and tighten the bolt. Remove the water pump mounting bolts, separate the pump from the water inlet pipe and remove the pump from the engine.

To install:

5. Install the pump with a new gasket to the engine. Torque the water pump mounting bolts to 20 ft. lbs. (27 Nm).

6. If not already done, position both camshafts so the marks align with those on the alternator bracket (rear bank) and inner

timing cover (front bank). Rotate the crankshaft so the timing mark aligns with the mark on the oil pump.

7. Install the timing belt on the crankshaft sprocket and while keeping the belt tight on the tension side (right side), install the belt on the front camshaft sprocket.

8. Install the belt on the water pump pulley, then the rear camshaft sprocket and the tensioner.

9. Rotate the front camshaft counterclockwise to tension the belt between the front camshaft and the crankshaft. If the timing marks became misaligned, repeat the procedure.

10. Install the crankshaft sprocket flange.

11. Loosen the tensioner bolt and allow the spring to tension the belt.

12. Turn the crankshaft 2 full turns in the clockwise direction only until the timing marks align again. Now that the belt is properly tensioned, torque the tensioner lock bolt to 21 ft. lbs. (29 Nm).

13. Refill the cooling system. Connect the negative battery cable and road test the vehicle.

Thermostat

Removal and Installation

1468CC ENGINE

1. Disconnect the negative battery cable. Remove the air cleaner.

2. Drain the cooling system to a point below the level of the tubes in the top tank of the radiator.

3. Disconnect the hose at the thermostat water pipe.

4. Remove the water pipe support bracket nut.

5. Unbolt and remove the thermostat housing and pipe.

6. Lift out the thermostat. Discard the gasket.

7. Clean the mating surfaces of the housing and manifold thoroughly.

8. Install the thermostat with the spring facing downward and position a new gasket. The jiggle valve in the thermostat should be on the manifold side.

9. Install the housing and pipe assembly. Torque the housing bolts to 10 ft. lbs.; the intake manifold nut to 14 ft. lbs.

10. Refill the cooling system. Connect the negative battery cable.

2351CC ENGINE

1. Connect the negative battery cable. Remove the air cleaner.

2. Drain the cooling system down well below the level of the tubes in the top tank of the radiator.

3. Disconnect the hose at the thermostat water pipe.

4. Unbolt and remove the thermostat housing.

5. Lift out the thermostat. Discard the gasket.

6. Clean the mating surfaces of the housing and manifold thoroughly.

To install:

7. Install the thermostat with the spring facing downward and position a new gasket.

8. Install the housing. Torque the housing bolts to 14 ft. lbs.

9. Refill the cooling system. Connect the negative battery cable.

2972CC ENGINE

1. Connect the negative battery cable. Remove the air cleaner.

2. Drain the cooling system down well below the level of the tubes in the top tank of the radiator.

3. Disconnect the hose at the thermostat water pipe.

4. Unbolt and remove the thermostat housing.

5. Lift out the thermostat. Discard the gasket.

6. Clean the mating surfaces of the housing and manifold thoroughly.

To install:

7. Install the thermostat with the spring facing downward and position a new gasket.

8. Install the housing. Torque the housing bolts to 14 ft. lbs.

9. Refill the cooling system. Connect the negative battery cable.

Cooling System Bleeding

After working on the cooling system, even to replace the thermostat, the system must bled. Air trapped in the system will prevent proper filling and leave the radiator coolant level low, causing a risk of overheating.

1. To bleed the system, start with the system cool, the radiator cap off and the radiator filled to about an inch below the filler neck.

2. Start the engine and run it at slightly above normal idle speed. This will insure adequate circulation. If air bubbles appear and the coolant level drops, fill the system with a mixture of anti-freeze and water to bring the level back to the proper level.

3. Run the engine this way until the thermostat opens. When this happens, the coolant will move abruptly across the top of the radiator and the temperature of the radiator will suddenly rise.

4. At this point, air is often expelled and the level may drop quite a bit. Keep refilling the system until the level is near the top of the radiator and remains constant.

5. If the vehicle has an overflow tank, fill the radiator to the top of the filler neck.

FUEL SYSTEM

Fuel System Service Precautions

Safety is the most important factor when performing not only fuel system maintenance but any type of maintenance. Failure to conduct maintenance and repairs in a safe manner may result in serious personal injury or death. Maintenance and testing of the vehicle's fuel system components can be accomplished safely and effectively by adhering to the following rules and guidelines.

• To avoid the possibility of fire and personal injury, always disconnect the negative battery cable unless the repair or test procedure requires that battery voltage be applied.

• Always relieve the fuel system pressure prior to disconnecting any fuel system component (injector, fuel rail, pressure regulator, etc.), fitting or fuel line connection. Exercise extreme caution whenever relieving fuel system pressure to avoid exposing skin, face and eyes to fuel spray. Please be advised that fuel under pressure may penetrate the skin or any part of the body that it contacts.

• Always place a shop towel or cloth around the fitting or connection prior to loosening to absorb any excess fuel due to spillage. Ensure that all fuel spillage (should it occur) is quickly removed from engine surfaces. Ensure that all fuel soaked cloths or towels are deposited into a suitable waste container.

• Always keep a dry chemical (Class B) fire extinguisher near the work area.

• Do not allow fuel spray or fuel vapors to come into contact with a spark or open flame.

• Always use a backup wrench when loosening and tightening fuel line connection fittings. This will prevent unnecessary stress and torsion to fuel line piping. Always follow the proper torque specifications.

• Always replace worn fuel fitting O-rings with new. Do not substitute fuel hose or equivalent where fuel pipe is installed.

Relieving Fuel System Pressure

1. Remove the fuel pump fuse from the fuse block.

2. Start the engine and let it run until the remaining fuel in the lines is consumed.

3. Crank engine again to make sure any fuel in the lines has been removed.

4. With the ignition **OFF** replace the fuel pump fuse.

5. Disconnect the negative battery cable.

Fuel Filter

Removal and Installation
CARBURETED ENGINE

The fuel filter is of the inline type. The filter is located at low center of the firewall.

NOTE: Remove the fuel tank cap to release pressure in the fuel lines.

1. Turn off the engine and allow it to cool. Loosen the screws in the fuel line clamps (at the filter) and then, using a pair of pliers, force open the clamps on the fuel lines and back them away from the connections.

2. Work the fuel lines back and off the filter connections. If they are difficult to remove, pull them off with a twisting motion. Remove the filter from its mounting clip.

3. Inspect the fuel lines for cracks or breaks and replace, if necessary.

4. Install the new filter in the same position the old one was in in the clamp. Connect the inlet fuel line to the inlet fitting on the bottom of the filter. Connect the outlet to the outlet fitting on top. Make sure the hoses are fully installed over the bulged-out portions of the fittings. Then, with pliers, move the clamps over the filter fittings so they are beyond the bulged-out sections of the fittings but a small distance away from the ends of the hoses.

FUEL INJECTED ENGINE

If equipped with fuel injection, relieve fuel system pressure before replacing the filter. An electric fuel pump is used on these vehicles and the filter is in the engine compartment. A connec-

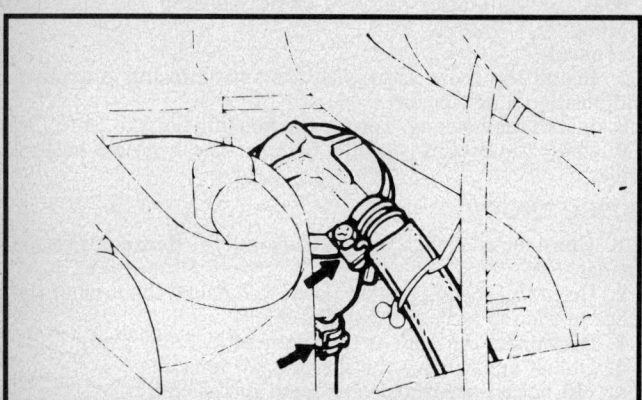

View of the fuel pump retaining clamps

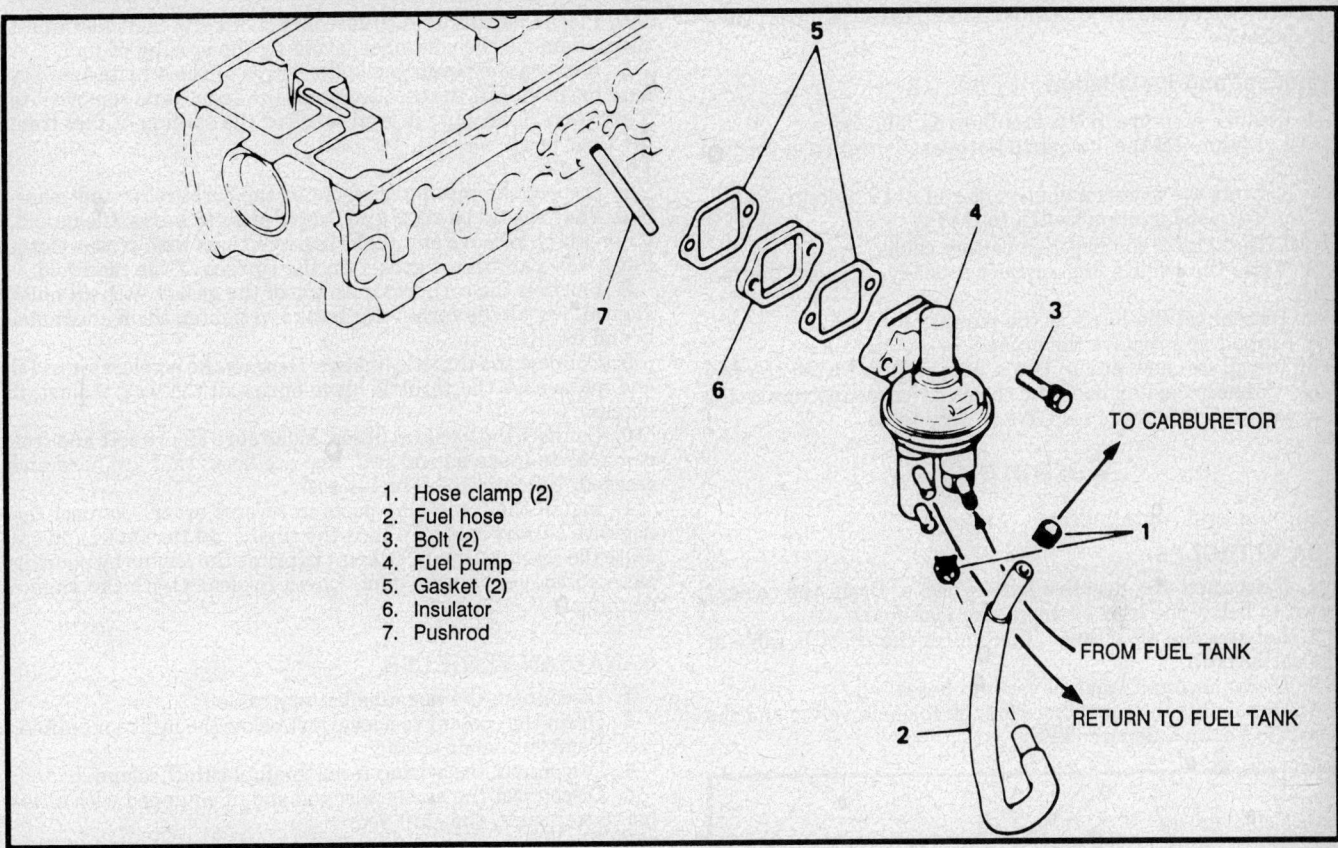

1. Hose clamp (2)
2. Fuel hose
3. Bolt (2)
4. Fuel pump
5. Gasket (2)
6. Insulator
7. Pushrod

TO CARBURETOR

FROM FUEL TANK

RETURN TO FUEL TANK

Mechanical fuel pump

tor, for checking the fuel function, is located under the battery tray. With the engine running, disconnect the connector, when the engine stops no pressure will remain in the system.

NOTE: Cover the fuel line fittings with a shop towel before loosening the eye bolts securing the fuel lines to the fuel filter.

1. Hold the fuel filter nuts securely and loosen the eye bolts securing the fuel lines to the fuel filter and remove the fuel lines from the filter ends.
2. Unclip the filter from the mounting bracket.
3. Installation is the reverse order of the remove procedure.
4. Install a new filter. Start the engine and check for leaks.
5. If a clogged filter is suspected, remove the filter and blow compressed air through the inlet and outlet fittings, reinstall the filter. Replace the old filter.

Mechanical Fuel Pump

Pressure Testing

1. Disconnect the inlet line, coming from the filter, at the pump.
2. Connect a vacuum gauge to the pump nipple.
3. Remove the high tension cable at the coil. Crank the engine and observe the gauge reading.
4. A vacuum of 2.7–3.7 psi should be produced. If there is a blow-back of pressure, the inlet valve on the pump is leaking and the unit must be replaced.

Removal and Installation

The mechanical fuel pump operates directly off of a camshaft eccentric. A fuel return valve is located in the upper body of the

pump. If the fuel temperature rises above 122°F (50°C), the valve opens and routes fuel back to the tank, preventing percolation.

1. Disconnect the negative battery cable. Remove the 2 screws and remove the plastic heat shield.
2. Disconnect the 3 fuel pump lines.
3. Unscrew the retaining nuts and remove the fuel pump and pushrod.
4. Remove the gasket, insulator and gasket.
5. Clean the fuel pump.
6. Apply non-hardening sealer to both sides of the gaskets. Position a gasket, the insulator and the other gasket on the head studs.
7. Set the No. 1 piston at TDC of the compression stroke and insert the pushrod into the head. Install the pump and torque the nuts to 25 ft. lbs.
8. Connect the negative battery cable.

Electric Fuel Pump

All fuel injected vehicles are equipped with an electric fuel pump. The fuel pump is in the gas tank.

Pressure Testing

If the fuel pump does not work:
1. Check the fuse.
2. Check all wiring connections.
3. Check the control relay which is located in the engine compartment, next to the ignition coil. If the engine starts when the ignition switch is turned to **START**, but stops when it is turned to **ON**, the relay is defective. Jumper terminals 1 and 2 of the test connecter, the fuel pump should operate. If the pump fails

to operate when the the jumper is connected, the pump is probably defective.

Removal and Installation

1. Reduce pressure in the fuel lines as follows:
   a. Disconnect the fuel pump harness connection at the fuel tank.
   b. Start the engine and allow it run until it stalls.
   c. Turn the ignition switch to **OFF**.
   d. Disconnect the negative battery cable.
2. Raise the vehicle and support it safely. Remove the fuel tank.
3. Disconnect the hoses at the pump.
4. Unbolt and remove the pump.
5. Install the new pump. Use a new gasket. Install the fuel tank. Connect the fuel lines and the electrical connectors to the fuel pump. Connect the negative battery cable.

Carburetor

Removal and Installation
USA VEHICLES

1. Disconnect the negative battery cable. Drain the coolant down to below the level of the intake manifold.
2. Remove the air cleaner. Disconnect the throttle cable at the carburetor.
3. Disconnect and label all vacuum hoses.
4. Disconnect the connectors for the solenoid valves and the Throttle Position Sensor (TPS).

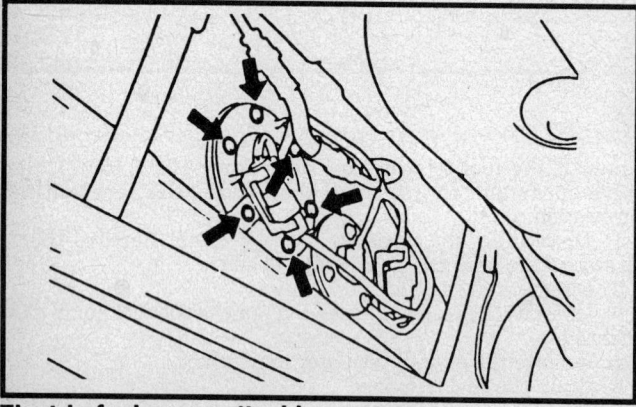

Electric fuel pump attaching screws

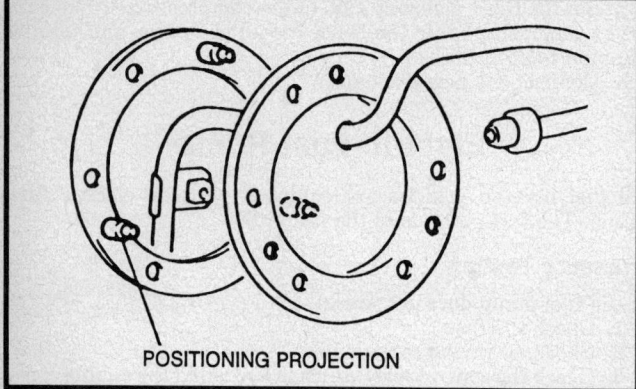

PROSITIONING PROJECTION

During electric fuel pump installation, make sure that positioning studs on the packing collar are properly positioned

5. Place a pan under the fuel connections and then disconnect them. Remove the container, avoiding the spilling of fuel.
6. Remove the mounting bolts. Three of the 4 bolts are very hard to get at. Lift the carburetor off the engine and remove it to a workbench, keeping it level to avoid the spilling of fuel from the float bowl.

To install:

7. Inspect the mating surfaces of the carburetor and manifold. They should be clean and free of nicks or burrs. Clean and, if necessary, remove any slight imperfections with crocus cloth. Put a new carburetor gasket on the surface of the manifold.
8. Position the carburetor on top of the gasket with all holes aligned. Install the carburetor bolts and tighten them alternately and evenly.
9. Connect the throttle linkage. Depress the accelerator pedal and make sure the throttle blade opens all the way. Adjust, if necessary.
10. Connect the vacuum hoses. Make sure all are soft and free of cracks to make a good seal. Replace hoses that are hard and cracked. Reconnect the fuel hoses.
11. Install the remaining parts in reverse order. Connect the negative battery cable. To start the engine, set the choke and operate the starter. Do not attempt to prime the engine by pouring gas into the carburetor inlet. Check for leaks with the engine running.

CANADIAN VEHICLES

1. Disconnect the negative battery cable.
2. Drain the coolant to a level just below the intake manifold.
3. Remove the air cleaner.
4. Disconnect the wiring from the fuel cutoff solenoid.
5. Disconnect the accelerator rod and, if equipped with automatic transaxle, the shift rod.
6. Tag and disconnect the vacuum hoses from the carburetor.
7. Place suitable rags or a container under the fuel inlet and return hoses to catch any leaking fuel and disconnect the hoses.
8. Disconnect the water hose which runs between the carburetor and the cylinder head.
9. Unscrew the 4 retaining nuts and remove the carburetor. Hold the carburetor level to avoid a fuel spill.
10. Mount the carburetor on the intake manifold and attach the choke water hose.
11. Reconnect the fuel lines and vacuum hoses to the carburetor.
12. Connect the accelerator or shift rod.
13. Reconnect the fuel cut-off solenoid and replace the air cleaner.
14. Refill the system with coolant. Connect the negative battery cable.

Idle Speed Adjustment

The idle speed is adjusted periodically to compensate for engine wear or after engine work is performed. Idle mixture adjustments are not required as a matter of routine but only when major carburetor work is required. The emission control system compensates as required to ensure a stable idle mixture. If a rough idle is apparent, check the idle mixture with a CO meter, if one is available.

Also, Hyundais have an idle-up solenoid that operates to prevent stalling under certain conditions. This does not require adjustment as a matter of routine either but may be adjusted, if the system is not functioning properly.

NOTE: The idle mixture adjustment is preset at the factory. The mixture adjusting screw is inaccessible without removing and modifying the carburetor. Since this adjustment is preset, it should not be changed unless major, unscheduled maintenance has been performed on the carburetor. This adjustment can only be made with a CO meter.

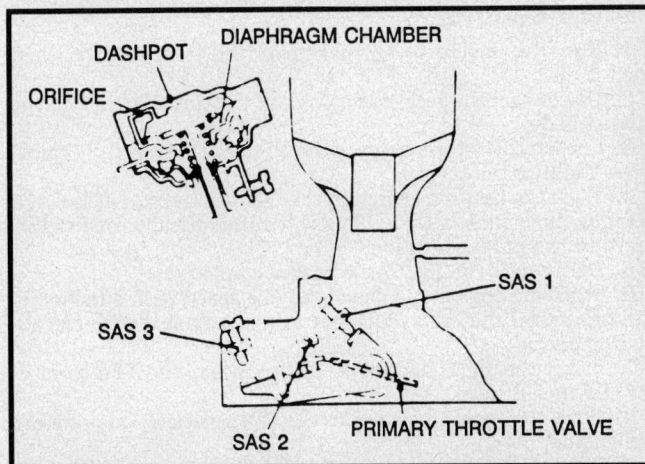

Idle speed adjustment points for carbureted engines

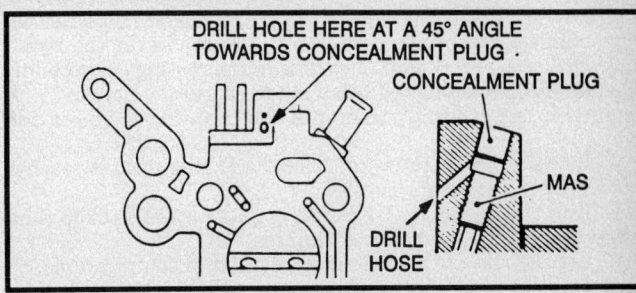

Drilling out the concealment plug to adjust CO

The idle adjustment is made under the following conditions:
  Lights Off
  All accessories Off
  Electric cooling fan Off
  Transaxle in neutral and parking brake applied

1. Start and run the engine at idle until normal operating temperature is reached.

2. Check the underhood decal or the tune-up specification charts for the correct curb idle speed.

3. Connect a tachometer, according to the manufacturer's instructions and adjust the idle speed screw until the correct rpm is reached.

4. Run the engine for at least 5 seconds at 2000–3000 rpm. Then, reduce the speed to idle rpm for at least 2 minutes.

5. If the idle speed is not at the specified rpm, turn the idle speed adjusting screw until the proper rpm is reached.

6. Check the underhood specifications sticker for the correct idle speed rpm.

Idle Mixture Adjustment

USA VEHICLES

1. Disconnect the negative battery cable. Remove the carburetor. The idle mixture screw is located in the base of the carbu-

retor, just to the left of the PCV hose. Mount the carburetor, carefully, in a soft-jawed vise, protecting the gasket surface and with the mixture adjusting screw facing upward.

2. Drill a $5/64$ in. (2mm) hole through the casting from the underside of the carburetor. Make sure the hole intersects the passage leading to the mixture adjustment screw just behind the plug. Now, widen that hole with a 3mm ($1/8$ in.) drill bit.

3. Insert a blunt punch into the hole and tap out the plug. Install the carburetor on the engine and connect all hoses, lines, etc. Connect the negative battery cable.

4. Start the engine and run it at fast idle until it reaches normal operating temperature. Make sure all accessories are OFF and the transaxle is in neutral. Turn the ignition switch **OFF** and disconnect the negative battery cable for about 3 seconds, then, reconnect it. Disconnect the oxygen sensor.

5. Start the engine and run it for at least 5 seconds at 2000–3000 rpm. Then, allow the engine to idle for about 2 minutes.

6. Connect a tachometer and allow the engine to operate at the specified curb idle speed. Adjust it, if necessary, to obtain this speed. Connect a CO meter to the exhaust pipe. A reading of 0.1–0.3 percent is necessary. Adjust the mixture screw to obtain the reading. If, during this adjustment, the idle speed is varied more than 100 rpm in either direction, reset the idle speed and readjust the CO until both specifications are met simultaneously. Shut off the engine, reconnect the oxygen sensor and install a new concealment plug.

CANADIAN VEHICLES

1. Disconnect the negative battery cable. Turn off all of the electrical accessories and place the transaxle in the neutral position. Then remove the carburetor from the engine.

2. Position the carburetor in a vise with idle mixture adjust-

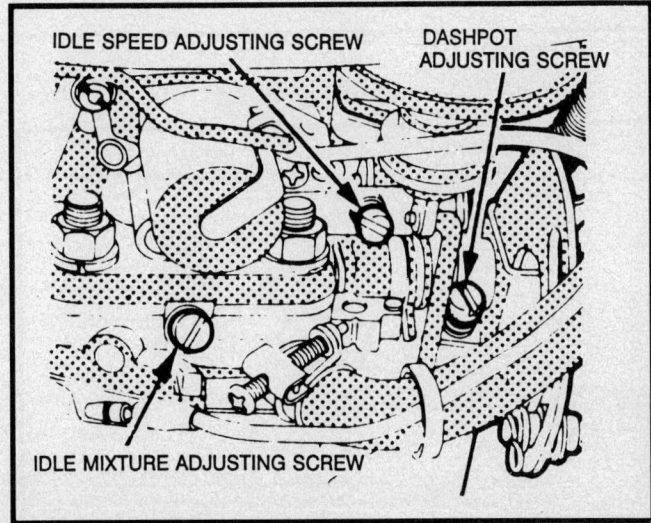

Carburetor adjustment points

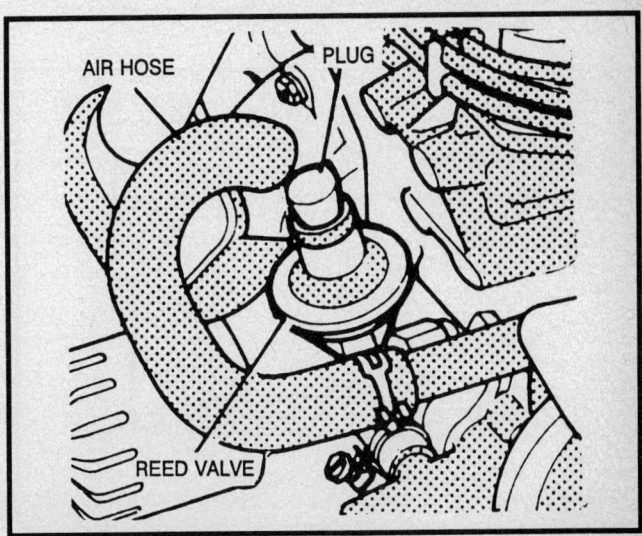

Air hose removal (typical)

ing screw facing up. Make sure the gasket surface does not become damaged when the carburetor is placed in the the vise.

3. Drill a $\frac{5}{64}$ in. (2mm) pilot hole in the casting surrounding the idle mixture adjusting screw, then redrill the hole to $\frac{1}{8}$ in. (3mm). Insert a blunt punch into the hole and drive out the plug.

4. Reinstall the carburetor. Run the engine until it reaches normal operating temperature.

5. Run the engine for 5 seconds or more at 2000–3000 rpm. Allow the engine to idle for 2 minutes.

6. Set the idle CO and the engine speed to specifications, by adjusting the idle speed adjusting screw No. 1 (SAS-1) and the idle mixture adjusting screw. Idle CO should be 1.8 percent when the curb idle speed is set between 850–900 rpm.

7. Install the concealment plug to seal the idle mixture adjusting screw.

For further information, please refer to "Chilton's Electronic Engine Control's Manual" for additional coverage.

Idle Speed Adjustment

NOTE: This adjustment must be made any time the Idle Speed Control (ISC) servo, Throttle Position Sensor (TPS), mixing body or throttle body has been removed. A digital voltmeter is essential for this operation.

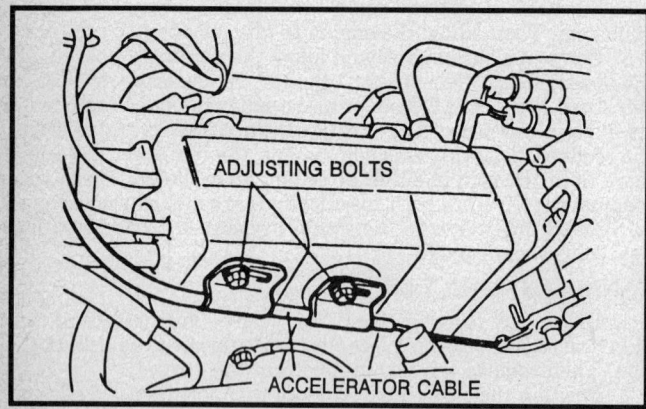

ISC control cable adjusting points

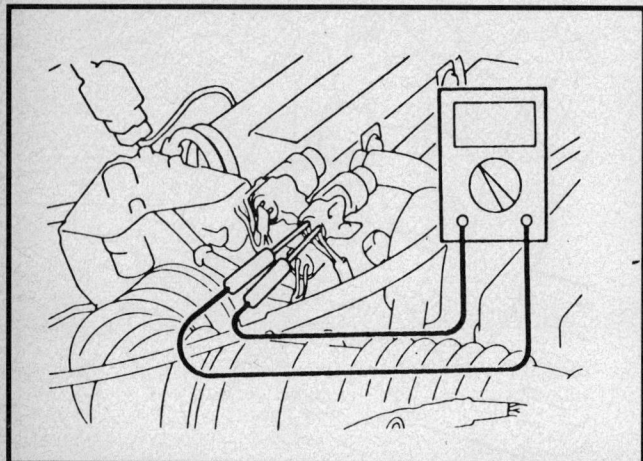

Multi-tester connections for the ISC adjustment

EXCEPT SCOUPE

1. Run the engine to normal operating temperature, then turn it off.

2. Disconnect the accelerator cable at the throttle lever on the mixing body.

3. Loosen the screws holding the TPS and turn it fully clockwise. Tighten the screws.

4. Turn the ignition switch to the **ON** position for at least 15 seconds, then turn it **OFF**. This will automatically set the ISC servo to the proper position.

5. Disconnect the ISC servo wiring connector.

6. Start the engine and check the idle speed with a tachometer. Idle speed should be 600 rpm. If not, adjust it with the adjusting screw.

7. Insert the digital voltmeter test probes in the TPS connector GW and B holes.

8. Turn the ignition switch to the **ON** position. Do not start the engine.

9. Read the voltage. If indicated voltage is not 0.45 0.51 volts, loosen the TPS mounting screws and turn the sensor clockwise or counterclockwise until the indicated voltage is 0.48 volts. Tighten the screws and apply a thread-locking sealant.

10. Open the throttle valve fully and allow it close. Recheck the indicated voltage. Adjust, if necessary.

11. Remove the voltmeter and reconnect the wiring.

12. Start the engine. Recheck the idle speed. Adjust, if necessary and stop the engine.

13. Turn the ignition switch to the **ON** position for at least 15 seconds, then turn it **OFF**.

14. Reconnect the cable and adjust, if necessary, to remove any slack, using the adjusting nut at the throttle lever.

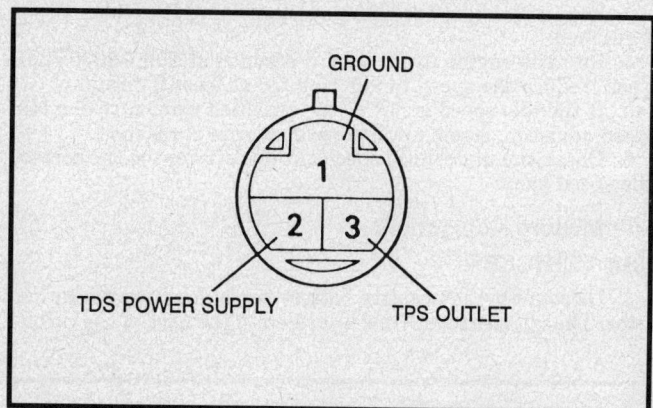

TPS connector

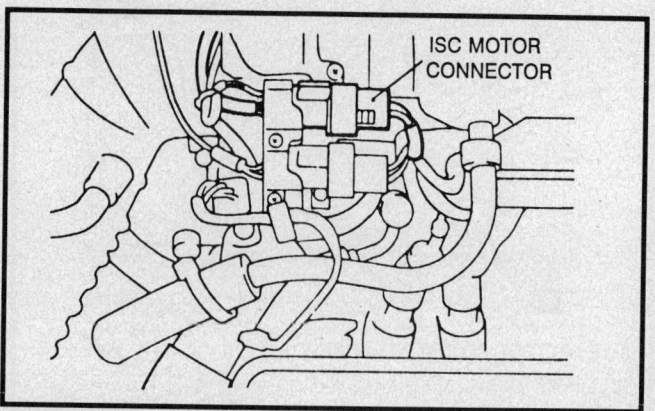

ISC motor connector

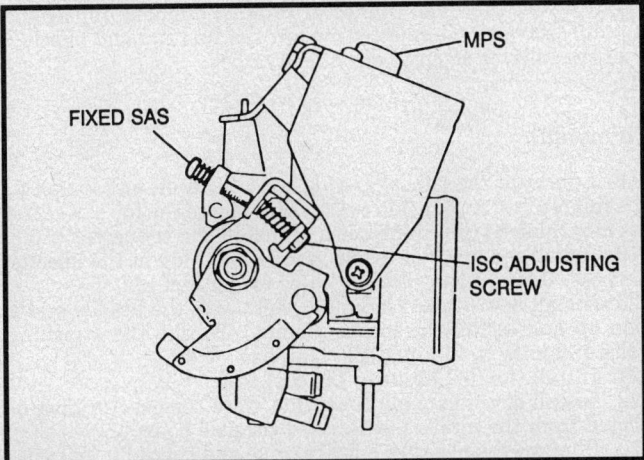

Speed control screws for fuel injected engines

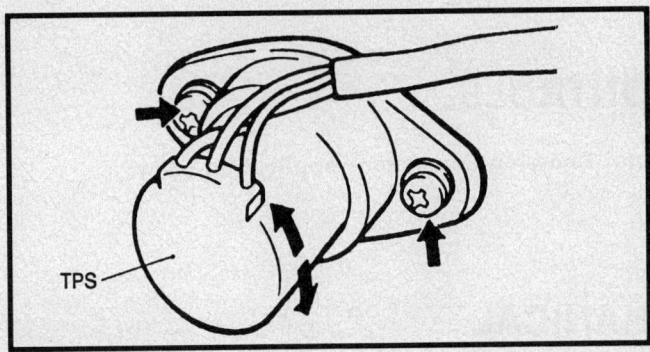

TPS adjustment

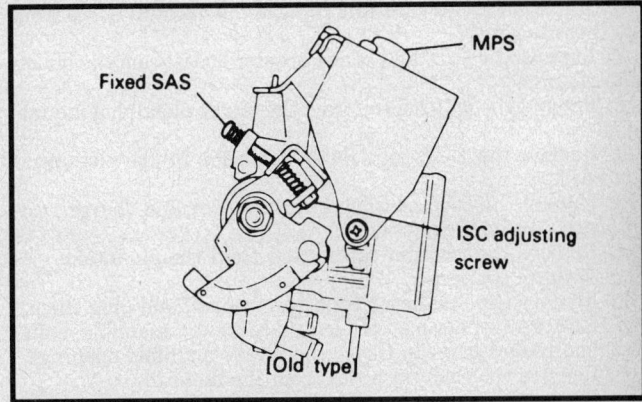

Idle adjust screw—Scoupe

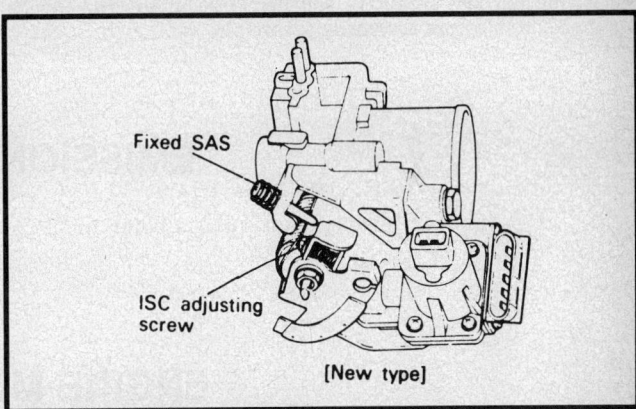

Idle adjust screw—Scoupe

SCOUPE

1. Loosen the accelerator cable.
2. Connnect the multi-use tester to the diagnosis connector in the fuse box. If using a digital voltmeter, connect the voltmeter between terminals 1 and 2 of the throttle position sensor.

NOTE: Do not disconnect the TPS connector from the throttle body.

3. Turn the ignition switch to the **ON** position for at least 15 seconds. Check to see that the ISC servo is fully retracted to the curb idle position.

NOTE: When the ignition switch is turned to the ON position, the ISC plunger extends to the fast idle position opening. After 15 seconds, it retracts to the fully closed (curb idle) position.

4. Turn the ignition switch to the **OFF** position.
5. Disconnect the ISC motor connector and secure the ISC motor at the fully retracted position.
6. In order to prevent the throttle valve from sticking, open it 2 or 3 times, then allow it to click shut and loosen the fixed SAS sufficiently.
7. Start the engine and allow it to run at idle speed. Ensure that the engine is running at idle speed of 700 rpm ± 100. Adjust as necessary by turning the ISC adjust screw.
8. Tighten the fixed SAS until the engine speed starts to increase. Then, loosen the screw until the engine speed ceases to drop (touch point) and loosen an additional ½ turn.
9. Turn the ignition switch to the **OFF** position.
10. Turn the ignition switch to the **ON** position and check TPS output voltage. The output voltage should be 0.48–0.52 volts.
11. If the voltage is out of specification, loosen the TPS mounting screws and adjust by turning the TPS.
12. Turn the ignition switch to the **OFF** position.
13. Adjust the accelerator cable to 0–0.04 in. (0–1mm) for a manual transaxle and 0.08–0.12 in. (2–3mm) for an automatic transaxle.
14. Connect the ISC motor connector.
15. Disconnect the voltmeter and connect the TPS connector.
16. Start the engine and check to be sure that the idle speed is correct.
17. Turn the ignition switch to the **OFF** and disconnect the negative battery cable for 15 seconds and re-connect.

Idle Mixture Adjustment

The fuel mixture is controlled and governed by the Electronic Control Unit (ECU). No mixture adjustment is necessary on the system.

Fuel Injector

Removal and Installation

1. Disconnect the negative battery cable.
2. Relieve the fuel pressure.
3. Remove the air cleaner-to-throttle body hose.
4. Disconnect the throttle cable from the throttle body and disconnect the kickdown linkage. Remove the throttle cable bracket attaching bolts.
5. Disconnect the connectors to the throttle body.

6. Matchmark and carefully remove the vacuum hoses from the throttle body.

7. Remove the PCV and brake booster hoses from the air intake plenum.

8. Remove the ignition coil from the intake plenum, if mounted there.

9. Remove the EGR tube flange from the intake plenum, if equipped.

10. Unplug the coolant temperature sensor and charge temperature sensor, if equipped.

11. Remove the vacuum connection from the air intake plenum vacuum connector.

12. Remove the fuel hoses from the fuel rail and plug them.

13. Remove the air intake plenum-to-intake manifold bolts, the plenum and gaskets. Cover the intake manifold openings.

14. Remove the vacuum hoses from the fuel rail.

15. Disconnect the fuel injector wiring harness.

16. Remove the fuel rail attaching bolts and the fuel rail with the wiring harness from the vehicle. Position the rail upside down so the injectors are easily accessible.

17. Remove the small connector retainer clip and unplug the injector. Remove the injector clip off the fuel rail and injector. Pull the injector straight out of the rail.

To install:

18. Lubricate the rubber O-ring with clean oil and install to the rail receiver cap. Install the injector clip to the top slot of the injector, plug in the connector and install the connector clip.

19. Install the fuel rail to the vehicle and plug in the injector harness. Connect the vacuum hoses to the fuel rail.

20. Install new intake plenum gaskets with the beaded sealer side up and install the intake plenum. Torque the attaching bolts and nuts to 115 inch lbs. (13 Nm).

21. Install the fuel hoses to the fuel rail.

22. Install or connect all items that were removed or disconnected from the intake plenum and throttle body.

23. Connect the negative battery cable and check for leaks using the DRB I or II to activate the fuel pump.

EMISSION CONTROLS

For further information, please refer to "Professional Emission Component Application Guide".

ENGINE MECHANICAL

NOTE: Disconnecting the negative battery cable on some vehicles may interfere with the functions of the on board computer systems and may require the computer to undergo a relearning process, once the negative battery cable is reconnected.

Engine Assembly

Removal and Installation

NOTE: The factory recommends that the engine and transaxle be removed as a unit.

1. Disconnect the negative battery cable. Remove the air cleaner assembly. Disconnect the purge control vacuum hose from the purge valve. Remove the purge control valve mounting bracket. Remove the windshield washer reservoir, radiator tank and carbon canister.

2. Drain the coolant from the radiator. Disconnect the upper and lower radiator hoses and then remove the radiator assembly with the electric cooling fan attached. Be sure to disconnect the fan wiring harness.

3. Disconnect the electrical connectors for the back-up lights and engine harness, located near the battery tray. If equipped with a 5 speed transaxle, disconnect the select control valve connector. Disconnect the alternator harness connectors and the oil pressure sending unit.

4. Label and disconnect the automatic transaxle oil cooler hoses. Avoid spilling oil and cap the openings.

5. Label and disconnect all low tension wires and the one high tension wire going to the coil from the distributor. Disconnect the engine ground.

6. Disconnect the brake booster vacuum hose at the intake manifold.

7. Disconnect the fuel supply, return and vapor hoses at the side of the engine. Avoid spilling fuel.

8. Disconnect the heater hoses from the side of the engine. Disconnect the accelerator cable at the engine side.

9. Remove the clutch control cable for manual transaxle or transaxle shifter control cable for automatic transaxles from the transaxle.

10. Unscrew and disconnect the speedometer cable at the transaxle. Disconnect the air conditioning compressor mounting bracket.

11. Raise and safely support the vehicle. Remove the splash shield. Remove the drain plug and drain the transaxle fluid. Dis-

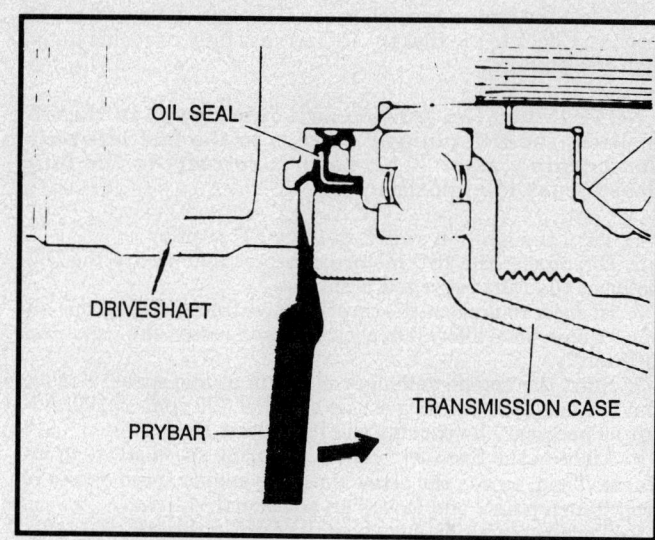

Removing the driveshafts

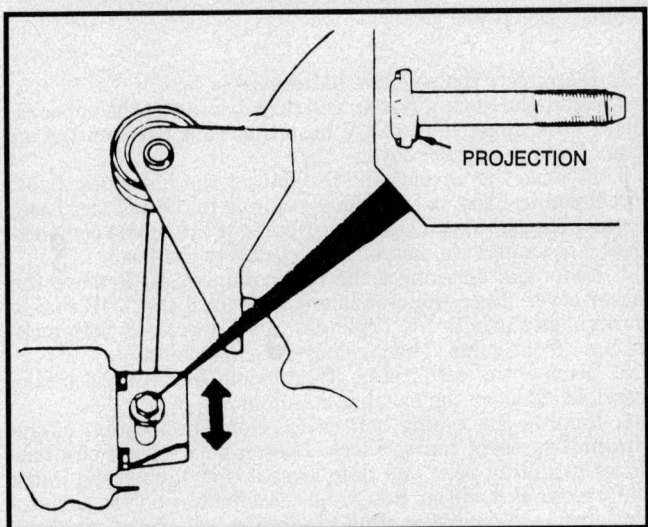

Installing the lower bolt on the roll stopper

Remove the front roll stop nut and the bolt; or, you may remove the attaching bolts from the engine damper

connect the exhaust pipe at the manifold. Then, suspend the pipe securely with wire.

12. If equipped with a manual transaxle, remove the shift control rod and extension rod.

13. Disconnect the stabilizer bar at both lower control arms. Remove the bolts that attach the lower control arms to the body on either side. Support the arms from the body.

14. Disconnect the halfshafts at the transaxle on both sides. Then, seal off the openings in the transaxle. Be sure to replace the circlips holding the halfshafts in the transaxle. Support the halfshafts from the body.

15. Attach a suitable lift, via chains or cables, to both the engine lifting hooks. Put just a little tension on the cables. Then, remove the nut and bolt from the front roll stopper; unbolt the brace from the top of the engine damper.

16. Separate the rear roll stopper from the No. 2 crossmember. Remove the attaching nut from the left mount insulator bolt, but do not remove the bolt.

17. Raise the engine just enough that the crane is supporting its weight. Check that everything is disconnected from the engine.

18. Remove the blind cover from the inside of the right fender inner shield. Remove the transaxle mounting bracket bolts.

19. Remove the left mount insulator bolt. Then, press downward on the transaxle while lifting the engine/transaxle assembly to guide it up and out of the vehicle.

NOTE: Make sure the transaxle does not hit the battery bracket during engine and transaxle removal.

To install:

20. Using a lifting device, lower the engine and transaxle carefully into position and loosely install the mounting bolts. Temporarily tighten the front and rear roll control rods mounting bolts. Lower the full weight of the engine and transaxle onto the mounts and tighten the nuts and bolts. Loosen and retighten the roll control rods.

21. Install the transaxle mounting bracket bolts. Install the blind cover to the inside of the right fender inner shield.

22. Assemble the rear roll stopper to the No. 2 crossmember. Install retaining nut and bolt.

23. Install new circlips on the halfshafts prior to installing. Connect the halfshafts at the transaxle on both sides.

24. Attach the lower control arms to the body on either side. Connect the stabilizer bar to both lower control arms.

25. If equipped with a manual transaxle, install the shift control rod and extension rod.

26. Raise the vehicle and support it safely. Connect the exhaust pipe at the manifold. Install the splash shield.

27. Connect the speedometer cable at the transaxle. Connect the air conditioning compressor mounting bracket.

28. Install the clutch control cable, for manual transaxle, or shifter control cable, for automatic transaxle, to the transaxle.

29. Lower the vehicle. Connect the heater to the engine. Connect the accelerator cable at the engine side.

30. Connect the fuel supply, return and vapor hoses at the side of the engine.

31. Connect the brake booster vacuum hose at the intake manifold.

32. Connect all low tension wires and the high tension wire going to the coil from the distributor. Connect the engine ground.

33. Connect the automatic transaxle oil cooler hoses.

34. Connect the electrical connectors for the back-up lights and engine harness, located near the battery tray. If equipped with 5 speed, connect the select control valve connector. Connect the alternator harness connectors and the oil pressure sending unit.

35. Install the radiator and electric cooling fan assembly. Connect the upper and lower radiator hoses. Observe the following torque values:

Left mount large insulator nut – 65–80 ft. lbs.
Left mount small insulator nut – 22–29 ft. lbs.
Left mount bracket-to-engine nuts/bolts – 36–47 ft. lbs.
Transaxle mount insulator nut – 65–80 ft. lbs.
Transaxle insulator bracket-to-side frame bolts – 22–29 ft. lbs.
Transaxle bracket assembly-to-automatic transaxle nuts – 65–80 ft. lbs.
Transaxle mount bracket to manual transaxle bolts – 40–43 ft. lbs.
Rear roll insulator nut – 33–43 ft. lbs.
Rear roll stopper bracket-to-crossmember assembly bolts – 22–29 ft. lbs.
Front roll insulator nut – 33–43 ft. lbs.
Front roll stopper bracket-to-crossmember assembly bolts – 33–40 ft. lbs.
Lower roll insulator-to-roll damper bracket bolt – 22–29 ft. lbs.
Center crossmember-to-body bolts – 43–58 ft. lbs.

36. Replenish all fluids. Adjust the transaxle and accelerator linkages. Start the engine and check for leaks as well as proper gauge operation. Replace the hood and the air conditioning system.

Engine Mounts

Removal and Installation

The engine mounts can be removed and installed by supporting the engine and transaxle assembly from below.

1. Disconnect the negative battery cable.
2. Remove the upper mount-to-body bracket bolts.
3. Using an engine holding fixture tool, support the engine.
4. Raise and safely support the vehicle.
5. Remove the left side inner fender shield.
6. Remove the lower engine mount-to-body bracket bolt.
7. Raise the engine, slightly, and remove the engine mount through bolt.
8. Remove the lower engine mount-to-engine bracket bolt and the mount.

To install:

9. Support the engine from below. To protect the engine, place a board between the support and the engine.
10. Install the lower engine mount and mount-to-engine bracket bolt.
11. Raise or lower the engine slightly, to install engine mount through bolt.
12. Install the left side inner fender shield.
14. Install the upper mount and mount-to-body bracket bolts.
15. Lower the vehicle and connnect the negative battery cable.

Cylinder Head

Removal and Installation

NOTE: Never remove the cylinder head unless the engine is cold, a hot cylinder head will warp.

1468CC ENGINE

1. Disconnect the negative battery cable.
2. Drain the cooling system and then disconnect the upper radiator hose. Remove the PCV hose that runs between the air cleaner and the rocker cover.
3. Remove the air cleaner. Disconnect the fuel lines. Label and disconnect any vacuum lines running to the cylinder head, manifold or carburetor from other parts of the engine compartment. Disconnect the heater hoses going to the head.
4. Label and disconnect the spark plug wires. Remove the rocker cover. Turn the crankshaft over until the TDC timing marks align and both No. 1 cylinder valves are closed, both rockers are off the cams. Then, remove the distributor.
5. Remove the carburetor, if equipped. Remove the intake manifold. Remove the exhaust manifold.
6. Remove the timing belt cover. Note the location of the camshaft sprocket timing mark. Loosen both timing belt tensioner mounting bolts and then lever it over toward the water pump as far as it will go. Retighten the adjusting bolt to hold the tensioner in this position. Pull the timing belt off the camshaft sprocket but leave it engaged with the other sprockets.
7. Using a hex type wrench, loosen the head bolts in the proper sequence. When all have been loosened, remove them. Then, pull the head off the engine block, rocking it slightly to break it loose.
8. Inspect the head with a straight-edge and a flat feeler gauge of 0.002 in. (0.05mm) thickness. The tolerance for warping of a used head is 0.002 in. (0.05mm). The block deck must be flat within the same tolerance. The height of the head should be 3.5 in. (89mm) with a maximum machining limit of 0.012 in. (0.3mm).

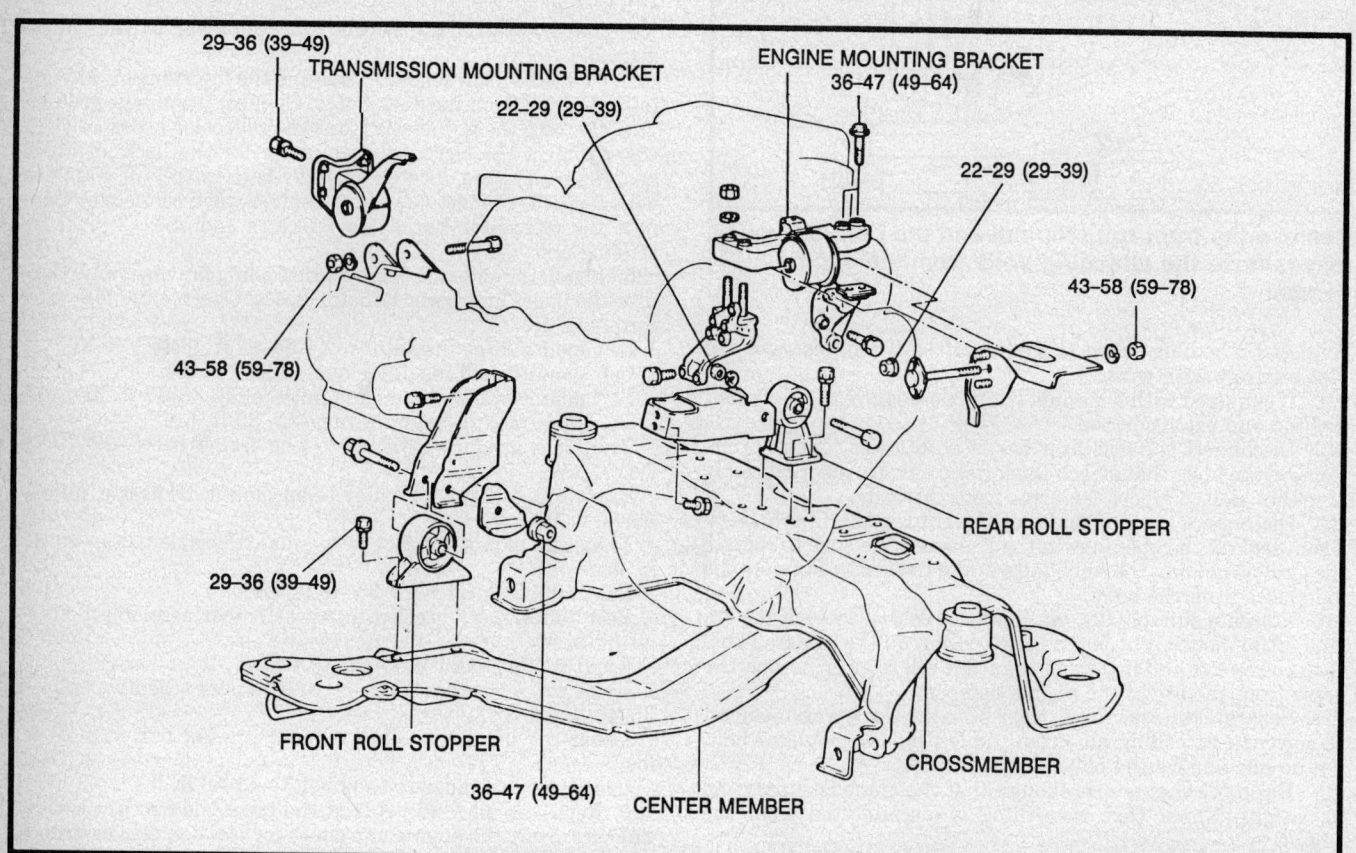

Sonata engine mounts

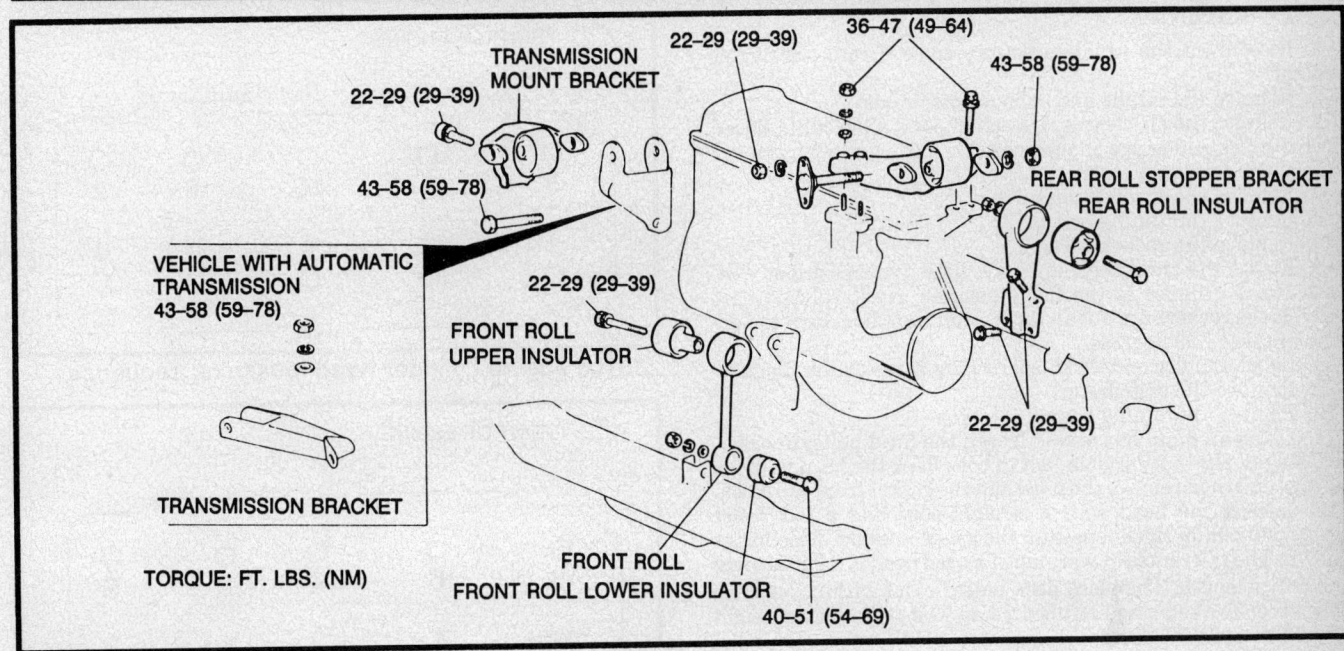

Excel engine mounts

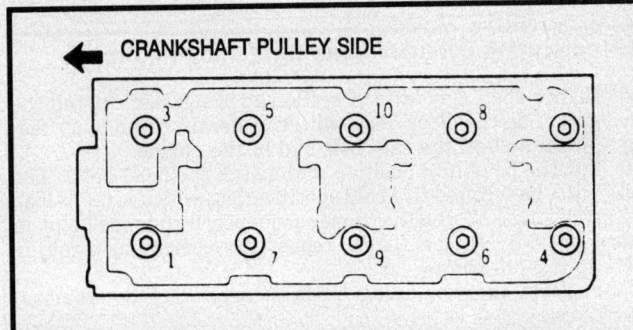

Cylinder head removal sequence for the 1468cc engine

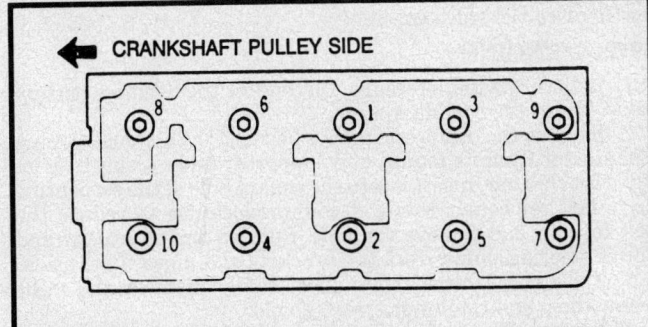

Cylinder head torque sequence for the 1468cc engine

To install:

9. Clean the combustion chambers of carbon with a scraper that is not excessively sharp, being carefully not to damage the aluminum surface. Sharp edges in the combustion chambers can cause detonation.

10. The oil and water passages should be cleaned thoroughly. Also, blow compressed air through all the small oil passages to ensure that they are clear. Check that the EGR and air pump passages are also clear. Both gasket surfaces must be completely free of dirt.

11. Install a new head gasket, without sealant, and position the head on the cylinder block. Install all the bolts finger tight. Torque the bolts in sequence. First to 25 ft. lbs. (35 Nm). Then, torque again, in sequence, to 51–54 ft. lbs. (69–74 Nm).

12. Install the timing belt on the camshaft tensioner and rotate the camshaft sprocket backward so the belt is tight on what is normally the tension side. Make sure all the timing marks are now aligned. That is, timing marks on the crankshaft sprocket and front case must align; and the marks on the camshaft sprocket and the tab on the cylinder head must be simultaneously aligned with the side of the belt away from the tensioner under tension. Now, loosen the timing belt tensioner adjusting bolt and allow spring tension to tension the belt. Make sure all timing marks are still aligned. If not, the belt is out of time and must be shifted with the tensioner shifted back toward the water pump and locked there. Now, torque the adjusting bolt, on the right side and working through a slot, to 15–18 ft. lbs. After the tensioner adjusting bolt is torqued, torque the hinged mounting bolt located on the opposite side. Don't torque the mounting bolt first or the tension on the belt will be too great.

13. Turn the crankshaft 1 full turn in the normal direction of rotation. Loosen first the tensioner pivot bolt and then the adjusting bolt. Now torque them exactly as before, adjusting bolt, working in the slot. This extra step is necessary to ensure the timing belt is properly seated before final tension is adjusted.

14. Install the cylinder head cover and tighten the bolts to 13–16 inch lbs. (1.5–2.0 Nm).

15. Install the timing belt cover.

16. Install the intake manifold using a new gasket and tighten the bolts and nut to 12–14 ft. lbs. (16–19 Nm).

17. Install the exhaust manifold using a new gasket and tighten the nuts to 12–17 ft. lbs. (16–19 Nm).

18. Install the carburetor.

19. Install the distributor. Connect all hoses, lines and the air cleaner.

20. Refill the cooling system. Operate the engine and check for leaks. After the engine has reached normal operating temperature, turn it off and remove the air cleaner and rocker cover. Retighten the cylinder head bolts to 58–61 ft. lbs. (78–83 Nm), in the sequence.

21. Reinstall the rocker cover and the air cleaner.

2351CC ENGINE

1. Disconnect the negative battery cable. Drain the engine coolant.
2. Remove the intake and exhaust manifolds.
3. Remove the air cleaner. Detach and tag all vacuum hoses, heater hoses and gauge connectors which connect with the cylinder head or would obstruct its removal.
4. Remove the throttle air valve body.
5. Remove the timing belt cover.
6. Remove the rocker cover.
7. Rotate the crankshaft until the timing marks are at TDC with No. 1 cylinder at the firing position, front valves closed fully. If the rockers are not all the way off the cams, turn the engine another 360 degrees.
8. Label and disconnect all spark plug wires at the plugs.
9. Remove the distributor.
10. Remove the timing belt.
11. Using an 8mm hex socket loosen the head bolts, in order, in 3 stages, alternating from bolt to bolt. Rock the head to break it loose and then remove the head and the gasket from the block.
12. Inspect the head with a straight-edge and a flat feeler gauge of 0.10mm thickness. Run the gauge in every direction as shown. The tolerance for warping of a used head is 0.05mm over the entire length. The block deck must be flat within the same tolerance. The refacing limit is 0.2mm. The overall head height should be 89.9–90.1mm.

To install:

13. Clean the combustion chambers of carbon with a scraper that is not excessively sharp and use it carefully to avoid damaging the relatively soft aluminum surface.
14. The oil and water passages should be cleaned thoroughly, Blow compressed air through all the small oil passages to ensure that they are clear. Check that the EGR and air pump passages are also clear. Both gasket surfaces must be completely free of dirt.

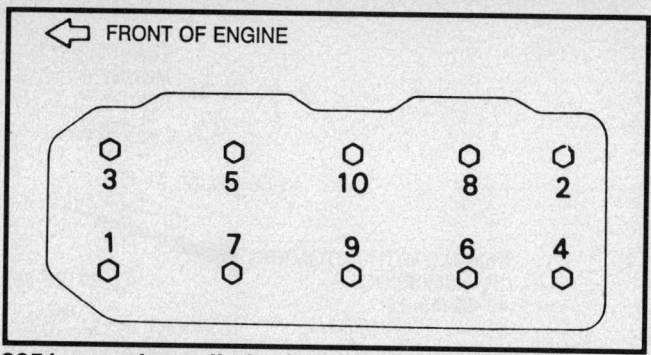

2351cc engine cylinder head loosening sequence

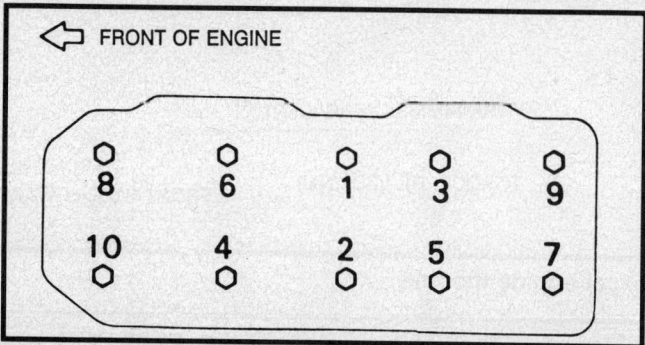

2351cc engine cylinder head tightening sequence

15. Do not apply any kind of sealant to the gasket. Install the head gasket on the block deck, with the identification mark facing upward and on the cam belt end of the engine.
16. Put the head into position and install the head bolts. The bolts must be torqued to a cold specification, which is 69 ft. lbs., in 2 equal stages. Using the proper sequence, torque the bolts, in order, to 33-36 ft. lbs. Then, repeat the operation, torquing them to the full torque.
17. Perform the remaining steps in reverse of the removal procedure.
18. Connect the negative battery cable.
19. Start the engine, check for leaks and run the engine to normal operating temperature. Stop the engine. Remove the valve cover and torque the head bolts, warm, in sequence, to 72–80 ft. lbs. Replace the valve cover.

2972CC ENGINE

1. Relieve the fuel pressure. Disconnect the negative battery cable. Drain the cooling system.
2. Remove the compressor drive belt and the air conditioning compressor from its mount and support it aside. Using a ½ in. drive breaker bar, insert it into the square hole of the serpentine drive belt tensioner, rotate it counterclockwise to reduce the belt tension and remove the belt. Remove the alternator and power steering pump from the brackets and move them aside.
3. Raise the vehicle and support safely. Remove the right front wheel and the inner splash shield.
4. Remove the crankshaft pulleys and the torsional damper.
5. Lower the vehicle. Using a floor jack and a block of wood positioned under the oil pan, raise the engine slightly. Remove the engine mount bracket from the timing cover end of the engine and the timing belt covers.
6. To remove the timing belt, perform the following procedures:
   a. Rotate the crankshaft to position the No. 1 cylinder on the TDC of its compression stroke; the crankshaft sprocket timing mark should align with the oil pan timing indicator and the camshaft sprockets timing marks (triangles) should align with the rear timing belt covers timing marks.

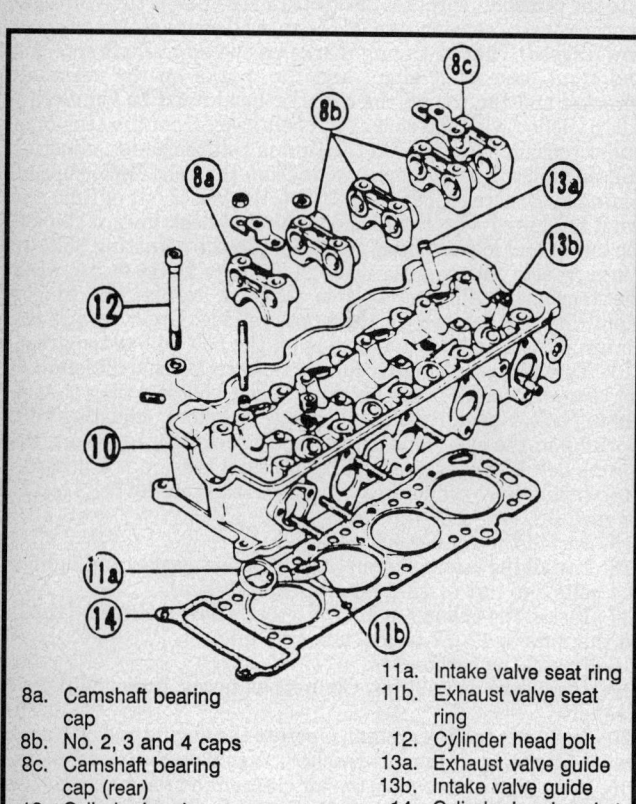

8a. Camshaft bearing cap	11a. Intake valve seat ring
8b. No. 2, 3 and 4 caps	11b. Exhaust valve seat ring
8c. Camshaft bearing cap (rear)	12. Cylinder head bolt
10. Cylinder head	13a. Exhaust valve guide
	13b. Intake valve guide
	14. Cylinder head gasket

Exploded view of the cylinder head—2351cc engine

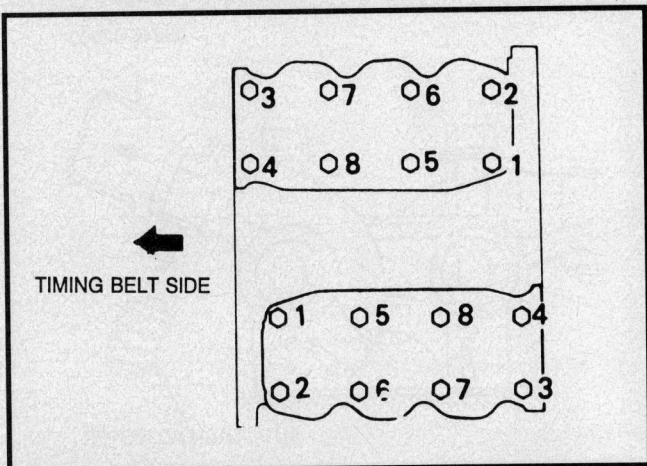

Cylinder head bolt loosening sequence—2972cc engine

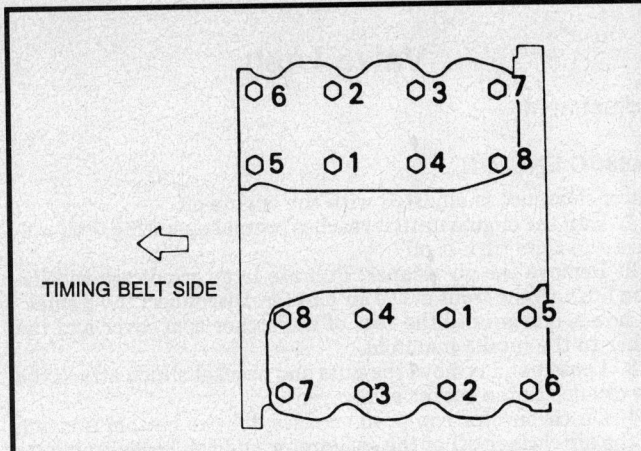

Cylinder head bolt torque sequence—2972cc engine

b. Mark the timing belt in the direction of rotation for reinstallation purposes.

c. Loosen the timing belt tensioner and remove the timing belt.

NOTE: When removing the timing belt from the camshaft sprocket, make sure the belt does not slip off of the other camshaft sprocket. Support the belt so it can not slip off of the crankshaft sprocket and opposite side camshaft sprocket.

7. Remove the air cleaner assembly. Label and disconnect the spark plug wires and the vacuum hoses.

8. Remove the valve cover.

9. Install auto lash adjuster retainer tools MD998443 or equivalent, on the rocker arms.

10. If removing the front cylinder head, matchmark the distributor rotor to the distributor housing and the housing to distributor extension locations. Remove the distributor and the distributor extension.

11. Remove the camshaft bearing assembly to cylinder head bolts but do not remove the bolts from the assembly. Remove the rocker arms, rocker shafts and bearing caps as an assembly, as required. Remove the camshafts from the cylinder head and inspect them for damage.

12. Remove the intake manifold assembly.

13. Remove the exhaust manifold.

14. Remove the cylinder head bolts, starting from the outside and working inward. Remove the cylinder head from the engine.

15. Clean the gasket mounting surfaces and check the heads for warpage; maximum warpage is 0.008 in. (0.20mm).

To install:

16. Install the new cylinder head gasket over the dowels on the engine block.

17. Install the cylinder head(s) on the engine and torque the cylinder head bolts, in sequence, using 3 even steps, to 70 ft. lbs. (95 Nm).

18. Install or connect all items that were removed or disconnected during the removal procedure.

19. When installing the timing belt over the camshaft sprocket, use care not to allow the belt to slip off the opposite camshaft sprocket.

20. Make sure the timing belt is installed on the camshaft sprocket in the same position as when removed.

21. Refill the cooling system. Connect the negative battery cable. Start the engine and check for leaks using the DRB I or II to activate the fuel pump.

22. Adjust the timing, as required.

Valve Lash Adjuster

The lash adjuster is similar to a hydraulic lifter that maintains a 0 lash adjustment. The lash adjuster is incorporated in the rocker arm and is removable. Though the lash adjuster is non-adjustable, if an abnormal tapping noise is heard during idling, air in the lash adjuster may be the problem. The adjuster can be bled and rechecked for noise.

Removal and Installation

2351CC AND 2972CC ENGINES

1. Disconnect the negative battery cable. Remove the air cleaner assembly.

2. Remove the valve cover.

NOTE: The lash adjuster is incorporated in the rocker arm on the side of the valve spring. When removing the rocker arm, a special tool must be used the prevent the lash adjuster from falling out.

3. Using the lash adjuster retainer tools MD998443 or equivalent, install them on the rocker arms.

4. On the right side cylinder head, remove the distributor extension.

5. Hold the rear end of the camshaft down. If the rear of the camshaft cannot be held down, the belt will dislodge and the valve timing will be lost. Loosen the camshaft cap bolts but do not remove them from the caps. Remove the caps, arms, shafts and bolts all as an assembly.

6. Remove the lifter(s) from the rocker arm(s).

7. Lubricate the lifter(s) and their bore(s) with clean engine oil.

8. The installation is the reverse of the removal procedure.

9. Connect the negative battery cable and check the lifters for proper operation.

Bleeding The Lash Adjusters

If the lash adjuster is removed and the diesel fuel contained inside is spilled, submerge the adjuster in clean diesel fuel and compress it several times to expel the air. If air is still trapped after assembly and installation and a clattering noise is heard when the engine is started, the air can be bled by increasing engine speed from idle to 3000 rpm and back to idle over a minute period. Do this several times, or until the clattering stops. If this does not stop the clattering, remove and submerge the lifter in clean diesel fuel, compressing it several times. If clattering continues, replace the lash adjuster.

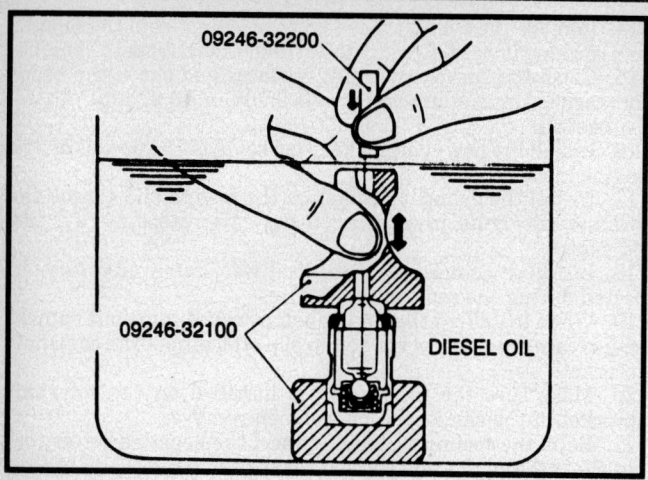

Bleeding the lash adjuster—2351cc and 2972oo engines

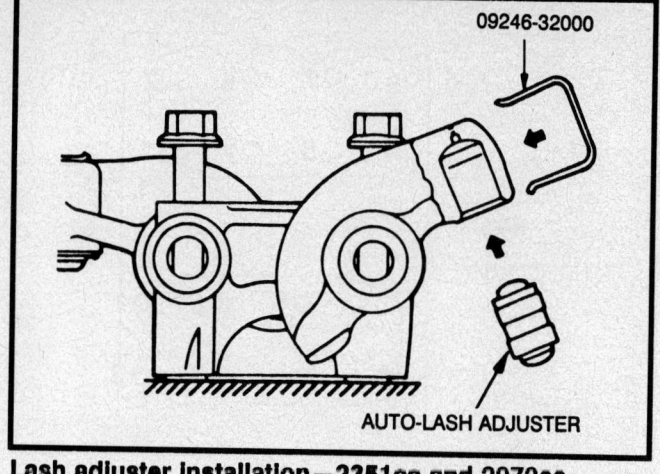

Lash adjuster installation—2351cc and 2972cc engines

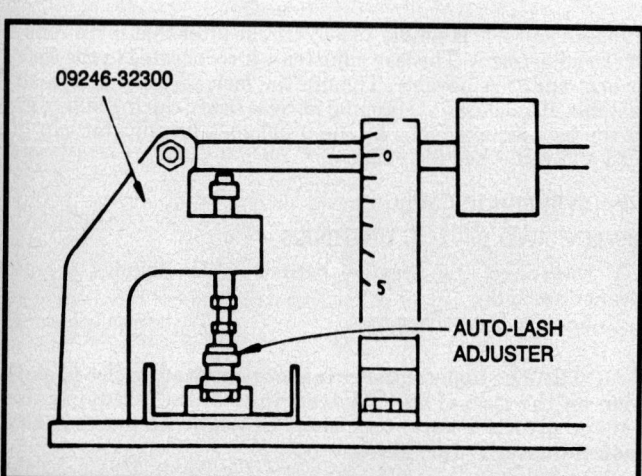

Lash adjuster leak-down—2351cc and 2972cc engines

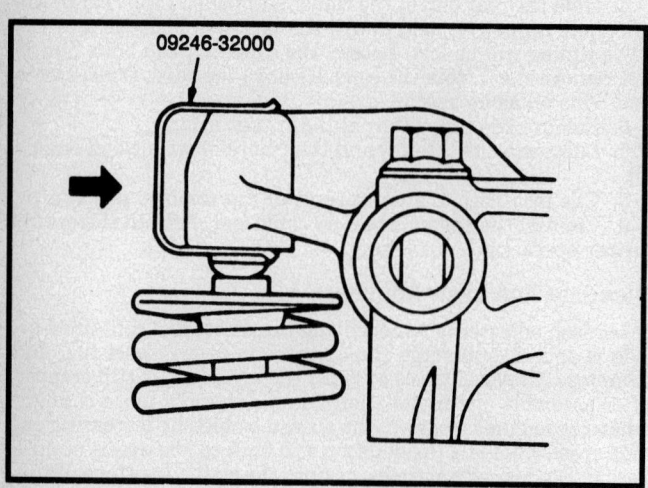

Lash adjuster holding tool installed—2351cc and 2972cc engines

Valve Lash

Adjustment

1468CC ENGINE

Valve clearance is adjusted with the engine off.

1. Run the engine until it reaches normal operating temperature and then turn it off.

2. Remove the air cleaner. Pull the large crankcase ventilation hose off the front of the air cleaner. Disconnect the 2 smaller hoses, one goes to the rear of the rocker arm cover and the other to the intake manifold.

3. Loosen and remove the nuts and bracket which attach the air cleaner to the rocker arm cover.

4. On carburetor equipped vehicles, lift the bottom housing of the air cleaner off of the carburetor and the hose coming up from the exhaust manifold heat stove.

5. Remove the spark plug wires from their clips on the rocker arm cover.

6. Using a deep socket or box wrench, remove the rocker arm cover bolts.

7. Carefully lift the rocker arm cover off the cylinder head. Using an $^5/_{16}$ in. (8mm) Allen socket and a torque wrench, make sure the cylinder head bolts are all tightened to specification.

8. Hot valve clearance is 0.006 in. (0.15mm) for the intake valves and (0.010 in. (0.25mm) for the exhaust.

9. Turn the crankshaft pulley to bring the piston to TDC of the compression stroke on the cylinder being adjusted.

10. Loosen the rocker arm adjusting screw locknuts.

11. Using the correct thickness feeler gauge, turn the adjusting screw until the gauge just snaps through the valve stem and the rocker arm.

12. Repeat the procedure to adjust the valves of each cylinder.

NOTE: Loose valve clearances will result in excessive wear and valve train chatter. Tight valve clearance will result in burnt valve seats. Make sure to set the valve clearance to the exact specifications.

13. Apply non-hardening sealer to the rocker arm cover gasket. Always use a new gasket.

14. Install the cover, hoses, spark plug wires and the air cleaner in the reverse order of removal. Tighten the rocker arm cover bolts to 48–60 inch lbs.

15. Start the engine and check for leaks.

2351CC ENGINE

Valve clearance is normally adjusted with the engine stopped and at normal operating temperature. However, after the engine has been rebuilt or a valve job done, the valves should first be set and adjusted with the engine cold. The basic procedure is the same, hot or cold, the only differences being the engine temperature and the valve clearance setting. The cold setting is 0.003 in. (0.08mm) for intake valves; 0.007 in. (0.18mm) for exhaust valves. The hot setting is 0.006 in. (0.15mm) for intake valves; 0.010 in. (0.25mm) for exhaust valves.

1. Start the engine and allow it to reach normal operating temperature.

2. Turn the engine off and disconnect the negative battery cable. Remove the air cleaner. Disconnect the large crankcase ventilation hose from the front of the air cleaner. Disconnect the smaller hoses from the rear of the rocker arm cover and the intake manifold.

3. Loosen and remove the nuts and bracket which secure the air cleaner to the rocker arm cover.

4. Lift the bottom housing of the air cleaner off of the carburetor, with the hose from the exhaust manifold heat stove attached.

5. Unsnap the spark plug wires from their clips on the rocker arm cover.

6. Remove the rocker arm cover bolts.

7. Carefully lift the rocker arm cover off the cylinder head. Using an $^5/_{16}$ in. (8mm) Allen socket and a torque wrench, torque the cylinder head bolts. Turn each bolt, in sequence, back just until it breaks loose and then torque it to 58–61 ft. lbs. After the first bolt, in sequence, has been torqued, move on to the second one, repeating the procedure. Continue, in order, until all the bolts have been torqued. Make sure the cylinder head bolts are all tightened, in sequence, to specification.

8. Remove the spark plugs.

9. Remove the distributor cap.

NOTE: A crankshaft pulley access hole is located on the left side frame member. Remove the covering plug and use a ratchet extension to turn the crankshaft when adjusting the valves.

10. Rotate the crankshaft until the No. 1 cylinder is at TDC of the compression stroke. Turn the engine by using a wrench on the bolt in the front of the crankshaft until the **TDC or 0** timing mark on the timing cover lines up with the notch in the front pulley. Observe the valve rockers for No. 1 cylinder. If both are in identical positions with the valves up, the engine is in the right position. If not, rotate the engine exactly 360 degrees until the **TDC or 0** degree timing mark is again aligned. Each jet valve is associated with an intake valve that is on the same rock-

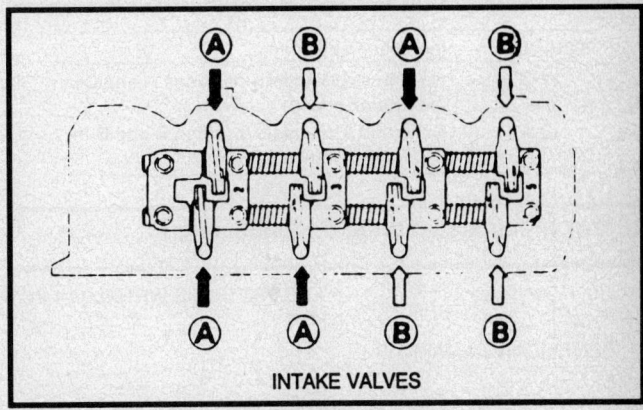

"A" and "B" valve adjusting positions—2351cc engine

er lever. In this position, adjust all the valves marked A, including associated jet valves, which are located on the rockers on the intake side only.

11. To adjust the appropriate jet valves, first loosen the regular (larger) intake valve adjusting stud by, loosening the locknut and backing the stud off 2 turns. Now, loosen the jet valve (smaller) adjusting stud locknut, back the stud out slightly and insert an 0.25mm feeler gauge between the jet valve and stud. Make sure the gauge lies flat on the top of the jet valve. Being careful not to twist the gauge or otherwise depress the jet valve spring, rotate the jet valve adjusting stud back in until it just touches the gauge. Now, tighten the locknut. Make sure the gauge still slides very easily between the stud and jet valve and they both are still just touching the gauge. Readjust, if necessary. Note that, especially with the jet valve, the clearance must not be too tight. Repeat entire the procedure for the other jet valves associated with rockers labeled A. Then, repeat the procedure for the intake valves labeled A (0.15mm).

12. Repeat the basic adjustment procedure for exhaust valves labeled A using a 0.25mm feeler gauge.

13. Turn the engine exactly 360 degrees, until the timing marks are again aligned at **TDC or 0**. First, perform the adjustment procedure for all the jet valves on rockers labeled B, intake side only. Complete the adjustment procedure for the regular intake valves labeled B. Finally, repeat the adjustment procedure for the exhaust valves labeled B.

NOTE: Loose valve clearances will result in excessive wear and valve train chatter; tight valve clearance will result in burnt valve seats.

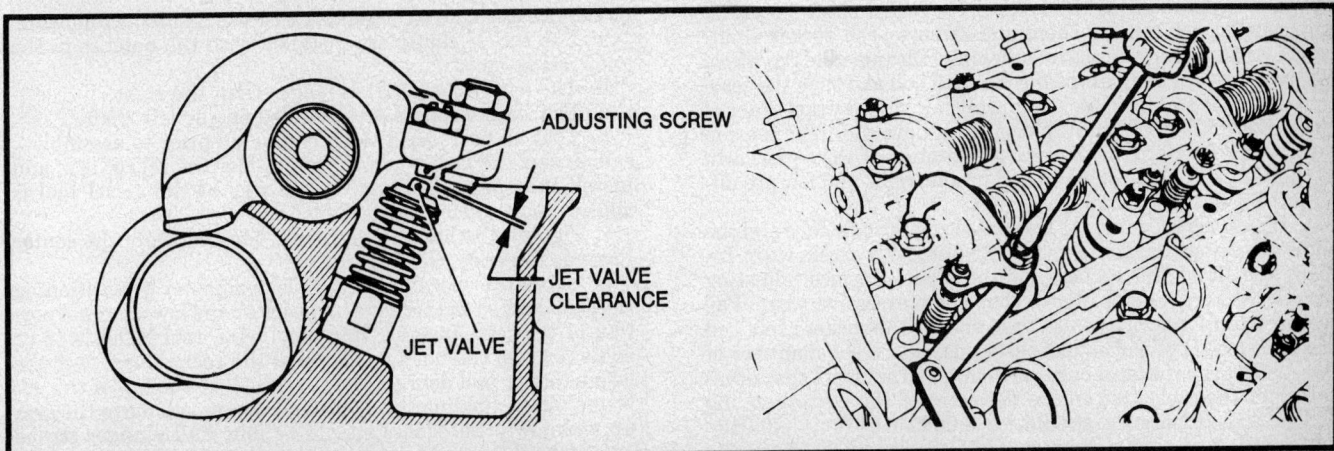

Jet valve clearance adjustment—2351cc engine

Identification	Installation position
1-3	No. 1 and 3 cylinders (positions A and C in illustration shown below)
2-4	No. 2 and 4 cylinders (position B and D in illustration shown below)

Rocker arm installation and identification

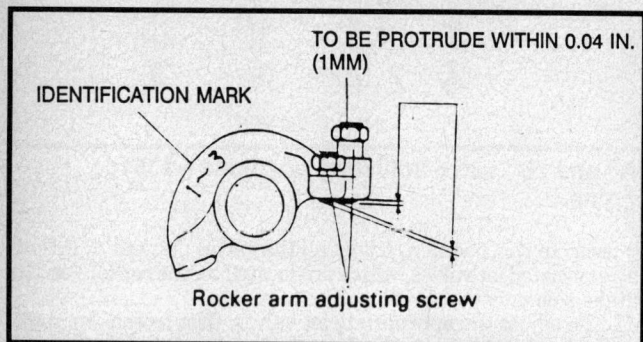

Rocker arm adjusting screw

14. Apply non-hardening sealer to the rocker arm cover gasket. Always use a new gasket.

15. Install the cover, hoses, spark plug wires and the air cleaner in the reverse order of removal. Tighten the rocker arm cover bolts to 48–60 inch lbs.

16. Start the engine and check for leaks. It's best to install new gaskets and seals wherever they are used and to observe torque specifications for the cam cover bolts.

2972CC ENGINE

The 2972cc engine uses hydraulic lash adjusters, no valve adjustment is necessary.

Rocker Arms/Shafts

Removal and Installation

1468CC ENGINE

1. Disconnect the negative battery cable. Remove the PCV hose running from the rocker cover and the air cleaner. Remove the air cleaner.

2. Remove the upper timing belt cover. Remove the rocker cover.

3. Loosen the bearing cap bolts or the rocker shaft mounting bolts but do not remove them and remove each rocker shaft, rocker arms and springs as an assembly. Disassemble the whole assembly by progressively removing each bolt and then the associated springs and rockers, keeping all parts in the exact order of disassembly. The left and right springs have different tension ratings and free length. Observe the location of the rocker arm as they are removed. Exhaust and intake, right and left are different. Do not mix them up.

4. Check the rocker arm face contacting the cam lobe and the adjusting screw that contacts the valve stem for excess wear. Inspect the fit of the rockers on the shaft. Replace adjusting screws, rockers, and/or shafts that show excessive wear. Pay special attention to the contact pad ends of the rocker arms and the ball surface of the adjustings studs. Check the diameter of the shaft at the rocker mounting points and subtract that number from the measured inside diameter of the corresponding rocker arm. Clearance should be 0.0005–0.0017 in. (0.013–0.043mm). The service limit is 0.004 in. (0.1mm). Check the rocker shaft bend. Total rocker shaft bend should be 0.002 in.

(0.05mm). Check the spring free length. Maximum free length should be 2.1 in. (53.3mm) for the exhaust side springs; 2.6 in. (66mm) for intake side springs.

To install:

5. Assemble all the parts, noting the differences between intake and exhaust parts. The intake rocker shaft is much longer; the intake rocker shaft springs are over 3 in. long, while those for the exhaust side are less than 2 in. long; intake rockers have the extra adjusting screw for the jet valve; rockers are labeled 1–3 and 2–4 for the cylinder with which they are associated. Torque the rocker shaft mounting bolts to 15–19 ft. lbs. (20–26 Nm).

6. Adjust the valve clearances. This step may be omitted only if all parts are being reused.

7. Install the rocker cover with a new gasket, torquing the bolts to 12–18 inch lbs. (1.5–2.0 Nm).

8. Install the air cleaner and PCV valve.

9. Run the engine at idle speed until it is hot. Then, unless valves did not require adjustment, remove the valve cover again and adjust the valve clearances with the engine hot.

10. Replace the rocker cover and timing belt cover, air cleaner and PCV valve.

2351CC ENGINE

NOTE: A special tool 09246-32000, is required to retain the automatic lash adjusters in this procedure.

1. Disconnect the negative battery cable. Remove the rocker cover and gasket and the timing belt cover.

2. Turn the crankshaft so the No. 1 piston is at TDC compression. At this point, the timing mark on the camshaft sprocket and the timing mark on the head to the left of the sprocket will be aligned.

3. Remove the camshaft bearing cap bolts.

4. Install the automatic lash adjuster retainer tool 09246-32000 or equivalent, to keep the adjuster from falling out of the rocker arms.

5. Lift off the bearing caps and rocker arm assemblies.

6. The rocker arms may now be removed from the shafts.

NOTE: Keep all parts in the order in which they were removed. None of the parts are interchangeable. The lash adjusters are filled with diesel fuel, which will spill out if they are inverted. If any diesel fuel is spilled, the adjusters must be bled.

7. Check all parts for wear or damage. Replace any damaged or excessively worn part.

8. Service as required, assemble all parts. Note the following:

   a. The rocker shafts are installed with the notches in the ends facing up.

   b. The left rocker shaft is longer than the right.

   c. The wave washers are installed on the left shaft.

   d. Coat all parts with clean engine oil prior to assembly.

   e. Insert the lash adjuster from under the rocker arm and install the special holding tool. If any of the diesel fuel is spilled, the adjuster must be bled.

   f. Tighten the bearing cap bolts, working from the center towards the ends, to 15 ft. lbs.

   g. Check the operation of each lash adjuster by positioning the camshaft so the rocker arm bears on the low or round portion of the cam. Insert a thin steel wire, tool MD998442 or equivalent, in the hole in the top of the rocker arm, over the lash adjuster and depress the check ball at the top of the adjuster. While holding the check ball depressed, move the arm up and down. Looseness should be felt. Full plunger stroke should be 2.2mm. If not, remove, clean and bleed the lash adjuster.

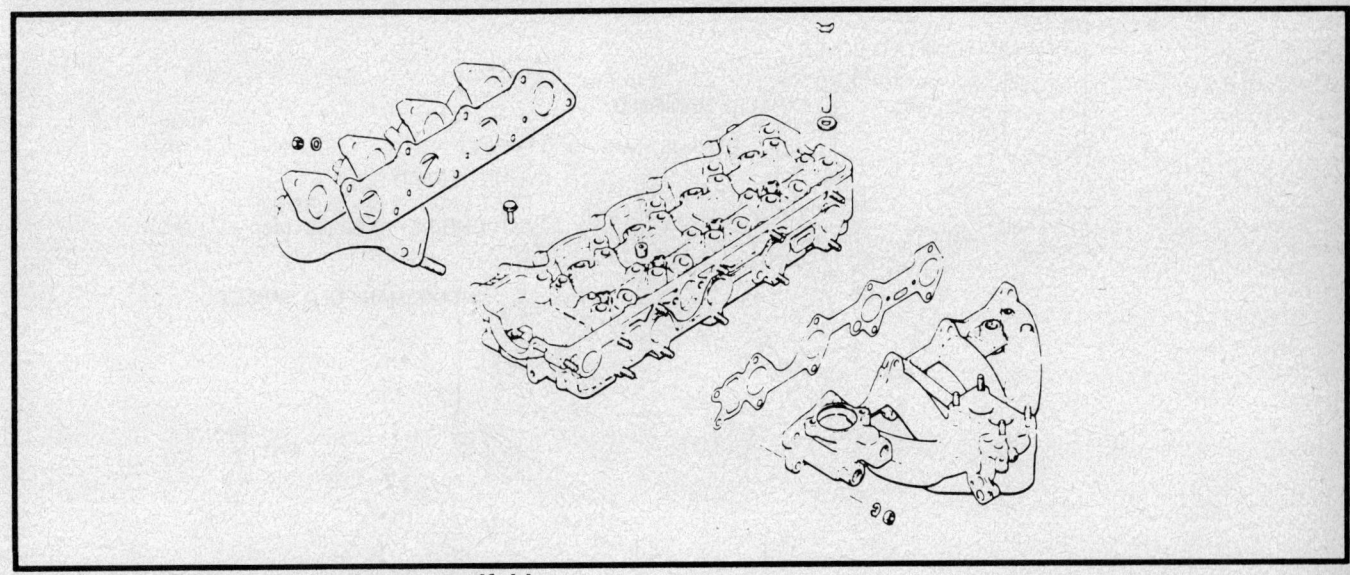

1468cc engine intake and exhaust manifolds

Intake Manifold

Removal and Installation

1468CC ENGINE

1. Disconnect the negative battery cable. Remove the air cleaner assembly.
2. Disconnect the fuel line and the EGR lines, if equipped with EGR. Tag and disconnect all vacuum hoses.
3. Disconnect the throttle positioner and fuel cut-off solenoid wires.
4. Disconnect the throttle linkage.
5. If equipped with an automatic transaxle, disconnect the shift cable linkage.
6. Disconnect the power brake booster vacuum line.
7. Drain the cooling system.
8. Disconnect the choke water hose at the manifold.
9. Remove the heater and water outlet hoses, disconnect the water temperature sending unit.
10. Remove the mounting nuts that hold the manifold to the cylinder head. Remove the intake manifold.

To install:

11. Clean all mounting surfaces. Before installing the manifold, coat both sides of a new gasket with a gasket sealer.

NOTE: If equipped with jet air system, take care not to get any sealer into the jet air intake passage.

12. Install the intake manifold assembly to the engine block.
13. Reconnect the heater and water outlet hoses. Connect the water temperature sending unit.
14. Connect the brake booster vacuum line. Connect the choke hose at the manifold.
15. Connect the throttle and shift cable linkages, the fuel lines and all vacuum hoses. Install the air cleaner.
16. Refill the engine with coolant. Connect the negative battery cable.

2351CC ENGINE

1. Disconnect the negative battery cable. Remove the air cleaner assembly.
2. Release fuel system pressure. Disconnect the fuel line and the EGR lines. Tag and disconnect all vacuum hoses.
3. Disconnect the throttle positioner and fuel cut-off solenoid wires.

4. Disconnect the throttle linkage. If equipped with automatic transaxle, disconnect the shift cable linkage.
5. Remove the heater and water outlet hoses, disconnect the water temperature sending unit. Disconnect the oxygen sensor connecter, power transistor connecter, ISC connector, ignition coil connector, etc. and the distributor.
7. Remove the mounting nuts that hold the manifold to the cylinder head. Remove the intake manifold lower and upper sections with injector assembly as a unit.
8. Clean all mounting surfaces. Before installing the manifold, coat both sides with a gasket sealer.

To install:

9. Clean all mounting surfaces. Before installing the manifold, coat both sides of a new gasket with a gasket sealer.

NOTE: If equipped with jet air system, take care not to get any sealer into the jet air intake passage.

10. Install the intake manifold lower and upper sections with injector assembly as a unit. Install the mounting nuts that hold the manifold to the cylinder head.
11. Install the heater and water outlet hoses, disconnect the water temperature sending unit. Connect the oxygen sensor connecter, power transistor connecter, ISC connector, ignition coil connector, etc. and the distributor.
12. Connect the throttle linkage. If equipped with automatic transaxle, connect the shift cable linkage.
13. Connect the throttle positioner and fuel cut-off solenoid wires.
14. Connect the fuel line the EGR lines. Connect all vacuum hoses.
15. Refill the engine with coolant. Connect the negative battery cable.

2972CC ENGINE

1. Disconnect the negative battery cable. Relieve the fuel system pressure.
2. Drain the cooling system.
3. Remove the throttle body to air cleaner hose.
4. Remove the throttle body and transaxle kickdown linkage.
5. Remove the AIS motor and TPS wiring connectors from the throttle body.
6. Remove and label the vacuum hose harness from the throttle body.

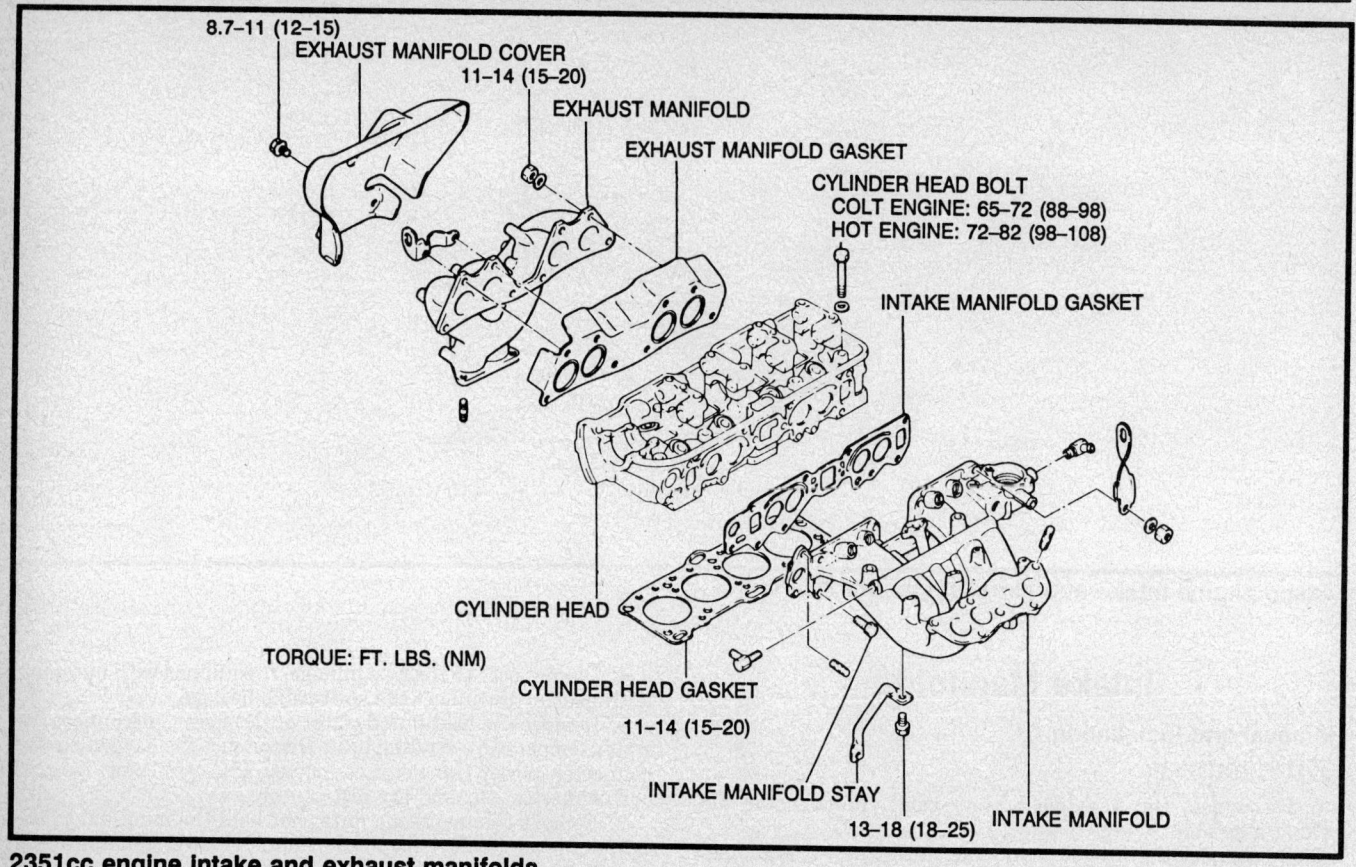

8.7–11 (12–15)
EXHAUST MANIFOLD COVER
11–14 (15–20)
EXHAUST MANIFOLD
EXHAUST MANIFOLD GASKET
CYLINDER HEAD BOLT
COLT ENGINE: 65–72 (88–98)
HOT ENGINE: 72–82 (98–108)
INTAKE MANIFOLD GASKET
CYLINDER HEAD
TORQUE: FT. LBS. (NM)
CYLINDER HEAD GASKET
11–14 (15–20)
INTAKE MANIFOLD STAY
13–18 (18–25)
INTAKE MANIFOLD

2351cc engine intake and exhaust manifolds

7. From the air intake plenum, remove the PCV and brake booster hoses and the EGR tube flange.

8. Disconnect and label the charge and temperature sensor wiring at the intake manifold.

9. Remove the vacuum connections from the air intake plenum vacuum connector.

10. Remove the fuel hoses from the fuel rail.

11. Remove the air intake plenum mounting bolts and the plenum.

12. Remove the vacuum hoses from the fuel rail and pressure regulator.

13. Disconnect the fuel injector wiring harness from the engine wiring harness.

14. Remove the fuel pressure regulator mounting bolts and the regulator from the fuel rail.

15. Remove the fuel rail mounting bolts and the fuel rail from the intake manifold.

16. Separate the radiator hose from the thermostat housing and heater hoses from the heater pipe.

17. Remove the intake manifold mounting bolts and the manifold from the engine.

18. Clean the gasket mounting surfaces on the engine and intake manifold.

To install:

19. Using new gaskets, position the intake manifold on the engine and install the mounting nuts and washers.

20. Torque the mounting nuts gradually and evenly, in sequence, to 15 ft. lbs. (20 Nm).

21. Make sure the injector holes are clean. Lubricate the injector O-rings with a drop of clean engine oil and install the injector assembly onto the engine.

22. Install and torque the fuel rail mounting bolts to 10 ft. lbs. (14 Nm).

23. Install the fuel pressure regulator onto the fuel rail.

24. Install the fuel supply and return tube and the vacuum crossover hold-down bolt.

25. Connect the fuel injection wiring harness to the engine wiring harness.

26. Connect the vacuum harness to the fuel pressure regulator and fuel rail assembly.

27. Remove the cover from the lower intake manifold and clean the mating surface.

28. Place the intake plenum gasket with the beaded sealant side up, on the intake manifold. Install the air intake plenum and torque the mounting bolts gradually and evenly, in sequence, to 10 ft. lbs. (14 Nm).

29. Connect or install all remaining items that were disconnected or removed during the removal procedure.

30. Refill the cooling system. Connect the negative battery cable and check for leaks using the DRB I or II to activate the fuel pump.

Exhaust Manifold

Removal and Installation

1468CC ENGINE

1. Disconnect the negative battery cable. Remove the air cleaner. Remove the heat stove and/or heat shield on the exhaust manifold, if equipped. With the manifold cool, soak all manifold nuts and studs with a liquid penetrant.

2. Disconnect the exhaust pipe at the exhaust manifold. Disconnect and remove the oxygen sensor. If there is a secondary air line connected to the exhaust manifold, disconnect it. First remove the exhaust pipe, then the secondary air supply pipe.

3. Support the manifold and remove all attaching nuts and washers. Slide the manifold from the cylinder head. Remove the converter mounting bolts. When the converter is disconnected,

remove the exhaust manifold, if necessary, rock it to break it loose.

4. Thoroughly clean the sealing surfaces on the cylinder head and manifold. Replace any nuts, washers or studs that are excessively rusted or may have been damaged during removal. Use a straight-edge to check the manifold and cylinder head sealing surfaces for flatness. Correct problems by replacing the manifold or machining the cylinder head surface.

To install:

5. Install new gaskets in such a way that all bolt holes and ports are aligned.

6. Make sure all the nuts turn freely, oiling them lightly, if necessary. Also, make sure all the studs are screwed all the way into the block.

7. Place the manifold in position and support it, install all washers and nuts hand tight.

8. Torque the exhaust manifold-to-cylinder head nuts to 14 ft. lbs. (20 Nm), alternately and in several stages.

9. Install piping, heat stoves and shields. Connect the exhaust pipe or primary catalytic converter.

10. Connect the negative battery cable. Operate the engine and check for leaks.

2351CC ENGINE

1. Disconnect the negative battery cable. Remove the air cleaner assembly.

2. Disconnect any EGR or heat lines. Disconnect the reed valve, if equipped.

3. Remove the exhaust pipe support bracket from the engine block, if equipped.

4. Remove the exhaust pipe from exhaust manifold by removing the exhaust pipe flange nuts. It may be necessary to remove 1 nut or bolt from underneath the vehicle.

5. If equipped with a catalytic converter mounted between the exhaust manifold and exhaust pipe, remove the exhaust pipe and the secondary air supply pipe.

6. Remove the nuts mounting the exhaust manifold to the cylinder head. Slide the manifold from the cylinder head, to provide enough room to remove the converter mounting bolts. When the converter is disconnected, remove the exhaust manifold.

To install:

7. Installation is the reverse order of the removal procedure. Install the exhaust manifold with new gaskets. New gaskets should be used and on some engines, port liner gaskets are used.

8. Torque the exhaust manifold-to-cylinder head bolts to 14 ft. lbs. (20 Nm).

2972CC ENGINE

1. Disconnect the negative battery cable. Raise the vehicle and support safely.

2. Disconnect the exhaust pipe from the rear exhaust manifold at the articulated joint.

3. Disconnect the EGR tube from the rear manifold and unplug the oxygen sensor wire.

4. Remove the crossover pipe to manifold bolts.

5. Remove the rear manifold to cylinder head nuts and the manifold.

6. Lower the vehicle and remove the heat shield from the manifold.

7. Remove the front manifold-to-cylinder head nuts and the manifold.

8. Clean the gasket mounting surfaces. Inspect the manifolds for cracks, flatness and/or damage.

To install:

9. When installing, the numbers 1–3–5 on the gaskets are used with the rear cylinders and 2–4–6 are on the gasket for the front cylinders. Torque the manifold-to-cylinder head nuts to 14 ft. lbs. (20 Nm).

10. Install the crossover pipe to the manifold.

11. Connect the EGR tube and oxygen sensor wire.

12. Connect the exhaust pipe to the rear exhaust manifold, at the articulated joint.

13. Connect the negative battery cable and check the manifolds for leaks.

Timing Belt Cover, Sprockets, Tensioner and Timing Belt

Removal and Installation

1468CC ENGINE

1. Disconnect the negative battery cable. Remove the timing belt cover.

2. Turn the crankshaft until the timing marks on the camshaft sprocket and cylinder head are aligned. Loosen the tensioning bolt, it runs in the slotted portion of the tensioner, and the pivot bolt on the timing belt tensioner. Move the tensioner as far as it will go toward the water pump. Tighten the adjusting bolt. Mark the timing belt with an arrow showing direction of rotation.

3. Pull the timing belt off the camshaft sprocket. Remove the camshaft sprocket.

4. Remove the crankshaft pulley. Then, remove the timing belt.

5. Remove the crankshaft sprocket bolts and remove the crankshaft sprocket and flange, noting the direction of installation for each. Remove the timing belt tensioner.

6. Inspect the belt thoroughly. The back surface must be pliable and rough. If it is hard and glossy, the belt should be replaced. Any cracks in the belt backing or teeth or missing teeth mean the belt must be replaced. The canvas cover should be intact on all the teeth. If rubber is exposed anywhere, the belt should be replaced.

7. Inspect the tensioner for grease leaking from the grease seal and any roughness in rotation. Replace a tensioner for either defect.

8. The sprockets should be inspected and replaced, if there is any sign of damaged teeth or cracking anywhere. Do not immerse sprockets in solvent, as solvent that has soaked into the metal may cause deterioration of the timing belt later. Do not clean the tensioner in solvent either, as this may wash the grease out of the bearing.

To install:

9. Install the flange and crankshaft sprocket. The flange must go on first with the chamfered area outward. The sprocket is installed with the boss forward and the studs for the fan belt pulley outward. Install and torque the crankshaft sprocket bolt to 37–43 ft. lbs. (49–58 Nm) on 1987 engines or 51–72 ft. lbs. (69–98 Nm) on 1988–91 engines. Install the camshaft sprocket and bolt, torquing it to 47–54 ft. lbs. (64–74 Nm).

10. Align the timing marks of the camshaft sprocket. Check that the crankshaft timing marks are still in alignment (the locating pin on the front of the crankshaft sprocket is aligned with a mark on the front case).

11. Mount the tensioner, spring and spacer with the bottom end of the spring free. Then, install the bolts and tighten the adjusting bolt slightly with the tensioner moved as far as possible away from the water pump. Install the free end of the spring into the locating tang on the front case. Position the belt over the crankshaft sprocket and then over the camshaft sprocket. Slip the back of the belt over the tensioner wheel. Turn the camshaft sprocket in the opposite of its normal direction of rotation until the straight side of the belt is tight and make sure the timing marks align. If not, shift the belt 1 tooth at a time in the appropriate direction until this occurs.

12. Loosen the tensioner mounting bolts so the tensioner works, without the interference of any friction, under spring pressure. Make sure the belt follows the curve of the camshaft pulley so the teeth are engaged all the way around.

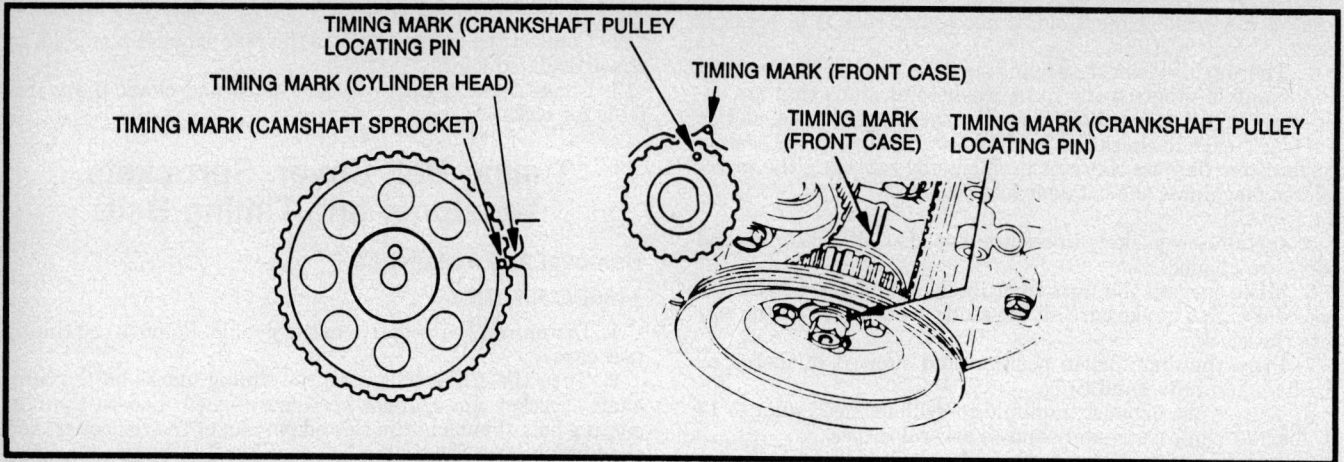

Installing the crankshaft and camshaft sprockets on the 1468cc engine

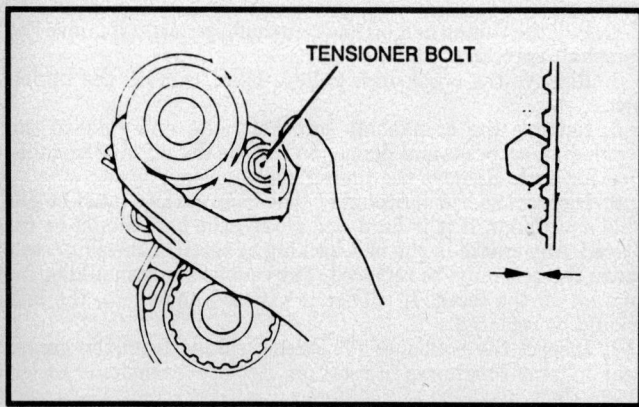

Checking belt tension on the 1468cc engine

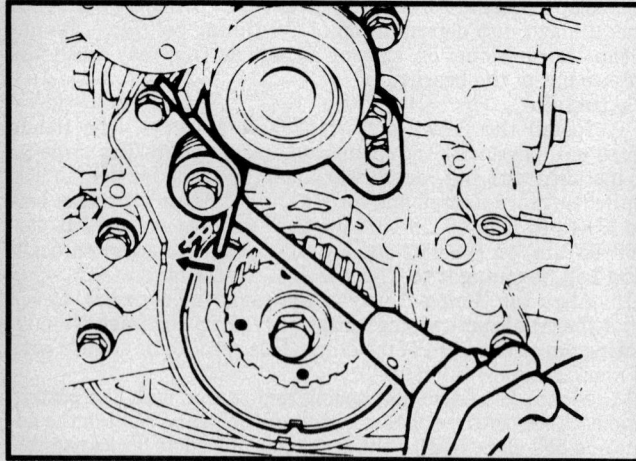

Installing the belt tensioner spring on the 1468cc engine

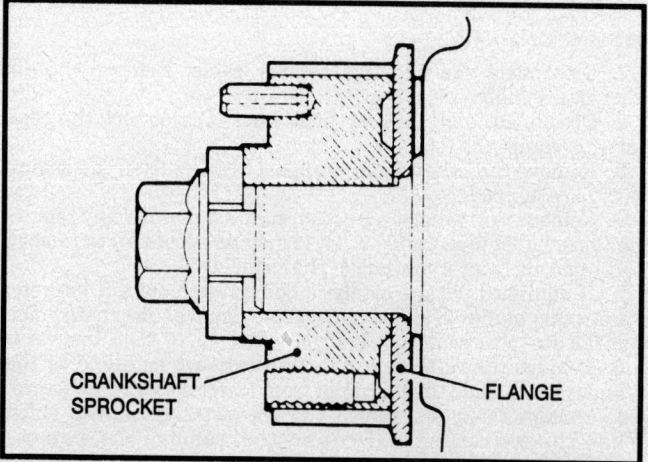

Installing the crankshaft sprocket on the 1468cc engine

13. Correct the path of the belt, if necessary. Torque the tensioner adjusting bolt to 15–18 ft. lbs. (20–26 Nm). Then, torque the tensioner pivot bolt to the same figure. Bolts must be torqued, in order, or tension won't be correct.

14. Turn the crankshaft 1 turn clockwise until timing marks again align to seat the belt. Loosen both tensioner attaching bolts and let the tensioner position itself under spring tension as before. Torque the bolts in order. Check belt tension by putting a finger on the water pump side of the tensioner wheel and pull the belt toward it. The belt should move toward the pump until the teeth are about ¼ of the way across the head of the tensioner adjusting bolt. Retension the belt, if necessary.

15. Install the timing belt covers.

16. Install the crankshaft pulley, making sure the pin on the crankshaft sprocket fits through the hole in the rear surface of the pulley. Install the bolts and torque to 7.5–8.5 ft. lbs. (9–12 Nm). Connect the negative battery cable.

2351CC ENGINE

NOTE: An 8mm diameter metal bar is needed for this procedure.

1. Disconnect the negative battery cable. Remove the water pump drive belt and pulley.

2. Remove the crank adapter and crankshaft pulley.

3. Remove the upper and lower timing belt covers.

4. Move the tensioner fully in the direction of the water pump and temporarily secure it there.

5. Make a paint mark on the belt to indicate the direction of rotation. Slip the belt from the sprockets.

NOTE: Place the belt in an area where it will not be contacted by oil or other petroleum distillates.

6. Remove the camshaft sprocket bolt and pull the sprocket from the camshaft.

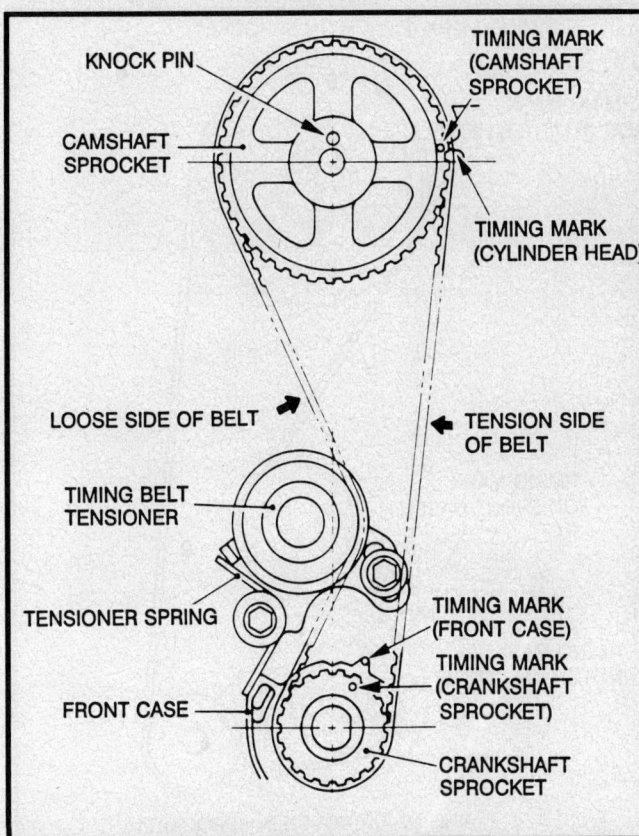

1468cc engine timing belt installation and timing mark alignment

7. Remove the crankshaft sprocket bolt and pull the crankshaft sprocket and flange from the crankshaft.
8. Remove the plug on the left side the block and insert an 8mm diameter metal bar in the opening to keep the silent shaft in position.
9. Remove the oil pump sprocket retaining nut and the oil pump sprocket.
10. Loosen the right silent shaft sprocket mounting bolt until it can be turned by hand.
11. Remove the silent shaft belt tensioner and slip the silent shaft belt off its sprockets.

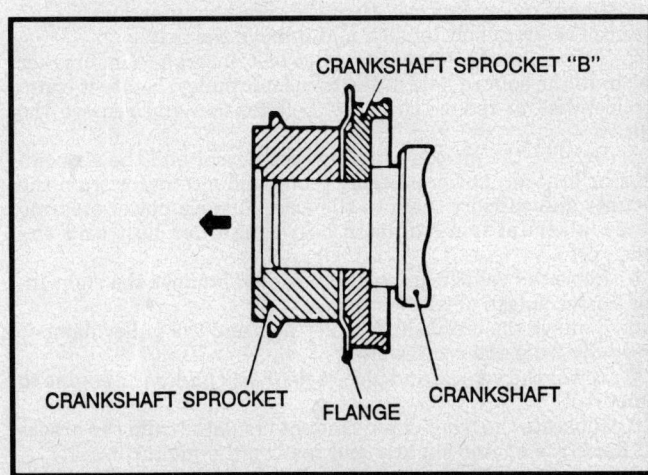

Crankshaft sprocket installation on the 2351cc

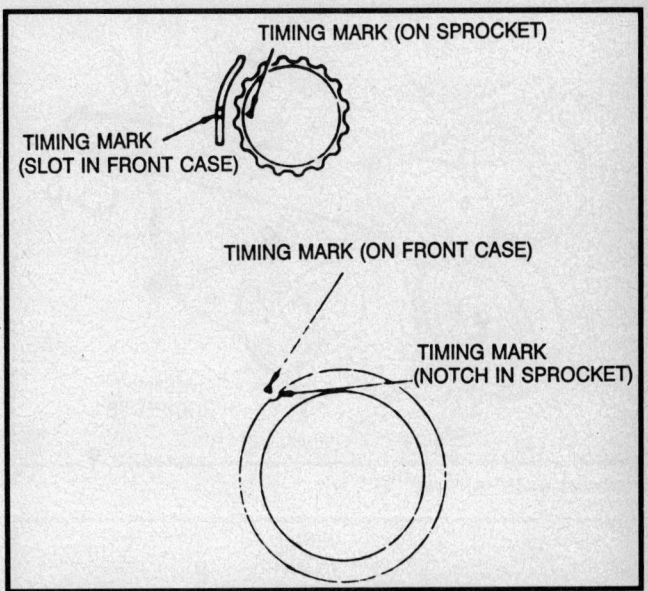

2351cc right counterbalance shaft timing mark alignment

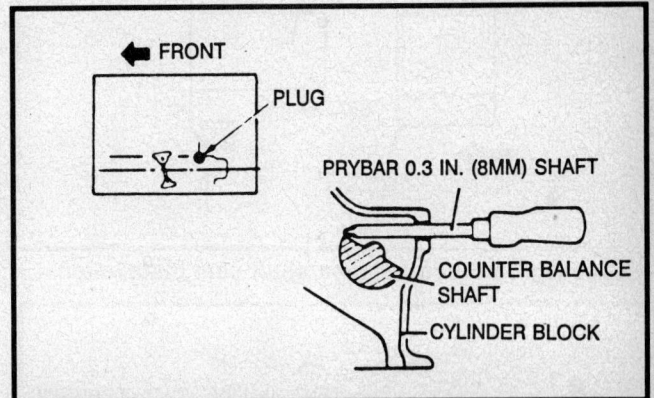

Holding the counterbalance shaft with an 8mm bar

NOTE: Do not attempt to turn the silent shaft sprocket or loosen its bolt while the belt is off.

12. Remove the silent shaft belt sprocket from the crankshaft.
13. Check the belt for wear, damage or glossing. Replace it if any cracks, damage, brittleness or excessive wear are found.
14. Check the tensioners for a smooth rate of movement.
15. Replace any tensioner that shows grease leakage through the seal.
To install:
16. Install the silent shaft belt sprocket on the crankshaft, with the flat face toward the engine.
17. Apply light engine oil on the outer face of the spacer and install the spacer on the right silent shaft. The side with the rounded shoulder faces the engine.
18. Install the sprocket on the right silent shaft and install the bolt finger tight.
19. Install the silent shaft belt and adjust the tension, by moving the tensioner into contact with the belt, tight enough to remove all slack. Tighten the tensioner bolt to 21 ft. lbs.
20. Tighten the silent shaft sprocket bolt to 28 ft. lbs.
21. Install the flange and crankshaft sprocket on the crankshaft. The flange conforms to the front of the silent shaft sprocket and the timing belt sprocket is installed with the flat face toward the engine.

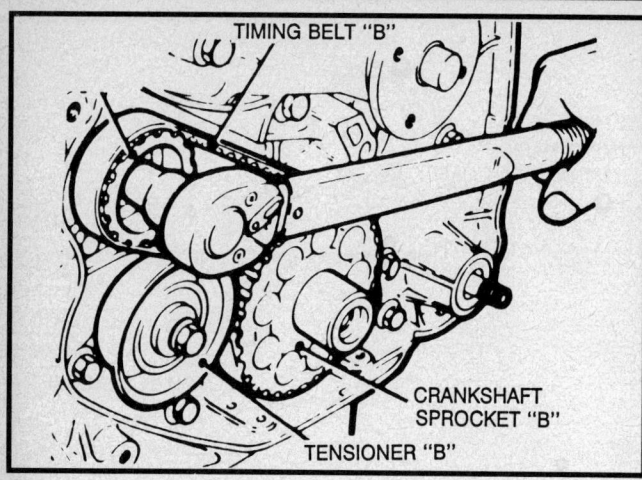

Removing tensioner "B"

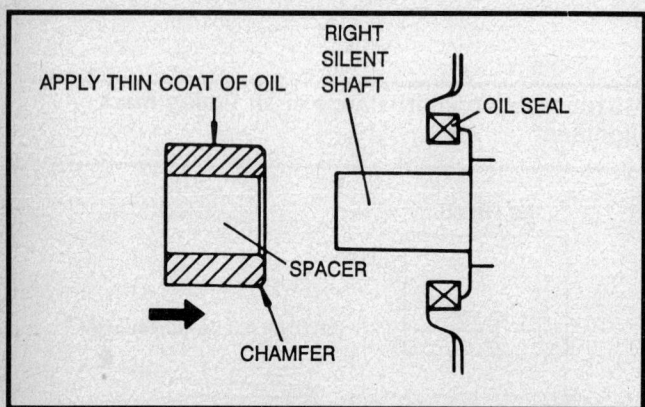

2351cc right counterbalance shaft seal installation

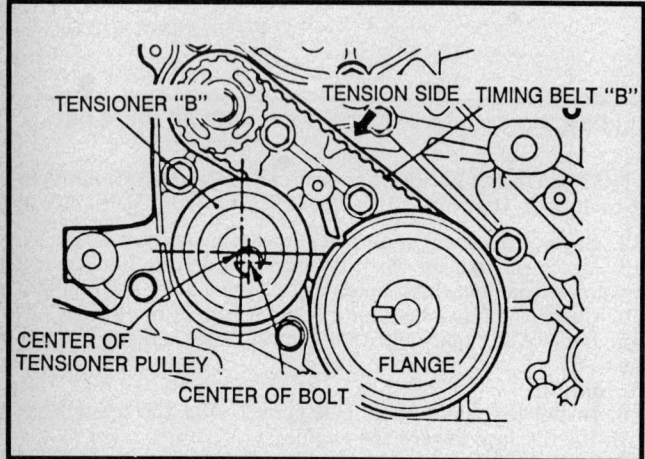

Checking timing belt tension on the 2351cc

NOTE: The flange must be installed correctly or a broken belt will be the result.

22. Install the washer and bolt in the crankshaft and torque it to 94 ft. lbs.
23. Install the camshaft sprocket and bolt and torque the bolt to 72 ft. lbs.
24. Install the timing belt tensioner, spacer and spring.
25. Align the timing mark on each sprocket with the corresponding mark on the front case.

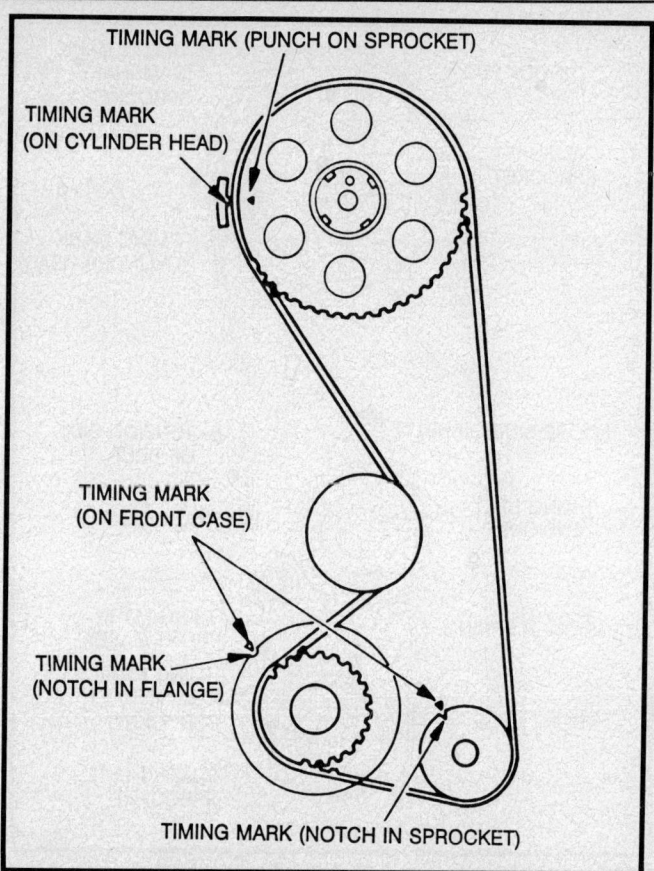

2351cc timing belt installation

26. Install the timing belt on the sprockets and move the tensioner against the belt with sufficient force to allow a deflection of 5–7mm along its longest straight run.
27. Tighten the tensioner bolt to 21 ft. lbs.
28. Install the upper and lower covers, the crankshaft pulley and the crank adapter. Tighten the bolts to 21 ft. lbs.
29. Remove the 8mm bar and install the plug.

2972CC ENGINE

1. Disconnect the negative battery cable.
2. To remove the air conditioning compressor belt, loosen the adjustment pulley locknut, turn the screw counterclockwise to reduce the drive belt tension and remove the belt.
3. To remove the serpentine drive belt, insert a ½ in. breaker bar in to the square hole of the tensioner pulley, rotate it counterclockwise to reduce the drive belt tension and remove the belt.
4. Remove the air conditioning compressor and the air compressor bracket, power steering pump and alternator from the mounts and support them to the side. Remove power steering pump/alternator automatic belt tensioner bolt and the tensioner.
5. Raise the vehicle and support safely. Remove the right inner fender splash shield.
6. Remove the crankshaft pulley bolt and the pulley/damper assembly from the crankshaft.
7. Lower the vehicle and place a floor jack under the engine to support it.
8. Separate the front engine mount insulator from the bracket. Raise the engine slightly and remove the mount bracket.
9. Remove the timing belt cover bolts and the upper and lower covers from the engine.

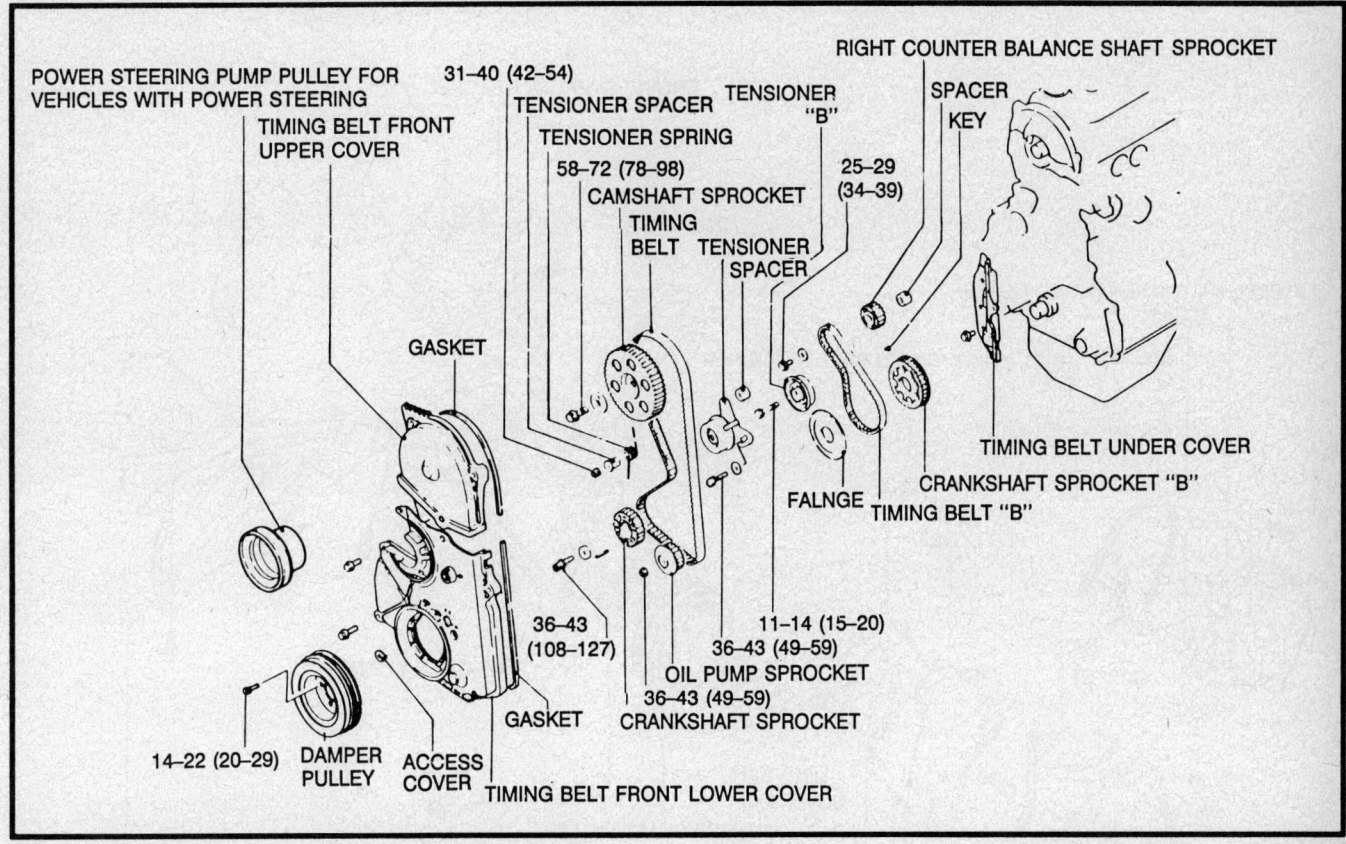

2351cc timing belt, cover and related components

10. Turn the crankshaft until the timing marks on the camshaft sprocket and cylinder head are aligned.

11. Loosen the tensioning bolt, it runs in the slotted portion of the tensioner, and the pivot bolt on the timing belt tensioner.

12. Move the tensioner as far as it will go toward the water pump. Tighten the adjusting bolt.

13. Mark the timing belt with an arrow showing direction of rotation.

14. Pull the timing belt off the camshaft sprocket.

15. Remove the crankshaft pulley. Then, remove the timing belt. Remove the timing belt tensioner.

16. Inspect the belt thoroughly. The back surface must be pliable and rough. If it is hard and glossy, the belt should be replaced. Any cracks in the belt backing or teeth or missing teeth mean the belt must be replaced. The canvas cover should be intact on all the teeth. If rubber is exposed anywhere, the belt should be replaced.

17. Inspect the tensioner for grease leaking from the grease seal and any roughness in rotation. Replace a tensioner for either defect.

18. The sprockets should be inspected and replaced if there is any sign of damaged teeth or cracking anywhere.

19. Do not immerse sprockets in solvent, as solvent that has soaked into the metal may cause deterioration of the timing belt later.

20. Do not clean the tensioner in solvent either, as this may wash the grease out of the bearing.

To install:

21. Align the timing marks of the camshaft sprocket. Check that the crankshaft timing marks are still in alignment, the locating pin on the front of the crankshaft sprocket is aligned with a mark on the front case.

22. Mount the tensioner, spring and spacer with the bottom end of the spring free. Then, install the bolts and tighten the adjusting bolt slightly with the tensioner moved as far as possible away from the water pump. Install the free end of the spring into the locating tang on the front case. Position the belt over the crankshaft sprocket and then over the camshaft sprocket. Slip the back of the belt over the tensioner wheel. Turn the camshaft sprocket in the opposite of its normal direction of rotation until the straight side of the belt is tight and make sure the timing marks align. If not, shift the belt 1 tooth at a time in the appropriate direction until this occurs.

23. Loosen the tensioner mounting bolts so the tensioner works, without the interference of any friction, under spring pressure. Make sure the belt follows the curve of the camshaft pulley so the teeth are engaged all the way around.

24. Correct the path of the belt, if necessary. Torque the tensioner adjusting bolt to 16–21 ft. lbs. (22–29 Nm). Then, torque the tensioner pivot bolt to the same figure. Bolts must be torqued in that order, or tension won't be correct.

25. Turn the crankshaft 1 turn clockwise until timing marks again align to seat the belt. Then loosen both tensioner attaching bolts and let the tensioner position itself under spring tension as before. Finally, torque the bolts in the proper order exactly as before. Check belt tension by putting a finger on the water pump side of the tensioner wheel and pull the belt toward it. The belt should move toward the pump until the teeth are about ¼ of the way across the head of the tensioner adjusting bolt. Retension the belt, if necessary.

26. Install the timing belt covers.

27. Install the crankshaft pulley, making sure the pin on the crankshaft sprocket fits through the hole in the rear surface of the pulley. Install the retaining bolt and torque to 108–116 ft. lbs. (147–157 Nm).

28. Install the engine mount bracket. The engine mount through bolt must be torqued to 75 ft. lbs. (102 Nm) on 1988 ve-

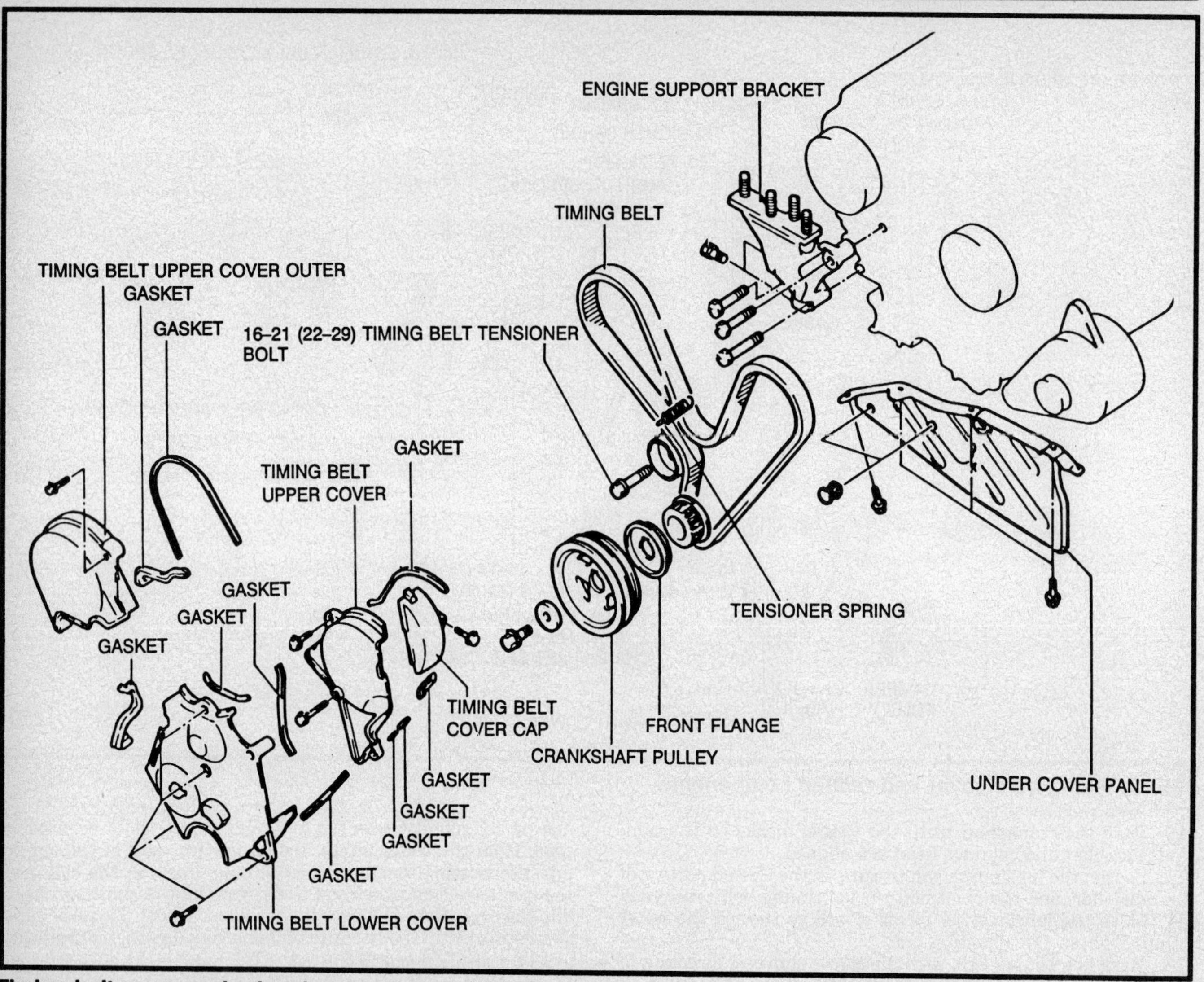

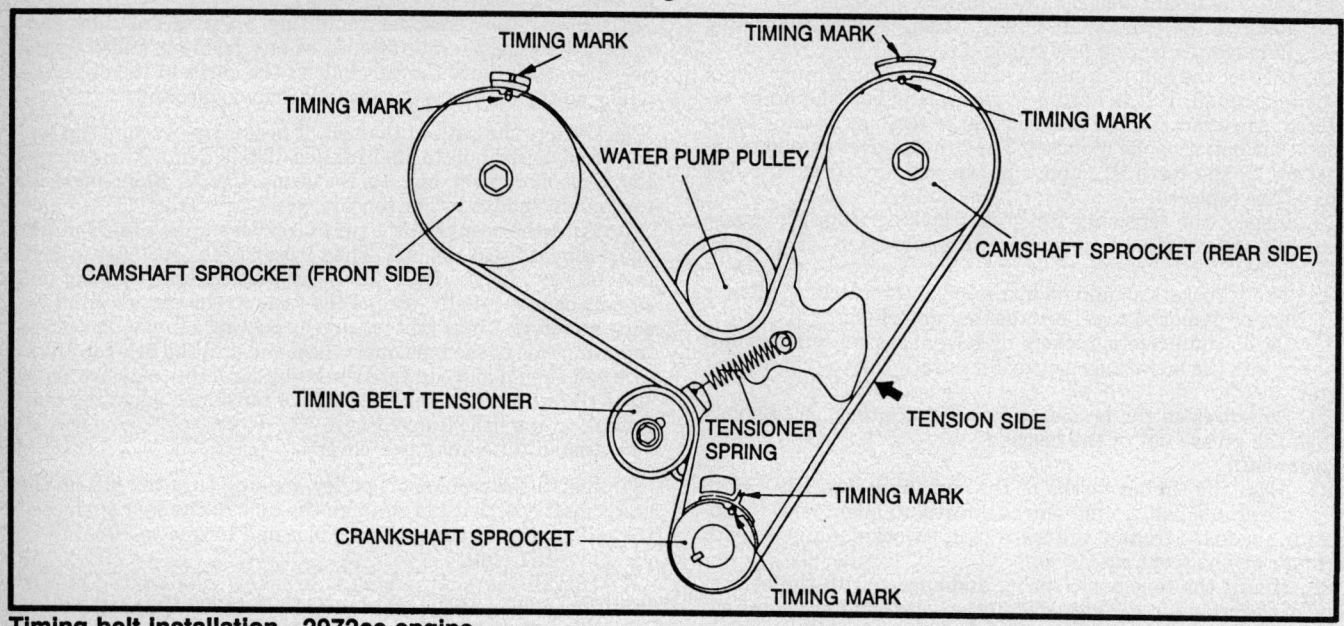

Timing belt cover and related components—2972cc engine

Timing belt installation—2972cc engine

hicles or 100 ft. lbs. (136 Nm) on 1989–91 vehicles, with the engine support removed and the engine's weight on the mount.

29. Install the pulley damper assembly to the crankshaft. Torque the bolt to 110 ft. lbs. (149 Nm). Install the splash shield.

30. Install the power steering pump/alternator automatic belt tensioner.

31. Install the air conditioning compressor bracket, compressor, power steering pump and alternator.

32. Install the belts.

33. Connect the negative battery cable and check all disturbed components for proper operation.

Oil Seal Replacement

1. Disconnect the negative battery cable.

2. Remove the air pump and alternator drive belts. Remove the air pump mounting bracket.

3. Raise and safely support the vehicle. Remove the right inner splash shield.

4. Remove the crankshaft pulley bolt and washer and remove the pulley.

5. Install a seal remover tool over crankshaft nose and turn it tightly into the seal.

6. Tighten the thrust screw to remove the seal.

NOTE: If the front cover is removed from the engine, tap the side of the thrust screw to remove the seal.

To install:

7. Using a oil seal installation tool, drive the new seal into the front cover.

8. Install the crankshaft pulley, washer and retaining bolt.

9. Install the right inner splash shield and lower the vehicle.

10. Install the air pump mounting bracket, air pump and alternator drive belts.

11. Connect the negative battery cable.

Timing Sprockets

Removal and Installation

1. Disconnect the negative battery cable. Remove the timing belt cover upper and lower covers.

2. Turn the crankshaft until the timing marks on the camshaft sprocket and cylinder head are aligned.

3. Loosen the tensioning bolt, it runs in the slotted portion of the tensioner, and the pivot bolt on the timing belt tensioner.

4. Move the tensioner as far as it will go toward the water pump. Tighten the adjusting bolt.

5. Mark the timing belt with an arrow showing direction of rotation.

6. Remove the timing belt from the camshaft sprocket. Remove the camshaft sprocket retaining bolt. Remove the camshaft sprocket.

7. Remove the crankshaft pulley. Remove the timing belt completely.

8. Remove the crankshaft sprocket retaining bolt and remove the crankshaft sprocket and flange, noting the direction of installation for each.

9. The sprockets should be inspected and replaced if there is any sign of damaged teeth or cracking anywhere.

10. Do not immerse sprockets in solvent, as solvent that has soaked into the metal may cause deterioration of the timing belt later.

To install:

11. Install the camshaft sprocket and retaining bolt. Make sure the timing marks are alignment. Observe the following torque values:

1468cc engine – 54 ft. lbs. (74 Nm)
2351cc engine – 72 ft. lbs. (98 Nm)
2972cc engine – 72 ft. lbs. (98 Nm).

12. Install the flange and crankshaft sprocket. The flange must go on first with the chamfered area outward. The sprocket is installed with the boss forward and the studs for the fan belt pulley outward.

13. Install the crankshaft sprocket and install the retaining bolt. Observe the following torque values:

1987 vehicles equipped with 1468cc engine – 43 ft. lbs. (58 Nm)

1988–91 vehicles equipped with 1468cc engine – 72 ft. lbs. (98 Nm)

2351cc engine – 94 ft. lbs. (127 Nm)

2972cc engine – 116 ft. lbs. (157 Nm).

14. Install the timing belt over the crankshaft and camshaft pulleys.

15. Align the timing marks of the camshaft sprocket. Check that the crankshaft timing marks are still in alignment, the locating pin on the front of the crankshaft sprocket is aligned with a mark on the front case.

16. Install the crankshaft pulley, making sure the pin on the crankshaft sprocket fits through the hole in the rear surface of the pulley. Install the bolt. Adjust the timing belt tension.

17. Install the upper and lower timing covers. Install the splash shield.

18. Install the power steering pump/alternator automatic belt tensioner.

19. Install the air conditioning compressor bracket, compressor, power steering pump and alternator.

20. Install the belts.

21. Connect the negative battery cable and check all disturbed components for proper operation.

Camshaft

Removal and Installation

1468CC ENGINE

1. Remove the rocker cover. Remove the timing belt cover. Remove the distributor.

2. Loosen the 2 bolts and move the timing belt tensioner toward the water pump as far as it will go, then retighten the timing belt tensioner adjusting bolt. Disengage the timing belt from the camshaft sprocket and unbolt and remove the sprocket. The timing belt may be left engaged with the crankshaft sprocket and tensioner.

3. Remove the rocker shaft assembly. Remove the small, square cover that sits directly behind the camshaft on the transaxle side of the head. Remove the camshaft thrust case tightening bolt that sits on the top of the head right near that cover.

4. Carefully, slide the camshaft out of the head through the

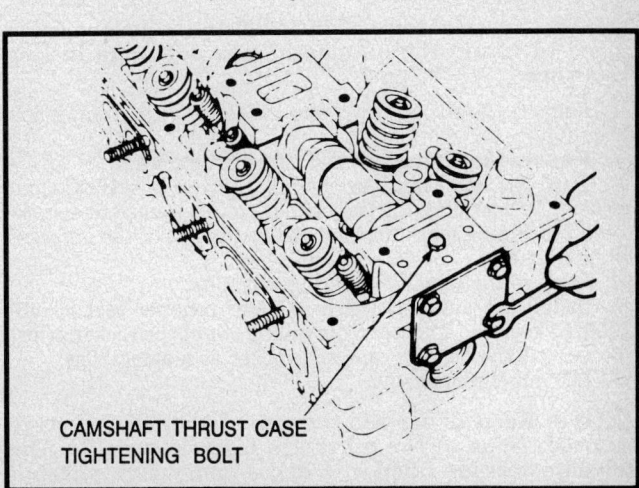

CAMSHAFT THRUST CASE
TIGHTENING BOLT

Rear camshaft cover on the 1468cc engine

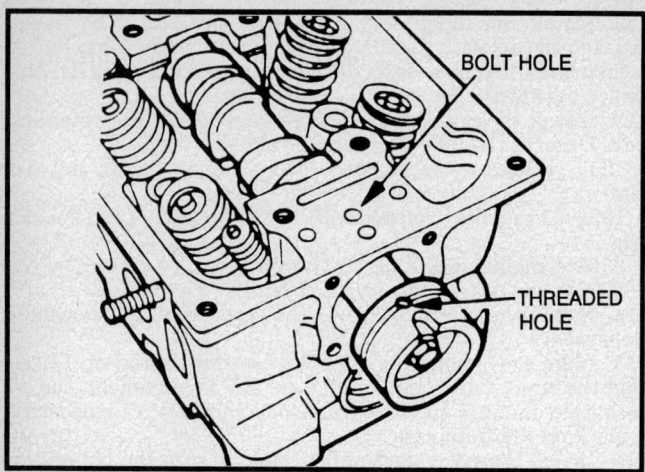

Camshaft installation on the 1468cc engine

hole in the camshaft side of the head, being careful that the cam lobes do not strike the bearing bores in the head.

To install:

5. Lubricate all journal and thrust surfaces with clean engine oil.

6. Carefully, insert the camshaft into the engine. Make sure the camshaft goes in with the threaded hole in the top of the thrust case straight upward.

7. Align the bolt hole in the trust case and the cylinder head surface.

8. Install the thrust case bolt and tighten firmly.

9. Install the rear cover with a new gasket and install and tighten the bolts.

10. Coat the external surface of the front oil seal with engine oil.

11. Using special installer tool MD 998306-01 or equivalent, drive the a new front camshaft oil seal into the clearance between the cam and head at the forward end, making sure the seal seats fully.

12. Install the camshaft sprocket and torque the bolt to 47–54 ft. lbs. (64–74 Nm).

13. Reconnect the timing belt, check the timing and adjust the belt tension.

14. Reinstall the rocker shaft assembly. Adjust the valves and install the rocker and timing belt covers.

2351CC ENGINE

NOTE: A special tool 09246-32000 or equivalent, is required to retain the automatic lash adjusters in this procedure.

1. Remove the rocker cover and gasket and the timing belt cover.

2. Remove the timing belt and camshaft sprocket.

3. Turn the crankshaft so the No. 1 piston is at TDC compression. At this point, the timing mark on the camshaft sprocket and the timing mark on the head to the left of the sprocket will be aligned.

4. Remove the camshaft bearing cap bolts.

5. Install the automatic lash adjuster retainer tool 09246-32000, to keep the adjuster from falling out of the rocker arms.

6. Lift off the bearing caps and rocker arm assemblies.

7. Lift out the camshaft.

NOTE: Keep all parts in the order in which they were removed. None of the parts are interchangeable. The lash adjusters are filled with diesel fuel, which will spill out if they are inverted. If any diesel fuel is spilled, the adjusters must be bled.

8. Check all parts for wear or damage. Replace any damaged or excessively worn part.

9. Coat the camshaft with clean engine oil and place it on the head.

10. Assemble all parts. Note the following:

a. The rocker shafts are installed with the notches in the ends facing up.

b. The left rocker shaft is longer than the right.

c. The wave washers are installed on the left shaft.

d. Coat all parts with clean engine oil prior to assembly.

e. Insert the lash adjuster from under the rocker arm and install the special holding tool. If any of the diesel fuel is spilled, the adjuster must be bled.

f. Tighten the bearing cap bolts, working from the center towards the ends, to 15 ft. lbs.

g. Check the operation of each lash adjuster by positioning the camshaft so the rocker arm bears on the low or round portion of the cam, pointed part of the can faces straight down. Insert a thin steel wire, or tool MD998442 or equivalent, in the hole in the top of the rocker arm, over the lash adjuster and depress the check ball at the top of the adjuster. While holding the check ball depressed, move the arm up and down. Looseness should be felt. Full plunger stroke should be 2.2mm. If not, remove, clean and bleed the lash adjusters.

2972CC ENGINE

1. Disconnect the negative battery cable. Remove the air cleaner assembly and valve covers.

2. Install auto lash adjuster retainer tools MD998443 or equivalent on the rocker arms.

3. If removing the right side (front) camshaft, remove the distributor extension.

4. Remove the camshaft bearing caps but do not remove the bolts from the caps.

5. Remove the rocker arms, rocker shafts and bearing caps, as an assembly.

6. Remove the camshaft from the cylinder head.

7. Inspect the bearing journals on the camshaft, cylinder head and bearing caps.

To install:

8. Lubricate the camshaft journals and camshaft with clean engine oil and install the camshaft in the cylinder head.

9. Align the camshaft bearing caps with the arrow mark depending on cylinder numbers and install in numerical order.

10. Apply sealer at the ends of the bearing caps and install the assembly.

11. Torque the rocker arm and shaft assembly bolts to 15 ft. lbs. (21 Nm).

12. Install the distributor extension, if removed.

13. Install the valve cover and all related parts. Torque the valve cover retaining bolts to 7 ft. lbs. (10 Nm).

14. Connect the negative battery cable and road test the vehicle.

Counterbalance Shafts

Removal and Installation

2351CC ENGINE

1. Disconnect the negative battery cable.

2. Remove the alternator and accessory belts. Remove the belt cover.

3. Rotate the crankshaft to bring No. 1 piston to TDC on the compression stroke. Align the notch on the crankshaft pulley with the T mark on the timing indicator scale and the timing mark on the upper under cover of the timing belt with the mark on the camshaft sprocket.

4. Remove the crankshaft pulley and bolt.

5. Remove the timing belt covers, upper front and lower front.

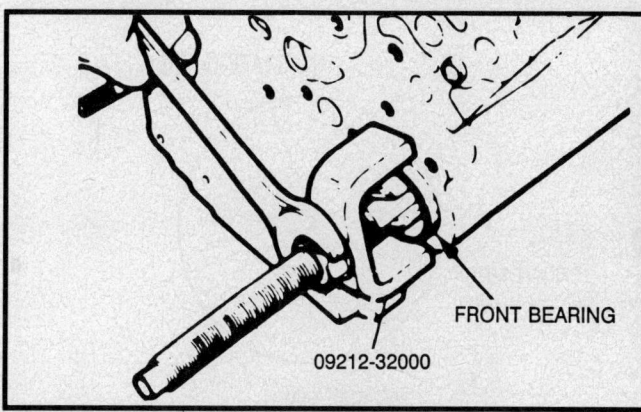

Removing the right counterbalance shaft

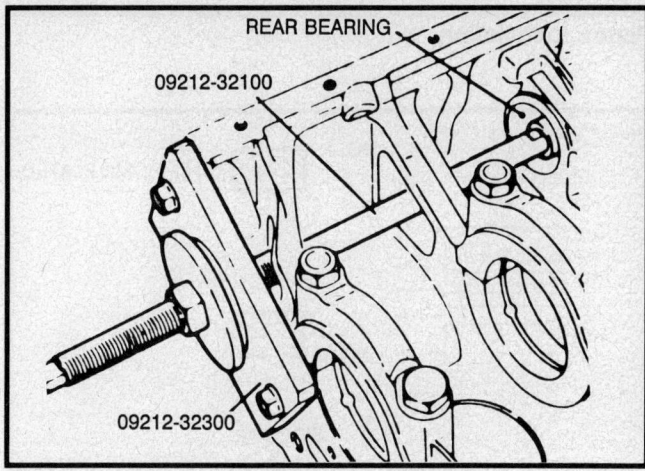

Removing the left counterbalance shaft

6. Remove the crankshaft sprocket bolt.

7. Loosen the tensioner mounting nut and bolt. Move the tensioner away from the belt and retighten the nut to keep the tensioner in the off position. Remove the tensioner.

8. Remove the camshaft sprocket, crankshaft sprocket, flange and tensioner.

9. Loosen the counterbalance shaft sprocket mounting bolt.

10. Remove the belt tensioner and remove the timing belt.

11. Remove the crankshaft sprocket (inner) and counterbalance shaft sprocket.

12. Remove the upper and lower under timing belt covers.

13. Remove the oil pump sprocket and cover.

14. Remove the plug at the bottom of the left side of the cylinder block and insert an 8mm metal bar to keep the left counter balance shaft in position while removing the sprocket nut.

15. Remove the front cover and oil pump as a unit, with the left counter shaft attached.

16. Remove the oil pump gear and left counterbalance shaft.

NOTE: To aid in removal of the front cover, a driver groove is provided on the cover, above the oil pump housing. Avoid prying on the thinner parts of the housing flange or hammering on it to remove the case.

17. Remove the right counterbalance shaft from the engine block.

To install:

18. Install a new front seal in the cover. Install the oil pump drive and driven gears in the front case, aligning the timing marks on the pump gears.

19. Install the left counterbalance shaft in the driven gear and temporarily tighten the bolt.

20. Install the right counterbalance shaft into the cylinder block.

21. Install an oil seal guide on the end of the crankshaft and install a new gasket on the front of the engine block for the front cover.

22. Install a new front case packing.

23. Insert the left counterbalance shaft into the engine block and at the same time, guide the front cover into place on the front of the engine block.

24. Insert an 8mm metal bar at the bottom of the left side of the block and hold the left counterbalance shaft and tighten the bolt. Install the hole plug.

25. Install an O-ring on the oil pump cover and install it on the front cover.

26. Tighten the oil pump cover bolts and the front cover bolts to 11–13 ft. lbs.

27. Install the upper and lower under covers.

28. Install the spacer on the end of the right counterbalance shaft, with the chambered edge toward the rear of the engine.

29. Install the counterbalance shaft sprocket and temporarily tighten the bolt.

30. Install the inner crankshaft sprocket and align the timing marks on the sprockets with those on the front case.

31. Install the inner tensioner (B) with the center of the pulley on the left side of the mounting bolt and with the pulley flange toward the front of the engine.

32. Lift the tensioner by hand, clockwise, to apply tension to the belt. Tighten the bolt to secure the tensioner.

33. Check that all alignment marks are in their proper places and the belt deflection is approximately ¼–½ in. on the tension side.

NOTE: When the tensioner bolt is tightened, make sure the shaft of the tensioner does not turn with the bolt. If the belt is too tight there will be noise and if the belt is too loose, the belt and sprocket may come out of mesh.

34. Tighten the counterbalance shaft sprocket bolt to 22–28.5 ft. lbs.

35. Install the flange and crankshaft sprocket. Tighten the bolt to 43–50 ft. lbs.

36. Install the camshaft spacer and sprocket. Tighten the bolt to 44–57 ft. lbs.

37. Align the camshaft sprocket timing mark with the timing mark on the upper inner cover.

38. Install the oil pump sprocket, tightening the nut to 25–28 ft. lbs. Align the timing mark on the sprocket with the mark on the case.

NOTE: To be assured that the phasing of the oil pump sprocket and the left counterbalance shaft is correct, a metal rod should be inserted in the plugged hole on the left side of the cylinder block. If it can be inserted more than 60mm, the phasing is correct. If the tool can only be inserted approximately 25mm, turn the oil pump sprocket through 1 turn and realign the timing marks. Keep the metal rod inserted until the installation of the timing belt is completed. Remove the tool from the hole and install the plug, before starting the engine.

39. Install the tensioner spring and tensioner. Temporarily tighten the nut. Install the front end of the tensioner spring (bent at right angles) on the projection of the tensioner and the other end (straight) on the water pump body.

40. If the timing belt is correctly tensioned, there should be about 12mm clearance between the outside of the belt and the edge of the belt cover. This is measured about halfway down the side of the belt opposite the tensioner.

41. Complete the assembly by installing the upper and lower front covers.

42. Install the crankshaft pulley, alternator and accessory belts and adjust to specifications.

43. Install the radiator, fill the cooling system and start the engine.

Pistons and Connecting Rods

Positioning

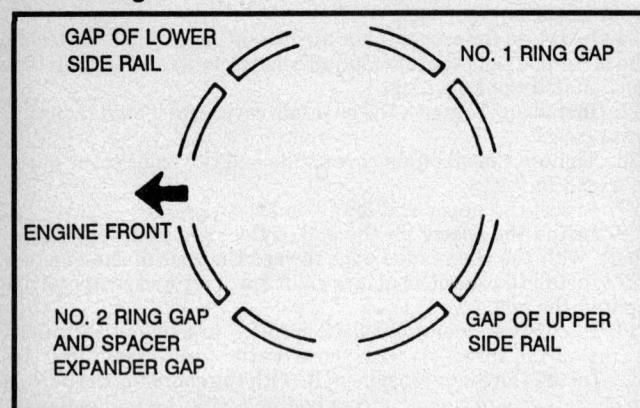

Piston ring positioning

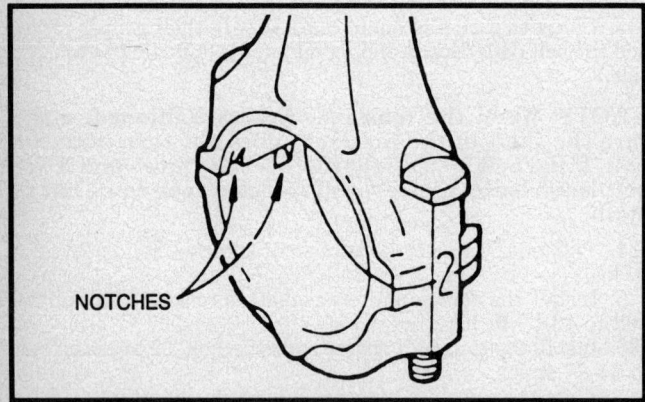

Connecting rod cap installation

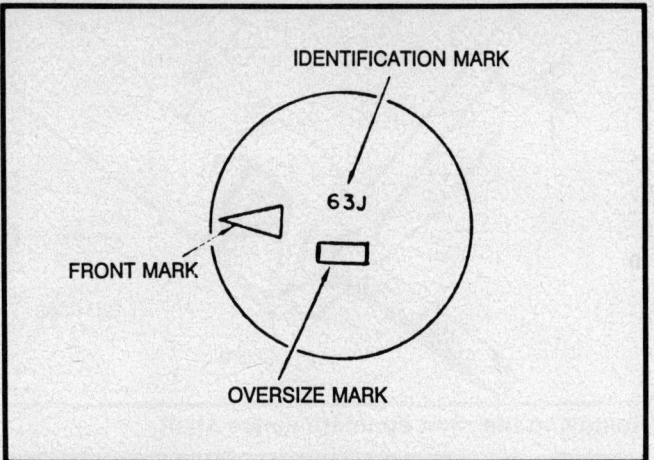

Piston Installation

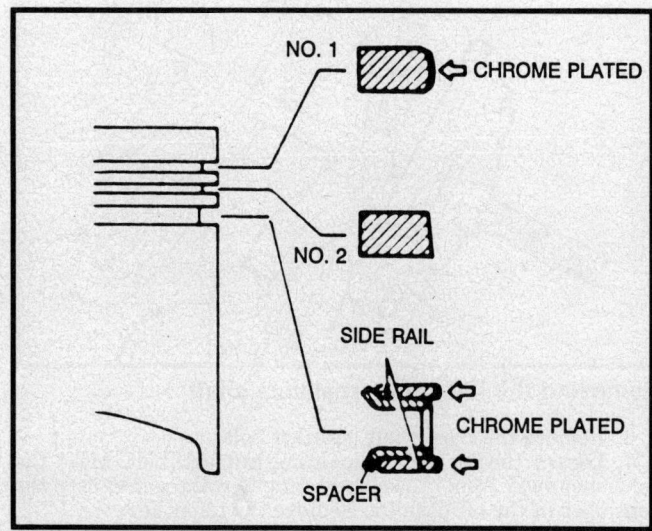

Piston ring installation

ENGINE LUBRICATION

Oil Pan

Removal and Installation

1468CC ENGINE

1. Disconnect the negative battery cable. Raise the vehicle and support it safely.
2. Drain the oil.
3. Remove the underbody splash shield.
4. Remove the oil pan bolts, drop the pan and slide it out from under the vehicle.
5. Clean the mating surfaces of the oil pan and the engine block.
6. Apply a ⅛ in. (3mm) bead of RTV sealer along the groove in the oil pan.

To install:

7. Using non-hardening sealer, glue a new gasket to the oil pan.

8. Install the oil pan. Hand tighten the retaining bolts.
9. Starting at one end of the pan, gradually tighten the retaining bolts to 48–72 inch lbs. in a criss-cross pattern.
10. Lower the engine and tighten the mount retaining nuts.
11. Install the oil pan drain plug.
12. Install the splash shield and lower the vehicle.
13. Refill the crankcase with oil. Start the engine and check for leaks.

2351CC ENGINE

1. Disconnect the negative battery cable. Raise the vehicle and support it safely.
2. Drain the oil.
3. Remove the underbody splash shield.
4. Remove the oil pan bolts, drop the pan and slide it out from under the vehicle.
5. Clean the mating surfaces of the oil pan and the engine block.

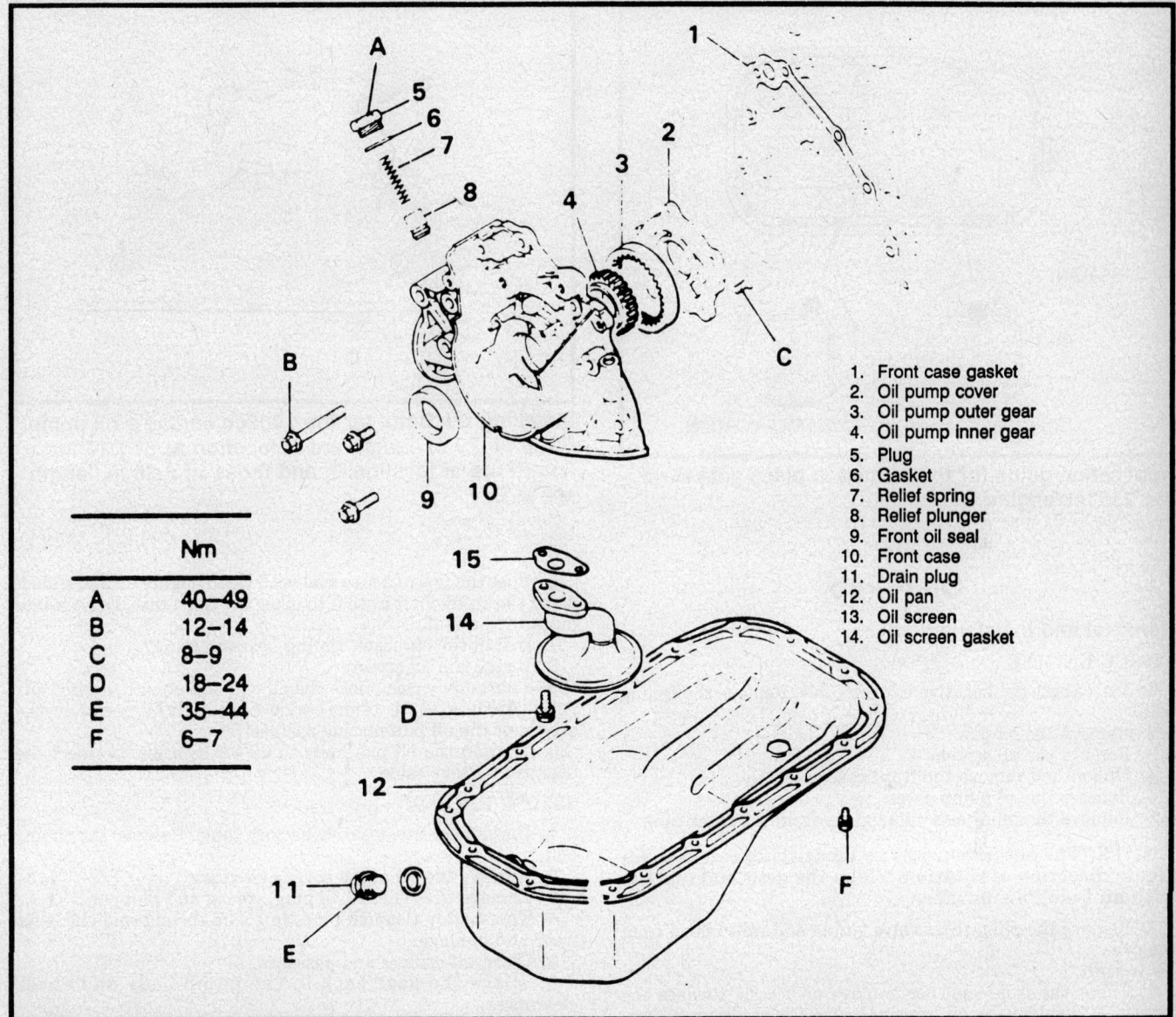

	Nm
A	40—49
B	12—14
C	8—9
D	18—24
E	35—44
F	6—7

1. Front case gasket
2. Oil pump cover
3. Oil pump outer gear
4. Oil pump inner gear
5. Plug
6. Gasket
7. Relief spring
8. Relief plunger
9. Front oil seal
10. Front case
11. Drain plug
12. Oil pan
13. Oil screen
14. Oil screen gasket

1468cc engine pan and front case

To install:
6. Apply sealer to the engine block at the block-to-chain case and block-to-rear oil seal case joint faces.
7. Use a non-hardening sealer and secure a new gasket to the oil pan.
8. Install the oil pan. Hand-tighten the retaining bolts.
9. Starting at one end of the pan, tighten the pan bolts to 48–72 inch lbs. in a criss-cross pattern.
10. Install the oil pan drain plug.
11. Install the splash shield and lower the vehicle.
12. Fill the crankcase with the proper amount of oil. Connect the negative battery cable. Start the engine and check for leaks.

2972CC ENGINE
1. Disconnect the negative battery cable.
2. Raise the vehicle and support safely.
3. Remove the torque converter bolt access cover.

4. Drain the engine oil.
5. Remove the oil pan retaining screws and remove the oil pan and gasket.

To install:
6. Thoroughly clean and dry all sealing surfaces, bolts and bolt holes.
7. Apply silicone sealer to the chain cover to block mating seam and the rear main seal retainer to block seam, if equipped.
8. Install a new pan gasket or apply silicone sealer to the sealing surface of the pan and install to the engine.
9. Install the retaining screws and torque to 50 inch lbs. (6 Nm).
10. Install the torque converter bolt access cover, if equipped. Lower the vehicle.
11. Install the dipstick. Fill the engine with the proper amount of oil.
12. Connect the negative battery cable and check for leaks.

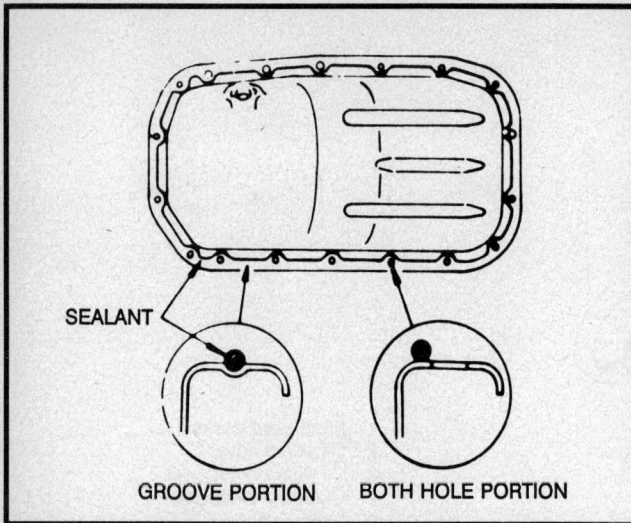

SEALANT

GROOVE PORTION   BOTH HOLE PORTION

Application guide for the formed-in-place gasket on the 2351cc engine oil pan

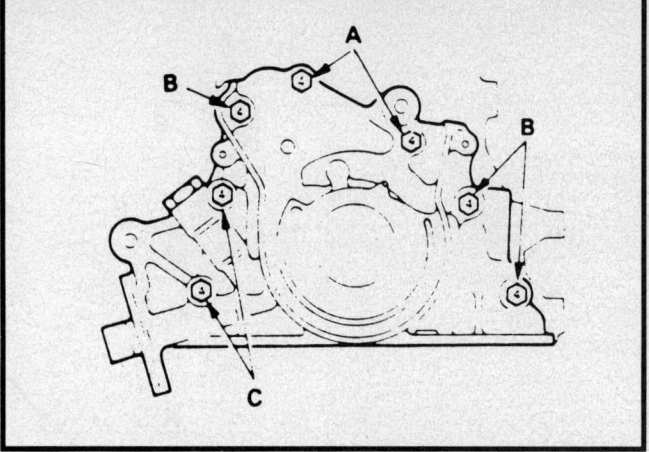

Installing the bolts for the 1468cc engine's oil pump. Bolts of .79 in. length are at location A; of 1.18 in. length are at location B; and those of 2.36 in. length are at C.

Oil Pump

Removal and Installation

1468CC ENGINE

1. Disconnect the negative battery cable. Remove the timing belt.
2. Remove the oil pan.
3. Remove the oil screen.
4. Unbolt and remove the front case assembly.
5. Remove the oil pump cover.
6. Remove the inner and outer gears from the front case.

NOTE: The outer gear has no identifying marks to indicate direction of rotation. Clean the gear and mark it with an indelible marker.

7. Remove the plug, relief valve spring and relief valve from the case.

To install:

8. Check the front case for damage or cracks. Replace the front seal. Replace the oil screen O-ring. Clean all parts thoroughly with a safe solvent.
9. Check the pump gears for wear or damage. Clean the gears thoroughly and place them in position in the case to check the clearances. There is a crescent-shaped piece between the 2 gears.
10. Check that the relief valve can slide freely in the case.
11. Check the relief valve spring for damage. The relief valve free length should be 1.8 in. (47mm). Load length should be 13.4 lbs. at 1.6 in. (40mm).
12. Throughly coat both oil pump gears with clean engine oil and install them in the correct direction of rotation.
13. Install the pump cover and torque the bolts to 6–7 ft. lbs. (8–10 Nm).
14. Coat the relief valve and spring with clean engine oil, install them and tighten the plug to 30–36 ft. lbs (39–49 Nm).
15. Position a new front case gasket, coated with sealer, on the engine and install the front case. Torque the bolts to 10 ft. lbs. Note that the bolts have different shank lengths. Use the following guide to determine which bolts go where.
Bolts marked:
   A: 0.08 in. (20mm)
   B: 1.2 in. (30mm)
   C: 2.4 in. (60mm)

16. Coat the lips of a new seal with clean engine oil and slide it along the crankshaft until it touches the front case. Drive it into place with a seal driver.
17. Install the sprocket, timing belt and pulley.
18. Install the oil screen.
19. Thoroughly clean both the oil pan and engine mating surfaces. Apply a ⅛ in. (3mm) wide bead of RTV sealer in the groove of the oil pan mating surface.
20. Tighten the oil pan bolts to 60–72 inch lbs. Connect the negative battery cable.

2351CC ENGINE

1. Disconnect the negative battery cable. Remove the timing belt.
2. Remove the oil pump cover and gears.
3. Remove the relief valve plug, spring and plunger.
4. Thoroughly clean all parts in a safe solvent and check for wear and damage.
5. Clean all orifices and passages.
6. Place the gear back in the pump body and check clearances.
   Gear teeth-to-body—0.10–0.15mm
   Driven gear endplay—0.06–0.12mm
   Drive gear-to-bearing (front end)—0.020–0.045mm
   Drive gear-to-bearing (rear end)—0.043–0.066mm.

NOTE: If gear replacement is necessary, the entire pump body must be replaced.

7. Check the relief valve spring for wear or damage. Free length should be 47mm; load/length should be 9.5 lbs. at 40mm.

To install:

8. Assembly the pump components. Make sure the gears are installed with the mating marks aligned.
9. Install the timing belt. Connect the negative battery cable.

2972CC ENGINE

1. Disconnect the negative battery cable. Remove the dipstick.
2. Raise the vehicle and support safely. Remove the timing belt, drain the engine oil and remove the oil pan from the engine. Remove the oil pickup.
3. Remove the oil pump mounting bolts and remove the pump from the front of the engine. Note the different length bolts and their position in the pump for installation.

To install:

4. Clean the gasket mounting surfaces of the pump and engine block.

5. Prime the pump by pouring fresh oil into the pump and turning the rotors. Using a new gasket, install the oil pump on the engine and torque all bolts to 11 ft. lbs. (15 Nm).

6. Install the balancer and crankshaft sprocket to the end of the crankshaft.

7. Clean out the oil pickup or replace, if necessary. Replace the oil pickup gasket ring and install the pickup to the pump.

8. Install the timing belt, oil pan and all related parts.

9. Install the dipstick. Fill the engine with the proper amount of oil.

10. Connect the negative battery cable and check the oil pressure.

Checking

1. If foreign matter is present, determine it's source.

2. Check the pump cover and housing for cracks, scoring and/or damage; if necessary, replace the housings.

3. Inspect the idler gear shaft for looseness in the housing; if necessary, replace the pump or timing chain, depending on the vehicle.

4. Inspect the pressure regulator valve for scoring or sticking; if burrs are present, remove them with an oil stone.

5. Inspect the pressure regulator valve spring for loss of tension or distortion; if necessary, replace it.

6. Inspect the suction pipe for looseness, if pressed into the housing and the screen for broken wire mesh; if necessary, replace them.

7. Inspect the gears for chipping, galling and/or wear; if necessary, replace them.

8. Inspect the driveshaft and driveshaft extension for looseness and/or wear; if necessary, replace them.

Rear Main Bearing Oil Seal

Removal and Installation

NOTE: The rear main seal is located in a housing on

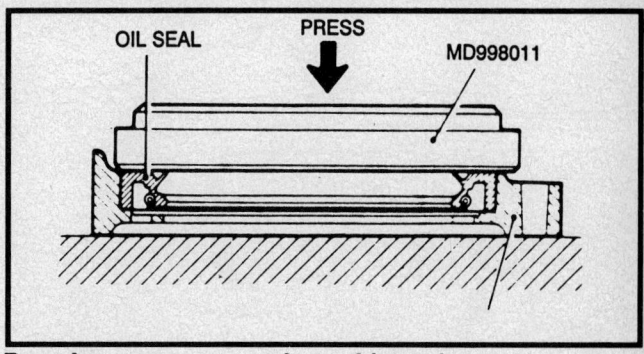
Pressing a new rear main seal into place

the rear of the block. To replace the seal, it is necessary to remove the transaxle and perform the work from underneath the vehicle or remove the engine and perform the work on an engine stand.

1. Raise the vehicle and support it safely. Remove the transaxle from the vehicle.

2. Unscrew the retaining bolts and remove the housing from the cylinder block. Remove the separator from the housing.

3. Using a small prybar, pry out the old seal.

4. Clean the housing and the separator.

5. Lightly oil the replacement seal. Tap the seal into the housing. The oil seal should be installed so the seal plate fits into the inner contact surface of the seal case.

6. Install the separator into the housing so the oil hole faces down.

7. Oil the lips of the seal and install the housing on the rear of the engine block.

8. Install the transaxle in the vehicle.

9. Lower the vehicle. Start the engine and check for leaks.

MANUAL TRANSAXLE

For further information, please refer to "Professional Transmission Repair Manual" for additional coverage.

Transaxle Assembly

Removal and Installation

1. Disconnect the negative battery cable. Remove the battery and battery tray.

2. On 5 speed transaxles, disconnect the electrical connector for the selector control valve.

NOTE: The actuator-to-shaft coupling pin collar is not reusable; replace it.

3. Disconnect and remove the speedometer cable. If equipped with a cable operated clutch, disconnect the clutch cable. If equipped with a hydraulically operated clutch, remove the clevis pin connecting the slave cylinder to the release fork shaft and remove the slave cylinder mounting bolts and the bolts attaching the hydraulic line support bracket to the transaxle. Support the slave cylinder assembly with a length of mechanics wire.

4. Disconnect the back-up lamp electrical connector. Remove the starter motor electrical harness.

5. Remove the 6 transaxle mounting bolts accessible from the top side of the transaxle.

6. Unbolt and remove the starter motor.

7. Raise the vehicle and support it safely. Then, remove the splash shield from under the engine. Drain the transaxle fluid.

8. Disconnect the extension rod and the shift rod at the transaxle end and lower them.

9. Disconnect the stabilizer bar at the lower control arm.

10. Remove the halfshafts.

11. Support the transaxle from below with a floor jack. Make sure the support is widely enough spread that the transaxle pan will not be damaged. Then, remove the attaching bolts and remove the bell housing cover.

12. Remove the lower bolts attaching the transaxle to the engine.

13. Remove the transaxle insulator mount bolt. Remove the cover from inside the right fender shield and remove the transaxle support bracket.

14. Remove the transaxle mount bracket.

15. Pull the assembly away from the engine and lower it from the vehicle.

To install:

16. Installation is the reverse of removal. Observe the following torques:

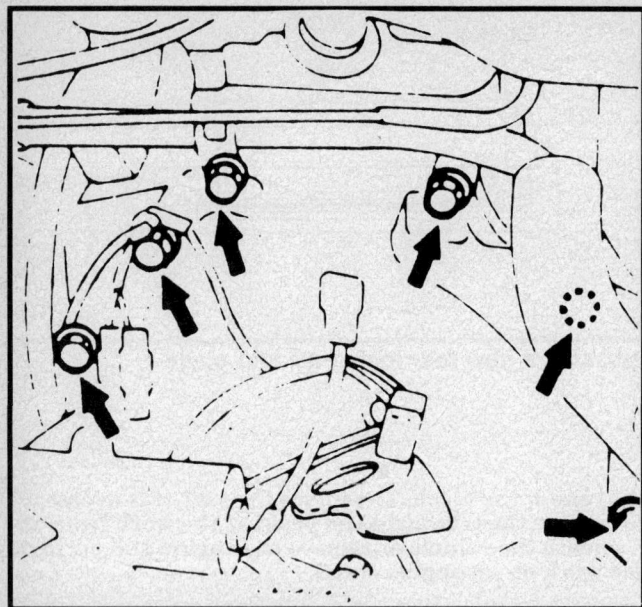

Upper transaxle bolt locations

M10–7T engine-to-transaxle bolts—35 ft. lbs.
M8–10T engine-to-transaxle bolts—25 ft. lbs
M8–20T bell housing cover bolts—15 ft. lbs.
M8–14T bell housing cover bolts—9 ft. lbs.
Transaxle mounting bracket bolt—40 ft. lbs.
  17. Refill the transaxle with the specified fluid to the level of the filler plug.
  18. If equipped, adjust the clutch cable. If equipped with a hydraulic clutch, install the slave cylinder mounting bolts and the

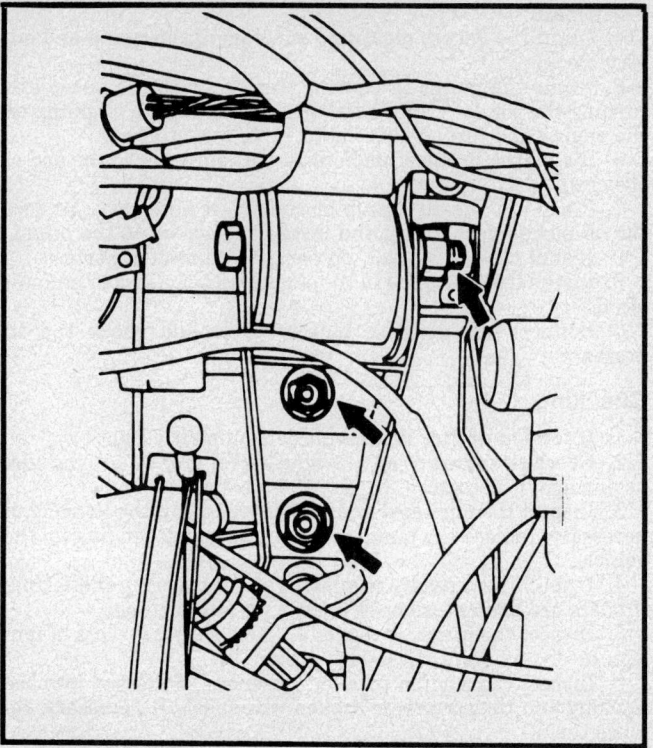

Transaxle mount insulator bolt locations

bolts attaching the hydaraulic line support bracket. Install the clevis pin.
  19. Make sure the gearshift lever works correctly.

CLUTCH

Clutch Assembly

Removal and Installation

——————— CAUTION ———————
The clutch driven disc contains asbestos, which has been determined to be a cancer causing agent. Never clean clutch surfaces with compressed air. Avoid inhaling any dust from any clutch surface! When cleaning clutch surfaces, use a commercially available brake cleaning fluid.

  1. Remove the transaxle. Insert the forward end of an old transaxle input shaft or a clutch disc guide tool into the splined center of the clutch disc, pressure plate and the pilot bearing in the crankshaft. This will keep the disc from dropping when the pressure plate is removed from the flywheel.
  2. Loosen the clutch mounting bolts alternately and diagonally in very small increments, no more than 2 turns at a time, so as to avoid warping the cover flange. When all bolts are free, remove the pressure plate and disc.
  3. Remove the snapring. Remove the clevis pin.
  4. Remove the return clip and then remove the release bearing.
  5. Use a center punch and hammer to remove the spring pins from the clutch release fork and shaft. Discard the spring pins.
  6. Remove the release shaft. Remove the release fork, seals and return spring.

If the clutch disc is not being replaced, examine it for the following before re-using it.
    a. Loose rivets
    b. Burned facing
    c. Oil or grease on the facing
    d. Less than 0.3mm left between the rivet head and the top of the facing.
  Check the pressure plate and replace it, if any of the following conditions exist:
    a. Scored or excessively worn face.
    b. Bent or distorted diaphragm spring.
    c. Loose rivets.
To install:
  7. Grease the bearing areas for the release shaft. Install the release shaft, seals, return spring and the release fork. Apply grease to the throw-out bearing contacting surfaces of the release fork.
  8. Align the lock pin holes of the release fork and shaft and drive in 2 new spring pins. Make sure the spring pin slot is at right angles to the centerline of the control shaft.
  9. Apply grease into the groove in the release bearing and install it into the front bearing retainer in the transaxle. Install the return clip to the release bearing and fork.
  10. Make sure the surfaces of the pressure plate and flywheel are wiped clean of grease and lightly sand them with crocus cloth. Lightly grease the clutch disc and transaxle input shaft splines.

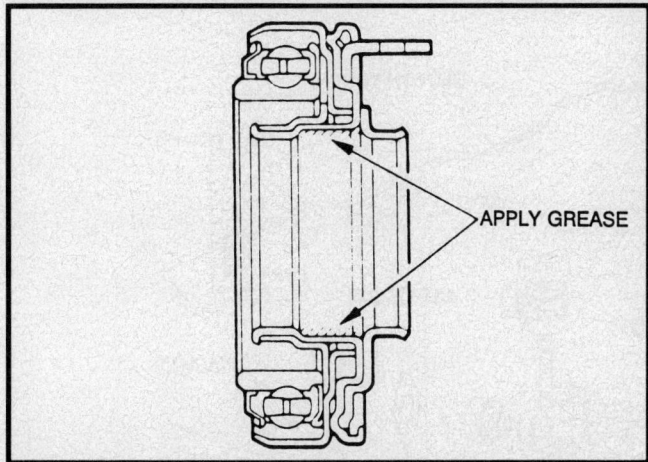

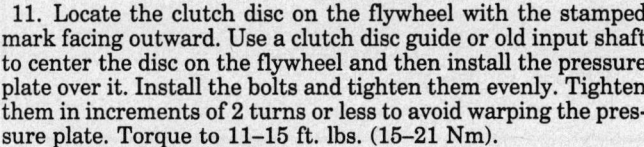

Grease the groove in the throwout bearing as shown

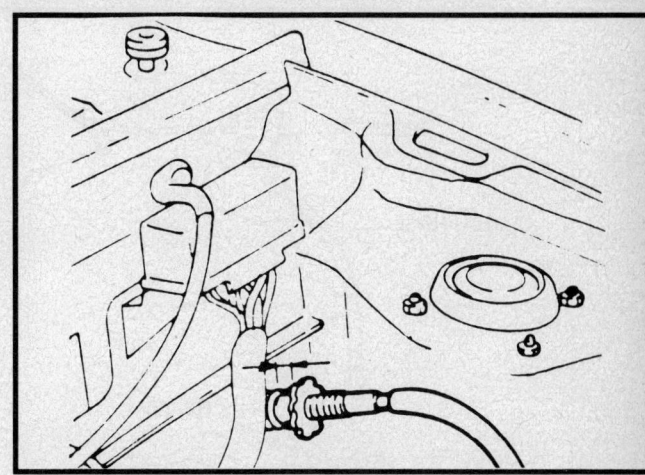

Clutch pedal height adjustment

11. Locate the clutch disc on the flywheel with the stamped mark facing outward. Use a clutch disc guide or old input shaft to center the disc on the flywheel and then install the pressure plate over it. Install the bolts and tighten them evenly. Tighten them in increments of 2 turns or less to avoid warping the pressure plate. Torque to 11–15 ft. lbs. (15–21 Nm).

12. Remove the clutch disc centering tool. Install the transaxle. Adjust the clutch free-play.

Pedal Height Adjustment

EXCEL

Measure the pedal height from the top of the pedal pad to the closest point on the floor. The distance should be 7.3–7.6 in. (185–192mm). Loosen the clutch switch locknut and move the pedal stop bolt. Then, tighten the locknut.

SONATA

Measure the pedal height from the face of the pedal to the floorboard. Pedal height should be 6.97–7.17 in. (177–182mm). If not:

1. Disconnect the clutch switch wiring.
2. Loosen the locknut and turn the switch, as required.
3. Tighten the locknut.

SCOUPE

Measure the pedal height from the top of the pedal pad to the closest point on the floor. The distance should be 7 in. (178mm). Loosen the clutch switch locknut and move the pedal stop bolt. Then, tighten the locknut.

Clevis Pin Play Adjustment

SONATA

Clevis pin play is measure at the pedal while observe the pin. Play should be 0.04–0.12 in. (1–3mm). If not, loosen the locknut and turn the pushrod, as required. Tighten the locknut.

Free-Play Adjustment

EXCEL

Slightly pull the cable away from the firewall. Turn the adjusting wheel on the cable until the play between the wheel and the cable retainer is 0.20–0.25 in. (5–6mm). Release the cable and make sure the end of the tension spring engages the adjusting wheel, so the wheel won't turn. Check the clutch pedal free-play. Free-play should be 0.8–1.2 in. (20–30mm). If it is outside specification, adjust it by means of the adjusting wheel on the cable.

SONATA

Check this adjustment after checking pedal height and clevis play. Free-play should be 0.24–0.51 in. (6–13mm). If not, there is air in the system which must be bled. If air persists, there is a leak and the system must be repaired.

Clutch Cable

Removal and Installation

EXCEL

1. Completely back-off the cable adjusting wheel in the engine compartment.
2. Raise the vehicle and support it safely.
3. Pull out the split pin from the end of the clutch control lever and disconnect the cable from the lever.
4. Disconnect the cable at the clutch pedal.

To install:

5. Installation is the reverse of removal. Make sure the cable does not touch any hot or moving parts. Lubricate the cable with clean engine oil. Adjust the clutch.

Clutch Master Cylinder

Removal and Installation

1. Loosen the bleeder screw on the slave cylinder and drain the system.
2. Disconnect the pushrod from the clutch pedal.
3. Disconnect the clutch pedal from the pedal bracket.
4. Disconnect the fluid line from the master cylinder.
5. Unbolt and remove the master cylinder.
6. Install the master cylinder and bleed the system.

Clutch Slave Cylinder

Removal and Installation

1. Disconnect the clutch hose from the slave cylinder.
2. Unbolt and remove the cylinder from the clutch housing.
3. Install the slave cylinder and bleed the system.

Hydraulic Clutch System Bleeding

1. Raise the vehicle and support it safely.
2. Loosen the bleeder screw at the slave cylinder.
3. Make sure the master cylinder is full.

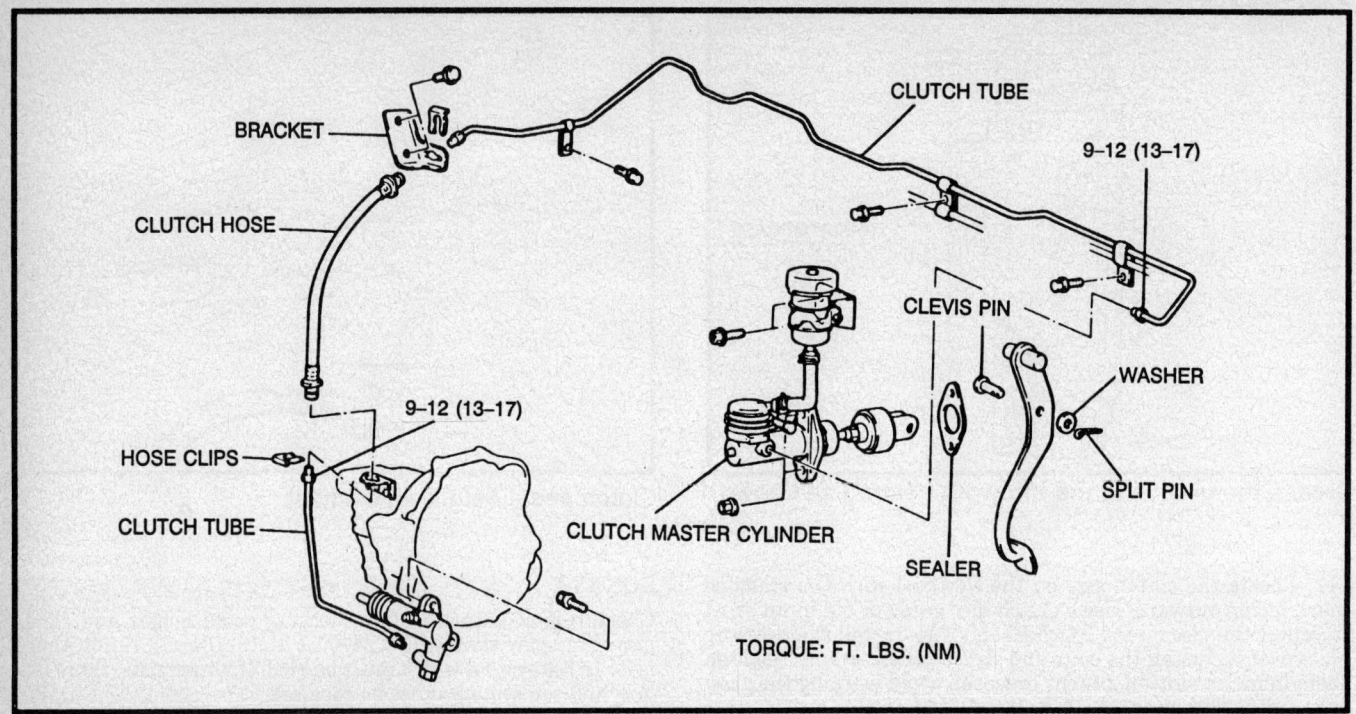

CLUTCH TUBE

9–12 (13–17)

BRACKET

CLUTCH HOSE

CLEVIS PIN

WASHER

9–12 (13–17)

SPLIT PIN

HOSE CLIPS

CLUTCH TUBE

CLUTCH MASTER CYLINDER

SEALER

TORQUE: FT. LBS. (NM)

Sonata hydraulic clutch components

4. Attach a length of rubber hose to the bleeder screw nipple and place the other end in a glass jar half full of clean brake fluid.

5. Have an assistant push the clutch pedal down slowly to the floor. If air is in the system, bubbles will appear in the jar as the pedal is being depressed.

6. When the pedal is at the floor, have an assistant hold it there. Tighten the bleeder screw.

7. Repeat Steps 5 and 6 until no bubbles are found. Check the master cylinder level frequently to make sure you don't run low on fluid.

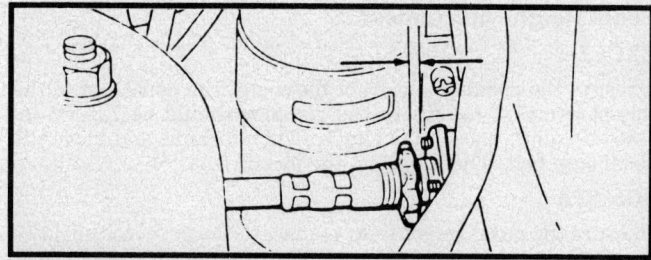

Clutch cable adjustment

AUTOMATIC TRANSAXLE

For further information, please refer to "Professional Transmission Repair Manual" for additional coverage.

Transaxle Assembly

Removal and Installation

NOTE: The transaxle and torque converter must be removed and installed as an assembly.

1. Disconnect the negative battery cable. Remove the battery and battery tray. Remove the air cleaner and housing.

2. Disconnect the throttle control cable and the manual control cable. Loosen the locknut which uses a star washer and locates the cable housing on the bracket. Also, remove the locknut at the very end of the cable, where it connects with the neutral safety switch.

3. Disconnect the inhibitor switch connector, pulse generator connector, oil cooler hoses, solenoid valve connector and speedometer cable from the transaxle. Immediately install clean caps

in the open ends of the hoses. Keep the hoses pointed up so fluid will not escape until the caps are installed.

4. Remove the 5 bolts attaching the converter housing to the engine that are accessible from above.

5. Raise the vehicle and support it safely. Label and then disconnect the starter motor wiring. Then, remove the mounting bolts and the starter.

6. Remove the front wheels. Remove the engine splash shield.

7. Drain the transaxle fluid by removing the drain plug. Remove the transaxle pan bolts and remove the pan and drain it.

8. Remove the undercover. Disconnect the strut bars and stabilizer bar from the lower control arm. Disconnect the lower arm at the crossmember.

9. Disconnect both halfshafts from the transaxle and suspend them in a secure manner.

10. Remove the bell housing cover. Turn the engine for access and remove the bolts connecting the drive plate to the front of the torque converter. Make sure to push the converter as far as it will go toward the transaxle after the bolts have been removed.

11. Support the weight of the engine from above, using a chain hoist. Support the transaxle from underneath with a floor jack in such a way that the support will be spread out and will not dent the transaxle pan. Remove the remaining bolts connecting the transaxle to the engine.

NOTE: Never support the full weight of the transaxle on the engine driveplate.

12. Remove the transaxle mount insulator bolts. Remove the transaxle insulator mount bracket from the transaxle.

13. Slide the transaxle and converter away from the engine, to the right and then lower and remove it as an assembly.

14. Installation is the reverse of removal. Observe the following torques:
Torque converter-to-driveplate mounting bolts—34–38 ft. lbs.
Transaxle assembly mounting bolts—35 ft. lbs.
Engine-to-transaxle bolts—35 ft. lbs.
Engine-to-transaxle bolts—25 ft. lbs.

15. Adjust the throttle control cable and neutral safety switch. Test the neutral safety switch.

16. Refill the transaxle to the proper level. Make sure the neutral safety switch wiring does not rub against the insulator mount bracket.

17. Connect the negative battery cable.

18. Start the engine and allow to come to normal operating temperature. Check fluid level in the transaxle.

Throttle Control Cable Adjustment

EXCEL

1. Make sure the engine is warm with the throttle in normal idling position.

2. Loosen the lower cable bracket mounting bolt. Pull the small rubber cover located near the transaxle back toward the housing to expose the nipple. Now, move the cable bracket until the distance between the nipple and the outer end of the cover next to the bracket is 0.02–0.06 in. (0.5–1.5mm). Then, torque

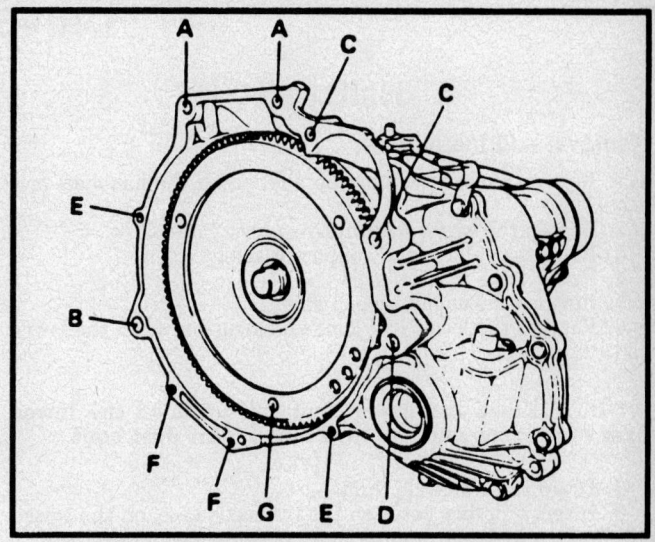

Bolt torques in ft. lbs. for the automatic transaxle:
A—31–40; B—31–40; C—16–23; D—22–25; E—7–9; F—11–16; G—25–30

the bracket mounting bolt to 9–10.5 ft. lbs. (12–14 Nm).

3. With the engine off, open the throttle all the way and hold it there. Then, pull the cable further upward to make sure it still has freedom of movement; that it has not bottomed out. If necessary, repeat the adjustment.

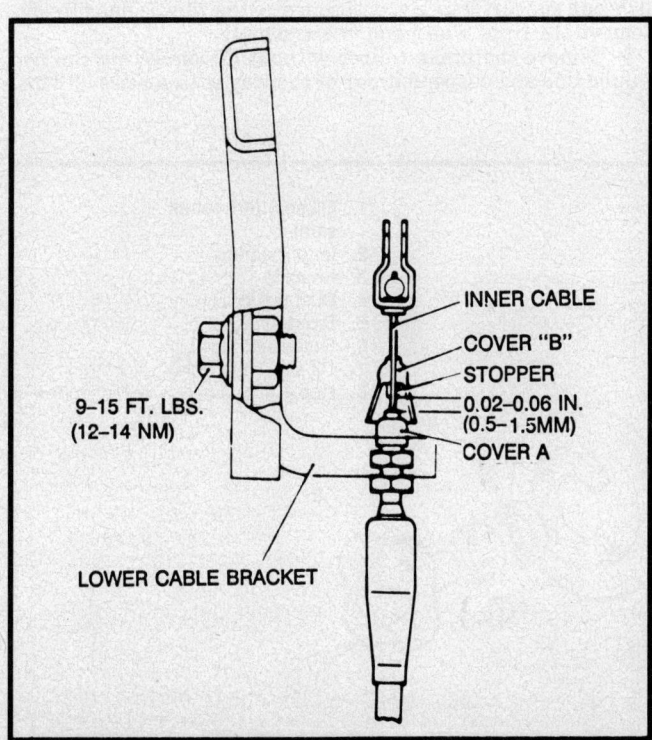

Excel throttle cable adjustment

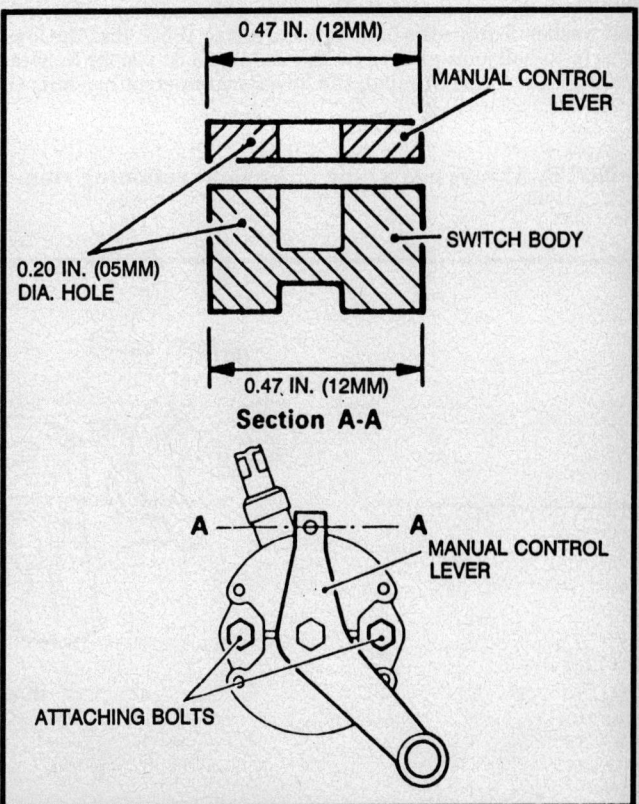

Disconnecting the throttle control cable at the transaxle

DRIVE AXLE

Halfshaft

Removal and Installation

1. Remove the hub center cap and loosen the halfshaft end nut.
2. Loosen the wheel lug nuts.
3. Raise the vehicle and support it safely.
4. Remove the front wheels.
5. Remove the engine splash shield.
6. Remove the lower ball joint and strut bar from the lower control arm.

NOTE: Place the lower arm ball joint on the lower arm to prevent damage to the ball joint dust boot.

7. Drain the transaxle fluid.
8. Insert a prybar between the transaxle case, on the raised rib, and the halfshaft inner joint case. Move the bar to the right to withdraw the left halfshaft; to the left to remove the right halfshaft.

NOTE: Do not insert the prybar too deeply (7mm) or the oil seal will be damaged.

9. Plug the transaxle case with a clean rag to prevent dirt from entering the case.
10. Use a puller/driver mounted on the wheel studs to push the halfshaft from the front hub. Take care to prevent the spacer shims from falling out of place.
11. Installation is the reverse of removal. Insert the halfshaft into the hub, first, then install the transaxle end. Install the hub nut washer. Torque the halfshaft end nut to 185 ft. lbs.; the lower arm-to-ball joint nuts to 87 ft. lbs. (42–53 ft. lbs. for Sonata, 1990-91 Excel and Scoupe); the lower arm-to-strut bar nuts to 87 ft. lbs.

NOTE: Always use a new inner joint retaining ring.

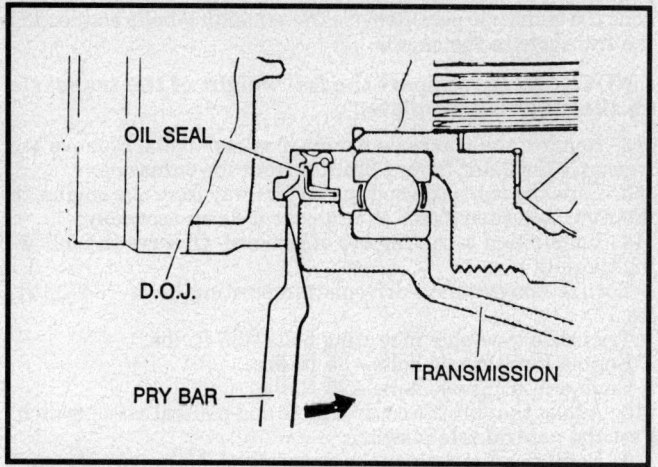

Halfshaft removal

Front Wheel Hub, Knuckle and Bearings

Removal and Installation

NOTE: The following procedure requires the use of a number of special tools. Always replace bearings and races as a set. Never replace just an inner or outer bearing. If either is in need of replacement, both sets must be replaced.

1. Remove the center hub cap and halfshaft nut. Raise the vehicle and support it safely, positioned so the wheels hang freely. Remove the front wheel and tire assembly.
2. Remove the brake caliper without disconnecting the hydraulic line and suspend it out of the way with a piece of wire.

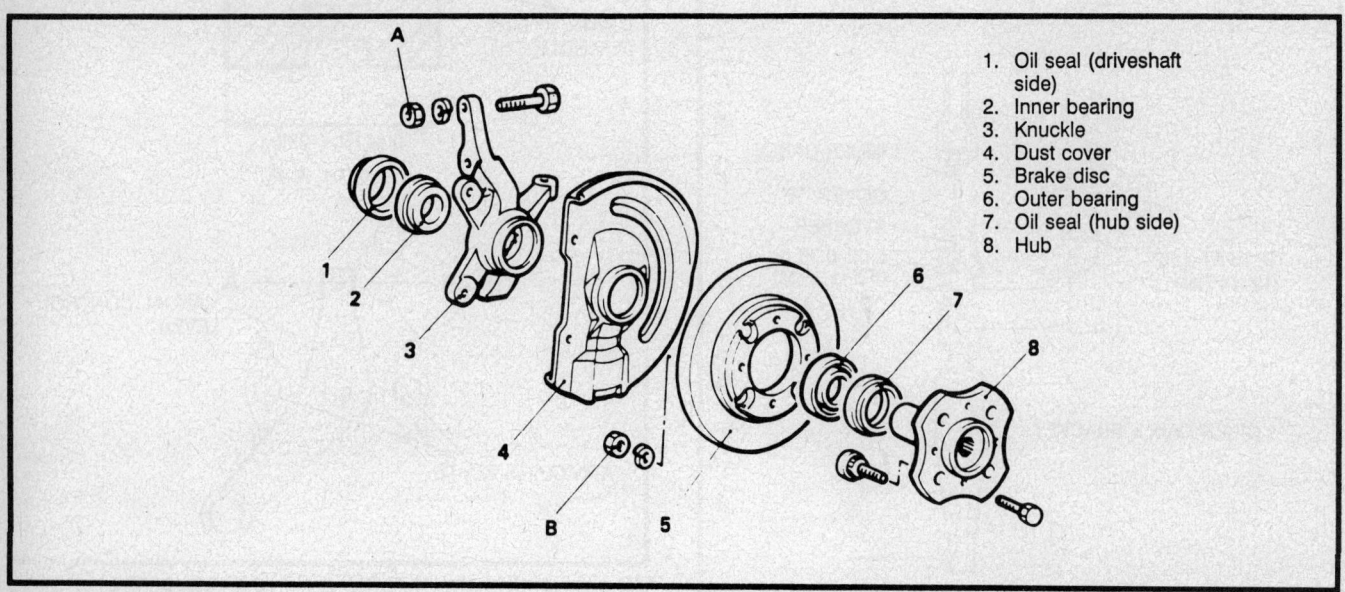

1. Oil seal (driveshaft side)
2. Inner bearing
3. Knuckle
4. Dust cover
5. Brake disc
6. Outer bearing
7. Oil seal (hub side)
8. Hub

Front hub and knuckle

3. Disconnect the stabilizer bar and strut bar from the lower control arm. Disconnect the ball joint at the steering knuckle. Disconnect the tie rod end ball joint at the steering knuckle as well.

4. Remove the halfshaft from the transaxle and press the halfshaft out of the hub with a 2 jawed puller.

5. Unbolt and remove the hub and knuckle from the bottom of the strut and remove the hub and knuckle assembly from the vehicle.

6. Several special tools are required to press the hub and disc from the steering knuckle and to remount them. Use 09517–21600 or equivalent. Do not attempt to hammer the parts apart, or damage to the bearing may result. Install the arm of the special tool then the body onto the knuckle and tighten the nut manually. Using special tool 09517–21500, separate the hub from the knuckle. Pull the bearings out, noting their positions and direction of installation (smaller diameter inward).

7. Matchmark the relationship between the brake disc and hub. Then place the knuckle in a vise and separate the rotor from the hub by removing the 4 attaching bolts.

8. Special tools 09532–1100, 09532–11301 (pulling ring and pulling collar) and 09517–21100 (stepped plate) or equivalent are needed. Fit the pulling lips of the collets onto the inner race and secure the pulling collar to the collets with the bolts provided. Then, attach the stepped plate to the hub.

9. Attach the pulling ring to the assembly, turning it and moving it up and down so the top of the pulling collar fits into the groove on the ring. Then, use an open-end wrench to keep the special tools from turning, while removing the bolt at the top of the assembly downward with another wrench. This will press the inner race out of the hub. Do this for both inner races.

10. Drive the oil seal and inner bearing inner race from the knuckle with a brass drift.

11. Using a brass drift and a hammer, tap the bearing outer races out of the knuckle.

12. Thoroughly clean and inspect all parts. Any suspect part should be replaced.

To install:

13. Apply multi-purpose grease to the outside surfaces of the bearing outer races to make them easy to press in. Using special tools 09500–21000, 09517–21300 and 09517–21200 or equivalents, install the outer races.

14. Install rotor on the hub and torque the mounting bolts to 36–43 ft. lbs. (49–59 Nm).

15. Drive the outer bearing inner race into position. Coat the outer ring and lip of the oil seal and drive the hub side oil seal into place, using a seal driver.

16. Mount the knuckle in a vise. Place the hub and knuckle together. Then use 09517–21500 or equivalent, to tighten the hub to the knuckle, torquing to 147–192 ft. lbs. (167 ft. lbs. for Scoupe). Then, rotate the hub to seat the bearing.

17. With the hub still in the vise, check the turning torque of the bearing with an inch lbs. torque wrench and tool 09517–21500. Starting torque should be 11.5 inch lbs. If the starting

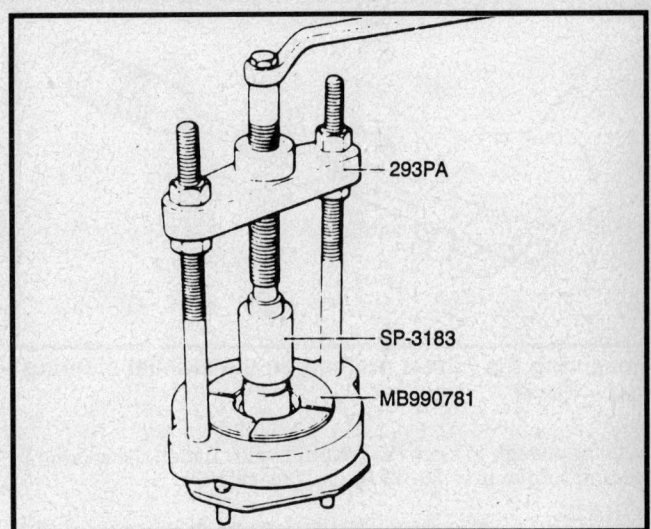

Removing the outer bearing inner race from the hub

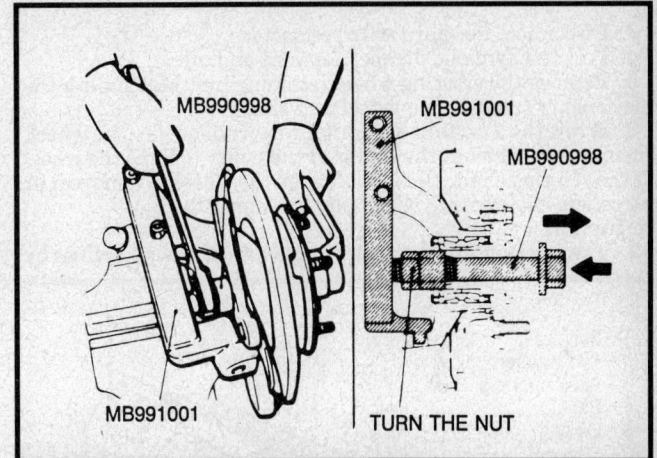

Removing the hub from the knuckle

torque is 0, measure the hub bearing axial play with a dial indicator. If axial play exceeds 0.004 in. (0.1mm), while the nut is tightened, the parts have been assembled incorrectly.

18. Remove the special tool. Place the outer bearing in the hub and drive the seal into place. Lower strut-to-knuckle mounting bolts are torqued to 54–65 ft. lbs. The remaining procedures are the reverse of removal except that the final torquing of the lower arm-to-ball joint connecting bolt should be accomplished after the vehicle is on the ground.

STEERING

Steering Wheel

Removal and Installation

EXCEL

1. Disconnect the negative battery cable. Pull off the horn cover at the center of the wheel by grasping the upper edge. Then, disconnect the horn wire connector.

2. Remove the steering wheel retaining nut. Matchmark the relationship between the wheel and shaft.

3. Remove the steering wheel dynamic dampener.

4. Screw the 2 bolts of a steering wheel puller into the wheel. Then, turn the bolt at the center of the puller to force the wheel off the steering shaft. Do not pound on the wheel to remove it or the collapsible steering shaft may be damaged.

To install:

5. The steering wheel can be pushed onto the shaft splines by

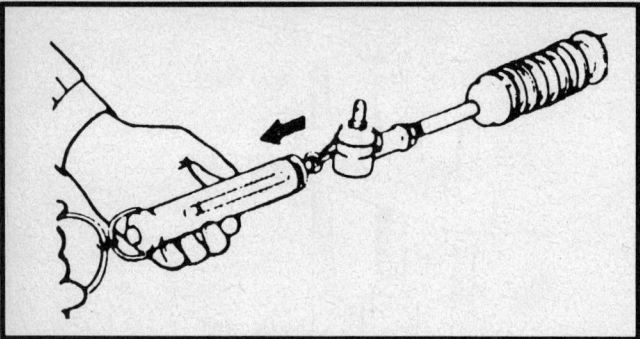

Measuring the pinion preload on the manual steering rack—Excel

hand far enough to start the retaining nut. Install the retaining nut and torque it to 26–32 ft. lbs. (34–44 Nm).

SONATA

1. Disconnect the negative battery cable.
2. Remove the screws from the back of the horn pad and lift it off.
3. Disconnect the horn wire connector.
4. Pull the dynamic damper forward and off.
5. Remove the steering wheel retaining nut. Matchmark the relationship between the wheel and shaft.
6. Screw the 2 bolts of a steering wheel puller into the wheel. Then, turn the bolt at the center of the puller to force the wheel off the steering shaft. Do not pound on the wheel to remove it or the collapsible steering shaft may be damaged.

To install:

7. The steering wheel can be pushed onto the shaft splines by

hand far enough to start the retaining nut. Install the retaining nut and torque it to 29–36 ft. lbs. (39–49 Nm).

Steering Column

Removal and Installation

1. Disconnect the negative battery cable. Remove the steering wheel.
2. Remove the lower column trim cover and the upper column trim cover.
3. Remove the light switch and wiper and washer switch. Disconnect the harness connectors.
4. Disconnect the steering column mounting bolts and lay the column down.
5. Remove the bolts securing the steering shaft coupling and universal joint. Pull the coupling and the universal joint from the rack and pinion.
6. Remove the dust cover retaining bolts at the firewall and remove the column from the vehicle.

To install:

7. Lower the steering column through the firewall and connect the steering column to the rack and pinion. Install the retaining bolt. Do not tighten at this time.
8. Install both upper and lower steering column mounting bolts. Tighten the steering column mounting bolts as follows:
   a. On Sonata, tighten the upper column to column member mounting bolts to 9–13 ft. lbs. (13–18 Nm) and the lower column to column member mounting bolts to 6–9 ft. lbs (8–12 Nm).
   b. On 1987–89 Excel, tighten the column and shaft assembly mounting bracket bolts to 7 ft. lbs. (10 Nm) and 1990–91 Excel and Scoupe to 9–13 ft. lbs. (13–18 Nm).
9. Tighten the steering shaft and joint bolt to 11–14 ft. lbs. (15–20 Nm).

1. Bellows
2. Tab washer
3. Rack bushing
4. Rack
5. Oil seal
6. Snapring
7. Snapring
8. Bearing
9. Pinion
10. Support yoke
11. Cushion rubber
12. Locking nut
13. Yoke plug
14. Yoke spring
15. Gear housing
16. Mounting bracket
17. Mounting rubber
18. Tie rod
19. Band
20. Clip
21. Tie rod end
22. Dust cover
23. Clip ring

	Nm	ft. lbs.
A	60–80	43–58
B	50–70	36–51
C	80–100	58–72
D	50–55	36–40
E	24–34	17–25

Manual rack and pinion steering assembly

10. Install the light switch and wiper and washer washer switch. Connect the harness connectors.

10. Install the upper column trim cover and the lower column trim cover.

11. Install the steering wheel. Connect the negative battery cable.

Manual Rack and Pinion

Adjustment

1. Mount the rack and pinion assembly in a soft jawed vise, clamping on the rack mounting area, only.

2. Using a spline adapter on an inch-pound torque wrench, turn the pinion shaft at the rate of 1 full turn every 4–6 seconds, turning the steering from lock-to-lock. Measure the total preload lock-to-lock. Preload should be 3.6–9.6 inch lbs.

3. Place a pull scale on each tie rod end, in turn and pull straight away. The rack starting force should be 11–66 lbs.

4. If the specifications in either Steps 2 or 3 are not met, the rubber cushion and yoke spring behind the pinion shaft nut will have to be replaced.

Removal and Installation

EXCEL AND SCOUPE

1. Loosen the lug nuts.
2. Raise the vehicle and support it safely.
3. Remove the wheels.
4. Remove the steering shaft-to-pinion coupling bolt.
5. Disconnect the tie rod ends with a separator.
6. Removing the clamps securing the rack to the crossmember and remove the unit from the vehicle. The tie rod ends can now be removed. Prior to removal, count the exact number of exposed threads on the tie rod ends, then loosen the locknut and unscrew the tie rod end. When installing new tie rod ends, oil the threads and screw them into place so the previously noted number of threads is visible with the locknut tight. As a further reference, the distance between the end of the tie rod boot and the centerline of the tie rod ball stud should be 9.6 in. (243.5mm). Torque the locknut to 38 ft. lbs.

7. Install the rubber mount for the gear box with the slit on the downside. The remainder of installation is the reverse of removal. Observe the following torques:

Rack-to-crossmember bolts—22–29 ft. lbs. for 1987–89 models, 43–58 ft. lbs. for 1990–91

Coupling bolt—11–14 ft. lbs.

Tie rod end slotted nuts—11–25 ft. lbs.

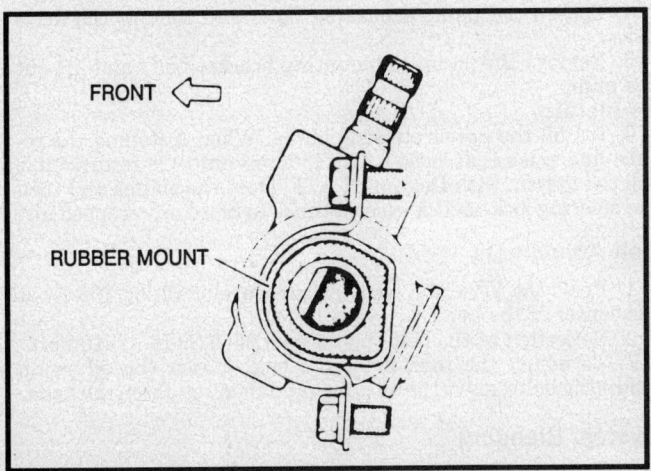

Install the rubber gearbox mount as shown—Excel

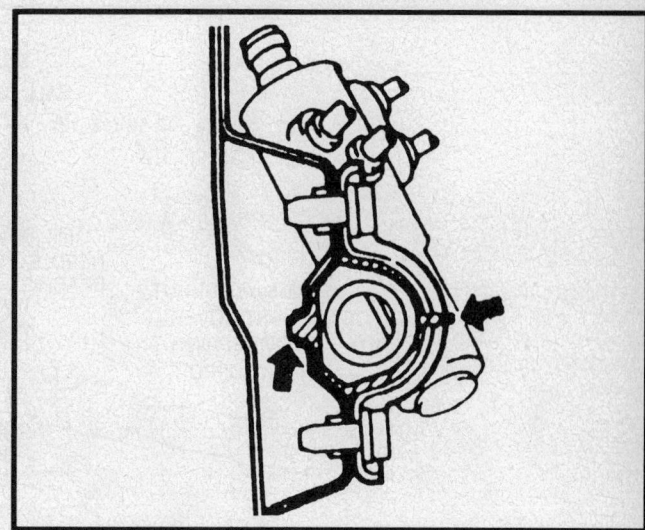

Rubber isolator alignment on the power steering rack—Excel

Power Rack and Pinion

Adjustment

1. Mount the rack in a soft jawed vise, clamping the vise on the rack mounting areas, only.

2. Using a spline adapter on an inch-pound torque wrench, rotate the pinion shaft several times, lock-to-lock and note the total pinion preload. Preload should be 5–11 inch lbs.

3. If the preload is note within specifications, adjust the position of the rack support cover and recheck the preload. If it does not work, the rack support cover components are defective.

Removal and Installation

EXCEL AND SCOUPE

1. Loosen the lug nuts.
2. Raise the vehicle and support it safely.
3. Remove the wheels.
4. Remove the steering shaft-to-pinion coupling bolt.
5. Disconnect the tie rod ends with a separator.
6. Drain the fluid.
7. Disconnect the hoses from the gear box.
8. Remove the band from the steering joint cover.
9. Unbolt and remove the stabilizer bar.
10. Remove the rear roll stopper-to-center member bolt and move the rear roll stopper forward, as required.
11. Remove the rack unit mounting clamp bolts and take the unit out the left side of the vehicle. The tie rod ends can now be removed. Prior to removal, count the exact number of exposed threads on the tie rod ends, then loosen the locknut and unscrew the tie rod end. When installing new tie rod ends, oil the threads and screw them into place so the previously noted number of threads is visible with the locknut tight. As a further reference, the distance between the end of the tie rod boot and the point at which the locknut touches the tie rod ball socket body should be 6.1–6.2 in. (155.5–157.5mm); 6.9–7.0 in. (174.3–176.3mm) for Scoupe. Torque the locknut to 38 ft. lbs.

12. When installing the power steering rack, make sure the rubber isolators have their nubs aligned with the holes in the clamps. Apply rubber cement to the slits in the gear mounting grommet. Tighten the clamp bolt to 43–58 ft. lbs., the tie rod end slotted nuts to 11–25 ft. lbs. and the coupling bolt to 11–14 ft. lbs.

13. Fill the system with Dexron®II ATF.

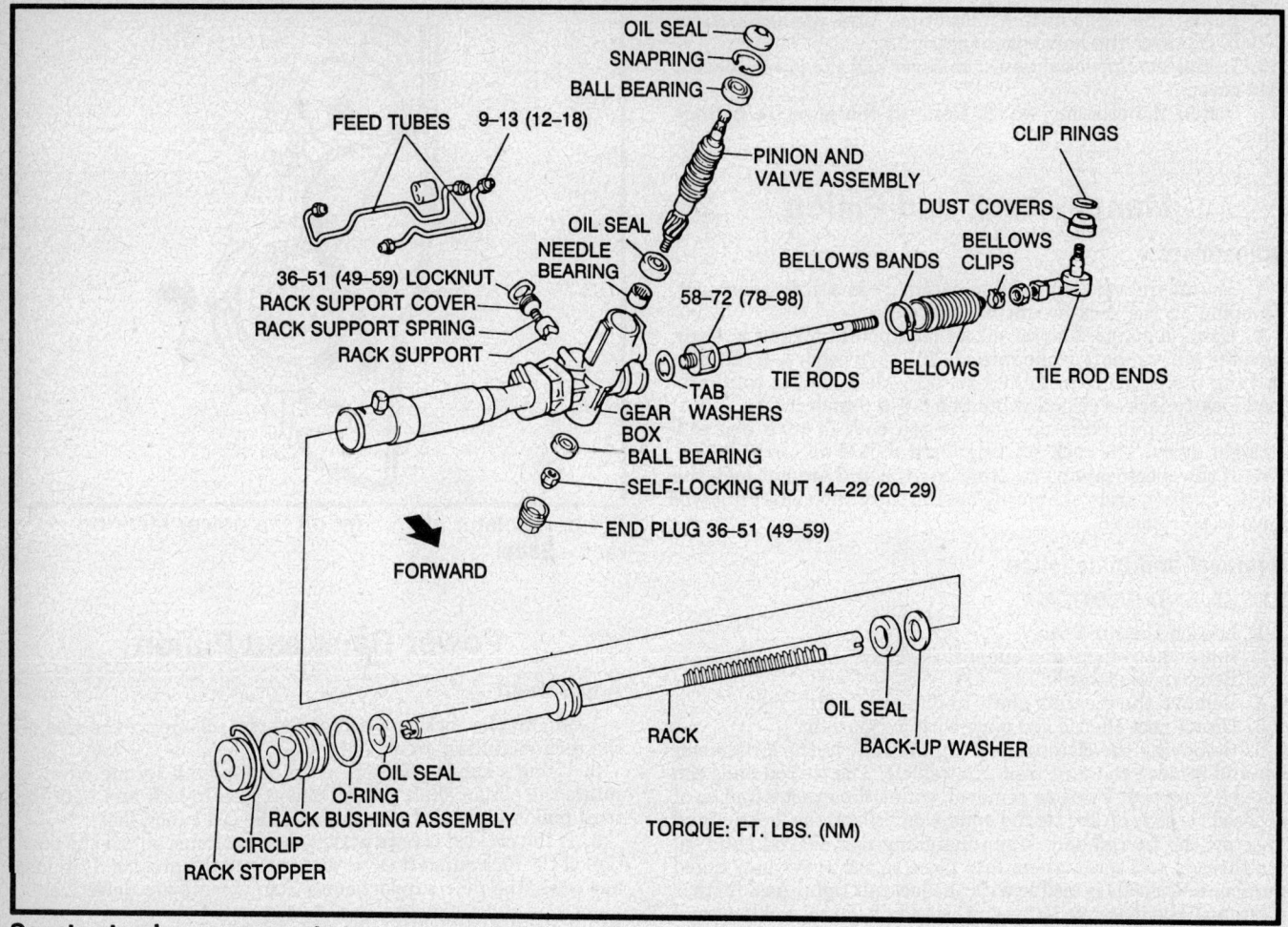

Sonata steering components

SONATA

1. Loosen the lug nuts.
2. Raise the vehicle and support it safely.
3. Remove the wheels.
4. Remove the steering shaft-to-pinion coupling bolt.
5. Disconnect the tie rod ends with a separator.
6. Drain the fluid.
7. Disconnect the hoses from the gear box.
8. Remove the center member and temporarily retighten the front muffler.
9. Unbolt and remove the stabilizer bar.
10. Remove the rack unit mounting clamp bolts and take the unit out the right side of the vehicle. The tie rod ends can now be removed. Prior to removal, count the exact number of exposed threads on the tie rod ends, then loosen the locknut and unscrew the tie rod end. When installing new tie rod ends, oil the threads and screw them into place so the previously noted number of threads is visible with the locknut tight. As a further reference, the distance between the end of the tie rod boot and the point at which the locknut touches the tie rod ball socket body should be 187.4mm. Torque the locknut to 38 ft. lbs.
11. When installing the power steering rack, make sure the rubber isolators have their nubs aligned with the holes in the clamps. Apply rubber cement to the slits in the gear mounting grommet. Tighten the clamp bolt to 43–58 ft. lbs., the tie rod nuts to 11–25 ft. lbs. and the coupling bolt to 22–25 ft. lbs.
12. Fill the system with Dexron®II ATF.

Power Steering Pump

Removal and Installation

1. Place a drain pan under the pump.
2. Disconnect the pressure hose from the pump.
3. Disconnect the return hose from the pump.
4. Loosen the pump mounting bolts and remove the drive belt.
5. Remove the pump-to-mounting bracket bolts and lift out the pump.

To install:

6. Install the power steering pump. When installing the return line, push it at least 1.2 in. (30mm) onto the return tube. Fill the system with Dexron®II ATF, start the engine and turn the steering lock-to-lock several times to bleed any trapped air.

Belt Adjustment

1. Press the V-belt by applying pressure of 22 lbs. (98 N) at the center of the belt.
2. Deflection of the belt should be 0.28–0.39 in. (7–10mm).
3. To adjust the tension of the belt, loosen the oil pump mounting bolts, move the oil pump and then retighten the bolts.

System Bleeding

1. Ensure that the reservoir is full of Dexron II® automatic transmission fluid.

2. Raise and safely support the front wheels of the vehicle.

3. Turn the steering wheel from lock to lock 5 or 6 times.

4. Disconnect the coil wire and connect to a solid ground. Operate the starter motor intermittently for 15 to 20 seconds and turn the steering wheel from lock to lock 5 or 6 times.

NOTE: Ensure that the reservoir is full during air bleeding to prevent the fluid level from falling below the lower position of the filter.

5. Connect the coil wire and start the engine.

6. Turn the steering wheel from lock to lock until no more air bubbles are visible in the reservoir.

7. Confirm that the oil is not milky and that the fluid level is correct.

8. Confirm that there is little change in the fluid level when the steering wheel is turned to the left and right.

NOTE: An abrupt rise in the fluid level after stopping the engine is a sign of incomplete bleeding. If this occurs, repeat the bleeding procedure.

Tie Rod Ends

Removal and Installation

1. Raise the vehicle and support it safely. Remove the front wheels.

2. Remove the cotter pin and then remove the ball stud retaining nut. Use a vise-like tool MB991113 or equivalent, to press the ball stud down and out of the steering knuckle.

3. Using a back-up wrench on the flats at the inner end of the tie rod end, loosen the nut that retains the end to the tie rod coming out of the steering box. Now, unscrew the tie rod end, counting the turns required to remove it.

To install:

4. Install the new tie rod end in reverse order. Torque the castellated nut retaining the ball stud to 11–25 ft. lbs. (15–33 Nm). Then, turn it just far enough to align the castellations with the hole in the stud and install a new cotter pin. Torque the inner nut to 36–40 ft. lbs. (49–54 Nm).

BRAKES

Master Cylinder

Removal and Installation

1. Disconnect the negative battery cable. Disconnect the fluid level sensor.

2. Disconnect the brake tubes from the master cylinder and cap them immediately.

3. Unbolt and remove the master cylinder from the booster.

4. Position the master cylinder to the booster and install the mounting bolts. Torque the mounting bolts to 6–9 ft. lbs. (8–12 Nm); 10–16 ft. lbs. (14–22 Nm) for Scoupe.

5. Connect the brake tubes to the master cylinder. Torque the tubes to 9–12 ft. lbs. (13–17 Nm).

6. Bleed the brake system. Connect the negative battery cable. Road test the vehicle.

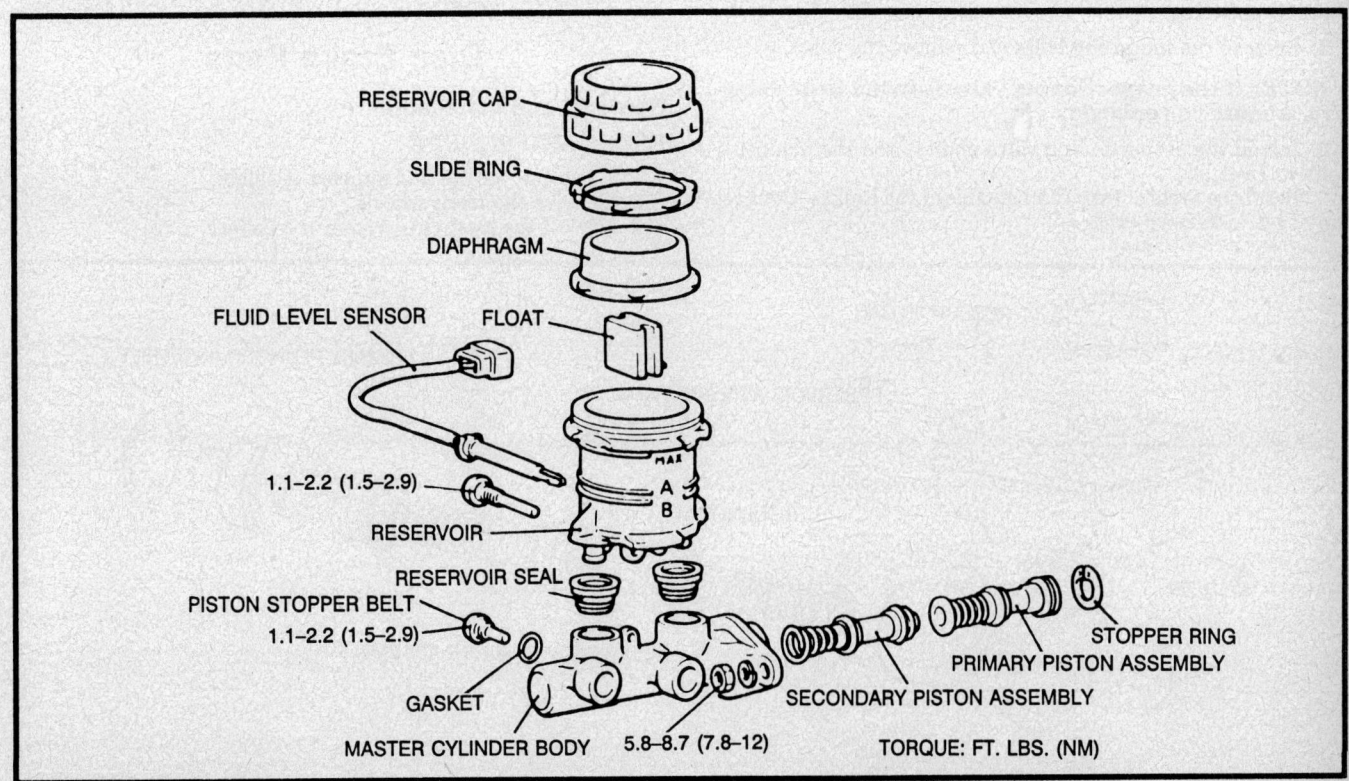

RESERVOIR CAP

SLIDE RING

DIAPHRAGM

FLUID LEVEL SENSOR   FLOAT

1.1–2.2 (1.5–2.9)

RESERVOIR

RESERVOIR SEAL

PISTON STOPPER BELT

1.1–2.2 (1.5–2.9)

GASKET

MASTER CYLINDER BODY   5.8–8.7 (7.8–12)

STOPPER RING

PRIMARY PISTON ASSEMBLY

SECONDARY PISTON ASSEMBLY

TORQUE: FT. LBS. (NM)

Excel master cylinder

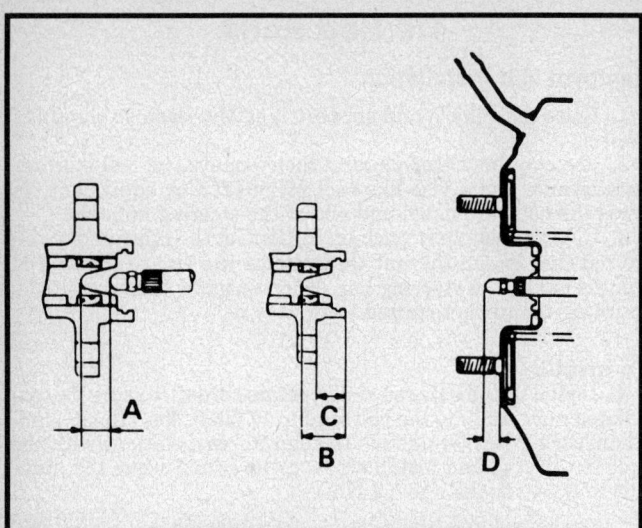

Determining brake booster pushrod clearance

Proportioning Valve

On Excel and Sonata, the proportioning valve is located under the master cylinder and supported by the brake lines to which it is connected and a through bolt. On Scoupe the proportioning valve is integral to the master cylinder. It does not require routine check or adjustment.

Removal and Installation

1. Disconnect the negative battery cable. Disconnect the brake lines at the valve.

NOTE: Use a flare nut wrench to avoid damage to the lines and fittings.

2. Remove the mounting bolts and remove the valve.

NOTE: If the proportioning valve is found to be defective, it must be replaced.

3. Install the proportioning valve and tighten the mounting bolts to 15 ft. lbs.
4. Refill the system with fluid and bleed the brakes. Connect the negative battery cable.

Power Brake Booster

Removal and Installation

1. Disconnect the negative battery cable. Slide back the clip and disconnect the vacuum supply line at the brake booster. Pull gently in order to avoid damaging the check valve.
2. Remove the master cylinder.
3. Disconnect the pushrod at the brake pedal. This requires pulling the lockpin out of the pedal clevis pin and then pulling the latter out of the pedal lever and clevis rod.
4. Remove the mounting bolts and nuts from the firewall and remove the booster.

To install:

5. Installation is the reverse order of the removal procedures. Install the brake booster on the firewall and tighten the mounting nuts to 72–108 inch lbs. (8–12 Nm); 10–12 ft. lbs. (13–17 Nm) for Scoupe. Bleed the system.

Brake Caliper

Removal and Installation

1. Raise the vehicle and support safely.
2. Remove the tire and wheel assembly.
3. Remove the caliper mounting pin(s).
4. Lift the caliper off of the rotor. Remove the outer pad from the caliper.
5. Remove the brake hose retaining bolt from the caliper.

To install:

6. Install the brake hose to the caliper using new copper washers.
7. Position the caliper over the rotor so the caliper engages the adaptor correctly. Install the mounting pin(s). Install the hold-down spring, if equipped.
8. Fill the master cylinder and bleed the brakes.
9. Install the wheel and tire assemby.
10. Lower the vehicle.

Disc Brake Pads

Removal and Installation
EXCEL AND SCOUPE

1. Raise the vehicle and support it safely.
2. Remove the front wheels.
3. Pry off the dust shield from the caliper.

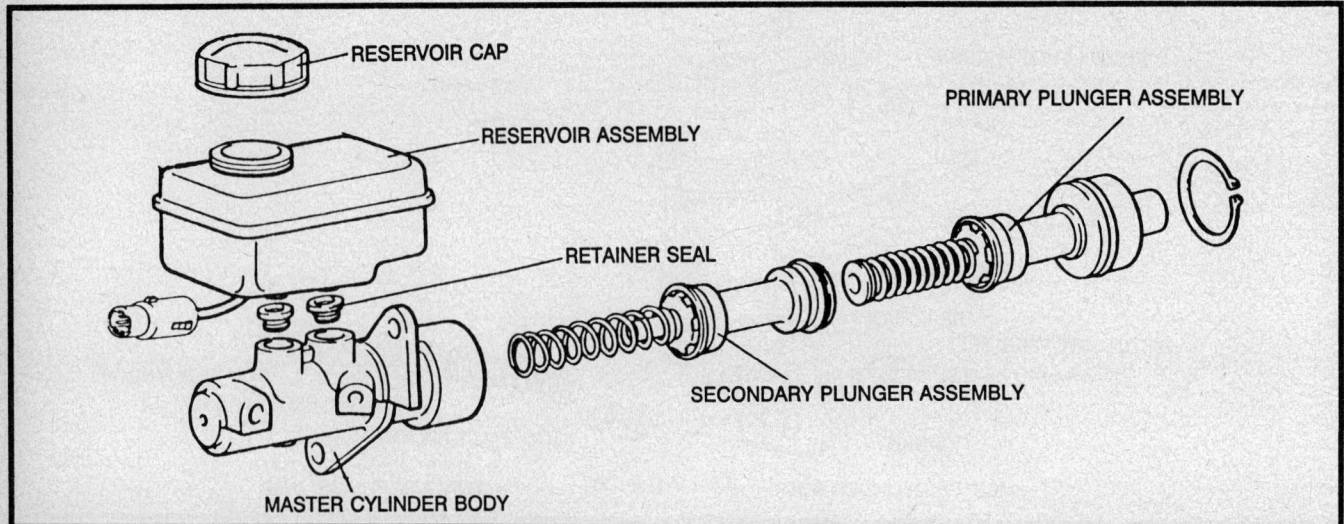

Sonata master cylinder

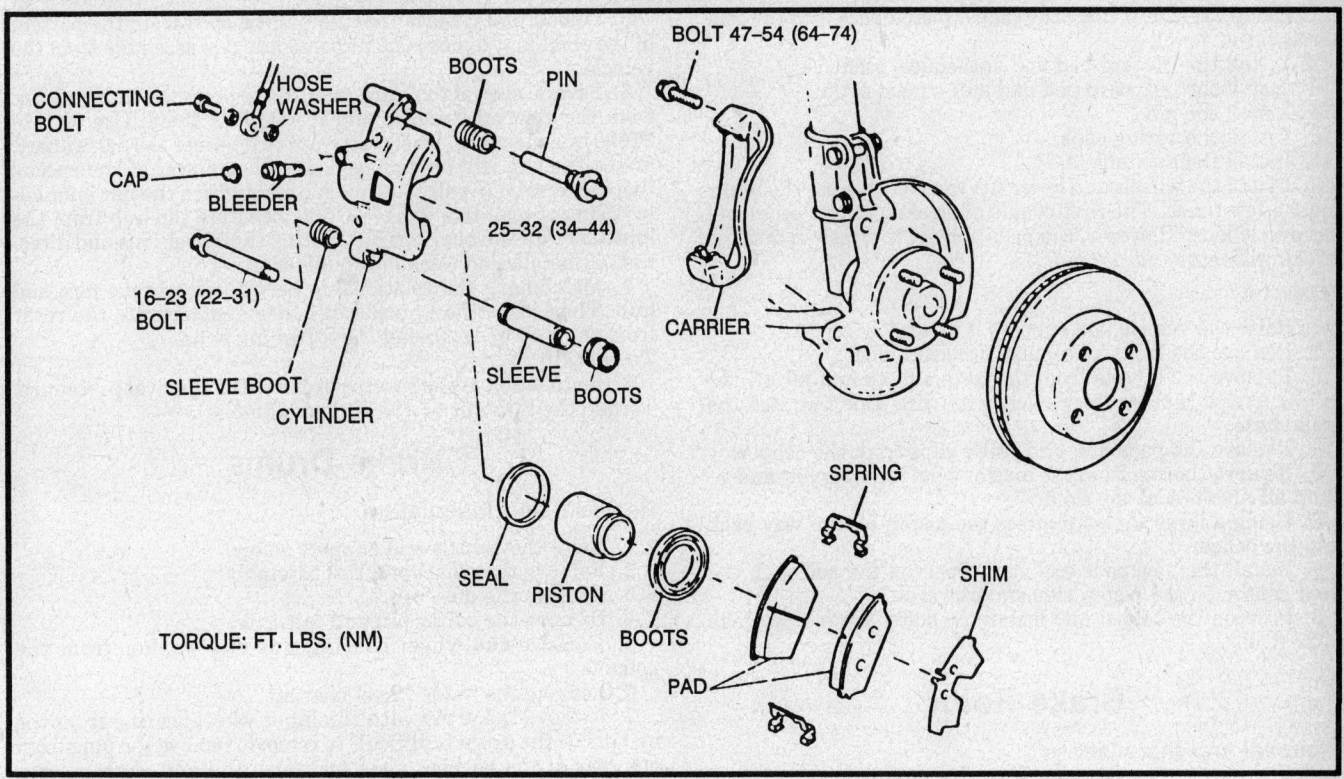

Excel front disc brake components

4. Depress the center of the outboard spring clip and remove the clip by slipping the ends from the pins.
5. Remove the inboard spring clip with pliers.
6. Using pliers, pull the retaining pins from the caliper.
7. Lift the pads and anti-squeal shims from the caliper.
8. Clean all caliper parts, especially the torque plate shafts, with a solvent made for brake parts.

NOTE: Replace all brake pads at the same time. Never replace the pads on 1 wheel only.

9. If the dust protector or spring clips are weak, damaged or deformed, replace them.
10. Remove the cap from the master cylinder reservoir and, using a clean suction gun, remove about 6mm of fluid.

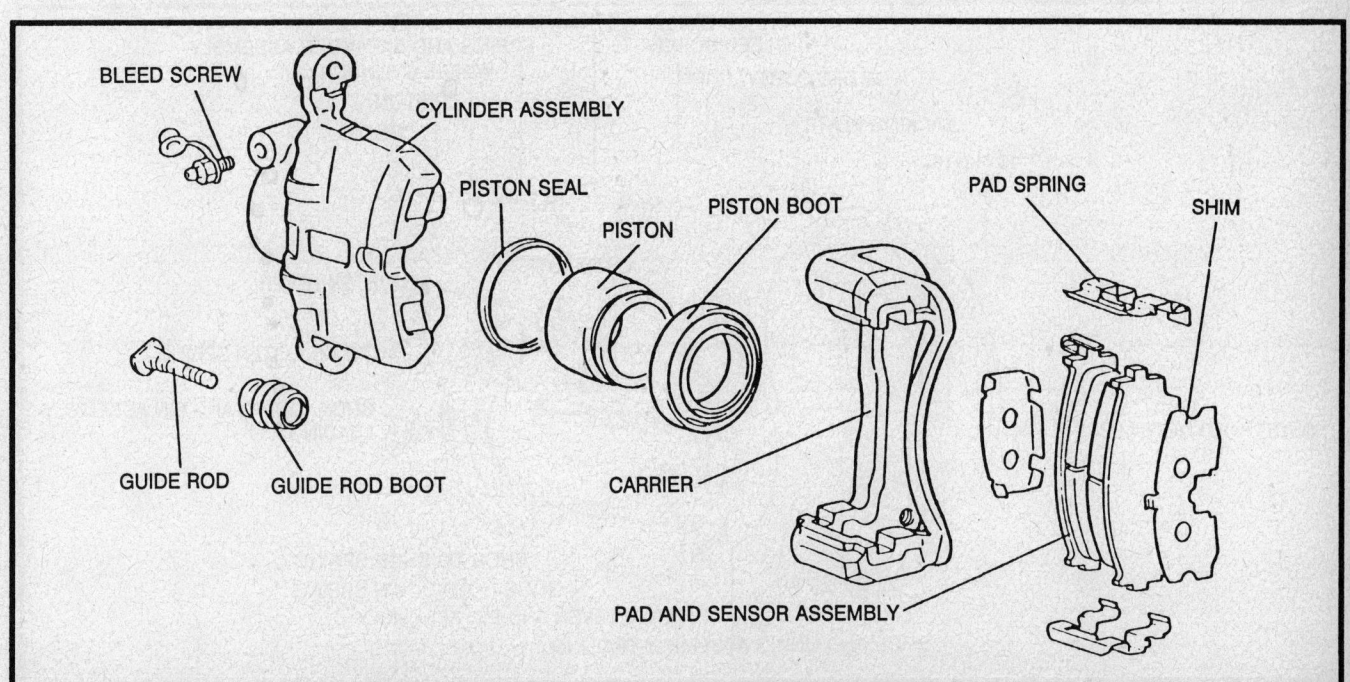

Sonata front disc brake components

11. Using a C-clamp, force the caliper piston back into the caliper as far as it will go.

12. Install the inboard pad and anti-squeal shim.

13. Install the outboard pad and anti-squeal shim.

14. Install the pins.

15. Install the spring clips.

16. Install the dust shield.

17. Install the wheels and lower the vehicle. Depress the brake pedal a few times. The first couple of strokes on the pedal will feel overly long. However, the pads will set themselves and the stroke will return to normal.

SONATA

1. Raise the vehicle and support it safely.

2. Remove the front wheel and tire assemblies.

3. Remove the 2 bolts from the torque plate and lift off the caliper. Suspend the caliper safely with wire. Don't stretch the brake hose.

4. Remove the pads and anti-rattle clips from the caliper.

5. Remove the cap from the master cylinder reservoir and siphon off about ⅓ of the fluid.

6. Using a large C-clamp, press the piston all the way back into the caliper.

7. Install the new pads and clips. Position the pad with the wear sensor on the piston side and upwards.

8. Position the caliper and install the bolts. Torque the bolts to 23 ft. lbs.

Brake Rotor

Removal and Installation

1. Remove the center hub cap and halfshaft nut. Then raise the vehicle and support it safely. Allow the wheels to hang freely. Then remove the front wheel.

2. Remove the brake caliper without disconnecting the hydraulic line and suspend it out of the way with a piece of wire.

3. Disconnect the stabilizer bar and strut bar from the lower control arm.

4. Remove the halfshaft from the transaxle and press the halfshaft out of the hub with a 2 jawed puller.

5. Unbolt and remove the hub and knuckle from the bottom of the strut and remove the hub and knuckle assembly from the vehicle.

6. Several special tools are required to press the hub and disc from the steering knuckle and to remount them. Use 09517–21600 or equivalent. Do not attempt to hammer the parts apart, or the bearing will be damaged. Install the arm of the special tool then the body onto the knuckle and tighten the nut manually. Using special tool 09517–21500, separate the hub from the knuckle. Pull the bearings out, noting their positions and direction of installation (smaller diameter inward).

7. Matchmark the relationship between the brake disc and hub. Then place the knuckle in a vise and separate the rotor from the hub by removing the attaching bolts.

To install:

8. Installation is the reverse order of the removal procedure. Torque the hub nut to 188 ft. lbs. (255 Nm).

Brake Drums

Removal and Installation

1. Raise the vehicle and support safely.

2. Remove the wheel and tire assembly.

3. Remove the dust cap.

4. Remove the cotter pin and nut lock.

5. Remove the wheel bearing nut and washer from the spindle.

6. Remove the outer wheel bearing.

7. Remove the drum with the inner wheel bearing from the spindle. If the drum is difficult to remove, remove the plug from the rear of the backing plate and push the self adjuster lever away from the star wheel. Rotate the star wheel to retract the shoes. Remove the grease seal.

To install:

8. Lubricate and install the inner wheel bearing. Install a new grease seal.

9. Install the drum to the spindle.

10. Lubricate and install the outer wheel bearing, washer and nut. When the bearing preload is properly set, install the nut lock and a new cotter pin.

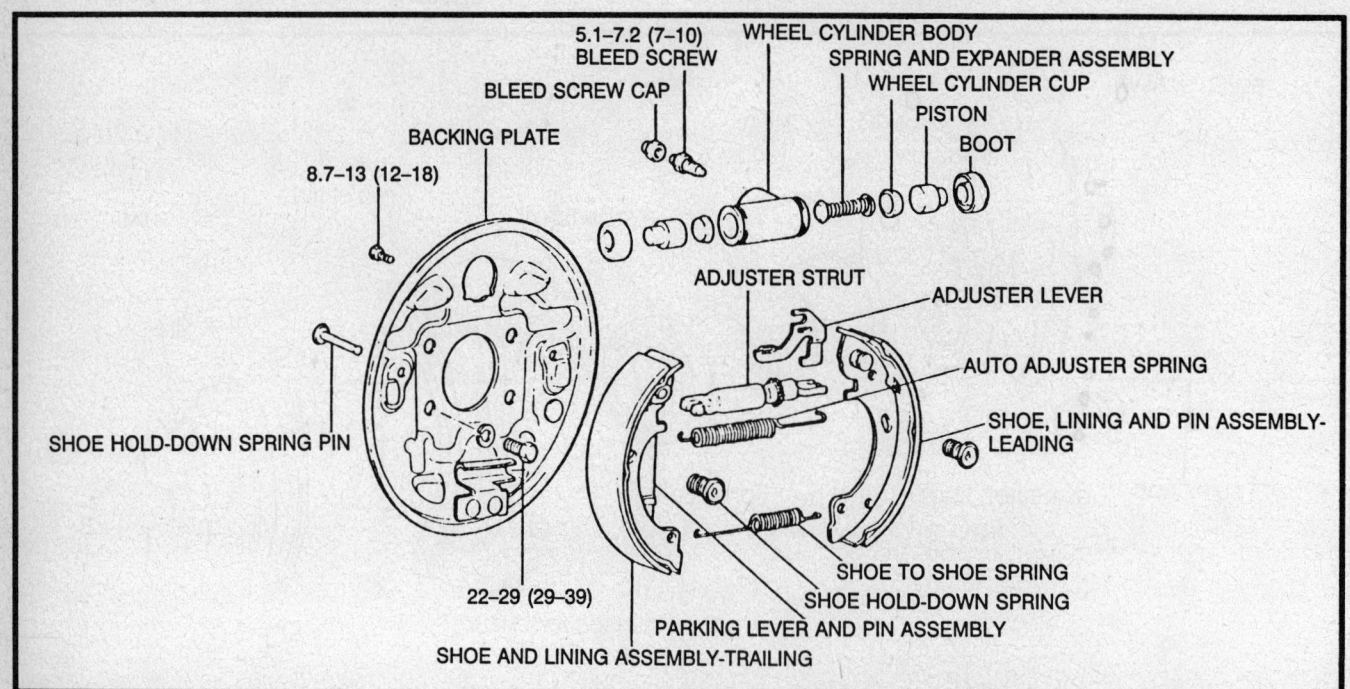

Excel rear brake components

11. Install the grease cap.
12. Install the wheel and tire assembly. Adjust the rear brakes as required.

Brake Shoes

Removal and Installation
EXCEL AND SCOUPE

1. Raise the vehicle and support it safely.
2. Remove the rear wheels.
3. Pry off the hub grease cap.
4. Remove the cotter pin, lock cap and bearing adjusting nut.
5. Remove the outer bearing and pull the hub and drum assembly from the spindle.
6. Thoroughly clean the spindle.
7. Remove the lower pressed metal spring clip, the shoe return spring, the large 1 piece spring between the 2 shoes, and the shoe hold-down springs.
8. Remove the shoes and adjuster as an assembly.
9. Disconnect the parking brake cable from the lever.
10. Remove the spring between the shoes and the lever from the rear (trailing) shoe.
11. Disconnect the adjuster retaining spring and remove the adjuster, turn the star wheel in to the adjuster body after cleaning and lubricating the threads.
To install:
12. Clean the backing plate with solvent made for cleaning brakes.
13. Lubricate all contact points on the backing plate, anchor plate, wheel cylinder to shoe contact and parking brake strut joints and contacts with lithium based grease.
14. Installation of the brake shoes, from this point, is the reverse of removal after the lever has been transferred to the new rear (trailing) shoe.
15. Pre-adjustment of the brake shoe can be made by turning the adjuster star wheel out until the drum will just slide on over the brake shoes. Before installing the drum make sure the parking brake is not adjusted too tightly, if it is, loosen it, or the adjustment of the rear brakes will not be correct.
16. Position the hub assembly on the spindle.
17. Insert the packed outer bearing, retaining washer and adjusting nut.

18. While rotating the hub, tighten the adjusting nut to 15 ft. lbs., then back it off until loose.
19. Torque the nut again, this time to 48 inch lbs.
20. Install the lock cap and turn the nut counterclockwise just enough to align the cap and cotter pin hole. Insert a new cotter pin. Never back the nut off more than 15 degrees to align the cotter pin hole. If more is necessary, repeat the entire adjustment procedure.
21. The brakes shoes are adjusted by pumping the brake pedal and applying and releasing the parking brake. Adjust the parking brake stroke. Road test the vehicle.

SONATA

1. Raise the vehicle and support it safely.
2. Remove the wheels.
3. Remove the hub nut, outer bearing and brake drum.
4. Thoroughly clean the spindle.
5. Clean the brake shoes and backing plate with a commercially available solvent.
6. Remove the lower spring.
7. Remove the upper spring.
8. Remove the hold-down springs.
9. Remove the shoes and adjuster.
10. Disconnect the parking brake cable from the adjuster arm.
To install:
11. Apply a thin coating of lithium based grease to the backing plate pads.
12. Connect the parking brake cable to the adjuster.
13. Position the shoes on the backing plate and install the hold-down springs and pins.
14. Install the upper spring, then the lower spring and adjuster spring.
15. Install the drum and adjust the wheel bearings.

Wheel Cylinder

Removal and Installation

1. Raise the vehicle and support it safely. Remove the tire and wheel assembly.
2. Remove the brake drums and shoes.

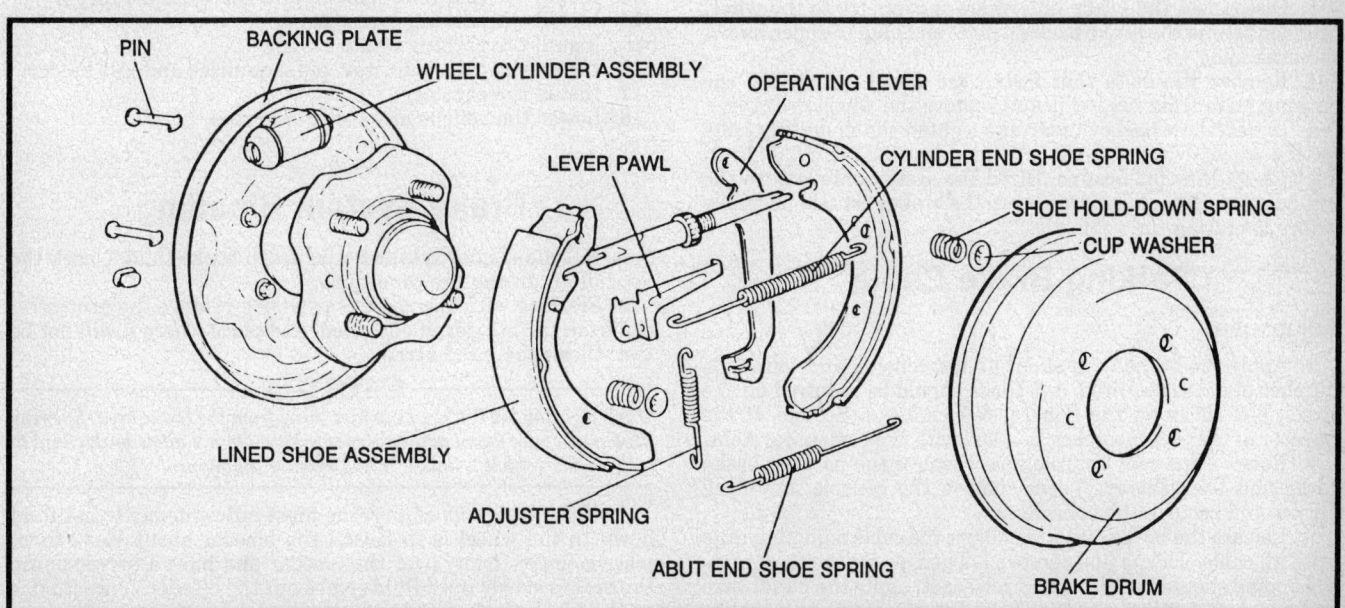

PIN   BACKING PLATE   WHEEL CYLINDER ASSEMBLY   OPERATING LEVER
LEVER PAWL   CYLINDER END SHOE SPRING
SHOE HOLD-DOWN SPRING
CUP WASHER
LINED SHOE ASSEMBLY
ADJUSTER SPRING
ABUT END SHOE SPRING
BRAKE DRUM

Sonata rear brake components

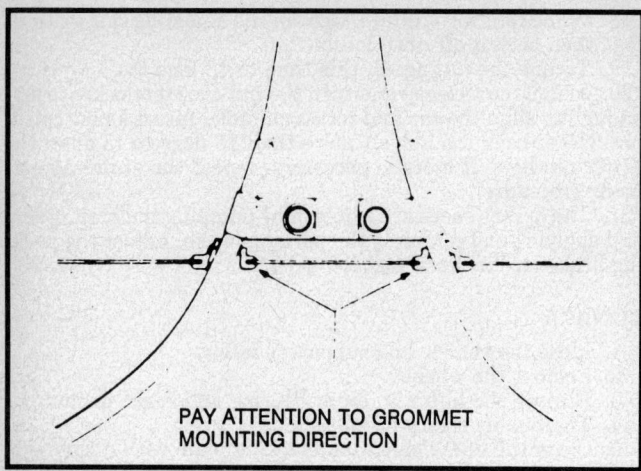

PAY ATTENTION TO GROMMET
MOUNTING DIRECTION

Parking brake cable grommet positioning

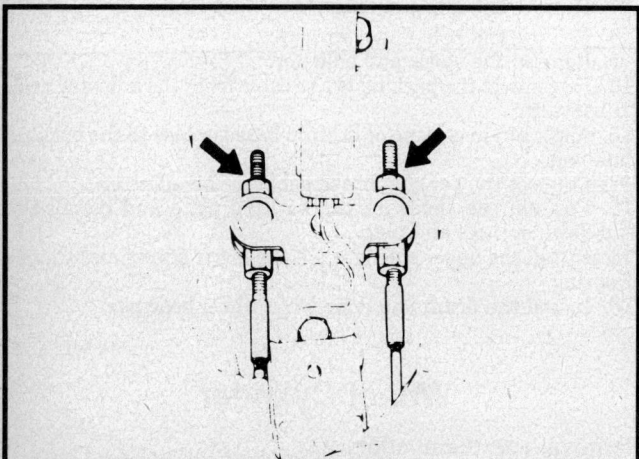

Parking brake cable adjusting nuts

3. Disconnect the brake line where it connects to the wheel cylinder behind the brake backing plate and plug the open end of the brake line.

4. Remove the bolts that fasten the wheel cylinder to the backing plate from behind it and remove the wheel cylinder.

5. Install the wheel cylinder and tighten the mounting bolts for the wheel cylinder to 72–108 inch lbs. (8–12 Nm); 9–13 ft. lbs. (12–18 Nm) for Scoupe. Bleed the system. Make sure the self-adjusters have taken up play so the brakes actuate normally before operating the vehicle.

Parking Brake Cable

Adjustment

1. Apply the brake with about 45 lbs. tension and count the number of clicks required. 5–7 clicks should be required on the Excel; 8–9 clicks on the Sonata; 6–7 clicks on Scoupe. If the number of clicks is incorrect, proceed with the remaining steps.

2. Remove the rear console box. Remove the parking brake cover and the ashtray. Then, remove the console mounting screws and remove the console.

3. Release the brake and then adjust the cable adjusting nuts until all cable slack is just removed. Then, apply the footbrake, the engine should be idling, and release it, apply the handbrake and release it, apply the footbrake and release it, etc. in a continuous cycle until the automatic adjusters stop clicking.

4. Recheck the number of clicks required to apply the brake, adjust the cable adjuster and repeat the check until the number of clicks required is correct.

5. Reinstall the console in reverse of the removal procedure.

6. Raise the vehicle and support it safely. Release the hand brake and rotate each rear wheel to make sure the brakes are not dragging.

Removal and Installation

EXCEL AND SCOUPE

1. Raise the vehicle and support it safely. Remove the rear wheels and brake drums.

2. Remove the console box and rear seat.

3. Release the hand brake and then disconnect the cable connectors at the equalizer. It may be necessary to loosen the cable adjusting nuts to do this.

4. Disconnect all cable clamps from the body. Remove the mounting bolts for the large mounting clamp located just forward of where the cables pass through the body grommets.

5. Pull the cables and grommets out of the body.

6. Disconnect the cables at the rear brakes.

To install:

7. When installing the cables, make sure the grommets are installed in the body completely and that the concave side faces to the rear. Adjust the hand brake mechanism. Adjust the switch for the indicator light so the light comes on when the lever is pulled 1 notch.

SONATA

1. Raise the vehicle and support it safely.

2. Remove the console.

3. Remove the cable adjuster, pin, equalizer and nut holder.

4. Remove the parking brake switch.

5. Remove the parking brake lever.

6. Remove the rear seat cushion and roll back the carpet.

7. Remove the brake cable clamp and grommet.

8. Remove the brake drums and shoes.

9. Disconnect the brake cables from the adjusting arms.

10. Remove the retaining clips and push the cable out of the backing plates.

To install:

11. Connect the brake cables to the adjusting arms.

12. Install the brake shoes and drums.

13. Install the rear seat cushion and roll back the carpet.

14. Install the parking brake lever.

15. Install the parking brake switch.

16. Install the cable adjuster, pin, equalizer and nut holder.

17. Install the console.

18. Lower the vehicle and test the brakes.

Brake System Bleeding

1. Fill the master cylinder with fresh brake fluid. Check the level often during the procedure.

2. Starting with the right rear wheel, remove the protective cap from the bleeder, if equipped, and place where it will not be lost. Clean the bleed screw.

——— CAUTION ———

When bleeding the brakes, keep face away from the brake area. Spewing fluid may cause facial and/or visual injury. Do not allow brake fluid to spill on the vehicle's finish; it will remove the paint.

3. If the system is empty, the most efficient way to get fluid down to the wheel is to loosen the bleeder about ½–¾ turn, place a finger firmly over the bleeder and have a helper pump the brakes slowly until fluid comes out the bleeder. Once fluid is at the bleeder, close it before the pedal is released inside the vehicle.

NOTE: If the pedal is pumped rapidly, the fluid will churn and create small air bubbles, which are almost impossible to remove from the system. These air bubbles will eventually congregate and a spongy pedal will result.

4. Once fluid has been pumped to the caliper or wheel cylinder, open the bleed screw again, have an assistant press the brake pedal to the floor, lock the bleeder and have an assitant slowly release the pedal. Wait 15 seconds and repeat the procedure, including the 15 second wait, until no more air comes out of the bleeder upon application of the brake pedal. Remember to close the bleeder before the pedal is released inside the vehicle each time the bleeder is opened. If not, air will be induced into the system.

5. If a helper is not available, connect a small hose to the bleeder, place the end in a container of brake fluid and proceed to pump the pedal from inside the vehicle until no more air comes out the bleeder. The hose will prevent air from entering the system.

6. Repeat the procedure on remaining wheel cylinders in order:
   a. Left rear
   b. Right front
   c. Left front

7. Hydraulic brake systems must be totally flushed, if the fluid becomes contaminated with water, dirt or other corrosive chemicals. To flush, bleed the entire system until all fluid has been replaced with the correct type of new fluid.

8. Install the bleeder cap(s) on the bleeder to keep dirt out. Always road test the vehicle.

FRONT SUSPENSION

MacPherson Strut

Removal and Installation

1. Raise the vehicle and support it safely. Remove the front wheels. Detach the brake hose bracket at the strut.
2. Remove the nuts securing the strut to the fender well.
3. Unbolt the strut lower end from the knuckle.
4. Remove the strut from the vehicle.
5. To install, reposition the strut and tighten the bolts. Observe the following torques:
   Strut-to-knuckle bolts—55–65 ft. lbs. for Excel.
   Strut-to-knuckle bolts—65–76 ft. lbs. for Sonata.
   Strut-to-knuckle bolts—54–64 ft. lbs. for Scoupe.
   Strut-to-fender well nuts—7–11 ft. lbs. for Excel.
   Strut-to-fender well nuts—18–25 ft. lbs. for Sonata.
   Strut-to-fender well nuts—11–14 ft. lbs. for Scoupe.

Lower Ball Joints

Inspection

Raise the vehicle and support it safely. Disconnect the ball joint at the lower end of the strut. Install the nut back onto the ball stud. Then, with an inch lbs., torque wrench, measure the torque required to start the ball joint rotating. The figures are 26–86 inch lbs. If the figures are within specification, the ball joint is satisfactory. If the figure is too high, the joint should be replaced. If the figure is too low, reuse the joint, provided its rotation is smooth and even. If there is roughness or play, it must be replaced.

Removal and Installation
EXCEL AND SCOUPE

1. Raise the vehicle and support it safely.
2. Unbolt the ball joint from the control arm.
3. Remove the stud retaining nut.
4. Use a ball joint removing tool and separate the ball joint from the steering knuckle.
5. Replace the ball joint and tighten the ball joint to control arm to 69–87 ft. lbs. (99–118 Nm). Torque the ball joint stud nut 43–52 ft. lbs. (59–71 Nm).

SONATA

1. Raise the vehicle and support it safely. Remove the tire and wheel and tire assemblies.
2. Remove the lower control arm from the vehicle.

3. Remove the ball joint dust cover. Using a special tool, press the ball joint from the control arm.
To install:
4. Apply grease to the lip of the control arm and to the ball joint contact surfaces.
5. Place the ball joint in the control arm. Using a special tool, press the ball joint into the control arm. The ball joint must be pressed evenly into the control arm.

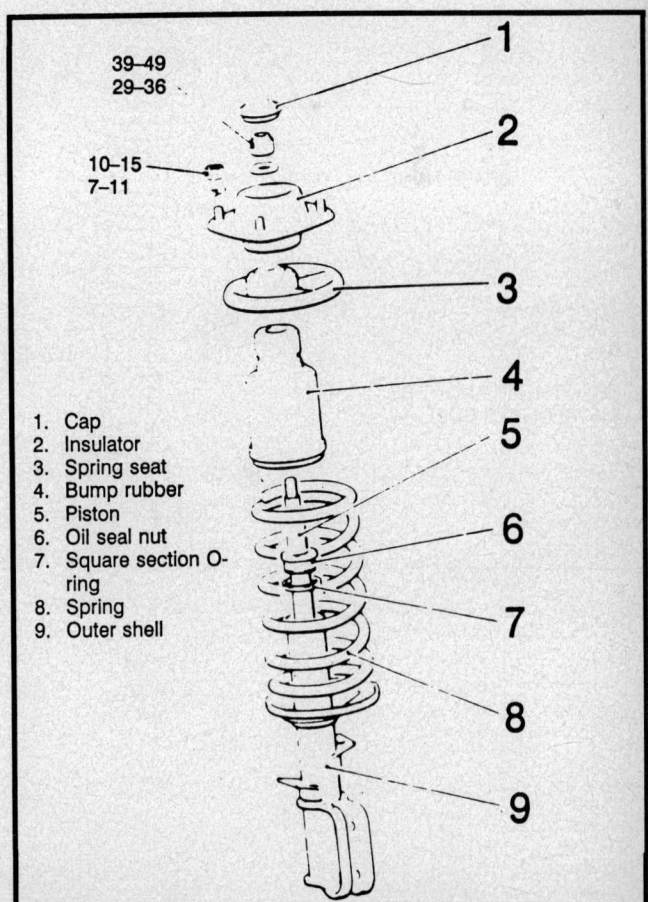

39–49
29–36
10–15
7–11

1. Cap
2. Insulator
3. Spring seat
4. Bump rubber
5. Piston
6. Oil seal nut
7. Square section O-ring
8. Spring
9. Outer shell

Excel front strut

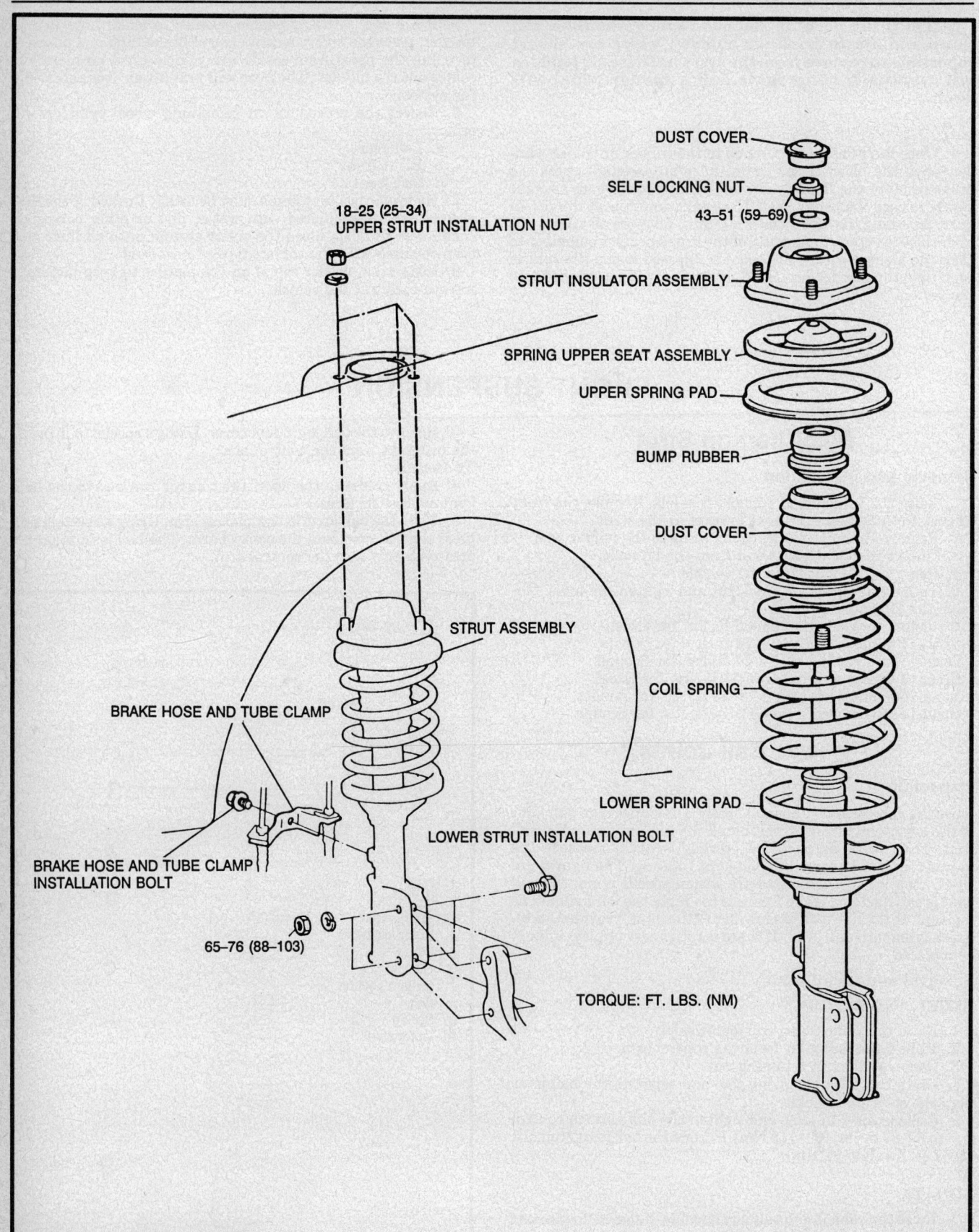

DUST COVER

SELF LOCKING NUT

43–51 (59–69)

18–25 (25–34)
UPPER STRUT INSTALLATION NUT

STRUT INSULATOR ASSEMBLY

SPRING UPPER SEAT ASSEMBLY

UPPER SPRING PAD

BUMP RUBBER

DUST COVER

STRUT ASSEMBLY

COIL SPRING

BRAKE HOSE AND TUBE CLAMP

BRAKE HOSE AND TUBE CLAMP
INSTALLATION BOLT

LOWER STRUT INSTALLATION BOLT

LOWER SPRING PAD

65–76 (88–103)

TORQUE: FT. LBS. (NM)

Sonata front strut

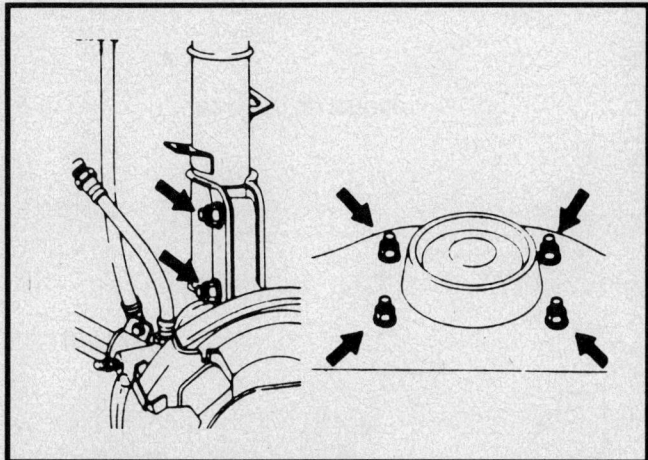

Excel strut attachment points

6. Install a new dust cover on the ball joint. Install the control arm assembly into the vehicle. Torque the ball joint-to-steering knuckle retaining nut to 52 ft. lbs. (71 Nm).

7. Install the wheel and tire assembly. Lower the vehicle.

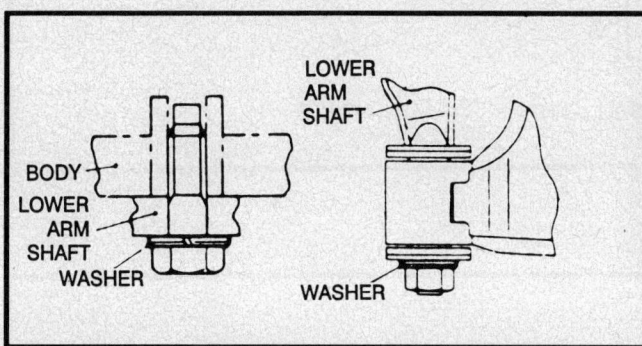

Lower control arm installation on the Excel

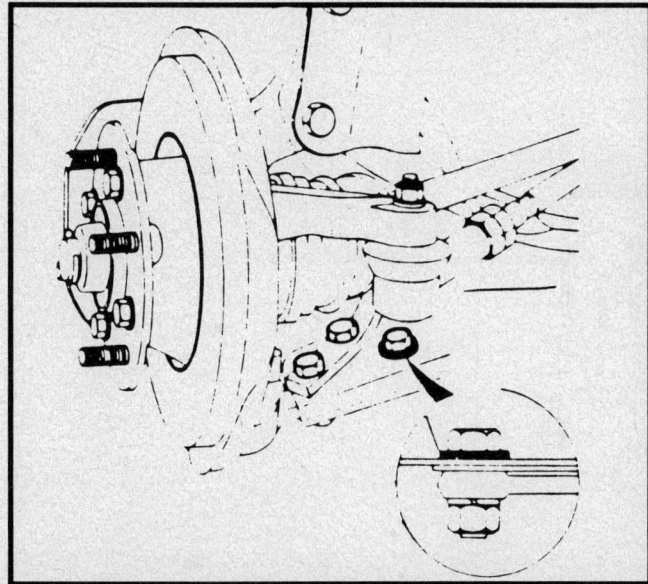

On the Excel, install a flat washer after the ball joint is mounted in the control arm

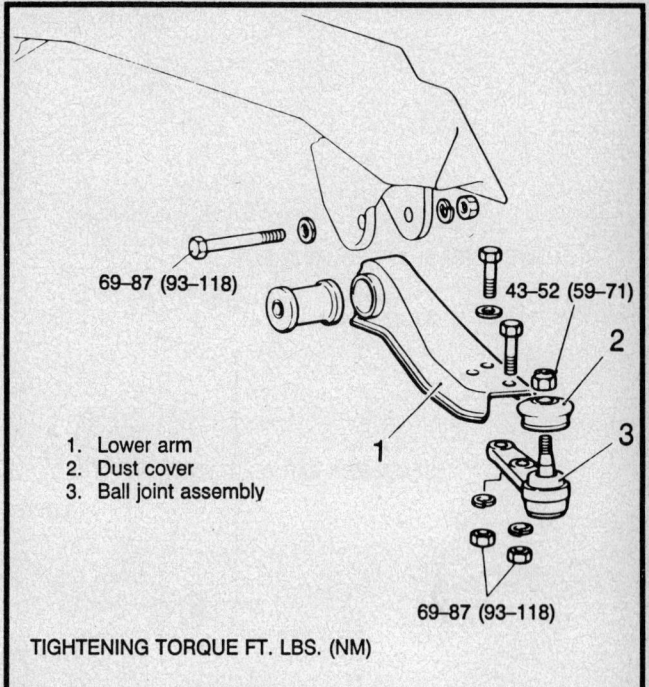

1. Lower arm
2. Dust cover
3. Ball joint assembly

TIGHTENING TORQUE FT. LBS. (NM)

Excel lower control arm

Lower Control Arms

Removal and Installation

EXCEL

1. Raise the vehicle and support it safely. Remove the front wheel and tire assembly.

2. Remove the undercover.

3. Disconnect the stabilizer bar from the lower arm. Remove the nut from under the control arm and take off the washer and spacer.

4. Remove the ball joint stud nut and press the tool off with a tool such as MB991113 or equivalent.

5. Remove the bolts which retain the spacer at the rear and the nut and washers on the front of the lower arm shaft (at the front). Slide the arm forward, off the shaft and out of the bushing.

6. Replace the dust cover on the ball joint. The new cover must be greased on the lip and inside with 2 EP multi-purpose grease or equivalent, and pressed on, with special tool MB990800 or equivalent, until it is fully seated.

To install:

7. When installing the control arm, the nut on the stabilizer bar bolt must be torqued until the link shows 0.8–0.9 in. (21–23mm) of threads below the bottom of the nut. Also, the washer for the lower arm must be installed as shown. The left side arm shaft has a left hand thread. Tighten the all fasteners with the vehicle on the ground. Observe the following torques:

Knuckle-to-strut—54–65 ft. lbs.
Lower arm shaft-to-body—69–87 ft. lbs.
Stabilizer bar-to-body—22–29 ft. lbs.
Stabilizer bar-to-strut bar—48–60 inch lbs.
Ball joint-to-knuckle—44–53 ft. lbs.
Lower arm-to-strut bar—70–88 ft. lbs.
Strut bar-to-body—55–60 ft. lbs.
Strut bar inner locknut—55–60 ft. lbs.

SONATA

1. Raise the vehicle and support it safely.

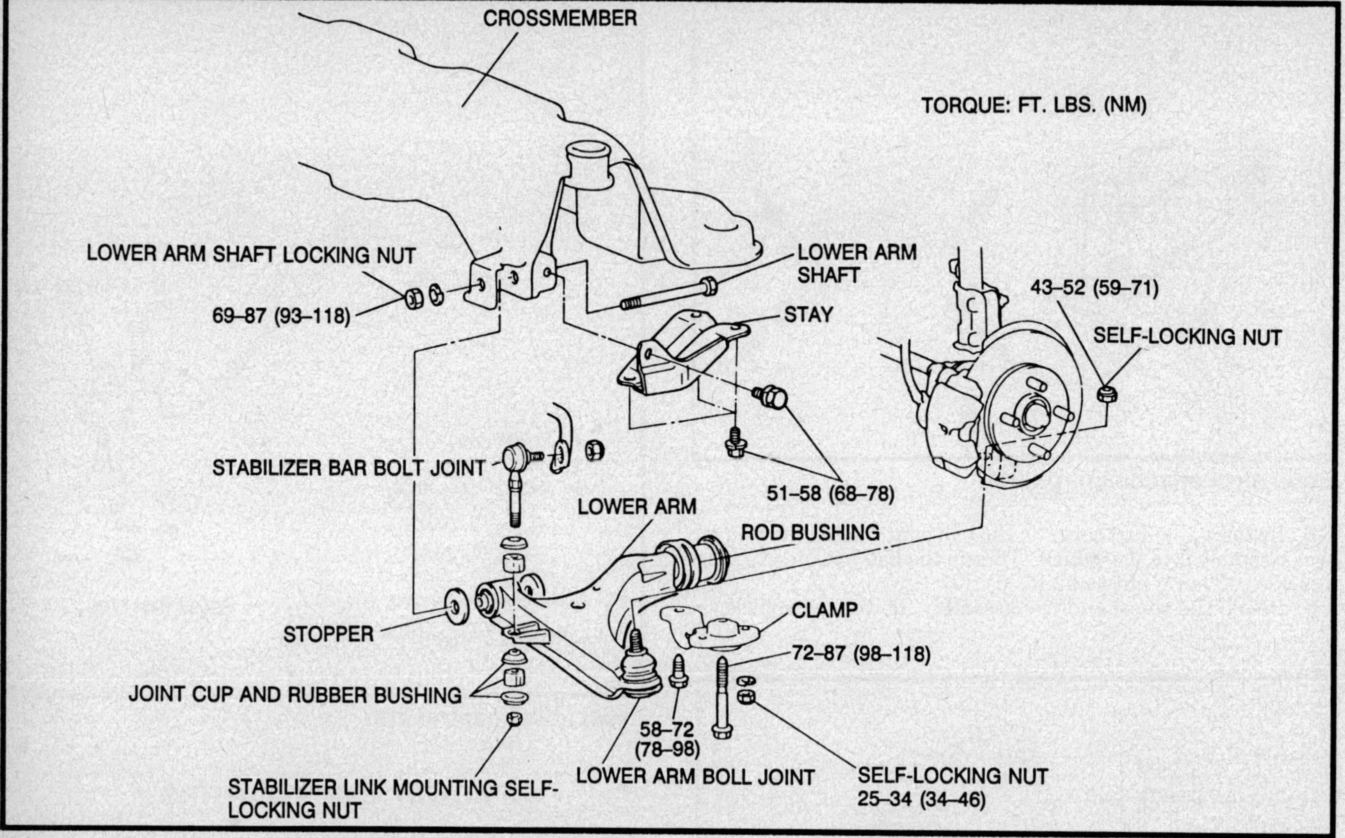

CROSSMEMBER

TORQUE: FT. LBS. (NM)

LOWER ARM SHAFT LOCKING NUT

69–87 (93–118)

LOWER ARM SHAFT

STAY

43–52 (59–71)

SELF-LOCKING NUT

STABILIZER BAR BOLT JOINT

LOWER ARM

ROD BUSHING

51–58 (68–78)

STOPPER

CLAMP

72–87 (98–118)

JOINT CUP AND RUBBER BUSHING

58–72 (78–98)

LOWER ARM BOLL JOINT

SELF-LOCKING NUT
25–34 (34–46)

STABILIZER LINK MOUNTING SELF-LOCKING NUT

Sonata lower control arm and related components

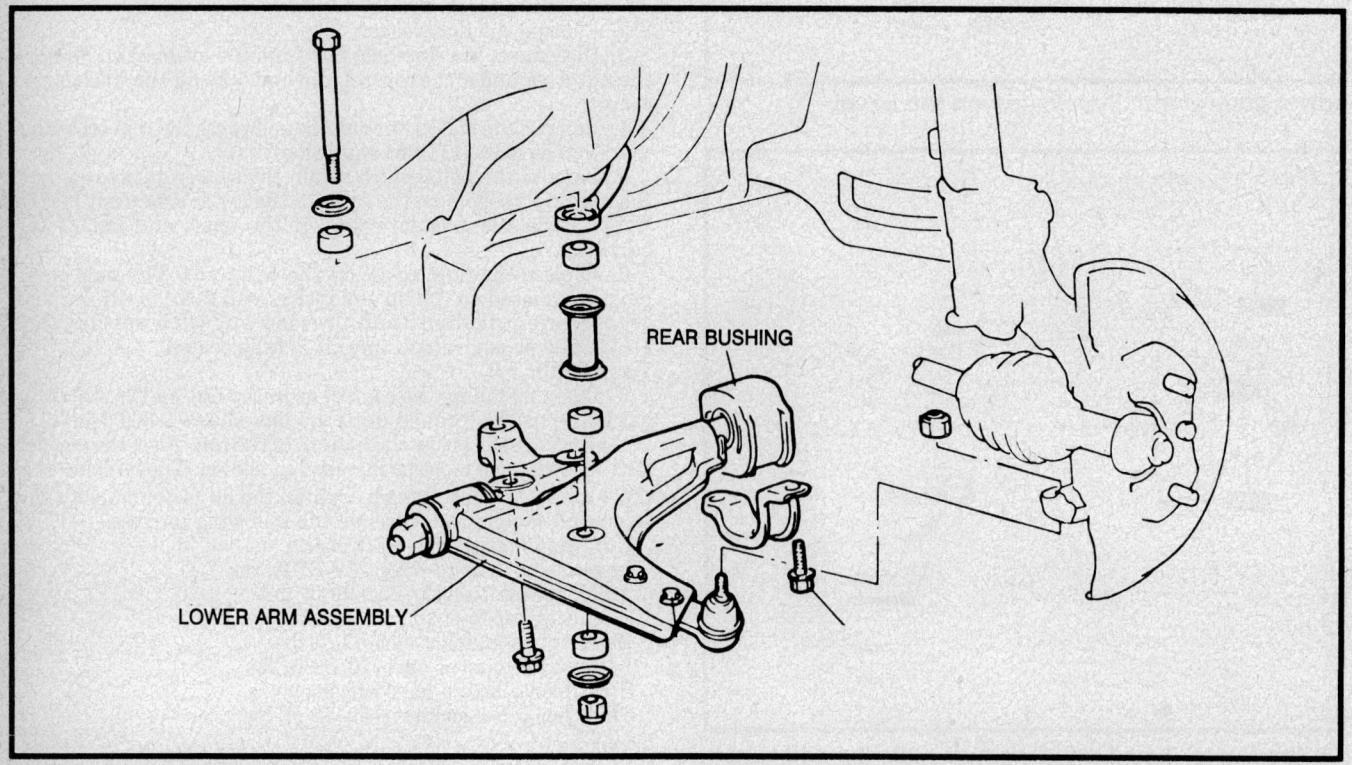

REAR BUSHING

LOWER ARM ASSEMBLY

Lower control arm assemlby—Scoupe

2. Loosen the ball joint nut and, using special tool 09568-3100 or equivalent. Disconnect the joint from the knuckle. Be sure to secure the tool's cord to a nearby part.

3. Once the ball joint is free, remove the nut.

4. Remove the stabilizer bar.

5. Remove the control arm-to-crossmber bolt.

To install:

6. Installation is the reverse of removal. Torque the control arm-to-crossmember bolt to 70–87 ft. lbs. Install the stabilizer bar link nut until 5–7mm of threads show beneath the nut. Torque the ball joint stud nut to 50 ft. lbs.

SCOUPE

1. Raise and safely support the vehicle.

2. Remove the tire and wheel assembly.

3. Using special tool 09545–21000 or equivalent, disconnect the lower arm ball joint from the knuckle.

4. Remove the stabilizer bar mounting bolt and nut and detach the stabilizer bar from the lower arm.

5. Detach the lower arm bracket. Remove the lower arm mounting shaft bolts and separate.

6. Remove the lower arm.

7. Install the lower control arm by reversing the removal procedure observing the following torque values:

Lower arm shaft-to-body – 69–87 ft. lbs.
Lower arm rear bushing bracket-to-body – 43–58 ft. lbs.
Stabilizer bar-to-body – 12–19 ft. lbs.
Ball joint-to-knuckle – 43–52 ft. lbs.
Ball joint-to-lower arm – 69–87 ft. lbs.

Stabilizer Bar

Removal and Installation

EXCEL

1. Raise the vehicle and support it safely.

2. Unbolt the stabilizer clamps from the crossmember.

3. Unbolt the stabilizer bar from the strut bar.

4. Examine the bushings for cracks and wear, if one is worn or cracked all the bushings must be replaced.

To install:

5. Installation is the reverse order of the removal procedures. Reposition the stabilizer bar and tighten the chassis clamp bolts to 29 ft. lbs.; the strut bar clamps to 50 inch lbs.

SONATA

1. Raise the vehicle and support it safely.

2. Remove the stabilizer bar brackets from the crossmember.

3. Lower the rear of the center member and lower the stabilizer bar.

4. Disconnect the end links and remove the stabilizer.

5. Installation is the reverse order of the removal procedures. Torque the end link nuts to 45 ft. lbs.; the bracket bolts to 30 ft. lbs.

SCOUPE

1. Raise and safely support the vehicle.

2. Remove the tire and wheel assembly.

3. Disconnect the tie rod end ball joint from the knuckle using special tool 09568–31000 or equivalent.

4. Remove the rear roll stopper mounting bolt and rear roll bracket asembly mounting bolt.

5. Pull the rear roll bracket assembly forward.

6. Loosen the stabilizer link bolt and nut, then separate the stabilizer bar from the lower arm.

7. Loosen the stabilizer bar mounting bolts through the steering gear box access opening provided on the vehicle body.

8. Remove the stabilizer through the access opening.

9. Detach the upper and lower bracket, then remove the bushing.

10. Install the stabilizer bar by reversing the removal procedure, observing the following torque values:

Stabilizer bar bracket bolts – 12–19 ft. lbs.
Ball joint-to-knuckle – 43–52 ft. lbs.

Strut Bar

Removal and Installation

EXCEL

1. Raise the vehicle and support it safely.

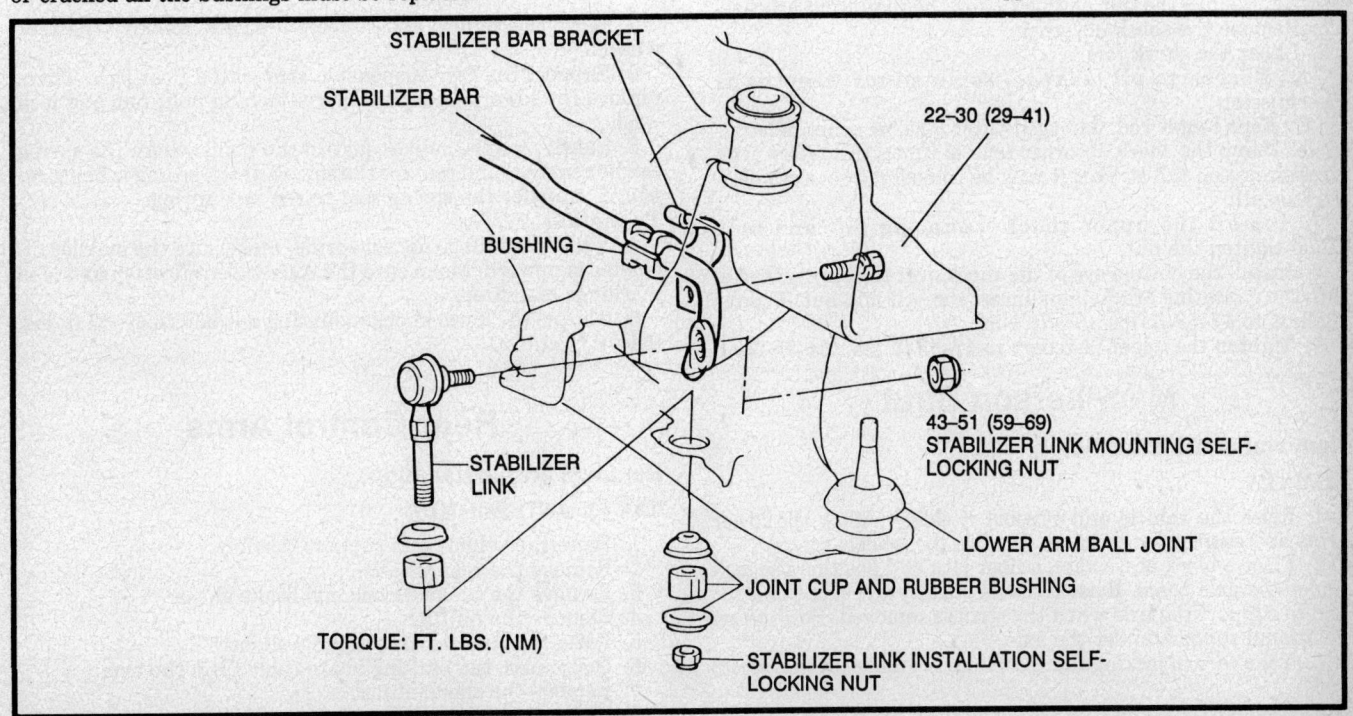

Sonata front stabilizer bar components

STABILIZER BAR BRACKET
STABILIZER BAR
BUSHING
22–30 (29–41)
STABILIZER LINK
43–51 (59–69)
STABILIZER LINK MOUNTING SELF-LOCKING NUT
LOWER ARM BALL JOINT
JOINT CUP AND RUBBER BUSHING
STABILIZER LINK INSTALLATION SELF-LOCKING NUT
TORQUE: FT. LBS. (NM)

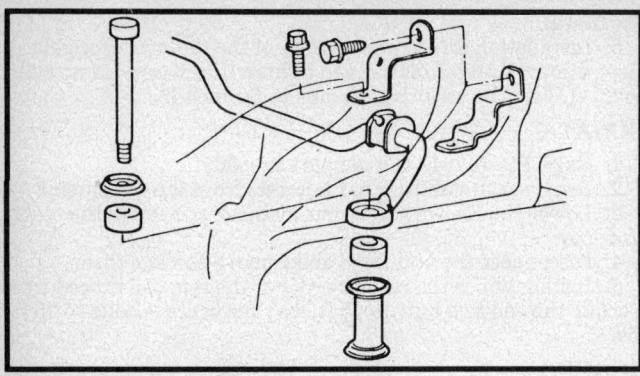

Stabilizer bar installation—Scoupe

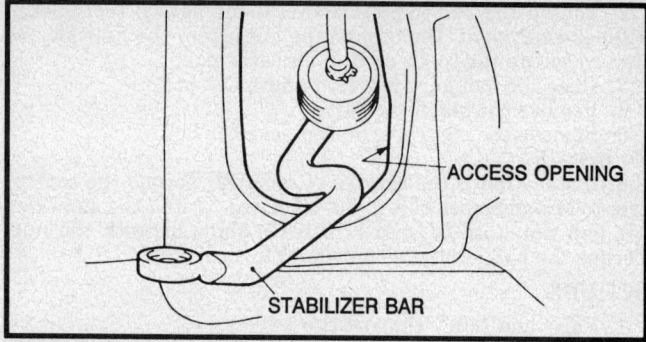

Stabilizer bar removal—Scoupe

2. Unbolt the stabilizer bar from the strut bar.
3. Remove the bolts securing the strut bar to the control arm.
4. Remove the strut bar-to-frame bracket outer nut and pull the bar from the bracket.
5. Inspect all parts and replace any cracked, dry or deformed parts. The strut bar bend must not exceed 3mm over its entire length.

To install:
6. Installation is the reverse order of the removal procedures. Note that the left side bar is identified with a dab of white paint. When installing the strut bar at the strut bar bracket, the distance between the inner locknut and the end of the strut bar must be 80.5mm. Torque the stabilizer bar-to-strut bar clamp bolts to 50 inch lbs.; the strut bar-to-control arm bolts to 87 ft. lbs.; the strut bar-to-bracket nut to 60 ft. lbs.

REAR SUSPENSION

Shock Absorbers

Removal and Installation
EXCEL AND SCOUPE

1. Remove the wheel cover. Loosen the lug nuts.
2. Raise the vehicle and support it safely. Remove the wheel.
3. Remove the upper mounting bolt/nut or nut.
4. While holding the bottom stud mount nut with one wrench, remove the locknut with another wrench, or on some vehicles, remove the nut and bolt from the mounting bracket.
5. Remove the shock absorber.
6. Check the shock for:
   a. Excessive oil leakage, some minor weeping is permissible;
   b. Bent center rod, damaged outer case, or other defects;
   c. Pump the shock absorber several times, if it offers even resistance on full strokes it may be considered serviceable.

To install:
7. Install the upper shock mounting nut and bolt. Hand-tighten the nut.
8. Install the bottom eye of the shock over the spring stud or into the mounting bracket and insert the bolt and nut. Tighten the nut to 47–58 ft. lbs. (64–78 Nm).
9. Tighten the upper fasteners to 47–58 ft. lbs. (64–78 Nm).

MacPherson Strut

Removal and Installation
SONATA

1. Raise the vehicle and support it safely. Allow the lower arms and suspension to hang. Remove the wheels.
2. Place a block of wood on a floor jack and position the jack under the axle beam. Raise the axle slightly to relax the strut and to support the axle when the strut is removed. Position an additional support under the axle.
3. Take care in jacking that no contact is made on the lateral rod.
4. Remove the upper dust cover cap from the strut assembly.
5. Remove the upper mounting nuts. Remove the lower mounting bolt and nut.

6. Remove the strut.
To install:
7. Installation is the reverse order of the removal procedures. Torque the lower mounting bolt and nut to 58–72 ft. lbs.; The upper mounting nuts to 18–25 ft. lbs.

Coil Springs

Removal and Installation
EXCEL AND SCOUPE

1. Raise the vehicle and support it safely. Remove the rear wheels.
2. Support the rear suspension arm with a floor jack. Then, remove the lower shock absorber attaching bolt, nut and lock washer.
3. Slowly, lower the jack just to the point where the spring can be removed and remove the spring. If the spring is being replaced, transfer the spring seat to the new spring.
To install:
4. When installing the coil spring, make sure the smaller diameter is upward. Make sure the spring identification and load markings match up.
5. Torque the lower shock mounting nut/bolt to 47–58 ft. lbs. (64–78 Nm).

Rear Control Arms

Removal and Installation
EXCEL AND SCOUPE

1. Raise the vehicle and support it safely.
2. Remove the rear wheels.
3. Remove the brake drums and brake shoes.
4. Remove the muffler.
5. Raise the suspension assembly slightly.
6. Disconnect the parking brake cable from the arm.
7. Remove the shock absorber.
8. Disconnect the brake hoses from their clips on the suspension members.
9. Lower the suspension. Remove the coil spring.

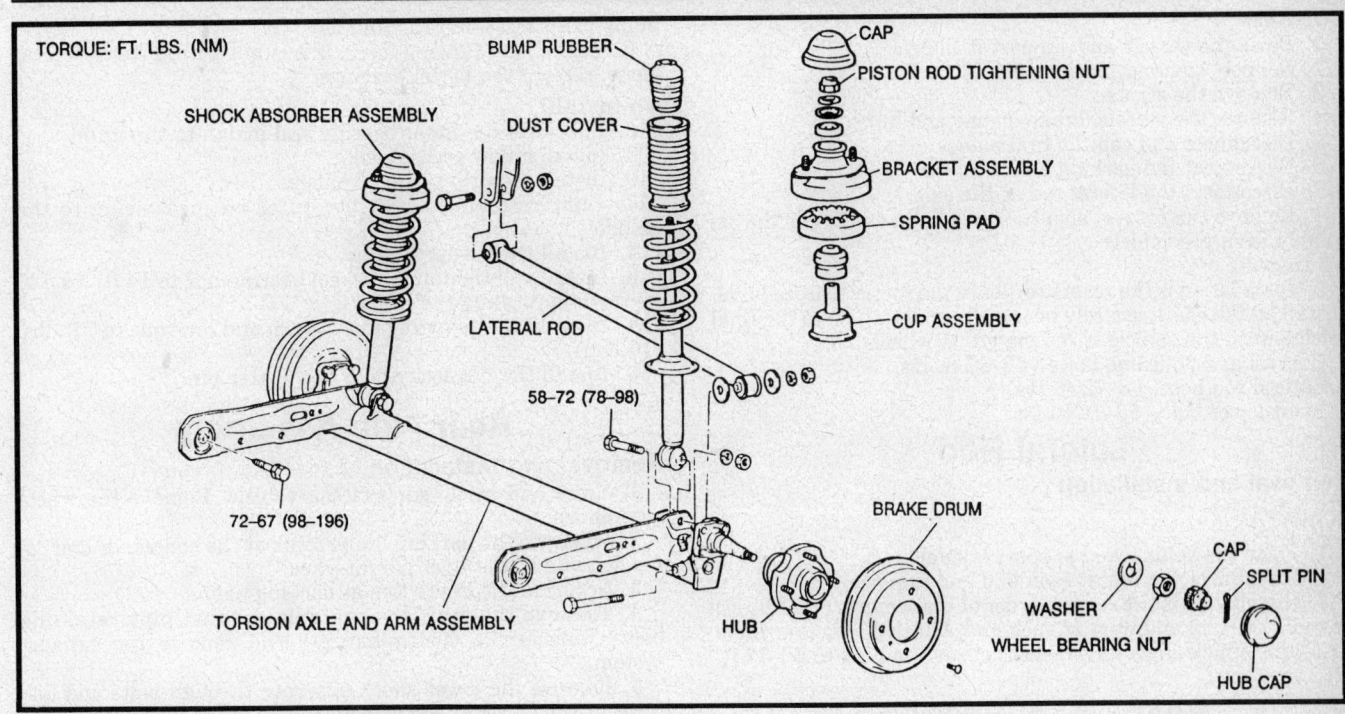

TORQUE: FT. LBS. (NM)

BUMP RUBBER

CAP

PISTON ROD TIGHTENING NUT

SHOCK ABSORBER ASSEMBLY

DUST COVER

BRACKET ASSEMBLY

SPRING PAD

CUP ASSEMBLY

LATERAL ROD

58–72 (78–98)

BRAKE DRUM

72–67 (98–196)

CAP

SPLIT PIN

WASHER

WHEEL BEARING NUT

HUB CAP

TORSION AXLE AND ARM ASSEMBLY

HUB

Sonata rear suspension components

1. Suspension arm (R.H.)
2. Dust cover
3. Clamp
4. Bushing A
5. Bushing B
6. Rubber stopper
7. Suspension arm (L.H.
8. Rubber bushing (inner)
9. Rubber stopper
10. Fixture
11. Rubber bushing (outer)
12. Washer
13. Stabilizer bar
14. Spring seat
15. Coil spring
16. Shock absorber
17. Bump stopper

	Nm	ft. lbs.
A	65–80	46–56
B	50–70	36–51
C	80–100	56–70
D	18–25	13–18

Excel rear suspension

10. Remove the rear suspension from the vehicle as an assembly.

11. Matchmark all parts for assembly reference; this is extremely important! If equipped with stabilizer bars, make a mark on the bar in line with the punch mark on the bracket.

12. Remove the dust cover clamp.

13. Remove the nuts securing the control arms and pull them apart. Leave the dust cover attached to the right arm.

14. Remove the rubber stopper from the right arm.

15. Using a flat bladed chisel, drive bushing from right the arm.

16. Using a brass drift, drive bushing out from the left arm.

17. Coat the inside of the left arm and the outside of the bushing with chassis lube and drive it into place with a suitable driver such as tools 09555-21100 and 09555-21000 or equivalent. Drive the bushing in until the notch on 09555-21000 or equivalent, reaches the end of the arm.

18. Coat the inside of the arm and the outside of the bushing with chassis lube and drive it into the arm until it is fully seated.

19. Install the dust cover to the center position of the right arm, about 400mm.

20. Apply chassis lube to the surface of the right arm and install the rubber stopper.

21. Align all matchmarks, including the stabilizer bar and slowly push the suspension halves together.

22. Install all remaining bushing, washers and attaching parts.

NOTE: The toothed sides of the washers face the bushings.

23. Install the end nuts and torque them loosely at this time.
To install:

24. Jack the assembly into position and torque the suspension-to-body bolts to 50 ft. lbs.

25. Install the coil springs and loosely install the shock absorbers.

26. Install the rear brake assembly.

27. Attach the parking brake cable and brake hoses to their clips on the suspension.

28. Install the wheels.

29. Lower the vehicle and tighten the suspension arm end nuts to 50 ft. lbs.; the shock bolts to 47–58 ft. lbs.

SONATA

1. Raise the vehicle and support it safely.
2. Support the rear torsion axle.
3. Remove the struts.
4. Remove the wheels, brake drums and hubs.
5. Disconnect and cap the brake lines.
6. Disconnect the parking brake cables.
7. Disconnect the lateral rod at the axle.
8. Remove the control arm-to-frame bolts and lower the assembly from the vehicle.

To install:

9. Installation is the reverse order of the removal procedures. Install all fasteners securely but don't tighten them to the final torque until the vehicle is resting on its wheels.

Control arm-to-frame bolts—72–87 ft. lbs.
Lateral rod bolt—58–72 ft. lbs.
Strut lower bolt—58–72 ft. lbs.

Lateral Rod
Removal and Installation
SONATA

1. Raise the vehicle and support it safely.
2. Disconnect the rod at each end and remove it.
3. Installation is the reverse order of the removal procedures. Install the bolts and nuts at each end, but don't tighten them until the vehicle is on its wheels. Torque the nuts to 58–72 ft. lbs.

Rear Wheel Bearings
Removal and Installation

1. Loosen the lug nuts. Safely raise and support the rear of the vehicle.
2. Remove the grease cap, cotter pin serrated nut cap, axle shaft nut and washer.
3. Pull outward on the brake drum slightly to remove the bearing. Pull the drum off completely.
4. Pry the inner grease seal from the hub and discard it.
5. Remove the inner bearing. If the bearings are being replaced, drive the bearing races from the hub.
6. Clean all old grease from the hub and bearings. If the old bearing are beings reused, clean them in a safe solvent and inspect them thoroughly.
7. If the bearings are being replaced, coat the new races with EP lithium wheel bearing grease and drive them into the hub, making sure they are fully and squarely seated.
8. Pack the hub cavity with new EP lithium wheel bearing grease, until the cavity is full.
9. Pack the bearings completely.
10. Install the inner bearing and drive a new grease seal into place.
11. Install the drum on the spindle and install the outer bearing, washer and shaft nut. Tighten the nut to 15 ft. lbs. while turning the drum, to seat the bearings. Back off on the nut until it is loose, then torque it to 48 inch lbs.
12. Install the serrated nut cap and a new cotter pin. If the cotter pin holes have to be aligned, back off on the nut no more than 15 degrees; if not, repeat the adjustment procedure.

Adjustment
EXCEL AND SCOUPE

1. Raise the vehicle and support it safely. Remove the rear wheel assembly.
2. Remove dust cover from the hub. Remove excess grease from adjustment nut.
3. Loosen the self locking nut. Torque the nut to 145 ft. lbs. (196 Nm).
4. Fill the dust cap with grease and install.
5. Using a cable and tension gauge tool, check the brake drum turning force. The service limit is 11 inch lbs. before the drum starts to move. If the turning force exceeds the limit, loosen the

adjustment nut and retighten it.

6. Recheck the turning force, if it is not within the specifications, replace the wheel bearings.

To install:

8. Lubricate the inner bearing and install to the drum.
9. Install a new grease seal.
10. Install the drum to the vehicle.
11. Lubricate and install the outer wheel bearing to the spindle.
12. Install the thrust washer.
13. Install and tighten the wheel bearing nut to 14 ft. lbs. (20 Nm) while rotating the drum.
14. Back off the adjusting nut ¼ turn and retorque to 7 ft. lbs. (10 Nm).
15. Install the nut lock and a new cotter pin.

Rear Axle Assembly
Removal and Installation

1. Raise and safely support the vehicle. Remove the wheel assemblies.
2. Separate the parking brake cable at the connector and cable housing at the floor pan bracket.
3. Separate the brake line at backing plate.
4. Remove the muffler-to-middle exhaust pipe retaining bolts, remove the O-ring hangers and remove the exhaust system.
5. Remove the lower shock absorber through bolts and disconnect the shock at the axle end.
6. Lower the axle until the spring and isolator assemblies can be removed.
7. Remove the axle assembly from the vehicle.

To Install:

8. Using floor jacks, position the rear axle assembly under vehicle.
9. Install the springs and isolators and carefully raise the axle assembly.
10. Install the shock absorber and through bolts, do not tighten.
11. Position brake support to the axle while routing the parking brake cable through the support. Lock it into place.
12. Connect the brake line fitting to the backing wheel cylinder. Torque to 9–12 ft. lbs. (13–17 Nm).
13. Install the hub and drum, if removed.
14. Route the parking brake cable through the fingers in the bracket and lock housing end into the floor pan bracket. Install the cable end into the intermediate connector.
15. Install the exhaust system and hangers. Torque the muffler-to-middle exhaust pipe retaining bolts to 22–29 ft. lbs. (30–40 Nm).

SONATA

1. Raise the vehicle and support safely.
2. Remove the rear wheel assembly.
3. Remove the dust cap.
4. Remove the cotter pin, nut lock and nut.
5. Remove the thrust washer and the outer wheel bearing.
6. Remove the drum with the inner wheel bearing and the grease seal.
7. Remove the grease seal and remove the inner bearing.

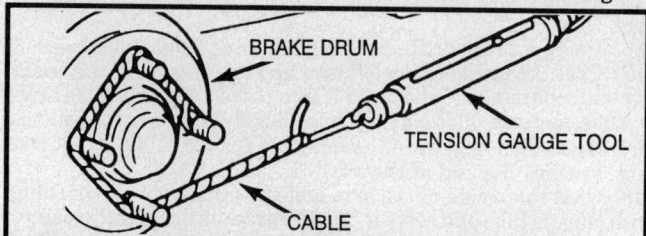

Checking brake drum turning force with a tension gauge tool

SERIAL NUMBER IDENTIFICATION

Vehicle Identification Plate

The vehicle identification plate can be viewed from in the engine compartment, at the upper left corner of the firewall.

Engine Number

The engine number is located at the rear of the engine block. It is centrally positioned on Q45 and slightly right of center on M30.

Vehicle Identification Number

The vehicle identification number plate is located on the upper left corner of the dash panel. It can be viewed through the windshield at that location.

Chassis Number

The chassis number plate can be viewed from in the engine compartment, toward the the upper right portion of the firewall.

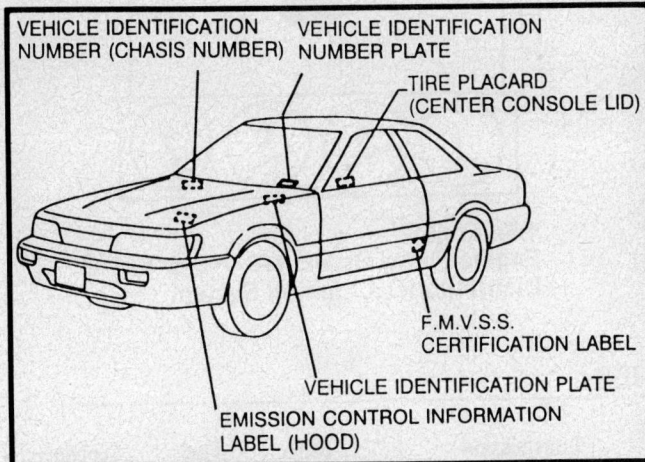

Vehicle identification plate locations—M30

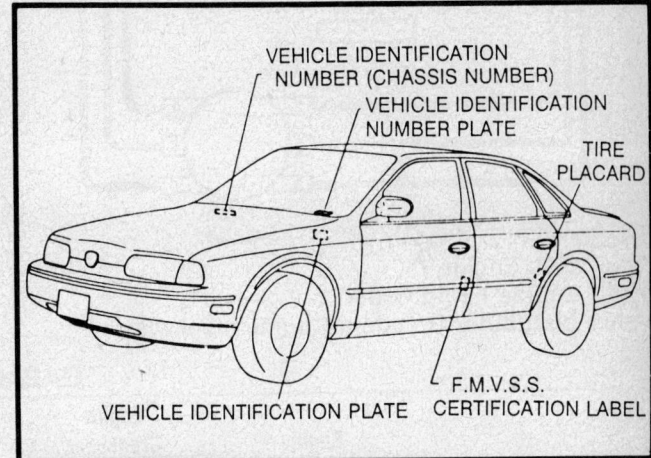

Vehicle identification plate locations—Q45

SPECIFICATIONS

ENGINE IDENTIFICATION

Year	Model	Engine Displacement cu. in. (cc/liter)	Engine Series Identification	No. of Cylinders	Engine Type
1990–91	Q45	274 (4494/4.5)	VH45DE	8	DOHC
	M30	181 (2960/3.0)	VG30	6	SOHC

GENERAL ENGINE SPECIFICATIONS

Year	Model	Engine Displacement cu. in. (cc)	Fuel System Type	Net Horsepower @ rpm	Net Torque @ rpm (ft. lbs.)	Bore × Stroke (in.)	Compression Ratio	Oil Pressure @ rpm
1990–91	Q45	274 (4494)	MPFI	278 @ 6000	280 @ 4000	3.66 × 3.26	10.2:1	67–81 @ 3000
	M30	181 (2960)	MPFI	162 @ 5200	180 @ 3600	3.43 × 3.27	9.0:1	53–67 @ 3200

GASOLINE ENGINE TUNE-UP SPECIFICATIONS

Year	Model	Engine Displacement cu. in. (cc)	Spark Plugs Type	Spark Plugs Gap (in.)	Ignition Timing (deg.) MT	Ignition Timing (deg.) AT	Compression Pressure (psi)	Fuel Pump (psi)	Idle Speed (rpm) MT	Idle Speed (rpm) AT	Valve Clearance In.	Valve Clearance Ex.
1990–91	Q45	274 (4494)	PFR6B-11	0.040	—	15B	185 @ 300 rpm	34	—	750	Hyd.	Hyd.
	M30	181 (2960)	PFR6B-11	0.040	—	15B	173 @ 300 rpm	43	—	800	Hyd.	Hyd.

FIRING ORDERS

NOTE: To avoid confusion, always replace spark plug wires one at a time.

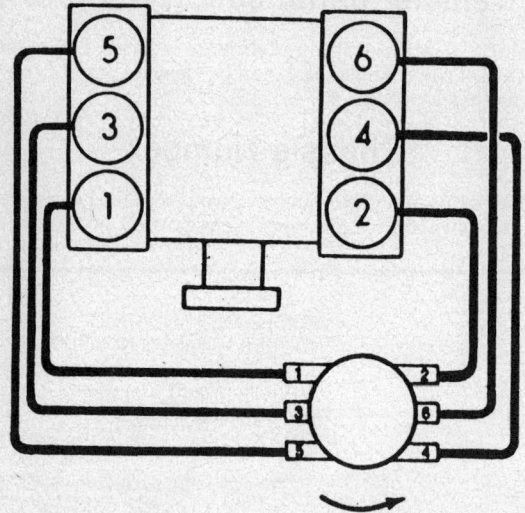

3.0L Engine
Engine Firing Order: 1-2-3-4-5-6
Distributor Rotation: Counterclockwise

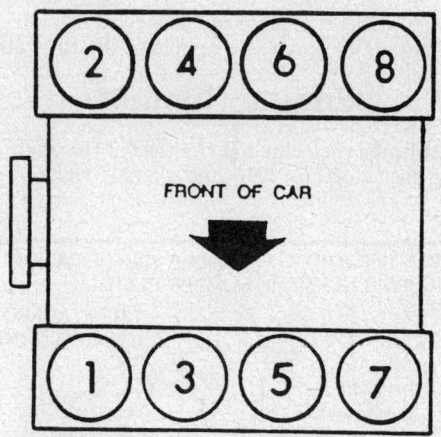

4.5L Engine
Engine Firing Order: 1-8-7-3-6-5-4-2
Distributorless Ignition System

CAPACITIES

Year	Model	Engine Displacement cu. in. (cc)	Engine Crankcase with Filter	Engine Crankcase without Filter	Transmission (pts.) 4-spd	Transmission (pts.) 5-Spd	Transmission (pts.) Auto.	Drive Axle (pts.)	Fuel Tank (gal.)	Cooling System (qts.)
1990–91	Q45	274 (4494)	6½	6	—	—	18¼	3⅛	22½	11
	M30	181 (2960)	4½	4¼	—	—	17½	2¾	16	9½

CAMSHAFT SPECIFICATIONS

All measurements given in inches.

Year	Engine Displacement cu. in. (cc)	Journal Diameter 1	Journal Diameter 2	Journal Diameter 3	Journal Diameter 4	Journal Diameter 5	Lobe Lift [1] In.	Lobe Lift [1] Ex.	Bearing Clearance	Camshaft End Play
1990–91	274 (4494)	1.0211–1.0218	1.0211–1.0218	1.0211–1.0218	1.0211–1.0218	—	1.4929–1.5004	1.3889–1.3964	0.0018–0.0059	0.0028–0.0079
	181 (2960)	1.8866–1.8874	1.8472–1.8480	1.8472–1.8480	1.8472–1.8480	1.6701–1.6709	1.5566–1.5641	1.5566–1.5641	0.0024–0.0041	0.0012–0.0024

CRANKSHAFT AND CONNECTING ROD SPECIFICATIONS

All measurements are given in inches.

Year	Engine Displacement cu. in. (cc)	Crankshaft Main Brg. Journal Dia.	Crankshaft Main Brg. Oil Clearance	Crankshaft Shaft End-play	Thrust on No.	Connecting Rod Journal Diameter	Connecting Rod Oil Clearance	Connecting Rod Side Clearance
1990–91	274 (4494)	[1]	0.0005–0.0020	0.0039–0.0118	3	[2]	0.0008–0.0026	0.0079–0.0157
	181 (2960)	[3]	0.0011–0.0035	0.0020–0.0118	4	1.9667–1.9675	0.0006–0.0035	0.0079–0.0157

[1] Grade No. 0—2.5180–2.5183
Grade No. 1—2.5178–2.5180
Grade No. 2—2.5176–2.5178
Grade No. 3—2.5173–2.5176

[2] Grade No. 0—2.0460–2.0462
Grade No. 1—2.0457–2.0460
Grade No. 2—2.0455–2.0457

[3] Grade No. 0—2.4790–2.4793
Grade No. 1—2.4787–2.4790
Grade No. 2—2.4784–2.4787

VALVE SPECIFICATIONS

Year	No. Cylinder Displacement cu. in. (cc)	Seat Angle (deg.)	Face Angle (deg.)	Spring Test Pressure (lbs.)	Spring Installed Height (in.)	Stem-to-Guide Clearance (in.) Intake	Exhaust	Stem Diameter (in.) Intake	Exhaust
1990-91	274 (4494)	45.25	44.75	120.4	1.86①	0.0017②	0.0018②	0.275	0.314
	181 (2960)	45.25	45	③	④	0.0039	0.0039	0.274	0.314

① Free height
② Miximum
③ Inner—57.3
  Outer—117.7
④ Inner—1.74
  Outer—2.02

PISTON AND RING SPECIFICATIONS

All measurements are given in inches.

Year	Engine Displacement cu. in. (cc)	Piston Clearance	Ring Gap Top Compression	Bottom Compression	Oil Control	Ring Side Clearance Top Compression	Bottom Compression	Oil Control
1990-91	274 (4494)	0.0004–0.0012	0.0106–0.0390	0.0154–0.0390	0.0079–0.0390	0.0016–0.0040	0.0012–0.0040	—
	181 (2960)	0.0010–0.0018	0.0083–0.0390	0.0071–0.0390	0.0079–0.0390	0.0016–0.0040	0.0012–0.0040	—

TORQUE SPECIFICATIONS

All readings in ft. lbs.

Year	Engine Displacement cu. in. (cc)	Cylinder Head Bolts	Main Bearing Bolts	Rod Bearing Bolts	Crankshaft Pulley Bolts	Flywheel Bolts	Manifold Intake	Exhaust	Spark Plugs
1990-91	274 (4494)	①	②	③	260–275	61–69	12–15	20–23	15–20
	181 (2960)	④	67–74	③	90–98	61–69	12–14	13–16	15–20

① ⓐ Tighten bolts to 29 N·m (3.0 kg-m, 22 ft-lb).
  ⓑ Tighten bolts to 93 N·m (9.5 kg-m, 69 ft-lb).
  ⓒ Loosen bolts completely.
  ⓓ Tighten bolts to 25 to 34 N·m (2.5 to 3.5 kg-m, 18 to 25 ft-lb).

  ⓔ Turn bolts 90 to 95 degrees clockwise or if angle wrench is not available, tighten bolts to 93 to 98 N·m (9.5 to 10.0 kg-m, 69 to 72 ft-lb).
② See text
③ Step 1: 10–12 ft. lbs.
  Step 2: An additional 60–65° or tighten to a final torque of 28–33 ft. lbs.

④ Step 1: 22 ft. lbs.
  Step 2: 43 ft. lbs.
  Step 3: Loosen all bolts completely
  Step 4: 22 ft. lbs.
  Step 5: An additional 60–65 ° or tighten to a final torque of 40–47 ft. lbs.

BRAKE SPECIFICATIONS

All measurements in inches unless noted.

Year	Model	Lug Nut Torque (ft. lbs.)	Master Cylinder Bore	Brake Disc Minimum Thickness	Maximum Runout	Standard Brake Drum Diameter	Minimum Lining Thickness Front	Rear
1990-91	Q45	72–87	1.06	①	0.003	—	0.08	0.08
	M30	76–90	1	②	0.003	—	0.08	0.08

① Front: 1.024
  Rear: 0.315
① Front: 0.787
  Rear: 0.354

WHEEL ALIGNMENT

Year	Model		Caster		Camber		Toe-in (in.)	Steering Axis Inclination (deg.)
			Range (deg.)	Preferred Setting (deg.)	Range (deg.)	Preferred Setting (deg.)		
1990–91	Q45	front	$5^3/_4$P–$7^1/_4$P	$6^1/_2$P	$1^1/_2$N–0	$^3/_4$N	$^1/_{32}$	12–$13^1/_2$
		rear	—	—	$1^1/_2$N–$^1/_2$N	1N	$^1/_8$	—
	M30	front	4P–$5^1/_2$P	$4^3/_4$P	$^1/_2$N–1P	$^3/_4$P	0	12–$13^1/_2$
		rear	—	—	1N–$^1/_4$P	$^3/_8$N	$^1/_{16}$	—

ENGINE ELECTRICAL

NOTE: Disconnecting the negative battery cable on some vehicles may interfere with the functions of the on board computer systems and may require the computer to undergo a relearning process, once the negative battery cable is reconnected.

Distributor

Removal

M30

1. Disconnect the negative battery cable.
2. Remove the splash shield. Disconnect the distributor connectors.
3. Unscrew the distributor cap hold-down screws and lift off the distributor cap with all ignition wires still connected.
4. Matchmark the rotor to the distributor housing and the distributor housing to the engine.

NOTE: Do not crank the engine during this procedure. If the engine is cranked, the matchmark must be disregarded.

5. Remove the hold-down bolt.
6. Remove the distributor from the engine.

Installation

TIMING NOT DISTURBED

1. Install a new distributor housing O-ring.
2. Install the distributor in the engine so the rotor is aligned with the matchmark on the housing and the housing is aligned with the matchmark on the engine. Make sure the distributor is fully seated and the distributor gear is fully engaged.
3. Install and snug the hold-down bolt.
4. Connect the distributor pickup lead wires.
5. Install the distributor cap and tighten the screws. Install the splash shield.
6. Connect the negative battery cable.
7. Adjust the ignition timing and tighten the hold-down bolt.

TIMING DISTURBED

1. Install a new distributor housing O-ring.
2. Position the engine so the No. 1 piston is at TDC of its compression stroke and the mark on the vibration damper is aligned with 0 on the timing indicator.
3. Install the distributor in the engine so the rotor is aligned with the position of the No. 1 ignition wire on the distributor cap and the housing is aligned with the matchmark on the engine. Make sure the distributor is fully seated and that the distributor shaft is fully engaged.

NOTE: There are distributor cap runners inside the cap on 3.0L engine. Make sure the rotor is pointing to where the No. 1 runner originates inside the cap.

4. Install and snug the hold-down bolt.
5. Connect the distributor pickup lead wires.
6. Install the distributor cap and tighten the screws. Install the splash shield, if equipped.
7. Connect the negative battery cable.
8. Adjust the ignition timing and tighten the hold-down bolt.

Distributorless Ignition

Removal and Installation

Q45

Power Transistor Unit

1. Disconnect the negative battery cable.
2. Remove the air intake duct, if necessary.

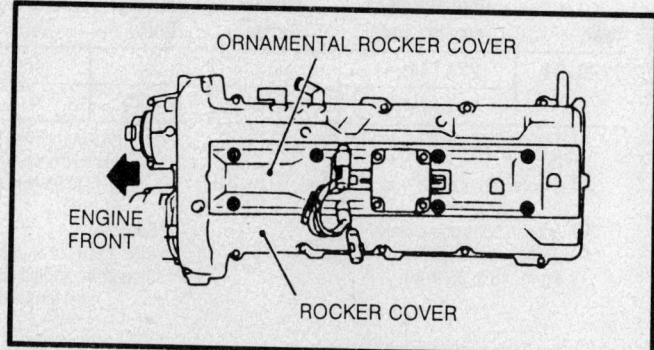

Ornamental rocker cover—4.5L engine

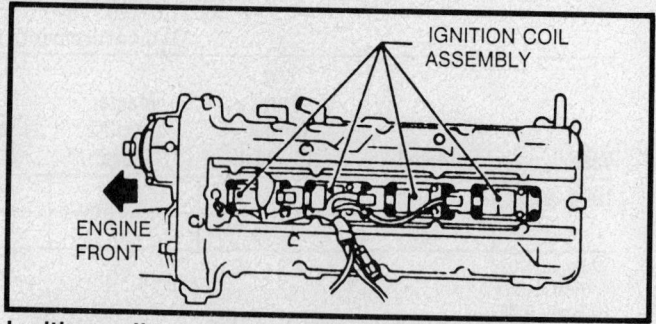

Ignition coil assembly—4.5L engine

3. Disconnect the connector.
4. Remove the bolts that attach the unit to the ornamental rocker cover.
5. Remove the unit from the engine.
6. The installation is the reverse of the removal procedure.

Ignition Coil

1. Disconnect the negative battery cable.
2. Remove the air intake duct, if necessary.
3. Disconnect the power transistor unit connector.
4. Remove the ornamental rocker cover.
5. Remove the ignition coil bracket mounting bolts and pull out the bracket with the ignition coils.
6. Separate the coil from the bracket and remove from the engine.
7. The installation is the reverse of the removal procedure.

Crank Angle Sensor

1. Disconnect the negative battery cable.
2. Remove the air intake duct.
3. Matchmark the position of the crankshaft sensor assembly to the head.
4. Disconnect the connector, remove the mounting bolts and remove the crank angle sensor from the engine.
5. The installation is the reverse of the removal procedure.
6. Check the ignition timing and adjust, if necessary.

Ignition Timing

Adjustment

1. Start the engine, set the parking brake and run the engine until at normal operating temperature. Keep all lights and accessories off.
2. Connect a timing light to the No. 1 cylinder spark plug wire.
3. Use the Nissan Consult System Checking tool in the Data Monitor mode to check engine rpm. Adjust, if necessary.
4. Aim the timing light at the timing scale.
5. On the M30, loosen the distributor hold-down bolt just enough so the distributor can be rotated. On the Q45, do the same with the crank angle sensor, which is used the set the timing.
6. Turn the distributor or crank angle sensor in the proper direction until the timing is 15 degrees BTDC. Tighten the hold-down bolt and recheck the timing and idle speed.

Alternator

Precautions

Several precautions must be observed with alternator equipped vehicles to avoid damage to the unit.
● If the battery is removed for any reason, make sure it is reconnected with the correct polarity. Reversing the battery connections may result in damage to the one-way rectifiers.
● When utilizing a booster battery as a starting aid, always connect the positive to positive terminals and the negative terminal from the booster battery to a good engine ground on the vehicle being started.
● Never use a fast charger as a booster to start vehicles.
● Disconnect the battery cables when charging the battery with a fast charger.
● Never attempt to polarize the alternator.
● Do not use test lamps of more than 12 volts when checking diode continuity.
● Do not short across or ground any of the alternator terminals.

● The polarity of the battery, alternator and regulator must be matched and considered before making any electrical connections within the system.
● Never separate the alternator on an open circuit. Make sure all connections within the circuit are clean and tight.
● Disconnect the battery ground terminal when performing any service on electrical components.
● Disconnect the battery if arc welding is to be done on the vehicle.

Belt Tension Adjustment

M30

1. Disconnect the negative battery cable.
2. Loosen the nut that secures the T-bolt to the slotted adjustment bracket.
3. Turn the adjustment bolt until the belt deflects approximately 0.3 in. at its widest expanse.
4. Tighten the T-bolt nut to 11 ft. lbs. (15 Nm).
5. Connect the negative battery cable.

Q45

1. Disconnect the negative battery cable.
2. Loosen the nut that secures the T-bolt to the alternator belt idler pulley.
3. Turn the adjustment bolt until the belt deflects approximately 0.3 in. at its widest expanse.
4. Tighten the T-bolt nut to 24 ft. lbs. (32 Nm).
5. Connect the negative battery cable.

Removal and Installation

M30

1. Disconnect the negative battery cable.
2. Loosen the alternator belt and remove from the pulley.
3. Remove the adjusting bracket.
4. Disconnect the harness connector and cable from the rear of the alternator.

NOTE: The front mounting bolt cannot be removed separately because of insufficient clearance between the alternator and engine coolant inlet tube.

5. Remove the rear mounting bolt loosen the front mounting bolt.
6. Remove the alternator with the front mounting bolt.
7. The installation is the reverse of the removal procedure. Torque the mounting bolts to 15 ft. lbs. (20 Nm).
8. Adjust the belt so it deflects approximately 0.3 in. at its widest expanse.
9. Connect the negative battery cable and check the alternator for proper operation.

Q45

1. Disconnect the negative battery cable.
2. Remove the radiator shroud and cooling fan.
3. Drain a sufficient amount of coolant and remove the upper radiator hose.
4. Remove the upper alternator bracket and the air conditioner pipe mounting bracket.
5. Remove the idler pulley and belt.
6. Remove the 2 power steering cooler pipe mounting screws.
7. Remove the mounting through bolt.
8. Pull the alternator toward the radiator and remove the harness heat shield.
9. Disconnect the wires from the rear of the alternator and remove from the vehicle.
To install:
10. Position the alternator and connect the wires. Install the heat shield.

11. Install the mounting through bolt loosely.

12. Install the 2 power steering cooler pipe mounting screws.

13. Install the idler pulley and belt.

14. Install the air conditioner pipe mounting bracket and upper alternator bracket. Tighten the through bolt.

15. Adjust the belt so it deflects approximately 0.3 in. at its widest expanse.

16. Install the upper radiator hose and refill the cooling system.

17. Install the cooling fan and radiator shroud.

18. Connect the negative battery cable and check the alternator for proper operation.

Starter

Removal and Installation

1. Disconnect the negative battery cable.

2. Raise the vehicle and support safely.

3. Remove the engine undercover.

4. Remove exhaust components, as required, in order to gain access to the starter.

5. Remove the starter mounting bolts and remove the starter.

6. The installation is the reverse of the removal procedure. Torque the mounting bolts to 25 ft. lbs. (34 Nm).

7. Connect the negative battery cable and check the starter for proper operation.

CHASSIS ELECTRICAL

CAUTION

It is possible for the air bag to inflate for 10 minutes after the battery has been disconnected. Therefore, disconnect the negative battery cable and wait 10 minutes before working on the system. Failure to do so may result in deployment of the air bag and possible personal injury.

Heater Blower Motor

Removal and Installation

1. Disconnect the negative battery cable. Remove the lower right side instrument panel cover.

2. Remove the screws that attach the blower housing to the intake unit.

3. Remove the housing and remove the blower motor from the housing.

4. The installation is the reverse of the removal procedure.

5. Connect the negative battery cable and check the climate control system for proper operation.

Windshield Wiper Motor

Removal and Installation

1. Disconnect the negative battery cable.

2. Disconnect the leads at the motor.

3. Remove the motor mounting bolts.

4. Pull the motor out and remove the wiper motor linkage attaching nut.

5. Remove the motor from the firewall.

6. The installation is the reverse of the removal procedure.

7. Connect the negative battery cable and check all windshield wiper and washer functions for proper operation.

Windshield Wiper Switch

Removal and Installation

M30

1. Disconnect the negative battery cable.

2. Remove the steering column covers. Disconnect the connector.

3. Remove the windshield wiper switch mounting screws and remove the switch from the switch base.

4. The installation is the reverse of the removal procedure.

5. Connect the negative battery cable and check all windshield wiper and washer functions for proper operation.

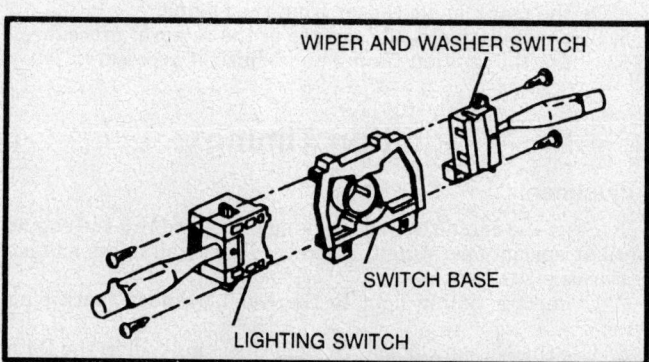

Combination switch assembly—M30

Instrument Cluster

Removal and Installation

M30

1. Disconnect the negative battery cable.

2. Remove the steering column covers.

3. Remove the screws that fasten the cluster lid to the instrument panel and remove the lid.

4. Remove the screws that fasten the instrument cluster to the instrument panel, pull the cluster out, disconnect all connectors and remove the cluster.

5. Disassemble the cluster, as required.

6. The installation is the reverse of the removal procedure.

7. Connect the negative battery cable and check all gauges for proper operation.

Q45

1. Disconnect the negative battery cable.

2. Remove the steering column covers.

3. Remove the gear shifter bezel from the console.

4. Remove the ash tray assembly.

5. Remove the screws that fasten the radio and climate control switch bezel to the instrument panel. Pull the bezel down and out, disconnect the rear window defogger switch and remove the bezel.

6. Remove the cruise control main switch/outside mirror control switch assembly.

7. Remove the screws that fasten the cluster lid to the instrument panel and remove the lid.

8. Remove the screws that attach the instrument cluster to the instrument panel, pull the cluster out, disconnect all connectors and remove the cluster.

9. Disassemble the cluster, as required.

To install:

10. Assemble the cluster, connect all connectors and install to the instrument panel.

11. Connect the negative battery cable and check all gauges for proper operation. If everything is operating properly, disconnect the negative battery cable and proceed.

12. Install the cluster lid and cruise control main switch/outside mirror control switch assembly.

13. Install the radio and climate control switch bezel to the instrument panel.

14. Install the ash tray and gear shifter bezel.

15. Install the steering column covers.

16. Connect the negative battery cable and check all gauges for proper operation.

Combination Switch

Removal and Installation

M30

On the M30, the combination switch refers to the turn signal, dimmer and headlight switch assembly.

1. Disconnect the negative battery cable.

2. Remove the steering column covers. Disconnect the connector.

3. Remove the combination switch mounting screws and remove the switch from the switch base.

4. The installation is the reverse of the removal procedure.

5. Connect the negative battery cable and check all functions of the combination switch for proper operation.

Q45

On the Q45, the combination switch assembly cannot be disassembled and refers to all column-mounted stalk switches as a singe unit.

Before replacing the switch, unplug the existing switch and plug in the replacement one to make sure all functions operate properly.

NOTE: Since this vehicle is equipped with an air bag, it is imperative that the exact steering wheel removal and installation procedure under Steering is followed. The air bag module is a fragile component. Always place it with the pad side facing upward. Do not allow oil, grease or water to come in cantact with the module. Do not drop the module; if it is damaged in any way, do not reinstall it to the steering wheel.

1. Make sure the wheels are pointing straight ahead. Disconnect the negative battery cable and allow 10 minutes to elapse.

2. Remove the steering wheel.

3. Disconnect all combination switch connectors from underneath the steering column.

4. Remove the screws that fasten the combination switch to the steering column and remove from the vehicle.

5. The installation is the reverse of the removal procedure.

6. Connect the negative battery cable and check all functions of the combination switch for proper operation.

Combination Switch Base

Removal and Installation

M30

NOTE: Since this vehicle is equipped with an air bag, it is imperative that the exact steering wheel removal and installation procedure under Steering is followed. The air bag module is a fragile component. Always place it with the pad side facing upward. Do not allow oil, grease or water to come in contact with the module. Do not drop the module; if it is damaged in any way, do not reinstall it to the steering wheel.

1. Make sure the wheels are pointing straight ahead. Disconnect the negative battery cable and allow 10 minutes to elapse.

2. Remove the steering wheel.

3. Disconnect all combination and windshield wiper switch connectors and remove the switches from the switch base.

4. To remove the combination switch base, remove the base attaching screw and turn after pushing it.

5. The installation is the reverse of the removal procedure.

6. Connect the negative battery cable and check all functions of the combination and windshield wiper switches for proper operation.

Ignition Lock/Switch

Removal and Installation

NOTE: Since this vehicle is equipped with an air bag, it is imperative that the exact steering wheel removal and installation procedure under Steering is followed. The air bag module is a fragile component. Always place it with the pad side facing upward. Do not allow oil, grease or water to come in contact with the module. Do

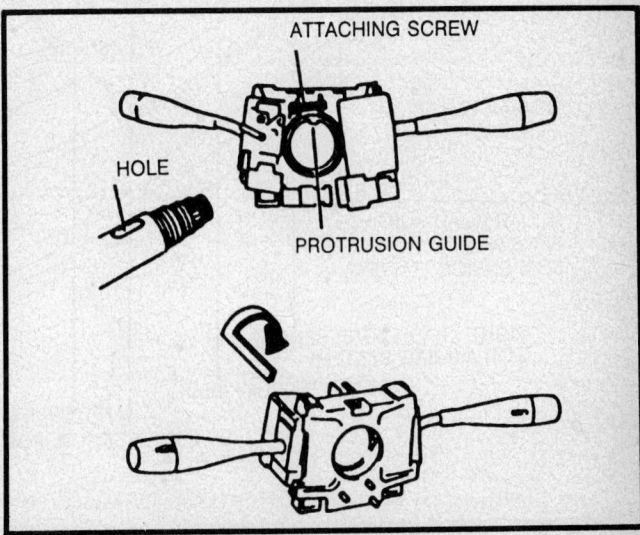

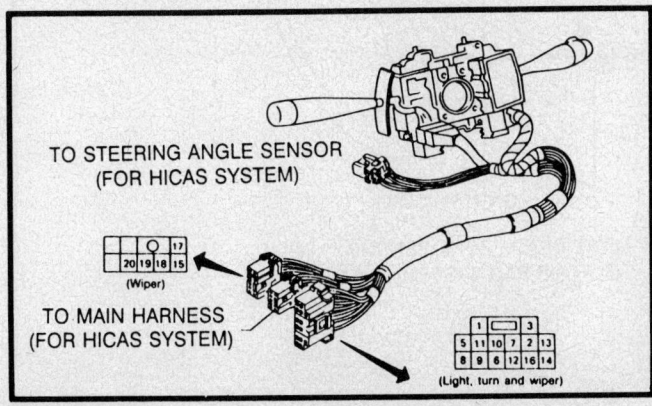

Combination switch assembly – Q45

Combination switch base removal – M30

not drop the module; if it is damaged in any way, do not reinstall it to the steering wheel.

1. Make sure the wheels are pointing straight ahead. Disconnect the negative battery cable and allow 10 minutes to elapse.
2. Remove the steering wheel and combination switch or switch base.
3. Disconnect the ignition switch wiring.
4. Lower the steering column.
5. Using a hacksaw blade, cut a groove into the heads of the special self-shearing screws and remove the screws.
6. Remove the assembly from the column.

To install:

7. With the key inserted in the switch, install the assembly onto the column with new self-shearing screws. Tighten the screws gradually, testing the key for binding often. Tighten the screws until the heads shear off.
8. Raise and secure the steering column.
9. Install the combination switch or switch base, and steering wheel.
10. Connect the negative battery cable and check the ignition switch for proper operation in all positions.

Stoplight Switch

Adjustment

1. Measure the free height of the brake pedal at its bottom edge. The specification is 8.0 in. (205mm) for M30 and 7.4 in. (190mm) for Q45. Adjust by loosening the booster input rod locknut and turning the input rod.
2. The stoplight switch is to the right of the cruise control cancel switch on the bracket above the brake pedal. Adjust both switches during this procedure.
3. Measure the clearance between the threaded end of the switches and the pedal stopper. The specification is 0.025 in. (0.06mm) for both.
4. Adjust be loosening the locknut and turning each switch.
5. Check the pedal free-play. The specification is 0.08 in. (2.0mm).
6. Make sure the brake lights illuminate when the pedal is depressed and they go out when the pedal is released.
7. Also, make sure the cruise control cancels when the brake pedal is depressed.

Removal and Installation

1. Disconnect the negative battery cable.

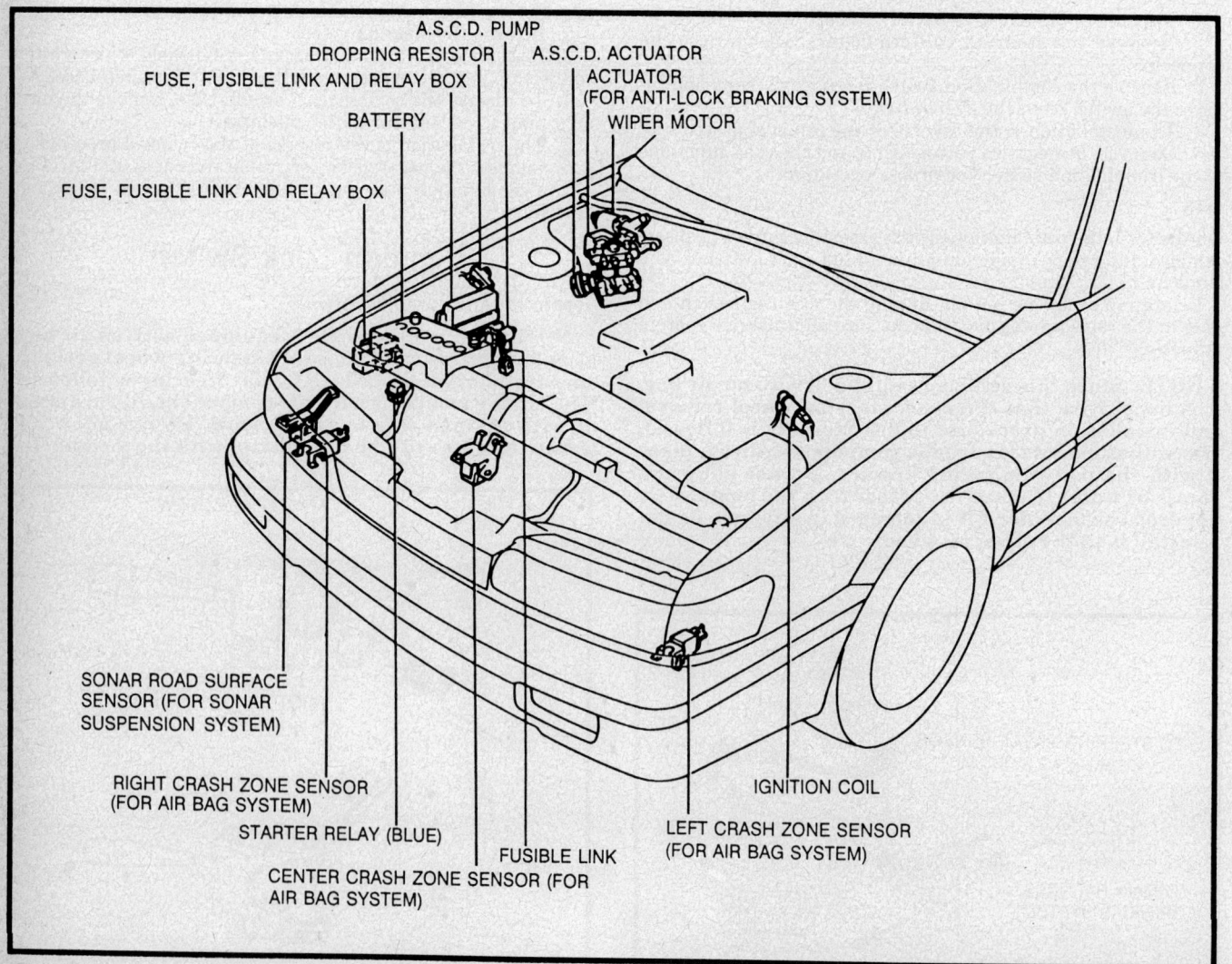

Engine compartment electrical component locations—M30

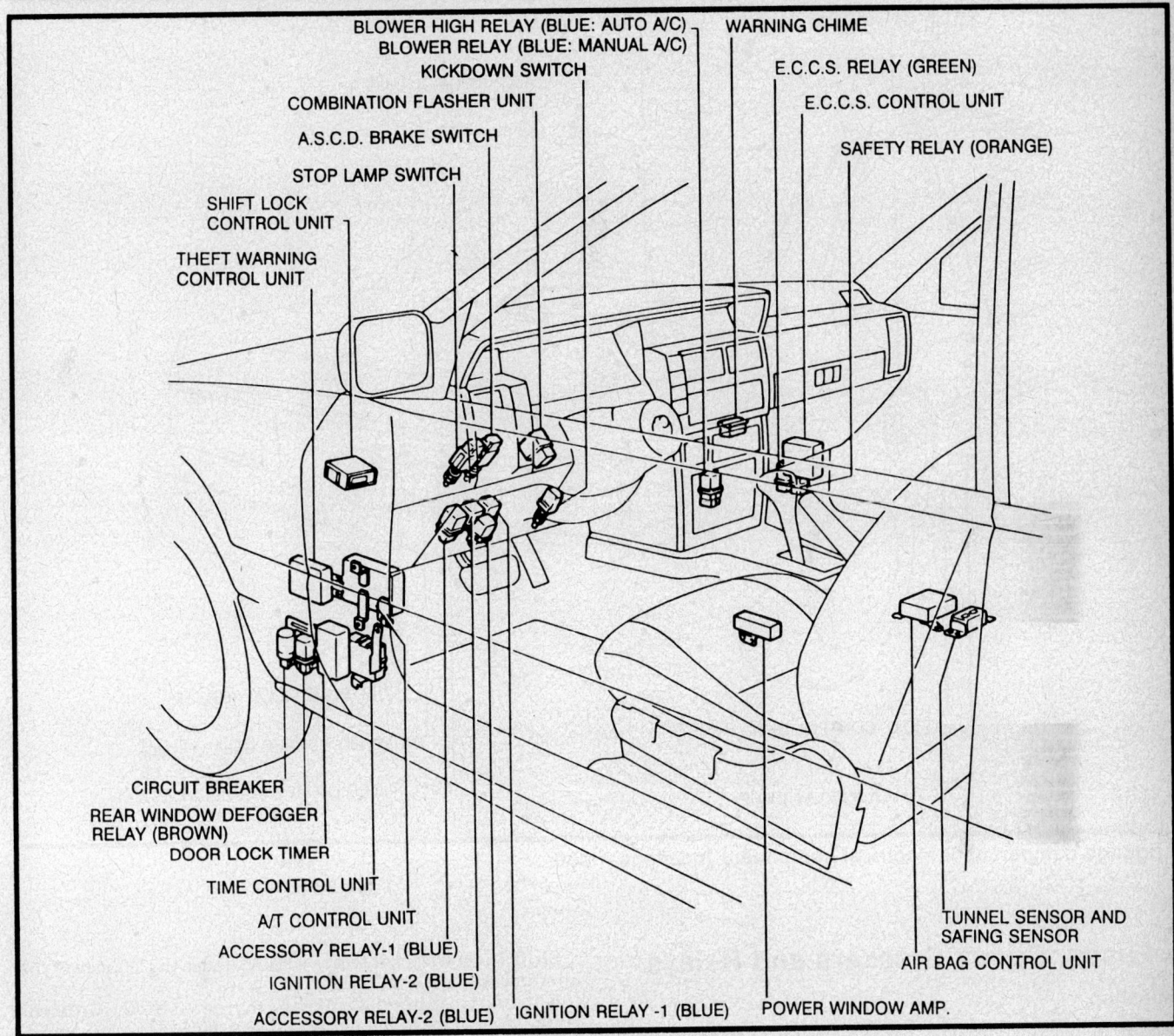

BLOWER HIGH RELAY (BLUE: AUTO A/C)
BLOWER RELAY (BLUE: MANUAL A/C)
KICKDOWN SWITCH

COMBINATION FLASHER UNIT

A.S.C.D. BRAKE SWITCH

STOP LAMP SWITCH

SHIFT LOCK
CONTROL UNIT

THEFT WARNING
CONTROL UNIT

WARNING CHIME

E.C.C.S. RELAY (GREEN)

E.C.C.S. CONTROL UNIT

SAFETY RELAY (ORANGE)

CIRCUIT BREAKER

REAR WINDOW DEFOGGER
RELAY (BROWN)

DOOR LOCK TIMER

TIME CONTROL UNIT

A/T CONTROL UNIT

ACCESSORY RELAY-1 (BLUE)

IGNITION RELAY-2 (BLUE)

ACCESSORY RELAY-2 (BLUE)   IGNITION RELAY -1 (BLUE)   POWER WINDOW AMP.

TUNNEL SENSOR AND
SAFING SENSOR

AIR BAG CONTROL UNIT

Passenger compartment electrical component locations — M30

2. Remove the locknut.
3. Remove the switch from the bracket above the brake pedal.
4. The installation is the reverse of the removal procedure.
5. Adjust the switch.
6. Connect the negative battery cable and check the switch for proper operation.

Neutral Safety Switch

Adjustment

1. Disconnect the negative battery cable.
2. Raise the vehicle and support safely.
3. Disconnect the manual control linkage from the manual shift shaft.
4. Set the manual shift shaft in the **N** detent.
5. Loosen the neutral safety switch mounting bolts.

6. Align the switch with the shift shaft by inserting a suitable pin in the alignment holes.
7. Tighten the switch mounting bolts and connect the control linkage.
8. Make sure the vehicle does not start in any gear except **P** or **N** and does start in both **P** and **N**.

Removal and Installation

1. Disconnect the negative battery cable.
2. Raise the vehicle and support safely.
3. Disconnect the wires to the switch.
4. Remove the switch mounting screws.
5. Remove the switch from the transmission.
6. The installation is the reverse of the removal procedure.
7. Adjust the switch.
8. Make sure the vehicle does not start in any gear except **P** or **N** and does start in both **P** and **N**.

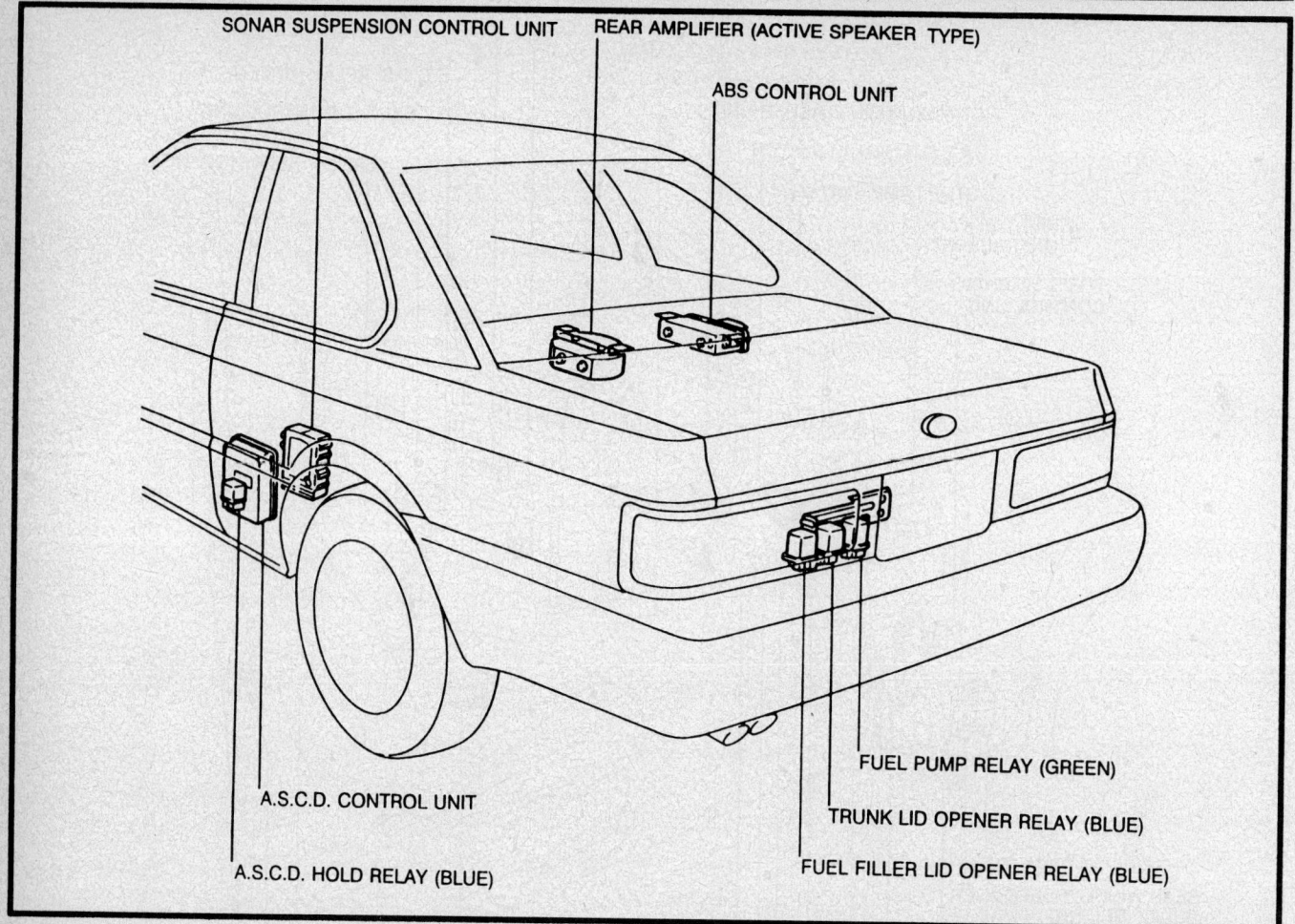

Luggage compartment electrical component locations—M30

Fuses, Circuit Breakers and Relays

Location

A fuse, fusible link and relay box is located in the engine compartment, near the battery. Release the latch and remove the protective covering to access the desired component. The radio has its own fuse behind it. Other various relays are located throughout the vehicle.

There is a second fuse box located behind an access door to the left of the steering column on the instrument panel. The circuit breaker for the power door locks and seats is located near this fuse box. The circuit breaker for the power windows and the sunroof is located behind the left side kick panel.

Computers

Location

M30

Sonar Suspension Control Unit—located to the left of the rear seat, behind the trim panel

Automatic Transmission Control Unit—located on the left side kick panel.

Time Control Unit—located on the left side kick panel.

Shift Lock Control Unit—located under the left side of the instrument panel.

Automatic Speed Control Device (ASCD) Control Unit—located to the left of the rear seat, behind the trim panel.

Theft Warning Control Unit—located on the left side kick panel.

Anti-Lock Brake System (ABS) Control Unit—located in the top front of the trunk.

Electronic Concentrated Control System (ECCS) Unit (for engine control)—located on the right side kick panel.

Air Bag Control Unit—located in the rear of the console.

Q45

Fuel Pump Control Module—located at the top front of the trunk.

High Captivity Actively Controlled Steering (HICAS) Control Unit (for 4WS)—located at the top front of the trunk.

Automatic Transmission Control Unit—located on the left side kick panel.

Time Control Unit—located on the left side kick panel.

Shift Lock Control Unit—located on the left side kick panel.

Automatic Drive Positioner Control Unit—located to the left of the steering column.

Automatic Speed Control Device (ASCD) Control Unit—located to the left of the console.

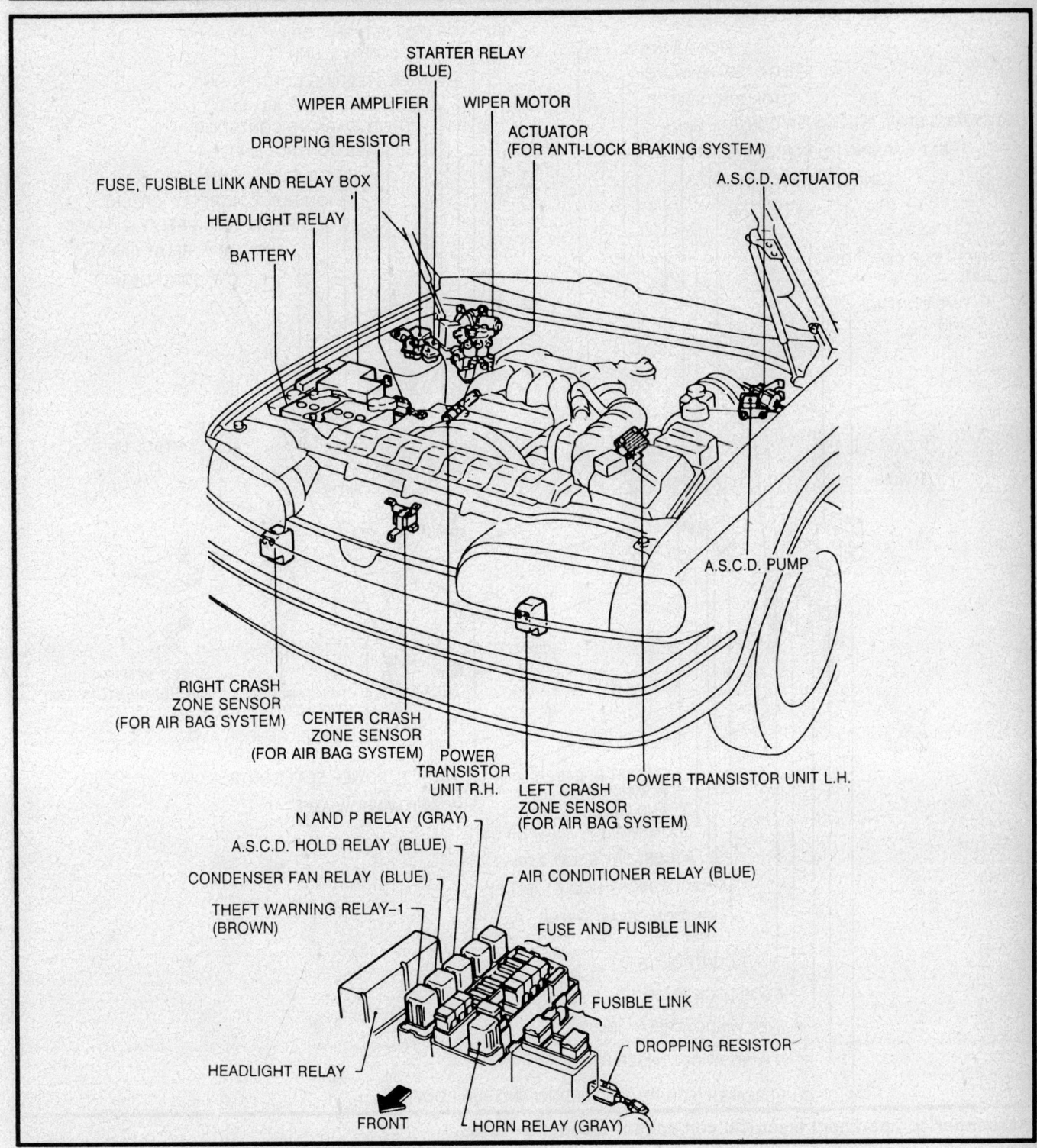

STARTER RELAY (BLUE)

WIPER AMPLIFIER   WIPER MOTOR

DROPPING RESISTOR   ACTUATOR (FOR ANTI-LOCK BRAKING SYSTEM)

FUSE, FUSIBLE LINK AND RELAY BOX   A.S.C.D. ACTUATOR

HEADLIGHT RELAY

BATTERY

A.S.C.D. PUMP

RIGHT CRASH ZONE SENSOR (FOR AIR BAG SYSTEM)

CENTER CRASH ZONE SENSOR (FOR AIR BAG SYSTEM)   POWER TRANSISTOR UNIT R.H.

LEFT CRASH ZONE SENSOR (FOR AIR BAG SYSTEM)

POWER TRANSISTOR UNIT L.H.

N AND P RELAY (GRAY)

A.S.C.D. HOLD RELAY (BLUE)

CONDENSER FAN RELAY (BLUE)   AIR CONDITIONER RELAY (BLUE)

THEFT WARNING RELAY-1 (BROWN)   FUSE AND FUSIBLE LINK

FUSIBLE LINK

DROPPING RESISTOR

HEADLIGHT RELAY

FRONT   HORN RELAY (GRAY)

Engine compartment electrical component locations—Q45

Power Steering Control Unit—located to the left of the console.

Theft Warning Control Unit—located behind the glove box.

Anti-Lock Brake System (ABS) Control Unit—located behind the glove box.

Electronic Concentrated Control System (ECCS) Unit (for engine control)—located on the right side kick panel.

Right Side Power Seat Control Unit—located under the right front seat.

Left Side Power Seat Control Unit—located under the left front seat.

Air Bag Control Unit—located in the rear of the console.

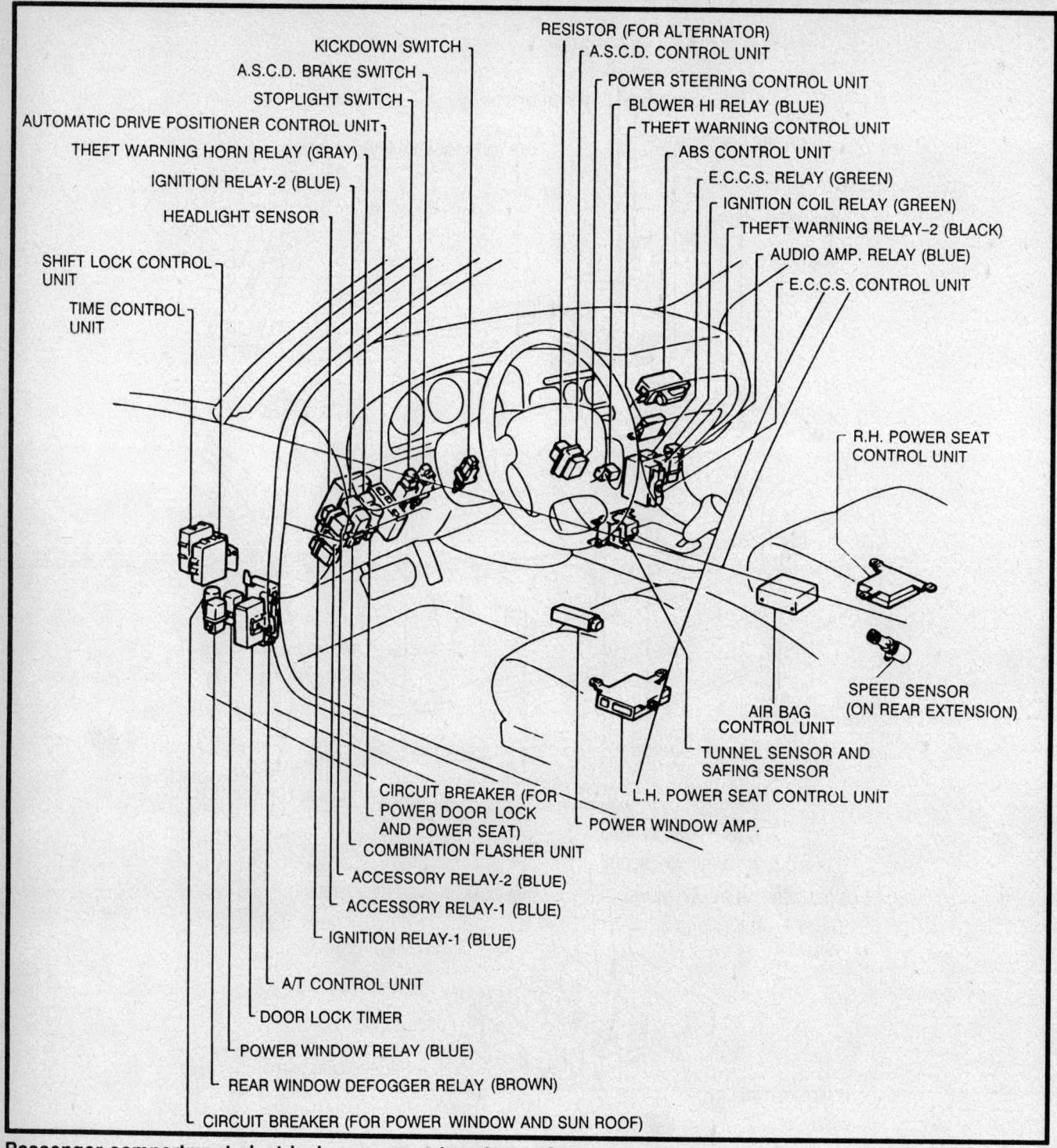

KICKDOWN SWITCH
A.S.C.D. BRAKE SWITCH
STOPLIGHT SWITCH
AUTOMATIC DRIVE POSITIONER CONTROL UNIT
THEFT WARNING HORN RELAY (GRAY)
IGNITION RELAY-2 (BLUE)
HEADLIGHT SENSOR
SHIFT LOCK CONTROL UNIT
TIME CONTROL UNIT

RESISTOR (FOR ALTERNATOR)
A.S.C.D. CONTROL UNIT
POWER STEERING CONTROL UNIT
BLOWER HI RELAY (BLUE)
THEFT WARNING CONTROL UNIT
ABS CONTROL UNIT
E.C.C.S. RELAY (GREEN)
IGNITION COIL RELAY (GREEN)
THEFT WARNING RELAY–2 (BLACK)
AUDIO AMP. RELAY (BLUE)
E.C.C.S. CONTROL UNIT

R.H. POWER SEAT CONTROL UNIT

SPEED SENSOR (ON REAR EXTENSION)

AIR BAG CONTROL UNIT
TUNNEL SENSOR AND SAFING SENSOR
L.H. POWER SEAT CONTROL UNIT
POWER WINDOW AMP.

CIRCUIT BREAKER (FOR POWER DOOR LOCK AND POWER SEAT)
COMBINATION FLASHER UNIT
ACCESSORY RELAY-2 (BLUE)
ACCESSORY RELAY-1 (BLUE)
IGNITION RELAY-1 (BLUE)
A/T CONTROL UNIT
DOOR LOCK TIMER
POWER WINDOW RELAY (BLUE)
REAR WINDOW DEFOGGER RELAY (BROWN)
CIRCUIT BREAKER (FOR POWER WINDOW AND SUN ROOF)

Passenger compartment electrical component locations—Q45

Flasher

Location

The combination flasher unit is located under the instrument panel to the right of the steering column on the M30 and near the interior fuse box on the Q45.

Cruise Control

For further information, please refer to "Chilton's Chassis Electronics Service Manual" for additional coverage.

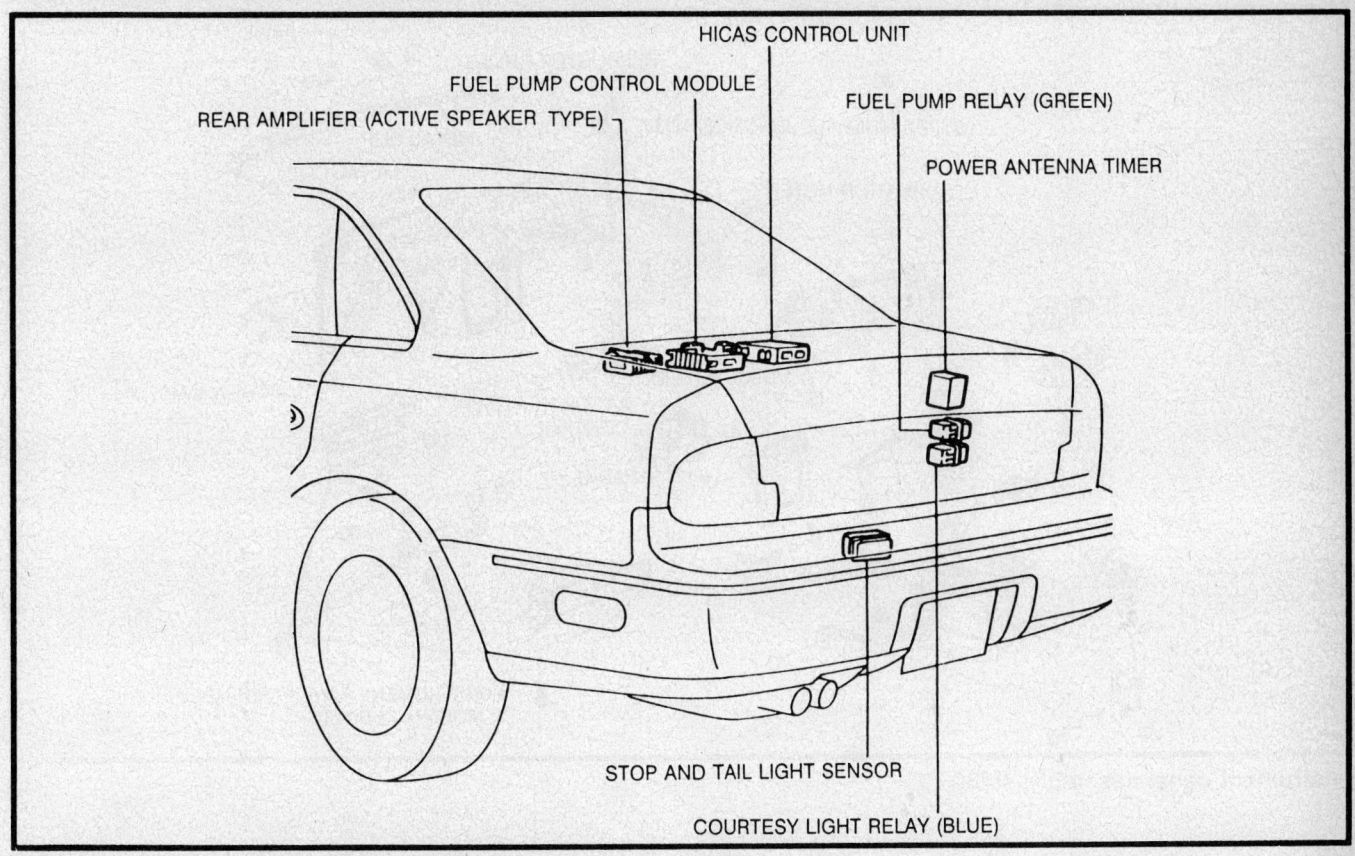

HICAS CONTROL UNIT

FUEL PUMP CONTROL MODULE

FUEL PUMP RELAY (GREEN)

REAR AMPLIFIER (ACTIVE SPEAKER TYPE)

POWER ANTENNA TIMER

STOP AND TAIL LIGHT SENSOR

COURTESY LIGHT RELAY (BLUE)

Luggage compartment electrical component locations – Q45

Adjustment

1. Adjust the throttle cable so it has 0.08 in. (2mm) free-play.

2. With no play in the cruise control cable, loosen the locknut and turn the adjusting nut ½–1 turn to prevent response delay.
3. Tighten the locknut.

ENGINE COOLING

Radiator

Removal and Installation

1. Disconnect the negative battery cable.
2. Drain the coolant.
3. On the Q45, remove the plastic cover over the radiator. Remove the upper hose and coolant reserve tank hose from the radiator.
4. Unbolt the shroud and move it backward in order to remove the fan and coupling. Remove the fan to water pump bolts and remove the fan, coupling, water pump pulley and shroud.
5. Raise the vehicle and support safely. Remove the lower hose from the radiator.
6. Disconnect and plug the automatic transmission cooler hoses. Disconnect the coolant thermo switch. Lower the vehicle.
7. Remove the mounting brackets or unbolt the radiator from the support and carefully lift out of the engine compartment.
To install:
8. Lower the radiator into position.
9. Install the mounting brackets or bolts.
10. Raise the vehicle and support safely. Connect the automatic transmission cooler lines and the thermo switch connector.
11. Connect the lower hose. Lower the vehicle.

12. Install the shroud, pulley, coupling and fan. Torque the water pump pulley nuts to 7 ft. lbs. (10 Nm). Adjust the belt.
13. Connect the upper hose and coolant reserve tank hose.
14. On the M30, open the air release plug. Fill the cooling system and check for leaks.
15. Connect the negative battery cable, run the vehicle until the thermostat opens, fill the radiator completely and check the automatic transmission fluid level. Recheck for coolant leaks.
16. Once the vehicle has cooled, recheck the coolant level.

Heater Core

For further information, please refer to "Chilton's Heating and Air Conditioning Manual" for additional coverage.

Removal and Installation

M30

1. Disconnect the negative battery cable and allow 10 minutes to elapse before entering the vehicle.
2. Drain the coolant.
3. Disconnect the heater hoses from the heater core tubes and plug them.

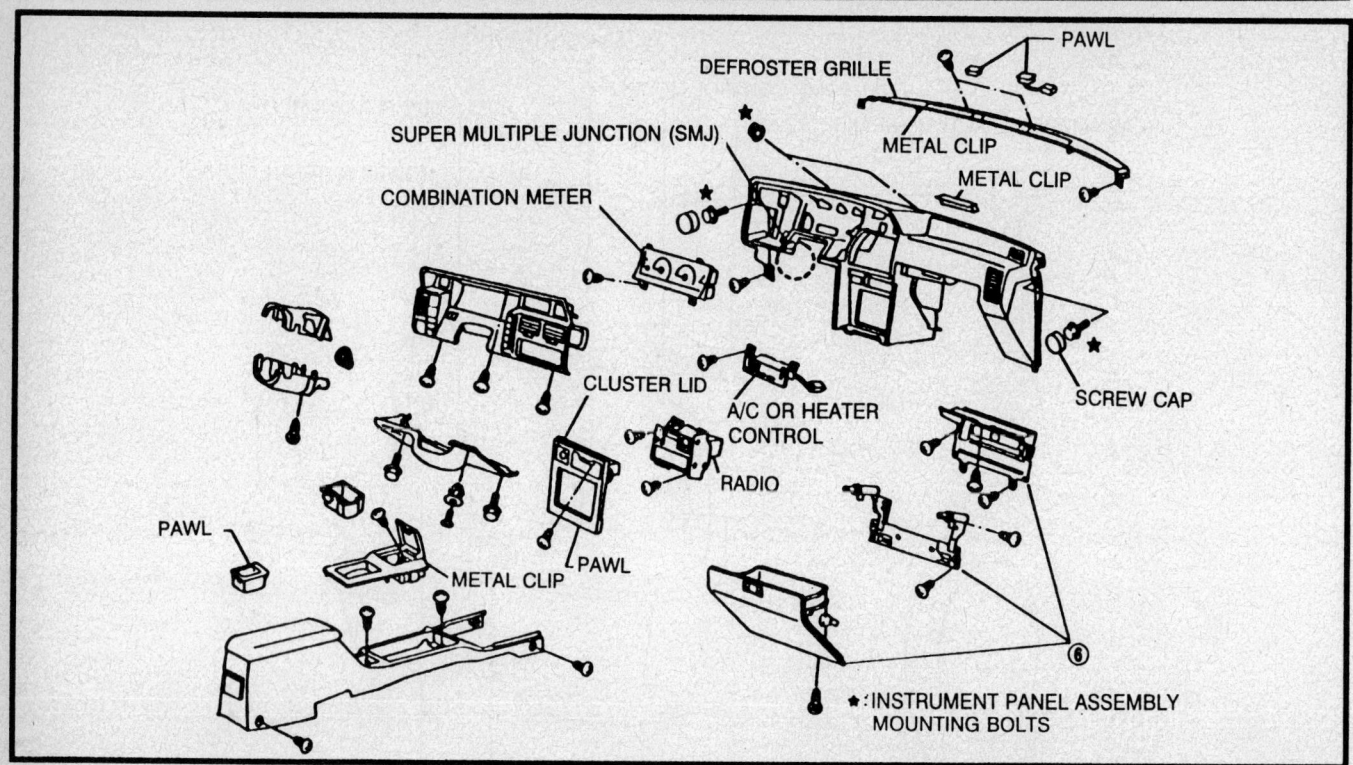

DEFROSTER GRILLE

PAWL

METAL CLIP

METAL CLIP

SUPER MULTIPLE JUNCTION (SMJ)

COMBINATION METER

SCREW CAP

CLUSTER LID

A/C OR HEATER CONTROL

RADIO

PAWL

METAL CLIP

PAWL

★ **INSTRUMENT PANEL ASSEMBLY MOUNTING BOLTS**

Instrument panel assembly—M30

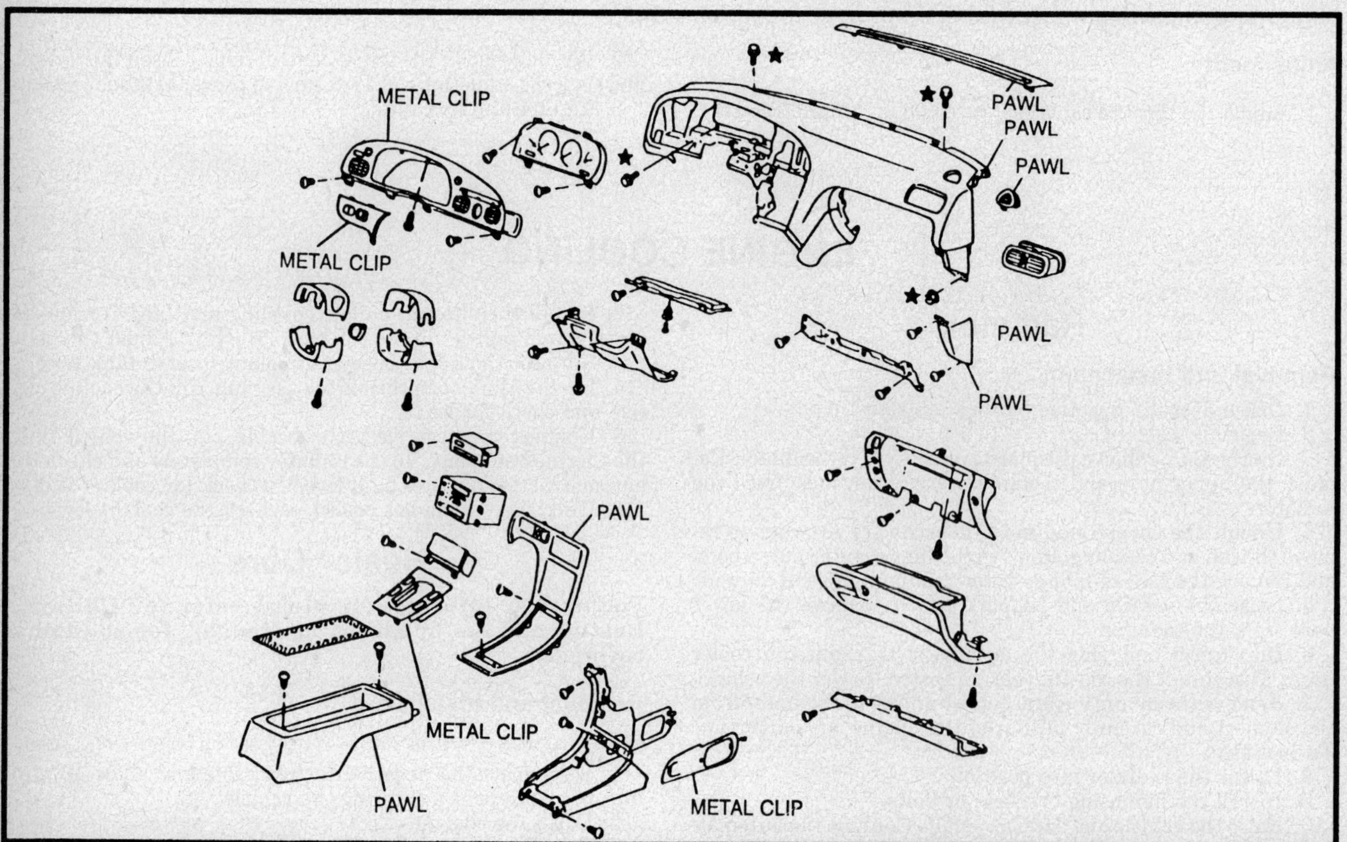

METAL CLIP

METAL CLIP

PAWL
PAWL
PAWL
PAWL
PAWL

PAWL

METAL CLIP

PAWL

METAL CLIP

Instrument panel assembly—Q45

4. Remove the steering column covers.

5. Remove the front pillar garnish and lower instrument covers.

6. Remove the cluster lid and instrument cluster.

7. Remove the radio bezel, radio and climate control switch assembly.

8. Remove the glove box.

9. Remove the instrument reinforcement and the shift lever cover.

10. Remove the console assembly.

11. Remove the defroster grille and sensors.

12. Remove the hood lock cable bracket and rear heater ducts.

13. Remove the fuse block and disconnect the Super Multiple Junction (SMJ).

14. Remove the steering column mounting bolts and lower the column.

15. Remove the caps that cover the instrument panel securing screws, remove the screws and remove the instrument panel assembly.

16. Remove the air distribution ducts from the heater unit.

17. Disconnect all wires and cables that connect to the unit.

18. Remove the mounting bolts and nuts and remove the heater unit from the vehicle.

19. Disassemble and remove the heater core from the unit.

To install:

20. Clean the inside of the unit out, install the heater core and assemble the unit.

21. Install the unit to the vehicle and connect all wires and cables. Install the air distribution ducts.

22. Install the instrument panel assembly and snap the screw caps in place.

23. Raise and secure the steering column.

24. Connect the SMJ and install the fuse block.

25. Install the rear heater ducts and hood lock cable bracket.

26. Install the defroster grille and sensors.

27. Install the console assembly and shift lever cover.

28. Install the instrument reinforcement and glove box.

29. Install the climate control switch assembly, radio and bezel.

30. Install the instrument cluster and lid.

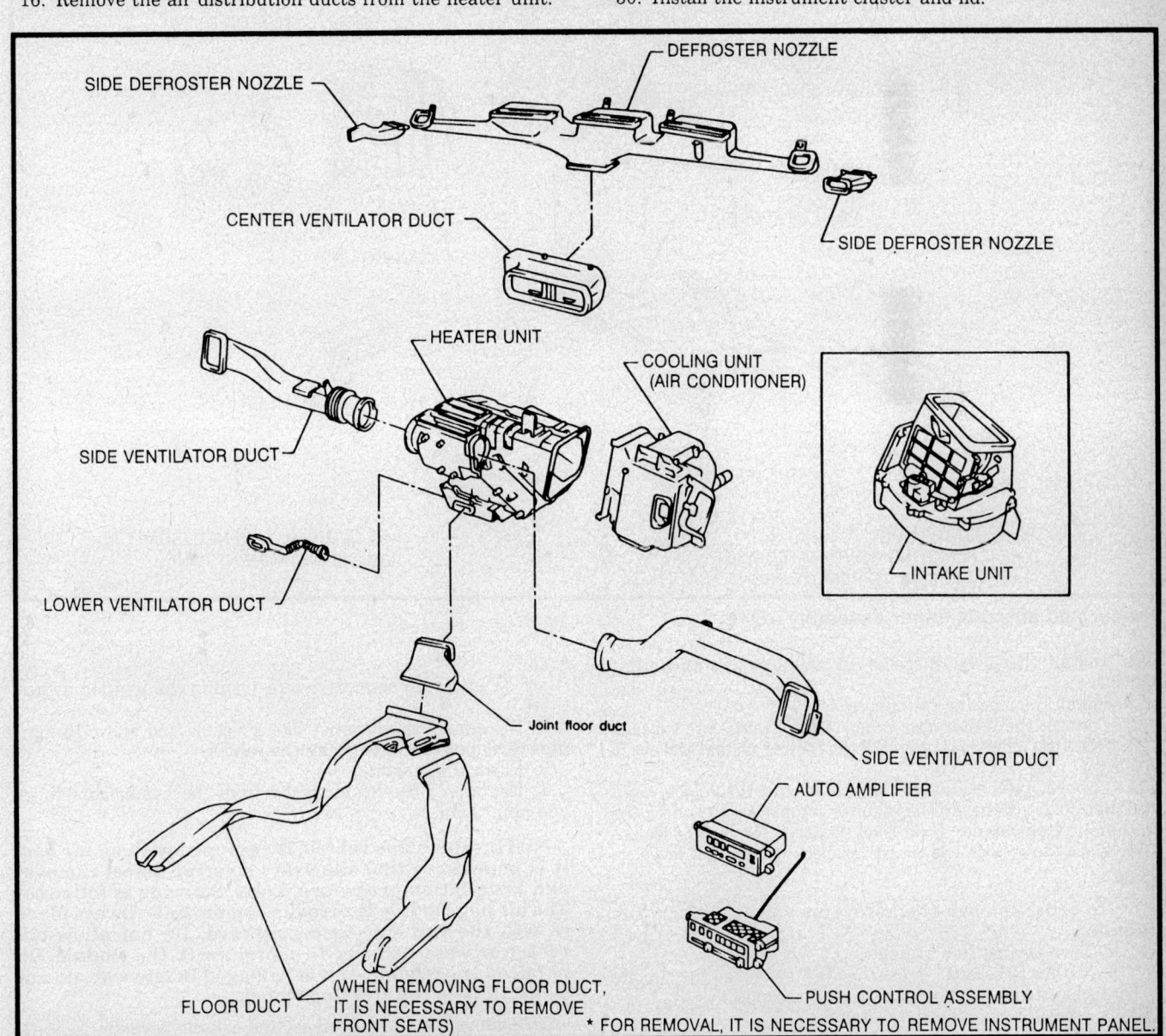

Heater and air conditioner assembly—M30

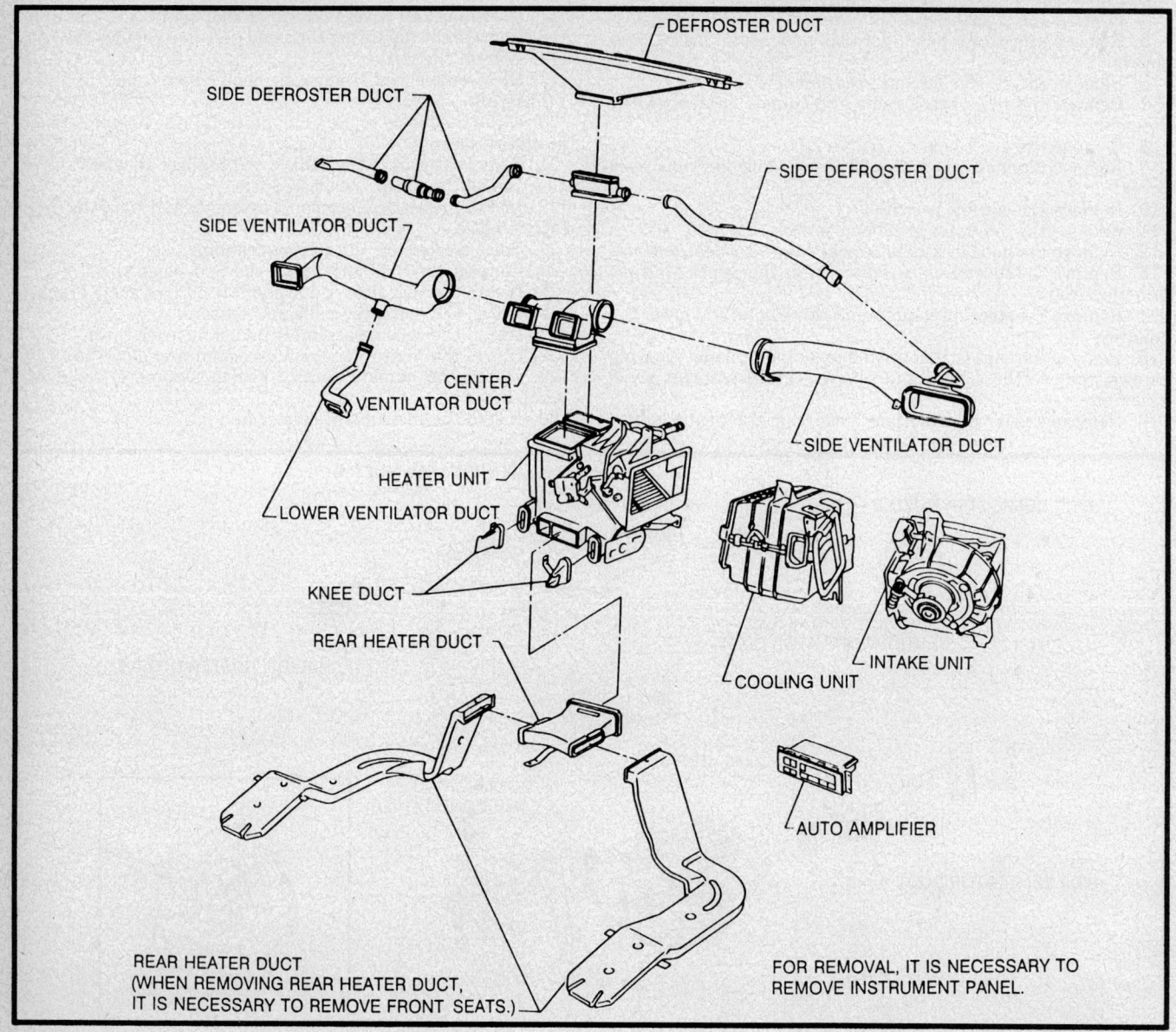

DEFROSTER DUCT

SIDE DEFROSTER DUCT

SIDE DEFROSTER DUCT

SIDE VENTILATOR DUCT

CENTER VENTILATOR DUCT

SIDE VENTILATOR DUCT

HEATER UNIT

LOWER VENTILATOR DUCT

KNEE DUCT

INTAKE UNIT

COOLING UNIT

REAR HEATER DUCT

AUTO AMPLIFIER

REAR HEATER DUCT
(WHEN REMOVING REAR HEATER DUCT,
IT IS NECESSARY TO REMOVE FRONT SEATS.)

FOR REMOVAL, IT IS NECESSARY TO
REMOVE INSTRUMENT PANEL.

Heater and air conditioner assembly—Q45

31. Install the lower instrument panel covers and pillar garnish.
32. Install the steering column covers.
33. Connect the heater core tubes to the heater core tubes.
34. Open the air release plug. Fill the cooling system and check for leaks.
35. Connect the negative battery cable, run the vehicle until the thermostat opens, fill the radiator completely and check the automatic transmission fluid level. Recheck for coolant leaks.
36. Once the vehicle has cooled, recheck the coolant level.

Q45

1. In order to open the hot water valve, perform the following:
  a. Turn the ignition switch to the **ON** position.
  b. Within 10 seconds, press the **OFF** switch on the climate control switch assembly for at least 5 seconds.
  c. Press the temp-hotter switch 3 times.
  d. Press the defroster switch 2 times.
  e. The air conditioning switch panel should display Code 43.
  f. Wait for 10 seconds before turning the ignition switch off.
2. Disconnect the negative battery cable and allow 10 minutes to elapse before entering the vehicle.
3. Drain the coolant.
4. Disconnect the heater hoses from the heater core tubes and plug them.

NOTE: Since this vehicle is equipped with an air bag, it is imperative that the exact steering wheel removal and installation procedure under Steering is followed. The air bag module is a fragile component. Always place it with the pad side facing upward. Do not allow oil, grease or water to come in contact with the module. Do not drop the module; if it is damaged in any way, do not reinstall it to the steering wheel.

5. Remove the steering wheel and column covers.
6. Remove the shifter lever bezel.
7. Remove the ash tray assembly.

8. Remove the radio and climate control switch bezel.
9. Remove the lower instrument panel covers.
10. Remove the front and rear floor console assemblies.
11. Remove the cruise control main switch/outside mirror control switch assembly.
12. Remove the cluster lid and instrument cluster.
13. Remove the glove box and glove box cover.
14. Remove the cover on the lower right side of the instrument panel.
15. Remove the defroster grille.
16. Remove the radio and climate control switch assemblies.
17. Remove the remaining mounting screws remove the instrument panel assembly.
18. Remove the air distribution ducts from the heater unit.
19. Disconnect all wires and cables that connect to the unit.
20. Remove the mounting bolts and nuts and remove the heater unit from the vehicle.
21. Disassemble and remove the heater core from the unit.
To install:
22. Clean the inside of the unit out, install the heater core and assemble the unit. Connect the heater hoses.
23. Install the unit to the vehicle and connect all wires and cables. Install the air distribution ducts.
24. Install the instrument panel assembly. Install the cover on the lower right side.
25. Install the radio and climate control switch assemblies.
26. Install the defroster grille.
27. Install the glove box cover and glove box assembly.
28. Install the instrument cluster and cluster lid.
29. Install the cruise control main switch/outside mirror control switch assembly.
30. Install the console assemblies.
31. Install the lower instrument panel covers.
32. Install the radio and climate control switch bezel.

33. Install the ash tray assembly.
34. Install the shifter lever bezel.
35. Install the steering wheel and column covers.
36. Fill the cooling system and check for leaks.
37. Connect the negative battery cable, run the vehicle until the thermostat opens, fill the radiator completely and check the automatic transmission fluid level. Recheck for coolant leaks.
38. Once the vehicle has cooled, recheck the coolant level.

Water Pump

Removal and Installation

M30

1. Disconnect the negative battery cable.
2. Drain the coolant from the radiator and from the drain plugs on both sides of the cylinder block.
3. Remove the timing belt covers.

NOTE: Use the proper precautions to avoid getting coolant on the timing belt.

4. Note the positioning of the clamp and disconnect the hose from the water pump.
5. Remove the water pump mounting bolts and remove the pump from the engine.
To install:
6. Thoroughly clean and dry the mating surfaces, bolts and bolt holes.
7. Apply liquid gasket to the water pump and install to the engine. Torque the bolts to 14 ft. lbs. (19 Nm).
8. Connect the hose and install the clamp in the same position as when it was removed to provide adequate clearance between it and the timing belt cover.

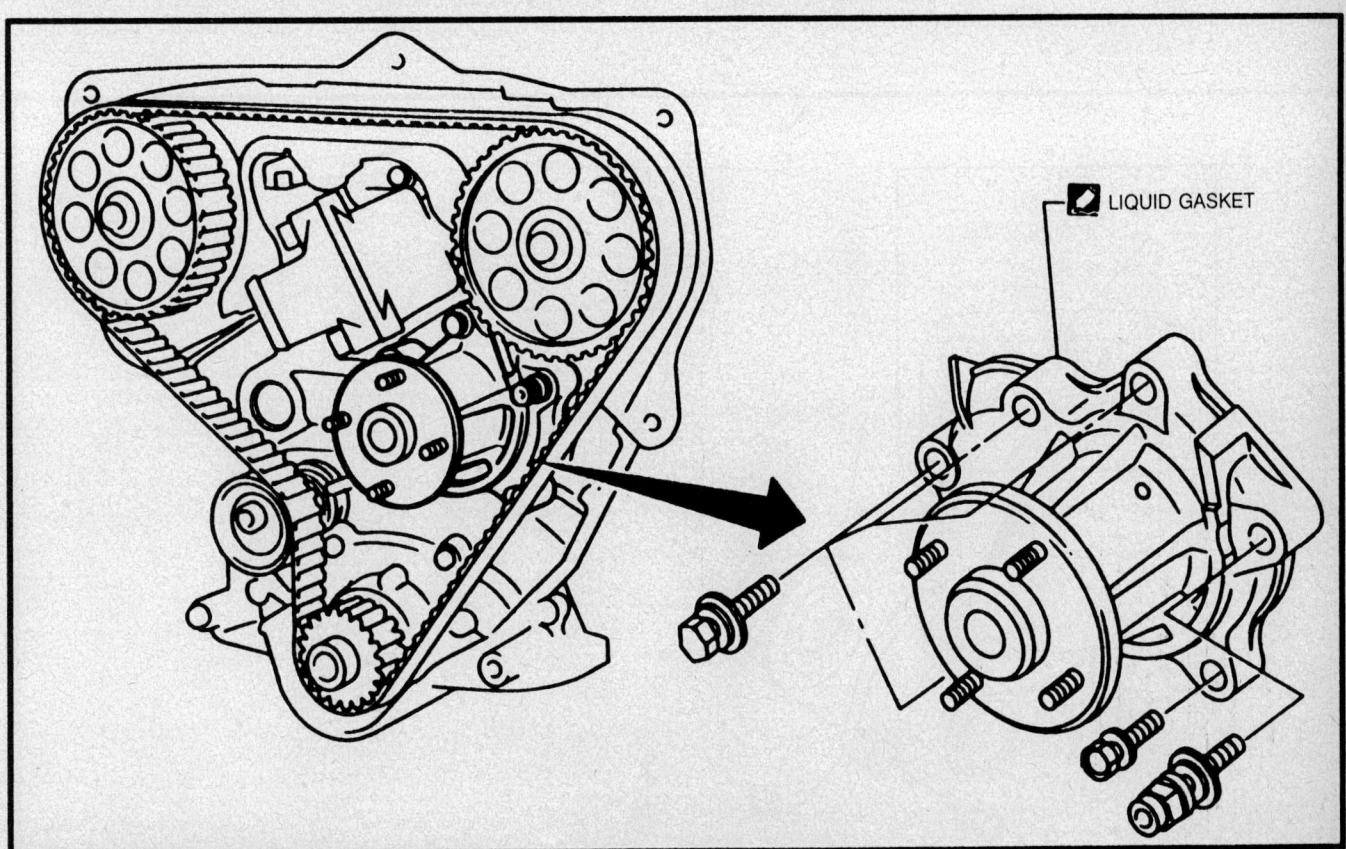

LIQUID GASKET

Water pump location—M30

9. Open the air release plug. Fill the cooling system and check for leaks using a pressure tester before continuing.

10. Install the timing belt covers and all related parts.

11. Connect the negative battery cable, run the vehicle until the thermostat opens and fill the radiator completely. Recheck for coolant leaks.

12. Once the vehicle has cooled, recheck the coolant level.

Q45

1. Disconnect the negative battery cable.

2. Drain the coolant from the radiator and from the drain cocks on both sides of the cylinder block.

3. Unbolt the shroud and move it backward in order to remove the fan and coupling. Remove the fan to water pump bolts and remove the fan, coupling, water pump pulley and shroud.

4. Remove all necessary accessories to gain access to the water pump.

5. Note the positioning of the clamp and disconnect the hose from the water pump.

6. Remove the water pump mounting bolts and remove the pump from the engine.

To install:

7. Thoroughly clean and dry the mating surfaces, bolts and bolt holes.

8. Apply liquid gasket to the water pump and install to the engine. Torque the bolts to 14 ft. lbs. (19 Nm).

9. Connect the hose and install the clamp in the same position as when it was removed. Fill the cooling system and check for leaks using a pressure tester before continuing.

10. Install all removed accessories.

11. Install the shroud, pulley, coupling and fan. Torque the water pump pulley nuts to 7 ft. lbs. (10 Nm). Adjust all belts.

12. Connect the negative battery cable, run the vehicle until the thermostat opens and fill the radiator completely. Recheck for coolant leaks.

13. Once the vehicle has cooled, recheck the coolant level.

Thermostat
Removal and Installation

M30

1. Disconnect the negative battery cable. Drain the cooling system to below thermostat level.

2. Disconnect the upper radiator hose from the thermostat housing.

3. Remove the thermostat housing and thermostat.

To install:

4. Thoroughly clean and dry the mating surfaces, bolts and bolt holes.

5. Install the thermostat with the **UPR** mark and arrow at the top.

6. Apply liquid gasket to the thermostat housing. Install the housing and torque the bolts to 14 ft. lbs. (19 Nm).

7. Open the air release plug and fill the cooling system.

8. Connect the negative battery cable, run the vehicle until the thermostat opens and fill the radiator completely. Recheck for coolant leaks.

9. Once the vehicle has cooled, recheck the coolant level.

Q45

1. Disconnect the negative battery cable. Drain the cooling system to below thermostat level.

2. Remove the front ornament cover.

3. Disconnect the upper hose from the coolant inlet.

4. Remove the inlet and thermostat.

To install:

5. Thoroughly clean and dry the mating surfaces, bolts and bolt holes.

6. Install the thermostat with the jiggle valve at the top.

7. Apply liquid gasket to the inlet. Install and torque the bolts to 14 ft. lbs. (19 Nm).

8. Fill the cooling system.

9. Connect the negative battery cable, run the vehicle until

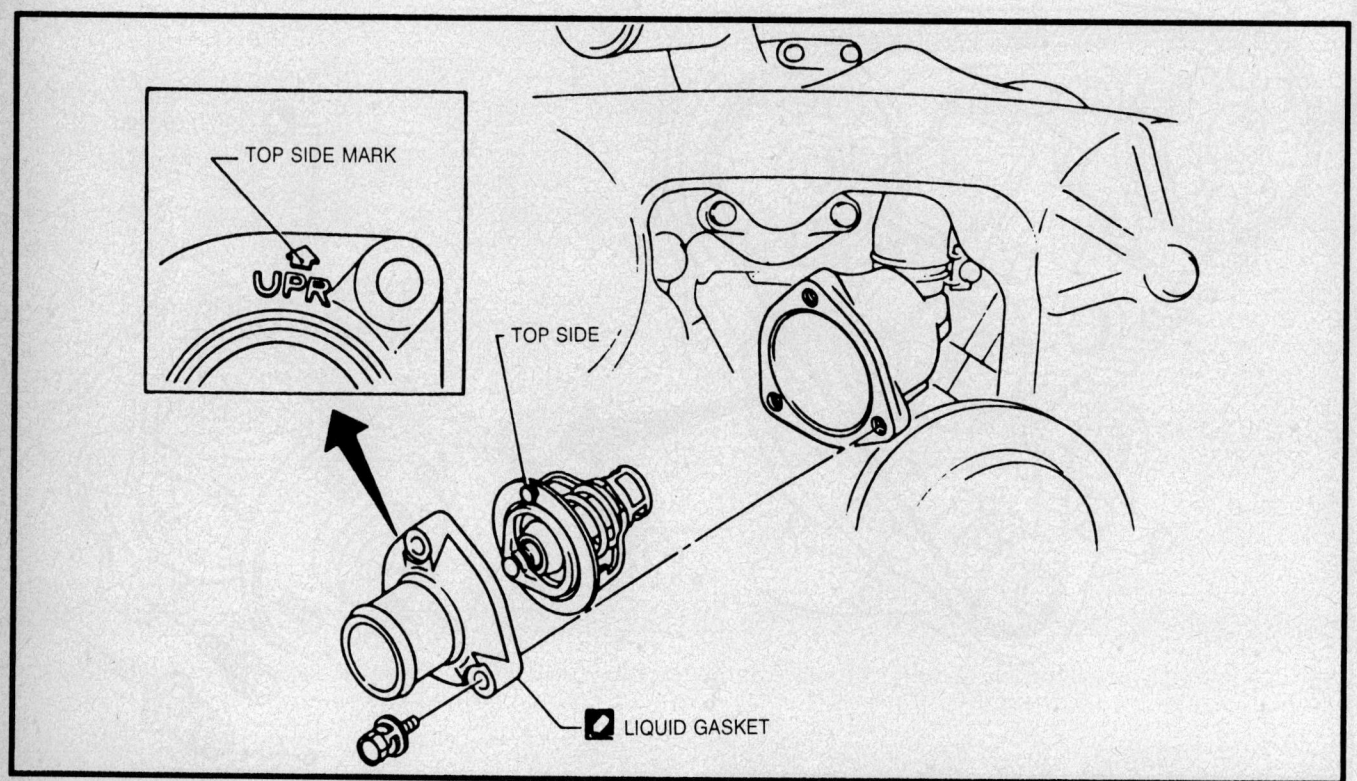

Thermostat location—M30

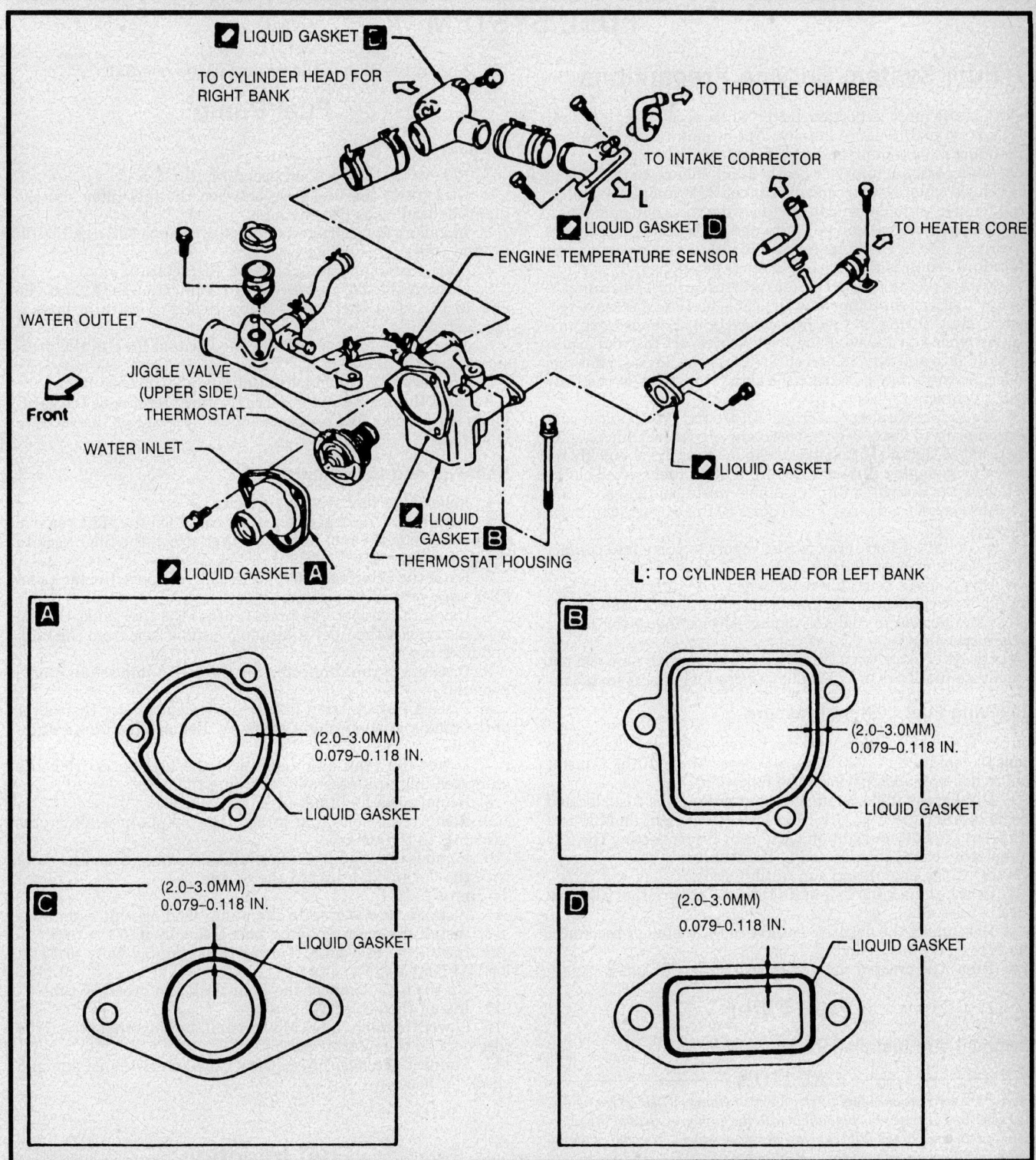

LIQUID GASKET C

TO CYLINDER HEAD FOR
RIGHT BANK

TO THROTTLE CHAMBER

TO INTAKE CORRECTOR

L

LIQUID GASKET D

TO HEATER CORE

ENGINE TEMPERATURE SENSOR

WATER OUTLET

JIGGLE VALVE
(UPPER SIDE)

Front

THERMOSTAT

WATER INLET

LIQUID GASKET

LIQUID
GASKET B

THERMOSTAT HOUSING

LIQUID GASKET A

L: TO CYLINDER HEAD FOR LEFT BANK

A

(2.0–3.0MM)
0.079–0.118 IN.

LIQUID GASKET

B

(2.0–3.0MM)
0.079–0.118 IN.

LIQUID GASKET

C

(2.0–3.0MM)
0.079–0.118 IN.

LIQUID GASKET

D

(2.0–3.0MM)
0.079–0.118 IN.

LIQUID GASKET

Thermostat location — Q45

the thermostat opens and fill the radiator completely. Recheck for coolant leaks.

10. Once the vehicle has cooled, recheck the coolant level.

Cooling System Bleeding

The M30 is equipped with a air release plug in line with a cool-ant hose on the right side of the ornamental collector cover. When filling the coolant system open the plug to bleed air from the system.

The Q45 uses a thermostat which is equipped with a jiggle valve. This valve bleeds air as the system is being filled, thus the cooling system requires no further bleeding.

FUEL SYSTEM

Fuel System Service Precautions

Safety is the most important factor when performing not only fuel system maintenance but any type of maintenance. Failure to conduct maintenance and repairs in a safe manner may result in serious personal injury or death. Maintenance and testing of the vehicle's fuel system components can be accomplished safely and effectively by adhering to the following rules and guidelines.

• To avoid the possibility of fire and personal injury, always disconnect the negative battery cable unless the repair or test procedure requires that battery voltage be applied.

• Always relieve the fuel system pressure prior to disconnecting any fuel system component (injector, fuel rail, pressure regulator, etc.), fitting or fuel line connection. Exercise extreme caution whenever relieving fuel system pressure to avoid exposing skin, face and eyes to fuel spray. Please be advised that fuel under pressure may penetrate the skin or any part of the body that it contacts.

• Always place a shop towel or cloth around the fitting or connection prior to loosening to absorb any excess fuel due to spillage. Ensure that all fuel spillage (should it occur) is quickly removed from engine surfaces. Ensure that all fuel soaked cloths or towels are deposited into a suitable waste container.

• Always keep a dry chemical (Class B) fire extinguisher near the work area.

• Do not allow fuel spray or fuel vapors to come into contact with a spark or open flame.

• Always use a backup wrench when loosening and tightening fuel line connection fittings. This will prevent unnecessary stress and torsion to fuel line piping. Always follow the proper torque specifications.

• Always replace worn fuel fitting O-rings with new. Do not substitute fuel hose or equivalent where fuel pipe is installed.

Relieving Fuel System Pressure

On the Q45, the fuel pressure can be released using the Nissan Consult tool in the Fuel Pressure Release Mode. If the Consult tool is not available, perform the following:

1. Disable the fuel system either by pulling the fuse, located in the interior fuse box, 4th from the bottom right on M30 and 6th from the bottom right on Q45, or by disconnecting the fuel pump relay or module located in the trunk.
2. Start the engine and run until it stalls.
3. Crank the engine 2–3 more times to ensure that all pressure is relieved.
4. Disconnect the negative battery cable. Install or reconnect the fuse, relay or module.
5. Erase the created code when servicing is finished.

Fuel Filter

Removal and Installation

————————— CAUTION —————————

Do not use conventional fuel filters, hoses or clamps when servicing this fuel system. They are not compatible with the high pressures of the injection system and could fail, causing personal injury. Use only components specifically designed for fuel injection.

————————————————————————————

1. Relieve the fuel system pressure.
2. Disconnect the negative battery cable.
3. Disconnect the fuel hoses from the fuel filter, located in the right side of the engine compartment.
4. Remove the filter mounting screws and remove from the vehicle.
5. Inspect all hoses and clamps for damage of any type. Replace parts, as required.

6. The installation is the reverse of the removal.

Fuel Pump

Pressure Testing

1. Relieve the fuel system pressure.
2. Disconnect the fuel hose between the fuel filter and the fuel tube leading to the engine.
3. Install an appropriate fuel pressure gauge between the filter and tube.
4. Start the engine and check for fuel leaks.
5. Observe the fuel pressure. The specification is 34 psi at idle and 43 psi when the fuel pressure regulator vacuum hose is pinched off.
6. Stop the engine, disconnect the vacuum hose to the pressure regulator and plug it.
7. Connect a hand-held vacuum pump to the regulator.
8. Start the engine and observe the fuel pressure as the vacuum is varied. The fuel pressure should decrease as the vacuum is increased.

Removal and Installation

1. Relieve the fuel system pressure.
2. Disconnect the negative battery cable. On the M30, remove the bolts inside the fuel filler door that attach the filler neck to the quarter panel.
3. Raise the vehicle and support safely. Remove the tank and filler neck protective plates.
4. Using the proper equipment, drain the fuel tank. On the Q45, disconnect the filler tube and overflow tube from the tank and plug them.
5. Disconnect the connector for the fuel pump/sending unit assembly.
6. Place a transmission jack or equivalent, under the center of the tank and apply slight pressure. Remove the tank retaining bolts.
7. Lower the tank and disconnect the fuel hoses from the pump/sending unit assembly and plug them.
8. Remove the fuel tank from the vehicle.
9. Remove the bolts that attach the fuel pump/sending unit assembly to the tank.
10. Remove the pump/sending unit assembly from the tank with the O-ring and discard the O-ring.

To install:

11. Install a new O-ring to the pump/sending unit assembly.
12. Install the pump/sending unit assembly into the tank.
13. Install the fuel tank. Torque the retaining bolts to 24 ft. lbs. (33 Nm).
14. On the Q45, connect the filler neck and overflow tube.
15. Install the protective plates.
16. Lower the vehicle. On M30, install the bolts that attach the filer neck to the quarter panel.
17. Connect the negative battery cable, start the engine and check for leaks.

Fuel Injection

For further information, please refer to "Chilton's Electronic Engine Control's Manual" for additional coverage.

Idle Speed Adjustment

The idle speed is controlled by the ECCS control unit. Adjustment is not required.

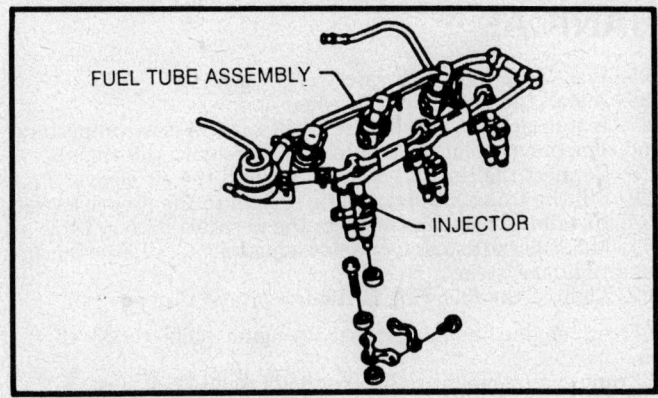

Fuel tube assembly—M30

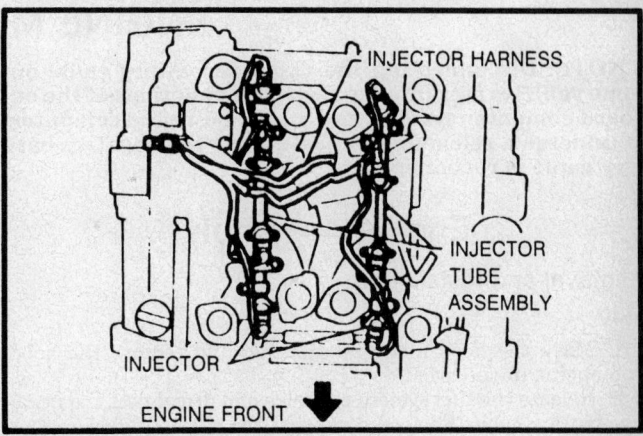

Fuel tube assembly—Q45

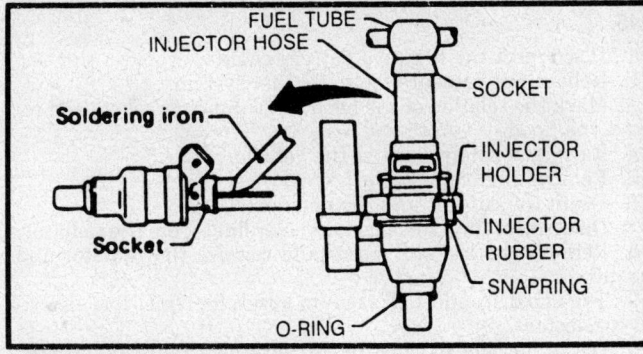

Injector assembly—M30

Idle Mixture Adjustment

The idle mixture is controlled by the ECCS control unit. Adjustment is not required.

Fuel Injector

Removal and Installation

M30

1. Relieve the fuel system pressure. Disconnect the negative battery cable.
2. Disconnect the cruise control and throttle cables from the throttle body.
3. Remove the intake manifold collector.
4. Disconnect the vacuum hose from the fuel pressure regulator.
5. Disconnect and plug the fuel hoses.
6. Disconnect all injector harness connectors.
7. Disconnect the fuel temperature sensor connector.
8. Remove the injector fuel fuel tube assembly retaining bolts and remove the assembly from the engine.

9. Remove the injector(s) and short fuel hose(s) from the fuel tube. Do not reuse the rubber hose(s).

To install:
10. Wet the inside of the new rubber hose(s) with fuel.
11. Push the end of the rubber hose with hose sockets into the injector tail piece and fuel tube end as far as they will go. Clamps are not used at these connections.
12. Install the injector fuel tube assembly.
13. Connect the fuel temperature sensor connector.
14. Connect all injector harness connectors.
15. Connect the fuel hoses and the regulator vacuum hose.
16. Install the intake manifold collector.
17. Connect the cruise control and throttle cables to the throttle body.
18. Connect the negative battery cable and check for leaks.

Q45

1. Relieve the fuel system pressure. Disconnect the negative battery cable.
2. Drain the coolant.
3. Remove the EGR control valve.
4. Remove the intake manifold collector.
5. Disconnect the harness connector(s) from the fuel injector(s).
6. Remove the injector(s) from the injector tube assembly. Do not reuse the O-ring(s).

To install:
7. Using new O-ring(s), install the injector(s) to the injector tube.
8. Connect the harness connector(s).
9. Install the intake manifold collector.
10. Install the EGR control valve.
11. Fill the cooling system.
12. Connect the negative battery cable and check for leaks.

EMISSION CONTROLS

For further information, please refer to "Professional Emission Component Application Guide".

ENGINE MECHANICAL

NOTE: **Disconnecting the negative battery cable on some vehicles may interfere with the functions of the on board computer systems and may require the computer to undergo a relearning process, once the negative battery cable is reconnected.**

Engine Assembly

Removal and Installation

M30

1. Mark the hood hinge relationship and remove the hood and engine undercover.
2. Release the fuel system pressure and disconnect the negative battery cable. Raise and support the vehicle safely.
3. Drain the cooling system and the oil pan.
4. Remove the air cleaner and disconnect the throttle cable.
5. Disconnect or remove the following:
    Drive belts
    Ignition wire from the coil to the distributor
    Ignition coil ground wire and the engine ground cable
    Block connector from the distributor
    Fusible links
    Engine harness connectors
    Fuel and fuel return hoses
    Upper and lower radiator hoses
    Heater inlet and outlet hoses
    Engine vacuum hoses
    Carbon canister hoses and the air pump air cleaner hose
    Any interfering engine accessory:power steering pump, air conditioning compressor or alternator
6. Remove the air pump air cleaner.
7. Remove the carbon canister.
8. Remove the auxiliary fan, washer tank, grille and radiator (with fan assembly).
9. Disconnect the speedometer cable.
10. Remove the spring pins from the transaxle gear selector rods.
11. Install engine slingers to the block and connect a suitable lifting device to the slingers.
12. Disconnect the exhaust pipe at both the manifold connection and the clamp holding the pipe to the engine.
13. Drain the transaxle gear oil.
14. Lower the shifter and selector rods and remove the bolts from the motor mount brackets. Remove the nuts holding the front and rear motor mounts to the frame.
15. Lift the engine/transaxle assembly up and away from the vehicle.

To install:

16. Lower the engine and transaxle assembly into the vehicle. When lowering the engine onto the frame, make sure to keep it as level as possible.
17. Check the clearance between the frame and transaxle and make sure the engine mount bolts are seated in the groove of the mounting bracket.
18. After installing the motor mounts, adjust and install the buffer rods. The front should be 3.50–3.58 in. (89–91mm), and the rear, 3.90–3.98 in. (99–101mm).
19. Raise the shifter and selector rods to their normal operating positions.
20. Connect the exhaust pipe to the manifold connection and the clamp holding the pipe to the engine.
21. Disconnect the lifting device and remove the engine slingers.
22. Insert the spring pins into the transaxle gear selector rods.
23. Connect the speedometer cable.
24. Install the auxiliary fan, washer tank, grille and radiator (with fan assembly).

25. Install the carbon canister.
26. Install the air pump air cleaner.
27. Install or connect all hoses, belts, harnesses, connectors and components that were necessary to remove the engine.
28. Connect the throttle cable and install the air cleaner.
29. Fill the transaxle and cooling system to the proper levels.
30. Install the hood and connect the negative battery cable.
31. Make all the necessary engine adjustments. Charge the air conditioning system.
32. Tighten the following to the the proper torque:
    Front engine mount bracket-to-engine bolts to 33–43 ft. lbs.
    Front engine mount-to-bracket bolts to 29–36 ft. lbs.
    Rear engine mount-to-crossmember bolts to 16–21 ft. lbs.
    Rear crossmember-to-transaxle bolts to 32–41 ft. lbs.

Q45

1. Disconnect the negative battery cable.
2. Relieve the pressure from the fuel system.
3. Mark the relation of the hood to the hinge brackets and remove the hood.
4. Raise and safely support the vehicle.
5. Remove the engine splash shield.
6. Drain the coolant and the engine oil.
7. Disconnect the transmission cooler lines from the radiator.
8. Remove the radiator hoses and remove the radiator and shroud.
9. Tag and disconnect all vacuum hoses, fuel lines and electrical connectors.
10. Disconnect the exhaust pipes from the exhaust manifolds.
11. Mark the position of the driveshaft on the flanges and remove the driveshaft.
12. Remove the accessory drive belts.
13. Remove the alternator, air conditioning compressor and power steering pump.
14. Remove the lower steering joint.
15. Remove the sway bar, transverse link and tension rod with bracket.
16. Place a suitable jack under the transmission and disconnect the transmission rear mount.
17. Remove the suspension member attaching bolts.
18. Remove the engine mounting bolts.
19. Attach a suitable hoist to the engine. Lower the transmission jack and the hoist and lower the engine and transmission from under the vehicle.

To install:

20. Raise the engine and transmission into position.
21. Install the engine mounting nuts and bolts and tighten to 41 ft. lbs. (55 Nm).
22. Install the suspension member bolts.
23. Install and tighten the rear mount-to-body bolts to 41 ft. lbs. (55 Nm).
24. Remove the hoist and the transmission jack.
25. Install the sway bar, transverse link and the tension rod with bracket.
26. Install the lower steering joint.
27. Install the alternator, air conditioning compressor and power steering pump.
28. Install and adjust the accessory drive belts.
29. Install the radiator and shroud. Install the radiator hoses.
30. Install the driveshaft, aligning the marks that were made during the removal procedure.
31. Connect the exhaust pipes to the exhaust manifolds.
32. Connect all electrical connectors, fuel lines and vacuum hoses.
33. Fill the crankcase with the proper type of engine oil to the required level. Fill the cooling system with the proper type and quantity of coolant.

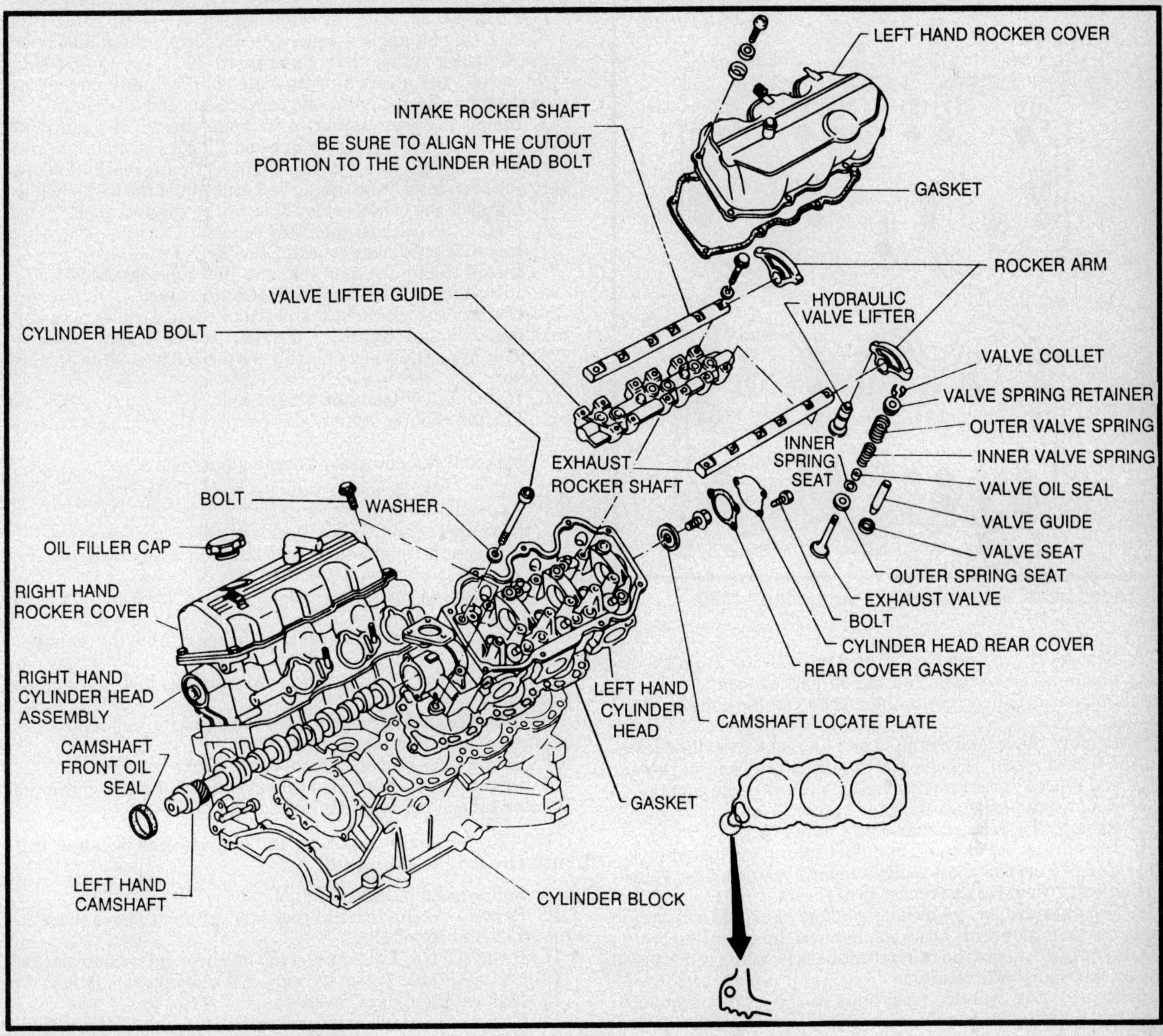

LEFT HAND ROCKER COVER

INTAKE ROCKER SHAFT

BE SURE TO ALIGN THE CUTOUT
PORTION TO THE CYLINDER HEAD BOLT

GASKET

VALVE LIFTER GUIDE

ROCKER ARM

CYLINDER HEAD BOLT

HYDRAULIC
VALVE LIFTER

VALVE COLLET

VALVE SPRING RETAINER

OUTER VALVE SPRING

INNER VALVE SPRING

INNER
SPRING
SEAT

VALVE OIL SEAL

EXHAUST
ROCKER SHAFT

VALVE GUIDE

BOLT

WASHER

VALVE SEAT

OIL FILLER CAP

OUTER SPRING SEAT

RIGHT HAND
ROCKER COVER

EXHAUST VALVE

BOLT

RIGHT HAND
CYLINDER HEAD
ASSEMBLY

LEFT HAND
CYLINDER
HEAD

CYLINDER HEAD REAR COVER

REAR COVER GASKET

CAMSHAFT LOCATE PLATE

CAMSHAFT
FRONT OIL
SEAL

GASKET

LEFT HAND
CAMSHAFT

CYLINDER BLOCK

Cylinder head components—M30

34. Install the hood, aligning the marks that were made during the removal procedure.

35. Connect the negative battery cable, start the engine and check for leaks.

Cylinder Head

Removal and Installation

M30

1. Relieve the fuel system pressure and disconnect the negative battery cable.
2. Drain the cooling system.
3. Remove the timing belt.

NOTE: Do not rotate either the crankshaft or camshaft from this point onward or the valves could be bent by hitting the tops of the pistons.

4. Disconnect and tag all vacuum and water hoses connected to the intake collector.

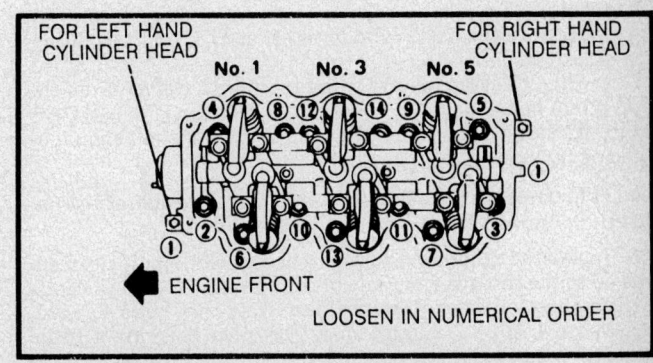

FOR LEFT HAND
CYLINDER HEAD

FOR RIGHT HAND
CYLINDER HEAD

No. 1   No. 3   No. 5

ENGINE FRONT

LOOSEN IN NUMERICAL ORDER

Cylinder head bolt removal sequence—M30

5. Remove the distributor, ignition wires and disconnect the accelerator and cruise control (ASCD) cables from the intake manifold collector.

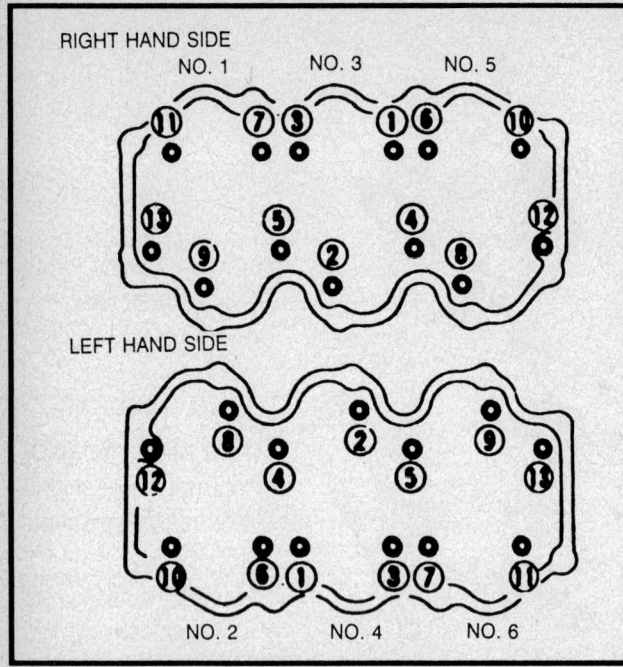

RIGHT HAND SIDE

NO. 1   NO. 3   NO. 5

LEFT HAND SIDE

NO. 2   NO. 4   NO. 6

Cylinder head bolt tightening sequence—M30

6. Remove the collector cover and the collector from the intake manifold. Disconnect and tag all harness connectors and vacuum lines to gain access to the cover retaining bolts on these models.

7. Remove the intake manifold and fuel tube assembly. Loosen the intake manifold bolts starting from the front of the engine and proceed in criss-cross pattern towards the center.

8. Remove the exhaust collector bracket.

9. Remove the exhaust manifold covers.

10. Disconnect the exhaust manifold from the exhaust pipe.

11. Remove the camshaft pulleys and the rear timing cover securing bolts. Remove the rocker arm covers.

12. Separate the air conditioning compressor and alternator from the their mounting brackets. Remove the mounting brackets. Do not disconnect the refrigerant lines from the compressor or serious injury will result.

13. Remove the cylinder head bolts in the correct sequence. Lift the cylinder head off the engine block with the exhaust manifolds attached. It may be necessary to tap the head lightly with a rubber mallet to loosen it.

To install:

14. Make sure the No. 1 cylinder is set at TDC on its compression stroke as follows:

    a. Align the crankshaft timing mark with the mark on the oil pump housing.

    b. The knock pin in the front end of the camshaft should be facing upward.

NOTE: Do not rotate crankshaft and camshaft separately because valves will hit piston head.

15. Install the cylinder head with a new gasket. Apply clean engine oil to the threads and seats of the bolts and install the bolts with washers in the correct position. Note that bolts 4, 5, 12, and 13 are 4.95 in. (127mm) long. The other bolts are 4.13 in. (106mm) long.

16. Torque the bolts in the proper sequence as follows:

    a. Torque all bolts, in sequence, to 22 ft. lbs. (29 Nm).

    b. Torque all bolts, in sequence, to 43 ft. lbs. (58 Nm).

    c. Loosen all bolts completely.

    d. Torque all bolts, in sequecne, to 22 ft. lbs. (29 Nm).

    e. Torque all bolts, in sequence, to 40–47 ft. lbs (54–64 Nm). Using an angle torque wrench, torque them 60–65 degrees tighter rather than going to 40–47 ft. lbs. (54–64 Nm)

17. Install the alternator and air conditioner compressor mounting brackets. Mount the compressor and alternator.

18. Install the rear timing cover bolts. Install the camshaft pulleys. Make sure the pulley marked R3 goes on the right and that marked L3 goes on the left. Align the timing marks if necessary and then install the timing belt and adjust the belt tension.

19. Connect the exhaust manifold to the exhaust pipe.

20. Install the exhaust manifold covers.

21. Install the exhaust collector bracket.

22. Install the intake manifold and fuel tube assembly.

23. Install the intake manifold collector cover.

24. Connect the accelerator and cruise control cables to the intake manifold and install the distributor and ignition wires.

25. Connect the vacuum and water hoses to the intake collector.

26. Install and tension the timing belt.

27. Fill the cooling system and connect the negative battery cable.

28. Make all the necessary engine adjustments.

Q45

1. Disconnect the negative battery cable.

2. Remove the engine and transmission assembly from the vehicle.

3. Remove the suspension member and engine mounts from the engine.

4. Remove the air compressor bracket and the exhaust manifolds.

5. Remove the cooling fan with coupling and the engine gusset.

6. Separate the engine from the transmission and mount the engine on a suitable workstand.

7. Remove the oil pan. Remove the intake collector.

8. Disconnect the injector harness connector and remove the injector tube assembly with injector.

NOTE: Be careful not to let the rubber washer fall into the intake manifold.

9. Remove the intake manifold.

10. Remove the ornamental rocker cover and remove the ignition coils and spark plugs.

11. Bring the No. 1 piston to TDC on the compression stroke.

12. Use a suitable puller to remove the crankshaft pulley.

13. Remove the rocker cover.

14. Remove the crank angle sensor and the Valve Timing Control (VTC) solenoid.

15. Remove the chain tensioners and the upper front covers.

16. Remove the front timing chain cover.

NOTE: The timing chain will not be disengaged or dislocated from the crankshaft sprocket unless the front cover is removed. The cast portion of the front cover is located on the lower side of the crankshaft sprocket so the timing chain is not disengaged from the sprocket.

17. Remove the VTC assembly and the camshaft sprocket.

18. Remove the oil pump chain and the timing chains.

NOTE: Do not attempt to disassemble the VTC assembly since they are difficult to reassemble accurately in the field. If it should be disassembled, the VTC assembly must be replaced with a new one.

19. Remove the camshaft brackets and the camshafts. Mark the parts so they can be reinstalled in their original positions.

20. Remove the rocker arm and hydraulic lash adjuster. Be sure to identify each adjuster so it can be reinstalled in it's original position.

21. Remove the cylinder head and gasket. Loosen the head

bolts in 2–3 steps working from the outside bolts in towards the center bolts.

To install:

22. Make sure all mating surfaces are clean before installation.

23. Check the cylinder head surface for warpage using a feeler gauge and a suitable straightedge. If the cylinder head is warped more than 0.004 in. (0.1mm) it must be resurfaced or replaced. The total amount machined from the head or head and block combined, cannot total more than 0.008 in. (0.2mm).

24. Make sure the No. 1 piston is still at TDC of the compression stroke, then turn the crankshaft until the No. 1 piston is at approximately 45 degrees before TDC on the compression stroke. At this point, the No. 3 piston will be at the same height as the No. 1 piston to prevent interference of the valves and pistons.

25. Install the cylinder heads with new gaskets. Temporarily tighten the cylinder head bolts to avoid damaging the cylinder head gaskets. Be sure to install washers between the bolts and the cylinder heads. Do not rotate the crankshaft or camshaft separately or the valves will hit the pistons.

26. Install the hydraulic lash adjusters and check them as follows:

   a. When the rocker arm can be moved at least 0.04 in. (1.0mm) by pushing at the hydraulic lash adjuster location, it indicates that there is air in the high pressure chamber. Noise will be emitted from the hydraulic lash adjuster if the engine is started without bleeding the air.

   b. Remove the hydraulic lash adjuster and dip in a container filled with engine oil. While pushing the top of the plunger down, insert a suitable thin rod through the hole in the top of the plunger and lightly push the check ball. Air is completely bled when the plunger no longer moves.

NOTE: Air cannot be bled from the lash adjusters by running the engine.

27. Install the rocker arms, camshafts and camshaft brackets on the right bank.

28. Install the VTC assembly and the exhaust cam sprocket on the right bank.

29. After making sure the camshafts are still correctly positioned, turn the crankshaft clockwise to bring the No. 1 piston to TDC on the compression stroke.

30. Install the timing chain on the right bank, aligning the mating marks on the chain with those on the crankshaft and camshaft sprockets.

31. Install the chain tensioner on the right bank.

32. Turn the crankshaft approximately 120 degrees clockwise from the point where the No. 1 piston is at TDC on the compression stroke. At this point, the valves on the left bank still remain unlifted.

33. Correctly position the camshafts for the left cylinder head. Install the VTC assembly and the exhaust cam sprocket.

34. Install the timing chain on the left bank, aligning the mating marks on the chain with those on the crankshaft and camshaft sprockets.

35. Install the oil pump chain and sprockets.

36. Install the oil pump chain guides. Place a 0.04 in. (1.0mm) feeler gauge between the upper chain guide and chain before assembling the chain guides. The force applied to the chain is equivalent to the upper chain guide weight.

37. Apply suitable sealer and install the front covers.

38. Install the chain tensioner for the left bank.

39. Apply suitable sealer to the rubber plugs and install them on the cylinder head.

40. Install the crank angle sensor, VTC solenoid, rocker cover and crank pulley.

41. Bring the piston in No. 1 cylinder to TDC on the compression stroke.

42. Tighten the cylinder head bolts in the proper torque sequence as follows:

   a. Tighten the bolts in sequence to 22 ft. lbs. (29 Nm).

   b. Tighten the bolts in sequence to 69 ft. lbs. (93 Nm).

   c. Loosen the bolts completely.

   d. Tighten the bolts in sequence to 18–25 ft. lbs. (25–34 Nm).

   e. Turn the bolts in sequence 90–95 degrees or 69–72 ft. lbs. (93–98 Nm).

43. Install the intake manifold bolts in their proper positions on the cylinder head and lightly tighten the mounting bolts.

44. Connect the injector tube assemblies, including the fuel injectors, to the intake manifolds and lightly tighten the mounting bolts.

NOTE: Be careful not to let the rubber washer fall into the intake manifold.

45. Install the intake collector and lightly tighten the mounting bolts.

46. Tighten the intake manifold mounting bolts at the cylinder head, remove the intake collectors and tighten the intake manifolds to 12–15 ft. lbs. (16–21 Nm).

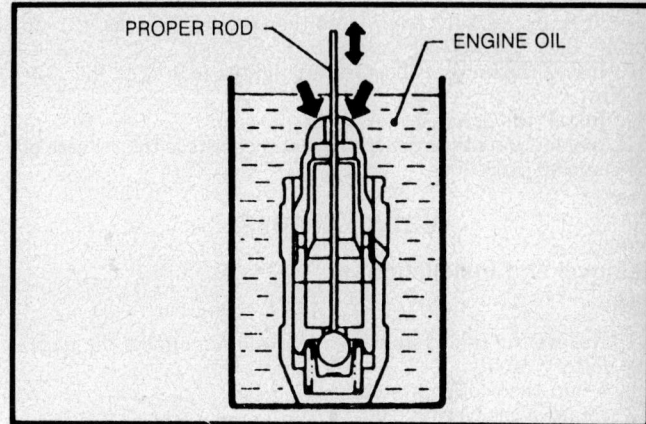

Hydraulic lash adjuster bleeding—Q45

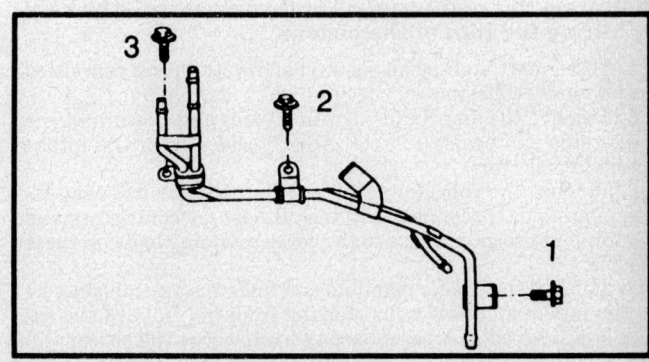

Sub-fuel tubes torque sequence

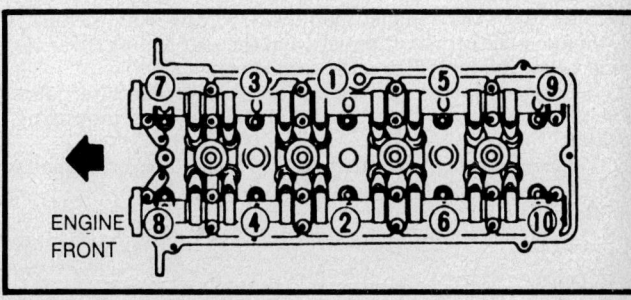

Cylinder head torque sequence—Q45

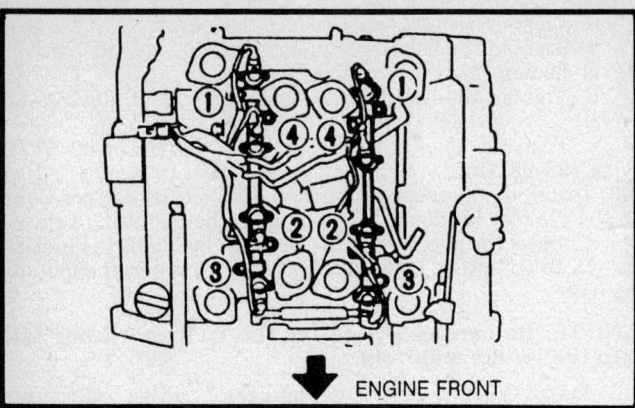

ENGINE FRONT

Injector tube torque sequence

47. Tighten the sub-fuel tubes, in sequence, first to 3.1–4.3 ft. lbs. (4.2–5.9 Nm) and then to 6.2–8.0 ft. lbs. (8.4–10.8 Nm).

48. Tighten the injector tube assemblies, in sequence, first to 6.9–8.0 ft. lbs. (9.3–10.8 Nm) and then to 15–20 ft. lbs. (21–26 Nm).

49. Install the intake collectors and tighten to 9–11 ft. lbs. (12–15 Nm).

50. Install the exhaust manifolds.

51. Installation of the remaining components is the reverse of the removal procedure.

Valve Lifters

Removal and Installation

M30

1. Relieve the fuel system pressure and disconnect the negative battery cable.

2. Drain the cooling system.

3. Remove the timing belt.

NOTE: Do not rotate either the crankshaft or camshaft from this point onward or the valves could be bent by hitting the tops of the pistons.

4. Disconnect and tag all vacuum and water hoses connected to the intake collector.

5. Remove the distributor, ignition wires and disconnect the accelerator and cruise control (ASCD) cables from the intake manifold collector.

6. Remove the collector cover and the collector from the intake manifold. Disconnect and tag all harness connectors and vacuum lines to gain access to the cover retaining bolts on these models.

7. Remove the intake manifold and fuel tube assembly. Loosen the intake manifold bolts starting from the front of the engine and proceed in criss-cross pattern towards the center.

8. Remove the exhaust collector bracket.

9. Remove the exhaust manifold covers.

10. Disconnect the exhaust manifold from the exhaust pipe.

11. Remove the camshaft pulleys and the rear timing cover securing bolts. Remove the rocker arm covers.

12. Separate the air conditioning compressor and alternator from the their mounting brackets. Remove the mounting brackets.

13. Remove the rocker shafts with the rocker arms. The bolts should be loosened in 2–3 steps.

14. Remove the hydraulic valve lifters and the lifter guide. Hold the valve lifter with wire so they do not fall from the lifter guide.

To install:

15. Install the valve lifters into the valve lifter guide.

16. Assemble the lifters to their original position and hold all the lifters with wire to prevent the lifters from falling out. After installing them, remove the wire.

17. Install the rocker shafts with the rocker arms. Tighten the bolts gradually in 2–3 stages. Before tightening, be sure to set camshaft lobe at the position where lobe is not lifted or the valve closed. Set each cylinder 1 at a time or follow the procedure below. The cylinder head, intake manifold, collector and timing belt must be installed:

   a. Set No. 1 piston at TDC of the compression stroke and tighten rocker shaft bolts for Nos. 2, 4 and 6 cylinders.

   b. Set No. 4 piston at TDC of the compression stroke and tighten rocker shaft bolts for Nos. 1, 3 and 5 cylinders.

   c. Torque specification for the rocker shaft retaining bolts is 13–16 ft. lbs. (18–22 Nm).

18. Install the alternator and air conditioner compressor mounting brackets. Mount the compressor and alternator.

19. Install the rear timing cover bolts. Install the camshaft pulleys. Make sure the pulley marked R3 goes on the right and that marked L3 goes on the left. Align the timing marks if necessary and then install the timing belt and adjust the belt tension.

20. Connect the exhaust manifold to the exhaust pipe.

21. Install the exhaust manifold covers.

22. Install the exhaust collector bracket.

23. Install the intake manifold and fuel tube assembly.

24. Install the intake manifold collector cover.

25. Connect the accelerator and cruise control cables to the intake manifold and install the distributor and ignition wires.

26. Connect the vacuum and water hoses to the intake collector.

27. Install and tension the timing belt.

28. Fill the cooling system and connect the negative battery cable.

29. Make all the necessary engine adjustments.

Hydraulic Lash Adjusters

Removal and Installation

Q45

1. Disconnect the negative battery cable.

2. Remove the engine and transmission assembly from the vehicle.

3. Remove the suspension member and engine mounts from the engine.

4. Remove the air compressor bracket.

5. Remove the cooling fan with coupling and the engine gusset.

6. Separate the engine from the transmission and mount engine on a suitable workstand.

7. Remove the oil pan.

8. Remove the ornamental rocker cover and remove the ignition coils and spark plugs.

9. Bring the No. 1 piston to TDC on the compression stroke.

10. Use a suitable puller to remove the crankshaft pulley.

11. Remove the rocker cover.

12. Remove the crank angle sensor and the Valve Timing Control (VTC) solenoid.

13. Remove the chain tensioners and the upper front covers.

14. Remove the front timing chain cover.

NOTE: The timing chain will not be disengaged or dislocated from the crankshaft sprocket unless the front cover is removed. The cast portion of the front cover is located on the lower side of the crankshaft sprocket so the timing chain is not disengaged from the sprocket.

15. Remove the VTC assembly and the camshaft sprocket.

16. Remove the oil pump chain and the timing chains.

NOTE: Do not attempt to disassemble the VTC assembly since they are difficult to reassemble accurately in the field. If it should be disassembled, the VTC assembly must be replaced with a new one.

17. Remove the camshaft brackets and the camshafts. Mark the parts so they can be reinstalled in their original positions.

18. Remove the rocker arm and hydraulic lash adjuster. Be sure to identify each adjuster so it can be reinstalled in it's original position.

To install:

19. Make sure all mating surfaces are clean before installation.

20. Install the hydraulic lash adjusters and check them as follows:

   a. When the rocker arm can be moved at least 0.04 in. (1.0mm) by pushing at the hydraulic lash adjuster location, it indicates that there is air in the high pressure chamber. Noise will be emitted from the hydraulic lash adjuster if the engine is started without bleeding the air.

   b. Remove the hydraulic lash adjuster and dip in a container filled with engine oil. While pushing the top of the plunger down, insert a suitable thin rod through the hole in the top of the plunger and lightly push the check ball. Air is completely bled when the plunger no longer moves.

NOTE: Air cannot be bled from the lash adjusters by running the engine.

21. Install the rocker arms, camshafts and camshaft brackets on the right bank.

22. Install the VTC assembly and the exhaust cam sprocket on the right bank.

23. Make sure the camshafts are still correctly positioned and the piston in the No. 1 cylinder is still at TDC.

24. Install the timing chain on the right bank, aligning the mating marks on the chain with those on the crankshaft and camshaft sprockets.

25. Install the chain tensioner on the right bank.

26. Turn the crankshaft approximately 120 degrees clockwise from the point where the No. 1 piston is at TDC on the compression stroke. At this point, the valves on the left bank still remain unlifted.

27. Correctly position the camshafts for the left cylinder head. Install the VTC assembly and the exhaust cam sprocket.

28. Install the timing chain on the left bank, aligning the mating marks on the chain with those on the crankshaft and camshaft sprockets.

29. Install the oil pump chain and sprockets.

30. Install the oil pump chain guides. Place a 0.04 in. (1.0mm) feeler gauge between the upper chain guide and chain before assembling the chain guides. The force applied to the chain is equivalent to the upper chain guide weight.

31. Apply suitable sealer and install the front covers.

32. Install the chain tensioner for the left bank.

33. Apply suitable sealer to the rubber plugs and install them on the cylinder head.

34. Install the crank angle sensor, VTC solenoid, rocker cover and crank pulley.

35. Installation of the remaining components is the reverse of the removal procedure.

Rocker Arms

Removal and Installation

M30

1. Relieve the fuel system pressure and disconnect the negative battery cable.

2. Drain the cooling system.

3. Remove the timing belt.

NOTE: Do not rotate either the crankshaft or camshaft from this point onward or the valves could be bent by hitting the tops of the pistons.

4. Disconnect and tag all vacuum and water hoses connected to the intake collector.

5. Remove the distributor, ignition wires and disconnect the accelerator and cruise control (ASCD) cables from the intake manifold collector.

6. Remove the collector cover and the collector from the intake manifold. Disconnect and tag all harness connectors and vacuum lines to gain access to the cover retaining bolts on these models.

7. Remove the intake manifold and fuel tube assembly. Loosen the intake manifold bolts starting from the front of the engine and proceed in criss-cross pattern towards the center.

8. Remove the exhaust collector bracket.

9. Remove the exhaust manifold covers.

10. Disconnect the exhaust manifold from the exhaust pipe.

11. Remove the camshaft pulleys and the rear timing cover securing bolts. Remove the rocker arm covers.

12. Separate the air conditioning compressor and alternator from the their mounting brackets. Remove the mounting brackets.

13. Remove the rocker shafts with the rocker arms. The bolts should be loosened in 2–3 steps.

To install:

14. Install the rocker shafts with the rocker arms. Tighten the bolts gradually in 2–3 stages. Before tightening, be sure to set camshaft lobe at the position where lobe is not lifted or the valve closed. Set each cylinder 1 at a time or follow the procedure below. The cylinder head, intake manifold, collector and timing belt must be installed:

   a. Set No. 1 piston at TDC of the compression stroke and tighten rocker shaft bolts for Nos. 2, 4 and 6 cylinders.

   b. Set No. 4 piston at TDC of the compression stroke and tighten rocker shaft bolts for Nos. 1, 3 and 5 cylinders.

   c. Torque specification for the rocker shaft retaining bolts is 13–16 ft. lbs. (18–22 Nm).

15. Install the alternator and air conditioner compressor mounting brackets. Mount the compressor and alternator.

16. Install the rear timing cover bolts. Install the camshaft pulleys. Make sure the pulley marked R3 goes on the right and that marked L3 goes on the left. Align the timing marks, if necessary, and then install the timing belt and adjust the belt tension.

17. Connect the exhaust manifold to the exhaust pipe.

18. Install the exhaust manifold covers.

19. Install the exhaust collector bracket.

20. Install the intake manifold and fuel tube assembly.

21. Install the intake manifold collector cover.

22. Connect the accelerator and cruise control cables to the intake manifold and install the distributor and ignition wires.

23. Connect the vacuum and water hoses to the intake collector.

24. Install and tension the timing belt.

25. Fill the cooling system and connect the negative battery cable.

26. Make all the necessary engine adjustments.

Q45

1. Disconnect the negative battery cable.

2. Remove the engine and transmission assembly from the vehicle.

3. Remove the suspension member and engine mounts from the engine.

4. Remove the air compressor bracket.

5. Remove the cooling fan with coupling and the engine gusset.

6. Separate the engine from the transmission and mount the engine on a suitable workstand.

7. Remove the oil pan.

8. Remove the ornamental rocker cover and remove the ignition coils and spark plugs.

9. Bring the No. 1 piston to TDC on the compression stroke.

10. Use a suitable puller to remove the crankshaft pulley.

11. Remove the rocker cover.

12. Remove the crank angle sensor and the Valve Timing Control (VTC) solenoid.

13. Remove the chain tensioners and the upper front covers.

14. Remove the front timing chain cover.

NOTE: The timing chain will not be disengaged or dislocated from the crankshaft sprocket unless the front cover is removed. The cast portion of the front cover is located on the lower side of the crankshaft sprocket so the timing chain is not disengaged from the sprocket.

15. Remove the VTC assembly and the camshaft sprocket.

16. Remove the oil pump chain and the timing chains.

NOTE: Do not attempt to disassemble the VTC assembly since they are difficult to reassemble accurately in the field. If it should be disassembled, the VTC assembly must be replaced with a new one.

17. Remove the camshaft brackets and the camshafts. Mark the parts so they can be reinstalled in their original positions.

18. Remove the rocker arms. Be sure to identify each rocker arm so it can be reinstalled in it's original position.

To install:

19. Make sure all mating surfaces are clean before installation.

20. Install the rocker arms, camshafts and camshaft brackets on the right bank. Properly lubricate the rocker arms and camshafts prior to installation.

21. Install the VTC assembly and the exhaust cam sprocket on the right bank.

22. Make sure the camshafts are still correctly positioned and the piston in the No. 1 cylinder is still at TDC.

23. Install the timing chain on the right bank, aligning the mating marks on the chain with those on the crankshaft and camshaft sprockets.

24. Install the chain tensioner on the right bank.

25. Turn the crankshaft approximately 120 degrees clockwise from the point where the No. 1 piston is at TDC on the compression stroke. At this point, the valves on the left bank still remain unlifted.

26. Correctly position the camshafts and rocker arms for the left cylinder head. Properly lubricate the rocker arms and camshafts prior to installation. Install the VTC assembly and the exhaust cam sprocket.

27. Install the timing chain on the left bank, aligning the mating marks on the chain with those on the crankshaft and camshaft sprockets.

28. Install the oil pump chain and sprockets.

29. Install the oil pump chain guides. Place a 0.04 in. (1.0mm) feeler gauge between the upper chain guide and chain before assembling the chain guides. The force applied to the chain is equivalent to the upper chain guide weight.

30. Apply suitable sealer and install the front covers.

31. Install the chain tensioner for the left bank.

32. Apply suitable sealer to the rubber plugs and install them on the cylinder head.

33. Install the crank angle sensor, VTC solenoid, rocker cover and crank pulley.

34. Installation of the remaining components is the reverse of the removal procedure.

Intake Manifold

Removal and Installation

M30

1. Relieve the fuel system pressure, disconnect the negative battery cable and drain the cooling system.

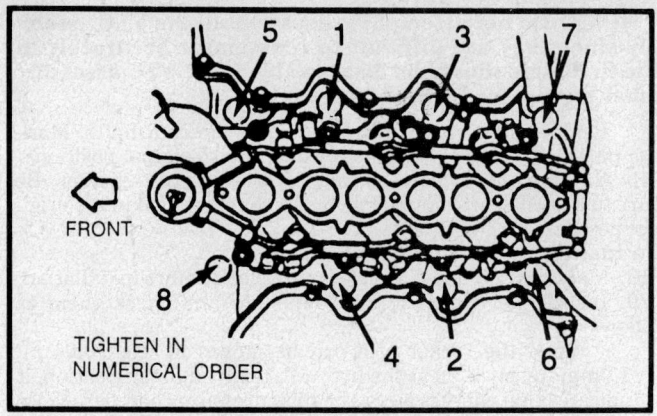

Intake manifold installation torque sequence—M30

2. Remove the distributor and the ignition wires.

3. Disconnect the ASCD and accelerator wires from the intake manifold collector.

4. Disconnect the harness connectors for the AAC valve, throttle sensor and idle switch.

5. Disconnect the air cut out valve water hose.

6. Disconnect the PCV valve hoses.

7. Disconnect the vacuum hoses from the vacuum gallery, swirl control valve, master brake cylinder, EGR control valve and EGR flare tube.

8. Loosen the upper collector cover bolts in proper sequence and remove the upper intake manifold collector from the engine. Remove the collector gasket.

9. Disconnect the engine ground harness.

10. Loosen the lower collector bolts, in sequence, and remove the lower intake manifold collector from the engine.

11. Disconnect the harness connectors for all injectors, engine temperature switch and sensor, power valve control solenoid valve, EGR control solenoid valve, EGR. temperature sensor (California only).

12. Disconnect the vacuum gallery hoses.

13. Disconnect the pressure regulator valve vacuum hose, heater hose, fuel feed and return hose.

14. Remove the intake manifold and fuel tube assembly. Loosen intake manifold bolts in numerical order.

To install:

15. Install the intake manifold and fuel tube assembly with a new gasket. Tighten the manifold bolts and nuts, in 2–3 stages, in sequence.

16. Connect the hoses and electrical wires to the intake manifold and fuel tube.

17. Install the upper and lower collector and collector cover with new gaskets. Tighten collector to intake manifold bolts, in 2–3 stages, by reversing the removal sequence.

18. Connect the vacuum lines, hoses, cables and brackets to the collector cover and collector assembly.

19. Install the distributor and ignition wires.

20. Fill the cooling system to the proper level and connect the negative battery cable.

21. Make all the necessary engine adjustments.

Q45

1. Disconnect the negative battery cable.

2. Properly relieve the fuel system pressure.

3. Drain the cooling system.

4. Tag and disconnect the fuel lines, vacuum hoses and electrical connectors. Disconnect the throttle linkage.

5. Remove the intake manifold collector.

6. Remove the injector tube assembly and remove the intake manifolds.

To install:

7. Make sure all mating surfaces are clean prior to installation.

8. Install the intake manifold bolts, in their proper positions, on the cylinder head and lightly tighten the mounting bolts.

9. Connect the injector tube assemblies, including the fuel injectors, to the intake manifolds and lightly tighten the mounting bolts.

NOTE: Be careful not to let the rubber washer fall into the intake manifold.

10. Install the intake collector and lightly tighten the mounting bolts.

11. Tighten the intake manifold mounting bolts at the cylinder head, remove the intake collectors and tighten the intake manifolds to 12–15 ft. lbs. (16–21 Nm).

12. Tighten the sub-fuel tubes, in sequence, first to 3.1–4.3 ft. lbs. (4.2–5.9 Nm) and then to 6.2–8.0 ft. lbs. (8.4–10.8 Nm).

13. Tighten the injector tube assemblies, in sequence, first to 6.9–8.0 ft. lbs. (9.3–10.8 Nm) and then to 15–20 ft. lbs. (21–26 Nm).

14. Install the intake collector and tighten to 9–11 ft. lbs. (12–15 Nm).

15. Install the remaining components in the reverse order of their removal.

Exhaust Manifold

Removal and Installation

M30

1. Disconnect the negative battery cable. Raise and support the vehicle safely.

2. Remove the undercover and dust covers, if equipped.

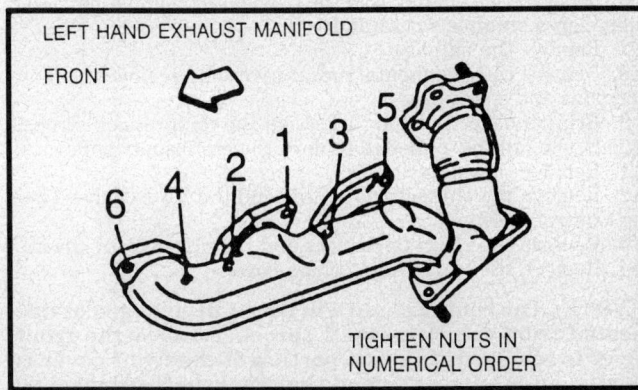

Left hand exhaust manifold installation torque sequence—M30

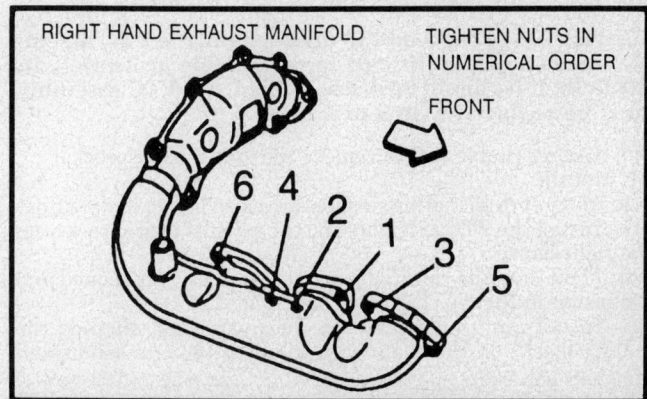

Right hand exhaust manifold installation torque sequence—M30

3. Remove the air cleaner or collector assembly, if necessary for access.

4. Remove the heat shield(s), if equipped.

5. Disconnect the exhaust pipe from the exhaust manifold.

6. Remove or disconnect the temperature sensors, oxygen sensors, air induction pipes, bracketry and other attachments from the manifold.

7. Loosen and remove the exhaust manifold attaching nuts and remove the manifold(s) from the block. Discard the exhaust manifold gaskets and replace with new.

8. Clean the gasket surfaces and check the manifold for cracks and warpage.

To install:

9. Install the exhaust manifold with a new gasket. Torque the manifold fasteners from the center outward in several stages.

10. Install or connect the temperature sensors, oxygen sensors, air induction pipes, bracketry and other attachments to the manifold.

11. Connect the exhaust pipe to the manifold or turbo outlet using a new gasket.

12. Install the heat shields.

13. Install the air cleaner or collector assembly.

14. Install the under covers and dust covers.

15. Connect the negative battery cable.

Q45

1. Disconnect the negative battery cable.

2. Remove the engine and transmission assembly from the vehicle.

3. Remove the exhaust manifold nuts and remove the exhaust manifold.

4. Installation is the reverse of the removal procedure. Make sure all mating surfaces are clean prior to installation. Tighten the exhaust manifold nuts to 20–23 ft. lbs. (27–31 Nm).

Timing Chain Front Cover

Removal and Installation

Q45

1. Disconnect the negative battery cable.

2. Remove the engine and transmission assembly from the vehicle.

3. Remove the suspension member and engine mounts from the engine.

4. Remove the air compressor bracket.

5. Remove the cooling fan with coupling and the engine gusset.

6. Separate the engine from the transmission and mount the engine on a suitable workstand.

7. Remove the oil pan.

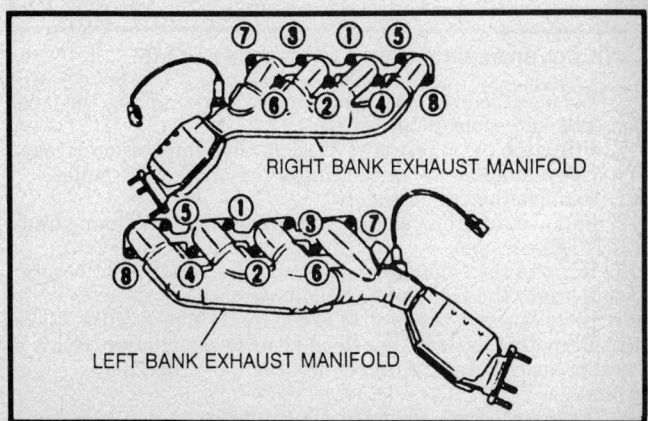

Exhaust manifold torque sequence—Q45

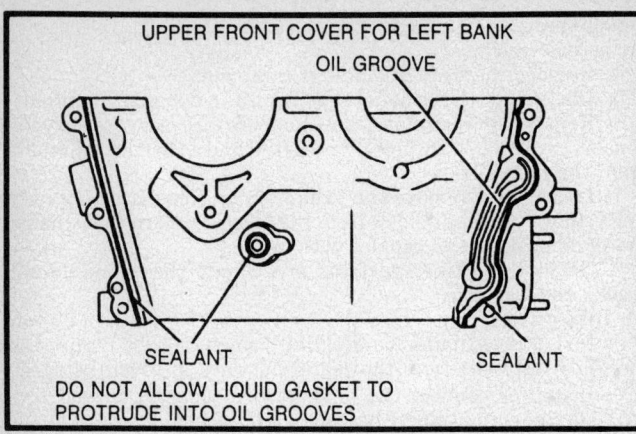

Upper front left cover sealant application areas—Q45

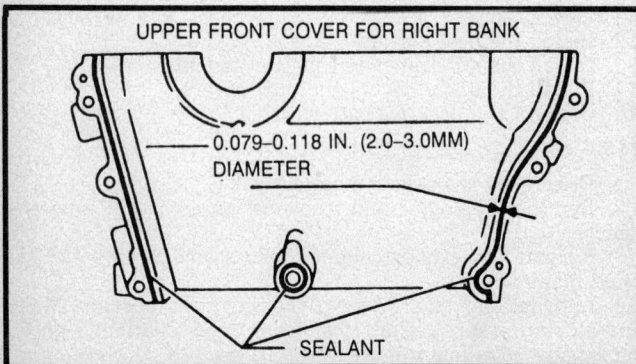

Upper front right cover sealant application areas—Q45

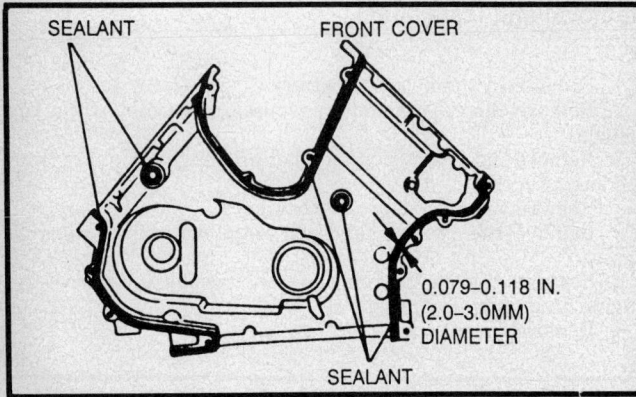

Front cover sealant application areas—Q45

8. Remove the ornamental rocker cover and remove the ignition coils and spark plugs.

9. Bring the No. 1 piston to TDC on the compression stroke.

10. Use a suitable puller to remove the crankshaft pulley.

11. Remove the rocker cover.

12. Remove the crank angle sensor and the Valve Timing Control (VTC) solenoid.

13. Remove the chain tensioners and the upper front covers.

14. Remove the front timing chain cover.

15. Installation is the reverse of the removal procedure. Make sure all mating surfaces are clean prior to installation. Apply a suitable sealant to the proper locations on the timing chain covers.

16. Tighten the cover bolts to 4.6–6.1 ft. lbs. (6.3–8.3 Nm) and the crankshaft pulley bolt to 260–275 ft. lbs. (353–373 Nm).

Front Cover Oil Seal

Replacement

Q45

1. Disconnect the negative battery cable.
2. Raise and safely support the vehicle.
3. Remove the engine splash shield.
4. Remove the cooling fan and the engine gusset.
5. Remove the necessary accessory drive belts.
6. Remove the lower rear plate in order to remove the crankshaft pulley bolt.
7. Remove the crankshaft pulley bolt and the crankshaft pulley.
8. Use a suitable tool to remove the front cover oil seal.
9. Installation is the reverse of the removal procedure. Lubricate the seal lip prior to installation. Tighten the crank pulley bolt to 260–275 ft. lbs. (353–373 Nm).

Timing Chain and Sprockets

Removal and Installation

Q45

1. Disconnect the negative battery cable.
2. Remove the engine and transmission assembly from the vehicle.
3. Remove the suspension member and engine mounts from the engine.
4. Remove the air compressor bracket.
5. Remove the cooling fan with coupling and the engine gusset.
6. Separate the engine from the transmission and mount the engine on a suitable workstand.
7. Remove the oil pan.
8. Remove the ornamental rocker cover and remove the ignition coils and spark plugs.
9. Bring the No. 1 piston to TDC on the compression stroke.
10. Use a suitable puller to remove the crankshaft pulley.
11. Remove the rocker cover.
12. Remove the crank angle sensor and the VTC (Valve Timing Control) solenoid.
13. Remove the chain tensioners and the upper front covers.
14. Remove the front timing chain cover.

NOTE: The timing chain will not be disengaged or dislocated from the crankshaft sprocket unless the front cover is removed. The cast portion of the front cover is located on the lower side of the crankshaft sprocket so the timing chain is not disengaged from the sprocket.

15. Remove the VTC assembly and the camshaft sprocket.
16. Remove the oil pump chain and the timing chains.

NOTE: Do not attempt to disassemble the VTC assembly since they are difficult to reassemble accurately in the field. If it should be disassembled, the VTC assembly must be replaced with a new one.

17. Use a suitable tool to remove the crankshaft sprocket.

To install:

18. Make sure all mating surfaces are clean before installation.
19. Install the VTC assembly and the exhaust cam sprocket on the right bank.
20. Make sure the camshafts are still correctly positioned and the piston in the No. 1 cylinder is still at TDC.
21. Install the timing chain on the right bank, aligning the mating marks on the chain with those on the crankshaft and camshaft sprockets.
22. Install the chain tensioner on the right bank.
23. Turn the crankshaft approximately 120 degrees clockwise from the point where the No. 1 piston is at TDC on the compres-

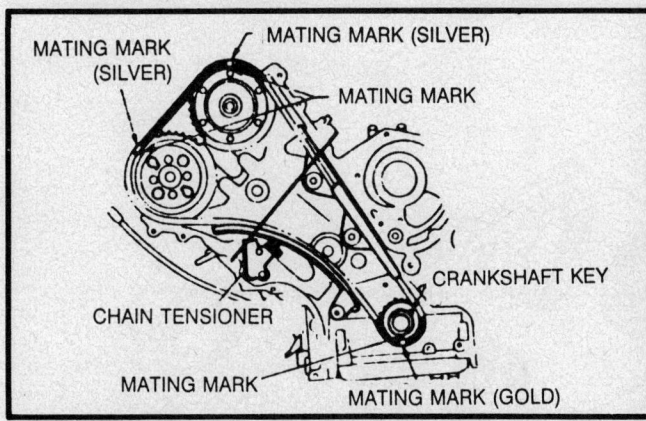

Right bank timing chain alignment—Q45

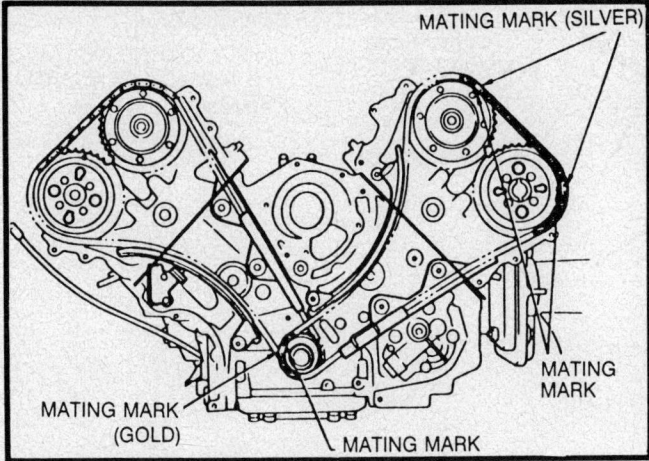

Left bank timing chain alignment—Q45

sion stroke. At this point, the valves on the left bank still remain unlifted.

24. Correctly position the camshafts and rocker arms for the left cylinder head. Properly lubricate the rocker arms and camshafts prior to installation. Install the VTC assembly and the exhaust cam sprocket.

25. Install the timing chain on the left bank, aligning the mating marks on the chain with those on the crankshaft and camshaft sprockets.

26. Install the oil pump chain and sprockets.

27. Install the oil pump chain guides. Place a 0.04 in. (1.0mm) feeler gauge between the upper chain guide and chain before assembling the chain guides. The force applied to the chain is equivalent to the upper chain guide weight.

28. Apply suitable sealer and install the front covers.

29. Install the chain tensioner for the left bank.

30. Apply suitable sealer to the rubber plugs and install them on the cylinder head.

31. Install the crank angle sensor, VTC solenoid, rocker cover and crank pulley.

32. Installation of the remaining components is the reverse of the removal procedure.

Timing Belt Front Cover

Removal and Installation

M30

1. Disconnect the negative battery cable.
2. Raise and support the front of the vehicle safely.

3. Remove the engine undercovers.
4. Drain the cooling system.
5. Remove the right front wheel.
6. Remove the engine side cover.
7. Remove the alternator, power steering and air conditioning compressor drive belts from the engine. When removing the power steering drive belt, loosen the idler pulley from the right side wheel housing.
8. Remove the upper radiator and water inlet hoses; remove the water pump pulley.
9. Remove the idler bracket of the compressor drive belt.
10. Remove the crankshaft pulley with a suitable puller.
11. Remove the upper and lower timing belt covers and gaskets.

To install:

12. Install the upper and lower timing belt covers with new gaskets.
13. Install the crankshaft pulley. Torque the pulley bolt to 90–98 ft. lbs. (123–132 Nm).
14. Install the compressor drive belt idler bracket.
15. Install the water pump pulley and torque the nuts to 12–15 ft. lbs. (16–21 Nm); install the upper radiator and water inlet hoses.
16. Install the drive belts.
17. Install the engine side cover.
18. Mount the front right wheel.
19. Install the engine undercovers.
20. Lower the vehicle.
21. Fill the cooling system and connect the negative battery cable.

Oil Seal Replacement

M30

1. Disconnect the negative battery cable.
2. Remove the timing belt.
3. Remove the crankshaft sprocket.
4. Remove the oil pan and oil pump.
5. Using a suitable tool, pry the oil seal from the front cover.

NOTE: When removing the oil seal, be careful not the gouge or scratch the seal bore or crankshaft surface.

6. Wipe the seal bore with a clean rag.
7. Lubricate the lip of the new seal with clean engine oil.
8. Install the seal into the front cover with a suitable seal installer.
9. Install the oil pump and oil pan.
10. Install the crankshaft sprocket.
11. Install the timing belt.
12. Connect the negative battery cable.

Timing Belt and Tensioner

Adjustment

M30

1. Disconnect the negative battery cable.
2. Remove timing belt front covers.
3. Set engine to TDC No. 1 cylinder on its compression stroke.
4. Loosen the tensioner locknut, keeping the tension steady with the hexagonal wrench.
5. Turn tensioner 70–80 degrees clockwise with the hexagonal wrench. Temporarily tighten locknut.
6. Turn crankshaft clockwise at least 2 times, then slowly set the engine to TDC No. 1 cylinder on its compression stroke.
7. Push the middle of the timing belt between the right hand camshaft sprocket and tensioner pulley with a force of 22 lbs. (98 N).
8. Loosen the tensioner locknut, keeping the tensioner steady with the hexagonal wrench.

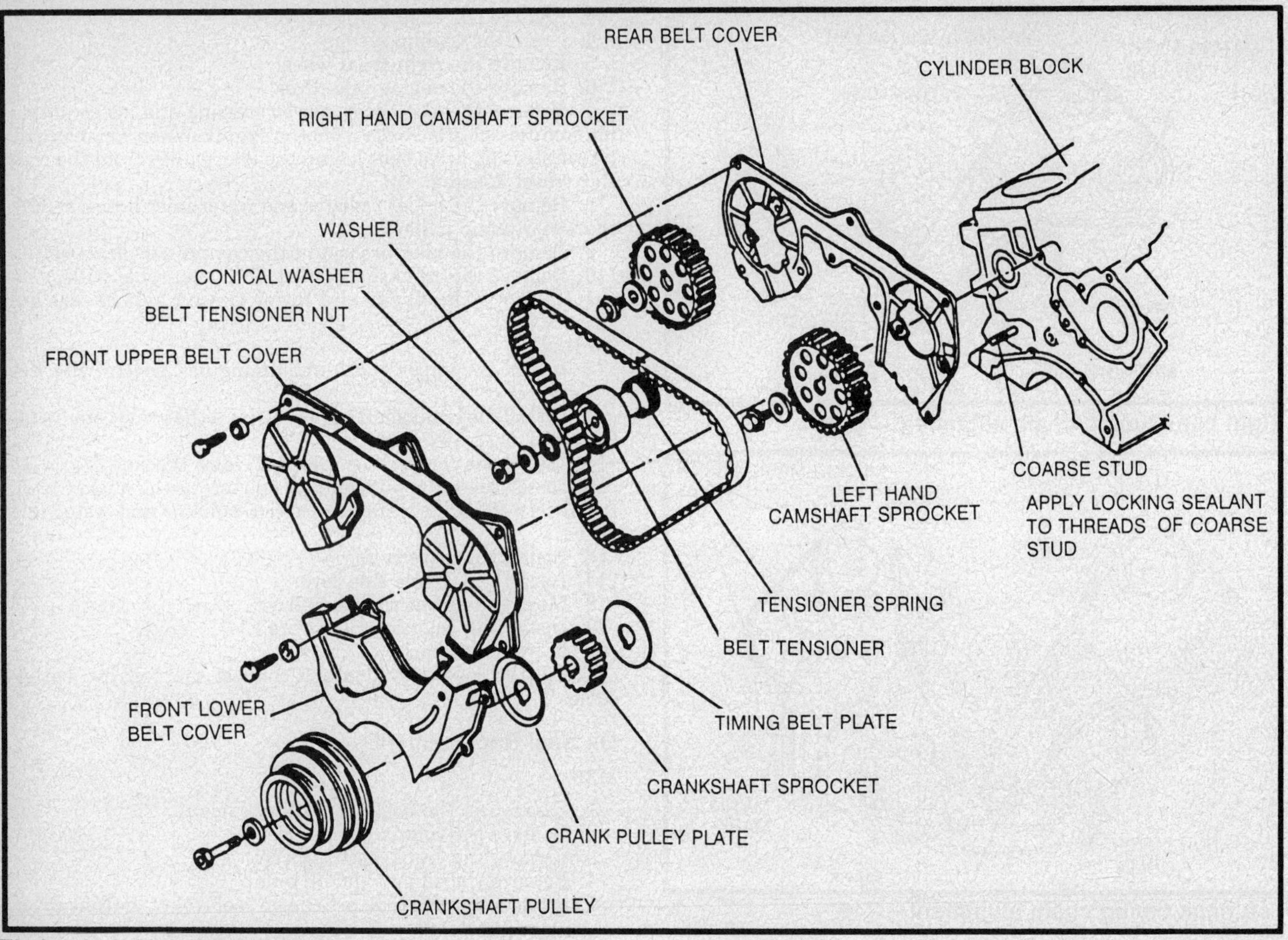

REAR BELT COVER

CYLINDER BLOCK

RIGHT HAND CAMSHAFT SPROCKET

WASHER

CONICAL WASHER

BELT TENSIONER NUT

FRONT UPPER BELT COVER

COARSE STUD

APPLY LOCKING SEALANT TO THREADS OF COARSE STUD

LEFT HAND CAMSHAFT SPROCKET

TENSIONER SPRING

BELT TENSIONER

TIMING BELT PLATE

FRONT LOWER BELT COVER

CRANKSHAFT SPROCKET

CRANK PULLEY PLATE

CRANKSHAFT PULLEY

Timing belt installation—M30

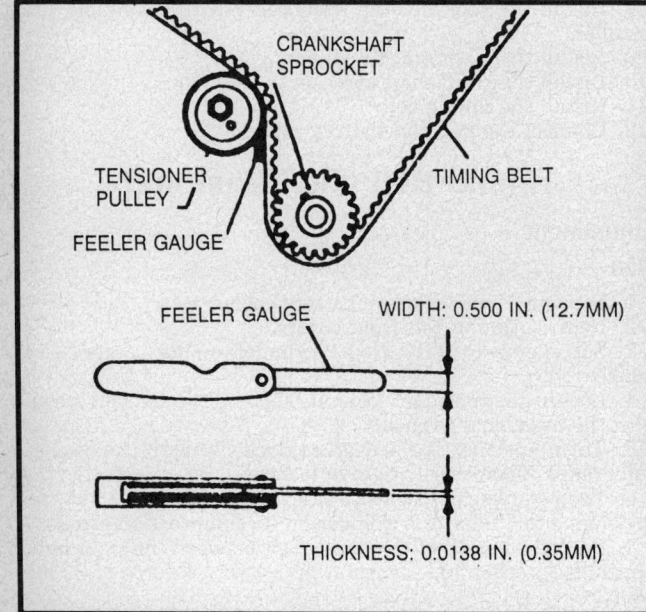

CRANKSHAFT SPROCKET

TENSIONER PULLEY

FEELER GAUGE

TIMING BELT

FEELER GAUGE

WIDTH: 0.500 IN. (12.7MM)

THICKNESS: 0.0138 IN. (0.35MM)

Setting timing belt tension—M30

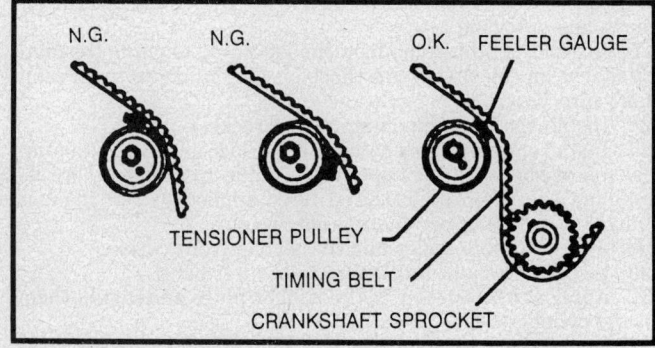

N.G.   N.G.   O.K.   FEELER GAUGE

TENSIONER PULLEY

TIMING BELT

CRANKSHAFT SPROCKET

Proper feeler gauge position for setting timing belt tension—M30

9. Set a feeler gauge 0.0138 in. (0.35mm) thick and 0.500 in. (12.7mm) wide between the timing belt and the tensioner pulley.

10. Turn the crankshaft clockwise and until the feeler gauge is on the tensioner pulley behind the timing belt.

11. Tighten the tensioner locknut, keeping tensioner steady with the hexagonal wrench.

12. Turn the crankshaft clockwise to remove the feeler gauge.

13. Turn the crankshaft clockwise at least 2 times, then slowly set the engine to TDC No. 1 on its compression stroke.

14. Install the timing belt covers.

15. Connect negative battery cable.

Removal and Installation

1. Disconnect the negative battery cable.
2. Raise and support the front of the vehicle safely.
3. Remove the engine undercovers.
4. Drain the cooling system.
5. Remove the front right side wheel.
6. Remove the engine side cover.
7. Remove the alternator, power steering and air conditioning compressor drive belts from the engine. When removing the power steering drive belt, loosen the idler pulley from the right side wheel housing.
8. Remove the upper radiator and water inlet hoses; remove the water pump pulley.
9. Remove the idler bracket of the compressor drive belt.
10. Remove the crankshaft pulley with a suitable puller.
11. Remove the upper and lower timing belt covers and gaskets.
12. Rotate the engine with a socket wrench on the crankshaft pulley bolt to align the punch mark on the left hand camshaft pulley with the mark on the upper rear timing belt cover; align the punchmark on the crankshaft with the notch on the oil pump housing; temporarily install the crankshaft pulley bolt to allow for crankshaft rotation.
13. Use a hex wrench to turn the belt tensioner clockwise and tighten the tensioner locknut just enough to hold the tensioner in position. Then, remove the timing belt.

To install:

14. Before installing the timing belt confirm that No. 1 cylinder is at TDC of the compression stroke. Install tensioner and tensioner spring. If stud is removed apply locking sealant to threads before installing.
15. Swing tensioner fully clockwise with hexagon wrench and temporarily tighten locknut.
16. Point the arrow on the timing belt toward the front belt cover. Align the white lines on the timing belt with the punch marks on all 3 pulleys.

NOTE: There are 133 total timing belt teeth. If timing belt is installed correctly there will be 40 teeth between left hand and right hand camshaft sprocket timing marks. There will be 43 teeth between left hand camshaft sprocket and crankshaft sprocket timing marks.

17. Loosen tensioner locknut, keeping tensioner steady with a hexagon wrench.
18. Swing tensioner 70–80 degrees clockwise with hexagon wrench and temporarily tighten locknut.
19. Turn crankshaft clockwise 2–3 times, then slowly set No. 1 cylinder at TDC of the compression stroke.
20. Push middle of timing belt between right hand camshaft sprocket and tensioner pulley with a force of 22 lbs.
21. Loosen tensioner locknut, keeping tensioner steady with a hexagon wrench.
22. Insert a 0.138 in. (0.35mm) thick and 0.5 in. (12.7mm) wide feeler gauge between the bottom of tensioner pulley and timing belt. Turn crankshaft clockwise and position gauge completely between tensioner pulley and timing belt. The timing belt will move about 2.5 teeth.
23. Tighten tensioner locknut, keeping tensioner steady with a hexagon wrench.
24. Turn crankshaft clockwise or counterclockwise and remove the gauge.
25. Rotate the engine 3 times, then set No. 1, to TDC, on its compression stroke.
26. Install the upper and lower timing belt covers with new gaskets.

27. Install the crankshaft pulley. Torque the pulley bolt to 90–98 ft. lbs. (123–132 Nm).
28. Install the compressor drive belt idler bracket.
29. Install the water pump pulley and torque the nuts to 12–15 ft. lbs. (16–21 Nm). Install the upper radiator and water inlet hoses.
30. Install the drive belts.
31. Install the engine side cover.
32. Mount the front right wheel.
33. Install the engine undercovers.
34. Lower the vehicle.
35. Fill the cooling system and connect the negative battery cable.

Timing Sprockets

Removal and Installation

M30

1. Disconnect the negative battery cable.
2. Set the No. 1 piston to TDC of the compression stroke.
3. Remove the timing belt covers.
4. Remove the timing belt.
5. Using a suitable spanner wrench and a socket wrench, remove the camshaft pulley bolt and washer. Remove the front plate, O-ring and spring from the right (intake) camshaft to gain access to the sprocket bolt. The left camshaft sprocket is held in place by plate and 4 bolts.
6. Using a suitable puller, remove the crankshaft gear and timing belt plates from the crankshaft. Be careful not to gouge or scratch the surface of the crankshaft when removing the gear.
7. Inspect the timing gear teeth for wear and replace, as necessary.

To install:

8. Install the crankshaft gear with new Woodruff® keys.
9. Install the camshaft sprockets. Torque the sprocket bolts to 58–65 ft. lbs. (78–88 Nm); 90–98 ft. lbs. (123–132 Nm) for right (intake) and 10–14 ft. lbs. (14–19 Nm) for the left (exhaust).

NOTE: The right hand and left hand camshaft pulleys are different. Install them in their correct positions. The right hand pulley has an R3 identification mark and the left hand pulley has an L3.

10. Install the timing belt.
11. Install the timing belt covers.
12. Connect the negative battery cable.

Camshaft

Removal and Installation

M30

1. Disconnect the negative battery cable.
2. Drain the cooling system.
3. Remove the timing belt.
4. Remove the collector assembly.
5. Remove the intake manifold.
6. Remove the cylinder head.
7. Remove the rocker shafts with rocker arms. Bolts should be loosened in several steps in the proper sequence.
8. Remove hydraulic valve lifters and lifter guide. Hold hydraulic valve lifters with wire so they will not drop from lifter guide.
9. Using a dial gauge measure the camshaft endplay. If the camshaft endplay exceeds the limit (0.0012–0.0024 in.), select the thickness of a cam locate plate so the endplay is within specification. For example: if camshaft endplay measures 0.0031 in. (0.08mm) with shim 2 used, then change shim 2 to shim 3 so the

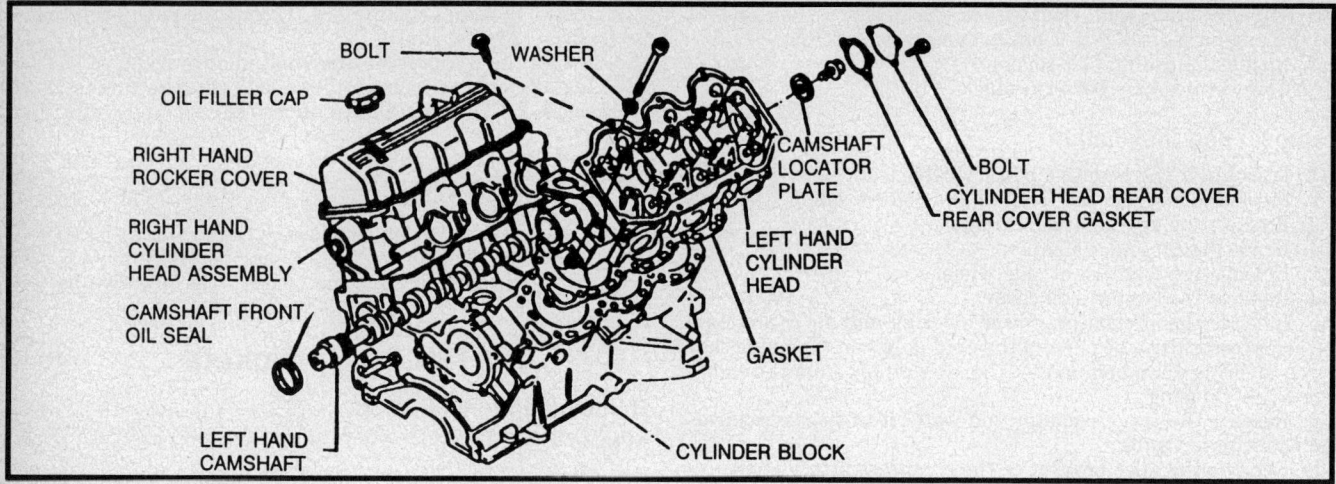

Camshaft installation — M30

camshaft endplay is 0.0020 in. (0.05mm).

10. Remove the camshaft front oil seal and slide camshaft out the front of the cylinder head assembly.

To install:

11. Install camshaft, locater plates, cylinder head rear cover and front oil seal. Set camshaft knock pin at 12 o'clock position. Install cylinder head with new gasket to engine.

12. Install valve lifter guide assembly. Assemble valve lifters in their original position. After installing them in the correct location remove the wire holding them in lifter guide.

13. Install rocker shafts in correct position with rocker arms. Tighten bolts, in 2–3 stages, to 13–16 ft. lbs. (18–22 Nm). Before tightening, be sure to set camshaft lobe at the position where lobe is not lifted or the valve closed. Set each cylinder 1 at a time or follow the procedure below. The cylinder head, intake manifold, collector and timing belt must be installed:

   a. Set No. 1 piston at TDC of the compression stroke and tighten rocker shaft bolts for Nos. 2, 4 and 6 cylinders.

   b. Set No. 4 piston at TDC of the compression stroke and tighten rocker shaft bolts for Nos. 1, 3 and 5 cylinders.

   c. Torque specification for the rocker shaft retaining bolts is 13–16 ft. lbs. (18–22 Nm).

14. Fill the cooling system to the proper level.

15. Connect the negative battery cable.

Q45

1. Disconnect the negative battery cable.

2. Remove the engine and transmission assembly from the vehicle.

3. Remove the suspension member and engine mounts from the engine.

4. Remove the air compressor bracket.

5. Remove the cooling fan with coupling and the engine gusset.

6. Separate the engine from the transmission and mount the engine on a suitable workstand.

7. Remove the oil pan.

8. Remove the ornamental rocker cover and remove the ignition coils and spark plugs.

9. Bring the No. 1 piston to TDC on the compression stroke.

10. Use a suitable puller to remove the crankshaft pulley.

11. Remove the rocker cover.

12. Remove the crank angle sensor and the Valve Timing Control (VTC) solenoid.

13. Remove the chain tensioners and the upper front covers.

14. Remove the front timing chain cover.

NOTE: The timing chain will not be disengaged or dislocated from the crankshaft sprocket unless the front cover is removed. The cast portion of the front cover is located on the lower side of the crankshaft sprocket so the timing chain is not disengaged from the sprocket.

15. Remove the VTC assembly and the camshaft sprocket.

16. Remove the oil pump chain and the timing chains.

NOTE: Do not attempt to disassemble the VTC assembly since they are difficult to reassemble accurately in the field. If it should be disassembled, the VTC assembly must be replaced with a new one.

17. Remove the camshaft brackets and the camshafts. Mark the parts so they can be reinstalled in their original positions.

18. Remove the rocker arms. Be sure to identify each rocker arm so it can be reinstalled in it's original position.

To install:

19. Make sure all mating surfaces are clean before installation.

20. Install the rocker arms, camshafts and camshaft brackets on the right bank. Properly lubricate the rocker arms and camshafts prior to installation. Tighten the camshaft bracket bolts to 9–10 ft. lbs. (12–14 Nm) in the proper sequence.

21. Install the VTC assembly and the exhaust cam sprocket on the right bank.

22. Make sure the camshafts are still correctly positioned and the piston in the No. 1 cylinder is still at TDC.

23. Install the timing chain on the right bank, aligning the mating marks on the chain with those on the crankshaft and camshaft sprockets.

24. Install the chain tensioner on the right bank.

25. Turn the crankshaft approximately 120 degrees clockwise from the point where the No. 1 piston is at TDC on the compression stroke. At this point, the valves on the left bank still remain unlifted.

26. Correctly position the camshafts and rocker arms for the left cylinder head. Properly lubricate the rocker arms and camshafts prior to installation. Tighten the camshaft bracket bolts to 9–10 ft. lbs. (12–14 Nm) in the proper sequence. Install the VTC assembly and the exhaust cam sprocket.

27. Install the timing chain on the left bank, aligning the mating marks on the chain with those on the crankshaft and camshaft sprockets.

28. Install the oil pump chain and sprockets.

29. Install the oil pump chain guides. Place a 0.04 in. (1.0mm) feeler gauge between the upper chain guide and chain before assembling the chain guides. The force applied to the chain is equivalent to the upper chain guide weight.

30. Apply suitable sealer and install the front covers.
31. Install the chain tensioner for the left bank.
32. Apply suitable sealer to the rubber plugs and install them on the cylinder head.
33. Install the crank angle sensor, VTC solenoid, rocker cover and crank pulley.
34. Installation of the remaining components is the reverse of the removal procedure.

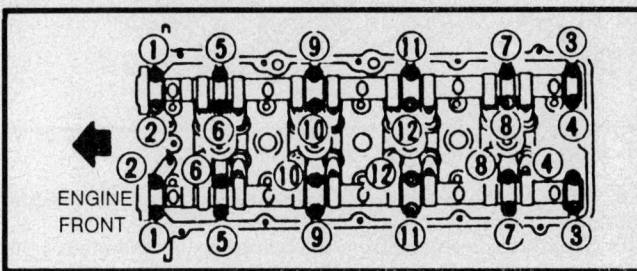

Camshaft bracket torque sequence—Q45

Piston and Connecting Rod

Positioning

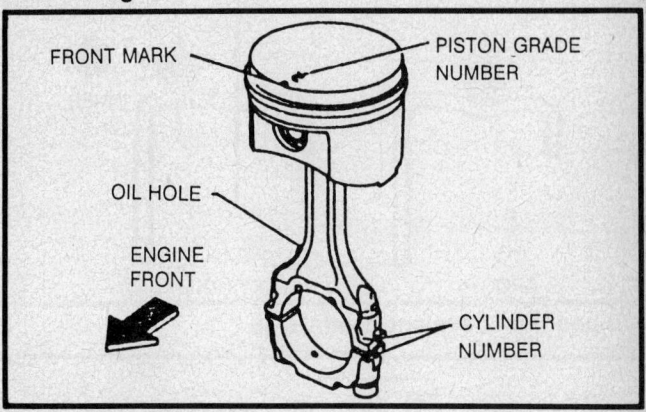

Piston positioning—Q45

ENGINE LUBRICATION

Oil Pan

Removal and Installation

M30

1. Raise and safely support the vehicle.
2. Drain the engine oil in a suitable container. Remove the oil level gauge.
3. Remove the air duct.

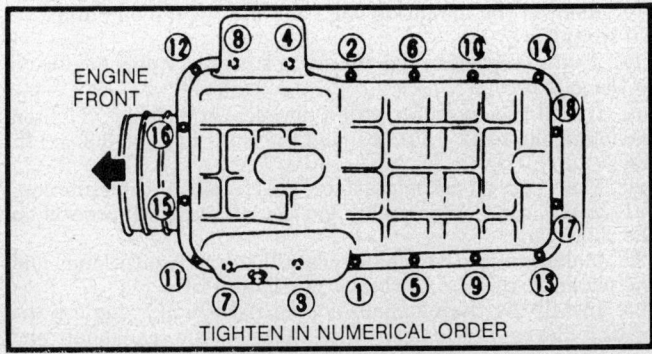

Oil pan bolt loosening sequence—M30

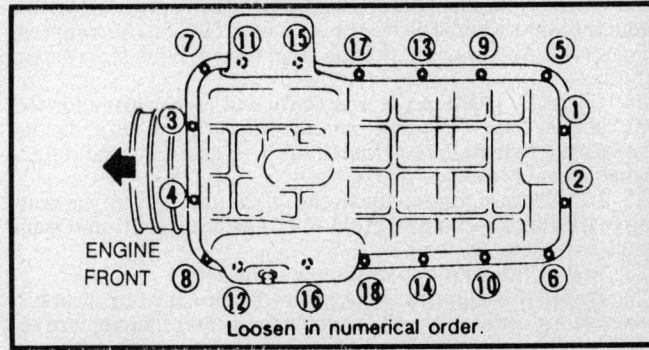

Oil pan bolt tightening sequence—M30

4. Disconnect the air conditioning and brake booster vacuum hoses from their mounting brackets.
5. Remove the upper radiator mounting bolts and the automatic transmission oil cooler line mounting bolts.
6. Remove the oil pan mounting bolts, loosen them in numerical order. remove the oil pan using the proper tool to remove.
7. Loosen the front exhaust tube mounting bolts and remove the front stabilizer bar mounting brackets. Remove the right side stabilizer mounting bolt.
8. Loosen the left side stabilizer mounting bolt. Position a suitable transmission jacking device under the transmission case.
9. Remove the engine mounting bolts. Slowly, raise the transmission jack and remove the oil pan.
10. Thoroughly clean the mounting surfaces. Apply the proper sealant to the oil pump gasket, the rear oil seal retainer and the oil pan mounting surface.
11. The installation is the reverse of the removal procedure. Install the bolts in the reverse order of the removal. Tighten to 5.1–5.8 ft. lbs.

Q45

1. Disconnect the negative battery cable.
2. Raise the vehicle and support safely.
3. Remove the engine undercover.
4. Drain the engine oil.
5. Remove the fan coupling with the fan.
6. Remove the drive belts, alternator, air compressor and engine gusset.
7. Remove the steering lower joint.
8. Support the transmission.
9. Attach a suitable lifting device and raise the engine.
10. Remove the suspension member assembly.
11. Remove the oil pan bolts and nuts.
12. Remove the oil pan from the engine block. Be careful not to damage the mating surface on the engine block.

To install:

13. Remove all gasket material from mating surfaces on the block and oil pan.

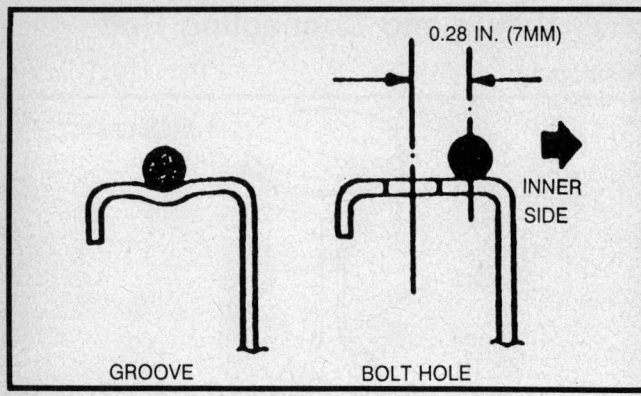

Oil pan liquid sealant bead—Q45

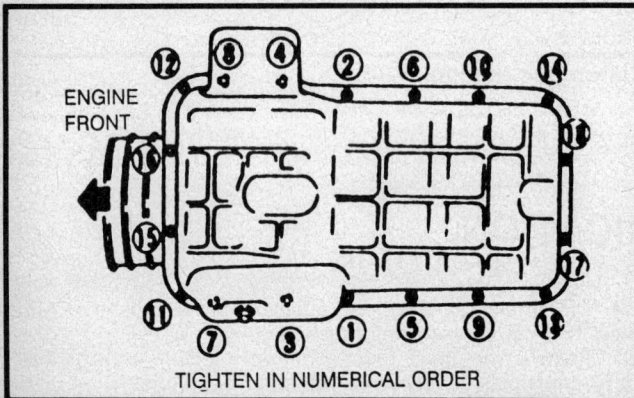

Oil pan installation torque sequence—Q45

14. Apply a continuous bead of liquid gasket to the mating surface on the oil pan. Ensure that the bead is 0.138–0.177 in. (3.5–4.5mm) wide.

15. Install the oil pan. Install attaching bolts and nuts in sequence.

16. Complete the installation of the oil pan by reversing the removal procedure.

17. Allow gasket material to set for 30 minutes before filling the engine with oil.

Oil Pump

Removal and Installation

M30

1. Raise and safely support the vehicle.
2. Drain the engine oil in a suitable container. Remove the oil level gauge.
3. Remove the oil pan.
4. Remove the oil pump mounting bolts and lift out the oil pump.
5. Always replace with a new oil seal and gasket. Apply oi to the inner and outer gears when installing.
6. The installation is the reverse of the removal procedure. Tighten the long mounting bolt to 9–12 ft. lbs. and the short bolts to 4.3–5.1 ft. lbs.

Q45

1. Disconnect the negative battery cable.
2. Remove the engine and transmission assembly from the vehicle.
3. Remove the suspension member and engine mounts from the engine.
4. Remove the air compressor bracket.

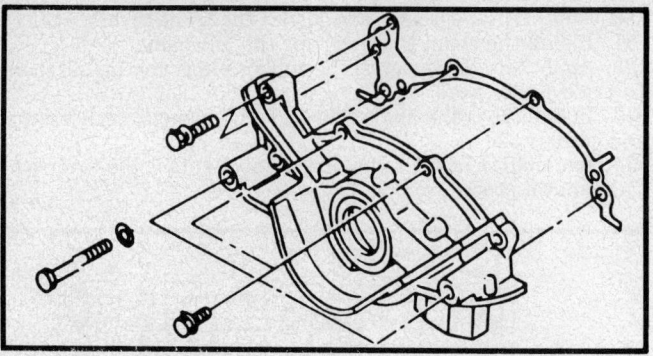

Oil pump assembly—M30

5. Remove the cooling fan with coupling and the engine gusset.
6. Separate the engine from the transmission and mount the engine on a suitable workstand.
7. Remove the oil pan.
8. Remove the ornamental rocker cover and remove the ignition coils and spark plugs.
9. Bring the No. 1 piston to TDC on the compression stroke.
10. Use a suitable puller to remove the crankshaft pulley.
11. Remove the rocker cover.
12. Remove the crank angle sensor and the Valve Timing Control (VTC) solenoid.
13. Remove the chain tensioners and the upper front covers.
14. Remove the front timing chain cover.

NOTE: The timing chain will not be disengaged or dislocated from the crankshaft sprocket unless the front cover is removed. The cast portion of the front cover is located on the lower side of the crankshaft sprocket so the timing chain is not disengaged from the sprocket.

15. Remove the VTC assembly and the camshaft sprocket.
16. Remove the oil pump chain and the timing chains.
17. Remove the mounting bolts and lift out the oil pump.
To install:
18. Thoroughly clean the mounting surfaces. Apply engine oil to the gears.
19. Install the oil pump with a new seal and gasket. Tighten the long bolts to 12–15 ft. lbs. and the short bolts to 3.3–4.3 ft. lbs.
20. Make sure all mating surfaces are clean before installation.
21. Install the VTC assembly and the exhaust cam sprocket on the right bank.
22. Make sure the camshafts are still correctly positioned and the piston in the No. 1 cylinder is still at TDC.
23. Install the timing chain on the right bank, aligning the mating marks on the chain with those on the crankshaft and camshaft sprockets.
24. Install the chain tensioner on the right bank.
25. Turn the crankshaft approximately 120 degrees clockwise from the point where the No. 1 piston is at TDC on the compression stroke. At this point, the valves on the left bank still remain unlifted.
26. Correctly position the camshafts and rocker arms for the left cylinder head. Properly lubricate the rocker arms and camshafts prior to installation. Install the VTC assembly and the exhaust cam sprocket.
27. Install the timing chain on the left bank, aligning the mating marks on the chain with those on the crankshaft and camshaft sprockets.
28. Install the oil pump chain and sprockets.
29. Install the oil pump chain guides. Place a 0.04 in. (1.0mm) feeler gauge between the upper chain guide and chain before assembling the chain guides. The force applied to the chain is equivalent to the upper chain guide weight.

30. Apply suitable sealer and install the front covers.

31. Install the chain tensioner for the left bank.

32. Apply suitable sealer to the rubber plugs and install them on the cylinder head.

33. Install the crank angle sensor, VTC solenoid, rocker cover and crank pulley.

34. Installation of the remaining components is the reverse of the removal procedure.

Checking

M30

1. Check the following clearances with a suitable feeler gauge:

    a. The body-to-outer gear clearance 0.0043–0.0079 in. (0.11–0.20mm).

    b. The inner gear-to-crescent clearance 0.0047–0.0091 in. (0.12–0.23mm).

    c. The outer gear-to-crescent clearance 0.0083–0.0126 in. (0.21–0.32mm).

    d. The housing -to-inner gear clearance 0.0020–0.0035 in. (0.05–0.09mm).

    e. The housing-to-outer gear clearance 0.0020–0.0043 in. (0.05–0.11mm).

2. If any clearance exceeds the limit, replace the gear set or the entire gear assembly.

Q45

1. Check the following clearances with a suitable feeler gauge:

    a. The driveshaft-to-oil pump cover and housing clearance 0.0009–0.0027 in. (0.24–0.69mm).

    b. The driven gear-to-driven shaft clearance 0.0010–0.0025 in. (0.25–0.64mm).

    c. The drive and driven gear-to-oil pump housing clearance 0.0031–0.0051 in. (0.08–0.13mm).

    d. The drive and driven gear-to-oil pump housing clearance 0.0049–0.0096 in. (0.125–0.245mm).

2. If any clearance exceeds the limit, replace the gear set or the entire gear assembly.

Rear Main Bearing Oil Seal

The rear main oil seal is a solid type seal located in the rear oil seal retainer at the rear of the engine.

Removal and Installation

1. Raise and safely support the vehicle. Remove the transmission.

2. Remove the flywheel or drive plate.

3. Remove the rear oil seal retainer from the block.

4. Using a suitable prying tool, remove the oil seal from the retainer.

5. Thoroughly scrape the surface of the retainer to remove any traces of the existing sealant or gasket material.

6. Wipe the seal bore with a clean rag.

7. Apply clean engine oil to the new oil seal and carefully install it into the retainer using the proper seal installation tool.

8. Install the rear oil seal retainer into the engine, along with a new gasket.

9. Install the driveplate and transmission. Lower the vehicle.

AUTOMATIC TRANSMISSION

For further information, please refer to "Professional Transmission Repair Manual" for additional coverage.

Transmission Assembly

Removal and Installation

1. Disconnect the negative battery cable.

2. Raise the vehicle and support safely.

3. Remove the exhaust tube.

4. Remove the fluid charging line.

5. Remove the oil cooler line.

6. Plug fluid charging and oil cooler fittings after removing lines.

7. Remove the control linkage from the selector lever.

8. Disconnect the neutral safety switch and solenoid harness connectors.

9. Disconnect the speedometer cable.

10. Remove the driveshaft. Insert plug into rear seal opening to prevent loss of fluid.

11. Remove the starter motor.

12. Support the transmission safely.

13. Remove the gusset securing the transmission to the engine. Remove the bolts attaching the transmission to the engine.

    NOTE: The bolts securing the transmission to the engine are of differing lengths. Note the length of the bolts as they are removed.

14. Remove the bolts securing the torque converter to the flexplate.

15. Support the engine safely. Avoid jacking directly under the oil pan drain plug.

16. Remove the transmission from the vehicle.

To install:

17. Position the transmission in the vehicle and install the torque converter-to-flexplate bolts. Tighten to 33–43 ft. lbs. (44–59 Nm).

18. Secure the transmission to the engine. Torque the:

    60mm bolts to 29–36 ft. lbs. (39–49 Nm)

    50mm bolts to 29–36 ft. lbs. (39–49 Nm)

    45mm bolts to 29–36 ft. lbs. (39–49 Nm)

    25mm bolts to 22–29 ft. lbs. (29–39 Nm)

    20mm gusset bolts to 22–29 ft. lbs. (29–39 Nm)

19. Install the starter motor.

20. Install the driveshaft.

21. Connect the speedometer cable.

22. Connect the neutral safety switch and solenoid harness connectors.

23. Install the control linkage to the selector lever.

24. Install the fluid charging and oil cooler lines.

25. Connect the exhaust tube.

26. Lower the vehicle.

27. Connect negative battery cable.

Shift Linkage Adjustment

1. Place the selector lever in **P** range.

2. Loosen the locknuts.

3. Without pushing the button, pull selector lever toward **R** and tighten locknut X until it touches trunnion.

4. Back off locknut X one turn and tighten locknut Y to 8–11 ft. lbs. (11–15 Nm).

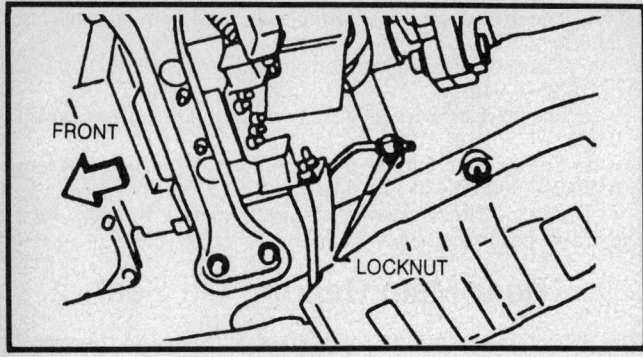

Manual control linkage locknut

Throttle Linkage Adjustment

Adjust throttle wire endplay to 0.04–0.12 in. (1–3mm). Tighten locknut to 6–7 ft. lbs. (8–10 Nm).

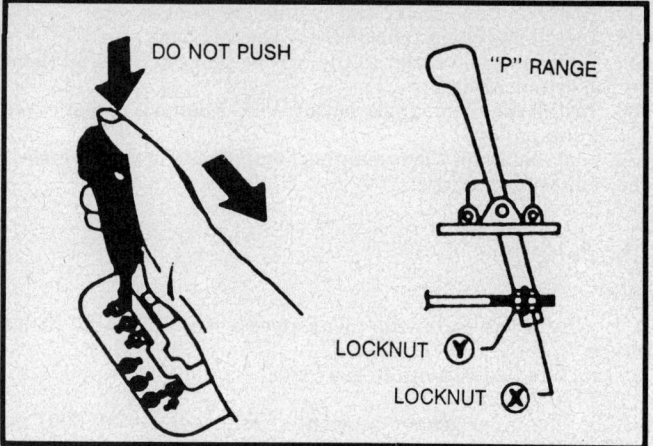

Manual control linkage adjustment

DRIVE AXLE

Halfshaft

Removal and Installation

M30

1. Raise the vehicle and support safely.
2. Remove the 6 bolts and nuts attaching the outer CV-joint to the companion flange.
3. Remove the inner CV-joint from the differential carrier by prying with a suitable tool.

To install:

4. Install the inner CV-joint into the differential carrier.
5. Connect the outer CV-joint to the companion flange with the 6 bolts and nuts. Tighten to 20–27 ft. lbs. (27–37 Nm).
6. Lower the vehicle.

Q45

1. Raise the vehicle and support safely.
2. Remove the rear wheel.
3. Remove the differential side flange bolts and nuts and separate shaft.

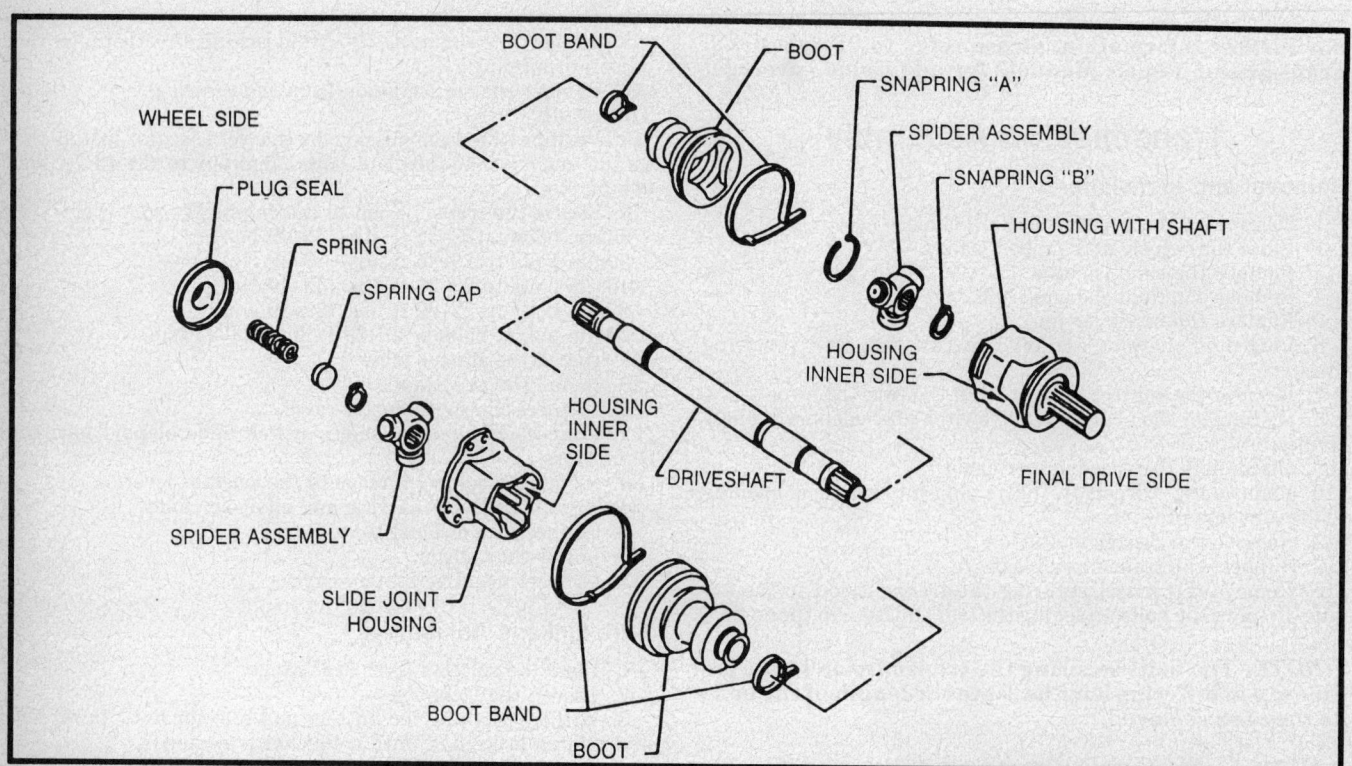

Halfshaft assembly exploded view—M30

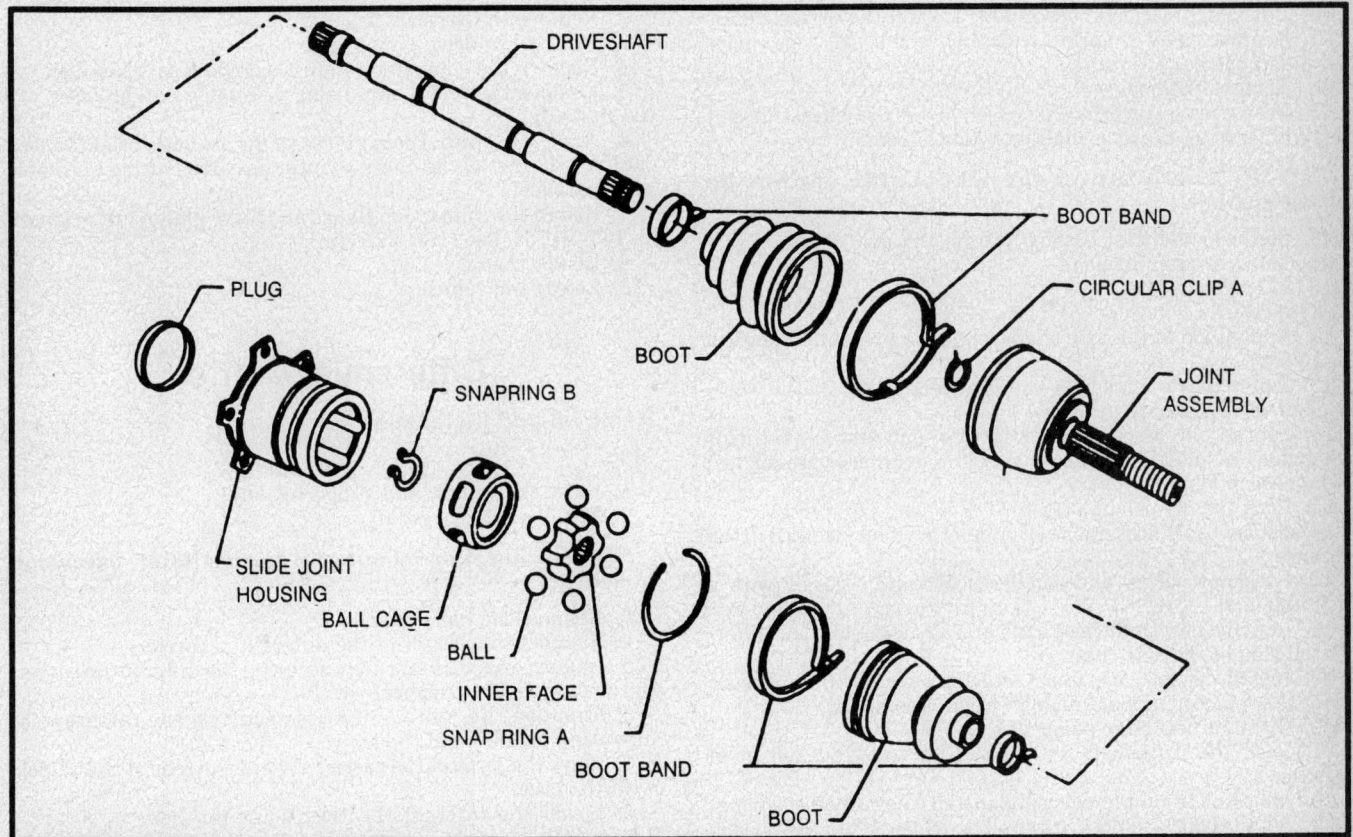

Halfshaft assembly exploded view—Q45

4. Remove the cotter pin, adjusting cap, insulator, wheel bearing locknut and washer from axle shaft.

5. Remove the axle shaft by lightly tapping it with a copper hammer.

6. Remove the halfshaft assembly from the vehicle.

To install:

7. Insert driveshaft into wheel hub and install washer and wheel bearing locknut. Temporarily tighten the locknut.

8. Connect the driveshaft with the differential side flange. Install the nuts and bolts and tighten to 25–33 ft. lbs. (34–44 Nm).

9. Tighten the wheel bearing locknut to 152–203 ft. lbs. (206–275 Nm). Install the insulator, adjusting cap and a new cotter pin.

10. Install the rear wheel.

11. Lower the vehicle.

CV-Boot

Removal and Installation

M30

1. Raise the vehicle and support safely.

2. Remove the halfshaft from the vehicle and place in a vise.

3. Remove the plug seal from the slide joint housing by lightly tapping around the slide joint housing.

4. Remove the boot bands.

5. Put matchmarks on the slide joint housing, driveshaft and spider assembly before separating the joint assembly.

6. Remove the snapring on the axle shaft and remove spider assembly.

7. Remove the CV-joint housing.

8. Remove the boot from the shaft.

NOTE: Cover the shaft splines with tape to protect the boot.

To install:

9. Install boot onto shaft.

10. Install CV-joint housing onto shaft.

11. Install spider assembly onto shaft observing matchmarks made on disassembly. Ensure that the spider assembly chamfer faces the shaft.

12. Install snapring onto shaft.

13. With the CV-joint housing held vertically in the vise, install the coil spring, spring cap and new plug seal.

NOTE: The CV-joint housing is held vertically to prevent the coil spring from tilting or falling over.

14. Pack the driveshaft with the 6.52–6.88 oz. (185–195 g) of grease.

15. Set the boot so it does not swell or deform when installed.

16. Install a new large boot band and lock in place.

17. Install a new small boot band and lock in place.

18. Install halfshaft assembly in vehicle.

19. Lower vehicle.

Q45

1. Raise the vehicle and support safely.

2. Remove the halfshaft assembly from the vehicle and place in a vise.

3. Remove the boot bands on both inner and outer joints.

4. Put matchmarks on the slide joint housing and inner race before separating the joint assembly.

5. Remove large snapring retaining slide joint and remove slide joint from axle shaft.

6. Put matchmarks on the inner race and the driveshaft.

7. Remove small snapring and remove the ball cage, inner race and balls as a unit.

8. Remove the boot.

9. Before separating the joint assembly on the wheel side, put matchmarks on the axle shaft and joint assembly.

NOTE: The joint on the wheel side cannot be disassembled.

10. Separate the joint assembly from the axle shaft using a slide hammer or equivalent.

11. Remove the boot.

To install:

12. Apply tape to the axle shaft splines to prevent damage to the boots.

13. Install a new small boot band and a new boot on the wheel side of the axle shaft.

14. Set the joint assembly onto the axle shaft and seat the joint by lightly tapping it. Ensure that the matchmarks are aligned when assembling.

15. Pack the driveshaft with 6.00–6.70 oz. (170–190 g).

16. Set boot so it does not swell or deform when installed in the vehicle.

17. Lock new larger and smaller boot band securely with a suitable tool.

18. Install a new small boot band and a new boot on the differential side of the axle shaft.

19. Install the ball cage, inner race and balls as a unit. Ensure that the matchmarks are aligned when assembling.

20. Install a new large snapring.

21. Pack the driveshaft with 6.35–7.05 oz. (180–200 g) of grease.

22. Install slide joint housing and install a new small snapring.

23. Set the boot so it does not swell or deform when installed in the vehicle.

24. Lock the new larger and smaller boot bands securely with a suitable tool.

25. Install the halfshaft assembly in the vehicle.

26. Install the rear wheel.

27. Lower the vehicle.

Driveshaft and U-Joints

Removal and Installation

1. Raise the vehicle and support safely.

2. Put matchmarks on the flanges and separate driveshaft from the differential carrier.

3. Remove driveshaft from the transmission and plug the rear opening of the extension housing.

4. Remove the bolts attaching the center bearing bracket.

5. Remove driveshafts from vehicle.

6. Inspect driveshaft runout. Runout should not exceed 0.024 in. (0.6mm).

To install:

7. Temporarily install the differential companion flange to the flange yoke. Observe the alignment marks made during removal.

8. Turn the driveshaft until alignment marks face straight upward. Securely fasten the driveshaft so the lower side wall of the concave flange yoke touches the lower side wall of the convex companion flange.

9. Remove the plug in the rear extension housing and install the driveshaft into the transmission.

10. Install the bolts attaching the center bearing bracket.

Pinion Seal

Removal and Installation

1. Raise the vehicle and support safely.

2. Remove the driveshaft.

3. Loosen the drive pinion nut.

4. Remove the companion flange using a suitable puller.

5. Remove the pinion seal using a suitable seal puller.

To install:

6. Apply a multi-purpose grease to the sealing lips of the new pinion seal. Install the new seal into the carrier using a suitable seal installer.

7. Install the companion flange and drive pinion nut. Tighten to 137–217 ft. lbs. (186–294 Nm).

8. Install the driveshaft.

9. Lower the vehicle.

Differential Carrier

Removal and Installation

M30

1. Raise the vehicle and support safely.

2. Remove the driveshaft.

NOTE: Plug rear opening in transmission extension housing.

3. Remove the halfshafts.

4. Support the weight of the differential carrier.

5. Remove the nuts and bolts securing the differential carrier to the suspension member.

6. Remove the bolts and nuts securing the differential mounting insulator to the body.

7. Move the differential carrier toward the rear of the vehicle with the jack.

8. Lower the differential carrier using the jack.

To install:

9. Position the differential carrier in the vehicle.

10. Install bolts and nuts securing the differential mounting insulator to the body. Tighten bolts to 22–29 ft. lbs. (29–39 Nm). Tighten the nuts to 43–58 ft. lbs. (59–78 Nm).

11. Install the differential carrier to the suspension member. Tighten the nuts to 43–65 ft. lbs. (59–88 Nm).

12. Remove the jack.

13. Install the halfshafts.

14. Install the driveshaft.

15. Install the exhaust tube.

16. Lower the vehicle.

Q45

1. Raise the vehicle and support safely.

2. Remove the exhaust tube.

3. Remove the driveshaft.

NOTE: Plug rear opening in transmission extension housing.

4. Remove the halfshafts.

5. Remove the nuts securing the differential carrier rear cover to suspension member.

6. Support the weight of the differential carrier.

7. Remove the differential carrier mounting member from the front of the differential carrier.

8. Move the differential carrier forward together with the jack. Remove the rear cover stud bolts from the suspension member.

9. Lower the differential carrier using the jack.

To install:

10. Position the differential carrier in the vehicle.

13. Install the nuts securing the differential carrier rear cover to the suspension member. Tighten to 72–87 ft. lbs. (98–118 Nm).

12. Install the differential carrier mounting member to the front of the differential carrier. Tighten to 72–87 ft. lbs. (98–118 Nm).

14. Remove the jack.

15. Install the halfshafts.
16. Install the driveshaft.
17. Install the exhaust tube.
18. Lower the vehicle.

STEERING

Steering Wheel

────────── CAUTION ──────────

On vehicles equipped with an air bag, the negative battery cable must be disconnected, before working on the system. Failure to do so may result in deployment of the air bag and possible personal injury.

─────────────────────────────

Removal and Installation

1. Make sure the wheels are pointing straight ahead. Disconnect the negative battery cable and allow 10 minutes to elapse.
2. Remove the lower lid from the steering colun and disconnect the air bag module connector.

NOTE: The air bag module is a fragile component. Always place it with the pad side facing upward. Do not allow oil, grease or water to come in cantact with the module. Do not drop the module; if it is damaged in any way, do not reinstall it to the steering wheel.

3. Remove the side access lids, remove the left and right T50H Torx® bolts and discard them. These bolts are specially coated and should not be reused.
4. Carefully remove the air bag module and place in a safe location with the pad side facing upward.
5. Disengage the spiral cable and disconnect the horn connector. Remove the steering wheel hold-down nut.
6. Using an appropriate puller, remove the steering wheel.
7. Attach the spiral cable to the stopper.
8. Remove the steering column covers.
9. Disconnect the connector, remove the 4 mounting screws and remove the spiral cable.
10. Disconnect all combination switch connectors from underneath the steering column.
11. Remove the screws that fasten the combination switch to the steering column and remove from the vehicle.

To install:
12. Feed the wires down the column and install the combination switch to the steering column.
13. Connect the spiral cable connectors and install to the column. Disengage the stopper by pulling the 2 pin guides on the spiral cable unit.
14. Pull the spiral cable through the steering wheel opening and install the steering wheel, setting the pin guides.
15. Connect the horn connector and engage the spiral cable with the pawls in the steering wheel.
16. Install the hold-down nut and torque to 25 ft. lbs. (34 Nm).
17. Carefully position the air bag module. Install new Torx® bolts and torque to 15 ft. lbs. (20 Nm). Connect the air bag module connector.
18. Install the 3 access lids and the column covers.
19. Connect the negative battery cable.
20. Using the Nissan Consult System Checking tool, conduct self-diagnosis to ensure the system is operating properly.
21. If the Consult tool is not available, perform the following:
   a. From the passanger seat, turn the ignition switch to the **ON** position.
   b. Observe the **AIR BAG** warning light on the instrument cluster.
   c. The warning light should illuminate for about 7 seconds, then go out.
   d. If the warning light illuminates in any sequence except the above, perform the proper diagnostics before continuing.

Steering Column

Removal and Installation

1. Disconnect the negative battery cable.
2. Remove the steering wheel.
3. Remove the upper and lower steering column covers.
4. Disconnect the steering column multi-function switch connectors.
5. Remove the bolts attaching the lower steering column bracket to the firewall.
6. Remove the set bolt from the steering column lower joint.
7. Remove the bolts attaching the steering column to the instrument panel.
8. Remove the steering column from the vehicle.

To install:
9. Position the steering column in the vehicle.

NOTE: Ensure that the lower steering column engages in the lower joint before the steering column is permanently attached.

10. Install and finger-tighten the bolts attaching the steering column to the instrument panel.
11. Tighten steering column-to-lower joint set bolt.

NOTE: When attaching the coupling, ensure that set bolt faces the cutout portion in the splines of the lower steering column shaft.

12. Install the bolts attaching the lower steering column bracket to the firewall. Tighten to 5.8–7.2 ft. lbs. (24–29 Nm).
13. Tighten the steering column-to-instrument panel bolts to 9–13 ft. lbs. (13–18 Nm).
14. Install the steering wheel.
15. Install the negative battery cable.

Power Steering Rack

Adjustment

1. With rack assembly removed from the vehicle and installed in a vise, set the rack to the neutral position without fluid in the gear.
2. Coat the adjusting screw with locking sealant and install the screw.
3. Lightly tighten the locknut.
4. Tighten the adjusting screw to 43–52 ft. lbs. (4.9–5.9 Nm).
5. Loosen the adjusting screw and retighten to 1.7 inch lbs. (0.2 Nm).
6. Move rack over its entire stroke several times.
7. Measure pinion rotating torque with the range of 180 degrees from the neutral position. Stop the gear at the point of maximum torque.
8. Loosen the adjusting screw, the retighten to 43 inch lbs. (4.9 Nm).

9. Loosen the adjusting screw 70–110 degrees.

10. Prevent the adjusting screw from turning and tighten the locknut to specified torque.

11. Measure the pinion rotating torque. Within ±100 from the neutral position: Average rotating torque should be 6.9–11.3 inch lbs. (0.8–1.3 Nm). Maximum torque deviation is 3.5 inch lbs. (0.4 Nm).

12. Check rack sliding force as follows:

a. Install the steering gear in the vehicle., but do not connect the tie rod-to-knuckle arm.

b. Connect all piping and fill with steering fluid.

c. Start the engine and bleed the air completely.

d. Disconnect the steering column lower joint from the gear.

e. Keep the engine at idle and make sure steering fluid has reached normal operating temperature.

f. While pulling tie rod slowly in the ±0.453 in. (±11.5mm) range from the neutral position, make sure the rack sliding force is within specification. On M30, the average rack sliding force should be 53–64 lbs. (235–284 N). On Q45, the average rack sliding force should be 37–51 lbs. (167–226 N).

g. Check sliding force outside the above range. Maximum allowable sliding force is not more than 9 lbs. (39 N) above the normal value.

Removal and Installation

1. Disconnect the negative battery cable.

2. Raise the vehicle and support safely.

3. Remove the front wheels.

4. Disconnect the outer tie rods from the steering knuckle.

5. Remove the set screw from the lower steering column universal joint. Disconnect the shaft from the joint.

6. Remove the power steering fluid lines from the rack assembly.

7. Remove the bolts attaching the power steering rack assembly to the body.

8. Remove the rack assembly from the vehicle.

9. Complete the installation of the power steering rack assembly by reversing the removal procedure. Pay close attention to the following:

a. Tighten the rack mounting bolts to 62–80 ft. lbs. (84–108 Nm).

b. Initially, tighten the tie rod-to-steering knuckle nuts bolts to 22–29 ft. lbs. (29–39 Nm). Tighten the nut further to expose first pin hole and install a new cotter pin.

c. Tighten the pinion shaft-to-universal joint set screw to 17–21 ft. lbs. (24–29 Nm).

d. On M30 models, tighten low pressure power steering lines to 20–29 ft. lbs. (27–39 Nm). Tighten high pressure lines to 11–18 ft. lbs. (15–25 Nm).

e. On Q45 models, tighten low pressure power steering lines to 27–30 ft. lbs. (36–40 Nm). Tighten high pressure lines to 22–26 ft. lbs. (30–35 Nm).

Power Steering Pump

Removal and Installation

1. Disconnect the negative battery cable.

2. Remove the power steering belt pump drive belt.

3. Disconnect the power steering fluid lines.

4. Remove the power steering pump mounting bolts and remove the pump.

5. Complete the installation of the power steering pump by reversing the removal procedure.

Belt Adjustment

1. Loosen the power steering pump tension locknut.

2. On the M30, using a suitable belt tension gauge, adjust the belt tension to 0.55–0.63 in. (14–16mm) with a force of 22 lbs. (98 N) applied at the midpoint of the belt run between the crankshaft and power steering pump pulleys.

3. On the Q45, using a suitable belt tension gauge, adjust the belt tension to 0.35–0.39 in. (9–10mm) with a force of 22 lbs. (98 N) applied at the midpoint of the belt run between the crankshaft and power steering pump pulleys for vehicles without Super HICAS. Vehicles with Super HICAS, adjust the tension to 0.28–0.31 in. (7–8mm) with a force of 22 lbs. (98 N) applied at the midpoint of the belt run between the crankshaft and power steering pump pulleys.

4. Tighten the power steering pump tension locknut.

System Bleeding

1. Raise the front of the vehicle until the front wheels are clear of the ground.

2. Ensure that the reservoir is full.

3. Quickly turn the wheels from side to side lightly touching the steering stops.

4. Repeat steps 2 and 3 until the fluid level no longer decreases in the reservoir.

5. Start the engine.

6. Air in the system may cause one or all of the following:

a. Air bubbles to appear in the reservoir.

b. Generation of a clicking noise in the oil pump.

c. Excessive buzzing in the oil pump.

Tie Rod Ends

Removal and Installation

1. Raise the vehicle and support safely.

2. Remove the front wheel.

3. Matchmark the position of tie rod end locknut on the threaded section of the tie rod.

4. Loosen the tie rod end locknut.

5. Remove the cotter pin and tie rod end nut.

6. Separate the tie rod end from the steering knuckle using a suitable tool.

7. Remove the tie rod end from the tie rod.

To install:

8. Install the new tie rod end on the tie rod.

9. Install the tie rod end on the steering knuckle. Initially, tighten the tie rod-to-steering knuckle nuts bolts to 22–29 ft. lbs. (29–39 Nm). Tighten the nut further to expose first pin hole and install a new cotter pin.

10. Adjust the toe-in to the matchmark made on the threaded section of the tie rod. Tighten the locknut.

11. Install the front wheel.

12. Lower the vehicle.

13. Check alignment to verify proper toe-in setting.

BRAKES

Master Cylinder

Removal and Installation

NOTE: Prevent brake fluid from coming in contact with painted surfaces. Clean up any spills immediately.

1. Loosen the brake line flare nuts and remove brake lines from master cylinder fittings.
2. Remove the master cylinder mounting nuts.
3. Remove the master cylinder.
To install:
4. Bench bleed the master cylinder.
5. Install the master cylinder in the vehicle.
6. Connect the brake lines to the master cylinder and finger-tighten the flare nuts.
7. Bleed the air from the brake lines. Tighten the flare nuts.

Proportioning Valve

The proportioning valve is integral to the master cylinder and cannot be serviced or removed separately.

Power Brake Booster

Removal and Installation

1. Remove the master cylinder.
2. Remove the clevis pin connecting the brake pedal to the booster input rod.
3. Remove the brake pedal bracket to booster mounting nuts.
4. Remove the brake booster.
5. Complete the installation of the brake booster by reversing the removal procedure.

Brake Caliper

Removal and Installation

NOTE: Prevent brake fluid from coming in contact with painted surfaces. Clean up any spills immediately.

1. Raise the vehicle and support safely.
2. Remove the wheel.
3. Loosen the brake hose connecting bolt.
4. Remove the bolts connecting the caliper to the torque member.
5. Slide the caliper out from the rotor and remove the pad, shim and shim cover.
6. Remove the brake hose connecting bolt from the caliper.
7. Remove the caliper from the vehicle.
8. Complete the installation of the brake caliper by reversing the removal procedure. Bleed the air from the system.

Disc Brake Pads

Removal and Installation

1. Remove the cap from the master cylinder reservoir and extract a small amount of brake fluid from the reservoir.
2. Raise the vehicle and support safely.
3. Remove the wheel.
4. On Q45 models, if servicing the right front brake, disconnect the sensor harness by pushing the connector pin and pulling the connector. Remove the bracket from the cylinder body. If servicing the right rear brake, remove the sensor harness by

pushing it toward the pad, turning it counterclockwise and removing it.
5. Remove the lower pin bolt.
6. Pivot the caliper body upward and remove pad retainers, inner and outer shims and pads.
7. Place the old pad in place over the caliper cylinders. Use a C-clamp to compress the cylinder pistons to allow for the added thickness of the new pads.
8. Complete the installation of the disc brake pads by reversing the removal procedure. Check level of brake fluid in the reservoir and add as necessary.

Brake Rotor

Removal and Installation

1. Raise the vehicle and support safely.
2. Remove the wheel.
3. Remove the caliper from the torque member and support using a length of mechanics wire.
4. Remove the bolts attaching the torque member and remove.
5. Remove the rotor from the hub assembly.
6. Complete the installation of the brake rotor by reversing the removal procedure.

Parking Brake Cable

Adjustment
SHOE CLEARANCE

1. Remove adjuster hole plug and turn the adjuster wheel down until the brake is locked.

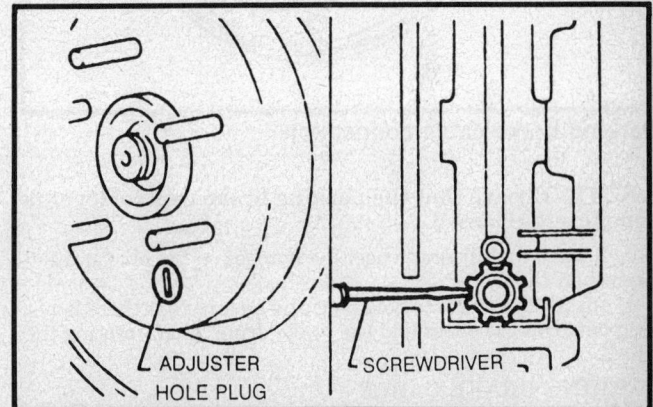

Adjusting parking brake shoe clearance

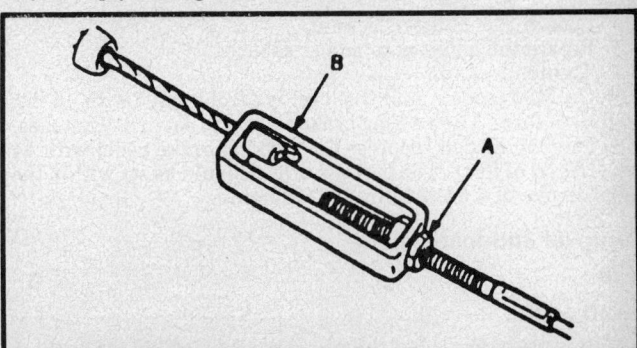

Parking brake cable adjustment

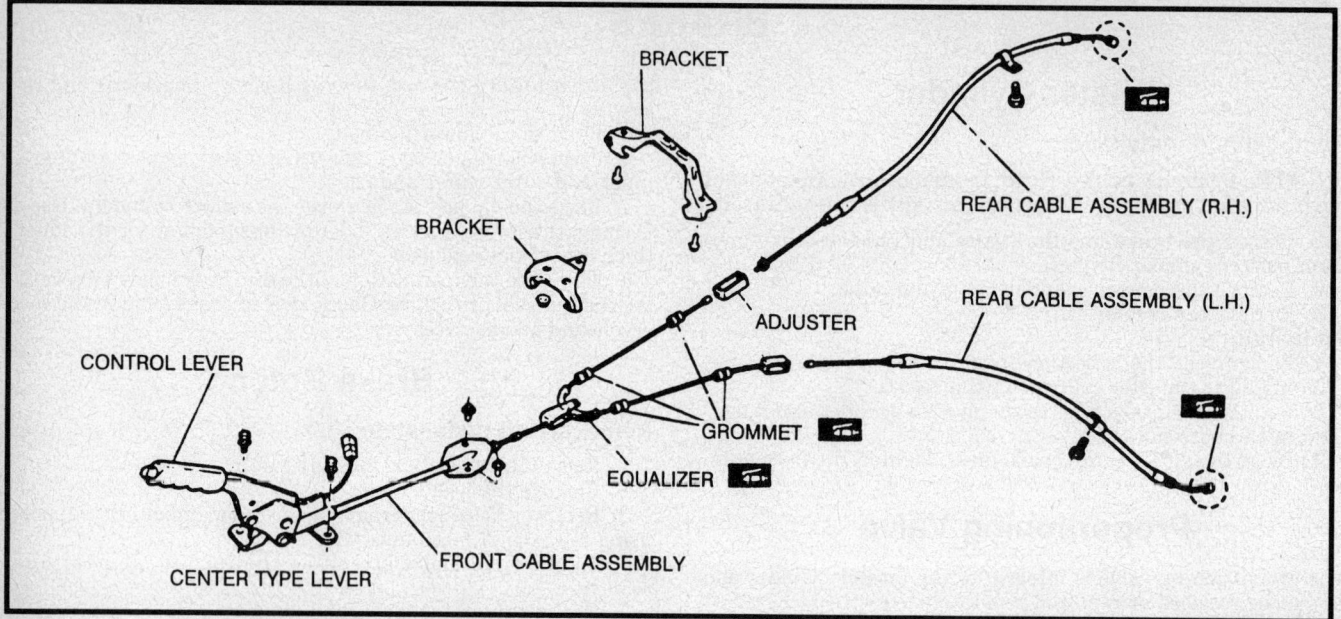

M30 parking brake cable assembly

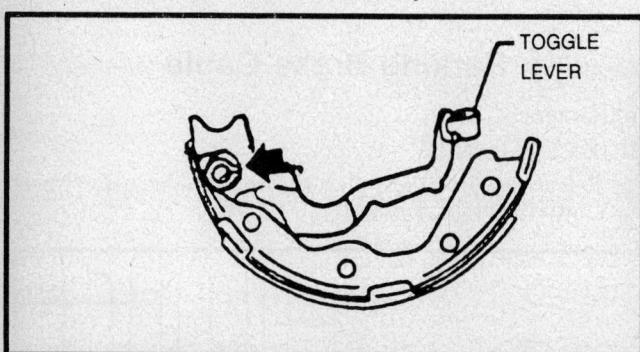

Parking brake cable connection

NOTE: Ensure that the parking brake control lever is completely released.

2. Return the adjuster wheel 7–8 notches on the M30 and 5–6 latches on the Q45.

3. Install the adjuster hole plug and ensure that there is not drag between the shoes and the brake drum when rotating the wheel.

PARKING BRAKE CABLE

1. Adjust shoe clearance before adjusting the parking brake cable.
2. Loosen the adjuster locknut.
3. Rotate the adjuster to adjust cable.
4. Tighten locknut.
5. On M30 models, pull the lever control handle with 44 lbs. (196 N) of force. The parking brake should be set in 8–9 notches.
6. On Q45 models, depress the parking brake pedal with 44 lbs. (194 N) of force. The parking brake should be set within the pedal stroke of 3.54–4.13 in. (90–105mm).

Removal and Installation

M30

Front Cable

1. It is necessary to cut the carpet directly behind the parking brake handle in order to access the front cable.

2. Remove the bolts attaching the parking brake handle and disconnect the parking brake front cable.
3. Remove the bolts attaching the bracket at the point where the cable passes through the floor.
4. Raise the vehicle and support safely.
5. Pull the cable through the hole in the floor and disconnect from the rear cable.
6. Connect the new cable and feed into the hole.
7. Connect the cable to the parking brake lever and install the floor bracket and parking brake handle bolts.
8. Adjust cable.

Rear Cable

1. Raise the vehicle and support safely.
2. Remove rear wheels.
3. Remove the bolts attaching the rear disc brake caliper mounting bracket. Remove bracket with caliper attached. Support using a length of mechanics wire.
4. Remove 2 bolts attaching rear brake rotor and remove rotor.
5. Disconnect parking brake cable end from toggle lever. Remove cable from backing plate mounting.
6. Remove cable brackets.
7. Disconnect rear cable from equalizer.
8. Complete the installation of the rear parking brake cable by reversing the removal procedure. Pay close attention to the following:

    a. Install the rear parking brake cable into the backing plate by tapping the flanged section of the cable cover with a hammer and punch.

    b. Check the shoe clearance adjustment before adjusting the cable.

    c. Adjust parking brake cable.

Q45

Front Cable

NOTE: It is possible to remove the front parking brake cable without removing the pedal assembly.

1. Raise the vehicle and support safely.
2. Disconnect the front cable from the equalizer.
3. Lower the vehicle.
4. Remove the clip retaining the cable end to the pedal assembly.

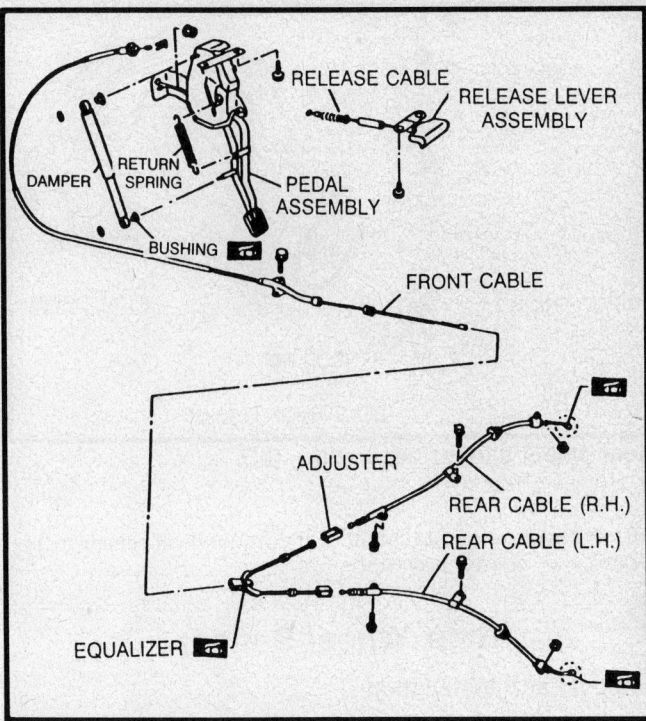

Q45 parking brake cable assembly

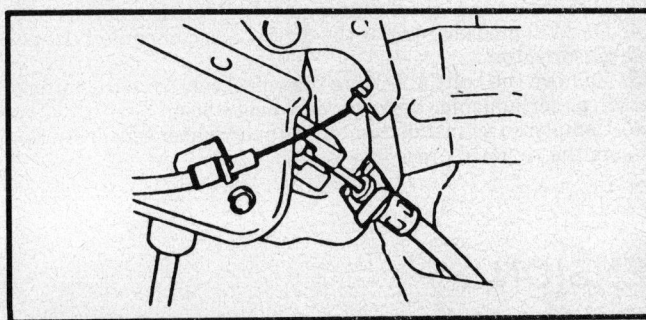

Front cable connection at pedal assembly—Q45

5. Remove the center console.
6. Remove the cable brackets and remove the cable from the floor grommet.
7. Complete the installation of the front parking brake cable by reversing the removal procedure.

Rear Cable

1. Raise the vehicle and support safely.
2. Remove rear wheels.
3. Remove the bolts attaching the rear disc brake caliper mounting bracket. Remove bracket with caliper attached. Support using a length of mechanics wire.
4. Remove 2 bolts attaching rear brake rotor and remove rotor.
5. Disconnect parking brake cable end from toggle lever. Remove cable from backing plate mounting.
6. Remove cable brackets.
7. Disconnect rear cable from equalizer.
8. Complete the installation of the rear parking brake cable by reversing the removal procedure. Pay close attention to the following:
    a. Install the rear parking brake cable into the backing plate by tapping the flanged section of the cable cover with a hammer and punch.

    b. Check the shoe clearance adjustment before adjusting the cable.
    c. Adjust parking brake cable.

Brake System Bleeding

1. Fill the brake master cylinder reservoir with brake fluid.
2. Raise and safely support the vehicle.
3. Connect a length of vinyl hose to the bleeder plug.
4. Submerge one end of the vinyl hose in a container filled with brake fluid. Connect the other end of the vinyl hose to the wheel cylinder bleeder plug.
5. Have an assistant slowly depress the brake pedal and hold it.
6. Open the bleeder plug of the right rear wheel cylinder ⅓–½ turn until the bubbles stop coming out of the tube. Close the bleeder plug.
7. Have the assistant release the brake pedal.

NOTE: The assistant must keep the brake pedal depressed until the bleeder plug is closed.

8. Continue the above procedure until air bubbles are no longer observed in the brake fluid.
9. Remove the vinyl tube and replace the bleeder plug cap.
10. Bleed the system without anti-lock brakes in the following order:
    a. Left rear
    b. Right rear
    c. Left front
    d. Right front
11. Bleed the system with anti-lock brakes in the following order:
    a. Left rear
    b. Right rear
    c. Left front
    d. Right front
    e. Front air bleed on ABS actuator
    f. Rear air bleed on ABS actuator
12. Check the brake fluid level in the master cylinder reservoir frequently during the bleeding operation.

Anti-Lock Brake System Service

Precautions

● Carefully monitor the brake fluid level in the master cylinder at all times during the bleeding procedure. Keep the reservoir full at all times.
● Only use brake fluid that meets or exceeds DOT 3 specifications.
● Place a suitable container under the master cylinder to avoid spillage of brake fluid.
● Do not allow brake fluid to come in contact with any painted surface.
● Make sure to use the proper bleeding sequence.

Relieving Anti-Lock Brake System Pressure

To relieve the pressure from the ABS system, turn the ignition switch to the **OFF** position. Disconnect the connectors from the ABS actuator. Wait a few minutes to allow for the system to bleed down, then disconnect the negative battery cable.

Actuator

Removal and Installation

1. Disconnect the negative battery cable.
2. Drain the brake fluid.
3. Disconnect the actuator electrical connectors.
4. Disconnect the brake lines from the actuator.
5. Remove the actuator attaching nuts.

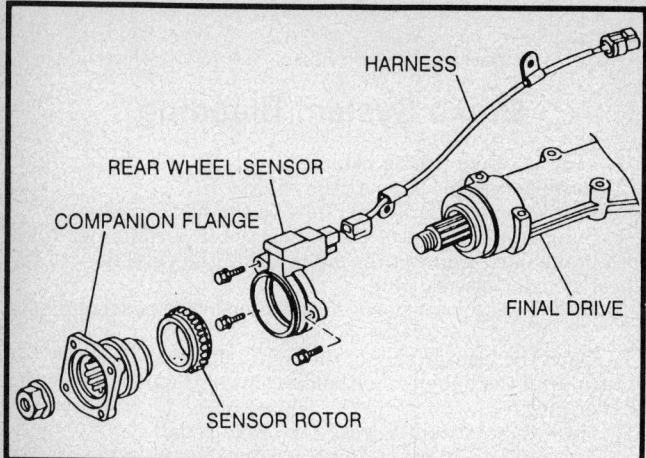

Rear wheel sensor assembly—M30

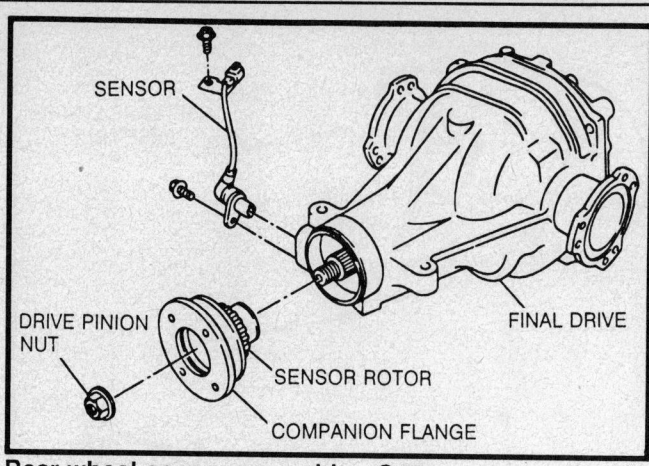

Rear wheel sensor assembly—Q45

To install:
6. Mount the new actuator and install the attaching nuts.
7. Connect the brake lines.
8. Connect the electrical connectors.
9. Bleed the air from the system.
10. Connect negative battery cable.

Front Wheel Sensor

Removal and Installation

1. Disconnect the negative battery cable.
2. Raise the vehicle and support safely.
3. Remove the front wheel.
4. Disconnect the wheel sensor harness connector.
5. Remove the bolts attaching the harness clamps and the sensor to the sensor bracket. Remove the sensor.

6. Complete the installation of the front wheel sensor by reversing the removal procedure.

Rear Wheel Sensor

Removal and Installation

1. Disconnect the negative battery cable.
2. Raise the vehicle and support safely.
3. Disconnect the wheel sensor electrical harness connector.
4. On M30 models, remove the driveshaft, companion flange and sensor rotor.
5. Remove the bolts attaching the wheel sensor to the differential carrier housing. Remove the wheel sensor.
6. Complete the installation of the rear wheel sensor by reversing the removal procedure.

FRONT SUSPENSION

Shock Absorbers

Removal and Installation

Q45

1. Remove the upper shock absorber mounting insulator bolts.
2. Raise and safely support the vehicle.
3. Remove the lower shock mounting bolt and lift out the shock assembly.
4. Lower the vehicle.
5. The installation is the reverse of the removal procedure. Keep the following torques in mind:
   a. Tighten the upper mounting bolts to 30–35 ft. lbs.
   b. Tighten the piston rod locknut to 13–17 ft. lbs.
   c. Tighten the lower mounting bolt to 80–94 ft. lbs.

MacPherson Strut

Removal and Installation

M30

1. Disconnect the negative battery cable.
2. Disconnect the sub-harness connector strut actuator mounting bolt.

3. Remove the strut assembly mounting nut. Do not remove the piston rod locknut on the vehicle.
4. Raise and safely support the vehicle. Remove the tension rod nuts and the strut-to-steering knuckle mounting bolts. Make sure the brake hose is not twisted.
5. Remove the strut assembly.
6. The installation is the reverse of the removal procedure. Keep the following torques in mind:
   a. Tighten the upper mounting bolts to 30–35 ft. lbs.
   b. Tighten the piston rod locknut to 13–17 ft. lbs.
   c. Tighten the lower mounting bolt to 80–94 ft. lbs.

Coil Springs

Removal and Installation

M30

1. Disconnect the negative battery cable.
2. Disconnect the sub-harness connector strut actuator mounting bolt.
3. Remove the strut assembly mounting nut. Do not remove the piston rod locknut on the vehicle.
4. Raise and safely support the vehicle. Remove the tension rod nuts and the steering knuckle mounting bolts. Make sure the brake hose is not twisted.

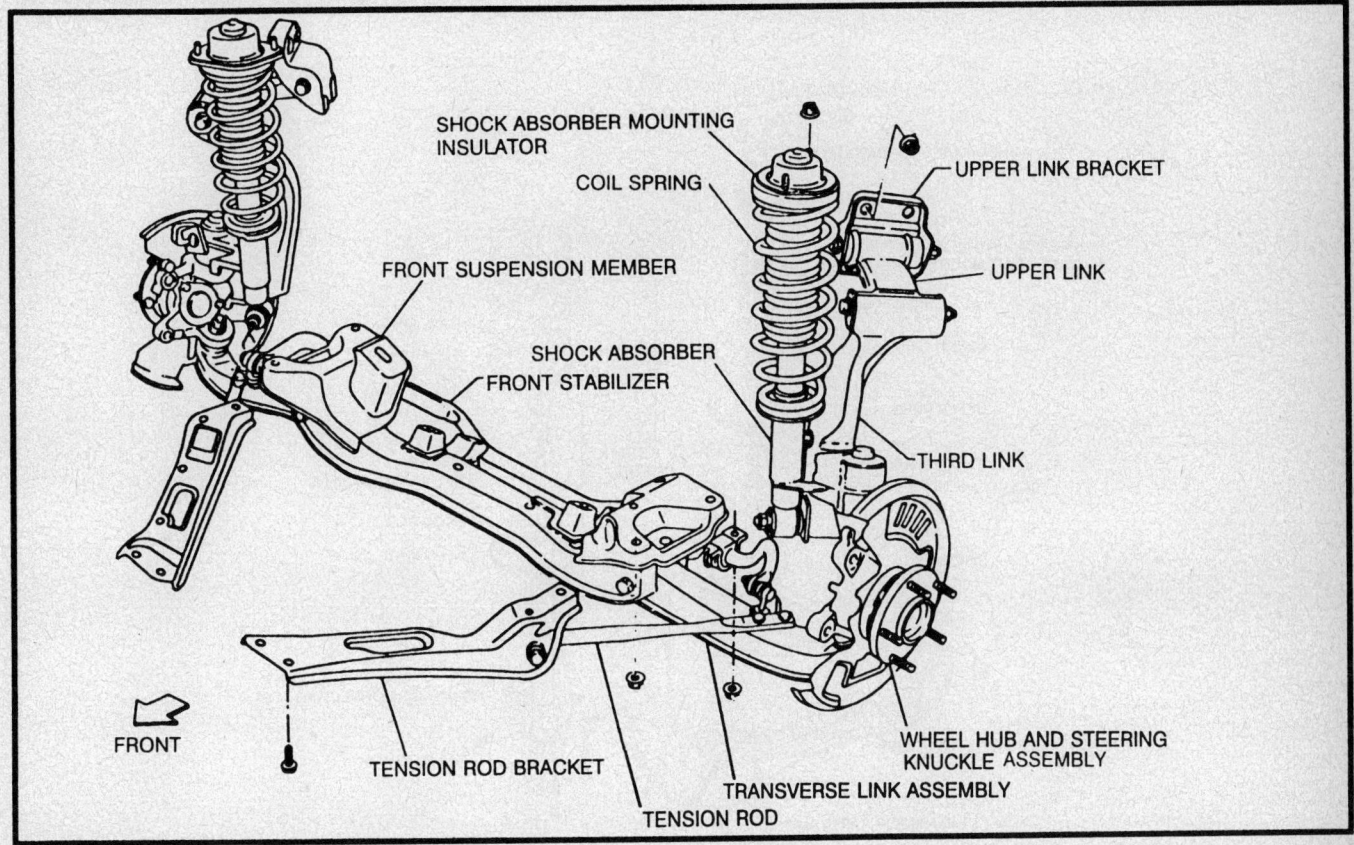

SHOCK ABSORBER MOUNTING INSULATOR
COIL SPRING
UPPER LINK BRACKET
UPPER LINK
FRONT SUSPENSION MEMBER
SHOCK ABSORBER
FRONT STABILIZER
THIRD LINK
FRONT
TENSION ROD BRACKET
TRANSVERSE LINK ASSEMBLY
TENSION ROD
WHEEL HUB AND STEERING KNUCKLE ASSEMBLY

Front suspension components—Q45

5. Secure the strut assembly in suitable holding fixture and loosen the piston rod locknut. Do not remove it.

6. Compress the spring with the proper tool so the shock absorber mounting insulator can be turned by hand.

7. Remove the piston rod locknut and the coil spring assembly.

8. Remove the gland packing with the proper tool. Retract the piston, by pushing it down until it bottoms.

9. Slowly, remove the piston rod from the cylinder together with the piston guide.

10. Inspect the rubber parts for deterioration.

11. Lubricate the sealing lip of the gland packing.

12. Install the gland packing while covering the piston rod with tape so not to damage the oil sealing lip.

13. Tighten the gland packing to 51–94 ft. lbs. without the special tool.

14. The installation is the reverse of the removal procedure. The flat portion of the spring goes in the top position.

15. Install the spring seat with it's cutout facing the outer side of the vehicle. Tighten the following:

    a. The upper cover mounting bolts to 22–29 ft. lbs.

    b. The upper piston rod locknut to 43–58 ft. lbs.

    c. The lower strut-to-knuckle arm mounting bolts to 53–72 ft. lbs.

Q45

1. Remove the upper shock absorber mounting insulator bolts.

2. Raise and safely support the vehicle.

3. Remove the lower shock mounting bolt and lift out the shock assembly.

4. Secure the shock absorber in a suitable holding fixture.

5. Loosen the piston rod locknut. Do not remove the locknut.

6. Compress the spring with the proper tool so the shock absorber mounting insulator can be turned by hand.

7. Remove the piston rod locknut. Remove the spring assembly, dust cover and rubber seat.

8. Remove the shock absorber. Inspect the rubber parts for deterioration.

9. The installation is the reverse of the removal procedure. Keep the following torques in mind:

    a. Tighten the upper mounting bolts to 30–35 ft. lbs.

    b. Tighten the piston rod locknut to 13–17 ft. lbs.

    c. Tighten the lower mounting bolt to 80–94 ft. lbs.

NOTE: When installing the coil spring, be careful not to reverse the top and bottom direction. The top end is flat.

Kingpins

Removal and Installation

THIRD LINK AND UPPER LINK

Q45

1. Raise and safely support the vehicle. Support the wheel assembly with a suitable jacking device.

2. Remove the cap and the upper kingpin mounting nut. Do not remove the lower nut.

3. Remove the shock absorber mounting nut and the upper link mounting bolts.

4. Remove the third link and the upper link.

5. The installation is the revere of the removal procedure. Upper link bushings cannot be disassembled.

6. Always install the upper link with the A facing the axle and the side without a character facing the vehicle body.

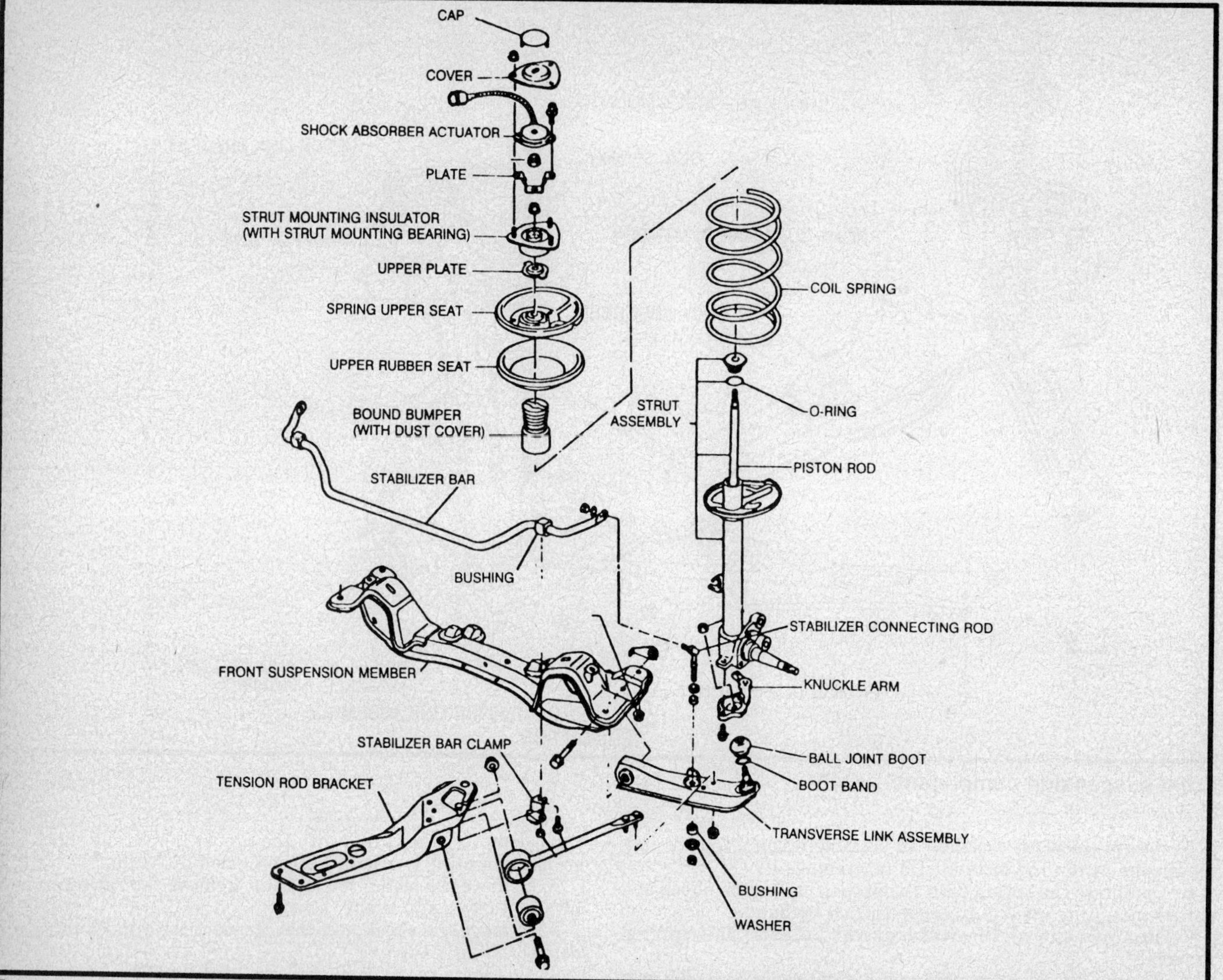

CAP

COVER

SHOCK ABSORBER ACTUATOR

PLATE

STRUT MOUNTING INSULATOR
(WITH STRUT MOUNTING BEARING)

UPPER PLATE

SPRING UPPER SEAT

UPPER RUBBER SEAT

BOUND BUMPER
(WITH DUST COVER)

STABILIZER BAR

BUSHING

FRONT SUSPENSION MEMBER

STABILIZER BAR CLAMP

TENSION ROD BRACKET

COIL SPRING

STRUT ASSEMBLY

O-RING

PISTON ROD

STABILIZER CONNECTING ROD

KNUCKLE ARM

BALL JOINT BOOT

BOOT BAND

TRANSVERSE LINK ASSEMBLY

BUSHING

WASHER

Front suspension components — M30

7. Tighten the upper kingpin mounting nut to 72–87 ft. lbs. and the lower kingpin mounting nut to 65–80 ft. lbs.

Lower Ball Joints

The lower ball joints are part of the the lower transverse arm and replaced as an assembly.

Inspection

1. Turn the ball joint at least 10 revolutions before checking.

2. Measure the swing force using the proper tool. The Q45 should be 1.8–11.9 ft. lbs. and the M30 should read 5.5–18.1 ft. lbs.

3. The turning torque should read 4.3–30.4 inch lbs. on the Q45 and 13–43 inch lbs. on the M30.

4. The vertical endplay should be 0 in. (0mm) on the Q45 and 0.004–0.051 in. (0.1–1.3mm) on the M30.

5. After inspecting, if the play exceeds these specifications replace the transverse arm.

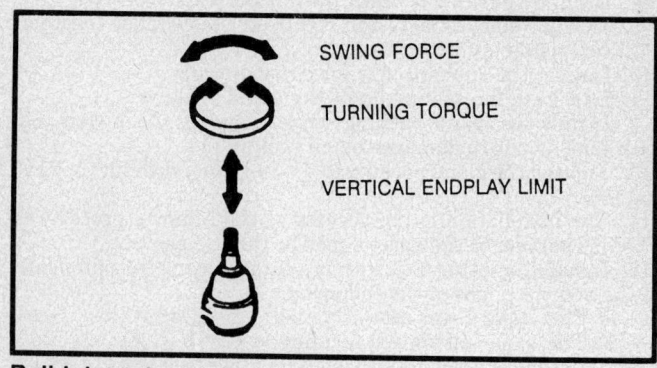

SWING FORCE

TURNING TORQUE

VERTICAL ENDPLAY LIMIT

Ball joint tolerances

Lower Control Arm

Removal and Installation

M30

1. Raise and safely support the vehicle.
2. Remove the bolts and disconnect the the tension and stabilizer bar.

3. Remove the bolt and disconnect the transverse arm from the knuckle arm, using the proper tool.

4. Remove the transverse arm and joint assembly.

5. Install the stabilizer bar with the ball joint socket in a straight position, not cocked.

6. The installation is the reverse of the removal procedure. Tighten the following to:
    a. The stabilizer bar mounting bolt to 14–22 ft. lbs.
    b. The tension rod mounting bolts to 35–43 ft. lbs.
    c. The steering knuckle mounting bolt to 71–88 ft. lbs.

Q45

1. Raise and safely support the vehicle. Support the wheel assembly with a suitable jacking device.

2. Remove the mounting bolts and disconnect the tension rod and stabilizer bar.

3. Remove the bolt and disconnect the transverse arm from the knuckle arm, using the proper tool.

4. Remove the transverse arm and joint assembly.

5. The installation is the reverse of the removal procedure. The final tightening must be at curb weight with the tires on the ground.

6. Tighten the following to:
    a. The stabilizer bar mounting bolt to 14–22 ft. lbs.
    b. The tension rod mounting bolts to 72–87 ft. lbs.
    c. The steering knuckle mounting bolt to 65–80 ft. lbs.

Front Wheel Bearings

Preload Adjustment

M30

1. Thoroughly clean all parts to prevent dirt entry.

2. Apply the recommended multi-purpose grease to the following components:
    a. The rubbing surface of the spindle.
    b. The contact surface between the lock washer and the outer wheel bearing.
    c. The inside of the dust cap.
    d. The grease seal lip.

3. Tighten the wheel bearing lock to 25–29 ft. lbs. Turn the wheel hub several times in both directions to seat the wheel bearing correctly.

4. Again, tighten the wheel bearing to the specified torque. Turn back the wheel bearing locknut 90 degrees.

5. Install the adjusting cap and the locknut. Do not turn the nut back for cotter pin insertion. Align the cotter pin by re-tightening the nut within 15 degrees.

6. Measure the wheel bearing preload and the axle endplay limit with the proper tool. The wheel bearing preload, measure at the wheel hub bolt should be 3.1 lbs. or less. The axle endplay limit is 0.0020 in. (0.05mm).

7. Repeat procedure until the correct bearing preload is obtained.

Removal and Installation

M30

1. Raise and safely support the vehicle. Remove the brake caliper assembly and the brake rotor. The brake line need not be disconnected.

2. Remove the wheel hub and the wheel bearing from the spindle.

3. Secure the hub in a suitable holding fixture. Drive out the outer race with the proper tool.

4. Inspect all the components for damage or excessive wear.

5. Install the bearing outer race with the proper tool until it seat in the hub.

6. Coat the bearing with the recommended multi-purpose

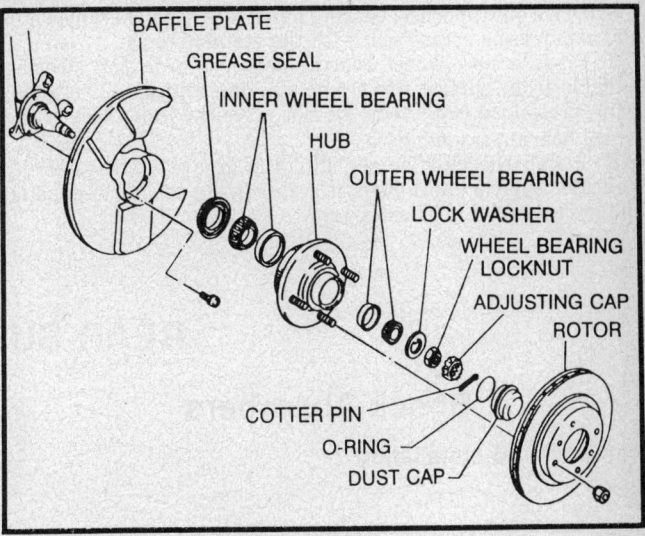

Front axle hub assembly—M30

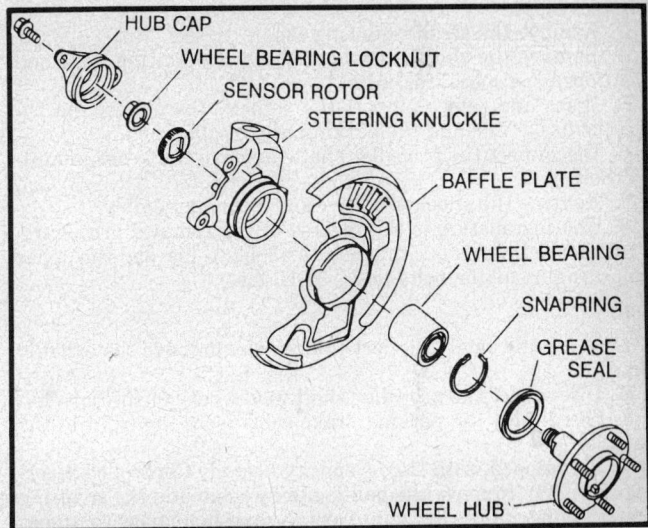

Front axle hub assembly—Q45

grease and install. Pack the grease seal lip with the recommended grease.

7. Install the seal with the proper tool until it seats in the hub. Pack the hub and dust cap with the recommended grease.

8. Adjust the wheel bearing preload.

9. The remainder of the installation is the reverse of the removal procedure.

Q45

1. Raise and safely support the vehicle. Remove the brake caliper assembly and the brake rotor. The brake line need not be disconnected.

2. Disconnect the tie rod and transverse arm from the steering knuckle assembly with the proper tool.

NOTE: The steering knuckle is made from aluminum alloy, Be careful not to hit the knuckle.

3. Remove the kingpin lower nut and the steering knuckle assembly. Secure the steering knuckle in a suitable holding fixture.

4. Remove the dust cap and the wheel bearing locknut. Remove the wheel hub with the proper tool.

5. Remove the circular clip and press out the bearing assembly from the steering knuckle with the proper tools.

6. Drive out the wheel bearing inner race from the wheel hub and remove the grease seal with the suitable tools.

7. Press a new wheel bearing assembly into the steering knuckle from outside the of the steering knuckle. The maximum press load is 3.9 tons. Do not press the inner race of the wheel bearing assembly.

8. Install the circular clip into the groove of the steering knuckle. Apply a multi-purpose grease to the sealing and install the grease seal and splash guard.

9. Press the wheel hub onto the steering knuckle with the proper tool. The maximum press load is 3.3 tons.

10. Tighten the wheel bearing locknut to 152–210 ft. lbs.

11. Stake the wheel bearing locknut and install the dust cap.

12. The remainder of the installation is the reverse of the removal procedure.

REAR SUSPENSION

Shock Absorbers

Removal and Installation

M30

1. Disconnect the negative battery cable.
2. Remove the rear parcel shelf. Disconnect the sub-harness connector.
3. Remove the strut mounting cap.
4. Remove the shock absorber actuator mounting bolts and the upper end mounting nuts.
5. Raise and safely support the vehicle. Disconnect the hydraulic brake line and the parking brake cable.
6. Disconnect the propeller shaft. Remove the lower mounting bolt.
7. Remove the shock absorber and spring assembly.
8. The installation is the reverse of the removal procedure. Tighten the lower mounting bolt to 43–58 ft. lbs. and the upper mounting insulator bolts to 23–31 ft. lbs.

Q45

1. Raise and safely support the vehicle. Remove the exhaust tube.
2. Disconnect the propeller shaft at the rear of the vehicle.
3. Disconnect the parking brake cable from the front of the vehicle.
4. If equipped, with High Capacity Actively Controlled Steering (HICAS). Remove the ball joints by removing the snapring and pressing out the ball joint from the axle housing with proper tools.
5. Remove the tire and wheel assembly. Remove the brake caliper assembly. It is not neccessary to disconnect the brake line.
6. Remove the upper shock absorber end nuts. Do not remove the piston rod nut.
7. Remove the rear suspension mounting nuts. Draw out the rear axle and rear suspension assembly.
8. Remove the shock absorber upper and lower mounting nuts. Do not remove the piston rod nut.
9. Remove the shock absorber and spring assembly.
10. The installation is the reverse of the removal procedure.

tighten the lower shock mounting bolt to 57–72 ft. lbs. and the upper spring seat mounting bolts to 12–14 ft. lbs.

Rear Control Arm

Removal and Installation

M30

1. Raise and support the vehicle. Remove the axle shaft assembly.
2. Remove the stabilizer bar bolt and disconnect the parking brake cable.
3. Disconnect the lower shock absorber bolt.
4. Matchmark the suspension arm to the pin and remove the pin.
5. Remove the lower suspension arm.
6. The installation is the reverse of the removal procedure. Adjust the rear alignment after installing the lower arm.
7. When installing, tighten the suspension arm pin to 72–87 ft. lbs. after installing the wheels and placing the vehicle on the ground under the unladen condition.

Q45

1. Raise and safely support the vehicle. Remove the exhaust tube.
2. Disconnect the propeller shaft at the rear of the vehicle.
3. Disconnect the parking brake cable from the front of the vehicle.
4. If equipped, with High Capacity Actively Controlled Steering (HICAS). Remove the ball joints by removing the snapring and pressing out the ball joint from the axle housing with proper tools.
5. Remove the tire and wheel assembly. Remove the brake caliper assembly. It is not neccessary to disconnect the brake line.
6. Remove the upper shock absorber end nuts. Do not remove the piston rod nut.
7. Remove the rear suspension mounting nuts. Draw out the rear axle and rear suspension assembly.
8. The installation is the reverse of the removal procedure. Tighten the lower arm adjusting pin bolts to 57–72 ft. lbs.

SERIAL NUMBER IDENTIFICATION

Vehicle Identification Plate

The vehicle identification number is embossed on a plate, that is attached to the top left corner of the instrument panel. The number is visible through the windshield from the outside of the vehicle. The 8th digit of the number, indicates the engine model and the 10th digit represents the model year; example is K for 1989, L for 1990 or M for 1991.

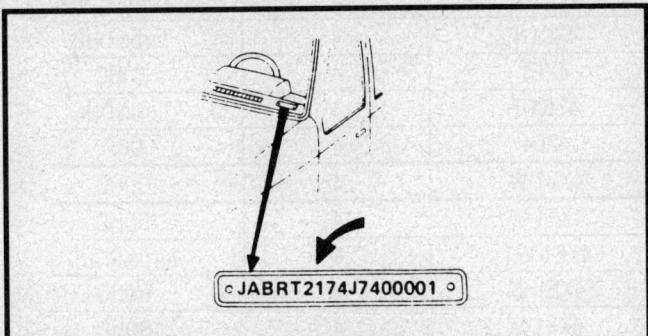

Vehicle identification plate location

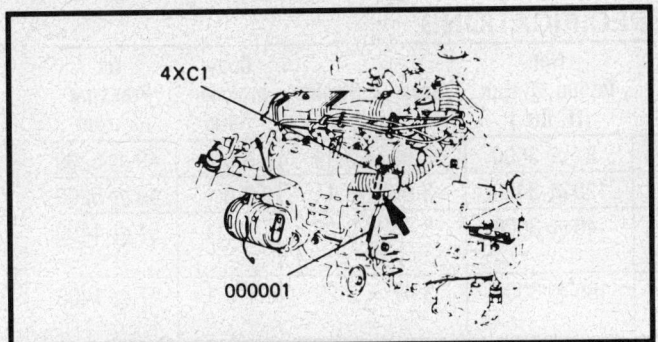

4XC1-T engine serial number location

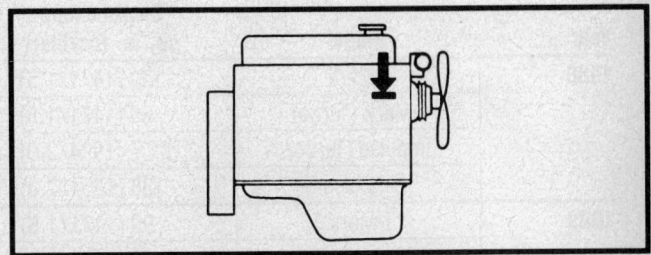

G200Z engine serial number location

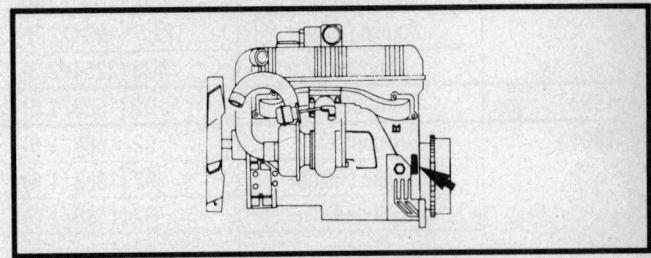

4ZC1-T and 4ZD1 engine serial number location

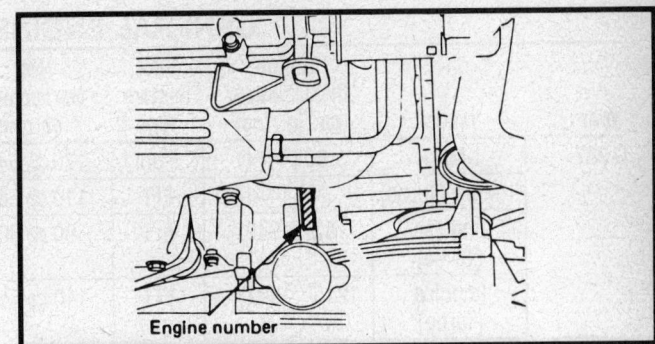

4XE1 engine serial number location

Engine Number

The Impulse equipped with the G200Z engine, has the engine serial number stamped on the top right corner of the engine block. The Impulse equipped with the 4ZC1-T and 4ZD1 engine, has the number stamped on the left rear corner of the engine block, near the engine to transaxle mounting. The Impulse equipped with the 4XE1-W, 4XE1-WT and 4XE1-V engine and all I-Marks, have the number stamped on the flange near the transaxle mounting, toward the front of the vehicle.

Vehicle Identification Number

The Vehicle Identification Number (VIN) appears on the vehicle identification plate and on the driver's door post pillar.

SPECIFICATIONS

ENGINE IDENTIFICATION

Year	Model	Engine Displacement cu. in. (cc/liter)	Engine Series Identification	No. of Cylinders	Engine Type
1987	I-Mark	90 (1471/1.5)	4XC1-U	4	OHC
	I-Mark (Turbo)	90 (1471/1.5)	4XC1-T	4	OHC
	Impulse	118.9 (1949/1.9)	G200Z	4	OHC
	Impulse (Turbo)	121.7 (1994/2.0)	4ZC1-T	4	Turbo OHC

ENGINE IDENTIFICATION

Year	Model	Engine Displacement cu. in. (cc/liter)	Engine Series Identification	No. of Cylinders	Engine Type
1988	I-Mark	90 (1471/1.5)	4XC1-U	4	OHC
	I-Mark (Turbo)	90 (1471/1.5)	4XC1-T	4	Turbo OHC
	Impulse (Turbo)	121.7 (1994/2.0)	4ZC1-T	4	Turbo OHC
	Impulse	138 (2254/2.3)	4ZD1	4	OHC
1989	I-Mark	90 (1471/1.5)	4XC1-U	4	OHC
	I-Mark (Turbo)	90 (1471/1.5)	4XC1-T	4	Turbo OHC
	I-Mark (DOHC)	92 (1588/1.6)	4XE1	4	DOHC
	Impulse (Turbo)	121.7 (1994/2.0)	4ZC1-T	4	Turbo OHC
	Impulse	138 (2254/2.3)	4ZD1	4	OHC
1990	Impulse	92 (1588/1.6)	4XE1-W	4	DOHC
1991	Impulse	92 (1588/1.6)	4XE1-W	4	DOHC
	Impulse (Turbo)	92 (1588/1.6)	4XE1-WT	4	Turbo DOHC
	Stylus	92 (1588/1.6)	4XE1-W	4	DOHC
	Stylus	92 (1588/1.6)	4XE1-V	4	SOHC

GENERAL ENGINE SPECIFICATIONS

Year	Model	Engine Displacement cu. in. (cc)	Fuel System Type	Net Horsepower @ rpm	Net Torque @ rpm (ft. lbs.)	Bore × Stroke (in.)	Compression Ratio	Oil Pressure @ rpm
1987	I-Mark	90 (1471)	2 bbl	70 @ 5400	87 @ 3400	3.03 × 3.11	9.6:1	49 @ 5200
	I-Mark (Turbo)	90 (1471)	EFI	110 @ 5400	120 @ 3400	3.03 × 3.11	8.0:1	49 @ 5200
	Impulse (Turbo)	118.9 (1949)	EFI	90 @ 5000	146 @ 3000	3.43 × 3.29	9.2:1	57 @ 1400
	Impulse (Turbo)	121.7 (1994)	EFI	140 @ 5400	166 @ 3000	3.47 × 3.29	7.9:1	57 @ 1400
1988	I-Mark	90 (1471)	2 bbl	70 @ 5400	87 @ 3400	3.03 × 3.11	9.6:1	49 @ 5200
	I-Mark (Turbo)	90 (1471)	EFI	110 @ 5400	120 @ 3400	3.03 × 3.11	8.0:1	49 @ 5200
	Impulse (Turbo)	121.7 (1994)	EFI	140 @ 5400	166 @ 3000	3.46 × 3.29	7.9:1	57 @ 1400
	Impulse	138 (2254)	EFI	110 @ 5000	127 @ 3000	3.52 × 3.54	8.6:1	57 @ 1400
1989	I-Mark	90 (1471)	2 bbl	70 @ 5400	87 @ 3400	3.03 × 3.11	9.6:1	49 @ 5200
	I-Mark (Turbo)	90 (1471)	EFI	110 @ 5400	120 @ 3400	3.03 × 3.11	8.0:1	49 @ 5200
	I-Mark (DOHC)	92 (1588)	EFI	125 @ 6800	138 @ 5400	3.15 × 3.11	9.8:1	49 @ 5200
	Impulse (Turbo)	121.7 (1994)	EFI	140 @ 5400	166 @ 3000	3.46 × 3.29	7.9:1	57 @ 1400
	Impulse	138 (2254)	EFI	110 @ 5000	127 @ 3000	3.52 × 3.54	8.6:1	57 @ 1400
1990	Impulse	92 (1588)	EFI	125 @ 6800	138 @ 5400	3.15 × 3.11	9.8:1	49 @ 5200
1991	Impulse	92 (1588)	EFI	130 @ 6600	102 @ 4600	3.15 × 3.11	9.8:1	49 @ 5200
	Impulse	92 (1588)	EFI	160 @ 6600	150 @ 4800	3.15 × 3.11	8.5:1	49 @ 5200
	Stylus	92 (1588) ①	EFI	95 @ 5800	97 @ 3400	3.15 × 3.11	9.1:1	49 @ 5200
	Stylus	92 (1588) ②	EFI	130 @ 6600	102 @ 4600	3.15 × 3.11	9.8:1	49 @ 5200

① SOHC
② DOHC

GASOLINE ENGINE TUNE-UP SPECIFICATIONS

Year	Model	Engine Displacement cu. in. (cc)	Spark Plugs Type	Gap (in.)	Ignition Timing (deg.) MT	AT	Compression Pressure (psi)	Fuel Pump (psi)	Idle Speed (rpm) MT	AT	Valve Clearance In.	Ex.
1987	I-Mark	90 (1471)	BPR6ES11	.040	3B	3B	177.8	3.8–4.7	750	1000	.006	.010
	I-Mark (Turbo)	90 (1471)	BPR6ES11	.040	15B	NA	171.0	28.4①	950	NA	.006	.010
	Impulse	118.9 (1949)	BPR6ES11	.040	12B	12B	178.0	36①	900②	900②	.006	.010
	Impulse (Turbo)	121.7 (1994)	BPR6ES11	.040	12B	12B	178.0	36①	900②	900②	.006	.010
1988	I-Mark	90 (1471)	BPR6ES11	.040	3B	3B	177.8	3.8–4.7	750	1000	.006	.010
	I-Mark (Turbo)	90 (1471)	BPR6ES11	.040	15B	NA	171.0	28.4①	950	NA	.006	.010
	Impulse (Turbo)	121.7 (1994)	BPR6ES11	.040	12B	12B	178.0	35.6①	900②	900②	.006	.010
	Impulse	138 (2254)	BPR6ES11	.040	12B	12B	178.0	35.6①	900②	900②	.008	.008
1989	I-Mark	90 (1471)	BPR6ES11	.040	3B	3B	177.8	3.8–4.7	750	1000	.006	.010
	I-Mark (Turbo)	90 (1471)	BPR6ES11	.040	15B	NA	171.0	28.4①	950	NA	.006	.010
	I-Mark (DOHC)	92 (1588)	BPR6ES11	.040	16B	—	171.0	28.4①	950	—	Hyd.	Hyd.
	Impulse (Turbo)	121.7 (1994)	BPR6ES11	.040	12B	12B	178.0	35.6①	900②	900②	.006	.010
	Impulse	138 (2254)	BPR6ES11	.040	12B	12B	178.0	35.6①	900②	900②	.008	.008
1990	Impulse	92 (1588)	BKR6E11	.041	10B	10B	185	35–38	850	850	.006	.010
1991	Impulse	92 (1588)	BKR6E11	.041	10B	10B	185	35–38	850	850	.006	.010
	Impulse (Turbo)	92 (1588)	BKR6E	.030	10B	10B	185	35–38	900	900	.006	.010
	Stylus③	92 (1588)	BPR6ES11	.041	10B	10B	185	35–38	850	940	.006	.010
	Stylus④	92 (1588)	BKR6E11	.041	10B	10B	185	35–38	850	850	.006	.010

① At 900 rpm with vacuum hose of the pressure regulator connected   ② ±50 rpm   ③ SOHC   ④ DOHC

FIRING ORDERS

NOTE: To avoid confusion, always replace spark plug wires one at a time.

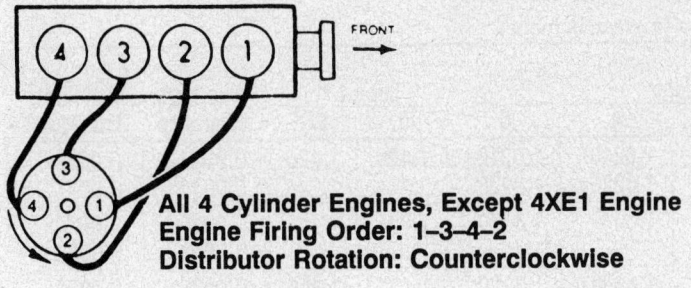

FRONT →

All 4 Cylinder Engines, Except 4XE1 Engine
Engine Firing Order: 1–3–4–2
Distributor Rotation: Counterclockwise

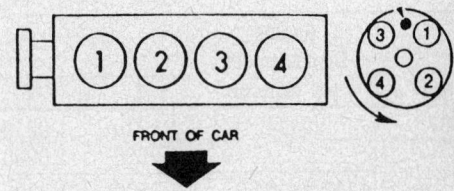

FRONT OF CAR

1.6L (4XE1) SOHC and DOHC Engines
Engine Firing Order: 1–3–4–2
Distributor Rotation: Counterclockwise

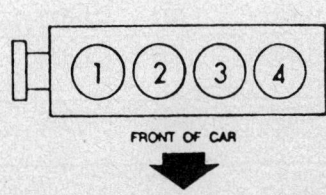

FRONT OF CAR

1.6L (4XE1) DOHC Turbo Engine
Engine Firing Order: 1–3–4–2
Distributorless Ignition System

CAPACITIES

Year	Model	Engine Displacement cu. in. (cc)	Engine Crankcase (qts.) with Filter	without Filter	Transmission (pts.) 4-Spd	5-Spd	Auto.	Drive Axle (pts.)	Fuel Tank (gal.)	Cooling System (qts.)
1987	I-Mark	90 (1471)	3.4③	3.0	—	5.6	13.6	NA	11.1	6.8
	I-Mark (Turbo)	90 (1471)	3.4③	3.0	—	5.0	NA	NA	11.1	7.5
	Impulse	118.9 (1949)	3.8①	3.4	—	3.3	14②	3.2	15.1	9.3
	Impulse	121.7 (1994)	3.8①	3.4	—	3.3	14②	3.2	15.1	9.5
1988	I-Mark	90 (1471)	3.4③	3.0	—	5.0	13.6	NA	11.1	6.8
	I-Mark (Turbo)	90 (1471)	3.4③	3.0	—	5.0	NA	NA	11.1	7.5
	Impulse (Turbo)	121.7 (1994)	3.8①	3.4	—	3.3	13.7	3.2	15.1	9.5
	Impulse	138 (2254)	3.8①	3.4	—	3.3	13.7	3.2	15.1	9.3
1989	I-Mark	90 (1471)	3.4③	3.0	—	5.0	13.6	NA	11.1	6.8
	I-Mark (Turbo)	90 (1471)	3.4③	3.0	—	5.0	NA	NA	11.1	7.5
	I-Mark (DOHC)	92 (1588)	3.2	3.0	—	5.0	—		11.1	6.8
	Impulse (Turbo)	121.7 (1994)	3.8①	3.4	—	3.3	13.7	3.2	15.1	9.5
	Impulse	138 (2254)	3.8①	3.4	—	3.3	13.7	3.2	15.1	9.3
1990	Impulse	92 (1588)	4.6	4.0	—	4.0	14.0	—	12.4	④
1991	Impulse	92 (1588)	4.6	4.0	—	4.0	14.0	⑤	12.4	④
	Impulse Turbo	92 (1588)	4.6	4.0	—	4.0	14.0	⑤	12.4	7.9
	Stylus ⑥	92 (1588)	3.2	3.6	—	4.0	14.0	—	12.4	④
	Stylus ⑦	92 (1588)	4.6	4.0	—	4.0	14.0	—	12.4	7.3

① The original fill is 5.0 qts.
② 21.8 pts. when transmission has been overhauled and torque converter serviced or replaced
③ Original fill 3.7 qts.
④ Manual transaxle—7.3 pts. Automatic transaxle—7.8 pts.
⑤ Rear axle—1.38 pts.
⑥ SOHC
⑦ DOHC

CAMSHAFT SPECIFICATIONS

All measurements given in inches.

Year	Engine Displacement cu. in. (cc)	Journal Diameter 1	2	3	4	5	Lobe Lift In.	Ex.	Bearing Clearance	Camshaft End Play
1987	90 (1471)	1.0210–1.0220	1.0210–1.0220	1.0210–1.0220	1.0210–1.0220	1.0210–1.0220	1.426	1.426	0.0024–0.0044	0.0039–0.0071
	118.9 (1949)	1.3390	1.3390	1.3390	1.3390	1.3390	1.451	1.451	0.0030–0.0043	0.0020–0.0060
	121.7 (1994)	1.3390	1.3390	1.3390	1.3390	1.3390	1.451	1.451	0.0026–0.0043	0.0002–0.0059
1988	90 (1471)	1.021–1.022	1.021–1.022	1.021–1.022	1.021–1.022	1.021–1.022	1.426	1.426	0.0024–0.0044	0.0039–0.0071
	138 (2254)	1.339	1.339	1.339	1.339	1.339	1.451	1.451	0.0033–0.0051	0.0002–0.0059
	121.7 (1994)	1.339	1.339	1.339	1.339	1.339	1.451	1.451	0.0033–0.0051	0.0002–0.0059

ISUZU

I-MARK • IMPULSE • STYLUS

11 SECTION

CAMSHAFT SPECIFICATIONS

All measurements given in inches.

Year	Engine Displacement cu. in. (cc)	Journal Diameter 1	2	3	4	5	Lobe Lift In.	Ex.	Bearing Clearance	Camshaft End Play
1989	90 (1471)	1.021–1.022	1.021–1.022	1.021–1.022	1.021–1.022	1.021–1.022	1.426	1.426	0.0024–0.0044	0.0039–0.0071
	92 (1588)	1.021–1.022	1.021–1.022	1.021–1.022	1.021–1.022	1.021–1.022	1.536	1.536	0.0024–0.0044	0.002–0.006
	138 (2254)	1.339	1.339	1.339	1.339	1.339	1.451	1.451	0.0033–0.0051	0.0002–0.0059
	121.7 (1994)	1.339	1.339	1.339	1.339	1.339	1.451	1.451	0.0033–0.0051	0.0002–0.0059
1990	92 (1588)	1.021–1.022	1.021–1.022	1.021–1.022	1.021–1.022	1.021–1.022	1.503	1.503	0.0011–0.0031	0.002–0.006
1991	92 (1588) ①	1.021–1.022	1.021–1.022	1.021–1.022	1.021–1.022	1.021–1.022	1.503	1.503	0.0011–0.0031	0.002–0.006
	92 (1588) ②	1.021–1.022	1.021–1.022	1.021–1.022	1.021–1.022	1.021–1.022	1.525	1.525	0.0011–0.0031	0.002–0.006
	92 (1588) ③	1.021–1.022	1.021–1.022	1.021–1.022	1.021–1.022	1.021–1.022	1.426	1.426	0.0023–0.0044	N/A

① DOHC   ② Turbocharged   ③ SOHC

CRANKSHAFT AND CONNECTING ROD SPECIFICATIONS

All measurements are given in inches.

Year	Engine Displacement cu. in. (cc)	Crankshaft Main Brg. Journal Dia.	Main Brg. Oil Clearance	Shaft End-play	Thrust on No.	Connecting Rod Journal Diameter	Oil Clearance	Side Clearance
1987	90 (1471)	1.8865–1.8873	0.0008–0.0020	0.0024–0.0095	2	1.5720–1.5726	0.0010–0.0023	0.0079–0.0138
	118.9 (1949)	2.2016–2.2022	0.0008–0.0025	0.0024–0.0094	3	1.929	0.0007–0.0029	0.0078–0.0130
	121.7 (1994)	2.2032–2.2038	0.0009–0.0020	0.0024–0.0099	3	1.9276–1.9282	0.0012–0.0024	0.0078–0.0130
1988	90 (1471)	1.8865–1.8873	0.0008–0.0020	0.0024–0.0095	2	1.5720–1.5726	0.0010–0.0023	0.0079–0.0138
	138 (2254)	2.2032–2.2038	0.0009–0.0020	0.0024–0.0099	3	1.9276–1.9282	0.0012–0.0024	0.0078–0.0130
	121.7 (1994)	2.2032–2.2038	0.0009–0.0020	0.0024–0.0099	3	1.9276–1.9282	0.0012–0.0024	0.0078–0.0130
1989	90 (1471)	1.8865–1.8873	0.0008–0.0020	0.0024–0.0095	2	1.5720–1.5726	0.0010–0.0023	0.0079–0.0138
	92 (1588)	1.8861–1.9171	0.0008–0.0020	0.0024–0.0095	2	1.5718–1.5728	0.0013–0.0024	0.0079–0.0138
	138 (2254)	2.2032–2.2038	0.0009–0.0020	0.0024–0.0099	3	1.9276–1.9282	0.0012–0.0024	0.0078–0.0130
	121.7 (1994)	2.0232–2.2038	0.0009–0.0020	0.0024–0.0099	3	1.9276–1.9282	0.0012–0.0024	0.0078–0.0130
1990	92 (1588)	2.0439–2.0448	0.0008–0.0020	0.0024–0.0095	2	1.5724–1.5728	0.0010–0.0023	0.0079–0.0138
1991	92 (1588) ①	2.0243	0.0008–0.0020	0.0024–0.0099	2	1.5526	0.0010–0.0023	0.0074–0.0138
	92 (1588) ②	2.0439–2.0448	0.0008–0.0020	0.0024–0.0099	2	1.5724–1.5728	0.0010–0.0023	0.0079–0.0138

① SOHC   ② DOHC

11–7

VALVE SPECIFICATIONS

Year	Engine Displacement cu. in. (cc)	Seat Angle (deg.)	Face Angle (deg.)	Spring Test Pressure (lbs.)	Spring Installed Height (in.)	Stem-to-Guide Clearance (in.) Intake	Stem-to-Guide Clearance (in.) Exhaust	Stem Diameter (in.) Intake	Stem Diameter (in.) Exhaust
1987	90 (1471)	45	45	49 @ 1.57	1.57	0.0009–0.0022	0.0012–0.0025	0.274–0.275	0.2740–0.2744
	118.9 (1949)	45	45	55 @ 1.60	1.60	0.0009–0.0022	0.0015–0.0031	0.315	0.3150
	121.7 (1994)	45	45	55 @ 1.62	1.62	0.0009–0.0022	0.0015–0.0031	0.315	0.3150
1988	90 (1471)	45	45	47 @ 1.57	1.57	0.0009–0.0022	0.0012–0.0025	0.274–0.275	0.2740–0.2744
	138 (2254)	45	45	55.3 @ 1.62	1.62	0.0009–0.0022	0.0015–0.0031	0.315	0.3150
	121.7 (1994)	45	45	55.3 @ 1.62	1.62	0.0009–0.0022	0.0015–0.0031	0.315	0.3150
1989	90 (1471)	45	45	47 @ 1.57	1.57	0.0009–0.0022	0.0012–0.0025	0.274–0.275	0.2740–0.2744
	92 (1588)	45	45	52 @ 44	1.52	0.0009–0.0022	0.0018–0.0025	0.234–0.235	0.2340–0.2350
	138 (2254)	45	45	55.3 @ 1.62	1.62	0.0009–0.0022	0.0015–0.0031	0.315	0.3150
	121.7 (1994)	45	45	55.3 @ 1.62	1.62	0.0009–0.0022	0.0015–0.0031	0.315	0.3150
1990	92 (1588)	45	45	44.1 @ 1.504	1.504	0.0009–0.0022	0.0012–0.0025	0.2348–0.2356	0.2346–0.2352
1991	92 (1588) ②	45	45	44.0 @ 1.50	1.504	0.0009–0.0022	0.0012–0.0025	0.2348–0.2356	0.2346–0.2352
	92 (1588) ③	45	45	①	1.504	0.0009–0.0022	0.0012–0.0025	0.2348–0.2356	0.2346–0.2352

① Intake—44.1 @ 1.50 ② DOHC
Exhaust—44.7 @ 1.50 ③ SOHC

PISTON AND RING SPECIFICATIONS

All measurements are given in inches.

Year	Engine Displacement cu. in. (cc)	Piston Clearance	Ring Gap Top Compression	Ring Gap Bottom Compression	Ring Gap Oil Control	Ring Side Clearance Top Compression	Ring Side Clearance Bottom Compression	Ring Side Clearance Oil Control
1987	90 (1471)	0.0010–0.0190	0.0098–0.0138	NA	0.0039–0.0236	0.0010–0.0025	NA	NA
	118.9 (1949)	0.0018–0.0026	0.0120–0.0180	0.0100–0.0160	0.0080–0.0280	0.0010–0.0024	0.0010–0.0024	0.0008
	121.7 (1994)	0.0018–0.0026	0.0120–0.0180	0.0100–0.0160	0.0080–0.0280	0.0010–0.0024	0.0010–0.0024	NA
1988	90 (1471)	0.0011–0.0019	0.0098–0.0138	NA	0.0039–0.0236	0.0010–0.0025	NA	NA
	90 (1471) Turbo	0.0011–0.0019	0.0106–0.0153	0.0098–0.0145	0.0039–0.0236	0.0010–0.0026	0.0008 0.0024	NA
	138 (2254)	0.0016–0.0024	0.0120–0.0180	0.0100–0.0160	0.0080–0.0280	0.0010–0.0024	0.0010–0.0024	NA
	121.7 (1994)	0.0008 0.0016	0.0120–0.0180	0.0100–0.0160	0.0080–0.0280	0.0010–0.0024	0.0010–0.0024	NA

PISTON AND RING SPECIFICATIONS

All measurements are given in inches.

Year	Engine Displacement cu. in. (cc)	Piston Clearance	Ring Gap			Ring Side Clearance		
			Top Compression	Bottom Compression	Oil Control	Top Compression	Bottom Compression	Oil Control
1989	90 (1471)	0.0011–0.0019	0.0098–0.0138	NA	0.0039–0.0236	0.0010–0.0025	NA	NA
	90 (1471) Turbo	0.0011–0.0019	0.0106–0.0153	0.0098–0.0145	0.0039–0.0236	0.0010–0.0026	0.0008–0.0024	NA
	92 (1588)	0.0019–0.0027	0.0110–0.0157	0.0177–0.0236	0.0039–0.0236	0.0018–0.0032	0.0008 0.0024	NA
	138 (2254)	0.0016–0.0024	0.0120–0.0180	0.0100–0.0160	0.0080–0.0280	0.0010–0.0024	0.0010–0.0024	NA
	121.7 (1994)	0.0008 0.0016	0.0120–0.0180	0.0100–0.0160	0.0080–0.0280	0.0010–0.0024	0.0010–0.0024	NA
1990	92 (1588)	0.0019–0.0027	0.0110–0.0157	0.0177–0.0236	0.0039–0.0236	0.0018–0.0032	0.0008–0.0024	NA
1991	92 (1588)	0.0011–0.0019	0.0110–0.0157	0.0177–0.0236	0.0039–0.0236	0.0018–0.0032	0.0008–0.0024	NA

TORQUE SPECIFICATIONS

All readings in ft. lbs.

Year	Engine Displacement cu. in. (cc)	Cylinder Head Bolts	Main Bearing Bolts	Rod Bearing Bolts	Crankshaft Pulley Bolts	Flywheel Bolts	Manifold		Spark Plugs
							Intake	Exhaust	
1987	90 (1471)	③	68	25	108	22④	17	17	11–14
	118.9 (1949)	①	65–79	42–45	87	72–79	13–18	16	11–14
	121.7 (1994)	①	72	43	87	43	13–18	16	11–14
1988	90 (1471)	③	68	25	108	22④	17	17	11–14
	138 (2254)	①	72	43	87	43	13–18	16	11–14
	121.7 (1994)	①	72	43	87	40	13–18	16	11–14
1989	90 (1471)	③	68	25	108	22④	17	17	11–14
	92 (1588)	③	65	⑤	123	⑥	17	30	11–14
	138 (2254)	①	72	43	87	43	13–18	16	11–14
	121.7 (1994)	①	72	43	87	40	13–18	16	11–14
1990	92 (1588)	③	65②	⑤	109	⑥	17	30	11–14
1991	92 (1588)	③	65②	⑤	123	⑥	17	30	11–14

① 1st step—62 ft. lbs.
　2nd step—72 ft. lbs.
② 1st step—35 ft. lbs.
　2nd step—65 ft. lbs.
③ 1st step—29 ft. lbs.
　2nd step—58 ft. lbs.
④ Turn the bolt an additional 45 degrees
⑤ 1st step—11 ft. lbs.
　2nd step—turn an additional 45-60 degrees
⑥ 1st step—22 ft. lbs.
　2nd step—turn an additional 45-60 degrees

BRAKE SPECIFICATIONS

All measurements in inches unless noted.

Year	Model	Lug Nut Torque (ft. lbs.)	Master Cylinder Bore	Brake Disc		Standard Brake Drum Diameter	Minimum Lining Thickness	
				Minimum Thickness	Maximum Runout		Front	Rear
1987	I-Mark	65①	0.810	0.378	0.0059	7.09	0.039	0.039
	Impulse	80–94	0.874	0.654	0.0051	NA	0.120	0.120

BRAKE SPECIFICATIONS
All measurements in inches unless noted.

Year	Model	Lug Nut Torque (ft. lbs.)	Master Cylinder Bore	Brake Disc Minimum Thickness	Brake Disc Maximum Runout	Standard Brake Drum Diameter	Minimum Lining Thickness Front	Minimum Lining Thickness Rear
1988	I-Mark	65①	0.810	0.378	0.0059	7.09	0.039	0.039
	I-Mark (Turbo)	65①	0.875	0.378	0.0059	7.09	0.039	0.039
	Impulse	87	0.875	0.654	0.0051	NA	0.120	0.120
	Impulse (Turbo)	87	0.875	0.654	0.0051	NA	0.120	0.120
1989	I-Mark	65①	0.810	0.378	0.0059	7.09	0.039	0.039
	I-Mark (Turbo)	65①	0.875	0.378	0.0059	7.09	0.039	0.039
	I-Mark (DOHC)	65①	0.875	0.378	0.0059	7.09	0.039	0.039
	Impulse	87	0.875	0.654	0.0051	NA	0.120	0.120
	Impulse (Turbo)	87	0.875	0.654	0.0051	NA	0.120	0.120
1990	Impulse	87	0.875	②	0.0059	—	0.039	0.039
1991	Impulse	87	0.875	0.866③	0.0050	—	0.039	0.039
	Stylus	87	0.875	0.866③	0.0050	7.87	0.039	0.039

① Aluminum wheels—86 ft. lbs.
② Front—0.81
Rear—0.29
③ Rear—0.30

WHEEL ALIGNMENT

Year	Model	Caster Range (deg.)	Caster Preferred Setting (deg.)	Camber Range (deg.)	Camber Preferred Setting (deg.)	Toe-in (in.)	Steering Axis Inclination (deg.)
1987	I-Mark	$1^3/_4$P–$2^3/_4$P	$2^1/_4$P	$^{11}/_{16}$N–$1^5/_{16}$P	$^5/_{16}$P	0	$11^{13}/_{16}$
	Impulse	$3^1/_2$P–6P	$4^3/_4$P	1N–$^1/_2$P	0	$^1/_{16}$	8
1988	I-Mark	$1^3/_4$P–$2^3/_4$P	$2^1/_4$P	$^{11}/_{16}$P–$1^5/_{16}$P	1P	0	$11^{13}/_{16}$
	I-Mark (Turbo)	$1^3/_4$P–$2^3/_4$P	$2^1/_4$P	$^1/_2$P–$1^1/_2$P	1P	0	$12^1/_8$
	Impulse	$1^3/_4$P–$2^3/_4$P	3P	$^1/_2$N–$^1/_2$P	0	0	8
	Impulse (Turbo)	$4^3/_4$P–$5^1/_4$P	5P	$^1/_2$N–$^1/_2$P	0	0	8
1989	I-Mark	$1^3/_4$P–$2^3/_4$P	$2^1/_4$P	$^{11}/_{16}$P–$1^5/_{16}$P	1P	0	$11^{13}/_{16}$
	I-Mark (Turbo)	$1^3/_4$P–$2^3/_4$P	$2^1/_4$P	$^1/_2$P–$1^1/_2$P	1P	0	$12^1/_8$
	I-Mark (DOHC)	$1^3/_4$P–$2^3/_4$P	$2^1/_4$P	$^1/_2$P–$1^1/_2$P	1P	0	$12^1/_8$
	Impulse	$1^3/_4$P–$2^3/_4$P	3P	$^1/_2$N–$^1/_2$P	0	0	8
	Impulse (Turbo)	$4^3/_4$P–$5^1/_4$P	5P	$^1/_2$N–$^1/_2$P	0	0	8
1990	Impulse	2P–4P	3P	$1^1/_4$N–$^1/_4$P	$^1/_2$N	0	NA
1991	Impulse	2P–4P	3P	$1^1/_4$N–$^1/_4$P	$^1/_2$N	$^1/_{32}$–$^3/_{32}$	NA
	Stylus	2P–4P	3P	$1^1/_4$N–$^1/_4$P	$^1/_2$N	$^1/_{32}$–$^3/_{32}$	NA

NOTE: Caster angle is pre-set and cannot be serviced
N Negative
P Positive

ENGINE ELECTRICAL

NOTE: Disconnecting the negative battery cable on some vehicles may interfere with the functions of the on board computer systems and may require the computer to undergo a relearning process, once the negative battery cable is reconnected.

Distributor

Removal

1. Turn the engine over and bring the No. 1 piston up to TDC on the compression stroke.
2. Disconnect the negative battery cable.
3. Remove the distributor cap and disconnect the electrical connectors from the distributor.
4. Mark the position of the distributor rotor in relation to the distributor housing and the distributor housing in relation to the cylinder head or block.
5. Remove the distributor hold-down bolt and remove the distributor.

Installation

TIMING NOT DISTURBED

1. Install the distributor, aligning the marks that were made during the removal procedure.
2. Install the distributor hold-down bolt and tighten temporarily.
3. Connect the distributor electrical connectors and install the distributor cap.
4. Connect the negative battery cable, start the engine, check the ignition timing and adjust, as necessary. Tighten the distributor hold-down bolt.

TIMING DISTURBED

1. Disconnect the spark plug wire and remove the spark plug from the No. 1 cylinder.
2. Place a finger over the spark plug hole and rotate the crankshaft until compression is felt.
3. Align the notched line on the crankshaft pulley with the **0** mark on the timing scale of the timing cover.
4. Install the distributor so the distributor rotor points to the No. 1 spark plug wire tower of the distributor cap.
5. Install the distributor hold-down bolt and tighten temporarily.
6. Connect the distributor electrical connectors and install the distributor cap.
7. Install the No. 1 spark plug and connect the No. 1 spark plug wire.
8. Connect the negative battery cable, start the engine and adjust the ignition timing. Tighten the distributor hold-down bolt.

Camshaft Sensor

Removal

1. Rotate the engine and bring up the No. 1 cylinder to top dead center of its compression stroke.

NOTE: To bring the engine to TDC of the No. 1 compression stroke, remove the spark plug for the No. cylinder. With the engine cool, turn the crankshaft over until compression is forced out of the spark plug hole. Watch the crankshaft damper while feeling for compression. When compression is felt, align the mark on the crankshaft damper with the O° mark on the timing cover.

2. Disconnect the negative battery cable. Disconnect and tag (if necessary) all the electrical connectors along with the spark plug wires from the distributor.

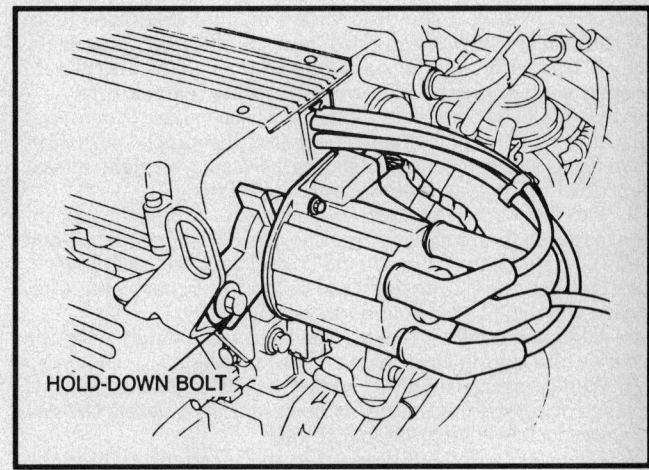

Distributor location—4XE1 engine

3. Remove the intercooler and disconnect the sensor electrical connector.
4. Remove the mounting bolt and camshaft angle sensor.

Installation

1. Install the sensor to its original position and install the mounting bolt.
2. Connect the wiring connectors.
3. Install the intercooler and connect the battery cable.
4. Start the engine and adjust the timing.

Ignition Timing

Adjustment

NOTE: The timing marks are located at the front of the crankshaft pulley and consist of a graduated scale attached to the timing cover and a notch in the crankshaft pulley.

G200Z, 4ZC1-T AND 4ZD1 ENGINES

1. Locate and clean off the timing marks. Highlight the marks with paint or chalk.
2. Connect the timing light lead to the No. 1 spark plug wire.
3. Start the engine and allow it to reach operating temperature. Make sure the engine idle speed is correct.
4. Aim the timing light at the marks and check the position of the crankshaft pulley notch on the timing scale. If necessary, adjust the timing by loosening the distributor hold-down bolt and turning the distributor to the correct specification.
5. After timing is set to specifications, tighten the distributor hold-down bolt and remove the timing light connections.

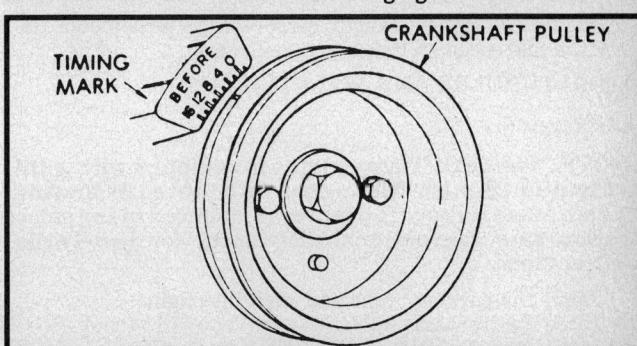

Timing mark alignment—G200Z engine

4XC1-U ENGINE

1. Set the parking brake and block the drive wheels. Place the selector lever in **N** if equipped with a manual transaxle. Place the select lever in **P** if equipped with an automatic transaxle. The air cleaner should be installed and the choke valve should be open and the engine at normal operating temperature.

2. Turn all electrical equipment off. If the vehicle is equipped with air conditioning it should be off also. If equipped with power steering the front wheels should be facing straight ahead. Wait until the engine cooling fan stops rotating.

3. The distributor vacuum line from the carburetor and intake manifold, the canister purge line, the EGR vacuum line and the ITC valve vacuum line should be disconnected and plugged.

4. Connect the timing light lead to the No. 1 spark plug wire. Loosen the distributor hold-down bolt (slightly).

5. Align the notched line on the crankshaft pulley with the mark on the timing cover using the timing light.

6. While aligning the notched line on the crankshaft pulley, advance or retard the timing, as necessary, by turning the distributor clockwise or counterclockwise.

7. After the timing has been set to specifications, tighten the distributor hold-down bolt and re-check the timing.

NOTE: Be sure the distributor body does not move together with the hold-down bolt.

8. Reconnect all vacuum lines and remove all test equipment, except for the tachometer.

9. Re-check the idle speed and adjust, as necessary.

4XC1-T AND 1989 I-MARK 4XE1 ENGINES

1. Check the ECM for trouble codes. If codes are found, repair or replace the problem sensor or circuit, as necessary.

2. Check all the vacuum lines for the proper routing.

3. Set the parking brake and block the drive wheels. Place the selector lever in **N**. The engine should be at normal operating temperature.

4. Turn all electrical equipment off. If equipped with air conditioning it should be off also. If equipped with power steering the front wheels should be facing straight ahead. Wait until the engine cooling fan stops rotating.

5. Connect the timing light lead to the No. 1 spark plug wire. Loosen the distributor hold-down bolt (slightly).

6. Align the notched line on the crankshaft pulley with the mark on the timing cover using the timing light.

7. While aligning the notched line on the crankshaft pulley, advance or retard the timing, as necessary, by turning the distributor clockwise or counterclockwise.

8. After the timing has been set to specifications, tighten the distributor hold-down bolt and re-check the timing.

NOTE: Be sure the distributor body does not move together with the hold-down bolt. The ignition timing is controlled by the ECM according to the engine operating conditions. Therefore, there are no external vacuum lines to the distributor.

9. Remove all test equipment, except for the tachometer. Re-check the idle speed and adjust, as necessary.

1990–91 IMPULSE AND 1991 STYLUS

4XE1 Engine

NOTE: The 4XE1 Turbo engine is equipped with a Direct Ignition System. Timing can be adjusted by moving the cam angle sensor. The sensor is mounted in the same location as a conventional distributor for non-Turbo 4XE1 engines.

1. Apply the parking brake and start the engine.
2. Place the transaxle in **N**.
3. Make sure the CHECK ENGINE light is not on.
4. Locate the ALDL connector under the right hand side of the instrument panel. Connect the terminals on both ends of the ALDL connector with a jumper wire.

5. Connect the timing light lead to the No. 1 spark plug wire.

6. Using the timing light, check that the center of fluctuation of a white notched line on the crankshaft pulley against the scale on the timing cover is between 9–11 degrees BTDC. If the fluctuation is too large, open the throttle valve a little to increase the engine speed to 1500–2000 rpm. The fluctuation will be reduced so the timing can be confirmed.

7. If the timing is incorrect, loosen the hold-down bolt on the distributor or cam angle sensor and turn the assembly clockwise or counterclockwise to adjust the timing. After adjustment, tighten the bolt to 17 ft. lbs. (24 Nm).

NOTE: When tightening the distributor or cam angle sensor hold-down bolt, make sure the assembly body does not rotate together with the mounting bolt.

8. Remove the jumper wire from the ALDL connector.

Alternator

Precautions

Several precautions must be observed with alternator equipped vehicles to avoid damage to the unit.

• If the battery is removed for any reason, make sure it is reconnected with the correct polarity. Reversing the battery connections may result in damage to the one-way rectifiers.

• When utilizing a booster battery as a starting aid, always connect the positive to positive terminals and the negative terminal from the booster battery to a good engine ground on the vehicle being started.

• Never use a fast charger as a booster to start vehicles.

• Disconnect the battery cables when charging the battery with a fast charger.

• Never attempt to polarize the alternator.

• Do not use test lamps of more than 12 volts when checking diode continuity.

• Do not short across or ground any of the alternator terminals.

• The polarity of the battery, alternator and regulator must be matched and considered before making any electrical connections within the system.

• Never separate the alternator on an open circuit. Make sure all connections within the circuit are clean and tight.

• Disconnect the battery ground terminal when performing any service on electrical components.

• Disconnect the battery if arc welding is to be done on the vehicle.

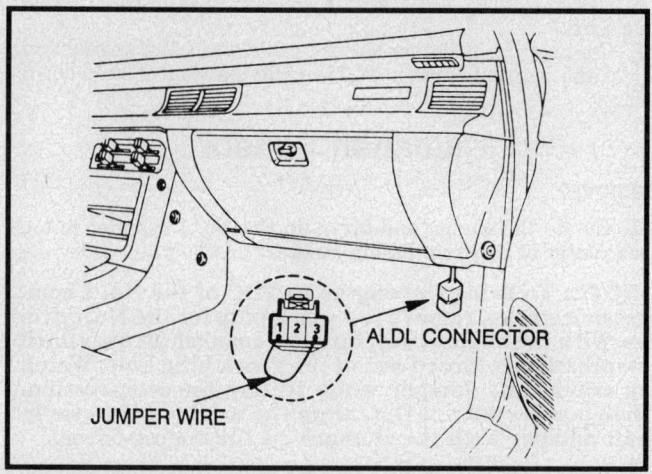

ALDL connector location—1990–91 Impulse and 1991 Stylus

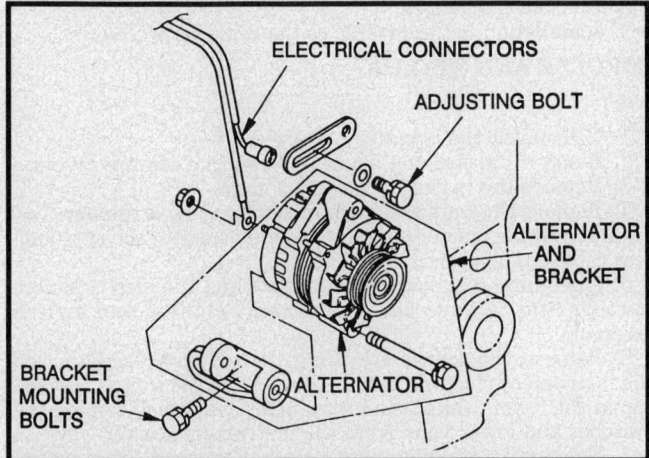

ELECTRICAL CONNECTORS

ADJUSTING BOLT

ALTERNATOR AND BRACKET

ALTERNATOR

BRACKET MOUNTING BOLTS

Alternator Installation—1990–91 Impulse and 1991 Stylus

Belt Tension Adjustment

I-MARK, 1990–91 IMPULSE AND 1991 STYLUS

1. Check the belt tension between the pulleys using a suitable belt tension gauge. The tension should be 70–110 lbs.
2. If the tension is incorrect, loosen the alternator pivot and adjusting bolts. Pry on the alternator until the proper belt tension is obtained.

1987–89 IMPULSE

1. Check the belt tension by applying approximately 22 lbs. (10 kg) of finger pressure to the belt between the pulleys and measuring the belt deflection. The belt should deflect 0.4 in. (10mm) on G200Z engines or 0.16–0.2 in. (4–5mm) on all others.
2. If the tension is incorrect, loosen the alternator pivot and adjusting bolts. Pry on the alternator until the proper belt deflection is obtained.

Removal and Installation

I-MARK AND 1987–89 IMPULSE

1. Disconnect the negative battery cable.
2. Disconnect the electrical connections at the back of the alternator and tag the wires for reassembly.
3. Loosen the pivot and adjusting bolts and remove the alternator belt.
4. Remove the mounting bolts and the alternator.
5. Installation is the reverse of the removal procedure. Adjust the belt tension.

1990–1991 STYUS AND IMPULSE

1. **Disconnect the negative (−) battery cable.**
2. Remove the right tie rod end, lower ball joint and driveshaft (4WD only).
3. Remove the adjuster plate bolt.
4. Disconnect the electrical connector.
5. Remove the alternator bracket bolts, alternator and bracket.

To install:

6. Install the alternator bracket bolts, alternator and bracket.
7. Connect the electrical connector.
8. Install the adjuster plate bolt.
9. Install the right tie rod end, lower ball joint and driveshaft (4WD only).
10. Connect the negative (−) battery cable.

Starter

Removal and Installation

1. Disconnect the negative battery cable.
2. Disconnect the electrical connectors at the starter.
3. Remove the starter mounting nuts or bolts and remove the starter.
4. Installation is the reverse of the removal procedure.

CHASSIS ELECTRICAL

—————— CAUTION ——————

On vehicles equipped with an air bag, the negative battery cable must be disconnected, before working on the system. Failure to do so may result in deployment of the air bag and possible personal injury.

Heater Blower Motor

Removal and Installation

1. Disconnect the negative battery cable.
2. Disconnect the wire connector from the blower motor.
3. Disconnect the rubber hose on vehicles equipped with air conditioning.
4. Remove the retaining clip and the blower motor.
5. Installation is the reverse of the removal procedure.

Windshield Wiper Motor

Removal and Installation
FRONT

1. Disconnect the negative battery cable.
2. Remove the wiper arm cap, nut and the wiper arm and blade.
3. Remove the cowl cover, if equipped.
4. Disconnect the wiper motor from the wiper linkage.
5. Disconnect the electrical connectors.
6. Remove the mounting bolts and the wiper motor.
7. Installation is the reverse of the removal procedure. Be sure to apply grease to the crank arm ball joint.

REAR

1. Disconnect the negative battery cable.
2. Remove the cover, nut and rear wiper arm and blade.
3. Remove the rear hatch trim panel, if equipped.
4. Disconnect the electrical connector at the wiper motor.
5. On I-Mark, remove the wiper motor mounting bolts, disconnect the wiper motor from the wiper linkage and remove the wiper motor.
6. On Impulse, remove the nut, cap washer and seal. Remove the wiper motor mounting bolts and remove the wiper motor.
7. Installation is the reverse of the removal procedure.

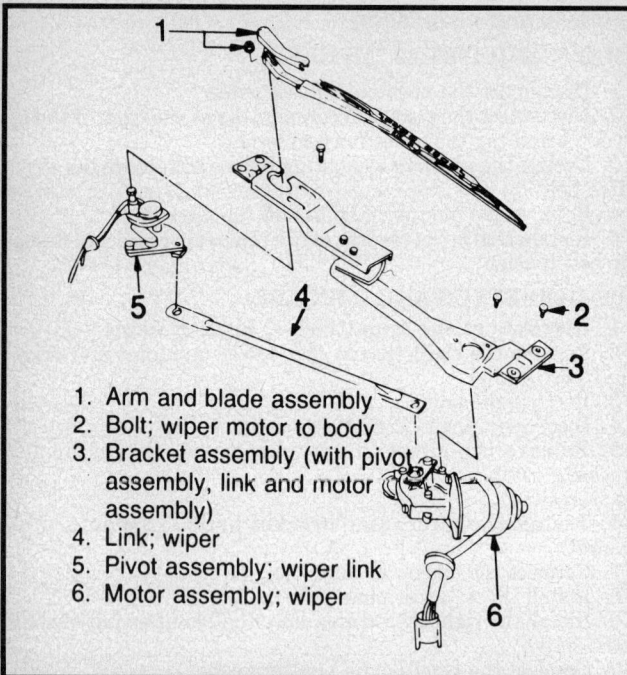

1. Arm and blade assembly
2. Bolt; wiper motor to body
3. Bracket assembly (with pivot assembly, link and motor assembly)
4. Link; wiper
5. Pivot assembly; wiper link
6. Motor assembly; wiper

Front wiper motor and linkage—1987–89 Impulse

Windshield Wiper Switch

Removal and Installation

I-MARK, 1990–91 IMPULSE AND 1991 STYLUS

1. Disconnect the negative battery cable.
2. Remove the instrument cluster hood attaching screws. Disconnect the electrical connectors so the hood can be removed.
3. Remove the instrument cluster, if necessary.
4. Remove the windshield wiper switch.
5. Installation is the reverse of the removal procedure.

1987–89 IMPULSE

1. Disconnect the negative battery cable.
2. Remove the instrument cluster and switch assembly.
3. Remove the screws attaching the switch and the instrument cluster lower hood.
4. Remove the switch harness clip located at the lower rear of the instrument cluster.
5. Remove the lower hood and switch together and separate them.
6. Installation is the reverse of the removal procedure.

Instrument Cluster

Removal and Installation

I-MARK

1. Disconnect the negative battery cable.
2. Remove the instrument cluster hood attaching screws and the instrument cluster hood.
3. Disconnect the electrical connectors at the instrument cluster.
4. Remove the instrument cluster attaching screws and the instrument cluster.
5. Remove the trip meter reset knob and the instrument cluster screen.
6. Remove the gauge surround and the buzzer, if equipped.
7. Remove the sockets and bulbs.

8. Remove the gauges.
9. Installation is the reverse of the removal procedure.

IMPULSE AND STYLUS

1987

1. Disconnect the negative battery cable.
2. Remove the steering wheel and steering column covers.
3. Remove the instrument cluster hood.
4. Remove the nuts and bolts retaining the instrument cluster and pull the cluster outward to gain access to the speedometer cable and electrical connectors.
5. Disconnect the speedometer cable and the electrical connectors and remove the instrument cluster and switch assembly.
6. Remove the screws attaching the switch assemblies and the instrument cluster lower hood. Remove the switch harness clip at the lower rear of the instrument cluster and remove the switches and lower hood from the instrument cluster.
7. Remove the trip meter reset knob. Remove the instrument cluster screen by unlocking the hooks. Remove the gauge surround by unlocking the hooks.
8. Remove the speedometer by removing the retaining nuts and screws.
9. Installation is the reverse of the removal procedure.

1988–89

1. Disconnect the negative battery cable.
2. Remove the steering wheel.
3. Remove the front console and radio assembly.
4. Remove the lower instrument panel cover and hood lock release lever.
5. Remove the left knee pad and the steering column covers.
6. Remove the instrument cluster hood.
7. Remove the nuts and bolts retaining the instrument cluster and pull the cluster outward to gain access to the speedometer cable and electrical connectors.
8. Disconnect the speedometer cable and the electrical connectors and remove the instrument cluster and switch assembly.
9. Remove the screws attaching the switch assemblies and the instrument cluster lower hood. Remove the switch harness clip at the lower rear of the instrument cluster and remove the switches and lower hood from the instrument cluster.
10. Remove the trip meter reset knob. Remove the instrument cluster screen by unlocking the hooks. Remove the gauge surround by unlocking the hooks.
11. Remove the speedometer by removing the retaining nuts and screws.
12. Installation is the reverse of the removal procedure.

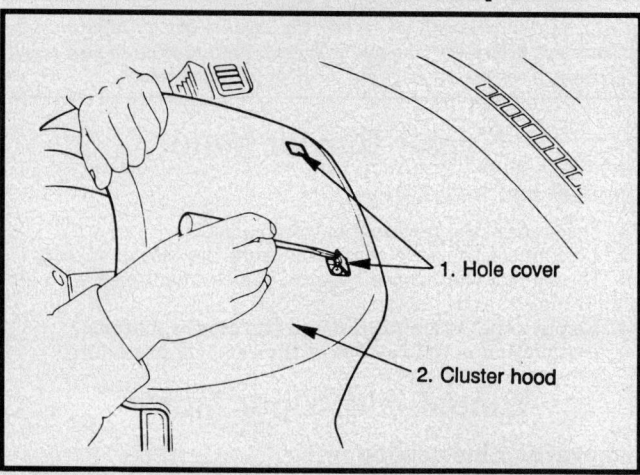

1. Hole cover
2. Cluster hood

Removing cluster hood screw covers—1990–91 Impulse and 1991 Stylus

1990–91

1. Disconnect the negative battery cable.
2. Remove the instrument cluster hood screw hole covers and remove the hood attaching screws.
3. Disconnect the lighting and windshield wiper switch connectors and remove the instrument cluster hood.
4. Disconnect the speedometer cable and electrical connectors from the instrument cluster.
5. Remove the instrument cluster.
6. Remove the trip meter and clock reset knob and the gauge screen.
7. Remove the instrument cluster bezel and remove the speedometer from the gauge case.
8. Installation is the reverse of the removal procedure.

Concealed Headlights

Manual Operation

1. Raise the hood and disconnect the electrical connector at the headlight cover motor.
2. Turn the manual operation knob located on the headlight cover motor to open or close the headlight covers.

Headlight Switch

Removal and Installation

I-MARK, 1990–91 IMPULSE AND 1991 STYLUS

1. Disconnect the negative battery cable.
2. Remove the instrument cluster hood attaching screws. Disconnect the electrical connectors so the hood can be removed.

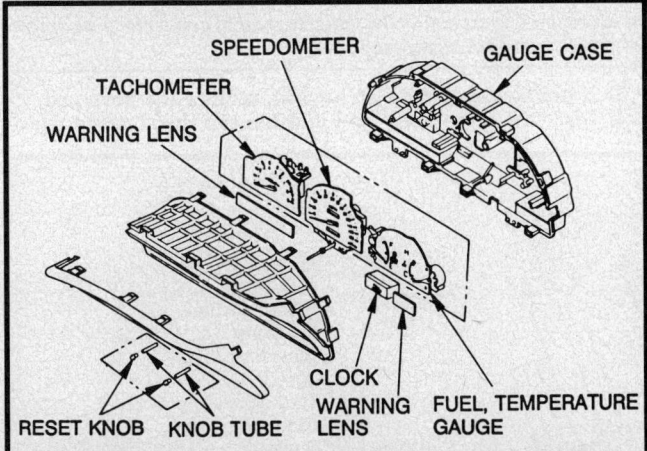

Instrument cluster assembly—1990–91 Impulse and 1991 Stylus

Headlight cover manual operation—1987 Impulse

3. Remove the instrument cluster, if necessary.
4. Remove the headlight switch.
5. Installation is the reverse of the removal procedure.

1987–89 IMPULSE

1. Disconnect the negative battery cable.
2. Remove the instrument cluster and switch assembly.
3. Remove the screws attaching the switch and the instrument cluster lower hood.
4. Remove the switch harness clip located at the lower rear of the instrument cluster.
5. Remove the lower hood and switch together and separate them.
6. Installation is the reverse of the removal procedure.

Dimmer Switch

Removal and Installation

I-MARK

1. Disconnect the negative battery cable.
2. Remove the steering wheel.
3. Remove the upper and lower steering column covers.
4. Disconnect the switch electrical connector from the harness.
5. Remove the switch attaching screws and remove the switch.

1987–89 IMPULSE

1. Disconnect the negative battery cable.
2. Remove the instrument cluster and switch assembly.
3. Remove the screws attaching the switch and the instrument cluster lower hood.
4. Remove the switch harness clip located at the lower rear of the instrument cluster.
5. Remove the lower hood and switch together and separate them.
6. Installation is the reverse of the removal procedure.

1990–91 IMPULSE AND 1991 STYLUS

1. Disconnect the negative battery cable.
2. Place the front wheels in the straight ahead position and the ignition key in the **LOCK** position.
3. From the lower side of the steering wheel, remove the 4 bolts holding the Supplemental Inflatable Restraint (SIR) module to the steering wheel. Disconnect the module connector and remove the SIR module.

----------- CAUTION -----------
The SIR module should always be carried with the urethane cover away from the body and should always be laid on a flat surface with the urethane side up. This is necessary because a free space is provided to allow the air cushion to expand in the unlikely event of accidental deployment. Otherwise, personal injury may result.

4. Disconnect the horn lead and remove the steering wheel nut. Use a suitable steering wheel puller to remove the steering wheel.
5. Remove the knee pad and the steering column cover.
6. Disconnect the electrical connector from the coil/switch assembly.
7. Remove the retaining screws and the coil/switch assembly.
8. Separate the coil from the switch.
9. Installation is the reverse of the removal procedure.

NOTE: Whenever the coil/switch assembly is be replaced, the vehicle's front wheels must be straight ahead. Failure to do so will cause the coil assembly to be removed without being centered. Installing an uncentered coil assembly can cause damage to the coil assembly.

Turn Signal Switch

Removal and Installation

I-MARK

1. Disconnect the negative battery cable.
2. Remove the steering wheel.
3. Remove the upper and lower steering column covers.
4. Disconnect the switch electrical connector from the harness.
5. Remove the switch attaching screws and remove the switch.

1987–89 IMPULSE

1. Disconnect the negative battery cable.
2. Remove the instrument cluster and switch assembly.
3. Remove the screws attaching the switch and the instrument cluster lower hood.
4. Remove the switch harness clip located at the lower rear of the instrument cluster.
5. Remove the lower hood and switch together and separate them.
6. Installation is the reverse of the removal procedure.

1990–91 IMPULSE AND 1991 STYLUS

1. Disconnect the negative battery cable.
2. Place the front wheels in the straight ahead position and the ignition key in the **LOCK** position.
3. From the lower side of the steering wheel, remove the 4 bolts holding the Supplemental Inflatable Restraint (SIR) module to the steering wheel. Disconnect the module connector and remove the SIR module.

—————————— CAUTION ——————————

The SIR module should always be carried with the urethane cover away from the body and should always be laid on a flat surface with the urethane side up. This is necessary because a free space is provided to allow the air cushion to expand in the unlikely event of accidental deployment. Otherwise, personal injury may result.

4. Disconnect the horn lead and remove the steering wheel nut. Use a suitable steering wheel puller to remove the steering wheel.
5. Remove the knee pad and the steering column cover.
6. Disconnect the electrical connector from the coil/switch assembly.
7. Remove the retaining screws and the coil/switch assembly.
8. Separate the coil from the switch.
9. Installation is the reverse of the removal procedure.

NOTE: Whenever the coil/switch assembly is be replaced, the vehicle's front wheels must be straight ahead. Failure to do so will cause the coil assembly to be removed without being centered. Installing an uncentered coil assembly can cause damage to the coil assembly.

Ignition Lock/Switch

Removal and Installation

1. Disconnect the negative battery cable.
2. If equipped with an air bag, perform the following procedure:
   a. Place the front wheels in the straight ahead position and the ignition key in the **LOCK** position.
   b. From the lower side of the steering wheel, remove the 4 bolts holding the Supplemental Inflatable Restraint (SIR) module to the steering wheel. Disconnect the module connector and remove the SIR module.

—————————— CAUTION ——————————

The SIR module should always be carried with the urethane cover away from the body and should always be laid on a flat surface with the urethane side up. This is necessary because a free space is provided to allow the air cushion to expand in the unlikely event of accidental deployment. Otherwise, personal injury may result.

3. If not equipped with an air bag, remove the horn pad.
4. Disconnect the horn lead and remove the steering wheel

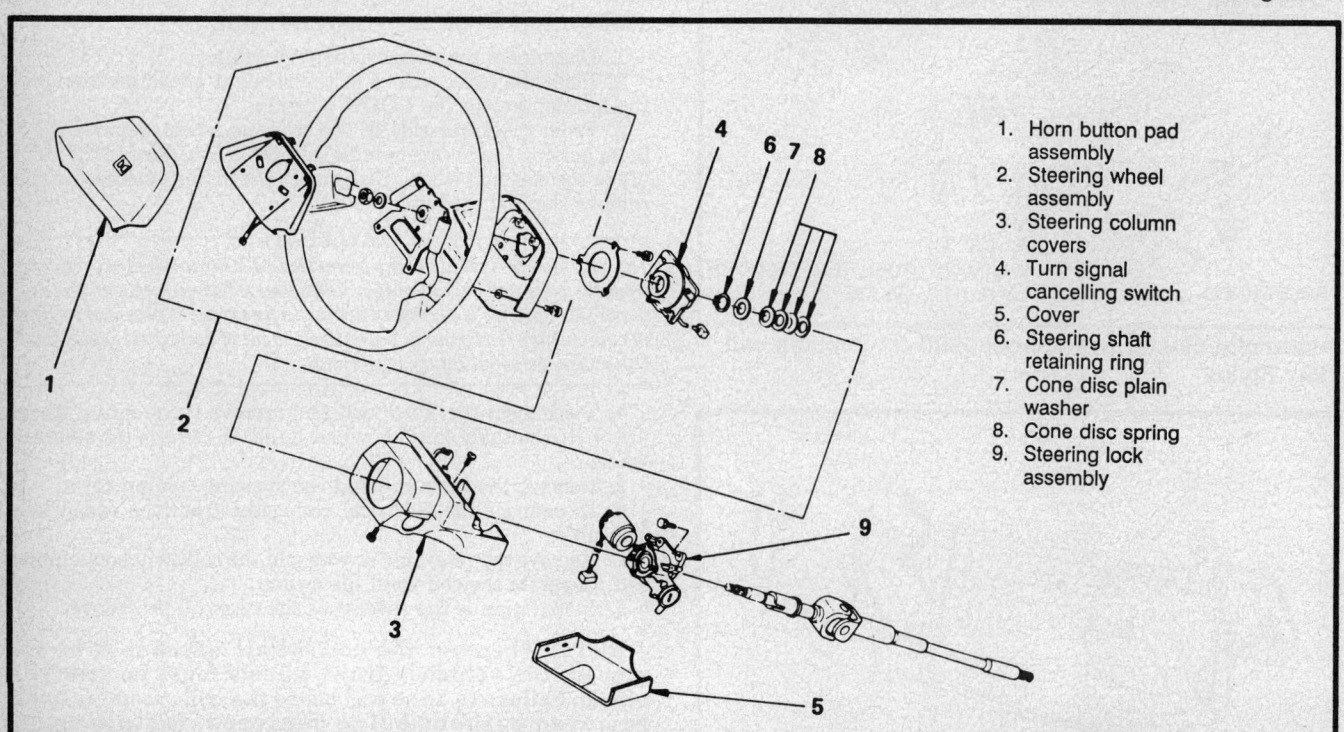

1. Horn button pad assembly
2. Steering wheel assembly
3. Steering column covers
4. Turn signal cancelling switch
5. Cover
6. Steering shaft retaining ring
7. Cone disc plain washer
8. Cone disc spring
9. Steering lock assembly

Steering column assembly—1987–89 Impulse

nut. Use a suitable steering wheel puller to remove the steering wheel.

5. Remove the knee pad on 1990–91 Impulse and 1991 Stylus.

6. Remove the steering column covers.

7. Disconnect the electrical connector and remove the turn signal/dimmer switch assembly on I-Mark. On 1987–89 Impulse, disconnect and remove the turn signal cancelling switch. On 1990–91 Impulse and 1991 Stylus, remove the coil/switch assembly.

8. Remove the steering shaft retaining ring and washer.

9. Disconnect the ignition switch electrical connector, remove the steering lock retaining screws and remove the lock/switch assembly.

10. Installation is the reverse of the removal procedure.

NOTE: Whenever the coil/switch assembly is be replaced, the vehicle's front wheels must be straight ahead. Failure to do so will cause the coil assembly to be removed without being centered. Installing an uncentered coil assembly can cause damage to the coil assembly.

Stoplight Switch

Adjustment

I-MARK, 1990–91 IMPULSE AND 1991 STYLUS

1. Loosen the locknut.
2. Place the tip of the switch so it rests gently against the rubber stopper on the pedal arm.
3. Rotate the stoplight switch until the switch housing contacts lightly with the pedal stopper.

NOTE: Do not attempt to force the brake pushrod into position during the stoplight switch adjustment procedure.

4. Tighten the locknut.

1987–89 IMPULSE

1. Adjust the brake pedal height to 5.630 in. (143mm) with the brake pedal pushrod.
2. Adjust the stoplight switch so the clearance between the switch and the brake pedal is 0.0039 in. (0.1mm).
3. On all except 1987–88 vehicles equipped with 4ZC1-T engine and automatic transmission and all 1989 vehicles, turn the stoplight switch ½ turn and lock into position, so the pedal height is reduced from 5.630 in. (143mm) to 5.52 in. (140mm).

Removal and Installation

1. Disconnect the negative battery cable.
2. Disconnect the electrical connector from the switch.
3. Loosen the locknuts and remove the switch.
4. Installation is the reverse of the removal procedure. Adjust the switch according to the proper procedure.

Clutch Switch

Removal and Installation

1. Disconnect the negative battery cable.
2. Disconnect the electrical connector at the switch.
3. Remove the switch retaining screws and the switch.
4. Installation is the reverse of the removal procedure.

Neutral Safety Switch

Removal and Installation

1. Raise and safely support the vehicle.

2. Disconnect the electrical connector to the switch.
3. Remove the switch from the transmission.
4. Installation is the reverse of the removal procedure.

This adjustment is necessary only if the engine will start with the shift selector in any range except N or P.

5. Loosen the neutral start switch bolt and set the shift selector into the N range.
6. Align the groove and the neutral basic line.
7. Hold it in position and torque the bolt to 9 ft. lbs. (12 Nm).

Fuses

Location

The fuse box is located in the lower left hand corner of the dashboard on all I-Mark and 1987 Impulse. On 1988–89 Impulse, the the fuse box is located on the left kick panel. On 1990–91 Impulse and 1991 Stylus, fuses are located in both the junction block located on the left kick panel and in the relay and fuse box located in the left side of the engine compartment.

All I-Marks except those equipped with the 4XC1-U engine have the air conditioning compressor fuse located behind the left side of the dashboard. The 1988–89 Impulse has the blower fan fuse located under the blower fan case.

Circuit Breakers

Location

All 1988–89 Impulse have a 20A circuit breaker for the power windows and a 30A circuit breaker for the Automatic seat belts located in the fuse box. The 1990–91 Impulse and 1991 Stylus have 2 circuit breaker locations on the junction box, with only 1 being used for the power windows.

Relays

Location

I-MARK

FICD Relay—located in right rear corner of engine compartment.

EFE Heater Relay—located in right rear corner of engine compartment.

Automatic Choke Relay—located in right rear corner of engine compartment.

Fog Lamp Relay—located in left front corner of engine compartment.

Cooling Fan Relay—located in left front corner of engine compartment.

E-Light Relay—located under left side of dashboard.

Convertible Top Relay—located under left side of dashboard.

Rear Defroster Relay—located under left side of dashboard.

Main Relay—located under left side of dashboard.

Restart Relay—located under left side of dashboard.

Air Conditioning Relay—located under left side of dashboard.

Timer Relay—located under dashboard to the right of instrument cluster.

Condenser Fan Relay—4XC1-T engine—located in right front corner of engine compartment.

Fuel Pump Relay—4XC1-T engine—located in right rear of engine compartment.

Air Conditioning Sub Relay—4XC1-T and 4XE1 engines—located in right rear of engine compartment.

IMPULSE

1987–89

Tail Light Relay—located in relay box in right front of engine compartment.

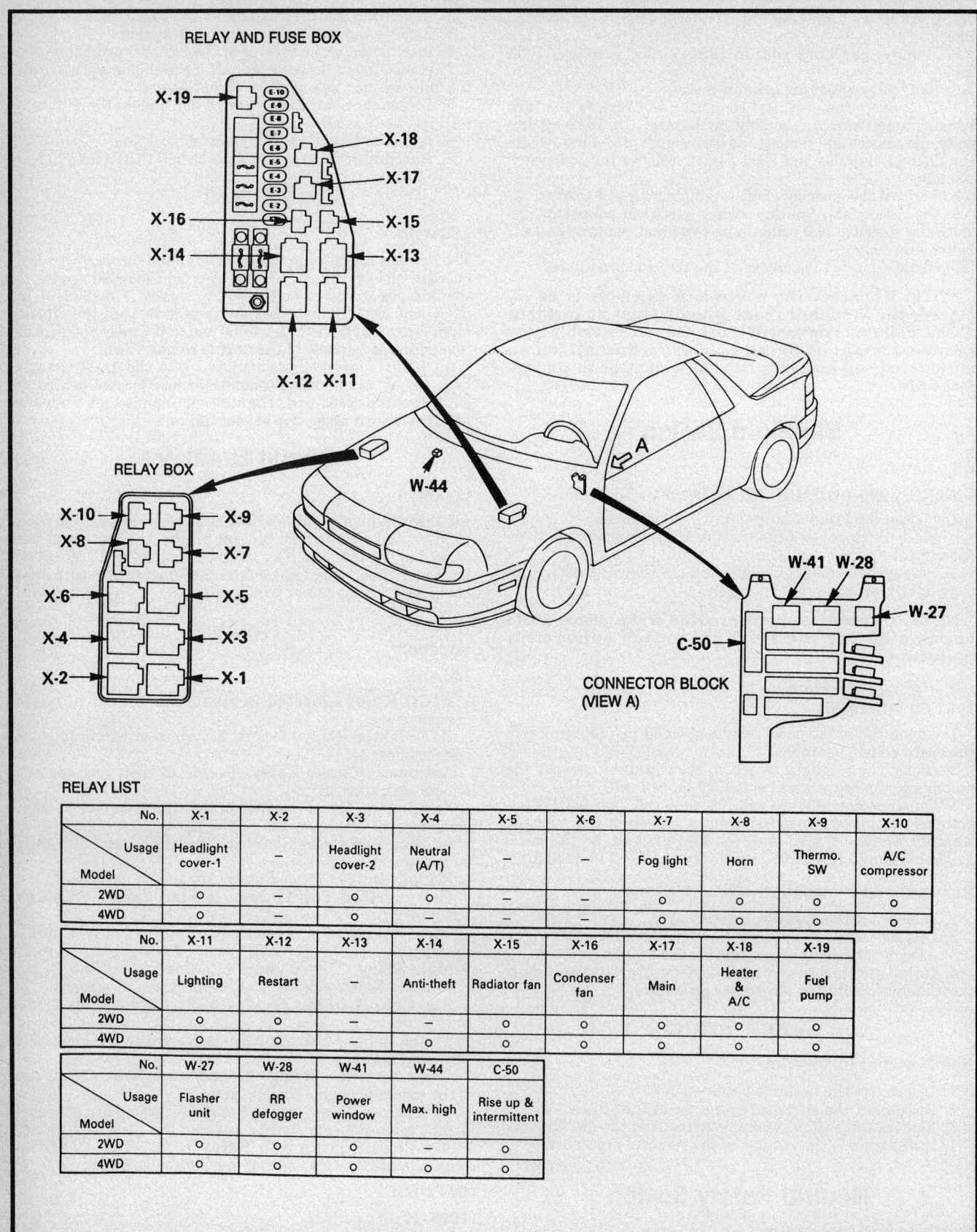

RELAY AND FUSE BOX

RELAY BOX

CONNECTOR BLOCK
(VIEW A)

RELAY LIST

No.	X-1	X-2	X-3	X-4	X-5	X-6	X-7	X-8	X-9	X-10
Usage / Model	Headlight cover-1	–	Headlight cover-2	Neutral (A/T)	–	–	Fog light	Horn	Thermo. SW	A/C compressor
2WD	○	–	○	○	–	–	○	○	○	○
4WD	○	–	○	–	–	–	○	○	○	○

No.	X-11	X-12	X-13	X-14	X-15	X-16	X-17	X-18	X-19
Usage / Model	Lighting	Restart	–	Anti-theft	Radiator fan	Condenser fan	Main	Heater & A/C	Fuel pump
2WD	○	○	–	–	○	○	○	○	○
4WD	○	○	○	–	○	○	○	○	○

No.	W-27	W-28	W-41	W-44	C-50
Usage / Model	Flasher unit	RR defogger	Power window	Max. high	Rise up & intermittent
2WD	○	○	○	–	○
4WD	○	○	○	○	○

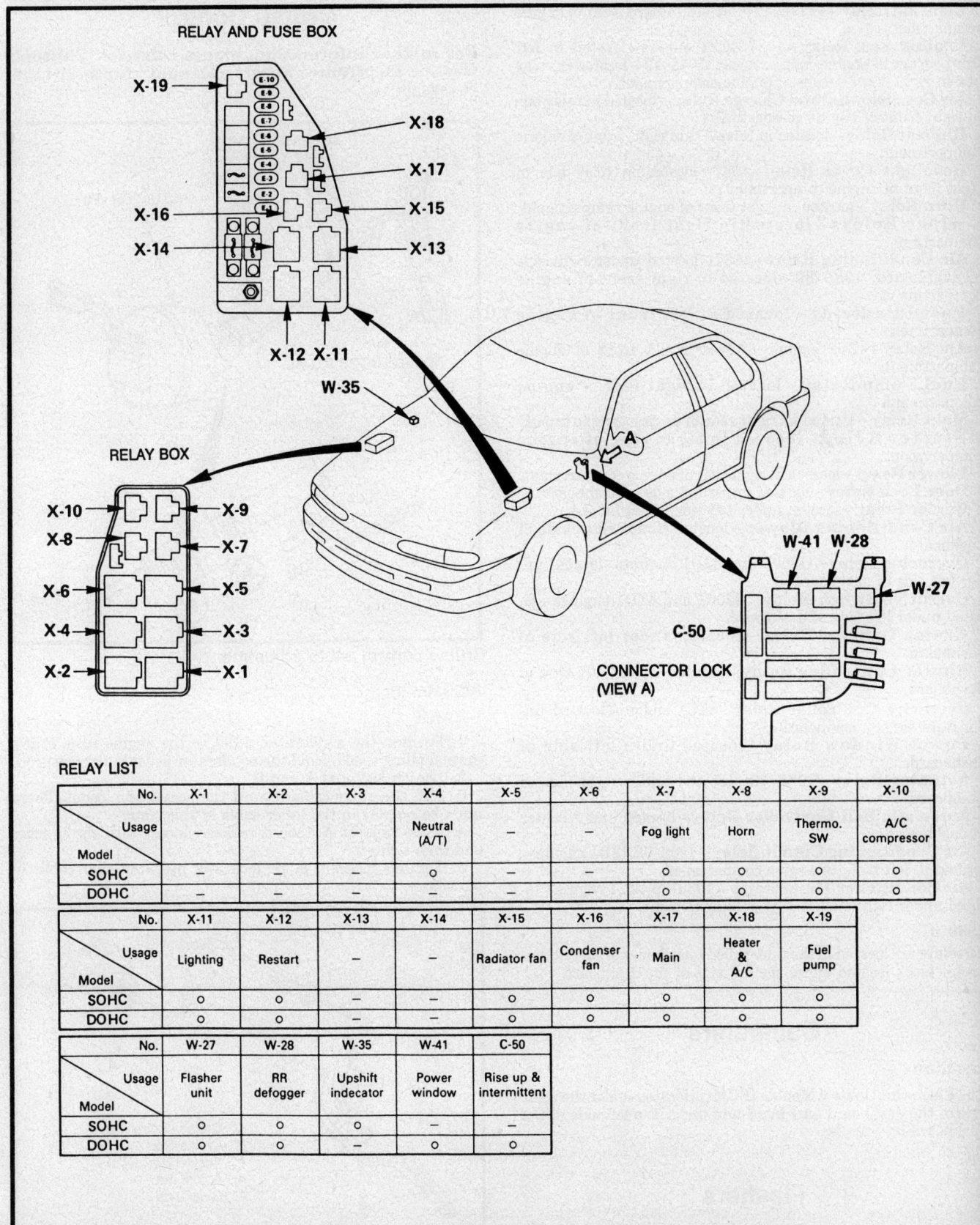

RELAY AND FUSE BOX

X-19
X-18
X-17
X-16
X-14
X-15
X-13
X-12 X-11
W-35

RELAY BOX

X-10   X-9
X-8   X-7
X-6   X-5
X-4   X-3
X-2   X-1

W-41 W-28
W-27
C-50

CONNECTOR LOCK
(VIEW A)

RELAY LIST

No.	X-1	X-2	X-3	X-4	X-5	X-6	X-7	X-8	X-9	X-10
Usage / Model	–	–	–	Neutral (A/T)	–	–	Fog light	Horn	Thermo. SW	A/C compressor
SOHC	–	–	–	○	–	–	○	○	○	○
DOHC	–	–	–	–	–	–	○	○	○	○

No.	X-11	X-12	X-13	X-14	X-15	X-16	X-17	X-18	X-19
Usage / Model	Lighting	Restart	–	–	Radiator fan	Condenser fan	Main	Heater & A/C	Fuel pump
SOHC	○	○	–	–	○	○	○	○	○
DOHC	○	○	–	–	○	○	○	○	○

No.	W-27	W-28	W-35	W-41	C-50
Usage / Model	Flasher unit	RR defogger	Upshift indecator	Power window	Rise up & intermittent
SOHC	○	○	○	–	–
DOHC	○	○	–	○	○

Relay location–1991 Stylus

Lighting Relay—located in relay box in right front of engine compartment.

Cooling Fan Relay—1987 4CZ1 engine—located in left front corner of engine compartment. 1988–89—located in relay box in right front corner of engine compartment.

Air Conditioning and Charge Relay—located in relay box in right front of engine compartment.

Dimmer Relay—located in relay box in right front of engine compartment.

Headlight Cover Relay—1987—located in relay box in right front of engine compartment.

Horn Relay—located in right front of engine compartment.

Wiper Relays—located in right front of engine compartment.

Air Conditioning Relay—1987—located under right side of dashboard. 1988–89—located in right front of engine compartment.

Fast Idle Relay—located in left front of engine compartment.

Air Relay—4ZC1 engine—located in left front of engine compartment.

Fuel Pump Relay—located in right rear of engine compartment.

Main Relay—located in right rear of engine compartment.

Starter Relay—located in right rear of engine compartment.

Blower Relay—located in right rear of engine compartment.

Door Lock Relay—located under left side of dashboard.

Buzzer Relay—located under left side of dashboard.

Air Conditioning Blower—located under right side of dashboard.

Overdrive Relay—G200Z and 4ZD1 engines—located under left side of dashboard.

Overdrive Switch Relay—G200Z and 4ZD1 engines—located under left side of dashboard.

Cruise Control Relay—located under left side of dashboard.

Blower Controller Relay—located under left side of dashboard.

Overdrive Controller Relay—4ZC1 engine—located under right side of dashboard.

Power Window Relay—located under left side of dashboard.

Actuator Relay—1988–89—located under right side of dashboard.

Automatic Belt Controller Relay—located under center of dashboard.

Air Conditioning Cutout Relay—1988–89 4ZD1 engine—located in left front of engine compartment.

Air Conditioner Timer Relay—1988–89 4ZC1 engine—located under right side of engine compartment.

1990–91

All relays are located in the underhood relay boxes or on the connector block located under the left side of the dashboard.

Computers

Location

The Electronic Control Module (ECM) is located under the right side of the dashboard on I-Mark and under the left side of the dashboard on Impulse.

Flashers

Location

Flashers are located under the left side of the dashboard.

Cruise Control

For further information, please refer to "Chilton's Chassis Electronics Service Manual" for additional coverage.

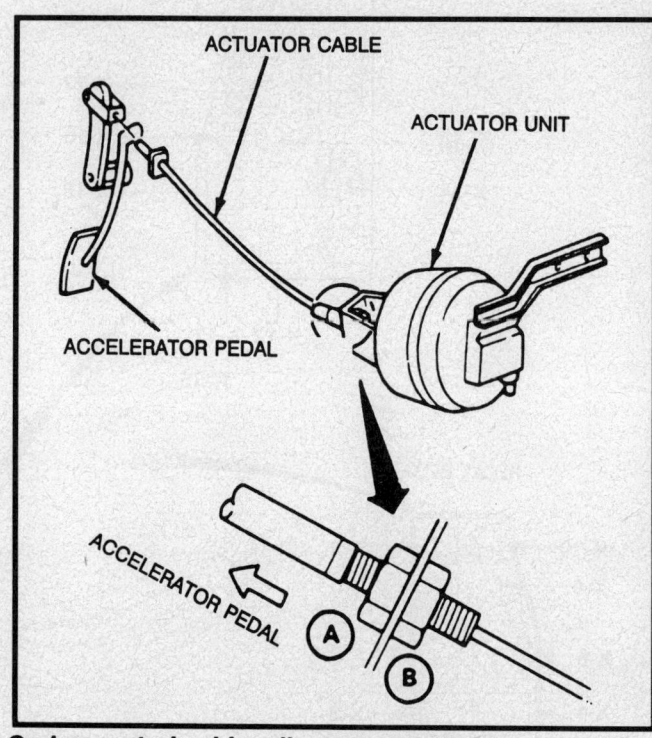

Cruise control cable adjustment—I-Mark

Adjustment

I-MARK

1. Position the accelerator pedal so the engine runs at it's normal idling speed. Hold the accelerator pedal in this position.
2. Loosen locknuts **A** and **B**.
3. Pull the outer cable toward the accelerator pedal. There must be no play in the inner cable at this time.
4. Move locknut **A** until it makes contact with the bracket and then tighten.
5. Tighten locknut **B** to lock the actuator side cable in position.

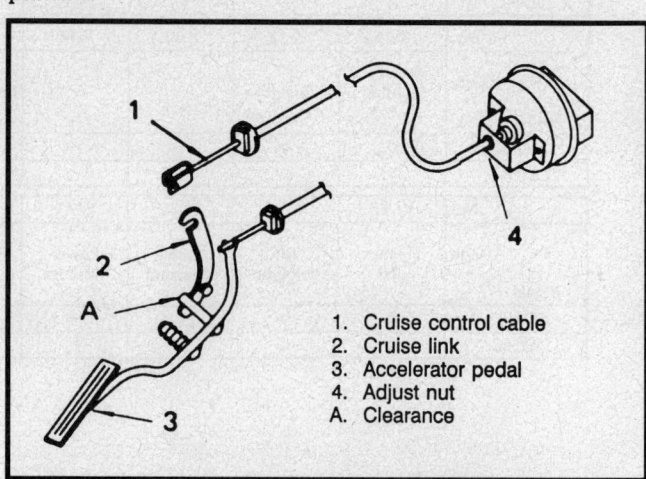

1. Cruise control cable
2. Cruise link
3. Accelerator pedal
4. Adjust nut
A. Clearance

Cruise control cable adjustment—1987–89 Impulse

IMPULSE AND STYLUS

1987–89

1. Loosen the adjust nut.
2. Adjust the cable with the "U" fitting connected to the cruise link, so the clearance A is adjusted to zero and the accelerator pedal is not being pushed by the cruise link.
3. Tighten the adjust nut.

1990–91

1. Position the accelerator pedal so the engine runs at normal idling speed. Hold the accelerator pedal in this position.

2. Loosen the actuator attaching bolts.
3. Relocate the actuator so a clearance between the leading end of the slide plate on the actuator and guide pin is within 0.079 in. (2.0mm).
4. Tighten the actuator attaching bolts.

NOTE: When tightening the bolts, be careful not to tilt the actuator, which would cause an excessive force to be applied to the cable.

ENGINE COOLING

Radiator

Removal and Installation

I-MARK, 1990–91 IMPULSE AND 1991 STYLUS

1. Disconnect the negative battery cable.
2. Remove the radiator cap and loosen the drain plug to drain the radiator.
3. Disconnect the fan motor and thermo switch connectors.
4. Disconnect the radiator and surge tank hoses from the radiator.
5. Disconnect the transaxle cooler hoses, if equipped.
6. Remove the radiator mounting bolts and the radiator and fan assembly.
7. Separate the cooling fan from the radiator.
8. Installation is the reverse of the removal procedure. Fill the radiator with enough water and anti-freeze to provide the required cooling, freezing and corrosion protection.

1987–89 IMPULSE

1. Disconnect the negative battery cable.
2. Remove the radiator cap and loosen the drain plug to drain the radiator.
3. Disconnect the radiator and surge tank hoses from the radiator. Disconnect the turbocharger water hose on vehicles equipped with the 4CZ1-T engine.
4. Remove the fan shroud and the stay.
5. Remove the radiator mounting bolts and the radiator.
6. Installation is the reverse of the removal procedure. Fill the radiator with enough water and anti-freeze to provide the required cooling, freezing and corrosion protection.

Electric Cooling Fan

Testing

1. Disconnect the negative battery cable.
2. Disconnect the electrical connector at the cooling fan motor.
3. Connect 1 end of a jumper wire to 1 of the terminals of the cooling fan motor connector and the other end to the positive terminal of the battery.
4. Connect 1 end of a jumper wire to the other terminal of the connector and the other end of the wire to the negative battery cable.
5. The cooling fan motor should run smoothly. If it does not, the cooling fan motor must be replaced.

Removal and Installation

1. Disconnect the negative battery cable.
2. Disconnect the electrical connector at the cooling fan motor.

3. Drain the coolant from the radiator and disconnect the upper radiator hose.
4. Remove the cooling fan mounting bolts and the cooling fan.
5. Installation is the reverse of the removal procedure.

Condenser Cooling Fan

Testing

Use the electric cooling fan procedures.

Removal and Installation

1. Disconnect the negative (−)battery cable.
2. Discharge the air conditioning system.
3. Remove the condenser from the vehicle.
4. Remove the fan shroud, guide and motor assembly.
5. Installation is the reverse of the removal procedure. Evacuate, recharge and leak test the air conditioning system.

Heater Core

For further information, please refer to "Chilton's Heating and Air Conditioning Manual" for additional coverage.

Removal and Installation

WITHOUT AIR CONDITIONING

I-Mark

1. Disconnect the negative battery cable.
2. Drain the cooling system.
3. Disconnect and plug the heater hoses at the heater core.
4. Remove the retaining clips holding the lower heater unit case and remove the lower case.
5. Remove the heater core assembly.
6. Installation is the reverse of the removal procedure. Fill the cooling system with the proper type and quantity of coolant.

Impulse

1987–89

1. Disconnect the negative battery cable.
2. Drain the cooling system.
3. Remove the instrument panel as follows:
   a. Remove the steering wheel and the gearshift knob.
   b. Remove the front console and the radio.
   c. On 1987 vehicles, remove the lap vent grille assembly. On 1988–89 vehicles, remove the lower dash panel, hood release lever and knee pad.
   d. Remove the instrument cluster hood and the steering column covers.

e. Remove the instrument cluster and switch assembly.

f. Remove the instrument panel front cover and the front pillar trim cover.

g. Remove the glove box.

h. Remove the instrument panel grille and the instrument panel cover assembly.

4. Disconnect and plug the heater hoses at the heater core and disconnect the electrical connectors from the heater unit.

5. Remove the heater unit mounting bolts and the heater unit.

6. Disassemble the heater unit and remove the heater core.

7. Installation is the reverse of the removal procedure. Fill the cooling system with the proper type and quantity of coolant.

1990–91 Impulse and 1991 Stylus

1. Disconnect the negative (−) battery cable.
2. Drain the engine coolant into a suitable container.
3. Disconnect the heater hoses. Be careful not to damage the core by pulling on the hose to remove. Cut the hoses if they will not come off easily.
4. Remove the instrument panel.
5. Disconnect the resistor assembly.
6. Remove the duct (non air conditioning) or the evaporator housing (air conditioning). If equipped with air conditioning, refer to Section 1 for discharging, evacuating and recharging the air conditioning system.
7. Remove the center vent duct and heater unit.
8. Disassemble the heater unit by removing the duct, mode control case, core assembly and heater core.

To install:

9. Install the heater core, making sure all the seals are in place.
10. Assemble the heater unit, making sure all the seals are in place.
11. Install the center vent duct and heater unit.
12. Install the duct (non air conditioning) or the evaporator housing (air conditioning). If equipped with air conditioning, refer to Section 1 for discharging, evacuating and recharging the air conditioning system.
13. Connect the resistor assembly.
14. Install the instrument panel.
15. Connect the heater hoses. Be careful not to damage the core by pulling on the hose to remove. Cut the hoses if they will not come off easily.
16. Refill the engine coolant.
17. Connect the negative (−) battery cable and check for leaks.

WITH AIR CONDITIONING

I-Mark

1. Disconnect the negative battery cable.
2. Drain the cooling system.
3. Disconnect and plug the heater hoses at the heater core.
4. Remove the retaining clips holding the lower heater unit case and remove the lower case.
5. Remove the heater core assembly.
6. Installation is the reverse of the removal procedure. Fill the cooling system with the proper type and quantity of coolant.

1987–89 Impulse

1. Disconnect the negative battery cable.
2. Drain the cooling system and properly discharge the air conditioning system.
3. Remove the instrument panel as follows:
   a. Remove the steering wheel and the gearshift knob.
   b. Remove the front console and the radio.
   c. On 1987 vehicles, remove the lap vent grille assembly.
   On 1988–89 vehicles, remove the lower dash panel, hood release lever and knee pad.
   d. Remove the instrument cluster hood and the steering column covers.

e. Remove the instrument cluster and switch assembly.

f. Remove the instrument panel front cover and the front pillar trim cover.

g. Remove the glove box.

h. Remove the instrument panel grill and the instrument panel cover assembly.

4. Disconnect and plug the heater hoses at the heater core and disconnect the electrical connectors from the heater unit.

5. Disconnect and plug the air conditioning lines and disconnect the electrical connectors at the evaporator.

6. Remove the foot air duct, if equipped.

7. Remove the evaporator mounting nuts and the evaporator.

8. Remove the heater unit mounting bolts and the heater unit.

9. Disassemble the heater unit and remove the heater core.

10. Installation is the reverse of the removal procedure. Fill the cooling system with the proper type and quantity of coolant. Evacuate and charge the air conditioning system.

1990–91 Impulse and 1991 Stylus

1. Disconnect the negative battery cable.
2. Drain the cooling system and properly discharge the air conditioning system.
3. Remove the instrument panel as follows:
   a. Pull the switch bezel out and disconnect the switch connectors.
   b. Pull the cigarette lighter bezel out and disconnect the electrical connectors, then remove the bezel.
   c. Disconnect the engine hood opener cable.
   d. Remove the knee pad assembly.
   e. Remove the 2 hinge pins from inside the glove box and remove the glove box.
   f. Remove the front console bracket.
   g. Remove the instrument cluster hood and the instrument cluster.
   h. Remove the front hole covers and the front cover.
   i. Remove the instrument panel assembly.
4. Disconnect and plug the heater hoses at the heater core.
5. Disconnect the resistor connector.
6. Disconnect and plug the air conditioning lines at the evaporator.
7. Disconnect the hose and the electrical connectors at the evaporator.
8. Remove the 3 mounting nuts and the evaporator.
9. Remove the center ventilator duct.
10. Remove the heater unit.
11. Disassemble the heater unit and remove the heater core.

To install:

12. Assemble the heater unit.
13. Install the heater unit into the vehicle.
14. Install the center ventilator duct.
15. Install the 3 mounting nuts and the evaporator.
16. Connect the hose and the electrical connectors at the evaporator.
17. Connect and plug the air conditioning lines at the evaporator.
18. Connect the resistor connector.
19. Connect the heater hoses at the heater core.
20. Install the instrument panel as follows:
   a. Install the instrument panel assembly.
   b. Install the front hole covers and the front cover.
   c. Install the instrument cluster and hood.
   d. Install the front console bracket.
   e. Install the 2 hinge pins to the inside of the glove box.
   f. Install the knee pad assembly.
   g. Connect the engine hood opener cable.
   h. Push the cigarette lighter and bezel.
   i. Install the switch bezel.
21. Refill the cooling system and properly evacuate and recharge the air conditioning system.
22. Connect the negative battery cable.

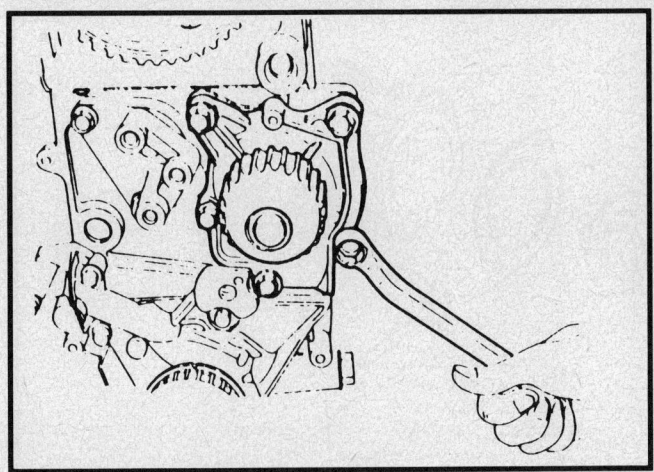

Water pump installation—I-Mark

Water Pump

Removal and Installation

I-MARK

1. Disconnect the negative battery cable.
2. Drain the cooling system.
3. Place a wooden block over a suitable floor jack and jack up the oil pan slightly.
4. Remove the rear side torque rod.
5. Remove the right side engine mount, then remove the body side and engine side brackets.
6. Remove all necessary drive belts.
7. Remove the crank pulley and the timing cover.
8. Turn the crank pulley hub bolt to bring the No. 1 cylinder to TDC.
9. Remove the crank pulley hub bolt and the pulley hub, being careful not to disturb the position of the crank.
10. Loosen the tension pulley bolts, turn the tension pulley clockwise and remove the timing belt.
11. Remove the tension pulley and spring and remove the water pump.

To install:

12. Installation is the reverse of the removal procedure. Make sure all gasket mating surfaces are clean prior to installation. Tighten the water pump bolts to 17 ft. lbs. (24 Nm).
13. Properly adjust the timing belt tension and tighten the tension pulley bolt to 37 ft. lbs. (51 Nm). Tighten the crank pulley hub bolt to 108 ft. lbs. (150 Nm).
14. Fill the cooling system with the proper type and quantity of coolant.

IMPULSE AND STYLUS

1987–89

1. Disconnect the negative battery cable.
2. Drain the cooling system.
3. Remove the necessary drive belts and the cooling fan and pulley.
4. Remove the water pump.
5. Installation is the reverse of the removal procedure. Make sure all gasket mating surfaces are clean prior to installation. Tighten the water pump mounting bolts to 17 ft. lbs. (24 Nm) on the G200Z engine and 13 ft. lbs. (19 Nm) on all others.

1990–91

1. Disconnect the negative battery cable.
2. Drain the cooling system.
3. Place a wooden block on a suitable floor jack and support the engine under the oil pan.
4. Remove the right side engine mount.
5. Remove the necessary drive belts.
6. Remove the crank pulley and the timing cover.
7. Bring the No. 1 cylinder to TDC.
8. Loosen the tension pulley lock bolt, turn the tension pulley clockwise and remove the timing belt.
9. Remove the water pump.

To install:

10. Make sure all gasket mating surfaces are clean prior to installation. Tighten the water pump mounting bolts to 17 ft. lbs. (24 Nm).
11. Properly adjust the timing belt tension and tighten the tension pulley bolt to 31 ft. lbs. (42 Nm). Tighten the crank pulley bolt to 109 ft. lbs. (147 Nm).
12. Fill the cooling system with the proper type and quantity of coolant.

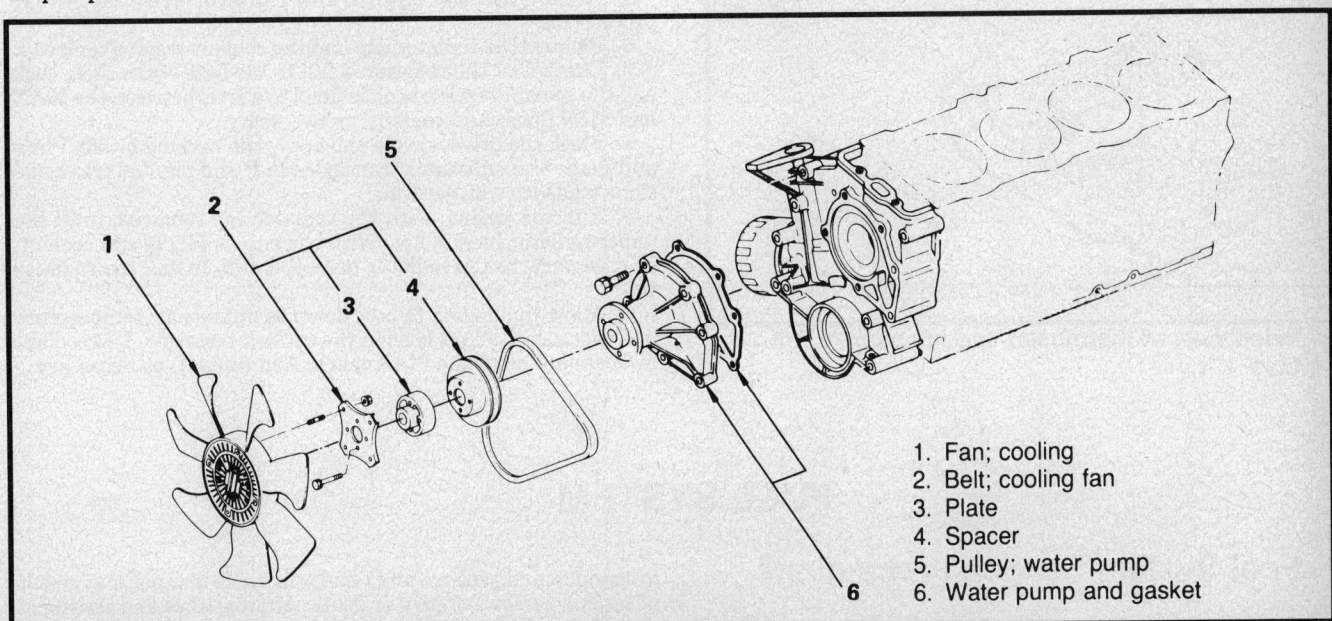

1. Fan; cooling
2. Belt; cooling fan
3. Plate
4. Spacer
5. Pulley; water pump
6. Water pump and gasket

Water pump installation—1987 Impulse with G200Z engine

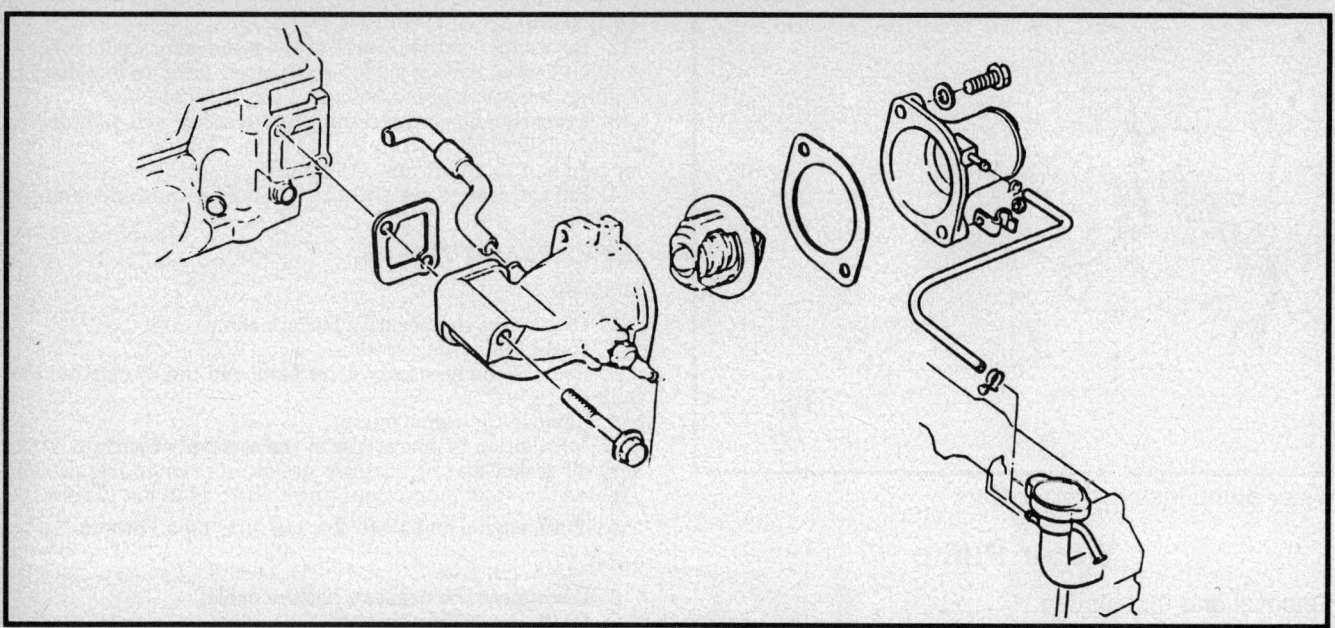

Exploded view of thermostat and housing—I-Mark except 4XE1 engine

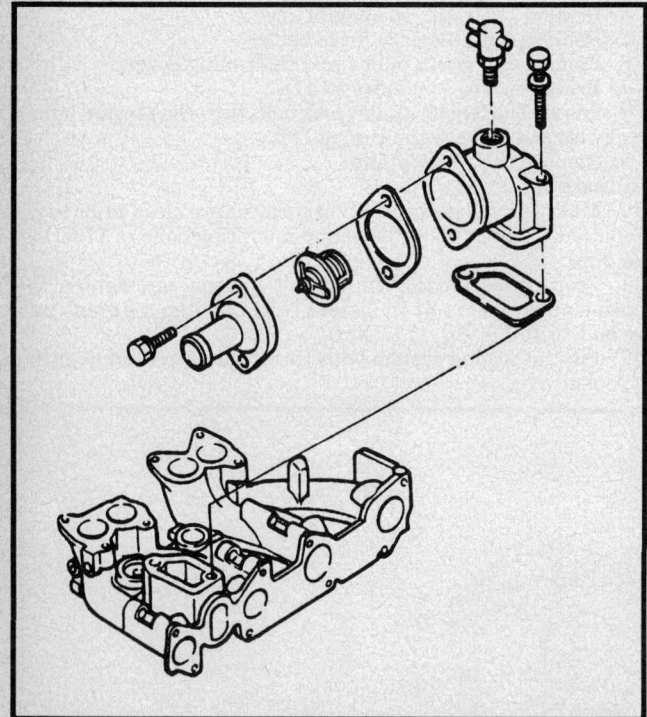

Exploded view of thermostat and housing—1988–89 Impulse

Thermostat

Removal and Installation

1. Disconnect the negative battery cable.
2. Drain the cooling system.
3. Disconnect the radiator hose from the water outlet.
4. Remove the water outlet from the thermostat housing and remove the thermostat.
5. Installation is the reverse of the removal procedure. Make sure all gasket mating surfaces are clean prior to installation. Install the thermostat with the jiggle valve toward the water outlet and the spring toward the thermostat housing.

Cooling System Bleeding

1. Make sure the engine and radiator are cold before proceeding.
2. Remove the radiator cap and the coolant reserve tank cap.
3. Check that the radiator is full to the base of the filler neck and the coolant reserve tank is filled to a level between the **MAX** and **MIN** lines. Add coolant, as necessary.
4. Block the drive wheels and apply the parking brake. Place automatic transmissions/transaxles in **P** and manual transmissions/transaxles in neutral.
5. Run the engine, with the radiator cap removed, until the upper radiator hose is hot. With the engine idling, add coolant, as necessary, to the radiator until it is full. Install the radiator cap.
6. Allow the engine to cool down to outside air temperature and check the coolant level in the coolant reservoir. The coolant level should be at the MAX mark. Add coolant, as necessary.

FUEL SYSTEM

Fuel System Service Precautions

Safety is the most important factor when performing not only fuel system maintenance but any type of maintenance. Failure to conduct maintenance and repairs in a safe manner may result in serious personal injury or death. Maintenance and testing of the vehicle's fuel system components can be accomplished safely and effectively by adhering to the following rules and guidelines.

• To avoid the possibility of fire and personal injury, always disconnect the negative battery cable unless the repair or test procedure requires that battery voltage be applied.

• Always relieve the fuel system pressure prior to disconnecting any fuel system component (injector, fuel rail, pressure regulator, etc.), fitting or fuel line connection. Exercise extreme caution whenever relieving fuel system pressure to avoid exposing skin, face and eyes to fuel spray. Please be advised that fuel under pressure may penetrate the skin or any part of the body that it contacts.

• Always place a shop towel or cloth around the fitting or connection prior to loosening to absorb any excess fuel due to spillage. Ensure that all fuel spillage (should it occur) is quickly removed from engine surfaces. Ensure that all fuel soaked cloths or towels are deposited into a suitable waste container.

• Always keep a dry chemical (Class B) fire extinguisher near the work area.

• Do not allow fuel spray or fuel vapors to come into contact with a spark or open flame.

• Always use a backup wrench when loosening and tightening fuel line connection fittings. This will prevent unnecessary stress and torsion to fuel line piping. Always follow the proper torque specifications.

• Always replace worn fuel fitting O-rings with new. Do not substitute fuel hose or equivalent where fuel pipe is installed.

Relieving Fuel System Pressure

1. Remove the fuel pump fuse from the fuse block or disconnect the harness connector at the tank.
2. Start the engine. It should run and then stall when the fuel in the lines is exhausted. When the engine stops, crank the starter for about 3 seconds to make sure all pressure in the fuel lines is released.
3. Install the fuel pump fuse after repair is made.

Fuel Filter

Removal and Installation

1. Disconnect the negative battery cable.
2. Relieve the fuel system pressure and remove the fuel filler cap.
3. On 1990–91 Impulse and 1991 Stylus, disconnect the engine harness connector and remove the air duct with the air cleaner cover.
4. Disconnect and plug the fuel lines at the fuel filter.
5. On Impulse, loosen the filter clamp bolt.
6. Remove the fuel filter.
7. Installation is the reverse of the removal procedure. Make sure the filter is installed in the proper direction of fuel flow.
8. Start the engine and check for leaks.

Mechanical Fuel Pump

Pressure Testing

1. Disconnect the negative battery cable.
2. Remove the fuel inlet hose from the carburetor.
3. Connect a fuel pump pressure gauge between the inlet hose and the carburetor, using a tee fitting. Reconnect the negative battery cable.
4. Start the engine and run it at 750 rpm. Note the reading on the pressure gauge.
5. Stop the engine and disconnect the negative battery cable. Remove the pressure gauge and tee fitting.
6. Place the open end of the fuel line into a graduated container. Reconnect the negative battery cable.
7. Crank the engine for 30 seconds. Note the amount of gasoline delivered to the container, then safely dispose of the fuel.
8. Connect the fuel inlet line to the carburetor. Compare the results of the these tests to the specifications below:

Fuel pressure – 3.84–4.70 psi.
Fuel delivery – 0.428 qts. in 30 seconds.
9. If the fuel pump fails these tests, it should be replaced.

Removal and Installation

1. Disconnect the fuel delivery and return hoses from the fuel pump.
2. Remove the bolts, fuel pump and heat insulator assembly.
3. After removing the fuel pump, cover the mounting face of the cylinder head to prevent oil discharge.
4. To install, reverse the removal procedures. Clean all mating surfaces prior to installation. Replace the heat insulator assembly.

Electric Fuel Pump

Pressure Testing

I-MARK AND 1987–89 IMPULSE

1. Relieve the fuel system pressure.
2. Disconnect the fuel hose between the pressure regulator and fuel distributor pipe.
3. Connect a suitable fuel pressure gauge across the pressure regulator and fuel distributor pipe correctly.

NOTE: On Impulse engines disconnect the Vacuum Switching Valve (VSV) harness at the connector.

4. Start the engine and measure the fuel pressure under the following conditions:
   a. Vacuum hose of the pressure regulator disconnected (Intake manifold side end of hose must be plugged). The pressure should read 35.6 psi. on I-Mark and 42.6 psi. on Impulse.
   b. Vacuum hose of the pressure regulator connected, at idling speed of 900 rpm. The pressure should read 28.4 psi. on I-Mark and 35.6 psi. on Impulse.

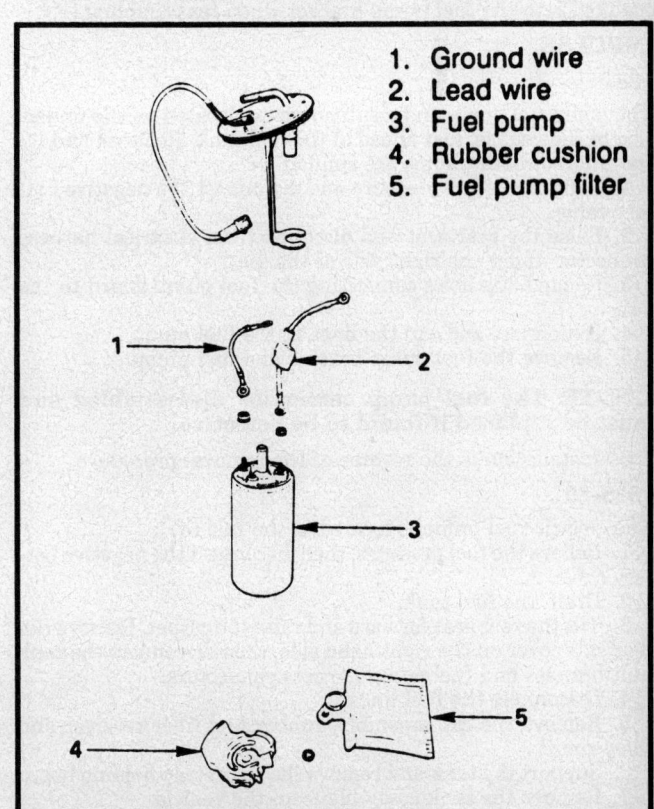

1. Ground wire
2. Lead wire
3. Fuel pump
4. Rubber cushion
5. Fuel pump filter

Exploded view of electric fuel pump – I-Mark

5. Remove the fuel pressure gauge and reconnect the fuel hose.

1990–91 IMPULSE AND 1991 STYLUS

1. Relieve the fuel system pressure.
2. Install a suitable fuel pressure gauge between the fuel filter and the fuel distributor pipe.
3. Disconnect the vacuum hose from the pressure regulator.
4. Make sure the ignition has been **OFF** for at least 10 seconds and the air conditioning is off.
5. Turn the ignition **ON**. The fuel pump should run for about 2 seconds. The fuel pressure reading should be 35–38 psi.
6. Turn the ignition **OFF** and disconnect the fuel pressure gauge.

Removal and Installation

I-MARK

The electric fuel pump is located in the fuel tank.
1. Relieve the fuel pressure, then disconnect the negative battery cable.
2. Raise and support the vehicle safely. Drain fuel tank.
3. Disconnect all fuel line and electrical connectors.
4. Remove the filler neck hose and clamp.
5. Remove the breather hose and clamp.
6. Disconnect the fuel tank hose to evaporator pipe. Place a suitable floor jack with a piece of wood on it under the fuel tank.
7. Remove the fuel tank mounting bolts and lower the tank from the vehicle. At this point disconnect the hose from the pump to the fuel filter.
8. Remove the fuel pump bracket plate and fuel pump as an assembly.
9. Remove the pump bracket, rubber cushion and fuel pump filter.
10. To install, reverse the removal procedures. Be careful to push the lower side of the fuel pump, together with the rubber cushion, into the fuel pump bracket when reassembling.

IMPULSE

1987

The main fuel pump and a sub pump are located on the underside of the vehicle, just ahead of the fuel tank. Removal and installation of both pumps are similar.
1. Relieve the fuel pressure and disconnect the negative battery cable.
2. Raise the rear seat and disconnect the electrical harness connector under the right side of the seat.
3. Remove the bolts connecting the fuel pump guard to the body.
4. Disconnect and cap the lines at the fuel pump.
5. Remove the fuel pump bracket and fuel pump.

NOTE: The fuel pump cannot be disassembled and must be replaced if found to be defective.

6. Installation is the reverse of the removal procedure.

1988–89

The electric fuel pump is located in the fuel tank.
1. Relieve the fuel pressure, then disconnect the negative battery cable.
2. Drain the fuel tank.
3. Tilt the rear seat forward and raise the carpet. Remove the rear side cover on the right hand side, then disconnect the tank unit harness and fuel pump harness connectors.
4. Disconnect the fuel lines.
5. Remove the cap assembly, rubber fuel filler receiver and filler guard.
6. Support the tank and remove the tank strap holding bolts.
7. Remove the tank assembly from the vehicle.
8. Remove the fuel pump bracket plate and fuel pump as an assembly.

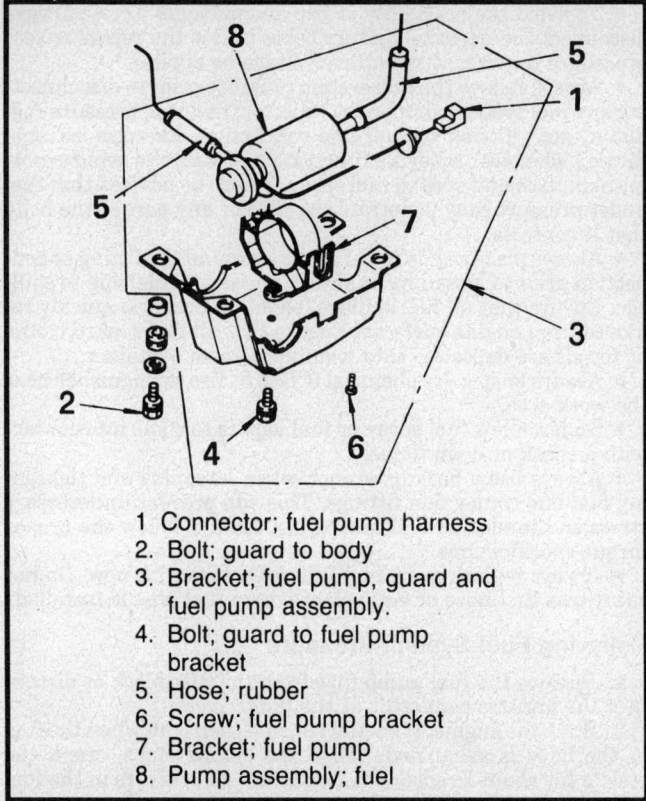

1 Connector; fuel pump harness
2 Bolt; guard to body
3 Bracket; fuel pump, guard and fuel pump assembly.
4 Bolt; guard to fuel pump bracket
5 Hose; rubber
6 Screw; fuel pump bracket
7 Bracket; fuel pump
8 Pump assembly; fuel

Exploded view of electric fuel pump and attaching parts—1987 Impulse

9. Remove the pump bracket, rubber cushion and fuel pump sock or filter.
10. To install, reverse the removal procedure. Be careful, to push the lower side of the fuel pump, together with the rubber cushion, into the fuel pump bracket when reassembling.

1990–91 IMPULSE AND STLYUS

The electric fuel pump is located in the fuel tank.
1. Relieve the fuel system pressure, then disconnect the negative battery cable.
2. Loosen the fuel filler cap and drain the fuel system.
3. Remove the fuel filler and air breather hoses and disconnect the fuel lines.
4. Remove the parking brake cable brackets and the parking brake return spring.
5. Disconnect the fuel gauge and fuel pump harness connectors.
6. Support the fuel tank and remove the mounting bolts. Lower the tank onto the exhaust pipe.
7. Peel off the harness fixing tape. Remove the fuel pump assembly attaching screws and pull the fuel pump assembly out of the tank.
8. Installation is the reverse of the removal procedure.

Carburetor

Removal and Installation

1. Disconnect the negative battery terminal from the battery.
2. Remove the air cleaner.
3. Disconnect the harness connector and hoses.
4. Remove the accelerator cable from the carburetor.
5. Remove the bolts securing the carburetor to the intake manifold. Remove the carburetor and place a cover over the intake manifold.

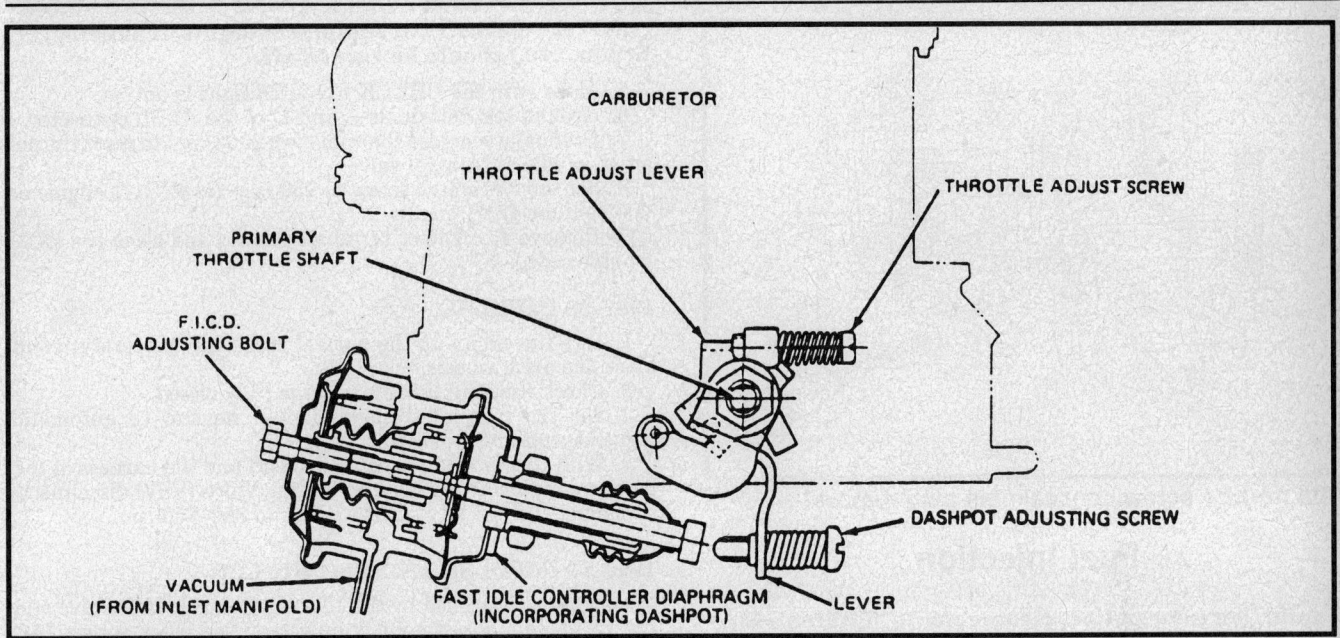

Carburetor adjusting screw locations

6. To install, reverse the removal procedures and torque carburetor fixing bolts to 7.2 ft. lbs. then start the engine and check for leaks.

Idle Speed Adjustment

NOTE: Before adjusting the idle speed, be sure to check the ignition timing. If the ignition timing is off, adjust it to the proper specification before adjusting the idle speed.

1. Set the parking brake and block the drive wheels.
2. Place manual transaxles in neutral or automatic transaxles in **P** and start the engine.
3. Let the engine run until it reaches normal operating temperature. Leave the air cleaner installed and disconnect the distributor vacuum line from the carburetor, canister purge line, the EGR vacuum line and the Inlet Air Temperature Compensator (ITC) valve. Plug and mark all lines.
4. With the proper tachometer installed, the air conditioning and all electrical equipment turned off, check the idle speed and adjust, as necessary, by turning the throttle adjustment screw.
5. The idle speed should be 750 rpm for manual transaxle or 1000 rpm for automatic transaxle.
6. Disconnect and plug the vacuum advance hoses from the intake manifold and the carburetor. Maintain the engine speed between 1900–2100 rpm and set the dashpot to contact the dashpot shaft and with the adjust screw of the throttle lever.
7. If equipped with air conditioning, turn it ON and set the temperature control level to **MAX COLD**. Set the blower to its highest position.
8. Using the Fast Idle Control Device (FICD) adjusting screw, located at the tip of the carburetor lever, set the fast idle speed. It should be 850 rpm for manual transaxle or 980 rpm for automatic transaxle.

Idle Mixture Adjustment

1. Set the parking brake and block the drive wheels.
2. Place manual transaxle in neutral or automatic transaxle in **P** and start the engine.
3. Remove the carburetor assembly.
4. Remove the idle mixture adjusting screw plug as follows:
   a. Cover the primary and secondary bores and other ports to prevent metal chips from entering the carburetor.

b. Mark the center of the plug with a punch.
c. Drill a hole in the plug to a depth less than 0.39 in. (10mm) and then thread a screw into the hole. Pull on the screw to remove the plug.
d. Remove the chips from the surroundings of the mixture screw with compressed air. Remove and inspect the idle mixture adjusting screw. Replace the screw if it is deformed or damaged from the drilling procedure.
e. Reinstall the idle mixture screw. Lightly seat the screw, then back it out 3 turns from fully closed for manual transaxle or 2 turns from fully closed on automatic transaxle.

NOTE: Do not overtighten the idle mixture screw.

5. Reinstall the carburetor and the air cleaner.
6. Adjust the idle speed.
7. Disconnect the idle set connector, located in the harness to right of the carburetor assembly. The CHECK ENGINE lamp will come on.
8. Adjust the throttle adjust screw to 750 rpm for manual transaxle or 1000 rpm for automatic transaxle.
9. Connect the positive lead of a suitable dwell meter to the duty monitor lead, located in the harness to the right of the carburetor assembly. Connect the negative lead of the dwell meter to ground. Place the meter dial on the 4 cylinder scale or 6 cylinder scale. Turn the idle mixture screw until the dwell meter reads 45 degrees on the 4 cylinder scale or 30 degrees on the 6 cylinder scale.
10. Reconnect the idle set connector, the CHECK ENGINE lamp should go out.
11. Readjust the throttle adjust screw to 750 rpm for manual transaxle or 1000 rom for automatic transaxle.
12. Check the idle speed and readjust, if necessary, using the throttle adjust screw. Readjust the dashpot, if necessary.
13. If equipped with air conditioning, turn it ON and set the temperature control lever to **MAX COLD**. Set the blower to it's highest position. Use the Fast Idle Control Device (FICD) adjusting screw at the tip of the carburetor throttle lever to set the fast idle speed to 850 rpm for manual transaxle or 980 rpm for automatic transaxle.

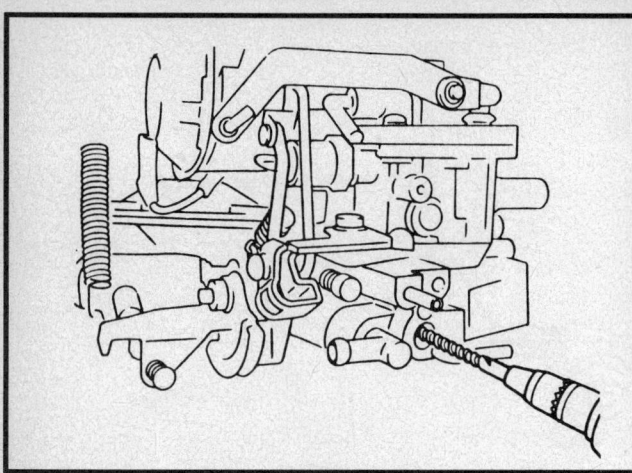

Idle mixture screw concealment plug removal

Fuel Injection

For further information, please refer to "Chilton's Electronic Engine Control's Manual" for additional coverage.

Idle Speed Adjustment

I-MARK

NOTE: Before adjusting the idle speed, be sure to check the ignition timing. If the ignition timing is off, adjust it to the proper specification before adjusting the idle speed.

1. Set the parking brake.
2. Block the front wheels.
3. Place the select lever in neutral.
4. Make the idling speed adjustment with the engine at normal operating temperature, with the air conditioning off and front wheels facing straight ahead.

NOTE: All electrical equipment (lights, rear defogger, heater, etc.) should be turned off.

5. Make sure the CHECK ENGINE light is not on.
6. Ground test terminals A and C of the ALDL connector.
7. Gradually increase the rpm over 2000 rpm to reset the position of idle air control valve.
8. Set the idle adjust screw to 950 rpm for 4XC1-T engine or 900 rpm for 4XE1 engine.
9. Remove ALDL test terminal ground and clear the ECM trouble code.

1987-89 IMPULSE

1. Run the engine to the normal operating temperature and block the drive wheels.
2. Check that the throttle valve is fully closed.
3. Set the manual transmission in neutral or automatic transmission in **P** position.
4. With the air conditioner turned off and the harness of the pressure regulator Variable Switching Valve (VSV) disconnected, adjust the idle adjustment screw to 850–950 rpm.

1990-91 IMPULSE AND 1991 STYLUS

Idle speed is controlled by the Idle Air Control (IAC) valve and the ECM. Idle adjustment is only required when a new IAC valve is installed.

1. Set the parking brake and block the drive wheels.
2. Place the transaxle in neutral.
3. The air conditioning must be off and the front wheels facing straight ahead. All electrical equipment should be turned off.
4. Ground the test terminals of the ALDL connector.
5. Start the engine and increase rpm slightly to reset the pintle position of the IAC valve. A throttle opening of 10 percent or more should correspond to an engine speed of 2000 rpm or more.
6. Continue to run the engine until it reaches normal operating temperature. Check the ignition timing and adjust as necessary.
7. Set the idle adjust screw to 950 rpm.
8. Remove the test terminal ground and clear the ECM trouble code.

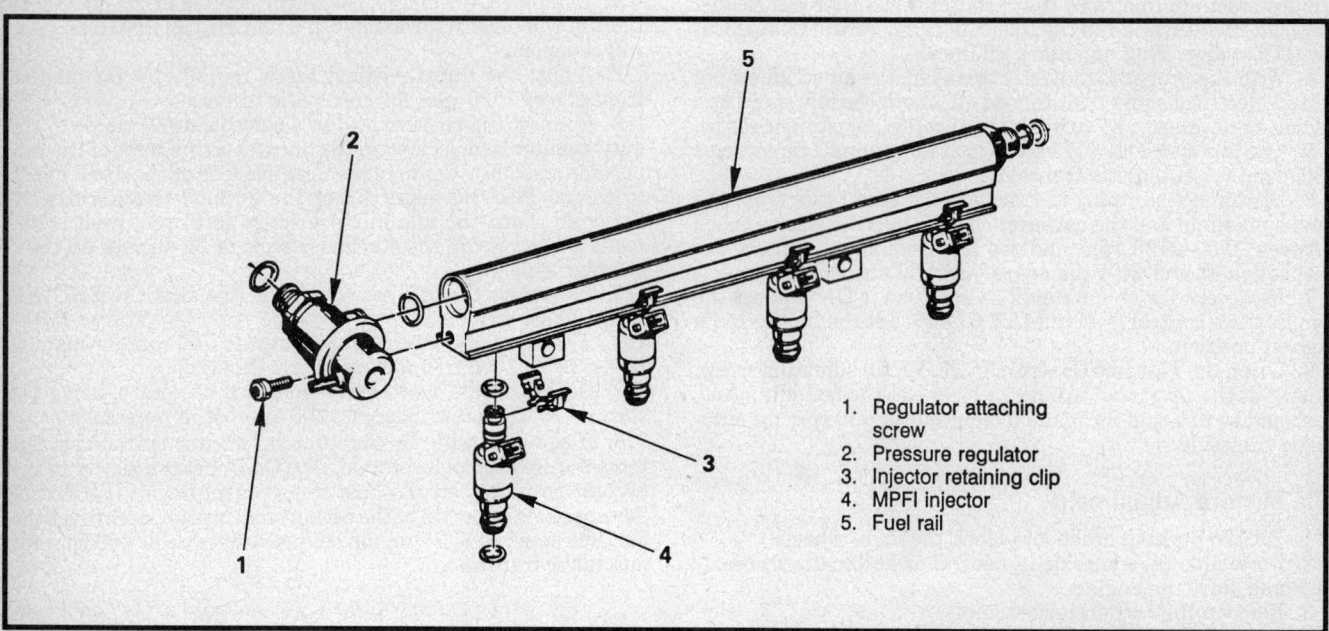

1. Regulator attaching screw
2. Pressure regulator
3. Injector retaining clip
4. MPFI injector
5. Fuel rail

Fuel rail and injector

Idle Mixture Adjustment

Idle mixture is controlled electronically by the fuel injection system. No adjustments are necessary.

Fuel Injector

Removal and Installation

1. Disconnect the negative battery cable. Remove the air cleaner and duct.
2. Relieve the fuel system pressure.

3. Remove the intercooler assembly, Turbo only.
4. Disconnect the throttle cable, hoses and electrical connectors from the throttle body and remove the throttle body.
5. Disconnect the vacuum line at the pressure regulator and the electrical connectors at the fuel injectors.
6. Disconnect the fuel lines at the fuel rail.
7. Remove the fuel rail mounting bolts and remove the fuel rail and injectors.
8. Installation is the reverse of the removal procedure. Replace all O-rings with new ones. Lubricate O-rings with engine oil during installation.

EMISSION CONTROLS

For further information, please refer to "Professional Emission Component Application Guide".

Emission Warning Lamps

Isuzu vehicles do not employ emission warning lamps that

would indicate scheduled component replacement. A CHECK ENGINE lamp is used to indicate component malfunction. When the CHECK ENGINE lamp comes on, the vehicle should be checked as soon as possible, using the proper diagnostic procedure, to locate the malfunction.

ENGINE MECHANICAL

NOTE: Disconnecting the negative battery cable on some vehicles may interfere with the functions of the on board computer systems and may require the computer to undergo a relearning process, once the negative battery cable is reconnected.

Engine Assembly

Removal and Installation

I-MARK

Except 4XE1 Engine

1. Relieve the fuel pressure and disconnect the battery cables. Scribe the position of the hood on the hood brackets and remove the hood.
2. Drain the oil from the transaxle case and engine oil pan into a suitable drain pan.
3. Drain the cooling system and if equipped with air conditioning, discharge the refrigerant from the air conditioning system.
4. Remove the air cleaner assembly and the throttle cable at the carburetor, on non-turbocharged model.
5. Remove, plug and tag the fuel pump inlet and return hoses on non-turbocharged model.
6. Remove the power steering hoses, air conditioning hose assembly, radiator and heater hoses and automatic transaxle cooler hoses, if equipped.
7. Remove the brake booster hose, clutch cable and select/shift cables, if equipped, speedometer cable and high tension cable.
8. Remove and tag all necessary electrical wires and remove the distributor from the engine.
9. Remove the battery and battery tray. Remove all the necessary wiring connectors from their respective sensor. Be sure to tag all connectors.
10. Remove and tag all necessary vacuum lines and remove the engine control cable.
11. Remove the halfshafts as follows:
    a. Raise and safely support the front of the vehicle. Remove the front wheels.

b. Disconnect the tie rod end ball joints from the steering knuckles using special remover tool J-21687-02 or equivalent.
c. Disconnect the lower arm end ball joints from the lower arm. Loosen but do not remove the nuts attaching the strut to the body.
d. Using a suitable tool, pull out the halfshafts, being careful not to damage the oil seals.
12. Remove the front exhaust pipe. On turbocharged engine remove the exhaust pipe at wastegate manifold and vacuum line at the wastegate control valve. Attach a suitable engine chain hoist to the engine hanger located on the top of the engine.
13. Raise the engine just enough to remove the weight from the engine mounts and disconnect the mounts from the vehicle.
14. Remove the torque rod from the side of the body.
15. Making sure all hoses and wires are aside, carefully and slowly raise the engine and transaxle assembly out of the vehicle. Place the assembly on a suitable engine stand or equivalent.
16. Remove the torque rod with bracket from the engine. Remove the main wire harness assembly from the engine.
17. Place a suitable transmission jack or equivalent under the transaxle and separate the transaxle assembly from the engine.
To install:
18. Installation is the reverse of the removal procedure. Make all necessary adjustments and refill the engine, transaxle, cooling system, power steering reservoir and recharge the air conditioning system with the proper lubricants and to the specified amount.
19. When installing the engine pay close attention to the following torque specifications.
    a. Transaxle-to-engine mounting bolts—56 ft. lbs. (77 Nm).
    b. Torque rod bracket-to-frame bolt—40 ft. lbs. (56 Nm).
    c. Torque rod-to-bracket bolt—56 ft. lbs. (77 Nm).
    d. Engine mount bracket-to-block—28 ft. lbs. (39 Nm).
    e. Front and rear engine mounting through bolts and nuts—60 ft. lbs. (84 Nm). Always use new bolts and nuts.
    f. Right hand mounting rubber on body side—30 ft. lbs. (41 Nm). Right hand mounting rubber on engine side—45 ft. lbs. (62 Nm).
    g. Torque rod to body frame—42 ft. lbs. (58 Nm).

h. Strut-to-body nuts—40 ft. lbs. (56 Nm).

i. Tie rod end-to-steering knuckle ball joints—29 ft. lbs. (40 Nm).

20. After the installation is completed, road test the vehicle and then re-check the fluid levels and check for any leaks.

4XE1 Engine

1. Relieve the fuel pressure and disconnect the battery cables.

2. Remove the battery. Scribe lines on the inside of the engine hood and remove the engine hood.

3. Drain the engine coolant and the transaxle fluid into suitable drain pans.

4. Remove the air intake duct from the common chamber and the breather hose from the rear of the valve cover.

5. Remove the fast idle vacuum hose from the air intake duct and the pulse air hose from the reed valve side.

6. Remove the 3 air cleaner fixing bolts and remove the air cleaner and air cleaner bracket from the engine.

7. Remove and tag the following vacuum lines:

a. The EGR vacuum hoses.

b. Canister hose from the throttle valve side of the vacuum switching valve.

c. Remove the MAP sensor hose from the common chamber side.

d. Remove the pulse air hose from the common chamber side.

e. Remove the canister hoses from the common chamber side.

f. Remove the master vacuum hose from the master VAC tube at the common chamber side.

8. Disconnect the following wiring harness:

a. On the electronic control gas injection harness, disconnect the 2 ECM ground connectors from the bracket located on top of the common chamber. Disconnect the 2 green and black multi-pin connectors on the top of the common chamber.

b. Remove the high tension cable from the ignition coil. Remove the 2 primary connections from the coil. Disconnect the condenser plug. Remove the ignition coil with bracket.

c. Disconnect 2 engine harness multi-pin plugs, near the battery tray. Remove the engine harness ground cable from the drivers inner fender. Disconnect the connector from the slow blow fuse.

d. Disconnect the connectors from the EGR temperature sensor, throttle position sensor, MAT sensor, oxygen sensor and remove the engine ground from the valve cover.

9. Working from the left side of the engine, remove the clutch cable by loosening the 2 adjusting nuts.

10. Remove the 2 transaxle shift cables by disconnecting the cotter pin and removing the clip from the shift cable bracket.

11. Disconnect the speedometer cable from the transaxle.

12. Disconnect the heater hoses from the engine. Disconnect the upper radiator hose from the engine.

13. Disconnect the accelerator cable from the throttle body and at the common chamber.

14. Disconnect the fuel feed hose at the fuel filter outlet and disconnect the return fuel line near the fuel filter.

15. Working from the front of the engine, remove the coolant reservoir.

16. Remove the 2 bolts from the power steering pump bracket, without disconnecting the feed lines and position the pump aside from the engine.

17. Disconnect the lower radiator hose from the radiator.

18. Remove the air conditioner compressor bolts and without disconnecting the air conditioning lines, secure the compressor away from the engine.

19. Remove the cooling fan and shroud as one assembly.

20. Raise and support the vehicle safely. Remove both front wheels.

21. Loosen the strut tower nuts on both sides but do not remove.

22. Remove the stabilizer bar. Disconnect the control arms on both sides from the body.

23. Remove the front air deflector, if equipped.

24. Remove the tension rod fixing nut from both sides and remove the rod out of the bracket.

25. Remove the passenger side halfshaft fixing bracket from the engine block and pull the halfshaft out of the transaxle. Pull the halfshaft on the drivers side out of the transaxle.

26. Remove the exhaust pipe from the exhaust manifold.

27. Remove the engine by using a suitable engine hoist. Remove the passenger side engine mount from the body.

28. Disconnect the torque rod at the firewall. Remove both lower engine mounting bolts.

29. Remove the engine and transaxle out of the vehicle together as an assembly.

To install:

30. Installation is the reverse of the removal procedure.

31. Tighten the engine mount bolts to the following specifications:

a. Lower engine mount-to-block bolts—28 ft. lbs. (39 Nm).

b. Lower engine mount through bolts and nuts—60 ft. lbs. (84 Nm).

c. Front and rear engine mount bracket-to-engine bolts—28 ft. lbs. (39 Nm).

d. Passenger side engine mount bracket-to-bracket bolts—29 ft. lbs. (41 Nm).

e. Passenger side mount-to-bracket bolts—29 ft. lbs. (41 Nm).

f. Passenger side mount-to-body bolt—60 ft. lbs. (84 Nm).

g. Torque rod through bolts—40 ft. lbs. (56 Nm).

32. Fill the engine and transaxle with the proper type and quantity of oil.

33. Fill the cooling system with the proper type and quantity of coolant.

34. Start the engine and check for leaks.

1987-89 IMPULSE

1. Relieve the fuel pressure, remove the battery cables, the battery clamp and the battery.

2. On 1987 vehicles, disconnect the headlight cover motor harness.

3. Scribe the location of the hood on the hood hinges and remove the hood.

4. Raise and safely support the vehicle.

5. Remove the engine splash shield and drain the cooling system.

6. Remove the air duct from the air cleaner to the throttle valve on non-turbocharged vehicles or the air ducts from the air cleaner to the turbocharger, turbocharger to intercooler and intercooler to throttle body on turbocharged vehicles.

7. Remove the radiator hoses and disconnect the overflow hose.

8. Remove the nuts attaching the fan blade and the fan pulley and remove the radiator stay and radiator mounting nuts.

9. Remove the radiator with the fan.

10. Remove the air cleaner intake duct on non-turbocharged vehicles or the intercooler and air duct on turbocharged vehicles.

11. Disconnect the wiring and cooler pipes on the condenser and remove the condenser with the receiver dryer and fan.

12. Disconnect the starter wires.

13. Disconnect the following hoses:

a. VSV (vacuum switch valve) to common chamber.

b. Fast idle solenoid to common chamber.

c. Throttle valve to 3 way.

d. Fast idle solenoid to pipe.

e. 2 from the VSV to the throttle valve on turbocharged vehicles.

f. Canister to common chamber.

g. Common chamber to brake master cylinder.

h. Injector blower duct to pipe.

i. Common chamber to automatic cruise actuator.

14. Disconnect and plug the power steering hoses.

15. On turbocharged vehicles, disconnect and plug the oil cooler hoses at the oil filter adapter.

16. If equipped with automatic transmission, disconnect and plug the transmission cooler lines at the radiator.

17. Disconnect the fuel lines and remove the injector blower duct.

18. Disconnect and plug the air conditioning compressor hoses.

19. Remove the clip clamping the battery cables and disconnect the engine wiring cables at the connectors inside the relay box.

20. Disconnect the knock sensor wiring, the dropping resister wiring and the crank angle sensor wiring.

21. Disconnect the ground cables at the engine and remove the right side engine mount nut.

22. Disconnect the alternator wires, the oxygen sensor wires and the transmission switch wires.

23. Disconnect the accelerator control cable and the heater hoses.

24. On turbocharged vehicles, remove the air switching valve with hoses, disconnect the turbocharger water hose, remove the turbocharger heat protector and disconnect the control cable.

25. Remove the engine left side mount nut.

26. If equipped with a manual transmission, remove the gear shift knob, the front console assembly and the gear shift lever boot.

27. Remove the heat protector at the exhaust pipe flange, disconnect the exhaust pipe at the flange and the front exhaust pipe bracket from the transmission bracket.

28. Remove the clutch slave cylinder and disconnect the shift linkage at the link joint on vehicles with manual transmission.

29. Disconnect the speedometer cable.

30. Remove the driveshafts and install a plug to the transmission rear cover.

31. Attach a suitable lifting device and lift the engine slightly. Remove the rear engine mounting bracket bolts.

32. Check to make sure all parts have been removed or disconnected from the engine.

33. Raise the engine toward the front of the vehicle and remove the engine and transmission assembly from the vehicle.

34. Disconnect the transmission from the engine.

To install:

35. Attach the transmission to the engine.

36. Position the engine and transmission assembly in the vehicle and install the engine mount bolts.

37. Install the driveshaft and connect the shift linkage.

38. Connect the speedometer cable and on manual transmission vehicles, install the clutch slave cylinder.

39. Connect the exhaust pipe and the bracket and install the heat protector.

40. If equipped with a manual transmission, install the gear shift lever boot, the console assembly and the gear shift knob.

41. On turbocharged vehicles, connect the control cable, install the turbocharger heat protector, connect the turbocharger water hose and install the air switching valve with the hoses.

42. Connect the heater hoses and the accelerator control cable.

43. Connect the air conditioning compressor hoses and install the injector blower duct.

44. Connect the fuel lines.

45. If equipped with an automatic transmission, connect the transmission cooler lines at the radiator.

46. Connect the oil cooler hoses at the oil filter adapter on turbocharged vehicles.

47. Connect the power steering hoses.

48. Install the condenser with the receiver dryer and fan.

49. Connect the wiring and cooler pipes on the condenser.

50. On turbocharged vehicles, install the intercooler and air duct. On all others, install the air cleaner intake duct.

51. Install the radiator with the fan blade, the radiator mounting nuts and radiator stay, the fan blade and pulley attaching nuts and the radiator and overflow hoses.

52. Connect all wiring and vacuum lines.

53. Install the air cleaner to throttle valve duct on non-turbocharged vehicles and the air cleaner to turbocharger, turbocharger to intercooler and intercooler to throttle valve ducts on turbocharged vehicles.

54. Install the engine splash shield.

55. Install the hood, aligning the marks that were made during the removal procedure.

56. Install the battery.

57. Fill the cooling system with the proper type and quantity of coolant. Fill the crankcase with the proper type of oil to the required level.

58. Connect the negative battery cable, start the engine and check for leaks.

59. Fill the power steering reservoir with fluid and bleed the system.

60. Evacuate and charge the air conditioning system.

1990–91 IMPULSE AND 1991 STYLUS

1. Relieve the fuel system pressure, disconnect the battery cables and remove the battery and battery tray.

2. Mark the position of the hood on the hood hinges and remove the hood.

3. Raise and safely support the vehicle.

4. Drain the coolant from the radiator and the oil from the transaxle. Remove the left and right undercovers.

5. Disconnect the accelerator cable from the throttle valve and the common chamber.

6. Disconnect the breather hose from the intake air duct side and remove the intake air duct from the throttle valve.

7. Remove the intercooler and breather hose, Turbo only.

8. Remove the air cleaner cover and element and the air cleaner body.

9. Disconnect the MAP sensor hose from the MAP sensor side, the vacuum hose from the vacuum booster side and the 2 canister vacuum hoses from the common chamber and throttle valve.

10. Remove the bracket which supports the 2 canister pipes and the MAP sensor pipe from the common chamber.

11. Disconnect the following electrical connectors and tag them for reassembly:

a. 2 cable harness connectors near the left front strut tower.

b. Ignition wire from the ignition coil side.

c. Bonding cable connector from the terminal at the thermostat housing flange.

d. Both primary connections from the ignition coil.

e. Ground cable from the driver's side inner fender.

f. Positive cable terminal in fuse box.

g. Cooling fan harness connector.

h. Both harness connectors at the front of the battery.

i. Oxygen sensor harness connector.

j. Ground cable terminals from the right side of the common chamber.

k. Bonding cable terminal from the right side of the induction control assembly.

l. If equipped with an automatic transaxle, the 4 connectors of the automatic transaxle control system on the automatic transaxle assembly.

m. Disconnect the oil cooler pipes, Turbo only.

12. Remove the ignition coil with the battery bracket.

13. If equipped with a manual transaxle, loosen both adjusting nuts and remove the clutch cable and disconnect the cotter pin and clip from the shift cable bracket.

14. If equipped with an automatic transaxle, disconnect the cotter pin and joint from the shift cable lever.

15. Disconnect the heater hoses, radiator hoses, fuel lines and speedometer cable.

16. Remove the coolant reservoir tank.

17. Remove the power steering pump and air conditioning compressors and position them aside without disconnecting their lines.

18. If equipped with an automatic transaxle, disconnect the oil cooler lines from the radiator.

19. Remove the cooling fan and the shroud.

20. Remove the front wheel and tire assemblies.

21. Loosen but do not remove, the strut tower nuts.

22. Disconnect the lower ball joints and tie rod ends and remove the halfshafts.

23. Remove the engine splash shield and disconnect the exhaust pipe.

24. Attach a suitable engine hoist to the engine/transaxle assembly and lift the engine slightly to take weight off of the mounts.

25. Disconnect the torque rod from the center beam.

26. Remove the center bolt of the rear side engine mounting after removing the damper weight.

27. Remove the left side engine mount.

28. Remove the cruise control pump and VSV assembly and remove the right side engine mount.

29. If equipped with a manual transaxle, disconnect the axle shaft center bearing support bracket from the cylinder bracket.

30. Remove the engine/transaxle assembly.

31. Separate the engine from the transaxle.

To install:

32. Connect the transaxle to the engine and position the assembly in the vehicle.

33. Connect the axle shaft center bearing support bracket to the cylinder bracket.

34. Install the right side engine mount. Tighten the mount attaching bolt to 89 ft. lbs. (121 Nm), the mount attaching nut to 37 ft. lbs. (50 Nm) and the through bolt to 51 ft. lbs. (69 Nm).

35. Install the left side engine mount and tighten the through bolt to 51 ft. lbs. (69 Nm).

36. Install the rear side engine mount. Tighten the through bolt to 76 ft. lbs. (103 Nm) and the damper weight to 37 ft. lbs. (50 Nm).

37. Install the torque rod. Tighten the center beam side bolt to 51 ft. lbs. (69 Nm) and the engine side bolt to 95 ft. lbs. (128 Nm).

38. Connect the exhaust pipe and install the engine splash shield.

39. Install the halfshafts and connect the tie rods and lower ball joints. Tighten the lower ball joint nuts to 48 ft. lbs. (66 Nm) and the tie rod nuts to 29 ft. lbs. (39 Nm).

40. Tighten the strut tower nuts to 51 ft. lbs. (69 Nm) and install the front wheel and tire assemblies.

41. Install the cooling fan and shroud. On automatic transaxle vehicles, connect the transaxle cooling lines.

42. Install the power steering pump and air conditioning compressor, install and adjust the drive belts.

43. Install the coolant reservoir tank.

44. Connect the radiator and heater hoses, the fuel lines and the speedometer cable. Install the intercooler and hoses. Connect the oil cooler lines, Turbo only.

45. Connect the transaxle shift cable and on manual transaxle vehicles, connect the clutch cable.

46. Install the ignition coil with the battery bracket.

47. Connect all electrical connectors.

48. Install the bracket that supports the 2 canister pipes and the MAP sensor pipe to the common chamber.

49. Connect all vacuum hoses.

50. Install the air cleaner body and the element and cover.

51. Install the intake air duct and connect the breather hose to the intake air side.

52. Connect the accelerator cable and install the hood, aligning the marks that were made during the removal procedure.

53. Install the battery tray and the battery.

54. Fill the cooling system with the proper type and quantity of coolant. Fill the crankcase with the proper type of oil to the required level.

55. Connect the battery cables, start the engine and check for leaks. Adjust the clutch cable.

Cylinder Head

Removal and Installation

I-MARK

Except 4XE1 Engine

1. Relieve the fuel system pressure, disconnect the negative battery cable and drain the cooling system into a suitable drain pan.

2. Remove the air cleaner assembly and disconnect the flex hose along with the oxygen sensor at the exhaust manifold.

3. Disconnect the exhaust pipe bracket at the block and the exhaust pipe at the manifold. On turbocharged model remove exhaust pipe at wastegate manifold, and remove vacuum line for turbocharger control.

4. Disconnect the spark plug wires and remove the thermostat housing.

5. Rotate the engine until the engine is at TDC on the compression stroke of the No. 1 cylinder. Remove distributor cap and mark the distributor rotor to housing position and housing to cylinder head. Remove the distributor hold-down bolt and remove the distributor.

6. Remove the vacuum advance hoses and the ground cable at the cylinder head.

7. Disconnect the fuel lines at the fuel pump and at the carburetor and remove the secondary hoses and throttle cable on non-turbocharged model.

8. Remove engine wiring harness assembly from fuel injectors and fuel line from fuel injector pipe on turbocharged model.

9. Disconnect the vacuum switching valve electrical connector and the heater hoses.

10. Remove the alternator, power steering pump and air conditioning adjusting bolts, brackets and drive belts. Remove and tag all necessary electrical and vacuum lines.

11. Support the engine using a suitable vertical hoist. Remove the right hand motor mount and the bracket at the front cover.

12. Remove the crankshaft bolt and remove the boss and the crank pulley.

13. Remove the timing cover and be sure the mark on the cam pulley is aligned with the upper surface of the cylinder head. Also the dowel pin on the camshaft should be positioned at the top.

14. Disconnect the PCV hoses and remove the valve cover. If the cover sticks to the head, carefully strike the valve cover with a soft mallet.

15. Insert a hex wrench into the tension pulley hexagonal hole. Loosen the timing belt tension by rotating the tension pulley clockwise and remove the timing belt.

16. Remove the fuel pump, on non-turbocharged model, and disconnect the intake manifold coolant hoses.

17. Remove the cylinder head bolts, remove the bolts from both ends at the same time, working toward the middle and remove the cylinder head. Remove the manifolds from the cylinder head.

To install:

18. Installation is the reverse of the removal procedure. Make sure all gasket mating surfaces are clean prior to installation.

19. Check the cylinder head for flatness before installing, using a suitable straight-edge and feeler gauge. If the head is warped more than 0.008 in. (0.2mm) it must be resurfaced. If the head is warped more than 0.016 in. (0.4mm) it must be replaced.

20. Using new seals and gaskets, apply oil to the head bolt

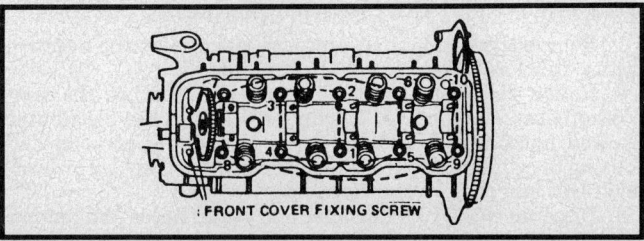

: FRONT COVER FIXING SCREW

Cylinder head bolt torque sequence—I-Mark except 4XE1 engine

threads and torque the head bolts. The head bolts are tightened, in 2 steps, first to 29 ft. lbs. (40 Nm), in sequence, and finally to 58 ft. lbs. (80 Nm), in sequence.

21. Properly adjust the timing belt tension and adjust the valve clearance.

4XE1 Engine

1. Relieve the fuel system pressure and disconnect the negative battery cable.
2. Mark the position of the hood on the hinge brackets and remove the hood.
3. Drain the cooling system.
4. Remove the accelerator cable from the throttle valve and common chamber.
5. Disconnect the breather hose from the intake air duct side.
6. Disconnect the MAP sensor hose from the MAP sensor side, the vacuum booster hose from the vacuum booster and the 2 canister hoses from the pipes on the common chamber.
7. Remove the bracket that supports the 2 canister pipes and MAP sensor pipe from the common chamber.
8. Disconnect the following electrical connectors and tag them for reassembly:
    a. Oxygen sensor.
    b. Ignition wire from the coil side.
    c. Bonding cable connector from the terminal at the thermostat housing flange.
    d. Temperature sensor and thermometer unit connector at the thermostat housing.
    e. Ground cable terminals from the right side of the common chamber.
    f. Bonding cable terminal from the right side of the induction control assembly.
    g. The 2 cable harness connectors near the left front strut tower.
9. Disconnect the heater hose, upper radiator hose, throttle valve heating hose and the fuel lines.
10. Remove the coolant by-pass stay pipe from the cylinder head.
11. Raise and safely support the vehicle.
12. Remove the engine splash shield and disconnect the exhaust pipe.
13. Use a suitable device to support the engine and remove the right side engine mount.
14. Remove the coolant recovery tank with the bracket.
15. Remove the accessory drive belts.
16. Remove the 2 bolts from the power steering pump bracket, without disconnecting the feed lines and position the pump and bracket aside.
17. Remove the engine mounting bridge bracket and the cylinder head center cover.
18. Disconnect the spark plug wires from the spark plugs, ignition coil and clips and the PCV hose from the cylinder head cover.
19. Remove the upper timing belt cover, the power steering pump bracket and the cylinder head cover.
20. Remove the tension adjusting hole cover and align the camshaft pulley timing marks even with the top edge of the cylinder head.

21. Loosen the tension pulley lock bolt and turn the tension pulley clockwise to loosen the timing belt. Remove the timing belt from the camshaft pulleys.
22. Remove the cylinder head bolts, starting at each end of the cylinder head and working toward the center.
23. Raise the cylinder head and remove the coolant hose from the oil cooler.
24. Remove the cylinder head assembly.

To install:

25. Installation is the reverse of the removal procedure, taking note of the following points.
26. Make sure all mating surfaces are clean prior to installation.
27. Check the cylinder head for flatness before installing. If the head is warped more than 0.008 in. (0.2mm), it must be resurfaced. If the head is warped more than 0.016 in. (0.4mm), it must be replaced.
28. Use a new gasket and align the cylinder head on the block dowel pins. Apply engine oil to the threads and seating faces of the cylinder head bolts.
29. Tighten the bolts, in 2 steps, following the proper sequence. First, tighten the bolts to 29 ft. lbs. (40 Nm), in sequence, and finally to 59 ft. lbs. (79 Nm), in sequence.
30. Apply a 0.08–0.12 in. (2–3mm) width bead of sealant to the arched area of the No. 1 and No. 5 camshaft bearing caps. Tighten the cylinder head cover bolts to 27 inch lbs. (3 Nm) in the proper sequence.
31. Properly adjust the timing belt after installation.
32. Be sure to torque the following components to specification:
    Upper timing cover—7 ft. lbs. (10 Nm).
    Engine mounting bridge bracket—30 ft. lbs. (40 Nm).
    Right side engine mount through bolt—51 ft. lbs. (69 Nm).
    Right side engine mount nut—37 ft. lbs. (50 Nm).
    Right side engine mount bolt—89 ft. lbs. (121 Nm).
    Exhaust pipe nuts—42 ft. lbs. (57 Nm).

IMPULSE AND STYLUS

G200Z Engine

1. Relieve the fuel system pressure and disconnect the negative battery cable.
2. Raise and safely support the vehicle.
3. Drain the cooling system.
4. Disconnect the exhaust pipe from the exhaust manifold.
5. Disconnect the upper radiator hose and heater hoses.
6. Disconnect the fuel lines and the accelerator cable.
7. Disconnect all necessary electrical connectors and vacuum hoses and tag them for reassembly.
8. Remove the cylinder head cover.
9. Bring the No 1 cylinder to TDC of the compression stroke.
10. Release the timing chain tension as follows:
    a. Using a suitable tool, depress the lock lever on the automatic adjuster rearward.
    b. Push in on the automatic adjuster shoe and lock it in the retracted position by releasing the lever.
11. Remove the timing sprocket-to-camshaft bolt and remove the sprocket from the camshaft. Do not remove the sprocket from the chain. Keep it in position on the chain using mechanics wire.
12. Remove the cylinder head to timing cover bolts. Remove the cylinder head bolts beginning with the outside bolts and working towards the center on both sides.
13. Remove the cylinder head.

To install:

14. Installation is the reverse of the removal procedure.
15. Make sure all mating surfaces are clean prior to installation.
16. Check the cylinder head surface for flatness before installing. If the head is warped more than 0.008 in. (0.2mm), it must

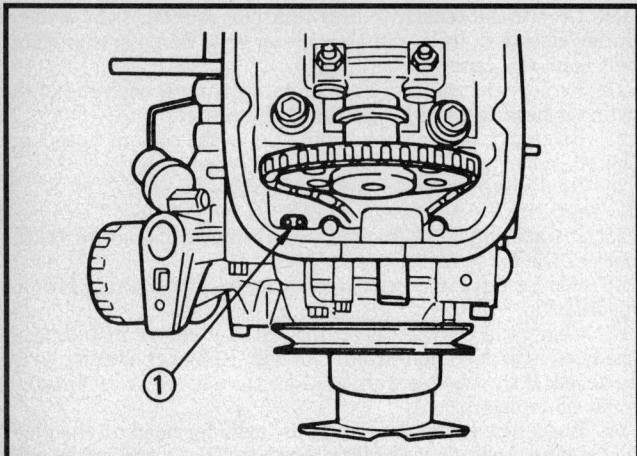

Timing chain automatic adjuster lock lever—G200Z engine

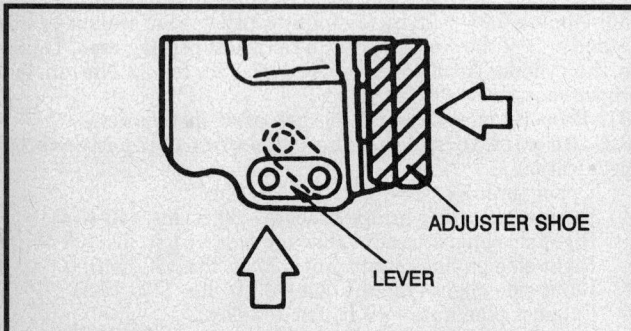

ADJUSTER SHOE

LEVER

Timing chain automatic adjuster shoe and lever—G200Z engine

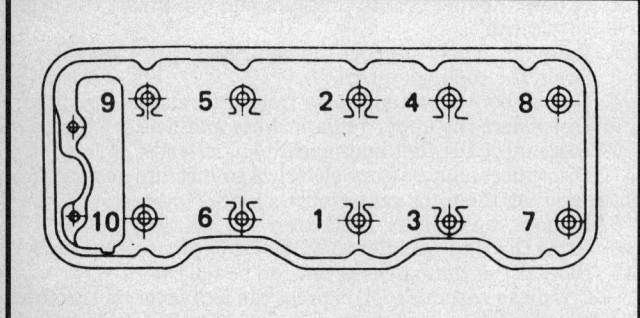

Cylinder head bolt torque sequence—G200Z engine

be resurfaced. If the head is warped more than 0.016 in. (0.4mm), it must be replaced.

17. Install a new cylinder head gasket and the cylinder head, aligning them on the dowels on the cylinder block.

18. Apply a thin coat of engine oil to the cylinder head bolt threads and install the bolts. Tighten them, in 2 steps, in sequence. First, tighten to 43 ft. lbs. (60 Nm), in sequence, and then to 72 ft. lbs. (100 Nm), in sequence.

19. Install the camshaft sprocket on the camshaft and tighten the bolt to 58 ft. lbs. (80 Nm). Set the automatic adjuster by turning the adjuster slide pin 90 degrees counterclockwise using a suitable tool.

20. Tighten the cylinder head cover bolts to 3.6 ft. lbs. (5 Nm).

4ZD1, 4ZC1-T and 4XE1 (SOHC) Engines

1. Relieve the fuel system pressure, disconnect the negative battery cable and drain the cooling system.

2. Rotate the engine until the engine is at TDC on the compression stroke of the No. 1 cylinder. Remove the distributor cap and mark the distributor rotor to housing position and housing to cylinder head position. Remove the distributor hold-down bolt and remove the distributor.

3. Disconnect the radiator inlet and outlet hoses and remove the radiator.

4. Remove the alternator and the air conditioner drive belts. Remove the engine cooling fan.

5. Remove the crankshaft pulley center bolt and remove the pulley and hub assembly.

6. Remove the air pump belt and move the air pump aside. If equipped, remove the air conditioning compressor and lay it to one side. Remove the compressor mounting bracket.

7. Remove the water pump pulley. Remove the top section of the front cover and the water pump.

8. Remove the lower section of the front cover.

9. Remove the tension spring. Loosen the top bolt of the tension pulley and draw the tension pulley fully to the water pump side.

10. Remove the timing belt.

11. Remove cam cover.

12. Sequentially, loosen and remove the rocker arm shaft tightening nuts from the outermost one and remove the rocker arm shaft with the bracket as an assembly.

13. Raise and safely support the vehicle and disconnect the exhaust pipe at the exhaust manifold. On turbocharged vehicles, disconnect the exhaust pipe from the wastegate manifold and remove the control cable for the turbocharger.

14. Lower the vehicle and disconnect all necessary lines, hoses and electrical connectors and tag them for reassembly.

15. Disconnect the accelerator linkage. On turbocharged vehicles remove the engine wiring harness assembly from the fuel injectors and fuel line from fuel injector pipe.

16. Remove the cylinder head bolts beginning with the outer bolts and working in towards the center on both sides.

17. Remove the cylinder head.

To install:

18. Installation is the reverse of the removal procedure.

19. Make sure all mating surfaces are clean prior to installation.

20. Check the cylinder head surface for flatness before installing. If the head is warped more than 0.008 in. (0.2mm), it must be resurfaced. If the head is warped more than 0.016 in. (0.4mm), it must be replaced.

21. Install a new cylinder head gasket and the cylinder head, aligning them on the dowels on the cylinder block.

22. Apply a thin coat of engine oil to the cylinder head bolt threads and install the bolts. Tighten them, in 2 steps, in sequence. First tighten to 58 ft. lbs. (80 Nm), in sequence, and then to 72 ft. lbs. (100 Nm), in sequence.

23. Properly adjust the timing belt tension.

4XE1 (DOHC) Engine

1. Relieve the fuel system pressure and disconnect the negative battery cable.

2. Mark the position of the hood on the hinge brackets and remove the hood.

3. Drain the cooling system.

4. Remove the accelerator cable from the throttle valve and common chamber.

5. Disconnect the breather hose from the intake air duct side.

6. Disconnect the MAP sensor hose from the MAP sensor side, the vacuum booster hose from the vacuum booster and the 2 canister hoses from the pipes on the common chamber.

7. Remove the bracket that supports the 2 canister pipes and MAP sensor pipe from the common chamber.

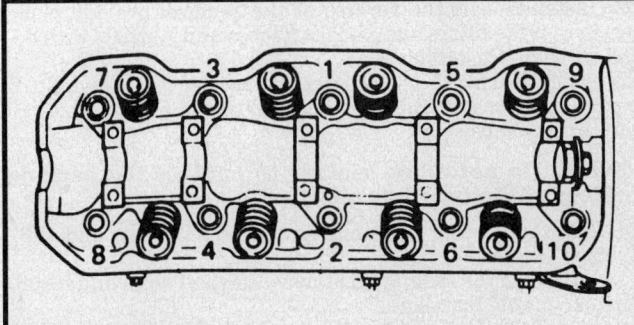

Cylinder head bolt torque sequence—4ZD1 and 4ZC1-T engines

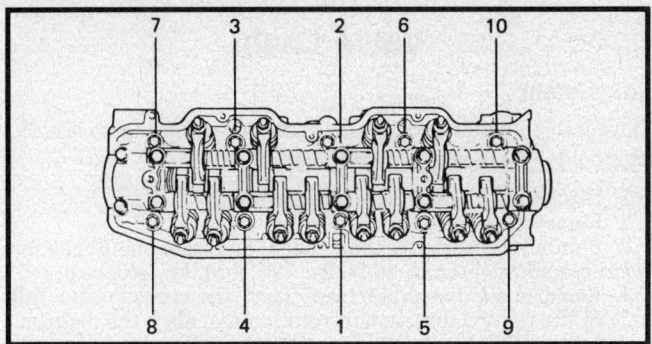

Cylinder head bolt torque sequence—4XE1 (SOHC) engine

8. Disconnect the following electrical connectors and tag them for reassembly:
   a. Oxygen sensor.
   b. Ignition wire from the coil side.
   c. Bonding cable connector from the terminal at the thermostat housing flange.
   d. Temperature sensor and thermometer unit connector at the thermostat housing.
   e. Ground cable terminals from the right side of the common chamber.
   f. Bonding cable terminal from the right side of the induction control assembly.
   g. The 2 cable harness connectors near the left front strut tower.
9. Disconnect the heater hose, upper radiator hose, throttle valve heating hose and the fuel lines.
10. Remove the coolant by-pass stay pipe from the cylinder head.
11. Raise and safely support the vehicle.
12. Remove the engine splash shield and disconnect the exhaust pipe.
13. Use a suitable device to support the engine and remove the right side engine mount.
14. Remove the coolant recovery tank with the bracket.
15. Remove the accessory drive belts.
16. Remove the 2 bolts from the power steering pump bracket, without disconnecting the feed lines and position the pump and bracket aside.
17. Remove the engine mounting bridge bracket and the cylinder head center cover.
18. Disconnect the spark plug wires from the spark plugs, ignition coil and clips and the PCV hose from the cylinder head cover.
19. Remove the upper timing belt cover, the power steering pump bracket and the cylinder head cover.

20. Remove the tension adjusting hole cover and align the camshaft pulley timing marks even with the top edge of the cylinder head.
21. Loosen the tension pulley lock bolt and turn the tension pulley clockwise to loosen the timing belt. Remove the timing belt from the camshaft pulleys.
22. Remove the cylinder head bolts, starting at each end of the cylinder head and working toward the center.
23. Raise the cylinder head and remove the coolant hose from the oil cooler.
24. Remove the cylinder head assembly.
To install:
25. Installation is the reverse of the removal procedure, taking note of the following points.
26. Make sure all mating surfaces are clean prior to installation.
27. Check the cylinder head for flatness before installing. If the head is warped more than 0.008 in. (0.2mm), it must be resurfaced. If the head is warped more than 0.016 in. (0.4mm), it must be replaced.
28. Use a new gasket and align the cylinder head on the block dowel pins. Apply engine oil to the threads and seating faces of the cylinder head bolts.
29. Tighten the bolts, in 2 steps, in sequence. First, tighten the bolts to 29 ft. lbs. (40 Nm), in sequence, and finally to 59 ft. lbs. (79 Nm), in sequence.
30. Apply a 0.08–0.12 in. (2–3mm) width bead of sealant to the arched area of the No. 1 and No. 5 camshaft bearing caps. Tighten the cylinder head cover bolts to 27 inch lbs. (3 Nm) in the proper sequence.

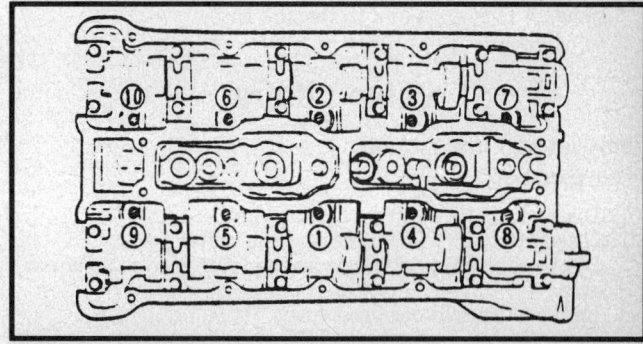

Cylinder head bolt torque sequence—4XE1 (DOHC) engine

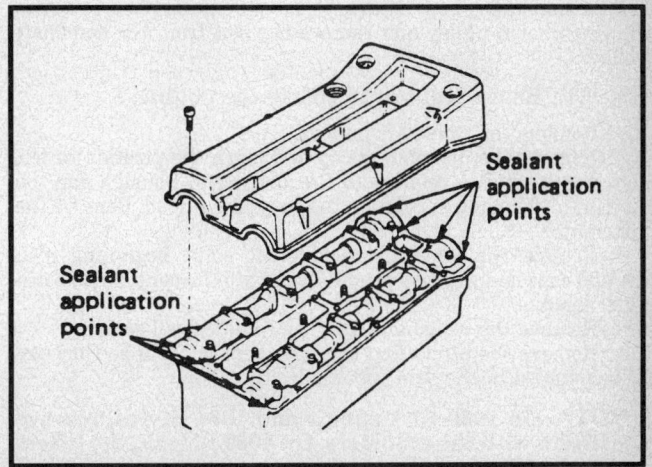

Sealant application points

Sealant application points

Installing the cylinder head cover—4XE1 (DOHC) engine

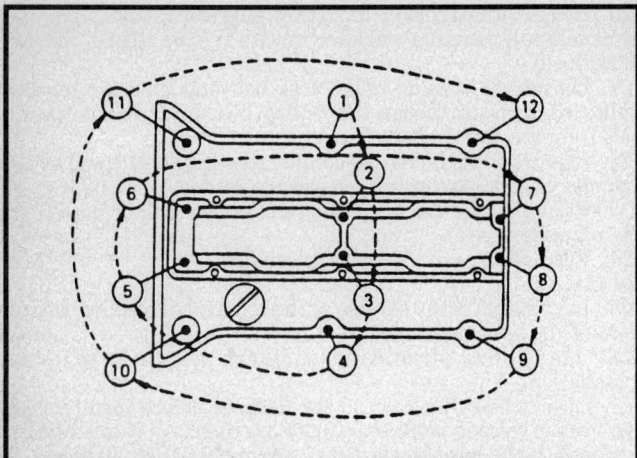

Cylinder head cover bolt torque sequence—4XE1 (DOHC) engine

31. Properly adjust the timing belt after installation.
32. Be sure to torque the following components to specification:
   Upper timing cover—7 ft. lbs. (10 Nm).
   Engine mounting bridge bracket—30 ft. lbs. (40 Nm).
   Right side engine mount through bolt—51 ft. lbs. (69 Nm).
   Right side engine mount nut—37 ft. lbs. (50 Nm).
   Right side engine mount bolt—89 ft. lbs. (121 Nm).
   Exhaust pipe nuts—42 ft. lbs. (57 Nm).

Valve Lifters

Removal and Installation

4XE1 ENGINE

1. Disconnect the negative battery cable.
2. Disconnect the PCV hoses and the center cover.
3. Disconnect the spark plug wires and remove the upper timing cover.
4. Remove the cylinder head cover.
5. Bring the No. 1 cylinder to TDC of the compression stroke. The timing marks on the camshafts should be even with the top edge of the cylinder head.
6. Loosen the camshaft pulley bolts and loosen the timing belt tension pulley bolt ½ turn. Loosen the timing belt by rotating the tension pulley and remove the belt from the camshaft pulleys.

NOTE: Be careful not to rotate the engine.

7. Remove the camshaft pulleys.
8. Remove the distributor cap and mark the position of the distributor rotor in relation to the distributor housing and the distributor housing in relation to the cylinder head. Remove the distributor.
9. Remove the camshaft bearing cap bolts, beginning with the end caps and working gradually toward the center of the cylinder head.
10. Remove the camshafts and the camshaft oil seals.
11. Remove the lifters and arrange them in order so they can be reinstalled in the same position.

NOTE: On 1990–91 Impulse and 1991 Stylus, remove the lifters with the adjusters. On 1989 I-Mark, the lifters are hydraulic and should be submerged in engine oil when removed. This will prevent air from mixing with the oil in the lifter and causing noise when reinstalled.

12. Installation is the reverse of the removal procedure. Be sure to coat the lifters and camshaft lobes and journals with engine oil before installing.
13. Apply sealant to the contact surfaces of No. 1 and No. 5 bearing caps. Install the caps and tighten to 89 inch lbs. (10 Nm), in sequence.

NOTE: Do not allow sealant to contact the bearing surfaces of the bearing cap.

14. Adjust the valve clearance on 1990–91 Impulse and 1991 Stylus.
15. Lubricate the sealing lip of new camshaft seals and install using a suitable installer.
16. Tighten the camshaft pulleys to 43 ft. lbs. (59 Nm), install the timing belt and properly adjust the tension.
17. Tighten the cylinder head cover bolts to 27 inch lbs. (3 Nm), in sequence.

Valve Lash

Adjustment

Valve lash adjustments must be made when the engine is cold.

EXCEPT 4XE1 (DOHC) ENGINE

1. Disconnect the negative battery cable.
2. Remove the cylinder head cover.
3. Before proceeding further, check the rocker shaft bolts for looseness and tighten to 16 ft. lbs. (22 Nm), as necessary.
4. Remove the distributor cap. Turn the crankshaft 1 full turn in the normal direction of rotation and align the distributor rotor with the No. 1 cylinder spark plug wire on the distributor cap and align the notched line on the crank pulley with the **0** mark on the timing gear case cover.
5. The following valves can be adjusted: Intake—No. 1 and No. 2. Exhaust—No. 1 and No. 3.
6. Measure the clearance between the rocker arm and the valve stem using a suitable feeler gauge. Adjust by loosening the

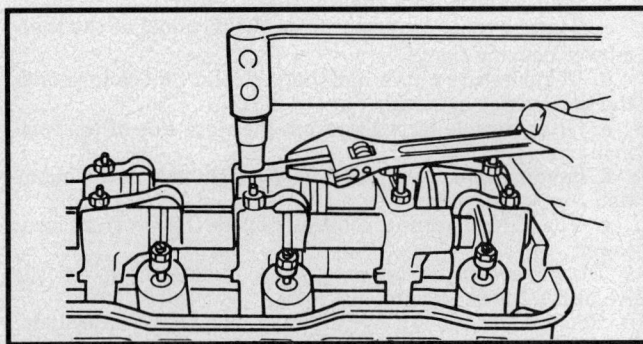

Checking rocker shaft for tightness

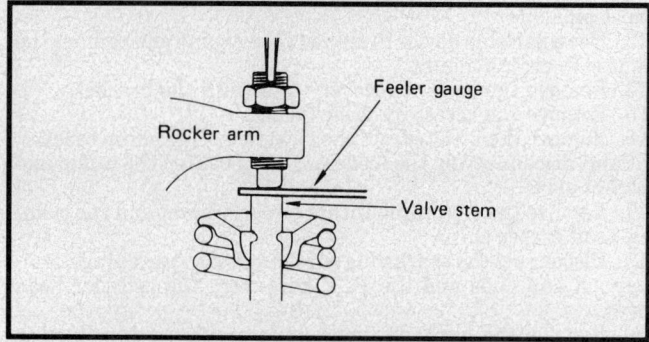

Adjusting the valve clearance

locknut and turning the adjustment stud until a slight drag is felt on the feeler gauge.

7. Adjust the valve clearance to the following specifications:
Except 4ZD1 and 4XE1 (SOHC) engine: Intake—0.006 in. (0.15mm), Exhaust—0.010 in. (0.25mm).
4ZD1 engine: Intake—0.008 in. (0.20mm), Exhaust—0.008 in. (0.20mm).
4XE1 (SOHC) engine: Intake—0.004–0.008 in. (0.10–0.20mm), Exhaust—0.008–0.012 in. (0.20–0.30mm).

8. After adjustment is completed, rotate the engine 1 revolution until the notched line on the crank pulley is aligned with the **0** mark on the timing gear case cover and the distributor rotor is aligned with the No. 4 spark plug wire on the distributor cap.

9. The remaining valves can now be adjusted.

10. After all valves have been adjusted, install the remaining components in the reverse of their removal procedure.

4XE1 (DOHC) ENGINE

NOTE: **The 4XE1 engine in 1989 I-Mark uses hydraulic lifters which require no adjustment.**

1. Disconnect the negative battery cable.
2. Remove the cylinder head cover and remove the spark plugs.
3. Check the torque of the camshaft bearing cap bolts and tighten to 89 inch lbs. (10 Nm), as necessary.
4. Rotate the engine and align the notched line on the crank pulley with the **0** mark on the timing cover. The lifters on the No. 1 cylinder should have play and the lifters on the No. 4 cylinder should not. If not, rotate the engine 1 more revolution and

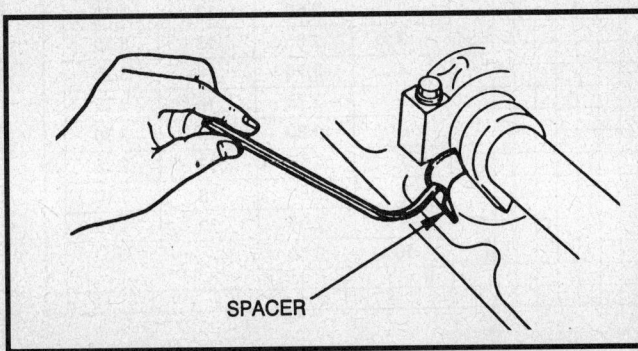

Installing valve adjustment spacer tool—Impulse with 4XE1 (DOHC) engine

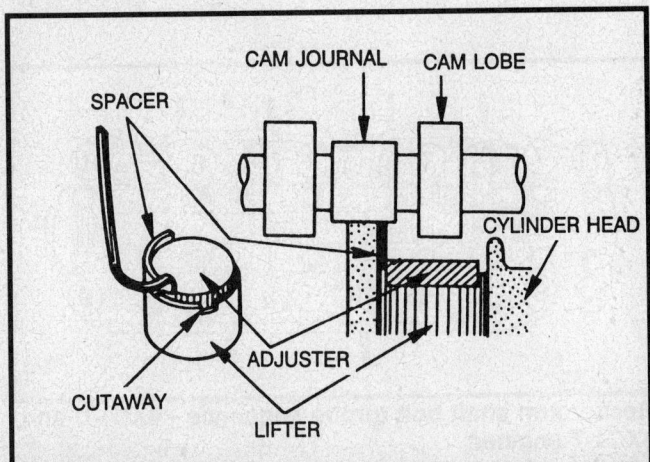

Valve adjuster shim removal—Impulse with 4XE1 (DOHC) engine

align the marks again. The No. 1 cylinder is on TDC of the compression stroke.

5. The following valves can be measured for valve clearance: Intake—No. 1 and No. 2. Exhaust—No. 1 and No. 3.
6. Measure the clearance using a suitable feeler gauge and record the measurements of those that are out of adjustment.
7. Rotate the engine 1 revolution until the No. 4 cylinder is at TDC and measure the clearance of the remaining valves. Record the measurements of those that are out of adjustment.
8. Adjust the valve clearance by replacing the adjuster shim as follows:
a. Turn the camshaft and use the cam lift to press down the lifter.
b. Place spacer J–38413–2 or J–38413–3 or equivalent, on the upper circumference of the lifter from outside the cylinder head.
c. Release the cam lift by turning the camshaft and hold the lifter down with the spacer. Remove the adjuster shim to the spark plug side using a suitable tool.

NOTE: **Before pressing down the lifter, turn the cutaway of the lifter toward the position at which the adjuster shim is easily removed.**

d. Measure the thickness of the adjuster shim using a suitable micrometer. Calculate the needed thickness of the replacement shim by adding the thickness of the original shim to the required clearance. Select the available adjuster shim with a thickness as close as possible to the calculated values.

NOTE: **Adjuster shims are available in 19 sizes in thickness increments of 0.05mm, ranging from 2.55–3.45mm.**

e. Place the selected adjuster shim on the lifter and press down the lifter by turning the camshaft and removing the spacer.
9. After valve adjustment is completed, install the remaining components in the reverse order of their removal.

Rocker Arms/Shafts

Removal and Installation

EXCEPT G200Z ENGINE

1. Disconnect the negative battery cable.
2. Remove the cylinder head cover and the timing belt cover.
3. Bring the No. 1 cylinder to TDC on the compression stroke.
4. On I-Mark, loosen the bolts attaching the timing belt tension pulley. Turn the tension pulley clockwise to loosen the timing belt and tighten the attaching bolts to hold the tension pulley in place.
5. On Impulse, remove the tension spring and loosen the bolt. Draw the timing cover tension pulley fully to the water pump side to loosen the timing belt.
6. Loosen and remove the rocker arm shaft tightening bolts starting with the outermost one and working toward the center of the cylinder head.

To install:

7. Remove the rocker arm shafts.
8. Inspect the rocker arms and shafts for wear and replace, as necessary. When disassembling, label the components and keep them in order so they may be reinstalled in their original positions. Apply engine oil to the rocker arms and shafts when reassembling.
9. Installation is the reverse of the removal procedure.
10. On I-Mark, remove any oil from the contact surfaces on the No. 1 and No. 5 rocker brackets and apply sealant to the contact surfaces before installation.
11. On Impulse, remove any oil from the contact surface of the

Intake adjuster shim chart—4XE1 (DOHC) engine

Measured clearance mm	inch	2.52	2.54	2.56	2.58	2.60	2.62	2.64	2.66	2.68	2.70	2.72	2.74	2.76	2.78	2.80	2.82	2.84	2.86	2.88	2.90	2.92	2.94	2.96	2.98	3.00	3.02	3.04	3.06	3.08	3.10	3.12	3.14	3.16	3.18	3.20	3.22	3.24	3.26	3.28	3.30	3.32	3.34	3.36	3.38	3.40	3.42	3.44	3.46	3.48
0.000~0.025	0.000~0.001																	1	1	2	2	2	3	3	4	4	5	5	6	6	6	7	7	8	8	8	9	9	9	10	10	10	11	11	12	13	13	14	15	16	17
0.026~0.050	0.001~0.002							1	1	1	2	2	3	3	3	4	4	5	5	5	6	6	7	7	7	8	8	9	9	10	10	11	11	11	12	13	13	13	14	14	15	15	16	16	17	17
0.051~0.075	0.002~0.003				1	1	1	2	2	3	3	3	4	4	5	5	5	6	6	7	7	7	8	8	9	9	10	10	11	11	11	12	13	13	13	14	15	15	15	16	17	17	18
0.076~0.100	0.003~0.004			1	1	2	2	2	3	3	4	4	5	5	6	6	6	7	8	8	9	9	10	10	10	11	11	12	12	13	13	14	14	15	15	16	16	16	17	18	18	18
0.101~0.200	0.004~0.008																	Replacement not to be required
0.201~0.225	0.008~0.009	2	2	2	3	3	4	4	5	5	6	6	6	7	8	8	8	9	9	10	10	10	11	11	12	13	13	14	14	15	15	16	16	16	17	18	18	18	19	19
0.226~0.250	0.009~0.010	2	3	3	3	4	4	5	5	5	6	6	7	7	7	8	8	9	9	9	10	11	11	12	12	13	13	13	14	14	15	15	15	16	16	17	17	18	18	18	19	19	19
0.251~0.275	0.010~0.011	3	3	3	4	4	5	5	5	6	7	7	7	8	8	9	9	10	11	11	11	12	13	13	13	14	14	15	15	16	16	17	17	17	18	19	19	19
0.276~0.300	0.011~0.012	3	4	4	4	5	5	6	6	6	7	7	8	8	8	9	9	10	10	10	11	12	12	13	13	14	14	15	15	16	16	16	17	18	18	18	19	19
0.301~0.325	0.012~0.013	4	4	4	5	5	6	6	6	7	7	8	8	9	9	10	10	10	11	12	12	13	13	14	14	14	15	15	16	16	17	17	18	18	18	19	19
0.326~0.350	0.013~0.014	4	5	5	5	6	6	7	7	7	8	8	9	9	10	10	11	11	11	12	13	13	13	14	14	15	15	16	16	17	17	17	18	19	19	19
0.351~0.375	0.014~0.015	5	5	5	6	6	7	7	7	8	9	9	9	10	10	11	11	11	12	13	13	13	14	15	15	16	16	16	17	17	18	18	19	19
0.376~0.400	0.015~0.016	5	6	6	6	7	7	8	8	8	9	9	10	10	10	11	12	12	12	13	13	14	14	15	15	16	16	16	17	18	18	18	19
0.401~0.425	0.016~0.017	6	6	6	7	7	8	8	9	9	10	10	11	11	12	12	12	13	14	14	14	15	15	16	16	16	17	17	18	18	19	19
0.426~0.450	0.017~0.018	6	7	7	7	8	8	9	9	10	10	11	11	11	12	13	13	13	14	14	15	15	16	16	17	17	17	18	19	19	19
0.451~0.475	0.018~0.019	7	7	7	8	8	9	9	9	10	11	11	12	12	13	13	13	14	14	15	15	16	16	17	17	18	18	19	19
0.476~0.500	0.019~0.020	7	8	8	8	9	9	10	10	11	11	12	12	13	13	14	14	15	15	16	16	16	17	18	18	18	19
0.501~0.525	0.020~0.021	8	8	8	9	9	10	10	11	11	12	12	13	13	14	14	15	15	16	16	16	17	17	18	18	19	19
0.526~0.550	0.021~0.022	8	9	9	9	10	11	11	11	12	13	13	13	14	14	15	15	16	16	17	17	18	18	19	19
0.551~0.575	0.022~0.023	9	9	9	10	10	11	11	12	12	13	13	14	14	15	15	16	16	17	17	18	18	19	19
0.576~0.600	0.023~0.024	9	10	10	10	11	11	12	12	13	13	14	14	15	15	16	16	17	17	18	18	19	19
0.601~0.625	0.024~0.025	10	10	10	11	11	12	12	13	13	14	14	15	15	16	16	17	17	18	18	19	19
0.626~0.650	0.025~0.026	10	11	11	11	12	12	13	13	14	14	15	15	16	16	17	17	18	18	19	19
0.651~0.675	0.026~0.027	11	11	11	12	12	13	13	14	14	15	15	16	16	17	17	18	18	19	19
0.676~0.700	0.027~0.028	11	12	12	12	13	13	14	14	15	15	16	16	17	17	18	18	19	19
0.701~0.725	0.028~0.029	12	12	12	13	13	14	14	15	15	16	16	17	17	18	18	19	19
0.726~0.750	0.029~0.030	12	13	13	13	14	14	15	15	16	16	17	17	18	18	19	19
0.751~0.775	0.030~0.031	13	13	13	14	14	15	15	16	16	17	17	18	18	19	19
0.776~0.800	0.031~0.032	13	14	14	14	15	15	16	16	17	17	18	18	19	19
0.801~0.825	0.032~0.033	14	14	14	15	15	16	16	17	17	18	18	19	19
0.826~0.850	0.033~0.034	14	15	15	15	16	16	17	17	18	18	19	19
0.851~0.875	0.034~0.035	15	15	15	16	16	17	17	18	18	19	19
0.876~0.900	0.035~0.036	15	16	16	16	17	17	18	18	19	19
0.901~0.925	0.036~0.037	16	16	16	17	17	18	18	19	19
0.926~0.950	0.0365~0.0374	16	17	17	17	18	18	19	19
0.951~0.975	0.037~0.038	17	17	17	18	18	19	19
0.976~1.000	0.038~0.039	17	18	18	18	19	19
1.001~1.025	0.039~0.040	18	18	18	19	19
1.026~1.050	0.040~0.041	18	19	19	19
1.051~1.075	0.041~0.042	19	19	19
1.076~1.100	0.042~0.043	19

Thickness of available adjuster (Shim)

NO in Chart	Thickness (mm)	NO in Chart	Thickness (mm)
1	2.55	11	3.05
2	2.60	12	3.10
3	2.65	13	3.15
4	2.70	14	3.20
5	2.75	15	3.25
6	2.80	16	3.30
7	2.85	17	3.35
8	2.90	18	3.40
9	2.95	19	3.45
10	3.00		

No. 1 rocker arm bracket and apply sealant to the contact surface before installation.

12. Tighten the rocker arm shaft bolts on I-Mark to 16 ft. lbs. (22 Nm) in the proper sequence.

13. On Impulse, tighten the rocker arm shaft bolts to 16 ft. lbs. (22 Nm) with the exception of the 2 small bolts at the front of the No. 1 bearing cap which are tightened to 5 ft. lbs. (8 Nm).

14. Properly adjust the timing belt tension.

G200Z ENGINE

1. Disconnect the negative battery cable.
2. Remove the cylinder head cover.
3. Release the timing chain tension as follows:
   a. Using a suitable tool, depress the lock lever on the automatic adjuster rearward.
   b. Push in on the automatic adjuster shoe and lock it in the retracted position by releasing the lever.
4. Loosen the rocker arm shaft bracket nuts starting with the outer ones and working in towards the center of the cylinder head.

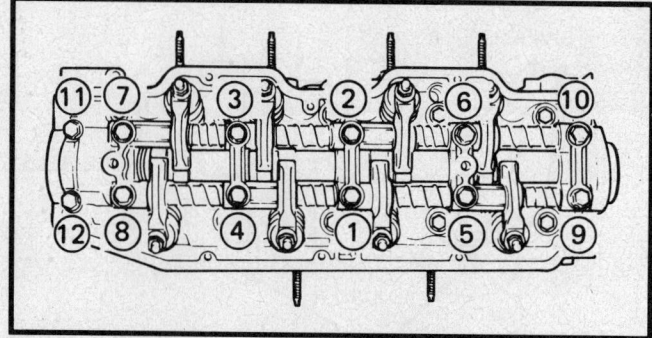

Rocker arm shaft bolt torque sequence—4XC1-U and 4XC1-T engines

5. Remove the rocker arm shaft assembly.
6. Inspect the rocker arms and shafts for wear and replace, as

Measured clearance		\ Original Adjuster (Shim) Thickness (mm)																																													
mm	inch	2.52	2.54	2.56	2.58	2.60	2.62	2.64	2.66	2.68	2.70	2.72	2.74	2.76	2.78	2.80	2.82	2.84	2.86	2.88	2.90	2.92	2.94	2.96	2.98	3.00	3.02	3.04	3.06	3.08	3.10	3.12	3.14	3.16	3.18	3.20	3.22	3.24	3.26	3.28	3.30	3.32	3.34	3.36	3.38	3.40	3.42	3.44	3.46	3.48
0.000~0.025	0.000~0.001														1	1	2	2	2	3	3	4	4	4	5	5	6	6	6	7	7	8	8	8	9	9	10	10	10	11	11	12	12	12	13	13	14	14	14	15
0.026~0.050	0.001~0.002												1	1	1	2	2	3	3	3	4	4	5	5	5	6	6	7	7	7	8	8	9	9	9	10	10	11	11	11	12	12	13	13	13	14	14	15	15	15
0.051~0.075	0.002~0.003											1	1	1	2	2	3	3	3	4	4	5	5	5	6	6	7	7	7	8	8	9	9	9	10	10	11	11	11	12	12	13	13	13	14	14	15	15	15	16
0.076~0.100	0.003~0.004										1	1	2	2	2	3	3	4	4	4	5	5	6	6	6	7	7	8	8	8	9	9	10	10	10	11	11	12	12	12	13	13	14	14	14	15	15	16	16	16
0.101~0.125	0.004~0.005									1	1	2	2	2	3	3	4	4	4	5	5	6	6	6	7	7	8	8	8	9	9	10	10	10	11	11	12	12	12	13	13	14	14	14	15	15	16	16	16	17
0.126~0.150	0.005~0.006							1	1	1	2	2	3	3	3	4	4	5	5	5	6	6	7	7	7	8	8	9	9	9	10	10	11	11	11	12	12	13	13	13	14	14	15	15	15	16	16	17	17	17
0.151~0.175	0.006~0.007						1	1	1	2	2	3	3	3	4	4	5	5	5	6	6	7	7	7	8	8	9	9	9	10	10	11	11	11	12	12	13	13	13	14	14	15	15	15	16	16	17	17	17	18
0.176~0.200	0.007~0.008					1	1	2	2	2	3	3	4	4	4	5	5	6	6	6	7	7	8	8	8	9	9	10	10	10	11	11	12	12	12	13	13	14	14	14	15	15	16	16	16	17	17	18	18	18
0.201~0.300	0.008~0.012	Replacement not to be required																																																
0.301~0.325	0.012~0.013	2	2	2	3	3	4	4	4	5	5	6	6	6	7	7	8	8	8	9	9	10	10	10	11	11	12	12	12	13	13	14	14	14	15	15	16	16	16	17	17	18	18	18	19	19				
0.326~0.350	0.013~0.014	2	3	3	3	4	4	5	5	5	6	6	7	7	7	8	8	9	9	9	10	10	11	11	11	12	12	13	13	13	14	14	15	15	15	16	16	17	17	17	18	18	19	19	19					
0.351~0.375	0.014~0.015	3	3	3	4	4	5	5	5	6	6	7	7	7	8	8	9	9	9	10	10	11	11	11	12	12	13	13	13	14	14	15	15	15	16	16	17	17	17	18	18	19	19	19						
0.376~0.400	0.015~0.016	3	4	4	4	5	5	6	6	6	7	7	8	8	8	9	9	10	10	10	11	11	12	12	12	13	13	14	14	14	15	15	16	16	16	17	17	18	18	18	19	19								
0.401~0.425	0.016~0.017	4	4	4	5	5	6	6	6	7	7	8	8	8	9	9	10	10	10	11	11	12	12	12	13	13	14	14	14	15	15	16	16	16	17	17	18	18	18	19	19									
0.426~0.450	0.017~0.018	4	5	5	5	6	6	7	7	7	8	8	9	9	9	10	10	11	11	11	12	12	13	13	13	14	14	15	15	15	16	16	17	17	17	18	18	19	19	19										
0.451~0.475	0.018~0.019	5	5	5	6	6	7	7	7	8	8	9	9	9	10	10	11	11	11	12	12	13	13	13	14	14	15	15	15	16	16	17	17	17	18	18	19	19	19											
0.476~0.500	0.019~0.020	5	6	6	6	7	7	8	8	8	9	9	10	10	10	11	11	12	12	12	13	13	14	14	14	15	15	16	16	16	17	17	18	18	18	19	19													
0.501~0.525	0.020~0.021	6	6	6	7	7	8	8	8	9	9	10	10	10	11	11	12	12	12	13	13	14	14	14	15	15	16	16	16	17	17	18	18	18	19	19														
0.526~0.550	0.021~0.022	6	7	7	7	8	8	9	9	9	10	10	11	11	11	12	12	13	13	13	14	14	15	15	15	16	16	17	17	17	18	18	19	19	19															
0.551~0.575	0.022~0.023	7	7	7	8	8	9	9	9	10	10	11	11	11	12	12	13	13	13	14	14	15	15	15	16	16	17	17	17	18	18	19	19	19																
0.576~0.600	0.023~0.024	7	8	8	8	9	9	10	10	10	11	11	12	12	12	13	13	14	14	14	15	15	16	16	16	17	17	18	18	18	19	19																		
0.601~0.625	0.024~0.025	8	8	8	9	9	10	10	10	11	11	12	12	12	13	13	14	14	14	15	15	16	16	16	17	17	18	18	18	19	19																			
0.626~0.650	0.025~0.026	8	9	9	9	10	10	11	11	11	12	12	13	13	13	14	14	15	15	15	16	16	17	17	17	18	18	19	19	19																				
0.651~0.675	0.026~0.027	9	9	9	10	10	11	11	11	12	12	13	13	13	14	14	15	15	15	16	16	17	17	17	18	18	19	19	19																					
0.676~0.700	0.027~0.028	9	10	10	10	11	11	12	12	12	13	13	14	14	14	15	15	16	16	16	17	17	18	18	18	19	19																							
0.701~0.725	0.028~0.029	10	10	10	11	11	12	12	12	13	13	14	14	14	15	15	16	16	16	17	17	18	18	18	19	19																								
0.726~0.750	0.029~0.030	10	11	11	11	12	12	13	13	13	14	14	15	15	15	16	16	17	17	17	18	18	19	19	19																									
0.751~0.775	0.030~0.031	11	11	11	12	12	13	13	13	14	14	15	15	15	16	16	17	17	17	18	18	19	19	19																										
0.776~0.800	0.031~0.032	11	12	12	12	13	13	14	14	14	15	15	16	16	16	17	17	18	18	18	19	19																												
0.801~0.825	0.032~0.033	12	12	12	13	13	14	14	14	15	15	16	16	16	17	17	18	18	18	19	19																													
0.826~0.850	0.033~0.034	12	13	13	13	14	14	15	15	15	16	16	17	17	17	18	18	19	19	19																														
0.851~0.875	0.034~0.035	13	13	13	14	14	15	15	15	16	16	17	17	17	18	18	19	19	19																															
0.876~0.900	0.035~0.036	13	14	14	14	15	15	16	16	16	17	17	18	18	18	19	19																																	
0.901~0.925	0.036~0.037	14	14	14	15	15	16	16	16	17	17	18	18	18	19	19																																		
0.926~0.950	0.0365~0.0374	14	15	15	15	16	16	17	17	17	18	18	19	19	19																																			
0.951~0.975	0.037~0.038	15	15	15	16	16	17	17	17	18	18	19	19	19																																				
0.976~1.000	0.038~0.039	15	16	16	16	17	17	18	18	18	19	19																																						
1.001~1.025	0.039~0.040	16	16	16	17	17	18	18	18	19	19																																							
1.026~1.050	0.040~0.041	16	17	17	17	18	18	19	19	19																																								
1.051~1.075	0.041~0.042	17	17	17	18	18	19	19	19																																									
1.076~1.100	0.042~0.043	17	18	18	18	19	19																																											
1.101~1.125	0.043~0.044	18	18	18	19	19																																												
1.126~1.150	0.044~0.045	18	19	19	19																																													
1.151~1.175	0.045~0.046	19	19	19																																														
1.176~1.200	0.046~0.047	19																																																

Thickness of available adjuster (Shim)

NO in Chart	Thickness (mm)	NO in Chart	Thickness (mm)
1	2.55	11	3.05
2	2.60	12	3.10
3	2.65	13	3.15
4	2.70	14	3.20
5	2.75	15	3.25
6	2.80	16	3.30
7	2.85	17	3.35
8	2.90	18	3.40
9	2.95	19	3.45
10	3.00		

Note; Thickness mark is printed on the surface to be contacted with tappet.

Exhaust adjuster shim chart—4XE1 (DOHC) engine

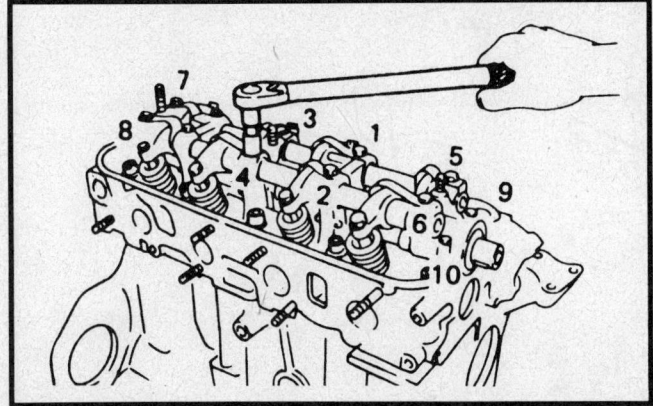

Rocker arm shaft bolt torque sequence—4ZD1 and 4ZC1-T engines

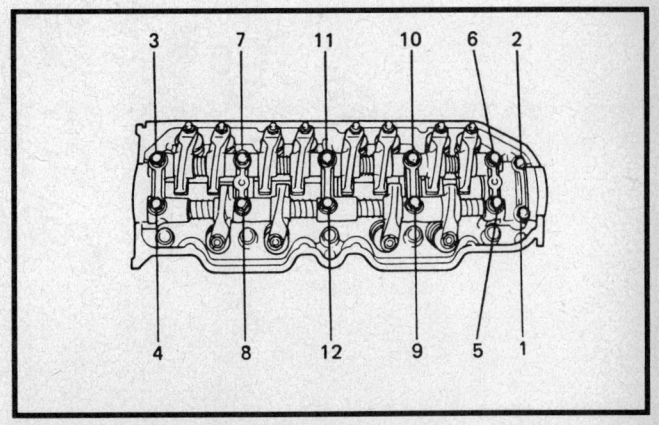

Rocker arm shaft bolt torque sequence—4XE1 (SOHC) engine

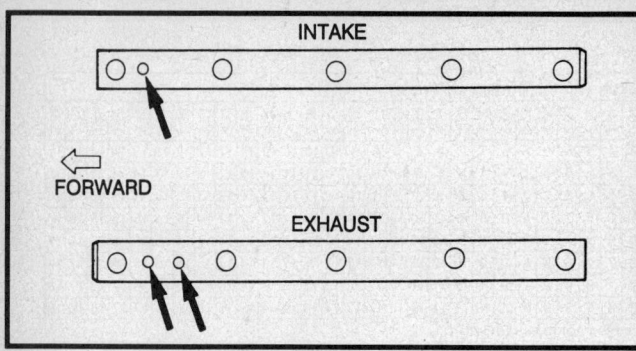

INTAKE

FORWARD

EXHAUST

Rocker arm shaft positioning

necessary. When disassembling, label the components and keep them in order so they may be reinstalled in their original positions. Apply engine oil to the rocker arms and shafts when reassembling.

Installation is the reverse of the removal procedure.

8. Tighten the rocker arm shaft nuts to 16 ft. lbs. (22 Nm). Tighten the nuts starting with the center ones and working towards the ends of the cylinder head.

9. Properly set the timing chain tension.

Intake Manifold

Removal and Installation

I-MARK
4XC1-U Engine

1. Disconnect the negative battery cable and drain the coolant into a suitable drain pan.

2. Remove the bolt securing the alternator adjusting plate to the engine.

3. Disconnect and tag all hoses attached to the air cleaner assembly and remove the air cleaner.

4. Disconnect the air inlet temperature switch wiring connector. Disconnect and tag all the hoses, electrical connectors and control cable attached to the carburetor.

5. If equipped with air conditioning, disconnect the fast idle control vacuum hose, the pressure tank control valve hose, the distributor/3-way connector hose and the vacuum switching valve wiring connector.

6. Remove the carburetor attaching bolts, which are located underneath the intake manifold. Remove the carburetor and the EFE heater.

7. At the intake manifold, remove the PCV hose, the water bypass hose, the two heater hoses, the EGR valve canister hose, the distributor vacuum advance hose and the ground wires.

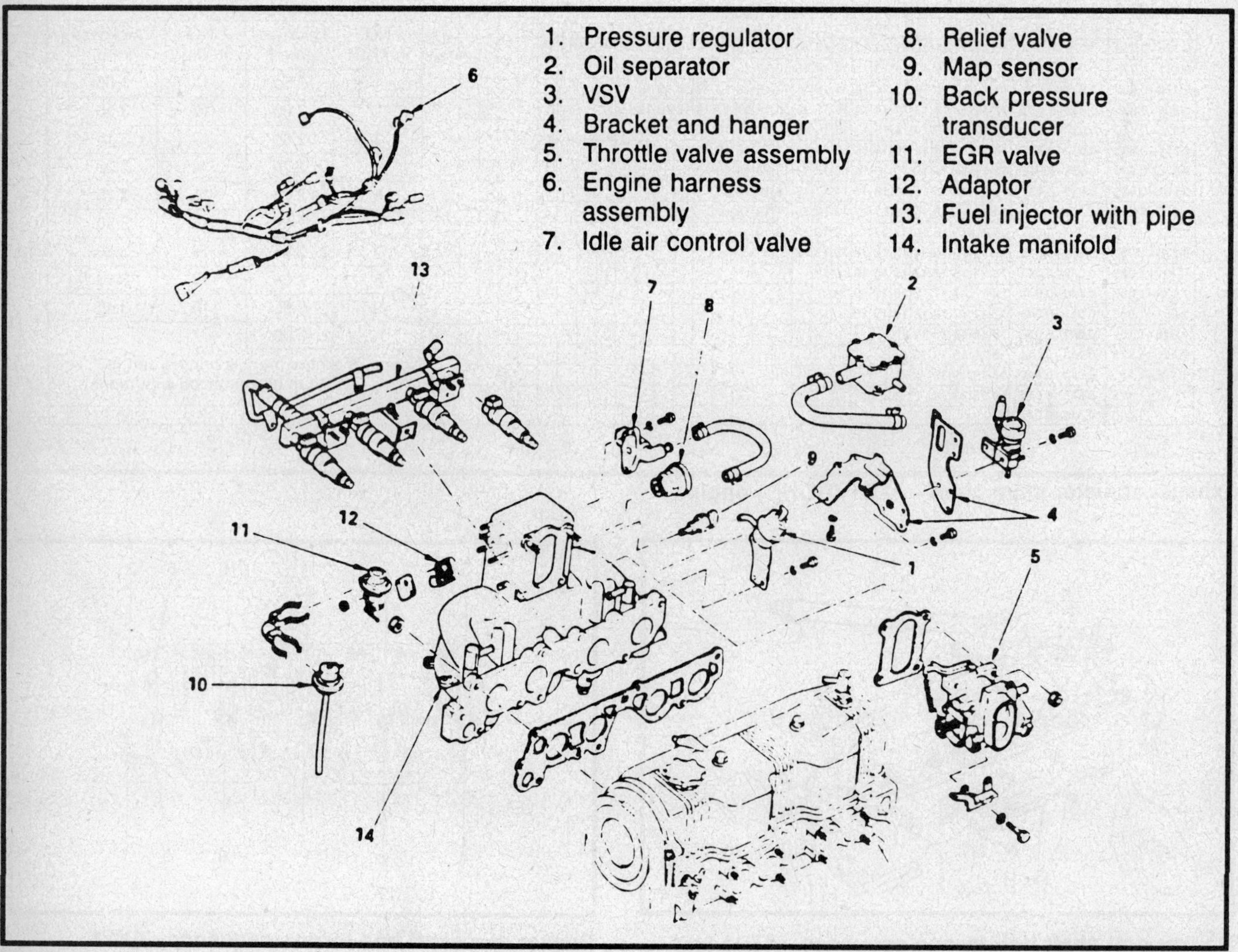

1. Pressure regulator
2. Oil separator
3. VSV
4. Bracket and hanger
5. Throttle valve assembly
6. Engine harness assembly
7. Idle air control valve
8. Relief valve
9. Map sensor
10. Back pressure transducer
11. EGR valve
12. Adaptor
13. Fuel injector with pipe
14. Intake manifold

Intake manifold assembly—I-Mark with 4XC1-T engine

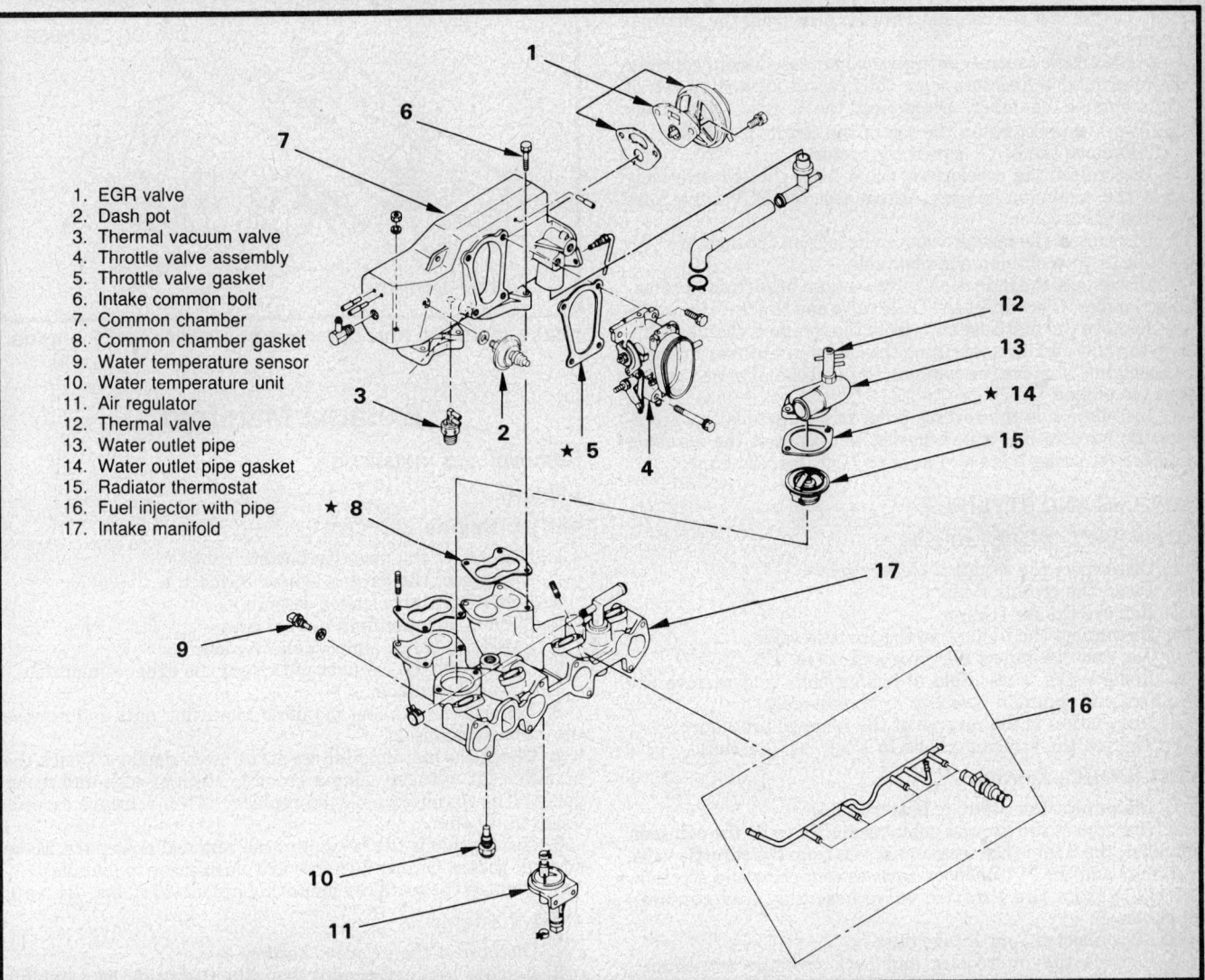

1. EGR valve
2. Dash pot
3. Thermal vacuum valve
4. Throttle valve assembly
5. Throttle valve gasket
6. Intake common bolt
7. Common chamber
8. Common chamber gasket
9. Water temperature sensor
10. Water temperature unit
11. Air regulator
12. Thermal valve
13. Water outlet pipe
14. Water outlet pipe gasket
15. Radiator thermostat
16. Fuel injector with pipe
17. Intake manifold

Intake manifold and common chamber—G200Z engine

8. Disconnect the thermometer unit switch wiring connector, if equipped.

9. Remove the intake manifold attaching nuts and bolts and remove the intake manifold.

10. Clean the sealing surfaces of the intake manifold and the cylinder head.

11. Use a straight-edge and a feeler gauge to check the surfaces containing the cylinder head for excessive warpage. The inlet manifold must be replaced if the warpage is in excess of 0.0157 in. (0.4mm).

12. To install, use new gaskets and reverse the removal procedure. Torque the intake manifold to 17 ft. lbs. (24 Nm); then adjust the engine control cable and the alternator belt tension. Refill the engine with coolant, run the engine and check for leaks. Make all necessary adjustments and road test the vehicle, be sure to check for vacuum leaks around the intake manifold sealing surfaces.

4XC1-T Engine

1. Disconnect the negative battery terminal.

2. Remove pressure regulator and oil separator.

3. Disconnect vacuum line from VSV and remove vacuum switching valve from bracket.

4. Remove oil separator/VSV bracket and hanger as an assembly.

5. Remove throttle valve assembly and engine harness assembly, mark or tag harness connections, if necessary.

6. Remove Idle Air Control Valve (IACV), Relief Valve and Map sensor.

7. Disconnect vacuum line from Back Pressure transducer and unclip transducer from hold-down bracket.

8. Remove EGR valve and adaptor plate.

9. Remove fuel injectors and fuel pipe connected to rail as one unit and position out of way then remove Intake Manifold with common chamber

10. To install, use new gaskets and reverse the removal procedures. Torque the intake manifold to 17 ft. lbs. (24 Nm). Start the engine and check for vacuum leaks.

4XE1 Engine

1. Disconnect negative battery cable and drain cooling system. Remove the air cleaner duct hose from the common chamber.

2. Disconnect and tag the following vacuum lines and wiring harness:

a. Fast idle vacuum hose from the air duct hose.

b. The MAP sensor vacuum hose from the common chamber.

c. Disconnect the TPC valve vacuum hose from the common chamber.

d. Disconnect the canister vacuum hose from the common chamber.

e. Electronic control gas injection harness, disconnect the 2 ECM ground connectors from the bracket located on top of the common chamber. Disconnect the 2 green and black multi-pin connectors on the top of the common chamber.

f. Remove the MAT sensor connector.

3. Disconnect the accelerator cable from the throttle body and at the common chamber. Disconnect the PCV valve hose from the valve cover.

4. Disconnect the master vacuum hose from the master vacuum tube at the common chamber side.

5. Disconnect the induction valve vacuum hose from the common chamber. Disconnect the EGR valve and the throttle valve.

6. Remove the fuel hose clips from the common chamber. Remove the bolt and nuts retaining the common (intake) chamber to the engine. Remove the common (intake) chamber and gasket from the engine.

7. Installation is the reverse order of the installation procedure. Be sure to use a new gasket and tighten the common chamber retaining bolts and nuts to 17 ft. lbs. (24 Nm).

IMPULSE AND STYLUS

Except 4XE1 (DOHC) Engine

1. Disconnect the negative battery cable.
2. Drain the cooling system.
3. Remove the air cleaner.
4. Disconnect the linkage to the throttle valve.
5. Tag and disconnect all wires and hoses.
6. Remove the 8 manifold attaching bolts and remove the manifold and common chamber as an assembly.
7. Installation is the reverse of the removal procedure.
8. Tighten the attaching bolts to 17 ft. lbs. (24 Nm).

4XE1 (DOHC) Engine

1. Disconnect the negative battery cable.
2. Disconnect the ground cable terminals from the common chamber, the 2 cable harness connectors from the throttle valve assembly and the MAT sensor harness connector and accelerator cable from the throttle valve assembly and common chamber.
3. Disconnect the air intake duct.
4. Remove the intercooler and back pressure transducer, Turbo only.
5. Disconnect the PCV hose, MAP sensor hose, fuel pressure regulator vacuum hose, the canister hoses and the vacuum booster hose.
6. Remove the canister pipes and the MAP sensor pipe with the bracket.
7. Disconnect the throttle valve assembly with the throttle valve heating hoses from the common chamber.
8. Remove the intercooler rear bracket and breather hoses, Turbo only.
9. Loosen the EGR pipe and valve retainers and clip.
10. Disconnect the induction control vacuum hose and the alternator harness clip.
11. Disconnect the common chamber bracket and the engine hanger from the common chamber and remove the common chamber.
12. Disconnect the VSV cable harness connector and the oil cooler pipe bracket from the bosses beneath the intake manifold.
13. Remove the EGR transducer and the VSV bracket.
14. Disconnect the fuel lines and remove the fuel injector harness and the fuel rail with the fuel injectors.
15. Remove the intake manifold.
16. Installation is the reverse of the removal procedure. Make sure all gasket mating surfaces are clean prior to installation.
15. Tighten the common chamber and intake manifold mounting nuts and bolts to 17 ft. lbs. (24 Nm).

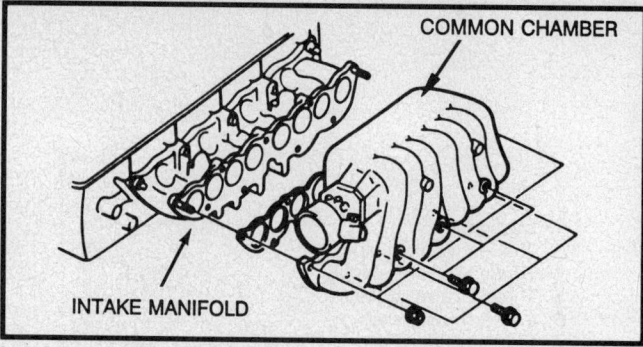

Intake manifold and common chamber—4XE1 engine

Exhaust Manifold

Removal and Installation

I-MARK

4XC1-U Engine

1. Disconnect the negative battery cable.
2. Disconnect the oxygen sensor connector.
3. Remove the air cleaner assembly.
4. Remove the manifold hot air cover.
5. Raise and safely support the vehicle.
6. Disconnect the exhaust pipe from the exhaust manifold.
7. Lower the vehicle.
8. Remove the exhaust manifold mounting nuts and remove the exhaust manifold.
9. Check the manifold for cracks or other damage. Check the manifold for flatness using a suitable straight-edge and feeler gauge. The manifold must be replaced if the warpage exceeds 0.016 in. (0.4mm).
10. Installation is the reverse of the removal procedure. Make sure all gasket mating surfaces are clean prior to installation.
11. Tighten the manifold mounting nuts to 17 ft. lbs. (24 Nm).

4XC1-T Engine

1. Disconnect the negative battery cable.
2. Remove the heat shields from the turbocharger assembly and remove the manifold heat protector.
3. Disconnect the vacuum pipe from the wastegate and position aside.
4. Disconnect the water lines and the oil return and delivery lines.
5. Raise and safely support the vehicle.
6. Disconnect the exhaust pipe from the wastegate manifold.
7. Lower the vehicle.
8. Remove the turbocharger and wastegate as an assembly.
9. Remove the exhaust manifold mounting nuts and remove the exhaust manifold.
10. Check the manifold for cracks or other damage. Check the manifold for flatness using a suitable straightedge and feeler gauge. The manifold must be replaced if the warpage exceeds 0.016 in. (0.4mm).
11. Installation is the reverse of the removal procedure. Make sure all gasket mating surfaces are clean prior to installation.
12. Tighten the manifold mounting nuts to 17 ft. lbs. (24 Nm).

4XE1 Engine

1. Disconnect the negative battery cable.
2. Raise and safely support the vehicle.
3. Disconnect the oxygen sensor connector.
4. Remove the pulse air bracket with the pipe and remove the heat protector and the EGR pipe.
5. Disconnect the exhaust pipe from the exhaust manifold.
6. Remove the mounting nuts and the exhaust manifold.

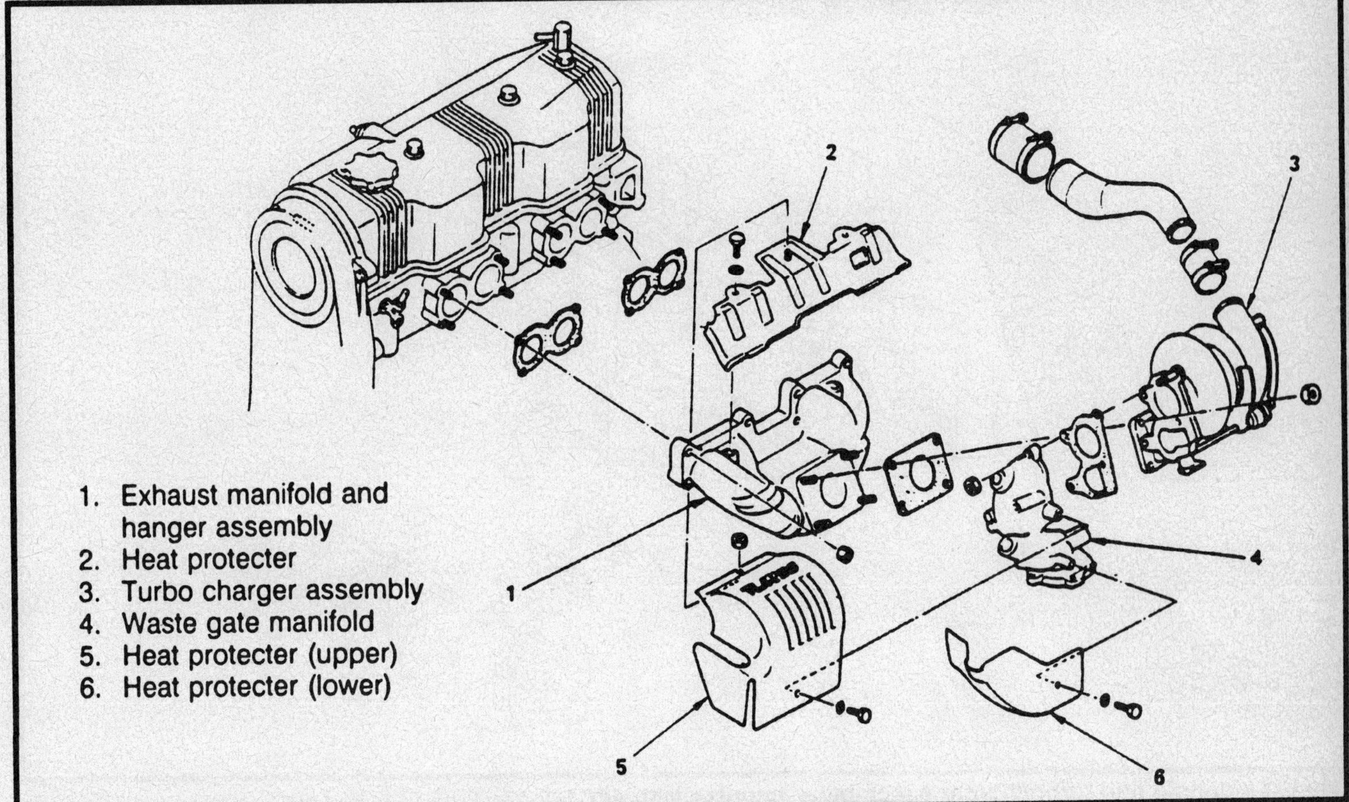

1. Exhaust manifold and hanger assembly
2. Heat protecter
3. Turbo charger assembly
4. Waste gate manifold
5. Heat protecter (upper)
6. Heat protecter (lower)

Exhaust manifold and turbocharger assembly—I-Mark with 4XC1-T engine

7. Check the manifold for cracks or other damage. Check the manifold for flatness using a suitable straightedge and feeler gauge. The manifold must be replaced if the warpage exceeds 0.016 in. (0.4mm).

8. Installation is the reverse of the removal procedure. Make sure all gasket mating surfaces are clean prior to installation.

9. Tighten the manifold mounting nuts to 30 ft. lbs. (41 Nm).

IMPULSE AND STYLUS

G200Z and 4ZD1 Engines

1. Disconnect the negative battery cable.
2. Disconnect the oxygen sensor connector and EGR pipe.
3. Remove the heat protector.
4. Raise and safely support the vehicle.
5. Disconnect the exhaust pipe from the exhaust manifold.
6. Lower the vehicle.
7. Remove the exhaust manifold nuts and the exhaust manifold.
8. Check the manifold for cracks or other damage. Check the manifold for flatness using a suitable straightedge and feeler gauge. The manifold must be replaced if the warpage exceeds 0.016 in. (0.4mm).
9. Installation is the reverse of the removal procedure. Make sure all gasket mating surfaces are clean prior to installation.
10. Tighten the manifold mounting nuts to 16 ft. lbs. (22 Nm).

4ZC1-T Engine

1. Disconnect the negative battery cable.
2. Remove the heat protector.
3. Disconnect the hoses from the air cleaner and intercooler at the turbocharger.
4. Disconnect the oxygen sensor connector, the control cable and the vacuum hose from the turbocharger.
5. Disconnect the oil delivery pipe.

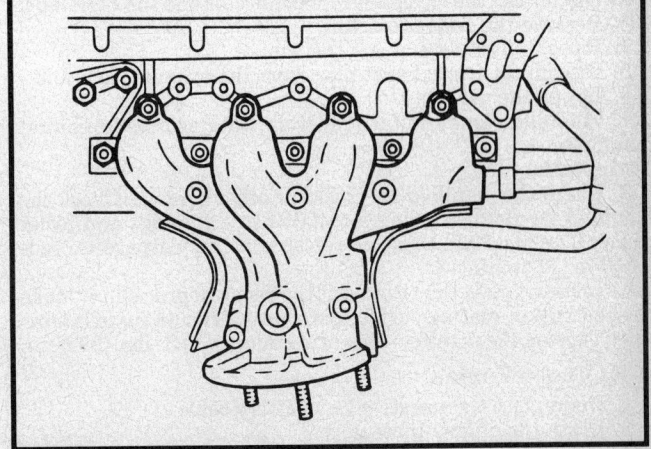

Exhaust manifold—4XE1 engine

6. Raise and safely support the vehicle.
7. Disconnect the oil return hose, the water lines and the exhaust pipe from the turbocharger.
8. Lower the vehicle.
9. Remove the turbocharger from the exhaust manifold.
10. Remove the mounting nuts and the exhaust manifold.
11. Check the manifold for cracks or other damage. Check the manifold for flatness using a suitable straightedge and feeler gauge. The manifold must be replaced if the warpage exceeds 0.016 in. (0.4mm).
12. Installation is the reverse of the removal procedure. Make sure all gasket mating surfaces are clean prior to installation.
13. Tighten the manifold mounting nuts to 16 ft. lbs. (22 Nm).

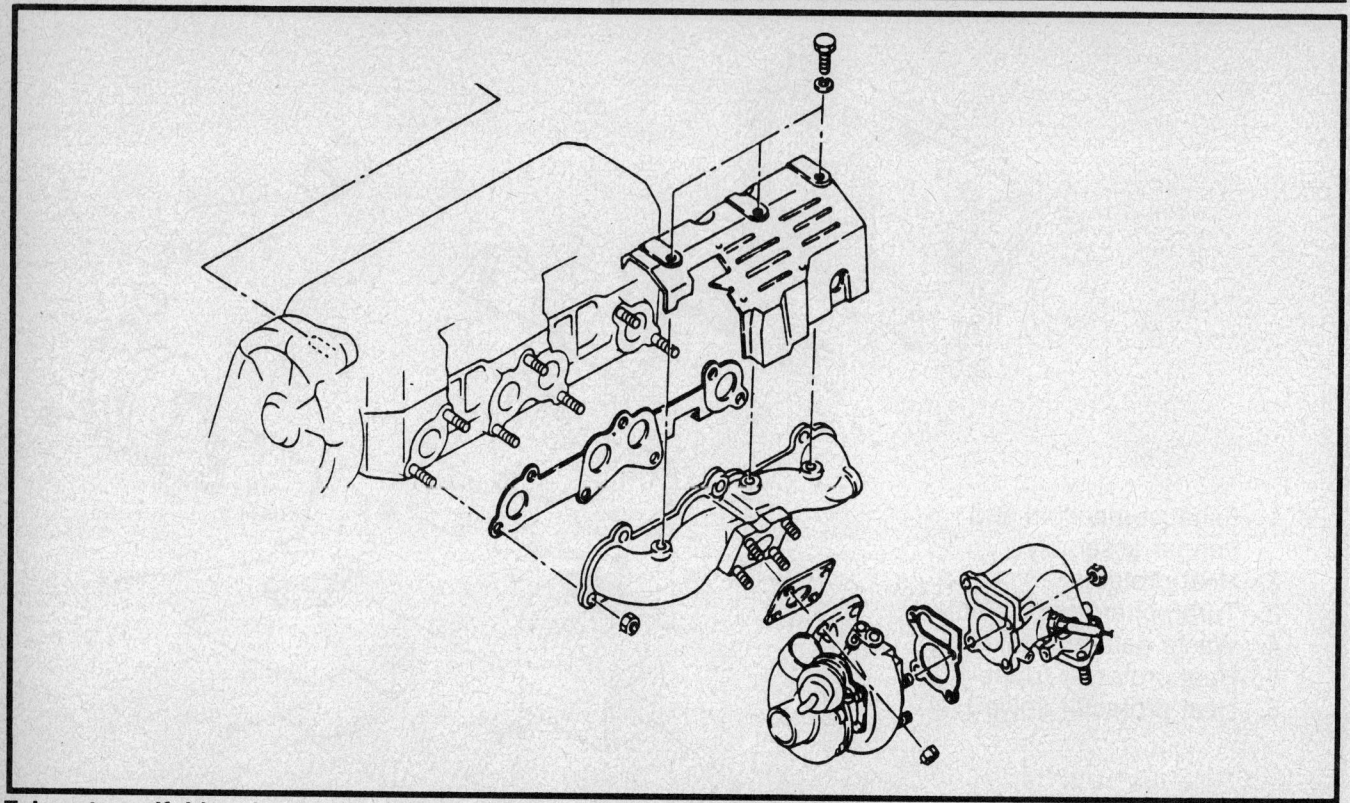

Exhaust manifold and turbocharger assembly— Impulse with 4ZC1-T

4XE1 Engine

1. Disconnect the negative battery cable.
2. Disconnect the oxygen sensor connector and the EGR pipe.
3. Remove the heat protector.
4. Raise and safely support the vehicle.
5. Disconnect the exhaust pipe from the exhaust manifold.
6. Lower the vehicle.
7. Remove the exhaust manifold nuts and the exhaust manifold.

To install:

8. Check the manifold for cracks or other damage. Check the manifold for flatness using a suitable straight-edge and feeler gauge. The manifold must be replaced if the warpage exceeds 0.016 in. (0.4mm).
9. Installation is the reverse of the removal procedure. Make sure all gasket mating surfaces are clean prior to installation.
10. Tighten the manifold mounting nuts to 30 ft. lbs. (39 Nm).

4XE1 Turbo Engine

1. Disconnect the negative (−) battery cable.
2. Drain the engine coolant.
3. Remove the intercooler, left and right undercovers, front exhaust from manifold, intake ducts from turbocharger and remove the power steering pump and move out of the way. Do not disconnect the lines.
4. Remove the bracket from the wastegate and heat protector from the turbocharger.
5. Disconnect the turbo coolant and oil lines.
6. Remove the bracket from the manifold convertor.
7. Remove the EGR pipe and clip.
8. Remove the exhaust manifold with the turbocharger and manifold convertor as an assembly.
9. Remove all necessary components from the manifold.

To install:

10. Make sure all gasket mating surfaces are clean prior to installation.

11. Install the manifold and turbocharger and torque the bolts to 43 ft. lbs. (59 Nm).
12. Install the wastegate manifold and torque the bolts to 21 ft. lbs. (28 Nm).
13. Install the EGR pipe and torque to 21 ft. lbs. (28 Nm).
14. Installation is the reverse of the removal procedure.

Turbocharger

Removal and Installation

I-MARK

4XC1-T Engine

1. Disconnect the negative battery cable.
2. Remove the heat shields from the turbocharger assembly and remove the manifold heat protector.
3. Disconnect the vacuum pipe from the wastegate and position aside.
4. Disconnect the water lines and the oil return and delivery lines.
5. Raise and safely support the vehicle.
6. Disconnect the exhaust pipe from the wastegate manifold.
7. Lower the vehicle.
8. Remove the turbocharger and wastegate as an assembly.
9. Installation is the reverse of the removal procedure. Make sure all gasket mating surfaces are clean prior to installation. Tighten the turbocharger mounting nuts to 21 ft. lbs. (29 Nm).

IMPULSE

4ZC1-T Engine

1. Disconnect the negative battery cable.
2. Remove the heat protector.
3. Disconnect the hoses from the air cleaner and intercooler at the turbocharger.

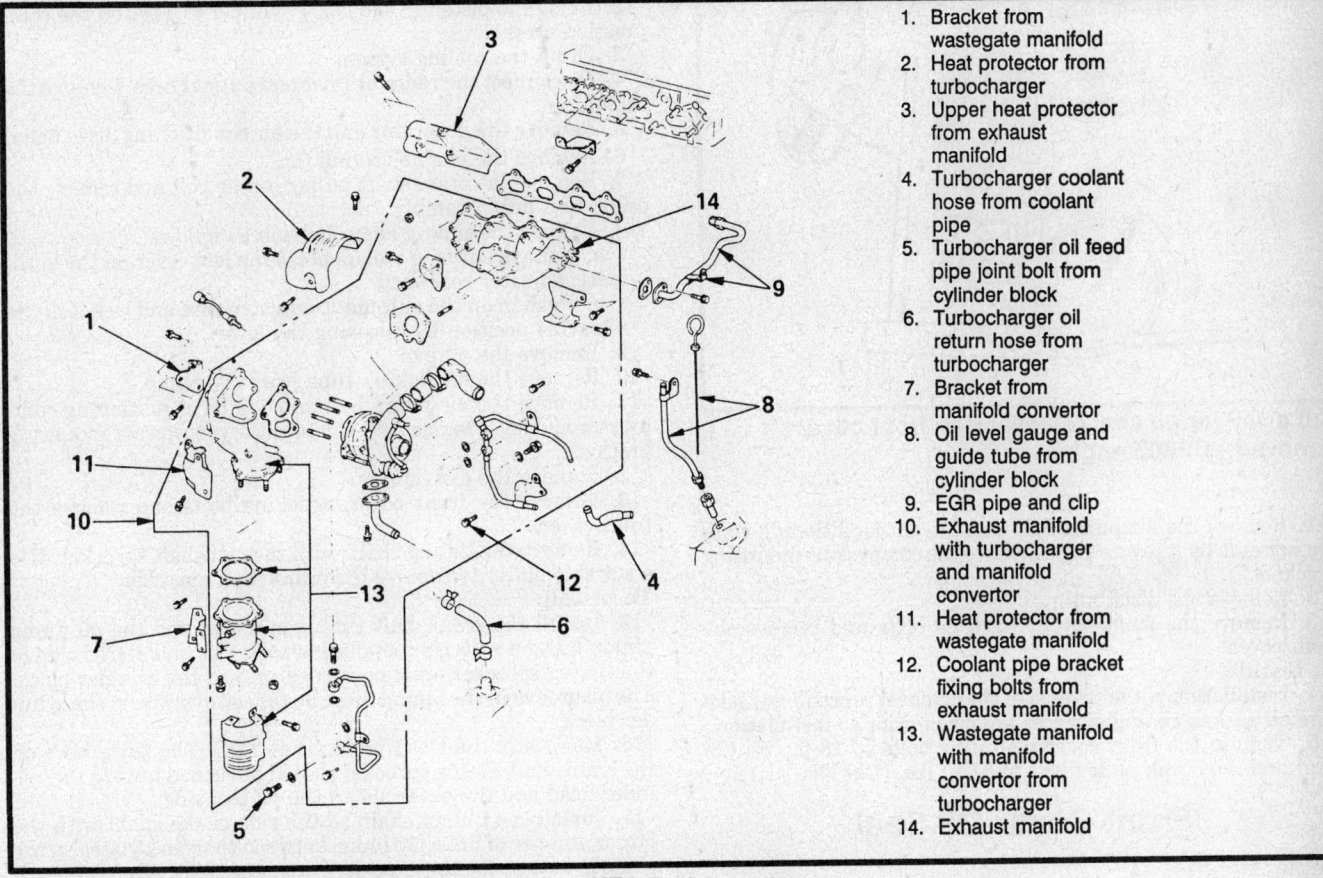

1. Bracket from wastegate manifold
2. Heat protector from turbocharger
3. Upper heat protector from exhaust manifold
4. Turbocharger coolant hose from coolant pipe
5. Turbocharger oil feed pipe joint bolt from cylinder block
6. Turbocharger oil return hose from turbocharger
7. Bracket from manifold convertor
8. Oil level gauge and guide tube from cylinder block
9. EGR pipe and clip
10. Exhaust manifold with turbocharger and manifold convertor
11. Heat protector from wastegate manifold
12. Coolant pipe bracket fixing bolts from exhaust manifold
13. Wastegate manifold with manifold convertor from turbocharger
14. Exhaust manifold

Exhaust manifold and turbocharger assembly—4XE1 Turbo engine

4. Disconnect the oxygen sensor connector, the control cable and the vacuum hose from the turbocharger.

5. Disconnect the oil delivery pipe.

6. Raise and safely support the vehicle.

7. Disconnect the oil return hose, the water lines and the exhaust pipe from the turbocharger.

8. Lower the vehicle.

9. Remove the turbocharger from the exhaust manifold.

To install:

10. Before reinstalling the turbocharger, connect a suitable pressure gauge and make sure the pressure is 430–466mm Hg with the control rod moved 2mm.

11. Installation is the reverse of the removal procedure. Make sure all gasket mating surfaces are clean prior to installation. Tighten the turbocharger mounting nuts to 21 ft. lbs. (29 Nm).

12. Adjust the control cable after installation by turning the adjust nuts so the clearance between the stopper screw and lever is 0.02 in. (0.5mm).

13. Install the pressure gauge to the wastegate and apply approximately 360mm Hg to the wastegate. The rod should begin to move when this pressure is applied. Do not allow the pressure applied to the wastegate to exceed 600mm Hg.

4XE1 Engine

1. Disconnect the negative battery cable.

2. Remove the air cleaner and air duct.

3. Disconnect the intake and exhaust hoses from the turbocharger.

4. Disconnect the oil lines from the turbocharger.

5. Remove the turbocharger-to-exhaust manifold nuts, the turbocharger assembly-to-exhaust pipe nuts and the turbocharger assembly.

6. Installation is the reverse of the removal procedure. Clean the gasket mounting surfaces. Refill the turbocharger with clean engine oil.

7. Using a new gasket, install the turbocharger-to-exhaust manifold nuts to 16–23 ft. lbs. (21–33 Nm) and the turbocharger assembly-to-exhaust pipe nuts to 16–23 ft. lbs. (21–33 Nm).

Timing Chain Front Cover

Removal and Installation

G200Z ENGINE

1. Relieve the fuel system pressure and disconnect the negative battery cable.

2. Drain the cooling system.

3. Disconnect the radiator inlet and outlet hoses. Remove the radiator.

4. Remove the alternator and the air conditioning drive belts.

5. Remove the engine cooling fan.

6. Remove the crankshaft pulley center bolt and remove the pulley and hub assembly.

7. Mark the position of the distributor rotor in relation to the distributor housing and the distributor housing in relation to the timing chain cover. Remove the distributor.

8. Release the timing chain tension as follows:

   a. Using a suitable tool, depress the lock lever on the automatic adjuster rearward.

   b. Push in on the automatic adjuster shoe and lock it in the retracted position by releasing the lever.

9. Remove the cylinder head and the oil pan.

10. Remove the oil pick-up tube from the pump.

Cut away for oil seal removal with front cover removed—G200Z engine

11. Remove the air pump belt and the air conditioning compressor and lay it to one side. Remove the compressor mounting brackets.

12. Remove the distributor.

13. Remove the front cover attaching bolts and remove the front cover.

To install:

14. Installation is the reverse of the removal procedure. Make sure all gasket mating surfaces are clean prior to installation.

15. Tighten the front cover mounting bolts to 18 ft. lbs. (25 Nm) and the crank pulley bolt to 87 ft. lbs. (120 Nm).

Front Cover Oil Seal

Replacement

G200Z ENGINE

Cover Installed

1. Disconnect the negative battery cable.
2. Drain the cooling system.
3. Disconnect the radiator hoses and remove the radiator.
4. Remove the accessory drive belts and remove the fan.
5. Remove the crank pulley bolt and remove the pulley and hub.
6. Using a suitable tool, pry out the seal being careful not to damage the crank sealing surface or the front cover.
7. Lubricate the lip of a new seal with grease and install using a suitable installation tool.
8. Installation of the remaining components is the reverse of the removal procedure. Tighten the crankshaft pulley bolt to 87 ft. lbs. (120 Nm).

Cover Removed

1. Disconnect the negative battery cable.
2. Remove the timing chain front cover.
3. Remove the oil seal by driving the edge of a suitable tool into the cutaway portion at the rear of the front cover.
4. Lubricate the lip of a new seal with grease and install using a suitable installation tool.
5. Install the timing chain cover and the remaining components in the reverse order of their removal.

Timing Chain and Sprockets

Removal and Installation

G200Z ENGINE

1. Relieve the fuel system pressure and disconnect the negative battery cable.

2. Bring the piston in the No. 1 cylinder to TDC on the compression stroke.

3. Drain the cooling system.

4. Disconnect the radiator inlet and outlet hoses. Remove the radiator.

5. Remove the generator and the air conditioning drive belts.

6. Remove the engine cooling fan.

7. Remove the crankshaft pulley center bolt and remove the pulley and hub assembly.

8. Release the timing chain tension as follows:

   a. Using a suitable tool, depress the lock lever on the automatic adjuster rearward.

   b. Push in on the automatic adjuster shoe and lock it in the retracted position by releasing the lever.

9. Remove the oil pan.

10. Remove the oil pick-up tube from the pump.

11. Remove the air pump belt and the air conditioning compressor and lay it to one side. Remove the compressor mounting brackets.

12. Remove the distributor.

13. Remove the front cover attaching bolts and remove the front cover.

14. Remove the timing chain with the camshaft sprocket. Use a suitable puller to remove the crankshaft sprocket.

To install:

15. Install the crankshaft timing sprocket and the oil pump pinion using a suitable installation tool. The chamfered side of the timing sprocket must be turned toward the cylinder block. The oil groove in the pinion must be turned away from the cylinder block.

16. Make sure the No. 1 piston is at TDC. The key groove on the crankshaft timing sprocket should be turned toward the cylinder head and the outer slit to the oil pan side.

17. Install the timing chain so the side of the chain with the larger number of links (50 links) between the mark plates on the chain is toward the chain guide. When installing, align the mark plate on the chain with the slit on the crankshaft timing sprocket.

18. Install the camshaft timing sprocket onto the timing chain, aligning the remaining mark plate on the chain with the triangular mark on the camshaft sprocket. Keep the chain engaged in position on the sprockets during the remaining installation steps, until the camshaft sprocket can be installed on the camshaft.

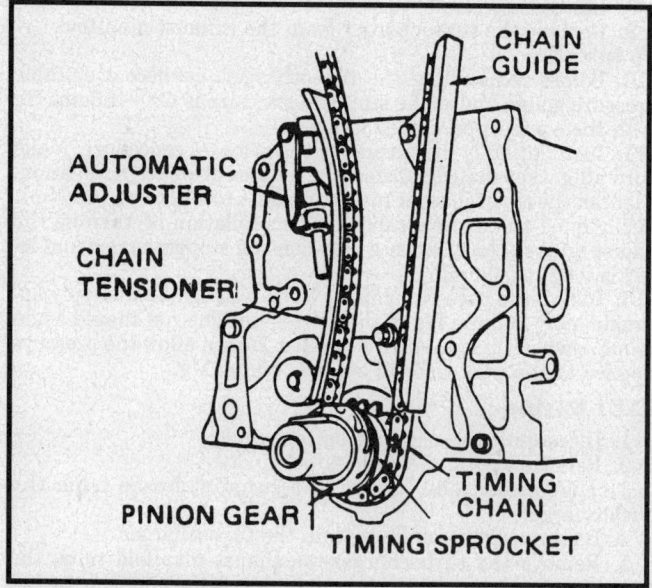

Removing the timing chain

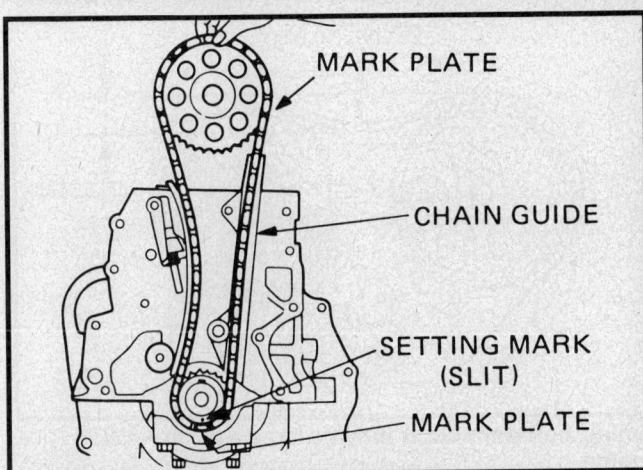

Timing chain alignment—G200Z engine

19. Turn the punch mark on the oil pump drive gear toward the oil filter and bring the center of the dowel pin on the gear into alignment with the mark on the oil pump case.

20. Install the front cover and check that the punch mark on the oil pump drive gear is turned rearward as viewed through the clearance between the cylinder block and front cover. Make sure the slot in the oil pump shaft is parallel with the front face of the cylinder block and that the slot is offset to the front side as viewed from the distributor hole. Tighten the front cover mounting bolts to 18 ft. lbs. (25 Nm).

21. Install the remaining components in the reverse order of their removal.

22. Before installing the camshaft sprocket onto the camshaft, make sure the marks on the front rocker arm shaft bracket and on the camshaft are in alignment and that the **0** mark on the front cover is aligned with the slot in the crank pulley.

23. Install the camshaft sprocket and tighten the bolt to 58 ft. lbs. (80 Nm).

24. Set the automatic timing chain adjuster by turning the adjuster slide pin 90 degrees counterclockwise with a suitable tool.

25. Check the ignition timing.

Timing Belt Front Cover

Removal and Installation

4XC1-U AND 4XC1-T ENGINES

1. Disconnect the negative battery cable.
2. Place a wooden block on a suitable floor jack and position the jack under the oil pan. Raise the engine slightly.
3. Remove the rear side torque rod.
4. Remove the right side engine mount, then remove the body side bracket and engine side bracket.
5. Remove the necessary accessory drive belts.
6. Remove the 4 crank pulley bolts and the crank pulley.
7. Remove the 6 timing belt cover bolts and the timing belt cover.

To install:

8. Installation is the reverse of the removal procedure. Tighten the timing belt cover bolts and the crank pulley bolts to 7 ft. lbs. (10 Nm).
9. Tighten the body side engine mount bolts to 29 ft. lbs. 41 Nm) and the engine side engine mount bolts to 44 ft. lbs. (62 Nm). Tighten the torque rod bolt to 42 ft. lbs. (58 Nm).

4ZD1 AND 4ZC1-T ENGINES

1. Disconnect the negative battery cable.
2. Drain the cooling system.
3. Disconnect the radiator hoses and remove the radiator.

4. Remove the necessary accessory drive belts and remove the engine cooling fan and pulley.
5. Remove the crank pulley bolt and the crank pulley.
6. Remove the timing belt cover.
7. Installation is the reverse of the removal procedure. Tighten the timing cover bolts to 5 ft. lbs. (8 Nm) and the crank pulley bolt to 86 ft. lbs. (120 Nm).

4XE1 ENGINE

1. Disconnect the negative battery cable.
2. On 1989 I-Mark, disconnect the clip securing the high pressure air conditioning line to the strut tower.
3. Use a suitable device to support the engine and remove the right side engine mount.
4. Remove the necessary accessory drive belts.
5. Remove the right side engine mounting bridge bracket and the torque rod.
6. Remove the crank pulley bolt and the crank pulley.
7. On 1990–91 Impulse and 1991 Stylus, remove the front exhaust pipe, the stud from the transaxle housing, the stiffener and the flywheel dust cover.
8. Remove the upper and lower timing belt covers.
9. Installation is the reverse of the removal procedure. Tighten the timing belt cover bolts to 89 inch lbs. (10 Nm). Tighten the crank pulley bolt to 123 ft. lbs. (170 Nm) on 1989 I-Mark or to 109 ft. lbs. (147 Nm) on 1990–91 Impulse and 1991 Stylus.

Oil Seal Replacement

1. Disconnect the negative battery cable.
2. Remove the timing belt cover and the timing belt.
3. Use a suitable tool to remove the crankshaft timing sprocket.
4. Remove the oil seal using a suitable removal tool.
5. Lubricate the lip of a new oil seal and install it using a suitable installation tool.
6. Install the remaining components in the reverse order of their removal.

Timing Belt and Tensioner

Adjustment

4XC1-U, 4XC1-T AND 4XE1 (SOHC) ENGINES

1. Disconnect the negative battery cable.
2. Remove the timing belt cover.
3. Loosen the tension pulley bolt.
4. Insert an Allen wrench into the tension pulley hexagonal

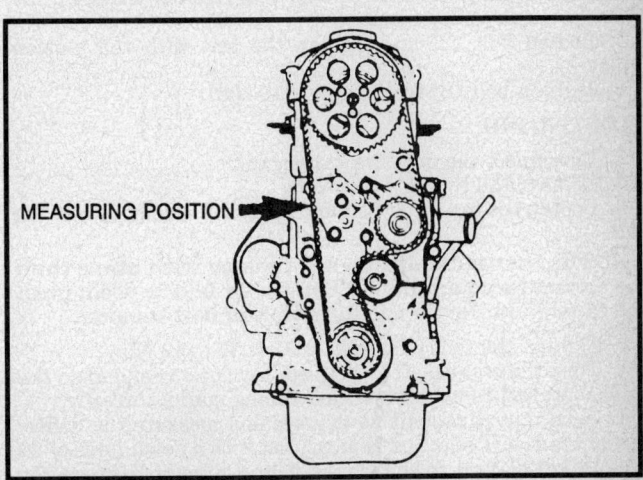

Timing belt tension measuring position—4XC1-U, 4XC1-T and 4XE1 (SOHC) engines

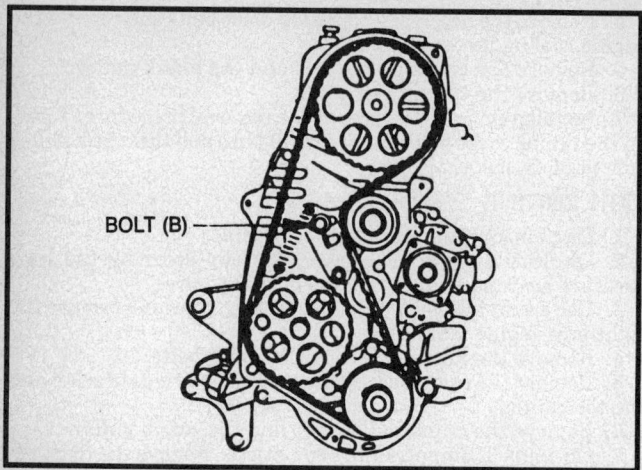

Timing belt tensioner bolt location—4ZD1 and 4ZC1-T engines

hole. Hold the pulley stationary and temporarily tighten the bolt.

5. Turn the crankshaft 2 complete revolutions in the reverse direction of normal rotation and align the crankshaft timing sprocket groove with the mark on the oil pump.

6. Loosen the tension pulley bolt and apply tension to the belt.

7. Insert the Allen wrench into the tension pulley hexagonal hole. Hold the pulley stationary and tighten the bolt to 37 ft. lbs. (51 Nm).

8. Move the crankshaft back to about 50 degrees BTDC and then turn the crankshaft 2 complete revolutions in the reverse direction of normal rotation and align the crank timing sprocket groove with the mark on the oil pump.

9. Use a suitable belt tension gauge to check the timing belt tension at the required measuring position. The tension should be 39.6–48.4 lbs. (18–22 kg).

4ZD1 AND 4ZC1-T ENGINES

1. Disconnect the negative battery cable.
2. Remove the timing belt cover.
3. Loosen bolt (B) to allow the tension spring to tighten the belt.
4. Temporarily tighten bolt (B).
5. Temporarily attach the crank pulley.
6. Turn the crankshaft 2 revolutions in the opposite direction of normal rotation to bring the oil seal retainer mark in line with the crank pulley mark.
7. Loosen bolt (B) and tighten the belt with the tension pulley.
8. Tighten bolt (B) to 13 ft. lbs. (19 Nm).

4XE1 ENGINE

1. Disconnect the negative battery cable.
2. Remove the timing belt covers.
3. Loosen the tensioner bolt and apply the spring force to the belt.

NOTE: On used belts, do not tension with other than the spring force applied. When a new belt is used, push the tension pulley in the direction of belt tension.

4. Tighten the tensioner bolt to 31 ft. lbs. (42 Nm).
5. Turn the crankshaft 2 complete revolutions and align the crankshaft and camshaft sprocket timing marks correctly.
6. Turn the crankshaft 60 degrees and measure the deflection of the belt. Deflection is measured with a down force of 22 lbs. (10 kg) applied to the timing belt at a point between the camshaft sprockets. The deflection should be 0.28–0.33 in. (7–8.5mm) for a new belt and 0.35–0.41 in. (9–10.5mm) for a used belt.

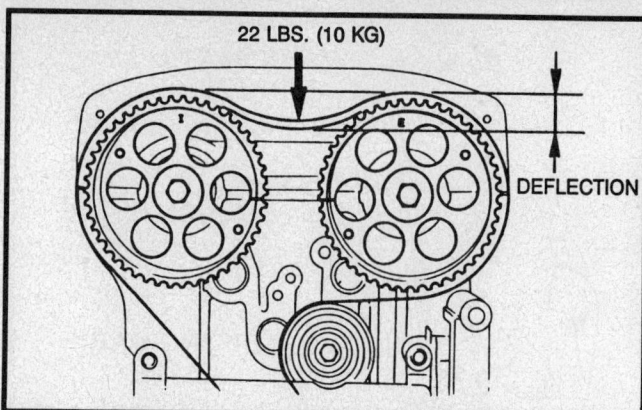

Timing belt deflection measuring position—4XE1 engine

Removal and Installation

4XC1-U, 4XC1-T AND 4XE1 (SOHC) ENGINES

1. Disconnect the negative battery cable.
2. Remove the timing belt cover.
3. Bring the piston in No. 4 cylinder to TDC on the compression stroke. The crankshaft sprocket timing mark should be aligned with the triangular mark on the oil pump housing and the notch on the camshaft sprocket should be aligned with the left upper corner of the cylinder head and the dowel pin in the up position.
4. Remove the crank pulley bolt and the crank pulley, being careful not to disturb the position of the crankshaft.
5. Loosen the bolts retaining the tension pulley. Use a suitable Allen wrench to turn the tension pulley clockwise and relieve the tension on the timing belt.
6. Mark the direction of rotation on the timing belt and remove the timing belt from the vehicle.
To install:
7. If a new belt is used, set the letters marked on the belt in the direction of engine rotation. If the old belt is used, install it in the same direction as before, as indicated by the mark that was made during the removal procedure.
8. Install the belt over the crankshaft sprocket, camshaft sprocket, water pump pulley and tension pulley, in that order.

NOTE: There must be no slack in the belt after it has been installed. The teeth of the belt and the teeth of the pulley must be in perfect alignment.

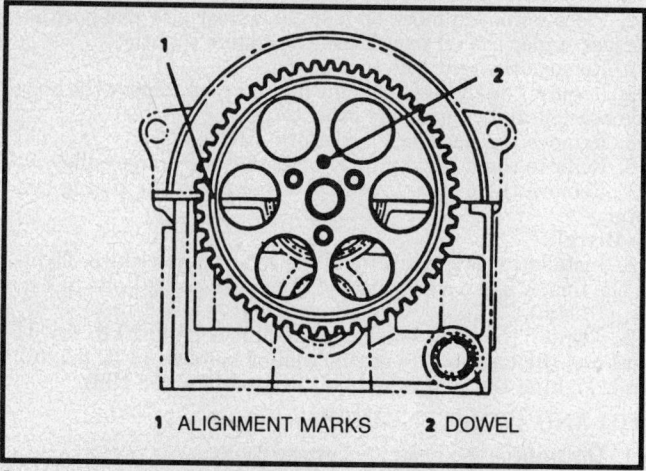

1 ALIGNMENT MARKS **2** DOWEL

Camshaft sprocket alignment—4XC1-U, 4XC1-T and 4XE1 (SOHC) engines

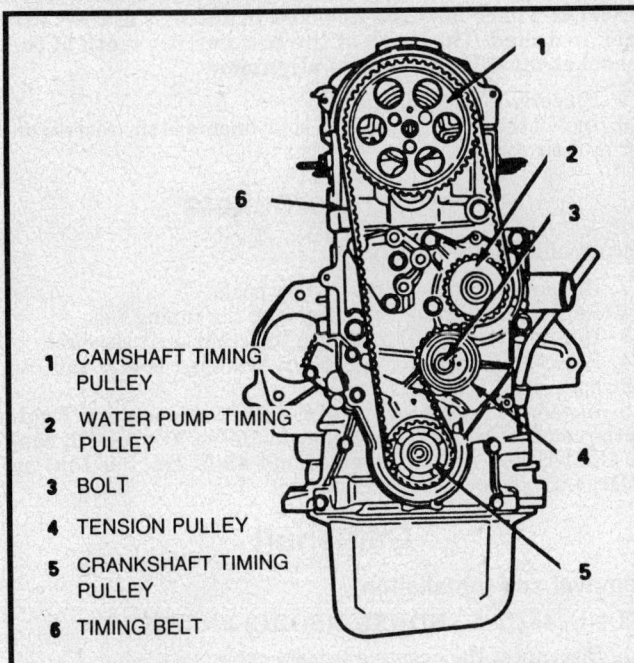

1 CAMSHAFT TIMING PULLEY
2 WATER PUMP TIMING PULLEY
3 BOLT
4 TENSION PULLEY
5 CRANKSHAFT TIMING PULLEY
6 TIMING BELT

Timing belt installed—4XC1-U, 4XC1-T and 4XE1 (SOHC) engines

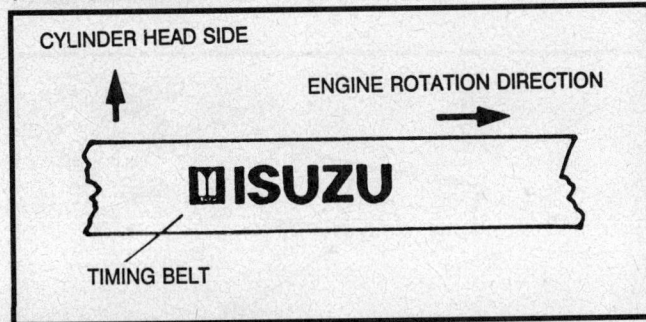

CYLINDER HEAD SIDE

ENGINE ROTATION DIRECTION

ISUZU

TIMING BELT

New timing belt positioning—4XC1-U, 4XC1-T and 4XE1 (SOHC) engines

9. Properly tension the timing belt.
10. Install the crankshaft pulley hub with the taper face to the belt. Tighten the crank pulley bolt to 108 ft. lbs. (150 Nm).
11. Install the remainder of the components in the reverse order of their removal.

4ZD1 AND 4ZC1-T ENGINES

1. Disconnect the negative battery cable.
2. Remove the timing belt cover.
3. Bring the piston in No. 4 cylinder to TDC on the compression stroke. The mark on the crankshaft timing sprocket should be aligned with the mark on the front seal retainer and the mark on the camshaft sprocket should be aligned with the mark on the front plate.
4. Remove the tension spring, loosen bolt (B) and draw the tension pulley fully to the water pump side. Tighten bolt (B).
5. Mark the rotational direction of the timing belt and remove the timing belt from the vehicle.

To install:
6. Make sure the timing marks are still aligned.
7. Install the timing belt, laying it over the crank sprocket, oil pump pulley, camshaft sprocket and tension pulley, in that order. If the old belt is being used, make sure it is installed in the

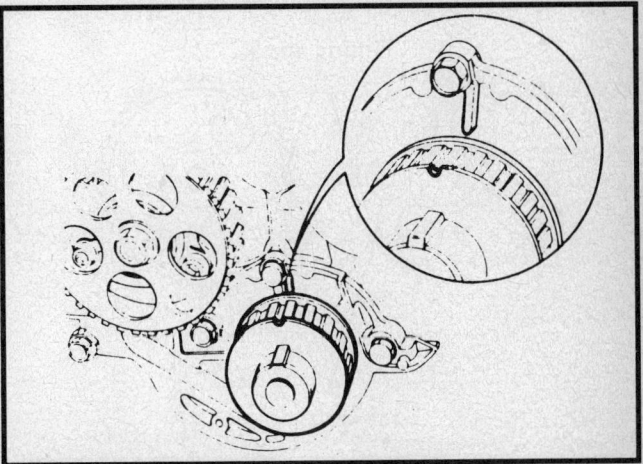

Aligning the crankshaft sprocket timing mark—4ZD1 and 4ZC1-T engines

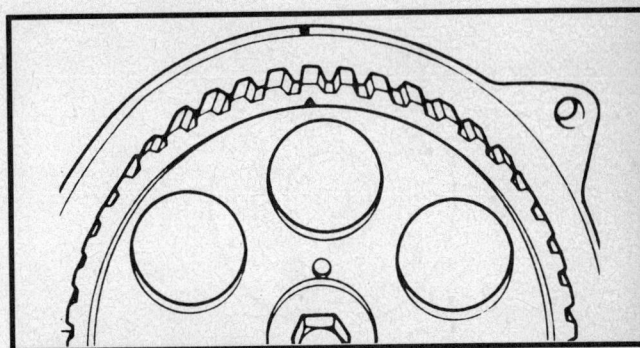

Aligning the camshaft sprocket timing marks—4ZD1 and 4ZC1-T engines

rotational direction that was marked during the removal procedure.
8. Properly tension the timing belt.
9. Install the remainder of the components in the reverse order of their removal.

4XE1 (DOHC) ENGINE

1. Disconnect the negative battery cable.
2. Remove the timing belt cover.
3. Rotate the crankshaft to align the timing marks. The mark on the crankshaft timing sprocket should be aligned with the triangular mark on the oil pump and the keyway should be at the top of the crankshaft, towards the cylinder head. The marks on the camshaft sprockets should be directly across from one another, aligned with the top edge of the cylinder head.
4. Loosen the tension pulley attaching bolt ½ turn. Insert a suitable hex wrench into the tension pulley hexagonal hole and loosen the timing belt by rotating the tension pulley.
5. Mark the rotational direction of the timing belt and remove it from the vehicle.

To install:
6. Make sure the timing marks are still in alignment.
7. Lock the camshaft sprockets in position by inserting 6mm bolts through the camshaft sprockets and into the cylinder heads.
8. Install the timing belt. A new belt is installed correctly if the lettering can be read while viewing it from the passenger side fender. If the old belt is being used, it must be installed in the same direction as was marked during the removal procedure. The belt must be installed in the following order:
   a. Crankshaft timing sprocket.

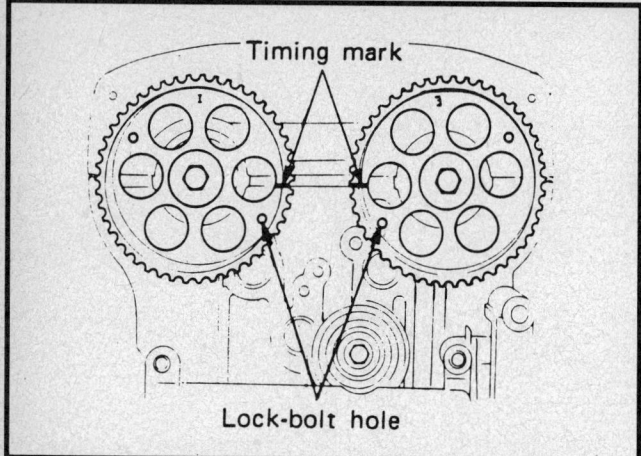

Aligning the camshaft sprocket timing marks—4XE1 (DOHC) engine

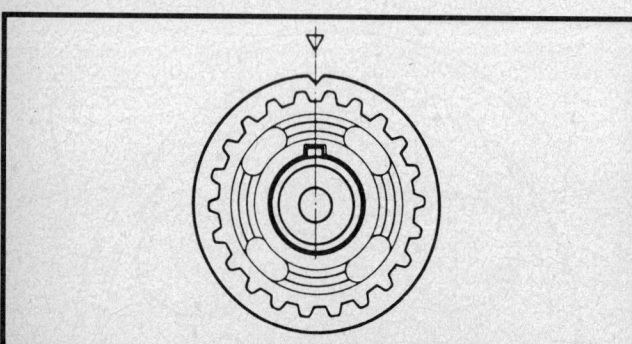

Aligning the crankshaft sprocket timing marks—4XE1 engine

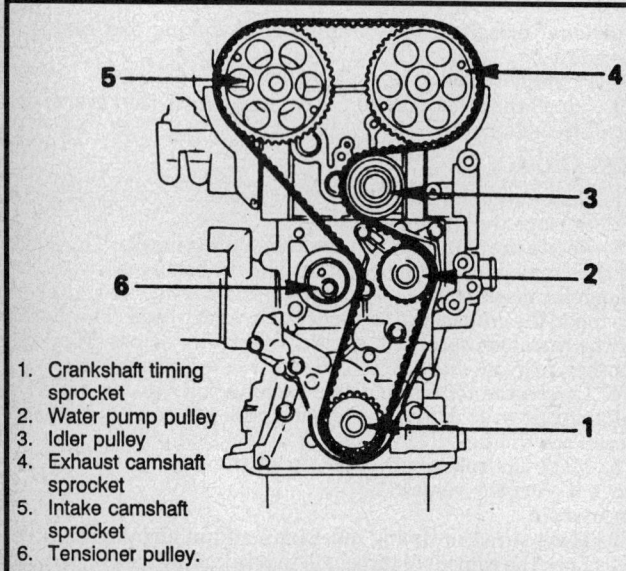

1. Crankshaft timing sprocket
2. Water pump pulley
3. Idler pulley
4. Exhaust camshaft sprocket
5. Intake camshaft sprocket
6. Tensioner pulley.

Timing belt installed—4XE1 (DOHC) engine

  b. Water pump pulley.
  c. Idler pulley.
  d. Exhaust camshaft sprocket.
  e. Intake camshaft sprocket.
  f. Tensioner pulley.

NOTE: There must be no slack in the belt after it has been installed. The teeth of the belt and the teeth of the sprocket must be in perfect alignment.

9. Properly tension the belt.
10. Install the remainder of the components in the reverse order of their removal.

Timing Sprockets

Removal and Installation

1. Disconnect the negative battery cable.
2. Remove the timing belt cover and the timing belt.
3. Use a suitable tool to remove the crankshaft sprocket.
4. Remove the camshaft sprocket retaining bolt(s) and the camshaft sprocket(s).
5. Installation is the reverse of the removal procedure. Tighten the camshaft sprocket retaining bolt(s) to 7 ft. lbs. (10 Nm) on 4XC1-U and 4XC1-T engines and 43 ft. lbs. (59 Nm) on 4ZD1, 4ZC1-T and 4XE1 engines.

Camshaft

Removal and Installation

4XC1-U, 4XC1-T AND 4XE1 (SOHC) ENGINES

1. Disconnect the negative battery cable.
2. Remove the cylinder head cover.
3. Remove the timing belt cover.
4. Align the timing marks properly and remove the timing belt.

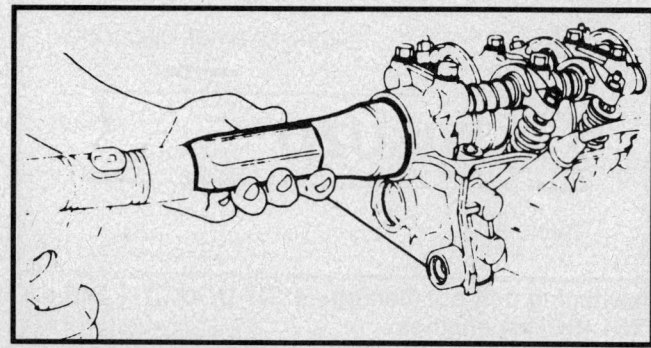

Installing the camshaft oil seal—4XC1-U, 4XC1-T and 4XE1 (SOHC) engines

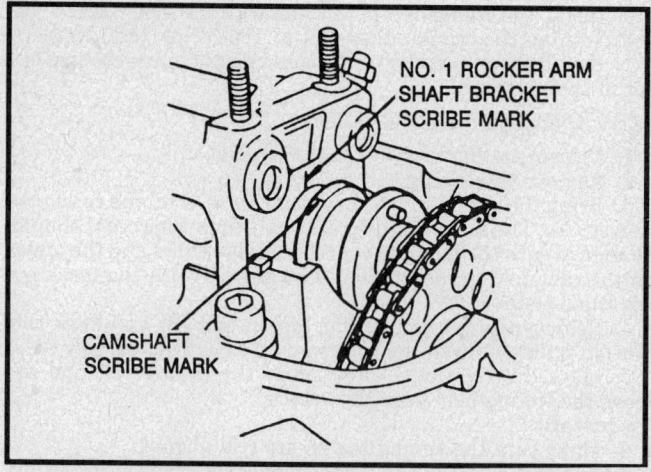

Aligning camshaft and No. 1 rocker arm shaft bracket scribe marks—G200Z engine

5. Mark the position of the distributor rotor in relation to the distributor housing and the distributor housing in relation to the cylinder head. Remove the distributor.

6. Remove the camshaft sprocket.

7. Remove the rocker arm shafts and remove the camshaft and seal.

To install:

8. Installation is the reverse of the removal procedure. Lubricate the camshaft lobes and journals and install the camshaft with the dowel pin in the UP position.

9. Lubricate the lip of a new camshaft seal and install it using a suitable installation tool.

10. Properly tension the timing belt, adjust the valve lash and check the ignition timing.

G200Z ENGINE

1. Disconnect the negative battery cable.

2. Remove the cylinder head cover.

3. Bring the piston in the No. 1 cylinder to TDC on the compression stroke.

4. Release the tension of the automatic timing chain adjuster as follows:

   a. Using a suitable tool, depress the lock lever on the automatic adjuster rearward.

   b. Push in on the automatic adjuster shoe and lock it in the retracted position by releasing the lever.

5. Remove the timing sprocket retaining bolt. Remove the timing sprocket, but leave it in position between the chain guide and chain tensioner. Keep the timing chain in position on the sprocket using mechanics wire.

6. Remove the rocker arm shaft assembly and remove the camshaft.

To install:

7. Installation is the reverse of the removal procedure. Lubricate the lobes and journals of the camshaft thoroughly before installation.

8. Install the rocker arm shaft assembly. Align the scribe mark on the No. 1 rocker arm shaft bracket with the mark on the camshaft.

9. Install the camshaft sprocket on the camshaft, taking care not to disturb the position of the chain on the sprocket. Tighten the camshaft sprocket to 58 ft. lbs. (80 Nm).

10. Set the automatic adjuster by turning the adjuster slide pin 90 degrees counterclockwise using a suitable tool.

11. Adjust the valve lash.

4ZD1 AND 4ZC1-T ENGINES

1. Disconnect the negative battery cable.

2. Remove the cylinder head cover.

3. Remove the timing belt cover.

4. Bring the piston in No. 4 cylinder to TDC on the compression stroke and align the timing marks.

5. Remove the timing belt and the camshaft sprocket.

6. Mark the position of the distributor rotor in relation to the distributor housing and the distributor housing in relation to the cylinder head. Remove the distributor.

7. Sequentially loosen and remove the rocker arm shaft nuts starting with the outermost one and remove the rocker arm shaft/bracket assembly.

8. Remove the camshaft.

To install:

9. Installation is the reverse of the removal procedure. Lubricate the lobes and journals of the camshaft before installing. Install the camshaft with the mark just behind the thrust surface in the UP position.

10. Install the rocker arm shaft assembly. Apply oil to the lip of a new camshaft seal and install, using a suitable installation tool.

11. Properly tension the timing belt, adjust the valve lash and check the ignition timing.

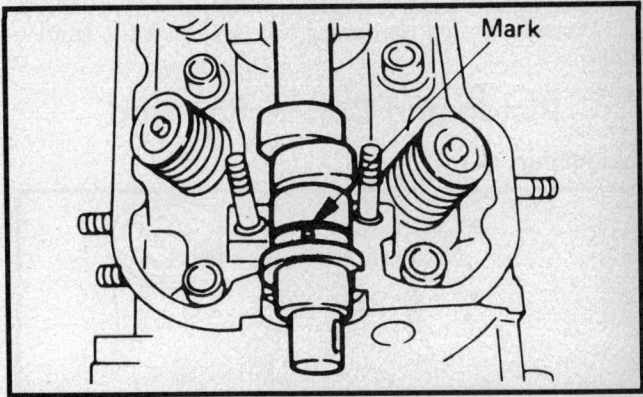

Camshaft alignment mark—4ZD1 and 4ZC1-T engines

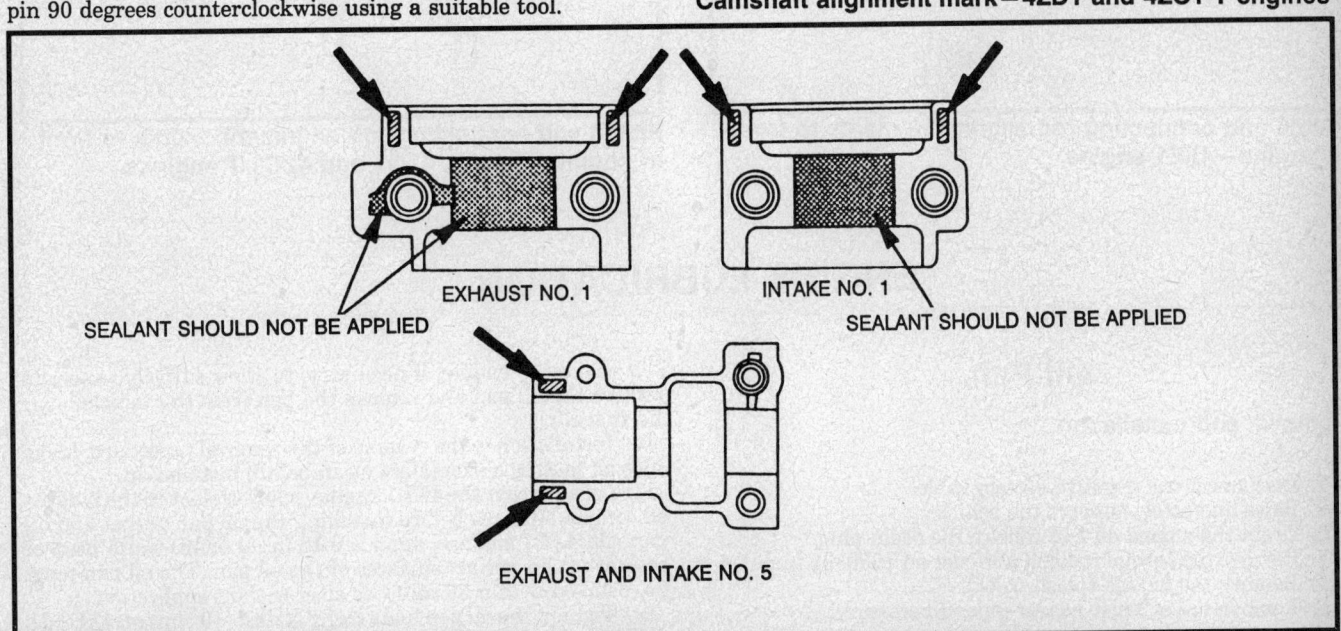

Sealant application points—4XE1 engine

4XE1 (DOHC) ENGINE

1. Disconnect the negative battery cable.
2. Remove the cylinder head cover.
3. Bring the piston in the No. 1 cylinder to TDC on the compression stroke.
4. Remove the timing belt cover.
5. Loosen the camshaft sprocket bolts and loosen the timing belt tension.
6. Remove the camshaft sprockets.
7. Mark the position of the distributor rotor in relation to the distributor housing and the distributor housing in relation to the cylinder head. Remove the distributor.
8. Remove the camshaft bearing caps working from the outside caps toward the center of the cylinder head.
9. Remove the camshafts and camshaft oil seals.

To install:

10. Installation is the reverse of the removal procedure. Lubricate the lobes and journals of the camshafts thoroughly before installation. Install the camshafts with the dowel pins in the UP position.
11. Remove any oil from the contact surfaces of the No. 1 and No. 5 bearing caps and the cylinder head. Apply sealant to the contact surfaces. Do not get sealant on the bearing surface.
12. Install the bearing caps and tighten to 89 inch lbs. (10 Nm). Adjust the valve clearance.
13. Lubricate the sealing lip of the new camshaft seals and install them using a suitable installation tool.
14. Properly tension the timing belt and check the ignition timing.

Piston and Connecting Rod

Positioning

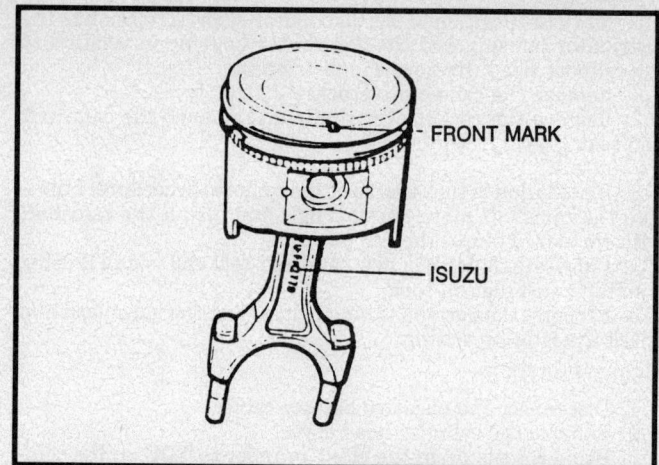

Piston and connecting rod alignment: marks to front of engine—4XC1-U and 4XC1-T engines

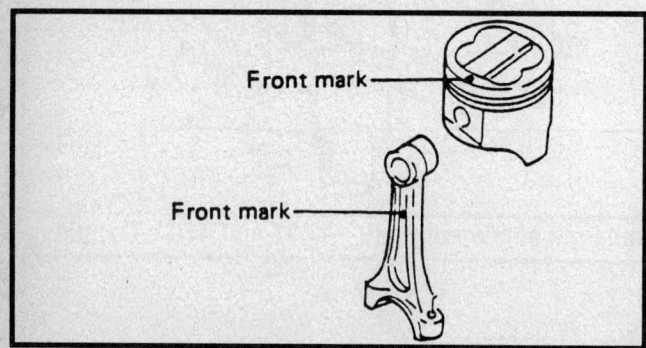

Piston and connecting rod alignment: marks to front of engine—4XE1 engine

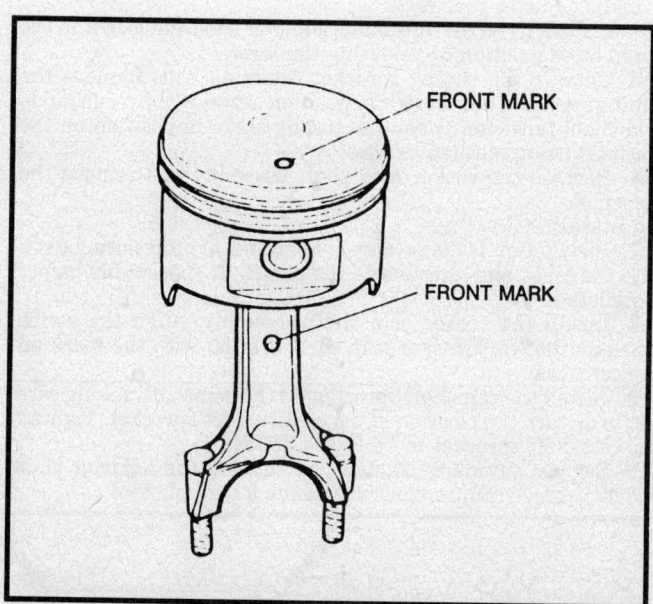

Piston and connecting rod alignment: marks to front of engine—G200Z, 4ZD1 and 4ZC1-T engines

ENGINE LUBRICATION

Oil Pan

Removal and Installation

1. Disconnect the negative battery cable.
2. Raise and safely support the vehicle.
3. Drain the engine oil and replace the drain plug.
4. Remove the torque rod and stiffener on 1990–91 Impulse.
5. Remove the engine splash shield.
6. Remove the exhaust header pipe, if necessary.
7. Remove the flywheel dust shield.
8. Remove the oil pan retaining bolts.

9. Raise the engine, if necessary, to allow sufficient room to remove the oil pan and remove the pan from the vehicle.

To install:

10. Installation is the reverse of the removal procedure. Make sure all mating surfaces are clean before installation.
11. On all except the 4XE1 engine, apply sealant to the indicated contact surfaces before installing the oil pan gasket and oil pan. On 4XE1 engines, apply a 0.18 in. (4.5mm) width bead of sealant to the contact surfaces of the oil pan. The oil pan must be installed within 30 minutes after sealant application.
12. Tighten the oil pan bolts to 7.2 ft. lbs. (10 Nm) on 4XC1-U, 4XC1-T and 4XE1 engines, 3.6 ft. lbs. (5 Nm) on G200Z engines and 13 ft. lbs. (18 Nm) on 4ZD1 and 4ZC1-T engines.

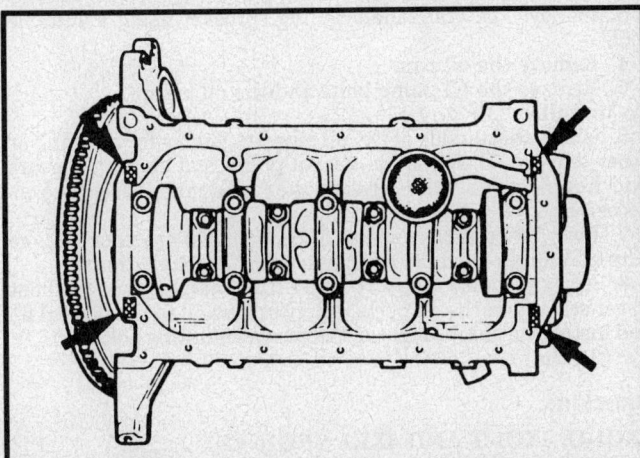

Sealant application points—4XC1-U, 4XC1-T and 4XE1 engines

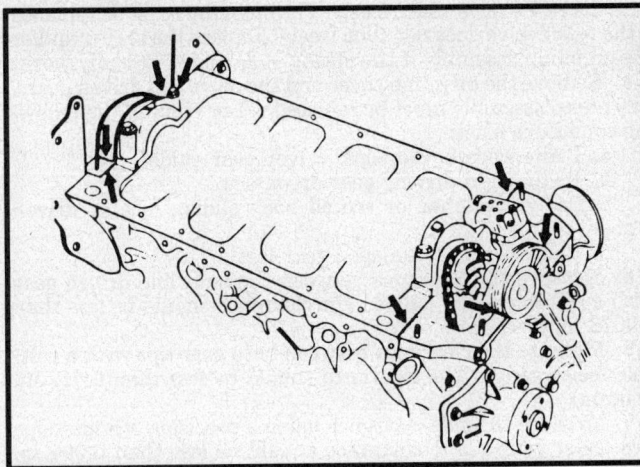

Sealant application points—G200Z engine

Sealant application points—4ZD1 and 4ZC1-T engines

Oil Pump

Removal and Installation

4XC1-U, 4XC1-T AND 4XE1 (SOHC) ENGINES

1. Disconnect the negative battery cable, raise and safely support the vehicle and drain the engine oil.

2. Place a wooden block on a suitable floor jack and place the jack under the oil pan. Slightly raise the engine.

3. Remove the rear side torque rod while the engine is slightly lifted.

4. Remove the right side engine mount, then remove the body side bracket and the engine side bracket.

5. Remove the necessary accessory drive belts.

6. Remove the 4 crank pulley bolts with the engine slightly lifted.

7. Remove the 6 timing cover bolts and remove the timing belt cover.

8. Make sure the crankshaft timing mark on the crankshaft pulley hub is aligned with the top dead center mark and the notch on the camshaft pulley hub is aligned with the left upper corner of the cylinder head.

9. Remove the crank pulley hub bolt and the crank pulley hub.

10. Loosen the bolts attaching the tension pulley. Turn the tension pulley clockwise with a suitable Allen wrench, then remove the timing belt.

11. Use a suitable tool to remove the crankshaft timing sprocket.

12. Temporarily reinstall the right side engine mount brackets and mount. Lower the engine, remove the jack and remove the oil pan.

13. Remove the oil pump retaining bolts and remove the oil pump assembly.

14. Check the outside of the oil pump assembly for cracking or other damage. Disassemble the oil pump and check the gears and housing for wear and proper clearance. Replace as necessary.

To install:

15. Installation is the reverse of the removal procedure. Make sure all mating surfaces are clean before installation.

16. Apply oil to the sealing lip of the oil seal and apply sealant to the pump fitting face. Install the pump and tighten the retaining bolts to 7.2 ft. lbs. (10 Nm).

G200Z ENGINE

1. Disconnect the negative battery cable, raise and safely support the vehicle and drain the engine oil.

2. Remove the cylinder head cover and the distributor.

3. Remove the oil pan.

4. Remove the bolt attaching the oil pick-up tube to the block and remove the tube from the oil pump.

5. Remove the oil pump mounting bolts and the oil pump.

To install:

6. Align the scribe mark on the camshaft with the scribe mark on the No. 1 rocker arm shaft bracket and the notch in the crankshaft pulley with the **0** mark on the timing chain cover.

7. Install the oil pump by aligning the marks, so the punched mark is away from the water pump.

8. After the oil pump is installed, make sure the punched

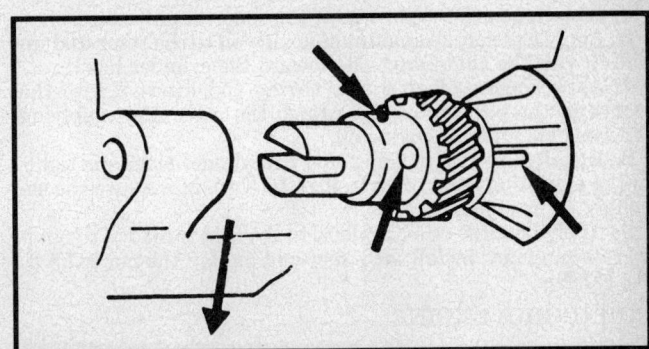

Oil pump installation alignment marks—G200Z engine

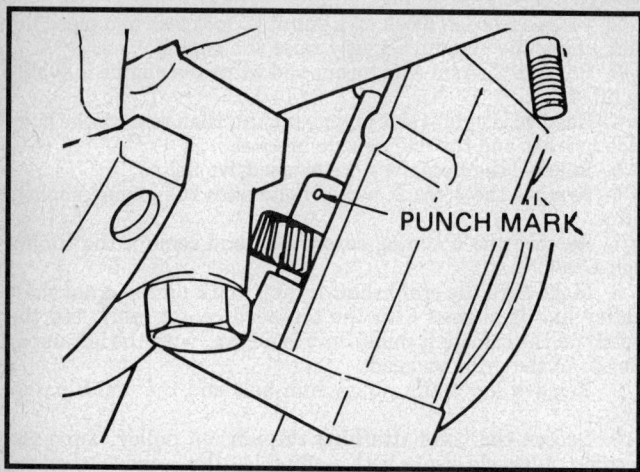

Checking oil pump alignment—G200Z engine

View through the distributor mounting hole—G200Z engine

mark on the pump driveshaft is away from the water pump as viewed through the clearance between the cylinder block and front cover. Make sure the slot at the end of the driveshaft is parallel to the front face of the cylinder block and is offset forward as viewed through the distributor mounting hole.

9. Install the oil pump pick-up tube.

10. Installation of the remaining components is the reverse of the removal procedure. Be sure to check the ignition timing.

4ZD1 AND 4ZC1-T ENGINES

1. Disconnect the negative battery cable.

2. Remove the timing belt cover and the timing belt.

3. Use a suitable tool to hold the oil pump pulley in position and remove the pulley bolt. Remove the oil pump pulley.

4. Remove the oil pump retaining bolts and the oil pump.

To install:

5. Installation is the reverse of the removal procedure.

6. Apply a generous amount of engine oil to the rotor and install it with the chamfered side toward the cylinder block.

7. Apply engine oil to a new O-ring and insert it into the groove in the pump housing. Attach the rotor after applying generous amounts of engine oil.

8. Install the pump housing onto the cylinder block and tighten the mounting bolts to 13 ft. lbs. (19 Nm). Make sure the assembly turns smoothly.

9. Apply Loctite® or equivalent, to the first thread of the pulley retaining nut, install the pulley and tighten the nut to 55 ft. lbs. (77 Nm).

4XE1 (DOHC) ENGINE

1. Disconnect the negative battery cable, raise and safely support the vehicle and drain the engine oil.

2. Remove the timing belt cover and the timing belt.

3. Remove the crankshaft timing sprocket using a suitable tool.

4. Remove the oil pan.

5. Remove the oil pump bolts and the oil pump.

To install:

6. Check the outside of the oil pump assembly for cracking or other damage. Disassemble the oil pump and check the gears and housing for wear and proper clearance. Replace as necessary.

7. Installation is the reverse of the removal procedure. Make sure all mating surfaces are clean prior to installation.

8. Apply sealant to the oil pump fitting face, being careful not to get sealant on the oil ports. Apply engine oil to the oil seal lip and install the pump. Tighten the pump mounting bolts to 17 ft. lbs. (24 Nm).

Checking

4XC1-U, 4XC1-T AND 4XE1 ENGINES

1. Disconnect the negative battery cable.

2. Remove the oil pump from the vehicle.

3. Remove the plug, spring and pressure relief valve. Make sure the relief valve slides freely. The oil pump must be replaced if the relief valve does not slide freely. Replace the spring and/or the oil pump assembly if the spring is damaged or badly worn.

4. Remove the oil pump cover and the drive and driven gears. The pump assembly must be replaced if 1 or more of the following conditions exist:

    a. Badly worn or damaged driven gear guide.

    b. Badly worn driving gear drive face.

    c. Badly scratched or scored body sliding face or driven gear.

    d. Badly worn or damaged gear teeth.

5. Measure the clearance between the body and driven gear with a suitable feeler gauge. The clearance should be less than 0.0078 in. (0.2mm).

6. Measure the clearance between both gear tips with a suitable feeler gauge. The clearance should be less than 0.012 in. (0.3mm).

7. Measure the side clearance using a precision straightedge and feeler gauge. The clearance should be less than 0.004 in. (0.10mm).

8. Check the oil pump pick-up for cracking or scoring and replace, as necessary.

9. If the oil pump assembly passes inspection, reassemble as follows:

    a. Coat the gears with engine oil and install them in the housing.

    b. Install the oil pump cover and semi-tighten all of the attaching screws. Then tighten the screws to 7 ft. lbs. (10 Nm). Make sure the gear rotates smoothly.

    c. Apply engine oil to the relief valve and install it with the spring and the plug. Tighten the plug to 27 ft. lbs. (37 Nm).

10. Check the oil seal and replace, as necessary.

11. Install the oil pump assembly.

G200Z ENGINE

1. Disconnect the negative battery cable.

2. Remove the oil pump from the vehicle.

3. Disassemble the oil pump and check the relief valve and spring, pump body and cover and the drive gear for wear or damage.

4. Check the clearance between the driven rotor and the pump body using a suitable feeler gauge. The clearance should be less than 0.00985 in. (0.25mm).

5. Check the clearance between the drive rotor and driven rotor using a suitable feeler gauge. The clearance should be less than 0.00788 in. (0.2mm).

6. Check the clearance between the drive rotor, driven rotor and oil pump cover using a suitable depth gauge. The clearance should be less than 0.00591 in. (0.15mm).

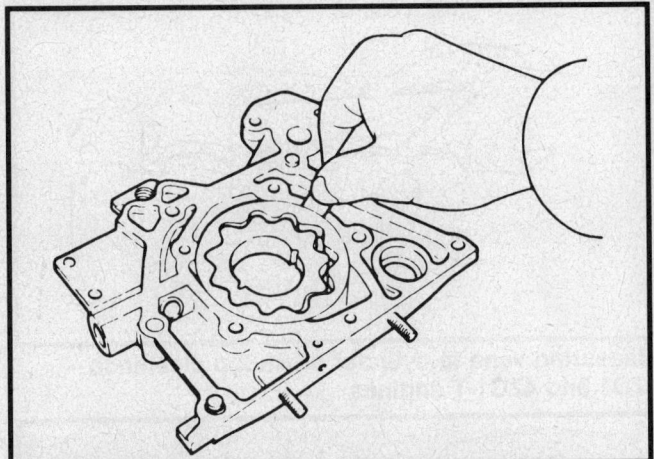

Measuring oil pump body to driven gear clearance—4XC1-U, 4XC1-T and 4XE1 engines

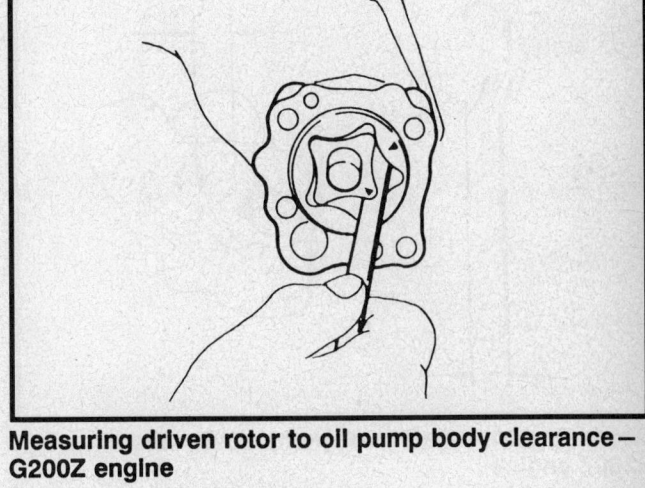

Measuring driven rotor to oil pump body clearance—G200Z engine

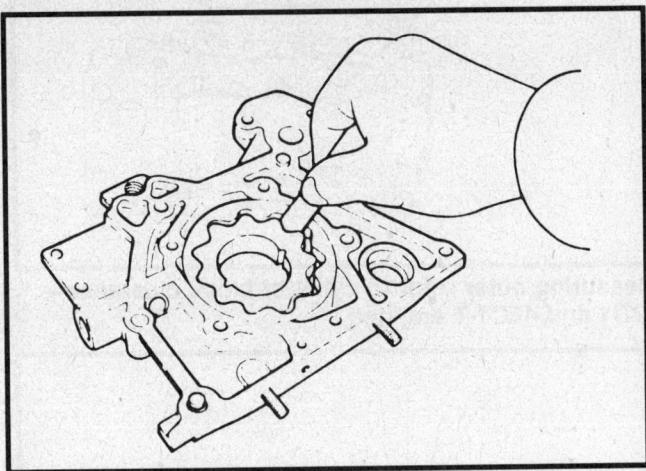

Measuring oil pump gear teeth clearance—4XC1-U, 4XC1-T and 4XE1 engines

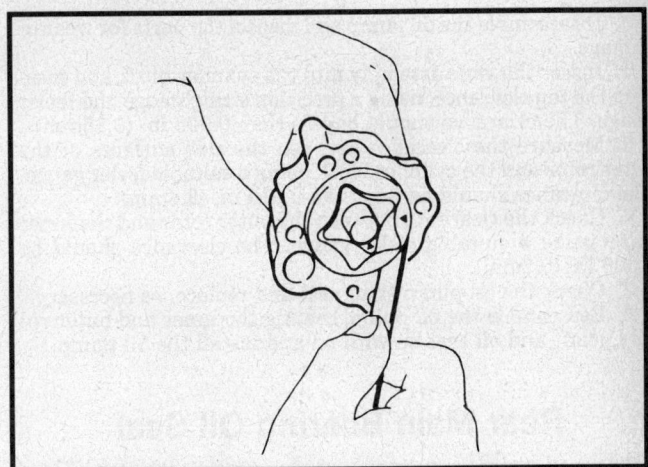

Measuring drive rotor to driven rotor clearance—G200Z engine

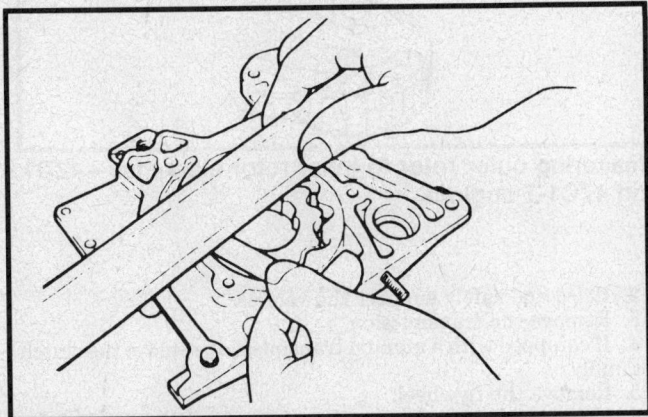

Measuring oil pump gear side clearance—4XC1-U, 4XC1-T and 4XE1 engines

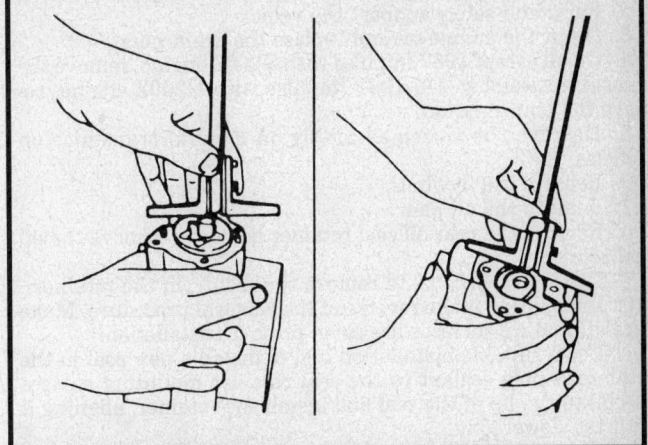

Measuring drive and driven rotor to oil pump cover clearance—G200Z engine

7. Check the clearance between the driveshaft and pump cover. The clearance should be less than 0.00985 in. (0.25mm).

8. If the pump passes inspection, coat the drive and driven rotors and the pressure relief valve with oil and reassemble the pump.

9. Install the oil pump assembly.

4ZD1 AND 4ZC1-T ENGINES

1. Disconnect the negative battery cable.
2. Remove the oil pump assembly from the vehicle.

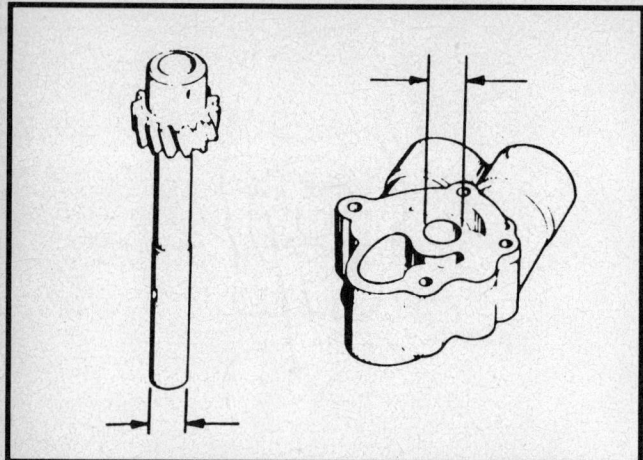

**Measuring driveshaft to oil pump cover clearance—
G200Z engine**

3. Disassemble the oil pump and inspect the parts for wear or damage.

4. Insert the vane assembly into the cylinder block and measure the top clearance, using a precision straightedge and feeler gauge. The clearance should be less than 0.006 in. (0.15mm).

5. Measure the clearance between the side surfaces of the outer rotor and the cylinder block using a suitable feeler gauge. The clearance should be less than 0.016 in. (0.4mm).

6. Check the clearance between the outer rotor and the inner rotor using a suitable feeler gauge. The clearance should be 0.008 in. (0.2mm).

7. Check the oil pump shaft seal and replace, as necessary.

8. Reassemble the oil pump, coating the inner and outer rotors, shaft and oil seal lip with oil and install the oil pump.

Rear Main Bearing Oil Seal

Removal and Installation

EXCEPT 4ZD1 AND 4ZC1-T ENGINES

1. Disconnect the negative battery cable.
2. Raise and safely support the vehicle.
3. Drain the engine oil and replace the drain plug.
4. On all except 1987 Impulse with G200Z engine, remove the transaxle assembly. On 1987 Impulse with G200Z engine, remove the transmission.
5. Remove the clutch assembly on manual transmission vehicles.
6. Remove the flywheel.
7. Remove the oil pan.
8. Remove the rear oil seal retainer bolts and remove the oil seal retainer.
9. Use a suitable tool to remove the seal from the retainer.
10. Installation is the reverse of the removal procedure. Make sure all mating surfaces are clean prior to installation.
11. Use a suitable installation tool to install a new seal in the retainer. Apply sealant to the seal retainer mounting surface and oil to the lip of the seal and install the retainer, aligning it with the dowel pins.

4ZD1 AND 4ZC1-T ENGINES

1. Disconnect the negative battery cable.

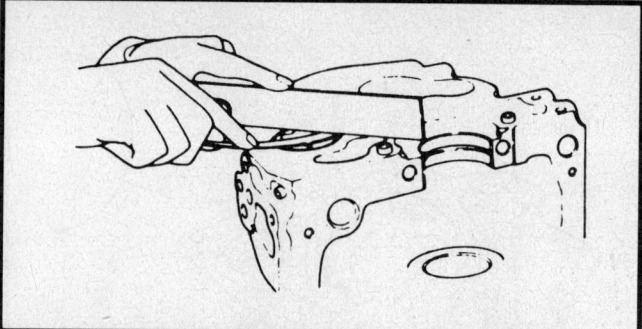

**Measuring vane to cylinder block top clearance—
4ZD1 and 4ZC1-T engines**

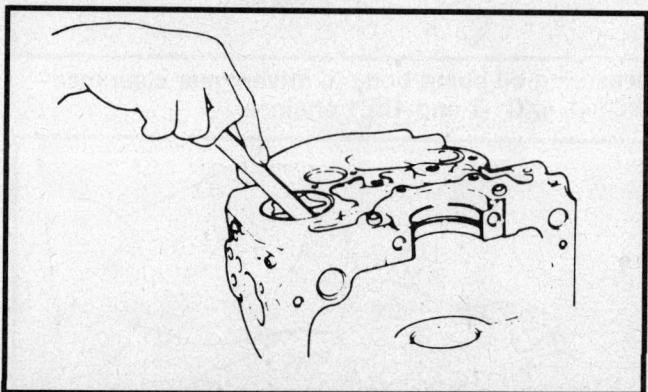

**Measuring outer rotor to cylinder block clearance—
4ZD1 and 4ZC1-T engines**

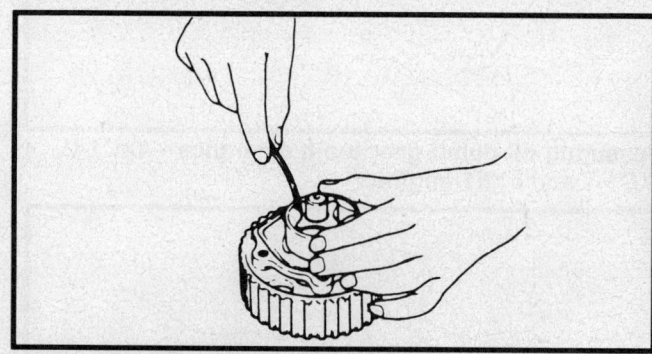

**Measuring outer rotor to inner rotor clearance—4ZD1
and 4ZC1-T engines**

2. Raise and safely support the vehicle.
3. Remove the transmission.
4. If equipped with a manual transmission, remove the clutch assembly.
5. Remove the flywheel.
6. Using a suitable prying tool, remove the rear main seal. Be careful not to damage the sealing surface of the crankshaft or the seal housing surface of the cylinder block.
7. Installation is the reverse of the removal procedure. Apply engine oil to the lip of the seal and install, using a suitable installation tool.

MANUAL TRANSMISSION

For further information, please refer to "Professional Transmission Repair Manual" for additional coverage.

Transmission Assembly

Removal and Installation

1987–89 IMPULSE

1. Disconnect the negative battery cable. Raise and support the vehicle safely.
2. Drain the transmission oil.
3. Remove the gearshift control lever knob, cover assembly and console.
4. Remove the front exhaust pipe.
5. Remove the driveshaft.
6. Disconnect the speedometer cable assembly.
7. Disconnect the clutch slave cylinder.
8. Remove the flywheel dust shield.
9. Position a jack under the transmission case, remove the engine rear mounting nuts, lower the transmission case slightly, then remove the bolts attaching the quadrant box cover to the transmission case.
10. Disconnect all electrical harness connectors.
11. Remove the control box assembly.
12. Remove the transmission-to-engine retaining bolts.

NOTE: The starter assembly is mounted in position with the bolts that are used for installing the transmission assembly to the engine. It may be necessary to move the starter assembly forward to prevent it from falling out when the bolts are removed.

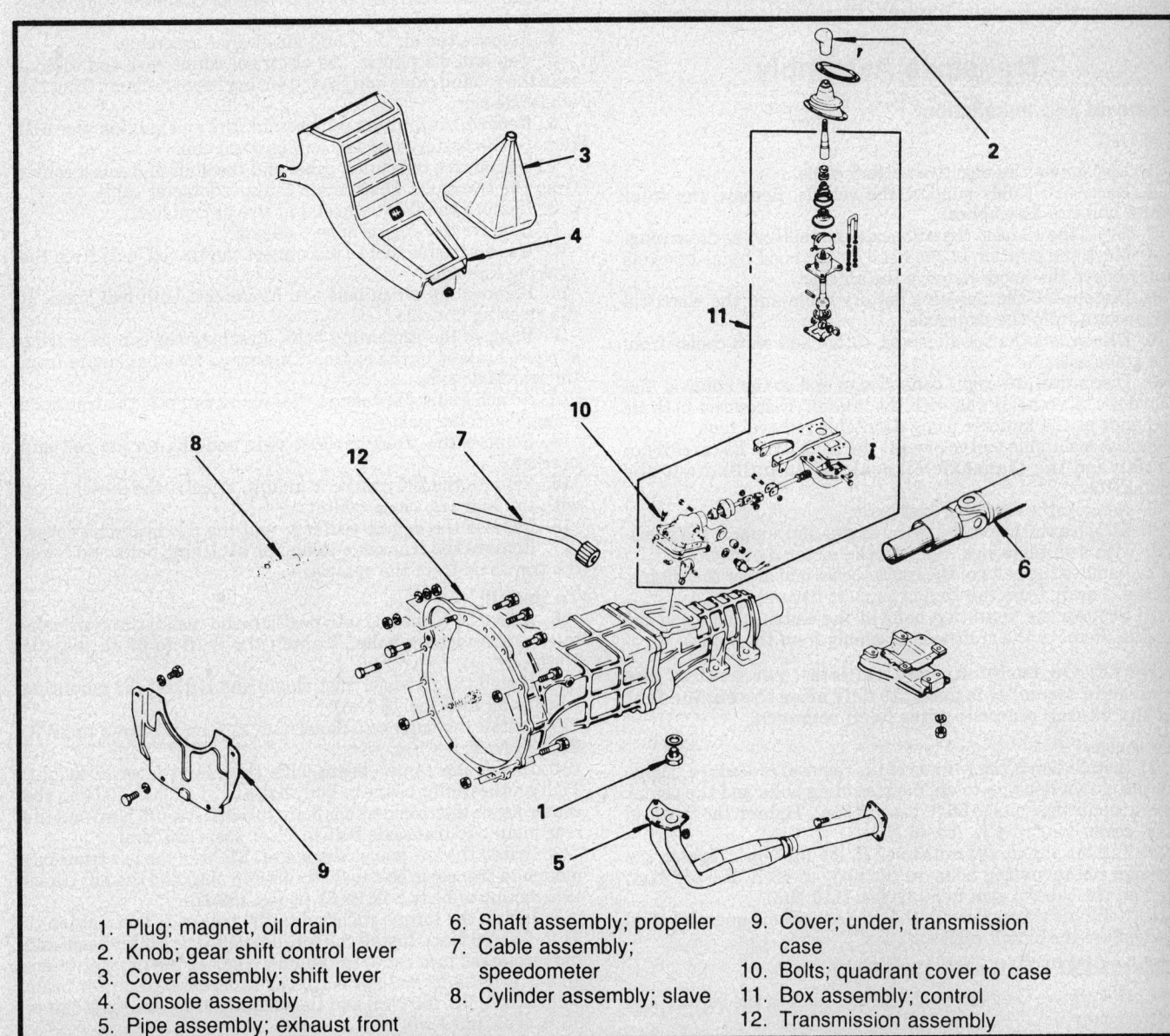

1. Plug; magnet, oil drain
2. Knob; gear shift control lever
3. Cover assembly; shift lever
4. Console assembly
5. Pipe assembly; exhaust front
6. Shaft assembly; propeller
7. Cable assembly; speedometer
8. Cylinder assembly; slave
9. Cover; under, transmission case
10. Bolts; quadrant cover to case
11. Box assembly; control
12. Transmission assembly

Manual transmission removal—1987–89 Impulse

To install:

13. Installation is the reverse of removal with the following exceptions:

   a. Position the transmission assembly with the speedometer cable fitting face turned downward and slide the assembly forward, guiding the gear shaft into the pilot bearing.

   b. Install and tighten the quadrant box cover to the transmission case bolts with a gasket fitted in position between the quadrant box cover and the transmission case, then install the engine rear mount.

   c. When reconnecting the driveshaft, install the bolts from the extension shaft side and the nuts and washers on the driveshaft side and tighten to 26 ft. lbs. (36 Nm).

   d. After tightening the rear engine mounting nuts to 14 ft. lbs. (19 Nm), raise the tab of the washers to prevent the nuts from loosening.

   e. Install and tighten the drain plug to 29 ft. lbs. (40 Nm). Remove the filler plug and fill the transmission with the proper oil. The capacity is approximately 3.28 pints. Tighten the filler plug to 29 ft. lbs. (40 Nm).

Linkage Adjustment

The shift lever is mounted on top of the transmission extension housing. All linkage is inside the transmission and requires no adjustment.

MANUAL TRANSAXLE

For further information, please refer to "Professional Transmission Repair Manual" for additional coverage.

Transaxle Assembly

Removal and Installation

I-MARK

1. Disconnect the negative battery cable.
2. Raise and safely support the vehicle. Remove the front wheel and tire assemblies.
3. Drain the oil from the transaxle and replace the drain plug.
4. Mark the position of the hood on the hood hinge brackets and remove the hood. Remove the air duct.
5. Disconnect the negative battery cable and the electrical connectors from the transaxle.
6. Disconnect the speedometer, clutch and shift cables from the transaxle.
7. Disconnect the right control arm end at the knuckle. Remove the left tension rod with the bracket. Disconnect both tie rod ends at the knuckle using a suitable removal tool.
8. Use a suitable tool to pry out the halfshafts. Be careful not to damage the transaxle oil seals when pulling out the halfshafts.
9. Remove the flywheel dust cover.
10. Attach a suitable hoist to the engine and support the transaxle with a suitable jack. Remove the motor mount bolts.
11. Remove the bolts of the center beam and lower the engine, tilting it away from the engine support fixture.
12. Remove the mounting bolts of the clutch housing to the engine. Remove the transaxle assembly from the vehicle.

NOTE: On turbocharged vehicles, removal of the transaxle assembly is possible only after the engine foot of the engine mounting has been removed.

To install:

13. Installation is the reverse of the removal procedure. Tighten the clutch housing-to-engine mounting bolts and the center beam mounting bolts to 56 ft. lbs. (77 Nm). Tighten the flywheel dust cover bolts to 4 ft. lbs. (6 Nm).
14. Tighten the tie rod nuts to 42 ft. lbs. (58 Nm). Tighten the tension rod mounting bolts on the body to 48 ft. lbs. (67 Nm) and on the control arm to 80 ft. lbs. (110 Nm).
15. Refill the transaxle with the proper type and quantity of oil and adjust the clutch cable.

1990–91 IMPULSE AND 1991 STYLUS

1. Disconnect the battery cables and remove the battery and battery tray.
2. Mark the position of the hood on the hinge brackets and remove the hood.
3. Raise and safely support the vehicle. Drain the oil from the transaxle and replace the drain plug.
4. Remove the air duct and air cleaner assembly.
5. Tag and disconnect the electrical connectors and disconnect the ground cable and engine wiring harness clamp from the transaxle side.
6. Remove the ignition coil ground wire and ignition wire and remove the battery bracket and ignition coil.
7. Disconnect the clutch cable and the shift and select cables from the transaxle. Disconnect the speedometer cable.
8. Remove the front wheel and tire assemblies.
9. Remove the engine splash shield.
10. Use a suitable tool to disconnect the tie rod ends from the steering knuckles.
11. Remove the pinch bolt and disconnect both ball joints at the steering knuckle.
12. Remove the remaining bolts attaching the center bearing support bracket to the engine. Disengage both halfshafts from the transaxle side.
13. Attach a suitable hoist to the engine. Support the transaxle using a suitable jack.
14. Remove the front exhaust pipe and the torque rod and bracket.
15. Remove the left transaxle mount. Remove the center beam with the rear transaxle mount.
16. Remove the engine stiffener and the flywheel dust cover.
17. Remove the transaxle-to-engine attaching bolts and lower the transaxle from the vehicle.

To install:

18. Raise the transaxle into position and install the transaxle-to-engine attaching bolts. Tighten the bolts to 69 ft. lbs. (94 Nm).
19. Install the flywheel dust shield and tighten the mounting bolts to 53 inch lbs. (6 Nm).
20. Install the engine stiffener and tighten the bolts to 28 ft. lbs. (38 Nm).
21. Install the center beam with the rear transaxle mount. Tighten the center beam-to-body bolts to 37 ft. lbs. (50 Nm), the center beam-to-crossmember bolts to 56 ft. lbs. (76 Nm) and the rear mount-to-transaxle bolt to 76 ft. lbs. (103 Nm).
22. Install the left transaxle mount. Tighten the left transaxle mount-to-transaxle bolt to 35 ft. lbs. (48 Nm) and the left transaxle mount-to-body bolt to 51 ft. lbs. (69 Nm).
23. Install the torque rod stud to the transaxle and tighten to 71 ft. lbs. (96 Nm). Install the torque rod to the center beam and the torque rod bracket to the engine. Tighten the bracket-to-engine bolt to 28 ft. lbs. (38 Nm), the torque rod-to-center beam bolt to 51 ft. lbs. (69 Nm) and the torque rod-to-transaxle bolt to 95 ft. lbs. (129 Nm).
24. Install the front exhaust pipe and tighten the pipe-to-manifold bolts to 49 ft. lbs. (67 Nm).

25. Install the halfshafts. Tighten the ball joint nuts to 48 ft. lbs. (65 Nm). Tighten the tie rod end nuts to 29 ft. lbs. (39 Nm).

26. Install the remainder of the components in the reverse order of their removal. Fill the transaxle with the proper type and quantity of oil. Adjust the clutch cable and shift linkage.

ALL WHEEL DRIVE IMPULSE

1. Disconnect the negative (−) battery cable.
2. Remove the battery and battery bracket.
3. Remove the intercooler, air duct and air cleaner.
4. Disconnect all electrical harnesses and cables from the transaxle.
5. Remove the transfer case.
6. Disconnect the torque rod and bracket to the lower control arm.
7. Remove the left mounting rubber.
8. Place a transmission jack under the transaxle and raise the engine with an engine holding fixture.
9. Remove the transaxle-to-engine bolts.
10. Lower the transaxle case from the vehicle.

To install:
11. Raise the transaxle case into the vehicle.
12. Install the transaxle-to-engine bolts.
13. Install the left mounting rubber and remove the transmission jack.
14. Connect the torque rod and bracket to the lower control arm.
15. Install the transfer case.
16. Connect all electrical harnesses and cables to the transaxle.
17. Install the intercooler, air duct and air cleaner.
18. Install the battery and battery bracket.
19. Connect the negative (−) battery cable and check operation.

Linkage Adjustment

1. Place the transaxle in neutral. Turn the adjusting nuts on the driver's side of the shift housing, until the gearshift lever is at right angle to the pivot case, as viewed from the side of the gear control.
2. After the adjustment tighten the 2 adjusting nuts securely.
3. Turn the adjusting nuts on the passenger's side of the shift

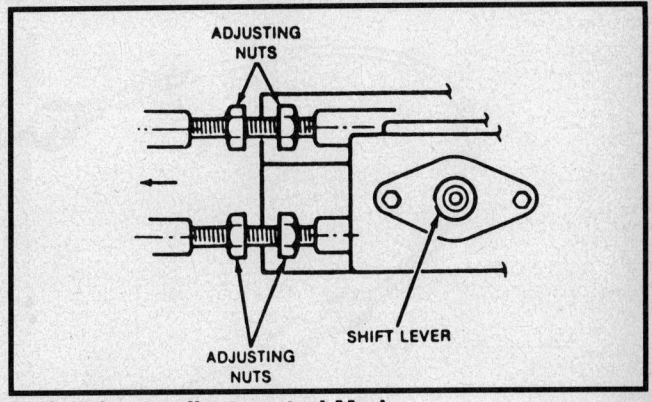

Shift linkage adjustment—I-Mark

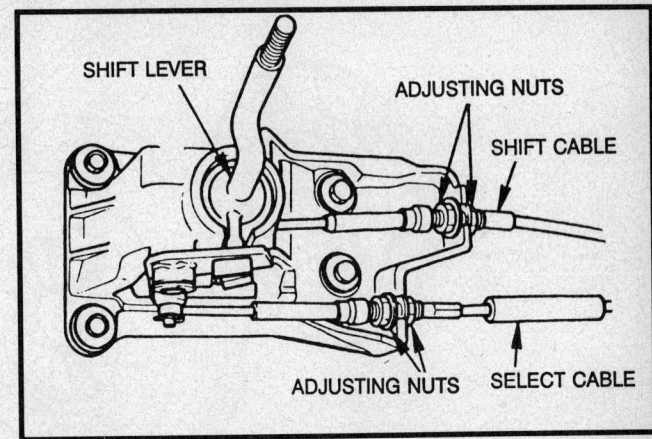

Shift linkage adjustment—1990–91 Impulse and 1991 Stylus

housing, until the gearshift lever is at right angle to the pivot case as viewed from the rear of the gear control.
4. After the adjustment tighten the 2 adjusting nuts securely.

CLUTCH

Clutch Assembly

Removal and Installation

1. Disconnect the negative battery cable.
2. Raise and safely support the vehicle.
3. Remove the transmission/transaxle assembly.
4. Mark the position of the pressure plate on the flywheel and remove the pressure plate and the clutch disc.
5. Remove the release bearing from the clutch fork.
6. Inspect the flywheel for scoring or heat cracks and resurface or replace, as necessary.
7. Inspect the pressure plate and clutch disc for wear or scoring and replace, as necessary.
8. Inspect the release bearing for wear or binding and replace, as necessary.

To install:
9. Install the flywheel if it was removed. Make sure the crank flange and the mating surface of the flywheel are clean. Tighten the flywheel bolts in a criss-cross pattern.

10. Tighten the bolts on 4XC1-U, 4XC1-T and 4XE1 engines in 2 steps, first to 22 ft. lbs. (29 Nm) and then repeat the pattern turning the bolts another 45 degrees each. Tighten the bolts on G200Z engines to 76 ft. lbs. (105 Nm). Tighten the bolts on 4ZD1 engines to 43 ft. lbs. (60 Nm). Tighten the bolts on 4ZC1-T engines to 40 ft. lbs. (55 Nm).
11. Lubricate the pilot bearing with a suitable grease. Install a suitable clutch alignment tool.
12. Install the clutch disc and the pressure plate on the flywheel. If the old pressure plate is used, make sure it is installed in the position that was marked during the removal procedure. Tighten the pressure plate bolts in a criss-cross pattern in 2–3 steps to avoid warping the pressure plate. The final bolt torque should be 13 ft. lbs. (18 Nm).
13. Remove the clutch alignment tool.
14. Apply suitable grease to the sliding surface of the release bearing and the contact surface of the clutch fork. Install the release bearing.
15. Install the remaining components in the reverse order of their removal. Adjust the clutch cable or pedal height, as required.

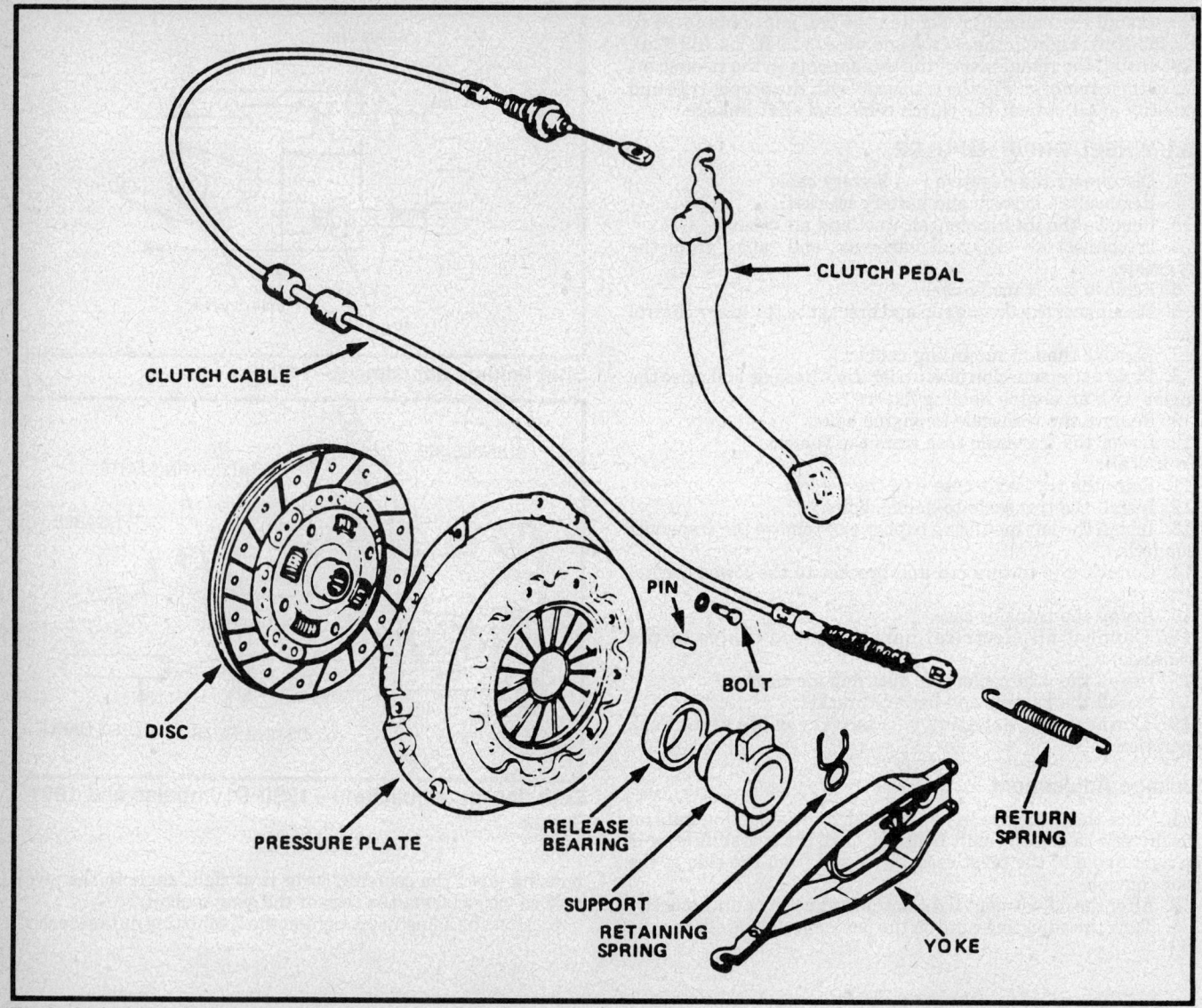

Exploded view of clutch components—except 1987- 89 Impulse

Pedal Height/Free-Play Adjustment

1987–89 IMPULSE

1. Loosen the clutch switch locknut.
2. Turn the clutch switch until the clearance between the clutch switch and the pedal is 0.020–0.059 in. (0.5–1.5mm).
3. Tighten the locknut.

NOTE: After adjustment, make sure the pushrod is in contact with the piston in the master cylinder. The clutch pedal free-play and pedal stroke are self-adjusted.

Clutch Cable

Adjustment

1. Pull the clutch cable to the rear until the adjusting nut turns freely.
2. Turn the adjusting nut either clockwise or counterclockwise to adjust the cable length.
3. On 1990–91 Impulse and 1991 Stylus, repeat Step 2 so the play between the clutch release arm and the clutch cable is 0.04–0.12 in. (1–3mm).
4. The pedal free-play should be 0.39–0.79 in. (10–20mm) on SOHC vehicles or 0.19–0.59 in. (15–25mm) on DOHC vehicles.

Removal and Installation

1. Disconnect the negative battery cable.
2. Raise and support safely the front of the vehicle.
3. Disconnect the clutch cable from the clutch housing and transaxle. Remove all necessary snaprings and locknuts to free the clutch cable.
4. Remove the clutch cable from the clutch pedal and pull the cable out from the engine compartment.
5. Installation is the reverse of the removal procedure. Adjust the clutch cable.

Clutch Master Cylinder

Removal and Installation

1. Disconnect the negative battery cable.

2. Disconnect clutch pedal return spring and joint pin from clutch pedal.

3. Disconnect and plug the hydraulic line and the hose at the clutch master cylinder.

4. Remove 2 hold-down nuts from inside of passenger compartment.

5. Remove clutch master cylinder from engine compartment.

6. Installation is the reverse of the removal procedure. Bleed the hydraulic system.

Clutch Slave Cylinder

Removal and Installation

1. Disconnect the negative battery cable.
2. Raise and safely support the vehicle.
3. Disconnect and plug the hydraulic line at the slave cylinder.
4. Remove the slave cylinder mounting bolts and disconnect the pushrod from the clutch fork. Remove the slave cylinder.

5. Installation is the reverse of the removal procedure. Bleed the hydraulic system.

Hydraulic Clutch System Bleeding

1. Fill the clutch fluid reservoir with brake fluid and keep it filled during the bleeding operation.

2. Remove the bleeder rubber cap and connect a clear plastic length of hose to the bleeder. Submerge the other end of the hose in a transparent container half filled with brake fluid.

3. Pump the clutch pedal several times and hold the pedal depressed.

4. With the pedal depressed, loosen the bleeder ½ turn to release brake fluid with air and tighten it immediately.

5. Repeat Steps 3 and 4 until air bubbles disappear completely from the fluid being forced out.

6. After bleeding is completed, check for pedal free-play and clutch disengagement, then check the brake fluid level in the reservoir.

AUTOMATIC TRANSMISSION

For further information, please refer to "Professional Transmission Repair Manual" for additional coverage.

Transmission Assembly

Removal and Installation

1. Disconnect the negative battery cable.
2. Raise and safely support the vehicle. Drain the transmission and replace the drain plug.
3. Disconnect the throttle cable at the engine side. Remove the transmission dipstick.
4. Disconnect the electrical connectors and remove the starter.
5. Mark the position of the driveshaft on the differential flange and remove the driveshaft.
6. Disconnect the link rod at the shift lever side. Disconnect the speedometer cable.
7. Remove the exhaust header pipe.
8. Disconnect the transmission cooler lines from the transmission. Secure the lines close to the body to prevent damage during transmission removal.
9. Remove the flywheel dust cover and the engine splash shield.
10. Remove the 6 bolts attaching the converter to the flywheel. Rotate the engine at the crankshaft pulley to gain access to all of the bolts.
11. Support the transmission using a suitable jack. Support the rear of the engine to hold it in position when the transmission is removed.
12. Remove the rear transmission mount and remove the transmission-to-engine mounting bolts.
13. Remove the transmission, taking care not to let the torque converter slip out of the transmission.
To install:
14. Installation is the reverse of the removal procedure. Tighten the transmission-to-engine mounting bolts to 47 ft. lbs. (65 Nm) and the converter attaching bolts to 13 ft. lbs. (19 Nm).
15. Install the driveshaft, aligning the marks that were made during the removal procedure. Tighten the bolts to 26 ft. lbs. (36 Nm).
16. Tighten the drain plug to 15 ft. lbs. (21 Nm). Adjust the link rod and the throttle cable.

17. Lower the vehicle and fill the transmission with approximately 4.2 qts. of the proper fluid. Start the engine and add fluid, as necessary, to bring the fluid to the proper level. Avoid racing the engine.

Shift Linkage Adjustment

1. Remove the adjustment nut attaching the select lever link to the control lever.
2. Move the manual valve lever forward to stop, then return to the **N** position (3rd stop).
3. Depress the manual valve lever toward the **R** position lightly and tighten the adjust nut.
4. Check that the control lever moves smoothly and that the position indicator works correctly.

Throttle Linkage Adjustment

1. Check that the throttle valve is held closed completely.
2. Adjust the setting of the adjustment nut, as necessary, so the clearance A between the inner cable stopper and the end of the rubber boot on the outer cable is adjusted to 0.032–0.059 in. (0.8–1.5mm).
3. Open the throttle valve fully and check that the inner cable stroke B is within the range of 1.30–1.34 in. (33–34mm).

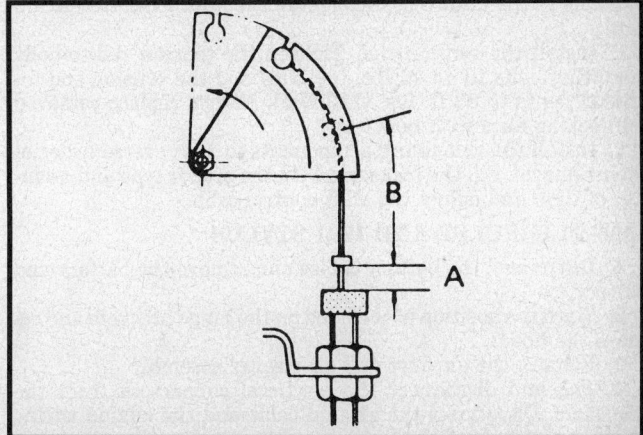

Throttle cable adjustment—1987–89 Impulse

AUTOMATIC TRANSAXLE

For further information, please refer to "Professional Transmission Repair Manual" for additional coverage.

Transaxle Assembly

Removal and Installation

I-MARK

1. Disconnect the negative battery cable.
2. Mark the position of the hood on the hinge brackets and remove the hood.
3. Raise and safely support the vehicle.
4. Drain the transaxle and replace the drain plug.
5. Tag and disconnect the electrical connectors from the transaxle. Disconnect the negative battery cable from the transaxle.
6. Disconnect the speedometer and the control cable from the transaxle.
7. Disconnect and plug the transaxle cooler lines at the transaxle. Disconnect the vacuum diaphragm hose from the transaxle.
8. Remove the air duct.
9. Remove the front wheel and tire assemblies.
10. Disconnect the right control arm end at the knuckle and remove the left tension rod with the bracket. Use a suitable removal tool to disconnect the tie rod ends at the steering knuckles.
11. Use a suitable tool to pry out the halfshafts. Be careful not to damage the transaxle seals when pulling out the halfshafts.
12. Attach a suitable hoist to the engine and support the transaxle with a suitable jack.
13. Disconnect the engine mounts and remove the center support. Remove the 3 upper transaxle-to-engine mounting bolts.
14. Remove the flywheel dust cover. Remove the 4 converter-to-flywheel mounting bolts.
15. Tilt the engine and lower the transaxle from the vehicle.

To install:

16. Raise the transaxle into position and install the transaxle-to-engine mounting bolts. Tighten the bolts to 56 ft. lbs. (77 Nm).
17. Install the converter-to-flywheel bolts and tighten to 30 ft. lbs. (41 Nm). Install the flywheel dust shield.
18. Install the center support and tighten the bolts to 56 ft. lbs. (77 Nm).
19. Install both lower engine mounts and tighten to 61 ft. lbs. (84 Nm).
20. Install the halfshafts into the transaxle. Connect the tie rod ends to the knuckles and tighten the nuts to 42 ft. lbs. (58 Nm).
21. Install the tension rod. Tighten the tension rod-to-body mounting bolts to 48 ft. lbs. (67 Nm) and the tension rod-to-knuckle nuts to 80 ft. lbs. (110 Nm). Always replace removed self-locking nuts with new ones.
22. Install the remaining components in the reverse order of their removal. Fill the transaxle with the proper type and quantity of fluid and adjust the shift control cable.

1990–91 IMPULSE AND 1991 STYLUS

1. Disconnect the battery cables and remove the battery and battery tray.
2. Mark the position of the hood on the hinge brackets and remove the hood.
3. Remove the air duct and air cleaner assembly.
4. Tag and disconnect the electrical connectors from the transaxle. Disconnect the ground cable and the engine wiring harness clamp from the transaxle side.
5. Disconnect the breather hose from the transaxle side.

6. Disconnect the ignition coil ground wire and ignition wire and remove the battery bracket and ignition coil.
7. Disconnect the shift cable from the transaxle side.
8. Raise and safely support the vehicle.
9. Disconnect the speedometer cable.
10. Remove the front wheel and tire assemblies.
11. Remove the engine splash shield. Disconnect the transaxle cooler lines from the radiator side.
12. Remove the pinch bolt and disconnect both ball joints at the steering knuckle.
13. Use a suitable tool to disconnect the tie rod ends from the steering knuckle.
14. Use a suitable tool to disengage both halfshafts from the transaxle side.
15. Attach a suitable hoist to the engine and support the transaxle with a suitable jack.
16. Remove the exhaust header pipe and the torque rod and bracket.
17. Remove the left transaxle mount and the center beam with the rear transaxle mount.
18. Remove the engine stiffener and the flywheel dust shield.
19. Remove the flywheel-to-converter attaching bolts.
20. Remove the transaxle-to-engine bolts and lower the transaxle from the vehicle.

To install:

21. Raise the transaxle into position and install the transaxle-to-engine bolts. Tighten the bolts to 69 ft. lbs. (94 Nm).
22. Install the flywheel-to-converter bolts and tighten to 33 ft. lbs. (44 Nm). Install the flywheel dust shield and tighten the mounting bolts to 53 inch lbs. (6 Nm).
23. Install the engine stiffener and tighten the bolts to 28 ft. lbs. (38 Nm).
24. Install the center beam with the rear transaxle mount. Tighten the center beam-to-body bolts to 37 ft. lbs. (50 Nm), the center beam-to-crossmember bolts to 56 ft. lbs. (76 Nm) and the rear mount-to-transaxle bolt to 76 ft. lbs. (103 Nm).
25. Install the left transaxle mount. Tighten the left transaxle mount-to-transaxle bolt to 35 ft. lbs. (48 Nm) and the left transaxle mount-to-body bolt to 51 ft. lbs. (69 Nm).
26. Install the torque rod stud to the transaxle and tighten to 71 ft. lbs. (96 Nm). Install the torque rod to the center beam and the torque rod bracket to the engine. Tighten the bracket-to-engine bolt to 28 ft. lbs. (38 Nm), the torque rod-to-center beam bolt to 51 ft. lbs. (69 Nm) and the torque rod-to-transaxle bolt to 95 ft. lbs. (129 Nm).
27. Install the front exhaust pipe and tighten the pipe-to-manifold bolts to 49 ft. lbs. (67 Nm).

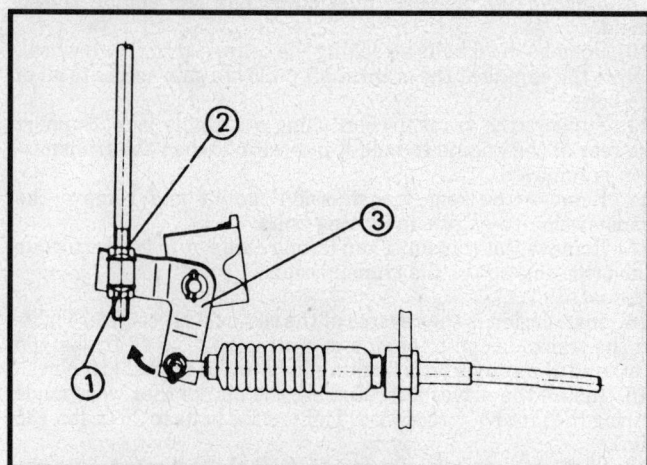

Shift link and cable end—I-Mark

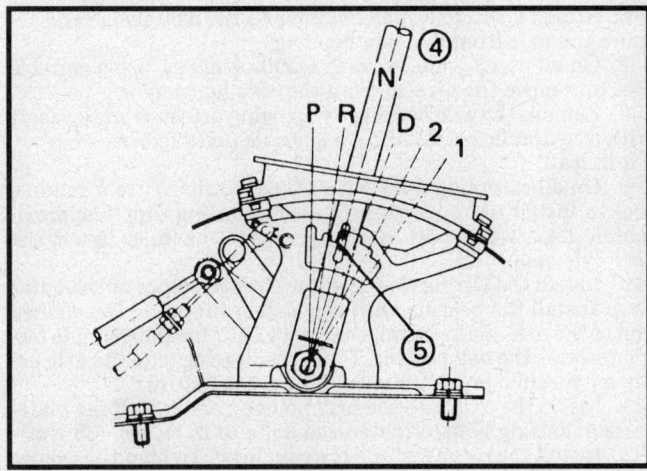

Shift lever assembly—I-Mark

28. Install the halfshafts. Tighten the ball joint nuts to 48 ft. lbs. (65 Nm). Tighten the tie rod end nuts to 29 ft. lbs. (39 Nm).
29. Install the remainder of the components in the reverse or-

der of their removal. Fill the transaxle with the correct quantity of Dexron® II ATF. Adjust the shift linkage.

Shift Cable Adjustment
I-MARK

1. Loosen locknuts (1) and (2).
2. Place the link assembly (3) on the transaxle in the **N** position.
3. Move the shift lever to the **N** range.
4. Rotate the link assembly (3) clockwise.
5. The shift lever detent pin (4) must be pressing against the **N** wall (5).
6. Temporarily tighten nut (1).
7. Tighten nut (2).

IMPULSE AND STYLUS

1. Loosen the 2 adjusting nuts at the selector lever.
2. Shift the transaxle into the **N** detent.
3. Place the shift lever into the **N** position.
4. Hand tighten the front adjusting nut fully against the selector lever boss and then back it off approximately ½ turn.
5. Tighten the rear adjusting nut fully against the selector lever boss to 19 ft. lbs. (26 Nm).

DRIVE AXLE

Halfshaft

Removal and Installation

1. Raise and safely support the vehicle. Drain the oil from the transaxle and replace the drain plug.
2. Remove the front wheel and tire assembly.
3. Remove the hub nut.
4. Disconnect the tie rod end from the steering knuckle using a suitable removal tool.
5. Loosen the pinch bolt and disconnect the lower control arm from the knuckle.
6. Pull out the hub and knuckle assembly from the halfshaft carefully. When pulling the hub assembly, pull just enough to push the shaft off. If necessary, strike the end of the halfshaft with a suitable plastic hammer.
7. To detach the snapring, fitted on the spline of the inboard CV-joint, from the differential side gear, pry out the inboard joint using a suitable tool.

NOTE: Never pull out the halfshaft, to prevent damaging the CV-joint. To prevent damage to the CV-boots, be careful not to bring them into contact with other parts when removing the halfshaft assembly.

8. Installation is the reverse of the removal procedure. Tighten the ball joint pinch bolt to 48 ft. lbs. (65 Nm). Tighten the tie rod end nut to 29 ft. lbs. (39 Nm).
9. Replace the locking nub nut with a new one. Apply grease to the hub nut fitting surfaces and the shaft threads. Tighten the nut to 137 ft. lbs. (186 Nm) and stake the nut.

CV-Boot

Removal and Installation

1. Raise and safely support the vehicle.
2. Remove the halfshaft assembly.
3. Mount the halfshaft in a suitable vice.

NOTE: The outer CV-joint cannot be disassembled. The inboard CV-joint must be removed to replace either CV-joint boot. The 1990–91 Impulse, Stylus and I-Mark equipped with automatic transaxle, on the right halfshaft only, a tripod inboard CV-joint used. All other inboard CV-joints are the double offset type. A different removal and installation procedure is used for each.

4. Remove the double offset CV-joint as follows:
   a. Mark the position of the case in relation to the shaft using paint or ink. Do not use a punch.
   b. Remove the big end band clip.
   c. Remove the circular clip and remove the outer case.
   d. Turn the ball guide on an angle and move it to the center shaft side. Remove the balls.
   e. Remove the snapring. Mark the position of the ball retainer in relation to the shaft and remove the ball retainer.
   f. Remove the ball guide and small end band clip. Remove the boot.
   g. If the outer boot is to be replaced, remove the band clips and remove the outer boot.
5. Installation of the CV-joint is the reverse of the removal procedure. When assembling, apply special grease to ½ of the space within the double offset joint. Make sure the band clips are securely tightened and the boot is not twisted.
6. Remove the tripod CV-joint as follows:
   a. Mark the position of the case in relation to the shaft using paint or ink. Do not use a punch.
   b. Remove the big end band clip.
   c. Remove the case.
   d. Remove the snapring.
   e. Mark the position of the tripod in relation to the shaft. Push the tripod off of the shaft using a suitable brass drift, being careful not to hit the roller.
   f. Remove the small end band clip and remove the boot.
   g. If the outer boot is to be replaced, remove the band clips and remove the outer boot.
7. Installation of the CV-joint is the reverse of the removal procedure. When installing the tripod, make sure the shorter spline is positioned to the outside. Apply special grease into the

tripod housing. Make sure the band clips are securely tightened and the boot is not twisted.

8. Install the halfshaft and lower the vehicle.

Driveshaft and U-Joints

Removal and Installation

EXCEPT G200Z ENGINE

1. Raise and safely support the vehicle.
2. Mark the position of the rear driveshaft in relation to both the center bearing flange and the differential flange.
3. Remove the rear driveshaft mounting nuts and bolts and remove the rear driveshaft.
4. Remove the center bearing bracket bolts and remove the center bearing bracket.
5. Remove the front driveshaft. Install a plug or equivalent in the rear of the transmission to prevent fluid loss.
6. Installation is the reverse of the removal procedure. Tighten the center bearing bracket bolts to 13 ft. lbs. (19 Nm). Tighten the driveshaft-to-flange bolts to 24 ft. lbs. (33 Nm).

G200Z ENGINE

1. Raise and safely support the vehicle.
2. Remove the parking brake cable adjustment nut and the rear cable from the front cable.
3. Remove the parking brake cable-to-body clip.
4. Remove the center exhaust pipe.
5. Mark the position of the driveshaft in relation to the flange and remove the flange bolts. Remove the driveshaft.
6. Installation is the reverse of the removal procedure. Make sure the coil spring is in position at the front of the driveshaft. Install the flange bolts from the extension shaft side and tighten to 24 ft. lbs. (33 Nm).

ALL WHEEL DRIVE IMPULSE

1. Raise and safely support the vehicle.
2. Apply alignment marks on the flange at the center bearing.
3. Remove the bolts at the rear axle side and center bearing.
4. Remove the shaft from the vehicle.
5. Installation is the reverse of the removal procedure. Align the marks and install the bolts. Torque the center bearing bolts to 14 ft. lbs. (19 Nm) and the rear bolts to 26 ft. lbs. (35 Nm).

Rear Axle Shaft, Bearing and Seal

Removal and Installation

1. Raise and safely support the vehicle.
2. Remove the rear wheel and tire assembly.
3. Remove the 2 caliper attaching bolts and remove the caliper from the rotor. Support the caliper with a length of wire, do not let it hang from the brake hose.
4. Remove the disc brake rotor.
5. Working through the access hole, remove the plate-to-axle housing bolts.

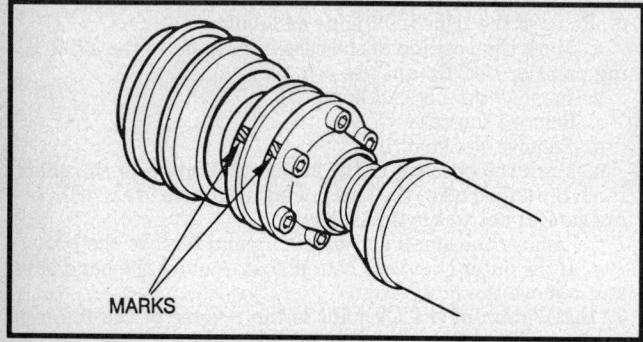

Driveshaft alignment marks—All Wheel Drive Impulse

6. Attach a suitable slide hammer to the axle flange and remove the axle from the axle housing.
7. On all except vehicles with G200Z engines, use a suitable tool to remove the oil seal from the axle housing.
8. Remove the axle bearing by applying pressure on the shaft with a hydraulic press, using a suitable press fixture.

To install:

9. On all except vehicles with G200Z engines, use a suitable tool to install the oil seal in the axle housing. Apply approximately 1.4 ozs. of wheel bearing grease to the inner face of the rear axle case.
10. Install the O-ring on the outer circumference of the outer race. Install the bearing with the O-ring turned to the splined end of the axle shaft. Install the sleeve with the flanged side facing towards the ball bearing. Press the bearing onto the axle using a hydraulic press and a suitable press fixture.
11. Insert the axle into the axle housing and install the plate-to-axle housing bolts. Tighten the bolts to 27 ft. lbs. (38 Nm).
12. Install the rotor and the brake caliper. Tighten the caliper bolts to 36 ft. lbs. (50 Nm).
13. Install the wheel and tire assembly and lower the vehicle.

Front Wheel Hub, Knuckle and Bearings

Removal and Installation

NOTE: Do not remove the hub from the knuckle unless it is absolutely necessary.

1. Raise and safely support the vehicle.
2. Remove the front wheel and tire assembly.
3. Remove the brake caliper and support it with a length of wire. Do not let the caliper hang from the brake hose.
4. Remove the disc brake rotor.
5. Pry the hub nut open and remove it from the end of the halfshaft.
6. Attach a suitable slide hammer to the hub and remove the hub from the vehicle.
7. Remove the dust shield.
8. Disconnect the tie rod end from the knuckle, using a suitable removal tool.
9. Remove the tension arm-to-control arm nuts and separate the control arm from the knuckle on I-Mark. On 1990–91 Impulse and 1991 Stylus, remove the pinch bolt and separate the ball joint from the knuckle.
10. Remove the bolts from the strut and remove the knuckle assembly.
11. Remove the inner and outer seals. On I-Mark, remove both snaprings. On 1990–91 Impulse and 1991 Stylus, remove the 1 inner snapring.
12. On I-Mark, mount the knuckle in a hydraulic press and press out the inside inner race and bearing, using a suitable press fixture. Mount the hub in the press and, using a suitable fixture, press out the outside inner race.
13. On 1990–91 Impulse and 1991 Stylus, mount the knuckle in a hydraulic press and press out the bearing, using a suitable fixture.

To install:

14. On I-Mark, install the outer snapring and mount the knuckle in a hydraulic press. Using a suitable fixture, press in a new hub bearing and inner and outer races. Do not remove the inner race fixed cover which is attached to the inside of the bearing inner race. When forcing the hub bearing onto the knuckle, apply pressure to the bearing outer race.
15. On 1990–91 Impulse and 1991 Stylus, mount the knuckle in a hydraulic press and, using a suitable fixture, press in a new bearing.
16. Install the inner snapring and the inner and outer seals. Install the dust cover.
17. Mount the knuckle in a hydraulic press and press the hub

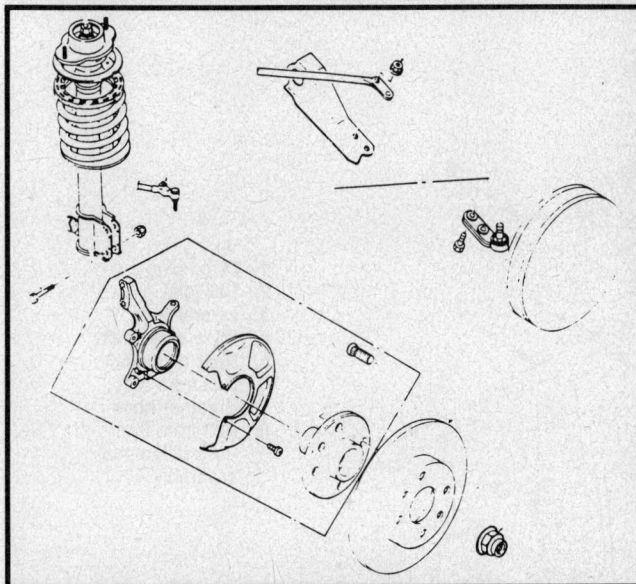

Front suspension components—I-Mark

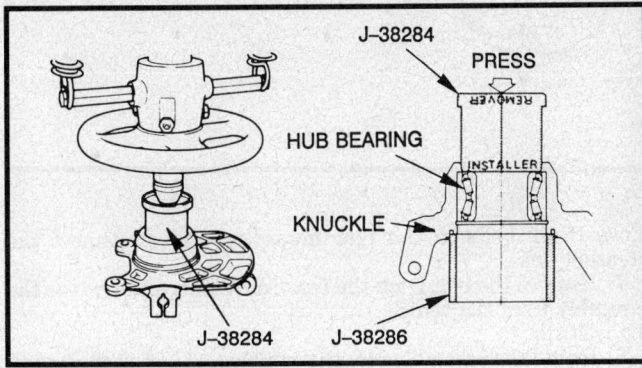

Removing front hub bearings

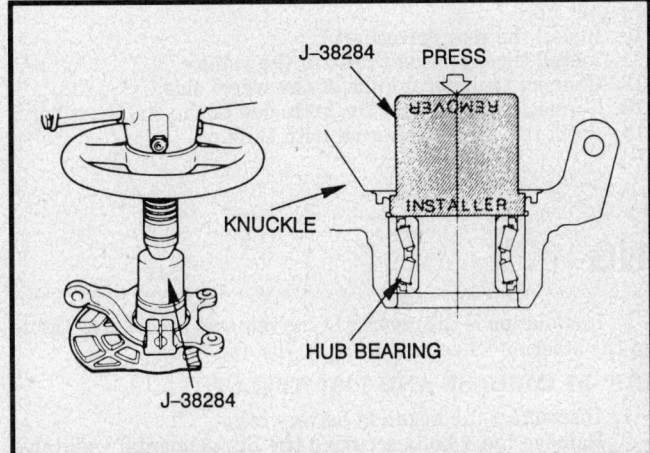

Installing front hub bearings

onto the knuckle, using a suitable fixture. On I-Mark, the bearing inner race mounting cover must be removed before the hub can be forced onto the knuckle. Push the mounting cover down and away from the hub to remove it.

18. Install the hub and knuckle assembly onto the halfshaft and tighten the hub nut temporarily.

19. Install the strut bolts and tighten to 87 ft. lbs. (120 Nm) on I-Mark and 115 ft. lbs. (156 Nm) on 1990–91 Impulse and 1991 Stylus.

20. On I-Mark, connect the control arm to the tension arm and install the nuts. Tighten the nuts to 79 ft. lbs. (110 Nm). Always replace a used self-locking nut with a new one.

21. On 1990–91 Impulse and 1991 Stylus, connect the ball joint to the knuckle and tighten the pinch bolt to 48 ft. lbs. (65 Nm).

22. Connect the tie rod end to the knuckle and tighten the nut to 29 ft. lbs. (39 Nm).

23. Remove the hub nut and apply grease to the halfshaft's thread. Install the hub nut and tighten it to 137 ft. lbs. (186 Nm). Stake the nut after installation.

24. Install the brake rotor and the caliper.

25. Install the wheel and tire assembly and lower the vehicle.

Pinion Seal

Removal and Installation

1. Raise and safely support the vehicle.

2. If equipped with the G200Z engine, remove the driveshaft and the extension shaft assembly. On all others, remove the driveshaft and the differential flange.

3. Use a suitable tool to pry out the pinion seal.

4. Installation is the reverse of the removal procedure. Lubricate the lip of the seal after installation.

5. Tighten the extension shaft nut on G200Z engine equipped vehicles to 87 ft. lbs. (120 Nm). On all others, tighten the flange nut to 130–202 ft. lbs. (180–280 Nm).

Differential Carrier

Removal and Installation

IMPULSE WITH 4ZD1 AND 4ZC1-T ENGINES

1. Raise and safely support the vehicle.

2. Drain the axle housing and replace the drain plug.

3. Remove the driveshaft.

4. Remove the axle shafts.

5. Remove the differential carrier mounting bolts and remove the differential carrier.

6. Installation is the reverse of the removal procedure. Tighten the carrier mounting bolts to 18 ft. lbs. (25 Nm). Fill the axle housing with the proper type and quantity of oil.

Axle Housing

Removal and Installation

EXCEPT ALL WHEEL DRIVE IMPULSE

1. Raise and safely support the vehicle.

2. Remove the rear wheel and tire assemblies.

3. Remove the driveshaft. On G200Z engine equipped vehicles, remove the extension shaft assembly.

4. Remove the calipers and support them with a length of wire. Do not let the calipers hang by the brake hoses. Disconnect the parking brake cables.

5. Remove the exhaust pipe and muffler, if necessary.

6. Disconnect the sway bar from the axle housing.

7. Support the axle housing with a suitable jack.

8. Remove the panhard rod.

9. Disconnect the shock absorbers from the axle housing.

10. Lower the axle housing slowly, enough to remove the coil springs.

11. Disconnect the control arms from the axle housing and lower the axle housing from the vehicle.

12. Installation is the reverse of the removal procedure.

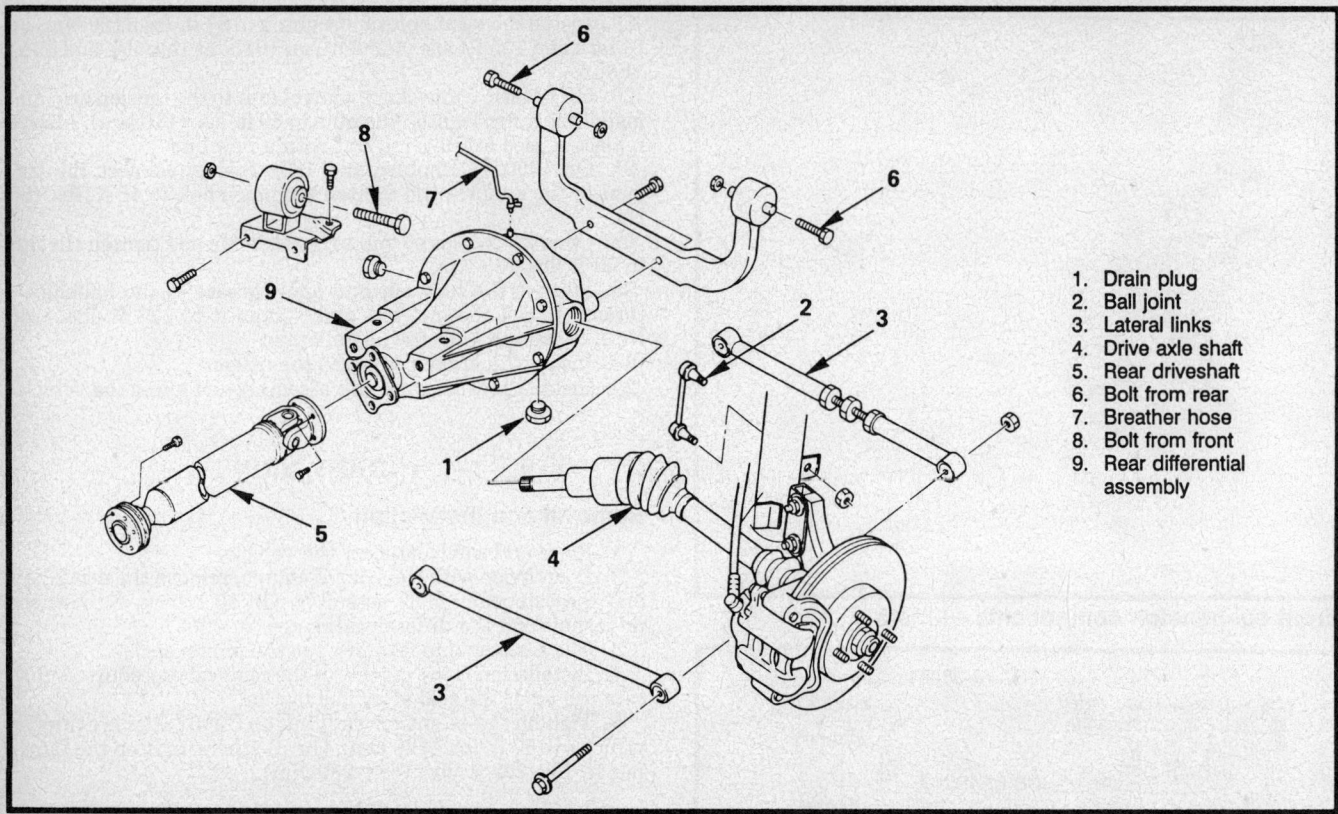

1. Drain plug
2. Ball joint
3. Lateral links
4. Drive axle shaft
5. Rear driveshaft
6. Bolt from rear
7. Breather hose
8. Bolt from front
9. Rear differential assembly

Rear differential assembly—All Wheel Drive Impulse

ALL WHEEL DRIVE IMPULSE
1. Drain the rear differential fluid.
2. Disconnect the ball joint for both side of the stabilizer bar.
3. Disconnect the lateral links at the wheel side.

NOTE: Never pull out the driveshaft. Damage to the boots and joints may result.

4. Pry the inboard joint against the differential housing to dislodge the snapring inside the differential assembly using a suitable prybar. Remove the rear axle shafts from the vehicle.
5. Remove the rear driveshaft.
6. Support the differential assembly using a suitable jack. Re-

move the 2 bolts in the rear mounting and disconnect the breather hose.
7. Remove the bolt from the front mounting and remove the assembly from the vehicle.
To install:
8. Install the assembly into the vehicle and install the bolt to the front mounting.
9. Install the 2 bolts in the rear mounting and connect the breather hose.
10. Install the rear driveshaft.
11. Install the rear axle shafts to the vehicle.
12. Connect the lateral links at the wheel side.
13. Connect the ball joint for both side of the stabilizer bar.
14. Refill the rear differential with fluid.

STEERING

Steering Wheel

— CAUTION —

On vehicles equipped with an air bag, the negative battery cable must be disconnected, before working on the system. Failure to do so may result in deployment of the air bag and possible personal injury.

Removal and Installation
EXCEPT 1990–91 IMPULSE AND 1991 STYLUS
1. Disconnect the negative battery cable.
2. Remove the horn pad.
3. Remove the steering wheel nut.
4. Use a suitable puller to remove the steering wheel.

5. Installation is the reverse of the removal procedure. Tighten the steering wheel nut to 25 ft. lbs. (35 Nm).
1990–91 IMPULSE AND 1991 STYLUS
1. Disconnect the negative battery cable.
2. Remove the 4 bolts securing the Supplemental Inflatable Restraint (SIR) module to the steering wheel.
3. Disconnect the module connector and remove the SIR module.

— CAUTION —

The SIR module should always be carried with the urethane cover away from the body. It should always be laid on a flat surface with the urethane side up. This is necessary because a free space is provided to allow the air cushion to expand in the unlikely event of accidental deployment. Otherwise, personal injury may result.

4. Disconnect the horn connector and remove the steering wheel nut.

5. Use a suitable puller to remove the steering wheel.

To install:

6. Mount the steering wheel on the column and tighten the steering wheel nut to 25 ft. lbs. (35 Nm).

NOTE: Be careful not to damage the harness section of the coil when installing the steering wheel. At this time, the cancel cam for the turn signal switch must be closely inserted into a boss hole in the steering wheel.

7. Support the SIR module and carefully connect the module connector. Pass the lead wire through the tabs on the plastic cover (wire protector) of the inflator to prevent the lead wire from being pinched.

8. Install the module retaining bolts and tighten them to 3.6 ft. lbs. (5 Nm).

9. Connect the negative battery cable. Turn the ignition switch to **ON** while watching the warning light. The light should flash 7–9 times and then go off. If the light does not operate correctly, there is a problem in the SIR system.

Steering Column

Removal and Installation

I-MARK

1. Disconnect the negative battery cable.
2. Remove the horn button pad assembly.
3. Remove the steering wheel nut. Use a suitable puller to remove the steering wheel.
4. Remove the upper and lower steering column covers.
5. Disconnect the ignition switch and turn signal switch connectors and remove the turn signal switch.
6. Remove the steering column protector.
7. Remove the steering joint bolt.
8. Remove the steering column mounting bolts and remove the steering column and shaft assembly.

To install:

9. Align the serrated notches of the stub shaft and the intermediate shaft. Tighten the bolt to 19 ft. lbs. (26 Nm).
10. Align the serrated notches of the steering shaft and the intermediate shaft. Partially tighten the steering shaft side joint part before tightening the steering column upper and lower brackets.
11. Pull the steering column rearward as the upper bracket bolt is tightened to 11 ft. lbs. (15 Nm). Tighten the lower bracket bolt to 11 ft. lbs. (15 Nm). Finish tightening the steering shaft side joint bolt to 19 ft. lbs. (26 Nm).
12. The remaining components are installed in the reverse order of their removal. Tighten the steering wheel nut to 25 ft. lbs. (35 Nm).

IMPULSE

1987

1. Disconnect the negative battery cable.
2. Remove the horn button and pad assembly.
3. Remove the steering wheel nut and use a suitable puller to remove the steering wheel.
4. Remove the upper and lower steering column covers.
5. Remove the lap vent grille assembly.
6. Remove the 2nd shaft-to-universal joint bolt.
7. Disconnect the electrical connectors from the steering column.
8. Remove the steering stay and remove the steering column bracket bolts.
9. Remove the steering column.
10. Installation is the reverse of the removal procedure. Tighten the upper bracket bolt to 13 ft. lbs. (18 Nm) and the lower bracket bolts to 4.3 ft. lbs. (6 Nm). Tighten the 2nd shaft-to-uni-

versal joint bolt to 18 ft. lbs. (25 Nm) and the steering wheel nut to 22 ft. lbs. (30 Nm).

1988–89

1. Disconnect the negative battery cable.
2. Remove the screw from the lower side of the horn button pad assembly. Slide the horn button pad towards the front of the vehicle and disconnect the electrical connector.
3. Remove the front console and the radio assembly.
4. Remove the lower dash panel and the hood lock release lever.
5. Remove the left knee pad and the steering column cover.
6. Remove the 2nd shaft-to-universal joint bolt and the steering stay instrument panel nut.
7. Disconnect the electrical connectors from the steering column.
8. Remove the steering column bracket nuts and bolts and remove the steering column and shaft assembly.
9. Installation is the reverse of the removal procedure. Tighten the column-to-instrument panel nut to 13 ft. lbs. (18 Nm) and the steering column support bracket bolt to 4.3 ft. lbs. (6 Nm). Tighten the 2nd shaft-to-universal joint bolt to 18 ft. lbs. (25 Nm). Tighten the left knee pad bolts to 29 ft. lbs. (40 Nm) and the steering column nut to 25 ft. lbs. (35 Nm).

1990–91 IMPULSE AND 1991 STYLUS

NOTE: The wheels of the vehicle must be in the straight ahead position and the steering column in the LOCK position before disconnecting the steering column or steering shaft from the steering gear. Failure to do so will cause the coil assembly to become uncentered which will cause damage to the coil assembly.

——————— CAUTION ———————

The SIR module should always be carried with the urethane cover away from the body. It should always be laid on a flat surface with the urethane side up. This is necessary because a free space is provided to allow the air cushion to expand in the unlikely event of accidental deployment. Otherwise, personal injury may result.

1. Disconnect the negative battery cable.
2. Remove the steering wheel according to the proper procedure.
3. Remove the steering column cover.
4. Remove the knee pad.
5. Disconnect the electrical connectors from the steering column.
6. If equipped with an automatic transaxle, remove the steering lock fixing pin.
7. Remove the steering shaft bolt from the steering unit side. Loosen the bolt on the steering column side, then remove the spline shaft from the steering unit side.
8. Remove the column mounting nuts and bolts and remove the column assembly.
9. Installation is the reverse of the removal procedure. Tighten the column mounting nuts and bolts to 11 ft. lbs. (15 Nm). Tighten the steering spline shaft bolt to 30 ft. lbs. (40 Nm).

Manual Steering Rack

Adjustment

I-MARK

1. Raise and safely support the vehicle. Remove the steering rack from the vehicle.
2. Remove the adjusting plug and apply grease to the sliding surfaces of the plunger, spring seat and the inside of the adjusting plug. Replace the adjusting plug and tighten to 3.6 ft. lbs. (5 Nm).
3. Loosen the adjusting plug.
4. Repeat Steps 2 and 3.

5. Back down the adjusting plug by a maximum of 25 degrees. Hold the adjusting plug with a locknut. If the pinion shaft starting torque does not equal 0.4–0.9 ft. lbs. (0.6–1.2 Nm), the adjusting plug must be readjusted.

6. Tighten the adjusting plug locknut to 49 ft. lbs. (68 Nm).

Removal and Installation

I-MARK

1. Disconnect the negative battery cable. Mark the position of the hood in relation to the hinge brackets and remove the hood.

2. Raise and safely support the vehicle. Remove both front wheel and tire assemblies.

3. Use a suitable tool to remove the tie rod ends from the steering knuckles.

4. Using a suitable engine hoist, slightly raise the engine. Support the lower part of the engine with a suitable jack.

5. Remove the engine mounting bolts.

6. Remove the front exhaust pipe hanger mounting rubber nut. Detach the mounting rubber from the beam. Remove the beam. Remove the intermediate shaft mounting bolt (steering shaft side bolt).

7. Remove the bracket nut(s) holding the manual steering unit.

8. Remove the steering unit and when removing the right and left steering unit boots through the body, be careful not to damage the boots.

9. Installation is the reverse of the removal procedure. Be sure to use the following torque specifications when installing the steering unit.

    a. Steering unit bracket nut – 30 ft. lbs.
    b. Steering shaft side bolt – 19 ft. lbs.
    c. Support beam bolts – 56 ft. lbs.
    d. Engine mounting bolts – 61 ft. lbs.
    e. Tie rod end nut – 29 ft. lbs.

Power Steering Rack

Adjustment

I-MARK

1. Raise and safely support the vehicle. Remove the steering rack from the vehicle.

2. Loosen the adjusting plug.

3. Tighten the adjusting plug to 3.6 ft. lbs. (5 Nm).

4. Loosen the adjusting plug.

5. Repeat Steps 3 and 4.

6. Tighten the adjusting plug to 3.6 ft. lbs. (5 Nm).

7. Back off on the adjusting plug 30–35 degrees.

8. Hold the adjusting plug with a locknut.

9. If the pinion shaft starting torque is different from 0.43–1.01 ft. lbs. (0.6–1.4 Nm), the adjusting plug must be readjusted. Tighten the adjusting plug locknut to 49 ft. lbs. (68 Nm).

1987–89 IMPULSE

1. Raise and safely support the vehicle. Remove the steering rack from the vehicle.

2. Loosen the adjustment plug, then tighten it to 5.42 ft. lbs. (7.5 Nm).

3. Back off the adjustment plug 30–35 degrees.

4. Make sure the rack shaft operates smoothly. Tighten the locknut to 50 ft. lbs. (70 Nm).

1990–91 IMPULSE AND 1991 STYLUS

1. Raise and safely support the vehicle. Remove the steering rack from the vehicle.

2. Loosen the adjustment plug.

3. Tighten the plug to 43.4 inch lbs. (4.9 Nm), loosen the plug and then tighten it again to 43.4 inch lbs. (4.9 Nm).

4. Back off the plug 26 degrees, then tighten the locknut.

5. Check the pinion shaft preload. It should be 5.3–14.1 inch lbs. (0.6–1.6 Nm). If the preload is not within specification, loosen the locknut and readjust the plug.

6. Tighten the locknut to 49 ft. lbs. (66 Nm).

Removal and Installation

I-MARK

1. Disconnect the negative battery cable. Mark the position of the hood on the hinge brackets and remove the hood.

2. Raise and safely support the vehicle. Remove the front wheel and tire assemblies.

3. Use a suitable tool to disconnect the tie rod ends from the steering knuckle.

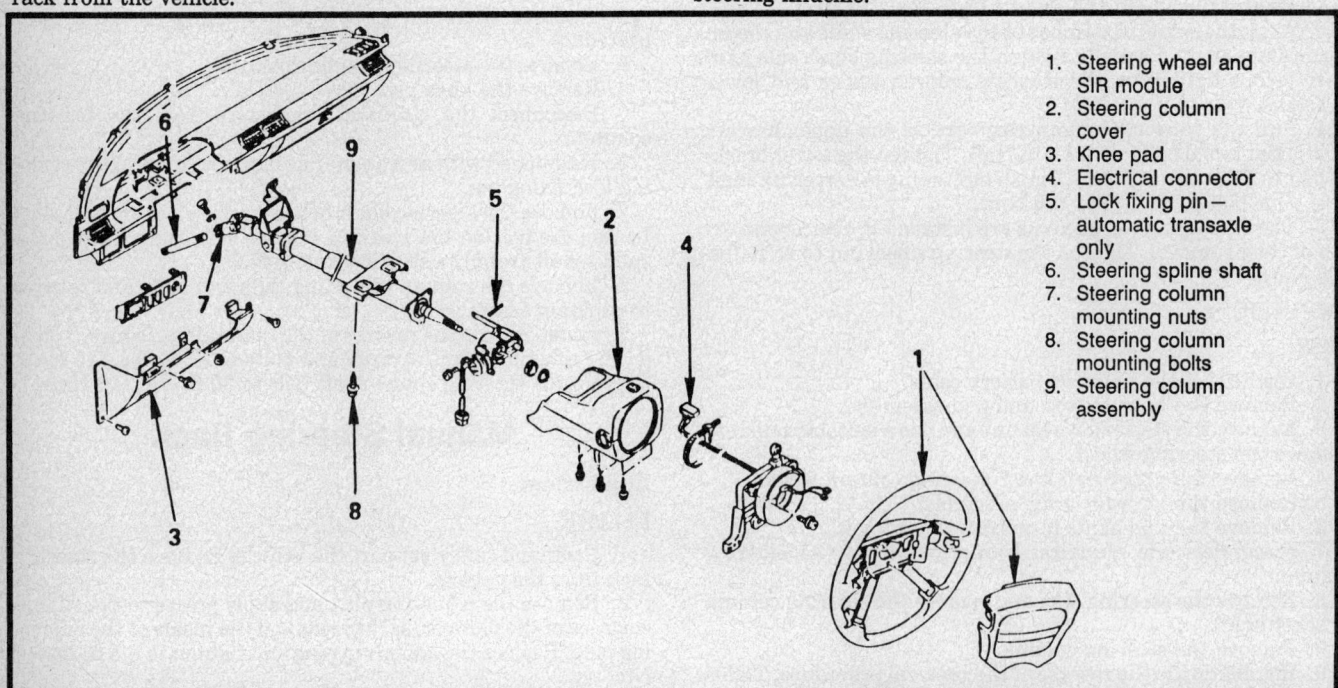

1. Steering wheel and SIR module
2. Steering column cover
3. Knee pad
4. Electrical connector
5. Lock fixing pin – automatic transaxle only
6. Steering spline shaft
7. Steering column mounting nuts
8. Steering column mounting bolts
9. Steering column assembly

Steering column assembly – 1990–91 Impulse and 1991 Stylus

4. Attach a suitable hoist to the engine and raise the engine slightly. Support the lower part of the engine with a suitable jack. Remove the engine mounting bolts.

5. Remove the exhaust pipe hanger rubber mounting nut. Separate the mounting rubber and the beam. Remove the beam.

6. Remove the steering column protector and the steering shaft bolt. Remove the intermediate shaft mounting bolt and the intermediate shaft.

7. Disconnect the power steering lines from the rack.

8. Remove the steering rack mounting bolts and remove the rack from the vehicle.

To install:

9. Installation is the reverse of the removal procedure. Make sure the serrated notches on the intermediate shaft are aligned. Tighten the steering shaft bolt to 19 ft. lbs. (26 Nm).

10. Tighten the beam mounting bolts to 56 ft. lbs. (77 Nm). Tighten the engine mounting bolts to 61 ft. lbs. (84 Nm). Tighten the tie rod nuts to 29 ft. lbs. (40 Nm).

11. Fill the reservoir with the proper type of fluid and bleed the air from the system.

1987–89 IMPULSE

1. Raise and safely support the vehicle. Remove the front wheel and tire assemblies.

2. Remove the front disc brake calipers and support them with a length of wire. Do not let them hang from the brake hoses.

3. Remove the hub and rotor assembly and the brake dust shield.

4. Use a suitable tool to disconnect the tie rod ends from the steering knuckles.

5. Disconnect the steering shaft from the steering column.

6. Disconnect the power steering lines from the rack.

7. Remove the rack mounting bolts and remove the rack assembly.

To install:

8. Installation is the reverse of the removal procedure. After tightening the rack mounting bolts, lock each bolt securely by bending the washer at 2 opposed points.

9. Fill the reservoir with the proper type of fluid and bleed the air from the system.

1990–91 IMPULSE AND 1991 STYLUS

1. Disconnect the negative battery cable. Mark the position of the hood on the hinge brackets and remove the hood.

2. Remove the column protector and remove the spline shaft pinch bolts. Remove the steering shaft boot nuts.

3. Raise and safely support the vehicle. Remove the front wheel and tire assemblies.

4. Attach a suitable hoist to the engine and support it.

5. Remove the exhaust header pipe. Place a suitable drain pan below the steering rack and disconnect the power steering lines.

6. Use a suitable tool to disconnect the tie rod ends from the steering knuckle.

7. Disconnect the ball joints from the steering knuckle and remove the crossmember assembly. Separate the steering rack from the crossmember.

To install:

8. Installation is the reverse of the removal procedure. Tighten the following components to specification:

    a. Steering rack-to-chassis bolts—37 ft. lbs. (50 Nm).

    b. Crossmember assembly—137 ft. lbs. (186 Nm).

    c. Front beam-to-chassis bolts—37 ft. lbs. (50 Nm).

    d. Ball joint—48 ft. lbs. (65 Nm).

    e. Tie rod ends—40 ft. lbs. (54 Nm).

    f. Exhaust pipe—49 ft. lbs. (67 Nm).

    g. Spline shaft pinch bolt—30 ft. lbs. (40 Nm).

9. Fill the reservoir with the proper type of fluid and bleed the air from the system.

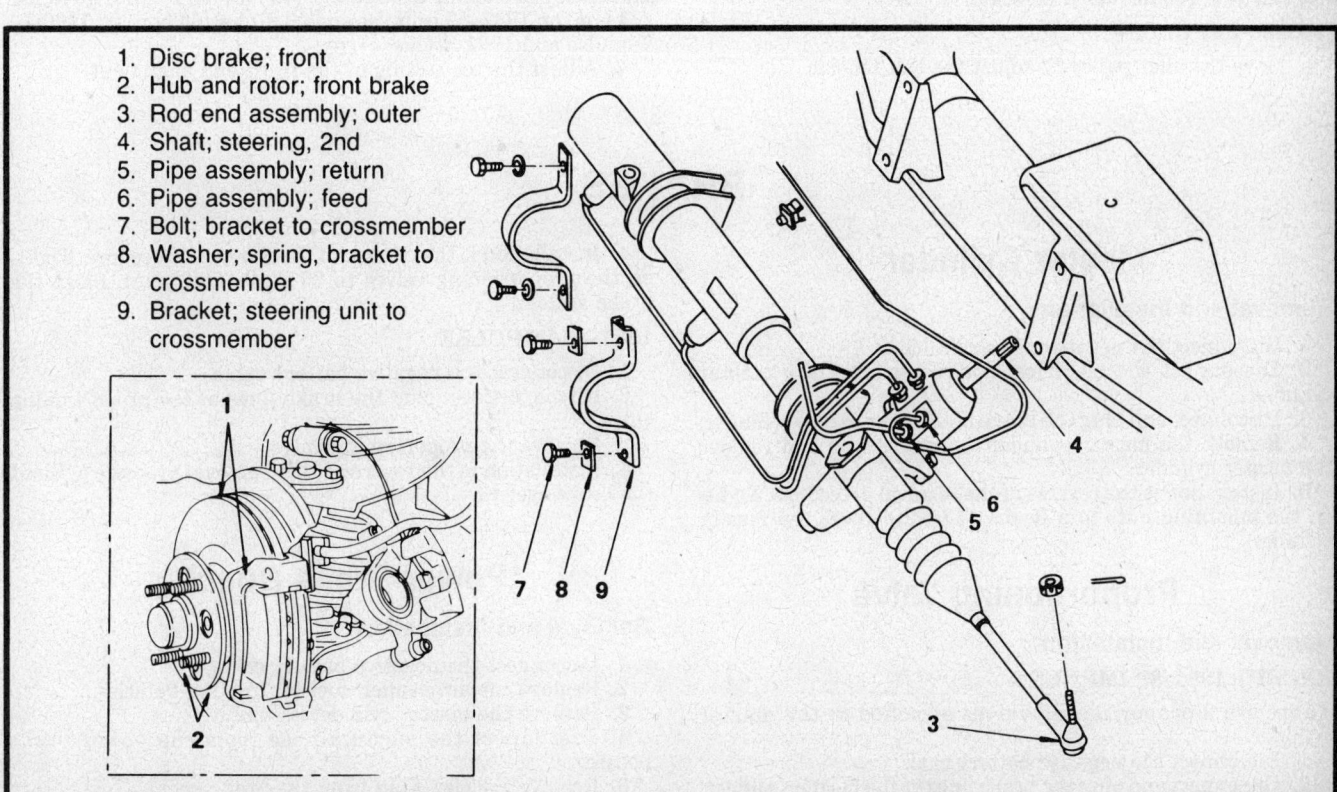

1. Disc brake; front
2. Hub and rotor; front brake
3. Rod end assembly; outer
4. Shaft; steering, 2nd
5. Pipe assembly; return
6. Pipe assembly; feed
7. Bolt; bracket to crossmember
8. Washer; spring, bracket to crossmember
9. Bracket; steering unit to crossmember

Power steering rack installation—1987–89 Impulse

Power Steering Pump

Removal and Installation

1. Disconnect the negative battery cable.
2. On 1987 Impulse equipped with the G200Z engine, remove the engine splash shield.
3. Disconnect the pressure and return lines from the pump.
4. Remove the drive belt from the pump pulley.
5. On 1987–89 Impulse, remove the pump pulley (and idler pulley except G200Z engine) and then remove the pump and bracket assembly. On all others, remove the pump and bracket assembly and then remove the pulley and bracket from the pump.

NOTE: On 1987 Impulse equipped with the G200Z engine, remove the sway bar or hold the engine assembly lifted by approximately 1.2 in. when removing the pump assembly. This will prevent interference between the pump bracket and the sway bar.

6. Installation is the reverse of the removal procedure. Adjust the drive belt, fill the reservoir with the proper type of fluid and bleed the air from the system.

Belt Adjustment

EXCEPT 1987–89 IMPULSE

1. Loosen the pump adjusting bolt and the pivot bolt. Use a suitable tool to force the pump away from the engine until the correct belt tension is reached.
2. On all except 4XE1 engine equipped vehicles, exert a force of approximately 22 lbs. to the belt at a point midway between the pump pulley and the crank pulley. The belt tension is correct if the belt deflects 0.2–0.4 in. when this force is applied.
3. On 4XE1 engine equipped vehicles, use a suitable belt tension gauge and set the belt tension to 120–150 lbs. for a used belt and 130–160 lbs. for a new belt.

1987–89 IMPULSE

1. Move the idler pulley to adjust the belt tension.

2. The belt tension is correct if the belt deflects 0.4 in. when a force of approximately 22 lbs. is applied midway between the pulleys.

System Bleeding

1. Turn the wheels to the extreme left.
2. With the engine stopped, add power steering fluid to the MIN mark on the fluid indicator.
3. Start the engine and run it for 15 seconds at fast idle.
4. Stop the engine, recheck the fluid level and refill to the MIN mark.
5. Start the engine and turn the wheels from side to side 3 times.
6. Stop the engine and check the fluid level.

NOTE: If air bubbles are still present in the fluid, the procedure must be repeated.

Tie Rod Ends

Removal and Installation

1. Raise and safely support the vehicle. Remove the front wheel and tire assembly.
2. Remove the nut from the tie rod end stud. Using a suitable removal tool, separate the tie rod from the steering knuckle.
3. Disconnect the retaining wire from the inner boot and pull back the boot.
4. Using a suitable tool, straighten the staked part of the locking washer between the tie rod and the rack.
5. Remove the tie rod from the rack.
6. Installation is the reverse of the removal procedure. Tighten the tie rod end nut to 30 ft. lbs. (40 Nm) on I-Mark, 60 ft. lbs. (84 Nm) on 1987–89 Impulse and 40 ft. lbs. (54 Nm) on 1990–91 Impulse and 1991 Stylus.
7. Adjust the toe setting of the front end alignment.

BRAKES

Master Cylinder

Removal and Installation

1. Disconnect the negative battery cable.
2. Disconnect the electrical connector from the master cylinder.
3. Disconnect and plug the brake lines at the master cylinder.
4. Remove the master cylinder mounting nuts and remove the master cylinder.
5. Installation is the reverse of the removal procedure. Tighten the mounting nuts to 9 ft. lbs. (13 Nm). Bleed the master cylinder.

Proportioning Valve

Removal and Installation

EXCEPT 1987–89 IMPULSE

There are 2 proportioning valves attached to the master cylinder.
1. Disconnect the negative battery cable.
2. Disconnect and plug the brake lines at the master cylinder.
3. Remove the proportioning valves from the master cylinder.

4. Installation is the reverse of the removal procedure. Tighten the proportioning valves to 30 ft. lbs. (40 Nm). Bleed the brake system.

1987–89 IMPULSE

1. Disconnect the negative battery cable.
2. Disconnect and plug the brake lines at the proportioning valve.
3. Remove the proportioning valve.
4. Installation is the reverse of the removal procedure. Bleed the brake system.

Power Brake Booster

Removal and Installation

1. Disconnect the negative battery cable.
2. Remove the air cleaner duct on Impulse vehicles.
3. Remove the master cylinder assembly.
4. Disconnect the vacuum hose from the power brake booster.
5. Remove the clevis pin from the brake pedal.
6. Remove the booster attaching nuts and remove the booster.

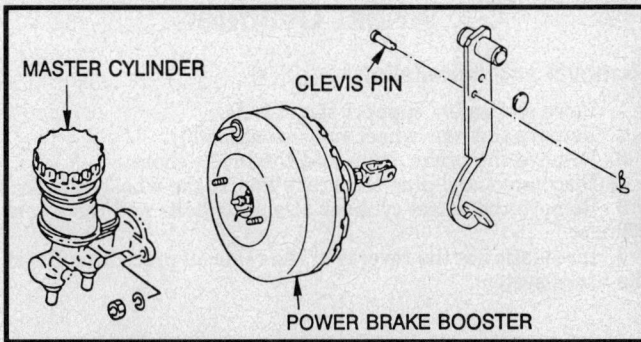

Master cylinder and power brake booster assembly—1990–91 Impulse and 1991 Stylus

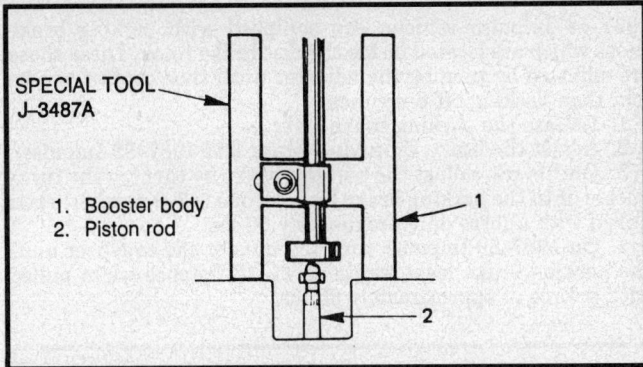

SPECIAL TOOL
J–3487A

1. Booster body
2. Piston rod

1

2

Adjusting pushrod length using special tool—1990–91 Impulse and 1991 Stylus

To install:

7. Installation is the reverse of the removal procedure. Tighten the booster attaching nuts to 13 ft. lbs. (18 Nm) for all, except 1987–89 Impulse or 9 ft. lbs. (13 Nm) for 1987–89 Impulse.

8. If a different booster is installed than was removed, or if the booster has been rebuilt, the pushrod must be adjusted before the master cylinder is installed. Adjust as follows:

  a. 1987–89 Impulse—Measure the distance from the flange face of the booster to the end of the pushrod. It should be 0.709–0.717 in. (18.0–18.2mm). Adjust, if necessary, by turning the locknut at the end of the pushrod.

  b. All other vehicles—Place pushrod gauge J–34873–A or equivalent, on the master cylinder and lower the pin until it's tip slightly touches the piston. Turn the pushrod gauge upside down and set it on the power brake booster. Adjust the pushrod length until the pushrod lightly touches the pin head.

  c. 1990–91 Impulse and 1991 Stylus—Measure the distance from the flange face of the booster to the end of the pushrod using a pushrod gauge J–34873–A. Turn the locknut at the end of the pushrod.

Brake Caliper

Removal and Installation

FRONT

1. Raise and safely support the vehicle.
2. Remove the front wheel and tire assemblies.
3. Disconnect and plug the brake hose at the caliper.
4. Remove the caliper slide pin(s) and remove the caliper.
5. Installation is the reverse of the removal procedure. Tighten the slide pin(s) to 36 ft. lbs. (50 Nm) for all, except on 1987–89 Impulse or 27 ft. lbs. (37 Nm) for 1987–89 Impulse. Bleed the brake system.

REAR

1. Raise and safely support the vehicle.
2. Remove the rear wheel and tire assemblies.
3. Disconnect and plug the brake hose at the caliper.

NOTE: On 1990–91 Impulse and 1991 Stylus, the banjo bolt retaining the brake hose on the right hand side has left hand thread.

4. On 1990–91 Impulse and 1991 Stylus, disconnect the rear parking brake cable from the front cable, remove the brake cable from the cable support bracket and disconnect the brake cable from the brake lever.

5. Remove the lower slide pin and remove the caliper assembly.

6. Installation is the reverse of the removal procedure. Tighten the slide pin to 14 ft. lbs. (20 Nm) on 1987–89 Impulse or 32 ft. lbs. (43 Nm) on 1990–91 Impulse. Bleed the brake system. On 1990–91 Impulse and 1991 Stylus, adjust the parking brake.

Disc Brake Pads

Removal and Installation

1. Remove ½ brake fluid from the master cylinder.
2. Raise and safely support the vehicle.
3. Remove the wheel and tire assemblies.
4. Remove the brake caliper without disconnecting the brake line. Support the caliper with a length of wire. Do not let the caliper hang from the brake hose.
5. Remove the brake pads and shims. Inspect the brake rotor and machine or replace, as necessary. Check the minimum thickness specification when machining.

To install:

6. Use a suitable tool to push the caliper piston into it's bore. On 1990–91 Impulse and 1991 Stylus rear calipers, push the piston in by rotating it clockwise until it stops, then set the piston, aligning the uneven section on the piston surface with the caliper center.

7. Apply a thin coat of grease to the rear face of the brake pad and install the shim. Install the brake pads. On 1990–91 Impulse and 1991 Stylus rear calipers, the brake pad is provided with a pinion. The automatic adjuster becomes inoperative when the pinion is not placed correctly into the indentation of the piston.

8. Install the calipers. Install the wheel and tire assemblies and lower the vehicle.

9. Apply the brakes several times to seat the pads. Check the fluid in the master cylinder and add, as necessary.

Brake Rotor

Removal and Installation

EXCEPT FRONT—1987–89 IMPULSE

1. Raise and safely support the vehicle.
2. Remove the wheel and tire assembly.
3. Remove the caliper and the caliper bracket.
4. Remove the brake rotor.
5. Installation is the reverse of the removal procedure.

FRONT—1987–89 IMPULSE

The rotor is part of the wheel hub on 1987–89 Impulse and must be removed as a unit.

1. Raise and safely support the vehicle.
2. Remove the front wheel and tire assembly.
3. Remove the caliper and the caliper bracket.
4. Remove the dust cap and cotter pin. Remove the castle nut, washer and the outer wheel bearing.
5. Remove the rotor/hub assembly with the inner wheel bearing.

6. If the rotor is machined while removed, the wheel bearings must be removed and the hub thoroughly cleaned before installation.

7. Installation is the reverse of the removal procedure. Properly adjust the wheel bearings and install a new cotter pin.

Brake Drums

Removal and Installation

1. Raise and safely support the vehicle.
2. Remove the rear wheel and tire assembly.
3. Remove the dust cap and cotter pin. Remove the castle nut, washer and outer wheel bearing.
4. Remove the brake drum/hub assembly with the inner wheel bearing.
5. Installation is the reverse of the removal procedure. Properly adjust the wheel bearings and install a new cotter pin.

Brake Shoes

Removal and Installation

1. Raise and safely support the vehicle.
2. Remove the rear wheel and tire assemblies.
3. Remove the brake drums.
4. Remove the brake return springs.
5. Remove the leading shoe holding pin and spring and the leading shoe.
6. Remove the self adjuster and the adjuster lever.
7. Remove the trailing shoe holding pin and spring.
8. Disconnect the parking brake cable from the trailing shoe and remove the trailing shoe. Remove the parking brake lever from the trailing shoe.

To install:

9. Installation is the reverse of the removal procedure. Apply a thin coat of suitable high temperature grease to the shoe contact pads on the brake backing plate prior to installation.
10. Check the brake drum for scoring or other wear and machine or replace, as necessary. Check the maximum brake drum diameter specification when machining. If the drum is machined, the wheel bearings must be removed and the hub thoroughly cleaned before reinstalling.
11. Adjust the brake shoes.

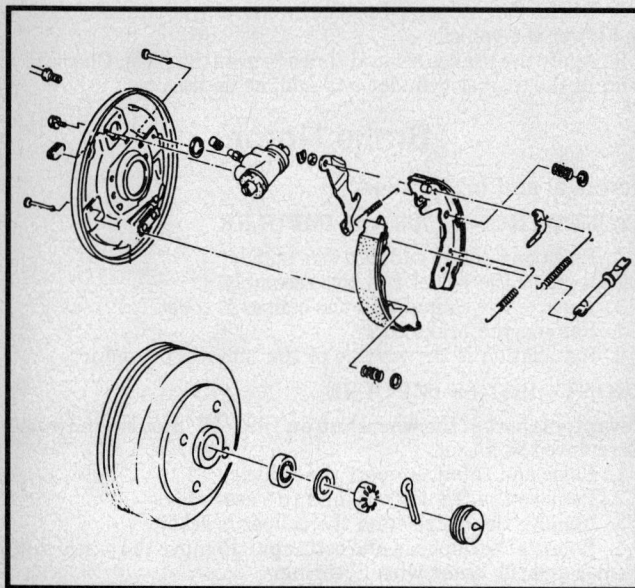

Drum brake assembly—I-Mark

Wheel Cylinder

Removal and Installation

1. Raise and safely support the vehicle.
2. Remove the rear wheel and tire assembly.
3. Remove the brake drum and the brake shoes.
4. Disconnect and plug the brake line at the wheel cylinder.
5. Remove the wheel cylinder attaching bolts and the wheel cylinder.
6. Installation is the reverse of the removal procedure. Bleed the brake system.

Parking Brake Cable

Adjustment

1987–89 Impulse vehicles are equipped with parking brake shoes which are located inside the disc brake rotor. These shoes are adjusted by turning the adjuster until shoe contact can be felt, then backing off 6 notches.

1. Release the parking brake lever.
2. Adjust the brake shoes on I-Mark and 1987–89 Impulse.
3. On I-Mark, adjust the parking brake by turning the turnbuckle until the parking brake lever stroke is 7–9 notches when pulled with a force of approximately 66 lbs.
4. On 1987–89 Impulse, turn the nuts at the equalizer until the parking brake lever stroke is 11–13 notches when pulled with a force of approximately 66 lbs.

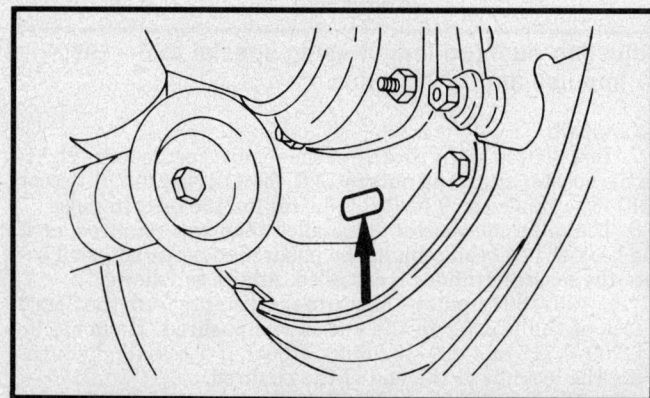

Parking brake shoe adjuster hole—1987–89 Impulse

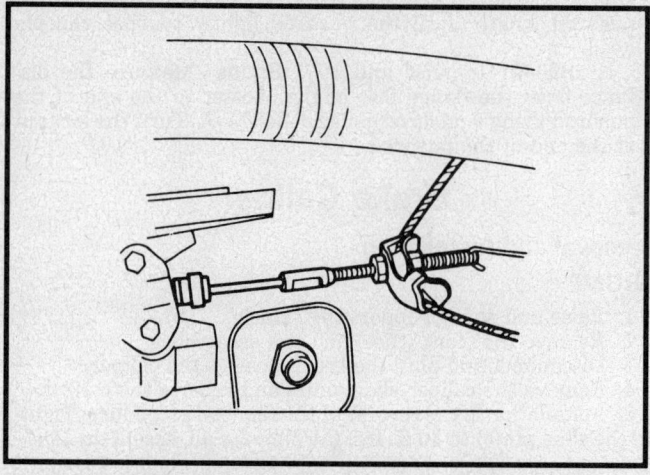

Parking brake cable adjusting nuts—1987–89 Impulse

NOTE: The parking brake shoes on 1987–89 Impulse must be broken down periodically or after replacement of the shoes or rotor in order to ensure effective operation. Drive the vehicle at about 30 mph on a safe, dry and level surface. Pull the brake lever up with a force of approximately 20 lbs. with the brake release button depressed. Drive the vehicle approximately ¼ mile with the parking brake partly applied. Repeat this operation 2–3 times.

5. On 1990–91 Impulse and 1991 Stylus, adjust the cable by turning the adjust nuts until the parking brake lever stroke is 7–8 notches when pulled with a force of approximately 66 lbs.

Removal and Installation

I-MARK

1. Raise and safely support the vehicle.
2. Remove the rear wheel and tire assemblies.
3. Remove the brake drums.
4. Disconnect the rear cables from the parking brake levers and the brake backing plates.
5. Disconnect the front parking brake cable from the parking brake lever. Disconnect the front cable from the rear cables and remove the tension spring from the rear axle.
6. Remove the cable-to-body mounting bolts and remove the cables.
7. Installation is the reverse of the removal procedure. Adjust the parking brake.

1987–89 IMPULSE

1. Raise and safely support the vehicle.
2. Remove the rear wheel and tire assemblies.
3. Remove the rear disc brake calipers and the rotors. Disconnect the rear cable from the parking brake levers and the brake backing plate.
4. Remove the return spring and the rear nut at the equalizer.
5. Remove the clips and the cable mounting bolts and remove the rear cable.
6. Remove the rear console assembly and the parking brake lever cover.
7. Remove the parking brake cable bolt from the parking brake lever.

NOTE: The parking brake cable bolt has left hand thread.

8. Remove the front cable mounting bolts and remove the front cable.
9. Installation is the reverse of the removal procedure. Adjust the parking brake.

1990–91 IMPULSE AND 1991 STYLUS

1. Raise and safely support the vehicle.
2. Remove the rear wheel and tire assemblies.
3. Loosen the adjusting nuts at the left side rear cable.
4. Remove the right side rear cable from the bracket and disconnect it from the front cable.
5. Disconnect the rear cables from the parking brake levers at the disc brake assemblies.
6. Remove the cable mounting bolts and remove the rear cables.
7. Remove the console box.
8. Disconnect the front parking brake cable from the parking brake lever, remove the mounting nuts and remove the front cable.
9. Installation is the reverse of the removal procedure. Adjust the parking brake.

Brake System Bleeding

1. Set the parking brake and start the engine.

NOTE: The vacuum booster will be damaged if the bleeding operation is performed with the engine off.

2. Remove the master cylinder reservoir cap and fill the reservoir with brake fluid. Keep the reservoir at least half full during the bleeding operation.
3. If the master cylinder is replaced or overhauled, first bleed the air from the master cylinder and then from each caliper or wheel cylinder. Bleed the master cylinder as follows:
   a. Disconnect the left front wheel brake line from the master cylinder.
   b. Have an assistant depress the brake pedal slowly once and hold it depressed.
   c. Seal the delivery port of the master cylinder where the line was disconnected with a finger, then release the brake pedal slowly.
   d. Release the finger from the delivery port when the brake pedal returns completely.
   e. Repeat Steps c–e until the brake fluid comes out of the delivery port during Step c.
   f. Reconnect the brake line to the master cylinder.
   g. Have an assistant depress the brake pedal slowly once and hold it depressed.
   h. Loosen the front wheel brake line at the master cylinder.
   i. Retighten the brake line, then release the brake pedal slowly.
   j. Repeat Steps g–i until no air comes out from the port when the brake line is loosened.
   k. Bleed the air from the right front wheel brake line connection by repeating Steps a–j.
4. Bleed the air from each wheel in the following order: Left front caliper, Right rear caliper or wheel cylinder, Right front caliper, Left rear caliper or wheel cylinder. Bleed the air as follows:
   a. Place the proper size box wrench over the bleeder screw.
   b. Cover the bleeder screw with a transparent tube and submerge the free end of the tube in a transparent container containing brake fluid.
   c. Have an assistant pump the brake pedal 3 times, then hold it depressed.
   d. Remove the air along with the brake fluid by loosening the bleeder screw.
   e. Retighten the bleeder screw, then release the brake pedal slowly.
   f. Repeat Steps c–e until the air is completely removed. It may be necessary to repeat the bleeding procedure 10 or more times for front wheels and 15 or more times for rear wheels.
   g. Go to the next wheel in sequence after each wheel is bled.
5. Depress the brake pedal to check if sponginess is felt after the air has been removed from all wheel cylinders and calipers. If the pedal feels spongy, the entire bleeding procedure must be repeated.
6. After the bleeding operation is completed on each individual wheel, check the level of brake fluid in the reservoir and replenish up to the **MAX** level, if necessary.
7. Install the master cylinder reservoir cap and stop the engine.

Anti-lock Brake System Service

Some diagnostic procedures require the installation of a pinout box tool J–35592 in order to prevent damage to the 35-pin EBCM connector. The pinout box should be installed prior to probing any circuit with a digital multi-meter.

Pinout Box Installation

1. Ensure that the ignition switch is in the OFF position when removing the 35-pin EBCM connector.
2. Disconnect the connector by depressing the locking plate and rotating the connector toward the front of the vehicle.

3. Inspect the 35-pin connector for damage. Install the pinout box tool J–35592 on the connector.
4. Proceed with self-diagnostic test.

System Self-Diagnosis

The ABS is equipped with a self diagnostic capability which is used to isolate ABS failures.

Electrical failures in the ABS are detected by the ECBM, located under the passenger seat, and result in the Anti-Lock warning light illuminating. The Anti-Lock warning light is intended to inform the driver that a condition exists which results in the ABS being disabled. The Anti-Lock warning light is connected to a Light Emitting Diode (LED) on the EBCM. The LED assists the individual servicing the system by flashing trouble codes which pinpoint the defective component.

NOTE: If more than one failure in the system is detected, the first failure to occur will be flashed in code on the LED. Once this failure has been corrected, the next failure code will be will be flashed.

The EBCM enters diagnostic mode any time a trouble code is set; the Anti-Lock light illuminates. To read the ABS trouble code, count the number of times the LED on the EBCM turns ON and OFF. Trouble codes are erased from the EBCM memory when the ignition key is turned OFF.

Service Precautions

• Do not use rubber hoses or other parts not specifically specified for the RWAL system. When using repair kits, replace all parts included in the kit. Partial or incorrect repair may lead to functional problems.
• Lubricate rubber parts with clean, fresh brake fluid to ease assembly. Do not use lubricated shop air to clean parts; damage to rubber components may result.
• Use only brake fluid from an unopened container. Use of suspect or contaminated brake fluid can reduce system performance and/or durability.
• A clean repair area is essential. Perform repairs after components have been thoroughly cleaned; use only denatured alcohol to clean components. Do not allow components to come into contact with any substance containing mineral oil; this includes used shop rags.
• The RWAL ECU is a microprocessor similar to other computer units in the vehicle. Insure that the ignition switch is OFF before removing or installing controller harnesses. Avoid static electricity discharge at or near the controller.
• Never disconnect any electrical connection with the ignition switch ON unless instructed to do so in a test.
• Avoid touching module connector pins.
• Leave new components and modules in the shipping package until ready to install them.
• To avoid static discharge, always touch a vehicle ground after sliding across a vehicle seat or walking across carpeted or vinyl floors.
• Never allow welding cables to lie on, near or across any vehicle electrical wiring.
• Do not allow extension cords for power tools or droplights to lie on, near or across any vehicle electrical wiring.
• If welding is to be performed on the vehicle using an electric arc welder, the EBCM and valve block connectors should be disconnected.
• Hydraulic units of the Anti-Lock Brake System are not separately serviceable and must be replaced as assemblies. Do not disassemble any component which is designated as non-serviceable.

Relieving Anti-lock Brake System Pressure

1. Set the parking brake and start the engine.

NOTE: The vacuum booster will be damaged if the bleeding operation is performed with the engine off.

2. Remove the master cylinder reservoir cap and fill the reservoir with brake fluid. Keep the reservoir at least half full during the bleeding operation.
3. If the master cylinder is replaced or overhauled, first bleed the air from the master cylinder and then from each caliper or wheel cylinder. Bleed the master cylinder as follows:
   a. Disconnect the left front wheel brake line from the master cylinder.
   b. Have an assistant depress the brake pedal slowly once and hold it depressed.
   c. Seal the delivery port of the master cylinder where the line was disconnected with a finger, then release the brake pedal slowly.
   d. Release the finger from the delivery port when the brake pedal returns completely.
   e. Repeat Steps C–E until the brake fluid comes out of the delivery port during Step C.
   f. Reconnect the brake line to the master cylinder.
   g. Have an assistant depress the brake pedal slowly once and hold it depressed.
   h. Loosen the front wheel brake line at the master cylinder.
   i. Retighten the brake line, then release the brake pedal slowly.
   j. Repeat Steps G–I until no air comes out from the port when the brake line is loosened.
   k. Bleed the air from the right front wheel brake line connection by repeating Steps A–J.
4. Bleed the air from each wheel in the following order: Left front caliper, Right rear caliper or wheel cylinder, Right front caliper, Left rear caliper or wheel cylinder. Bleed the air as follows:
   a. Place the proper size box wrench over the bleeder screw.
   b. Cover the bleeder screw with a transparent tube and submerge the free end of the tube in a transparent container containing brake fluid.
   c. Have an assistant pump the brake pedal 3 times, then hold it depressed.
   d. Remove the air along with the brake fluid by loosening the bleeder screw.
   e. Retighten the bleeder screw, then release the brake pedal slowly.
   f. Repeat Steps C–E until the air is completely removed. It may be necessary to repeat the bleeding procedure 10 or more times for front wheels and 15 or more times for rear wheels.
   g. Go to the next wheel in sequence after each wheel is bled.
5. Depress the brake pedal to check if sponginess is felt after the air has been removed from all wheel cylinders and calipers. If the pedal feels spongy, the entire bleeding procedure must be repeated.
6. After the bleeding operation is completed on each individual wheel, check the level of brake fluid in the reservoir and replenish up to the **MAX** level, if necessary.
7. Install the master cylinder reservoir cap and stop the engine.

Hydraulic Unit

Removal and Installation

1. Disconnect negative battery cable.
2. Raise and support vehicle safely.
3. Remove under cover to gain access to hydraulic unit.
4. Remove tire if needed and remove inner fender liner.
5. Disconnect harness connectors from hydraulic unit.
6. Remove radiator reservoir tank.
7. Remove brake lines using a *flare nut* wrench. Cap or tape brake line ends to prevent entry of foreign matter.
8. Disconnect hydraulic motor ground cable.

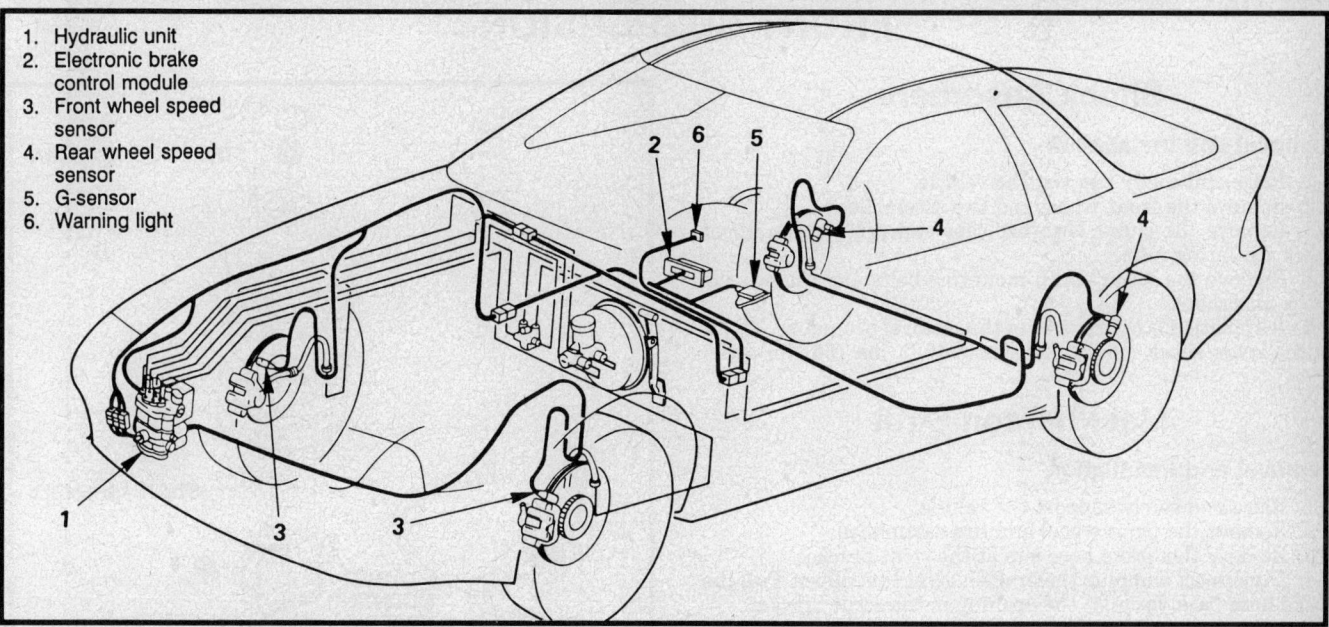

1. Hydraulic unit
2. Electronic brake control module
3. Front wheel speed sensor
4. Rear wheel speed sensor
5. G-sensor
6. Warning light

Anti-Lock Brake System components

9. Remove bracket attaching bolt, hydraulic unit attaching nut, bracket and hydraulic unit.
To install:
10. Installation is the reverse of removal. Torque hydraulic unit attaching nut, bracket attaching bolt and ground cable bolt to 17 ft. lbs. Torque brake line to 9 ft. lbs.
11. Bleed the brake system.

NOTE: Replace all components included in repair kits used to service this system. Lubricate rubber parts with clean, fresh brake fluid to ease assembly. Do not use lubricated shop air to clean parts, as damage to rubber components may result. Always bleed the braking system after repairing or replacing hydraulic components.

Electric Brake Control Unit (EBCM)

Removal and Installation

The EBCM is located under the passenger side seat on the Impulse.
1. Disconnect the negative battery cable.
2. It may be necessary to move the passenger seat out of the way to gain access to the EBCM. If so, remove the seat attaching bolts and move the seat.
3. Remove the EBCM attaching bolts.
4. Remove the EBCM wiring harness connector. Remove the EBCM.
5. Installation is the reverse of removal. Tighten EBCM attaching bolts to 62 inch lbs. (7.0 Nm).

G-Sensor

Removal and Installation

1. Disconnect negative battery cable.
2. Remove center console.
3. Remove G-Sensor wiring harness connector.
4. Remove G-Sensor attaching bolt. Remove the G-Sensor.
5. Place G-Sensor on a known level surface and check continuity between terminals. If no continuity, replace the G-Sensor.

6. Incline the G-Sensor to a 30 degree angle and retest for continuity. If continuity exists, replace the G-Sensor.

NOTE: Ensure that G-Sensor is installed in the correct direction.

7. Installation is the reverse of removal. Torque attaching bolts to 53 inch lbs. (5.4 Nm).

Speed Sensor

Removal and Installation

1. Disconnect negative battery cable.
2. Raise and support vehicle safely.
3. Remove wheel assembly. Remove inner fender liner.
4. Disconnect speed sensor wire connector.
5. Remove sensor cable attaching bolts and screws.
6. Remove sensor attaching bolts. Remove sensor.
To install:
7. Inspect the speed sensor for damage.
   a. Check speed sensor pole piece for dirt and remove.
   b. Check the pole piece for damage and replace, if necessary.
   c. Check for continuity while flexing the sensor cable. Replace sensor cable, if a short or open is found.
   d. Check the sensor rotor for damage including tooth chipping. Replace the driveshaft assembly, if sensor rotor is damaged.
8. Install the speed sensor taking care not to damage the pole piece. Tighten the attaching bolt to 62 inch lbs. (6.8 Nm).
9. Check the clearance between the speed sensor pole piece and the rotor. Clearance should be 0.0079–0.0315 in. (0.20–0.80mm).
10. Install the sensor cable fixing bolt, tighten to 13 ft. lbs. (17 Nm) and screw to 9 ft. lbs. (12 Nm).
11. Ensure the white line marked on the cable is not twisted. If so, loosen connections and straighten cable.
12. Reconnect sensor wire connector, install inner liner, install wheel, lower vehicle and reconnect negative battery cable.

FRONT SUSPENSION

Shock Absorbers

Removal and Installation

1. Raise and safely support the vehicle.
2. Remove the front wheel and tire assemblies.
3. Remove the shock absorber caps and remove the upper shock mounting nuts.
4. Remove the lower shock mounting bolts and remove the shock absorbers.
5. Installation is the reverse of the removal procedure. Tighten the lower shock mounting bolts to 40 ft. lbs. (56 Nm).

MacPherson Strut

Removal and Installation

1. Raise and safely support the vehicle.
2. Remove the front wheel and tire assemblies.
3. Remove the brake hose clip at the strut bracket.
4. Disconnect and plug the brake hose at the caliper. Pull the brake hose back through the opening in the strut bracket.
5. Remove the strut-to-knuckle bolts.
6. Remove the strut mounting nuts and remove the strut.

To install:

7. Installation is the reverse of the removal procedure. Tighten the strut mounting nuts to 40 ft. lbs. (56 Nm) on I-Mark or 50 ft. lbs. (68 Nm) on 1990–91 Impulse and 1991 Stylus. Tighten the strut-to-knuckle bolts to 86 ft. lbs. (120 Nm) on I-Mark or 115 ft. lbs. (156 Nm) on Impulse and Stylus.
8. Bleed the brake system.

Coil Springs

Removal and Installation

1. Raise and safely support the vehicle.
2. Remove the front wheel and tire assembly.
3. Remove the disc brake caliper assembly. Support the caliper with a length of wire. Do not let the caliper hang from the brake hose.
4. Mark the position of the nuts on the front of the strut bar for reassembly, these nuts control the caster setting, and remove the strut bar.
5. Remove the sway bar brackets on both sides of the vehicle. Remove the bolt, tube and grommets holding the sway bar to the lower control arm. Move the sway bar aside.
6. Use a suitable tool to disconnect the tie rod end from the steering knuckle. Turn the steering wheel to move the tie rod end aside.
7. Place a suitable hydraulic floor jack under the lower control arm and apply slight upward pressure.

NOTE: Install a safety chain through 1 coil at the top of the spring and attach it to the upper control arm to prevent the spring from coming out unexpectedly.

8. Install a spring compressor tool J-36567 or equivalent, and slightly compress the spring.
9. Remove the upper and lower ball joint nuts. Using a suitable removal tool, disconnect the upper and lower ball joints from the steering knuckle. Remove the steering knuckle from the vehicle.
10. Slowly lower the lower control arm until the spring is free of the lower control arm. Slowly and evenly release the spring compressor until the spring is fully extended. Remove the safety chain and the coil spring.

To install:

11. Installation is the reverse of the removal procedure. Make

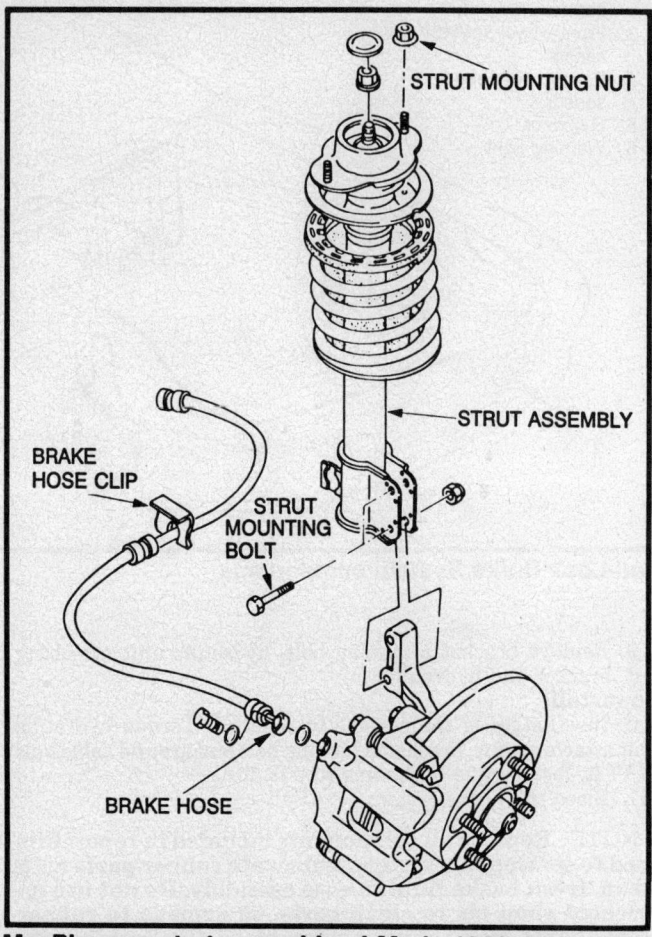

MacPherson strut assembly—I-Mark, 1990–91 Impulse and 1991 Stylus similar

sure the lower end of the coil spring is aligned with the notch in the lower control arm.
12. Install new self-locking nuts on the upper and lower ball joint studs and tighten the upper ball joint nut to 39 ft. lbs. (54 Nm) and the lower ball joint nut to 58 ft. lbs. (80 Nm).
13. Install a new self-locking nut on the sway bar end link and tighten to 19 ft. lbs. (26 Nm). Tighten the sway bar bracket bolt to 14 ft. lbs. (19 Nm).
14. Install the strut bar to the chassis and tighten the locknuts. Install the strut bar-to-lower arm bolts, aligning the marks that were made during the removal procedure. Tighten the small bolt to 47 ft. lbs. (65 Nm) and the large bolt to 114 ft. lbs. (158 Nm).
15. Tighten the tie rod end nut to 60 ft. lbs. (84 Nm). Check the front end alignment.

Upper Ball Joints

Inspection

1. Raise and safely support the vehicle.
2. Place a suitable jack under the lower control arm. Raise the jack enough to slightly compress the coil spring.
3. Have an assistant grasp the front wheel and attempt to move the top of the wheel in and out toward the inside of the wheel well. If any play is observed in the ball joint during this procedure, the ball joint must be replaced.

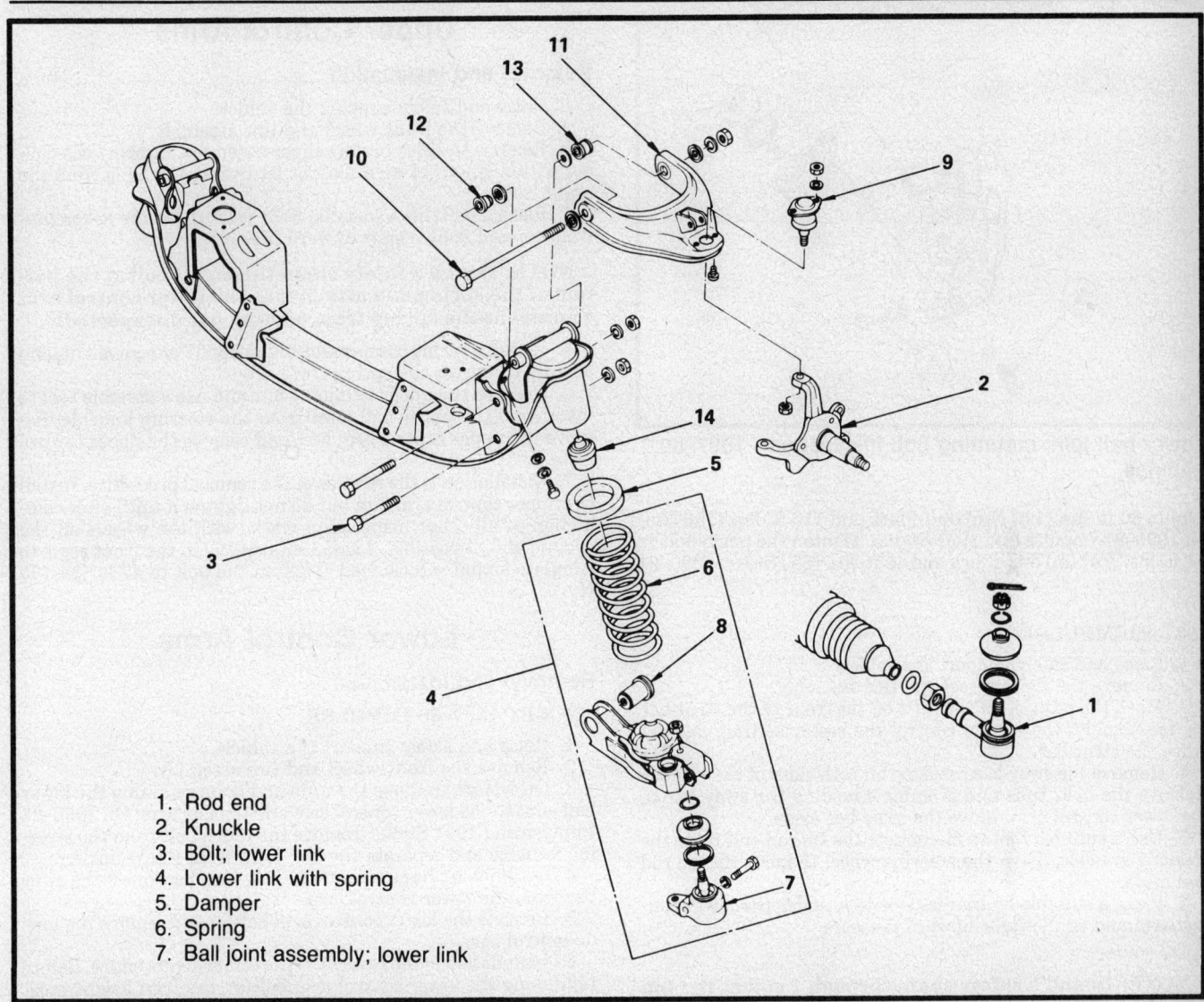

1. Rod end
2. Knuckle
3. Bolt; lower link
4. Lower link with spring
5. Damper
6. Spring
7. Ball joint assembly; lower link

Front suspension assembly—1987–89 Impulse

Removal and Installation

1. Raise and safely support the vehicle.
2. Remove the front wheel and tire assembly.
3. Remove the disc brake caliper assembly. Support the caliper with a length of wire. Do not let the caliper hang from the brake hose.
4. Place a suitable hydraulic floor jack under the lower control arm and apply slight upward pressure.

NOTE: Install a safety chain through 1 coil at the bottom of the spring and attach it to the lower control arm to prevent the spring from coming out unexpectedly.

5. Install a spring compressor tool J-36567 or equivalent, and slightly compress the spring.
6. Remove the upper ball joint nut and use a suitable tool to disconnect the upper ball joint from the steering knuckle.
7. Remove the upper ball joint from the upper control arm.
8. Installation is the reverse of the removal procedure. Install the ball joint with the cutaway portion turned outward. Tighten the ball joint mounting nuts to 40 ft. lbs. (56 Nm). Install a new self-locking nut on the upper ball joint stud and tighten to 39 ft. lbs. (54 Nm).

Lower Ball Joints

Inspection

1. Raise and safely support the vehicle.
2. On 1987–89 Impulse, place a suitable jack under the lower control arm. Raise the jack enough to slightly compress the coil spring.
3. Have an assistant grasp the front wheel and attempt to move the bottom of the wheel in and out toward the inside of the wheel well. If any play is observed in the ball joint during this procedure, the ball joint must be replaced.

Removal and Installation

EXCEPT 1987–89 IMPULSE

1. Raise and safely support the vehicle.
2. Remove the front wheel and tire assembly.
3. Remove the pinch bolt and nut from the steering knuckle.
4. Remove the nuts and bolts retaining the lower ball joint to the lower control arm and remove the lower ball joint.
5. Installation is the reverse of the removal procedure. Tighten the bolts retaining the lower ball joint to the lower control

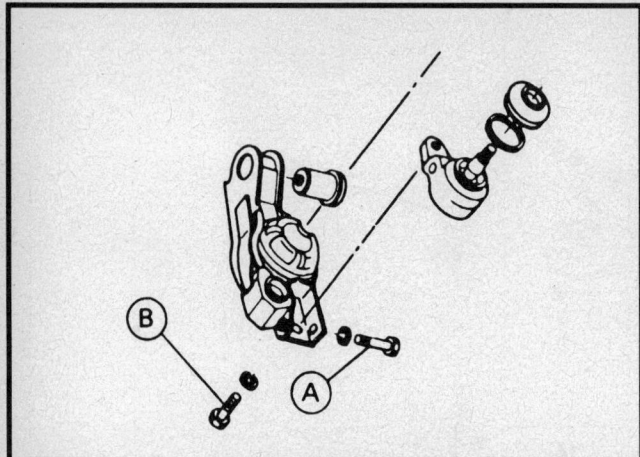

Lower ball joint mounting bolt installation — 1987–89 Impulse

arm to 80 ft. lbs. (110 Nm) on I-Mark and 115 ft. lbs. (156 Nm) on 1990–91 Impulse and 1991 Stylus. Tighten the pinch bolt to 51 ft. lbs. (70 Nm) on I-Mark and 48 ft. lbs. (65 Nm) on 1990–91 Impulse.

1987–89 IMPULSE

1. Raise and safely support the vehicle.
2. Remove the front wheel and tire assembly.
3. Mark the position of the nuts on the front of the strut bar for reassembly, these nuts control the caster setting, and remove the strut bar.
4. Remove the sway bar brackets on both sides of the vehicle. Remove the bolt, tube and grommets holding the sway bar to the lower control arm. Move the sway bar aside.
5. Use a suitable tool to disconnect the tie rod end from the steering knuckle. Turn the steering wheel to move the tie rod end aside.
6. Place a suitable hydraulic floor jack under the lower control arm and apply slight upward pressure.

NOTE: Install a safety chain through 1 coil at the top of the spring and attach it to the upper control arm to prevent the spring from coming out unexpectedly.

7. Install a spring compressor tool J-36567 or equivalent, and slightly compress the spring.
9. Remove the lower ball joint nut. Using a suitable removal tool, disconnect the lower ball joint from the steering knuckle.
10. Slowly lower the lower control arm until the ball joint stud is clear of the knuckle. Remove the lower ball joint mounting bolts and remove the lower ball joint.

To install:

11. Installation is the reverse of the removal procedure. Tighten lower ball joint mounting bolt (A) to 76 ft. lbs. (105 Nm) and bolt (B) to 47 ft. lbs. (65 Nm). Tighten the lower ball joint nut to 58 ft. lbs. (80 Nm).
12. Install a new self-locking nut on the sway bar end link and tighten to 19 ft. lbs. (26 Nm). Tighten the sway bar bracket bolt to 14 ft. lbs. (19 Nm).
13. Install the strut bar to the chassis and tighten the locknuts. Install the strut bar-to-lower arm bolts, aligning the marks that were made during the removal procedure. Tighten the small bolt to 47 ft. lbs. (65 Nm) and the large bolt to 114 ft. lbs. (158 Nm).
14. Tighten the tie rod end nut to 60 ft. lbs. (84 Nm). Check the front end alignment.

Upper Control Arms

Removal and Installation

1. Raise and safely support the vehicle.
2. Remove the front wheel and tire assembly.
3. Remove the disc brake caliper assembly. Support the caliper with a length of wire. Do not let the caliper hang from the brake hose.
4. Place a suitable hydraulic floor jack under the lower control arm and apply slight upward pressure.

NOTE: Install a safety chain through 1 coil at the bottom of the spring and attach it to the lower control arm to prevent the spring from coming out unexpectedly.

5. Install a spring compressor tool J-36567 or equivalent, and slightly compress the spring.
6. Remove the upper ball joint nut and use a suitable tool to disconnect the upper ball joint from the steering knuckle. Remove the upper control arm bolt and remove the upper control arm.
7. Installation is the reverse of the removal procedure. Install the upper control arm bolt but do not tighten it until after completion of all other installation work, with the wheels on the ground and, if possible, 2 assistants sitting in the front seats to simulate actual vehicle load. Tighten the bolt to 47 ft. lbs. (65 Nm).

Lower Control Arms

Removal and Installation

EXCEPT 1987–89 IMPULSE

1. Raise and safely support the vehicle.
2. Remove the front wheel and tire assembly.
3. On I-Mark, remove the nuts and bolts retaining the lower ball joint to the lower control arm and tension arm. On 1990–91 Impulse and 1991 Stylus, remove the pinch bolt from the steering knuckle and separate the ball joint from the knuckle.
4. On 1990–91 Impulse and 1991 Stylus, disconnect the sway bar from the lower control arm.
5. Remove the lower control arm bolt(s) and remove the lower control arm.
6. Installation is the reverse of the removal procedure. Before tightening the lower control arm bolt(s), the trim height must be set. Raise the lower control arm with a suitable jack and set the trim height to 15.2 in. (386mm) on I-Mark and 3 in. (77mm) from the center of the front lower control arm bushing to the center of the wheel hub on 1990–91 Impulse and 1991 Stylus.

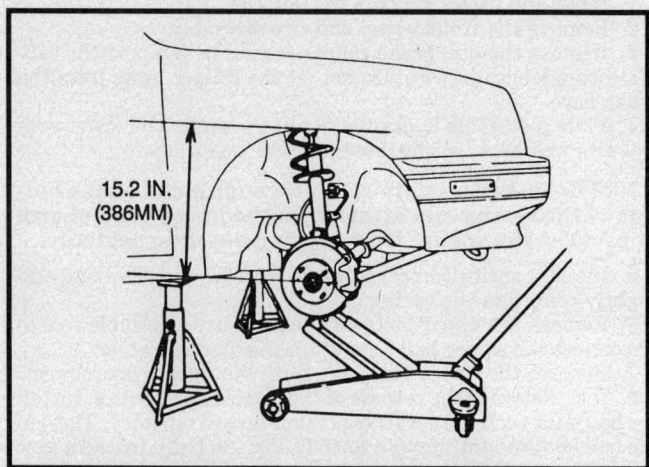

Trim height setting — I-Mark front suspension

15.2 IN. (386MM)

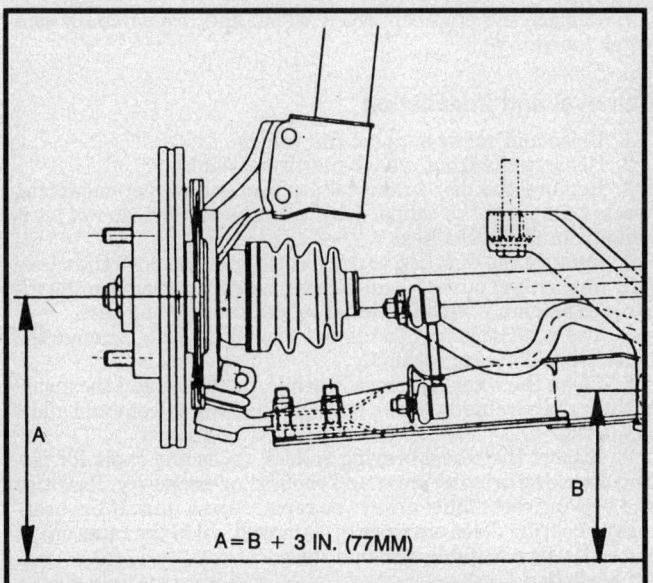

Trim height setting—1990–91 Impulse and 1991 Stylus front suspension

A = B + 3 IN. (77MM)

7. Tighten the lower control arm bolt to 41 ft. lbs. (56 Nm) on I-Mark. On 1990–91 Impulse and 1991 Stylus, the torque is 50 ft. lbs. (68 Nm) on the rear bolt and 94 ft. lbs. (128 Nm) on the front bolt.

1987–89 IMPULSE

1. Raise and safely support the vehicle.
2. Remove the front wheel and tire assembly.
3. Mark the position of the nuts on the front of the strut bar for reassembly (these nuts control the caster setting) and remove the strut bar.
4. Remove the sway bar brackets on both sides of the vehicle. Remove the bolt, tube and grommets holding the sway bar to the lower control arm. Move the sway bar aside.
5. Use a suitable tool to disconnect the tie rod end from the steering knuckle. Turn the steering wheel to move the tie rod end aside.
6. Place a suitable hydraulic floor jack under the lower control arm and apply slight upward pressure.

NOTE: Install a safety chain through 1 coil at the top of the spring and attach it to the upper control arm to prevent the spring from coming out unexpectedly.

7. Install a spring compressor tool J-36567 or equivalent, and slightly compress the spring.
9. Remove the lower ball joint nut. Using a suitable removal tool, disconnect the lower ball joint from the steering knuckle.
10. Slowly lower the lower control arm. Remove the lower control arm bolt and remove the lower control arm.
To install:
11. Installation is the reverse of the removal procedure. Install the lower control arm bolt but do not tighten it until all components are reassembled and the vehicle is on the ground, preferably with a driver and passenger in the front seats to simulate average load. Tighten the bolt to 68 ft. lbs. (94 Nm).
12. Tighten the lower ball joint nut to 58 ft. lbs. (80 Nm).
13. Install a new self-locking nut on the sway bar end link and tighten to 19 ft. lbs. (26 Nm). Tighten the sway bar bracket bolt to 14 ft. lbs. (19 Nm).
14. Install the strut bar to the chassis and tighten the locknuts. Install the strut bar-to-lower arm bolts, aligning the marks that were made during the removal procedure. Tighten

the small bolt to 47 ft. lbs. (65 Nm) and the large bolt to 114 ft. lbs. (158 Nm).
15. Tighten the tie rod end nut to 60 ft. lbs. (84 Nm). Check the front end alignment.

Sway Bar

Removal and Installation
I-MARK

1. Raise and safely support the vehicle.
2. Remove the sway bar from the tension rod.
To install:
3. Install the sway bar when the vehicle is at no load.
4. Install the mounting rubbers and brackets to the tension rod. Align the front mounting rubbers with the rear side of the tension rod paint mark. Align the rear mounting rubbers rear end with the end of the sway bar.
5. Install the sway bar to the mounting rubbers and brackets on the right side of the vehicle. Loosely close and temporarily tighten the right hand side mounting rubbers and brackets.
6. Push the sway bar toward the vehicle center to install it to the left rear mounting rubber and bracket.
7. Install the sway bar to the left front mounting rubber and bracket.
8. Tighten the nuts to 6 ft. lbs. (8 Nm).
9. Lower the vehicle.

1987–89 IMPULSE

1. Raise and safely support the vehicle.
2. Remove the engine splash shield.
3. Remove the sway bar link assemblies from the ends of the sway bar and the lower control arms.
4. Remove the sway bar-to-body brackets and remove the sway bar.
5. Installation is the reverse of the removal procedure. Tighten the sway bar link nuts to 19 ft. lbs. (26 Nm) and the bracket bolts to 14 ft. lbs. (19 Nm).

1990–91 IMPULSE AND 1991 STYLUS

1. Raise and safely support the vehicle.
2. Remove the exhaust header pipe.
3. Disconnect and plug the power steering lines at the steering rack.
4. Remove the steering shaft boot nuts from inside the vehicle. Remove the steering shaft bolt.
5. Remove the pinch bolts and disconnect the lower ball joints from the steering knuckles.
6. Using a suitable tool, disconnect the tie rod ends from the steering knuckle.
7. Place a suitable jack under the engine and raise it to support the engine.
8. Disconnect the engine torque rod at the center beam.
9. Disconnect the rear engine mount. Remove 2 bolts at the center beam and 4 bolts at the crossmember. Lower the crossmember assembly with the steering rack carefully.
10. Remove the steering rack, then remove the sway bar from the crossmember.

NOTE: The sway bar cannot be removed unless the crossmember assembly is removed, however the sway bar bushings can be replaced without removing the crossmember.

11. Installation is the reverse of the removal procedure. Tighten the 4 crossmember bolts to 137 ft. lbs. (186 Nm) and the 2 center beam bolts to 37 ft. lbs. (50 Nm). Tighten the lower ball joint pinch bolts to 48 ft. lbs. (65 Nm) and the steering shaft bolt to 30 ft. lbs. (40 Nm). Tighten the tie rod nuts to 40 ft. lbs. (54 Nm).

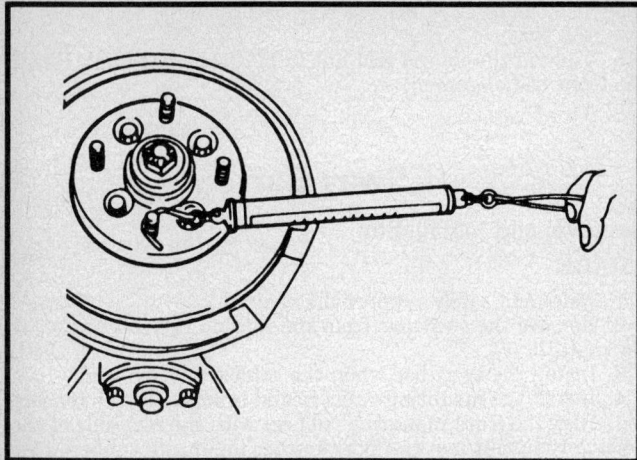

Front wheel bearing adjustment procedure – 1987–89 Impulse

Front Wheel Bearings

Adjustment

1. Raise and safely support the vehicle. Remove the front wheel and tire assembly.
2. Remove the dust cap and the cotter pin. Make sure the wheel bearings are clean and adequately greased before proceeding further.
3. Tighten the hub nut to 22 ft. lbs. (30 Nm) and turn the hub 2–3 turns in fore and aft directions to set the bearings.
4. Loosen the hub nut just enough, so it can be turned by hand. Hand tighten the hub nut using a suitable socket wrench and check that the hub has no play in it.
5. Attach a suitable pull scale to one of the hub studs. Adjust the tightness of the hub nut, so the hub begins to rotate when the pull scale is pulled forward with a force of 1.1–3.3 lbs.
6. Install the cotter pin. If the cotter pin holes are not aligned, further turn the nut the minimum amount necessary in the direction of tightening.

7. Replace the dust cap, front wheel and tire assembly and lower the vehicle.

Removal and Installation

1. Raise and safely support the vehicle.
2. Remove the front wheel and tire assembly.
3. Remove the disc brake caliper and the caliper mounting bracket. Support the caliper with a length of wire, do not let it hang from the brake hose.
4. Remove the dust cap and the cotter pin. Remove the castle nut, washer and outer wheel bearing assembly. Remove the rotor/hub assembly with the inner wheel bearing and seal.
5. Use a suitable tool to remove the wheel seal. Remove the inner wheel bearing assembly.
6. Clean the wheel bearings, washer, castle nut and the inside of the hub thoroughly with a suitable cleaning solvent and allow to air dry.
7. Inspect the wheel bearing rollers, cages and races for pitting, cracking or other wear and replace, as necessary. Bearings and bearing races must always be replaced as a unit. If the bearings or bearing races are worn or damaged, drive the races out of the hub using suitable removal tools.

To install:

8. If the bearing races were removed, drive the new races into the hub using suitable installation tools. Make sure the inside of the hub is clean before installation.
9. Pack the wheel bearings using a suitable high temperature wheel bearing grease. If a bearing packer is not available, the bearings may be packed by hand, but care must be taken that grease thoroughly penetrates behind the bearing rollers.
10. Place a quantity of wheel bearing grease inside the hub between the races and coat the races with grease. Install the inner wheel bearing.
11. Use a suitable tool to install a new wheel seal.
12. Install the rotor/hub assembly onto the spindle and install the outer wheel bearing, washer and the castle nut. Adjust the wheel bearings, install a new cotter pin and install the dust cap.
13. Install the disc brake caliper mounting bracket and the disc brake caliper.
14. Install the front wheel and tire assembly and lower the vehicle.

REAR SUSPENSION

Shock Absorbers

Removal and Installation

1. Raise and safely support the vehicle.
2. Support the rear axle using a suitable jack.
3. Remove the shock tower cover or trim plate cover, as necessary.
4. Remove the upper shock mounting nuts, washers and grommets.
5. Remove the lower shock mounting bolts, washers and grommets and remove the shock absorbers.
6. Installation is the reverse of the removal procedure. Tighten the lower shock mounting bolts to 30 ft. lbs. (41 Nm) on I-Mark and 20 ft. lbs. (28 Nm) on 1987–89 Impulse.

MacPherson Strut

Removal and Installation

1. Raise and safely support the vehicle.
2. Remove the rear wheel and tire assembly.

3. Remove the brake line clip at the strut. Disconnect and plug the brake hose at the strut.
4. Disconnect the sway bar end. Remove the strut-to-knuckle bolts.
5. Open the rear hatch and remove the strut tower cover. Remove the strut mounting nuts and remove the strut.
6. Installation is the reverse of the removal procedure. Tighten the strut mounting nuts to 51 ft. lbs. (69 Nm) and the strut-to-knuckle bolts to 116 ft. lbs. (157 Nm).

Coil Springs

Removal and Installation

1. Raise and safely support the vehicle.
2. Support the rear axle with a suitable jack.
3. Remove the lower shock mounting bolts and disconnect the shocks from the axle assembly.
4. Slowly lower the rear axle with the jack until the coil springs can be removed.

NOTE: Do not stress the brake hoses when lowering the rear axle.

1. Lower control arm
2. Lower control arm-to-body bolt
3. Lower control arm-to-rear axle bolt
4. Upper control arm
5. Upper control arm-to-body bolt
6. Upper control arm-to-rear axle bolt
7. Bushing
8. Panhard rod
9. Cover
10. Nut and spring washer
11. Bolt
12. Nut and spring washer
13. Lower spring insulator
14. Spring
15. Upper spring insulator
16. Sway bar
17. Shackle bolts
18. Sway bar-to-rear axle bolts
19. Washer and grommet
20. Shock absorber
21. Washer and grommet
22. Nuts
23. Washer and grommet
24. Shock absorber
25. Washer and grommet
26. Nuts
27. Bushing and washer
28. Spring washer, cover and bushing
29. Bolt
30. Bushing and washer
31. Spring washer, cover and bushing
32. Bolt

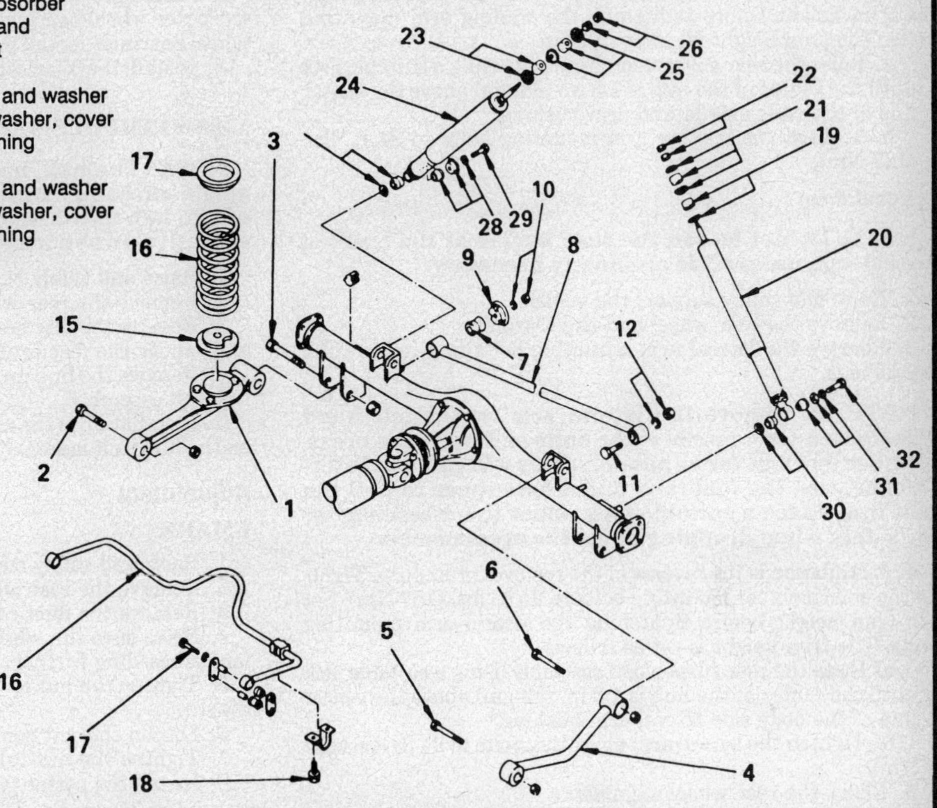

Rear axle and suspension assembly—1987–89 Impulse except G200Z engine

5. Installation is the reverse of the removal procedure. Tighten the lower shock mounting bolts to 30 ft. lbs. (41 Nm) on I-Mark and 20 ft. lbs. (28 Nm) on 1987–89 Impulse.

Rear Control Arms

Removal and Installation

1987–89 IMPULSE

NOTE: Only the upper arm removal and installation procedure applies to G200Z engine equipped vehicles. The lower arm is not removable on these vehicles.

Upper Arm

1. Raise and safely support the vehicle.
2. Remove the rear wheel and tire assembly.

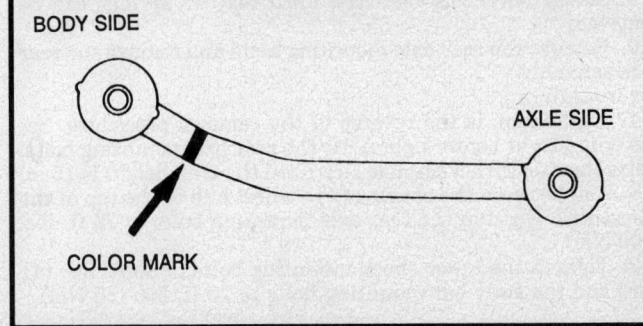

Upper control arm identification mark—1987–89 Impulse except G200Z engine

3. Remove the upper arm mounting bolts and remove the upper control arm.
4. Installation is the reverse of the removal procedure. The upper arms are color coded to indicate whether they are to be installed on the right hand or left hand side. Upper arms for right side installation are red and upper arms for left side installation are blue.
5. Tighten the upper control arm mounting bolts to 98 ft. lbs. (136 Nm).

Lower Arm

1. Raise and safely support the vehicle.
2. Remove the rear wheel and tire assembly.
3. Support the rear axle assembly with a suitable jack.
4. Remove the lower shock mounting bolts and disconnect the shock absorbers from the axle assembly.
5. Slowly lower the rear axle with the jack until the coil springs can be removed.

NOTE: Do not stress the brake hoses when lowering the rear axle.

6. Remove the lower control arm mounting bolts and remove the lower control arm.
7. Installation is the reverse of the removal procedure. Tighten the lower control arm mounting bolts to 118 ft. lbs. (163 Nm) and the lower shock mounting bolts to 20 ft. lbs. (28 Nm).

1990–91 IMPULSE AND 1991 STYLUS

Trailing Arm

1. Raise and safely support the vehicle.
2. Remove the rear wheel and tire assembly.
3. Remove the trailing arm mounting bolts and remove the trailing arm.

4. Installation is the reverse of the removal procedure. Set the trim height before tightening the trailing arm mounting bolts. The trim height is set as follows:

a. Raise the rear suspension assembly using a suitable jack until the center of the hub is 1.3 in. (33mm) above the center line of the body side lateral arm bushing.

b. Tighten the trailing arm mounting bolts to 94 ft. lbs. (127 Nm).

Lateral Arm

NOTE: Do not loosen the turn buckle of the trailing lateral arm unless it is absolutely necessary.

1. Raise and safely support the vehicle.
2. Remove the rear wheel and tire assembly.
3. Remove the lateral arm mounting bolts and remove the lateral arm.

NOTE: To remove the lateral arm on the left hand side, loosen the crossmember bolts and push the cross-member down as far as possible. This will prevent interference with the fuel tank and create space to pull the bolt free. Place a suitable jack under the crossmember for safety when dropping down the crossmember.

4. Installation is the reverse of the removal procedure. Tighten the crossmember mounting bolts to 94 ft. lbs. (127 Nm). Set the trim height before tightening the lateral arm mounting bolts. The trim height is set as follows:

a. Raise the rear suspension assembly using a suitable jack until the center of the hub is 1.3 in. (33mm) above the center line of the body side lateral arm bushing.

b. Tighten the lateral arm mounting bolts to 94 ft. lbs. (127 Nm).

5. Check the rear wheel alignment.

Rear Wheel Bearings

Removal and Installation

I-MARK

1. Raise and safely support the vehicle.
2. Remove the rear wheel and tire assembly.
3. Remove the dust cap and the cotter pin. Remove the castle nut, washer and outer wheel bearing assembly. Remove the drum/hub assembly with the inner wheel bearing and seal.
4. Use a suitable tool to remove the wheel seal. Remove the inner wheel bearing assembly.
5. Clean the wheel bearings, washer, castle nut and the inside of the hub thoroughly with a suitable cleaning solvent and allow to air dry.
6. Inspect the wheel bearing rollers, cages and races for pitting, cracking or other wear and replace, as necessary. Bearings and bearing races must always be replaced as a unit. If the bearings or bearing races are worn or damaged, drive the races out of the hub using suitable removal tools.

To install:

7. If the bearing races were removed, drive the new races into the hub using suitable installation tools. Make sure the inside of the hub is clean before installation.
8. Pack the wheel bearings using a suitable high temperature wheel bearing grease. If a bearing packer is not available, the bearings may be packed by hand, but care must be taken that grease thoroughly penetrates behind the bearing rollers.
9. Place a quantity of wheel bearing grease inside the hub between the races and coat the races with grease. Install the inner wheel bearing.
10. Use a suitable tool to install a new wheel seal.

11. Install the drum/hub assembly onto the spindle and install the outer wheel bearing, washer and the castle nut. Adjust the wheel bearings, install a new cotter pin and install the dust cap.
12. Install the rear wheel and tire assembly and lower the vehicle.

1990–91 IMPULSE AND 1991 STYLUS

NOTE: The hub, hub bearing and the spindle are a single unit and cannot be disassembled. Replace the entire hub unit assembly if the hub axial play is excessive or abnormal noise occurs.

1. Raise and safely support the vehicle.
2. Remove the rear wheel and tire assembly.
3. Remove the disc brake caliper and caliper mounting bracket. Remove the disc brake rotor.
4. Remove the hub unit assembly mounting bolts and remove the hub assembly.
5. Installation is the reverse of the removal procedure. Tighten the hub unit assembly mounting bolts to 49 ft. lbs. (66 Nm).

Adjustment

I-MARK

1. Raise and safely support the vehicle.
2. Remove the rear wheel and tire assembly.
3. Remove the dust cap and the cotter pin.
4. Make sure the wheel bearings are adequately greased before proceeding further.
5. Tighten the nut to 22 ft. lbs. (30 Nm). Rotate the hub 2–3 times.
6. Loosen the nut completely.
7. Tighten the nut fully by hand.
8. Install the cotter pin.

NOTE: If the cotter pin holes are not aligned, tighten the nut just enough to align the holes.

Rear Axle Assembly

Removal and Installation

I-MARK

1. Raise and safely support the vehicle.
2. Remove the rear wheel and tire assemblies.
3. Remove the brake drums.
4. Disconnect the parking brake cable from the parking brake levers and the brake backing plates. Remove the parking brake cable mounting bolts.
5. Remove the brake hose clip. Disconnect and plug the brake hose.
6. Remove the sway bar.
7. Support the rear axle with a suitable jack.
8. Remove the lower shock mounting bolts and disconnect the shocks from the rear axle.
9. Slowly lower the rear axle until the coil springs can be removed.
10. Remove the rear axle mounting bolts and remove the rear axle assembly.

To install:

11. Installation is the reverse of the removal procedure. Set the trim height before tightening the rear axle mounting bolts. Raise the axle with a suitable jack until the trim height is 15 in. (381mm) between the center of the wheel hub to the top of the wheel well. Tighten the rear axle mounting bolts to 72 ft. lbs. (100 Nm).
12. Tighten the lower shock mounting bolts to 30 ft. lbs. (41 Nm) and the sway bar mounting bolts to 20 ft. lbs. (28 Nm).

SPECIFICATIONS

ENGINE IDENTIFICATION

Year	Model	Engine Displacement cu. in. (cc/liter)	Engine Series Identification	No. of Cylinders	Engine Type
1987	XJ6	213 (3590/3.6)	AJ6	6	DOHC
	XJS-6	213 (3590/3.6)	AJ6	6	DOHC
	XJS-12	326 (5345/5.3)	V12	12	DOHC
1988	XJ6	213 (3590/3.6)	AJ6	6	DOHC
	XJS-6	213 (3590/3.6)	AJ6	6	DOHC
	XJS-12	326 (5345/5.3)	V12	12	DOHC
1989	XJ6	213 (3590/3.6)	AJ6	6	DOHC
	XJS-6	213 (3590/3.6)	AJ6	6	DOHC
	XJS-12	326 (5345/5.3)	V12	12	DOHC
1990–91	XJ6	213 (3590/3.6)	AJ6	6	DOHC
	XJS-6	213 (3590/3.6)	AJ6	6	DOHC
	XJS-12	326 (5345/5.3)	V12	12	DOHC

GENERAL ENGINE SPECIFICATIONS

Year	Model	Engine Displacement cu. in. (cc)	Fuel System Type	Net Horsepower @ rpm	Net Torque @ rpm (ft. lbs.)	Bore × Stroke (in.)	Compression Ratio	Oil Pressure @ rpm
1987	XJ6	213 (3590)	FI	195 @ 5000	232 @ 4000	3.58 × 3.62	9.6:1	40 @ 3000
	XJS-6	213 (3590)	FI	195 @ 5000	232 @ 4000	3.58 × 3.62	9.6:1	40 @ 3000
	XJS-12	326 (5345)	EFI	263 @ 5350	288 @ 3200	3.54 × 2.76	11.5:1	40 @ 3000
1988	XJ6	213 (3590)	FI	195 @ 5000	232 @ 4000	3.58 × 3.62	9.6:1	40 @ 3000
	XJS-6	213 (3590)	FI	195 @ 5000	232 @ 4000	3.58 × 3.62	9.6:1	40 @ 3000
	XJS-12	326 (5345)	EFI	263 @ 5350	288 @ 3200	3.54 × 2.76	11.5:1	40 @ 3000
1989	XJ6	213 (3590)	FI	195 @ 5000	232 @ 4000	3.58 × 3.62	9.6:1	40 @ 3000
	XJS-6	213 (3590)	FI	195 @ 5000	232 @ 4000	3.58 × 3.62	9.6:1	40 @ 3000
	XJS-12	326 (5345)	EFI	263 @ 5350	288 @ 3200	3.54 × 2.76	11.5:1	40 @ 3000
1990–91	XJ6	213 (3590)	FI	195 @ 5000	232 @ 4000	3.58 × 3.62	9.6:1	40 @ 3000
	XJS-6	213 (3590)	FI	195 @ 5000	232 @ 4000	3.58 × 3.62	9.6:1	40 @ 3000
	XJS-12	326 (5345)	EFI	263 @ 5350	288 @ 3200	3.54 × 2.76	11.5:1	40 @ 3000

EFI—Electronic Fuel Injection
FI—Fuel Injection

ENGINE TUNE-UP SPECIFICATIONS

Year	Model	Engine Displacement cu. in. (cc)	Spark Plugs Type	Gap (in.)	Ignition Timing (deg.) MT	AT	Compression Pressure (psi)	Fuel Pump (psi)	Idle Speed (rpm) MT	AT	Valve Clearance In.	Ex.
1987	XJ6	213 (3590)	NC9YC	0.035	—	18B @ 2000	①	45	—	750	0.012–0.014	0.012–0.014
	XJS-6	213 (3590)	NC9YC	0.035	—	18B @ 2000	①	45	—	750	0.012–0.014	0.012–0.014
	XJS-12	326 (5345)	RS9YC	0.025	—	18B @ 2000	②	45	—	750	0.010–0.012	0.010–0.012

ENGINE TUNE-UP SPECIFICATIONS

Year	Model	Engine Displacement cu. in. (cc)	Spark Plugs Type	Gap (in.)	Ignition Timing (deg.) MT	AT	Compression Pressure (psi)	Fuel Pump (psi)	Idle Speed (rpm) MT	AT	Valve Clearance In.	Ex.
1988	XJ6	213 (3590)	NC9YC	0.035	—	18B @ 2000	①	45	—	750	0.012–0.014	0.012–0.014
	XJS-6	213 (3590)	NC9YC	0.035	—	18B @ 2000	①	45	—	750	0.012–0.014	0.012–0.014
	XJS-12	326 (5345)	RS9YC	0.025	—	18B @ 2000	②	45	—	750	0.010–0.012	0.010–0.012
1989	XJ6	213 (3590)	NC9YC	0.035	—	18B @ 2000	①	45	—	750	0.012–0.014	0.012–0.014
	XJS-6	213 (3590)	NC9YC	0.035	—	18B @ 2000	①	45	—	750	0.012–0.014	0.012–0.014
	XJS-12	326 (5345)	RS9YC	0.025	—	18B @ 2000	②	45	—	750	0.010–0.012	0.010–0.012
1990–91	XJ6	213 (3590)	NC9YC	0.035	—	18B @ 2000	①	45	—	750	0.012–0.014	0.012–0.014
	XJS-6	213 (3590)	NC9YC	0.035	—	18B @ 2000	①	45	—	750	0.012–0.014	0.012–0.014
	XJS-12	326 (5345)	RS9YC	0.025	—	18B @ 2000	②	45	—	750	0.010–0.012	0.010–0.012

① Non-Catalyst = 160–170 psi
  Catalyst = 150–160 psi
② Non-Catalyst = 210–230 psi
  Catalyst = 200–220 psi

FIRING ORDERS

NOTE: To avoid confusion, always replace spark plug wires one at a time.

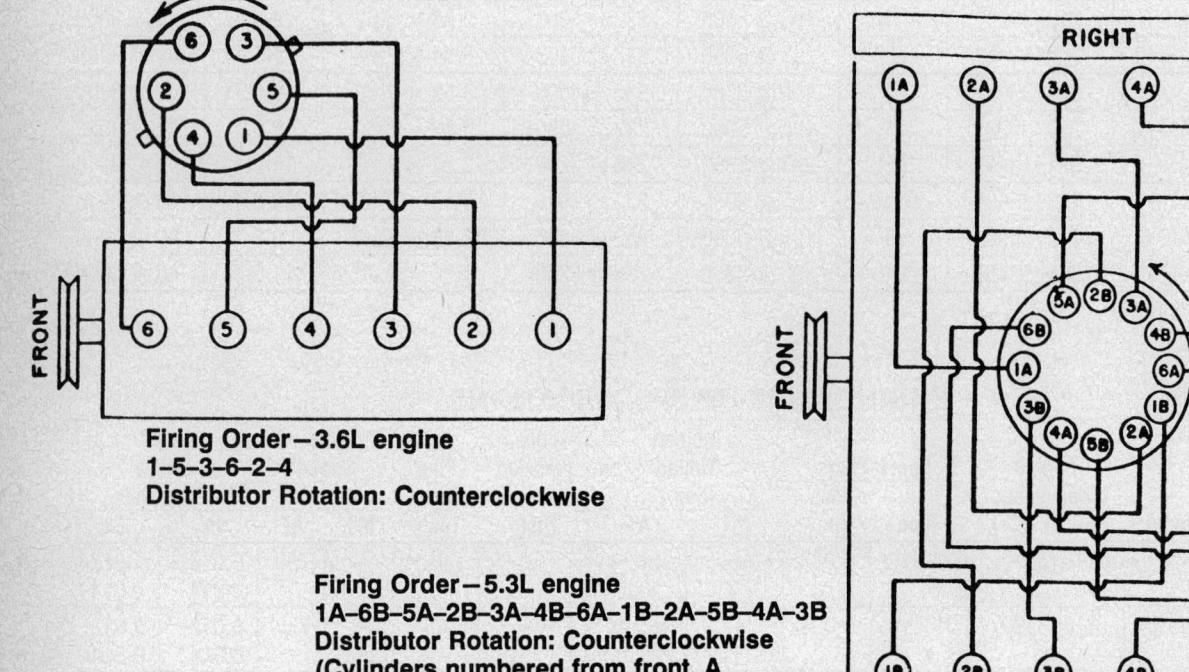

Firing Order—3.6L engine
1–5–3–6–2–4
Distributor Rotation: Counterclockwise

Firing Order—5.3L engine
1A–6B–5A–2B–3A–4B–6A–1B–2A–5B–4A–3B
Distributor Rotation: Counterclockwise
(Cylinders numbered from front. A is right and B is left bank, as viewed from the rear of vehicle.)

CAPACITIES

Year	Model	Engine Displacement cu. in. (cc)	Engine Crankcase with Filter	Engine Crankcase without Filter	Transmission (pts.) 4-Spd	Transmission (pts.) 5-Spd	Transmission (pts.) Auto.	Drive Axle (pts.)	Fuel Tank (gal.)	Cooling System (qts.)
1987	XJ6	213 (3590)	8.4	7.9	—	—	12.8②	4.4	23.2	13.0
	XJS-6	213 (3590)	11.0	10.5	—	—	12.8②	4.4	23.2	13.0
	XJS-12	326 (5345)	11.0	10.5	—	—	40.8②	3.3	①	21.0
1988	XJ6	213 (3590)	8.4	7.9	—	—	12.8②	4.4	23.2	13.0
	XJS-6	213 (3590)	11.0	10.5	—	—	12.8②	4.4	23.2	13.0
	XJS-12	326 (5345)	11.0	10.5	—	—	40.8②	3.3	①	21.0
1989	XJ6	213 (3590)	8.4	7.9	—	—	12.8②	4.4	23.2	13.0
	XJS-6	213 (3590)	11.0	10.5	—	—	12.8②	4.4	23.2	13.0
	XJS-12	326 (5345)	11.0	10.5	—	—	40.8②	3.3	①	21.0
1990–91	XJ6	213 (3590)	8.4	7.9	—	—	12.8②	4.4	23.2	13.0
	XJS-6	213 (3590)	11.0	10.5	—	—	12.8②	4.4	23.2	13.0
	XJS-12	326 (5345)	11.0	10.5	—	—	40.8②	3.3	①	21.0

① Coupe   24.0 gals.
   Convertible   21.6 gals.
② Refill

CRANKSHAFT AND CONNECTING ROD SPECIFICATIONS

All measurements are given in inches.

Year	Engine Displacement cu. in. (cc)	Crankshaft Main Brg. Journal Dia.	Crankshaft Main Brg. Oil Clearance	Crankshaft Shaft End-play	Crankshaft Thrust on No.	Connecting Rod Journal Diameter	Connecting Rod Oil Clearance	Connecting Rod Side Clearance
1987	213 (3590)	3.001	0.0016–0.0033	0.004–0.010	4	2.086	0.0016–0.0033	0.005–0.009
	326 (5345)	3.001–3.007	0.0015–0.0030	0.004–0.006	4	2.2994–2.3000	0.0015–0.0034	0.007–0.013
1988	213 (3590)	3.001	0.0016–0.0033	0.004–0.010	4	2.086	0.0016–0.0033	0.005–0.009
	326 (5345)	3.001–3.007	0.0015–0.0033	0.004–0.010	4	2.2994–2.3000	0.0015–0.0034	0.007–0.013
1989	213 (3590)	3.001	0.0016–0.0033	0.004–0.010	4	2.086	0.0016–0.0033	0.005–0.009
	326 (5345)	3.001–3.007	0.0015–0.0033	0.004–0.010	4	2.2994–2.3000	0.0015–0.0034	0.007–0.013
1990–91	213 (3590)	3.001	0.0016–0.0033	0.004–0.010	4	2.086	0.0016–0.0033	0.005–0.009
	326 (5345)	3.001–3.007	0.0015–0.0033	0.004–0.010	4	2.2994–2.3000	0.0015–0.0034	0.007–0.013

VALVE SPECIFICATIONS

Year	Cylinder Displacement cu. in. (cc)	Seat Angle (deg.)	Face Angle (deg.)	Spring Test Pressure (lbs.)	Spring Free Length (in.)	Stem-to-Guide Clearance (in.) Intake	Stem-to-Guide Clearance (in.) Exhaust	Stem Diameter (in.) Intake	Stem Diameter (in.) Exhaust
1987	213 (3590)	44.5	—	—	①	0.001–0.004	0.001–0.004	0.310–0.311	0.310–0.311
	326 (5345)	44.5	—	—	①	0.0020–0.0023	0.0020–0.0023	0.311–0.312	0.311–0.312

VALVE SPECIFICATIONS

Year	Cylinder Displacement cu. in. (cc)	Seat Angle (deg.)	Face Angle (deg.)	Spring Test Pressure (lbs.)	Spring Free Length (in.)	Stem-to-Guide Clearance (in.)		Stem Diameter (in.)	
						Intake	Exhaust	Intake	Exhaust
1988	213 (3590)	44.5	—	—	①	0.001–0.004	0.001–0.004	0.310–0.311	0.310–0.311
	326 (5345)	44.5	—	—	①	0.0020–0.0023	0.0020–0.0023	0.311–0.312	0.311–0.312
1989	213 (3590)	44.5	—	—	①	0.001–0.004	0.001–0.004	0.310–0.311	0.310–0.311
	326 (5345)	44.5	—	—	①	0.0020–0.0023	0.0020–0.0023	0.311–0.312	0.311–0.312
1990–91	213 (3590)	44.5	—	—	①	0.001–0.004	0.001–0.004	0.310–0.311	0.310–0.311
	326 (5345)	44.5	—	—	①	0.0020–0.0023	0.0020–0.0023	0.311–0.312	0.311–0.312

① Inner 1.734 inch
Outer 2.103 inch

PISTON AND RING SPECIFICATIONS

All measurements are given in inches.

Year	Engine Displacement cu. in. (cc)	Piston Clearance	Ring Gap			Ring Side Clearance		
			Top Compression	Bottom Compression	Oil Control	Top Compression	Bottom Compression	Oil Control
1987	213 (3590)	0.0007–0.0016	0.015–0.025	0.015–0.025	0.012–0.022	0.0025	0.0025	0.0040
	326 (5345)	0.0012–0.0170	0.014–0.020	0.010–0.015	0.015–0.045	0.0029	0.0034	0.0055–0.0065
1988	213 (3590)	0.0007–0.0016	0.015–0.025	0.015–0.025	0.012–0.022	0.0025	0.0025	0.0040
	326 (5345)	0.0012–0.0170	0.014–0.020	0.010–0.015	0.015–0.045	0.0029	0.0034	0.0055–0.0065
1989	213 (3590)	0.0007–0.0016	0.015–0.025	0.015–0.025	0.012–0.022	0.0025	0.0025	0.0040
	326 (5345)	0.0012–0.0170	0.014–0.020	0.010–0.015	0.015–0.045	0.0029	0.0034	0.0055–0.0065
1990–91	213 (3590)	0.0007–0.0016	0.015–0.025	0.015–0.025	0.012–0.022	0.0025	0.0025	0.0040
	326 (5345)	0.0012–0.0170	0.014–0.020	0.010–0.015	0.015–0.045	0.0029	0.0034	0.0055–0.0065

Piston clearance is measured at bottom of skirt, 90 degrees to wrist pin axis.

TORQUE SPECIFICATIONS

All readings in ft. lbs.

Year	Engine Displacement cu. in. (cc)	Cylinder Head Bolts	Main Bearing Bolts	Rod Bearing Bolts	Crankshaft Pulley Bolts	Flywheel Bolts	Manifold		Spark Plugs
							Intake	Exhaust	
1987	213 (3590)	38–41	100–105	38–41	150	72	17–20	17–20	17–20
	326 (5345)	①	②	40	127–152	66	17–20	17–20	7–9

TORQUE SPECIFICATIONS
All readings in ft. lbs.

Year	Engine Displacement cu. in. (cc)	Cylinder Head Bolts	Main Bearing Bolts	Rod Bearing Bolts	Crankshaft Pulley Bolts	Flywheel Bolts	Manifold Intake	Manifold Exhaust	Spark Plugs
1988	213 (3590)	38–41	100–105	38–41	150	72	17–20	17–20	17–20
	326 (5345)	①	②	40	127–152	66	17–20	17–20	7–9
1989	213 (3590)	38–41	100–105	38–41	150	72	17–20	17–20	17–20
	326 (5345)	①	②	40	127–152	66	17–20	17–20	7–9
1990–91	213 (3590)	38–41	100–105	38–41	150	72	17–20	17–20	17–20
	326 (5345)	①	②	40	127–152	66	17–20	17–20	7–9

① 9/16" Bolts = 27 ft. lbs.
   5/8" Bolts = 52 ft. lbs.
② 3/8" Bolts = 27–28 ft. lbs.
   1/2" Bolts = 62 ft. lbs.

BRAKE SPECIFICATIONS
All measurements in inches unless otherwise noted.

Year	Model	Lug Bolt Torque (ft. lbs.)	Master Cylinder Bore	Front Brake Rotor Original Thickness	Front Brake Rotor Minimum Thickness	Rear Brake Rotor Original Thickness	Rear Brake Rotor Minimum Thickness	Allowable Rotor Run-Out (max.)	Minimum Lining Thickness Front	Minimum Lining Thickness Rear
1987	XJS	65–75	0.937	0.945	0.885	0.500	0.450	0.004	0.125	0.125
	XJ6	①	0.875	0.950	0.890	0.500	0.440	0.004	0.125	0.125
1988	XJS	65–75	0.937	0.945	0.885	0.500	0.450	0.004	0.125	0.125
	XJ6	①	0.875	0.950	0.890	0.500	0.440	0.004	0.125	0.125
1989	XJS	65–75	0.937	0.945	0.885	0.500	0.450	0.004	0.125	0.125
	XJ6	①	0.875	0.950	0.890	0.500	0.440	0.004	0.125	0.125
1990–91	XJS	65–75	0.937	0.945	0.885	0.500	0.450	0.004	0.125	0.125
	XJ6	①	0.875	0.950	0.890	0.500	0.440	0.004	0.125	0.125

① Steel wheel 48–63 ft. lbs.
   Alloy wheel 65–75 ft. lbs.

WHEEL ALIGNMENT

Year	Model	Caster Range (deg.)	Caster Preferred Setting (deg.)	Camber Range (deg.)	Camber Preferred Setting (deg.)	Toe-in (in.)	Steering Axis Inclination (deg.)
1987	XJ6	3 1/2–4 1/2P	4P	0–1/2N	1/4P	1/16	NA①
	XJS	3 1/2 ± 1/4P	3 1/2P	± 1/2N	1/2N	0–1/8	NA①
1988	XJ6	3 1/2–4 1/2P	4P	0–1/2N	1/4P	1/16	NA①
	XJS	3 1/2 ± 1/4P	3 1/2P	± 1/2N	1/2N	0–1/8	NA①
1989	XJ6	3 1/2–4 1/2P	4P	0–1/2N	1/4P	1/16	NA①
	XJS	3 1/2 ± 1/4P	3 1/2P	± 1/2N	1/2N	0–1/8	NA①
1990–91	XJ6	3 1/2–4 1/2P	4P	0–1/2N	1/4P	1/16	NA①
	XJS	3 1/2 ± 1/4P	3 1/2P	± 1/2N	1/2N	0–1/8	NA①

① NA—Not available

ENGINE ELECTRICAL

NOTE: Disconnecting the negative battery cable on some vehicles may interfere with the functions of the on board computer systems and may require the computer to undergo a relearning process, once the negative battery cable is reconnected.

Distributor

Removal and Installation
TIMING NOT DISTURBED
3.6L ENGINE

1. Disconnect the negative battery cable.
2. Remove the air cleaner assembly and distributor cap.
3. Raise and support the vehicle safely.
4. Rotate the engine until its at TDC on No. 1 cylinder, then mark the position of the rotor arm relevant to the distributor housing.
5. Remove the distributor hold-down bolt and lift the distributor assembly from the engine.

To install:
6. Align the rotor arm with the mark indicating No. 1 cylinder, then fit the distributor into the engine.
7. Install the distributor hold-down bolt.
8. Install the distributor cap and air cleaner assembly.
9. Reconnect the negative battery cable. Recheck the ignition timing.

Alternator

Precautions

To avoid damage to the alternator unit, the following precautions must be observe:
- If the battery is removed for any reason, make sure it is reconnected with the correct polarity. Reversing the battery connections may result in damage to the one-way rectifiers.
- When utilizing a booster battery as a starting aid, always connect the positive to positive terminals and the negative terminal from the booster battery to a good engine ground on the vehicle being started.
- Never use a fast charger as a booster to start vehicles.
- Disconnect the battery cables when charging the battery with a fast charger.
- Never attempt to polarize the alternator.
- Do not use test lamps of more than 12 volts when checking diode continuity.
- Do not short across or ground any of the alternator terminals.
- The polarity of the battery, alternator and regulator must be matched and considered before making any electrical connections within the system.
- Never separate the alternator on an open circuit. Make sure all connections within the circuit are clean and tight.
- Disconnect the battery ground terminal when performing any service on electrical components.
- Disconnect the battery if arc welding is to be done on the vehicle.

Belt Tension

Check the tension by applying the specified pressure at right angle to the belt, in the longest straight run between pulleys, then measure the belt's deflection. Specification is as followed:
3.6L ENGINE
Air pump—apply a force of 3.3 lbs. (1.5kg). Deflection should not exceed 0.180 in. (4.4mm)
Compressor—apply a force of 6.4 lbs. (2.9kg). Deflection should not exceed 0.170 in. (4.6mm)

Alternator—apply a force of 3.3 lbs. (1.5kg). Deflection should not exceed 0.170 in. (4.6mm)

5.3L ENGINE
Pwr. Str./Water pump—apply a force of 6.5 lbs. (3.0kg). Deflection should not exceed 0.160 in. (4.1mm)
Alternator—apply a force of 3.2 lbs. (1.0kg). Deflection should not exceed 0.170 in. (4.4mm)
Compressor/Air pump—apply a force of 6.4 lbs. (2.9kg). Deflection should not exceed 0.220 in. (5.6mm)
Fan belt—apply a force of 6.4 lbs. (2.9kg). Deflection should not exceed 0.130 in. (3.3mm)

Adjustment
3.6L ENGINE
Air Pump Drive Belt

1. Loosen the air pump adjuster block retaining bolt, air pump pivot bolt and adjuster link locknuts.
2. Tighten the lower adjuster link locknut until the specified tension is obtained.
3. Tighten the upper adjuster link locknut, adjuster block retaining bolt and air pump pivot bolt.
4. Recheck the belt tension.

Air Conditioning Compressor Drive Belt

1. Loosen the compressor adjuster block retaining bolt and upper adjuster link locknut.
2. Raise the vehicle and support it safely.
3. Loosen the compressor pivot bolt.
4. Tighten the lower adjuster link locknut until the specified tension is obtained, then tighten the compressor pivot bolt.
5. Lower the vehicle, then tighten the upper adjuster link locknut and adjuster block retaining bolt.
6. Recheck the belt tension.

Alternator Drive Belt

1. Loosen the alternator adjuster block retaining bolt and the alternator pivot bolt.
2. Loosen the adjusting rod to water pump retaining nut and adjuster link locknuts.

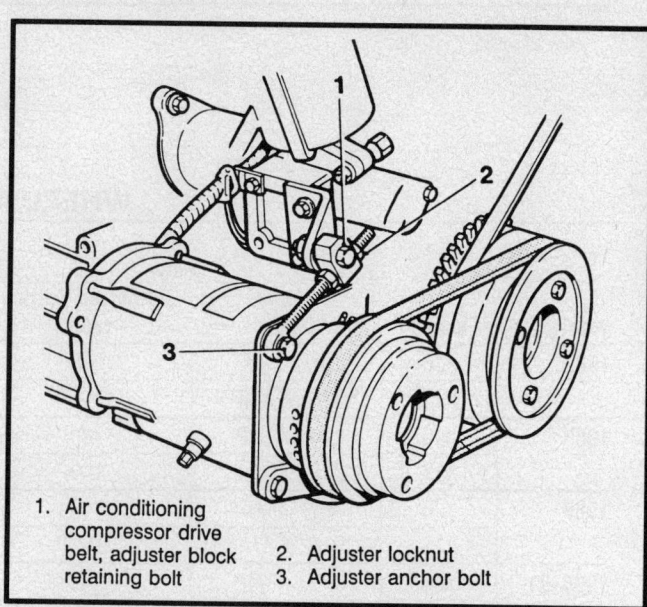

1. Air conditioning compressor drive belt, adjuster block retaining bolt
2. Adjuster locknut
3. Adjuster anchor bolt

Air conditioning compressor drive belt adjustment—3.6L engine

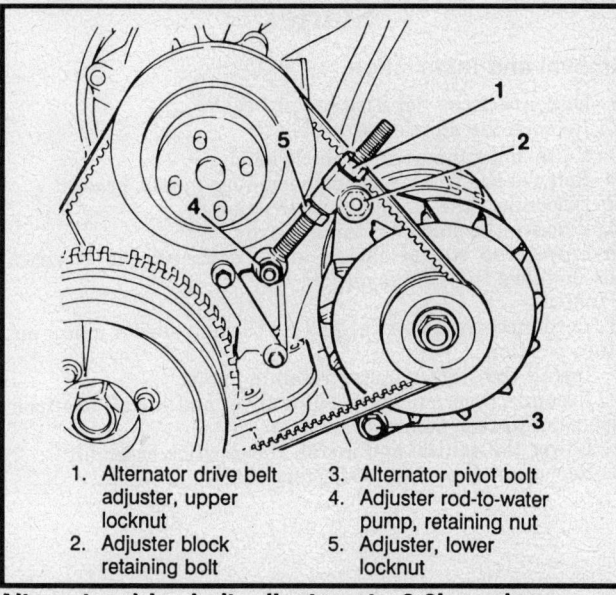

1. Alternator drive belt adjuster, upper locknut
2. Adjuster block retaining bolt
3. Alternator pivot bolt
4. Adjuster rod-to-water pump, retaining nut
5. Adjuster, lower locknut

Alternator drive belt adjustment—3.6L engine

3. Tighten the lower adjuster link locknut until the specified tension is obtained, then tighten the compressor pivot bolt.

4. Tighten the adjusting rod to water pump retaining nut, adjuster block retaining bolt and the alternator pivot bolt.

5. Recheck the belt tension.

5.3L ENGINE

Front Fan Drive Belt

1. Loosen the jockey pulley carrier retaining bolt and nuts at the adjuster block and link, as required.

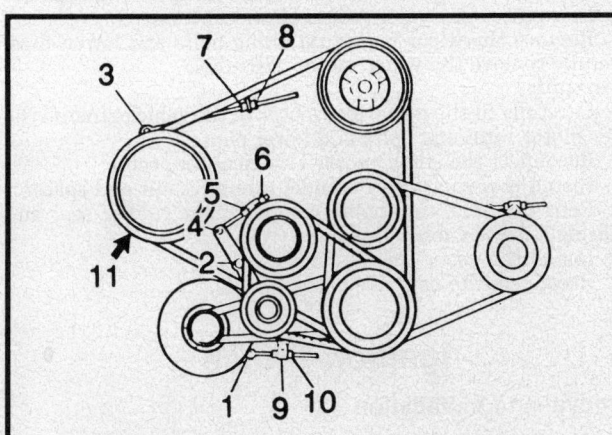

1. Alternator adjuster link
2. Jockey pulley carrier bolt
3. Adjuster pulley or air pump (where fitted) adjuster link securing bolt
4. Adjuster link retaining nut
5. Adjuster link lower locknut
6. Adjuster link upper locknut
7. Adjuster pulley or air pump (where fitted) adjuster link locknut
8. Adjuster pulley or air pump (where fitted) adjuster link locknut
9. Alternator adjuster link locknut
10. Alternator adjuster link locknut
11. Adjuster pulley or air pump (where fitted)

Drive belts, exploded view—5.3L engine

2. Tighten the appropriate adjuster link locknut(s) until the specified tension is obtained.

3. Tighten the nuts at the adjusting link and jockey pulley carrier, as required.

4. Recheck the belt tension.

Removal and Installation

3.6L ENGINE

Drive Belts

1. Loosen the air pump adjuster block retaining bolt, air pump pivot bolt and adjuster link locknuts, as required.

2. Loosen the air conditioning compressor adjuster block retaining bolt and upper adjuster link locknut, as required.

NOTE: If the air conditioning compressor drive belt is to be replaced, the vehicle must be raised and supported safely.

3. Loosen the alternator adjuster block retaining bolt and the alternator pivot bolt, as required.

4. Maneuver the belt(s) past the fan blades.

5. If necessary, install a new belt(s).

6. Tighten the appropriate adjuster link locknuts until the specified tension is obtained.

7. Recheck the belt(s) tension.

5.3L ENGINE

1. Loosen the jockey pulley carrier retaining bolt and nuts at the adjuster block and link.

2. Loosen the appropriate adjuster link locknuts, then maneuver the belt(s) past the fan blades.

3. If the power steering/water pump drive belt is being replace, the driving belt (front belt) must first be removed.

4. If the air conditioning drive belt is being replace, the the driving belt (front belt) and power steering/water pump drive belt must first be removed.

NOTE: If the alternator drive belt (rear belt) is to be replaced, the vehicle must be raised and supported safely.

5. If necessary, install a new belt(s).

6. Tighten the appropriate adjuster link locknuts until the specified tension is obtained.

7. Recheck the belt(s) tension.

Alternator

Removal and Installation

3.6L ENGINE

1. Disconnect the negative battery cable.

2. Remove the alternator adjuster block retaining bolt and the alternator pivot bolt.

3. Loosen the adjusting rod to water pump retaining nut and adjuster link locknuts.

4. Remove the alternator belt

6. Disconnect the alternator electrical connections and remove the alternator.

To install:

7. Fit the alternator into position and reconnect the electrical connections.

8. Install the alternator pivot bolt and adjuster block retaining bolt.

9. Refit the alternator belt.

10. Tighten the lower adjuster link locknut until the specified tension is obtained, then tighten the compressor pivot bolt.

11. Tighten the adjusting rod to water pump retaining nut, adjuster block retaining bolt and the alternator pivot bolt.

12. Recheck the belt tension.

5.3L ENGINE

1. Disconnect the negative battery cable.
2. Remove the power steering and air conditioning compressor drive belts.
3. Raise the vehicle and support it safely.
4. From beneath the vehicle, remove the alternator pivot bolt, adjuster link and trunnion.
5. Disconnect the alternator electrical connections and remove the alternator belt.
6. Remove the alternator from the vehicle.

To install:

7. Fit the alternator into position and install the alternator pivot bolt, adjuster link and trunnion.
8. Reconnect the alternator electrical connections, install the drive belt and adjust to specification.
9. Lower the vehicle.
10. Install and adjust the air conditioning compressor drive belt and power steerings.
11. Reconnect the negative battery cable.

Starter

Removal and Installation

1. Disconnect the negative battery cable.
2. Remove the dipstick assembly.
3. Raise and support the vehicle safely.
4. Remove the front suspension-to-rear mount bracket.
5. Disconnect the engine ground strap.
6. Remove the starter retaining bolts.
7. Lower the starter motor and disconnect the electrical leads. Remove the starter motor.

To install:

8. Reconnect the electrical leads to the new starter motor and fit into position.
9. Install the starter motor retaining bolts.
10. Reconnect the engine ground strap and install the front suspension-to-rear mount bracket.
11. Lower the vehicle and install the dipstick assembly.
12. Reconnect the negative battery cable.

CHASSIS ELECTRICAL

Heater Blower Motor

Removal and Installation

1. Disconnect the negative battery cable.
2. Remove the dash liner and glove box.
3. Remove the the central processor and retaining bracket, as required.
4. Remove the blower motor retaining screws.
5. Disconnect the multi-plug connector cable harness, in-car sensor and vacuum lines from the servo.
6. Remove the blower motor assembly.

To install:

7. Fit the blower motor into position, using a new gasket with glue. Do not tighten the retaining screws at this time.
8. Reconnect the multi-plug connector cable harness, in-car sensor and vacuum lines to the servo.
9. Tighten the blower motor retaining screws.
10. Install the central processor.
11. Install the dash liner and glove box.
12. Reconnect the negative battery cable.

Windshield Wiper Motor

Removal and Installation

1. Disconnect the negative battery cable.
2. Remove the wiper arm assembly.

3. Remove the engine compartment rubber seal and windshield lower rubber finish.
4. Remove the valance retaining screws and position it aside.
5. Remove the wiper drive spindle retaining nut and spacer.
6. Disconnect the wiper motor electrical connector.
7. Remove the wiper motor retaining bolts and lower clips. Carefully remove the wiper motor assembly.

To install:

8. Carefully fit the new wiper motor to the vehicle. Install the wiper motor retaining bolts and lower clips.
9. Reconnect the wiper motor electrical connector.
10. Install the wiper drive spindle retaining nut and spacer.
11. Refit the valance, engine compartment rubber seal and windshield lower rubber finish.
12. Install the wiper arm assembly.
13. Reconnect the negative battery cable.

Ignition Switch

Removal and Installation

1. Disconnect the negative battey cable.
2. Remove the steering wheel.
3. Remove the dimmer switch control knob.
4. Remove the lower cowl.
5. Remove the ignition switch retaining screws.

6. Disconnect the switch harness connector and remove the switch.

To install:

7. Fit the harness connector to the replacement switch.

8. Fit the switch into position and install the retaining screws.

9. Refit the lower cowl, dimmer switch control knob and steering wheel.

10. Reconnect the negative battey cable.

Stoplight Switch

Removal and Installation

1. Disconnect the negative battery cable.

2. Remove the stoplight switch retaining screws and disconnect the switch electrical connector.

3. Remove the switch assembly.

4. Remove the mounting plate and gasket.

To install:

5. Fit the new switch to the mounting plate.

6. Install the switch assembly, using a new mounting plate gasket.

7. Reconnect the electrical connector to the switch.

8. Reconnect the negative battery cable.

9. Depress the brake pedal and check the operation to the switch. Slacken the screws retaining the switch and adjust the switch, as required.

Fuses, Circuit Breakers and Relays

Location

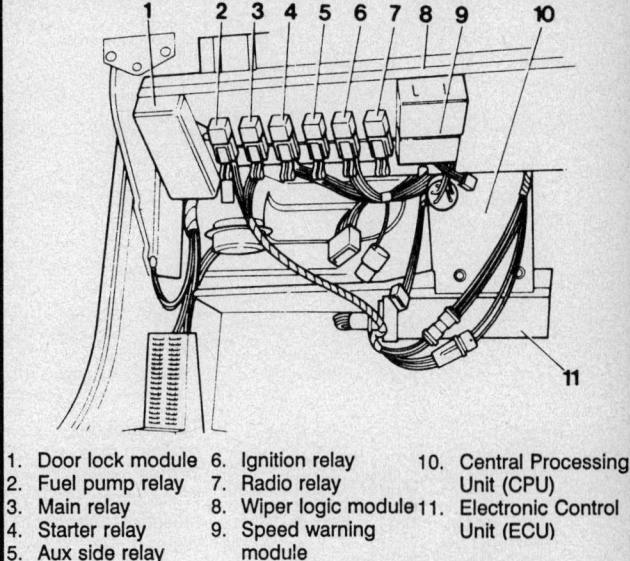

1. Door lock module
2. Fuel pump relay
3. Main relay
4. Starter relay
5. Aux side relay
6. Ignition relay
7. Radio relay
8. Wiper logic module
9. Speed warning module
10. Central Processing Unit (CPU)
11. Electronic Control Unit (ECU)

Control system, components location—XJ6

ENGINE COOLING

Radiator

Removal and Installation

1. Disconnect the negative battery cable.

2. Place a suitable container beneath the radiator. Loosen the radiator drain plug, remove the radiator cap and drain the cooling system.

3. Remove the air cleaner assembly.

4. Remove the cooling fan assembly.

5. Remove the fan shroud retaining clips, then remove lift out the fan shroud and fan assembly.

6. Disconnect the power steering and transmission cooler lines to the radiator, as necessary. Plug the lines.

7. Remove the expansion tank hose and upper and lower radiator hoses.

8. Remove the top rail and lift the radiator from the vehicle.

To install:

9. Fit the radiator mounting rubbers in place, then position the radiator into the vehicle.

10. Install the top rail.

11. Install the expansion tank hose and upper and lower radiator hoses.

12. Reconnect the power steering and transmission cooler lines to the radiator, as necessary.

13. Install the fan and shroud assembly. Make certain the paint spots on the fan assembly and fan pulley are aligned.

14. Install the air cleaner assembly.

15. Retighten the radiator drain plug, fill the cooling system and install the radiator cap.

16. Start the engine and check for leaks.

Water Pump

Removal and Installation

1. Disconnect the negative battery cable.

2. Remove the air cleaner element.

3. Place a drain pan beneath the radiator and open the drain plug. Remove the radiator cap.

4. Remove the torquatrol unit-to-water pump retaining nuts.

5. Remove the fan cowl retaining clips, then lift both the fan assembly and fan cowl from the vehicle.

6. Remove the alternator drive belt.

7. Place a protective board against the radiator.

8. Remove the water pump retaining bolts and remove the water pump assembly.

To install:

9. Apply sealant, Hylosil 102 or equivalent, to the water pump mating surfaces. Place the pump into position and install the retaining bolts. Torque the bolts 17–20 ft. lbs. (23–27 Nm).

10. Remove the protective board from the radiator and install the alternator belt.

11. Install the fan unit assembly and fan cowl into the vehicle.

12. Align the 2 paint spots, one on the torquatrol unit and one on the drive belt pulley assembly, then install the retaining nuts. Torque the retaining nuts 10 ft. lbs. (13.5 Nm).

13. Secure the fan cowl with the retaining clips.

14. Reconnect the negative battery cable.

15. Tighten the drain plug and refill the cooling system. Start the engine and check for leaks.

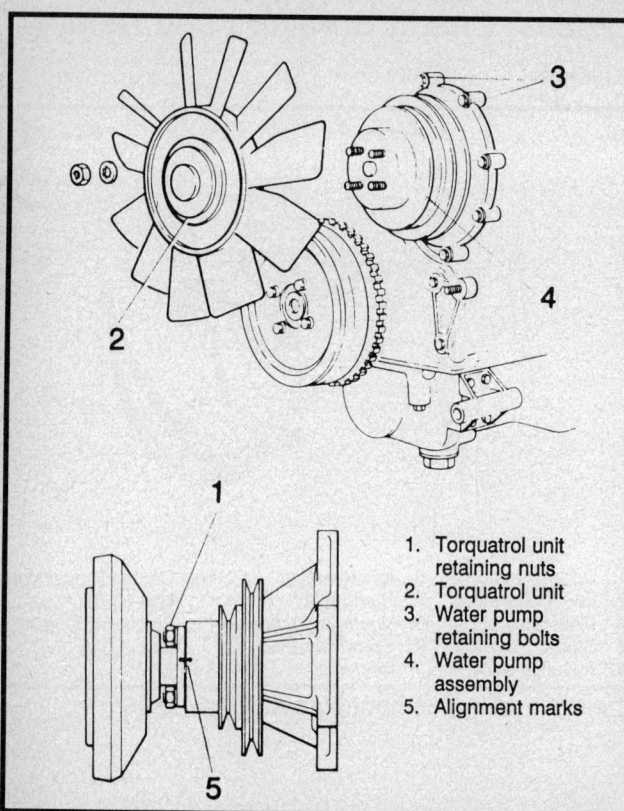

1. Torquatrol unit retaining nuts
2. Torquatrol unit
3. Water pump retaining bolts
4. Water pump assembly
5. Alignment marks

Water pump and torquatrol unit, exploded view—3.6L engine

Thermostat

Removal and Installation

1. Disconnect the negative battery cable.
2. Remove the air cleaner element.
3. Place a drain pan beneath the radiator and open the drain plug. Remove the radiator cap.
4. Remove the thermostat cover retaining bolts and remove the thermostat.

To install:

5. Fit a new O-ring to the thermostat and position the thermostat in the housing.
6. Apply sealant, Hylosil 102 or equivalent, to the thermostat cover and housing mating surfaces and install the thermostat cover. Torque the retaining bolts 17-20 ft. lbs. (23–27 Nm).
7. Reconnect the negative battery cable.
8. Tighten the drain plug and refill the cooling system. Start the engine and check for leaks.

Cooling System Bleeding

Whenever the coolant is drained from the cooling system or any cooling system part(s) have been replaced. All air must be purge from the system. To bleed the system, proceed as follow:

1. Refill the cooling system and install the radiator cap.
2. Move the heater selector lever to the **HOT** position.
3. Refit the expansion tank cap and run the engine until the thermostat is open.
4. Turn the engine OFF. Remove the expansion tank cap and refill the system.
5. Install the expansion tank cap.

FUEL SYSTEM

Fuel System Service Precautions

Safety is the most important factor when performing not only fuel system maintenance but any type of maintenance. Failure to conduct maintenance and repairs in a safe manner may result in serious personal injury or death. Maintenance and testing of the vehicle's fuel system components can be accomplished safely and effectively by adhering to the following rules and guidelines.

• To avoid the possibility of fire and personal injury, always disconnect the negative battery cable unless the repair or test procedure requires that battery voltage be applied.

• Always relieve the fuel system pressure prior to disconnecting any fuel system component (injector, fuel rail, pressure regulator, etc.), fitting or fuel line connection. Exercise extreme caution whenever relieving fuel system pressure to avoid exposing skin, face and eyes to fuel spray. Please be advised that fuel under pressure may penetrate the skin or any part of the body that it contacts.

• Always place a shop towel or cloth around the fitting or connection prior to loosening to absorb any excess fuel due to spillage. Ensure that all fuel spillage (should it occur) is quickly removed from engine surfaces. Ensure that all fuel soaked cloths or towels are deposited into a suitable waste container.

• Always keep a dry chemical (Class B) fire extinguisher near the work area.

• Do not allow fuel spray or fuel vapors to come into contact with a spark or open flame.

• Always use a backup wrench when loosening and tightening fuel line connection fittings. This will prevent unnecessary stress and torsion to fuel line piping. Always follow the proper torque specifications.

• Always replace worn fuel fitting O-rings with new. Do not substitute fuel hose or equivalent where fuel pipe is installed.

Relieving Fuel System Pressure

1. Open the passenger door and remove the right side dash liner.
2. Remove the Fuel pump relay from the yellow block cable connector.
3. Crank the engine for 10 seconds, then turn the ignition switch **OFF**.
4. Re-install the relay and right side dash liner.

Fuel Filter

Removal and Installation

1. Depressurize the fuel system pressure.
2. Disconnect the negative battery cable.
3. Raise and support the vehicle safely.
4. Position a suitable container below the fuel filter.
5. Remove the filter feed hose banjo bolt. Remove the hose from the filter and plug the openings. Be careful not to loose the copper washers from the banjo bolt.
6. Remove the fuel pump-to-filter hose union nut and remove the hose. Plug the openings.

7. Loosen the filter retaining clamp and remove the filter assembly.

8. Remove the pump-to-filter adaptor piece, front plastic cover and foam pad from the filter.

To install:

9. Refit the pump-to-filter adaptor piece, front plastic cover and foam pad to the new filter.

10. Install the filter assembly to the retaining clamp.

11. Install the fuel pump-to-filter hose and tighten the union nut.

12. Install the filter feed hose. Make certain the copper washers are fitted to the banjo bolt.

13. Lower the vehicle and reconnect the negative battery cable.

14. Start the engine and check for leaks.

Electric Fuel Pump

Removal and Installation

1. Depressurize the fuel system pressure.
2. Disconnect the negative battery cable.
3. Raise and support the vehicle safely.
4. Remove the right side wheel assembly.
5. Cut and remove the straps securing the fuel pump feed hose to the axle carrier.
6. Fit a clamps to the fuel feed hose. Remove the retaining clip and disconnect the fuel feed hose. Plug the hose.
7. Loosen the union nut at the pump and reposition the hose. Plug the hose.
8. Remove the fuel pump-to-axle carrier mounting nuts.
9. Remove the electrical harness from the fuel pump and remove the pump assembly.
10. Remove the fuel pump mounting assembly from the fuel pump. Remove the non-reture valve.

To install:

11. Assemble the new pump to the fuel pump mounting assembly. Refit the non-return valve.
12. Reconnect the electrical harness to the fuel pump.
13. Install the pump assembly to the carrier.
14. Fit the union nut and fuel feed hose to the pump.
15. Install the right side wheel assembly.
16. Lower the vehicle and reconnect the negative battery cable.

Fuel Injector

Removal and Installation

1. Depressurize the fuel system.
2. Disconnect the negative battery cable.
3. Disconnect the injector connectors.
4. Place a rag into position to catch any fuel leakage. Release the fuel feed hose from the union nut and remove the fuel rail.
5. Carefully remove the fuel rail from the manifold and pressure regulator. Plug all openings to prevent dirt and foreign materials.
6. Place the fuel rail on a clean work bench. Separate the injector(s) from the fuel rail by removing the injector retaining clips.

To install:

7. Clean the injector rail, then fit the new injector(s) to the fuel rail. Secure each injector with its retaining clip.
8. Carefully fit the injector rail to the manifold. Be certain all injectors are fully seated.
9. Connect the fuel rail to the pressure regulator and fuel feed hose.
10. Reconnect the injector electrical connectors.
11. Reconnect the negative battery cable.

Pressure Regulator

Removal and Installation

1. Depressurize the fuel system.
2. Disconnect the negative battery cable.
3. Place a rag under the pressure regulator to catch any fuel leakage.
4. Disconnect the fuel hose and vacuum hose from the pressure regulator. Plug the fuel hose opening to prevent dirt and foreign materials.
5. Separate the pressure regulator from the fuel rail and mounting bracket.
6. Remove the pressure regulator. Plug all openings to prevent dirt and foreign materials.

To install:

7. Fit the new regulator to the mounting bracket and fuel rail. Tighten the regulator union nut.
8. Reconnect the vacuum hose and fuel feed hose to the pressure regulator.
9. Reconnect the negative battery cable.

ENGINE MECHANICAL

NOTE: Disconnecting the negative battery cable on some vehicles may interfere with the functions of the on board computer systems and may require the computer to undergo a relearning process, once the negative battery cable is reconnected.

Engine Assembly

Removal and Installation

3.6L ENGINE

1. Depressurize the fuel system.
2. Disconnect the negative battery cable.
3. From the engine compartment, remove the right side insulation pad.
4. Disconnect the underhood lamp.
5. Apply tape to the forward edge of the hood behind the grille surrounding.
6. Disconnect the hood support struts and hood assembly.
7. Remove the air cleaner assembly and drain the cooling system.
8. Remove the front grille.
9. If equipped with air conditioning, drain the air conditioning system. Remove the air conditioning compressor and receiver/drier. Be certain to plug all openings.
10. Disconnect the heater hoses and radiator hoses. Remove the cooling fan shroud, radiator and auxiliary electric fan.
11. Disconnect and tag all electrical connectors and vacuum hoses, as required.
12. Remove horn assembly and the tie bars at front of engine.
13. On automatic transmission, disconnect and plug the cooler lines from the radiator.
14. Disconnect the engine oil cooler pipes and remove the oil cooler radiator.
15. Disconnect and plug the fuel lines.
16. Disconnect the power steering pump/drive and remove the coupling.

17. Remove the throttle cable and throttle support bracket at the intake manifold.
18. Support the engine weight, using tool 18G 1465 and MS 53B or their equivalent.
19. Raise the vehicle and support it safely.
20. Remove the front exhaust pipe.
21. On manual transmission, disconnect the gear lever linkage and switch multi-plugs. Disconnect the clutch slave cylinder from the bell housing.
21. On automatic transmission, disconnect the gear selector cable from the selector shaft and mounting bracket.
22. Remove the transmission center mount.
23. Remove the rear heat shield and propeller shaft.
24. Lower the vehicle and fit a suitable engine removal tool.
25. Remove the engine and transmission assembly from the vehicle; being careful not to damage the steering rack.
26. Mount the engine to a suitable engine stand.

To install:

27. Fit the engine and transmission assembly to the engine hoist and carefully lower the engine into the vehicle.
28. Position a jack under the transmission to support the weight.
29. Install tool MS 53B or equivalent. Tighten the hook nut to take the weight of the engine.
30. Install the rear mount spring assembly and the mount. Remove the jack.
31. Install the driveshaft.
32. Slacken off the hook nut to release the weight of the engine and remove the hook. Remove tool MS 53B or equivalent.
33. Install the transmission mount.
34. Reconnect the electrical harness and vacuum hoses, as required.
35. Reconnect the heater hoses.
36. Install the throttle cable support bracket and cable. Slack-

en off the locknut and adjust the cable to obtain the correct tension.
37. Install the fuel hoses to the manifold and pressure regulator.
38. Clean the power steering mating face and fit the coupling to the pump. Align the pump shaft with the distributor driveshaft, then connect the pump assembly.
39. Install the air conditioning compressor.
40. Install the oil cooler pipes, receiver/drier and oil cooler radiator.
41. Install the horn assembly, condenser and brackets. Make certain the condenser is secured by the mounting brackets and that the pipes run along the inner wing.
42. Install the fan and frame assembly. Reconnect the fan electrical connector.
43. Install the fan cowl assembly and radiator. Connect the lower radiator hose.
44. Install the front grille, air cleaner element and hood struts.
45. Remove tool 18G 1465 or equivalent and refill the cooling system.
46. Install the hood and reconnect the negative battery cable.
47. On automatic transmission, check and adjust the downshift cable initial setting.
48. Check and adjust all fluid levels. Start the engine and check for leaks.

5.3L ENGINE

1. Depressurize the fuel system.
2. Disconnect the negative battery cable.
3. Disconnect the underhood light and remove the hood assembly.
4. Remove the lower grille.
5. If equipped with air conditioning, drain the air condition-

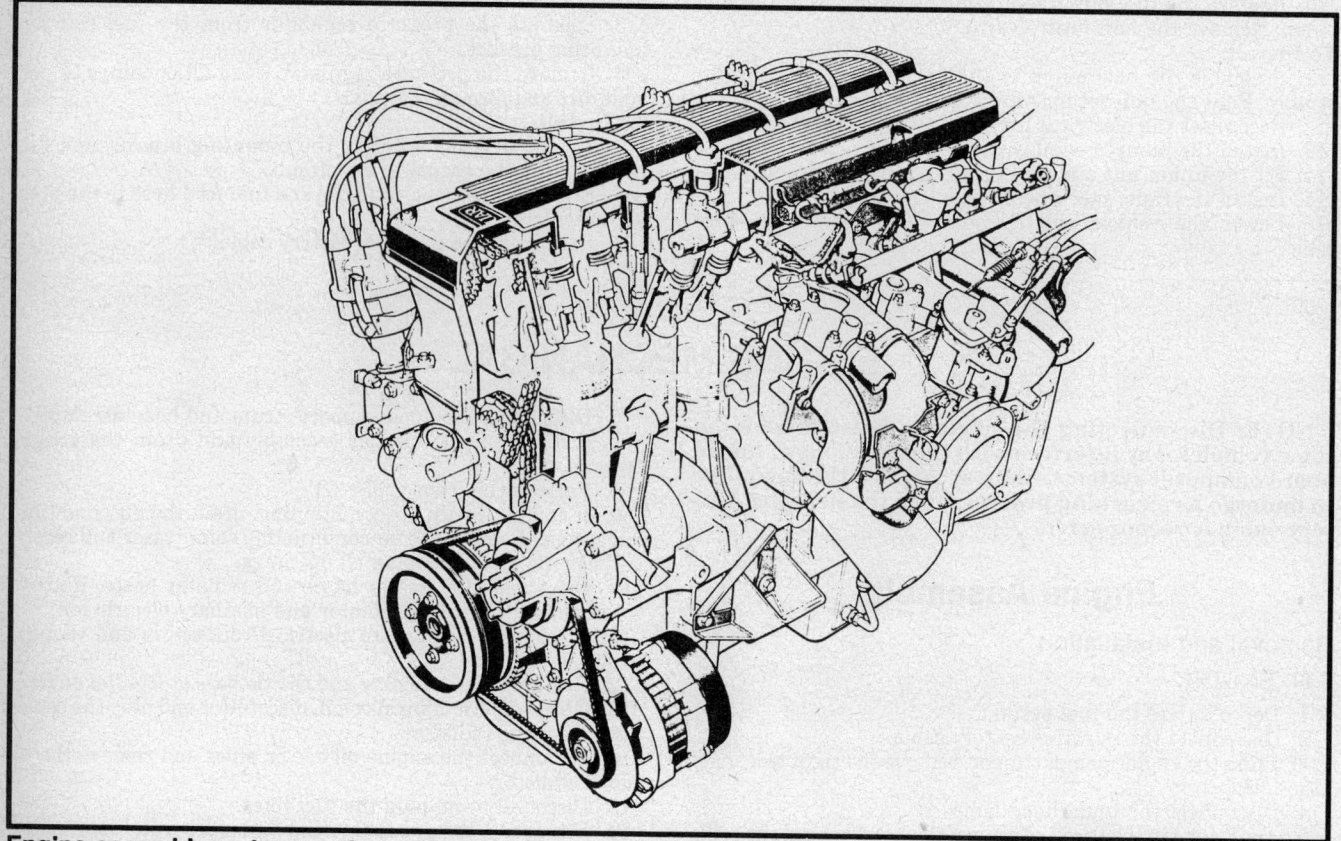

Engine assembly, cut-away view—3.6L engine

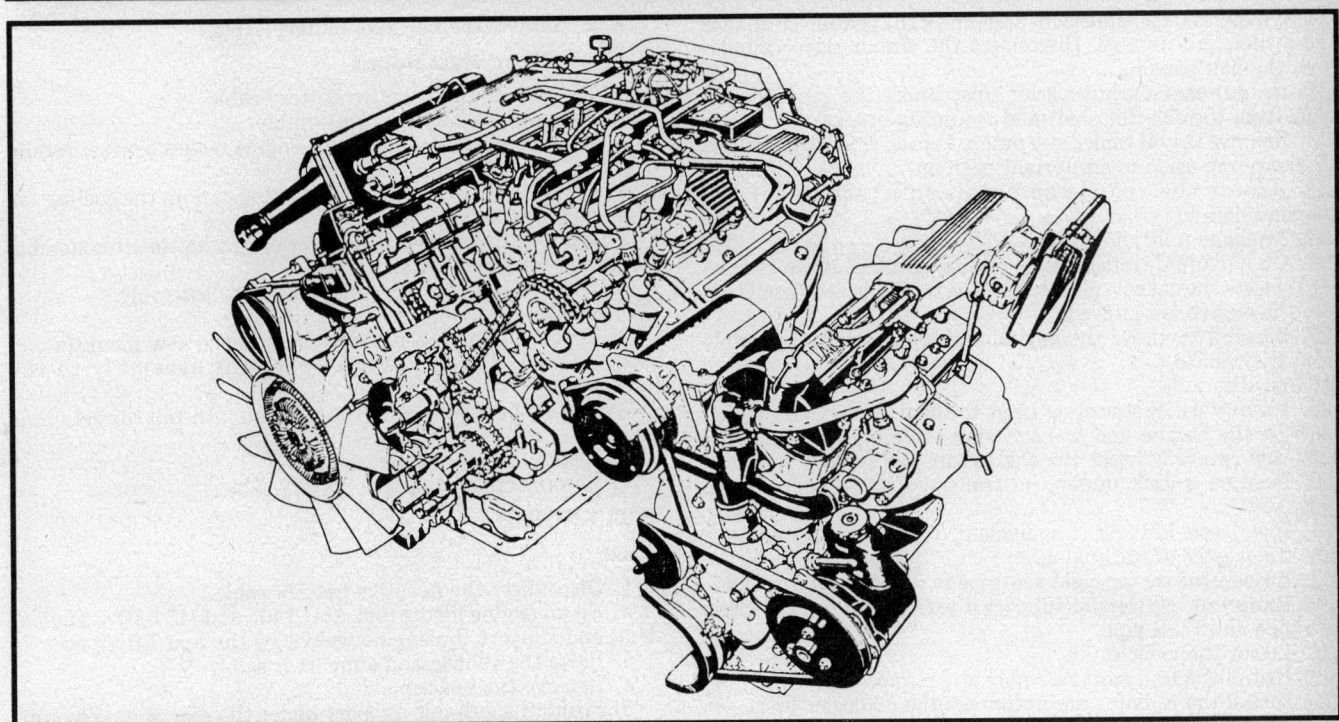

Engine assembly, cut-away view—5.3L engine

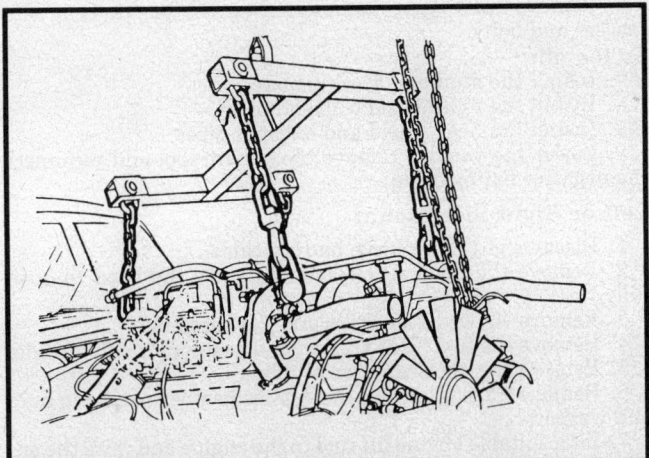

Engine and transmission assembly installation—5.3L engine shown

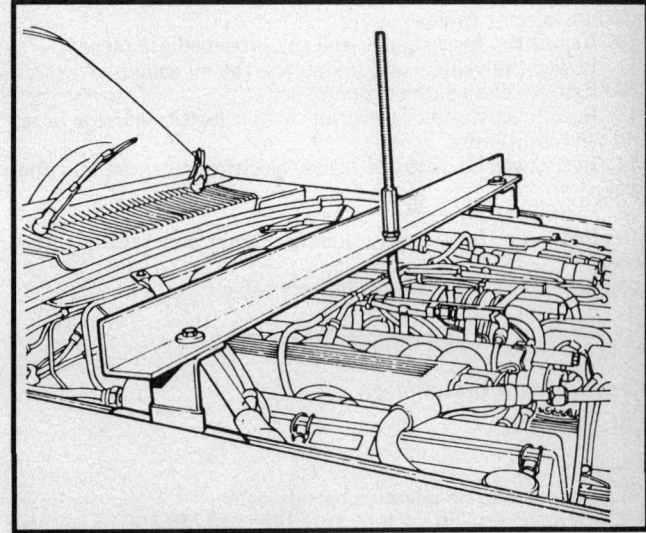

Engine support assembly

ing system and separate the hoses, as required. Be certain to plug all openings.

6. Remove the left and right side air cleaner assembly and drain the cooling system.

7. Disconnect and label all electrical connectors and vacuum hoses, as required. Disconnect the starter harness at the bulkhead connector.

8. Disconnect the throttle cable, heater hoses and radiator hoses.

9. Disconnect and plug the fuel feed hose.

10. If equipped with an automatic transmission, disconnect and plug the transmission oil cooler lines.

11. Remove the radiator top rail, then disconnect and plug the outlet pipe from the reciever/drier.

12. Remove the condenser pipe retaining clips.

13. Remove the radiator top rail completely with the evaporator and receiver/drier unit.

14. Disconnect the low coolant sensor and oil cooler pipes from the radiator. Plug the oil cooler pipes.

15. Carefully remove the radiator, fan cowl and electric fan.

16. Fit an engine lifting tool, MS 53B or equivalent, and support the engine weight.

17. Raise the vehicle and safely support it.

18. Disconnect the front exhaust pipes. Remove the heat shields.

19. Support the transmission and remove the transmission mount; note the position of the spacers and bolts to facilitate reassemble.

20. Remove the driveshaft.

21. On manual transmission, disconnect the gear lever linkage and switch multi-plugs. Disconnect the clutch slave cylinder from the bell housing.

22. On automatic transmission, disconnect the gear selector cable from the selector shaft and mounting bracket.

23. Remove the oil cooler and pump. Loosen the drive belt and lay the pump aside in an upright position.

24. Lower the vehicle and position a jack under the transmission.

25. Attached a lifting chain.

26. On a manual transmission vehicle, check that the gear lever is below the console and clear of the transmission tunnel before the engine is removed.

27. Carefully remove the engine and transmission assembly from the vehicle.

To install:

28. Fit new exhaust sealing rings to the front exhaust pipes.

29. Fit the engine and transmission assembly to the engine hoist and carefully lower the engine into the vehicle.

30. Position a jack under the transmission to support the weight.

31. Install tool MS 53B or equivalent. Tighten the hook nut to take the weight of the engine.

32. Loosely secure the right side pipe to the exhaust manifold.

33. Raise the vehicle and support it safely. Tighten the right side pipe and EGR pipe.

34. Lower the vehicle.

35. Install the fan, cowl assembly and pump.

36. Install the radiator and reconnect the oil cooler lines.

37. Raise the vehicle and support it safely.

38. Raise the engine and install the rear mount.

39. Reconnect the driveshaft, speedometer cable and transmission selector cable.

40. Install the heat shields and the intermediate pipes.

41. Lower the vehicle and install the the oil cooler.

42. Remove the engine support.

43. Reconnect the receiver/drier, heater hoses, radiator hoses and air conditioning hoses.

44. Reconnect all vacuum hoses, electrical harness and fuel lines.

45. Install the air cleaner(s) assembly.

46. Recharge the air conditioning system and refill all fluid levels.

47. Reconnect the negative battery cable.

Engine Mounts

Removal and Installation

3.6L ENGINE

Rear

1. Disconnect the negative battery cable.

2. Fit an engine lifting tool, 18G 1465 and MS 53B or equivalent, and support the engine weight by the rear lifting eye.

3. Raise the vehicle and support it safely.

4. Remove the intermediate heat shield.

5. Remove the retaining nut from the rear engine mount.

6. Remove the crash bracket from the transmission.

7. Remove the weight from the rear mounting using a suitable support. Remove the retaining bolts and remove the rear mount assembly.

To install:

8. Fit the replacement rear mount assembly into position and install the retaining bolts. Torque the retaining bolts 15–18 ft. lbs. (20–25 Nm).

9. Remove the support.

10. Install the crash bracket.

11. Install the center retaining nut to the rear engine mount.

12. Install the intermediate heat shield.

13. Lower the vehicle and remove the engine support tools.

14. Reconnect the negative battery cable.

Left or Right Side Mount

1. Disconnect the negative battery cable.

2. Remove the air cleaner assembly.

3. Remove the left or right side engine mount bracket retaining nut.

4. Carefully, raise the engine, making certain the cooling fan does nor hit the fan cowl.

5. Remove the engine mount lower bracket-to-crossmember retaining nuts and bolts.

6. Remove the mount(s) and bracket(s) assembly.

To install:

7. Transfer the spacer and bracket to the new mount(s).

8. Install the bracket and mount assembly to the crossmember.

9. Lower the engine onto the mount(s). Install the retaining bolts.

10. Install the air cleaner assembly.

11. Reconnect the negative battery cable.

5.3L ENGINE

Rear

1. Disconnect the negative battery cable.

2. Fit an engine lifting tool, 18G 1465 and MS 53B or equivalent, and support the engine weight by the rear lifting eye.

3. Raise the vehicle and support it safely.

4. Remove the heat shield(s).

5. Position a suitable support under the rear engine mounting plate, remove the mounting-to-body bolts and lower the support.

6. Remove the engine mount, noting the positions of the spacers and bolts.

To install:

7. Install the stud and seating plate.

8. Install the mount and collision plate.

9. Install the heat shield and exhaust pipes.

10. Lower the vehicle, remove the service tool and reconnect the negative battey cable.

Left or Right Side Mount

1. Disconnect the negative battery cable.

2. Remove the hood stay clamps to allow the hood to open fully.

3. Remove the radiator grille and fan assembly.

4. Remove the fuel filter bracket and position the filter aside.

5. Remove the air cleaner assembly.

6. Remove the engine mount-to-crossmember retaining nuts and washers.

7. Fit a suitable engine lift tool to the engine and raise the engine sufficiently to remove the mount(s).

To install:

8. Install the replacement mount into position and tighten the retaining nuts.

9. Lower the engine and remove the service tool.

10. Refit the fuel filter and fan to the spindle.

11. Refit the air cleaner, hood stay clamps and radiator grille.

12. Reconnect the negative battery cable.

Cylinder Head

Removal and Installation

3.6L ENGINE

1. Depressurize the fuel system.

2. Disconnect the negative battery cable.

3. Remove the intake manifold and the thermostat housing.

4. Remove the distributor cap and rotate the engine until No. 1 cylinder is at TDC.

5. Raise and support the vehicle safely.

6. Remove the front exhaust pipe retaining bracket from the transmission. Remove the front pipe retaining bolts and disconnect the exhaust system.

7. Lower the vehicle.

8. Disconnect the high tension leads from the spark plugs and coil.

9. Remove the valve cover.

10. Remove the upper timing chain tensioner clamp bolt and remove the clamp.

11. Mark the relationship of the rotor arm to the distributor housing, then remove the distributor.

12. Bend the tabs back from the camshafts sprocket retaining bolts. Remove the bolts and washers.

13. Remove the upper timing chain tensioner valve, then relieve the tension by turning clockwise with an Allen key.

14. Remove the tensioner retaining bolts and remove the tensioner.

15. Remove the camshaft sprockets.

16. Position the timing chain between the upper dampers and fit an elastic band to retain the dampers and chain.

17. Remove the retaining bolts from the from the front of the cylinder head.

18. Move the hydraulic pump hose and harness mounting bracket aside.

19. Remove the remaining nuts and bolts and upper static damper support from the cylinder head. Remove the cylinder head.

20. Remove and discard the cylinder head gasket and exhaust manifold sealing rings.

21. Clean and inspect the cylinder head.

To install:

22. Install new exhuast manifold sealing rings and cylinder head gasket into position.

23. Carefully install the cylinder head to the engine. Make certain no hoses or cables are trapped.

24. Refit the upper static damper assembly.

25. Fit the harness clip and hose bracket to the front cylinder head bolts. Install the cylinder head bolts. Tighten and torque to specification, using the following sequence.

26. Check to ensure the camshaft is still on TDC using tool 18G 1433 or equivalent.

27. Raise the timing chain from between the upper dampers and remove the elastic band. Position the chain over the camshafts.

28. Install the sprockets to the chain and camshaft.

29. Move all the chain free-play to the tensioner side. Install tool 18G 1436 or equivalent, to the upper chain, then tighten the tool retaining bolts. Tension the timing chain.

30. Remove the inner sprocket retaining clip and remove the inner sprocket. Align the retaining bolt holes and install the tab washers and retaining bolts. Tighten the camshaft sprocket to camshaft retaining bolts 17-20 ft. lbs. (23–27 Nm). Lock over the tabs and re-install the inner sprocket retaining clip.

31. Repeat Step 30 for the opposite sprocket.

32. Release the tension on the timing chain. Slacken off the chain tensioner tool retaining bolts and remove the tensioner tool.

33. Clean the tensioner assembly and gasket surfaces.

34. Lubricate a new O-ring. Fit the O-ring and housing gasket into position.

35. Install the tensioner assembly to the cylinder head and tighten the tensioner assembly retaining bolt.

36. Using an Allen key, release the tensioner by turning it counter-clockwise.

37. Clean the tensioner valve and fit it with a new O-ring. Lubricate the tensioner valve and install it into place.

38. Install the tensioner clamp and retaining bolt.

39. Fit a new O-ring to the distributor. Lubricate the O-ring and driven gear.

40. Align the rotor arm with the mark made on the distributor housing, then install the distributor.

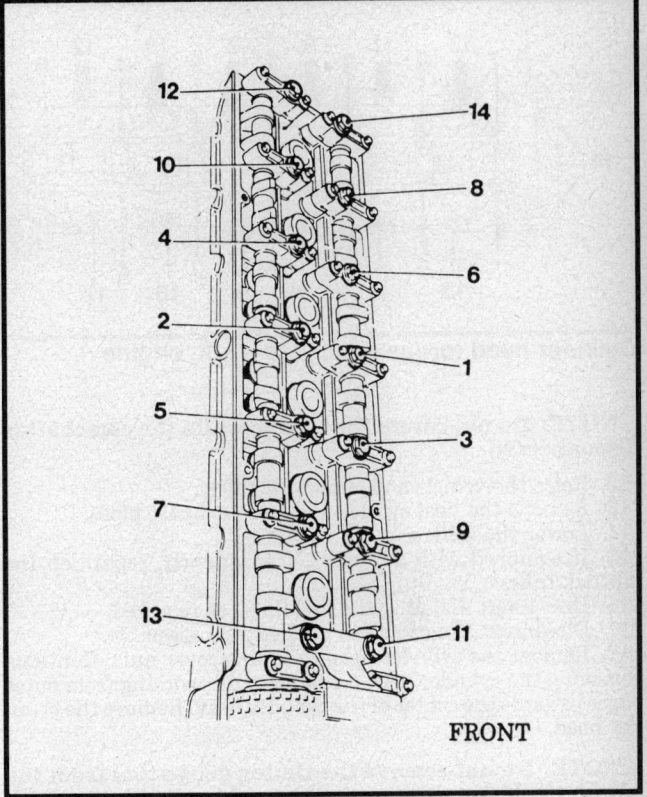

Cylinder head torque sequence—3.6L engine

41. Apply sealant to the half moon seals and fit them to the cylinder head.

42. Install a new valve cover gasket and new plug well seals.

43. Install the valve cover and tighten the retaining bolts.

44. Install the distributor cap. Reconnect the high tension leads to the coil and spark plugs.

45. Install the thermostat housing to the cylinder head using a new gasket.

46. Install the intake manifold.

47. Refill the cooling system and reconnect the negative battery cable.

48. Start the engine and check for leaks.

5.3L ENGINE

1. Depressurize the fuel system.

2. Disconnect the negative battery cable. Drain the cooling system.

3. Remove the valve covers.

4. Remove the air conditioning compressor and position aside, if necessary.

5. Remove the thermostat housing and position aside. Remove the fan assembly.

6. Rotate the engine and install the timing gauge tool tool C 3993 or equivalent to the right side camshaft recess.

7. Remove the rubber grommet from the front of the timing. Release the locking catch on the timing chain tensioner, using tool JD 50 or equivalent.

8. Remove both service tools.

9. Note the 2 uppermost camshaft sprocket retaining bolts. and rotate the engine until the 2 lower camshaft sprocket retaining bolts become accessible. Remove the 2 lower camshaft sprocket retaining bolts.

10. Rotate the engine until the timing gauge can be re-inserted and refit the gauge.

11. Remove the 2 retaining bolts and install the camshaft sprocket retainer tool, JD 40 or equivalent.

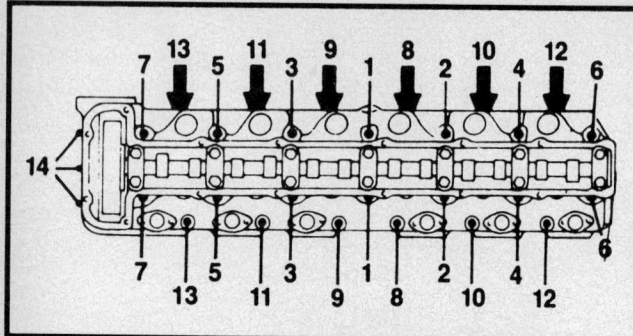

Cylinder head torque sequence—5.3L engine

NOTE: **Do not rotate the engine while the camshaft is disconnected.**

12. Raise the vehicle and support it safely.
13. Remove the heat shields and front exhaust pipes.
14. Lower the vehicle.
15. If equipped with automatic transmission, reposition the dipstick tube.
16. Disconnect and plug the fuel lines, as required.
17. Disconnect the camshaft oil feed pipe assembly.
18. Remove the cylinder head-to-timing cover nuts. Continue removing the cylinder head retaining nuts, working from outer edges towards the center of the cylinder head. Remove the cylinder head.

NOTE: **Do not remove the timing gauge tool from the camshaft. If for any reason the engine must be rotated, install the cylinder liner retaining bracket, service tool JD 41 or equivalent, into position.**

To install:
19. Fit a new head gasket to the cylinder block, with the side marked TOP facing upwards.

NOTE: **Do not use any grease of sealing compound on the cylinder head gasket.**

20. Fit the cylinder head on the cylinder block. Install the cylinder head retaining nuts and torque, in sequence, to the specified value.
21. Remove the camshaft sprocket retainer tool and install the 2 sprocket retaining bolts, using new tab washers. If the camshaft sprocket holes are not in alignment, use the following procedure:
   a. Remove the coupling-to-sprocket retaining circlip.
   b. Disengage the coupling from the splines, at the same time pressed the sprocket on the camshaft shoulder.
   c. Rotate the coupling until alignment is obtained.
22. Remove the timing gauge tool and install the 2 remaining sprocket retaining bolts, using new tab washers. Torque the retaining bolts 17–20 ft. lbs. (23–27 Nm).
23. Install the camshaft oil feed pipe assembly and amplifier unit.
24. Reconnect the dipstick tube and fuel hoses.
25. Raise the vehicle and support it safely.
26. Reconnect the exhaust pipes and heat shields.
27. Lower the vehicle.
28. Install the timing chain tension retainer tool and release the locking catch, allowing the tensioner to expand. Remove the service tool.
29. Adjust the valve clearance.
30. Install the fan unit, making certain the paint marks are aligned.
31. Install the thermostat housing and air valve assembly.
32. Install the valve cover and induction manifolds.

33. Refit the air conditioning compressor, as required. Charge the system, if necessary.
34. Install the air cleaner and reconnect the negative battery cable.
35. Check and adjust the engine oil level and cooling system.
36. Adjust the ignition timing.

Valve Cover

Removal and Installation
3.6 ENGINE
1. Disconnect the negative battery cable.
2. Remove the distributor cap and high tension wires.
3. Remove the breather hose from the valve cover.
4. Remove the valve cover retaining bolts and remove the cover.

To install:
5. Clean the valve cover and mating surfaces, then install a new gasket and half moon seals.
6. Install the valve cover.
7. Reconnect the breather hose.
8. Install the distributor cap and high tension leads.
9. Reconnect the negative battery cable.

5.3L ENGINE
1. Depressurize the fuel system.
2. Disconnect the negative battery cable.
3. ove the air cleaner assembly.
4. Remove the breather hose, fuel pipes and vacuum hoses, as required.
5. Disconnect the throttle cable, kickdown switch, fuel injectors and cold start injector.
6. Remove the induction manifold stud spacers and carefully remove the manifold assembly from the cylinder head. Fit plugs to the inlet ports.
7. Reposition the electrical harness.
8. Disconnect the cross pipe hose from the auxiliary air valve. Disconnect the air rail, as required.
9. Remove the valve cover retaining bolts and remove the cover.
To install:
10. Apply sealant to the radial edge of the new half moon seal and install the valve cover, using a new gasket.
11. Reconnect the cross pipe hose to the auxiliary air valve and air rail.
12. Reconnect the electrical harness.
13. Install the induction manifold, using a new gasket. Install the stud spacers.
14. Reconnect the throttle cable, kickdown switch, fuel injectors and cold start injector.
15. Install the breather hose, fuel pipes and vacuum hoses, as required.

Valve Lash

Adjustment
3.6L ENGINE
1. Disconnect the negative battery cable.
2. Remove the distributor cap and high tension leads.
3. Remove the valve cover.
4. Measure the valve clearance between the heel of the camshaft and the cam follower, turning the engine over as necessary to measure all the clearance.
5. Make a note of the actual clearances.
6. If any of the clearances are incorrect, remove the camshaft caps, camshaft(s) and followers.
7. Remove all the shims requiring adjustment. Check the size of the existing shims with a micrometer and note the readings.

EXCESSIVE CLEARANCE	INCHES
Size of existing shim	0.100
Plus the actual clearance noted	0.019
	0.119
Less the specified valve clearance	0.013
= required shim size	0.106
INSUFFICIENT CLEARANCE	INCHES
Size of existing shim	0.107
Plus the actual clearance noted	0.010
	0.117
Less the specified valve clearance	0.013
= required shim size	0.104

Calculating valve clearance—3.6L and 5.3L engines

8. Calculate the size of the shim required, as follow:
Shims available sizes are as follow:

A—0.085
B—0.086
C—0.087
D—0.088
E—0.089
F—0.090
G—0.091
H—0.092
I—0.093
J—0.094
K—0.095
L—0.096
M—0.097
N—0.098
O—0.099
P—0.100
Q—0.101
R—0.102
S—0.103
T—0.104
U—0.105
V—0.106
W—0.107
X—0.108
X—0.109
X—0.110

9. After refitting the correct shim(s), install the cam followers, camshaft(s) and camshaft caps.
10. Recheck the valve clearances.

5.3L ENGINE

1. Disconnect the negative battery cable.
2. Remove the valve cover.
3. Measure the valve clearance between the heel of the camshaft and the cam follower, turning the engine over as necessary to measure all the clearance. Make a note of the actual clearances.
4. If any of the clearances are incorrect, remove the rubber grommet from the front of the timing cover.
5. Remove the left side camshaft, cam followers and shims.

Check the size of each shim with a micrometer and note the reading.
6. Calculate the size of the shim required. When the correct shim sizes have been obtained, refit the shims and cam followers to the carrier.
Shims available sizes are as follow:

A—0.085
B—0.086
C—0.087
D—0.088
E—0.089
F—0.090
G—0.091
H—0.092
I—0.093
J—0.094
K—0.095
L—0.096
M—0.097
N—0.098
O—0.099
P—0.100
Q—0.101
R—0.102
S—0.103
T—0.104
U—0.105
V—0.106
W—0.107
X—0.108
X—0.109
X—0.110

7. Install the camshaft using the camshaft timing tool. Install the camshaft bearing caps.
8. Recheck the valve clearances. Readjust, if necessary.
9. With the timing gauge in position, refit the camshaft sprocket.
10. Repeat the valve clearance adjustment procedure for the right side camshaft.
11. Refit service tool, JD 50 or equivalent, and release the locking catch, allowing the tensioner to expand.
12. Install the rubber grommet to the front to the timing cover and install the valve cover.
13. Reconnect the negative battery cable.

Intake Manifold

Removal and Installation

3.6 ENGINE

1. Depressurize the fuel system.
2. Disconnect the negative battery cable. Remove the air cleaner assembly and drain the cooling system.
3. Disconnect the hoses at intake elbow hose to throttle housing, breather hose from intake elbow and intake elbow hose from the throttle orifice control housing.
4. Remove the intake manifold-to-distick tube retaining bolt.
5. Remove the oil filler tube-to-upper mounting bracket retaining bolt. Separate the oil filler tube from the lower housing.
6. Remove the breather hose from the valve cover.
7. Disconnect the inlet heater hose from the cylinder head.
8. Remove the intake manifold retaining nuts and bolts.

NOTE: One of the intake manifold retaining bolt is located behind the oil filler tube.

9. Remove the engine ground strap and oil filler tube upper mounting bracket.
10. Carefully lift the intake manifold from the cylinder head. Remove the gasket and discard.
11. Clean the intake manifold and cylinder head mating surfaces.

To install:

12. Fit a new intake manifold gasket into position and a new seal to the oil filler tube housing.

13. Position the intake manifold over the studs and tighten the hidden bolt behind the oil filler tube.

14. Install the filer tube and upper mounting bracket.

15. Fit the engine wiring harness channel mounting brackets to the intake manifold studs and the starter solenoid harness bracket to the rear bolt hole.

16. Install and tighten the intake manifold bolts and nuts to specification.

17. Reconnect the heater hose to the cylinder head and breather hose to the valve cover.

18. Install the oil filler tube upper mounting bracket and dipstick tube mounting bracket retaining bolts.

19. Reconnect the throttle housing hose to the intake elbow, breather hose to the breather pipe and air valve hose to the intake elbow.

20. Raise the vehicle and support it safely.

21. Reconnect the exhaust system to the exhaust manifold and exhaust pipe mounting bracket to the transmission.

22. Lower the vehicle.

23. Install the air cleaner assembly.

24. Fill the cooling system and reconnect the negative battery cable.

25. Start the engine and check for leaks.

Exhaust Manifold

Removal and Installation

3.6 ENGINE

1. Disconnect the negative battery cable.
2. Raise and support the vehicle safely.
3. Remove the front pipe-to-bell housing mounting bracket retaining nuts and bolts. Remove the bracket.
4. Remove the front pipe-to-manifold retaining nuts and lower the exhaust system.
5. Lower the vehicle, then remove the heat shield retaining bolts and remove the heat shield.
6. Remove the manifold-to-cylinder head retaining nuts and remove the exhaust manifold assembly.
7. Discard the exhaust manifold gasket and front pipe sealing rings.

To install:

8. Fit the exhaust manifold with a new gasket, then install the manifold to the cylinder head.
9. Install the retaining nuts and tighten to specification.
10. Install the heat shield and retaining bolts. Torque to 17–20 ft. lbs. (23–27 Nm).
11. Raise and support the vehicle safely.
12. Fit the front pipe with new sealing rings and lift into position. Install the retaining nuts. Torque to 22–26 (30–35Nm).
13. Install the front pipe-to-bell housing mounting bracket retaining nuts and bolts.
14. Lower the vehicle and reconnect the negative battery cable.

Timing Chain Front Cover

Removal and Installation

3.6L ENGINE

1. Depressurize the fuel system.
2. Disconnect the negative battery cable.
3. Drain the radiator and engine oil.
4. Remove the air cleaner assembly.
5. Remove the cylinder head.
6. Remove the sump-to-timing cover retaining bolts.
7. Disconnect the harness connections and top hose from the thermostat housing.

8. Remove the water pump hoses and expansion hoses from the thermostat housing.

9. Remove the fan assembly and power steering pump from the timing cover.

10. Remove the pump drive plastic coupling.

11. Remove the drive plate center retaining bolt. Remove the drive plate from the shaft, using a prybar.

12. Remove the distributor and alternator drive belt.

13. Install the front pulley lock tool 18G 1437 or equivalent to the crankshaft damper. Loosen the crankshaft damper retaining bolt and remove the service tool.

14. Install the crankshaft damper removal tool 18G 1436 or equivalent and remove the damper.

15. Remove the crankshaft sensor retaining bolts and remove the sensor. Position the sensor aside.

16. Remove the expansion tank hose, bottom hose and heater return hose from the water pump.

17. Remove the water pump assembly from the timing cover.

18. Remove the alternator link arm assembly.

19. Remove the timing cover retaining bolts and timing pointer. Remove the timing cover assembly.

20. Remove the damper woodruff key and oil seal spacer form the crankshaft.

21. Remove the old oil seal from the cover. Clean all gasket surfaces, oil seal spacer and pointer.

To install:

22. Install a new oil seal into the timing cover using tool JD 129 or equivalent and a suitable press. Lubricate the oil seal and bearing surface.

23. Apply sealant Hylosil 102 or equivalent, to the gasket faces and the outer edge of the sump face.

24. Install the timing cover to the cylinder block. Tighten the retaining bolts to 17–20 ft. lbs. (23–27 Nm), but do not tighten the timing pointer bolt at this time.

25. Install the oil seal spacer to the crankshaft and into the oil seal.

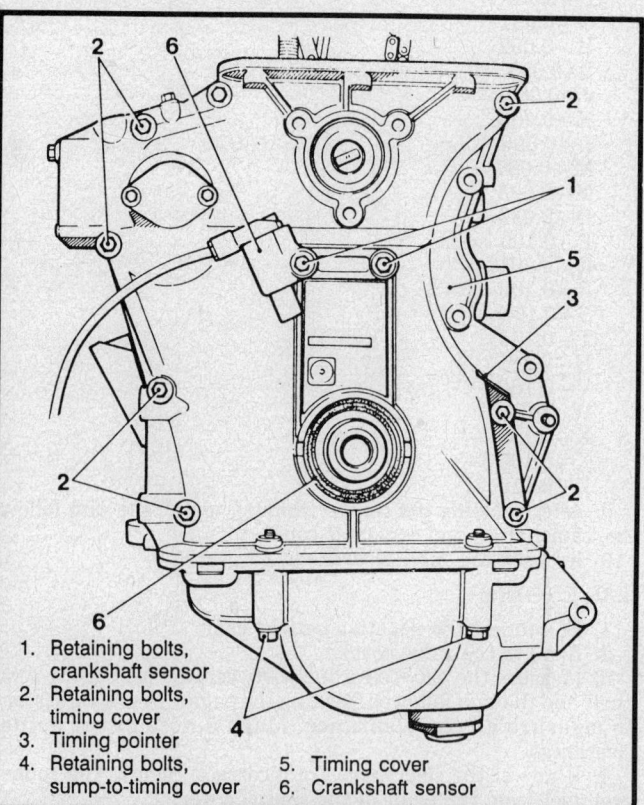

1. Retaining bolts, crankshaft sensor
2. Retaining bolts, timing cover
3. Timing pointer
4. Retaining bolts, sump-to-timing cover
5. Timing cover
6. Crankshaft sensor

Timing cover exploded view—3.6L engine

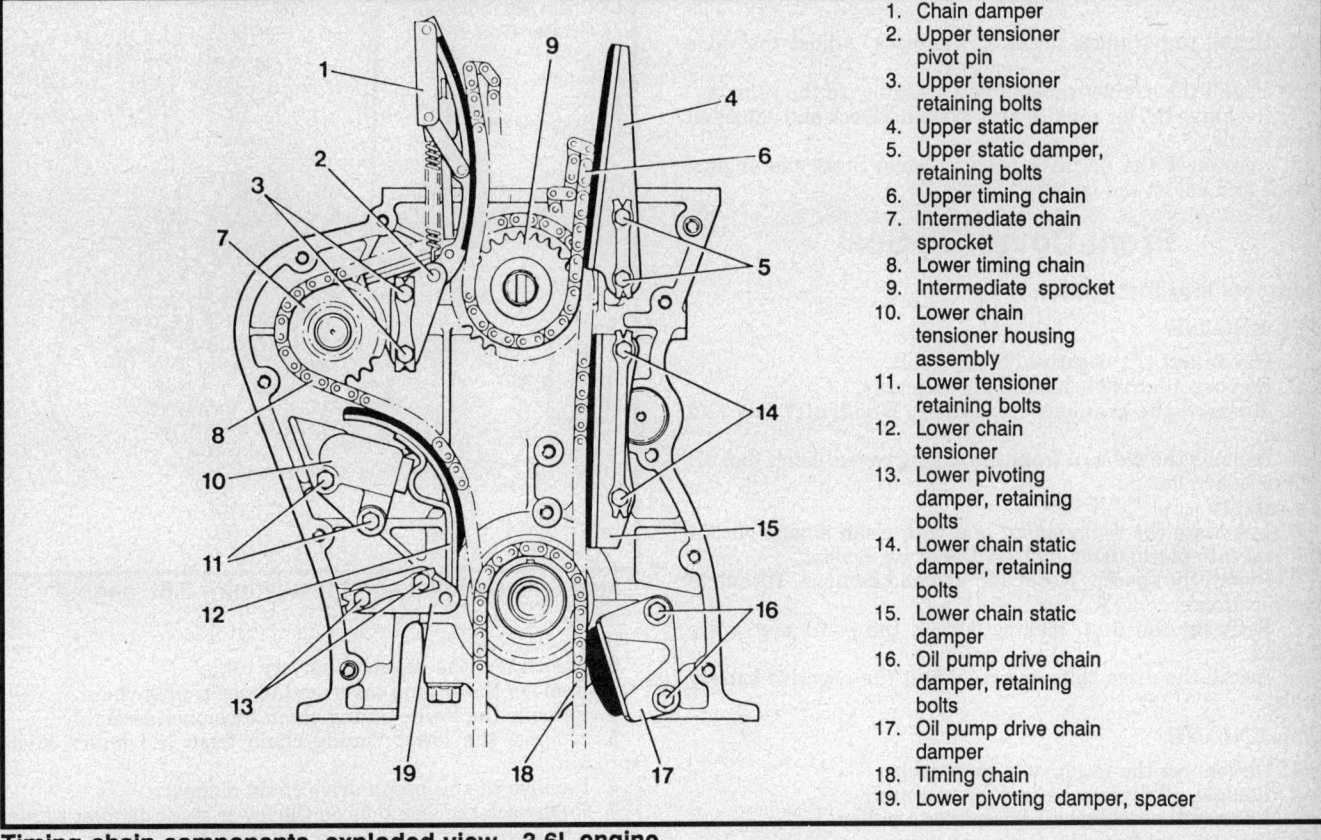

1. Chain damper
2. Upper tensioner pivot pin
3. Upper tensioner retaining bolts
4. Upper static damper
5. Upper static damper, retaining bolts
6. Upper timing chain
7. Intermediate chain sprocket
8. Lower timing chain
9. Intermediate sprocket
10. Lower chain tensioner housing assembly
11. Lower tensioner retaining bolts
12. Lower chain tensioner
13. Lower pivoting damper, retaining bolts
14. Lower chain static damper, retaining bolts
15. Lower chain static damper
16. Oil pump drive chain damper, retaining bolts
17. Oil pump drive chain damper
18. Timing chain
19. Lower pivoting damper, spacer

Timing chain components, exploded view—3.6L engine

26. Secure the Woodruff® key into the crankshaft and install the damper to the crankshaft. Torque to specification.
27. Align the timing pointer to TDC and tighten the pointer retaining bolt.
28. Install the damper retaining bolt.
29. Install the alternator link arm assembly, but do not tighten the trunnion bolt at this time.
30. Install the water pump. Tighten the retaining bolts to 17-20 ft. lbs. (23–27 Nm).
31. Reconnect the expansion tank hose, bottom hose and heater return hose to the water pump.
32. Install the crankshaft sensor to the timing cover. Secure the harness with the P-clip.
33. Install and adjust the alternator drive belt, then tighten the trunnion bolt 17-20 ft. lbs. (23–27 Nm).
34. Install the crankshaft pulley and balance weights. Install the retaining bolt and tighten to 150 ft. lbs. (203.5 Nm).
35. Clean the power steering pump drive coupling and mating faces, then install the driveplate to the shaft. Apply locite to the drive plate retaining bolts, then install.
36. Install and align the coupling to the pump. Install the pump to the driveshaft.
37. Fit a new O-ring to the distributor, then lubricate the O-ring and driven gear. Install the distributor assembly being certain the rotor arm is aligned to the proper position.
38. Install the fan unit assembly, being certain the paint spots are align together.
39. Install the water pump hose, expansion and top hose to the thermostat housing. Reconnect the thermostat housing sensor connections.
40. Install the cylinder head assembly.
41. Install the air cleaner assembly.
42. Fill the engine crankcase and cooling system.

43. Reconnect the negative battery cable, start the engine and check for leaks.

5.3L ENGINE

1. Depressurize the fuel system and discharge the air conditioning system, cap all openings.
2. Disconnect the negative battery cable.
3. Remove the engine/transmission assembly from the vehicle and fit it to suitable stand.
4. Remove the cylinder heads from the cylinder block.

NOTE: Immediately after the cylinder heads has been removed, the cylinder liner brackets tool JD 41 or equivalent must be fitted to the engine. Failure to do so will result in the Hylomar seal being broken, causing water leakage into the sump.

5. Drain the engine oil and remove the oil sump.
6. Remove the suction elbow and sandwich plate, noting the different stud lengths.
7. Remove the alternator, power steering pump, air pump, air conditining compressor and water pump.
8. Remove the crankshaft pulley and Woodruff® key.
9. Remove the timing cover retaining bolts, noting the different bolts lengths and location. Remove the timing cover assembly.
To install:
10. Dip the new oil seal in clean engine oil and press the seal into the timing cover.
11. Install the timing cover using a new gasket.
12. Install the crankshaft pulley and Woodruff® key.
13. Install the alternator, power steering pump, air pump, air conditining compressor and water pump.

14. Refit the sandwich plate assembly and install the sump pan.

15. Install the cylinder heads to the block. Adjust the valve clearance.

16. Install the engine/transmission assembly to the vehicle.

17. Recharge the air conditioning system. Check and adjust all fluid levels.

18. Reconnect the negative battery cable. Start the engine. Check and adjust the ignition timing.

Front Cover Oil Seal

Removal and Installation

3.6L ENGINE

1. Disconnect the negative battery cable.
2. Remove all drive belts and fan assembly.
3. Remove the crankshaft damper, Woodruff® key and spacer.
4. Remove the old seal from the timing cover, using tool JD 128 or equivalent.

To install:

5. Lubricate the replacement seal with clean engine oil. Fit the seal into place, using tool JD 129 or equivalent.
6. Install the spacer, Woodruff® key and damper. Torque to specification.
7. Refit the fan unit, making certain the paint marks are aligned.
8. Install the drive belts and reconnect the negative battery cable.

5.3L ENGINE

1. Disconnect the negative battery cable.
2. Remove all drive belts and fan assembly.
3. Remove the crankshaft damper and pulley.
4. Pry the seal from the timing cover.
5. Withdraw the crankshaft spacer.
6. Clean the seal recess.

To install:

7. Lubricate the replacement seal with clean engine oil.
8. Position the seal squarely in the recess and tap gently with a rubber mallet.
9. Install the crankshaft damper and pulley. Torque to specification.
10. Refit the fan unit, making certain the paint marks are aligned.
11. Install the drive belts and reconnect the negative battery cable.

Timing Chain and Sprocket

Removal and Installation

3.6 ENGINE

Upper

1. Depressurize the fuel system.
2. Disconnect the negative battery cable.
3. Remove the timing cover.
4. Remove the upper tensioner retaining bolts and remove the tensioner.
5. Remove the upper timing chain.

To install:

6. Lubricate and install the upper timing chain to the intermediate sprocket.
7. Position the timing chain between the upper dampers and fit an elastic band to retain the dampers and chain.
8. Install the timing cover.
9. Reconnect the negative battery cable.

Lower

1. Depressurize the fuel system.

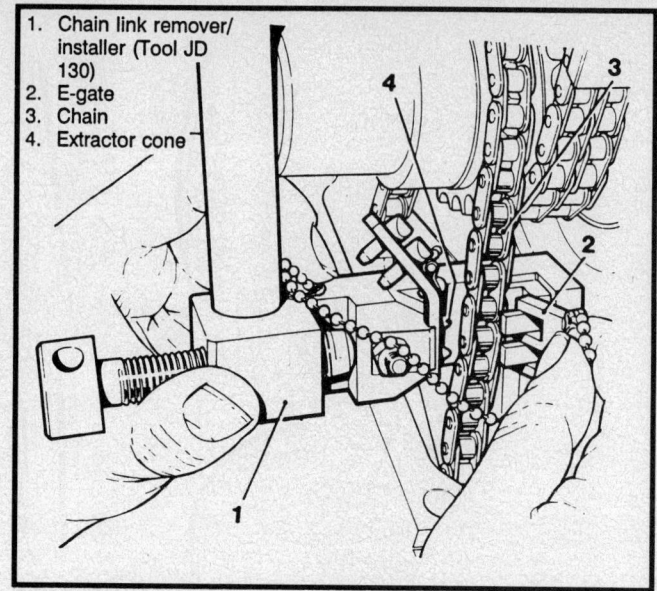

1. Chain link remover/installer (Tool JD 130)
2. E-gate
3. Chain
4. Extractor cone

Chain link, removal and installation—3.6L engine

2. Disconnect the negative battery cable.
3. Remove the timing cover and upper timing chain.
4. Remove the lower timing chain tensioner assembly.
5. Remove the lower timing chain from the intermediate sprocket.
6. Remove the oil pump drive chain damper.
7. Push back the lock tabs on the lower static damper retaining bolts. Remove the retaining bolts and the damper.
8. Locate the master link on the chain. Rotate the engine, is necessary.
9. Install the chain link remover/installer, tool JD 130 or equivalent, to the master link, then position the E gate to the tool and seat behind the chain.
10. Tighten the tool handle making certain the extractor cones line up with the link pins and extract the link.
11. Carefully slacken the tool handle and remove the oil pump chain. Make certain that no components fall into the sump.
12. Remove the lower timing chain.

To install:

13. Lubricate and install the lower timing chain over the auxiliary drive shaft and crankshaft sprocket.
14. Lubricate and install a new oil pump drive chain over the oil pump and crank sprocket. Make certain the drive chain ends are on the damper side of the sprocket.

NOTE: Never reuse the old oil pump drive chain.

15. Install a new link to the drive chain and align a link plate to the removal/installation tool. Make certain the link and tool clamp holes are aligned.
16. Install the E gate to the tool and chain link. Make certain the chain is center to the tool. Tighten the center bolt on the tool, fully seating the plate on the link.
17. Loosen the tool center bolt.
18. Re-position the tool and locate the link riveting head on the clamp. Tighten the center bolt on the tool finger-tight, then make an additional 1/2–3/4 turn.
19. Remove the tool.
20. Rotate the engine and set No. 1 piston on TDC. Mount a magnetic dial indicator with the pointer resting on the top of the piston.
21. Install the lower static damper and tighten the retaining bolts 17–20 ft. lbs. (23–27 Nm). Lock the tab washers over the retaining bolts.

22. Install the oil pump chain damper into position, but do not tighten the retaining bolts at this time.

23. Push the damper, using hand pressure, to remove any slack from the chain. Tighten the damper retaining bolts.

24. Lubricate the intermediate sprocket bearing. Fit the sprocket to the chain and install the sprocket into the bearing.

25. Install the lower tensioner assembly.

26. Lubricate the upper chain and fit it on the intermediate sprocket.

27. Install the upper static damper and upper tensioner assembly.

28. Install the timing cover.

29. Refill the cooling system and engine crankcase.

30. Reconnect the negative battery cable.

5.3L ENGINE

1. Disconnect the negative battery cable.

2. Remove the timing cover.

3. Fit the sprocket retainer tool, JD 39 or equivalent, to the jackshaft.

4. Disconnect the timing chain form the camshaft and jackshaft sprockets.

5. Remove the crankshaft sprocket and timing chain.

NOTE: Do not rotate the engine while the chain/sprocket assembly are disconnected.

To install:

6. Fit the replacement chain to the crankshaft sprocket.

7. Install the sprocket/chain assembly to the camshaft and jackshaft sprockets.

8. Remove the sprocket retainer tool and install the timing cover.

9. Reconnect the negative battery cable.

Intermediate Sprocket and Crankshaft Timing Sprocket

Removal and Installation

3.6L ENGINE

1. Depressurize the fuel system.

2. Disconnect the negative battery cable.

3. Remove the timing cover, upper timing chain and the oil pump drive chain damper.

4. Remove the lower timing chain assembly from the intermediate sprocket.

5. Remove the intermediate sprocket.

6. Remove the crankshaft timing gear, using a suitable drift.

To install:

7. Install the replacement timing gear to the crankshaft.

8. Install the crankshaft pulley retaining bolt.

9. Using a straight edge, check the alignment of the oil pump drive sprocket and the crankshaft sprocket.

10. If the alignment is not correct, use the following procedure:

   a. Remove the oil pump drive sprocket retaining bolt. Rotate the sprocket and remove the remaining bolt.

   b. Remove the oil pump drive sprocket and shims. Calculate the thickness of the shim(s) which would be required for correct alignment.

   c. Install a dummy stud to the oil pump drive flange. Align and install the shim(s), flange, sprocket, tab washer and 1 retaining bolt. Tighten the retaining bolt, but do not lock over the tab washer at this time.

NOTE: Never reuse the old tab washers. Always use new one.

   d. Install and tighten the second retaining bolt, then lock over both tab washers.

   e. Remove the dummy stud and install the remaining bolt. Lock over the tab washer.

   f. Recheck the alignment of the oil pump drive sprocket and the crankshaft sprocket. Readjust, if necessary.

11. Install the intermediate sprocket.

12. Install the lower timing chain assembly.

13. Install the oil pump drive chain and damper.

NOTE: Never reuse the old oil pump drive chain.

14. Install the upper timing chain and the timing cover.

15. Reconnect the negative battery cable.

Camshafts

Removal and Installation

3.6L ENGINE

1. Depressurize the fuel system.

2. Disconnect the negative battery cable and drain the cooling system.

3. Remove the distributor cap and high tension wires.

4. Remove the breather hose from the valve cover and remove the valve cover.

5. Using tool 18G 1433 or equivalent, rotate the engine and set No. 1 cylinder at TDC.

6. Remove the distributor and block off the opening.

7. Push back the lock tabs from the camshaft sprocket retaining bolts and loosen the bolts.

8. Remove the upper chain tensioner valve clamp retaining bolt, clamp and valve.

9. Turn the tensioner clockwise, using a 3mm Allen key, until it engages the park position.

10. Remove the tensioner housing retaining bolt and remove the tensioner assembly.

11. Remove the camshaft sprocket retaining bolt and tab washers, then remove the sprockets.

12. From the left side camshaft, remove the cylinder head bolt, cap retaining bolts and cap from No. 2 cap.

13. Install spacer tool 18G 1435 or equivalent to the head and re-install the cylinder head bolt at No. 2 cap. Repeat this procedure for No. 3, 4, 5 and 6 caps of the left side camshaft.

14. Alternately remove the cylinder head bolts from No. 7 and No. 1 caps of the left side camshaft until the camshaft is free.

15. Remove the camshaft from the cylinder head and install

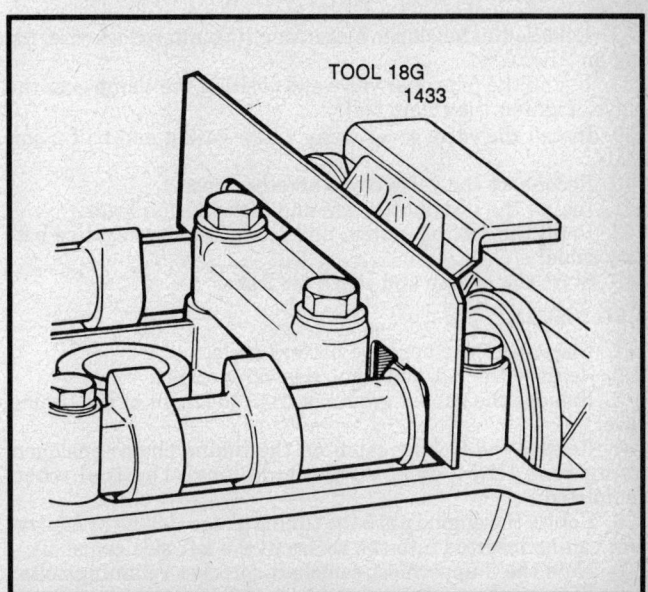

Checking camshafts TDC alignment—3.6L engine

spacer tool 18G 1435 or equivalent to the head. Re-install the cylinder head bolt at No. 7 cap.

16. If the right side camshaft is to be removed, repeat Steps 11–14.

To install:

17. Lubricate the new camshaft and position it at TDC on the cylinder head.

18. Lubricate No. 1 and No. 7 caps. Install No. 1 cap assembly. Do not tighten the retaining bolt.

19. Remove the No. 7 cap cylinder head retaining bolt and spacer, then install the No. 7 cap assembly. Do not tighten the retaining bolt.

20. Alternately tighten the No. 1 and No. 7 retaining bolts.

NOTE: Tighten the camshaft cap to cylinder head bolts 17-20 ft. lbs. (23–27 Nm).

21. Remove the No. 4 cap cylinder head retaining bolt and spacer. Lubricate and install the No. 4 cap assembly. Tighten the retaining bolt.

22. Install and tighten No. 4 cap cylinder head bolt.

23. Repeat Steps 20 and 21 for No. 2, 3, 5 and 6 of the left side camshaft.

24. Set the left side camshaft at TDC.

25. If necessary, repeat Steps 16–23 for the right side camshaft.

26. Install and align the camshaft sprockets to the chain and the camshaft. Move all slack in the chain to the tensioner side.

27. Install the chain tensioner tool, 18G 1436 or equivalent, and tension the cam chain.

28. Remove the inner sprocket retaining clip and inner sprocket, then align the retaining bolt holes.

29. Install the tab washers and retaining bolts. Tighten the camshaft sprocket to camshaft retaining bolts 17-20 ft. lbs. (23–27 Nm). Lock over the tabs.

30. Reinstall the inner sprocket retaining clip.

31. Repeat Steps 27–29 for the opposite sprocket.

32. Check and adjust the valve clearances.

33. Slacken off the chain tensioner tool retaining bolts and remove the tensioner tool.

34. Clean the tensioner assembly and gasket surfaces, then lubricate and install a new O-ring.

35. Install the tensioner assembly to the cylinder head. Tighten the tensioner assembly retaining bolt, but do not tighten the valve clamp bolt.

36. Clean the tensioner valve and fit a new O-ring on the valve. Lubricate the valve.

37. Release the tensioner by turning it counter-clockwise, using an Allen key.

38. Install the tensioner valve and position the clamp over the valve. Tighten the clamp bolt.

39. Install the valve cover using a new gasket and half moon seals.

40. Reconnect the valve cover breather hose.

41. Install the distributor, cap and high tension leads.

42. Refill the cooling system and reconnect the negative battery cable.

43. Start the engine and check for leaks.

5.3L ENGINE

1. Disconnect the negative battery cable.

2. Remove the left and right side valve covers.

3. Remove the rubber grommet from the front of the timing cover.

4. Release the locking catch on the timing chain tensioner, using tool JD 50 or equivalent. Remove the tool when completed.

5. Rotate the engine until the timing gauge C 3993 or equivalent can be inserted into the recess in the left side camshaft.

6. Note the 2 uppermost camshaft sprocket retaining bolts.

7. Remove the timing gauge tool and rotate the engine until the 2 lower camshaft sprocket retaining bolts is accessible.

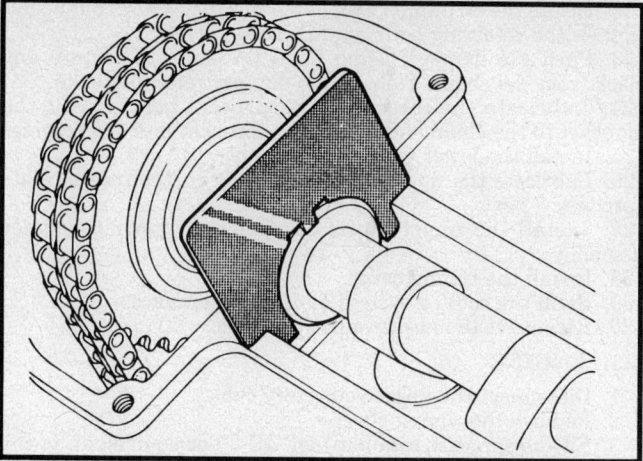
Checking camshafts TDC alignment—5.3L engine

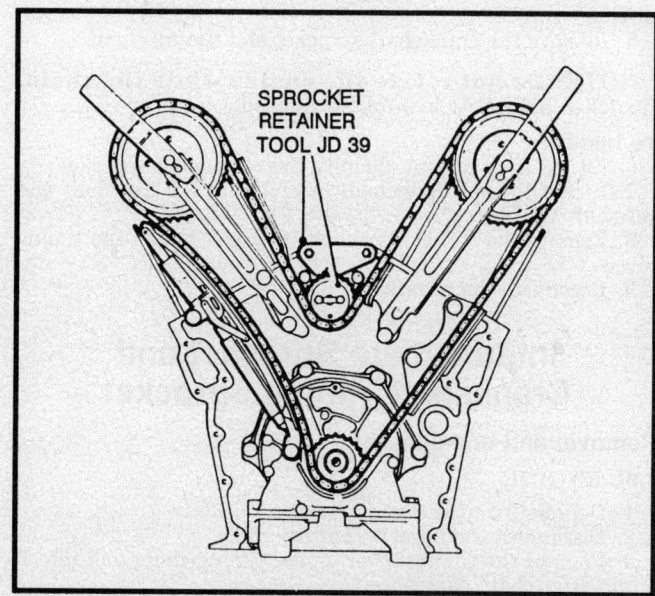
Positioning the sprocket retainer tool—5.3L engine

8. Remove the 2 retaining bolts.

9. Rotate the engine until the timing gauge can be re-inserted and refit the gauge.

10. Remove the remaining 2 camshaft sprocket retaining bolts and fit the sprocket retainer tool, JD 40 or equivalent.

NOTE: Do not rotate the engine while the camshaft is disconnected.

11. Gradually, loosen each camshaft cap retaining nut until the all tension is relieved from the valve springs.

12. Remove the camshaft caps, noting the position of each.

13. Remove the left side camshaft.

To install:

14. Install the camshaft using the camshaft timing tool.

15. Install the camshaft bearing caps. Progressively tighten the retaining nuts 8–10 ft. lbs. (11–13.5 Nm), working from the center outwards.

16. With the timing gauge in position, refit the camshaft sprocket.

17. Refit service tool, JD 50 or equivalent, and release the locking catch, allowing the tensioner to expand.

18. Install the rubber grommet to the front to the timing cover and install the valve cover.

19. Check and adjust the valve clearance.
20. Install the valve cover and reconnect the negative battery cable.

Auxiliary Drive Shaft

Removal and Installation

3.6L ENGINE

1. Disconnect the negative battery cable.
2. Remove the cylinder head assembly.
3. Remove the timing cover.
4. Remove the pulley Woodruff® key and remove the oil seal spacer from the crankshaft.
5. Remove the elastic band from the upper dampers, then push back the lock tabs on the tensioner retaining bolts.
6. Remove the upper tensioner retaining bolts and washers and tensioner pivot pin, then remove the upper tensioner assembly and chain damper.
7. Push back the lock tabs on the upper static damper retaining bolts, then remove the bolts, washers, upper damper and upper timing chain.
8. Remove the lower chain tensioner retaining bolts, then remove the lower tensioner assembly.
9. Remove the intermediate sprocket and chain from the block.
10. Remove the power steering pump housing-to-auxiliary shaft housing retaining bolts.
11. Remove the power steering pump drive coupling.
12. Remove the auxiliary shaft rear oil seal, using tool JD 118 ,18G 1468 or equivalent.
13. Remove the driveshaft retaining circlip using the appropriate tool.
14. Remove the timing chain from the intermediate sprocket, then remove the shaft and retrieve the thrust washer.

To install:

15. Install a new gasket on the auxiliary shaft housing, then install the retaining bolt.
16. Lubricate the shaft and install it into the housing, engaging the chain with the gears as it is fitted.
17. Lubricate and install the thrust washer. Secure it using the circlip.
18. Lubricate and install the rear oil seal, using tool 18G 1469 or equivalent. Do not remove the plastic seal insert prior to fitting the seal.
19. Install the drive coupling to the power steering pump.
20. Align the pump shaft with the auxiliary shaft and connect the pump shaft to the driveshaft.
21. Install the pump housing retaining bolts.
22. Lubricate the intermediate sprocket bearing and fit the chain to the sprocket, then install the assembly into the bearing.
23. Assembly the plunger, spring and base to the guide. Lubricate the assembly and install it into the tensioner housing.
24. Reposition the chain damper to provide access, but be certain no loose links are left below the crankshaft, then install tensioner assembly into position with the guide facing downwards.
25. Install the tensioner retaining bolt finger-tight, then push the guide into the housing to release the base and align with the damper.
26. Align the damper with the lower bolt hole, then install the lower tensioner retaining bolt. Tighten the lower and upper tensioner retaining bolts (11).
27. Fill the tensioner oil reservoir with oil and work the tensioner allowing it to prime. Refill and continue to work the tensioner until the tensioner is fully primed.
28. Lubricate the upper timing chain and install it to the intermediate sprocket.
29. Install the upper static damper, washer and retaining bolt. Lock the tabs over the washers.

30. Install a new tensioner to the upper support, then install the pivot pin.
31. Install the tensioner retaining bolt and washer.
32. Align the damper to the tensioner and install the damper/tensioner assembly to the engine. Be certain that the damper does not interfere with the distributor drive shaft sprocket. Then, tighten the retaining bolts and lock the tab over the washers.
33. Reposition the upper tensioner and use an elastic band to secure the upper dampers.
34. Remove and install a new oil seal into the timing cover, using tool JD 129 or equivalent, and a press.
35. Apply Hylosil 102 or equivalent to the timing cover gasket faces and the outer edge of the sump face.
36. Lubricate the oil seal and bearing surfaces, then install the timing cover assembly to the cylinder block.
37. Install the cylinder head assembly.
38. Refill the cooling system and engine crank case.
39. Reconnect the negative battery cable.

Oil Pump Drive Chain Damper

Removal and Installation

3.6L ENGINE

1. Disconnect the negative battery cable.
2. Remove the timing cover.
3. Remove the drive chain damper retaining bolts and remove the damper.

To install:

4. Install the new damper, but do not tighten the retaining bolts at this time.
5. Push the damper towards the center of the engine, using hand pressure only. This will take any slack out of the chain. Tighten the damper retaining bolts.
6. Install the timing cover.
7. Reconnect the negative battery cable.

Timing Chain Tensioner

Removal and Installation

3.6L ENGINE

Lower

1. Disconnect the negative battery cable.
2. Remove the timing cover.
3. Remove the lower timing chain tensioner retaining bolts and remove the tensioner assembly.

To install:

4. Assemble the plunger, spring and base to the guide. Lubricate the assembly.
5. Assemble the guide, valve and O-ring to the tensioner housing.
6. Move the chain damper to provide for access, but be certain no loose links are left below the crankshaft.
7. Install the tensioner assembly with the guide facing downwards.
8. Install the tensioner upper retaining bolt, but do not tighten at this time.
9. Push the guide into the housing to release the base and align with the damper.
10. Align the damper with the lower bolt hose, then install the lower tensioner retaining bolt. Tighten both bolts 17-20 ft. lbs. (23–27 Nm).
11. Fill the tensioner oil reservoir with oil and be certain that the tensioner is fully primed.
12. Install the timing cover.
13. Reconnect the negative battery cable.

Upper

1. Depressurize the fuel system.
2. Disconnect the negative battery cable.
3. Remove the distributor cap, high tension wires and amplifier block connector.
4. Mark the position of the rotor arm in relationship to the distributor housing. Remove the distributor and block off the opening.
5. Remove the upper chain tensioner valve.
6. Turn the tensioner clockwise, using a 3mm Allen key, to release the tension.
7. Remove the tensioner housing retaining bolt and remove the tensioner assembly.
8. Remove the gasket and O-ring from the tensioner assembly.
9. Remove the guide, plunger, spring and base from the housing as an assembly.
10. Release the spring tension, then remove the base, spring and plunger from the guide. Remove the O-ring from the valve.

To install:
11. Lubricate the plunger, spring and base, then assemble them the guide. Make certain the base is seated correctly.
12. Lubricate the guide and fit it into the housing.
13. Fit a new gasket and O-ring to the housing. Install the assembly into the cylinder head damper, then install the retaining bolt.
14. Clean the tensioner valve and fit it with a new O-ring.
15. Turn the tensioner counter-clockwise, using a 3mm Allen key. Lubricate and install the valve.
16. Install the clamp over the valve and tighten the retaining bolt.
17. Install a new O-ring to the distributor. Lubricate the O-ring and driven gear.
18. Install the distributor making certain the rotor is aligned with the mark made on the housing.
19. Install the distributor cap and high tension cables.
20. Reconnect the amplifier block connector and vacuum hoses, as necessary.
21. Reconnect the negative battery cable.
22. Start engine, then check and adjust the timing.

Crankshaft

Removal and Installation

3.6L ENGINE

1. Disconnect the negative battery cable and drain the cooling system.
2. Remove the engine/transmission assembly from the vehicle.
3. Fit the engine to a stand and separate the transmission from the engine.
4. Remove the cylinder head.
5. Hold the crankshaft damper, using tool 18G 1437 or equivalent, and remove the damper retaining bolt.
6. Remove the crankshaft damper, using tool 18G 1436 or equivalent.
7. Remove the sump retaining bolts and remove the sump.
8. Remove the oil transfer housing.
9. Remove the oil pump pick-up pipe assembly, crankshaft windage trays and the oil pump.
10. Remove the engine timing cover assembly.
11. Loosen the oil pump drive chain damper retaining bolts and position the damper away from the chain.
12. Remove the oil pump drive chain, elastic band from the upper dampers and the upper timing chain.
13. Remove the lower tensioner bolts and remove the tensioner.
14. Push the lock tabs from the lower chain fixed damper retaining bolt. Remove the bolt, damper and tab washer. Repeat

this procedure for the remaining fixed and pivot dampers, then remove the lower chain and intermediate sprocket.
15. Remove the seal/crankshaft damper spacer and crank damper Woodruff® key. Oil the crankshaft sprockets and inner Woodruff® key.
16. Remove the rear oil seal housing retaining bolts and remove the housing.
17. Remove the connecting rod cap retaining nuts and remove the bearing caps in pairs (example: 1–6, 2–5, 3–4). Mark the position of caps as they are removed, to facilitate re-assemble. As each cap is removed, push the related piston assembly away from the crankshaft, enabling the crankshaft to be rotated.

NOTE: Be careful not push the piston assembly too far upwards in the cylinder bore, as this may cause the piston rings to release.

18. Remove the main bearing cap bolts and remove the bearing caps. Mark the position of caps as they are removed, to facilitate re-assemble.
19. Carefully remove the crankshaft from the cylinder block.
20. Remove the bearing shell halves and thrust washers.

To install:
21. Assemble the new bearing shell halves to the cylinder block and lubricate with clean engine oil.
22. Lubricate the crankshaft and carefully position it in the cylinder block.
23. Install the thrust washers, making certain the steel side of the washer is mated to the cylinder block.
24. Check to ensure the crankshaft turns freely.
25. Assemble the main bearing shells into the main bearing caps. Lubricate and install the bearing caps to the cylinder block.
26. Install the main bearing cap bolts. Lightly tap the main bearing caps to ensure they are seated in the cylinder block.
27. Tightening the main bearing cap bolts. Rotate the crankshaft after tightening each cap to ensure it turns freely. Torque the bolts to specification.
28. When completed, check that the crankshaft endplay is between 0–0.010 in. (254mm). If the endplay is not within specification, oversize thrust washers are available in 0.005 in. (127mm) and 0.010 in. (254mm).

5.3L ENGINE

1. Disconnect the negative battery cable and drain the cooling system.
2. Remove the engine/transmission assembly from the vehicle.
3. Separate the transmission from the engine and fit the engine to a stand.
4. Remove the timing cover and timing chain.
5. Remove the oil sump.
6. Remove the suction elbow and sandwich plate.
7. Remove the delivery pipe elbow-to-oil pump casing retaining bolts.

NOTE: Leave the bolt at the outboard elbow fastening in position in the oil pump casing. If this bolt is removed, it must be refitted in a downward direction.

8. Remove the crankshaft sprocket and Woodruff® key.
9. Remove the oil pump retaining bolts and remove the pump, drive gear and Woodruff® key.
10. Remove the connecting rod caps, starting with No. 1 and 5 cylinder. Remove the main bearing cap starting from the center bearing. Note the location of each part as they are removed.
11. Displace the connecting rods from the crankshaft and lift the crankshaft from the cylinder block.

To install:
12. Fit new sealing strips to the grooves of the rear main bearing casting.
13. Apply 1 drop of Red Hermatite or equivalent, into the

crankshaft rear oil seal grooves, at top and bottom. Fit the seal halves.

14. Install the rear main bearing casting to the cylinder block.
15. Pre-size the rear oil seal, using tool JD 17B and adaptor JD 17B-1 or their equivalent.
16. Remove the rear main bearing casting.
17. Lubricate the rear oil seal with Dag Colloidal Graphite or equivalent.
18. Refit the crankshaft into the cylinder block.
19. Lubricate the main bearing caps and fit to the cylinder block. Check the crankshaft endplay.
20. Lubricate and fit the connecting rod bearing caps.
21. Install the oil pump drive gear and Woodruff® key. Install the oil pump.
22. Install the crankshaft sprocket, using a new Woodruff® key.
23. Install the delivery pipe elbow and suction pipe, using new O-rings.
24. Install the sandwich plate and oil sump.
25. Install the timing chain and timing cover.
26. Install the engine/transmission assembly to the vehicle.
27. Reconnect the negative battery cable.

Piston and Connecting Rod

All pistons are marked FRONT. Be sure the marking faces the front of the engien.

Positioning

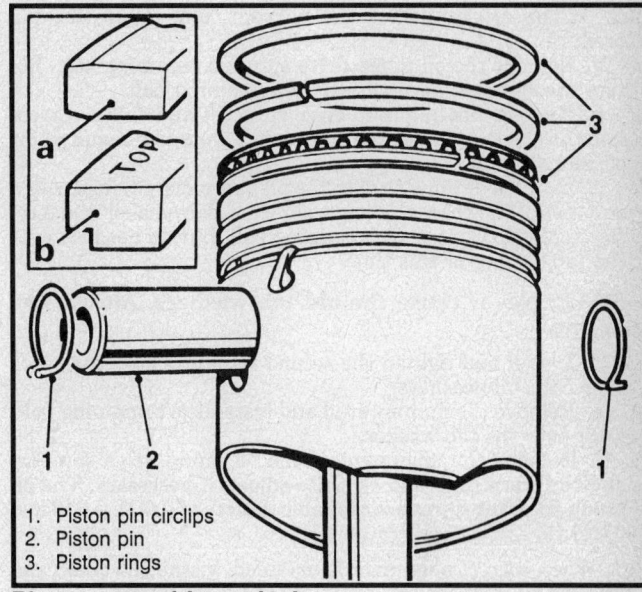

1. Piston pin circlips
2. Piston pin
3. Piston rings

Piston assembly, typical

ENGINE LUBRICATION

Oil Pan

Removal and Installation

3.6L ENGINE

1. Disconnect the negative battery cable.
2. Remove the dipstick housing and the alternator.
3. Raise the vehicle and support it safely.
4. Drain the engine oil.
5. Remove the front crossmember.
6. Remove the rear spacers and move the power steering pipes for access.
7. Loosen the union retaining the oil drain back tube to the sump and pull the tube clear of the sump.
8. If equipped with automatic transmission, remove the oil cooler lines-to-sump retaining clamp.
9. Remove the bell housing to sump retaining bolts, then remove the remaining sump bolts. Lower the sump.
10. Remove the alternator mounting bracket, sump baffle and oil drain-back adaptor plug from the sump.

To install:

11. Refit the sump baffle, oil drain-back adaptor plug and alternator mounting bracket.
12. Apply sealant, Hylosil 102 or equivalent, to the sump mating surfaces. Fit a new gasket and install the sump.
13. Install the oil cooler lines-to-sump retaining clamp, as required.
14. Refit the oil drain back tube and power steering pipes.
15. Install the front crossmember.
16. Refill the engine crankcase.
17. Reconnect the negative battery cable.

5.3L ENGINE

1. Disconnect the negative battery cable.
2. Remove the oil sump drain plug and drain the oil into a suitable container.

3. Remove the oil sump retaining bolts, noting the position of the transmission oil cooler pipe clip.
4. Lower and remove the oil pan.

To install:

5. Lightly coat the new gasket with Hylomar or equivalent.
6. Place the oil sump into position and install the retaining bolts.
7. Secure the transmission oil cooler pipe clip.
8. Refill the crankcase.
9. Reconnect the negative battery cable.

Oil Pump

Removal and Installation

3.6L ENGINE

1. Disconnect the negative battery cable.
2. Remove the oil sump.
3. Place a suitable drain pan under the oil transfer housing are and remove the transfer housing.
4. Remove the oil pump pick-up pipes.
5. Push the tabs away from the oil pump sprocket retaining bolts and remove the bolts.
6. Remove the oil pump drive sprocket. Retrieve the tab washers and shims.
7. Remove the oil pump retaining bolts and remove the pump assembly.

To install:

8. Lubricate the pressure relief valve assembly, install it into the pump, then tighten the cap.
9. Position the oil pump assembly to the engine and install the retaining bolts. Tighten the retaining bolts 17-20 ft. lbs. (23–27 Nm).
10. Move the drive chain as far rearward as possible, then fit a shim pack of 0.015 in. thickness to the oil pump flange. Align the bolt holes and install the sprocket.

11. Using a straight-edge, check the alignment of the oil pump drive sprocket and the crankshaft sprocket.

12. If the alignment is not correct, use the following procedure:

a. Remove the oil pump drive sprocket retaining bolt. Rotate the sprocket and remove the remaining bolt.

b. Remove the oil pump drive sprocket and shims. Calculate the thickness of the shim(s) which would be required for correct alignment.

c. Install a dummy stud to the oil pump drive flange. Align and install the shim(s), flange, sprocket, tab washer and 1 retaining bolt. Tighten the retaining bolt, but do not lock over the tab washer at this time.

NOTE: Never reuse the old tab washers. Always use new one.

d. Install and tighten the second retaining bolt, then lock over both tab washers.

e. Remove the dummy stud and install the remaining bolt. Lock over the tab washer.

f. Recheck the alignment of the oil pump drive sprocket and the crankshaft sprocket. Re-adjust, if necessary. The oil pump sprocket shims are available in sizes of 0.005, 0.010 and 0.020 in.

13. When correct alignment is obtained, install the chain and shims to the sprocket and assemble to the oil pump.

14. Install the tab washers and retaining bolts. Lock the tab washers over the retaining bolts.

15. Fit new O-rings to the oil pump pick-up pipes. Lubricate and install the pipes to the pump.

16. Apply sealant, Hylosil 102 or equivalent, to the transfer housing gasket face. Fit the gasket to the housing and install the housing to the engine.

17. Install the sump.

5.3L ENGINE

1. Disconnect the negative battery cable.

2. Remove the engine/transmission assembly and mount to a suitable stand.

3. Drain the engine oil and remove the timing cover.

4. Remove the timing chain.

5. Remove the oil sump.

6. Remove the suction elbow and sandwich plate.

7. Remove the delivery pipe elbow-to-oil pump casing retaining bolts.

NOTE: Leave the bolt at the outboard elbow fastening in position in the oil pump casing. If this bolt is removed, it must be refitted in a downward direction.

8. Remove the crankshaft sprocket and Woodruff® key.

9. Remove the oil pump retaining bolts and remove the pump, drive gear and Woodruff® key.

To install:

10. Install the oil pump drive gear and Woodruff® key. Install the oil pump.

11. Install the crankshaft sprocket, using a new Woodruff® key.

12. Install the delivery pipe elbow and suction pipe, using new O-rings.

13. Install the sandwich plate and oil sump.

14. Install the timing chain and timing cover.

15. Install the engine/transmission assembly to the vehicle.

16. Reconnect the negative battery cable.

Rear Oil Seal

Removal and Installation

3.6L ENGINE

1. Disconnect the negative battery cable.

2. Remove the engine/transmission assembly and position on a suitable stand.

3. Separate the engine from the transmission.

4. On manual transmission, remove the clutch assembly.

5. Remove the flywheel or driveplate, as required.

6. Remove the rear oil seal housing retaining bolts and remove the housing.

NOTE: Do not remove the plastic O-ring protector from the seal prior to fitting to the housing.

7. Carefully remove the oil seal from the housing.

To install:

8. Install the replacement seal to the housing, using a suitable tool JD 550-3 and 18G 134 or their equivalent.

9. Place the plastic protector O-ring on the end of the crankshaft.

10. Coat the housing gasket face with Hylosil 102 or equivalent. Fit the seal housing over the crankshaft and up to the rear cylinder block face.

11. Remove the plastic protector O-ring.

12. Install the rear seal housing retaining bolts, check that the sump face is flush with the cylinder block. Tighten and torque the retaining bolts 17-20 ft. lbs. (23–27 Nm).

13. Install the flywheel or driveplate and torque to specification.

14. On manual transmission, install the clutch assembly to the flywheel. Make certain the flywheel side of the driveplate faces the flywheel. Align the clutch assembly and torque the retaining bolts 17-20 ft. lbs. (23–27 Nm). Install the clutch housing.

15. Install the engine/transmission assembly into the vehicle.

16. Reconnect the negative battery cable.

5.3L ENGINE

1. Disconnect the negative battery cable.

2. Remove the engine/transmission assembly and position on a suitable stand.

3. Separate the engine from the transmission and drain the oil from the engine.

4. Remove the crankshaft from the cylinder block.

5. Remove the crankshaft seal halves from the bearing casting and cylinder block.

To install:

6. Fit new sealing strips to the grooves of the rear main bearing casting.

7. Apply 1 drop of Red Hermatite or equivalent, into the crankshaft rear oil seal grooves, at top and bottom. Fit the seal halves.

8. Install the rear main bearing casting to the cylinder block.

9. Pre-size the rear oil seal, using tool JD 17B and adaptor JD 17B-1 or equivalent.

10. Remove the rear main bearing casting.

11. Lubricate the rear oil seal with Dag Colloidal Graphite or equivalent.

12. Refit the crankshaft into the cylinder block.

13. Install the engine/transmission assembly to the vehicle.

14. Adjust the fluid levels and reconnect the negative battery cable.

Auxilliary Shaft Rear Seal

Removal and Installation

3.6L ENGINE

1. Disconnect the negative battery cable.

2. Remove the timing cover.

3. Remove the pulley woodruff key and remove the oil seal spacer from the crankshaft.

4. Remove the upper tensioner assembly, chain damper and upper timing chain.

5. Remove the lower chain tensioner retaining bolts, then remove the lower tensioner assembly.

6. Remove the intermediate sprocket and chain from the block.

7. Remove the power steering pump housing-to-auxiliary shaft housing retaining bolts.

8. Remove the power steering pump drive coupling.

9. Remove the auxiliary shaft rear oil seal, using tool JD 118, 18G 1468 or equivalent.

To install:

10. Lubricate the new seal and mating faces.

11. Lubricate and install the rear oil seal, using Tool 18G 1469

or equivalent. Do not remove the plastic seal insert prior to fitting the seal.

12. Install the power steering pump drive coupling and pump.

13. Install the power steering pump housing-to-auxiliary shaft housing retaining bolts.

14. Install intermediate sprocket and chain to the block.

15. Install the lower tensioner assembly.

16. Install the upper tensioner assembly, chain damper and upper timing chain.

17. Install the timing cover.

18. Reconnect the negative battery cable.

MANUAL TRANSMISSION

Transmission Assembly

Removal and Installation

3.6L ENGINE

1. Depressurize the fuel system.

2. Disconnect the negative battery cable.

3. From the engine compartment, remove the right side insulation pad.

4. Disconnect the underhood lamp.

5. Apply tape to the forward edge of the hood behind the grille surrounding.

6. Disconnect the hood support struts and hood assembly.

7. Remove the air cleaner assembly and drain the cooling system.

8. Remove the front grille.

9. If equipped with air conditioning, drain the air conditioning system. Remove the air conditioning compressor and receiver/drier. Be certain to plug all openings.

10. Disconnect the heater hoses and radiator hoses. Remove the cooling fan shroud, radiator and auxiliary electric fan.

11. Disconnect and tag all electrical connectors and vacuum hoses, as required.

12. Remove horn assembly and the tie bars at front of engine.

13. On automatic transmission, disconnect and plug the cooler lines from the radiator.

14. Disconnect the engine oil cooler pipes and remove the oil cooler radiator.

15. Disconnect and plug the fuel lines.

16. Disconnect the power steering pump/drive and remove the coupling.

17. Remove the throttle cable and throttle support bracket at the intake manifold.

18. Support the engine weight, using tool 18G 1465 and MS 53B or their equivalent.

19. Raise the vehicle and support it safely.

20. Remove the front exhaust pipe.

21. On manual transmission, disconnect the gear lever linkage and switch multi-plugs. Disconnect the clutch slave cylinder from the bell housing.

21. On automatic transmission, disconnect the gear selector cable from the selector shaft and mounting bracket.

22. Remove the transmission center mount.

23. Remove the rear heat shield and propeller shaft.

24. Lower the vehicle and fit a suitable engine removal tool.

25. Remove the engine and transmission assembly from the vehicle; being careful not to damage the steering rack.

26. Mount the engine to a suitable engine stand.

To install:

27. Fit the engine and transmission assembly to the engine hoist and carefully lower the engine into the vehicle.

28. Position a jack under the transmission to support the weight.

29. Install tool MS 53B or equivalent. Tighten the hook nut to take the weight of the engine.

30. Install the rear mount spring assembly and the mount. Remove the jack.

31. Install the driveshaft.

32. Slacken off the hook nut to release the weight of the engine and remove the hook. Remove tool MS 53B or equivalent.

33. Install the transmission mount.

34. Reconnect the electrical harness and vacuum hoses, as required.

35. Reconnect the heater hoses.

36. Install the throttle cable support bracket and cable. Slacken off the locknut and adjust the cable to obtain the correct tension.

37. Install the fuel hoses to the manifold and pressure regulator.

38. Clean the power steering mating face and fit the coupling to the pump. Align the pump shaft with the distributor driveshaft, then connect the pump assembly.

39. Install the air conditioning compressor.

40. Install the oil cooler pipes, receiver/drier and oil cooler radiator.

41. Install the horn assembly, condenser and brackets. Make certain the condenser is secured by the mounting brackets and that the pipes run along the inner wing.

42. Install the fan and frame assembly. Reconnect the fan electrical connector.

43. Install the fan cowl assembly and radiator. Connect the lower radiator hose.

44. Install the front grille, air cleaner element and hood struts.

45. Remove tool 18G 1465 or equivalent and refill the cooling system.

46. Install the hood and reconnect the negative battery cable.

47. On automatic transmission, check and adjust the downshift cable initial setting.

48. Check and adjust all fluid levels. Start the engine and check for leaks.

5.3L ENGINE

1. Depressurize the fuel system.

2. Disconnect the negative battery cable.

3. Disconnect the underhood light and remove the hood assembly.

4. Remove the lower grille.

5. If equipped with air conditioning, drain the air conditioning system and separate the hoses, as required. Be certain to plug all openings.

6. Remove the left and right side air cleaner assembly and drain the cooling system.

7. Disconnect and label all electrical connectors and vacuum hoses, as required. Disconnect the starter harness at the bulkhead connector.

8. Disconnect the throttle cable, heater hoses and radiator hoses.

9. Disconnect and plug the fuel feed hose.

10. If equipped with an automatic transmission, disconnect and plug the transmission oil cooler lines.

11. Remove the radiator top rail, then disconnect and plug the outlet pipe from the reciever/drier.

12. Remove the condenser pipe retaining clips.

13. Remove the radiator top rail completely with the evaporator and receiver/drier unit.

14. Disconnect the low coolant sensor and oil cooler pipes from the radiator. Plug the oil cooler pipes.

15. Carefully remove the radiator, fan cowl and electric fan.

16. Fit an engine lifting tool, MS 53B or equivalent, and support the engine weight.

17. Raise the vehicle and safely support it.

18. Disconnect the front exhaust pipes. Remove the heat shields.

19. Support the transmission and remove the transmission mount; note the position of the spacers and bolts to facilitate reassemble.

20. Remove the driveshaft.

21. On manual transmission, disconnect the gear lever linkage and switch multi-plugs. Disconnect the clutch slave cylinder from the bell housing.

22. On automatic transmission, disconnect the gear selector cable from the selector shaft and mounting bracket.

23. Remove the oil cooler and pump. Loosen the drive belt and lay the pump aside in an upright position.

24. Lower the vehicle and position a jack under the transmission.

25. Attached a lifting chain.

26. On a manual transmission vehicle, check that the gear lever is below the console and clear of the transmission tunnel before the engine is removed.

27. Carefully remove the engine and transmission assembly from the vehicle.

To install:

28. Fit new exhaust sealing rings to the front exhaust pipes.

29. Fit the engine and transmission assembly to the engine hoist and carefully lower the engine into the vehicle.

30. Position a jack under the transmission to support the weight.

31. Install tool MS 53B or equivalent. Tighten the hook nut to take the weight of the engine.

32. Loosely secure the right side pipe to the exhaust manifold.

33. Raise the vehicle and support it safely. Tighten the right side pipe and EGR pipe.

34. Lower the vehicle.

35. Install the fan, cowl assembly and pump.

36. Install the radiator and reconnect the oil cooler lines.

37. Raise the vehicle and support it safely.

38. Raise the engine and install the rear mount.

39. Reconnect the driveshaft, speedometer cable and transmission selector cable.

40. Install the heat shields and the intermediate pipes.

41. Lower the vehicle and install the the oil cooler.

42. Remove the engine support.

43. Reconnect the receiver/drier, heater hoses, radiator hoses and air conditioning hoses.

44. Reconnect all vacuum hoses, electrical harness and fuel lines.

45. Install the air cleaner(s) assembly.

46. Recharge the air conditioning system and refill all fluid levels.

47. Reconnect the negative battery cable.

CLUTCH

Clutch Assembly

Removal and Installation

1. Disconnect the negative battery cable.

2. Remove the transmission/engine assembly from the vehicle.

3. Separate the transmission and remove the clutch assembly.

To install:

4. Fit the replacement clutch assembly to the flywheel. Make certain the flywheel side of the clutch plate faces the flywheel. Align the clutch assembly and install the clutch cover-to-flywheel retaining bolts. Tighten the retaining bolts 17–20 ft. lbs. (23–27 Nm).

5. Install the transmission/engine assembly into the vehicle.

6. Reconnect the negative battery cable.

Clutch Master Cylinder

Removal and Installation

1. Disconnect the negative battery cable.

2. Disengage the return spring from the pedal. Remove the spring clip, washer and clevis pin.

3. Remove the master cylinder-to-pedal box retaining nuts.

4. Remove the master cylinder-to-piller setscrew nut and washers, if equipped.

5. Remove the brake fluid reservoir bracket and withdraw the master cylinder and shims.

To install:

6. Refit the brake fluid reservoir, replacement master cylinder and shims into place. Tighten the retaining nuts 16–21 ft. lbs. (22–28 Nm).

7. Install the clevis pin, washer, spring clip and return spring to the pedal.

8. Reconnect the negative battery cable.

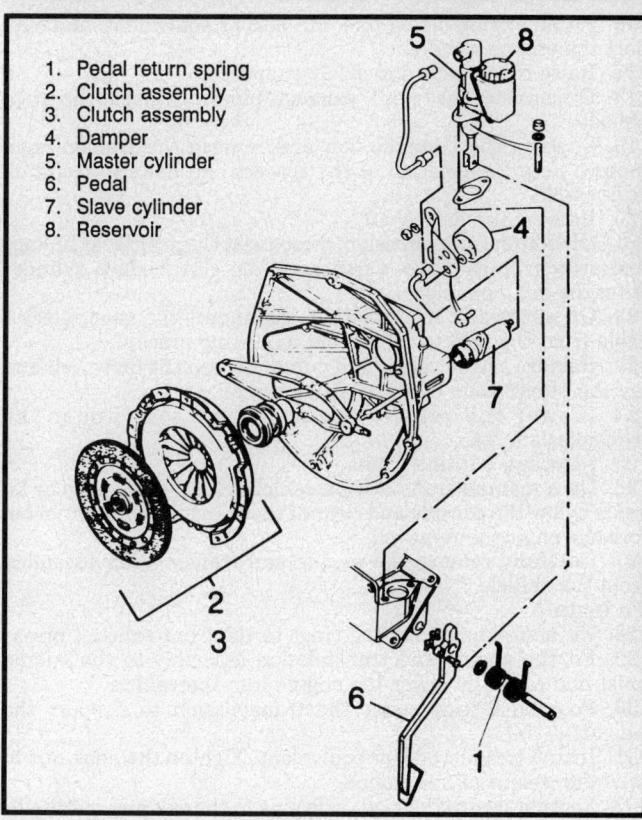

1. Pedal return spring
2. Clutch assembly
3. Clutch assembly
4. Damper
5. Master cylinder
6. Pedal
7. Slave cylinder
8. Reservoir

Clutch assembly, exploded view

Clutch Slave Cylinder

Removal and Installation

1. Disconnect the negative battery cable.
2. Remove the hydraulic pipe from the slave cylinder and plug it to prevent dirt or other foreign materials from entering.
3. Remove the slave cylinder retaining nuts and remove the slave cylinder from its mounting studs.

To install:

4. Install the pushrod and rubber boot to the replacement slave cylinder, if required.
5. Fit the slave cylinder to its mounting studs and install the retaining nuts.
6. Reconnect the pipe to the slave cylinder.
7. Reconnect the negative battery cable.

Hydraulic Clutch System Bleeding

1. Disconnect the negative battery cable.
2. Remove the reservoir filler cap. Adjust the fluid level, if required.
3. Attach one end of a bleed tube to the slave cylinder bleed nipple. Partially fill a clean container with brake fluid and immerse the other end of the tube into a the container.
4. Loosen the bleed nipple on the end of the slave cylinder.
5. Bleed the trap air from the clutch system by slowly pumping the clutch pedal. Be certain to pause between each pedal stroke. Check the reservoir level constantly while bleeding the system, after every 3 stroke.
6. Pump the pedal until it become firm, then tighten the slave cylinder bleed nipple.

NOTE:Use only Castrol-Girling brake fluid in the clutch system. Never reuse the fluid that have been bled from the system.

AUTOMATIC TRANSMISSION

Transmission Assembly

Removal and Installation

3.6L ENGINE

1. Depressurize the fuel system.
2. Disconnect the negative battery cable.
3. From the engine compartment, remove the right side insulation pad.
4. Disconnect the underhood lamp.
5. Apply tape to the forward edge of the hood behind the grille surrounding.
6. Disconnect the hood support struts and hood assembly.
7. Remove the air cleaner assembly and drain the cooling system.
8. Remove the front grille.
9. If equipped with air conditioning, drain the air conditioning system. Remove the air conditioning compressor and receiver/drier. Be certain to plug all openings.
10. Disconnect the heater hoses and radiator hoses. Remove the cooling fan shroud, radiator and auxiliary electric fan.
11. Disconnect and tag all electrical connectors and vacuum hoses, as required.
12. Remove horn assembly and the tie bars at front of engine.
13. On automatic transmission, disconnect and plug the cooler lines from the radiator.
14. Disconnect the engine oil cooler pipes and remove the oil cooler radiator.

15. Disconnect and plug the fuel lines.
16. Disconnect the power steering pump/drive and remove the coupling.
17. Remove the throttle cable and throttle support bracket at the intake manifold.
18. Support the engine weight, using tool 18G 1465 and MS 53B or their equivalent.
19. Raise the vehicle and support it safely.
20. Remove the front exhaust pipe.
21. On manual transmission, disconnect the gear lever linkage and switch multi-plugs. Disconnect the clutch slave cylinder from the bell housing.
21. On automatic transmission, disconnect the gear selector cable from the selector shaft and mounting bracket.
22. Remove the transmission center mount.
23. Remove the rear heat shield and propeller shaft.
24. Lower the vehicle and fit a suitable engine removal tool.
25. Remove the engine and transmission assembly from the vehicle; being careful not to damage the steering rack.
26. Mount the engine to a suitable engine stand.

To install:

27. Fit the engine and transmission assembly to the engine hoist and carefully lower the engine into the vehicle.
28. Position a jack under the transmission to support the weight.
29. Install tool MS 53B or equivalent. Tighten the hook nut to take the weight of the engine.

30. Install the rear mount spring assembly and the mount. Remove the jack.
31. Install the driveshaft.
32. Slacken off the hook nut to release the weight of the engine and remove the hook. Remove tool MS 53B or equivalent.
33. Install the transmission mount.
34. Reconnect the electrical harness and vacuum hoses, as required.
35. Reconnect the heater hoses.
36. Install the throttle cable support bracket and cable. Slacken off the locknut and adjust the cable to obtain the correct tension.
37. Install the fuel hoses to the manifold and pressure regulator.
38. Clean the power steering mating face and fit the coupling to the pump. Align the pump shaft with the distributor driveshaft, then connect the pump assembly.
39. Install the air conditioning compressor.
40. Install the oil cooler pipes, receiver/drier and oil cooler radiator.
41. Install the horn assembly, condenser and brackets. Make certain the condenser is secured by the mounting brackets and that the pipes run along the inner wing.
42. Install the fan and frame assembly. Reconnect the fan electrical connector.
43. Install the fan cowl assembly and radiator. Connect the lower radiator hose.
44. Install the front grille, air cleaner element and hood struts.
45. Remove tool 18G 1465 or equivalent and refill the cooling system.
46. Install the hood and reconnect the negative battery cable.
47. On automatic transmission, check and adjust the downshift cable initial setting.
48. Check and adjust all fluid levels. Start the engine and check for leaks.

5.3L ENGINE

1. Depressurize the fuel system.
2. Disconnect the negative battery cable.
3. Disconnect the underhood light and remove the hood assembly.
4. Remove the lower grille.
5. If equipped with air conditioning, drain the air conditioning system and separate the hoses, as required. Be certain to plug all openings.
6. Remove the left and right side air cleaner assembly and drain the cooling system.
7. Disconnect and label all electrical connectors and vacuum hoses, as required. Disconnect the starter harness at the bulkhead connector.
8. Disconnect the throttle cable, heater hoses and radiator hoses.
9. Disconnect and plug the fuel feed hose.
10. If equipped with an automatic transmission, disconnect and plug the transmission oil cooler lines.
11. Remove the radiator top rail, then disconnect and plug the outlet pipe from the reciever/drier.
12. Remove the condenser pipe retaining clips.
13. Remove the radiator top rail completely with the evaporator and receiver/drier unit.
14. Disconnect the low coolant sensor and oil cooler pipes from the radiator. Plug the oil cooler pipes.
15. Carefully remove the radiator, fan cowl and electric fan.

16. Fit an engine lifting tool, MS 53B or equivalent, and support the engine weight.
17. Raise the vehicle and safely support it.
18. Disconnect the front exhaust pipes. Remove the heat shields.
19. Support the transmission and remove the transmission mount; note the position of the spacers and bolts to facilitate reassemble.
20. Remove the driveshaft.
21. On manual transmission, disconnect the gear lever linkage and switch multi-plugs. Disconnect the clutch slave cylinder from the bell housing.
22. On automatic transmission, disconnect the gear selector cable from the selector shaft and mounting bracket.
23. Remove the oil cooler and pump. Loosen the drive belt and lay the pump aside in an upright position.
24. Lower the vehicle and position a jack under the transmission.
25. Attached a lifting chain.
26. On a manual transmission vehicle, check that the gear lever is below the console and clear of the transmission tunnel before the engine is removed.
27. Carefully remove the engine and transmission assembly from the vehicle.

To install:
28. Fit new exhaust sealing rings to the front exhaust pipes.
29. Fit the engine and transmission assembly to the engine hoist and carefully lower the engine into the vehicle.
30. Position a jack under the transmission to support the weight.
31. Install tool MS 53B or equivalent. Tighten the hook nut to take the weight of the engine.
32. Loosely secure the right side pipe to the exhaust manifold.
33. Raise the vehicle and support it safely. Tighten the right side pipe and EGR pipe.
34. Lower the vehicle.
35. Install the fan, cowl assembly and pump.
36. Install the radiator and reconnect the oil cooler lines.
37. Raise the vehicle and support it safely.
38. Raise the engine and install the rear mount.
39. Reconnect the driveshaft, speedometer cable and transmission selector cable.
40. Install the heat shields and the intermediate pipes.
41. Lower the vehicle and install the the oil cooler.
42. Remove the engine support.
43. Reconnect the receiver/drier, heater hoses, radiator hoses and air conditioning hoses.
44. Reconnect all vacuum hoses, electrical harness and fuel lines.
45. Install the air cleaner(s) assembly.
46. Recharge the air conditioning system and refill all fluid levels.
47. Reconnect the negative battery cable.
The engine and transmission is remove as a unit. Mount the engine to a suitable support and separate the engine and transmission assembly. See engine removal procedure.

Kickdown Cable Adjustment

1. Loosen the cable locknut and manually open the throttle linkage to full throttle position.
2. Measure the distance from the outer cable to the crimp.
3. Adjust the outer cable locknuts until the distance between the crimp and the outer cable is 1½ in. (39mm).
4. Tighten the cable locknut.

DRIVE AXLE

Driveshaft

Removal and Installation

1. Disconnect the negative battery cable.
2. If equipped with manual transmission, select a forward gear.
3. Raise and support the vehicle safely.
4. Remove the split pin and clevis pin securing the parking brake cable adjuster to the compensator.
5. Remove the driveshaft flange-to-differential drive flange retaining nuts.
6. Remove the center mounting plate.
7. Remove the driveshaft from the differential flange, slide it rearwards and remove it from the vehicle. Fit a plug to the transmission to prevent spillage.
To install:
8. Lubricate the shaft splines and fit it to the vehicle.
9. Install the center mounting plate. Stand at the rear of the vehicle and eye the driveshaft center bearing. Position the mounting just to the left of the center and tighten the mounting plate bolts.
10. Refit the parking brake cable assembly.
11. Lower the vehicle and reconnect the negative battery cable.

Halfshafts

Removal and Installation

1. Disconnect the negative battery cable.
2. Raise and support the vehicle safely.
3. Before removing the wheels, scribe a mark on the wheel and 1 wheel nut to facilitate installation. Remove the rear wheel(s) assembly.
4. Cut the strap retaining the wear pad sensor harness and disconnect the block connector.
5. Remove the rear brake pads. Remove the rear caliper retaining bolts and secure the caliper aside, with a piece of wire.
6. Remove the clevis pin retaining the parking brake expander to the parking brake cable.
7. Remove the retaining nut from the rear hub-to-halfshaft.
8. Install the threaded protector, tool JD 1D/7 or equivalent, to the driveshaft threads.

9. Install the hub remover, tool JD 1D or equivalent, and remove the hub assembly.
10. Remove the parking brake cable from the hub and lower the hub from the driveshaft.
11. Remove the driveshaft-to-differential retaining nuts and bolts. Remove the driveshaft assembly.
To install:
12. Fit the driveshaft into position and install the retaining nuts and bolts.
13. Lubricate the hub splines and fit the hub assembly to the driveshaft.
14. Secure the parking brake cable assembly.
15. Install the rear brake caliper and pads.
16. Reconnect the pad sensor harness connector.
17. Install the wheel(s) assembly and lower the vehicle.
18. Reconnect the negative battery cable.

Pinion Seal

Removal and Installation

1. Disconnect the negative battery cable.
2. Raise and support the vehicle safely.
3. Reposition the propeller shaft from the final differential flange.
4. Measure the torque required to turn the pinion through the back lash, using a torque wrench. Make certain the pinion is reset before each measurement.
5. Mark the pinion flange retaining nut to the pinion shaft.
6. Remove the pinion shaft retaining nut, using tool 18G 1205 or equivalent.
7. Remove the pinion shaft flange, using tool 18G 2 or equivalent.
8. Remove the pinion seal, using a suitable tool.
To install:
9. Lubricate the pinion seal and fit it into position, using Tool 18G 1428A or equivalent.
10. Lubricate and seat the flange.
11. Install the flange retaining nut to the mark made previously. Set the pinion back lash and preload at 35–55 inch lbs., using a torque wrench.
12. Refit the propeller shaft.
13. Lower the vehicle and reconnect the negative battery cable.

STEERING

Steering Wheel

CAUTION

On vehicles equipped with an air bag, the negative battery cable must be disconnected, before working on the system. Failure to do so may result in deployment of the air bag and possible personal injury.

Removal and Installation

1. Disconnect the negative battery cable.
2. Place the front wheels in straight forward position.
3. Remove the steering wheel pad.
4. Loosen the steering wheel retaining nut, pull the steering wheel to release it from the shaft, then remove the retaining nut.
5. Remove the cancelation boss and remove the steering wheel assembly.

To install:
6. Lubricate the split collars on the steering column shaft.
7. Install the steering wheel to the shaft in it's original position.
8. Install the steering wheel retaining nut. Torque the nut 26–33 ft. lbs. (35–45 Nm).
9. Install the steering wheel pad.
10. Reconnect the negative battery cable.

Steering Column

Removal and Installation

1. Disconnect the negative battery cable.
2. Place the front wheels in straight forward position.
3. Remove the steering wheel.
4. Remove the dash liner.

5. Disconnect the steering column switch assembly block connector.

6. Remove the universal joint-to-upper column retaining nut and bolt.

7. Remove the steering column lower bearing-to-bracket retaining bolt.

8. Remove the steering column-to-upper mounting nuts and carefully lower the column. Remove the column from the vehicle.

To install:

9. Fit the steering column to the vehicle, using new steering lock retaining bolts.

10. Refit the dash liner. Align the heater duct prior to securing the liner.

11. Install the steering wheel.

12. Reconnect the negative battery cable.

Power Steering Rack Pinion

Adjustment

1. Remove the outer tie rod assembly closest to the pinion from the steering arm.

2. Remove the grease nipple from the rack damper threaded plug and insert the stem of a dial indicator through the grease nipple hole to contact the back of the rack shaft. Secure the gauge to the rack and zero the indicator.

3. Firmly, grip the inner tie rod assembly, nearest to the pinion and move it away from the pinion, towards the rack damper assembly. Note the reading.

4. The maximum clearance between the rack and the pinion should not exceed 0.010 in. (0.25mm). If the clearance is excessive and adjustment is required, proceed as follow:

 a. Loosen the locknut and screw in the plug until firm resistance is felt.

 b. Back off the plug $\frac{1}{6}$ of a turn and tighten the locknut.

 c. Recheck the pinion to rack clearance.

5. Move the rack through its full travel and check for binding.

6. If binding occurs at any point, slightly increase the clearance and recheck.

7. When the correct clearance is obtained, fully tighten the locknut and install the grease nipple.

8. Install the outer tie rod assembly to the steering arm and recheck the front wheel alignment.

Removal and Installation

1. Disconnect the negative battery cable.

2. Loosen the power steering fluid reservoir filler cap.

3. Raise and support the vehicle safely.

NOTE: To assist in the initial setting of the front wheel alignment prior to dismantling, measure the distance between the center of the inner and outer ball joints.

4. Before removing the wheels, scribe a mark on the wheel and 1 wheel nut to facilitate installation. Remove the wheel(s) assembly.

5. Place a suitable container beneath the steering rack. Disconnect and plug both hoses from the pinion housing.

6. If equipped with the 5.3L engine, remove the right side heat shield.

7. Separate the outer tie-rod assembly, using tool JD 24 or equivalent.

8. Separate the lower steering column universal joint, from the rack pinion.

9. If equipped with the 5.3L engine, remove the pinch bolts retaining the universal joint to the lower and upper column, at the driver's footwell. Separate the universal joint from the upper column and lower shaft.

NOTE: Record the number and position of the packing washers for installation.

To install:

10. Remove the steering rack mounting bolts, washers and self locking nuts. Remove the steering rack from the crossmember.

11. Set the steering wheel in the straight-ahead position and fit the rack into the vehicle.

12. Fit the lower coupling to the pinion. Make certain the single rack mounting lug is shimmed so it is centered between the cross-beam brackets, as followed:

 a. Fit the shims between the faces of the steel/rubber washers and the bracket.

 b. Check that a gap of 0.10–0.12 in. (2.5–3.0mm) exists between the face of the rubber thrust washers and the single lug of the rack.

13. Install the mounting bolts, but do not fully tighten at this time.

14. Loosen the clips securing the rubber boots to the rack housing and pull the boot clear of the inner assembly.

15. To obtain an approximate setting prior to checking the front wheel alignment, assemble a steering rack checking fixture, tool JD 36A or equivalent. Adjust the position of the rack, until both legs are in contact with the rack shaft. Tighten the rack mounting bolts and remove the service tool.

16. Re-fit the rubber boots and tie-rod assembly.

17. On vehicles equipped with the 5.3L engine, install the right side heat shield.

18. Reconnect the hoses to the pinion housing.

19. On vehicles equipped with the 5.3L engine, refit the universal joint to the upper column and lower shaft.

20. Refit the lower steering column universal joint to the rack pinion.

21. Lower the vehicle and reconnect the negative battery cable.

22. Refill and bleed the system.

23. Check and adjust the front wheel alignment.

Power Steering Pump

Removal and Installation

1. Disconnect the negative battery cable.

2. Place a suitable container beneath the pump and remove the reservoir-to-pump hose. Plug the hose.

3. Remove the pump retaining bolts and remove the pump.

4. Remove the drive coupling from the pump.

To install:

5. Fit the pump and drive coupling to the engine.

6. Reconnect the reservoir-to-pump hose. Plug the hose.

7. Refill the system with fluid and bleed the system.

8. Reconnect the negative battery cable.

Bleeding the System

1. Check and adjust the power steering reservoir fluid level.

2. Start the engine and turn the steering from stop-to-stop without stopping.

3. Position the wheels in straight ahead position and recheck the fluid level.

4. Allow the engine to idle for a few minutes, then turn the engine **OFF**. Allow the system to settle and recheck the fluid level.

BRAKES

Master Cylinder

Removal and Installation

XJS

1. Disconnect the negative battery cable.
2. Pull back the rubber cover from the top of the reservoir and disconnect the electrical connector from the fluid level indicator switch.
3. Remove the reservoir cap and siphon the fluid using a suitable syringe.
4. Disconnect the fluid lines from the master cylinder and plug the lines to prevent dirt and other foreign materials.

NOTE: Before removing the master cylinder, pump the pedal at least 10 times, to ensure there is no vacuum effect left in the booster (servo). Do not depress the pedal with the master cylinder removed, as damage to the booster can occur.

5. Remove the master cylinder retaining nuts and remove the master cylinder.
To install:
6. Lubricate the operating rod socket with grease and install the replacement cylinder to the booster unit.
7. Install the brake lines.
8. Fill the master cylinder reservoir to the correct fluid level. Use Jaguar brake and clutch fluid or Castrol Girling Universal to DOT 4.
9. Install the cap and bleed the system.
10. Reconnect the negative battery cable.

Power Brake Booster

Removal and Installation

XJS

1. Disconnect the negative battery cable.
2. Remove the vacuum hose from the booster.
3. Remove the master cylinder and master cylinder reservoir.
4. If equipped with automatic transmission, disconnect the throttle cable from the turntable.
5. Remove the pedal housing retaining nuts and bolts, then lift the pedal box and booster assembly from the vehicle.
6. Place the assembly on a workbench and separate the pedal box from the booster.
To install:
7. Secure the replacement booster to the pedal box and fit the assembly into the vehicle.
8. Install the master cylinder to the booster.
9. Install the reservoir and vacuum hose.
10. Install the throttle cable and reconnect the electrical connectors to the kickdown switch, if required.
11. Reconnect the negative battery cable.

Disc Brake Pads

Removal and Installation

1. Disconnect the negative battery cable.
2. Raise the vehicle and support it safely.
3. Before removing the wheels, scribe a mark on the wheel and 1 wheel nut to facilitate installation. Remove the wheel(s) assembly.
4. Remove the spring clip which secures the retaining pins to the caliper and remove the retaining pins.
5. Remove the inner and outer anti-rattle springs and remove the brake pads.

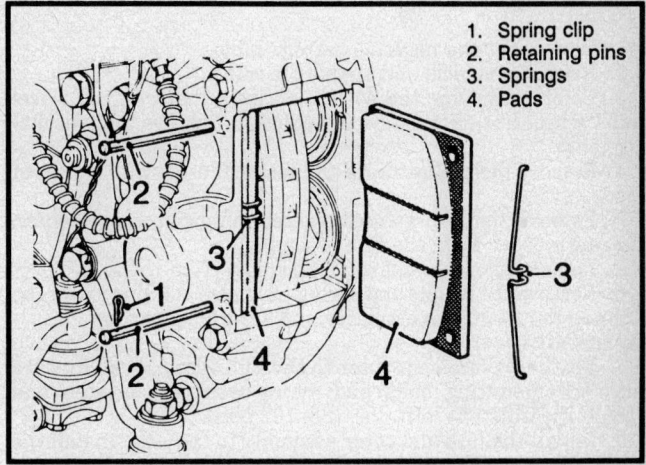

1. Spring clip
2. Retaining pins
3. Springs
4. Pads

Front brake assembly—XJS

To install:
6. Check the master cylinder fluid level. If necessary, reduce the brake fluid level.
7. Bottom the caliper pistons into the bores, using tool 64932392 or equivalent.
8. Install the new pads and fit the retaining pins. The lower retaining pin goes through the first pad only.
9. Install the anti-rattle springs.
10. Install the retaining pins and pin clips.
11. Install the wheels.
12. Lower the vehicle and reconnect the negative battery cable.

Brake Caliper

Removal and Installation

1. Disconnect the negative battery cable.
2. Raise the vehicle and support it safely.
3. Before removing the wheels, scribe a mark on the wheel and 1 wheel nut to facilitate installation. Remove the wheel(s) assembly.
4. Remove the brake pads.
5. Disconnect the brake line to the caliper, at the support bracket. Plug the line to prevent dirt and other foreign materials.
6. Cut the lock wire and remove the mounting bolts that secures the brake caliper to the axle carrier stud.

NOTE: Record the value of shim(s) located between the steering arm and the brake caliper. Under no circumstances should the bolts securing the caliper halves together be removed.

7. Remove the caliper assembly.
To install:
8. Fit the caliper assembly to the axle carrier stud, being certain the correct value of shim(s) are repositioned.
9. Install and torque the caliper mounting bolts 50–60 ft. lbs. (68–81 Nm).
10. Reconnect the brake line.
11. Install the brake pads.
12. Install the wheels and bleed the brake system.
13. Reconnect the negative battery cable.

Brake Rotor

Removal and Installation

FRONT

1. Disconnect the negative battery cable.
2. Raise the vehicle and support it safely.
3. Before removing the wheels, scribe a mark on the wheel and 1 wheel nut to facilitate installation. Remove the wheel(s) assembly.
4. Remove the brake caliper and secure it aside with a piece of wire.
5. Remove the hub grease cap, retaining pin, cap retainer, nut and washer from the hub assembly.
6. Remove the hub and rotor assembly from the axle.
7. Remove the 5 bolts and spring washers retaining the brake rotor to the front hub assembly and separate the rotor.

To install:

8. Fit the replacement rotor to the hub assembly and secure with the mounting bolts and spring washers. Tighten and torque the nuts 65–75 ft. lbs. (88–102 Nm).
9. Install the hub and rotor assembly to the axle. Install the nut and washer and adjust the bearing clearance as follow:

    a. Mount a dial indicator gauge with the plunger against the hub.

    b. Set the dial indicator to zero.

    c. Tighten the nut until the bearing clearance is 0.001–0.003 in. (0.03–0.08mm). If a dial indicator is not available, tighten the nut until there is no clearance, rotation of the hub is slightly restricted, then slacken off the nut 1 flat.

NOTE: When tightening the nut, do not exceed a maximum of 5 ft. lbs. as damage to the bearing can occur.

10. Install the cap retainer, retaining pin and grease cap.
11. Install the caliper and wheel(s) assembly.
12. Lower the vehicle and reconnect the negative battery cable.

REAR

1. Disconnect the negative battery cable.
2. Raise the vehicle and support it safely.
3. Before removing the wheels, scribe a mark on the wheel and 1 wheel nut to facilatate installation. Remove the wheel(s) assembly.
4. Remove the nut and bolts retaining the tie-plate to the rear suspension unit, then remove the tie-plate.
5. Loosen the parking brake adjusting and lock nut at the parking brake lever.
6. Release the springs form the parking brake caliper arms and detach the cable form the arms.
7. Remove the brake rotor.
8. Remove the hub carrier shaft grease nipple to prevent damaging the nipple.
9. Remove the radius arm bolt and separate the arm from the anchor on the body.
10. Support the hub carrier assembly.
11. Remove the nuts and washers retaining the rear dampers to the lower wishbone.
12. Drive out the damper mounting pin and recover the front damper spacer collar.
13. Loosen the clip retaining the driveshaft inner U-joint cover and position the cover aside.
14. Remove the driveshaft flange-to-brake rotor retaining nuts and carefully separate the driveshaft flange from the brake rotor. Recover the camber angle shims from the disc mounting bolts. Make a note of the shims to aid during re-assemble.
15. Remove the rotor.

NOTE: Do not distrub the shims mounted between the final drive flange and the brake rotor.

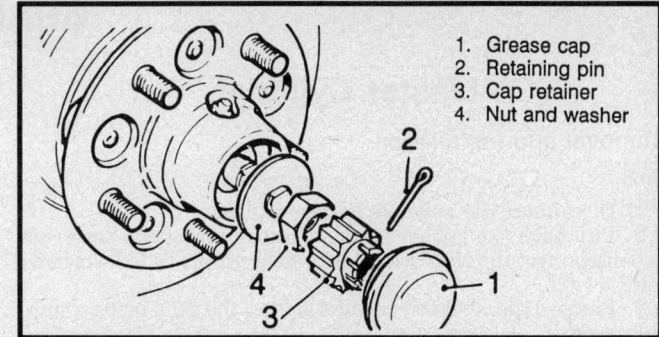

1. Grease cap
2. Retaining pin
3. Cap retainer
4. Nut and washer

Brake rotor assembly

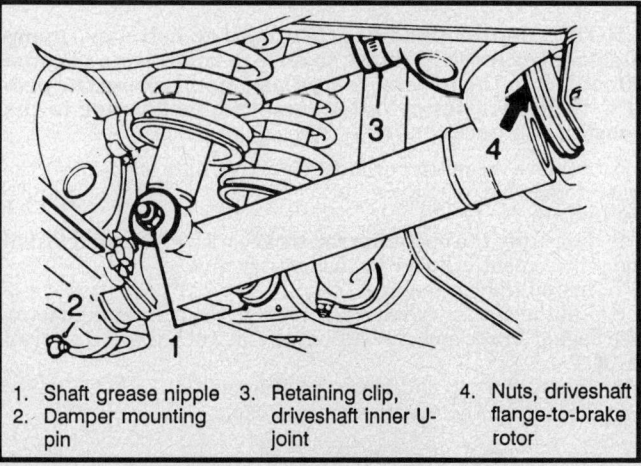

1. Shaft grease nipple
2. Damper mounting pin
3. Retaining clip, driveshaft inner U-joint
4. Nuts, driveshaft flange-to-brake rotor

Removing rear brake rotor assembly

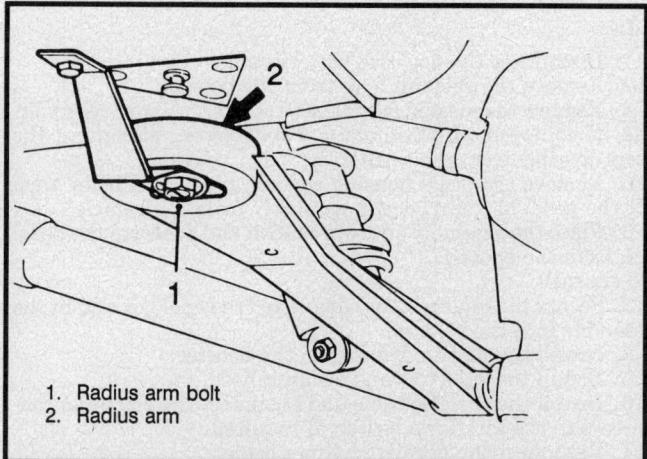

1. Radius arm bolt
2. Radius arm

Radius arm assembly

To install:

16. Position the replacement rotor on the mounting bolts and install the camper angle shims.
17. Install the driveshaft flange over the shims on the top of the mounting bolts. Secure the driveshaft flange to the brake rotor.
18. Clamp a dial indicator to the crossmember, with its plunger against the rotor face and check the rotor run-out.
19. Check that the rotor is centered in the caliper by measuring the gap between the caliper supports and the rotor face. The gap on either sides may differ by up to 0.010 in. (0.25mm). How-

ever, the gap between the upper and lower support on one side must be equal.

20. If adjustment is necessary, remove the caliper and rotor. Add or remove shims from between the axle output shaft flange and the brake rotor. Note the thickness of shims added or removed.

21. After the rotor is centered, add or remove the same value of shims from the camber angle shim pack, between the brake rotor and the driveshaft flange, as follows:

    a. If, for example, a 0.004 shim was removed to center the rotor, then add the same value to the camber angle shim pack.

    b. If a 0.004 shim was added to center the rotor, then remove the same value to the camber angle shim pack.

22. Tighten the caliper mounting bolts and install the lock wire.

23. Lubricate the body spigot, fit the radius arm into position and install the retaining bolt.

24. Fit the U-joint cover into place and tighten the retaining clip.

25. Install the parking brake caliper.

26. Install the parking brake cable into the levers and install the return spring. Operate the parking brake actuating lever until the adjuster ratchet cease to click. The pads are now adjusted.

27. Install the suspension tie plate and adjust the parking brake.

28. Lower the vehicle and reconnect the negative battery cable.

Parking Brake Cable

Adjustment

XJS

1. Disconnect the negative battery cable.
2. Release the parking brake lever. Lift the carpet adjacent to the parking brake lever.
3. Loosen the parking brake cable adjusting and locknuts.
4. Adjust the parking brake cable so there is a small amount of slack in the cable, with the parking brake lever fully OFF.

NOTE: If the parking brake cable is adjusted to a point where all slack is removed from the cable, binding of the parking brake caliper may result.

5. Tighten the cable adjusting and locknuts.
6. Refit the carpet and reconnect the negative battery cable.

XJ6

1. Release the parking brake lever.
2. Disconnect the negative battery cable.
3. Raise and support the vehicle safely.
4. Loosen the parking brake cable adjuster locknut and tighten the adjuster to remove any slack from the cable, then tighten the locknut. The parking brake should be fully ON between 3–5 clicks.
5. Lower the vehicle and reconnect the negative battery cable.

Removal and Installation

XJS

1. Disconnect the negative battery cable.
2. Remove the driver's seat from the vehicle.
3. Remove the parking brake lever cover, lift the carpet and loosen the cable adjusting and locknuts.
4. Remove the adjustable nipple from the end of the parking brake cable.
5. Raise the vehicle and support it safely.
6. Disconnect the nipple, inner cable and outer cable from the operating arm of the caliper.

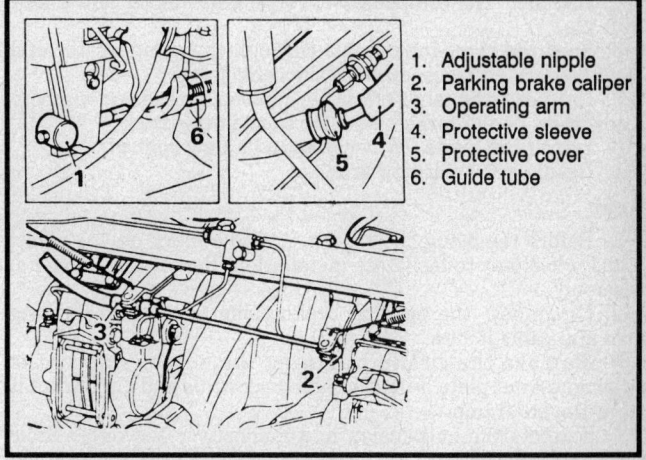

1. Adjustable nipple
2. Parking brake caliper
3. Operating arm
4. Protective sleeve
5. Protective cover
6. Guide tube

Parking brake cable assembly

7. Cut the retaining clips from the protective sleeve-to-outer cable.
8. Remove the protective cover from the point where the outer cable goes through the body.
9. Lower the vehicle. From inside the vehicle, pull the cable from the body guide tube and remove the cable.
To install:
10. Transfer the adjusting nut and guide tube to the new cable.
11. Install the cable into position.
12. Raise and support the vehicle safely.
13. Fit the outer cables to the operating arm, install the inner cable and the nipple to the other operating arm.
14. Install the protective cover and sleeve. Use a new retaining clip.
15. Lower the vehicle. From inside the vehicle, attach the cable to the lever mounting point, then install the adjustable nipple to the cable end.
16. Adjust the parking brake.
17. Refit the parking brake cover and install the seat assembly.
18. Reconnect the negative battery cable.

XJ6
Front

1. Release the parking brake lever.
2. Disconnect the negative battery cable.
3. Raise and support the vehicle safely.
4. Remove the parking brake lever split pin and clevis pin.
5. Remove the washer and cable assembly from the relay lever.
To install:
6. Lubricate the lever and clevis pin. Install the cable, washer, clevis pin and split pin.
7. Loosen the adjuster locknut and tighten the adjuster to remove any slack from the cable.

Intermediate

1. Remove the split pin and clevis pin from the intermediate cable to relay lever.
2. Remove the compensator, intermediate cable and adjuster assembly.
3. Loosen the forked adjuster from the threaded part of the intermediate cable assembly and unscrew the locknut.
4. Remove the split pin and clevis pin from the compensator to intermediate cable.
5. Remove the clevis pin, washer and intermediate cable.
To install:
6. Assemble the locknut and forked adjuster to the threaded part of the replacement cable. Do not fully tighten at this time.

7. Assemble the compensator, clevis pin, washer and a new split pin.

8. Feed the right inner cable through the compensator and reconect the left inner cable at the cable joiner.

9. Lubricate the cable, clevis pin adjuster thread and compensator, then fit the forked adjuster to the relay lever.

10. Install the clevis pin, washer and a new split pin.

11. Readjust the parking brake.

Rear

1. Before removing the wheels, scribe a mark on the wheel and 1 wheel nut to facilatate installation. Remove the wheel(s) assembly.

2. Disconnect the parking brake cable from the operating arm and cable joiner.

3. Remove the circlip retaining the outer cable to the subframe front plate. Pull the cable rearwards and disconnect it from the subframe.

4. Support the suspension and manoeuvor the outer cable from the hub carrier.

To install:

5. Lightly lubricate the ring on the cable. Install the cable to the hub carrier, using a twisting action.

6. Remove the support from the suspension and fit the cable through the mounting hole in the subframe. Secure it a new circlip.

7. Lubricate the cables and compsnsator. Check that the left side cable is correctly positioned in the compensator and reconnect the right side cable to the joiner.

8. Reconnect the cable to the parking brake operating arm. Install the clevis pin and a new split pin.

9. Readjust the parking brake.

10. Install the wheels and lower the vehicle.

11. Reconnect the negative battery cable.

Brake System Bleeding

1. Disconnect the negative battery cable.

2. Check the master cylinder fluid level and adjust, as necessary.

3. Raise the vehicle and support it safely.

NOTE: Never allow brake fluid to contact the vehicle paint work. If a spill occurs, rinse immediately with running water.

Start the bleeding operation with the wheel furthest away from the master cylinder.

During the bleeding operation, check that the level of the fluid in the reservoir is keep at an appropriate level, to avoid drawing more air into the brake system.

4. Remove the dust cap from bleed screw and attach one end of a bleed tube to the bleed screw. Partially fill a small jar with fresh brake fluid and immerse the other end into the jar.

5. Loosen the bleed screw ½ of a turn.

6. Slowly pump the brake pedal until clear, air-free fluid flows from the bleed screw.

7. Tighten the bleed screw and and remove the bleed hose. Recheck the master cylinder fluid level.

8. Repeat Steps 4–7 at the remaining wheels.

Anti-Lock Brake System Service

Precautions

Failure to observe the following precautions may result in system damage:

• Never disassemble any component of the Anti-Lock Brake System (ABS) which is designated non-servicable; the component must be replaced as an assembly.

• Do not allow the pump motor to run continuously for more that 2 minutes. If, for any reason, the motor overrun the 2 min-

ute time limit, immediately turn the ignition switch **OFF**. Allow the motor to cool for at least 10 minutes before continuing with the bleeding procedure.

Brake System Bleeding

EXCEPT THE MOTOR, PUMP UNIT, FLUID INTAKE HOSE OR ACTUATION UNIT

Front

1. Position the vehicle on a level surface.

2. With the ignition switch **OFF**, operate the brake pedal, approximately 20 times, until the pedal goes hard.

3. Fill the master cylinder reservoir approximately ¾ inch below the bottom of the filler neck.

4. Bleed the caliper furthest away from the actuation unit.

NOTE: The following procedure must be done at a rate not faster than 3 seconds per cycle.

5. Open the bleed nipple, then have a helper fully depress the brake pedal and hold.

6. Close the bleed nipple, then have the helper release the pedal slowly.

7. Repeat Steps 6 and 7 until clear air-free fluid flows from the bleed nipple.

8. Repeat the procedure for the opposite caliper.

Rear

1. Position the vehicle on a level surface.

2. With the ignition switch **OFF**, operate the brake pedal, approximately 20 times, until the pedal goes hard.

3. Fill the master cylinder reservoir approximately ¾ inch below the bottom of the filler neck.

4. Open the bleed nipple, then have a helper fully depress the brake pedal and hold.

5. Turn the ignition switch **ON** and wait, approximately 15 seconds, until clear air-free fluid flows from the bleed nipple.

6. Close the bleed nipple, then have the helper release the pedal slowly.

7. Turn the ignition switch **OFF**.

8. Repeat the procedure for the opposite caliper.

NOTE: Do not allow the master cylinder reservoir to drop more than ⅜ inch below the maximum mark during the bleeding procedure.

MOTOR, PUMP UNIT, FLUID INTAKE HOSE OR ACTUATION UNIT

1. Position the vehicle on a level surface.

2. Turn the ignition switch **OFF**.

3. Fill the master cylinder reservoir approximately ¾ inch below the bottom of the filler neck.

4. Disconnect the fluid intake hose at the pump and allow the fluid to flow into a container until all air has been removed.

5. Check that the plastic O-ring is not damaged, then reconnect the intake hose while the fluid is flowing.

6. Turn the ignition switch **ON** and depressed the brake pedal several times.

7. If the motor/pump unit is charging, the fluid level in the reservoir will decrease. The upper cut-out point should be reached in less that 60 seconds.

8. After bleeding is completed, turn the ignition switch **ON**. Wait until the accumulator is charged to the upper cut-out point and adjust the reservoir to the maximum level.

System Components

CAUTION

The anti-lock brake system operates under high hydraulic pressure. To avoid personal injury, special care must be exercised when servicing or repairing the system.

ACTUATION UNIT

Removal and Installation

1. Position the vehicle on a level surface.
2. Disconnect the negative battery cable.
3. With the ignition switch **OFF**, operate the brake pedal, approximately 20 times, until the pedal goes hard.
4. Place a suitable container beneath the reservoir area. Wrap a shop rag around the low pressure hose. Disconnect the hose and drain the fluid.
5. Disconnect the reservoir multi-plug and remove the reservoir.
6. Disconnect the actuation unit multi-plug and remove the fluid lines from the valve block.
7. Remove the high pressure line.
8. Remove the pedal box-to-bulkhead retaining bolts and remove the actuation unit and pedal box assembly. Remove the split pin and clevis pin.
9. Remove the actuation unit-to-pedal box retaining bolts and separate the unit.

To install:

10. Fit and secure the actuation unit to the pedal box. Connect the brake pedal and install the clevis and split pins.
11. Install the assembly into position and connect the lines to the valve block.
12. Install the pedal box retaining bolts.
13. Reconnect the high pressure pipe and mlti-plug connector.
14. Re-fit the reservoir into position and connect the low pressure hose, using a new O-ring.
15. Bleed the hydraulic system.
16. Turn the ignition switch **ON**. Wait until the accumulator is charged to the upper cut-out point and adjust the reservoir to the maximum level.

ACCUMULATOR

Removal and Installation

1. Position the vehicle on a level surface.
2. Disconnect the negative battery cable.

3. With the ignition switch **OFF**, operate the brake pedal, approximately 20 times, until the pedal goes hard.
4. Place a suitable container beneath the accumulator area.
5. Slacken off and remove the accumulator.

To install:

6. Re-fit the accumulator, using a new O-ring.
7. Re-connect the negative battery cable.
8. Turn the ignition switch **ON**. Wait until the accumulator is charged to the upper cut-out point and the ABS warning light goes **OFF**.
9. Turn the ignition switch **OFF**.

MOTOR AND PUMP UNIT

Removal and Installation

1. Position the vehicle on a level surface.
2. Disconnect the negative battery cable.
3. With the ignition switch **OFF**, operate the brake pedal, approximately 20 times, until the pedal goes hard.
4. Place a suitable container beneath the reservoir area. Wrap a shop rag around the low pressure hose. Disconnect the hose and drain the fluid.
5. Disconnect the pressure warning switch and multi-plug.
6. Disconnect the pipe at the end of the motor/pump unit.
7. Remove the motor/pump unit special retaining bolt and remove the unit.
8. Remove the accumulator and pressure warning switch from the unit.

To install:

9. Install the pressure warning switch to the motor/pump unit, using a new O-ring.
10. Install the accumulator, using a new O-ring.
11. Install the unit into the vehicle, using a new special bolt.
12. Install the low pressure hose, using a new O-ring.
13. Reconnect the pipe and multi-plug connector to the motor/pump unit.
14. Bleed the hydraulic system.
15. Turn the ignition switch **ON**. Wait until the accumulator is charged to the upper cut-out point and adjust the reservoir to the maximum level.

FRONT SUSPENSION

Shock Absorbers

Removal and Installation

XJ6

1. Disconnect the negative battery cable.
2. Raise the vehicle and safely support it with axle stands.
3. Before removing the wheels, scribe a mark on the wheel and 1 wheel nut to facilitate installation. Remove the wheel assembly.
4. Remove the weight from the suspension, using tool JD 133 or equivalent.
5. Remove the shock absorber upper retaining locknut, then remove the washers and rubber insulators.
6. Remove the anti-roll bar lower link arm to provide access, then remove the shock absorber lower retaining nuts and bolts.
7. Remove the shock absorber from the vehicle. Remove the washers and rubber insulators.

To install:

8. Assemble the rubber insulators and washers to the replacement shock, then fit it into the vehicle.
9. Install the lower retaining bolts and nuts.
10. Install the anti-roll bar lower link arm.

11. Secure the shock upper mounting stud, then remove tool JD 133 or equivalent.
12. Install the wheel to the vehicle.
13. Lower the vehicle and reconnect the negative battery cable.

XJS

1. Disconnect the negative battery cable.
2. If necessary, remove the air cleaner assembly to gain access.
3. Remove the locknut, nut, outer washer, rubber buffer and inner washer from the shock mounting.
4. Raise the vehicle and safely support it with axle stands.
5. Remove the locknut and bolts from the bottom of the shock.
6. Remove the shock from the vehicle.

To install:

7. Before installing the replacement shock, it is advisable to purge the air from the pressure chamber, as follow:
    a. Hold the shock absorber vertically and make several half-way strokes, then extend the shock absorber to its full length once or twice.
    b. Keep the shock in an upright position until the shock is installed on the vehicle.

8. Assemble the lower washers and rubber buffer to the shock stem, then fit the shock into position and install the retaining bolts and locking nut.

9. Lower the vehicle.

10. Install the upper washers, rubber buffer, nut and locknut.

11. If removed, install the air cleaner assembly.

12. Reconnect the negative battery cable.

Coil Springs

Removal and Installation

XJ6 AND XJS

1. Disconnect the negative battery cable.

2. Raise the vehicle and safely support it with axle stands.

3. Before removing the wheels, scribe a mark on the wheel and 1 wheel nut to facilitate installation. Remove the wheel(s) assembly.

4. Compress the spring, using tool, JD 115, JD6G or equivalent.

5. Remove the spring support retaining bolts, then carefully loosen the spring compressor to release the spring tension.

6. Remove the tool, spring and spring plates.

To install:

7. Assemble the spring and spring plates to the compressor tool, then fit the assembly into position. Make certain the tool is seated properly.

8. Tighten the tool to compress the spring. Install guide bolts as the spring is being compressed.

9. After the spring support is completely seated, remove the guide bolts and install new retaining bolts.

NOTE: Do not reuse the old spring support retaining bolts.

Upper Ball Joints

Removal and Installation

XJ6

1. Disconnect the negative battery cable.

2. Raise the vehicle and safely support it with axle stands.

3. Before removing the wheels, scribe a mark on the wheel and 1 wheel nut to facilatate installation. Remove the wheel(s) assembly.

4. Remove the upper ball joint retaining bolts from the control arm. Note the position of the castor shims and recover them.

5. Separate the upper control arm.

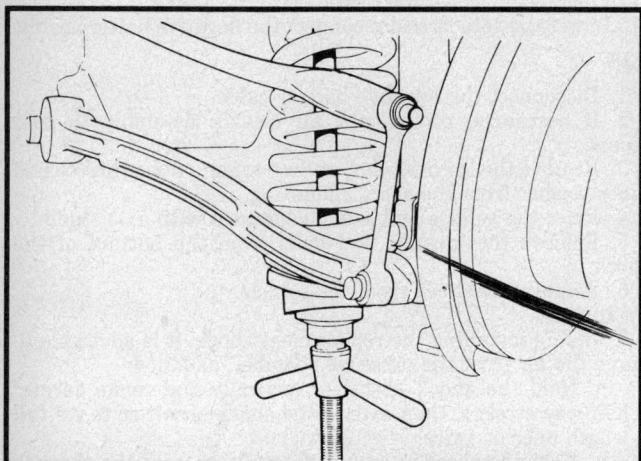

Front spring, removal and installation

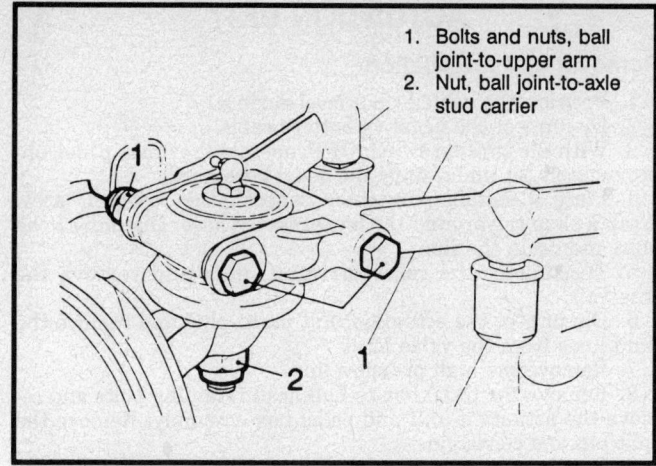

1. Bolts and nuts, ball joint-to-upper arm
2. Nut, ball joint-to-axle stud carrier

Upper ball joint assembly—XJS shown

6. Remove the upper ball joint to steering knuckle retaining nut and separate the ball joint.

7. Remove the ball joint and tool.

To install:

8. Fit the replacement ball joint into place but do not tighten the retaining nut at this time.

9. Fit the ball joint retaining bolts into position and install the castor shims. Torque the retaining 55–60 ft. lbs. (75–80 Nm).

10. Torque the ball joint-to-knuckle retaining nut 35–50 ft. lbs. (47–68 Nm).

11. Install the wheel(s) assembly, lower the vehicle and reconnect the negative battery cable.

12. Check and adjust the front wheel alignment.

XJS

1. Disconnect the negative battery cable.

2. Raise the vehicle and safely support it.

3. Before removing the wheels, scribe a mark on the wheel and 1 wheel nut to facilitate installation. Remove the wheel(s) assembly.

4. Compress the spring, using tool JD 6G or equivalent.

5. Wire the stub axle carrier aside.

6. Remove the nuts, bolts and washers retaining the ball joint to the upper arm. Note the position of the castor shims and recover them.

7. Remove the self-locking nut and washer retaining the ball joint to the spindle assembly, then separate the ball joint using tool JD 100 or equivalent.

To install:

8. Fit the replacement ball joint into place and tighten the locknut.

9. Fit the ball joint to the upper arm, being certain that the shims are correctly positioned. Install and tighten the nuts, bolts and washers.

10. Remove the service tool and install the wheel(s) assembly.

11. Lower the vehicle and reconnect the negative battery cable.

12. Check and adjust the front wheel alignment.

Lower Ball Joints

Removal and Installation

XJ6

1. Disconnect the negative battery cable.

2. Raise the vehicle and safely support it.

3. Before removing the wheels, scribe a mark on the wheel

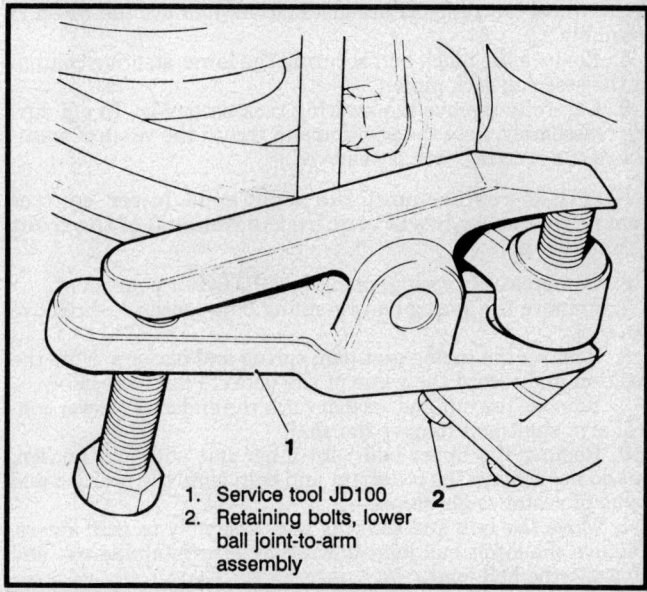

1. Service tool JD100
2. Retaining bolts, lower
   ball joint-to-arm
   assembly

Separating track rod end from lower arm

and 1 wheel nut to facilitate installation. Remove the wheel(s) assembly.

4. Disconnect the left side parking brake pad wear sensor block connector.

5. Remove the brake caliper and position it aside.

6. Remove the retaining nut that secures the steering arm to the tie rod end. Assemble tool JD 100 or equivalent, to the track rod end joint and break the taper.

7. Remove the upper ball joint retaining bolts. Note the position of the caster shims and recover them.

8. Remove the lower ball joint-to-spindle assembly retaining nut. Fit tool JD 100 or equivalent, into position and separate the ball joint.

9. Remove the steering arm assembly from the lower arm.

10. Remove the lower ball joint-to-arm assembly retaining bolts and remove the ball joint assembly.

To install:

11. Fit the replacement lower ball joint into position and install the retaining bolts. Tighten and torque 45–55 ft. lbs. (61–75 Nm).

12. Install the steering arm assembly to the lower arm.

13. Install the upper ball joint, but do not tighten the retaining nut at this time.

14. Install the ball joint retaining bolts into position and install the castor shims. Torque the retaining 55–60 ft. lbs. (75–80 Nm).

15. Reconnect the tie-rod end to the steering arm.

16. Install the brake caliper and re-connect the left side parking brake pad wear sensor block connector.

17. Install the wheel(s) assembly and lower the vehicle.

18. Reconnect the negative battery cable.

19. Check and adjust the front wheel alignment.

XJS

1. Disconnect the negative battery cable.

2. Raise the vehicle and safely support it.

3. Before removing the wheels, scribe a mark on the wheel and 1 wheel nut to facilitate installation. Remove the wheel(s) assembly.

4. Compress the spring, using tool JD 6G or equivalent.

5. Remove the nut retaining the outer ball joint to the steering arm, using tool JD 24, JD 100 or equivalent.

6. Remove the upper ball joint inner nut and bolt. Loosen, but do not remove the outer nut and bolt.

7. Remove the lower ball joint-to-arm retaining nut.

8. Support the hub and disc assembly and separate the ball joint from the steering arm assembly.

9. Remove the lower ball joint-to-arm (4) retaining bolts and remove the ball joint.

To install:

10. Fit the replacement lower ball joint into place and install the retaining bolts.

11. Fit the lower ball joint to the steering arm assembly.

12. Install the upper ball joint inner bolt. Tighten both inner and outer bolts.

13. Remove the spring compressor.

14. Install the wheel(s) assembly and lower the vehicle.

15. Reconnect the negative battery cable.

16. Check and adjust the front wheel alignment.

Upper Control Arms

Removal and Installation

XJ6

1. Disconnect the negative battery cable.

2. Raise the vehicle and safely support it.

3. Before removing the wheels, scribe a mark on the wheel and 1 wheel nut to facilitate installation. Remove the wheel(s) assembly.

4. Remove the upper ball joint retaining bolts from the control arm. Note the position of the castor shims and recover them.

5. Remove the accumulator clamp and bracket retaining bolt, then reposition the accumulator for access.

6. Remove the nut, washers and bolt from the rear and front of the upper control arm. Remove the upper control arm.

To install:

7. Fit the replacement upper control arm into position and install the bolt, washers and nut to the front and rear of the control arm.

8. Re-fit the accumulator.

9. Re-fit the upper ball joint-to-control arm retaining bolts. Be certain to locate the castor shims in their proper positions.

10. Install the wheel(s) assembly and lower the vehicle.

11. Reconnect the negative battery cable.

12. Check and adjust the front wheel alignment.

XJS

1. Disconnect the negative battery cable.

2. Raise the vehicle and safely support it.

3. Before removing the wheels, scribe a mark on the wheel and 1 wheel nut to facilitate installation. Remove the wheel(s) assembly.

4. Compress the spring, using tool JD 6G or equivalent.

5. Separate the upper ball joint from the steering arm assembly. Note the position of the castor angle shims and recover them.

6. Wire up the steering arm assembly so the brake hose is not damaged.

7. Remove the (2) bolts that retains the upper control arm shaft. Note the position of the camber angle shims and recover them.

8. Remove the upper arm.

To install:

9. Fit the upper arm to the suspension, making certain that the camber angle shims are correctly positioned.

NOTE: Do not tighten the control arm shaft retaining nuts until the full weight of the vehicle is resting on the suspension.

10. Resecure the upper ball joint, making certain that the castor angle shims are correctly positioned.

11. Remove the spring compressor tool and install the wheel(s).

12. Lower the vehicle and tighten the control arm shaft retaining nuts.
13. Reconnect the negative battery cable.
14. Check and adjust the front wheel alignment.

Lower Control Arms

Removal and Installation
XJ6

1. Disconnect the negative battery cable.
2. Raise the vehicle and safely support it.
3. Before removing the wheels, scribe a mark on the wheel and 1 wheel nut to facilitate installation. Remove the wheel(s) assembly.
4. Compress the spring, using tool JD 115 or equivalent.
5. Remove the spring pan retaining bolt, loosen and remove the tool.
6. Remove the caliper and wire it aside.
7. Separate the upper ball joint from the steering arm assembly. Note the position of the castor angle shims and recover them.
8. Separate the tie-rod from the steering arm.
9. Remove the shock absorber lower retaining bolts and nuts.
10. Lower the control arm and steering arm assembly.
11. Maneuver the steering rack to gain access, then remove the lower control arm retaining bolts, nuts and washers. Remove the lower control arm.

To install:

12. Install the lower control arm to the vehicle.
13. Install the shock absorber lower retaining bolts and nuts.
14. Install the tie-rod.
15. Resecure the upper ball joint, making certain that the castor angle shims are correctly positioned.
16. Install the caliper assembly.
17. Fit tool JD 115 or equivalent into place and secure the spring pan.
18. Install the wheel(s) assembly and lower the vehicle.
19. Reconnect the negative battery cable.
20. Check and adjust the front wheel alignment.

XJS

1. Disconnect the negative battery cable.
2. Raise the vehicle and safely support it.
3. Before removing the wheels, scribe a mark on the wheel and 1 wheel nut to facilatate installation. Remove the wheel(s) assembly.
4. Remove the pinch bolt securing the lower steering column to the steering rack pinion.
5. Carefully remove the steering rack assembly. To aid during reassembly, note the position and record the value of washers as the steering rack is removed.

NOTE: If replacement the right side lower control arm is necessary, it will require the removal of the front exhaust pipe.

6. Compress the spring, using tool JD 6G or equivalent.
7. Remove the spring pan retaining bolt, loosen and remove the tool.
8. Remove the spring seat pan, spring and packers. Note the position and record the value of the packers for reassembly.
9. Remove the nut and washer form the end of the lower control arm shaft and remove the shaft.
10. Remove the upper ball joint inner nut and bolt. Loosen, but do not remove the outer nut and bolt. Note the position and value of castor angle shims.
11. Move the hub and steering arm assembly to gain access. Remove the lower ball joint-to-steering arm retaining nut and separate the ball joint.
12. Remove the bolts retaining the front damper and anti-roll bar brackets to the lower control arm.
13. Remove the shock absorber.
14. Remove the lower control arm.

To install:

15. Install the lower control arm to the vehicle.
16. Install the damper and anti-roll bar brackets.
17. Resecure the lower ball joint to the steering axle.
18. Refit the upper ball joint. Make certain the shims are correctly positioned.
19. Refit the lower control arm shaft, washer and nut.

NOTE: Do not tighten the control arm shaft retaining nuts until the full weight of the vehicle is resting on the suspension.

20. Install the spring seat pan, spring and packers.
21. If required, install the exhaust down pipe.
22. Install the steering rack. Make certain to correctly positioned the washers.
23. Install the steering column pinch bolt.
24. Install the wheels and lower the vehicle.
25. Reconnect the negative battery cable.
26. Check and adjust the front wheel alignment.

REAR SUSPENSION

Spring and Shock Absorber Assembly

Removal and Installation
XJ6

1. Disconnect the negative battery cable.
2. Raise the vehicle and safely support it.
3. Before removing the wheels, scribe a mark on the wheel and 1 wheel nut to facilitate installation. Remove the wheel(s) assembly.
4. Remove the brake caliper and position it aside.
5. Remove the shock absorber lower retaining nut and bolt.
6. Remove the shock absorber to body retaining bolts and remove the spring assembly.
7. Compress the spring, using tool JD 125 or equivalent.
8. Remove the cotters and release the spring.
9. Remove the collar, spring seat and spring.

To install:

10. Compress the spring assembly and fit the collar, new spring seat and cotters.
11. Check to ensure the cotters are properly seated, then release the spring tension.
12. Fit the assembly to the vehicle.
13. Install the caliper assembly.
14. Install the wheel(s) assembly.
15. Lower the vehicle and reconnect the negative battery cable.

SERIAL NUMBER IDENTIFICATION

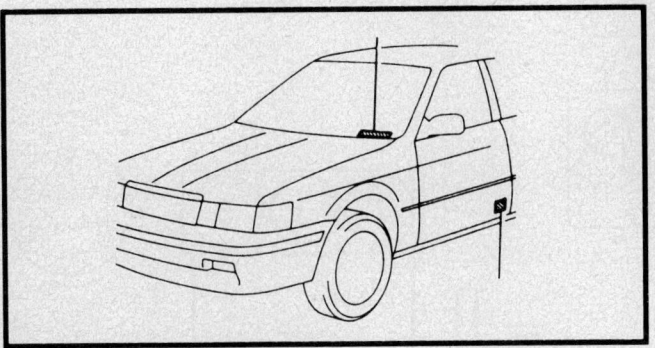

Vehicle identification plate

Engine serial number—ES250

Engine serial number—LS400

Vehicle Identification Plate

The vehicle identification plate is located at the top of the left instrument panel.

Engine Number

The engine identification on the side of the engine block on the ES250 and the top of the engine block on the LS400.

Vehicle Identification Number

The vehicle identification number is also located on the left front door.

SPECIFICATIONS

ENGINE IDENTIFICATION

Year	Model	Engine Displacement cu. in. (cc/liter)	Engine Series Identification	No. of Cylinders	Engine Type
1990–91	ES250	153 (2508/2.5)	2V2-FE	6	DOHC
	LS400	242.1 (3969/4.0)	1V2-FE	8	DOHC

GENERAL ENGINE SPECIFICATIONS

Year	Model	Engine Displacement cu. in. (cc)	Fuel System Type	Net Horsepower @ rpm	Net Torque @ rpm (ft. lbs.)	Bore × Stroke (in.)	Compression Ratio	Oil Pressure @ rpm
1990–91	ES250	153 (2508)	EFI	156 @ 5600	160 @ 4400	3.44 × 2.74	9.0:1	43–78 @ 3000
	LS400	242.1 (3969)	EFI	250 @ 5600	260 @ 4400	3.44 × 3.25	10.0:1	36–71 @ 3000

GASOLINE ENGINE TUNE-UP SPECIFICATIONS

Year	Model	Engine Displacement cu. in. (cc)	Spark Plugs Type	Spark Plugs Gap (in.)	Ignition Timing (deg.) MT	Ignition Timing (deg.) AT	Compression Pressure (psi)	Fuel Pump (psi)	Idle Speed (rpm) MT	Idle Speed (rpm) AT	Valve Clearance In.	Valve Clearance Ex.
1990	ES250	153 (2508)	①	0.043	10B	10B	142	38–44	600–700	650–750	③	③
	LS400	242.1 (3969)	②	0.043	8–12B	8–12B	142	38–44	600–700	600–700	④	④
1991		SEE UNDERHOOD SPECIFICATIONS STICKER										

① BCPR6EP11
② BKR6EP11

③ Intake—0.005 in. cold
  Exhaust—0.015 in. cold

④ Intake—0.006–0.010 in. cold
  Exhaust—0.010–0.014 in. cold

FIRING ORDERS

NOTE: To avoid confusion, always replace spark plug wires one at a time.

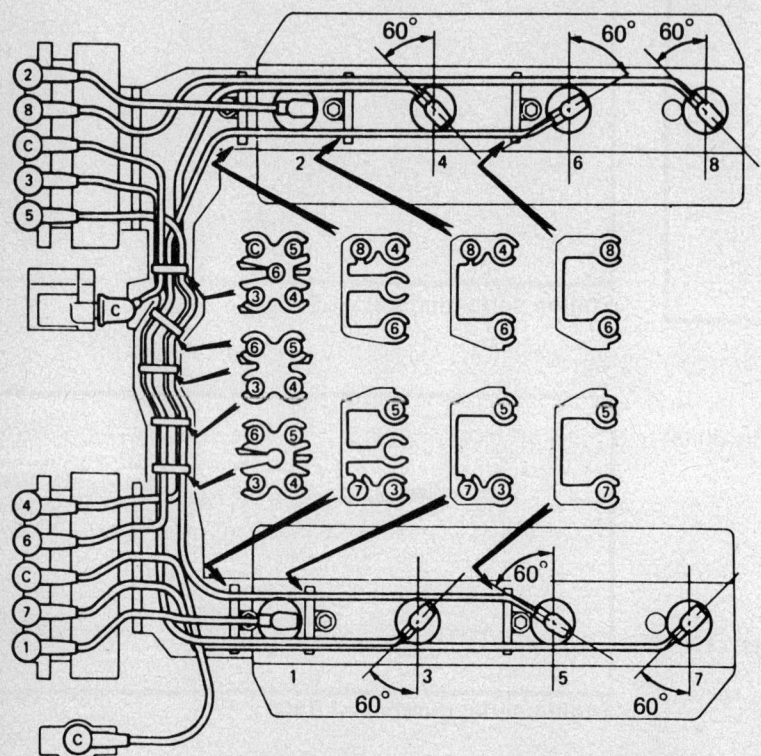

4.0L Engine
Engine Firing Order: 1–8–4–3–6–5–7–2
Distributorless Ignition System

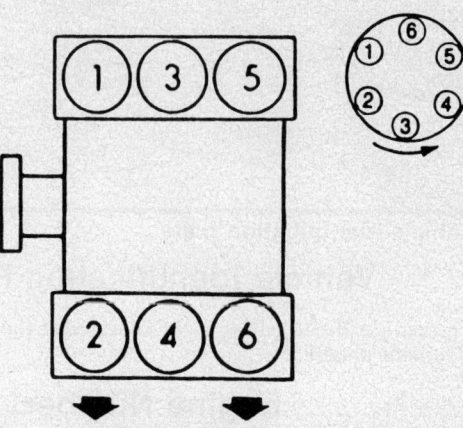

Front of car

2.5L Engine
Engine Firing Order: 1-2-3-4-5-6
Distributor Rotation: Counterclockwise

CAPACITIES

Year	Model	Engine Displacement cu. in. (cc)	Engine Crankcase (qts.) with Filter	without Filter	Transmission (pts.) 4-Spd	5-Spd	Auto.	Drive Axle (pts.)	Fuel Tank (gal.)	Cooling System (qts.)
1990-91	ES250	153 (2508)	4.1	3.9	—	4.4	2.6	1.1	15.9	①
	LS400	242.1 (3969)	5.3	5	—	—	2.1	1.3	22.5	11.2

① MT—10.0 qts.
AT—9.9 qts.

CAMSHAFT SPECIFICATIONS

All measurements given in inches.

Year	Engine Displacement cu. in. (cc)	Journal Diameter 1	2	3	4	5	Lobe Lift In.	Ex.	Bearing Clearance	Camshaft End Play
1990-91	153 (2508)	1.0610-1.0616	1.0610-1.0616	1.0610-1.0616	1.0610-1.0616	1.0610-1.0616	1.5555-1.5594	1.5339-1.5378	0.0014-0.0028	0.0012-0.0031
	242.1 (3969) ①	1.0612-1.0618	1.0612-1.0618	1.0612-1.0618	1.0612-1.0618	1.0612-1.0618	1.6421-1.6461	1.6500-1.6539	0.0012-0.0026	0.0016-0.0035

① The exhaust camshaft thrust portion of journal diameter is 0.9433-0.9439 in.

CRANKSHAFT AND CONNECTING ROD SPECIFICATIONS

All measurements are given in inches.

Year	Engine Displacement cu. in. (cc)	Crankshaft				Connecting Rod		
		Main Brg. Journal Dia.	Main Brg. Oil Clearance	Shaft End-play	Thrust on No.	Journal Diameter	Oil Clearance	Side Clearance
1990–91	153 (2508)	2.5191–2.5197	0.0011–0.0022	0.0008–0.0087	3	1.8892–1.8898	0.0011–0.0026	0.0059–0.0130
	242.1 (3969)	2.6373–2.6378	0.0010–0.0018	0.0008–0.0087	3	2.0465–2.0472	0.0011–0.0021	0.0063–0.0114

VALVE SPECIFICATIONS

Year	Engine Displacement cu. in. (cc)	Seat Angle (deg.)	Face Angle (deg.)	Spring Test Pressure (lbs.)	Spring Installed Height (in.)	Stem-to-Guide Clearance (in.)		Stem Diameter (in.)	
						Intake	Exhaust	Intake	Exhaust
1990–91	153 (2508)		44.5	41.0–47.2	1.677	0.0010–0.0024	0.0012–0.0026	0.2350–0.2356	0.2348–0.2354
	242.1 (3969)		44.5	41.9–46.3	1.717	0.0010–0.0024	0.0012–0.0026	0.2350–0.2356	0.2348–0.2354

PISTON AND RING SPECIFICATIONS

All measurements are given in inches.

Year	Engine Displacement cu. in. (cc)	Piston Clearance	Ring Gap			Ring Side Clearance		
			Top Compression	Bottom Compression	Oil Control	Top Compression	Bottom Compression	Oil Control
1990–91	153 (2508)	0.0018–0.0026	0.0118–0.0213	0.0138–0.0244	0.0079–0.0224	0.0004–0.0031	0.0012–0.0028	—
	242.1 (3969)	0.0008–0.0016	0.0098–0.0177	0.0138–0.0236	0.0059–0.0197	0.0008–0.0024	0.0006–0.0022	—

TORQUE SPECIFICATIONS

All readings in ft. lbs.

Year	Engine Displacement cu. in. (cc)	Cylinder Head Bolts	Main Bearing Bolts	Rod Bearing Bolts	Crankshaft Pulley Bolts	Flywheel Bolts	Manifold		Spark Plugs
							Intake	Exhaust	
1990–91	153 (2508)	①	②	③	181	61	13	29	13
	242.1 (3969)	④	⑤	③	181	72	13	29	13

① Tighten in 3 steps:
1—tighten to 25 ft. lbs.
2—turn 90 degrees
3—turn 90 degrees
② Tighten in 2 steps:
1—tighten to 45 ft. lbs.
2—turn 90 degrees
③ Tighten in 2 steps:
1—tighten to 18 ft. lbs.
2—turn 90 degrees
④ Tighten in 2 steps:
1—tighten to 29 ft. lbs.
2—turn 90 degrees
⑤ Tighten in 2 steps:
1—tighten to 20 ft. lbs.
2—turn 90 degrees

BRAKE SPECIFICATIONS
All measurements in inches unless noted.

Year	Model	Lug Nut Torque (ft. lbs.)	Master Cylinder Bore	Brake Disc Minimum Thickness	Brake Disc Maximum Runout	Standard Brake Drum Diameter	Minimum Lining Thickness Front	Minimum Lining Thickness Rear
1990-91	ES250	76	NA	0.945②	0.0028③	NA	0.039	0.039
	LS400	76	NA	0.906①	0.0020	NA	0.039	0.039

NA—Not available
① Rear—0.591 in.
② Rear—0.354 in.
③ Rear—0.0059 in.

WHEEL ALIGNMENT

Year	Model	Caster Range (deg.)	Caster Preferred Setting (deg.)	Camber Range (deg.)	Camber Preferred Setting (deg.)	Toe-in (in.)	Steering Axis Inclination (deg.)
1990-91	ES250 Front	$^{11}/_{12}$P–$2^5/_{12}$P	$1^2/_3$P	$^1/_4$N–$1^1/_4$P	$^1/_2$P	$^1/_{16}$N–$^3/_4$	22
	Rear	—	—	$1^5/_{12}$N–$^1/_4$P	$^2/_3$N	$^{13}/_{32}$–$^{15}/_{16}$	—
	LS400 Front	$8^1/_2$P–10P②	$9^1/_4$P	$^2/_3$N–$1^5/_6$P①	$^1/_{12}$P	0–$^{13}/_{16}$	$32^2/_3$③
	Rear	—	—	$^3/_4$N–$^3/_4$P	0④	0–$^{13}/_{16}$⑤	—

① W/air suspension $^5/_6$N–$^2/_3$P—Range
   $^1/_{12}$N—Preferred
② W/air suspension $9^1/_4$P–$10^7/_{12}$P—Range
   $9^5/_6$P—Preferred
③ W/air suspension $32^1/_2$ degree
④ W/air suspension $1^1/_2$N–0—Range
   $^3/_4$N—Preferred
⑤ W/air suspension $^{11}/_{32}$–$^7/_8$ in.

ENGINE ELECTRICAL

NOTE: Disconnecting the negative battery cable on some vehicles may interfere with the functions of the on board computer systems and may require the computer to undergo a relearning process, once the negative battery cable is reconnected.

Distributor

Removal

ES250

1. Disconnect the negative battery cable. Remove the upper bracket.
2. Remove the air cleaner top. Disconnect the air flow meter and the air cleaner hose.
3. Remove the wires from the distributor cap and disconnect the distributor wire connector.
4. Remove the hold-down bolts and pull out the distributor. Remove the O-ring.
5. Remove the distributor.

LS400

Right

1. Disconnect the negative battery cable. Remove the air duct assembly.
2. Disconnect the air flow meter connector and air hose.
3. Remove the air flow meter assembly and the throttle body cover.
4. Disconnect the ISC and power steering idle-up air hose. Remove the No. 1 air hose.
5. Remove the high tension cable upper cover and the right side engine wire cover.

6. Disconnect the mounting bolts and remove the No. 3 timing belt cover.
7. Disconnect the sensor connector. Remove the mounting bolts, the wire cover and take off the No. 2 timing belt cover.
8. Disconnect the electrical wires from the distributor cap.
9. Remove the distributor cap and the rotor.
10. Remove the mounting bolts and lift out the distributor housing.

Left

1. Disconnect the negative battery cable. Drain the cooling system and remove the engine wire cover.
2. Remove the No. 2 junction block cover and the No. 3 timing belt cover.
3. Disconnect the water inlet housing hose and the reservoir tank hose.
4. Remove the mounting bolts and the water pipe from the No. 2 timing belt cover.
5. Disconnect the sensor connector, the connector boot and remove the No. 2 timing belt cover.
6. Disconnect the electrical connections from the cap and the housing. Remove the distributor cap and the rotor.
7. Remove the mounting screws and lift out the distributor housing.

Installation

TIMING NOT DISTURBED

ES250

1. Install a new O-ring in the housing. Lubricate the O-ring with engine oil.
2. Align the cutout marks of the coupling and the housing.

3. Insert the distributor, aligning the line of the distributor housing with the cutout of the distributor attachment bearing cap. Tighten the left side hold-down bolts.

4. Install the rotor and the distributor cap. Connect the cables to the distributor cap. Align the spline of the distributor cap with the spline groove of the holder.

5. Connect the electrical connections to the distributor. Replace the air cleaner cap, air flow meter and the air cleaner hose.

6. Install the upper bracket and connect the negative battery cable.

7. Adjust the timing.

LS400—Right

1. Install the distributor housing. Replace the rotor and the distributor cap.

2. Connect the ignition cables to the distributor cap.

3. Connect the sensor connector. Install the No. 2 timing belt cover and boots.

4. Install the No. 3 timing belt cover and engine wire cover. Tighten the mounting bolts.

5. Install the electrical connection upper cover and the upper throttle body cover.

6. Replace the No. 1 air hose, the PS idle-up air hose and the ISC air hose.

7. Install the air flow meter assembly and connect the air hose and the meter connector.

8. Connect the negative battery cable. Adjust the timing.

LS400—Left

1. Install the distributor housing and tighten the mounting bolts.

2. Install the rotor and replace the distributor cap.

3. Connect the ignition cables to the distributor cap.

4. Connect the sensor connector. Install the No. 2 timing belt cover and boots.

5. Connect the water inlet housing hose and the reservoir tank hose.

4. Replace the water pipe to the No. 2 timing belt cover.

6. Install the No. 3 timing belt cover and replace the No. 2 junction block cover.

7. Install the engine wire cover and tighten the mounting bolts.

8. Refill the cooling system and connect the negative battery cable. Adjust the timing.

TIMING DISTURBED

1. Turn the crankshaft pulley and the groove on the pulley with the timing mark 0 of the No. 1 timing belt cover.

2. Check that the timing marks of the camshaft timing pulleys and the No. 3 timing belt cover are aligned. If not, turn the crankshaft 1 revolution (360 degrees).

3. Position the slit of the intake camshaft (right side cylinder head) in the proper position.

4. Install the distributor following the proper procedure.

Ignition Timing

Adjustment

1. Allow the engine to reach normal operating temperature.

2. Connect a tachometer to terminal IG (−) of the check connector.

3. Check the idle speed, 650–750 rpm on the ES250 or 600–700 rpm on the LS400.

4. Connect the proper tool to terminals TE1 and E1 of the check connector.

5. Connect the timing light to No. 1 clyinder on the ES250 and No. 6 cylinder on the LS400.

6. Start the engine and check the timing with the transmission in N position.

7. The ignition timing should be 10 degrees BTDC at idle on the ES250 or 8–12 degrees BTDC at idle on the LS400.

8. If not within specifications, loosen the hold-down bolts and adjust the timing by turning the distributor.

9. Tighten the hold-down bolts and recheck the timing.

Alternator

Precautions

Several precautions must be observed with alternator equipped vehicles to avoid damage to the unit.

• If the battery is removed for any reason, make sure it is reconnected with the correct polarity. Reversing the battery connections may result in damage to the one-way rectifiers.

• When utilizing a booster battery as a starting aid, always connect the positive to positive terminals and the negative terminal from the booster battery to a good engine ground on the vehicle being started.

• Never use a fast charger as a booster to start vehicles.

• Disconnect the battery cables when charging the battery with a fast charger.

• Never attempt to polarize the alternator.

• Do not use test lamps of more than 12 volts when checking diode continuity.

• Do not short across or ground any of the alternator terminals.

• The polarity of the battery, alternator and regulator must be matched and considered before making any electrical connections within the system.

• Never separate the alternator on an open circuit. Make sure all connections within the circuit are clean and tight.

• Disconnect the battery ground terminal when performing any service on electrical components.

• Disconnect the battery if arc welding is to be done on the vehicle.

Belt Tension Adjustment

A belt tensioner is used to maintain the proper amount of pressure on the drive belt on the LS400. On the ES250:

1. Disconnect the negative battery cable.

2. Loosen the adjusting lock bolt and the pivot bolt.

3. Move the alternator to adjust the belt tension to 5 lbs. on a new belt or 20 lbs. on a used belt.

4. Tighten the adjusting and pivot bolts.

5. Connect the negative battery cable.

Removal and Installation

ES250

1. Disconnect the negative battery cable.

NOTE: Work must be started after approximately 20 seconds or longer from the time the ignition switch is turned to the LOCK position and the negative battery cable is disconnected.

2. Remove the mounting bolts and disconnect the electrical connections at the alternator.

3. Disconnect the wiring harness from the mounting clip.

4. Remove the drive belt.

5. Remove the adjusting lock bolt, the pivot bolt and remove the alternator.

To install:

6. Mount the alternator on the alternator bracket with the pivot bolt and the adjusting bolt. Do not tighten.

7. Install the drive belt and adjust the belt tension.

8. Connect the electrical connections at the alternator and the wiring harness to the mounting clip.
9. Replace the mounting bolts and tighten to 64 ft. lbs.
10. Connect the negative battery cable.

LS400

1. Disconnect the negative battery cable.
2. Remove the drive belt and the engine undercover.
3. Disconnect the electrical connections at the alternator.
4. Remove the through bolt and nut. Remove the alternator.
5. The installation is the reverse of the removal procedure.

Starter

Removal and Installation

ES250

1. Disconnect both battery cables. Remove the battery and battery tray.

NOTE: Work must be started after approximately 20 seconds or longer from the time the ignition switch is turned to the LOCK position and the negative battery cable is disconnected.

2. Disconnect the noise filter connector, the igniter connector, the coil wire and the ground strap.
3. Disconnect the harness clamp and remove the igniter bracket.

4. Disconnect the electrical connections at the starter.
5. Remove the mounting bolts and the starter motor.
To install:
6. Install the starter and tighten the mounting bolts to 29 ft. lbs.
7. Connect the electrical connections at the starter.
8. Install the igniter bracket and connect the harness clamp.
9. Connect noise filter connector, igniter connector, the coil wire and the ground strap.
10. Install the battery tray and the battery.
11. Connect the battery cables.

LS400

1. Disconnect the negative battery cable.

NOTE: Work must be started after approximately 20 seconds or longer from the time the ignition switch is turned to the LOCK position and the negative battery cable is disconnected.

2. Remove the intake chamber and the intake manifold.
3. Disconnect the electrical connections at the starter.
4. Remove the mounting bolts and the starter motor.
To install:
5. Install the starter and tighten the mounting bolts to 29 ft. lbs.
6. Connect the electrical connections at the starter.
7. Install the intake manifold and the intake manifold.
8. Connect the negative battery cable.

CHASSIS ELECTRICAL

CAUTION

On vehicles equipped with an air bag, the negative battery cable must be disconnected, before working on the system. Failure to do so may result in deployment of the air bag and possible personal injury.

Heater Blower Motor

Removal and Installation

ES250

1. Disconnect the negative battery cable.
2. Disconnect the electrical connection at the blower motor.
3. Remove the mounting bolts and the blower motor.
4. The installation is the reverse of the removal procedure.

LS400

1. Disconnect the negative battery cable. Remove the right side instrument panel cover.
2. Properly discharge the air conditioning system. Remove the cruise control actuator.
3. Remove the bolt and disconnect the actuator tubes.
4. Disconnect both the liquid and the suction tubes for the air conditioner.
5. Remove the cover plate to the control assembly.

NOTE: Cap the open tubes to keep moisture out of the system.

6. Disconnect the drain hose clamp. Remove the mirror control electronic unit.
7. Disconnect the electrical connections and the mounting bracket from the blower control.
8. Disconnect the vehicle side wire harness from the blower unit.

9. Remove the mounting nuts and screws and remove the blower control unit.
10. The installation is the reverse of the removal procedure. Evacuate and recharge the air conditioning system.

Windshield Wiper Motor

Removal and Installation

ES250

1. Disconnect the negative battery cable. Remove the wiper arm and blade assembly.
2. Disconnect the electrical connections at the wiper motor.
3. Remove the mounting bolts and disconnect the wiper arm.
4. Remove the wiper motor.
5. The installation is the reverse of the removal procedure.

LS400

1. Disconnect the negative battery cable. Remove the wiper arm and blade assembly.
2. Remove the hood to cowl seal and remove the cowl louver.

NOTE: Raise the front side of the cowl louver up to remove the louver.

3. Remove the mounting bolts and disconnect the electrical connection.
4. Raise the front side of the wiper motor and link assembly up. Remove the wiper motor and link assembly.
5. Remove the wiper motor cover.
6. The installation is the reverse of the removal procedure. Tighten the mounting bolts to 48 inch lbs.

NOTE: With the front side of the louver raised, install the protector on the glass, then push the louver down.

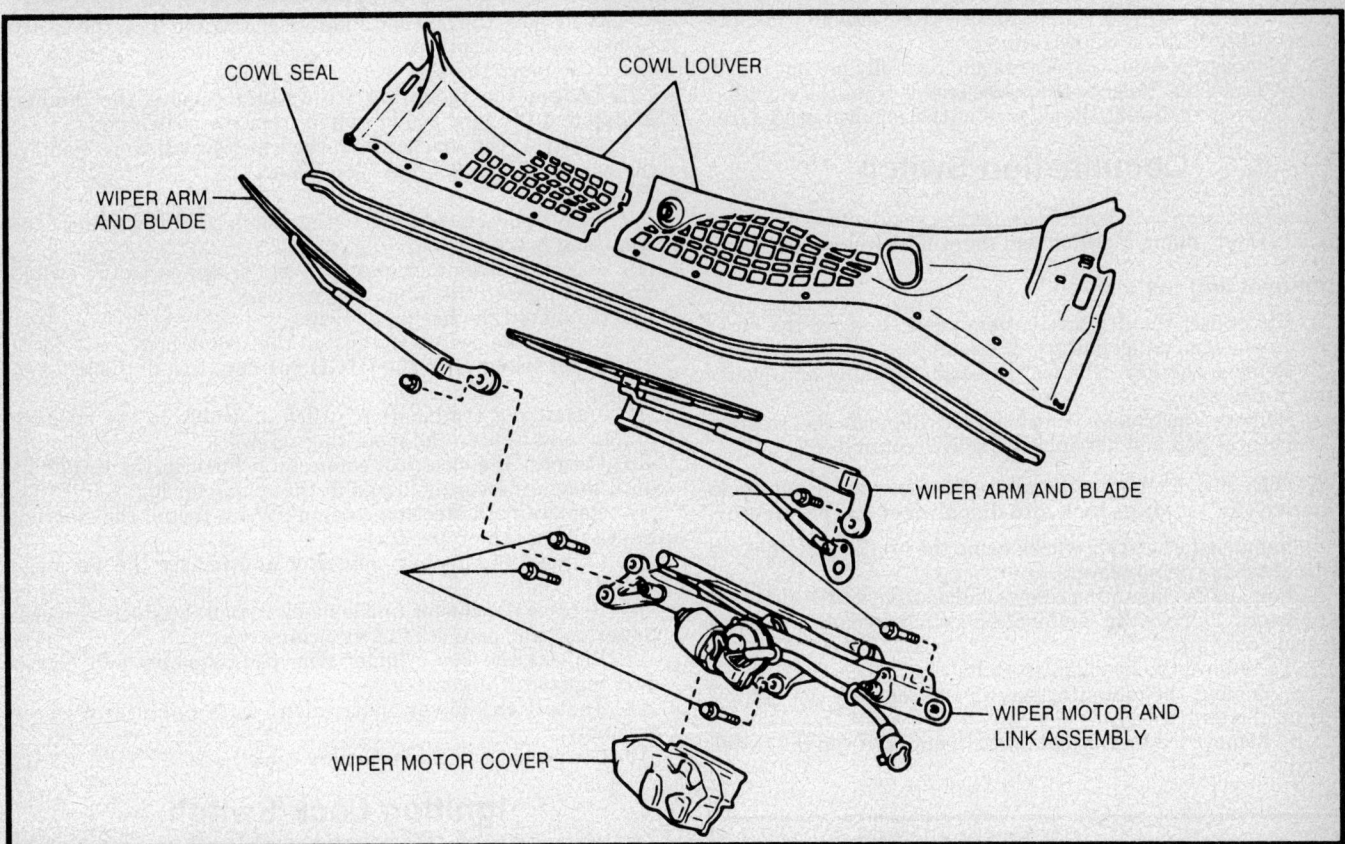

COWL SEAL

COWL LOUVER

WIPER ARM
AND BLADE

WIPER ARM AND BLADE

WIPER MOTOR AND
LINK ASSEMBLY

WIPER MOTOR COVER

Wiper motor location—LS400

Windshield Wiper Switch

Removal and Installation

1. Disconnect the negative battery cable.
2. Remove the combination switch assembly.
3. Remove the mounting screws and separate the bracket from the switch body.
4. Remove the mounting screws and the switch from the switch body.
5. Remove the boot.
6. The installation is the reverse of the removal procedure.

Instrument Cluster

Removal and Installation

ES250

1. Disconnect the negative battery cable.

NOTE: Work must be started after approximately 20 seconds or longer from the time the ignition switch is turned to the LOCK position and the negative battery cable is disconnected.

2. Remove the steering wheel.
3. Pry out the clips and pull the front pillar molding upward and remove.
4. Remove the left lower dash panel. Disconnect the hood release lever and remove the panel cover.
5. Pry out the switch bases and the speaker panel with the proper tool. Remove the mounting screws and lower the lower column panel.

6. Remove the mounting screws and the cluster panel. Disconnect the electrical connections.
7. Remove the steering column cover.
8. Disconnect the mounting screws, the speedometer cable and the electrical connections. Remove the instrument cluster and the speedometer.
9. The installation is the reverse of the removal procedure.

LS400

1. Disconnect the negative battery cable.

NOTE: Work must be started after approximately 20 seconds or longer from the time the ignition switch is turned to the LOCK position and the negative battery cable is disconnected.

2. Remove the steering wheel. Remove the left and right front pillar moldings.
3. Remove the steering column cover and the upper console panel, with the proper tool, to prevent damaging the cover.
4. Remove the front ash receptacle and disconnect the electrical connection.
5. Pry out the front side of the lower console cover and remove by sliding the cover forward.
6. Remove the mounting screws and pry out the lower console box. Remove the cup holder.
7. Pry out the rear end panel and disconnect the wire connector. Remove the console box.
8. Remove the left lower trim panel. Remove the hood release lever and disconnect the cable from the lever.
9. Remove the mounting bolts and the left trim pad. Disconnect the wire connections and hose from the pad.
10. Remove the key cylinder pad and disconnect the park

brake lever. Remove the outer mirror switch assembly and disconnect the electrical connection.

11. Remove the mounting screws and carefully pry out the instrument cluster. Remove the speedometer from the cluster.

12. The installation is the reverse of the removal procedure.

Combination Switch

The combination switch incorporates the headlight switch, turn signal switch, dimmer switch and the windshield wiper switch.

Removal and Installation

1. Disconnect the negative battery cable. Remove the lower instrument trim panel and cover assembly.

2. Remove the key cylinder trim pad assembly and heater duct, if necessary.

3. Remove the cluster finish panel. Remove the steering wheel center pad and disconnect the wire connector.

NOTE: Since the air bag connector has a 2-stage lock, remove the 1st stage lock and disconnect the connector.

4. Remove the steering wheel, using the proper tool. Remove both steering column covers.

5. Remove the mounting screws and disconnect the electrical connectors. Remove the combination switch assembly from the steering column.

6. To remove the headlight switch:
   a. Remove the mounting screws and separate the bracket from the switch body.
   b. Remove the screws and the ball set plate from the switch body.

c. Remove the ball and slide out the switch from the switch body with the spring.
   d. Remove the boot.

7. Loosen the mounting screws and remove the dimmer switch and the turn signal switch from the switch body.

8. Separate the bracket from the wiper switch body. Remove the wiper switch from the switch body.

To install:

9. Install the wiper switch to the switch body and connect the mounting bracket.

10. Install the dimmer and turn signal switch to the switch body and tighten the mounting screws.

11. To install the headlight switch:
   a. Slide the switch and install the switch body.
   b. Set the lever in the **HIGH** position. Install the ball and plate.

12. Install the combination switch assembly to the steering column and tighten the mounting screws.

13. Connect the electrical connectors. Push in the terminals until they are securely locked in the connector lug.

14. Replace both steering column covers. Install the steering wheel, using the proper tool.

15. Connect the air bag connector and replace the 1st stage lock.

16. Replace the cluster finish panel. Install the steering wheel center pad and connect the wire connector.

17. Replace the key cylinder trim pad assembly and heater duct register, if necessary.

18. Install the lower instrument trim panel and cover assembly.

19. Connect the negative battery cable.

Ignition Lock/Switch

Removal and Installation

1. Disconnect the negative battery cable.

2. Remove the lower trim panel and pad assembly, if necessary.

3. Remove the key cylinder trim panel and pad assembly. Disconnect the key cylinder lamp assembly.

4. Remove the trim panel mounting bracket and the heater duct register, if necessary.

5. Remove the mounting screws and disconnect the electrical connections. Remove the ignition switch.

6. The installation is the reverse of the removal procedure.

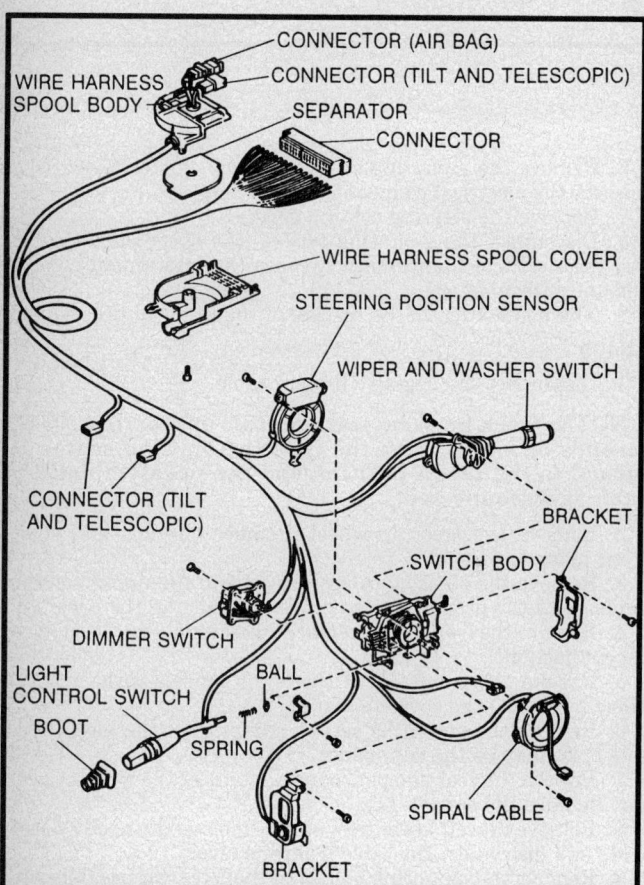

Exploded view of the combination switch—LS400

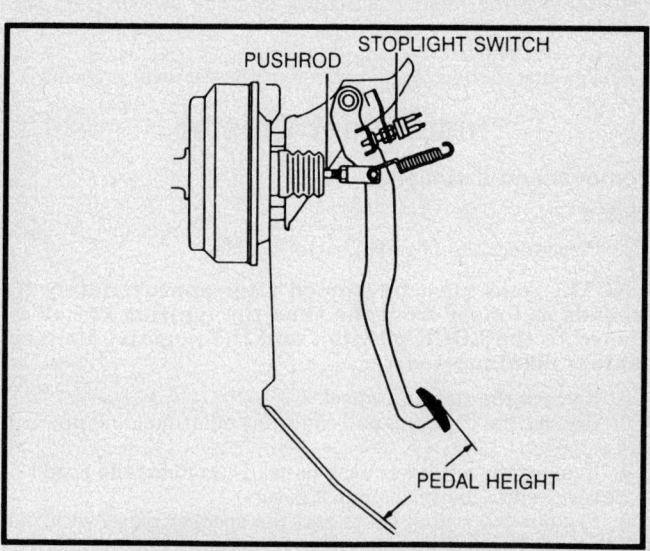

Stoplight switch adjustment

Stoplight Switch

Adjustment

1. Disconnect the negative battery cable.
2. Remove the instrument panel undercover, the lower trim panel and air duct, if necessary.
3. Remove the power steering computer, if equipped. Disconnect the connector from the stoplight switch.
4. Loosen the stoplight switch locknut, the switch and the pushrod locknut.
5. Adjust the pedal height by turning the pushrod. Return the stoplight switch until it contacts the pedal stopper.
6. Tighten the stoplight switch locknut, the switch and the pushrod locknut. Connect the electrical connection at the switch.
7. Connect the negative battery cable.
8. Check that the stoplights light when the brake pedal is depressed. It goes off when the pedal is released.

Removal and Installation

1. Disconnect the negative battery cable.
2. Remove the instrument panel undercover, the lower trim panel and air duct, if necessary.
3. Remove the power steering computer, if equipped. Disconnect the connector from the stoplight switch. Loosen the pushrod locknut.
4. Remove the stoplight switch locknut and the stoplight switch.
To install:
5. Install the stoplight switch and replace the locknut, do not tighten.
6. Adjust the pedal height by turning the pushrod. Return the stoplight switch until it contacts the pedal stopper.
7. Tighten the stoplight switch locknut, the switch and the pushrod locknut. Connect the electrical connection at the switch.
8. Connect the negative battery cable.
9. Check that the stoplights light when the brake pedal is depressed and off when the pedal is released.

Clutch Switch

Adjustment

ES250

1. Disconnect the negative battery cable.
2. Remove the lower dash trim panel and disconnect the air duct.
3. Loosen the locknut and disconnect the connection at the clutch switch. Turn the clutch switch until the pedal height is 7.52–7.91 in. from stop.
4. Tighten the locknut and connect the electrical connection at the switch.
5. Connect the air duct and replace the lower dash panel.
6. Connect the negative battery cable.

Neutral Safety Switch

Adjustment

1. Disconnect the negative battery cable. Raise and safely support the vehicle.
2. Loosen the neutral start switch bolt and place the shift lever in the **N** position.
3. Align the groove and the neutral basic line.
4. Hold in position and tighten the bolt to 9 ft. lbs.
5. Lower the vehicle and connect the negative battery cable.

Removal and Installation

1. Disconnect the negative battery cable. Raise and safely support the vehicle.
2. Remove the front exhaust pipe on the LS400.
3. Disconnect the neutral start switch connector.
4. Remove the control shaft shift lever. Pry off the washer and remove the nut.
5. Remove the bolt(s) and pull out the neutral start switch.
6. The installation is the reverse of the removal procedure.
7. Lower the vehicle and connect the negative battery cable.

Fuses, Circuit Breakers and Relays

Location

There is a fuse block, relay center and circuit breaker center located on the left lower portion of the instrument panel. There is a fuse block and relay center located on the right lower portion of the instrument panel. There is a fuse block and relay center located in the engine compartment on the driver's side.

Computers

Location

The Total Diagnostic Communication Link (TDCL) is located inside the vehicle under the left side instrument panel.

ES250

Theft Deterrent and **Door Lock Control ECU**—located behind the dash panel on the right side.
Progressive Power Steering ECU—located behind the dash panel on the right side.
Engine and Transmission Control ECU—located under the middle section of the center console.

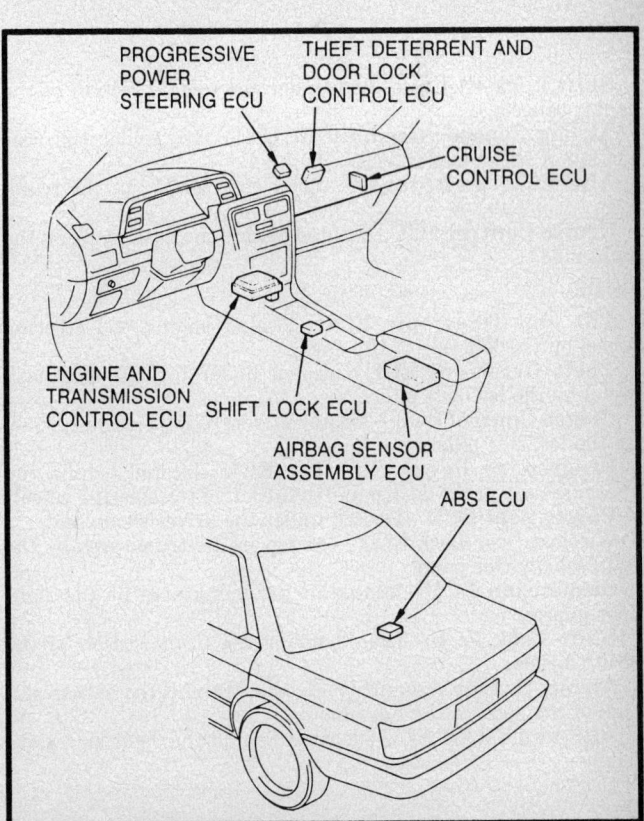

ECU unit locations—ES250

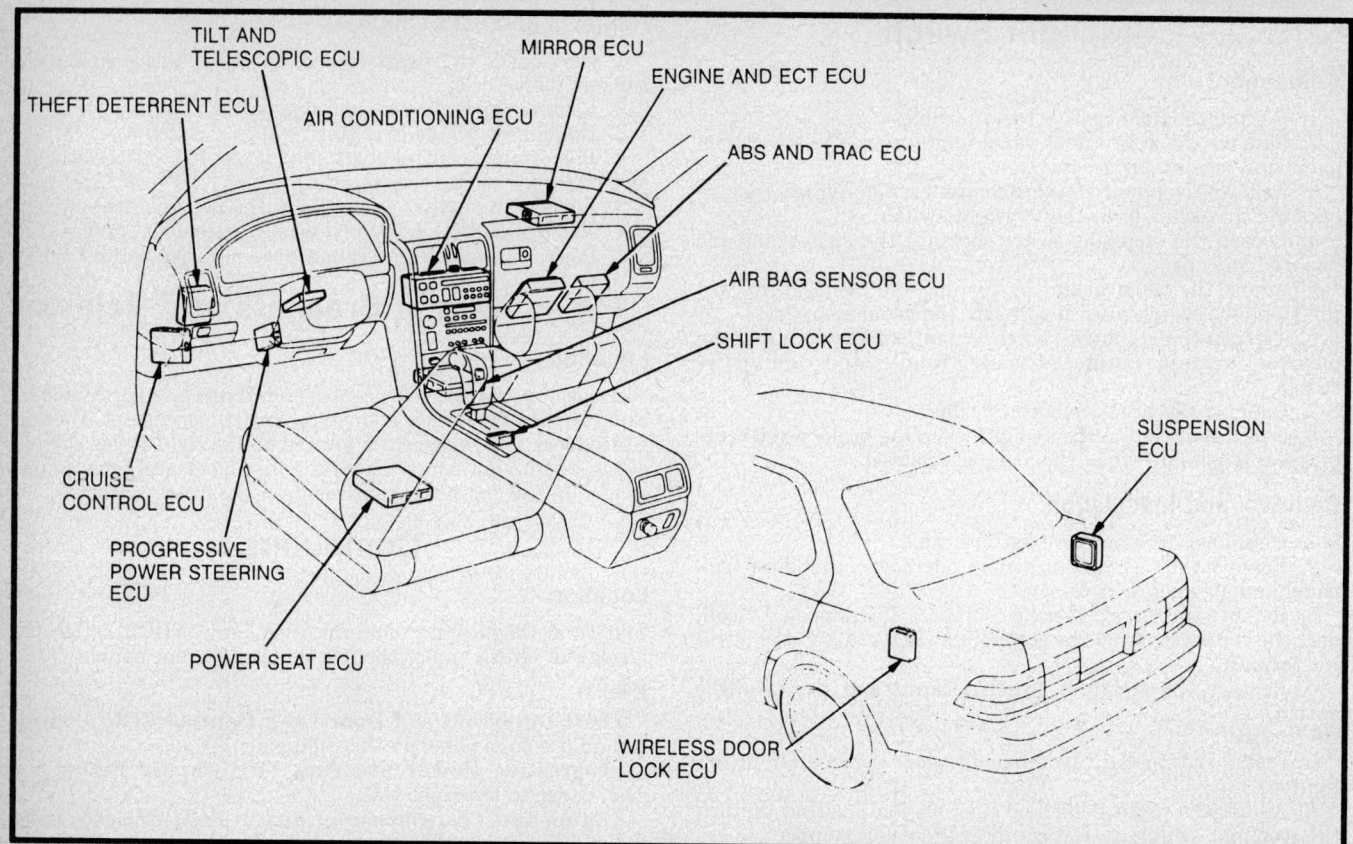

ECU unit locations—LS400

Shift Lock ECU—located under the middle section of the center console.

Airbag Sensor Assembly ECU—located under the rear section of the center console.

ABS ECU—located in the upper rear section of the trunk area.

Cruise Control ECU—located behind the dash panel on the right side.

LS400

Tilt and Telescopic ECU—located behind the steering wheel on the left side of the dash.

Theft Deterrent ECU—located under the left side dash panel by the left side pillar.

Cruise Control ECU—located under the left side dash panel by the left side pillar.

Progressive Power Steering ECU—located behind the center section of the dash panel to the left of the steering wheel.

Power Seat ECU—located under the driver's side seat.

Wireless Door Lock ECU—located in the trunk area by the left rear quarter panel.

Suspension ECU—located in the trunk area by the right rear quarter panel.

Shift Lock ECU—located under the front section of the shift console.

Airbag Sensor Assembly—located behind the center section of the dash at the bottom.

ABS and TRAC ECU—located behind the right side glove box.

Engine and ECT ECU—located behind the right side glove box.

Mirror ECU—located behind the right side dash panel above the glove box.

Air Conditioning ECU—located behind the center section of the dash panel above the radio.

Flashers

Location

The turn signal and hazard flashers are located on the left lower section of the instrument panel.

Cruise Control

For further information, please refer to "Chilton's Chassis Electronics Service Manual" for additional coverage.

Adjustment

1. Measure the cable stroke on the actuator to where the throttle valve begins to open.
2. The control cable free-play should be 0.39 in. with a slight amount of free-play.
3. Adjust the cable to the proper specifications.

ENGINE COOLING

Radiator

Removal and Installation

ES250

1. Disconnect both battery cables and remove the battery. Drain the cooling system.
2. Remove the ignition coil, igniter and bracket assembly.
3. Disconnect the radiator reservoir hose and the radiator hoses.
4. Remove the engine undercover and disconnect the cooling fan connectors.
5. Disconnect and plug the oil cooler lines, if equipped with an automatic transaxle.
6. Remove the mounting bolts, the supports and the radiator with the cooling fans attached.
7. Disconnect the cooling fans from the radiator.
8. The installation is the reverse of the removal procedure.

LS400

1. Disconnect the negative battery cable. Drain the cooling system.
2. Remove the air intake duct and disconnect and plug the automatic transmission lines.
3. Disconnect the cooling fan motor connector.
4. Disconnect the water hose from the coolant reservoir and remove both radiator hoses.
5. Remove the radiator supports and the radiator.
6. Remove both fan shrouds.
7. The installation is the reverse of the removal procedure.

Electric Cooling Fan

Testing

1. Disconnect the fan motor connector.
2. Connect a suitable jumper wire between the battery and the fan motor connector.
3. If the fan does not run, replace the motor.

Removal and Installation

ES250

1. Disconnect both battery cables and remove the battery. Drain the cooling system.
2. Remove the ignition coil, igniter and bracket assembly.
3. Disconnect the radiator reservoir hose and the radiator hoses.
4. Remove the engine undercover and disconnect the cooling fan connectors.
5. Disconnect and plug the oil cooler lines, if equipped with an automatic transaxle.
6. Remove the mounting bolts, the supports and the radiator with the cooling fans attached.
7. Disconnect the cooling fans from the radiator.
8. The installation is the reverse of the removal procedure.

LS400

1. Disconnect the negative battery cable. Remove the air cleaner cover on the right side.
2. Remove the clearance light and disconnect the electrical connector.
3. Remove the mounting bolts and nut. Remove the headlight together with the fog light.
4. Remove the parking light and disconnect the wire connector. Remove the engine undercover.
5. Disconnect the tube from the wind guide. Remove the mounting screws and lift off the guide.

6. Disconnect the mounting bolts. Remove the bumper and bumper retainer.
7. Remove the bumper reinforcement and both horn assemblies.
8. Disconnect the fan motor connectors.
9. Remove the mounting bolts and disconnect the wire from the mounting brackets. Remove the cooling fan(s).

To install:

10. Install the cooling fan(s) and tighten the mounting bolts. Connect the wire to the mounting brackets.
11. Connect the fan motor connector. Install the horn assemblies.
12. Replace the bumper reinforcement and replace the bumper and retainer.
13. The remainder of the installation is the reverse of the removal procedure.

Heater Core

Removal and Installation

ES250

1. Disconnect the negative battery cable. Drain the cooling system.
2. Remove the console, if equipped, by removing the shift knob (manual), wiring connector and console attaching screws.
3. Remove the carpeting from the tunnel.
4. If necessary, remove the cigarette lighter and ash tray.
5. Remove the package tray, if access to the heater core is difficult.
6. Remove the bottom cover/intake assembly screws and withdraw the assembly.
7. Remove the cover from the water valve.
8. Remove the water valve.
9. Remove the hose clamps and remove the hoses from the core.
10. Remove the heater core.
11. Installation is the reverse of the removal procedure. Fill the cooling system to the proper level. Operate the heater and check for leaks.

LS400

1. Disconnect the negative battery cable. Drain the cooling system.
2. Properly discharge the air conditioning system.
3. Disconnect the mounting nuts and hoses. Remove the heater valve.
4. Remove the cooling and blower unit.
5. Disconnect the inlet and outlet water hoses. Remove the mounting nuts and the insulator retainer.
6. Remove the instrument cluster and the radio assembly with the air conditioning control attached.
7. Remove the undercover.
8. Remove the glove box by performing the following:
   a. Remove the glove box compartment panel and disconnect the left side check arm from the door.
   b. Remove the retaining clips. Insert the proper tool between the upper side of the compartment and the safety pad, pry out the compartment to remove.
   c. Disconnect the connector from the glove box compartment.
9. Disconnect the mounting bolts and remove the right side lower pad. remove the connectors from the pad.
10. Remove the glove box door. Disconnect the connectors and remove the ABS Electronic Control Unit (ECU).
11. Remove the air ducts.

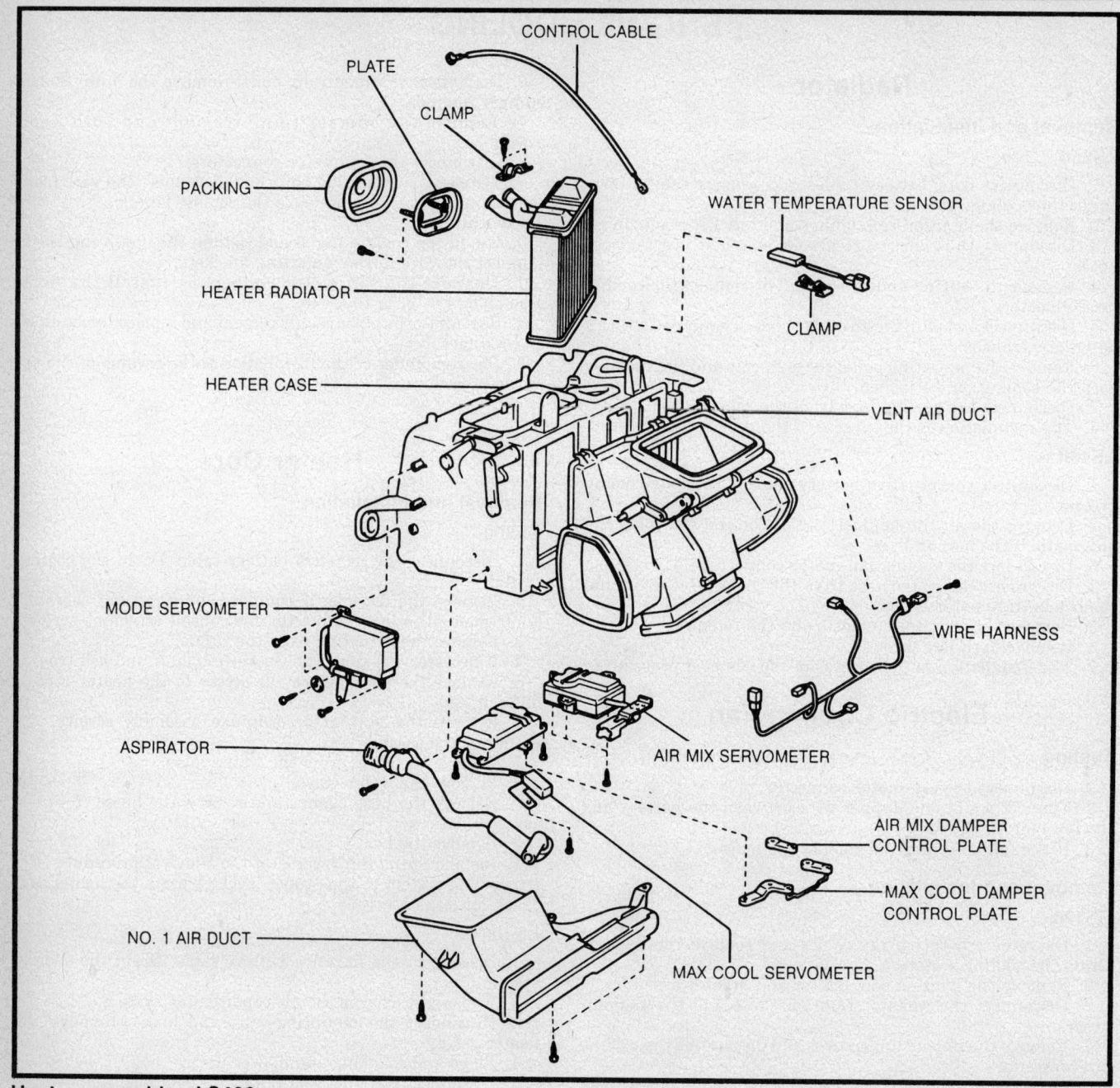

CONTROL CABLE

PLATE

CLAMP

PACKING

WATER TEMPERATURE SENSOR

HEATER RADIATOR

CLAMP

HEATER CASE

VENT AIR DUCT

MODE SERVOMETER

WIRE HARNESS

AIR MIX SERVOMETER

ASPIRATOR

AIR MIX DAMPER
CONTROL PLATE

MAX COOL DAMPER
CONTROL PLATE

NO. 1 AIR DUCT

MAX COOL SERVOMETER

Heater assembly—LS400

12. On the driver's side, loosen the lock bolt and disconnect the junction block. Disconnect the retaining clips at the floor. Remove the combination switch.

13. On the passenger side, disconnect the connectors and the bond cable. Disconnect the retaining clips at the floor carpet.

14. Remove the bolts and nut from the safety pad and lift out the pad.

15. Remove the heater ducts.

16. Remove the mounting screws and lift out the heater unit. Disconnect the connector and remove the servo motor.

17. Remove the mounting screws and remove the aspirator.

18. Remove the packing, screw, plate and the retaining screws. Pull out the heater core assembly.

To install:

19. Install the heater core. Replace the retaining screws, plate, screw and install the packing.

20. Install the aspirator and the servo motor. Connect the connector.

21. Install the heater unit and tighten the retaining screws. Replace the heater ducts.

22. Install the safety pad and tighten the mounting bolts and nut.

23. On the passenger side, connect the connectors and the bond cable. Connect the retaining clips at the floor carpet.

24. On the driver's side, connect the junction block and tight-

en the lock bolt. Connect the retaining clips at the floor. Replace the combination switch.

25. Replace the glove box door. Connect the connectors and replace the ABS Electronic Control Unit (ECU).

26. Install the air ducts.

27. Replace the right side lower pad and tighten the mounting bolts. Replace the connectors to the pad.

28. Replace the glove box by performing the following:

   a. Connect the connector to the glove box compartment.

   b. Install the glove box and replace the retaining clips.

   c. Replace the glove box compartment panel and connect the left side check arm from the door.

29. Install the undercover.

30. Replace the instrument cluster and the radio assembly with the air conditioning control attached.

31. Connect the inlet and outlet water hoses. Replace the mounting nuts and the insulator retainer.

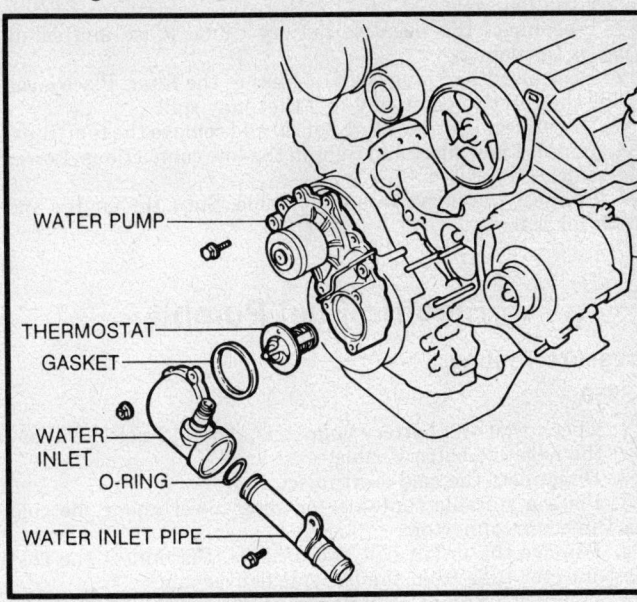

Water pump assembly—ES250

32. Replace the cooling and blower unit.

33. Install the heater valve. Connect the mounting nuts and hoses.

34. Properly, evacuate and recharge the air conditioning system.

35. Refill the cooling system and connect the negative battery cable. Run the engine and check for leaks.

Water Pump

Removal and Installation

1. Disconnect the negative battery cable. Drain the cooling system.

2. Disconnect the radiator inlet hose from the inlet pipe. Remove the timing belt from the water pump pulley.

3. Remove the right side ignition coil on the LS400.

4. Disconnect the water inlet pipe on the ES250.

5. Remove the water inlet housing and thermostat, if necessary.

6. Remove the mounting bolts and studs. Lift out the water pump by carefully prying between the pump and the cylinder head.

7. Remove all the old packing and clean the mounting surfaces.

To install:

8. Install new seal packing to the water pump groove and a new O-ring to the water bypass pipe.

9. Install the water pump and tighten the mounting bolts to 13–14 ft. lbs.

10. Install the water inlet housing and thermostat, if necessary.

11. Install the water inlet pipe with a new O-ring on the ES250. Tighten the mounting bolt to 14 ft. lbs.

12. Replace the ignition coil on the LS400.

13. Install the timing belt and connect the inlet hose to the inlet pipe.

14. Refill the cooling system and connect the negative battery cable.

15. Run the engine and check for leaks.

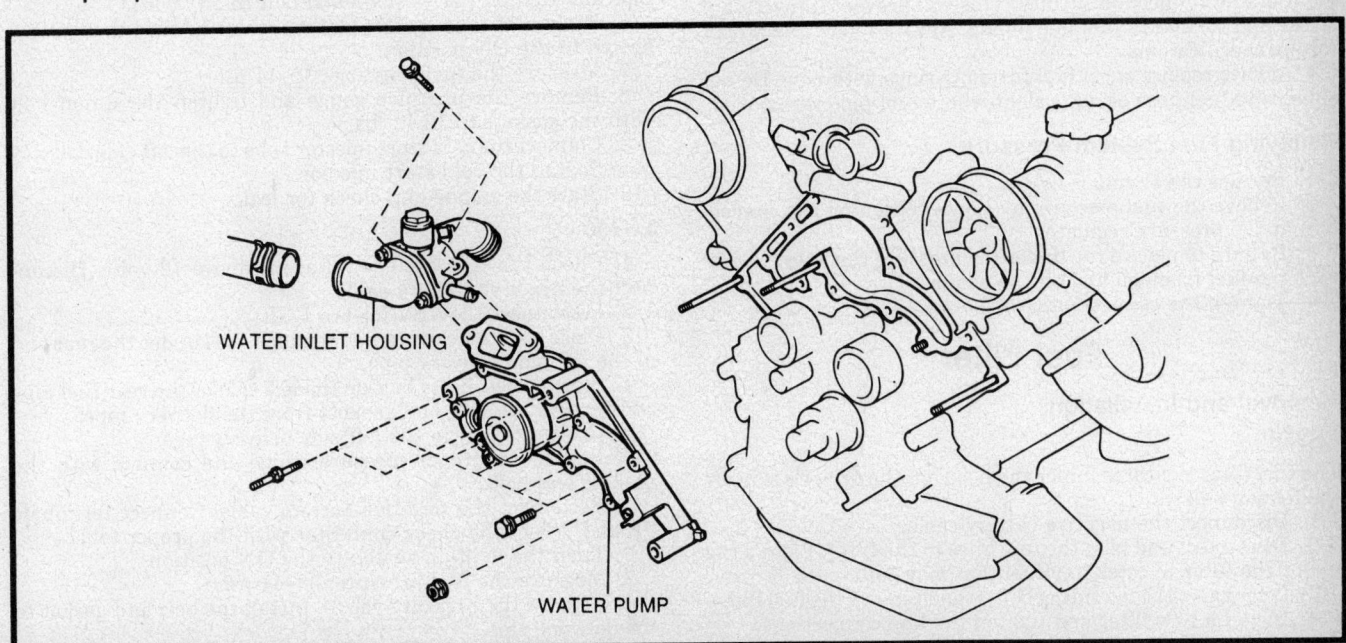

Water pump assembly—LS400

Thermostat

Removal and Installation

1. Disconnect the negative battery cable. Drain the cooling system.

2. Remove the water inlet pipe and disconnect the water temperature sensor on the ES250.

3. Remove the water inlet from the inlet housing.

4. Remove the thermostat and gasket.

5. Clean the mounting surfaces. Install the thermostat, using a new gasket.

6. The installation is the reverse of the removal procedure. Tighten the water inlet bolts to 13–14 ft. lbs.

FUEL SYSTEM

Fuel System Service Precautions

Safety is the most important factor when performing not only fuel system maintenance but any type of maintenance. Failure to conduct maintenance and repairs in a safe manner may result in serious personal injury or death. Maintenance and testing of the vehicle's fuel system components can be accomplished safely and effectively by adhering to the following rules and guidelines.

• To avoid the possibility of fire and personal injury, always disconnect the negative battery cable unless the repair or test procedure requires that battery voltage be applied.

• Always relieve the fuel system pressure prior to disconnecting any fuel system component (injector, fuel rail, pressure regulator, etc.), fitting or fuel line connection. Exercise extreme caution whenever relieving fuel system pressure to avoid exposing skin, face and eyes to fuel spray. Please be advised that fuel under pressure may penetrate the skin or any part of the body that it contacts.

• Always place a shop towel or cloth around the fitting or connection prior to loosening to absorb any excess fuel due to spillage. Ensure that all fuel spillage (should it occur) is quickly removed from engine surfaces. Ensure that all fuel soaked cloths or towels are deposited into a suitable waste container.

• Always keep a dry chemical (Class B) fire extinguisher near the work area.

• Do not allow fuel spray or fuel vapors to come into contact with a spark or open flame.

• Always use a backup wrench when loosening and tightening fuel line connection fittings. This will prevent unnecessary stress and torsion to fuel line piping. Always follow the proper torque specifications.

• Always replace worn fuel fitting O-rings with new. Do not substitute fuel hose or equivalent where fuel pipe is installed.

Relieving Fuel System Pressure

1. Be sure the engine is cold.
2. Relieve the fuel pressure by slowly loosening the connection at the pressure regulator.
3. Be sure to place a rag under the pressure regulator to prevent the fuel from spilling on the engine.
4. Tighten the connection.

Fuel Filter

Removal and Installation

ES250

The fuel filter is located under the hood, on the driver's side, by the fender well.

1. Disconnect the negative battery cable.
2. Disconnect and plug the fuel lines to the filter. Place a rag under the filter to catch any fuel that may spill.
3. Disconnect the mounting bolt(s) and remove the fuel filter.
4. Install a new filter and tighten the line connections.
5. Connect the negative battery cable. Start the engine and check for leaks.

LS400

The fuel filter is located under the vehicle on the driver's side before the rear axle.

1. Disconnect the negative battery cable. Raise and safely support the vehicle.
2. Disconnect and plug the fuel lines to the filter. Place a rag under the filter to catch any fuel that may spill.
3. Disconnect the mounting bolt(s) and remove the fuel filter.
4. Install a new filter and tighten the line connections. Lower the vehicle.
5. Connect the negative battery cable. Start the engine and check for leaks.

Electric Fuel Pump

Pressure Testing

ES250

1. Check that the battery voltage is above 12 volts. Disconnect the negative battery cable.
2. Disconnect the cold start injector.
3. Place a suitable container or shop towel under the cold start injector connector.
4. Remove the union bolt and gaskets. Disconnect the cold start injector tube from the left side delivery pipe.
5. Install the proper pressure gauge to the left side delivery pipe and tighten the washers and bolt to 13 ft. lbs.
6. Reconnect the negative battery cable and turn the ignition switch to the ON position.
7. Measure the fuel pressure; 38–44 psi.
8. Remove the pressure gauge and tighten the union bolt with the gaskets to 13 ft. lbs.
9. Connect the cold start injector tube to the left side delivery pipe. Install the cold start injector.
10. Start the engine and check for leaks.

LS400

1. Check that the battery voltage is above 12 volts. Disconnect the negative battery cable.
2. Disconnect the VSV for the EGR.
3. Place a suitable container or shop towel under the rear end of the left side delivery pipe.
4. Slowly, loosen the bolt on the left side of the rear fuel pipe and remove the bolt and gaskets from the delivery pipe.
5. Drain the fuel in the left side delivery pipe.
6. Install the proper pressure gauge and connect with the gaskets and bolt.
7. Reconnect the negative battery cable. Connect terminals FP and +B of the check connector with the proper tool.
8. Turn the ignition switch to the ON position.
9. Measure the fuel pressure; 38–44 psi.
10. Remove the pressure gauge. Install the bolt and gasket to the delivery pipe.
11. Connect the VSV for the EGR. Start the engine and check for leaks.

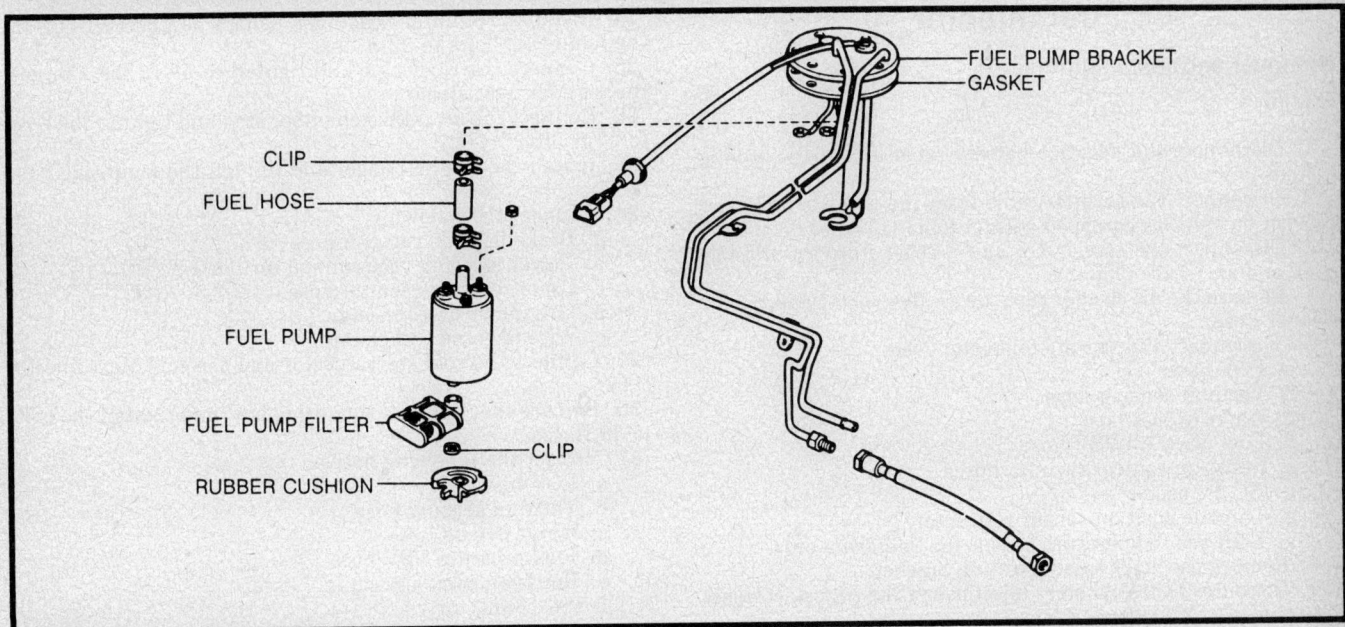

Fuel pump assembly—ES250

Removal and Installation

ES250

1. Disconnect the negative battery cable. Raise and safely support the vehicle.
2. Drain the fuel from the fuel tank. Disconnect and clamp the fuel lines.
3. Remove both fuel tank protector shields. Support the tank with a suitable jacking device.
4. Remove the mounting bolts and take down both tank band straps. Lower the tank and disconnect the electrical connections.
5. Remove the fuel tank.
6. Remove the fuel pump bracket. Disconnect the fuel line and electrical connector.
7. Remove the mounting nuts and the pump assembly.

To install:

8. Install the fuel pump to the mounting bracket. Connect the mounting nuts, fuel line and electrical connectors.

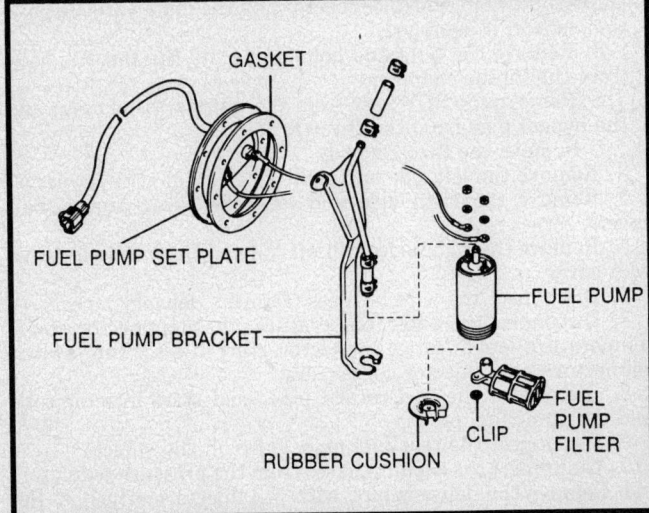

Fuel pump assembly—LS400

9. Raise the fuel tank and connect the electrical connections.
10. Install the tank band straps and tighten the strap bolts to 29 ft. lbs.
11. Install both fuel tank protector shields. Connect the fuel lines.
12. Remove the jacking device. Lower the vehicle.
13. Connect the negative battery cable. Fill the fuel tank.

LS400

1. Disconnect the negative battery cable. Drain the fuel from the fuel tank.
2. Remove the front trim panel from inside the trunk.
3. Remove the seat back assembly by performing the following:
   a. Disconnect the hook and remove the clips, using the proper tool.
   b. Disconnect the wire harness clamp and connectors.
   c. Disconnect the side hooks and remove the mounting bolts and seat back assembly.
4. Remove the partition panel plug. Disconnect the fuel pump connector.
5. Remove the mounting bolts and the fuel pump set plate. Move the clips aside and disconnect and plug the fuel hose.
6. Remove the mounting bolts and the fuel pump assembly.
7. The installation is the reverse of the removal procedure. Tighten the fuel pump mounting bolts to 48 inch lbs. and the fuel pump set plate bolts to 26 inch lbs.
8. Connect the negative battery cable.

Fuel Injection

For further information, please refer to "Chilton's Electronic Engine Control's Manual" for additional coverage.

Idle Speed Adjustment

The idle speed adjustment is controlled by the Electronic Control Unit (ECU).

Idle Mixture Adjustment

The idle mixture adjustment is controlled by the Electronic Control Unit (ECU).

Fuel Injector

Removal and Installation
ES250

1. Disconnect the negative battery cable. Drain the cooling system.
2. Disconnect the throttle cable from the throttle body and bracket on vehicles equipped with automatic transaxle.
3. Disconnect the accelerator and bracket from the throttle body and air intake chamber.
4. Remove the air cleaner cap, the air flow meter and the air cleaner hose.
5. .Disconnect and tag the following hoses:
   a. PCV hoses
   b. Vacuum sensing hose
   c. Water bypass hose
   d. Fuel pressure VSV hose
   e. Emission control vacuum hoses
   f. ISC connector
   g. Throttle position sensor connector
   h. EGR gas temperature sensor for California only.
6. Remove the right side mounting bracket.
7. Disconnect the cold start injector and the cold start injector tube.
8. Disconnect and tag the following:
   a. Brake booster vacuum hose
   b. Power steering vacuum and air hoses
   c. Cruise control vacuum hose
   d. Ground strap connector
   e. Wire harness and clamp
9. Disconnect the EGR pipe. Disconnect the engine hanger and the air intake chamber stay from the air intake chamber.
10. Remove the air intake chamber. Disconnect and tag the cold start injector connector, water temperature sensor connector and the 6 injector connectors.
11. Disconnect the wire harness from the left side delivery pipe.
12. Disconnect the fuel inlet and return hoses. Remove the fuel line.
13. Remove the 2 bolts and the left side delivery pipe with the 3 injectors. Remove the 3 bolts and the right side delivery pipe with the fuel pipe and the injectors attached.
14. Pull out the 6 injectors from the delivery pipe. Remove the 6 insulators and the 4 spacers from the intake manifold.

To install:
15. Install a new grommet and O-ring to the injector. Apply a light coat of gasoline to the new O-ring.
16. Install the injectors to the delivery pipes, while turning to left and right.
17. Place the insulators and the spacers in the proper position on the intake manifold.
18. Install the 3 injectors together with the right side delivery pipe and the fuel pipe in the proper position on the intake manifold.
19. Install the 3 injectors together with the left side delivery pipe in the proper position on the intake manifold.

NOTE: Make sure the injectors rotate smoothly. If the injectors do not rotate smoothly, the probable cause is the incorrect installation of the O-rings. Replace the O-rings.

20. Position the injector connector upward and install the mounting bolts. Tighten to 9 ft. lbs.
21. Install the No. 2 fuel pipe with new gaskets. Tighten the mounting bolts to 24 ft. lbs.
22. Connect the fuel inlet and return hoses. Connect the wire harness clamps to the left side delivery pipe.
23. Connect the 6 injector connectors, the cold start injector connector and the water temperature connector.

24. Install the air intake chamber, using a new gasket. Tighten the mounting bolts to 32 ft. lbs.
25. Connect the EGR pipe and tighten to 58 ft. lbs. Connect the wire harness clamp.
26. Connect the air intake chamber stay and tighten the bolts to 27 ft. lbs.
27. Install the engine hanger and tighten the mounting bolts to 27 ft. lbs.
28. Connect the following:
   a. Brake booster vacuum hose
   b. Power steering vacuum and air hoses
   c. Cruise control vacuum hose
   d. Ground strap connector
   e. Wire harness and clamp
29. Connect the cold start injector and the cold start injector tube.
30. Replace the right side mounting stay and tighten the bolts to 38 ft. lbs.
31. Connect the following hoses:
   a. PCV hoses
   b. Vacuum sensing hose
   c. Water bypass hose
   d. Fuel pressure VSV hose
   e. Emission control vacuum hoses
   f. ISC connector
   g. Throttle position sensor connector
   h. EGR gas temperature sensor for California only.
32. Replace the air cleaner cap, the air flow meter and the air cleaner hose.
33. Connect the accelerator and bracket to the throttle body and air intake chamber.
34. Connect the throttle cable and bracket, if equipped with automatic transaxle.
35. Refill the cooling system. Connect the negative battery cable.

LS400
Right

1. Disconnect the negative battery cable. Remove the air cleaner with the air flow meter.
2. Remove the throttle body by performing the following:
   a. Disconnect the vacuum hoses from the throttle body and the pressure regulator.
   b. Remove the upper electrical wire cover and the bypass pipe from the ISC valve.
   c. Disconnect the throttle valve motor connector, the sub-throttle position sensor connector and the main throttle position sensor, if equipped.
   d. Remove the nuts and bolts. Separate the throttle body from the intake chamber.
   e. Remove the PCV hose from the cylinder head cover and the bypass pipe from the throttle body.
   f. Remove the throttle body.
3. Remove the left side and right side engine wire covers.
4. Remove the right side and left side No. 3 timing belt covers.
5. Remove the right side ignition coil and the lower electrical wire cover.
6. Disconnect the wire harness from the delivery pipe.
7. Disconnect the water temperature sensor connector, water temperature sender gauge connector, start injector time switch connector and 4 injector connectors.
8. Disconnect the fuel return pipe, cold start injector tube and the front fuel pipe.
9. Disconnect the rear fuel pipe, leave on the vehicle.
10. Disconnect the vacuum hoses from the pressure regulator.
11 Remove the delivery pipe with the injectors attached. Remove the insulators from the intake manifold.
12. Remove the injectors from the delivery pipe.

To install:

13. Install a new grommet and O-ring to the injector. Apply a light coat of gasoline to the new O-ring.
14. Install the injectors to the delivery pipes, while turning to left and right. Make sure the injectors rotate smoothly.
15. Place the insulators and the spacers in the proper position on the intake manifold.
16. Install the injectors together with the delivery pipe in the proper position on the intake manifold.

NOTE: Make sure the injectors rotate smoothly. If the injectors do not rotate smoothly, the probable cause is the incorrect installation of the O-rings. Replace the O-rings.

17. Temporarily, install the rear fuel pipe and the front fuel pipe. Tighten the delivery pipe first, then the front and rear fuel pipes. Tighten the delivery pipe to 13 ft. lbs. and the front and rear fuel pipes to 22 ft. lbs.
18. Connect the cold start injector tube, tighten to 11 ft. lbs. Install the fuel return pipe and tighten the union bolt to 22 ft. lbs.
19. Connect the fuel injector connectors, the start injector time switch connector, the water temperature sensor connector and the water temperature sender gauge connector.
20. Install the wire harness to the delivery pipe and tighten the mounting bolts to 74 inch lbs.
21. Install the lower electrical wire cover and the right side ignition coil.
22. Install the right side and left side No. 3 timing covers.
23. Install the throttle body by performing the following:
   a. Install the bypass hoses and the PCV hose. Install a new gasket to the air intake chamber.
   b. Connect the PCV hose to the cylinder head cover and the bypass hose to the throttle body.
   c. Install the throttle body to the air intake chamber. Tighten the nuts and bolts to 13 ft. lbs.
   d. Connect the main throttle position sensor connector to the throttle body. Connect the sub-throttle position sensor and the throttle valve motor connector, if equipped.
   e. Install the bypass hose to the ISC valve and the upper electrical wire cover.
   f. Connect the vacuum hoses to the throttle body and the pressure regulator.
24. Install the intake air connector pipe and tighten to 45 inch lbs.
25. Install the air cleaner and the air flow meter. Refill the engine coolant.
26. Connect the negative battery cable. Run the engine and check for leaks.

Left

1. Disconnect the negative battery cable. Drain the cooling system.
2. Disconnect the PCV hose. Remove the upper electrical wire cover and the left side wire cover.
3. Disconnect the following hoses:
   a. Vacuum hoses from the air pipe
   b. Vacuum hose from the BVSV
   c. Vacuum hose from the VSV for the EGR
   d. EGR vacuum modulator hose
4. Remove the EGR vacuum modulator with the mounting bracket. Disconnect the check connector from the bracket.
5. Disconnect the connectors and remove the mounting bolts from the 2 VSV's. Remove the VSV's.

6. Remove the water bypass pipes.
7. Disconnect the engine wire from the delivery pipe.
8. Disconnect the following connectors:
   a. Distributor connector
   b. Engine speed sensor connector
   c. EGR gas temperature sensor connector, California only
   d. Injector connectors
9. Remove the bolt, pulsation damper and disconnect the fuel inlet hose from the delivery pipe.
10. Disconnect the front fuel pipe and disconnect the rear fuel pipe.
11. Remove the delivery pipe with the injectors attached. Remove the insulators from the intake manifold.
12. Remove the injectors from the delivery pipe.

To install:

13. Install a new grommet and O-ring to the injector. Apply a light coat of gasoline to the new O-ring.
14. Install the injectors to the delivery pipes, while turning to left and right. Make sure the injectors rotate smoothly.
15. Place the insulators and the spacers in the proper position on the intake manifold.
16. Install the injectors together with the delivery pipe in the proper position on the intake manifold.

NOTE: Make sure the injectors rotate smoothly. If the injectors do not rotate smoothly, the probable cause is the incorrect installation of the O-rings. Replace the O-rings.

17. Temporarily, install the rear fuel pipe and the front fuel pipe. Tighten the delivery pipe first, then the front and rear fuel pipes. Tighten the delivery pipe to 13 ft. lbs. and the front and rear fuel pipes to 22 ft. lbs.
18. Connect the cold start injector tube, tighten to 11 ft. lbs. Install the fuel return pipe and tighten the union bolt to 22 ft. lbs.
19. Connect the fuel inlet hose to the delivery pipe and replace the pulsation damper and bolt. Tighten the damper to 22 ft. lbs. and the bolt to 69 inch lbs.
20. Connect the following connectors:
   a. Distributor connector
   b. Engine speed sensor connector
   c. EGR gas temperature sensor connector, California only
   d. Injector connectors
21. Connect the engine wire to the delivery pipe and tighten the mounting bolts to 74 inch lbs.
22. Install the water bypass pipes.
23. Install the VSV's and tighten the bolts to 13 ft. lbs. Connect the connectors.
24. Connect the check connector to the bracket. Replace the EGR vacuum modulator with the mounting bracket.
25. Connect the following hoses:
   a. Vacuum hoses from the air pipe
   b. Vacuum hose from the BVSV
   c. Vacuum hose from the VSV for the EGR
   d. EGR vacuum modulator hose
26. Connect the PCV hose. Replace the upper electrical wire cover and the left side wire cover.
27. Refill the cooling system. Connect the negative battery cable.
28. Run the engine and check for leaks.

EMISSION CONTROLS

For further information, please refer to "Professional Emission Component Application Guide".

ENGINE MECHANICAL

NOTE: Disconnecting the negative battery cable on some vehicles may interfere with the functions of the on board computer systems and may require the computer to undergo a relearning process, once the negative battery cable is reconnected.

Engine Assembly

Removal and Installation

ES250

1. Disconnect the negative battery cable. Disconnect the positive battery cable.
2. Remove the hood assembly. Remove the battery from the vehicle and disconnect the ground cable.
3. Remove the engine undercovers and drain the cooling system.
4. Raise and safely support the vehicle. Drain the engine oil in a suitable container. Lower the vehicle.
5. Remove the suspension upper brace.
6. Disconnect the igniter connector, noise filter connector and the high tension electrical cord.
7. Remove the ignition coil, igniter and bracket assembly.
8. Remove the radiator, alternator, alternator belt and the adjusting bar.
9. Remove the radiator reservoir tank and disconnect the accelerator cable from the throttle body.
10. Disconnect the throttle cable from the throttle body, on vehicles equipped with automatic transaxle.
11. Remove the cruise control actuator.
12. Disconnect the air flow meter connector, ISC valve air hose and the vacuum pipe air hose.
13. Disconnect the air cleaner hose, air cleaner cap, hoses and the air flow meter. Remove the mounting bolts and the air cleaner assembly.
14. Disconnect the following:
    a. Check connector
    b. Ground straps from the left side fender apron
    c. Connectors from the relay box
    d. Engine compartment wire connector.
15. Disconnect the following hoses:
    a. Brake booster vacuum hose to the air intake chamber
    b. Air conditioning control valve vacuum hose
    c. Charcoal canister vacuum hose
16. Disconnect the ground strap from the transaxle.
17. Disconnect the heater hoses and the fuel line hoses. Use a suitable container to catch any excess fuel.
18. Remove the starter, if equipped with manual transaxle.
19. Remove the clutch release cylinder and tube clamp, do not disconnect the tube, if equipped with manual transaxle.
20. Disconnect the speedometer cable and the transaxle control cable(s).
21. Remove the engine undercover and glove compartment box.
22. Disconnect the following connectors:
    a. 3 engine and ECT Electronic Control Unit (ECU) connectors
    b. Circuit opening relay connector
    c. Cowl wire connector
    d. Instrument panel wire connector
23. Remove the engine wire from the cowl panel.
24. Raise and safely support the vehicle. Remove the bolts and the suspension lower crossmember.
25. Disconnect the front exhaust pipe.
26. Disconnect the air conditioning wire connectors and remove the mounting bolts. Position and support the compressor aside.
27. Remove the halfshafts.

28. Remove the power steering pump and support. Do not disconnect the hoses.
29. Remove the mounting bolts and the engine cross member. Support the engine with a suitable jacking device.
30. Remove the front, center and rear engine mounting insulators and brackets.
31. Remove the power steering reservoir tank, without disconnecting the hoses. Remove the ground strap.
32. Remove the mounting brackets on both sides of the engine assembly. Lower the vehicle, keeping the engine supported.
33. Attach a suitable engine hoist to the engine hangers. Disconnect the clamps of the power steering oil cooler lines.
34. Remove the mounting insulators on both sides of the engine. Lift the engine and transaxle out of the vehicle.
35. Remove the starter, if equipped with automatic transaxle.
36. Separate the engine from the transaxle.

To install:

37. Assemble the engine to the transaxle. Install the starter, if equipped with an automatic transaxle. Tighten the mounting bolts to 29 ft. lbs.
38. Lower the engine and the transaxle into the vehicle with a suitable engine hoist. Tilt the transaxle downward to clear the left side mounting bracket.
39. Align the right side and the left side mounting with the body bracket. Attach the right side mounting insulator to the mounting bracket and install the bolts.
40. Install the left side mounting bracket to the transaxle case and tighten the mounting bolts to 38 ft. lbs.
41. Attach the left side mounting insulator to the mounting bracket. Tighten the mounting bolts to 38 ft. lbs. and the through bolt to 64 ft. lbs.
42. Tighten the nuts and bolts of the right side mounting insulator. Tighten the bolts to 47 ft. lbs. Tighten the bracket nuts to 38 ft. lbs. and the body nuts to 65 ft. lbs.
43. Remove the engine hoist from the engine and connect the power steering cooler line clamp.
44. Connect the right side engine mounting brackets. Tighten the bolts to 38–48 ft. lbs. and the nut 38 ft. lbs.
45. Connect the left side engine mounting bracket. Tighten the bolt to 14 ft. lbs. and the nuts to 38 ft. lbs.
46. Install the automatic transaxle mounting bracket, if equipped. Tighten the 12mm nut to 15 ft. lbs. and the 14mm nut to 38 ft. lbs.
47. Install the power steering reservoir tank and connect the ground strap.
48. Install the front engine mounting bracket and insulator. Tighten the bolts to 57 ft. lbs.
49. Install the center mounting bracket and insulator. Tighten the mounting bolts to 38 ft. lbs.
50. Install the rear engine mounting bracket and insulator. Tighten the mounting bolts to 57 ft. lbs.
51. Install the engine mounting cross member and tighten the bolts to 29 ft. lbs.
52. Install and tighten the bolts holding the insulators to the cross member. Tighten the bolts to 54 ft. lbs. Tighten the mounting insulator through bolts to 64 ft. lbs.
53. Install the power steering pump and the halfshafts.
54. Install the air conditioning compressor and tighten the mounting bolts. Connect the electrical connection.
55. Raise and safely support the vehicle. Install the front exhaust pipe . Tighten the manifold nuts to 46 ft. lbs. and the converter nuts 32 ft. lbs.
56. Install the suspension cross member and tighten the bolts and nuts to 153 ft. lbs. Lower the vehicle.
57. Push in the engine wire through the cowl panel.
58. Connect the following connectors:
    a. 3 engine and ECT Electronic Control Unit (ECU) connectors

b. Circuit opening relay connector
c. Cowl wire connector
d. Instrument panel wire connector

59. Install the glove compartment box and the engine undercover.

60. Connect the transaxle control cables and the speedometer cable.

61. Install the clutch release cylinder and tube clamp, if equipped with manual transaxle.

62. Install the starter, if equipped with manual transaxle.

63. Connect the heater hoses and fuel line hoses. Connect the ground strap to the transaxle case.

64. Connect the following hoses:
   a. Brake booster vacuum hose to the air intake chamber
   b. Air conditioning control valve vacuum hose
   c. Charcoal canister vacuum hose

65. Connect the following:
   a. Check connector
   b. Ground straps from the left side fender apron
   c. Connectors from the relay box
   d. Engine compartment wire connector

66. Install the air cleaner case and tighten the mounting bolt. Connect the air cleaner hose, air cleaner cap, hoses and the air flow meter.

67. Install the cruise control actuator.

68. Install the throttle control cable and adjust, if equipped with automatic transaxle.

69. Install the accelerator cable and adjust. Replace the radiator reservoir tank.

70. Install the alternator belt adjusting bar, the alternator and belt.

71. Install the radiator assembly.

72. Replace the ignition coil, igniter and bracket assembly. Connect the igniter connector, noise filter connector and the high tension electrical cord.

73. Install the suspension upper brace and tighten the mounting bolts to 47 ft. lbs.

74. Install the battery and refill the cooling system. Fill the engine crankcase to the proper oil level.

75. Install the engine undercovers and the hood assembly.

76. Connect the battery cables. Start the engine and check for leaks. Check the ignition timing. Adjust, if necessary. Recheck the cooling system and the oil level.

LS400

1. Disconnect the negative battery cable and the positive battery cable. Remove the hood assembly.

2. Remove the dust covers and the air duct above the radiator assembly. Drain the cooling system.

3. Remove the battery from the vehicle. Raise and safely support the vehicle.

4. Remove the engine undercover and drain the engine oil, in a suitable container. Lower the vehicle.

5. Disconnect the radiator upper hose from the water inlet. Loosen the nuts holding the fluid coupling to the fan bracket.

6. Loosen the drive belt tension by turning the belt tensioner counterclockwise. Remove the drive belt.

7. Remove the radiator assembly.

8. Disconnect the air flow meter connector, the mounting bolts and the the air cleaner hose. Remove the air cleaner, the air flow meter and hose assembly.

9. Remove the igniter cover and disconnect the igniter connectors.

10. Remove the bolts, nut and the throttle body cover. Disconnect the accelerator and cruise control actuator cables.

11. Disconnect the air hose from the ISC valve and the power steering air control valve.

12. Disconnect the air connector pipe from the throttle body and remove the air connector pipe. Remove the bolt and connector pipe bracket.

13. Disconnect the air hose from the air intake chamber. Remove the power steering pump mounting bolts and nut. Position the pump aside.

14. Disconnect the coolant level sensor connector and remove the radiator reservoir tank. Remove the mounting bolts and reservoir tank bracket.

15. Disconnect the following hoses:
   a. Heater and bypass hoses
   b. Fuel hoses (plug the open end and catch the fuel in a suitable container)
   c. Vacuum hose from the brake booster on the air intake chamber
   d. Air conditioning control valve vacuum hoses
   e. EVAP and BVSV vacuum hoses

16. Remove the relay box cover. Disconnect the connector and ground cables from the engine compartment relay box. Remove the ground straps from under the fender aprons.

17. Remove the cruise control actuator cover.

18. Remove the instrument panel undercover and the lower the trim panel the ECU for the engine and transmission.

19. Disconnect the glove box door, the glove box light and remove the glove box assembly.

20. Disconnect the ABS ECU and the heater air duct.

21. Disconnect the following connectors:
   a. The 3 engine and Electronic Controlled Transmission (ECT) ECU connectors
   b. Ciruit opening relay connector
   c. Cowl wire connector
   d. Instrument panel wire connector

22. Remove the mounting bolts and pull out the engine wire from the cowl panel.

23. Raise and safely support the vehicle.

24. Remove the mounting bolts and disconnect the power steering oil cooler pipe from the oil pan.

25. Remove the mounting bolts and the steering damper.

26. Disconnect the grommet from the floor and the sub-oxygen sensor from the exhaust pipe. Disconnect the 2 sub-oxygen sensors.

27. Remove the sub-oxygen sensor covers and the exhaust pipe. Remove the exhaust pipe support brackets.

28. Remove the catalytic converters and the exhaust pipe heat insulator.

29. Remove the center floor crossmember braces. Remove the driveshaft.

30. Disconnect the shift control rod from the shift lever. Lower the vehicle.

31. Attach a suitable engine hoist to the engine hangers and support the engine.

32. Remove the nuts holding the engine mounting insulators to the front suspension crossmember.

33. Remove the rear engine mounting member. Disconnect the ground strap.

34. Lift out the engine with the transmission attached. Place the engine assembly on a suitable holding fixture. Separate the engine from the transmission.

To install:

35. Connect the engine to the transmission. Attach a suitable engine hoist to the engine hangers.

36. Lower the engine assembly into the vehicle. Insert the stud bolts of the front engine mounting brackets into the stud bolt holes of the front suspension crossmember.

37. Install the rear engine mounting member and tighten the bolts to 19 ft. lbs. and the nuts to 10 ft. lbs. Install the ground strap.

38. Remove the engine hoist. Raise and safely support the vehicle.

39. Install the nuts holding the engine mounting brackets to the front suspension crossmember. Tighten the nuts to 43 ft. lbs.

40. Connect the transmission control rod to the shift lever. Install the propeller shaft.

41. Install the center floor crossmember braces. Tighten the bolts to 9 ft. lbs.
42. Install the exhaust pipe heat insulator. Replace the catalytic converters and tighten the bolts to 46 ft. lbs.
43. Install the front exhaust pipe and the sub-oxygen sensor covers. Tighten the bolts to 32 ft. lbs. Install the sub-oxygen sensors to the exhaust pipe and tighten to 33 ft. lbs.
44. Install the steering damper and tighten the mounting bolts to 20 ft. lbs. Connect the engine wire to the wire bracket on the front suspension crossmember.
45. Install the power steering oil cooler pipe to the engine oil pan. Lower the vehicle.
46. Push in the engine wire through the cowl panel and install the wire retainer.
47. Connect the following connectors:
  a. 3 engine and ECT ECU connectors
  b. Circuit opening relay connector
  c. Cowl wire connector
  d. Instrument panel wire connector
48. Install the heater duct and the glove compartment.
49. Install the right side lower instrument panel pad and the engine and ECT electronic control units. Replace the right side instrument panel undercover.
50. Install the cruise control actuator. Connect the connectors and ground cables to the relay box.
51. Install the upper cover to the relay box. Connect the 2 ground straps to the underside of the fender aprons.
52. Connect the following hose:
  a. The heater bypass water hoses
  b. Fuel hoses
  c. Vacuum hose to the brake booster on the air intake chamber
  d. Vacuum hose to the EVAP BVSV
53. Install the air conditioning compressor. Tighten the bolts to 36 ft. lbs. and the nut to 22 ft. lbs. Connect the electrical connectors.
54. Install the radiator reservoir tank bracket, the reservoir and connect the coolant level sensor connector.
55. Install the power steering pump and tighten the mounting bolts to 29 ft. lbs. and the nuts to 32 ft. lbs. Connect the air hose to the air intake manifold.
56. Connect the air connector pipe to the throttle body. Connect the air hose to the ISC valve and the power steering control valve.
57. Connect the accelerator cable and the cruise control actuator cable to the throttle body. Install the throttle body cover.
58. Connect the igniter connectors and install the igniter cover.
59. Connect the air cleaner hose to the intake air connector pipe.
60. Install the air cleaner, the air flow meter and hose assembly. Connect the air flow meter connector.
61. Install the radiator.
62. Temporarily install the fan pulley, the fan and the fluid coupling assembly. Install the drive belt by turning the belt tensioner counterclockwise.
63. Tighten the bolts holding the fluid coupling to the fan bracket to 16 ft. lbs.
64. Install the battery. Replace the air ducts and dust covers.
65. Refill the cooling system and the crankcase to the proper levels.
66. Install the engine undercover and hood assembly.
67. Connect the battery cables. Start the engine and check for leaks. Check the timing.
68. Recheck the fluid levels.

Engine Mounts

Removal and Installation

ES250

Front
1. Raise and safely support the vehicle.
2. Support the engine with a suitable jacking device.
3. Remove the nut and the through bolt.
4. Remove the insulator. Remove the mounting bolts and the bracket, if necessary.
5. The installation is the reverse of the removal procedure. Tighten the bolts to 57 ft. lbs.

Center
1. Raise and safely support the vehicle.
2. Support the engine with a suitable jacking device.
3. Remove the nut and the through bolt.
4. Remove the insulator. Remove the mounting bolts and the bracket, if necessary.
5. The installation is the reverse of the removal procedure. Tighten the bolts to 38 ft. lbs.

Rear
1. Raise and safely support the vehicle.
2. Support the engine with a suitable jacking device.
3. Remove the nut and the through bolt.
4. Remove the insulator. Remove the mounting bolts and the bracket, if necessary.
5. The installation is the reverse of the removal procedure. Tighten the bolts to 57 ft. lbs. Remove the jacking device and lower the vehicle.

LS400
1. Raise and safely support the vehicle.
2. Support the engine with a suitable jacking device.
3. Remove the mounting nuts and the mounting insulator. Remove the mounting bracket, if necessary.
4. The installation is the reverse of the removal procedure. Tighten the bolts to 19 ft. lbs. and the nuts to 10 ft. lbs. Remove the jacking device and lower the vehicle.

Cylinder Head

Removal and Installation
ES250
1. Disconnect the negative battery cable. Drain the cooling system.
2. Remove the suspension upper brace. Disconnect the throttle cable from the throttle body, if equipped with an automatic transaxle.
3. Disconnect the accelerator cable from the throttle body. Remove the cruise control actuator and the vacuum pump.
4. Disconnect the ISC hose, the vacuum pipe hose and the air cleaner hose.
5. Raise and safely support the vehicle. Remove the right side engine undercover.
6. Remove the suspension lower crossmember and the front exhaust pipe. Lower the vehicle.
7. Remove the alternator, the ISC valve and the throttle body.
8. Remove the EGR pipe, the EGR valve and the vacuum modulator.
9. Disconnect the (4) BVSV vacuum hoses, the fuel pressure VSV hose and the air conditioning control valve hose.
10. Remove the distributor and the exhaust crossover pipe.
11. Disconnect the cold start injector connector and remove the cold start injector tube.
12. Disconnect the following hoses:
  a. PCV hose

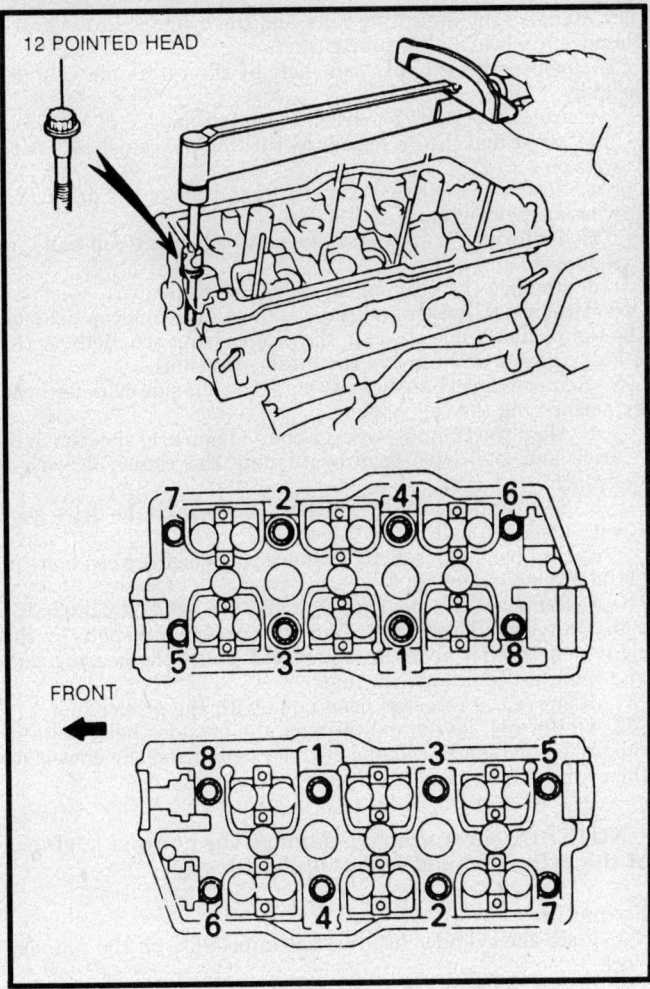

Cylinder head tightening sequence—ES250

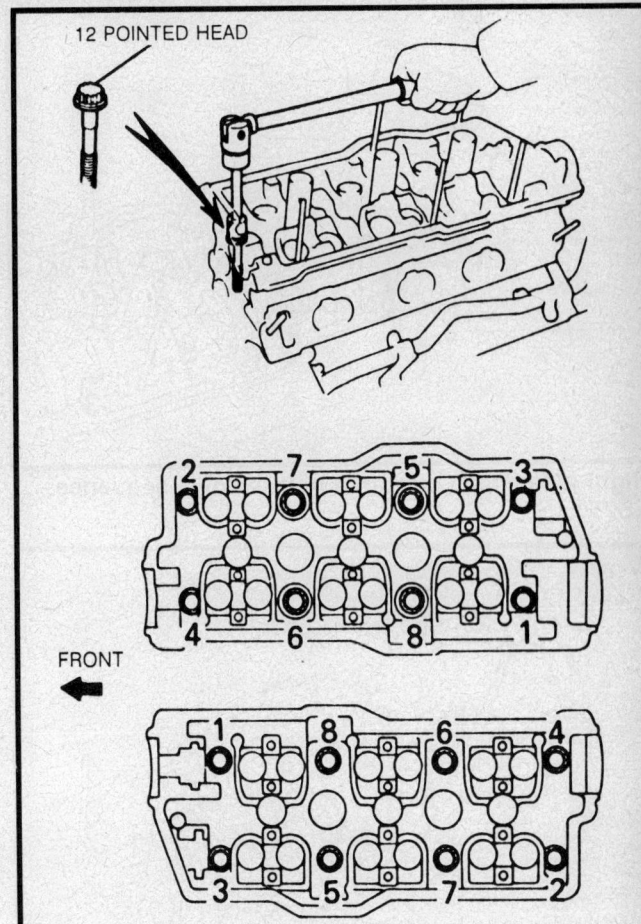

Cylinder head bolt removal sequence—ES250

b. Vacuum sensing hose
c. Fuel pressure VSV hose
d. Air conditioning control valve vacuum hose
e. EGR gas temperature sensor connector—California only
13. Remove the mounting bolts and the brackets from the intake chamber. Remove the air intake chamber.
14. Remove the delivery pipes and the injectors.
15. Disconnect the water temperature sensor connector and the upper radiator hose. Remove the water outlet.
16. Disconnect the following connectors and hose:
a. Cold start injector time switch connector
b. Water temperature sensor connector
c. Heater water bypass hose
17. Remove the water bypass outlet. Remove the crossover pipe insulator from the water bypass outlet.
18. Remove the cylinder head rear plate and the idler pulley bracket.
19. Remove the mounting bolts and nuts. Lift off the intake manifold.
20. Disconnect the main oxygen sensor connector. Remove outside heat insulator.
21. Remove the mounting nuts and the right side exhaust manifold. Remove the inside heat insulator.
22. Remove the heat insulator, the mounting nuts and the left side exhaust manifold.
23. Remove the spark plugs.

24. Remove the timing belt, camshaft pulleys and the No. 2 idler pulley.
25. Remove the No. 3 timing cover.

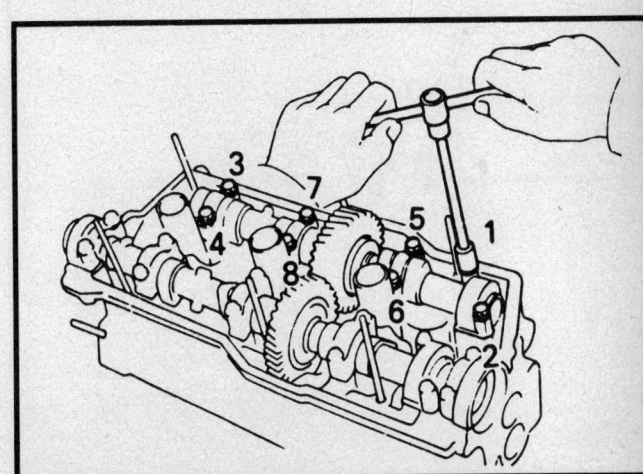

Right side exhaust camshaft bolt removal sequence—ES250

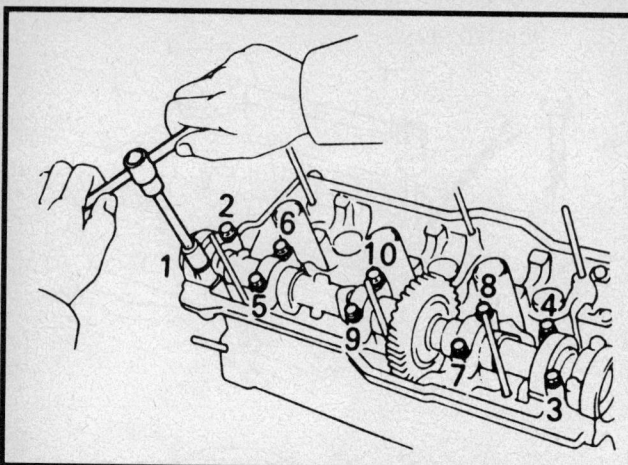

Right side intake camshaft bolt removal sequence—
ES250

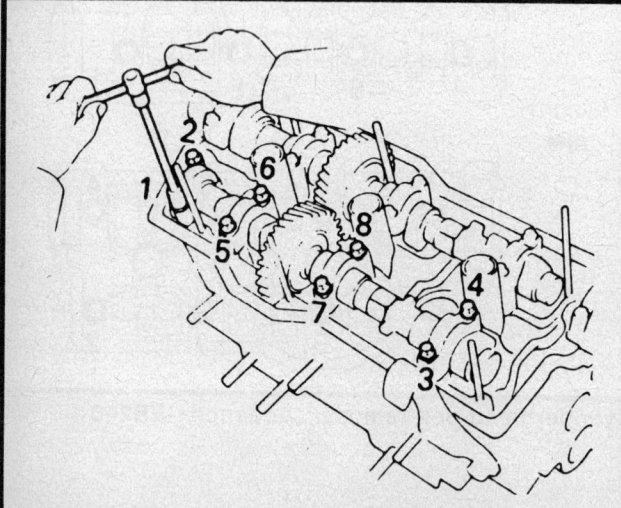

Left side exhaust camshaft bolt removal sequence—
ES250

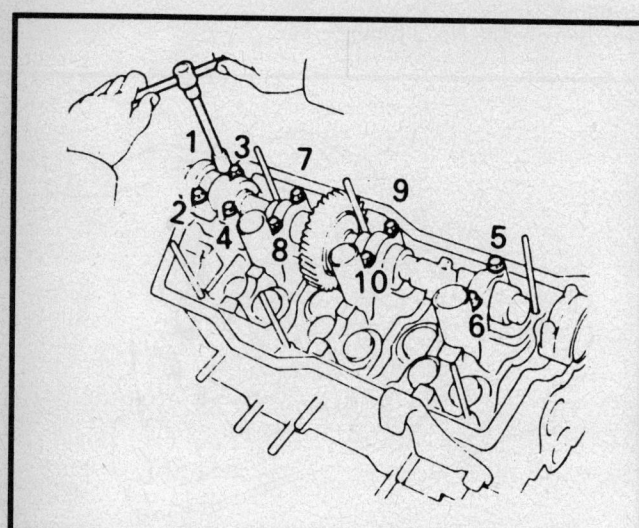

Left side intake camshaft bolt removal sequence—
ES250

26. Remove the mounting nuts and the cylinder head covers. Remove the spark plug tube gaskets.

27. Remove the exhaust camshaft of the right side cylinder head by:

    a. Align the timing marks, 2 pointed marks, of the camshaft drive and the drive gear by turning the camshaft with a wrench.

    b. Secure the exhaust camshaft sub-gear to the drive gear with a service bolt.

    c. Uniformly, loosen and remove the bearing cap bolts, in sequence.

    d. Remove the bearing caps and the camshaft.

28. Uniformly, loosen and remove the 10 bearing cap bolts on the right side cylinder head in the proper sequence. Remove the 5 bearing caps and remove the intake camshaft.

29. Remove the exhaust camshaft of the left side cylinder head by performing the following:

    a. Align the timing marks, 1 pointed mark, of the camshaft drive and the drive gear by turning the camshaft with a wrench.

    b. Secure the exhaust camshaft sub-gear to the drive gear with a service bolt.

    c. Uniformly, loosen and remove the 8 bearing cap bolts in the proper sequence.

    d. Remove the 4 bearing caps and the exhaust camshaft.

30. Uniformly, loosen and remove the bearing cap bolts on the right side cylinder head, in sequence. Remove the bearing caps and remove the intake camshaft.

31. Remove the recessed head bolts with the proper tool.

32. Uniformly, loosen and remove the cylinder head bolts in the proper sequence. Lift the cylinder head from the dowels on the cylinder block and place on wooden blocks.

NOTE: Be careful not to damage the contact surfaces of the cylinder head and cylinder block.

To install:

33. Place the cylinder head gasket in position on the cylinder block.

34. Install the cylinder head onto the cylinder block, aligning the dowels.

35. Install the head bolts and tighten, in sequences, using 3 steps:

    a. Apply a light coat of engine oil on the threads of the bolts and install. Uniformly, tighten the cylinder head bolts in several passes, in sequence, to 25 ft. lbs.

    b. Mark the front of the cylinder head bolt with paint. Retighten the cylinder head bolts 90 degrees in the proper sequence.

    c. Retighten the cylinder head bolts by an additional 90 degrees.

36. Apply a light coat of engine oil on the recessed head bolts. Install the head bolts and tighten to 13 ft. lbs.

37. Install the left side engine hanger and tighten to 27 ft. lbs.

NOTE: Since the thrust clearance of the camshaft is small, the camshaft must be held level while it is being installed. If the camshaft is not level, the portion of the cylinder head receiving the shaft thrust may crack or be damaged, causing the camshaft to seize or break.

38. Install the intake camshaft of the right side cylinder head by:

    a. Apply a suitable multi-purpose grease to the thrust portion of the camshaft.

    b. Apply seal packing to the No. 1 bearing cap. Install the bearing caps.

    c. Apply a light coat of oil on the threads of the bearing cap bolts.

    d. Install and uniformly tighten the bearing cap bolts to 12 ft. lbs.

39. Install the exhaust camshaft of the right side cylinder head by:

    a. Apply a suitable multi-purpose grease to the thrust portion of the camshaft.

    b. Align the timing marks, 2 pointed marks, of the camshaft and the drive gears.

    c. Place the camshaft on the cylinder head and install the bearing caps.

    d. Apply a light coat of oil on the threads of the bearing cap bolts.

    e. Install and uniformly tighten the bearing cap bolts to 12 ft. lbs. Remove the service bolt.

40. Install the intake camshaft on the left side cylinder head by:

    a. Apply a suitable multi-purpose grease to the thrust portion of the camshaft.

    b. Place the intake camshaft at a 90 degree angle of the timing mark on the cylinder head, 1 pointed mark.

    c. Apply seal packing to the No. 1 bearing cap. Install the bearing caps.

    d. Apply a light coat of oil on the threads of the bearing cap bolts.

    e. Install and uniformly tighten the bearing cap bolts to 12 ft. lbs.

41. Install the exhaust camshaft on the left side cylinder head by:

    a. Apply MP grease to the thrust portion of the camshaft.

    b. Align the timing marks, 1 pointed mark, of the camshaft and the drive gears.

    c. Place the camshaft on the cylinder head and install the bearing caps.

    d. Apply a light coat of oil on the threads of the bearing cap bolts.

    e. Install and uniformly tighten the bearing cap bolts to 12 ft. lbs. Remove the service bolt.

42. Turn the camshaft and position the cam lobe upward. Check and adjust the valve clearance.

43. Apply a suitable multi-purpose grease to the the new camshaft oil seals and install with the proper tool.

44. Install the spark plug tube gaskets. Install the proper seal packing to the cylinder heads.

45. Install the cylinder head cover gasket and install with the seal washers and nuts. Tighten to 52 inch lbs.

46. Install the No. 3 timing belt cover and tighten the bolts 65 inch lbs.

47. Install the No. 2 idler pulley, the camshaft timing pulleys and the timing belt.

48. Install the spark plugs and tighten to 13 ft. lbs.

49. Install the right side heat insulator and the right side exhaust manifold with a new gasket. Tighten the nuts to 29 ft. lbs.

50. Install the outside heat insulator and connect the oxygen sensor connector.

51. Install the left side exhaust manifold with a new gasket and tighten the nuts to 29 ft. lbs. Install the heat insulator.

52. Install the intake manifold with new gaskets. Tighten the nuts and bolts to 13 ft. lbs.

53. Install the No. 2 idler pulley bracket and tighten to 13 ft. lbs. Replace the rear cylinder head plate.

54. Install the crossover pipe heat insulator. Replace the water bypass outlet and tighten the mounting bolts to 14 ft. lbs.

55. Connect the heater water bypass hose, cold start injector time switch connector and the water temperature switch.

56. Connect the upper radiator hose, the water temperature sensor connector and install the water oulet with a new gasket. Tighten the bolts to 73 inch lbs.

57. Install the fuel injectors and the delivery pipes.

58. Install the air intake chamber with new gaskets and tighten the mounting bolts to 32 ft. lbs.

59. Install the intake chamber brackets.

60. Connect the following hoses:

    a. PCV hose

    b. Vacuum sensing hose

    c. EGR gas temperature sensor connector (California only)

    d. Air conditioning control valve air hose

61. Install the cold start injector tube and connect the cold start injector connector.

62. Install the exhaust crossover pipe with new gaskets and tighten the mounting bolts to 25 ft. lbs. and the nuts to 29 ft. lbs.

63. Install the distributor.

64. Install the vacuum pipe and connect the BVSV vacuum hoses and the air conditioning control valve vacuum hose.

65. Install the EGR valve and vacuum modulator. Tighten the mounting bolts to 13 ft. lbs. Install the vacuum pipe hoses.

66. Install the EGR pipe with a new gasket and tighten the mounting bolts to 13 ft. lbs. and the nut to 58 ft. lbs.

67. Install the throttle body and ISC valve.

68. Raise and support the vehicle. Install the front exhaust pipe and the right side engine undercover. Lower the vehicle.

69. Install the air cleaner hose and cruise control actuator.

70. Install the accelerator cable and connect the throttle cable, if equipped with an automatic transaxle.

71. Install the suspension upper brace and fill the cooling system.

72. Connect the negative battery cable. Run the engine and check for leaks.

73. Adjust the timing. Recheck the fluid levels.

LS400

1. Disconnect the negative battery cable. Drain the cooling system.

2. Remove the camshaft timing pulleys.

3. Disconnect the accelerator cable, the throttle control cable, if equipped with automatic transmission and the cruise control actuator cable.

4. Remove the high tension cord cover and the right side ignition coil.

5. Remove the water inlet housing mounting bolts and disconnect the water bypass hose from the ISC valve.

6. Remove the water inlet and inlet housing assemblies. Remove the O-ring from the water inlet housing.

7. Remove the EGR pipe.

8. Disconnect the following:

    a. VSV connector

    b. Vacuum pipe hose

    c. EGR water bypass pipe

    d. Fuel pressure VSV

9. Disconnect the EGR vacuum hoses and remove the EGR VSV.

10. Disconnect the following hoses:

    a. Water bypass pipe hose from the ISC valve.

    b. Water bypass joint hose.

    c. Vacuum pipe hoses.

11. Disconnect the EGR gas temperature sensor (California only). Remove the EGR valve adapter.

12. Disconnect the following:

    a. Fuel pressure regulator vacuum hose.

    b. Air intake chamber vacuum hose.

    c. Vacuum hose from the EVAP BVSV.

13. Remove the mounting bolts, hoses and the vacuum pipe.

14. Remove the ISC valve.

15. Remove the throttle body sensor connectors and the water bypass pipe from the rear water bypass joint.

16. Remove the mounting bolts/nuts and disconnect the PCV valve. Remove the throttle body and gasket.

17. Disconnect the accelerator cable bracket and the brake booster vacuum union and hose.

18. Disconnect the cold start injector connector and the cold start injector tube from the right side delivery pipe.

19. Disconnect the check connector from the intake chamber and remove the mounting nuts and bolts.

20. Remove the air intake chamber and the cold start injector, tube and wire assembly.

21. Disconnect the engine wire from the intake manifold and from the right side cylinder head. Disconnect the heater hoses.

22. Remove the delivery pipes and the fuel injectors. Remove the mounting bolts and nuts. Lift up the intake manifold.

23. Remove the front and rear water bypass joint.

24. Raise and safely support the vehicle. Remove the front exhaust pipe and the main catalytic converters. Lower the vehicle.

25. Disconnect the right side oxygen sensor. Remove the mounting bolts and nuts and remove the right side exhaust manifold.

26. Remove the oil dipstick and guide. Disconnect the left side oxygen sensor.

27. Remove the mounting bolts and nuts and remove the left side exhaust manifold.

28. Remove the 2 engine hangers and the wire brackets from the right side cylinder head.

29. Remove the bolts, washers and the cylinder head cover. Remove the semi-circular plugs, if necessary.

30. Remove the exhaust camshaft of the right side cylinder head by:

  a. Position the service bolt hole of the drive sub-gear to the upright position. Secure the camshaft sub-gear to drive gear with a service bolt.

  b. Set the timing mark, 1 pointed mark, of the camshaft drive gear at approximately 10 degrees, by turning the camshaft with the proper tool.

  c. Alternately, loosen and remove the bearing cap bolts holding the intake camshaft side of the oil feed pipe to the cylinder head.

  d. Uniformly, loosen and remove the bearing cap bolts in sequence.

  e. Remove the oil feed pipe and the bearing caps. Remove the camshaft.

31. Remove the intake camshaft from the right side cylinder head by:

  a. Set the timing mark, 1 pointed mark, of the camshaft drive gear at approximately 45 degrees, by turning the camshaft with the proper tool.

  c. Uniformly, loosen and remove the bearing cap bolts in the proper sequence.

  d. Remove the bearing caps, oil seal and the intake camshaft.

32. Remove the exhaust camshaft of the left side cylinder head by:

  a. Position the service bolt hole of the drive sub-gear to the

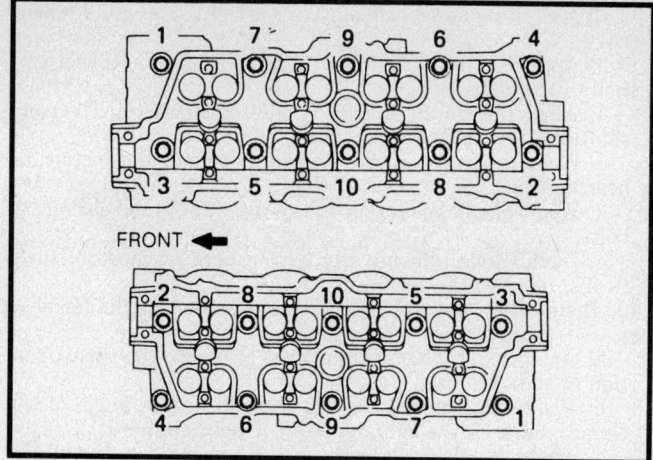

Cylinder head bolt removal sequence – LS400

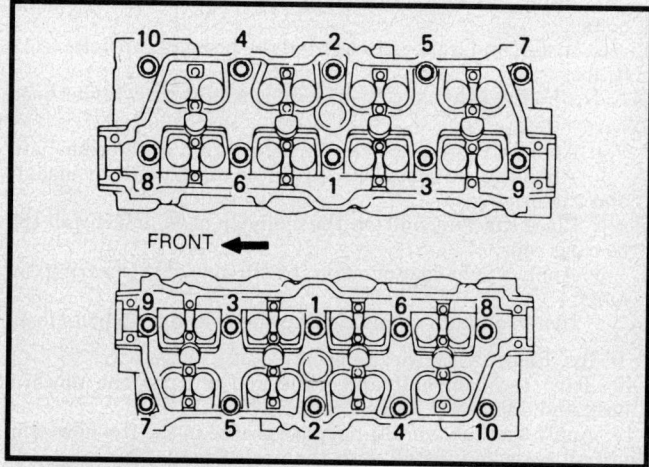

Cylinder head tightening sequence – LS400

upright position. Secure the camshaft sub-gear to drive gear with a service bolt.

NOTE: When removing the camshaft, make sure the torsional spring force of the sub-gear has been eliminated.

  b. Set the timing mark, 2 pointed marks, of the camshaft drive gear at approximately 15 degrees, by turning the camshaft with the proper tool.

  c. Alternately, loosen and remove the bearing cap bolts holding the intake camshaft side of the oil feed pipe to the cylinder head.

  d. Uniformly, loosen and remove the bearing cap bolts in the proper sequence.

  e. Remove the oil feed pipe and the bearing caps. Remove the camshaft.

33. Remove the intake camshaft from the left side cylinder head by:

  a. Set the timing mark, 1 pointed mark, of the camshaft drive gear at approximately 60 degrees, by turning the camshaft with the proper tool.

  c. Uniformly, loosen and remove the bearing cap bolts in the proper sequence.

  d. Remove the bearing caps, oil seal and the intake camshaft.

34. Disconnect the ground straps and clamp of the engine wire from the rear of the cylinder heads.

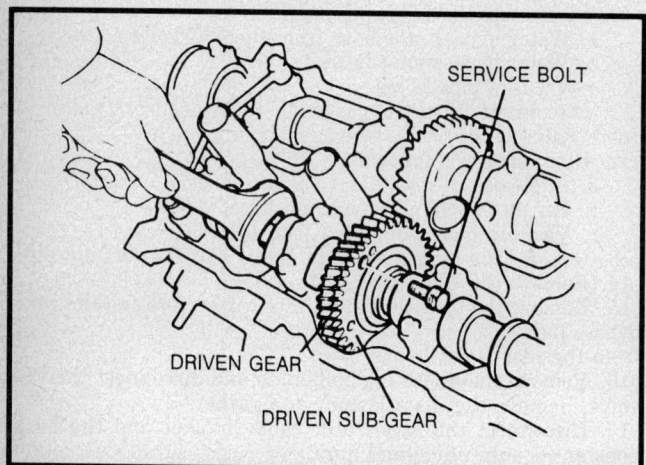

Securing the camshaft gears – LS400

35. Uniformly, loosen the head bolts of 1 side of the cylinder head then on the other side. Remove the head bolts and washers.

36. Lift out the cylinder head from the dowels on the cylinder block and place on a suitable holding fixture. Remove the gasket and clean the mounting surface.

To install:

37. Place new cylinder gasket into position on the cylinder block. Install the cylinder head.

38. The cylinder head bolts are tightened in 2 steps:

a. Apply a light coat of engine oil on the threads of the bolts. Temporarily, install the washers and bolts. Uniformly, tighten the head bolts one 1 side of the cylinder head in the proper sequence then the other side. Tighten the bolts to 29 ft. lbs.

b. Mark the front the cylinder head bolt with paint. Re-tighten the cylinder head bolts in the proper sequence 90 degrees. Check that the painted mark is at a 90 degree angle to the front.

39. Connect the engine wire to the cylinder head(s), tighten the clamps.

40. Install the circular plugs on the cylinder head with the cup side facing forward.

41. Remove any old packing and apply new seal packing to the bearing caps.

42. Install the bearing cap on the right side cylinder head, marked I1, in position with the arrow mark facing the rear. Install the bearing cap on the left side cylinder head, marked I6, in position with the arrow mark facing the front.

43. Apply a light coat of oil on the threads of the cap bolts. Install the nearing cap bolts with new washers and tighten to 12 ft. lbs.

44. Install the right side cylinder head intake camshaft by:

a. Apply MP grease to the thrust portion of the camshaft.

b. Place the intake camshaft at a 45 degree angle of the timing mark, 1 pointed mark, on the cylinder head.

c. Remove any old packing and apply new seal packing to the bearing cap marked I6 and install the front bearing cap, marked I6 with the arrow facing rearward.

d. Align the arrows at the front and rear of the cylinder head with the bearing cap.

e. Install the remaining bearing caps in the proper sequence with the arrow mark facing rearward. Install the oil feed pipe and the mounting bolts.

f. Uniformly, tighten the bearing cap bolts in the proper sequence to 12 ft. lbs.

45. Install the right side cylinder head exhaust camshaft by:

a. Set the timing mark, 1 pointed mark, of the camshaft

drive gear at a 10 degree angle by turning the intake camshaft with the proper tool.

b. Apply MP grease to the thrust portion of the camshaft.

c. Align the timing marks, 1 pointed mark, of the camshaft drive and driven gears.

d. Place the exhaust camshaft ion the cylinder head. Install the rear bearing cap with the arrow mark facing rearward.

e. Align the arrow marks at the front and rear of the cylinder head with the mark on the bearing cap. Apply a light coat of oil on the threads of the bearing cap bolts.

f. Uniformly, tighten the bearing cap bolts in the proper sequence to 12 ft. lbs.

g. Bring the service bolt installed upward by turning the camshaft with the proper tool. Remove the service bolt.

46. Install the left side cylinder head intake camshaft by:

a. Apply MP grease to the thrust portion of the camshaft.

b. Place the intake camshaft at a 60 degree angle of the timing mark (1 pointed mark) on the cylinder head.

c. Remove any old packing and apply new seal packing to the bearing cap marked I6 and install the front bearing cap, marked I1 with the arrow facing rearward.

d. Align the arrows at the front and rear of the cylinder head with the bearing cap. Apply a light coat of oil on the threads of the bearing cap bolts.

e. Install the remaining bearing caps in the proper sequence with the arrow mark facing rearward. Install the oil feed pipe and the mounting bolts.

f. Uniformly, tighten the bearing cap bolts in the proper sequence to 12 ft. lbs.

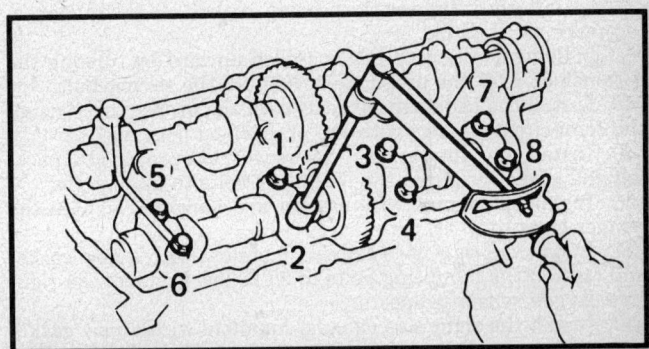

Right side exhaust camshaft bearing cap bolt tightening sequence—LS400

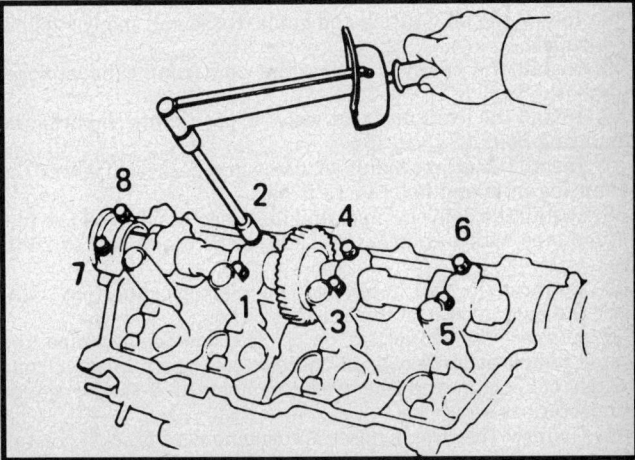

Left side intake camshaft bearing cap bolt tightening sequence—LS400

Right side intake camshaft bearing cap bolt tightening sequence—LS400

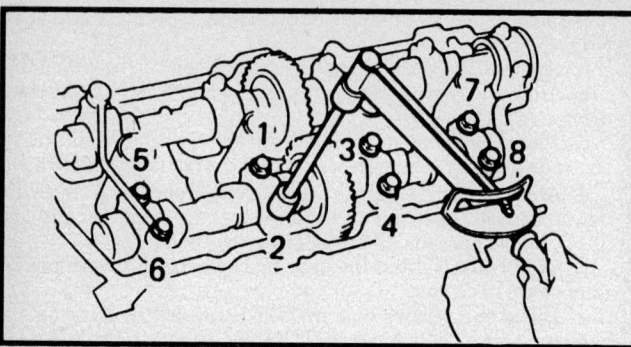

Left side exhaust camshaft bearing cap bolt tightening sequence — LS400

47. Install the left side cylinder head exhaust camshaft by:

a. Set the timing mark, 2 dot marks, of the camshaft drive gear at a 15 degree angle by turning the intake camshaft with the proper tool.

b. Apply MP grease to the thrust portion of the camshaft.

c. Align the timing marks, 2 dot marks, of the camshaft drive and driven gears.

d. Place the exhaust camshaft ion the cylinder head. Install the rear bearing cap with the arrow mark facing rearward.

e. Align the arrow marks at the front and rear of the cylinder head with the mark on the bearing cap. Apply a light coat of oil on the threads of the bearing cap bolts.

f. Uniformly, tighten the bearing cap bolts in the proper sequence to 12 ft. lbs.

g. Bring the service bolt installed upward by turning the camshaft with the proper tool. Remove the service bolt.

48. Install the camshaft oil seals with the proper tool. Install the semi-circular plugs with the proper seal packing.

49. Install the cylinder head covers with the proper seal packing and gasket. Tighten the mounting bolts to 52 inch lbs.

50. Install the engine wire bracket and hangers. Tighten the hanger bolts to 27 ft. lbs.

51. Install the right side exhaust manifold with a new gasket and tighten the mounting bolts to 29 ft. lbs. Connect the right side oxygen sensor connector.

52. Install the right side exhaust manifold with a new gasket and tighten the mounting bolts to 29 ft. lbs. Connect the right side oxygen sensor connector.

53. Install the left side exhaust manifold with a new gasket and tighten the mounting bolts to 29 ft. lbs. Connect the left side oxygen sensor connector.

54. Install the oil dipstick and guide. Raise and safely support the vehicle.

55. Install the catalytic converters and front exhaust pipe. Lower the vehicle.

56. Install the front and rear water bypass joints. Tighten the mounting bolts to 13 ft. lbs.

57. Install the intake manifold, using new gaskets. Tighten the mounting nuts and bolts to 13 ft. lbs.

58. Install the delivery pipes and fuel injectors. Install the fuel return pipe with new gaskets. Tighten the union bolt to 26 ft. lbs.

59. Connect the fuel hoses and the injector connectors. Connect the engine wire to the delivery pipes.

60. Connect the connectors on the left side delivery pipe, the water temperature sensor connector, cold start injector time switch connector and the water temperature sender gauge connector.

61. Connect the heater hoses and engine wire bracket. Install the engine wire to the bracket.

62. Install the cold start injector, tube and wire assembly. Tighten the mounting bolts to 69 inch lbs.

63. Install the air intake chamber with new gaskets and tighten the mounting bolts to 13 ft. lbs.

64. Connect the cold start injector tube to the right side delivery pipe and tighten the union bolt to 11 ft. lbs.

65. Connect the cold start injector connector. Install the accelerator cable bracket.

66. Install the brake booster union and connect the vacuum hose. Tighten the union bolt to 22 ft. lbs.

67. Connect the water bypass hose to the throttle body and the PCV hose to the cylinder head cover.

68. Install the throttle body, using a new gasket. Tighten the mounting bolts to 13 ft. lbs.

69. Install the water bypass pipe and connect the sensor connectors. Install the ISC valve and tighten the mounting bolts to 13 ft. lbs. Connect the water bypass hose.

70. Install the vacuum pipe and the following hoses:

a. Fuel pressure regulator vacuum hose.

b. Vacuum hose to the upper port of the EVAP BVSV.

c. Air intake chamber vacuum hose.

d. Trottle body vacuum hoses.

71. Install the EGR valve adapter with a new gasket. Tighten the mounting bolts to 13 ft. lbs.

72. Connect the EGR gas temperature sensor connector (California only).

73. Install the EGR valve and vacuum modulator. Connect the water bypass hoses and the vacuum hoses.

74. Install the EGR and fuel pressure VSV and connect the hoses and connectors. Replace the EGR pipe and tighten the mounting bolts to 13 ft. lbs.

75. Install the timing belt rear plates and tighten the bolts to 69 inch lbs. Install the water inlet and inlet hosing and tighten the bolts to 13 ft. lbs.

76. Install the right side ignition coil and the high tension cord cover.

77. Connect and adjust the accelerator cable, the automatic transmission throttle cable and the cruise control actuator cable. Install the camshaft timing pulley.

78. Fill the cooling system and connect the negative battery cable. Start the engine and check for leaks.

79. Recheck all the fluid levels and check the ignition timing.

Valve Lifters

Removal and Installation

1. Disconnect the negative battery cable.
2. Remove the cylinder head from the cylinder block.
3. Remove the lifters and the adjusting shims, using the proper tool.
4. Install the valve lifters and shims.
5. Check that the valve lifter rotates smoothly.
6. Install the cylinder head.
7. Connect the negative battery cable.

Valve Lash

Adjustment

ES250

NOTE: Adjust the valve clearance when the engine is cold.

1. Disconnect the negative battery cable.
2. Remove the air intake chamber. Remove the cylinder head covers.
3. Turn the crankshaft pulley and align it's groove with the timing mark 0 of the No. 1 timing cover.
4. Check that the valve lifters on the No. 1 intake and exhaust are tight.
5. Measure the clearance between the valve lifter and the camshaft. Record the measurements on valves No. 1, 2, 3 and 6.

6. Turn the crankshaft ⅔ of a revolution and check the clearance on valves No. 2, 3, 4 and 5 and record.

7. Turn the crankshaft another ⅔ of a revolution and check valves; 1, 4, 5 and 6 and record.

8. Remove the adjusting shim and turn the crankshaft to position the cam lobe of the camshaft on the adjusting valve upward. Press down the valve lifter with the proper tool and place the proper tool between the camshaft and the valve lifter. Remove the tool.

9. Remove the adjusting shim with the proper tool.

10. Install the specified valve shim on the valve lifter with the proper tool.

11. Recheck the valve clearance.

12. Install the cylinder head covers and intake chamber.

13. Connect the negative battery cable.

LS400

1. Disconnect the negative battery cable.

2. Remove the No. 3 timing belt covers.

3. Disconnect the spark plug wires and remove the cylinder head covers.

4. Turn the crankshaft pulley and align it's groove with the timing mark 0 of the No. 1 timing cover. Check that the timing marks of the camshaft timing pulleys and timing belt rear plates are aligned. If not, turn the crankshaft 1 revolution (360 degrees) and align the mark.

5. Measure the clearance between the valve lifter and the camshaft on the valves in step 1 and record.

6. Turn the crankshaft 1 full revolution (360 degrees) and align the mark.

7. Measure the clearance between the valve lifter and the camshaft on the valves in step 2 and record.

8. Remove the adjusting shim and turn the crankshaft to position the cam lobe of the camshaft on the adjusting valve upward. Press down the valve lifter with the proper tool and place

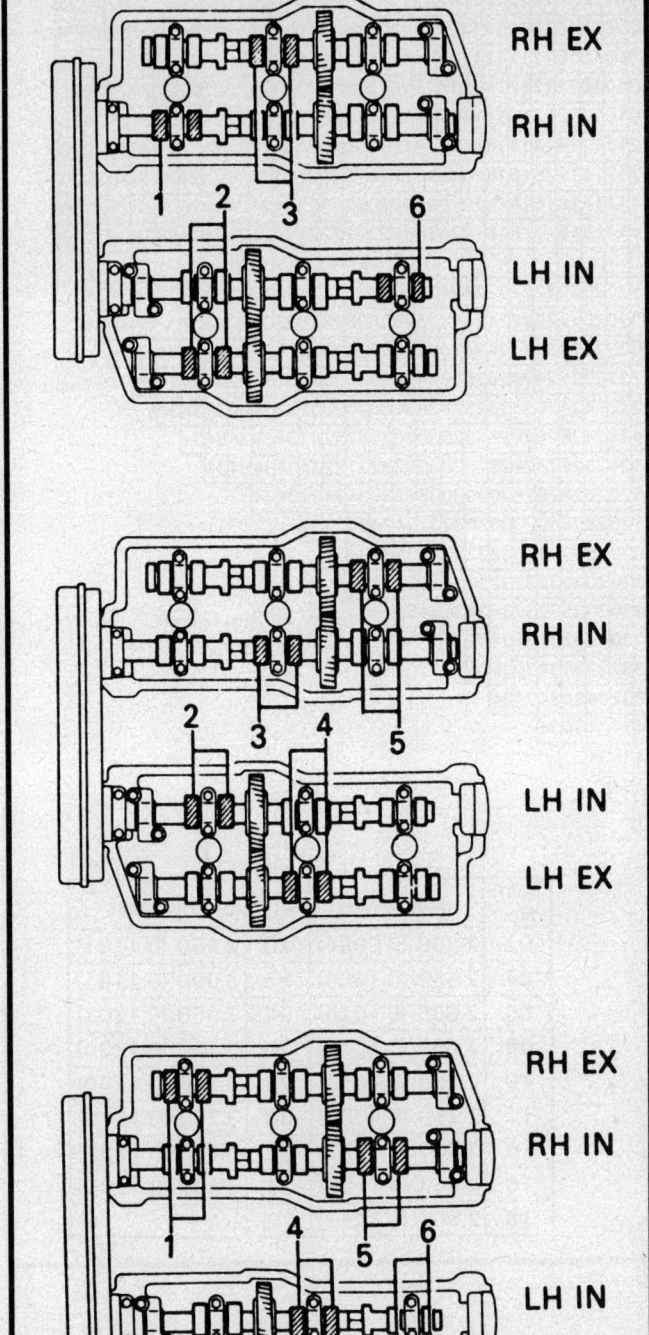

Valve adjusting sequence—ES250

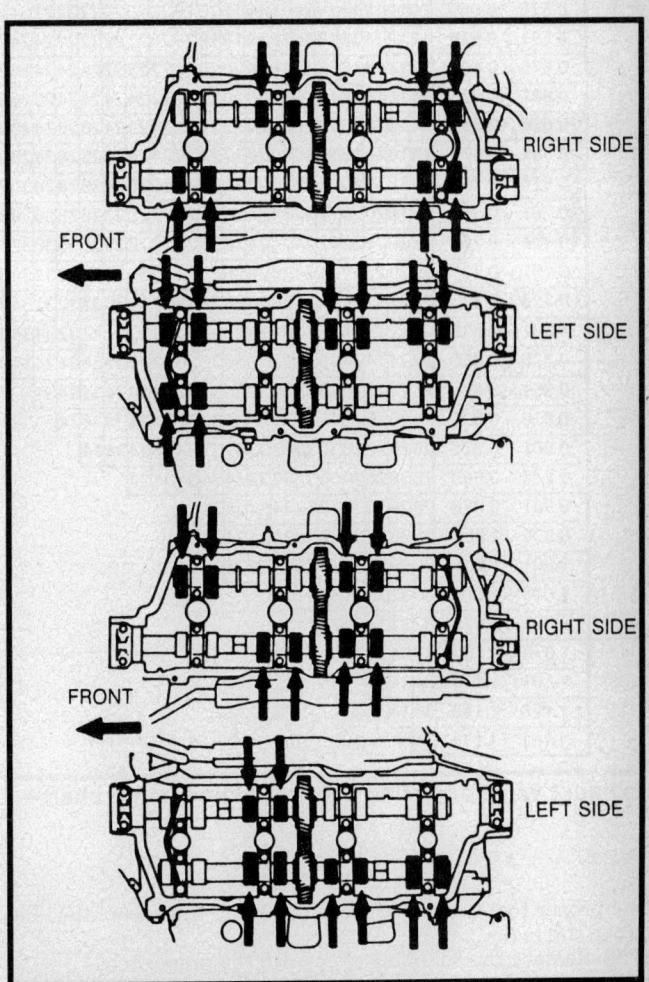

Valve adjusting sequence—LS400

Exhaust valve adjusting shim selection using chart — LS400

Measured clearance (mm)	Installed Shim thickness (mm)																																														
	2.500	2.525	2.550	2.575	2.600	2.620	2.640	2.650	2.660	2.680	2.700	2.720	2.740	2.750	2.760	2.780	2.800	2.820	2.840	2.850	2.860	2.880	2.900	2.920	2.940	2.950	2.960	2.980	3.000	3.020	3.040	3.050	3.060	3.080	3.100	3.120	3.140	3.150	3.160	3.180	3.200	3.225	3.250	3.275	3.300
0.000 – 0.025																	02	02	02	02	02	04	04	04	06	06	08	08	08	10	10	12	12	12	14	14	16	16	16	16	18	18	20	20	22
0.026 – 0.050																02	02	02	02	02	02	04	04	06	06	06	08	08	08	10	10	10	12	12	12	14	14	14	16	16	18	18	18	20	20
0.051 – 0.075															02	02	02	02	02	02	04	04	06	06	06	06	08	10	10	10	10	12	12	14	14	14	14	16	16	18	18	18	18	20	20
0.076 – 0.100														02	02	02	02	02	02	04	04	04	06	06	06	08	08	08	10	10	12	12	12	14	14	16	16	16	16	18	18	20	20	22	22
0.101 – 0.125													02	02	02	02	02	02	04	04	04	06	06	08	08	08	08	10	10	12	12	12	12	14	14	16	16	16	16	18	18	20	20	20	22
0.126 – 0.150												02	02	02	02	02	02	04	04	04	06	06	06	08	08	08	10	10	12	12	12	14	14	14	16	16	18	18	18	20	20	20	22	22	24
0.151 – 0.175											02	02	02	02	02	02	04	04	06	06	06	08	08	10	10	10	10	12	12	14	14	14	14	16	16	18	18	18	18	20	20	22	22	24	24
0.176 – 0.200										02	02	02	02	02	04	04	04	06	06	06	08	08	08	10	10	12	12	12	14	14	14	16	16	18	18	18	20	20	20	22	22	24	24	26	26
0.201 – 0.225									02	02	02	02	02	04	04	04	04	06	08	08	08	08	10	10	12	12	12	12	14	14	16	16	16	18	18	18	20	20	22	22	24	24	24	26	26
0.226 – 0.250								02	02	02	02	04	04	04	06	06	06	08	08	08	10	10	12	12	12	14	14	14	16	16	18	18	18	20	20	22	22	24	24	24	26	26	28	28	30
0.251 – 0.269							02	02	02	04	04	06	06	06	08	08	10	10	10	12	12	14	14	14	16	16	18	18	18	20	20	22	22	22	24	24	26	26	28	28	30	30	32		
0.270 – 0.370																																													
0.371 – 0.375	04	06	06	08	08	08	10	10	10	12	12	12	14	14	14	16	16	16	18	18	18	20	20	20	22	22	22	24	24	24	26	26	28	28	28	30	30	30	32	32	34	34	34		
0.376 – 0.400	04	06	06	08	08	10	10	10	12	12	12	14	14	14	16	16	16	18	18	18	20	20	20	22	22	24	24	24	26	26	28	28	28	30	30	30	32	32	32	34	34	34			
0.401 – 0.425	06	06	08	08	10	10	12	12	12	14	14	16	16	16	16	18	18	20	20	20	22	22	24	24	24	26	28	28	28	30	30	32	32	32	32	34	34	34							
0.426 – 0.450	06	08	08	10	10	12	12	12	14	14	14	16	16	18	18	18	20	20	20	22	22	24	24	24	26	26	28	28	28	30	30	30	32	32	32	34	34	34							
0.451 – 0.475	08	08	10	10	12	12	14	14	14	16	16	18	18	18	20	20	22	22	22	22	24	26	26	26	28	28	30	30	30	32	32	32	34	34	34	34									
0.476 – 0.500	08	10	10	12	12	14	14	14	16	16	16	18	18	20	20	20	22	22	24	24	24	26	26	28	28	28	30	30	30	32	32	32	34	34	34	34									
0.501 – 0.525	10	10	12	12	14	14	16	16	16	18	18	20	20	20	22	22	24	24	24	26	26	28	28	28	30	30	32	32	32	34	34	34	34												
0.526 – 0.550	10	12	12	14	14	16	16	16	18	18	18	20	20	22	22	22	24	24	26	26	26	28	28	30	30	30	32	32	32	34	34	34	34												
0.551 – 0.575	12	12	14	14	16	16	18	18	18	20	20	22	22	22	24	24	26	26	26	28	28	30	30	30	32	32	34	34	34	34															
0.576 – 0.600	12	14	14	16	16	18	18	18	20	20	22	22	24	24	24	26	26	26	28	28	30	30	30	32	32	32	34	34	34	34															
0.601 – 0.625	14	14	16	16	18	18	20	20	20	22	22	24	24	24	26	26	28	28	28	30	30	32	32	32	34	34	34	34																	
0.626 – 0.650	14	16	16	18	18	20	20	20	22	22	22	24	24	26	26	26	28	28	30	30	30	32	32	32	34	34	34	34																	
0.651 – 0.675	16	16	18	18	20	20	22	22	22	24	24	26	26	26	28	28	30	30	30	32	32	32	34	34	34	34																			
0.676 – 0.700	16	18	18	20	20	22	22	22	24	24	24	26	26	28	28	28	30	30	32	32	32	34	34	34	34																				
0.701 – 0.725	18	18	20	20	22	22	24	24	24	26	26	28	28	28	30	30	32	32	32	34	34	34	34																						
0.726 – 0.750	18	20	20	22	22	24	24	24	26	26	28	28	28	30	30	30	32	32	32	34	34	34	34																						
0.751 – 0.775	20	20	22	22	24	24	26	26	26	28	28	30	30	30	30	32	32	34	34	34	34	34																							
0.776 – 0.800	20	22	22	24	24	26	26	26	28	28	30	30	30	30	32	32	32	34	34	34	34																								
0.801 – 0.825	22	22	24	24	26	26	28	28	28	30	30	32	32	32	32	34	34	34	34																									
0.826 – 0.850	22	24	24	26	26	28	28	28	30	30	30	32	32	32	34	34	34	34																										
0.851 – 0.875	24	24	26	26	28	28	30	30	30	30	32	32	34	34	34	34	34																											
0.876 – 0.900	24	26	26	28	28	30	30	30	32	32	32	34	34	34	34																													
0.901 – 0.925	26	26	28	28	30	30	32	32	32	32	34	34	34	34																														
0.926 – 0.950	26	28	28	30	30	32	32	32	34	34	34	34																																
0.951 – 0.975	28	28	30	30	32	32	34	34	34	34																																		
0.976 – 1.000	28	30	30	32	32	34	34	34	34																																			
1.001 – 1.025	30	30	32	32	34	34	34	34																																				
1.026 – 1.050	30	32	32	34	34	34	34																																					
1.051 – 1.075	32	32	34	34	34																																							
1.076 – 1.100	32	34	34	34																																								
1.101 – 1.125	34	34	34																																									
1.126 – 1.150	34	34																																										
1.151 – 1.170	34																																											

New shim thicknesses   mm (in.)

Shim No.	Thickness	Shim No.	Thickness
02	2.500 (0.0984)	20	2.950 (0.1161)
04	2.550 (0.1004)	22	3.000 (0.1181)
06	2.600 (0.1024)	24	3.050 (0.1201)
08	2.650 (0.1043)	26	3.100 (0.1220)
10	2.700 (0.1063)	28	3.150 (0.1240)
12	2.750 (0.1083)	30	3.200 (0.1260)
14	2.800 (0.1102)	32	3.250 (0.1280)
16	2.850 (0.1122)	34	3.300 (0.1299)
18	2.900 (0.1142)		

the proper tool between the camshaft and the valve lifter. Remove the tool.

9. Remove the adjusting shim with the proper tool.

10. Install the specified valve shim on the valve lifter with the proper tool.

11. Recheck the valve clearance. Install the cylinder head covers.

12. Connect the spark plug wires and install the No. 3 timing belt covers.

13. Connect the negative battery cable.

Installed shim thickness (mm)

Measured clearance (mm)	2.500	2.525	2.550	2.575	2.600	2.620	2.640	2.650	2.660	2.680	2.700	2.720	2.740	2.750	2.760	2.780	2.800	2.820	2.840	2.850	2.860	2.880	2.900	2.920	2.940	2.950	2.960	2.980	3.000	3.020	3.040	3.050	3.060	3.080	3.100	3.120	3.140	3.150	3.160	3.180	3.200	3.225	3.250	3.275	3.300
0.000 – 0.025						02	02	02	02	02	04	04	04	06	06	06	08	08	10	10	10	12	12	14	14	14	16	16	16	18	18	18	20	20	20	22	22	22	24	24	24	26	26	26	28
0.026 – 0.050					02	02	02	02	02	04	04	06	06	06	06	08	08	10	10	10	10	12	12	14	14	14	16	16	18	18	18	18	20	20	20	22	22	22	24	24	26	26	26	28	28
0.051 – 0.075				02	02	02	02	02	04	04	04	06	06	06	08	08	08	10	10	10	12	12	12	14	14	14	16	16	16	18	18	18	20	20	20	22	22	22	24	24	26	26	28	28	30
0.076 – 0.100			02	02	02	04	04	04	06	06	08	08	08	08	10	10	12	12	12	12	14	14	16	16	16	16	18	18	20	20	20	20	22	22	24	24	24	26	26	28	28	30	30
0.101 – 0.125	02	02	02	04	04	04	06	06	06	08	08	08	10	10	10	12	12	12	14	14	14	16	16	18	18	18	20	20	20	22	22	22	24	24	26	26	28	28	30	30	32
0.126 – 0.129	02	02	04	04	06	06	06	08	08	08	10	10	10	12	12	12	14	14	14	16	16	16	18	18	18	20	20	20	22	22	22	24	24	26	26	26	28	28	28	30	30	32
0.130 – 0.230																																													
0.231 – 0.250	04	06	06	08	08	10	10	10	10	12	12	14	14	14	14	16	16	18	18	18	18	20	20	22	22	22	22	24	24	26	26	26	28	28	30	30	30	30	32	32	34	34	34
0.251 – 0.275	06	06	08	08	10	10	10	12	12	12	14	14	16	16	16	18	18	18	20	20	20	22	22	22	24	24	26	26	28	28	28	30	30	30	32	32	32	34	34	34
0.276 – 0.300	06	08	08	10	10	12	12	12	14	14	16	16	16	18	18	20	20	20	22	22	24	24	24	26	26	28	28	28	30	30	32	32	32	34	34	34
0.301 – 0.325	08	08	10	10	12	12	12	14	14	16	16	16	18	18	18	20	20	22	22	22	24	24	26	26	26	28	28	30	30	30	32	32	34	34	34	34
0.326 – 0.350	08	10	10	12	12	14	14	14	16	16	18	18	18	20	20	22	22	22	24	24	26	26	26	28	28	30	30	30	32	32	34	34	34
0.351 – 0.375	10	10	12	12	14	14	16	16	16	18	18	18	20	20	22	22	22	24	24	26	26	26	28	28	30	30	30	32	32	32	34	34	34	34
0.376 – 0.400	10	12	12	14	14	16	16	16	18	18	20	20	20	22	22	24	24	24	26	26	28	28	28	30	30	32	32	32	34	34	34
0.401 – 0.425	12	12	14	14	16	16	16	18	18	20	20	20	22	22	24	24	24	26	26	28	28	28	30	30	30	32	32	34	34	34	34
0.426 – 0.450	12	14	14	16	16	18	18	18	20	20	22	22	22	24	24	26	26	26	28	28	30	30	30	32	32	34	34	34	34
0.451 – 0.475	14	14	16	16	18	18	20	20	20	22	22	22	24	24	26	26	28	28	28	30	30	32	32	32	34	34	34	34
0.476 – 0.500	14	16	16	18	18	20	20	20	22	22	24	24	24	26	28	28	28	30	30	32	32	32	34	34	34	34
0.501 – 0.525	16	16	18	18	20	20	20	22	22	24	24	26	26	26	28	28	30	30	30	32	32	34	34	34	34
0.526 – 0.550	16	18	18	20	20	22	22	22	22	24	24	26	26	26	28	28	30	30	30	32	32	34	34	34	34
0.551 – 0.575	18	18	20	20	22	22	22	24	24	24	26	26	26	28	28	30	30	32	32	32	34	34	34	34
0.576 – 0.600	18	20	20	22	22	24	24	24	26	26	28	28	28	28	30	30	32	32	32	34	34	34	34
0.601 – 0.625	20	20	22	22	24	24	24	26	26	28	28	28	30	30	30	32	32	34	34	34	34
0.626 – 0.650	20	22	22	24	24	26	26	26	28	28	30	30	30	30	32	32	34	34	34	34
0.651 – 0.675	22	22	24	24	26	26	26	28	28	30	30	30	32	32	32	34	34	34	34
0.676 – 0.700	22	24	24	26	26	28	28	28	30	30	32	32	32	32	34	34	34	34
0.701 – 0.725	24	24	26	26	28	28	28	30	30	32	32	32	34	34	34	34
0.726 – 0.750	24	26	26	28	28	30	30	30	30	32	32	34	34	34	34
0.751 – 0.775	26	26	28	28	30	30	30	32	32	32	34	34	34	34
0.776 – 0.800	26	28	28	30	30	32	32	32	32	34	34	34	34
0.801 – 0.825	28	28	30	30	32	32	32	34	34	34	34
0.826 – 0.850	28	30	30	32	32	32	34	34	34	34
0.851 – 0.875	30	30	32	32	34	34	34	34
0.876 – 0.900	30	32	32	34	34	34	34
0.901 – 0.925	32	32	34	34	34	34
0.926 – 0.950	32	34	34	34	34
0.951 – 0.975	34	34	34	34
0.976 – 1.000	34	34	34
1.001 – 1.025	34	34
1.026 – 1.030	34

New shim thicknesses   mm (in.)

Shim No.	Thickness	Shim No.	Thickness
02	2.500 (0.0984)	20	2.950 (0.1161)
04	2.550 (0.1004)	22	3.000 (0.1181)
06	2.600 (0.1024)	24	3.050 (0.1201)
08	2.650 (0.1043)	26	3.100 (0.1220)
10	2.700 (0.1063)	28	3.150 (0.1240)
12	2.750 (0.1083)	30	3.200 (0.1260)
14	2.800 (0.1102)	32	3.250 (0.1280)
16	2.850 (0.1122)	34	3.300 (0.1299)
18	2.900 (0.1142)		

Intake valve adjusting shim selection using chart— LS400

Intake Manifold

Removal and Installation

ES250

1. Disconnect the negative battery cable. Drain the cooling system.

2. Remove the suspension upper brace. Disconnect the throttle cable from the throttle body, if equipped with an automatic transaxle.

3. Disconnect the accelerator cable from the throttle body. Remove the cruise control actuator and the vacuum pump.

4. Disconnect the ISC hose, the vacuum pipe hose and the air cleaner hose.

New shim thickness   mm (in.)

Shim No.	Thickness	Shim No.	Thickness
01	2.50 (0.0984)	38	2.95 (0.1161)
63	2.55 (0.1004)	43	3.00 (0.1181)
06	2.60 (0.1024)	48	3.05 (0.1201)
66	2.65 (0.1043)	51	3.10 (0.1220)
13	2.70 (0.1063)	77	3.15 (0.1240)
18	2.75 (0.1083)	56	3.20 (0.1260)
23	2.80 (0.1102)	80	3.25 (0.1280)
28	2.85 (0.1122)	61	3.30 (0.1299)
33	2.90 (0.1142)		

Installed shim thickness mm (in.) — top axis:

2.50 (0.0984), 2.52 (0.0992), 2.54 (0.1000), 2.55 (0.1004), 2.56 (0.1008), 2.58 (0.1016), 2.60 (0.1024), 2.62 (0.1031), 2.64 (0.1039), 2.65 (0.1043), 2.66 (0.1047), 2.67 (0.1051), 2.68 (0.1055), 2.69 (0.1059), 2.70 (0.1063), 2.71 (0.1067), 2.72 (0.1071), 2.73 (0.1075), 2.74 (0.1079), 2.75 (0.1083), 2.76 (0.1087), 2.77 (0.1091), 2.78 (0.1094), 2.79 (0.1098), 2.80 (0.1102), 2.81 (0.1106), 2.82 (0.1110), 2.83 (0.1114), 2.84 (0.1118), 2.85 (0.1122), 2.86 (0.1126), 2.87 (0.1130), 2.88 (0.1134), 2.89 (0.1138), 2.90 (0.1142), 2.91 (0.1146), 2.92 (0.1150), 2.93 (0.1154), 2.94 (0.1157), 2.95 (0.1161), 2.96 (0.1165), 2.97 (0.1169), 2.98 (0.1173), 2.99 (0.1177), 3.00 (0.1181), 3.01 (0.1185), 3.02 (0.1189), 3.03 (0.1193), 3.04 (0.1197), 3.05 (0.1201), 3.06 (0.1205), 3.08 (0.1213), 3.10 (0.1220), 3.12 (0.1228), 3.14 (0.1236), 3.15 (0.1240), 3.16 (0.1244), 3.18 (0.1252), 3.20 (0.1260), 3.22 (0.1268), 3.24 (0.1276), 3.25 (0.1280), 3.26 (0.1283), 3.28 (0.1291), 3.30 (0.1299)

Measured clearance mm (in.) — left axis:

mm	(in.)
0.000 – 0.020	(0.0000 – 0.0008)
0.021 – 0.040	(0.0008 – 0.0016)
0.041 – 0.060	(0.0016 – 0.0024)
0.061 – 0.080	(0.0024 – 0.0031)
0.081 – 0.100	(0.0032 – 0.0039)
0.101 – 0.120	(0.0040 – 0.0047)
0.121 – 0.140	(0.0048 – 0.0055)
0.141 – 0.160	(0.0056 – 0.0063)
0.161 – 0.180	(0.0063 – 0.0071)
0.181 – 0.200	(0.0071 – 0.0079)
0.201 – 0.220	(0.0079 – 0.0087)
0.221 – 0.240	(0.0087 – 0.0094)
0.241 – 0.249	(0.0095 – 0.0098)
0.250 – 0.350	(0.0098 – 0.0138)
0.351 – 0.360	(0.0138 – 0.0142)
0.361 – 0.380	(0.0142 – 0.0150)
0.381 – 0.400	(0.0150 – 0.0157)
0.401 – 0.420	(0.0158 – 0.0165)
0.42 – 0.440	(0.0166 – 0.0173)
0.441 – 0.460	(0.0174 – 0.0181)
0.461 – 0.480	(0.0181 – 0.0189)
0.481 – 0.500	(0.0189 – 0.0197)
0.501 – 0.520	(0.0197 – 0.0205)
0.521 – 0.540	(0.0205 – 0.0213)
0.541 – 0.560	(0.0213 – 0.0220)
0.561 – 0.580	(0.0221 – 0.0228)
0.58 – 0.600	(0.0229 – 0.0236)
0.601 – 0.620	(0.0237 – 0.0244)
0.621 – 0.640	(0.0244 – 0.0252)
0.644 – 0.660	(0.0252 – 0.0260)
0.661 – 0.680	(0.0260 – 0.0268)
0.68 – 0.700	(0.0268 – 0.0276)
0.701 – 0.720	(0.0276 – 0.0283)
0.721 – 0.740	(0.0284 – 0.0291)
0.741 – 0.760	(0.0292 – 0.0299)
0.761 – 0.780	(0.0300 – 0.0307)
0.781 – 0.800	(0.0307 – 0.0315)
0.801 – 0.820	(0.0315 – 0.0323)
0.821 – 0.840	(0.0323 – 0.0331)
0.841 – 0.860	(0.0331 – 0.0339)
0.861 – 0.880	(0.0339 – 0.0346)
0.881 – 0.900	(0.0347 – 0.0354)
0.901 – 0.920	(0.0355 – 0.0362)
0.921 – 0.940	(0.0363 – 0.0370)
0.941 – 0.960	(0.0370 – 0.0378)
0.961 – 0.980	(0.0378 – 0.0386)
0.981 – 1.000	(0.0386 – 0.0394)
1.001 – 1.020	(0.0394 – 0.0402)
1.021 – 1.040	(0.0402 – 0.0409)
1.041 – 1.060	(0.0409 – 0.0417)
1.061 – 1.080	(0.0418 – 0.0425)
1.081 – 1.100	(0.0426 – 0.0433)
1.101 – 1.120	(0.0433 – 0.0441)
1.121 – 1.140	(0.0441 – 0.0449)
1.141 – 1.150	(0.0449 – 0.0453)

Exhaust valve adjusting shim selection using chart — ES250

New shim thickness — mm (in.)

Shim No.	Thickness	Shim No.	Thickness
01	2.50 (0.0984)	38	2.95 (0.1161)
63	2.55 (0.1004)	43	3.00 (0.1181)
06	2.60 (0.1024)	48	3.05 (0.1201)
66	2.65 (0.1043)	51	3.10 (0.1220)
13	2.70 (0.1063)	77	3.15 (0.1240)
18	2.75 (0.1083)	56	3.20 (0.1260)
23	2.80 (0.1102)	80	3.25 (0.1280)
28	2.85 (0.1122)	61	3.30 (0.1299)
33	2.90 (0.1142)		

Intake valve adjusting shim selection using chart — ES250

5. Raise and safely support the vehicle. Remove the right side engine undercover.

6. Remove the suspension lower crossmember and the front exhaust pipe. Lower the vehicle.

7. Remove the alternator, the ISC valve and the throttle body.

8. Remove the EGR pipe, the EGR valve and the vacuum modulator.

9. Disconnect the (4) BVSV vacuum hoses, the fuel pressure VSV hose and the air conditioning control valve vacuum hose.

10. Remove the distributor and the exhaust crossover pipe.

11. Disconnect the cold start injector connector and remove the cold start injector tube.

12. Disconnect the following hoses:
    a. PCV hose
    b. Vacuum sensing hose
    c. Fuel pressure VSV hose
    d. Air conditioning control valve vacuum hose
    e. EGR gas temperature sensor connector – California only

13. Remove the mounting bolts and the brackets from the intake chamber. Remove the air intake chamber.

14. Remove the delivery pipes and the injectors.

15. Disconnect the water temperature sensor connector and the upper radiator hose. Remove the water outlet.

16. Disconnect the following connectors and hose:
    a. Cold start injector time switch connector
    b. Water temperature sensor connector
    c. Heater water bypass hose

17. Remove the water bypass outlet. Remove the crossover pipe insulator from the water bypass outlet.

18. Remove the cylinder head rear plate and the idler pulley bracket.

19. Remove the mounting bolts and nuts. Lift off the intake manifold.

To install:

20. Install the intake manifold with new gaskets. Tighten the nuts and bolts to 13 ft. lbs.

21. Install the No. 2 idler pulley bracket and tighten to 13 ft. lbs. Replace the rear cylinder head plate.

22. Install the crossover pipe heat insulator. Replace the water bypass outlet and tighten the mounting bolts to 14 ft. lbs.

23. Connect the heater water bypass hose, cold start injector time switch connector and the water temperature switch.

24. Connect the upper radiator hose, the water temperature sensor connector and install the water outlet with a new gasket. Tighten the bolts to 73 inch lbs.

25. Install the fuel injectors and the delivery pipes.

26. Install the air intake chamber with new gaskets and tighten the mounting bolts to 32 ft. lbs.

27. Install the intake chamber brackets.

28. Connect the following hoses:
    a. PCV hose
    b. Vacuum sensing hose
    c. EGR gas temperature sensor connector (California only)
    d. Air conditioning control valve air hose

29. Install the cold start injector tube and connect the cold start injector connector.

30. Install the exhaust crossover pipe with new gaskets and tighten the mounting bolts to 25 ft. lbs. and the nuts to 29 ft. lbs.

31. Install the distributor.

32. Install the vacuum pipe and connect the BVSV vacuum hoses and the air conditioning control valve vacuum hose.

33. Install the EGR valve and vacuum modulator. Tighten the mounting bolts to 13 ft. lbs. Install the vacuum pipe hoses.

34. Install the EGR pipe with a new gasket and tighten the mounting bolts to 13 ft. lbs. and the nut to 58 ft. lbs.

35. Install the throttle body and ISC valve.

36. Raise and support the vehicle. Install the front exhaust pipe and the right side engine undercover. Lower the vehicle.

37. Install the air cleaner hose and cruise control actuator.

38. Install the accelerator cable and connect the throttle cable, if equipped with automatic transaxle.

39. Install the suspension upper brace and fill the cooling system.

40. Connect the negative battery cable. Run the engine and check for leaks.

41. Adjust the timing. Recheck the fluid levels.

LS400

1. Disconnect the negative battery cable. Drain the cooling system.

2. Remove the camshaft timing pulleys.

3. Disconnect the accelerator cable, the throttle control cable, if equipped with automatic transmission and the cruise control actuator cable.

4. Remove the high tension cord cover and the right side ignition coil.

5. Remove the water inlet housing mounting bolts and disconnect the water bypass hose from the ISC valve.

6. Remove the water inlet and inlet housing assemblies. Remove the O-ring from the water inlet housing.

7. Remove the EGR pipe.

8. Disconnect the following:
    a. VSV connector
    b. Vacuum pipe hose
    c. EGR water bypass pipe
    d. Fuel pressure VSV

9. Disconnect the EGR vacuum hoses and remove the EGR VSV.

10. Disconnect the following hoses:
    a. Water bypass pipe hose from the ISC valve.
    b. Water bypass joint hose.
    c. Vacuum pipe hoses.

11. Disconnect the EGR gas temperature sensor, California only. Remove the EGR valve adapter.

12. Disconnect the following:
    a. Fuel pressure regulator vacuum hose.
    b. Air intake chamber vacuum hose.
    c. Vacuum hose from the EVAP BVSV.

13. Remove the mounting bolts, hoses and the vacuum pipe.

14. Remove the ISC valve.

15. Remove the throttle body sensor connectors and the water bypass pipe from the rear water bypass joint.

16. Remove the mounting bolts/nuts and disconnect the PCV valve. Remove the throttle body and gasket.

17. Disconnect the accelerator cable bracket and the brake booster vacuum union and hose.

18. Disconnect the cold start injector connector and the cold start injector tube from the right side delivery pipe.

19. Disconnect the check connector from the intake chamber and remove the mounting nuts and bolts.

20. Remove the air intake chamber and the cold start injector, tube and wire assembly.

21. Disconnect the engine wire from the intake manifold and from the right side cylinder head. Disconnect the heater hoses.

22. Remove the delivery pipes and the fuel injectors. Remove the mounting bolts and nuts. Lift up the intake manifold.

To install:

23. Install the intake manifold, using new gaskets. Tighten the mounting nuts and bolts to 13 ft. lbs.

24. Install the delivery pipes and fuel injectors. Install the fuel return pipe with new gaskets. Tighten the union bolt to 26 ft. lbs.

25. Connect the fuel hoses and the injector connectors. Connect the engine wire to the delivery pipes.

26. Connect the connectors on the left side delivery pipe, the water temperature sensor connector, cold start injector time switch connector and the water temperature sender gauge connector.

27. Connect the heater hoses and engine wire bracket. Install the engine wire to the bracket.

28. Install the cold start injector, tube and wire assembly. Tighten the mounting bolts to 69 inch lbs.

29. Install the air intake chamber with new gaskets and tighten the mounting bolts to 13 ft. lbs.

30. Connect the cold start injector tube to the right side delivery pipe and tighten the union bolt to 11 ft. lbs.

31. Connect the cold start injector connector. Install the accelerator cable bracket.

32. Install the brake booster union and connect the vacuum hose. Tighten the union bolt to 22 ft. lbs.

33. Connect the water bypass hose to the throttle body and the PCV hose to the cylinder head cover.

34. Install the throttle body, using a new gasket. Tighten the mounting bolts to 13 ft. lbs.

35. Install the water bypass pipe and connect the sensor connectors. Install the ISC valve and tighten the mounting bolts to 13 ft. lbs. Connect the water bypass hose.

36. Install the vacuum pipe and the following hoses:
    a. Fuel pressure regulator vacuum hose.
    b. Vacuum hose to the upper port of the EVAP BVSV.
    c. Air intake chamber vacuum hose.
    d. Throttle body vacuum hoses.

37. Install the EGR valve adapter with a new gasket. Tighten the mounting bolts to 13 ft. lbs.

38. Connect the EGR gas temperature sensor connector (California only).

39. Install the EGR valve and vacuum modulator. Connect the water bypass hoses and the vacuum hoses.

40. Install the EGR and fuel pressure VSV and connect the hoses and connectors. Replace the EGR pipe and tighten the mounting bolts to 13 ft. lbs.

41. Install the timing belt rear plates and tighten the bolts to 69 inch lbs. Install the water inlet and inlet hosing and tighten the bolts to 13 ft. lbs.

42. Install the right side ignition coil and the high tension cord cover.

43. Connect and adjust the accelerator cable, the automatic transmission throttle cable and the cruise control actuator cable. Install the camshaft timing pulley.

44. Fill the cooling system and connect the negative battery cable. Start the engine and check for leaks.

45. Recheck all the fluid levels and check the ignition timing.

Exhaust Manifold

Removal and Installation

ES250

1. Disconnect the negative battery cable. Drain the cooling system.

2. Remove the suspension upper brace. Disconnect the throttle cable from the throttle body, if equipped with an automatic transaxle.

3. Disconnect the accelerator cable from the throttle body. Remove the cruise control actuator and the vacuum pump.

4. Disconnect the ISC hose, the vacuum pipe hose and the air cleaner hose.

5. Raise and safely support the vehicle. Remove the right side engine undercover.

6. Remove the suspension lower crossmember and the front exhaust pipe. Lower the vehicle.

7. Remove the alternator, the ISC valve and the throttle body.

8. Remove the EGR pipe, the EGR valve and the vacuum modulator.

9. Disconnect the (4) BVSV vacuum hoses, the fuel pressure VSV hose and the air conditioning control valve vacuum hose.

10. Remove the distributor and the exhaust crossover pipe.

11. Disconnect the cold start injector connector and remove the cold start injector tube.

12. Disconnect the following hoses:
    a. PCV hose
    b. Vacuum sensing hose
    c. Fuel pressure VSV hose
    d. Air conditioning control valve vacuum hose
    e. EGR gas temperature sensor connector – California only

13. Remove the mounting bolts and the brackets from the intake chamber. Remove the air intake chamber.

14. Remove the delivery pipes and the injectors.

15. Disconnect the water temperature sensor connector and the upper radiator hose. Remove the water outlet.

16. Disconnect the following connectors and hose:
    a. Cold start injector time switch connector
    b. Water temperature sensor connector
    c. Heater water bypass hose

17. Remove the water bypass outlet. Remove the crossover pipe insulator from the water bypass outlet.

18. Remove the cylinder head rear plate and the idler pulley bracket.

19. Remove the mounting bolts and nuts. Lift off the intake manifold.

20. Disconnect the main oxygen sensor connector. Remove outside heat insulator.

21. Remove the mounting nuts and the right side exhaust manifold. Remove the inside heat insulator. It may be necessary to remove the cylinder on the right side to provide ample clearance.

22. Remove the heat insulator, the mounting nuts and the left side exhaust manifold.

To install:

23. Install the right side heat insulator and the right side exhaust manifold with a new gasket. Tighten the nuts to 29 ft. lbs.

24. Install the outside heat insulator and connect the oxygen sensor connector.

25. Install the left side exhaust manifold with a new gasket and tighten the nuts to 29 ft. lbs. Install the heat insulator.

26. Install the intake manifold with new gaskets. Tighten the nuts and bolts to 13 ft. lbs.

27. Install the No. 2 idler pulley bracket and tighten to 13 ft. lbs. Replace the rear cylinder head plate.

28. Install the crossover pipe heat insulator. Replace the water bypass outlet and tighten the mounting bolts to 14 ft. lbs.

29. Connect the heater water bypass hose, cold start injector time switch connector and the water temperature switch.

30. Connect the upper radiator hose, the water temperature sensor connector and install the water outlet with a new gasket. Tighten the bolts to 73 inch lbs.

31. Install the fuel injectors and the delivery pipes.

32. Install the air intake chamber with new gaskets and tighten the mounting bolts to 32 ft. lbs.

33. Install the intake chamber brackets.

34. Connect the following hoses:
    a. PCV hose
    b. Vacuum sensing hose
    c. EGR gas temperature sensor connector (California only)
    d. Air conditioning control valve air hose

35. Install the cold start injector tube and connect the cold start injector connector.

36. Install the exhaust crossover pipe with new gaskets and tighten the mounting bolts to 25 ft. lbs. and the nuts to 29 ft. lbs.

37. Install the distributor.

38. Install the vacuum pipe and connect the BVSV vacuum hoses and the air conditioning control valve vacuum hose.

39. Install the EGR valve and vacuum modulator. Tighten the mounting bolts to 13 ft. lbs. Install the vacuum pipe hoses.

40. Install the EGR pipe with a new gasket and tighten the mounting bolts to 13 ft. lbs. and the nut to 58 ft. lbs.

41. Install the throttle body and ISC valve.

42. Raise and support the vehicle. Install the front exhaust pipe and the right side engine undercover. Lower the vehicle.

43. Install the air cleaner hose and cruise control actuator.

44. Install the accelerator cable and connect the throttle cable, if equipped with an automatic transaxle.

45. Install the suspension upper brace and fill the cooling system.

46. Connect the negative battery cable. Run the engine and check for leaks.

47. Adjust the timing. Recheck the fluid levels.

LS400

1. Disconnect the negative battery cable. Drain the cooling system.

2. Remove the camshaft timing pulleys.

3. Disconnect the accelerator cable, the throttle control cable, if equipped with automatic transaxle and the cruise control actuator cable.

4. Remove the high tension cord cover and the right side ignition coil.

5. Remove the water inlet housing mounting bolts and disconnect the water bypass hose from the ISC valve.

6. Remove the water inlet and inlet housing assemblies. Remove the O-ring from the water inlet housing.

7. Remove the EGR pipe.

8. Disconnect the following:
    a. VSV connector
    b. Vacuum pipe hose
    c. EGR water bypass pipe
    d. Fuel pressure VSV

9. Disconnect the EGR vacuum hoses and remove the EGR VSV.

10. Disconnect the following hoses:
    a. Water bypass pipe hose from the ISC valve.
    b. Water bypass joint hose.
    c. Vacuum pipe hoses.

11. Disconnect the EGR gas temperature sensor, California only. Remove the EGR valve adapter.

12. Disconnect the following:
    a. Fuel pressure regulator vacuum hose.
    b. Air intake chamber vacuum hose.
    c. Vacuum hose from the EVAP BVSV.

13. Remove the mounting bolts, hoses and the vacuum pipe.

14. Remove the ISC valve.

15. Remove the throttle body sensor connectors and the water bypass pipe from the rear water bypass joint.

16. Remove the mounting bolts/nuts and disconnect the PCV valve. Remove the throttle body and gasket.

17. Disconnect the accelerator cable bracket and the brake booster vacuum union and hose.

18. Disconnect the cold start injector connector and the cold start injector tube from the right side delivery pipe.

19. Disconnect the check connector from the intake chamber and remove the mounting nuts and bolts.

20. Remove the air intake chamber and the cold start injector, tube and wire assembly.

21. Disconnect the engine wire from the intake manifold and from the right side cylinder head. Disconnect the heater hoses.

22. Remove the delivery pipes and the fuel injectors. Remove the mounting bolts and nuts. Lift up the intake manifold.

23. Remove the front and rear water bypass joint.

24. Raise and safely support the vehicle. Remove the front exhaust pipe and the main catalytic converters. Lower the vehicle.

25. Disconnect the right side oxygen sensor. Remove the mounting bolts and nuts and remove the right side exhaust manifold.

26. Remove the oil dipstick and guide. Disconnect the left side oxygen sensor.

27. Remove the mounting bolts and nuts and remove the left side exhaust manifold.

To install:

28. Install the right side exhaust manifold with a new gasket and tighten the mounting bolts to 29 ft. lbs. Connect the right side oxygen sensor connector.

29. Install the left side exhaust manifold with a new gasket and tighten the mounting bolts to 29 ft. lbs. Connect the left side oxygen sensor connector.

30. Install the oil dipstick and guide. Raise and safely support the vehicle.

31. Install the catalytic converters and front exhaust pipe. Lower the vehicle.

32. Install the front and rear water bypass joints. Tighten the mounting bolts to 13 ft. lbs.

33. Install the intake manifold, using new gaskets. Tighten the mounting nuts and bolts to 13 ft. lbs.

34. Install the delivery pipes and fuel injectors. Install the fuel return pipe with new gaskets. Tighten the union bolt to 26 ft. lbs.

35. Connect the fuel hoses and the injector connectors. Connect the engine wire to the delivery pipes.

36. Connect the connectors on the left side delivery pipe, the water temperature sensor connector, cold start injector time switch connector and the water temperature sender gauge connector.

37. Connect the heater hoses and engine wire bracket. Install the engine wire to the bracket.

38. Install the cold start injector, tube and wire assembly. Tighten the mounting bolts to 69 inch lbs.

39. Install the air intake chamber with new gaskets and tighten the mounting bolts to 13 ft. lbs.

40. Connect the cold start injector tube to the right side delivery pipe and tighten the union bolt to 11 ft. lbs.

41. Connect the cold start injector connector. Install the accelerator cable bracket.

42. Install the brake booster union and connect the vacuum hose. Tighten the union bolt to 22 ft. lbs.

43. Connect the water bypass hose to the throttle body and the PCV hose to the cylinder head cover.

44. Install the throttle body, using a new gasket. Tighten the mounting bolts to 13 ft. lbs.

45. Install the water bypass pipe and connect the sensor connectors. Install the ISC valve and tighten the mounting bolts to 13 ft. lbs. Connect the water bypass hose.

46. Install the vacuum pipe and the following hoses:
    a. Fuel pressure regulator vacuum hose.
    b. Vacuum hose to the upper port of the EVAP BVSV.
    c. Air intake chamber vacuum hose.
    d. Throttle body vacuum hoses.

47. Install the EGR valve adapter with a new gasket. Tighten the mounting bolts to 13 ft. lbs.

48. Connect the EGR gas temperature sensor connector (California only).

49. Install the EGR valve and vacuum modulator. Connect the water bypass hoses and the vacuum hoses.

50. Install the EGR and fuel pressure VSV and connect the hoses and connectors. Replace the EGR pipe and tighten the mounting bolts to 13 ft. lbs.

51. Install the timing belt rear plates and tighten the bolts to 69 inch lbs. Install the water inlet and inlet hosing and tighten the bolts to 13 ft. lbs.

52. Install the right side ignition coil and the high tension cord cover.

53. Connect and adjust the accelerator cable, the automatic transmission throttle cable and the cruise control actuator cable. Install the camshaft timing pulley.

54. Fill the cooling system and connect the negative battery cable. Start the engine and check for leaks.

55. Recheck all the fluid levels and check the ignition timing.

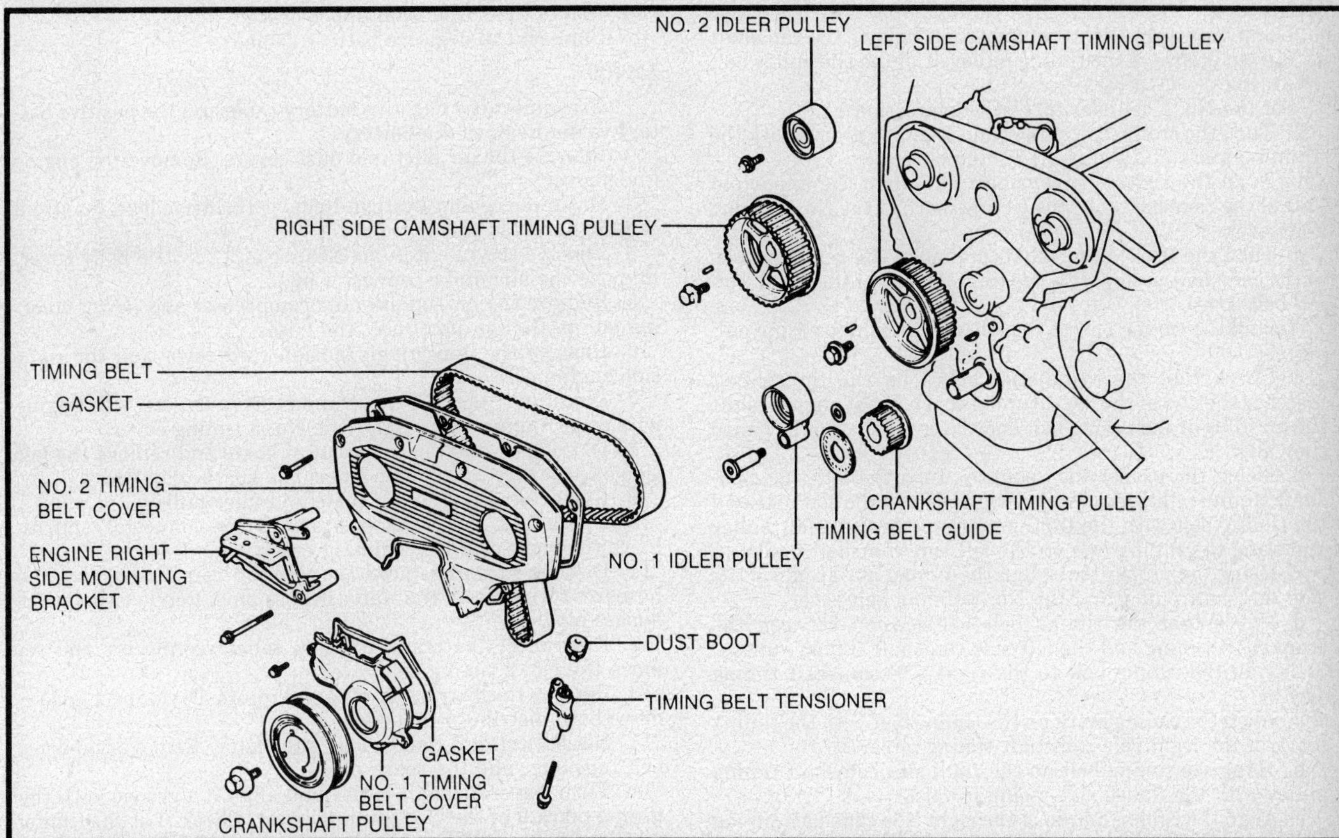

NO. 2 IDLER PULLEY

LEFT SIDE CAMSHAFT TIMING PULLEY

RIGHT SIDE CAMSHAFT TIMING PULLEY

TIMING BELT

GASKET

NO. 2 TIMING BELT COVER

ENGINE RIGHT SIDE MOUNTING BRACKET

NO. 1 IDLER PULLEY

CRANKSHAFT TIMING PULLEY

TIMING BELT GUIDE

DUST BOOT

TIMING BELT TENSIONER

GASKET

NO. 1 TIMING BELT COVER

CRANKSHAFT PULLEY

Exploded view of the timing belt assembly—ES250

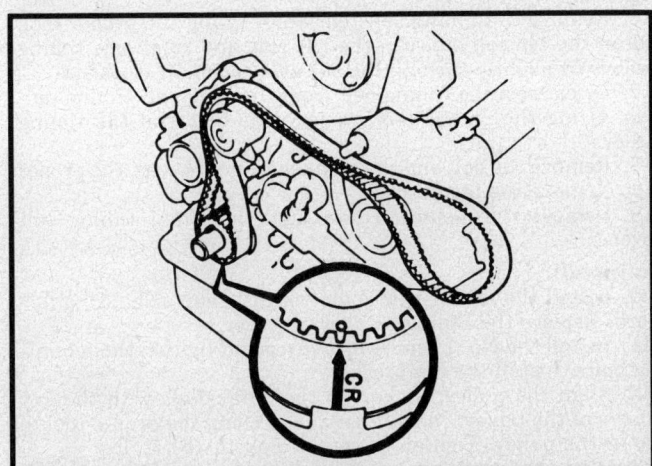

Aligning the timing belt—ES250

Timing Belt Front Cover

Removal and Installation

ES250

1. Disconnect the negative battery cable. Remove the suspension upper brace.
2. Remove the cruise control actuator.
3. Remove the power steering oil reservoir tank. Do not disconnect the hoses.
4. Raise and safely support the vehicle. Remove the right front tire and wheel assembly. Lower the vehicle.

5. Remove the alternator and power steering belts. Remove the right side fender apron seal.
6. Remove the right side engine support brackets. Raise the engine enough to remove the weight from the engine mounting on the right side, using a suitable jacking device.
7. Disconnect the power steering oil cooler lines and remove the right side engine mount.
8. Remove the air intake chamber and remove the spark plugs.
9. Remove the No. 2 timing belt cover and the right side engine mount bracket.
10. Turn the crankshaft pulley and align it's groove with the timing mark 0 of the No. 1 timing cover. Check that the timing marks of the camshaft timing pulleys and the No. 3 timing belt cover are aligned. If not, turn the crankshaft 1 full revolution (360 degrees).
11. Remove the timing belt tensioner and dust boot. Using the proper tool, loosen the tension between the left side and right side timing pulleys by slightly turning the right side camshaft timing pulley clockwise.
12. Remove the timing belt from the camshaft pulleys.
13. Remove the bolt, timing pulley and lock pin with the proper tool. Remove the 2 timing pulleys.
14. Remove the bolt and the No. 2 idler pulley.
15. Remove the crankshaft pulley bolt and the pulley, using the proper tool.
16. Remove the No. 1 timing cover.
To install:
17. Install the No. 1 timing belt cover and gasket.
18. Install the crankshaft pulley by aligning the pulley set key with the key groove of the pulley. Install the bolt with the proper tool and tighten to 181 ft. lbs.
19. Install the No. 2 idler pulley and tighten the bolt to 29 ft. lbs.

20. Install the left side camshaft timing pulley with the flange side facing outward. Align the knock pin hole of the camshaft with the pin groove of the timing pulley. Tighten the pulley bolt to 80 ft. lbs.

21. Set the No. 1 cylinder to TDC compression by:

a. Turn the crankshaft pulley and align it's groove with the 0 timing mark and the No. 1 timing cover.

b. Turn the right side camshaft and align the knock pin hole of the camshaft with the timing mark of the No. 3 timing belt cover.

c. Turn the left side camshaft and align the timing marks of the camshaft pulley with the timing mark of the No. 3 timing belt cover.

22. Install the timing belt to the left side camshaft timing pulley by:

a. Check that the installation mark on the timing belt matches the end of the No. 1 timing cover. If not aligned, shift the meshing of the timing belt and the crankshaft pulley until they align.

b. Using the proper tool, slightly, turn the left side camshaft timing pulley clockwise. Align the installation mark on the timing belt with the timing mark of the camshaft pulley and hang the timing belt on the left side camshaft pulley.

c. Using the proper tool, align the timing marks of the left side camshaft pulley and the No. 3 timing belt cover.

d. Check that the timing belt has tension between the crankshaft timing and the left side camshaft timing pulleys.

23. Install the timing belt to the right side camshaft timing pulley by:

a. Align the timing mark on the timing belt with the timing mark of the right side camshaft timing pulley.

b. Hang the timing belt on the right side camshaft timing pulley with the flange side facing inward.

c. Align the timing marks of the right side camshaft timing pulley and the No. 3 timing belt cover.

24. Slide the right side camshaft timing pulley on the camshaft. Align the knock pin hole of the camshaft with the knock pin groove of the pulley and install the knock pin. Tighten the bolt to 55 ft. lbs.

25. The timing belt tensioner must be set prior to installation. The tensioner can be set by:

a. Place a plate washer between the tensioner and a block. Using a suitable press, press in the pushrod using 220–2205 lbs. of pressure.

b. Align the holes of the pushrod and housing, pass the proper tool through the holes to keep the setting position of the pushrod.

c. Release the press and install the dust boot to the tensioner.

26. Install the tensioner and tighten the bolts to 20 ft. lbs. Remove the tool from the tensioner.

27. Turn the crankshaft pulley 2 revolutions from TDC to TDC. Always turn the crankshaft clockwise. Check that each pulley aligns with the timing marks.

28. Install the right side engine mounting bracket and tighten the bolts to 30 ft. lbs.

29. Install the No. 2 timing belt cover and gasket. Install the spark plugs and tighten to 13 ft. lbs.

30. Install the air intake chamber.

31. Install the right side engine mount and tighten the nut-to-bracket to 38 ft. lbs. and the nut-to-body to 65 ft. lbs. Do not tighten the mounting bolt.

32. Lower the engine. Install the right side engine mounting brackets and tighten the bolts. Fasten the power steering cooler pipes and tighten the engine mount bolt to 47 ft. lbs.

33. Install the alternator and power steering belts. Replace the right side fender apron seal.

34. Raise and safely support the vehicle. Install the RF tire and wheel assembly. Lower the vehicle.

35. Install the power steering reservoir tank and cruise control actuator.

36. Install the suspension upper brace.

37. Connect the negative battery cable.

LS400

1. Disconnect the negative battery cable and the positive battery cable. Remove the battery.

2. Remove the air duct and dust covers. Remove the engine undercover.

3. Drain the cooling system. Remove the drive belt, fan, fluid coupling and fan pulley.

4. Remove the radiator, air cleaner and throttle body cover. Remove the air intake connector pipe.

5. Remove the air conditioning compressor and power steering pump. Do not disconnect the hoses.

6. Remove the upper high tension cord cover and the right side engine wire cover.

7. Disconnect the PCV hose and remove the left side engine wire cover. Remove the right side No. 3 timing cover.

8. Disconnect and tag the vacuum hoses and remove the left side engine wire cover. Disconnect the spark plug wires.

9. Remove the bolt, cover plate and idler pulley.

10. Disconnect the crank position sensor connector and remove the right side No. 2 timing belt cover.

11. Disconnect and remove the ignition coil. Disconnect the hoses and wires from the water bypass pipe. Remove the water bypass pipe.

12. Disconnect the crank position sensor connector and remove the No. 2 timing belt cover.

13. Remove the distributor caps and rotors. Disconnect and remove both distributor housings.

14. Disconnect and remove the alternator. Remove the drive belt tensioner and the spark plugs.

15. Turn the crankshaft pulley and align it's groove with the timing mark **0** of the No. 1 timing cover. Check that the timing marks of the camshaft timing pulleys and timing belt rear plates are aligned. If not, turn the crankshaft 1 full revolution (360 degrees).

16. Remove the timing belt tensioner. Using the proper tool, loosen the tension between the left side and right side timing pulleys by slightly turning the left side camshaft clockwise.

17. Disconnect the timing belt from the camshaft timing pulleys. Using the proper tool, remove the bolt and the timing pulleys.

18. Remove the bolt and the crankshaft pulley with the proper tool. Remove the fan bracket.

19. Remove the mounting bolts and the No. 1 timing belt cover.

To install:

20. Install the timing belt guide with the cup side facing forward. Replace the timing belt cover spacer.

21. Install the No. 1 timing belt cover and tighten the mounting bolts. Install the fan bracket.

22. Align the pulley set key on the crankshaft with the key groove of the pulley. Install the pulley, using the proper tool to tap in the pulley. Tighten the pulley bolt to 181 ft. lbs.

23 Align the knock pin on the right side camshaft with the knock pin of the timing pulley. Slide on the timing pulley with the right side mark facing forward. Tighten the bolt to 80 ft. lbs.

24. Align the knock pin on the left side camshaft with the knock pin of the timing pulley. Slide on the timing pulley with the left side mark facing forward. Tighten the bolt to 80 ft. lbs.

25. Turn the crankshaft pulley and align it's groove with the0 timing mark on the No. 1 timing belt cover. Using the proper tool, turn the crankshaft timing pulley and align the timing marks of the camshaft timing pulley and the timing belt rear plate.

26. Install the timing belt to the left side camshaft timing pulley by:

a. Using the proper tool, slightly turn the left side timing pulley clockwise. Align the installation mark of the timing belt with the timing mark of the camshaft timing pulley and hang the timing belt on the left side camshaft pulley.

    b. Using the proper tool, align the timing marks of the left side camshaft pulley and the timing belt rear plate.

    c. Check that the timing belt has tension between crankshaft timing pulley and the left side camshaft pulley.

27. Install the timing belt to the right side camshaft timing pulley by:

    a. Using the proper tool, slightly turn the right side timing pulley clockwise. Align the installation mark of the timing belt with the timing mark of the camshaft timing pulley and hang the timing belt on the right side camshaft pulley.

    b. Using the proper tool, align the timing marks of the right side camshaft pulley and the timing belt rear plate.

    c. Check that the timing belt has tension between crankshaft timing pulley and the right side camshaft pulley.

28. The timing belt tensioner must be set prior to installation. The tensioner can be set by:

    a. Place a plate washer between the tensioner and a block. Using a suitable press, press in the pushrod using 220–2205 lbs. of pressure.

    b. Align the holes of the pushrod and housing, pass the proper tool through the holes to keep the setting position of the pushrod.

    c. Release the press and install the dust boot to the tensioner.

29. Install the tensioner and tighten the bolts to 20 ft. lbs. Remove the tool from the tensioner.

30. Turn the crankshaft pulley 2 revolutions from TDC to TDC. Always turn the crankshaft clockwise. Check that each pulley aligns with the timing marks.

31. Install the spark plugs and tighten to 13 ft. lbs. Install the drive belt tensioner and tighten the bolt to 12 ft. lbs.

32. Install the alternator and engine wire bracket. Tighten the nut and bolt to 26 ft. lbs. Connect the electrical connections at the alternator.

33. Install both distributor housings and tighten the mounting bolts to 13 ft. lbs. Replace the distributor rotors and caps.

34. Install the right side No. 2 timing belt cover and tighten the 10mm bolts to 69 inch lbs. and the 12mm bolts to 12 ft. lbs. Connect the crank position sensor connector.

35. Install the left side No. 2 timing belt cover and connect the crank position sensor connector.

36. Install the water bypass pipe and connect the hoses and connectors.

37. Replace the left side ignition coil and connect the coil connector. Install the idler pulley and cover plate. Tighten the bolt to 27 ft. lbs.

38. Install and secure the ignition wires. Install the right side No. 3 timing belt cover.

39. Install the left side No. 3 timing belt cover and connect the vacuum hose and connectors. Install the right side engine wire cover.

40. Install the left side engine wire cover and connect the vacuum hoses.

41. Install the upper high tension cord covers. Fit the front side claw groove of the upper cover to claw of the lower cover.

42. Install the power steering pump and the air conditioning compressor.

43. Install the throttle body cover and the air cleaner.

44. Install the radiator, fan pulley, fan coupling, fan and drive belt.

45. Install the engine undercover and replace the battery.

46. Install the air ducts and dust covers. Connect the battery cables.

47. Refill the cooling system. Check the ignition timing.

Timing Belt and Tensioner

Removal and Installation

ES250

1. Disconnect the negative battery cable. Remove the suspension upper brace.

2. Remove the cruise control actuator.

3. Remove the power steering oil reservoir tank. Do not disconnect the hoses.

4. Raise and safely support the vehicle. Remove the right front tire and wheel assembly. Lower the vehicle.

5. Remove the alternator and power steering belts. Remove the right side fender apron seal.

6. Remove the right side engine support brackets. Raise the engine enough to remove the weight from the engine mounting on the right side, using a suitable jacking device.

7. Disconnect the power steering oil cooler lines and remove the right side engine mount.

8. Remove the air intake chamber and remove the spark plugs.

9. Remove the No. 2 timing belt cover and the right side engine mount bracket.

10. Turn the crankshaft pulley and align it's groove with the timing mark **0** of the No. 1 timing cover. Check that the timing marks of the camshaft timing pulleys and the No. 3 timing belt cover are aligned. If not, turn the crankshaft 1 full revolution (360 degrees).

11. Remove the timing belt tensioner and dust boot. Using the proper tool, loosen the tension between the left side and right side timing pulleys by slightly turning the right side camshaft timing pulley clockwise.

12. Remove the timing belt from the camshaft pulleys.

13. Remove the bolt, timing pulley and lock pin with the proper tool. Remove the 2 timing pulleys.

14. Remove the bolt and the No. 2 idler pulley.

15. Remove the crankshaft pulley bolt and the pulley, using the proper tool.

16. Remove the No. 1 timing cover.

17. Remove the timing belt guide and lift off the timing belt.

To install:

18. Align the installation mark on the timing belt with the drilled mark of the crankshaft timing pulley. Install the timing belt on the crankshaft timing pulley, No. 1 idler pulley and the No. 2 idler pulley.

19. Install the timing belt guide with the cup side facing outward.

20. Install the No. 1 timing belt cover and gasket.

21. Install the crankshaft pulley by aligning the pulley set key with the key groove of the pulley. Install the bolt with the proper tool and tighten to 181 ft. lbs.

22. Install the No. 2 idler pulley and tighten the bolt to 29 ft. lbs.

23. Install the left side camshaft timing pulley with the flange side facing outward. Align the knock pin hole of the camshaft with the pin groove of the timing pulley. Tighten the pulley bolt to 80 ft. lbs.

24. Set the No. 1 cylinder to TDC compression by:

    a. Turn the crankshaft pulley and align it's groove with the 0 timing mark and the No. 1 timing cover.

    b. Turn the right side camshaft and align the knock pin hole of the camshaft with the timing mark of the No. 3 timing belt cover.

    c. Turn the left side camshaft and align the timing marks of the camshaft pulley with the timing mark of the No. 3 timing belt cover.

25. Install the timing belt to the left side camshaft timing pulley by:

    a. Check that the installation mark on the timing belt matches the end of the No. 1 timing cover. If not aligned, shift

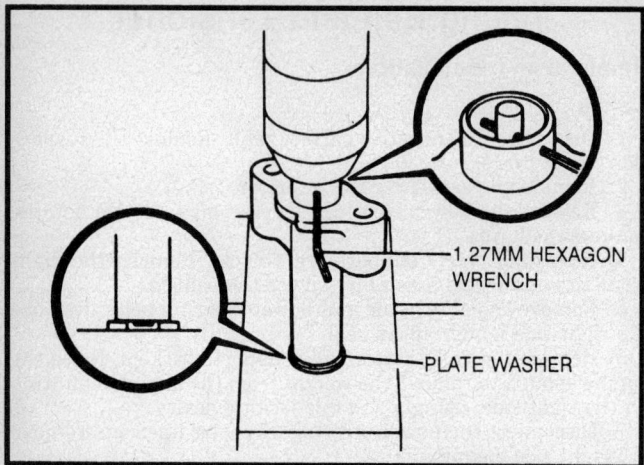

Setting the timing belt tensioner—ES250

the meshing of the timing belt and the crankshaft pulley until they align.

b. Using the proper tool, slightly, turn the left side camshaft timing pulley clockwise. Align the installation mark on the timing belt with the timing mark of the camshaft pulley and hang the timing belt on the left side timing pulley.

c. Using the proper tool, align the timing marks of the left side camshaft pulley and the No. 3 timing belt cover.

d. Check that the timing belt has tension between the crankshaft timing and the left side camshaft timing pulleys.

26. Install the timing belt to the right side camshaft timing pulley by:

a. Align the timing mark on the timing belt with the timing mark of the right side camshaft timing pulley.

b. Hang the timing belt on the right side camshaft timing pulley with the flange side facing inward.

c. Align the timing marks of the right side camshaft timing pulley and the No. 3 timing belt cover.

27. Slide the right side camshaft timing pulley on the camshaft. Align the knock pin hole of the camshaft with the knock pin groove of the pulley and install the knock pin. Tighten the bolt to 55 ft. lbs.

28. The timing belt tensioner must be set prior to installation. The tensioner can be set by:

a. Place a plate washer between the tensioner and a block. Using a suitable press, press in the pushrod using 220–2205 lbs. of pressure.

b. Align the holes of the pushrod and housing, pass the proper tool through the holes to keep the setting position of the pushrod.

c. Release the press and install the dust boot to the tensioner.

29. Install the tensioner and tighten the bolts to 20 ft. lbs. Remove the tool from the tensioner.

30. Turn the crankshaft pulley 2 revolutions from TDC to TDC. Always turn the crankshaft clockwise. Check that each pulley aligns with the timing marks.

31. Install the right side engine mounting bracket and tighten the bolts to 30 ft. lbs.

32. Install the No. 2 timing belt cover and gasket. Install the spark plugs and tighten to 13 ft. lbs.

33. Install the air intake chamber.

34. Install the right side engine mount and tighten the nut-to-bracket to 38 ft. lbs. and the nut-to-body to 65 ft. lbs. Do not tighten the mounting bolt.

35. Lower the engine. Install the right side engine mounting brackets and tighten the bolts. Fasten the power steering cooler pipes and tighten the engine mount bolt to 47 ft. lbs.

36. Install the alternator and power steering belts. Replace the right side fender apron seal.

37. Raise and safely support the vehicle. Install the RF tire and wheel assembly. Lower the vehicle.

38. Install the power steering reservoir tank and cruise control actuator.

39. Install the suspension upper brace.

40. Connect the negative battery cable.

LS400

1. Disconnect the negative battery cable and the positive battery cable. Remove the battery.

2. Remove the air duct and dust covers. Remove the engine undercover.

3. Drain the cooling system. Remove the drive belt, fan, fluid coupling and fan pulley.

4. Remove the radiator, air cleaner and throttle body cover. Remove the air intake connector pipe.

5. Remove the air conditioning compressor and power steering pump. Do not disconnect the hoses.

6. Remove the upper high tension cord cover and the right side engine wire cover.

7. Disconnect the PCV hose and remove the left side engine wire cover. Remove the right side No. 3 timing cover.

8. Disconnect and tag the vacuum hoses and remove the left side engine wire cover. Disconnect the spark plug wires.

9. Remove the bolt, cover plate and idler pulley.

10. Disconnect the crank position sensor connector and remove the right side No. 2 timing belt cover.

11. Disconnect and remove the ignition coil. Disconnect the hoses and wires from the water bypass pipe. Remove the water bypass pipe.

12. Disconnect the crank position sensor connector and remove the No. 2 timing belt cover.

13. Remove the distributor caps and rotors. Disconnect and remove both distributor housings.

14. Disconnect and remove the alternator. Remove the drive belt tensioner and the spark plugs.

15. Turn the crankshaft pulley and align it's groove with the timing mark 0 of the No. 1 timing cover. Check that the timing marks of the camshaft timing pulleys and timing belt rear plates are aligned. If not, turn the crankshaft 1 full revolution (360 degrees).

16. Remove the timing belt tensioner. Using the proper tool, loosen the tension between the left side and right side timing pulleys by slightly turning the left side camshaft clockwise.

17. Disconnect the timing belt from the camshaft timing pulleys. Using the proper tool, remove the bolt and the timing pulleys.

18. Remove the bolt and the crankshaft pulley with the proper tool. Remove the fan bracket.

19. Remove the mounting bolts and the No. 1 timing belt cover.

20. Remove the timing belt guide and lift off the timing belt.

To install:

21. Align the installation mark on the timing belt with the drilled mark of the crankshaft timing pulley. Install the timing belt on the crankshaft timing pulley, No. 1 idler pulley and the No. 2 idler pulley.

22. Install the timing belt guide with the cup side facing forward. Replace the timing belt cover spacer.

23. Install the No. 1 timing belt cover and tighten the mounting bolts. Install the fan bracket.

24. Align the pulley set key on the crankshaft with the key groove of the pulley. Install the pulley, using the proper tool to tap in the pulley. Tighten the pulley bolt to 181 ft. lbs.

25. Align the knock pin on the right side camshaft with the knock pin of the timing pulley. Slide the timing pulley with the right side mark facing forward. Tighten the bolt to 80 ft. lbs.

26. Align the knock pin on the left side camshaft with the

knock pin of the timing pulley. Slide on the timing pulley with the left side mark facing forward. Tighten the bolt to 80 ft. lbs.

27. Turn the crankshaft pulley and align it's groove with the 0 timing mark on the No. 1 timing belt cover. Using the proper tool, turn the crankshaft timing pulley and align the timing marks of the camshaft timing pulley and the timing belt rear plate.

28. Install the timing belt to the left side camshaft timing pulley by:

   a. Using the proper tool, slightly turn the left side timing pulley clockwise. Align the installation mark of the timing belt with the timing mark of the camshaft timing pulley and hang the timing belt on the left side camshaft pulley.

   b. Using the proper tool, align the timing marks of the left side camshaft pulley and the timing belt rear plate.

   c. Check that the timing belt has tension between crankshaft timing pulley and the left side camshaft pulley.

29. Install the timing belt to the right side camshaft timing pulley by:

   a. Using the proper tool, slightly turn the right side timing pulley clockwise. Align the installation mark of the timing belt with the timing mark of the camshaft timing pulley and hang the timing belt on the right side camshaft pulley.

   b. Using the proper tool, align the timing marks of the right side camshaft pulley and the timing belt rear plate.

   c. Check that the timing belt has tension between crankshaft timing pulley and the right side camshaft pulley.

30. The timing belt tensioner must be set prior to installation. The tensioner can be set by:

   a. Place a plate washer between the tensioner and a block. Using a suitable press, press in the pushrod using 220–2205 lbs. of pressure.

   b. Align the holes of the pushrod and housing, pass the proper tool through the holes to keep the setting position of the pushrod.

   c. Release the press and install the dust boot to the tensioner.

31. Install the tensioner and tighten the bolts to 20 ft. lbs. Remove the tool from the tensioner.

32. Turn the crankshaft pulley 2 revolutions from TDC to TDC. Always turn the crankshaft clockwise. Check that each pulley aligns with the timing marks.

33. Install the spark plugs and tighten to 13 ft. lbs. Install the drive belt tensioner and tighten the bolt to 12 ft. lbs.

34. Install the alternator and engine wire bracket. Tighten the nut and bolt to 26 ft. lbs. Connect the electrical connections at the alternator.

35. Install both distributor housings and tighten the mounting bolts to 13 ft. lbs. Replace the distributor rotors and caps.

36. Install the right side No. 2 timing belt cover and tighten the 10mm bolts to 69 inch lbs. and the 12mm bolts to 12 ft. lbs. Connect the crank position sensor connector.

37. Install the left side No. 2 timing belt cover and connect the crank position sensor connector.

38. Install the water bypass pipe and connect the hoses and connectors.

39. Replace the left side ignition coil and connect the coil connector. Install the idler pulley and cover plate. Tighten the bolt to 27 ft. lbs.

40. Install and secure the ignition wires. Install the right side No. 3 timing belt cover.

41. Install the left side No. 3 timing belt cover and connect the vacuum hose and connectors. Install the right side engine wire cover.

42. Install the left side engine wire cover and connect the vacuum hoses.

43. Install the upper high tension cord covers. Fit the front side claw groove of the upper cover to claw of the lower cover.

44. Install the power steering pump and the air conditioning compressor.

45. Install the throttle body cover and the air cleaner.

46. Install the radiator, fan pulley, fan coupling, fan and drive belt.

47. Install the engine undercover and replace the battery.

48. Install the air ducts and dust covers. Connect the battery cables.

49. Refill the cooling system. Check the ignition timing.

Timing Sprockets

Removal and Installation

ES250

1. Disconnect the negative battery cable.
2. Remove the timing belt.
3. Remove the idler pulley with the proper tool.
4. Remove the crankshaft pulley.

NOTE: If the pulley cannot be removed by hand, carefully pry off the pulley with a suitable pry bar.

To install:

5. Align the crankshaft timing pulley set key with the groove on the timing pulley. Slide on the crankshaft pulley with the flange side facing inward.
6. Install the No. 1 idler pulley, using the proper adhesive on the threads of the mounting bolt end. Install the bolt and washer with the proper tool. Tighten the bolt to 25 ft. lbs. Check that the pulley bracket moves smoothly.
7. Align the installation mark on the timing belt with the drilled mark on the crankshaft pulley.
8. Install the timing belt.
9. Connect the negative battery cable.

LS400

1. Disconnect the negative battery cable.
2. Remove the timing belt.
3. Remove the pulley bolt and the No. 2 idler pulley. Using the proper tool, remove the bolt and No. 1 idler pulley.
4. Remove the crankshaft timing pulley with the proper tool.

To install:

5. Align the pulley set key on the crankshaft with the key groove on the timing pulley. Using the proper tool, tap in the timing pulley with the flange side facing to the rear.
6. Install the No. 1 idler pulley, using a suitable adhesive on the threads of the pulley bolt end. Tighten the pulley bolt to 25 ft. lbs.
7. Turn the crankshaft and align the timing marks of the crankshaft timing pulley and the oil pump body.
8. Align the installation mark on the timing belt with the drilled mark of the crankshaft timing pulley.
9. Install the timing belt and connect the negative battery cable

Camshaft

Removal and Installation

ES250

1. Disconnect the negative battery cable.

NOTE: Since the thrust clearance of the camshaft is small, the camshaft must be held level while it is being removed. If the camshaft is not kept level, the portion of the camshaft head receiving the shaft thrust may crack or be damaged, causing the camshaft to seize or break.

2. Remove the suspension upper brace. Disconnect the throttle cable from the throttle body, if equipped with an automatic transaxle.
3. Disconnect the accelerator cable from the throttle body. Remove the cruise control actuator and the vacuum pump.

4. Disconnect the ISC hose, the vacuum pipe hose and the air cleaner hose.

5. Raise and safely support the vehicle. Remove the right side engine undercover.

6. Remove the suspension lower crossmember and the front exhaust pipe. Lower the vehicle.

7. Remove the alternator, the ISC valve and the throttle body.

8. Remove the EGR pipe, the EGR valve and the vacuum modulator.

9. Disconnect the (4) BVSV vacuum hoses, the fuel pressure VSV hose and the air conditioning control valve vacuum hose.

10. Remove the distributor and the exhaust crossover pipe.

11. Disconnect the cold start injector connector and remove the cold start injector tube.

12. Disconnect the following hoses:
   a. PCV hose
   b. Vacuum sensing hose
   c. Fuel pressure VSV hose
   d. Air conditioning control valve vacuum hose
   e. EGR gas temperature sensor connector – California only

13. Remove the mounting bolts and the brackets from the intake chamber. Remove the air intake chamber.

14. Remove the delivery pipes and the injectors.

15. Disconnect the water temperature sensor connector and the upper radiator hose. Remove the water outlet.

16. Disconnect the following connectors and hose:
   a. Cold start injector time switch connector
   b. Water temperature sensor connector
   c. Heater water bypass hose

17. Remove the water bypass outlet. Remove the crossover pipe insulator from the water bypass outlet.

18. Remove the cylinder head rear plate and the idler pulley bracket.

19. Remove the mounting bolts and nuts. Lift off the intake manifold.

20. Disconnect the main oxygen sensor connector. Remove outside heat insulator.

21. Remove the mounting nuts and the right side exhaust manifold. Remove the inside heat insulator.

22. Remove the heat insulator, the mounting nuts and the left side exhaust manifold.

23. Remove the spark plugs.

24. Remove the timing belt, camshaft pulleys and the No. 2 idler pulley.

25. Remove the No. 3 timing cover.

26. Remove the mounting nuts and the cylinder head covers. Remove the spark plug tube gaskets.

27. Remove the exhaust camshaft of the right side cylinder head by:
   a. Align the timing marks, 2 pointed marks, of the camshaft drive and the drive gear by turning the camshaft with a wrench.
   b. Secure the exhaust camshaft sub-gear to the drive gear with a service bolt.
   c. Uniformly, loosen and remove the 8 bearing cap bolts in the proper sequence.
   d. Remove the 4 bearing caps and the camshaft.

28. Uniformly, loosen and remove the 10 bearing cap bolts on the right side cylinder head, in sequence. Remove the 5 bearing caps and remove the intake camshaft.

29. Remove the exhaust camshaft of the left side cylinder head by performing the following:
   a. Align the timing marks, 1 pointed mark, of the camshaft drive and the drive gear by turning the camshaft with a wrench.
   b. Secure the exhaust camshaft sub-gear to the drive gear with a service bolt.
   c. Uniformly, loosen and remove the 8 bearing cap bolts in the proper sequence.
   d. Remove the 4 bearing caps and the exhaust camshaft.

30. Uniformly, loosen and remove the 10 bearing cap bolts on the right side cylinder head, in sequence. Remove the 5 bearing caps and remove the intake camshaft.

To install:

31. Install the intake camshaft of the right side cylinder head by:
   a. Apply a suitable multi-purpose grease to the thrust portion of the camshaft.
   b. Apply seal packing to the No. 1 bearing cap. Install the bearing caps.
   c. Apply a light coat of oil on the threads of the bearing cap bolts.
   d. Install and uniformly tighten the bearing cap bolts to 12 ft. lbs.

32. Install the exhaust camshaft of the right side cylinder head by:
   a. Apply a suitable multi-purpose grease to the thrust portion of the camshaft.
   b. Align the timing marks (2 pointed marks) of the camshaft and the drive gears.
   c. Place the camshaft on the cylinder head and install the bearing caps.
   d. Apply a light coat of oil on the threads of the bearing cap bolts.
   e. Install and uniformly tighten the bearing cap bolts to 12 ft. lbs. Remove the service bolt.

33. Install the intake camshaft on the left side cylinder head by:
   a. Apply MP grease to the thrust portion of the camshaft.
   b. Place the intake camshaft at a 90 degree angle of the timing mark on the cylinder head, 1 pointed marrk.
   c. Apply seal packing to the No. 1 bearing cap. Install the bearing caps.
   d. Apply a light coat of oil on the threads of the bearing cap bolts.
   e. Install and uniformly tighten the bearing cap bolts to 12 ft. lbs.

34. Install the exhaust camshaft on the left side cylinder head by:
   a. Apply a suitable multi-purpose grease to the thrust portion of the camshaft.
   b. Align the timing marks, 1 pointed mark, of the camshaft and the drive gears.
   c. Place the camshaft on the cylinder head and install the bearing caps.
   d. Apply a light coat of oil on the threads of the bearing cap bolts.
   e. Install and uniformly tighten the bearing cap bolts to 12 ft. lbs. Remove the service bolt.

35. Turn the camshaft and position the cam lobe upward. Check and adjust the valve clearance.

36. Apply a suitable multi-purpose grease to the the new camshaft oil seals and install with the proper tool.

37. Install the spark plug tube gaskets. Install the proper seal packing to the cylinder heads.

38. Install the cylinder head cover gasket and install with the seal washers and nuts. Tighten to 52 inch lbs.

39. Install the No. 3 timing belt cover and tighten the bolts 65 inch lbs.

40. Install the No. 2 idler pulley, the camshaft timing pulleys and the timing belt.

41. Install the spark plugs and tighten to 13 ft. lbs.

42. Install the right side heat insulator and the right side exhaust manifold with a new gasket. Tighten the nuts to 29 ft. lbs.

43. Install the outside heat insulator and connect the oxygen sensor connector.

44. Install the left side exhaust manifold with a new gasket and tighten the nuts to 29 ft. lbs. Install the heat insulator.

45. Install the intake manifold with new gaskets. Tighten the nuts and bolts to 13 ft. lbs.

46. Install the No. 2 idler pulley bracket and tighten to 13 ft. lbs. Replace the rear cylinder head plate.

47. Install the crossover pipe heat insulator. Replace the water bypass outlet and tighten the mounting bolts to 14 ft. lbs.

48. Connect the heater water bypass hose, cold start injector time switch connector and the water temperature switch.

49. Connect the upper radiator hose, the water temperature sensor connector and install the water outlet with a new gasket. Tighten the bolts to 73 inch lbs.

50. Install the fuel injectors and the delivery pipes.

51. Install the air intake chamber with new gaskets and tighten the mounting bolts to 32 ft. lbs.

52. Install the intake chamber brackets.

53. Connect the following hoses:
   a. PCV hose
   b. Vacuum sensing hose
   c. EGR gas temperature sensor connector, California only
   d. Air conditioning control valve air hose

54. Install the cold start injector tube and connect the cold start injector connector.

55. Install the exhaust crossover pipe with new gaskets and tighten the mounting bolts to 25 ft. lbs. and the nuts to 29 ft. lbs.

56. Install the distributor.

57. Install the vacuum pipe and connect the BVSV vacuum hoses and the air conditioning control valve vacuum hose.

58. Install the EGR valve and vacuum modulator. Tighten the mounting bolts to 13 ft. lbs. Install the vacuum pipe hoses.

59. Install the EGR pipe with a new gasket and tighten the mounting bolts to 13 ft. lbs. and the nut to 58 ft. lbs.

60. Install the throttle body and ISC valve.

61. Raise and support the vehicle. Install the front exhaust pipe and the right side engine undercover. Lower the vehicle.

62. Install the air cleaner hose and cruise control actuator.

63. Install the accelerator cable and connect the throttle cable, if equipped with an automatic transaxle.

64. Install the suspension upper brace and fill the cooling system.

65. Connect the negative battery cable. Run the engine and check for leaks.

66. Adjust the timing. Recheck the fluid levels.

LS400

1. Disconnect the negative battery cable. Drain the cooling system.

2. Remove the camshaft timing pulleys.

3. Disconnect the accelerator cable, the throttle control cable, if equipped with automatic transmission and the cruise control actuator cable.

4. Remove the high tension cord cover and the right side ignition coil.

5. Remove the water inlet housing mounting bolts and disconnect the water bypass hose from the ISC valve.

6. Remove the water inlet and inlet housing assemblies. Remove the O-ring from the water inlet housing.

7. Remove the EGR pipe.

8. Disconnect the following:
   a. VSV connector
   b. Vacuum pipe hose
   c. EGR water bypass pipe
   d. Fuel pressure VSV

9. Disconnect the EGR vacuum hoses and remove the EGR VSV.

10. Disconnect the following hoses:
   a. Water bypass pipe hose from the ISC valve.
   b. Water bypass joint hose.
   c. Vacuum pipe hoses.

11. Disconnect the EGR gas temperature sensor, California only. Remove the EGR valve adapter.

12. Disconnect the following:
   a. Fuel pressure regulator vacuum hose.
   b. Air intake chamber vacuum hose.
   c. Vacuum hose from the EVAP BVSV.

13. Remove the mounting bolts, hoses and the vacuum pipe.

14. Remove the ISC valve.

15. Remove the throttle body sensor connectors and the water bypass pipe from the rear water bypass joint.

16. Remove the mounting bolts/nuts and disconnect the PCV valve. Remove the throttle body and gasket.

17. Disconnect the accelerator cable bracket and the brake booster vacuum union and hose.

18. Disconnect the cold start injector connector and the cold start injector tube from the right side delivery pipe.

19. Disconnect the check connector from the intake chamber and remove the mounting nuts and bolts.

20. Remove the air intake chamber and the cold start injector, tube and wire assembly.

21. Disconnect the engine wire from the intake manifold and from the right side cylinder head. Disconnect the heater hoses.

22. Remove the delivery pipes and the fuel injectors. Remove the mounting bolts and nuts. Lift up the intake manifold.

23. Remove the front and rear water bypass joint.

24. Raise and safely support the vehicle. Remove the front exhaust pipe and the main catalytic converters. Lower the vehicle.

25. Disconnect the right side oxygen sensor. Remove the mounting bolts and nuts and remove the right side exhaust manifold.

26. Remove the oil dipstick and guide. Disconnect the left side oxygen sensor.

27. Remove the mounting bolts and nuts and remove the left side exhaust manifold.

28. Remove the 2 engine hangers and the wire brackets from the right side cylinder head.

29. Remove the bolts, washers and the cylinder head cover. Remove the semi-circular plugs, if necessary.

30. Remove the exhaust camshaft of the right side cylinder head by:
   a. Position the service bolt hole of the drive sub-gear to the upright position. Secure the camshaft sub-gear to drive gear with a service bolt.
   b. Set the timing mark, 1 pointed mark, of the camshaft drive gear at approximately 10 degrees, by turning the camshaft with the proper tool.
   c. Alternately, loosen and remove the bearing cap bolts holding the intake camshaft side of the oil feed pipe to the cylinder head.
   d. Uniformly, loosen and remove the bearing cap bolts, in sequence.
   e. Remove the oil feed pipe and the bearing caps. Remove the camshaft.

31. Remove the intake camshaft from the right side cylinder head by:
   a. Set the timing mark, 1 pointed mark, of the camshaft drive gear at approximately 45 degrees, by turning the camshaft with the proper tool.
   c. Uniformly, loosen and remove the bearing cap bolts in the proper sequence.
   d. Remove the bearing caps, oil seal and the intake camshaft.

32. Remove the exhaust camshaft of the left side cylinder head by:
   a. Position the service bolt hole of the drive sub-gear to the upright position. Secure the camshaft sub-gear to drive gear with a service bolt.

NOTE: When removing the camshaft, make sure the torsional spring force of the sub-gear has been eliminated.

   b. Set the timing mark, 2 pointed marks, of the camshaft

drive gear at approximately 15 degrees, by turning the camshaft with the proper tool.

   c. Alternately, loosen and remove the bearing cap bolts holding the intake camshaft side of the oil feed pipe to the cylinder head.

   d. Uniformly, loosen and remove the bearing cap bolts in the proper sequence.

   e. Remove the oil feed pipe and the bearing caps. Remove the camshaft.

33. Remove the intake camshaft from the left side cylinder head by:

   a. Set the timing mark, 1 pointed mark, of the camshaft drive gear at approximately 60 degrees, by turning the camshaft with the proper tool.

   c. Uniformly, loosen and remove the bearing cap bolts, in sequence.

   d. Remove the bearing caps, oil seal and the intake camshaft.

To install:

34. Remove any old packing and apply new seal packing to the bearing caps.

35. Install the bearing cap on the right side cylinder head, marked I1, in position with the arrow mark facing the rear. Install the bearing cap on the left side cylinder head, marked I6, in position with the arrow mark facing the front.

36. Apply a light coat of oil on the threads of the cap bolts. Install the nearing cap bolts with new washers and tighten to 12 ft. lbs.

37. Install the right side cylinder head intake camshaft by:

   a. Apply MP grease to the thrust portion of the camshaft.

   b. Place the intake camshaft at a 45 degree angle of the timing mark (1 pointed mark) on the cylinder head.

   c. Remove any old packing and apply new seal packing to the bearing cap marked I6 and install the front bearing cap, marked I6 with the arrow facing rearward.

   d. Align the arrows at the front and rear of the cylinder head with the bearing cap.

   e. Install the remaining bearing caps in the proper sequence with the arrow mark facing rearward. Install the oil feed pipe and the mounting bolts.

   f. Uniformly, tighten the bearing cap bolts in the proper sequence to 12 ft. lbs.

38. Install the right side cylinder head exhaust camshaft by:

   a. Set the timing mark, 1 pointed mark, of the camshaft drive gear at a 10 degree angle by turning the intake camshaft with the proper tool.

   b. Apply MP grease to the thrust portion of the camshaft.

   c. Align the timing marks, 1 pointed mark, of the camshaft drive and driven gears.

   d. Place the exhaust camshaft ion the cylinder head. Install the rear bearing cap with the arrow mark facing rearward.

   e. Align the arrow marks at the front and rear of the cylinder head with the mark on the bearing cap. Apply a light coat of oil on the threads of the bearing cap bolts.

   f. Uniformly, tighten the bearing cap bolts in the proper sequence to 12 ft. lbs.

   g. Bring the service bolt installed upward by turning the camshaft with the proper tool. Remove the service bolt.

39. Install the left side cylinder head intake camshaft by:

   a. Apply MP grease to the thrust portion of the camshaft.

   b. Place the intake camshaft at a 60 degree angle of the timing mark, 1 pointed mark, on the cylinder head.

   c. Remove any old packing and apply new seal packing to the bearing cap marked I6 and install the front bearing cap, marked I1 with the arrow facing rearward.

   d. Align the arrows at the front and rear of the cylinder head with the bearing cap. Apply a light coat of oil on the threads of the bearing cap bolts.

   e. Install the remaining bearing caps in the proper sequence with the arrow mark facing rearward. Install the oil feed pipe and the mounting bolts.

   f. Uniformly, tighten the bearing cap bolts in the proper sequence to 12 ft. lbs.

40. Install the left side cylinder head exhaust camshaft by:

   a. Set the timing mark, 2 dot marks, of the camshaft drive gear at a 15 degree angle by turning the intake camshaft with the proper tool.

   b. Apply MP grease to the thrust portion of the camshaft.

   c. Align the timing marks, 2 dot marks, of the camshaft drive and driven gears.

   d. Place the exhaust camshaft ion the cylinder head. Install the rear bearing cap with the arrow mark facing rearward.

   e. Align the arrow marks at the front and rear of the cylinder head with the mark on the bearing cap. Apply a light coat of oil on the threads of the bearing cap bolts.

   f. Uniformly, tighten the bearing cap bolts in the proper sequence to 12 ft. lbs.

   g. Bring the service bolt installed upward by turning the camshaft with the proper tool. Remove the service bolt.

41. Install the camshaft oil seals with the proper tool. Install the semi-circular plugs with the proper seal packing.

42. Install the cylinder head covers with the proper seal packing and gasket. Tighten the mounting bolts to 52 inch lbs.

43. Install the engine wire bracket and hangers. Tighten the hanger bolts to 27 ft. lbs.

44. Install the right side exhaust manifold with a new gasket and tighten the mounting bolts to 29 ft. lbs. Connect the right side oxygen sensor connector.

45. Install the right side exhaust manifold with a new gasket and tighten the mounting bolts to 29 ft. lbs. Connect the right side oxygen sensor connector.

46. Install the left side exhaust manifold with a new gasket and tighten the mounting bolts to 29 ft. lbs. Connect the left side oxygen sensor connector.

47. Install the oil dipstick and guide. Raise and safely support the vehicle.

48. Install the catalytic converters and front exhaust pipe. Lower the vehicle.

49. Install the front and rear water bypass joints. Tighten the mounting bolts to 13 ft. lbs.

50. Install the intake manifold, using new gaskets. Tighten the mounting nuts and bolts to 13 ft. lbs.

51. Install the delivery pipes and fuel injectors. Install the fuel return pipe with new gaskets. Tighten the union bolt to 26 ft. lbs.

52. Connect the fuel hoses and the injector connectors. Connect the engine wire to the delivery pipes.

53. Connect the connectors on the left side delivery pipe, the water temperature sensor connector, cold start injector time switch connector and the water temperature sender gauge connector.

54. Connect the heater hoses and engine wire bracket. Install the engine wire to the bracket.

55. Install the cold start injector, tube and wire assembly. Tighten the mounting bolts to 69 inch lbs.

56. Install the air intake chamber with new gaskets and tighten the mounting bolts to 13 ft. lbs.

57. Connect the cold start injector tube to the right side delivery pipe and tighten the union bolt to 11 ft. lbs.

58. Connect the cold start injector connector. Install the accelerator cable bracket.

59. Install the brake booster union and connect the vacuum hose. Tighten the union bolt to 22 ft. lbs.

60. Connect the water bypass hose to the throttle body and the PCV hose to the cylinder head cover.

61. Install the throttle body, using a new gasket. Tighten the mounting bolts to 13 ft. lbs.

62. Install the water bypass pipe and connect the sensor connectors. Install the ISC valve and tighten the mounting bolts to 13 ft. lbs. Connect the water bypass hose.

63. Install the vacuum pipe and the following hoses:

   a. Fuel pressure regulator vacuum hose.

b. Vacuum hose to the upper port of the EVAP BVSV.
c. Air intake chamber vacuum hose.
d. Throttle body vacuum hoses.

64. Install the EGR valve adapter with a new gasket. Tighten the mounting bolts to 13 ft. lbs.

65. Connect the EGR gas temperature sensor connector (California only).

66. Install the EGR valve and vacuum modulator. Connect the water bypass hoses and the vacuum hoses.

67. Install the EGR and fuel pressure VSV and connect the hoses and connectors. Replace the EGR pipe and tighten the mounting bolts to 13 ft. lbs.

68. Install the timing belt rear plates and tighten the bolts to 69 inch lbs. Install the water inlet and inlet housing and tighten the bolts to 13 ft. lbs.

69. Install the right side ignition coil and the high tension cord cover.

70. Connect and adjust the accelerator cable, the automatic transmission throttle cable and the cruise control actuator cable. Install the camshaft timing pulley.

71. Fill the cooling system and connect the negative battery cable. Start the engine and check for leaks.

72. Recheck all the fluid levels and check the ignition timing.

Piston and Connecting Rod

Positioning

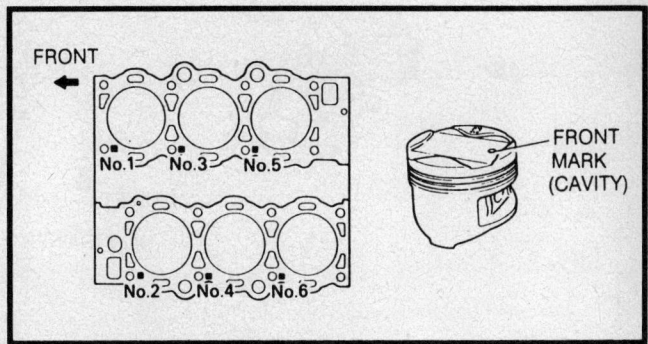

Piston location—ES250

ENGINE LUBRICATION

Oil Pan

Removal and Installation

ES250

1. Disconnect the negative battery cable. Remove the hood assembly.

2. Raise and safely support the vehicle. Remove the engine undercovers.

3. Drain the engine oil, using a suitable container. Remove the suspension lower crossmember.

4. Disconnect the front exhaust pipe and remove the center engine support mount. Remove the front engine mount and bracket.

5. Remove the stiffener plate. Remove the oil dipstick.

6. Remove the mounting bolts and the oil pan assembly. Remove any old packing or sealer from the mounting surfaces.

7. The installation is the reverse of the removal procedure. Tighten the oil pan mounting bolts to 52 inch lbs. Tighten the stiffener plate mounting bolts to 27 ft. lbs.

LS400

1. Disconnect the negative battery cable.

2. Raise and safely support the vehicle. Remove the engine undercover.

3. Drain the engine oil, using a suitable container.

4. Remove the mounting bolts and drop down the oil pan. Remove any old packing or sealer from the mounting surfaces.

5. The installation is the reverse of the removal procedure. Tighten the oil pan mounting bolts to 69 inch lbs.

Oil Pump

Removal and Installation

ES250

1. Disconnect the negative battery cable. Remove the oil pan.

2. Remove the oil strainer and gasket.

2. Raise the engine using a suitable chain hoist. Remove the timing belt and pulleys.

3. Remove the alternator and the air conditioning compressor and bracket. Do not disconnect the refrigerant lines.

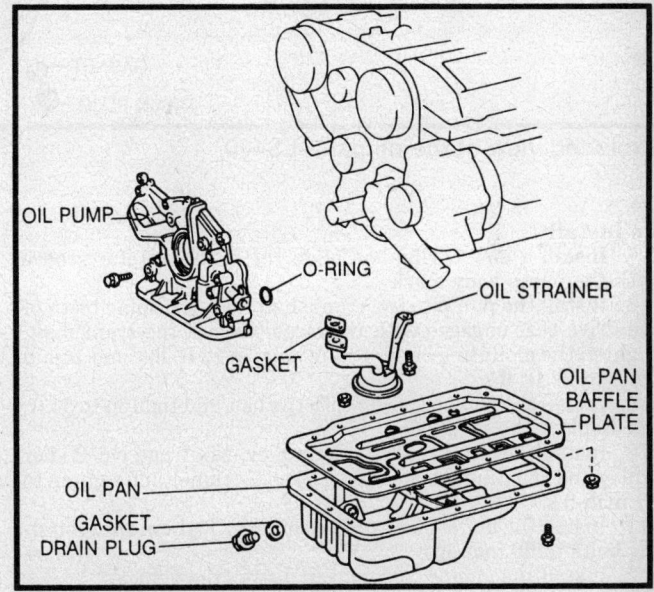

Oil pump assembly—ES250

4. Remove the oil pump from the engine.

5. Installation is the reverse of the removal procedure.

LS400

1. Disconnect the negative battery cable. Raise and safely support the vehicle.

2. Remove the engine undercover.

3. Drain the oil, using a suitable container. Remove the oil dipstick.

4. Remove the mounting bolts and pull down the oil pan. Remove the baffle plate and the oil strainer.

5. Remove the timing belt, No. 1 and No. 2 idler and crankshaft pulleys. Remove the bolt and pickup sensor.

6. Remove the stud bolts and mounting bolts. Remove the oil pump with the proper tool to pry away from the cylinder block. Clean and remove any packing from the mounting surfaces.

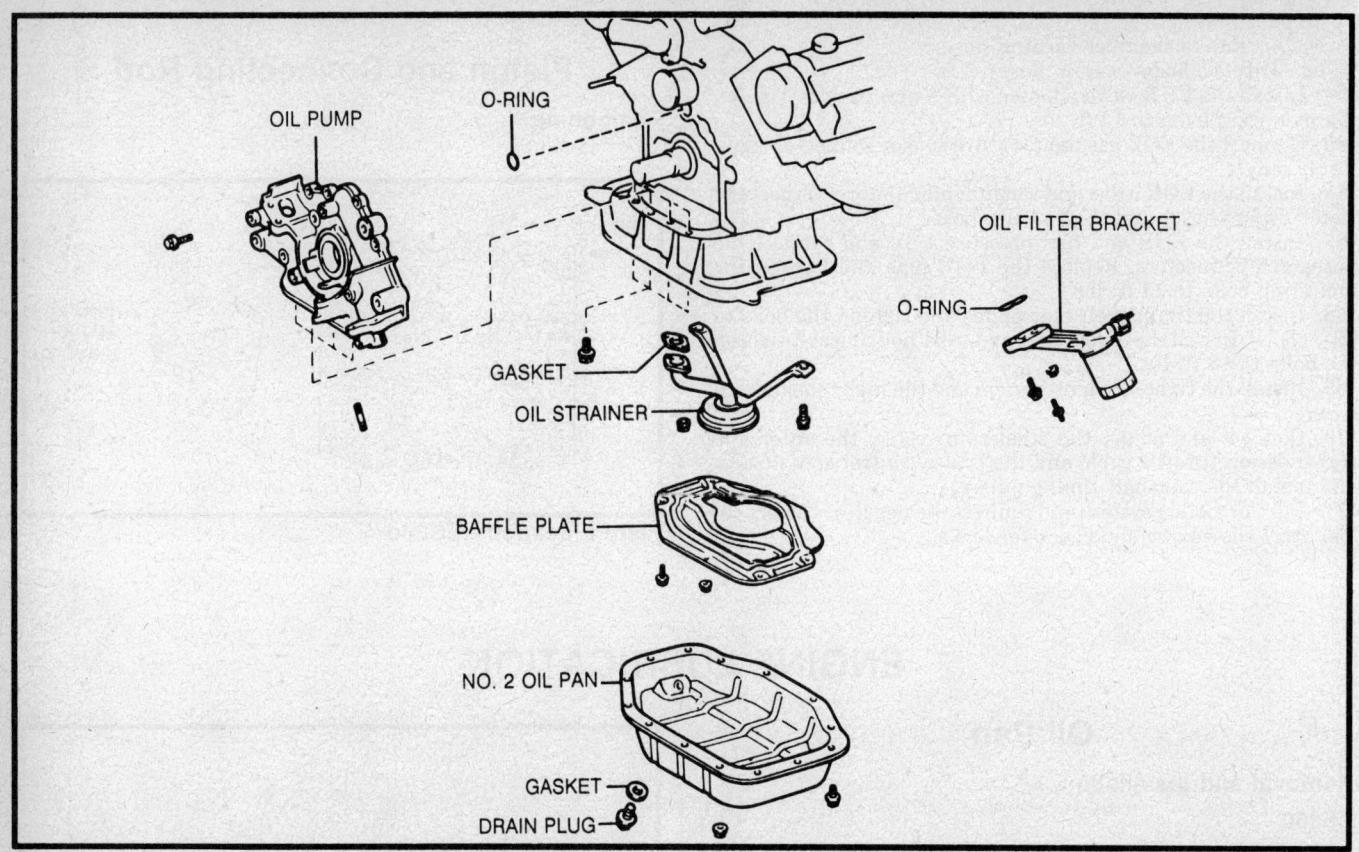

Exploded view of the oil pan—LS400

To install:

7. Install a new O-ring and align the oil drive rotor groove with the pump body mark.

8. Install the pump to the crankshaft with the spine teeth of the drive gear engaged with the large teeth of the crankshaft. Tighten the mounting bolts; 12mm bolts to 12 ft. lbs. and 14mm bolts to 22 ft. lbs.

9. Install the pickup sensor with the bolt and tighten to 56 ft. lbs. Replace the stud bolt.

10. Install the crankshaft timing pulley, No. 1 and No. 2 idler pulley and the timing belt. Install the oil strainer and tighten to 69 inch lbs.

11. Install the baffle plate and the oil pan. Tighten the mounting bolts to 69 inch lbs.

12. Install the engine undercover. Lower the vehicle.

13. Install the dipstick and refill the crankcase.

Checking

1. Measure the body clearance between the driven motor and the pump body with the proper tool. The standard body clearance is 0.0039–0.0069 in. The maximum clearance is 0.0118 in. If the body clearance is greater then maximum replace the rotors as a set.

2. Measure the rotor tip clearance between the drive and the driven gears with the proper tool. The standard clearance is 0.0043–0.0118 in. The maximum clearance is 0.0138 in.

3. Measure the side clearance between the rotors, using the proper tool. The standard side clearance is 0.0012–0.0035 in. The maximum side clearance is 0.0059 in. If the side clearance is greater than maximum, replace the rotors as set. If necessary, replace the oil pump assembly.

Rear Main Bearing Oil Seal

Removal and Installation

1. Disconnect the negative battery cable. Raise and safely support the vehicle.

2. Remove the transmission.

3. Remove the clutch cover assembly and flywheel, if equipped with manual transaxle. Remove the drive plate, if equipped with an automatic transmission or transaxle.

4. Remove the oil seal retaining plate, complete with the oil seal.

5. Using a suitable tool pry the old seal from the retaining plate. Be careful not to damage the plate. The seal is solid type seal.

6. Install the new seal, carefully, by using a block of wood to drift it into place. Do not damage the seal as a leak will result.

7. Lubricate the lips of the seal with multipurpose grease. Installation is the reverse of removal.

MANUAL TRANSAXLE

For further information, please refer to "Professional Transmission Repair Manual" for additional coverage.

Transaxle Assembly

Removal and Installation

ES250

1. Disconnect the negative battery cable. Remove the clutch release cylinder and tube clamp. Remove the clutch tube bracket.

2. Disconnect the control cables. Disconnect the back-up light switch electrical connector. Remove the ground strap.

3. Remove the starter assembly. Remove the transaxle upper mounting bolts.

4. Raise and support the vehicle safely. Remove the undercovers. Drain the transaxle fluid. Disconnect the speedometer cable.

5. Remove the suspension lower crossmember. Remove the engine mounting center member.

6. Disconnect both halfshafts. Remove the center halfshaft. Disconnect the left steering knuckle from the lower control arm. Remove the stabilizer bar.

7. Properly support the engine and remove the left engine mount.

8. Properly support the transaxle assembly. Remove the engine-to-transaxle bolts, lower the left side of the engine and

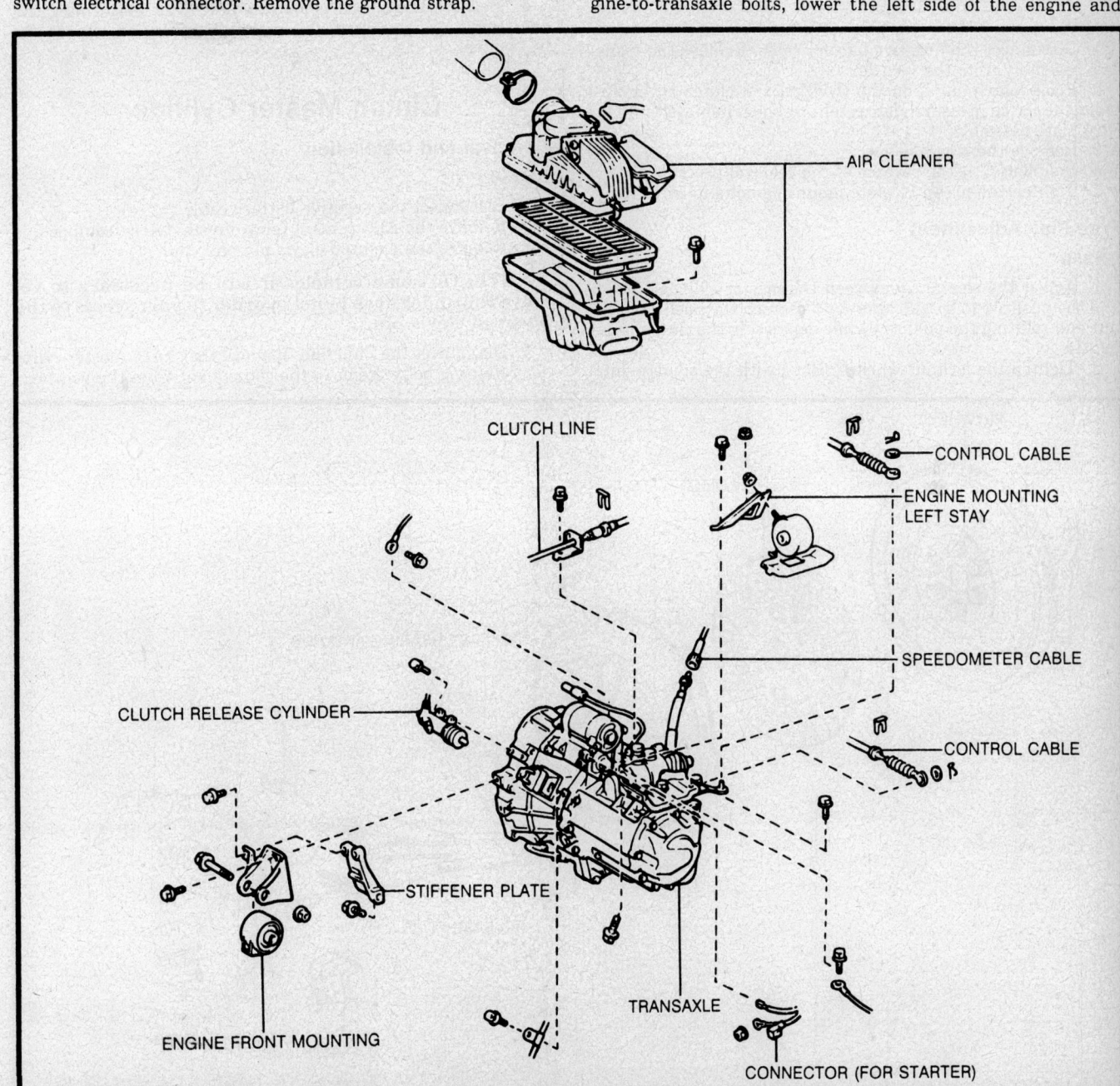

Manual transaxle assembly—ES250

carefully ease the transaxle out of the engine compartment.

9. Installation is the reverse of the removal procedure. Please note the following:

    a. Tighten the 12mm mounting bolts to 47 ft. lbs. (64 Nm) and the 10mm bolts to 34 ft. lbs. (46 Nm).

    b. Tighten the left engine mount to 38 ft. lbs. (52 Nm).

    c. Tighten the 4 center engine mount bolts to 29 ft. lbs. (39 Nm).

    d. Tighten the front and rear engine mount bolts to 32 ft. lbs. (43 Nm).

    e. Tighten the lower crossmember bolts to 153 ft. lbs. (207 Nm)—4 outer bolts; and, 29 ft. lbs. (39 Nm)—2 inner bolts.

CLUTCH

Clutch Assembly

Removal and Installation

ES250

1. Disconnect the negative battery cable. Remove the transaxle assembly from the vehicle.

2. Place matchmarks on the flywheel and clutch cover. Remove the clutch pressure plate retaining bolts. Remove the pressure plate assembly.

3. Remove the clutch disc.

4. Installation is the reverse of the removal procedure.

5. Tighten the pressure plate mounting bolts to 14 ft. lbs.

Free-Play Adjustment

ES250

1. Adjust the clearance between the master cylinder piston and the pushrod to specification by loosening the pushrod locknut and rotating the pushrod while depressing the clutch pedal lightly.

2. Tighten the locknut when finished with the adjustment.

3. Adjust the release cylinder free-play by loosening the release cylinder pushrod locknut and rotating the pushrod until proper specification is obtained.

4. Measure the clutch pedal free-play after performing the adjustments. If it fails to fall within specification, repeat the procedure.

Clutch Master Cylinder

Removal and Installation

ES250

1. Disconnect the negative battery cable.

2. Remove the ABS control relay on vehicles so equipped.

3. Remove the pushrod clevis pin and clip.

NOTE: On some vehicles it will be necessary to remove the under dash panel in order to gain access to the pushrod clevis pin.

5. Disconnect the fluid line. Remove the clutch master cylinder retaining bolts. Remove the component from the vehicle.

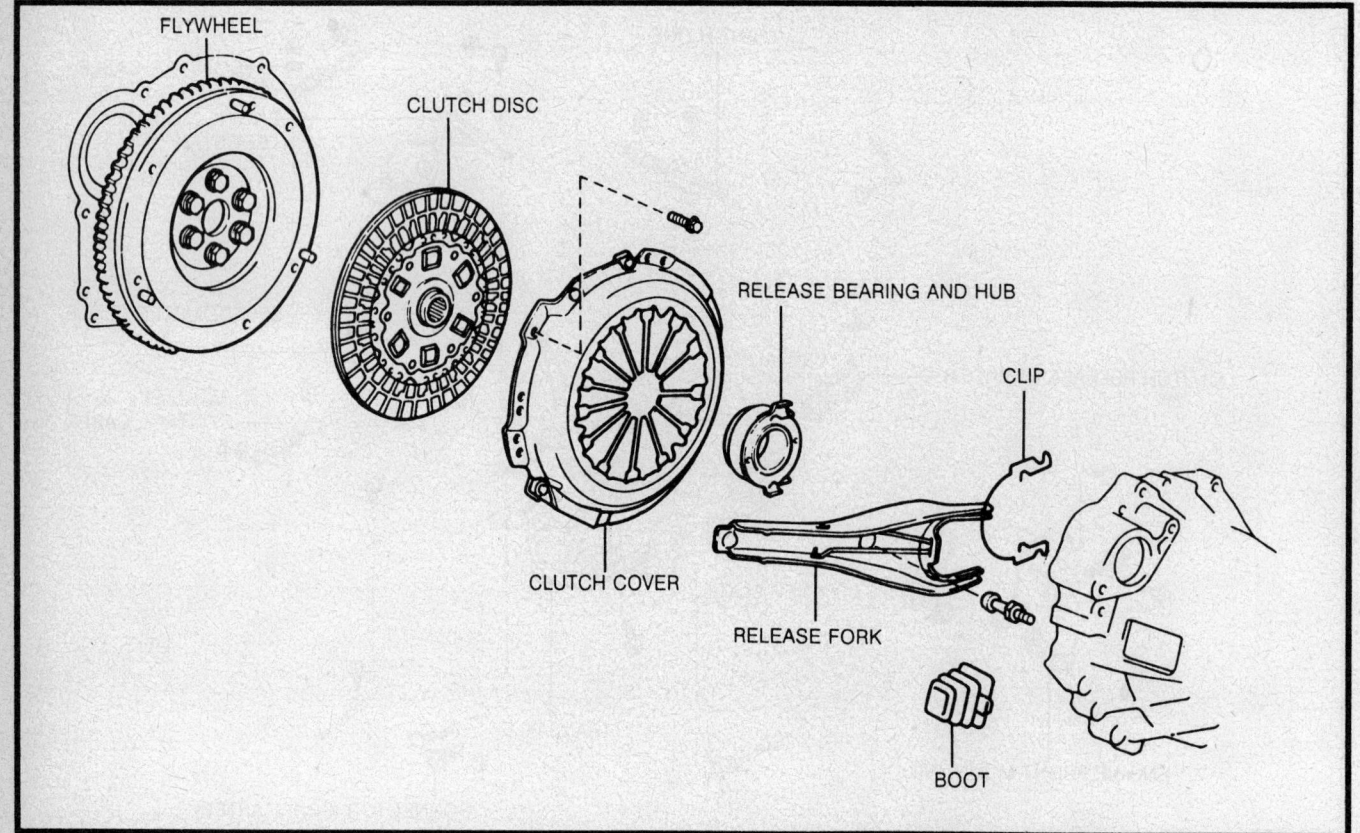

Exploded view of the clutch assembly—ES250

6. Installation is the reverse of the removal procedure. Bleed the system as required.

Clutch Slave Cylinder

Removal and Installation

ES250

1. Disconnect the negative battery cable. Raise and support the vehicle safely.
2. Remove the gravel shield, if equipped. Disconnect the fluid line from the assembly.
3. Remove the slave cylinder retaining bolts. Remove the clutch slave cylinder from the vehicle.
4. Installation is the reverse of the removal procedure. Bleed the system as required.

Hydraulic Clutch System Bleeding

ES250

1. Check and fill the clutch fluid reservoir to the specified level as necessary. During the bleeding process, continue to check and replenish the reservoir to prevent the fluid level from getting lower than ½ the specified level.
2. Remove the dust cap from the bleeder screw on the clutch slave cylinder and connect a tube to the bleeder screw and insert the other end of the tube into a clean glass or metal container.

NOTE: Take precautionary measures to prevent the brake fluid from getting on any painted surfaces.

3. Pump the clutch pedal several times, hold it down and loosen the bleeder screw slowly.
4. Tighten the bleeder screw and release the clutch pedal gradually. Repeat this operation until air bubbles disappear from the brake fluid being expelled out through the bleeder screw.
5. Repeat until all evidence of air bubbles completely disappears from the fluid being pumped out of the tube.
6. When the air is completely removed, tighten the bleeder screw and replace the dust cap.
7. Check and refill the master cylinder reservoir as necessary.
8. Depress the clutch pedal several times to check the operation of the clutch and check for leaks.

AUTOMATIC TRANSMISSION

For further information, please refer to "Professional Transmission Repair Manual" for additional coverage.

Transmission Assembly

Removal and Installation

LS400

1. Disconnect the negative battery cable. Remove the air cleaner assembly. Disconnect the transmission throttle cable.
2. Raise and support the vehicle safely. Drain the transmission fluid. Remove the driveshaft along with the center bearing.
3. Remove the exhaust pipe together with the catalytic converter. Disconnect the manual shift linkage. Remove the speedometer cable.
4. Disconnect the oil cooler lines. As necessary, remove the transmission oil filler tube. As required, remove the starter assembly. Remove the speedometer cable.
5. Remove both stiffener plates and the catalytic converter cover from the transmission housing and cylinder block.
6. Support the engine and transmission using the proper jacking device. Remove the rear crossmember.
7. Remove the torque converter cover. Remove the torque converter-to-engine retaining bolts.
8. Remove the bolts retaining the transmission to the engine. Carefully remove the transmission from the vehicle.

9. Installation is the reverse of the removal procedure. Tighten the transmission housing bolts to 47 ft. lbs. (64 Nm). Tighten the torque converter bolts to 20 ft. lbs. (27 Nm).

Shift Linkage Adjustment

1. Loosen the nut on the shift linkage. Push the selector lever all the way to the rear of the vehicle.
2. Return the lever 2 notches to the **N** shift position.
3. While holding the selector lever slightly toward the **R** shift position, tighten the connecting rod nut.

Throttle Cable Adjustment

1. Remove the air cleaner.
2. Confirm that the accelerator linkage opens the throttle fully. Adjust the linkage as necessary.
3. Peel the rubber dust boot back from the throttle cable.
4. Loosen the adjustment nuts on the throttle cable bracket (cylinder head cover) just enough to allow cable housing movement.
5. Have an assistant depress the accelerator pedal fully.
6. Adjust the cable housing so the distance between its end and the cable stop collar is 0.04 in.
7. Tighten the adjustment nuts. Make sure the adjustment hasn't changed. Install the dust boot and the air cleaner.

AUTOMATIC TRANSAXLE

For further information, please refer to "Professional Transmission Repair Manual" for additional coverage.

Transaxle Assembly

Removal and Installation

ES250

1. Disconnect the negative battery cable. Remove the air flow meter and the air cleaner assembly.

2. Disconnect the transaxle wire connector. Disconnect the neutral safety switch electrical connector.
3. Disconnect the transaxle ground strap. Disconnect the throttle cable from the throttle linkage.
4. Remove the transaxle case protector. Disconnect the speedometer cable. Disconnect the control cable.
5. Disconnect the oil cooler hoses. Remove the upper starter retaining bolts, as required remove the starter assembly. Remove the upper transaxle housing bolts. Remove the engine rear mount insulator bracket set bolt.

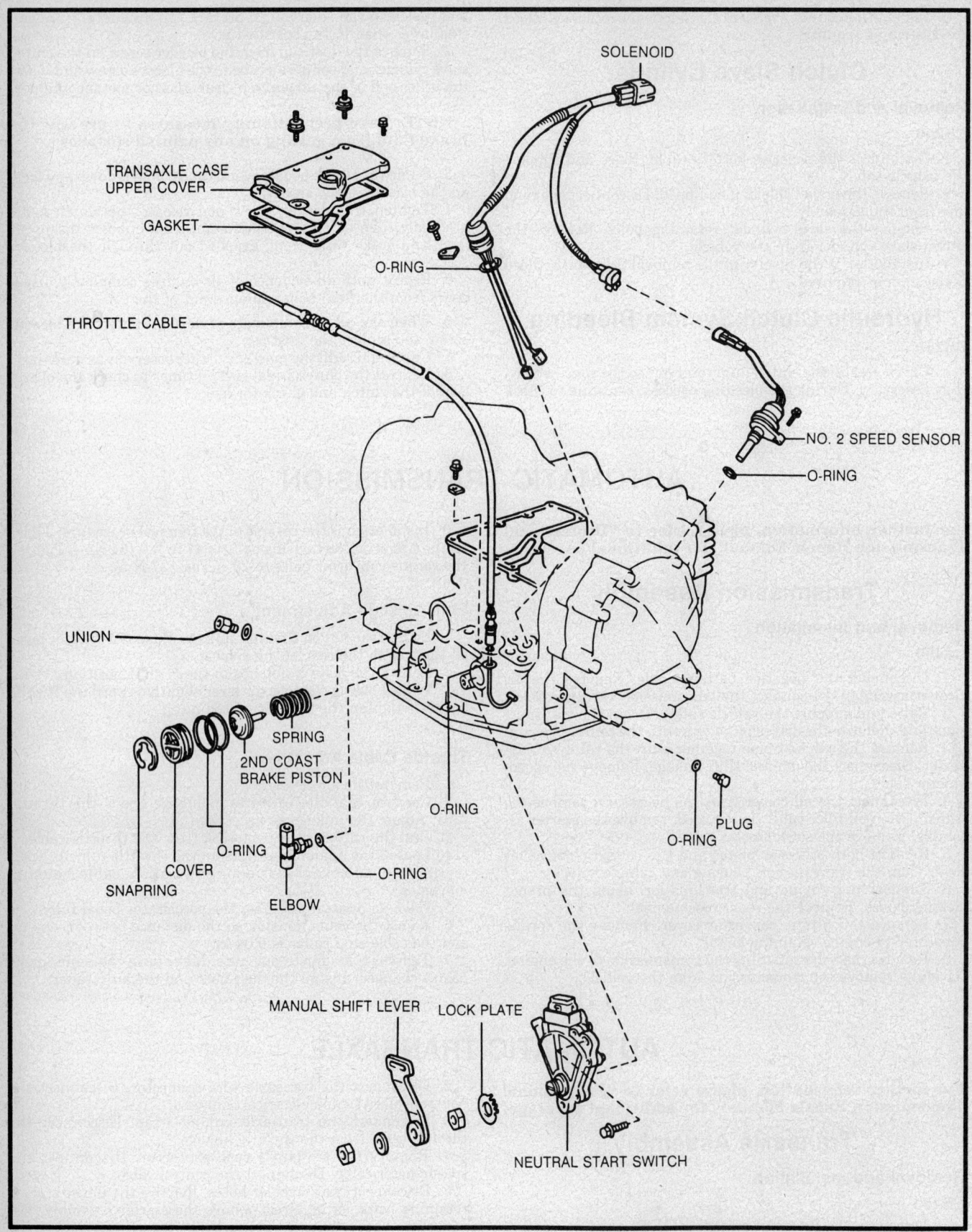

SOLENOID

TRANSAXLE CASE
UPPER COVER

GASKET

O-RING

THROTTLE CABLE

NO. 2 SPEED SENSOR

O-RING

UNION

SPRING

2ND COAST
BRAKE PISTON

O-RING

COVER

SNAPRING

ELBOW

O-RING

O-RING

PLUG

O-RING

MANUAL SHIFT LEVER   LOCK PLATE

NEUTRAL START SWITCH

Automatic transaxle assembly—ES250

6. Raise and support the vehicle safely. Drain the transaxle fluid.

7. Remove the left front fender apron seal. Disconnect both halfshafts.

8. Remove the suspension lower crossmember assembly. Remove the center halfshaft.

9. Remove the engine mounting center crossmember. Remove the stabilizer bar. Remove the left steering knuckle from the lower control arm.

10. Remove the torque converter cover. Remove the torque converter retaining bolts.

11. Properly support the engine and transaxle assembly. Remove the rear engine mounting bolts. Remove the remaining transaxle-to-engine retaining bolts.

12. Carefully remove the transaxle assembly from the vehicle.

13. Installation is the reverse of the removal procedure. Tighten the 12mm transaxle housing bolts to 47 ft. lbs. (64 Nm); tighten the 10mm bolts to 34 ft. lbs. (46 Nm). Tighten the rear engine mount set bolts to 38 ft. lbs. (52 Nm). Tighten the torque converter mounting bolts to 20 ft. lbs. (27 Nm).

Shift Cable Adjustment

ES250

1. Loosen the swivel nut on the selector lever.
2. Push the lever fully toward the right side of the vehicle.
3. Return the lever 2 notches to the **N** position.
4. Set the shift lever in the **N** position.
5. While holding the selector lever slightly toward the **R** shift position tighten the swivel nut to 48 inch lbs. (5.4 Nm).

Throttle Cable Adjustment

ES250

1. Remove the air cleaner.
2. Confirm that the accelerator linkage opens the throttle fully. Adjust the linkage as necessary.
3. Peel the rubber dust boot back from the throttle cable.
4. Loosen the adjustment nuts on the throttle cable bracket (cylinder head cover) just enough to allow cable housing movement.

5. Depress the accelerator pedal fully.
6. Adjust the cable housing so the distance between its end and the cable stop collar is 0.04 in.
7. Tighten the adjustment nuts. Make sure the adjustment hasn't changed. Install the dust boot and the air cleaner.

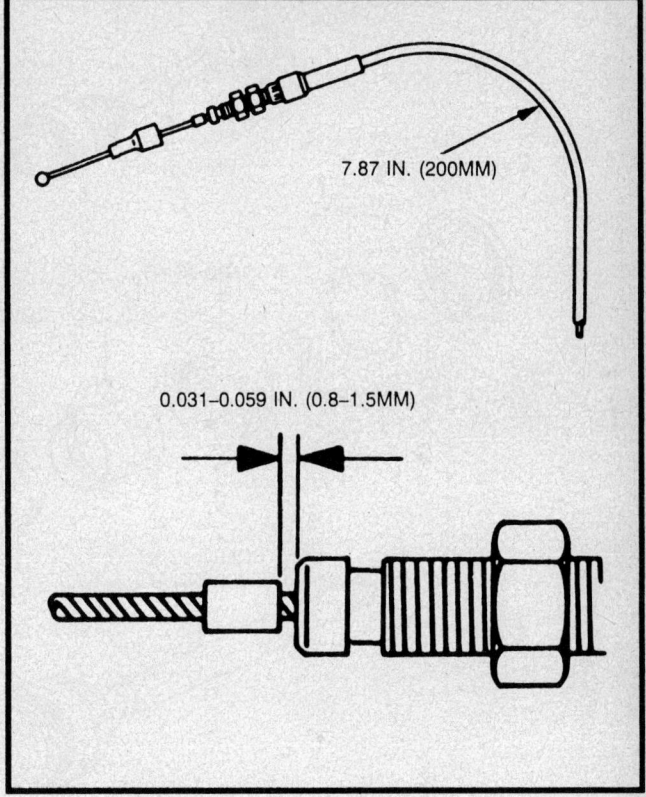

7.87 IN. (200MM)

0.031–0.059 IN. (0.8–1.5MM)

Throttle cable adjustment—ES250

DRIVE AXLE

Halfshaft

Removal and Installation

ES250

Front

1. Raise and safely support the vehicle. Remove the front tire and wheel assembly.
2. Disconnect the steering knuckle from the lower ball joint with the proper tool.
3. Disconnect the tie rod end from the steering knuckle with the proper tool.
4. Place matchmarks on the halfshaft and center halfshaft. Using the proper tool, loosen the mounting bolts.

NOTE: Do not remove the bolts. Finger tighten them so the halfshaft does not fall.

5. Disconnect the halfshaft from the axle hub. Remove the left side halfshaft and the joint cover gasket.
6. Remove the bearing lock bolt and the snapring with the proper tool. Pull out the left side halfshaft with the center halfshaft.

NOTE: If the halfshaft cannot be pulled out, tap out the driveshaft with the proper tool.

7. Push the side gear shaft to the differential, in order to replace. Measure and note the distance between the transaxle case and the side gear shaft. Remove the side gear shaft with the proper tool.
8. If necessary, replace the side gear gear shaft oil seal.
To install:
9. Install the left side gear shaft, using a suitable tool to tap in the driveshaft until it makes contact with the pinion shaft. Ensure a new snapring is positioned securely in the groove of the side gear shaft.
10. Check that the side gear will not come out by hand. Push the side gear shaft to the differential and measure the distance between side gear shaft and the transaxle case. Make sure the distance is the same measurement taken before removing the side gear shaft.
11. Pack the side gear shaft with a suitable grease.
12. Align the matchmarks on the side gear shaft and the halfshaft. Install the left side halfshaft and finger tighten the bolts.

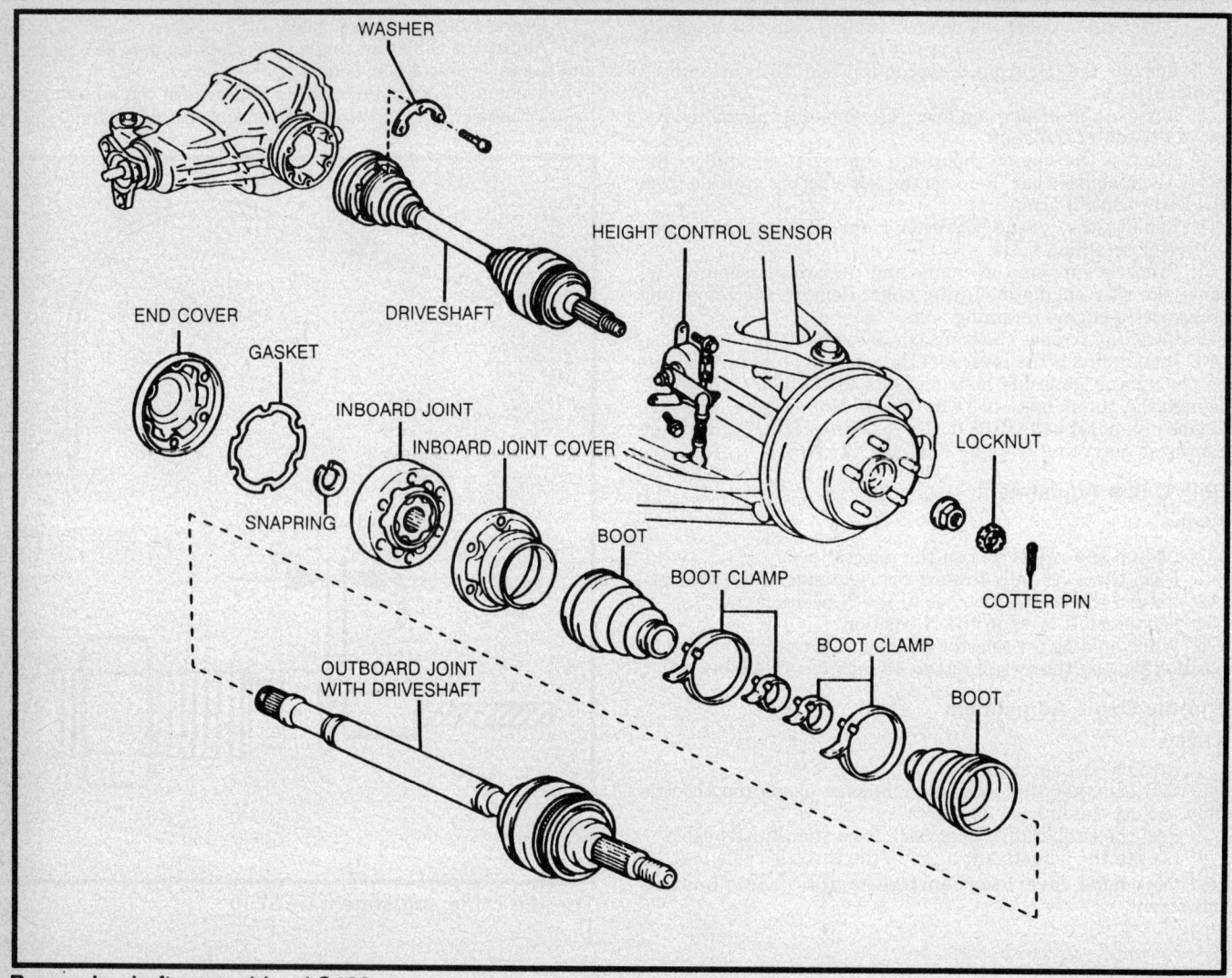

Labels on diagram: WASHER, HEIGHT CONTROL SENSOR, END COVER, DRIVESHAFT, GASKET, INBOARD JOINT, INBOARD JOINT COVER, LOCKNUT, SNAPRING, BOOT, BOOT CLAMP, COTTER PIN, BOOT CLAMP, OUTBOARD JOINT WITH DRIVESHAFT, BOOT

Rear axle shaft assembly—LS400

13. Install the right side halfshaft with the center halfshaft to the transaxle through the bearing bracket. Install the snapring.

14. Install the outboard joint side of the halfshaft to the axle hub. Temporarily, connect the steering knuckle to the lower ball joint.

15. Connect the tie rod end to the steering knuckle and tighten the bolt to 36 ft. lbs. Tighten the lower ball joint mounting bolts to 83 ft. lbs.

16. Tighten the hexagon bolts to 48 ft. lbs.

17. Replace the front tire and wheel assembly. Lower the vehicle.

LS400

Rear

1. Raise and safely support the vehicle. Remove the rear tire and wheel assembly.

2. Remove the tail pipe O-rings and suspend the tail pipe, using a piece of wire.

3. Disconnect the height control sensor, if equipped.

4. Place matchmarks on the driveshaft and the side gear shaft. Remove the hexagon bolts and washers with the proper tool.

5. Hold the inboard joint side of the halfshaft so the outboard joint side does not bend too much. Tap the end of the halfshaft with the proper tool and disengage the axle hub.

6. Remove the halfshaft.

To install:

7. Insert the outboard joint side of the halfshaft and align the matchmarks on the side gear shaft and the halfshaft.

8. Install the hexagon bolts and tighten to 61 ft. lbs.

9. Connect the height control sensor, if equipped. Replace the O-rings supporting the tail pipe.

10. Install the bearing locknut and tighten to 253 ft. lbs. Replace the rear tire and wheel assembly.

11. Lower the vehicle.

CV-Boot

Removal and Installation

ES250

Front

1. Raise and safely support the vehicle. Remove the front tire and wheel assembly.

2. Disconnect the center halfshaft from the right side halfshaft, using the proper tool. Remove the inboard joint clamp.

3. Place matchmarks on the inboard joint and the halfshaft. Remove the snapring with the proper tool.

4. Remove the inboard joint from the halfshaft, using the

proper tool to press out the joint.

5. Remove the inboard joint from the inboard joint cove. When lifting the inboard joint, hold on to the inner race and outer race.

6. Remove the inboard joint boot and the outboard joint boot.

7. Reverse the removal procedure for installation. Pack the boot with a suitable grease prior to installation.

LS400
Rear

1. Raise and safely support the vehicle. Remove the rear tire and wheel assembly.

2. Remove the tail pipe O-rings and suspend the tail pipe, using a piece of wire.

3. Disconnect the height control sensor, if equipped.

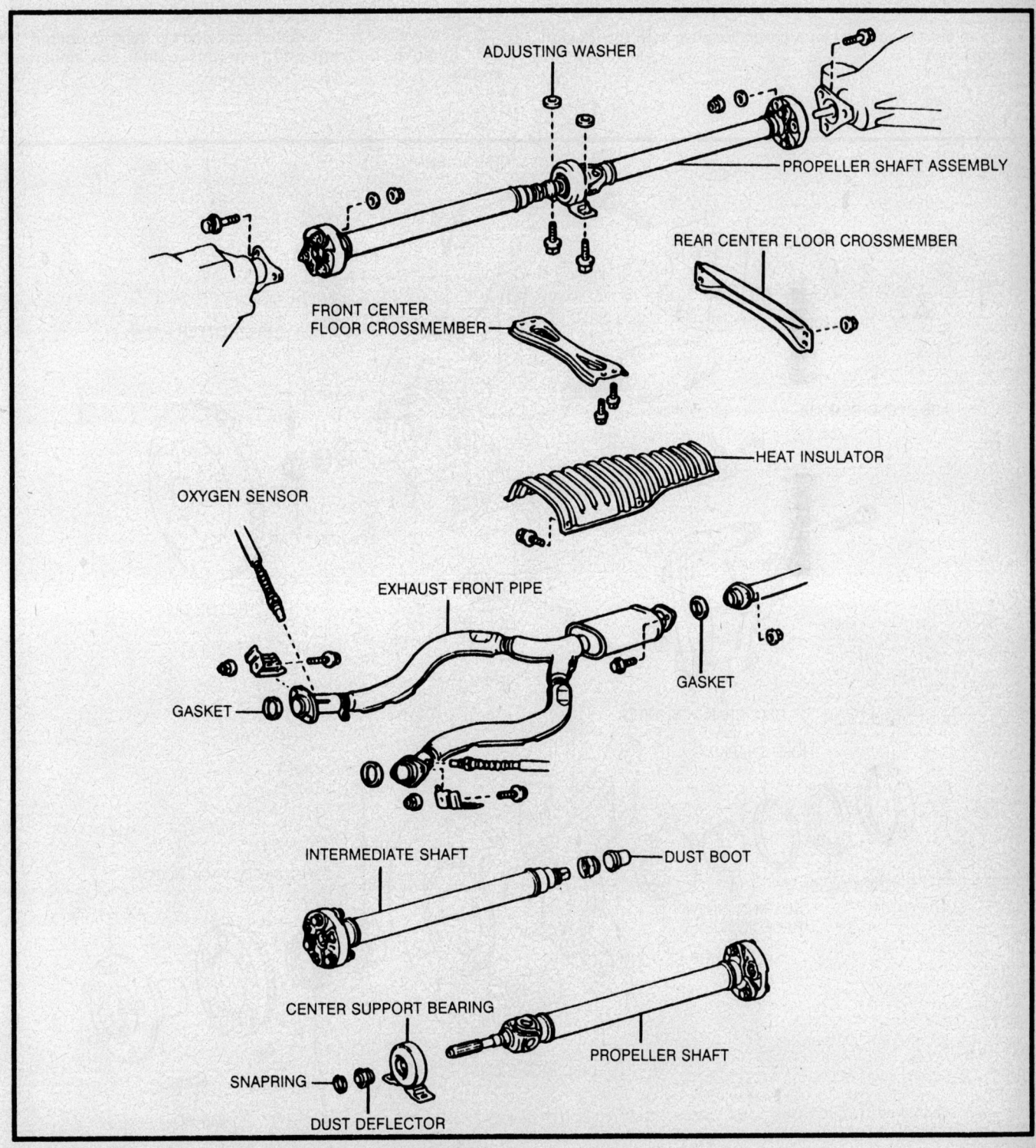

ADJUSTING WASHER

PROPELLER SHAFT ASSEMBLY

REAR CENTER FLOOR CROSSMEMBER

FRONT CENTER FLOOR CROSSMEMBER

HEAT INSULATOR

OXYGEN SENSOR

EXHAUST FRONT PIPE

GASKET

GASKET

INTERMEDIATE SHAFT

DUST BOOT

CENTER SUPPORT BEARING

PROPELLER SHAFT

SNAPRING

DUST DEFLECTOR

Exploded view of the driveshaft assembly—LS400

4. Remove the halfshaft.
5. Secure the halfshaft in a suitable holding fixture. Tap out the end cover with the proper tools.
6. Remove the boot clamps from the inboard and outboard joint boots.
7. Place matchmarks on the inboard joint and halfshaft. Remove the snapring , using the proper pliers.
8. Press out the inboard joint from the halfshaft with the proper tools. Secure the inboard joint in a suitable holding fixture.
9. Tap out the inboard joint cover. Remove both the inboard and outboard
joint boots.

10. The installation is the reverse of the removal procedure. Pack the boots and the end cover with a suitable grease prior to installation.

Driveshaft and U-Joints

Removal and Installation

LS400
1. Raise and safely support the vehicle.
2. Remove the front exhaust pipe and the heat insulator.
3. Remove the front and rear center floor crossmember braces.

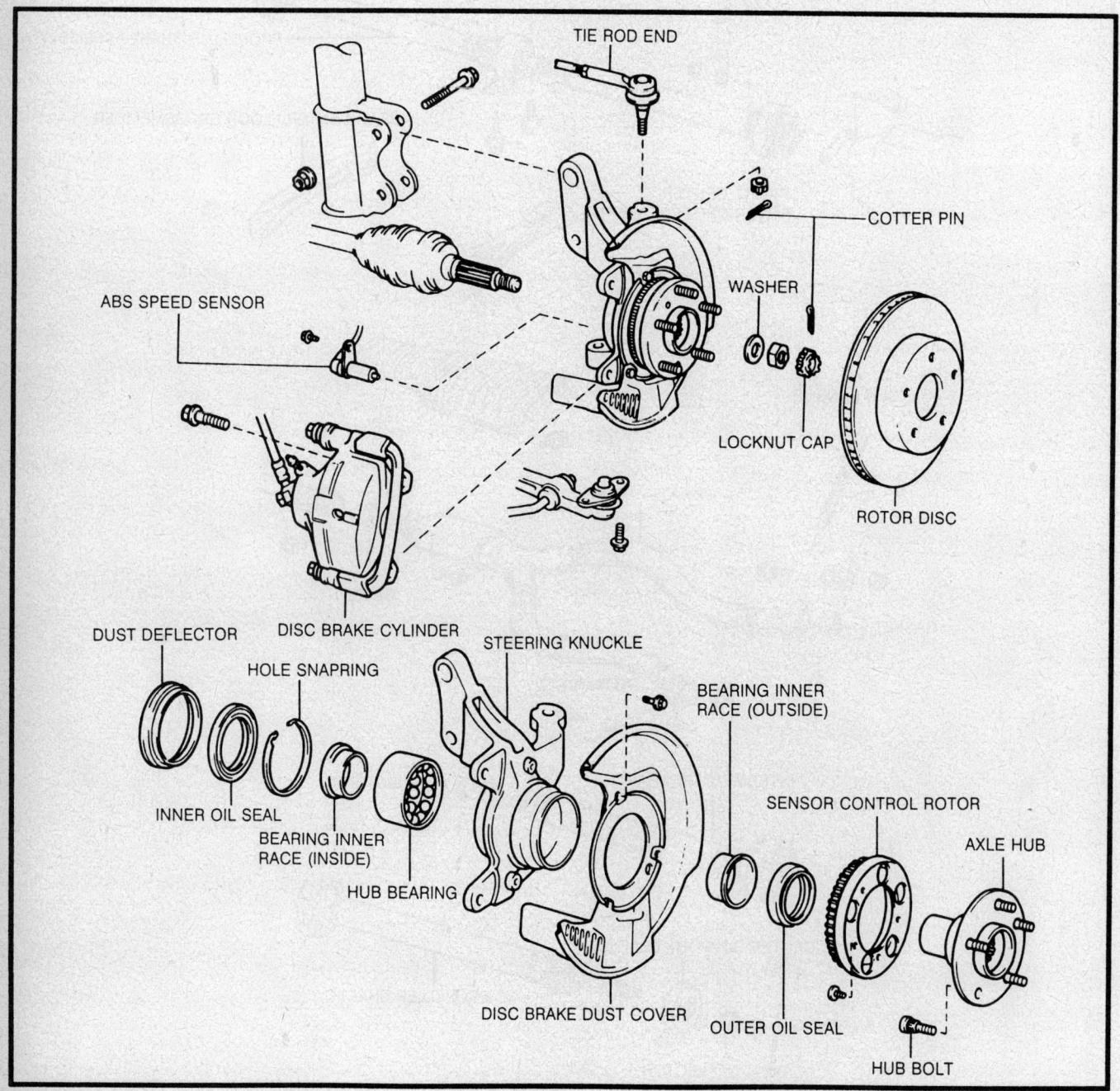

Front axle hub assembly—ES250

4. Using the proper tool, loosen the adjusting nut on the driveshaft. Place matchmarks on the transmission flange and the flexible coupling.

5. Remove the bolts inserted from the transmission side.

NOTE: The bolts inserted from the driveshaft side should not be removed.

6. Place matchmarks on the differential flange and the flexible coupling.

7. Remove the bolts inserted from the differential side. Separate the flexible couplings from the transmission and the differential.

8. Remove the center support bearing set bolts and the adjusting washers, if equipped.

NOTE: When removing the set bolts, support the center support bearing so the transmission and intermediate shaft and the driveshaft and differential remain in straight line.

9. Push the rear driveshaft forward to compress the driveshaft and pull out the driveshaft from the centering pin of the differential.

10. Remove the driveshaft by pulling out toward the rear of the vehicle.

To install:

11. Apply a suitable grease to the flexible coupling centering bushings.

12. Insert the propeller shaft from the rear of the vehicle and connect the transmission and differential.

13. Temporarily, install the center support bearing set bolts with the adjusting washers, if equipped.

14. Align the matchmarks and connect the propeller shaft to the transmission. Insert the bolts from the transmission side and tighten to 58 ft. lbs.

15. Align the matchmarks and install the driveshaft to the differential. Insert the bolts from the differential side and tighten to 58 ft. lbs.

16. Tighten the center bearing support bolts to 27 ft. lbs. Tighten the adjusting nut with the proper tool.

17. Install the front and rear crossmember braces and tighten to 9 ft. lbs.

18. Install the heat insulator and the front exhaust pipe.

19. Lower the vehicle.

Front Wheel Hub, Knuckle and Bearings

Removal and Installation

ES250

1. Raise and safely support the vehicle. Remove the front tire and wheel assembly.

2. Remove the brake caliper and support, using a piece of wire. Place match marks on the rotor disc and the axle hub. Remove the rotor.

3. Disconnect the ABS speed sensor.

4. Disconnect the lower ball joint from the steering knuckle with the proper tool. Disconnect the tie rod end from the steering knuckle.

5. Disconnect the steering knuckle from the shock absorber.

6. Remove the steering knuckle with the axle hub from the halfshaft.

7. Remove the dust protector and pry out the inner oil seal with the proper tool.

8. Remove the snapring from the steering knuckle and separate the dust cover from the steering knuckle.

9. Push out the axle hub and remove the inner race (inside) from the bearing, using the proper tool.

10. Remove the sensor control rotor from the axle hub. Remove the bearing inner race (outside) from the axle hub.

11. Pry out the oil seal with the proper tool and tap out the bearing.

To install:

12. Install the sensor control rotor to the axle hub and press in a new bearing into the steering knuckle.

13. Install the outer oil seal and the disc brake dust cover.

14. Apply a suitable multi-purpose grease between the oil seal lip, the oil seal and the bearing. Install the axle hub into the steering knuckle, using the proper tool.

15. Install the snapring into the steering knuckle.

16. Install the oil seal into the steering knuckle with a suitable seal installer tool. Apply a suitable multi-purpose grease to the oil seal lip.

17. Tap the dust deflector into the steering knuckle

18. Install the steering knuckle with the axle hub to the halfshaft. Tighten the lower mounting nuts to 224 ft. lbs.

19. Connect the tie rod end to the steering knuckle and tighten the bolts to 36 ft. lbs.

20. Tighten the lower ball joint mounting bolts to 83 ft. lbs. Connect the ABS speed sensor.

21. Align the matchmarks and install the brake rotor. Replace the brake caliper and tighten the mounting bolts to 79 ft. lbs.

22. Tighten the bearing locknut to 137 ft. lbs. Replace the tire and wheel assembly.

23. Lower the vehicle.

LS400

1. If equipped with air suspension, move the height control switch in the trunk area to the **OFF** position.

2. Raise and safely support the vehicle. Remove the front tire and wheel assembly.

3. Disconnect the brake caliper from the steering knuckle and support with a piece of wire.

4. Place matchmarks on the disc brake rotor and the axle hub. Remove the brake rotor.

5. Remove the speed sensor from the steering knuckle. Loosen the axle shaft nut.

6. Remove the steering knuckle from the lower ball joint, using the proper tool. Remove the steering knuckle from the upper ball joint.

7. Remove the steering knuckle with the axle hub.

8. Remove the nut and the speed sensor rotor. Using the proper tool, remove the axle hub from the steering knuckle.

9. Remove the outside inner race from the axle and the oil seal from the steering knuckle, using the proper tools.

10. Remove the snapring and remove the bearing from the steering knuckle.

To install:

11. Using the proper tool, install the bearing to the steering knuckle. Replace the snapring.

12. Install the inner race (outside) and press in a new oil seal until it is flush with the end surface of the steering knuckle.

13. Install the brake dust cover to the steering knuckle and using the proper tools, press the axle hub to the steering knuckle.

14. Install the speed sensor. Install the steering knuckle to the lower ball joint and temporarily, tighten the bolts.

15. Install the steering knuckle to the upper arm and tighten the nut to 48 ft. lbs.

16. Align the matchmarks and install disc rotor to the axle hub. Install the brake caliper and tighten the mounting bolts top 87 ft. lbs.

17. Tighten the axle shaft nut to 147 ft. lbs. Install the speed sensor to the steering knuckle.

18. Replace the front tire and wheel assembly. Lower the vehicle.

19. If equipped with air suspension, turn the height control switch to the **ON** position.

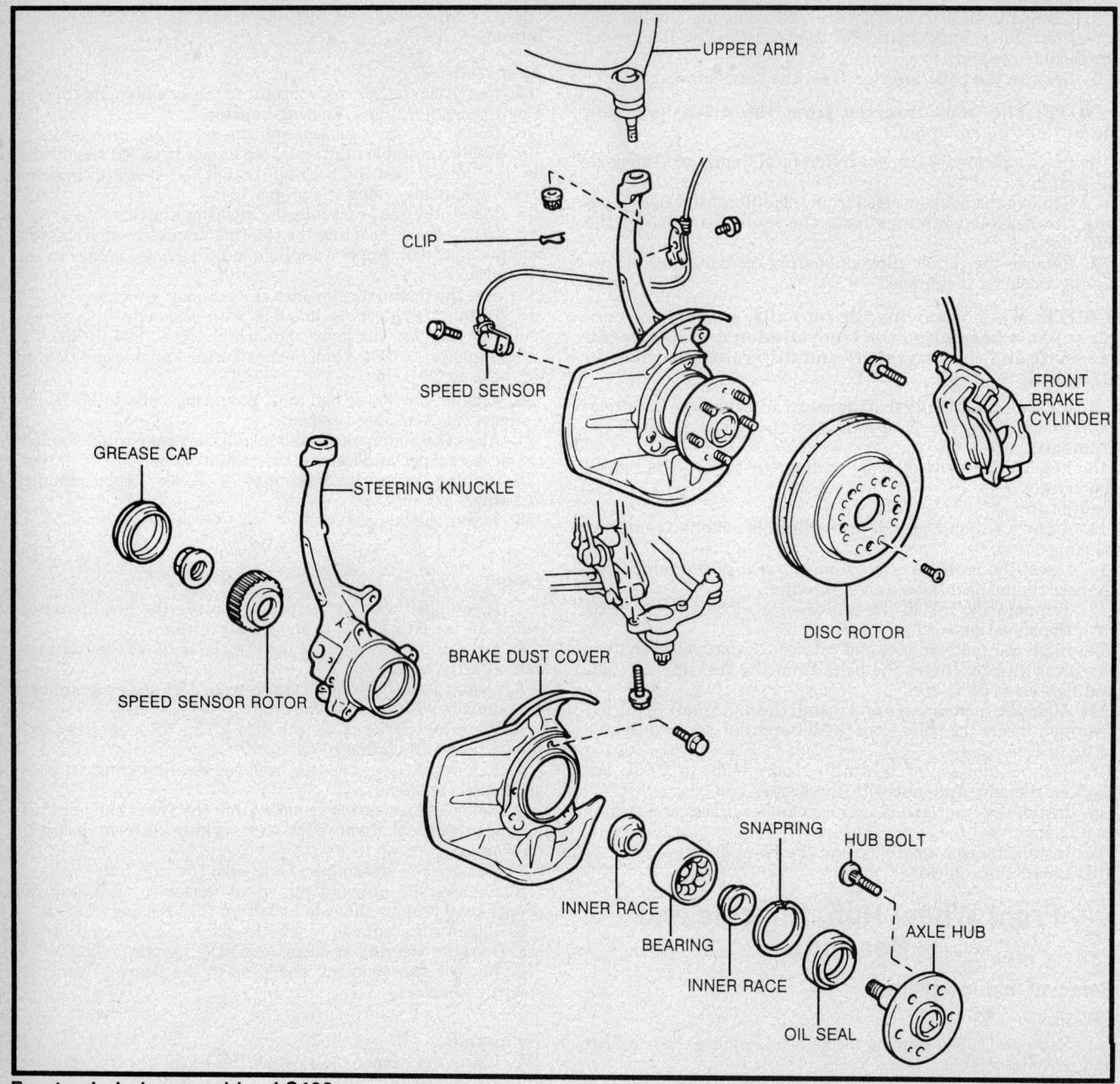

UPPER ARM

CLIP

SPEED SENSOR

GREASE CAP

STEERING KNUCKLE

SPEED SENSOR ROTOR

BRAKE DUST COVER

FRONT BRAKE CYLINDER

DISC ROTOR

INNER RACE

BEARING

INNER RACE

OIL SEAL

SNAPRING

HUB BOLT

AXLE HUB

Front axle hub assembly—LS400

Rear Axle Shaft Bearing and Seal

Removal and Installation

LS400

1. If equipped with air suspension, move the height control switch in the trunk area to the **OFF** position.
2. Raise and safely support the vehicle. Remove the rear tire and wheel assembly.
3. Disconnect the brake caliper from the rear axle carrier and support with a piece of wire.
4. Place matchmarks on the disc brake rotor and the axle hub. Remove the brake rotor.
5. Remove the speed sensor. Remove the strut rod and lower suspension rods.

6. Remove the nut on the lower side of the shock absorber. Do not remove the bolt.
7. Remove the upper arm set bolts and the bolt on the lower side of the shock absorber. Remove the axle with the arm.
8. Remove the upper arm and the dust deflector, using the proper tools. Remove the inner oil seal.
9. Remove the axle hub and the backing plate. Remove the inner race (outside) from the axle hub.
10. Pry out the outer oil seal. Remove the snapring and the bearing, using the proper tools.

To install:

11. Install the bearing to the axle carrier.

NOTE: If the inner races come loose from the bearing outer race, be sure to install them on the same side as before.

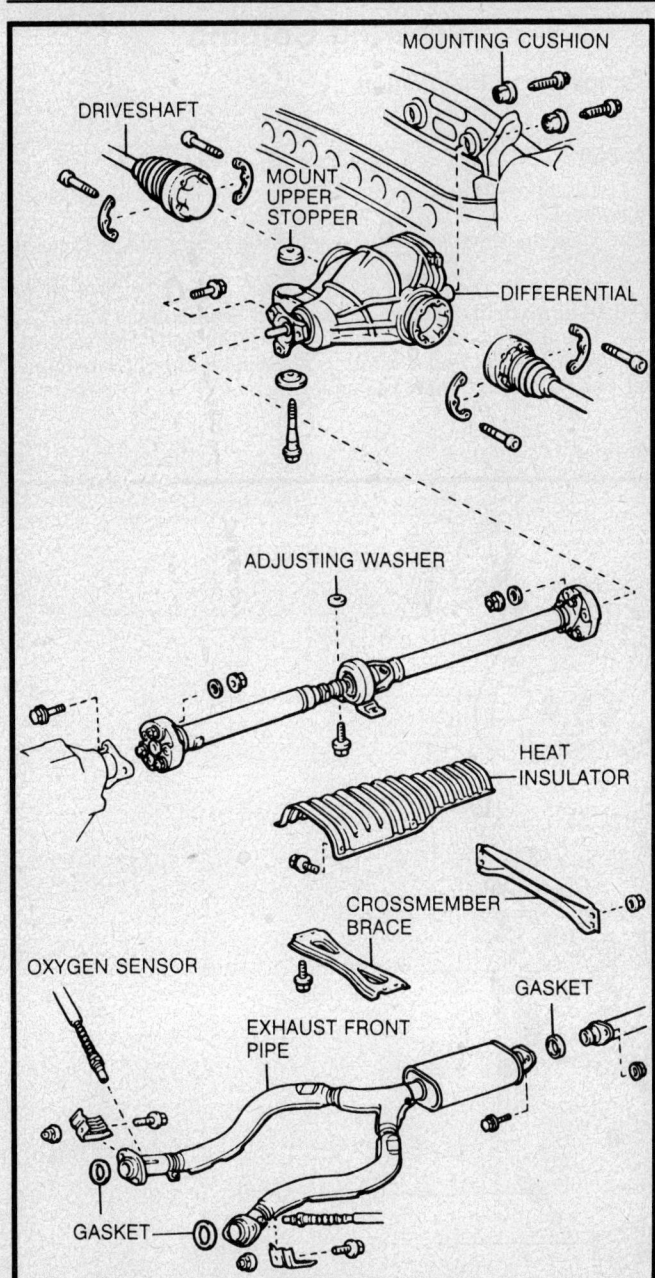

Exploded view of the rear differential—LS400

12. Install the snapring. Replace the backing plate to the axle carrier and tighten the mounting bolts 43 ft. lbs.

13. Install the inner race (outside) and a new oil seal.

14. Install the inner race (inside) and press in the axle hub with the proper tools.

15. Install the inner oil seal. Align the holes for the speed sensor in the dust deflector and axle carrier. Install the dust deflector.

16. Install the upper arm to the axle carrier. Tighten the nut and bolt to 80 ft. lbs.

17. Replace the nut on the lower side of the shock absorber.

18. Install the speed sensor. Replace the strut rod and lower suspension rods.

19. Install the brake rotor. Connect the brake caliper to the rear axle carrier.

20. Replace the rear tire and wheel assembly. Lower the vehicle.

Differential Carrier

Removal and Installation

LS400

1. Raise and safely support the vehicle. Remove the front exhaust pipe.

2. Remove the driveshaft. Drain the differential oil in a suitable container.

3. Place matchmarks on the driveshafts and side gear shafts. Using the proper tool, disconnect the driveshafts from the differential.

4. Support the driveshafts, using a piece of wire.

5. Support the differential with a suitable jacking device. Remove the bolts and lower the differential.

6. Remove the mount upper stopper from the differential carrier.

NOTE: Some vehicles have the adjusting shim for adjusting the driveshaft joint angle installed on the mount upper stopper.

To install:

7. Install the mount upper stopper on the differential carrier. Install the adjusting shim, if equipped.

8. Support the differential with a proper jacking device and install the washer and bolt. Tighten to bolt to 87 ft. lbs.

9. Tighten the upper mounting bolts to 90 ft. lbs.

10. Align the matchmarks and connect the driveshafts to the differential. Tighten the bolts to 61 ft. lbs.

11. Install the driveshaft and connect the front exhaust pipe. Refill the differential to the specified level.

12. Lower the vehicle

STEERING

Steering Wheel

CAUTION

On vehicles equipped with an air bag, the negative battery cable must be disconnected, before working on the system. Failure to do so may result in deployment of the air bag and possible personal injury.

Removal and Installation

1. Disconnect the negative battery cable. Position the front wheels in a straight ahead position.

2. Loosen the screw until the groove along the screw circumference catches on the screw case.

3. Pull the wheel pad away from the steering wheel and disconnect the air bag connector.

NOTE: When removing the wheel pad, take care not to pull the air bag harness connector.

4. Disconnect the wire connector and remove the set nut. Place matchmarks on the steering wheel and main shaft.

5. Remove the steering with a suitable puller.

To install:

6. Check that the front wheels are facing straight ahead. Center the spiral cable.

7. Align the matchmarks and install the steering wheel. Tighten the set nut to 26 ft. lbs.

8. Connect the connector.

9. Install the steering wheel pad after confirming that the circumference groove of the screws is caught on the screw case.

10. Tighten the screws to 65 inch lbs. Connect the negative battery cable.

Steering Column

Removal and Installation

ES250

1. Disconnect the negative battery cable. Remove the steering wheel.

2. Using a centering punch, mark the center of the tapered-head bolts.

3. Drill into the tapered-head bolts, using a 0.12–0.16 in. (0.3–0.4mm) drill. Remove the tapered-head bolts.

4. Use a screw extractor and remove the bolts and separate the upper bracket and column tube. Remove the thrust stopper set bolts and disconnect the snapring.

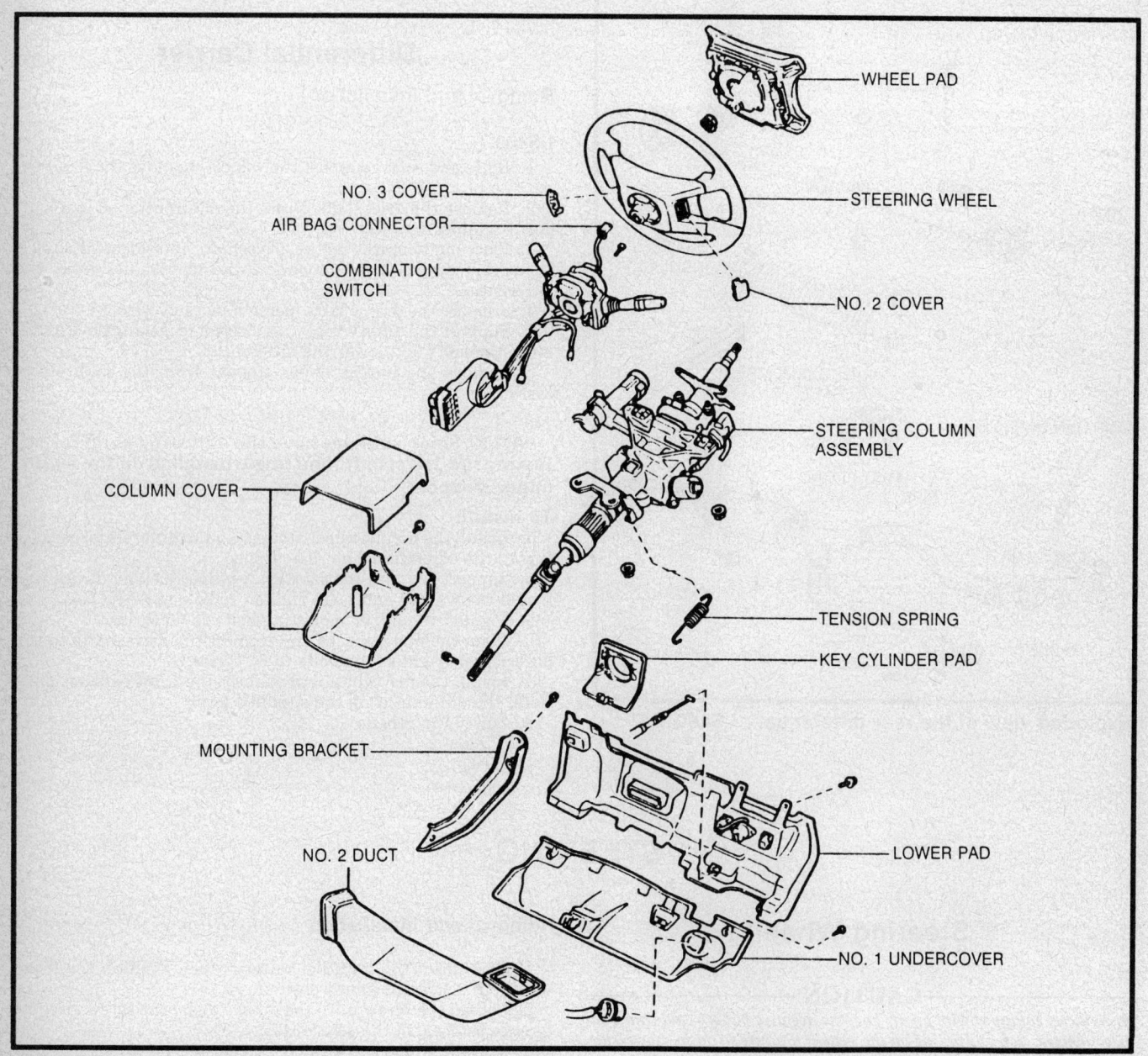

WHEEL PAD

NO. 3 COVER

AIR BAG CONNECTOR

COMBINATION SWITCH

STEERING WHEEL

NO. 2 COVER

STEERING COLUMN ASSEMBLY

COLUMN COVER

TENSION SPRING

KEY CYLINDER PAD

MOUNTING BRACKET

NO. 2 DUCT

LOWER PAD

NO. 1 UNDERCOVER

Steering column assembly—LS400

5. Remove the main shaft. Using the proper tool, remove the snapring and thrust stopper.

6. The installation is the reverse of the removal procedure. Tighten the thrust stopper bolts to 9 ft. lbs.

LS400

1. Disconnect the negative battery cable. Remove the steering wheel.

2. Disconnect the ignition key light. Remove the No. 2 intermediate shaft.

3. Remove the lower dust cover and gasket. Remove the tilt position sensor.

4. Remove the turn signal bracket, the lower shield protectors and connector bracket.

5. Using a centering punch, mark the center of the tapered-head bolts.

6. Drill into the tapered-head bolts, using a 0.16–0.20 in. (0.4–0.5mm) drill. Remove the tapered-head bolts.

7. Use a screw extractor and remove the bolts and separate the upper bracket and the break-away bracket.

8. Remove the nuts, spacers, springs, bushings and bond cable. Using the proper tool, remove the 2, No. 2 tilt steering shafts.

9. Remove the tilt steering gear assembly. Disconnect the nut and telescopic lever serration attachment.

10. Install a double nut on the lock bolt and remove the lock bolt. Remove the steering column tube upper stop bolt.

11. Remove the snapring from the mainshaft. Disconnect the break away bracket from the main shaft.

12. Remove the No. 1 and No. 2 telescopic spring seats and compression ring from the lower tube.

13. Remove the steering shaft thrust stopper from the break-away bracket. Remove the lock wedges from the break-away bracket.

14. Remove the upper tube with the main shaft and the tilt housing support.

15. Remove the main shaft using the proper tool to compress the mainshaft spring and remove the snapring.

16. Remove the main shaft from the upper tube. Remove the spring, thrust collar and bearing.

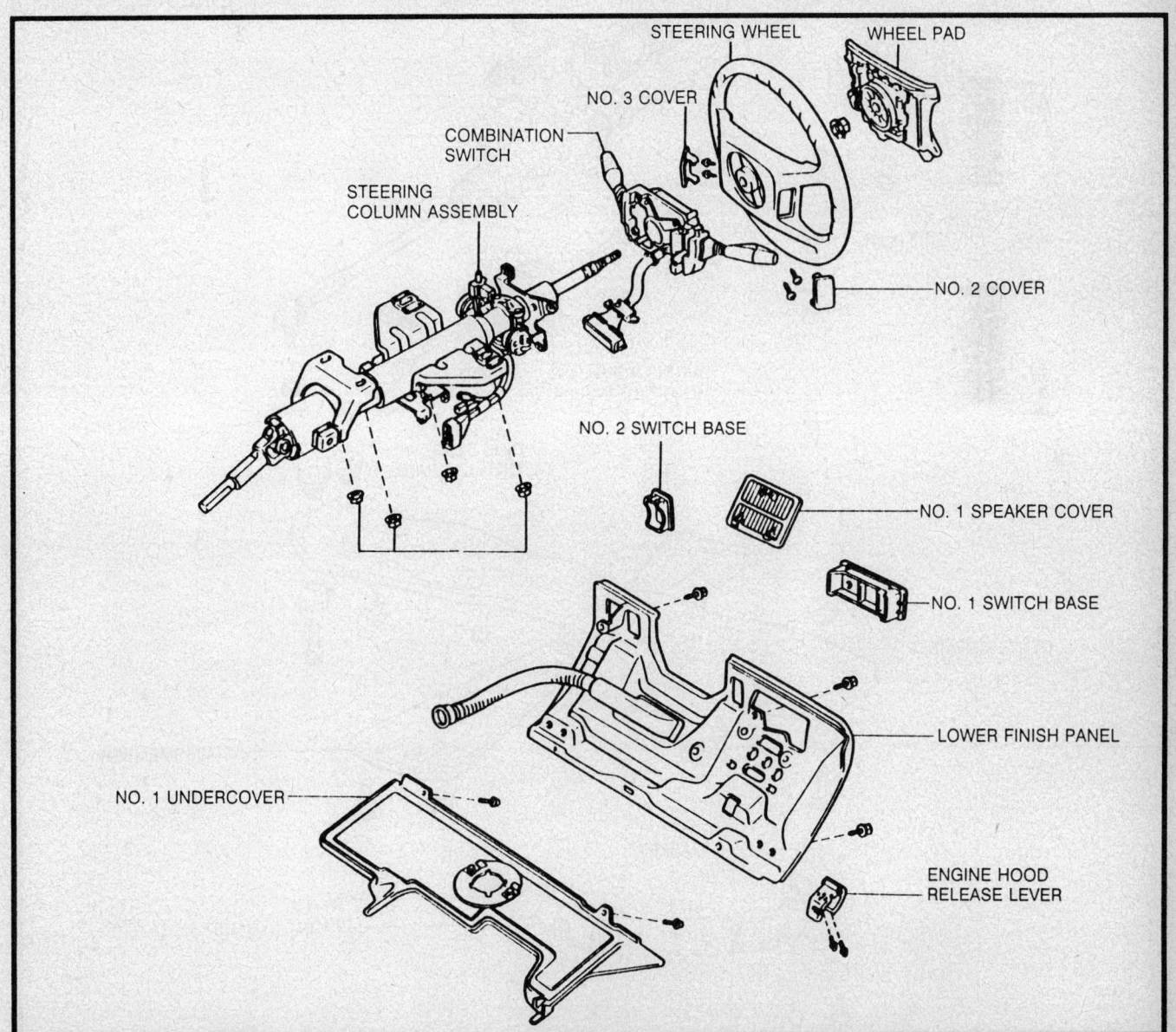

Steering column assembly—ES250

To install:

17. Install the spring, thrust collar and spring to the main shaft. Insert the main shaft in the upper tube.

18. Using the proper tool, compress the main shaft spring and install the snapring.

19. Install the tilt steering upper housing support. Tighten to 9 ft. lbs.

20. Insert the upper tube and the mainshaft into the lower tube. Press in the 2 tilt steering shafts.

21. Replace the lock wedges to the break-away bracket. Install the steering shaft thrust stopper to the break-away bracket.

22. Install the No. 1 and No. 2 telescopic spring seats and compression spring. Install the break-away bracket to the main shaft.

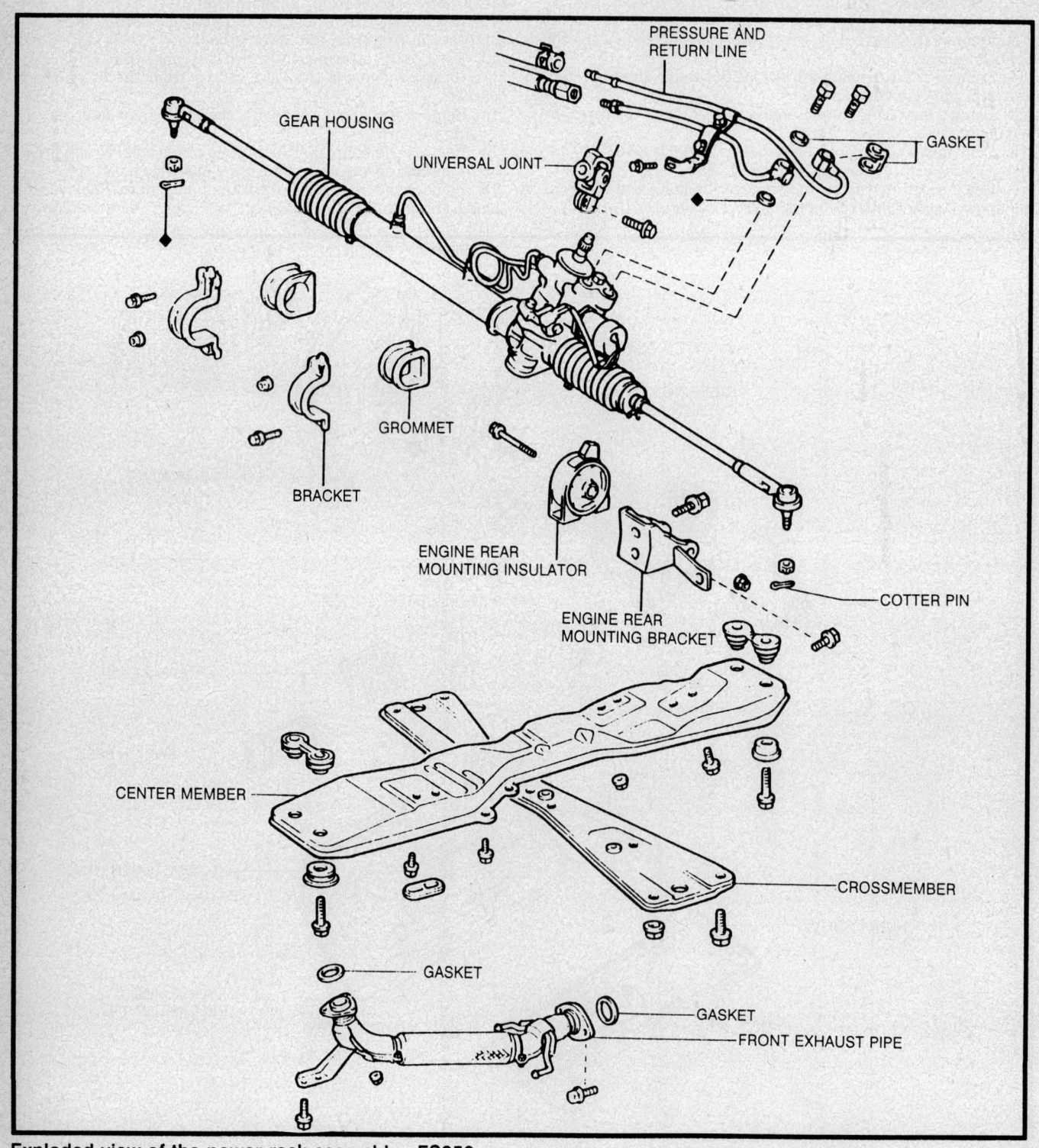

Exploded view of the power rack assembly—ES250

23. Install the snapring to the main shaft and the steering column tube stopper bolt. Tighten the bolt to 14 ft. lbs.

24. Pull the steering column away from the break-away bracket and facing the body installation surface of the break-away bracket upward, temporarily install the lock bolt.

25. Install a double nut on the lock bolt. Tighten to 12 ft. lbs., loosen once, then tighten again to 65 inch lbs.

26. Install the compression spring and ball, washer, lever, collar and bolt. Tighten the bolt to 19 ft. lbs. with the depression of the lever matching the depression of the ball.

27. Rotate the telescopic lever until it touches the break-away bracket. Install the serration attachment so the alignment marks on the telescopic lever align with the serration attachment. Tighten to 9 ft. lbs.

28. Install the tilt steering gear assembly with the motor by:
    a. Install the bushings and support stopper bolts.
    b. Press in the 2, No. 2 tilt steering shafts, using the proper tools.
    c. Install the bushing, spring and spacer to each stopper bolt.
    d. Install the bond cable and the locknuts. Tighten to 26 inch lbs.

29. Install the upper bracket and tighten the tapered-head bolts until the bolt heads break off.

30. Install the connector bracket and tighten to 43 inch lbs. Replace both protective covers.

31. Install the turn signal bracket so the upper surface is parallel with thew upper surface of the capsule of the break-away bracket.

32. Install the tilt position sensor. Install the lower dust cover, using the proper tool to press in the dust seal.

33. Install the No. 2 intermediate shaft and tighten to 26 ft. lbs. Replace the ignition key cylinder lamp.

34. Check that there is no axial play when the lever is turned fully counterclockwise.

35. Check that the main shaft moves smoothly when the lever is turned clockwise

Power Steering Rack

Removal and Installation

ES250

1. Place the front wheels in a straight ahead position, secure the steering wheel with a suitable device to prevent the wheel from turning.

2. Place matchmarks in the universal joint and control valve shaft. Disconnect the joint.

3. Disconnect and plug the hydraulic lines to rack assembly.

4. Raise and safely support the vehicle. Disconnect the front exhaust pipe.

5. Remove the center support member and the crossmember.

6. Matchmark and disconnect the tie rod ends from the steering knuckle with the proper tool.

7. Remove the rear engine mount and mounting bracket. Raise the front of the engine with a suitable jacking device.

NOTE: Do not over-tilt the engine

8. Remove the mounting brackets and slide the gear housing to the right side to put the tie rod end in the body panel.

9. Pull the gear housing out through the opening in the left side lower side of the vehicle body.

NOTE: Do not damage the turn pressure tube and the transmission control cables.

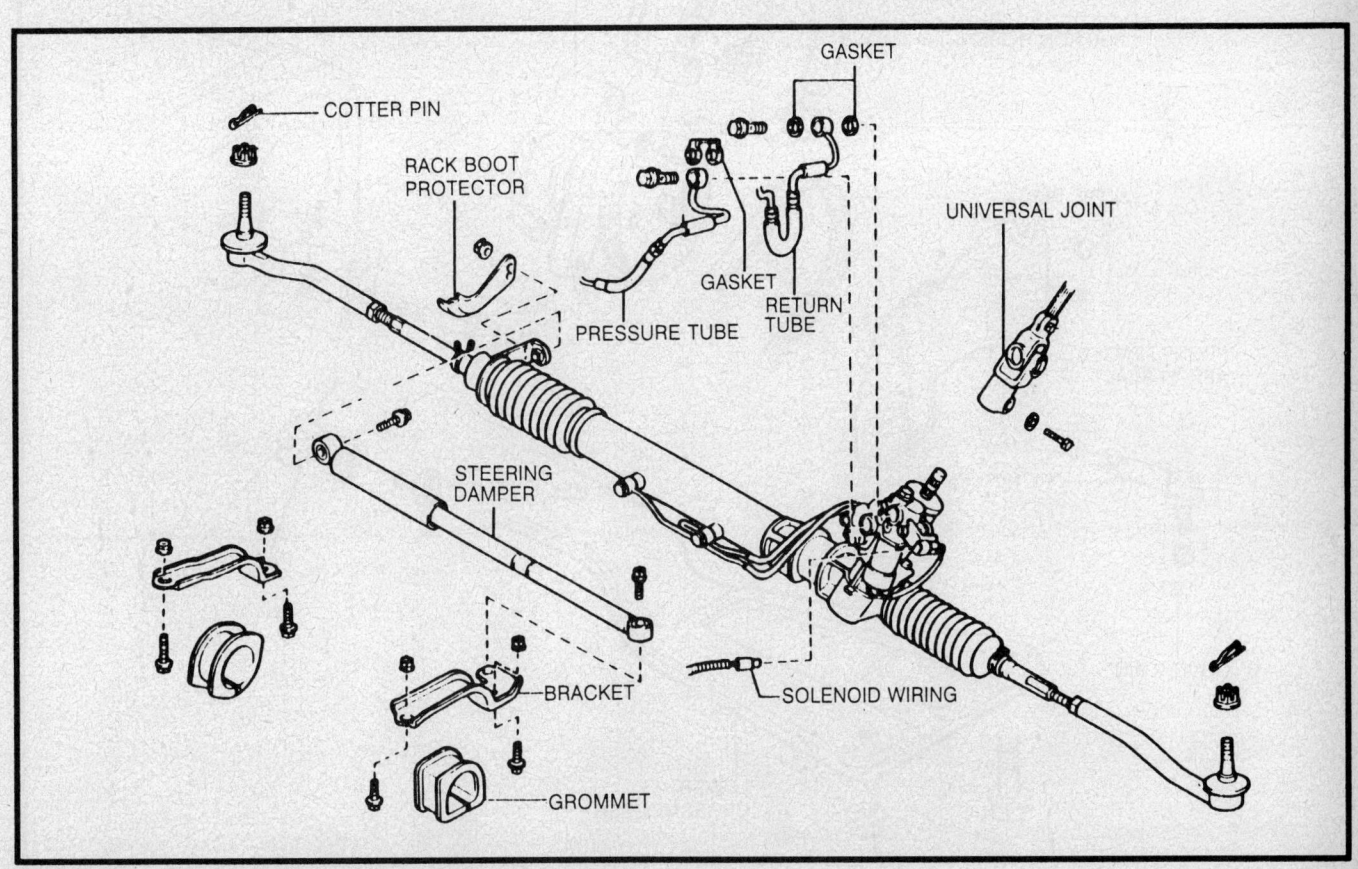

Exploded view of the power rack assembly—LS400

10. Secure the gear housing in a suitable holding fixture. Remove the return and pressure tubes.

To install:

11. Connect the hydraulic tubes to the rack assembly and tighten to 38 ft. lbs. Insert the rack assembly into position.

12. Replace the mounting brackets and tighten to 43 ft. lbs.

13. Replace the rear engine mount and mounting bracket. Tighten the the through bolt to 64 ft. lbs. and the mounting bolts to 38 ft. lbs. Lower the front of the engine with a suitable jacking device. Remove the jacking device.

14. Connect the tie rod ends to the steering knuckle. Tighten to 36 ft. lbs.

15. Replace the center support member and the crossmember. Tighten the crossmember bolts to 153 ft. lbs. and the center member support bolts to 29 ft. lbs.

16. Install the front exhaust pipe and lower the vehicle.

17. Connect the hydraulic lines to the rack assembly.

18. Align the matchmarks on the universal joint and the control valve shaft and connect. Tighten the connecting bolt to 26 ft. lbs.

19. Check the steering wheel center point and the toe-in. Refill the power steering reservoir.

LS400

1. Disconnect the negative battery cable.

2. Place the front wheels in a straight ahead position, secure the steering wheel with a suitable device to prevent the wheel from turning.

3. Place matchmarks in the universal joint and control valve shaft. Disconnect the joint.

4. Disconnect and plug the hydraulic lines to rack assembly.

5. Raise and safely support the vehicle. Disconnect the brake caliper and support with a piece of wire.

6. Disconnect the tie rod end from the steering knuckle with the proper tool.

7. Remove the steering damper and rack boot protector.

8. Disconnect the solenoid wiring and remove the mounting grommets and brackets. Remove the rack assembly.

9. The installation is the reverse of the removal procedure. Follow the following torque specifications:

   a. Joint connecting bolt — 26 ft. lbs.
   b. Tie rod end nuts — 43 ft. lbs.
   c. Steering damper bolts — 20 ft. lbs.
   d. Mounting bracket bolts — 56 ft. lbs.

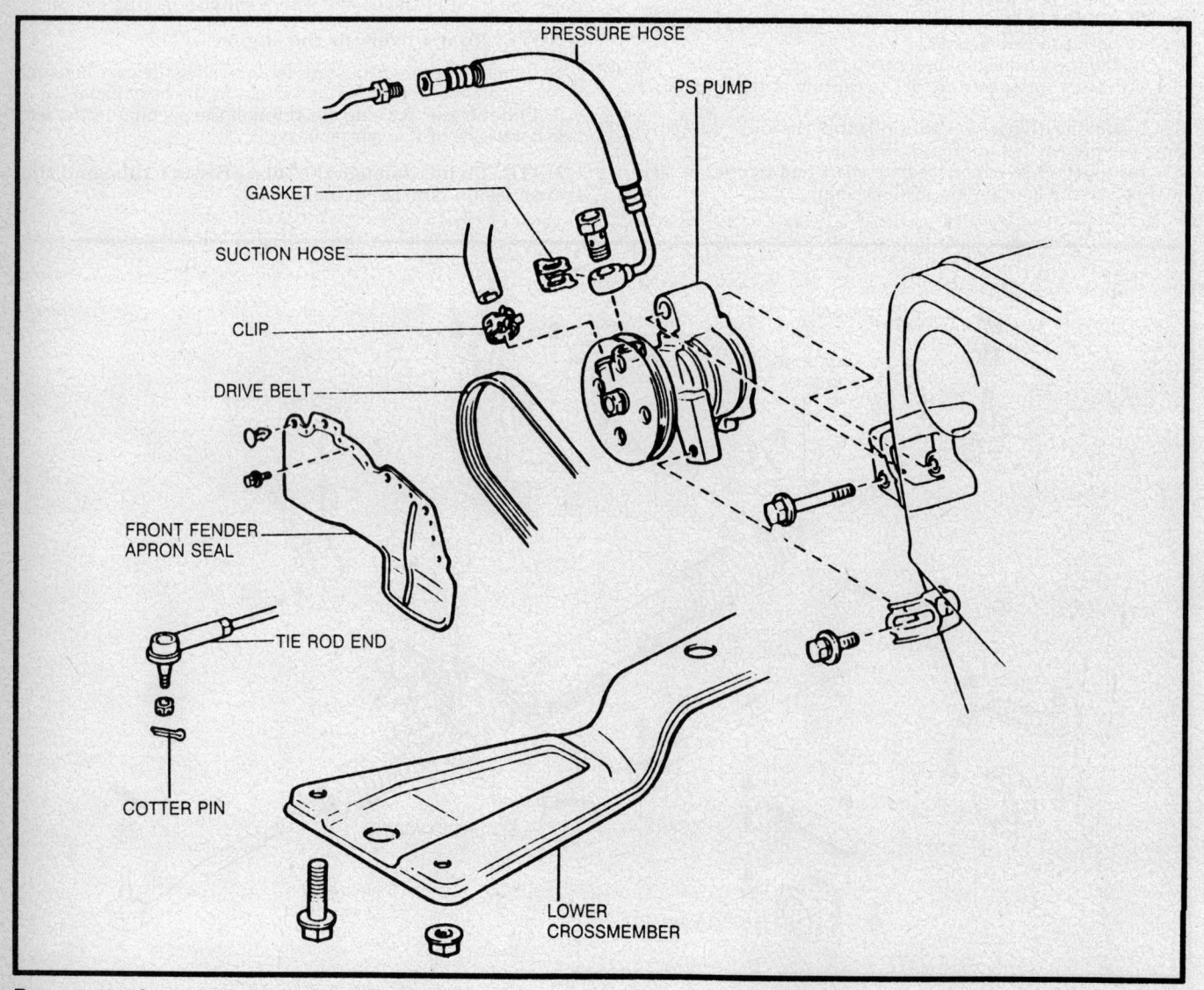

Power steering pump location — ES250

Power Steering Pump

Removal and Installation

ES250

1. Disconnect the negative battery cable. Disconnect the hydraulic lines at the pump assembly.
2. Raise and safely support the vehicle. Disconnect the right side tie rod end with the proper tool.
3. Remove the lower crossmember and the front fender apron seal.
4. Loosen the adjusting and through bolt and push the power steering pump forward. Remove the drive belt.
5. Remove the adjusting bolt and through bolt, then remove the power steering pump.
6. Remove the pressure hose from the pump.
7. The installation is the reverse of the removal procedure. Follow the following torque specifications:
    a. Power steering pump mounting bolts—29 ft. lbs.
    b. Lower crossmember bolts—153 ft. lbs.
    c. Tie rod end nuts—36 ft. lbs.
    d. Pressure line fitting—27-33 ft. lbs.

LS400

1. Disconnect the negative battery cable.
2. Remove the air cleaner cover, air duct and battery cover.
3. Turn the drive belt tensioner counterclockwise and remove the drive belt. Remove the pump pulley with the proper tool.
4. Raise and safely support the vehicle. Remove the engine undercover.

5. Disconnect the hydraulic and vacuum lines at the pump assembly.
6. Remove the pump mounting bolts and the pump assembly.
7. The installation is the reverse of the removal procedure. Follow the following torque specifications:
    a. Pump mounting bolts—29 ft. lbs.
    b. Pump pulley bolt—32 ft. lbs.
    c. Pressure line fitting—36 ft. lbs.
8. Bleed the power steering system.

Belt Adjustment

On the LS400, a belt tensioner is used. There is no need for belt adjustment.

ES250

1. Disconnect the negative battery cable.
2. Loosen the power steering pump adjusting bolt and the through bolt.
3. Using the proper tool, move the pump assembly to attain the proper belt tension.
4. Tighten the pump mounting bolts.
5. Connect the negative battery cable.

System Bleeding

1. Check that the fluid level in the reservoir tank is at the maximum level.
2. Start the engine and turn the steering wheel from lock to lock until the air bubbles are removed from the fluid.
3. Stop the engine and measure the fluid level.
4. Make sure the rise of the fluid is not over 0.020 in.

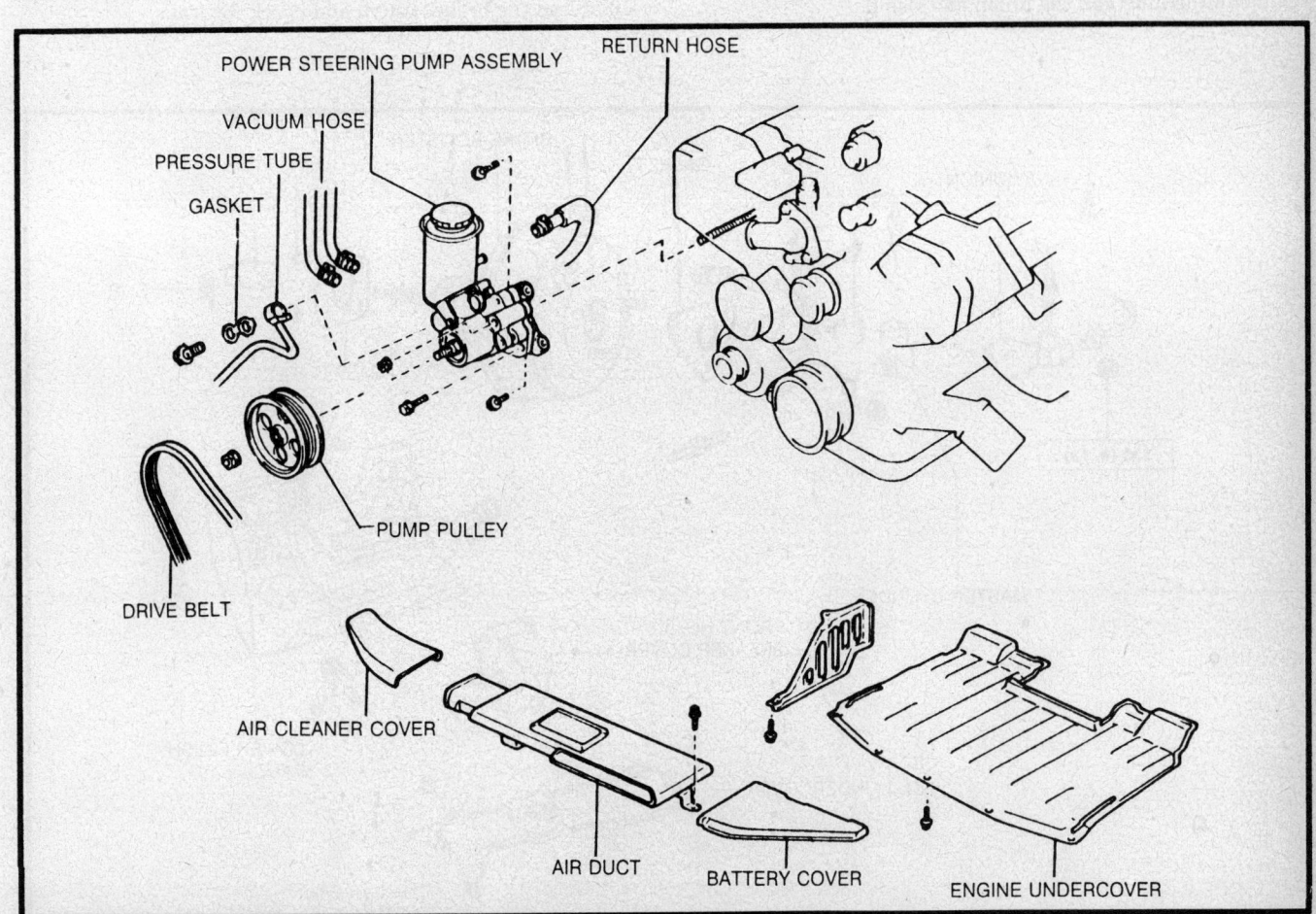

RETURN HOSE
POWER STEERING PUMP ASSEMBLY
VACUUM HOSE
PRESSURE TUBE
GASKET
PUMP PULLEY
DRIVE BELT
AIR CLEANER COVER
AIR DUCT
BATTERY COVER
ENGINE UNDERCOVER

Power steering pump location—LS400

Tie Rod Ends

Removal and Installation

1. Raise and safely support the vehicle.
2. Place matchmarks on the threads of the tie rod end and the rack end.
3. On LS400, disconnect the brake caliper and suspend with a piece of wire. Do not disconnect the lines.
4. Remove the cotter pin and nut. Disconnect the tie rod end from the steering knuckle with the proper tool.

5. Unscrew the tie rod end from the rack end.

To install:

6. Install the tie rod end to the rack end, counting the same number of threads as were removed.
7. Connect the tie rod end to the steering knuckle. Tighten the nut to 41–43 ft. lbs.
8. Connect the caliper, if removed.
9. Lower the vehicle. Check the toe-in.

BRAKES

Master Cylinder

Removal and Installation

ES250

1. Disconnect the negative battery cable. Remove the charcoal canister.
2. Remove the fluid from the reservoir, using a suitable syringe.
3. Disconnect and plug the hydraulic lines to the master cylinder.
4. Disconnect the level warning switch connector. Remove the mounting nuts and the union and clamp.

5. Remove the master cylinder from the booster and remove the gasket.

To install:

6. Adjust the length of the booster pushrod before installing the master cylinder.
7. Install the master cylinder with a new gasket. Replace the union, clamp and tighten the mounting nuts to 9 ft. lbs.
8. Connect the brake lines with the proper tool and tighten the union nuts to 11 ft. lbs.
9. Connect the level warning switch connector. Fill the reservoir with brake fluid.
10. Bleed the brake system and check for leaks.

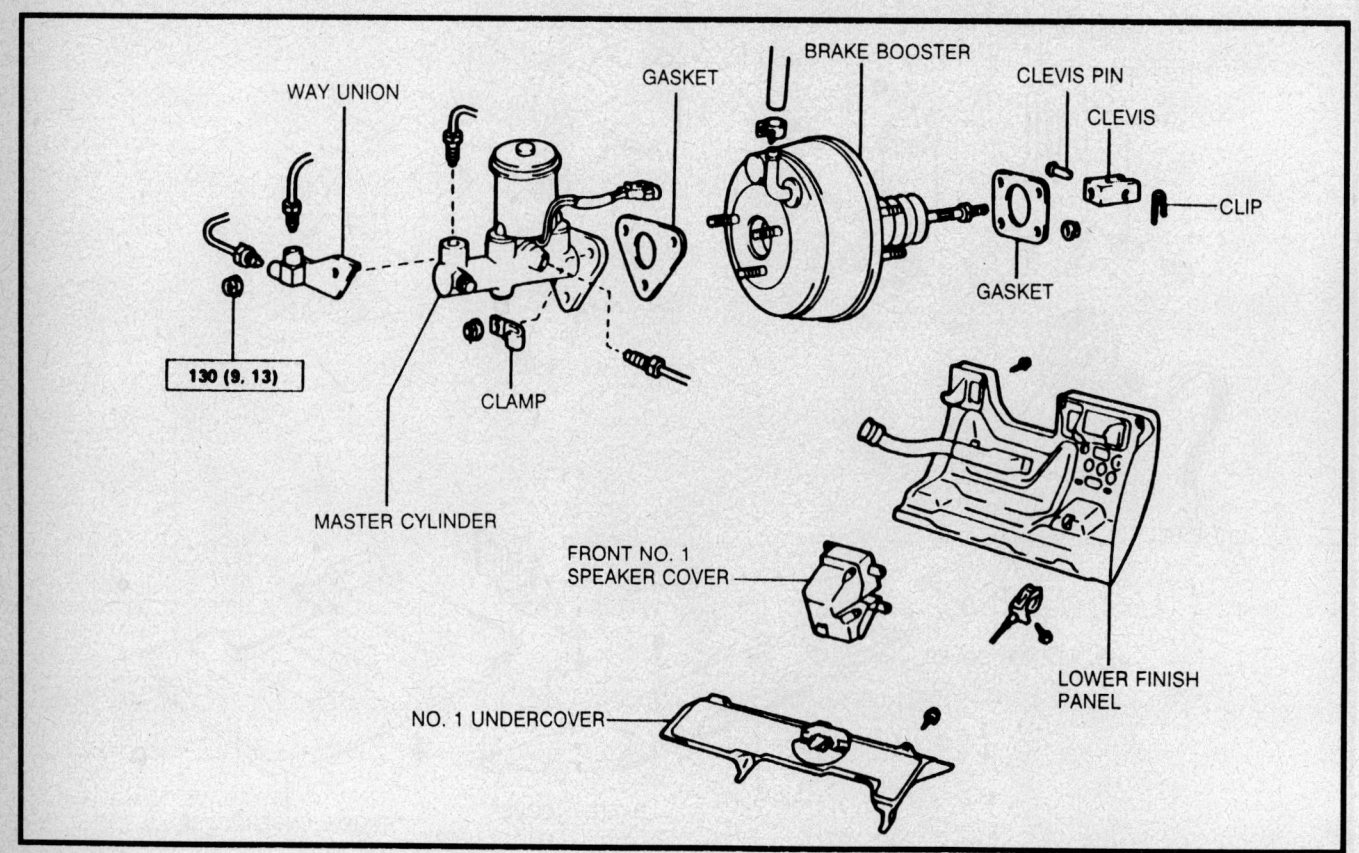

Brake master cylinder and booster location—ES250

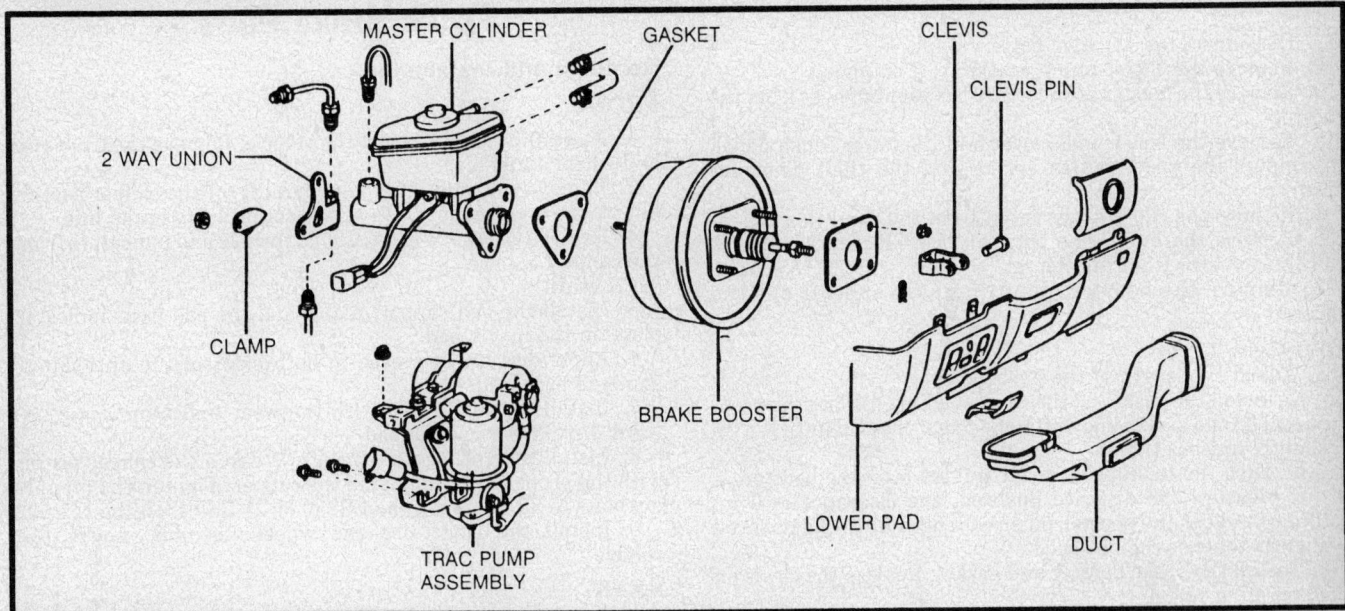

Brake master cylinder and booster location—LS400

LS400

1. Disconnect the negative battery cable.
2. If equipped with a Traction Control System (TRAC), perform the following procedure:
   a. Remove the air cleaner.
   b. Connect a vinyl tube from a container to the bleeder plug of the TRAC actuator, then loosen the bleeder plug with the ignition in the **OFF** position.
   c. Tighten the plug when the fluid stops flowing out.

NOTE: The fluid is under high pressure and could spray out with great force, use caution.

3. Remove the fluid from the reservoir, using a suitable syringe.
4. If equipped with a TRAC, disconnect the hydraulic lines, mounting bolts and connector. Remove the TRAC pump assembly.
5. Disconnect the brake lines from the master cylinder.
6. Remove the mounting nuts and 2-way union. Remove the master cylinder and gasket from the brake booster.
To install:
7. Adjust the length of the booster pushrod before installation.
8. Install the master cylinder and replace the 2-way union. Tighten the mounting nuts to 9 ft. lbs.
9. Connect the brake lines to the master cylinder and the 2-way union. Tighten the nuts to 11 ft. lbs.
10. Install the TRAC pump assembly, if equipped.
11. Bleed the brake system and the TRAC system, if equipped.
12. Check for leaks. Check and adjust the brake pedal, if needed.

Proportioning Valve

Removal and Installation

1. Disconnect the brake line from the valve union. Use caution if under pressure.
2. Remove the valve mounting bolts and remove the valve assembly.
3. The installation is the reverse of the removal procedure.
4. Bleed the brake system. Check for leaks.

Power Brake Booster

Removal and Installation

ES250

1. Disconnect the negative battery cable. Remove the master cylinder and the vacuum hose.
2. Remove the No. 1 undercover and the lower finish panel. Disconnect the pedal return spring and the theft deterrent horn.
3. Remove the clip and clevis pin from the operating rod.
4. Remove the pedal bracket mounting bolt, the steering support nuts and the break-away bracket nuts. Lower the steering column.
5. Remove the mounting nuts and pull out the booster and gasket.
To install:
6. Adjust the length of the pushrod by:
   a. Install the gasket on the master cylinder. Place the proper tool on the gasket and lower the pin of the tool until it's tip slightly touches the pin.
   b. Turn the tool upside down and set it on the booster.
   c. Measure the distance pushrod, the clearance is 0 in. (0mm). Adjust the booster pushrod length until the pushrod slightly touches the pin head.
7. Install the booster and gasket. Replace the clevis pin to the operating rod.
8. Install and tighten the mounting nuts to 9 ft. lbs.
9. Insert the clevis pin to the clevis and brake pedal. Install the clip to the clevis pin.
10. Lift up the steering column and install the steering support nuts and break-away nuts. Tighten to 19 ft. lbs.
11. Install the pedal bracket mounting bolt and tighten to 13 ft. lbs. Replace the pedal return spring.
12. Install the master cylinder and connect the vacuum hose to the brake booster.
13. Fill the reservoir with brake fluid and bleed the brake system. Check for leaks.
14. Check and adjust the brake pedal. Tighten the clevis locknut to 19 ft. lbs.
15. Install the lower finish panel and No. 1 undercover. Connect the negative battery cable.

LS400

1. Disconnect the negative battery cable.
2. Remove the TRAC pump assembly, if equipped.
3. Remove the master cylinder and the vacuum hose from the booster.
4. Remove the No. 1 undercover and the lower finish panel. Disconnect the pedal return spring and the theft deterrent horn.
5. Remove the clip and clevis pin from the operating rod.
6. Remove the brake line between the TRAC accumulator and the actuator from the clamp.
7. Remove the booster mounting nuts and lift out the booster.

To install:

8. Adjust the length of the pushrod by:
   a. Install the gasket on the master cylinder. Place the proper tool on the gasket and lower the pin of the tool until it's tip slightly touches the pin.
   b. Turn the tool upside down and set it on the booster.
   c. Measure the distance pushrod, the clearance is 0 in. (0mm). Adjust the booster pushrod length until the pushrod slightly touches the pin head.
9. Install the brake booster and gasket. Replace the clevis on the operating rod.
10. Install and tighten the mounting nuts to 9 ft. lbs.
11. Insert the clevis pin into the clevis and brake pedal and install the clip on the clevis pin.
12. If equipped with a TRAC, install the brake tube between the TRAC accumulator and actuator to the No. 2 clamp.
13. Install the No. 1 undercover and lower finish panel.
14. Install the master cylinder and connect the vacuum hose to the booster.
15. Replace the TRAC pump, if equipped.
16. Fill the brake reservoir with brake fluid and bleed the brake system.
17. Check and adjust the brake pedal. Check for leaks.
18. Connect the negative battery cable.

Brake Caliper

Removal and Installation

FRONT

1. Raise and safely support the vehicle. Remove the front tire and wheel assembly.
2. Disconnect and plug the brake line at the caliper.
3. Remove the mounting bolts and the caliper assembly.
4. Remove the brake pads, shims, springs and indicators from the caliper.
5. The installation is the reverse of the removal procedure.
6. Tighten the mounting bolts to 29 ft. lbs. on the ES250 or 25 ft. lbs. on the LS400.
7. Bleed the brake system.

REAR

1. Raise and safely support the vehicle. Remove the rear tire and wheel assembly.
2. Disconnect and plug the brake line at the caliper.
3. Remove the mounting bolts and the caliper assembly.
4. Remove the brake pads, shims, springs and indicators from the caliper.
5. The installation is the reverse of the removal procedure.
6. Tighten the mounting bolts to 29 ft. lbs. on the ES250 or 25 ft. lbs. on the LS400.
7. Bleed the brake system.

Disc Brake Pads

Removal and Installation

FRONT

1. Raise and safely support the vehicle. Remove the front tire and wheel assembly.
3. Remove the mounting bolts and lift off the caliper assembly. Support the caliper. Do not disconnect the brake line.
4. Remove the brake pads, shims, springs and indicators from the caliper.

To install:

5. Install the pad support plates and the pad wear indicator plate on the inside pad.
6. Apply disc brake grease to both sides of the anti-squeal shims to each pad.
7. Install the inside pad with the wear indicator facing upward. Install the outside pad.
8. Install the anti-squeal springs. Press in the caliper piston with the proper tool and install the caliper. Tighten the mounting bolts to 29 ft. lbs. on the ES250 or 25 ft. lbs. on the LS400.
9. Install the front tire and wheel assembly. Lower the vehicle.

REAR

1. Raise and safely support the vehicle. Remove the rear tire and wheel assembly.
3. Remove the mounting bolts and lift off the caliper assembly. Support the caliper. Do not disconnect the brake line.
4. Remove the brake pads, shims, springs and indicators from the caliper.

To install:

5. Install the pad support plates and the pad wear indicator plate on the inside pad.
6. Apply disc brake grease to both sides of the anti-squeal shims to each pad.
7. Install the inside pad with the wear indicator facing upward. Install the outside pad.
8. Install the anti-squeal springs. Press in the caliper piston with the proper tool and install the caliper. Tighten the mounting bolts to 29 ft. lbs. on the ES250 or 25 ft. lbs. on the LS400.
9. Install the rear tire and wheel assembly. Lower the vehicle.

Brake Rotor

Removal and Installation

FRONT

1. Raise and safely support the vehicle. Remove the front tire and wheel assembly.
2. Remove the mounting bolts and lift off the caliper assembly. Support the caliper. Do not disconnect the brake line.
3. Remove the torque plate from the steering knuckle, if equipped.
4. Remove the hub bolts and pull the brake rotor.
5. The installation is the reverse of the removal procedure. Tighten the hub bolts to 79 ft. lbs. on the ES250 or 87 ft. lbs. on the LS400.

Parking Brake Cable

Adjustment

ES250

1. Pull the parking brake lever all the way up and count the number of clicks, should be 5–8 clicks.
2. Before adjusting the parking brake, make sure the rear parking brake shoe clearance is adjusted. Adjust by:
   a. Raise and safely support the vehicle. Remove the rear tire and wheel assembly.
   b. Remove the hole plug.

c. Turn the adjuster and expand the shoes until the rotor locks.

d. Return the adjuster 8 notches.

e. Install the hole plug. Replace the tire and wheel assembly.

f. Lower the vehicle.

3. Remove the console box.

4. Loosen the locknut and turn the adjusting nut until the lever travel is correct.

5. Tighten the locknut to 48 inch lbs. Install the console box.

LS400

1. Depress the parking brake all the way and count the number of clicks, should be 5–7 clicks.

2. Before adjusting the parking brake, make sure the rear parking brake shoe clearance is adjusted. Adjust by:

a. Raise and safely support the vehicle. Remove the rear tire and wheel assembly.

b. Remove the hole plug.

c. Turn the adjuster and expand the shoes until the rotor locks.

d. Return the adjuster 8 notches.

e. Install the hole plug. Replace the tire and wheel assembly.

f. Lower the vehicle.

3. Raise and safely support the vehicle.

4. Loosen the lock adjuster locknut and adjuster until the parking brake pedal travel is correct. Tighten the locknut.

5. The installation is the reverse of the removal procedure.

Brake System Bleeding

1. Fill the reservoir to the maximum level with brake fluid.

2. To bleed the master cylinder:

a. Disconnect the brake lines from the master cylinder.

b. Depress the brake pedal and hold it.

c. Block off the outer holes with your fingers and release the brake pedal. Repeat 2–3 times.

3. To bleed the wheels:

a. Start bleeding the brakes from the farthest point.

b. Connect a vinyl tube to the brake cylinder bleeder plug and insert the other end of the tube in a ½ full container of brake fluid.

c. Press on the brake pedal and loosen the bleeder plug until brake fluid comes out.

d. Repeat until there is no more air bubbles in the fluid. Tighten the bleeder screw.

e. Repeat the procedure for each wheel.

4. To bleed TRAC Control System:

a. Remove the air cleaner, then temporarily reinstall it so the engine can be started.

b. Connect a vinyl tube to the bleeder plug of the TRAC actuator, then loosen the bleeder plug.

c. Start the engine, then operate the TRAC pump motor until all the air has been bled out of the fluid.

d. Tighten the bleeder screw and stop the engine. Install the air cleaner.

Anti-Lock Brake System Service

The ABS system controls the hydraulic pressure of all 4 wheels during sudden braking and braking on slippery road surfaces, preventing the wheels from locking.

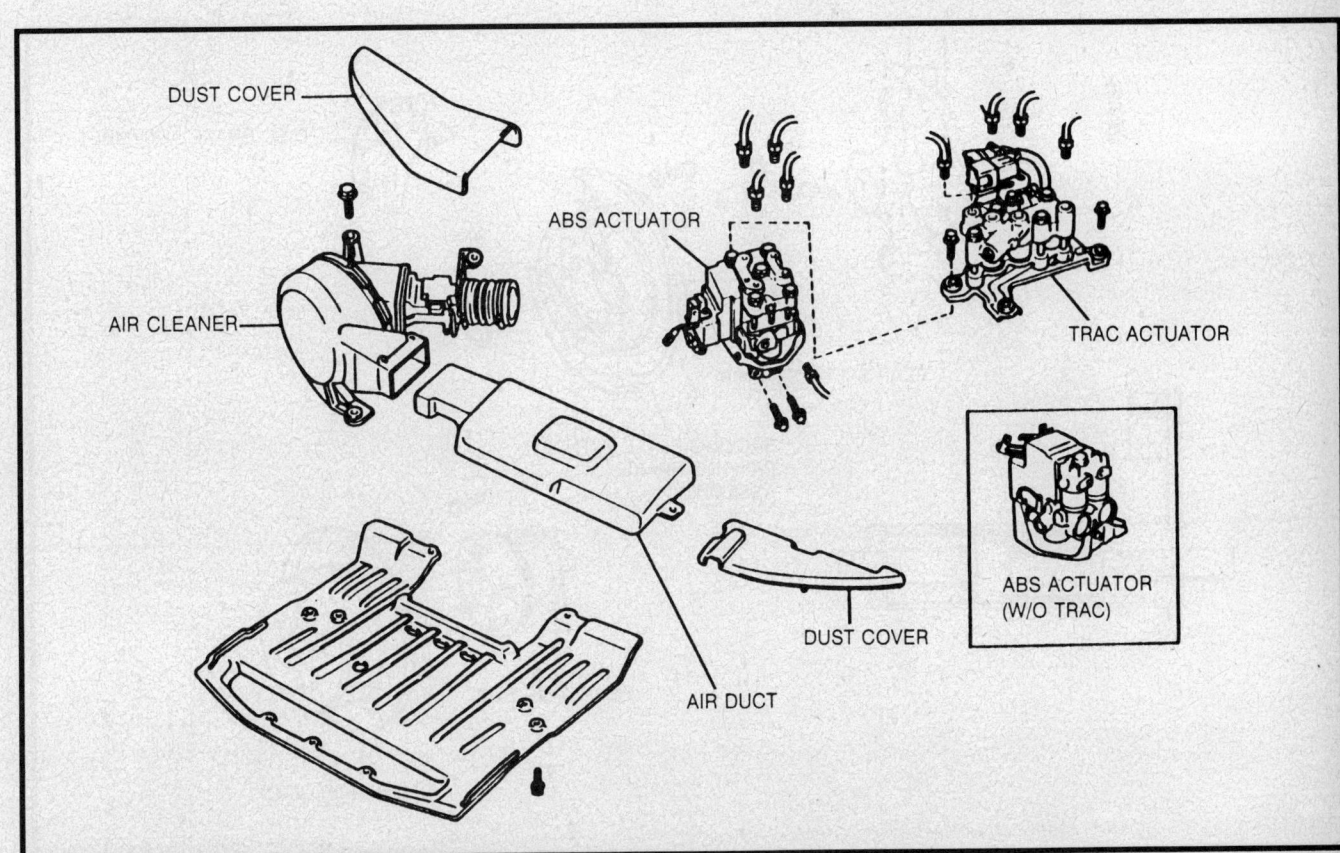

Exploded view of the ABS actuator—LS400

ABS Actuator

Removal and Installation
ES250

1. Disconnect the negative battery cable. Remove brake fluid using a proper syringe.
2. Remove the actuator cover and disconnect the connectors from the actuator.
3. Remove the cover bracket and stud bolt.
4. Disconnect the brake tubes from the actuator, mounting nuts, wave washers and washers.
5. Remove the actuator from the actuator bracket.

To install:

6. Install the actuator to the actuator bracket. Replace the washers, wave washers and tighten the mounting nuts to 48 inch lbs.
7. Connect the brake tubes to the actuator with the proper tool and tighten to 11 ft. lbs.
8. Connect the connectors to the actuator. Install the stud and bracket.
9. Install the actuator cover.
10. Fill the brake reservoir to the proper level and bleed the brake system.
11. Connect the negative battery cable. Check for leaks.

LS400

1. Disconnect the negative battery cable. Remove brake fluid using a proper syringe.
2. Disconnect the dust cover, air cleaner and the air duct.
3. Disconnect the brake line from the ABS, actuator with the proper tool. Disconnect the brake lines from the TRAC actuator, if equipped.

4. Remove the mounting bolts from the ABS actuator or TRAC actuator, if equipped.
5. Disconnect the connectors and remove the actuator.

To install:

6. Install the ABS actuator or TRAC actuator, if equipped. Tighten the mounting bolts to 9 ft. lbs. Connect the actuator connectors.
7. Using the proper tool, connect the brake lines to the actuator and tighten to 11 ft. lbs.
8. Connect the dust cover, air cleaner and the air duct.
9. Bleed the brake system and connect the negative battery cable.
10. Check for leaks.

Front Speed Sensor

Removal and Installation
ES250

1. Disconnect the negative battery cable.
1. Raise and safely support the vehicle. Remove the tire and wheel assembly.
2. Disconnect the speed sensor connector.
3. Remove the front hub and steering knuckle assembly.
4. Remove the nut and the speed sensor rotor. Do not scratch the serrations of the speed sensor rotor.
5. The installation is the reverse of the removal procedure.

LS400

1. Disconnect the negative battery cable.
2. Raise and safely support the vehicle. Remove the tire and wheel assembly.
3. Disconnect the speed sensor connector.

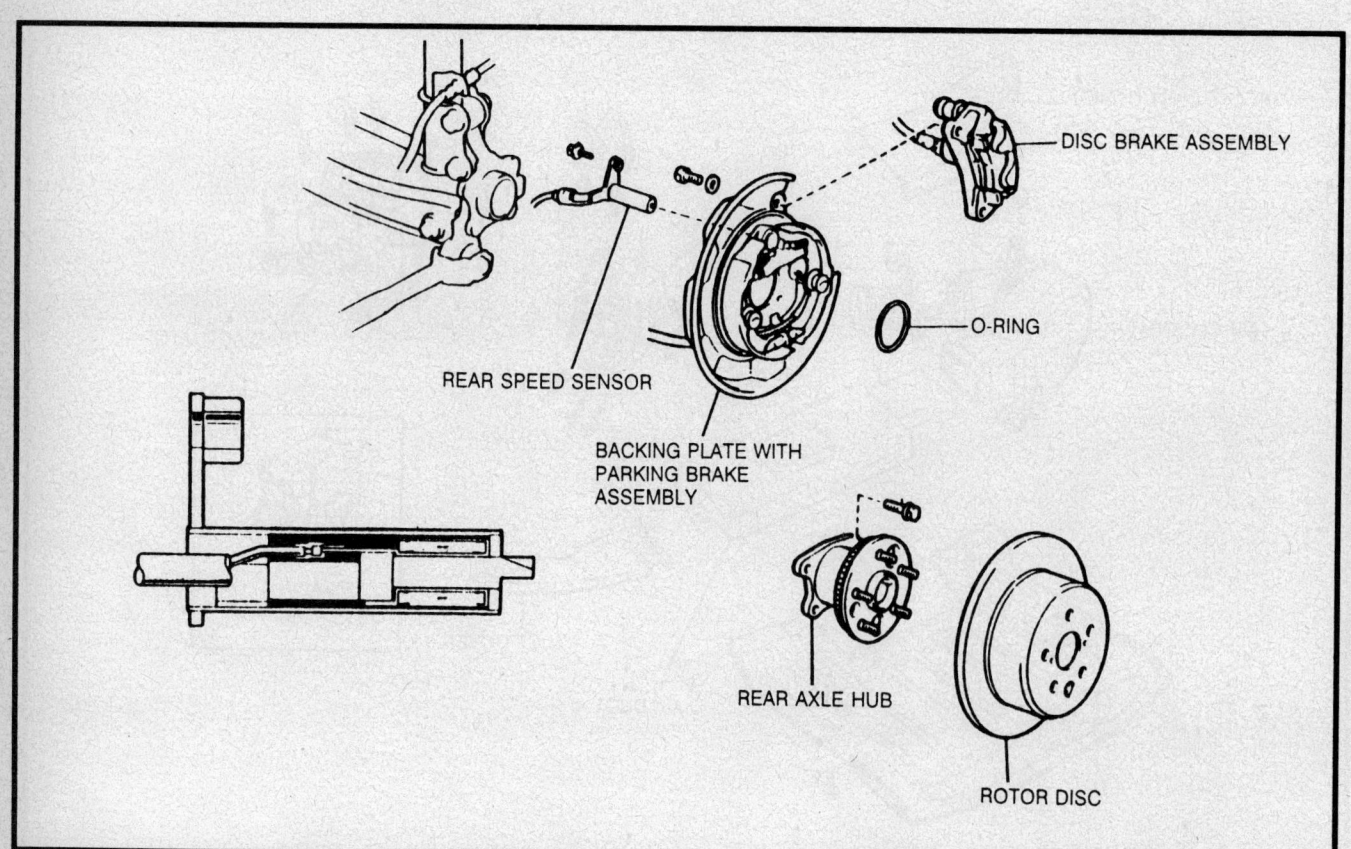

DISC BRAKE ASSEMBLY

O-RING

REAR SPEED SENSOR

BACKING PLATE WITH
PARKING BRAKE
ASSEMBLY

REAR AXLE HUB

ROTOR DISC

Exploded view of the ABS rear wheel speed sensor

4. Remove the front axle hub from the steering knuckle. Remove the sensor control rotor from the axle hub with the proper tool.

5. The installation is the reverse of the removal procedure.

Rear Speed Sensor

Removal and Installation

1. Disconnect the negative battery cable.

2. Raise and safely support the vehicle. Remove the tire and wheel assembly.

3. Disconnect the speed sensor connector.

4. Remove the rear axle hub and backing plate.

5. Remove the mounting bolts and the speed sensor from the backing plate.

6. The installation is the reverse of the removal procedure.

FRONT SUSPENSION

Shock Absorbers

Removal and Installation

LS400

1. Raise and safely support the vehicle. Remove the tire and wheel assembly.

2. Remove the steering knuckle from the upper ball joint with the proper tool. Support the steering knuckle using a piece of wire.

3. Disconnect the shock assembly from the lower shock bracket. Remove the plug from the upper shock mount.

4. Loosen the nut on the middle of the shock mount support. Do not remove it.

5. Remove the other 3 mounting nuts and remove the shock assembly with the coil spring from the vehicle.

6. The installation is the reverse of the removal procedure. Tighten the upper shock mount nuts to 27 ft. lbs. and the lower shock mount nut to 106 ft. lbs.

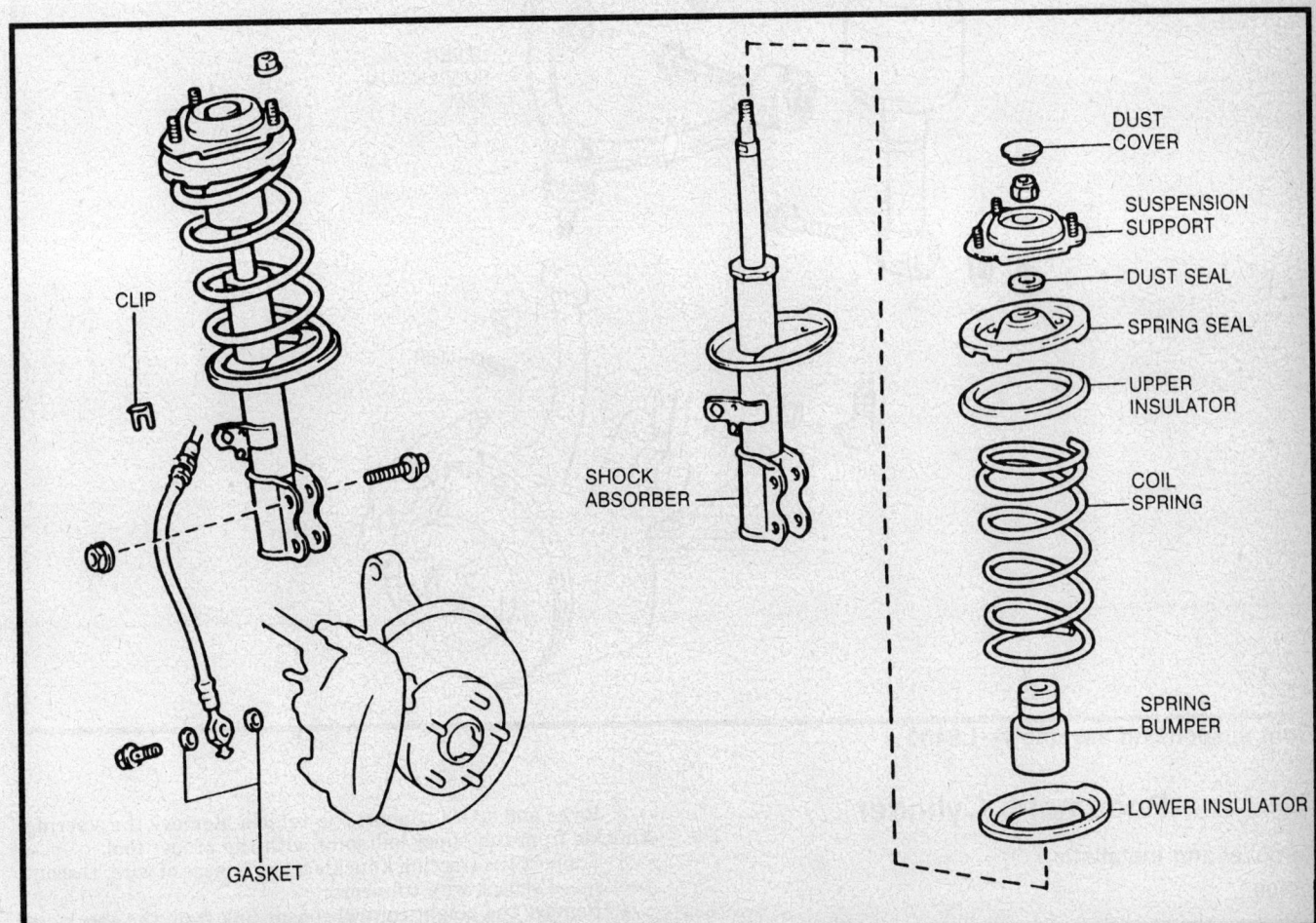

CLIP

SHOCK ABSORBER

GASKET

DUST COVER

SUSPENSION SUPPORT

DUST SEAL

SPRING SEAL

UPPER INSULATOR

COIL SPRING

SPRING BUMPER

LOWER INSULATOR

Front strut assembly—ES250

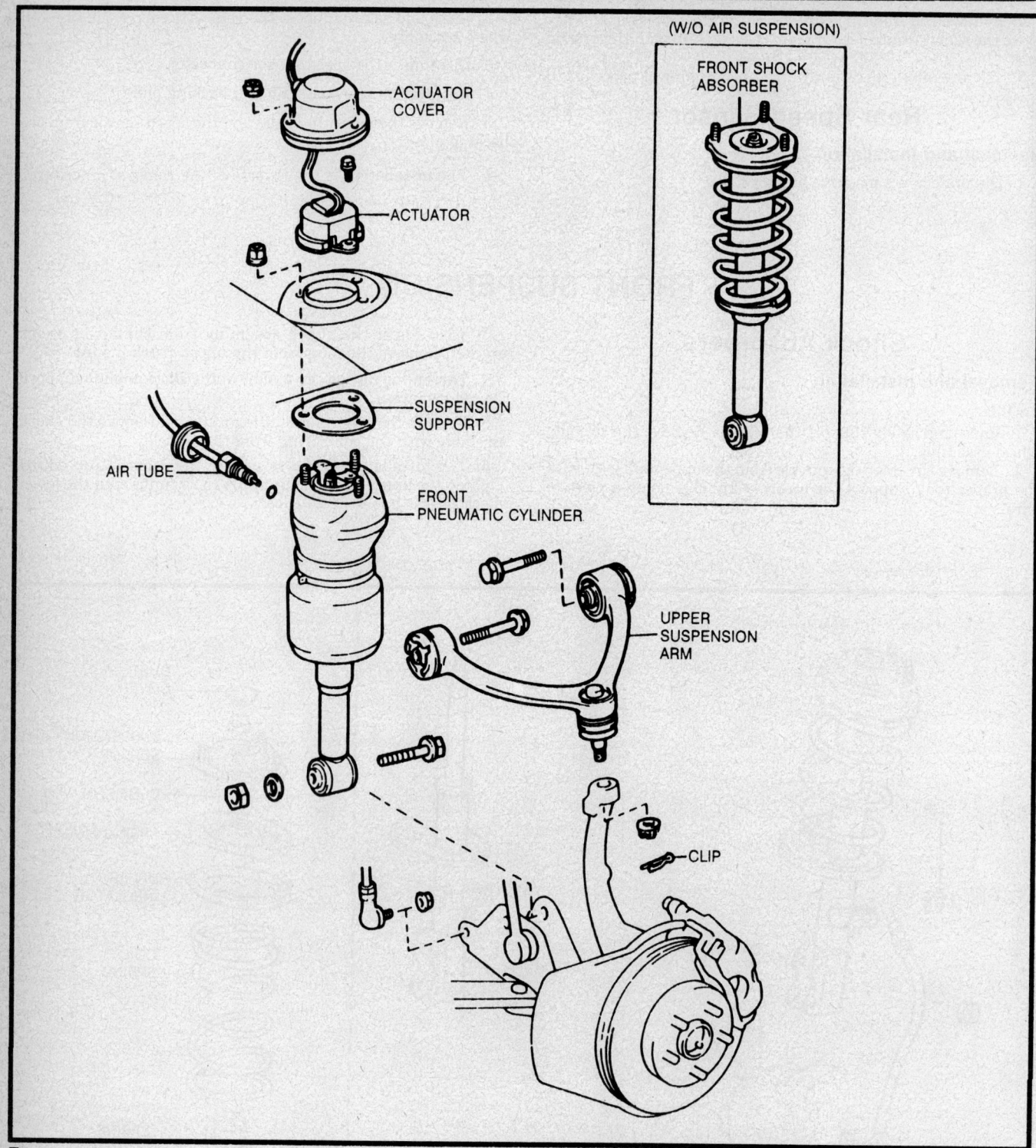

Front suspension assembly—LS400

Pneumatic Cylinder

Removal and Installation

LS400

1. Move the height control switch, located in the trunk area to the **OFF** position.

2. Raise and safely support the vehicle. Remove the steering knuckle from the upper ball joint with the proper tool.

3. Support the steering knuckle using a piece of wire. Disconnect speed sensor wire connector.

4. Remove the height control sensor link from the shock absorber lower bracket.

5. Disconnect the shock absorber from the lower mounting

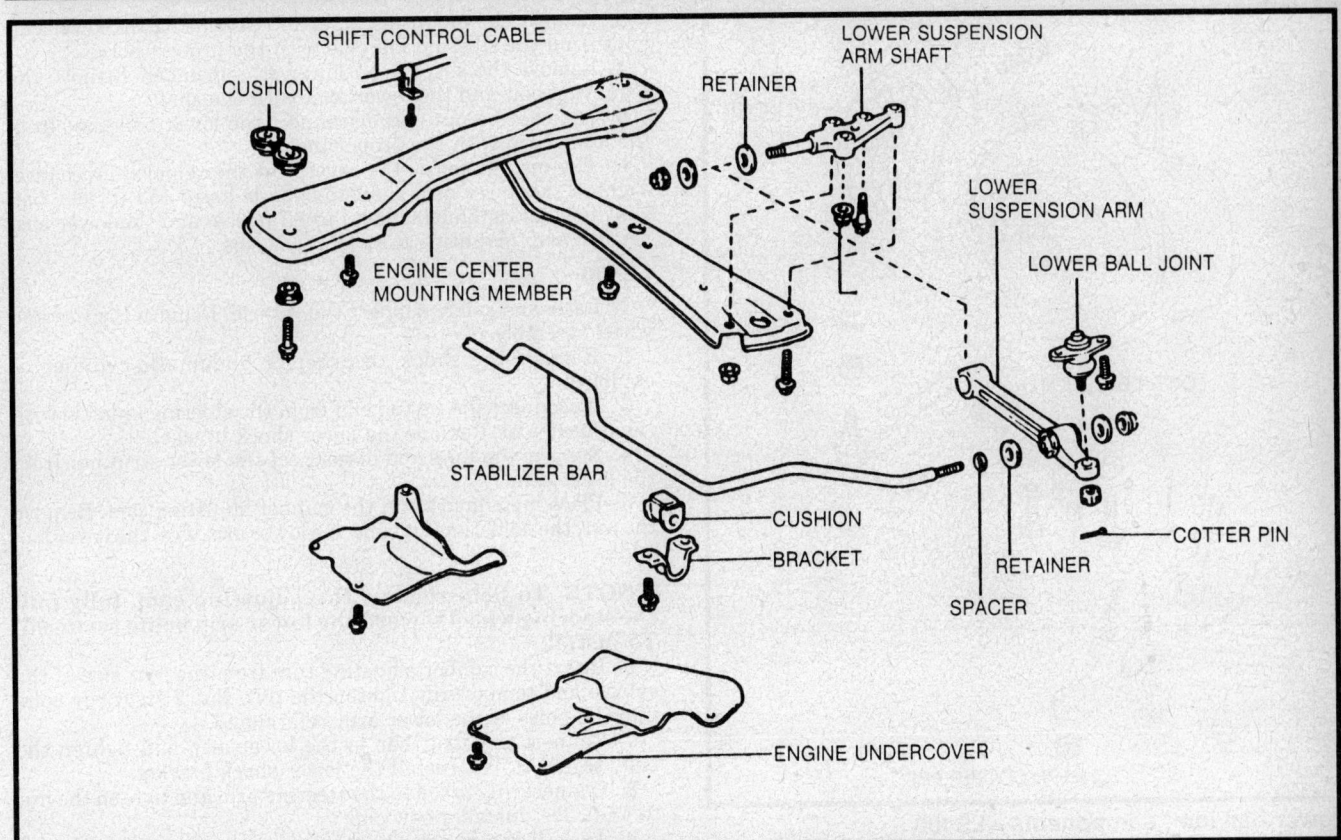

Front suspension components—ES250

bracket. Remove the grommet and disconnect the air tube from the shock absorber.

6. Remove the mounting bolts and the actuator cover. Remove the mounting bolts and the actuator.

7. Remove the 3 upper mounting nuts and remove the shock absorber from the vehicle.

8. The installation is the reverse of the removal procedure. Tighten the upper mounting nuts to 27 ft. lbs., actuator cover mounting nuts to 27 ft. lbs. and the lower shock mount nut to 106 ft. lbs.

MacPherson Strut

Removal and Installation

ES250

1. Raise and safely support the vehicle. Remove the tire and wheel assembly.

2. Disconnect the ABS speed sensor connector. Disconnect the brake hose from the brake caliper.

3. Disconnect the steering knuckle and the strut assembly from the lower mount.

4. Remove the upper mounting nuts from the top suspension mount and remove the strut assembly.

5. The installation is the reverse of the removal procedure. Tighten the upper strut mount nuts to 47 ft. lbs. and the lower strut mount nuts to 224 ft. lbs.

Lower Ball Joints

Inspection

1. Raise and safely support the vehicle. Place a wooden block under the tire and wheel assembly.

2. Lower the jacking device until there is about ½ the load on the front spring.

3. Make sure the front wheels are in a straight forward position and block the wheel with wheel chocks.

4. Move the lower arm up and down and check that the ball joint has no excessive play. The ball joint vertical play limit is 0 in. (0mm) on the ES250 or 0.012 in. (0.3mm) on the LS400.

Removal and Installation

ES250

1. Raise and safely support the vehicle. Remove the tire and wheel assembly.

2. Loosen the nut holding the stabilizer bar to the lower suspension arm.

3. Loosen the nut holding the lower suspension arm to the lower suspension arm shaft.

4. Disconnect thew lower ball joint from the lower suspension arm with the proper tool.

5. Remove the mounting bolts and using a suitable prybar, push down the lower suspension arm, the remove the ball joint.

6. The installation is the reverse of the removal procedure. Tighten the ball joint mounting bolts to 83 ft. lbs., the castle nut to 90 ft. lbs., the stabilizer bar—lower suspension arm nuts to 156 ft. lbs. and the lower arm shaft—lower suspension arm nuts to 156 ft. lbs.

7. Check the front wheel alignment.

LS400

1. If equipped with air suspension, move the height control switch, located in the trunk area to the **OFF** position.

2. Raise and safely support the vehicle. Remove the tire and wheel assembly.

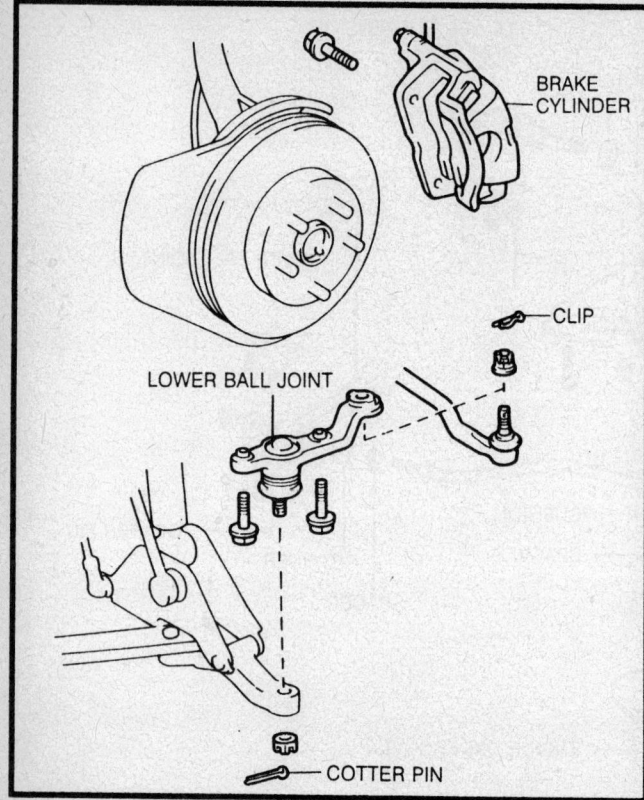

Lower ball joint components—LS400

3. Disconnect the brake caliper and support, using a piece of wire.

4. Loosen the lower mounting bolts. Do not remove.

5. Disconnect the tie rod end from the steering arm with the proper tool. Remove the bolts and disconnect the lower ball joint from the steering knuckle.

6. Remove the nut and disconnect the lower ball joint from the lower arm with the proper tool.

7. The installation is the reverse of the removal procedure. Tighten the ball joint castle nut to 112 ft. lbs., the tie rod end nut to 43 ft. lbs. and the lower ball joint bolts to 83 ft. lbs.

Upper Control Arms

Removal and Installation

LS400

1. Raise and safely support the vehicle. Remove the tire and wheel assembly.

2. Remove the shock absorber or pneumatic cylinder, if equipped.

3. Remove the mounting bolts and the upper suspension arm.

4. Install the upper suspension arm and tighten the mounting bolts to 83 ft. lbs.

5. Reverse the remainder of the procedures for installation.

Lower Control Arms

Removal and Installation

ES250

1. Raise and safely support the vehicle.

2. Remove the nut holding the stabilizer to the lower suspension arm. Remove the nut holding the lower suspension arm to the lower suspension arm shaft.

3. Remove the mounting bolts and disconnect the lower ball joint from the steering knuckle with the proper tool.

4. Remove the suspension lower crossmember. Remove the mounting bolt and the lower arm with the shaft.

5. Remove the nut and disconnect the lower ball joint from the lower arm with the proper tool.

6. The installation is the reverse of the removal procedure. Tighten the lower arm shaft-to-body bolts to 153 ft. lbs., ball joint-to-steering knuckle bolts to 83 ft. lbs. and the lower suspension arm mounting nuts to 156 ft. lbs.

LS400

1. Raise and safely support the vehicle. Remove the tire and wheel assembly.

2. Remove the shock absorber or pneumatic cylinder, if equipped.

3. Disconnect the tie rod end from the steering knuckle with the proper tool. Remove the lower shock bracket.

4. Remove the nuts and disconnect the lower strut bar from the lower arm.

5. Place matchmarks on the camber adjusting cam. Remove the nut, the adjusting cam and the lower arm with the lower ball joint.

NOTE: To help remove the adjusting cam, fully pull the steering wheel toward the lower arm being removed. To install:

6. Insert the camber adjusting cam from the rear side of the vehicle and temporarily tighten the nut. Put 2 strut bar bolts into the holes of the lower arm beforehand.

7. Connect the strut bar to the lower arm and tighten the bolts to 121 ft. lbs. Install the lower shock bracket.

8. Connect the tie rod to the steering arm and tighten the nut to 43 ft. lbs. Install a new clip.

9. Install the shock absorber or pneumatic cylinder, if equipped.

10. Install the steering knuckle with the axle hub. Replace the tire and wheel assembly.

11. Lower the vehicle and stabilize the suspension.

12. Support the lower arm with a suitable jacking device and remove the tire and wheel assembly.

13. Align the matchmarks and tighten the nut to 185 ft. lbs. Replace the tire and wheel assembly. Remove the jacking device.

14. Check the front end alignment.

Sway Bar

Removal and Installation

ES250

1. Raise and safely support the vehicle. Remove the suspension lower crossmember.

2. Remove the mounting nuts and retainers holding the suspension bar to the lower suspension arms.

3. Remove the stabilizer bar brackets.

4. Remove the 2 engine undercovers and the automatic transaxle control cables from the engine center mounting member.

5. Remove the bolts and lower the engine center mounting member. Pull the stabilizer bar from the suspension arms.

6. Remove the retainers and the spacers from the stabilizer bar.

7. The installation is the reverse of the removal procedure. Tighten the stabilizer bar brackets to 94 ft. lbs., the engine center mounting member to 29–32 ft. lbs., the lower crossmember to 153 ft. lbs. and the stabilizer bar mounting nuts to 156 ft. lbs.

8. Check the front wheel alignment.

LS400

1. Raise and safely support the vehicle. Remove the steering knuckle with the axle hub.

2. Remove the shock absorber or pneumatic cylinder, if equipped.

3. Remove the stabilizer bar links and the lower shock bracket.

4. Disconnect the strut bar from the lower arm and remove the strut bar and cushion.

5. Remove the stabilizer bar bushings.

6. Remove the strut bar bracket and the stabilizer bar.

7. The installation is the reverse of the removal procedure. Tighten the strut bar bracket bolts to 53 ft. lbs., the strut bar cushion bolts to 59 ft. lbs. and stabilizer links to 70 ft. lbs.

Front Wheel Bearings

Removal and Installation

LS400

1. Raise and safely support the vehicle. Remove the tire and wheel assembly.

2. Remove the steering knuckle with the axle hub. Remove the nut and the speed sensor rotor.

3. Remove the 4 bolts and shift the brake dust cover towards the hub side (outside). Remove the axle shaft from the steering knuckle with the proper tool.

4. Using the proper tool, remove the inner race (outside) from the axle shaft. Pry out the oil seal from the steering knuckle with the proper tool.

5. Remove the snapring and press out the bearing from the steering knuckle with the proper tools.

To install:

6. Using the proper tool, press the new bearing into the steering knuckle. Install the snapring, using suitable snapring pliers.

7. Install the inner race (outside) and press in the new oil seal until it is flush with the end surface of the steering knuckle.

8. Install the brake dust cover to the steering knuckle. Press the axle hub to the steering knuckle with the proper tool.

9. Install the speed sensor rotor and the steering knuckle.

10. Replace the tire and wheel assembly. Lower the vehicle.

REAR SUSPENSION

Shock Absorbers

Removal and Installation

LS400

1. Remove the rear seat cushion and seat back. Remove the rear scuff plates and the roof side inner trim panel and the speaker panel.

2. Raise and safely support the vehicle. Remove the tire and wheel assembly.

3. Remove the rear halfshaft and disconnect the stabilizer links.

4. Disconnect and support the brake caliper. Do not disconnect the brake line.

5. Remove the nut on the lower side of the shock. Do not remove the bolt.

6. Support the rear axle assembly with a suitable jacking device. Remove the 3 nuts and the shock absorber cap.

7. Loosen the nut in the middle of the suspension support. Do not remove it.

8. Remove the other 3 mounting bolts. Lower the rear axle assembly and remove the bolt on the lower side of the shock assembly.

9. Remove the shock absorber with the coil spring.

To install:

10. Install the shock absorber with the coil spring to the vehicle and tighten the nuts to 47 ft. lbs. Tighten the nut in the middle of the suspension support to 20 ft. lbs.

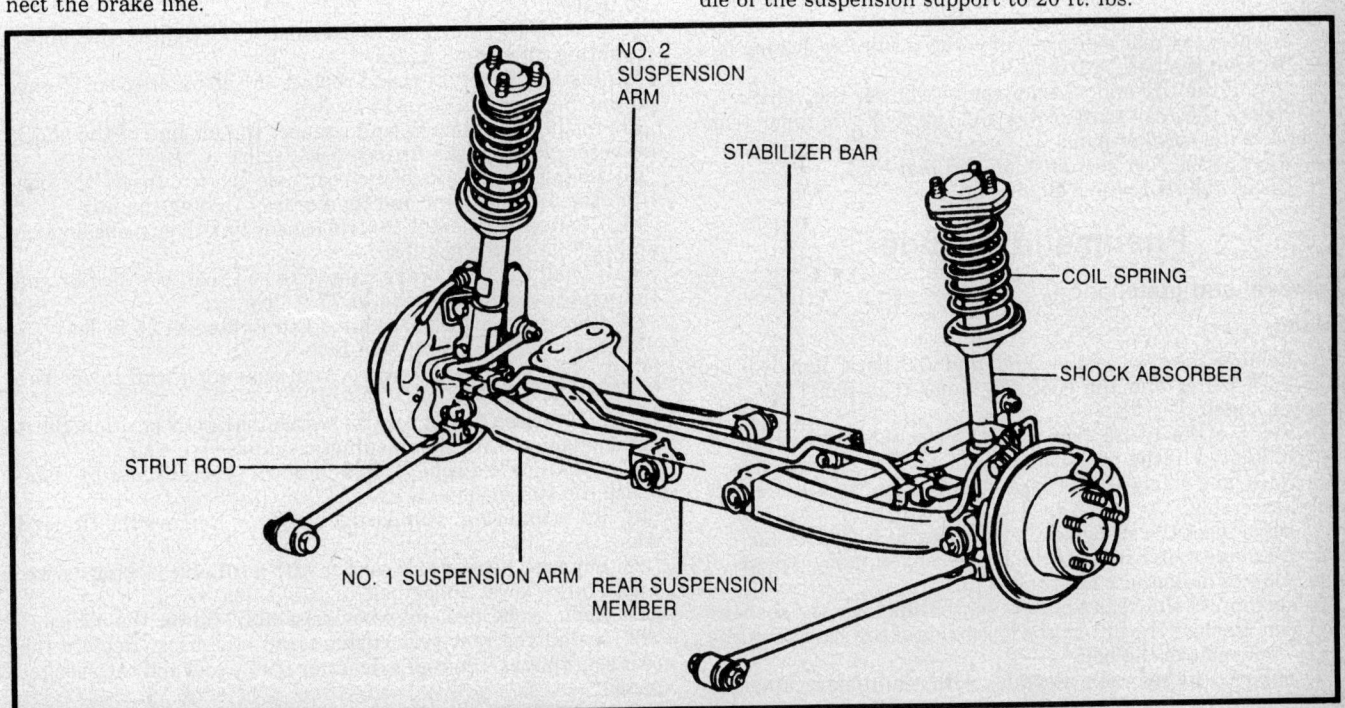

Rear suspension—ES250

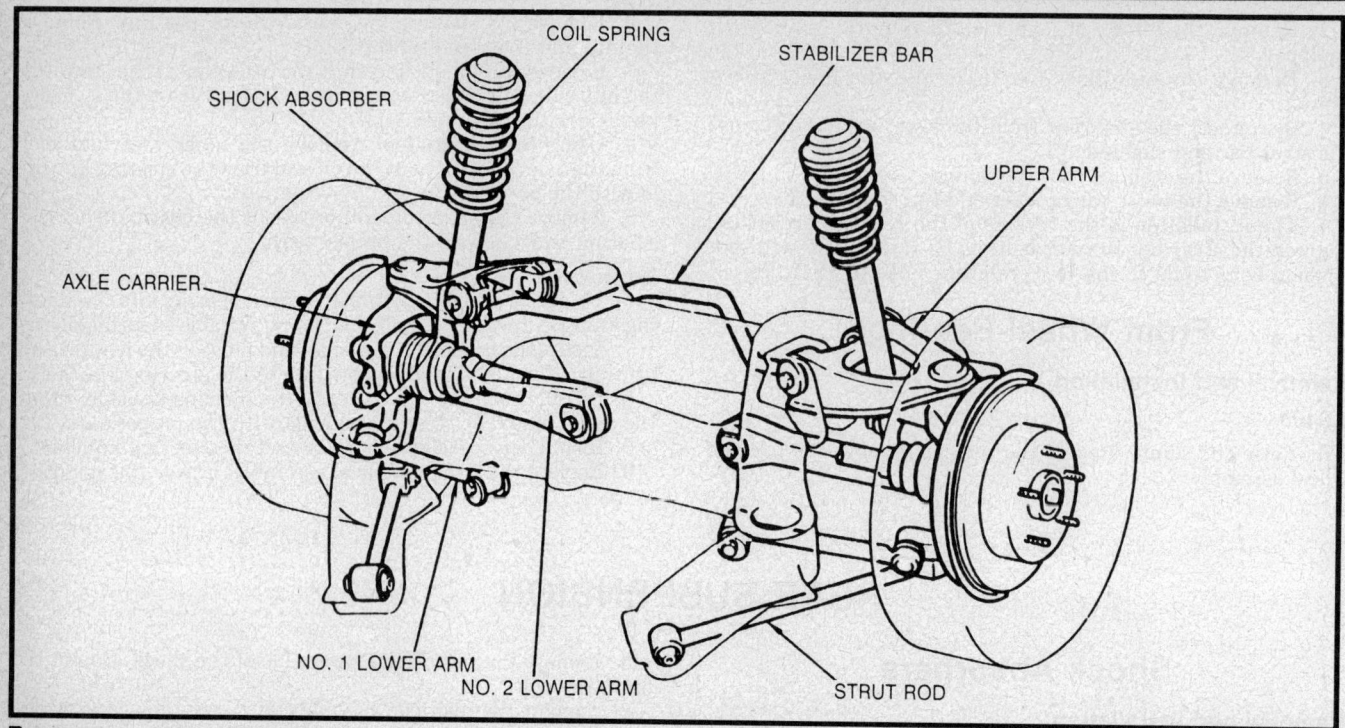

Rear suspension—LS400

11. Install the shock to the rear axle carrier. Install the bolt from the rear of the vehicle and temporarily tighten the nut.

12. Install the brake caliper and tighten the mounting bolts to 77 ft. lbs. Connect the stabilizer links and tighten to 26 ft. lbs.

13. Install the rear halfshaft. Replace the tire and wheel assembly. Lower the vehicle.

14. Bounce the vehicle up and down to stabilize the suspension.

15. Raise and safely support the vehicle. Remove the tire and wheel assembly.

16. Support the rear axle assembly with a suitable jacking device. Tighten the bolt to 101 ft. lbs.

17. Install the tire and wheel assembly. Lower the vehicle.

18. Relace the rear scuff plates and the roof side inner trim panel and the speaker panel.

19. Replace the rear seat cushion and seat back.

20. Check the rear wheel alignment.

Pneumatic Cylinder

Removal and Installation

LS400

1. Remove the rear seat cushion and seat back. Remove the rear scuff plates and the roof side inner trim panel and the speaker panel.

2. Remove the trunk trim panel. Move the height control switch, located in the trunk area to the **OFF** position.

3. Raise and safely support the vehicle. Remove the tire and wheel assembly.

4. Disconnect the stabilizer links from the stabilizer bar.

5. Disconnect and support the brake caliper, using a piece of wire. Do not disconnect the brake line.

6. Disconnect the height control sensor link from the suspension arm. Remove the nut on the lower side of the shock absorber. Do not remove the bolt.

7. Support the rear axle assembly with a suitable jacking device. Remove the grommet and disconnect the air tube from the shock absorber.

8. Remove the mounting bolts and the actuator cover. Remove the mounting bolts and the actuator.

9. Remove the upper mounting nuts and lower the rear axle assembly. Remove the bolt on the lower side of the shock absorber.

10. Remove the shock absorber.

To install:

11. Install the shock to the vehicle and tighten the upper mounting nuts to 43 ft. lbs.

12. Install the actuator and replace the actuator cover. Tighten the mounting nuts to 13 ft. lbs.

13. Install new O-rings and connect the air line to the shock absorber. Tighten the fitting to 13 ft. lbs.

14. Install the shock to the rear axle carrier. Insert the bolt from the vehicle's rear and temporarily tighten the nut.

15. Connect the height control sensor link to suspension arm and tighten to 48 inch lbs.

16. Install the rear brake caliper to the rear axle carrier and tighten the mounting bolts to 77 ft. lbs.

17. Connect the stabilizer links and tighten to 26 ft. lbs.

18. Stabilize the suspension by:

   a. Install the tire and wheel assembly and lower the vehicle.

   b. Move the height control switch to the **ON** position. Start the engine an fill the pneumatic cylinder with air.

   c. Bounce the vehicle up and down several times to stabilize the suspension.

19. Raise and safely support the vehicle. Remove the tire and wheel assembly.

20. Support the rear axle carrier with a suitable jacking device. Tighten the lower shock bolt to 101 ft. lbs.

21. Replace the tire and wheel assembly. Lower the vehicle.

22. Install the rear seat cushion and seat back. Replace the rear scuff plates, the roof side inner trim panel and the speaker panel.

23. Install the trunk trim panel. Check the rear wheel alignment.

MacPherson Strut

Removal and Installation

LS250

1. Raise and safely support the vehicle. Remove the tire and wheel assembly.
2. Disconnect and plug the brake line from the strut assembly.
3. Disconnect the stabilizer link from the strut assembly.
4. Remove the rear seat back and package tray trim. Remove the dust cover from the upper suspension support. Loosen the nut but do not remove.
5. Remove the strut mounting bolts and disconnect the strut assembly. Remove the upper mounting bolts and remove the strut assembly.
6. The installation is the reverse of the removal procedure. Tighten the upper mounting bolts to 29 ft. lbs., lower strut-to-axle bolts to 166 ft. lbs., upper center mounting nut to 36 ft. lbs. and the stabilizer link top 47 ft. lbs.

Rear Control Arms

Removal and Installation

LS400

Upper

1. Raise and safely support the vehicle. Remove the tire and wheel assembly.
2. Remove the rear axle carrier with the upper arm assembly.
3. Install the axle carrier in a suitable holding fixture.

4. Disconnect the upper control arm from the axle carrier.
5. The installation is the reverse of the removal procedure. Tighten the upper arm-to-axle bolt to 80 ft. lbs.

Rear Wheel Bearings

Removal and Installation

ES250

1. Raise and safely support the vehicle. Remove the tire and wheel assembly.
2. Remove the rear brakes and rotor assembly.
3. Remove the axle hub mounting bolts and remove the axle hub with the parking brake assembly.
4. Using the proper tool, unstake the locknut and remove.
5. Push the rear axle shaft off the axle hub with the proper tool. Remove the bearing inner race (inside) with the proper tool.
6. Using the proper tool, pull off the bearing inner race (outside) from the axle shaft. Remove the oil seal.
7. Install the inner race (outside) of the bearing to be removed, using the proper tool, press out the bearing.

NOTE: Always replace the bearing as an assembly.

To install:
8. Apply a suitable multi-purpose grease to the outer race of a new bearing. Press the bearing into the axle hub with the proper tool.
9. Install a new bearing inner race (outside) and drive in a new oil seal with the proper tool. Apply a suitable multi-purpose grease to the seal lip.

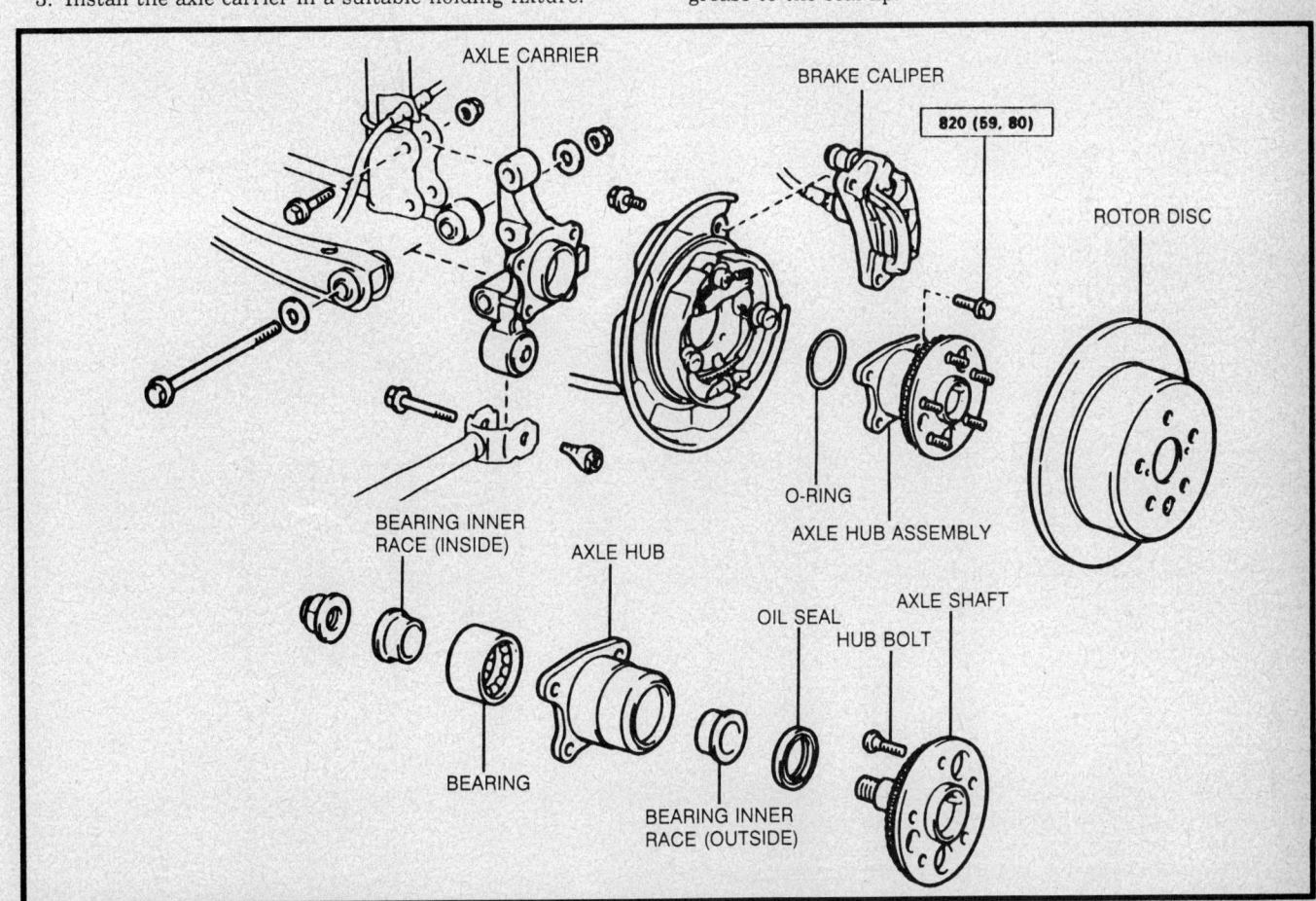

Rear axle bearing assembly—ES250

10. Install a new bearing inner race (inside) and press the inner races onto the axle shaft, using the proper tool. Install and tighten the locknut to 90 ft. lbs. Stake the nut.

11. Install the parking brake assembly and a new oil seal to the axle carrier.

12. Install the axle hub and tighten the bolts to 59. lbs.

13. Install the tire and wheel assembly. Lower the vehicle.

Rear Axle Assembly

Removal and Installation

ES250

1. Raise and safely support the vehicle. Remove the tire and wheel assembly.

2. Remove the rear brakes and rotor assembly.

3. Remove the axle hub mounting bolts and remove the axle hub with the parking brake assembly. Remove the O-ring from the axle carrier.

NOTE: Be careful not to damage the sensor control rotor.

4. Remove the strut rod nut and bolt from the axle carrier. Remove the suspension arm mounting bolts from the axle carrier.

5. Supporting the axle carrier, remove the axle carrier mounting bolt and nut from the strut assembly. Remove the axle carrier assembly.

To install:

6. Place the axle carrier into position.

7. Install the axle carrier mounting bolt and nut to the strut assembly. Tighten to 166 ft. lbs.

8. Temporarily, connect the suspension arms to axle carrier. Temporarily, connect the strut rod to the axle carrier.

9. Install the parking brake assembly and a new oil seal to the axle carrier.

10. Install the axle hub and tighten the mounting bolts to 59 ft. lbs.

11. Install the rotor and disc brake assembly. Stabilize the suspension.

12. Tighten the axle carrier-to strut rod mounting bolts to 83 ft. lbs. and the suspension arm-to- axle carrier bolts to 134 ft. lbs. Tighten with the vehicle weight on the supension.

13. Check the rear wheel alignment.

SERIAL NUMBER IDENTIFICATION

Vehicle Identification Plate

The serial number is on a plate located on the driver's side windshield pillar and is visible through the glass.

A Vehicle Identification Number (VIN) plate, bearing the serial number and other data, is attached to the cowl.

Engine Number

The engine number is located on a plate which is attached to the engine housing, just behind or below the distributor or on a machined pad at the right front side of the engine block.

The engine number consists of an identification number followed by a 6-digit production number.

The 626, MX-6 and RX-7 engine serial number is located on the rear of the alternator bracket, stamped on the engine block. The 323 and Protege engine serial number is stamped on the left side of the engine block, just below the cylinder head. The 929 engine serial number is stamped on the cylinder block, just below the distributor. The Miata engine serial number is stamped on the cylinder block, right in front of the intake manifold.

Vehicle Identification Label

In addition to the serial numbers, other important vehicle information and specifications can be found on the underhood emission sticker, vacuum hose routing diagram, tire pressure label and motor vehicle safety certification label.

Transmission/Transaxle Number

The transmission/transaxle model and serial number are either stamped on a plate that is bolted to the transmission case or stamped directly on the case. The location varies from model-to-model.

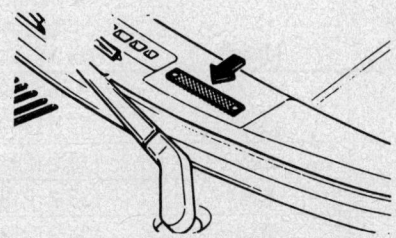

Vehicle identification plate location

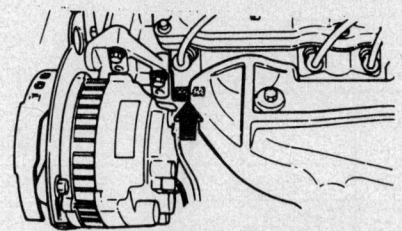

Engine number location

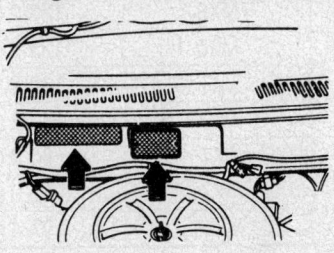

Chassis number (left) and model plate (right) location

SPECIFICATIONS

ENGINE IDENTIFICATION

Year	Model	Engine Displacement cu. in. (cc/liter)	Engine Series Identification	No. of Cylinders	Engine Type
1987	323	97.4 (1597/1.6)	B6	4	SOHC
	626	121.9 (1998/2.0)	FE	4	SOHC
	626	121.9 (1998/2.0)	FE	4	SOHC-Turbo
	RX7	80.0 (1308/1.3)	13B	—	Rotary
	RX7	80.0 (1308/1.3)	13B	—	Rotary-Turbo
1988	323	97.4 (1597/1.6)	B6	4	SOHC
	323	97.4 (1597/1.6)	B6	4	DOHC
	626	133.2 (2184/2.1)	F2	4	SOHC
	626	133.2 (2184/2.1)	F2	4	SOHC-Turbo
	MX6	133.2 (2184/2.1)	F2	4	SOHC
	MX6	133.2 (2184/2.1)	F2	4	SOHC-Turbo
	RX7	80.0 (1308/1.3)	13B	—	Rotary
	RX7	80.0 (1308/1.3)	13B	—	Rotary-Turbo
	929	180.2 (2954/2.9)	JE	6	DOHC

ENGINE IDENTIFICATION

Year	Model	Engine Displacement cu. in. (cc/liter)	Engine Series Identification	No. of Cylinders	Engine Type
1989	323	97.4 (1597/1.6)	B6	4	SOHC
	323	97.4 (1597/1.6)	B6	4	DOHC-Turbo
	626	133.2 (2184/2.1)	F2	4	SOHC
	626	133.2 (2184/2.1)	F2	4	SOHC-Turbo
	MX6	133.2 (2184/2.1)	F2	4	SOHC
	MX6	133.2 (2184/2.1)	F2	4	SOHC-Turbo
	RX7	80.0 (1308/1.3)	13B	—	Rotary
	RX7	80.0 (1308/1.3)	13B	—	Rotary-Turbo
	929	180.2 (2954/2.9)	JE	6	SOHC
1990-91	323	97.4 (1597/1.6)	B6	4	SOHC
	Protege	112.2 (1839/1.8)	BP	4	SOHC
	Protege	112.2 (1839/1.8)	BP	4	DOHC
	626	133.2 (2184/2.1)	F2	4	SOHC
	626	133.2 (2184/2.1)	F2	4	SOHC-Turbo
	MX6	133.2 (2184/2.1)	F2	4	SOHC
	MX6	133.2 (2184/2.1)	F2	4	SOHC-Turbo
	929	180.2 (2954/3.0)	JE	6	SOHC
	929	180.2 (2954/3.0)	JE	6	DOHC
	RX7	80.0 (1308/1.3)	13B	—	Rotary
	RX7	80.0 (1308/1.3)	13B	—	Rotary-Turbo
	Miata	97.4 (1597/1.6)	B6	4	DOHC

SOHC Single Overhead Cam
DOHC Double Overhead Cam

GENERAL ENGINE SPECIFICATIONS

Year	Model	Engine Displacement cu. in. (cc)	Fuel System Type	Net Horsepower @ rpm	Net Torque @ rpm (ft. lbs.)	Bore × Stroke (in.)	Compression Ratio	Oil Pressure @ rpm
1987	323	97.4 (1597)	EFI①	82 @ 5000	92 @ 2500	3.07 × 3.29	9.3:1	43–57
	626	121.9 (1998)	EFI	93 @ 5000	115 @ 2500	3.39 × 3.39	8.6:1	43–57
	626 Turbo	121.9 (1998)	EFI	120 @ 5000	115 @ 3000	3.39 × 3.39	7.8:1	43–57
1988	323	97.4 (1597)	EFI	82 @ 5000	92 @ 2500	3.07 × 3.29	9.3:1	50–64
	323 Turbo	97.4 (1597)	EFI	132 @ 6000	136 @ 3000	3.07 × 3.29	7.9:1	50–64
	626	133.2 (2184)	EFI	97 @ 5000	120 @ 2500	3.39 × 3.70	8.6:1	43–57
	626 Turbo	133.2 (2184)	EFI	125 @ 5000	155 @ 3500	3.39 × 3.70	7.8:1	43–57
	MX6	133.2 (2184)	EFI	97 @ 5000	120 @ 2500	3.39 × 3.70	8.6:1	43–57
	MX6 Turbo	133.2 (2184)	EFI	125 @ 5000	155 @ 3500	3.39 × 3.70	7.8:1	43–57
	929	180.2 (2954)	EFI	158 @ 5500	170 @ 4000	3.54 × 3.05	8.5:1	50–64
1989	323	97.4 (1597)	EFI	82 @ 5000	92 @ 2500	3.07 × 3.29	9.3:1②	50–64
	323 Turbo	97.4 (1597)	EFI	132 @ 6000	136 @ 3000	3.07 × 3.29	7.9:1	50–64
	626	133.2 (2184)	EFI	110 @ 4700	130 @ 3000	3.39 × 3.70	8.6:1	43–57

GENERAL ENGINE SPECIFICATIONS

Year	Model	Engine Displacement cu. in. (cc)	Fuel System Type	Net Horsepower @ rpm	Net Torque @ rpm (ft. lbs.)	Bore × Stroke (in.)	Compression Ratio	Oil Pressure @ rpm
1989	626 Turbo	133.2 (2184)	EFI	145 @ 4300	190 @ 3500	3.39 × 3.70	7.8:1	43–57
	MX6	133.2 (2184)	EFI	110 @ 4700	130 @ 3000	3.39 × 3.70	7.8:1	43–57
	MX6 Turbo	133.2 (2184)	EFI	145 @ 4300	110 @ 3500	3.39 × 3.70	8.6:1	43–57
	929	180.2 (2954)	EFI	158 @ 5500	170 @ 4000	3.54 × 3.05	8.5:1	41–61
1990–91	323②	97.4 (1597)	EFI	82 @ 5000	92 @ 2500	3.07 × 3.29	9.3:1②	50–64
	Protege③	112.2 (1839)	EFI	103 @ 5500	111 @ 4000	3.27 × 3.35	8.9:1	
	626	133.2 (2184)	EFI	110 @ 4700	130 @ 3000	3.39 × 3.70	8.6:1	43–57
	626 Turbo	133.2 (2184)	EFI	145 @ 4300	190 @ 3500	3.39 × 3.70	7.8:1	43–57
	MX6	133.2 (2184)	EFI	110 @ 4700	130 @ 3000	3.39 × 3.70	8.6:1	43–57
	MX6 Turbo	133.2 (2184)	EFI	145 @ 4300	190 @ 3500	3.39 × 3.70	7.8:1	43–57
	929②	180.2 (2954)	EFI	158 @ 5500	170 @ 4000	3.54 × 3.05	8.5:1	53–75
	929③	180.2 (2954)	EFI	190 @ 5600	191 @ 4500	3.54 × 3.05	8.5:1	45.5–71.1
	Miata③	97.4 (1597)	EFI	116 @ 6500	100 @ 5500	3.10 × 3.30	9.4:1	43–57

NA Not available
DFI Diesel Fuel Injection
EFI Electronic Fuel Injection
① Canadian models use 2 bbl carburetor
② SOHC engine
③ DOHC engine

GENERAL ENGINE SPECIFICATIONS—ROTARY ENGINE

Year	Model	Engine Displacement cu. in. (cc)	Fuel System Type	Net Horsepower @ rpm	Net Torque @ rpm (ft. lbs.)	Rotor Displacement (cu. in.)	Compression Ratio	Oil Pressure @ 3000 rpm
1987	RX7	80 (1308)	EFI	146 @ 6500	138 @ 3500	40	9.4:1	64–78
	Turbo	80 (1308)	EFI	182 @ 6500	183 @ 3500	40	8.5:1	64–78
1988	RX7	80 (1308)	EFI	146 @ 6500	138 @ 3500	40	9.4:1	64–78
	Turbo	80 (1308)	EFI	182 @ 6500	183 @ 3500	40	8.5:1	64–78
1989	RX7	80 (1308)	EFI	146 @ 6500	138 @ 3500	40	8.5:1	64–78
	Turbo	80 (1308)	EFI	182 @ 6500	183 @ 3500	40	9.4:1	64–78
1990–91	RX7	80 (1308)	EFI	160 @ 7000	140 @ 4000	40	9.7:1	64–78
	Turbo	80 (1308)	EFI	200 @ 6500	196 @ 3500	40	9.0:1	64–78

EFI Electronic Fuel Injection

GASOLINE ENGINE TUNE-UP SPECIFICATIONS

Year	Model	Engine Displacement cu. in. (cc)	Spark Plugs Type	Gap (in.)	Ignition Timing (deg.) MT	Ignition Timing (deg.) AT	Compression Pressure (psi)	Fuel Pump (psi)	Idle Speed (rpm) MT	Idle Speed (rpm) AT	Valve Clearance In.	Valve Clearance Ex.
1987	323	97.4 (1597)	BPR5ES-11	0.040	2B①	2B	NA	②	800–900	900–1050	③	③
	626	121.9 (1998)	BPR5ES	0.031	6B	6B	NA	64–85	750	900	③	③
	626 Turbo	121.9 (1998)	BPR6ES	0.031	6B	6B	NA	64–85	750	900	③	③

GASOLINE ENGINE TUNE-UP SPECIFICATIONS

Year	Model	Engine Displacement cu. in. (cc)	Spark Plugs Type	Gap (in.)	Ignition Timing (deg.) MT	AT	Compression Pressure (psi)	Fuel Pump (psi)	Idle Speed (rpm) MT	AT	Valve Clearance In.	Ex.
1988	323	97.4 (1597)	BPR5ES-11 ④	0.040	2B⑤	2B⑤	NA	64–85	850	850	Hyd.	Hyd.
	626	133.2 (2194)	ZFR5A-11	0.040	6B	6B	NA	64–85	750	750	Hyd.	Hyd.
	626 Turbo	133.2 (2184)	ZFR5A-11	0.040	9B	9B	NA	64–85	750	750	Hyd.	Hyd.
	MX6	133.2 (2184)	ZFR5A-11	0.040	6B	6B	NA	64–85	750	750	Hyd.	Hyd.
	MX6 Turbo	133.2 (2184)	ZFR5A-11	0.040	9B	9B	NA	64–85	750	750	Hyd.	Hyd.
	929	180.2 (2954)	ZFR5A-11	0.040	15B	15B	NA	64–85	650	650	Hyd.	Hyd.
1989	323	97.4 (1597)	BPR5ES-11	0.041	2B	2B	135–192	64–85	650	650	Hyd.	Hyd.
	323 Turbo	97.4 (1597)	BCPR-6ES11	0.041	12B	12B	109–156	64–85	850	850	Hyd.	Hyd.
	626	133.2 (2194)	ZFR5A-11	0.041	6B	6B	114–162	64–85	750	750	Hyd.	Hyd.
	626 Turbo	133.2 (2184)	ZFR5A-11	0.041	9B	9B	98–139	64–85	750	750	Hyd.	Hyd.
	MX6	133.2 (2184)	ZFR5A-11	0.041	6B	6B	114–162	64–85	750	750	Hyd.	Hyd.
	MX6 Turbo	133.2 (2184)	ZFR5A-11	0.041	9B	9B	98–139	64–85	750	750	Hyd.	Hyd.
	929	180.2 (2954)	ZFR5A-11	0.041	15B	15B	114–164	64–85	650	650	Hyd.	Hyd.
1990	323⑥	97.4 (1597)	BPR5ES-11	0.041	7B	7B	135–192	64–85	750⑧	750⑧	Hyd.	Hyd.
	Protege⑥	112.2 (1839)	BKR5E-11	0.041	5B	5B	121–173	64–85	750⑧	750⑧	Hyd.	Hyd.
	Protege⑦	112.2 (1839)	BKR5E-11	0.041	10B	10B	128–182	64–85	750	750	Hyd.	Hyd.
	626	133.2 (2184)	ZFR5A-11	0.041	6B	6B	114–162	64–85	750	750	Hyd.	Hyd.
	626 Turbo	133.2 (2184)	ZFR5A-11	0.041	9B	9B	98–139	64–85	750	750	Hyd.	Hyd.
	MX6	133.2 (2184)	ZFR5A-11	0.041	6B	6B	114–162	64–85	750	750	Hyd.	Hyd.
	MX6 Turbo	133.2 (2184)	ZFR5A-11	0.041	9B	9B	98–139	64–85	750	750	Hyd.	Hyd.
	929⑥	180.2 (2954)	ZFR5A-11	0.041	15B	15B	114–164	64–85	650	650	Hyd.	Hyd.
	929⑦	180.2 (2954)	ZFR5A-11	0.041	8B	8B	125–179	64–85	700	700	Hyd.	Hyd.
	Miata⑦	97.4 (1597)	BKR5E-11	0.041	10B	10B	135–192	64–85	850	850	Hyd.	Hyd.
1991†				SEE UNDERHOOD SPECIFICATION STICKER								

NA Not available
B Before top dead center
① 7B with the vacuum hose connected to EFI models
② Carburetor—4.0–5.0 psi
   EFI—64–85 psi
③ Valve side—0.012 in.
   Cam side—0.008 in.
④ DOHC turbocharged engine—DCPR6E11
⑤ DOHC turbocharged engine—12 degrees BTDC
⑥ SOHC engine
⑦ DOHC engine
⑧ Canada—800 rpm

TUNE-UP SPECIFICATIONS—ROTARY ENGINE

Year	Engine Displacement cu. in. (cc)	Spark Plugs Type	Gap (in.)	Distributor	Ignition Timing (degrees) Leading	Trailing	Idle Speed (rpm) MT	AT①
1987	80 (1308)	S-29A② S-31③	0.080	Electronic	5A	20A	750	750
1988	80 (1308)	SD10A② SD11③	0.080	Electronic	5A	20A	750	750

TUNE-UP SPECIFICATIONS—ROTARY ENGINE

Year	Engine Displacement cu. in. (cc)	Spark Plugs Type	Gap (in.)	Distributor	Ignition Timing (degrees) Leading	Ignition Timing (degrees) Trailing	Idle Speed (rpm) MT	Idle Speed (rpm) AT ①
1989	80 (1308)	SD10A② SD11A③	0.080	Electronic	5A	20A	750	750
	80 (1308)	SD10A② SD11A③	0.080	Electronic	5A	20A	750	750
1990-91	80 (1308)	BUR7EQ② BUR9EQ③	0.043-0.067	Electronic	5A	20A	750	750

A After top dead center
① Transmission in Drive
② Leading
③ Trailing

FIRING ORDERS

NOTE: To avoid confusion, always replace spark plug wires one at a time.

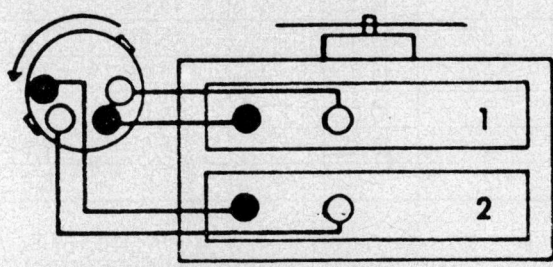

1.3L Rotary Engine
Distributorless Ignition System

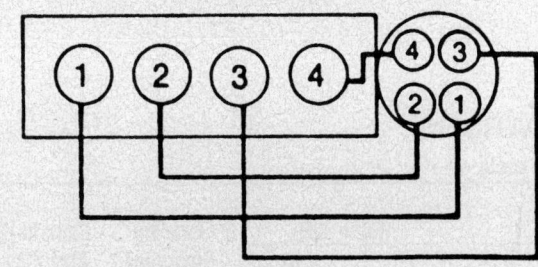

1.6L, 1.8L, 2.0L, 2.1L Engines
Engine Firing Order: 1–3–4–2
Distributor Rotation: Counterclockwise

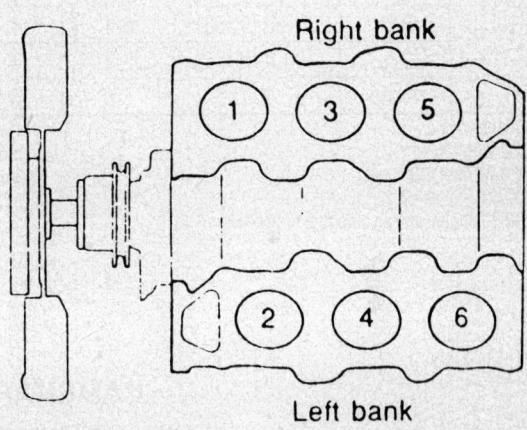

Right bank

Left bank

2.9L Engine
Engine Firing Order: 1–2–3–4–5–6
Distributorless Ignition

CAPACITIES

Year	Model	Engine Displacement cu. in. (cc)	Engine Crankcase (qts.) with Filter	Engine Crankcase (qts.) without Filter	Transmission (pts.) 4-spd	Transmission (pts.) 5-Spd	Transmission (pts.) Auto.	Drive Axle (pts.)	Fuel Tank (gal.)	Cooling System (qts.)
1987	323	97.4 (1597)	3.2	2.9	6.8	6.8	12.0	—	11.9	6.3
	626	121.9 (1998)	5.0	4.5	—	7.0	12.0	—	15.6	7.4
	RX7	80 (1308)	5.0	4.5	—	4.2	15.8	2.8	16.6	9.2

CAPACITIES

Year	Model	Engine Displacement cu. in. (cc)	Engine Crankcase (qts.) with Filter	Engine Crankcase (qts.) without Filter	Transmission (pts.) 4-spd	Transmission (pts.) 5-Spd	Transmission (pts.) Auto.	Drive Axle (pts.)	Fuel Tank (gal.)	Cooling System (qts.)
1988	323	97.4 (1597)	3.6①	3.2①	—	6.8②	13.2	2.8	12.7	5.3③
	626	133.2 (2184)	4.9	4.1	—	7.2⑤	13.2	NA	15.9④	7.9
	MX6	133.2 (2184)	4.9	4.1	—	7.2⑤	13.2	NA	15.9④	7.9
	RX7	80 (1308)	6.1	4.7	—	5.2	15.8	2.8	16.6	9.2⑥
	929	180.2 (2954)	5.7	4.8	—	5.2	15.4	2.8	18.5	9.9
1989	323	97.4 (1597)	3.6①	3.2①	—	7.6⑧⑨	13.4	—	12.7	5.3⑨
	626	133.2 (2184)	4.9	4.1	—	7.0⑤	14.4	—	15.9④	7.9
	MX6	133.2 (2184)	4.9	4.1	—	7.0⑤	14.4	—	15.9④	7.9
	RX7	80 (1308)	6.1	4.7	—	5.2	15.8	1.3	16.6	9.2⑥
	929	180.2 (2954)	5.7	9.8	—	5.2	15.4	—	18.5	9.9④
1990–91	323	97.4 (1597)	3.6①	3.2①	—	7.6	13.4	—	12.7	5.3⑨
	Protege	112.2 (1839)	3.8	3.4	—	7.1	12.2	—	13.2⑩	5.3⑨
	626	133.2 (2184)	4.9	4.1	—	7.0⑤	14.4	—	15.9④	7.9
	MX6	133.2 (2184)	4.9	4.1	—	7.0⑤	14.4	—	15.9④	7.9
	RX7	80 (1308)	6.1	4.7	—	5.2	15.8	1.3	16.6	9.2⑥
	929	180.2 (2954)	5.7	9.8	—	5.2	15.4	—	18.5	9.9④
	Miata	97.4 (1597)	4.0	3.5	—	4.2	—	—	11.9	6.3

① DOHC engine
  3.8 with filter
  3.4 without filter
② DOHC engine—7.2
③ DOHC engine and all automatic transaxle—6.3
④ 4 wheel steering—15.0
⑤ Turbocharged engine—7.8
⑥ Non-turbocharged engine—7.7
⑦ Turbocharged engine—7.6 pts.
⑧ With 4WD
  Transaxle capacity—7.6 pts.
  Transfer carrier capacity—1 pt.
⑨ Automatic—6.3
⑩ Sedan, 14.5 gal.

CAMSHAFT SPECIFICATIONS

All measurements given in inches.

Year	Engine Displacement cu. in. (cc)	Journal Diameter 1	Journal Diameter 2	Journal Diameter 3	Journal Diameter 4	Journal Diameter 5	Lobe Lift In.	Lobe Lift Ex.	Bearing Clearance	Camshaft End Play
1987	97.4 (1597)	1.710–1.711	1.709–1.710	1.709–1.710	1.709–1.710	1.710–1.711	1.439–1.443	1.439–1.443	0.001–0.003 ①	0.002–0.007
	121.9 (1998)	1.257–1.258	1.256–1.257	1.256–1.257	1.256–1.257	1.257–1.258	1.5023	1.5024	0.0014–0.0033 ②	0.003–0.006 ③
1988	97.4 (1597)	1.710–1.711	1.709–1.710	1.709–1.710	1.709–1.710	1.710–1.711	1.434–1.438	1.434–1.438	0.001–0.003 ①	0.002–0.007
	97.4 (1597) ④	1.021–1.022	1.021–1.022	1.021–1.022	1.021–1.022	1.021–1.022	1.6098	1.6098	0.0014–0.0032	0.0028–0.0075
	133.2 (2184)	1.2575–1.2585	1.2563–1.2573	1.2563–1.2573	1.2563–1.2573	1.2575–1.2585	1.6256–1.6295	1.6455–1.6495	0.0014–0.0033 ⑤	0.003–0.006
	180.2 (2954)	1.9268–1.9274	1.9258–1.9266	1.9258–1.9266	1.9258–1.9274	—	1.6163	1.6257	0.0024–0.0035 ⑥	0.002–0.007

CAMSHAFT SPECIFICATIONS

All measurements given in inches.

Year	Engine Displacement cu. in. (cc)	Journal Diameter					Lobe Lift		Bearing Clearance	Camshaft End Play
		1	2	3	4	5	In.	Ex.		
1989	97.4 (1597)	1.710–1.711	1.710–1.711	1.709–1.711	1.710–1.711	1.710–1.711	1.4321–1.4380	1.4321–1.4380	0.0013–0.0045 ①	0.0020–0.0071
	97.4 (1597) ④	1.0213–1.0222	1.0213–1.0222	1.0213–1.0222	1.0213–1.0222	1.0213–1.0222	1.6098	1.6098	0.0014–0.0032	0.0028–0.0075
	133.2 (2184)	1.2575–1.2585	1.2563–1.2573	1.2563–1.2573	1.2563–1.2573	1.2575–1.2585	1.6256–1.6295	1.6197	0.0014–0.0033 ⑤	0.003–0.006
	180.2 (2954)	1.9268–1.9274	1.9258–1.9266	1.9255–1.9266	1.9268–1.9274	—	1.6163	1.6257	0.0024–0.0035 ⑥	0.0020–0.0071
1990-91	97.4 (1597)	1.7102–1.7112	1.7102–1.7112	1.7091–1.7100	1.7102–1.7112	1.7102–1.7112	1.4272–1.4351	1.4272–1.4351	⑧	0.0020–0.0071
	112.2 (1839) ⑦	1.7102–1.7110	1.7096–1.7106	1.7091–1.7100	1.7096–1.7106	1.7102–1.7110	1.4092–1.4170	1.4202–1.4281	⑨	0.0024–0.0079
	112.2 (1839) ④	1.0213–1.0222	1.0213–1.0222	1.0213–1.0222	1.0213–1.0222	1.0213–1.0222	1.7281–1.7360	1.7480–1.7560	0.0014–0.0032	0.0028–0.0075
	133.2 (2184)	1.2575–1.2585	1.2563–1.2573	1.2563–1.2573	1.2563–1.2573	1.2575–1.2585	1.6256–1.6295	1.6197	0.0014–0.0033 ⑦	0.003–0.006
	180.2 (2959) ⑦	1.9268–1.9274	1.9258–1.9266	1.9255–1.9266	1.9268–1.9274	—	1.6163	1.6257	0.0024–0.0035 ⑧	0.0020–0.0071
	180.2 (2959) ④	1.1787–1.1797	1.1776–1.1785	1.1776–1.1785	1.1787–1.1797	—	1.5898–1.5976	1.5856–1.5935	⑩	0.0012–0.0063

① Center clearance—0.0026-0.0045
② Center clearance—0.0026-0.0043
③ Wear limit—0.008
④ DOHC engine
⑤ Nos. 2, 3 & 4—0.0026-0.0045
⑥ Nos. 2 & 3—0.0031-0.0045
⑦ SOHC engine
⑧ Nos. 1, 2, 4, 5—0.0014-0.0030; No. 3—0.0020-0.0037
⑨ Nos. 1 & 5—0.0016-0.0030; Nos. 2 & 4—0.0014-0.0031; No. 3—0.0020-0.0037
⑩ Nos. 1 & 4—0.0014-0.0032; Nos. 2 & 3—0.0026-0.0044

CRANKSHAFT AND CONNECTING ROD SPECIFICATIONS

All measurements are given in inches.

Year	Engine Displacement cu. in. (cc)	Crankshaft				Connecting Rod		
		Main Brg. Journal Dia.	Main Brg. Oil Clearance	Shaft End-play	Thrust on No.	Journal Diameter	Oil Clearance	Side Clearance
1987	97.4 (1597)	1.9662–1.9668	0.0011–0.0027	0.0031–0.0071	4	1.7693–1.7699	0.0011–0.0027	0.0043–0.0103
	121.9 (1998)	2.359–2.360	0.0012–0.0019	0.0031–0.0071	3	2.005–2.006	0.0010–0.0026	0.004–0.010
1988	97.4 (1597)	1.9961–1.9668	0.0009–0.0017 ②	0.0031–0.0111	4	1.7693–1.7699	0.0011–0.0027	0.0043–0.0103
	133.2 (2184)	2.3597–2.3604	0.0010–0.0017 ①	0.0031–0.0071	3	2.0055–2.0061	0.0011–0.0026	0.004–0.010
	180.2 (2954)	2.4385–2.4392	0.0010–0.0015	0.0031–0.0111	NA	2.0842–2.0848	0.0009–0.0025	0.007–0.013

CRANKSHAFT AND CONNECTING ROD SPECIFICATIONS

All measurements are given in inches.

Year	Engine Displacement cu. in. (cc)	Crankshaft Main Brg. Journal Dia.	Crankshaft Main Brg. Oil Clearance	Crankshaft Shaft End-play	Crankshaft Thrust on No.	Connecting Rod Journal Diameter	Connecting Rod Oil Clearance	Connecting Rod Side Clearance
1989	97.4 (1597)	1.9961–1.9668	0.0009–0.0017 ②	0.0031–0.0111	4	1.8898–1.8904	0.0011–0.0027	0.0043–0.0103
	133.2 (2184)	2.3597–2.3604	0.0010–0.0017 ①	0.0031–0.0071	3	2.1261–2.1266	0.0011–0.0026	0.012
	180.2 (2954)	2.4385–2.4392	0.0010–0.0015	0.0031–0.0111	NA	2.2047–2.2053	0.0009–0.0025	0.007–0.013
1990–91	97.4 (1597)	1.9961–1.9668	0.0007–0.0014	0.0031–0.0111	4	1.7693–1.7699	0.0011–0.0027	0.0043–0.0103
	112.2 (1839)	1.9961–1.9668	0.0007–0.0014	0.0031–0.0111	4	1.7693–1.7699	0.0011–0.0027	0.0043–0.0103
	133.2 (1839)	2.3597–2.3604	0.0010–0.0017 ①	0.0031–0.0071	3	2.1261–2.1266	0.0011–0.0026	0.012
	180.2 (2954)	2.4385–2.4392	0.0010–0.0015	0.0031–0.0111	NA	2.2047–2.2053	0.0009–0.0025	0.007–0.013

① Bearing No. 3—0.0012–0.0019
② DOHC engine—0.0010–0.0017

VALVE SPECIFICATIONS—PISTON ENGINE

Year	Engine Displacement cu. in. (cc)	Seat Angle (deg.)	Face Angle (deg.)	Spring Squareness limit	Spring Free Length Outer	Spring Free Length Inner	Stem-to-Guide Clearance Intake	Stem-to-Guide Clearance Exhaust	Stem Diameter Intake	Stem Diameter Exhaust
1987	97.4 (1597)	45	45	0.059	1.717	1.717	0.0018–0.0051	0.0019–0.0053	0.2740–0.2750	0.2740–0.2750
	121.9 (1998)	45	45	0.071	2.047	1.732	0.0010–0.0024	0.0010–0.0024	0.3177–0.3185	0.3159–0.3165
1988	97.4 (1597)	45	45	0.059	1.720	1.720	0.0010–0.0024	0.0011–0.0026	0.2744–0.275	0.2744–0.275
	97.4 (1597) ①	45	45	NA	1.858	1.858	0.0010–0.0024	0.0012–0.0026	0.2350–0.2360	0.2350–0.2360
	133.2 (2184)	45	45	0.067	1.949	1.949	0.0010–0.0024	0.0012–0.0026	0.2740–0.2750	0.2740–0.2750
	180.2 (2954)	45	45	②	③	③	0.0010–0.0024	0.0012–0.0026	0.2740–0.2750	0.2760–0.2770
1989	97.4 (1597)	45	45	0.059	1.720	1.720	0.0010–0.0024	0.0011–0.0026	0.274–0.275	0.274–0.275
	97.4 (1597) ①	45	45	0.062	1.858	1.858	0.0010–0.0024	0.0012–0.0026	0.2350–0.2356	0.2348–0.2354
	133.2 (2184)	45	45	0.067	1.949	1.949	0.0010–0.0024	0.0012–0.0026	0.2744–0.2750	0.2742–0.2748
	180.2 (2954)	45	45	②	④	③	0.0010–0.0024	0.0012–0.0026	0.2744–0.2750	0.3159–0.3165

VALVE SPECIFICATIONS—PISTON ENGINE

Year	Engine Displacement cu. in. (cc)	Seat Angle (deg.)	Face Angle (deg.)	Spring Square-ness limit	Spring Free Length Outer	Inner	Stem-to-Guide Clearance Intake	Exhaust	Stem Diameter Intake	Exhaust
1990-91	97.4 (1597)	45	45	0.060	1.720	1.720	0.0010–0.0024	0.0012–0.0026	0.2744–0.2750	0.2742–0.2748
	112.2 (1839)	45	45	0.060 ⑤	0.815	1.717	0.0010–0.0024	0.0012–0.0026	0.2350–0.2356	0.2348–0.2354
	112.2 (1839) ①	45	45	0.064	0.821	1.821	0.0010–0.0024	0.0012–0.0026	0.2350–0.2356	0.2348–0.2354
	133.2 (2184)	45	45	0.067	1.949	1.984	0.0010–0.0024	0.0012–0.0026	0.2744–0.2750	0.2742–0.2748
	180.2 (2954)	45	45	④	⑤	⑤	0.0010–0.0024	0.0012–0.0026	0.2744–0.2750	0.3159–0.3165

① DOHC engine
② Intake
    Outer—0.070
    Inner—0.064
  Exhaust
    Outer—0.083
    Inner—0.074

③ Intake
    Outer—2.0000
    Inner—1.9835
  Exhaust
    Outer—2.382
    Inner—2.130

④ Intake
    Outer—2.000
    Inner—1.835
  Exhaust
    Outer—2.295
    Inner—2.091
⑤ Intake, 0.063
⑥ Exhaust, 1.902

PISTON AND RING SPECIFICATIONS

All measurements are given in inches.

Year	Engine Displacement cu. in. (cc)	Piston Clearance	Ring Gap Top Compression	Bottom Compression	Oil Control	Ring Side Clearance Top Compression	Bottom Compression	Oil Control
1987	97.4 (1597)	0.0015–0.0020	0.0080–0.0160	0.0060–0.0120	0.0120–0.0350	0.0010–0.0030	0.0010–0.0030	—
	121.9 (1998)	0.0014–0.0030	0.008–0.014	0.006–0.012	0.012–0.035	0.0012–0.0028	0.0012–0.0028	—
1988	97.4 (1597)	0.0010–0.0026	0.0079–0.0157	0.059–0.0118	0.008–0.028	0.0012–0.0026	0.0012–0.0026	—
	133.2 (2184)	0.0014–0.0030	0.0080–0.0138	0.006–0.012	0.0080–0.0276 ①	0.0012–0.0028	0.0012–0.0028	—
	180.2 (2954)	0.0019–0.0026	0.0080–0.0138	0.006–0.012	0.008–0.028	0.0012–0.0028	0.0012–0.0028	—
1989	97.4 (1597)	0.0010–0.0026	0.0079–0.0157	0.00579–0.0587	0.008–0.028	0.0012–0.0026	0.0012–0.0026	—
	133.2 (2184)	0.0014–0.0030	0.008–0.0138	0.006–0.012	0.008–0.0276 ①	0.0012–0.0028	0.0012–0.0028	—
	180.2 (2954)	0.0019–0.0026	0.008–0.014	0.006–0.012	0.008–0.028	0.001–0.003	0.001–0.003	—
1990-91	97.4 (1597)	0.0015–0.0020	0.006–0.012	0.006–0.012	0.008–0.028	0.0012–0.0026 ②	0.0012–0.0026 ②	—
	112.2 (1839)	0.0015–0.0020	0.006–0.012	0.006–0.012	0.008–0.028	0.0012–0.0026	0.0012–0.0026	—
	133.2 (2184)	0.0014–0.0030	0.008–0.0138	0.006–0.012	0.008–0.0276	0.0012–0.0028	0.0012–0.0028	—
	180.2 (2954)	0.0019–0.0026	0.008–0.014	0.006–0.012	0.008–0.028	0.001–0.003	0.001–0.003	—

① Turbocharged engine—0.012–0.0354   ② DOHC engine—0.0012–0.0028

TORQUE SPECIFICATIONS

All readings in ft. lbs.

Year	Engine Displacement cu. in. (cc)	Cylinder Head Bolts	Main Bearing Bolts	Rod Bearing Bolts	Crankshaft Pulley Bolts	Flywheel Bolts	Manifold Intake	Manifold Exhaust	Spark Plugs
1987	97.4 (1597)	56–60	40–43	37–41	36–45	71–76	14–19	12–17	11–17
	121.9 (1998)	59–64 ①	61–65	37–41	108–112	71–76	14–19	16–20	11–17
1988	97.4 (1597)	56–60	40–43	35–38 ②	36–45	71–76	14–19	12–17 ③	11–17
	133.2 (2184)	59–64	61–65	48–51	36–45	71–76	14–22	14–22	11–17
	180.2 (2954)	④	⑤	⑥	116–123	76–81	14–19	16–21	11–17
1989	97.4 (1597)	56–60	40–43	35–38 ②	9–13	71–76	14–19	12–17 ③	11–17
	133.2 (2184)	59–64	61–65	48–51	36–45	71–76	14–22	14–22	11–17
	180.2 (2954)	④	⑤	⑥	7–11	76–81	14–19	16–21	11–17
1990–91	97.4 (1597)	56–60	40–43	35–38	9–13	71–76	14–19	12–17 ③	11–17
	112.2 (1839)	56–60	40–43	36–38	9–13	71–76	14–19	12–17 ⑦	11–17
	133.2 (2184)	59–64	61–65	48–51	36–45	71–76	14–22	14–22	11–17
	180.2 (2954)	④	⑤	⑥	7–11	76–81	14–19	16–21	11–17

① Warm—69–80
② DOHC Engine—48–51
③ DOHC Engine—29–42
④ 14 ft. lbs.
Paint a mark on each bolt head. Using the mark as a reference, tighten the bolts 90 degrees in the proper sequence. Retighten each bolt another 90 degrees in the proper sequence.
⑤ 14 ft. lbs.
Paint a mark on each bolt head. Using the mark as a reference, tighten the bolts 90 degrees. Tighten the bolts again 45 degrees.
⑥ 22 ft. lbs.
Paint a mark on each bolt head. Using the mark as a reference, tighten the bolts 90 degrees.
⑦ DOHC Engine—28–34

TORQUE SPECIFICATIONS—ROTARY ENGINE

Engine Displacement cu. in. (cc)	Front Cover	Bearing Housing	Rear Stationary Gear	Eccentric Shaft Pulley Bolt	Flywheel-to-Eccentric Shaft Nut	Manifolds Intake	Manifolds Exhaust	Oil Pan	Tension Bolts
80 (1308)	12–17	12–17	12–17	80–98	290–360	14–19	23–34	6–8	23–29

BRAKE SPECIFICATIONS

All measurements in inches unless noted.

Year	Model	Lug Nut Torque (ft. lbs.)	Master Cylinder Bore	Brake Disc Minimum Thickness	Brake Disc Maximum Runout	Standard Brake Drum Diameter	Minimum Lining Thickness Front	Minimum Lining Thickness Rear
1987	323	65–87	0.8750	0.630 ①	0.0030	7.8700	0.120	0.040
	626	65–87	0.8750	0.710 ①	0.0040	7.8700	0.118	0.040
	RX7	65–87	0.8750	0.790 ②	0.0040	—	0.120	0.040
1988	323	65–87	0.8750	0.390 ③	0.0030	7.8700	0.120	0.040
	626	65–87	0.8750	0.940 ①	0.0040	9.0000	0.039	0.031
	MX6	65–87	0.8750	0.940 ①	0.0040	9.0000	0.039	0.031
	929	65–87	0.8750	0.870 ①	0.0040	—	0.039	0.031
	RX7	65–87	0.8750	0.870 ②	0.0040	—	0.035 ②	0.031
1989	323	65–87	0.8750	0.390 ④	0.0040	7.8700	0.039	0.039 ③
	626	65–87	0.8750	0.870 ④	0.0040	9.0000	0.039	0.040
	MX6	65–87	0.8750	0.870 ④	0.0040	9.0000	0.039	0.040
	929	65–87	0.8750	0.870 ④	0.0040	—	0.039	0.031
	RX7	65–87	0.8750	0.870 ②	0.0040	—	0.035 ②	0.031

BRAKE SPECIFICATIONS
All measurements in inches unless noted.

Year	Model	Lug Nut Torque (ft. lbs.)	Master Cylinder Bore	Brake Disc Minimum Thickness	Brake Disc Maximum Runout	Standard Brake Drum Diameter	Minimum Lining Thickness Front	Minimum Lining Thickness Rear
1990-91	323	65–87	0.8750	0.390④	0.0040	7.8700	0.039	0.039③
	Protege	65–87	0.8750	0.390④	0.0040	7.8700	0.039	0.039③
	626	65–87	0.8750	0.870④	0.0040	9.0000	0.039	0.040
	MX6	65–87	0.8750	0.870④	0.0040	9.0000	0.039	0.040
	929	65–87	0.8750	0.870④	0.0040	—	0.039	0.031
	RX7	65–87	0.8750	0.870⑤	0.0040	—	0.035②	0.031
	Miata	65–87	0.8750	0.630⑥	0.0040	—	0.040	0.040

NOTE: Minimum lining thickness is as recommended by the manufacturer. Due to variations in state inspection regulations, the minimum allowable thickness may be different than specified.

① Rear disc—0.350
② Rear disc
    14 in. wheels—0.310

15 in. wheels—0.710
③ Rear disc—0.31
④ Rear disc—0.39

⑤ Rear disc—14 in. wheel—0.040
    15 in. wheel—0.79
⑥ Rear disc—0.280 in.

WHEEL ALIGNMENT

Year	Model	Caster Range (deg.)	Caster Preferred Setting (deg.)	Camber Range (deg.)	Camber Preferred Setting (deg.)	Toe-in (in.)	Steering Axis Inclination (deg.)
1987	323	$^1/_{16}$P–$1^9/_{16}$P	$3^1/_{16}$P	$1^3/_{16}$P–$2^5/_{16}$P	$1^9/_{16}$P	$^3/_{64}$–$^{13}/_{16}$	$12^3/_8$
	323 Wagon	$^3/_4$N–$^3/_4$P	0	—	—	$^3/_{64}$–$^{13}/_{64}$	$12^3/_8$
	626	$^3/_{16}$N–$1^1/_{16}$P	$^5/_{16}$P	$^{15}/_{16}$P–$2^7/_{16}$P	$1^{11}/_{16}$P	0–$^1/_4$①	$12^{15}/_{16}$
	RX-7	②	$^5/_{16}$P	$4^5/_8$P	—	0–$^1/_4$③	$13^3/_4$
1988	323 (2WD)	$1^3/_{16}$P–$2^5/_{16}$P	$1^9/_{16}$P	$^5/_{16}$P–$1^5/_{16}$P	$1^3/_{16}$P	$^3/_{64}$–$^{13}/_{64}$	$12^3/_8$
	323 (4WD)	$1^1/_{16}$P–$2^9/_{16}$P	$1^{13}/_{16}$P	$^9/_{16}$P–$1^9/_{16}$P	$^1/_{16}$P	$^3/_{64}$–$^{13}/_{64}$	12
	626④	$^5/_{16}$P–$1^5/_{16}$P	$1^3/_{16}$P	$^7/_{16}$N–$1^1/_{16}$P	$^5/_{16}$P	0–$^1/_4$	$12^{13}/_{16}$
	MX6④	$^5/_{16}$P–$1^{15}/_{16}$P	$1^3/_{16}$P	$^7/_{16}$N–$1^1/_{16}$P	$^5/_{16}$P	0–$^1/_4$	$12^{13}/_{16}$
	929	$3^3/_4$P–$5^1/_4$P	$4^1/_2$P	$^1/_4$P–$1^3/_4$P	1P	0–$^1/_4$	$12^{11}/_{16}$
	RX-7	$3^{15}/_{16}$P–$5^7/_{16}$P	$4^5/_8$P	$^3/_{16}$N–$1^3/_{16}$P	$^5/_{16}$P	0–$^1/_4$	$13^3/_4$
1989	323 (2WD)	$1^3/_{16}$P–$2^5/_{16}$P	$1^9/_{16}$P	$^5/_{16}$P–$1^5/_{16}$P	$1^3/_{16}$P	$^3/_{64}$–$^{13}/_{36}$	$12^3/_8$
	323 (4WD)	$1^1/_{16}$P–$2^9/_{16}$P	$1^{13}/_{16}$P	$^9/_{16}$P–$1^9/_{16}$P	$1^1/_{16}$P	$^3/_{64}$–$^{13}/_{64}$	12
	626④	$^5/_{16}$P–$1^5/_{16}$P	$1^3/_{16}$P	$^7/_{16}$N–$1^1/_{16}$P	$^5/_{16}$P	0–$^1/_4$	$12^{13}/_{16}$
	MX6⑤	$^5/_{16}$P–$1^{15}/_{16}$P	$1^3/_{16}$P	$^7/_{16}$N–$1^1/_{16}$P	$^5/_{16}$P	0–$^1/_4$	$12^{13}/_{16}$
	929	$3^3/_4$P–$5^1/_4$P	$4^1/_2$P	$^1/_4$P–$1^3/_4$P	1P	0–$^1/_4$	$12^{11}/_{16}$
	RX-7	$3^{15}/_{16}$P–$5^7/_{16}$P	$4^5/_8$P	$^3/_{16}$N–$1^3/_{16}$P	$^5/_{16}$P	0–$^1/_4$	$13^3/_4$
1990-91	323 (2WD)	$1^{15}/_{16}$P–$2^{13}/_{16}$P	$2^1/_6$P	$^{13}/_{16}$N–$1^1/_{16}$P⑥	$^1/_{16}$N⑦	$^1/_{32}$–$^7/_{32}$	$12^7/_{16}$
	Protege	$1^5/_{16}$P–$2^{13}/_{16}$P	$2^1/_6$P	$^{13}/_{16}$N–$1^1/_{16}$P⑥	$^1/_{16}$N⑦	$^1/_{32}$–$^7/_{32}$	$12^7/_{16}$
	626④	$1^5/_{16}$P–$1^{15}/_{16}$P	$1^3/_{16}$P	$^7/_{16}$N–$1^1/_{16}$P	$^5/_{16}$P	0–$^1/_4$	$12^{13}/_{16}$
	MX6④	$^5/_{16}$P–$1^{15}/_{16}$P	$1^3/_{16}$P	$^7/_{16}$N–$1^1/_{16}$P	$^5/_{16}$P	0–$^1/_4$	$12^{13}/_{16}$
	929	$3^3/_4$P–$5^1/_4$P	$4^1/_2$P	$^1/_4$P–$1^3/_4$P	1P	0–$^1/_4$	$12^{11}/_{16}$
	RX-7	$3^{15}/_{16}$P–$5^7/_{16}$P	$4^5/_8$P	$^3/_{16}$N–$1^3/_{16}$P	$^5/_{16}$P	0–$^1/_4$	$13^3/_4$
	Miata	$3^3/_4$P–$5^1/_4$P	$4^1/_2$P	$^3/_8$N–$1^1/_8$P⑧	$^3/_8$P⑨	0–$^1/_4$	$11^5/_{16}$

① Rear—$^1/_8$ in.
② Rear—$1^1/_4$N–$^1/_4$N–$^3/_4$ preferred
③ Rear—0 in.
④ Rear Alignment
    2 Wheel Steering

Camber—$1^1/_4$N–$^1/_4$P
Toe In—$^1/_4$N–$^1/_4$P
4 Wheel Steering
Camber—$^3/_4$N–$^3/_4$P
Toe In—0–$^1/_2$P

⑤ Rear—$^7/_{16}$N–$^9/_{16}$P
⑥ Rear—$1^1/_{16}$N–$^7/_{16}$P
⑦ Rear $^5/_{16}$P
⑧ Rear—$1^1/_4$N–$^1/_4$N
⑨ Rear—$^3/_4$N

ECCENTRIC SHAFT SPECIFICATIONS—ROTARY ENGINE

All measurements are given in inches.

Engine Type	Journal Diameter		Oil Clearance		Eccentric Shaft End-play		Minimum Shaft Run-out
	Main Bearing	Rotor Bearing	Main Bearing	Rotor Bearing	Normal	Limit	
13B	1.6918–1.6923	2.9122–2.9128	0.0016–0.0031	0.0016–0.0031	0.0016–0.0028	0.0035	0.0047

ROTOR AND HOUSING SPECIFICATIONS—ROTARY ENGINE

All measurements are given in inches.

Engine Type	Rotor			Housings					
	Side ① Clearance	Width		Front and Rear		Rotor		Intermediate	
				Distortion Limit	Wear Limit	Width	Distortion Limit	Distortion Limit	Wear Width
13B	0.0047–0.0083	3.142–3.144		0.0016	0.0039	3.1485–3.1500	0.0024	0.0016	0.0039

① New

SEAL CLEARANCES—ROTARY ENGINE

All measurements are given in inches.

Engine Type	Apex Seals				Side Seal			
	To Side Housing		To Rotor Groove		To Rotor Groove		To Corner Seal	
	Normal	Limit	Normal	Limit	Normal	Limit	Normal	Limit
13B	0.0051–0.0075	—	0.0024–0.0040	0.0059	0.0011–0.0031	0.0039	0.0020–0.0059	0.0160

ENGINE ELECTRICAL

NOTE: Disconnecting the negative battery cable on some vehicles may interfere with the functions of the on board computer systems and may require the computer to undergo a relearning process, once the negative battery cable is reconnected.

If equipped with Audio Anti-Theft system, before performing any repairs, the Personal Code Number (PCN) must be obtained.

Distributor

Removal

323 AND PROTEGE

1. Disconnect the negative battery cable to prevent accidental cranking once the distributor is removed. Disconnect the spark plug wires from the distributor cap and route aside.
2. Disconnect and label the vacuum hose(s) and the electrical connector from the distributor.
3. Rotate the engine with a socket wrench on the pulley until the No. 1 piston is at TDC mark, pulley mark aligned with **T** mark on the timing belt cover.
4. Remove the distributor hold-down bolt and withdraw the distributor from the cylinder head.
5. Remove the O-ring seal and discard it.

626 AND MX-6

1. Disconnect the negative battery cable to prevent accidental cranking once the distributor is removed. Disconnect the spark plug wires from the distributor cap.
2. On the non-turbocharged engine, disconnect the vacuum

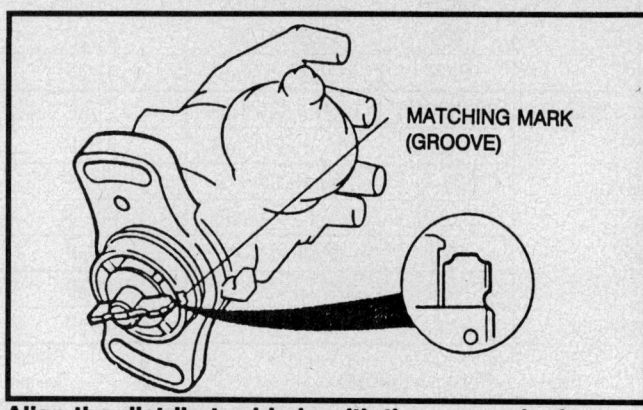

MATCHING MARK (GROOVE)

Align the distributor blade with the groove in the housing—323 with turbocharger

hoses and wiring. On the turbocharged engine, disconnect the electrical coupler.

3. Rotate the engine with a socket wrench on the pulley until the No. 1 piston is at TDC.

4. Loosen the lock bolts and remove the distributor.

5. Remove the O-ring from the coupling shaft and discard it.

929

1. Disconnect the negative battery cable to prevent accidental cranking once the distributor is removed. Disconnect the spark plug wires from the distributor cap.

2. Disconnect the distributor electrical connector.

3. Rotate the engine with a socket wrench on the pulley until the No. 1 piston is at TDC, yellow mark on pulley aligned with **T** mark on the timing scale.

4. Loosen the lock bolt and remove the distributor.

5. Remove the O-ring from the distributor shaft and discard it.

Installation
TIMING NOT DISTURBED
323 and Protege

1. Coat the new O-ring seal with a light film of clean engine oil and fit it into the cylinder head opening.

NOTE: Make sure the No. 1 piston is at TDC before installing the distributor.

2. On non-turbocharged engines, turn the distributor blade so it aligns with the small oil holes in the bottom of the distributor. On turbocharged engines, align the distributor blade with the grooved matchmark on the body.

3. Install the distributor and reconnect the wiring connector, vacuum hose(s) and spark plug wires. Connect the negative battery cable.

4. Set the ignition timing.

626 and MX-6

1. Install a new O-ring onto the coupling shaft and apply a coat of clean engine oil to the O-ring to the driven gear.

2. On 1987 vehicles, align the dimple on the distributor drive gear with the mark cast into the base of the distributor body by rotating the shaft. On 1988–91 vehicles, align the shaft coupling blade with the alignment marks on the distributor body, rotate the distributor and check that the rotor is properly aligned.

3. Install the distributor and connect the wiring connector, vacuum hose(s) and spark plug wires. Connect the negative battery cable.

4. Set the ignition timing.

929

1. Install the new O-ring over the distributor shaft and lightly oil both the O-ring and the driven gear with clean engine oil.

2. Align the match marks on the distributor housing with the driven gear.

3. Install the distributor and connect the electrical connector

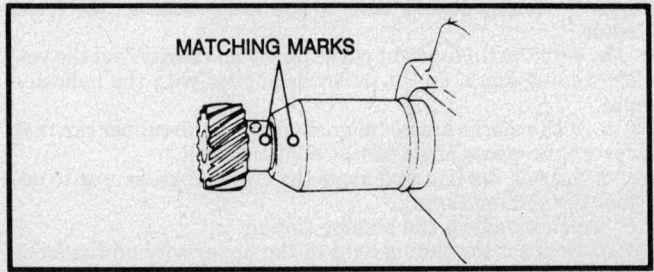
Distributor housing and drive gear alignment marks—929

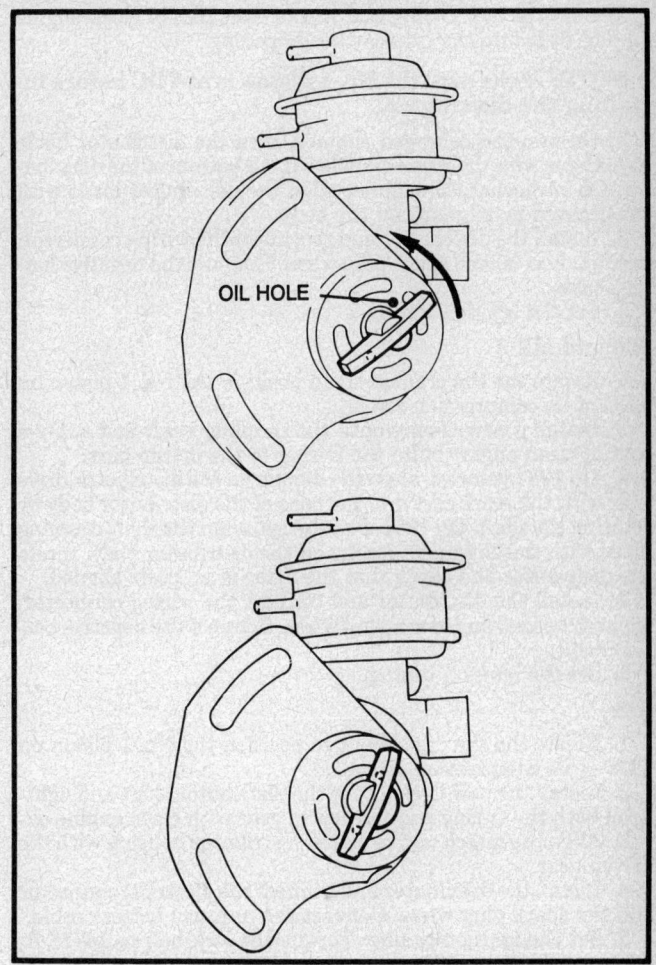
Align the blade with the oil hole before installing the distributor—323 without turbocharger

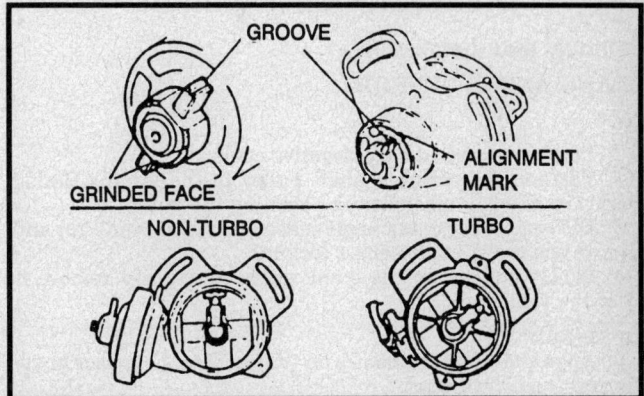
Distributor shaft coupling and rotor alignment—626 and MX-6

and the spark plug wires. Connect the negative battery cable.

4. Set the ignition timing. Torque the lock bolt to 14–18 ft. lbs. once the timing is set.

TIMING DISTURBED
323 and Protege

1. Rotate the the crankshaft to position the No. 1 piston on TDC of its compression stroke.

2. Coat the new O-ring seal with a light film of clean engine oil and fit it into the cylinder head opening.

NOTE: Make sure the No. 1 piston is at TDC before installing the distributor.

3. On non-turbocharged engines, turn the distributor blade so it aligns with the small oil holes in the bottom of the distributor. On turbocharged engines, align the distributor blade with the grooved matchmark on the body.

4. Install the distributor and reconnect the wiring connector, vacuum hose(s) and spark plug wires. Connect the negative battery cable.

5. Set the ignition timing.

626 and MX-6

1. Rotate the the crankshaft to position the No. 1 piston on TDC of its compression stroke.

2. Install a new O-ring onto the coupling shaft and apply a coat of clean engine oil to the O-ring to the driven gear.

3. On 1987 vehicles, align the dimple on the distributor drive gear with the mark cast into the base of the distributor body by rotating the shaft. On 1988–91 vehicles, align the shaft coupling blade with the alignment marks on the distributor body, rotate the distributor and check that the rotor is properly aligned.

4. Install the distributor and connect the wiring connector, vacuum hose(s) and spark plug wires. Connect the negative battery cable.

5. Set the ignition timing.

929

1. Rotate the the crankshaft to position the No. 1 piston on TDC of its compression stroke.

2. Install the new O-ring over the distributor shaft and lightly oil both the O-ring and the driven gear with clean engine oil.

3. Align the match marks on the distributor housing with the driven gear.

4. Install the distributor and connect the electrical connector and the spark plug wires. Connect the negative battery cable.

5. Set the ignition timing. Torque the lock bolt to 14–18 ft. lbs. once the timing is set.

Distributorless Ignition

Removal and Installation

CRANK ANGLE SENSOR

RX-7

1. Disconnect the battery negative cable.

2. Position the eccentric shaft pulley to the leading timing mark, usually painted yellow, by turning the pulley.

3. Disconnect the crank angle sensor electrical connector and remove the crank angle sensor locknut.

4. Slowly pull up on the crank angle sensor and remove it from the vehicle.

To install:

5. Align the matching marks on the crank angle sensor housing and the driven gear.

6. Make sure the eccentric shaft pulley is set to the leading timing mark.

7. Install the crank angle sensor locknut.

8. Connect the battery negative cable and check the ignition timing. Tighten locknut to 70–90 inch lbs.

IGNITION COIL

Miata

1. Disconnect the battery negative cable.

2. Disconnect the spark plug wires and the ignition coil electrical connector.

3. Remove the ignition coil-to-engine bolts and the ignition

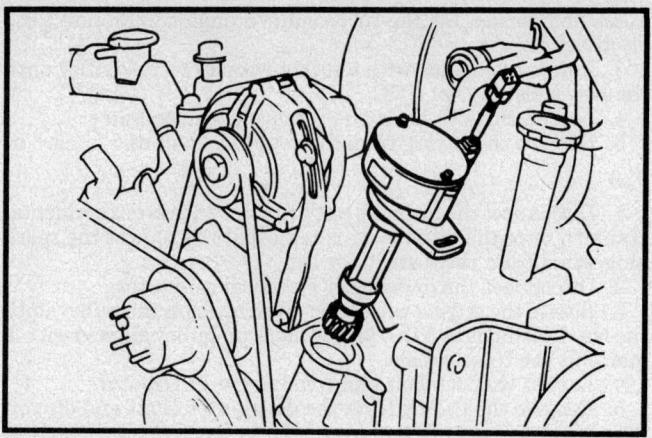

Crank angle sensor removal and installation—RX-7

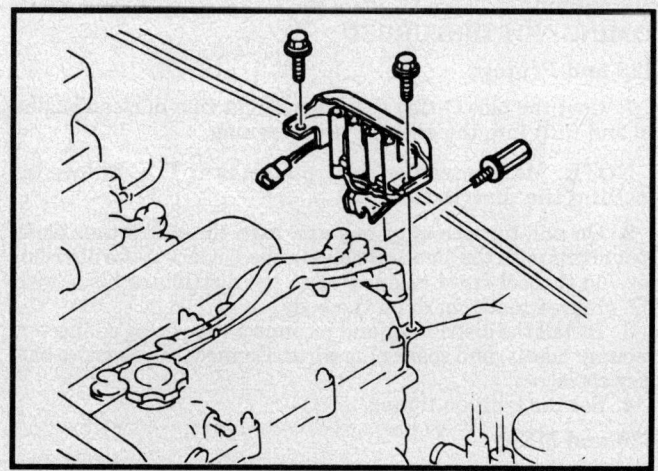

Removing ignition coil—Miata

coil assembly from the vehicle.

4. Reverse procedure to install. Torque ignition mounting bolts to 14–19 ft. lbs. (19–25 Nm).

Ignition Timing

Adjustment

RX-7

1. Warm up the engine to normal operating temperature.

2. Stop the engine and connect a tachometer. Turn all the electrical accessories to the **OFF** position.

3. Start the engine and verify that the engine is running at normal idle speed. If not, adjust idle speed to specification.

4. To check/adjust the leading timing:

   a. Connect a timing light to the lower wire on the front rotor.

   b. Aim the timing light at the pulley and verify that the yellow timing mark, on the pulley, is aligned with the indicator pin.

   c. If the marks are not aligned, remove the rubber cap that covers the crank angle sensor adjusting bolt.

   d. Loosen the bolt and move the crank angle sensor to adjust the leading timing.

5. To check/adjust the trailing timing:

   a. Connect the timing light to the upper wire on the front rotor.

   b. Check that the red mark on the pulley is aligned with the indicator pin.

c. If not, loosen the adjusting bolt and rotate the crank angle sensor to align the marks.

d. Tighten the crank angle sensor adjusting bolt and install the rubber cap.

1987 626

1. Warm up the engine to normal operating temperature.
2. Stop the engine and turn all the accessories OFF.
3. Connect a timing light and a tachometer to the engine.
4. Start the engine. Check the idle speed and adjust, as necessary.
5. Disconnect and plug both vacuum hoses from the vacuum control unit.
6. Aim the timing light at the crankshaft pulley and check that the yellow mark on the pulley is aligned with the mark on the timing belt cover.
7. If the marks are not aligned, loosen the distributor bolt and rotate the distributor housing until the timing marks are properly aligned.
8. Tighten the distributor bolt and connect the vacuum hoses to the control unit.
9. Disconnect the timing light and the tachometer.

1988–90 626 AND MX-6

1. Warm up the engine to normal operating temperature.
2. Turn all electrical accessories OFF.

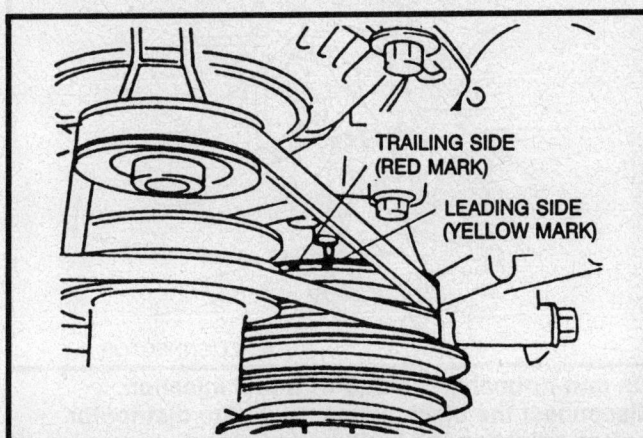

Rotary engine timing marks—all vehicles

Turn the crank angle sensor to adjust the ignition timing—RX-7

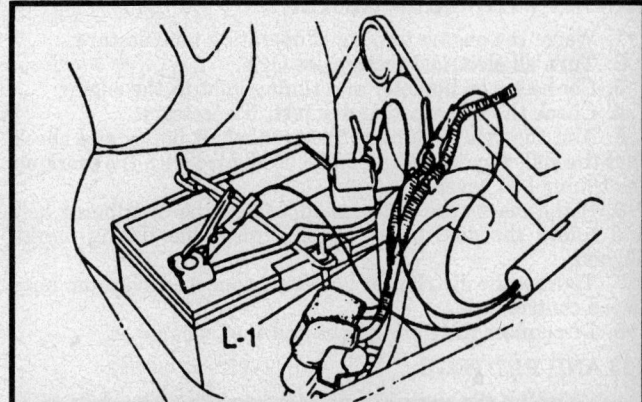

When checking the rotary engine timing connect the timing light to the "L-1" high tension lead

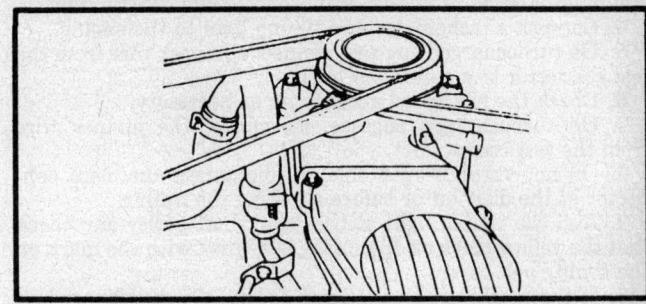

Timing marks—626 and MX-6

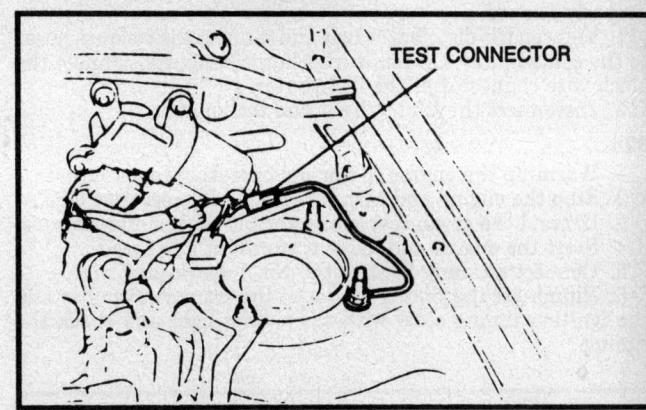

Grounding the test connector for ignition timing adjustment—626 and MX-6

3. Connect a tachometer and timing light to the engine.
4. Connect a jumper wire from the test connector to a suitable ground.
5. Check the idle speed and adjust, as necessary.
6. On non-turbocharged engines, disconnect and plug both vacuum hoses from the vacuum control unit; leave the test connector grounded.
7. Aim the timing light at the crankshaft pulley and check that the yellow mark on the pulley is aligned with the mark on the timing belt cover.
8. If the marks are not aligned, loosen the distributor bolt and rotate the distributor housing until the timing marks are properly aligned.
9. Tighten the distributor bolt and connect the vacuum hoses to the control unit, non-turbocharged engines.
10. Disconnect the timing light and the tachometer.

1987 323 WITH CARBURETOR

1. Warm the engine to normal operating temperature.
2. Turn all electrical accessories OFF.
3. Connect a tachometer and timing light to the engine.
4. Check the idle speed and adjust, if necessary.
5. Aim the timing light at the crankshaft pulley and check that the yellow mark on the pulley is aligned with the mark on the timing belt cover.
6. If the marks are not aligned, loosen the distributor bolt and rotate the distributor housing until the timing marks aligned.
7. Tighten the distributor bolt and connect the vacuum hose to the control unit.
8. Disconnect the timing light and the tachometer.

323 AND PROTEGE

1. Warm up the engine to normal operating temperature.
2. Turn all electrical accessories OFF.
3. On both turbo and non-turbocharged engines, disconnect and plugthe vacuum hose(s) from the vacuum control unit.
4. Connect a tachometer and timing light to the engine.
5. On turbocharged engines, connect a jumper wire from the test connector to a suitable ground.
6. Check the idle speed and adjust, as necessary.
7. On turbocharged engines, disconnect the jumper wire from the test connector.
8. On non-turbocharged engines, disconnect the black connector at the distributor before checking the timing.
9. Aim the timing light at the crankshaft pulley and check that the yellow mark on the pulley is aligned with the mark on the timing belt cover.
10. If the marks are not aligned, loosen the distributor bolt and rotate the distributor housing until the timing marks are properly aligned.
11. Tighten the distributor bolt and connect the vacuum hoses to the control unit. On non-turbocharged engines, connect the black wire connector at the distributor.
12. Disconnect the timing light and tachometer.

929

1. Warm up the engine to normal operating temperature.
2. Stop the engine and turn all electrical accessories OFF.
3. Ground the green test connector pin with a jumper wire.
4. Start the engine and allow it to run at idle speed.
5. Connect a timing light to the No. 1 spark plug wire.
6. Illuminate the timing marks on the crankshaft pulley and the ignition timing scale with the timing light and check the timing.

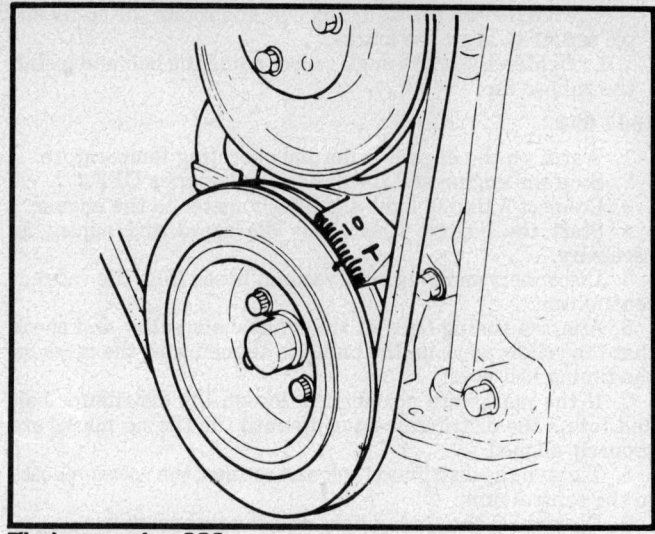

Timing marks—323

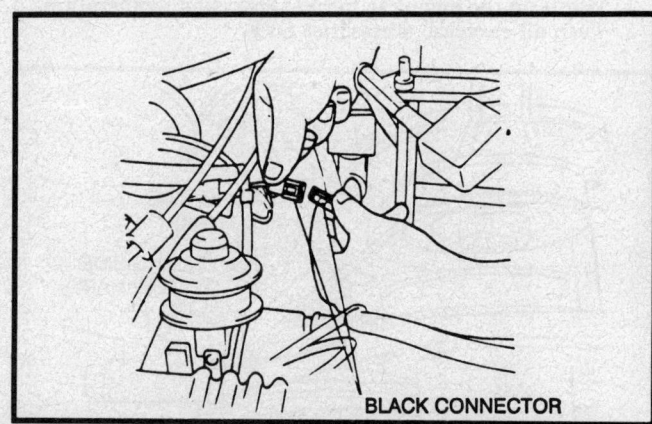

BLACK CONNECTOR

On non-turbocharged 323 with fuel injection, disconnect the black connector at the distributor before adjusting the ignition timing

TEST CONNECTOR (GREEN: 1-PIN)

Grounding the test connector for ignition timing adjustment—929

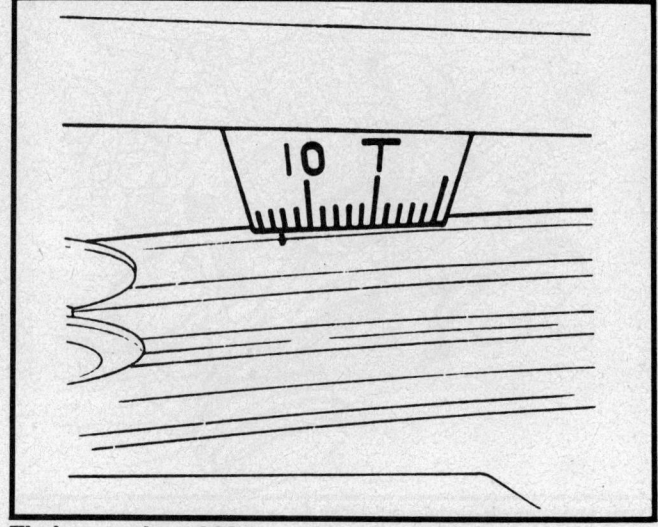

Timing marks—929

7. If the timing is not within specification, loosen the distributor bolt and rotate the distributor housing to adjust the timing.

8. When the timing is correct, tighten the distributor bolt.

9. Disconnect the timing light and remove the jumper wire from the test connector.

MIATA

1. PLace the vehicle in neutral, block the drive wheels and apply the emergency brake. Make sure all the accessories are turned OFF

2. Start the engine allow it to reach normal operating temperature. Connect a timing light and tachometer to the diagnosis connector terminal **1G.''**

NOTE: When using an externally powered timing light and/or tachometer, connect it to the power connector, blue: 1–pin.

3. Connect the System Selector 49–B019–9A0 to the diagnosis connector and set the **TEST SW** to the **SELF TEST** position.

NOTE: If the System Selector is not available, connect a jumper wire between terminals No. 10 and ground on the diagnostic connector. Take care when making connections to the diagnostic connector, as a mistaken connection will cause a malfunction or damage to the ECU.

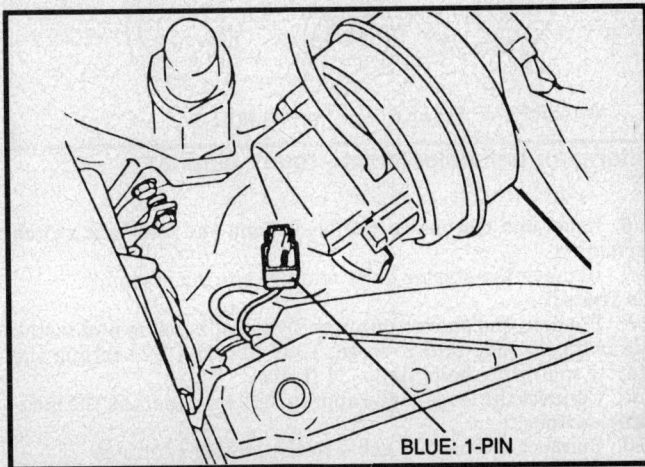

Power connector location—Miata

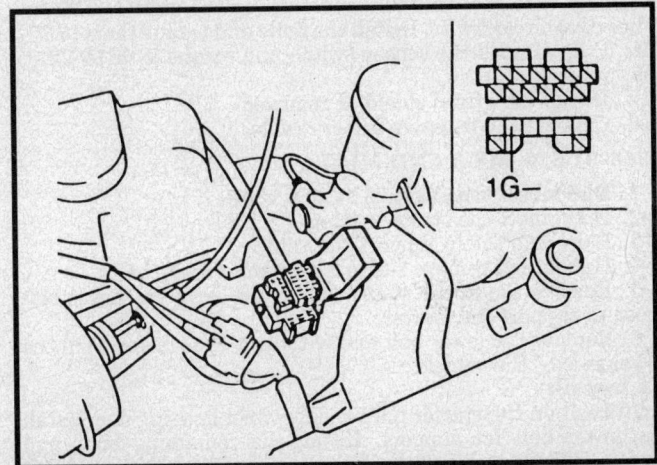

Diagnosis connector location—Miata

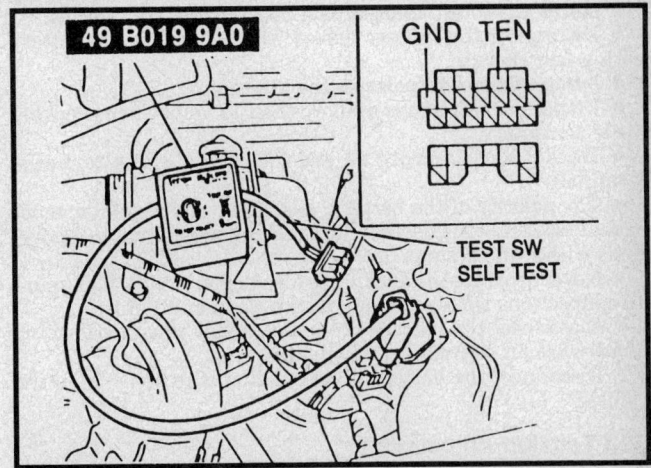

Installing system selector for checking ignition Timing—Miata

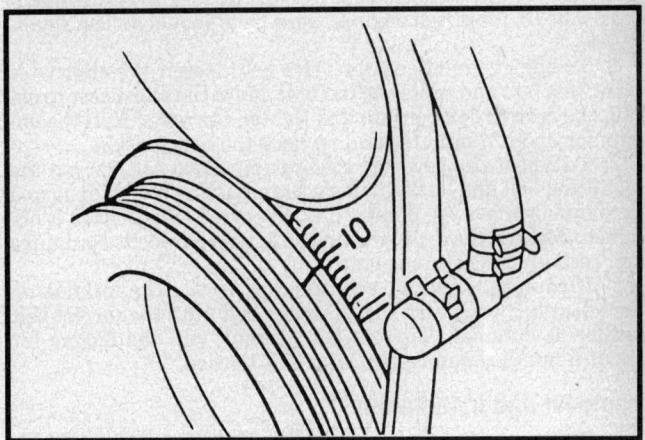

Timing mark location—Miata

4. Check that the idle speed is within specification; if not, adjust the idle speed.

5. Point the timing light at the timing marks, on the crankshaft pulley and timing belt cover. If the timing marks, usually a yellow mark, are difficult to see, use chalk or a dab of paint to make them more visible.

6. With the engine idling, ignition timing should be 9–11 degrees BTDC at 800–900 rpm.

7. If ignition timing is not as specified, loosen the crank angle sensor hold-down bolt and rotate the crank angle sensor to advance or retard the timing, as necessary.

8. Disconnect the System Selector and reconnect the electrical connectors. Disconnect the timing light and tachometer.

Alternator

Precautions

Several precautions must be observed with alternator equipped vehicles to avoid damage to the unit.

• If the battery is removed for any reason, make sure it is reconnected with the correct polarity. Reversing the battery connections may result in damage to the one-way rectifiers.

• When utilizing a booster battery as a starting aid, always connect the positive to positive terminals and the negative terminal from the booster battery to a good engine ground on the vehicle being started.

- Never use a fast charger as a booster to start vehicles.
- Disconnect the battery cables when charging the battery with a fast charger.
- Never attempt to polarize the alternator.
- Do not use test lamps of more than 12 volts when checking diode continuity.
- Do not short across or ground any of the alternator terminals.
- The polarity of the battery, alternator and regulator must be matched and considered before making any electrical connections within the system.
- Never separate the alternator on an open circuit. Make sure all connections within the circuit are clean and tight.
- Disconnect the battery ground terminal when performing any service on electrical components.
- Disconnect the battery if arc welding is to be done on the vehicle.

Belt Tension Adjustment

Check tension by using a suitable belt tension gauge, installed midway between the eccentric shaft and alternator pulleys. Used belts should deflect about 0.55–67 in. for rotary engines or 0.31–0.35 in. for piston engines. New belts should deflect slightly less.

1. To adjust the alternator drive belt, loosen the alternator mounting bolt and adjusting bar bolt. Move the alternator to obtain the correct belt tension and tighten the bolts. Run the engine for about 5 minutes and recheck the belt tension.
2. To adjust the power steering pump drive belt, loosen the mounting bolt and locknut. Turn the adjusting bolt, if equipped or manually move the pump until the correct belt tension is obtained. Tighten the locknut, run the engine for about 5 minutes and recheck the belt tension.
3. If equipped with air conditioning, loosen the locknut on the idler pulley and turn the adjusting bolt until the correct belt tension is obtained. Tighten the locknut, run the engine for about 5 minutes and recheck the belt tension.

Removal and Installation

1. Disconnect the negative battery cable. Label and disconnect all electrical leads from the alternator.
2. Remove the alternator adjusting link bolt. Do not remove the adjusting link.
3. Lift the alternator belt from the pulley. Remove the alternator. On some vehicles the alternator is removed from under the vehicle.
4. Installation is the reverse the removal procedure. Adjust the drive belt tension.
5. Connect the negative battery cable. Run the engine for about 5 minutes and recheck the belt tension.

Starter

Removal and Installation

EXCEPT RX-7, 1988–90 626 AND MX-6

1. Disconnect the negative battery cable from the battery.
2. If equipped with the lower mounted starter, remove the gravel shield from under the engine. If equipped with an automatic transmission, remove both starter bracket-to-transmission bolts.
3. Raise and support the vehicle safely, as required.
4. On 1989–91 323 and Protege with 4WD, remove the differential lock assembly from the transaxle by removing the sensor switch and the retaining bolts. Insert a suitable tool into the shift rod housing and turn the shift rod 90 degrees clockwise to disengage the differential lock assembly from the transaxle.
5. Remove the battery cable from the starter terminal.

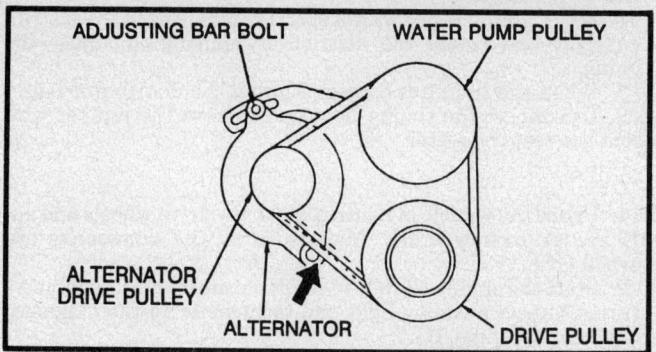

Alternator belt adjustment—piston engines

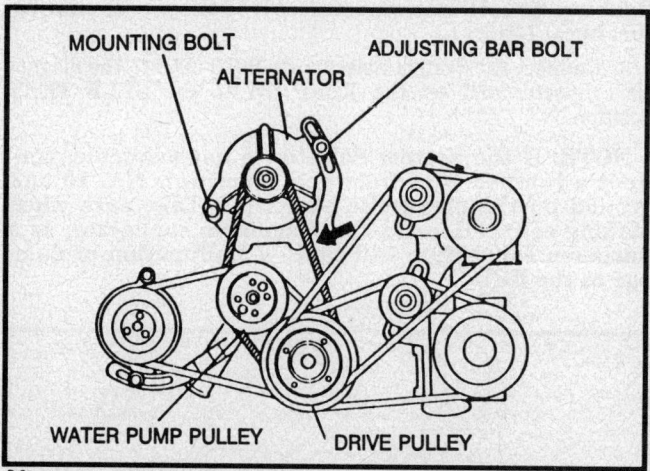

Alternator belt adjustment—rotary engines

6. Label and disconnect the leads from the magnetic switch terminals.
7. Remove the starter bolts and the starter assembly.
To install:
8. Position the starter onto the flywheel housing and install the bolts. On 323 and Protege, 1987 626 and 929 torque the starter mounting bolts to 23–34 ft. lbs.
9. Connect the leads to the appropriate terminals on the magnetic switch.
10. Connect the battery cable to the starter terminal.
11. On 1989–91 323 and Protege with 4WD, install the center differential lock assembly onto the transaxle by positioning the assembly onto the transaxle and turning the shift rod 90 degrees counterclockwise. Install the bolts and torque them to 78–122 ft. lbs. Install the sensor switch and torque it to 14–22 ft. lbs.
12. Install the gravel shield, if removed.
13. Connect the negative battery cable.

1988–91 626, MX-6 AND MIATA

1. Disconnect the negative battery cable.
2. Disconnect the starter wiring.
3. Raise and safely support the vehicle.
4. Unbolt and remove the intake manifold bracket.
5. Remove the upper starter bolts and leave the lower bolt loose to support the starter.
6. Remove the lower bolt and withdraw the starter from the lower side of the vehicle.
To install:
7. Position the starter onto the flywheel housing and install the lower bolt for support. Install the remaining bolts and torque all bolts to 27–38 ft. lbs.
8. Install the intake manifold bracket. Torque the bracket

bolt to 27–38 ft. lbs. and the nut to 14–19 ft. lbs.
9. Lower the vehicle.
10. Connect the starter wiring.
11. Connect the negative battery cable.

RX-7

The starter is mounted on the driver's side bottom of the engine.
1. Disconnect the negative battery cable.
2. Raise the vehicle and support it safely.
3. Disconnect the heavy battery cable from the terminal marked **B** on the magnetic switch.
4. Disconnect the thinner ignition switch wire from the terminal marked **S** on the solenoid.
5. If equipped with an automatic transmissions, remove the front starter motor bracket bolts and the bracket. Remove both starter bolts and the starter.
To install:
6. Support the starter and position it onto the flywheel housing. Install the mounting bolts. Torque the bolts to 24–33 ft. lbs. Install the front starter bracket, if removed.
7. Connect the starter wiring to the appropriate terminals on

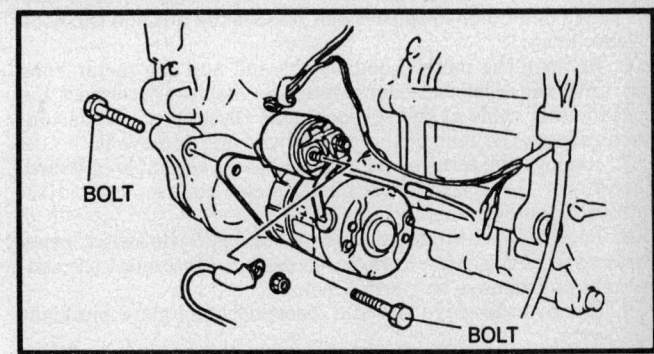

Starter removal and Installation—RX-7

the magnetic switch. Torque the "B" terminal (battery cable) nut to 8 ft. lbs.
8. Lower the vehicle.
9. Connect the negative battery cable.

CHASSIS ELECTRICAL

— **CAUTION** —

If equipped with an air bag, the negative battery cable must be disconnected, before working on the system. Failure to do so may result in deployment of the air bag and possible personal injury.

Heater Blower Motor

Removal and Installation

1. Disconnect the negative battery cable.
2. Remove the dash undercover which is located on the passenger side of the vehicle, if equipped. Remove the glove box. Disconnect the multi-connector to the blower motor.
3. Remove the stay of the steel plate provided in the upper part of the glove box. Remove the right side defroster hose for clearance, if necessary.
4. Remove the air duct in between the blower unit and the heater unit. If equipped with sliding heater controls, move the control to the **HOT** position and disconnect the control wire, if necessary.
5. On 323 and Protege, remove the mounting screws and remove the Fresh-Rec air selector wire harness connector. Remove the screws and the blower motor.
6. Installation is the reverse of removal.

Windshield Wiper Motor

Removal and Installation

1. Disconnect the negative battery cable. Remove the wiper arms.
2. Remove the cowl plate screws, move the cowl plate up at the front and disconnect the washer hose. Remove the cowl plate.
3. Disconnect the wires from the wiper motor.
4. Unbolt and remove the motor.
5. Installation is the reverse of removal. Check the system for proper operation.

Instrument Cluster

Removal and Installation

RX-7

The instrument cluster front bezel contains the switches for headlights and lighting, cruise control, turn signals and high beams, windshield wiper controls and dimmer knobs. The bezel and switch assembly is removed by unscrewing the attaching screws, then pulling the cluster gently and disconnecting the instrument cluster wiring harness from the switch assemblies. Once the bezel is removed, the switch assemblies can be removed from the rear of the unit. The gauges can be removed once the bezel is clear by unscrewing the screws and disconnecting the speedometer cable and wiring connectors.

1987 626

1. Disconnect the negative battery cable. Tilt the steering wheel downward.
2. Disconnect the speedometer cable from the rear of the cluster by reaching up behind the cluster and unscrewing the collar.
3. Remove the 4 screws from the underside of the instrument cluster assembly where it attaches to the underside of the dash and the 3 from the underside of the hood.
4. Remove the upper cluster-to-hood screws. Pull the assembly slightly outward and disconnect the wiring connectors; to disconnect the plugs, depress the retaining (clip) and remove the cluster assembly.
5. Install the instrument cluster in reverse order.

1988–91 626 AND MX-6

1. Disconnect the negative battery cable.
2. If equipped with an automatic transaxle, remove both shift knob-to-shaft screws and the shift lever knob.
3. Remove the rear console screws, pull the console rearward and remove it.
4. Remove the front console screws and pry the ornament from the steering wheel pad. Remove the steering wheel.
5. Remove the screws and separate the upper and lower column covers. Remove the undercover screws and the under cov-

er. Reach behind hood release and remove the nut and the hood release knob.

6. Remove the meter hood screws and pull the meter hood out until the electrical connectors are visible. Disconnect the speedometer cable at the speedometer. Disconnect all the connectors from the rear of the meter hood and remove it.

7. Remove the screws and pull the meter assembly outward. Disconnect the speedometer cable, meter connectors and remove the meter assembly.

8. Remove the switch panel screws and pull the switch panel forward until the connectors are accessible. Disconnect the connectors and remove the switch panel.

9. Remove the glove box and disconnect the glove box light connector.

10. Remove the center panel. Remove the screws and slide the heater control assembly from the instrument panel. On lever control type instrument panels, disconnect the control cables from the **DEF**, **MAX-COLD** and **REC** lever positions. On Logicon type panels, disconnect the electrical connectors from the rear of the panel.

11. Remove the protective cap that covers the instrument panel center mounting bolt. Remove the center and side instrument panel mounting and bracket bolts. Remove the steering shaft mounting bolts.

12. Disconnect the harness connectors from the rear of the dash and remove the instrument panel.

13. Installation is the reverse of the removal procedure.

1987 323

1. Disconnect the negative battery cable. Remove the 3 screws from under the top edge of the instrument hood.

2. Pull the hood out for access, unplug the electrical connectors to the cluster switches on either side and remove it.

3. Remove the screw located near the bottom of the cluster on either side and the cluster from the dash.

4. Installation is the reverse of removal.

1988–91 323 AND PROTEGE

1. Remove the steering wheel, upper and lower column covers and the combination switch assembly.

2. Remove the screws and remove the meter hood.

3. Remove the meter hood screws and pull the meter hood out until the electrical connectors are visible. Disconnect the

speedometer cable at the speedometer. Disconnect all the connectors from the rear of the meter hood and remove it.

4. Remove the screws and separate the side wall from the front gear shift console on both sides. Remove the rear console (1 bolt), the front console and slide it forward. Disconnect the antenna feeder wire from the back of the radio.

5. Remove the hardware and the passenger's and driver's side undercovers.

6. Remove the lower panel screws. Remove the lower louver with the reinforcement. Remove the duct and disconnect the hood release wire.

7. Remove the covers from the center and side panel bolts. Remove the driver's and passenger's side covers along with the bolts.

8. Remove the glove box insert and the center bracket bolts.

9. Remove the nut from both sides of the side bracket and remove the ashtray screws.

10. Unscrew and remove the center panel. Disconnect the cigarette lighter connector and remove the light.

11. Disconnect and remove the cables from the heater control and blower units.

12. Unscrew and remove the lower cover. Remove the bolts from the instrument panel support bracket. Pull the instrument panel forward and disconnect the harness connectors from the rear of the unit. Remove the instrument panel from the rear of the vehicle.

13. Installation is the reverse of the removal procedure.

929

1. Disconnect the negative battery cable. Disconnect the speedometer cable at the transmission. Remove the shifter knob and dash upper plate.

2. Remove the ashtray and disconnect the cigarette lighter connector. If equipped with a manual transmission, apply the parking brake and remove the support bracket. Remove the screws, pull the console rearward and remove it.

3. Remove the steering wheel. Remove the steering wheel upper and lower cover assemblies.

4. Unscrew and pull the switch panel from the dash. Disconnect the electrical connectors and remove the switch panel.

5. Remove the meter hood screws and pull the meter hood out until the electrical connectors are visible. Disconnect the speedometer cable at the speedometer. Disconnect all the con-

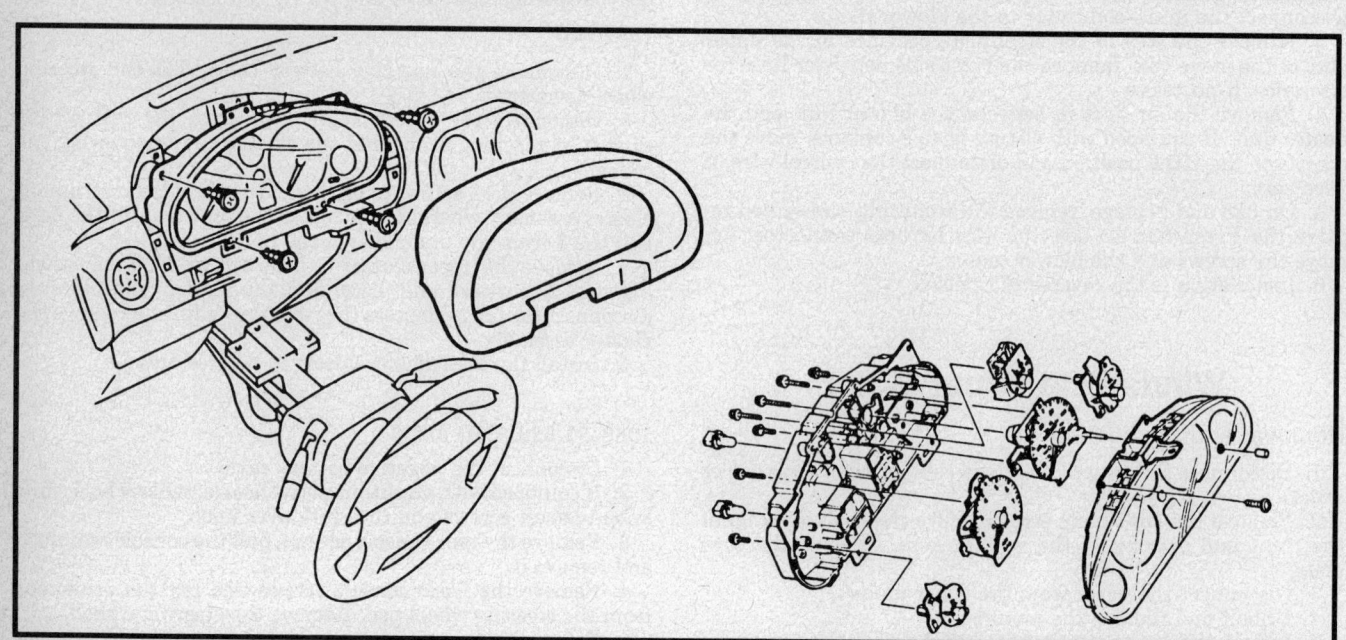

Exploded view of instrument cluster—Miata

nectors from the rear of the meter hood and remove it.

6. Remove the left and right ducts by releasing the clips and fasteners.

7. Unscrew and remove the center lower panel. Remove the hood release knob.

8. If equipped with an automatic transmission, remove the locking screw and the parking brake release knob and remove the nut from the parking brake release cable.

9. Unscrew and slide the air conditioning panel from the dash. Disconnect the connectors from the rear of the panel.

10. Remove the front header, left and right side trim. Remove the protective cap from the center instrument panel bolt and remove the bolt. Pull the side panel out carefully until the installation bolts are visible. Remove the side panel installation bolts.

11. Locate the bolts at the instrument panel center bracket and remove them. Remove the bolts from the steering shaft. Pull the instrument panel forward and disconnect the connectors that bridge the instruments and the harnesses. Remove the instrument panel from the vehicle.

12. Installation is the reverse of the removal procedure.

MIATA

1. Disconnect the battery negative cable.

2. Remove the steering column bracket bolts and lower the steering column carefully.

3. Remove the instrument cluster bezel.

4. Remove the instrument cluster bolts, disconnect the electrical connectors and remove the instrument cluster from the vehicle.

5. Remove the speedometer screws and the speedometer assembly from the instrument cluster.

6. Reverse the removal procedure to install.

Concealed Headlights

Manual Operation

RX-7 AND MIATA

1. Open hood.

2. Disconnect the battery negative cable.

NOTE: On Miata, the Personal Code Number (PCN) must be obtained before disconnecting the battery negative cable.

3. Turn the knob, located on the headlight motor, to open or close the the headlight, as necessary.

4. Reconnect the battery negative cable.

Combination Switch

Removal and Installation

1. Disconnect the negative battery cable.
2. Remove the steering wheel.
3. Remove the steering column covers.
4. Disconnect the electrical connectors.
5. Remove the stop ring from the shaft.
6. Remove the switch retaining screws. Remove the combination switch from its mounting.
7. Installation is the reverse of the removal procedure. On all vehicles except 323, once the combination switch is in place and the covers are installed, set the front wheels straight and align the combination switch and steering angle sensor marks.

Ignition Lock/Switch

Removal and Installation

EXCEPT RX-7

1. Disconnect the negative battery cable.
2. Remove the steering wheel.

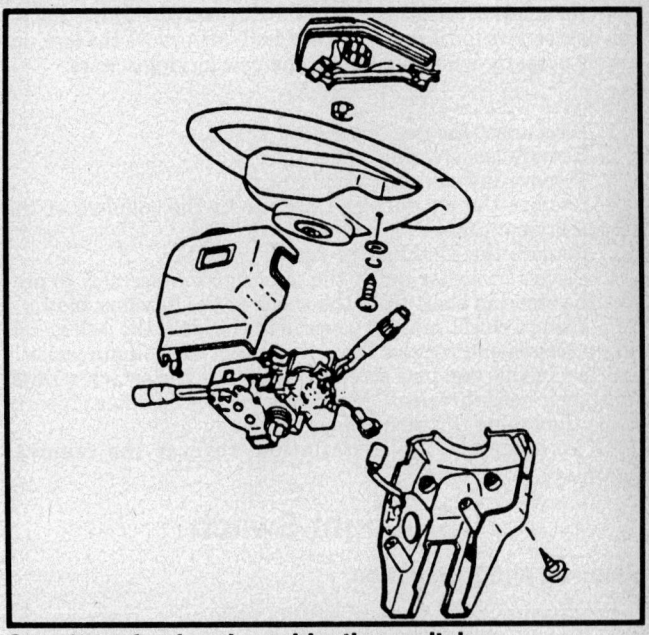

Steering wheel and combination switch components—323

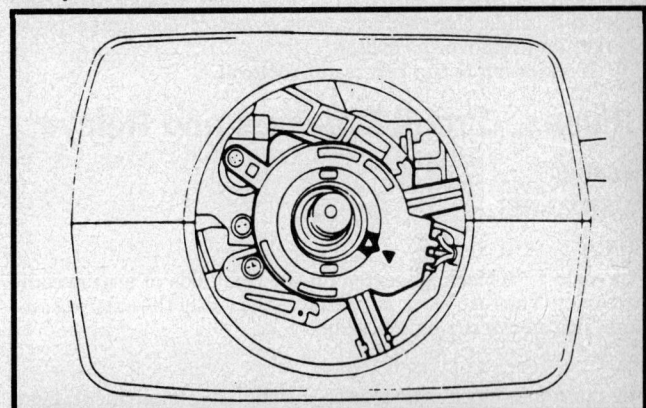

Combination switch and angle sensor alignment marks—626, MX-6 and 929

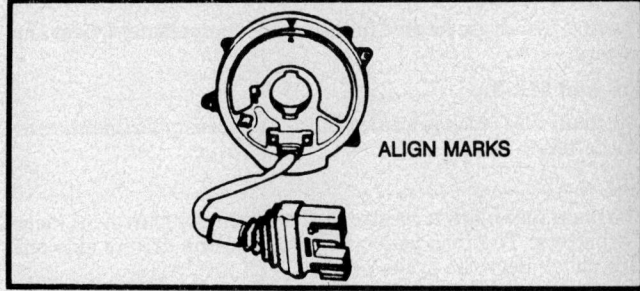

ALIGN MARKS

Aligning marks on the clock spring connector and the outer housing—RX-7

3. Remove the steering column covers.

4. Disconnect the electrical connectors.

5. Remove the stop ring from the shaft.

6. Remove the switch screws and the combination switch.

7. Remove the instrument frame brace. Disconnect the switch wires.

8. Use a chisel to make slots in the lock screws. Remove the screws.

9. Installation is the reverse of the removal procedure. Install the new screws until the head twists off. Make sure the lock operates properly while tightening the new locking screws.

RX-7

1. Disconnect the negative battery cable.
2. Remove the steering wheel.
3. Remove the steering wheel covers.
4. Remove the air duct and disconnect the couplers of the combination switch.
5. Remove the combination switch assembly.
6. Place a protector under the steering lock assembly to protect the steering shaft from the shock of the hammer blows.
7. Using a chisel, make grooves in the heads of the lock installation screws and remove the screws from the column jacket.
8. To install, use new screws and tighten the switch screws, until their heads break off. Make sure the lock operates properly while tightening the new locking screws.
9. To complete the installation, reverse the removal procedure.

Stoplight Switch

Removal and Installation

1. Disconnect the negative battery cable.
2. Disconnect the stoplight switch wire connector from the switch.
3. Remove the switch retainer and outer washer from the pedal pin. Slide the stoplight switch out of the brake pedal bracket and remove the switch.
4. Installation is the reverse of removal.

Fuses, Circuit Breakers and Relays

Location

FUSE PANEL

Miata

The main fuse block is located on the right side of engine compartment. The fuse block is located to the left of the steering column, just above the clutch pedal.

RX-7

The main fuse block is located in the engine compartment, near the radiator support. The fuse panel and joint box, are located behind the drivers side left kick panel.

323 and Protege

The fuse blocks are located in the engine compartment, near the battery.

626 and MX-6

The main fuse block is located in the engine compartment, near the battery.

929

The main fuse block is located in the engine compartment, near the battery. The fuse panel, is located on the drivers side left kick panel, near the brake pedal.

CIRCUIT BREAKERS

Various circuit breakers are located either in the main fuse block or the fuse panel.

RELAYS

RX-7

Cooling Fan Relay—located in front of engine near radiator.
Power Antenna Relay—located in rear of vehicle, near antenna.

Dimmer Relay—located in front of engine near radiator.

323 and Protege

Horn Relay—located in engine compartment, on left fender.
Headlight Relay—located in engine compartment, on left fender.
Windshield Wiper Relay—located in engine compartment, on left fender.

929

Various relays can be found in the relay box, located in the engine compartment near the battery.

Miata

Horn Relay—located behind the instrument panel, on the driver's side.
Cooling Fan Relay—located in the engine compartment, on the right fender.
Headlight Relay—located in the engine compartment, on the left fender.

626 and MX-6

Various relays can be found in the relay boxes, located in the engine compartment on the firewall and under the instrument panel on the drivers side.

Computers

Location

RX-7

Central Processing Unit (CPU)—located behind the drivers side kick panel, near the fuse block.
Anti-Lock Brake Control Unit—located under the right hand side of the instrument panel.

323 AND PROTEGE

Cruise Control Unit—located under the left side of the instrument, near the instrument panel relay box.
Engine RPM Control Unit—located in the center of the instrument panel, near the EGI control unit.

626 AND MX-6

Anti-Lock Brake Control Unit—located under the driver's front seat.
EGI Electronic Control Unit—located below the center of the instrument panel.
Electronic Control Unit (ECU)—located in the engine compartment, on the right fender.

929

Anti-Lock Brake Control Unit—located behind the passenger's side front kick panel.
Engine Control Unit—located in the engine compartment, on the right fender.

MIATA

Cruise Control Unit—located behind the driver's side kick panel, near the instrument panel.

Flashers

Location

RX-7

The turn signal/hazard flasher unit is located in the left kick panel, on the bottom of the CPU.

323 AND PROTEGE

The turn signal/hazard flasher unit is located on the instrument panel relay box.

626 AND MX-6

The turn signal/hazard flasher unit is located below the left side side of the instrument panel.

929

The turn signal/hazard flasher unit is located in the relay box, under the instrument panel on the steering column.

MIATA

The turn signal/hazard flasher unit is located behind the center of the instrument panel.

ENGINE COOLING

Radiator

Removal and Installation

RX-7

1. Position a drain under the radiator, loosen the drain plug and drain the radiator.
2. Remove the cooling fan from the water pump pulley.
3. Remove the air inlet pipe.
4. Disconnect the cables from the battery and remove the battery and bracket.
5. Disconnect the heater and upper hose from the radiator.
6. Disconnect the coolant level sensor and the radiator switch connectors.
7. If equipped with an automatic transmission, disconnect the radiator cooling hoses from the bottom of the radiator and plug the ends to prevent leakage.
8. Remove the radiator and the radiator cowling.

To install:

9. Install the radiator cowling and the radiator. Leave the cowling bolts snug and complete the installation of the remaining components in reverse of installation.
10. Once the cooling fan is bolted to the water pump pulley, check the clearance between the blades of the cooling fan and the fan shroud. If the clearance is not sufficient to allow the blades to turn without contacting the cowling, adjust the cowling and the cowling bolts.
11. Fill the cooling system to the proper level. Start the engine and check for coolant leaks.

EXCEPT RX-7

1. Disconnect the negative battery cable. Drain the radiator.
2. Remove the fan blades and shroud or disconnect the electrical harness from the electric fan motor and remove the fan and cowling mount. On 929, disconnect the vacuum hoses from the fresh air duct and remove the duct.
3. Remove the upper and lower hoses and coolant reservoir tank hose. Disconnect the transmission cooler lines, if equipped.
4. Remove the radiator bolts and the radiator.
5. Install the radiator by reversing the removal procedure. Refill the cooling system.

Electric Cooling Fan

Testing

1. Disconnect the cooling fan electrical connector.
2. Apply battery voltage to the cooling fan connector.
3. Fan should operate, if not, replace fan.

Removal and Installation

1. Disconnect the battery negative cable.
2. Drain cooling system.
3. Disconnect the cooling fan electrical connector(s).
4. Remove the radiator, if necessary.
5. Remove the fan motor bolts and the fan motor.
6. Reverse procedure to install. Connect battery negative cable.

Heater Core

For further information, please refer to "Chilton's Heating and Air Conditioning Manual" for additional coverage.

Removal and Installation

1. Disconnect the negative battery cable. Drain the coolant.
2. Disconnect the heater hoses at the engine firewall.
3. On 1988–91 323, 626 and MX-6, disconnect the duct between the heater box and the blower motor or depending on the vehicle, remove the crash pad and instrument panel pad from the dash.
4. Disconnect the defroster hoses, if necessary, set the control to the **DEF** and **HOT** position and disconnect the control wires if they are in the way.
5. Unfasten the screws that secure the halves of the heater box together or remove the heater unit and bracket. Separate the heater box for access to the heater core.
6. Detach the hoses if not already disconnected. Remove the mounting clips and the heater core. Plugs the open inlet and outlet connections to prevent the leakage of coolant onto the interior. Installation is the reverse of the removal procedure.

Water Pump

Removal and Installation

RX-7

1. Disconnect the negative battery cable. Remove the air cleaner and disconnect the water temperature switch wiring from the radiator.
2. Remove the air conditioner, air pump, power steering and alternator drive belts. Remove the alternator and the air pump.
3. Remove the cooling fan and drive assembly. On the 13B en-

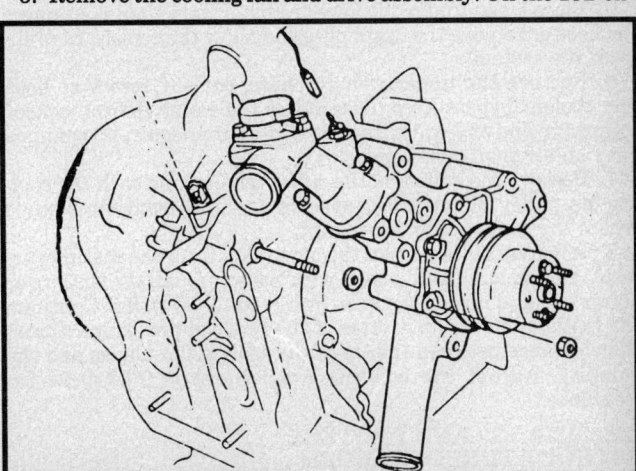

Water pump removal and installation—RX-7

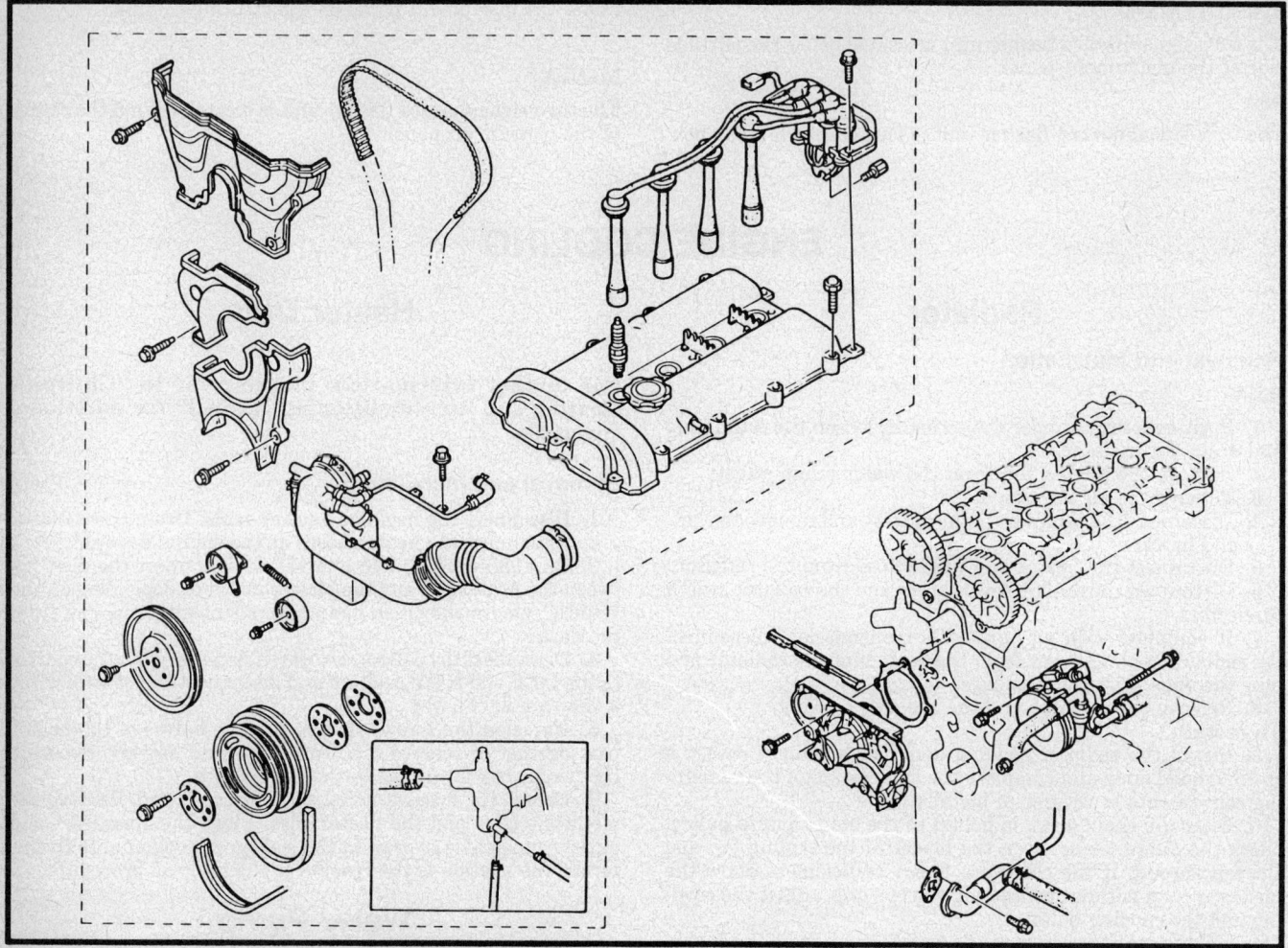

Exploded view of the water pump assembly—Miata

gine, turn the eccentric shaft so the top mark of the pulley is aligned with the indicator pin.

4. Remove the drive pulley for the air conditioner compressor from in front of the alternator/air pump drive pulleys. It is the pulley on the eccentric shaft, not the one on the front of the compressor.

5. Place a pan under the lower radiator hose then disconnect the hose or remove the drain plug and allow the coolant to drain from the system.

6. Remove the upper radiator hose, coolant reservoir hose and coolant bypass hose. Disconnect the water thermo sensor connector and the water thermo switch connector, if equipped with an automatic transmission.

7. Remove the bolts and the water pump along with the cooling fan pulley. Retrieve the spacers or shims from the 2 studs where the gasket does not mount.

8. When installing, clean the old gasket from the mating surfaces, and install a new gasket with sealer. Install the spacers or shims and and torque the bolts evenly to 13–20 ft. lbs. Continue the installation in the reverse of the removal procedure. Check the clearance between the tip of the cooling fan blades and the cowling. Adjust the cowling until there is 0.63–0.94 in. clearance.

626, MX-6, 323 AND PROTEGE WITHOUT TURBOCHARGER

NOTE: Use special tool 49E301060 or equivalent, on

the engine flywheel gear to stop the engine from rotating during removal and installation of the crankshaft pulley.

1. Disconnect the negative battery cable. Drain the cooling system. Turn the crankshaft so the No. 1 cylinder piston is at TDC on the compression stroke.

2. Remove the front cover assembly, timing belt and pulleys.

3. Remove the water inlet pipe from the water pump.

4. Remove the water pump bolts and the water pump.

5. Installation is the reverse of the removal procedure. Use new O-rings and gaskets. On 1988–90 626 and MX-6, use an O-ring and 3 rubber seals. Fill the cooling system and check the timing.

323 WITH TURBOCHARGER

1. Disconnect the negative battery cable. Drain the cooling system. Position the engine at TDC on the compression stroke.

2. Remove the drive belts. Remove the water pump pulley. Remove the crankshaft pulley. Remove the baffle plate.

3. Remove the middle and lower timing belt covers. Remove the belt tensioner. Remove the tensioner spring. Remove the timing belt.

4. Remove the coolant inlet pipe. Remove the water pump bolts and the water pump.

5. Installation is the reverse of the removal procedure. Be sure to use new gaskets or RTV sealant, as required. Torque the water pump bolts to 14–19 ft. lbs.

929

1. Disconnect the negative battery cable. Drain the cooling system. Position the engine at TDC on the compression stroke.

2. Remove the drive belts, the timing belt cover assembly and the timing belt.

3. Remove the water pump bolts and the water pump.

4. Installation is the reverse of the removal procedure. Be sure to use new gaskets or RTV sealant, as required.

MIATA

1. Disconnect the battery negative cable and drain the cooling system.

2. Remove the ignition coil pack assembly and the spark plug wires.

3. Remove the cylinder head cover bolts and the cylinder head cover.

4. Remove the intake air pipe assembly.

5. Remove the timing belt.

6. Remove the power steering oil pump and the water pump inlet pipe.

7. Remove the water pump bolts and the water pump.

8. Reverse procedure to install. Torque the water pump bolts to 14–19 ft. lbs. (19–25 Nm).

Thermostat

Removal and Installation

RX-7

1. Disconnect the negative battery cable. Drain the engine coolant. Remove the upper hose from thermostat housing.

2. Disconnect the water thermo switch connector. Remove the thermostat housing and the thermostat.

3. Installation is the reverse or removal procedure, always install a new mounting gasket. When installing the thermostat, make sure the jiggle pin is facing up. Align the marks on the upper hose with the cover marks during installation.

EXCEPT RX-7

1. Disconnect the negative battery cable. Drain the cooling system.

2. Disconnect the radiator hose and the coolant temperature switch lead from the thermostat housing.

3. Remove the thermostat housing bolts, housing, gasket and thermostat.

4. Clean all gasket surfaces. Install the new thermostat with the temperature sensing pellet downwards or toward the engine block. Use a new mounting gasket and install the housing.

Thermostat removal and installation—RX-7

THE JIGGLE PIN SHOULD BE ON THE UPPER SIDE

SEAL PRINT SIDE SHOULD FACE THE CYLINDER HEAD

Thermostat assembly—323

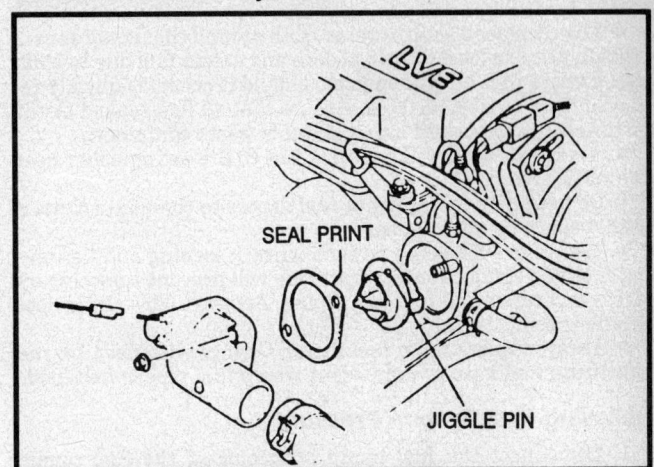

SEAL PRINT

JIGGLE PIN

Thermostat assembly—626 and MX-6

Thermostat housing positioning—929

5. To complete the installation, reverse the removal procedure. When installing the thermostat into the housing, be sure the jiggle pin is positioned upward. On 929, install the thermostat housing so the mark is facing the front of the engine. Fill the cooling system.

FUEL SYSTEM

Fuel System Service Precautions

Safety is the most important factor when performing not only fuel system maintenance but any type of maintenance. Failure to conduct maintenance and repairs in a safe manner may result in serious personal injury or death. Maintenance and testing of the vehicle's fuel system components can be accomplished safely and effectively by adhering to the following rules and guidelines.

• To avoid the possibility of fire and personal injury, always disconnect the negative battery cable unless the repair or test procedure requires that battery voltage be applied.

• Always relieve the fuel system pressure prior to disconnecting any fuel system component (injector, fuel rail, pressure regulator, etc.), fitting or fuel line connection. Exercise extreme caution whenever relieving fuel system pressure to avoid exposing skin, face and eyes to fuel spray. Please be advised that fuel under pressure may penetrate the skin or any part of the body that it contacts.

• Always place a shop towel or cloth around the fitting or connection prior to loosening to absorb any excess fuel due to spillage. Ensure that all fuel spillage (should it occur) is quickly removed from engine surfaces. Ensure that all fuel soaked cloths or towels are deposited into a suitable waste container.

• Always keep a dry chemical (Class B) fire extinguisher near the work area.

• Do not allow fuel spray or fuel vapors to come into contact with a spark or open flame.

• Always use a backup wrench when loosening and tightening fuel line connection fittings. This will prevent unnecessary stress and torsion to fuel line piping. Always follow the proper torque specifications.

• Always replace worn fuel fitting O-rings with new. Do not substitute fuel hose or equivalent where fuel pipe is installed.

Relieving Fuel System Pressure

1. Disconnect the fuel pump connector at the fuel pump, while the engine is running.
2. Allow the engine to stall. Turn the ignition switch OFF.
3. Disconnect the negative battery cable. Allow the engine to cool.
4. Carefully, loosen but do not remove, the fuel hose clamp located at the distribution pipe inlet.
5. Place a rag around the end of the fuel inlet hose and slide the clamp away from the distribution pipe inlet opening.
6. With the rag still in place, carefully work the fuel hose from the inlet opening to relieve any system pressure. Drain excess fuel in a suitable container.

Fuel Filter

Removal and Installation

RX-7

1. Relieve the fuel system pressure. Disconnect the negative battery cable. Raise and support the vehicle safely.
2. Loosen the clips at both ends of the filter and place a collection pan under it to catch excess fuel.
3. Disconnect the fuel filter lines and remove the filter from its retainer.
4. Install the new filter, paying close attention to the direction of the filter in relation to the direction of the fuel flow.
5. Turn the starter to ON to activate the fuel pump and check the fuel filter connections for leaks.

EXCEPT RX-7

1. Properly relieve the fuel system pressure. Disconnect the negative battery cable. Remove the screw and wire retainer bracket.
2. Remove the inlet and outlet fuel lines.
3. Remove the fuel filter. On some vehicles, it may be necessary to remove the bracket with the fuel filter.
4. Installation is the reverse of the removal procedure. Install the filter in the proper direction. If the fuel filter is equipped with union bolt fittings, use new metal crush gaskets. Start the engine and check for leaks.

Electric Fuel Pump

Pressure Testing

1. On electric fuel pumps with carburetor engines, connect a suitable tee connection to the fuel filter hose and attach a pressure gauge. Install a jumper wire to connect the terminals of the fuel pump test connection, then turn the ignition ON and read the fuel pressure. Compare it to specification.
2. On electric fuel pumps with fuel injection, connect a suitable pressure gauge to the main fuel line from the fuel pump. Install a jumper wire to connect the terminals of the test connector, then turn the ignition ON and read the fuel pump output pressure. Compare it to specification.
3. Install a tee connector in the fuel line from the filter and attach the pressure gauge. Remove the jumper wire from the test connector and disconnect the vacuum line at the fuel pressure regulator. Start the engine and read the fuel pressure at idle. Compare it to specification.
4. Reconnect the vacuum hose to the pressure regulator and again read the fuel pressure. Compare it to specification.
5. Stop the engine and allow it to cool before disconnecting the pressure regulator after testing.

Removal and Installation

EXTERNAL CHASSIS MOUNTED

Except RX-7

1. Relieve the fuel system pressure. Disconnect the negative battery cable.
2. Disconnect the fuel pump lead wire in the luggage compartment.
3. Raise and support the vehicle safely.
4. Disconnect the fuel pump bracket.
5. Disconnect the fuel inlet and outlet hoses and remove the fuel pump.
6. Installation is the reverse of removal. Use new gaskets as required.

RX-7

1. Relieve the fuel system pressure. Disconnect the negative battery cable. Remove the rear floor mat and floor plate.
2. Disconnect the fuel pump electrical connection under the floor plate.
3. Raise and support the vehicle safely.
4. Remove the fuel pump protecting cover. Remove inlet and outlet lines. Remove the pump.
5. Installation is the reverse of removal.

INTERNAL TANK MOUNTED

1. Relieve the fuel system pressure. Disconnect the negative battery cable. Depending on the vehicle, lifting of the rear mat or removal of the rear seat will be required in order to gain access to the fuel pump cover plate.
2. Disconnect the electrical connector.
3. Remove the fuel pump cover screws and lift off the cover.
4. Disconnect the fuel feed and return hoses. Wrap a clean rag around the fuel lines when disconnect to catch any fuel

spray, then plug the lines to prevent leakage.

5. Remove the mounting screws and lift the fuel pump and gauge assembly from the fuel tank.

6. Installation is the reverse of the removal procedure. Be careful not to allow any dirt or other foreign material to contaminate the fuel tank while the unit is removed. Use a new cover plate gasket, as required.

Carburetor

Removal and Installation

1. Disconnect the negative battery cable. Remove the air cleaner assembly.

2. Disconnect the accelerator cable assembly. Disconnect the cruise control cable, if necessary. Remove all necessary wiring and vacuum lines.

3. Disconnect the fuel supply and fuel return lines. As required, disconnect the air/fuel solenoid harness at the wiring connector and the bullet connector.

4. Remove the connector for the bimetal choke heater, if equipped. Disconnect the choke cable, if equipped.

5. Disconnect the leads from the throttle solenoid and deceleration valve at the quick disconnects. Disconnect the throttle return spring.

6. Remove the carburetor bolts and the carburetor assembly.

7. Installation is the reverse of the removal procedure. Be sure to use a new carburetor base gasket.

Idle Speed Adjustment

1. Warm the engine. Turn the headlights and other accessories OFF.

2. Make sure the check valve is fully open. Check the ignition timing and adjust, as required. Disconnect the electric cooling fan motor before setting the idle speed.

3. Connect a tachometer to the engine. Apply the parking brake and block the wheels. The transmission should be in N.

4. Turn the throttle adjusting screw to adjust the idle speed.

5. On 1987 323, the dash pot must be adjusted as follows:

   a. Start the engine and warm to normal operating temperature. Leave the tachometer connected.

   b. Increase the engine speed to 3000 rpm.

   c. Slowly reduce the engine speed and make sure the dash pot rod contacts the lever at 2400–2600 rpm.

   d. If not as described, loosen the locknut and adjust the rod by turning the dash pot.

Idle Mixture Adjustment

1987 323

NOTE: Do not fix the spring pin to lock the mixture adjust screw until the adjustment is performed. Before adjusting the idle mixture, check/adjust the idle speed.

1. Start the engine and allow it to reach normal operating temperature. Connect a tachometer to the engine. On the 323, disconnect and plug the secondary hoses from the reed valves.

2. Connect a dwell meter (90 degrees, 4 cylinder) to the Y wire in the check connector of the A/F solenoid valve and read the meter.

3. The reading should be 32–40 degrees at idle. If the reading is not within specification, adjust the idle mixture by turning the idle mixture adjustment screw.

NOTE: If the adjustment cannot be made, it is probably because of a faulty oxygen sensor, a broken wire or a short in the wiring between the oxygen sensor and the control unit.

4. Insert an exhaust gas analyzer probe into the secondary air hose and seal the opening to prevent exhaust gas leakage. Adjust the CO to 1.5–2.5 percent by turning the idle mixture screw.

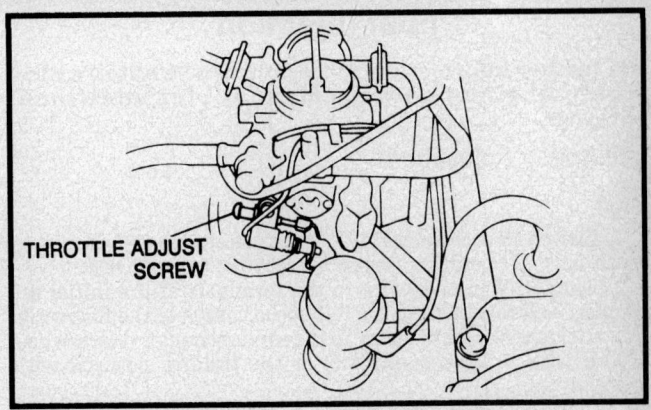

Adjusting the idle speed—1987 323 carbureted engines

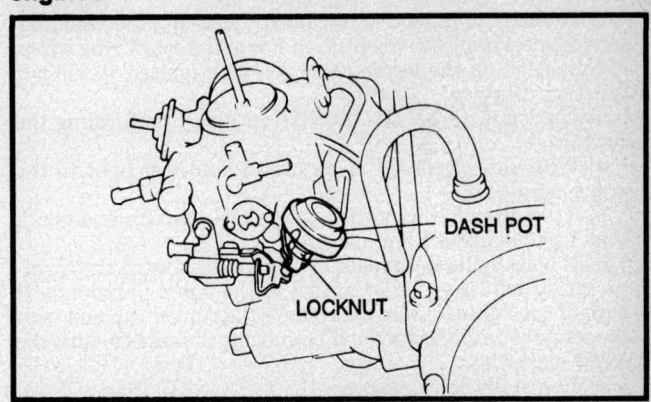

Dash pot adjustment—1987 323

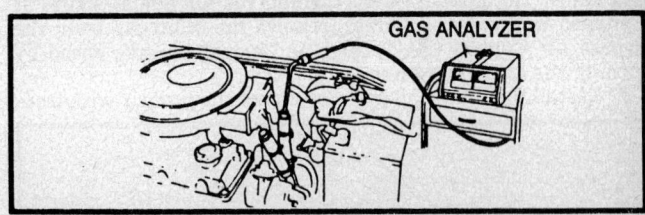

Adjusting idle mixture on 1987 323 vehicle. Insert the probe into the secondary air hose as shown

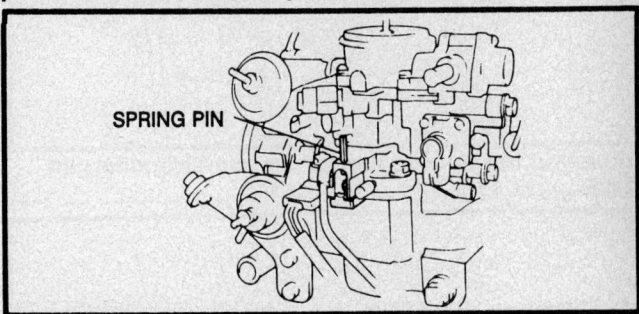

Location of spring pin on carburetor—1987 323

5. Be sure the idle speed is set at specification. If not, adjust, as necessary, by using the throttle adjust screw. Fix the spring pin to lock the mixture adjustment screw.

Fuel Injection

For further information, please refer to "Chilton's Electronic Engine Control's Manual" for additional coverage.

Idle Speed Adjustment

RX-7

1. Switch all accessories OFF. Start the engine and allow it to reach normal operating temperature, then turn it OFF.
2. Connect a jumper wire to the terminals of the initial set coupler. Before adjusting the idle speed complete the following.
   a. Connect a tachometer to the service coupler (black/white wire with a black connector) at the trailing side coil with igniter.
   b. If the tachometer does not function correctly on the trailing side coil with igniter, reconnect at the leading side coil with igniter (black/white terminal).
   c. If using an inductive (secondary pick-up type tachometer), connect it only at the trailing side of the spark plug wires. If connected on the leading side coil with igniter, it will not function properly.
3. Inspect and adjust the throttle sensor by performing the following:
   a. With the engine OFF, connect a dual test light to the green connector.
   b. Turn the ignition switch to the **ON** position and check that 1 of the lights illuminate.
   c. If both lights illuminate or neither does, turn the throttle sensor adjusting screw until 1 of the lights illuminate. If both of the lights illuminate, remove the rubber cap and turn the screw counterclockwise. If both lights illuminate, turn the screw clockwise.
   d. Reinstall the rubber cap.
4. If not equipped with a turbocharger, remove the blind cap and adjust the idle speed by turning the air adjust screw. If equipped with a turbocharger, remove the blind cap from the Bypass Air Control (BAC) valve and adjust the idle speed by turning the air adjust screw.
5. Install the blind cap and disconnect the jumper wire from

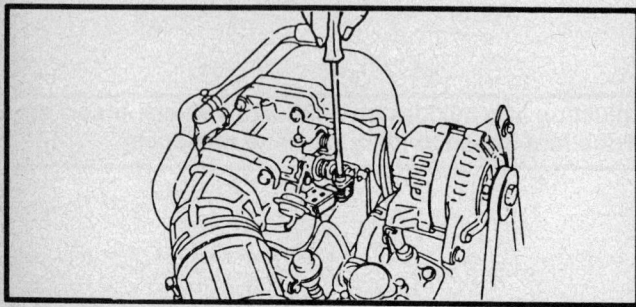

Adjusting the throttle sensor on non-turbocharged RX-7

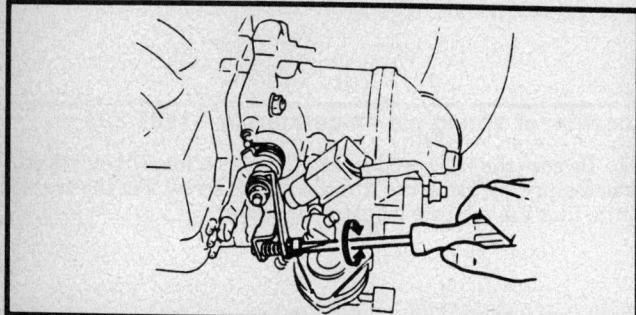

Adjusting the throttle sensor on turbocharged RX-7

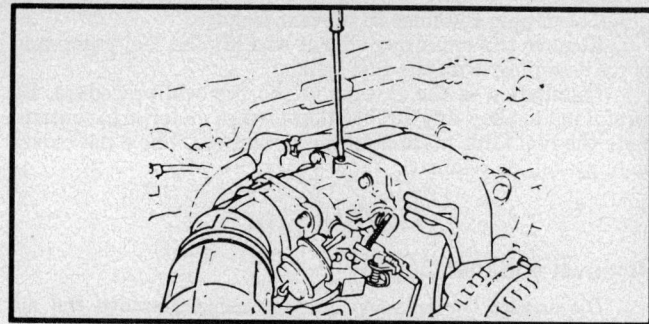

Idle speed adjustment screw location on non-turbocharged RX-7

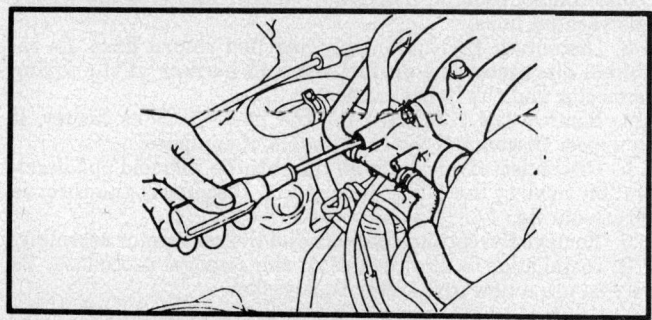

Idle speed adjustment screw location on turbocharged RX-7

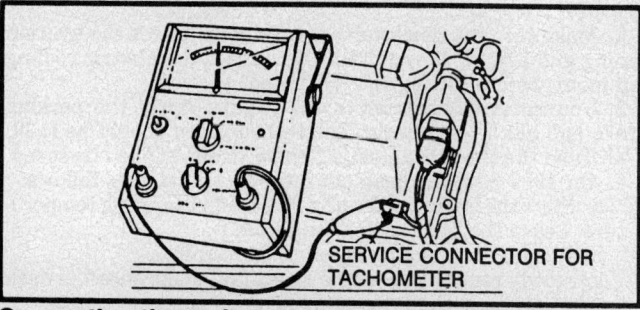

SERVICE CONNECTOR FOR TACHOMETER

Connecting the tachometer to the check connector—323, Protege, 626 and MX-6

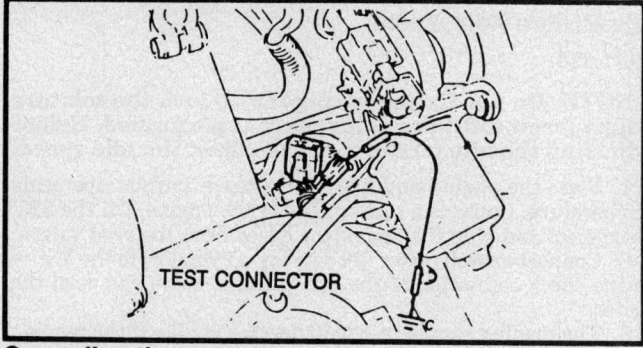

TEST CONNECTOR

Grounding the green test connector for the idle speed adjustment—323, Protege, 626 and MX-6

the initial coupler. Be sure to remove the jumper wire, otherwise the engine performance will be reduced.

323, PROTEGE, 626 AND MX-6

1. Connect a tachometer to the white engine check connector. Start the engine and allow it to run for 3 minutes in neutral for manual transmissions/transaxles or **P** for automatic transmis-

sions/transaxles, in the 2500–3000 rpm range.

2. Make sure all accessories are switched OFF. On 1987 vehicles, make sure the electric cooling fan is OFF, if not run the engine at idle until the cooling fan stops.

3. Check the initial ignition timing and adjust, as necessary.

4. On 1988–91 vehicles, connect a jumper wire from pin 1 of the green test connector to ground.

5. Make sure the idle speed is within specification.

6. If the idle speed is not within specification, remove the blind cap and adjust it by turning the air adjusting screw in the throttle body.

7. Install the blind cap. On 1988–91 vehicles, disconnect the jumper wire.

8. Disconnect the tachometer.

MIATA

1. Ensure that all accessories OFF. Start the engine and allow it to reach normal operating temperature.

2. Connect a tachometer to the diagnostic connector terminal IG.

NOTE: When using an externally powered tachometer, connect it to the power connector, Blue: 1-pin. Do not ground the power connector terminal, Blue: 1-pin or the fuse will be burned.

3. Connect SST 49–B019–9A0 or equivalent, to the diagnostic connector terminals TEN and GND and set the SST tester to SELF TEST.

4. Idle speed should be between 800–900 rpm.

5. If specifications are not as indicated, remove the blind cap from the air adjusting screw and adjust the idle speed, as necessary.

6. After adjustment, replace the blind cap and remove tachometer and SST tester.

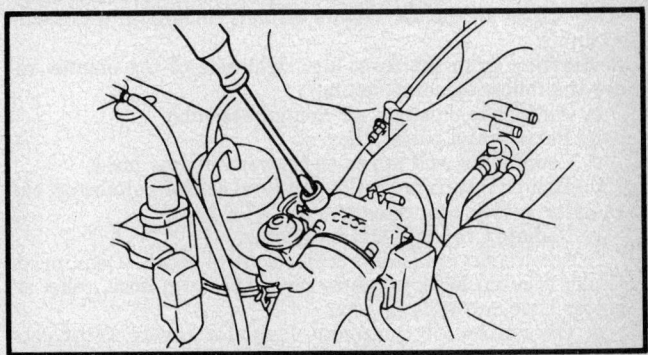

Adjusting the idle speed—Miata

Idle Mixture Adjustment

Because a automatic compensation function of the air fuel mixture has been built into the the Electronic Gasoline Injection (EGI) control unit, it is not necessary to check or adjust the idle mixture.

Fuel Injector

Removal and Installation

1. Depressurize the fuel system.
2. Disconnect the battery negative cable.
3. Remove the injector harness from the delivery pipe.
4. Remove the intake manifold, if necessary.
5. Remove the delivery pipe bolts, the delivery pipe with injectors and the pressure regulator.
6. Reverse procedure to install. Connect the battery negative cable.

ROTARY ENGINE MECHANICAL

Engine Assembly

Removal and Installation

RX-7

Without Turbocharger

1. Relieve the fuel system pressure. Disconnect the negative battery cable. Scribe mark the hinge locations and remove the hood. Drain the coolant and engine oil.

2. As required, discharge the air conditioning system, using the proper equipment.

3. From the left side of the engine compartment, remove the spark plug wires, distributor cap and the rotor. Disconnect the oil pressure gauge and oil temperature gauge wire harnesses. Disconnect the accelerator cable, fuel lines and evaporator lines. Plug the lines to prevent leakage and contamination.

4. Disconnect the air conditioner compressor drive belt and remove the compressor. Remove the power steering pump and mounting brackets. Remove the rear oil hose and drain the engine oil into a container. Remove the starter wire harness bracket. Disconnect the heater hoses and temperature gauge unit wiring.

5. From the right side of the engine remove or disconnect the air pump hose, the air funnel, air flow meter connector and the air cleaner assembly. Remove the radiator hoses and heater hoses.

6. Disconnect the fan harness. Remove the fan and cover. Disconnect the coolant level sensor. Remove the radiator. Dis-

connect the oil cooler hoses. Disconnect the cruise control cable and the oil pump metering rod connector. Remove water hoses, brake booster hose and air pump hoses.

7. From the top of the engine, remove or disconnect the 8 vacuum sensor tubes from the chamber to sensing pipes. Disconnect the intake air sensor connector, the air supply valve connector and the throttle sensor. Remove the mounting nut and disconnect the terminal cover wire. Remove the dynamic chamber from the engine.

8. Disconnect the following wiring connectors. Oxygen sensor, injectors, water temperature sensor, vacuum control solenoid valve, pressure regulator control solenoid, vent solenoid, vacuum valve solenoid, engine ground and the alternator harness and wires.

9. Raise and support the vehicle safely. Remove the exhaust pipe front cover, catalytic converter cover, exhaust pipe bracket, exhaust pipe, disconnect the starter motor harness and remove the starter motor.

10. Remove the converter cover and remove the converter-to-flywheel bolts. Remove the transmission-to-engine bolts and engine mount nuts.

11. Lower the vehicle, attach a suitable lifting sling to a hoist and carefully remove the engine after pulling it forward slightly to disengage the transmission.

12. Installation is the reverse of the removal procedure. Replace the coolant and lubricant. Check the ignition timing.

With Turbocharger

1. Relieve the fuel system pressure. Disconnect the negative

battery cable. Drain the engine oil and coolant into suitable containers.

2. Starting from the front and right side of the engine, remove the following components.

    a. Air intake pipe and air cleaner assembly

    b. Battery and battery box

    c. Cooling fan and upper and lower radiator hoses

    d. Heater return hose. Coolant level sensor connector, the radiator switch connector and the ATF hose.

    e. Radiator, cowling and intercooler

    f. Accelerator cable and cruise control cable, if equipped. Brake vacuum hose, pressure sensor vacuum hose, relief silencer hose and spilt air pipe

    g. Oxygen sensor connector. Insulator covers, front converter upper nut and engine harness connector

3. Working from the left side of the engine, remove the following components.

    a. Power steering pump and drive belt. Leave the hoses connected to the power steering pump and secure it aside.

    b. Air conditioning compressor and drive belt. Leave the hoses connected to the compressor and secure it aside.

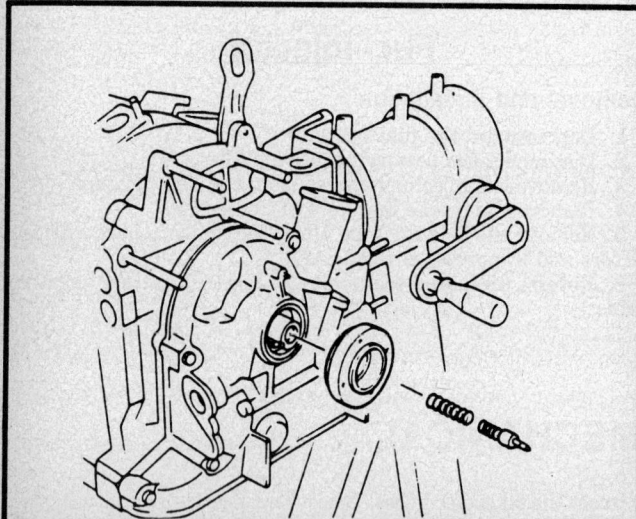

Eccentric shaft bypass valve, spring and pulley boss removal and installation—1.3L rotary engine

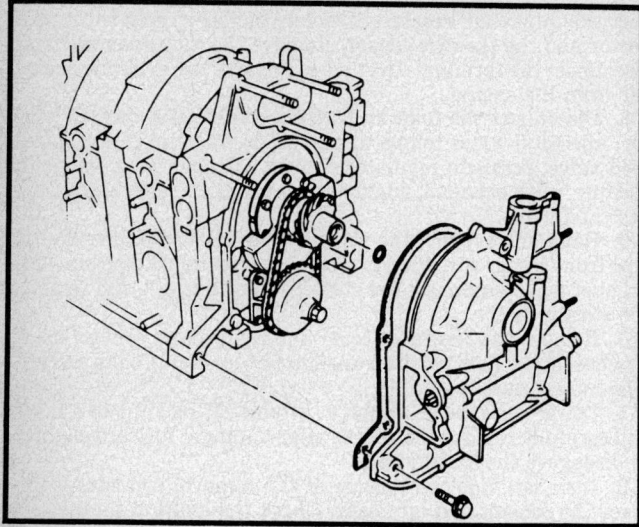

Front cover removal and installation—1.3L rotary engine

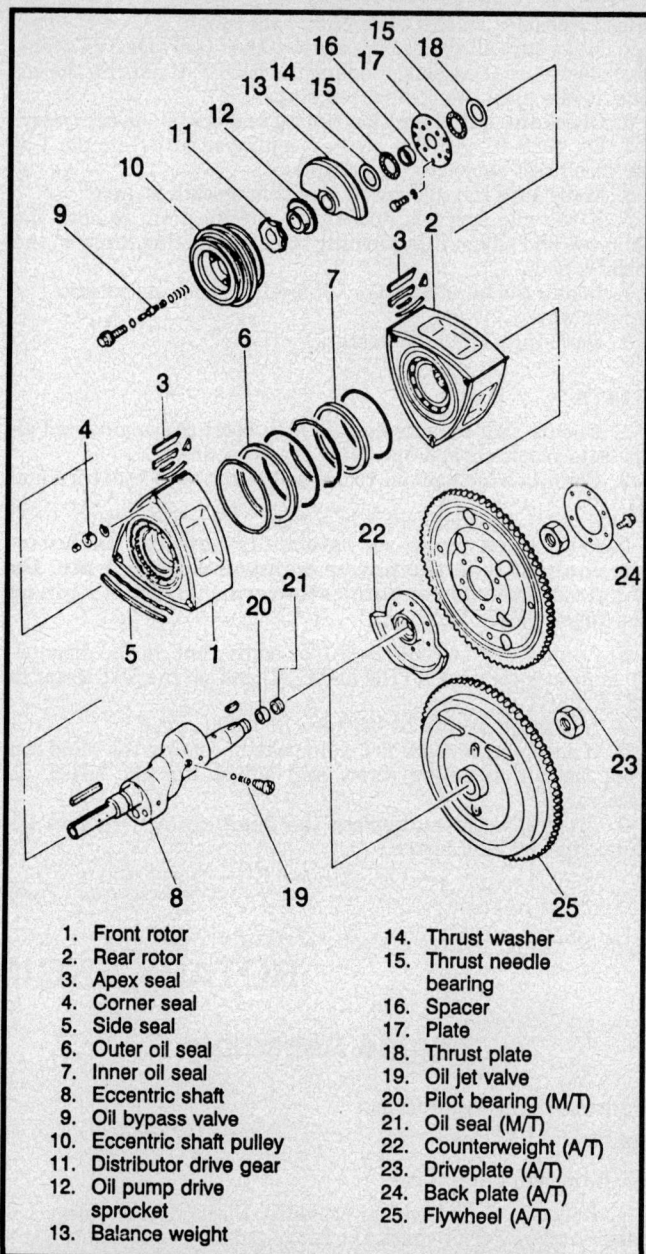

1. Front rotor	14. Thrust washer
2. Rear rotor	15. Thrust needle
3. Apex seal	bearing
4. Corner seal	16. Spacer
5. Side seal	17. Plate
6. Outer oil seal	18. Thrust plate
7. Inner oil seal	19. Oil jet valve
8. Eccentric shaft	20. Pilot bearing (M/T)
9. Oil bypass valve	21. Oil seal (M/T)
10. Eccentric shaft pulley	22. Counterweight (A/T)
11. Distributor drive gear	23. Driveplate (A/T)
12. Oil pump drive	24. Back plate (A/T)
sprocket	25. Flywheel (A/T)
13. Balance weight	

Engine rotating components—1.3L rotary engine

    c. Remove the spark plug wires, crank angle sensor connector and alternator connector.

    d. Remove the canister hose. Remove and plug the fuel hose.

    e. Remove the oil pressure connector, heater hose, clutch release cylinder, engine ground and oil cooler pipe and bracket.

4. Raise and support the vehicle safely. Remove the under cover, catalytic converter insulator, split air pipe, exhaust pipe bracket and catalytic converter. Remove the exhaust pipe and front converter, starter, transmission bolts and engine mounting nuts.

5. Lower the vehicle, attach a suitable lifting sling to a hoist and carefully remove the engine after pulling it forward slightly to disengage the transmission.

6. Installation is the reverse of the removal procedure. Replace the coolant and lubricant. Check the ignition timing.

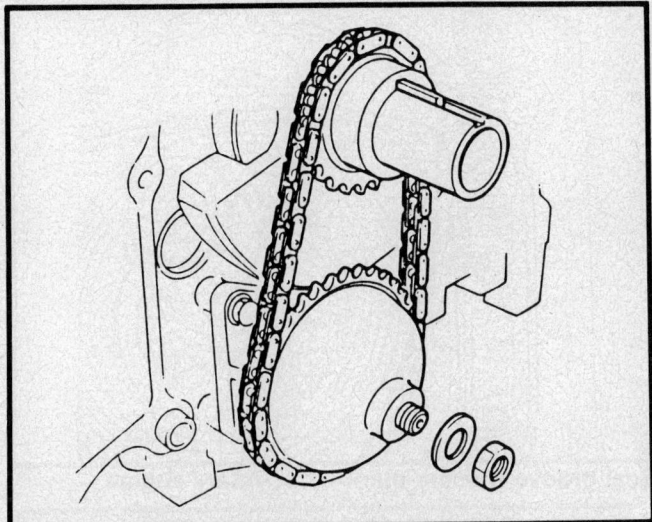

Oil pump drive gear, driven gear and chain removal and installation—1.3L rotary engine

Disassembly

NOTE: Because of the design of the rotary engine, it is not practical to attempt component removal and installation. It is best to disassemble and assemble the entire engine or go as far as necessary with the disassembly and assembly procedure as needed.

1. Mount the engine on a stand.
2. Mark or label all components for assembly reference.
3. Remove the air conditioning compressor and the power steering pump bracket.
4. Remove the left engine mount, spark plugs, oil level gauge, oil filler pipe, oil filter and filter body.
5. Remove the oil pressure gauge, crank angle sensor, air pump and drive belt, air pump bracket, alternator and drive belt, clutch cover and clutch disc.
6. Remove the metering oil connecting rod, 2nd vacuum piping, throttle and dynamic chamber.
7. Primary fuel injector and distribution pipe. Air control valve, switching actuator, water pipe and air hose.
8. Housing oil nozzle and manifold oil nozzle, intake manifold, exhaust manifold and insulator.
9. Metering oil pump, eccentric shaft pulley, water pump, dynamic chamber bracket, engine harness and vacuum piping and the oil inlet pipe.
10. Invert the engine.
11. Remove right engine mount and the oil pan.
12. Remove the oil strainer and gasket.
13. Identify the front and rear rotor housing with a felt tip pen. These are common parts and must be identified to be assembled in their respective locations.
14. Turn the engine on the stand so the top of the engine is up.
15. Remove the engine mounting bracket from the front cover.
16. Remove the eccentric shaft pulley. Remove the eccentric shaft bypass valve and spring. Remove the O-ring from the eccentric shaft lock bolt and discard it. Remove the eccentric shaft pulley boss.
17. Turn the engine on a stand so the front end of the engine is up.
18. Remove the front cover with the oil pressure control valve.
19. Remove the O-ring from the oil passage on the front housing.
20. Remove the oil slinger and distributor drive gear from the shaft.
21. Unbolt and remove the chain adjuster.
22. Remove the locknut and washer from the oil pump driven sprocket.
23. Slide the oil pump drive sprocket and driven sprocket, together with the drive chain off the eccentric shaft and oil pump, simultaneously.
24. Remove the baffle plate for turbocharged engines only. Remove the keys from the eccentric and oil pump shaft. Remove the oil pump.
25. Slide the balance weight, thrust washer and needle bearing from the shaft.
26. Unbolt the bearing housing and slide the bearing housing, needle bearing, spacer and thrust plate off the shaft.
27. Turn the engine on the stand so the top of the engine is up.
28. If equipped with a manual transmission, remove the clutch pressure plate and clutch disc. Remove the flywheel with a puller. Remove the key from the shaft.
29. If equipped with an automatic transmission, remove the driveplate. Remove the counterweight. Block the weight and remove the mounting nut. Remove the counterweight with a puller.
30. Working at the rear of the engine, loosen the tension bolts. Loosen the bolts, evenly, in small stages to prevent distortion. Mark tension bolts to replace in original holes during reassembly.
31. Lift the rear housing off the shaft.

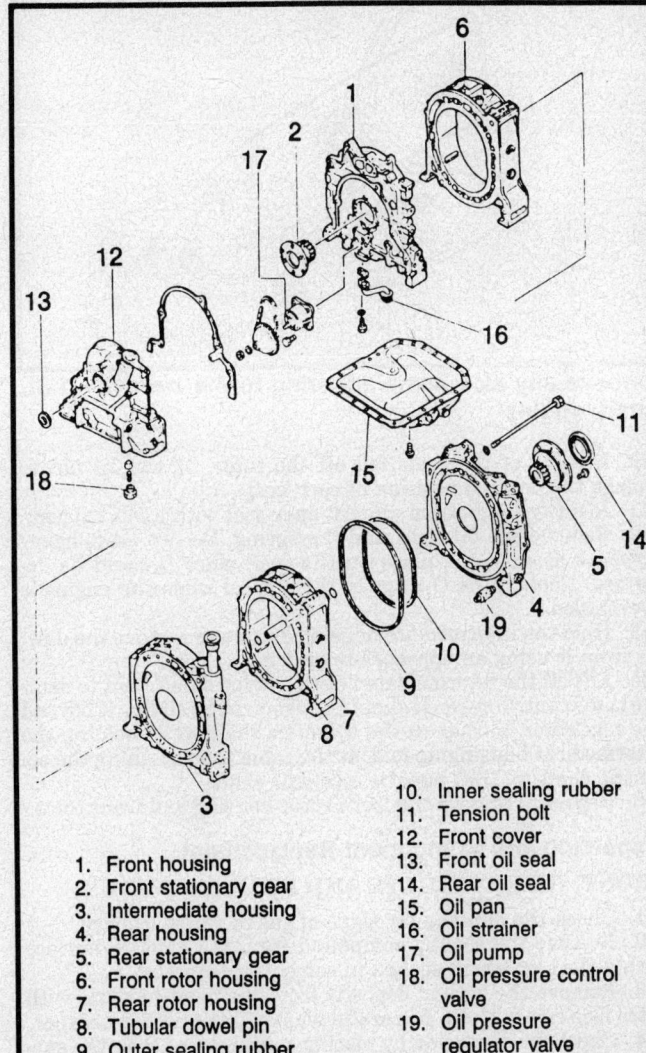

1. Front housing
2. Front stationary gear
3. Intermediate housing
4. Rear housing
5. Rear stationary gear
6. Front rotor housing
7. Rear rotor housing
8. Tubular dowel pin
9. Outer sealing rubber
10. Inner sealing rubber
11. Tension bolt
12. Front cover
13. Front oil seal
14. Rear oil seal
15. Oil pan
16. Oil strainer
17. Oil pump
18. Oil pressure control valve
19. Oil pressure regulator valve

Engine housing components—1.3L rotary engine

32. Remove any seals that are stuck to the rotor sliding surface of the rear housing and reinstall them in their original locations.

33. Remove all the corner seals, corner seal spring, side seal and side seal springs from the rear side of the rotor. Mazda has a special tray which holds all the seals and keeps them segregated to prevent mistakes during reassembly. Each seal groove is marked with numbers near the grooves on the rotor face to prevent confusion.

34. Remove both rubber seals, both O-rings or oil seal from the rear rotor housing. Remove the pressure regulator and the rear rotor housing side pieces.

35. Remove the tubular dowels from the rear rotor housing using the appropriate puller.

36. Lift the rear rotor housing away from the rear rotor, being careful not to drop the apex seals on the rear rotor. Remove the O-ring from the upper dowel hole.

37. Remove each apex seal, side piece and spring from the rear rotor and segregate them.

38. Remove the rear rotor from the eccentric shaft and place it upside down on a clean rag; do not place the rotor on a hard surface.

39. Remove each seal and spring from the other side of the rotor and segregate them.

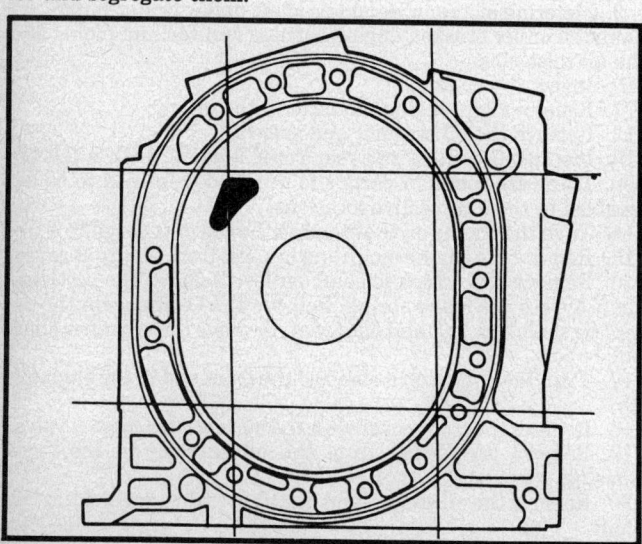

Measure housing distortion along the lines—1.3L rotary engine

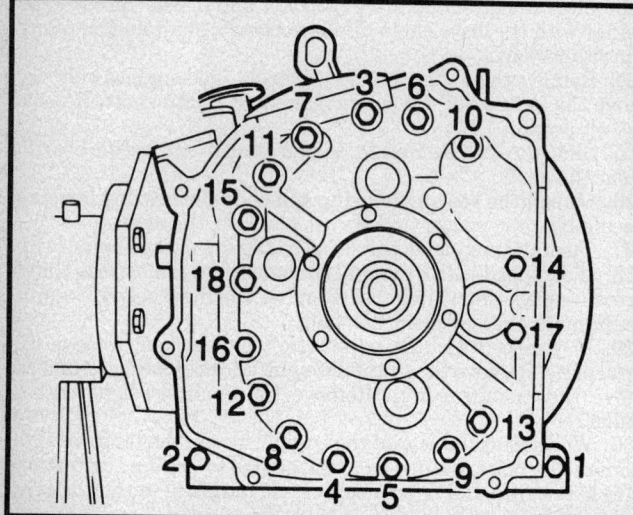

Tension bolt loosening sequence—1.3L rotary engine

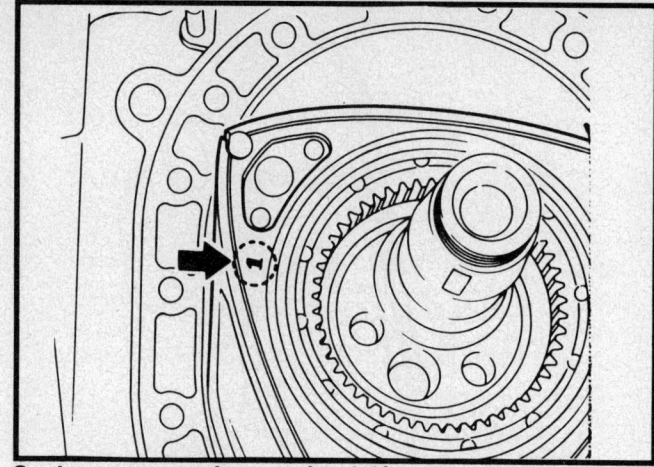

Seal groove number mark—1.3L rotary engine

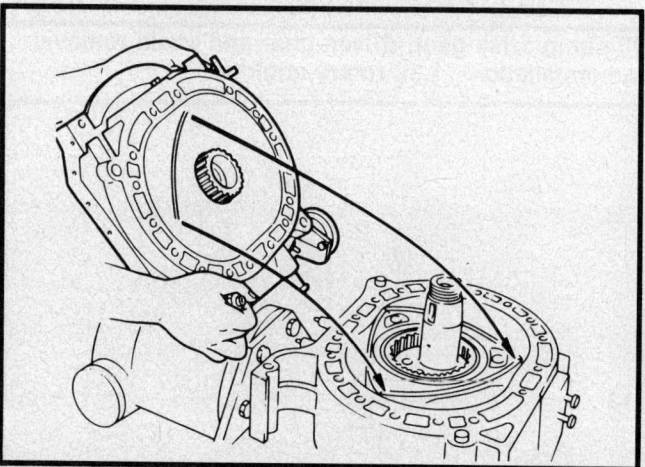

Remove any side seals adhering to the surface—1.3L rotary engine

40. If some of the seals fall off the rotor, be careful not to change the original position of each seal.

41. Identify the bottom of each apex seal with a felt tip pen.

42. Remove the oil seals and the spring. Do not exert heavy pressure at only one place on the seal, since it could be deformed. Replace the O-rings in the oil seal when the engine is overhauled.

43. Hold the intermediate housing down and remove the dowels from it using an appropriate puller.

44. Lift off the intermediate housing being careful not to damage the eccentric shaft. It should be removed by sliding it beyond the rear rotor journal on the eccentric shaft while holding the intermediate housing up and, at the same time, pushing the eccentric shaft up. Lift out the eccentric shaft.

45. Repeat to remove the front rotor housing and front rotor.

Inspection and Component Replacement

FRONT, INTERMEDIATE AND REAR HOUSINGS

1. Check the housing for signs of gas or water leakage.

2. Remove the sealing compound from the housing surface with a cloth or brush soaked in solvent or thinner.

3. Remove the carbon deposits from the front housing with extra fine emery cloth. Be careful when using a carbon scraper.

4. Check for distortion by placing a straight-edge on the surface of the housing. Measure the clearance between the straight-edge and the housing with a feeler gauge. If the clearance is greater than 0.0016 in. at any point, replace the housing.

5. Use a dial indicator to check for wear on the rotor contact surfaces of the housing. If the wear is greater than 0.004 in., replace the housing.

NOTE: The wear at either end of the minor axis is greater than at any other point on the housing. However, this is normal and should be not cause for concern.

FRONT STATIONARY GEAR AND MAIN BEARING

1. Examine the teeth of the stationary gear for wear or damage.
2. Be sure the main bearing shows no signs of excessive wear, scoring or flaking.
3. Check the main bearing to eccentric journal clearance by measuring the journal with a vernier caliper and the bearing with a pair of inside calipers. The standard clearance is 0.0016–0.0031 in.

Main Bearing Replacement

1. Unfasten the securing bolts, if used. Remove stationary gear and main bearing assembly, out of the housing, using puller tool 49–0813–235 or equivalent.
2. Press the main bearing from the stationary gear.
3. Press a new main bearing into the stationary gear so it is in the same position of the old bearing.
4. Align the slot in the stationary gear flange with the dowel pin in the housing and press the gear into place. On later engines, align the bearing lug with the slot in the gear. Install the securing bolts, if required.

REAR STATIONARY GEAR AND MAIN BEARING

Inspect the rear stationary gear and main bearing in a similar manner to the front. In addition, examine the O-ring, which is located in the stationary gear, for signs of wear or damage. Replace the O-ring, if necessary. To replace the stationary gear, use the following procedure.

1. Remove the rear stationary gear securing bolts.
2. Drive the stationary gear from the rear housing with a brass drift.
3. Apply a light coating of grease to a new O-ring and fit it into the groove on the stationary gear.
4. Apply sealer to the flange of the stationary gear.
5. Install the stationary gear on the housing so the slot on its flange aligns with the pin on the rear housing. On later engines align the bearing lug with the housing slot. Use care not to damage the O-ring during installation.
6. Tighten the stationary gear bolts, evenly, in several stages, to 12–17 ft. lbs.

ROTOR HOUSINGS

1. Examine the inner margin of both housings for signs of gas or water leakage.

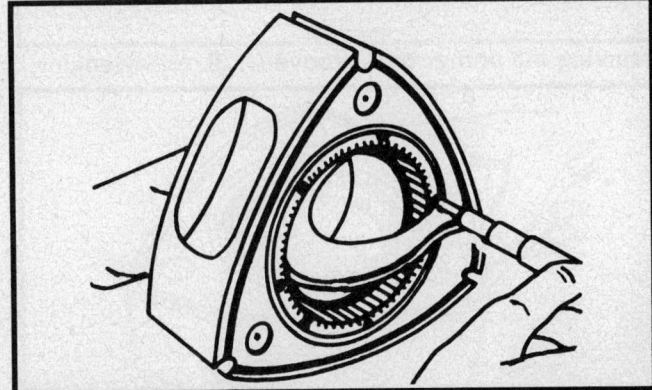

Measure the rotor width at the point indicated—1.3L rotary engine

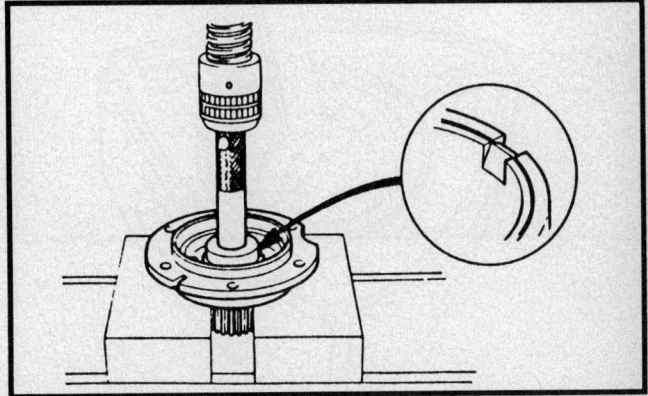

Main bearing replacement—1.3L rotary engine

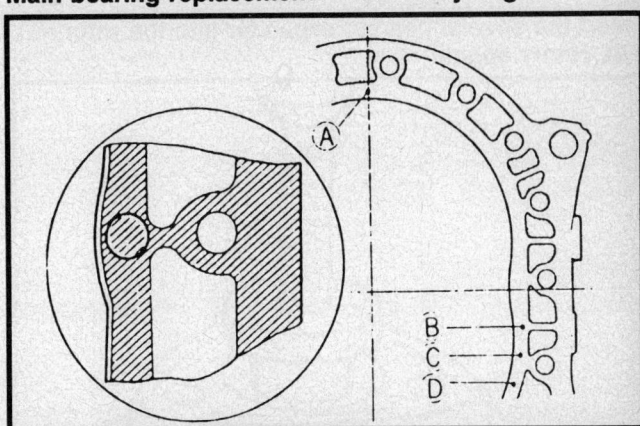

Measure the rotor housing width at the indicated points—1.3L rotary engine

Checking the rotor housing width—1.3L rotary engine

2. Wipe the inner surface of each housing with a clean cloth to remove the carbon deposits.
3. Clean all of the rust deposits out of the cooling passages of each rotor housing.
4. Remove the old sealer using the proper removal solvent.
5. Examine the chromium plated inner surfaces for scoring, flaking or other signs of damage. If any are present, the housing must be replaced.
6. Check the rotor housings for distortion by placing a straight-edge on the axes.
7. If distortion exceeds 0.002 in., replace the rotor housing.
8. Check the widths of both rotor housings, at a minimum of

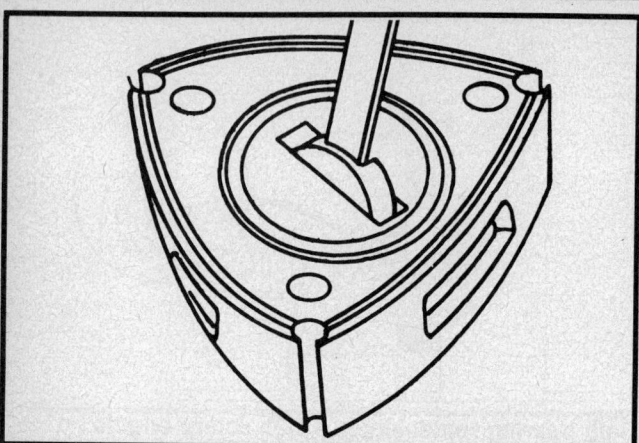

Insert the special bearing expander into the rotor—
1.3L rotary engine

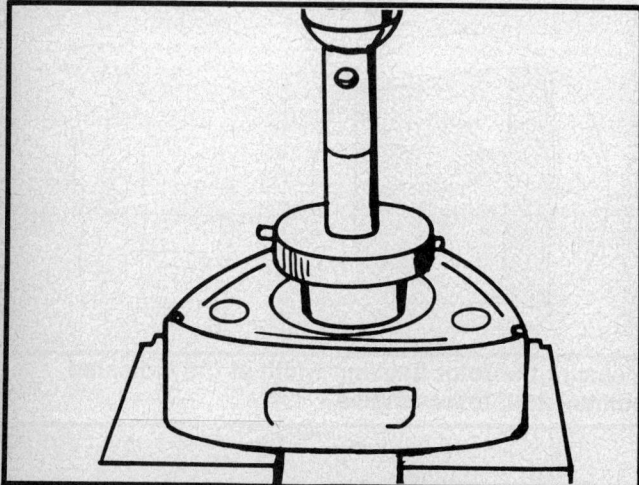

Installing a new rotor bearing—1.3L rotary engine

a. Measure the rotor width with a vernier caliper.
b. Compare the rotor width against the width of the rotor housing which was measured above.
c. Replace the rotor, if the difference between both measurements is not within 0.0047–0.0083 in.
8. Check the rotor bearing for flaking, wearing or scoring.

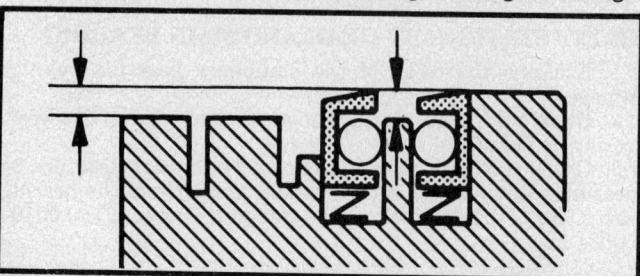

Measuring the oil seal protrusion—1.3L rotary engine

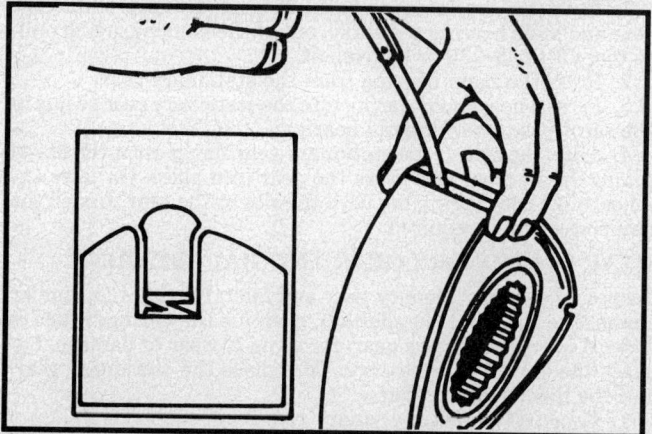

Check the gap between the apex seal and groove with a feeler gauge—1.3L rotary engine

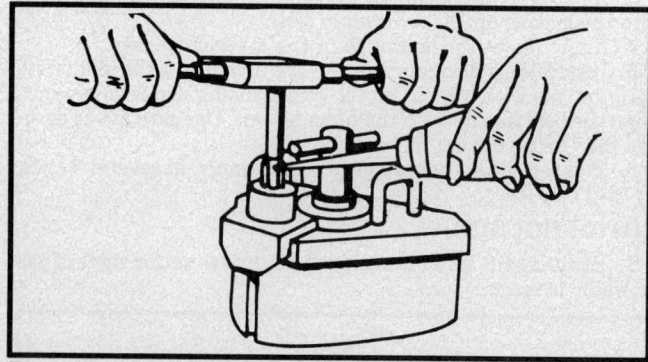

Reaming the corner seal groove—1.3L rotary engine

Corner seal installation—1.3L rotary engine

8 points near the trochoid surfaces of each housing, using a vernier caliper.

9. If the difference between the maximum and minimum values obtained is greater than 0.0024 in., replace the housing. A housing in this condition will be prone to gas and coolant leakage.

ROTORS

1. Check the rotor for signs of blow-by around the side and corner seal areas.

2. The color of the carbon deposits on the rotor should be brown, just as in a piston engine. Usually the carbon deposits on the leading side of the rotor are brown, while those on the trailing side tend toward black, as viewed from the direction of rotation.

3. Remove the carbon on the rotor with a scraper or extra fine emery paper. Use the scraper carefully when doing the seal grooves so no damage is done to them.

4. Wash the rotor in solvent and blow it dry with compressed air.

5. Examine the internal gear for cracks or damaged teeth. If the internal gear is damaged, the rotor and gear must be replaced as a single assembly.

6. With the oil seal removed, check the land protrusions by placing a straight-edge over the lands. Measure the gap between the rotor surface and the straight-edge with a feeler gauge.

7. Check the gaps between the housings and the rotor on both of its sides.

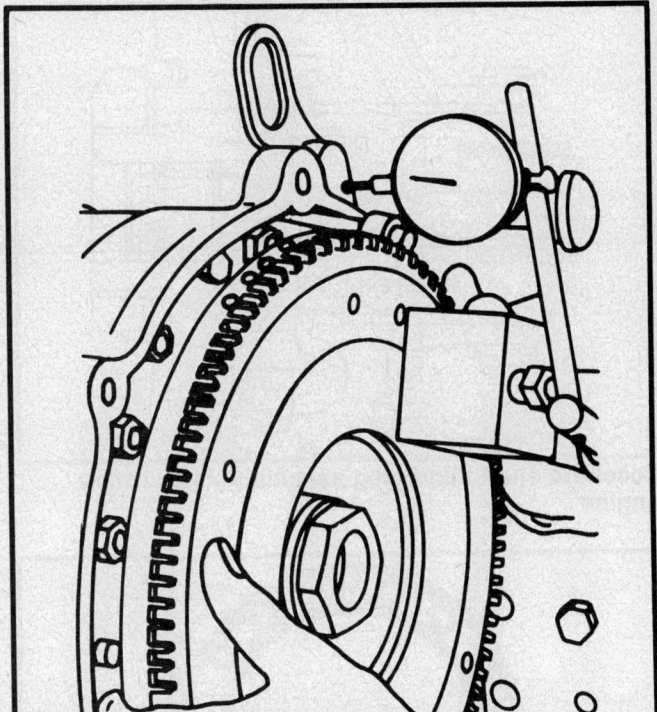

Use a dial indicator attached to the flywheel to measure eccentric shaft endplay—1.3L rotary engine

Position the dial indicator to measure the shaft runout—1.3L rotary engine

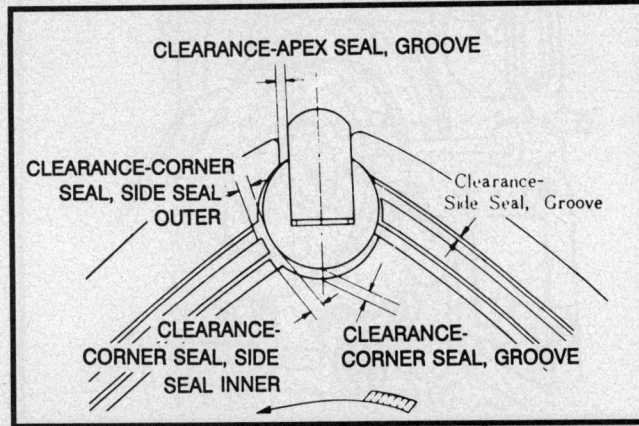

Check the clearance of the seals at the points indicated—1.3L rotary engine

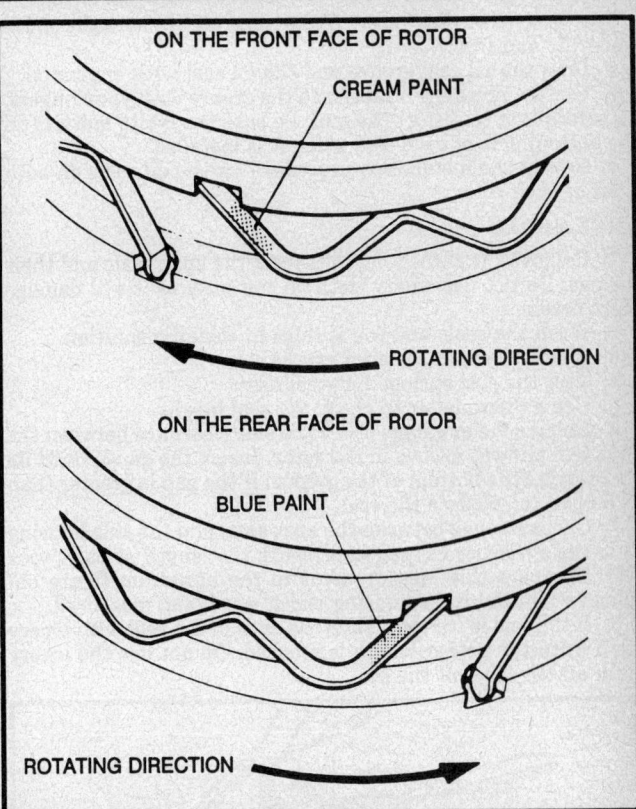

The oil seal springs are identified by a painted mark—1.3L rotary engine

ROTOR BEARING REPLACEMENT

1. Check the clearance between the rotor bearing and the rotor journal on the eccentric shaft. Measure the inner diameter of the rotor bearing and the outer diameter of the journal. The wear limit is 0.0039 in., replace the bearing, if it exceeds specification.
2. Place the rotor on the support so the internal gear is facing downward. Using the puller tool 49–0813–240 without adaptor ring, press the bearing from the rotor; being careful not to damage the internal gear.
3. Place the rotor on the support with internal gear faced upward. Place the new rotor bearing on the rotor so the bearing lug is aligned with the slot of the rotor bore.
4. Remove the adaptor ring-to-special tool screws. Using the special tool and adaptor ring, press fit the new bearing until the bearing is flush with the rotor boss.

Oil Seal Inspection

1. Examine the oil seal while it is mounted in the rotor.
2. If the width of the oil seal lip is greater than 0.020 in., replace the oil seal.
3. If the protrusion of the oil seal is greater then 0.020 in., replace the seal.

Oil Seal Replacement

1. Pry the seal out by inserting a small prybar into the slots on the rotor. Be careful not to deform the lip of the oil seal if it is to be reinstalled.
2. Fit both the oil seal springs into their respective grooves, so the ends are facing upward and their gaps are opposite each other on the rotor.
3. Insert a new O-ring into each of the oil seals. Before installing the O-rings into the oil seals, fit each of the seals into its

proper groove on the rotor. Make sure all of the seals move smoothly and freely.

4. Coat the oil seal groove and the oil seal with engine oil.

5. Gently, press the oil seal into the groove with your fingers. Be careful not to distort the seal. Be sure the white mark is on the bottom side of each seal when it is installed.

6. Repeat the installation procedure for the oil seals on both sides of each rotor.

APEX SEALS

1. Remove the carbon deposits from the apex seals and their springs. Do not use emery cloth on the seals as it will damage their finish.

2. Wash the seals and the springs in cleaning solution.

3. Check the apex seals for cracks.

4. Test the seal springs for weakness.

5. Use a micrometer to check the seal height.

6. Using a feeler gauge, check the side clearance between the apex seal and the groove in the rotor. Insert the gauge until its tip contacts the bottom of the groove. If the gap is greater than or 0.0059 in., replace the seal.

7. Check the gap between the apex seals and the side housing by using a vernier caliper to measure the length of each apex seal. Compare this measurement to the minimum figure obtained when the rotor housing width was being measured.

8. If the seal is too long, sand the ends of the seal with emery cloth until the proper length is reached. Do not use the emery cloth on the faces of the seal.

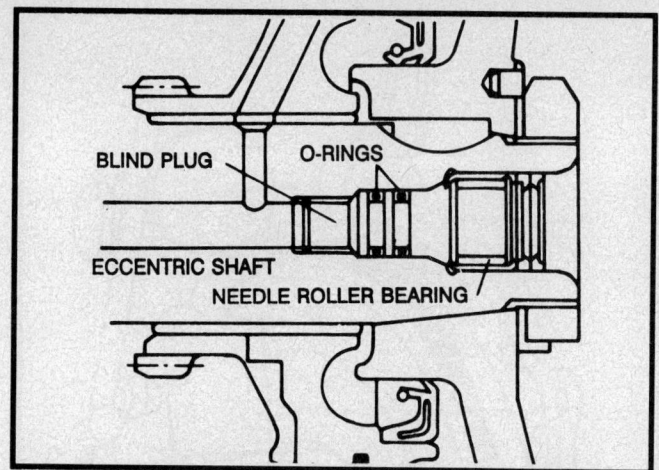

Eccentric shaft blind plug assembly—1.3L rotary engine

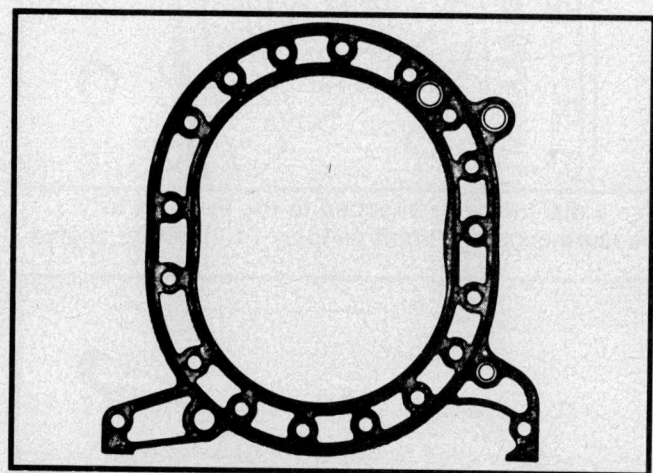

Apply sealer to the grey shadowed areas of the rotor housing—1.3L rotary engine

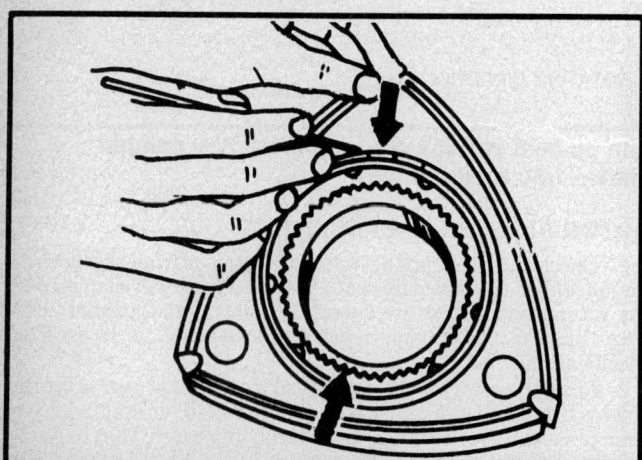

Position the oil seal spring gaps at the arrows—1.3L rotary engine

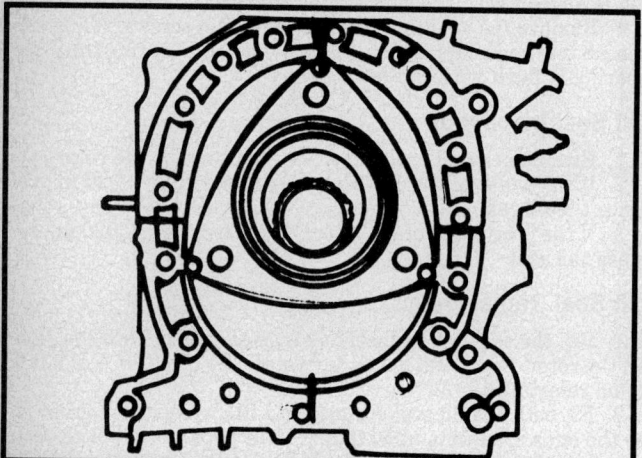

The rear rotor must be positioned as shown during engine assembly—1.3L rotary engine

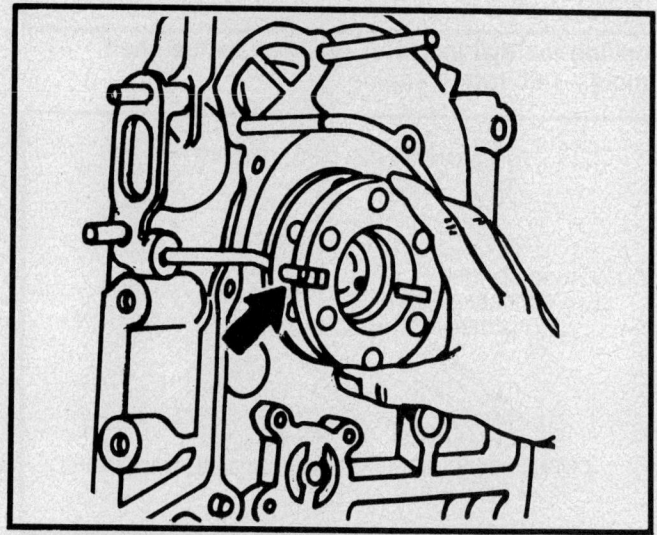

Align the slot in the stationary gear flange with the pin in the housing (arrow)—1.3L rotary engine

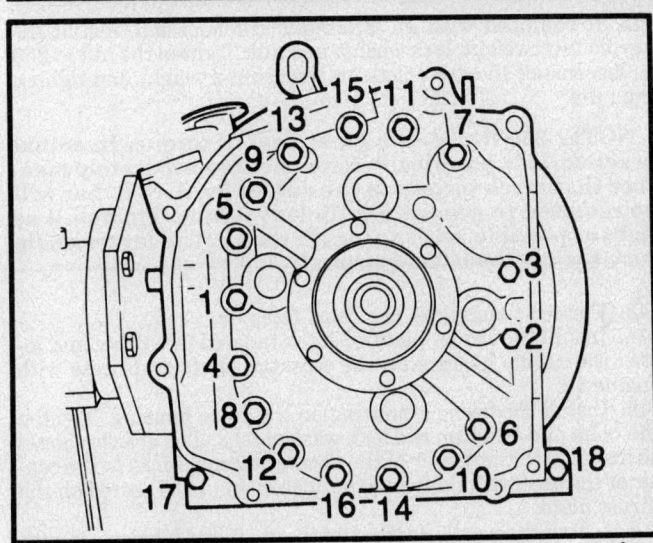

Tension bolt tightening sequence—1.3L rotary engine

SIDE SEALS

1. Remove the carbon deposits from the side seals and their springs.
2. Check the side seals for cracks.
3. Check the clearance between the side seals and their grooves with a feeler gauge.
4. Check the clearance between the side seals and the corner seals with both installed in the rotor. Insert a feeler gauge between the end of the side seal and the corner seal. Insert the gauge against the direction of the rotor's rotation. Check the side seal protrusion; acceptable minimum protrusion is 0.020 in.
5. Replace the side seal if the clearance is greater than 0.016 in.
6. If the side seal is replaced, adjust the clearance between it and the corner seal as follows. File the side seal on its reverse side, in the same rotational direction of the rotor, along the outline made by the corner seal.
7. The clearance obtained should be 0.002–0.006 in. If it exceeds this, the performance of the seals will deteriorate.

NOTE: There are 4 different types of side seals, depending upon location. Do not mix the seals up and be sure to use the proper type of seal for replacement.

CORNER SEALS

1. Clean the carbon deposits.
2. Examine each of the seals.
3. Measure the clearance between the corner seal and its groove. The clearance should be 0.008–0.0019 in. The wear limit of the gap is 0.031 in.
4. If the wear between the corner seal and the groove is uneven, check the clearance with special tool 49–0839–165. This tool has a go/no go function.
5. If neither end of the gauge goes into the groove, the clearance is within specification.
6. If the go end of the gauge fits into the groove but the no go end does not, replace the corner seal with 1 that is 0.0012 in. oversize.
7. If both ends of the gauge fit into the groove, then the groove must be reamed. Replace the corner seal with one which is 0.0072 in. oversize, after reaming. Take the measurement of the groove in the direction of maximum wear, i.e., that of rotation.

SEAL SPRINGS

Check the seal springs for damage or weakness. Be exceptionally careful when checking the spring areas which contact either the rotor or the seal.

ECCENTRIC SHAFT

1. Wash the eccentric shaft in solvent and blow the oil passages dry with compressed air.
2. Check the shaft for wear, cracks or other signs of damage; make sure none of the oil passages are clogged.
3. Measure the shaft journals; replace the shaft if any journals show excessive wear.
4. Check eccentric shaft run-out. Rotate the shaft slowly and note the dial indicator reading. If run-out is greater than specification, replace the eccentric shaft.
5. Check the blind plug at the end of the shaft. If it is loose or leaking, remove it with an Allen wrench and replace the O-ring.
6. Check the operation of the needle roller bearing for smoothness by inserting a mainshaft into the bearing and rotating it. Examine the bearing for signs of wear or damage. Check the oil jet for spring weakness, sticking or ball damage.
7. Replace the bearings, if necessary, with the special bearing replacer tools 49–0823–073 and 49–0823–072.

NEEDLE BEARING AND THRUST PLATE

1. Inspect the needle bearing for wear and damage.
2. Inspect the bearing housing and the thrust plate for wear and damage.

OIL PUMP DRIVE CHAIN AND SPROCKET

1. Lay the chain on a flat surface and check the entire length for broken links.
2. Check the oil pump drive and driven sprockets for missing and broken teeth.
3. Replace, as necessary.

Assembly

1. Replace all O-rings, rubber seals and gaskets with new parts. Place the rotor on a rubber pad or cloth.
2. Install the oil seal rings in their respective grooves in the rotors with the edge of the spring in the stopper hole. The oil seal springs are painted cream or blue in color. The cream colored springs must be installed on the front faces of both rotors. The blue colored springs must be installed on the rear faces of both rotors. When installing each oil seal spring, the painted side, square side, of the spring must face upward toward the oil seal.
3. Install a new O-ring in each groove. Place each oil seal in the groove so the square edge of the spring fits in the stopper hole of the oil seal. Push the head of the oil seal slowly with the fingers, being careful that the seal is not deformed. Be sure the oil seal moves smoothly in the groove before installing the O-ring.
4. Lubricate each oil seal and groove with engine oil. Check the movement of the seal. It should move freely when the head of the seal is pressed.
5. Check the oil seal protrusion and install the seals on the other side of each rotor.
6. Install the apex seals without springs and side pieces into their respective grooves so each side piece positions on the side of each rotor.
7. Install the corner seal springs and corner seals into their respective grooves.
8. Install the side seal springs and side seals into their respective grooves.
9. Apply engine oil to each spring and check each spring for smooth movement.
10. Check each seal protrusion.
11. Invert the rotor, being careful that the seals do not fall out, and install the oil seals on the other side in the same manner.
12. Mount the front housing on a workstand so the top of the housing is up.

13. Lubricate the internal gear of the rotor with engine oil.

14. Hold the apex seals with used O-ring to keep the apex seals installed and place the rotor on the front housing. Be careful not to drop the seals. Turn the front housing so the sliding surface faces upward.

15. Mesh the internal and stationary gears so one of the rotor apexes is at any one of the 4 places shown and remove the old O-ring which is holding the apex seals in position.

16. Lubricate the front rotor journal of the eccentric shaft with engine oil and lubricate the eccentric shaft main journal.

17. Insert the eccentric shaft. Be careful not to damage the rotor bearing and main bearing.

18. Apply sealing agent to the front side of the front rotor housing.

19. Apply a light coat of petroleum jelly onto new O-rings and rubber seals and install the O-rings and rubber seals on the front side of the rotor housing.

NOTE: The inner rubber seal is of the square type. The wider white line of the rubber seal should face the combustion chamber and the seam of the rubber seal should be positioned as such. Do not stretch the rubber seal.

20. If the engine is being overhauled, install the seal protector to only the inner rubber seal to improve durability.

21. Invert the front rotor housing, being careful not to let the rubber seals and O-rings fall from their grooves, and mount it on the front housing.

22. Lubricate the dowels with the engine oil and insert them through the front rotor housing holes and into the front housing.

23. Apply sealer to the front side of the rotor housing.

24. Install new O-rings and rubber seals on the front rotor housing in the same manner.

25. Insert each apex spring seal, making sure the seal is installed in the proper direction.

26. Install each side piece in its original position and be sure the springs seat on the side piece.

27. Lubricate the side pieces with engine oil. Make sure the front rotor housing is free of foreign matter and lubricate the sliding surface of the front housing with engine oil.

28. Turn the front housing assembly with the rotor, so the top of the housing is up. Pull the eccentric shaft about 1 in.

29. Position the eccentric portion of the eccentric shaft diagonally, to the upper right.

30. Install the intermediate housing over the eccentric shaft onto the front rotor housing. Turn the engine so the rear of the engine is up.

31. Install the rear rotor and rear rotor housing following the same steps as for the front rotor and the front housing.

32. Lubricate the stationary gear and main bearing.

33. Install the rear housing onto the rear rotor housing.

34. If necessary, turn the rear rotor slightly to mesh the rear housing stationary gear with the rear rotor internal gear.

35. Install a new washer on each tension bolt, and lubricate each bolt with engine oil.

36. Install the tension bolts and tighten them evenly, in several stages and in sequence. The specified torque is 23–27 ft. lbs. Be sure bolts are installed in their original positions; longer bolts are used in later engines and are not interchangeable.

37. After tightening the bolts, turn the eccentric shaft to be sure the shaft and rotors turn smoothly and easily.

38. Lubricate the oil seal in the rear housing.

39. If equipped with a manual transmission, install the flywheel on the rear of the eccentric shaft so the flywheel keyway fits the key on the shaft.

40. Apply sealer to both sides of the flywheel lock washer and install the lock washer.

41. Install the flywheel locknut. Hold the flywheel securely and tighten the nut to 350 ft. lbs.

42. If equipped with an automatic transmission, install the key, counterweight, lock washer and nut. Tighten the nut to 350 ft. lbs. Install the driveplate on the counterweight and tighten the nuts.

NOTE: 350 ft. lbs. is a great deal of torque. In actual practice, it is practically impossible to accurately measure that much torque on the nut. At least a 3 ft. bar will be required to generate sufficient torque. Tighten it as tight as possible, with no longer than 3 ft. of leverage. Be sure the engine is held securely.

43. Turn the engine so the front faces up.

44. Install the thrust plate with the tapered face down and install the needle bearing on the eccentric shaft. Lubricate with engine oil.

45. Install the bearing housing on the front housing. Tighten the bolts and bend up the lock washer tabs. The spacer should be installed so the center of the needle bearing comes to the center of the eccentric shaft and the spacer should be seated on the thrust plate.

46. Install the needle bearing on the shaft and lubricate it with engine oil.

47. Install the balancer and thrust washer on the eccentric shaft.

48. Install the oil pump drive chain over both of the sprockets. Install the sprocket and chain assembly over the eccentric shaft and oil pump shaft simultaneously. Install the key on the eccentric shaft. Be sure both of the sprockets are engaged with the chain before install them over the shafts.

49. Install the distributor drive gear onto the eccentric shaft with the F mark on the gear facing the front of the engine. Slide the spacer and oil slinger onto the eccentric shaft.

50. Align the keyway and install the eccentric shaft pulley. Tighten the pulley bolt to 72–87 ft. lbs.

51. Turn the engine until the top of the engine faces up.

52. Check the eccentric shaft endplay in the following manner.

　a. Attach a dial indicator to the flywheel. Move the flywheel forward and backward.

　b. Note the reading on the dial indicator, it should be 0.0016–0.0028 in.

　c. If the endplay is not within specification, adjust it by replacing the front spacer. Spacers come in 4 sizes, ranging from 0.3150–0.3181 in. If necessary, a spacer can be ground on a surface plate with emery paper.

　d. Recheck the endplay; if it is now within specification, proceed with the next Step.

53. Remove the pulley from the front of the eccentric shaft. Tighten the oil pump drive sprocket nut and bend the lock tabs on the lock washer.

54. Fit a new O-ring over the front cover oil passage.

55. Install the chain tensioner, if equipped, and tighten its securing bolts.

56. Position the front cover gasket and the front cover on the front housing, then secure the front cover with its bolts.

57. Install the eccentric shaft pulley again. Tighten its bolt to required torque.

58. Turn the engine so the bottom faces up.

59. Cut off the excess gasket on the front cover along the mounting surface of the oil pan.

60. Install the oil strainer gasket and strainer on the front housing and tighten the bolts.

61. Apply sealer to the joint surfaces of each housing.

62. Install the oil pan.

63. Turn the engine so the top is up.

64. Install the water pump and tighten the nuts in a crisscross sequence. Tighten to 13–20 ft. lbs. Be sure to use shims on the side housing contact surfaces. If shims are not used, coolant will leak.

65. Attach 2 O-rings to the oil filter body. Install the oil filter body.

66. Align the leading timing mark (yellow painted) on the eccentric shaft pulley with the indicator pin on the front cover.

67. Align the tally marks on the distributor housing and driven gear. Install the distributor and locknut. Turn the distributor housing until the projection of the signal rotor aligns with core of the leading side pick-up coil. Tighten the locknut. Install the distributor rotor and cap.

68. Place the exhaust manifold gasket in position and install the exhaust manifold. Tighten to 23–34 ft. lbs.

69. Install the hot air duct and absorber plate.

70. Install the intake manifold auxiliary ports. Installation should be made so the bigger sides of the auxiliary port valve shaft align the matching mark on the gasket as shown in the figure.

71. Install the O-rings. Install the intake manifold and gasket.

72. Connect the metering oil pump pipes. Tighten to 14–19 ft. lbs.

73. Install the fuel injection nozzles.

74. Install the delivery pipe assembly, the chamber and the emission device assembly as 1 piece. Tighten delivery pipe body to 14–19 ft. lbs., emission device assembly to 14–19 ft. lbs.

75. Install the vacuum sensing tube. Install the alternator belt. Install the air pump. Install the engine hanger bracket.

76. Remove the engine from the stand and install it in the vehicle.

Intake Manifold

Removal and Installation

1. Remove the dynamic chamber by removing or disconnecting the following parts.
   a. On turbocharged engines, drain the cooling system.
   b. Negative battery cable, air funnel, intercooler (turbo only), oil filler pipe (turbo only), accelerator cable and throttle sensor connector.
   c. Metering oil pump connecting rod and water hoses.
   d. Terminal cover, vacuum sensing tubes.
   e. Air supply connector, intake air temperature sensor connector.
   f. Retaining bolts and nuts and the dynamic chamber.

2. Cover the intake manifold port opening with a clean cloth to prevent dust or dirt from entering the engine.

3. Remove the incline check valve assemblies and vacuum lines.

4. Remove the air hoses from the manifold mounted solenoids.

5. Remove the actuator from the intake manifold.

6. Remove the nuts and bolts that mount the intake manifold to the engine, remove the manifold. Clean all gaskets mounting surfaces.

7. Remove the auxiliary port valve. Check the valve for cracks and breakage.

8. Install the auxiliary valve. Make sure the bigger side of the valve shafts align with the matching mark on the mounting gasket.

9. Install the remaining parts in the reverse order of removal. Fill the cooling system and perform all the necessary adjustments.

Exhaust Manifold

Removal and Installation

13B NON-TURBOCHARGED ENGINE

1. Disconnect the negative battery cable.

2. Remove the air intake manifold (throttle and dynamic chamber).

3. Remove the exhaust absorber plate.

4. Disconnect the oxygen sensor connector and route the wiring so it will be readily removed with the exhaust manifold.

5. Raise and support the front end. Remove the exhaust pipe front cover, catalytic converter cover, exhaust pipe bracket and disconnect the exhaust exhaust pipe from the exhaust manifold.

6. Loosen and remove the exhaust manifold nuts and lock washers.

7. Separate the manifold and insulator from the engine and pull the manifold from the engine mounting studs. Remove the gasket and discard it.

8. Throughly clean the exhaust manifold contact surfaces and check the exhaust manifold for warpage with a metal straight-edge.

9. Install a new manifold gasket onto the engine and install the exhaust manifold assembly over the mounting studs and make it flush with the gasket. Install the mounting nuts and lock washers and torque them to 23–34 ft. lbs.

10. Connnect all the exhaust manifold components using new gaskets, as required.

11. Connect the oxygen sensor connector. Install the absorber plate and torque the retaining screws to 6–8 ft. lbs.

12. Complete the installation of the intake manifold in reverse of the removal procedure.

13. Start the engine and allow it to reach normal operating temperature and check for exhaust leaks.

13B TURBOCHARGED ENGINE

1. Remove the turbocharger from the engine. Seal all the turbocharger openings to prevent the entry of foreign matter.

2. Remove the insulator covers from the exhaust manifold. Loosen and remove the exhaust manifold nuts and lock washers.

3. Remove the exhaust manifold and waste gate actuator assembly from the engine. Remove the gasket and discard it.

4. Throughly clean the exhaust manifold and turbocharger contact surfaces and check the exhaust manifold for warpage with a metal straight-edge.

5. Install a new manifold gasket onto the engine and install the exhaust manifold/actuator assembly over the mounting studs and make it flush with the gasket. Install the mounting nuts and lock washers and torque them to 23–34 ft. lbs.

6. Install a new turbocharger gasket onto the exhaust manifold and carefully guide the turbo over the mounting studs and onto the gasket. Install the nuts and lock washers. Torque the nuts to 33–40 ft. lbs. Once the nuts are torqued, crimp the tabs on the nut retaining plate to prevent the nuts from loosening.

7. Complete the remainder of the turbocharger installation procedure in reverse of the removal procedure. Use new gaskets where required. Fill the cooling system and connect the negative battery cable. Start the engine and check for leaks. Make all the necessary adjustments.

Turbocharger

Removal and Installation

1. Disconnect the negative battery cable. Drain the cooling system.

2. Disconnect the air hoses from the air pump and remove the air pump from the engine.

3. Loosen the hose clamps and disconnect the air funnel and air hose from the air cleaner and the turbocharger. Remove the air funnel and air hose from the engine.

4. Disconnect the connector from the air control valve and remove the valve from the engine.

5. Disconnect the split air pipe from the engine and remove the pipe along with the gasket.

6. Disconnect the water hose and the water pipe from the engine and remove them.

7. Disconnect the supply and return oil pipes from the turbo and cover the openings.

8. Remove the front converter insulator covers and disconnect the front converter from the exhaust manifold. Remove the

gasket and discard it.

9. Unstake the retainer tabs from the retainer plate with a small prying tool. Remove the nuts and washers that secure the turbocharger to the exhaust manifold studs and remove the turbocharger from the engine. Cover all the turbo openings to prevent the entry of dirt and foreign matter. Remove the turbocharger gasket and discard it.

10. Remove the insulator covers from the exhaust manifold. Loosen and remove the exhaust manifold retaining nuts and lock washers.

11. Remove the exhaust manifold and wastegate actuator assembly from the engine. Remove the gasket and discard it.

12. Thoroughly clean the exhaust manifold and turbocharger contact surfaces and check the exhaust manifold for warpage with a metal straight-edge.

13. Install a new manifold gasket onto the engine and install the exhaust manifold/actuator assembly over the mounting studs and make it flush with the gasket. Install the nuts and lock washers and torque them to 23–34 ft. lbs.

14. Install a new turbocharger gasket onto the exhaust manifold and carefully guide the turbo over the mounting studs and onto the gasket. Install the nuts and lock washers. Torque the nuts to 33–40 ft. lbs. Once the nuts are torqued, crimp the tabs on the nut retaining plate to prevent the nuts from loosening. Remove the protective covers from the turbo openings.

15. Connect the front converter to the exhaust manifold with a new gasket. Torque the nuts to 33–40 ft. lbs.

16. Install the remaining components in reverse of the removal procedure. If any part requires a new gasket, install one:
    a. Insulator covers.
    b. Oil pipes.
    c. Water pipe and water hose.
    d. Split air pipe.
    e. Air control valve.
    f. air funnel and air hose.
    g. air pump and air hoses.

17. Fill the cooling system and connect the negative battery cable. Start the engine and check for leaks. Make all the necessary adjustments.

PISTON ENGINE MECHANICAL

NOTE: Disconnecting the negative battery cable on some vehicles may interfere with the functions of the on board computer systems and may require the computer to undergo a relearning process, once the negative battery cable is reconnected.

Engine Assembly

Removal and Installation

323 AND PROTEGE EXCEPT TURBOCHARGED

1. Relieve the fuel system pressure. Disconnect the negative battery cable. Drain the engine oil, transaxle oil and coolant into suitable drain pans.

2. Remove the battery and battery box. Remove the air cleaner assembly, oil level gauge and cooling fan with the radiator assembly. If equipped with an automatic transaxle, just remove the radiator shroud, do not remove the radiator.

3. Remove the accelerator cable and cruise control cable, if equipped. Remove the speedometer cable and fuel hoses. If equipped with an automatic transaxle, remove the upper and lower radiator hoses.

4. Remove the heater hose, brake vacuum hose, 3-way solenoid vacuum hoses, canister hose and the engine harness connectors along with the engine ground.

5. Remove the upper and lower radiator hoses. Remove the exhaust pipe. If equipped with an automatic transaxle, remove the secondary air pipe.

6. Remove the air conditioning compressor and power steering pump, if equipped. Do not disconnect the high and low pressure hoses from the compressor. Secure the compressor in the fender well area with a piece of wire or rope. Do not remove the pressure and return hoses from the pump. Raise the pump and move it aside.

7. Remove the driveshafts, clutch control cable, shift control rod, engine undercover and side cover.

8. Install a suitable engine hoist to the engine and lift the engine slightly. Remove the engine mounts.

9. Carefully, remove the engine and transaxle.

10. Installation is the reverse of removal. Refill the engine coolant, engine oil and transaxle fluid.

323 AND PROTEGE WITH TURBOCHARGED ENGINE

1. Properly relieve the fuel system pressure. Disconnect the negative battery cable. Remove the hood. Drain the cooling system. Drain the engine oil.

2. Remove the battery and battery holder. Remove the air cleaner assembly. Disconnect the body-to-transaxle ground wire, back-up light and engine harness connectors.

3. Disconnect all the necessary vacuum hoses. Disconnect the clutch release cylinder.

4. Disconnect the shift control cables. Disconnect the speedometer cable. Disconnect the accelerator cable.

5. Disconnect the heater hoses from the engine. Remove the radiator hoses, the radiator and the intercooler assembly.

6. Remove the air conditioning compressor bolts and position the compressor aside, as required; do not disconnect the refrigerant lines.

7. Remove the power steering pump bolts. Remove the power steering pump and position aside, as required.

8. Raise and support the vehicle safely. Remove the tire and wheel assemblies. Remove the engine undercover and side cover. Remove the control unit.

9. Disconnect the exhaust system at the exhaust manifolds. Remove the driveshafts. If equipped with 4WD, remove the propeller shaft.

10. Remove the engine crossmember assembly. Remove the No. 2 and 3 engine mounts. If equipped with 4WD, remove the No. 4 engine mount.

11. Properly support the transaxle assembly, using the required equipment. Properly support the engine using the required equipment.

12. Remove the engine to transaxle retaining bolts. Lower the vehicle. Remove any and all retaining brackets required for engine removal.

13. Install the engine lifting device and carefully remove the engine from the vehicle.

14. Installation is the reverse of the removal procedure. Refill the engine, transaxle and cooling system to the proper levels.

626 AND MX-6

1. Relieve the fuel system pressure. Remove the hood. Disconnect the negative battery cable. Remove the battery, if necessary.

2. Loosen the front wheel lugs. Drain the coolant, engine oil and transaxle fluid.

3. Remove the air cleaner assembly. Remove the radiator hoses. Remove the radiator shroud and electric fan assembly.

Remove the washer tank and the radiator overflow.

4. Remove the fuel hose, fuel return hose, accelerator cable and speedometer cable. If equipped with a turbocharger, remove the inner cooler pipe and hose.

5. If equipped with a manual transaxle, remove the clutch cable along with the clutch slave cylinder, and if equipped with an automatic transaxle, remove the control cable.

6. Remove the engine ground wire, engine harness, power brake vacuum hose and 3-way valve vacuum switch with bracket. Remove the heater hoses, duty solenoid valve and the vacuum sensor.

7. Remove any additional engine or transaxle wiring. Remove the air vent hose and vacuum canister hose.

8. If equipped with air conditioning, remove the air conditioning compressor and position it aside. Do not disconnect the high and low pressure hoses from the compressor.

9. Raise and support the vehicle safely. Remove the splash shield. Remove the tire and wheel assembly.

10. Remove the power steering pump and position it aside. Do not remove the pressure and return hoses from the pump.

11. Remove the drive axles and change rod, using the proper tools.

12. Disconnect the shift control rod, if equipped with a manual transaxle. Remove the shift control extension bar. Install a suitable engine hoist to the engine and lift the engine slightly.

13. Remove the transaxle and engine mounting bolts and nuts. Disconnect the exhaust pipe and turbocharger, if equipped.

14. Remove the torque stopper mount from the right wheel housing area and inside the engine compartment.

15. Carefully, remove the engine and transaxle from the vehicle. Separate the engine from the transaxle.

16. Installation is the reverse of removal. Refill the engine coolant, engine oil and transaxle fluid.

929

1. Relieve the fuel system pressure. Disconnect the negative battery cable and drain the engine oil and the cooling system.

2. Matchmark and remove the hood.

3. Remove the fresh air duct and the air cleaner assembly.

4. Disconnect the accelerator cable from the throttle body.

5. Remove the cooling fan pulley bolts, the cooling fan and cowling.

6. Remove the drive belts, spark plug wires and spark plugs.

7. Disconnect the evaporative canister and brake hoses.

8. Disconnect and plug the fuel hoses the fuel rails.

9. Remove the heater hoses and disconnect the engine harness.

10. Working from under the vehicle, remove the engine undercover.

11. Remove the upper and lower radiator hoses.

12. If equipped with an automatic transmission, disconnect the automatic transmission fluid hoses from the radiator.

13. Disconnect the radiator harness and remove the radiator.

14. Remove the alternator and the alternator strap.

15. If equipped, disconnect the air conditioning compressor and bracket from it's mounting and tie the unit off to side of the vehicle with the lines in tact and connected. Position the power steering pump in the same manner as the air conditioner, if equipped.

16. Remove the section of exhaust pipe that runs from the catalytic converter to the exhaust manifold.

17. Connect a lifting strap to the engine lifting bracket and attach a hoist to the sling and tension the hoist. Support and remove the transmission.

18. Remove the engine mounting nuts and lift the engine from the vehicle.

19. Installation is the reverse of the removal procedure. Fill the engine, transmission and cooling system to the proper levels.

MIATA

1. Relieve the fuel system pressure and disconnect the negative battery cable.

2. Drain cooling system and remove the undercover.

3. Remove the air cleaner assembly and disconnect the accelerator cable.

4. Disconnect the upper and lower radiator hoses and the coolant reservoir hose.

5. Disconnect the cooling fan electrical connector and remove the cooling fan and radiator as an assembly.

6. Remove the power steering, air conditioning and alternator drive belts.

7. Remove the power steering oil pump with the hoses connected and position pump assembly aside.

8. Remove the air conditioning assembly with the hoses still connected and position it aside.

9. Disconnect all electrical connectors and hoses necessary for engine removal. Cap all openings to prevent entry of dirt.

10. Disconnect the exhaust pipe from the exhaust manifold.

11. Remove the clutch release cylinder.

12. Remove the center console and the shift knob assembly.

13. Disconnect the transmission electrical connectors.

14. Disconnect the speedometer cable and driveshaft from the transmission.

15. Remove the transmission-to-frame bolts.

16. Install a engine lifting device onto the engine. Remove the engine mount nuts and the engine and transmission as an assembly from the vehicle. Separate the transmission from the engine.

To install:

17. Install the engine and transmission assembly into the engine compartment.

18. Torque the engine mount nuts to 42–58 ft. lbs. (57–78 Nm).

19. Connect the transmission assembly electrical connectors and the driveshaft.

20. Connect the speedometer cable and shift knob assembly.

21. Install the clutch release cylinder assembly and torque bolts to 14–19 ft. lbs. (19–25 Nm).

22. Connect all electrical connectors and hoses that were disconnected during removal.

23. Install the air conditioning compressor and the power steering oil pump.

24. Install drive belts.

25. Install the radiator and cooling fan assembly. Connect cooling fan electrical connector.

26. Install the upper and lower radiator hoses and connect the accelerator cable.

27. Install the air cleaner assembly and the undercover.

28. Connect the battery negative cable and refill the cooling system. Start engine and check for leaks.

Cylinder Head

Removal and Installation

1987 626

1. Disconnect the negative battery cable. Turn the crankshaft so the piston of the No. 1 cylinder is at TDC of its compression stroke. Drain the coolant.

2. Remove the accelerator cable, secondary air pipe, distributor and rear housing.

3. Remove the air hose, secondary air pipe, oil pipe and insulator No. 1, 2 and 3.

4. If equipped, remove the turbocharger bracket and the front catalytic converter.

5. Remove the oil return hose, water inlet hose, water outlet hose and the EGR pipe.

6. Remove the exhaust manifold bolts and the exhaust manifold. If equipped with a turbocharger, remove the exhaust mani-

fold and the turbocharger as an assembly.

7. Remove the intake manifold retaining bolts. Remove the intake manifold assembly and gasket.

8. Remove the timing belt cover and timing belt.

NOTE: Before removing the timing belt, turn the crankshaft to align the timing mark (A) of the camshaft pulley with the front timing mark. Be sure to mark the direction of rotation on the timing belt. The reason to mark the belt is so the belt can be reinstalled in the same direction. If the camshaft pulley has to be removed, use a suitable tool to lock the pulley in place so as to keep it from turning and remove the pulley retaining nut or bolt.

9. Remove the cylinder head cover and gaskets. Remove the cylinder head bolts. Loosen the head bolts in reverse of the torque sequence.

10. Remove the cylinder head and cylinder head gasket.

11. Clean and inspect the gasket mating surfaces and check the cylinder head for warpage. Check for wear and damage, replace defective parts, as necessary.

To install:

12. Use new gaskets and reverse the removal procedure. Torque the cylinder head bolts to specifications. Do not forget to insert the plain washer, as necessary. Adjust the valves, as required.

1988–91 626 AND MX-6

1. Disconnect the negative battery cable and drain the cooling system.

2. Disconnect the spark plug wires and remove the spark plugs.

3. Disconnect the accelerator cable. If equipped with automatic transaxle, disconnect the throttle cable.

4. Remove the air intake pipe.

5. Remove the air intake pipe and fuel hose. Cover the fuel hose to prevent leakage.

6. Remove the upper radiator hose, water bypass hose, heater hose, oil cooler hose (turbo only) and brake vacuum hose.

7. Remove the 3-way and EGR solenoid valve assemblies.

8. Disconnect the engine harness connector and ground wire.

9. Remove the vacuum chamber and exhaust manifold insulator.

10. Remove the EGR pipe, turbo oil pipes, if equipped, and exhaust pipe.

11. Remove the exhaust manifold and the turbocharger, if equipped.

12. Remove the intake manifold bracket and the intake manifold.

13. Remove the distributor.

14. Loosen the air conditioning compressor and bracket and position and tie it aside; do not disconnect the refrigerant lines.

15. Remove the upper timing belt cover and the timing belt tensioner spring.

16. To remove the timing belt, perform the following:

a. Rotate the crankshaft so the 1 on the camshaft pulley is aligned with the timing mark on the front housing.

b. When timing marks are aligned, loosen the timing belt tensioner lock bolt. Pull the tensioner as far out as it will go and temporarily tighten the lock bolt.

c. Lift the timing belt from the camshaft pulley and position it aside.

17. Remove the cylinder head cover and gasket.

18. Loosen the cylinder head bolts, in sequence, and remove the cylinder head and head gasket.

To install:

19. Thoroughly clean the cylinder head and cylinder block contact surfaces to remove any dirt or oil. Check the cylinder head for warpage and cracks. The maximum allowable contact distortion is 0.006 in. Inspect the cylinder head bolts for damaged

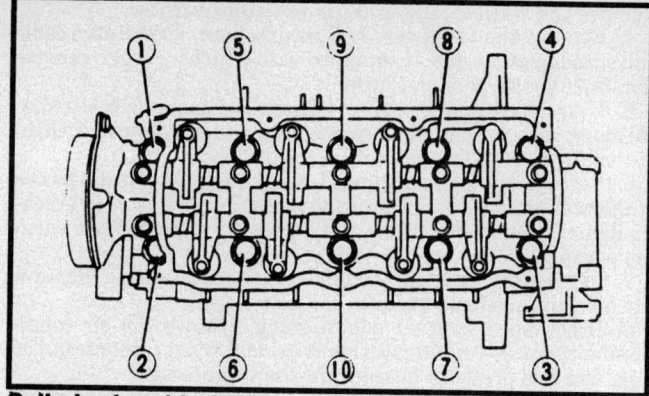

Cylinder head bolt loosening sequence — 626 and MX-6

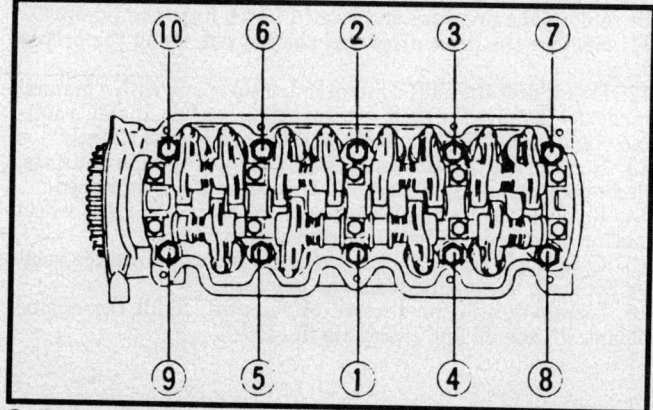

Cylinder head bolt torque sequence — 626 and MX-6

threads and make sure they are free from grease and dirt.

20. Lay the new gasket on the surface of the block.

NOTE: Turbocharged and non-turbocharged engines use different cylinder head gaskets. To ensure proper sealing and compression, make sure the proper type gasket is being installed.

21. Set the cylinder head on the gasket.

22. Coat the bolt threads and seat surfaces with clean engine oil and torque the bolts, in sequence, to 59–64 ft. lbs., in 3 stages.

23. Apply sealant to the 4 corners of the cylinder head and install the cover with a new gasket. Torque the cover nuts to 52–69 inch lbs.

24. Make sure the camshaft pulley and front housing timing marks are still aligned and install the timing belt.

25. Complete the remainder of the installation by reversing the removal procedure. Fill the cooling system to the proper level and connect the negative battery cable.

323 AND PROTEGE

Without Turbocharger

1. Disconnect the negative battery cable. Turn the crankshaft so the piston of the No. 1 cylinder is at TDC of its compression stroke. Drain the coolant.

2. Remove the air cleaner assembly and remove the following components:

a. Remove the oil level gauge, accelerator cable and cruise control cable, if equipped.

b. Remove the fuel hoses, heater hoses, brake vacuum hose and canister hose. If equipped with a carburetor, remove the fuel pump.

c. Remove the engine harness connectors, spark plug wires, distributor, spark plugs and secondary air pipe assembly for carbureted vehicles.

d. Remove the front hanger and engine ground wire. Remove the upper radiator hose, water bypass hose and bracket.

e. Remove the intake manifold assembly. Remove the exhaust manifold insulator and the exhaust manifold.

f. Remove the engine side cover. Remove the upper and lower timing belt cover. Remove the timing belt tensioner with spring and remove the timing belt.

NOTE: Before removing the timing belt, turn the crankshaft to align the timing matching mark on the camshaft pulley with the matching mark on the cylinder head cover. Be sure to mark the direction of rotation on the timing belt. The reason to mark the belt is so the belt can be reinstalled in the same direction.

g. To remove the camshaft pulley, use a suitable tool to lock the pulley in place to keep it from turning and remove the pulley nut or bolt.

h. Remove the rear engine hanger, cylinder head cover and gaskets.

i. Remove the cylinder head bolts; loosen the head bolts in reverse of the torque sequence.

j. Remove the cylinder head and cylinder head gasket.

To install:

3. Clean and inspect the gasket mating surfaces. Check for wear and damage, replace defective parts, as necessary.

4. Use new gaskets and reverse the removal procedure. Torque the cylinder head bolts to specification. Do not forget to insert the plain washer. Adjust the valve clearance, as required. Check the timing. Refill the cooling system.

5. Be sure to install the camshaft pulley onto the dowel pin and keyway with the matching mark straight up, so the timing marks on the camshaft pulley and cylinder head align. Tighten the camshaft pulley to 36–45 ft. lbs.

With Turbocharger

1. Relieve the fuel system pressure. Disconnect the negative battery cable. Drain the cooling system. Remove the air cleaner assembly. Remove the distributor, distributor wires and spark plugs.

2. Remove the air intake pipe, air pipe, air bypass valve and hoses.

3. Remove the radiator.

4. Remove the engine side cover and the engine undercover.

5. Disconnect the exhaust pipe at the exhaust manifold. Remove the turbocharger mounting bracket and the exhaust manifold and turbocharger insulators. Remove the exhaust manifold retaining bolts. Remove the exhaust manifold and the turbocharger assembly from the engine.

6. Remove the radiator hose and coolant bypass pipe. Disconnect the accelerator cable. Disconnect all required electrical connections, vacuum hoses and fuel line couplings.

7. Remove the surge tank and bracket.

8. Remove the cylinder head cover bolts and the cylinder head cover from the engine.

9. Remove the timing cover assembly bolts, the timing cover assembly and the timing belt.

10. Remove the cylinder head bolts, the cylinder head and the intake manifold assembly from the engine. Remove the thermostat and the thermostat cover.

11. Thoroughly, clean the cylinder head and cylinder block contact surfaces to remove any dirt or oil. Check the cylinder head for warpage and cracks. The maximum allowable contact distortion is 0.006 in. Inspect the cylinder head bolts for damaged threads and make sure they are free from grease and dirt.

To install:

12. Installation is essentially the reverse of the removal procedure but pay attention to the following:

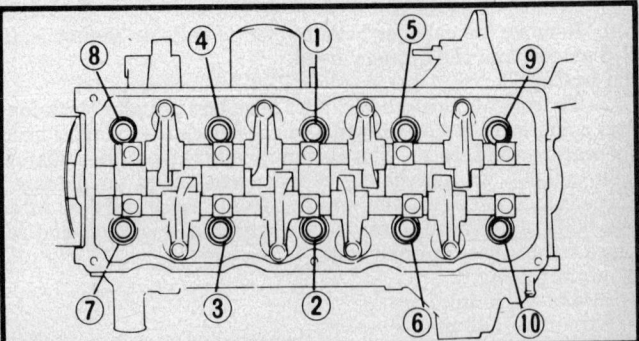

Cylinder head bolt torque sequence—323 and Protege with SOHC engine

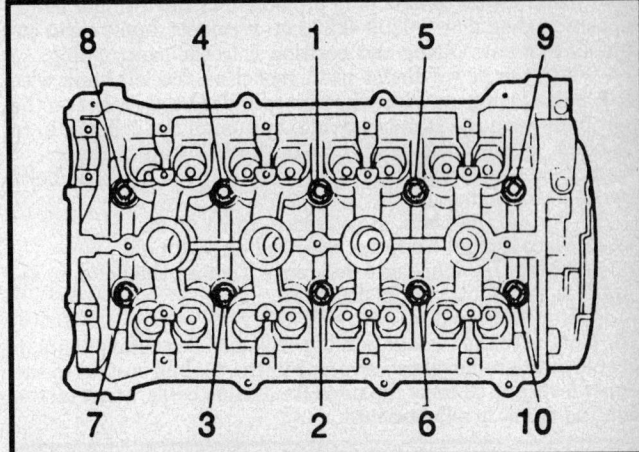

Cylinder head bolt torque sequence—323, Protege and Miata with DOHC engine

a. Install the thermostat with the jiggle pin facing upward and the printed side of the gasket facing the thermostat.

b. Be sure to torque the cylinder head bolts to specifications, in sequence, to 56–60 ft. lbs., in several stages.

c. Use a new cylinder head cover gasket and apply sealant to the cover. Torque the cover bolts to 26–35 inch lbs.

d. Fill the cooling system to the proper level and perform the necessary tune-up adjustments.

929

1. Relieve the fuel system pressure. Disconnect the negative battery cable. Remove the air cleaner assembly. Drain the coolant.

2. Position the engine at TDC on the compression stroke so all the pulley matchmarks are aligned. Remove the timing cover assembly and the timing belt; mark the direction of rotation if it is to be re-used.

3. Disconnect and plug canister, brake vacuum and fuel hoses. If equipped with an automatic transmission, disconnect the vacuum hose.

4. Remove the 3-way solenoid valve assembly and disconnect all engine harness connector and grounds.

5. If equipped with an automatic transmission, remove the dipstick. Disconnect the required vacuum hoses and the accelerator linkage.

6. Remove the distributor and the EGR pipe.

7. Remove the extension manifold. Remove the intake manifold, by loosening the retaining bolts, in sequence.

8. Remove the cylinder head cover.

9. Remove the center exhaust pipe insulator and pipe. Disconnect the exhaust manifold bolts and the exhaust manifold with insulator.

10. Remove the seal plate.

11. Remove the cylinder head-to-engine bolts, in sequence, in 2–3 stages, and the cylinder head.

To install:

12. Thoroughly clean the cylinder head and cylinder block contact surfaces to remove any dirt or oil. Check the cylinder head for warpage and cracks. The maximum allowable contact distortion is 0.004 in. Inspect the cylinder head bolts for damaged threads and make sure they are free from grease and dirt. After the bolts are cleaned, measure the length of each bolt and replace out of specifications bolts, as required.

Minimum Length:
  Intake—4.25 in.
  Exhaust—5.43 in.
Maximum Length:
  Intake—4.29 in.
  Exhaust—5.47 in.

13. Check the oil control plug projection at the cylinder block. Projection should be 0.0209–0.224 in. If correct, apply clean engine oil to a new O-ring and position it to the control plug.

14. Place the new cylinder head gasket on the left bank with the **L** mark facing up. Place the new cylinder head gasket on the right bank with the **R** mark facing up. Install the cylinder onto the block. Tighten the head bolts in the following manner:

  a. Coat the threads and the seating faces of the head bolts with clean engine oil.

  b. Torque the bolts, in sequence, to 14 ft. lbs.

  c. Place a paint mark on the head of each bolt.

  d. Using this mark as a reference, tighten the bolts, in sequence, an additional 90 degrees.

  e. Repeat Step d.

15. Complete the installation of the remaining components in reverse of the removal procedure. Fill the cooling system to the proper level and connect the negative battery cable. Make all the required tune-up adjustments.

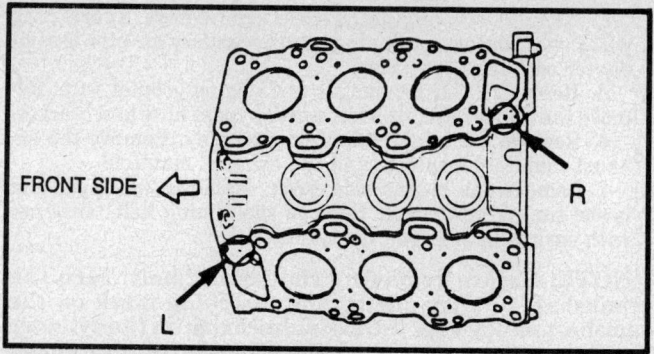

Cylinder head gasket installation—929

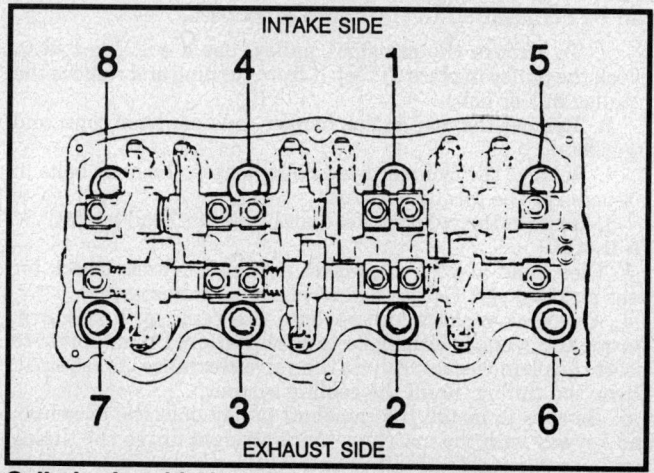

Cylinder head bolt torque sequence—929

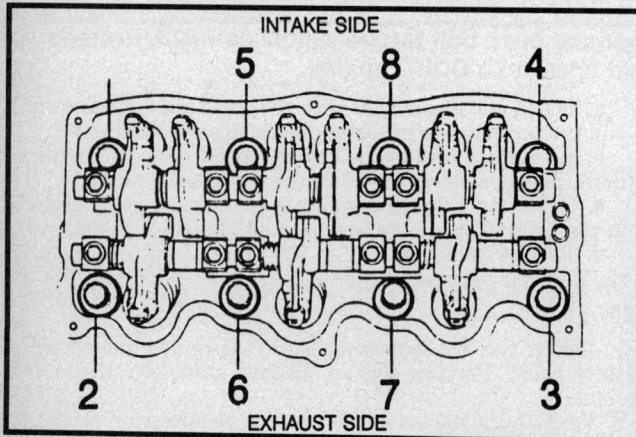

Cylinder head bolt removal sequence—929

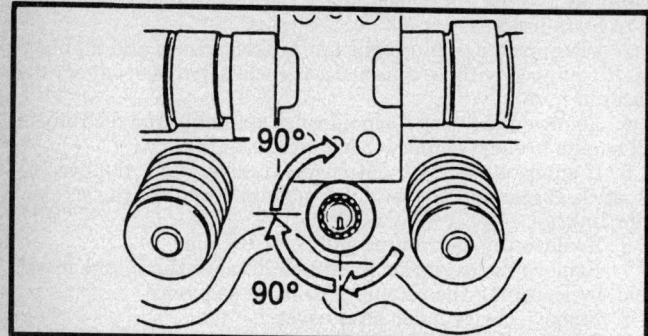

On 929 use paint mark as a reference, then torque cylinder head bolts by using the angular method

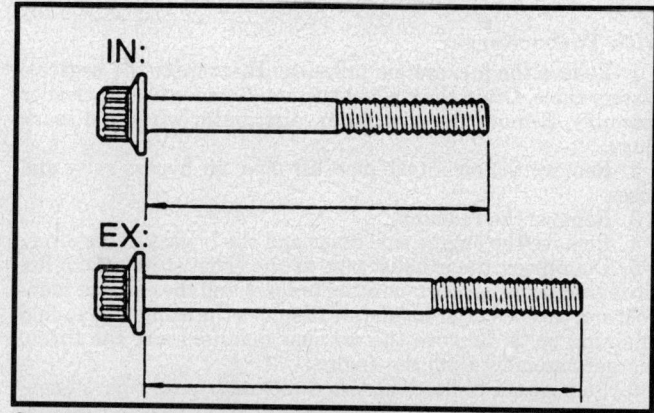

On 929, measure the length of each cylinder head bolt before installation

MIATA

1. Disconnect the battery negative cable and drain engine cooling system.

2. Remove the air cleaner assembly and disconnect the accelerator cable.

3. Disconnet the fuel, heater, cruise control, brake vacuum and purge control hoses.

4. Disconnect and tag all electrical connectors necessary for cylinder head removal.

5. Remove the exhaust manifold insulator cover and disconnect the water bypass pipe.

6. Remove the ignition coil pack assembly with the spark plug wires and the cylinder head cover.

7. Remove the timing belt front cover and the timing belt.

8. Disconnect the exhaust pipe from the exhaust manifold and the manifold bracket.

9. Remove the cylinder head bolts, in sequence, the cylinder head and gasket from the vehicle.

To install:

10. Install new gasket on cylinder block and coat bolt threads with clean engine oil.

11. Install cylinder head onto block. Torque bolts, in 2–3 steps, in sequence, to 56–60 ft. lbs. (76–81 Nm).

12. Install manifold bracket and connect the exhaust pipe to the exhaust manifold.

13. Install the timing belt and the front cover assembly.

14. Install the cylinder head cover and the ignition coil pack assembly with spark plug wires.

15. Install the water bypass pipe and the exhaust manifold insulator cover.

16. Connect all electrical connectors and hoses that were disconnected during removal.

17. Connect the accelerator cable and the air cleaner assembly.

18. Connect the battery negative cable and fill cooling system. Start engine and check for leaks.

Valve Lash

Adjustment

1987 323 AND 626

1. Start and allow engine to reach normal operating temperature.

2. Remove the cylinder head cover.

3. Rotate engine to bring the No. 1 cylinder to TDC on its compression stroke. On 323, adjust the No. 1 and 2 intake and No. 1 and No. exhaust valves to 0.012 in. (0.30mm). On 626, adjust the No. 3 and 4 intake valves and No. 2 and 4 exhaust valves to 0.012 in. (0.30mm).

4. Rotate the crankshaft 1 complete turn so the No. 4 cylinder is at TDC on its compression stroke. Adjust the remaining valves to 0.012 in. (0.30mm).

5. Install cylinder head cover. Start engine and check for leaks.

Rocker Arms/Shafts

Removal and Installation

626 AND MX-6

1. Disconnect the negative battery cable. Remove the air cleaner assembly.

2. Remove the necessary components in order to gain access to the cylinder head cover bolts. Remove the cylinder head cover.

3. As necessary, remove the camshaft pulley, front housing assembly, distributor and rear housing assembly.

4. Loosen the rocker arm assembly bolts, a little at a time,

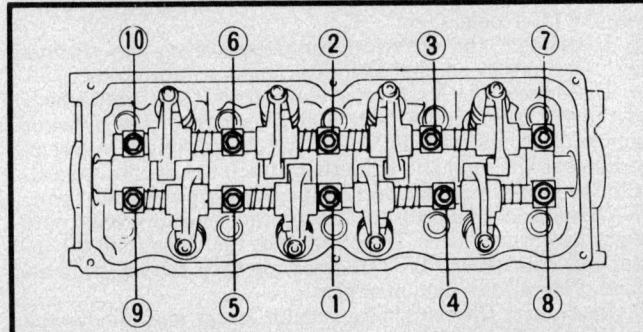

Rocker shaft torque sequence—323, Protege, 626 and MX-6

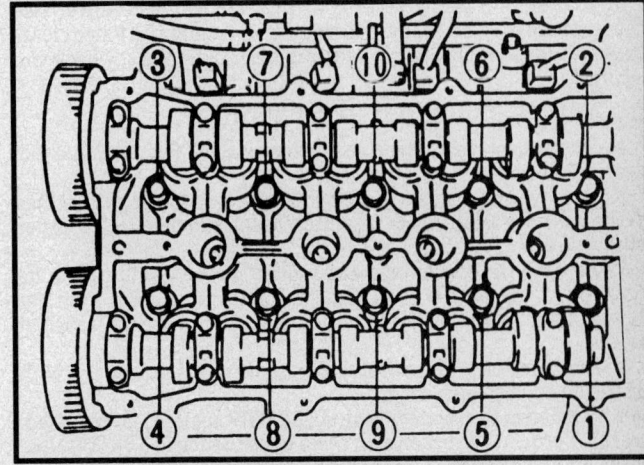

Cylinder head loosening sequence—Miata

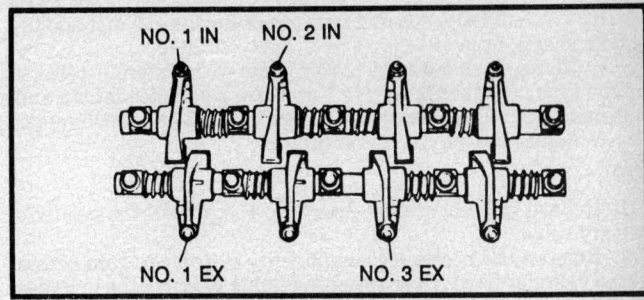

Rocker arms and shafts—1987 323

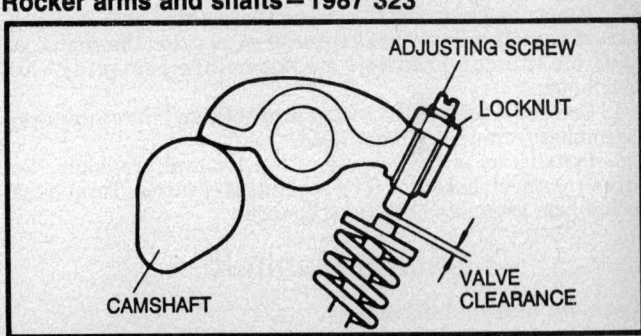

Adjusting valve clearance—1987 323

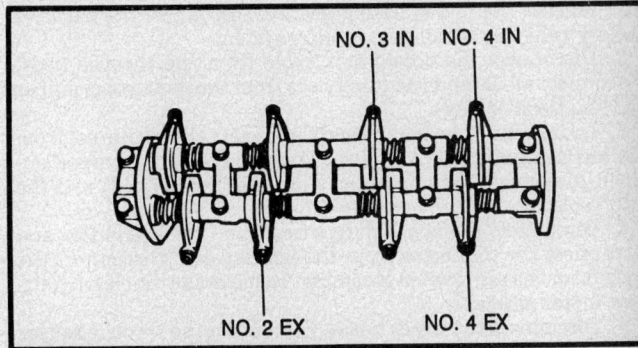

Rocker arms and shafts—1987 626

from the outer ends toward the center, reverse of torque sequence; do not remove the bolts, remove them with the rocker arm assembly.

5. Inspect the parts for wear and damage, replace, as necessary. Clean and inspect the gasket mounting surfaces.

6. Installation is the reverse of the removal procedure. Use new gaskets or RTV sealant, as required. Adjust the valve clearances, if not equipped with hydraulic lash adjusters. Check the timing.

323 AND PROTEGE WITHOUT TURBO

1. Disconnect the negative battery cable. Remove the air cleaner assembly.

2. Remove the necessary components in order to gain access to the cylinder head cover retaining bolts. Remove the cylinder head cover.

3. Remove the rocker arm and rocker shaft assembly from its mounting. Tag and bag all the components as what cylinder they belong to and whether they are for intake or exhaust service.

4. Installation is the reverse of the removal procedure with attention to the following:
   a. Be sure to use new gaskets or RTV sealant, as required.
   b. Torque the rocker arm bolts in sequence to 16–21 ft. lbs.
   c. Make sure both rocker arm shaft bolt holes face downward when installing.
   d. The bolt holes spacing is different for the exhaust and intake shafts.
   e. There are 2 types of rocker arms with different offsets. One type of rocker is for No.1 and No. 2 cylinder intake and exhaust and the other type belongs to No. 3 and 4 cylinders.
   f. Adjust the valves, as required.

929

1. Relieve the fuel system pressure. Disconnect the negative battery cable.

2. Remove the necessary components in order to gain access to the cylinder head cover retaining bolts. Remove the cylinder head cover.

3. It may be necessary to remove the distributor in order to remove the left cylinder head cover; if so, position the engine at TDC on the compression stroke before removing the distributor.

4. Carefully, remove the rocker arm bolts and the rocker arm assemblies from the cylinder head.

5. Installation is the reverse of the removal procedure. Be sure to use new gaskets or RTV sealant, as required. Torque the rocker arm assembly bolts, in sequence.

Intake Manifold

Removal and Installation

323 AND PROTEGE

1. Release the fuel system pressure. Disconnect the negative battery cable and drain the cooling system.

2. Disconnect the accelerator cable from the throttle body. Disconnect all air and vacuum hoses from the dynamic chamber and the throttle body.

3. Loosen the hose clamps and disconnect the air funnel from the airflow meter and the throttle body. On turbocharged engines, disconnect the air funnel from the throttle body and the intercooler.

4. Disconnect the spark plug wires from the distributor and disconnect the connector from the ignition coil. Disconnect the hose from the air cleaner assembly. Remove the air cleaner/airflow meter assembly.

5. Disconnect the water hoses. Disconnect the throttle sensor connector. Remove the retaining nuts and bolts from the throttle body and separate the throttle body from the intake manifold.

6. Disconnect the hoses and remove the BAC valve. On turbocharged engines, disconnect the water hose for the oil cooler. Plug the opening to prevent leakage.

7. On turbocharged engines, unbolt the intake manifold and dynamic chamber assembly from the cylinder block and lift it

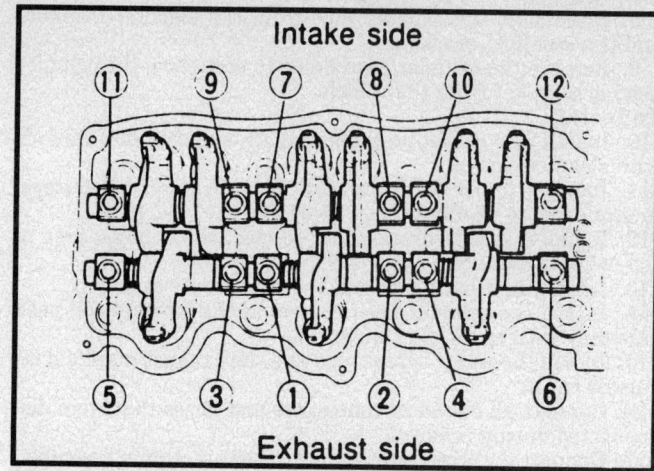

Rocker arm bolt torque sequence—929

from the vehicle. On non-turbocharged engines, unbolt the dynamic chamber from the intake manifold and remove it along with the gasket, then remove the intake manifold. Remove the intake manifold gasket from the cylinder block. Cover or plug the intake ports to prevent anything from falling into the engine.

8. Thoroughly, clean the intake manifold and cylinder block gasket mating surfaces. Visually inspect the intake manifold and dynamic chamber for cracks.

9. Place a new gasket on the cylinder block and lower the intake manifold onto the gasket. On turbo-charged engines, attach the dynamic chamber to the intake manifold with a new gasket. Install the retaining nuts and bolts and torque to 14–19 ft. lbs.

10. Install the remaining components in the reverse order of removal.

11. Refill the cooling system to the proper level and connect the negative battery cable.

626 AND MX-6

1. Release the fuel pressure. Disconnect the negative battery cable and drain the cooling system.

2. Disconnect the airflow meter connector. Remove the air cleaner duct (1987 only), secondary air hoses, air control vacuum hoses and remove the air cleaner. On 1988–89 vehicles, remove the air duct and disconnect and No. 1 resonance chamber.

3. Remove the air flow meter and attendant air hoses. On 1988–89 non-turbocharged engines, disconnect and remove the No. 2 resonator which is connected to the bottom of the flex air hose.

4. On 1988–89 turbocharged engines, trace the upper hose on the intercooler to the air bypass valve and disconnect the hoses. Unbolt and remove the valve from its mounting bracket. Remove the intercooler.

5. Disconnect the electrical connectors from the throttle body. Disconnect and plug the water and vacuum hoses.

6. Disconnect the accelerator cable from the throttle body and remove the throttle body and gasket from the dynamic chamber. Disconnect the PCV hose and the vacuum pipe assembly. Remove the nuts and bolts that attach the dynamic chamber to the intake manifold and remove it along with the gasket.

7. Disconnect connectors from the fuel injectors and route the wiring harness aside. Disconnect the fuel hose from the injector rail and remove the rail assembly with the injectors attached. Plug all the fuel openings.

8. Disconnect the remaining vacuum hoses and remove the EGR pipe.

9. Remove the intake manifold bracket. Remove the intake manifold and the gasket. Cover or plug the intake ports to pre-

vent anything from falling into the engine.

10. Thoroughly, clean the intake manifold and cylinder block gasket mating surfaces with a gasket scraper and solvent. Visually inspect the intake manifold and dynamic chamber for cracks.

11. Place a new gasket on the cylinder block and lower the intake manifold onto the gasket. Install the nuts and torque them to 14–22 ft. lbs.

12. Install the remaining components in the reverse order of removal.

13. Refill the cooling system to the proper level and connect the negative battery cable. Check the accelerator cable deflection.

929

1. Release the fuel system pressure. Disconnect the negative battery cable. Disconnect and plug the water hoses. The coolant will be drained from the radiator just before the intake manifold is ready to be removed.

2. Disconnect the air inlet duct from the air cleaner and disconnect the air flow meter connector.

3. Disconnect the vacuum hoses from the TICS and purge air control solenoid valves. These valves are bolted to the front of the air cleaner assembly.

4. Remove the air cleaner, air cleaner element, air flow meter and air funnel.

5. Disconnect the Bypass Air Control (BAC) valve connector, water hoses and remove the valve.

6. Disconnect the throttle sensor connector and the accelerator cable. Remove the throttle body and gasket.

7. Disconnect all vacuum hoses, EGR pipe, EGR position sensor connector, water hose and ground wire.

8. Remove the wiring harness bracket.

9. Disconnect the air intake pipe from the dynamic chamber with the gasket.

10. Mark the extension manifolds right and left for assembly reference as they are not interchangeable. Remove the 6 extension manifolds with their gaskets from the dynamic chamber.

11. Disconnect the intake air thermo sensor connector, vacuum hoses and ground connectors.

12. Remove the nuts and lift the dynamic chamber from the intake manifold studs. Drain the radiator and disconnect all remaining connectors, fuel hoses and water hoses.

13. Using sequence, loosen the intake manifold nuts, in 2 stages. Lift the intake manifold from the engine and remove both intake manifold gaskets. Cover the intake ports to prevent anything from falling into the engine.

14. Visually inspect the intake manifold for cracks, warpage or any other type of damage and replace, as necessary. Remove all gasket material from the seating surface on the manifold and the engine.

NOTE: Forward of one of the studs that secure the dynamic chamber is an O-ring that seals the manifold to the chamber. Remove this O-ring and replace it with a new one.

15. Place the new intake manifold gaskets onto the cylinder block and lower the manifold over the gaskets. Install the intake manifold washers with the white paint marks facing up. Install the retaining nuts and torque, in 2 stages, to 14–18 ft. lbs., in sequence.

16. Install the remaining components in reverse of the removal procedure. Fill the cooling system to the proper level. Connect the negative battery cable. Start the engine and check for leaks.

MIATA

1. Relieve fuel system pressure.
2. Disconnect the battery negative cable.
3. Disconnect the accelerator cable and remove the throttle body bolts and the throttle body from the vehicle.
4. Remove the air valve and disconnect the vacuum and fuel

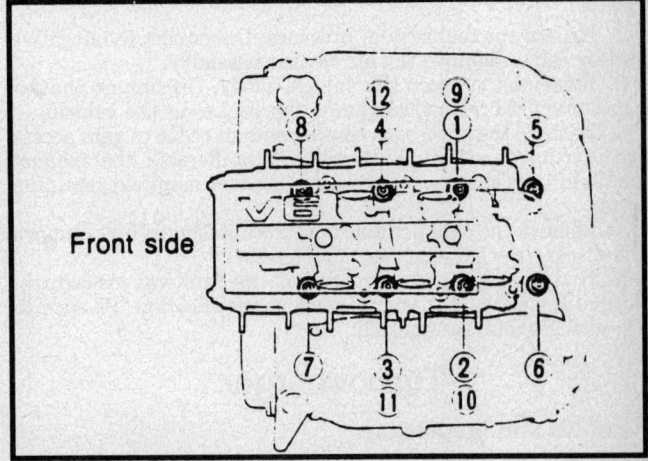
Intake manifold torque sequence—929

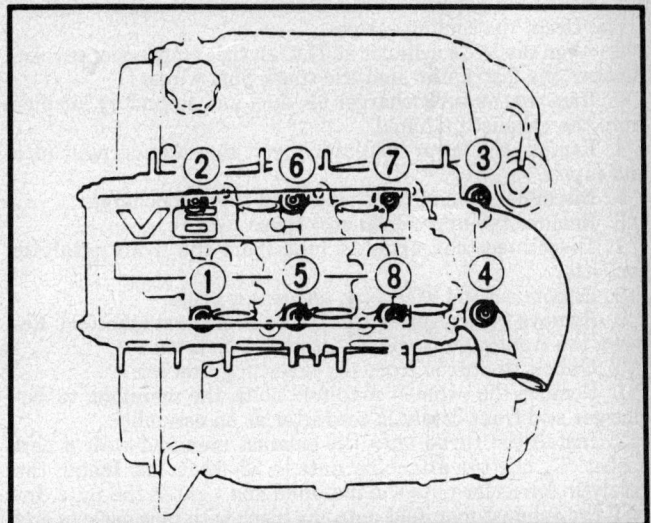
Intake manifold loosening sequence—929

hoses. Plug all openings.

5. Disconnect the electrical connectors from the injectors and remove the injectors and delivery pipe as an assembly.

6. Remove the injector harness attaching bolts and the injector harness from the vehicle.

7. Remove the intake manifold bracket and the intake manifold from the vehicle.

8. Reverse procedure to install. Use a new gasket and torque intake manifold and delivery pipe bolts to 14–19 ft. lbs. (19–25 Nm).

Exhaust Manifold

Removal and Installation

EXCEPT 929

1. Disconnect the negative battery cable. Remove the heat shield cover, if equipped. Remove the 2 attaching nuts from the exhaust pipe at the manifold.

2. If equipped with a turbocharger, remove the air duct and turbocharger-to-manifold mounting bolts.

3. Remove all necessary exhaust brackets and hangers. Remove the exhaust manifold retaining bolts. Remove the manifold from the engine.

4. Installation is the reverse of the removal procedure. Torque the exhaust manifold to specification. Use new gaskets.

929

1. Relieve the fuel system pressure. Disconnect the negative battery cable. Remove the air cleaner assembly.
2. Raise and support the vehicle safely. Disconnect the exhaust manifold from the exhaust flange. Lower the vehicle.
3. Remove the necessary components in order to gain access to the exhaust manifold retaining bolts. Remove the exhaust manifold heat shields. Remove the exhaust manifold retaining bolts.
4. Remove the exhaust manifold from its mounting. Remove and discard the exhaust manifold gasket.
5. Installation is the reverse of the removal procedure. Torque the exhaust manifold nuts to specification. Be sure to use new gaskets, as required.

Turbocharger

Removal and Installation

1987 626

1. Be sure the engine is cold. Disconnect the negative battery cable. Drain the cooling system.
2. Align the No. 1 cylinder at TDC on the compression stroke. Remove the distributor and the spark plug wires.
3. Remove the turbocharger air duct and secondary air pipe from the exhaust manifold.
4. Remove the lower insulator cover, the secondary air pipe and nipple.
5. Disconnect the oil feed pipe from the turbocharger.
6. Remove the upper insulator cover.
7. Disconnect the exhaust pipe from the front catalytic converter.
8. Disconnect the EGR pipe and water hoses.
9. Remove the oxygen sensor from the exhaust manifold. Remove the front pipe from the catalytic converter.
10. Unbolt the turbo from the mounting bracket.
11. Remove the exhaust manifold bolts, the manifold, turbocharger and front catalytic converter as an assembly.
12. Install the turbo onto the exhaust manifold with a new gasket. Torque the attaching nuts to 23–32 ft. lbs. Install the catalytic converter onto the manifold and tighten the nuts. Install the exhaust manifold onto the block with new gaskets and torque the nuts to 16–21 ft. lbs.
13. Installation is the reverse or removal. Add 25cc of oil to the turbocharger oil passage before installing and replace all gaskets or sealant. Disconnect the coil and crank the engine for 20 seconds to insure that oil reaches the center bearings. Reconnect the coil and start the engine, allow it idle for 30 seconds to ensure the proper operation of the turbocharger.

1988–91 626 AND MX-6

NOTE: When replacing the turbocharger, always check the oil level and the condition of the oil and the turbo oil inlet and outlet lines. If the oil is dirty or the lines are damaged, replace them.

1. Disconnect the negative battery cable and drain the cooling system.
2. Remove the air hoses and the air bypass hose.
3. Remove the exhaust manifold insulators.
4. Disconnect the oil inlet and return pipes from the turbocharger and plug the ends.
5. Disconnect and plug the water hoses from the water pipe.
6. Disconnect the EGR pipe from the exhaust manifold.
7. Remove the oxygen sensor.
8. Disconnect the front pipe from the turbocharger and set the gasket aside. Remove the bolt from the turbocharger joint pipe.
9. Support the turbocharger and remove the exhaust manifold nuts. Remove the turbo and the manifold as an assembly.

Cover the exhaust manifold ports with a clean rag or masking tape to prevent the entry of foreign matter.

NOTE: Do not drop the turbocharger carry it around by the actuating handle. When laying the unit down, do so with the turbine shaft in the horizontal position. Do not bend the actuator mounting or rod.

10. Remove all the sealant and gasket material from the turbocharger and exhaust manifold mating surfaces. Use all new gaskets.
11. Pour 25cc of clean engine oil into the opening for the turbo oil line.
12. Attach the turbo to the exhaust manifold and torque the nuts to 20–29 ft. lbs. Attach the assembly to the engine using new gaskets and torque the nuts to specification. Torque the turbocharger joint pipe bolt to 27–46 ft. lbs. and the turbocharger bracket bolts to 23–30 ft. lbs.
13. Install the front pipe and the oxygen sensor.
14. Connect the EGR pipe to the exhaust manifold and the water hose to the inlet pipe.
15. Connect the oil inlet and return pipes to the turbo connections. Install the exhaust manifold insulators.
16. Install the air bypass valve and air hoses.
17. Fill the cooling system to the proper level and connect the negative battery cable.
18. Disconnect the connector from the igniter and crank the engine for 20 seconds. Reconnect the connector and start the engine. Run the engine at idle for 20 seconds. Stop the engine and disconnect the negative battery cable. Depress and hold the brake pedal in for 5 seconds to clear the malfunction code from the control unit.

323 AND PROTEGE

NOTE: When replacing the turbocharger, always check the oil level and the condition of the oil and the turbo oil inlet and outlet lines. If the oil is dirty or the lines are damaged, replace them.

1. Disconnect the negative battery cable.
2. From under the vehicle, remove the engine undercover.
3. Disconnect the 2 air hoses attached to the throttle body inlet hose and remove the air pipe.
4. Remove the exhaust manifold insulator covers.
5. Remove the water hoses.
6. Remove the oil pipe and the oil return hose.
7. Support the turbocharger and remove the nuts and bolts from the exhaust manifold. Remove the turbocharger and the exhaust manifold as an assembly. Remove the mounting gasket.
8. Remove the nuts and lift the turbocharger from the exhaust manifold studs. Cover the exhaust manifold ports to prevent the entry of foreign matter. If the gasket is bent or cracked, replace it. If the turbocharger mounting nuts are damaged, replace them with factory made replacement nuts only.

NOTE: Be careful to avoid dropping the turbocharger or handling it roughly. Be careful not to bend the wastegate actuator mounting and rod.

9. Installation is the reverse of removal.

Timing Belt Cover, Belt and Tensioner

Removal and Installation

1987 626

1. Disconnect the negative battery cable. Remove the alternator belt and the power steering pump belt. Remove the upper and the lower timing belt cover.
2. Turn the crankshaft to position the A mark on the camshaft pulley with the mark on the housing. Remove the crankshaft pulley mounting bolts and the pulley.

3. Remove the tensioner pulley lock bolt, the pulley and the spring. Remove the timing belt and mark an arrow in the direction of rotation on the timing belt.

4. To remove the camshaft pulley, insert a T-wrench through the camshaft pulley onto a housing bolt, place another wrench on the pulley center bolt, hold the T-wrench securely and remove the pulley center bolt.

5. Pull the camshaft pulley from the camshaft. To remove the crankshaft pulley, remove the center bolt and the pulley.

6. Install the timing belt and be sure the timing mark on the timing belt pulley is aligned with the matching mark. Make sure the mark (A) of the camshaft pulley is aligned with the timing mark. If it is not, turn the camshaft to align it.

7. Install the timing belt tensioner and spring. Temporarily secure it as the spring is fully extended.

8. Install the timing belt, if using the old timing belt, be sure it is reinstalled in the same direction of previous rotation. Also make sure there is no oil, grease or dirt on the timing belt.

9. Loosen the tensioner lock bolt. Turn the crankshaft twice in the direction of rotation. Align the timing marks. Tighten the timing belt tensioner lock bolt to 28–38 ft. lbs. Check the timing belt tension. The timing belt deflection should be 0.43–0.51 in. at 22 lbs.

626 AND MX-6

1. Disconnect the negative battery cable and remove the spark plug wires and spark plugs.

2. Remove the engine side cover and the drive belts.

3. Unbolt the crankshaft pulley and remove the upper and lower timing belt covers. Remove the crankshaft pulley baffle plate and make a note of how it is installed. The curved side should be facing out.

4. Turn the crankshaft until the **1** mark on the camshaft is aligned with the mark on top of the front housing. Unbolt and remove the tensioner and the tensioner spring.

5. Remove the timing belt. If the timing belt is to be reused, mark the direction of rotation, prior to removal.

6. Inspect the belt and replace it, if it is oil soaked or shows excessive wear, peeling, cracking or hardening. Inspect the tensioner for free and smooth rotation and replace it, if it does not turn smoothly. Replace all damaged components, as necessary.

7. Align the timing mark on the timing belt pulley with the matchmark on the lower front housing. Recheck the camshaft pulley and and front housing alignment marks. Turn the camshaft as necessary to re-align the marks.

8. Install the spring and tensioner with the bolt. Move the tensioner until the spring is fully extended and temporarily tighten the tensioner bolt to hold it in place.

9. Install the timing belt. Make sure there is no slack at the

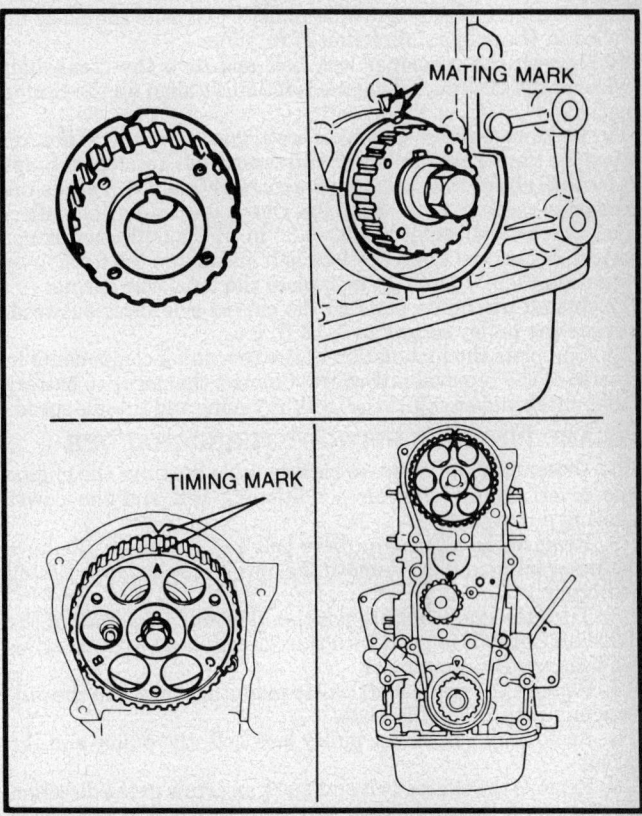

Timing belt alignment marks—1987 626

1. High-tension lead and spark plug
2. Engine side cover
3. Drive belt
4. Crankshaft pulley
5. Upper timing belt cover
6. Lower timing belt cover
7. Baffle plate
8. Timing belt tensioner
9. Timing belt tensioner spring
10. Timing belt

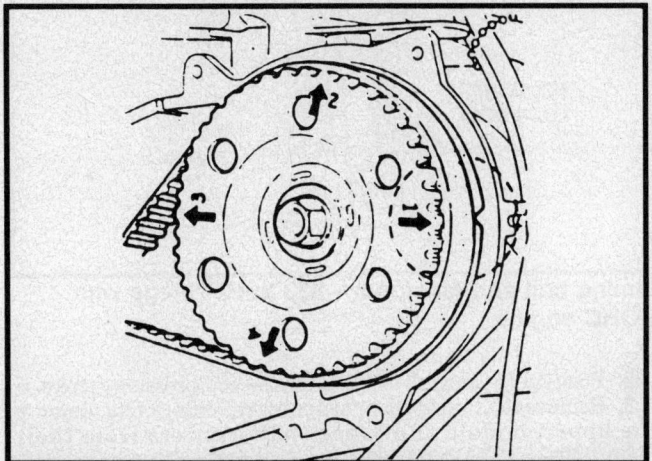

Camshaft pulley and front housing timing mark alignment—1988–91 626 and MX-6

Timing belt and related components—1988–91 626 and MX-6

side of the water pump and idler pulleys. Old belts should be installed in the original direction of rotation.

10. Loosen the tensioner lock bolt and turn the crankshaft twice, in the direction of engine rotation, to align all the timing marks.

11. Make sure all timing marks are aligned correctly. If not, remove the timing belt tensioner and timing belt and repeat Steps 7–10 until all the timing marks are correctly aligned. Torque the tensioner lock bolt to 27–38 ft. lbs. Check the timing belt deflection. Correct deflection is 0.30–0.33 in. If the deflection is not correct, loosen the tensioner lock bolt and adjust the tension by repeating Steps 10 and 11 or replace the tensioner spring.

12. Install the baffle plate so the curved side faces outward. Torque the pulley screws to 9–13 ft. lbs.

13. Complete the installation of the remaining components in reverse of the removal procedure. Connect the negative battery cable, check and/or adjust the ignition timing and the idle speed.

323 AND PROTEGE WITHOUT TURBOCHARGER

1. Disconnect the negative battery cable. Remove the engine side cover. Remove the air conditioning belt and the power steering pump belt.

2. Remove the alternator drive belt and alternator. Remove the water pump pulley. Remove the upper and the lower timing belt cover.

3. Turn the crankshaft to position the matching mark of the camshaft pulley is aligned with the cylinder head and the cylinder head cover timing mark.

4. Remove the crankshaft pulley mounting bolts and the pulley along with the baffle plate.

5. Remove the tensioner pulley lock bolt, the pulley and the spring.

6. Remove the timing belt and mark an arrow in the direction of rotation on the timing belt.

7. To remove the camshaft (water pump) pulley, use a suitable tool to lock the pulley in place to keep it from turning and remove the pulley retaining nut or bolt. To remove the crankshaft pulley, remove the center bolt and the pulley.

8. Reinstall the camshaft and crankshaft pulleys, if they where removed. Install the timing belt as follows:

   a. Be sure the timing mark on the timing belt pulley is aligned with the matching mark.

   b. Make sure the matching mark of the camshaft pulley is aligned with the cylinder head and the cylinder head cover timing mark.

   c. If it is not, turn the camshaft to align it.

9. Install the timing belt tensioner and spring. Temporarily secure it as the spring is fully extended.

10. Install the timing belt, if using the old timing belt, be sure it is reinstalled in the same direction of previous rotation. Also make sure there is no oil, grease or dirt on the timing belt.

11. Loosen the tensioner lock bolt. Turn the crankshaft twice in the direction of rotation. Align the timing marks.

12. Make sure the timing marks are correctly aligned, if they are not aligned, remove the timing belt tensioner and timing belt and repeat Steps 8–12.

13. Tighten the timing belt tensioner lock bolt to 14–19 ft. lbs. Check the timing belt tension. The timing belt deflection should be 0.35–0.51 in. at 22 lbs.

14. Complete the installation by reversing the removal procedure.

323 AND PROTEGE WITH TWINCAM ENGINE

1. Disconnect the negative battery cable. Remove the engine side cover. Remove the required drive belts. Remove the water pump pulley and crankshaft pulley.

NOTE: Remove the No. 3 engine mount installation bolts, then lower the engine to remove the air conditioning pulley, power steering pulley and the crankshaft pulley.

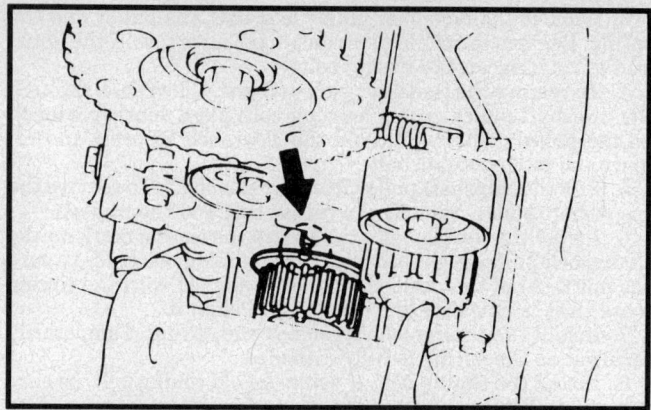

Timing belt pulley and front housing alignment marks—1988–91 626 and MX-6

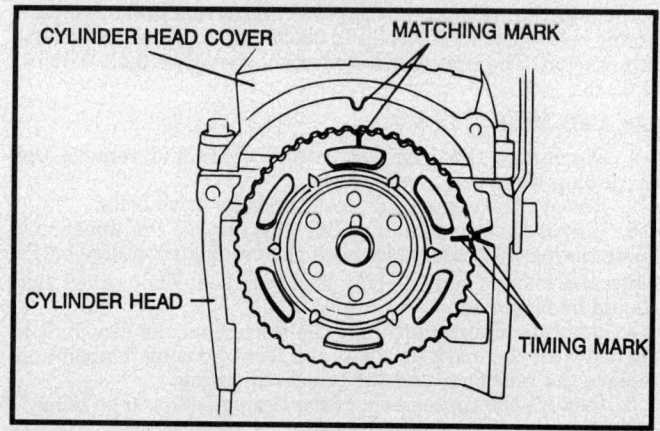

Timing mark alignment—323 and Protege with SOHC engine

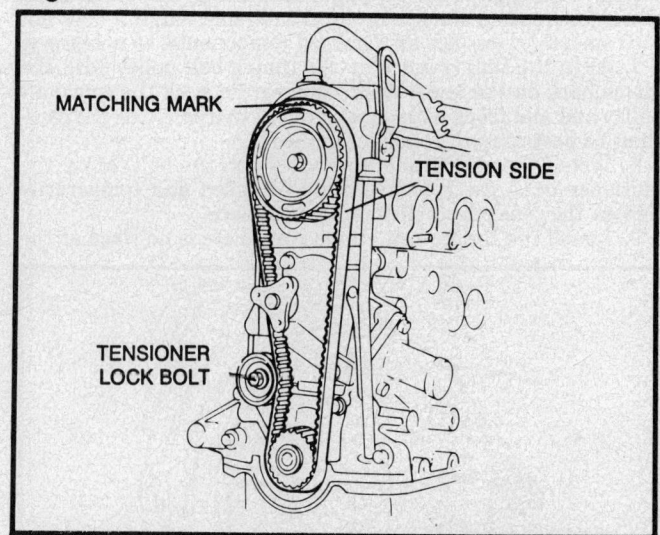

Timing belt and tensioner—323 and Protege with SOHC engine

2. Position the engine at TDC on the compression stroke.

3. Remove the timing cover assembly retaining bolts. Remove the upper, middle and lower timing covers from their mountings.

4. Remove the baffle plate. Remove the timing belt tensioner and spring. Remove the timing belt from the engine. If the old

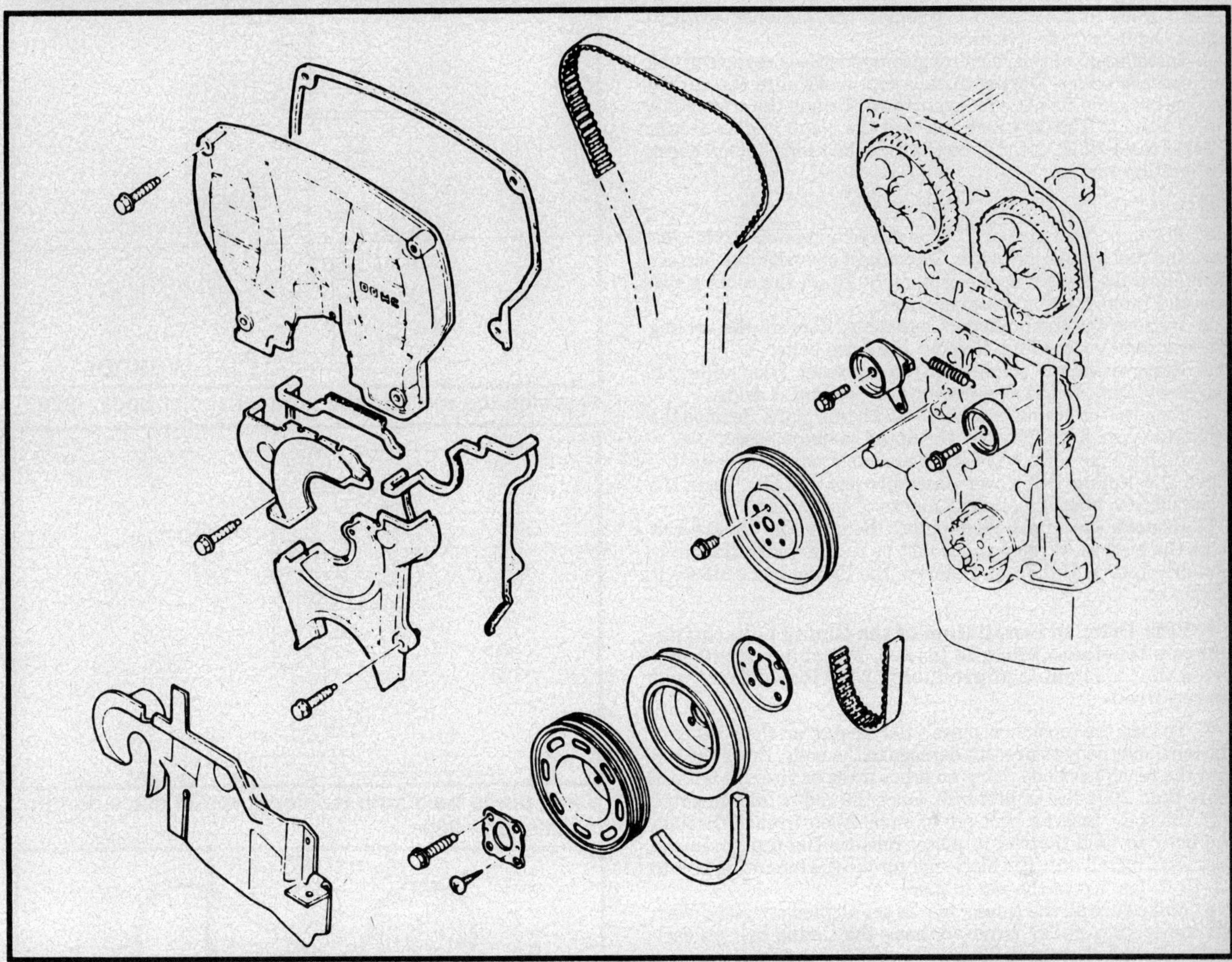

Timing belt cover and related components—323 and Protege with DOHC engine

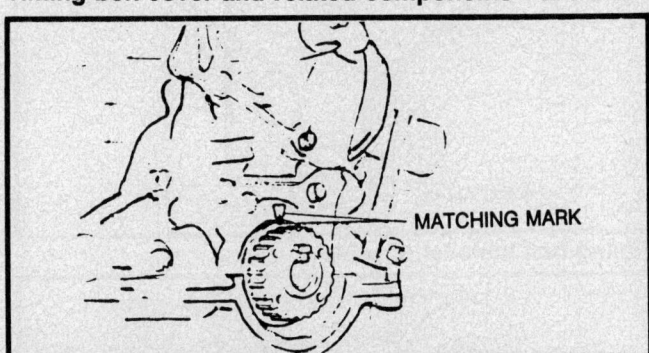

MATCHING MARK

Crankshaft gear timing mark alignment—323 and Protege with DOHC engine

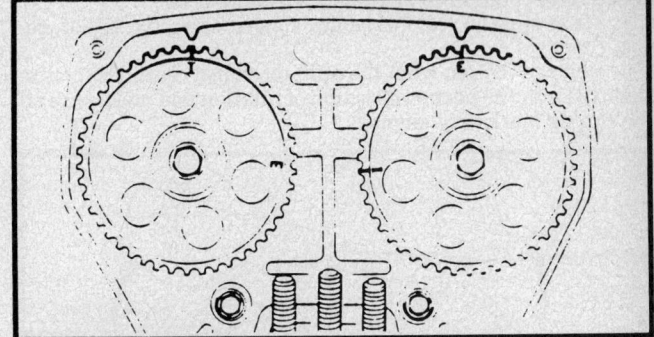

Camshaft gear timing mark alignment—323 and Protege with DOHC engine

belt is being reused, mark the direction of rotation. Be sure the timing mark on the timing belt pulley is aligned with the mark on the engine. Be sure the camshaft pulleys are properly aligned.

5. Install the spring and tensioner with the bolt. Move the tensioner until the spring is fully extended and temporarily tighten the tensioner bolt to hold it in place.

6. Install the timing belt by keeping the right side of the belt as tight as possible. Old belts must be installed in the original di-

rection of rotation.

7. Turn the crankshaft twice in the normal direction of rotation and make sure all the timing marks are aligned. Loosen the tensioner lock bolt and apply tension to the belt.

8. Torque the tensioner lock bolt to 27–38 ft. lbs. and turn the crankshaft twice in the normal direction of rotation to ensure all the timing marks are aligned correctly.

9. Measure the tension between the camshaft pulleys. The deflection should be between 0.33–0.45 in. between the pulleys.

If not correct, repeat Steps 5–8 or replace the tensioner spring to adjust the tension to specification.

10. Installation of the remaining components is reverse of the removal procedure. During installation, make sure the curved surface of the baffle plate faces outward. Torque the crankshaft pulley bolts to 109–152 inch lbs. and the No. 3 engine mount bracket to 44–63 ft. lbs. Adjust the drive belt tension and check the ignition timing.

929

1. Position the engine at TDC on the compression stroke. Relieve the fuel system pressure. Disconnect the negative battery cable. Remove the air cleaner assembly. Drain the cooling system and remove the spark plug wires.

2. Remove the fresh air duct assembly. Remove the cooling fan and radiator cowling. Remove the drive belts.

3. Remove the air conditioning compressor idler pulley. If necessary, remove the compressor and position it aside.

4. Remove the crankshaft pulley and baffle plate. Remove the coolant bypass hose. Remove the upper radiator hose.

5. Remove the timing belt cover assembly retaining bolts. Remove the timing belt cover assembly and gasket. Turn the crankshaft to align the mating marks of the pulleys.

6. Remove the upper idler pulley. Remove the timing belt from the pulleys. If reusing the belt be sure to mark the direction of rotation. Unbolt and remove the timing belt automatic tensioner.

NOTE: Prior to installation of the timing belt, the automatic tensioner must be loaded. For this operation a press that is capable of producing 2000 lbs. of force will be required.

7. To load the tensioner, place a flat washer on the bottom of the tensioner body to prevent damage to the body. Press the rod into the tensioner body using an arbor press or vise. Do not use more than 2000 lbs. of pressure. Once the rod is fully inserted into the body, insert a bent pin or small Allen wrench through the body to hold the rod in place. Remove the unit from the press and install onto the block and torque the mounting bolt to 14–19 ft. lbs. Leave the pin in place.

8. Make sure all the timing marks are aligned properly. With the upper idler pulley removed, hang the timing belt on each pulley. Install the upper idler pulley and torque the mounting bolt to 27–38 ft. lbs. Rotate the crankshaft twice in the normal direction of rotation to align all the timing marks.

9. Make sure all the marks are aligned correctly. If not, repeat Step 8.

10. Remove the pin from the auto tensioner. Turn the crankshaft twice in the normal direction of rotation and make sure all the timing marks are aligned.

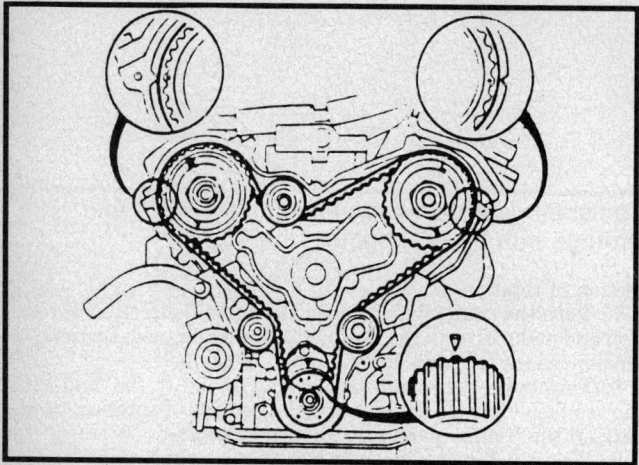

Timing belt alignment marks—929

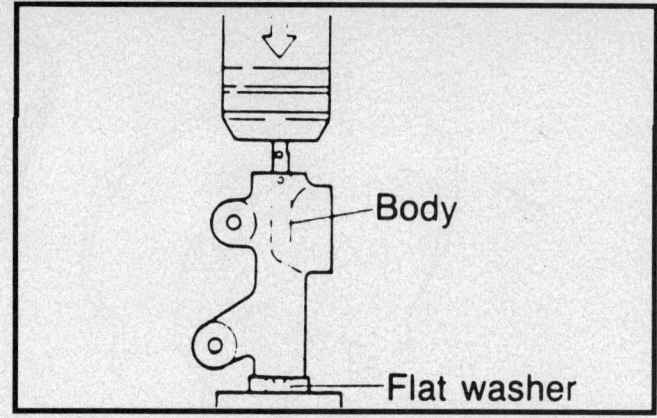

Pressing the rod into the auto tensioner body—929

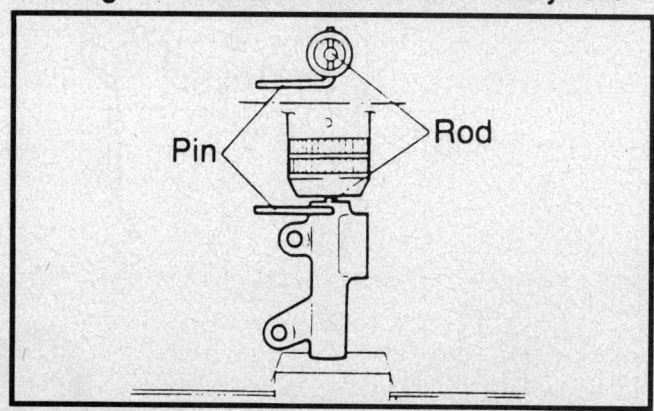

Using pin to hold auto tensioner rod in place during installation—929

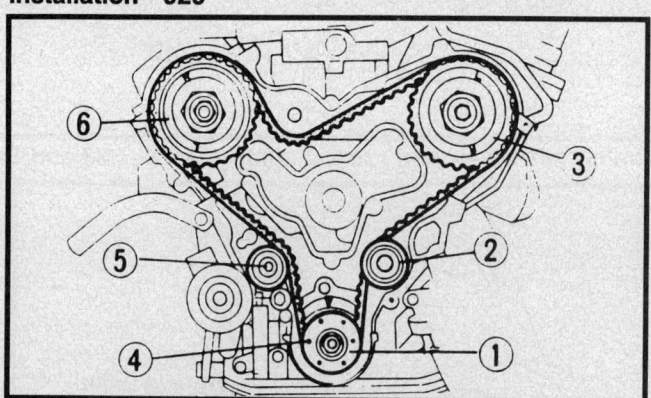

Timing belt installation—929

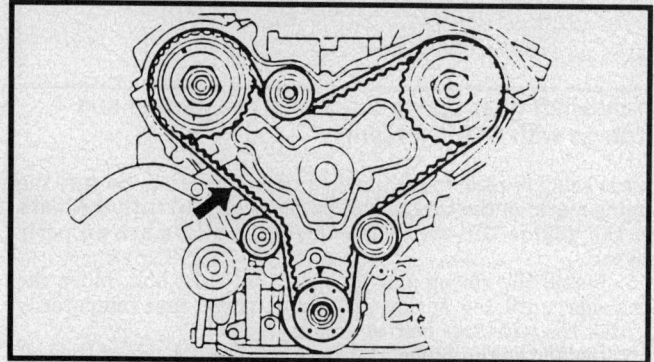

Checking timing belt deflection—929

11. Check the timing belt deflection. If the deflection is not 0.20–0.28 in. repeat the adjustment procedure.

NOTE: Excessive belt deflection is caused by auto tensioner failure or an excessively stretched timing belt.

12. Complete the installation of the remaining components in reverse of the removal procedure. Fill the cooling system to the proper level. Adjust the belt tension. Check and/or adjust the ignition timing and the idle speed.

MIATA

1. Disconnect the battery negative cable and drain the cooling system.
2. Remove the air intake pipe and the upper radiator hose.
3. Remove the water hoses from the thermostat housing.
4. Remove the power steering, air conditioning and alternator drive belts.
5. Remove the water pump pulley and the crankshaft pulley.
6. Remove the timing belt inner and outer guide plates.
7. Remove the ignition coil pack assembly and spark plug wires.
8. Remove the cylinder head cover.
9. Remove the upper, middle and lower timing belt covers.
10. Align the marks on the camshaft pulleys with the engine block.
11. Remove the timing belt tensioner bolt and the timing belt tensioner and spring.
12. Remove the timing belt.

To install:

13. Install the timing belt tensioner and spring.
14. Check the the mark on the crankshaft pulley is aligned.
15. Check that the marks on the camshaft pulleys are aligned with the marks on the block.
16. Install the timing belt so there is no looseness on the idler side or between the 2 camshaft pulleys. Note mark on timing belt for proper installation.
17. Rotate the crankshaft clockwise, 2 complete turns, and align the crankshaft timing marks. Check that the camshaft timing marks align.
18. Loosen the tensioner and apply pressure to the timing belt and tighten the tensioner lock bolt to 27–38 ft. lbs. (37–52 Nm).
19. Check the timing belt deflection. Deflection should be 0.35–0.45 in. (9–11.5mm).
20. Install the timing belt covers and the cylinder head cover.
21. Install the ignition coil pack assembly and the spark plug wires.
22. Install the inner and outer timing belt guide plates.
23. Install the water pump pulley and the crankshaft pulley.
24. Install the air conditioning, power steering and alternator drive belts.
25. Install the upper radiator hose and the air intake pipe. Connect the battery negative cable and refill cooling system.

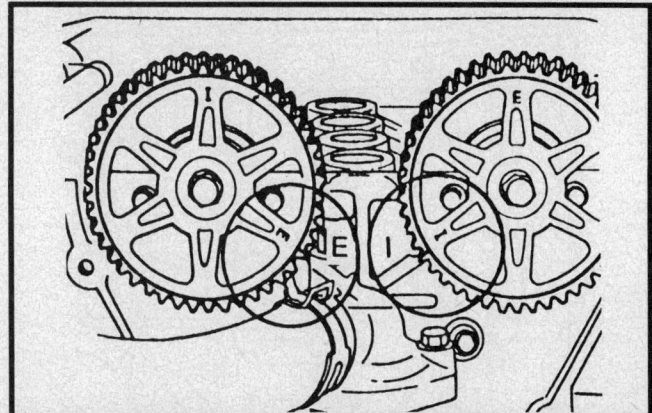

Aligning camshaft timing sprockets—Miata

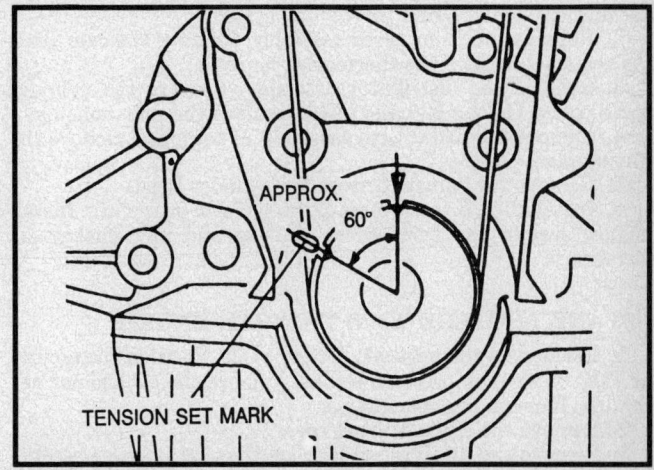

Aligning the timing belt pulley mark with the tension set mark—Miata

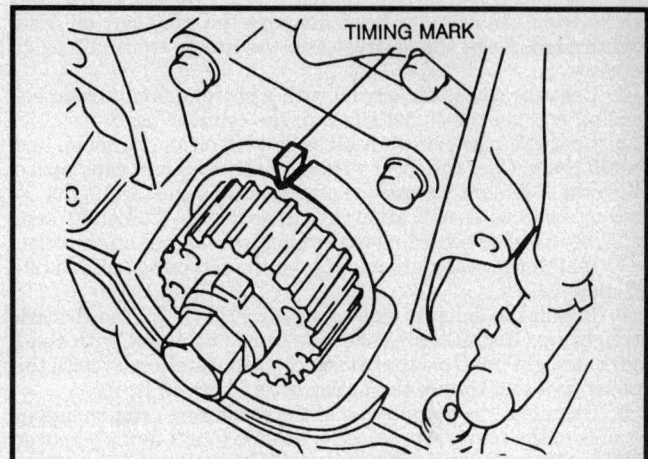

Aligning timing belt pulley—Miata

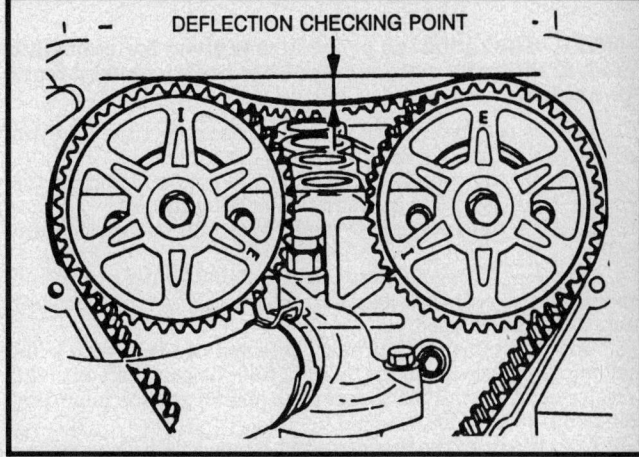

Measuring timing belt deflection—Miata

Camshaft

Removal and Installation

626, MX-6, 323 AND PROTEGE EXCEPT TWINCAM ENGINE

1. Disconnect the negative battery cable. Remove the air

cleaner assembly. Drain the cooling system.

2. Remove the front cover assembly. Remove the cam gear. As required remove the thermostat housing.

3. Remove the distributor assembly. Remove the cylinder head cover. On the 626 and MX-6, remove the rear housing.

4. Remove the rocker arm assembly. If equipped, remove the thrust plate.

5. Remove the camshaft from the cylinder head.

6. Installation is the reverse of the removal procedure. Install a new seal in the front cover housing and new gaskets as necessary.

323 AND PROTEGE WITH TWINCAM ENGINE

1. Disconnect the negative battery cable. Position the engine at TDC on the compression stroke. Remove the air cleaner assembly. Remove the spark plugs.

2. Remove the cylinder head cover.

3. Remove the distributor. Remove the timing cover assembly. Remove the timing belt and camshaft pulleys. Remove the seal plate.

4. Remove the camshaft retaining bolts. Remove the camshafts from the cylinder head. Remove the camshaft oil seals and discard. Keep the exhaust and the intake camshaft parts separate.

5. Coat the camshaft journal with a liberal amount clean engine oil and lay the camshafts into the cylinder head.

6. Coat the new camshaft oil seals with clean engine oil and install them. Coat the front surface of the camshaft caps with a thin coat of sealant. Install the camshaft caps and torque the retaining bolts to specification and in sequence. Camshaft caps must be installed according to the number stamped on the caps.

7. Install the seal plate and torque the retaining bolts to 69–95 inch lbs.

8. Install the exhaust side camshaft pulley with the **E** mark straight up. Install the intake side camshaft pulley with the **I** mark straight up. Hold the camshaft journal stationary with the proper tool and torque the pulley bolts to 36–45 ft. lbs.

9. Complete the installation of the remaining components in reverse of the removal procedure. Be sure to use new gaskets or RTV sealant, as required.

929

NOTE: The following procedure is given for camshaft removal after the cylinder head has been removed from the engine.

1. Relieve the fuel system pressure. Disconnect the negative battery cable. Remove the air cleaner assembly.

2. Remove the cylinder head from the engine. Position the cylinder head assembly in a suitable holding fixture.

3. Remove the rocker arm shaft bolts and the rocker arm shafts.

4. Remove the camshaft sprocket and and gently pry the oil seals from the cylinder head. Carefully withdraw the camshaft from the cylinder head.

5. Coat the camshaft journals, lobes and bearings with a liberal amount of clean engine oil and slide the camshaft into the cylinder head. Install the thrust plate and torque the mounting bolt to 69–95 inch lbs.

6. Coat the lip of the new camshaft oil seals with clean engine oil and drive the seals into the head using a seal installation tool.

7. Complete the installation of the cylinder head in reverse of the removal procedure. When installing the camshaft pulleys, align the left and right camshaft so the keyways are facing up. The camshaft pulleys are stamped **L** and **R** for the left and right banks respectively. Make sure these marks are facing outward during installation. Torque the pulley bolts to 52–59 ft. lbs. Be sure to use new gaskets or RTV sealant, as required. Torque the cylinder head to specification and in sequence.

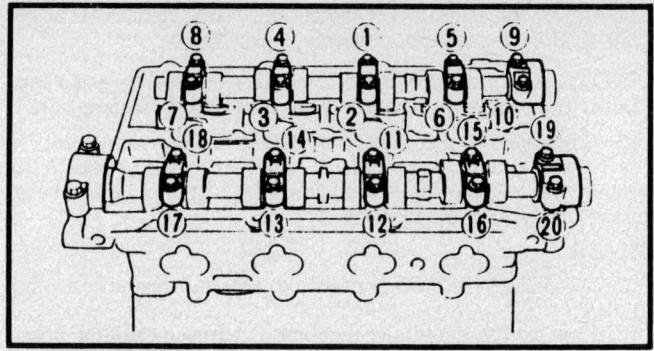

Camshaft bolt torque sequence—323 and Protege with DOHC engine

MIATA

1. Disconnect the battery negative cable.

2. Drain the cooling system

3. Remove the timing belt.

4. Remove the crank angle sensor

5. Remove the ignition coil assembly along with the spark plug wires.

6. Remove the cylinder head cover.

7. Hold the camshaft with a wrench and remove the camshaft pulley lock bolt and the camshaft pulley.

8. Loosen the camshaft cap bolts, in 2–3 steps, in sequence.

9. Remove the camshaft caps, camshaft and camshaft seal from the vehicle.

To install:

10. Reverse the removal procedure to install, noting the following:

  a. Apply clean engine oil to the camshaft journals and bearings. Install camshaft into position.

  b. Install the camshaft cap bolts. Torque the cap bolts to 100–126 inch lbs. (11.3–14.2 Nm).

  c. Apply clean engine oil to lip of the new camshaft seal. Install the seal so it is flush with the edge of the camshaft cap.

  d. Rotate the camshafts until the camshaft dowel pin face straight up. Install the camshaft pulleys with the I mark, intake side or E mark, exhaust side, face straight up.

  d. Hold the camshaft with a wrench and install the camshaft bolts. Torque bolts to 36–45 ft. lbs. (49–61 Nm).

  e. Install new O-ring onto the crank angle sensor. Apply grease to O-ring. Install the crank angle sensor.

  f. Connect the battery negative cable and refill the cooling system. Start the engine and check for leaks. Check the ignition timing.

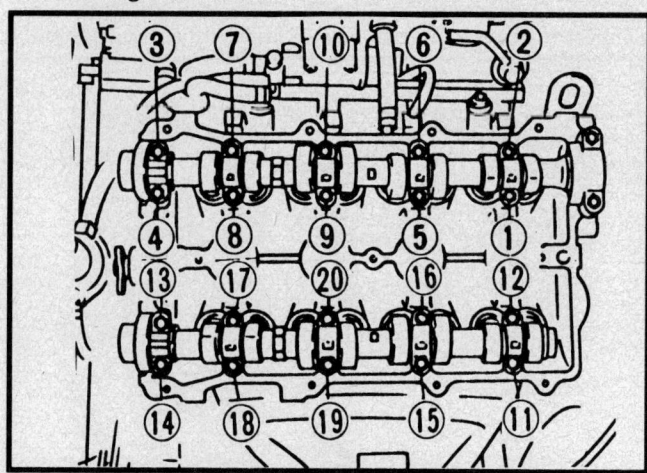

Camshaft cap bolts loosening sequence—Miata

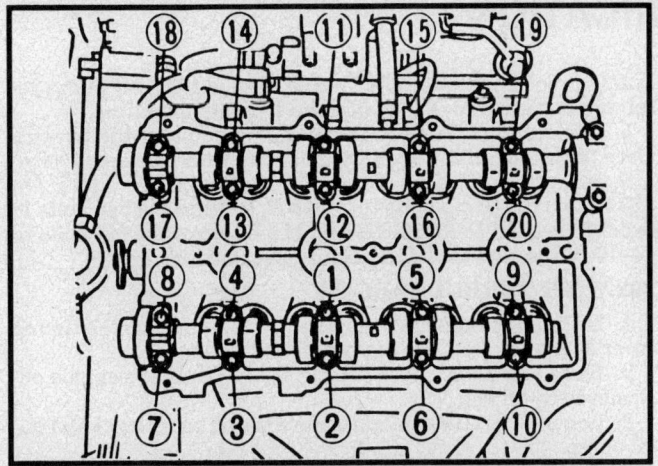

Camshaft cap bolts tightening sequence—Miata

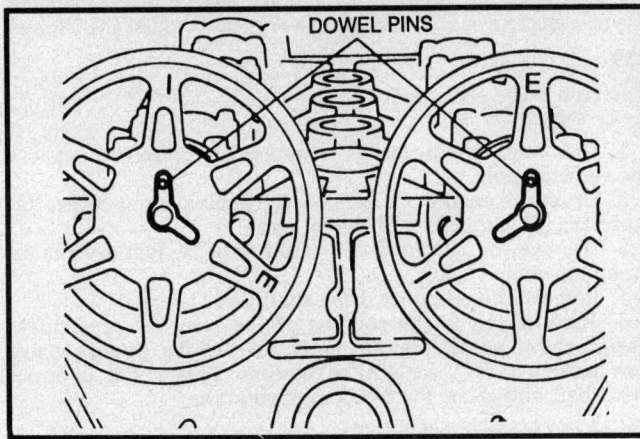

Installing camshaft timing sprockets—Miata

Piston and Connecting Rod

Positioning

The "F" marks (arrow) face the front of the engine

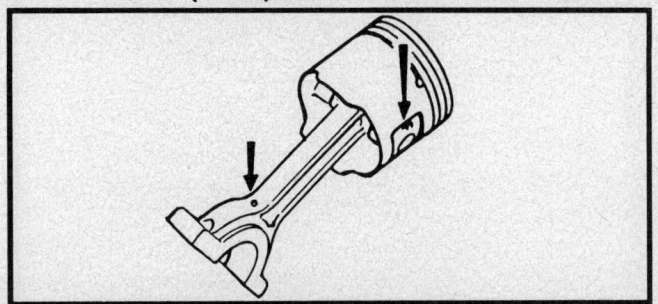

Piston and connecting rod positioning

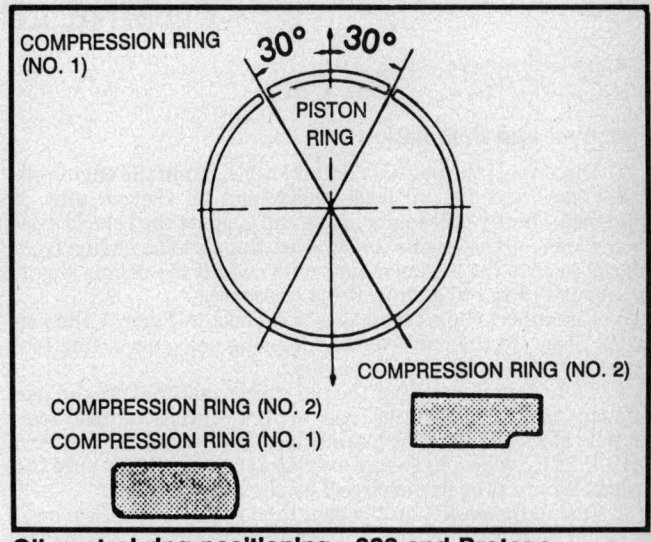

Oil control ring positioning—323 and Protege

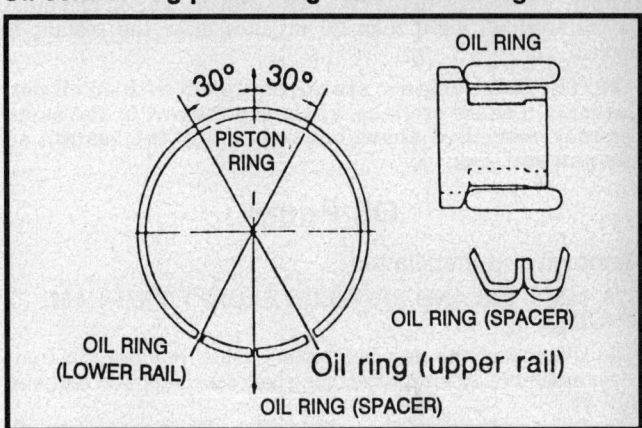

Compression ring positioning—323 and Protege

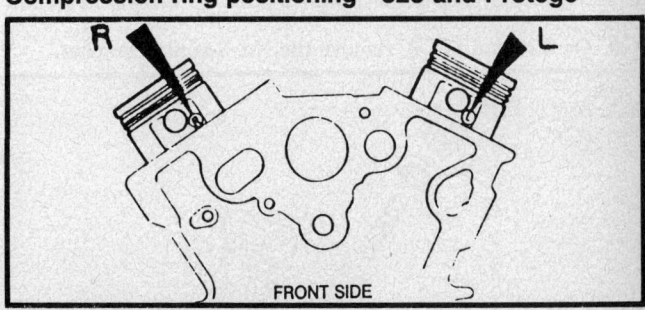

Piston positioning—929

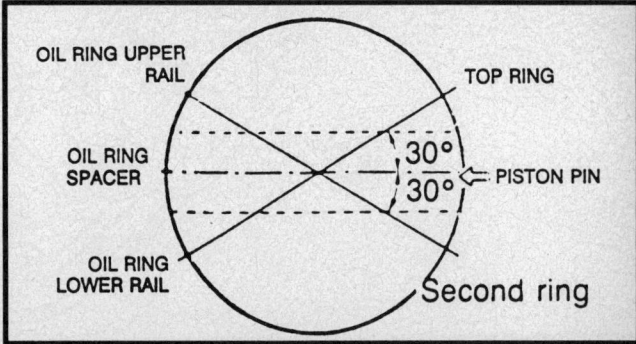

Piston ring positioning—all except 323 and Protege

ENGINE LUBRICATION

Oil Pan

Removal and Installation

1. Disconnect the negative battery cable. Drain the engine oil.
2. Disconnect the oil level sensor and oil thermo unit, if equipped. On the 13B engine, raise and support the vehicle safely and remove the engine undercover. Support the engine from above, remove the engine mount nuts and lift the engine slightly, about 2–3 in., to gain working clearance.
3. Disconnect the oil level sensor connector. Remove the pan bolts. Separate the pan from the housing using an prying tool and lower the pan from the engine.
4. To install, clean all of the old gasket material off the pan and engine mating surfaces then, apply a continuous bead sealer, part 8527 77 739 to the pan surface. The bead should be from 0.16–0.24 in. wide and should overlap at the end. Make sure the bolt holes are properly encircled by the sealant bead.
5. Install the gasket on the pan, then apply an identical bead of sealer on top of the gasket. Install the gasket and torque the bolts to 6–8 ft. lbs. Fill the crankcase with oil. The oil pan must be installed no more than 30 minutes after the sealant is applied.

NOTE: Some engines are not equipped with an oil pan gasket. On these engines, apply the sealant in the same manner described above but only apply the sealant to the pan surface.

Oil Pump

Removal and Installation

626, MX-6, 323 AND PROTEGE EXCEPT TWINCAM ENGINE

1. Disconnect the negative battery cable. Remove the front cover assembly. Remove the timing belt, tensioner and required pulleys.
2. Raise and support the vehicle safely. Drain the engine oil. Remove the oil pan. Remove the oil pump strainer and pickup tube.
3. On 626 and MX-6, remove the No. 3 engine bracket.

4. As required, lower the vehicle. Remove the oil pump retaining bolts. Remove the oil pump from its mounting.
5. Replace the oil seal in the oil pump and coat the lip with clean engine oil. Fill the oil pump cavity with petroleum jelly.
6. Installation is the reverse of the removal procedure. On 323 torque the pump bolts to 14–19 ft. lbs. and the pan bolts to 6–6.5 ft. lbs. On 1988–89 626 and MX-6 torque the M8 bolts to 14–19 ft. lbs. and the M10 bolts to 27–38 ft. lbs.

323 WITH TURBOCHARGER

1. Disconnect the negative battery cable. Remove the timing cover assembly. Remove the timing belt pulley.
2. Raise and support the vehicle safely. Drain the engine oil. Remove the oil pan.
3. Remove the oil strainer. Remove the oil pump bolts and the oil pump.
4. Installation is the reverse of the removal procedure. Torque the oil pump retaining bolts to 14–19 ft. lbs. Be sure to use new gaskets or RTV sealant, as required. Adjust the timing.

929

Positive Displacement Gear Type

1. Disconnect the negative battery cable. Raise and support the vehicle safely.
2. Drain the engine oil. Remove the engine under cover. Remove the oil pan bolts and the oil pan.
3. Remove the oil pump and strainer bolts. Remove the oil pump assembly.
4. Remove the oil pump drive shaft and O-ring.
5. Installation is the reverse of the removal procedure. Torque the oil pump retaining bolts to 6–8 ft. lbs. Be sure to use new gaskets or RTV sealant, as required. Engage the oil pump driveshaft and check for freedom of rotation.

Trochoid Gear Type

NOTE: The trochoid gear type oil pump is not used on 1988 vehicles.

1. Disconnect the negative battery cable. Raise and support the vehicle safely.

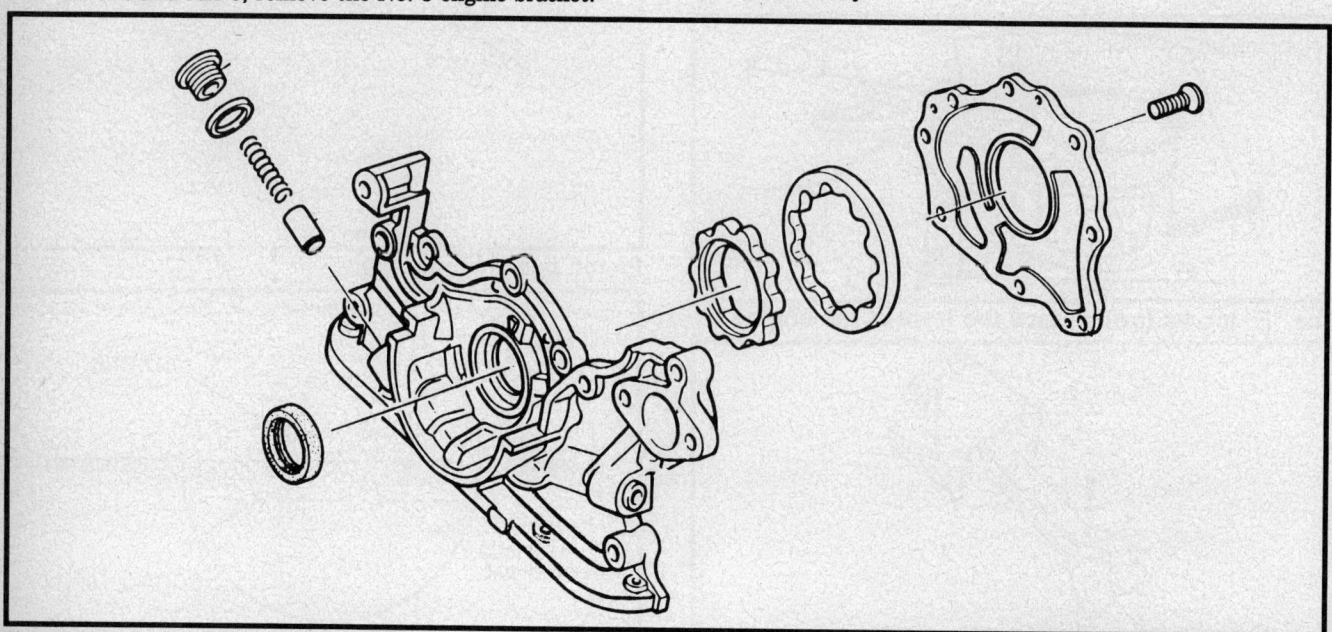

Trochold gear type oil pump–929

2. Drain the engine oil and the cooling system.

3. Remove the timing belt, the timing belt pulley and key. Remove the thermostat and gasket.

4. Remove the oil pan, oil strainer and O-ring.

5. Unbolt and remove the oil pump and gasket.

6. Installation is the reverse of the removal procedure. Press in a new oil seal and coat the seal lip with oil. Use a new gasket, O-ring and sealant, as required. Torque the oil pump retaining bolts to 14–19 ft. lbs.

Rear Main Bearing Oil Seal

Removal and Installation

323, PROTEGE, 626 AND MX-6

1. Disconnect the negative battery cable. Raise and support the vehicle safely. Remove the transaxle.

2. If equipped with a manual transaxle, remove the pressure plate, the clutch disc and the flywheel. If equipped with an automatic transaxle, remove the driveplate from the crankshaft.

3. Remove the rear oil pan-to-seal housing bolts.

4. Remove the rear main seal housing bolts and the housing from the engine.

5. Remove the oil seal from the rear main housing.

6. Clean the gasket mounting surfaces.

7. To install, use a new seal, coat the seal and the housing with oil. Press the seal into the housing, using an arbor press.

8. To complete the installation, use new gaskets, apply sealant to the oil pan mounting surface and reverse the removal procedure. Torque the rear seal housing bolts to 6–8 ft. lbs.

929

1. Raise and support the vehicle safely. Remove the transmission from the vehicle.

2. If equipped with a manual transmission, remove the clutch pressure plate and flywheel.

3. If equipped with automatic transmission, remove the flywheel assembly.

4. Drain the engine oil. Remove the engine oil pan.

5. Remove the rear main seal cover retaining bolts. Remove the rear main seal cover. Remove the seal from the rear cover.

6. Installation is the reverse of the removal procedure. Apply clean engine oil to the seal before pressing it into the cover.

7. After installing the rear cover cut away the portion of the gasket that projects out toward the oil pan side.

MIATA

1. Disconnect the battery negative cable.

2. Raise and safely support the vehicle.

3. Remove the transmission.

4. Remove the clutch cover and disc.

5. Remove the flywheel bolts and the flywheel.

6. Cut the oil seal lip, then remove the oil seal from the vehicle.

7. Reverse procedure to install. Apply a coat of clean engine oil to the lip of the new seal before installation. Torque flywheel bolts to 71–76 ft. lbs. (96–103 Nm).

MANUAL TRANSMISSION

For further information, please refer to "Professional Transmission Repair Manual" for additional coverage.

Transmission Assembly

Removal and Installation

MIATA

1. Disconnect the battery negative cable.

2. Raise and safely support the vehicle.

3. Remove the shift lever knob and the console.

4. Remove the shift lever assembly and the engine undercover.

5. Remove the exhaust system, if necessary.

6. Remove the drive shaft and the clutch release cylinder from the transmission.

7. Remove the starter motor bolts and the starter.

8. Disconnect the speedometer cable from the transmission.

9. Remove the power plant frame from the transmission and the differential.

10. Disconnect the electrical connectors from the transmission.

11. Remove the transmission bolts and the transmission.

To install:

12. Install the transmission. Torque the bolts to to 47–66 ft. lbs. (64–89 Nm). Connect the transmission electrical connectors.

13. Install the power plant frame. Torque the bolts to 77–91 ft. lbs. (104–123 Nm).

14. Connect the speedometer cable to the transmission.

15. Install the starter and the clutch release cylinder.

16. Install the driveshaft and the exhaust system, if removed.

17. Install the engine undercover.

18. Install the shift lever, console and the shift lever knob.

19. Connect the battery negative cable. Check transmission fluid. Start the engine and check for leaks.

RX-7

1. Disconnect the negative battery cable. Raise the vehicle and support safely. Drain the transmission.

2. Remove the console box and the gearshift lever.

3. Unbolt the clutch release cylinder from the transmission but do not disconnect the hydraulic line. Route the assembly aside.

4. Disconnect the exhaust pipe and remove the converter covers.

5. Disengage the driveshaft from the transmission. Disconnect the speedometer cable. Disconnect the neutral and 5th/reverse switch connectors.

6. Disconnect the electrical wiring and remove the starter. Remove the crossmember.

7. Support the transmission with a transmission jack using a block of wood to protect the oil pan and remove the transmission case-to-engine bolts.

8. Slide the transmission rearward until the main shaft clears the clutch disc and carefully remove the transmission from under the vehicle.

9. Installation is the reverse order of the removal procedure. Adjust the clutch and shift linkage. Refill the transmission and road test the vehicle.

MANUAL TRANSAXLE

For further information, please refer to "Professional Transmission Repair Manual" for additional coverage.

Transaxle Assembly

Removal and Installation

1987 626

1. Disconnect the negative battery cable. Remove the speedometer cable from the transaxle.
2. Remove the clutch cable bracket bolts and disconnect the clutch cable from the release lever.
3. Remove the ground wire and wiring harness clip. Remove any pipe brackets attached to the case.
4. Remove the starter.
5. Install the engine support tool 49–G030–025 and support the weight of the engine.
6. Remove all of the transaxle-to-engine bolts, except the lower 2.
7. Raise and support the vehicle safely. Drain the transaxle oil.
8. Remove the front wheels and the splash shields.
9. Remove the stabilizer bar control link. Remove the undercover, if equipped.
10. Remove the lower arm ball joint and the knuckle coupling bolt, pull the arm downward and separate the lower arm from the knuckle.
11. Remove the left side halfshaft from the transaxle. Insert a lever between the halfshaft and the transaxle case. Tap the end of the lever to uncouple the halfshaft from the differential side gear. Pull the front hub forward and separate the halfshaft from the transaxle.

NOTE: **Do not insert the lever too deeply between the shaft and the case or the oil seal lip could be damaged. To avoid damage to the oil seal, hold the CV-joint at the differential and pull the halfshaft straight out.**

12. Remove the right side halfshaft and joint shaft. Insert a lever between the driveshaft and the joint shaft. Pry the lever to uncouple the shafts.
13. Pull the front hub forward and then separate the halfshaft from the joint shaft.
14. Remove the joint shaft bracket mounting bolts. Remove the joint shaft and bracket from the transaxle as an assembly.
15. Remove the transaxle mounting bracket nuts at the crossmember.
16. Remove the crossmember and the left lower arm as an assembly.
17. Separate the shift change control rod from the shift change rod.
18. Remove the shift control extension bar from the transaxle. Remove the transaxle undercover.
19. Position the proper removal equipment under the transaxle assembly.
20. Remove the 2 remaining transaxle-to-engine bolts and separate the transaxle from the engine. Lower the assembly to the floor.
21. Remove the transaxle brackets from the transaxle.
22. Installation is the reverse of the removal procedure.

1988–91 626 AND MX-6

1. Remove the battery and battery carrier.
2. Disconnect the main fuse block, distributor lead and air flow meter connector. Remove the air cleaner assembly.
3. On turbocharged engines, disconnect the intercooler hoses. On non-turbocharged engines, remove the resonance chamber.

4. Disconnect the speedometer cable and the transaxle grounds.
5. Raise and support the vehicle safely and remove the front wheels and splash shield. Drain the transaxle oil.
6. Remove the clutch release cylinder and disconnect the tie rod ends using the proper tool.
7. Remove the stabilizer control links. Remove the nuts and bolts from the lower control arm ball joints and pull the lower control arms downward to separate them from the steering knuckles. Be careful not to damage the ball joint dust boots.
8. Insert a small prybar between the left driveshaft and the transaxle case and tap the end of the lever to uncouple the driveshaft from the differential side gear. Pull the front hub forward and separate the driveshaft from the transaxle. Remove the left joint shaft bracket. Separate the right driveshaft and joint shaft in the same manner as the left.

NOTE: **Do not insert the lever too deeply between the shaft and the case or the oil seal lip could be damaged. To avoid damage to the oil seal, hold the CV-joint at the differential and pull the driveshaft straight out.**

9. Once both drive and joint shafts are removed, install differential side gear holders 49–G030–455 (turbo), 49–G027–003 or their equivalents, in the differential side gears to hold them in place and prevent misalignment.
10. Remove the gusset plates and under cover. Remove the extension bar and the control rod. Remove the surge tank bracket and the starter.
11. Suspend the engine from the engine hanger with a suitable lifting device or engine support fixture.
12. Remove the No. 4 and No. 2 engine mounts and bracket. Disconnect the rubber hanger from the crossmember, then remove the crossmember and left side lower control arm as an assembly.
13. Lean the engine towards the transaxle and support the transaxle with a jack. Remove the trasaxle-to-engine bolts and slide the transaxle from under the vehicle.
14. Installation is the reverse of the removal procedure. Fill the transaxle to the proper level.

323 AND PROTEGE

Without 4WD

1. Disconnect the negative battery cable. Remove the air cleaner. Loosen the front wheel lug nuts.
2. Disconnect the speedometer from the transaxle. Disconnect the clutch cable from the release lever and remove the clutch cable bracket bolts.
3. Remove the ground wire installation boot. Remove the water pipe bracket. Remove the secondary air pipe and the EGR pipe bracket.
4. Remove the wire harness clip. Disconnect the coupler for the neutral switch and back-up light switch. Disconnect the body ground connector.
5. Remove the 2 upper transaxle mounting bolts. Mount the engine support tool 49–ER301–025A or equivalent, to the engine hanger.
6. Raise and support the vehicle safely. Drain the transaxle oil into a suitable container and remove the front wheels.
7. Remove the engine undercover and side covers. Remove the front stabilizer.
8. Remove the lower arm ball joints and the knuckle clinch bolts, pull the lower arm downward and separate the lower arms from the knuckles.
9. Separate the driveshaft by pulling the front hub outward. Make sure not to use too much force at once, increase the force gradually. Be sure the driveshaft's ball joint is bent to its maxi-

mum extent. Do not allow the halfshafts to drop. Damage may occur to the ball and socket joints and to the rubber boots. Wire the shafts to the vehicle body when released from the differential.

10. Remove the transaxle crossmember. Separate the change control rod from the transaxle. Remove the extension bar from the transaxle. Remove the wiring and the starter motor.

11. Remove the end plates. Lean the engine toward the transaxle side to lower the transaxle by loosening the engine support hook bolt. Support the transaxle with a suitable transaxle jack.

12. Remove the necessary engine brackets. Remove the remaining transaxle mounting bolt and No. 2 engine bracket. Lower the jack and slide the transaxle from under the vehicle.

13. To install, reverse the removal procedure. Adjust clutch and shift linkage. Refill the transaxle with the proper grade of gear oil.

With 4WD

1. Remove the battery and the air cleaner assembly. Disconnect the speedometer cable in the center. Remove the clutch release cylinder bolt, clip and the clutch release cylinder. Raise and support the vehicle safely and drain the transaxle and engine oil.

2. Disconnect the neutral safety switch, back-up light switch, differential lock sensor switch and differential lock motor electrical connectors. Disconnect the transaxle shift and select control cables from the transaxle by removing the pins and cable retaining clips. Route the cables aside.

3. Mount the engine support tool 49–8017–5A0 or equivalent, to the engine hanger. Remove the No. 4 engine mount bracket and the the front wheels.

4. Remove the side cover and undercover. Remove the oil filter and differential lock assembly. Disconnect the starter wiring and remove the starter and stabilizer bar.

5. Disconnect the tie rod end from the lower control arm. Insert a small prybar between the driveshaft and the transaxle case and tap the end of the lever to uncouple the driveshaft from the differential side gear. Remove the remaining driveshaft in the same manner. Insert differential side gear holder 49–B027–001 or equivalent, to hold the side gears in place and prevent misalignment.

6. Remove the end plate bolts and connect a suitable hoist and lifting strap to the transaxle. Lift the transaxle and transfer carrier assembly out of the engine.

7. Installation is the reverse of the removal procedure. Fill the crankcase. Fill the transaxle to the proper level through the speedometer drive gear opening. Adjust the shift and select control cables.

Linkage Adjustment

323 AND PROTEGE WITH 4WD

1. Set the transaxle shift lever to the **NEUTRAL** position.
2. On the transaxle make sure the shift and select levers are also in the **NEUTRAL** position.
3. Remove the shift lever console.
4. Disconnect the shift and select cables from the control levers by removing the pins, flat washers and spring clips. The clips must be replaced.
5. Make sure the select cable end hole aligns with the select lever pin. If not aligned, loosen cable adjusting nut "A" and ro-

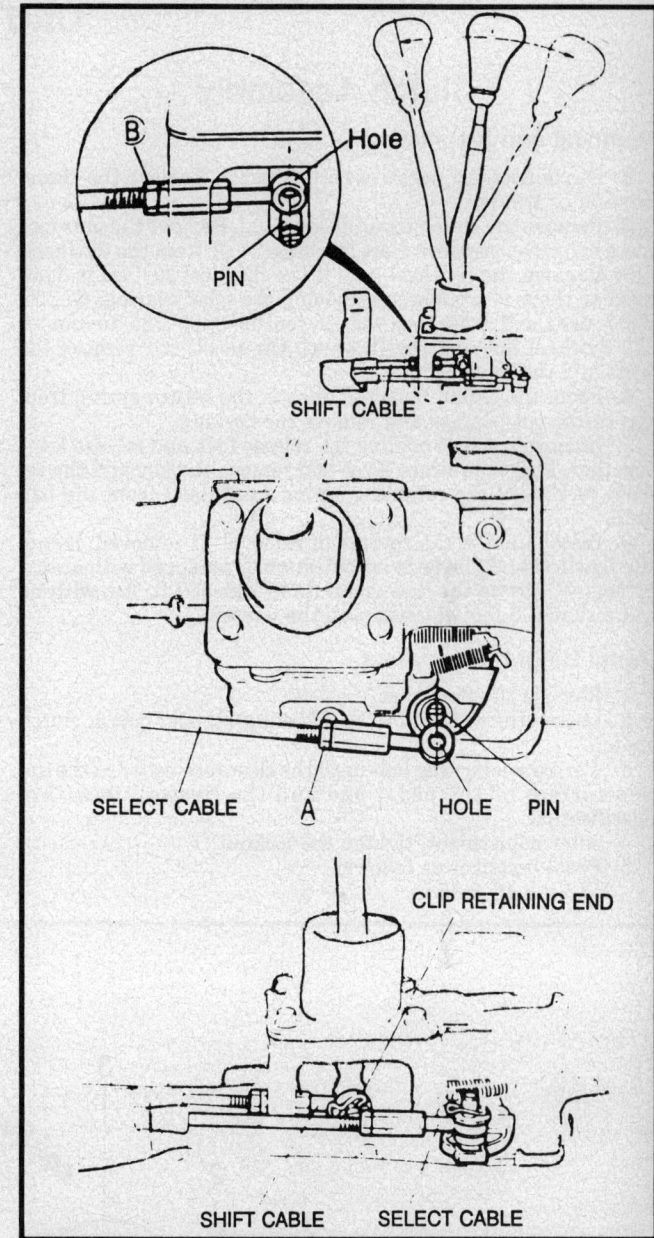

Shift control cable adjustment—323 with 4WD

tate the cable end until the holes are aligned.

6. Place the shift lever at the center of its front-to-rear stoke.
7. Make sure the select cable end hole aligns with the select lever pin. If not aligned, loosen cable adjusting nut "B" and rotate the cable end until the holes are aligned.
8. Connect the cables.

CLUTCH

Clutch Assembly

Removal and Installation

1. Disconnect the negative battery cable. Remove the transmission or transaxle.

2. Remove the clutch cover, if equipped. Remove the pressure plate bolts, the pressure plate and clutch disc from the flywheel.

3. Remove the flywheel only if the flywheel surface is damaged or there is trouble in removing the pilot bearing. On the RX-7, use the flywheel box wrench tool 49–0820–035, to remove the flywheel nut and the flywheel. On all others, remove the bolts and the flywheel.

4. From the clutch housing, unhook the return spring from the throw out bearing and remove the bearing.

5. Remove the bolt holding the release fork and release lever together. Pull the release lever and remove the key and the release fork until the retaining spring frees itself from the ball stud.

6. Installation is the reverse of removal. If removed, install the flywheel and torque to specification. If equipped with a rotary engine, torque the flywheel nuts to 289–362 ft. lbs. with no more than a 3 foot extension on the wrench.

Pedal Height Adjustment

1. Remove the floor mat.

2. Loosen the locknut on the adjusting, stopper bolt or clutch switch.

3. Turn the adjusting bolt until the clearance between the upper surface of the pedal pad and the firewall is within specification.

4. After adjustment, tighten the locknut.

5. Pedal height is as follows:
   RX-7 – 8.46–8.86 in.

1987–88 626 – 8.44–8.64 in.
1988–91 626 and MX-6 – 8.52–8.72 in.
323 and Protege (cable type) – 8.44–8.64 in.
323 and Protege (hydraulic type) – 9.02–9.22 in.
929 – 8.46–8.66 in.
Miata – 6.89–7.28 in.

Pedal Free-Play Adjustment

CABLE CLUTCH

Except 323 and Protege

1. Depress the clutch pedal lightly and measure the free-play.

2. Loosen the locknut and pull the outer cable away from the engine side of the firewall.

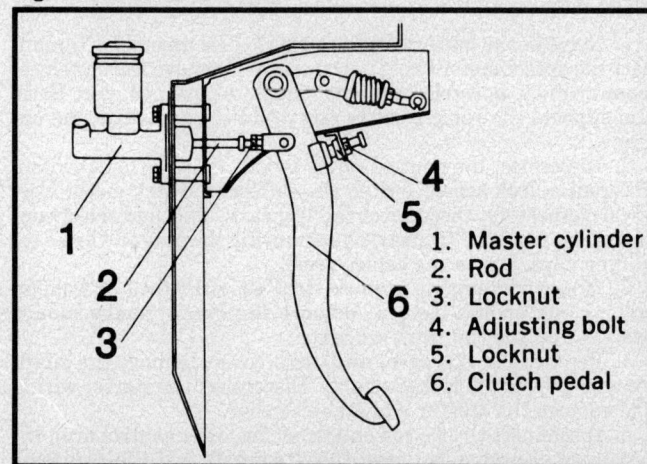

1. Master cylinder
2. Rod
3. Locknut
4. Adjusting bolt
5. Locknut
6. Clutch pedal

Clutch pedal height adjustment

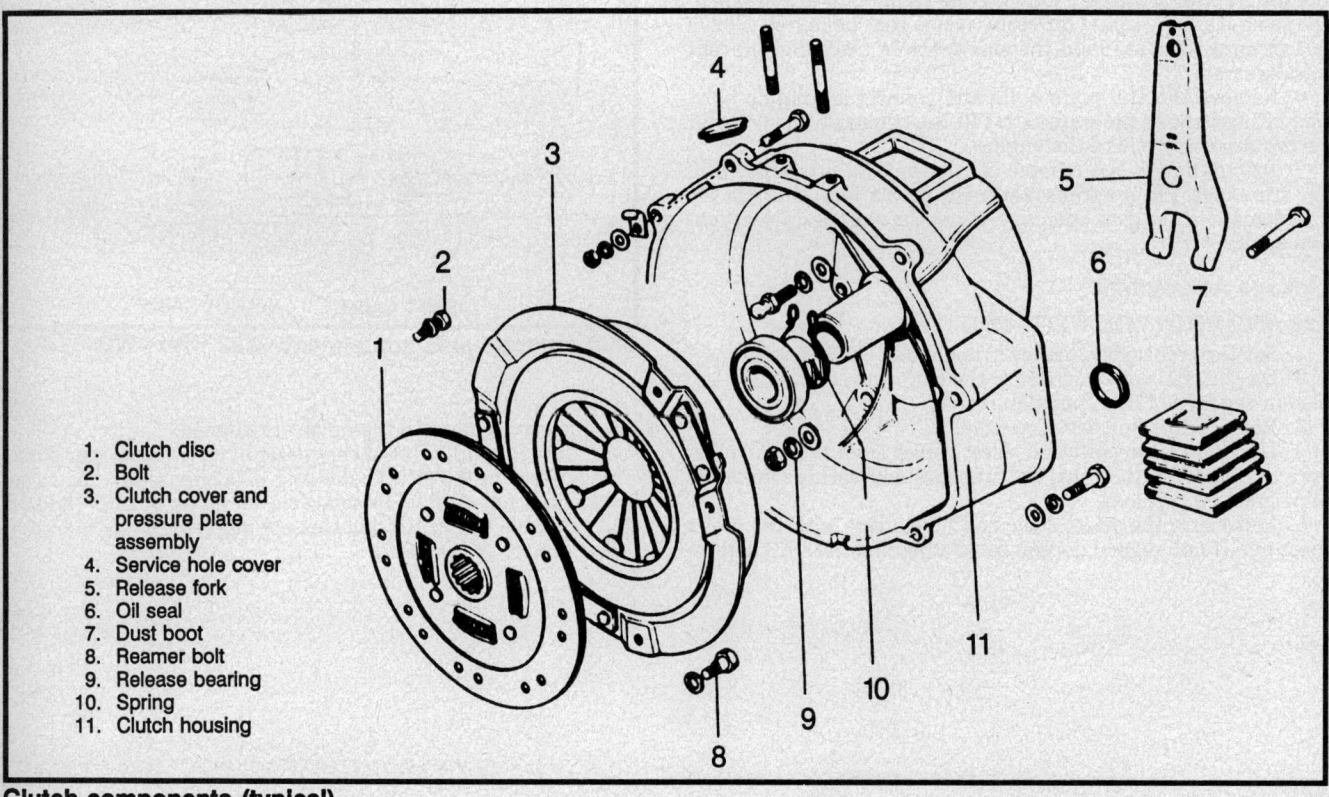

1. Clutch disc
2. Bolt
3. Clutch cover and pressure plate assembly
4. Service hole cover
5. Release fork
6. Oil seal
7. Dust boot
8. Reamer bolt
9. Release bearing
10. Spring
11. Clutch housing

Clutch components (typical)

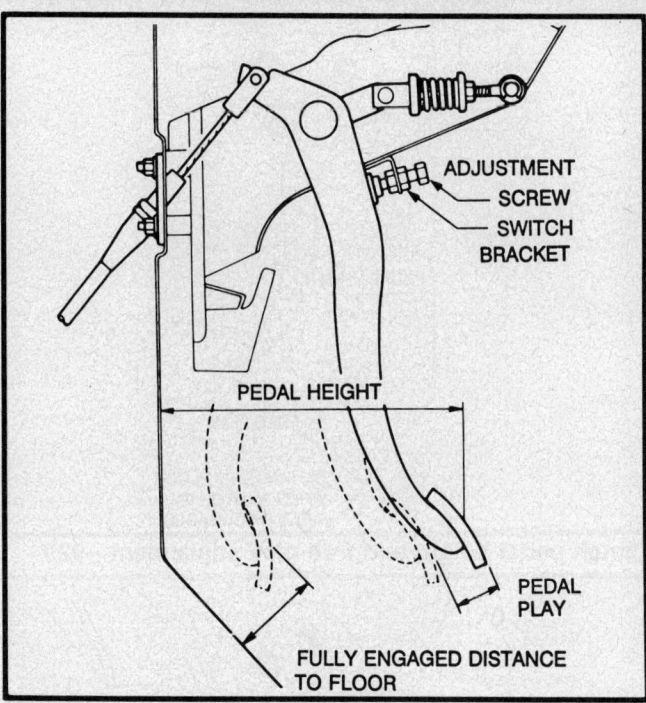

Clutch pedal height and free-play adjustment—1987 626

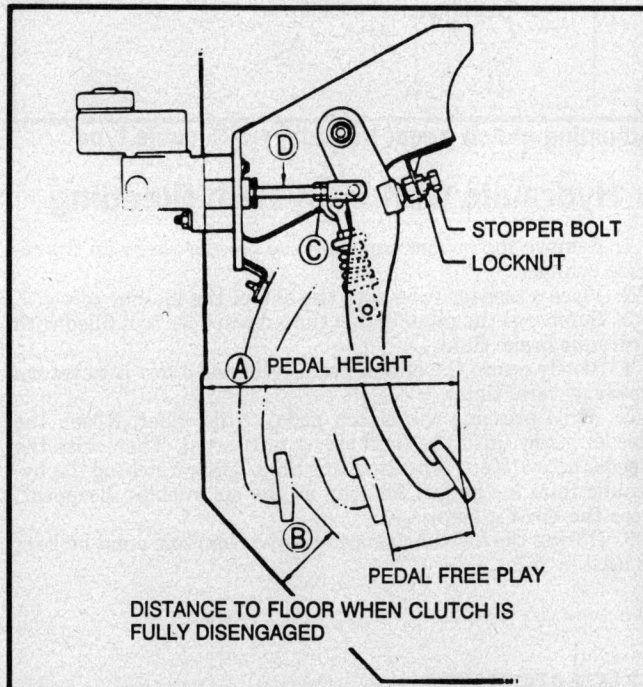

Clutch pedal height adjustment—1988–91 626 and MX-6

323 and Protege

Depress the pedal lightly and measure the free-play. The free-play should be from 0.35–0.59 in. If not within specification, adjust the free-play as follows:

1. On 1988–91 vehicles, depress the clutch pedal 7 times and straighten the clutch cable in the cable bracket.

2. Depress the release lever and pull the pin away from the lever then adjust the clearance between the pin and the adjusting lever by turning the adjusting nut. On 1987 vehicles, the clearance should be between 0.06–0.10 in. On 1988–91 vehicles, the clearance should be between 0.08 in.

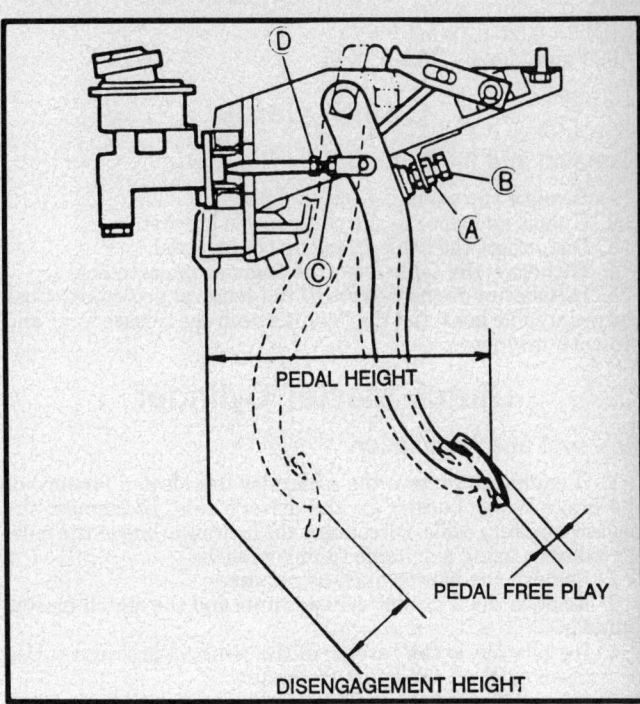

Clutch pedal height and free-play adjustment—323 cable type

3. Turn the adjusting nut on the cable to obtain a 0.06–0.010 in. clearance between the adjusting nut and the firewall.

4. Tighten the locknut. Adjust the free-play to specification.

5. Pedal free-play is as follows:

626—0.43–0.67 in. except turbocharger
626—0.20–0.51 in. turbocharger
MX-6—0.20–0.51 in.
RX-7—0.02–0.12 in. at the pedal

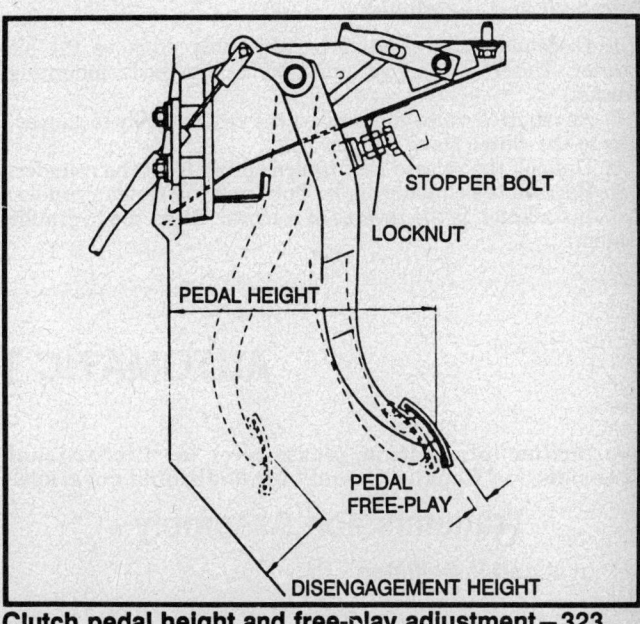

Clutch pedal height and free-play adjustment—323 and Protege hydraulic type

3. After adjustment, ensure that when the clutch is disengaged, the distance between the floor and the upper center of the pedal is 3.3 in.

4. Recheck the pedal height and adjust, if necessary.

HYDRAULIC CLUTCH

Loosen the locknut on the clutch master cylinder pushrod. Turn the pushrod to obtain 0.02–0.12 in. free-play between the pedal and the pushrod. Tighten the locknut on the pushrod.

323 — 0.20–0.51 in.
626 — 0.08–0.12 in. except turbocharger
626 — 0.20–0.51 in. turbocharger
MX-6 — 0.20–0.51 in.
RX-7 — 0.02–0.12 in.
929 and Miata — 0.02–0.12 in.

Clutch Cable

Removal and Installation

1. Remove the adjusting nut and pin.
2. Unbolt and remove the clutch cable bracket.
3. Disconnect the cable from the clutch pedal.
4. Withdraw the cable from the engine compartment.
5. Installation is the reverse of the removal procedure. Coat the pedal cable hook and the joint between the release lever and pin with lithium grease.

Clutch Master Cylinder

Removal and Installation

1. If equipped, remove the ABS relay box located forward of the brake power booster on the driver's side. Disconnect the negative battery cable. Disconnect the hydraulic line at the master cylinder using a suitable tubing wrench.
2. Remove the blower duct, as required.
3. Remove the 2 master cylinder nuts and the clutch master cylinder.
4. Installation is the reverse of the removal procedure. Use new gaskets. Bleed the hydraulic system.

Clutch Slave Cylinder

Removal and Installation

1. Disconnect the negative battery cable. Remove the air cleaner. Unscrew the hydraulic line at the body mounting bracket.
2. As required, raise and support the vehicle safely to gain access to the clutch slave cylinder bolts.
3. Unhook the release fork return spring from the cylinder.
4. Remove the clutch cylinder bolts and the clutch cylinder.
5. Installation is the reverse of removal. Bleed the hydraulic system.

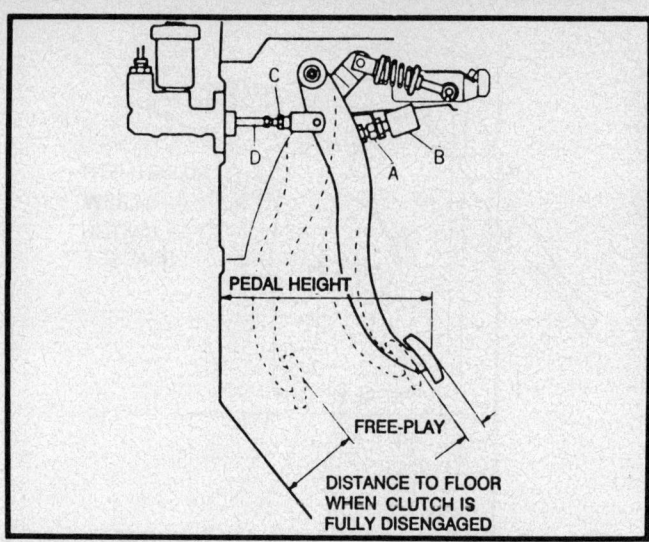

Clutch pedal height and free-play adjustment — 929

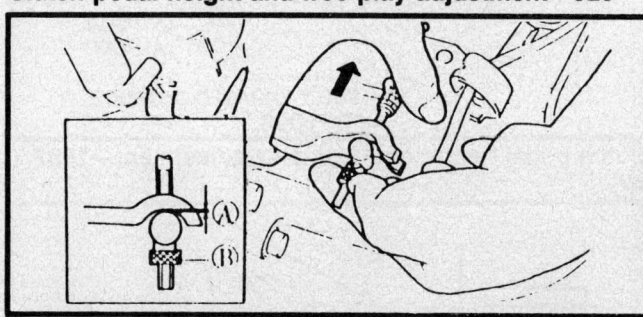

Adjusting clutch pedal free-play — 323 cable type

Hydraulic Clutch System Bleeding

1. Remove the rubber cap from the bleeder screw on the release cylinder.
2. Place a bleeder tube over the end of the bleeder screw.
3. Submerge the other end of the tube in a jar half filled with hydraulic brake fluid.
4. Slowly pump the clutch pedal fully and allow it to return slowly, several times.
5. While pressing the clutch pedal to the floor, loosen the bleeder screw until the fluid starts to run out. Then close the bleeder screw. Keep repeating this Step, while watching the hydraulic fluid in the jar. As soon as the air bubbles disappear, close the bleeder screw.
6. During the bleeding procedure the reservoir must be kept at least ¾ full.

AUTOMATIC TRANSMISSION

For further information, please refer to "Professional Transmission Repair Manual" for additional coverage.

Transmission Assembly

Removal and Installation

RX-7

1. Disconnect the negative battery cable. Raise the vehicle

and support safely.
2. Remove the exhaust pipe with the heat insulator.
3. Matchmark and disconnect the propeller shaft. Install the turning holder tool 49–0259–440 to the extension housing, to prevent the fluid from leaking from the housing.
4. Remove the vacuum and oil pipes and plug the ends to prevent leakage.
5. Remove the starter bracket and starter.
6. Disconnect the speedometer cable.

7. Disconnect the shift rod from the transmission.

8. Remove the oil level gauge and filler pipe.

9. Disconnect the harness coupler.

10. Remove the service hole coupler.

11. Support the transmission with a jack and remove the transmission mounting bolts. Slide the transmission rearward, until the input shaft clears the eccentric shaft, then remove the transmission/torque converter assembly from under the vehicle.

12. Installation is the reverse of the removal procedure.

929

1. Disconnect the negative battery cable. Remove the transmission oil dipstick.

2. Raise and support the vehicle safely. Disconnect the shift rod. Remove the front exhaust pipe. Remove the heat insulator.

3. Matchmark and remove the driveshaft. Remove the starter. Disconnect the speedometer cable.

4. Disconnect the inhibitor switch connector, the turbine sensor connector, the lock-up solenoid connector and the solenoid valve connector.

5. Remove the oil pipe and the vacuum pipe. Remove the undercover assembly.

6. Support the engine using the proper equipment. Support the transmission assembly, using the proper equipment. Remove the crossmember assembly.

7. Remove the flywheel cover. Remove the transmission-to-torque converter bolts.

8. Remove the transmission-to-engine bolts and the transmission from the vehicle.

9. Installation is the reverse of the removal procedure.

Shift Linkage Adjustment

RX-7

1. Remove the shifter cover.

2. Turn locknuts A and B to the proper adjusting position.

3. Move the shifter level to the **P** position.

4. Shift the transmission. Make sure the vehicle is supported safely when working underneath.

5. Turn locknut A until it just touches the shifter lever, then back it off 1 full turn.

6. Torque locknut B to 8 ft. lbs.

7. Move the shifter and make sure there is a click at each gear when shifting from **P** through **1ST**. The positions of the selector lever and the indicator should be exact. The release button should return smoothly when used to shift the selector.

929

1. Remove the console shifter cover assembly. Position the transmission selector lever in the **P** detent.

2. Loosen the locknuts A and B. Move the selector from the **P** range and back into the **P** range.

3. Using a feeler gauge, check the clearance between the first locknut, behind the shifter bracket. Adjust the shift lever and locknut to 0.039 in.

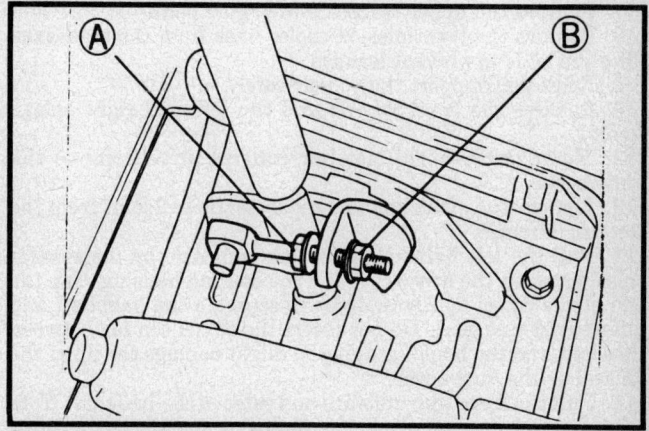

Shifter adjustment—RX-7

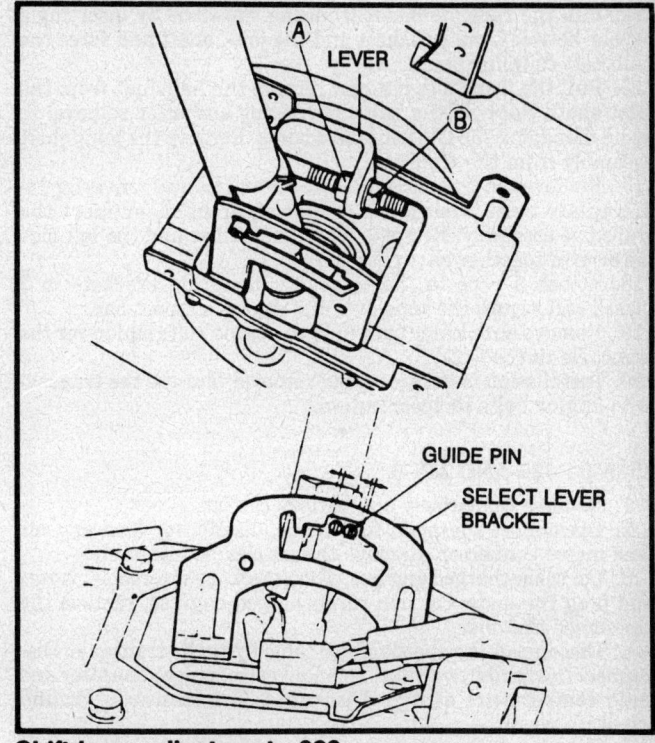

Shift lever adjustment—929

4. Remove the feeler gauge and tighten the locknut B.

5. Move the selector lever through the other gear ranges and check to be sure there is clearance between the selector lever bracket and the guide pin.

6. If clearance does not exist, readjust both locknuts.

AUTOMATIC TRANSAXLE

For further information, please refer to "Professional Transmission Repair Manual" for additional coverage.

Transaxle Assembly

Removal and Installation

1987 626

1. Disconnect the negative battery cable and drain the trans-axle. Disconect the speedometer cable.

2. Remove the shift control cable from the transaxle.

3. Disconnect the ground wire, the inhibitor switch and the kickdown solenoid.

4. Remove the starter motor.

5. Attach the engine support tool 49–G030–025 and suspend the engine.

6. Remove the line connected to the vacuum diaphragm.

7. Remove the upper transaxle-to-engine bolts.

8. Remove the transmission cooler lines from the transaxle. Plug the ends to prevent leakage.

9. Raise and support the vehicle safely.

10. Remove the front wheels and the left and right splash shields.

11. Remove the stabilizer bar control link. Remove the undercover.

12. Remove the pinch bolt and separate the ball joint from the steering knuckle.

13. Pull the left halfshaft from the transaxle by inserting a chisel between the driveshaft and the bearing housing. Tap the end of the chisel lightly in order to separate the halfshaft and differential side gear. Do not insert the chisel too far between the shaft and the housing, doing so might damage the lip of the oil seal or the dust cover.

14. Pull the front hub outward and remove the halfshaft from the transaxle. Support the halfshaft during and after removal to avoid damaging the CV-joints and boots.

15. Pull the right halfshaft from the transaxle by inserting a prybar between the halfshaft and the joint shaft and force the halfshaft coupling open.

16. Pull the front hub out and remove the halfshaft from the joint shaft. Support the halfshaft during and after removal to avoid damaging the CV-joints and boots. Remove the joint shaft assembly from the transaxle.

17. Remove the transaxle undercover and torque converter-to-driveplate bolts. Using the proper equipment, support the transaxle assembly. Remove the crossmember and the left side lower arm together as an assembly.

18. Attach a rope to the transaxle mounting brackets in 2 places and secure the rope over the engine support bar.

19. Remove both lower transaxle-to-engine bolts and lower the transaxle to the floor.

20. Installation is the reverse of removal. Torque the transaxle-to-engine bolts to specification.

1988–91 626 AND MX-6

1. Remove the battery and battery carrier.

2. Disconnect the main fuse block, distributor lead and air flow meter connector. Remove the air cleaner assembly.

3. On turbocharged engines, disconnect the intercooler hoses and plug the ends. On non-turbocharged engines, remove the resonance chamber.

4. Disconnect the speedometer cable from the transaxle. Disconnect the inhibitor switch, solenoid valve, pulse generator and fluid temperature switch. Disconnect the transaxle ground wires.

5. Disconnect the selector and throttle cables from the transaxle selector lever.

6. Raise and support the vehicle safely. Remove the front wheels and splash shield. Drain the transaxle fluid. Disconnect the inlet and outlet hoses from the oil cooler and plug the ends to prevent leakage.

7. Separate the tie rod ends using the proper tool.

8. Remove the stabilizer control links. Remove the nuts and bolts from the lower control arm ball joints and pull the lower control arms downward to separate them from the steering knuckles. Be careful not to damage the ball joint dust boots.

9. Insert a small prybar between the left driveshaft and the transaxle case and tap the end of the lever to uncouple the driveshaft from the differential side gear. Pull the front hub forward and separate the driveshaft from the transaxle. Remove the left joint shaft bracket. Separate the right driveshaft and joint shaft in the same manner as the left.

NOTE: Do not insert the lever too deeply between the shaft and the case or the oil seal lip could be damaged. To avoid damage to the oil seal, hold the CV-joint at the differential and pull the halfshaft straight out.

10. Once both drive and joint shafts are removed, install differential side gear holders 49–G030–455 or equivalent, in the differential side gears to hold them in place and prevent misalignment.

11. Remove the exhaust pipe hanger, gusset plates and undercover. Remove the torque converter nuts.

12. Remove the manifold bracket and the starter.

13. Suspend the engine from the engine hanger with suitable lifting device or special engine support fixture 49–G017–5A0.

14. Remove the No. 4 and No. 2 engine mounts and bracket. Remove the crossmember and left side lower control arm as an assembly.

15. Lean the engine towards the transaxle and support the transaxle with a jack. Remove the transaxle-to-engine bolts and slide the transaxle from under the vehicle.

16. Installation is the reverse of the removal procedure. Fill the transaxle to the proper level. Adjust the throttle cable and selector cables.

1987 323

1. Disconnect the negative battery cable. Remove the air cleaner and loosen the front wheel lug nuts.

2. Disconnect the speedometer and throttle cable from the transaxle. Disconnect the change control cable from the transaxle.

3. Remove the ground wire installation boot. Remove the water pipe bracket. Remove the secondary air pipe and the EGR pipe bracket.

4. Remove the wire harness clip. Disconnect the coupler for the inhibitor switch, the kickdown solenoid and any other necessary solenoids or switches. Disconnect the body ground connector and selector cable.

5. Remove the upper transaxle mounting bolts. Disconnect the neutral switch connector and the vacuum line from the vacuum diaphragm. Disconnect the transaxle oil cooler lines. Mount the engine support tool 49–ER301–025A or equivalent, to the engine hanger.

6. Raise and support the vehicle safely. Drain the transaxle oil into a suitable container and remove the front wheels.

7. Remove the engine undercover and side covers. Remove the front stabilizer.

8. Remove the lower arm ball joints and the knuckle clinch bolts, pull the lower arm downward and separate the lower arms from the knuckles.

9. Separate the driveshaft from the transaxle by prying with a suitable prybar inserted between the shaft and the case. Be sure not to damage the oil seals.

10. Using the proper equipment, support the transaxle assembly. Remove the transaxle crossmember. Remove the wiring and the starter motor.

11. Remove the end plates. Lean the engine toward the transaxle side to lower the transaxle by loosening the engine support hook bolt. Support the transaxle with a suitable transaxle jack.

12. Remove the necessary engine brackets. Remove the remaining transaxle bolt, lower the jack and slide the transaxle from under the vehicle.

13. To install, reverse the removal procedure. Adjust the shift linkage. Refill the transaxle with the proper grade of gear oil.

1888–91 323 AND PROTEGE

1. Disconnect the negative battery cable. Raise the vehicle and support safely. Drain the transxle.

2. Disconnect the lead wire from the distributor. Disconnect the air flow meter connector and remove the air cleaner assembly.

3. Disconnect the speedometer and throttle selector cables from the selector lever.

4. Disconnect the inhibitor switch and overdrive release solenoid connectors. Disconnect the transaxle case grounds and route the wiring aside.

5. Unbolt and remove the selector cable from the transaxle case.

6. Remove the heater pipe and disconnect the oil hose from the connection on the transaxle. Plug the end of the hose to prevent leakage.

7. Suspend the engine from the hanger bracket with special support fixture 49-G017-5A0 or equivalent.

8. Remove the front wheels. Remove the splash shield and engine undercover.

9. Remove the lower arm ball joints and the knuckle clinch bolts, pull the lower arm downward and separate the lower arms from the knuckles.

10. Separate the driveshaft from the transaxle by prying with a suitable prybar. Install special differential side gear holding tool 49-B027-006 or equivalent, to prevent misalignment of the side gears. Disconnect the other driveshaft in the same manner. Remove the clips from the ends of the driveshafts and replace with new.

11. Remove the starter, No. 2 engine mount and the crossmember. Remove the gusset and end plates.

12. Lock the flywheel with the proper tool and remove the torque converter bolts. Lean the engine towards the transaxle by loosening the support hook bolt on the support fixture.

13. Support the transaxle with a jack. Remove the transaxle bolts and the transaxle from under the engine.

14. Installation is essentially the reverse of the removal procedure. Torque the transaxle mounting bolts to 41–59 ft. lbs., torque converter and driveplate bolts to 25–36 ft. lbs. Adjust the throttle and selector cables.

TRANSFER CASE

Transfer Case Assembly

Removal and Installation

1. Disconnect both battery cables. Remove the battery from the vehicle and the air cleaner assembly.

2. Disconnect the speedometer cable. Disconnect the clutch release cylinder. Disconnect the neutral switch, back-up lamp switch, body ground wire and the control cable.

3. Proper support the engine, using tool 49-B0175-A0 or equivalent. Remove the front engine mount-to-frame bolts and the mount assembly from the vehicle. Disconnect the center differential lock sensor electrical connector.

4. Raise and safely support the vehicle. Remove the left tire and wheel assembly. Drain the engine oil and remove the oil filter. Drain the transaxle and the transfer case.

5. Remove the side cover and the engine undercover. Remove the driveshaft.

6. Remove the center differential lock assembly. Remove the starter. Remove the front stabilizer bar. Remove the left tie rod end.

7. Remove the left lower control arm. Remove the front driveshaft. Remove the lower mounting member. Remove the inspection plate.

8. Using the proper equipment, remove the transaxle and the transfer case from the vehicle.

9. Installation is the reverse of the removal procedure.

DRIVE AXLE

Halfshaft

Removal and Installation

1987 626, 323 AND PROTEGE

1. Raise and support the vehicle safely. Drain the transaxle fluid and remove the splash shield.

2. Operate the brakes to secure the wheel hub and loosen the halfshaft locknut but do not remove it. Remove the front wheels. Raise the tabs before loosening the locknut.

3. Remove the stabilizer bar control link from the lower arm.

4. Remove the pinch bolt and the ball joint from the steering knuckle.

5. Remove the left side halfshaft.

   a. On manual transaxles, insert a prybar between the halfshaft and the transaxle case. Remove the halfshaft from the side gear by lightly tapping the end of the prybar. Do not insert the prybar too far, doing so, could damage the lip of the oil seal or the dust cover.

   b. For automatic transaxle, insert a prybar between the halfshaft and the bearing housing. Tap the end of the prybar in order to uncouple the halfshaft and differential side gear.

   c. After removing the halfshaft locknut, pull the front hub outward and toward the rear. Disconnect the halfshaft from the wheel and the transaxle.

6. Remove the right side halfshaft and joint shaft.

   a. Insert a prybar between the halfshaft and the joint shaft and separate them.

   b. Remove the halfshaft locknut and pull the front hub outward and to the rear, disconnecting the halfshaft from the front hub. Remove the halfshaft from the joint shaft.

   c. If the driveshaft is stuck to the front hub and cannot be removed, install bearing puller tool 49-0839-425C or equivalent, to push the shaft out. After removing the driveshaft, install differential side gear holder tool 49G-030-455 into the transaxle, this prevents dirt from getting into the transaxle.

7. Install differential side gear holder 49-G030-455 to prevent misalignment of the side gears.

8. Installation is the reverse of removal.

1988–91 626 AND MX-6

NOTE: Removal and installation of the halfshafts is the same for manual and automatic transaxles.

1. Drain the transaxle oil. Raise the the vehicle and support safely.

2. Remove the front wheels and the splash shields. Apply the brakes and unstake the driveshaft locknut using a small cold chisel. Loosen the locknut but do not remove it.

3. Using the proper tool, disconnect the tie rod ends. Remove the stabilizer control links.

4. Remove the nuts and bolts from the lower control arm ball joints and pull the lower control arm downward to separate it from the steering knuckle. Be careful not to damage the ball joint dust boots.

5. Remove the locknut and insert a small prybar between the left driveshaft and the transaxle case. Tap the end of the lever to

uncouple the driveshaft from the differential side gear. Pull the front hub forward and separate the driveshaft from the transaxle. If the hub is difficult to remove, use a puller to separate it from the driveshaft. Remove the left joint shaft bracket and shaft.

NOTE: Do not insert the lever too deeply between the shaft and the case or the oil seal lip and the boot could be damaged. To avoid damage to the oil seal and the boot, hold the CV-joint at the differential and pull the driveshaft straight out.

6. Separate and remove the right driveshaft and joint shaft in the same manner as the left.

7. Once both drive and joint shafts are removed, install differential side gear holders 49-G030-455 (non-turbo), 49-H027-003 (turbo) or equivalents, in the differential side gears to hold them in place and prevent misalignment.

8. Installation is essentially the reverse of removal. Use new clips on the spline shafts. Before installing the driveshafts, inspect the oil seal for damage. Coat the seal with clean transaxle oil prior to installation. Lock the stabilizer nut so approximately 0.8 in. of the through bolt thread is exposed. Torque the wheel hub locknut to 174–235 ft. lbs.

CV-Boot

Removal and Installation

1. Disconnect the battery negative cable.
2. Raise and support the vehicle safely.
3. Remove the tire and wheel assembly.
4. Remove the halfshaft.
5. Place the halfshaft assembly into a suitable vise.
6. Note matching marks on the tri-pod joint and the outer ring. Remove the clip and the outer ring. Remove the boot bands.
7. Remove the snapring. Note match marks on the halfshaft and the tripod joint. Using a hammer and suitable prybar remove tri-pod joint and the outer boot.
8. To remove the inner boot, unclip boot bands, remove the shaft and ball joint assembly and the boot.
9. Reverse procedure to install.

Driveshaft and U-Joints

Removal and Installation

RX-7, 929 AND MIATA

1. Raise and support the vehicle safely. Matchmark the flanges on the driveshaft and pinion so they may be installed in their original position.

2. Remove all necessary exhaust components. On 929, remove the all the nuts, bolts, lock washers, spacers and bushings from the center support bearing. Remove the nuts that attach the driveshaft to the companion flange of the rear axle. Lower the back end of the driveshaft and slide the front end out of the transmission.

3. Plug up the hole in the transmission with the main shaft turning holder tool 49-0259-440 or 49-S120-440, to prevent fluid from leaking.

4. Driveshaft installation is the reverse of removal. On RX-7, if the driveshaft was replaced and unusual noise and vibration is noticed, correct the problem with balance washers positioned on various places on the companion flange. If noise and vibration is exhibited on the 929, the problem may be corrected by using different size bolts and spacers on the center bearing support. On 929, torque the center bearing bolts to 28–38 ft. lbs.

323 AND PROTEGE WITH 4WD

1. Raise and support the vehicle safely.
2. Matchmark the front and rear flanges for assembly refer-

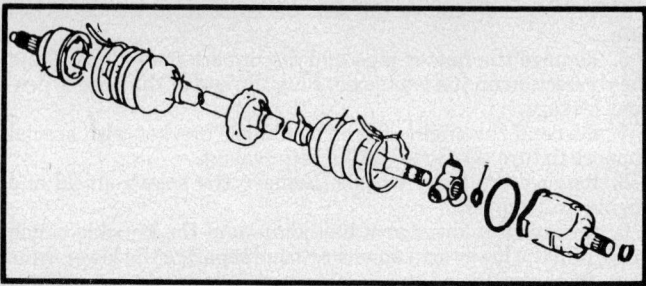

Drive axle—exploded view

ence. Stuff a rag in the double offset joint to prevent damage to the boot by the propeller shaft. Remove the front and rear retaining bolts and nuts.

3. Remove the nuts, bolts, shims and bushings from the center bearing support and remove the support bracket.

4. Lower and remove the driveshaft from the vehicle.

5. Installation is the reverse of the removal procedure. Torque the rear flange bolts to 27–38 ft. lbs. Torque the front flange bolts to 20–22 ft. lbs. Check that the front and rear shafts are aligned. If not, adjust the height of the center bearing support with shims. Both shims must be the same thickness.

Rear Axle Shaft, Bearing and Seal

Removal and Installation

RX-7

1. Raise the vehicle and support it safely.
2. Remove the rear tire. Using a blunt drift or small cold chisel, uncrimp the locknut on the halfshaft. Depress the brake pedal to hold the hub secure and then remove the axle nut.
3. Remove the caliper assembly and tie it back with a piece of rope. Remove the setting screws and the disc.
4. Remove the knuckle assembly.
5. Remove the nuts attaching the driveshaft to the companion flange on the transaxle and remove the driveshaft.
6. When installing, insert the wheel side of the driveshaft to the axle flange and then install the differential side of the driveshaft. Tighten the driveshaft attaching nuts 40–47 ft. lbs.
7. The rest of the installation procedure is the reverse order of the removal procedure. If equipped with ABS, check the clearance between the speed sensor and the rotor. The clearance should be between 0.016–0.039 in. Torque the locknut to 174–231 ft. lbs. Be sure to measure the play of the wheel bearing. If the play exceeds the 0.004 in. or less, replace the wheel bearing. Crimp the driveshaft locknut to the driveshaft groove.

929

1. Raise and support the vehicle safely. Remove the rear tire and wheel assembly. Remove the rear driveshaft.
2. Remove the caliper and position it aside. Remove the locknut and washer. Remove the rotor.
3. Remove the brake shoes. Disconnect the parking brake cable. Remove the wheel speed sensor assembly, if equipped with ABS.
4. Disconnect and remove the rear trailing arm. Remove the rear shock absorber.
5. Disconnect the stabilizer control link. Disconnect the upper control link using the proper tool. Disconnect the lower link in front of the assembly using the proper tool. Disconnect the lower link behind the assembly.
6. Matchmark the driveshaft and flange for assembly reference and remove the rear hub and support assembly from its mounting. Measure the play of the wheel bearing and, if necessary, replace the wheel bearing.
7. Installation is the reverse of the removal procedure.

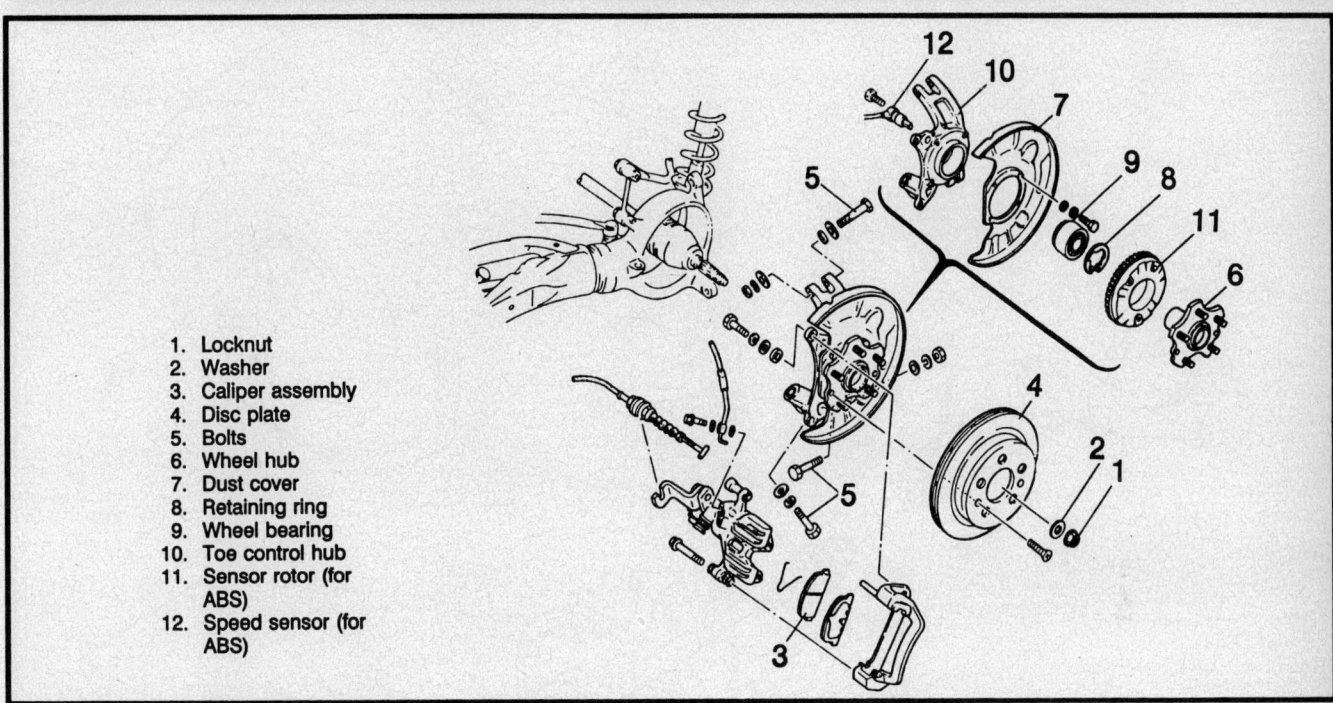

1. Locknut
2. Washer
3. Caliper assembly
4. Disc plate
5. Bolts
6. Wheel hub
7. Dust cover
8. Retaining ring
9. Wheel bearing
10. Toe control hub
11. Sensor rotor (for ABS)
12. Speed sensor (for ABS)

Rear axle hub components—RX-7

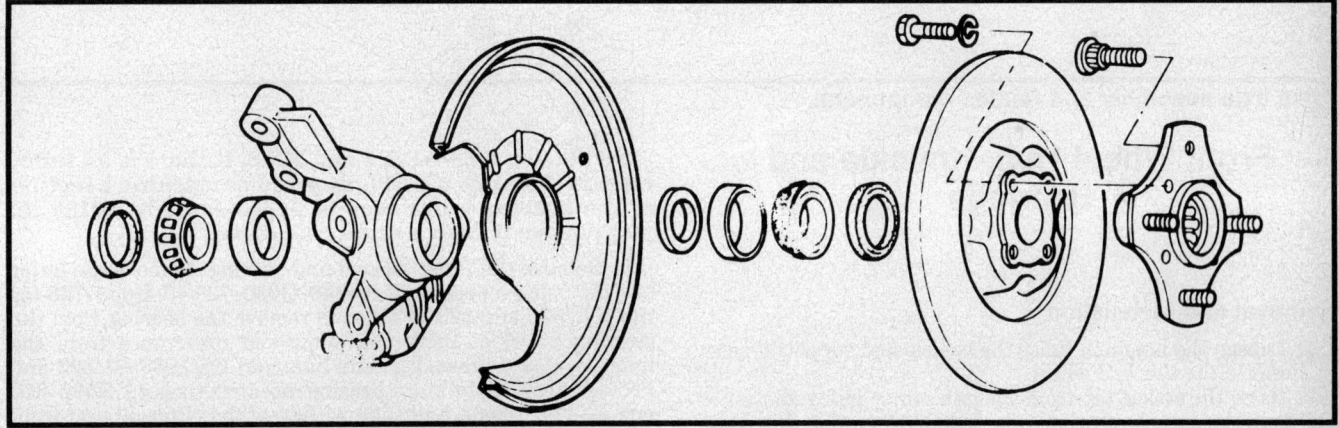

Rear axle hub components—323 with 4WD

Torque the lower front and rear and upper links to 40–55 ft. lbs., rear hub support to 69–86 ft. lbs., caliper assembly to 33–50 ft. lbs. and driveshaft flange bolts to 40–47 ft. lbs. Check the rear bearing endplay. Maximum allowable endplay is 0.08 in. Torque the disc locknut to 174–231 ft. lbs. Use a new locknut. Adjust the rear toe-in.

323 AND PROTEGE WITH 4WD

1. Raise and support the vehicle safely. Remove the rear tire and wheel assembly.
2. Remove the dust cap. Unstake the locknut and remove. To remove the right rear locknut, turn it clockwise.
3. Remove the caliper and position it aside. Remove the driveshaft, using tool 490–8394–25C.
4. Disconnect the lateral link. Disconnect the trailing link. Remove the lower arm retaining bolts that hold the strut assembly to the lower arm.

5. Remove the hub and knuckle assembly from its mounting.
6. Installation is the reverse of the removal procedure. Check the rear wheel bearing endplay. There must be no endplay. Replace wheel bearing if necessary. Torque the locknuts to 116–174 ft. lbs.

MIATA

1. Raise and safely support the vehicle.
2. Remove the tire and wheel assembly.
3. Remove the driveshaft locknut.
4. Remove the driveshaft-to-differential bolts and the driveshaft from the vehicle. If the driveshaft is stuck to the wheel hub, install a used locknut and tap end using a plastic hammer.
5. Reverse procedure to install. Torque driveshaft-to-differential bolts to 40–47 ft. lbs. (54–64 Nm). Torque the driveshaft locknut to 159–217 ft. lbs. (216–294 Nm).

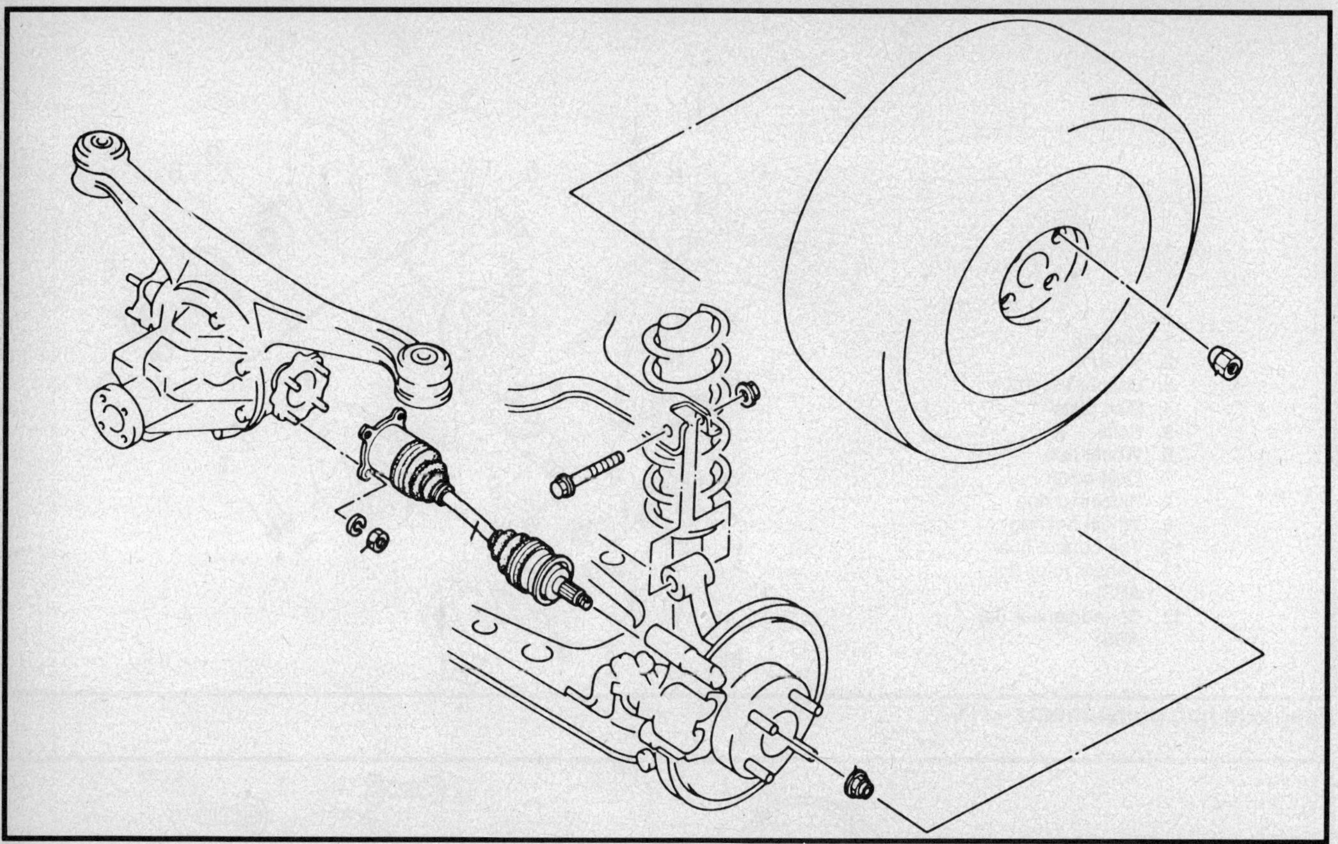

Drive axle assembly and related components

Front Wheel Hub, Knuckle and Bearings

Removal and Installation

1. Loosen the lug nuts. Raise the vehicle and support it safely. Remove the tire and wheel.

2. Raise the staked tab from the hub center nut, remove the nut from the axle. Apply the brake to hold the rotor while loosening the nut.

3. Using ball joint puller tool 49–0118–850C or equivalent, separate the tie rod end from the steering knuckle. Disconnect the horseshoe clip that retains the brake line to the strut. On the 626 and MX-6, remove the stabilizer bar control link from the control arm.

4. Remove the mounting bolts that hold the caliper assembly to the knuckle. Wire the caliper aside, do not allow the caliper to be supported by the brake hose, support it with wire.

5. Remove the thru bolt and nut that retains the lower ball joint to the steering knuckle and disconnect the ball joint.

6. Remove the 2 strut-to-steering knuckle nuts and bolts. Separate the steering knuckle and hub from the strut and halfshaft. On 626 and MX-6 with ABS, remove the speed sensor from the strut bracket.

7. The hub is pressed through the wheel bearings into the knuckle. Replacement of the hub and removal requires wheel hub puller tool 49–B001–726 for the GLC and tool 49–G030–725/49–G030–727 or equivalent, pulley assembly for the 1987 626 and 323 or G49–G033–102, 104 and 105 for 1988–91 626 and MX-6 in order to separate the hub from the steering knuckle.

NOTE: On 1988–91 626 and MX-6, if there is an inner race on the front wheel hub, grind or machine a section of the bearing inner race to approximately 0.0197 in. and remove it with a small cold chisel.

8. Remove the inner oil seal and bearing. Remove the outer bearing using a press and tool 49–G030–725/49–G030–728 for the 1987 626 and 323 in order to remove the bearing from the steering knuckle. Drive the outer and inner race from the knuckle with a brass drift and hammer. On 1988–91 323 and Protege, remove the outer bearing race with tools 49–B092–372 and 49–F401–366A and then withdraw the outer oil seal from the front hub. On 1988–91 323 and Protege, remove the bearing

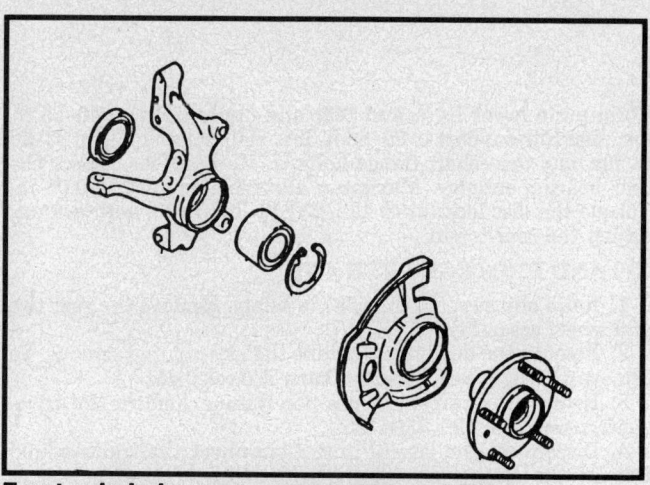

Front axle hub components—626 and MX-6

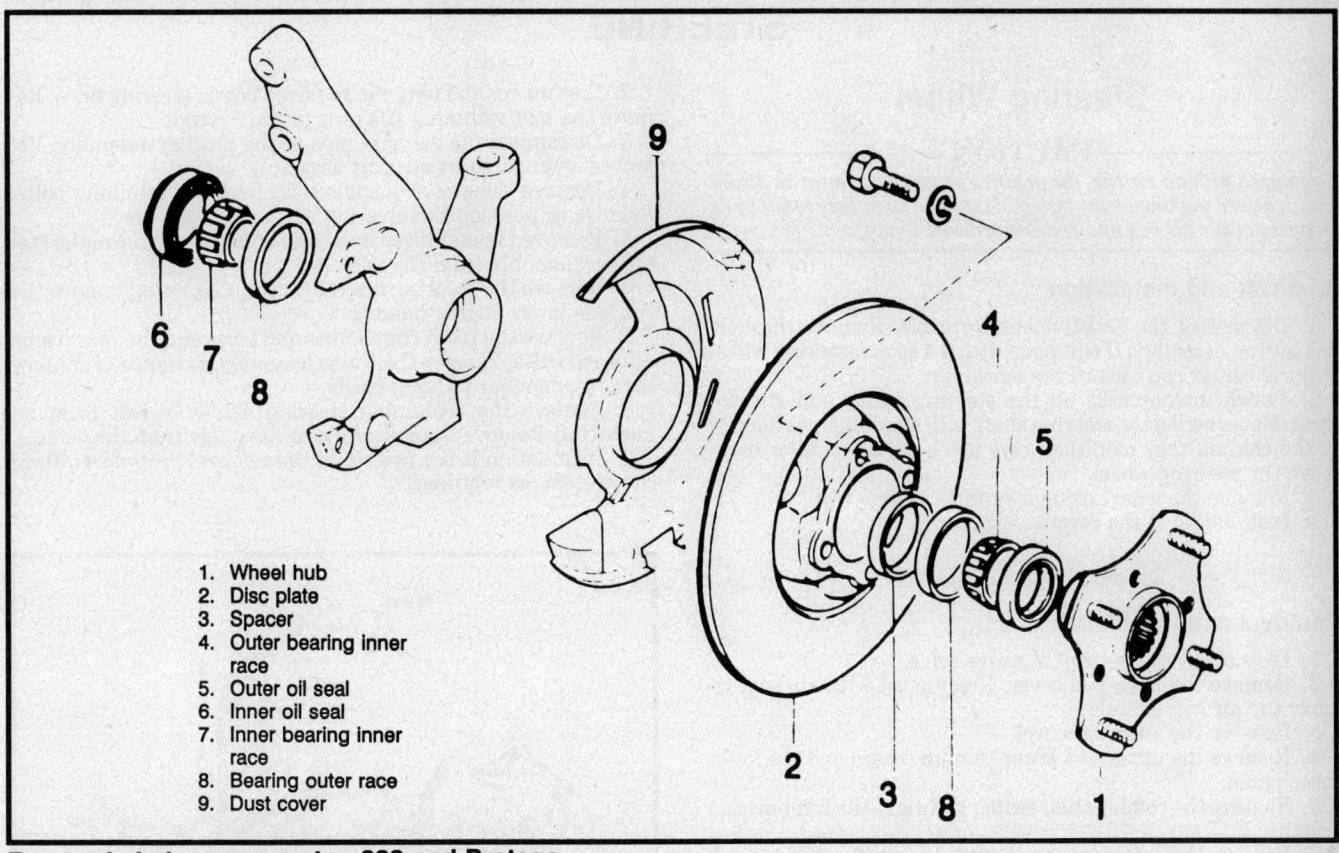

1. Wheel hub
2. Disc plate
3. Spacer
4. Outer bearing inner race
5. Outer oil seal
6. Inner oil seal
7. Inner bearing inner race
8. Bearing outer race
9. Dust cover

Front axle hub components—323 and Protege

outer race with tool 49–FT01–361 and a press and remove the wheel bearing. On 1988–91 626 and MX-6, press the bearing from the hub using tools, 49–G033–102, 104 and 106.

9. Install new inner and outer races, as required. Make sure the edge of the race contact the steering knuckle. Pack the inner and outer bearing and install in knuckle. Use tool 49–G030–728 for the 1987 626 and 323 to press the hub into the steering knuckle. On 1988–91 323 and Protege, use tool 49–V001–795 to seat the bearing in the hub. On 1988–91 626 and MX-6, use tools 49–G030–797, 49–F027–007 and 49–H026–103 to install the wheel bearing.

10. On 1987 vehicles, measure the preload with a scale connected to the caliper mounting hole on the knuckle. Various spacers are available to increase or decrease the preload. Preload should be 1.7–6.9 ft. lbs.

11. On 1988–91 323 and Protege, measure/adjust the preload as follows:

a. Insert the bearing and spacer into the steering knuckle and install tool 49–B001–727. Tighten the tool to 145 ft. lbs.

b. Connect a spring scale to caliper mounting bolt hole on the dust cover and pull on the scale to measure the bearing preload (starting rotation torque). This preload should be 0.53–2.55 lbs. for 13 inch wheels and 0.48–2.35 lbs. for 14 inch wheels. When tightening the preload tool, torque in 36 ft. lbs. increments.

c. If the preload is not within specification, spacers are available in a variety of thicknesses to adjust it. Increase the the spacer thickness when the preload is too high and decrease the thickness if too low.

12. Install the inner and outer grease seals. Press fit the hub through the bearings into the knuckle.

13. Installation of the knuckle and hub is in the reverse order of removal. Always use a new axle locknut. On the 323 and Protege, torque halfshaft locknut to 116–174 ft. lbs. On the 626 and MX-6 torque the locknut to 116–124 ft. lbs. Stake the locknut after tightening.

Differential Carrier

Removal and Installation

1. Raise and safely support the vehicle.
2. Remove the tire and wheel assembly.
3. Disconnect the right and left driveshaft from the differential carrier.
4. Disconnect the propeller shaft from the differential carrier.
5. Remove the differential carrier nuts and bolts and the differential from the vehicle.
6. Reverse procedure to install.

STEERING

Steering Wheel

— CAUTION —

If equipped with an air bag, the negative battery cable must be disconnected, before working on the system. Failure to do so may result in deployment of the air bag and possible personal injury.

Removal and Installation

1. Disconnect the negative battery cable. Remove the horn pad button assembly. If equipped with a 4 spoke steering wheel, pull the center cap toward the wheel top.
2. Punch matchmarks on the steering wheel and steering shaft. Never strike the steering shaft with a hammer, as damage to the column may result. Always use a suitable puller to remove the steering wheel.
3. Remove the wheel using a suitable puller.
4. Installation is the reverse of removal.

Steering Column

Removal and Installation

1. Disconnect the battery negative cable.
2. Remove the horn pad cover. If equipped with air bag, remove the air bag module.
3. Remove the steering wheel.
4. Remove the upper and lower column covers and the lower cover panel.
5. Remove the combination switch bolts and the combination switch.
6. Remove the intermediate shaft bolt and the steering column bolts and the steering column from the vehicle.
7. Reverse procedure to install.

Steering Gear

Removal and Installation
323, PROTEGE, 626 AND MX-6

NOTE: The following information does not pertain to 1988–90 626 and MX-6 equipped with 4 wheel steering.

1. Disconnect the negative battery cable. Raise the vehicle and support it safely. If equipped with 4WD, remove the battery and battery tray.
2. Raise and support the vehicle safely. Remove the tire and wheel assemblies. Remove the undercovers.
3. Remove the steering gear to steering column coupler pinch bolt and separate the coupler from the steering gear. Disconnect the tie rod end nuts and cotter pin. Remove the knuckle arm/tie rod connections.
4. If equipped with power steering, remove and plug the pressure hose going to the power steering pump. Matchmark the pressure pipe union nuts to ensure proper installation and sealing. Oil will leak from the pressure and return pipes. Have a container on hand to collect the excess fluid.
5. Remove the boot band and all bolts from the steering gear. Remove the gear and linkage from the engine compartment through the tie rod hole.
6. Installation is the reverse of removal. Be sure to bleed the air from the system if equipped with a power steering pump.

626 AND MX-6 WITH FWS
Front Steering Gear

1. Disconnect the negative battery cable. Raise and support the vehicle safely. Remove the tire and wheel assemblies.

2. Disconnect and plug the required power steering lines. Remove the bolt retaining the unit to the firewall.
3. Disconnect the exhaust pipe at the muffler assembly. Remove the undercover support assembly.
4. Remove the steering angle transfer shaft retaining bolts. Remove or position the steering angle assembly aside
5. Remove the stabilizer link bolts and nuts. Remove the stabilizer assembly from the vehicle.
6. Remove the steering assembly retaining nuts. Remove the left side lower engine mount.
7. Remove the front frame nuts and bolts and the rear frame nuts and bolts. Remove the frame assembly, as required or allow the crossmember to hang freely.
8. Remove the remaining steering assembly bolt from its mounting. Remove the steering gear assembly from the vehicle.
9. Installation is the reverse of the removal procedure. Bleed the system, as required,

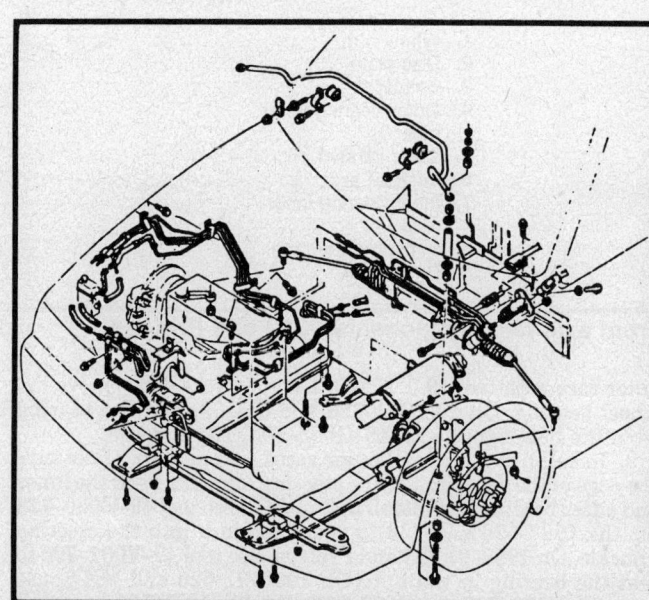

Front wheel steering front rack assembly—626 and MX-6

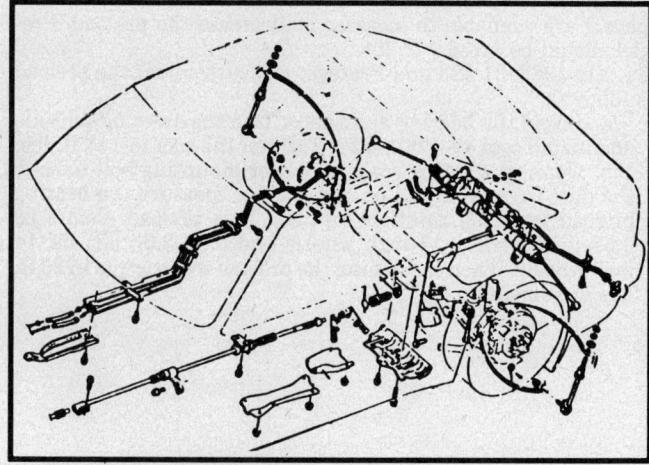

Front wheel steering rear rack assembly—626 and MX-6

Rear Steering Gear

1. Disconnect the negative battery cable. Raise and support the vehicle safely. Remove the rear tire assemblies, as required for working clearance.
2. Disconnect the electrical connector from the steering gear assembly. Remove the electrical harness retaining bolts.
3. Remove the steering angle transfer shaft cover. Disconnect the universal joint and bolts from the steering angle transfer shaft assembly. Remove the lower cover and the brake line joint block.
4. Disconnect and cap all required fluid lines. Disconnect the lower spring link retaining bolts. Remove the solenoid valve, which is mounted on the steering gear assembly.
5. Using the proper tool, disconnect the tie rod ends from the knuckles. Remove the mounting bolts from the left and right sub frames. Allow the components to hang freely.
6. Remove the rear steering gear bolts and the rear steering gear assembly from the vehicle.
7. Installation is the reverse of the removal procedure. Bleed the system, as required.

929 AND RX-7

1. Disconnect the negative battery cable. Raise and support the vehicle safely. Remove the tire and wheel assemblies.
2. Remove the lower steering gear assembly cover. Remove the steering damper.
3. Disconnect and plug the power steering fluid lines. Remove the control valve assembly. Remove the pressure switch.
4. Separate the tie rod ends from their mountings. Remove the steering gear from the vehicle.
5. Installation is the reverse of the removal procedure. Bleed the system, as required.

MIATA

1. Loosen the wheel lug nuts. Raise and safely support the vehicle.
2. Remove the tire and wheel assembly and the engine undercover.
3. If equipped with power steering, disconnect the hydraulic lines from the steering gear. Plug all openings.
4. Remove the tie rod cotter pin and nut and separate the tie rod from the knuckle.
5. Remove the intermediate shaft bolt and steering gear assembly bolts and the steering gear assembly from the vehicle.
6. Reverse procedure to install. Torque steering gear mounting bolts to 34–43 ft. lbs. (46–59 Nm), tie rod nut to 22–29 ft. lbs.

(29-39 Nm) and intermediate shaft bolt to 13–20 ft. lbs. (18–26 Nm).

Power Steering Pump

Removal and Installation

1. Disconnect the negative battery cable. Disconnect and plug the fluid hoses from the pump.
2. Remove all necessary drive belts. Remove the alternator and or the air conditioning compressor, if necessary.
3. Loosen the pump belt adjusting bolt, slide the pump aside and remove the belt. On some vehicles, it may be necessary to remove the pump pulley before removing the pump. On 626, MX-6 and 929 use tool 49–W023–585 or equivalent, to hold the pulley stationary while the pulley lock bolt is removed.
4. Support the pump, remove the mounting bolts and lift out the pump.
5. Installation is the reverse of removal.

Belt Adjustment

Adjust belt to give approximately a ½ in. deflection at the midpoint of its longest stretch.

System Bleeding

1. Check the fluid level. Add fluid, as required.
2. Turn the steering wheel full cycle, in both directions, 5 times with the engine OFF.
3. Recheck the fluid level again and add, as required.
4. Start the engine and allow to warm up at idle. Turn the steering wheel full cycle, in both directions, 5 times with the engine running.
5. Turn the steering wheel completely to the left and the right, several times until the air bubbles leave the oil.
6. Top off the fluid reservoir.

Tie Rod Ends

Removal and Installation

1. Raise and support the vehicle safely.
2. Place alignment marks on the tie rod end, adjusting nut and shaft. Disconnect the tie rod end from the center link and knuckle arm, using the proper removal tool.
3. Remove the tie rod end from the vehicle.
4. Install the tie rod end to the center link and knuckle arm. Be sure to use new cotter pins.

BRAKES

Master Cylinder

Removal and Installation

NOTE: If equipped with a fluid reservoir located separately from the master cylinder, remove the lines which run between the 2 and plug the lines to prevent leakage.

1. Disconnect the negative battery cable. Disconnect the oil level sensor, if equipped. If equipped, disconnect the electrical connector from the assembly.
2. Using a suitable wrench, disconnect and plug the brake fluid lines from the master cylinder; if equipped with ABS, "banjo" type fittings are used. Collect all the excess fluid in a small container.
3. Remove the proportioning bypass valve attaching bolts and valve, if equipped.

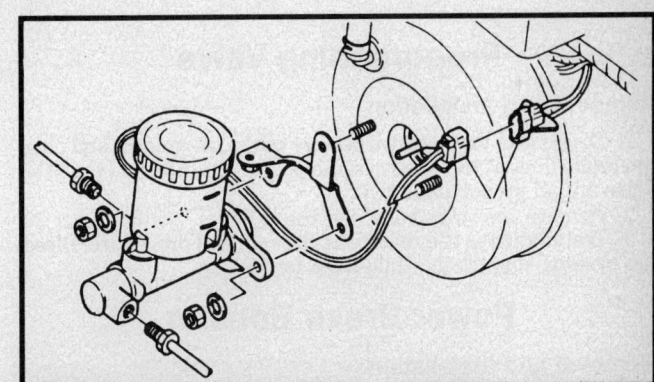

Master cylinder removal and installation—626 and MX-6

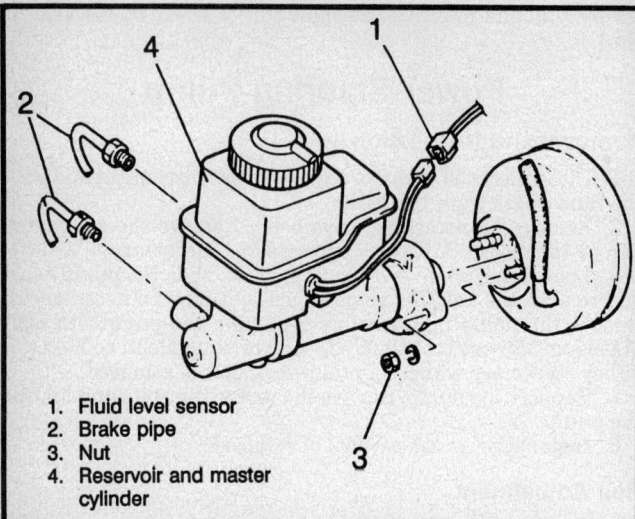

1. Fluid level sensor
2. Brake pipe
3. Nut
4. Reservoir and master cylinder

Master cylinder removal and installation—323 and Protege

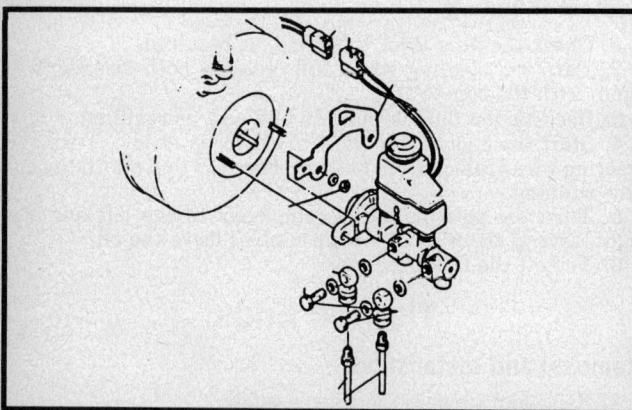

Master cylinder removal and installation—929

4. Remove the master cylinder-to-power brake unit bolts and the master cylinder from the vehicle. Remove the clutch pipe holder, if equipped.

5. Installation is the reverse of removal. Bleed the brake system. If equipped with ABS, use new crush washers on the banjo fittings.

Proportioning Valve

Removal and Installation

1. Disconnect the negative battery cable. Disconnect and plug the brake lines at the valve assembly. The 323, 626 and the MX-6 use a dual proportioning valve.

2. Remove the valve bolts and the valve.

3. Installation is the reverse of the removal procedure. Bleed the system. Inspect the fluid lines for leakage.

Power Brake Booster

Removal and Installation

1. Disconnect the negative battery cable. Remove the blower air duct, if equipped. Disconnect the vacuum hose from the pow-

er booster assembly.

2. On some vehicles, it may be possible to remove the power brake booster without disconnecting the brake fluid lines from the master cylinder; if so, remove the cylinder and position it aside.

3. As required, disconnect the master cylinder fluid lines and remove it from the vehicle.

4. Remove the cotter pin and disconnect the clevis pin from the booster yoke at the brake pedal.

5. Remove the booster nuts and the booster from the vehicle.

6. Installation is the reverse of removal. Use a new gasket. Bleed the system.

Brake Caliper

Removal and Installation

1. Raise and safely support the vehicle.

2. Remove the tire and wheel assembly.

3. Disconnect and plug the brake line.

4. Disconnect the brake cable, if equipped.

5. Remove the caliper attaching bolts, and/or lock pin bolt, and the caliper assembly from the vehicle.

6. To install, reverse the removal procedures. Bleed the brake system.

Disc Brake Pads

Removal and Installation

FRONT

Except RX-7

1. Raise and safely support the vehicle. Remove the front wheels.

2. Remove both caliper bolts or the lower lock pin bolt for 929 and pull the caliper off the disc. Tie the caliper up to prevent putting tension and stress on the brake hose.

3. Remove the outer pad by using a suitable prying tool to release the clip. Then, remove the inner pad.

4. Remove about ½ the brake fluid from the reservoir in the master cylinder. Use a C-clamp or special holding tool 49–0221–600C with an old pad to depress the caliper piston back into the caliper to allow the new thicker pad to be installed.

5. Reverse the removal procedure to install. If either or both pads shows excessive wear, replace both pads. Before reattaching the caliper, push the sleeve toward the outside of the caliper so the sleeve boot does not get pinned between the caliper and steering knuckle and get torn. On 929, torque the lower lock pin bolt to 61–69 ft. lbs.

RX-7

1. Raise the vehicle and support it safely.

2. Remove the wheels.

3. Remove the lock pin bolt and lift the caliper. Tie the caliper up to prevent putting tension and stress on the brake hose.

4. Remove the anti-rattle spring and remove the brake pads and shims.

5. Use special tool 49–0221–600C to push the piston inward and hold it in place to accept the new thicker pad.

6. Install new brake pads. Be sure to fit the shims in the proper positions and attach the anti-rattle spring.

7. Fit the caliper in place. If the piston in the caliper is out too far to allow installation of the caliper with the new brake pads, remove master cylinder reservoir cap and siphon some (by not all) of the brake fluid out of the reservoir, then press in the piston. If the piston will not press in, submerge an end of a piece of hose in brake fluid, attach the other end of the caliper bleeder valve, open the valve and push in the piston. When the piston is in far enough, close the valve.

8. Remaining assembly is the reverse of removal. Torque the lock bolt to 23–30 ft. lbs.

REAR

Except RX-7 and 929

1. Loosen the rear wheel lug nuts. Raise and safely support the vehicle. Release the parking brake and remove the rear wheels.
2. Disconnect the parking brake cable mounting bracket and the cable operating lever.
3. Remove the upper caliper bolt and pivot the caliper assembly downward and position it aside.
4. Release the V-springs. Remove the inner and outer pads with the shims.
5. Coat the new shims with grease and attach them to the pads.
6. Using special tool 49–FA18–602 turn the piston fully inward in a clockwise rotation. Install the inner pad and align the piston groove with the inner pad alignment pin using the special tool. Again, this alignment must be accomplished with the inner pad installed.
7. Complete the installation in reverse of the removal procedure. Torque the caliper mounting bolt to 12–17 ft. lbs. When connecting the parking brake cable on 626 and MX-6, there must be no clearance between the cable end and the operating lever. When the wheels are installed apply the brakes a few times and check that there is no excessive brake drag when the wheels are turned.

RX-7

1. Raise and safely support the vehicle.
2. Remove the rear wheels.
3. Remove the lock pin bolts from the caliper and support the caliper with wire to prevent placing stress and tension on the brake hose.
4. Release the V-spring and remove the brake pads from the mounting support.
5. Complete the installation in reverse of the removal procedure. Torque the caliper lock pin bolts to 20–30 ft. lbs. Depress the brake pedal to adjust the parking brake cable play.

Brake Rotor

Removal and Installation

1. Raise and safely support the vehicle. Remove the wheel.
2. Disconnect and plug the brake line.
3. Remove the caliper.
4. Remove the rotor screws and the rotor from the vehicle.
5. Reverse procedure to install. Bleed brake system.

Brake Drums

Removal and Installation

1. Loosen the lug nuts. Raise and safely support the vehicle.
2. Remove the tire and wheel assembly.
3. To ease removal of the leading shoe and installation of the return spring later, insert a suitable prybar into the gap between the quadrant of the automatic adjuster mechanism and twist it in the arrowed direction to release tension.
4. Remove the brake drum from the vehicle.
5. Reverse procedure to install.

Brake Shoes

Removal and Installation

626, MX-6, 323 AND PROTEGE

1. Raise the vehicle and support safely. Remove the wheels and the brake drum. Clean the dirt from the brake components with a dry brush.
2. To ease removal of the leading shoe and installation of the

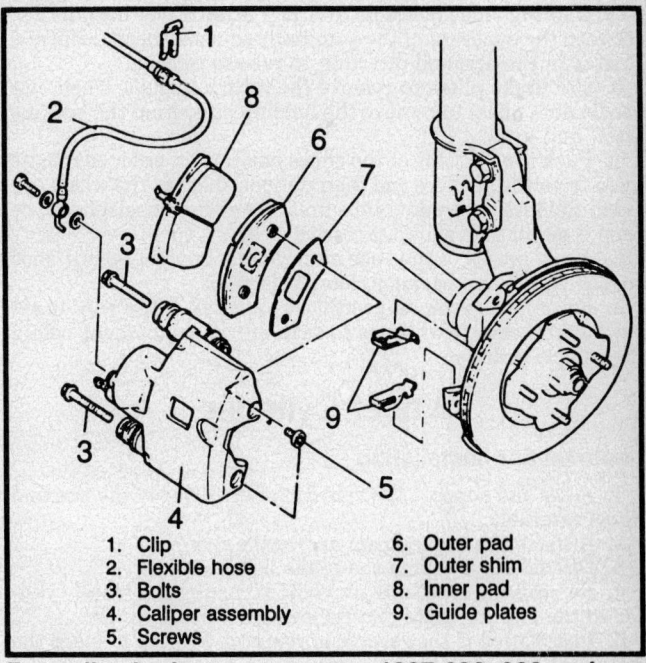

1. Clip
2. Flexible hose
3. Bolts
4. Caliper assembly
5. Screws
6. Outer pad
7. Outer shim
8. Inner pad
9. Guide plates

Front disc brake components—1987 626, 323 and Protege

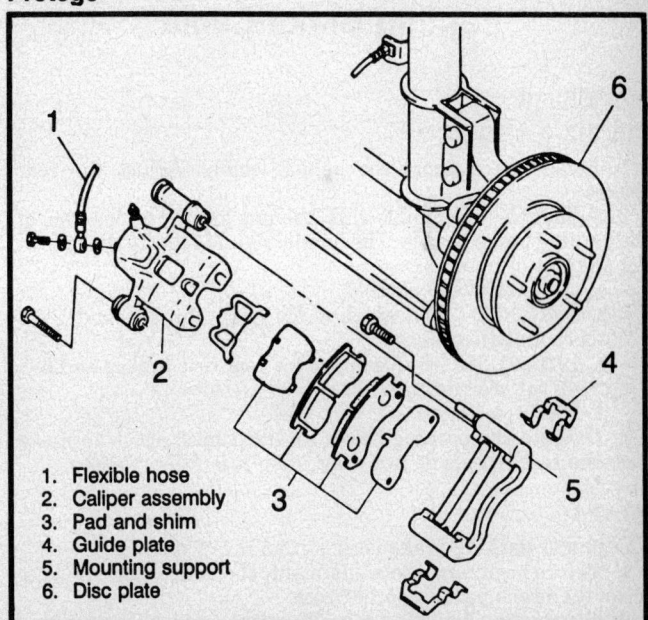

1. Flexible hose
2. Caliper assembly
3. Pad and shim
4. Guide plate
5. Mounting support
6. Disc plate

Front disc brake components—1988–91 626 and MX-6

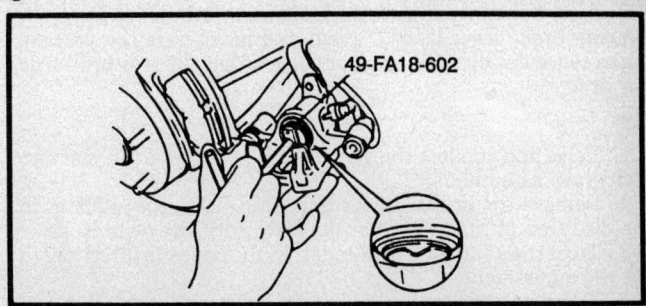

49-FA18-602

Aligning the piston groove using special tool

return spring later, insert an ordinary screwdriver into the gap between the quadrant of the automatic adjuster mechanism and twist it in the arrowed direction to release tension.

3. Use brake pliers to remove the return springs. Then, use needle nose pliers to remove the holding pins, from the backing plate, and clips.

4. Push the bottoms of the shoes outward in order to release them from the anchors and then unhook them at the wheel cylinder. Remove the leading shoe first. Both rear wheels should be done if either side shows excessive wear.

5. Apply grease to the shoe and cylinder contact points, shoe anchor points and backing plate projections.

6. Reverse the removal procedure to install. Make sure to apply the brakes several times to take up the adjustment before the vehicle is driven.

Wheel Cylinder

Removal and Installation

1. Raise and support the vehicle safely. Remove the tire and wheel assembly.

2. Remove the brake drum and brake shoes.

3. Disconnect and plug the brake lines.

4. Remove the stud nuts and bolt attaching the wheel cylinder to the backing plate and remove the wheel cylinder.

5. Installation is the reverse of removal. Be sure to bleed the system after installation.

Parking Brake Cable

Adjustment

626, MX-6 AND RX-7

1. Raise and support the vehicle safely. Adjust the rear brakes.

2. Adjust the front cable with the nut located at the rear of the parking brake handle. The handle should require the following amount of notches:

    a. 1987 626—7–9 notches.

    b. 1987 323—7–11 notches for drum brakes and 9–15 notches for disc brakes.

    c. 1988–91 323—5–7 notches for rear disc brakes and 6–8 notches for rear drum brakes.

    d. RX-7—4–5 notches.

3. Operate the parking brake several times, check to make sure the rear wheels do not drag when it is fully released.

MIATA

The proper parking brake lever stroke is 5–7 notches.

1. Before beginning the adjustment, start the engine and depress the brake pedal several times.

2. Remove the adjusting nut clip at the front of the parking brake cable and rotate the adjusting nut until the lever stroke is within specification.

3. After adjustment, turn the ignition switch ON and pull the parking brake lever back 1 notch and make sure the parking brake reminder light illuminates. Check that the rear brakes do not drag.

929

1. Raise and support the vehicle safely. Remove the rear tire and wheel assembly.

2. Remove the brake service hole plug. Turn the adjuster in the direction of the arrow, on the disc, until the plate locks.

3. Turn the adjuster 3–5 notches, in the opposite direction, to set the adjustment.

4. Make sure the brakes do not drag. Check the functions of the parking brake assembly.

Removal and Installation

FRONT CABLE

1. Disconnect the negative battery cable. Remove the console assembly, as required.

2. Remove the adjusting nut. Remove the mounting bracket assembly.

3. Remove the parking brake lever assembly.

4. Remove the front cable.

5. Installation is the reverse of the removal procedure. Adjust the parking brake cable, as required.

REAR CABLE

1. Disconnect the negative battery cable. Remove the rear console assembly, as required.

2. Remove the bracket assembly. Disconnect the cable from its mounting.

3. Raise and support the vehicle safely. Remove the rear tire and wheel assembly.

4. On all except 929, disconnect the brake cable from its mounting and remove it from the vehicle.

5. On the 929, remove the disc brake caliper assembly and position it aside. Remove the rotor. Remove the parking brake shoe assembly, then remove the cable from its mounting.

6. Installation is the reverse of the removal procedure. Adjust the parking brake, as required.

Brake System Bleeding

1. Clean all dirt from around the master cylinder reservoir cap.

2. If a bleeder tank is used, follow the manufacturer's instruction.

3. Remove the filler cap and fill the master cylinder reservoir to the lower edge of the filler neck.

4. Clean off the bleeder connections at all of the wheel cylinders and disc brake calipers. Attach a bleeder hose and fixture to the right wheel cylinder bleeder screw and place the end of the hose in a suitable glass jar, submerged in clean brake fluid.

5. Open the bleeder valve ½–¾ of a turn. Have an assistant depress the brake pedal and allow it to return slowly. Continue this pumping action, stopping with each up and down motion, to force any air from the system.

6. When bubbles cease to appear at the end of the bleeder hose, close the bleeder valve and remove the hose. Check the level of the brake fluid in the master cylinder reservoir and add fluid, if necessary.

7. After the bleeding operation at each caliper or wheel cylinder has been completed, fill the master cylinder reservoir and replace the filler cap.

Anti-Lock Brake System Service

Precaution

Failure to observe the following precautions may result in system damage.

• Before preforming any arc welding on the vehicle, disconnect the Electronic Brake Control Module.

• When preforming painting work on the vehicle, do not expose the Electronic Brake Control Module to temperatures in excess of 185°F (85°C) for longer than 2 hrs.

• Never disconnect or connect Electronic Brake Control Module or its components connectors with the ignition switch ON.

• Never disassemble any component of the Anti-Lock Brake System (ABS) which is designated non-serviceable; the component must be replaced as an assembly.

Relieving Anti-Lock Brake System Pressure

NOTE: Unless otherwise specified, the hydraulic accumulator should be depressurized before disassembling any portion of the hydraulic system.

1. With the ignition switch in the OFF position and the battery negative cable disconnected, pump the brake pedal a minimum of 25 times using approximately 50 lbs. of pedal force. When a noticeable change in pedal feel occurs, the accumulator is discharged.

2. When a definite increase in pedal effort is felt, stroke the pedal a few additional times.

Hydraulic Unit

Removal and Installation

1. Disconnect the battery negative cable.
2. Depressurize the Anti-Lock system brake pressure.
3. Disconnect the connectors from the hydraulic unit.
4. Disconnect and plug the brake lines and hoses from the hydraulic unit.
5. Remove the hydraulic unit attaching bolt and the hydraulic unit from the vehicle.

Speed Sensor and Sensor Rotor

Removal and Installation
FRONT
626 and MX-6

1. Disconnect the battery negative cable and depressurize the brake system.
2. Raise and safely support the vehicle. Remove the tire and wheel assembly.
3. Remove the speed sensor bolts and the speed sensor from the vehicle. Remove the hub dust cap and locknut. Remove the halfshaft.
4. Place the halfshaft into a vise. Using a prybar, remove the sensor rotor from the halfshaft.
5. Reverse procedure to install. Torque hub nut to 174–235 ft. lbs. (235–319 Nm).

929

1. Disconnect the battery negative cable and depressurize the brake system.
2. Raise and safely support the vehicle. Remove the tire and wheel assembly.
3. Remove the caliper, hub dust cap and the hub nut and washer.
4. Remove the rotor and the sensor rotor from the rotor.
5. Remove the speed sensor bolt and the speed sensor from the vehicle.
6. Reverse procedure to install. Torque the hub nut to 72–130 ft. lbs. (98–177 Nm).

RX-7

1. Disconnect the battery negative cable and depressurize the brake system.
2. Raise and safely support the vehicle. Remove the tire and wheel assembly.
3. Disconnect and plug the brake line from the caliper and remove the caliper.
4. Remove the hub dust cap, cotter pin, locknut and washer. Remove the rotor screw and the rotor.
5. Remove the hub bearing, race and the hub. Remove the sensor rotor.
6. Remove the speed sensor bolt and the speed sensor.
7. Reverse procedure to install. Torque hub nut to 174–231 ft. lbs. (235–314 Nm).

REAR
626 and MX-6

1. Disconnect the battery negative cable, depressurize brake system. Raise and safely support the vehicle.
2. Remove the tire and wheel assembly.
3. Remove the hub dust cap and locknut.
4. Remove the caliper from the rotor; do not disconnect the brake hose and position aside.
5. Remove the rotor and the sensor rotor from the rotor.
6. Remove the speed sensor bolt and the speed sensor.
7. Reverse procedure to install. Torque the locknut to 72–130 ft. lbs. (98–177 Nm).

RX-7

1. Disconnect the battery negative cable, depressurize brake system. Raise and safely support the vehicle.
2. Remove the tire and wheel assembly.
3. Disconnet the parking brake cable. Remove the caliper; do not disconnect the brake line.
4. Remove the hub nut, rotor screw and the rotor from the vehicle.
5. Remove the speed sensor bolt and the speed sensor.
6. Remove the hub-to-hub control assembly bolts and the hub. Remove the sensor rotor from the hub.
7. Reverse procedure to install. Torque the hub nut to 174–231 ft. lbs. (235–314 Nm).

929

1. Disconnect the battery negative cable, depressurize brake system. Raise and safely support the vehicle.
2. Remove the tire and wheel assembly.
3. Remove the driveshaft nut and washer and the driveshaft from the vehicle.
4. Remove the speed sensor bolt and the speed sensor from the vehicle.
5. Place the driveshaft in a vise. Using a prybar, remove the sensor rotor from the driveshaft.
6. Reverse procedure to install. Torque driveshaft nut to 174–231 ft. lbs. (235–314 Nm).

FRONT SUSPENSION

MacPherson Strut

Removal and Installation

1. Unfasten the nuts which secure the upper strut mount to the top of the wheel arch. If equipped, remove the Adjustable Shock Aborbers (ASA) rubber cap, electrical connectors and actuator assembly from its mounting before removing the strut retaining nuts.

2. Raise and support the vehicle safely. Remove the tire and wheel assembly.
3. As required, remove the disc brake caliper. Remove the brake line clip from the strut assembly. If equipped, remove the ABS harness bracket.
4. Unfasten the 2 bolts that secure the lower end of the strut to the steering knuckle arm.
5. Remove the strut assembly from the vehicle.
6. Installation is the reverse of the removal procedure. Install

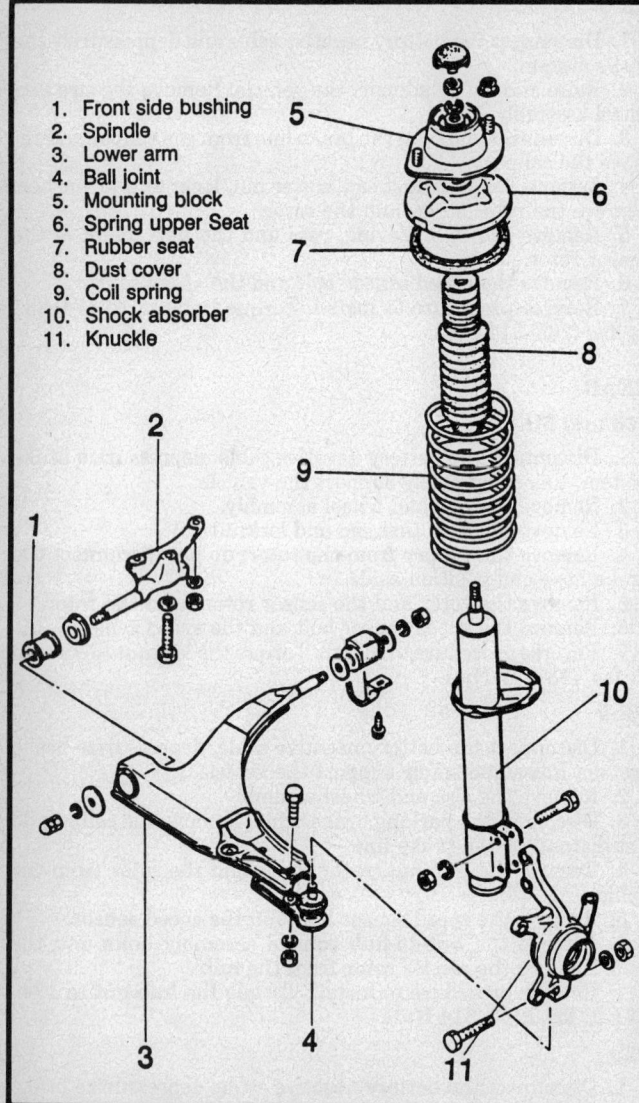

1. Front side bushing
2. Spindle
3. Lower arm
4. Ball joint
5. Mounting block
6. Spring upper Seat
7. Rubber seat
8. Dust cover
9. Coil spring
10. Shock absorber
11. Knuckle

Typical front suspension assembly—front wheel drive vehicles

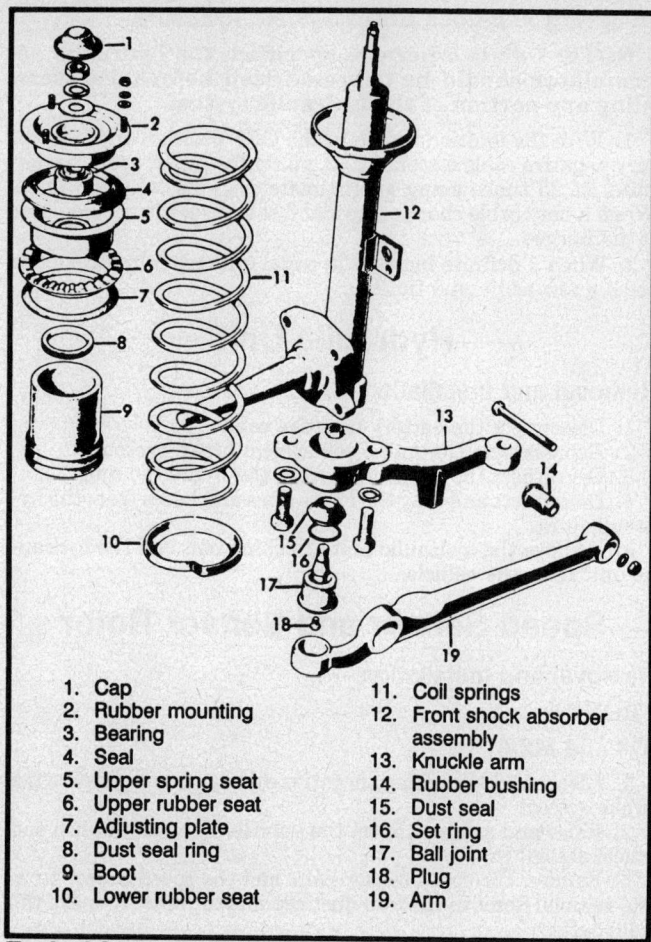

1. Cap
2. Rubber mounting
3. Bearing
4. Seal
5. Upper spring seat
6. Upper rubber seat
7. Adjusting plate
8. Dust seal ring
9. Boot
10. Lower rubber seat
11. Coil springs
12. Front shock absorber assembly
13. Knuckle arm
14. Rubber bushing
15. Dust seal
16. Set ring
17. Ball joint
18. Plug
19. Arm

Typical front suspension assembly—rear wheel drive vehicles

the strut mounting block so the white paint mark faces the inside of the vehicle.

Upper Ball Joints

Inspection

MIATA

With the upper control arm removed from the vehicle, connect a suitable pull scale to the ball joint stud. Pull the spring scale until the arm just begins to turn. Spring scale should read 2.9–8.8 lbs. (3.9–11.8 N).

Removal and Installation

Replacement of the ball joint dust boot is accomplished by removing the upper control arm from the vehicle and chiseling the off old boot. Coat the inside of the new dust boot with lithium grease and press it into the ball joint using the proper tool. Check the ball joint stud threads for damage and repair, as necessary. Check the ball joint preload and install the lower control arm by reversing the removal procedure.

Lower Ball Joints

Inspection

1. Raise and support the vehicle safely. Remove the wheel.
2. Remove the cotter pin and nut, which secure the tie rod end, from the knuckle arm, then use a puller to separate them.
3. Unbolt the lower end of the shock absorber.
4. Remove the nut, then withdraw the rubber bushing and washer which secure the stabilizer bar to the control arm.
5. Unfasten the nut and bolt which secure the control arm to the frame member.
6. Check the ball joint dust boot.
7. Shake the ball joint stud a couple of times before measuring the preload. Check the amount of pressure required to turn the ball stud, by hooking a pull scale into the tie rod hole in the knuckle arm. On RX-7, a special attachment tool 49–0180–510B must be installed onto the ball joint stud and then the spring scale is connected to the loop on the attachment. Pull the spring scale until the arm just begins to turn, this should require 4.4–7.7 lbs. on the 626, MX-6 and RX-7, 1–2.2 lbs. on the 1987 323, 4.0–6.8 lbs. on 1988–91 323 and Protege, 1.1–2.6 lbs. on the 929 or 1.7–3.3 lbs. on the Miata.
8. If specification is not as indicated, replace the ball joint.

Removal and Installation

RX-7

1. Raise and support the vehicle safely. Remove the control arm.

2. Remove the set ring and the dust boot.

3. Press the ball joint out of the control arm.

4. Clean the ball joint mounting bore and coat the inside of the new ball joint dust boot with lithium grease.

5. Press the ball joint into the control arm use the appropriate tool.

NOTE: If the pressure required to press the new ball joint into place is less than 3300 lbs., the bore is worn and the control arm must be replaced.

Except RX-7

Replacement of the ball joint dust boot is accomplished by removing the lower control arm from the vehicle and chiseling the off old boot. Coat the inside of the new dust boot with lithium grease and press it into the ball joint using the proper tool. Check the ball joint stud threads for damage and repair, as necessary. Check the ball joint preload and install the lower control arm by reversing the removal procedure.

NOTE: If replacement of the ball joint is required, the entire lower control arm assembly must be replaced.

Upper Control Arms

Removal and Installation

MIATA

1. Raise and safely support the vehicle.

2. Remove the engine undercover.

3. Remove the tire and wheel assembly.

4. Using tool 49–0118–850C, separate the ball joint from the steering knuckle.

5. Remove the lower shock absorber nut and the upper control arm through bolt. Remove the upper control arm and bushings from the vehicle.

6. Reverse procedure to install. Torque through bolt to 75–102 ft. lbs. (102–138 Nm) and ball joint nut to 30–46 ft. lbs. (41–62 Nm).

Lower Control Arms

Removal and Installation

RX-7

1. Raise the vehicle and support it safely.

2. Remove the lower splash shield.

3. Disconnect the front stabilizer link from the control arm.

4. Remove the pinch bolt, then separate the lower ball joint from the steering knuckle.

5. Remove the front control arm mounting bolt.

6. Remove the control arm bushing bracket bolts and lower the control arm from the vehicle.

7. Installation is the reverse of removal. Check the ball joint preload and inspect the dust boot for damage. Check the front end alignment after the installation is complete.

323, PROTEGE, 626 AND MX-6

1. Raise and support the vehicle safely. Remove the tire and wheel assembly.

2. Remove the splash shield. If equipped, remove the compression rod bolts.

3. Remove the stabilizer link from the control arm through bolt. Remove the lower control arm-to-frame bolts.

4. Properly support the control arm assembly. Remove the pinch bolt and separate the ball joint from the steering knuckle.

5. Remove the lower control arm. On 1988–90 626 and MX-6, disconnect the lower arm spindle from the lower arm first and then remove the lower arm.

6. Installation is the reverse of the removal procedure. When

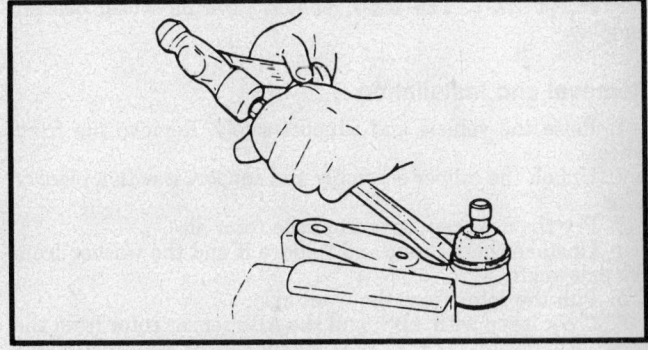

Ball joint dust boot removal

tightening of the lower control bolts and nuts is required, lower the vehicle and then tighten the bolts and nuts. The vehicle must be unloaded. On 1988–90 626 and MX-6, tighten the link nut until approximately 0.8 in. of the through bolt is exposed.

929

1. Raise and support the vehicle safely. Remove the tire and wheel assembly.

2. Remove the stabilizer link assembly. Remove the tie rod end from its mounting.

3. Remove the compression rod bolts. Position the compression rod assembly aside.

4. Remove the knuckle arm. Properly support the lower control arm.

5. Remove the lower control arm bolt and the lower control arm from the vehicle.

6. Installation is the reverse of the removal procedure.

Stabilizer Bar

Removal and Installation

1. Raise and safely support the vehicle.

2. Remove the stabilizer bracket bolts and stabilizer control link bolts.

3. On 323 and Protege, remove the stabilizer bar-to-steering gear box bolts.

4. Remove the stabilizer bar from the vehicle.

5. Reverse procedure to install. On Miata and RX-7, torque stabilizer mounting bolts to 13–20 ft. lbs. (18–26 Nm) and the stabilizer control link bolts to 27–40 ft. lbs. (36–54 Nm) on Miata or 27–37 ft. lbs. (36–50 Nm) on RX-7. On 626 and MX-6, torque stabilizer mounting bolts to 27–40 ft. lbs. (36–54 Nm), and tighten the control link nuts so there is 0.71–0.87 in. of thread exposed. On 929, torque the stabilizer mounting bolts to 37–45 ft. lbs. (50–61 Nm) and the control link nuts so there is 0.59 in. (15mm) of thread exposed. On 323 and Protege, torque the stabilizer bar mounting bolts to 69–93 ft. lbs. (93–127 Nm), the stabilizer nut so 0.067–0.75 in. (17–19mm) of thread is exposed and the stabilizer bar to steering gear box to 27–38 ft. lbs. (37–52 Nm).

Front Wheel Bearings

Adjustment

1. Raise and support the vehicle safely. Remove the tire and wheel assembly.

2. Remove the caliper assembly and position it aside.

3. Position a dial indicator gauge against the dust cap. Push and pull the disc in the axial direction.

4. Measure the endplay of the wheel bearing. If endplay is greater than specification, replace the wheel bearing.

5. Wheel bearing endplay should not exceed 0.002 in. on vehi-

cles except RX-7. The RX-7, should have no wheel bearing endplay.

Removal and Installation

1. Raise the vehicle and support safely. Remove the front wheels.
2. Unbolt the caliper assembly and support it with a piece of wire.
3. Pry the dust cap loose from the rotor disc.
4. Unstake the locknut and remove it and the washer from the axle shaft.
5. Pull the rotor from the front axle.
6. If equipped with ABS, pull the ABS sensor rotor from the disc using a 2-jawed puller. Remove the oil seal.
7. Remove the bearing retaining ring. Using tools 49–B001–797 and 49–H033–101, press the front wheel bearing from the disc.
8. Press the ABS sensor rotor into the disc using the proper tool. Press the rotor in evenly to avoid damaging the teeth.
9. Press the bearing into the disc using the proper tool. Install the bearing retainer.
10. Install a new oil seal and coat the lip of the seal with grease. Complete the installation of the disc in reverse of the removal procedure. Torque the disc locknut to 72–130 ft. lbs. Adjust the bearing preload and check the endplay. Wheel bearing endplay should exceed 0.002 in. except RX-7; RX-7, should have no wheel bearing endplay.

REAR SUSPENSION

MacPherson Strut

Removal and Installation
EXCEPT RX-7 AND MIATA

1. As required, remove the side trim panels from the inside of the trunk or the rear seat and trim; then, loosen and remove the top mounting nuts from the strut mounting block assembly.
2. Raise the vehicle and safely support it safely. Remove the tire and wheel assemblies, as required to gain working clearance.
3. Remove the rubber protective cover and than disconnect and remove the Adjustable Shock Absorber (ASA) assembly. Remove the top strut retaining bolts. Disconnect the flexible brake hose and clip from the strut. On 626 and MX-6, remove the ABS harness/bracket assembly and the trunk side trim.
4. As required, disconnect the trailing arm from the lower side of the strut. Separate the lateral link and strut by removing the bolt assembly. On 626 and MX-6 disconnect the strut bar from the strut bar bracket and remove the strut bar bracket from the strut cap.
5. Remove the lower strut retaining bolts. On 626 and MX-6 with 2 wheel steering, remove the upper cap nuts also. Remove the strut assembly from the vehicle.
6. Installation is the reverse of the removal procedure.

RX-7 AND MIATA

1. Raise the the vehicle and support it safely.
2. Remove the 2 top strut flange mounting bolts, actuator, nut and actuator bracket.
3. Remove the bottom strut absorber bolt, the strut and spring assembly from the vehicle. If equipped, disconnect the electrical connector from the strut assembly.
4. Installation is the reverse of the removal procedure.

Rear Control Arms

Removal and Installation

1. Raise and safely support the vehicle.
2. Remove the tire and wheel assembly.
3. Remove the shock absorber bolt. Remove the stabilizer control link bolt, if equipped.
4. Remove the control arm(s) bolts and the control arm(s) from the vehicle.
5. Reverse procedure to install.

Rear Wheel Bearings

Removal and Installation

1. Raise and support the vehicle safely. Remove the tire and wheel assembly.
2. Remove the rear brake drum or rotor and lift out the bearing cage assembly. Remove the bearing retainer, as required.
3. Use a blunt drift to knock the bearing race out, then press in a new race using a bench press and suitable mandrel.
4. Continue the installation in the reverse of the removal procedure. Replace the oil seal, as required.

Adjustment
626 AND MX-6

1. Raise and support the vehicle safely. Remove the tire and wheel assembly.
2. Remove and properly support the caliper assembly.
3. Position a dial indicator gauge against the dust cap. Push and pull the disc brake rotor or brake drum in the axial direction and measure the endplay of the wheel bearing.
4. Endplay should be 0.0079 in. Correct by replacing the wheel bearing.

323 AND PROTEGE

1. Raise and support the vehicle safely. Remove the tire and wheel assembly.
2. Remove the dust cap and torque the locknut to 18–21 ft. lbs.
3. Turn the wheel assembly to seat the bearing properly. Loosen the locknut until it can be turned by hand.
4. Hook a spring seal to a wheel lug stud in order to measure the oil seal drag. Pull the spring scale squarely.
5. Take the oil seal drag value when the wheel hub starts to turn and record the measurement.
6. Add the oil seal drag value to the standard bearing preload of 0.6–1.9 lbs. Turn the locknut slowly until the standard bearing preload is obtained.

Rear Axle Assembly

Removal and Installation

1. Raise and safely support the vehicle.
2. Remove the tire and wheel assembly.
3. Remove the hub dust cap and locknut and disconnect the parking brake cable.
4. Remove the caliper, rotor and the dust cover.
5. If equipped with drum brakes, remove the backing plate with shoes as an assembly.
6. Disconnect the control arms. Remove the stabilizer bar bracket, if equipped.
7. If equipped with ABS, disconnect the speed sensor.
8. Remove the tie-rod and shock absorber and the knuckle spindle from the vehicle.
9. Reverse procedure to install. Torque the hub locknut to 73–130 ft. lbs. (98–117 Nm) for the 626 and MX-6 or 130–174 ft. lbs. (177–235 Nm) for the 323 and Protege.

SERIAL NUMBER IDENTIFICATION

Vehicle Identification Plate

The Vehicle Identification Plate is located in the left window post and consists of a 17 digit number.

Engine Number

The Engine Number is located in rear of the engine block and consists of a 10 digit number.

Transmission Number

Mercedes-Benz vehicles for the U.S. market have been equipped with either a 5 speed manual transmission or with a fully automatic 4 speed unit. The automatic transmissions are equipped with a torque converter.

Serial numbers on the manual transmission are located on a pad on the side cover of the transmission (left side).

Automatic transmission serial numbers are located on a metal plate which is attached to the driver's side of the transmission.

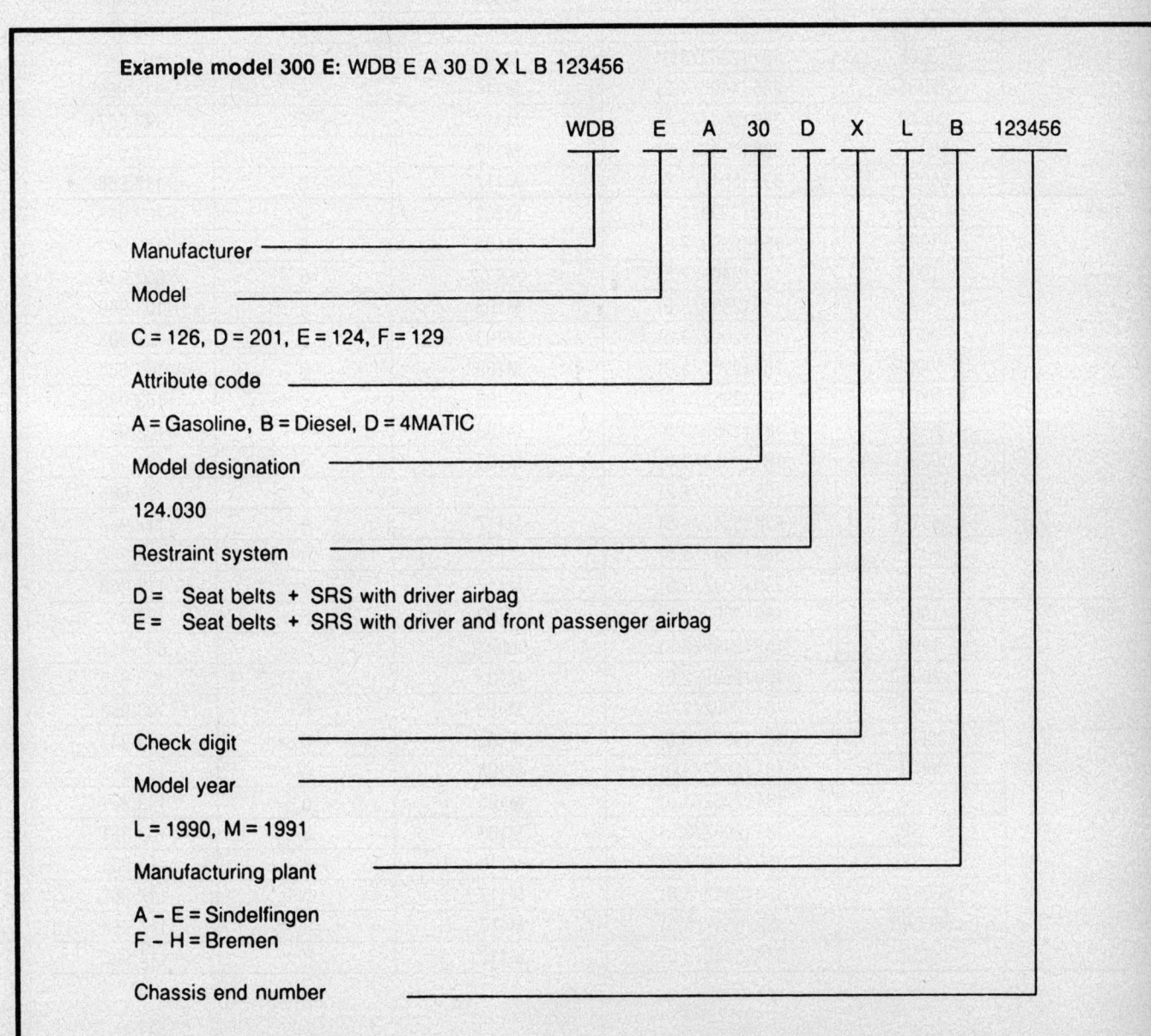

Example model 300 E: WDB E A 30 D X L B 123456

| WDB | E | A | 30 | D | X | L | B | 123456 |

Manufacturer

Model

C = 126, D = 201, E = 124, F = 129

Attribute code

A = Gasoline, B = Diesel, D = 4MATIC

Model designation

124.030

Restraint system

D = Seat belts + SRS with driver airbag
E = Seat belts + SRS with driver and front passenger airbag

Check digit

Model year

L = 1990, M = 1991

Manufacturing plant

A – E = Sindelfingen
F – H = Bremen

Chassis end number

SPECIFICATIONS

ENGINE IDENTIFICATION

Year	Model	Engine Displacement cu. in. (cc/liter)	Engine Series Identification	No. of Cylinders	Engine Type
1987	190D	152 (2497/2.5)	OM602	5	602.911
	190D	152 (2497/2.5)	OM602	5	602.961
	190E	140 (2299/2.3)	M102	4	102.985
	190E	159 (2599/2.6)	M103	6	103.942
	190E-16	140 (2299/2.3)	M102	4	102.983
	260E	159 (2599/2.6)	M103	6	103.940
	300D	183 (2996/3.0)	M603	6	603.962
	300SDL	183 (2996/3.0)	M603	6	603.961
	300TD	183 (2996/3.0)	M603	6	603.962
	300E	181 (2962/3.0)	M103	6	103.983
	420SEL	256 (4196/4.2)	M116	8	116.965
	560SL	338 (5547/5.6)	M117	8	117.967
	560SEC	338 (5547/5.6)	M117	8	117.968
	560SEL	338 (5547/5.6)	M117	8	117.968
1988	190E	140 (2299/2.3)	M102	4	102.985
	190E	159 (2599/2.6)	M103	6	103.942
	190D	152 (2497/2.5)	OM602	5	602.911
	260E	159 (2599/2.6)	M103	6	103.940
	300E	181 (2962/3.0)	M103	6	103.983
	300CE	181 (2962/3.0)	M103	6	103.983
	300TE	181 (2962/3.0)	M103	6	103.983
	300SE	181 (2962/3.0)	M103	6	103.981
	300SEL	181 (2962/3.0)	M103	6	103.981
	420SEL	256 (4196/4.2)	M116	8	116.965
	560SEL	338 (5547/5.6)	M117	8	117.967
	560SEC	338 (5547/5.6)	M117	8	117.968
	560SL	338 (5547/5.6)	M117	8	117.968
1989	190E	159 (2599/2.6)	M103	6	103.942
	190D	152 (2497/2.5)	OM602	5	602.911
	260E	159 (2599/2.6)	M103	6	103.940
	300E	181 (2962/3.0)	M103	6	103.983
	300CE	181 (2962/3.0)	M103	6	103.983
	300TE	181 (2962/3.0)	M103	6	103.983
	300SE	181 (2962/3.0)	M103	6	103.981
	300SEL	181 (2962/3.0)	M103	6	103.981
	420SEL	256 (4196/4.2)	M116	8	116.965
	560SEL	338 (5547/5.6)	M117	8	117.967
	560SEC	338 (5547/5.6)	M117	8	117.968
	560SL	338 (5547/5.6)	M117	8	117.968

ENGINE IDENTIFICATION

Year	Model	Engine Displacement cu. in. (cc/liter)	Engine Series Identification	No. of Cylinders	Engine Type
1990–91	190E	159 (2599/2.6)	M103	6	103.942
	300E	181 (2962/3.0)	M103	6	103.983
	300CE	181 (2962/3.0)	M103	6	104.980
	300SE	181 (2962/3.0)	M103	6	103.981
	300SL	181 (2962/3.0)	M104	6	104.981
	300TE	181 (2962/3.0)	M103	6	103.983
	300SEL	181 (2962/3.0)	M103	6	103.981
	420SEL	256 (4196/4.2)	M116	8	116.965
	500SL	304 (4973/5.0)	M119	8	119.960
	560SEC	338 (5547/5.6)	M117	8	117.968
	560SEL	338 (5547/5.6)	M117	8	117.968

GENERAL ENGINE SPECIFICATIONS

Year	Model	Engine Displacement cu. in. (cc)	Fuel System Type	Net Horsepower @ rpm	Net Torque @ rpm (ft. lbs.)	Bore × Stroke (in.)	Compression Ratio	Oil Pressure @ 2000 rpm
1987	190D	152 (2497)	DFI	93 @ 4600	122 @ 2400	3.43 × 3.31	22:1	55
	190D	152 (2497)	Turbo	123 @ 4600	168 @ 2400	3.43 × 3.31	22:1	55
	190E	140 (2299)	CIS	130 @ 5100	146 @ 3600	3.76 × 3.16	9.0:1	55
	190E	159 (2599)	CIS	158 @ 5800	162 @ 4600	3.26 × 3.16	9.2:1	55
	190E-16	140 (2299)	CIS	167 @ 5800	162 @ 4750	3.76 × 3.16	9.7:1	55
	260E	159 (2599)	CIS	158 @ 5800	162 @ 4600	3.26 × 3.16	9.2:1	55
	300D	181 (2962)	Turbo	148 @ 4600	201 @ 2400	3.43 × 3.31	22:1	55
	300E	183 (2996)	CIS	177 @ 5700	188 @ 4400	3.48 × 3.16	9.2:1	55
	300SDL	183 (2996)	Turbo	148 @ 4600	201 @ 2400	3.43 × 3.31	22:1	55
	300TD	183 (2996)	Turbo	148 @ 4600	201 @ 2400	3.43 × 3.31	22:1	55
	420SEL	256 (4196)	CIS	201 @ 5200	228 @ 3600	3.62 × 3.11	9.0:1	55
	560SEL	338 (5547)	CIS	227 @ 4750	279 @ 3250	3.80 × 3.73	9.0:1	55
	560SEC	338 (5547)	CIS	238 @ 4800	287 @ 3500	3.80 × 3.73	9.0:1	55
	560SEL	338 (5547)	CIS	238 @ 3500	287 @ 3500	3.80 × 3.73	9.0:1	55
1988	190D	152 (2497)	DFI	93 @ 4600	122 @ 2400	3.43 × 3.31	22:1	55
	190E	140 (2299)	CIS	130 @ 5100	146 @ 3500	3.76 × 3.16	9.0:1	55
	190E	159 (2599)	CIS	158 @ 5800	162 @ 4600	3.26 × 3.16	9.2:1	55
	260E	159 (2599)	CIS	158 @ 5800	162 @ 4600	3.26 × 3.16	9.2:1	55
	300E	181 (2962)	CIS	177 @ 5700	188 @ 4400	3.48 × 3.16	9.2:1	55
	300CE	181 (2962)	CIS	177 @ 5700	188 @ 4400	3.48 × 3.16	9.2:1	55
	300SE	181 (2962)	CIS	177 @ 5700	188 @ 4400	3.48 × 3.16	9.2:1	55
	300SEL	181 (2962)	CIS	177 @ 5700	188 @ 4400	3.48 × 3.16	9.2:1	55
	300TE	181 (2962)	CIS	177 @ 5700	188 @ 4400	3.48 × 3.16	9.2:1	55
	420SEL	256 (4196)	CIS	201 @ 5200	228 @ 3600	3.62 × 3.11	9.0:1	55
	560SEC	338 (5547)	CIS	238 @ 4800	287 @ 3500	3.80 × 3.73	9.0:1	55
	560SEL	338 (5547)	CIS	238 @ 4800	287 @ 3500	3.80 × 3.73	9.0:1	55
	560SL	338 (5547)	CIS	227 @ 4750	279 @ 3250	3.80 × 3.73	9.0:1	55

MERCEDES-BENZ
190 • 260 • 300 • 420 • 500 • 560

GENERAL ENGINE SPECIFICATIONS

Year	Model	Engine Displacement cu. in. (cc)	Fuel System Type	Net Horsepower @ rpm	Net Torque @ rpm (ft. lbs.)	Bore × Stroke (in.)	Compression Ratio	Oil Pressure @ 2000 rpm
1989	190D	152 (2497)	DFI	93 @ 4600	122 @ 2400	3.43 × 3.31	22:1	55
	190E	159 (2599)	CIS	158 @ 5800	162 @ 4600	3.26 × 3.16	9.2:1	55
	260E	159 (2599)	CIS	158 @ 5800	162 @ 4600	3.26 × 3.16	9.2:1	55
	300E	181 (2962)	CIS	177 @ 5700	188 @ 4400	3.48 × 3.16	9.2:1	55
	300CE	181 (2962)	CIS	177 @ 5700	188 @ 4400	3.48 × 3.16	9.2:1	55
	300SE	181 (2962)	CIS	177 @ 5700	188 @ 4400	3.48 × 3.16	9.2:1	55
	300SEL	181 (2962)	CIS	177 @ 5700	188 @ 4400	3.48 × 3.16	9.2:1	55
	300TE	181 (2962)	CIS	177 @ 5700	188 @ 4400	3.48 × 3.16	9.2:1	55
	420SEL	256 (4196)	CIS	201 @ 5200	228 @ 3600	3.62 × 3.11	9.0:1	55
	560SEC	338 (5547)	CIS	238 @ 4800	287 @ 3500	3.80 × 3.73	9.0:1	55
	560SEL	338 (5547)	CIS	238 @ 4800	287 @ 3500	3.80 × 3.73	9.0:1	55
	560SL	338 (5547)	CIS	227 @ 4750	279 @ 3250	3.80 × 3.73	9.0:1	55
1990–91	190E	159 (2599)	CIS	158 @ 5800	162 @ 4600	3.26 × 3.16	9.2:1	55
	300E	181 (2962)	CIS	177 @ 5700	188 @ 4400	3.48 × 3.16	9.2:1	55
	300CE	181 (2962)	CIS	177 @ 5700	188 @ 4400	3.48 × 3.16	9.2:1	55
	300SE	181 (2962)	CIS	177 @ 5700	188 @ 4400	3.48 × 3.16	9.2:1	55
	300SL	181 (2962)	CIS	228 @ 6300	201 @ 4600	3.48 × 3.16	10.0:1	55
	300TE	181 (2962)	CIS	177 @ 5700	188 @ 4400	3.48 × 3.16	9.2:1	55
	300SEL	181 (2962)	CIS	177 @ 5700	188 @ 4400	3.48 × 3.16	9.2:1	55
	420SEL	256 (4196)	CIS	201 @ 5200	228 @ 3600	3.62 × 3.11	9.0:1	55
	500SL	304 (4973)	CIS	322 @ 5500	332 @ 4000	3.80 × 3.35	10.0:1	55
	560SEC	338 (5547)	CIS	238 @ 4800	287 @ 3500	3.80 × 3.73	9.0:1	55
	560SEL	338 (5547)	CIS	238 @ 4800	287 @ 3500	3.80 × 3.73	9.0:1	55

GASOLINE ENGINE TUNE-UP SPECIFICATIONS

Year	Model	Engine Displacement cu. in. (cc)	Spark Plugs Type	Gap (in.)	Ignition Timing (deg.) MT	Ignition Timing (deg.) AT	Compression Pressure (psi)	Fuel Pump (psi)	Idle Speed (rpm) MT	Idle Speed (rpm) AT	Valve Clearance In.	Valve Clearance Ex.
1987	190E	140 (2299)	S9YC	.032	10B	10B	125	91–94	750	750	Hyd.	Hyd.
	190E	159 (2599)	S12YC	.032	9B	9B	125	91–94	700	700	Hyd.	Hyd.
	190E-16	140 (2299)	S7YC	.032	TDC	TDC	125	91–94	890	890	.006	.012
	260E	159 (2599)	S12YC	.032	9B	9B	125	91–94	700	700	Hyd.	Hyd.
	300E	181 (2962)	S9YC	.032	TDC	TDC	125	91–94	650	650	Hyd.	Hyd.
	420SEL	256 (4196)	N9YC	.032	—	5B	125	91–94	650	650	Hyd.	Hyd.
	560SL	338 (5547)	N9YC	.032	—	5B	125	91–94	650	650	Hyd.	Hyd.
	560SEC	338 (5547)	N9YC	.032	—	5B	125	91–94	650	650	Hyd.	Hyd.
	560SEL	338 (5547)	N9YC	.032	—	5B	125	91–94	650	650	Hyd.	Hyd.
1988	190E	140 (2299)	S9YC	.032	10B	10B	125	91–94	750	750	Hyd.	Hyd.
	190E	159 (2599)	S12YC	.032	9B	9B	125	91–94	700	700	Hyd.	Hyd.
	260E	159 (2599)	S12YC	.032	9B	9B	125	91–94	700	700	Hyd.	Hyd.
	300E	181 (2962)	S9YC	.032	TDC	TDC	125	91–94	650	650	Hyd.	Hyd.

GASOLINE ENGINE TUNE-UP SPECIFICATIONS

Year	Model	Engine Displacement cu. in. (cc)	Spark Plugs Type	Gap (in.)	Ignition Timing (deg.) MT	AT	Compression Pressure (psi)	Fuel Pump (psi)	Idle Speed (rpm) MT	AT	Valve Clearance In.	Ex.
	300CE	181 (2962)	S9YC	.032	—	TDC	125	91–94	—	650	Hyd.	Hyd.
	300SE	181 (2962)	S9YC	.032	—	TDC	125	91–94	—	650	Hyd.	Hyd.
	300SEL	181 (2962)	S9YC	.032	—	TDC	125	91–94	—	650	Hyd.	Hyd.
	300TE	181 (2962)	S9YC	.032	—	TDC	125	91–94	—	650	Hyd.	Hyd.
	420SEL	256 (4196)	N9YC	.032	—	TDC	125	91–94	—	650	Hyd.	Hyd.
	560SEC	338 (5547)	N9YC	.032	—	TDC	125	91–94	—	650	Hyd.	Hyd.
	560SEL	338 (5547)	N9YC	.032	—	TDC	125	91–94	—	650	Hyd.	Hyd.
	560SL	338 (5547)	N9YC	.032	—	TDC	125	91–94	—	650	Hyd.	Hyd.
1989	190E	159 (2599)	S12YC	.032	9B	9B	125	91–94	700	700	Hyd.	Hyd.
	260E	159 (2599)	S12YC	.032	9B	9B	125	91–94	700	700	Hyd.	Hyd.
	300E	181 (2962)	S9YC	.032	TDC	TDC	125	91–94	650	650	Hyd.	Hyd.
	300CE	181 (2962)	S9YC	.032	—	TDC	125	91–94	—	650	Hyd.	Hyd.
	300SE	181 (2962)	S9YC	.032	—	TDC	125	91–94	—	650	Hyd.	Hyd.
	300SEL	181 (2962)	S9YC	.032	—	TDC	125	91–94	—	650	Hyd.	Hyd.
	300TE	181 (2962)	S9YC	.032	—	TDC	125	91–94	—	650	Hyd.	Hyd.
	420SEL	256 (4196)	N9YC	.032	—	TDC	125	91–94	—	650	Hyd.	Hyd.
	560SEC	338 (5547)	N9YC	.032	—	TDC	125	91–94	—	650	Hyd.	Hyd.
	560SEL	338 (5547)	N9YC	.032	—	TDC	125	91–94	—	650	Hyd.	Hyd.
	560SL	338 (5547)	N9YC	.032	—	TDC	125	91–94	—	650	Hyd.	Hyd.
1990–91	190E	159 (2599)	S12YC	.032	9B	9B	125	91–94	700	700	Hyd.	Hyd.
	300E	181 (2962)	S9YC	.032	—	TDC	125	91–94	—	650	Hyd.	Hyd.
	300CE	181 (2962)	S9YC	.032	—	TDC	125	91–94	—	650	Hyd.	Hyd.
	300SE	181 (2962)	S9YC	.032	—	TDC	125	91–94	—	650	Hyd.	Hyd.
	300SL	181 (2962)	C12YCC	.032	TDC	TDC	125	91–94	—	—	Hyd.	Hyd.
	300TE	181 (2962)	S9YC	.032	—	TDC	125	91–94	—	650	Hyd.	Hyd.
	300SEL	181 (2962)	S9YC	.032	—	TDC	125	91–94	—	650	Hyd.	Hyd.
	420SEL	256 (4196)	N9YC	.032	—	TDC	125	91–94	—	650	Hyd.	Hyd.
	500SL	304 (4973)	C10YCC	.032	—	TDC	125	91–94	—	700	Hyd.	Hyd.
	560SEC	338 (5547)	N9YC	.032	—	TDC	125	91–94	—	650	Hyd.	Hyd.
	560SEL	338 (5547)	N9YC	.032	—	TDC	125	91–94	—	650	Hyd.	Hyd.

DIESEL ENGINE TUNE-UP SPECIFICATIONS

Year	Engine Displacement cu. in. (cc)	Valve Clearance Intake Type	Exhaust (in.)	Intake Valve Opens (deg.)	Injection Pump Setting (deg.)	Injection Nozzle Pressure (psi) New	Used	Idle Speed (rpm)	Cranking Compression Pressure (psi)
1987	152 (2497)	Hyd.	Hyd.	12A	15A	1564–2103	1740	660–700	284–327
	152 (2497)	Hyd.	Hyd.	12A	15A	1564–2103	1740	660–700	284–327
	183 (2996)	Hyd.	Hyd.	12A	15A	1958–2103	1740	610–650	284–327

DIESEL ENGINE TUNE-UP SPECIFICATIONS

Year	Engine Displacement cu. in. (cc)	Valve Clearance Intake Type	Exhaust (in.)	Intake Valve Opens (deg.)	Injection Pump Setting (deg.)	Injection Nozzle Pressure (psi) New	Used	Idle Speed (rpm)	Cranking Compression Pressure (psi)
	183 (2996)	Hyd.	Hyd.	12A	15A	1958–2103	1740	610–650	284–327
	183 (2996)	Hyd.	Hyd.	12A	15A	1958–2103	1740	610–650	284–327
1988	152 (2497)	Hyd.	Hyd.	12A	15A	1564–2103	1740	660–700	284–327
1989	152 (2497)	Hyd.	Hyd.	12A	15A	1564–2103	1740	660–700	284–327
1990	152 (2497)	Hyd.	Hyd.	12A	15A	1564–2103	1740	660–700	284–327

FIRING ORDERS

NOTE: To avoid confusion, always replace spark plug wires one at a time.

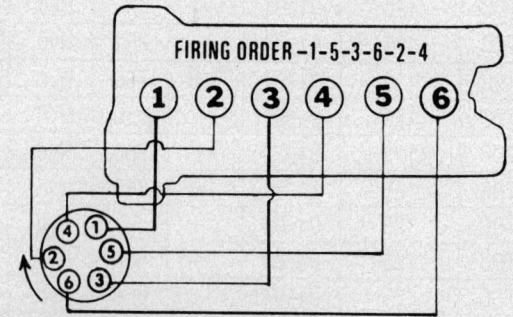

2.6L and 3.0L Gasoline Engine
Engine Firing Order: 1–5–3–6–2–4
Distributor Rotation: Counterclockwise

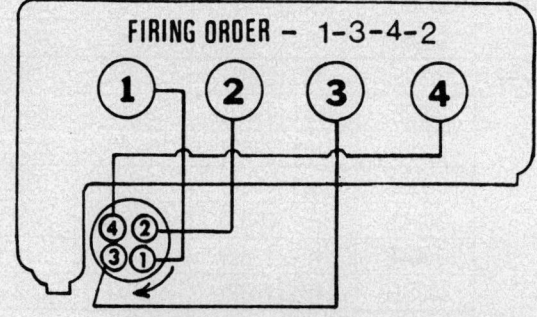

2.3L Gasoline Engine
Engine Firing Order: 1–3–4–2
Distributor Rotation: Counterclockwise

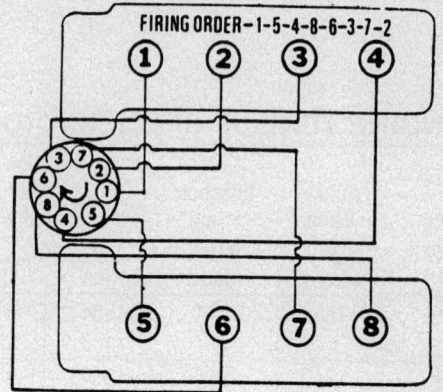

4.2L, 5.0L and 5.6L Gasoline Engine
Engine Firing Order: 1–5–4–8–6–3–7–2
Distributor Rotation: Counterclockwise

CAPACITIES

Year	Model	Engine Displacement cu. in. (cc)	Engine Crankcase with Filter	without Filter	Transmission (pts.) 4-Spd	5-Spd	Auto.	Drive Axle (pts.)	Fuel Tank (gal.)	Cooling System (qts.)
1987	190D	152 (2497)	8.0	7.5	—	3.2	11.6	1.5	14.5	8.5
	190E	140 (2299)	4.8	4.3	—	3.2	12.7	2.3	14.5	9.0
	190E	159 (2599)	6.4	5.9	—	3.2	12.7	2.3	14.5	9.5
	190E-16	140 (2299)	5.3	4.8	—	3.4	12.6	2.3	18.5	8.5
	260E	159 (2599)	6.4	5.9	—	3.2	13.1	2.3	18.5	9.5
	300E	181 (2962)	6.4	5.9	—	3.2	13.1	2.3	18.5	8.5
	300D	183 (2996)	8.5	8.0	—	—	13.1	2.3	18.5	10.6
	300TD	183 (2996)	8.5	8.0	—	—	13.1	2.3	19.0	10.6
	300SDL	183 (3996)	8.5	8.0	—	3.2	13.1	2.3	23.8	13.3
	420SEL	256 (4196)	8.5	8.0	—	—	16.2	2.7	23.8	13.8
	560SL	338 (5547)	8.5	8.0	—	—	16.2	2.7	22.4	13.8
	560SEL	338 (5547)	8.5	8.0	—	—	16.2	2.7	23.8	13.8
	560SEC	338 (5547)	8.5	8.0	—	—	16.2	2.7	23.8	13.8
1988	190D	152 (2497)	8.0	7.5	—	—	11.6	1.5	14.5	8.5
	190E	140 (2299)	4.8	4.3	—	3.2	12.7	2.2	14.5	9.0
	190E	159 (2599)	6.4	5.9	—	3.2	12.7	2.3	14.5	9.5
	260E	159 (2599)	6.4	5.9	—	3.2	13.1	2.3	18.5	9.5
	300E	181 (2962)	6.4	5.9	—	3.2	13.1	2.3	18.5	8.5
	300CE	181 (2962)	6.4	5.9	—	—	13.1	2.3	18.5	10.6
	300SE	181 (2962)	6.4	5.9	—	—	13.1	2.3	23.8	10.6
	300SEL	181 (2962)	6.4	5.9	—	—	13.1	2.3	23.8	10.6
	300TE	181 (2962)	6.4	5.9	—	—	13.1	2.3	19.0	10.6
	420SEL	256 (4196)	8.5	8.0	—	—	16.2	2.7	23.8	13.8
	560SEC	338 (5547)	8.5	8.0	—	—	16.2	2.7	23.8	13.8
	560SEL	338 (5547)	8.5	8.0	—	—	16.2	2.7	23.8	13.8
	560SL	338 (5547)	8.5	8.0	—	—	16.2	2.7	22.4	13.8
1989	190D	152 (2497)	8.0	7.5	—	—	11.6	1.5	14.5	8.5
	190E	159 (2599)	6.4	5.9	—	3.2	12.7	2.3	14.5	9.5
	260E	159 (2599)	6.4	5.9	—	3.2	13.1	2.3	18.5	9.5
	300E	181 (2962)	6.4	5.9	—	3.2	13.1	2.3	18.5	8.5
	300CE	181 (2962)	6.4	5.9	—	—	13.1	2.3	18.5	10.6
	300SE	181 (2962)	6.4	5.9	—	—	13.1	2.3	23.8	10.6
	300SEL	181 (2962)	6.4	5.9	—	—	13.1	2.3	23.8	10.6
	300TE	181 (2962)	6.4	5.9	—	—	13.1	2.3	19.0	10.6
	420SEL	256 (4196)	8.5	8.0	—	—	16.2	2.7	23.8	13.8
	560SEC	338 (5547)	8.5	8.0	—	—	16.2	2.7	23.8	13.8
	560SEL	338 (5547)	8.5	8.0	—	—	16.2	2.7	23.8	13.8
	560SL	338 (5547)	8.5	8.0	—	—	16.2	2.7	22.4	13.8

CAPACITIES

Year	Model	Engine Displacement cu. in. (cc)	Engine Crankcase with Filter	Engine Crankcase without Filter	Transmission (pts.) 4-Spd	Transmission (pts.) 5-Spd	Transmission (pts.) Auto.	Drive Axle (pts.)	Fuel Tank (gal.)	Cooling System (qts.)
1990-91	190E	159 (2599)	6.4	5.9	—	3.2	12.7	2.3	14.5	9.5
	300E	181 (2962)	6.4	5.9	—	—	13.1	2.3	18.5	8.5
	300CE	181 (2962)	6.4	5.9	—	—	13.1	2.3	18.5	10.6
	300SE	181 (2962)	6.4	5.9	—	—	13.1	2.3	23.8	10.6
	300SL	181 (2962)	8.0	7.5	—	3.4	12.6	2.8	21.1	12.2
	300TE	181 (2962)	6.4	5.9	—	—	13.1	2.3	19.0	10.6
	300SEL	181 (2962)	6.4	5.9	—	—	13.1	2.3	23.8	10.6
	420SEL	256 (4196)	8.5	8.0	—	—	16.2	2.7	23.8	13.8
	500SL	304 (4973)	8.5	8.0	—	—	16.2	2.8	21.1	15.9
	560SEC	338 (5547)	8.5	8.0	—	—	16.2	2.7	23.8	13.8
	560SEL	338 (5547)	8.5	8.0	—	—	16.2	2.7	23.8	13.8

CAMSHAFT SPECIFICATIONS

All measurements given in inches.

Year	Engine Displacement cu. in. (cc)	Journal Diameter 1	Journal Diameter 2	Journal Diameter 3	Journal Diameter 4	Journal Diameter 5	Lobe Lift In.	Lobe Lift Ex.	Bearing Clearance	Camshaft End Play
1987	140 (2299)	1.260	1.260	1.260	1.260	1.260	NA	NA	NA	NA
	140 (2299)	1.102	1.102	1.102	1.102	1.102	NA	NA	NA	NA
	159 (2599)	1.378	1.831	1.831	1.831	1.831	0.394	0.413	0.002	0.004
	152 (2497)	1.260	1.260	1.260	1.260	1.260	NA	NA	NA	NA
	159 (2599)	1.378	1.831	1.831	1.831	1.831	0.394	0.413	0.002	0.004
	181 (2962)	1.378	1.831	1.831	1.831	1.831	0.394	0.413	0.002	0.004
	183 (2996)	1.378	1.831	1.831	1.831	1.831	0.394	0.413	0.002	0.004
	256 (4196)	1.377	1.936	1.936	1.944	1.944	NA	NA	0.0016	0.004
	338 (5547)	1.377	1.936	1.936	1.944	1.944	NA	NA	0.0016	0.004
1988	140 (2299)	1.260	1.260	1.260	1.260	1.260	NA	NA	NA	NA
	152 (2497)	1.260	1.260	1.260	1.260	1.260	NA	NA	NA	NA
	159 (2599)	1.378	1.831	1.831	1.831	1.831	0.394	0.413	0.002	0.004
	181 (2962)	1.378	1.831	1.831	1.831	1.831	0.394	0.413	0.002	0.004
	256 (4196)	1.377	1.936	1.936	1.944	1.944	NA	NA	0.0016	0.004
	338 (5547)	1.377	1.936	1.936	1.944	1.944	NA	NA	0.0016	0.004
1989	152 (2497)	1.260	1.260	1.260	1.260	1.260	NA	NA	NA	NA
	159 (2599)	1.378	1.831	1.831	1.831	1.831	0.394	0.413	0.002	0.004
	181 (2962)	1.378	1.831	1.831	1.831	1.831	0.394	0.413	0.002	0.004
	256 (4196)	1.377	1.936	1.936	1.944	1.944	NA	NA	0.0016	0.004
	338 (5547)	1.377	1.936	1.936	1.944	1.944	NA	NA	0.0016	0.004
1990-91	159 (2599)	1.378	1.831	1.831	1.831	1.831	0.394	0.413	0.002	0.004
	181 (2962)	1.378	1.831	1.831	1.831	1.831	0.394	0.413	0.002	0.004
	256 (4196)	1.377	1.936	1.936	1.944	1.944	NA	NA	0.0016	0.004
	338 (5547)	1.377	1.936	1.936	1.944	1.944	NA	NA	0.0016	0.004
	304 (4973)	1.377	1.936	1.936	1.944	1.944	NA	NA	0.0016	0.004

CRANKSHAFT AND CONNECTING ROD SPECIFICATIONS

All measurements are given in inches.

Year	Engine Displacement cu. in. (cc)	Crankshaft				Connecting Rod		
		Main Brg. Journal Dia.	Main Brg. Oil Clearance	Shaft End-play	Thrust on No.	Journal Diameter	Oil Clearance	Side Clearance
1987	140 (2299)	2.281–2.282	0.001–0.003	0.004–0.010	①	1.887–1.888	0.001–0.003	NA
	159 (2599)	2.360–2.361	NA	NA	①	2.031–2.032	0.001–0.002	NA
	152 (2497)	2.281–2.282	0.001–0.003	0.004–0.010	①	1.887–1.888	0.001–0.003	NA
	181 (2962)	2.360–2.361	NA	NA	①	2.031–2.032	0.001–0.002	NA
	183 (2996)	2.754–2.755	0.002–0.003	0.004–0.009	①	2.045–2.046	0.001–0.002	0.004–0.010
	256 (4196)	2.517–2.518	0.002–0.003	0.004–0.009	①	1.887–1.888	0.004–0.009	0.009–0.014
	338 (5547)	2.517–2.518	0.002–0.003	0.004–0.009	①	1.887–1.888	0.004–0.009	0.009–0.014
1988	140 (2299)	2.281–2.282	0.001–0.003	0.004–0.010	①	1.887–1.888	0.001–0.003	NA
	152 (2497)	2.281–2.282	0.001–0.003	0.004–0.010	①	1.887–1.888	0.001–0.003	NA
	159 (2599)	2.360–2.361	NA	NA	①	2.031–2.032	0.001–0.002	NA
	181 (2962)	2.360–2.361	NA	NA	①	2.031–2.032	0.001–0.002	NA
	256 (4196)	2.517–2.518	0.002–0.003	0.004–0.009	①	1.887–1.888	0.004–0.009	0.009–0.014
	338 (5547)	2.517–2.518	0.002–0.003	0.004–0.009	①	1.887–1.888	0.004–0.009	0.009–0.014
1989	152 (2497)	2.281–2.282	0.001–0.003	0.004–0.010	①	1.887–1.888	0.001–0.003	NA
	159 (2599)	2.360–2.361	NA	NA	①	2.031–2.032	0.001–0.002	NA
	181 (2962)	2.360–2.361	NA	NA	①	2.031–2.032	0.001–0.002	NA
	256 (4196)	2.517–2.518	0.002–0.003	0.004–0.009	①	1.887–1.888	0.004–0.009	0.009–0.014
	338 (5547)	2.517–2.518	0.002–0.003	0.004–0.009	①	1.887–1.888	0.004–0.009	0.009–0.014
1990–91	159 (2599)	2.360–2.361	NA	NA	①	2.031–2.032	0.001–0.002	NA
	181 (2962)	2.360–2.361	NA	NA	①	2.031–2.032	0.001–0.002	NA
	256 (4196)	2.517–2.518	0.002–0.003	0.004–0.009	①	1.887–1.888	0.004–0.009	0.009–0.014
	338 (5547)	2.517–2.518	0.002–0.003	0.004–0.009	①	1.887–1.888	0.004–0.009	0.009–0.014
	304 (4973)	2.517–2.518	0.002–0.003	0.004–0.009	①	1.887–1.888	0.004–0.009	0.009–0.014

NA Not available
① Center main on 5 main bearing engines; rear main on 7 main bearing engines; 3rd from front on 300D (5 cylinder)

VALVE SPECIFICATIONS

Year	Engine Displacement cu. in. (cc)	Seat Angle (deg.)	Face Angle (deg.)	Spring Test Pressure (lbs.)	Spring Installed Height (in.)	Stem-to-Guide Clearance (in.)		Stem Diameter (in.)	
						Intake	Exhaust	Intake	Exhaust
1987	140 (2299)	45①	45①	191	1.929	0.004	0.004	0.314	0.353
	140 (2299)	45	45	191	1.929	0.004	0.004	0.274	0.313
	152 (2497)	45①	45①	169	2.000	0.004	0.004	0.314	0.353
	159 (2599)	45	45	NA	NA	0.004	0.004	0.314	0.353
	183 (2996)	45	45	191	1.929	0.004	0.004	0.314	0.353
	181 (2962)	45	45	NA	NA	0.004	0.004	0.314	0.352
	256 (4196)	45	45	194	1.200	0.004	0.004	0.353	0.352
	338 (5547)	45	45	194	1.200	0.004	0.004	0.353	0.352
1988	140 (2299)	45①	45①	191	1.929	0.004	0.004	0.314	0.353
	152 (2497)	45①	45①	169	2.000	0.004	0.004	0.314	0.353
	159 (2599)	45	45	NA	NA	0.004	0.004	0.314	0.353
	183 (2996)	45	45	191	1.929	0.004	0.004	0.274	0.313
	181 (2962)	45	45	NA	NA	0.004	0.004	0.314	0.353
	256 (4196)	45	45	194	1.200	0.004	0.004	0.353	0.352
	338 (5547)	45	45	194	1.200	0.004	0.004	0.353	0.352
1989	152 (2497)	45①	45①	169	2.000	0.004	0.004	0.314	0.353
	159 (2599)	45	45	NA	NA	0.004	0.004	0.314	0.353
	181 (2962)	45	45	NA	NA	0.004	0.004	0.314	0.352
	256 (4196)	45	45	194	1.200	0.004	0.004	0.353	0.352
	338 (5547)	45	45	194	1.200	0.004	0.004	0.353	0.352
1990-91	159 (2599)	45	45	NA	NA	0.004	0.004	0.314	0.353
	181 (2962)	45	45	NA	NA	0.004	0.004	0.314	0.352
	256 (4196)	45	45	194	1.200	0.004	0.004	0.353	0.352
	338 (5547)	45	45	194	1.200	0.004	0.004	0.353	0.352
	304 (4973)	45	45	194	1.200	0.004	0.004	0.315	0.354

NA Not available
① Plus 15"

PISTON AND RING SPECIFICATIONS
All measurements are given in inches.

Year	Engine Displacement cu. in. (cc)	Piston Clearance	Ring Gap			Ring Side Clearance		
			Top Compression	Bottom Compression	Oil Control	Top Compression	Bottom Compression	Oil Control
1987	140 (2299)	0.001–0.002	0.008–0.016	0.008–0.016	0.008–0.016	0.004–0.005	0.002–0.003	0.001–0.003
	152 (2497)	0.001–0.002	0.008–0.016	0.008–0.016	0.008–0.016	0.004–0.005	0.003–0.004	0.001–0.002
	159 (2599)	0.001–0.002	0.008–0.016	0.008–0.016	0.008–0.016	0.004–0.005	0.003–0.004	0.001–0.002
	181 (2962)	0.001–0.002	0.008–0.016	0.008–0.016	0.010–0.016	0.004–0.005	0.003–0.004	0.001–0.002
	183 (2996)	0.001–0.002	0.008–0.016	0.008–0.016	0.010–0.016	0.004–0.005	0.003–0.004	0.001–0.002
	256 (4196)	0.001	0.008–0.016	0.008–0.016	0.010–0.016	0.004–0.005	0.003–0.004	0.001–0.002
	338 (5547)	0.001	0.010–0.017	0.010–0.017	0.010–0.016	0.004–0.005	0.001–0.002	0.001–0.002

PISTON AND RING SPECIFICATIONS

All measurements are given in inches.

Year	Engine Displacement cu. in. (cc)	Piston Clearance	Ring Gap			Ring Side Clearance		
			Top Compression	Bottom Compression	Oil Control	Top Compression	Bottom Compression	Oil Control
1988	140 (2299)	0.001–0.002	0.008–0.016	0.008–0.016	0.008–0.016	0.004–0.005	0.002–0.003	0.001–0.003
	152 (2497)	0.001–0.002	0.008–0.016	0.008–0.016	0.008–0.016	0.004–0.005	0.003–0.004	0.001–0.002
	159 (2599)	0.001–0.002	0.008–0.016	0.008–0.016	0.010–0.016	0.004–0.005	0.003–0.004	0.001–0.002
	181 (2962)	0.001–0.002	0.008–0.016	0.008–0.016	0.010–0.016	0.004–0.005	0.003–0.004	0.001–0.002
	256 (4196)	0.001	0.008–0.016	0.008–0.016	0.010–0.016	0.004–0.005	0.003–0.004	0.001–0.002
	338 (5547)	0.001	0.010–0.017	0.010–0.017	0.010–0.016	0.004–0.005	0.001–0.002	0.001–0.002
1989	152 (2497)	0.001–0.002	0.008–0.016	0.008–0.016	0.010–0.016	0.004–0.005	0.003–0.004	0.001–0.002
	159 (2599)	0.001–0.002	0.008–0.016	0.008–0.016	0.010–0.016	0.004–0.005	0.003–0.004	0.001–0.002
	181 (2962)	0.001–0.002	0.008–0.016	0.008–0.016	0.010–0.016	0.004–0.005	0.003–0.004	0.001–0.002
	256 (4196)	0.001	0.008–0.016	0.008–0.016	0.010–0.016	0.004–0.005	0.003–0.004	0.001–0.002
	338 (5547)	0.001	0.010–0.017	0.010–0.017	0.010–0.016	0.004–0.005	0.001–0.002	0.001–0.002
1990-91	159 (2599)	0.001–0.002	0.008–0.016	0.008–0.016	0.010–0.016	0.004–0.005	0.003–0.004	0.001–0.002
	181 (2962)	0.001–0.002	0.008–0.016	0.008–0.016	0.010–0.016	0.004–0.005	0.003–0.004	0.001–0.002
	256 (4196)	0.001	0.008–0.016	0.008–0.016	0.010–0.016	0.004–0.005	0.003–0.004	0.001–0.002
	338 (5547)	0.001	0.010–0.017	0.010–0.017	0.010–0.016	0.004–0.005	0.001–0.002	0.001–0.002
	304 (4973)	0.001	0.010–0.017	0.010–0.017	0.010–0.016	0.004–0.005	0.001–0.002	0.001–0.002

TORQUE SPECIFICATIONS

All readings in ft. lbs.

Year	Engine Displacement cu. in. (cc)	Cylinder Head Bolts	Main Bearing Bolts	Rod Bearing Bolts	Crankshaft Pulley Bolts	Flywheel Bolts	Manifold Intake	Manifold Exhaust	Spark Plugs
1987	140 (2299)	51⑦	65	⑥	145	25	NA	NA	15
	152 (2497)	④①	40	⑤	218	25	18	NA	—
	159 (2599)	70⑩	65	22	217	22	NA	NA	15
	181 (2962)	65⑨	65	33	218	⑥	NA	18	15
	183 (2996)	65⑨	65	33	218	⑥	18	18	—
	256 (4196)	44⑧	③	33	289	⑥	NA	NA	15
	338 (5547)	44⑧	②	33	187	⑥	NA	20	15

TORQUE SPECIFICATIONS
All readings in ft. lbs.

Year	Engine Displacement cu. in. (cc)	Cylinder Head Bolts	Main Bearing Bolts	Rod Bearing Bolts	Crankshaft Pulley Bolts	Flywheel Bolts	Manifold Intake	Manifold Exhaust	Spark Plugs
1988	140 (2299)	51⑦	65	⑥	145	25	NA	NA	15
	152 (2497)	④ ①	40	⑤	218	25	18	NA	—
	159 (2599)	70⑩	65	22	217	22	NA	NA	15
	181 (2962)	65⑨	65	33	218	⑥	NA	18	15
	256 (4196)	44⑧	③	33	289	⑥	NA	NA	15
	338 (5547)	44⑧	②	33	187	⑥	NA	20	15
1989	152 (2497)	④ ①	40	⑤	218	25	18	NA	—
	159 (2599)	70⑩	65	22	217	22	NA	NA	15
	181 (2962)	65⑨	65	33	218	⑥	NA	18	15
	256 (4196)	44⑧	③	33	289	⑥	NA	NA	15
	338 (5547)	44⑧	②	33	187	⑥	NA	20	15
1990–91	159 (2599)	70⑩	65	22	217	22	NA	NA	15
	181 (2962)	65⑨	65	33	218	⑥	NA	18	15
	256 (4196)	44⑧	③	33	289	⑥	NA	NA	15
	338 (5547)	44⑧	②	33	187	⑥	NA	20	15
	304 (4973)	75⑪	②	33	187	⑥	NA	20	15

NA Not available
① See text
② M 10 bolts—37 ft. lbs.
  M 12 bolts—72 ft. lbs.
③ M 10 bolts—43 ft. lbs.
  M 12 bolts—58 ft. lbs.
④ M 10 bolts:
  1st step—18 ft. lbs.
  2nd step—29 ft. lbs., setting time 10 minutes
  3rd step—90 degrees torquing angle
  4th step—29 degrees torquing angle
  M 8 bolts—18 ft. lbs.
⑤ 1st step—22–25 ft. lbs.
  2nd step—90–100 degrees torquing angle
⑥ 1st step—22–25 ft. lbs.
  2nd step—90–100 degrees torquing angle
⑦ M 12 bolts:
  1st step—29 ft. lbs.
  2nd step—51 ft. lbs., setting time 10 minutes
  3rd step—90 degrees torquing angle
  4th step—90 degrees torquing angle
  M 8 bolts—18 ft. lbs.
⑧ 1st step—22 ft. lbs.
  2nd step—44 ft. lbs., setting time 10 minutes
  3rd step—Loosen bolts and retighten to 44 ft. lbs.
⑨ 1st step—29 ft. lbs.
  2nd step—51 ft. lbs., setting time 10 minutes
  3rd step—90 degrees torquing angle
  4th step—90 degrees torquing angle
⑩ 1st step—70 ft. lbs.
  2nd step—90 degrees torquing angle
  3rd step—90 degrees torquing angle
⑪ 1st step—75 ft. lbs.
  2nd step—90 degrees torquing angle
  3rd step—90 degrees torquing angle

BRAKE SPECIFICATIONS
All measurements in inches unless noted.

Year	Model	Lug Nut Torque (ft. lbs.)	Master Cylinder Bore	Brake Disc Minimum Thickness	Brake Disc Maximum Runout	Standard Brake Drum Diameter	Minimum Lining Thickness Front	Minimum Lining Thickness Rear
1987	190D	75	④	0.35⑥	0.005⑦	—	0.08	0.08
	190E	75	④	0.35⑥	0.005⑦	—	0.08	0.08
	190E-16	75	④	0.35⑥	0.005⑦	—	0.08	0.08
	260E	75	②	① ⑤	0.005⑦	—	0.08	0.08
	300D	75	②	① ⑤	0.005⑦	—	0.08	0.08
	300E	75	②	① ⑤	0.005⑦	—	0.08	0.08
	300TD	75	②	① ⑤	0.005⑦	—	0.08	0.08
	300SDL	75	②	③ ⑤	0.005	—	0.08	0.08
	420SEL	75	②	③ ⑤	0.005	—	0.08	0.08
	560SL	75	②	③ ⑤	0.005	—	0.08	0.08
	560SEC	75	②	③ ⑤	0.005	—	0.08	0.08
	560SEL	75	②	③ ⑤	0.005	—	0.08	0.08

BRAKE SPECIFICATIONS
All measurements in inches unless noted.

Year	Model	Lug Nut Torque (ft. lbs.)	Master Cylinder Bore	Brake Disc Minimum Thickness	Brake Disc Maximum Runout	Standard Brake Drum Diameter	Minimum Lining Thickness Front	Minimum Lining Thickness Rear
1988	190D	75	④	0.35⑥	0.005⑦	—	0.08	0.08
	190E	75	④	0.35⑥	0.005⑦	—	0.08	0.08
	260E	75	②	①⑤	0.005⑦	—	0.08	0.08
	300E	75	②	①⑤	0.005⑦	—	0.08	0.08
	300CE	75	②	①⑤	0.005⑦	—	0.08	0.08
	300SE	75	②	③⑤	0.005	—	0.08	0.08
	300SEL	75	②	③⑤	0.005	—	0.08	0.08
	300TE	75	②	①⑤	0.005⑦	—	0.08	0.08
	420SEL	75	②	③⑤	0.005	—	0.08	0.08
	560SEC	75	②	③⑤	0.005	—	0.08	0.08
	560SEL	75	②	③⑤	0.005	—	0.08	0.08
	560SL	75	②	③⑤	0.005	—	0.08	0.08
1989	190D	75	④	0.35⑥	0.005⑦	—	0.08	0.08
	190E	75	④	0.35⑥	0.005⑦	—	0.08	0.08
	260E	75	②	①⑤	0.005⑦	—	0.08	0.08
	300E	75	②	①⑤	0.005⑦	—	0.08	0.08
	300CE	75	②	①⑤	0.005⑦	—	0.08	0.08
	300SE	75	②	③⑤	0.005	—	0.08	0.08
	300SEL	75	②	③⑤	0.005	—	0.08	0.08
	300TE	75	②	①⑤	0.005⑦	—	0.08	0.08
	420SEL	75	②	③⑤	0.005	—	0.08	0.08
	560SEC	75	②	③⑤	0.005	—	0.08	0.08
	560SEL	75	②	③⑤	0.005	—	0.08	0.08
	560SL	75	②	③⑤	0.005	—	0.08	0.08
1990-91	190E	75	④	0.35⑥	0.005⑦	—	0.08	0.08
	300E	75	②	①⑤	0.005⑦	—	0.08	0.08
	300CE	75	②	①⑤	0.005⑦	—	0.08	0.08
	300SE	75	②	③⑤	0.005	—	0.08	0.08
	300SL	75	②	⑧	0.005	—	0.08	0.08
	300TE	75	②	①⑤	0.005⑦	—	0.08	0.08
	300SEL	75	②	③⑤	0.005	—	0.08	0.08
	420SEL	75	②	③⑤	0.005	—	0.08	0.08
	500SL	75	②	⑧	0.005	—	0.08	0.08
	560SEC	75	②	③⑤	0.005	—	0.08	0.08
	560SEL	75	②	③⑤	0.005	—	0.08	0.08

① Caliper with 57mm piston diameter—0.44 in. caliper with 60mm piston diameter—0.42 in.
② Pushrod circuit—15/16 in. Floating circuit—3/4 in.
③ Caliper with 57mm piston diameter—0.81 in. Caliper with 60mm piston diameter—0.79 in.
④ Pushrod circuit—7/8 in. Floating circuit—11/16 in.
⑤ Rear disc—0.33 in.
⑥ Rear disc—0.30 in.
⑦ Rear disc—0.006 in.
⑧ Front disc—1.10 in. Rear disc—0.35 in.

WHEEL ALIGNMENT

Year	Model	Caster Range (deg.)	Caster Preferred Setting (deg.)	Camber Range (deg.)	Camber Preferred Setting (deg.)	Toe-in (in.)	Steering Axis Inclination (deg.)
1987	190D	10–11	$10^1/_2$	$^1/_2$N–0	$^3/_{16}$N	$^3/_{32}$	NA
	190E	10–11	$10^1/_2$	$^1/_2$N–0	$^3/_{16}$N	$^3/_{32}$	NA
	190E-16	10–11	$10^1/_2$	$^{11}/_{16}$N–$^5/_{16}$P	$^5/_{16}$N	$^3/_{32}$	NA
	300D	$9^{11}/_{16}$–$10^{11}/_{16}$	$10^3/_{16}$	$^5/_{16}$N–$^3/_{16}$P	0	$^3/_{16}$	NA
	300E	$9^{11}/_{16}$–$10^{11}/_{16}$	$10^3/_{16}$	$^5/_{16}$N–$^3/_{16}$P	0	$^3/_{16}$	NA
	300SDL	10–11	$10^1/_2$	$^1/_2$N–0	$^3/_{16}$N	$^3/_{32}$	NA
	300TD	10–11	$10^1/_2$	$^1/_2$N–0	$^3/_{16}$N	$^3/_{32}$	NA
	420SEL	10–11	$10^1/_2$	$^1/_2$N–0	$^3/_{16}$N	$^3/_{32}$	NA
	560SL	10–11	$10^1/_2$	$^1/_2$N–0	$^3/_{16}$N	$^3/_{32}$	NA
	560SEC	10–11	$10^1/_2$	$^1/_2$N–0	$^3/_{16}$N	$^3/_{32}$	NA
	560SEL	10–11	$10^1/_2$	$^1/_2$N–0	$^3/_{16}$N	$^3/_{32}$	NA
1988	190D	10–11	$10^1/_2$	$^1/_2$N–0	$^3/_{16}$N	$^3/_{32}$	NA
	190E	10–11	$10^1/_2$	$^1/_2$N–0	$^3/_{16}$N	$^3/_{32}$	NA
	260E	$9^{11}/_{16}$–$10^{11}/_{16}$	$10^3/_{16}$	$^5/_{16}$N–$^3/_{16}$P	0	$^3/_{16}$	NA
	300E	$9^{11}/_{16}$–$10^{11}/_{16}$	$10^3/_{16}$	$^5/_{16}$N–$^3/_{16}$P	0	$^3/_{16}$	NA
	300CE	$9^{11}/_{16}$–$10^{11}/_{16}$	$10^3/_{16}$	$^5/_{16}$N–$^3/_{16}$P	0	$^3/_{16}$	NA
	300SE	10–11	$10^1/_2$	$^1/_2$N–0	$^3/_{16}$N	$^3/_{32}$	NA
	300SEL	10–11	$10^1/_2$	$^1/_2$N–0	$^3/_{16}$N	$^3/_{32}$	NA
	300TE	$9^{11}/_{16}$–$10^{11}/_{16}$	$10^3/_{16}$	$^5/_{16}$N–$^3/_{16}$P	0	$^3/_{16}$	NA
	420SEL	10–11	$10^1/_2$	$^1/_2$N–0	$^3/_{16}$N	$^3/_{32}$	NA
	560SEC	10–11	$10^1/_2$	$^1/_2$N–0	$^3/_{16}$N	$^3/_{32}$	NA
	560SEL	10–11	$10^1/_2$	$^1/_2$N–0	$^3/_{16}$N	$^3/_{32}$	NA
	560SL	10–11	$10^1/_2$	$^1/_2$N–0	$^3/_{16}$N	$^3/_{32}$	NA
1989	190D	10–11	$10^1/_2$	$^1/_2$N–0	$^3/_{16}$N	$^3/_{32}$	NA
	190E	10–11	$10^1/_2$	$^1/_2$N–0	$^3/_{16}$N	$^3/_{32}$	NA
	260E	$9^{11}/_{16}$–$10^{11}/_{16}$	$10^3/_{16}$	$^5/_{16}$N–$^3/_{16}$P	0	$^3/_{16}$	NA
	300E	$9^{11}/_{16}$–$10^{11}/_{16}$	$10^3/_{16}$	$^5/_{16}$N–$^3/_{16}$P	0	$^3/_{16}$	NA
	300CE	$9^{11}/_{16}$–$10^{11}/_{16}$	$10^3/_{16}$	$^5/_{16}$N–$^3/_{16}$P	0	$^3/_{16}$	NA
	300SE	10–11	$10^1/_2$	$^1/_2$N–0	$^3/_{16}$N	$^3/_{32}$	NA
	300SEL	10–11	$10^1/_2$	$^1/_2$N–0	$^3/_{16}$N	$^3/_{32}$	NA
	300TE	$9^{11}/_{16}$–$10^{11}/_{16}$	$10^3/_{16}$	$^5/_{16}$N–$^3/_{16}$P	0	$^3/_{16}$	NA
	420SEL	10–11	$10^1/_2$	$^1/_2$N–0	$^3/_{16}$N	$^3/_{32}$	NA
	560SEC	10–11	$10^1/_2$	$^1/_2$N–0	$^3/_{16}$N	$^3/_{32}$	NA
	560SEL	10–11	$10^1/_2$	$^1/_2$N–0	$^3/_{16}$N	$^3/_{32}$	NA
	560SL	10–11	$10^1/_2$	$^1/_2$N–0	$^3/_{16}$N	$^3/_{32}$	NA
1990-91	190E	10–11	$10^1/_2$	$^1/_2$N–0	$^3/_{16}$N	$^3/_{32}$	NA
	300E	$9^{11}/_{16}$–$10^{11}/_{16}$	$10^3/_{16}$	$^5/_{16}$N–$^3/_{16}$P	0	$^3/_{16}$	NA
	300CE	$9^{11}/_{16}$–$10^{11}/_{16}$	$10^3/_{16}$	$^5/_{16}$N–$^3/_{16}$P	0	$^3/_{16}$	NA
	300SE	10–11	$10^1/_2$	$^1/_2$N–0	$^3/_{16}$N	$^3/_{32}$	NA
	300SL	10–11	$10^1/_2$	$^3/_4$N–$^1/_4$N	$^1/_2$N	$^1/_4$	NA
	300SEL	10–11	$10^1/_2$	$^1/_2$N–0	$^3/_{16}$N	$^3/_{32}$	NA
	300TE	$9^{11}/_{16}$–$10^{11}/_{16}$	$10^3/_{16}$	$^5/_{16}$N–$^3/_{16}$P	0	$^3/_{16}$	NA
	420SEL	10–11	$10^1/_2$	$^1/_2$N–0	$^3/_{16}$N	$^3/_{32}$	NA

WHEEL ALIGNMENT

Year	Model	Caster Range (deg.)	Caster Preferred Setting (deg.)	Camber Range (deg.)	Camber Preferred Setting (deg.)	Toe-in (in.)	Steering Axis Inclination (deg.)
1990-91	500SL	10–11	10¹/₂	³/₄N–¹/₄N	¹/₂N	¹/₄	NA
	560SEC	10–11	10¹/₂	¹/₂N–0	³/₁₆N	³/₃₂	NA
	560SEL	10–11	10¹/₂	¹/₂N–0	³/₁₆N	³/₃₂	NA

ENGINE ELECTRICAL

NOTE: Disconnecting the negative battery cable on some vehicles may interfere with the functions of the on board computer systems and may require the computer to undergo a relearning process, once the negative battery cable is reconnected.

Distributor

Removal and Installation

NOTE: The distributor on the 190E with 2.6L engine, 260E, 300E, 300CE, 300SE, 300TE and 300SEL is part of the cylinder head. With the exception of the cap and rotor, it is not readily removable.

The removal and installation procedures for all distributors on Mercedes-Benz vehicles are basically similar. Certain minor differences may exist from model-to-model.

1. The distributor is usually located on the front side or front of the engine.
2. Disconnect the negative battery cable. Remove the dust, cover, distributor cap, cable plug connections and vacuum line.
3. Rotating the engine in the normal direction, crank it until the distributor rotor points to the mark on the rim of the distributor housing. This indicates the No. 1 cylinder.
4. The engine can be cranked with a socket wrench on the balancer bolt or with a prybar inserted in the balancer.
5. Matchmark the distributor body and the engine so the distributor can be returned to its original position.
6. Remove the distributor hold-down bolt and withdraw the distributor from the engine.

NOTE: Do not crank the engine while the distributor is removed.

7. Installation is the reverse of removal. Insert the distributor so the matchmarks on the distributor and engine are aligned.
8. Tighten the clamp bolt and check the dwell angle and ignition timing.

Ignition Timing

Adjustment

Before attempting to set the timing, read the "Ignition Timing Specifications" chart carefully and determine at what speed the timing should be set and whether the vacuum should be connected or disconnected.

NOTE: It is a good idea to paint the appropriate timing mark with dayglow or white paint to make it quickly and easily visible.

On engines with transistorized coil ignition, the timing light may or may not work depending on the construction of the light.

GASOLINE ENGINES

NOTE: All gasoline engines utilize the new EZL electronic ignition system. Although service checking of ignition timing is possible, no adjustment is either possible or necessary.

1. Raise the hood and connect a tachometer.
2. Connect a timing light.
3. Run the engine at the specified speed and read the firing point on the balancing plate or vibration damper while shining the light on it.

NOTE: The balancer on some engines has 2 timing scales. If in doubt as to which scale to use, rotate the crankshaft, in the direction of rotation only, until the distributor rotor is aligned with the notch on the distributor housing (No. 1 cylinder). In this position, the timing pointer should be at TDC on the proper timing scale.

4. Adjust the ignition timing by loosening the distributor clamp bolt and rotating the distributor. To advance the timing, rotate the distributor in the opposite direction of normal rotation. To retard the timing, rotate the distributor in the direction of normal rotation.
5. Once the timing has been adjusted, recheck the timing once more to be sure it has not been disturbed.
6. Remove the timing light and tachometer and connect any wires that were removed.

DIESEL ENGINES

The diesel uses no distributor, so requires no ignition timing adjustment.

Alternator

Precautions

Several precautions must be observed with alternator equipped vehicles to avoid damage to the unit.
● If the battery is removed for any reason, make sure it is reconnected with the correct polarity. Reversing the battery connections may result in damage to the one-way rectifiers.
● When utilizing a booster battery as a starting aid, always connect the positive to positive terminals and the negative terminal from the booster battery to a good engine ground on the vehicle being started.

- Never use a fast charger as a booster to start vehicles.
- Disconnect the battery cables when charging the battery with a fast charger.
- Never attempt to polarize the alternator.
- Do not use test lights of more than 12 volts when checking diode continuity.
- Do not short across or ground any of the alternator terminals.
- The polarity of the battery, alternator and regulator must be matched and considered before making any electrical connections within the system.
- Never separate the alternator on an open circuit. Make sure all connections within the circuit are clean and tight.
- Disconnect the battery ground terminal when performing any service on electrical components.
- Disconnect the battery if arc welding is to be done on the vehicle.

Belt Tension Adjustment

All alternator dive belts should be tensioned to approximately ½ in. deflection under thumb pressure at the middle of the longest span.

NOTE: All models utilize a single V-belt with automatic tensioning. No adjustment is necessary.

Removal and Installation

Viewing the engine from the front, the alternator is located on either side, usually down low. Because of the location, it is sometimes easier to remove the alternator from under the vehicle. The following is a general procedure for all models.
1. Disconnect the negative battery cable. Locate the alternator and disconnect and identify all wires.
2. Loosen the adjusting (pivot) bolt or the adjusting mechanism and swing the alternator in toward the engine.
3. Remove the drive belt from the alternator pulley.
4. The alternator can now be removed from its mounting bracket or the bracket and alternator can be removed from the engine.
5. Installation is the reverse of removal.
6. Tighten all of the drive belts that were loosened.

Poly V-Belt

Removal and Installation

1. Disconnect the negative battery cable. Remove fan and remove together with fan cover.
2. On 190D with 2.5L engine, remove radiator with 1-piece fan cover.
3. On 190D with 2.5L engine with split fan cover, open cover and remove. For this purpose, place rear part on fan. Pull holding clamp form front part. Remove both parts 1 after the other.
4. On 190D with 2.5L engine and 300D, 300TD and 300SDL, loosen fan cover and place above fan. Remove viscous fan clutch, using prybar element 103 589 01 09 00 or equivalent, torque wrench 001 589 72 21 00 or equivalent and counter holder 603 589 00 40 00 or equivalent, for this purpose.
5. Remove nut.
6. Slacken draw spring. For this purpose, swivel lever clockwise.
7. Remove poly V-belt. For this purpose, push back tensioning roller.
8. Check pulley profiles and tensioning device for damage and contamination and replace, if required, worn out bearing points of tensioning device, dents in pulleys, etc.
9. Mount poly V-belt. Slightly pull up tensioning roller. Turn poly V-belt on its back, make a small loop and slip between coolant pump pulley and crankshaft pulley.

To install:
10. Press poly V-belt with left hand tightly against coolant pump pulley and rotate pulley counterclockwise, until the poly V-belt has run up on tensioning roller.
11. Place poly V-belt on tensioning roller and on crankshaft pulley. Turn free poly V-belt part around and place on refrigerant compressor, power steering pump, coolant pump and alternator pulley.
12. Tension poly V-belt and mount tensioning device reverse order of removal.
13. On 190D and 300D and 300TD, install fan or viscous fan clutch with a fan and fan cover. The tightening torque of viscous fan clutch fastening screw is 33.2 ft. lbs. (45 Nm) on 190D with 2.5L engine and 300D, 300TD and 300SDL. For tightening viscous fan clutch fastening screw, prybar element 103 589 01 09 00 or equivalent, torque wrench 001 589 72 21 00 or equivalent and counter holder 603 589 00 40 00 or equivalent.

Poly V-belt Tensioner

Removal and Installation

1. Disconnect the negative battery cable. Remove poly V-belt.
2. Remove tensioning roller. For this purpose, remove closing cap and remove hex head socket screw.
3. Remove pulley for coolant pump.
4. Remove hex head screws and remove shock absorber.
5. Disengage draw spring.
6. On first version, remove closing cover on tensioning lever. Take off hex head socket screw and remove together with lock washer and tensioning lever.
7. Remove bearing bolt.
8. On second version, remove closing cap.
9. Remove fitted screw together with tensioning lever.
10. Check bearing bolt and tensioning lever for wear. If one part is worn out replace both parts.
11. Clean threads in timing housing cover and on bearing bolt with activator. Coat threads on bearing bolt with adhesive Omnifit 100 M orange 002 989 23 71 or equivalent, and tighten bearing bolt to 73.8 ft. lbs. (100 Nm).
To install:
12. Reverse removal procedure.
13. Check shock absorber for function prior to installation.
14. Install poly V-belt.

Starter

Removal and Installation
260E, 300E, 300CE AND 300TE

1. Disconnect negative battery terminal.
2. Remove complete air cleaner.
3. Remove holder on intake manifold.
4. Remove engine compartment enclosure.
5. Disconnect electric wires for oil level and oil pressure sensor.
6. Remove starter.
To install:
7. Reverse removal procedure.

ALL OTHER MODELS

1. Remove all wires from the starter and tag them for location.
2. Disconnect the battery cable.
3. Unbolt the starter from the bell housing and remove the ground cable.
4. Remove the starter from under the vehicle.
5. Installation is the reverse of removal. Be sure to replace all wires and washers in their original location.

CHASSIS ELECTRICAL

─── **CAUTION** ───

On vehicles equipped with an air bag, the negative battery cable must be disconnected, before working on the system. Failure to do so may result in deployment of the air bag and possible personal injury.

Heater Blower Motor

Removal and Installation

260E, 300D, 300E, 300SE, 300TE, 300SEL AND 300TD

1. Disconnect the negative battery cable. Remove the cover from under the right side of the instrument panel.
2. Disconnect the plug from the blower motor.
3. Unscrew the contact plate screw, lift the contact plate and disconnect both wires to the series resistor.
4. Loosen the blower motor flange screws and lift out the blower motor.
5. Installation is in the reverse order or removal.

560SL

1. Disconnect the negative battery cable. Working in the engine compartment, unscrew the 8 mounting screws and remove the panel which covers the blower motor.
2. Disconnect the plug from the series resistor at the firewall.
3. Remove the mounting bolts and remove the series resistor.
4. Unscrew the 4 blower motor retaining nuts and lift out the motor.
5. Installation is in the reverse order of removal. Be sure the rubber sealing strip is not damaged.

420SEL, 560SEC AND 560SEL

1. Disconnect the negative battery cable. Remove the cover from under the right side of the instrument panel.
2. Remove the cover for the blower motor and disconnect the 2-prong plug.
3. Remove the blower motor flange bolts and the blower motor.
4. Installation is in the reverse order of removal.

190D AND 190E

1. Disconnect the negative battery cable. Open the hood to a 90 degree position and remove the wiper arms.
2. Disconnect the retaining clips for the air intake cover at the firewall.
3. Remove the rubber sealing strip from the cover and remove the retaining screw. Slide the cover from the lower windshield trim strip and remove it.
4. Disconnect the vacuum line from the heater valve.
5. Remove the heater cover retaining screws.
6. Pull up the rubber sealing strip from the engine side of the defroster plenum (firewall), unscrew the retaining screws and pull up and out on the blower motor cover.
7. Loosen the cable straps on the connecting cable and disconnect the plug.
8. Unscrew the mounting bolts and remove the blower motor.
9. Installation is in the reverse order of removal.

Windshield Wiper Motor and Linkage

Removal and Installation

300D AND 300TD

1. Disconnect the negative battery cable. Remove the wiper arms.
2. Remove the air intake grille on the right side.

3. Remove the covering cap and nut on the left and right side bearing shafts.
4. Remove the 4 expanding rivets and the left side air intake grille.
5. Remove the center air plenum cover; 4 expanding rivets and a Phillips screw.
6. Carefully, pull the left and right side connecting rods off the wiper motor crank.
7. Remove the water drain tube from the right side bearing shaft.
8. Disconnect the coupler plug in the engine compartment. Unclip the plug from the firewall and pull it all the way through.
9. Unbolt the wiper motor and remove it toward the right side.
10. Installation is in the reverse order of removal.

300SE, 420SEL, 560SEC AND 560SEL

1. Disconnect the negative battery cable. Remove the wiper arms.
2. Remove the air intake cover. Unscrew the fastening screws and disconnect the front plug connector.
3. Compress the mounting flange on the rear plug connector. Push the plug from the firewall toward the front of the vehicle, twist it and insert it toward the rear of the vehicle.
4. Remove the wiper motor and linkage.
5. Unscrew the nut on the wiper motor shaft.
6. Swivel the wiper linkage and unscrew the bolts for the wiper motor underneath.
7. Remove the wiper motor.
To install:
8. Mount the wiper motor in the base plate.
9. Push the crank arm on the wiper motor shaft and position the nut. Make sure the lever on the right hand wiper shaft is pointing down.
10. Align the crank arm so the upper edge is parallel with the wiper motor shaft.
11. Tighten the nut on the wiper motor shaft.
12. Attach the wiper motor and linkage assembly to the vehicle.
13. Installation of the remaining components is in the reverse order of removal.

260E, 300E, 300CE, 300SE, 300TE AND 300SEL

1. Disconnect the negative battery cable. Open the hood.
2. Remove the air inlet cover.
3. Pry open the cover plate on the lower end of the wiper arm and remove the Allen screw.
4. Pull the wiper arm off the shaft.
5. Remove the motor assembly mounting nuts and clamp.
6. Disconnect the electrical lead and remove the wiper assembly.
7. Unscrew the nut on the motor shaft and pry off the driver lever.
8. Unbolt the wiper motor and remove it.
9. Tighten the wiper motor-to-mount bracket nuts to 4 ft. lbs. (5 Nm). The motor must be in the **PARK** position; if unsure, connect the electrical lead temporarily and operate the switch to the **PARK** position. Disconnect the lead.
10. Position the drive arm onto the motor shaft and tighten the nut to 14 ft. lbs. (19 Nm).
11. Installation of the remaining components is the reverse order of removal.

190D AND 190E

1. Open the hood and disconnect the battery.
2. Remove the wiper arm.
3. Remove the round cover from the wiper shaft.
4. Remove the 2 clips, the rubber seal, the 2 screws and the air intake cover.

5. Pull the 3-piece air intake pan from the windshield and remove it.

6. Unscrew the wiper motor/linkage assembly.

7. Remove the cover and unscrew the 4 mounting bolts for the fuse box. Pull the fuse box slightly forward and up and unplug the wiper motor connection.

8. Remove the wiper motor/linkage assembly.

9. Remove the nut on the wiper motor shaft and pull off the crank arm and linkage.

10. Unscrew and remove the wiper motor.

To install:

11. Attach the wiper motor to the base plate.

12. Press the crank arm onto the wiper motor shaft. Make sure the crank arm and the pushrod are parallel.

13. Attach the crank arm to the wiper motor and install the wiper motor/linkage assembly.

14. Installation of the remaining components is in the reverse order of removal.

Instrument Cluster

Removal and Installation

190D, 190E, 420SEL, 560SEC, 560SEL AND 560SL

1. Disconnect the negative battery cable. Remove the cover under the left side of the instrument panel.

2. Disconnect the defroster ducting which runs behind the instrument cluster.

3. Unscrew the speedometer cable from below and push the cluster out far enough to disconnect all connections on the back of the instrument cluster.

4. Remove the 5 clips which secure the instrument cluster and remove it.

5. Installation is in the reverse order of removal.

260E, 300E, 300CE, 300SE, 300TE AND 300SEL

1. Disconnect the negative battery cable. Remove the instrument panel undercover.

2. Remove the speedometer cable from the slips on the panel under the instrument cluster. This will allow the cable come out when the cluster is removed.

3. Fabricate a removal tool (hook) and insert it between the padding and the cluster at the top of the left side of the cluster. Rotate the tool and pull out until it rests against the detent.

4. Pull the instrument cluster out evenly on both sides. Be sure the speedometer cable slides into the recess on the brake pedal cover.

5. Reach behind the cluster, unscrew the speedometer cable. Label and disconnect all electrical leads.

6. Remove the instrument cluster.

7. When installing, position the cluster and reconnect the speedometer cable and all electrical leads.

8. Push the cluster backwards into its recess.

NOTE: Be certain the speedometer cable slides back into the footwell area without buckling behind the cluster.

300D AND 300TD

1. Disconnect the negative battery cable.

2. Remove the instrument cluster slightly by hand. Don't pull on the edge of the glass.

3. A removal hook can be fabricated and inserted between the instrument cluster and the dashboard.

4. Guide the removal hook up to the right to the recess and pull the instrument cluster out.

5. Pull it out as far as possible and disconnect the speedometer cable, electrical connections and oil pressure line.

To install:

6. Reconnect the electrical connections, oil pressure line and speedometer cable. To avoid speedometer cable noise, guide it into the largest radius possible.

7. Push the instrument cluster firmly into the dashboard.

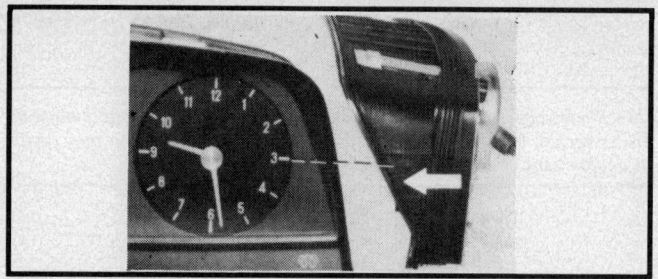

Recess slot in the instrument cluster

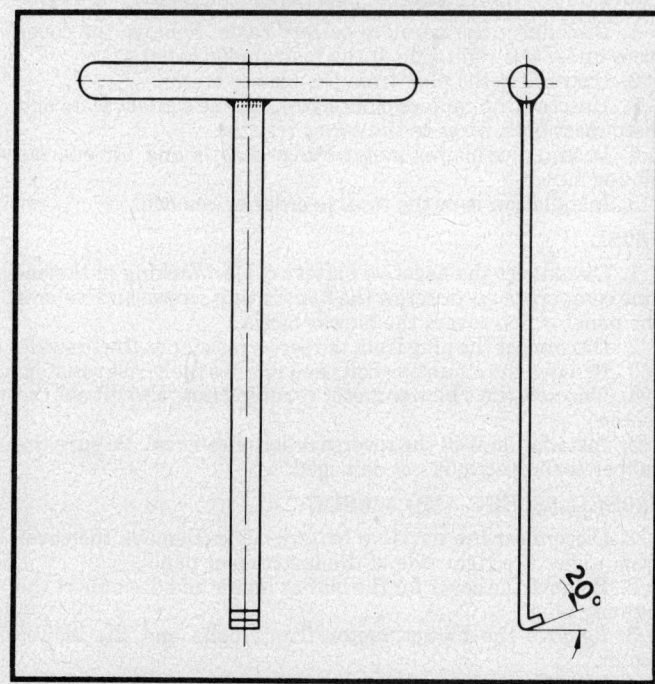

Fabricated tool for removing the instrument cluster

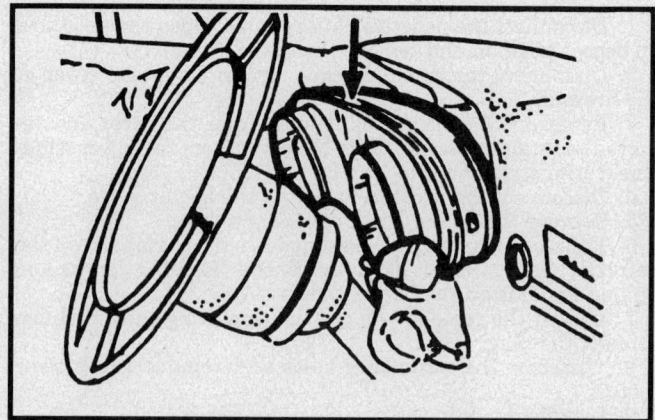

Instrument panel removal showing rubber retaining strip

Combination Switch

Removal and Installation

190D, 190E, 260E, 300D, 300E, 300CE, 300SE, 300TE, 300SEL, 300TD AND 560SL

1. Disconnect the negative battery cable. Remove the rubber sleeve on the switch and unscrew the retaining screws.

2. Pull the switch out slightly, loosen the screws for the cable connection of the twin carbon contacts and pull out the cable.

3. Remove the cover under the left side of the instrument panel.

4. Disconnect the plug and remove the switch.

5. Installation is in the reverse order of removal.

420SEL, 560SEC AND 560SEL

1. Disconnect the negative battery cable. Remove the steering wheel.

2. Remove the cover under the left side of the instrument panel.

3. Unscrew the switch retaining screws.

4. Disconnect the 14-prong plug under the instrument panel.

5. Remove the switch.

6. Installation is in the reverse order of removal.

Ignition Switch

Removal and Installation

WITH IGNITION SWITCH IN DASHBOARD

Except 190D, 190E, 260E, 300E, 300CE, 300SE, 300TE and 300SEL

1. Disconnect the negative battery cable. Remove the instrument cluster.

2. Remove the right cover plate from under the dashboard.

3. Remove the plug connection from the ignition switch.

4. Remove the ignition switch-to-lock cylinder screws and the switch.

To install:

5. Attach the plug connection, after fastening the switch to the steering lock.

6. Install the instrument cluster.

7. Check the switch for proper function and install the lower cover.

190D, 190E, 260E and 300E

1. Disconnect the negative battery cable. Remove the cover plate under the left side of the instrument panel.

2. Remove the steering wheel. Remove the instrument cluster.

3. Pry the cylinder rosette (trim ring) upwards and remove it.

4. Insert the ignition key and turn it to position 1.

5. Disconnect the plug at the rear of the ignition switch.

NOTE: The plug can only be disconnected when the key is in position No. 1.

6. Loosen the screws and remove the steering column jacket (upper and lower halves).

7. Release the clamp on the jacket tube. Press in the lock-pin in position 1 and pull the steering lock out slightly from the jacket tube holder.

8. Pull off the ignition key at the right bottom section, slightly to the rear. Swivel the steering lock so the lock cylinder clears its hole in the instrument panel.

9. Unscrew the retaining screws and remove the ignition switch from the back of the steering lock.

10. Installation is in the reverse order of removal. Remember to reconnect the switch to the steering lock.

Lock Cylinder

Removal and Installation

KEY CAN BE REMOVED IN POSITION NO. 1

1. Disconnect the negative battery cable. Turn the key to position 1 and remove the key.

2. Pry the cover sleeve from the lock cylinder with a small prybar.

3. Using a bent paper clip, hook onto the cover sleeve and remove the sleeve. Do not remove the rosette in the dashboard.

4. Insert the paper clip between the rosette and the steering lock and push in the lock pin. Remove the lock cylinder slightly with the key.

5. Insert the paper clip into the locking hole and pull the lock cylinder completely out.

6. Installation is the reverse or removal. Turn the lock cylinder to position 1 and insert it into the steering lock, make sure the lock pin engages. Push the cover sleeve into position 1.

7. Make sure the cylinder operates properly.

KEY CANNOT BE REMOVED IN POSITION NO. 1

Except 190D, 190E, 260E, 300E, 300CE, 300SE, 300TE and 300SEL

Because of legal requirements, the lock was changed from the previous version, so the key can only be removed in position 0.

1. Disconnect the negative battery cable. Turn the key to position 1.

2. Lift the cover sleeve to the edge of the key and turn the key to position 0.

3. Remove the key and cover sleeve.

4. Insert the key into the lock cylinder and turn to position 1 (90 degrees to the right), push in the lock pin and remove the lock cylinder.

To install:

5. Turn the lock cylinder to position 1 and insert the lock cylinder, make sure the locking pin engages.

6. Turn the key to position 0 and remove the key.

7. Place the cover sleeve on the steering lock, insert and turn the key and push in the cover sleeve in position 1.

8. Check the locking cylinder for proper function.

190D, 190E, 260E, 300E, 300CE, 300SE, 300TE and 300SEL

1. Disconnect the negative battery cable. Pry the cylinder rosette (trim ring) upwards and remove it.

2. Insert the ignition key and turn it to position 1.

3. Using a bent paper clip, insert each end into the holes on either side of the lock cylinder. Press the clip ends inward; the pressure will unlock the cylinder from the steering lock.

4. Grasp the key and with pressure still on the paper clip, pull the ignition key/lock cylinder assembly from the steering lock.

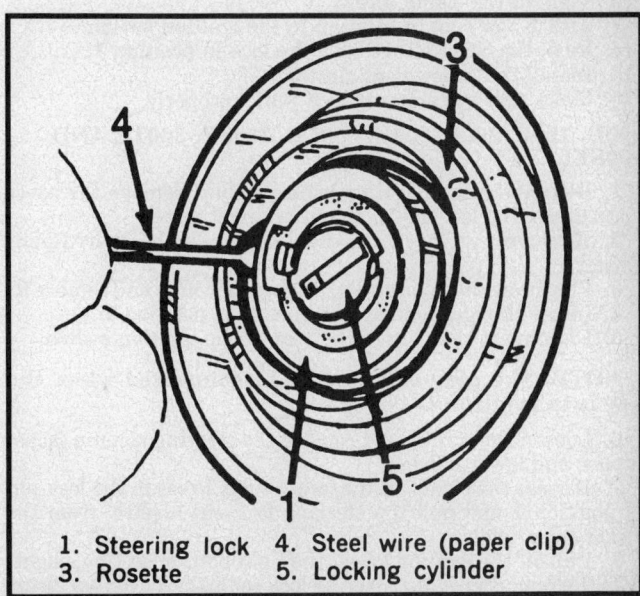

1. Steering lock	4. Steel wire (paper clip)
3. Rosette	5. Locking cylinder

Ignition lock cylinder removal from the instrument panel (both types)

5. Remove the paper clip, turn the key to position **0** and remove it. Slide the lock cylinder from the cover.

To install:

6. Insert the lock cylinder just enough so the ridge on the cylinder body engages the groove in the steering lock.

7. Slide the cover onto the lock cylinder so the detent is on the left side.

8. Insert the ignition key, turn it to position **1**, push the lock cylinder and its cover into the steering lock.

NOTE: When the ignition key is in position 1 and is aligned with the mark on the cover, the detent on the cover is also aligned with the ridge on the steering lock. This is the only manner in which the lock cylinder/cover can be installed in the steering lock.

9. Check that the lock cylinder functions properly, if so, install the rosette.

Steering Lock

Removal and Installation

EXCEPT 190D, 190E, 260E, 300E, 300CE, 300SE, 300TE AND 300SEL

1. Disconnect the ground cable from the battery.

2. Remove the instrument cluster.

3. Remove the plug connection from the ignition switch behind the dashboard.

4. Pull the ignition key to position **1**.

5. Loosen the attaching screw for the steering lock.

6. Remove the cover sleeve from the steering lock.

7. Pull the connection for the warning buzzer.

8. Push in the lock pin with a small punch.

9. Turn the steering lock and remove it from the holder in the column jacket. Be sure the rosette is not damaged.

NOTE: The lock pin can only be pushed in when the cylinder is in position 1.

To install:

10. Connect the warning buzzer, if equipped.

11. Place the steering lock in position **1** and insert the lock into the steering column while pushing the lock pin in; be sure the lock pin engages.

12. Tighten the clamp screw.

13. Attach the plug connection to the ignition switch.

14. Push the cover sleeve onto the lock in position **1**.

15. Install the instrument cluster.

16. Make sure the steering lock works properly.

190D, 190E, 260E, 300E, 300CE, 300SE, 300TE AND 300SEL

1. Disconnect the negative battery cable. Remove the cover plate under the left side of the instrument panel.

2. Remove the steering wheel. Remove the instrument cluster.

3. Pry the cylinder rosette (trim ring) upwards and remove it.

4. Insert the ignition key and turn it to position **1**.

5. Disconnect the plug at the rear of the ignition switch.

NOTE: The plug can only be disconnected when the key is in position 1.

6. Loosen the screws and remove the steering column jacket (upper and lower halves).

7. Release the clamp on the jacket tube. Press in the lock-pin in position **1** and pull the steering lock out slightly from the jacket tube holder.

8. Pull off the ignition key at the right bottom section, slightly to the rear. Swivel the steering lock so the lock cylinder clears its hole in the instrument panel.

9. Remove the screws and the ignition switch from the back of the steering lock.

10. Unplug the switch and remove the steering lock.

11. Installation is in the reverse order of removal.

Stoplight Switch

Removal and Installation

1. Disconnect the negative battery cable. Disconnect electrical connector from stoplight switch.

2. Remove locknut.

3. Remove stoplight switch.

To install:

4. Screw switch into bracket.

5. Adjust switch so the stoplight is 7–20mm, measured to center of pedal plate and tighten locknuts.

Starter Lockout and Back-Up Light Switch

Adjustment

1. Disconnect the selector rod and move the shift selector, on the transmission, to position **N**.

2. Tighten the clamping screw prior to making adjustments.

3. Loosen the adjusting screw and insert the locating pin through the driver into the locating hole in the shift housing.

4. Tighten the adjusting screw and remove the locating pin.

5. Move the selector lever to position **N** and connect the selector rod so there is no tension.

6. Make sure the engine cannot be started in **N** or **P**.

Fuses

A listing of the protected equipment and the amperage of the fuse is printed in the lid of the fuse box. Spare fuses and a tool

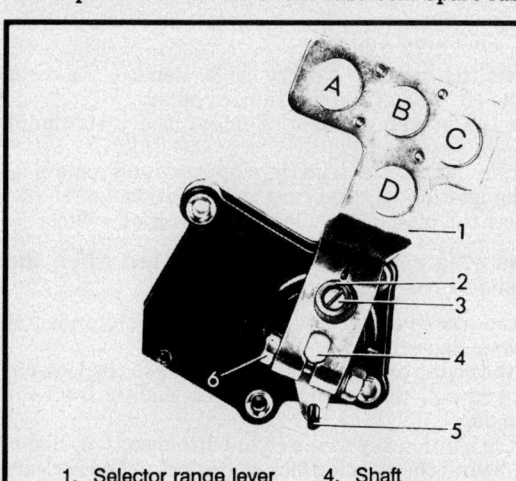

1. Selector range lever
2. Washer
3. Adjusting screw
4. Shaft
5. Locating pin
6. Clamping screw

a. Column shaft for left-hand and right-hand drive vehicles 220/8, 220 D/8, 230/8, 280 S/8, 280 SE/8 and 300 SEL/8.

b. Steering wheel shift for left-hand drive vehicles (220/8, 220 D/8, 230/8, 250/8)

c. Steering wheel shift for right-hand drive vehicles (220/8, 220 D/8, 230/8, 250/8)

d. Steering wheel shift for left-hand drive vehicles (280S/8, 280 SE/8, 300 SEL/8, 280 SE/3.5 and 300 SEL/3.5

Starter lockout and backup light switch adjustment

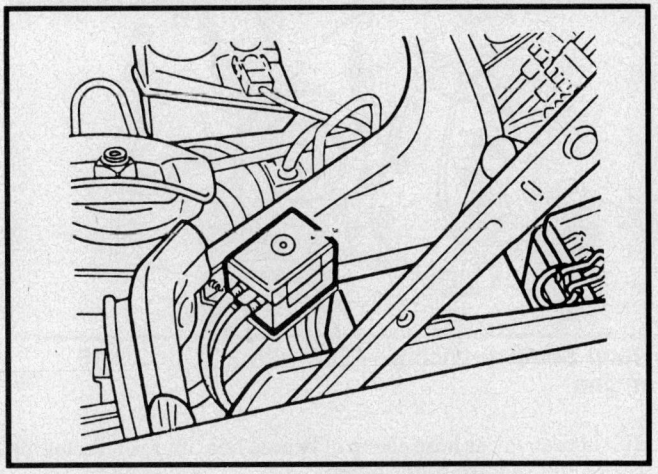

Auxiliary fuse box—190D with 2.5L engine

for removing and installing fuses are contained in the vehicle's tool kit.

Location

300D AND 300TD

The fuse box is located in the engine compartment on the driver's side, next the brake master cylinder. Some models have separate fuse boxes or inline fuses for additional equipment. The radio is usually fused with a separate inline glass fuse behind the radio and the ignition is unfused.

190D, 190E, 260E, 300E, 300CE, 300SE, 300TE, 300SEL, 300SD, 420SEL, 560SEC, 560SEL AND 560SEC

The fuse box is located in the engine compartment, on the driver's side, next to the brake master cylinder. Some models may have separate fuse boxes or inline fuses in the engine compartment for additional equipment. The radio is usually fused with a separate inline glass fuse behind the radio and the ignition is unfused. The fuse box also contains various relays.

ENGINE COOLING

Radiator

Removal and Installation

190D, 300D, 300TD AND 300SDL

1. Disconnect the negative battery cable. If equipped with an automatic transmission, pinch oil lines from or to transmission with special tool 000 589 40 37 00 or equivalent, displacing coil spring slightly laterally and removing from radiator for this purpose.
2. Disconnect coolant hoses on radiator.
3. Pull out flat contour springs for fan cover, slightly lift fan cover and place over fan.
4. On 300D and 300TD models, remove expanding rivets for lateral radiator paneling right and left.
5. On some models, pull off holding clamps at right and left below.

6. Pull out flat contour springs for radiator and lift out radiator.

To install:

7. Reverse the removal procedure. Take note that the fastening mounts of the radiator are correctly introduced into rubber grommets of lower holders and the holders of the fan cover into holding lugs on radiator.
8. Fill with coolant, pressure test cooling system with tester and check for leaks.

EXCEPT 190D, 300D, 300TD AND 300SDL

1. Disconnect the negative battery cable. Remove the radiator cap.
2. Unscrew the radiator drain plug and drain the coolant from the radiator. If all of the coolant in the system is to be drained, move the heater controls to **WARM** and open the drain cocks on the engine block.

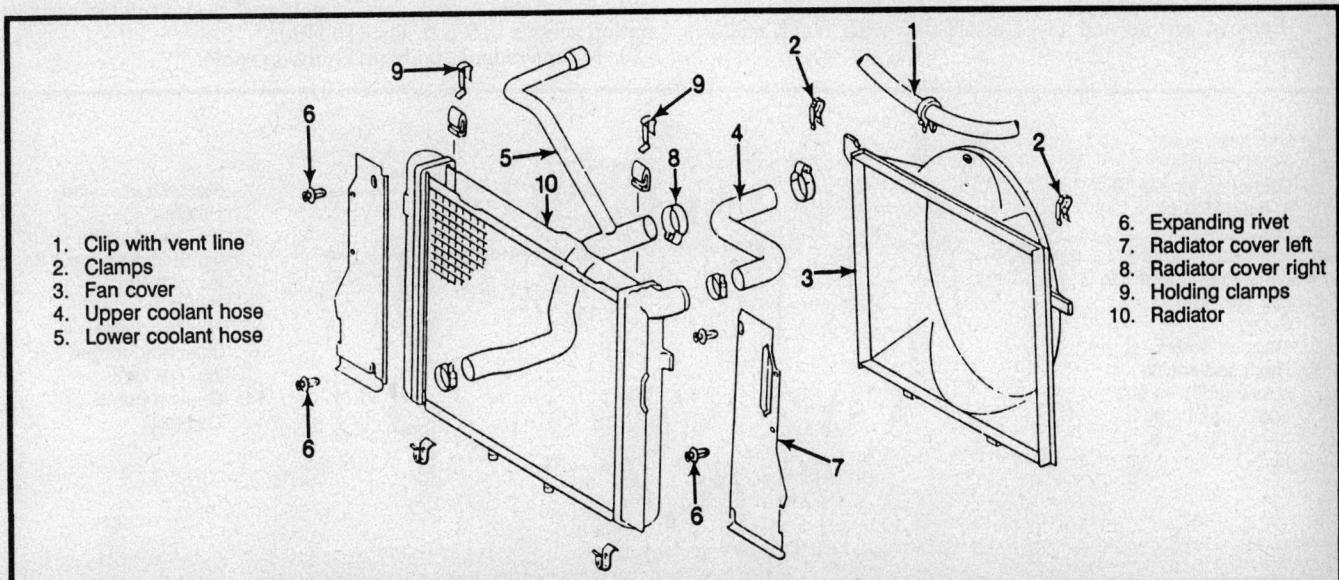

1. Clip with vent line
2. Clamps
3. Fan cover
4. Upper coolant hose
5. Lower coolant hose

6. Expanding rivet
7. Radiator cover left
8. Radiator cover right
9. Holding clamps
10. Radiator

Radiator servicing—190D, 300D and 300SDL

3. If equipped with an oil cooler, drain the oil from the cooler.

4. If equipped, loosen the radiator shell.

5. Loosen the hose clips on the top and bottom radiator hoses and remove the hoses from the connections on the radiator.

6. Unscrew and plug the bottom line on the oil cooler.

7. If equipped with an automatic transmission, unscrew and plug the lines on the transmission cooler.

8. Disconnect the right and left side rubber loops and pull the radiator up and from the body.

To install:

9. Inspect and replace any hoses which have become hardened or spongy.

10. Install the radiator shell and radiator, if the shell was removed, from the top and connect the top and bottom hoes to the radiator.

11. Bolt the shell to the radiator.

12. Attach the rubber loops or position the retaining spring, as applicable.

13. Position the hose clips on the top and bottom hoses.

14. Attach the lines to the oil cooler.

15. If equipped with an automatic transmission, connect the lines to the transmission cooler.

16. Move the heater levers to the **WARM** position and slowly add coolant, allowing air to escape.

17. Check the oil level and fill if necessary. Run the engine for about 1 minute at idle with the filler neck open.

18. Add coolant to the specified level. Install the radiator cap and turn it until it seats in the 2nd notch. Run the engine and check for leaks.

Water Pump

Removal and Installation

190E WITH 2.3L ENGINE

1. Disconnect the negative battery cable. Drain coolant.

2. Remove air cleaner.

3. Remove radiator.

4. Loosen hose clamps and disconnect heater return line and coolant hose from coolant pump.

5. Remove fan.

6. Remove pulley of water pump.

7. Remove hex socket screws, slacken water pump V-belt and remove.

8. Pull cable from magnetic body, remove fastening screws and remove magnetic body.

9. Remove screws and place alternator with front holder aside.

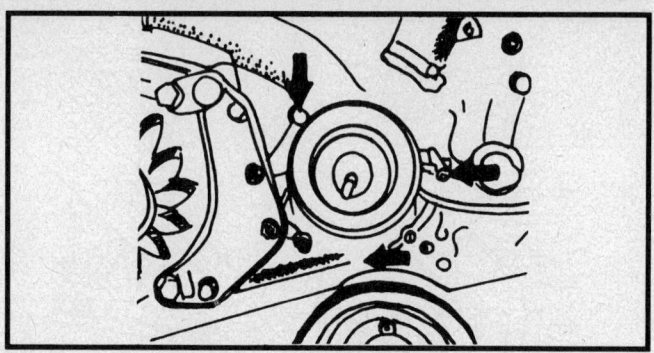

Water pump servicing—190E with 2.3L or 2.3-16 engine

10. Loosen lower hose clamp of bypass line, unscrew fastening screws and remove water pump.

11. Carefully clean sealing surfaces on water pump housing and timing housing cover.

To install:

12. Apply gasket adhesive to gasket and pump.

13. Install pump and torque bolts to 7.5 ft. lbs. (10 Nm).

14. Complete installation by reversing removal procedure. Fill coolant system and check for leaks.

190D, 300D, 300TD AND 300SDL

1. Disconnect the negative battery cable. Remove fan and remove together with fan cover, if necessary.

2. On 190D with 2.5L engine and 300D, 300TD and 300SDL, loosen fan cover and place on fan. Remove viscous fan clutch using prybar element 103 589 01 09 00 or equivalent, torque wrench 001 589 72 21 00 or equivalent, and counter holder 603 589 00 40 00 or equivalent, for this purpose.

3. Remove fastening screws and pulley.

4. Remove hex nuts and magnet body.

5. The magnet carrier is glued to the water pump housing and should not be pulled off.

6. Remove water pump housing.

7. Clean sealing surfaces.

To install:

8. Insert water pump with a new gasket and tighten combination screws to 7.5 ft. lbs. (10 Nm).

9. Mount water pump with a new gasket and tighten combination screws to 7.5 ft. lbs. (10 Nm).

10. Mount magnet body and plug on cable.

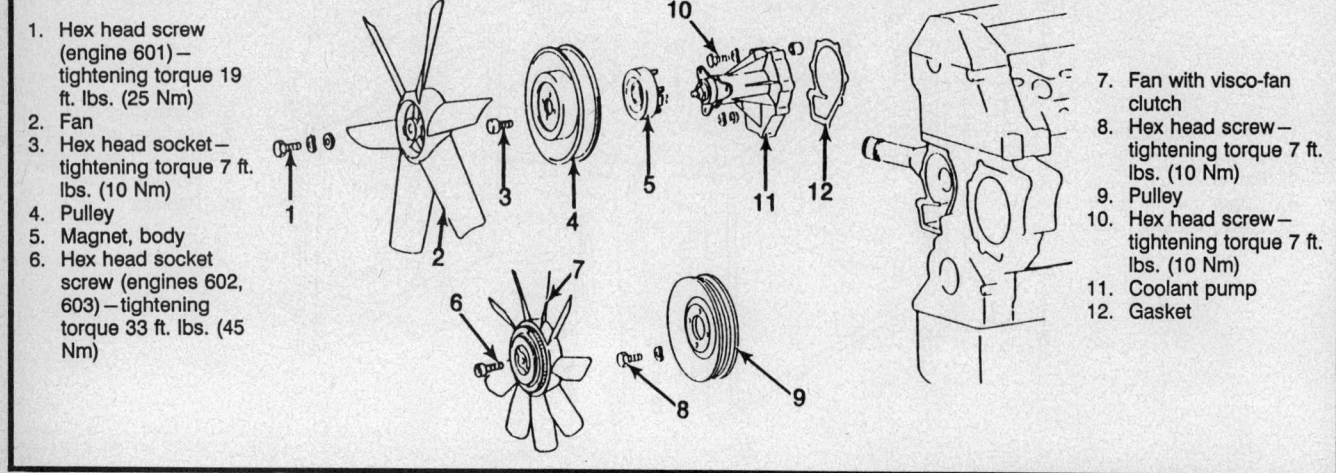

1. Hex head screw (engine 601)—tightening torque 19 ft. lbs. (25 Nm)
2. Fan
3. Hex head socket—tightening torque 7 ft. lbs. (10 Nm)
4. Pulley
5. Magnet, body
6. Hex head socket screw (engines 602, 603)—tightening torque 33 ft. lbs. (45 Nm)
7. Fan with visco-fan clutch
8. Hex head screw—tightening torque 7 ft. lbs. (10 Nm)
9. Pulley
10. Hex head screw—tightening torque 7 ft. lbs. (10 Nm)
11. Coolant pump
12. Gasket

Water pump servicing—190D, 300D, 300TD and 300SDL

11. Mount pulley and tighten fastening screws to 7.5 ft. lbs. (10 Nm).

12. Complete installation by reversing removal procedure.

V8 MODELS

1. Disconnect the negative battery cable. Drain the water from the radiator and block.

2. Remove the air cleaner.

3. Loosen and remove the drive belt.

4. Disconnect the upper water hose from the radiator and thermostat housing.

5. Remove the fan and coupling.

6. Remove the hose from the intake (top) connection of the water pump.

7. Set the engine at TDC. Matchmark the distributor and engine and remove the distributor. Crank the engine with a socket wrench on the crankshaft pulley bolt or with a small prybar inserted in the balancer. Crank in the normal direction of rotation only.

8. Turn the balancer so the recesses provide access to the mounting bolts. Remove the mounting bolts. Rotate the engine in the normal direction of rotation only.

9. Remove the water pump.

To install:

10. Clean the mounting surfaces of the water pump and block.

11. Installation is the reverse of removal. Always use a new gasket. Set the engine at TDC and install the distributor rotor points to the notch on the distributor housing. Fill the cooling system and check and adjust the ignition timing.

ALL OTHER MODELS

1. Disconnect the negative battery cable. Drain the water from the radiator.

2. Loosen the radiator shell and remove the radiator.

3. Remove the fan with the coupling and set it aside in an upright position.

4. Loosen the belt around the water pump pulley and remove the belt.

5. Remove the harmonic balancer bolts, the balancer and pulley.

6. Unbolt and remove the water pump.

7. Installation is the reverse of removal. Tighten the belt and fill the cooling system.

Water Pump Housing

Removal and Installation

190D, 300D, 300TD AND 300SDL

1. Disconnect negative terminal on battery.

2. Remove alternator and place it aside.

3. Remove alternator carrier.

4. Remove return line on crankcase and pull from water pump housing.

5. Remove water pump housing.

6. Clean sealing surfaces.

To install:

7. Renew O-ring on return line.

NOTE: Keep O-ring free of grease. For better assembly, immerse O-ring into coolant.

8. Plug coolant pump housing on return line and screw with a gasket to crankcase, tighten to 7.5 ft. lbs. (10 Nm).

9. Screw return line to crankcase.

10. Mount alternator carrier and tighten screws to 18.5 ft. lbs. (25 Nm).

11. Mount alternator and tighten screw to 33 ft. lbs. (45 Nm). Connect negative battery terminal.

Thermostat

Removal and Installation

EXCEPT V8 ENGINES

The thermostat housing is a light metal casting attached directly to the cylinder head, except on the 190D where it is attached to the side of the water pump housing; and the 190E with the 2.6L engine, 260E, 300E, 300CE, 300SE, 300TE and 300SEL where it is under a plastic cover atop the water pump.

1. Disconnect the negative battery cable. Open the radiator cap and depressurize the system.

2. Open the radiator drain cock and partially drain the coolant. Drain enough coolant to bring the coolant level below the level of the thermostat housing.

3. Remove the thermostat housing cover bolts and cover.

4. Note the installation position of the thermostat and remove it.

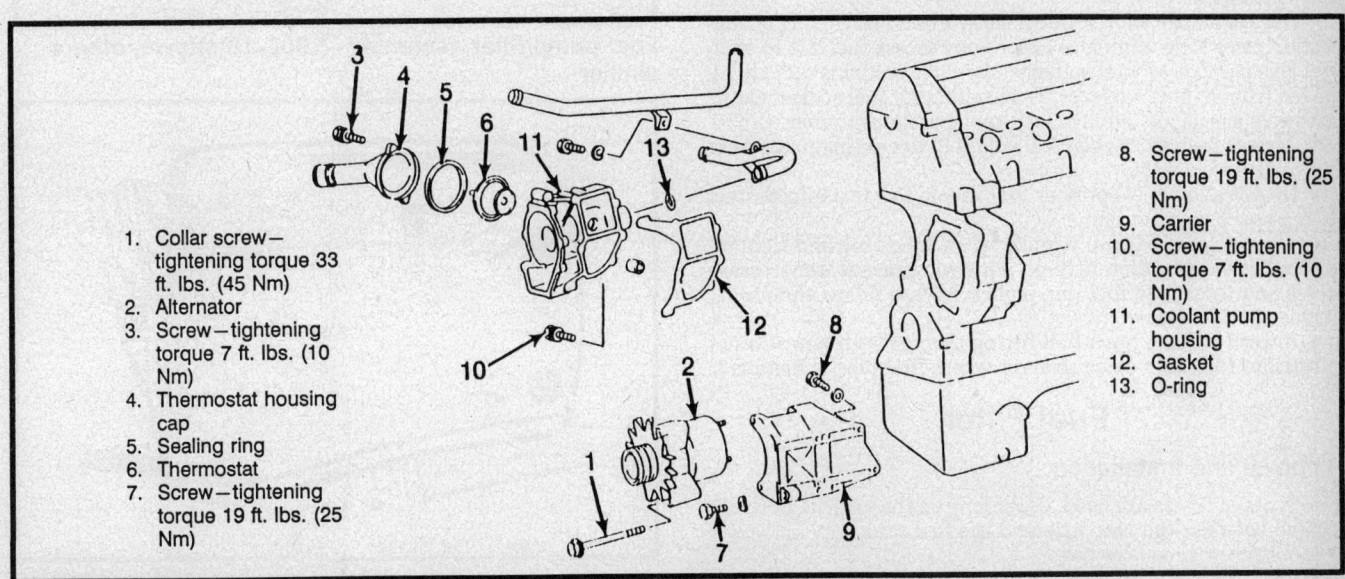

1. Collar screw—tightening torque 33 ft. lbs. (45 Nm)
2. Alternator
3. Screw—tightening torque 7 ft. lbs. (10 Nm)
4. Thermostat housing cap
5. Sealing ring
6. Thermostat
7. Screw—tightening torque 19 ft. lbs. (25 Nm)
8. Screw—tightening torque 19 ft. lbs. (25 Nm)
9. Carrier
10. Screw—tightening torque 7 ft. lbs. (10 Nm)
11. Coolant pump housing
12. Gasket
13. O-ring

Water pump housing servicing—190D, 300D, 300TD and 300SDL

Aligning the thermostat on the 190D

To install:

5. Installation is the reverse of removal. Be sure the thermostat is positioned with the ball valve at the highest point and the bolts are tightened evenly against the seal. On the 190D, the recess in the thermostat casing should be located above the lug in the thermostat housing. On the 190E with 2.6L engine, 260E, 300E, 300CE, 300SE, 300TE and 300SEL, the ball valve must be at its highest point in the housing to allow complete venting of gas bubbles.

6. Refill the cooling system and check for leaks.

NOTE: When refilling the coolant system on the 300E, 300CE, 300SE, 300TE and 300SEL, always remove the hex-head plug on the left side of the cylinder head and fill the hole with coolant until it overflows. Install the plug and fill the coolant system. When filling the coolant system on the 190E with 2.6L and the 260E, open the vent screw on top of the thermostat housing approximately 2 turns, start the engine run the engine at idle.

V8 ENGINES

1. Drain the coolant from the radiator and block.
2. Remove the air cleaner.
3. Disconnect the battery and remove the alternator.
4. Unscrew the housing cover on the side of the water pump and remove the thermostat.
5. If a new thermostat is to be installed, always install a new sealing ring.
6. Installation is the reverse of removal. Be sure to tighten the screws on the housing cover evenly to prevent leaks. Refill the cooling system and check of leaks.

GASOLINE FUEL SYSTEM

Fuel System Service Precautions

Safety is the most important factor when performing not only fuel system maintenance but any type of maintenance. Failure to conduct maintenance and repairs in a safe manner may result in serious personal injury or death. Maintenance and testing of the vehicle's fuel system components can be accomplished safely and effectively by adhering to the following rules and guidelines.

• To avoid the possibility of fire and personal injury, always disconnect the negative battery cable unless the repair or test procedure requires that battery voltage be applied.

• Always relieve the fuel system pressure prior to disconnecting any fuel system component (injector, fuel rail, pressure regulator, etc.), fitting or fuel line connection. Exercise extreme caution whenever relieving fuel system pressure to avoid exposing skin, face and eyes to fuel spray. Please be advised that fuel under pressure may penetrate the skin or any part of the body that it contacts.

• Always place a shop towel or cloth around the fitting or connection prior to loosening to absorb any excess fuel due to spillage. Ensure that all fuel spillage (should it occur) is quickly removed from engine surfaces. Ensure that all fuel soaked cloths or towels are deposited into a suitable waste container.

• Always keep a dry chemical (Class B) fire extinguisher near the work area.

• Do not allow fuel spray or fuel vapors to come into contact with a spark or open flame.

• Always use a backup wrench when loosening and tightening fuel line connection fittings. This will prevent unnecessary stress and torsion to fuel line piping. Always follow the proper torque specifications.

• Always replace worn fuel fitting O-rings with new. Do not substitute fuel hose or equivalent where fuel pipe is installed.

Fuel Filter

Removal and Installation

Two types of filters are used, depending on the vehicle. Both are located between the rear axle and the fuel tank.

1. Unscrew the cover box.
2. Remove the pressure hoses.
3. Loosen the screws and remove the filter. Remove the con-

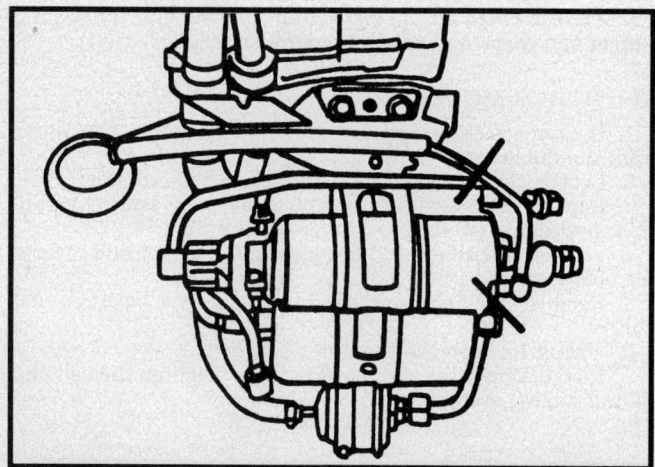

Fuel pump/filter assembly—190E-16 shown, others similar

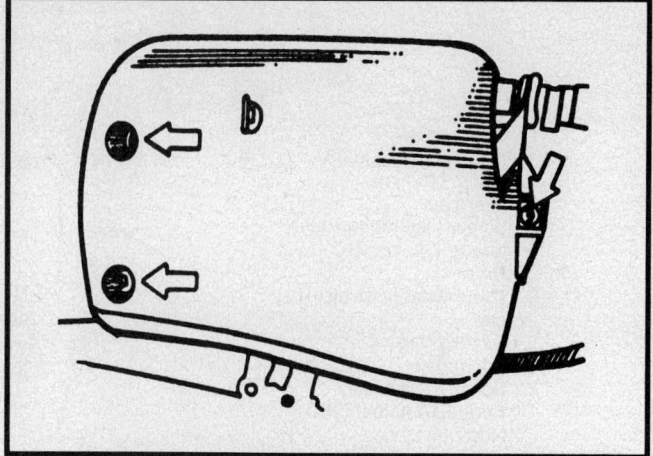

Fuel pump package cover—190 series, 260E, 300E, 300CE, 300SEL and 300TE

necting plug from the old filter and install it on a new filter using a new gasket.

To install:

4. Install a new filter in the direction of flow.
5. Replace the attaching screws.
6. Install the pressure hoses.
7. Install the fuel filter in the holder by positioning it in the center of the transparent holder. Be sure the plastic sleeve between the fuel filter and fuel pump is installed. Galvanic corrosion may occur in cases of direct contact between these components.
8. Replace the cover box and check for proper sealing.

Testing Delivery

1. Remove the wire from the coil to prevent starting.
2. Connect a pressure gauge into the output line of the fuel pump.
3. Crank the engine and read the delivery pressure on the pressure gauge. The pressure should be a constant 1.5–2.5 psi.
4. If the pressure is not within specifications or is erratic, remove the pump for service or for replacement with a new or rebuilt unit. No adjustment is provided.

Electric Fuel Pump

NOTE: Do not confuse the electric fuel pump with the injection pump.

All Mercedes-Benz fuel injected engines are equipped with electric fuel pumps. The electric fuel pump is located under the rear floor panel. The fuel return line was also eliminated and a check ball installed in its place. The fuel pump uses a replaceable check valve on the outside of the pump which can be replaced separately.

Two types of fuel pumps have been used. One, the large pump, has been replaced with a new small design which has a bypass system to prevent vapor lock.

Testing Fuel Pump Delivery Pressure

Remove the fuel return hose from the fuel distributor. Connect a fuel line and hold the end in the measuring cup. Disconnect the plug from the safety switch on the mixture regulator and turn **ON** the ignition for 30 seconds. If the delivery rate is less than 1 liter in 30 seconds, check the voltage at the fuel pump it should be 11.5V, and the fuel lines for kinks. Disconnect the leak off line between the fuel accumulator and the suction damper. Check the delivery rate again. If it is low, replace the accumulator.

Replace the fuel filter and test again. If still low, replace the fuel pump.

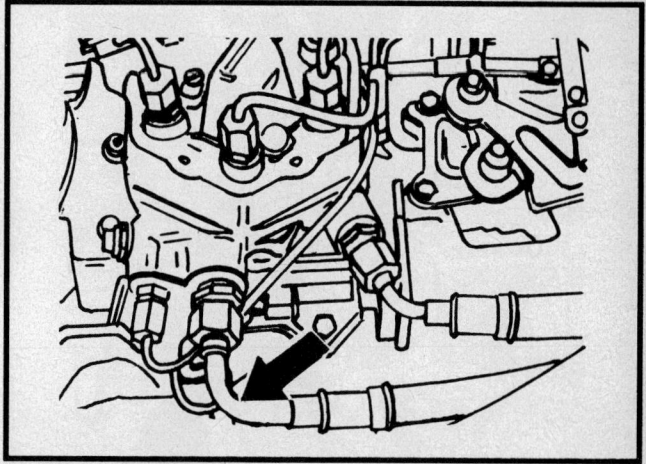

Testing fuel pump pressure

Removal and Installation

1. Disconnect the negative battery cable. Raise and safely support the vehicle.
2. Remove and plug the intake, outlet and bypass lines from the pump.
3. Disconnect the electrical leads.
4. Unbolt and remove the fuel pump and vibration pads.

NOTE: The V8 engines utilize 2 fuel pumps connected in series.

5. Install the fuel pump in the reverse order of removal. Be sure the electrical leads are connected to the proper terminals. The negative wire (brown) is connected to the negative terminal (brown plastic plate) and the positive wire (black/red) is connect to the positive terminal (red plastic plate). If the terminals are reversed, the pump will operate in the reverse direction of normal rotation and will deliver no fuel.

Fuel Injection

For further information, please refer to "Chilton's Electronic Engine Control's Manual" for additional coverage.

Adjustments

These engines have electronically controlled idle speed, using a solenoid connected to the control unit. Idle speed and mixture adjustments are not recommended.

DIESEL FUEL SYSTEM

Fuel Filter

Replacement
MAIN FUEL FILTER

Loosen the center bolt and remove the filter cartridge downward. Lubricate the new filter gasket with clean diesel fuel and install a new filter cartridge.

To bleed the fuel filter: Loosen the bleed bolt on the fuel filter housing and release the manually operated delivery pump. Operate the delivery pump until the fuel emerges free of bubbles at the bleed screw. Close the bleed bolt and operate the pump until the overflow valve on the injection pump opens, a buzzing noise

will be heard. Close the manual pump before starting the engine. To bleed the injection pump on 4 cylinder diesels, loosen the bleed screw on the injection pump and keep pumping the hand pump until fuel emerges free of bubbles.

NOTE: The 190D uses a self-bleeding fuel pump, therefore the hand pump has been eliminated. No bleeding is necessary.

DIESEL PRE-FILTER

Diesel engines use a pre-filter in addition to the main fuel filter, since even the most minute particle of dirt will clog the injection system. The pre-filter is located in the line just before it enters the injection pump.

Some diesel injection pumps have a manually operated delivery pump (1)

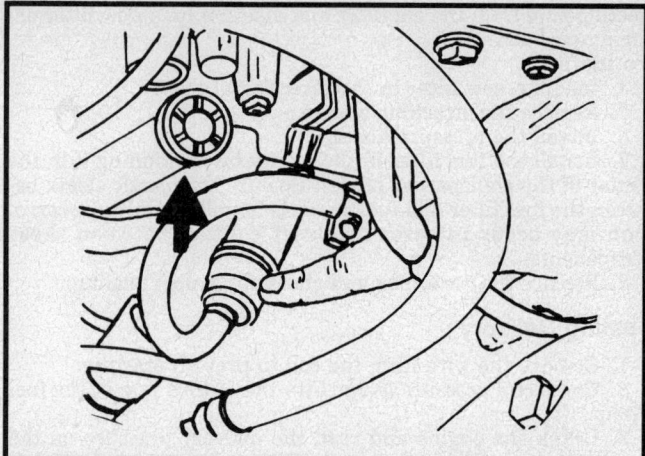

Diesel engines use a pre-filter in addition to the main fuel filter. The arrow indicates the hard operated delivery pump

To replace it, simply unscrew the clamps on each end and remove the old filter. Install a new filter and bleed the system.

Idle Speed Adjustment

All engines are equipped with an electronic idle speed control system. The rpm sensor picks up the engine speed and transmits it in the form of AC voltage to the EDS control unit. The EDS control unit processes the rpm signal and performs a nominal-actual value comparison. The idle speed is held constant by the magnetic actuator independent of engine load. Provisions for adjustment are not provided.

EMISSION CONTROLS

For further information, please refer to "Professional Emission Component Application Guide".

Emission Warning Lights

Resetting

560 SERIES

1. The instrument cluster must be partially removed on certain models. Using a steel wire with a small hook on the end, slip the wire between the right side of the cluster and the dashboard. Turn the hook to engage the cluster and the dashboard. Turn the hook to engage the cluster and gently pull the edge of the cluster from the retaining clips.
2. Remove the oxygen sensor bulb at the extreme lower corner of the cluster. Press the cluster back into position. No reset switch is provided.

GASOLINE ENGINE MECHANICAL

NOTE: Disconnecting the negative battery cable on some vehicles may interfere with the functions of the on board computer systems and may require the computer to undergo a relearning process, once the negative battery cable is reconnected.

Also, note that care should be taken when working on Mercedes-Benz engines, since there are many aluminum parts which can be damaged, if carelessly handled.

Engine Assembly

Removal and Installation

NOTE: In all cases, Mercedes-Benz engines and transmissions are removed as a unit.

----- CAUTION -----
Air conditioner lines should not be indiscriminately disconnected without taking proper precautions. It is best to swing the compressor aside while still connected to its hoses. Never do any welding around the compressor-heat may cause an explosion. Also, the refrigerant, while inert at normal room temperature, breaks down under high temperature into hydrogen fluoride and phosgene (among other products), which are highly poisonous.

EXCEPT V8 ENGINES

1. Remove the hood, drain the cooling system and disconnect the battery. While not strictly necessary, it is better to remove the battery completely to prevent breakage by the engine as it is lifted out.
2. Remove the fan shroud and radiator.
3. Disconnect all heater hoses and oil cooler lines. Plug all openings to keep out dirt.

4. Remove the air cleaner and all fuel, vacuum and oil hoses (e.g., power steering and power brakes). Plug all openings to keep out dirt.

5. Remove the viscous coupling and fan.

6. Disconnect the accelerator linkage.

7. Disconnect all ground straps and electrical connections; it is a good idea to tag each wire for easy reassembly.

8. Detach the gearshift linkage and the exhaust pipes from the manifolds.

9. Loosen the steering relay arm and move it aside, along with the center steering rod and hydraulic steering damper.

10. The hydraulic engine shock absorber should be removed.

11. Remove the hydraulic line from the clutch housing and the oil line connectors from the automatic transmission.

12. Unbolt the clutch slave cylinder from the bell housing after removing the return spring.

13. Remove the exhaust pipe bracket from the transmission. Support bellhousing or place a cable sling under the oil pan, to support the engine.

14. Mark the position of the rear engine support and unbolt the 2 outer bolts, remove the top bolt at the transmission and pull the support out.

15. Disconnect the speedometer cable and the front driveshaft U-joint. Push the driveshaft back and wire it aside.

16. Unbolt the engine mounts on both sides and, on 4 cylinder engines, the front limit stop.

17. Unbolt the power steering fluid reservoir and swing it aside; then, using a chain hoist and cable, lift the engine and transmission upward and outward. An angle of about 45 degrees will allow the vehicle to be pushed backward while the engine is coming up.

18. Reverse the procedure to install, making sure to bleed the hydraulic clutch, power steering, power brakes and fuel system.

V8 ENGINES

NOTE: Removal of a V8 engine equipped with air conditioning, may require discharging the air conditioning system. Use caution; Freon is lethal.

1. Remove the hood.
2. Drain the cooling system.
3. Remove the radiator and fan shroud.
4. Remove the cable plug from the temperature switch.
5. Remove the battery, battery frame and air filter.
6. Drain the power steering reservoir and windshield washer reservoir.
7. Disconnect and plug the high pressure and return lines on the power steering pump.
8. Detach the fuel lines from the fuel filter, pressure regulator, and pressure sensor.
9. If equipped, loosen the line to the supply and anti-freeze tanks. If equipped, disconnect the lines to the hydro-pneumatic suspension.
10. Disconnect the cables from the ignition coil and transistor ignition switchbox.
11. Disconnect the brake vacuum lines.
12. Detach the cable connections for the following:
   a. Venturi control unit
   b. Temperature sensor
   c. Distributor
   d. Temperature switch
   e. Cold start valve
13. Remove the regulating shaft by pushing it in the direction of the firewall.
14. Disconnect the thrust and pullrods.
15. Disconnect the heater lines.
16. Detach the lines to the oil pressure and temperature gauges.
17. Remove the ground strap from the vehicle.
18. Detach the cables from the alternator, terminal bridge, and battery. Remove the battery.

19. Position a lifting sling on the engine and take up the slack in the chain.

20. Remove the left side engine mount and loosen the hex nut on the right side mount.

21. Remove the exhaust system. Remove the connecting rod chain on the rear level control valve and loosen the torsion bar slightly. Raise the vehicle slightly at the rear and remove the exhaust system in the rearward direction.

22. Disconnect the hand brake cable.

23. Remove the shield plate from the transmission tunnel.

24. Place a block of wood between the transmission and cross-yoke so the engine will not sag when the rear mount is removed.

25. Loosen the driveshaft intermediate bearing and the drive-shaft slide.

26. Support the transmission.

27. Mark the installation of the crossmember and remove the crossmember. Remove the rear engine carrier with the engine mount.

28. Unbolt the front U-joint flange on the transmission and push it back. Do not loosen the clamp nut on the intermediate bearing. Support the driveshaft.

29. Disconnect the speedometer shaft, shift rod, control pressure rod, regulating linkage, for automatic transmissions, kickdown switch cable, starter lockout switch cable, and the cable for the back-up light switch.

30. Remove the front engine mounting bolt and remove the engine at approximately a 45 degree angle.

31. Installation is the reverse of removal. Lower the engine until it is behind the front axle carrier. Support the transmission and lower the engine into its compartment. While lowering the engine, install the right-hand shock mount.

32. Fill the engine with all required fluids and start the engine. Check for leaks.

Cylinder Head

Removal and Installation

4 CYLINDER ENGINE

Except 190E-16 (DOHC)

This is fairly straight forward but some caution must be observed to ensure that the valve timing is not disturbed.

1. Disconnect the negative battery cable. Drain the radiator and remove all hoses and wires. Tag all wires to ensure easy reassembly.

2. The cylinder head cover on the 190E is removed with the spark plug cables and distributor cap still attached to it.

3. The rockers and their supports must be removed together.

4. Mark the chain, sprocket and cam for ease of assembly.

5. Using a suitable puller, remove the camshaft sprocket.

6. Remove the sprocket and chain and wire it aside.

7. Make sure the chain is securely wired so it will not slide into the engine.

8. Unbolt the manifolds and exhaust header pipe and push them aside.

9. Loosen the cylinder head hold-down bolts in the reverse order of that shown in torque diagrams for each model. It is good practice to loosen each bolt a little at a time, working around the head, until all are free. This prevents unequal stresses in the metal.

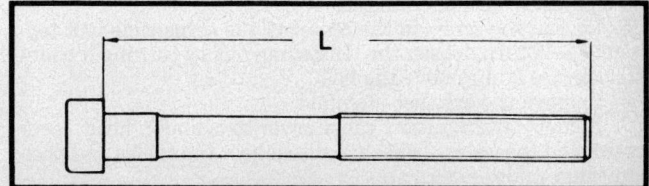

Cylinder head bolt stretch is measured at "L"

The timing marks on the camshaft bearing cap (1) and the camshaft (2) should be in alignment when the No. 1 cylinder is at TDC

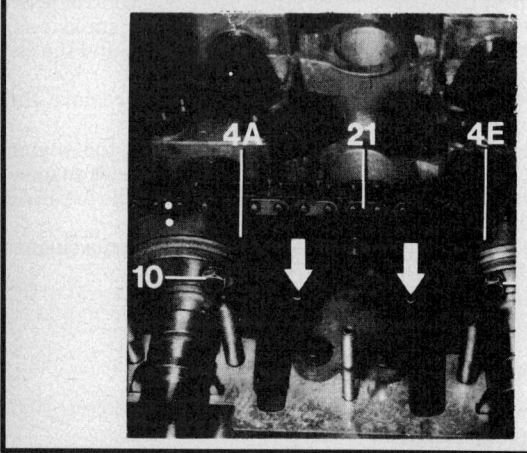

When the 2 punch marks are in alignment on the 190E-16 camshaft sprockets, the engine is at TDC

10. Reach into the engine compartment and gradually work the head loose from each end by rocking it. Never, under any circumstances, use a prybar between the head and block to pry, as the head will be scarred badly and may be ruined.
11. Installation is the reverse of removal.

190E-16 (DOHC)

1. Disconnect the negative battery cable. Drain the engine coolant and disconnect the radiator and heater hoses at the cylinder head.
2. Tag and disconnect the intake air temperature sensor lead and the crankcase ventilation hose where they connect to the air cleaner.
3. Remove the 2 air cleaner mounting nuts. Lift the housing at the rear until it releases from its holding studs, slide it backwards slightly and remove it from the air flow sensor.
4. Loosen the oil dipstick mounting bracket screw and pull the dipstick from the crankcase.
5. Loosen the screw in the center of the serpentine belt tensioner ¼–½ turn, loosen the tensioning nut by turning it counterclockwise and remove the belt.
6. Remove the exhaust manifold.
7. Remove the ignition cable cover-to-cylinder head cover screws and the cover. Label and disconnect the cables and position them aside.
8. Loosen the clamp on the rear heater hose and pull it off the water outlet.

9. Disconnect the breather line at the cylinder head cover.
10. Remove the 6 mounting nuts and lift up the cylinder head cover.

NOTE: If the cylinder head cover sticks to the head, do not use a hammer to loosen it as it may crack. Try to break the seal by pushing at both corners on 1 side or the other by hand.

11. Set the No. 1 piston to TDC, of the compression stroke, by turning the crankshaft in the directions of normal engine rotation. When the 2 punch marks in the camshaft sprockets are aligned, the engine will be at TDC.
12. Place matchmarks on the camshaft sprocket and the timing chain.
13. Remove the alternator air duct. Label and disconnect the electrical leads. Pull the harness through the component compartment wall and position it aside. Remove the alternator.
14. Using a 32mm wrench, unscrew the chain tensioner.
15. Label and disconnect the two pump lines and remove the pump from the exhaust side camshaft. Remove the 3 screws and pull the pump flange from the end of the camshaft.
16. Remove the 2 mounting nuts and lift the chain slide from the front of the engine.

NOTE: If equipped, remove the sheet metal bracket that is attached to the 2 front cylinder head bolts and the 2 eyes at the timing chain housing cover.

17. Remove the 4 mounting screws from each camshaft sprocket. Knock the camshaft back slightly with a rubber mallet; be careful. Remove the front bearing caps and pull off the 2 sprockets.

NOTE: Secure the timing chain so it will not slip into the crankcase.

18. Loosen the water bypass hose clamp. Remove the mounting screws and pull out the water inlet/thermostat housing.
19. Use a Allen wrench to remove the 2 return pipe mounting screws and pull it from the cylinder head. If the pipe sticks, rotate it clockwise slightly and force it out with a suitable prybar.
20. Unbolt the intake manifold and push it aside.
21. Loosen the cylinder head bolts in the reverse order of the tightening sequence. Loosen each bolt, a little at a time, working around the head until all are free; this will prevent unequal stress on the aluminum head.
22. Reach into the engine compartment and gradually work the head loose from the cylinder block. Never use a prybar to pry the head free.
23. Installation is in the reverse order of removal. Please note the following:
   a. Measure the cylinder head bolts prior to installation. A new bolt is 110mm long from the bottom of bolt head to the end of the bolt. If it has stretched to more than 113mm, replace it.
   b. Tighten the cylinder head bolts, a little at a time, in seqthe uence.
   c. Use new O-rings and a new flange gasket when installing the return pipe.
   d. Install the intake camshaft sprocket first; right side when facing the vehicle. Be certain that the matchmarks are aligned.
   e. Make sure the 2 punch marks in the sprockets are in alignment.

6 CYLINDER SOHC

NOTE: The cylinder head on the 190E with 2.6L engine, 260E, 300E, 300CE, 300SE, 300TE and 300SEL should be removed cold, with the camshaft, intake and exhaust manifolds attached.

1. Disconnect the negative battery cable. Remove the engine undercovers from below.

2. Drain the engine coolant. Drain the engine oil.
3. Remove the air filter.
4. Remove the distributor cap mounting bolts. Unbolt the cylinder head cover and remove it with the ignition wires and distributor cap still attached.

NOTE: Distributor cap removal will require a 5mm T-shaped Allen wrench about 80mm in length.

5. Loosen the 3 Allen screws and lift off the distributor rotor.
6. Using a 6mm Allen wrench, unscrew the distributor driver and remove it. Carefully, pry off the protective cover.
7. Remove the mounting screws for the cylinder head front cover and carefully knock the cover off with a rubber mallet.
8. Rotate the crankshaft so the No. 1 cylinder is set at TDC of the compression stroke.
9. Unscrew the timing chain tensioner plug and remove the compression spring.
10. Use a 17mm Allen-head socket and unscrew the tensioner threaded ring.
11. Insert an M8 screw into the tensioner bore, tilt it slightly and ease the tensioner from the bore. If the tensioner is difficult to remove, loosen the socket head screw above the tensioner bore slightly; this should facilitate removal.
12. Matchmark the camshaft sprocket to the camshaft by putting a dab of paint next to the hole in the sprocket with the dowel pin.
13. Matchmark the camshaft sprocket to the timing chain.
14. Remove the mounting screws and pull off the camshaft sprocket. Secure the timing chain so it will not slip into the crankcase.
15. Remove the slide rail bolt with an impact puller.
16. Unscrew the oil dipstick guide tube bracket and pull out the dipstick and tube.
17. Unscrew the upper intake manifold mounting bolt. Loosen the lower bolt.
18. Loosen the hose clamp and remove the coolant hose at the water pump.
19. Unscrew the exhaust pipe at both flanges.
20. Disconnect the automatic transmission dipstick tube at the cylinder head and position it aside.
21. Tag and disconnect all wiring, electrical leads and vacuum hoses connected to or in the way of the cylinder head.
22. Disconnect the fuel feed and return lines, plug them and position them aside.
23. Disconnect the accelerator pedal Bowden cable.
24. Loosen the cylinder head bolts in the reverse order of the tightening sequence. Loosen each bolt, a little at a time, working around the head until all bolts are free; this will prevent unequal stress on the aluminum head.
25. Reach into the engine compartment and gradually work the head loose from the cylinder block. Never use a prybar to pry the head free.

To install:
26. Position a new cylinder head gasket on the cylinder block.
27. Connect the water pump coolant hose to the head and position the head on the block. There are 2 dowel pins for locating purposes.
28. Measure the length of the cylinder head bolts from the underside of the bolt head to the end of the bolt. If the length exceeds 108.4mm, the bolts must be replaced with new stretch bolts.
29. Install the cylinder head bolts and tighten them a little at a time, in sequence.
30. Install the camshaft sprocket and tighten the bolts to 8 ft. lbs. (11 Nm). Be sure the dowel pin is in the hole marked previously and that the matchmarks on the timing chain and sprocket are aligned.
31. Slide the chain tensioner housing into the bore. Screw in the threaded ring and tighten it to 22 ft. lbs. (30 Nm). Install the thrust bolt with the detent spring. Position the compression spring and a new seal. Tighten the plug to 37 ft. lbs. (50 Nm).

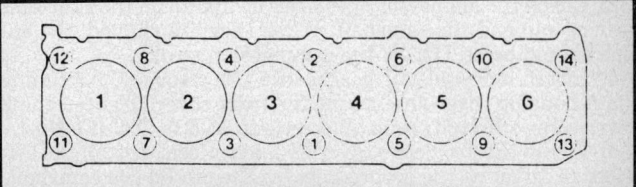

Cylinder head bolt torque sequence—6 cylinder engines

Matchmark the camshaft sprocket on the 260E, 300E, 300CE, 300SEL and 300TE

The groove (arrow) on the driver (5) must engage the pin in the camshaft—260E, 300E, 300CE, 300SE, 300SEL and 300TE

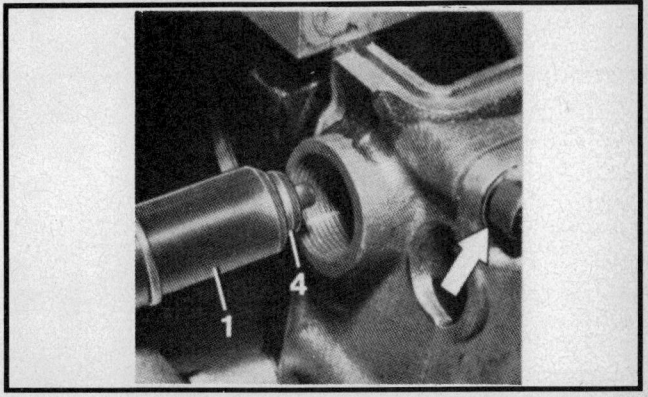

Removing the chain tensioner on the 260E, 300E, 300CE, 300SE, 300SEL and 300TE

32. Check the alignment of the timing marks on the camshaft bearing cap and the camshaft. When they are aligned, the engine should be at TDC of the compression stroke.

33. Install a new elastic gasket into the groove of the timing chain housing cover and mount the front cover. Tighten the 2 lower screws first. Torque all screws to 15.5 ft. lbs. (21 Nm).

34. Install the protective cover with a new seal. Install the distributor driver so the groove engages the pin on the camshaft. Tighten the screw to 15.5 ft. lbs. (21 Nm).

35. Installation of the remaining components is in the reverse order of removal.

NOTE: When refilling the coolant system on the 300E, 300CE, 300SE, 300TE and 300SEL, always remove the hex head plug on the left side of the cylinder head and fill the hole with coolant until it overflows. Install the plug and fill the coolant system. When filling the coolant system on the 190E with 2.6L engine and 260E, open the vent screw approximately 2 turns, start the engine and run at idle.

V8 ENGINES

NOTE: Before removing the cylinder head from a V8, obtain the 4 special tools necessary to torque the head bolts; without them it will be impossible. Do not confuse the left and right side head gaskets. The left side has 2 attaching holes in the timing chain cover, the right side has only 1 hole.
Cylinder heads can only be removed with the engine cold.

1. Drain the cooling system.
2. Remove the battery.
3. Remove the air cleaner. Remove the fan and fan shroud.
4. Pull the cable plug from the temperature sensor.
5. Detach the vacuum hose from the venturi control unit.
6. Remove the following electrical connections:
   a. Injection valves.
   b. Distributor
   c. Venturi control unit
   d. Temperature sensor and temperature switch
   e. Starting valve
   f. Temperature switch for the auxiliary fan.
7. Loosen the ring line on the fuel distributor.
8. Loosen the screws on the injection valves and pressure regulator or mixture regulator. Remove the ring line with the injection valves and pressure regulator.
9. Plug the holes for the injection valves in the cylinder head.

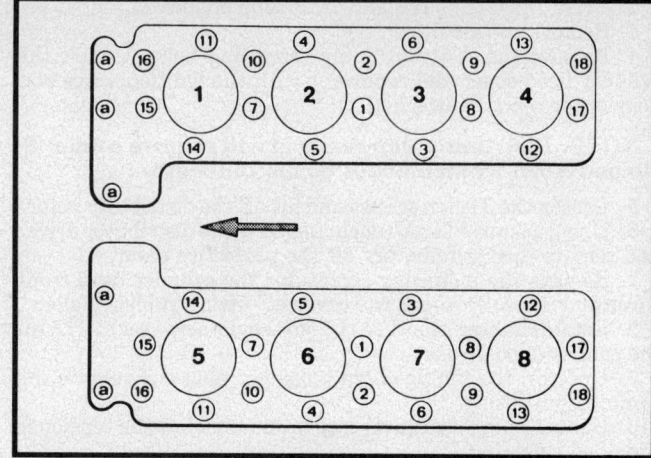

Cylinder head torque sequence — V8 engines

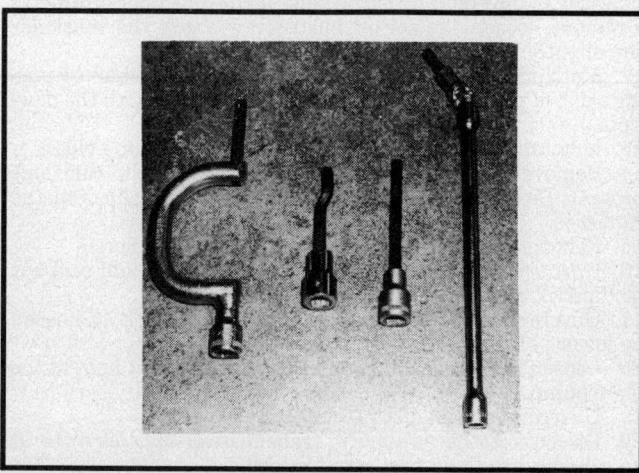

Without these tools, it is practically impossible to service the V8 cylinder head.

10. Remove the regulating shaft by disconnecting the pull rod and the thrust rod.
11. Remove the ignition cable plug.
12. Loosen the vacuum connection on the intake manifold.

Be careful removing the cylinder head bolts on a V8 engine. The inner row of cam bolts are the only bolts NOT holding the head on. Note the angle of the bolts

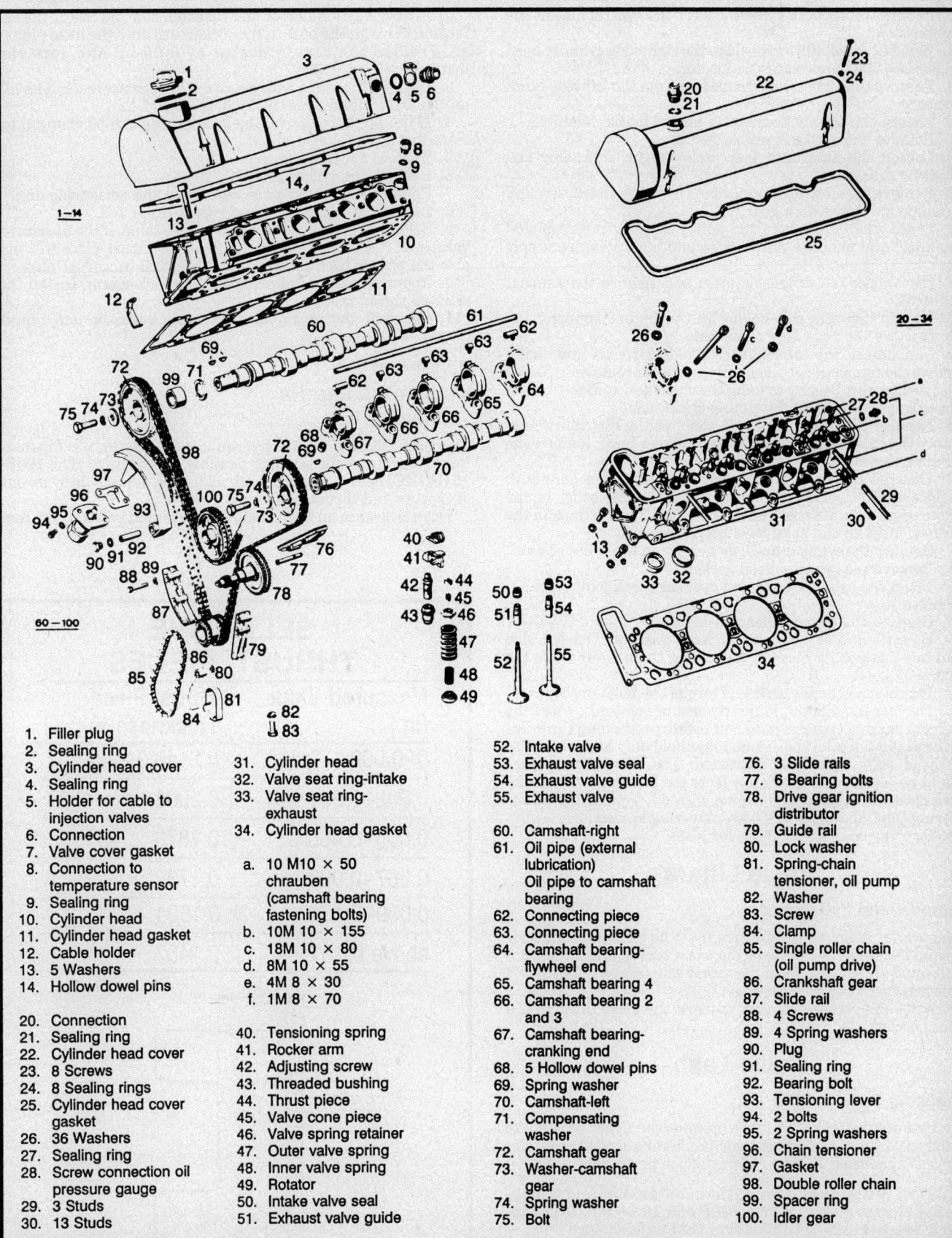

1. Filler plug
2. Sealing ring
3. Cylinder head cover
4. Sealing ring
5. Holder for cable to injection valves
6. Connection
7. Valve cover gasket
8. Connection to temperature sensor
9. Sealing ring
10. Cylinder head
11. Cylinder head gasket
12. Cable holder
13. 5 Washers
14. Hollow dowel pins

20. Connection
21. Sealing ring
22. Cylinder head cover
23. 8 Screws
24. 8 Sealing rings
25. Cylinder head cover gasket
26. 36 Washers
27. Sealing ring
28. Screw connection oil pressure gauge
29. 3 Studs
30. 13 Studs

31. Cylinder head
32. Valve seat ring-intake
33. Valve seat ring-exhaust
34. Cylinder head gasket

a. 10 M10 × 50 chrauben (camshaft bearing fastening bolts)
b. 10M 10 × 155
c. 18M 10 × 80
d. 8M 10 × 55
e. 4M 8 × 30
f. 1M 8 × 70

40. Tensioning spring
41. Rocker arm
42. Adjusting screw
43. Threaded bushing
44. Thrust piece
45. Valve cone piece
46. Valve spring retainer
47. Outer valve spring
48. Inner valve spring
49. Rotator
50. Intake valve seal
51. Exhaust valve guide

52. Intake valve
53. Exhaust valve seal
54. Exhaust valve guide
55. Exhaust valve

60. Camshaft-right
61. Oil pipe (external lubrication)
Oil pipe to camshaft bearing
62. Connecting piece
63. Connecting piece
64. Camshaft bearing-flywheel end
65. Camshaft bearing 4
66. Camshaft bearing 2 and 3
67. Camshaft bearing-cranking end
68. 5 Hollow dowel pins
69. Spring washer
70. Camshaft-left
71. Compensating washer
72. Camshaft gear
73. Washer-camshaft gear
74. Spring washer
75. Bolt

76. 3 Slide rails
77. 6 Bearing bolts
78. Drive gear ignition distributor
79. Guide rail
80. Lock washer
81. Spring-chain tensioner, oil pump
82. Washer
83. Screw
84. Clamp
85. Single roller chain (oil pump drive)
86. Crankshaft gear
87. Slide rail
88. 4 Screws
89. 4 Spring washers
90. Plug
91. Sealing ring
92. Bearing bolt
93. Tensioning lever
94. 2 bolts
95. 2 Spring washers
96. Chain tensioner
97. Gasket
98. Double roller chain
99. Spacer ring
100. Idler gear

Exploded view of the V8 cylinder head

13. Loosen the vacuum connection for the central lock at the transmission.

14. Remove the oil filler tube from the right side cylinder head and remove the temperature connector.

15. Remove the oil pressure gauge line from the left side cylinder head.

16. Loosen the coolant connection on the intake manifold.

17. Remove the intake manifold bolts.

18. Loosen the alternator belt. Remove the alternator and mounting bracket.

19. Remove the electrical connections from the distributor and electronic ignition switch gear.

20. Drain some fluid from the power steering reservoir and disconnect and plug the return hose and high pressure supply line.

21. Disconnect the exhaust system and remove the exhaust manifolds.

22. Loosen the right side holder for the engine damper.

23. Remove the right side chain tensioner.

24. Matchmark the camshaft, camshaft sprocket and chain. Remove the camshaft sprocket and chain after removing the cylinder head cover. Be sure to hang the chain and sprocket to prevent it from falling into the timing chain case.

25. Remove the upper slide rail. Remove the distributor and remove the inner slide rail on the left cylinder head. Remove the rail after the camshaft sprocket.

26. Unscrew the cylinder head bolts; this should be done with a cold engine. Unscrew the bolts in the reverse order of the torque sequences. Unscrew all the bolts, a little at a time, in the manner, until all the bolts have been removed.

27. Remove the cylinder head; do not pry on the cylinder head.

28. Remove the cylinder head gasket.

29. Clean the cylinder head and cylinder block joint faces.

To install:

30. Position the cylinder head gasket.

31. Do not confuse the cylinder head gaskets. The left side head has 2 attaching holes in the timing chain cover while the right side has 3.

32. Install the cylinder head and torque the bolts in sequence.

33. Further installation is the reverse of removal. Insert the rear cam bearing cylinder head bolt before positioning the cylinder head. Also, install the exhaust manifold only after the cylinder head bolts have been tightened. The camshaft sprocket should be installed so the flange faces the camshaft. Check the valve clearance and fill the engine with oil. Top off the power steering tank and bleed the power steering system.

34. Run the engine and check for leaks.

Valve Lifters

Removal and Installation

Temporarily removed valve lifters must be reinstalled in their original locations. When replacing worn rocker arms, the camshaft must also be replace. If the rocker arm or hydraulic lifter is replaced, check the base setting.

Remove the rocker arm and unscrew the valve lifter with a 24mm socket.

Valve Lash

Checking Base Setting

The base setting is the clearance between the upper edge of the cylindrical part of the plunger and the lower edge of the retaining cap (dimension A) when the cam lobe is vertical.

NOTE: A dial indicator with an extension and a measuring thrust piece (MBNA *100 589 16 63 00), 0.187 in. thick are necessary to perform this adjustment.

1. Turn the cam lobe to a vertical position, relative to the rocker arm.

2. Attach a dial indicator and tip extension and insert the extension through the bore in the rocker arm onto the head plunger. Preload the dial indicator by 0.08 in. and zero the instrument.

3. Depress the valve with a valve spring compressor. The lift on the dial indicator should be 0.028–0.075 in.

4. If the lift is excessive, the base setting can be changed by installing a new thrust piece.

5. Remove the dial indicator.

6. Remove the rocker arm.

7. Remove the thrust piece and insert the measuring disc.

8. Install the rocker arm and repeat Steps 1–3.

9. Select a thrust piece according to the table. If the measured valve was 0–0.002 in. and the 0.2146 in. thrust piece will not give the proper base setting, use the 0.2283 in. thrust piece.

10. Remove the dial indicator and the rocker arm. Install the selected thrust piece.

11. Reinstall the rocker arm and dial indicator and repeat Steps 1–3.

Adjustment

4 CYLINDER ENGINE

190 Series

The 190E (SOHC) utilizes hydraulic valve clearance compensation. No adjustment is either possible or necessary. The 190E-16 (DOHC) uses mechanical lash adjusters, adjustable by means of tappets and thrust washers.

Valve clearance on the 190E-16 is measured between the cam

SELECTIVE THRUST PIECES

Measured Value (in.)	Thrust Piece Thickness(s) (in.)
0–0.002	0.2146/0.2283
0.002–0.034	0.2008
0.035–0.066	0.1870
0.067–0.099	0.1732
0.099–0.131	0.1594
above 0.131	0.1457

Thrust piece thickness

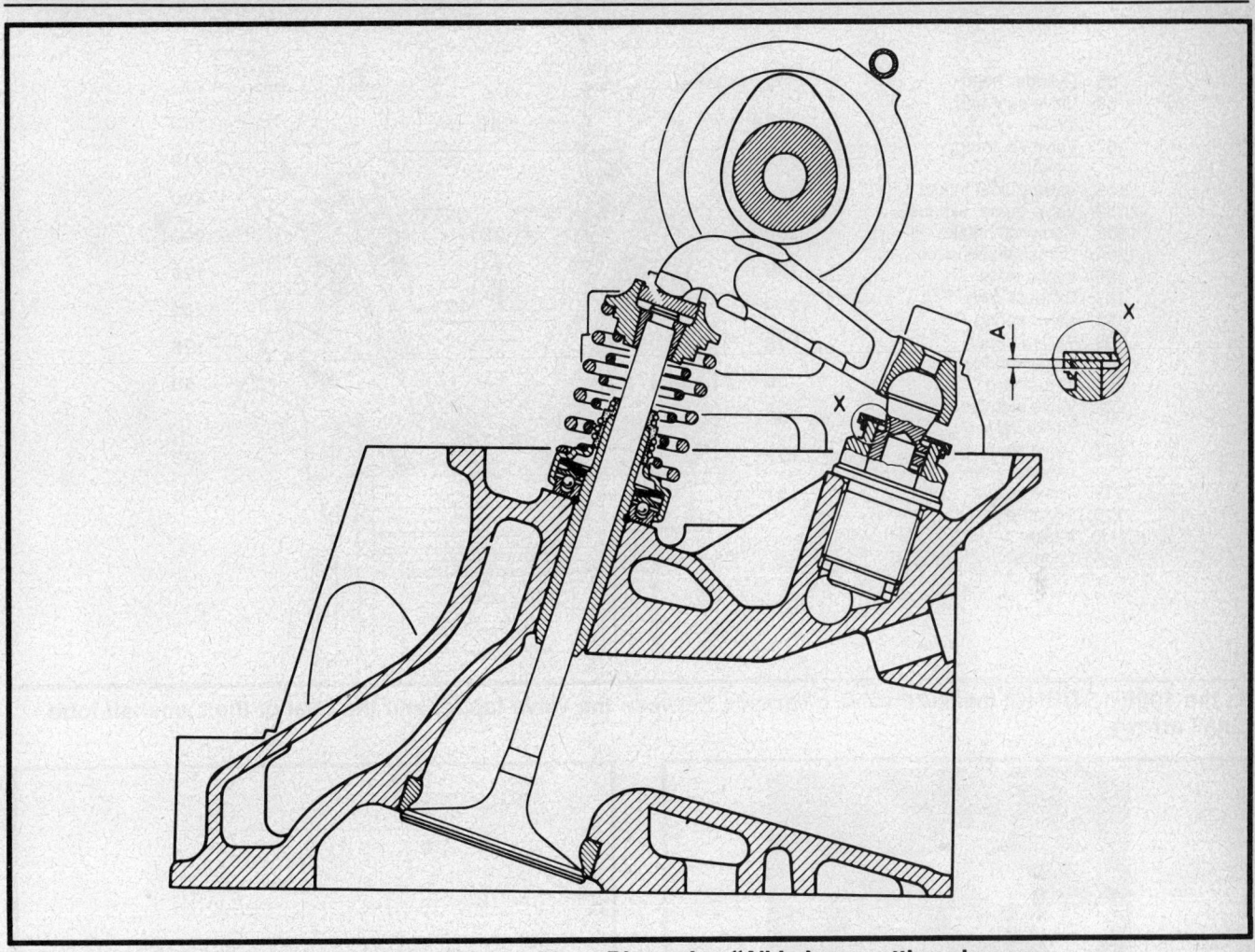

Cutaway of valve train showing hydraulic valve lifter. Dimension "A" is base setting clearance.

base circle and the cup-type valve tappet.

1. Tag and disconnect the spark plug wires and position them aside.

2. Remove the spark plugs and the cylinder head cover.

3. Note the position of the intake and exhaust valves. Viewed from the front of the vehicle, the exhaust valves are on the left and the intake valves are on the right.

4. Using a wrench on the crankshaft pulley bolt, rotate the crankshaft until the heel of the camshaft lobe is in the position.

NOTE: Do not rotate the engine using the camshaft sprocket bolt. The strain will distort the timing chain tensioner rail. Always rotate the engine in the direction of normal rotation only.

5. To measure the valve clearance, insert a feeler gauge of the specified thickness between the heel of the camshaft lobe and the top of the valve tappet. Clearance is correct if the blade can be inserted and withdrawn with a very slight drag.

6. If all measured clearances are within specifications, install the cylinder head cover, spark plugs and their wires. If any clearances are not within specifications, continue checking and record the actual clearance.

7. Remove the camshafts.

8. Lift out the valve tappet. Directly under the tappet is a thrust plate. The thrust plate is held in place by means of the valve keepers; it is also what changes the tappet height and thus the valve clearance.

9. Pry the thrust plate from the valve keepers and check to see what thickness it is; it should be stamped on the surface.

10. Check what the clearance was from Step 6 for the valve that is being worked on. The difference between the measured clearance and the specified clearance is amount by which the existing thrust plate thickness must be increased to obtain the proper valve clearance. New thrust plates are available in increments of 0.05mm.

11. When the proper thickness of the new thrust plate has been determined, press it into the valve keepers and drop the tappet into position over the valve stem/spring.

12. Install the camshafts and recheck the valve clearance.

13. Install the remaining components.

6 CYLINDER ENGINES

NOTE: The 190E with 2.6L engine, 260E, 300E, 300CE, 300SE, 300TE and 300SEL utilizes hydraulic valve clearance compensation. No adjustment is either possible or necessary.

V8 ENGINES

NOTE: V8 engines use hydraulic valve lifters and require no periodic adjustment.

The valve clearance is measured between the sliding surface of the rocker arm and the heel of the camshaft

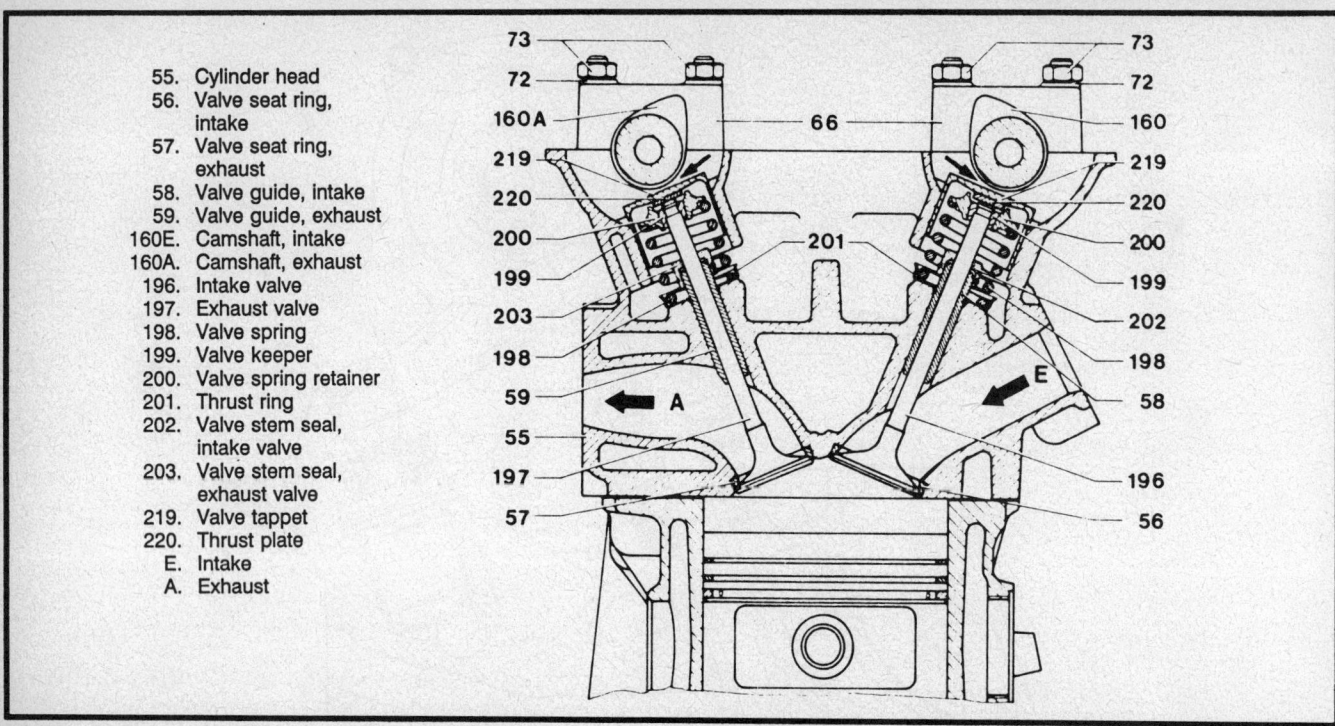

55. Cylinder head
56. Valve seat ring, intake
57. Valve seat ring, exhaust
58. Valve guide, intake
59. Valve guide, exhaust
160E. Camshaft, intake
160A. Camshaft, exhaust
196. Intake valve
197. Exhaust valve
198. Valve spring
199. Valve keeper
200. Valve spring retainer
201. Thrust ring
202. Valve stem seal, intake valve
203. Valve stem seal, exhaust valve
219. Valve tappet
220. Thrust plate
E. Intake
A. Exhaust

On the 190E-16 DOHC, measure valve clearance between the valve tappet and the heal of the camshaft lobe (small arrow)

A valve adjusting wrench (crow's foot) is required to accurately measure torque on all models

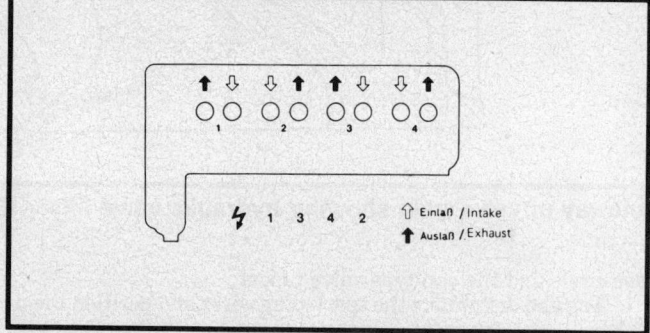

Valve location—SOHC 4 cylinder engines

lobe. The highest point of the camshaft lobe should be at a 90 degree angle to the sliding surface of the rocker arm.

1. Disconnect the negative battery cable. Loosen the venting line and remove the regulating linkage. Remove the valve cover.
2. Disconnect the cable from the ignition coil.
3. Identify all of the valves as intake or exhaust.
4. Begin with the No. 1 cylinder, crank the engine with the starter to position the heel of the camshaft approximately over the sliding surface of the rocker arm.
5. Rotate the crankshaft by means of a socket wrench on the crankshaft pulley bolt until the heel of the camshaft lobe is perpendicular to the sliding surface of the rocker arm.

NOTE: Do not rotate the engine using the camshaft sprocket bolt. The strain will distort the timing chain tensioner rail. Always rotate the engine in the direction of normal rotation only.

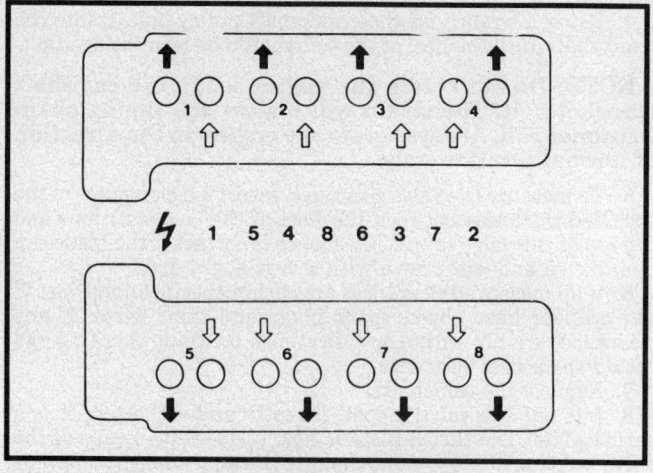

Valve location—V8 engine

6. Some models have holes in the vibration damper plate to assist in crankshaft rotation. In this case, a small prybar can be used to carefully rotate the crankshaft.

7. To measure the valve clearance, insert a feeler blade of the specified thickness between the heel of the camshaft lobe and the sliding surface of the rocker arm. The clearance is correct if the blade can be inserted and withdrawn with a very slight drag.

8. If adjustment is necessary, it can be done by turning the ball pin head at the hex collar. If the clearance is too small, increase it by turning the ball pin head in. If the clearance is too large, turn the ball pin head out.

NOTE: If the adjuster turns very easily or it the proper clearance can't be obtained, check the torque on the adjuster using a special adapter (crow's foot).

9. When the ball pin head is turned, the adjusting torque should be 14–29 ft. lbs. (19–39 Nm). If the torque is lower, either the adjusting screw, the threaded bolt or both will have to be replaced. If the valve clearance is too small and the ball pin head cannot be screwed in far enough to correct it, a thinner pressure piece should be installed in the spring retainer. To replace the pressure piece, the rocker arm must be removed.

10. Install the regulating linkage, valve cover gasket, and valve cover. Be sure the gasket is seated properly.

11. Connect the cable to the coil and the venting line. Run the engine and check for leaks at the valve cover.

Rocker Arms

Removal and Installation

EXCEPT 190E, 260E, 300E, 300CE, 300SE, 300TE AND 300SEL

Before removing the rocker arm(s), be sure they are identified as to their position relative to the camshaft lobe. They should be installed in the same place as they were before disassembly.

Be very careful removing the thrust pieces; they can easily fall into the engine.

1. Disconnect the negative battery cable. Remove the rocker arm cover or covers.

2. Force the clamping spring from the notch in the top of the rocker arm. Slide it in an outward direction across the ball socket or the rocker arm.

NOTE: Turn the engine over each time to relieve any load from the rocker arm.

3. On V8 models, the clamping spring must be forced from the adjusting screw with a small prybar.

4. Force the valve down to remove load from the rocker arm.

NOTE: Do not depress the spring too far. When the piston is up as it should be, the valve will hit the piston. As the spring goes down, the thrust piece will fall into the engine.

5. Lift the rocker arm from the ball pin and remove the rocker arm.

To install:

6. Force the rocker arm down until the rocker arm and its ball socket can be installed in the top of the pin.

7. Install the rocker arms.

8. Slide the clamping spring across the ball socket of the rocker arm until it rests in the notch of the rocker arm.

9. On V8 models, engage the clamping spring into the recess of the adjusting screw.

10. Check and, if necessary, adjust the valve clearance.

11. After completion of the adjustment, check to be sure the clamping springs are correctly seated.

12. Install the rocker arm cover and connect any hoses or lines that were disconnected.

13. Run the engine and check for leaks at the rocker arm cover.

190E, 260E, 300E, 300CE, 300SE, 300TE AND 300SEL

NOTE: The 190E-16 utilizes double overhead camshafts acting directly on valve tappets. There are no rocker arms on this engine.

Rocker arms on this engine are individually mounted on rocker arm shafts that fit into either side of the camshaft bearing brackets.

1. Disconnect the negative battery cable. Remove the cylinder head cover. The cover is removed with the spark plug wires and distributor cap still connected.

2. Tag each rocker arm and shaft so they are identified as to their position relative to the camshaft. They should always be install in the same place as they were before disassembly.

3. The rocker arm shaft is held axially and rotationally by a bearing bracket fastening bolt. Remove the bolt on the side of the bearing bracket that allows access to the exposed end of the rocker shaft.

4. Thread a bolt (M8) into the end of the rocker arm shaft and slowly ease the shaft from the bearing bracket.

NOTE: Support the rocker arm/lifter assembly while removing the shaft so it will not drop onto the cylinder head.

Carefully, forcing the valve down with a small prybar will remove the load on the hydraulic valve tappet and ease the removal of the shaft. Do not depress the spring too far. When the piston is up as it should be, the valve will hit the piston. As the spring goes down the thrust piece will fall into the engine.

5. Replace the bearing bracket bolt and tighten it to 11 ft. lbs. (15 Nm) until ready to replace the rocker shaft.

To install:

6. Position the rocker arm between the 2 bearing brackets and slide the shaft into place.

NOTE: The circular groove on the end of the rocker shaft must align with the mounting bolt shank to ensure proper positioning.

7. Replace the bearing bracket mounting bolt.

8. Repeat Steps 3–7 for all remaining rocker arm/shaft assemblies. Turn the engine over each time to relieve any load from the rocker arm.

9. Replace the cylinder head cover.

To remove the rocker shaft on the 190E SOHC, thread a bolt into the hole (D). On installation, the dished groove (arrow) must always line up with the mounting bolt shank

Intake Manifold

Removal and Installation

190E WITH 2.3L ENGINE

1. Disconnect the negative battery cable. Remove mixture control unit with air guide housing.
2. Disconnect fuel lines.
3. Remove holder for starter cable.
4. Remove electric lines and vacuum lines.
5. Remove supporting holder for intake manifold.
6. Remove engine suspension eye.
7. Remove fastening nuts and bolt.
8. Remove intake manifold.
9. Clean and test flange surfaces with straight-edge, machine on surface plate, if required.

To install:

10. Use new gasket and reverse removal procedure. Check idle.

V8 ENGINE

1. Disconnect the negative battery cable. Partially drain the coolant.
2. Remove the air cleaner.
3. Disconnect the regulating linkage and remove the longitudinal regulating shaft.
4. Pull off all cable plug connections.
5. Disconnect and plug the fuel lines on the pressure regulator and starting valve.

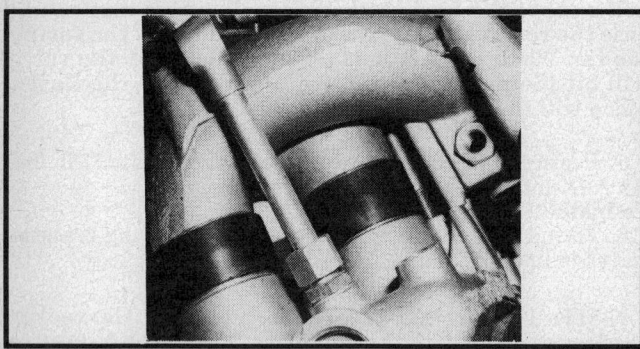

Replace the rubber connecting pieces on the intake manifold, anytime the manifold is removed

6. Unscrew the nuts on the injection valves and set the injection valves aside.
7. Remove the 16 attaching bolts from the intake manifold.
8. Loosen the hose clip on the thermostat housing hose and disconnect the hose.
9. Remove the intake manifold. If a portion of the manifold must be replaced, disassembly the intake manifold. Replace the rubber connections during reassembly.
10. Intake manifold installation is the reverse of removal. Replace all seals and gaskets. Adjust the linkage and idle speed.

Exhaust Manifold

Removal and Installation

V8 ENGINE

1. Disconnect the negative battery cable. Unbolt the exhaust pipes from the manifolds.
2. Disconnect the rubber mounting ring from the exhaust system.
3. Loosen the shield plate on the exhaust manifold.
4. When removing the left side exhaust manifold, remove the shield plate for the engine mount together with the engine damper.
5. Unbolt the manifold from the engine.
6. Pull the manifold off of the mounting.
7. Installation is the reverse of removal.

Timing Chain Tensioner

Removal and Installation

4 CYLINDER ENGINE

There are 2 kinds of timing chain tensioners. One uses an O-ring seal and the other a flat gasket. Do not install a flat gasket on a tensioner meant to be use with an O-ring.

Chain tensioners should be replaced as a unit if defective.

1. Disconnect the negative battery cable. Drain the coolant. If equipped with an air conditioner, disconnect the compressor and mounting bracket and lay it aside; do not disconnect the refrigerant lines.
2. Remove the thermostat housing.
3. Loosen and remove the chain tensioner; be careful of loose O-rings. On the 190, remove the tensioner cap nut and the ten-

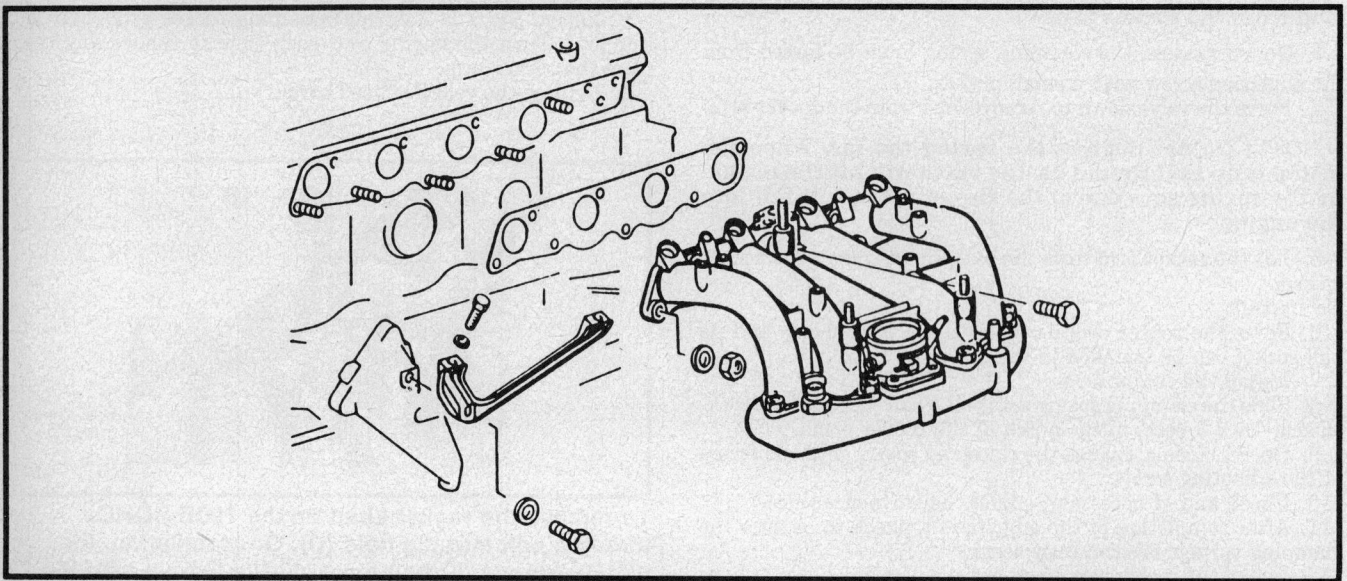

Intake manifold servicing—190E with 2.3L or 2.3-16 engine

15. Valve connection
16. Nut
17. Washer
18. Gasket
19. Idle speed air line
20. Screw connection
21. Sealing ring
22. Upper intake manifold
23. Holder
24. Hex bolt
25. Connection
26. Sealing ring
27. Gasket
28. Screw connection
29. Sealing ring
30. Screw connection
31. Sealing ring
32. Bottom intake manifold
33. Rubber connecting piece
34. Hex bolt
35. Hex bolt
36. Sealing ring
37. Plug
38. Hose

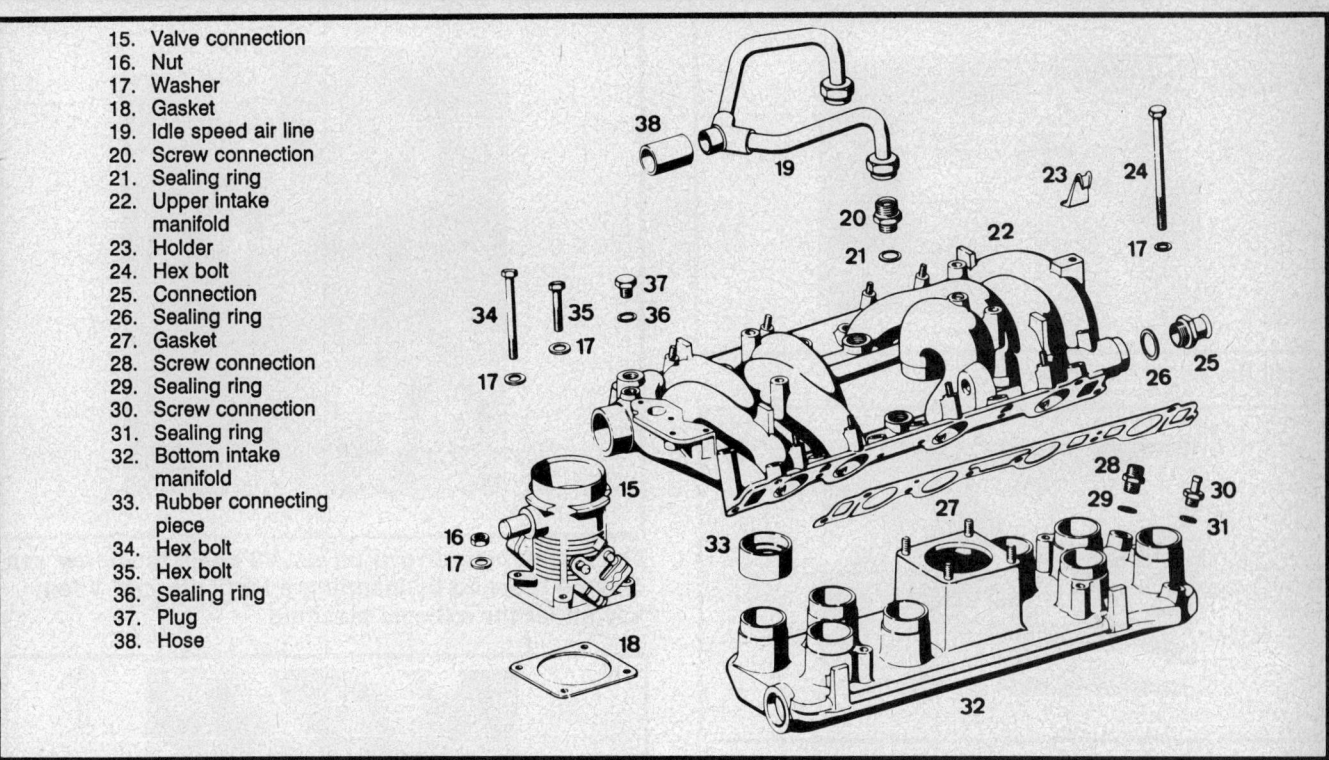

V8 intake manifold

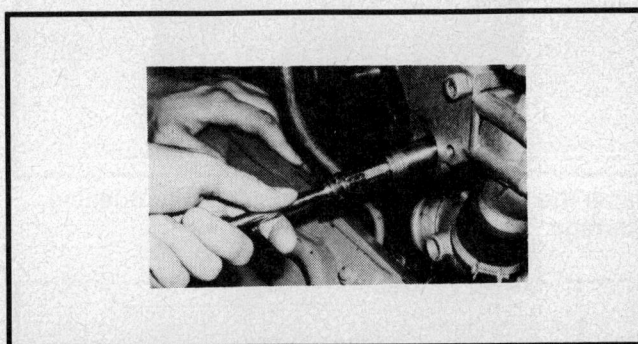

Remove the chain tensioner with a 10mm Allen key

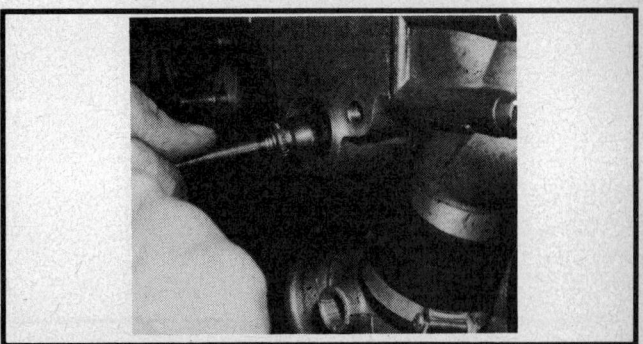

Tighten the tensioner until it "clicks"

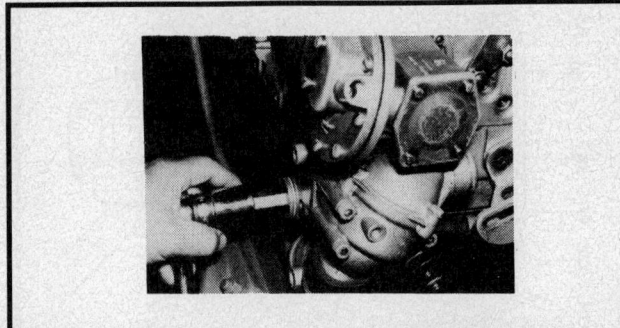

Remove the plug with a 17mm Allen key

Crank the engine by hand until the new chain has come all the way through the engine. Be sure to keep tension on chain

sion spring; the tensioner body can be unscrewed with an Allen wrench.

4. Check the O-rings or gasket and replace, if necessary.

5. To fill the chain tensioner, place the tensioner, pressure bolt down, in a container of SAE 10 engine oil, at least up to the flat flange. Using a drill press, depress the pressure bolt slowly,

about 7–10 times; be sure this is done slowly and uniformly.

6. Install the chain tensioner. Tighten the bolts evenly. Tighten the cap nut on the 190 to 51 ft. lbs. (70 Nm).

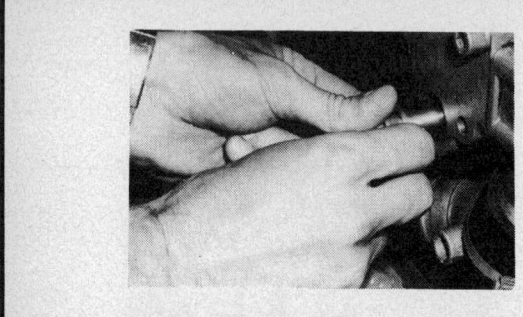

Install the chain tensioner

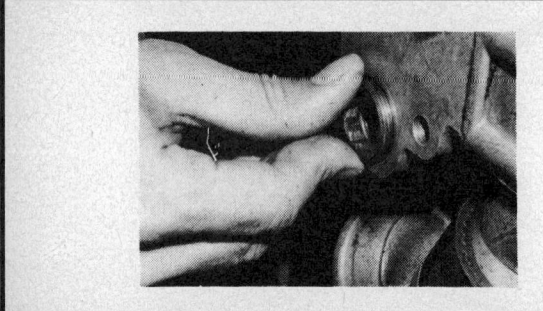

Remove the threaded plug

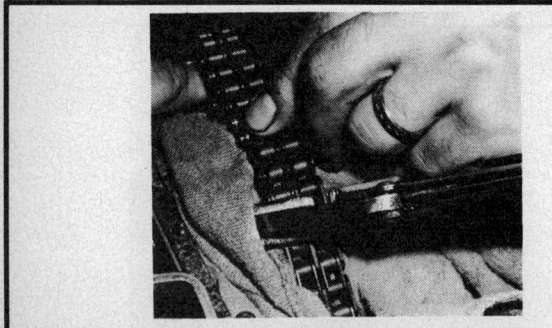

Clamp the chain again, cover the opening and remove the old chain from the master link. Connect both ends of the new chain

The inside bolt (arrow) on the V8 chain tensioner can only be reached by inserting a long, straight Allen key under the exhaust manifold

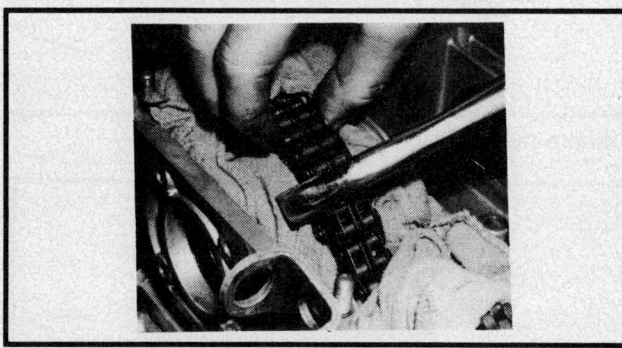

Clamp the chain to the gear and cover the opening with rags

V8 ENGINES

The chain tensioner is connected to the engine oil circuit. Bleeding occurs once oil pressure has been established and the tensioner is filling with oil.

A venting hole has been installed in the tensioner to prevent oil foaming. If there is a lot of timing chain noise, use this type of tensioner, which is identified by a white paint dot on the cap.

Service procedures for tensioners and rails on the different V8's are similar. Arrangement and shape and size of parts however, is slightly different.

1. Disconnect the negative battery cable. On California models, disconnect the line from the tensioner.

2. Remove the bolts and the tensioner; the inside bolts will probably require a long, straight 6mm Allen key to bypass the exhaust manifold. It is a tight fit.

3. Place the tensioner vertically in a container of engine oil. Operate the pressure bolt to fill the tensioner. After filling, it should permit compression very slowly under considerable force. If not, replace the tensioner with a new unit.

4. Install the tensioner and tighten the bolts evenly.

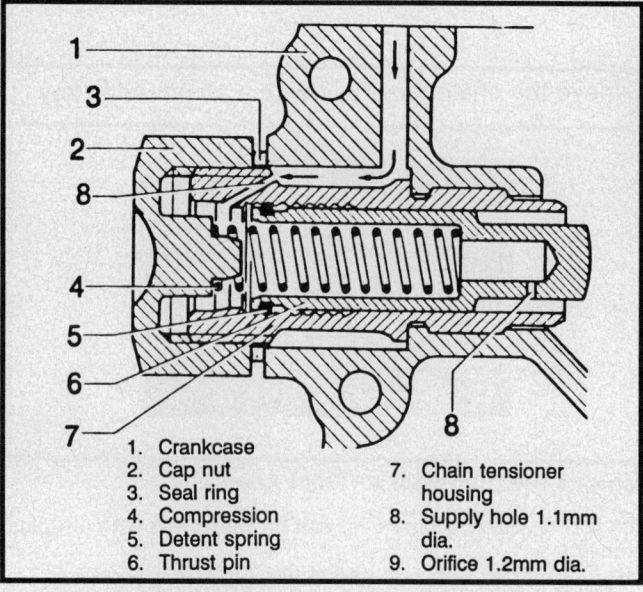

1. Crankcase
2. Cap nut
3. Seal ring
4. Compression
5. Detent spring
6. Thrust pin
7. Chain tensioner housing
8. Supply hole 1.1mm dia.
9. Orifice 1.2mm dia.

Cross-section of the timing chain tensioner—190E—190D similar

Timing Chain

Replacement

An endless timing chain is used on production engines but a split chain with a connecting link is used for service. The endless chain can be separated with a "chain breaker." Only 1 master link (connecting link) should be used on a chain.

1. Disconnect the negative battery cable. Remove the spark plugs.
2. Remove the valve cover(s).
3. Clamp the chain to the camshaft gear and cover the opening of the timing chain case with rags. On 6 cylinder and V8 engines, remove the rocker arms from the right side camshaft.
4. Separate the chain with a chain breaker.

To install:

5. Attach a new timing chain to the old chain with a master link.
6. Using a socket wrench on the crankshaft, slowly rotate the engine in the direction of normal rotation. Simultaneously, pull the old chain through until the master link is uppermost on the camshaft sprocket; be sure to keep tension on the chain throughout this procedure.
7. Disconnect the old timing chain and connect the ends of the new chain with the master link. Insert the new connecting link from the rear so the lock washers can be seen from the front.
8. Rotate the engine until the timing marks align. Check the valve timing. Once the new chain is assembled, rotate the engine, by hand, through a least 1 complete revolution to be sure everything is Okay

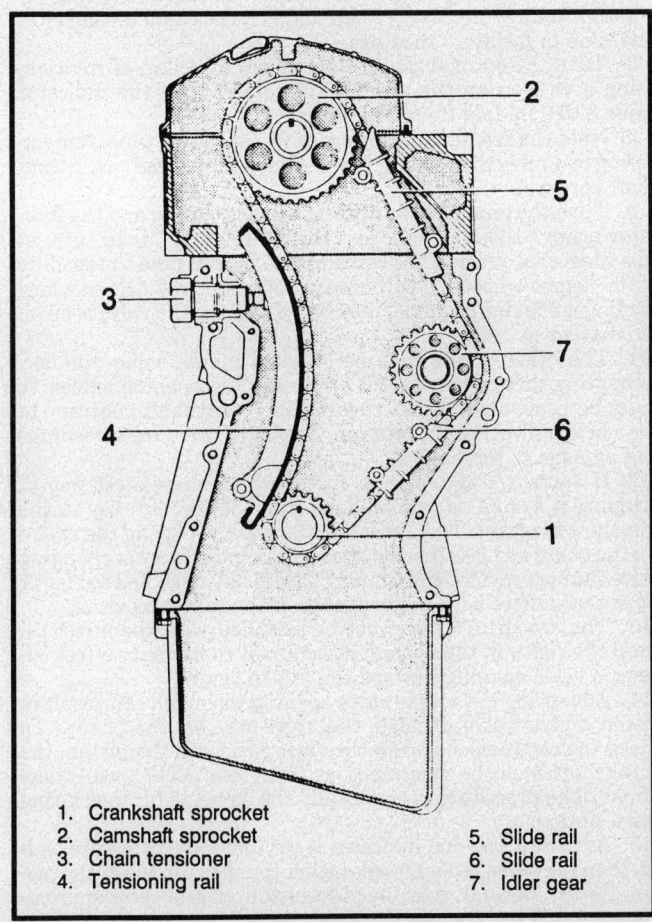

1. Crankshaft sprocket
2. Camshaft sprocket
3. Chain tensioner
4. Tensioning rail
5. Slide rail
6. Slide rail
7. Idler gear

Timing chain assembly—190E SOHC

Camshaft

Removal and Installation

190E

NOTE: On the 190E it is always a good idea to replace the rocker arms and shafts whenever the camshaft is replaced.

1. Disconnect the negative battery cable. Remove the valve cover.
2. Remove the chain tensioner.
3. Remove the rocker arms and shafts.
4. Set the crankshaft at TDC for the No. 1 piston and make sure the timing marks on the camshaft are in alignment.
5. Using a 24mm open-end wrench, hold the rear of the camshaft, flats are provided, loosen and remove the camshaft bolt. Carefully, slide the gear and chain off the shaft and wire them securely so they won't slip into the case.

NOTE: Be careful not to lose the Woodruff® key while removing the gear.

6. The camshaft is secured on the cylinder head by means of the bearing caps. Remove them and keep them in order. Each cap is marked by a number punched into its side; this number must match the number cast into the cylinder head.

NOTE: When removing the bearing caps, loosen the center 2 first and move on to the outer ones.

7. Remove the camshaft.
8. Installation is in the reverse order of removal. Always make sure the No. 1 cylinder is at TDC and all timing marks are aligned. Tighten the bearing caps to 15 ft. lbs. (21 Nm). The camshaft gear retaining bolt should be tightened to 58 ft. lbs. (80 Nm).

NOTE: Be certain not to forget the Woodruff® key.

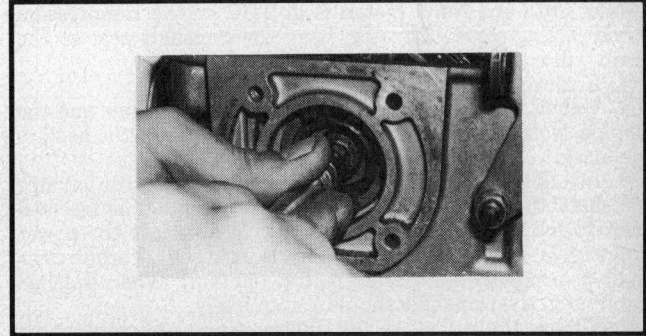

Loosen the camshaft bolts

On the 190E SOHC, the mark (arrow) on the camshaft collar (B) must always be aligned

Check the oil pipes (arrow)—V8 engine

V8 ENGINES

Experience shows that the right side camshaft is always the 1st one to require replacement. When the V8 camshaft is removed, keep the pedestals with the camshaft. In particular, make sure the 2 left side rear cam pedestals are not swapped. The result will be no oil pressure. Always replace the oil gallery pipe with the camshaft.

1. Disconnect the negative battery cable. Remove the valve cover.

2. Remove the tensioning springs and rocker arms.

3. Using a wrench on the crankshaft pulley, crank the engine around until the No. 1 piston is at TDC on the compression stroke. Using some stiff wire, hang the camshaft gear so the chain will not slip off the gears.

4. Remove the camshaft gear.

5. Unbolt the camshaft, camshaft bearing pedestals and the oil pipe. Note the angle of the bolts that do not hold the head to the block.

6. Install the bearing pedestals and camshaft. On the left side camshaft, the outer bolt on the rear bearing must be inserted prior to installing the bearings or it will not clear the power brake until. Tighten the bolts from the inside out. Torque camshaft bearing cap bolts to 37 ft. lbs. (50 Nm). When finished tightening, the camshaft should rotate freely.

7. Check the oil pipes for obstructions and replace, if necessary.

8. When install the oil pipes, also check the 3 inner connecting pipes.

9. Install the compensating washer so the keyway below the notch slides over the Woodruff® key of the camshaft.

10. Install the rocker arms and tensioning springs.

11. Adjust the valve clearance and check the valve timing.

Valve Timing

Ideally, this operation should be performed by a dealer who is equipped with the necessary tools and knowledge to do the job properly.

Checking valve timing is too inaccurate at the standard tappet clearance; therefore timing values are given for an assumed tappet clearance of 0.4mm. The engines are not measured at 0.4mm but rather at 2mm.

1. To check the timing, remove the rocker arm cover and spark plugs. Remove the tensioning springs. On the 6 cylinder engine, install the testing thrust pieces. Eliminate all valve clearance.

2. Install a degree wheel.

NOTE: If the degree wheel is attached to the camshaft as shown, values read from it must be doubled.

3. A pointer must be made from a bent section of $\frac{3}{16}$ in. brazing rod or coat hanger wire and attached to the engine.

4. With a 22mm wrench on the crankshaft pulley, turn the engine, in the direction of rotation, until the TDC mark on the vibration damper registers with the pointer and the distributor rotor points to the No. 1 cylinder mark on the housing. The camshaft timing marks should align at this point.

NOTE: Due to the design of the chain tensioner on V8 engines, the right side of the chain travels slightly farther than the left side. This means the right side cam will be almost 7 degrees retarded compared to the left side and both marks will not simultaneously align.

5. Turn the loosened degree wheel until the pointer aligns with the 0 degree (OT) mark and tighten it in this position.

6. Continue turning the crankshaft in the direction of rotation until the camshaft lobe of the associated valve is vertical, e.g., point away from the rocker arm surface. To take up tappet clearance, insert a feeler gauge, thick enough to raise the valve slightly from its seat, between the rocker arm cone and the pressure piece.

7. Attach the indicator to the cylinder head so the feeler rests against the valve spring retainer of the No. 1 cylinder intake valve. Preload the indicator at least 0.008 in. and set to 0, make sure the feeler is exactly perpendicular on the valve spring retainer. It may be necessary to bleed down the chain tensioner at this time to facilitate readings.

8. Turn the crankshaft, in the normal direction of rotation, using a wrench on the crankshaft pulley, until the indicator reads 0.016 in. less than 0 reading.

9. Note the reading of the degree wheel at this time, remembering to double the reading, if the wheel is mounted to the camshaft sprocket.

10. Turn the crankshaft until the valve is closing and the indicator again reads 0.016 in. less than 0 reading. Make sure, at this time, that preload has remained constant, note the reading of the degree wheel. The difference between the 2 degree wheel reading is the timing angle, number of degrees the valve is open, for that valve.

11. The other valves may be checked in the same manner, comparing them against each other and the opening values. It must be remembered that turning the crankshaft contrary to the normal direction of rotation results in inaccurate readings and damage to the engine.

12. If valve timing is not to specification, the easiest way of bringing it in line, is to install an offset Woodruff® key in the camshaft sprocket. This is far simpler than replacing the entire timing chain and it is the factory-recommended way of changing valve timing provided the timing chain is not stretched too far or worn out. Offset keys are available in the following sizes:

13. The Woodruff® key must be installed with the offset toward the right, in the normal direction of rotation, to effect advanced valve opening; toward the left to retard.

14. Advancing the intake valve opening too much can result in piston and/or valve damage, the valve will hit the piston. To check the clearance between the valve head and the piston, the crankshaft must be positioned at 5 degrees ATDC, on intake stroke. The procedure is essentially the same as for measuring valve timing.

15. As before, the dial indicator is set to 0 after being preloaded, then the valve is depressed until it touches the top of the piston. As the normal valve head-to-piston clearance is approximately 0.035 in., the dial indicator must be preloaded at least 0.042 in. so there will be enough movement for the feeler.

VALVE TIMING OFFSET KEYS

Offset	Part No.	For a Correction at Crankshaft of
2° (0.7)	621 991 04 67	4°
3°20+ (0.9)	621 991 02 67	6½°
4° (1.1)	621 991 01 67	8°
5° (1.3)	621 991 00 67	10°

Valve Timing Offset Keys

Note that the timing marks on the right-hand cam do not exactly align. This is because the timing chain travels farther on the right side than on the left

The V8 timing marks on the left-hand cam

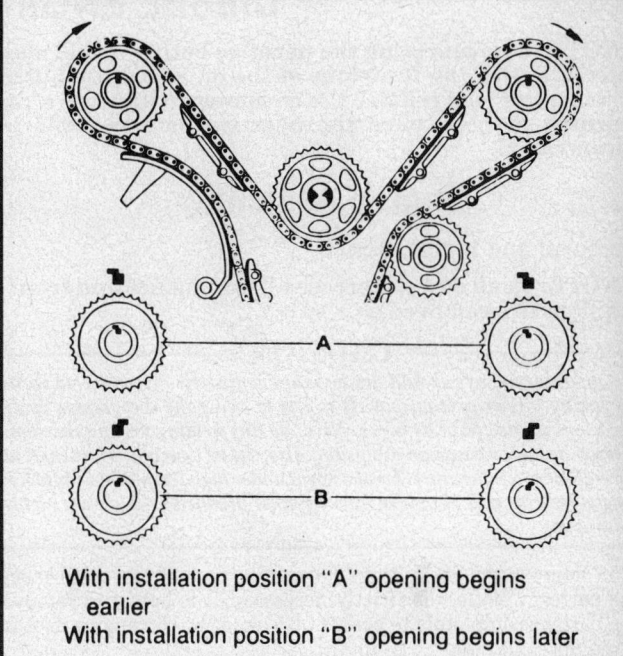

With installation position "A" opening begins earlier
With installation position "B" opening begins later

Offset Woodruff® keys—V8 engine

16. If the clearance is much less than 0.035 in., the cylinder head must be removed and checked for carbon deposits. If none exist, the valve seat must be cut deeper into the head. Always set the ignition timing after installing an offset key.

Piston and Connecting Rod

Positioning

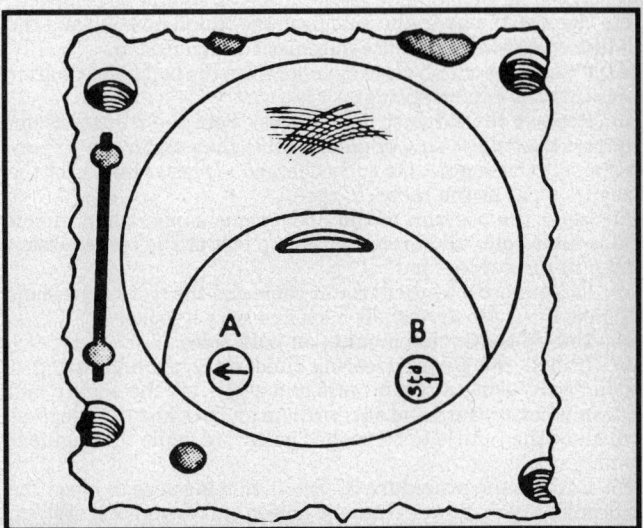

Pistons normally are marked with an arrow (a) indicating front and a weight or size marking (b).

DIESEL ENGINE MECHANICAL

NOTE: Disconnecting the negative battery cable may interfere with the functions of the on board computer systems and may require the computer to undergo a re-learning process, once the negative battery cable is reconnected.

Engine Assembly

Removal and Installation

NOTE: In all cases, Mercedes-Benz engines and transmissions are removed as a unit.

——————— CAUTION ———————

Air conditioner lines should not be indiscriminately disconnected without taking proper precautions. It is best to swing the compressor aside while still connected to its hoses. Never do any welding around the compressor-heat may cause an explosion. Also, the refrigerant, while inert at normal room temperature, breaks down under high temperature into hydrogen fluoride and phosgene (among other products), which are highly poisonous.

1. Remove the hood, drain the cooling system and disconnect the battery. While not strictly necessary, it is better to remove the battery completely to prevent breakage by the engine as it is lifted out.
2. Remove the fan shroud, radiator and disconnect all heater hoses and oil cooler lines.
3. Remove the air cleaner and all fuel, vacuum and oil hoses, e.g., power steering and power brakes.
4. Plug all openings to keep out dirt.
5. Remove the viscous coupling and fan.
6. Disconnect the accelerator linkage.
7. Disconnect all ground straps and electrical connections. It is a good idle to tag each wire for easy reassembly.
8. Detach the gearshift linkage and the exhaust pipes from the manifolds.
9. Loosen the steering relay arm and pull it aside, along with the center steering rod and hydraulic steering damper.
10. The hydraulic engine shock absorber should be removed.
11. Remove the hydraulic line from the clutch housing and the oil line connectors from the automatic transmission.
12. Unbolt the clutch slave cylinder from the bell housing after removing the return spring.
13. Remove the exhaust pipe bracket from the transmission. Support the bellhousing or place a cable sling under the oil pan, to support the engine. On turbocharged models, disconnect the exhaust pipes at the turbocharger.
14. Mark the position of the rear engine support and unbolt the 2 outer bolts, then remove the top bolt at the transmission and pull the support out.
15. Disconnect the speedometer cable and the front driveshaft U-joint. Push the driveshaft back and wire it aside.
16. Unbolt the engine mounts on both sides.
17. Unbolt the power steering fluid reservoir and swing it aside; then, using a chain hoist and cable, lift the engine and transmission upward and outward. An angle of about 45 degrees will allow the vehicle to be pushed backward while the engine is coming up.
18. Reverse the procedure to install, making sure to bleed the hydraulic clutch, power steering, power brakes and fuel system.

Cylinder Head

Removal and Installation

5 CYLINDER ENGINE

This is fairly straight forward but some caution must be observed to ensure that the valve timing is not disturbed.

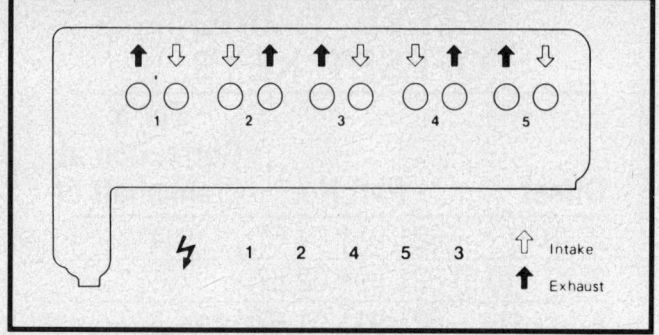

Cylinder head bolt torque sequence—5 cylinder engines. Tighten bolts "A" and "B" with a hex bit.

1. Disconnect the negative battery cable. Drain the radiator and remove all hoses and wires. Tag all wires to ensure easy reassembly.
2. Remove the camshaft cover and associated throttle linkage.
3. Remove the camshaft sprocket nut.
4. Remove the rockers and their supports must be removed together.
5. Mark the chain, sprocket and cam for ease of assembly.
6. Using a suitable puller, remove the camshaft sprocket.
7. Remove the sprocket and chain and wire it aside.

NOTE: Make sure the chain is securely wired so it will not slide into the engine.

8. Unbolt the manifolds and exhaust header pipe and push them aside.
9. Loosen the cylinder head hold-down bolts, in the reverse order of the torque sequence. It is good practice to loosen each bolt, a little at a time, working around the head, until all are free. This prevents unequal stresses in the metal.
10. Reach into the engine compartment and gradually work the head loose from each end by rocking it. Never use a prybar between the head and block to pry, as the head will be scarred badly and may be ruined.
11. Installation is the reverse of removal.

NOTE: All diesel engines utilize cylinder head stretch-bolts. These bolts undergo a permanent stretch each time they are tightened. When a maximum length is reached, they must be discarded and replace with new bolts. When tightening the head bolts on these engines, it is imperative that the steps listed under "Torque Specifications" are followed exactly.

Valve Lash

Adjustment

1. Disconnect the negative battery cable. Remove the valve cover and note the position of the intake and exhaust valves.
2. Turn the engine with a socket and breaker bar on the crankshaft pulley or by using a remote starter, hooked to the battery (+) terminal and the large, uppermost starter solenoid terminal. Due to the extremely high compression pressures, it will be considerably easier to use a remote starter. If a remote starter is not available, the engine can be bumped into position with the normal starter.

NOTE: Do not turn the engine backwards or use the camshaft sprocket bolt to rotate the engine.

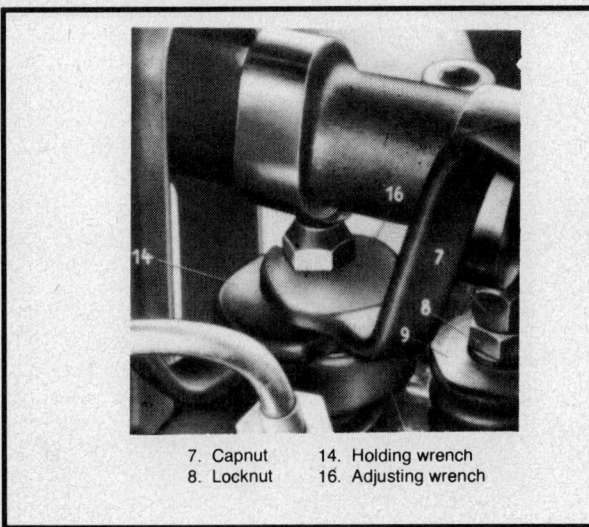

7. Capnut	14. Holding wrench
8. Locknut	16. Adjusting wrench

Adjusting valve clearance on diesel engine

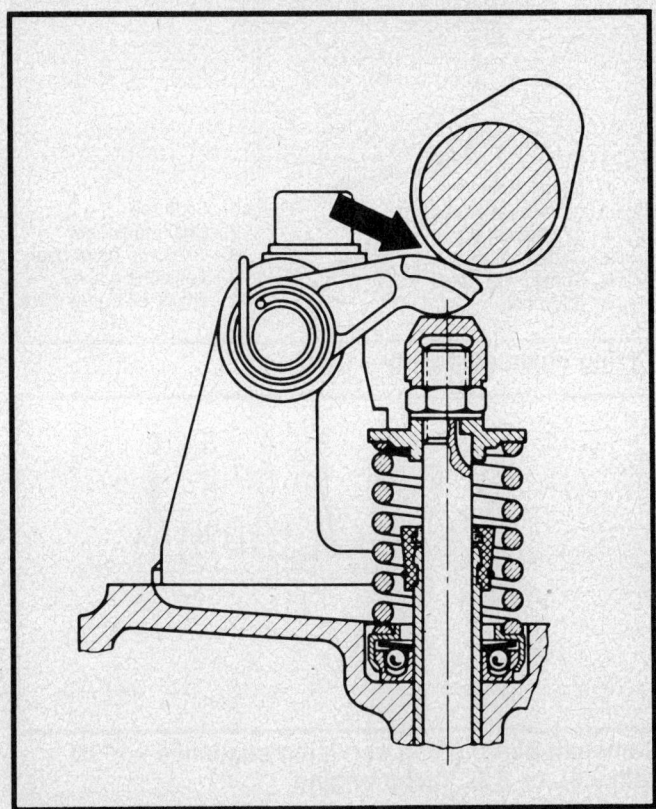

Measure valve clearance on diesel engines at arrow

3. Measure the valve clearance when the heel of the camshaft lobe is directly over the sliding surface of the rocker arm. The lobe of the camshaft should be vertical to the surface of the rocker arm. The clearance is correct when the specified feeler gauge can be pulled through with a very slight drag.

4. To adjust the clearance, loosen the cap nut while holding the hex nut. Adjust the valve clearance by turning the hex nut.

5. After adjustment, hold the cap nut and lock it in place with the hex nut. Recheck the clearance.

6. Check the gasket and install the rocker arm cover.

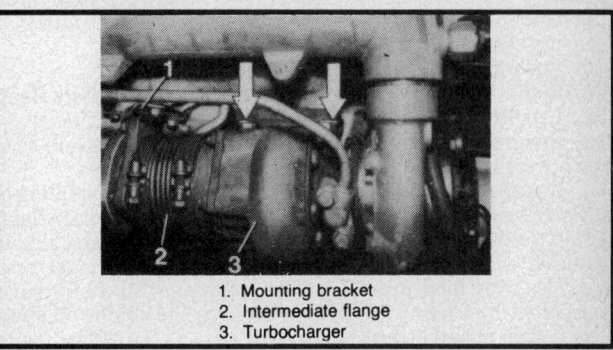

1. Mounting bracket
2. Intermediate flange
3. Turbocharger

Remove the mounting nuts (arrow) to remove the turbocharger

Rocker Arms

Removal and Installation

NOTE: The 190D does not use rocker arms. The camshaft acts directly on the hydraulic valve tappet.

Rocker arms can only be removed as a unit with the respective rocker arm blocks.

1. Disconnect the negative battery cable. Detach the connecting rod for the venturi control unit from the bearing bracket lever and remove the bearing bracket from the rocker arm cover.

2. Remove the air vent line from the rocker arm cover and the rocker arm cover.

3. Remove the stretch-bolts from the rocker arm blocks and the blocks with the rocker arms. Turn the crankshaft in each case so the camshaft does not put any load on the rocker arms.

NOTE: Turn the crankshaft with a socket wrench on the crankshaft pulley bolt. Do not rotate the engine by turning the camshaft sprocket.

4. Before installing the rocker arms, check the sliding surfaces of the ball cup and rocker arms. Replace any defective parts.

To install:

5. Assembly the rocker arm blocks and insert new stretch-bolts.

6. Tighten the stretch-bolts. In each case, position the camshaft so there is no load on the rocker arms.

7. Check to be sure the tension clamps have engaged with the notches of the rocker arm blocks.

8. Adjust the valve clearance.

9. Reinstall the rocker arm cover, air vent line and bearing bracket for the reverse lever. Attach the connecting rod for the venturi control unit to the reversing lever.

10. Make sure during acceleration, the control cable can move freely without binding.

11. Start the engine and check the rocker arm cover for leaks.

Turbocharger

Removal and Installation

1. Disconnect the negative battery cable. Remove the air filter.

2. Disconnect the electrical cable from the temperature switch.

3. Loosen the lower hose clamp on the air duct that connects the air filter with the compressor housing.

4. Remove the vacuum line and crankcase breather pipe.

5. Remove the air filter and air intake duct.

6. Disconnect the oil line at the turbocharger.

7. Remove the air filter mounting bracket.

8. Disconnect the turbocharger at the exhaust flange.

9. Disconnect and remove the pipe bracket on the automatic transmission.

10. Push the exhaust pipe rearward.

11. Remove the mounting bracket at the intermediate flange.

12. Unbolt and remove the turbocharger.

13. Remove the intermediate flange and oil return line at the turbocharger.

14. Installation is the reverse of removal. Before installing the turbocharger, install the oil return line and intermediate flange. Install the flange gasket between the turbocharger and exhaust manifold with the reinforcing bead toward the exhaust manifold. Use only heat proof nuts and bolts and fill a new turbocharger with ¼ pint of engine oil through the engine oil supply bore before operating.

Timing Chain Tensioner

Filling

1. Place chain tensioner with thrust pin in downward direction in engine oil SAE 10 up to above collar on hex head.

2. Slowly press thrust pin 7–10 times up to stop by means of a press or an upright drill press.

3. Upon filling, the chain tensioner should permit compressing very slowly only, uniformly and at considerable force.

4. To prevent peak pressures of chain tensioner against tensioning rail, a modified valve disk will be installed in chain tensioner.

Removal and Installation

5 CYLINDER ENGINE

There are 2 kinds of timing chain tensioners. One uses an O-ring seal and the other a flat gasket. Do not install a flat gasket on a tensioner meant to be use with an O-ring.

Chain tensioners should be replaced as a unit, if defective.

1. Disconnect the negative battery cable. Drain the coolant. If equipped with air conditioning, disconnect the compressor, mounting bracket and lay it aside. Do not disconnect the refrigerant lines. Drain the coolant from the block.

2. Remove the thermostat housing.

3. Loosen and remove the chain tensioner; be careful of loose O-rings. On the 190, remove the tensioner cap nut and the tension spring. The tensioner body can be unscrewed with an Allen wrench.

4. Check the O-rings or gasket and replace, if necessary.

5. To fill the chain tensioner, place the tensioner, pressure bolt down, in a container of SAE 10 engine oil, at least up to the flat flange. Using a drill press, depress the pressure bolt slowly, about 7–10 times. Be sure this is done slowly and uniformly.

6. Install the chain tensioner. Tighten the bolts evenly. Tighten the cap nut on the 190 to 51 ft. lbs. (70 Nm).

Timing Chain

Replacement

1. Disconnect the negative battery cable. Remove cylinder head cover.

2. Remove injection nozzles.

3. Remove chain tensioner.

4. Remove fan and fan cover.

5. Connect new timing chain with connecting link to old timing chain.

6. Slowly, rotate crankshaft in rotating direction of engine, while simultaneously pulling up the old timing chain until the connecting link comes to rest against uppermost point of camshaft timing gear.

NOTE: Timing chain should remain in mesh while rotating camshaft and crankshaft timing gears.

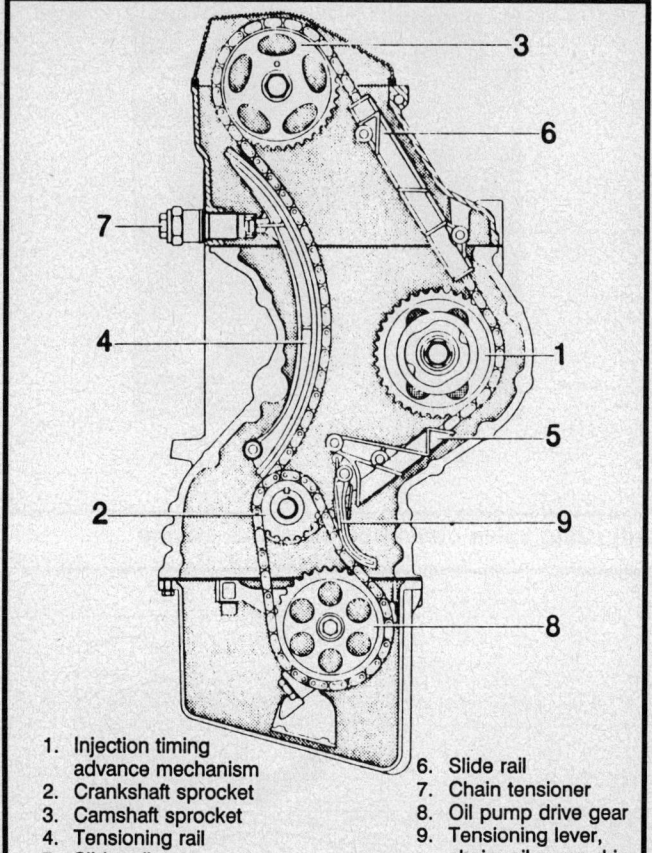

1. Injection timing advance mechanism
2. Crankshaft sprocket
3. Camshaft sprocket
4. Tensioning rail
5. Slide rail
6. Slide rail
7. Chain tensioner
8. Oil pump drive gear
9. Tensioning lever, chain, oil pump drive

Timing chain assembly—190D

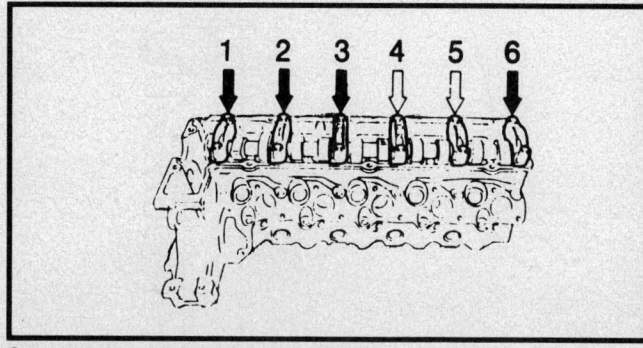

Camshaft bearing cap servicing sequence—190D with 2.5L or 2.5L Turbo engine

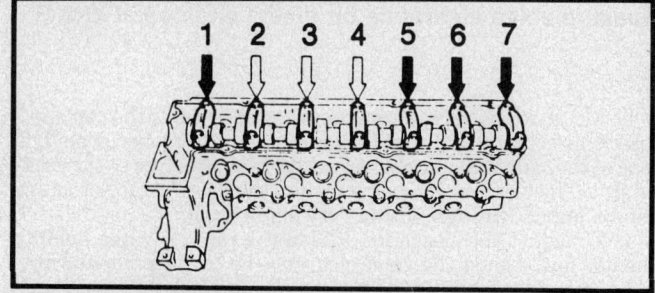

Camshaft bearing cap servicing sequence—300D and 300SCL

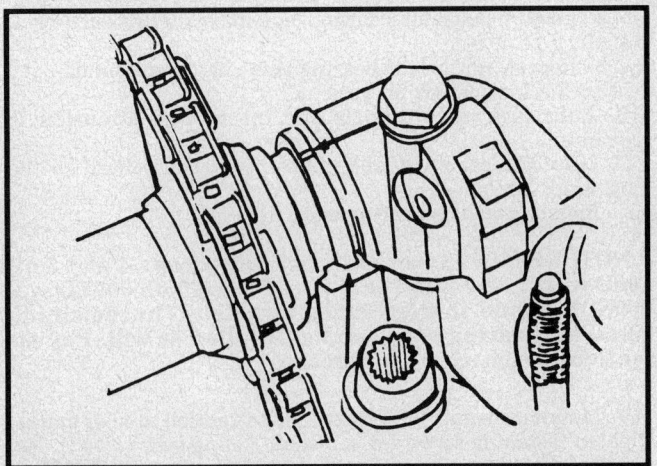

Camshaft alignment marks—190D, 300D and 300SDL

7. Take off old timing chain and connect ends of new timing chain with connecting link. For this purpose, secure chain ends with wire on camshaft timing gear.

To install:

NOTE: Use only a rivet-type connecting link. Do not use connecting link that use a retaining spring.

8. Insert connecting link from the rear into timing chain.

9. Put separately enclosed outer flange of connecting link, with punched in IWIS identification, into pressing-on tool. The outer flange is held magnetically.

10. Place pressing-on tool on connecting link and press on flange up to stop, while holding pressing-on tool on vertical level.

11. Rearrange plunger, of assembly tool, so the notch is pointing forward.

12. Hold assembly tool on handle and rivet chain bolts individ-

ually. Tightening torque of spindle approximately 22–26 ft. lbs. (30–35 Nm).

13. Check chain bolt rivet and rivet again, if required.

14. Install chain tensioner.

15. Rotate crankshaft and check adjusting mark at TDC position of engine.

NOTE: If the adjusting mark is wrong, check timing of camshaft and begin of delivery of injection pump.

16. Install cylinder head cover and tighten to 7.5 ft. lbs. (10 Nm).

17. Install fan and fan cover.

Camshaft

Removal and Installation

1. Disconnect the negative battery cable. Remove cylinder head cover.

2. Set crankshaft to TDC of No. 1 cylinder.

NOTE: Do not rotate the engine on the fastening screw of the camshaft timing gear; do not rotate engine in reverse.

3. Remove chain tensioner.

4. Mark the camshaft timing gear and timing chain in relation to each other.

5. Remove camshaft timing gear. To loosen screws, apply counter hold on camshaft by means of a mandrel.

6. If equipped with level control, remove pressure oil pump and place aside with lines connected.

7. To prevent damage to camshafts, be sure to apply the following sequence during assembly:

   a. 190 with 2.5L engine—remove both screws on camshaft bearing 1, 2, 3 and 6. Loosen both screws on camshaft bearing 4 and 5 alternately and in steps only until counter-pressure has been eliminated.

   b. 300D, 300TD and 300SDL—remove both screws on

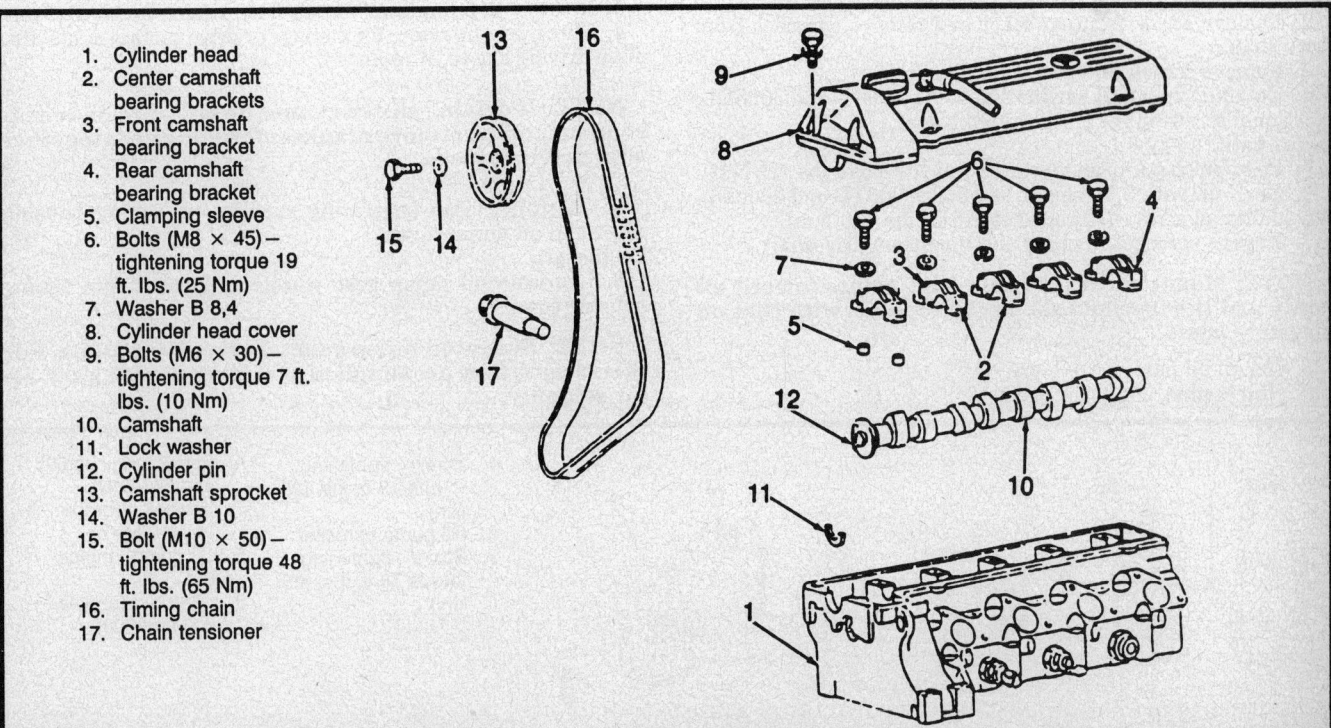

1. Cylinder head
2. Center camshaft bearing brackets
3. Front camshaft bearing bracket
4. Rear camshaft bearing bracket
5. Clamping sleeve
6. Bolts (M8 × 45)— tightening torque 19 ft. lbs. (25 Nm)
7. Washer B 8,4
8. Cylinder head cover
9. Bolts (M6 × 30)— tightening torque 7 ft. lbs. (10 Nm)
10. Camshaft
11. Lock washer
12. Cylinder pin
13. Camshaft sprocket
14. Washer B 10
15. Bolt (M10 × 50)— tightening torque 48 ft. lbs. (65 Nm)
16. Timing chain
17. Chain tensioner

Camshaft servicing—190D, 300D and 300SDL

camshaft bearing 1, 5, 6 and 7. Loosen both screws for camshaft bearing 2, 3, and 4 alternately and in steps only until counter-pressure has been eliminated.

8. Remove camshaft in upward direction.
9. Remove circlip for axial locating for camshaft longitudinal alignment and check for condition.
10. Pull out valve tappet by means of solenoid lifter tool 102 589 03 40 00 or equivalent.
11. Check valve tappet for condition, visual checkup, and renew, if required.

To install:

NOTE: **Install valve tappets only at the same spot where they were installed. If a new camshaft has been installed or if the cylinder head has been machined, check camshaft for easy operation.**

12. Insert circlip for axial locating into cylinder head.
13. Lubricate camshaft and place into cylinder head, without valve tappet.
14. Tighten camshaft bearing caps uniformly to 18.5 ft. lbs. (25 Nm). Pay attention to identification of bearing caps.
15. When checking for easy operation, the camshaft can be rotated by means of a hex socket screw M10 × 30, which is screwed in through camshaft timing gear instead of fastening screw. If the camshaft can be rotated with effort only, proceed as follows:

a. Loosen camshaft bearing caps individually. Turn camshaft, if required.
b. Repeat, until tight bearing point has been found.
c. Check camshaft for runout.
16. Lubricate valve tappets and insert. Pay attention to sequence.
17. Lubricate camshaft and place into cylinder head so the TDC mark is vertical.
18. Install camshaft bearing caps.

NOTE: **Screw in camshaft bearing screws 4 and 5 on 190D with 2.5L engine or 2, 3, and 4 on 300D, 300TD and 300SDL engine, in steps, and alternately. The remaining camshaft bearing caps can be installed at will. Pay attention to tightening torques.**

19. Mount camshaft timing gear. Pay attention to color marks. Tighten fastening screw for camshaft timing gear to 48 ft. lbs. (65 Nm). For this purpose, apply counter hold to camshaft timing gear by means of a steel pin or suitable tool.
20. Install chain tensioner.
21. If equipped with level control, mount pressure oil pump and driver.
22. Check engine for TDC marks.
23. Mount cylinder head cover.
24. Run engine, check for leaks.

ENGINE LUBRICATION

Oil Pump

Removal and Installation

190D AND 300D, 300TD AND 300SDL

1. Disconnect the negative battery cable. Remove oil pan.
2. Remove screw from sprocket and remove sprocket from drive shaft.
3. Remove screws and remove oil pump.
4. On 190D with 2.5L engine and 300D, 300TD and 300SDL, additional screw on intake manifold holder.

To install:
5. Position oil pump and torque screw to 18.5 ft. lbs. (25 Nm).
6. On 190D with 2.5L engine and 300D, 300TD and 300SDL, the additional screw is torqued to 7.5 ft. lbs. (10 Nm).
7. Engage sprocket in chain and mount on driveshaft.

NOTE: **Mount sprocket so the rise points toward oil pump and the trochoid shape corresponds with that on oil pump shaft.**

8. Install oil pan.
9. Run engine, check for leaks.

190E WITH 2.3L ENGINE

1. Disconnect the negative battery cable. Remove timing housing cover.
2. Remove screw and oil suction pipe with oil strainer, as well as oil pump cover.
3. Remove oil pump gear wheels from timing housing cover.
4. Check driving sleeve for damage or drive surface dents. Replace driving sleeve, if required.

NOTE: **If driving sleeve cannot be pulled from crankshaft manually, remove crankshaft timing gear together with driving sleeve.**

5. Carefully, clean separating surfaces on timing housing cover and oil pump cover.
To install:
6. Lubricate oil pump gear wheels and insert into timing housing cover.

NOTE: **Renew oil pump gear wheels only in pairs. For this reason, they are supplied as a spare part in a set, rotor set, only.**

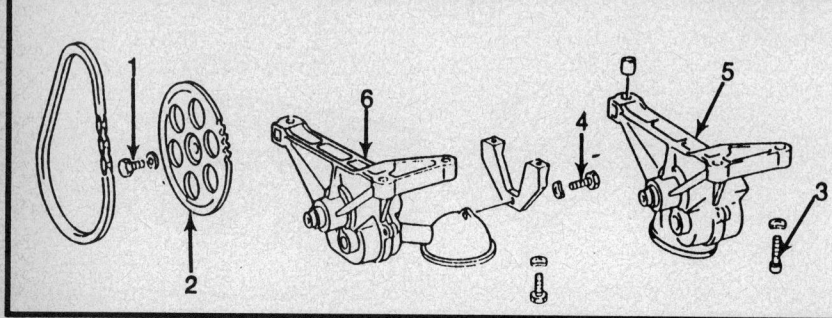

1. Screw—tightening torque 19 ft. lbs. (25 Nm)
2. Oil pump sprocket
3. Screw—tightening torque 19 ft. lbs. (25 Nm)
4. Screw (engines 602 and 603 only)—tightening torque 7 ft. lbs. (10 Nm)
5. Oil pump (engine 601)
6. Oil pump (engine 602 and 603)

Oil pump servicing—190D, 300D and 300SDL

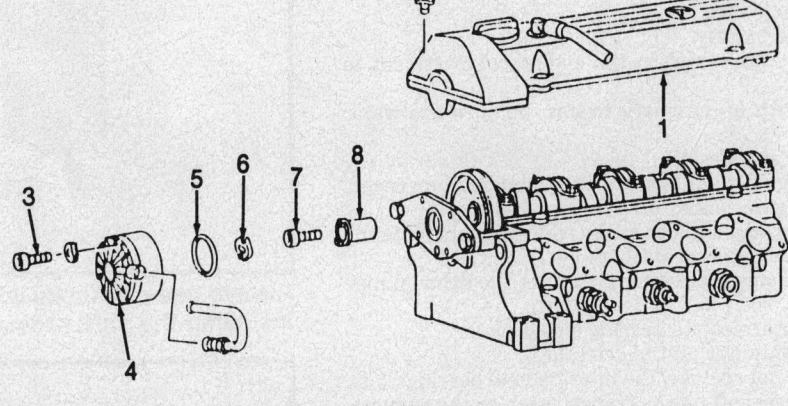

1. Cylinder head cover
2. Screw—tightening torque 7 ft. lbs. (10 Nm)
3. Screw
4. Hydraulic oil pump
5. O-ring
6. Driven plate
7. Hex. head sprocket screw
8. Drive sleeve

Hydraulic oil pump servicing—190D, 300D and 300SDL

7. Renew sealing ring on connection of oil pump cover.
8. Mount oil pump cover on timing housing cover. Position oil suction pipe with oil strainer and with new gasket on oil pump cover. Screw in fastening screws and tighten to 7.5 ft. lbs. (10 Nm).

NOTE: Pay attention to correct installation of gasket between flange of oil suction pipe and oil pump cover.

9. Check oil pump for easy operation.
10. Slip driving sleeve on crankshaft.
11. Install timing housing cover.
12. Check for leaks with engine running.

560SL

1. Disconnect the negative battery cable. Drain engine oil.
2. Remove oil pan.
3. Place compensating weight of first crankpin in horizontal position.
4. Remove fastening screw, tilt oil pump forward, remove drive chain from drive sprocket and remove oil pump.
To install:
5. Tilt oil pump forward and place drive chain on drive sprocket, screw-in fastening screw and tighten to 18.5 ft. lbs. (25 Nm).
6. Install oil pan with new gasket and tighten fastening screws to 7.5 ft. lbs. (10 Nm) for M6 bolts or 18.5 ft. lbs. (25 Nm) for M8 bolts.

7. Fill with engine oil.
8. Run engine and check for leaks.

420SEL, 560SEL AND 560SEC

1. Disconnect the negative battery cable. Drain engine oil.
2. Remove oil pan lower half.
3. Place compensating weight of first crankpin in horizontal position.
4. Remove screws.
5. Loosen screw on drive sprocket, tilt oil pump toward rear and remove screw.
6. Push drive sprocket away from oil pump by means of a suitable tool and remove oil pump.
7. Lift drive sprocket from drive chain.
8. Engage drive sprocket in drive chain.
9. Push oil pump on drive sprocket. Dowel sleeve in drive sprocket should enter cutout in driveshaft.
10. Tilt oil pump to rear, screw-in screw and tighten to 21 ft. lbs. (28 Nm).
11. Screw-in fastening screws and tighten to 18.5 ft. lbs. (25 Nm).
12. Install oil pan lower half with new gasket and tighten fastening screw to 7.5 ft. lbs. (10 Nm) for M6 bolts or 18.5 ft. lbs. (25 Nm) for M8 bolts.
13. Fill with engine oil.
14. Run engine and check for leaks.

MANUAL TRANSMISSION

For further information, please refer to "Professional Transmission Repair Manual" for additional coverage.

Transmission Assembly

Removal and Installation

WITH ENGINE

The transmission should only be removed with the engine as a unit, since the transmission-to-clutch housing bolts can only be reached from the inside. Once the engine/transmission unit has been removed from the vehicle, the transmission and bellhousing must be separated from the engine, as follows:

See the "Engine" section to remove the engine/transmission.

1. After removing the engine/transmission unit, unbolt the bellhousing from the engine. The bolts which hold the transmission to the bellhousing cannot be reached except from inside the bellhousing.
2. Remove the starter from its mounting position and pull the transmission and bellhousing from the engine.
3. The bolts which secure the bellhousing to the transmission are now visible and can be removed to separate the bellhousing and transmission.
To install:
4. Connect the engine, bellhousing and transmission, after coating the splines of the mainshaft with grease.
5. Install the starter.
6. Further installation is the reverse of removal.

WITHOUT ENGINE

190D, 190E, 260E, 300E, 300CE, 300SE, 300TE and 300SEL

1. Disconnect the battery.
2. Cover the insulation mat in the engine compartment to prevent damage.
3. If equipped with an auxiliary heater, be sure the water hose is aside.
4. Support the transmission.
5. Unbolt the engine mounts at the rear transmission cover.
6. Unbolt the engine carrier on the floor frame.
7. Unscrew the exhaust holder at the transmission. Note the number and positioning of all washers.
8. Unscrew the clamping strap and remove the exhaust pipe holder.
9. Remove the intermediate bearing shield plate.
10. Loosen the clamp nut on the driveshaft.
11. Loosen but do not remove, the intermediate bearing bolts.
12. Unbolt the driveshaft on the transmission so the companion plate remains with the driveshaft.
13. Carefully push the driveshaft as far to the rear as permitted.

NOTE: On the 190E, the fitted sleeves on the universal flange must be loosened before separating the flange from the companion plate. This will require a cylindrical mandrel.

14. Disconnect the exhaust system at the rear suspension and suspend it with wire.
15. Loosen and remove the input shaft for the tachometer.
16. Loosen and remove the tachometer drive shaft on the rear transmission case cover. Unclip the clip for the tachometer drive shaft from its holder.
17. Unscrew the holder for the line to the clutch housing. Unscrew the clutch slave cylinder and move it toward the rear until the pushrod is clear of the housing.
18. Push off the clip locks and remove the shift rods from the intermediate levers on the shift bracket. Note the position of the disc springs.

NOTE: When the shift rods are disconnected, do not move the shift lever into reverse or the back-up light switch could be damaged.

19. Unbolt the starter and remove it.
20. Remove all transmission-to-intermediate flange screw. Remove the upper 2 last.
21. Rotate the transmission approximately 45 degrees to the left, slide it from the clutch plate and remove it downward.

NOTE: Make sure the input shaft has cleared the clutch plate before tilting the transmission.

To install:
22. Lightly grease the centering lug and splines on the transmission input shaft.

NOTE: Position the clutch slave cylinder and line above the transmission before beginning installation.

23. Move the transmission into the clutch so one gear step engages. Rotate the mainshaft back and forth until the splines on the input shaft and clutch plate are aligned.
24. Move the transmission all the way in and tighten the transmission-to-intermediate flange screws.
25. Install the starter.
26. Install the clutch slave cylinder with the proper plastic shims.
27. Installation of the remaining components is in the reverse order of removal. Please note the following:
    a. After installing the driveshaft, roll the vehicle back and forth and tighten the intermediate bearing free of tension.

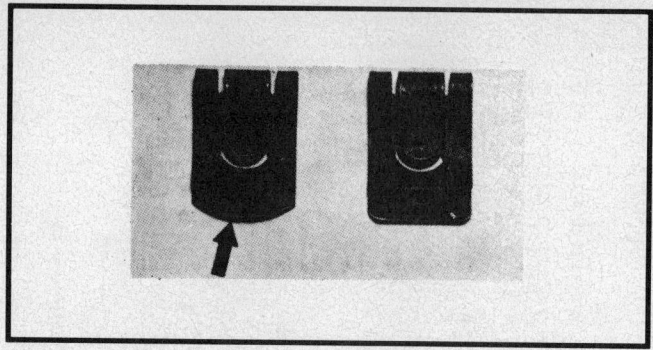

Always use clip locks with curved edges when installing the shift rods on the 190

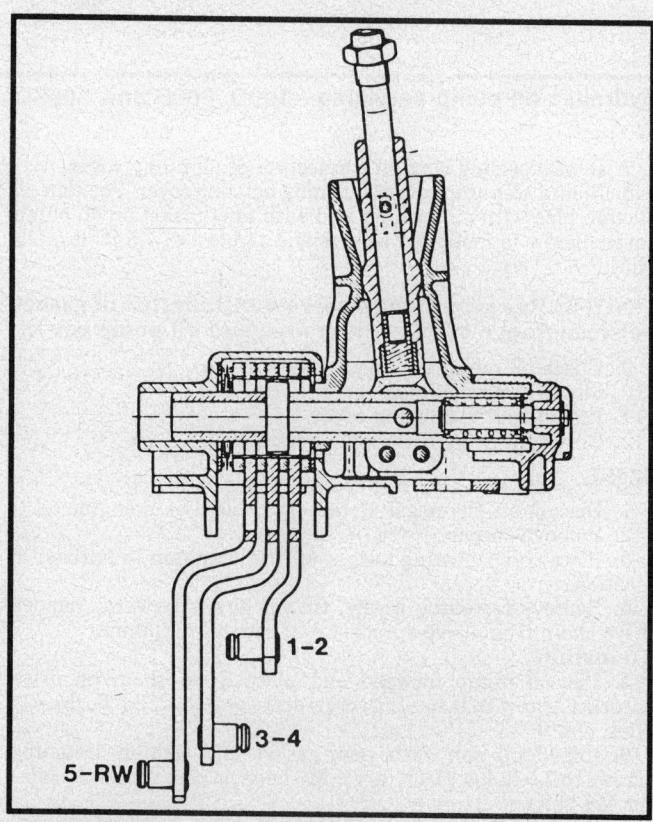

Intermediate lever positioning on the 5 speed 190

b. Tighten the driveshaft clamp nut to 22–29 ft. lbs. (30–40 Nm).
c. Make sure of the proper positioning of all washers, spacers and shims.

Linkage Adjustment

The only type of shifter used is a floor mounted type.

NOTE: On all types of transmissions, never hammer or force a new shift knob on with the shifter installed, as the plastic bushing connected to the lever will be damaged and caused hard shifting.

Proper adjustment of the shift linkage is dependent on both the position of the shift levers at the transmission and the length of the shift rods. The shift levers, rods and bearing block are all located under the floor tunnel; the driveshaft shield may have to be removed to gain access to them.

1. With the transmission in **N** and the driveshaft shield removed, if equipped, remove the clip locks and disconnect the shift rods from the intermediate shift levers under the floor shift bearing bracket.

2. With the shifter still in the **N** position, lock the 3 intermediate shift levers by inserting a 0.2156 in. rod, a No. 3 drill bit will do, or any other tool of approximately the same diameter, through the levers and the holes in the bearing bracket.

3. Check the position of the shift levers at the transmission. Adjust by loosening the clamp bolts and moving the levers.

4. With the intermediate levers locked and the shift levers adjusted properly, try hooking the shift rods back onto their respective intermediate levers. The shift rods may be adjusted by loosening the locknut and turning the ball socket on the end until they are the proper length.

NOTE: When hooking up the shift rods to the intermediate levers, be very careful not to move the transmission shift levers from their adjusted position.

When reattaching the shift rods on 190 models, use only clip locks which have a radius edge. If the old style clip locks with a square edge are used, there is a possibility that the locks will pop out and the shift rods will drop.

5. Remove the locking rod from the bearing bracket, start the engine and shift through the gears a few times. Occasionally, slight binding may call for very slight further adjustments.

CLUTCH

Removal and Installation

1. To remove the clutch, first remove the transmission.

2. Loosen the clutch pressure plate hold-down bolts, evenly, 1–1½ turns at a time, until tension is relieved. Never remove 1 bolt at a time, as damage to the pressure plate is possible.

3. Examine the flywheel surface for blue heat marks, scoring or cracks. If the flywheel is to be machined, always machine both sides.

To install:

4. Coat the splines with high temperature grease and place the clutch disc against the flywheel, centering it with a clutch pilot shaft. A wooden shaft, available at automotive jobbers, is satisfactory but an old transmission mainshaft works best.

5. Tighten the pressure plate hold-down bolts evenly, 1–1½ turns at a time, until tight, then remove the pilot shaft.

NOTE: Most clutch plates have the flywheel side marked Kupplungsseite. Do not assume the pressure springs always face the transmission.

Clutch

Adjustment

WITHOUT BRAKE BLEEDING DEVICE

1. Loosen locknut on adjusting screw on master cylinder.

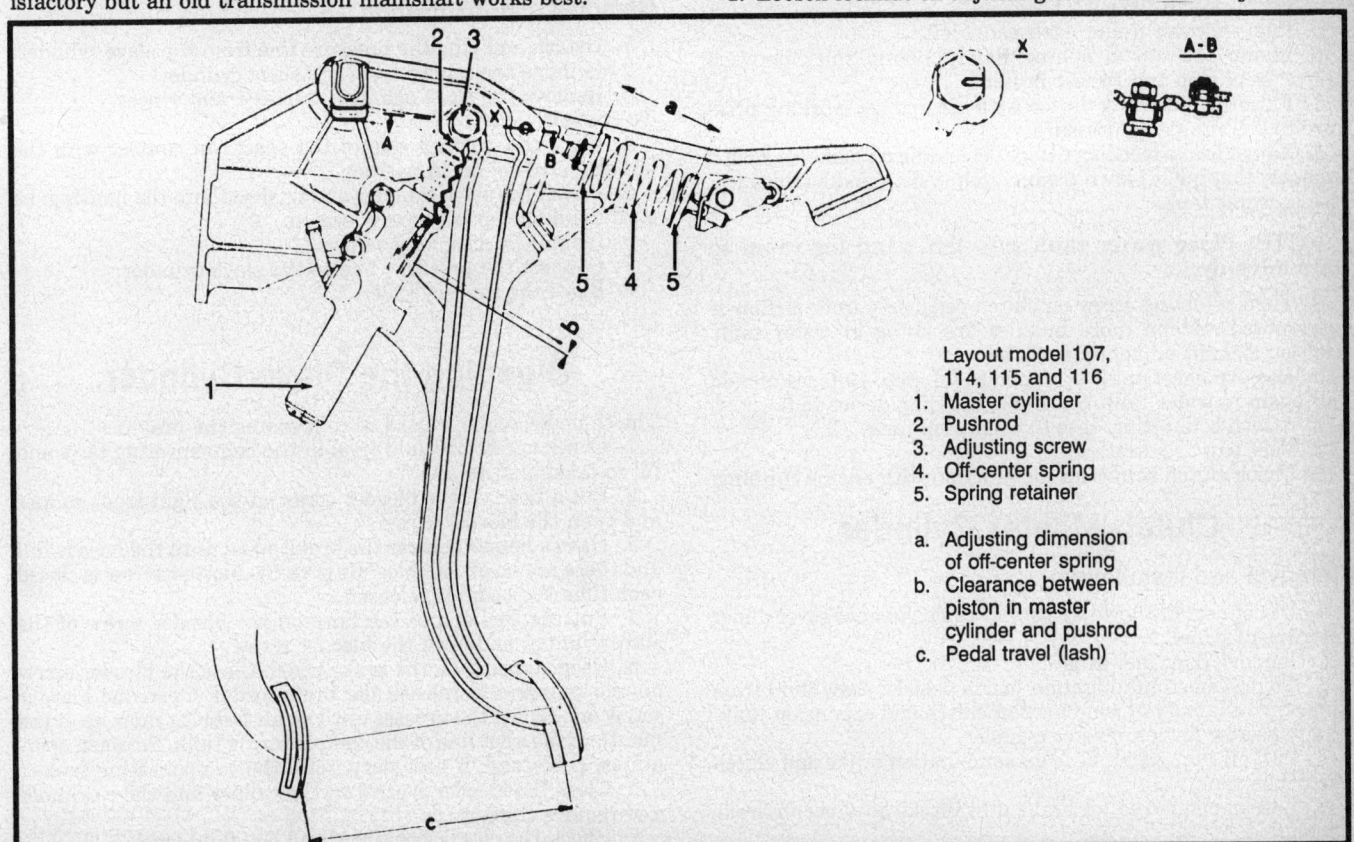

Layout model 107, 114, 115 and 116
1. Master cylinder
2. Pushrod
3. Adjusting screw
4. Off-center spring
5. Spring retainer

a. Adjusting dimension of off-center spring
b. Clearance between piston in master cylinder and pushrod
c. Pedal travel (lash)

Clutch adjustment

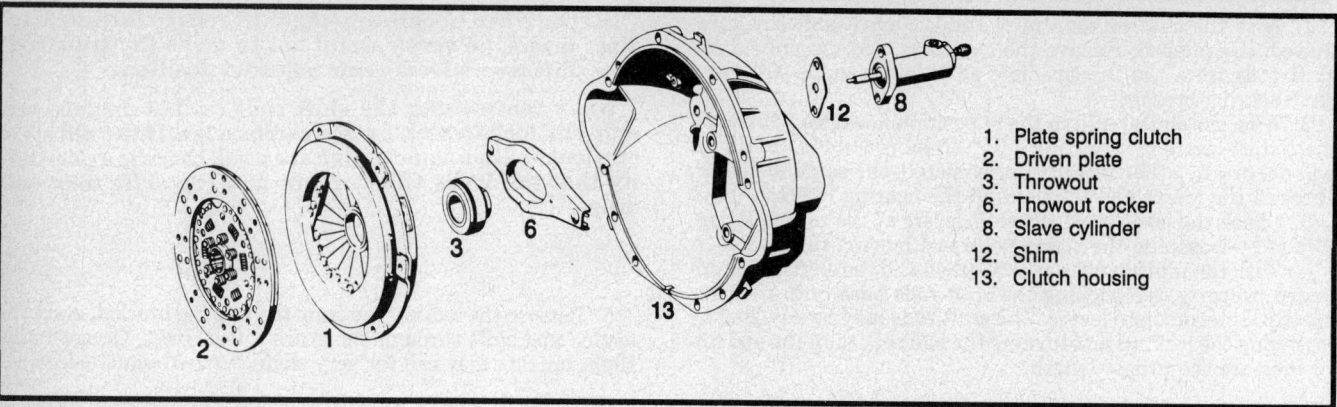

1. Plate spring clutch
2. Driven plate
3. Throwout
6. Thowout rocker
8. Slave cylinder
12. Shim
13. Clutch housing

Exploded view of clutch

2. Turn adjusting screw in such a manner that pushrod will travel the idle path **b** up to piston first when pedal is actuated. If a line mark is shown on head of adjusting screw, make sure during inspection or during adjustment that this line mark is pointing toward the rear.

WITH BRAKE BLEEDING DEVICE

1. Draw brake fluid from expansion tank up to connection for clutch actuation.
2. Pull connecting hose to master cylinder from expansion tank.
3. Open venting screw on clutch sleeve cylinder and evacuate clutch system by stepping repeatedly on clutch pedal.
4. Insert plastic hose of approximately 1 meter in length, 8mm in diameter, into connecting hose and immerse other end into a container filled with water.
5. Remove cover under dash panel left.
6. Clamp sheetmetal approximately 1.5mm thick between upper pedal stop and rubber buffer.
7. Fill brake bleeding device with air and set working pressure to 0.5 bar gauge pressure.
8. Adjust brake bleeding device depending on make, in such a manner, that air is blown from clutch system and bubbles will rise in water tank.

NOTE: Place water tank into left hand leg room to gain advantage.

9. Turn adjusting screw on clutch pedal only until airflow is interrupted and no more bubbles are rising in water tank. Tighten locknut on adjusting screw.
10. Remove sheetmetal at upper pedal stop. Bubbles should rise again in water tank. Set brake bleeding device to 0.
11. Attach connecting hose to expansion tank.
12. Vent clutch actuation.
13. Check clutch actuation for function with engine running.

Clutch Master Cylinder

Removal and Installation

1. Disconnect the negative battery cable. Remove cover under instrument panel at left.
2. Remove floor mat at left.
3. To prevent contamination inside vehicle, draw fluid from respective chamber of combination clutch and expansion tank.
4. Unscrew line on master cylinder.
5. Pull off connecting hose on combination brake and clutch expansion tank.
6. Loosen piston rod for brake unit (brake booster) on brake pedal.

7. Pull cable plug from stop light switch.
8. Unscrew nuts for attaching pedal carrier to fire wall.
9. Move pedal assembly to the rear until screw plate of pedal carrier is free from threaded bolt of brake unit (brake booster) and holder at top on water tank.
10. Remove pedal assembly in downward direction, while paying attention to connecting hose for master cylinder and remove master cylinder.
To install:
11. Return any fallen rubber mounts, reverse removal procedure and bleed clutch actuation.

Clutch Slave Cylinder

Removal and Installation

1. Detach and plug the pressure line from the slave cylinder.
2. Remove the screws from the slave cylinder.
3. Remove the slave cylinder, pushrod and spacer.
To install:
4. Place the grooved side of the spacer in contact with the housing and hold it in position.
5. Install the slave cylinder and pushrod into the housing; be sure the dust cap is properly seated.
6. Install the attaching screws.
7. Connect the pressure line to the slave cylinder.
8. Bleed the slave cylinder.

Bleeding the Slave Cylinder

The same principle is used as in bleeding the brakes.
1. Check the brake fluid level in the compensating tank and fill to maximum level.
2. Put a hose on the bleeder screw of the right front caliper and open the bleeder screw.
3. Have a helper depress the brake pedal until the hose is full and there are no air bubbles. Be sure the bleeder screw is closed each time the pedal is released.
4. Put the free end of the hose on the bleeder screw of the slave cylinder and open the bleeder screw.
5. Keep stepping on the brake pedal. Close the bleeder screw on the caliper and release the brake pedal. Open the bleeder screw and repeat the process until no air bubbles show up at the mouth of the inlet line of the compensating tank. Between operations, check and, if necessary, refill the compensating tank.
6. Close the bleeder screws on the caliper and slave cylinder and remove the hose.
7. Check the clutch operation and the fluid level.

AUTOMATIC TRANSMISSION

For further information, please refer to "Professional Transmission Repair Manual" for additional coverage.

Transmission Assembly

Removal and Installation

722.3 (W4A040) TRANSMISSION

Except 190D, 190E and 260E

1. Disconnect negative battery terminal.
2. Remove holder for oil filler pipe on cylinder head.
3. Disengage engine longitudinal regulating shaft.
4. Force off ball socket.
5. Disconnect control wire for control pressure.
6. If equipped with an injected engine, pull out lock and loosen control wire.
7. If equipped with a carburetor engine, compress both plates on plastic clip with pliers and pull out control wire.
8. Raise and safely support the vehicle.
9. Remove cross yoke center place.
10. Remove drain plug on oil pan and drain oil.
11. Remove drain plug on torque converter and drain oil.
12. Remove cover plate.
13. Remove screws for driving plate torque converter.
14. Place a fitting wooden block between engine oil pan and cross yoke.
15. Loosen exhaust system on plug connection and remove.
16. Remove crossbeam together with rear engine mount.
17. Remove cable strap and cable on kickdown solenoid valve. Remove fastening screw for impulse transmitter and pull out impulse transmitter.

NOTE: Disconnect tachometer shaft, if equipped with a mechanical tachometer.

18. Remove exhaust support.
19. Remove exhaust shielding plate.
20. Loosen propeller shaft clamping nut and contract propeller shaft, as much as possible.

21. Remove plug for starter lock out switch.

NOTE: Starter lock out switch plug is secured by a lock, white plastic ring. Prior to pushing off plug, turn lock in upward direction. Carefully, push off plug at cable outlet and tongue, by means of 2 suitable tools.

22. Pull off plug.
23. Disconnect control rod on range selector lever.
24. Remove holder and pull off vacuum line.
25. Remove oil cooler feed line.
26. Remove oil cooler return line.
27. Remove fastening screw for oil filler pipe and push oil filler pipe in upward direction.
28. Remove all fastening screw except for 2 lateral screws.
29. Slightly, lift transmission with mount 116 589 06 62 00 or equivalent, for pit lift.
30. Remove lateral screws.
31. Push transmission to rear as far as propeller shaft permits and lower carefully.

To install:

32. Reverse removal procedure taking attention to the following:
   a. Replace sealing rings for forward and return flow lines.
   b. Torque propeller shaft clamping nuts to 22 ft. lbs. (30 Nm).
   c. Torque driveplate screw to 31 ft. lbs. (42 Nm).
   d. Screw in drain plug on oil pan and on torque converter and torque to 10.5 ft. lbs. (14 Nm).
   e. Replace self-locking screws on cross yoke center piece and torque to 33 ft. lbs. (45 Nm).
   f. Adjust cable for control pressure.

722.4 (W4A020) TRANSMISSION

190D, 190E and 260E

NOTE: Attach a 300mm square sheetmetal panel to unit compartment wall to protect insulating mat during all jobs where the transmission is lowered at the rear. Disconnect exhaust assembly at rear mounting bracket

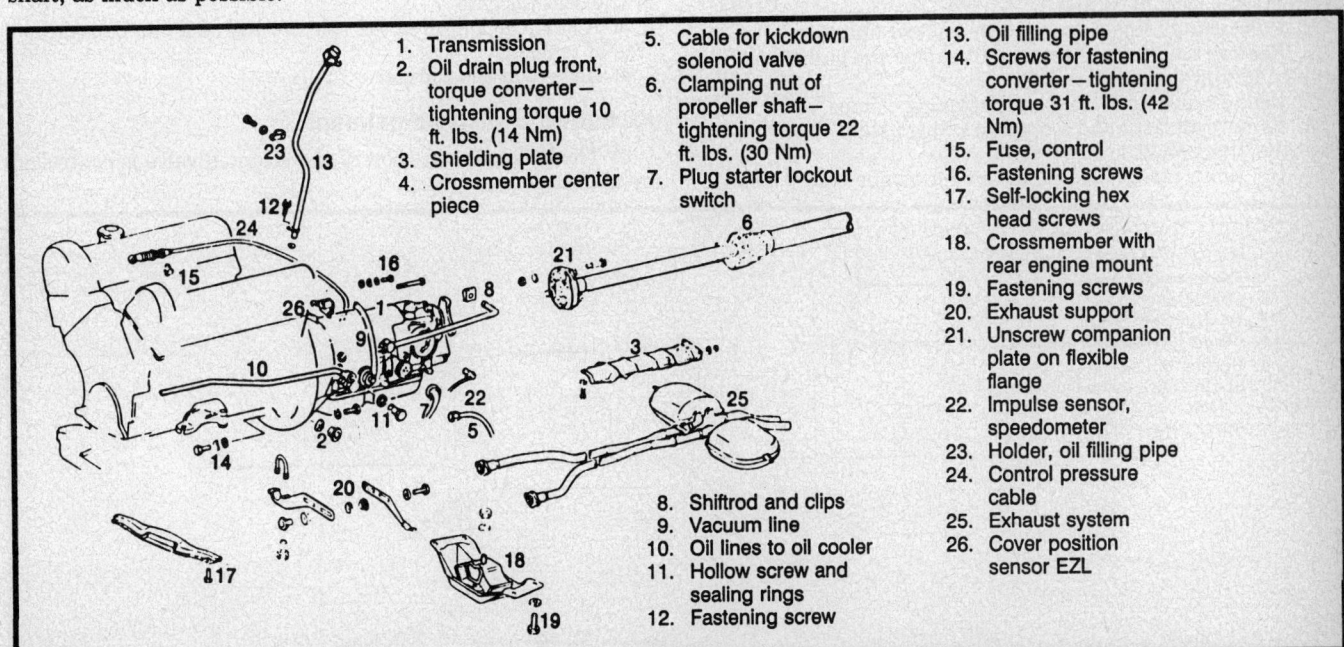

1. Transmission
2. Oil drain plug front, torque converter—tightening torque 10 ft. lbs. (14 Nm)
3. Shielding plate
4. Crossmember center piece
5. Cable for kickdown solenoid valve
6. Clamping nut of propeller shaft—tightening torque 22 ft. lbs. (30 Nm)
7. Plug starter lockout switch
8. Shiftrod and clips
9. Vacuum line
10. Oil lines to oil cooler
11. Hollow screw and sealing rings
12. Fastening screw
13. Oil filling pipe
14. Screws for fastening converter—tightening torque 31 ft. lbs. (42 Nm)
15. Fuse, control
16. Fastening screws
17. Self-locking hex head screws
18. Crossmember with rear engine mount
19. Fastening screws
20. Exhaust support
21. Unscrew companion plate on flexible flange
22. Impulse sensor, speedometer
23. Holder, oil filling pipe
24. Control pressure cable
25. Exhaust system
26. Cover position sensor EZL

Automatic transmission and related components— 300D, 300E, 300CE, 300TE, 300SE, 300SEL, 300TD, 420SEL, 560SL, 560SEL and 560SEC

and fasten by means of a wire approximately 50cm lower. If equipped with an auxiliary heater, make sure the water hose is not damaged when lowering transmission. On 123 models, disconnect engine throttle control.

1. Disconnect negative cable on battery.
2. Remove holder for oil filling pipe on cylinder head and holder on valve cover.
3. If equipped with a fuel injection engine:
    a. Force off ball socket.
    b. Disconnect cable control for control pressure. Pull out lock and remove cable control.
    c. Force plastic ball socket apart by means of a prybar and pull holding bracket from slotted lever.
4. If equipped with a carburetor, force off ball socket. Compress holding clips and disengage cable control for control pressure.
5. On 190D and 300D and 300TD, force off ball socket, remove holding clips and disengage control pressure cable control.
6. Raise and safely support the vehicle.
7. Remove drain plug on oil pan as well as torque converter and drain oil.
8. Install drain plug with new seals and tighten to 10.5 ft. lbs. (14 Nm).
9. Remove screw for driven plate torque converter.
10. Remove crossmember with rear engine mount.
11. Remove exhaust support. Remove companion plate with articulated flange-transmission.

NOTE: Remove tangentially soft companion plate installed at transmission end with a mandrel.

12. Disconnect exhaust system on rear suspension.
13. Remove shielding plate.
14. Remove propeller shaft clamping nut and run together propeller shaft, as much as possible.
15. Pull off cable on kickdown solenoid valve.
16. Remove speedometer shaft. If equipped with an electronic speedometer, remove impulse transmitter.
17. Disconnect control rod on floor shift.
18. Remove fastening clip for speedometer shaft.
19. Swivel locking bracket in upward direction and pull plug from starter lockout switch.
20. Pull vacuum line form vacuum control unit.
21. Remove socket screw from oil filler pipe and pull out oil filler pipe in upward direction.
22. Remove oil cooler lines and fastening clamps.
23. Remove all fastening screws on transmission-to-engine except the 2 screws at left and right.
24. On 190D, insert holding device for torque converter into vent grille cutout and screw in stud until it is entering the socket of oil drain plug.
25. Slightly lift transmission with mounting for pit lift.
26. Remove remaining screws.
27. Slide transmission, to the extent propeller shaft permits, to the rear and carefully lower.
To install:
28. Reverse the removal procedure and pay particular attention to the following:
    a. Install new sealing rings on oil cooler line.
    b. Torque driven plate-to-converter screws to 31 ft. lbs. (42 Nm).

Selector Rod Linkage Adjustment

NOTE: Before performing this adjustment on any vehicle, be sure it is resting on its wheels. No part of the vehicle may be raised for this adjustment.

COLUMN MOUNTED LINKAGE

W4A 040

1. Loosen the counter nut on the rear selector rod while holding both recesses of the front selector rod with an open end wrench.
2. Disconnect the selector rod from the selector lever.
3. Set the selector lever on the transmission and on the column to **N**.
4. Adjust the selector rod until the bearing pin is aligned with the bearing bushing in the selector lever.
5. Connect the rear selector lever to the selector rod and secure it with the lock. Be sure the clearance of the selector lever in **D** and **S** is equal.
6. Tighten the locknut on the rear selector rod while holding the front selector rod as in Step 1.

FLOOR MOUNTED LINKAGE

NOTE: The vehicle must be standing with the weight normally distributed on all 4 wheels.

1. Disconnect the selector rod from the selector lever.
2. Set the selector lever in **N** and make sure there is approximately 1mm clearance between the selector lever and the **N** stop of the selector gate.
3. Adjust the length of the selector rod so it can be attached free of tension.
4. Retighten the counter nut.

Kickdown Switch Adjustment

1. The kickdown position of the solenoid valve is controlled by the accelerator pedal.

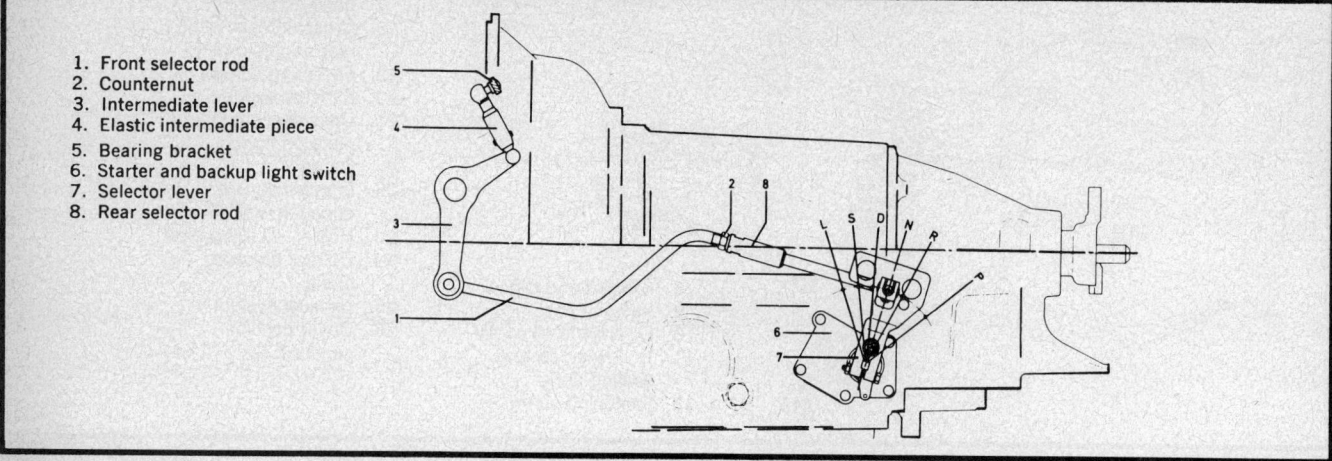

1. Front selector rod
2. Counternut
3. Intermediate lever
4. Elastic intermediate piece
5. Bearing bracket
6. Starter and backup light switch
7. Selector lever
8. Rear selector rod

Selector rod linkage on the W4A 040 and W4B 025

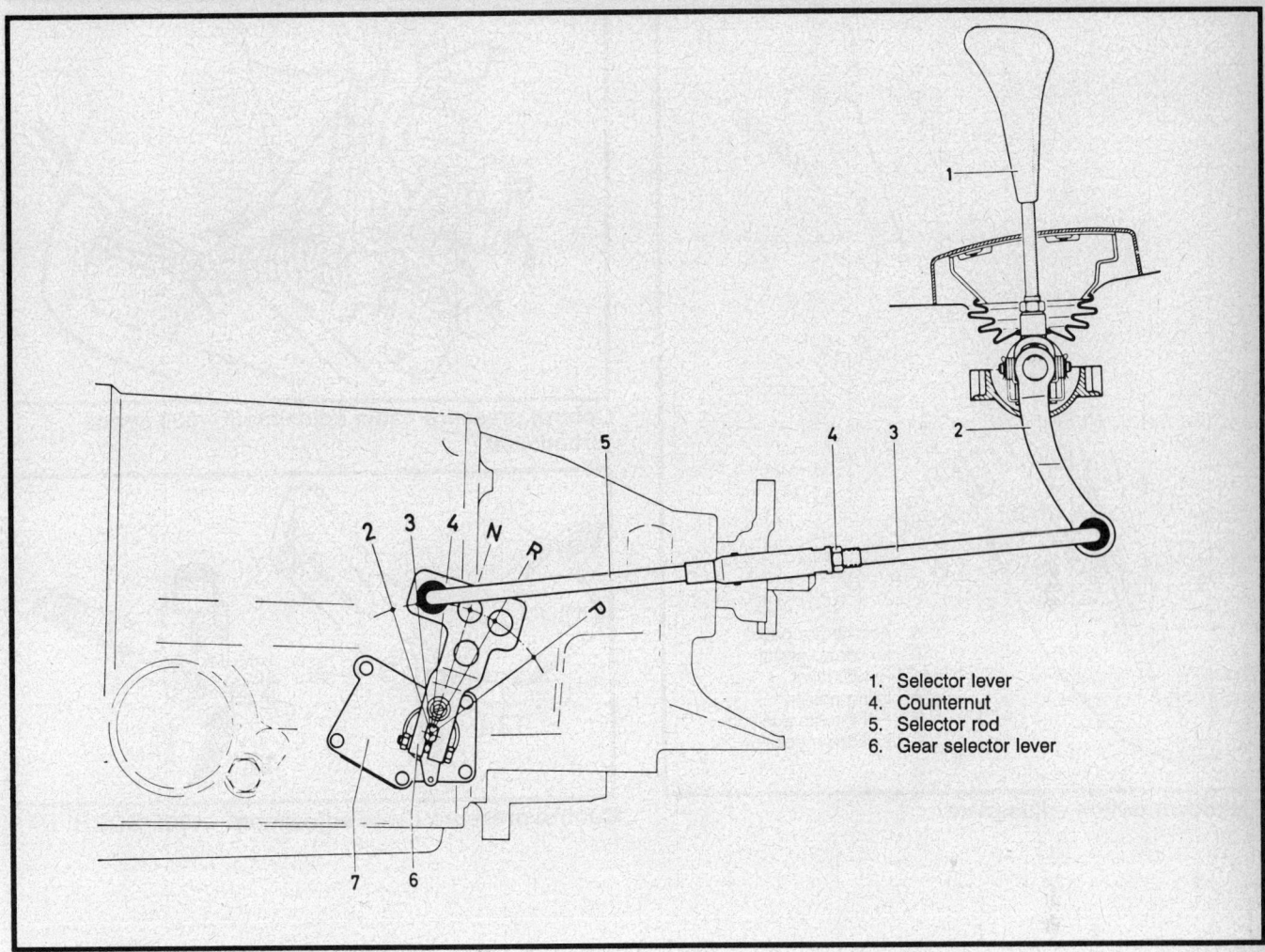

1. Selector lever
4. Counternut
5. Selector rod
6. Gear selector lever

Floor mounted selector rod linkage

2. Push the accelerator pedal against the kickdown limit stop. In this position the throttle lever should rest against the full load stop of the venturi control unit.

3. Adjustments are made by loosening the clamping screw on the return lever on the accelerator pedal shaft and turning the shaft. Tighten the clamping screw again.

Control Pressure Cable Adjustment

300SE, 300SEL, 420SEL, 560SEC, 560SEL AND 560SL

1. Remove the air cleaner.
2. Loosen the clamping screw.
3. Push the ball socket back and pull carefully forward until a slight resistance is felt. At this point, tighten the clamp screw.
4. Install the air cleaner.

TURBODIESELS

1. Pry off the ball socket.
2. Push the ball socket back and pull carefully forward until a slight resistance is felt.
3. Hold the ball socket above the ball head. The drag lever should rest against the stop.
4. Adjust the cable at the adjusting screw so the ball socket can be attached with no strain.

190D

1. Remove the ball socket and extend the telescoping rod to its full length.
2. Pull the control cable forward until a slight resistance is felt. Hold the ball socket over the ball head and engage tension free.
3. Adjust by using the telescoping rod, if required.

190E AND 190E-16

1. Turn the adjusting screw inward until the compression nipple on the spacing sleeve has approximately 1mm of play left.
2. Unscrew the adjusting screw until the tip of the pointer rests directly above the groove on the adjusting screw.

260E, 300E, 300CE AND 300TE

1. Disconnect the ball socket.
2. Pull the control pressure cable forward until a slight resistance is felt. In this position, hold the ball socket above the ball and engage the 2, free of tension.
3. Adjust by turning the screw, if required.

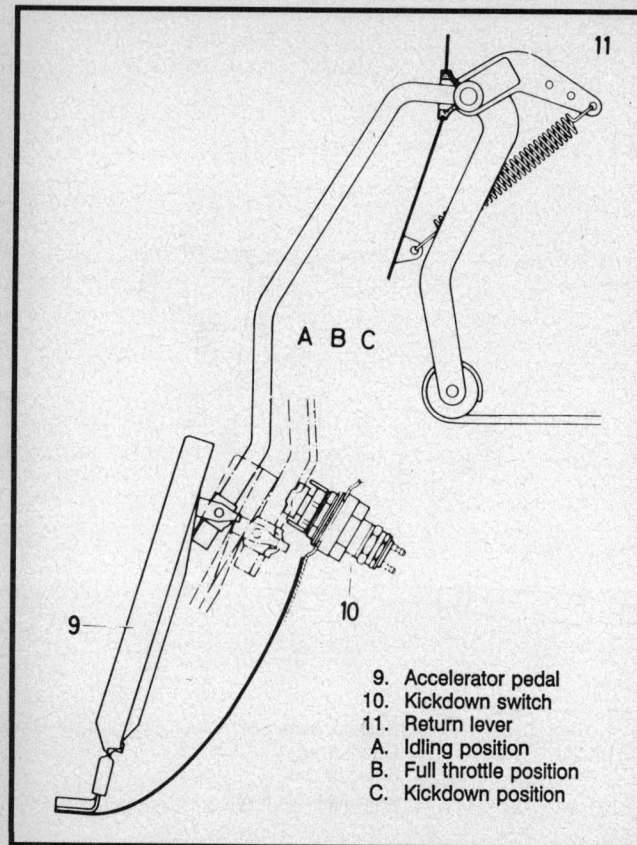

9. Accelerator pedal
10. Kickdown switch
11. Return lever
A. Idling position
B. Full throttle position
C. Kickdown position

Kickdown switch adjustment

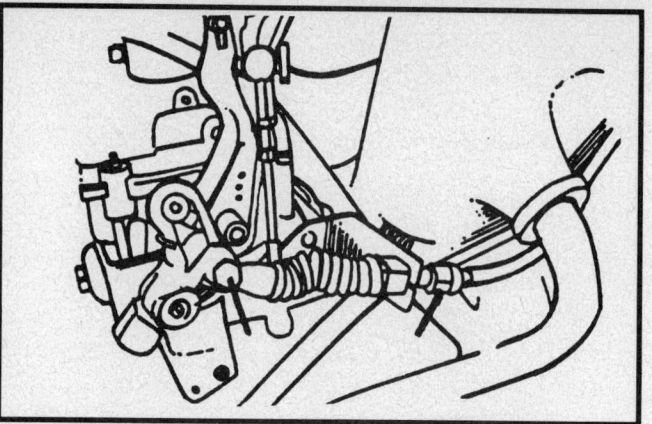

Control pressure cable adjustment—300 series turbodiesel

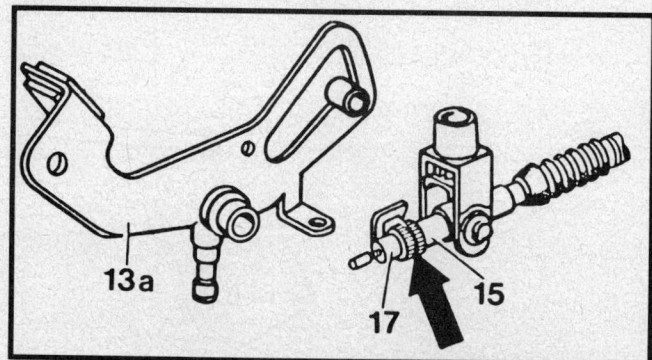

Control pressure cable adjustment—190E SOCH

DRIVE AXLE

These vehicles use either 2 or 3 piece driveshaft to connect the transmission to a hypoid independent rear axle. All models covered in this book use independent rear suspension with open or enclosed driveshaft to the rear wheels.

Driveshaft and U-Joints

Removal and Installation

NOTE: Steps 1–3 apply to 4 cylinder and V8 engines. Matchmark all driveshaft connections prior to removal.

1. Fold the torsion bar down after disconnecting the level control linkage, if equipped.
2. Remove the exhaust system.
3. Remove the heat shield from the frame.
4. Support the transmission and remove the rear engine mount crossmember.
5. Without sliding the rubber sleeve back, loosen the clamp nut approximately 2 turns, the rubber sleeve will slide along.

NOTE: On 3 piece driveshafts, only the front clamp nut need be loosened.

6. Unscrew the U-joint mounting flange from the U-joint plate.
7. Bend back the locktabs and remove the driveshaft-to-rear axle pinion yoke bolts.

8. Remove the intermediate bearing(s)-to-frame bolts, push the driveshaft together slightly and remove it from the vehicle.
9. Try not to separate the driveshafts. If necessary, matchmark all components so they can be reassembled in the same order.
10. Installation is the reverse of removal. Always use new self-locking nuts. After the driveshaft is installed, rock the vehicle back and forth, several times, to settle the driveshaft. Make sure neither intermediate shaft is binding against either intermediate bearing and the clearance between the intermediate bearing and the driveshaft is the same at both ends.

Rear Axle Shafts

NOTE: The rubber covered joints are filled with special oil. If they are disassembled for any reason, they must be refilled with special oil.

Removal and Installation

EXCEPT 190D, 190E, 260E, 300D, 300TD, 300E, 300CE, 300SE, 300TE, 300SEL, 300SDL, 420SEL, 560SEC AND 560SEL

Without Torque Compensator (Torsion Bar)

Most models do not use a torque compensator (torsion bar) which is actually a steel bar used to locate the rear axle under

Removing the lock-ring (26) from the axle shaft with pliers (1)

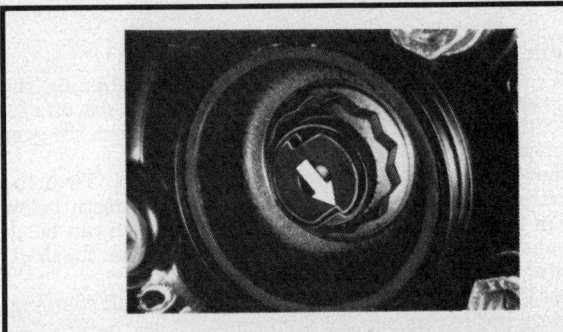

Lock the collar nut on the 190 at the crush flange (arrow)

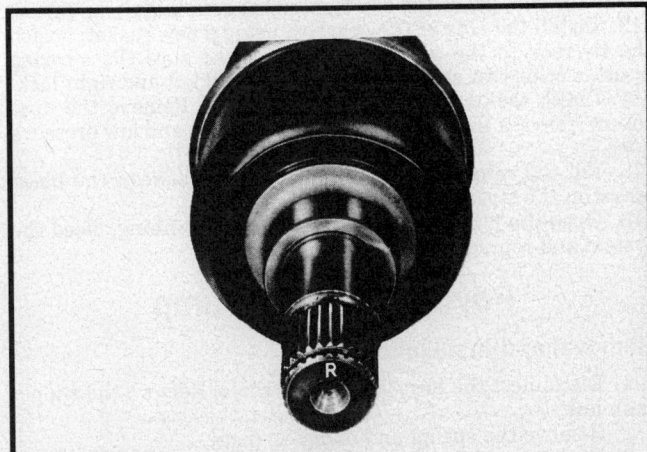

Axle shaft markings (r)

acceleration. In general, only the large sedans use a torque compensator but it is wise to check for one prior to servicing the axle shaft. The illustrations apply to either type.

1. Raise and safely support the vehicle. Remove the wheel and center axle hold-down bolt (in hub).
2. Remove the brake caliper and suspend it from a hook.
3. Drain the differential oil and support the differential housing.
4. Unbolt the rubber mount from the chassis and the differ-

ential housing and remove the differential housing cover to expose the ring and pinion gears.

5. Press the shaft from the axle flange. If necessary, loosen the shock absorber.
6. Using a prybar, remove the axle lock ring inside the differential case.
7. Pull the axle from the housing by pulling the splined end from the side gears, with the spacer.

NOTE: Axle shafts are stamped R and L for right and left units. Always use new lock rings.

8. Installation is the reverse of removal. Fill the rear axle. New radial seal rings are used on all models. Lubricate the outside diameter of rubber covered radial sealing rings with hypoid gear lubricant prior to installation.

NOTE: Check endplay of the lock ring in the groove. If necessary, install a thicker lock ring or spacer to eliminate all endplay, while still allowing the lock ring to rotate. Do not allow the joints in the axle shaft to hang free or the joint bearing may be damaged and leak.

With Torque Compensator (Torsion Bar)

1. Drain the oil from the rear axle.
2. Disconnect and plug the brake lines.
3. Loosen the connecting rod and unscrew the torsion bar bearing bracket. Lower the exhaust system slightly and remove the torsion bar.
4. Loosen the shock absorber.
5. Remove the bolt which attaches the rear axle shaft to the rear axle shaft flange.
6. Disconnect the brake cable control. Remove the bracket from the wheel carrier, remove the rubber sleeve and push back the cover.
7. Force the rear axle shaft from the flange with a suitable tool.
8. Support the rear axle.
9. Remove the rubber mount.
10. Clean the axle housing and remove the cover fan from the housing.

NOTE: The axle shafts are the floating type and can be compressed in the constant velocity joints.

11. Remove the locking ring from the end of the axle shafts which engage the side gears in the differential.
12. Disengage the axle shaft from the side gear and remove the axle shaft together with the spacer.

NOTE: Do not hang the outer constant velocity joint in a free position, unsupported, as the shaft may be damaged and the constant velocity joint housing may leak.

13. Installation is the reverse of removal.
14. If either axle shaft is replace, be sure the proper replacement shaft is installed. Axle shafts are marked L and R for left and right.
15. Check the endplay between the lock ring on the axle shaft and the side gear. There should be no noticeable endplay but the lock ring should be able to turn in the groove.
16. Be sure to bleed the brakes and fill the rear axle with the proper quantity and type of lubricant. New radial seal rings are used on all models. Lubricate the outside diameter of rubber covered radial seal rings with hypoid gear lubricant prior to installation.

190D, 190E, 260E, 300D, 300TD, 300E, 300CE, 300SE, 300TE, 300SEL, 300SDL, 420SEL, 560SEC AND 560SEL

1. Loosen but do not remove, the axle shaft collar nut.
2. Raise and safely support the vehicle.
3. Disconnect the axle shaft from the hub assembly. On the

190, make sure while loosening the locking screws, the bit is seated properly in the multi-tooth profile of the screws.

4. Remove the self-locking screws that attach the inner CV-joint to the connecting flange on the differential. Always loosen the screws in a crosswise manner.

NOTE: Make sure the end cover on the inner CV-joint is not damaged when separated from the connecting flange.

5. While supporting the axle shaft, use a slide hammer or the like and press the axle shaft from the hub assembly.
6. Tilt the axle shaft down and remove it.

NOTE: Make sure the CV-joint boots are not damaged during the removal process.

7. Installation is in the reverse order of removal. Please note the following:

a. Always clean the connecting flanges before installation.

b. Always use new self-locking screws. Lubricate the screw threads and contact faces with oil before installing.

c. 190, 260E, 300E, 300CE and 300TE—tighten the screws to 51 ft. lbs. (70 Nm).

d. 300D, 300SE, 300SEL, 300TD, 300SDL, 420SEL, 560SEC and 560SEL—tighten the screws to 51 ft. lbs. (70 Nm) for M10 bolts or 100 ft. lbs. (135 Nm) for M12 × 1.5 bolts.

e. All other models—tighten the screws to 90–105 ft. lbs. (125–145 Nm). Always tighten the screws in a criss-cross pattern.

f. Tighten the axle shaft collar nut to 203–230 ft. lbs. (280–320 Nm) on the 190 or 22 ft. lbs. (30 Nm) on the others. On the 190, lock the collar nut at the crush flange.

STEERING

Steering Wheel

CAUTION

Some vehicles are equipped with a Supplemental Restraint System (SRS). Improper maintenance, including incorrect removal and installation of related components, can lead to personal injury caused by unintentional activation of the Airbag. Related components on these models should be serviced only by authorized service technicians.

Removal and Installation

WITHOUT SRS

1. Disconnect the negative battery cable. On 560SL, pry the 3-pointed star trademark from the center padding. On all other models, remove the padded plate. Pull at one corner near the wheel spokes.
2. Unscrew the hex nut from the steering shaft and remove the spring washer and the steering wheel.

NOTE: All models use an Allen screw in place of the hex nut. The Allen screw must be replaced, if removed.

3. Installation is the reverse of removal. Be sure the alignment mark on the steering shaft is pointing upward and be sure the slightly curved spoke of the steering wheel is down.

Power Steering Gear

Removal and Installation

1. Remove the oil from the power steering reservoir using a syringe.
2. Detach the high-pressure hose and oil return hose from the steering assembly.
3. Cap both lines to prevent entry of dirt and remove the clamp screw from the lower part of the coupling flange.
4. Remove the rubber plug from the cover plate and remove the U-joint socket screw. On LS90 power steering units, remove the steering spindle. Pull the steering spindle up only until the coupling is no longer engaged with the worn gear.
5. The tail pipe and left side exhaust pipe may have to be removed for access.
6. Detach the tie rod and center tie rod or drag link and track rod, from the pitman arm, using pullers or a tie rod splitter.
7. Remove the hex-head bolts that hold the gearbox to the frame, press the worm shaft stub from the steering coupling and remove the gearbox from under the vehicle.

To install:

8. First install the pitman arm, if removed, aligning the matchmarks. Tighten the pitman arm nut to 110 ft. lbs. and install the cotter pin. Use new self-locking nuts to attach the gear to the frame.
9. Remove the screw plug from the steering box. Turn the worm shaft until the center of the power piston is directly below the bore in the housing. Check dimension (a) which can be altered by changing the position of the pitman arm on its shaft.
10. Center the steering wheel.
11. Press the worm shaft stub into the steering shaft coupling, making sure not to damage the serrations.

NOTE: Install assembly pin as for manual steering.

12. Install and tighten the hex-head screws that hold the gearbox to the chassis, install and tighten the coupling clamp screw.
13. Install the plug in the gearbox, using a new gasket; attach the tie rods to the pitman arm and make sure the steering knuckle arms rest against their stops at full left and right lock.
14. Check toe-in and correct if necessary. Remove the dust covers from the fluid lines, reconnect the high and low pressure lines.
15. Fill the reservoir and connect a hose between the bleed screw on the steering and the reservoir.
16. Open the bleed screw and, with engine running, bleed the system and top up.

Power Steering Pump

Removal and Installation

1. Disconnect the negative battery cable. Remove the supply tank nut.
2. Remove the spring and damping plate.
3. Drain the oil from the tank with a syringe.
4. Loosen and remove the expanding and return hoses from the pump. Plug all connections and pump openings.
5. If necessary for clearance, loosen the radiator shell. Loosen the mounting bolts and move the pump toward the engine by using the toothed wheel. Remove the belt. Remove the pulley and the pump.
6. Loosen the plate nut and the support bolt.
7. Push the pump toward the engine and remove the belts from the pulley.
8. Unscrew the mounting bolts and remove the pump and carrier.
9. Installation is the reverse of removal.

BRAKES

Master Cylinder

Removal and Installation

1. Disconnect the negative battery cable. To remove the master cylinder, first open a bleed screw at one front and one rear wheel.
2. Pump the pedal to empty the reservoir completely. Make sure both reservoirs are completely drained.
3. Disconnect the switch connectors using a small prybar. Disconnect the brake lines at the master cylinder. Plug the ends with bleed screw caps or the equivalent.
4. Unbolt the master cylinder from the power brake unit and remove; do not loose the O-ring in the flange groove of the master cylinder.
5. Installation is the reverse of removal. Be sure to replace the O-ring between the master cylinder and the power brake unit, since this must be absolutely tight. Torque the nuts to 12–15 ft. lbs. Be sure both chambers are completely filled with brake fluid and bleed the brakes.

Power Brake Booster

Removal and Installation

300SDL, 300SE, 300SEL, 420SEL, 560SEC AND 560SEL

1. Disconnect the negative battery cable. If equipped with a manual transmission, remove hose to master cylinder.
2. Remove master cylinder.
3. Loosen vacuum line to brake unit.
4. Remove cover under dash panel on driver's side.
5. Remove lock and remove collar bolt to release pushrod.
6. Remove nuts for fastening booster unit to front end and remove booster unit.

NOTE: Care must be taken when handling brake unit, for it is made of plastic and may break.

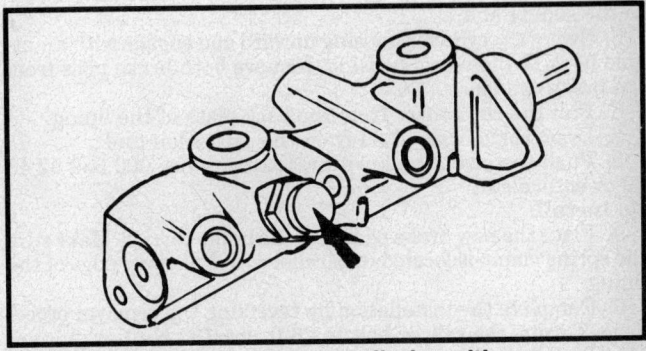

Reset pin (arrow) on master cylinder with pressure warning differential

To install:

7. Position brake unit to front end and install attaching nuts. Torque to 11 ft. lbs. (15 Nm).
8. Install collar bolt and lock to pushrod and brake pedal.
9. Install cover under dash panel.
10. Connect vacuum line to brake unit and torque nut to 22 ft. lbs. (30 Nm).
11. Install master cylinder.
12. If equipped with a manual transmission, connect hose to master cylinder on expansion tank.

Disc Brake Pads

Removal and Installation

190D, 190E, 260E, 300E, 300CE AND 300TE

Front Axle

1. Raise and safely support the vehicle.
2. Remove the front wheel assemblies.
3. Lift the 2 holding lugs located laterally on the cover of the plug connection by means of a suitable tool and open the cover.

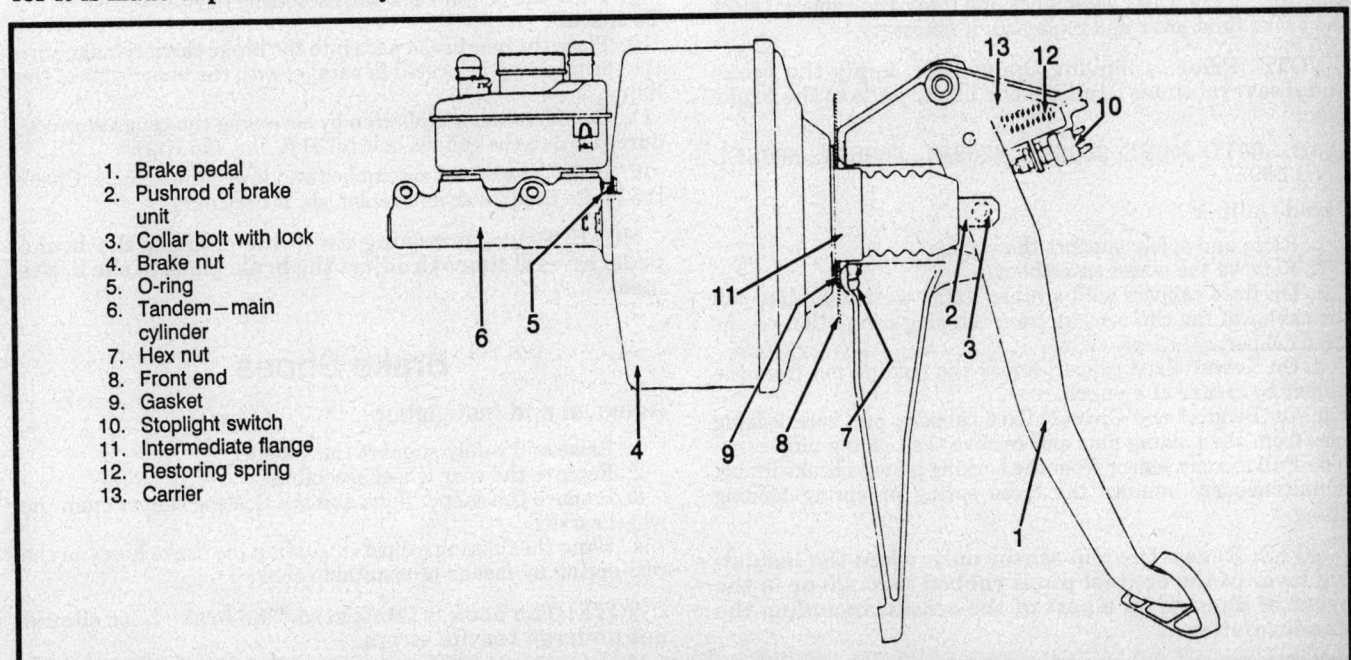

1. Brake pedal
2. Pushrod of brake unit
3. Collar bolt with lock
4. Brake nut
5. O-ring
6. Tandem—main cylinder
7. Hex nut
8. Front end
9. Gasket
10. Stoplight switch
11. Intermediate flange
12. Restoring spring
13. Carrier

Power braking system—300SDL, 300SE, 300SEL, 420SEL, 560SEC and 560SEL

Do not use force. Remove the cable of clip sensor from the plug connection on the floating caliper. Do not pull on the cable.

4. Remove the lower caliper bolt while applying counter hold to the sliding bolt.

5. Swing the cylinder housing upward and engage with a suitable hook to the wheel housing. Remove both brake pads from the brake carrier.

6. Pull the clip sensor from the back plate of the lining.

7. Draw some brake fluid from the expansion tank.

8. Push the piston back with resetting device 000 589 52 43 00 or equivalent.

To install:

9. Place the new brake pads into the brake carrier. Make sure the spring clamp is located in parallel with the upper edge of the lining.

10. Complete the installation by reversing the removal procedure. Torque the caliper bolt to 26 ft. lbs. (35 Nm).

11. Install the wheel assemblies and lower the vehicle. Check the brake fluid lever and replenish, if necessary.

NOTE: Prior to moving the vehicle, apply the brake pedal several times to adjust the brake pads to the brake disc.

Rear Axle

1. Raise and safely support the vehicle.
2. Remove the rear wheel assemblies.
3. Knock the holding pin from the fixed caliper by means of a punch. Remove the cross spring.
4. Push the brake pads from the fixed caliper by means of a pushing lever.

NOTE: If the brake pads are rusted, use a puller for removal of the stuck brake pads.

5. Clean the guide surface for the brake pad in the fixed caliper with a brake caliper brush.
6. Draw some brake fluid from the expansion tank.
7. Push both the pistons back with a resetting device.

To install:

8. Place the new brake pads into the brake carrier.
9. Complete the installation by reversing the removal procedure.
10. Install the wheel assemblies and lower the vehicle. Check the brake fluid lever and replenish, if necessary.

NOTE: Prior to moving the vehicle, apply the brake pedal several times to adjust the brake pads to the brake disc.

300D, 300TD 300SE, 300SEL, 420SEL, 560SEC, 560SEL AND 560SL

Fixed Caliper

1. Raise and safely support the vehicle.
2. Remove the wheel assemblies.
3. On fixed calipers with a brake lining wear indicator, pull the cables of the clip sensors from the plug connection on the fixed caliper.
4. On Teves® fixed caliper, knock the holding pin from the caliper by means of a punch.
5. On Bendix® and Girling® fixed calipers, pull both locking eyes from the holding pins and remove the holding pins.
6. Pull the clip sensor from the backing plate or brake lining. Simultaneously, remove the cross spring or spring holding lining.

NOTE: Renew the clip sensor only, when the insulating layer of the contact pin is rubbed through or in the event of damage on a part of the sensor, including the line insulation.

7. Force the brake pads from the fixed caliper by means of the forcing lever.

NOTE: If the brake pad is rusted, use a puller for removal of the stuck brake pads.

8. Clean the guide for the brake pad in the fixed caliper with a brake caliper brush.
9. Draw a slight amount of brake fluid from the expansion tank.
10. Push both the pistons back with a resetting device.

To install:

11. Place the new brake pads into the brake carrier.
12. Complete the installation by reversing the removal procedure.
13. Install the wheel assemblies and lower the vehicle. Check the brake fluid lever and replenish, if necessary.

NOTE: Prior to moving the vehicle, apply the brake pedal several times to adjust the brake pads to the brake disc.

Floating Caliper

1. Raise and safely support the vehicle.
2. Remove the wheel assemblies.
3. Lift the 2 holding lugs located laterally on the cover of the plug connection by means of a suitable tool and open the cover. Do not use force. Remove the cable of clip sensor from the plug connection on the floating caliper; do not pull on the cable.
4. Remove the upper caliper bolt while applying counter hold to the sliding bolt.
5. Fold the cylinder housing in a downward direction and attach to the torsion bar by means of a suitable hook. Remove both brake pads from the brake carrier.
6. Pull the clip sensor from the lining backup plate.

NOTE: The wear indicator on the floating caliper is at inside the brake pad only. Renew the clip sensor only, when the insulating layer of the contact pin is rubbed through or in the event of damage on a part of the sensor, including the line insulation.

7. Clean the contact surface of the brake pads in the brake carrier.
8. Draw a slight amount of brake fluid from the expansion tank.
9. Push the piston back with resetting device.

To install:

10. Place the new brake pads into the brake carrier; make sure the spring clamp is located in parallel with the upper edge of the lining.
11. Complete the installation by reversing the removal procedure. Torque the caliper bolt to 26 ft. lbs. (35 Nm).
12. Install the wheel assemblies and lower the vehicle. Check the brake fluid lever and replenish, if necessary.

NOTE: Prior to moving the vehicle, apply the brake pedal several times to adjust the brake pads to the brake disc.

Brake Shoes

Removal and Installation

1. Raise and safely support the vehicle.
2. Remove the rear wheel assemblies.
3. Remove the caliper bolts and the floating caliper from the wheel carrier.
4. Hang the floating caliper, including the brake hose, on the rear spring by means of a suitable hook.

NOTE: The hook is fabricated. The brake hose should not undergo tensile stress.

5. Turn the rear axle shaft flange in such a manner that 1 tapped hole faces the spring. Compress the spring slightly with

installer, turn the tool by approximately 90 degrees, disconnect the spring from the covering ring and remove it.

6. Remove the spring on the other brake shoe.

7. Disconnect the return spring with the remover and installer from the brake shoes.

8. Pull both brake shoes apart until they can be removed over the rear axle flange.

9. Disconnect the return spring from the brake shoes and remove the adjusting device.

10. Push the bolt from the expanding lock and remove the expanding lock from the brake cable control.

To install:

11. Reverse the removal procedure. Torque the caliper bolts to 38 ft. lbs. (50 Nm).

Parking Brake Cable

Adjustment

260E, 300E, 300CE, 300SE, 300TE AND 300SEL

1. Loosen the parking brake cable slack adjusting screw. The expanders in the rear wheel should not be preloaded via the cable.

2. Raise and safely support the vehicle.

3. Remove 1 of the wheel bolts and rotate the wheel until the star wheel is accessible through the hole. Positioning of the hole should be around 2 o'clock.

4. Use a prybar to run the star wheel adjuster until wheel locks. Turn the adjuster back about 4–5 teeth until the wheel turns freely.

NOTE: To tighten the star wheel adjuster on the left wheel, move the prybar upwards; on the right wheel, move it downwards.

5. Turn the parking brake cable slack adjuster screw into the bracket until the cables have no slack.

6. Depress the parking brake hand (400 N), several times.

7. Turn the adjusting screw until the brake pedal can be depressed by one tooth at a force of approximately 170–200 N.

ALL OTHER MODELS

1. If the floor pedal can be depressed more than 2 notches before actuating the brakes. Raise and safely support the vehicle. Remove 1 lug bolt and adjust the star wheel with a prybar.

2. Move the prybar upward on the left (driver's) side, downward on the right (passenger's) side to tighten the shoes.

3. When the wheel is locked, back off about 2–4 clicks.

4. With this type system, the adjusting bolt on the cable relay lever only serves to equalize cable length; therefore, do not attempt to adjust the brakes by turning this bolt.

Removal and Installation

FRONT CABLE

190D, 190E, 260E, 300E, 300CE, 300SE, 300TE and 300SEL

1. Disconnect the return spring at the cable control compensator.

2. Unbolt the brake cable from the intermediate lever and pull the cable away.

3. Remove the parking brake lever.

4. Loosen the brake cable at the lever and pull it out toward the rear, through the floor.

5. Installation is in the reverse order of removal.

300D and 300TD

1. Remove the spring from the equalizer.

2. Back off the adjusting screw completely.

3. Detach the relay lever from the bracket on the frame and from the adjusting shackle.

4. Detach the cable from the relay lever by pulling the cotter pin from the bolt.

5. Remove the clip from the cable guide. Remove the clips from the chassis.

6. Detach the brake cable from the parking brake link. Remove the clip from the cable guide and detach the brake cable from the parking brake.

7. Pull the cable downward from the chassis.

8. Installation is in the reverse of removal.

560SL

1. Remove the exhaust system.

2. Disconnect the return spring.

3. Remove the guide-to-intermediate lever bolts and pull the cotter pin from the flange bolt. Remove the flange bolt.

4. Remove the spring clamp from the cable guide and remove the cable control from the bracket.

5. Remove the tunnel cover.

6. Disconnect the brake control from the parking brake and remove the spring clamp from the cable guide. Remove the cable control from the parking brake.

7. Remove the brake control cable from the frame toward the rear.

8. Installation is the reverse of removal.

420SEL, 560SEC and 560SEL

1. Disconnect return spring on bracket and back-off adjusting screw on adjusting bracket.

2. Loosen brake cable on intermediate lever, while pulling cotter pin from flange bolt and remove flange bolt.

3. Remove spring clip from cable guide on frame floor.

4. Remove floor mat and cover under dash panel.

5. Remove center console.

6. Disconnect brake cable from pedal plate. Remove spring clip from cable guide. Remove brake cable.

7. Loosen pipe clamp on pedal assemble.

8. Remove brake cable from accelerator pedal bearing.

9. Fold back passenger compartment carpet until cable is exposed. Slightly raise passenger compartment seat. Loosen plate and pipe clamp. Pull out brake cable.

10. Open cable band on shift bracket and pull brake cable ofrom heater box toward rear.

To install:

11. Route brake cable at rear past heater box and pull up to pedal of parking brake.

12. Attach brake cable to cable draw link of pedal and insert spring clamp.

13. Attach brake cable to accelerator pedal bearing and by means of pipe clamp to pedal assemble.

14. Route brake cable to rear through frame floor and attach to tunnel by means of plate, pipe clamp and by means of cable band to shift bracket.

15. Attach cable to frame floor by means of spring clamp.

16. Attach brake cable to intermediate lever by means of flange bolt and secure.

17. Attach return spring to bracket.

18. Adjust parking brake.

19. Install carpet and install center console.

20. Install cover under dash panel.

21. Install floor mat.

All Other Models

1. Remove the floor mat.

2. Remove the leg room cover (upper and lower).

3. Remove the air duct.

4. Disconnect the 4 rubber rings and lower and support the exhaust system.

5. Remove the shield above the exhaust pipes.

6. Disconnect and return spring from the bracket.

7. Back off the adjusting screw on the bracket.

8. Disconnect the intermediate lever from the adjusting bracket.

9. Loosen the brake cable controls on the intermediate lever while pulling the cotter pin from the flange bolt. Remove the flange bolt.

10. Remove the spring clip from the cable guide on the floor pan.

11. Disconnect the brake cable control from the parking brake bracket.

12. Remove the spring clip from the cable and the cable control from the parking brake.

13. Pull the cable away upward.

14. Installation is the reverse of removal. Adjust the parking brake.

REAR CABLE

190D and 190E

1. Remove brake shoes of parking brake.
2. Remove hex head screw from wheel carrier and brake cable.
3. Disconnect return spring from holder.
4. Back-off adjusting screw of adjusting bracket.
5. Remove front brake cable from intermediate lever.
6. Disconnect intermediate lever on bearing of frame floor.
7. Disconnect brake control from compensating lever.
8. Remove spring clamp, remove cable from holder.

To install:

9. Route cable through rubber grommet of holder on rear axle carrier.

NOTE: Make sure rubber grommets are not damaged, so no dirt can enter cable guide.

10. Fasten brake cable to wheel carrier.
11. Attach brake cable to compensating lever. Secure brake cable to holder by means of spring clamp.
12. Connect intermediate lever and install front brake cable. Attach return spring.
13. Install brake shoes and adjust parking brake.

420SEL, 560SEC and 560SEL

1. Remove brake shoes of parking brake.
2. If equipped with a diagonal swing axle, remove screw from wheel carrier and remove brake cable.
3. If equipped with a diagonal swing axle with starting torque compensation, remove both socket screws from wheel carrier and remove cable.
4. Disconnect return spring an bracket and back-off adjusting screw on adjusting bracket.
5. Disconnect intermediate lever on bearing of frame floor and remove adjusting bracket.
6. Disconnect brake cable from compensating lever.
7. Remove spring clamp, take cable from bracket.
8. Pull out brake cable toward rear through rubber grommet in semi-trailing arm.

To install:

9. Make sure rubber grommets are not damaged, so no dirt can enter cable guide.
10. Route brake cable through rubber grommet in semi-trailing arm and attach to wheel carrier or bracket, respectively.
11. Attach brake cable to compensating lever. Mount intermediate lever into bearing on frame floor.
12. Install brake shoes and adjust parking brake.

300D and 300TD

1. Remove the parking brake shoes after removing the wheel.
2. Remove the screws from the wheel support and detach the brake cable.
3. Back off the adjusting screw from the adjusting shackle.
4. Remove the spring clips, detach the cable and remove the equalizer.
5. Installation is the reverse of removal.

All Other Models

1. Remove the parking brake shoes.
2. Remove the bolt from the wheel carrier and remove the cable.
3. Remove the exhaust system. On some models the exhaust system can be lowered and supported after removing the rubber rings. If equipped, remove the heat shield from above the exhaust pipes.
4. Disconnect the draw spring from the holder.
5. Detach the guide from the intermediate lever.
6. Remove the adjusting screw from the bracket.
7. Disconnect the intermediate lever on the bearing and remove it from the adjusting bracket.
8. Remove the holder, compensating lever, cable control plates and intermediate lever from the tunnel.
9. Remove the spring clamps and disconnect the cable from the plate.
10. Installation is the reverse of removal.

Anti-Lock Brake System Service
Precautions

• When welding with an electric welding unit, unplug the electric control unit.

• During paint jobs, the electronic control unit may be exposed to a maximum of 203°F (95°C) for up to 2 hours or 185°F (85°C) if more time is needed.

• When removing the rear axle centerpiece, make sure the correct toothed wheel with the correct ratio for the wheel speed sensor is installed. If a wheel with the wrong number of teeth is installed, this fault will not show up when checking the system with the ABS tester. The stopping distance, however, will be increased during controlled braking.

• If work was done to non-ABS brake components, a simple operational test will be sufficient. This means that after driving about 5 mph, the yellow warning light on the instrument panel should go out if the ABS system is intact.

• If ABS components have been replaced, the entire system should be checked using the appropriate Bosch tester in combination with brake test bench or an adaptor in combination with a multimeter.

Anti-Lock Brake (ABS) Hydraulic Unit

Removal and Installation
420SEL, 560SEC AND 560SEL

1. With ignition switch **OFF**, disconnect battery negative terminal.
2. Disconnect brake lines from hydraulic unit and seal open lines with blind plugs.

NOTE: Do not loosen sealed center bolt and 2 socket screws.

3. Remove cover fastening screw and remove cover.
4. Disconnect grounding strap from pump motor.
5. Disconnect stress relief and remove plug.

NOTE: Two relays for pump motor or for solenoid valves can be replaced.

6. Remove mounting nuts and hydraulic unit.

To install:

7. Mount hydraulic unit on mounting bracket and attach 12 terminal plug and attach stress relief.
8. Install hydraulic unit cover and screw.
9. Connect brake lines to hydraulic unit. Torque line nuts to 10 ft. lbs. (14 Nm).

NOTE: Do not interchange brake lines.

10. Connect ground terminal of battery.

FRONT SUSPENSION

Shock Absorbers

Removal and Installation

560SL

1. Raise and safely support the vehicle.
2. When removing the shock absorbers, it is also wise to draw a simple diagram of the location of parts such as lock rings, rubber stops, locknuts and steel plates, since many shock absorbers require their own peculiar installation of these parts.
3. Raise the hood and locate the upper shock absorber mount.
4. Support the lower control arm.
5. Unbolt the mount for the shock absorber at the top. Remove the coolant expansion tank to allow access to the right front shock absorber.
6. Remove the nuts which secure the shock absorber to the lower control arm.
7. Push the shock absorber piston rod in, install the stirrup, and remove the shock absorber.
8. Remove the stirrup, since this must be install on replacement shock absorber.
9. Installation is the reverse of removal. Always use new bushing when installing replacement shock absorber.

EXCEPT 190D, 190E, 260E, 300E, 300CE, 300SE, 300TE AND 300SEL

1. Raise and safely support the vehicle. Support the lower control arm.
2. Loosen the nuts on the upper shock absorber mount. Remove the plate and ring.
3. Place the shock absorber vertical to the lower control arm and remove the lower mounting bolts.
4. Remove the shock absorber; be sure to disconnect and plug the pressure line on models with level control.
5. Installation is the reverse or removal. On Bilstein shocks, do not confuse the upper and lower plates.

Damper Strut

Removal and Installation

190D, 190E, 260E, 300E, 300CE, 300SE, 300TE AND 300SEL

1. Raise and safely support the vehicle. Remove the wheel.
2. Using a spring compressor, compress the spring until any load is removed from the lower control arm.

NOTE: When using a spring compressor, be sure a least 7½ coils are engaged before applying tension.

3. Support the lower control arm. Loosen the retaining bolt for the upper end of the damper strut by holding the inner piston rod with an Allen wrench and unscrew the nut. Never use an impact wrench on the retaining nut.

─────── **CAUTION** ───────

Never unscrew the nut with the axle half at full rebound the spring may fly out with considerable force, causing personal injury.

4. Unbolt the 2 screws and 1 nut and disconnect the lower damper strut from the steering knuckle.
5. Remove the strut down and forward. Be sure to disconnect and plug the pressure line on models with level control. Secure the steering knuckle in position so it won't tilt.
6. Installation is in the reverse order of removal. Please note the following:
    a. When attaching the lower end of the damper strut to the steering knuckle, first position all 3 screws; next tighten the 2 lower screws to 72 ft. lbs. (100 Nm); finally, tighten the nut on the upper clamping connection screw to 54 ft. lbs. (75 Nm).

    b. Tighten the retaining nut on the upper end of the damper strut to 44 ft. lbs. (60 Nm).

Coil Springs

Removal and Installation

190D, 190E, 260E, 300E, 300CE, 300SE, 300TE AND 300SEL

1. Raise and safely support the vehicle. Remove the wheel.
2. Remove the engine compartment lining under the vehicle, if equipped.
3. Install a spring compressor so at least 7½ coils are engaged.
4. Support the lower control arm and loosen the retaining nut at the upper end of the damper strut.

─────── **CAUTION** ───────

Never loosen the damper strut retaining nut unless the wheels are on the ground, the control arm is supported or the springs have been removed; personal injury may result.

5. Lower the control arm slightly and remove the spring toward the front.
6. On installation, position the spring between the control arm and the upper mount so when the control arm is raised, the end of the lower coil will be seated in the impression in the control arm.
7. Raise the control arm until the spring is held securely.
8. Using a new nut, tighten the upper end of the damper strut to 44 ft. lbs. (60 Nm).
9. Slowly ease the tension on the spring compressor until the spring is seated properly and remove the compressor.
10. Installation of the remaining components is in the reverse order of removal.

560SL

NOTE: Be extremely careful when attempting to remove the front springs as they are compressed and under considerable load.

1. Raise and safely support the vehicle. Remove the wheels.
2. Remove the front shock absorber and disconnect the sway bar.
3. Punchmark the position of the eccentric adjusters and loosen the hex bolts.
4. Support the lower control arm.
5. Knock out the eccentric pins and gradually lower the arm until spring tension is relieved.
6. The spring can now be removed.

NOTE: Check caster and camber after installing a new spring.

7. Installation is the reverse of removal.
8. For ease of installation, tape the rubber mounts to the springs.
9. If the eccentric adjusters were not match marked, install the eccentric bolts.

ALL OTHER MODELS

1. Raise and safely support the vehicle. Support the lower control arm.
2. Remove the wheel. Unbolt the upper shock absorber mount.
3. Install a spring compressor and compress the spring.
4. Remove the front spring with the lower mount.
5. Installation is the reverse of removal. Tighten the upper shock absorber suspension.

Steering Knuckle and Ball Joints

Inspection

1. Raise and safely support the vehicle. Check the steering knuckles or ball joints, by raising the front spring plate. This unloads the front suspension to allow the maximum play to be observed.

2. Late model ball joints need to be replaced only if dried out with plainly visible wear and/or play.

Removal and Installation

190D, 190E, 260E, 300E, 300CE, 300SE, 300TE AND 300SEL

1. Raise and safely support the vehicle. Remove the wheel.
2. Install a spring compressor on the spring.
3. Remove the brake caliper and wire it aside; be careful not to damage the brake line.
4. Remove the brake disc and wheel hub.

NOTE: If equipped equipped with ABS, remove the speed sensor.

5. Unscrew the 3 socket-head bolts and remove the brake backing plate from the steering knuckle.
6. Tighten the spring compressor until all tension and/or lead has been removed from the lower control arm.
7. Disconnect the steering knuckle arm from the steering knuckle; this is the arm attached to the tie rod.

CAUTION

There must be no tension on the lower control arm; otherwise personal injury may result.

---

8. Unscrew the 3 bolts and disconnect the lower end of the damper strut from the steering knuckle.
9. Remove the hex-head clamp nut at the supporting joint, lower ball joint.
10. Remove the steering knuckle.
11. Installation is in the reverse order of removal. Tighten the supporting joint clamp nut to 70 ft. lbs. (125 Nm).

560SL

1. This should only be done with the front shock absorber installed. If, however, the front shock absorber has been removed, the lower control arm should be supported and the spring should be clamped with a spring tensioner. In this case, the hex nut on the guide joint should not be loosened without the spring tensioner installed.
2. Raise and safely support the vehicle.
3. Remove the wheel.
4. Remove the brake caliper.
5. Unbolt the steering relay lever from the steering knuckle. For safety, install spring clamps on the front springs.
6. Remove the hex nuts from the upper and lower ball joints.
7. Remove the ball joints from the steering knuckle with the aid of a puller.
8. Remove the steering knuckle.
9. Installation is the reverse of removal. Be sure the seats for the pins of the ball joints are free of grease.
10. Bleed the brakes.

ALL OTHER MODELS

1. Raise and safely support the vehicle. For safety, install some type of clamp on the front spring. Support the lower control arms.
2. Remove the wheel.
3. Remove the steering knuckle arm from the steering knuckle.
4. Remove and suspend the brake caliper.
5. Remove the front wheel hub.

NOTE: If equipped equipped with ABS, disconnect the speed sensor.

6. Loosen the brake hose holder on the cover plate.
7. Loosen the guide joint nut and remove the joint from the steering knuckle.
8. Loosen the nut on the support joint.
9. Swivel the steering knuckle outward and force the ball joint from the lower control arm.
10. Remove the steering knuckle.
11. If necessary, remove the cover plate from the steering knuckle.
12. Installation is the reverse of removal. Use self-locking nuts and adjust the wheel bearings.

Upper Control Arm

NOTE: The 190D, 190E, 260E, 300E, 300CE, 300SE, 300TE and 300SEL models have no upper control arm.

Removal and Installation

EXCEPT 560SL

1. Raise and safely support the vehicle.
2. Remove the wheel.
3. Loosen the nut on the guide joint.
4. Remove the guide joint from the steering knuckle.
5. Secure the steering knuckle with a hook on the upper control arm stop to prevent it from tilting.
6. Loosen the clamp screw and separate the upper control arm from the torsion bar.
7. Loosen the upper control arm bearing at the front and remove the upper control arm.
8. Installation is the reverse of removal. Use new self-locking nuts and check the front wheel alignment.

560SL

1. The front shock absorbers should remain installed. Never loosen the hex nuts of the ball joints with the shock absorber removed, unless a spring clamp is installed.
2. Raise and safely support the vehicle. Remove the wheel.
3. Support the front end.
4. Remove the steering arm from the steering knuckle.
5. Separate the brake line and brake hose from each other and plug the openings.
6. Support the lower control arm and unscrew the nuts from the ball joints.
7. Remove the ball joints from the steering knuckle.
8. Loosen the bolts on the upper control arm and remove the upper control arm.
9. Installation is the reverse of removal.

NOTE: Mount the front hex bolt from the rear in a forward direction and the rear hex bolt from the front in a rearward direction.

10. Bleed the brakes.

Lower Control Arm

Removal and Installation

EXCEPT 190D, 190E, 260E, 300E, 300CE, 300SE, 300TE, 300SEL, AND 560SL

The lower control arm is the same as the front axle half. For safety install a spring compressor on the coil spring.
1. Raise and safely support the vehicle. Remove the wheels.
2. Remove the front shock absorber. Loosen the top mount first.
3. Remove the front springs.
4. Separate and plug the brake lines.
5. Remove the track rod from the steering knuckle arm.

6. Matchmark the position of the eccentric bolts on the bearing of the lower control arm in relation to the crossmember.

7. Remove the shield from the cross yoke.

8. Support the front axle half.

9. Loosen the eccentric bolt on the front and rear bearing of the lower control arm and knock them out.

10. Remove the bolt from the cross yoke bearing.

11. Loosen the screw at the opposite end of the cross yoke bearing.

12. Pull the cross yoke bearing down slightly.

13. Loosen the support of the upper control arm on the torsion bar. Remove the clamp screw from the clamp.

14. Remove the upper control arm bearing on the front end.

15. Remove the front axle half.

16. Installation is the reverse of removal. Tighten the eccentric bolts on the lower control arm bearing with the vehicle resting on the wheels. Bleed the brakes and check the front end alignment.

190D, 190E, 260E, 300E, 300CE, 300SE, 300TE AND 300SEL

1. Remove the engine compartment lining at the bottom of the vehicle, if equipped.

2. Raise and safely support the vehicle. Remove the wheel.

3. Support the lower control arm and disconnect the torsion bar bearing at the control arm.

4. Remove the spring.

5. Disconnect the tie rod at the steering knuckle and press out the ball joint with the proper tool.

6. Remove the brake caliper and position it aside; do not damage the brake line.

7. Remove the brake disc/wheel hub assembly.

8. Disconnect the lower end of the damper strut from the steering knuckle and remove the knuckle.

9. Mark the position of the inner eccentric pins, relative to the frame, on the bearing of the control arm.

10. Unscrew and remove the pins.

11. Remove the lower control arm.

12. Installation is in the reverse order of removal. Please note the following:

    a. Tighten the eccentric bolts on the inner arm to 130 ft. lbs. (180 Nm).

    b. To facilitate torsion bar installation, raise the opposite side of the lower control arm.

    c. Tighten the clamp nut on the tie rod ball joint to 25 ft. lbs. (35 Nm).

    d. When installing the rear torsion bar bushing, on the 300E, 300CE, 300SE, 300TE and 300SEL, the flats on the cone must be vertical.

560SL

1. Since the front shock absorber acts as a deflection stop for the front wheels, the lower shock absorber attaching point should not be loosened unless the vehicle is resting on the wheels or unless the lower control arm is supported.

2. Raise and safely support the vehicle.

3. Support the lower control arm.

4. Loosen the lower shock absorber attachment.

5. Unscrew the steering arm from the steering knuckle.

6. Separate the brake line and brake hose and plug the openings.

7. Remove the front spring.

8. Unscrew the hex nuts on the ball joints.

9. Remove the lower ball joint and remove the lower control arm.

10. Installation is the reverse of removal. Bleed the brakes and check the front end alignment.

Front Wheel Bearings

Adjustment

1. Tighten the clamp nut until the hub can just be turned.

2. Slacken the clamp nut and seat the bearings on the spindle by rapping the spindle sharply with a hammer.

3. Attach a dial indicator, with the pointer indexed, onto the wheel hub.

4. Check the endplay of the hub by pushing and pulling on the flange. The endplay should be approximately 0.0004–0.0008 in.

5. Make an additional check by rotating the washer between the inner race of the outer bearing and the clamp nut. It should be able to be turned by hand.

6. Check the position of the suppressor pin in the wheel spindle and the contact spring in the dust cap.

7. Pack the dust cap with 20–25 grams of wheel bearing grease and install the cap.

8. Install the brake caliper and bleed the brakes.

Removal and Installation

If the wheel bearing play is being checked for correct setting only, it is not necessary to remove the caliper. It is only necessary to remove the brake pads.

1. Remove the brake caliper.

2. Pull the cap from the hub with a pair of channel-lock pliers. Remove the radio suppression spring, if equipped.

3. Loosen the socket screw of the clamp nut on the wheel spindle. Remove the clamp nuts and washer.

4. Remove the front wheel hub and brake disc.

5. Remove the inner race with the roller cage of the outer bearing.

6. Using a brass or aluminum drift, carefully tap the outer race of the inner bearing until it can be removed with the inner race, bearing cage and seal.

7. In the same manner, tap the outer race of the bearing ofrom the hub.

8. Separate the front hub from the brake disc.

9. To assemble, press the outer races into the front wheel hub.

10. Pack the bearing cage with bearing grease and insert the inner race with the bearing into the wheel hub.

11. Coat the sealing ring with sealant and press it into the hub.

12. Pack the front wheel hub with 45–55 grams of wheel bearing grease. The races of the tapered bearing should be well packed and also apply grease to the front faces of the rollers. Pack the front bearings with the specified amount of grease. Too much grease will cause overheating of the lubricant and it may lose its lubricity. Too little grease will not lubricate properly.

13. Coat the contact surface of the sealing ring on the wheel spindle with Molykote paste.

14. Press the wheel hub onto the wheel spindle.

15. Install the inner race and cage of the outer bearing.

16. Install the steel washer and the clamp nut.

REAR SUSPENSION

Shock Absorbers
Removal and Installation
190D, 190E, 260E, 300E, 300CE, 300SE, 300TE, 300SEL AND 560SL

1. Raise and safely support the vehicle.
2. From inside the trunk (sedans), remove the rubber cap, locknut and hex nut from the upper mount of the shock absorber.
3. Unbolt the mounting for the rear shock absorber at the bottom and remove the shock absorber. Be sure to disconnect and plug the pressure line on the 190E-16.
4. Installation is the reverse of removal.

ALL OTHER MODELS
1. Remove the rear seat and backrest.
2. Remove the cover from the rear wall.
3. Raise and safely support the vehicle. Support the trailing arm.
4. Loosen the nuts on the upper mount. Remove the washer and rubber ring.
5. Loosen the lower mount and remove the shock absorber downward.
6. Installation is the reverse of removal. Tighten the upper mounting nut to the end of the threads.

Springs
Removal and Installation
190D, 190E, 260E, 300E, 300CE, 300SE, 300TE AND 300SEL

1. Raise and safely support the vehicle. Remove the wheel.
2. Disconnect the holding clamps for the spring link cover and remove the cover.
3. Install a spring compressor and compress the spring until the spring link is free of all load.
4. Disconnect the lower end of the shock absorber.
5. Increase the tension on the spring compressor and remove the spring.
6. Installation is in the reverse order of removal. Please note the following:
   a. Position the spring so the end of the lower coil is seated in the impression of the spring seat and the upper coil seats properly in the rubber mount in the frame floor.
   b. Do not release tension on the spring compressor until the lower end of the shock absorber is connected and tightened to 47 ft. lbs. (65 Nm).

560SL
1. Raise and safely support the vehicle.
2. Remove the rear shock absorber.
3. Raise the control arm to a horizontal position. Install a spring compressor to aid in this operation.
4. Carefully, lower the control arm until it contacts the stop on the rear axle support.
5. Remove the spring and spring compressor with great care.
6. Installation is the reverse of removal. For ease of installation, attach the rubber seats to the springs with masking tape.

ALL OTHERS
1. Raise and safely support the vehicle. Support the trailing arm.
2. Remove the rear shock absorber.
3. Be sure the upper shock absorber attachment is released first.
4. Compress the spring with a spring compressor.
5. Remove the rear spring with the rubber mount.
6. Installation is the reverse or removal. When installing the [shock absorber], tighten the lower mount first.

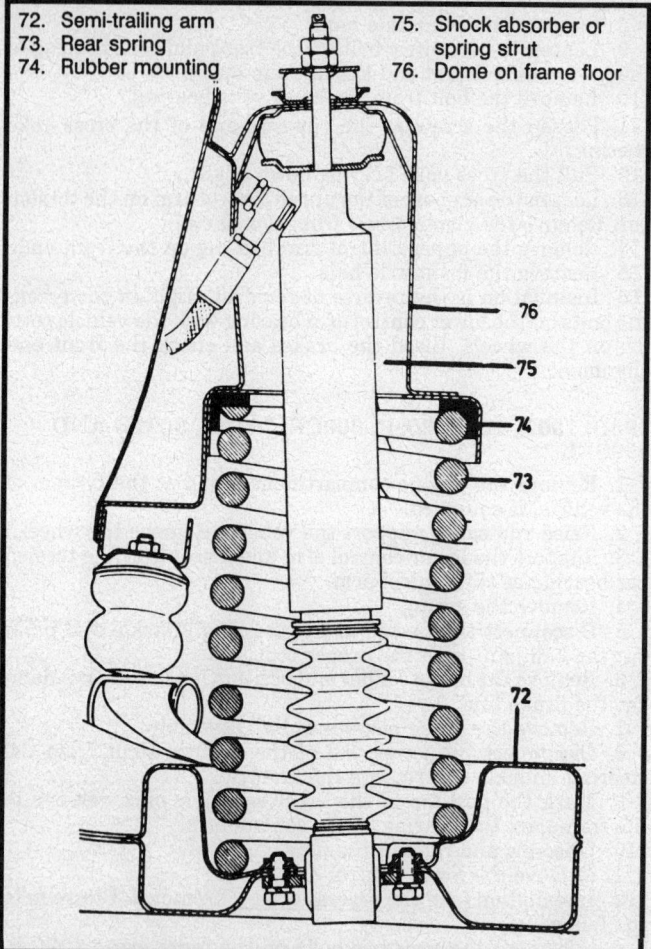

72. Semi-trailing arm
73. Rear spring
74. Rubber mounting
75. Shock absorber or spring strut
76. Dome on frame floor

Rear spring—except 190D, 190E, 260E, 300E, 300CE, 300TE and 560SL

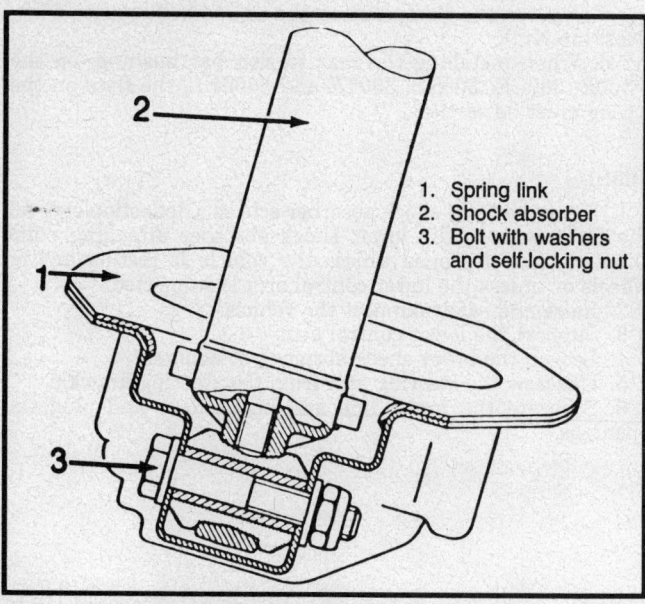

1. Spring link
2. Shock absorber
3. Bolt with washers and self-locking nut

Rear shock absorber lower mount—190D and 190E

SERIAL NUMBER IDENTIFICATION

Vehicle Identification Plate

The official Vehicle Identification Number (VIN) for title and registration purposes is stamped on a metal tab that is fastened to the instrument panel close to the windshield on the driver's side of the vehicle.

On the Scorpio, the VIN is also stamped on the floor pan of the passenger's door.

Engine Number

Refer to Vehicle Certification Label for engine identification and consecutive unit numbers. The engine calibration number is located on a sticker affixed to the front of the engine. Engine code information is also contained on this sticker.

On the 2.9L engine, the last 8 digits of the VIN number are stamped on the front, left side, next to the exhaust port and the upper right, rear side of the engine.

Vehicle Identification Label

The vehicle identification/certification label is attached to the left front door lock panel. The upper half of the label contains the name of the manufacturer, gross vehicle weight (GVWR) and gross axle weight (GAWR) ratings, and the certification statement. A 17 character VIN number is also shown. The number indicates; manufacturer, type of restraint system, line, series, body type, engine (8th position), model year (10th position) and consecutive unit number. The last 6 digits of the VIN label

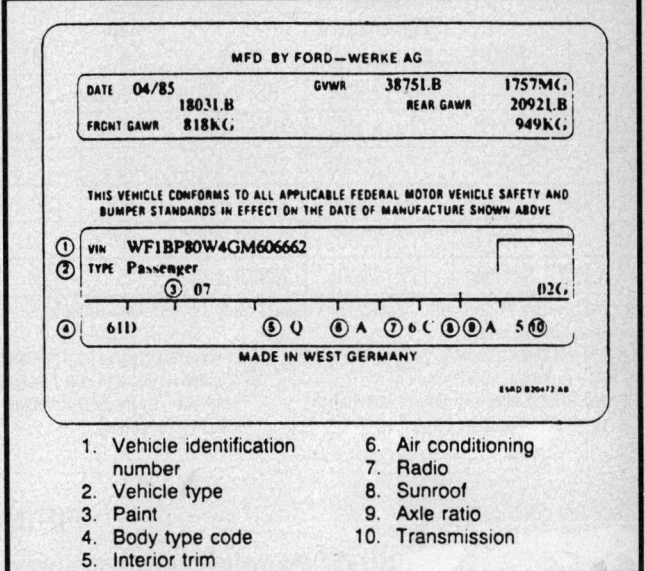

1. Vehicle identification number
2. Vehicle type
3. Paint
4. Body type code
5. Interior trim
6. Air conditioning
7. Radio
8. Sunroof
9. Axle ratio
10. Transmission

Typical Vehicle Identification Lable

indicate the consecutive unit number of each vehicle built at each assembly plant. Also shown on the label are the color code, body type and interior trim codes. The remaining numbers are special equipment, axle and transmission codes.

SPECIFICATIONS

ENGINE IDENTIFICATION

Year	Model	Engine Displacement cu. in. (cc/liter)	Engine Series Identification	No. of Cylinders	Engine Type
1987	XR4Ti	140 (2300/2.3)	W	4	SOHC
1988	XR4Ti	140 (2300/2.3)	W	4	SOHC
	Scorpio	177 (2900/2.9)	V	6	OHV
1989	XR4Ti	140 (2300/2.3)	W	4	SOHC
	Scorpio	177 (2900/2.9)	V	6	OHV
1990	Scorpio	177 (2900/2.9)	V	6	OHV

SOHC Single Overhead Camshaft
OHV Overhead Valves

GENERAL ENGINE SPECIFICATIONS

Year	Model	Engine Displacement cu. in. (cc)	Fuel System Type	Net Horsepower @ rpm	Net Torque @ rpm (ft. lbs.)	Bore × Stroke (in.)	Compression Ratio	Oil Pressure @ rpm
1987	XR4Ti	140 (2300)	EFI	175 @ 5000①	200 @ 3000②	3.78 × 3.12	8.0:1	50 @ 2000
1988	XR4Ti	140 (2300)	EFI	175 @ 5000①	200 @ 3000②	3.78 × 3.12	8.0:1	50 @ 2000
	Scorpio	177 (2900)	EFI	144 @ 5500	162 @ 3000	3.66 × 2.83	9.0:1	50 @ 2000
1989	XR4Ti	140 (2300)	EFI	175 @ 5000①	200 @ 3000②	3.78 × 3.12	8.0:1	50 @ 2000
	Scorpio	177 (2900)	EFI	144 @ 5500	162 @ 3000	3.66 × 2.83	9.0:1	50 @ 2000
1990	Scorpio	177 (2900)	EFI	144 @ 5500	162 @ 3000	3.66 × 2.83	9.0:1	50 @ 2000

EFI Electronic Fuel Injection ① 145 @ 4400 with automatic transaxle ② 180 @ 3000 with automatic transaxle

GASOLINE ENGINE TUNE-UP SPECIFICATIONS

Year	Model	Engine Displacement cu. in. (cc)	Spark Plugs Type	Gap (in.)	Ignition Timing (deg.) MT	Ignition Timing (deg.) AT	Compression Pressure (psi)	Fuel Pump (psi)	Idle Speed (rpm) MT	Idle Speed (rpm) AT	Valve Clearance In.	Valve Clearance Ex.
1987	XR4Ti	140 (2300)	BSFC-32	0.034	13B①	10B①	NA	39②	900①	900①	Hyd.	Hyd.
1988	XR4Ti	140 (2300)	AWSF-32C	0.034	13B①	10B①	NA	39②	900①	900①	Hyd.	Hyd.
	Scorpio	177 (2900)	AWSF-42C	③	③	③	NA	43.5	③	③	Hyd.	Hyd.
1989	XR4Ti	140 (2300)	AWSF-32C	0.034	13B①	10B①	NA	39②	900①	900①	Hyd.	Hyd.
	Scorpio	177 (2900)	AWSF-42C	③	③	③	NA	43.5	③	③	Hyd.	Hyd.
1990	Scorpio	177 (2900)	AWSF-42C	③	③	③	NA	43.5	③	③	Hyd.	Hyd.

NOTE: The Underhood Specifications sticker often reflects tune-up specification changes made in production. Sticker figures must be used if they disagree with those in this chart.

MT—Manual transmission
AT—Automatic transmission
NA—Not available at time of publication
B—Before Top Dead Center

Hyd.—Hydraulic valve lash adjusters
① Ignition timing and idle speed are computer-controlled by the EEC-IV engine control system. See text for details

② Specification is fuel system pressure. Two fuel pumps are used. See text for details
③ Refer to emissions decal

FIRING ORDER

NOTE: To avoid confusion, always replace spark plug wires one at a time.

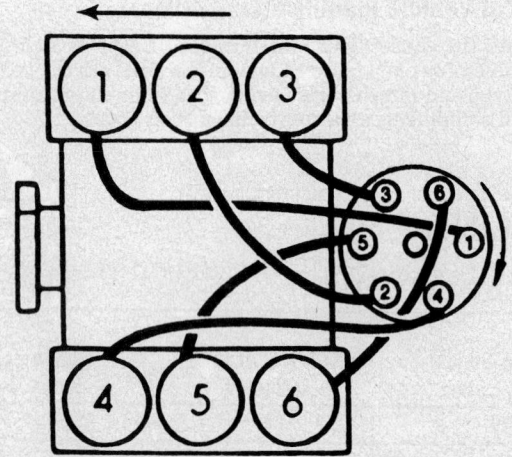

2900cc V6 Engine
Engine Firing Order: 1–4–2–5–3–6
Distributor Rotation: Clockwise

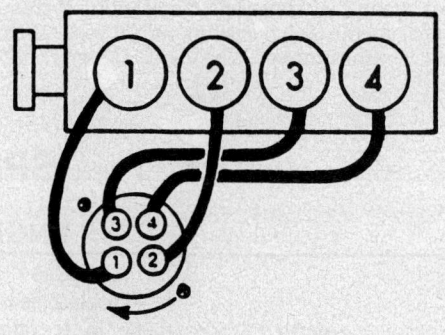

2300cc 4 Cyl. Engine
Engine Firing Order: 1–3–4–2
Distributor Rotation: Clockwise

CAPACITIES

Year	Model	Engine Displacement cu. in. (cc)	Engine Crankcase with Filter	Engine Crankcase without Filter	Transmission (pts.) 4-Spd	Transmission (pts.) 5-Spd	Transmission (pts.) Auto.	Drive Axle (pts.)	Fuel Tank (gal.)	Cooling System (qts.)
1987	XR4Ti	140 (2300)	5.0	4.5	—	2.6	16①	1.9	15	10.5
1988	XR4Ti	140 (2300)	5.0	4.5	—	2.6	16①	2.7	15	10.5
	Scorpio	177 (2900)	5.0	4.5	—	2.4	19①	2.8	17	9.0
1989	XR4Ti	140 (2300)	5.0	4.5	—	2.6	16①	2.7	15	10.5
	Scorpio	177 (2900)	5.0	4.5	—	2.4	19①	2.8	17	9.0
1990	Scorpio	177 (2900)	5.0	4.5	—	2.4	19①	2.8	17	9.0

① Specification is for total refill. Check fluid level with dipstick

CAMSHAFT SPECIFICATIONS

All measurements given in inches.

Year	Engine Displacement cu. in. (cc)	Journal Diameter 1	2	3	4	5	Lobe Lift In.	Ex.	Bearing Clearance	Camshaft End Play
1987	140 (2300)	1.7713–1.7720	1.7713–1.7720	1.7713–1.7720	1.7713–1.7720	—	0.400	0.400	0.0010–0.0030	0.0010–0.0070
1988	140 (2300)	1.7713–1.7720	1.7713–1.7720	1.7713–1.7720	1.7713–1.7720	—	0.400	0.400	0.0010–0.0030	0.0010–0.0070
	177 (2900)	1.7285–1.7293	1.7135–1.7143	1.6985–1.6992	1.6835–1.6842	—	0.373	0.373	0.0010–0.0026	0.0008–0.0040
1989	140 (2300)	1.7713–1.7720	1.7713–1.7720	1.7713–1.7720	1.7713–1.7720	—	0.400	0.400	0.0010–0.0030	0.0010–0.0070
	177 (2900)	1.7285–1.7293	1.7135–1.7143	1.6985–1.6992	1.6835–1.6842	—	0.373	0.373	0.0010–0.0026	0.0008–0.0040
1990	177 (2900)	1.7285–1.7293	1.7135–1.7143	1.6985–1.6992	1.6835–1.6842	—	0.373	0.373	0.0010–0.0026	0.0008–0.0040

CRANKSHAFT AND CONNECTING ROD SPECIFICATIONS

All measurements are given in inches.

Year	Engine Displacement cu. in. (cc)	Crankshaft Main Brg. Journal Dia.	Main Brg. Oil Clearance	Shaft End-play	Thrust on No.	Connecting Rod Journal Diameter	Oil Clearance	Side Clearance
1987	140 (2300)	2.3990–2.3982	0.0008–0.0015	0.004–0.008	3	2.0465–2.0472	0.0008–0.0015	0.004–0.011
1988	140 (2300)	2.3990–2.3982	0.0008–0.0015	0.004–0.008	3	2.0465–2.0472	0.0008–0.0015	0.004–0.011
	177 (2900)	2.2433–2.2441	0.0008–0.0015	0.004–0.008	3	2.1252–2.1260	0.0006–0.0016	0.004–0.011
1989	140 (2300)	2.3990–2.3982	0.0008–0.0015	0.004–0.008	3	2.0465–2.0472	0.0008–0.0015	0.004–0.011
	177 (2900)	2.2433–2.2441	0.0008–0.0015	0.004–0.008	3	2.1252–2.1260	0.0006–0.0016	0.004–0.011
1990	177 (2900)	2.2433–2.2441	0.0008–0.0015	0.004–0.008	3	2.1252–2.1260	0.0006–0.0016	0.004–0.011

VALVE SPECIFICATIONS

Year	Engine Displacement cu. in. (cc)	Seat Angle (deg.)	Face Angle (deg.)	Spring Test Pressure (lbs.)	Spring Installed Height (in.)	Stem-to-Guide Clearance (in.) Intake	Exhaust	Stem Diameter (in.) Intake	Exhaust
1987	140 (2300)	45	44	71–79 ①	1.5313–1.5938	0.0010–0.0027	0.0015–0.0032	0.3416–0.3423	0.3411–0.3418
1988	140 (2300)	45	44	71–79 ①	1.5313–1.5938	0.0010–0.0027	0.0015–0.0032	0.3416–0.3423	0.3411–0.3418
	177 (2900)	45	44	60–68 ②	1.5781–1.6093	0.0008–0.0025	0.0018–0.0035	0.3159–0.3167	0.3149–0.3156
1989	140 (2300)	45	44	71–79 ①	1.5313–1.5938	0.0010–0.0027	0.0015–0.0032	0.3416–0.3423	0.3411–0.3418
	177 (2900)	45	44	60–68 ②	1.5781–1.6093	0.0008–0.0025	0.0018–0.0035	0.3159–0.3167	0.3149–0.3156
1990	177 (2900)	45	44	60–68 ②	1.5781–1.6093	0.0008–0.0025	0.0018–0.0035	0.3159–0.3167	0.3149–0.3156

① @ 1.52 in.   ② @ 1.585 in.

PISTON AND RING SPECIFICATIONS

All measurements are given in inches

| Year | Engine Displacement cu. in. (cc) | Piston Clearance | Ring Gap | | | Ring Side Clearance | | |
			Top Compression	Bottom Compression	Oil Control	Top Compression	Bottom Compression	Oil Control
1987	140 (2300)	0.0030–0.0038	0.0100–0.0200	0.0100–0.0200	0.0150–0.0550	0.0020–0.0040	0.0020–0.0040	Snug
1988	140 (2300)	0.0030–0.0038	0.0100–0.0200	0.0100–0.0200	0.0150–0.0550	0.0020–0.0040	0.0020–0.0040	Snug
	177 (2900)	0.0011–0.0019	0.0150–0.0230	0.0150–0.0230	0.0150–0.0550	0.0020–0.0033	0.0020–0.0033	Snug
1989	140 (2300)	0.0030–0.0038	0.0100–0.0200	0.0100–0.0200	0.0150–0.0550	0.0020–0.0040	0.0020–0.0040	Snug
	177 (2900)	0.0011–0.0019	0.0150–0.0230	0.0150–0.0230	0.0150–0.0550	0.0020–0.0033	0.0020–0.0033	Snug
1990	177 (2900)	0.0011–0.0019	0.0150–0.0230	0.0150–0.0230	0.0150–0.0550	0.0020–0.0033	0.0020–0.0033	Snug

TORQUE SPECIFICATIONS

All readings in ft. lbs.

| Year | Engine Displacement cu. in. (cc) | Cylinder Head Bolts | Main Bearing Bolts | Rod Bearing Bolts | Crankshaft Pulley Bolts | Flywheel Bolts | Manifold | | Spark Plugs |
							Intake	Exhaust	
1987	140 (2300)	80–90 ①	80–90 ①	30–36 ②	100–120	56–64	14–21	16–23 ③	7–15
1988	140 (2300)	80–90 ①	80–90 ①	30–36 ②	100–120	56–64	14–21	16–23 ③	7–15
	177 (2900)	④	65–75	19–24	85–96	47–52	⑤	20–30	18–28
1989	140 (2300)	80–90 ①	80–90 ①	30–36 ②	100–120	56–64	14–21	16–23 ③	7–15
	177 (2900)	④	65–75	19–24	85–96	47–52	⑤	20–30	18–28
1990	177 (2900)	④	65–75	19–24	85–96	47–52	⑤	20–30	18–28

① Torque in 2 steps—1st to 50–60 and 2nd to 80–90
② Torque in 2 steps—1st to 25–30 and 2nd to 30–36
③ Torque in 2 steps—1st to 5–7 and 2nd to 16–23
④ Torque in 3 steps—1st to 22; 2nd to 51–55; 3rd an additional 90 degrees
⑤ Intake manifold (in sequence)
   Step 1—3–6 ft. lbs.
   Step 2—6–11 ft. lbs.
Step 3—11–15 ft. lbs.
Step 4—15–18 ft. lbs.
Step 5—warm engine and recheck torque
Upper intake (plenum)
   Step 1—7 ft. lbs.
   Step 2—15–18 ft. lbs.

BRAKE SPECIFICATIONS

All measurements in inches unless noted

| Year | Model | Lug Nut Torque (ft. lbs.) | Master Cylinder Bore | Brake Disc | | Standard Brake Drum Diameter | Minimum Lining Thickness | |
				Minimum Thickness	Maximum Runout		Front	Rear
1987	XR4Ti	75–105	1.000	0.900	0.0030	10.0	①	①
1988	XR4Ti	75–105	1.000	0.900	0.0030	10.0	①	①
	Scorpio	52–73	—	②	0.0039	—	①	①
1989	XR4Ti	75–105	1.000	0.900	0.0030	10.0	①	①
	Scorpio	52–73	—	②	0.0039	—	①	①
1990	Scorpio	52–73	—	②	0.0039	—	①	①

① ⅛ in. above metal shoe
   1/16 in. above rivets
② Front—0.900
   Rear—0.350

WHEEL ALIGNMENT

Year	Model	Caster Range (deg.)	Caster Preferred Setting (deg.)	Camber Range (deg.)	Camber Preferred Setting (deg.)	Toe-in (in.)	Steering Axis Inclination (deg.)
1987	XR4Ti	$^{15}/_{16}$P–$2^{15}/_{16}$P	$1^{15}/_{16}$P	$1^1/_2$N–$^1/_2$P	$^1/_2$N ①	②	$13^{11}/_{16}$
1988	XR4Ti	$^{15}/_{16}$P–$2^{15}/_{16}$P	$1^{15}/_{16}$P	$1^1/_2$N–$^1/_2$P	$^1/_2$N ①	②	$13^{11}/_{16}$
	Scorpio	1P–3P	2P	$1^1/_4$N–$1^1/_4$P	0 ③	④	—
1989	XR4Ti	$^{15}/_{16}$P–$2^{15}/_{16}$P	$1^{15}/_{16}$P	$1^1/_2$N–$^1/_2$P	$^1/_2$N ①	②	$13^{11}/_{16}$
	Scorpio	1P–3P	2P	$1^1/_4$N–$1^1/_4$P	0 ③	④	—
1990	Scorpio	1P–3P	2P	$1^1/_4$N–$1^1/_4$P	0 ③	④	—

① Rear—$2^3/_4$N–$2^3/_{16}$P; dependent upon ride height
② Front—$^1/_{16}$N–$^3/_4$P; dependent upon ride height
Rear—$^1/_{32}$N–$^5/_{16}$P; dependent upon ride height
③ Rear—$4^5/_{16}$N–$1^7/_8$P; dependent upon ride height
④ Rear—$^1/_2$N–$^5/_8$P; combined wheel-to-wheel

ENGINE ELECTRICAL

NOTE: Disconnecting the negative battery cable on some vehicles may interfere with the functions of the on board computer systems and may require the computer to undergo a relearning process, once the negative battery cable is reconnected.

Distributor

Removal and Installation

2.3L ENGINE

1. Disconnect the negative battery cable. Rotate the crankshaft until the No. 1 cylinder is on the TDC of it's compression stroke.
2. Disconnect the wiring harness to the TFI module on the side of the distributor. Disconnect the coil wire.
3. Loosen the hold-down screws, remove the distributor cap and position it aside with the spark plug wires attached.
4. Using chalk or paint, matchmark the rotor-to-distributor and the distributor housing-to-engine position.
5. Remove the rotor-to-distributor screws and the rotor.

6. Remove the distributor hold-down bolt and clamp, located under the distributor bowl between the distributor base and cylinder block. If the hold-down bolt has a Torx® head, a special wrench will be required.
7. Remove the distributor from the engine by grasping the base and pulling straight out. Check that the base O-ring is in position and not damaged or cut. Once the distributor is removed, the TFI module can be replaced by simply removing the mounting bolts and working the module back and forth until the pin connectors are free. Make sure there are no bent pin connectors when installing the TFI module.

NOTE: When installing a new TFI module, coat the metal base plate uniformly with a $^1/_{32}$ in. thick cover of silicone dielectric compound. Failure to do so will result in premature module failure due to excessive heat buildup.

To install:
8. Lubricate the base O-ring lightly with engine oil. To install, align the matckmarks and reverse the removal procedures.

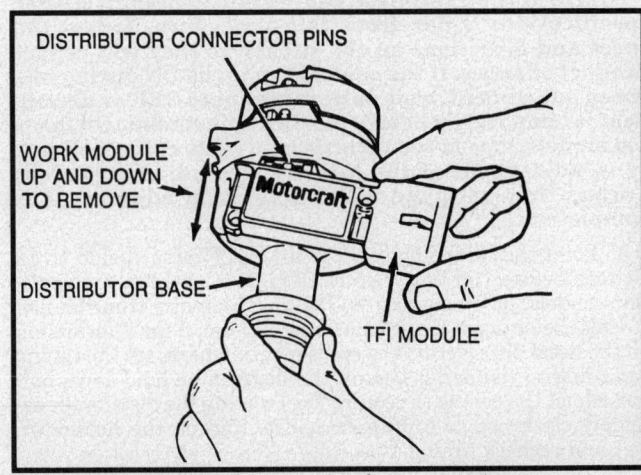

Removing the TFI module from the distributor. If attempting this with the distributor installed, be careful not to bend any connector pins

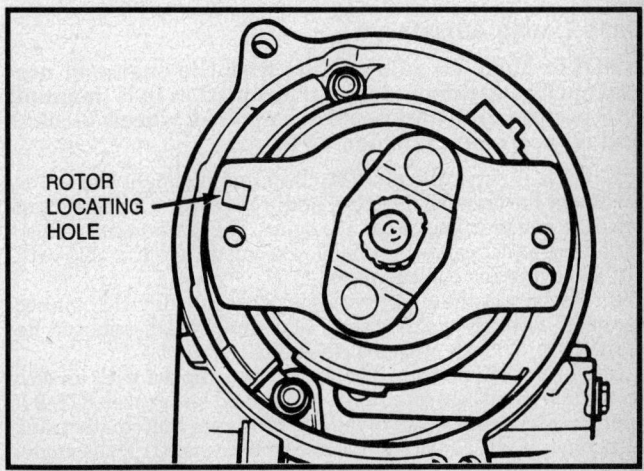

Note the position of the shaft plate, armature and rotor locating holes when removing the distributor

9. Install the hold-down clamp and bolt. Torque the bolt until the distributor can barely be rotated.

10. Install the rotor and distributor cap. Reconnect the coil wire and TFI harness connector, then reconnect the negative battery cable.

11. Start the engine, check and/or adjust the ignition timing as required. Once the ignition timing is set, torque the hold-down bolt to 6–8 ft. lbs. (8–11 Nm).

2.9L ENGINE

1. Disconnect the negative battery cable.
2. Remove the distributor cap, with plug wires attached and position the assembly aside.
3. Using chalk or paint, matchmark the rotor-to-distributor and the distributor housing-to-engine positions.
4. Rotate the crankshaft, in the normal direction of rotation, until No. 1 piston is at TDC on the compression stroke and the timing marks are aligned.
5. Remove the distributor rotor and disconnect the TFI electrical harness connector.
6. Remove the distributor hold-down bolt and the distributor.

To install:

7. Verify that the No. 1 piston is still at TDC of the compression stroke and the timing marks are aligned.
8. Rotate the distributor shaft until the rotor is pointing about 20 degrees counterclockwise from the No. 1 spark plug tower mark on the distributor body.
9. Install the rotor to the distributor. Hold the distributor with the TFI module parallel with the rear of the engine block and install it into the engine slowly. The rotor should be pointing to the distributor body mark after the drive gear is engaged and the distributor is seated into the engine.
10. Rotate the distributor in the engine until the leading edge of the vane is aligned with the vane switch. Make sure the rotor is pointing to the matchmark on the distributor body.
11. If the vane and vane switch cannot be aligned, pull the distributor out of the block enough to disengage the drive gear and rotate the shaft slightly until another drive tooth is engaged. Repeat as necessary to get proper alignment.
12. Install the bracket and mounting bolt, but do not tighten completely. Connect the TFI harness connector. Install the distributor cap and wires.
13. Start the engine, check and/or adjust the engine timing and secure the distributor.

Ignition Timing

Base Timing Adjustment

NOTE: Make all adjustments with the engine at normal operating temperature, transmission in N (manual) or P (automatic), parking brake applied, wheels blocked and all accessories turned OFF.

1. With engine turned **OFF**, clean and highlight the timing marks on the crankshaft pulley and front cover. Connect a timing light and tachometer to the engine. The ignition coil connector allows a tachometer connection using an alligator clip without removing the coil connector.
2. Disconnect the single wire spark output (SPOUT) connector near (within 6 inches of the TFI module) the distributor. Restart the previously warmed up engine.
3. Check the idle rpm. The engine is equipped with an electronic idle speed control and the idle should be between 825–975 rpm (manual transmission) or 925–1075 rpm (automatic transmissions). If idle adjustment is necessary, turn **OFF** the engine and disconnect the electrical connector at the idle bypass valve. Restart the engine and run at approximately 2000 rpm, briefly. Allow the engine to return to idle and adjust the idle speed to 725–775 rpm by turning the throttle plate stop screw. Turn

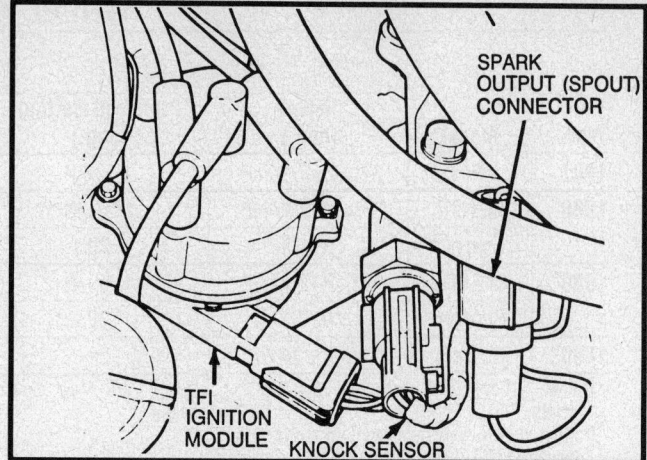

The SPOUT connector must be disconnected to set base timing

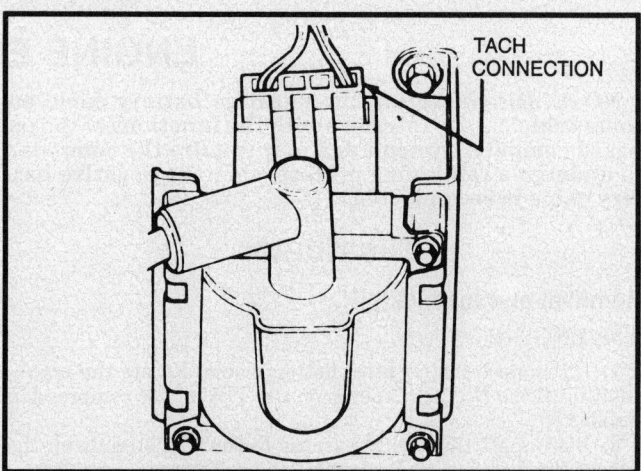

Tachometer connection

OFF the engine and reconnect the electrical connector to the bypass valve. Restart engine and proceed with ignition timing check.

NOTE: If the underhood calibration/emissions sticker specifications differ from this procedure, follow the specs and directions on the sticker as they will reflect product changes. If the cooling fan turns ON during idle speed adjustment, wait until turns shuts OFF or disconnect it temporarily before making adjustment. On Scorpio models, loosen the throttle cam plate roller bolt prior to adjustment of the throttle stop adjusting screw. Torque the cam plate roller bolt when adjustment is completed.

4. Point the timing light at the marks. Timing should be 13 degrees Before Top Dead Center (BTDC) for manual transmission models, or 10 degrees BTDC for automatic transmission models. Refer to the Emissions Control Decal, if the information on the decal differs from the specs mention here, set the timing according to the decal. Loosen the distributor hold-down bolt and adjust the timing as required by twisting the distributor assembly clockwise or counterclockwise. Torque the hold-down bolt and recheck timing.

NOTE: Some distributor hold-down bolts made have a special Torx® head which requires a special wrench.

5. After base timing has been set, turn **OFF** the engine and

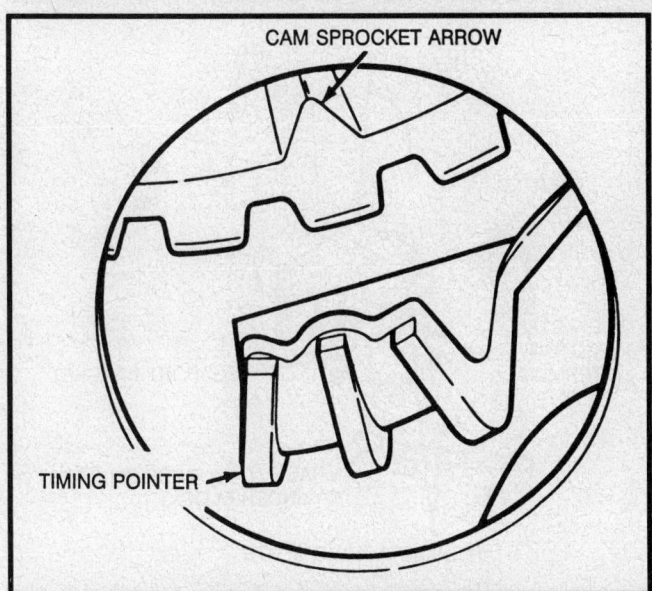

CAM SPROCKET ARROW

TIMING POINTER

Correct timing mark alignment as viewed through the access plug on the timing belt outer cover

remove all test equipment. Reconnect the single SPOUT wire harness at the distributor.

Initial Timing Check

2.3L ENGINE

An initial timing check should be performed if there is reason to believe the distributor is no longer timed to the engine. This condition can result from incorrect installation of the distributor or a timing belt that has jumped timing.

1. Remove the No. 1 spark plug from the engine.
2. Install a compression gauge in the No. 1 spark plug hole.
3. Connect a remote starter switch between the battery positive terminal and the starter relay **S** terminal.
4. Using the starter switch, bump the engine around until the compression gauge indicates the No. 1 piston is on its compression stroke.
5. Continue bumping the engine with the starter switch until the timing mark on the crankshaft (pulley notch) is aligned with the Top Dead Center (TDC) mark on the timing scale.
6. Remove the distributor cap and check that the rotor tip is pointing to the No. 1 spark plug wire terminal in the distributor cap. If the rotor and cap are correctly aligned, the initial timing is correct, proceed to the next step. If the rotor and distributor cap do not align, remove the distributor and reinstall it so the rotor is pointing to No. 1 plug tower.
7. Remove the access plug from the timing belt outer cover and check that the timing mark on the cam sprocket is aligned with the timing pointer. If the cam sprocket timing mark is aligned with the pointer, the engine is properly timed. If the cam sprocket timing mark does not align with the pointer, the timing belt has jumped time and must be replaced.
8. Check and/or readjust the base ignition timing.

Alternator

Precautions

Several precautions must be observed with alternator equipped vehicles to avoid damage to the unit.

• If the battery is removed for any reason, make sure it is reconnected with the correct polarity. Reversing the battery connections may result in damage to the 1 way rectifiers.

• When utilizing a booster battery as a starting aid, always connect the positive to positive terminals, and the negative terminal from the booster battery to a good engine ground on the vehicle being started.
• Never use a fast charger as a booster to start vehicles with alternating current (AC) circuits.
• Disconnect the battery cables when charging the battery with a fast charger.
• Avoid long soldering times when making alternator repairs. Prolonged heat will damage the alternator.
• Do not use test lights of more than 12 volts when checking diode continuity.
• Do not short across or ground any of the alternator terminals.
• The polarity of the battery, alternator and regulator must be matched and considered before making any electrical connections within the system.
• Never separate the alternator on an open circuit. Make sure all connections within the circuit are clean and tight.
• Disconnect the battery ground terminal when performing any service on electrical components.
• Disconnect the battery if arc welding is to be done on the vehicle.

Belt Tension Adjustment

Adjust the drive belt tension so there is approximately ⅛–⅜ in. of deflection on the longest span of belt between pulleys. Apply pressure to the square rib on the alternator housing using the proper size open end wrench to maintain pressure when adjusting belt tension. Torque the:
Adjuster pivot bolt—44–60 ft. lbs. (60–81 Nm)
Adjuster nut—30–46 ft. lbs. (40–62 Nm)

Removal and Installation

1. Disconnect the negative battery cable. Remove other drive belts that interfere with alternator removal.
2. Loosen the alternator pivot bolt and remove the adjustment arm-to-alternator bolt. Pivot the alternator to release belt tension.
3. Remove the drive belts.
4. Label and disconnect the wiring terminals from the alternator.
5. Remove the alternator pivot bolt and the alternator.
6. To install, reverse the removal procedures. Adjust the drive belt tension.

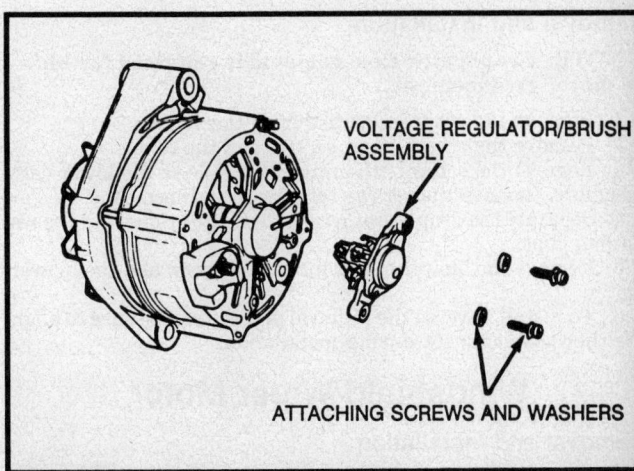

VOLTAGE REGULATOR/BRUSH ASSEMBLY

ATTACHING SCREWS AND WASHERS

Voltage regulator mounting at rear of alternator housing

Voltage Regulator

Removal and Installation

The voltage regulator is mounted to the rear of the alternator and contains the brushes as well as circuit control components. It is replaced as a unit by simply removing the mounting bolts and disconnecting the wiring connector.

Starter

Removal and Installation

2.3L ENGINE

1. Disconnect the negative battery cable.
2. Raise and safely support the vehicle.
3. Disconnect the electrical connectors from the starter.
4. Remove the heat shield-to-engine bolt.
5. Remove the starter-to-engine bolts, the heat shield rear support bracket, transmission-to-engine brace and the starter.
6. To install, reverse the removal procedures. Torque the mounting bolts to 15–20 ft. lbs. (20–27 Nm). Check the starter operation.

2.9L ENGINE

1. Disconnect the negative battery cable.
2. Raise and safely support the vehicle.
3. Disconnect the electrical connectors from the starter.
4. Disconnect the starter motor relay-to-solenoid wire.
5. Remove the starter-to-housing bolts and the starter.

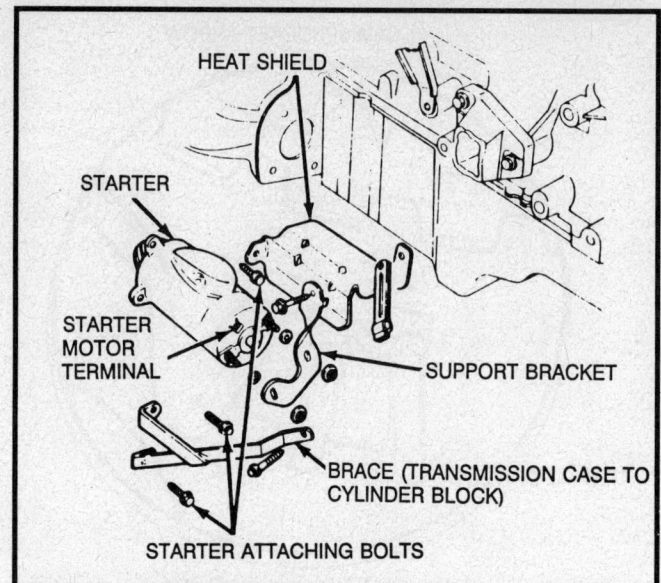

Typical starter motor mounting

To install:

6. Position the starter into the bell housing and torque the bolts to 20–25 ft. lbs. (27–34 Nm).
7. To complete the installation, reverse the removal procedures. Check the starter operation.

CHASSIS ELECTRICAL

NOTE: Disconnecting the negative battery cable on some vehicles may interfere with the functions of the on board computer systems and may require the computer to undergo a relearning process, once the negative battery cable is reconnected.

Heater Blower Motor

Removal and Installation

NOTE: Evaporator case removal is required for blower motor replacement.

1. Remove the evaporator case from the vehicle.
2. Remove the access cover screws and the cover.
3. Remove the screws retaining the scrolls to the lower case assembly. Remove the screws retaining the thermostat.
4. Separate the evaporator case halves after removing the retaining clips.
5. Remove the blower motor mounting screw and the blower motor.
6. To install, reverse the removal procedures; be sure to align the thermostat sensor during installation.

Windshield Wiper Motor

Removal and Installation

FRONT MOTOR

The internal magnets used in the wiper motor are a ceramic ma-

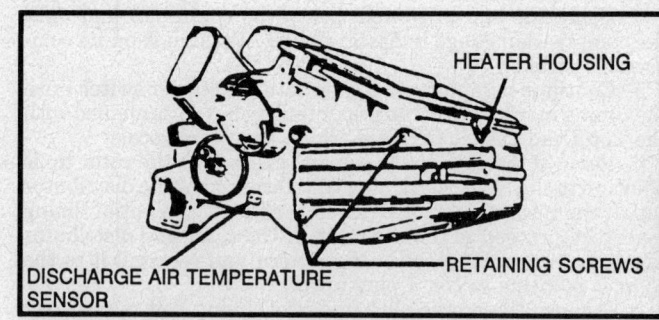

Heater core cover mounting points

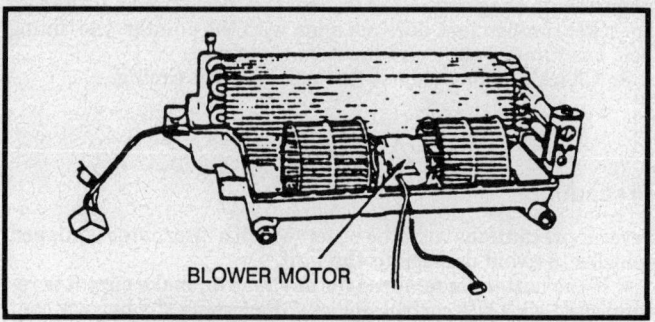

Blower motor location

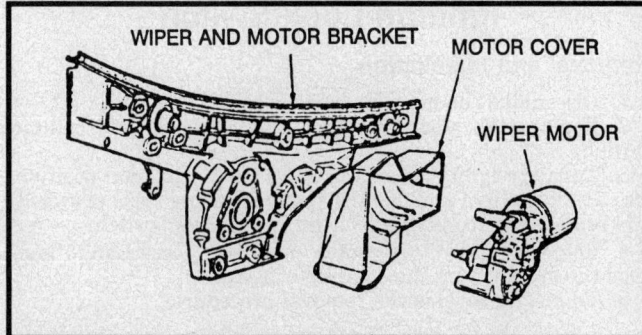

WIPER AND MOTOR BRACKET MOTOR COVER

WIPER MOTOR

Exploded view of the front windshield wiper motor assembly

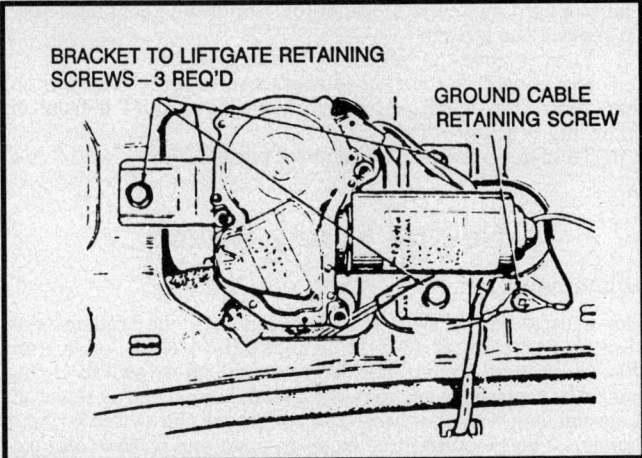

BRACKET TO LIFTGATE RETAINING SCREWS—3 REQ'D

GROUND CABLE RETAINING SCREW

Exploded view of the rear wiper motor assembly

terial. Exercise care when handling the motor to avoid damaging the magnets by dropping or striking with metal tools. The ceramic magnets cannot tolerate sharp impacts.

1. Operate the wiper motor and turn **OFF** key when the linkage mounting nut is exposed, then, remove the arm and blade assembly.
2. Disconnect the negative battery cable.
3. Remove the linkage-to-motor locknut and disconnect the linkage from the motor shaft.
4. Remove the motor-to-chassis bolts and the motor. Disconnect the electrical harness plug.
5. To install, reverse the removal procedures. Torque the:
   Motor bolts—7–9 ft. lbs. (10–12 Nm)
   Linkage locknut—13–15 ft. lbs. (18–20 Nm)

REAR MOTOR

1. Lift the plastic cover at the base of the wiper arm to expose the mounting nut. Remove the nut, then, lift the wiper arm and blade assembly from the pivot shaft.
2. Open the hatch and remove the trim panel by carefully prying out the panel clips from their locations.
3. Remove the wiper motor bracket-to-liftgate bolts. Remove the ground lead screw and disconnect the wire harness plug. Remove the motor and bracket as an assembly. Disconnect the rear washer supply hose from the wiper.
4. To install, reverse the removal procedures. Torque the:
   Wiper motor bracket bolts—4–5 ft. lbs. (6–7 Nm)
   Wiper arm attaching nut—7–9 ft. lbs. (10–12 Nm)

Windshield Wiper Switch

Removal and Installation

The windshield wiper/washer is a part of the combination switch.
1. Disconnect the negative battery cable.
2. Remove the steering wheel and the upper/lower steering column shrouds; there is a screw near the hazard flasher switch and 2 under the column, on either side of the hood release lever.
3. Remove the sound panels from the underside of the dash. Be careful to disconnect courtesy lights and radio speaker connectors before removing the column completely.
4. Remove the switch-to-column screws. Disengage the switch from the column, disconnect the wire connectors and remove the switch from the steering column.
5. To install, align the switch mounting holes with the corresponding holes in the housing and reverse the removal procedures.

Instrument Cluster

Removal and Installation

1. Disconnect the negative battery cable.
2. Remove the upper steering column shroud screws and the shroud.
3. Remove the rheostat and intermittent wiper control from the instrument panel, if equipped.
4. Remove the bezel screws and the bezel.
5. Remove the cluster panel-to-dash screws.
6. Pull the cluster forward and disconnect the speedometer cable and wiring harness connectors from the instrument cluster. Remove the cluster.
7. To install, reverse the removal procedures.

Headlight Switch

The headlight switch is a part the of the combination switch.

Removal and Installation

1. Disconnect the negative battery cable.
2. Remove the steering wheel and the upper/lower steering column shrouds; there is a screw near the hazard flasher switch and 2 under the column, on either side of the hood release lever.
3. Remove the sound panels from the underside of the dash. Be careful to disconnect courtesy lights and radio speaker connectors before removing the column completely.
4. Remove the switch-to-column screws. Disengage the switch from the column, disconnect the wire connectors and remove the switch from the steering column.
5. To install, align the switch mounting holes with the corresponding holes in the housing and continue in the reverse order of removal.

Turn Signal and Combination Switch

The combination switch contains the controls for windshield wiper/washer and headlight high beam operation. Although mounted next to each other in the steering column, the turn signal and combination switches are replaced separately.

Removal and Installation

1. Disconnect the negative battery cable.
2. Remove the steering wheel and the upper/lower steering column shrouds; there is a screw near the hazard flasher switch and 2 under the column, on either side of the hood release lever.
3. Remove the sound panels from the underside of the dash. Be careful to disconnect courtesy lights and radio speaker connectors before removing the column completely.

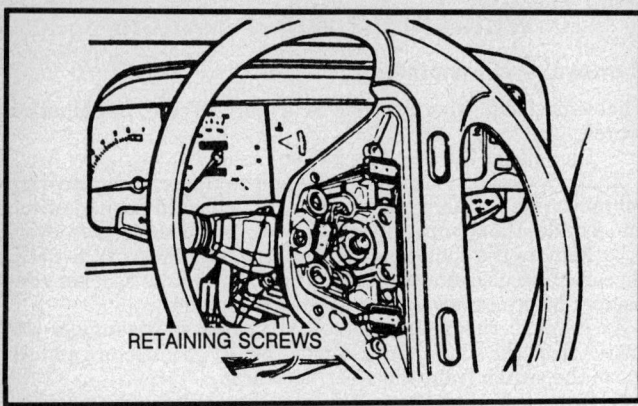

Combination switch mounting

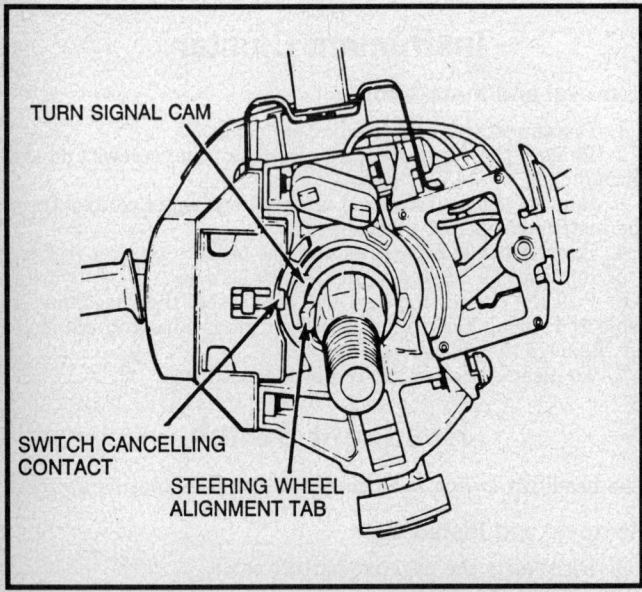

Make sure the turn signal cam is aligned with the cancelling lever before installing the steering wheel

4. Remove the switch-to-column screws. Disengage the switch from the column, disconnect the wire connectors and remove the switch from the steering column.

5. To install, align the switch mounting holes with the corresponding holes in the housing and continue in the reverse order of removal.

Ignition Lock/Switch

Removal and Installation

1. Disconnect the negative battery cable.
2. Remove the steering wheel, sound panels and column shrouds.
3. Turn the ignition key switch to the **I** (ignition) position. Use a suitable tool and depress the lock spring (hole provided) and remove the lock cylinder from the ignition switch.
4. Remove the ignition switch mounting screws and disengage the switch from the steering column.
5. To install, reverse the removal procedures.

Stoplight Switch

Removal and Installation

The stoplight switch is mounted on the brake pedal assembly. To replace the switch:
1. First remove the left lower instrument panel.
2. Disconnect the wiring harness connector at the switch, then twist the switch counterclockwise to remove it from its mounting bracket.
3. To install, reverse the removal procedures.

Neutral Safety Switch

Adjustment

The neutral safety switch is threaded into the transmission housing and torqued to 7–10 ft. lbs. (10–14 Nm). Aside from this, there is no adjustment. The neutral safety switch O-ring should be replaced every time the switch is removed or replaced. A special deep socket is necessary to remove the switch without damage. The twisting force from an open end wrench will collapse the switch housing. Make sure the electrical connector is clean and tight.

Fuses and Circuit Breakers

Location

The fuse box is located in the engine compartment on the driver's side cowl. Open the fuse box by pressing the retaining handle inward and removing the cover. Replace any blown fuse or relay with the same approved amp rating for that particular circuit. Replacing a blown fuse with 1 of a higher rating can lead to serious wiring damage and a possible fire.

ENGINE COOLING

Radiator

Removal and Installation

XR4Ti

1. Drain the cooling system.
2. Disconnect the upper, lower and overflow hoses at the radiator and overflow reservoir.
3. If equipped with an automatic transmission, disconnect and plug the fluid cooler lines at the radiator.
4. Remove the fan and shroud assembly. If the air conditioner condenser is attached to the radiator, remove the retaining bolts and position the condenser aside. Do not disconnect the refrigerant lines.
5. Remove the radiator attaching bolts or top brackets and lift out the radiator.

To install:

6. If a new radiator is to be installed, transfer the petcock from the old radiator to the new one. If equipped with an automatic transmission, transfer the fluid cooler line fittings from the old radiator.
7. Position the radiator and install, but do not torque, the radiator support bolts. If equipped with an automatic transmis-

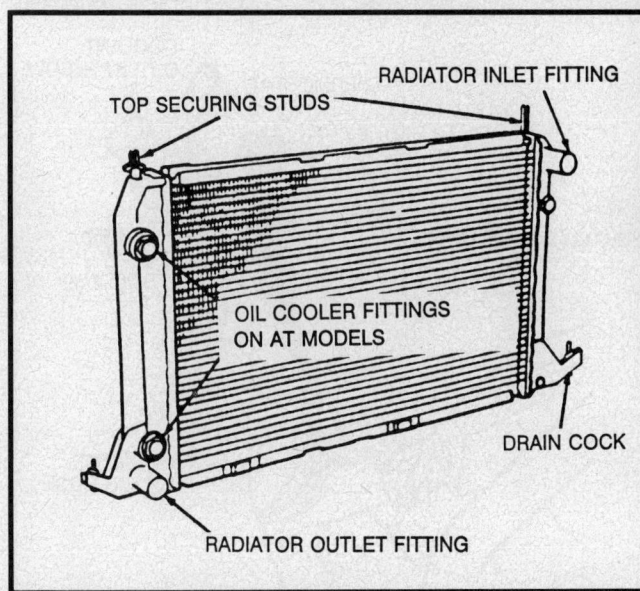

RADIATOR INLET FITTING
TOP SECURING STUDS
OIL COOLER FITTINGS ON AT MODELS
DRAIN COCK
RADIATOR OUTLET FITTING

Crossflow radiator components

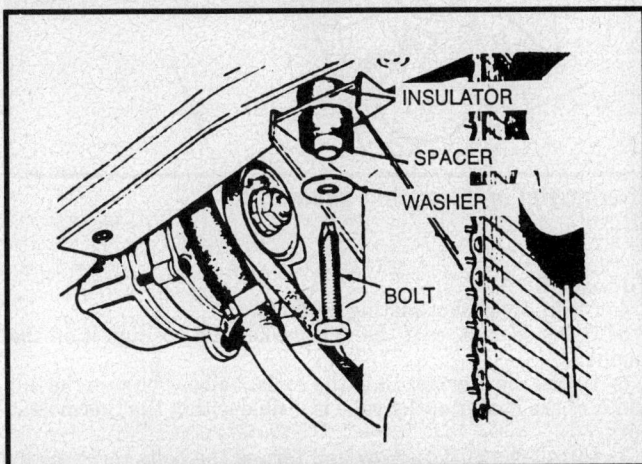

INSULATOR
SPACER
WASHER
BOLT

Lower radiator mounting

sion, connect the fluid cooler lines. Then, torque the radiator support bolts and install the fan and shroud assembly.

8. To complete the installation, reverse the removal procedures. Refill and bleed the cooling system.

9. Start the engine, allow it to reach normal operating temperatures and check for leaks.

10. If equipped with automatic transmission, check the cooler lines for leaks and interference. Check transmission fluid level.

SCORPIO

1. Disconnect the negative battery cable. Drain the cooling system.

2. Disconnect the upper and lower radiator hoses from the radiator.

3. If equipped with an automatic transmission, disconnect and plug the transmission oil cooler lines.

4. Disconnect the air conditioning cooling fan switch connector. Remove the upper fan shroud bolts and rivets. Drive out the center pin from the plastic shroud attaching rivets and remove the rivets. Remove the upper shroud.

5. Raise and safely support the vehicle.

6. Remove both bolts and washers from the lower radiator mounts. Disengage the upper securing studs by depressing the tabs. Remove the radiator from underneath the vehicle.

To install:

7. Make sure the mounting insulators are in position on the radiator studs. Position the radiator from below and install the upper mounting studs.

8. Install the mounting bolts from below. Position the insulating bushings, spacer and washers both above and below the brackets as the bolts are installed. Torque the bolts to 6–8 ft. lbs. (8–12 Nm).

9. To complete the installation, reverse the removal procedures. Refill and bleed the cooling system, run the engine and check for leaks.

Heater Core

Removal and Installation

1. Disconnect the negative battery cable.

2. Drain the cooling system. Remove the heater hoses from the heater core tubes at the firewall. Plug the core tubes.

3. Remove the tube cover screws, the cover and the plate from the firewall.

4. From inside the vehicle, remove the center console and move it rearward. Remove the right side footwell trim panel.

5. Disconnect the heater control lever. Disconnect the electrical leads from the glove compartment light, air conditioning blower switch and cigarette lighter.

6. Remove the ash tray, radio, ECA and anti-lock module, if equipped. Remove the right dash panel.

7. Remove all duct hoses from the heater housing.

8. Detach the control cables from the heater housing.

9. Remove the heater housing-to-firewall screws. Pull the heater into the vehicle until the core tubes are clear of the firewall and pull the housing toward the right side of the vehicle for removal.

10. Remove the heater core from the housing.

11. To install, reverse order of removal. Refill the cooling system. Start the engine, allow it to reach normal operating temperatures and check for leaks.

Water Pump

Removal and Installation

2.3L ENGINE

1. Drain the cooling system.

2. Disconnect the negative battery cable.

3. Remove all drive belts and the outer timing belt cover.

4. Disconnect the lower radiator hose and heater hose from the water pump.

5. Remove the electric fan and shroud assembly if necessary for clearance.

6. Remove the water pump retaining bolts and the water pump.

To install:

7. Clean the gasket mounting surfaces.

8. Using water resistant sealant, coat both sides of the new gasket.

9. To complete the installation, reverse the removal procedures. Torque the water pump mounting bolts to 14–21 ft. lbs. (19–29 Nm).

2.9L ENGINE

1. Disconnect the negative battery cable. Drain the cooling system.

2. Disconnect the radiator and heater hose from the water pump.

3. Remove the fan and clutch assembly. Special tool T88M-6312B fan hub wrench and T88M-6312A fan clutch wrench or equivalents are required.

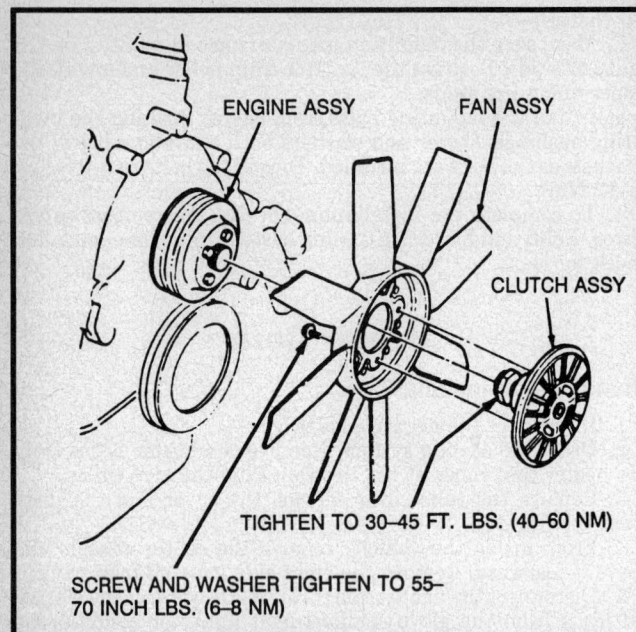

Scorpio cooling fan and clutch assembly

(labels in figure: ENGINE ASSY, FAN ASSY, CLUTCH ASSY, TIGHTEN TO 30–45 FT. LBS. (40–60 NM), SCREW AND WASHER TIGHTEN TO 55–70 INCH LBS. (6–8 NM))

NOTE: The fan clutch attaching nut is equipped with left hand threads; turn the nut clockwise to remove.

4. Loosen the alternator mounting bolts. Remove the drive belt and the alternator.
5. Remove the water pump drive pulley. Remove the water pump-to-engine bolts and the water pump.

NOTE: Two different length bolts are used, note their locations.

To install:
6. Clean all gasket mounting surfaces.
7. Using sealant, apply it to both sides of the new mounting gasket.
8. Position the gasket on the water pump and install the pump to the engine. Tighten the mounting bolts finger tight and torque them evenly.
9. To complete the installation, reverse the removal procedures. Refill and bleed the cooling system. Start the engine and check for leaks.

Thermostat

Removal and Installation

1. Open the drain cock and drain the radiator so the coolant level is below the coolant outlet elbow which houses the thermostat.
2. Remove the outlet elbow retaining bolts and position the elbow sufficient clear of the intake manifold or cylinder head to provide access to the thermostat. Remove the radiator and heater hoses if necessary.
3. Remove the thermostat and the gasket.

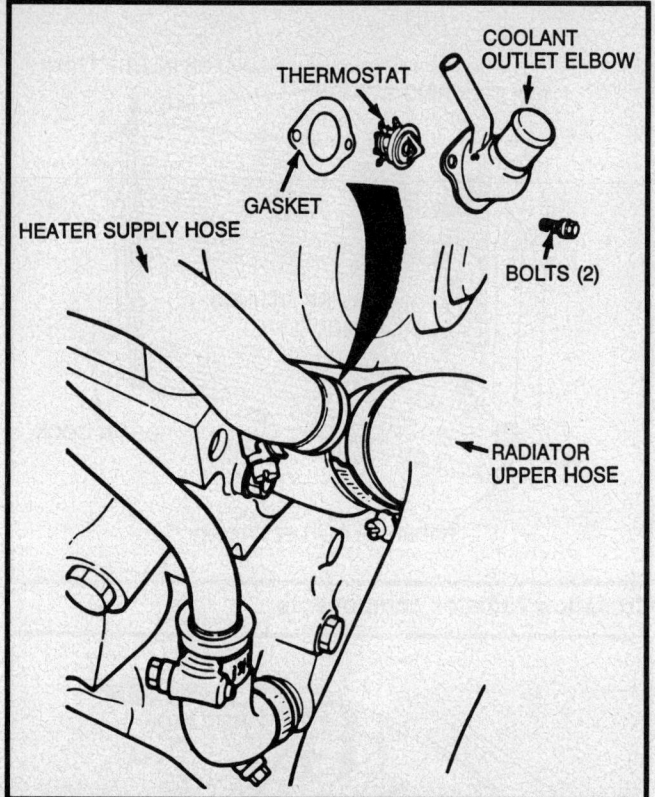

Thermostat and housing assembly

(labels in figure: THERMOSTAT, COOLANT OUTLET ELBOW, GASKET, HEATER SUPPLY HOSE, BOLTS (2), RADIATOR UPPER HOSE)

To install:
4. Clean the gasket mating surfaces.
5. Using sealant, coat the new gasket and position it on the engine.
6. Install the thermostat in the coolant elbow; be sure the full width of the heater outlet tube is visible within the thermostat port.
7. Install the outlet elbow and torque the bolts to 14–21 ft. lbs. (19–28 Nm).
8. Refill the radiator. Operate the engine, until normal operating temperatures are reached and check for leaks. Recheck the coolant level.

Cooling System Bleeding

1. Check all hose clamps for proper tightness.
2. Make sure the radiator draincock is closed. Place the heater control temperature selector in the **MAX HEAT** position.
3. Remove the pressure cap and refill the expansion tank to the **MAX** mark on the reservoir.
4. Leave the pressure cap off. Start and run the engine until normal operating temperatures are reached.
5. Stop the engine and add coolant to the expansion tank as necessary. Install the pressure cap.

FUEL SYSTEM

Fuel System Service Precaution

Safety is the most important factor when performing not only fuel system maintenance but any type of maintenance. Failure to conduct maintenance and repairs in a safe manner may result in serious personal injury or death. Maintenance and testing of the vehicle's fuel system components can be accomplished safely and effectively by adhering to the following rules and guidelines.

• To avoid the possibility of fire and personal injury, always disconnect the negative battery cable unless the repair or test procedure requires that battery voltage be applied.

• Always relieve the fuel system pressure prior to disconnecting any fuel system component (injector, fuel rail, pressure regulator, etc.), fitting or fuel line connection. Exercise extreme caution whenever relieving fuel system pressure to avoid exposing skin, face and eyes to fuel spray. Please be advised that fuel under pressure may penetrate the skin or any part of the body that it contacts.

• Always place a shop towel or cloth around the fitting or connection prior to loosening to absorb any excess fuel due to spillage. Ensure that all fuel spillage (should it occur) is quickly removed from engine surfaces. Ensure that all fuel soaked cloths or towels are deposited into a suitable waste container.

• Always keep a dry chemical (Class B) fire extinguisher near the work area.

• Do not allow fuel spray or fuel vapors to come into contact with a spark or open flame.

• Always use a backup wrench when loosening and tightening fuel line connection fittings. This will prevent unnecessary stress and torsion to fuel line piping. Always follow the proper torque specifications.

• Always replace worn fuel fitting O-rings with new. Do not substitute fuel hose or equivalent where fuel pipe is installed.

Relieving Fuel System Pressure

Depressurize the fuel system before disconnecting any fuel system lines or components or attempting any service procedures.

1. Connect a hand vacuum pump to the fuel pressure regulator vacuum connection.
2. Apply 25 in. Hg. for at least 3 minutes to allow the fuel system to depressurize.
3. Never replace high pressure fuel line with ordinary fuel hose and replace all clamps.

Quick Connect Fittings

"Quick Connect" (push) type fuel fittings are used on all models equipped with a pressurized fuel system. The fittings must be disconnected using proper procedures or the fitting may be damaged. Two types of retainers are used on the push connect fittings. Line sizes of ⅜ in. and ⁵⁄₁₆ in. use a "hairpin" clip retainer. ¼ in. line connectors use a "duck bill" clip retainer. In either case, a special connector tool must be used to separate the quick connect fittings or they may be damaged.

Removal and Installation
HAIRPIN CLIP

1. Clean all dirt and/or grease from the fitting. Spread the 2 clip legs about an ⅛ in. each to disengage from the fitting and pull the clip outward from the fitting. Use finger pressure only, do not use any tools.

2. Grease the fitting and hose assembly and pull away from the steel line. Twist the fitting and hose assembly slightly while pulling, if necessary, when a sticking condition exists.

To install:

3. Inspect the hairpin clip for damage; replace the clip, if necessary. Reinstall the clip in position on the fitting.
4. Inspect the fitting and inside of the connector to insure freedom of dirt or obstruction. Install fitting in to the connector and push together. A click will be heard when the hairpin snaps into proper connection. Pull on the line to ensure full engagement.

DUCK BILL CLIP

1. A special tool is available for removing the retaining clips, Ford tool T82L-9500-AH. If the tool is not available, see the next step. Align the slot on the push connector disconnect tool with either tab on the retaining clip. Pull the line from the connector.

2. If the special clip tool is not available, use a pair of narrow 6 in. channel lock pliers with a jaw width of 0.2 in. or less. Align the jaws of the pliers with the openings of the fitting case and compress the part of the retaining clip that engages the case. Compressing the retaining clip will release the fitting which may be pulled form the connector. Both sides of the clip must be compressed at the same time to disengage.

To install:

3. Inspect the retaining clip, fitting end and connector; replace the clip, if necessary.
4. Push the line into the steel connector until a click is heard, indicating clip is in place. Pull on line to check engagement.

Fuel Filter

Removal and Installation

Models equipped with EFI have 4 fuel filters: a nylon mesh "sock" at the fuel pump inlet in the fuel tank, a large paper element filter mounted in the fuel line under the vehicle, a small canister filter mounted in the engine compartment and an individual mesh filters at each injector fuel inlet. Of these, only the under car paper element filter is scheduled for regular replacement.

1. Filter replacement requires discharging of the fuel injection system pressure prior to filter change.
2. Discharge pressure, disconnect the fuel lines and remove the fuel filter retainer from it's mounting bracket beneath the fuel pump. Note the direction of the fuel flow arrow on filter.
3. To install the new filter, reverse the removal procedures; make sure the arrow points in the direction of fuel flow (toward the engine).
4. Start the engine and check for leaks.

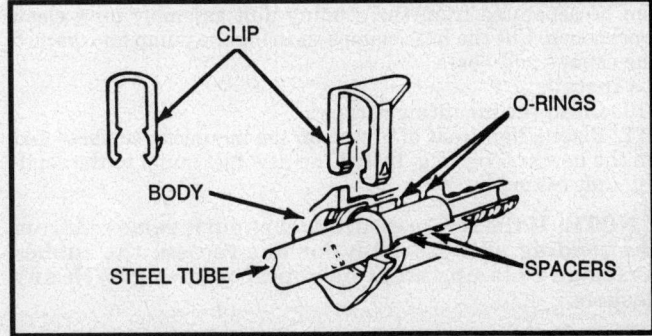

Hairpin clip fitting used on quick connect fuel lines

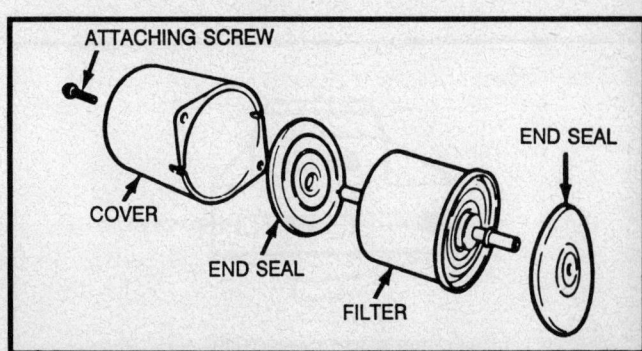

Exploded view of fuel filter showing location on fuel pump bracket

Electric Fuel Pump

Testing

2.3L ENGINE

1. Connect a compatible fuel pressure gauge to the Schrader valve on the fuel supply manifold. An adapter may be required to tap into the valve.

2. Start the engine. If the engine will not start, remove the fuel pump relay from the circuit protection panel.

NOTE: **If equipped with a 2.3L engine, connect a jumper wire from relay panel terminal 87 to the alternator output terminal.**

3. With the pump running, check the pressure reading on the gauge. Normal fuel pressure is 35–45 psi at idle.

4. Insert the test volume hose in a graduated container and open the flow control valve for 10 seconds; if the pump delivers 7.5 oz. in 10 seconds, the fuel volume is correct.

5. Disconnect the jumper wire to stop the pumps and observe the pressure gauge. If the pressure holds at a minimum of 30 psi, the system is holding pressure. Install the fuel pump relay and disconnect the pressure gauge.

2.9L ENGINE

1. Disconnect the electrical connector at the inertia switch, located at the rear center of the luggage compartment near the tailgate striker.

2. Crank the engine for at least 15 seconds to reduce the fuel pressure in the fuel lines.

3. Disconnect the fuel return line at the pressure regulator. Avoid fuel spillage.

4. Connect a hose from the fuel return fitting to a calibrated 2 quart container. Attach a fuel pressure gauge to the Schrader valve fitting on the fuel rail.

5. Connect a jumper wire to circuit 9-25 at the VIP test connector which is located on the **BLUE/red** wire near the ECA module.

6. Turn the ignition switch to the **RUN** position; do not start the engine. Touch the jumper wire to ground and observe the fuel pump pressure. Check the volume of fuel in the container.

7. Pump pressure should be 43.5 psi. Fuel flow should be 1.18–1.96 qts. per minute. Fuel pressure should remain at a minimum of 30 psi immediately after shutdown.

8. If the 3 tests are within specs, check the engine and electrical connectors. If the pressure specs are met but the flow is off; check for block fuel filters and supply lines. If both pressure and flow conditions are met, but the pressure will not maintain after de-energizing, check for leaking injectors or pressure regulator. If both are all right, replace the fuel pump.

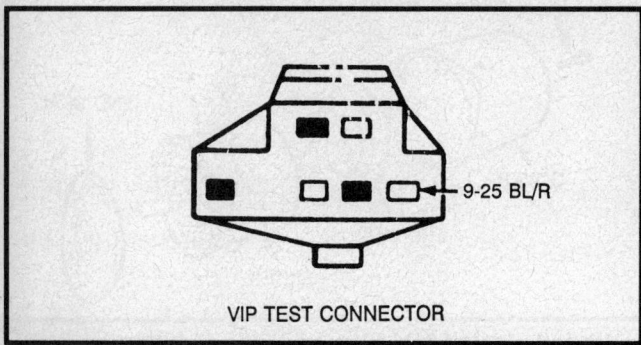

Scorpio VIP test connector identification

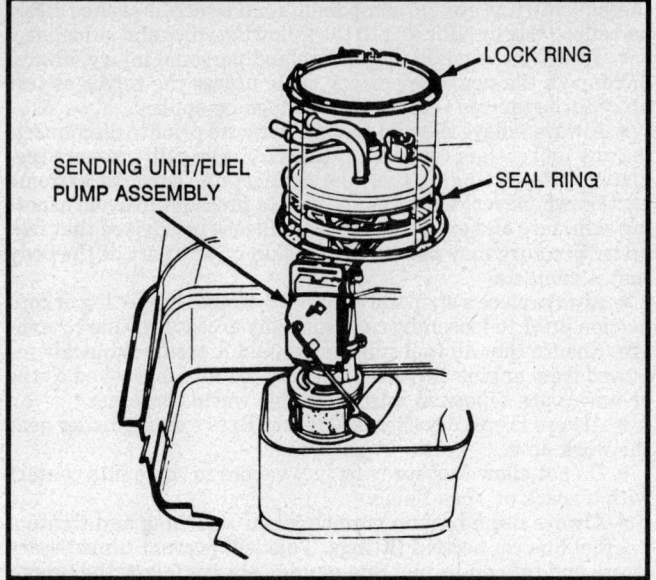

Low pressure fuel pump assembly located in the fuel tank

Removal and Installation

XR4Ti

Low Pressure Tank Pump

1. Run the vehicle until the fuel tank is about ¼ full. Disconnect the negative battery cable.

2. Depressurize the fuel system and drain as much gas from the tank by pumping it out through the filler neck into an approved safety container, then seal the can(s) tightly for temporary storage during service procedures. Place the gasoline away from the work area and take precautions to avoid the risk of fire.

3. Chock the front wheels. Raise and safely support the vehicle. Rock the vehicle a bit to make sure the vehicle is firmly supported before working underneath it.

4. Working under the vehicle at the rear frame rails near the fuel tank, disconnect the fuel supply, return and vent lines at the right and left side of the frame.

5. Disconnect the wiring to the fuel pump.

6. Support the fuel tank, loosen and remove the mounting straps, then lower the tank carefully.

7. Disconnect the fuel and vapor lines and wire harness connectors at the pump flange.

8. Clean the outside of the mounting flange and retaining ring. Turn the fuel pump lock ring counter-clockwise and remove it from the top of the tank.

9. Remove the seal ring, fuel pump and fuel sending unit as an assembly from the fuel tank. Once removed, the fuel pump can be separated from the sending unit assembly on a clean workbench. Cut the hose clamps securing the pump and discard the clamps and hoses.

To install:

10. Clean the mounting surfaces.

11. Place a light coat of grease on the mounting surfaces and on the new sealing ring. Install the new fuel pump to the sending unit assembly.

NOTE: **If the low pressure fuel pump is removed from the sending unit assembly for any reason, the rubber hoses and clamps must be replaced along with any gaskets.**

12. To install, reverse the removal procedures. Coat the seal ring with heavy duty grease before installing the pump and

sending unit and make sure the lock ring lugs are engaged properly.

13. After the tank is secured and all connections are complete, refill the tank with at least 10 gals. of fuel. Turn the ignition key **ON** for 3 seconds. Repeat 6–7 times until the fuel system is pressurized. Check for any fitting leaks.

14. Start the engine and check for leaks.

High Pressure Chassis Pump

1. Disconnect the negative battery cable.

2. Depressurize the fuel system by attaching a hand vacuum pump to the fuel pressure regulator and applying 25 in. Hg. of vacuum for 3 minutes.

3. Chock the front wheels, raise and safely support the vehicle. Rock the vehicle a bit to make sure the vehicle is firmly supported before working underneath it.

4. Working under the vehicle at the rear frame rail just ahead of the fuel tank, locate the external fuel pump and filter bracket and disconnect the inlet and outlet fuel lines. Separate the fuel pump electrical connector.

5. Remove the fuel pump bracket attaching screws and lower the fuel pump and bracket as an assembly. Working on a clean workbench, remove the pump and foam insulator from the mounting bracket. Disconnect the wiring harness from the pump.

To install:

6. To install, reverse the removal procedures; make sure the pump is indexed correctly in the mounting bracket insulator.

7. Position the insulator ends in the opening at the base of the mounting bracket. Route the wire harness between the insulator ends, then position the pump on the body mounting bracket and install the attaching bolts.

8. Reconnect the fuel lines and harness connectors. Refill the tank with at least 10 gals. of fuel. Turn the ignition key **ON** for 3 seconds.

9. Repeat 6–7 times until the fuel system is pressurized. Check for any fitting leaks. Start the engine and check for leaks.

SCORPIO

Fuel Tank Pump

1. Relieve the fuel system pressure. Disconnect the negative battery cable.

2. From in the luggage compartment, disconnect the fuel pump electrical connector (located near the right rear light assembly). Push the grommet and wiring harness from the luggage compartment.

3. Remove the fuel tank.

4. Clean any dirt that has built up from the fuel pump mounting flange. Remove the mounting clamp. Unscrew the fuel pump locking ring and remove.

5. Remove the fuel pump and sender assembly. Remove the sealing ring.

To install:

6. Clean the fuel tank pump mounting surface.

7. Install a new seal onto the fuel pump flange by assembling the seal around the fuel pump locking ring threads.

8. Lower the pump carefully into the tank; make sure the location arrows on the pump and tank are aligned.

9. Push the pump downward against the loading spring; visually make sure the sealing ring edges can be seen all around the flange.

10. Turn the locking ring clockwise while holding the pump in position.

11. Tighten the locking ring and install the lock ring. Install the fuel tank.

Fuel Injection

Idle Speed and Mixture Adjustment

Refer to the ignition timing procedure for checking and adjusting the idle speed. Mixture is controlled by the EEC IV (electronic engine control) system and is not adjustable. EEC IV system testing is required if an ignition or air/fuel mixture problem is suggested.

NOTE: If the engine speed is excessive while driving the vehicle with the throttle at the idle position, turn the ignition switch OFF and restart it. If the engine speed is still excessive, do not drive the vehicle until the condition is repaired.

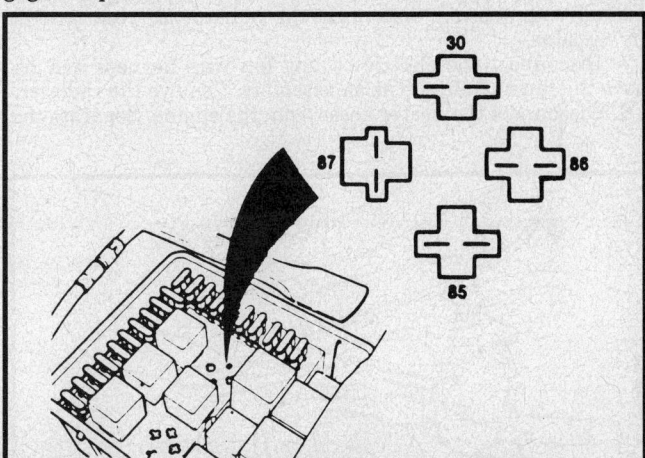

Location of the fuel pump relay and terminal identification for testing—XR4Ti

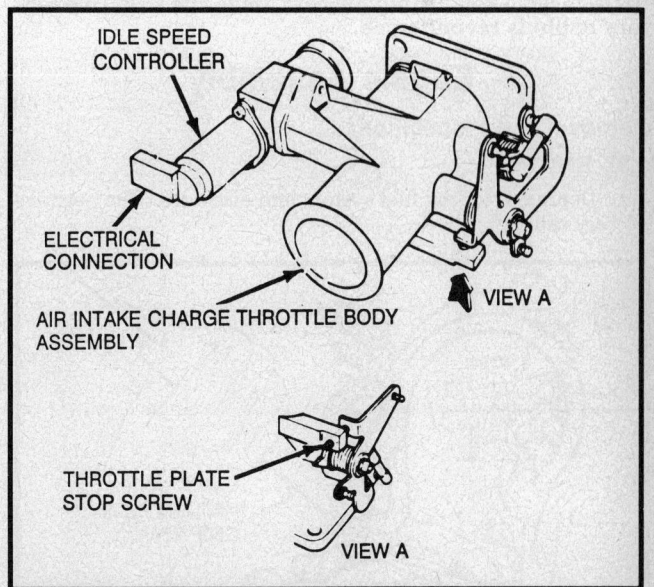

Adjust the idle speed by turning the throttle plate stop screw after unplugging the idle speed controller connector. Disconnect or reconnect all electrical connections with the ignition switch off.

EMISSION CONTROLS

For further information, please refer to "Professional Emission Component Application Guide".

Emission Warning Lamps

Resetting

1. Firmly apply the parking brake. Place the transmission into **P** (automatic) or **N** (manual).
2. Turn **OFF** all electrical loads.
3. Make sure the ignition switch is turned **OFF**.
4. Using a STAR tester, connect the color coded adapter leads to the tester. Connect the adapter leads to the 2 service connectors to the vehicle self-test connectors.
5. Place the ignition switch in the **RUN** position, to activate the self-test; do not depress the throttle during the test.

NOTE: The memory will activate the service code lists.

6. When the service codes begin, disconnect the STAR tester; this will the clear the memory of all codes.

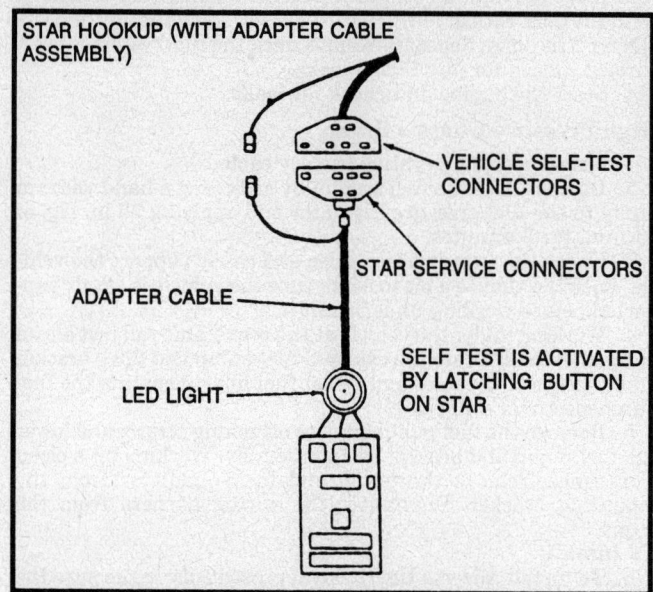

View of the STAR tester and the voltmeter connections for the electronic quick test

ENGINE MECHANICAL

NOTE: Disconnecting the negative battery cable on some vehicles may interfere with the functions of the on board computer systems and may require the computer to undergo a relearning process, once the negative battery cable is reconnected.

Engine Assembly

Removal and Installation

2.3L ENGINE

1. Depressurize the fuel system and disconnect the negative battery cable.

2. Label and disconnected the hoses, vacuum lines and wires.
3. Mark the hood hinge positions on the hood. Make sure the ground strap near the right hinge is disconnected, then remove the hood.
4. Disconnect the battery and remove it from the vehicle. Drain the cooling system.
5. Remove the air cleaner and duct assembly from the turbocharger.
6. Remove the upper and lower radiator hoses. If equipped with an automatic transmission, disconnect and plug the transmission fluid cooler lines from the radiator. If equipped with a manual transmission, disconnect the radiator air vent hose at the radiator.
7. Disconnect the electric cooling fan wire harness and remove the fan and shroud as an assembly. Remove the radiator.
8. Disconnect the heater hoses from the engine. Separate the

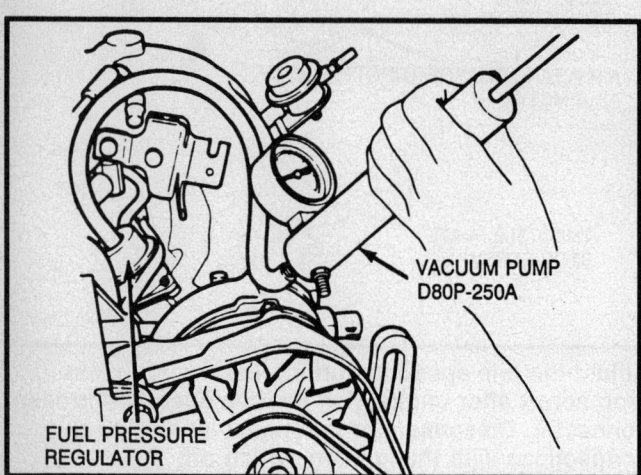

Depressurize the fuel system by applying vacuum to the fuel pressure regulator

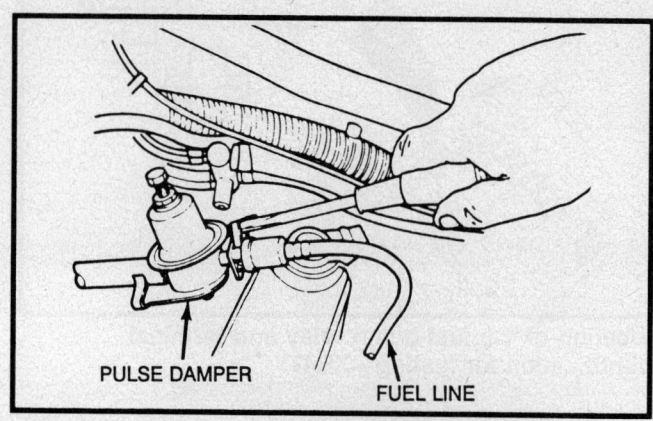

Disconnect the fuel line at the pulse damper

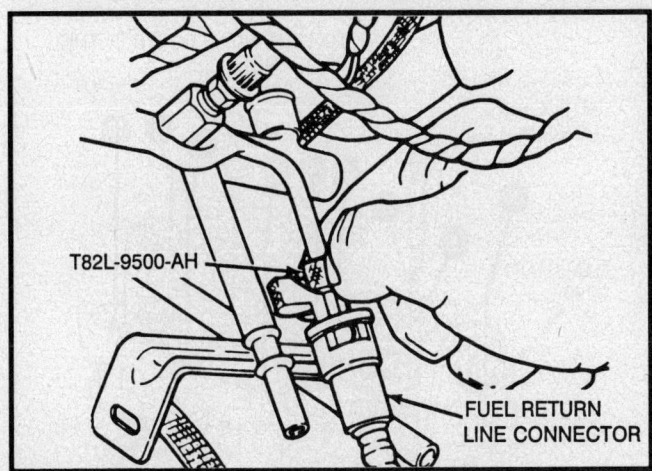

T82L-9500-AH

FUEL RETURN
LINE CONNECTOR

**Disconnecting the quick-connect fuel line with
removal tool**

oil level sensor wiring connector and remove the engine oil level
dipstick.

9. Disconnect the wiring form the alternator and starter motor. Disconnect the air bypass valve connector and throttle position sensor connector from the throttle body. Disconnect the vacuum hose at the EGR valve, then separate the fuel injection wiring harness connector located between the upper intake manifold and the engine oil dipstick.

10. Disconnect the throttle cable and transmission kickdown cable, if equipped, at the pivot ball connections on the bracket. Remove the accelerator cable bracket attaching screws and the bracket from the upper intake manifold, then place the bracket and the accelerator and kickdown cables aside.

11. Depressurize the fuel system, if not already done, and disconnect the fuel line at the pulse damper. Disconnect the fuel return line using quick connector removal tool T82L-9500-A or equivalent. Plug the fuel line and rail immediately to prevent contamination of the fuel system by dirt or grease during service.

12. Disconnect the wiring to the ignition coil, TFI module, oil pressure switch, temperature sending unit and all other sensors. Label all connectors for installation. Label and disconnect the supply hose at the vacuum tree mounted on the dash panel.

13. Remove the turbocharger air inlet tube, then disconnect the orange ground wire and vacuum hose at the turbocharger air inlet elbow.

14. Raise and safely support the vehicle. Remove the air conditioner compressor from the mounting brackets and move it aside.

15. Drain the engine oil. Remove the starter motor. Remove the flywheel or converter housing upper mounting bolts and the side braces.

16. Disconnect the muffler inlet pipe from the turbocharger. Disconnect any exhaust system mounting brackets from the engine. Remove the right and left side engine mount-to-crossmember studs and nuts.

17. Remove the flywheel or converter housing lower plate cover.

18. If equipped with a manual transmission, remove the lower flywheel housing mounting bolts. If equipped with an automatic transmission, disconnect the converter from the drive plate (turn the engine in normal direction of rotation to gain access to the mountings). Remove the converter housing lower mounting bolts.

19. Lower the vehicle. Support the transmission with a jack.

20. Attach an engine lifting sling to the existing engine lifting brackets. Slowly raise the engine and separate it from the trans-

mission. Be sure the converter (automatic transmission) remains on the input shaft.

21. Slowly raise the engine from the vehicle, being careful not to snag any hoses, lines or wire harness connectors on the way out. Watch for any engine sensor connectors that may not have been disconnected.

To install:

22. Reverse the removal procedures. If equipped with an automatic transmission, be sure the converter mounts are aligned with the flex plate and the converter hub fits flush into the crank pilot. If equipped with a manual transmission be sure the transmission mainshaft is aligned with the clutch disc. If necessary turn the engine with the transmission in gear until the shaft splines engage the disc.

NOTE: Whenever self-locking motor mount bolts are nuts are removed, they must be replaced with new self-locking nuts or bolts. Clean old locking adhesive from the bolt or hole threads prior To installation.

2.9L ENGINE

1. Disconnect the negative battery cable.
2. Drain the cooling system.
3. Disconnect the under hood light connector (black-to-gray), located on the inboard side of the battery.
4. Disconnect the windshield washer hose from the reservoir. Plug the reservoir.
5. Disconnect the hood ground strap. Mark the hood hinge locations and remove the hood.
6. Loosen the clamps and disconnect the inlet air hoses at the throttle body. Remove the air cleaner cover, air box and inlet air hoses.
7. Remove the upper radiator shroud and cooling fan.
8. Remove the power steering pump mounting bolts and position the pump aside.
9. Remove the alternator and thermactor pump, if equipped.
10. Disconnect the heater hoses from the firewall bulkhead.
11. Disconnect the coolant hoses at the water pump and thermostat housing.
12. Disconnect the throttle cable from the linkage on the throttle body. Remove the cable bracket from the upper manifold. Set the bracket to the side.
13. Release fuel system pressure at the pressure regulator. Disconnect the fuel supply and return lines.
14. Remove the distributor cap, rotor, distributor and plug wires. Label and disconnect the ignition coil electrical connectors.
15. Label and disconnect the vacuum hoses from the front and rear of the upper intake manifold and EGR fitting.
16. Remove the carbon canister, bracket and vacuum line.
17. Label and disconnect the air charge temperature (ACT) sensor; idle speed control valve; throttle position (TP) sensor; air conditioning compressor clutch wiring; fuel injectors; engine coolant (ECT) sensor and the oil pressure switch.
18. Remove the ground wire from the spade connector located on the left fender apron.
19. Lift the cowl weatherstrip and unclip the manifold absolute sensor (MAP) and set it to the side.
20. Raise and safely support the vehicle.
21. Remove the exhaust manifold to crossover pipe retaining nuts.
22. If equipped with an automatic transmission, disconnect and plug the transmission lines from the radiator.
23. Remove the radiator-to-chassis bolts, disengage the upper radiator clips by depressing the tabs and remove the radiator from under the vehicle.
24. Disconnect the starter motor wiring and remove the starter motor.
25. Remove the engine insulator lower retaining nuts and washers. Remove the lower side and lower clutch or converter housing to engine mounting bolts.

26. If equipped with an automatic transmission, remove the inspection plate. Remove the converter to flywheel mounting nuts.

27. Loosen the air conditioning compressor retaining and pivot bolts.

28. Lower the vehicle.

29. Attach an appropriate engine sling to the lifting brackets provided on the engine. Attach a hoist. Support the transmission with a suitable floor jack.

30. Remove both upper bell housing-to-engine bolts. Raise the engine slightly and remove the air conditioning compressor from the mounting brackets and wire the compressor (with hoses attached) aside.

31. Raise the engine enough to clear the mounts and pull the engine forward to clear the transmission. If equipped with an automatic transmission, make sure the converter is pushed back onto the transmission. Carefully raise the engine out of the vehicle to prevent damage to the engine compartment and engine components.

To install:

32. When installing the engine, remove the left engine support bracket to gain clearance.

33. Lower the engine into the compartment carefully. Make sure the exhaust manifolds are aligned with the exhaust pipe. If equipped with a manual transmission, start the transmission mainshaft into the clutch disc. It may be necessary to adjust the angle of the transmission with the floor jack if the mainshaft binds. Turn the engine slightly to engage the clutch disc splines. If equipped with an automatic transmission, align the converter studs with the flywheel mounting holes and start the converter pilot into the crankshaft.

34. Install the engine in the reverse order of removal. Torque the:

Upper bell housing-to-engine bolts—23–26 ft. lbs. (30–36 Nm)—automatic

Upper bell housing-to-engine bolts—30–38 ft. lbs. (40–51 Nm)—manual

35. Before lowering the engine completely, install the air conditioning compressor and install the left engine bracket. Proceed with the rest of the engine installation. Torque the remaining bell housing bolts to the same value as the upper.

Cylinder Head

Removal and Installation

2.3L ENGINE

NOTE: The engine should be COLD before removing the cylinder head to prevent warpage or distortion.

1. Relieve the fuel pressure. Disconnect the negative battery cable. Drain the cooling system.

2. Disconnected hoses and electrical connectors to assure proper assembly.

3. Rotate the crankshaft to position the No. 1 cylinder on TDC (top dead center) on the compression stroke with the timing marks aligned.

4. Disconnect the air intake cast tube from the turbocharger to the throttle body. Remove the valve rocker cover.

5. Remove the upper radiator hose and disconnect the heater hose if it interferes with cylinder head removal. Remove the alternator drive belts and the alternator and mounting brackets.

6. Remove the intake and exhaust manifolds from the cylinder head.

7. Remove the camshaft drive belt cover.

8. Loosen the drive belt tensioner and remove the drive belt.

9. Remove the water outlet from the cylinder head.

10. Remove the cylinder head bolts evenly, and remove the cylinder head.

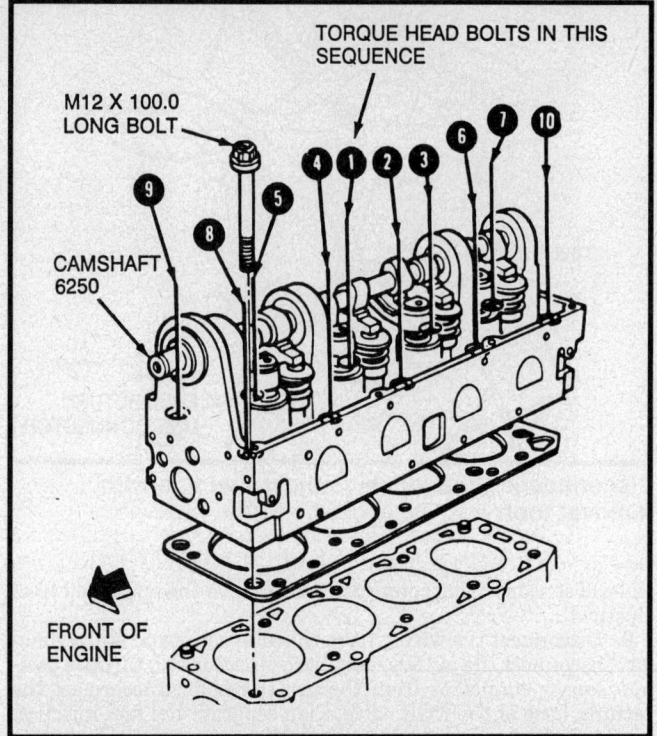

Exploded view of the cylinder head and torquing sequence—2.3L engine

To install:

11. Using a new cylinder head gasket, position it on the block. Rotate the camshaft so the drive sprocket locating pin is at the 5 o'clock position, to avoid valve or piston damage when reinstalling the cylinder head on the engine.

12. Position the cylinder head and camshaft assembly on the block. Install the bolts finger tight, then torque to specifications in 2 stages. The 1st to 50–60 ft. lbs. (68–81 Nm), the 2nd step to 80–90 ft. lbs. (108–122 Nm).

NOTE: If difficulty in positioning the head on the block is encountered, guide pins may be fabricated by cutting the heads off 2 extra cylinder head bolts.

13. Set the crankshaft at TDC (if rotated) and be sure the camshaft drive gear is positioned correctly.

14. Install the camshaft drive belt and release the tensioner. Rotate the crankshaft 2 full turns clockwise (facing the engine) to remove all slack from the belt. The timing marks should again be aligned. Torque the tensioner lockbolt and pivot bolts.

15. Install the camshaft drive belt cover.

16. Apply sealer to the water outlet and new gasket, and install.

17. Install the intake and exhaust manifolds and torque the mounting nuts and bolts to specifications.

18. Install a new valve cover gasket and install the valve cover.

19. Install all removed components, hoses and wiring.

20. To complete the installation, reverse the removal procedures.

2.9L ENGINE

1. Relieve the fuel pressure. Disconnect the negative battery cable.

2. Disconnected hoses and electrical connectors to assure proper assembly.

3. Rotate the crankshaft to position the No. 1 cylinder on TDC on the compression stroke with the timing marks aligned.

4. Drain the engine coolant.

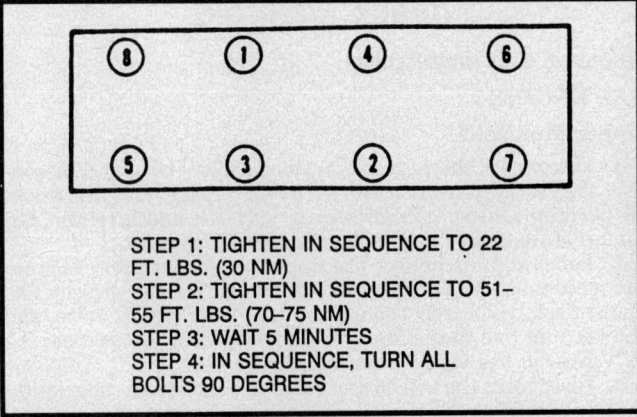

STEP 1: TIGHTEN IN SEQUENCE TO 22
FT. LBS. (30 NM)
STEP 2: TIGHTEN IN SEQUENCE TO 51–
55 FT. LBS. (70–75 NM)
STEP 3: WAIT 5 MINUTES
STEP 4: IN SEQUENCE, TURN ALL
BOLTS 90 DEGREES

Cylinder head torquing sequence—2.9L engine

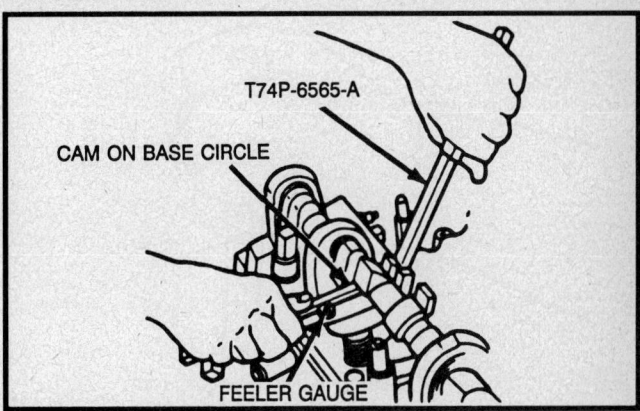

T74P-6565-A

CAM ON BASE CIRCLE

FEELER GAUGE

Compress the valve spring with spring compressor as shown to remove cam follower

5. Remove the intake hoses from the throttle body and disconnect the throttle linkage. Remove the distributor.

6. Remove the upper radiator hose. Remove the rocker arm (valve) covers Remove the rocker arm and shaft assemblies.

7. Remove the fuel line from the fuel rail. Remove the intake manifold.

8. Remove the pushrods. Keep the pushrods in correct sequence for proper assembly in the same position as removed.

9. Remove the exhaust manifolds from the cylinder heads.

10. Remove the cylinder head mounting bolts, starting from the outer edges toward the center. A No. 55 Torx® drive bit/socket is required.

11. Remove the cylinder heads.

To install:

12. Clean the gasket mounting surfaces.

13. Using new head gaskets, position them on the cylinder block; the gaskets are marked top and front and are not interchangeable.

14. Using old head bolts, cut the tops off and make alignment studs. Torque the cylinder head bolts, in sequence, using the following 4 steps:

Step 1—torque to 22 ft. lbs. (30 Nm)
Step 2—torque to 51–55 ft. lbs. (70–75 Nm)
Step 3—wait 5 minutes
Step 4—torque an additional 90 degrees

15. To complete the installation, reverse the remove procedures. Adjust the valves. Check and adjust the ignition timing.

Cam Follower

Removal and Installation

2.3L ENGINE

1. Loosen the clamp on the PCV hose at the oil separator on the rocker arm cover and disconnect the hose. Do not attempt to remove the oil separator from the valve cover; it is pressed into the cover and sealed with Loctite®.

2. Disconnect the coolant hose that passes over the rear of the rocker arm cover. Remove the coolant pipe retaining clip screw from the right, front side of the valve cover.

3. Remove the throttle body from the upper intake manifold. Label all connectors, hoses and linkage for installation in their original locations.

4. Disconnect the spark plug wires at the spark plugs and at the valve cover studs, then lay the wires aside.

5. Remove the remaining valve cover bolts, then lift the valve cover and gasket off the cylinder head. Tap the valve cover with a rubber mallet to break it loose, if necessary.

6. Rotate the camshaft so the base circle of the cam is against the cam follower you intend to remove.

7. Using a valve spring compressor tool T74P-6565-A or

equivalent, depress the valve spring and slide the cam follower over the lash adjuster and out from under the camshaft.

8. Once the cam follower is removed, the hydraulic lash adjuster can be lifted out, if necessary. Make sure the lash adjuster bore is clean before installing the adjuster into the cylinder head.

9. To install the cam follower, reverse the removal procedures. Make sure the lash adjuster is collapsed and released before rotating the camshaft.

Valve Lash

Hydraulic valve lash adjusters/lifters are used in the valve train. The lash adjusters on the OHC 4 cylinder engine, are placed at the fulcrum point of the rocker arms and operation is similar to the hydraulic lifters used in pushrod equipped 2.9L engine. Oil is provided to the lash adjusters under pressure via passages drilled in the cylinder head. The lash adjusters require no periodic manual adjustment.

Adjustment

2.3L ENGINE

If a lash adjuster becomes noisy or valve service has been performed on the cylinder head, valve train clearance should be checked as follows:

1. Remove the cam follower. Turn the crankshaft in the normal direction of rotation until the base circle (round part) of camshaft lobe is against the rocker arm of the valve being checked. Do not attempt to rotate the crankshaft backwards; if the base circle alignment is missed, rotate the crankshaft and try again.

2. Use a valve spring compressor tool T74P-6565-A or equivalent, to slowly apply pressure to the cam follower, until the lash adjuster is completely collapsed. Hold the rocker arm in this position and check the clearance between the base circle of the cam lobe and the rocker arm with a feeler gauge. Allowable clearance is 0.035–0.055 in. (0.89–1.4mm). Desired clearance is 0.040–0.050 in. (1.0–1.27mm).

3. If the clearance is excessive, remove the cam follower and inspect for wear. If the follower is not worn, measure the assembled height of the valve spring. If the assembled height of the spring is correct, check for camshaft wear. If the camshaft is not worn, the lash adjuster should be removed and checked.

4. Replace worn parts as required and recheck clearance.

2.9L ENGINE

1. Turn the crankshaft (in normal direction of rotation) until the lifters, of the cylinder to be adjusted, are in the base circle location of the camshaft; that is, after the intake valve has

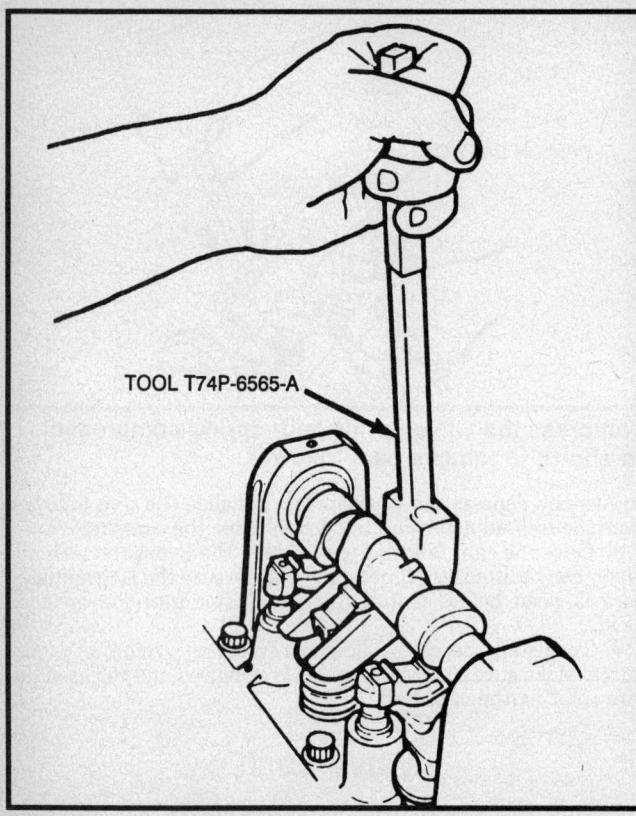

Measuring clearance between the base circle of the camshaft and the follower with a feeler gauge and spring compressor tool

opened and closed. Both the intake and exhaust valves should now be fully closed.

2. Loosen the adjusting screws until distinctive lash (clearance) between the rocker arm and valve tip is noticed.

3. Slowly, torque the adjusting screw until all clearance is taken out and the rocker arm is just touching the valve tip.

4. Torque the adjusting screw an additional 1½ turns to set the normal working position of the lifter plunger. Proceed to the next valve. Turn the crankshaft to the correct position for the next cylinder and adjust.

Rocker Arms/Shaft

Removal and Installation

2.9L ENGINE

1. Remove the rocker arm (valve) covers.

2. Remove the rocker arm stand mounting bolts from the ends, working toward the center. Loosen each bolt 2 turns at a time in sequence.

3. When all the bolts are loose, lift off the rocker arm shaft assembly.

4. Loosen each rocker arm adjusting screw several turns.

To install:

5. Clean the gasket mounting surfaces.

6. Install the oil baffle and guide the rocker arms into their pushrod sockets. Torque the rocker stand bolts, in sequence, starting from the center working toward the ends. Torque, 2 turns at a time, to 43–50 ft. lbs. (59–67 Nm).

7. Adjust the valves. Install the rocker arm (valve) covers. Apply a bead of RTV sealer to the covers. The covers must be installed within 15 minutes after RTV is applied.

Intake Manifold

Removal and Installation

2.3L ENGINE

Upper Manifold

1. Disconnect the negative battery cable. Label and disconnect the electronic connectors at the air bypass valve, the throttle position sensor, injector wiring harness, knock sensor, fan temperature sensor and coolant temperature sensor.

2. Label and disconnect the upper intake manifold vacuum fitting connections at the manifold fitting, the rear vacuum line at the dash panel tree, the vacuum line to the EGR valve, and the vacuum line to the fuel pressure regulator. Disconnect the PCV hose at the intake manifold fitting.

3. Disconnect the accelerator cable and kickdown cable (automatic only) from the throttle linkage at the pivot ball connection. Unbolt the accelerator cable bracket from the upper intake manifold, then lay the bracket and cables aside.

4. Loosen the hose clamps and remove the turbocharger outlet hose flexible connection to the throttle body.

5. Remove the EGR flange attaching bolts, then remove the flange and EGR valve as an assembly. Remove the flange gasket and discard.

6. Remove the nut attaching the pulse damper to its bracket, then disconnect the low oil level sensor and remove the engine oil level dipstick.

7. Remove the engine oil dipstick bracket mounting bolt. If necessary, cut the fuel injection wiring harness routing strap at the pulse damper bracket.

8. Remove the pulse damper bracket attaching nuts and remove the bracket.

9. The throttle body can either be removed at this point by re-

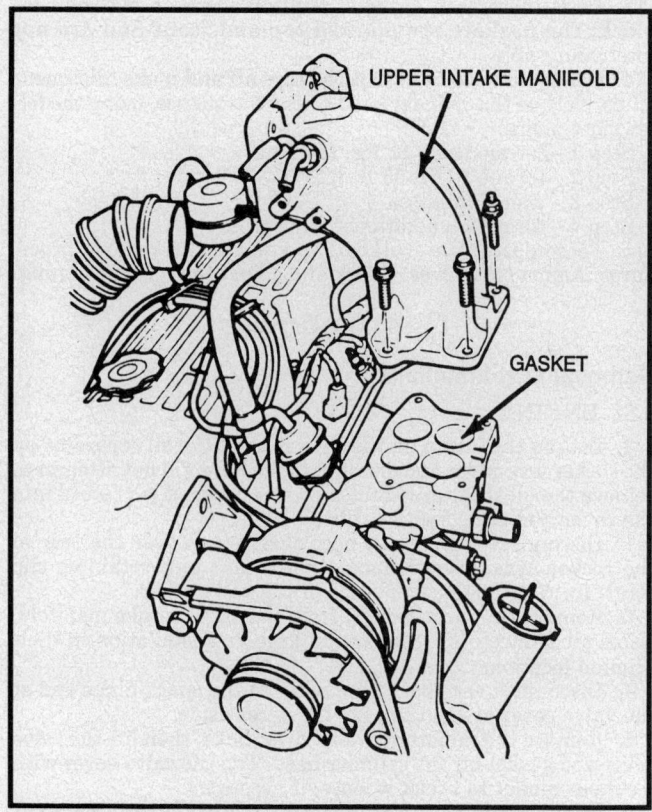

Exploded view of the upper intake manifold—2.3L engine

moving the mounting bolts, or left attached and removed with the upper intake manifold as an assembly.

10. Loosen and remove the upper intake manifold mounting bolts. Lift the upper intake manifold upward and off the lower intake manifold. Remove the gasket.

To install:

11. Clean the gasket mounting surfaces.

12. Reverse the removal procedures. Torque the:
   Upper intake manifold mounting nuts and bolts, in the sequence—15–22 ft. lbs. (18–26 Nm)
      EGR flange bolts—13–19 ft. lbs. (18–26 Nm)
      Throttle body bolts—12–15 ft. lbs. (16–20 Nm)

13. To complete the installation, reverse the removal procedures.

Lower Manifold

1. Drain the cooling system and disconnect the negative battery cable.

2. Label and disconnect the wire harness connectors at the knock sensor, fan temperature sensor, fuel injection wiring harness and coolant temperature sender. The sender is located on the left side at the rear of the cylinder block below the oil pressure sender/turbocharger oil feed fitting.

3. Disconnect the coolant bypass line from the lower intake manifold.

4. Depressurize the fuel system by connecting a hand vacuum pump to the fuel pressure regulator and applying 25 in. Hg. Disconnect the fuel supply line from the fuel supply manifold, then disconnect the push connect fuel return line.

5. Remove the nut attaching the pulse damper to its bracket and place the pulse damper and fuel supply line aside.

6. Remove the upper intake manifold as previously described.

7. Disconnect the coolant temperature sensor, then remove the upper and lower mounting bolts from the lower intake manifold and lift the manifold off the engine with the fuel injectors and fuel supply manifold installed.

8. Remove the manifold-to-cylinder head bolts and the manifold; the injectors can be removed at this time by exerting a slight twisting/pulling motion.

To install:

9. Clean the gasket mounting surfaces. Inspect the parts for damage.

10. Clean and oil all stud threads. Install a new mounting gasket over the studs.

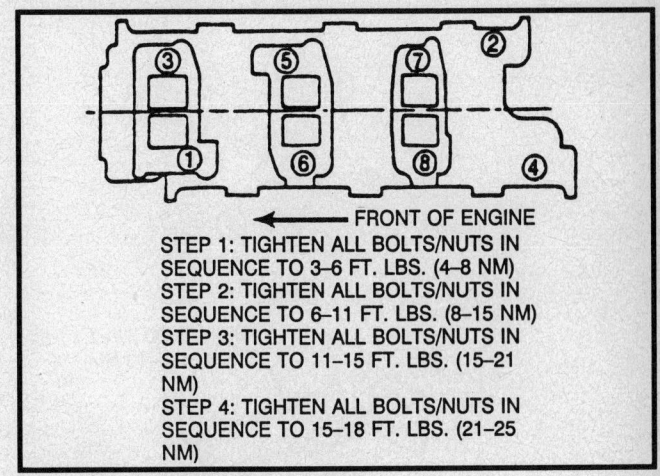

STEP 1: TIGHTEN ALL BOLTS/NUTS IN SEQUENCE TO 3–6 FT. LBS. (4–8 NM)
STEP 2: TIGHTEN ALL BOLTS/NUTS IN SEQUENCE TO 6–11 FT. LBS. (8–15 NM)
STEP 3: TIGHTEN ALL BOLTS/NUTS IN SEQUENCE TO 11–15 FT. LBS. (15–21 NM)
STEP 4: TIGHTEN ALL BOLTS/NUTS IN SEQUENCE TO 15–18 FT. LBS. (21–25 NM)

V6 intake manifold installation

11. Install the lower manifold-to-cylinder head, with lift bracket in position, and torque the bolts, in sequence, to 12–15 ft. lbs. (16–20 Nm).

12. To complete the installation, reverse the removal procedures.

2.9L ENGINE

1. Disconnect the negative battery cable.

2. Remove the air inlet hoses from the throttle body and air cleaner.

3. Disconnect the throttle cable from the linkage at the throttle body.

4. Disconnect the throttle cable bracket mounting bolts and position the bracket assembly aside.

5. Discharge the fuel pressure from the system. Remove the fuel lines from the fuel supply manifold and pressure regulator.

6. Disconnect the following connectors after labeling them: the air charge temperature sensor, the idle speed control valve, the throttle position sensor and the engine coolant temperature sensor. Note location and label all vacuum hoses from the front and rear of the intake manifold, manifold plenum and throttle body.

7. Drain the engine coolant. Remove the hose from the thermostat housing to radiator. Remove the EGR tube-to-throttle body mounting bolts. Remove the EGR tube from the throttle body.

8. Remove the plenum-to-intake manifold Torx® bolts and the throttle body/plenum assembly.

9. Remove the distributor. Remove the rocker arm (valve) covers.

10. Remove the intake manifold mounting bolts. Note the length and position of each bolt. Tap the manifold lightly with a plastic hammer to break the gasket seal and remove the intake manifold.

To install:

11. Clean the gasket mounting surfaces; make sure no gasket material falls into the intake passages.

12. Apply sealing compound to the gasket mounting joint surfaces.

13. Position a new gasket on the intake manifold and ensure the tab on the right cylinder head fits the cutout of the gasket.

14. Place the manifold carefully onto the engine. Install and hand tighten the mounting bolts. Follow the tightening sequence provides and progressively tighten the mounting bolts and nuts to the torque values shown.

15. To complete the installation, reverse the removal procedures.

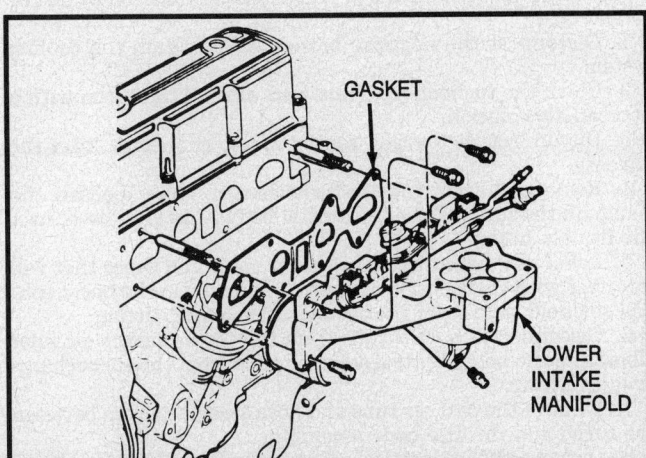

Exploded view of the lower intake manifold—2.3L engine

GASKET

LOWER INTAKE MANIFOLD

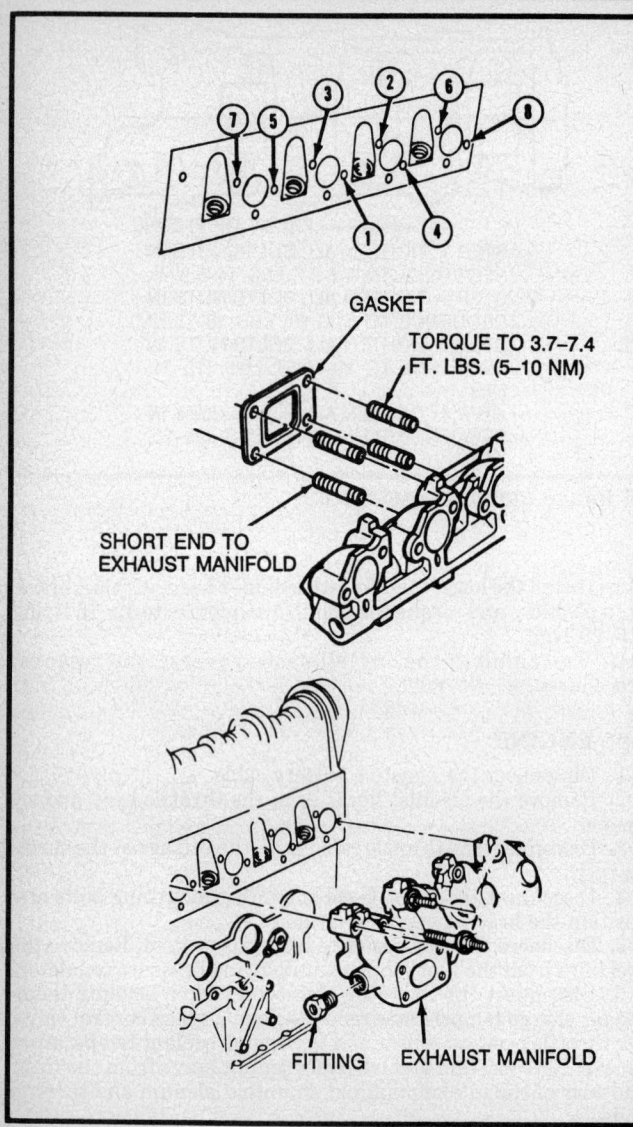

GASKET

TORQUE TO 3.7–7.4
FT. LBS. (5–10 NM)

SHORT END TO
EXHAUST MANIFOLD

FITTING   EXHAUST MANIFOLD

Exploded view of the exhaust manifold—2.3L engine

Exhaust Manifold

Removal and Installation

2.3L ENGINE

1. Loosen the cap on the coolant expansion tank and drain the cooling system.
2. Remove the heater return hose at the water pump. Remove the bolt attaching the coolant pipe routing bracket to the right, front side of the valve cover.
3. Disconnect the coolant pipe-to-expansion tank hose at the coolant pipe.
4. Disconnect the turbocharger oil supply line at the turbocharger. Disconnect the turbocharger coolant supply and return line at the turbocharger.
5. Disconnect the PCV tube at the turbo air inlet adapter, then remove the turbo-to-exhaust manifold nuts.
6. Remove the turbocharger support bracket.
7. Remove the exhaust manifold-to-cylinder head nuts/bolts and the manifold.
To install:
8. Clean the gasket mounting surfaces.

9. Install the exhaust manifold-to-cylinder head nuts and torque, in sequence, in 2 steps, to:
    Step 1 — 14–17 ft. lbs. (20–23 Nm)
    Step 2 — 20–30 ft. lbs. (27–41 Nm)
10. To complete the installation, reverse the removal procedures. Refill the cooling system and crank the engine a few times without starting to build oil pressure back up in the turbocharger. Start the engine and check for leaks.

2.9L ENGINE

Right Side

1. Disconnect the negative battery cable.
2. Remove the heat shield mounting bolts and remove the heat shield.
3. Remove the nuts that retain the crossover pipe. Remove the pipe.
4. Remove the thermactor air pipe to manifold, on models equipped.
5. Remove the manifold-to-cylinder head nuts and the manifold.
To install:
6. Clean the gasket mounting surfaces.
7. Using new gaskets, reverse the removal procedures. Torque the manifold mounting nuts to 20–30 ft. lbs. (26–40 Nm). Start the engine and check for leaks.

Left Side

1. Disconnect the negative battery cable.
2. Remove the EGR valve-to-manifold bolts. Remove the EGR tube-to-throttle body attaching screws and detach the tube.
3. Remove the heat shield. Remove the crossover pipe-to-manifold mounting nuts. Remove thermactor pipe, if equipped.
4. Remove the manifold-to-cylinder head nuts and the manifold.
To install:
5. Clean all gasket mounting surfaces.
6. Using new gaskets, reverse the removal procedures. Torque the exhaust manifold-to-cylinder head nuts to 20–30 ft. lbs. (26–40 Nm). Start the engine and check for leaks.

Turbocharger

Removal and Installation

Turbocharger servicing is by replacement only. Maintain clean as possible working conditions while removing and installing the turbocharger. When disconnecting lines and feed pipes always cover or plug openings to prevent contamination by dirt or grease.

1. Disconnect the negative battery cable. Drain the cooling system.
2. Clean the turbocharger and area around the turbo with a non-caustic solution.
3. Disconnect the oxygen sensor wiring connector from the harness.
4. Remove the air tube-to-turbocharger bolts. Loosen the clamp on the intake hose-to-throttle body bolts and disconnect the flexible hose.
5. Label and disconnect all vacuum hoses and tubes that will interfere with turbocharger removal. Disconnect the boost control solenoid hose from the turbocharger outlet fitting.
6. Disconnect the PCV tube from the turbocharger air inlet elbow and the boost control solenoid hose from the turbocharger inlet fitting.
7. Remove the cast air tube and hose assembly from between the turbo and throttle body assembly.
8. Disconnect the electrical ground wire from the turbocharger outlet fitting.
9. Disconnect the oil supply line routing bracket and line from the turbocharger. Disconnect the coolant outlet line from

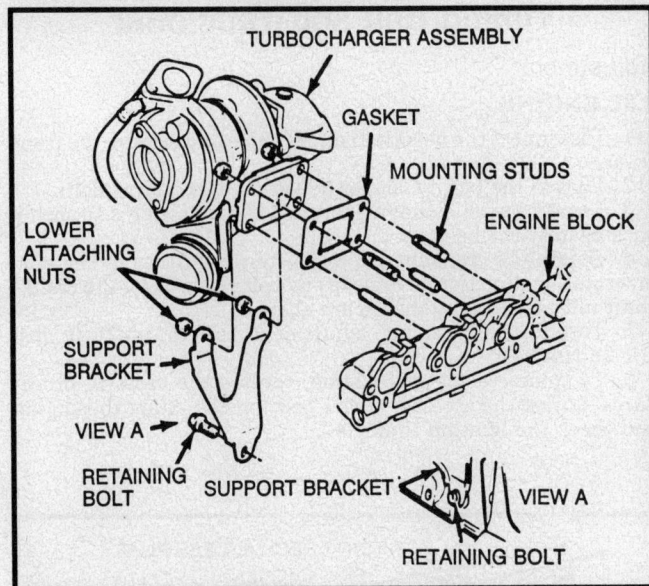

Exploded view of the turbocharger-to-exhaust manifold assembly—2.3L engine

the turbocharger housing. Loosen the hose clamp and disconnect the coolant inlet line from the turbocharger fitting.

10. Loosen the heat shield-to-upper right engine mount nut.

11. Raise and safely support the vehicle. Remove the transmission mount center plate.

12. Disconnect the exhaust pipe from the turbocharger. Disconnect the oil return line from the bottom of the turbocharger; be careful not kink or damage the line. Remove and discard the gasket.

13. Remove the lower turbocharger nuts/bolts, the lower turbocharger support bracket bolt and the bracket.

14. Lower the vehicle. If equipped with an automatic transmission, remove the nut and disconnect the dipstick tube support bracket from the cast tube flange.

15. Remove the upper turbocharger nuts.

16. Loosen the other turbocharger nuts, a little at a time, and slide the turbo on the mounting studs until the nuts can be removed. Remove the turbocharger, gasket, outlet tube and hose as an assembly. Continue disassembly on a clean workbench to transfer components to the new turbocharger.

To install:

17. Clean the gasket mounting surfaces.

18. To install, reverse the removal procedures. Use new mounting gasket on the turbo and oil return line. Use new mounting nuts when installing the turbocharger. Torque the:

  Lower bracket bolt—28–40 ft. lbs. (38–54 Nm)
  Oil return line—14–21 ft. lbs. (19–28 Nm)
  Exhaust pipe—25–35 ft. lbs. (34–47 Nm)
  Turbo mounting nuts—28–40 ft. lbs. (38–54 Nm)
  Cast air pipe to turbo—15–22 ft. lbs. (20–30 Nm)

Front Cover

Removal and Installation

2.3L ENGINE

1. Disconnect the negative battery cable.

NOTE: An access plug is provided in the cam drive belt cover so the camshaft timing can be checked without removing the drive belt cover.

2. Remove the access plug, turn the crankshaft until the timing mark on the crankshaft damper indicates TDC, and observe

that the timing mark on the camshaft drive sprocket is aligned with the pointer on the inner belt cover. Also, the rotor of the distributor must align with No. 1 cylinder firing position.

NOTE: Never turn the crankshaft of any of the overhead cam engines in the opposite direction of normal rotation. Backward rotation of the crankshaft may cause the timing belt to slip and alter the timing.

3. Loosen the adjustment bolts on the alternator and accessories and remove the drive belts. To provide clearance for removing the camshaft belt, remove the fan and shroud assembly.

4. Remove the water pump pulley attaching bolts and the pulley from the water pump shaft.

5. Remove the cover bolts and the timing belt outer cover.

To install:

6. To install, reverse the removal procedures. Adjust the accessory drive belt tension. Start the engine and check the ignition timing.

2.9L ENGINE

1. Disconnect the negative battery cable. Drain the engine coolant and remove the radiator.

2. Drain the engine oil. Remove the engine oil pan.

3. Remove the air conditioning compressor. Thermactor air pump and bracket.

4. Remove the power steering pump and bracket. Remove the alternator and drive belts.

5. Remove the radiator cooling fan assembly. Remove the water pump, heater hose and radiator hoses.

6. Remove the drive pulley from the crankshaft.

7. Remove the front cover mounting bolts. Tap the cover with a plastic hammer to loosen the gasket seal. Remove the front cover. Replace the oil seal after cleaning the cover and removing all gasket material from the mounting surfaces.

To install:

8. Using guide sleeves and a new gasket, position the front cover on the engine, start all mounting bolts 2–3 turns.

9. Using a front cover alignment tool, install the front cover to the engine.

NOTE: Make sure the front cover to oil pan mating flange aligns with the lower edge of the cylinder block.

10. To complete the installation, reverse the removal procedures.

Oil Seal Replacement

2.9L ENGINE

1. Drain the engine coolant and remove the radiator after disconnecting the negative battery cable.

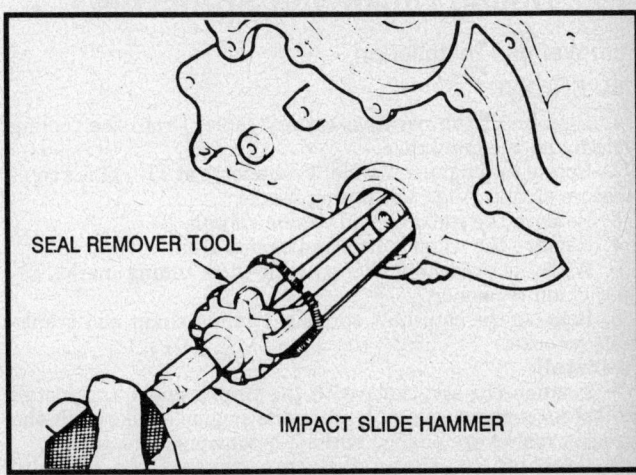

Scorpio front crankshaft seal removal

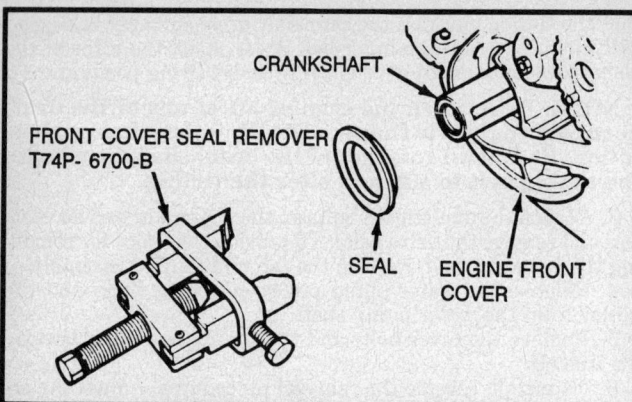

Front crankshaft oil seal showing remover tool

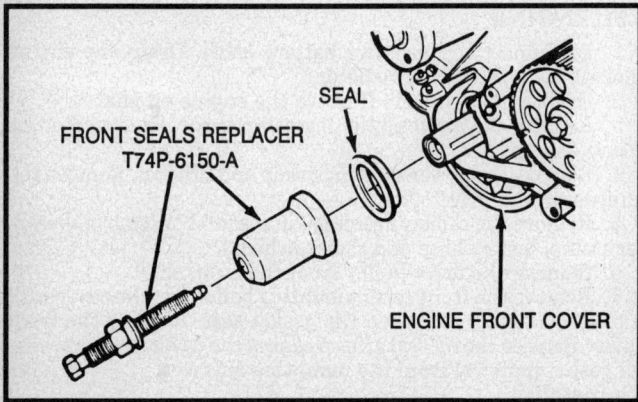

Install front cover oil seal using tool as shown

2. Remove the crankshaft pulley, the water pump and drive belt.

3. Use a suitable long jawed slide hammer puller with internal jaws. Position the puller inside the oil seal and remove the seal. Use care during the procedure.

To install:

4. Using a new oil seal, coat it with engine oil.

5. Using a seal driver tool, carefully, drive the new seal into the housing until it seats.

6. To complete the installation, reverse the removal procedures.

Timing Chain and Sprockets

Removal and Installation

2.9L ENGINE

1. Disconnect the negative battery cable. Drain the cooling system and the crankcase.

2. Rotate the engine until No. 1 cylinder is at TDC of it's compression stroke. Align the timing marks.

3. Remove the radiator and engine oil pan.

4. Remove the water pump and engine front cover.

5. With the sprockets aligned with their timing marks, release chain tensioner.

6. Remove the camshaft sprocket, timing chain and crankshaft sprocket.

To install:

7. Position the sprockets with the timing chain and install the sprocket/chain assembly onto the engine. Make sure the sprocket marks are aligned and apply tensioner pressure.

8. To complete the installation, reverse the removal procedures.

Timing Belt and Tensioner

Adjustment

2.3L ENGINE

1. Disconnect the negative battery cable and remove the front cover.

2. Loosen the belt tensioner adjustment and pivot bolts.

3. Loosen the tensioner adjustment bolt, allowing it to spring back against the belt.

4. Rotate the crankshaft 2 complete revolutions in the normal rotation direction to remove any belt slack. Turn the crankshaft until the timing marks are aligned.

5. Torque the tensioner adjustment bolt to 14–21 ft. lbs. (19–28 Nm).

6. To complete the installation, reverse the removal procedures. Adjust the accessory drive belt tension. Start the engine and check the ignition timing.

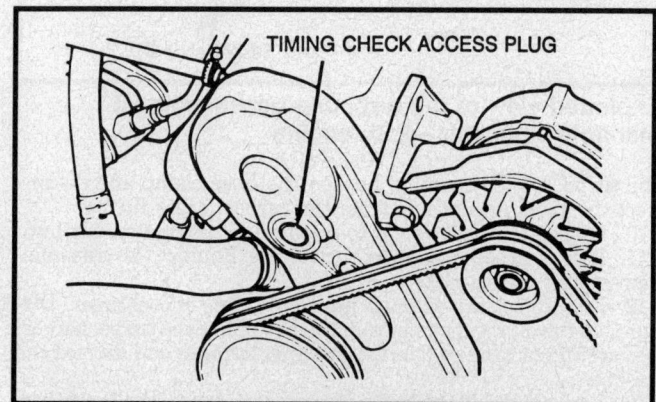

Location of access plug for checking valve timing visually

Correct timing mark alignment as viewed through the access hole

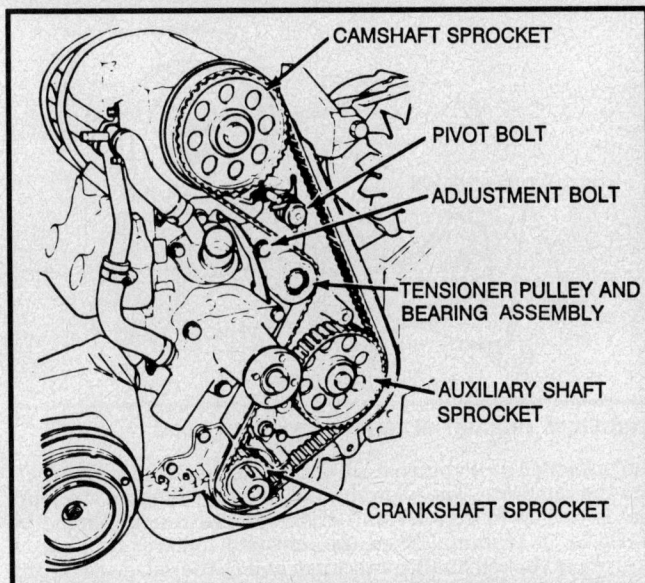

Location of timing belt tensioner, adjustment and pivot bolts

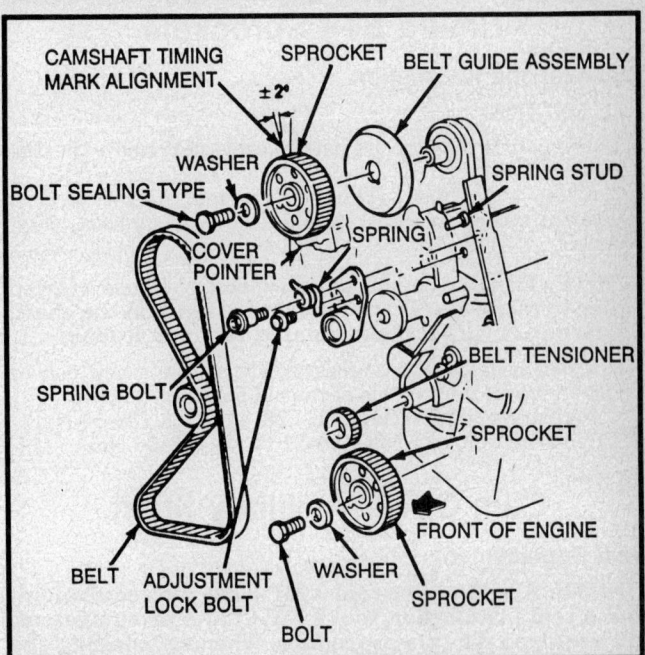

Exploded view of timing belt and sprocket assemblies

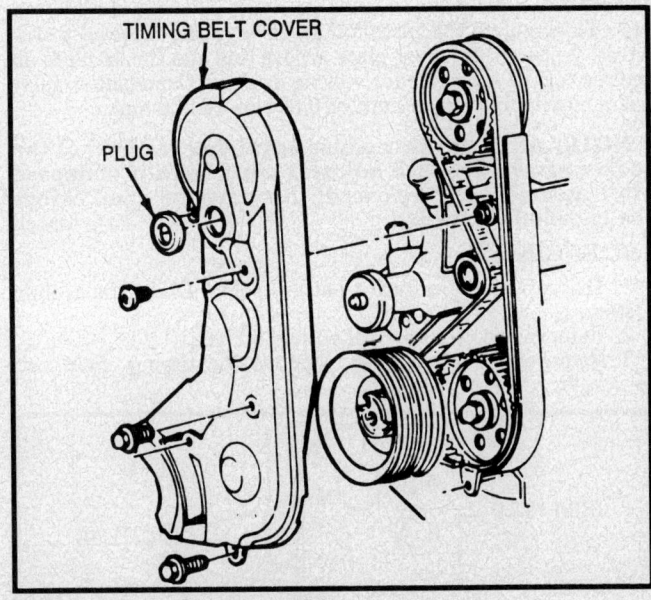

Timing belt cover assembly

Removal and Installation

2.3L ENGINE

Should the camshaft drive belt jump timing by a tooth or two, the engine could still run; but very poorly. To visually check for correct timing of the crankshaft, auxiliary shaft and the camshaft, follow this procedure.

An access plug is provided in the cam drive belt cover so the camshaft timing can be checked without removing the drive belt cover. Remove the access plug, turn the crankshaft until the timing mark on the crankshaft damper indicates TDC, and observe that the timing mark on the camshaft drive sprocket is aligned with the pointer on the inner belt cover. Also, the rotor of the distributor must align with No. 1 cylinder firing position.

CAUTION

Never turn the crankshaft of any of the overhead cam engines in the opposite direction of normal rotation. Backward rotation of the crankshaft may cause the timing belt to slip and alter the timing.

---

1. Set the engine at TDC as described above for checking valve timing. The crankshaft and camshaft timing marks should align with their respective pointers and the distributor rotor should point to the No. 1 plug tower.
2. Loosen the adjustment bolts on the alternator and accessories and remove the drive belts. To provide clearance for removing the camshaft belt, remove the fan and shroud assembly.
3. Remove the water pump pulley attaching bolts and the pulley from the water pump shaft. Remove the cover bolts and the timing belt outer cover.
4. Remove the crankshaft damper and pulley center bolt. Using a crankshaft damper puller tool T74P-6312-A or equivalent, remove the crankshaft damper from the crankshaft.
5. Loosen the belt tensioner adjustment and pivot bolts. Using the tensioner tool T74P-6254-A or equivalent, lever the tensioner away from the belt and retighten the adjustment bolt to hold it away.
6. Remove the camshaft drive belt.
To install:
7. Install the belt over the crankshaft pulley, then, counterclockwise over the auxiliary shaft sprocket and the camshaft sprocket. Adjust the belt so it is centered on the sprockets.
8. Loosen the tensioner adjustment bolt, allowing it to spring back against the belt.
9. Rotate the crankshaft 2 complete revolutions in the normal rotation direction to remove any belt slack. Turn the crankshaft until the timing marks are aligned. If the timing has slipped, remove the belt and repeat the procedure.
10. Torque the:
    Tensioner adjustment bolt—14–21 ft. lbs. (19–28 Nm)
    Pivot bolt—28–40 ft. lbs. (38–54 Nm)
11. Replace the belt guide and crankshaft pulley, belt outer cover, fan and pulley, drive belts and accessories. Adjust the accessory drive belt tension. Start the engine and check the ignition timing.

Timing Belt Sprockets

Removal and Installation

2.3L ENGINE

1. Disconnect the negative battery cable and remove the timing belt.
2. Using a sprocket holding/removal tool T74P-6256-B or equivalent, secure the sprockets and remove the sprocket center bolts.

NOTE: Do not hammer on the sprocket or use a jawed puller to remove it. If the sprocket is tight on the shaft, lightly tap it with a plastic mallet to break it loose.

3. When installing the sprockets, always use a new bolt or Teflon® tape on the threads of the old bolts. Torque the:
   Auxiliary shaft sprocket bolt—28–40 ft. lbs. (38–54 Nm)
   Camshaft sprocket bolt—50–71 ft. lbs. (68–96 Nm)

Cam Cover/Auxiliary Shaft

Seal Replacement

NOTE: A seal puller tool T74P-6700-B or equivalent, and a seal installation tool T74P-6150-A or equivalent, are required for this procedure. When reinstalling the drive sprockets, always use a new attaching bolt or Teflon® tape on the threads of the old bolts.

1. Disconnect the negative battery cable and remove the timing belt.
2. Remove the camshaft sprocket-to-camshaft bolt. Using a puller tool, remove the sprocket(s).

To install:

3. Install a seal puller and pull the seal from the bore.
4. Clean the mounting bore of the oil seal, take care not to damage the sealing surfaces.
5. Lubricate the inner and outer surfaces of the seal. Install the seal using the appropriate installation tool.
6. Reinstall the drive sprocket(s) and timing belt. Start the engine and check it's operation.

Camshaft

Removal and Installation

2.3L ENGINE

1. Disconnect the negative battery cable. Drain the cooling system.
2. Remove the camshaft drive belt, and the rocker arm (valve) cover (see various procedure sections).
3. Remove the fan and shroud assembly (if not previously removed). Remove the upper and lower radiator hoses. If equipped with an automatic transmission, disconnect and plug the transmission fluid cooler lines.
4. Raise and support the vehicle.
5. If clearance is a problem when removing the camshaft from the cylinder head, remove the front motor mount upper center nut. Position a piece of wood on a floor jack and raise the engine slowly as high as it will go. Place a piece of wood between the engine and mount brackets to support the engine in the raised position.
6. Lower the vehicle.
7. Remove the camshaft followers by compressing the valve springs and sliding them out from under the camshaft. Keep the followers in order so they may be installed in their original locations. Remove the camshaft sprocket and oil seal. Remove the camshaft retainer from the rear of the camshaft.
8. Slide the camshaft through the head supports carefully. Support the camshaft or bearing and lobe damage can occur. Inspect the camshaft for wear or damage and check the lobes and

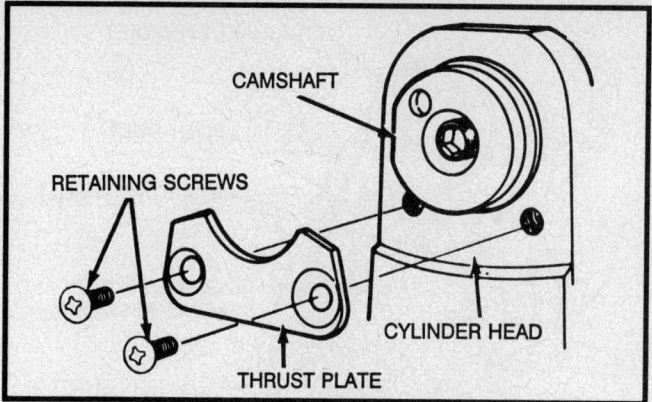

Camshaft retainer at rear of cylinder head

journals with a micrometer. All of the camshaft bearing journals are the same size. The allowable out-of-round limit on any journal is 0.0005 in. (0.0127mm) and the total runout should be 0.005 in. (0.127mm). Check the camshaft follower for wear or scoring at the camshaft contact pad and at the valve end. If any scoring or grooves are present, replace the follower.

To install:

9. Lubricate the camshaft lobes, bearings and bearing journals with heavy SF motor oil and reverse the removal procedures: be careful not to nick or scratch the camshaft bearings as the shaft is inserted.
10. To complete the installation, reverse the removal procedures. Inspect the thrust plate groove and the thrust plate on the rear of the camshaft for scoring or wear. Camshaft endplay has a maximum service limit of 0.009 in. (0.229mm).

NOTE: After any procedure requiring removal of the rocker arms, each lash adjuster must be fully collapsed after assembly and released; this must be done before the camshaft is turned.

2.9L ENGINE

1. Disconnect the negative battery cable. Drain the cooling system.
2. Remove the radiator and engine oil pan.
3. Remove the front cover. Remove the timing chain and sprockets.

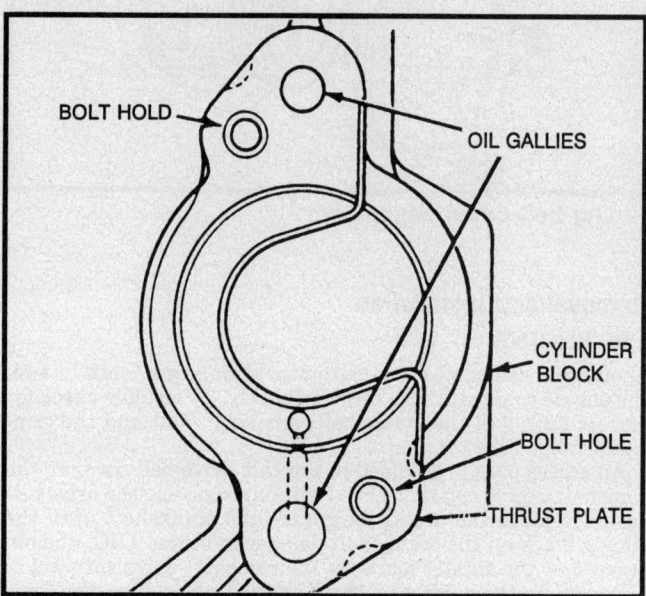

Installing the thrust plate—2.9L engine

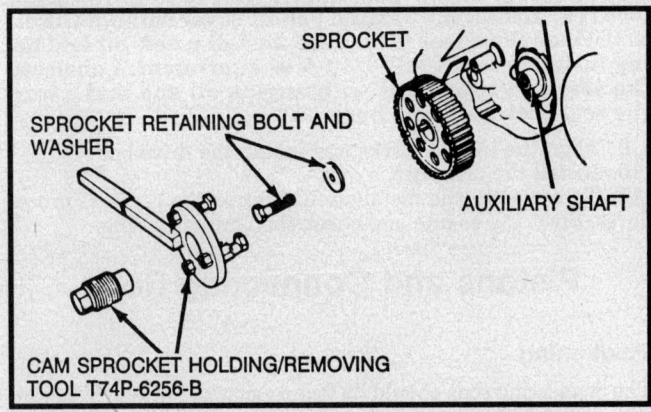

Auxiliary shaft sprocket removal showing puller/holder tool

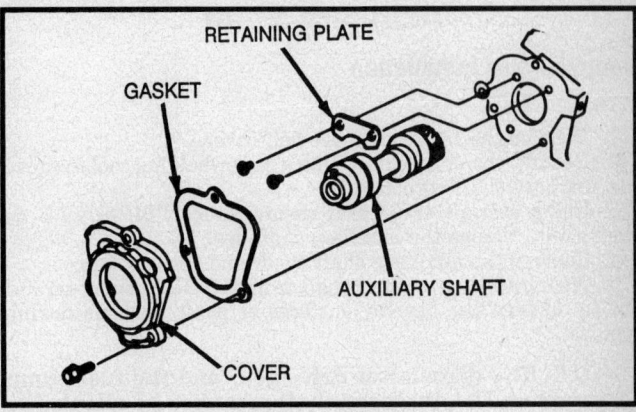

Auxiliary shaft and cover assembly

4. Loosen the air conditioning condenser mounting bolts. Remove the upper and lower engine insulator retaining nuts and washers.

5. Remove the grille retaining screws. Lift the grille upward to disengage the lower locating tabs and remove the grille.

6. Remove the air conditioning condenser retaining bolts and lower the condenser and electric fan assembly to the floor.

7. Remove the intake manifold, cylinder heads and valve tappets. Raise the engine enough, with a floor jack, to permit the camshaft to clear the upper edge of the front bumper. Remove the camshaft thrust plate mounting bolts and the camshaft.

To install:

8. Lubricate the camshaft journals and lobes with heavy SF oil. Install the camshaft carefully into the engine block.

9. Install the thrust plate, torque the mounting bolts to 13–16 ft. lbs. (17–21 Nm). Position the engine insulators and loosely install the upper washers and nuts.

10. Install the timing chain and sprockets.

11. Install the front cover, water pump etc.

12. To complete the installation, reverse the removal procedures. Adjust the valves. Check and adjust the ignition timing.

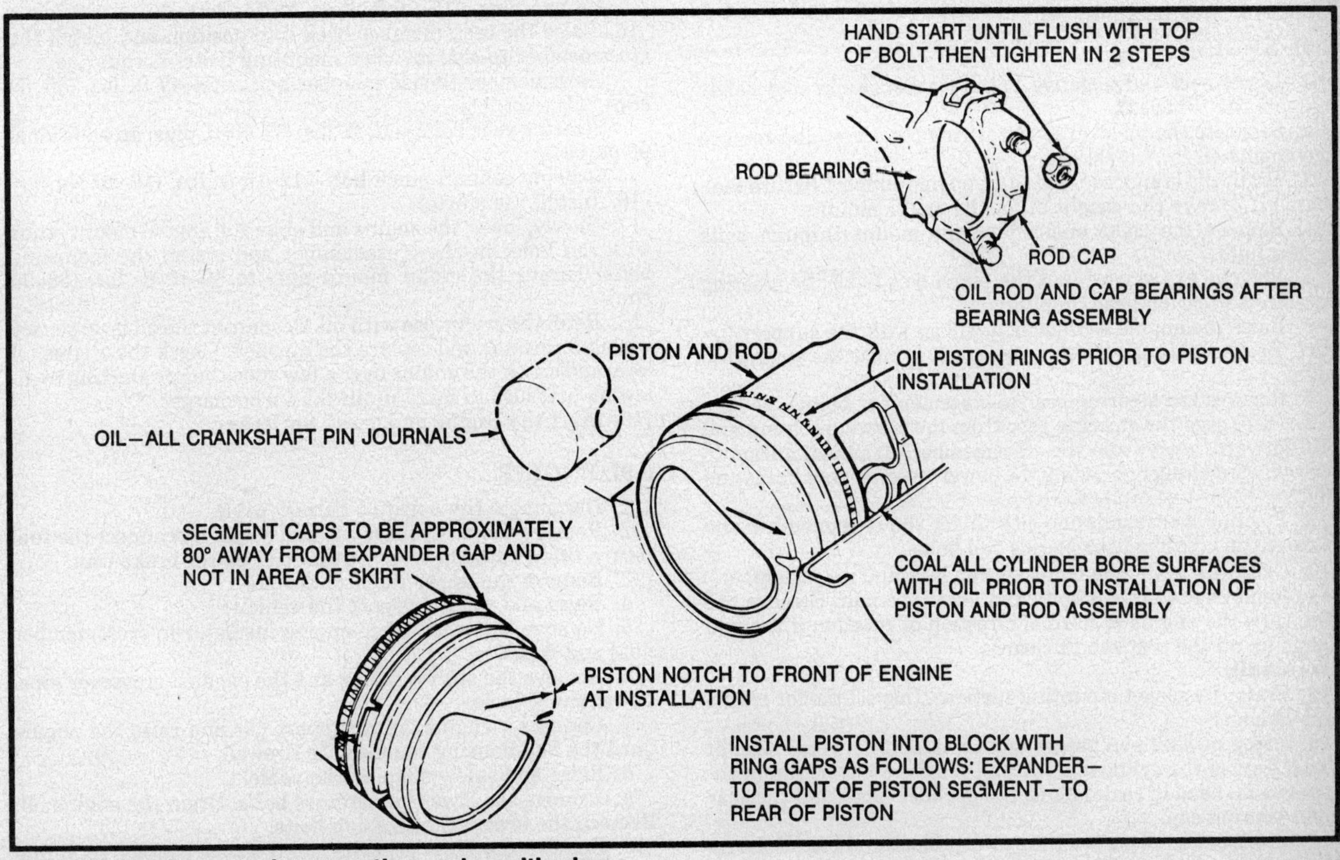

View of the piston and connecting rod positioning

Auxiliary Shaft

Removal and Installation

2.3L ENGINE

1. Remove the camshaft drive belt cover.
2. Remove the drive belt. Using a puller/holding tool, remove the auxiliary shaft sprocket.
3. Using a front cover seal remover tool T74P-6700-B or equivalent, remove the auxiliary shaft seal.
4. Remove the auxiliary shaft cover and thrust plate.
5. Withdraw the auxiliary shaft from the block, being careful not to damage the bearing surfaces or shaft journals during removal.

NOTE: The distributor drive gear and the fuel pump eccentric on the auxiliary shaft must not be allowed to touch the auxiliary shaft bearings during removal and installation.

To install:
6. Lubricate the shaft with heavy SF engine oil before sliding it into place.
7. Slide the auxiliary shaft into the housing and insert the thrust plate to hold the shaft.
8. Using a new gasket and auxiliary shaft cover, torque the cover bolts to 6–9 ft. lbs. (8–12 Nm).

NOTE: Install the auxiliary shaft cover without the oil seal. Once the cover is in place, install a new oil seal using installer tool T74P-6150-A or equivalent. Lubricate the seal and cover seat with engine oil and make sure the seal bottoms in its bore.

9. Align the timing marks and install the drive belt.
10. Install the drive belt cover.
11. To complete the installation, reverse the removal procedures. Start the engine and check the ignition timing.

Pistons and Connecting Rods

Positioning

The connecting rods should be factory marked with cylinder location numbers on the rod and bearing cap edges. If factory marks are not present, match mark both the rod and cap numerically and in sequence from the front to the back of the engine. The numbers not only tell from which cylinder the piston and rod came from but also insures that the rod caps are installed in correct matching position with the connecting rod. The piston is marked with a notch indicating front position for installation. Ring gaps should be spaced with the compression rings approximately 2 in. (50mm) apart on opposite sides of the oil ring gaps.

ENGINE LUBRICATION

Oil Pan

Removal and Installation

2.3L ENGINE

1. Disconnect the negative battery cable. Raise and safely support the vehicle.
2. Separate the oil level sensor wiring connector and remove the engine oil level dipstick.
3. Drain the crankcase. Using an engine support fixture tool, install it to take the weight off of the motor mounts.
4. Remove the right and left engine mount through bolts and/or nuts.
5. Remove the starter and the pinch bolt from the steering column-to-steering gear coupling.
6. Raise the engine as high as it will go with the support fixture. Be careful if using a shop crane not to raise the engine too high.
7. Remove the steering gear-to-crossmember bolts.
8. Disengage the steering gear from the steering column and pull forward, away from the crossmember. Exercise caution to prevent stretching or bending the power steering gear hoses and lines.
9. Position a transmission jack under the crossmember and remove the crossmember-to-side rail bolts.
10. Carefully lower the transmission jack and crossmember.
11. Remove the oil pan bolts and lower the pan. Remove the pan, turn the engine in normal direction of rotation if the pan hangs up on the crankshaft throws.
To install:
12. Clean the gasket mounting surfaces. Inspect the for cracks and damage.
13. Using new oil pan gasket and seals, apply a ¼ in. bead of sealant along the cylinder block and the front cover. Apply another ¼ in. bead of sealer along the cylinder block and the rear main bearing cap.
14. Position the oil pan on the cylinder block and install the retaining bolts. Torque the:

Oil pan-to-front cover bolts – 8–10 ft. lbs. (11–13 Nm)
Oil pan-to-cylinder block bolts – 6–8 ft. lbs. (8–11 Nm)
Oil pan plug – 15–25 ft. lbs. (20–34 Nm)
15. Raise the crossmember back into position and install the crossmember-to-side member mounting bolts. Torque the:
Crossmember-to-side member bolts – 38–47 ft. lbs. (56–64 Nm)
Steering gear bolts – 10 ft. lbs. (15 Nm), plus, an additional 90 degrees
Steering column pinch bolt – 12–15 ft. lbs. (16–20 Nm)
16. Install the starter.
17. Slowly, lower the engine and align the engine mount studs with the holes in the crossmember and install the mounting bolts. Torque the motor mount nuts to 50–70 ft. lbs. (68–95 Nm).
18. Refill the crankcase with oil. Reconnect the oil level sensor wiring connector and replace the dipstick. Check the engine oil level and crank the engine over a few times before starting to allow oil pressure to build up in the turbocharger.
19. Start the engine and check for leaks.

2.9L ENGINE

1. Disconnect the negative battery cable.
2. Remove the distributor cap and rotor. Disconnect the fuel return line located in front of the ABS power brake unit.
3. Remove the upper radiator shroud.
4. Raise and safely support the vehicle.
5. Remove the both lower engine insulator-to-crossmember nuts and washers.
6. Remove the starter motor and the exhaust crossover pipe. Lower the vehicle.
7. Connect a engine cross support bar and raise the engine until the bell housing touches the firewall.
8. Raise and safely support the vehicle.
9. Remove the lower heater hose bolts. Drain the engine oil. Remove the lower transmission bolts.
10. Remove the lower steering shaft flange coupler retaining nuts and bolts.

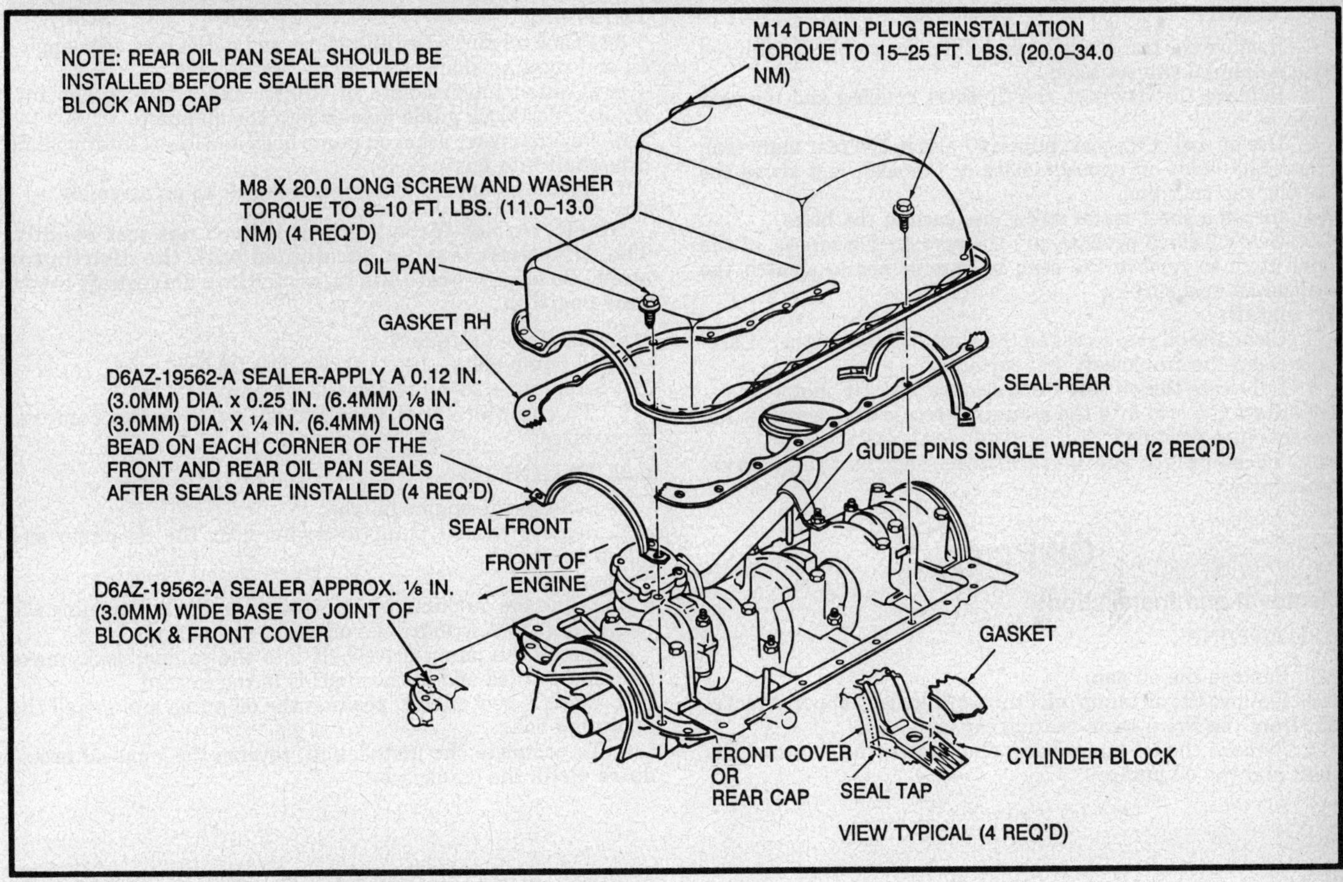

NOTE: REAR OIL PAN SEAL SHOULD BE INSTALLED BEFORE SEALER BETWEEN BLOCK AND CAP

M14 DRAIN PLUG REINSTALLATION TORQUE TO 15–25 FT. LBS. (20.0–34.0 NM)

M8 X 20.0 LONG SCREW AND WASHER TORQUE TO 8–10 FT. LBS. (11.0–13.0 NM) (4 REQ'D)

OIL PAN

GASKET RH

D6AZ-19562-A SEALER-APPLY A 0.12 IN. (3.0MM) DIA. x 0.25 IN. (6.4MM) ⅛ IN. (3.0MM) DIA. X ¼ IN. (6.4MM) LONG BEAD ON EACH CORNER OF THE FRONT AND REAR OIL PAN SEALS AFTER SEALS ARE INSTALLED (4 REQ'D)

SEAL-REAR

GUIDE PINS SINGLE WRENCH (2 REQ'D)

SEAL FRONT

FRONT OF ENGINE

D6AZ-19562-A SEALER APPROX. ⅛ IN. (3.0MM) WIDE BASE TO JOINT OF BLOCK & FRONT COVER

GASKET

FRONT COVER OR REAR CAP

SEAL TAP

CYLINDER BLOCK

VIEW TYPICAL (4 REQ'D)

Exploded view of the oil pan assembly—2.3L engine

11. Place a floor jack under the No. 1 crossmember. Remove the front flexible brake line attaching clips.

12. Remove the crossmember bolts and lower the crossmember 2 inches.

13. Remove the oil pan attaching nuts/bolts and the oil pan.

To install:

14. Clean the gasket mounting surfaces.

15. Apply sealant to the cylinder block. Install the bearing cap; be sure the bearing cap is installed flush with the cylinder block rear face.

16. Apply silicone rubber sealant to the oil pan surfaces and to the main bearing gasket wedges. Position the gasket wedges in the bearing cap grooves.

17. Using a new oil pan gasket, install the pan-to-cylinder block nuts and bolts.

18. To complete the installation, reverse the removal procedures.

Rear Main Oil Seal

Removal and Installation

2.3L ENGINE

1. Remove the transmission, clutch and flywheel or driveplate.

2. Punch 2 holes in the crankshaft rear oil seal on opposite sides of the crankshaft just above the bearing cap to cylinder block split line.

3. Install a sheet metal screw in each of the holes or use a small slide hammer and pry the crankshaft rear main oil seal from the block.

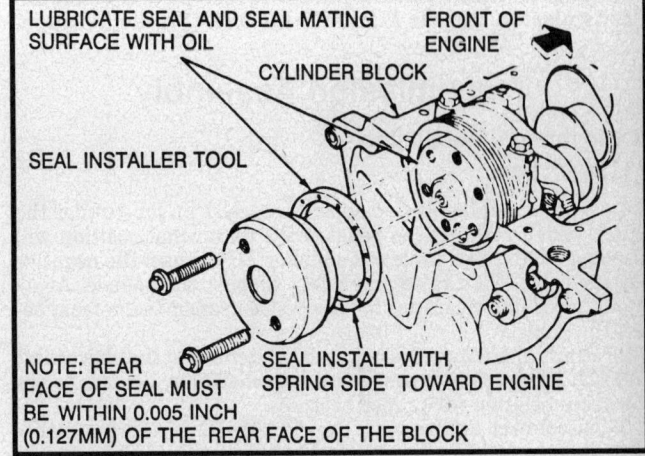

LUBRICATE SEAL AND SEAL MATING SURFACE WITH OIL

FRONT OF ENGINE

CYLINDER BLOCK

SEAL INSTALLER TOOL

NOTE: REAR FACE OF SEAL MUST BE WITHIN 0.005 INCH (0.127MM) OF THE REAR FACE OF THE BLOCK

SEAL INSTALL WITH SPRING SIDE TOWARD ENGINE

Rear main oil seal installation

NOTE: Use extreme caution not to scratch the crankshaft oil seal surface. Clean the oil seal recess in the cylinder block and main bearing cap.

To install:

4. Lubricate the seal and the seal mounting surfaces with oil.

5. Install the seal in the recess, driving it in place with an oil seal installation tool or a large socket.

6. To complete the installation, reverse the removal procedures.

2.9L ENGINE

1. Remove the transmission and clutch assembly, if equipped with a manual transmission.
2. Remove the flywheel, the flywheel housing and the rear plate.
3. Use an awl or ice pick, punch 2 holes in the rear main seal; punch the holes on opposite sides of the seal, just above the bearing cap split line.
4. Install a sheet metal screw into each of the holes.
5. Using 2 small prybars, pry outward on the screws, at the same time to remove the seal; be careful not to scratch the crankshaft seal surface.

To install:

6. Clean the oil seal recess an the block and bearing cap. Carefully clean the crankshaft seal surface.
7. Lubricate the oil seal block surface with SF motor oil.
8. Start the seal into the mounting recess and carefully tap the seal into position.
9. To complete the installation, reverse the removal procedures.

Oil Pump

Removal and Installation

2.3L ENGINE

1. Remove the oil pan.
2. Remove the oil pump inlet tube and screen support bracket nut from the No. 4 main bearing cap.
3. Remove the oil pump bolts, the gasket, the intermediate shaft and the oil pump.

To install:

4. Prime oil pump by filling inlet and outlet port with engine oil and rotating shaft of pump to distribute it.
5. Position intermediate driveshaft and retaining clip into the cylinder block guide hole or into the oil pump.
6. Position new gasket on pump body and insert intermediate driveshaft into pump body.
7. Install pump and intermediate shaft as an assembly.

NOTE: Do not force pump if it does not seat readily. The driveshaft may be misaligned with the distributor shaft. To align, rotate the intermediate driveshaft into a new position.

8. Install and torque the:
   Oil pump bolts — 14–21 ft. lbs. (19–28 Nm)
   Strap nut — 28–40 ft. lbs. (38–54 Nm)
9. To complete the installation, reverse the removal procedures.

2.9L ENGINE

1. Remove the engine oil pan.
2. Remove the oil pump-to-engine bolt, the oil pump and pump driveshaft.

To install:

3. Prime the oil pump by filling it with oil while turning the pump shaft to distribute the oil inside the pump.
4. Install the pump driveshaft into the engine block; make sure the pointed end of the shaft is facing inward.
5. Using a new gasket, position the oil pump and install the mounting bolts.
6. To complete the installation, reverse the removal procedures. Refill the crankcase.

MANUAL TRANSMISSION

For further information, please refer to "Professional Transmission Repair Manual" for additional coverage.

Transmission Assembly

Removal and Installation

2.3L ENGINE

1. Wedge a block of wood approximately 7 in. long under the clutch pedal. Holding the pedal above its normal position will disengage the clutch cable self adjuster. Disconnect the negative battery cable, then raise and safely support the vehicle. Allow enough working clearance to remove the transmission from below the vehicle.
2. Drain the transmission fluid. Matchmark the driveshaft and rear companion flange so the driveshaft may be installed in the same position for proper balance.
3. Disconnect and remove the driveshaft. Install a suitable plug in the extension housing seal to prevent fluid leakage during service.
4. Remove the nuts attaching the catalytic converter inlet pipe to the turbocharger. Remove the catalytic converter outlet-to-muffler inlet flange nuts and the catalytic converter support bracket. Remove the catalytic converter and inlet pipe as an assembly.

NOTE: If the engine is started for any reason just prior to transmission removal, allow sufficient time for the catalytic converter to cool before attempting removal procedures. The normal converter operating temperature can cause severe burns.

5. Remove the starter.
6. Remove the front stabilizer bar to body U-brackets and the body stiffener rod.
7. Remove the transmission air baffle, if equipped. Position a block of wood between the stabilizer bar and the body side rail.
8. Support the transmission with a floor jack. Remove the rear transmission mount to transmission mounting bolts. Remove the transmission support member.
9. Loosen the engine mount attaching nuts until only 2–3 threads are visible on the end of the stud. Position a block of wood against the engine oil pan and raise the engine. Raise engine until the stud nuts on the engine mounts contact the crossmember.
10. As the engine tilts downward, lower the transmission jack slightly and remove the Torx® bolts that mount the shift lever. Remove the shift lever from the extension housing.
11. Disconnect the back-up light and neutral safety switch wiring harness connectors. Remove the snapring and pull the speedometer cable out of the extension housing.
12. Remove the clutch release lever cover and pull rearward on the clutch release cable to disengage it from the release lever.
13. Remove the speedometer cable routing clip screws (2 places) and move the cable aside on the left side of the vehicle. Remove the transmission-to-flywheel housing bolts.
14. Slide the transmission rearward until the flywheel housing contacts the body. Raise the rear of the transmission and pull it rearward to clear the body, then, back and away from the engine and lower to the ground. Lower the engine slightly, if necessary for clearance.

To install:

15. Align the transmission input shaft with the clutch pressure plate and push the transmission forward until the flywheel

housing contacts the body. Raise the rear of the transmission as necessary to clear the body, lower it and push it into position. Rock the transmission slightly to align the input shaft and clutch disc splines.

NOTE: Exercise caution to prevent damage to the transmission pilot bearing in the end of the crankshaft.

16. Install the shifter into the extension housing and torque the mounting bolts to 16–19 ft. lbs. (21–26 Nm).

17. Continue installation and make sure the mounting surface of the transmission and flywheel housing are free of dirt and burrs.

18. Install 2 guide pins in the lower flywheel housing bolt holes (bolts with the heads cut off). Raise the transmission and move it forward on the guide pins until the input shaft splines enter the clutch hub splines and the case is against the flywheel housing. Torque the:

Flywheel housing-to-engine bolts – 28–38 ft. lbs. (38–51 Nm)

Engine mount stud nuts – 50–70 ft. lbs. (68–95 Nm)

Rear transmission mount – 25–35 ft. lbs. (34–48 Nm)

2.9L ENGINE

1. Disconnect the negative battery cable. Wedge a wood block approximately 7 inches long under the clutch pedal. Holding it the above its normal position will disengage the clutch cable self adjuster.

2. Disconnect the negative battery cable. Remove the distributor cap and rotor.

3. Unscrew and remove the gear shift lever knob. Remove the center console screws and the console. Remove the shift lever boot, the center console bracket, frame and noise dampening pad.

4. Remove the gear lever-to-extension housing screws and the gear shift lever assembly.

5. Disconnect the oxygen sensor wiring connector located in the engine compartment. Remove the wiring from the retaining clip.

6. Raise and safely support the vehicle. Drain the transmission fluid. Remove the stabilizer bar-to-side members bolts.

7. Remove the ground strap from the exhaust pipe. Remove the exhaust system from the exhaust manifolds to the front muffler. Remove the converter heat shield.

8. Scribe a mark on the rear driveshaft and differential yokes for installation reference. Remove the rear shaft mounting bolts. Remove the driveshaft center support bolts and slide the driveshaft from the back of the transmission.

9. Support the engine by placing a block of wood between the oil pan and floor jack. Remove the radio ground strap, the transmission rear mount nuts and the mount.

10. Disconnect the speedometer sensor, speedometer sensor ground strap, neutral gear start switch and the back-up light switch.

11. Disconnect the electrical connectors from the starter and remove the starter.

12. Pull the clutch lever dust boot aside and disconnect the clutch cable from the release lever. Remove the clutch cable and dust boot from the housing.

13. Remove the rear engine cover plate from the bell housing. Support the transmission with a jack. Remove the engine-to-bell housing bolts and the starter heat shield.

14. Lower the engine and transmission jacks slightly. Pull the transmission rearward. Adjust the jacks and pull the transmission until it separates from the engine. Lower the transmission and remove it from the vehicle.

To install:

15. Position the transmission and start the mainshaft into the clutch disc; adjust the supporting jacks, as necessary. Turn the engine slightly, if necessary, to engage the mainshaft with the clutch disc splines. Torque the:

Transmission-to-engine bolts – 28–38 ft. lbs. (38–51 Nm)

Transmission mount – 25–35 ft. lbs. (34–48 Nm)

Center driveshaft mount bolts – 13–17 ft. lbs. (18–23 Nm)

Rear driveshaft mounting bolts – 42–55 ft. lbs. (57–75 Nm)

CLUTCH

Clutch Assembly

Removal and Installation

1. Lift the clutch pedal to it's uppermost position to disengage the pawl and quadrant. Push the quadrant forward, unhook the clutch cable and allow the quadrant to slowly swing rearward.

2. Disconnect the negative battery cable. Raise and safely support the vehicle.

3. Disconnect the cable from the clutch release lever.

4. Remove the clutch cable from the flywheel housing.

5. Disconnect the starter motor cable and remove the starter motor. Remove the lower shield from the flywheel housing.

6. Remove the transmission.

7. Remove the flywheel housing. If the pressure plate is being reused, paint or scribe alignment marks on the pressure plate and flywheel so they may be assembled in their original positions.

8. Loosen the pressure plate-to-flywheel bolts, evenly, in rotation, to release the spring pressure gradually. Remove the pressure plate and clutch disc.

9. Remove the clutch release bearing from the release lever. Inspect the lever and bearing for wear and replace as necessary.

NOTE: The clutch release bearing is lubricated and permanently sealed during manufacture. Never wash or soak the bearing in cleaning solvent or it will ruin the bearing.

To install:

10. Using an alignment tool, install and align the clutch disc and pressure plate; make sure the clutch disc is installed with the correct side facing the flywheel.

NOTE: A new disc will be stamped flywheel to indicate the correct installation, but the disc is installed properly if the damper springs face away from the flywheel. The 3 dowel pins on the flywheel must be properly aligned with the pressure plate. Avoid touching the disc surface and start the pressure plate mounting bolts slowly and evenly to avoid distortion.

11. Torque the pressure plate-to-flywheel bolts, evenly, in sequence, to 15–19 ft. lbs. (20–25 Nm).

12. To complete the installation, reverse the removal procedures. Check and/or adjust the clutch operation.

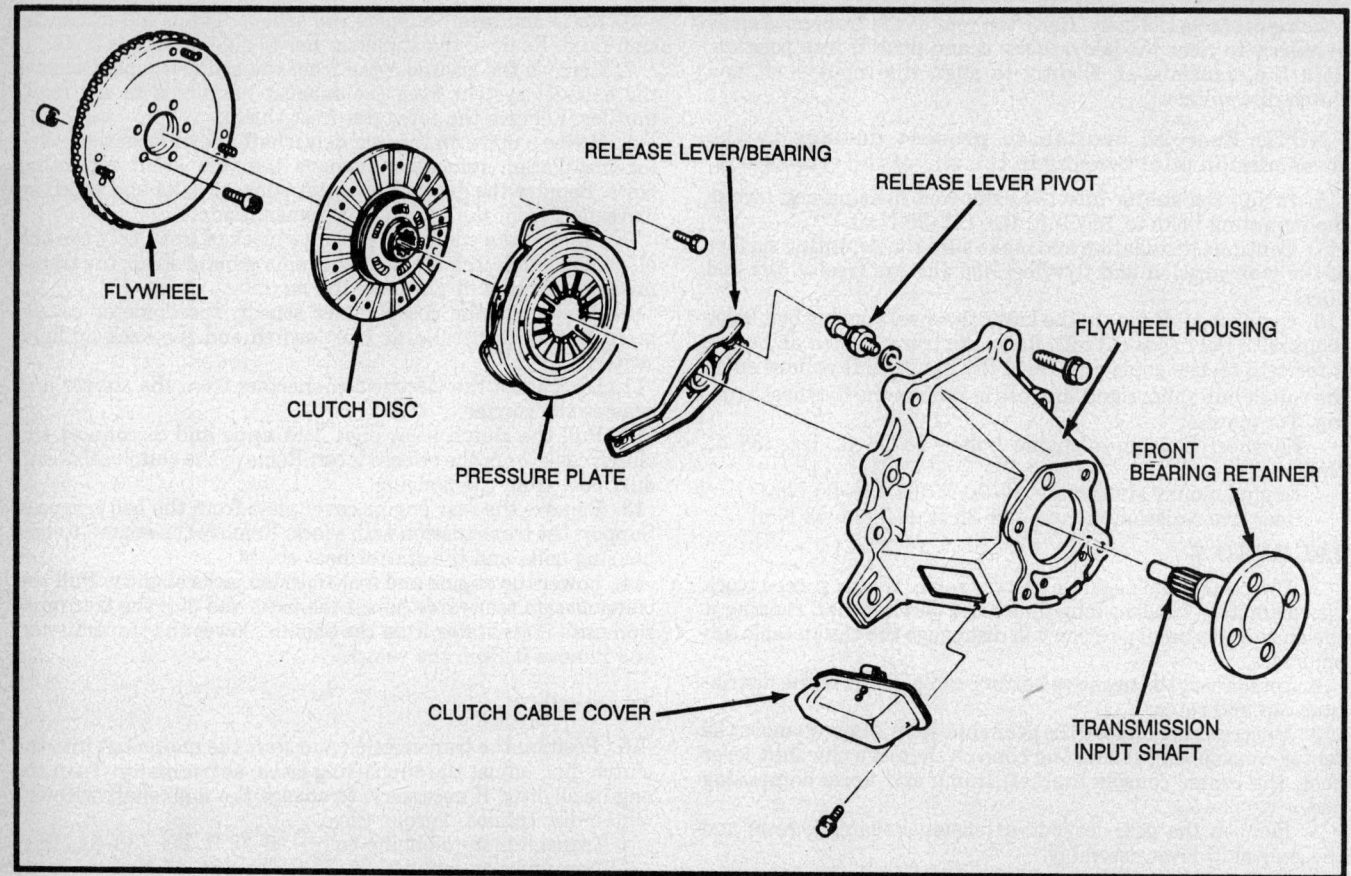

Exploded view of the clutch assembly—2.3L engine

Adjustments

The clutch free play is self adjusting during normal operation. The self adjusting feature should be checked every 5000 miles. This is accomplished by insuring that the clutch pedal travels to the top of it's upward position.

1. Grasp the clutch pedal by hand or place a foot under the pedal, then pull up on the pedal until it stops. Very little effort is required (about 10 lbs.).

2. During the application of upward pressure, a click may be heard which means an adjustment was necessary and has been accomplished.

Clutch Cable

Removal and Installation

1. Hold the clutch pedal above it's normal position to disengage the clutch cable self adjuster.
2. Raise and safely support the vehicle. Remove the clutch release lever cover.
3. Pull rearward on the cable to disengage it from the release lever. The sound panels under the left side of the dashboard must be removed to gain access to the clutch cable routing through the body.
4. Install the replacement cable using the same routing as the old cable, unless the reason for cable replacement was binding or wear due to sharp turns in the cable.

AUTOMATIC TRANSMISSION

For further information, please refer to "Professional Transmission Repair Manual" for additional coverage.

Transmission Assembly

Removal and Installation

1. Disconnect the negative battery cable and remove the transmission dipstick. Raise and safely support the vehicle.
2. Place a drain pan under the transmission fluid pan. Starting at the rear of the pan and working forward, loosen the bolts and allow the fluid to drain. Remove all of the oil pan bolts except 2 at the front, to allow the fluid to further drain. After all the fluid has drained, install 2 bolts on the rear side of the pan to temporarily hold it in place.
3. Disconnect the oxygen sensor harness and unclip the wires from the securing clip. Remove the starter motor. On 4 cylinder engines, remove the catalytic converter inlet pipe-to-turbocharger nuts. Remove the support bracket bolt and the catalytic converter and inlet pipe as an assembly. On V6 models remove the exhaust system from the exhaust manifolds to the front muffler. Remove the converter heat shield.

4. Remove the stabilizer bar U-brackets and the body stiffener rod, then, position a block of wood between the stabilizer bar and the body side rail.

5. Remove the torque converter drain plug access cover and adapter plate bolts from the lower end of the converter housing.

6. Remove the torque converter-to-drive plate nuts through the starter opening. Remove the converter drain plug and drain the converter. Reinstall the plug. Turn the engine in normal direction of rotation to gain access to the converter nuts and drain plug, using a wrench on the crankshaft pulley bolt.

NOTE: If equipped with a 2.3L engine, do not turn the engine counter-clockwise; backward rotation may cause the valve timing belt to jump time.

7. Remove the driveshaft and plug the extension housing to prevent dirt entry and fluid loss during service.

8. Using a floor jack, support the transmission and secure it with a safety chain. Remove the rear mount-to-transmission support bracket bolts. Remove the nuts attaching the rear mount to the body and remove the mount.

9. Disconnect the shift rod from the transmission lever and the downshift rod from the transmission downshift lever.

10. Disconnect the neutral start switch wires and the speedometer cable from the transmission.

11. Remove the vacuum line from the transmission vacuum modulator and the transmission filler tube.

12. Disconnect the transmission cooler lines using quick connect removal tool T82L-9500-AH or equivalent.

13. Remove the upper converter housing bolts.

14. Remove the crossmember-to-frame side support bolts and the crossmember.

15. Lower the transmission slightly. Place a piece of wood on a floorjack and support the engine.

16. Pull the transmission back and away from the engine slowly. Make sure the converter is mounted fully on the transmission and not stuck on the driveplate.

17. Lower the transmission and converter and remove it from beneath the vehicle.

To install:

18. Reverse the removal procedures: make sure the torque converter hub is fully engaged in the pump gear. Torque the:
    Converter housing-to-engine bolt—28–38 ft. lbs. (38–51 Nm)
    Torque converter-to-flywheel nuts—12–16 ft. lbs. (27–46 Nm)—2.3L engine
    Torque converter-to-flywheel nuts—22–30 ft. lbs. (29–41 Nm)—2.9L engine

19. If the transmission was completely drained, add 2 quarts of fluid before starting the engine. Start the engine, check the fluid level with the dipstick and top off as necessary.

Pan and Filter Service

1. Raise and safely support the vehicle.

2. Place a drain pan under the oil pan, then start at the rear of the pan and work forward loosening the pan bolts until the fluid starts to drain. Slowly remove the pan bolts, leaving 2 on 1 side for last, until the pan tilts down and the remaining fluid drains.

3. Remove the remaining bolts and lower the oil pan.

4. Remove the transmission filter attaching screws and lower the filter from the valve body.

To install:

5. Clean the gasket mating surfaces.

6. Install the oil filter gasket and the new oil filter. Torque the bolts to 6–8 ft. lbs. (8–11 Nm).

7. Install the oil pan and gasket. Torque the attaching bolts to 12–17 ft. lbs. (16–23 Nm). Refill the transmission.

Linkage Adjustments

XR4Ti

C3 Transmission

1. Raise and safely the vehicle.

2. Remove the retaining clip and disengage the shift rod from the selector lever.

3. Rotate the transmission shift lever forward, as far as possible; this is the **DRIVE 1** or **LOW** position.

4. Rotate the transmission shift lever 2 detent positions rearward; this is the **DRIVE** position.

5. Move the gearshift lever to the **DRIVE** position as indicated by the shifter. Without moving the transmission or gearshift levers, attempt to slide the shift rod clevis over the selector lever pin. If the clevis slides on the pin, the linkage is properly adjusted.

6. If the clevis does not slide onto the pin, loosen the locknut and thread the clevis in or out to obtain the proper fit. After making the adjustment, tighten the clevis locknut.

7. Install the selector rod retaining clip and lower the vehicle.

8. Check transmission in each selector position.

NOTE: Make sure the linkage adjustment has not affected the operation of the neutral safety switch. With the parking brake set and service brakes applied firmly, try to start the engine in each gearshift position. The engine should crank only in N and P positions; if the engine cranks in any other shifter position, check the linkage adjustment and neutral safety switch.

SCORPIO

A4LD Transmission

1. Position the selector lever in the **D** position.

2. Raise and safely support the vehicle.

3. Remove the retaining clip and disengage the shift rod from the selector lever.

4. Rotate the transmission shift lever forward, as far as possible; this is the **DRIVE 1** or **LOW** position.

5. Rotate the lever 3 detent positions rearward; this is the **DRIVE** or **D** position.

6. Without moving the transmission shift lever or selector lever, attempt to slide the shift rod clevis over the selector lever pin. If the clevis slides onto the pin, the linkage is in proper adjustment. If the clevis does not slide onto the pin, loosen the locknut and thread the clevis in or out to obtain proper fit.

7. After making the adjustment, tighten the locknut and install the selector rod retaining clip.

Kickdown Adjustment

1. Using a pair of pliers, remove the kickdown cable retaining clip located near the throttle body routing bracket.

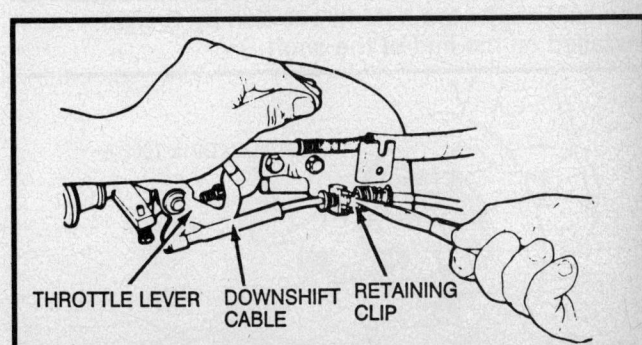

THROTTLE LEVER   DOWNSHIFT CABLE   RETAINING CLIP

Kickdown cable adjustment. Hold the throttle lever in the wide open position and install the cable clip, then release the lever

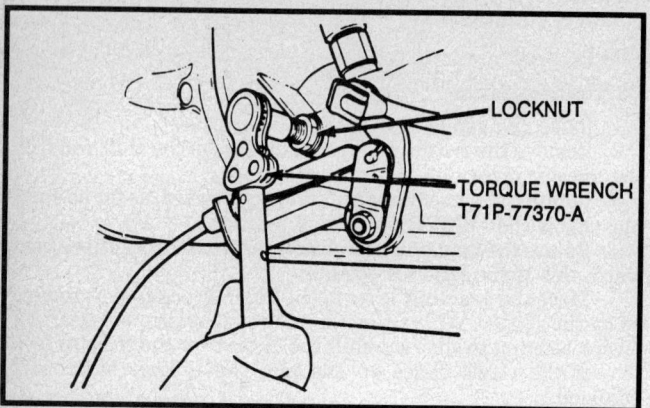

Front band adjustment

2. Rotate the throttle body lever to the wide open position and hold it there.

3. While holding the throttle open, install the cable retaining clip, then release the throttle lever.

Front Band Adjustment

XR4Ti

C3 Transmission

1. Raise and safely support the vehicle.
2. Clean all of the dirt and grease from around the band adjusting screw area.
3. Remove and discard the band adjusting screw locknut. Install a new locknut on the screw, but do not tighten it.
4. Using an accurate torque wrench, torque the adjusting screw to 10 ft. lbs. (14 Nm) and back it off 2 turns.
5. Hold the adjusting screw from turning and torque the locknut to 35–45 ft. lbs. (48–61 Nm).

DRIVE AXLE

Halfshafts

Power is transferred to the rear wheels by independent axle halfshafts. Each shaft is equipped with both an inner and an outer constant velocity joint. CV-joints require care during servicing to avoid causing damage to machined surfaces and splines. Never allow a CV-joint to hang by it's own weight; wire the shaft to the underbody to support it during service procedures.

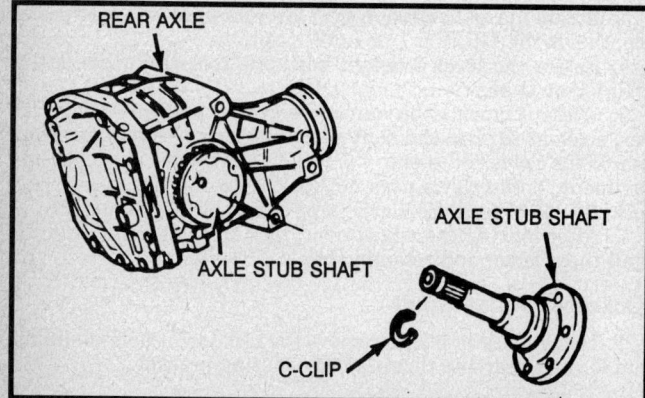

The axle shafts are held in position by C-clips installed on the end of the shaft

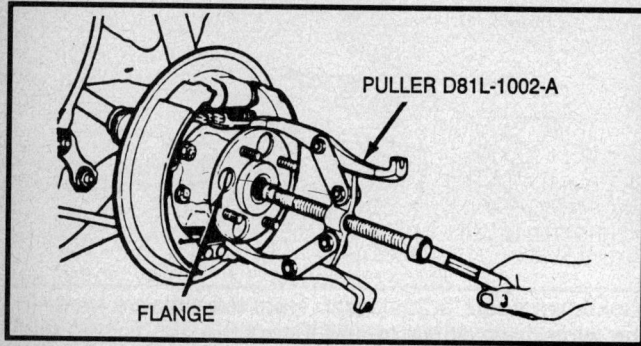

Remove the rear axle drive flange with a puller

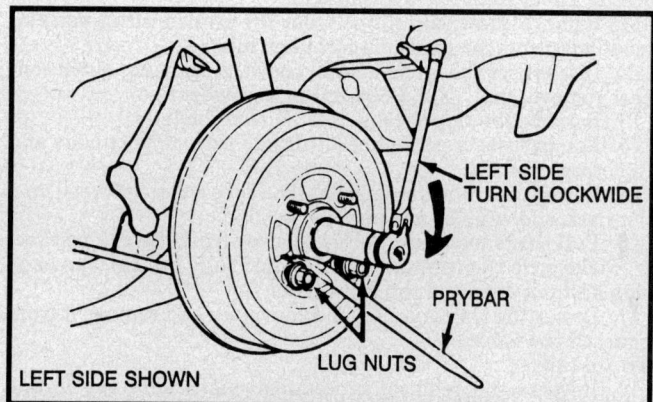

Use a prybar as shown when removing or installing the rear axle flange locknut

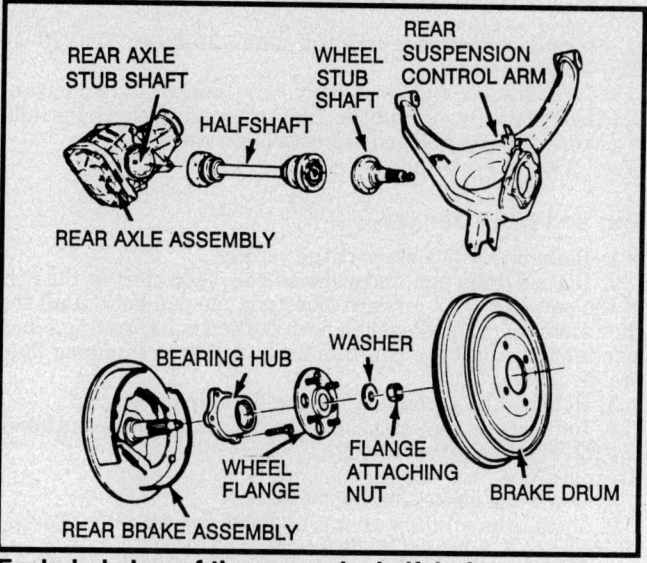

Exploded view of the rear axle, halfshaft and hub assembly

Removal and Installation

1. Raise and safely support the vehicle with the rear wheels hanging freely. Make sure the transmission is in **N** and the parking brake is fully released.
2. Remove the flange bolts on the outside joint at the wheel stub shaft. Rotate the halfshaft to bring the flange bolts around.
3. Remove the flange bolts at the differential stub shaft only after securing the outer end of the halfshaft with wire or rope to the vehicle underbody.
4. Use a wide, flat-blade prybar to separate the flanges, if necessary, but be careful not to damage any mating surfaces.
5. Carefully lower the axle driveshaft down and out. Handle the CV-joints with care; they can be damaged if dropped.

NOTE: The halfshafts are different lengths, so they must be installed on the correct side of the vehicle. Be careful not to confuse the 2; the longer shaft is installed on the right side of the vehicle.

6. Pack the constant velocity joints with grease before installation.
7. To install, reverse the removal procedures. Torque the halfshaft flange bolts to 28–31 ft. lbs. (38–43 Nm).

Driveshaft and U-Joints

Removal and Installation

1. Raise and safely support the vehicle.
2. Scribe alignment marks on the driveshaft and pinion flanges before removal.

NOTE: If the driveshaft is indexed improperly when installed, it could ruin driveline balance and cause vibrations.

3. Place the transmission gear selector in **N** to allow rotation of the driveshaft.
4. Detach any exhaust system components interfering with driveshaft removal.
5. Remove the pinion flange-to-driveshaft bolts.
6. Remove the center bearing support-to-floorpan bolts; be careful not to lose the spacers that are installed between the support bearing bracket and the floor pan.

NOTE: Note the position and number of the spacers so they may be installed in their original location. Failure to do so could result in driveline vibration.

7. Remove the driveshaft-to-transmission flange bolts.
8. To install the driveshaft, reverse the removal procedures. Torque the:
    Flange bolts—42–49 ft. lbs. (57–67 Nm)
    Center bearing support mounting bolts—13–17 ft. lbs. (18–23 Nm)

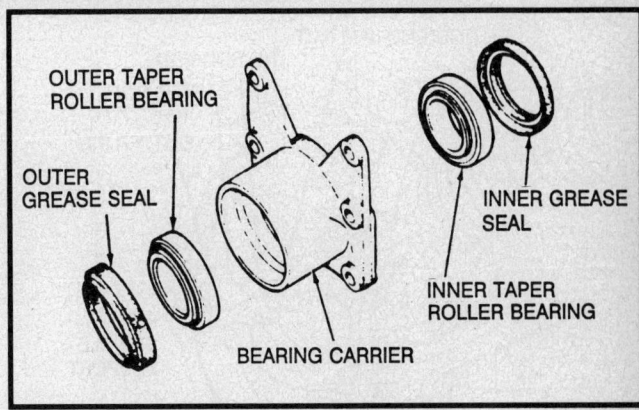

Rear axle bearing carrier components

Rear Axle Shaft and Bearing

Removal and Installation

NOTE: The rear axle flange locknuts are not interchangeable; they have different threads. The right side has right hand threads and the left side has left hand threads. Be sure to turn the nuts in the proper direction when removing or installing.

1. Prior to raising the vehicle, loosen the rear axle locknut and wheel lugs. Raise and safely support the vehicle.
2. Remove the rear wheel and the brake drum or rotor. If equipped with drum brakes, there is a drum retaining clip which must be removed. The self adjusters may have to be backed off in order to allow drum removal.
3. Remove the axle locknut. Using a 3 jawed puller and slide hammer, remove the rear axle flange from the halfshaft.
4. Remove the bearing hub bolts and the bearing hub.
5. The hub contains a set of inner and outer bearings and races similar to conventional front wheel bearings. The cups are replaceable and the inner and outer bearings should be packed with grease in the normal manner. A grease seal is installed on either side of the hub.
To install:
6. To install, reverse the removal procedures. Torque the hub mounting bolts to 45–48 ft. lbs. (52–64 Nm). Install the axle flange and brake drum.
7. Install a new locknut on the axle, being careful not to mix sides. Torque the locknuts to 185–214 ft. lbs. (250–290 Nm).

STEERING

Steering Wheel

Removal and Installation

1. Disconnect the negative battery cable.
2. Turn the ignition switch to the **RUN** position and center the steering wheel with the front tires in a straight-ahead position.
3. Remove the steering wheel hub cover assembly by carefully prying it up with a small prybar.
4. Loosen the center hub nut a few turns and pull the steer-

ing wheel straight up to release it from the tapered steering shaft.
5. Remove the wheel hub nut and lift off the steering wheel.
6. Make sure the turn signal cam is aligned with the turn signal switch canceling lever.

To install:
7. Position the steering wheel over the column shaft and align the slot on the underside of the steering wheel hub with the tab on the turn signal switch. Install the center hub nut on the shaft and torque it to 33–40 ft. lbs. (45–55 Nm).

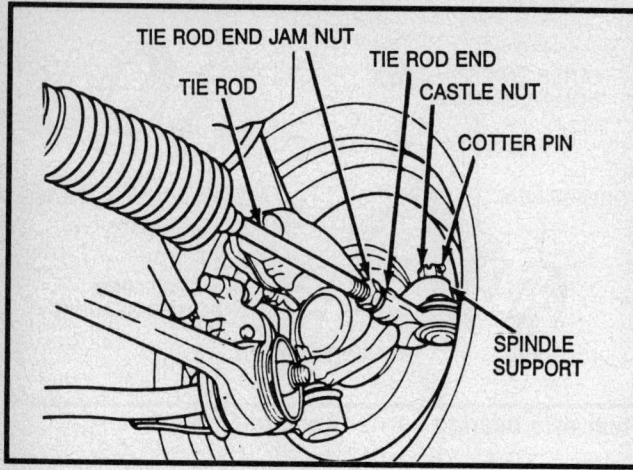

TIE ROD END JAM NUT

TIE ROD END

TIE ROD

CASTLE NUT

COTTER PIN

SPINDLE SUPPORT

Tie rod end and steering knuckle assembly

8. Turn the ignition key to **LOCK** and remove it, then check that the steering wheel locks properly. Install the hub trim pad and connect the negative battery cable. Verify that the horn functions.

Power Steering Gear

Removal and Installation

1. Disconnect the negative battery cable and turn the ignition switch to the **ON** position. Center the steering wheel with the front tires in the straight ahead position.
2. Raise and safely support the vehicle.
3. Remove the lower flexible coupler-to-steering gear input shaft pinch bolt.
4. Remove the front wheels.
5. Remove the cotter pin and castle nut from the tie rod ends. Disconnect the tie rod ends from the steering knuckles, using a puller.
6. Position a drain pan, then, disconnect the power steering pressure and return lines from the steering gear assembly by removing the routing clamp and the washer head pump line plate assembly-to-gear housing screw. Plug the lines and connections at the steering gear to prevent the entry of dirt or contaminants during service.
7. Remove the steering gear-to-crossmember bolts and the gear.
To install:
8. Reverse the removal procedures. Torque the:
  Mounting bolts—11 ft. lbs. (15 Nm), plus, an additional 90 degrees
  Steering shaft pinch bolt—18–22 ft. lbs. (25–30 Nm)

NOTE: Tie rod ends may be replaced by separating them from the steering knuckle after releasing the boot, loosening the locknut and unscrewing the tie rods from the gear assembly. Always count the number of turns for reinstallation reference.

9. Bleed the power steering system.

Adjustment

This procedure is not a serviceable adjustment; it is to be done only as part of a complete overhaul of the rack/pinion assembly.
1. Remove the rack/pinion assembly from the vehicle and position it in a soft jawed vise in the horizontal position. Position the rack/pinion in the straight ahead position.
2. Remove the yoke plug from the front side of the rack/pinion assembly.

3. Lubricate the yoke plug threads with Loctite® activator No. 764 or equivalent, and reinstall the yoke plug.
4. Using the yoke plug hex adapter tool T85M-3504-C or equivalent, torque the yoke plug to 30–35 inch lbs. (3.4–3.9 Nm).
5. Using the pinion shaft replacer/torque adapter tool, position it on the pinion shaft so the lock screws engage the shaft splines. Turn the pinion in 1 direction and then the opposite direction, until the rack has moved, twice, from stop-to-stop.
6. Retorque the yoke plug to 30–35 inch lbs. (3.4–3.9 Nm).
7. Using the pinion shaft torque adapter tool T85M-3504-B or equivalent, check the pinion shaft turning force; it should be at least 12 inch lbs. (1.35 Nm). If the turning force is less than 12 inch lbs. (1.35 Nm), repeat the torquing procedure.
8. When the pinion shaft rotation torque meets the specification, back off the yoke plug 22–27 degrees and recheck the turning force; it should not exceed 15 inch lbs. (1.7 Nm).
9. If the torque exceeds 15 inch lbs. (1.7 Nm), back off the yoke cover 5 degrees.
10. Using Loctite® 290 penetrating anaerobic sealant or equivalent, apply it to the yoke cover threads.
11. Stake the rack/pinion assembly housing in 3 places around the yoke plug; do not use the original staking positions.
12. Reinstall the rack/pinion assembly into the vehicle. Bleed the power steering system.

Power Steering Pump

Removal and Installation

NOTE: Special power steering pump pulley removal and installer tools are required for this procedure. The pulley remover is tool T69L-10300-B and the installer is tool T65P-3A733-E.

1. Disconnect the power steering fluid return line from the pump fitting and drain the fluid into a suitable container.
2. Remove the pressure line from the pump.
3. Remove the drive belts from the pump.
4. Remove the pump drive pulley using a suitable puller. Unbolt the pump from the mounting bracket and lift it clear.
To install:
5. Reverse the removal procedures; a pulley installer tool will be necessary to attach the pump pulley. Torque the:
  Pump mounting bolts—30–45 ft. lbs. (41–61 Nm)
  Pressure and return hose fittings—10–25 ft. lbs. (14–34 Nm)
6. Hose swivel and/or end play in the fitting is normal and does not indicate a loose fitting. Over torquing the tube nut can result in a leak and require replacement of the hose assembly.
7. Bleed the power steering system.

Belt Adjustment

Adjust the drive belt tension so that there is approximately ⅛–⅜ in. of deflection on the longest span of belt between pulleys. Apply pressure to the square rib on the alternator housing using the proper size open end wrench to maintain pressure when adjusting belt tension. Torque the:
  Adjuster pivot bolt—44–60 ft. lbs. (60–81 Nm)
  Adjuster nut—30–46 ft. lbs. (40–62 Nm)

System Bleeding

After any service procedure that requires draining the power steering pump, perform the following procedure to remove any trapped air in the system. Failure to bleed the power steering pump can cause excessively noisy operation.
1. Disconnect the ignition coil wire. Raise and safely support the vehicle with the front wheels off the ground.
2. Fill the power steering pump reservoir to the specified level with Type F power steering and transmission fluid.
3. Crank the engine with the starter while rotating the steering wheel from lock-to-lock. Crank the engine briefly and keep

checking the fluid level in the pump reservoir. Keep adding fluid until the level remains constant.

4. Reconnect the coil wire.

5. Start the engine and allow it to idle for several minutes. Rotate the steering wheel from lock-to-lock several times, then turn **OFF** the engine and recheck the fluid level. Add fluid as necessary.

Tie Rod Ends

Removal and Installation

1. Raise and safely support the vehicle. Remove the front wheels.

2. Remove the cotter pin and nut that secure the tie rod end to the steering knuckle. Release the boot clamps.

3. Use a puller and separate the tie rod end from the knuckle. Loosen the tie rod end locknut.

4. Turn the tie rod end out from the tie rod; count the number of turns for installation reference.

To install:

5. Screw in the new tie rod end, approximately the same number of turns as removed. Tighten the locknut.

6. To complete the installation, reverse the removal procedures. Check and/or adjust the alignment.

BRAKES

Master Cylinder

Removal and Installation

XR4Ti

1. Disconnect the low fluid indicator connector from the filler cap.

2. Disconnect the brake lines from the master cylinder.

3. Remove the master cylinder-to-brake booster nuts and lockwashers.

4. Remove the master cylinder from the booster.

To install:

5. Reverse the removal procedures. Torque the master cylinder mounting nuts to 16–20 ft. lbs. (21–27 Nm).

6. Refill the master cylinder reservoir with brake fluid and bleed the brake system.

SCORPIO

───── **CAUTION** ─────

Before servicing any components of the 4 Wheel Anti-Lock Brake System (ABS), it is mandatory that the high pressure in the system be discharged. To discharge the system: Turn the ignition switch to the Off Position and pump the brake pedal a minimum of 20 times until an increase in brake pedal force is clearly experienced.

1. Disconnect the negative battery cable.

2. Disconnect all of the electrical connectors from the reservoir cap, main valve, pressure switch, valve block, electric pump and ground connection.

3. Disconnect the hydraulic lines from the valve body and plug the lines to prevent dirt entry.

4. Remove the under dash trim panel and disconnect the brake pedal to unit pushrod by removing the retainer clip.

5. Support the hydraulic unit and remove the mounting nuts. Remove the unit from the vehicle and drain the reservoir.

6. Remove and replace the seal gasket (always use a new gasket) between the hydraulic unit and the dash panel.

To install:

7. Place the hydraulic unit into position and support it. Install the mounting nuts and torque them to 30–40 ft. lbs. (41–51 Nm.).

8. Install the pushrod to brake pedal retaining clip. Connect the fluid lines and electrical wiring to the unit. Refill the reservoir with new brake fluid. Bleed the front brake system.

9. Connect the negative battery cable. Turn the ignition switch to the **RUN** position and check the electric pump operation.

10. Do not operate the electric pump for more than 2 minutes at a time or it will overheat. Bleed the rear brake system. Install the under dash panel. Road test the vehicle to check brake operation.

Proportioning Valve

Removal and Installation

XR4Ti

1. Raise and safely support the vehicle.

2. Disconnect the brake lines from the proportioning valve, located just under the master cylinder/booster assembly.

3. Remove the attaching bolt and remove the proportioning valve from the vehicle.

4. To install, reverse of removal. Bleed the brake system.

Power Brake Booster

The XR4Ti models use a dual diaphragm booster.

Removal and Installation

1. Depress the brake pedal several times to deplete the vacuum reserve in the brake booster. Depressurize the fuel system by connecting a hand vacuum pump to the fuel pressure regulator and applying 25 in. Hg. of vacuum for about 3 minutes.

2. Disconnect the fuel line at the pulse damper. Disconnect the fuel return line using a quick disconnect tool.

3. Disconnect the low oil level sensor connector and remove the engine oil level dipstick. The dipstick connector is only used on 1985–86 models.

4. Remove the screw attaching the engine oil dipstick tube to the pulse damper bracket. Remove the pulse damper bracket-to-intake manifold stud nuts. Disconnect the pulse damper from the fuel manifold and remove the damper/bracket assembly.

5. Label and disconnect the vacuum lines at the vacuum tree. Disconnect the low fluid warning light connector from the master cylinder cap and pull the vacuum check valve from the booster body.

6. Working inside, below the instrument panel, disconnect booster valve operating rod from the brake pedal assembly. To do this, disconnect the stop light switch wires at the connector. Remove the hairpin retainer and nylon washer from the pedal pin. Slide the switch off, just enough for the outer arm to clear the pin. Remove the switch. Slide the booster push rod, bushing and inner nylon washer off the pedal pin.

7. Disconnect the brake lines at the master cylinder outlet fittings.

8. If equipped with speed control, remove the left cowl screen in the engine compartment. Remove speed control servo-to-firewall nuts and move the servo aside.

9. Remove the bracket-to-firewall bolts.

10. Remove the booster and bracket assembly from the firewall, sliding the valve operating rod out from the engine side.

11. To install, reverse of removal. Bleed the brakes system.

Disc Brake Pads

Removal and Installation

FRONT

1. Remove approximately ⅓ of the brake fluid from the master cylinder.

2. Raise and safely support the vehicle. Remove the front wheels.

3. Disconnect the electrical connector from the wear sensor; to disconnect, press the harness connector pads and pull apart.

4. Using a prybar, place it between the caliper and the outer pad, then, force the piston into the caliper.

5. Remove the caliper-to-caliper support bolts and the caliper; support it on a wire.

NOTE: When removing the caliper, the anti-rattle spring will fall out.

6. Remove the outboard pad and the inboard pad.

7. If the piston has not seated in the caliper, use a C-clamp to force it into the caliper.

To install:

8. Install the pads onto the caliper.

9. Position the caliper over the rotor; make sure the pads are properly engaged on the anchor plate.

NOTE: Make sure the sensor wire is positioned between the caliper and the anchor before install the caliper bolts.

10. Install the caliper-to-caliper support bolts and torque to 18–23 ft. lbs. (25–30 Nm).

11. Install the anti-rattle spring. Connect the wear sensor electrical connector; make sure the O-ring is in position before making the connection.

12. To complete the installation, reverse the removal procedures. Refill the master cylinder reservoir.

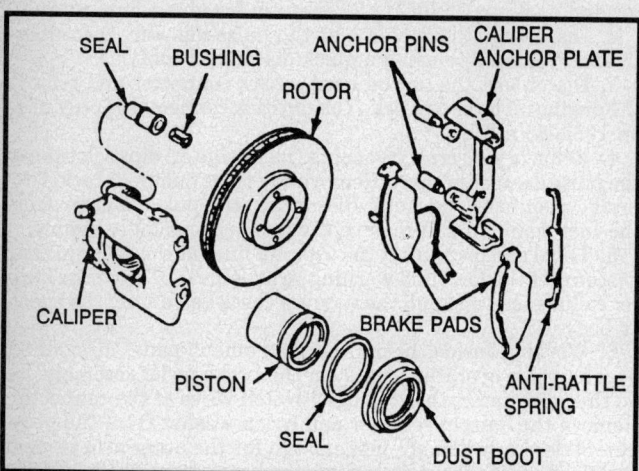

Exploded view of the front disc brake assembly

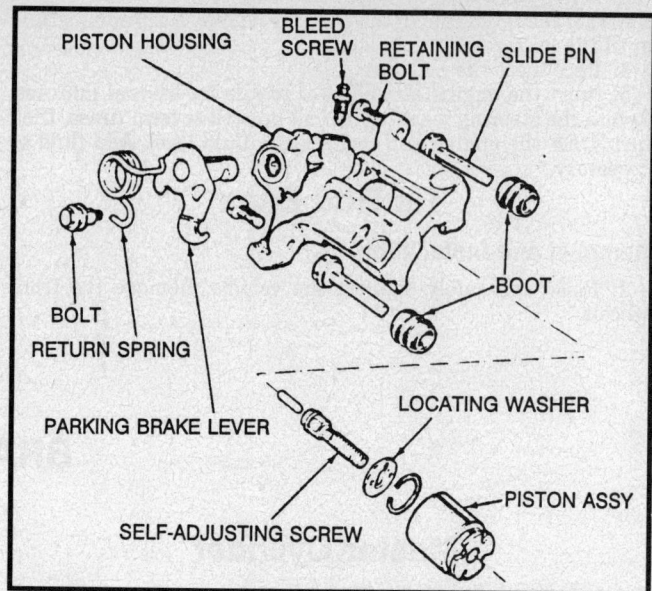

Exploded view of the rear disc brake assembly— Scorpio

REAR

Scorpio

1. Raise and safely support the vehicle. Remove the rear wheels.

2. Disengage the parking brake cable from the retaining bracket.

3. Using a prybar, place it between the caliper and the outer pad, then, force the piston into the caliper.

4. Remove the front caliper piston housing-to-anchor bracket slide pin bolt and lift the piston assembly up and away from the rotor.

5. Remove the brake pads from the carrier bracket.

6. If the piston has not seated in the caliper, use a C-clamp to force it into the caliper.

To install:

7. Install the brake pads onto the carrier bracket and the caliper over the rotor; position the piston's slot over the tab in the brake pad backing plate. Make sure the anti-rattle spring are correctly positioned in the piston housing.

8. Install the caliper-to-caliper bracket slide pin bolt and torque it to 23–25 ft. lbs. (31–35 Nm).

9. Connect the parking brake cable to the retainer bracket.

10. To complete the installation, reverse the removal procedures. Turn the ignition switch to the **RUN** position and pump the brake pedal prior to moving the vehicle, to pressurize the system and position the brake pads.

Brake Shoes

Removal and Installation

XR4Ti

1. Raise and safely support the vehicle. Remove the rear wheels.

2. Remove the brake drum and discard the retaining clip.

3. Should the brake drum be difficult to remove, perform the following procedures:

    a. Remove the wheel cylinder bolts

    b. Push the wheel cylinder away from the backing plate to provide access.

    c. Using a thin blade tool, insert it through the backing plate and rotate the self-adjuster cam to released position.

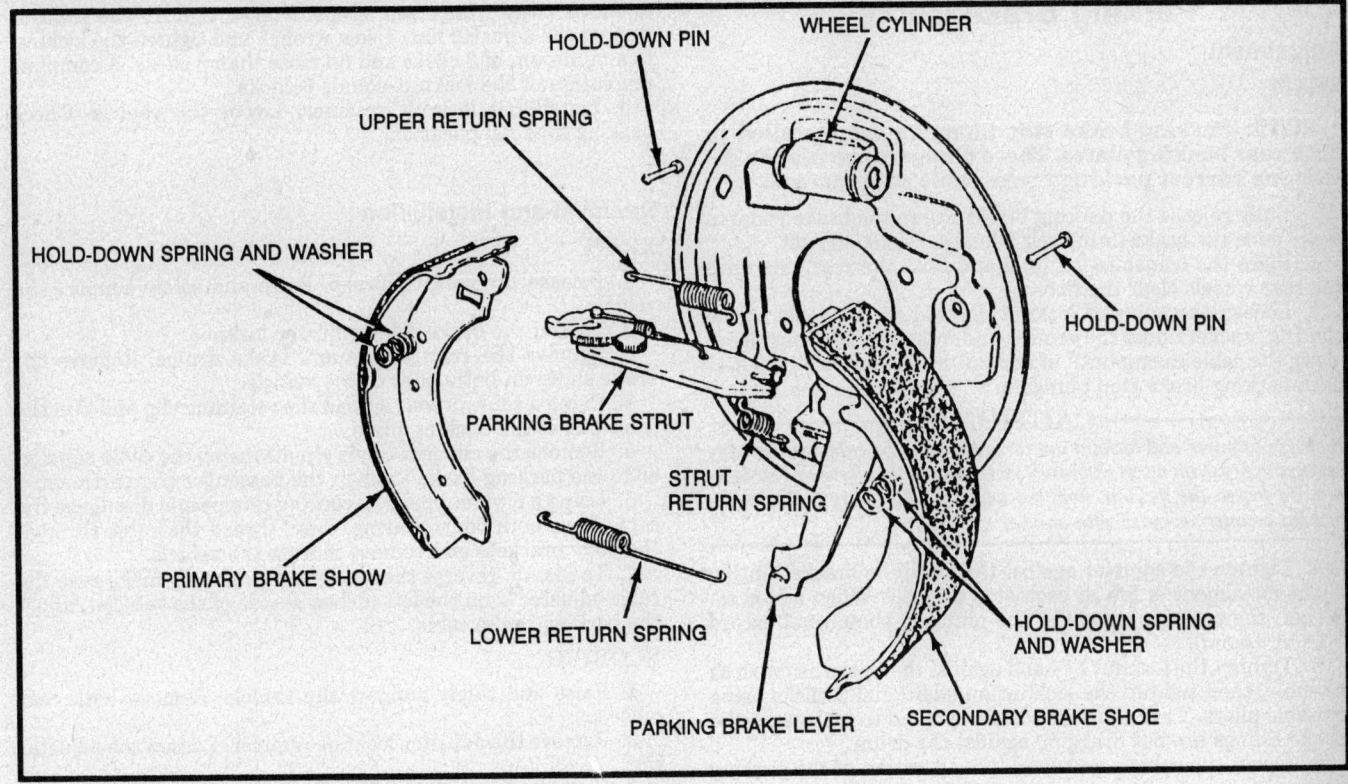

Exploded view of the rear drum brake assembly— Merkur

d. Remove the brake drum and torque the wheel cylinder bolts to 5–7 ft. lbs. (7–10 Nm).

4. Remove both brake drum hold-down springs.

5. Pry the lower end of the primary shoe from it's anchor and remove the lower spring.

6. Remove the shoes and strut by passing the strut between the wheel cylinder and the hub.

7. Pull the top of the primary shoe away from the secondary shoe to disconnect the strut from the secondary shoe.

8. Disconnect the parking brake cable from the secondary shoe lever.

9. Remove the strut return spring from the secondary shoe.

10. Remove the adjuster cam spring, pull the primary shoe away from the strut while rotating the cam to the fully released position.

11. Remove the primary shoe spring and the primary shoe spring from the strut.

To install:

12. Using high temperature brake grease, lubricate the 6 support ledges (where the brake shoes contact the backing plate).

13. Connect the parking brake cable to the secondary shoe lever.

NOTE: When properly installed, the plastic washer will be between the spring and the lever.

14. Position the secondary shoe and install the hold-down spring. Install the strut and cam assembly onto the primary shoe.

15. Rotate the cam to the fully released position. Install the cam adjuster spring and the primary shoe spring.

16. Install the strut spring onto the secondary shoe and the strut.

17. Position the strut onto the parking brake lever and move the primary shoe toward the backing plate.

NOTE: The strut will "click" into place over the parking brake lever and the secondary shoe web.

18. To complete the installation, reverse the removal procedures. Depress the brake pedal, twice, hard, to set the self-adjuster cam position. Adjust the parking brake cable as necessary.

Wheel Cylinder

Removal and Installation

XR4Ti

1. Raise and safely support the vehicle. Remove the wheel and brake drum.

2. Disconnect the brake line from the wheel cylinder. Plug the brake line to prevent any dirt from entering the system.

3. Pull the primary (front) shoe away from the wheel cylinder. The self adjuster cam will rotate outward to hold the brake shoes away from the wheel cylinder.

4. Remove the wheel cylinder mounting bolts, O-ring and the wheel cylinder from the brake backing plate.

To install:

5. To install, mount the O-ring on the wheel cylinder, then position the wheel cylinder on the brake backing plate and install the mounting bolts. Torque the bolts to 5–7 ft. lbs. (7–10 Nm). Connect the brake line.

6. Using a tool and push the adjuster cam to the release position.

7. Install the brake drum. Bleed the rear brakes and install the wheel.

NOTE: If a pressure bleeder is used, push the brake pedal hard twice to set the self adjuster cam position. The cam will make a ratcheting sound as it resets.

Parking Brake Cable

Adjustment

XR4Ti

NOTE: Parking brake stop plungers are installed in both rear backing plates. These plungers are used to determine correct parking brake cable adjustments.

1. Fully release the parking brake. Pump the brake pedal to make sure the brake lining self adjuster is properly set.
2. Place the transmission in N and raise the rear axle until the rear wheels clear the floor.
3. Loosen the adjuster locknut, located on the cable at the routing bracket under the vehicle, and rotate the adjuster sleeve along the cable casing until in and out movement can be felt at both parking brake stop plungers.

––––––––––––––––– CAUTION –––––––––––––––––
Both the adjuster and locknut are threaded onto the cable casing. Any attempt to pry them apart will result in damage to the sleeve and/or locknut. To loosen the locknut, hold the adjuster with pliers and turn the locknut counterclockwise with another set of pliers.

4. Tighten the adjuster against the retaining bracket until a slight movement is felt at each stop plunger. When added together, the total movement of the plungers should not exceed 0.16 in. (4mm).
5. Tighten the locknut by hand against the sleeve as much as possible, then tighten the locknut an additional 2 clicks using suitable pliers. Turn the rear wheels by hand to make sure the brake linings are not dragging against the drum.
6. Lower the vehicle and check the operation of the parking brake.

SCORPIO

1. Raise and safely support the vehicle. Release the parking brake lever.
2. Remove the adjusting locknut retainer. Loosen the adjuster locknut and adjuster nut until both parking brake levers have fully returned to the caliper stops.
3. Paint reference marks on both the caliper lever and housing for position reference.
4. Turn the adjuster nut until the parking brake levers start

to move away from their stops. Finger tighten the locknut against the adjuster nut. Use a wrench and tighten the locknut to a minimum of 3 clicks and no more than 6 clicks. A complete revolution of the locknut equals 6 clicks.
5. Install the locknut retainer. Lower the vehicle. Check parking brake application.

Removal and Installation

XR4Ti

1. Release the parking brake. Raise and safely support the vehicle.
2. Loosen the brake cable adjuster locknut.
3. Remove the rear wheels and brake drums. Remove the brake shoes on both sides of the vehicle.
4. Using a screwdriver, spread the retaining clip and pull the cable out of the backing plate.
5. Remove the clip and clevis pin attaching the cable equalizer to the parking brake lever in the passenger compartment.
6. Using a prybar, open the routing clamps and disengage the cable from both control arms, then, thread the cable through the body brackets and remove it from the vehicle.
7. To install, reverse the removal procedures; make sure the cable adjuster is on the left (driver's) side of the vehicle. Adjust the parking brake cable.

SCORPIO

1. Raise and safely support the vehicle. Remove both rear wheels.
2. Remove the adjuster locknut retainer. Loosen the adjuster nut.
3. Remove the circlip and clevis pin that attaches the cable yoke to the parking brake lever rod.
4. Remove the circlip that attaches the cable to the caliper levers. Remove the cable from the calipers and guide sleeves.
5. Remove the cable from the lower arm retaining clips.
6. Remove the circlip that retains the outer cable (non-adjusting) to the retaining bracket. Remove the cable from the bracket.
7. Pull the cable through the lower arm and remove the cable.
8. To install, reverse the removal procedures. Adjust the parking brake cable.

Parking brake adjustment

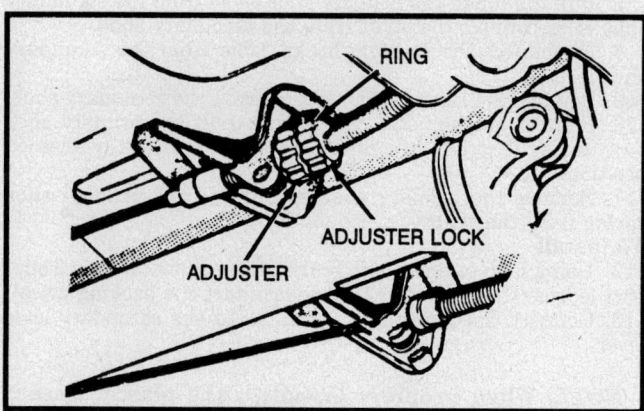
Scorpio parking brake adjustment points

FRONT SUSPENSION

MacPherson Strut

Removal and Installation

XR4Ti

1. Raise and safely support the vehicle, after loosening the front wheel lug nuts.
2. Remove the tire assembly and the caliper/anchor assembly. Position a floor jack under the lower control arm and raise it until it is slightly lower than the control arm.
3. Remove the strut-to-lower control arm pinch bolt. Use a small prybar to spread the mounting flange ears and push down on the lower control arm to separate the arm and strut. Lower the jack (if necessary) but do not allow the brake hose to stretch. When separated, rest the control arm on the jack.
4. Hold the top of the strut by inserting a 6mm hex wrench in the slot provided and remove the locknut.
5. Remove the strut assembly from the vehicle.
6. To install, reverse the removal procedures.

SCORPIO

1. Disconnect the negative battery cable. Loosen the wheel lugs, raise and safely support the vehicle.
2. Remove the front wheel. Remove the caliper and support it on a wire.
3. Remove the wheel sensor from the spindle carrier. Separate the tie rod end from the spindle.
4. To separate the control arm ball joint from the spindle, use a small prybar to pry down on the control arm and stabilizer bar. Pull the strut clear of the control arm.
5. Remove the brake pad sensor wire from the strut clip and the dust cover from the top strut mount on the inner fender.
6. Support the strut and spindle carrier. Remove the upper locknuts and washers. Lower the strut assembly from the upper mount.
7. Remove the pinch bolt from the spindle carrier. Insert spindle carrier lever tool T85M-3206A or equivalent, into the spindle carrier slot and rotate it 90 degrees. Slide the spindle carrier off of the strut.
8. To install, reverse the removal procedures. Torque the:
   Pinch bolt—59–66 ft. lbs. (80–90 Nm)
   Upper strut mounting—15–17 ft. lbs. (20–24 Nm)

Stabilizer Bar

Removal and Installation

1. Raise and safely support the vehicle. Remove the wheel assemblies.
2. Remove the attaching nuts and front washers/covers from the ends of the stabilizer bar.
3. Remove the both U-brackets and torque brace from the body.
4. Detach a control arm pivot bolt and pull the control arm from the crossmember.
5. Pull the stabilizer from the lower control arms and remove it from the vehicle. Remove the rear washers/covers from the stabilizer bar, along with the insulators.

To install:

6. Coat the inside of the stabilizer bar bushings and the bushing surfaces on the stabilizer bar with rubber lube; do not use engine oil. Install the insulators on the stabilizer bar.
7. Install the rear washers/covers on the stabilizer bar. The rear washer is black and has a shallower dish than the front washer, which is yellow. When the washer is installed, make sure the plastic cover is in place between the dished steel washer and the bushing. The dished side of the steel washer faces away from the bushing.
8. Install the stabilizer bar into the control arm bushings. Install the control arm into the crossmember with the pivot bolt, washer and nut. Snug the attaching nut but do not tighten.
9. Install the U-bolts on the insulators and install the attaching bolts. Torque the bolts to 42–52 ft. lbs. (57–70 Nm).
10. Install the front washers/covers on the stabilizer bar, making sure the dished side of the steel washer faces away from the bushing, with the plastic cover in place between the bushing and steel washer.
11. Install the stabilizer bar attaching nuts but just snug them; do not tighten to specifications.
12. Lower the vehicle and torque the:
    Stabilizer bar nut—52–81 ft. lbs. (70–110 Nm)
    Control arm pivot nut/bolt—11 ft. lbs. (15 Nm) and turn an additional 90 degrees

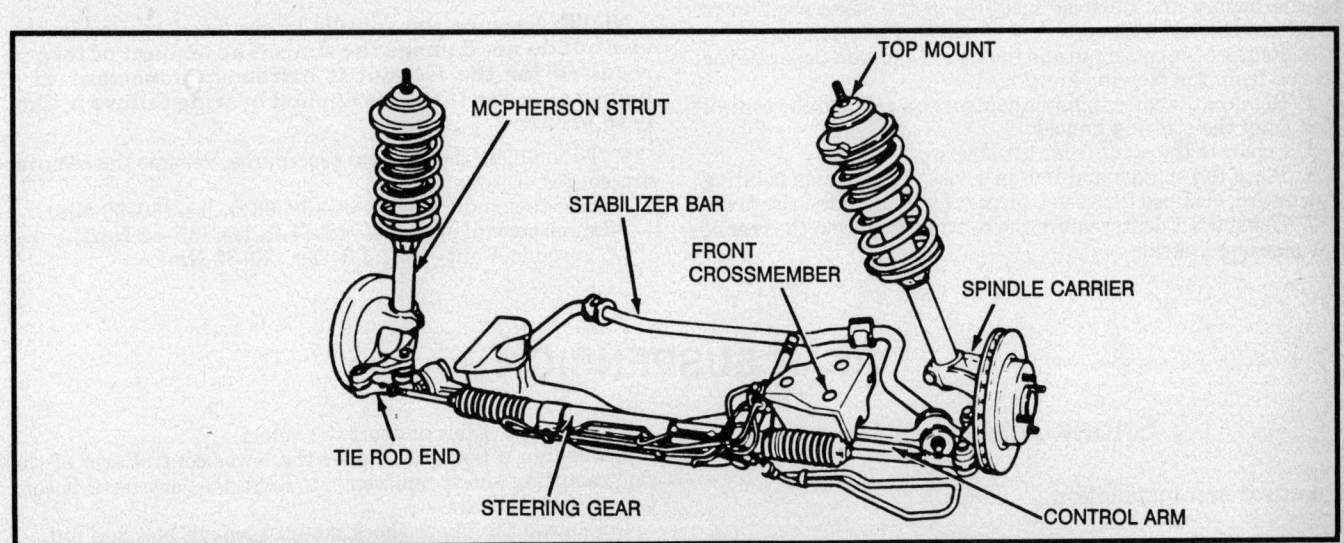

XR4Ti front suspension assembly

Lower Control Arm

Removal and Installation

1. Raise and safely support the vehicle.
2. Remove the front tire.
3. Remove the cotter pin and attaching nut. Separate the control arm from the spindle carrier.

NOTE: With the spindle carrier and control arm disconnected, the spindle carrier can easily cause damage to the control arm ball joint boot. The control arm and ball joint are replaced as an assembly if the ball joint is worn or damaged.

4. Remove the control arm-to-crossmember pivot bolt.
5. Remove the stabilizer bar-to-control arm nut.
6. Remove the front washer/cover from the end of the stabilizer bar.
7. Remove the control arm and bushing as an assembly. Remove the rear washer/cover from the end of the stabilizer bar. Remove the bushings if replacement is necessary; the bushings are pressed into the control arm.
To install:
8. Reverse the removal procedures.

NOTE: The stabilizer bar bushings are designed to allow the control arm to move forward and rearward somewhat; this movement should not be interpreted as a suspension problem.

9. Torque the control arm ball joint stud nut to 48–63 ft. lbs. (65–85 Nm) and install a new cotter pin; the castle nut may be tightened slightly to align the cotter pin hole with the castellations but do not loosen the nut for alignment.
10. If equipped with a 2.3L engine, torque the control arm pivot bolt to 11 ft. lbs. (15 Nm), plus, an additional 90 degrees.
11. If equipped with a 2.9L engine, install the front wheel and lower the vehicle. Torque the control arm pivot bolt to 22 ft. lbs. (30 Nm), plus, an additional ¼ turn.

Front Wheel Bearing

Removal and Installation

1. Raise and safely support the vehicle. Remove the front wheels and brake calipers; suspend the calipers on wire to prevent brake hose damage.
2. Matchmark the rotor and wheel stud. The unit is balanced by the factory and must be installed in the same position to maintain balance.
3. Remove the cotter pin and the tie rod end nut. Separate the tie rod from the steering knuckle.
4. Remove the cotter pin, the control arm nut and the control arm from the steering knuckle.
5. Separate the strut from the steering knuckle.
6. Place the spindle and hub in a vise, wheel studs pointing downward, clamped between 2 pieces of wood and the vise jaws.
7. Using a flat drift, remove the bearing plug from the rear of the steering knuckle.

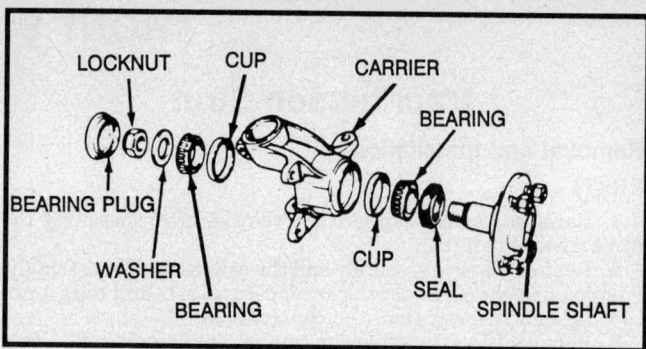

Exploded view of the front hub and bearing assembly

8. Remove the spindle bearing locknut.

NOTE: Spindles form the right side of the vehicle are equipped with left hand threads and are loosened by turning clockwise. Spindles from the left side of the vehicle are equipped with right hand threads which are loosened by turning counterclockwise. The spindles are marked with an R or L on the large hexagonal recess.

9. Lift the spindle carrier and inner bearing off the (hub) spindle shaft. Remove the inner bearing and splined washer. If the bearing is to be reused, label for location identification.
10. Clamp the spindle carrier (knuckle) in a vise and remove the grease seal using a flat prybar. Remove the outer bearing and label for location identification.
11. Remove bearing cups from the spindle, if necessary, using a bearing puller jaws on a slide hammer.
To install:
12. Clean and inspect all parts. Press new bearing cups into the spindle. Pack the wheel bearing with high temperature grease.
13. Install the outer bearing and grease seal in the spindle (knuckle). Install the spindle shaft (hub).
14. Install the inner bearing and splined washer. Install the spindle bearing locknut and torque to:
    2.3L engine—202–232 ft. lbs. (274–315 Nm)
    2.9L engine—288–331 ft. lbs. (390–450 Nm)
15. Install the bearing cover plug.

NOTE: Be sure the spindle is mounted secure in the vise but do not damage the studs. The amount of torque required for the locknut is extremely important. If a higher or lower torque is applied bearing failure is likely to occur.

16. To complete the removal procedures. Reverse the removal procedures. Torque the:
    Strut-to-spindle pinch bolt—59–66 ft. lbs. (80–90 Nm)
    Lower control arm nut—48–63 ft. lbs. (65–85 Nm)
    Tie rod end nut—15–23 ft. lbs. (20–32 Nm)

REAR SUSPENSION

Shock Absorber

Removal and Installation

1. Remove the rear parcel shelf or luggage compartment cover and remove the upper shock mount trim cover.

2. Raise and safely support the vehicle.
3. Position a floor jack under the lower control arm of the side requiring shock replacement. Raise the jack until it contacts the control arm.
4. Remove the upper shock mount through bolt and nut.
5. Remove the cap from the lower shock mount. Remove the through bolt/nut and the shock absorber.

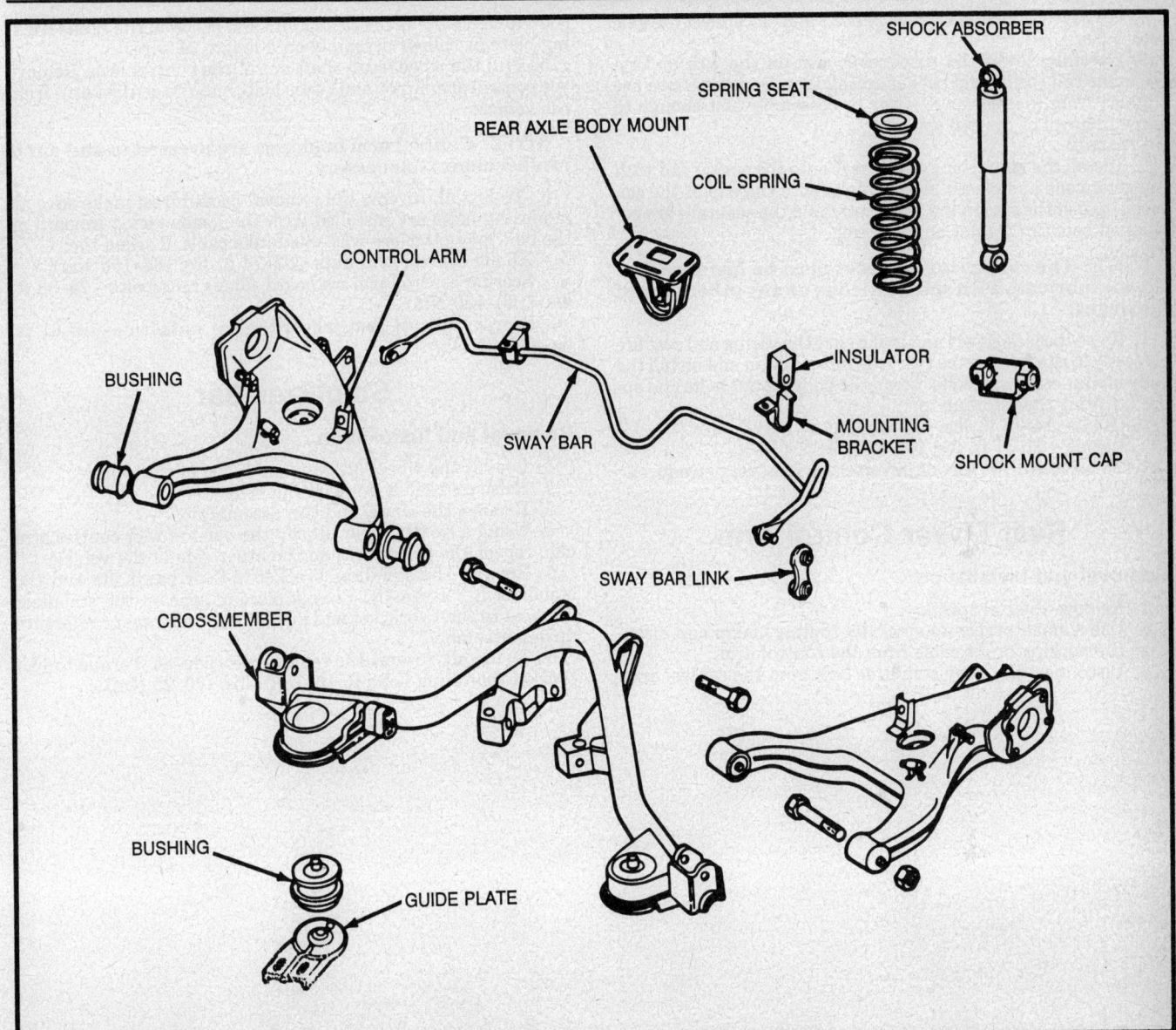

Exploded view of the rear suspension components

To install:

6. Install the replacement shock and reverse reverse the removal procedures. Install the lower through bolt with the head facing inboard, then, torque the:

Lower mounting head bolt — 33–40 ft. lbs. (45–55 Nm)
Lower mounting head nut — 30–37 ft. lbs. (40–50 Nm)
Upper mounting bolt and nut — 30–37 ft. lbs. (40–50 Nm)

Coil Spring

Removal and Installation

1. Loosen the rear wheel lug nuts. Raise and safely support the vehicle, with the rear suspension hanging freely. Remove the rear tire and the brake drum or rotor and caliper.

NOTE: The rear brake self adjusters may have to be backed off in order to remove the brake drum.

2. Position a floor jack under the rear control arm and take a slight amount of weight off of the spring.

3. Disconnect the rear brake hose at the body bracket (rubber line from steel line).

4. Remove the rear axle flange/brake backing plate-to-control arm bolts.

5. Remove the halfshaft. Secure the backing plate in it's installed position with 2 bolts to prevent damage to the steel brake line.

6. On Scorpio models, detach the stabilizer bar from the link rod. When removing the left spring, the brake line distribution block must be removed from the floor panel. Remove the brake line clip and disconnect the steel to rubber brake line.

7. Remove the lower shock mounting cap and the bolt that secures the lower mounting eye of the shock absorber to the control arm.

CAUTION

Make sure the lower arm and spring tension is securely supported by a floor jack before removing the lower shock absorber mounting bolt. Exercise caution, as the energy stored in a compressed coil spring is dangerous if suddenly released.

8. Remove the rear axle-to-body bolts and disconnect the axle vent tube.

9. Carefully lower the suspension arm on the jack and remove the coil spring and rubber spring seat. Do not remove the support from the rear axle; lower the assembly just enough to allow removal of the coil spring.

To install:

10. Install the rear spring upper seat onto the spring end with the color code and plastic sleeve. Make sure the end of the coil seats against the step in the spring seat and the seat tabs are positioned between the 1st and 2nd coil.

NOTE: The coil spring and seat must be installed dry. Do not lubricate with spray silicone or any other type of lubricant.

11. Raise the jack slowly and make sure the spring and seat are correctly located. Raise the rear axle into position and install the body mount attaching bolts. Clean the body mount bolts and apply Loctite®, then, torque to:
   XR4Ti—14–18 ft. lbs. (20–25 Nm)
   Scorpio—31–37 ft. lbs. (41–51 Nm)
12. To complete the install, reverse the removal procedures.

Rear Lower Control Arm

Removal and Installation

1. Remove the coil spring.
2. Use a small prybar to open the routing clamp and disengage the parking brake cable from the control arm.
3. Disconnect the sway stabilizer link from the control arm.
4. Remove the rear bearing hub and suspend the brake backing plate or caliper assembly on a length of wire.
5. Pull the wheel stub shaft out of the control arm. Remove the control arm inner and outer bolts and the control arm from the vehicle.

NOTE: Control arm bushings are pressed in and out if replacement is necessary.

6. To install, reverse the removal procedures; make sure all mounting bolts are installed with the heads facing inboard or the bolt may interfere with the brake cable. Torque the:
   XR4Ti control arm nuts—63–74 ft. lbs. (85–100 Nm)
   Scorpio control arm outboard (blue) nuts/bolts—74–88 ft. lbs. (100–120 Nm)
   Scorpio control arm inboard (gold) nuts/bolts—52–63 ft. lbs. (70–85 Nm)

Stabilizer Bar

Removal and Installation

1. Loosen the wheel lug nuts on 1 side of the vehicle.
2. Raise and safely support the vehicle.
3. Remove the wheel and tire assembly.
4. Using a small prybar, unclip the bar-to-lower control arm clip; repeat the procedures on the other side of the vehicle.
5. Remove the stabilizer bracket-to-floor pan bolts and the stabilizer bar assembly. Place a piece of tape on the stabilizer bar next to the U-bracket and insulator for alignment reference during assembly.
6. To install, reverse the removal procedures. Torque the U-bracket mounting bolts to 15–18 ft. lbs. (20–25 Nm).

SERIAL NUMBER IDENTIFICATION

Vehicle Identification Plate

The Vehicle Identification Number (VIN) is mounted on the instrument panel, adjacent to the lower corner of the windshield on the driver's side and is visible through the windshield.

A standard 17 digit VIN code is used, the 10th digit identifies model year:

H represents 1987
I represents 1988
J represents 1989
K represents 1990
L represents 1991

The 8th digit identifies the installed engine.

A vehicle information code plate is riveted onto the front of the right side wheel house or onto the firewall, depending on vehicle. The plate shows vehicle code, engine vehicle, transaxle vehicle and body color code.

A chassis number plate is located on the top center of the firewall in the engine compartment.

Engine Number

The engine vehicle and serial numbers in all cases are stamped on the block near the front of the engine. In most cases, they are located on the right side.

Engine codes for all years are as follows:
6G72 — 181.4 cu. in. (2972cc) engine
G45B — 155.9 cu. in. (2555cc) engine
G62B — 109.5 cu. in. (1795cc) engine
G63B — 121.9 cu. in. (1997cc) engine
G15B — 89.6 cu. in. (1468cc) engine
G32B — 97.4 cu. in. (1597cc) engine
G64B — 143.4 cu. in. (2350cc) engine

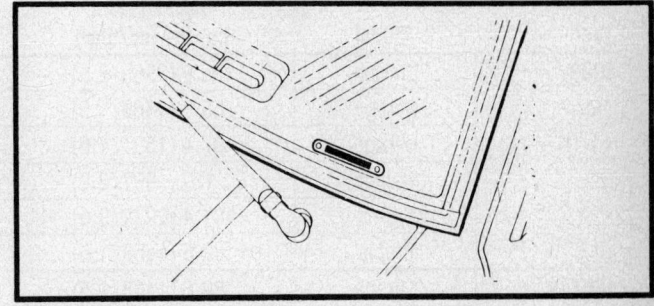

VIN location

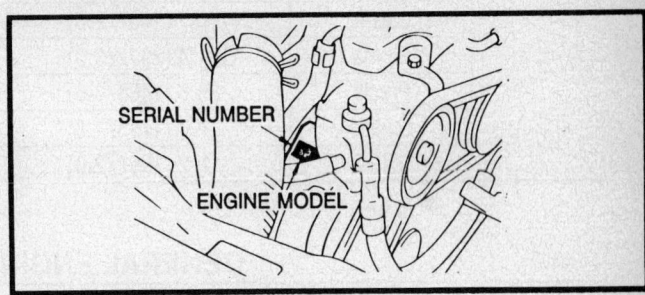

Engine number location

Transmission Number

The transmission identification number is located below the engine number on the vehicle information code plate.

ENGINE IDENTIFICATION

Year	Model	Engine Displacement cu. in. (cc/liter)	Engine Series Identification	No. of Cylinders	Engine Type
1987	Cordia	109.5 (1795/1.8)	G62B	4	SOHC
	Cordia	121.9 (1997/2.0)	G63B	4	SOHC
	Tredia	109.5 (1795/1.8)	G62B	4	SOHC
	Tredia	121.9 (1997/2.0)	G63B	4	SOHC
	Starion	155.9 (2555/2.5)	G54B	4	SOHC
	Mirage	89.6 (1468/1.5)	G15B	4	SOHC
	Mirage	97.4 (1597/1.6)	G32B	4	SOHC
	Galant	143.4 (2350/2.3)	G64B	4	SOHC
	Precis	89.6 (1468/1.5)	G15B	4	SOHC
1988	Cordia	109.5 (1795/1.8)	G62B	4	SOHC
	Cordia	121.9 (1997/2.0)	G63B	4	SOHC
	Tredia	109.5 (1795/1.8)	G62B	4	SOHC
	Tredia	121.9 (1997/2.0)	G63B	4	SOHC
	Starion	155.9 (2555/2.5)	G54B	4	SOHC
	Mirage	89.6 (1468/1.5)	G15B	4	SOHC
	Mirage	97.4 (1597/1.6)	G32B	4	SOHC
	Galant	143.4 (2350/2.3)	G64B	4	SOHC
	Galant	181.4 (2972/3.0)	6G72	6	SOHC
	Precis	89.6 (1468/1.5)	G15B	4	SOHC

ENGINE IDENTIFICATION

Year	Model	Engine Displacement cu. in. (cc/liter)	Engine Series Identification	No. of Cylinders	Engine Type
1989	Starion	155.9 (2555/2.5)	G64B	4	SOHC
	Mirage	89.6 (1468/1.5)	4G15	4	SOHC
	Mirage	97.4 (1597/1.6)	4G61	4	DOHC
	Galant	122 (1997/2.0)	4G63	4	SOHC & DOHC
	Sigma	181.4 (2972/3.0)	6G72	6	SOHC
	Precis	89.6 (1468/1.5)	G15B	4	SOHC
1990–91	Mirage	89.6 (1468/1.5)	4G15	4	SOHC
	Mirage	97.3 (1595/1.6)	4G61	4	DOHC
	Galant	122 (1997/2.0)	4G63	4	SOHC & DOHC
	Sigma	181.4 (2972/3.0)	6G72	6	SOHC
	Precis	89.6 (1468/1.5)	G15B	4	SOHC
	Eclipse	107 (1755/1.8)	4G37	4	SOHC
	Eclipse	122 (1997/2.0)	4G63	4	DOHC

GENERAL ENGINE SPECIFICATIONS

Year	Model	Engine Displacement cu. in. (cc)	Fuel System Type	Net Horsepower @ rpm	Net Torque @ rpm (ft. lbs.)	Bore × Stroke (in.)	Compression Ratio	Oil Pressure @ rpm
1987	Cordia	109.5 (1795)	ECI②	116 @ 5500	129 @ 3000	3.17 × 3.46	7.5:1	63①
	Cordia	121.9 (1997)	Carb.	88 @ 5000	108 @ 3500	3.35 × 3.46	8.5:1	63①
	Tredia	109.5 (1795)	ECI②	116 @ 5500	129 @ 3000	3.17 × 3.46	7.5:1	63①
	Tredia	121.9 (1997)	Carb.	88 @ 5000	108 @ 3500	3.35 × 3.46	8.5:1	63①
	Starion	155.9 (2555)	ECI②	145 @ 5000	185 @ 2500	3.59 × 3.86	7.0:1	63①
	Mirage	89.6 (1468)	Carb.	68 @ 5000	82 @ 3500	2.97 × 3.23	9.4:1	63①
	Mirage	97.4 (1597)	ECI②	102 @ 5500	122 @ 3000	3.03 × 3.39	7.6:1	63①
	Galant	143.4 (2350)	MPI③	110 @ 4500	138 @ 3500	3.41 × 3.94	8.5:1	63①
	Precis	89.6 (1468)	Carb.	68 @ 5000	82 @ 3500	2.97 × 3.23	9.4:1	63①
1988	Cordia	109.5 (1795)	ECI②	116 @ 5500	129 @ 3000	3.17 × 3.46	7.5:1	63①
	Cordia	121.9 (1997)	Carb.	88 @ 5000	108 @ 3500	3.35 × 3.46	8.5:1	63①
	Tredia	109.5 (1795)	ECI②	116 @ 5500	129 @ 3000	3.17 × 3.46	7.5:1	63①
	Tredia	121.9 (1997)	Carb.	88 @ 5000	108 @ 3500	3.35 × 3.46	8.5:1	63①
	Starion	155.9 (2555)	ECI②	145 @ 5000	185 @ 2500	3.59 × 3.86	7.0:1	63①
	Mirage	89.6 (1468)	Carb.	68 @ 5000	82 @ 3500	2.97 × 3.23	9.4:1	63①
	Mirage	97.4 (1597)	ECI②	102 @ 5500	122 @ 3000	3.03 × 3.39	7.6:1	63①
	Galant	143.4 (2350)	MPI③	110 @ 4500	138 @ 3500	3.41 × 3.94	8.5:1	63①
	Galant	181.1 (2972)	MPI③	142 @ 5000	168 @ 2500	3.59 × 2.99	8.9:1	63①
	Precis	89.6 (1468)	Carb.	68 @ 5500	82 @ 3500	2.97 × 3.23	9.4:1	63①
1989	Starion	155.9 (2555)	ECI②	145 @ 5000	185 @ 2500	3.59 × 3.86	7.0:1	63①
	Mirage	86.6 (1468)	Carb.	68 @ 5000	82 @ 3500	2.97 × 3.23	9.4:1	63①
	Mirage	97.4 (1597)	ECI②	102 @ 5500	122 @ 3000	3.03 × 3.39	7.6:1	63①
	Galant	122 (1997)④	MPI③	120 @ 5000	116 @ 4500	3.35 × 3.46	8.5:1	11.4 @ 750
	Galant	122 (1997)⑤	MPI③	135 @ 6000	125 @ 5000	3.35 × 3.46	9.0:1	11.4 @ 750
	Sigma	181.1 (2972)	MPI③	142 @ 5000	168 @ 2500	3.59 × 2.99	8.9:1	63①
	Precis	89.6 (1468)	Carb.	68 @ 5500	82 @ 3500	2.97 × 3.23	9.4:1	63①

GENERAL ENGINE SPECIFICATIONS

Year	Model	Engine Displacement cu. in. (cc)	Fuel System Type	Net Horsepower @ rpm	Net Torque @ rpm (ft. lbs.)	Bore × Stroke (in.)	Compression Ratio	Oil Pressure @ rpm
1990–91	Mirage	89.6 (1468)	MPI③	81 @ 5500	91 @ 3000	2.97 × 3.23	9.4:1	11.4 @ 750
	Mirage	97.3 (1595)	MPI③	113 @ 6500	99 @ 5000	3.24 × 2.95	9.2:1	11.4 @ 750
	Galant	122 (1997)④	MPI③	120 @ 5000	116 @ 4500	3.35 × 3.46	8.5:1	11.4 @ 750
	Galant	122 (1997)⑤	MPI③	135 @ 6000	125 @ 5000	3.35 × 3.46	9.0:1	11.4 @ 750
	Sigma	181.4 (2972)	MPI③	142 @ 5000	168 @ 2500	3.59 × 2.99	8.9:1	11.4 @ 750
	Precis	89.6 (1468)	MPI③	81 @ 5500	91 @ 3000	2.97 × 3.23	9.4:1	11.4 @ 750
	Eclipse	107 (1755)	MPI③	92 @ 5000	105 @ 3500	3.17 × 3.39	9.0:1	11.4 @ 750
	Eclipse	122 (1997)	MPI③	135 @ 6000	125 @ 3000	3.35 × 3.46	9.0:1	11.4 @ 750
	Eclipse	122 (1997)	MPI⑥③	190 @ 6000 ⑦	203 @ 3000	3.35 × 3.46	7.8:1	11.4 @ 750

① Relief valve opening pressure
② Electronic controlled injection
③ Multi-point injection
④ Single overhead camshaft
⑤ Double overhead camshaft
⑥ Turbocharged
⑦ GSX model-195

TUNE-UP SPECIFICATIONS

Year	Model	Engine Displacement cu. in. (cc)	Spark Plugs Type	Gap (in.)	Ignition Timing (deg.) MT	AT	Compression Pressure (psi)	Fuel Pump (psi)	Idle Speed (rpm) MT	AT	Valve Clearance ① In.	Ex.
1987	Cordia	109.5 (1795)	BUR7EZ-11	0.035–0.039	5B	5B	170③	35–47	750	750	0.006	0.010
	Cordia	121.9 (1997)	BPR6ES-11	0.035–0.039	5B	5B	170③	2.4–3.4	700②	750②	Hyd.	Hyd.
	Tredia	109.5 (1795)	BUR7EZ-11	0.035–0.039	5B	5B	170③	35–47	750	750	0.006	0.010
	Tredia	121.9 (1997)	BPR6ES-11	0.035–0.039	5B	5B	170③	2.4–3.4	700②	750②	Hyd.	Hyd.
	Starion	155.9 (2555)	BP6ES-11	0.039–0.043	10B	10B	170③	35–47	750	850	0.006	0.010
	Mirage	89.6 (1468)	W20EP-10	0.039–0.043	3B	3B	170③	—	700	750	0.006	0.010
	Mirage	97.4 (1597)	BUR7EZ-11	0.035–0.039	8B	8B	170③	36	700	—	0.006	0.010
	Galant	143.4 (2350)	BPR6ES-11	0.039–0.043	—	5B	170③	36	—	750	Hyd.	Hyd.
	Precis	89.6 (1468)	W20EP-10	0.039–0.043	3B	3B	170③	—	700	750	0.006	0.010
1988	Cordia	109.5 (1795)	BUR7EZ-11	0.035–0.039	5B	5B	170③	35–47	750	750	0.006	0.010
	Cordia	121.9 (1997)	BPR6ES-11	0.035–0.039	5B	5B	170③	2.4–3.4	700②	750②	Hyd.	Hyd.
	Tredia	109.5 (1795)	BUR7EZ-11	0.035–0.039	5B	5B	170③	35–47	750	750	0.006	0.010
	Tredia	121.9 (1997)	BPR6ES-11	0.035–0.039	5B	5B	170③	2.4–3.4	700②	750②	Hyd.	Hyd.
	Starion	155.9 (2555)	BP6ES-11	0.039–0.043	10B	10B	170③	35–47	750	850	0.006	0.010
	Mirage	89.6 (1468)	W20EP-10	0.039–0.043	3B	3B	170③	—	700	750	0.006	0.010
	Mirage	97.4 (1597)	BUR7EZ-11	0.035–0.039	8B	8B	170③	36	700	—	0.006	0.010
	Galant	143.4 (2350)	BPR6ES-11	0.039–0.043	—	5B	170③	36	—	750	Hyd.	Hyd.
	Galant	181.4 (2972)	PGR5A-11	0.039–0.043	5B	5B	170③	38	700	700	Hyd.	Hyd.
	Precis	89.6 (1468)	W20EP-10	0.039–0.043	3B	3B	164③	—	700	750	0.006	0.010
1989	Starion	155.9 (2555)	BP6ES-11	0.039–0.043	10B	10B	170③	35–47	750	850	0.006	0.010
	Mirage	89.6 (1468)	W20EP-10	0.039–0.043	3B	3B	170③	—	700	750	0.006	0.010
	Mirage	97.4 (1597)	BUR7EZ-11	0.035–0.039	8B	8B	170③	36	700	—	0.006	0.010
	Galant	122 (1997)	BPR6ES-11	0.039–0.043	5	5B	125	47–50	750	750	Hyd.	Hyd.
	Galant	122 (1997)	BPR6ES-11	0.039–0.043	5	5B	137	47–50	750	750	Hyd.	Hyd.
	Sigma	181.4 (2972)	PGR5A-11	0.039–0.043	5B	5B	170③	38	700	700	Hyd.	Hyd.
	Precis	89.6 (1468)	W20EP-10	0.039–0.043	5B	5B	164③	2.8–3.6	800	800	0.006	0.010

TUNE-UP SPECIFICATIONS

Year	Model	Engine Displacement cu. in. (cc)	Spark Plugs Type	Spark Plugs Gap (in.)	Ignition Timing (deg.) MT	Ignition Timing (deg.) AT	Compression Pressure (psi)	Fuel Pump (psi)	Idle Speed (rpm) MT	Idle Speed (rpm) AT	Valve Clearance ① In.	Valve Clearance ① Ex.
1990	Eclipse	107 (1755)	BPR6ES-11	0.039–0.043	5B	5B	131	47–50	700	700	Hyd.	Hyd.
	Eclipse	122 (1997)	BPR6ES	0.028–0.031	5B	5B	137	47–50	700	700	Hyd.	Hyd.
	Eclipse	122 (1997)	BPR6ES-11	0.039–0.043	5B	5B	114	36–38	700	700	Hyd.	Hyd.
	Mirage	89.6 (1468)	BPR6ES-11	0.040–0.043	5B	5B	137	47–50	750	750	0.006	0.010
	Mirage	97.3 (1595)	BPR6ES	0.028–0.031	8B	8B	170 ③	47–50	750	750	Hyd.	Hyd.
	Galant	122 (1997)	BPR6ES-11	0.039–0.043	5B	5B	125	47–50	750	750	Hyd.	Hyd.
	Galant	122 (1997)	BPR6ES-11	0.039–0.043	5	5B	137	47–50	750	750	Hyd.	Hyd.
	Sigma	181.4 (2972)	PGR5A-11	0.039–0.043	—	5B	119	47–53	—	700	Hyd.	Hyd.
	Precis	89.6 (1468)	W20EP-10	0.039–0.043	5B	5B	164 ③	—	800	800	0.006	0.010
1991	ALL		SEE UNDERHOOD SPECIFICATIONS STICKER									

① Jet Valve—0.010
② With air conditioning
    Manual transaxle—750
    Automatic transaxle—850
③ Standard Valve—136 Limit

FIRING ORDER

NOTE: To avoid confusion, always replace spark plug wires one at a time.

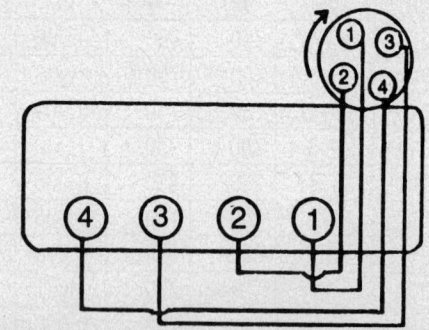

1.5L, 1.6L, 1.8L, 2.0L and 2.3L Engines
Engine Firing Order: 1–3–4–2
Distributor Rotation: Clockwise

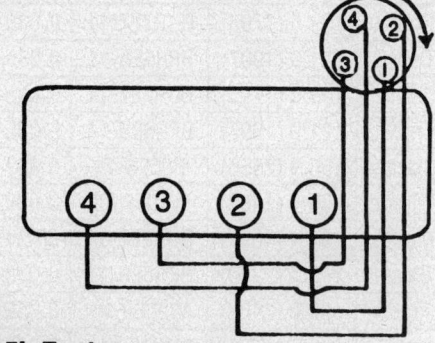

2.5L Engine
Engine Firing Order: 1–3–4–2
Distributor Rotation: Clockwise

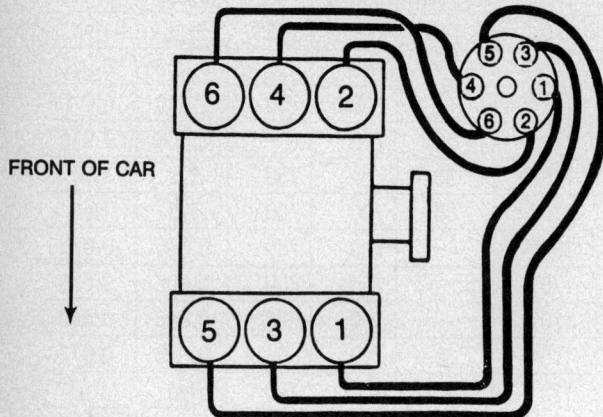

3.0L Engine
Engine Firing Order: 1–2–3–4–5–6
Distributor Rotation: Clockwise

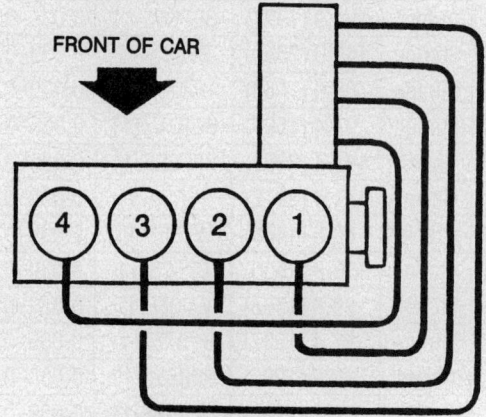

2.0L DOHC Engine
Engine Firing Order: 1–3–4–2
Distributorless Ignition System

CAPACITIES

Year	Model	Engine Displacement cu. in. (cc)	Engine Crankcase (qts.) with Filter	without Filter	Transmission (pts) 4-Spd	5-Spd	Auto.	Drive Axle (pts.)	Fuel Tank (gal.)	Cooling System (qts.)
1987	Cordia	109.5 (1795)	4.5	4.0	4.4	4.4	12.2	NA	13.2	7.4
	Cordia	121.9 (1997)	4.5	4.0	4.4	4.4	12.2	NA	13.2	7.4
	Tredia	109.5 (1795)	4.5	4.0	4.4	4.4	12.2	NA	13.2	7.4
	Tredia	121.9 (1997)	4.5	4.0	4.4	4.4	12.2	NA	13.2	7.4
	Starion	155.9 (2555)	5.0	4.5	4.8	—	14.8	2.7	19.8	9.7
	Mirage	89.6 (1468)	3.7	3.2	—	4.4	12.4	NA	11.9	5.3
	Mirage	97.4 (1597)	4.5	4.0	—	4.8	12.4	NA	11.9	5.3
	Galant	143.4 (2350)	4.5	4.0	—	—	12.4	NA	15.9	7.4
	Precis	89.6 (1468)	3.7	3.2	—	4.4	—	NA	11.9	5.3
1988	Cordia	109.5 (1795)	4.5	4.0	4.4	4.4	12.2	NA	13.2	7.4
	Cordia	121.9 (1997)	4.5	4.0	4.4	4.4	12.2	NA	13.2	7.4
	Tredia	109.5 (1795)	4.5	4.0	4.4	4.4	12.2	NA	13.2	7.4
	Tredia	121.9 (1997)	4.5	4.0	4.4	4.4	12.2	NA	13.2	7.4
	Starion	155.9 (2555)	5.0	4.5	4.8	—	14.8	2.7	19.8	9.7
	Mirage	89.6 (1468)	3.7	3.2	—	4.4	12.4	NA	11.9	5.3
	Mirage	97.4 (1597)	4.5	4.0	—	4.8	12.4	NA	11.9	5.3
	Galant	143.4 (2350)	4.5	4.0	—	—	12.4	NA	15.9	7.4
	Galant	181.4 (2972)	4.5	4.0	—	5.3	12.3	NA	15.9	9.7
	Precis	89.6 (1468)	3.7	3.2	—	4.4	—	NA	11.9	5.3
1989	Starion	155.9 (2555)	5.0	4.5	4.8	—	14.8	2.7	19.8	9.7
	Mirage	89.6 (1468)	3.7	3.2	—	4.4	12.4	NA	11.9	5.3
	Mirage	97.4 (1597)	4.5	4.0	—	4.8	12.4	NA	11.9	5.3
	Galant	122 (1997)	①	①	—	3.8②	12.8	④	15.9③	7.6
	Sigma	181.4 (2972)	4.5	4.0	—	5.3	12.3	NA	15.9	9.7
	Precis	89.6 (1468)	3.7	3.2	—	4.4	12.2	NA	11.9	5.3
1990-91	Elipse	107 (1955)	4.1	3.6	—	3.8	12.8	NA	15.9	6.6
	Elipse	122 (1997)	4.6	4.1	—	3.8	12.8	NA	15.9	7.6
	Elipse	122 (1997)	5.1	4.6	—	4.6②	12.8	④	15.9	7.6
	Mirage	89.6 (1468)	3.6	3.2	—	3.8	12.9	NA	13.2	5.3
	Mirage	97.3 (1595)	4.6	4.2	—	3.8	12.9	NA	13.2	5.3
	Galant	122 (1997)	①	①	—	3.8②	12.8	④	15.9③	7.6
	Sigma	181.4 (2972)	4.5	4.0	—	—	12.2	NA	15.9	9.7
	Precis	89.6 (1468)	3.7	3.2	—	4.4	12.2	NA	11.9	5.3

① SOHC
    Without filter—3.6 qts.
    With filter—4.1 qts.
  DOHC
    Without filter—4.1 qts.
    With filter—4.6 qts.
② 2WD; 4.8 on 4WD
③ 2WD; 16.4 on 4WD
④ 4WD model—transfer—1.26; Rear axle—1.48

CRANKSHAFT AND CONNECTING ROD SPECIFICATIONS
All measurements are given in inches.

Year	Engine Displacement cu. in. (cc)	Main Brg. Journal Dia.	Main Brg. Oil Clearance	Shaft End-play	Thrust on No.	Journal Diameter	Oil Clearance	Side Clearance
1987	109.5 (1795)	2.244	0.0008–0.0020	0.0020–0.0071	3	1.772	0.0008–0.0020	0.004–0.010
	121.9 (1997)	2.244	0.0008–0.0020	0.0020–0.0071	3	1.772	0.0008–0.0020	0.004–0.010
	155.9 (2555)	2.362	0.0008–0.0020	0.0020–0.0071	3	2.087	0.0008–0.0024	0.004–0.010
	89.6 (1468)	1.889	0.0008–0.0020	0.0020–0.0071	3	1.653	0.0004–0.0024	0.004–0.010
	97.4 (1597)	2.244	0.0008–0.0020	0.0020–0.0071	3	1.772	0.0004–0.0024	0.004–0.010
	143.4 (2350)	2.244	0.0008–0.0020	0.0020–0.0071	3	2.087	0.0008–0.0024	0.004–0.010
1988	109.5 (1795)	2.244	0.0008–0.0020	0.0020–0.0071	3	1.772	0.0008–0.0020	0.004–0.010
	121.9 (1997)	2.244	0.0008–0.0020	0.0020–0.0071	3	1.772	0.0008–0.0020	0.004–0.010
	155.9 (2555)	2.362	0.0008–0.0020	0.0020–0.0071	3	2.087	0.0008–0.0024	0.004–0.010
	89.6 (1468)	1.889	0.0008–0.0020	0.0020–0.0071	3	1.653	0.0004–0.0024	0.004–0.010
	97.4 (1597)	2.244	0.0008–0.0020	0.0020–0.0071	3	1.772	0.0004–0.0024	0.004–0.010
	143.4 (2350)	2.244	0.0008–0.0020	0.0020–0.0071	3	2.087	0.0008–0.0024	0.004–0.010
	181.4 (2972)	2.362	0.0008–0.0019	0.0020–0.0098	3	1.969	0.0006–0.0018	0.008–0.016
1989	121.9 (1997)	2.244	0.0008–0.0020	0.0020–0.0071	3	1.772	0.0008–0.0020	0.004–0.010
	155.9 (2555)	2.362	0.0008–0.0020	0.0020–0.0071	3	2.087	0.0008–0.0024	0.004–0.010
	89.6 (1468)	1.889	0.0008–0.0020	0.0020–0.0071	3	1.653	0.0004–0.0024	0.004–0.010
	97.4 (1597)	2.244	0.0008–0.0020	0.0020–0.0071	3	1.772	0.0008–0.0020	0.004–0.010
	181.4 (2972)	2.362	0.0008–0.0019	0.0020–0.0981	3	1.969	0.0006–0.0018	0.008–0.016
	181.4 (2972)	2.362	0.0008–0.0019	0.0020–0.0098	3	1.969	0.0006–0.0018	0.008–0.016
1990–91	107 (1755)	2.244	0.0008–0.0020	0.0020–0.0070	3	1.772	0.0008–0.0020	0.004–0.010
	122 (1997)	2.244	0.0008–0.0020	0.0020–0.0070	3	1.772	0.0008–0.0010	0.004–0.010
	121.9 (1997)	2.244	0.0008–0.0020	0.0020–0.0070	3	1.772	0.0008–0.0020	0.004–0.010
	89.6 (1468)	1.889	0.0008–0.0018	0.0020–0.0071	3	1.653	0.0006–0.0017	0.004–0.010
	97.3 (1595)	2.244	0.0008–0.0020	0.0020–0.0071	3	1.772	0.0008–0.0020	0.004–0.010
	181.4 (2972)	2.358	0.0008–0.0019	0.0020–0.0098	3	1.965	0.0006–0.0018	0.004–0.010

VALVE SPECIFICATIONS

Year	Engine Displacement cu. in. (cc)	Seat Angle (deg.)	Face Angle (deg.)	Spring Test Pressure (lbs. @ in.)	Spring Installed Height (in.)	Stem-to-Guide Clearance (in.)		Stem Diameter (in.)	
						Intake	Exhaust	Intake	Exhaust
1987	109.5 (1795)	45	45	62 @ 1.591	1.591	0.0010–0.0022	0.0020–0.0035	0.315	0.315
	121.9 (1997)	45	45	72 @ 1.591	1.591	0.0010–0.0022	0.0020–0.0035	0.315	0.315
	155.9 (2555)	45	45	72 @ 1.591	1.591	0.0012–0.0024	0.0020–0.0035	0.315	0.315
	89.6 (1468)	45	45	53 @ 1.469	1.417	0.0008–0.0020	0.0020–0.0035	0.315	0.315
	97.4 (1597)	45	45	62 @ 1.469	1.469	0.0012–0.0024	0.0020–0.0035	0.315	0.315
	143.4 (2350)	45	45	72 @ 1.591	1.591	0.0012–0.0024	0.0020–0.0035	0.322	0.315
1988	109.5 (1795)	45	45	62 @ 1.591	1.591	0.0010–0.0022	0.0020–0.0035	0.315	0.315
	121.9 (1997)	45	45	72 @ 1.591	1.591	0.0010–0.0022	0.0020–0.0035	0.315	0.315
	155.9 (2555)	45	45	72 @ 1.591	1.591	0.0012–0.0024	0.0020–0.0035	0.315	0.315
	89.6 (1468)	45	45	53 @ 1.469	1.417	0.0008–0.0020	0.0020–0.0035	0.315	0.315
	97.4 (1597)	45	45	62 @ 1.469	1.469	0.0012–0.0024	0.0020–0.0035	0.315	0.315
	143.4 (2350)	45	45	72 @ 1.591	1.591	0.0012–0.0024	0.0020–0.0035	0.322	0.315
	181.4 (2972)	44	45	74 @ 1.591	1.591	0.0012–0.0024	0.0020–0.0035	0.314	0.313
1989	121.9 (1997)	44	45	72 @ 1.591	1.591	0.0012–0.0024	0.0020–0.0035	0.315	0.315
	155.9 (2555)	45	45	72 @ 1.591	1.591	0.0012–0.0024	0.0020–0.0035	0.315	0.315
	89.6 (1468)	45	45	53 @ 1.469	1.417	0.0008–0.0020	0.0020–0.0035	0.315	0.315
	97.4 (1597)	45	45	62 @ 1.469	1.469	0.0012–0.0024	0.0020–0.0035	0.315	0.315
	143.4 (2350)	45	45	72 @ 1.591	1.591	0.0012–0.0024	0.0020–0.0035	0.322	0.315
	181.4 (2972)	44	45	74 @ 1.591	1.591	0.0012–0.0024	0.0020–0.0035	0.314	0.313
1990-91	107 (1755)	44	45	62 @ 1.469	1.469	0.0012–0.0024	0.0020–0.0035	0.315	0.315
	122 (1997)	44	45	66 @ 1.575	1.575	0.0008–0.0019	0.0020–0.0033	0.259	0.258
	121.9 (1997)	44	45	72 @ 1.591	1.591	0.0012–0.0024	0.0020–0.0035	0.315	0.315
	89.6 (1468)	44	45	53 @ 1.469	1.417	0.0008–0.0020	0.0020–0.0035	0.260	0.260
	97.3 (1595)	44	45	62 @ 1.469	1.469	0.0008–0.0019	0.0020–0.0033	0.259	0.258
	181.4 (2972)	44	45	74 @ 1.591	1.591	0.0012–0.0024	0.0020–0.0035	0.314	0.314

PISTON AND RING SPECIFICATIONS

All measurements are given in inches.

Year	Engine Displacement cu. in. (cc)	Piston Clearance	Ring Gap Top Compression	Ring Gap Bottom Compression	Ring Gap Oil Control	Ring Side Clearance Top Compression	Ring Side Clearance Bottom Compression	Ring Side Clearance Oil Control
1987	109.5 (1795)	0.0008–0.0016	0.0100–0.0180	0.0080–0.0160	0.0080–0.0200	0.002–0.004	0.001–0.002	—
	121.9 (1997)	0.0008–0.0016	0.0100–0.0180	0.0080–0.0160	0.0080–0.0200	0.002–0.004	0.001–0.002	—
	155.9 (2555)	0.0008–0.0016	0.0120–0.0200	0.0100–0.0160	0.0120–0.0310	0.002–0.004	0.001–0.002	—
	89.6 (1468)	0.0008–0.0016	0.0080–0.0160	0.0080–0.0160	0.0080–0.0280	0.0012–0.0028	0.0008–0.0024	—
	97.4 (1597)	0.0008–0.0016	0.0080–0.0160	0.0080–0.0160	0.0080–0.0280	0.0012–0.0028	0.0008–0.0024	—
	143.4 (2350)	0.0008–0.0016	0.0100–0.0180	0.0080–0.0160	0.0080–0.0280	0.0012–0.0028	0.0008–0.0024	—
1988	109.5 (1795)	0.0008–0.0016	0.0100–0.0180	0.0080–0.0160	0.0080–0.0200	0.002–0.004	0.001–0.002	
	121.9 (1997)	0.0008–0.0016	0.0100–0.0180	0.0080–0.0160	0.0080–0.0200	0.002–0.004	0.001–0.002	—
	155.9 (2555)	0.0008–0.0016	0.0120–0.0200	0.0100–0.0160	0.0120–0.0310	0.002–0.004	0.001–0.002	—
	89.6 (1468)	0.0008–0.0016	0.0080–0.0160	0.0080–0.0160	0.0080–0.0280	0.0012–0.0028	0.0008–0.0024	—
	97.4 (1597)	0.0008–0.0016	0.0080–0.0160	0.0080–0.0160	0.0080–0.0280	0.0012–0.0028	0.0008–0.0024	—
	143.4 (2350)	0.0008–0.0016	0.0100–0.0180	0.0080–0.0160	0.0080–0.0280	0.0012–0.0028	0.0008–0.0024	—
	181.4 (2972)	0.0008–0.0016	0.0118–0.0177	0.0098–0.0157	0.0079–0.0276	0.0012–0.0035	0.0008–0.0024	
1989	121.9 (1997)	0.0004–0.0012	0.0098–0.0157	0.0079–0.0138	0.0079–0.0276	0.0012–0.0028	0.0008–0.0024	—
	155.9 (2555)	0.0008–0.0016	0.0120–0.0200	0.0100–0.0160	0.0120–0.0310	0.002–0.004	0.001–0.002	—
	89.6 (1468)	0.0008–0.0016	0.0080–0.0160	0.0080–0.0160	0.0080–0.0280	0.0012–0.0028	0.0008–0.0024	—
	97.4 (1597)	0.0008–0.0016	0.0080–0.0160	0.0080–0.0160	0.0080–0.0280	0.0012–0.0028	0.0008–0.0024	—
	143.4 (2350)	0.0008–0.0016	0.0100–0.0180	0.0080–0.0160	0.0080–0.0280	0.0012–0.0028	0.0008–0.0024	—
1990–91	107 (1755)	0.0004–0.0012	0.0118–0.0177	0.0079–0.0138	0.0079–0.0276	0.0018–0.0033	0.0008–0.0024	—
	122 (1997)	0.0008–0.0016	0.0098–0.0177	0.0138–0.0197	0.0079–0.0276	0.0012–0.0028	0.0012–0.0028	—
	121.9 (1997)	0.0004–0.0012	0.0098–0.0157	0.0079–0.0138	0.0079–0.0276	0.0012–0.0028	0.0008–0.0024	—
	89.6 (1468)	0.0008–0.0016	0.0079–0.0138	0.0079–0.0138	0.0079–0.0276	0.0012–0.0028	0.0008–0.0024	—
	97.3 (1595)	0.0008–0.0016	0.0098–0.0157	0.0138–0.0197	0.0079–0.0276	0.0012–0.0028	0.0012–0.0028	—
	181.4 (2972)	0.0008–0.0016	0.0118–0.0177	0.0098–0.0157	0.0118–0.0354	0.0012–0.0035	0.0008–0.0024	—

TORQUE SPECIFICATIONS
All readings in ft. lbs.

Year	Engine Displacement cu. in. (cc)	Cylinder Head Bolts	Main Bearing Bolts	Rod Bearing Bolts	Crankshaft Pulley Bolts	Flywheel Bolts	Manifold Intake	Manifold Exhaust	Spark Plugs
1983	109.5 (1795)	73–79	38	37	80–94	94–101	11–14	11–14	14–22
	155.9 (2555)	73–79②	55–61	33	80–94	94–101	11–14	11–14	14–22
1984	109.5 (1795)	73–79	38	37	80–94	94–101	11–14	11–14	14–22
	121.9 (1992)	73–79	38	37	80–94	94–101	11–14	11–14	14–22
	155.9 (2555)	73–79②	55–61	33	80–94	94–101	11–14	11–14	14–22
1985	109.5 (1795)	73–79	38	37	80–94	94–101	11–14	11–14	14–22
	121.9 (1997)	73–79	38	37	80–94	94–101	11–14	11–14	14–22
	155.9 (2555)	73–79②	55–61	33	80–94	94–101	11–14	11–14	14–22
	89.6 (1468)	58–61	38	24	51–72	94–101	11–14	11–14	14–22
	97.4 (1597)	58–61	38	24	80–93	94–101	11–14	11–14	14–22
	143.4 (2350)	73–79	38	33	80–94	94–101	11–14	11–14	14–22
1986	109.5 (1795)	73–79	38	37	80–94	94–101	11–14	11–14	14–22
	121.9 (1997)	73–79	38	37	80–94	94–101	11–14	11–14	14–22
	155.9 (2555)	73–79②	55–61	33	80–94	94–101	11–14	11–14	14–22
	89.6 (1468)	58–61	38	24	51–72	94–101	11–14	11–14	14–22
	97.4 (1597)	58–61	38	24	80–93	94–101	11–14	11–14	14–22
	143.4 (2350)	73–79	38	33	80–94	94–101	11–14	11–14	14–22
1987	109.5 (1795)	73–79	38	37	80–94	94–101	11–14	11–14	14–22
	121.9 (1997)	73–79	38	37	80–94	94–101	11–14	11–14	14–22
	155.9 (2555)	73–79②	55–61	33	80–94	94–101	11–14	11–14	14–22
	89.6 (1468)	58–61	38	24	51–72	94–101	11–14	11–14	14–22
	97.4 (1597)	58–61	38	24	80–93	94–101	11–14	11–14	14–22
	143.4 (2350)	73–79	38	33	80–94	94–101	11–14	11–14	14–22
1988	109.5 (1795)	73–79	38	37	80–94	94–101	11–14	11–14	14–22
	121.9 (1997)	73–79	38	37	80–94	94–101	11–14	11–14	14–22
	155.9 (2555)	73–79②	55–61	33	80–94	94–101	11–14	11–14	14–22
	89.6 (1468)	58–61	38	24	51–72	94–101	11–14	11–14	14–22
	97.4 (1597)	58–61	38	24	80–93	94–101	11–14	11–14	14–22
	143.4 (2350)	73–79	38	33	80–94	94–101	11–14	11–14	14–22
	181.4 (2972)	73–79	55–61	38	109–115	53–55	11–14	11–16	14–22
1989	155.9 (2555)	73–79②	55–61	33	80–94	94–101	11–14	11–14	14–22
	89.6 (1468)	58–61	38	24	51–72	94–101	11–14	11–14	14–22
	97.4 (1597)	58–61	38	24	80–93	94–101	11–14	11–14	14–22
	122 (1997)③	65–72	36–40	36–38	80–94	94–101	11–14	11–14	14–22
	122 (1997)④	65–72	47–51	36–38	80–94	94–101	④	18–22	14–22
	181.4 (2972)	73–79	55–61	38	109–115	53–55	11–14	11–16	14–22
1990–91	107 (1755)	51–54	37–39	24–25	80–94	94–101	11–14	11–14	14–22
	122 (1997)	65–72	47–51	36–38	80–94	94–101	④	18–22	14–22
	155.9 (2555)	73–79②	55–61	33	80–94	94–101	11–14	11–14	14–22
	89.6 (1468)	51–54	36–40	③	51–72	94–101	13–18	11–14	14–22
	97.3 (1595)	65–72	47–51	36–38	80–93	94–101	②	18–22	14–22
	122 (1997)③	65–72	36–40	36–38	80–94	94–101	11–14	11–14	14–22
	122 (1997)④	65–72	47–51	36–38	80–94	94–101	④	18–22	14–22
	181.4 (2972)	66–72	55–61	38	130–137	53–55	11–14	11–16	14–22

① Single overhead camshaft
② Double overhead camshaft
③ Tighten to 14.5 ft. lbs.; 2nd back off; 3rd tighten to 14.5; 4th tighten additional ¼ turn
④ Torque bolts to 11–14 ft. lbs., torque nuts to 22–30 ft. lbs.

BRAKE SPECIFICATIONS
All measurements in inches unless noted.

Year	Model	Lug Nut Torque (ft. lbs.)	Master Cylinder Bore	Brake Disc Minimum Thickness	Brake Disc Maximum Runout	Maximum Brake Drum Diameter	Minimum Lining Thickness Front	Minimum Lining Thickness Rear
1987	Cordia	50–57②	0.87	—	0.650	8.000	0.040	0.040
	Tredia	50–57②	0.87	—	0.650	8.000	0.040	0.040
	Starion	50–57②	0.94	—	0.880	—	0.040	—
	Mirage	50–57②	0.81④	—	0.450③	7.100	0.040	0.040
	Galant	50–57②	0.94	—	0.650	8.000	0.040	0.040
	Precis	51–58①	0.81	—	0.450	7.100	0.040	0.040
1988	Cordia	50–57②	0.87	—	0.650	8.000	0.040	0.040
	Tredia	50–57②	0.87	—	0.650	8.000	0.040	0.040
	Starion	50–57②	0.94	—	0.880	—	0.040	—
	Mirage	50–57②	0.81④	—	0.450③	7.100	0.040	0.040
	Galant	43–52②	0.94	—	0.650		0.040	0.040
	Precis	51–58①	0.81	—	0.450		0.040	0.040
1989	Starion	50–57②	0.94	—	0.880	—	0.040	—
	Mirage	50–57②	0.81④	—	0.450③	7.100	0.040	0.040
	Galant	65–80②	⑨	0.882	0.003	8.100⑦	0.080	0.080
	Precis	69–78⑩	0.81	0.670	0.006	7.200	0.040	0.040
	Sigma	43–52②	0.94	—	0.004	—	0.079	0.039
1990–91	Eclipse	87–101②	0.87⑪	0.882	0.003	⑦	0.080	0.080
	Mirage⑤	65–80	0.81	0.449	0.006	7.200	0.080	0.080
	Mirage⑥	65–80	0.87	0.882	0.006	⑦	0.080	0.080
	Galant	65–80	⑨	0.882	0.003	8.100⑦	0.080	0.080
	Precis	69–78⑩	0.81	0.670	0.006	7.200	0.040	0.040
	Sigma	65–79	0.94	0.882	0.004	⑧	0.079	0.079

① With aluminum wheels—57–72
② With aluminum wheels—66–81
③ Turbo 0.650
④ Turbo 0.87
⑤ 1500 Engine
⑥ 1600 Engine
⑦ Rear disc minimum thickness—0.331
⑧ Rear disc minimum thickness—0.646
⑨ 2WD w/o ABS—0.87
   2WD w/ ABS—0.94
   4WD w/o ABS—0.94
   4WD w/ ABS—1.00
⑩ With aluminum wheels—78–98
⑪ Turbo 0.94

WHEEL ALIGNMENT

Year	Model	Caster Range (deg.)	Caster Preferred Setting (deg.)	Camber Range (deg.)	Camber Preferred Setting (deg.)	Toe-in (in.)	Steering Axis Inclination (deg.)
1987	Cordia	5/16–15/16P	13/16P	1/16N–5/16P	7/16P⑤	1/8N–1/8P	7 1/16
	Tredia	5/16–15/16P	13/16P	1/16N–15/16P	7/16P⑤	1/8N–1/8P	7 1/16
	Starion	5 5/16–6 5/16P	5 13/16P	1N–0P	1/2N	13/64P–13/64P	—
	Mirage	1/2–1 1/2P⑥	1P	1/2N–1/2P	0P①	1/8N–1/8P	5 3/4
	Galant	5/32–15/32P	21/32P	0–1P	1/2P	1/8N–1/8P	6 5/8
	Precis	1/2–1/8P	3/16P	0–1P	1/2P⑦	1/16P–5/32P	12 11/16
1988	Cordia	5/16–15/16P	13/16P	1/16N–5/16P	7/16P⑤	1/8N–1/8P	7 1/16
	Tredia	5/16–15/16P	13/16P	1/16N–15/16P	7/16P⑤	1/8N–1/8P	7 1/16
	Starion	5 5/16–6 5/16P	5 13/16P	1N–0P	1/2N	13/64P–13/64P	—
	Mirage	1/2–1 1/2P⑥	1P	1/2N–1/2P	0P①	1/8N–1/8P	5 3/4
	Galant	5/32–15/32P	21/32P	0–1P	1/2P⑧	1/8N–1/8P	6 5/8
	Precis	1/2–1/8P	3/16P	0–1P	1/2P⑦	1/16P–5/32P	12 11/16

WHEEL ALIGNMENT

Year	Model	Caster Range (deg.)	Caster Preferred Setting (deg.)	Camber Range (deg.)	Camber Preferred Setting (deg.)	Toe-in (in.)	Steering Axis Inclination (deg.)
1989	Starion	$5^5/_{16}$–$6^5/_{16}$P	$5^{13}/_{16}$P	1N-0P	$^1/_2$N	$^{13}/_{64}$P-$^{13}/_{64}$P	—
	Mirage	$^1/_2$-$1^1/_2$P ⑥	1P	$^1/_2$N-$^1/_2$P	0P ①	$^1/_8$N-$^1/_8$P	$5^3/_4$
	Galant	$1^1/_2$-$2^1/_2$P	2P	$^3/_{16}$N-$^{13}/_{16}$P	$^5/_{16}$P ⑧	$^1/_8$N-$^1/_8$P	—
	Precis	$^1/_2$-$1^1/_8$P	$^{13}/_{16}$P	0-1P	$^1/_2$P ⑦	$^1/_{16}$P-$^5/_{32}$P	$12^{11}/_{16}$
	Sigma	$3^1/_{16}$-$1^3/_{16}$P	$^{11}/_{16}$P	0-1P ⑨	$^1/_2$P ⑩	$^1/_8$N-$^1/_8$P	NA
1990-91	Eclipse ⑪	$1^{27}/_{32}$-$2^{27}/_{32}$P	$2^{11}/_{32}$P	$^1/_4$N-$^3/_4$P	$^1/_4$P ⑬	$^1/_8$N-$^1/_8$P	$14^3/_{32}$
	Eclipse ⑫	$1^{29}/_{32}$-$2^{29}/_{32}$P	$2^{13}/_{32}$P	$^{13}/_{32}$N-$^{19}/_{32}$P	$^3/_{32}$P ⑬	$^1/_8$N-$^1/_8$P	$14^3/_{32}$
	Mirage	$1^{11}/_{16}$-$2^{11}/_{16}$P	$2^3/_{16}$P	$^1/_2$N-$^1/_2$P	0P ①	$^1/_8$N-$^1/_8$P	—
	Galant	$1^1/_2$-$2^1/_2$P	2P	$^3/_{16}$N-$^{13}/_{16}$P	$^5/_{16}$P ⑧	$^1/_8$N-$^1/_8$P	—
	Precis	$^1/_2$-$1^1/_8$P	$^{13}/_{16}$P	0-1P	$^1/_2$P ⑦	$^1/_{16}$P-$^5/_{32}$P	$12^{11}/_{16}$
	Sigma	$^3/_{16}$-$1^3/_{16}$P	$^{11}/_{16}$P	0-1P ⑨	$^1/_2$P ⑩	$^1/_8$N-$^1/_8$P	—

N Negative
P Positive
① Rear—$^{11}/_{16}$N
② Rear—$^5/_{16}$P
③ Rear—$^9/_{16}$N
④ Rear—$^{21}/_{32}$N
⑤ Rear—$^{11}/_{16}$P
⑥ With power steering—$^{11}/_{16}$-$2^3/_{16}$
⑦ Rear—$^5/_8$N
⑧ Rear—$^3/_4$N
⑨ Rear—1N-$^1/_4$N
⑩ Rear—$^3/_4$N
⑪ 1.8L engine
⑫ 2.0L engine
⑬ Rear—$^3/_4$P

ENGINE ELECTRICAL

Distributor

Removal

1. Rotate the engine until the No. 1 piston is at TDC of the compression stroke. Disconnect the negative battery cable. Remove all necessary components in order to gain access to the distributor assembly.
2. Remove the distributor cap with the spark plug wires attached and position it out of the way. Disconnect the distributor wiring connector and vacuum hoses. Be sure to tag all the wires and vacuum lines for easy installation.
3. Remove the distributor base retaining nut. Remove the distributor.
4. Before installation check that the No. 1 piston is at TDC of the compression stroke, then align the marks on the bottom of the distributor housing, just above the drive gear, with the punch mark on the distributor drive gear.

Installation

TIMING NOT DISTURBED

1. To install, double check that the crankshaft mark and timing mark are still aligned and that the engine has not been turned. Align the mating mark on the distributor housing described above with the mating mark (punch) on the distributor driven gear.
2. Install the distributor assembly while aligning the mating mark on the distributor attaching flange with the center of the hold-down stud.
3. Connect all wiring and reinstall distributor cap and seal.
4. Connect the negative battery cable. Start engine and set timing. Then tighten distributor mounting nut.

TIMING DISTURBED

1. Remove the spark plug from No. 1 cylinder and position a compression gauge or a thumb over the spark plug hole.

2. Slowly crank the engine until compression pressure starts to build.
3. Continue cranking the engine so the timing marks align with the TDC mark.
4. Install the distributor assembly while aligning the mating mark on the distributor attaching flange with the center of the hold-down stud.
5. Connect all wiring and reinstall distributor cap and seal.
6. Connect the negative battery cable. Start engine and set timing. Then tighten distributor mounting nut.

NOTE: Some engines may be sensitive to the routing of the distributor sensor wires. If routed near the high-voltage coil wire or the spark plug wires, the electromagnetic field surrounding the high voltage wires could generate an occasional disruption of the ignition system operation.

Distributorless Ignition

Removal and Installation

NOTE: The 2.0L DOHC engine is used on the Eclipse.

CRANK ANGLE SENSOR

1. Disconnect the battery negative cable.
2. The crank sensor is driven off the back of the intake camshaft. To remove, turn the crankshaft by hand so the No. 1 cylinder piston is at TDC.
3. Disconnect the multi-wire connector.
4. Remove the retainer bolts and lift the sensor from the cylinder head.
To install:
5. At installation, align the punch mark on the crank angle sensor housing with the notch in the plate, then install the crank sensor. Make sure the flat drive tang registers into the slot in the camshaft.

6. Reconnect the multi-wire connector.

7. Reconnect the battery negative cable and check the timing.

IGNITION COIL

1. Disconnect the battery negative cable.

2. The ignition coil is mounted on the front of the intake manifold. Remove and tag the spark plug cables.

3. Remove the mounting bolts and remove from engine.

To install:

4. Install coil to manifold. Install bolt and tighten to 15–19 ft. lbs.

5. Install spark plug cables in the correct locations.

6. Reconnect the battery negative cable.

POWER TRANSISTOR

1. Disconnect the battery negative cable.

2. The power transistor is mounted on the front of the intake manifold. Remove and retaining screw and disconnect the wires to remove.

To install:

3. Install power transistor to manifold. Install screw and tighten.

4. Reconnect the battery negative cable.

5. Install the distributor to the cylinder head while aligning the mark on the base attaching flange with center of the hold-down stud. Install the retaining nut, distributor cap and vacuum hoses. Start the engine and adjust the ignition timing.

Ignition Timing

Adjustment

1. Run the engine until operating temperature is reached.

2. Leave the engine idling, apply the hand brake and position the gear selector in neutral, if equipped with a manual transmission, or **P**, if equipped with an automatic transmission. Turn **OFF** all accessories and stop the engine.

3. Install a tachometer, connecting the red lead to the (−) terminal of the coil and the black lead to a clean ground; on all vehicles, except the following:

a. 1988–90 Starion and Mirage with the 1.6L engine—disconnect the female connector from the ignition timing connector, connect a suitable jumper wire with an alligator clip to the ignition timing adjusting terminal to ground it.

b. 1988–91 Galant and Sigma—insert a suitable jumper wire, from the harness side, to the 1 pin connector located between the noise filter and the primary side of the ignition coil, and connect the tachometer. Be sure to insert the jumper wire along the terminal surface. If the connector is a male connector, the jumper wire should be inserted to the lock tab side. If the connector is a female connector, the jumper wire should be inserted opposite the lock tab side. Also using a alligator clip, connect a suitable jumper wire to the terminal for the ignition timing adjustment, located in the engine compartment, and ground it.

c. Eclipse—locate the wire connector on the ignition coil connector. Insert a paper clip behind the TACH terminal connector to act as a tach hookup adapter. Connect a tachometer to the paper clip.

4. Disconnect and plug the vacuum lines to the sub vacuum chamber at the distributor, if equipped. On the Cordia and Tredia 1.8L engine, disconnect the boost sensor connector, located in the engine compartment.

5. Start the engine and let it reach normal operating temperature. Check and verify that the engine idle speed is correct. If not within specifications, adjust it.

6. Stop the engine and connect the timing light according to manufacturers instructions. Disconnect and plug the vacuum advance hose, as required.

7. Start the engine and allow it to idle. Point the timing light at the mark on the front cover and read the timing by noting the

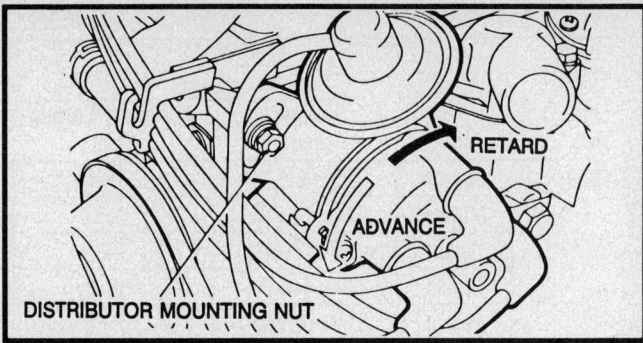

Adjusting ignition timing

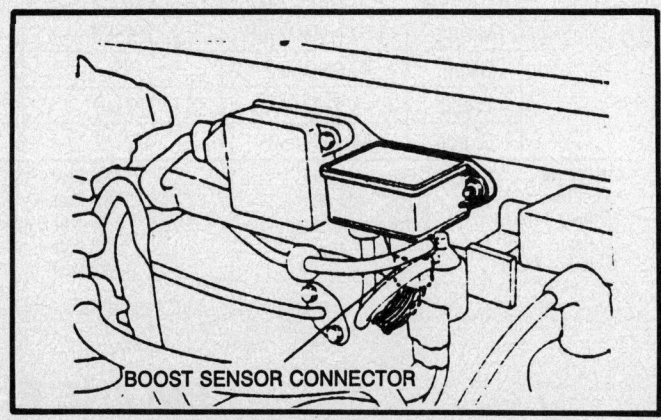

Boost sensor connector location—Cordia/Tredia

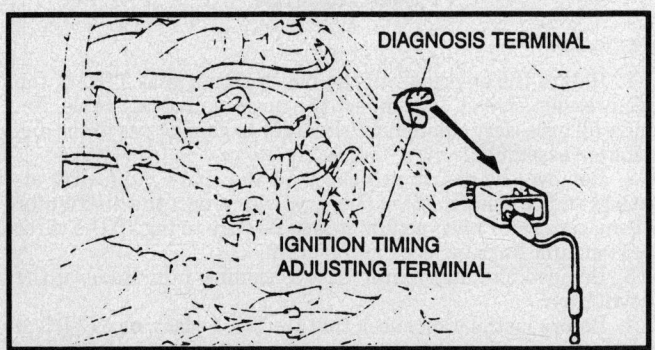

Jumping the ignition timing adjusting terminal— Mirage

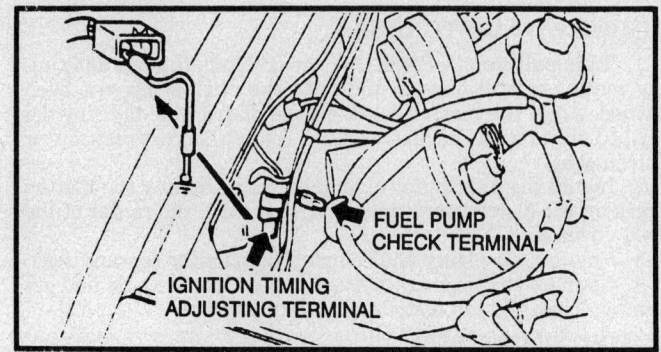

Jumping the ignition timing adjusting terminal— Starion

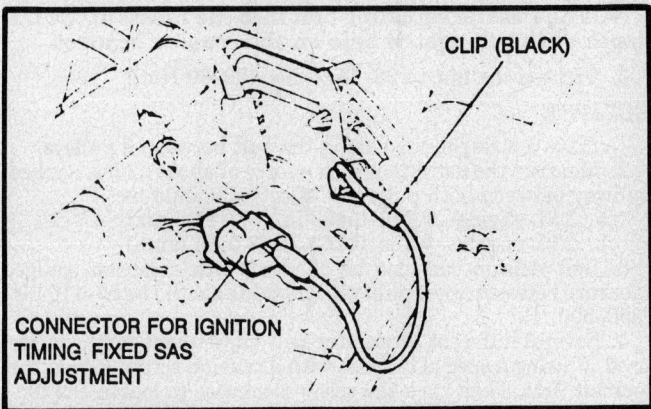

Jumping the ignition timing adjusting terminal—Galant

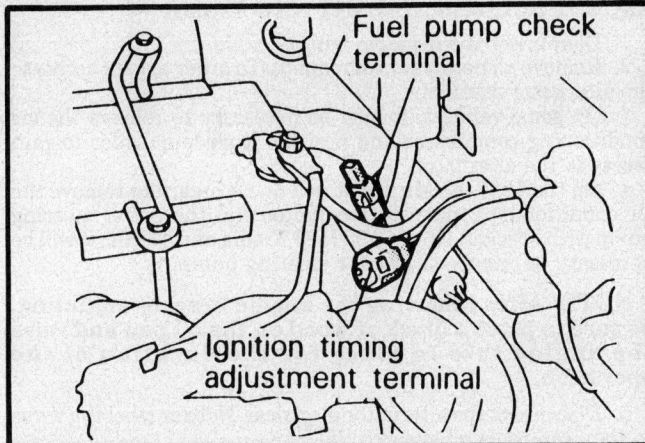

Ignition timing adjustment terminal location—Eclipse 1.8L engine

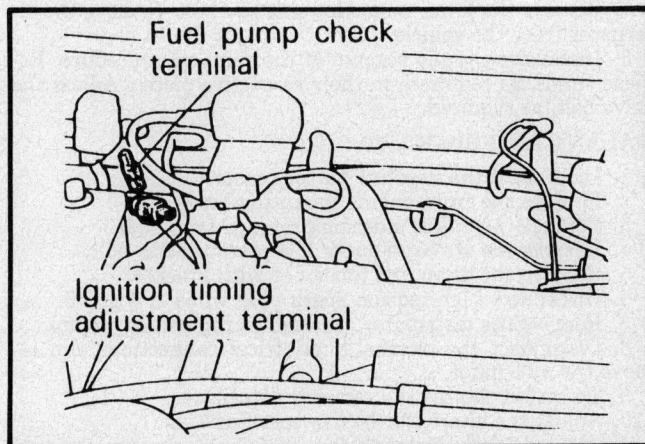

Ignition timing adjustment terminal location—Eclipse 2.0L engine

position of the groove in the front pulley in relation to the timing mark or scale on the front cover. If the timing is incorrect, on all except the Eclipse 2.0L engine, loosen the distributor mounting bolt. Turn the distributor slightly clockwise to retard the timing or counterclockwise to advance it. On the Eclipse 2.0L engine, loosen the crank angle sensor mounting nut and adjust by turning the crank angle sensor. The crank angle sen-

sor is located and driven by the back of the intake camshaft. Turning the sensor to the right advances the timing, to the left retards it.

8. When the reading is correct, tighten the distributor mounting bolt back up and verify that the setting has not changed.

9. Turn the engine **OFF**, disconnect the timing light and tachometer and, if necessary, reconnect all the vacuum lines and disconnect connectors. Remove all jumper wires. Recheck the idle speed and adjust, as necessary.

Alternator

Precautions

In order to prevent damage to the alternator observe the following precautions:

• Reversing the battery connections will result in damage to the diodes.

• Booster cables should be connected from positive to positive and the negative cable from the booster battery connected to a good ground on the engine of the vehicle with the dead battery.

• Never use a fast charger as a booster to start the vehicle.

• When servicing the battery with a fast charger always disconnect the battery cables.

• Never attempt to polarize an alternator.

• Avoid long soldering times when replacing diodes or transistors. Prolonged heat is damaging to alternators.

• Do not use test lamps of more than 12 volts for checking diode continuity.

• Do not short across or ground any of the alternator terminals.

• The polarity of the battery, alternator and regulator must be matched and considered before making any electrical connections within the system.

• Never operate the alternator on an open circuit. Make sure all connections within a circuit are clean and tight.

• Disconnect the negative (or both) battery terminals when performing any service on the electrical system.

• Disconnect the negative battery cable if arc welding is to be done on any part of the vehicle.

Belt Tension Adjustment

EXCEPT SIGMA AND ECLIPSE

1. Check the drive belt(s) for cracking, fraying or any other deterioration. Replace the drive belt if suspect.

2. Loosen the alternator pivot nut.

3. Loosen the lock bolt of the belt tension adjuster.

4. Using the adjustment bolt, adjust the belt tension to specification. Belt tension is proper when the belt can be deflected at midpoint $9/32-11/32$ in.

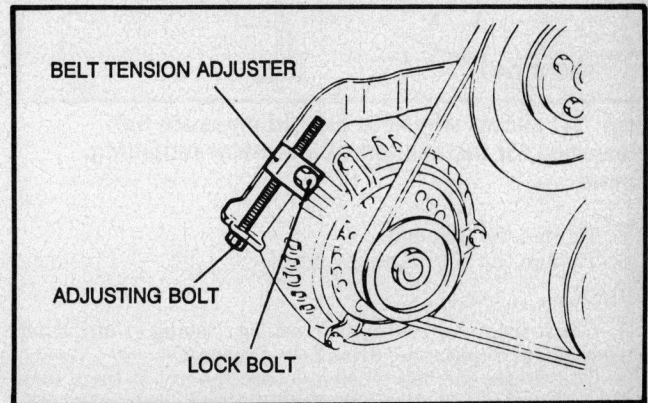

Alternator belt adjustment—except Sigma

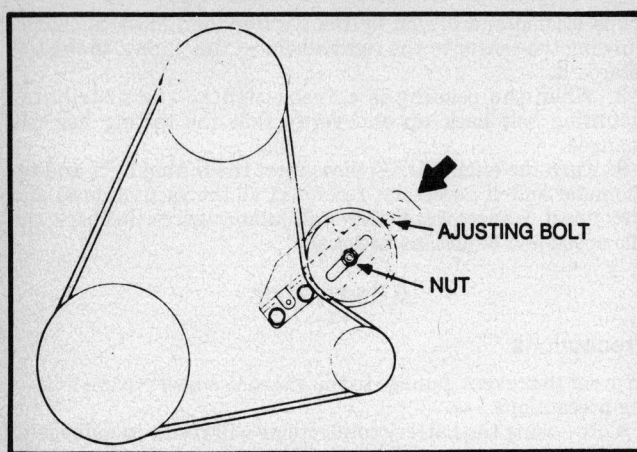

Alternator belt adjustment—Sigma

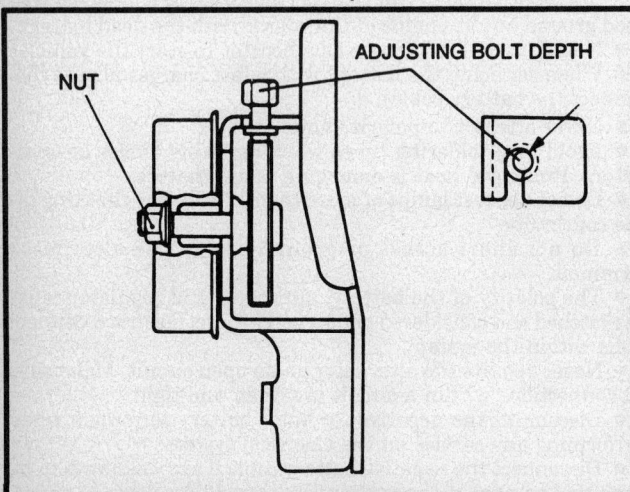

Tension pulley adjustment bolt

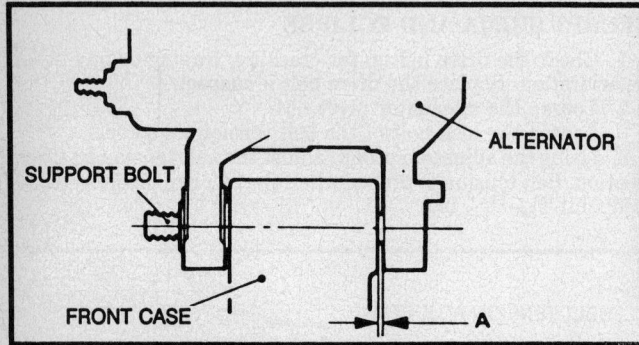

Gap "A" shows where to should measure the clearance for installation of alternator mounting shims

5. Tighten the lock bolt.
6. Tighten the alternator pivot nut.

SIGMA

1. Check the drive belt(s) for cracking, fraying or any other deterioration. Replace the drive belt if suspect.
2. To increase the belt tension, loosen the nut ⅛ turn, turn the left threaded adjusting bolt clockwise and displace the tension pulley slightly.

NOTE: Put the adjusting bolt into the recess at the far depth of the elongated hole on the tension bracket.

3. Tighten the nut to 28–43 ft. lbs. (39–60 Nm).

ECLIPSE

1. Place a straight-edge along the belt between 2 pulleys.
2. Measure the deflection with a force of about 22 lbs. applied midway between both pulleys. Deflection should be:
   a. 1.8L engine—0.315–0.433 in. (8.0–11.0mm)
   b. 2.0L engine—0.354–0.453 in. (9.0–11.5mm)
3. Belt tension can also be checked with a tension gauge. Measure between any 2 pulleys. The value should be 55–110 lbs. (250–500 N).
4. Several different alternator belt adjustment methods are used. If using a special bracket with a tension screw, loosen the locknut first. Then turn the screw clockwise to loosen the tension and counterclockwise to increase the tension.

Removal and Installation

EXCEPT ECLIPSE, GALANT AND SIGMA V6

1. Disconnect the negative battery cable.
2. Remove all necessary components in order to gain access to the alternator assembly.
3. On some vehicles, it may be necessary to remove the air conditioning compressor and position it aside in order to gain access to the alternator.
4. On the 1987–88 Mirage, it will be necessary to remove the air conditioning condenser fan motor and the power steering pump with bracket. On the 1987–88 Tredia and Cordia, it will be necessary to remove the power steering pump.

NOTE: After removing the engine bracket mounting, be sure to place a block of wood on the oil pan and raise the engine into to place for the duration of the operation.

5. Disconnect the alternator electrical. Note or label the wires so they can reinstalled correctly.
6. Remove the top mounting bolt. Loosen the lower mounting nut. Slide the alternator over in its attaching bracket and remove the fan belt.
7. Remove the lower mounting nut and bolt. Remove the alternator from the vehicle.
8. Installation is the reverse of the removal procedure. Replace shims, as required, in their respective places. Adjust the drive belt, as required.

GALANT AND SIGMA V6

1. Disconnect the negative battery cable.
2. Remove the front engine mounting bracket.
3. Remove the power steering pressure hose nut.
4. Remove the air conditioner low pressure line bolt.
5. Remove the drive belt tensioner with bracket.
6. Disconnect high tension spark plug wires 2, 4 and 6.
7. Remove the distributor cap and timing belt cover cap.
8. Disconnect the alternator electrical connections and remove the alternator.
9. To install reverse the removal procedure.
10. Adjust the alternator belt to specifications.

ECLIPSE

1.8L Engine

1. Disconnect the negative battery cable.
2. If equipped with air conditioning, remove condensor electric fan motor and shroud assembly. Then remove air conditioner compressor drive belt.
3. Remove alternator and water pump belts.
4. Remove both water pump pulleys.
5. Remove the alternator top brace, then disconnect the alternator wiring.

6. Remove alternator.

7. At installation, adjust drive belts, reconnect battery negative cable.

2.0L Engine

1. Disconnect the negative battery cable.

2. Remove the left cover panel from under the vehicle.

3. If equipped with air conditioning, remove condensor electric fan motor and shroud assembly.

4. Remove alternator and water pump belts.

5. Remove both water pump pulleys.

6. Remove the alternator top brace and disconnect the alternator wiring.

7. Remove alternator.

8. At installation, adjust belt tension, reinstall cover panel and reconnect battery negative cable.

Starter

Removal and Installation

EXCEPT ECLIPSE

1. Disconnect the negative battery cable.

2. Remove the necessary components in order to gain access to the starter assembly.

3. Disconnect the electrical connections from the starter motor.

4. Remove the starter motor to engine mounting bolts. Remove the starter motor from the vehicle.

5. If various components make starter motor removal difficult from the top of the engine compartment, raise and support the vehicle, then remove the starter from under after removing the splash shield.

6. Installation is the reverse of the removal procedure.

ECLIPSE

1. Disconnect both battery cables.

2. Remove the battery and battery tray.

3. Disconnect the speedometer cable on the transaxle end.

4. Remove the intake manifold brace on the 1.8L engine.

5. Disconnect the starter motor electrical connections.

5. Remove the starter motor bolts and the starter.

To install:

6. Position the starter motor and install the bolts.

7. Reconnect the electrical connections.

8. Install the intake manifold brace on the 1.8L engine and reconnect the speedometer cable.

9. Install the battery tray and battery.

10. Reconnect battery cables and check starter motor operation.

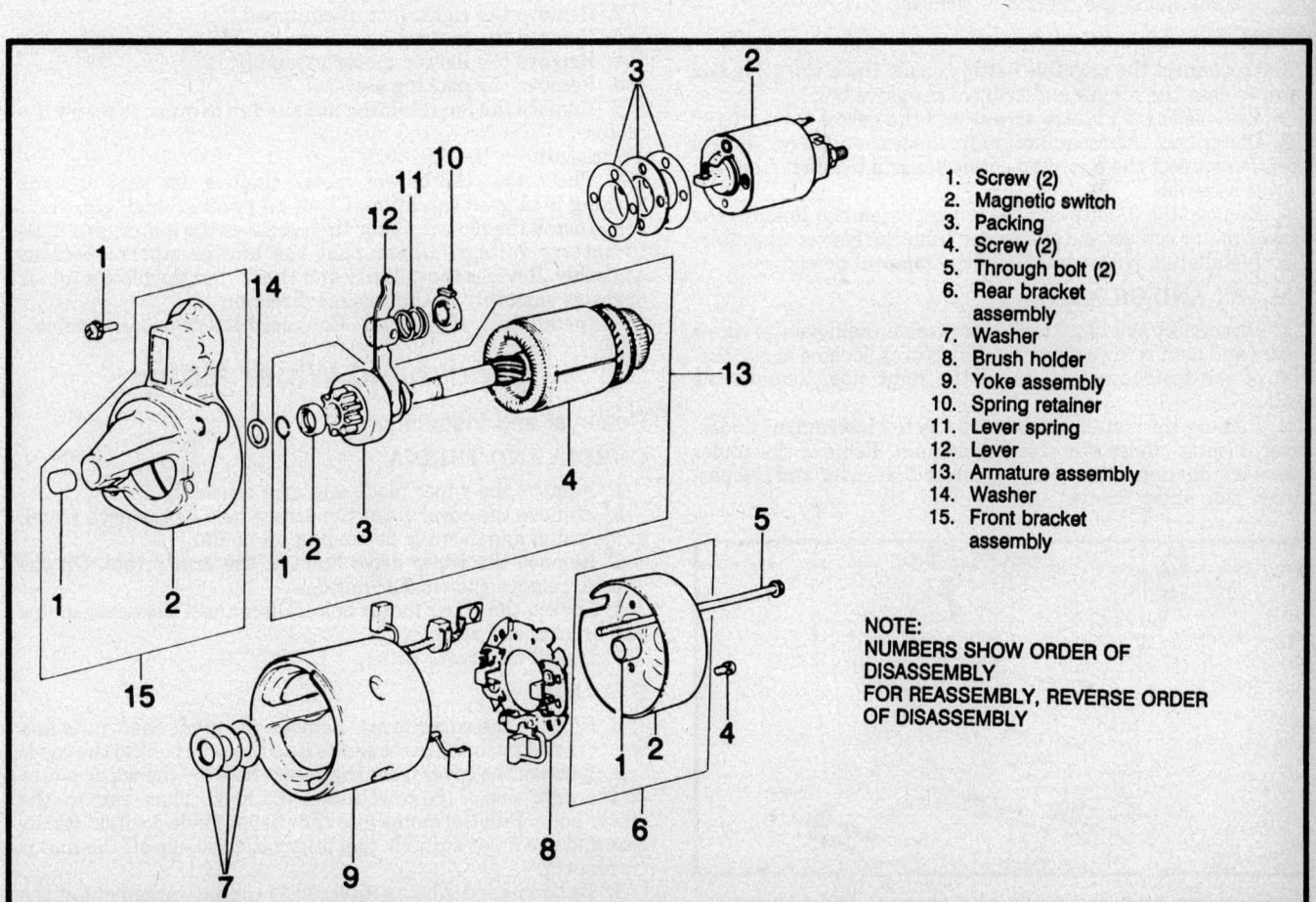

1. Screw (2)
2. Magnetic switch
3. Packing
4. Screw (2)
5. Through bolt (2)
6. Rear bracket assembly
7. Washer
8. Brush holder
9. Yoke assembly
10. Spring retainer
11. Lever spring
12. Lever
13. Armature assembly
14. Washer
15. Front bracket assembly

NOTE:
NUMBERS SHOW ORDER OF DISASSEMBLY
FOR REASSEMBLY, REVERSE ORDER OF DISASSEMBLY

Typical starter motor components

CHASSIS ELECTRICAL

Heater Blower Motor

Removal and Installation

CORDIA AND TREDIA

1. Disconnect the negative battery cable. Unscrew the 1 attaching bolt and remove the lower cover from under the right side of the instrument panel. Remove the mounting screws at the front and remove the glove box. Remove the cowl side trim.
2. Disconnect the air selector control wire. Disconnect the discharge duct at the blower.
3. Disconnect the electrical connector. Remove the 4 mounting bolts and remove the blower assembly.
4. Installation is the reverse of the removal procedure.

STARION

1. Disconnect the negative battery cable. Remove the under cover from the bottom of the dash panel, under the glove box. Then, open the glove box door and pull the glove box forward while pressing inward on both sides of the glove box. This will allow the door to drop.
2. Remove the screws attaching the glove box door hinge to the bottom of the dashboard and then remove the assembly.
3. Disconnect the fresh air/recirculated air change over cable from the blower housing. Disconnect the blower electrical connector.
4. Remove the 3 bolts and the blower assembly. The blower motor and fan may be removed from the case.
5. Installation is the reverse of removal.

MIRAGE

1. Disconnect the negative battery cable. Open the glove box door, release the hinges and remove the glove box.
2. Remove the 4 Phillips screws and the parcel tray.
3. Disconnect the recirculation/fresh air change over control wire. Disconnect the electrical connector and the duct from the blower assembly.
4. Remove the 3 bolts and the blower assembly. Remove the blower motor screws and the motor from the blower assembly.
5. Installation is the reverse of the removal procedure.

GALANT AND SIGMA

1. Disconnect the negative battery cable. Remove the screw covers and both screws from the undercover, located at the bottom of the instrument panel on the right side. Remove the undercover.
2. Remove the installation screws and the instrument undercover, located under the steering column. Remove the under frame installation screws located under that cover and the passenger side under frame.

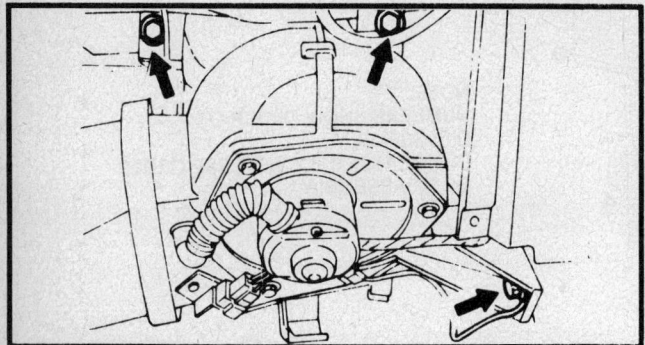

Remove the arrowed bolts and remove the blower motor—Cordia and Tredia

3. Remove both stops from the bottom of the glove box at the front. Remove the glove box installation screws and the glove box. Remove the duct leading into the blower unit, which is accessible through the glove box door.
4. Remove the 4 bolts and the blower assembly. Disconnect the electrical connector and the inside/outside air change over control vacuum hose before pulling the unit out.
5. Installation is the reverse of removal.

PRECIS

NOTE: To remove either the blower or core, the heater case must be removed.

1. Disconnect the battery ground.
2. Place the control in the **HOT** position.
3. Drain the cooling system.
4. Remove the heater hoses from the core tubes.
5. Remove the lower instrument panel section.
6. Remove the center console.
7. Disconnect the ducts at the heater case.
8. Disconnect the heater control cable at the case.
9. If equipped with air conditioning, discharge the system and remove the evaporator.
10. Unbolt and remove the heater case.
11. Installation is the reverse of removal. Adjust the control cable. If necessary, charge the refrigerant system.

ECLIPSE

1. Disconnect battery negative cable.
2. Remove the right duct, if equipped.
3. Remove the molded hose from the blower assembly.
4. Remove the blower motor assembly.
5. Remove the packing seal.
6. Remove the fan retaining nut and fan in order to renew the motor.

To install:

7. Check that the blower motor shaft is not bent and the packing is in good condition. Clean all parts of dust, etc.
8. Install the blower motor then connect the motor terminals to battery voltage. Check that the blower motor operates smoothly. Reverse the polarity and check that the blower motor operates smoothly in the reverse direction.
9. Install duct, if removed. Connect battery negative cable.

Windshield Wiper Motor

Removal and Installation

CORDIA AND TREDIA

1. Remove the wiper blade and arm assembly.
2. Remove the cover from the access hole or the deck panel, guide panel and garnish depending on mode.
3. Remove the wiper drive bolts at the arm pivots. On the Tredia, remove the washer nozzle.
4. Loosen the wiper motor bolts. Disconnect the wiper motor and linkage and remove.
5. Install in reverse order.

STARION

1. Remove the wiper arms. Remove the pivot shaft nuts and washers and push the pivot shafts into the area behind the cowl.
2. Remove the cover from the access hole for the wiper motor on the right side of the cowl, under the hood. Then, remove the motor bolts. Pull the motor into the best possible position for access and use a flat suitable tool to pry the linkage off the motor crank arm.
3. If the linkage is being replaced, it can be worked out of the cowl at this time. If the motor is being replaced, matchmark the position of the crank arm of the motor shaft of the new motor

and then remove the nut and crank arm, transferring both to the new motor.

4. Installation is the reverse of removal. Make sure the wiper blades stop about 0.5 in. from the lower windshield molding. Torque the wiper arm attaching nuts to 7–12 ft. lbs.

MIRAGE AND PRECIS

1. Remove the wiper arms. Remove the air inlet and cowl front center trim panels. Remove the 3 pivot shaft nuts and push the pivot shafts into the area under the cowl.

2. Remove the motor bolts. Pull the motor into the best possible position for access and use a flat suitable tool to pry the linkage off the motor crank arm. Remove the motor and then the linkage.

3. If the motor is being replaced, matchmark the position of the crank arm of the motor shaft of the new motor and then remove the nut and crank arm, transferring both to the new motor.

4. Installation is the reverse of removal. Torque the pivot shaft nuts to 4.3–5.8 ft. lbs. Position the wiper arms so the blades are about 0.6 in. above the lower windshield molding on the driver's side and 0.8 in. above it on the passenger's side. Torque the wiper arm nuts to 7.2–12 ft. lbs. Make sure the wiper motor is securely grounded.

GALANT AND SIGMA

1. Remove the wiper arms. Remove the front deck and inlet trim.

2. Remove the 3 bolts for each pivot shaft and push the shafts into the area behind the panel. Disconnect the electrical connector. Remove the 3 motor mounting bolts and the motor and linkage as an assembly.

3. If the motor is being replaced, matchmark the relationship between linkage and motor, as it is critical. If the linkage only is being replaced, pry the connection off the end of the motor crank arm with a flat suitable tool.

4. Install in reverse order. Make sure the wiper arms sit in their original positions when in parked position. Make sure the wiper motor is securely grounded.

ECLIPSE

Front

1. Disconnect the negative battery cable.

2. Remove the windshield wiper arms by unscrewing the cap nuts and lifting the arms from the linkage posts.

3. Remove the front garnish panel.

4. Remove the air inlet trim pieces.

5. Remove the hole cover.

6. Remove the wiper motor by loosening the bolts, removing the motor assembly and disconnecting the linkage.

NOTE: Because the installation angle of the crank arm and the motor has been factory set, do not remove them unless necessary. If they must be removed, remove them only after marking their positions.

To install:

7. Install the windshield wiper motor and connect the linkage.

8. Reinstall all the trim pieces and connect the negative battery cable.

9. Reinstall the wiper blades. Note that the driver's side wiper arm should be marked **D** and the passenger's side wiper arm should be marked **A**. The identification marks should be located at the base of the arm, near the pivot. Install the arms so the blades are 1 in. from the garnish molding when parked. Wet down the windshield glass and test wiper motor at all speeds.

Rear

1. Disconnect the negative battery cable.

2. Remove the rear wiper arm by removing the cover, unscrewing the nut and lifting the arm from the linkage post.

3. Remove the large interior trim panel. Use a plastic trim stick to unhook the trim clips of the liftgate trim.

4. If equipped with rear air spoiler, remove grommet.

5. Remove the rear wiper assembly; do not loose the grommet for the wiper post.

To install:

6. Install the motor and grommet. Mount the grommet so the arrow on the grommet is pointing upward.

7. Connect the negative battery cable.

8. Reinstall the wiper blade, wet down the rear glass and test the wiper motor.

9. If operation is satisfactory, fit the tabs on the upper part of the liftgate trim into the liftgate clips and secure the liftgate trim.

Windshield Wiper Switch

Removal and Installation

EXCEPT ECLIPSE, GALANT, MIRAGE AND SIGMA

1. Disconnect the negative battery cable.

2. Remove the steering column lower trim panel.

3. Remove the steering wheel and the steering column cable band.

4. Disconnect the electrical connections from the switch assembly.

5. Remove the switch screws and the switch assembly from the vehicle.

6. Installation is the reverse of the removal procedure.

GALANT, MIRAGE AND SIGMA

1. Disconnect the negative battery cable.

2. If equipped with tilt wheel lower the steering wheel to its lowest position.

3. Remove the steering wheel, the steering column lower trim panel, the steering column upper trim panel and the steering column cable band.

4. Disconnect the electrical connections from the switch assembly.

5. Remove the switch screws and the switch assembly from the vehicle.

6. Installation is the reverse of the removal procedure.

ECLIPSE

1. Disconnect the negative battery cable.

2. Remove the horn pad by removing the screw from behind the steering wheel and pressing the pad upward.

3. Remove the steering wheel.

NOTE: Make mating marks on the steering wheel and the steering wheel shaft. Use a steering wheel puller to remove the steering wheel; do not hammer on the steering wheel to remove it or the collapsible mechanism may be damaged.

4. Locate the rectangular plugs in the knee protector on either side of the steering column. Pry these plugs out, remove the screws. Remove the screws from the hood lock release lever and remove the knee protector.

5. Remove the upper and lower column covers.

6. Remove the lap cooler ducts.

7. Remove the band retaining the switch wiring.

8. Remove the column switch.

To install:

9. Installation is the reverse of the removal procedure. Take care that no wires are pinched or out of place.

10. Torque the steering wheel-to-column nut to 25–33 ft. lbs.

11. Check the steering wheel position with the wheels straight ahead.

12. Connect battery negative cable.

Instrument Cluster

Removal and Installation

CORDIA AND TREDIA

1. Disconnect the negative battery cable.
2. Remove the screws at the top of the instrument cluster trim panel. Remove the trim panel.
3. Disconnect the speedometer cable from the back of the speedometer.
4. Remove the cluster screws and pull the cluster forward.
5. Disconnect the electrical connectors and remove the cluster. Install in reverse order.

STARION

1. Disconnect the negative battery cable.
2. Remove the meter trim hood screws. Pull out and down on the side of the hood.
3. Disconnect the plug connectors on both sides of the cluster.
4. Remove the cluster screws and nuts. Pull the lower sides of the cluster up and disconnect the speedometer cable.
5. Disconnect the plug connectors at the rear of the cluster and remove the cluster. Install in reverse order.

MIRAGE

1. Disconnect the negative battery cable. Remove both meter hood attaching screws, located at the bottom and tile the lower meter hood outward. Pull the hood downward to release the locking tangs at the top and remove it.
2. Remove the 4 meter assembly screws, 2 at top and 2 at the bottom, and pull the unit outward. Disconnect the speedometer cable and all connectors and remove the unit.
3. Installation is the reverse of removal.

GALANT AND SIGMA

1. Disconnect the negative battery cable. Remove both meter hood screw covers located along the bottom of the hood using a suitable tool. Remove the screws and pull off the hood.
2. Remove the 4 meter assembly screws, 2 on each side, pull the assembly outward slightly and then disconnect the electrical connectors, speedometer cable and adapter. Remove the assembly.
3. Installation is the reverse of removal.

ECLIPSE

1. Disconnect the negative battery cable.
2. Remove the screw cover at the side of the bezel.
3. Remove the instrument cluster bezel.
4. Remove the instrument cluster.

NOTE: If the speedometer cable adapter must be serviced, disconnect the cable at the transaxle end. Pull the cable slightly toward the vehicle interior, release the lock by turning the adapter to the right or left, and then remove the adapter.

To install:
5. Installation is the reverse of the removal procedure. Use care not to damage the printed circuit board or any gauge components.
6. Connect battery negative cable.

Headlight Switch

Removal and Installation

EXCEPT ECLIPSE, GALANT, MIRAGE AND SIGMA

1. Disconnect the negative battery cable.
2. Remove the steering column lower trim panel.
3. Remove the steering wheel and the steering column cable band.

4. Disconnect the electrical connections from the switch assembly.
5. Remove the switch screws and the switch assembly from the vehicle.
6. Installation is the reverse of the removal procedure.

GALANT, MIRAGE AND SIGMA

1. Disconnect the negative battery cable.
2. If equipped with tilt wheel, lower the steering wheel to its lowest position.
3. Remove the steering wheel and the steering column lower trim panel. Remove the steering column upper trim panel and the steering column cable band.
4. Disconnect the electrical connections from the switch assembly.
5. Remove the switch retaining screws and the switch assembly from the vehicle.
6. Installation is the reverse of the removal procedure.

Combination Switch

Removal and Installation

EXCEPT ECLIPSE

1. Disconnect the negative battery cable. Remove the steering wheel and have the tilt handle in the lowest position.
2. Remove the combination meter and column covers.
3. Remove the connectors from the column switch and the column switch from the column tube.

NOTE: Some vehicles may have the turn signal and hazard switches mounted on a base plate. Removal of the attaching screws will allow these switches to be removed without removal of the remaining switches.

4. Switch installation is the reverse of removal. Be sure the switch is centered in the column or self canceling will be affected.

ECLIPSE

1. Disconnect the negative battery cable.
2. Remove the horn pad by removing the screw from behind the steering wheel and then pressing the pad upward.
3. Remove the steering wheel.

NOTE: Make mating marks on the steering wheel and the steering wheel shaft. Use a steering wheel puller to remove the steering wheel. Do not hammer on the steering wheel to remove it or the collapsible mechanism may be damaged.

4. Locate the rectangular plugs in the knee protector on either side of the steering column. Pry these plugs out and remove the screws. Remove the screws from the hood lock release lever and the knee protector.
5. Remove the upper and lower column covers.
6. Remove the lap cooler ducts.
7. Remove the band retaining the switch wiring.
8. Remove the column switch.
To install:
9. At installation, take care that no wires are pinched or out of place.
10. Torque the steering wheel-to-column nut to 25–33 ft. lbs.
11. Check the steering wheel position with the wheels straight ahead.
12. Connect battery negative cable.

Ignition Switch

Removal and Installation

EXCEPT ECLIPSE

1. Disconnect the negative battery cable. Cut a notch in the lock bracket bolt head with a hacksaw.
2. Remove the bolt and lock.
3. Remove the column cover and the ignition switch.
4. Install both lock and switch in reverse of removal.

NOTE: When installing lock, the bolt should be tightened until the head is crushed. When installing switch, install the switch bolt loosely and insert and work the key a few times to make sure everything checks out before tightening the bolt.

ECLIPSE

1. Disconnect the negative battery cable.
2. Remove the lower instrument panel knee protector.
3. Remove the lower steering column cover.
4. Remove the clip that holds the wiring against the steering column.
5. Unplug the ignition switch from the steering lock cylinder.
6. Insert the key into the steering lock cylinder and turn to the **ACC** position.
7. With a small pointed tool, push the lock pin of the steering lock cylinder inward and pull the lock out.

NOTE: Vehicles equipped with automatic transmission safety-lock systems will have a key interlock cable installed in a slide lever on the side of the key lock.

To install:

8. Installation is the reverse of the removal process. Make sure the lock pin snaps into place. Install the ignition switch plug carefully and make sure no wires are pinched.
9. Reconnect the negative battery cable.

Stoplight Switch

Adjustment

1. The stoplight switch works off the brake pedal lever. To adjust, disconnect the electrical connection and loosen the switch locknut.
2. Screw the switch inward until it contacts the stop on the brake pedal arm. Back out the switch ½–1 full turn. The gap between the switch plunger and the brake lever stop should be 0.020–0.040 in.
3. Tighten the locknut, connect the wires.
4. Check that the stoplights are not on unless the pedal is depressed.

Removal and Installation

1. Disconnect the negative battery cable.
2. Locate the stoplight switch above the brake pedal lever.
3. Disconnect the wiring connectors from the switch and unscrew the switch.
4. Installation is the reverse of the removal process. Install the replacement switch and adjust to 0.020–0.040 in. clearance.
5. Reconnect the stoplight wires.
6. Reconnect the negative battery cable.

Clutch Switch

Adjustment

The clutch interlock switch is located at the top of the clutch pedal arm. Note that there may be 2 switches; one will be a cruise control cut-out switch.

1. Clutch interlock switch adjustment is made with the pedal depressed its full stock of 6 in.
2. Measure the gap between the switch plunger and the arm stop. The gap should be 0.140 in.
3. If adjustment is necessary, loosen the locknut and turn and adjust.
4. After completing the adjustment, check that the pedal free-play, measured at the face of the pedal pad, is 0.240–0.510 in. The distance between the pedal pad and the firewall when the clutch is disengaged should be 2.80 in. or more. If these dimensions are not right, the hydraulic clutch system will probably need to be bled.

Removal and Installation

1. Disconnect the negative battery cable.
2. Locate the interlock switch above the clutch pedal lever.
3. Disconnect the wiring connectors from the switch and unscrew the switch.
4. Installation is the reverse of the removal procedure. Install the replacement switch and adjust to 0.140 in. clearance.
5. Reconnect the interlock wires.
6. Reconnect the negative battery cable.

Neutral Safety Switch

Adjustment

1. Locate the neutral safety switch on the top of the transaxle. Note that several different cable attaching methods have been used. The procedure here can be used as a general guide for all.
2. Place the selector lever in **N**.
3. Loosen both adjusting nuts to free up the cable and lever.
4. Place the safety switch manual control lever in **N**.
5. Note that one end of the safety switch manual control lever has a 12mm wide square end. There is also a 12mm wide tab on the switch body flange. Loosen both retaining bolts and turn the safety switch until these portions align. Tighten the bolts, making sure the switch doesn't move.
6. Loosen the adjuster nuts and gently pull the cable to remove any slack. Gently tighten adjusting nut until it just starts to contact the adjuster. Secure adjusting nut with its locknut then turn nut to lock.
7. Verify that the switch lever moves to positions corresponding to each position of the selector lever.
8. To test, apply the parking and service brake securely. Place the selector in **R**. Turn the ignition key to the **START** position. Slowly move the selector lever upward until it clicks and fits in the notch of the **P** range. If the starter motor operates when the lever makes a click the **P** position is correct. Slowly move the lever to the **N** range. Using the same procedure, if the starter operates when the selector fits in the **N** position, adjustment is correct. Also check that the vehicle doesn't begin to move and the lever doesn't stop between **P-R-N-D**.

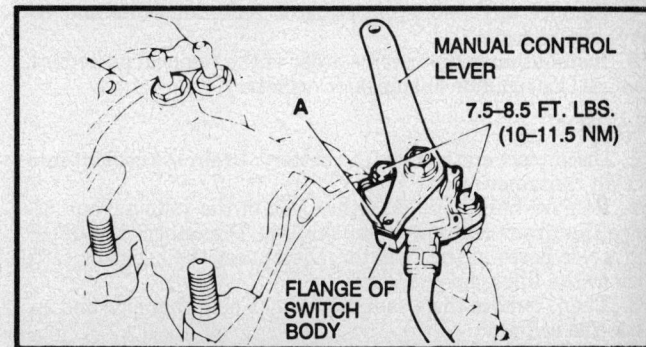

MANUAL CONTROL LEVER

7.5–8.5 FT. LBS. (10–11.5 NM)

A

FLANGE OF SWITCH BODY

Neutral start switch adjustment. "A" denotes the small end of the lever

Fuses, Circuit Breakers and Relays

Location

The fuse box on every vehicle is located under the instrument panel on the left (driver's side) above the cowl side trim. On the Galant and most other vehicles, there are also secondary fuses in the relay box in the engine compartment. The sun roof fuse is located in the electrical harness for the roof circuit at the extreme right side of the dashboard, directly behind the right windshield pillar. The radio fuse is located behind the radio and is accessible after the radio is removed.

There is a checker knob in the fuse box that make it easy to find a blown fuse. Slide the check knob until it is aligned with the fuse being checked. Turn on the ignition switch and lighting switch and the light will cone on, indicating the fuse is functioning.

ENGINE COOLING

Radiator

Removal and Installation

CORDIA, TREDIA, MIRAGE AND 1987 GALANT

1. Disconnect the negative battery cable. Disconnect the electrical connector for the fan motor. Drain the coolant into a clean container.
2. Disconnect the upper and lower radiator hoses and the overflow tank at the radiator. If equipped with an automatic transaxle, disconnect both hoses for the cooler at the lower tank and plug all openings. Then, remove both bolts from the rear of the radiator, lift the unit out of the bushings at the front crossmember and remove it. On Galant, note that the radiator is held at the top by 2 brackets which must be unbolted from the top of the panel in front of the radiator.
3. Remove the fan and electric motor from the radiator, transferring it to a new unit, if necessary.
4. Install the unit in reverse order, making sure the prongs on the lower tank fit securely into the bushings on the crossmember. Refill the radiator with clean coolant and run the engine until the thermostat opens. Refill the radiator with coolant as necessary, install the cap and then fill the overflow tank. If the vehicle has an automatic transaxle, check the fluid level and if necessary refill.

1988–91 GALANT AND SIGMA

1. Drain the engine coolant into a suitable container, remove the radiator cap while draining the coolant.
2. Remove the battery, coolant overflow tube and coolant reserve tank bracket and tank.
3. Remove the upper radiator hose. Disconnect the electrical fan motor connection, thermosensor connections on the condenser fan and the radiator fan.
4. Remove the oil cooler lines from the radiator, if equipped with an automatic transaxle.
5. Remove the radiator fan motor, lower radiator hose and radiator bracket.
6. Remove any remaining radiator retaining bolts and remove the radiator.
7. Installation is the reverse order of the removal procedure. Replace the radiator bushings, if necessary.

STARION

1. Disconnect and remove the battery. Drain the coolant into a clean container.
2. Remove both bolts on either side of the radiator and remove the upper and lower fan shrouds. Disconnect the upper and lower hoses at the radiator. Disconnect the overflow tank hose at the filler cap opening.
3. Then, remove the 4 radiator bolts, 2 on either side and remove the radiator.
4. Install the unit in reverse order. Refill the radiator with clean coolant and run the engine until the thermostat opens.

Refill the radiator with coolant as necessary, install the cap and then fill the overflow tank.

PRECIS

1. Disconnect the negative battery cable. Remove the splash shield from under the vehicle.
2. Drain the radiator.
3. Remove the fan shroud and disconnect the fan motor wiring harness.
4. Disconnect the radiator hoses and, if equipped, the automatic transmission cooler hoses.
5. Disconnect the expansion tank hose.
6. Remove the radiator bolts and lift out the radiator and fan assembly.
7. Installation is the reverse of removal.

ECLIPSE

1. Disconnect the negative battery cable.
2. Drain the cooling system.
3. Disconnect the overflow tube. Some vehicles may also require removal of the overflow tank.
4. Disconnect upper and lower radiator hoses.
5. Disconnect electrical connectors for cooling fan and air conditioning condensor fan, if equipped.
6. Disconnect thermo sensor wires.
7. Disconnect and plug automatic transmission cooler lines, if used.
8. Remove the upper radiator mounts and lift out the radiator/fan assembly.

To install:

9. At installation, use proper mix of coolant suitable for use in engines with aluminum components.
10. Reconnect the negative battery cable.
11. Check automatic transaxle fluid level and refill as necessary.

Heater Core

Removal and Installation

CORDIA, TREDIA, MIRAGE, GALANT AND SIGMA

1. Disconnect the battery ground cable.
2. Set the heater control lever to **WARM**.
3. Drain the cooling system.
4. Remove the instrument panel.
5. Remove the duct from between the heater unit and the blower case.
6. Disconnect the coolant hoses at the heater case.
7. Unbolt and remove the heater case.
8. Remove the hose and pipe clamps and remove the water valve, if equipped.
9. Remove the core from the case.
10. Set the mixing damper to the closed position and, with the damper in that position, install the rod so the water valve is fully closed.

11. Place the damper lever in the **VENT** position and adjust the linkage so the **FOOT/DEF** damper opens to the **DEF** side and the **VENT** damper is level with the separator.

12. Install the hoses. They are marked for flow direction.

13. The remainder of assembly is the reverse of disassembly.

STARION

1. Drain the cooling system and disconnect the negative battery cable.

2. Place the heater control in the **WARM** position.

3. Disconnect the heater hose at the engine firewall.

4. Remove the instrument panel and the center console.

5. Remove the center ventilator duct, defroster duct and lap duct.

6. Remove the center reinforcement and heater control assembly.

7. Remove the heater assembly bolts and the heater assembly.

8. Remove the heater core.

9. Install in reverse order.

ECLIPSE

1. Disconnect the negative battery cable.

2. Drain the cooling system.

3. Remove the floor console by first removing the plugs, then the screws retaining the side covers and the small cover piece in front of the shifter. Remove the shifter knob, manual transmission, and the cup holder. Remove both small pieces of upholstery to gain access to retainer screws. Disconnect the two electrical connectors at the front of the console. Remove the shoulder harness guide plates and remove the console assembly.

4. Remove the instrument panel assembly. Use the following procedure:

   a. Locate the rectangular plugs in the knee protector on either side of the steering column. Pry these plugs out, remove the screws. Remove the screws from the hood lock release lever and remove the knee protector.

   b. Remove the upper and lower column covers.

   c. Remove the narrow panel covering the instrument cluster cover screws, and take out the cover.

   d. Remove the radio panel and take out the radio.

   e. Remove the center air outlet assembly by reaching through the grill and pushing the side clips out with a small flat-tip tool while carefully prying the outlet free.

   f. Pull the heater control knobs off and remove the heater control panel assembly.

   g. Open the glove box, remove the plugs from the sides and remove the glove box assembly.

   h. Remove the instrument gauge cluster and the speedometer adapter by disconnecting the speedometer cable at the transaxle, pulling the cable sightly towards the vehicle interior, then giving a slight twist on the adapter to release it.

   i. Remove the left and right speaker covers from the top of the instrument panel.

   j. Remove the center plate below the heater controls.

   k. Remove the heater control assembly installation screws.

   l. Remove the lower air ducts.

   m. Drop the steering column by removing the bolts.

   n. Remove the instrument panel screws, bolts and the instrument panel assembly.

5. Remove both stamped steel reinforcement pieces.

6. Remove the lower duct work from the heater box.

7. Remove the upper center duct.

8. Vehicles without air conditioning will have a square duct in place of the evaporator. Remove this duct, if not equipped with air conditioning. If equipped with air conditioning, remove the evaporator assembly. Properly discharge the air conditioning system. Disconnect and cap the refrigerant lines at the evaporator. Remove the wiring harness connectors and the electronic control unit. Remove the drain hose and lift out the evaporator unit.

9. With the evaporator removed, take out the heater unit. To prevent bolts from falling inside the blower assembly, set the inside/outside air-selection damper to the position that permits outside air introduction.

10. Remove the cover plate around the heater tubes and remove the core fastener clips. Pull the heater core from the heater box, being careful not to damage the fins or tank ends.

To install:

11. Installation is the reverse of the removal procedure. Install the heater core to the heater box. Install the clips and cover.

12. Install the evaporator and the automatic transmission ELC box.

13. Install the heater box and connect the duct work.

14. Connect all wires and control cables.

15. Install the instrument panel assembly and the console.

16. Connect the battery negative cable, start engine and bleed cooling system. Recharge the air conditioning system.

Water Pump

Removal and Installation

CORDIA, TREDIA, MIRAGE, PRECIS AND 1987 GALANT

1. Disconnect the negative battery cable. Loosen the 4 bolts attaching the water pump pulley to the pulley flange. Loosen the alternator bolts, slide the alternator toward the engine and remove the belt. Drain the radiator.

2. Remove the 4 bolts attaching the water pump pulley to the pump flange and remove the pulley. Remove the timing belt covers and timing belt tensioner.

3. Remove the 5 water pump bolts. Remove the pump and gasket, disconnecting the outlet at the water pipe (don't lose the O-ring).

4. Clean gasket surfaces and coat a new gasket with sealer. Then, position the gasket on the front of the block with all bolt holes aligned. Replace the O-ring for the outlet water pipe.

5. Install the pump over a new gasket, connecting the outlet water pipe.

6. Install the remaining parts in reverse order. Final tightening of the water pump pulley bolts is done most easily after the V-belt has been installed and tensioned some what. Recheck tension after the pulley bolts are tightened. Close the radiator drain and refill the system. Run the engine until the thermostat opens and then add coolant until the level stabilizes before replacing the radiator cap. Check for leaks.

1988–91 GALANT AND SIGMA

1. Bring the No. 1 piston to TDC of its compression stroke. Disconnect the negative battery cable and drain the engine oil and coolant into a suitable containers.

2. Remove the timing belt covers, timing belt and sprockets and crankshaft sprocket as previously outlined in this section.

3. Remove the water pump bolts. Remove the pump and gasket, disconnecting the outlet at the water pipe (don't lose the O-ring).

4. Clean gasket surfaces and coat a new gasket with sealer. Then, position the gasket on the front of the block with all bolt holes aligned. Replace the O-ring for the outlet water pipe.

5. Install the pump over a new gasket, connecting the outlet water pipe.

6. Complete the installation by reversing the order of the removal procedure. Torque the water pump bolts to 14–19 ft. lbs.

STARION

1. Disconnect the negative battery cable. Drain the radiator.

2. Loosen the 4 nuts attaching the clutch fan to the water pump studs; then, loosen the adjusting and mounting bolts for the alternator, rock it toward the engine and remove the belt. Remove the 4 bolts for the fan shrouds from the rear of the radiator and remove the upper and lower shrouds. Loosen the nuts

and remove them together with the lockwashers. Remove the fan clutch unit, storing the fan clutch in its normal altitude to keep the fluid from migrating to the wrong portions of the unit. Remove the pulley from the studs.

3. Disconnect the lower radiator hose at the pump by loosening the clamp and pulling the hose off. Then, remove the mounting bolts from the pump and then remove the pump and gasket from the front of the block.

4. Clean both gasket surfaces thoroughly and coat both sides of a new gasket and both gasket surfaces with sealer.

5. Install the gasket onto the block and then position the water pump over the gasket. Install the bolts in the proper positions.

6. Install the remaining parts in reverse order.

7. Refill the radiator with clean antifreeze and water mixed 50/50. Run the engine until the thermostat opens, refill the radiator as necessary, install the cap and check for leaks.

ECLIPSE

1. Disconnect the negative battery cable.
2. Drain cooling system.
3. Remove engine under cover.
4. Remove the timing belt.
5. Remove the alternator bracket.
6. Remove the water pump, gasket and O-ring where the water inlet pipe joins the pump.

To install:

7. Installation is the reverse of the removal process. Clean both gasket surfaces of the water pump and block. Install the new O-ring into the groove on the front end of the water inlet pipe. Do not apply oils or grease to the O-ring. Wet with water only. Install the gasket and pump assembly and tighten the bolts. Note the marks on the bolt heads. Those marked **4** should be torqued to 9–11 ft. lbs. Those bolts marked **7** should be torqued from 14–20 ft. lbs.

8. Reinstall the alternator bracket.
9. Install the timing covers, drive pulleys and belts and the undercover.
10. Refill with coolant.
11. Reconnect the negative battery cable, start engine and bleed cooling system.

Thermostat

Removal and Installation

1. Disconnect the negative battery cable. Drain the coolant below the level of the thermostat.

2. Remove both retaining bolts and lift the thermostat housing off the intake manifold with the hose still attached. If careful, it is not necessary to remove the upper radiator hose.

3. Lift the thermostat out of the manifold.

4. Installation is the reverse of the removal procedure.

FUEL SYSTEM

Fuel System Service Precaution

Safety is the most important factor when performing not only fuel system maintenance but any type of maintenance. Failure to conduct maintenance and repairs in a safe manner may result in serious personal injury or death. Maintenance and testing of the vehicle's fuel system components can be accomplished safely and effectively by adhering to the following rules and guidelines.

• To avoid the possibility of fire and personal injury, always disconnect the negative battery cable unless the repair or test procedure requires that battery voltage be applied.

• Always relieve the fuel system pressure prior to disconnecting any fuel system component (injector, fuel rail, pressure regulator, etc.), fitting or fuel line connection. Exercise extreme caution whenever relieving fuel system pressure to avoid exposing skin, face and eyes to fuel spray. Please be advised that fuel under pressure may penetrate the skin or any part of the body that it contacts.

• Always place a shop towel or cloth around the fitting or connection prior to loosening to absorb any excess fuel due to spillage. Ensure that all fuel spillage (should it occur) is quickly removed from engine surfaces. Ensure that all fuel soaked cloths or towels are deposited into a suitable waste container.

• Always keep a dry chemical (Class B) fire extinguisher near the work area.

• Do not allow fuel spray or fuel vapors to come into contact with a spark or open flame.

• Always use a backup wrench when loosening and tightening fuel line connection fittings. This will prevent unnecessary stress and torsion to fuel line piping. Always follow the proper torque specifications.

• Always replace worn fuel fitting O-rings with new. Do not substitute fuel hose or equivalent, where fuel pipe is installed.

Relieving Fuel System Pressure
FUEL INJECTED

1. Disconnect the fuel pump harness connector at the fuel tank side.

2. Start the engine and after it stops by itself, turn the ignition switch to the **OFF** position.

3. Disconnect the negative battery terminal. Reconnect the fuel pump harness connector and then reconnect the negative battery terminal.

Fuel Filter

Removal and Installation

1. On carbureted vehicles, remove the inlet and outlet fuel lines from the filter connections after loosening the fuel line clamps. Remove the old filter. Install the new filter in the reverse order.

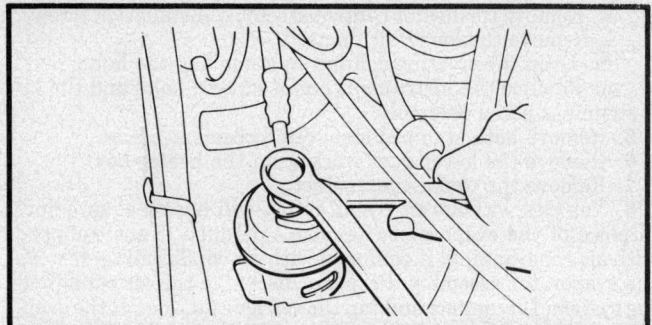

Fuel filter location—turbocharged and fuel injected engines

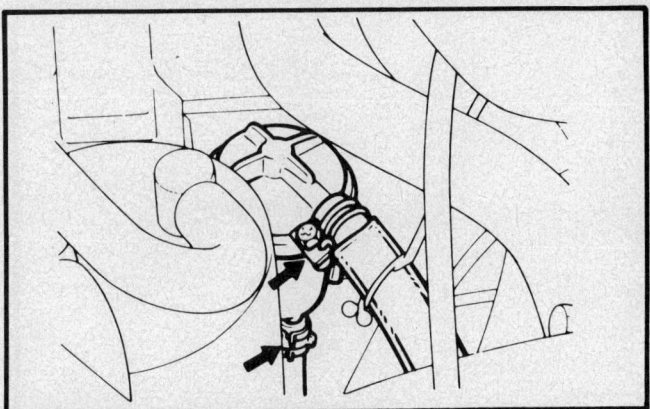

Fuel filter with carbureted engines

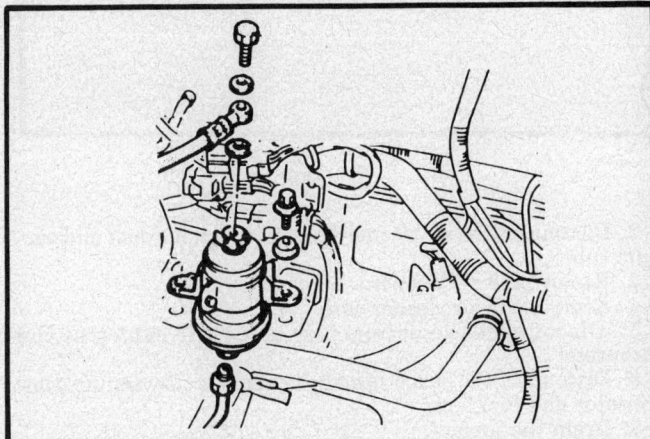

Fuel filter servicing—Eclipse

2. On fuel injected and turbocharged vehicles, the under hood filter is replaced after first reducing fuel line pressure. Hold the side filter nut securely and remove the mounts. Disconnect the lines and remove the filter.

3. On the 1988–91 Galant vehicles, remove the air cleaner assembly and the compressor for the electronic controlled suspension, if equipped.

4. Disconnect the fuel lines and remove the fuel filter mounting bolt and then remove the fuel filter assembly.

5. Install the new fuel filter in the reverse order of the removal procedure.

Mechanical Fuel pump

Pressure Testing

1. Disconnect the fuel line from the carburetor. Attach a pressure tester to the end of the line.

2. Crank the engine. If fuel pump pressure is not within specification replace the fuel pump.

Removal and Installation

1. Disconnect the negative battery cable. Remove the distributor cap to check the direction of the rotor, and then turn the engine over until the pointer near the front pulley is at Top Dead Center and the rotor points to the ignition wire for No. 1 cylinder, indicating that No. 1 is at firing position. Disconnect the negative battery cable.

2. Disconnect the fuel lines by using a pair of pliers to shift clamps away from the nipples on the pump and then pulling the lines off with a twisting motion. Note the locations at which lines connect.

3. Remove both bolts from the head, and then remove the pump, spacer and gasket(s) from the head. While pulling the pump off the head, catch the pushrod which is located just behind the pump.

4. Inspect the pump as follows: There is a small breather hole in the area of the pump above the diaphragm which vents the pump's upper chamber. Leakage of fuel or oil here indicates that the pump's diaphragm or oil seal is leaking and that the unit should be replaced. Also, inspect the end of the pushrod and the wear surface where the pushrod engages with the pump operating lever. Replace the pushrod or pump if there is obvious wear. If the camshaft end of the pushrod is badly worn, remove the cam cover and inspect the camshaft eccentric which operates the fuel pump for excessive wear.

5. Clean the gasket surfaces of the insulator, pump and cylinder head. Insert both bolts through the pump's base. Slide a new gasket, the insulator, and a second new gasket into position over both bolts. Turn the pump so its mounting surface faces the cylinder head.

6. Locate the pump pushrod against the cupped surface of the operating lever and angle it upward in the position it was in during removal. Hold the pushrod at that angle and insert it into the bore in the head. Once the pushrod is in the cylinder head bore, release it and move the pump toward the head following the installation angle of the pushrod. Start both bolts into the bores in the head and tighten them finger-tight.

7. Tighten the bolts alternately and evenly. Inspect the hoses for cracks (even hairline cracks can leak) and replace if necessary. Then, reconnect the fuel hoses. Make sure the hoses are installed all the way onto the nipples and then work the clamps into position. Make sure the clamps are located well past the bulged portion of the nipples but do not sit at the extreme inner ends of the hoses. Replace the distributor cap. Start the engine and check for leaks.

Electric Fuel Pump

Pressure Testing

1. Relieve the fuel pressure as follows:
    a. Disconnect the fuel pump harness connector at the fuel tank side.
    b. Start the engine and after it stops by itself, turn the ignition switch to the **OFF** position.
    c. Disconnect the negative battery terminal. Reconnect the fuel pump harness connector and then reconnect the negative battery terminal.

2. Install a suitable fuel pressure gauge to the fuel delivery pipe; be sure to tighten the bolt at 18–25 ft. lbs.

3. Apply voltage to the terminal for the fuel pump drive and activate the fuel pump; then, with fuel pressure thus applied,

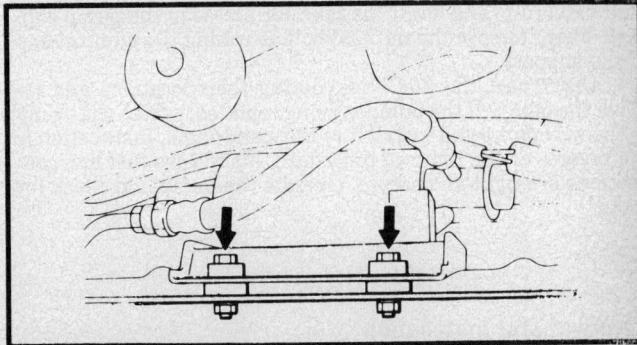

View of the externally mounted electric fuel pump mounting bolts

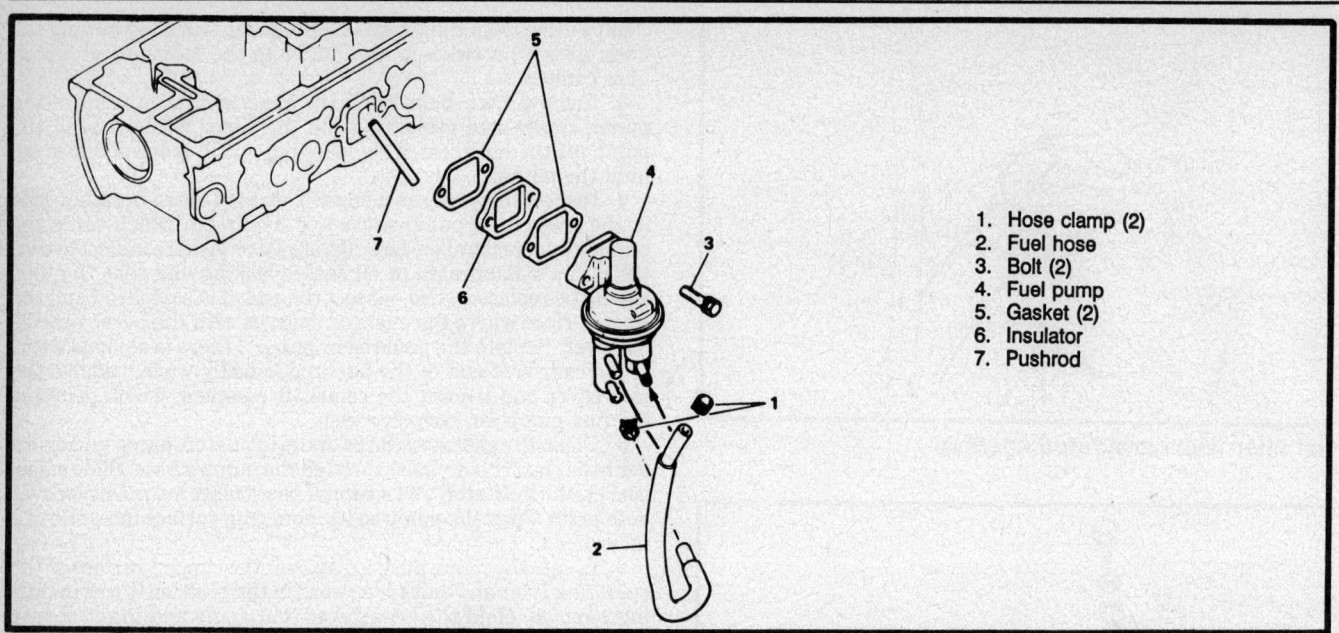

1. Hose clamp (2)
2. Fuel hose
3. Bolt (2)
4. Fuel pump
5. Gasket (2)
6. Insulator
7. Pushrod

Exploded view of the mechanical fuel pump

check the there is no fuel leakage from the pressure gauge or the special tool connection pipe.

4. Disconnect the vacuum hose from the pressure regulator and plug the hose end. Measure the fuel pressure during idling.

    a. All engines except 2.0L turbocharged engine: 38 psi at idle, vacuum hose connected to regulator, 47–50 psi at idle hose disconnected from regulator and plugged.

    b. 2.0L turbocharged engine: 27 psi at idle, vacuum hose connected to regulator, 36–38 psi at idle hose disconnected from regulator and plugged.

5. If the fuel pressure readings are not within specifications, determine the probable cause and make the necessary repairs.

6. Remove all test equipment, use a new gasket and tighten the bolt on the delivery pipe to 18–25 ft. lbs. Start the engine and check for fuel leaks.

Removal and Installation

1. Start the engine and allow it to idle. Disconnect the electric fuel pump connector (accessible by removing a panel in the floor of the trunk). Allow the engine to continue running until it stalls to relieve the pressure in the fuel lines.

2. If equipped with a drain plug, remove it and drain the fuel into a suitable container. Support the vehicle safely. Remove the left rear wheel.

3. Support the fuel tank with a floor jack. Loosen the fuel tank band nuts and lower the tank for access to the pump support. Then, remove the nut and bolt attaching the pump clamp to the support.

4. Disconnect the fuel lines, noting their locations and remove the pump. If the pump is being replaced, switch the clamp to the new pump and install it at the same angle. Installation is the reverse of the removal procedure. Make sure fuel line connections are tight and secure. Operate the pump and check for leaks.

Carburetor

Removal and Installation

1. Disconnect the negative battery cable. Remove the solenoid valve wiring.

2. Disconnect the air cleaner breather hose, air duct and vacuum tube.

3. Remove the air cleaner.

4. Remove the air cleaner case.

5. Disconnect the accelerator and shift cables at the carburetor.

6. Disconnect the purge valve hose; remove the vacuum compensator and fuel lines.

7. Drain the coolant.

8. Remove the water hose between the carburetor and the cylinder head.

9. Remove the carburetor.

10. Installation is the reverse of removal.

Accelerator Cable Adjustment

MIRAGE, PRECIS AND 1987–88 CORDIA AND TREDIA

1. The engine must be hot so the fast idle cam will not interfere with throttle position; warm it if necessary.

2. Inspect the inner cable to see if there is slack. If there is no slack, the adjustment is okay. If there is slack, loosen the adjusting nuts until the throttle is free to assume idle position with no effect by the accelerator cable.

3. Make sure there are no sharp bends in the cable. Then, turn the adjusting nut that's furthest away from the carburetor until the throttle starts to move; then back the nut off ½ a turn on Cordia and Tredia or 1 turn on Mirage. Secure the locknut.

Idle Speed Adjustment

NOTE: The throttle valve adjusting screw should not be tampered with unless the carburetor has been rebuilt. This screw is preset and determines the relationship between the throttle valve and the free lever, and has been accurately set at the factory. If this setting is disturbed, the throttle opener adjustment and or dashpot adjustment cannot be done accurately. Also the improper setting (throttle valve opening) will increase the exhaust gas temperature and deceleration, which in turn will reduce the life of the catalyst greatly and deteriorate the exhaust gas cleaning performance. It will also effect the fuel consumption and the engine braking.

1987–89

1. With the vehicle in **P**, the drive wheels blocked and all the accessories **OFF**. Run the engine until it reaches normal operating temperature.

2. Bring the engine rpm up to 2000–3000 rpm for about 10 seconds, then let the engine idle for at least 2 minutes.

3. Connect a tachometer to the engine and check the idling speed. If it does not meet specifications, readjust the idle speed to the nominal specification, using the idle speed adjusting screw, which is located closest to the primary throttle valve shaft.

Idle Speed Control Adjustment

1987–88 CORDIA AND TREDIA

NOTE: When replacing the ISC servo, the engine speed should be adjusted.

1. With the vehicle in **P**, the drive wheels blocked and all the accessories **OFF**. Run the engine until it reaches normal operating temperature.

2. Remove the carburetor from the engine. Remove the concealment plug from the carburetor.

3. Reinstall the carburetor onto the engine and relax the tension on the accelerator cable.

4. Place the ignition switch to the one position and wait for at least 18 seconds. Turn the ignition switch **OFF** and disconnect the ISC actuator connector and the oxygen sensor connector.

5. Start the engine check the ignition timing and adjust if necessary. Increase the engine speed between 2000–3000 rpm, 2–3 times and let the engine idle for 30 seconds.

6. Adjust the mixture adjusting screw for a concentration of 0.1–0.3 percent. Adjust the engine rpm to the specified speed by using the ISC adjustment screw.

7. Turn the idle mixture screw, secondary air supply screw, until the engine reaches its highest rpm. Turn the screw ⅔ of turn in the reverse direction from that point.

8. Race the engine 2–3 times. Check to be sure the CO and engine rpm are still adjusted to specifications. If they are not, readjust as necessary.

9. Adjust the tension of the accelerator cable. The cable should have enough play so as not to interfere with idle switch.

10. Reconnect the ISC actuator connector and the oxygen sensor connector.

PRECIS

1. Make sure the gear selector is in **N** or **P**. Run the engine at fast idle until the cooling system reaches 185°F or more, not to exceed 205°F. Then, race the engine at 2000–3000 rpm for more than 5 seconds. Release the throttle. All accessories including the electric cooling fan must be off.

2. Idle the engine for a full 2 minutes. Connect a tachometer between the (−) terminal of the coil and a good ground while the engine is idling. If the idle speed is not to the specification, adjust the idle speed screw (which is located closest to the primary throttle valve shaft) to obtain the proper idle speed specifications.

3. The idle speed should be as follows:
   a. Manual Transaxle—600–800 rpm
   b. Automatic Transaxle—650–850 rpm
   c. Canada—820–880 rpm

Idle-Up Speed Adjustment

1987–88 CORDIA, TREDIA, MIRAGE AND 1987–89 PRECIS

Without Air Conditioning

NOTE: Adjustment condition—lights, electric cooling fan and all accessories are OFF and transaxle is in N.

1. Make sure the curb idle speed is within specifications, adjust if necessary.

2. By using the auxiliary lead wire, activate the idle up solenoid valve. Apply the intake manifold vacuum to the throttle opener and activate the throttle opener.

3. Open the throttle slightly, to engine speed of about 2000 rpm, and then slowly close it.

4. Adjust the engine speed to the specifications with the idle-up adjusting screw.

5. After repeating Step 3, check the engine speed.

6. Remove the auxiliary lead wire used in Step 2 and reconnect the idle-up solenoid valve wiring.

With Air Conditioning

1. With the vehicle in **P**, the drive wheels blocked and all the accessories **OFF**. Run the engine until it reaches normal operating temperature.

2. Disconnect the electric cooling fan connector. If equipped with power steering, set the tires in the straight-ahead position to prevent the pump from being loaded. Set the steering wheel in the stationary position.

3. Be sure the curb idle speed is within the specifications, adjust, if necessary.

4. With the air conditioner on, adjust the engine speed to the specified speed with the throttle opener setting screw, idle-up adjusting screw.

5. Reconnect the electric cooling fan connector and turn the air conditioning **ON** and **OFF** several times to check the operation of the throttle opener.

Idle Mixture Adjustment

EXCEPT 1987–89 PRECIS AND 1987–88 CORDIA, TREDIA AND MIRAGE WITH AUTOMATIC TRANSAXLE

1. Remove the carburetor from the engine. The idle mixture screw is located in the base of the carburetor, just to the left of the PCV hose. Mount the carburetor, carefully, in a soft jawed vise, protecting the gasket surface and with the mixture adjusting screw facing upward.

2. Drill a hole through the casting from the underside of the carburetor. Make sure the hole intersects the passage leading to the mixture adjustment screw just behind the plug. Widen that hole with a ⅛ in. drill bit.

3. Insert a blunt punch into the hole and tap out the plug. Install the carburetor on the engine and connect all hoses, lines, etc.

4. Start the engine and run it at fast idle until it reaches normal operating temperature. Make sure all accessories are **OFF** and the transaxle is in **N**. Turn the ignition switch **OFF** and disconnect the battery ground cable for about 3 seconds, then, reconnect it. Disconnect the oxygen sensor.

5. Start the engine and run it for at least 5 seconds at 2000–3000 rpm. Then, allow the engine to idle for about 2 minutes.

6. Connect a tachometer and allow the engine to operate at the specified curb idle speed. Adjust it if necessary, to obtain this speed. Connect a CO meter to the exhaust pipe. A reading of 0.1–0.3 percent is necessary. Adjust the mixture screw to obtain the reading. If, during this adjustment, the idle speed is varied more than 100 rpm in either direction, reset the idle speed and readjust the CO until both specifications are met simultaneously. Shut **OFF** the engine, reconnect the oxygen sensor and install a new concealment plug.

1987–88 CORDIA, TREDIA AND MIRAGE WITH AUTOMATIC TRANSAXLE

1. Remove the carburetor from the engine and place the carburetor in a suitable fixture in order to remove the concealment plug.

2. Drill a ²/₆₄ in. (2mm) pilot hole in the casting surrounding

the idle mixture adjusting screw. Then redrill the hole to ⅛ in. (3mm) and insert a punch into the hole to drive out the concealment plug.

3. Reinstall the carburetor on the engine without the concealment plug.

4. With the vehicle in **P**, the drive wheels blocked and all the accessories **OFF**, run the engine until it reaches normal operating temperature.

5. Turn **OFF** the engine and disconnect the negative battery cable for about 3 seconds and reconnect the cable.

6. Disconnect the connector of the exhaust oxygen sensor. Run the vehicle for 5 minutes at a speed of 30 rpm or run the engine for more than 5 minutes at the engine speed of 2000–3000 rpm.

7. Run the engine at idle for 2 minutes and set the idle CO and the engine speed to specification (the idle CO: 0.1–0.3 percent at nominal curb idle speed).

8. Reconnect the oxygen sensor connector. Readjust the engine speed, if necessary and install the concealment plug into the hole to seal the idle mixture adjusting screw.

1987–89 PRECIS

1. Remove the carburetor. The idle mixture screw is located in the base of the carburetor, just to the left of the PCV hose. Mount the carburetor, carefully, in a soft jawed vise, protecting the gasket surface, and with the mixture adjusting screw facing upward.

2. Drill a small hole through the casting from the underside of the carburetor. Make sure the hole intersects the passage leading to the mixture adjustment screw just behind the plug. Widen the hole with a ⅛ in. drill bit.

3. Insert a blunt punch into the hole and tap out the plug. Install the carburetor on the engine and connect all hoses, lines, etc.

4. Start the engine and run it at fast idle until it reaches normal operating temperature. Make sure all accessories are **OFF** and the transaxle is in **N**. Turn the ignition switch **OFF** and disconnect the battery ground cable for about 3 seconds, then, reconnect it. Disconnect the oxygen sensor.

5. Start the engine and run it for at least 5 seconds at 2000–3000 rpm. Then, allow the engine to idle for about 2 minutes.

6. Connect a tachometer and allow the engine to operate at the specified curb idle speed. Adjust it, if necessary, to obtain this speed. Connect a CO meter to the exhaust pipe. A reading of 0.1–0.3 percent is necessary. Adjust the mixture screw to obtain the reading. If, during this adjustment, the idle speed is varied more than 100 rpm in either direction, reset the idle speed and readjust the CO until both specifications are met simultaneously. Shut **OFF** the engine, reconnect the oxygen sensor and install a new concealment plug.

Fuel Injection

Idle Speed Adjustment
EXCEPT ECLIPSE

1. Run the engine until normal operating temperature is reached. Make sure all lights and accessories are turned **OFF**.

2. Apply the parking brake and block the wheels. Position the gear selector in **N** and stop the engine.

3. Attach a tachometer and timing light. Start the engine and increase the engine speed to 2000–3000 rpm several times, return to idle and check the ignition timing, adjust if necessary.

4. Remove the rubber cap covering the idle speed adjuster switch, leaving the cable connector connected. The idle adjuster switch is located on the throttle linkage. Adjust the idle speed.

5. If the idle adjustment screw must be turned more than 1 turn during adjustment, disconnect the connector from the speed adjust switch and plug it into the dummy terminal on the

injector base. Adjust to correct idle speed and reconnect to the idle switch. Remove the tachometer and timing light.

1990–91 ECLIPSE
1.8L Engine

The electronic system controls the idle speed and adjustment of the idling speed is usually unnecessary. The idle speed may be checked using the following procedure:

1. Warm the engine to operating temperature, leave lights, electric cooling fan and accessories **OFF**. The transaxle should be in **N** or **P** for automatic transmission. The steering wheel in a neutral position for vehicles with power steering.

2. Check the ignition timing and adjust, if necessary.

3. Connect a tachometer to the CRC filter connector. Use a paper clip for a tach adapter.

4. Run the engine for more than 5 seconds at 2000–3000 rpm. Allow the engine to idle for 2 minutes. Check the idle rpm. Curb idle should be 600–800 rpm.

5. If adjustment is required, slacken the accelerator cable.

6. Connect a digital voltmeter between terminal 19 throttle position sensor output voltage) of the engine control unit and terminal 24 (ground).

7. Set the ignition switch to **ON**, without starting the engine, and hold it in that position for 15 seconds or more. Turn the ignition switch **OFF**.

8. Disconnect the connectors of the idle speed control servo and lock the idle speed control plunger at the initial position. Back out the fixed Speed Adjusting Screw (SAS).

9. Start the engine and allow to idle. Basic idle speed should be 650–750 rpm. A new engine may idle a little lower. If the vehicle stalls or has a very low idle speed, suspect a deposit buildup on the throttle valve which must be cleaned.

10. If the idle speed is wrong, adjust with the idle speed control adjusting screw. Use a hexagon wrench if possible. Turn in the fixed SAS until the engine speed rises. Then back out the fixed SAS until the Touch Point where the engine speed does not fall any longer, is found. Back out the fixed SAS an additional ½ turn from the touch point.

11. Stop the engine. Turn the ignition switch to **ON** but do not start engine. Check that the output voltage from the throttle position sensor is 0.48–0.52 volts. If it is out of specification, adjust by loosening the throttle position sensor screws and rotating the throttle position sensor. Turning the throttle position sensor clockwise increases the output voltage. After adjustment, tighten screws firmly.

12. Turn the ignition switch **OFF**.

13. Adjust the free-play of the accelerator cable, reconnect the connectors of the idle speed control servo and remove the voltmeter.

14. Start the engine and check the curb idle. It should be 600–800 rpm.

15. Turn the ignition switch to **OFF**, disconnect the negative battery cable for more than 10 seconds and reconnect. This clears any trouble codes introduced during testing.

16. Restart the engine, allow to run for 5 minutes and check for good idle quality.

2.0L Engine

The electronic system controls the idle speed and adjustment of the idling speed is usually unnecessary. The idle speed may be checked using the following procedure:

1. Warm the engine to operating temperature, leave lights, electric cooling fan and accessories **OFF**. The transaxle should be in **N**. The steering wheel in a neutral position for vehicles with power steering.

2. Check the ignition timing and adjust, if necessary.

3. Connect a tachometer to the special terminal under the hood.

4. Run the engine for more than 5 seconds at 2000–3000 rpm. Allow the engine to idle for 2 minutes. Check the idle rpm. Curb idle should be 650–850 rpm.

5. If adjustment is required, disconnect the waterproof female connector used for ignition timing adjustment. Connect this terminal to ground using a jumper wire.

6. Locate the self-diagnosis terminal under the dashboard and connect terminal No. 10 to ground with a jumper wire.

7. Start the engine and allow to idle. Check that the basic idle speed is 650–850 rpm. If the idle speed deviates from this speed, check the following:

a. A new engine will idle more slowly. Break-in should take approximately 300 miles.

b. If the vehicle stalls or has a very low idle speed, suspect a deposit buildup on the throttle valve which must be cleaned.

c. If the idle speed is high even though the speed adjusting screw is fully closed, check that the idle position switch, fixed speed adjusting screw, position has changed. if, adjust the idle position switch.

d. If after all these checks the idle is still out of specification, it is probable that there is leakage resulting from deterioration of the Fast-Idle Air Valve (FIAV) and the throttle body will need to be replaced.

8. Turn the ignition switch **OFF** and stop the engine. Disconnect the jumper wire from the diagnosis connector, disconnect the jumper wire from the ignition timing connector and reconnect the waterproof connector. Disconnect the tachometer.

9. Restart the engine, allow to run for 5 minutes and check for good idle quality.

Fuel Injector

Removal and Installation

1. Relieve fuel system pressure.
2. Disconnect the negative battery cable.
3. Remove the high pressure line where it connects to the delivery pipe, or fuel rail. The O-ring must be replaced. Do not reuse.
4. Remove the return line from the pressure regulator. Also remove the vacuum line from the regulator.
5. Remove the fuel pressure regulator. The O-ring must be replaced. Do not reuse.
6. Remove the injector electrical connectors.
7. Remove the delivery pipe/injector assembly. Use care. Do not let the injectors drop.
8. Pull injectors from the delivery pipe for replacement.
To install:
9. Injectors can be checked for electrical resistance between the terminals. Resistance should be 13–16 ohms. If out of specification, replace injector.
10. Install the grommets on the injector first, then the O-ring. Apply light oil to lubricate the O-rings. Install the injector by pushing into the delivery pipe while turning back and forth. The injector should turn smoothly. If it does not, the O-ring may be trapped or dislodged. Remove the injector, check and insert injector again.
11. The O-ring for the pressure regulator and high pressure line should also be lubed with light oil or gasoline.
12. After assembly, the fuel pressure should be checked.

EMISSION CONTROLS

For further information, please refer to "Professional Emission Component Application Guide".

ENGINE MECHANICAL

NOTE: **Disconnecting the negative battery cable on some vehicles may interfere with the functions of the on board computer systems and may require the computer to undergo a relearning process, once the negative battery cable is reconnected.**

Engine Assembly

Removal and Installation

NOTE: **All engine and transaxle assemblies are removed as a unit.**

CORDIA AND TREDIA

NOTE: **Use care when disconnecting the refrigerant lines. Escaping refrigerant will freeze any surface it contacts, including skin and eyes.**

1. Matchmark and then unbolt and remove the hood. Disconnect both battery connectors and remove the battery.
2. Drain the engine coolant and transaxle fluid. Disconnect the heater hoses from the engine, as required.
3. Disconnect the power steering fluid return hose at the reservoir and drain the fluid into a clean container.
4. Drain and remove the radiator overflow and windshield washer tanks.

5. Disconnect the upper and lower radiator hoses at both ends and remove them. If equipped with air conditioning, disconnect the hoses as close as possible to the condensor unit in front of the radiator and cap the openings securely. Then, remove the radiator or radiator and condensor assemble.
6. Remove the battery tray. Disconnect both heater hoses from the side of the engine.
7. Remove the air cleaner. On turbocharged vehicles, disconnect the turbocharger intake hose.
8. Disconnect the brake booster vacuum hose. On turbocharged vehicles, disconnect the oil cooler hoses at the engine. If equipped with an automatic transmission, disconnect the cooler lines.
9. If equipped with a manual transmission, disconnect the clutch cable. If equipped with an automatic transmission, disconnect the shift control cable. Disconnect the speedometer cable from the transaxle.
10. Disconnect the accelerator cable at the side of the engine. Disconnect the engine ground strap at the right front fender. If equipped with an air conditioner, disconnect the hoses at the compressor and cap all openings securely.
11. Disconnect the power steering hoses at the side of the pump. Cap all openings. Disconnect the coil low and high tension wires. Label the low tension wires for reassembly to the proper terminals. Disconnect the battery negative cable from the engine.

12. Label and disconnect the alternator connectors. Disconnect the oil pressure sending unit wire.

13. Remove the vacuum unit and solenoid valve screws and disconnect the electrical connector; move the unit aside.

14. Disconnect both smaller vacuum hoses from the purge control valve, remove the screw and move the unit aside.

15. Loosen the clamps and disconnect the vacuum hoses going to the evaporative emissions canister.

16. Disconnect the fuel return hose from the carburetor or injection mixer. Disconnect the fuel supply hose at the fuel filter.

17. Raise the vehicle and support it safely. Then, disconnect the exhaust pipe at the manifold. Fasten the exhaust pipe with wire to keep it from falling.

18. If equipped with a manual transmission, disconnect the shift control rod and extension and remove them.

19. Disconnect the left and right side strut bars and stabilizer bars where they connect to the lower control arms. Then, remove the bolts fastening the control arms on both sides to the rearward crossmember.

20. Disconnect the lower arm ball joint at the steering knuckle on both sides. Then, disconnect the strut bar and stabilizer bar at the lower control arm. Using a prybar inserted between the transaxle case and driveshaft, carefully pry the halfshaft out of the transaxle on each side. Plug the openings in the transaxle to prevent dirt from getting in.

21. Carefully lower all parts to the crossmember. Discard the retaining clips for the halfshafts. They must be replaced.

22. Attach a cable securely supported by a lift and pulley arrangement to each engine lifting point. Put tension on all the cables to support the engine securely.

23. Remove the nut from the left side engine mount insulator. Remove the 4 front roll bracket bolts located on the side of the front crossmember.

24. Remove the bolt from the rear roll insulator. Remove the nuts attaching the left engine mount insulator to the fender.

25. From inside the right fender shield, detach the protective cap and then remove the transaxle insulator bracket bolts. Remove the bolts connecting the transaxle mount insulator.

26. Remove the bolts to the shift control selector. Remove the wiring connector going to the transaxle. Disconnect vacuum hoses.

27. Remove the transaxle insulator bracket. Increase the tension on the lifting cables so the engine weight is supported entirely by the cables and none of the weight is on the mounts. Remove the bolts passing through the insulators of the rear roll stop and left bracket.

28. Make sure all items are disconnected from the engine/transaxle assembly. Press downward on the transaxle to guide the assembly and lift it carefully out of the vehicle.

29. Installation is the exact reverse of removal. When installing the engine, be careful to ensure that engine compartment wiring and hoses do not catch on engine wiring and hoses do not catch on engine parts. Torque bolts as follows:

Left engine mount insulator nut (large)—43–58 ft. lbs.
Left engine mount insulator nuts (small)—22–29 ft. lbs.
Left engine mount bracket-to-engine bolts/nuts—36–47 ft. lbs.
Transaxle mount insulator nut—43–58 ft. lbs.
Transaxle insulator bracket-to-fender shield bolts—manual 40–43 ft. lbs.
Transaxle insulator bracket-to-fender shield bolts—automatic 22–29 ft. lbs.
Transaxle mounting bracket-to-automatic transaxle nuts—43–58 ft. lbs.
Transaxle mounting bracket bolts—22–29 ft. lbs.
Rear roll stop insulator nut—22–29 ft. lbs.
Rear roll stop-to-rear crossmember nuts—43–58 ft. lbs.
Rear roll stop bracket-to-rear roll stop stay bolt—22–29 ft. lbs.
Front roll stop insulator nut—36–47 ft. lbs.
Front roll bracket-to-front crossmember nuts—29–36 ft. lbs.

30. After the engine is securely mounted, operate the engine checking carefully for leaks. Check all gauges for proper readings. Adjust clutch and shift linkage. Adjust the accelerator cable. Recharge the air conditioner.

STARION

NOTE: Use care when disconnecting the refrigerant lines. Escaping refrigerant will freeze any surface it contacts, including skin and eyes.

1. Matchmark and then unbolt and remove the hood. Drain the cooling system. Disconnect the accelerator cable at the injection mixer. Disconnect both battery cables.

2. Disconnect both heater hoses at the block and the brake booster vacuum hose at the intake manifold.

3. Disconnect the fuel hoses at the injection system.

4. Disconnect the high tension wire at the center of the distributor. Disconnect the temperature sensor wire. Disconnect the intake manifold ground cable connector. First label the wires for reassembly and then disconnect the starter motor wiring harness.

5. Disconnect the power steering pump hoses. Remove the power steering pump.

6. Unbolt and disconnect both engine oil cooler hoses at the oil filter adapter. Plug all openings to prevent the entry of dirt and leakage of oil.

7. Label and then disconnect the alternator wiring. Disconnect the engine ground cable. Disconnect both plugs for the electronic injection wiring harness.

8. Disconnect the vacuum hose from the boost sensor, located on the firewall.

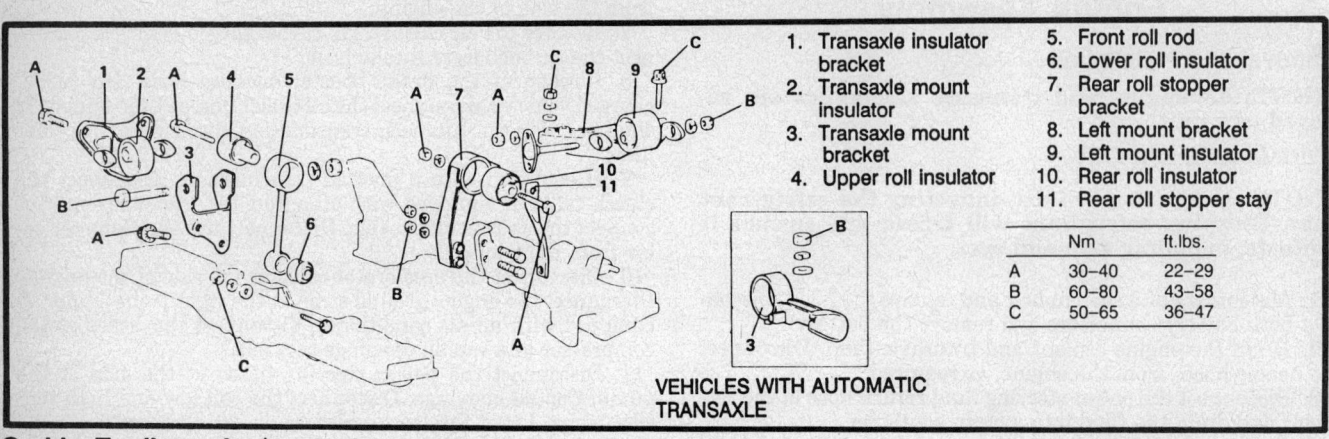

1. Transaxle insulator bracket
2. Transaxle mount insulator
3. Transaxle mount bracket
4. Upper roll insulator
5. Front roll rod
6. Lower roll insulator
7. Rear roll stopper bracket
8. Left mount bracket
9. Left mount insulator
10. Rear roll insulator
11. Rear roll stopper stay

VEHICLES WITH AUTOMATIC TRANSAXLE

	Nm	ft.lbs.
A	30–40	22–29
B	60–80	43–58
C	50–65	36–47

Cordia, Tredia engine/transaxle mounting

9. Remove the rear catalytic converter.

10. Unscrew and disconnect the speedometer cable at the transmission. Disconnect the wiring for the oil pressure gauge sending unit on the block.

11. If equipped with an automatic transmission, disconnect both oil cooler hoses and plug all openings. On all vehicles, disconnect the back-up light switch harness at the plug located under the transmission.

12. Remove the propeller shaft.

13. Remove the clutch slave cylinder.

14. Put the gearshift in N. Unbolt the gearshift lever assembly.

15. Securely support the engine using a suitable engine crane. Support the transmission with a jack. Then, remove the front and rear engine mounting nuts and bolts, and the rear crossmember. Raise the assembly slightly and remove all the front support brackets and insulators. Then, gradually lower the transmission jack and pull the engine and transmission assembly out by raising the front of the engine so the transmission will clear the firewall.

16. Install in exact reverse order. When reassembling mounts, make sure all holes are properly aligned and that mounts are not distorted. On both front insulators, make sure the locating boss and hole in the insulator are in alignment. Torques are as follows.

17. On the rear crossmember insulators torque the bolts to the following specifications: turn them until a flat will align with lockwasher tabs and then bend the tabs up against the flats to keep the bolts from unscrewing. Refill all fluids and adjust all linkages.

MIRAGE

NOTE: Use care when disconnecting the refrigerant lines. Escaping refrigerant will freeze any surface it contacts, including skin and eyes.

1. Remove the hood. Remove the air cleaner assembly. Disconnect both battery cables and then remove the batter. Unbolt and remove the battery tray.

2. Disconnect the electrical connectors for the backup lights and engine harness, located near the battery tray. If equipped with a 5 speed, disconnect the select control valve connector. Disconnect both alternator harness connectors and the oil pressure sending unit.

3. Label and then disconnect the automatic transmission oil cooler hoses. Avoid spilling oil and cap the openings.

4. Drain the cooling system. Then disconnect and remove the upper and lower hoses and remove them. Remove the radiator.

5. Label and then disconnect all low tension wires and the one high tension wire going to the coil from the distributor. Disconnect the engine ground.

6. Disconnect the brake booster vacuum hose at the intake manifold. Disconnect the cap power steering lines, as required. Remove pump as needed.

7. Disconnect the fuel supply, return and vapor hoses at the side of the engine.

8. If equipped with a turbocharger, the 3 electrical connectors must be disconnected—1 for the idle speed control system and 2 for the injection system. All are located on the injection mixer.

9. Disconnect the heater hoses from the side of the engine. Disconnect the accelerator cable at the side of the injection mixer and the block.

10. If equipped with a manual transmission, disconnect the clutch control cable. If equipped with an automatic transmission, disconnect the shift control cable from the transaxle.

11. Unscrew and disconnect the speedometer cable at the transaxle.

12. Raise and securely support the vehicle. Remove the drain plug and drain the transmission fluid. Disconnect the exhaust pipe at the manifold. Then, suspend the pipe securely with wire.

13. If equipped with a manual transmission, remove the shift control rod and extension rod.

14. Disconnect the stabilizer bar at both lower control arms. Remove the bolts that attach the lower control arms to the body on either side. Support the arms from the body.

15. If equipped with a turbocharger, disconnect and remove the oil cooler tube from the side of the engine.

16. Disconnect the halfshaft at the transaxle on both sides. Then, seal off the openings in the transaxle. Make sure to replace the circlips holding the driveshafts in the transaxle. Support the halfshafts from the body.

17. Attach a crane-type lift, via chains or cables, to both the engine lifting hooks. Put just a little tension on the cables. Then, remove the nut and bolt from the front roll stopper; unbolt the brace from the top of the engine damper.

18. Separate the rear roll stopper from the crossmember. Remove the attaching nut from the left mount insulator bolt, but do not remove the bolt.

19. Raise the engine just enough that the crane is supporting its weight. Check that everything is disconnected from the engine.

20. Remove the blind cover from the inside of the right fender inner shield. Then, remove the blind cover from the inside of the right front fender inner shied. Remove the transaxle bracket bolts.

21. Remove the left mount insulator bolt. Then, press downward on the transaxle while lifting the engine/transaxle assembly to guide it up and out of the vehicle.

22. Installation is generally performed in reverse of the removal procedure. During installation, first install all nuts and bolts with the weight of the engine carried by the crane. Tighten just slightly. Then, allow the weight of the engine to sit on the mounts and torque parts as follows.

23. Finally, replenish all fluids. Adjust the transaxle and accelerator linkages. Start the engine and check for leaks as well as proper gauge operation. Replace the hood and recharge the air conditioner, if necessary.

GALANT WITH 4 CYLINDER ENGINE

NOTE: Use care when disconnecting the refrigerant lines. Escaping refrigerant will freeze any surface it contacts, including skin and eyes.

1. Matchmark the position of the hood hinges on the hood and remove it. Drain the engine coolant. Remove the drain plug and drain the transaxle fluid.

2. Remove the air cleaner. Disconnect the battery cables, remove the battery and then unbolt and remove the battery tray.

3. Carefully label and then disconnect each of 3 connectors of the engine wiring harness.

4. Disconnect the ground wire at the right side wheelhouse. Drain the power steering fluid by disconnecting a hose at the low point of the system. Plug all openings.

5. If equipped with a electronically controlled suspension, remove the compressor and reserve tank.

6. Disconnect the transaxle control cable by moving the adjusting nut on the transaxle end of the cable and pulling the cable out of the fitting on the transaxle. Keep the rearward nut from moving to preserve the adjustment.

7. Disconnect the alternator connectors and the oil pressure sending unit. Disconnect the high tension cable at the coil.

8. Disconnect the engine ground cable at the firewall. Disconnect the brake booster vacuum hose.

9. Label and then disconnect the eight connectors for the sensors of the electronic fuel injection at the injection mixing body. Disconnect the accelerator and speed control cables nearby.

10. Disconnect the fuel supply and return hoses at the electronic injection mixing body.

11. Mark and then disconnect the transmission oil cooler hoses. Cap the openings to keep oil in and dirt out. Disconnect both radiator hoses and both heater hoses at the engine.

12. Unscrew and then disconnect the speedometer cable at the transaxle. Disconnect the power steering hoses at the pump and cap all openings.

13. Raise and securely support the vehicle. Disconnect the exhaust pipe at the exhaust manifold. Then, hang the pipe to the body with wire.

14. Disconnect the steering knuckles from the lower arm ball joints. Disconnect the tie rods from the steering knuckle. Remove the halfshafts from the transaxle. Make sure to cap all openings to keep fluid in and dirt out. Discard the retaining clips that hold the shafts in the transaxle and replace them.

15. Attach a lifting crane to both engine lifting hooks and put very slight tension on the chains or cables. Then remove the nut, but not the bolt, coupling the engine mount bracket to the body. Remove the upper installation nuts of the front and rear roll stopper brackets.

16. Detach the protective cap from inside the right fender shield and then remove the transaxle bracket bolts. Then, remove the bolts connecting the transaxle mount insulator to the bracket and remove the bracket.

17. Increase the tension on the engine lifting mechanism until the weight of the engine is borne by the lift instead of its mounts. Remove the bolts of the rear roll stopper bracket, the engine mount bracket and the front roll stopper bracket. Confirm that all cable, wires and linkages are disconnected.

18. Tilting the transaxle side downward, carefully life the engine/transaxle assemble out of the vehicle.

19. Install in exact reverse order. Make sure nothing gets pinched or bent when installing the engine. When installing rubber insulators, make sure they are not twisted. Observe the torque

20. Check the operation of all linkages, adjusting if necessary, Replenish all fluids and then operate the engine, checking for leaks.

GALANT AND SIGMA WITH V6 ENGINE

NOTE: Use care when disconnecting the refrigerant lines. Escaping refrigerant will freeze any surface it contacts, including skin and eyes.

1. Matchmark the position of the hood hinges on the hood and remove it. Drain the engine coolant. Remove the drain plug and drain the transaxle fluid.

2. Remove the air cleaner. Disconnect the battery cables, remove the battery and then unbolt and remove the battery tray.

3. Carefully label and then disconnect each of the connectors of the engine wiring harness.

4. Remove the accelerator cable bracket screws. Remove the accelerator cable and cruise control cable from the throttle body linkage.

5. Disconnect and plug the high pressure fuel lines and fuel return lines from the engine.

6. Open the cover of the fusible link box and disconnect the alternator wiring. Disconnect and tag all necessary wiring including the pulse generator connector, if equipped with an automatic transaxle.

7. If equipped with an automatic transaxle, disconnect the transaxle control cables. Remove the control cable bracket bolts and disconnect the transaxle control cables from the transaxle. Disconnect and plug the oil cooler lines.

8. If equipped with electronic controlled suspension, remove the air compressor.

9. If equipped with a manual transaxle, remove the clutch release cylinder bolts. Remove the clutch oil tube bracket and secure the clutch release cylinder and the clutch oil tube assembly on the chassis side with some wire.

10. Disconnect the speedometer. Disconnect and plug the heater hoses. Remove all the radiator hoses and remove the radiator.

11. Disconnect and plug the air conditioner lines from the compressor. Release the engine block section clamp and disconnect the discharge flexible hose. Remove the clip from the power steering oil pump section and disconnect the suction flexible hose.

12. Remove the engine under cover panels. Remove the stabilizer nut and tie rod end cotter pin. Using the special tie rod tool, disconnect the tie rod end from the steering knuckle. Using the suitable tool, disconnect the lower arm ball joint from the knuckle. Loosen the nut but do not remove it.

13. Remove the left side halfshaft (after removing the circlip, cotter pin and halfshaft nut) by inserting a suitable tool between the bearing bracket and the halfshaft and then pry the halfshaft from the bearing bracket. Be sure to pull the halfshaft out from the bearing bracket as an assembly with the hub knuckle and other parts. Suspend the removed halfshaft with a wire to prevent the joint section from bending sharply.

14. Remove the right side halfshaft circlip and locknut, then remove the halfshaft from the hub by using the special hub removal tool. Once the hub is remove, use a suitable tool and pull the halfshaft out from the transaxle.

15. Remove the rubber hangers from the exhaust system. Disconnect the oxygen sensor connector. Remove the bolts or nuts from the front exhaust pipe and remove the pipe from the engine. Be sure to suspend the disconnected exhaust pipe with a wire to keep it from bending sharply.

16. Remove the distributor cap and connect a suitable engine lifting device to the proper locations on the engine and raise the lifting device just enough to take the slack out of the cable.

17. Remove the front roll stopper bracket mount bolt, engine damper and rear roll stopper bracket mount bolt. Remove the bolts and nuts that fasten the engine mount bracket to the body.

18. To remove the transaxle mount bracket, first remove the 4 plugs from the fender shield. Remove the transaxle mount bracket bolts with care to prevent them from falling into the fender shield.

19. Check that all cables, hoses, electrical harness connections and wires are disconnected from the side of the engine. Slowly remove the engine and transaxle assembly upwards from the engine compartment with the engine lift. Once the engine and transaxle assembly has cleared the vehicle, place it on a suitable engine stand.

20. Installation is the reverse order of the removal procedure, except for the following:

   a. When installing the halfshaft nut, install the washer and wheel bearing nut in the proper direction. If the position of the cotter pin holes does not match, tighten the nut up to 188 ft. lbs. and then install the cotter pin in the first matching holes and bend it securely.

   b. After the installation is complete, check all the remove and disconnect components for proper operation and adjust or repair as necessary.

PRECIS

NOTE: Use care when disconnecting the refrigerant lines. Escaping refrigerant will freeze any surface it contacts, including skin and eyes.

1. Remove the air cleaner assembly by disconnecting all hoses, unbolting it and removing it. Disconnect both battery cables and then remove the battery. Unbolt and remove the battery tray.

2. Disconnect the electrical connectors for the back-up lights and engine harness, located near the battery tray. If equipped with a 5 speed, disconnect the select control valve connector. Disconnect both alternator harness connectors and the oil pressure sending unit.

3. First label and then disconnect the transmission oil cooler hoses. Avoid spilling oil and cap the openings.

4. Drain the cooling system through the cock on the bottom of the radiator and the plug in the block. Then disconnect and

remove the upper and lower hoses and remove them. Remove the radiator.

5. Label and then disconnect all low tension wires and the 1 high tension wire going to the coil from the distributor. Disconnect the engine ground.

6. Disconnect the brake booster vacuum hose at the intake manifold.

7. Disconnect the fuel supply, return, and vapor hoses at the side of the engine. Avoid spilling fuel.

8. Disconnect the heater hoses from the side of the engine.

9. If equipped with a manual transmission, disconnect the clutch control cable. If equipped with an automatic transmission, disconnect the shifter control cable from the transaxle.

10. Unscrew and disconnect the speedometer cable at the transaxle.

11. Raise and securely support the vehicle. Remove the drain plug and drain the transmission fluid. Disconnect the exhaust pipe at the manifold. Then, suspend the pipe securely with wire.

12. If equipped with a manual transaxle, remove the shift control rod and extension rod.

13. Disconnect the stabilizer bar at both lower control arms. Remove the bolts that attach the lower control arms to the body on either side. Support the arms from the body.

14. Disconnect the halfshafts at the transaxle on both sides. Then, seal off the openings in the transaxle. Make sure to replace the circlips holding the halfshafts in the transaxle. Support the halfshafts from the body.

15. Attach a crane-type lift, via chains or cables, to both the engine lifting hooks. Put just a little tension on the cables. Then, remove the nut and bolt from the front roll stopper; unbolt the brace from the top of the engine damper.

16. Separate the rear roll stopper from the crossmember. Remove the attaching nut from the left mount insulator bolt, but do not remove the bolt.

17. Raise the engine just enough that the crane is supporting its weight. Check that everything is disconnected from the engine.

18. Remove the blind cover from the inside of the right fender inner shield. Remove the transaxle bracket bolts.

19. Remove the left mount insulator bolt. Then, press downward on the transaxle while lifting the engine/transaxle assembly to guide it up and out of the vehicle.

20. Installation is generally performed in reverse of the removal procedure. During installation, first install all nuts and bolts with the weight of the engine carried by the crane. Tighten just slightly. Then, allow the weight of the engine to sit on the mounts, and torque parts as follows:

Left mount large insulator nut—65–80 ft. lbs.
Left mount small insulator nut—22–29 ft. lbs.
Left mount bracket-to-engine nuts/bolts—36–47 ft. lbs.
Transaxle mount insulator nut—65–80 ft. lbs.
Transaxle insulator bracket-to-side frame bolts—22–29 ft. lbs.
Transaxle bracket assembly-to-automatic transaxle nuts—65–80 ft. lbs.
Transaxle mount bracket-to-manual transaxle bolts—40–43 ft. lbs.
Rear roll insulator nut—33–43 ft. lbs.
Rear roll stopper bracket-to-crossmember assembly bolts—22–29 ft. lbs.
Front roll insulator nut—33–43 ft. lbs.
Front roll stopper bracket-to-crossmember assembly bolts—33–40 ft. lbs.
Lower roll insulator roll-to-damper bracket bolt—22–29 ft. lbs.
Center crossmember body—43–58 ft. lbs.

21. Finally, replenish all fluids. Adjust the transaxle and accelerator linkages. Start the engine and check for leaks as well as proper gauge operation. Replace the hood and have the air conditioner recharged.

ECLIPSE

1. Relieve fuel system pressure.
2. Disconnect the negative battery cable.
3. Matchmark hood and hinges and remove hood assembly.
4. Drain the engine coolant and remove the radiator assembly.
5. Remove the transaxle.
6. Disconnect and tag for assembly reference the connections for the accelerator cable, heater hoses, brake vacuum hose, connection for vacuum hoses, high pressure fuel line, fuel return line, oxygen sensor connection, coolant temperature gauge connection, coolant temperature sensor connector, connection for thermo switch sensor, if equipped with automatic transmission, the connection for the idle speed control, the motor position sensor connector, the throttle position sensor connector, the EGR temperature sensor connection (California vehicles), the fuel injector connectors, the power transistor connector, the ignition coil connector, the condensor and noise filter connector, the distributor and control harness, the connections for the alternator and oil pressure switch wires.
7. Remove the air conditioner drive belt and then the air conditioning compressor. Leave the hoses attached. Do not discharge the system. Wire the compressor aside.
8. Remove the power steering pump and wire back aside.
9. Remove the exhaust manifold to head pipe nuts. Discard the gasket.
10. Attach a hoist to the engine and take up the engine weight. Remove the engine mount bracket. Remove any torque control brackets (roll stoppers). Note that some engine mount pieces have arrows on them for proper assembly. Double check that all cables, hoses, harness connectors, etc., are disconnected from the engine. Lift the engine slowly from the engine compartment.

To install:
11. Installation is the reverse of the removal procedure. Install the engine and torque control brackets.
12. Install the exhaust pipe, power steering pump and air conditioning compressor.
13. Checking the tags installed at removal, reconnect all electrical and vacuum connections.
14. Install the transaxle.
15. Refill with engine oil, coolant, install the hood and adjust the drive belts.
16. Adjust the accelerator cable as required.

Engine Mounts

Removal and Installation

1. Disconnect the negative battery cable.
2. Raise and safely support the engine so it is not resting on the engine mount. One suggested way is a block of wood between a floor jack and the oil pan. Use care not to bend or damage any components.
3. Remove the engine mount bracket and body connection through bolt. Take note of the position of the arrow on the oval shaped stopper plate. This is important.
4. Remove the engine bracket. Some engines may use an additional small strap that should be removed.
5. Remove the stopper plate.

To install:
6. Installation is the reverse of the removal procedure. Note the arrows on the stopper plates and make sure they are installed properly. Torque the engine mount-to-body bolts as well as the engine mount-to-engine nuts to 36–47 ft. lbs. Torque the stopper through bolt to 33–43 ft. lbs.
7. Lower engine. Reconnect the negative battery cable.

Cylinder Head

Removal and Installation

4 CYLINDER EXCEPT 1.5L, 1.6L ENGINES AND ECLIPSE 1.8L AND 2.0L ENGINES

1. Turn the engine until the No. 1 piston is at TDC on the compression stroke. Disconnect the negative battery cable. Remove the air cleaner assembly.

2. Drain the engine coolant. Remove the upper radiator hose and disconnect the heater hoses.

3. Disconnect the fuel lines, wiring harnesses, distributor vacuum lines, spark plug wires (from plugs), purge valves, accelerator linkage and water temperature unit wire.

4. Remove the distributor and (if necessary) the fuel pump from the cylinder head.

5. Remove the nuts connecting the exhaust pipe to the manifold or turbocharger. Lower the exhaust pipe.

6. Remove the turbocharger and/or exhaust manifold.

7. Remove the intake manifold assembly.

8. On 1795cc, 1997cc and 2350cc engines:

   a. Remove the upper, outer front cover. Align the timing mark on the cylinder head with the mark on the camshaft sprocket, engine should already be on the No. 1 piston TDC of the compression stroke.

   b. Matchmark the timing belt with the timing mark on the camshaft sprocket using a felt tip marker.

   c. Remove the sprocket and insert a 2 in. piece of rubber or other material between the camshaft sprocket and sprocket holder on the lower front cover, to hold the sprocket and belt so the valve timing will not be changed.

   d. Remove the timing belt upper under cover and the rocker arm cover.

9. On 2555cc engines:

   a. Remove the rocker arm cover.

   b. Position the camshaft sprocket dowel pin at the 12 o'clock position with the timing mark TDC at the front of the timing case cover; engine should already be on the No. 1 piston TDC of the compression stroke.

   c. Match the timing chain with the timing mark on the camshaft sprocket. Take a soft piece of wire and secure the chain and sprocket together at the timing mark and opposite side.

   d. Remove the camshaft sprocket bolt, gear and sprocket from the camshaft.

10. Except on the Starion, a special hex head wrench will be needed. Mitsubishi part MD998051–01 or equivalent. Loosen and remove the cylinder head bolts in 2–3 stages to avoid cylinder head warpage. Follow the sequence shown in the appropriate illustration.

11. Remove the cylinder head from the engine.

12. Clean the cylinder head and block mating surfaces and install a new cylinder head gasket.

13. Position the cylinder head on the engine block, engage the dowel pins front and rear and install the cylinder head bolts.

14. The bolts must be torqued to cold specification, which is 65–72 ft. lbs. in 2 equal stages. Using the sequence shown in the appropriate illustration, torque the bolts in order to 32.5–36 ft. lbs. then, repeat the operation torquing them to the full torque. Note that on the Starion, the front head bolts, attaching the head only to the timing cover, are torqued to 11–15 ft. lbs. Torque them to about 7 ft. lbs. the first time around.

15. Install the timing belt upper undercover, 1795cc and 1997cc engines.

16. Locate the camshaft in original position. Pull the camshaft sprocket and belt or chain upward and install on the camshaft.

NOTE: If the dowel pin and the dowel pin hole does not align between the sprocket and the spacer or camshaft, move the camshaft by bumping either of both projections provided at the rear of No. 2 cylinder exhaust

cam of the camshaft, with a light hammer or other tool, until the hole and pin align. Be certain the crankshaft does not turn.

17. Install the camshaft sprocket bolt and the distributor gear and tighten.

18. Install the timing belt upper front cover and spark plug cable support.

19. Apply sealant to the intake manifold gasket on both sides. Position the gasket and install the intake manifold. Tighten the

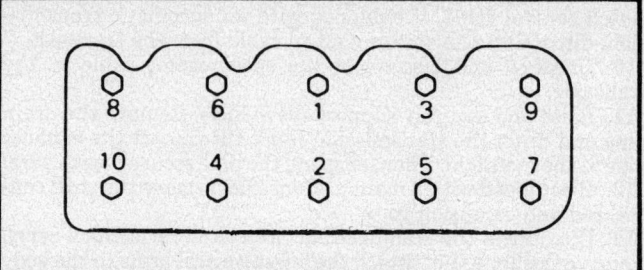

Engine head bolt torque sequence for 1795cc, 1997cc and 2350cc engines

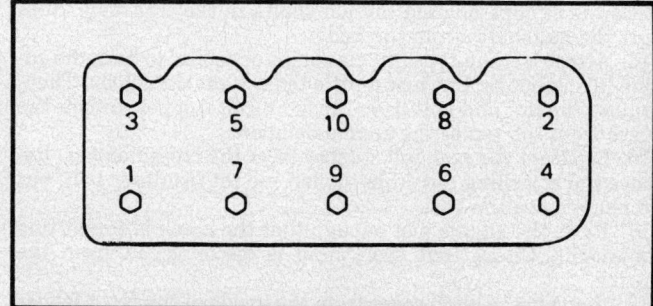

Engine head bolt torque removal sequence for 1795cc, 1997cc and 2350cc engines

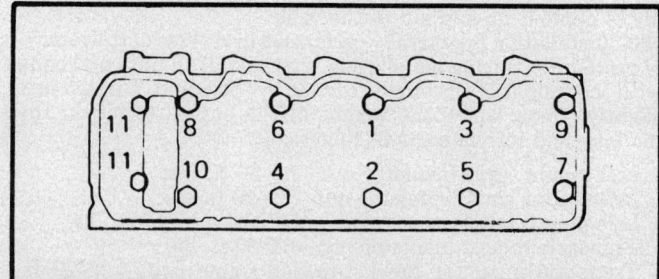

Engine head bolt torque sequence for the 2555cc engine

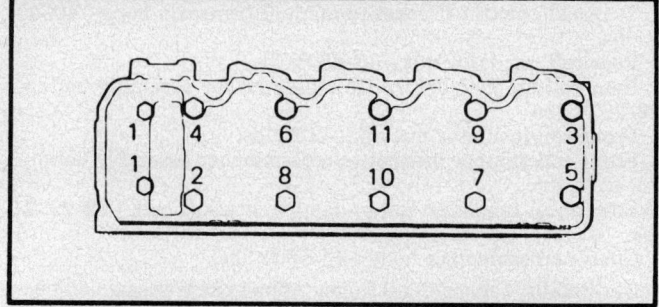

Engine head bolt removal sequence for the 2555cc engine

nuts to specifications. Be sure no sealant enters the jet air passages, when equipped.

20. Install the exhaust manifold gaskets and the manifold assembly. Tighten the nuts to specifications.

21. Connect the exhaust pipe to the exhaust manifold and install the fuel pump. Install the purge valve.

22. Install the water temperature gauge wire, heater hoses and the upper radiator hose.

23. Connect the fuel lines, accelerator linkage, vacuum hoses and the spark plug wires.

24. Fill the cooling system and connect the batter ground cable. Install the distributor.

25. Temporarily adjust the valve clearance to the cold engine specifications.

26. Install the gasket on the rocker arm cover and temporarily install the cover on the engine.

27. Start the engine and bring it to normal operating temperature. Stop the engine and remove the rocker arm cover.

28. Adjust the valves to hot engine specifications.

29. Reinstall the rocker arm cover and tighten securely.

30. Install the air cleaner, hoses, purge valve hose, and any other removed unit.

1.5L ENGINE

1. Disconnect the negative battery cable. Drain the cooling system and then disconnect the upper radiator hose. Remove the PCV hose that runs between the air cleaner and the rocker cover.

2. Remove the air cleaner. Disconnect the fuel lines. Label and disconnect any vacuum lines running to the cylinder head, manifold, or carburetor from other parts of the engine compartment. Disconnect the heater hoses going to the head.

3. Label and disconnect the spark plug wires. Remove the rocker cover. Turn the crankshaft over until the TDC timing marks align and both No. 1 cylinder valves are closed; both rockers are off the cams. Then, remove the distributor.

4. Remove the carburetor, intake manifold and the exhaust manifold.

5. Remove the timing belt cover. Note the location of the camshaft sprocket timing mark. Loosen both timing belt tensioner bolts and lever it toward the water pump as far as it will go. Retighten the adjusting bolt to hold the tensioner in this position. Pull the timing belt off the camshaft sprocket but leave it engaged with the other sprockets.

6. Using a hex-type wrench, part MD998360, loosen the head bolts in the sequence shown. When all have been loosened, remove them. Then, pull the head off the engine block, rocking it slightly to break it loose, if necessary.

7. Remove the gasket. If pieces of the gasket adhere to the head or block deck, scrape them off carefully, using a scraper that will not scratch the surfaces. Make sure none of the pieces gets into the engine.

8. Install a new head gasket (without any sealer) and then position the head on the block deck. Install all the bolts finger-tight. Torque them, in sequence, first to 25 ft. lbs., then, to 58–61 ft. lbs.

9. Install the timing belt on the camshaft tensioner and rotate the camshaft sprocket backward so the belt is tight on what is normally the tension side. Make sure all the timing marks are now aligned.

10. Loosen the timing belt tensioner adjusting bolt and allow spring tension to tension the belt. Make sure all timing marks are still aligned. If not, the belt is out of time and must be shifted with the tensioner shifted back toward the water pump and locked there. Torque the adjusting bolt (on the right side and working through a slot) to 15–18 ft. lbs. After the tensioner adjusting bolt is torqued, torque the hinged bolt located on the opposite side. Don't torque the bolt first or the tension on the belt will be too great.

11. Turn the crankshaft 1 full turn in the normal direction of rotation. Loosen first the tensioner pivot bolt and the adjusting

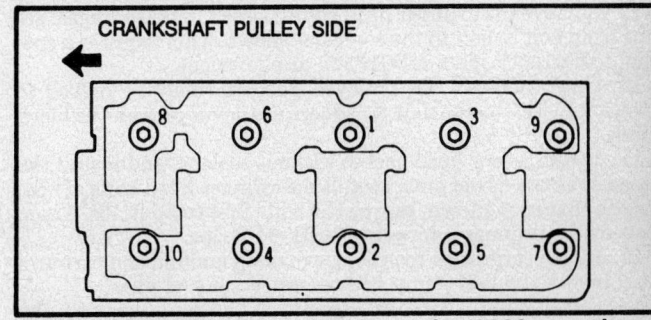

Engine head bolt torque sequence for 1468cc and 1597cc engines

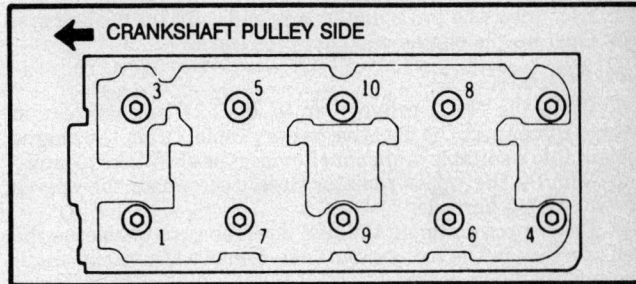

Engine head bolt removal sequence for 1468cc and 1597cc engines

bolt. Torque them exactly as before—adjusting bolt (working in the slot) first. This extra step is necessary to ensure the timing belt is properly seated before final tension is adjusted.

12. Install the intake and exhaust manifolds, carburetor, distributor, air cleaner, rocker cover, timing belt cover, and all hoses in reverse of the above procedures. Refill the cooling system. Operate the engine and check for leaks.

1.6L ENGINE

1. Disconnect the negative battery cable. Drain engine coolant and then disconnect the upper radiator hose at the thermostat. Remove PCV and canister purge hoses.

2. Remove the air cleaner. Disconnect the fuel line. Disconnect vacuum hoses at the distributor and canister purge control valve.

3. Label and then disconnect the spark plug wires. Remove the rocker cover. Turn the crankshaft over until the TDC timing marks align and both No. 1 cylinder valves are closed (both rockers are off the cams). Then, remove the distributor.

4. Disconnect the heater hose at the intake manifold. Disconnect the water hose leading from the cylinder head and carburetor water jacket.

5. Disconnect the temperature gauge sending unit wire at the head. Remove the fuel pump.

6. Remove the exhaust manifold. Turn the crankshaft until No. 1 piston is at TDC of its compression stroke. Align the timing mark on the upper cover at the rear of the timing belt with the mark on the camshaft sprocket to do this. Use some sort of marker to mark the relationship between the timing belt and the mark on the cam sprocket.

7. Remove the sprocket-to-camshaft bolt, hold the sprocket in position and work to keep the belt from slipping off. Then, rest the sprocket on the sprocket holder provided on the lower front cover. If necessary, slip a short piece of used timing belt or other thin, flexible object between the holder and the sprocket to keep tension and avoid losing belt timing. Be sure not to turn the crankshaft throughout this work.

8. Remove the bolts from the timing belt rear cover and remove the cover.

9. Remove the cylinder head bolts. Loosen in three stages, going from bolt to bolt in the sequence shown. This requires a special hex wrench, part MD998360 or equivalent.

10. Once the bolts are removed, the head may be rocked to break it loose. Do not slide it as there are dowel pins on the block deck.

11. Install a new head gasket without sealant, and install the head over the dowel pins. Install the cylinder head bolts. Then, in the sequence shown, torque the bolts first to 25 ft. lbs. Then, repeat the sequence, torquing to 51–54 ft. lbs.

12. Install the intake manifold, exhaust manifold and carburetor. Install the fuel pump and reconnect all fuel lines.

13. Install the distributor. Reconnect the plug wires in the proper firing order. Reconnect the temperature gauge wire and all water hoses. Reconnect the distributor, PCV and evaporative emissions system vacuum hoses.

14. Reconnect the top radiator hose and refill the cooling system. Operate the engine and check for leaks.

3.0L ENGINE

1. Bring the No. 1 cylinder up to **TDC** of its compression stroke. Disconnect the negative battery cable. Drain the engine coolant into a suitable drain pan. Remove the air intake plenum.

2. Remove the upper radiator hose. Disconnect the engine control wiring harness.

3. Disconnect and plug the fuel lines, be sure to release the fuel pressure in the fuel system first. Remove the intake manifold and manifold gasket.

4. Disconnect and tag the spark plug wires. Disconnect the oxygen sensor connector.

5. Remove the self-locking nuts from the exhaust pipe and then suspend the exhaust pipe with a piece of wire.

6. Remove the distributor assembly and the air intake plenum stay. Remove any bolts that attach hoses or pipes to the cylinder heads.

7. Remove the heat protector bolts, then remove the heat protector along with the exhaust manifolds.

8. Remove the oil level gauge guide and the exhaust manifold gaskets.

9. Remove the timing belt and camshaft sprocket. Use the camshaft special tool MB990767 or equivalent, to hold the camshaft sprocket still so as to break loose the camshaft sprocket bolt.

10. Remove the timing belt rear cover. Remove the small retaining bolt from the side of the cylinder heads.

11. Remove the rocker arm cover and rocker arm cover gasket.

12. Remove the cylinder head bolts, in sequence, in 2–3 cycles, and remove the cylinder heads and gaskets from the engine.

13. Installation is the reverse order of the removal procedure, except for the following:

    a. Using a suitable torque wrench, torque the head bolts, in sequence, using 2–3 steps, to a final torque of 73–79 ft. lbs. (hot) or 65–72 ft. lbs. (cold).

    b. Be sure to coat all O-rings with clean engine oil and apply a suitable sealant to the cut-out ends of the rocker arm covers.

    c. Be sure to use special tool MB990767 or equivalent, to hold the camshaft sprocket still so as to torque the camshaft sprocket bolt to 58–72 ft. lbs.

ECLIPSE

1.8L Engine

1. Relieve fuel system pressure. Drain the cooling system.

2. Disconnect the negative battery cable.

3. Remove the connections for the air intake hose and the breather hose.

4. Remove the connection for the accelerator cable. There will be 2 cables, if equipped with cruise control.

5. Remove the connection for the high pressure fuel line.

6. Remove the upper radiator hose, the water breather hose, the water bypass hose and the heater hose.

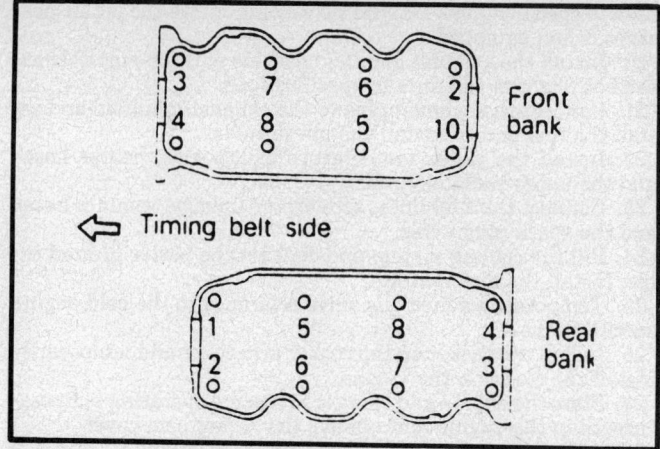

Cylinder head bolt removal sequence—3.0L engine

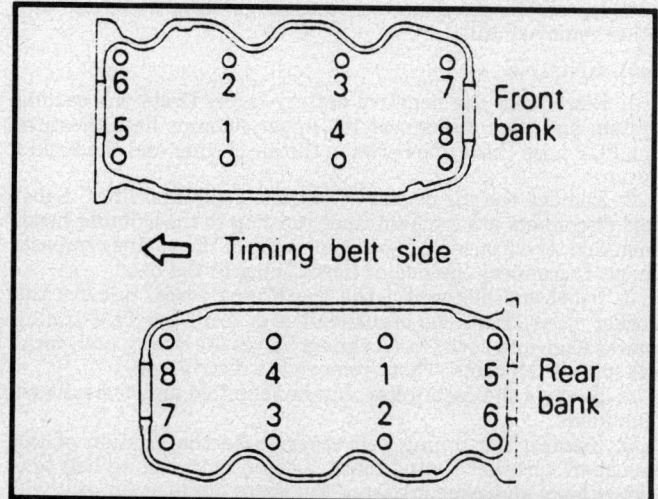

Cylinder head bolt torque sequence—3.0L engine

7. Remove the connector for the PCV hose.

8. Remove the spark plug cables.

9. Remove the fuel return line.

10. Remove the vacuum line for the brake booster.

11. Remove the electrical connections for the oxygen sensor, engine coolant temperature gauge unit and the water temperature sensor.

12. Remove the electrical connections for the ISC motor, throttle position sensor, distributor, MPS, fuel injectors, EGR temperature sensor (California vehicles), power transistor, condenser and ground cable.

13. Remove the engine control wiring harness.

14. Remove the clamp that holds the power steering pressure hose to the engine bracket.

15. Place a jack and wood block under the oil pan and carefully lift just enough to take the weight off the engine bracket and remove the bracket.

16. Remove the rocker cover, gasket and half-round seal.

17. Remove the timing belt front upper cover.

18. Remove the camshaft sprocket. First rotate the crankshaft clockwise until the timing marks on the sprocket align. Remove the sprocket with the timing belt attached and place on the timing belt front lower cover. Remove the timing belt rear upper cover.

19. Remove the exhaust pipe self-locking nuts and separate the exhaust pipe from the exhaust manifold. Discard the gasket.

20. Loosen the cylinder head bolts according to sequence in 2–3 steps and lift off the cylinder head assembly.

To install:

21. Installation is the reverse of the removal process. Check the cylinder head for cracks, damage or engine coolant leakage. Remove scale, sealing compound and carbon. Clean oil passages thoroughly. Check the head for flatness. End to end, the head should be within 0.002 in. normally with 0.008 in. the maximum allowed out of true. The total thickness allowed to be removed from the head and block is 0.008 in. maximum.

22. Place a new head gasket on the cylinder block with any identification marks facing upward.

23. Carefully install the cylinder head on the block. Tighten the bolts in sequence and torque in 3 steps to 51–54 ft. lbs.

24. Complete installation by reversing the removal procedure.

2.0L Engine

1. Relieve fuel system pressure. Drain the cooling system.
2. Disconnect the negative battery cable.
3. Remove the connection for the accelerator cable. There will be 2 cables, if equipped with cruise control.
4. Remove the electrical connections for the oxygen sensor, engine coolant temperature sensor, the engine coolant temperature gauge unit and the engine coolant temperature switch on vehicles with air conditioning.
5. Remove the electrical connections for the ISC motor, throttle position sensor, crankshaft angle sensor, fuel injectors, ignition coil, power transistor, noise filter, knock sensor on turbocharged engines, EGR temperature sensor (California vehicles) and ground cable.
6. Remove the engine control wiring harness.
7. Remove the upper radiator hose and the overflow tube.
8. Remove the connections for the air intake hose on turbocharged models, and the breather hose. Remove the large bellows-type air intake hose.
9. Remove the connection for the high pressure fuel line.
10. Remove the small vacuum hoses.
11. Remove the heater hose and water bypass hose.
12. Remove the PCV hose.
13. If turbocharged, remove the vacuum hoses, water line, eyebolt connection for the oil line for the turbo.
14. Remove the fuel return hose.
15. Remove the brake booster hose.
16. Remove the timing belt.
17. Remove the rocker cover and the half-round seal.
18. On non-turbo vehicles, remove the exhaust pipe self-locking nuts and separate the exhaust pipe from the exhaust manifold. Discard the gasket.
19. On turbocharged engines, remove the sheetmetal heat protector.
20. Loosen the cylinder head bolts according to sequence in 2–3 cycles and lift off the cylinder head assembly.

To install:

21. Installation is the reverse of the removal process. Check the cylinder head for cracks, damage or engine coolant leakage. Remove scale, sealing compound and carbon. Clean oil passages thoroughly. Check the head for flatness. End to end, the head should be within 0.002 in. normally with 0.008 in. the maximum allowed out of true. The total thickness allowed to be removed from the head and block is 0.008 in. maximum.

22. Place a new head gasket on the cylinder block with any identification marks facing upward.

23. Carefully install the cylinder head on the block. Tighten the bolts in sequence and torque in 3 steps to 65–72 ft. lbs.

24. Complete installation by reversing the removal procedure.

Valve Lash

Adjustment

Valve lash must be adjusted on all engines not equipped with automatic lash adjusters. Some engines have an unusual third valve of very small size called a jet valve. The jet valve must be adjusted, whether the engine uses automatic lash adjusters for the normal intake and exhaust valves or not. Thus, on some engines, there are 3 valves per cylinder that must be adjusted.

1. Run the engine until operating temperature is reached.
2. Turn **OFF** the engine and block the wheels.
3. Remove all necessary components in order to gain access to the rocker cover.
4. Remove the spark plugs from the cylinder head for easy operations.

   a. On Starion—remove the air intake pipe and remove the rocker cover.

   b. On Cordia and Tredia—disconnect the oxygen sensor connecting joint. Remove the engine bracket mounting, be sure to place a block of wood on the oil pan and raise it into place for the duration of the operation. Remove the upper front timing belt cover, remove the air cleaner assembly (2.0L engine) and the air intake pipe (1.8L engine) and remove the rocker cover.

   c. On all other vehicles—remove the air cleaner or air intake pipe assembly and remove the rocker cover.

5. Turn each cylinder head bolt in the sequence back just until it is loose. Torque the cylinder head bolts in the proper sequence to specification.

6. Position the engine at **TDC** with No. 1 cylinder at the firing position. Turn the engine by using a wrench on the bolt in the front of the crankshaft until the **0** degree timing mark on the timing cover aligns with the notch in the front pulley. On some vehicles turn the crankshaft clockwise until the notch on the pulley is aligned with the **T** mark on the timing belt lower cover.

7. Observe the valve rockers for No. 1 cylinder. If both are in identical positions with the valves up, the engine is in the right

Adjusting valve clearance

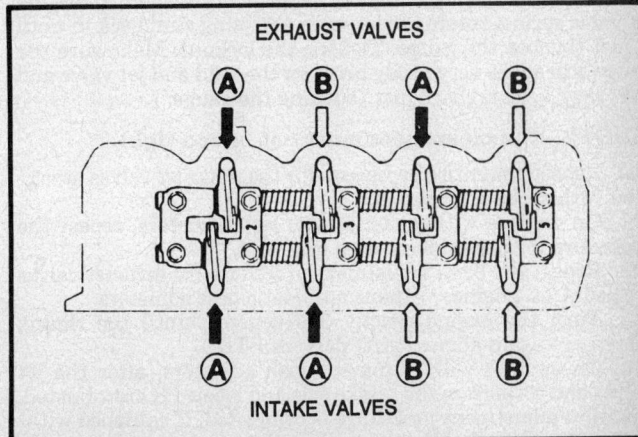

"A" and "B" valve adjusting positions

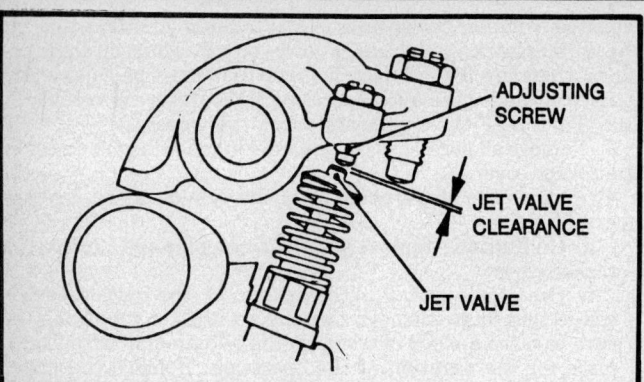

Jet valve adjusting

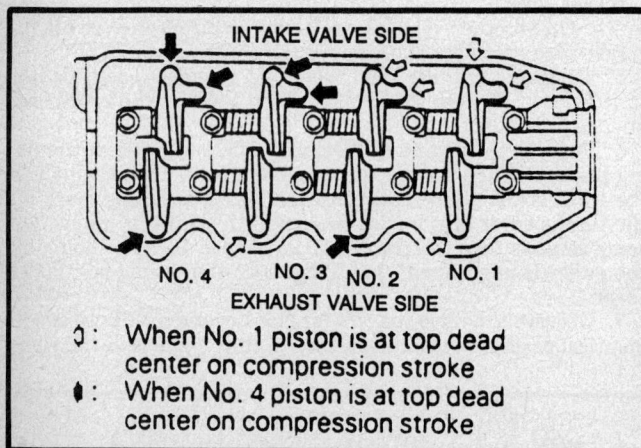

INTAKE VALVE SIDE

NO. 4   NO. 3   NO. 2   NO. 1
EXHAUST VALVE SIDE

◐ : When No. 1 piston is at top dead center on compression stroke

◑ : When No. 4 piston is at top dead center on compression stroke

Typical valve adjustment sequence

position. If not, rotate the engine exactly 360 degrees until the 0 degree timing mark is again aligned. Each jet valve is associated with an intake valve that is on the same rocker lever. In this position, adjust all the valves marked **A**, including associated jet valves which are located on the rockers on the intake side only.

8. To adjust the appropriate jet valves, first loosen the regular (larger) intake valve adjusting stud by loosening the locknut and backing the stud off 2 turns. Note that this particular step is not required on engines that have automatic lash adjusters.

9. Loosen the jet valve (smaller) adjusting stud locknut, back the stud out slightly and insert the feeler gauge between the jet valve and stud. Make sure the gauge lies flat on the top of the jet valve. Be careful not to twist the gauge or otherwise depress the jet valve spring, rotate the jet valve adjusting stud back in until it just touches the gauge. Tighten the locknut. Make sure the gauge still slides very easily between the stud and jet valve and that they both are still just touching the gauge.

NOTE: The clearances must not be too tight.

10. Repeat the entire procedure for the other jet valves associated with rockers labeled **A**.
11. On engines without automatic lash adjusters, repeat the procedure for the intake valves labeled **A**.
12. Repeat the basic adjustment procedure for exhaust valves labeled **A** on engines without automatic lash adjusters.
13. Turn the engine exactly 360 degrees, until the timing marks are again aligned at **O** degrees BTDC.
14. On engines with automatic lash adjusters, after the jet valves and rockers on the intake side and labeled **B** are adjusted, the valve adjustment procedure is completed. If equipped without automatic lash adjusters, adjust the regular intake and exhaust valves labeled **B**.

15. Reinstall the cam cover. Run the engine to check for oil leaks.

Jet Valve Adjustment

NOTE: An incorrect jet valve clearance would affect the emission levels and could also cause engine troubles, so the jet valve clearance must be correctly adjusted. Adjust the jet valve clearance before adjusting the intake valve clearance. Furthermore, the cylinder head bolts should be retightened before making this adjustment. The jet valve clearance should be adjusted with the adjusting screw on the intake valve side fully loosened.

1. Start the engine and let it run at idle until it reaches normal operating temperature.
2. Remove all spark plugs from the cylinder head for easy operation.
3. On Starion—remove the air intake pipe and remove the rocker cover.
4. On Cordia and Tredia—disconnect the oxygen sensor connecting joint. Remove the engine bracket mounting, be sure to place a block of wood on the oil pan and raise into to place for the duration of the operation. Remove the upper front timing belt cover, remove the air cleaner assembly (2.0L engine) and the air intake pipe (1.8L engine) and remove the rocker arm.
5. On all other vehicles—remove the air cleaner or air intake pipe assembly and remove the rocker cover.
6. Put the engine at TDC with No. 1 cylinder at the firing position. Turn the engine by using a wrench on the bolt in the front of the crankshaft until the **0** degree timing mark on the timing cover aligns with the notch in the front pulley; on some vehicles turn the crankshaft clockwise until the notch on the pulley is aligned with the **T** mark on the timing belt lower cover. This will bring both No. 1 and No. 4 cylinder pistons to **TDC**.

NOTE: Never turn the crankshaft counterclockwise.

7. Move the rocker arms on the No. 1 and No. 4 cylinders up and down by hand to determine if the piston in that cylinder is at TDC on the compression stroke. If the intake and exhaust rocker arms do not move, the piston in that cylinder is not at TDC on the compression stroke.
8. Measure the jet valve clearance at point **A**.

NOTE: Measure the valve clearance when the No. 1 cylinder or the No. 4 cylinder pistons are at TDC on the compression stroke. Then give the crankshaft 1 clockwise turn to bring the other cylinder piston to TDC on compression stroke.

9. If the jet valve clearance is not 0.010 in. (hot) and 0.007 in. (cold), loosen the rocker arm locknut of the intake valve and loosen the adjusting screw at least 2 turns or more.
10. Loosen the jet valve locknut and adjust the clearance using a feeler gauge while turning the adjusting screw.

NOTE: The jet valve spring has a small tension and the adjustment is somewhat delicate. Be careful not to push in the jet valve by turning the adjusting screw in too much.

11. Tighten the adjusting screw until it touches the feeler gauge. Turn the locknut to secure it, while holding the rocker arm adjusting screw with a suitable tool to keep it from turning.
12. Check the intake and exhaust valve clearance, if it is not within specifications, adjust the valves as follows:
   a. Loosen the locknut on the adjusting screw for the valve. Turn the adjusting screw counterclockwise and insert the proper size feeler gauge between the valve stem and the adjusting screw.
   b. Tighten the adjusting screw until it touches the feeler gauge. Turn the locknut to secure it, while holding the rocker

arm adjusting screw with a suitable tool to keep it from turning.

13. Turn the engine by using a wrench on the bolt in the front of the crankshaft 360 degrees until the **0** degree timing mark on the timing cover aligns with the notch in the front pulley; on some vehicles, turn the crankshaft clockwise until the notch on the pulley is aligned with the **T** mark on the timing belt lower cover.

14. Repeat Steps 9 through 13 on the other valves (marked **B**) for clearance adjustment.

15. Reinstall all the remove components in the reverse order of the removal procedure.

Rocker Arms/Shafts

Removal and Installation

4 CYLINDER ENGINES
EXCEPT 1.5L AND 1.6L ENGINES

NOTE: If equipped with hydraulic lash adjusters, 8 special holders, tool MD998443, are required to retain the hydraulic lash adjusters when disassembling the valve train.

1. Disconnect the negative battery cable.
2. Remove the rocker cover and, on Cordia, Tredia and Galant the upper timing belt cover.
3. Loosen the camshaft sprocket bolt until it can be turned by hand.
4. Turn the engine over until the camshaft sprocket timing mark aligns with the timing mark on the cylinder head on the Cordia, Tredia and Galant. On the Starion, the timing mark on the sprocket ends up on the extreme right of the sprocket bolt as viewed from the front. In both cases the TDC mark on the front crankshaft pulley must align with the timing scale on the front cover.
5. Remove the camshaft sprocket bolt and without allowing tension on the timing chain or belt to be lost, place the sprocket in the sprocket holder of the front cover or lower timing belt cover. Make sure the crankshaft is not turned throughout the work.
6. On 1987–88 Cordia, Tredia and Galant with hydraulic lash adjusters, put the special clips on the 8 hydraulic adjusters at the outer ends of all 8 rocker arms. Note that these clips go over the lash adjusters that actuate the large intake valves, not on the small adjusting screw for the smaller jet valves.
7. Loosen but do not remove the camshaft bearing cap bolts. After all bolts have been loosened, remove them and then, holding the ends so the assembly stays together, remove the rocker shaft assembly from the cylinder head. Note that the rear most cam bearing cap is not associated with the rocker shafts on the Starion and need not be removed.
8. Keep all parts in original order. Assemble the parts of the rocker assembly as follows:
   a. Cordia, Tredia and Galant install left and right side rocker shafts into the front bearing cap. Notches in the ends of the shaft must be upward.
   b. Install the bolts for the front cap to retain the shafts in place. Note that the left rocker shaft is longer than the right rocker shaft.
   c. Install the wave washer onto the left rocker shaft with the bulge forward.
   d. Coat the inner surfaces of the rockers and the upper bearing surfaces of the bearing caps with clean engine oil and assemble rockers, springs and the remaining bearing caps in the order in which removed. The intake rockers are the only ones with the jet valve actuators.

NOTE: The rockers are labeled for cylinders 1–3 and 2–4 because the direction the jet valve actuator faces changes. Use bolts to hold the caps in place after each is assembled.

To install:
9. When the assembly is complete, install it onto the head and start all bolts into the head and tighten finger-tight.
10. On the Starion install the right and left rocker shafts into the front bearing cap. Note that shafts can be identified by the fact that the rear end of the left side shaft has a notch. Align the mating marks of the front of the rocker shaft with that on the front bearing cap. Insert the front bolts.
11. Install the waved washers on both sides with the bulge in the washers facing forward.
12. Install the rockers, shafts, caps and bolts in their original positions, using the bolts to hold each cap in place after it is installed.
13. Oil the inner surfaces of the rockers and the upper bearing surfaces of the caps with clean engine oil prior to assembly. Note that the valve actuating ends of the rockers must face outward and that only the intake side rockers have the jet valve actuator.
14. When the assembly is complete, install it onto the head and start all the bolts into the threads, tightening them finger-tight.
15. Torque the attaching bolts for the rocprocket goes into the hole in the front of the cam.
17. Install the bolt. Torque it to 37–43 ft. lbs. on the Starion or 59–72 ft. lbs. on the Cordia, Tredia and Galant.
18. Adjust the valves.
19. Apply sealant to the top surface oker assembly 14–15 ft. lbs. going from the center outward.
16. Without removing tension from the timing chain or belt, lift the sprocket out of the holder and position it against the front of the cam. Make sure the locating tang on the sf the semi-circular seals in the head and then install the valve cover. Install the upper timing belt cover on the Cordia, Tredia and Galant.

1.5L ENGINE

1. Disconnect the negative battery cable. Remove the PCV hose running from the rocker cover and the air cleaner. Remove the air cleaner.
2. Remove the upper timing belt cover. Remove the rocker cover.
3. Loosen the rocker shaft bolts, but do not remove them. After all bolts are loosened remove the rocker shaft, rocker arms and springs as an assembly.
4. Be sure to keep all parts in original order, for reinstallation.

To install:
5. Assemble all the parts, noting the differences between intake and exhaust parts. The intake rocker shaft is much longer; the intake rocker shaft springs are over 3 in. long, while those for the exhaust side are less than 2 in. long; intake rockers have the extra adjusting screw for the jet valve; rockers are labeled 1–3 and 2–4 for the cylinder with which they are associated. Torque the rocker shaft bolts to 15–19 ft. lbs.
6. Adjust the valve clearances. This step may be omitted only if all parts are being reused. Install the rocker cover with a new gasket, torquing the bolts to 1–1.5 ft. lbs. Install the air cleaner and PCV valve. Remember that there is no timing belt cover in place and keep fingers clear. Run the engine at idle speed until it is hot. Then remove the valve cover again and adjust the valve clearances with the engine hot. Finally, replace the rocker cover and timing belt cover, air cleaner and PCV valve.

1.6L ENGINE

1. Disconnect the negative battery cable. Remove the air cleaner assembly. Label and then disconnect the spark plug high tension wires. Remove the upper front timing belt cover.
2. Turn the crankshaft until No. 1 piston is at TDC of its compression stroke. Align the timing mark on the upper cover at the rear of the timing belt with the mark on the camshaft sprocket; mark the relationship between the timing belt and the mark on the cam sprocket.
3. Remove the sprocket-to-camshaft bolt; hold the sprocket in position to keep the belt from slipping off. Then, rest the

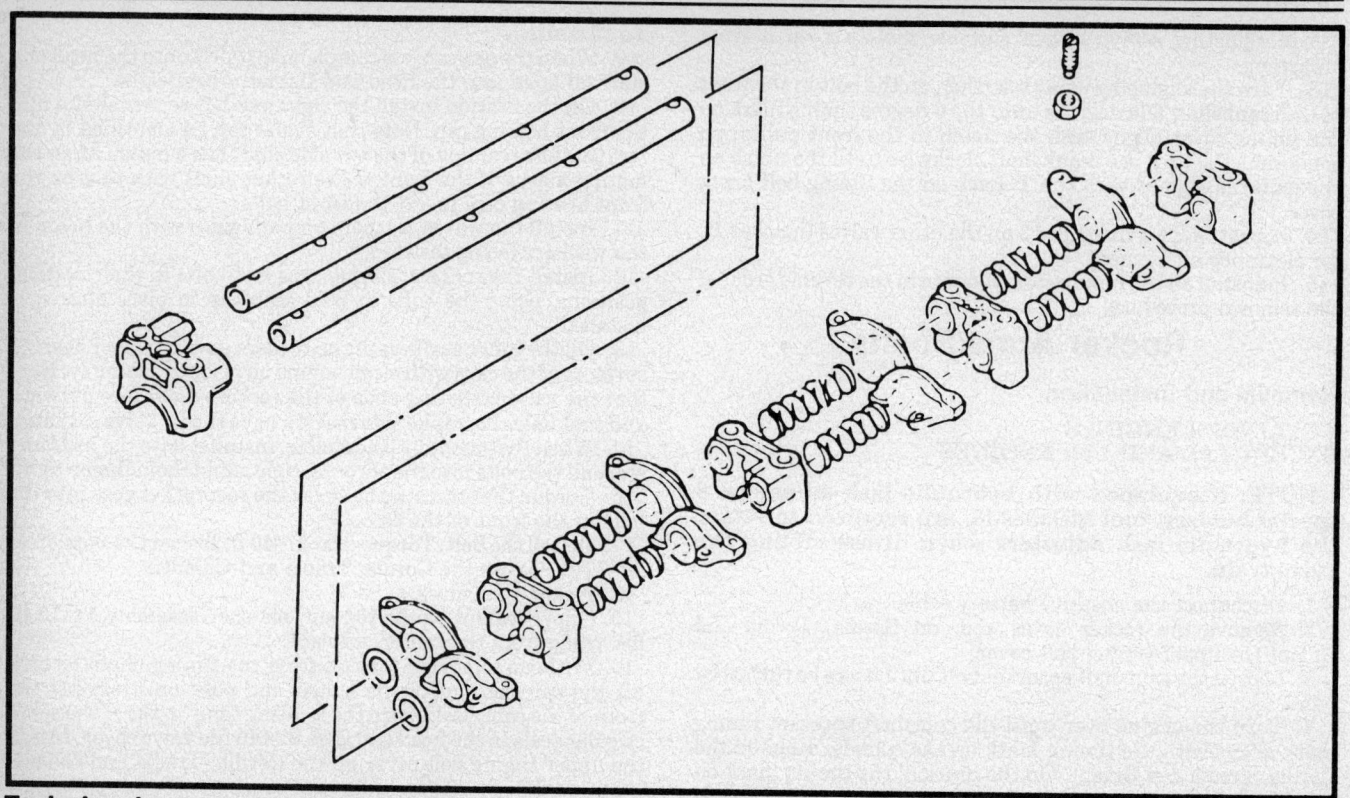

Typical rocker arm and shaft assembly

sprocket on the sprocket holder provided on the lower front cover. If necessary, slip a short piece of used timing belt or other thin, flexible object between the holder and the sprocket to keep tension and avoid losing belt timing. Be sure not to turn the crankshaft throughout this work.

4. Remove the upper cover located behind the timing belt. Remove the rocker cover. Loosen the camshaft bearing cap bolts without pulling them out of the caps and remove the caps, rockers and shafts as an assembly.

5. Be sure to keep all parts in original order, for reinstallation.

To install:

6. Lubricate all wear surfaces with clean engine oil and then insert both rocker shafts into the front bearing cap with the cuts at the top/front of the caps at the tops. Note that the longer shaft goes on the left side (facing the crankshaft pulley). Note that the intake rockers only have the jet valve actuators and that the waved washers are installed behind the last set of rockers with the bulge at the center of the washer facing the crankshaft pulley. After each cap goes on and the holes are aligned, install the bolts to keep it in place. Note that if the camshaft front oil seal has been damaged it must be replaced.

7. Lubricate the wear surfaces of the cam bearing caps and then install them. Torque the bolts to 14–15 ft. lbs.

8. Install the timing belt rear cover. Pull the camshaft sprocket upward and install it to the camshaft. Turn the camshaft slightly if necessary to make the dowel pin fit into the hole in the sprocket. Make sure the mating mark made when these parts were disassembled are still aligned so the camshaft will be in time. Make corrections as necessary. Install the sprocket bolt and torque it to 44–57 ft. lbs.

9. Install the timing belt upper cover and spark plug high tension wire supports. Adjust the valve clearances. Apply sealant to the top of the front bearing cap and rear of the head where the rocker cover seals and then install the rocker cover. Install new gaskets and install the rocker cover, torquing the bolts to 4–5 ft.

lbs. Reconnect the spark plug wires and install the air cleaner and PCV and evaporative emissions hoses. Run the engine at idle speed until it is hot. Then, remove the rocker cover and again set the valves with the engine hot.

3.0L ENGINE

1. Disconnect the negative battery cable. Remove the rocker arm covers. It may be necessary to refer to the cylinder head removal procedure as an aid in the rocker arm cover removal.

2. To remove the rocker arm assembly, remove the camshaft bearing cap retaining bolts and remove the rocker arm assembly from the cylinder head. Install tool MD998443–01 or equivalent, over the auto lash adjuster to keep it from falling out.

3. When disassembling the rocker arm shaft assembly, be sure to remove one rocker arm and spring at a time and keep all the parts in their original order.

4. Check the rocker arms and rocker arm shafts for any cracks, distortion, wear or heat damage and replace as necessary.

5. Reassemble the rocker arm shaft assemblies in the reverse order of disassembly. If the auto lash adjuster should fall out during disassembly, reinstall it from under the rocker arm, using caution so as not to spill the diesel fuel inside the adjuster. Install tool MD998443–01 or equivalent, over the auto lash adjuster to keep it from falling out.

6. Apply a small amount of a suitable sealant on the 4 corners of the cylinder head just in front of the bearing caps at the end of the rocker arm shaft.

NOTE: Be sure the sealant does not swell out onto the cam journal surface of the cylinder head. If it swells out, immediately wipe it off before it can dry.

7. Attach the rocker arm shaft assemblies so the arrow mark on the bearing cap faces in the same direction as the arrow on the cylinder head.

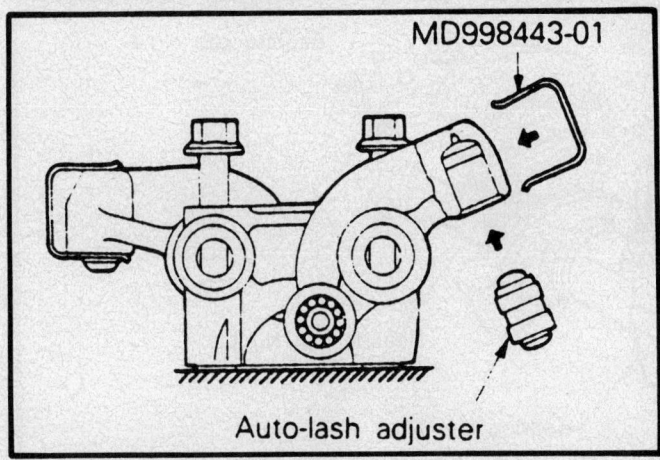

Auto lash adjuster installation—3.0L engine

NOTE: The arrow marks face each other on the rocker arm shaft assemblies. Since bearing caps number 1 and 4 look alike, check the number stamped on the cap. Be sure to coat the inside of the bearing cap and rocker arm with clean engine oil before assembling them.

8. Insert bearing cap No. 1 so the notch on the end of the shaft faces in the direction as shown in the illustration provided and insert the bolts. Be sure the oil groove faces downward and the oil port is located on the rocker shaft side **A**.

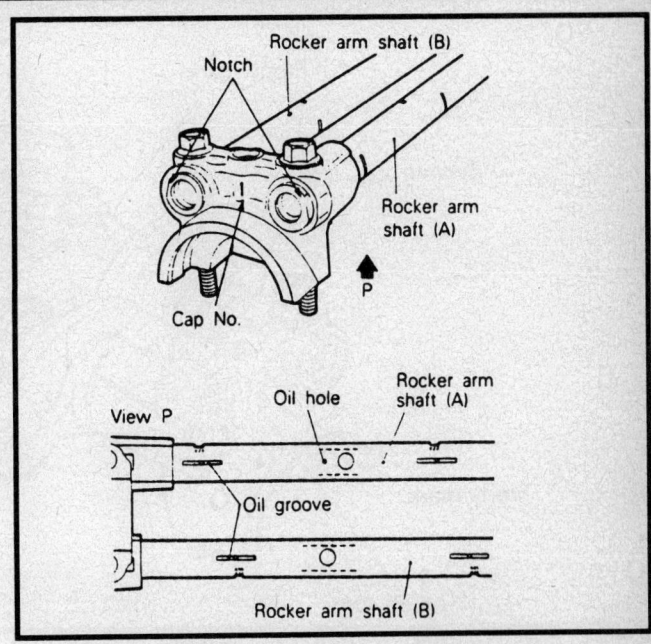

Installing the bearing cap No. 1—3.0L engine

9. Install all the bearing cap bolts and torque them to 15 ft. lbs. Remove the auto lash adjuster special tool.
10. Apply a suitable sealant to the rocker arm covers and in-

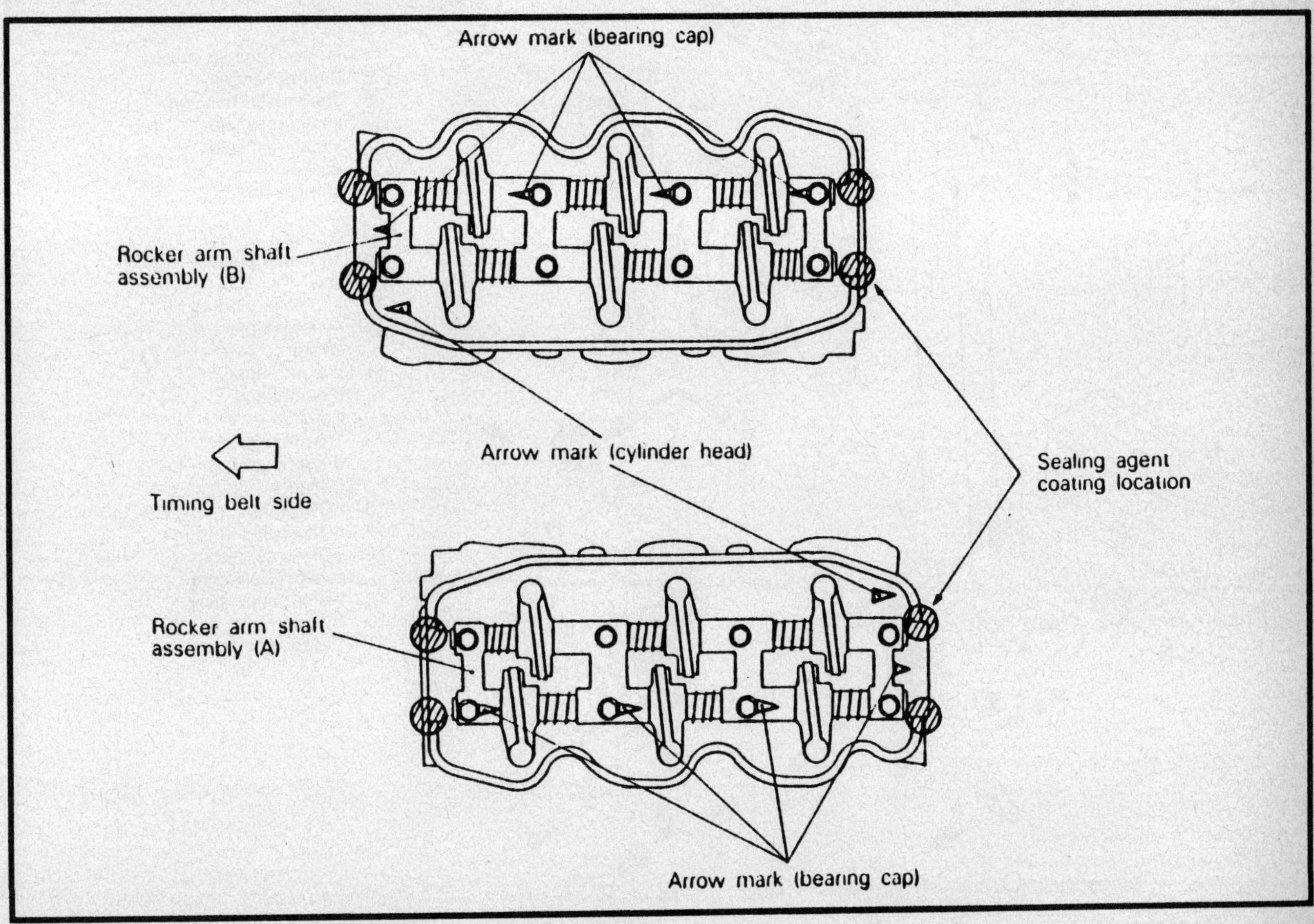

Rocker arm shaft assemblies installation—3.0L engine

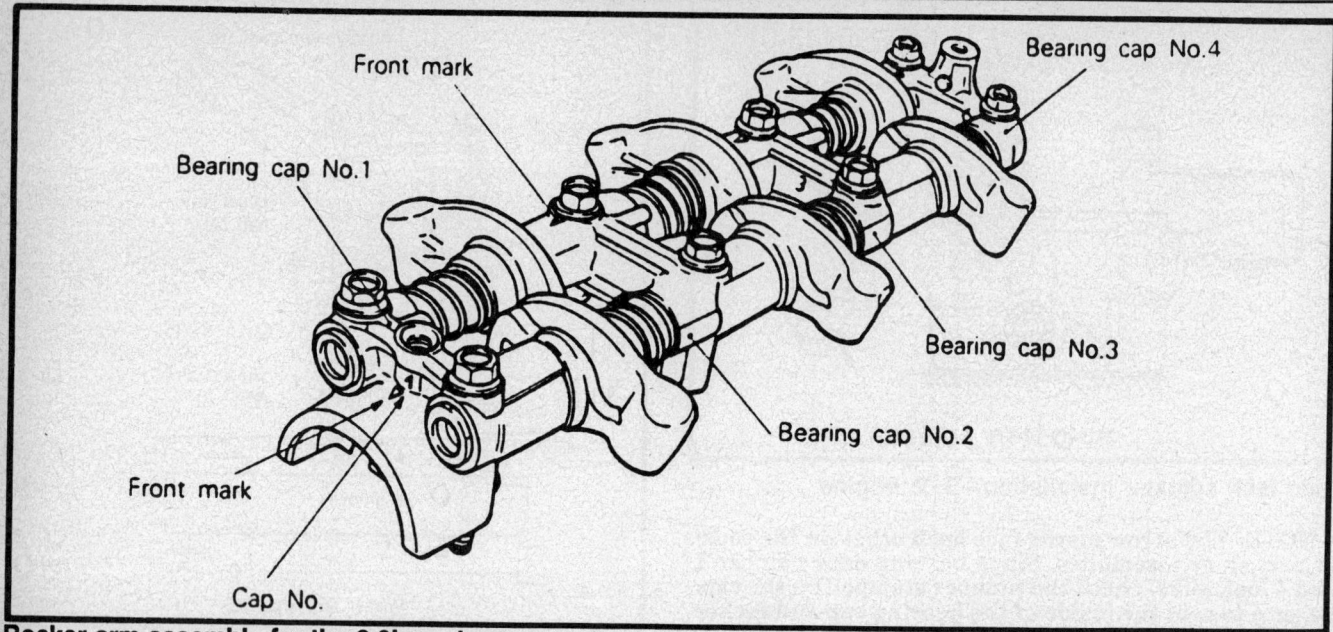

Bearing cap No.4

Bearing cap No.1

Front mark

Bearing cap No.3

Bearing cap No.2

Front mark

Cap No.

Rocker arm assembly for the 3.0L engine

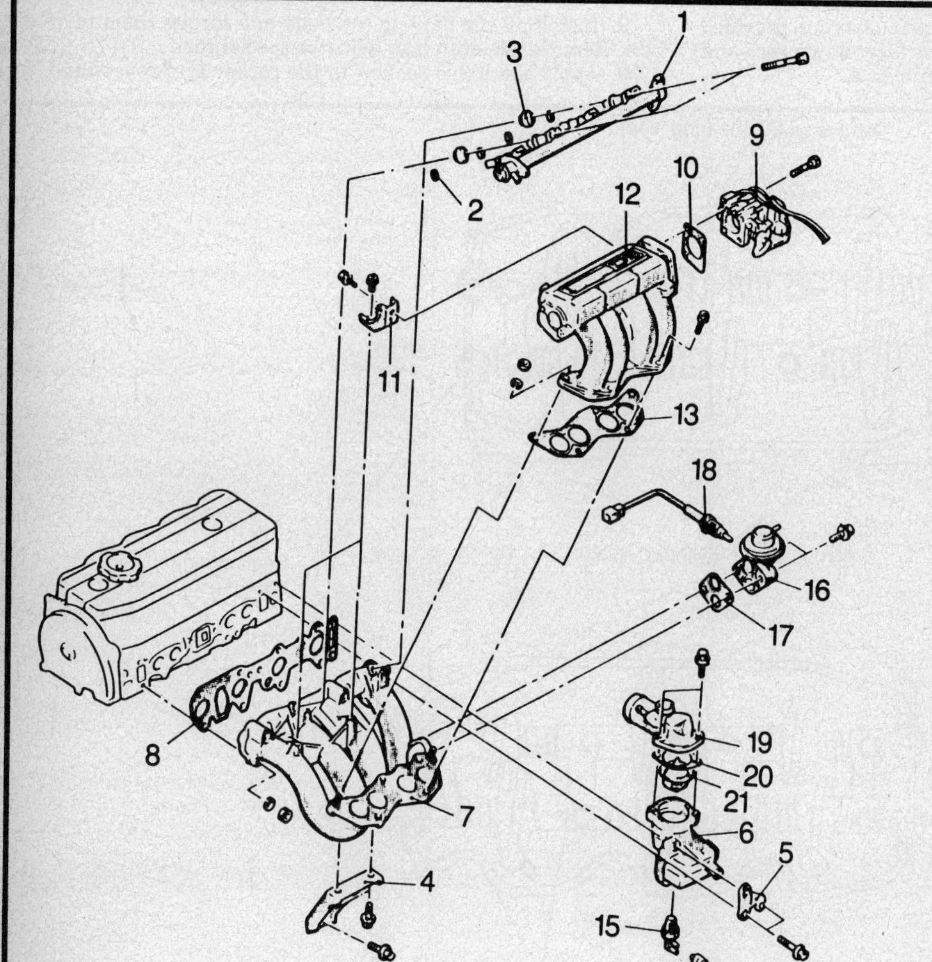

1. Fuel injector and pressure regulator deliver pipe
2. Insulator
3. Insulator
4. Intake manifold stay
5. Engine hanger
6. Thermostat housing
7. Intake manifold
8. Intake manifold gasket
9. Throttle body assembly
10. Gasket
11. Air intake plenum stay
12. Air intake plenum
13. Air intake plenum gasket
14. Vacuum hose (Federal and Canada)
15. Thermo valve (Federal and Canada)
16. EGR valve
17. EGR gasket
18. EGR temperature sensor (California)
19. Water outlet fitting
20. Gasket
21. Thermostat

Intake manifold servicing—Eclipse 1.8L engine

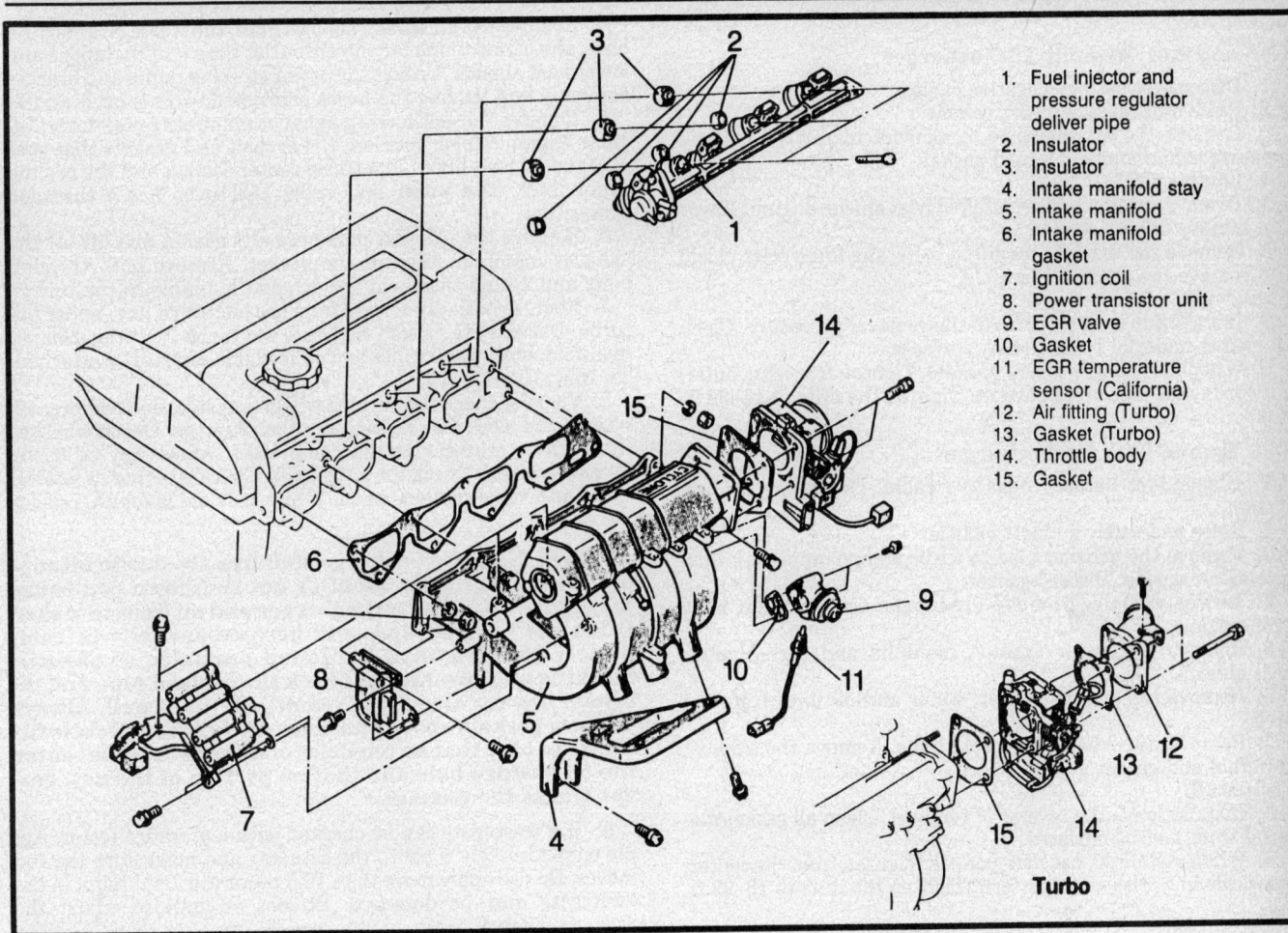

1. Fuel injector and pressure regulator deliver pipe
2. Insulator
3. Insulator
4. Intake manifold stay
5. Intake manifold
6. Intake manifold gasket
7. Ignition coil
8. Power transistor unit
9. EGR valve
10. Gasket
11. EGR temperature sensor (California)
12. Air fitting (Turbo)
13. Gasket (Turbo)
14. Throttle body
15. Gasket

Turbo

Intake manifold servicing — Eclipse 2.0L engine

stall the covers to the cylinder head. Reinstall any other removed components and reconnect the negative battery cable.

Intake Manifold

Removal and Installation

1. Disconnect the negative battery cable. Remove the air cleaner and duct hose assembly. Disconnect the air plenum assembly on fuel injected vehicles.

2. Disconnect the fuel line(s), EGR lines and other vacuum hoses and wire harness connectors. On the fuel injected vehicles, it is necessary to remove the fuel delivery pipe, fuel injectors and pressure regulator.

3. Disconnect the throttle positioner solenoid and fuel cutoff solenoid wires.

4. Disconnect the accelerator linkage and, if equipped with an automatic transmission, the shift cables at the carburetor/injector.

5. Drain the coolant.

6. Remove the water hose from carburetor and cylinder head. If necessary, disconnect the upper radiator hose.

7. Remove the heater and water outlet hoses. On some vehicles it may be necessary to remove the water outlet housing.

8. Disconnect the water temperature sending unit.

9. Remove the nuts/bolts from the ends toward the middle. Remove the manifold and carburetor/injector assembly. Remove the insulators and gaskets at this time as well, if equipped.

10. Clean all mounting surfaces. Before reinstalling the manifold, coat both sides with gasket sealer. Install nuts/bolts starting from the center toward the ends.

Exhaust Manifold

Removal and Installation

EXCEPT ECLIPSE 1.8L AND 2.0L ENGINES

1. Disconnect the negative battery cable. Remove the air cleaner and duct hose assembly. Disconnect the oxygen sensor connection, if equipped. If equipped with fuel injection, it may be necessary to remove the air plenum assembly.

2. Remove the manifold heat stove, heat protector and hose. Disconnect the EGR lines and reed valve, if equipped. On the 1988–91 Galant, when removing the front exhaust gasket, remove the oil level gauge guide. In order to remove the rear manifold, the air plenum assembly must be removed.

3. Disconnect the exhaust pipe bracket from the engine block.

4. Remove the exhaust pipe flange bolts from the manifold. It may be necessary to remove the exhaust pipe flange bolts from under the vehicle.

5. Remove the manifold flange stud nuts starting from the ends toward the middle and remove the manifold from the cylinder head.

6. Installation is the reverse of removal. Install nuts starting from the middle toward the ends. On the 1988–91 Galant, when installing the front exhaust manifold and be sure to coat the O-ring of the oil level gauge guide with clean engine oil, before inserting it into the cylinder block.

ECLIPSE

1.8L and 2.0L Without Turbocharger

1. Disconnect battery negative cable.
2. Raise and safely support vehicle.
3. Remove the exhaust pipe to exhaust manifold nuts and separate exhaust pipe. Discard gasket.
4. Lower vehicle.
5. Remove outer exhaust manifold heat shield, engine hanger and remove oxygen sensor.
6. Remove the exhaust manifold bolts, the inner heat shield and remove the exhaust manifold.

To install:

7. Installation is the reverse of the removal procedure. Clean all gasket material from mating surfaces.
8. When installing, use new gaskets. Tighten from the center, outwards in a criss-cross pattern. Tighten the nuts to 18–22 ft. lbs.

2.0L Engine With Turbocharger

1. Disconnect battery negative cable. Drain the cooling system.
2. Raise and safely support vehicle.
3. Remove the exhaust pipe to turbocharger nuts and separate exhaust pipe. Discard gasket.
4. Lower vehicle. Remove air intake and vacuum hose connections.
5. Remove the upper exhaust manifold and turbocharger heat shields.
6. Remove the engine hanger, water and oil lines from the turbo.
7. Remove the exhaust manifold bolts. Remove the exhaust manifold and gasket.

To install:

8. Installation is the reverse of removal. Clean all gasket material from mating surfaces.
9. When installing, use new gaskets. Tighten from the center, outwards in a criss-cross pattern. Tighten the nuts to 18–22 ft. lbs.

Turbocharger

Removal and Installation

EXCEPT 2.0L ENGINE

1. Disconnect the negative battery cable. Remove the air cleaner and turbocharger inlet ducting. Unbolt the turbocharger discharge hose going to the injection mixer.
2. Disconnect the oxygen sensor at the catalytic converter to protect it.
3. Unbolt and remove the large heat shield that covers the top of the turbocharger.
4. Remove the nuts fastening the turbo to the catalytic converter. On Cordia, Tredia and Mirage, disconnect the oil return pipe at the oil pan. On Starion, disconnect the oil return hose at the oil return pipe and the timing chain cover.
5. Disconnect the oil supply line at the turbo and at the oil filter bracket.
6. Disconnect the turbocharger from the exhaust manifold and remove the unit from the vehicle.
7. Installation is the reverse of the removal procedure. Replace all gaskets, as required. Pour clean engine oil into the oil supply fitting before connecting the oil supply pipe.

2.0L ENGINE

1. Disconnect negative battery cable.
2. Drain engine oil, cooling system and remove radiator. If equipped with air conditioning, remove the condensor fan assembly with the radiator.
3. Disconnect the oxygen sensor connector and remove sensor. Pull out oil dipstick and tube.

4. Remove the air intake bellows hose, the wastegate vacuum hose, the connections for the air outlet hose and the upper and lower heat shields. Unbolt the power steering pump and bracket assembly and leaving the hoses connected, wire it back aside.
5. Remove the self-locking exhaust manifold nuts, the triangular engine hanger bracket, the eyebolt and gaskets that connect the oil feed line to the turbo center section and the cooling water lines. The water line under the turbo has a threaded connection.
6. Remove the exhaust pipe nuts and gasket and lift off the exhaust manifold. Discard the gasket. Remove both through bolts and 2 nuts that hold the exhaust manifold to the turbo.
7. Remove both cap screws from the oil return line, under the turbo. Discard the gasket. Separate the turbo from the exhaust manifold. both water pipes and oil feed line can still be attached.

To install:

8. Visually check the turbine wheel (hot side) and compressor wheel (cold side) for cracking or other damage. Check whether the turbine wheel and the compressor wheel can be easily turned by hand. Check for oil leakage. Check whether or not the wastegate valve remains open. If any problem is found, replace the part.

NOTE: Many turbocharger failures are due to oil supply problems. Heat soak after hot shutdown can cause the engine oil in the turbocharger and oil lines to 'coke.' Often the oil feed lines will become partially or completely blocked with hardened particles of carbon, blocking oil flow. Always check the oil feed pipe and oil return line for clogging. Clean these tubes well. Always use new gaskets above and below the oil feed eyebolt fitting. Use care that no particles of dirt of old gasket enter the oil passage hole and that no portion of the new gasket blocks the passage.

9. The wastegate can be checked with a pressure tester. Apply approximately 9 psi to the actuator and make sure the rod moves. Do not apply more than 10.3 psi or the diaphragm in the wastegate may be damaged. Do not attempt to adjust the wastegate valve.
10. Installation is the reverse of the removal process. Note that the oil feed line should be primed with clean engine oil. None of the self-locking nuts should be reused. Replace all locking nuts. Before installing the threaded connection for the water inlet pipe, apply light oil to the inner surface of the pipe flange.
11. Fill the engine crankcase, cooling system and reconnect the battery negative cable.

Front Cover

Removal and Installation

EXCEPT 2.5L AND 3.0L ENGINES

1. Disconnect the negative battery cable. Remove the alternator drive belt.
2. Unbolt and remove the water pump drive pulley. Remove the bolt from the crankshaft pulley. Using a suitable puller, remove the crankshaft pulley.
3. Remove the bolts from the cover (1468cc—Mirage and Precis) or upper and lower covers and remove them. If the engine has 2 covers, the upper cover comes off first.
4. Install in reverse order, using new gaskets under the cover(s).

2.5L ENGINE

1. Disconnect the negative battery cable. Unbolt the clutch fan. Unbolt the fan shroud and then remove the shroud and clutch fan together. Remove the pulley and belt.
2. Remove the crankshaft bolt. With a puller, remove the crankshaft pulley.
3. Remove the rocker cover. Then, remove both front bolts

from the cylinder head; these screw into and seal the top of the timing cover.

4. Remove the oil pan bolts (front and side) that screw into the timing cover.

5. Drain the cooling system and remove the coolant hose leading to the water pump. Remove the alternator or other accessories that are in the way of the timing cover.

6. Unbolt and remove the timing cover.

7. Clean all the gasket surfaces. If the oil pan gasket was damaged in removing the front cover, carefully cut the oil pan gasket off flush with the front of the block on both sides and remove the cut off pieces of gasket.

8. Carefully pry the old oil seal out of the cover without scratching the bore into which the seal fits. Then, install a new seal with an installer such as parts MD998376–01 and MB990938–01.

9. Install new gaskets to the cylinder block. If necessary, cut an exact replacement for the oil pan gasket section that was removed from a new pan gasket. Insert this piece of gasket onto the front of the pan in the exact position of the old piece and use liquid sealer on the joint between both sections of gasket on both sides. Install the chain cover. Install the cover bolts and torque them to 9–10.5 ft. lbs. Lightly coat the outside diameter of the crankshaft pulley boss with clean engine oil. Then install the pulley onto the crankshaft, install the bolt and turn it to force the pulley all the way on. Torque it to 80–94 ft. lbs.

10. Install the front head bolts (2) and torque to 11–15 ft. lbs. Install the oil pan bolts and torque them to 4.5–5.5 ft. lbs.

11. Install all hoses and accessories and refill the cooling system.

3.0L ENGINE

1. Disconnect the negative battery cable. Disconnect the power steering oil pump pressure switch connector.

2. Remove the power steering pump hose bracket bolts from the engine.

3. Slightly raise the engine and support it safely and remove the engine bolt(s) from the engine bracket and remove the bracket.

4. Remove the air conditioning compressor belt and tension pulley bracket.

5. Remove the power steering pump and place it aside with the pressure lines still attached. Remove the tensioner pulley and pulley bracket.

6. Remove the outer upper timing belt cover and gaskets.

7. Remove the engine bolt(s) from the engine support bracket and remove the bracket. Be sure to take note of the different bolt sizes and the holes which they came from.

8. Remove the timing belt cover cap and the other outer upper timing belt cover with gaskets.

9. Remove the under cover panel. Remove the crankshaft pulley bolt and using a suitable pulley, remove the crankshaft pulley. Remove the front flange and then remove the lower timing belt cover(s). Be sure to take note of the different bolt sizes in the lower cover and the holes which they came from.

10. Installation is the reverse order of the removal procedure. Torque the crankshaft pulley bolt to 108–116 ft. lbs.

Timing Chain and Sprockets

Removal and Installation

2.5L ENGINE

1. Disconnect the negative battery cable.
2. Remove the rocker cover.
3. Put the engine on TDC No. 1 cylinder firing position by turning the crankshaft until the TDC timing marks align and both front valves are fully closed (rockers off the cams).
4. Remove the timing cover.
5. Unbolt and remove the three silent shaft chain guides.

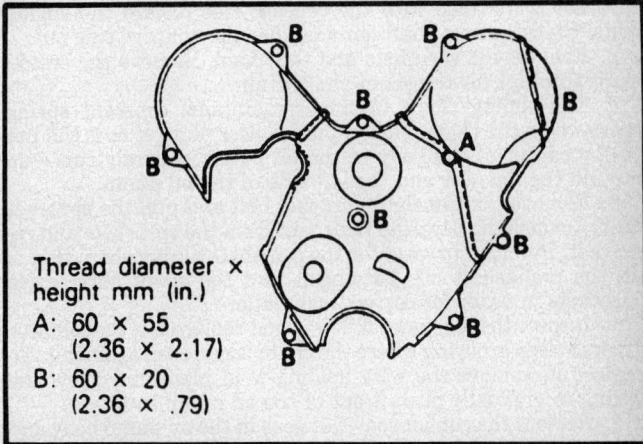

Thread diameter × height mm (in.)
A: 60 × 55 (2.36 × 2.17)
B: 60 × 20 (2.36 × .79)

Bolt diameter location on the timing cover—3.0L engine

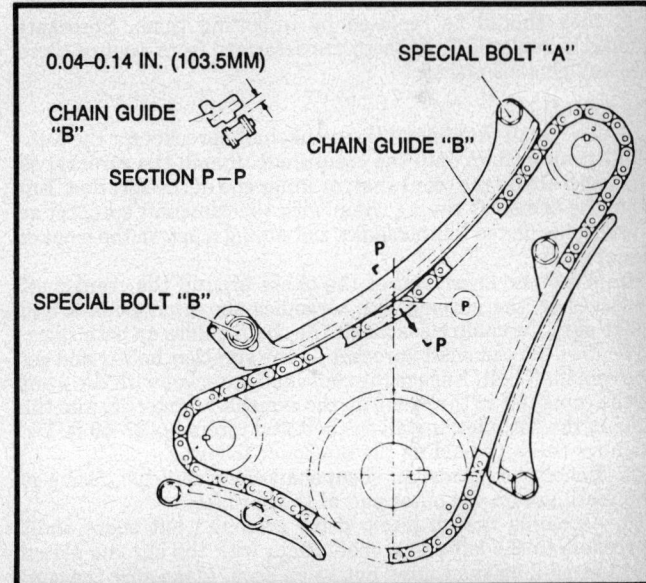

0.04–0.14 IN. (103.5MM)

CHAIN GUIDE "B"

SECTION P–P

SPECIAL BOLT "A"

CHAIN GUIDE "B"

SPECIAL BOLT "B"

2555cc silent shaft timing mark alignment

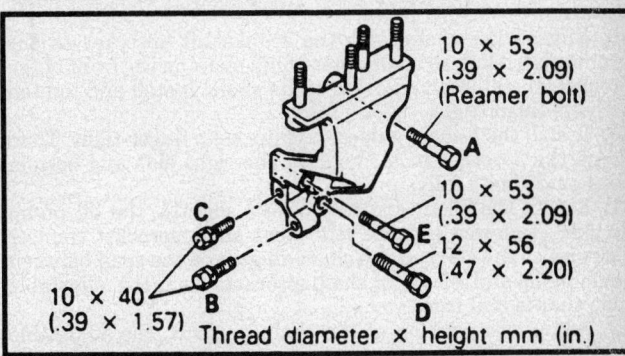

10 × 53 (.39 × 2.09) (Reamer bolt)

A

10 × 53 (.39 × 2.09)

12 × 56 (.47 × 2.20)

C

E

D

10 × 40 (.39 × 1.57)

B

Thread diameter × height mm (in.)

Bolt diameter location on the engine support bracket—3.0L engine

6. Unscrew and remove the oil pump drive sprocket bolt and the left silent shaft sprocket bolt.

7. When the bolts are removed, pull these 2 sprockets off and then disengage the chain from the crankshaft sprocket. Note that both sprockets are identical, but that the oil pump drive

sprocket is installed with the concave side toward the engine while the left silent shaft sprocket has the concave side out.

8. Remove the sprockets and the chain. Remove the crankshaft sprocket for the silent shaft chain.

9. The timing chain tensioner maintains constant spring pressure on the chain. Fasten the follower plunger so it will not be forced out of the body of the oil pump. Securely run wire around the follower and the left side of the oil pump.

10. Remove the camshaft sprocket bolt and pull the sprocket off the camshaft. Separate the chain from the sprockets and remove it. Pull the sprocket for the camshaft timing chain that is on the crankshaft off, keeping it and the silent shaft drive sprockets in order for correct installation.

11. Inspect the tensioner follower and replace it if the follower shows a deep grooving where the chain was ridden against it. To replace it, remove the wire holding it in place and allow the spring to gradually push it out of the oil pump body.

12. Replace the rubber seal that goes in the oil pump body and the spring behind it when replacing the tensioner follower. Make sure the thinner part of the follower faces downward. Wire the new follower in place just as the old one was.

13. If the timing chain right and left guides show heavy grooving, they should be replaced by unbolting them. Sprockets should be replaced if the teeth are deformed from wear or there are any obvious cracks.

To install:

14. To install first install the crankshaft sprocket for the camshaft timing chain onto the crankshaft. Install the sprocket so the teeth are on the crankshaft or inner end of the sprocket. Engage the camshaft timing chain with the camshaft sprocket so the chrome plated link straddles the timing mark on the front of the sprocket.

15. Wrap the lower end of the chain around the crankshaft sprocket so the chrome link straddles the timing mark and make sure the chain rides inside the chain guides on both sides.

16. Rest the camshaft sprocket on the sprocket holder and get the camshaft bolt. Engage the cam shaft sprocket with the front of the camshaft so the prong on the camshaft flange fits into the hole in the sprocket, install the bolt and torque to 37–43 ft. lbs. Remove the wire holding the tensioner follower.

17. Install the crankshaft silent shaft chain sprocket, facing so the teeth are on the outer end of the sprocket.

18. Assemble the oil pump drive gear and left silent shaft sprockets to the left silent shaft chain with the chrome plated links straddling the timing marks on each. Make sure the concave side of the oil pump sprocket is toward the oil pump, but that the concave side of the left silent shaft sprocket faces outward.

19. Engage the chain with the crankshaft sprocket so the chrome plated link straddles the timing mark on the front of the sprocket. Install each sprocket on its shaft. Install and tighten the bolts finger-tight.

20. Install the 3 chain guides, turning bolts finger-tight. Then torque the sprocket bolts. Tighten the right side and bottom chain guide bolts fully.

21. Rotate the silent shaft sprockets slightly, the oil pump sprocket clockwise and the left silent shaft sprocket counter clockwise so the slack in the chain all goes to the span between the oil pump and left silent shaft sprockets, near the adjustable guide that is still loose.

22. Adjust the position of the chain guide **B**, the adjustable guide, by positioning it and then tightening the bolts until the play in the center of the chain near the adjustable guide is 0.04–1.4 in. Pull the chain away from the guide at the center of the guide at the center of the guide and measure the distance between the outer edge of the guide and edge of the chain to do this. When the play is correct, torque, first, the guide adjusting bolt (the one that runs in the slot) to 11–15 ft. lbs. Then, torque the upper guide bolt to 6–7 ft. lbs.

23. Install the timing chain cover and front pulley.

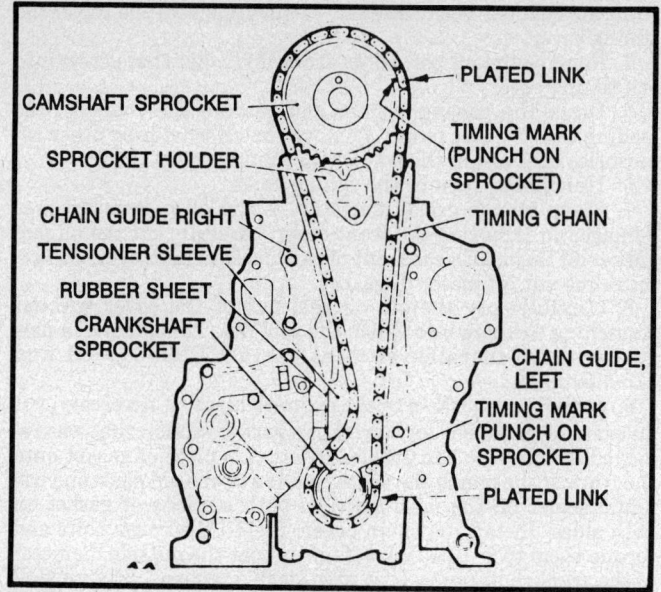

2555cc cam drive timing marks

24. Continue the installation in the reverse order of the removal.

Timing Belt Front Cover

Removal and Installation

1. Disconnect the negative battery cable.
2. Raise and safely support vehicle. Remove the under panel.

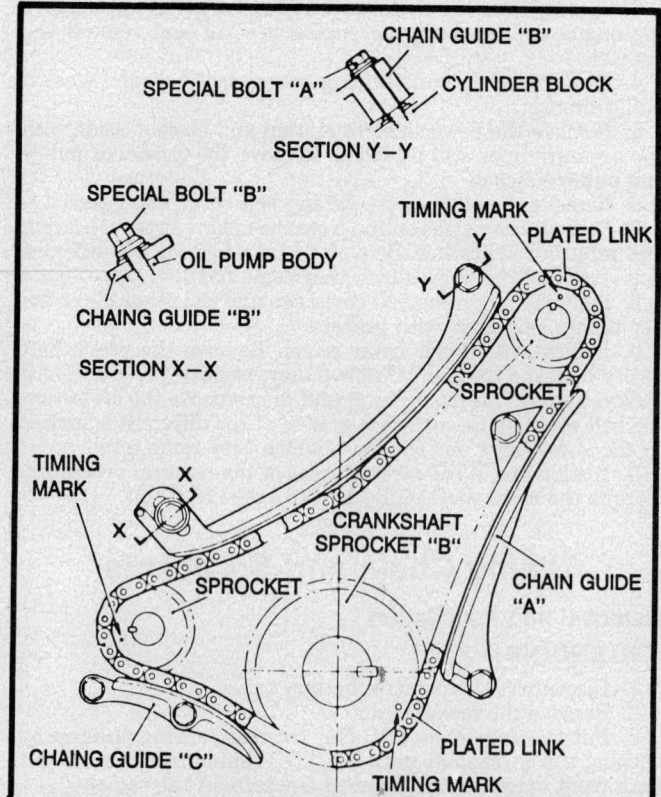

2555cc silent shaft chain timing marks

3. Place a wooden block between a jack and the oil pan. Slightly raise the engine and remove the engine mount bracket.

4. Remove all accessory drive belts, tension pulley bracket, water pump pulley, crankshaft compressor pulley and crankshaft pulley. The crankshaft pulley may be difficult to remove since the crankshaft will tend to turn when the center bolt is loosened. Use an old drive belt, wrap it around the pulley and draw it tight to hold the pulley.

5. Remove the upper and lower timing belt covers.

6. If removal of the front crank seal is necessary, pry the seal from the case cover.

To install:

7. Installation is the reverse of the removal process. Apply engine oil to the surface of the new seal. With a suitable pipe-like driver, tap the new seal into place.

8. Install the timing belt covers and the pulleys and drive belts. Adjust accessory drive belt tension.

9. Install the engine brackets, lower the engine connect the battery cable.

Timing Belt and Tensioner

Removal and Installation

4 CYLINDER EXCEPT 1.5L, 1.6L AND ECLIPSE 1.8L AND 2.0L ENGINES

NOTE: Timing belt and sprocket removal procedures are combined because the procedures are interrelated. Belts are kept in place to permit sprocket bolts to be loosened. If only replacing the belt(s), skip the steps related to removing or replacing the sprockets, unless it is noted that a sprocket must be removed to gain access to a belt related part.

1. Disconnect the negative battery cable. Remove the timing belt cover. Rotate the engine until the timing marks on the camshaft sprocket and cylinder head or rear belt cover and the crankshaft sprocket and front cover are perfectly aligned.

2. Loosen the timing belt tensioner adjusting bolt and the mounting bolt, shift the tensioner as far as it will go toward the left or water pump side (so belt tension is lost) and then retighten the adjusting bolt. If the belt is to be reused, draw an arrow on it in the direction of rotation. Remove the belt. Hold the tensioner in position to remove the tensioner adjusting bolt. Slowly release tension and remove the bolt the tension, spring and spacer.

3. Remove the bolt and the camshaft sprocket.

4. If replacing the inner timing belt, which drives the oil pump and right silent shaft, or need to remove the sprockets, proceed as follows; otherwise, proceed with Step 5:

a. Remove the crankshaft front sprocket bolt and remove the front crankshaft sprocket and flange. Remove the plug from the left side of the block. Insert a suitable tool about 0.3 in. in diameter and about 2.5 in. long or longer into the hole to keep the left silent shaft in position.

b. Remove the oil pump sprocket retaining nut and remove the nut and the sprocket. Loosen the right silent shaft sprocket bolt until it can be turn by hand.

c. Then, remove the inner tensioner bolts and remove the tensioner. Remove the inner timing belt. Then, remove the large crankshaft sprocket from the crankshaft and the right silent shaft bolt, sprocket and spacer.

5. Inspect all components as required. Replace defective parts as needed.

To install:

6. Install the larger crankshaft sprocket onto the crankshaft with the flatter or flanged side forward and the boss which is there to extend the sprocket forward from the front of the crankshaft at the rear. Align the timing mark on the sprocket with the mark on the front case. Apply a light coating of engine oil to the inner surface of the right silent shaft spacer and install the spacer. The chamfer must face inward, toward the engine. Then, install the right silent shaft sprocket and bolt and tighten the bolt finger-tight. Align the timing mark on this sprocket also with the timing mark on the front case.

7. Install the inner belt over the sprockets so the timing marks are in alignment and the upper side is under slight tension. Then, install the inner belt tensioner with the center of the pulley on the left side of the bolt and the flange of the pulley facing the front of the engine. Lift the tensioner until there is tension on the inner belt's upper length. Hold the tensioner in exactly this position and tighten the tensioner bolt. Make sure the turning of the bolt does not alter the position of the tensioner, or belt tension will be excessive. Then, tighten the right silent shaft retaining flange bolt to 25–28 ft. lbs.

8. Check to make sure the timing marks effected by this belt are in alignment. Shift the position of the belt's teeth and retension, if necessary. Depressing the belt's upper span should enable it to depress about 0.2–0.3 in. Adjust the tension again to product this amount of deflection, if necessary.

9. Torque the right silent shaft bolt to 25–28 ft. lbs. Then, install the flange and crankshaft sprocket onto the crankshaft. The concave (inner) side of the flange must face to the rear so as to fit the curved front of the inner crankshaft sprocket. The flat side of the outer crankshaft sprocket must face the flange, to the rear. Finally, install the washer and bolt to the front of the crankshaft and torque it to 80–94 ft. lbs.

10. Install the camshaft sprocket to the camshaft and torque the bolt to 58–72 ft. lbs.

11. Install the spacer and main timing belt tensioner, installing the bolts finger-tight. Install the spring between the locking tang on the right side of the tensioner and the tang on the right side of the water pump, just above the tensioner. This will force the tensioner to turn counterclockwise on the pivot bolt. Push the tensioner all the way toward the water pump and lock it by tightening the adjusting bolt.

12. Check alignment of all timing marks: the mark on the camshaft sprocket must align with the mark on the head; the mark on the crankshaft sprocket must align with that on the front case; and the mark on the oil pump sprocket must align with that on the front case.

13. Install the timing belt. The belt should be fitted over the sprockets in order: first the crankshaft, the oil pump and the camshaft sprocket. The (right) side of the belt which is normally straight must be straight during installation so the timing marks will remain aligned when the belt is actually tensioned. Remove the suitable tool installed to keep the silent shaft in position and replace the plug. Making sure there is no tension on the pivot bolt, loosen the tensioner adjusting bolt so the spring applies tension to the belt. Make sure the belt remains completely engaged with the teeth on the camshaft sprocket and that all timing marks remain aligned. Correct if necessary. Tighten the adjusting bolt. Finally, tighten the pivot bolt. Make sure to tighten the bolts in that order or tension will not be correct. Recheck alignment of the timing marks.

14. Turn the engine one full turn clockwise only. Loosen the tensioner pivot bolt and then the adjusting bolt. Allow the tensioner spring to again position the tensioner without interference from bolt friction. Tighten the adjusting bolt. Tighten the pivot bolt. Try to pry the belt outward by hand. The distance between the back of the belt and seal line will be about 0.55 in., if the tension is correct.

15. Continue the installation in the reverse order of the removal procedure.

1.5L ENGINE

1. Disconnect the negative battery cable. Remove the cooling fan, spacer, water pump pulley and belt. Remove the timing belt cover.

2. Turn the crankshaft until the timing marks on the camshaft sprocket and cylinder head are aligned. Loosen the tensioning bolt, it runs in the slotted portion of the tensioner, and

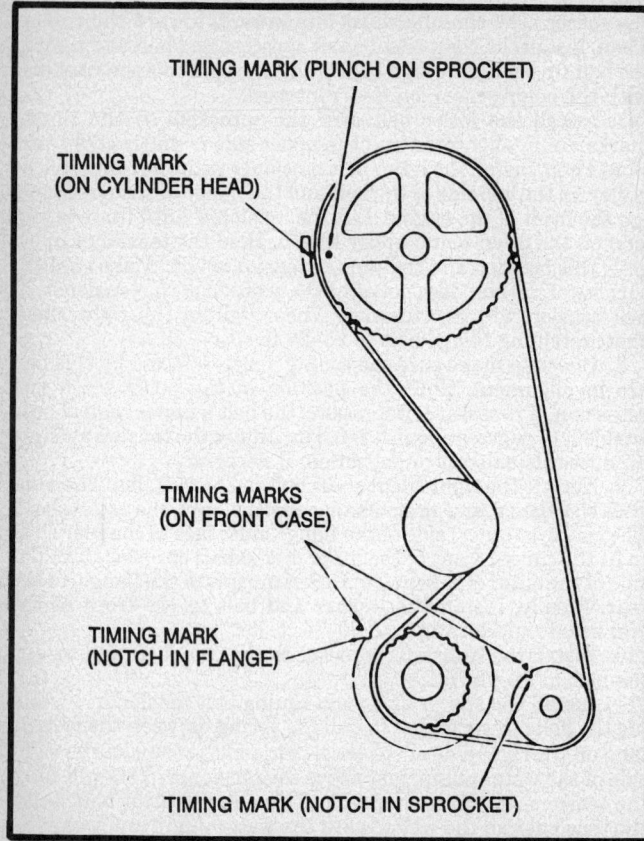

TIMING MARK (PUNCH ON SPROCKET)

TIMING MARK
(ON CYLINDER HEAD)

TIMING MARKS
(ON FRONT CASE)

TIMING MARK
(NOTCH IN FLANGE)

TIMING MARK (NOTCH IN SPROCKET)

1795cc and 1997cc engines (except Eclipse) camshaft drive belt timing marks

the pivot bolt on the timing belt tensioner and lever the tensioner as far as it will go toward the water pump. Tighten the adjusting bolt. Mark the timing belt with an arrow showing direction of rotation, if reusing it.

3. Pull the timing belt off the camshaft sprocket. Remove the camshaft sprocket.

4. Remove the crankshaft pulley. Then, remove the timing belt.

5. Remove the crankshaft sprocket bolts and remove the crankshaft sprocket and flange, noting the direction of installation for each. Remove the timing belt tensioner.

6. Inspect all components, as required. Replace defective parts as needed.

To install:

7. To install, first reinstall the flange and crankshaft sprocket. The flange must go on first with the chamfered area outward. The sprocket is installed with the boss forward and the studs for the fan belt pulley outward. Install and torque the crankshaft sprocket bolt to 51–72 ft. lbs. Install the camshaft sprocket and bolt, torque it to 47–54 ft. lbs.

8. Align the timing marks of the camshaft sprocket. Check that the crankshaft timing marks are still in alignment, the locating pin on the front of the crankshaft sprocket is aligned with a mark on the front case.

9. To install the tensioner assembly, mount the tensioner, spring and spacer with the bottom end of the spring free. Then, install the bolts and tighten the adjusting bolt slightly with the tensioner moved as far as possible away from the water pump. Install the free end of the spring into the locating tang on the front case. Position the belt over the crankshaft sprocket and then over the camshaft sprocket. Make sure the belt is straight on the right side, where there's no tensioner. Slip the back of the belt over the tensioner wheel. Turn the camshaft sprocket in the

opposite of its normal direction of rotation until the straight side of the belt is tight and make sure the timing marks align. If not, shift the belt one tooth at a time in the appropriate direction until this occurs.

10. Install the crankshaft pulley, making sure the pin on the crankshaft sprocket fits through the hole in the rear surface of the pulley. Install the bolts and torque to specification.

11. Loosen the tensioner bolts so the tensioner works, without the interference of any friction, under spring pressure. Make sure the belt follows the curve of the camshaft pulley so the teeth are engaged all the way around. Correct the path of the belt, if necessary. Torque the tensioner adjusting bolt to 15–18 ft. lbs. Torque the tensioner pivot bolt to the same figure. Bolts must be torqued in that order or tension won't be correct.

12. Turn the crankshaft 1 turn clockwise until timing marks again align to seat the belt. Loosen both tensioner bolts and let the tensioner position itself under spring tension as before. Finally, torque the bolts in the proper order exactly as before. Check belt tension by pulling the belt toward the water pump side of the tensioner wheel. The belt should move toward the pump until the teeth are about 1/4 of the way across the head of the tensioner adjusting bolt. Retension the belt, if necessary.

13. Install the timing belt covers and remaining cooling system parts in the reverse of the removal procedure.

1.6L ENGINE

1. Disconnect the negative battery cable. Remove the crankshaft pulley. Remove the upper and lower timing belt covers. Rotate the crankshaft until all timing marks are aligned. There is a pin on the crankshaft sprocket which serves as the timing mark. It aligns with a pin protruding from the block behind the sprocket.

2. Remove the crankshaft sprocket bolt and loosen the other sprocket bolts.

3. Loosen the tensioner and adjusting bolts, shift the tensioner all the way to the left and retighten the adjusting bolt. Mark the timing belt with an arrow in the direction of rotation if it may be reused. Remove the timing belt.

4. Remove the camshaft sprocket, crankshaft sprocket and flange. If necessary, the crankshaft sprocket may be pulled off with a puller such as Mitsubishi part MD998311.

5. Remove the tensioner.

6. Inspect all components, as required. Replace defective parts as required.

7. Install the spacer, flange and crankshaft sprocket. The spacer is installed with the larger opening to the rear, so it fits tightly over the crankshaft at the front. Then install the flange with the slightly concave side backward. Finally, install the sprocket with the flat side rearward and boss forward. Install the sprocket bolt and torque to 80–93 ft. lbs. Make sure the sprocket and block timing marks are still aligned. Also check the timing marks for the oil pump drive sprocket and make sure they are aligned.

8. Apply a thin coating of clean engine oil to the outer circumference of the camshaft spacer and install the spacer onto the camshaft. Install the camshaft sprocket and bolt to 44–57 ft. lbs. Make sure the timing marks are aligned. Then install the crankshaft pulley so the engine can be turned. The bolts may be finger-tight.

9. Install the tensioner by first installing the spring, then the tensioner itself and then by installing and tightening the nut (finger-tight) used for adjusting the tensioner. Make sure the bent end of the spring goes to the right. Rock the tensioner, as necessary, until the pivot hole and bolt hole in the block align and install the pivot bolt. The spring must be installed so the bent end will work against the tab on the tensioner and the straight end works against the tab on the water pump body. Engage the ends of the spring with the tabs. Push the tensioner as far as it will go toward the water pump and then tighten the adjusting nut.

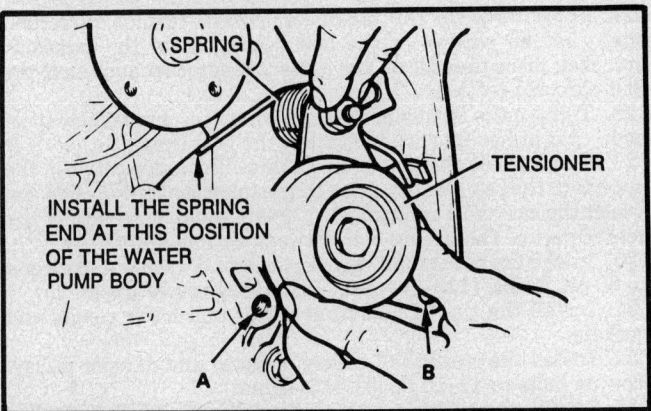

Installing belt tensioner spring — 1597cc engine

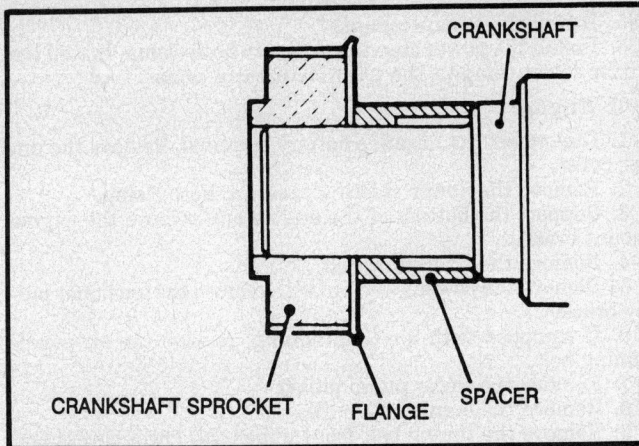

Installation of the crankshaft sprocket — 1597cc engine

10. Install the timing belt, first over the crankshaft sprocket and then onto the oil pump sprocket. With the right side straight, engage the belt with the camshaft sprocket. Then, loosen the tensioner adjusting nut so the tensioner will tension the belt.

11. Push the tensioner slightly toward the adjusting nut so the belt teeth will be forced to mesh with the sprocket teeth. Make sure all teeth have meshed. With the tensioner under spring tension only, tighten the adjusting nut and then the pivot bolt. Check to make sure all timing marks are in alignment and make corrections, if necessary.

12. Turn the crankshaft one full turn in the normal direction of rotation, until all timing marks again align. Turn the engine smoothly and do not allow it to turn backwards. Don't grab the belt to test tension during this procedure. Loosen the tensioner adjusting nut and mounting bolt, again allowing it to adjust under spring pressure along. Torque the tensioner adjusting nut to 16–21 ft. lbs. Finally, tighten the bolt.

13. Test the tension on the belt by grasping the right edge of the rear timing belt cover and pull the center of the belt span toward it. With reasonable pressure, the belt should move to within just under ½ in. (0.47 in.) from the seal line. Repeat Steps 11 and 12 if the tension isn't correct.

14. Remove the crankshaft pulley. Install the timing belt lower front cover. Then install the upper cover.

3.0L ENGINE

1. Bring the No. 1 piston to TDC of its compression stroke. Disconnect the negative battery cable. Disconnect the power steering oil pump pressure switch connector.

2. Remove the power steering pump hose bracket bolts from the engine.

3. Slightly raise the engine and support it safely and remove the engine mounting bolt(s) from the engine bracket and remove the bracket.

4. Remove the air conditioning compressor belt and tension pulley bracket.

5. Remove the power steering pump and place it aside with the pressure lines still attached. Remove the tensioner pulley and pulley bracket.

6. Remove the outer upper timing belt cover and gaskets.

7. Remove the engine mounting bolt(s) from the engine support bracket and the bracket. Be sure to take note of the different bolt sizes and the holes which they came from.

8. Remove the timing belt cover cap and the other outer upper timing belt cover with gaskets.

9. Remove the under cover panel. Remove the crankshaft pulley bolt and using a suitable pulley, remove the crankshaft pulley. Remove the front flange and then remove the lower timing belt cover(s) and gaskets. Be sure to take note of the different bolt sizes in the lower cover and the holes which they came from.

10. Loosen the timing belt tensioner bolt and turn the timing belt tensioner counterclockwise along the elongated hole. Remove the tensioner bolt, tensioner and timing belt.

NOTE: If the old timing belt is going to be reused, the direction of rotation should be marked on the belt before removing it.

11. Attach the tension and the timing bolt tensioner. Engage the top of the tensioner spring onto the water pump pin. Be sure the hook on the spring is facing outward. Turn the timing belt tensioner to the extreme counterclockwise along the elongated hole and temporarily fix the timing belt tensioner.

To install:

12. Install the timing belt as follows:

   a. Align the timing marks of the camshaft sprockets (on the front and rear sides) and the crankshaft sprocket. At the top dead point on the number 1 cylinder compression stroke.

   b. Route the timing belt on the crankshaft sprocket then on the camshaft sprocket on the side without slackness in the tight side.

   c. Run the timing belt onto the water pump pulley, the camshaft sprocket on the front side, and the timing belt tensioner.

   d. Apply force counterclockwise to the camshaft sprocket on the rear side. When the tight side of the belt is felt, check that the timing marks are aligned.

13. Attach the flange. Back off the fixing bolts of the temporarily tighten tension 1–2 turns and tighten the timing belt with tensioner spring force.

14. Using a suitable tool, turn the crankshaft 2 turns in the normal (clockwise) rotating direction. Never turn the engine counterclockwise.

15. Re-align the sprockets timing marks and tighten the tensioner fixing bolts. Using a belt tension gauge, check the belt tension. The belt tension should be 57–84 lbs.

16. Complete installation by reversing the order of the removal procedure. Torque the crankshaft pulley bolt to 108–116 ft. lbs.

ECLIPSE

1.8L Engine

1. Disconnect the negative battery terminal. Remove the under cover.

2. Remove the power steering pressure hose clamp.

3. Support the bottom of the engine and remove the engine mount bracket.

4. Remove the power steering belt.

5. If equipped with air conditioning, remove the air conditioning belt.

6. Remove the alternator belt.

7. Remove the water pump pulley.

8. Remove the crankshaft pulley, damper pulley and adapter.

9. Remove the timing belt front upper and lower covers and gaskets.

10. Remove the crankshaft sprocket bolt access cover and remove the crankshaft sprocket bolt and washer.

11. To remove the timing belt, turn the crankshaft clockwise and align the timing marks.

NOTE: The crankshaft must always be turned clockwise.

12. If the timing belt is to be reused, make a mark on the back of the timing belt to indicate the direction of rotation so it may be reassembled in the same direction.

13. Remove the timing belt tensioner, tensioner spacer and tensioner spring and remove the timing belt.

14. To remove timing belt "B", remove the timing belt "B" tensioner.

15. If the timing belt "B" is to be reused, make a mark on the back of the timing belt indicating the direction of rotation so it may be reassembled in the same direction.

16. Remove timing belt "B".

To install:

17. Ensure that the crankshaft sprocket "B" timing mark and silent shaft sprocket timing mark are aligned.

18. Fit the timing belt "B" over the crankshaft sprocket "B" and the silent shaft sprocket. Ensure that there is no slack in the belt.

19. Install the timing belt "B" tensioner and temporarily position the tensioner so the center of the tensioner pulley is to the left and above the center of the installation bolt, and temporarily attach the tensioner pulley so the flange is toward the front of the engine.

20. Hold the timing belt "B" tensioner up with a finger in the direction of the arrow, place pressure on the timing belt so the tension side of the belt is taut. Tighten the bolt to position the tensioner. When tightening the bolt, ensure that the tensioner pulley shaft does not rotate with the bolt. Allowing it to rotate with the bolt can cause excessive tension on the belt. Belt deflection should be 0.20–0.28 in. (5–7mm).

21. Install the timing belt tensioner spring, spacer and belt tensioner. Place the upper end of the tensioner spring against the water pump body. Move the tensioner fully toward the water pump and temporarily tighten the bolt.

22. Ensure that the timing marks of the camshaft sprocket, the crankshaft sprocket and the oil pump sprocket are all aligned. When aligning the timing mark of the oil pump sprocket, remove the plug of the cylinder block; then insert the shaft of a prybar with a shaft diameter of 0.31 in. (8mm) into the plug hole and be sure the prybar's shaft can be inserted at least 2.4 in. (60mm). Do not remove the prybar until the timing belt is completely attached. If the prybar's shaft can be inserted only to a depth of about 0.79–0.98 in. (20–25mm) because it contacts the silent shaft, turn the sprocket by one rotation and align the timing mark once again; then, check again to be sure the prybar's shaft can be inserted at least 2.4 in. (60mm).

23. Install the timing belt. While making sure tension side of the belt is not slackened, install the timing belt onto the crankshaft sprocket, oil pump sprocket and camshaft sprocket in that order. If reusing the timing belt, be sure to install the timing belt in the direction of the marked arrow.

24. Loosen the belt tensioner nut. This will apply pressure to the belt.

25. Be sure each sprocket's timing mark is aligned.

26. Turn the crankshaft clockwise by 2 teeth of the camshaft sprocket. This is to apply the proper amount of tension on the timing belt.

27. Apply force on the tensioner toward turning direction, such that no portion of the belt raises out of the camshaft sprocket, place the belt on the camshaft sprocket such that the belt sprocket teeth are fully engaged.

28. Tighten the tensioner installation bolt and tensioner spacer in that order. Be sure to tighten the bolt first.

29. Check to see that a 0.40 in. (12mm) clearance between the outside of the belt and the cover by grasping the tension side, between the camshaft sprocket and the oil pump sprocket, of the center part of the timing belt between thumb and finger.

30. Install the crankshaft sprocket bolt and washer and torque to 80–94 ft. lbs. (110–130mm). Install the access cover.

31. Install the timing belt front upper and lower covers and gaskets.

32. Install the crankshaft pulley, adapter and damper pulley. Torque bolts to 11–13 ft. lbs. (15–18mm).

33. Install the water pump pulley. Torque to 6–7 ft. lbs. (8–10mm).

34. Install all drive belts and adjust.

35. Install the engine mount.

36. Install the power steering pressure hose clamp. Install the under cover. Connect the negative battery cable.

2.0L Engine

1. Disconnect the negative battery terminal. Remove the under cover.

2. Remove the power steering pressure hose clamp.

3. Support the bottom of the engine and remove the engine mount bracket.

4. Remove the alternator belt.

5. Remove the power steering belt. Remove the tensioner pulley bracket.

6. If equipped with air conditioning, remove the air conditioning belt.

7. Remove the water pump pulley.

8. Remove the crankshaft pulley.

9. Remove the timing belt front upper and lower covers and gaskets.

10. Remove the center cover, breather hose, PCV hose, spark plug cables and rocker cover with the semi-circular gasket.

11. Remove the plug rubber.

12. Turn the crankshaft clockwise and align the timing marks. Remove the auto tensioner.

NOTE: The crankshaft must always be turned clockwise.

13. If the timing belt is to be reused, make a mark on the back of the timing belt to indicate the direction of rotation so it may be reassembled in the same direction.

14. Remove the timing belt tensioner pulley and arm and remove the timing belt.

15. To remove timing belt "B", remove the timing belt "B" tensioner.

16. If the timing belt "B" is to be reused, make a mark on the back of the timing belt indicating the direction of rotation so it may be reassembled in the same direction.

17. Remove timing belt "B".

To install:

18. Ensure that the crankshaft sprocket "B" timing mark and silent shaft sprocket timing mark are aligned.

19. Fit the timing belt "B" over the crankshaft sprocket "B" and the silent shaft sprocket. Ensure that there is no slack in the belt.

20. Install the timing belt "B" tensioner and temporarily position the tensioner so the center of the tensioner pulley is to the left and above the center of the installation bolt, and temporarily attach the tensioner pulley so the flange is toward the front of the engine.

21. Hold the timing belt "B" tensioner up with a finger in the direction of the arrow, place pressure on the timing belt so the tension side of the belt is taut. Tighten the bolt to position the

tensioner. When tightening the bolt, ensure that the tensioner pulley shaft does not rotate with the bolt. Allowing it to rotate with the bolt can cause excessive tension on the belt. Belt deflection should be 0.20–0.28 in. (5–7mm).

22. To install the auto tensioner, the tensioner should be reset.

    a. Keep the auto tensioner level and clamp it in a vice with soft jaws. If the plug at the bottom of the tensioner protrudes, install flat washers to prevent the plug from contacting the vise.

    b. Push in the rod little by little with the vise until the set hole in the rod is aligned with the hole in the cylinder.

    c. Install a 0.055 in. (1.4mm) wire into the set holes.

    d. Unclamp the tensioner from the vise.

23. Install the auto tensioner and tighten bolts to 14–20 ft. lbs. (20–27mm).

24. Install the tensioner pulley onto the arm. Position the pinholes in the tensioner pulley shaft to the left of the center bolt. Tighten the center bolt finger-tight. Do not remove the wire from the auto tensioner.

25. Ensure that the timing marks of the camshaft sprocket, the crankshaft and the oil pump sprockets are aligned. When aligning the timing mark of the oil pump sprocket, remove the plug of the cylinder block; then insert the shaft of a prybar with a shaft diameter of 0.31 in. (8mm) into the plug hole and be sure the prybar's shaft can be inserted at least 2.4 in. (60mm). Do not remove the prybar until the timing belt is completely attached. If the prybar's shaft can be inserted only to a depth of about 0.79–0.98 in. (20–25mm) because it contacts the silent shaft, turn the sprocket by one rotation and align the timing mark once again; then check again to be sure that the prybar's shaft can be inserted at least 2.4 in. (60mm).

26. Install the timing belt over the intake side camshaft sprocket and fix a clip to the hold the belt.

27. Install the timing belt over the exhaust side sprocket, aligning the timing marks with the cylinder head top surface using 2 wrenches and fix a clip to hold the belt.

28. Install the timing belt over the idler pulley, the oil pump sprocket, the crankshaft sprocket and the tension pulley in that order. Remove the clips.

29. Lift up the tensioner pulley in the direction of the arrow and tighten the center bolt.

30. Check to see that all timing marks are aligned. Remove the prybar and install the plug.

31. Turn the crankshaft ¼ turn counterclockwise. Then, turn it clockwise until the timing marks are aligned again.

32. To adjust the timing belt tension:

    a. Loosen the center bolt, and then attach special tool MD998752 and a torque wrench capable of measurement within a range of 0–2.5 ft. lbs. (0–3 Nm). Apply a torque of 1.88–2.03 ft. lbs. (2.6–2.8 Nm).

    b. Holding the tensioner pulley with the special tool and the torque wrench, tighten the center bolt to 31–40 ft. lbs. (43–55 Nm).

    c. Install special tool MD998738 into the engine left support bracket until its end makes contact with the tensioner arm. At that point, screw the special tool in some more and then remove the set wire attached to the auto tensioner. Remove the special tool.

    d. Rotate the crankshaft 2 complete turns clockwise and leave it as is for about 15 minutes. Then, measure the auto tensioner protrusion; distance between the tensioner arm and the auto tensioner body. Measurement should be 0.15–0.18 in. (3.8–4.5mm).

    e. If the clearance between the tensioner arm and the auto tensioner body cannot be measured, screw in the special tool MD998738 until it contacts the tensioner arm. From that point of contact, further the screw in the special tool, screwing it in until the pushrod of the auto tensioner body is caused to move backward and the tensioner arm contacts the auto tensioner body. Be sure the amount the special tool has been

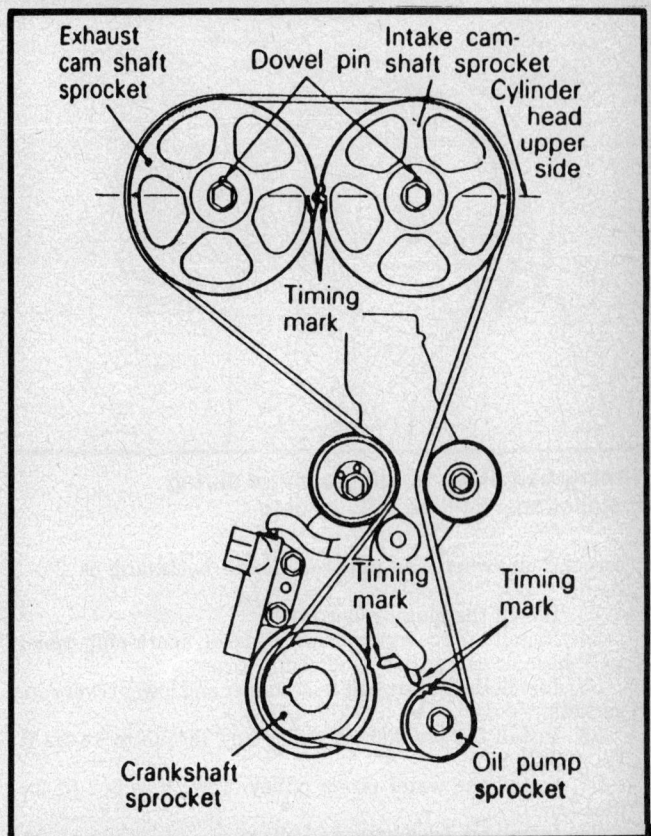

Timing belt alignment marks—Eclipse 2.0L engine

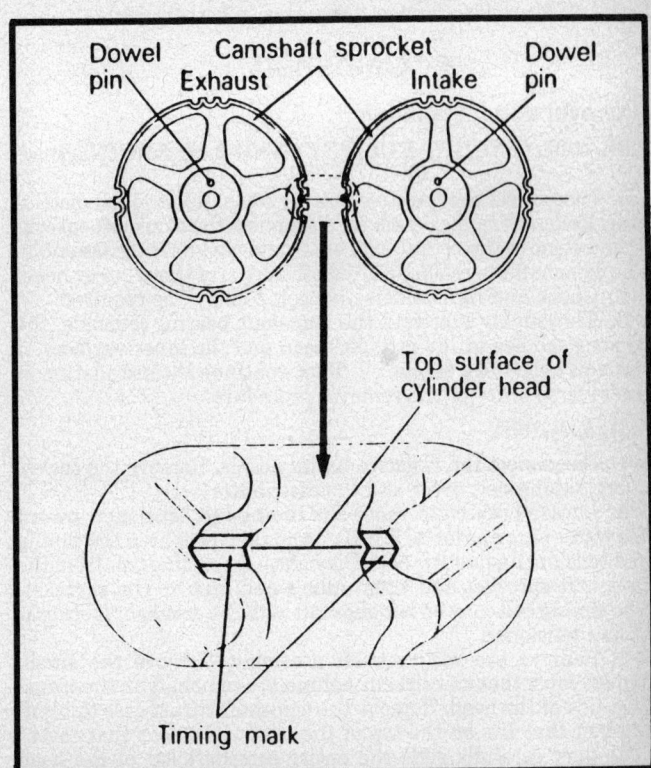

Camshaft sprocket alignment marks—Eclipse 2.0L engine

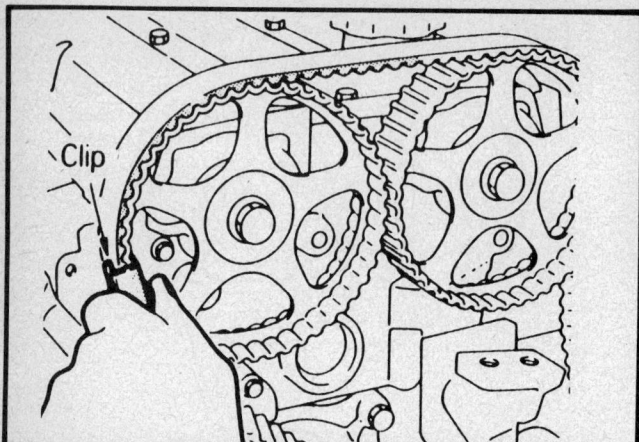

Clip

Timing belt place holding clamps during installation—Eclipse 2.0L engine

screwed in, when the pushrod moves backward, is 2½–3 turns.

33. Install the plug rubber.

34. Install the rocker cover with gasket, spark plug cables, PCV hose, breather hose and center cover.

35. Install the timing belt front upper and lower covers and gaskets.

36. Install the crankshaft pulley and torque to 14–22 ft. lbs. (20–30mm).

37. Install the water pump pulley. Torque to 6–7 ft. lbs. (8–10mm).

38. Install all drive belts and adjust.

39. Install the engine mount.

40. Install the power steering pressure hose clamp. Install the under cover. Connect the negative battery cable.

Camshaft

Removal and Installation

1.8L, 2.0L (EXCEPT ECLIPSE) AND 2.3L ENGINES

1. Disconnect the negative battery cable. Remove the distributor. Remove the rocker cover, disconnect the camshaft sprocket and remove the rocker arm shaft and cam bearing assembly. The camshaft may then be lifted off the top of the cylinder head.

2. Check and replace defective components, as required.

3. Thoroughly lubricate the camshaft bearing journals, the bearing saddles in the cylinder head and the inner surfaces of the caps with clean engine oil. Then continue the installation in the reverse order of the removal procedure.

1.5L ENGINE

1. Disconnect the negative battery cable. Remove the rocker cover, timing belt cover and the distributor.

2. Loosen both bolts, move the timing belt tensioner toward the water pump as far as it will go and then retighten the timing belt tensioner adjusting bolt. Disengage the timing belt from the camshaft sprocket and then unbolt and remove the sprocket. The timing belt may be left engaged with the crankshaft sprocket and tensioner.

3. Remove the rocker shaft assembly. Remove the small, square cover that sits directly behind the camshaft on the transaxle side of the head. Remove the camshaft thrust case tightening bolt that sits on the top of the head right near that cover.

4. Very carefully slide the entire camshaft out of the head through the hold in the camshaft side of the head, being sure the cam lobes do not strike the bearing bores in the head.

5. Check and replace defective components as required.

6. Lubricate all journal and thrust surfaces with clean engine oil and then insert the camshaft into the engine, again keeping the cam lobes from touching the bearing bores. Make sure the camshaft goes in with the threaded hole in the top of the thrust case straight upward and align the bolt hole in the thrust case and the cylinder head surface once the camshaft is all the way inside the head. Install the thrust case bolt and tighten firmly. Finally, install the rear cover with a new gasket and install and tighten the 4 bolts.

7. Coat the external surface of the front oil seal with engine oil. With a special installer part MD998306–01 or equivalent, drive the reusable or new front camshaft oil seal into the clearance between the cam and head at the forward end. Make sure the seal seats fully.

8. Install the camshaft sprocket and torque the bolt to 47–54 ft lbs. Reconnect the timing belt, check timing and adjust the belt tension. Reinstall the rocker shaft assembly. Adjust the valves. Install the rocker and timing belt covers.

1.6L ENGINE

1. Disconnect the negative battery cable. Remove the distributor and remove the rocker cover. Remove the upper timing cover. Turn the engine over until the timing mark on the rear timing belt cover aligns with the mark on the camshaft sprocket. It's a good idea to mark the timing belt itself to align with the marks on the sprocket and rear timing belt cover to make precise reassembly easier. Remove the camshaft sprocket from the camshaft and remove the rocker arms and shafts assembly.

2. Pull the camshaft front oil seal off the front of the camshaft. Remove the camshaft.

3. Check and replace defective components, as required.

4. Thoroughly lubricate the camshaft bearing journals, the bearing saddles in the cylinder head and the inner surfaces of the caps with clean engine oil.

5. Install the camshaft onto the cylinder head, being careful not to damage any of the camshaft journals. Install the rocker arm and shaft assembly to the head, torque the bolts to 14–15 ft. lbs.

6. Coat the outside diameter of the front end of the camshaft with clean engine oil. Then, with a special tool such as MD998354–01 or equivalent, tap a new front seal in, using a hammer. Install the rear timing belt cover.

7. Turn the camshaft so the dowel pin on the front aligns with the hole in the sprocket. If necessary to turn the cam, exert force on either of both projections behind the No. 2 cylinder exhaust valve cam. Reconnect the camshaft drive sprocket by lifting it off the rest and installing it to the camshaft with the dowel pin going through the hole in the sprocket. Torque the sprocket bolt to 44–57 ft. lbs.

8. Install the remaining parts and adjust the valves.

2.5L ENGINE

1. Disconnect the negative battery cable. Remove the distributor. Remove the rocker cover and rocker shaft assembly. Remove also the rear bearing cap bolts and the cap.

2. Remove the camshaft from the head.

3. Check and replace defective components as required.

4. Thoroughly lubricate the camshaft bearing journals, the bearing saddles in the cylinder head and the inner surfaces of the caps with clean engine oil. Install the camshaft onto the cylinder head, being careful not to damage any of the camshaft journals. Apply a sealer to the outside diameter of the circular seal for the rear bearing and install it in the head with one side directly in contact with the rear of the camshaft. The packing will end up under the rearmost portion of the rear bearing cap. Then, install and torque the rocker shaft/bearing cap assembly. Include the rear bearing cap, using the same torque. Refit the cam sprocket and chain to the camshaft.

5. Also inspect the semicircular seal that goes in the front of the timing chain cover and seal the top with an adhesive such as 3M Super Weatherstrip Adhesive 801k or equivalent.

6. Adjust the valve clearances. Install the rocker cover and all other parts removed earlier. Start the engine and idle it until after the temperature gauge indicates normal operating temperature. Remove the rocker cover again and adjust the valves with the engine hot.

3.0L ENGINE

1. Remove the rocker arm covers.
2. Using special tool MD9990767–01 or equivalent, remove the camshaft sprockets.
3. Remove the rocker arm shaft and cam bearing assemblies. Be sure to install the special tool MD99843–01 or equivalent, to assure that the auto lash adjuster does not fall out.
4. Carefully lift out the camshafts from their prospective heads, be sure to keep all removed parts in the proper order.
5. Check and replace defective components, as required.
6. Thoroughly lubricate the camshaft bearing journals, the bearing saddles in the cylinder head and the inner surfaces of the caps with clean engine oil.
7. Installation is the reverse order of the removal procedure. Torque the camshaft sprocket bolts to 58–72 ft. lbs. and the bearing cap retaining bolts to 15 ft. lbs. It may be necessary to use the cylinder head and the rocker arm procedure already outlined in this section as guide for an easier installation.

ECLIPSE

1.8L Engine

1. Relieve the fuel system pressure.
2. Disconnect the battery negative cable.
3. Remove the distributor.
4. Remove the rocker cover, timing belt cover and timing belt.
5. Remove the camshaft sprocket and oil seal.
6. Loosen both rocker arms assembly uniformly and remove.
7. Remove the camshaft rear cover, rear cover gasket, thrust plate and camshaft thrust case. Remove the camshaft.
8. After the camshaft has been removed, check the following:
   a. Check the camshaft journals for wear or damage.
   b. Check the fuel pump drive eccentric cam and distributor drive gear tooth surfaces.
   c. Check the cam lobes for damage. Also, check the cylinder head oil holes for clogging.

To install:

9. Lubricate the camshaft with heavy engine oil and slide it into the head.
10. Insert the camshaft thrust case in cylinder head with the threaded hole facing upward and align the threaded hole with the bolt hole in the cylinder head. Install and firmly tighten the attaching bolt.
11. Check the camshaft endplay between the thrust case and camshaft. The camshaft endplay should be 0.0020–0.0080 in. (0.5–0.20mm). If the endplay is not within specification, replace the camshaft thrust bearing.
12. When installing the oil seal, coat the external surface with engine oil. Position the seal on the camshaft end and drive into place using tool MD998306 or equivalent.
13. Complete installation by reversing the removal procedure.

2.0L Engine

1. Relieve the fuel system pressure.
2. Disconnect battery negative cable.
3. Remove the accelerator cable connection.
4. Remove the timing belt cover and timing belt.
5. Remove the center cover, breather and PCV hoses and spark plug cables.
6. Remove the rocker cover, semi-circular packing, throttle body stay, crankshaft angle sensor, both camshaft sprockets and oil seals.
7. Loosen the bearing cap bolts in 2–3 steps. Label and remove both camshaft bearing caps.

NOTE: If the bearing caps are difficult to remove, use a plastic hammer to gently tap the rear part of the camshaft.

8. Remove the intake and exhaust camshafts.
9. After the camshaft has been removed, check the following:
   a. Check the camshaft journals for wear or damage.
   b. Check the cam lobes for damage. Also, check the cylinder head oil holes for clogging.

To install:

10. To install, lubricate the camshafts with heavy engine oil and position the camshafts on the cylinder head.

NOTE: Do not confuse the intake camshaft with the exhaust camshaft. The intake camshaft has a split on its rear end for driving the crank angle sensor.

11. Make sure the dowel pin on both camshaft sprocket ends are located on the top.
12. Install the bearing caps. Tighten the caps, in sequence, in 2–3 steps. No. 2 and 5 caps are of the same shape. Check the markings on the caps to identify the cap number and intake/exhaust symbol. Only **L** (intake) or **R** (exhaust) is stamped on No. 1 bearing cap. Also, make sure the rocker arm is correctly mounted on the lash adjuster and the valve stem end.
13. Apply a coating of engine oil to the oil seal. Using tool MD998307 or equivalent, press-fit the seal into the cylinder head.
14. Align the punch mark on the crank angle sensor housing with the notch in the plate. With the dowel pin on the sprocket side of the intake camshaft at top, install the crank angle sensor on the cylinder head.

NOTE: The crank angle sensor can be installed with the punch mark positioned opposite the notch; however, that position will result in incorrect fuel injection and ignition timing.

15. Complete the installation by reversing the removal procedure.

Intermediate Shaft

Removal and Installation

ECLIPSE

1.8L Engine

1. Disconnect the negative battery cable.
2. Remove the oil filter, oil pressure switch, oil gauge sending unit and oil filter bracket and gasket.
3. Drain engine oil. Remove engine oil pan, oil screen and gasket.
4. Remove the front engine cover which is also the oil pump cover. Different length bolts are used. Take note of their locations. If the cover sticks to the block, look for a special slot provided and pry with a suitable tool. Discard the shaft seal and gasket.
5. Remove the oil pump driven gear flange bolt. When loosening this bolt, first insert a suitable tool approximately 3/8 in. diameter into the plug hole on the left side of the cylinder block to hold the silent shaft. Remove the oil pump gears and remove the front case assembly. Remove the threaded plug, the oil pressure relief spring and plunger.
6. Remove the silent shaft oil seals, the crankshaft oil seal and front case gasket.
7. Remove the silent shafts.

To install:

8. Installation is the reverse of the removal procedure. Use new gaskets and seals. Clean all mating surfaces well.
9. Use care to get the proper length bolt in the correct location on the timing cover as well as the oil pump cover.
10. Refill with engine oil. Install new filter. Check for leaks.

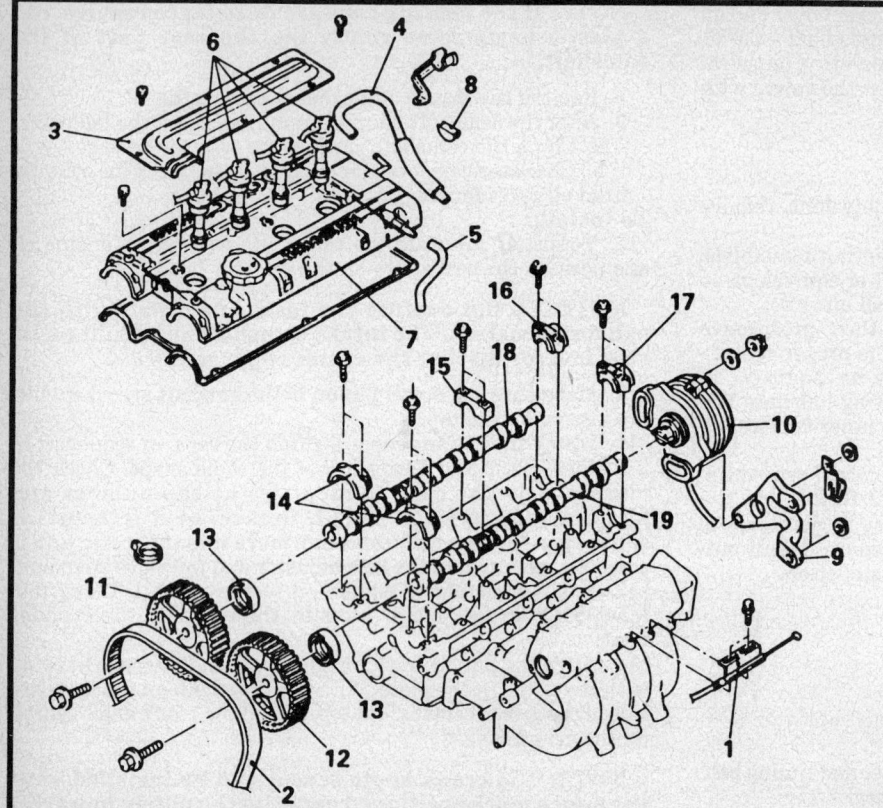

1. Connection for accelerator cable
2. Timing belt
3. Center cover
4. Connection for breather hose
5. Connection for PCV hose
6. Connection for spark plug cables
7. Rocker cover
8. Semi-circular packing
9. Throttle body stay
10. Crankshaft angle sensor
11. Exhaust camshaft sprocket
12. Intake camshaft sprocket
13. Camshaft oil seals
14. Front camshaft bearing caps
15. Camshaft bearing caps
16. Right-hand rear camshaft bearing cap
17. Left-hand rear camshaft bearing cap
18. Exhaust camshaft
19. Intake camshaft

Camshaft servicing—Eclipse 2.0L engine

Silent Shafts

Removal and Installation

4 CYLINDER ENGINES EXCEPT 2.5L ENGINE

NOTE: A special oil seal guide MD998285 or equivalent, is needed to complete this operation.

1. Disconnect the negative battery cable. Remove the timing belt covers, timing belts and sprockets.
2. Drain the oil and remove the oil filter. Then, remove the oil pan and gasket. Remove the oil pick-up and gasket.
3. Remove the oil pressure relief plunger plug and gasket, and then remove the spring and plunger from the oil filter bracket. Remove the 4 bracket bolts, the oil filter mount and gasket.
4. Remove the cap and gasket that cover the oil pump driven gear shaft. This is located on the right side of the front case at the front of the engine, just above the protruding silent shaft.
5. Using a long socket, remove the retaining bolt from the oil pump driven gear, behind the plug removed earlier.
6. Remove the front case bolts, the case and the gasket. Slide the silent shafts from the block, noting their installation angles.
7. Inspect the silent shaft bearing journals for signs of excessive wear of seizure. If there are signs of critical wear problems, the bushings should also be inspected. The bushings may be replaced by pulling them out and pressing new ones in, using special tools. This is done with the crankshaft removed, since it normally is required only at time of major engine overhaul.
8. Lubricate the silent shaft bearing journals with clean engine oil and install the shafts into the block. Insert the shafts into their original position, a suitable tool in the left side of the block will ensure that the left side shaft will be in position.

9. Install a special seal guide tool MD998285–01 or equivalent, onto the crankshaft, so the smaller diameter faces outward. Coat the outer diameter of the seal with clean engine oil. Install a new front case gasket. Install the front case by carefully positioning its crankshaft seal over the seal guide and lining up all bolt holes. Install all 8 bolts and tighten the bolts just finger-tight.
10. Install the oil filter bracket gasket, the bracket and 4 bolts; torque the front case bolts to 15–19 ft. lbs. and the oil filter bracket bolts to 11–15 ft. lbs.
11. Install the remaining parts in reverse of the removal procedure.

2.5L ENGINE

NOTE: Two long, 8mm bolts are needed to pull out the silent shaft thrust plates and 2 guides, made by cutting the heads off 6mm bolts about 2 in. long.

1. Disconnect the negative battery cable. Remove the timing cover, chains and sprockets. Before removing both sprocket bolts, put a wrench on the flange bolt which attaches the upper oil pump gear to the center of the right side silent shaft and turn it just enough to break it loose.
2. Screw 8mm bolts into the bolt holes in the thrust plate and turn them evenly to pull the thrust plate out of the block. Then, remove the left silent shaft.
3. Remove the oil pump bolts. Then, pull the oil pump and gasket straight off the front of the block. The right side silent shaft will come out with the pump. Be careful to support the pump and shaft in such a way that the rear shaft bearing will not be damaged. Remove the bolt from the center of the oil pump driven (upper) gear. Separate the silent shaft and key from the oil pump driven gear by sliding it out. Remove the oil pump gasket.

4. Inspect the silent shaft bearing journals for signs of excessive wear or seizure. If there are signs of critical wear problems, the bushings should also be inspected. The bushings may be replaced by pulling them out and pressing new ones in , using special tools. This is done with the crankshaft removed, since it normally is required only at time of major engine overhaul.

5. Lubricate the left silent shaft bearing journals with clean engine oil and install the shaft into the block. Insert the shaft into their original position, a suitable tool in the left side of the block will ensure that the shaft will be in position.

6. Screw both guides, made from 6mm headless bolts, into the holes in the block above and below the left side silent shaft. Install a new O-ring with engine oil. Then, install the thrust plate over the guides and into the block. Finally, remove the guides and install the thrust plate bolts, torquing to 7.5–8.5 ft. lbs.

7. Pull the cover off the oil pump housing and verify that the oil pump gears still positioned so the timing marks are aligned. Install the cover over the guide pins and pour about 0.6 cu. in. of clean engine oil into the oil pump outlet, which is at top right of the pump cover. Install the oil pump gasket to the rear of the pump, it may be necessary to use grease to hold it in position. Then, position the pump in its installed direction and engage the key of the right silent shaft to the slot in the oil pump driven gear. Slide the shaft all the way into the pump driven gear and then install the bolt and torque to 44–50 ft. lbs. Lubricate the right side silent shaft bearing journals with clean engine oil and then insert the shaft into the block and install the oil pump. Install the oil pump bolts and torque to 7.5–8.5 ft. lbs.

8. Install the sprockets, timing chains, tensioners and front cover.

Piston and Connecting Rod

Positioning

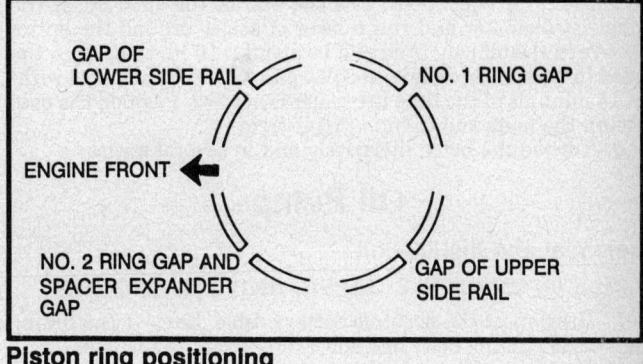

Piston ring positioning

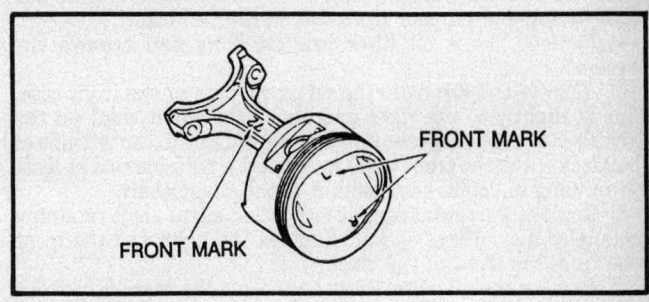

Piston installation identification marks—3.0L engine

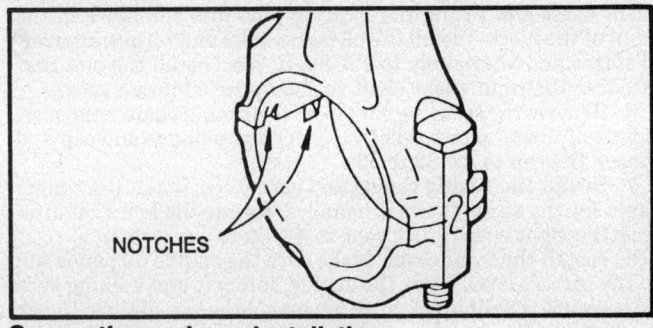

Connecting rod cap installation

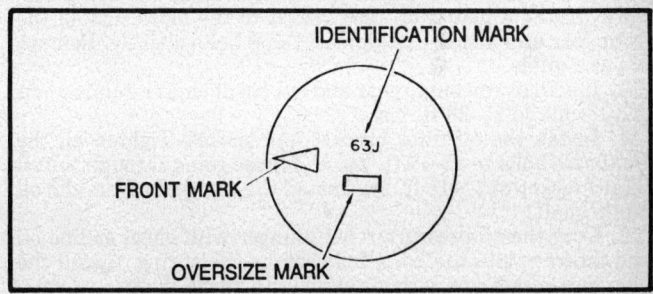

Piston installation

ENGINE LUBRICATION

Oil Pan

Removal and Installation

1. The oil pan must be pulled downward as much as 6 in. to clear the oil pickup. In nearly all applications, this requires that the engine mounts be disconnected and the engine raised to clear a crossmember under the shallower section of the pan. First, survey the area under the engine to determine whether or not there is clearance, in case, the engine can be left in place.

2. Disconnect the negative battery cable. Drain the oil pan into a suitable container. Disconnect all those hoses and wires that would prevent the engine from being lifted the required distance for removal of the pan. If necessary, remove the starter, transaxle mounts, bell housing and oil filter.

3. Raise and safely support the vehicle and remove the oil pan bolts. Hook a lift to the hooks on the cylinder head and support the engine.

4. Remove the through bolts from the engine mounts. Raise the engine far enough to gain clearance, as necessary. Remove the oil pan from the vehicle.

5. Installation is the reverse of the removal procedure.

6. On the Mirage 1597cc engine, coat the 4 seams on the gasket surface for the block with a liquid sealer. These are the joints between the front cover and block on the front and the rear oil seal case and the block at the rear.

7. If equipped with gasketless pans, use liquid sealer

MD997110 or equivalent. Cut the end of the tube off at the smallest diameter and run a bead of sealer around the entire groove in the oil pan. It should be about 0.16 in. thick. Run the head in back of the bolt holes. The pan should be installed within 15 minutes of the time the sealer is applied. Position the pan, install the bolts and tighten finger-tight.

8. Torque the bolts alternately and in several stages.

Oil Pump

Removal and Installation

1.8L, 2.0L (EXCEPT ECLIPSE) AND 2.3L ENGINES

1. Disconnect the negative battery cable. Remove the timing belt cover, timing belts and sprockets. Drain the oil pan.

2. The front oil pan bolts screw into the front case, onto which the oil pump is mounted using a seal. Remove the oil pan.

3. Remove the oil filter. Remove the oil screen and gasket. Remove the oil relief plunger plug and gasket. Then, remove the relief spring and plunger from the oil filter bracket.

4. Remove the 4 oil filter bracket bolts and remove the bracket.

5. Remove the cap from the oil pump area of the front case. This is slightly to the right and above the silent shaft on the driver's side of the vehicle. Remove the plug from the left side of the block (near the front case) and insert a suitable tool at least 2.4 in. long to retain the position of the silent shaft.

6. Remove the retaining bolt for the left silent shaft retaining bolts. Use a deep well socket. Remove the bolts and the front case from the front of the block.

7. Remove the oil pump cover bolts from the rear of the front case and remove the oil pump cover. Remove the gears from the front case.

8. Install the oil pump cover to the front case and torque the 5 bolts to 11–13 ft. lbs.

9. Install a special oil seal guide tool MD998285–01, to the front of the crankshaft, with the smaller diameter facing outward. Install a new front case gasket to the block. Install the front case and install and tighten the 8 bolts slightly. Remove the seal guide.

10. Install the oil pump gear and left silent shaft retaining bolt and torque to 25–28 ft. lbs.

11. Install the oil filter bracket and gasket. Tighten all the front case bolts to 15–19 ft. lbs. and those going through the oil filter bracket to 11–15 ft. lbs. Install the cap that covers the oil pump shaft.

12. Coat the oil pressure relief plunger with clean engine oil and insert it into the bore, followed by the spring. Install the plug and gasket and torque the plug to 29–36 ft. lbs.

13. Install the oil screen and gasket.

14. Install the oil pan in reverse of removal. Install the sprockets, tensioners and timing belts and tension them to specification. Install the timing covers and engine accessories. Make sure to refill the oil pan with the full capacity of clean engine oil. Idle the engine and make sure oil pressure builds up within a reasonable length of time.

1.5L AND 1.6L ENGINES

NOTE: On the 1468cc engine, the front case must be removed to gain access to the oil pump. On the Mirage with the 1597cc engine, the oil pump is bolted to the front of the front case. If necessary to leave the front case in place, remove the timing belt covers and belts to gain access to the pump. If doing a complete overhaul, follow the procedure in order to replace the oil pan gasket and other parts.

1. Disconnect the negative battery cable. Remove the timing belt cover and timing belt.

2. Drain the oil and then remove the oil pan. Unbolt the oil pick-up and screen from the front case and remove it.

3. Remove the front cover with the oil pump assembled to it. On the 1468cc engine, pull the cover straight off to avoid damaging the crankshaft seal.

4. Put the cover on a clean bench. Remove the oil pump relief valve plug and gasket, spring and plunger.

5. Remove the attaching nut and then remove the oil pump sprocket on the Mirage with the 1597cc engine. On the 1468cc engine, turn the cover over. Then, remove the bolts and remove the oil pump cover from the case.

6. Installation is the reverse of the removal procedure. Repair or replace defective components as required.

2.5L ENGINE

1. Disconnect the negative battery cable. Remove the front cover. Follow the procedure above for removal of timing chains and sprockets up to Step 3, but make sure to unscrew and remove the bolt for the right side silent shaft, just above the oil pump drive sprocket, before removing the chain. In other words, remove the timing chain for the silent shafts and securing the plunger for the camshaft timing chain tensioner, but don't disturb the camshaft timing chain. Leave the crankshaft sprocket that drives the silent shaft chain in place.

2. Remove the oil pump relief valve plug, spring and plunger. Remove the oil pump bolts and the pump assembly and gasket. Remove the cover from the rear of the oil pump.

3. Oil the oil pump gears and the inner walls of the pump housing thoroughly with engine oil. Install the gears into the oil pump housing with both timing marks directly across from one another. If the timing marks aren't aligned, the silent shaft will be out of phase and the engine will vibrate severely.

4. Install the pump cover over both pins on the rear of the pump. Pour about 0.6 cu. in. of oil into the pump outlet, at top right, looking at the rear cover. Place the gasket over both locator pins.

5. Install the pump onto the front of the block, engaging the keyway slot in the upper oil pump gear with the key on the right silent shaft and fitting the locating pins into the holes in the front of the block. Install the oil pump bolts and torque in several stages and alternately to 7.5–8.5 ft. lbs. Install the bolt that attaches the right silent shaft to the upper oil pump gear.

6. Remove the securing wire from the timing chain tensioner. Reinstall the oil pump relief valve spring, plunger and cap and torque the cap to 22–32 ft. lbs.

7. Install the timing chains and sprockets. When the timing chain for the silent shafts is installed, torque the bolt that attaches the right silent shaft gear to 44–50 ft. lbs.

8. Install the front cover. Make sure the engine oil pan is full to the correct level. Start the engine, idling it and making sure oil pressure is built up within a reasonable length of time. Check for leaks and repair, as necessary.

3.0L ENGINE

1. Bring the No. 1 piston to TDC of its compression stroke. Disconnect the negative battery cable and drain the engine oil into a suitable container.

2. Remove the timing belt covers, timing belt and sprockets.

3. Connect a suitable engine lift to the engine and take up the slack in the chain.

4. Remove the crankshaft sprocket. Remove the front 2 transaxle mounts.

5. Remove the oil pressure switch, oil filter, oil filter bracket and bracket gasket.

6. Remove the oil pan, oil pan gasket, oil pump screen and screen gasket.

7. Remove the oil pump pressure relief valve assembly. Remove the crankshaft front oil seal.

8. Remove the oil pump case, oil pump gasket, oil pump cover, oil pump outer rotor and oil pump inner rotor.

9. Installation is the reverse order of the removal procedure. Be sure to check all moving parts and replace, as necessary. Use new gaskets and O-rings when necessary, replace the front

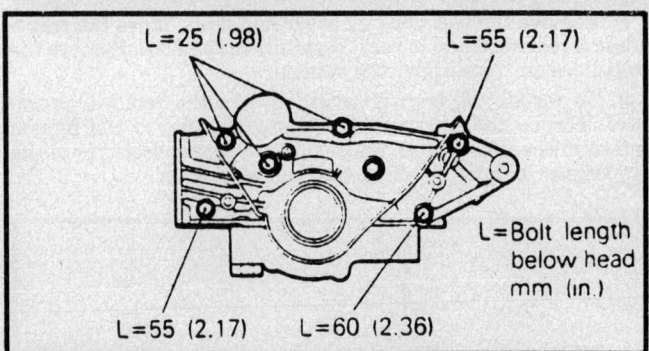

L=25 (.98)   L=55 (2.17)

L=55 (2.17)   L=60 (2.36)

L=Bolt length below head mm (in.)

Bolt diameter location on the oil pump assembly—3.0L engine

crankshaft seal with a new one. Apply a suitable sealant to the oil pan gasket and coat the threads of the oil pressure switch with a suitable sealant. Torque the oil pump bolts to 10 ft. lbs.

ECLIPSE

1.8L and 2.0L Engines

1. Disconnect the negative battery cable.
2. Remove the front engine mount bracket and accessory drive belts.
3. Remove timing belt upper and lower covers.
4. Remove the timing belt and crankshaft sprocket.
5. Remove the oil pan drain plug and drain the engine oil.
6. Remove the oil pan bolts and the oil pan.
7. Remove the oil screen and gasket.
8. Remove and tag the front cover bolts; the bolts are of different length.
9. Remove the front case cover and oil pump assembly.
10. Check the oil pump housing and gears for cracks, wear and other damage.
11. Remove the oil seal from the front cover.
12. Clean all gasket material from mounting surfaces.
13. To install, apply engine oil to the entire surface of the gears.
14. Assemble the front case cover and oil pump assembly to the engine block using a new gasket.
15. Complete installation by reversing the removal procedure. Connect battery, run engine and check for leaks.

Rear Main Bearing Oil Seal

Removal and Installation

CORDIA, TREDIA, GALANT, ECLIPSE, STARION AND SIGMA

1. Remove the transaxle or transmission and clutch from the vehicle. Remove the flywheel or driveplate and adapter plate.
2. Unbolt and remove the lower bell housing cover from the rear of the engine. Remove the rear plate from the upper portion of the rear of the block.
3. The lower surface of the oil seal case seals against the oil pan gasket or sealer at the rear. On engines with a gasket, care-

fully separate the gasket from the bottom of the seal case with a moderately sharp instrument. Loosen the oil pan bolts slightly at the rear to make it easier to separate both surfaces. If the gasket is damaged, the oil pan will have to be removed and the gasket replaced. If using sealant, unbolt and lower the oil pan and clean both surfaces, apply new sealer and reinstall the oil pan after Step 7 is completed.

4. Remove the oil seal case bolts and pull it straight off the rear of the crankshaft. Remove the case gasket.
5. Remove the seal retainer or oil separator from the case, and then pry out the seal. Inspect the sealing surface at the rear of the crankshaft. If a deep groove is worn into the surface, the crankshaft will have to be replaced. Lubricate the sealing surface with clean engine oil.
6. Using a seal installer such as MD998376–01 and MD990938–01, install the new seal into the bore of rear oil seal case in such a way that the flat side of the seal will face outward when the case is installed on the engine. The inside of the seal must be flush with the inside surface of the seal case.
7. Install the retainer or oil separator directly over the seal with the small hole located directly at the bottom. Then, install a new gasket onto the block surface and install the seal case to the rear of the block. Retorque pan bolts, as necessary. Refill the oil pan if necessary.
8. Install the rear plate and bell housing cover. Install the flywheel or driveplate and the transaxle in reverse of the removal procedure.

MIRAGE AND PRECIS

1. Remove the transaxle or manual transaxle and clutch from the vehicle. Remove the flywheel or driveplate and adapter plate.
2. Unbolt and remove the rear plate from the rear of the block. On the Mirage with the 1597cc engine, use a moderately sharp instrument and separate the rear portion of the oil pan gasket from the lower surface of the rear main seal case on the back of the block. Loosen the oil pan bolts slightly at the rear to make it easier to separate both surfaces. If the gasket is damaged, drain the oil pan and remove it. On the 1468cc engine, drain the oil pan and remove it, as the sealing surfaces must be cleaned and new sealer applied all around.
3. Unbolt the oil seal case and then pull it straight back and off the crankshaft. Remove the case gasket. Pry the old seal out of the case.
4. Inspect the sealing surface at the rear of the crankshaft. If a deep groove is worn into the surface, the crankshaft will have to be replaced. Press a new seal into the case with a special seal installing tool such as MD998011. The seal must be pressed in square until it bottoms in the case.
5. Oil the crankshaft sealing surfaces and the lips of the new seal. On the Mirage with the 1597cc engine spread a liquid sealer thoroughly around those areas which butt up against the block and oil pan gasket at the bottom surface and on the front at both sides. Then, install the seal, gasket and seal case straight over the crankshaft sealing surface. Install and tighten the 5 case bolts.
6. On the 1468cc engine, install sealer and reinstall the oil pan. On the Mirage with the 1597cc engine reinstall the pan with a new gasket, if necessary, or retorque pan bolts, as necessary.
7. Reinstall the transaxle. Make sure the engine oil pan is refilled with clean engine oil, if necessary.

MANUAL TRANSMISSION

Removal and Installation

1. Disconnect the negative battery cable. Remove the air cleaner. Remove the starter.

2. Remove the top transmission bolts from the bell housing.
3. From inside the vehicle, raise the console assembly and remove the dust cover retaining plate at the shift lever.

4. Place the transmission in the **N** position. Remove the control lever assembly.

5. Raise the vehicle and support it safely. Drain the transmission. Disconnect the speedometer and the backup light switch.

6. Remove the driveshaft. Disconnect the exhaust pipe. Remove the clutch cable or slave cylinder and linkage.

7. Support the engine and transmission and remove the engine rear support bracket. Drain the transmission, as required.

8. Remove the bell housing cover and bolts, move the transmission rearward and lower it carefully to the floor. Remove the transmission from under the vehicle.

9. To install the transmission, reverse the removal procedure. Torque the transmission to engine bolts to the figures shown in the illustration. Make sure the transmission is in the proper gear before installing the gear shift lever.

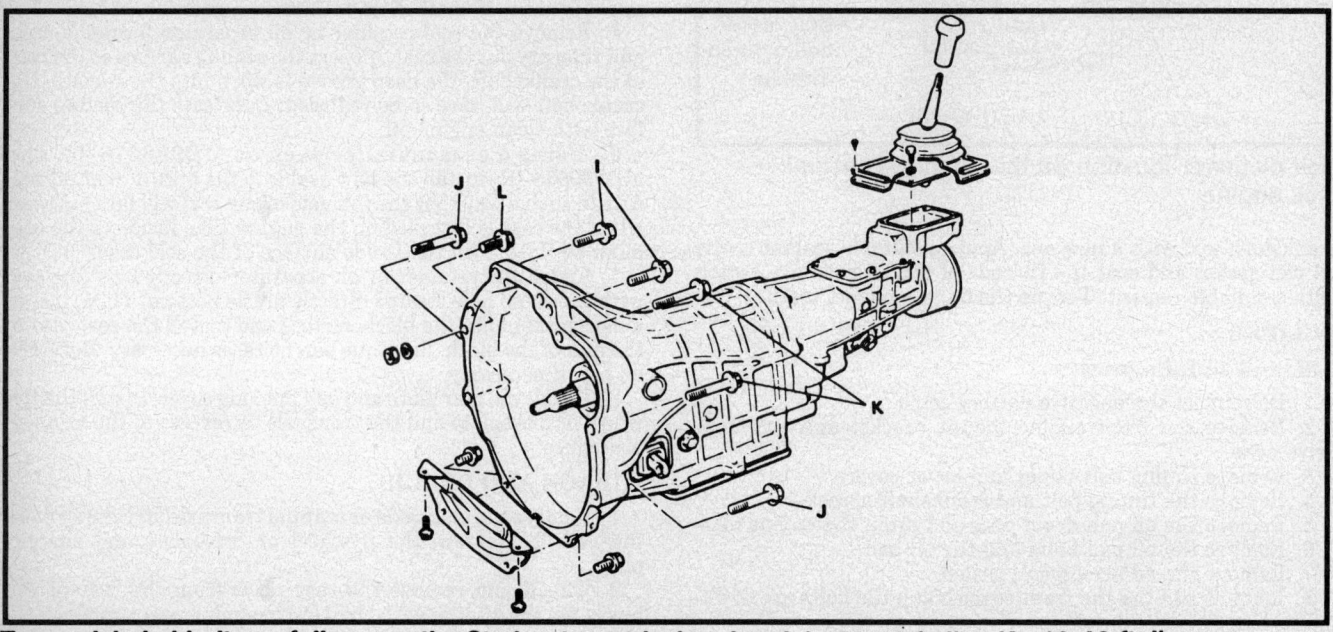

Torque labeled bolts as follows on the Starion transmission: I and J—31–40 ft. lbs; K—16–23 ft. lbs.; L—14–20 ft. lbs.

MANUAL TRANSAXLE

Removal and Installation

CORDIA, TREDIA AND 1987 GALANT

1. Disconnect the negative battery cable. Remove the battery and battery tray. Remove the coolant and windshield reservoir tanks. Remove the air cleaner and housing.

2. Disconnect from the transaxle; the clutch cable or slave cylinder, speedometer cable, back-up light harness, starter motor and the upper bolts connecting the engine to the transaxle.

3. Raise and support the vehicle safely.

4. Remove the front wheels, Remove the engine splash shield.

5. Remove the shift rod and extension. It may be necessary to remove any heat shields.

6. Drain the transaxle fluid.

7. Remove the right and left halfshafts from the transaxle case.

8. Disconnect the range selector cable, if equipped. Remove the engine rear cover.

9. Support the weight of the engine from above. Remove the bell housing cover. Support the transaxle and remove the remaining lower bolts.

10. Remove the transaxle mount insulator bolt and the cover from inside the front fender shield. Remove the insulator bracket bolts and remove the bracket. Remove the transaxle mount bracket.

11. Remove, slide away from the engine, and lower the transaxle.

12. Reverse the removal procedure in install. Torque the mounting bolts to specification. Use new driveshaft retaining rings. Adjust the gearshift lever and range selector lever.

1988–91 GALANT AND SIGMA

1. Disconnect the battery cables and remove the battery and battery tray.

2. Drain the engine coolant and the transaxle fluid into suitable containers.

3. Disconnect the connections for the air flow sensor, purge control solenoid valve and air cleaner assembly.

4. Disconnect the air intake hose and breather hose and remove the air cleaner assembly. Raise and support the vehicle safely.

5. Disconnect the transaxle control cables. Disconnect the lower radiator hose and the water inlet pipe **B**. Disconnect all the connections on the water pipe assembly.

6. Disconnect the back-up light switch connector and the engine wiring harness connector.

7. Place a suitable transaxle jack under the transaxle to support. Remove the transaxle mount bracket cap and the mount bracket.

8. Remove the air compressor from the vehicles equipped with electronic controlled suspension.

9. Disconnect the clutch release cylinder and the clutch tube bracket. Disconnect the speedometer cable. Remove the starter assembly.

10. Remove the engine under cover panel. Disconnect the tie rod end from the steering knuckle. Disconnect the lower arm ball joint.

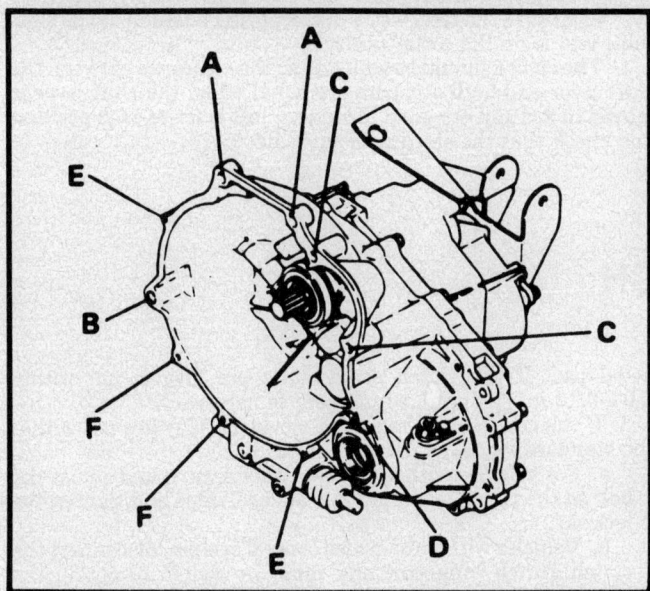

Torque Cordia/Tredia and Mirage transaxle bolts as follows: A—31–40 ft. lbs.; B—31–40 ft. lbs.; C—16–23 ft. lbs.; D—22–25 ft. lbs.; E—7–9 ft. lbs.; F—11–16 ft. lbs.

11. Disconnect the left side halfshaft and bearing bracket.

12. Remove the driveshaft nut from the right side shaft and remove the halfshaft, circlip, bolt, bearing bracket, shaft assembly and circlip.

13. Remove the transaxle stay (bracket). Remove the remaining transaxle retaining bolts, pull the transaxle clear from the engine and lower it away from the vehicle.

14. Reverse the removal procedure in install. Torque the mounting bolts to specification. Use new halfshaft retaining rings. Adjust the gearshift lever and range selector lever.

MIRAGE AND PRECIS

1. Remove the battery and battery tray. On turbocharged vehicles, remove the air cleaner housing assembly.

2. On 5 speed transaxles, disconnect the electrical connector for the selector control valve. On turbocharged vehicles, remove the actuator bolts, remove the actuator to shaft pin and then remove the actuator. Replace the collar with a new part.

3. Disconnect and remove the speedometer and clutch cables.

4. Disconnect the back-up lamp electrical connector. Remove the starter motor electrical harness.

5. Remove the 6 transaxle bolts accessible from the top side of the transaxle.

6. Unbolt and remove the starter motor.

7. Raise the vehicle and support it safely. Then, remove the splash shield from under the engine. Drain the transaxle fluid.

8. Disconnect the extension rod and the shift rod at the transaxle end and lower them.

9. Disconnect the stabilizer bar at the lower control arm.

10. Remove the halfshaft.

11. Support the transaxle from below with a floor jack or similar device. Make sure the support is widely enough spread that the transaxle pan will not be damaged. Then, remove the 5 attaching bolts and remove the bell housing cover.

12. Remove the lower bolts attaching the transaxle to the engine.

13. Remove the transaxle insulator mount bolt. Remove the cover from inside the right fender shield and remove the transaxle support bracket.

14. Remove the transaxle mount bracket.

15. Pull the assembly away from the engine and then lower it from the vehicle.

16. Installation is the reverse of removal. Refill the transaxle with the specified fluid to the level of the filler plug. Adjust the clutch cable. Make sure the gearshift lever works correctly.

ECLIPSE

1. Disconnect the negative and positive battery cables and remove the battery.

2. Remove the Auto-Cruise Actuator and bracket underhood, on the passenger side inner fender wall.

3. Drain the transaxle oil. On 4WD the transfer case also has a drain plug.

4. Remove the air intake hose.

5. Remove the cotter pin securing the select and shift cables and remove the cable ends from the transaxle.

6. Remove the connection for the clutch release cylinder and without disconnecting the hydraulic line, secure at the body side aside.

7. Disconnect the backup light switch and the speedometer cable.

8. Disconnect the starter electrical connections and remove the starter motor.

9. Remove the transaxle mount bracket.

10. Raise and safely support vehicle and remove the under cover.

11. Remove the cotter pin and disconnect the tie rod end from the steering knuckle.

12. Remove the self-locking nut and remove the lower arm ball joint.

13. Remove the halfshafts by inserting a prybar between the transaxle case and the driveshaft and prying the shaft from the transaxle. Do not pull on the driveshaft. Doing so damages the inboard joint. Use the prybar. Do not insert the prybar so far the oil seal in the case is damaged. On 4WD, remove the right halfshaft. The left halfshaft can be removed by tapping with a plastic hammer. Remove the shaft with the hub and knuckle as an assembly. Don't tap on the center bearing or it will be damaged. Tie the shafts back aside. Note the circle clip on the end of the inboard shafts. These should not be reused.

14. On 4WD, disconnect the front exhaust pipe.

15. On 4WD, remove the transfer case by removing the attaching bolts, moving the transfer case to the left and lowering the front side. Remove it from the rear driveshaft. Be careful of the oil seal. Do not allow the prop shaft to hang; tie it up. Cover the transfer case openings to keep out dirt.

16. Remove the underpan from the transaxle bell housing. On 4WD, also remove the crossmember and the triangular gusset.

17. Remove the transaxle lower coupling bolt. It is just above the halfshaft opening on 2WD or transfer case opening on 4WD.

18. Remove the transaxle assembly. On turbocharged equipped vehicles, take care to prevent damaging the lower radiator hose with the transaxle housing. Wind tape around the lower hose and put tape on the transaxle housing. Support the transaxle assembly, move the transaxle to the right and lower it.

To install:

19. Installation is the reverse of the removal procedure, with the following points to watch. When installing the halfshafts, always use new circlips on the axle ends. Take care to get the inboard joint parts straight, not bent relative to the axle. Care must be taken to ensure that the oil seal lip of the transaxle is not damaged by the serrated part of the driveshaft.

20. When bolting up the starter, make sure the ground cable is securely fastened.

21. Make sure the vehicle is level when refilling the transaxle. Use Hypoid gear oil or equivalent, GL-4 or higher. Check transaxle and transfer case on 4WD.

Linkage Adjustment

There are 2 cables, the select cable and the shift cable.

1. On the transaxle, put select lever in **N** and move the transaxle shift lever to put it in **4th** gear. Depress the clutch, if necessary, to shift.

2. Move the shift lever in the vehicle to the **4th** gear position until it contacts the stop.

3. Turn the adjuster turn buckle so the shift cable eye aligns with the eye in the gear shift lever. When installing the cable eye, make sure the flange side of the plastic bushing at the shift cable end is on the cotter pin side.

4. The cables should be adjusted so the clearance between the shift lever and both stoppers are equal when the shift lever is moved to 3rd and 4th gear. Move the shift lever to each position and check that the shifting is smooth.

CLUTCH

Removal and Installation

1. Disconnect the negative battery cable.

2. Remove the transmission. It is recommended that a clutch aligning tool be inserted in the clutch disc during disassembly.

3. Diagonally remove pressure plate bolts a little at a time each. Then remove the pressure plate and driven disc.

4. From inside the bell housing, remove the return spring clip and remove the release bearing assembly. On the Starion, remove the release fork by sliding it in the direction of the arrow to disengage the fulcrum from the clip. Attempting to remove it any other way will damage the clip.

5. If necessary, remove the release control lever and spring pin with a $^5/_{16}$ in. punch. Always replace spring pins, as they should not be reused. Remove the control lever shaft assembly and clutch shift arm, 2 felt packings and 2 return springs.

6. Installation is the reverse of removal. Torque the pressure plate bolts, diagonally, to 11–15 ft. lbs.

Free-Play Adjustment

CABLE TYPE

1. Depress the clutch pedal by hand, free-play, until tension is felt, should be 0.6–0.8 in.

2. If the free-play is too great or too little, turn the outer cable adjusting nut for adjustment.

3. After adjustment is made, depress the clutch pedal several times and recheck.

HYDRAULIC TYPE

Except Eclipse

1. Measure the clutch pedal clevis pin play at the pedal pad, it should be 6.9–7.1 in. for Cordia and Tredia or 7.4–7.6 in. for Starion.

2. Measure the clutch pedal height from the surface of the pad to the floor, it should be 0.04–0.12 in.

3. If adjustment is required, turn the clutch switch to adjust the pedal height then tighten the locknut.

4. To adjust the clevis pin play turn the pushrod and then tighten the locknut.

5. If adjustment can not be made there is probably either air in the system or the clutch cylinder or clutch disc is defective.

6. Bleed the air from the system as follows.

7. Loosen the bleeder screw at the clutch slave cylinder.

8. Push the clutch pedal down slowly while the bleeder screw is opened.

9. Hold the pedal down and tighten the bleeder screw.

10. Check the clutch master cylinder and refill with fluid, if necessary. Repeat the bleeding procedure several times until all air is dispelled from the system.

Eclipse

1. Measure the clutch pedal height from the face of the pedal pad to the firewall. If the pedal height is not within 6.70–6.89 in. (170–175mm), adjustment is necessary.

2. Measure the clutch pedal clevis pin play at the face of the pedal pad. If the clutch pedal clevis pin play is not within 0.04–0.12 in. (1–3mm), adjustment is necessary.

3. If the clutch pedal height or clevis pin play are not within the standard value, adjust as follows:

   a. For vehicles without cruise control, turn and adjust the bolt so the pedal height is the standard value and tighten the locknut.

   b. Vehicles with auto-cruise control system, disconnect the clutch switch connector and turn the switch to obtain the standard clutch pedal height. Then, lock with the locknut.

   c. Turn the pushrod to adjust the clutch pedal clevis pin play to agree with the standard value and secure the pushrod with the locknut.

NOTE: When adjusting the clutch pedal height or the clutch pedal clevis pin play, be careful not to push the pushrod toward the master cylinder.

   d. Check that when the clutch pedal is depressed all the way 5.9 in. (149mm), the interlock switch switches over from ON to OFF.

Clutch Master Cylinder

Removal and Installation

1. Disconnect the negative battery cable. Loosen the bleeder screw and drain the clutch fluid; on the Eclipse, it may be necessary to remove the air filter for access. Disconnect the pushrod at the clutch pedal by removing the cotter pin.

2. Disconnect the hydraulic tube at the master cylinder. Remove the clutch master cylinder.

3. Installation is the reverse of removal. Use a new cotter pin. Bleed the system. Torque the bolts or nuts to 7–11 ft. lbs. Torque the clutch tube connection at the master cylinder to 9.4–12.3 ft. lbs.

Clutch Slave Cylinder

Removal and Installation

1. Disconnect the negative battery cable. Loosen the bleeder screw and drain the fluid.

2. Disconnect the clutch tube or hose from the slave cylinder.

3. Unbolt and remove the slave cylinder.

4. Installation is the reverse of removal. Torque the clutch tube eye bolt to 14–18 ft. lbs.

Bleeding The Hydraulic Clutch System

Make sure the clutch master cylinder is filled with the correct fluid. Loosen the bleeder screw at the slave cylinder. Push the clutch pedal down slowly until all air is expelled and do not release, but hold it depressed. Retighten the bleeder screw. Release the clutch pedal. Refill the master cylinder to the correct level.

AUTOMATIC TRANSMISSION

Removal and Installation

1. Loosen the oil pan screws, tap the oil pan at one corner to break it loose and then allow the fluid to drain out one side. Remove the pan and remove the remaining fluid.

2. Disconnect the battery negative cable. Remove its attaching bolt and then remove the transmission pan filler tube by pulling it upward and out of the transmission case.

3. Raise and support the vehicle safely. Remove both top transmission attaching bolts from the converter housing.

4. Disconnect the starter wiring and remove the starter.

5. Disconnect the oil cooler hoses at the metal tubes near the engine block. Then, unbolt and remove the tubes and their mountings from the block.

6. Remove the 4 bolts and remove the converter housing cover. Remove the torque converter bolts.

7. Disconnect the speedometer cable. Disconnect the transmission control rod and the connection lever at the cross shaft assembly.

8. Disconnect the transmission ground cable. Remove the driveshaft.

9. Support the rear of the transmission with a floor jack. Unbolt the transmission rear support bracket by removing 2 bolts on either side. Then, unbolt the bracket from the transmission.

10. Remove the remaining bolts from the area of the converter housing. Separate the transmission from the engine and remove it.

11. Installation is the reverse of the removal procedure. Before beginning, check the distance between the front of the bell housing and the torque converter driveplate bolts with a straight-edge and ruler. The distance must be at least 1.38 in. After installation, refill the transmission with the approved fluid. Check that the transmission will start only in **N** and **P** positions and that the backup light lights in **R** position. Torque the driveplate to crankshaft bolts to 94–100 ft. lbs. Torque the converter housing to engine bolts to 31–39 ft. lbs.

Pan and Filter Replacement

1. Raise and support the vehicle safely.

2. Loosen and remove the transmission pan drain plug. As required, remove the splash shield.

3. Remove the pan bolts and pan. Remove the filter.

4. Install a new filter, as required. Reinstall the oil pan using a new gasket. Add the proper amount of transmission fluid after. Start the engine and move the selector lever through all positions. Allow the engine to run until normal operating temperature is reached.

5. Recheck the fluid level with the dipstick, add fluid, if necessary.

Kickdown Band Adjustment

1. Remove the transmission oil pan.

2. Loosen the band adjusting stem locknut and turn the stem outward. Then, turn the stem inward with a torque wrench until the required torque reaches 5–7 ft. lbs. Then, back the stem off exactly 2 turns.

3. Hold the adjustment and torque the locknut to 11–29 ft. lbs.

AUTOMATIC TRANSAXLE

Transaxle Assembly

Removal and Installation

EXCEPT ECLIPSE

NOTE: The transaxle and converter must be removed and installed as an assembly.

1. Disconnect the negative battery cable. Remove the battery tray. Remove the coolant reservoir and windshield washer tank. Remove the air cleaner and housing. Where so equipped, disconnect also the pulse generator connector and solenoid valve connector.

2. Disconnect the throttle control cable at the carburetor and the manual control cable at the transaxle.

3. Disconnect from the transaxle; the neutral safety switch connector, fluid cooler hose and the 4 upper bolts connecting the engine to the transaxle.

4. Raise and support the vehicle safely.

5. Remove the front wheels. Remove the engine splash shield.

6. Drain the transaxle fluid.

7. Remove the right and left halfshafts from the transaxle case. Remove the strut bars and the stabilizer bar from the lower arms.

8. Disconnect the speedometer cable. Disconnect and plug the oil cooler hoses. Remove the starter motor.

9. Remove the lower cover from the converter housing. Remove the 3 bolts that connect the converter to the engine drive plate.

NOTE: Never support the full weight of the transaxle on the engine driveplate.

10. Turn and force the converter back and away from the engine driveplate.

11. Support the weight of the engine from above. Support the transaxle and remove the remaining bolts.

12. Remove the transaxle mount insulator bolt.

13. Remove and lower the transaxle and converter as an assembly.

14. To install reverse the removal procedure. Torque the converter housing bolts according to the illustration. Torque the driveplate bolts to 25–30 ft. lbs. Be sure to connect all controls, wiring and hoses. Use new retaining rings when installing the drive axles. Refill the transaxle to the proper level with the recommended fluid.

ECLIPSE

1. Disconnect the battery cables and remove the battery.

2. On vehicle equipped with Auto-cruise, remove the control actuator and bracket.

3. Drain the transaxle fluid.

4. Remove the air cleaner assembly.

5. Remove the adjusting nut and disconnect the shift cable.

6. Disconnect and tag as required the electrical connectors for the solenoid, neutral safety switch (inhibitor switch), the pulse generator kickdown servo switch and oil temperature sensor.

7. Disconnect the speedometer cable and oil cooler lines.

8. Disconnect the wires to the starter motor and remove the starter.

9. Remove the upper transaxle to engine bolts.

10. Remove the transaxle bracket.

11. Raise and safely support vehicle and remove the sheet metal under guard.

12. Remove the tie rod ends and the ball joints from the steering knuckle.

13. Remove the halfshafts by inserting a prybar between the transaxle case and the driveshaft and prying the shaft from the transaxle. Do not pull on the driveshaft. Doing so damages the inboard joint. Use the prybar. Do not insert the prybar so far the oil seal in the case is damaged. Tie the halfshafts aside.

14. Remove the lower bell housing cover and remove the bolts holding the flexplate to the torque converter. These are special bolts. Do not loose. To remove, turn the engine crankshaft with a box wrench and bring the bolts into position one at a time. After removing the bolts, push the torque converter toward the transaxle so it doesn't stay on the engine side and allow oil to pour out the converter hub.

15. Remove the lower transaxle to engine bolts and remove the transaxle assembly.

To install:

16. Installation is the reverse of the removal process. After the torque converter has been mounted on the transaxle, install the transaxle assembly on the engine. If the torque converter is first mounted on the engine, a damaged oil seal in the transaxle could result. Tighten the driveplate bolts to 34–38 ft. lbs. Install the bell housing cover.

17. Install the halfshafts to the transaxle and connect the tie rods and ball joint connections.

18. Install the underguard and the bracket. Reconnect the cable controls, oil cooler lines and electrical connections.

19. Lower vehicle, refill with Dexron® or Dexron® II automatic transmission fluid. Start engine and allow to idle for 2 minutes. Apply parking brake and move selector through each gear position , ending in **N**. Recheck fluid level and add, if necessary. Fluid level should be between the marks in the **HOT** range.

Shift Linkage Adjustment

1. The shifter cable adjustment is done at the neutral safety switch (inhibitor switch). Locate the switch on the transaxle and not the alignment hole in the arm and the body of the switch. Place the selector lever in **N**. Place the manual lever of the transaxle in **N**.

2. Align the holes on the switch.

3. If the cable needs to be adjusted, loosen the nut on the cable end and pull the cable end by hand until the alignment holes match. Tighten the nut. Check that the transaxle shifts and conforms to the positions of the selector lever.

Throttle Linkage Adjustment

1. Check that the throttle lever is in the curb idle position, with the engine **OFF** but at normal operating temperature.

2. At the lower cable bracket, raise the cone shaped cover to uncover a small fitting on the cable. By loosening the locknut and adjuster nut, make the distance between the fitting on the cable and the lower collar 0.020–0.060 in.

3. With the throttle in the wide open position, check that the cable does not bind.

NOTE: Not all vehicles use a throttle linkage. The throttle position sensor on some vehicles feeds an electric signal to the transaxle so no linkage adjustment is required. If the throttle position sensor itself needs to be adjusted, use the following procedure:

Throttle Cable Adjustment

1. Run the engine to normal operating temperature and make sure the throttle lever on the carburetor is in the curb idle position.

2. Raise the cover on the throttle cable to expose the nipple.

3. Loosen the lower cable bolt.

4. Move the lower cable bracket until the distance between the nipple and the top of the cable end is 0.5mm.

5. Tighten the lower cable bracket bolt and check the adjustment by pulling the cable upward with the throttle plate in the wide open position. The cable should move freely.

Detent Cable Adjustment

1. Several special factory tools may be required for this operation. Locate the detent switch on the transaxle. Remove the road dirt from around it. Remove the snapring and pull out the kickdown servo switch.

2. To keep the piston in the transaxle from turning, the special tool has fingers or pawls that engage the slots in the piston to hold it while adjustment is made. Do not press in on the piston with the special tool or its equal. With the piston restrained from turning, loosen the locknut. Using the special tool, tighten to 7.2 ft. lbs. (10 Nm) and return or back off the adjustment 2 times. Then tighten to 3.6 ft. lbs. (5 Nm). Finally back off the adjustment 2–2¼ turns and making sure the piston does not turn, tighten the locknut.

3. Install a new O-ring into the groove in the switch, install the switch and fit the snapring in place.

TRANSFER CASE

Transfer Case

Removal and Installation

1. Disconnect the battery negative cable.
2. Raise and safely support vehicle.
3. Disconnect the front exhaust pipe.
4. Unbolt the transfer case assembly and remove by sliding it off the rear driveshaft. Be careful not to damage the oil seal in the transfer case output housing. Do not let the rear driveshaft hang. Tie up with wire. Cover the opening in the transaxle to keep oil from dripping and to keep dirt out.

To install:

5. Installation is the reverse of the removal procedure. Use care when installing the rear driveshaft to the transfer case output shaft. Tighten the transfer case to transaxle bolts to 40–43 ft. lbs.

6. Install the exhaust pipe using a new gasket.
7. Check oil levels in transaxle and transfer case.

Linkage Adjustment

There are 2 cables, the select cable and the shift cable.

1. On the transaxle, put select lever in **N** and move the transfer case shift lever to **N**.

2. Turn the adjuster turn buckle so the shift cable eye aligns with the eye in the select lever. When installing the cable eye, make sure the flange side of the plastic bushing at the shift cable end is on the cotter pin side.

3. The cables should be adjusted so the clearance between the shift lever and both stoppers are equal when the shift lever is moved to 3rd and 4th gear. Move the shift and select levers to each position and check that the shifting is smooth.

DRIVE AXLE

Halfshaft

Removal and Installation
EXCEPT CENTER BEARING

1. Remove the hub center cap and remove the cotter pin, then loosen the driveshaft (axle) nut. Loosen the wheel lug nuts.
2. Raise and safely support the vehicle. Remove the front wheels. Remove the drive axle (hub) nut and remove the engine splash shield.
3. Using the tools required, remove the tie rod ends, stabilizer bar nut, the lower arm ball joint nut and lower arm ball joint.
4. Disconnect the oxygen sensor connection, if necessary. Drain the transaxle fluid.
5. Remove any retaining circlips. Insert a suitable tool between the transaxle case, on the raised rib, and the halfshaft double offset joint case. Do not insert the tool too deeply or the seal may be damaged. Move the tool to the right to withdraw the left halfshaft; to the left to remove the right halfshaft.
6. Plug the transaxle case with a clean rag to prevent dirt from entering the case.
7. Use a puller driver mounted on the wheel studs to push the halfshaft from the front hub. Take care to prevent the spacer from falling out of place.
8. Assembly is the reverse of removal. Insert the halfshaft into the hub first, then install the transaxle end. Torque the drive axle nut, if equipped, to 144–188 ft. lbs.

NOTE: Always use a new DOJ retaining ring every time the driveshaft is removed.

CENTER BEARING

1. Remove the hub center cap and loosen the halfshaft (axle) nut. Loosen the wheel lug nuts.
2. Raise and safely support the vehicle. Remove the front wheels. Remove the engine splash shield.
3. Remove the lower ball joint and strut bar from the lower control arm.
4. Drain the transaxle fluid.
5. Before removing the halfshaft remove the center bearing snapring.
6. Remove the halfshaft from the transaxle by lightly tapping the outer race with a plastic hammer.
7. Do not insert a prybar between the transaxle case and the halfshaft, as damage to the dust cover of the shaft will occur.
8. If the halfshaft is pulled out from the birfield joint side there is danger of causing damage to the joint.
9. Drive the shaft out of the hub by lightly tapping the halfshaft end with a plastic hammer.

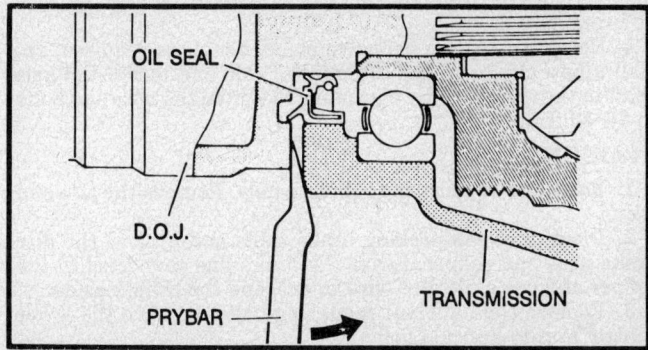

Half shaft removal—except Mirage with center bearing

10. Plug the transaxle case with a clean rag to prevent dirt from entering the case.
11. Use a puller driver mounted on the wheel studs to push the halfshaft from the front hub. Take care to prevent the spacer from falling out of place.
12. Assembly is reverse of removal. Insert the halfshaft into the hub first, then install the transaxle end. Always use a new DOJ retaining ring every time the halfshaft is removed.

CV-Boot

These vehicles used several different types of joints. Engine size, transmission type, whether the joint is an inboard or outboard joint, even which side of the vehicle is being serviced will make a difference in joint type. Proper identification is important when ordering parts. Be sure to properly identify the joint before attempting joint or boot replacement. Look for identification numbers at the big end of the boots and on the end of the metal retainer bands.

The 4 types of joints used are the Birfield Joint, (BJ), the Tripod Joint (TJ), the Double Offset Joint (DOJ) and the Rzeppa Joint (RJ). In addition, some left hand shafts will have a round dynamic damper installed on the shaft. Special grease is generally used with these joints and is often supplied with the replacement joint and/or boot. Do not use regular chassis grease.

In most cases, a specification is called out for the distance between the large and small boot bands. This is so the boot will not be installed either too loose or too tight which could cause early wear and cracking, allowing the grease to get out and water and dirt in, leading to early joint failure.

Removal and Installation
EXCEPT DOUBLE OFFSET JOINT

Although joint types vary, the basic procedures are the same, with the exception of the Double Offset Joint. The following is a general procedure which should apply to most applications.
1. Remove the halfshaft.
2. Remove the snapring next to the tripod joint spider from the halfshaft with snapring pliers and remove the spider from the shaft. Do not disassemble the spider and use care in handling.
3. Side cutter pliers can be used to cut the metal retaining bands.
4. If the boot is be reused, wrap vinyl tape around the spline part of the shaft so the boot will not be damaged when removed. Remove the dynamic damper, if used, and boots from the shaft.
To install:
5. Double check that the correct replacement parts are being installed. Wrap vinyl tape around the splines to protect the boot and install the boots and damper, if used, in the correct order.
6. Fill the inside of the boot with the specified grease. Often the grease supplied in the replacement parts kit is meant to be divided in half, with half being used to lube the joint and half being used inside the boot. Keep grease off the rubber part of the dynamic damper, if used.
7. Secure the boot bands with the halfshaft horizontal.

DOUBLE OFFSET JOINT

1. Remove the halfshaft. The Double Offset Joint (DOJ) is bigger than other joints and in these applications, is only used as an inboard joint.
2. Side cutter pliers can be used to cut the metal retaining bands.
3. Locate and remove the large circlip at the base of the joint. Remove the outer race, the body of the joint.
4. Makematch marks on the shaft, DOJ inner race and cage. Remove the joint balls and the small snapring from the shaft.

With a brass drift pin, tap lightly and evenly around the inner race to remove the race and then the inner cage from the shaft.

5. If the boot is to be reused, wipe the grease from the splines and wrap the splines in vinyl tape before sliding the boot from the shaft.

To install:

6. Be sure to tape the shaft splines before installing the boots. Fill the inside of the boot with the specified grease. Often the grease supplied in the replacement parts kit is meant to be divided in half, with half being used to lube the joint and half being used inside the boot.

7. Install the cage onto the halfshaft so the small diameter side of the cage is installed first. Align the matchmarks made at disassembly on the inner race and shaft. With a brass drift pin, tap lightly and evenly around the inner race to install the race until it comes into contact with the rib of the shaft. Apply the specified grease to the inner race and cage and fit them together aligning the matchmarks. Insert the balls into the cage.

8. Install the outer race, the body of the joint, after filling with the specified grease. The outer race should be filled with this grease.

9. Tighten the boot bands securely.

Driveshaft and U-Joints

Removal and Installation

EXCEPT 4WD

1. Raise and support the vehicle safely. Matchmark the rear flange yoke and the differential pinion flange.

2. Remove the bolts from the rear flange. Remove the driveshaft by pulling it from the rear of the transmission extension housing. Place a container under the transmission extension housing to collect any oil leakage when the driveshaft is removed.

3. To install the shaft, align the front sleeve yoke with the splines of the transmission output shaft and push the driveshaft into the extension housing.

NOTE: Be careful not to damage the rear transmission seal lip upon installation

4. Align the matchmarks on the rear yokes, install the bolts, and Torque to 36–43 ft. lbs.

5. Inspect the oil level of the transmission.

4WD

1. Raise and safely support vehicle

2. The rear driveshaft is a 3 piece unit, with a front, center and rear propeller shaft. Remove the nuts and insulators from the support bearings. Work carefully. There will be a number of spacers which will differ from vehicle to vehicle. Check the number of spacers and write down their locations for reference during reassembly.

3. Make matchmarks on the rear differential companion flange and the rear driveshaft flange yoke. Remove the companion shaft bolts and remove the driveshaft, keeping it as straight as possible so as to ensure that the boot is not damaged or pinched. Use care to keep from damaging the oil seal in the output housing of the transfer case.

NOTE: Damage to the boot can be avoided and work will be easier, if a piece of cloth or similar material is inserted in the boot.

4. Do not lower the rear of the vehicle or oil will flow from the transfer case. Cover the opening to keep out dirt.

To install:

5. Installation is the reverse of the removal process. The shafts should be checked for straightness. A dial indicator and V-blocks set as much as possible to the end of the shaft can be used. The limit is 0.024 in. Check the bearing for smooth operation.

6. At installation, match up the companion shaft marks made at removal.

7. Install the spacers and insulators where they were before or use new spacers of equal thickness. Torque the nuts to 22–29 ft. lbs.

8. Lower vehicle and test drive for signs of vibration.

Front Axle Shaft, Bearing and Seal

Removal and Installation

1. Remove the hub cotter pin, axle nut and washer.

2. Raise and safely support vehicle. Remove front wheels. Remove the brake caliper and hang by a wire.

3. Remove the ball joint from the lower arm and disconnect the tie rod end.

4. Remove the halfshaft.

5. Unbolt the lower end of the strut and remove the hub and steering knuckle assembly.

6. Set up a puller with the knuckle/hub in a vise and pull the hub from the knuckle. If the hub and knuckle are disassembled by hitting them with a hammer, the bearing will be damaged.

7. Once the hub and outer bearing inner race are removed with a puller, the bearing outer races can be removed by tapping out with a brass drift pin and a hammer.

To install:

8. Apply a thin coat of grease to the outside of the outer races and install into the hub with a bearing driver.

9. Apply multi-purpose grease to the bearings, inside surface of the hub and the lip of the grease seal. Place the outside bearing into the knuckle and install the seal with a driver.

10. The hub is assembled to the knuckle with a puller. Draw the parts together firmly to seat the bearings. Use a small torque wrench to check the bearing turning torque. It should be 11 inch lbs. or less. Check that the bearings feel smooth when rotated. A dial indicator is used to check endplay which should be 0.008 in. or less.

11. Apply a thin coat of grease to the lip of the halfshaft side axle seal and drive into place until it contacts the inner bearing outer race.

12. Installation of the hub assembly is the reverse of the removal procedure.

Rear Axle Shafts, Bearing and Seal

Removal and Installation

EXCEPT STARION

1. Raise and support the vehicle safely. Remove the tire and wheel.

2. Remove the brake drum and brake shoes. Remove the 4 wheel side flange nuts and bolts.

3. Connect a flanged slide hammer to the axle flange and pull the axle from the differential. Take care not to damage the side differential seals.

4. Repair or replace defective components, as required. Install a new circlip on the differential side and install the axle shaft in the reverse order of removal. Tighten the nuts and bolts to 36–43 ft. lbs.

STARION

1. Raise and support the vehicle safely. Remove the tire and wheel.

2. Disconnect the parking brake cable and remove the disc brake pads and caliper. Leave the brake line connected to the caliper and use a piece of wire to suspend the caliper aside.

3. Remove the halfshaft mounting bolts. Remove the lower control arm-to-knuckle bolt.

4. Remove the strut assembly retaining bolts and remove the axle housing assembly.

5. Remove the axle shaft from the axle housing as follows:

a. Remove the companion flange nut. Using a plastic hammer tap the axle shaft out of the axle housing.

b. Remove the spacer, outer bearing, dust cover, companion flange, dust cover, oil seal, inner bearing, axle housing and dust cover.

6. Reassemble the axle shaft into the axle housing and install the axle housing by reversing the removal procedure. Torque the companion flange nut to 188–217 ft. lbs. Torque the strut bolts to 36–51 ft. lbs., the halfshaft mounting bolt/nuts to 40–47 ft. lbs. and the lower control arm bolt/nut to 51–58 ft. lbs.

Front Wheel Hub, Knuckle and Bearings

Removal and Installation

1. Raise and support the vehicle safely. Remove the tire and wheel. Remove the grease cap and halfshaft nut.
2. Remove the brake caliper and suspend it from the body without disconnecting the hydraulic line.
3. Disconnect the stabilizer bar and strut bar from the lower arm.
4. Loosen but do not remove the ball joint stud nut and press the ball joint stud out of the knuckle; then remove the nut.
5. Press the halfshaft out of the hub.
6. Disconnect the tie rod end ball joint from the knuckle in the same way as the lower ball joint was disconnected.
7. Remove the nuts and bolts connecting the knuckle to the strut and remove the hub and knuckle.
8. The hub must now be pressed out of the knuckle using a special tool set such as MB990998–01 and MB991001.
9. Assembly is the reverse of removal.
10. Front wheel drive vehicles require no bearing adjustment. The axle washer must be installed, "taper side" facing out. Tighten the axle nut to 144–188 ft. lbs. Align the nearest cotter pin hole and install cotter pin.

Pinion Seal

Removal and Installation

ECLIPSE 4WD REAR DIFFERENTIAL

1. Raise and safely support vehicle.
2. Make matchmarks on the rear driveshaft and companion flange and remove the shaft. Don't let it hang from the transaxle. Tie it up to the underbody.
3. Remove the large self-locking nut in the center of the companion flange.
4. With a suitable puller, remove the flange. Pry the old seal out.

To install:

5. Installation is the reverse of the removal process. Apply a thin coat of multi-purpose grease to the seal lip and the companion flange seal contacting surface. Install the new seal with a suitable driver. Install the companion flange. Torque the locknut to 116–160 ft. lbs.
6. Install the propeller shaft, matching up the marks made at disassembly. Torque the bolts to 40–47 ft. lbs.

Differential Carrier

Removal and Installation

ECLIPSE 4WD REAR DIFFERENTIAL

1. Raise and safely support vehicle.
2. Drain the differential gear oil and remove the center exhaust pipe.
3. Make matchmarks on the rear propeller shaft and companion flange and remove the rear driveshaft. Don't let it hang from the transaxle. Tie it up to the under body.
4. Remove the halfshafts by unbolting the 3 bolts at the wheel hub and prying the inboard joint from the carrier housing.
5. The large differential carrier support plate-to-under body bolts use self-locking nuts. Before removing them, support the rear axle assembly in the middle. Remove the locknuts, the support plate and the square dynamic damper from the rear of the carrier.
6. Remove the large bolts and lower the differential carrier.

To install:

7. Installation is the reverse of the removal process. Clean all parts well. The large locknut that held the mounting plate to the under body should not be reused. The replacements should be torqued to 80–94 ft. lbs.
8. Use new circlips on the inboard joints and snap into place.
9. Install the rear driveshaft, matching up the marks made at disassembly. Torque the bolts to 40–47 ft. lbs.

STEERING

Steering Wheel

Removal and Installation

1. Disconnect the negative battery cable. Pry off the steering wheel center foam pad or remove the screws from the back, depending on vehicle. Disconnect the electrical connector for the horn.
2. Remove the steering wheel retaining nut after marking the wheel and shaft position.
3. Using a steering wheel puller, remove the steering wheel.
4. Installation is the reverse of the removal procedure. Be sure the front wheels are in a straight ahead position.

Steering Column

Removal and Installation

1. Disconnect the negative battery cable.
2. Remove the instrument panel under cover.
3. Remove the trim clip, foot shower duct and lap shower duct.
4. Remove the horn pad, steering wheel and column upper and lower cover.
5. Remove the band from the steering joint cover and remove the joint assembly and gear box connecting bolt.
6. Remove the lower and upper column brackets.
7. Remove the steering column assembly.
8. Installation is the reverse of the removal procedure.

Manual Steering Rack

Adjustment

1. Remove the rack and pinion assembly.
2. Mount rack in a vise and with a small torque wrench and an adapter to connect to the input shaft, position the rack at its center. Tighten the rack support cover, the bottom plug, to 11 ft. lbs. In the neutral position, rotate the shaft clockwise 1 turn in 4–6 seconds. Return the rack support cover 30–60 degrees

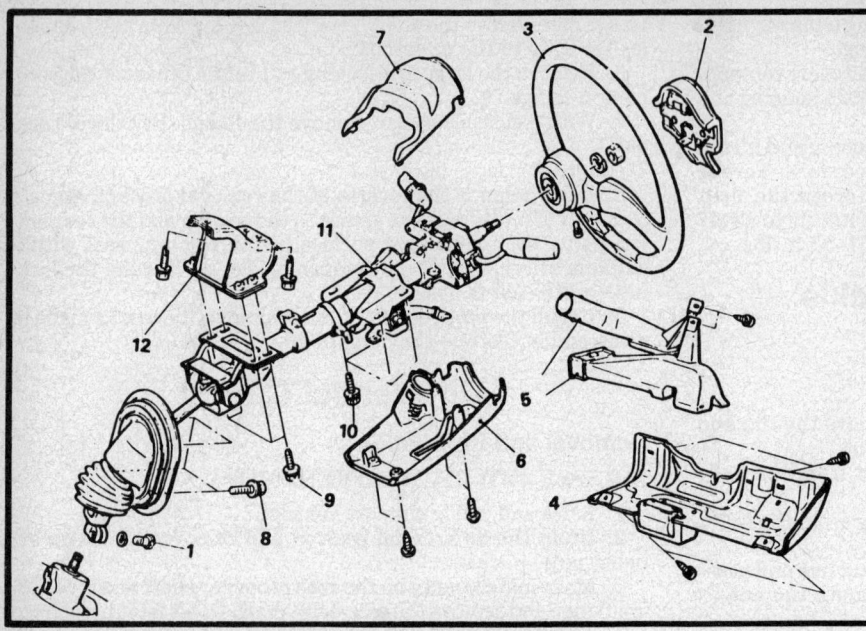

1. Joint assembly and gear box connecting bolt
2. Horn pad
3. Steering wheel
4. Instrument under cover
5. Foot shower duct and lap shower duct
6. Column cover lower
7. Column cover upper
8. Cover attaching bolt
9. Lower bracket installation bolt
10. Tilt bracket installation bolt
11. Steering column assembly
12. Column support

Steering wheel and column servicing—Eclipse

and adjust the torque from 0–90 degrees to 5–11 inch lbs. and from 90–650 degrees to 2–9 inch lbs.

3. When adjusting, set to the high side of the specification. Make sure there is no ratcheting or catching when operating the rack. If the rack cannot be adjusted to spec, check the rack support cover components or replace. After adjusting, lock the rack support cover with the locking nut.

Removal and Installation

CORDIA AND TREDIA

1. Raise and support the vehicle safely. Remove the front wheels.

2. Remove the bolt connecting the steering shaft universal joint with the steering gear. Before removing the bolt, mark its location and be sure the wheels are pointed straight.

3. Remove the tie rod ends from the hub knuckles. Disconnect bolts located near the inner tie rods on the crossmember. Remove right side sub-member from the No. 2 crossmember. Remove the gearbox from the No. 2 crossmember. Pull the gear box out from the right side of the vehicle.

4. Installation is the reverse of removal. Observe the following torques:
   Gear box-to-No. 2 crossmember—43–58 ft. lbs.
   Tie rod-to-rack—58–72 ft. lbs.
   Tie rod end locknut—36–40 ft. lbs.
   Tie rod-to-knuckle—17–25 ft. lbs.

MIRAGE

1. Support the vehicle. Remove front wheels.

2. Uncouple the shaft assembly from the gearbox from inside the passenger compartment.

3. Press the tie rod ends off the steering knuckles.

4. Cut the retaining band off the rubber boot that covers the joint connecting the box with the steering shaft.

5. Remove the 4 attaching bolts for both main steering box clamps. Pull the gearbox out toward the left side of the vehicle.

6. Install in reverse order, make sure the projections on the rubber mounting fit into the holes in the housing bracket and clamps.

7. Replace the band attaching the steering joint rubber boot. Make sure the steering wheel rotates smoothly throughout its travel. Adjust toe-in. Torque the steering box bolts to 43–58 ft. lbs. and the tie rod end attaching nuts to 11–25 ft. lbs.

PRECIS

1. Raise and support the vehicle safely. Remove the bolt which secures the universal joint in the steering shaft to the gearbox; inside the vehicle where the steering linkage passes through the toe board.

2. Remove the cotter pin from the tie rod end ball stud and loosen the nut. Press the ball stud out of the steering knuckle with a vice like tool such as MB991113 or equivalent; then remove the nut. Do the same on the other side.

3. Cut the band off the steering joint rubber boot.

4. Remove both attaching bolts from the gearbox housing clamp on either side and pull the gearbox out the left side of the vehicle. Work slowly to keep the unit from being damaged.

5. Install the unit in reverse order. There are rubber tabs on the inside and outside of the sleeve. The larger tab must go on the inside. Use a new band for the steering joint rubber boot. Adjust toe-in. Use the following torques: bracket attaching bolts, 43–58 ft. lbs.; ball stud nut, 17 ft. lbs., then turn farther to align castellations with the cotter pin hole and install a new cotter pin. Turn the steering wheel back and forth to test steering and support the vehicle safely.

ECLIPSE

1. Disconnect the negative battery cable. Raise and safely support vehicle.

2. Remove the bolt holding lower steering column joint to the rack and pinion input shaft.

3. Remove the cotter pins and disconnect the tie rod ends.

4. Locate the triangular brace near the stabilizer bar brackets on the crossmember and remove both the brace and the stabilizer bar brackets.

5. Remove the through bolt from the round roll stopper and remove the rear bolts from the center crossmember.

6. Disconnect the front exhaust pipe.

7. Remove the rack and pinion steering assembly and its rubber mounts. Move the rack to the right to remove from the crossmember. Use caution to avoid damaging the boots.

8. Installation is the reverse of the removal procedure. Note that none of the self-locking should be reused. Replace with new parts. When installing the rubber rack mounts, align the projection of the mounting rubber with the indentation in the crossmember. Check the steering wheel position with the front wheels straight ahead. Align the front end, if necessary.

Power Steering Rack

Adjustment

1. Disconnect the negative battery cable.
2. Raise and support the vehicle safely.
3. Remove the steering rack assembly.
4. Secure the steering rack assembly in a vise. Do not clamp the vise jaws on the steering housing tubes. Clamp the vise jaws only on the housing cast metal.
5. Remove the steering gear housing end plug from the steering gear shaft bore using tool 6103 or equivalent.
6. Remove the preload adjustment cap locknut from the steering gear housing bore using tool 6097 or equivalent.
7. Loosen the preload adjustment cap. Retorque the preload adjustment cap to 45–50 inch lbs. (5–6 Nm), then back off the plug by turning it 45–50 degrees counterclockwise.
8. Secure the preload adjustment cap with a new locknut using tool 6097 or equivalent. Do not allow the adjustment cap to rotate when tightening the locknut.
9. Install the end plug using tool 6103 or equivalent. Complete installation by reversing the removal procedure.

Removal and Installation
CORDIA AND TREDIA

1. Raise and support the vehicle safely. Remove the bolt attaching the steering shaft universal joint to the gearbox.
2. Remove the cotter pin from the tie rod end ball stud and then loosen the nut. Press the ball stud out of the steering knuckle with a vise like tool such as MB991113 or equivalent. Remove the nut and pull the stud out of the knuckle.
3. Place a drain pan under the gearbox and then disconnect the pressure and return hose connectors with a flare nut wrench and allow the fluid to drain.
4. Disconnect the hose from the bottom of the fuel filter and plug it.
5. Remove the fuel line clips to permit the fuel line to move.
6. Remove the brace from the rear engine roll stop.
7. Remove the crossmember support bracket from the No. 2 crossmember, located on the right side of the vehicle.
8. Unbolt and remove both bolts in each gearbox clamp, working from the engine compartment side.
9. Pull the gearbox out the right side of the vehicle, working carefully to keep the unit from being damaged.
10. Installation is the reverse of the removal procedure.

STARION

1. Raise and support the vehicle safely. Remove the clamp bolt which connects the steering box input shaft to the steering shaft.
2. Place a drain pan under, disconnect the pressure and return hoses at the gearbox.
3. Press the pitman arm off the gearbox with the special tool.
4. Remove the 4 attaching nuts and remove the steering box.
5. Install in reverse order, torquing the steering box mounting nuts/bolts to 25–29 ft. lbs. and the pitman arm shaft retaining nut to 25–33 ft. lbs. Fill the power steering pump with fluid, as required.

MIRAGE

1. Raise and support the vehicle safely. Remove the bolt which secures the universal joint in the steering shaft to the gearbox. It's just inside the vehicle where the steering linkage passes through the toe board.
2. Remove the cotter pin from the tie rod end ball stud and loosen the nut. Press the ball stud out of the steering knuckle with a vise like tool such as MB991113 or equivalent; then remove the nut. Do the same on the other side.
3. Cut the bad off the steering joint rubber boot. Place a drain pan under the steering box. Then, disconnect the pressure and return hoses at the gearbox.

4. Remove the stabilizer bar.
5. Remove the rear roll stopper-to-centermember bolt and move the rear roll stopper forward.
6. Remove both bolts in the clip on either side of the gearbox and remove the unit carefully out the left of the vehicle. Avoid damaging the rubber boots.
7. Installation is the reverse of the removal procedure.

GALANT AND SIGMA

1. Raise and support the vehicle safely. If equipped with electronically controlled suspension, remove the stabilizer bar.
2. Remove the cotter pin from the tie rod and ball stud and loosen the nut. Press the ball stud out of the steering knuckle with a vice like tool such as MB991113 or equivalent; then remove the nut. Do the same on the other side.
3. Drain the fluid from the system. Then, disconnect the pressure and return hoses at the gearbox.
4. Remove the bolt attaching the steering shaft universal joint to the gearbox. Disconnect the connector for the solenoid valve.
5. Remove the front bolt from the center crossmember. Remove the exhaust pipe hanger from the crossmember. Remove the front roll stopper bolt.
6. Disconnect the oxygen sensor connection. Disconnect the exhaust pipe at the front and lower it aside. Remove the stabilizer bar and bracket. Press the rear of the center crossmember downward.
7. Move the rack all the way to the right. Then, remove the bolts from the brackets. Tilt the gearbox downward and remove it toward the left. Avoid damaging the rubber boots.
8. Installation is the reverse of the removal procedure.

ECLIPSE

1. Disconnect the negative battery cable.
2. Raise the vehicle and support it safely.
3. Drain the power steering fluid.
4. Remove the bolt holding lower steering column joint to the rack and pinion input shaft.
5. Disconnect the return and high pressure lines from the rack assembly.
3. Remove the cotter pins and disconnect the tie rod ends.
4. Locate the triangular brace near the stabilizer bar brackets on the crossmember and remove both the brace and the stabilizer bar brackets.
5. Remove the through bolt from the round roll stopper and remove the rear bolts from the center crossmember.
6. Disconnect the front exhaust pipe.
7. Remove the rack and pinion steering assembly and its rubber mounts. Move the rack to the right to remove from the crossmember. Use caution to avoid damaging the boots.
8. Installation is the reverse of the removal procedure. Note that none of the self-locking nuts should be reused. Replace with new parts. When installing the rubber rack mounts, align the projection of the mounting rubber with the indentation in the crossmember.
9. Refill the system and bleed out the air. Check the steering wheel position with the front wheels straight ahead. Align the front end, if necessary.

Power Steering Pump

Removal and Installation

1. Disconnect the negative battery cable. Remove the reservoir cap and disconnect the return hose at the reservoir. Drain the fluid into a clean container.
2. As required, raise and support the vehicle safely. Loosen the pulley nut if the pulley is to be removed. Loosen the mounting bolts and remove the belt. Turn the pump over to pump remaining fluid into the container. Disconnect the pressure hose at the top of the pump. Disconnect the suction hose at the side of the pump and drain the fluid.

3. Remove the pump attaching bolts and lift the pump from the brackets.

4. Make sure the bracket bolts are tight and install the pump to the brackets.

5. If pulley had been removed, install it and tighten the nut securely. Bend the lock tab over the nut.

6. Install the drive belt and adjust to a tension of 22 lbs. at a deflection of 0.28–0.39 in. at the top center of the belt. Tighten the pump bolts securely to hold the tension.

7. Connect the pressure and return lines and fill the reservoir with approved fluid.

Belt Adjustment

1. Press the belt in about the center between the power steering pump pulley and the pulley it shares, usually the water pump pulley. With reasonable pressure applied, about 22 lbs., the belt should deflect about ¼–⅜ in.

2. Adjustment can be made by loosening the 3 bolts that hold the pump. Place a suitable bar or lever between the body of the pump and gently pry to get the desired tension.

3. Retighten the 3 bolts and check again.

System Bleeding

1. The reservoir should be full with the proper grade and type power steering fluid.

2. Raise and support the vehicle safely.

3. Turn the steering wheel fully to the right and left until no air bubbles appear in the fluid. Maintain the reservoir level.

4. Lower the vehicle and with the engine idling, turn the wheels fully to the right and left. Stop the engine.

5. If equipped, install a tube from the bleeder screw on the steering gear box to the reservoir.

6. Start the engine, turn the steering wheel fully to the left and loosen the bleeder screw.

7. Repeat the procedure until no air bubbles pass through the tube.

8. Tighten the bleeder screw and remove the tube. Refill the reservoir as needed and check that no further bubbles are present in the fluid. An abrupt rise in the fluid level after stopping the engine is a sign of incomplete bleeding. This will cause noise from the pump or control valve.

Tie Rod Ends

Removal and Installation

STARION

1. Raise and support the vehicle safely.

2. Remove the cotter pin and locknut from the tie rod end.

3. Using the proper tools separate the tie rod end from its mounting.

4. Unscrew the tie rod end from the relay rod.

5. Installation is the reverse of the removal procedure. Adjust the toe-in, as required.

ECLIPSE

1. Disconnect the battery negative cable.

2. Raise and safely support vehicle.

3. Wire brush the threads on the tie rod shaft and lubricate with penetrating oil. Loosen the locknut.

4. Remove the cotter pin and nut and press the tie rod end from the steering knuckle. Hold the tie rod shaft in locking pliers and turn the tie rod end off. Counting the exact number of turns and installing the replacement tie rod end the same number of turns will put the toe-in alignment close to specification.

5. It is possible to drive the dust cover from the joint and replace the joint end. Use high quality chassis grease. Use sealer on the boot when installing.

6. Install the tie rod end. Measure from the end of the rack and pinion boot to the inner part of the tie rod end. This dimension should be:

    c. Vehicles with manual rack and pinion: 7.24–7.32 in. (184–186mm).

    d. 2WD vehicles with power rack and pinion: 7.22–7.30 in. (183.4–185.4mm).

    e. 4WD vehicles with power rack and pinion: 7.07–7.15 in. (179.6–181.6mm).

7. When the tie rod is adjusted properly, lock with locking nut.

8. Reinstall tie rod ends in steering knuckle.

BRAKES

Master Cylinder

Removal and Installation

1. Disconnect the negative battery cable. On the Starion, Mirage with turbocharger and Precis, the brake fluid reservoir is separate from the master cylinder. Disconnect the hoses at the master cylinder and plug them or drain the fluid into a container.

2. Disconnect the electrical connector for the fluid level sensor. Remove the proportioning valve bracket, if equipped.

3. Disconnect all the brake tubes. Remove the nuts and lock washers attaching the master cylinder to the booster. Remove the master cylinder from the vehicle.

4. Install the reverse order, torquing the attaching nuts to 6–9 ft. lbs. Refill the reservoirs with approved, new fluid and bleed the system thoroughly.

Proportioning Valve

Removal and Installation

1. Disconnect battery negative cable.

2. On most vehicles the proportioning valve is located on the body under the master cylinder. Disconnect and tag for proper reassembly the brake lines, disconnect the electrical connector and unbolt the valve from the body.

To install:

3. Reverse the removal procedure to install. Use care not to cross thread any connections. Tighten flared brake lines to 9–12 ft. lbs. Add fluid and bleed brakes.

Power Brake Booster

Removal and Installation

1. Disconnect the negative battery cable. Disconnect the vacuum supply line from the brake booster.

2. Remove the master cylinder. It may be possible to position the master cylinder aside rather then disconnect the fluid lines.

3. Disconnect the pushrod from the brake pedal.

4. Remove the mounting bolts from the firewall. Remove the power brake booster.

5. Installation is the reverse of the removal procedure. Bleed the brake system.

Brake Caliper

Removal and Installation

FRONT

1. Disconnect the battery negative cable. Raise and safely support vehicle, remove appropriate wheel assembly.
2. Drain the brake fluid.
3. Disconnect the front brake hose. Hold the nut on the brake hose side, loosen the flared brake line nut.
4. Remove the caliper lock pins and remove the caliper.

To install:

5. Reverse the removal procedure to install. Make sure the brake hose is not twisted after installation. Refill brake fluid as required and bleed brakes.

REAR

1. Disconnect battery negative cable. Raise and safely support vehicle, remove appropriate wheel assembly.
2. Drain the brake fluid.
3. Disconnect the parking brake cable and the rear brake hose. Hold the nut on the brake hose side, loosen the flared brake line nut.
4. Remove the rear caliper assembly.

To install:

5. Reverse the removal procedure to install. Make sure the brake hose is not twisted after installation. Refill brake fluid as required and bleed brakes. Adjust parking brake if required.

Disc Brake Pads

Removal and Installation

1. Disconnect battery negative cable.
2. Raise and safely support vehicle.
3. Remove appropriate wheel assembly.
4. Remove the caliper from its bracket. Do not disconnect the brake line. Do not allow the caliper to hang by the brake line. Take note of the clips, pins, anti-squeak shims and other parts that are installed for assembly reference. These will vary from vehicle-to-vehicle.
5. If equipped with rear disc brakes, loosen the parking brake cable from inside the vehicle and disconnect the parking brake end from the rear caliper.

To install:

6. Reverse the removal procedure to install. Check for fluid contamination that might indicate leaking caliper seals.
7. Always replace disc brake pads in complete sets of 4. The limit for lining wear is 0.080 in. of lining remaining. On rear disc brake caliper, a special tool may be needed to retract the piston due to the parking brake mechanism. Note that these rear disc pads should have a projection on the back side of the shoe that fits into the rear caliper piston.
8. Make sure the brake hose is not twisted after installation.
9. Refill brake fluid as required and bleed brakes. Adjust parking brake, if required.

Brake Rotor

Removal and Installation

FRONT

1. Loosen the large driveshaft nut while the vehicle is still on the ground with the brakes applied. Then raise and safely support vehicle. Remove appropriate wheel assembly.
2. Remove the caliper from its bracket. Do not disconnect the brake line. Do not allow the caliper to hang by the brake line.
3. Remove the lower ball joint connection and the tie rod end.
4. Remove the halfshaft.
5. Remove the bolts from the lower strut and separate the hub/rotor assembly.

6. A puller can be set up to separate the hub from the knuckle freeing the rotor.

To install:

7. Installation is the reverse of the removal process. When installing the wheel hub, be sure to install the washer and halfshaft nut in the proper direction. After installing the wheel, lower the vehicle to the floor for final tightening. If the position of the cotter pin holes does not match, tighten the nut to 188 ft. lbs. maximum. Install the cotter pin and bend it securely.

REAR

1. Raise and safely support vehicle, remove appropriate wheel assembly.
2. Disconnect the parking brake cable. Remove the caliper from its bracket. Do not disconnect the brake line. Do not allow the caliper to hang by the brake line.
3. The rotor is held to the hub by 2 small bolts. Remove the bolts and pull off the rotor.

To install:

4. Installation is the reverse of the removal process.

Brake Drums

Removal and Installation

1. Raise and safely support vehicle, remove appropriate wheel assembly.
2. Remove the grease cap and remove the center wheel bearing nut.
3. Remove the outer bearing and brake drum assembly.

To install:

4. Installation is the reverse of the removal process. Check the drum inside diameter. The wear limit is 7.20 in. (182mm). Inspect the rear hub nut. Replace if unusable.

Brake Shoes

Removal and Installation

1. Raise the vehicle and support it safely.
2. Remove the wheel and tire assembly.
3. Remove the brake drum.
4. Remove the shoe-to-strut spring and the shoe-to-shoe spring.
5. Remove the shoe hold-down spring and the shoe retainer spring.
6. Remove the leading shoe.
7. Remove the parking brake cable from the lever and then remove the trailing shoe.
8. Install in the reverse order of removal.

Wheel Cylinder

Removal and Installation

1. Raise and support the rear of the vehicle. Remove the wheel and brake drum. Remove the brake shoes.
2. Place a container under the brake backing plate to catch the brake fluid that will run out of the wheel cylinder.
3. Disconnect the brake line and remove the cylinder mounting bolts. Remove the cylinder from the backing plate.
4. Installation is the reverse of the removal procedure. Bleed the brake system.

Parking Brake Cable

Adjustment

REAR DRUM BRAKES

1. Make sure the parking brake cable is free and is not frozen or sticking. With the engine running, forcefully depress the brake pedal 5–6 times. Check the parking brake stroke. It

should be 5-7 notches. If not, adjust using the following procedure.

2. Remove the floor console by prying out the coin holder, box tray and remote mirror switch or if not so equipped, the cover. Remove the small cover around the seat belt from the console side. The console is in 2 pieces. Remove the screws from the center section and remove the rear part of the console.

3. Loosen the locknut then loosen the adjusting to the end of the cable and free the parking brake cable. Repeat the procedure to pull the parking brake lever back with a force of about 44 lbs. until the lever stoke ceases to change. If the lever stroke does not change, the automatic adjustment mechanism is functioning normally and the clearance between the shoe and drum is correct.

4. Rotate the adjusting nut to adjust the parking brake stroke to the 5-7 notch setting. After making the adjustment check there is no looseness between the adjusting nut and the parking brake lever, then tighten the locknut.

NOTE: Do not adjust the parking brake too tight. If the number of notches is less than specification, the cable has been pulled too much and the automatic adjuster will fail. Use the 5-7 notch specification.

5. After adjusting the lever stroke, raise the vehicle. With the parking brake lever in the released position, turn the rear wheel to confirm that the rear brakes are not dragging.

REAR DISC BRAKES

1. Make sure the parking brake cable is free and is not frozen or sticking. With the engine running, forcefully depress the brake pedal 5-6 times. Check the parking brake stroke. It should be 5-7 notches. If not, adjust using the following procedure.

2. Remove the floor console by prying out the coin holder, box tray, and remote mirror switch, or if not so equipped, the cover. Remove the small cover around the seat belt from the console side. The console is in 2 pieces. Remove the screws from the center section and remove the rear part of the console.

3. Loosen the locknut then loosen the adjusting to the end of the cable and free the parking brake cable. Repeat the procedure to pull the parking brake lever back with a force of about 44 lbs. until the lever stoke ceases to change. If the lever stroke does not change, the automatic adjustment mechanism is functioning normally and the clearance between the shoe and drum is correct.

4. Check to be sure the distance between the stopper and the parking brake lever at the caliper side is 0.078 in. (2mm) or less. If the clearance between the parking lever, on the caliper, and the stopper exceeds 0.078 in., the probable causes are brake cable sticking, improper cable installation or a malfunction of the automatic adjuster in the caliper which will require disassembling the caliper.

5. Turn the adjusting nut to get the brake lever stroke to specification, 5-7 notches.

NOTE: Do not adjust the parking brake too tight. If the number of notches is less than specification, the cable has been pulled too much and the automatic adjuster will fail. Use the 5-7 notch specification.

6. After making the adjustment, check to be sure there is no

play between the adjusting nut and the parking brake lever, then tighten the locknut. After adjusting the lever stroke, raise the vehicle. With the parking brake lever in the released position, turn the rear wheel to confirm that the rear brakes are not dragging.

Removal and Installation
FRONT WHEEL DRIVE

1. Remove the floor console by prying out the coin holder, box tray and remote mirror switch, if equipped, or the cover. Remove the small cover around the seat belt from the console side. The console is in 2 pieces. Remove the screws from the center section and remove the rear part of the console.

2. Remove the rear seat cushion by pulling both levers at floor level and removing the seat cushion.

3. Remove the center cable clamp and grommet.

4. Raise and safely support vehicle.

5. At the rear wheel, remove the brake drum and disconnect the cable end from the parking brake strut lever and the snap ring which retains the cable to the back plate for rear drum brakes or cable end and clip for rear disc brakes. Unfasten any other frame retainers and remove the cables.

To install:

6. Installation is the reverse of the removal procedure. Check parking brake adjustment and adjust, as required.

REAR WHEEL DRIVE

1. As required, remove the console and rear seat.
2. Raise and support the rear of the vehicle.
3. Disconnect all clevis pin connecting and the cable ends.
4. Pull the cable through the floor.
5. Install in reverse order.
6. Adjust the cable. Apply sealer to the edge of the grommet at the floor opening. Check the parking brake indicator, the light should come on when the brake is applied 1 notch.

Brake System Bleeding

System Dry

1. If the master cylinder is dry, disconnect the brake tube from the master cylinder.

2. With an assistant, have one person slowly depressing the brake pedal and holding it down. The other person should use a finger to close the outlet port of the master cylinder and then the first person should release the pedal. Repeat these steps 3-4 times. Keep the cylinder full of brake fluid. This operation bleeds the master cylinder.

3. Connect the brake tube to the master cylinder.

4. Start the engine. Using the bleeder screws are the calipers and wheel cylinders, bleed the brakes at the wheels in the following sequence: right rear, left front, left rear, right front.

5. Do not allow the master cylinder reservoir to run out of fluid.

Normal Service Bleeding

1. Press the brake pedal several times until resistance is felt.
2. With the brake pedal depressed, loosen the bleeder screw $1/3$-$1/2$ turn and then tighten it before the fluid pressure is gone.
3. Release the brake pedal. Repeat this procedure until there are no more air bubbles in the brake fluid.

FRONT SUSPENSION

Shock Absorbers

Removal and Installation

EXCEPT CORDIA AND TREDIA

1. Disconnect the negative battery cable. Remove the shock absorber retaining nut from the upper control arm.
2. Raise and support the vehicle safely. Remove the front under cover spoiler.
3. Remove the shock absorber retaining nut and bolt from the lower control arm.
4. Remove the shock absorber from the vehicle.
5. Installation is the reverse of the removal procedure.

MacPherson Strut

Removal and Installation

CORDIA AND TREDIA

1. Raise and support the vehicle safely.
2. Remove the front wheel. Remove the brake line from the strut.
3. Disconnect the strut assembly from the steering knuckle by removing both bolts/nuts. Support the strut and remove both nuts and washers fastening it to the wheel well. Remove the strut.
4. Installation is the reverse of the removal procedure. When installing the strut, apply a non hardening sealer to the mating surfaces of the strut and knuckle arm.

STARION

1. Raise and support the vehicle safely. Remove the tire and wheel. Remove the caliper. Remove the front hub with disc and dust cover.
2. Disconnect the stabilizer linkage and the lower. Remove the strut assembly, knuckle arm and strut insulator retaining bolts and remove the strut assembly from the wheelhouse.
3. Installation is the reverse of the removal procedure. When installing the strut, apply a non hardening sealer to the mating surfaces of the strut and knuckle arm.

MIRAGE AND GALANT

1. Raise and support the vehicle safely. Remove the front wheels. On the Mirage, detach the brake hose bracket at the strut.
2. Remove both nuts, bolts and lockwashers attaching the lower end of the strut to the steering knuckle.
3. Remove the dust cover from the top of the strut on the wheel well. Support the strut from under. Install the socket wrench on the nut at the top of the strut and a box or open end wrench on the socket. Then, install the Allen wrench through the center of the socket, long part downward. Hold the Allen wrench in place, if necessary, by using a small diameter pipe as a cheater. Turn the socket to loosen the nut. Remove the nut and the lower and remove the strut.
4. To install, reverse the removal procedure. Torque the bolts attaching the bottom of the strut to the knuckle to 53–63 ft. lbs. on the Mirage or 65–76 ft. lbs. on the Galant. The nut at the top of the strut must be torqued with the shaft of the shock held from turning with the Allen wrench, as during the loosening process. Since it is not usually possible to use a torque wrench on the flats of a socket, estimate the torque; it should be 36–43 ft. lbs.

PRECIS

1. Raise and support the vehicle safely. Remove the front wheels. Detach the brake hose bracket at the strut.
2. Remove the 4 nuts securing the strut to the fender well.

3. Unbolt the strut lower end from the knuckle.
4. Remove the strut from the vehicle.
5. Installation is the reverse of removal. Torque the strut to knuckle bolts to 55–65 ft. lbs.; the strut to fender well nuts to 7–11 ft. lbs.

ECLIPSE

1. Raise and safely support vehicle.
2. Remove the brake hose and tube bracket. Do not pry the brake hose and tube clamp away when removing it.
3. Remove the strut lower bolts. Support the lower arm. Use a piece of wire to suspend the knuckle to keep the weight off the brake hose.
4. Before removing the top bolts, make matchmarks on the body and the strut insulator for proper reassembly. If this plate is installed improperly, the wheel alignment will be wrong. Remove the strut upper bolts and pull the strut/spring from the vehicle.
To install:
5. Inspect the strut for signs of oil leakage or damage. Installation is the reverse of the removal process. Check that the top plate is properly installed or alignment will be affected. Torque the strut to knuckle bolts to 80–94 ft. lbs.

Electronic Control Strut

Removal and Installation

GALANT AND SIGMA

1. Raise and support the vehicle safely. Remove the front wheels. Detach the brake hose bracket at the strut.
2. Remove the front height sensor bolt.
3. Remove the front strut lower bolts. When uncoupling the right strut assembly and knuckle, be sure to first disconnect the front height sensor rod from the lower control arm.
4. Disconnect the electronic control suspension air line joint, then the connector and the O-ring, then disconnect the air tube.
5. Remove the front strut upper nuts. Be careful not to strike the actuator or air line joint against the wheel house.
6. Remove the front strut assembly along with the actuator and the adaptor.
7. Installation is the reverse of removal. Torque the strut to knuckle bolts to 65–76 ft. lbs.

Torsion Bars

Removal and Installation

1. Raise and support the vehicle safely.
2. Remove the torsion bar locknut. Remove the torsion bar adjusting nut. Remove the seat holding nut.
3. Before removing the anchor bolt measure the protrusion through the assembly, this will aid in reinstallation of the assembly. Remove the anchor bolt that retains the torsion bar to its mounting on the frame.
4. Remove the nuts that retain the torsion bar to the control arm.
5. Remove the torsion bar from the vehicle.
6. Installation is the reverse of the removal procedure. Adjust the alignment and the torsion bar, as required.

Ball Joints

Removal and Installation

FRONT WHEEL DRIVE

1. Raise and support the vehicle safely. Remove the tire and wheel.

2. Disconnect the stabilizer bar and strut from the lower arm.

3. Remove the ball joint nut and separate the ball joint from the front knuckle. The ball joint stud must be pressed off; use special tool MB991113 or equivalent.

4. Remove the lower control arm by removing the bolt(s)/nut(s) attaching it to the crossmember.

5. Remove the dust cover from the ball joint. Remove the snapring.

6. Press the ball joint out of the lower control arm.

7. Press the new ball joint into place. Install a new snapring with snapring pliers.

8. Apply multipurpose grease to the lip and to the inside of the dust cover. Use a special tool (and hammer) such as MB990800-3-01 to drive a new dust cover. It must go in and make contact with the snapring.

9. Install the lower control arm to the crossmember, making sure there is not torque on it. Install and tighten the bolt and nut.

REAR WHEEL DRIVE

1. Raise and support the vehicle safely. Remove the tire and wheel.

2. Remove the strut end from the steering knuckle.

3. Remove the ball joint-to-knuckle arm nut. A tool is necessary, which can be bolted to the holes in the knuckle arm and which will then press downward on the center of the ball stud tool MB990241-01 or equivalent.

4. Remove the ball joint to control arm nuts and bolts and remove the ball joint.

5. Install in reverse order. Torques in ft. lbs.: ball joint bolts 43–51 ft. lbs., strut to knuckle arm bolts 58–72 ft. lbs., ball stud nut 43–52 ft. lbs.

Lower Control Arm

Removal and Installation

CORDIA AND TREDIA

1. Raise and support the vehicle. Remove the tire and wheel.

2. Disconnect the stabilizer bar and strut bar from the lower control arm by removing the 1 attaching bolt for the stabilizer bar and both bolts for the strut bar.

3. Remove the ball stud nut and then press the ball joint stud out of the knuckle with a tool such as MB991113.

4. Remove the nut and bolt attaching the inner end of the stabilizer bar to the crossmember and pull the stabilizer bar and bushing out of the crossmember.

5. Installation is the reverse of removal. Install all parts and tighten nuts and bolts just snug. Then, complete tightening, torquing the lower arm to crossmember attaching nut/bolt to 87–108 ft. lbs. and the ball joint stud nut to 43–52 ft. lbs. Torque the strut rod to stabilizer bar bolt/nut to 43–50 ft. lbs.

STARION

1. Raise and support the vehicle safely. Remove the tire and wheel.

2. Disconnect the stabilizer bar where the link bolts to the control arm by removing the nut under the arm. Remove the nut and bolt attaching the strut bar to the control arm.

3. Disconnect the tie rod at the knuckle arm. Use a fork like tool such as MB990778-01, a standard type tool for pulling ball joint studs. First, loosen the stud nut until it is near the top of the threads and then hammer the tool between the ball joint of the tie rod end and the knuckle arm. When the ball stud comes loose, remove the nut and disconnect the stud.

4. Unbolt the strut from the knuckle arm.

5. Unbolt the inner end of the ball joint assembly to disconnect it from the outer end of the control arm.

6. Remove the nut, bolt and lockwasher and pull the inner end of the control arm out of the crossmember.

7. Installation is the reverse of removal. Torque the bolt fastening the control arm to the crossmember to 58–69 ft. lbs.; the bolts attaching the ball joint to the outer end to 43–51 ft. lbs.; the ball stud nut to 43–52 ft. lbs.; and the strut bolts to 58–72 ft. lbs. Tighten the nut for the stabilizer bar link until 0.59–0.67 in. of thread shows below the bottom of the nut.

MIRAGE, GALANT AND SIGMA

1. Raise and support the vehicle safely. Remove the tire and wheel.

2. On the Mirage, remove the under cover.

3. Disconnect the stabilizer bar from the lower arm. On the Galant, remove the nut at the top and remove the washer and bushing, keeping them in order. On the Mirage, remove the nut from under the control arm and take off the washer and spacer.

4. On the Galant with electronically controlled suspension, if removing the right arm, disconnect the height sensor rod from the lower arm. Loosen the ball joint stud nut and then press the stud out of the control arm, using a fork like tool MB990778-01 and hammer on the Galant; on the Mirage, remove the stud nut and press the tool off with a tool such as MB991113.

5. On the Galant, remove the nuts and bolts which retain the bushings to the crossmember at the front and which retain the bushing retainer to the crossmember at the rear and pull the arm out. On the Mirage, remove the bolts which retain the spacer at the rear and the nut and washers on the front of the lower arm shaft (at the front). Slide the arm forward, off the shaft and out of the busing.

6. Replace the dust cover on the ball joint. The new cover must be greased on the lip and inside with No. 2 EP Multi-purpose grease and pressed on with a tool such as MB990800 and a hammer until it is fully seated.

7. Installation is the reverse of removal. On the Galant, make sure the nut on the stabilizer bar bolt is torqued to give 0.63–0.7 in. of thread exposed between the top of the nut and the end of the link. On the Mirage, the nut must be torqued until the link shows 0.83–0.91 in. of threads below the bottom of the nut. Also on the Mirage, the washer for the lower arm must be installed as shown. The left side arm shaft has a left hand thread. Finally tighten the arm shaft to the lower arm with the weight of the vehicle with no passengers or luggage on the front suspension. On the Mirage, torque the nut for the lower arm shaft to 69–87 ft. lbs.; the bolts for the spacer at the rear to 43–58 ft. lbs. and the ball stud nut to 43–52 ft. lbs. On the Galant, torque the nut for the nut/bolt to crossmember to 69–87 ft. lbs., the ball stud to 42–50 ft. lbs. and the bolt for retaining the rear bushing to the body to 58–72 ft. lbs.

PRECIS

1. Raise and support the vehicle safely. Remove the tire and wheel.

2. Remove the under cover.

3. Disconnect the stabilizer bar from the lower arm. Remove the nut from under the control arm and take off the washer and spacer.

4. Remove the ball joint stud nut and press the tool off with a tool such as MB991113.

5. Remove the bolts which retain the spacer at the rear and the nut and washers on the front of the lower arm shaft, at the front. Slide the arm forward, off the shaft and out of the bushing.

6. Replace the dust cover on the ball joint. The new cover must be greased on the lip and inside with No. 2 EP Multi-purpose grease and pressed on with a tool such as MB990800 and a hammer until it is fully seated.

7. Installation is the reverse of removal. The nut on the stabilizer bar bolt must be torqued until the link shows 21–23mm of threads below the bottom of the nut. Also, the washer for the lower arm must be installed as shown. The left side arm shaft has a left hand thread. Finally, tighten the arm shaft to the lower arm with the weight of the vehicle with no passengers or lug-

gage on the front suspension. Torque the nut for the lower arm shaft to 69–87 ft. lbs.; the bolts for the spacer at the rear to 43–58 ft. lbs.; the ball stud nut to 43–52 ft. lbs.

Front Wheel Bearings

NOTE: This section pertains to rear wheel drive vehicles only.

Adjustment

1. Remove the wheel and dust cover. Remove the cotter pin and lock cap from the nut.
2. Torque the wheel bearing nut to 14.5 ft. lbs. and then loosen the nut. Retorque the nut to 3.6 ft. lbs. and install the lock cap and cotter pin.
3. Install the dust cover and the wheel.

Removal and Installation

1. Raise and support the vehicle safely. Remove the tire and wheel. Remove the caliper.

2. Pry off the dust cap. Tap out and discard the cotter pin. Remove the locknut.
3. Being careful not to drop the outer bearing, pull off the brake disc and wheel hub.
4. Remove the grease inside the wheel hub.
5. Using a brass drift, carefully drive the outer bearing race out of the hub.
6. Remove the inner bearing seal and bearing.
7. Check the bearings for wear or damage and replace them, if necessary.
8. Coat the inner surface of the hub with grease.
9. Grease the outer surface of the bearing race and drift it into place in the hub.
10. Pack the inner and outer wheel bearings with grease. If the brake disc has been removed and/or replaced, tighten the retaining bolts to specification.
11. Install the inner bearing in the hub. Being careful not to distort it, install the oil seal with its lip facing the bearing. Drive the seal on until its outer edge is even with the edge of the hub.
12. Install the hub/disc assembly on the spindle, being careful not to damage the oil seal.
13. Install the outer bearing, washer and spindle nut. Adjust the bearing.

REAR SUSPENSION

Shock Absorbers

Removal and Installation

1. Raise and support the vehicle safely. Remove the tire and wheel.
2. Position a floor jack under the lower control arm. Remove the upper shock bolt and nut.
3. Compress the shock slightly and remove the lower mounting bolt.
4. Remove the shock absorber.
5. Installation is the reverse of the removal procedure.

MacPherson Strut

Removal and Installation

STARION

1. Raise and safely support the vehicle on the frame rails. Position a floor jack under the lower control arm and raise it slightly.
2. Disconnect the rear brake hose from the strut assembly.
3. Disconnect the axle shaft from the wheel side flange.
4. Remove the strut assembly to axle housing bolts. Separate the strut assembly from the axle housing. Lower the floor jack and push down on the housing while opening the coupling with a small prybar.
5. Remove the upper strut nuts from under the side trim in rear hatch.
6. Remove the strut assembly.
7. Install in reverse order. Tighten the top nuts to 18–25 ft. lbs. and the lower to 36–51 ft. lbs.

GALANT

1. Raise and safely support the vehicle. Remove the rear wheels.
2. Place a floor jack under the axle/arm assembly and raise it slightly. Remove the forward trim from the trunk and remove the cap and strut nuts and washers.
3. Remove the nut, pull the through bolt out where the strut connects with the axle/arm assembly and remove the strut assembly.

4. Installation is the reverse of removal. Torque the upper strut nuts to 33–40 ft. lbs. without Electronic Level Control (ELC) or 18–25 ft. lbs. with Electronic Level Control (ELC) and the lower through bolt to 72–87 ft. lbs. without Electronic Level Control (ELC) or 58–72 ft. lbs. with Electronic Level Control (ELC).

ECLIPSE

1. Remove the trim panel inside the trunk area for access to the top nuts.
2. Remove the top cap and nuts.
3. Raise and safely support vehicle.
4. Remove the brake tube bracket bolt, then remove the shock absorber lower bolt and remove the shock absorber/spring assembly from the vehicle.
To install:
5. Installation is the reverse of the removal procedure. It is recommended that the self-locking nuts used at the top and bottom mount not be reused, but replaced.

Coil Spring

Removal and Installation

1. Raise and support the vehicle safely allowing the rear axle to hang unsupported.
2. Place a jack under the work side control arm and remove the bottom bolts of the shock absorbers.
3. Lower the arm and remove the coil spring.
4. Installation is the reverse of removal.

Rear Control Arm

Removal and Installation

EXCEPT STARION AND ECLIPSE

1. Raise and safely support the vehicle. Remove the rear wheels. Remove the rear brake assemblies. As required, remove the muffler.
2. Disconnect the parking brake cable from the suspension arm on both sides.
3. Raise the suspension arm on both sides just slightly and re-

move both lower shock absorber attaching bolts. Lower the jack and when it can be disengaged, remove the spring. Keep the spring in the position it was in when installed so it can be installed in the same direction.

4. Disconnect the brake hoses at the suspension arms. Support the rear suspension assembly while removing both bolts on either side and remove the assembly.

5. Installation is the reverse of removal. Lower shock mounting bolts are torqued to 47–58 ft. lbs. Suspension assembly-to-body bolts are torqued to 51–65 ft. lbs. on Cordia and Tredia or 36–51 ft. lbs. on Mirage.

STARION

1. Raise and support the vehicle safely.
2. Disconnect the parking brake from the control arm brackets. Disconnect the stabilizer bar.
3. Remove the nut and bolt connecting the lower control arm to the front support.
4. Matchmark the relationship between the crossmember and the eccentric bushing so alignment can be restored at assembly. Remove the nut and bolt connecting the lower control arm to the crossmember.
5. Remove the lower control arm from the vehicle.
6. Install in reverse order.

ECLIPSE

1. Raise and safely support vehicle.
2. Remove the locknut for the lower arm ball joint.
3. Remove the rear stabilizer bar link to the lower arm.
4. Remove the inboard lower arm pivot bolt and separate the arm from the vehicle.

To install:

5. Installation is the reverse of the removal procedure. It is recommended that the self-locking nuts not be reused, but replaced. Torque the inboard pivot bolt and nut to 65–80 ft. lbs., and the ball joint stud nut to 43–52 ft. lbs.

Rear Wheel Bearings

Removal and Installation

EXCEPT THE MIRAGE AND ECLIPSE

1. Raise and support the vehicle safely. Inspect the play of the bearing, if there is excessive play in the wheel bearing, remove the hub cap, cotter pin and lock cap.
2. Loosen the locknut. Using a suitable torque wrench, tighten the locknut to 14 ft. lbs. and then loosen. Retorque the locknut to 4–7 ft. lbs.
3. Install the lock cap and the cotter pin.
4. If the position of the cotter pin is not matched with the holes in the lock cap, reposition the lock cap so the holes align. If this cannot be accomplished, back off the locknut 15 degrees. Align the lock cap and install the cotter pin.

MIRAGE

1. Raise and support the vehicle safely. Loosen the lug nuts.
2. Remove the tire and wheel. Remove the grease cap. Remove the nut.
3. Pull the drum off; the outer bearing will fall out while the drum is coming off, be sure to catch it.

4. Pry out the oil seal. Discard it. Remove the inner bearing.
5. Check the bearing races and bearings. If any scoring, heat checking or damage is noted, they should be replaced. When bearings or races need replacement, replace them as a set.
6. If the bearings and races are to be replaced, drive out the race with a brass drift.
7. Before installing new races, coat them with lithium based wheel bearing grease. The races are most easily installed using a driver made for that purpose. They can, however, be driven into place with a brass drift. Make sure they are fully seated.

To install:

8. Thoroughly pack the bearings with lithium based wheel bear grease. Pack the hub with grease.
9. Install the inner bearing and coat the lip and rim of the grease seal with grease. Drive the seal into place with a seal driver.
10. Mount the drum on the axleshaft. Install the outer bearing. Don't install the nut at this point.
11. Using a pull scale attached to one of the lugs, measure the starting force necessary to get the drum to turn. Starting force should be 5 lbs. If the starting torque is greater than specified, replace the bearings.
12. Install the nut on the axleshaft. Thread the nut on, by hand, to a point at which the back face of the nut is 2–3mm from the shoulder of the shaft, where the threads end.
13. Using an inch lb. torque wrench, turn the nut counterclockwise 2–3 turns, noting the average force needed during the turning procedure. Turning torque for the nut should be about 48 inch lbs. If turning torque is not within 5 inch lbs., either way, replace the nut.
14. Tighten the nut to 75–110 ft. lbs. Using a stand mounted gauge, check the axial play of the wheel bearings. Play should be less than 0.0079 in. If play cannot be brought within that figure, the unit may be assembled incorrectly. Pack the grease cap with wheel bearing grease and install it.

ECLIPSE

1. Raise and safely support vehicle.
2. Remove appropriate wheel and grease cap, if used. Remove the hub locking nut and remove the outer wheel bearing. Pull off the brake drum or hub, if rear disc, and remove the inner bearing.

To install:

3. Installation is the reverse of the removal procedure. Lube the wheel bearings with good quality wheel bearing grease. A new seal should be installed. It is recommended that the self-locking nut not be reused, but replaced. Fill the grease cap with wheel bearing grease.

Adjustment

1. Raise and safely support vehicle.
2. Remove appropriate wheel and grease cap, if used. Release the parking brake lever. If equipped with disc brakes, remove the caliper assembly and brake rotor.
3. Set up a dial indicator and measure the endplay while moving the hub or drum in and out. If the endplay exceeds the limit of 0.004 in. for Eclipse or 0.008 in. for others, retighten the locknut. Torque should be 144–188 ft. lbs. for Eclipse or 108–145 ft. lbs. for others, recheck. If the endplay is still beyond the limit, replace the wheel bearing.

SERIAL NUMBER IDENTIFICATION

Vehicle Identification Plate

The vehicle identification plate is attached to the hood ledge or the firewall. The VIN plate is mounted on the front of the left strut housing on the 1987–89 300ZX and on the radiator core on 1990–91 300ZX. The identification plate gives the vehicle type, model, engine displacement in cc, SAE horsepower rating, wheelbase, engine number and chassis number.

VIN location

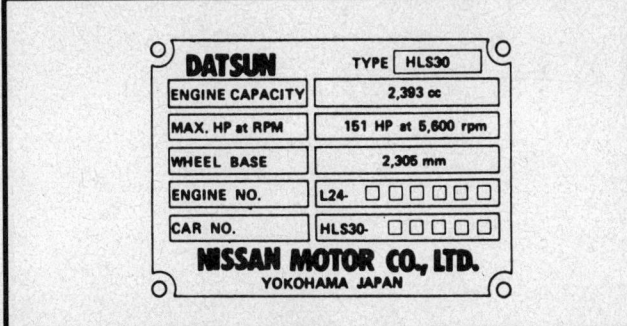

Vehicle identification plate

Engine identification number location—CA18ET, CA20E, E16i, GA16i, CA16DE and CA18DE

Engine Number

On most vehicles, the engine number is stamped on the right side top edge of the cylinder block. On the 1987–88 200SX (CA20E ad CA18ET engines), the number is stamped on the left rear edge of the block, next to the bell housing, looking from driver side seat. On 240SX, the number is stamped on the block just below the valve cover looking from the driver's seat. On the 300ZX, the number is stamped on the right rear edge of the right cylinder bank, looking from driver side seat. On the Maxima, the number can be found on the driver's side edge of the front cylinder bank, looking from driver's seat. On the 1990–91 Stanza, the number is stamped on the cylinder block just below the valve cover looking down at the front of the engine. The engine serial number is preceded by the engine model code.

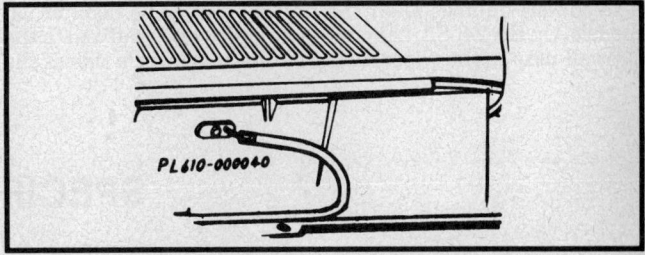

Chassis number location

Typical engine serial and code number location

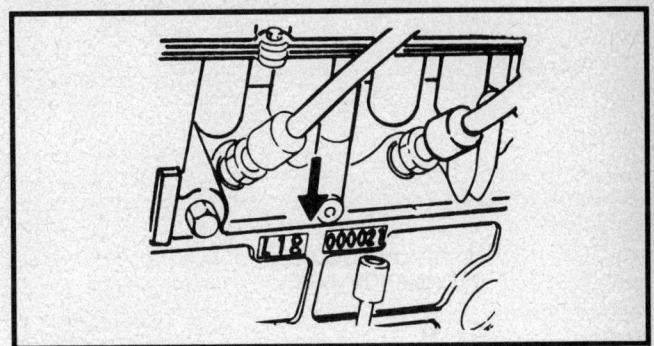

Engine serial and code number—all except V6, CD17 and CA20/CA18ET

Engine serial number location on 240SX and 1990–91 Stanza

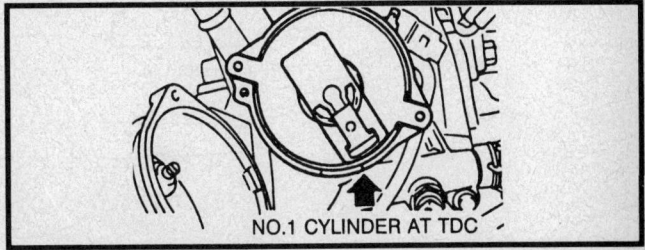

Distributor rotor at No. 1 cylinder TDC position—E16i engine

Chassis Number

The chassis number is on the firewall under the hood on all models. On the 240SX, the chassis number plate is affixed to the firewall next to the wiper motor on the passenger's side of the engine compartment. All vehicles also have the chassis number (vehicle identification number) on a plate attached to the top of the instrument panel on the driver's side, visible through the windshield. The chassis serial number is preceded by the model designation. All models have an Emission Control information label affixed to the firewall or on the underside of the hood.

SPECIFICATIONS

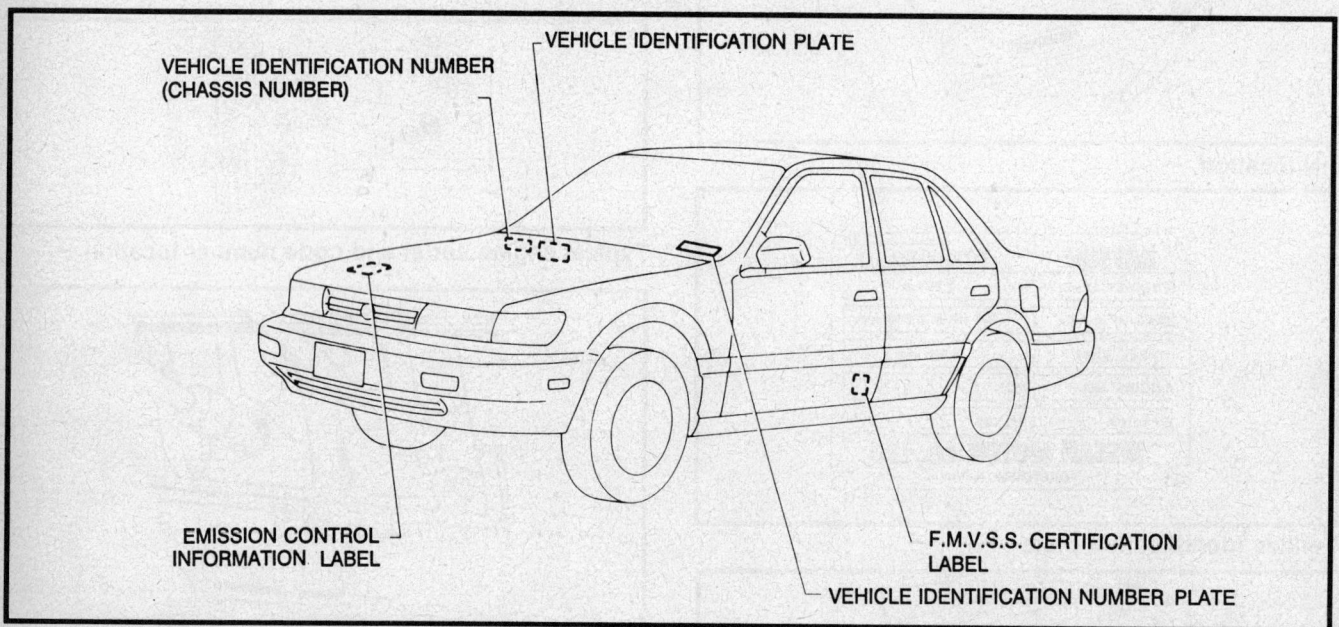

Vehicle identification—Stanza

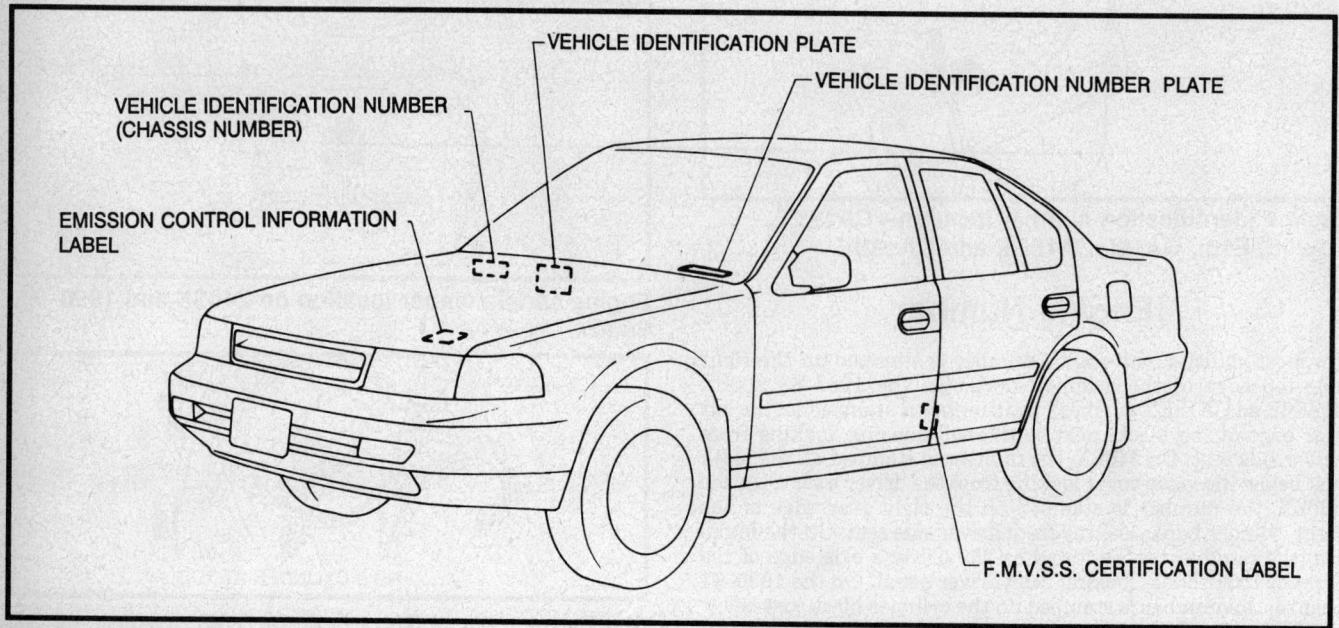

Vehicle identification—Maxima

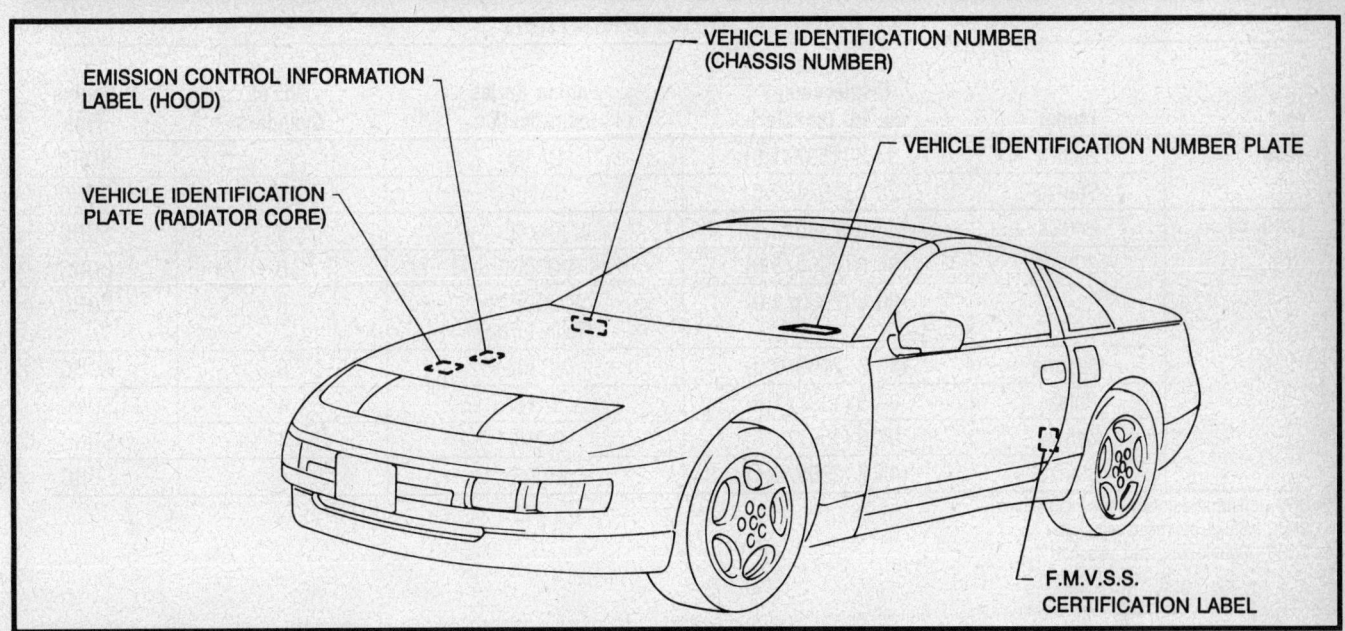

EMISSION CONTROL INFORMATION LABEL (HOOD)

VEHICLE IDENTIFICATION NUMBER (CHASSIS NUMBER)

VEHICLE IDENTIFICATION NUMBER PLATE

VEHICLE IDENTIFICATION PLATE (RADIATOR CORE)

F.M.V.S.S. CERTIFICATION LABEL

Vehicle identification—300ZX

ENGINE IDENTIFICATION

Year	Model	Engine Displacement cu. in. (cc/liter)	Engine Series Identification	No. of Cylinders	Engine Type
1987	200SX	110.3 (1809/1.8)	CA18ET (Turbo)	4	SOHC
		120.4 (1974/2.0)	CA20E	4	SOHC
		180.6 (2960/3.0)	VG30E	6	SOHC
	300ZX	180.6 (2960/3.0)	VG30E	6	SOHC
		180.6 (2960/3.0)	VG30ET (Turbo)	6	SOHC
	Maxima	180.6 (2960/3.0)	VG30E	6	SOHC
	Pulsar	97.4 (1597/1.6)	E16i	4	SOHC
		97.5 (1598/1.6)	CA16DE	4	DOHC
	Sentra	97.4 (1597/1.6)	E16S, E16i	4	SOHC
	Stanza	120.4 (1974/2.0)	CA20E	4	SOHC
1988	200SX	120.4 (1974/2.0)	CA20E	4	SOHC
		180.6 (2960/3.0)	VG30E	6	SOHC
	300SX	180.6 (2960/3.0)	VG30E	6	SOHC
		180.6 (2960/3.0)	VG30ET (Turbo)	6	SOHC
	Maxima	180.6 (2690/3.0)	VG30E	6	SOHC
	Pulsar	97.4 (1597/1.6)	E16i	4	SOHC
		110.3 (1809/1.8)	CA18DE	4	DOHC
	Sentra	97.4 (1597/1.6)	E16i	4	SOHC
	Stanza	120.4 (1974/2.0)	CA20E	4	SOHC
1989	240SX	145.8 (2389/2.4)	KA24E	4	SOHC
	300ZX	180.6 (2960/3.0)	VG30E	6	SOHC
		180.6 (2960/3.0)	VG30ET (Turbo)	6	SOHC
	Maxima	180.6 (2690/3.0)	VG30E	6	SOHC
	Pulsar	97.5 (1597/1.6)	GA16i	4	SOHC
		110.3 (1809/1.8)	CA18DE	4	DOHC

ENGINE IDENTIFICATION

Year	Model	Engine Displacement cu. in. (cc/liter)	Engine Series Identification	No. of Cylinders	Engine Type
1989	Sentra	97.5 (1597/1.6)	GA16i	4	SOHC
	Stanza	120.4 (1974/2.0)	CA20E	4	SOHC
1990-91	240SX	145.8 (2389/2.4)	KA24E	4	SOHC
	300ZX	180.6 (2960/3.0)	VG30DE	6	DOHC
		180.6 (2960/3.0)	VC30DETT (Twin Turbo)	6	SOHC
	Maxima	180.6 (2960/3.0)	VG30E	6	SOHC
	Pulsar	97.5 (1597/1.6)	GA16i	4	SOHC
	Sentra	97.5 (1597/1.6)	GA16i	4	SOHC
	Stanza	145.8 (2389/2.4)	KA24E	4	SOHC

OHV—Pushrod-activated overhead valves
SOHC—Single overhead camshaft
DOHC—Double overhead camshaft

GENERAL ENGINE SPECIFICATIONS

Year	Model	Engine Displacement cu. in. (cc)	Fuel System Type	Net Horsepower @ rpm	Net Torque @ rpm (ft. lbs.)	Bore × Stroke (in.)	Compression Ratio	Oil Pressure @ rpm
1987	200SX	120.4 (1974)	EFI	102 @ 5200	116 @ 3200	3.33 × 3.46	8.5:1	43 @ 2000
		110.3 (1809) ①	EFI	120 @ 5200	134 @ 3200	3.27 × 3.29	8.0:1	43 @ 2000
		180.6 (2960)	EFI	160 @ 5200	174 @ 4000	3.43 × 3.27	9.0:1	43 @ 2000
	300ZX	180.6 (2960)	EFI	160 @ 5200	174 @ 4000	3.43 × 3.27	9.0:1	43 @ 2000
		180.6 (2960) ①	EFI	200 @ 5200	227 @ 3600	3.43 × 3.27	7.8:1	43 @ 2000
	Maxima	180.6 (2960)	EFI	160 @ 5200	174 @ 4000	3.43 × 3.27	9.0:1	43 @ 2000
	Pulsar	97.4 (1597)	EFI	70 @ 5000	94 @ 2800	2.99 × 3.46	9.4:1	43 @ 1700
		97.5 (1598)	EFI	113 @ 6400	99 @ 4800	3.07 × 3.29	10.0:1	67 @ 2000
	Sentra	97.4 (1597)	2 bbl	70 @ 5000	92 @ 2800	2.99 × 3.46	9.4:1	43 @ 1700
	Stanza	120.4 (1974)	EFI	97 @ 5200	114 @ 3200	3.33 × 3.46	8.5:1	43 @ 2000
1988	200SX	120.4 (1974)	EFI	99 @ 5200	116 @ 2800	3.33 × 3.46	8.5:1	60.5 @ 3200
		180.6 (2960)	EFI	165 @ 5200	168 @ 3600	3.43 × 3.27	9.0:1	59 @ 3200
	300ZX	180.6 (2960)	EFI	165 @ 5200	174 @ 3600	3.43 × 3.27	9.0:1	59 @ 3200
		180.6 (2690) ①	EFI	205 @ 5200	227 @ 3600	3.43 × 3.27	8.3:1	58.5 @ 3200
	Maxima	180.6 (2960)	EFI	157 @ 5200	168 @ 3600	3.43 × 3.27	9.0:1	59 @ 3200
	Pulsar	97.4 (1597)	EFI	70 @ 5000	94 @ 2800	2.99 × 3.46	9.4:1	64 @ 3200
		110.3 (1809)	EFI	125 @ 6400	115 @ 4800	3.27 × 3.29	10.0:1	67 @ 2000
	Sentra	97.4 (1597)	EFI	70 @ 5000	94 @ 2800	2.99 × 3.46	9.4:1	64 @ 3000
	Stanza	120.4 (1974)	EFI	97 @ 5200	114 @ 2800	3.33 × 3.46	8.5:1	58 @ 3000
1989	240SX	145.8 (2389)	EFI	140 @ 5600	152 @ 4400	3.50 × 3.78	9.1:1	65 @ 3000
	300ZX	180.6 (2960)	EFI	165 @ 5200	174 @ 4000	3.43 × 3.27	9.0:1	59 @ 3200
		180.6 (2960) ①	EFI	205 @ 5200	227 @ 3600	3.43 × 3.27	8.3:1	58 @ 3200
	Maxima	180.6 (2690)	EFI	160 @ 5200	182 @ 2800	3.43 × 3.27	9.0:1	59 @ 3200
	Pulsar	97.5 (1597)	EFI	90 @ 6000	96 @ 3200	2.99 × 3.46	9.4:1	64 @ 3000
		110.3 (1809)	EFI	96 @ 3200	115 @ 4800	3.27 × 3.29	9.5:1	67 @ 2000
	Sentra	97.5 (1597)	EFI	90 @ 6000	96 @ 3200	2.99 × 3.47	9.4:1	64 @ 3000
	Stanza	120.4 (1974)	EFI	94 @ 5400	114 @ 2800	3.33 × 3.47	8.5:1	61 @ 3200

GENERAL ENGINE SPECIFICATIONS

Year	Model	Engine Displacement cu. in. (cc)	Fuel System Type	Net Horsepower @ rpm	Net Torque @ rpm (ft. lbs.)	Bore × Stroke (in.)	Compression Ratio	Oil Pressure @ rpm
1990–91	240SX	145.8 (2389)	EFI	140 @ 5600	152 @ 4400	3.50 × 3.78	8.6:1	60–70 @ 3000
	300ZX	180.6 (2960)	EFI	222 @ 6400	198 @ 4800	3.43 × 3.27	10.5:1	51–65 @ 3000
		180.6 (2960) ①	EFI	③	283 @ 3600	3.43 × 3.27	8.1:1	51–65 @ 3000
	Maxima	180.6 (2960)	EFI	160 @ 5200	181 @ 2800	3.43 × 3.27	9.0:1	53–65 @ 3200
	Pulsar	97.5 (1597)	EFI	90 @ 6000	96 @ 3200	2.99 × 3.47	9.4:1	57–71 @ 3000
	Sentra	97.5 (1597)	EFI	90 @ 6000	96 @ 3200	2.99 × 3.47	9.4:1	57–71 @ 3000
	Stanza	145.8 (2389)	EFI	138 @ 5600	148 @ 3200	3.50 × 3.78	8.6:1	60–70 @ 3000

EFI: Electronic Fuel Injection
① Turbo
② Twin Turbo
③ MT: 300 @ 6400
  AT: 280 @ 6400

ENGINE TUNE-UP SPECIFICATIONS

Year	Model	Engine Displacement cu. in. (cc)	Spark Plugs Type	Gap (in.)	Ignition Timing (deg.) MT	AT	Compression Pressure (psi)	Fuel Pump (psi)	Idle Speed (rpm) MT	AT	Valve Clearance In.	Ex.
1987	200SX	120.4 (1974)	②	0.039–0.043	15B	15B	171	37	750	700	Hyd.	Hyd.
		110.3 (1809) ①	②	0.039–0.043	15B	15B	171	37	750	—	0.012	0.012
		180.6 (2960)	BCPR6ES-11	0.039–0.043	20B	20B	173	37	700	700	Hyd.	Hyd.
	300ZX	180.6 (2960)	BCPR6ES-11	0.039–0.043	20B	20B	173	37	700	650	Hyd.	Hyd.
		180.6 (2960) ①	BCPR6E-11	0.039–0.043	15B	15B	165	37	700	650	Hyd.	Hyd.
	Maxima	180.6 (2960)	BCPR6ES-11	0.039–0.043	20B	20B	173	37	750	700	Hyd.	Hyd.
	Pulsar	97.4 (1597)	BPR5ES-11	0.039–0.043	7B	7B	181	14	800	700	0.011	0.011
		97.5 (1598)	PFR6A-11	0.039–0.043	15B	—	199	28	800	—	Hyd.	Hyd.
	Sentra	97.4 (1597)	BPR5ES-11	0.039–0.043	7B	7B	181	14③	800	700	0.011	0.011
	Stanza	120.4 (1974)	②	0.039–0.043	15B	15B	171	37	750	700	Hyd.	Hyd.
1988	200SX	120.4 (1974)	②	0.039–0.043	15B	15B ④	171	36⑥	750	750 ④	Hyd.	Hyd.
		180.6 (2690)	BCPR6ES-11	0.039–0.043	20B	20B	173	37④ ⑦	700	700	Hyd.	Hyd.
	300ZX	180.6 (2960)	BCPR6ES-11	0.039–0.043	15B	20B	173	37⑦	700 ④	700 ④	Hyd.	Hyd.
		180.6 (2690) ①	BCPR6E-11	0.039–0.043	10B	15B	169	44⑦	700	650 ④	Hyd.	Hyd.
	Maxima	180.6 (2960)	BCPR6ES-11	0.039–0.043	15B	20B	173	30⑤	750	700 ④	Hyd.	Hyd.
	Pulsar	97.4 (1597)	BPR6ES-11	0.039–0.043	7B	7B	181	14⑤	800	700 ④	Hyd.	Hyd.
		110.3 (1809)	PFR6A-11	0.039–0.043	15B	15B	199	36⑧	800	700 ④	Hyd.	Hyd.
	Sentra	97.4 (1597)	BPR6ES-11	0.039–0.043	7B	7B	181	14⑨	800	700 ④	0.011	0.011
	Stanza	120.4 (1974)	②	0.039–0.043	15B	15B	171	43.4	750	700	Hyd.	Hyd.

18–7

ENGINE TUNE-UP SPECIFICATIONS

Year	Model	Engine Displacement cu. in. (cc)	Spark Plugs Type	Spark Plugs Gap (in.)	Ignition Timing (deg.) MT	Ignition Timing (deg.) AT	Compression Pressure (psi)	Fuel Pump (psi)	Idle Speed (rpm) MT	Idle Speed (rpm) AT	Valve Clearance In.	Valve Clearance Ex.
1989	240SX	145.8 (2389)	ZFR5D-11	0.039–0.043	15B	15B	192	33⑧	750	750	Hyd.	Hyd.
	300ZX	180.6 (2690)	BCPR6ES-11	0.039–0.043	15B	20B	173	37⑦	700	700 ④⑩	Hyd.	Hyd.
		180.6 (2960)	BCPR6ES-11	0.039–0.043	10B	15B	169	44⑦	700	650	Hyd.	Hyd.
	Maxima	180.6 (2960)	BKR6ES-11	0.039–0.043	15B	15B	181	36⑧	750	700	Hyd.	Hyd.
	Pulsar	97.5 (1597)	BCPR5ES-11	0.039–0.043	7B ⑪	7B ⑪	181	43⑤	800 ⑯	750 ⑯	Hyd.	Hyd.
		110.3 (1809)	PFR6A-11	⑫	15B	15B	199	36⑧	800	700 ④	Hyd.	Hyd.
	Sentra	97.5 (1597)	BCPR5ES-11	0.039–0.043	7B	7B	181	43⑤	800 ⑪	700 ④⑪	Hyd.	Hyd.
	Stanza	120.4 (1974)	BCPR5ES-11	0.039–0.043	15B	15B	171	37⑧	750	700 ④	Hyd.	Hyd.
1990	240SX	145.8 (2389)	ZFRSE-11	0.039–0.043	15B	15B	175	⑮	750	750	Hyd.	Hyd.
	300ZX	180.6 (2960)	PFR6B-11	0.039–0.043	15B	15B	186	⑮	770	750	Hyd.	Hyd.
		180.6 (2960)	PFR5B-11B	0.039–0.043	15B	15B	186	⑮	770	750	Hyd.	Hyd.
	Maxima	180.6 (2960)	BRR6ES-11	0.039–0.043	15B	15B	173	⑮	750	700	Hyd.	Hyd.
	Pulsar	97.5 (1597)	BCPRSES-11	0.039–0.043	7B ⑪	7B ⑪	181	⑮	800 ⑯	900 ⑯	Hyd.	Hyd.
	Sentra	97.5 (1597)	BCPRSES-11	0.039–0.043	7B ⑪	7B ⑪	181	⑮	800 ⑯	900 ⑯	Hyd.	Hyd.
	Stanza	145.8 (2389)	ZFRSF-11	0.039–0.043	15B	15B	175	⑮	700	700	Hyd.	Hyd.
1991		SEE UNDERHOOD SPECIFICATIONS STICKER										

NOTE: The Underhood Specifications sticker often reflects tune-up specification changes made in production. Sticker figures must be used if they disagree with those in this chart.

MT Manual transmission
AT Automatic transmission
NA Not adjustable
A After Top Dead Center
B Before Top Dead Center
Hyd. Hydraulic valve lash adjusters
① Turbocharged model
② Intake side: BCPR6ES-11
  Exhaust side: BCPRSES-11
③ E16S—3.8 psi
④ In drive position
⑤ At idle speed

⑥ Fuel pressure is measured at idle speed between the fuel filter and injector body
⑦ The moment the gas pedal is fully depressed
⑧ Fuel pressure is measured at idle speed between the fuel filter and fuel pipe with the vacuum hose connected at the pressure regulator
⑨ 4WD model—36.6 psi at idle speed
⑩ 600 rpm at high altitudes
⑪ With throttle sensor harness connected
  With throttle sensor harness disconnected—7° BTDC ±5°

⑫ Spark plug gap not adjustable
⑬ Ignition timing tolerance: ±2°
⑭ Idle speed tolerance: ±50 rpm
⑮ Fuel pressure is measured at idle speed between the fuel filter and fuel pipe (engine) side
  36.3 psi—with pressure regulator vacuum hose connected
  43.4 psi—with pressure regulator vacuum hose disconnected
⑯ Idle speed is computer controlled; not adjustable

FIRING ORDERS

NOTE: To avoid confusion, always replace spark plug wires one at a time.

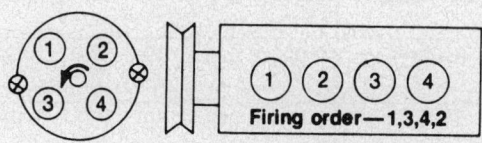

Firing order—1,3,4,2

E-Series, KA24E and GA16I Engines
Engine Firing Order: 1–3–4–2
Distributor Rotation: Counterclockwise

FIRING ORDERS

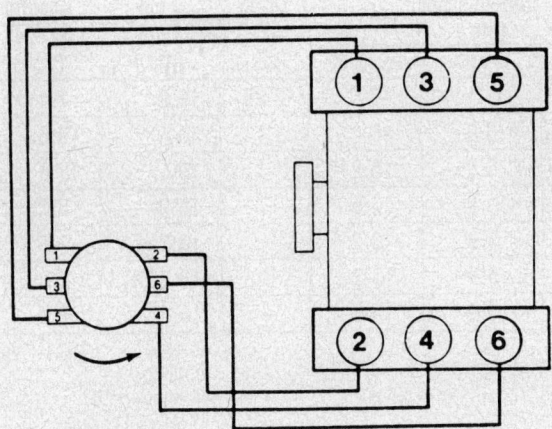

V6 Engines
Engine Firing Order: 1–2–3–4–5–6
Distributor Rotation: Counterclockwise

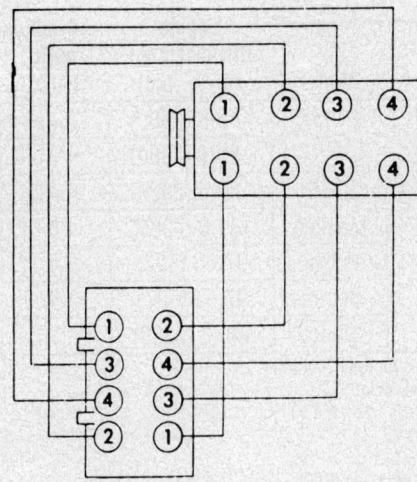

C-Series Engines
Engine Firing Order: 1–3–4–2
Distributorless Ignition System

CAPACITIES

Year	Model	Engine Displacement cu. in. (cc)	Engine Crankcase (qts.) with Filter	without Filter	Transmission (pts.) 4-Spd	5-Spd	Auto.■	Drive Axle (pts.)	Fuel Tank (gal.)	Cooling System (qts.)
1987	200SX	120.4 (1974)	3.9	3.4	—	4.25	14.8	①	14	9.1
		110.3 (1809)	3.9	3.4	—	4.25	14.8	①	14	9.1
		180.6 (2960)	4.5	4.0	—	4.25	14.8	2.75	14	9.6
	300ZX	180.6 (2960)	4.25	3.9	—	4.25	14.8	2.75	19	11.1②
	Maxima	180.6 (2960)	4.5	4.1	—	10.0	14.5	—	15.9	9.75
	Pulsar	97.4 (1597)	3.4	2.9	—	5.75	13.0	—	13.25	③
		97.5 (1598)	3.75	3.25	—	5.75	—	—	13.25	5.9
	Sentra	97.4 (1597)	3.5	3.0	—	5.75	13.0	—	13.75④	③
	Stanza	120.4 (1974)	3.75	3.25	—	10	14.5	—	15.9⑤	7.75
1988	200SX	120.4 (1974)	3.9	3.4	—	4.25	14.8	①	14	9.1
		180.6 (2690)	4.5	4.0	—	4.25	14.8	2.75	14	9.6
	300ZX	180.6 (2960)	4.25	3.9	—	4.25	14.8	2.75	19	11.1②
	Maxima	180.6 (2960)	4.5	4.1	—	10.0	14.5	—	15.9	9.75
	Pulsar	97.4 (1597)	3.4	2.9	—	5.75	13.2	—	13.25	③
		110.3 (1809)	3.7	3.3	—	10.0	14.4	—	13.25	⑥
	Sentra	97.4 (1597)	3.4	3.0	5.7	5.9	13.2	⑦	13.25⑧	③
	Stanza	120.4 (1974)	3.75	3.25	—	10	14.4	⑦	15.9⑤	7.75⑨
1989	240SX	145.8 (2389)	3.75	3.4	—	5.1	17.5	2.75	15.9	7.1⑪
	300ZX	180.6 (2960)	4.25	3.8	—	4.25⑫	14.8	2.75	19	11.1⑬
	Maxima	180.6 (2960)	4.5	4.1	—	10.0	15.5	—	15.9	8.75
	Pulsar	97.4 (1597)	3.4	3.0	—	5.75	6.6	—	13.25	⑭
		110.3 (1809)	3.75	3.25	—	10.0	7.25	—	13.25	5.9
	Sentra	97.5 (1597)	3.4	3.0	5.75	5.9	13.25	⑦	13.25⑧	⑮
	Stanza	120.4 (1974)	3.75	3.25	—	10.0	7.25	—	15.9	7.75

CAPACITIES

Year	Model	Engine Displacement cu. in. (cc)	Engine Crankcase (qts.) with Filter	without Filter	Transmission (pts.) 4-Spd	5-Spd	Auto.■	Drive Axle (pts.)	Fuel Tank (gal.)	Cooling System (qts.)
1990-91	240SX	145.8 (2389)	3.75	3.4	—	5.1	17.5	2.75	15.9	7.1⑪
		180.6 (2960)	4.4	3.9	—	5.9	16.2	3.1	19	10.6
	300ZX	180.6 (2960)	4.4⑯	3.9⑰	—	5.9	16.2	3.1	19	10.6
	Maxima	180.6 (2960)	4.5	4.1	—	10.0	15.5	—	15.9	8.75
	Pulsar	97.5 (1597)	3.4	3.0	—	5.9	13.2	—	13.25	⑭
	Sentra	97.5 (1597)	3.4	3.0	5.75	5.9	13.2	⑦	13.25⑧	
	Stanza	145.8 (2389)	3.75	3.25	—	10.0	15.8	—	16.4	7.9

■ Figure is for drain and refill
— Not applicable
① Solid rear axle—2.1
   IRS—2.75
② Turbo—11.5
③ MT—4.9; AT—5.5
④ 4WD—12.4
⑤ 4WD—13.25

⑥ MT—5.9; AT—6.1
⑦ Rear differential carrier on 4WD—2.1
   Transfer case on 4WD—2.2
⑧ 4WD—12.4
⑨ Station wagon with heater 7.1
   and without heater 6.1
⑩ Rear differential carrier on
   4WD—2.75

⑪ Reservoir Capacity—.75
⑫ Turbo—5.1
⑬ Turbo—11.6
⑭ MT—5.75
   AT—6.25
⑮ MT—5.75
   2WD w/AT—5.75
   4WD w/AT—6.25

CAMSHAFT SPECIFICATIONS
All measurements given in inches.

Year	Engine Displacement cu. in. (cc)	Journal Diameter 1	2	3	4	5	Lobe Lift In.	Ex.	Bearing Clearance	Camshaft End Play
1987	CA16DE 97.5 (1598)	1.0998–1.1006	1.0998–1.1006	1.0998–1.1006	1.0998–1.1006	1.0998–1.1006	0.335	0.335	0.0018–0.0035	0.0028–0.0059
	C-Series 110.3 (1809) 120.4 (1974)	1.8085–1.8092	1.8085–1.8092	1.8085–1.8092	1.8085–1.8092	1.8077–1.8085	0.354	0.354	0.0040 ①	0.0028–0.0055
	E-Series 97.4 (1597)	1.6515–1.6522	1.6498–1.6505	1.6515–1.6522	1.6498–1.6505	1.6515–1.6522	NA	NA	0.0014–0.0030 ②	0.0059–0.0114
	V-Series 180.6 (2960)	1.8472–1.8480	1.8472–1.8480	1.8472–1.8480	1.8472–1.8480	1.8472–1.8480	NA	NA	0.0024–0.0041	0.0012–0.0024
1988	CA20E 120.4 (1974)	1.8085–1.8092	1.8085–1.8092	1.8085–1.8092	1.8085–1.8092	1.8077–1.8055	0.335	0.374	0.0040 ①	0.0028–0.0055
	V-Series 180.6 (2960)	1.8866–1.8874	1.8472–1.8480	1.8472–1.8480	1.8472–1.8480	1.6701–1.6709	NA	NA	0.0018–0.0035	0.0012–0.0024
	E16i 97.4 (1597)	1.6515–1.6522	1.6498–1.6505	1.0515–1.6522	1.6498–1.6505	1.6515–1.6522	NA	NA	0.0014–0.0030	0.0059–0.0114
	CA18DE 110.3 (1809)	1.0998–1.1006	1.0998–1.1006	1.0998–1.1006	1.0998–1.1006	1.0998–1.1006	0.335	0.335	0.0018–0.0035	0.0028–0.0059
1989	CA20E 120.4 (1974)	1.8085–1.8092	1.8085–1.8092	1.8085–1.8092	1.8085–1.8092	1.8077–1.8055	0.335	0.374	0.0040 ①	0.0028–0.0055
	KA24E 145.8 (2389)	1.2967–1.2974	1.2967–1.2974	1.2967–1.2974	1.2967–1.2974	1.2967–1.2974	0.409	0.409	0.0018–0.0035	0.0028–0.0059
	V-Series 180.6 (2960)	1.8866–1.8874②	1.8472–1.8480	1.8472–1.8480	1.8472–1.8480	1.6701–1.6709	NA	NA	0.0018–0.0035	0.0012–0.0024
	GA16i 97.5 (1597)	1.6510–1.6518	1.6510–1.6518	1.6510–1.6518	1.6510–1.6518	1.6510–1.6518	NA	NA	0.0018–0.0035	0.0012–0.0059
	CA18DE 110.3 (1809)	1.0998–1.1006	1.0998–1.1006	1.0998–1.1006	1.0998–1.1006	1.0998–1.1006	0.335	0.335	0.0018–0.0035	0.0028–0.0059

CAMSHAFT SPECIFICATIONS

All measurements given in inches.

Year	Engine Displacement cu. in. (cc)	Journal Diameter					Lobe Lift		Bearing Clearance	Camshaft End Play
		1	2	3	4	5	In.	Ex.		
1990–91	GA16i 97.5 (1597)	1.6510–1.6518	1.6510–1.6518	1.6510–1.6518	1.6510–1.6518	1.6510–1.6518	NA	NA	0.0018–0.0035	0.0012–0.0051
	KA24E 145.8 (2389)	1.2967–1.2974	1.2967–1.2974	1.2967–1.2974	1.2967–1.2974	1.2967–1.2974	0.409	0.409	0.0018–0.0035	0.0028–0.0059
	VG30DE 180.6 (2960)	1.0998–1.1006	1.0998–1.1006	1.0998–1.1006	1.0998–1.1006	1.0998–1.1006	NA	NA	0.0018–0.0035	0.0018–0.0035
	VG30DETT 180.6 (2960)	1.0998–1.1006	1.0998–1.1006	1.0998–1.1006	1.0998–1.1006	1.0998–1.1006	NA	NA	0.0018–0.0035	0.0018–0.0035
	VG3DE 180.6 (2960)	1.8866–1.8874 ③	1.8472–1.8480	1.8472–1.8480	1.8472–1.8480	1.6732–1.6742	NA	NA	0.0024–0.0041	0.0012–0.0024

NA Not available
① Clearance limit
② Journals No. 1, 3 & 5
   No. 2 & 4. 0.0031–0.0047
③ Front of engine, left hand camshaft only

CRANKSHAFT AND CONNECTING ROD SPECIFICATIONS

All measurements are given in inches.

Year	Engine Displacement cu. in. (cc)	Crankshaft				Connecting Rod		
		Main Brg. Journal Dia.	Main Brg. Oil Clearance	Shaft End-play	Thrust on No.	Journal Diameter	Oil Clearance	Side Clearance
1987	CA16DE 97.5 (1598)	2.0847–2.0856	0.0008–0.0019	0.0120	3	1.7698–1.7706	0.0007–0.0018	0.0007–0.0018
	C-Series 110.3 (1809) 120.4 (1974)	2.0847–2.0852	0.0016–0.0024	0.0120 ②	3	1.7701–1.7706	0.0008–0.0024	0.0080–0.0120
	E-Series 97.4 (1597)	1.9661–1.9671	①	0.0020–0.0071	3	1.5730–1.5738	0.0004–0.0017	0.0040–0.0146
	V-Series 180.6 (2960)	2.4790–2.4793	0.0011–0.0022	0.0020–0.0067	4	1.9670–1.9675	0.0004–0.0020	0.0079–0.0138
1988	CA20E 120.4 (1974)	2.0847–2.0852	0.0016–0.0024	0.0120	3	1.7701–1.7706	0.0008–0.0024	0.0080–0.0120
	V-Series 180.6 (2960)	2.4790–2.4793	0.0011–0.0022	0.0020–0.0067	4	1.9760–1.9675	0.0006–0.0021	0.0079–0.0138
	E16i 97.4 (1597)	1.9661–1.9671	③	0.0020–0.0065	3	1.5733–1.5738	0.0004–0.0017	0.0040–0.0146
	CA18DE 110.3 (1809)	2.0847–2.0856	0.0008–0.0019	0.0020–0.0091	3	1.7698–1.7706	0.0007–0.0018	0.0079–0.0138
1989	CA20 120.4 (1974)	2.0847–2.0852	0.0008–0.0019	0.0020–0.0071	3	1.7701–1.7706	0.0004–0.0014	0.0080–0.0120
	KAE24 145.8 (2389)	2.3609–2.3612	0.0008–0.0019	0.0020–0.0071	3	1.9672–1.9675	0.0004–0.0017	0.0080–0.0160
	V-Series 180.6 (2960)	2.4790–2.4793	0.0011–0.0022	0.0020–0.0067	4	1.9667–1.9675	0.0006–0.0021	0.0079–0.0138
	GA16i 97.5 (1597)	1.9668–1.9671	0.0008–0.0017	0.0024–0.0071	3	1.5731–1.5738	0.0004–0.0014	0.0079–0.0185
	CA18DE 110.3 (1809)	2.0847–2.0856	0.0008–0.0019	0.0020–0.0071	3	1.7698–1.7706	0.0007–0.0018	0.0079–0.0138

CRANKSHAFT AND CONNECTING ROD SPECIFICATIONS

All measurements are given in inches.

Year	Engine Displacement cu. in. (cc)	Crankshaft				Connecting Rod		
		Main Brg. Journal Dia.	Main Brg. Oil Clearance	Shaft End-play	Thrust on No.	Journal Diameter	Oil Clearance	Side Clearance
1990–91	GA16i 97.5 (1597)	1.9668–1.9671	0.0008–0.0017	0.0024–0.0071	3	1.5731–1.5738	0.0004–0.0014	0.0079–0.0185
	KA24E 145.8 (2389)	2.3609–2.3612	0.0008–0.0019	0.0020–0.0071	3	1.7701–1.7706	0.0004–0.0014	0.0080–0.0120
	VG30DE 180.6 (2960)	2.4790–2.4793	0.0011–0.0022	0.0020–0.0071	4	1.9672–1.9675	0.0011–0.0019	0.0079–0.0138
	VG30DETT 180.6 (2960)	2.4790–2.4793	0.0011–0.0022	0.0020–0.0071	4	1.9672–1.9675	0.0011–0.0019	0.0079–0.0138
	VG30E 180.6 (2960)	2.4790–2.4793	0.0011–0.0022	0.0020–0.0067	4	1.9667–1.9675	0.0006–0.0021	0.0079–0.0138

① No. 1 & 5—0.0012–0.0022
  No. 2, 3 & 4—0.0012–0.0036
② CA18ET—0.0020–0.0071
③ No. 1, 3 & 5—0.0012–0.0022
  No. 2 & 4—0.0012–0.0036

VALVE SPECIFICATIONS

Year	Engine Displacement cu. in. (cc)	Seat Angle (deg.)	Face Angle (deg.)	Spring Test Pressure (lbs.)	Spring Installed Height (in.)	Stem-to-Guide Clearance (in.)		Stem Diameter (in.)	
						Intake	Exhaust	Intake	Exhaust
1987	CA16DE 97.5 (1598)	44°30′	45°30′	—	—	0.0008–0.0021	0.0016–0.0021	0.2348–0.2354	0.2341–0.2346
	C-Series 110.3 (1809) 120.4 (1974)	44°30′	45°30′	108 @ 1.16 ②	1.575 ①	0.0008–0.0021	0.0016–0.0029	0.2742–0.2748	0.2734–0.2740
	E-Series 97.4 (1597)	44°30′	45°30′	—	1.543	0.0008–0.0020	0.0018–0.0030	0.2744–0.2750	0.2734–0.2740
	V-Series 180.6 (2960)	44°30′	45°30′	118 @ 1.18 ②	1.575 ①	0.0008–0.0021	0.0016–0.0029	0.2742–0.2748	0.3128–0.3134
1988	CA20E 120.4 (1974)	45°	45°30′	129.9 ③	1.959 ④	0.0008–0.0021	0.0016–0.0029	0.2742–0.2748	0.2734–0.2740
	V-Series 180.6 (2960)	45°	45°30′	118 @ 1.18 ②	1.575 ①	0.0008–0.0021	0.0016–0.0029	0.2742–0.2748	0.3136–0.3138
	E16i 97.4 (1597)	45°	45°30′	—	1.543	0.0008–0.0020	0.0018–0.0030	0.2744–0.2750	0.2734–0.2740
	CA18DE 110.3 (1809)	45°	45°30′	⑤	⑥	0.0008–0.0021	0.0016–0.0029	0.2348–0.2354	0.2341–0.2346
1989	CAE20 120.4 (1974)	45°	45°30′	⑦	⑧	0.0008–0.0021	0.0016–0.0029	0.2742–0.2748	0.2734–0.2740
	KAE24 145.8 (2389)	45°	45°30′	⑨	⑩	0.0008–0.0021	0.0016–0.0028	0.2742–0.2748	0.3129–0.3134
	V-Series 180.6 (2960)	45°	45°30′	117.7 @ 1.181 ⑪	2.016 ⑤	0.0008–0.0021	0.0016–0.0029	0.2742–0.2748	0.3136–0.3138 ⑬
	GA16i 97.5 (1597)	45°	45°30′	⑫	1.634 ⑬	0.0008–0.0020	0.0008–0.0020	0.2348–0.2354	0.2582–0.2587
	CA18DE 110.3 (1809)	45°	45°30′	⑭	⑥	0.0008–0.0020	0.0008–0.0020	0.2348–0.2354	0.2582–0.2587

VALVE SPECIFICATIONS

Year	Engine Displacement cu. in. (cc)	Seat Angle (deg.)	Face Angle (deg.)	Spring Test Pressure (lbs.)	Spring Installed Height (in.)	Stem-to-Guide Clearance (in.) Intake	Exhaust	Stem Diameter (in.) Intake	Exhaust
1990-91	GA16i 97.5 (1597)	45°	45°15' 45°45'	⑫	⑬	0.0008-0.0020	0.0012-0.0022	0.2348-0.2354	0.2582-0.2587
	KA24E 145.8 (2389)	45°	45°	⑨	⑩	0.0008-0.0021	0.0016-0.0028	0.2742-0.2748	0.3129-0.3134
	VG30DE 180.6 (2960)	45°15' 45°45'	45°	⑮	⑥	0.0008-0.0021	0.0016-0.0028	0.2348-0.2354	0.2341-0.2346
	VG30DETT 180.6 (2960)	45°15' 45°45'	45°	⑮	⑥	0.0008-0.0021	0.0016-0.0028	0.2348-0.2354	0.2341-0.2346
	VG30E 180.6 (2960)	45°15' 45°45'	45°	⑯	⑰	0.0008-0.0021	0.0016-0.0029	0.2742-0.2748	0.3136-0.3138

① Outer; Inner—1.378
② Outer; Inner—57 @ 0.98
③ Outer; Inner—56 @ 0.965
④ Outer; Inner—1.736
⑤ 0.650 in. @ 121 lbs. of load
⑥ 1.697 in. free height
⑦ Outer—129.9 @ 2.32
　 Inner—66.6 @ 1.19
⑧ Free height:
　 Outer—1.959
　 Inner—1.736

⑨ Intake:
　 Outer—135.8 @ 1.480
　 Inner—63.9 @ 1.283
　 Exhaust.
　 Outer—144 @ 1.343
　 Inner—73.9 @ 1.146
⑩ Free height:
　 Intake—outer, 2.261, inner; 2.100
　 Exhaust—outer; 1.343, inner; 1.887
⑪ Outer; Inner—57.3 @ 0.9840
　 Maxima; 300ZX—0.3128-0.3134

⑫ Intake—110.0 @ 1.331
　 Exhaust—122.6 @ 1.346
⑬ Free height:
　 Intake—2.071
　 Exhaust—2.154
⑭ 162 @ 2.9
⑮ 26.5 @ 1.043
⑯ 25 @ 0.984
⑰ Free height:
　 Outer—2.016
　 Inner—1.736

PISTON AND RING SPECIFICATIONS

All measurements are given in inches.

Year	Engine Displacement cu. in. (cc)	Piston Clearance	Ring Gap Top Compression	Bottom Compression	Oil Control	Ring Side Clearance Top Compression	Bottom Compression	Oil Control
1987	CA16DE 97.5 (1598)	0.0006-0.0014	0.0087-0.0154	0.0075-0.0177	0.0079-0.0299	0.0016-0.0029	0.0012-0.0025	0.0010-0.0033
	CA18ET 110.3 (1809)	0.0010-0.0018	①	0.0059-0.0122	0.0079-0.0299	0.0016-0.0029	0.0012-0.0025	—
	CA20E 120.4 (1974)	0.0010-0.0018	0.0098-0.0201	0.0059-0.0122	0.0079-0.0299	0.0016-0.0029	0.0012-0.0025	—
	E16i 97.4 (1597)	0.0009-0.0017	②	③	0.0079-0.0236	0.0016-0.0029	0.0012-0.0025	④
	E16S 97.4 (1597)	0.0009-0.0017	0.0079-0.0138	0.0059-0.0118	0.0118-0.0354	0.0016-0.0029	0.0012-0.0025	0.0020-0.0057
	V-Series 180.6 (2960)	0.0010-0.0018	0.0083-0.0173	0.0071-0.0173	0.0079-0.0299	0.0016-0.0029	0.0012-0.0025	0.0006-0.0075
1988	CA20E 120.4 (1974)	0.0010-0.0018	0.0098-0.0201	0.0059-0.0122	0.0079-0.0299	0.0016-0.0029	0.0012-0.0025	—
	V-Series 180.6 (1960)	0.0010-0.0018	0.0083-0.0173 ⑤	0.0071-0.0173	0.0079-0.0299	0.0016-0.0029	0.0012-0.0025	0.0006-0.0075
	E16i 97.4 (1597)	0.0009-0.0017	②	③	0.0079-0.0236	0.0016-0.0029	0.0012-0.0025	④
	CA18DE 110.3 (1809)	0.0006-0.0014	0.0087-0.0154	0.0075-0.0177	0.0079-0.0299	0.0016-0.0029	0.0012-0.0025	0.0010-0.0033

PISTON AND RING SPECIFICATIONS

All measurements are given in inches.

Year	Engine Displacement cu. in. (cc)	Piston Clearance	Ring Gap			Ring Side Clearance		
			Top Compression	Bottom Compression	Oil Control	Top Compression	Bottom Compression	Oil Control
1989	CA20E 120.4 (1974)	0.0010–0.0018	0.0098–0.0201	0.0059–0.0122	0.0079–0.0299	0.0016–0.0029	0.0012–0.0025	—
	KAE24 145.8 (2389)	0.0008–0.0016	0.0110–0.0169	⑥	0.0079–0.0236	0.0016–0.0031	0.0012–0.0028	0.0026–0.0053
	V-Series 180.6 (2960)	0.0010–0.0018	0.0083–0.0173 ⑤	0.0071–0.0173	0.0079–0.0299	0.0016–0.0029	0.0012–0.0025	0.0006–0.0075
	GA16i 97.5 (1597)	0.0006–0.0014	0.0079–0.0138	0.0146–0.0205	0.0079–0.0236	0.0016–0.0031	0.0012–0.0028	
	CA18DE 110.3 (1809)	0.0010–0.0018	0.0098–0.0201	0.0059–0.0122	0.0079–0.0299	0.0016–0.0029	0.0012–0.0025	—
1990–91	GA16i 97.5 (1597)	0.0006–0.0014	0.0079–0.0138	0.0146–0.0205	0.0079–0.0236	0.0016–0.0031	0.0012–0.0028	
	KA24E 145.8 (2389)	0.0008–0.0016	0.0110–0.0169	⑥	0.0079–0.0236	0.0016–0.0031	0.0012–0.0028	—
	VG30DE 180.6 (2960)	0.0006–0.0014	0.0083–0.0157	0.0197–0.0299	0.0079–0.0299	0.0016–0.0029	0.0012–0.0025	—
	VG30DETT 180.6 (2960)	0.0010–0.0018	0.0083–0.0157	0.0197–0.0299	0.0079–0.0299	0.0016–0.0029	0.0012–0.0025	—
	VG30E 180.6 (2960)	0.0006–0.0014	0.0083–0.0173	0.0071–0.0173	0.0079–0.0299	0.0016–0.0029	0.0012–0.0025	—

① Piston grades No. 1 & No. 2:
  1984—0.0098–0.0126
  1985–88—0.0098–0.0150
  Piston grades No. 3, 4 & 5:
  1984—0.0075–0.0102
  1985–88—0.0110–0.0165

② Type 1: 0.0055–0.0102
  Type 2: 0.0079–0.0118
③ Type 1: 0.0110–0.0146
  Type 2: 0.0059–0.0098
④ Type 1: 0.0026–0.0055
  Type 2: 0.0002–0.0069

⑤ Turbocharged engine
  0.0083–0.0122
⑥ For rings punched with R or T—0.0177–0.0236
  For rings punched with N—0.0217–0.0276

TORQUE SPECIFICATIONS

All readings in ft. lbs.

Year	Engine Displacement cu. in. (cc)	Cylinder Head Bolts	Main Bearing Bolts	Rod Bearing Bolts	Crankshaft Pulley Bolts	Flywheel Bolts	Manifold		Spark Plugs
							Intake	Exhaust	
1987	CA16DE 97.5 (1598)	76 ③	33–40	30–33	105–112	61–69	14–19	27–35	14–22
	CA18ET, CA20E 110.3 (1809) 120.4 (1974)	②	33–40	24–27	90–98	72–80	14–19	14–22	14–22
	E-Series 97.6 (1597)	51–54	36–43	23–27	80–94	58–65	12–15	12–15	14–22
	V-Series 180.6 (2960)	40–47 ③	67–74	33–40	90–98	72–80	⑤	13–16	14–22
1988	CA20E 120.4 (1974)	⑤	33–40	24–27	90–98	72–80	14–19	14–22	14–22
	V-Series 180.6 (2960)	40–47 ③	67–74	⑥	90–98	72–80	④	13–16	14–22
	E16i 97.4 (1597)	⑦	36–43	23–27	80–94	58–65 ⑧	12–15	12–15	14–22
	CA18DE 110.3 (1809)	⑨	33–40	⑥	105–112	61–69	14–19	27–35	14–22

TORQUE SPECIFICATIONS
All readings in ft. lbs.

Year	Engine Displacement cu. in. (cc)	Cylinder Head Bolts	Main Bearing Bolts	Rod Bearing Bolts	Crankshaft Pulley Bolts	Flywheel Bolts	Manifold Intake	Manifold Exhaust	Spark Plugs
1989	CA20E 120.4 (1974)	⑤	33–40	24–27	90–98	72–80	14–19	14–22	14–22
	KAE24 145.8 (2389)	⑮	34–38	⑥	87–116	⑰	12–15	12–15	14–22
	V-Series 180.6 (2960)	③	67–74	⑥	90–98	72–80 ⑪	④	13–16	14–22
	GA16i 97.5 (1597)	③	34–38	⑫	132–152	69–76	12–15	12–15	14–22
	CA18DE 110.3 (1809)	⑨	33–40	⑬	105–112	61–69	12–15	12–15	14–22
1990–91	KA24E 145.8 (2389)	⑬	34–38	⑥	87–116	⑭	12–15	12–15	14–22
	V630DE 180.6 (2960)	③	64–74	⑥	159–174	61–69 ⑱	⑳	17–20	14–22
	V630DETT 180.6 (2965)	③	64–79	⑥	159–174	61–69 ⑱	⑯	20–23	14–22
	VC30E 180.6 (2960)	③	67–74	⑥	90–98	61–69 ⑮	⑯	13–16	14–22
	GA16i 97.5 (1597)	③	34–38	⑫	98–112	⑰	12–15	12–15	14–22

① Tighten in two steps:
  1st—33 ft. lbs.
  2nd—51-54 ft. lbs.
② Tighten in 2 steps:
  1st—22 ft. lbs.
  2nd—58 ft. lbs.
  Then loosen all bolts completely.
  Final torque is in 2 steps:
  1st—22 ft. lbs.
  2nd—54-61 ft. lbs.
  If angle torquing, turn all bolts
  90-95 degrees clockwise
③ See text
④ Intake bolt: 12-14 ft. lbs.
  Intake nut: 17-20 ft. lbs.
⑤ Tighten in 2 steps:
  1st—22 ft. lbs.
  2nd—58 ft. lbs.
  Then loosen all bolts completely.
  Final torque is in 2 steps:
  1st—22 ft. lbs.
  2nd—54-61 ft. lbs.
  (if angle torquing, tighten bolt 8 to
  83-88 degrees and all other bolts to
  75-80 degrees clockwise.)
  NOTE: No. 8 bolt is the longest bolt.

⑥ Tighten in 2 steps:
  1st—10-12 ft. lbs.
  2nd—28-33 ft. lbs.
  (If angle torquing, tighten bolts to
  60-65 degrees clockwise.)
⑦ Tighten in 2 steps:
  1st—22 ft. lbs.
  2nd—51 ft. lbs.
  Then loosen all bolts completely.
  Final torque in 2 steps:
  1st—22 ft. lbs.
  2nd—51-54 ft. lbs.
⑧ A/T Drive Plate: 69-76 ft. lbs.
⑨ Tighten in 2 steps:
  1st—22 ft. lbs.
  2nd—76 ft. lbs.
  Then loosen all bolts completely.
  Final torque in 2 steps:
  1st—22 ft. lbs.
  2nd—76 ft. lbs.
  (If angle torquing, tighten bolts to
  85-90 degrees clockwise.)
⑩ Tighten in 2 steps:
  1st—22 ft. lbs.
  2nd—58 ft. lbs.
  Then loosen all bolts completely.

Final torque in 2 steps:
  1st—22 ft. lbs.
  2nd—54-61 ft. lbs.
  (If angle torquing in 2nd step, turn
  all bolts 80 to 85 degrees clockwise
  with an angle torque wrench)
⑪ 300ZX Maxima—61 to 69
⑫ Tighten in 2 steps:
  1st—10 to 12 ft. lbs.
  2nd—17-21 ft. lbs.
  Then loosen all bolts completely.
  (If angle torquing in 2nd step, turn
  all bolts 35-40 degrees with an
  angle torque wrench.)
⑬ Tighten in 2 steps:
  1st—10-12 ft. lbs.
  2nd—30-33 ft. lbs.
  (If angle torquing in 2nd step, turn
  all nuts 60 to 65 degrees with an
  angle torque wrench.)
⑭ M/T Flywheel—105-112
  A/T Driveplate—69-76
⑮ Flywheel (M/T) or driveplate (A/T)
⑯ Tighten intake nut in two steps:
  1st—2.2-3.6 ft. lbs.
  2nd—17-20 ft. lbs.
  Tighten intake bolt in two steps:
  1st—2.2-3.6 ft. lbs.
  2nd—12-14 ft. lbs.
⑰ M/T Flywheel—61-69
  A/T driveplate—69-76

BRAKE SPECIFICATIONS
All measurements in inches unless noted.

Year	Model	Lug Nut Torque (ft. lbs.)	Master Cylinder Bore	Brake Disc Minimum Thickness	Brake Disc Maximum Runout	Standard Brake Drum Diameter	Minimum Lining Thickness Front	Minimum Lining Thickness Rear
1987	200SX	87–108	0.938	0.630 ①	0.0028 ②	—	0.080	0.080
	300ZX	72–87	0.938	0.787 ③	0.0028 ②	—	0.079	0.079
	Maxima	72–87	1.000	0.787 ①	0.0028 ②	—	0.079	0.079
	Pulsar	72–87	④	⑤	0.0028	8.000	0.079	0.059
	Sentra	72–87	④	⑤	0.0028	8.000 ⑥	0.079	0.059
	Stanza	72–87	④	0.787	0.0028	10.24 ⑦	0.079	0.059
1988	200SX	87–108	0.938	0.630 ①	0.0028 ②	—	0.080	0.080
	300SX	72–87	0.938	0.787 ③	0.0028 ②	—	0.080	0.080
	Maxima	72–87	1.000	0.787 ①	0.0028 ②	—	0.079	0.079
	Pulsar	72–87	④	⑤	0.0028	8.000	0.079	0.059
	Sentra	72–87	⑧	⑤	0.0028	8.000 ⑥	0.079	0.059
	Stanza	72–87	④	0.787	0.0028	9.000 ⑦	0.079	0.059
1989	240SX	72–87	0.875	0.709 ⑨	0.0028 ⑥	—	0.079	0.079
	300ZX	72–87	0.937	0.787 ⑯	0.0028 ⑥	—	0.079	0.079
	Maxima	72–87	1.000	0.787 ①	0.0028 ⑥	9.06	0.079	0.059
	Pulsar	72–87	⑩	⑪	0.0028	8.05	0.079	0.059
	Sentra	72–87	⑫	⑤	0.0028	8.05 ⑬	0.079	0.059
	Stanza	72–87	1.000	0.787	0.0028	9.06	0.079	0.059
1990–91	240SX	72–87	⑭	⑮	0.0028	—	0.079	0.059
	300ZX	72–87	⑯	⑰	0.0028	—	0.079	0.079
	300ZX Twin Turbo	72–87	—	⑱	0.0028	—	0.079	0.079
	Maxima	72–87	⑲	⑳	0.0028	9.000	0.079	㉑
	Pulsar	72–87	⑩	0.394	0.0028	8.000	0.079	0.059

BRAKE SPECIFICATIONS
All measurements in inches unless noted.

Year	Model	Lug Nut Torque (ft. lbs.)	Master Cylinder Bore	Brake Disc		Standard Brake Drum Diameter	Minimum Lining Thickness	
				Minimum Thickness	Maximum Runout		Front	Rear
1990-91	Sentra	72–87	⑫	㉒	0.0028	㉓	0.079	0.059
	Stanza	72–87	㉔	㉕	0.0028	9.000	0.079	㉑

NOTE: Minimum lining thickness is as recommended by the manufacturer. Due to variation in state inspection regulations, the minimum allowable thickness may be different than recommended.

—Not applicable

① Front disc on V6 models—0.787
  Rear disc on all models—0.354
② Rear disc—0.0028
③ Front disc on Turbo—0.945
  rear disc on all models—0.709
④ Pulsar
  with CA16DE—1.000
  with E16i—0.9380
  with CA18DE—1.000
  Sentra
  with gasoline engine—0.938
  Stanza
  All except 2WD wagon—1.000
  2WD wagon—0.9380
⑤ Pulsar
  with CA16DE—0.630
  with E16i—0.394
  with CA18DE—0.630
  Sentra
  Gasoline engine except wagon 0.394
  Gasoline engine wagon—0.630
  4WD wagon—0.630

⑥ 4WD—9.000
⑦ Wagon—9.000
⑧ 2WD wagon—0.938
  4WD wagon—1.000
⑨ Front; Rear—0.079
⑩ Pulsar
  with CA18DE
  large—1.000
  small—0.812
  With GA16i
  large—0.937
  Small—0.750
⑪ Pulsar
  with CA18DE 0.630
  with GA16i 0.394
⑫ Sentra 2WD and 4WD
  large—1.000
  small—0.812
⑬ 4WD—9.06
⑭ With ABS—0.937
  without ABS—0.575
⑮ Front disc:
  with ABS—0.709
  without ABS—0.787

Rear disc: 0.315
⑯ With ABS—0.941
  without ABS—0.937
⑰ Front disc—0.945
  Rear disc—0.630
⑱ Front disc—1.102
  Rear disc—0.630
⑲ GXE, SE (w/o ABS),
  GXE (with ABS)—0.937
  SE with ABS—1.000
⑳ Front disc—0.787
  Rear disc—0.354
㉑ Rear drum—0.059
  Rear disc—0.079
㉒ 2WD except wagon—0.394
  2WD wagon and all 4WD—0.630
㉓ 2WD—8.000
  4WD—9.000
㉔ With ABS—1.000
  without ABS—0.937
㉕ Front—0.787
  Rear—0.354

WHEEL ALIGNMENT

Year	Model	Caster		Camber		Toe-in (in.)	Steering Axis Inclination (deg.)
		Range (deg.)	Preferred Setting (deg.)	Range (deg.)	Preferred Setting (deg.)		
1987	200SX (Front)	$2\frac{3}{4}$P–$4\frac{1}{4}$P	—	$\frac{7}{16}$N–$1\frac{1}{16}$P	—	$\frac{1}{32}$N–$\frac{1}{32}$P	$11\frac{11}{16}$
	Rear	—	—	$1\frac{1}{4}$N–$\frac{1}{4}$P	—	$\frac{5}{64}$N–0	—
	300ZX (Front)	$5\frac{13}{16}$P–$7\frac{5}{16}$P	—	$\frac{9}{16}$N–$\frac{15}{16}$P	—	$\frac{1}{32}$N–$\frac{1}{8}$P	13
	Rear	—	—	$1\frac{15}{16}$N–$\frac{7}{16}$N	—	$\frac{1}{16}$N–$\frac{3}{32}$P	—
	Maxima (Front)	$1\frac{1}{4}$P–$2\frac{3}{4}$P	—	$\frac{7}{16}$N–$1\frac{1}{16}$P	—	$\frac{1}{32}$–$\frac{1}{8}$	$13\frac{3}{4}$
	Rear	—	—	$1\frac{3}{16}$N–$\frac{5}{16}$P	—	$\frac{5}{64}$–$\frac{15}{64}$	—
	Pulsar (Front)	$1\frac{3}{16}$P–$2\frac{11}{16}$P	—	$1\frac{1}{4}$N–$\frac{1}{4}$P	—	$\frac{1}{32}$N–$\frac{1}{32}$P	$14\frac{7}{16}$
	Rear	—	—	2N–$\frac{1}{2}$N	—	$\frac{1}{16}$N–$\frac{3}{32}$P	—
	Sentra—2wd (Front exc Cpe)	$1\frac{1}{16}$P–$2\frac{9}{16}$P	—	$\frac{15}{16}$N–$\frac{9}{16}$P	—	$\frac{1}{32}$N–$\frac{1}{32}$P	14
	(Front—Cpe)	$1\frac{1}{4}$P–$2\frac{3}{4}$P	—	$1\frac{1}{16}$N–$\frac{1}{4}$P	—	$\frac{1}{32}$N–$\frac{1}{32}$P	$14\frac{1}{4}$
	(Rear exc Cpe)	—	—	$1\frac{3}{4}$N–$\frac{1}{4}$N	—	$\frac{1}{32}$–$\frac{3}{16}$	—
	(Rear Cpe)	—	—	$1\frac{15}{16}$N–$\frac{7}{16}$N	—	$\frac{1}{32}$–$\frac{3}{16}$	—
	Sentra 4WD (Front)	$\frac{3}{16}$P–$1\frac{11}{16}$P	—	$1\frac{3}{16}$N–$\frac{11}{16}$P	—	$\frac{1}{32}$N–$\frac{1}{16}$P	$13\frac{9}{16}$
	(Rear)	—	—	$1\frac{15}{16}$N–$\frac{9}{16}$P	—	0–$\frac{5}{32}$	—
	Stanza (Front)	$1\frac{1}{4}$P–$2\frac{3}{4}$P	—	$\frac{1}{4}$N–$1\frac{1}{2}$P	—	$\frac{1}{32}$–$\frac{1}{8}$P	$14\frac{9}{16}$
	(Rear)	—	—	$1\frac{3}{16}$N–$\frac{5}{16}$P	—	$\frac{5}{64}$–$\frac{16}{64}$	—

WHEEL ALIGNMENT

Year	Model	Caster Range (deg.)	Caster Preferred Setting (deg.)	Camber Range (deg.)	Camber Preferred Setting (deg.)	Toe-in (in.)	Steering Axis Inclination (deg.)
1987	Stanza Wagon (Front 2WD)	3/4P–2 1/4P	—	1/4N–1 1/4P	—	1/16–1/8	12
	(Front 4WD)	9/16P–2 1/16P	—	7/16N–1 1/16P	—	1/32N–1/16P	11 3/4
	(Rear 2WD)	—	—	1N–1P	—	5/64–5/16	—
	(Rear 4WD)	—	—	0–1 1/2P	—	5/32N–0	—
1988	200SX (Front)	2 3/4P–4 1/4P	—	3/8N–1 1/16P	—	1/64P–1/10P	12 3/4
	Rear	—	—	1 1/4N–1/4P	—	5/64P–0	—
	300SX (Front)	5 13/16P–7 5/16P	—	9/16N–15/16P	—	1/32P–1/8P	13 11/16
	Rear	—	—	1 15/16N–7/16N	—	①	—
	Maxima (Front)	1 1/4P–2 3/4P	—	7/16N–1/16P	—	1/16P–1/4P	14 1/2
	Rear	—	—	1 3/16N–5/16P	—	3/32P–1/4P	—
	Pulsar (Front)	1 3/16P–2 11/16P	—	1 1/4N–1/4P	—	②	14 13/16
	Rear	—	—	2N–1/2N	—	①	—
	Sentra 2WD (Front—Cpe)	7/8P–2 3/8P	—	1 1/16N–7/16P	—	③	14 3/4
	(Rear Cpe)	—	—	1 15/16N–7/16N	—	1/32P–1/8P	—
	(Front exc Cpe)	3/4P–2 1/4P	—	15/16N–9/16P	—	③	14 1/2
	(Rear exc Cpe)	—	—	1 7/8N–3/8N	—	0–3/16P	—
	Sentra 4WD (Front)	1/8P–1 5/8P	—	7/8N–5/8P	—	④	13 15/16
	(Rear)	—	—	7/8N–5/8P	—	0–3/16P	—
	Stanza (Front)	1 1/4P–2 3/4P	—	7/16N–1 1/16P	—	1/32P–1/8P	14 5/8
	(Rear)	—	—	1 3/16N–5/16P	—	3/32P–1/4P	—
	Stanza Wagon (Front 2WD)	3/4P–2 1/4P	—	1/4N–1 1/4P	—	1/16P–9/64P	12
	(Rear 2WD)	—	—	1N–1P	—	⑤	—
	(Front 4WD)	9/16P–2 1/16P	—	1/2N–1 1/16P	—	1/64P–1/16P	11 3/4
	(Rear 4WD)	—	—	0–1 1/2P	—	⑥	—
1989	240SX (Front)	6P–7 1/2P	—	1 1/2N–0	—	0–3/16P	13 1/4
	Rear	—	—	2N–1/2N	—	1/16–3/32	—
	300ZX (Front)	5 13/16P	—	9/16N–15/16P	—	1/32–1/8	13 7/16
	Rear	—	—	1 15/16N–7/16N	—	1/16–3/32	—
	Maxima (Front)	1/2P–2P	—	1N–1/2P	—	1/32–1/8	14 3/8
	Rear	—	—	1 5/16N–3/16	—	1/32–1/8P	—
	Pulsar (Front)	1 3/16P–2 11/16P	—	1 1/4N–1/4P	—	⑦	14 13/16
	Rear	—	—	2N–1/2N	—	1/16–3/32	—
	Sentra 2WD (Front—Cpe)	7/8P–2 3/8P	—	1 1/16N–7/16P	—	1/32–1/16 ⑧	14 3/4
	(Rear Cpe)	—	—	1 15/16N–7/16N	—	1/32P–1/8P ⑨	—
	(Front exc Cpe)	3/4P–2 1/4P	—	15/16N–9/16P	—	1/32–1/16 ⑧	14 1/2
	(Rear exc Cpe)	—	—	1 7/8N–3/8N	—	0–3/16P	—
	Sentra 4WD (Front)	1/8P–1 5/8P	—	7/8N–5/8P	—	③	13 15/16
	(Rear)	—	—	7/8N–5/8P	—	0–3/16	—

WHEEL ALIGNMENT

Year	Model	Caster Range (deg.)	Caster Preferred Setting (deg.)	Camber Range (deg.)	Camber Preferred Setting (deg.)	Toe-in (in.)	Steering Axis Inclination (deg.)
1989	Stanza (Front)	1 5/16 P–2 13/16 P	—	7/16 N–1 1/16 P	—	1/16–5/32	14 5/8
	(Rear)	—	—	1 3/16 N–5/16 P	—	3/32–5/16 ⑤	—
1990-91	240SX (Front)	6°P–7°1/2	—	1 1/2 N–0	—	1/32–3/32	13 1/4
	(Rear)	—	—	1 5/8 N–5/8 N	—	1/32–3/16	—
	300ZX (Front)	9°P–10°1/2P	—	1 9/16 N–1/16 N	—	0–3/32	12 15/16
	(Rear)	—	—	1 5/8 N–5/8 N	—	1/64–3/16	—
	Maxima (Front)	1/2P–2°P	—	1N–1/2P	—	1/32–1/8	14 3/8
	(Rear)	—	—	1 5/16 N–3/16 P	—	0–5/32	—
	Pulsar (Front)	1 3/16 P–2 11/16 P	—	1 1/4 N–1/4 P	—	⑦	14 13/16
	(Rear)	—	—	2N–1/2N	—	①	—
	Sentra 2WD (Front—Cpe.)	7/8P–2 3/8 P	—	1 1/16 N–7/16 N	—	③	14 3/4
	(Rear—Cpe.)	—	—	2N–1/2N	—	①	—
	(Front Exc. Cpe.)	3/4P–2 1/4P	—	15/16 N–9/16 P	—	⑧	14 1/2
	(Rear Exc. Cpe.)	—	—	1 7/8 N–3/8 N	—	0–3/16	—
	Sentra 4WD (Front)	1/8P–1 5/8P	—	7/8N–5/8P	—	③	13 15/16
	(Rear)	—	—	7/8N–5/8P	—	0–3/16	—
	Stanza (Front)	5/8P–2 1/16P	—	1/2N–1P	—	1/16–1/8	14 1/2
	(Rear)	—	—	1 7/16 N–3/16	—	0–5/16	—

N—Negative
P—Positive
① 1/16 Toe Out–3/32 Toe In
② 1/16 Toe Out–1/16 Toe In
③ 1/32 Toe Out–1/16 Toe In
④ 1/32 Toe Out–1/32 Toe In
⑤ 3/32 Toe Out–5/16 Toe In
⑥ 5/32 Toe Out–0
⑦ 1/16 Toe Out–1/16 Toe In
⑧ 1/32 Toe Out–1/16 Toe In
⑨ 1/32 Toe Out–1/8 Toe In

ENGINE ELECTRICAL

NOTE: Disconnecting the negative battery cable on some vehicles may interfere with the functions of the on board computer systems and may require the computer to undergo a relearning process, once the negative battery cable is reconnected.

Distributor

NOTE: The CA16DE and CA18DE (used in the 1987–89 Pulsar) and VG30DE and VG30DETT engines (used in the 1990–91 300ZX) do not use a conventional distributor and high tension wires. Instead these engines use small ignition coils fitted directly to each spark plug. The ECU controls the coils by means of a crank angle sensor and other engine parameter gathering equipment.

Removal

1. Disconnect the negative battery cable.

2. Release the retaining clips and lift the distributor cap straight up. It will be easier to install the distributor if the wiring is not disconnected from the cap. If the wires must be removed from the cap, label the wires according to cylinder number to aid in installation and avoid confusion.

3. Disconnect the distributor wiring harness.

4. Disconnect and label the vacuum lines, if equipped.

5. Note the position of the rotor in relation to the base. Scribe a mark on the base of the distributor and on the engine block to facilitate reinstallation. Align the marks with the direction the rotor is pointing.

6. Remove the bolt(s) which hold the distributor to the engine.

7. Lift the distributor assembly from the engine.

NOTE: Once the distributor is removed, try not to disturb the position of the rotor.

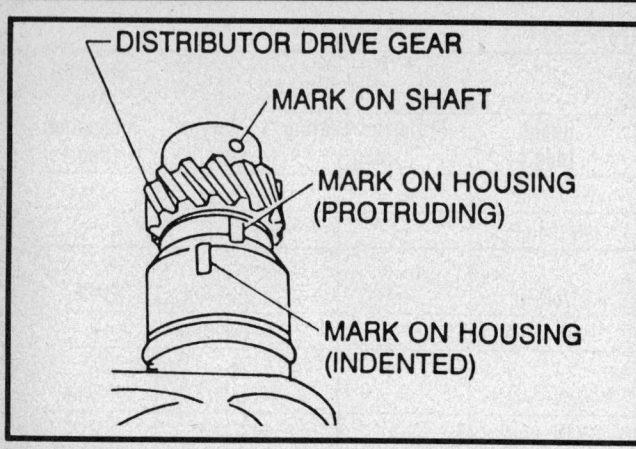

Distributor shaft and housing alignment marks—V-Series engines, except 1990–91 300ZX

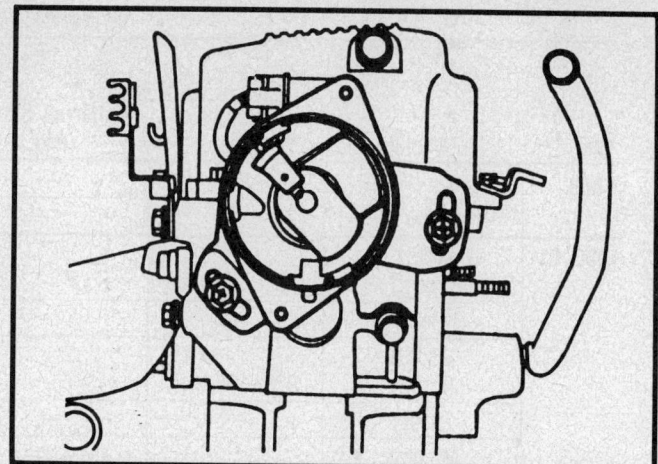

Distributor rotor at No. 1 cylinder TDC postion—1990–91 Stanza

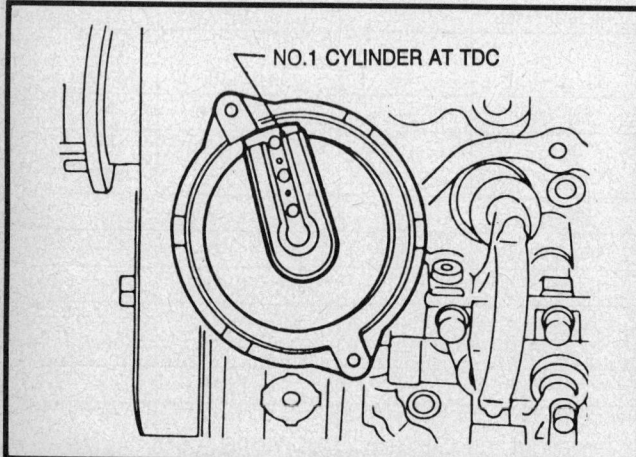

Distributor rotor at No. 1 cylinder TDC position—V-Series engines, except 1990–91 300ZX

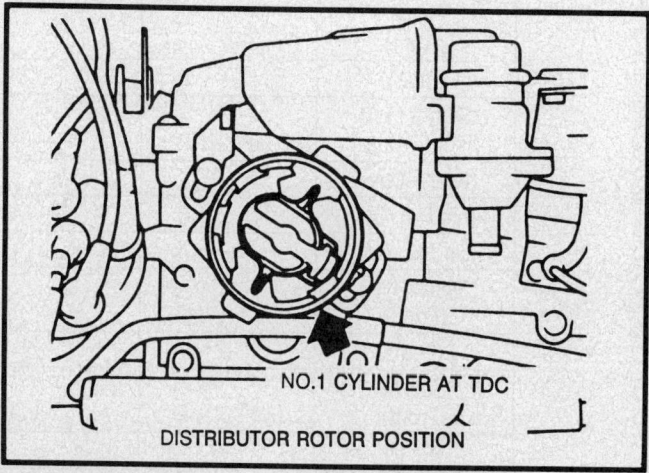

Distributor rotor at No. 1 cylinder TDC position—GA16i engine

Installation

TIMING NOT DISTURBED

1. Insert the distributor shaft and assembly into the engine.

2. Align the distributor and engine matchmarks with the rotor. Make sure the vacuum advance diaphragm is pointed in the same direction as it was pointed originally. This will be done automatically if the marks on the engine and the distributor are lined up with the rotor. On 240SX, make sure the distributor driving spindle is properly aligned before inserting the distributor into the front cover.

3. Install the distributor hold-down bolt and clamp. Leave the screw loose enough so the distributor can be moved with moderate hand pressure.

4. Connect the vacuum lines, if equipped.

5. Connect the primary wire to the coil.

6. Install the distributor cap on the distributor housing. Secure the distributor cap with the spring clips.

7. Install the spark plug wires if removed. Make sure the wires are pressed all the way into the top of the distributor cap and firmly onto the spark plug.

8. Set the ignition timing.

TIMING DISTURBED

NOTE: If the crankshaft has been turned or the engine disturbed in any manner (i.e., disassembled and re-built) while the distributor was removed or if the marks were not drawn, it will be necessary to initially time the engine. Follow the procedure given below.

1. It is necessary to place the No. 1 cylinder in the firing position to correctly install the distributor. To locate this position, the ignition timing marks on the crankshaft front pulley are used.

2. Remove the No. 1 cylinder spark plug. Turn the crankshaft until the piston in the No. 1 cylinder is moving up on the compression stroke. This can be determined by placing a thumb over the spark plug hole and feeling the air being forced out of the cylinder. Stop turning the crankshaft when the timing marks are aligned. On 240SX, the driving spindle must be properly aligned to accept the distributor.

3. Oil the distributor housing lightly where the distributor mounts to the block.

4. Install the distributor so the rotor, which is mounted on the shaft, points toward the No. 1 spark plug terminal tower position when the cap is installed. Lay the cap on top of the distributor and make a mark on the side of the distributor housing just below the No. 1 spark plug terminal. Make sure the rotor points toward that mark when installing the distributor.

5. When the distributor shaft has reached the bottom of the hole, move the rotor back and forth slightly until the driving lug on the end of the shaft enters the slots cut in the end of the oil pump shaft and the distributor assembly slides down into place.

6. When the distributor is correctly installed, the reluctor teeth should be aligned with the pick-up coil. This can be accomplished by rotating the distributor body after it has been installed in the engine. Once again, line up the marks made before the distributor was removed.

7. Install the distributor hold-down bolt.

8. Install the spark plug into the No. 1 spark plug hole and continue with the remainder of the distributor installation procedure.

Ignition Timing

NOTE: The 200SX (CA20E), 200SX Turbo (CA18ET) and 1987–89 Stanza models use a dual electronic ignition. The firing order is 1–3–4–2 and the rotor is designed with a 135 degree offset to fire both spark plugs at the same time.

Adjustment

200SX, 240SX, 1987–89 300ZX, MAXIMA, SENTRA AND STANZA

1. Locate the timing marks on the crankshaft pulley and the front of the engine.

2. Clean off the timing marks.

3. Use chalk or white paint to color the mark on the crankshaft pulley and the mark on the scale which will indicate the correct timing when aligned with the notch on the crankshaft pulley.

4. Connect a tachometer to the engine.

5. Attach a timing light to the engine, according to the manufacturer's instructions.

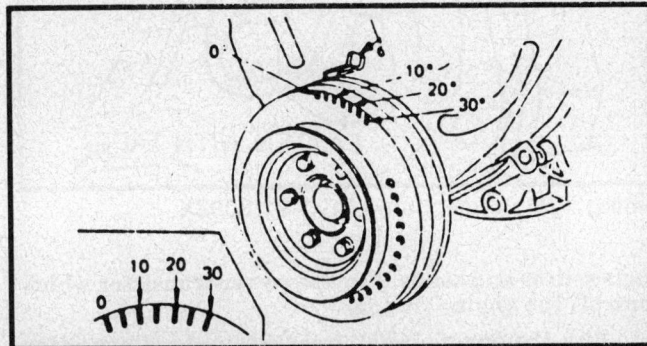

300ZX V6 timing marks

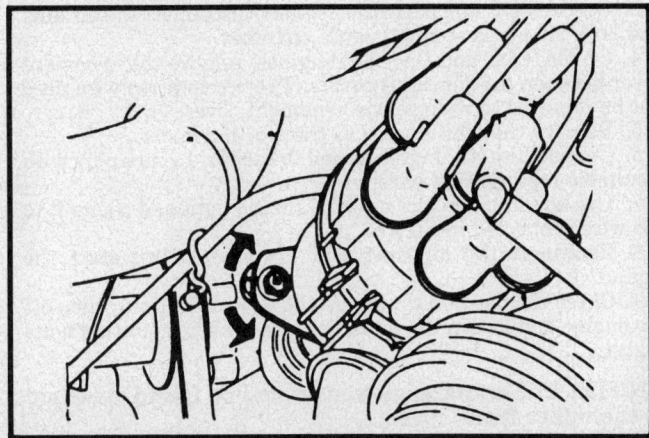

Loosen the distributor lockbolt and turn the distributor slightly to advance (upper arrow) or retard (lower arrow) the timing

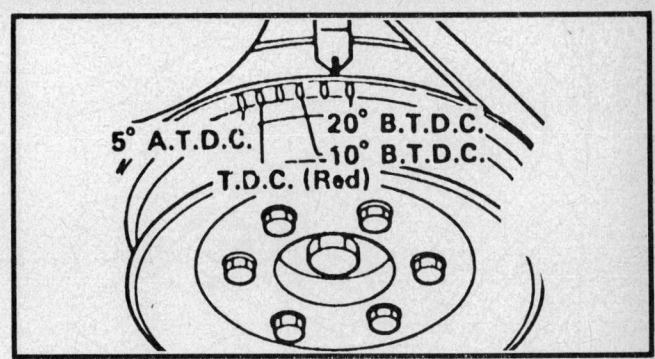

Ignition timing marks—240SX and 1990–91 Stanza

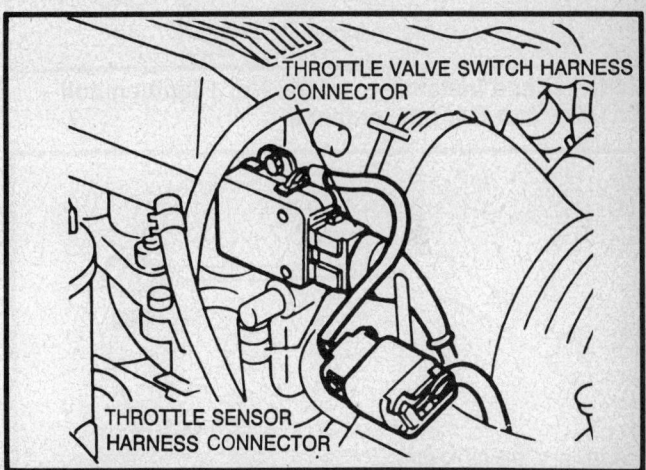

Throttle harness connector location on 240SX

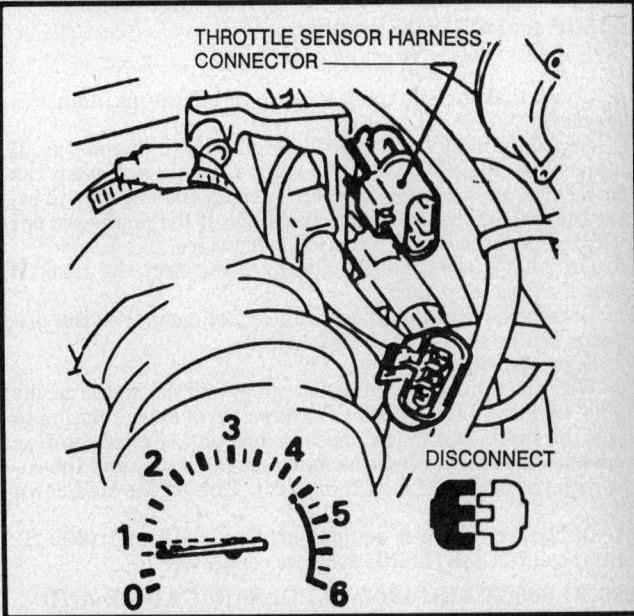

Throttle harness connector location on 1990–91 Stanza

6. Leave the vacuum line connected to the distributor vacuum diaphragm and disconnect and plug the hose on those models.

7. Start the engine and allow to reach normal operating temperature.

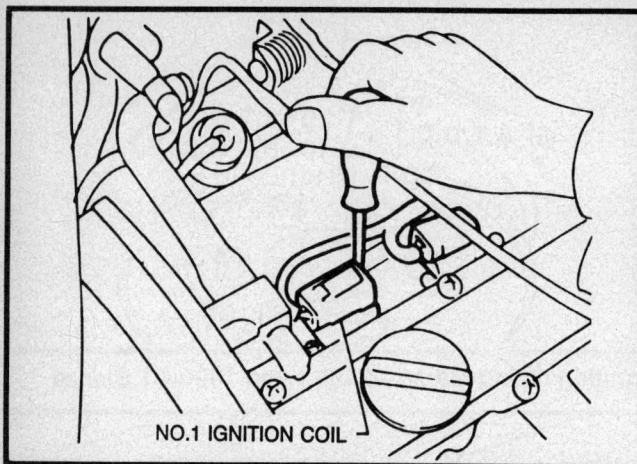

Removal and installation of the No. 1 ignition coil—CA16DE and CA18DE engines

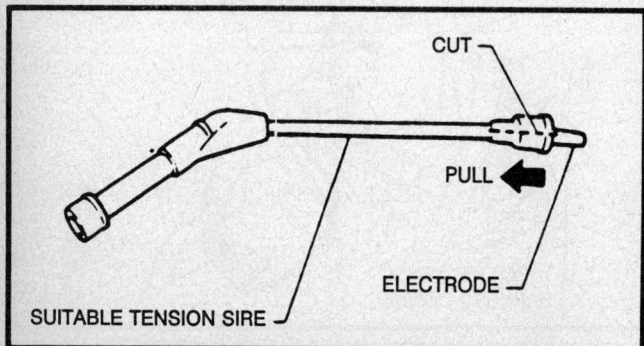

Suitable high tension wire for timing adjustment—CA16DE and CA18DE engines

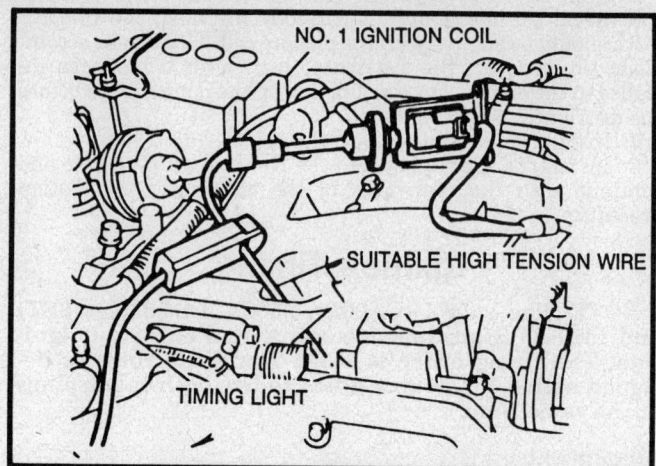

Timing licht connection—1990–91 300ZX

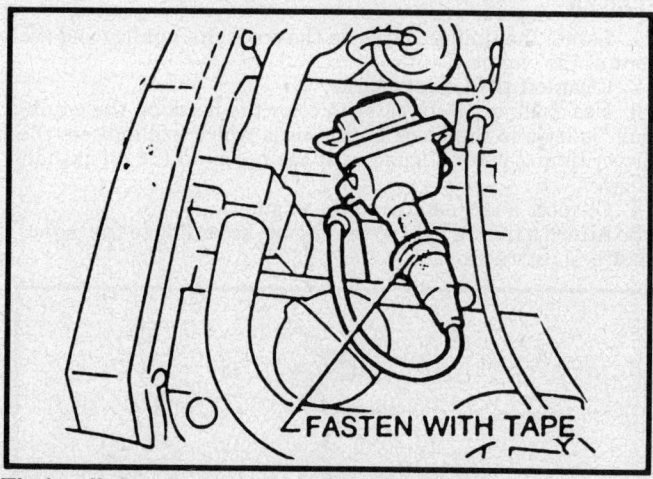

Timing light connection—1990–91 300ZX

8. Check that the idle speed is set to specifications. Adjust as necessary.

9. Aim the timing light and illuminate the timing marks. If the marks on the pulley and the engine are aligned when the light flashes, the timing is correct. Turn off the engine and remove the tachometer and the timing light. If the marks are not in alignment, proceed with the following steps.

10. On 240SX and 1990–91 Stanza, disconnect the throttle sensor harness connector.

11. Loosen the distributor lockbolt(s) just enough so the distributor can be turned with little effort.

12. Start the engine.

13. With the timing light aimed at pulley and the marks on the engine, turn the distributor in the direction of rotor rotation to retard the spark, and in the opposite direction of rotor rotation to advance the spark. Align the marks on the pulley and the engine with the flashes of the timing light. Tighten the hold-down bolt.

14. Disconnect the test equipment. On 240SX and 1990–91 Stanza, connect the throttle harness connector.

1990–91 300ZX AND 1987–89 PULSAR (CA16DE AND CA18DE ENGINES)

NOTE: The CA16DE, CA18DE, VG30DE and VG30DETT engines do not utilize a conventional distributor and high tension wires. Instead they use small ignition coils fitted directly to each spark plug. The ECU controls the coils by means of a crank angle sensor from which it receives piston position and engine speed information. The ECU takes the information from the crank angle sensor and sends it to the power transistor which controls the engine timing.

1. Run the engine until it reaches normal operating temperature.

2. Check the idle speed and adjust as necessary.

3. On CA16DE and CA18DE engines, disconnect the air duct and both air hoses at the throttle chamber.

4. On CA16DE and CA18DE engines, remove the ornament cover between the camshaft covers. The acceleration wire need not be removed to remove the ornament cover.

5. Remove the ignition coil at the No. 1 cylinder.

6. Connect the No. 1 ignition coil to the No. 1 spark plug with a suitable high tension wire.

7. Use an inductive pick-up type timing light and clamp it to the wire connected in Step 6.

8. Reconnect the air duct and hoses and then start the engine.

9. Check the ignition timing. If not to specifications, turn off the engine and loosen the 3 crank angle sensor mounting bolts slightly.

NOTE: The crank angle sensor can be found attached to the upper front cover.

10. Restart the engine and adjust the timing by turning the sensor body slightly until the timing is within specifications. Clockwise rotation retards the timing and counterclockwise rotation advances it.

1989–91 PULSAR AND SENTRA (GA16i ENGINE)

1. Run the engine until the water temperature indicator points to the middle of the gauge.
2. Run the engine for 1–2 minutes with no load; all electrical accessories in the **OFF** position.
3. Connect a timing light to the engine and illuminate the timing marks. If the timing is not within specification, proceed to adjust.
4. To adjust the timing, stop the engine and disconnect the throttle sensor connector. Loosen the distributor hold-down bolt just enough to allow the distributor to be turned by hand.
5. Start the engine and race it 2–3 times with no load and then allow the engine to run at idle speed.
6. Adjust the ignition timing by rotating the distributor either clockwise or counterclockwise.
7. Tighten the distributor hold-down bolt and stop the engine.
8. Connect the throttle sensor connector and remove the timing light.

Alternator

Precautions

The following precautions must be observed to prevent alternator and regulator damage:
- Be absolutely sure of correct polarity when installing a new battery or connecting a battery charger.
- Do not short across or ground any alternator or regulator terminals.
- Disconnect the battery ground cable before replacing any electrical unit.
- Never operate the alternator with any of the leads disconnected.
- When steam cleaning the engine, be careful not to subject the alternator to excessive heat or moisture.
- When charging the battery, remove it from the vehicle or disconnect the alternator output terminal.

Belt Tension Adjustment

The correct belt tension for all alternators is about ½–½ in. play on the longest span of the belt.
1. Loosen the alternator pivot and mounting bolts.
2. Pry the alternator toward or away from the engine until the tension is correct. Use a hammer handle or wooden prybar.
3. When the tension is correct, tighten the bolts and check the adjustment. Be careful not to over-tighten the belt, which will lead to alternator bearing failure.

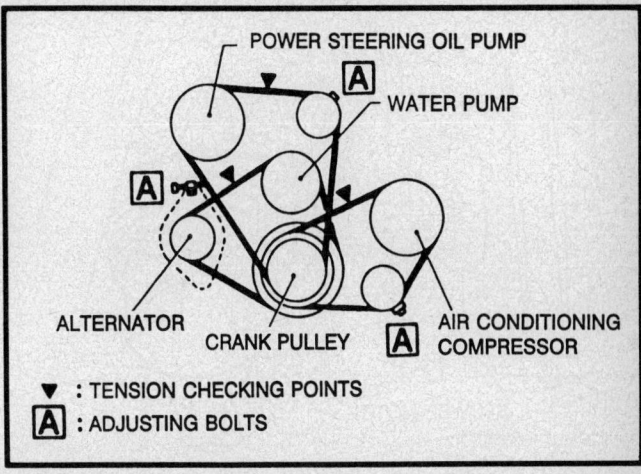

Drive belt arrangement—240SX and 1990–91 Stanza

Removal and Installation

1. Disconnect the negative battery cable.
2. Disconnect the 2 lead wires and harness connector from the alternator.
3. Loosen the drive belt adjusting bolt and remove the belt.
4. Unscrew the alternator attaching bolts and remove the alternator from the vehicle. On the 1987–89 300ZX, first remove the front stabilizer bar bolts and pull the stabilizer bar down. On 1990–91 300ZX, remove the lower radiator hose bracket and pull the hose upward to gain the clearance to remove the alternator.
5. Installation is in the reverse order of removal. Adjust the drive belt tension.

Starter

Removal and Installation

1. Disconnect the negative battery cable.
2. Remove the starter heat shield (300ZX) and harness clamps, if equipped. On 1990–91 Stanza with automatic transaxle, remove the harness connectors from the harness connector bracket.
3. Disconnect and label the wires from the terminals on the solenoid.
4. Remove the 2 bolts which secure the starter to the flywheel housing and pull the starter forward and out. To install, reverse the removal procedure. Check the starter for proper operation.

CHASSIS ELECTRICAL

CAUTION

On vehicles equipped with an air bag, the negative battery cable must be disconnected, before working on the vehicle. Failure to do so may result in deployment of the air bag and possible personal injury.

Heater Blower Motor

Removal and Installation

1. Disconnect the negative battery cable.
2. Remove all panels and ducting necessary to gain access to the blower motor.
3. Disconnnect the blower motor harness wiring connectors.
4. Remove the blower motor retaining screws and lower the motor/wheel from the intake housing. On some models, release the clips that attach the blower casing to the intake housing to remove the blower motor.

To install:
5. Transfer the old blower wheel to the shaft of the new motor.
6. Raise the blower/wheel assembly up and onto the intake housing. Use a new gasket, if required.
7. Install the blower motor retaining screws or lock the clips.
8. Connect the blower motor wiring.

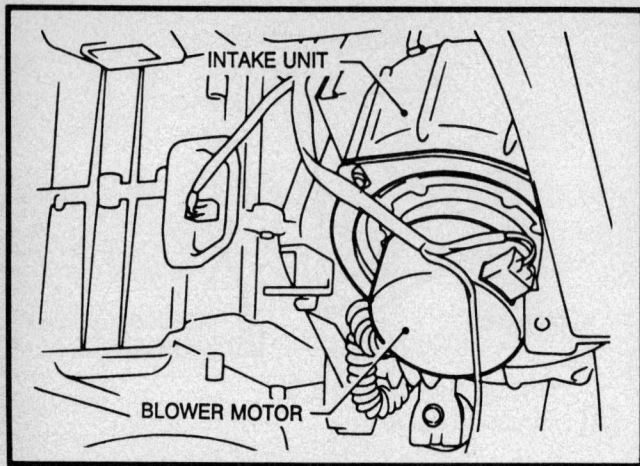

Typical blower motor mounting

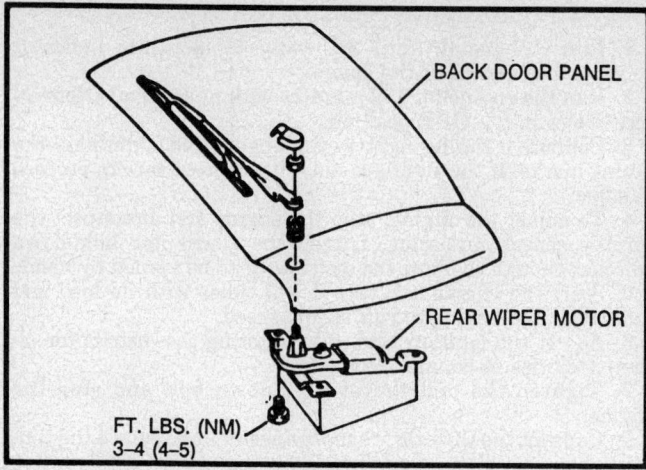

Rear wiper assembly—240SX

9. Install all ducting and panels.
10. Connect the negative battery cable.
11. Check the blower for proper operation at all speeds.

Windshield Wiper Motor

Removal and Installation

200SX, 240SX, STANZA AND STANZA WAGON

Front

1. Disconnect the negative battery cable and make sure the wiper switch is in the **OFF** position.
2. Remove the wiper arm.
3. Remove the cowl cover and disconnect the wiper harness connector(s).
3. Remove the wiper motor bolts.
4. Maneuver the wiper motor so the wiper motor link exits the oblong opening in the front cowl top panel. Then, pull the motor straight out and disconnect the ball joint from the motor and wiper links.
5. Remove the wiper motor.
6. Remove the wiper link pivot blocks on the driver's and passenger's sides.
7. Withdraw the wiper link and pivot blocks as one unit from the oblong opening on the left side (driver's) of the cowl top.

To install:

8. Lubricate the ball joints and pivot points with multi-purpose grease.
9. Position the wiper link and pivot block as one unit in the cowl top thorough the oblong hole.
10. Before installing the pivot blocks on the cowl top, hold the end of the motor side link at the hole in the front cowl top panel and insert the motor link ball pin into the wiper link hole.
11. Mount the wiper motor and install the bolts.
12. Connect the wiper motor wiring and install the cowl cover.
13. Attach the wiper arm. To reduce wiper arm looseness, prior to connecting the wiper arm, make sure the motor spline shaft and pivot area is completely free of debris and corrosion. Wire brush as necessary.

NOTE: On 200SX, one wiper arm is longer than the other. The driver's side arm is marked with a "D" and the passenger's side with an "A". Make sure they are installed on their respective sides.

14. Connnect the negative battery cable and check the wipers for proper operation.

Rear

1. Disconnect the negative battery cable.

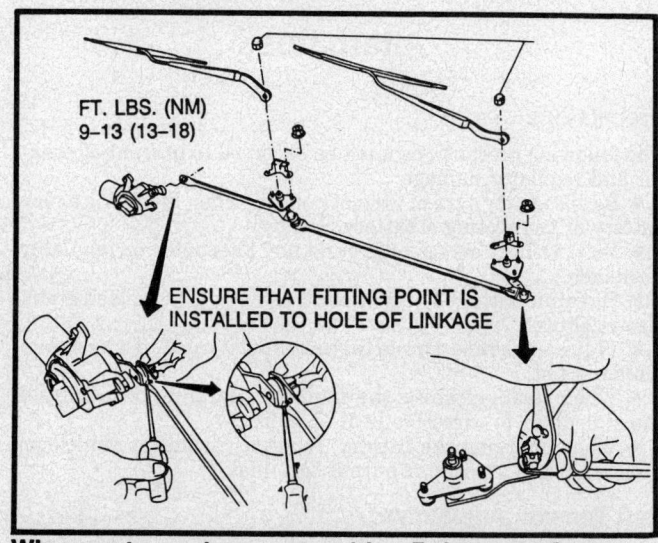

Wiper motor and arm assembly—Pulsar and Sentra

2. Lift up the rear hatch.
3. Separate the rear wiper arm from the motor shaft.
4. Disconnect the wiper motor wiring harness connector.
5. Unbolt and remove the rear wiper motor from the hatch.
6. Installation is the reverse of the removal procedure. Check the wipers for proper operation.

PULSAR AND SENTRA

The wiper motor is on the firewall under the hood. The operating linkage is on the firewall inside the vehicle.

1. Detach the motor wiring plug.
2. Working from inside the vehicle, remove the nut connecting the linkage to the wiper shaft.
3. Unbolt and remove the wiper motor from the firewall.
4. Installation is the reverse of the removal procedure. To reduce wiper arm looseness, prior to connecting the wiper arm, make sure the motor spline shaft and pivot area is completely free of debris and corrosion. Wire brush as necessary.

300ZX AND MAXIMA

The wiper motor and operating linkage is on the firewall under the hood.

1. Disconnect the negative battery cable.
2. Lift the wiper arms. Remove the securing nuts and detach the arms.

3. Remove the air intake grille.
4. Remove the nuts holding the wiper pivots to the body.
5. Open the hood and unscrew the motor from the firewall.
6. Disconnect the wiring connector and remove the wiper motor with the linkage.
7. Installation is the reverse of the removal procedure. To reduce wiper arm looseness, prior to connecting the wiper arm, make sure the motor spline shaft and pivot area is completely free of debris and corrosion. Wire brush as necessary.

NOTE: If the wipers do not park correctly, adjust the position of the automatic stop cover on the wiper motor.

Windshield Wiper Switch

Removal and Installation
FRONT
The windshield wiper switch is part of the combination switch, which is mounted on the steering column.

REAR

200SX, 240SX, 300ZX, Stanza and Sentra
On Stanza wagon the rear window wiper/washer is located left-side of the instrument panel. On Sentra wagon the rear window wiper/washer is located right-side of the instrument panel. On all other vehicles, the rear window wiper switch is located on the right side of the instrument panel.
1. Remove the instrument cluster.
2. Remove the nut that attaches the combination switch to the dash.
3. Disconnect the electrical connectors from the rear of the switch, then remove it.
4. Installation is the reverse of the removal procedure.

Instrument Cluster

Removal and Installation
200SX AND 240SX

NOTE: On 240SX, when removing the Head-Up Display (HUD) finisher, be careful not to scratch the HUD's reflective surface. To prevent this, cover the finisher and reflective surface with a protective covering.

1. Disconnect the negative battery cable.
2. Remove the steering wheel and steering wheel covers, as required.
3. Remove the screws holding the cluster lid in place and remove the lid.
4. On 200SX, remove the 2 screws and 7 pawls to release the cluster. On 240SX, the cluster is held with 3 screws.
5. Carefully withdraw the cluster from the instrument panel and disconnect the speedometer cable (analog) and electrical wiring from the rear of the cluster. Make sure the wiring is labeled clearly to avoid confusion during installation.
6. Remove the cluster. Be careful not to damage the printed circuit.
7. Installation is the reverse of the removal procedure.

300ZX

1. Disconnect the negative battery cable.
2. Remove the steering wheel and steering wheel covers.
3. To remove the combination switch, first remove the combination switch lower mounting nut, then remove the switch.
4. Remove the left and right instrument switches by removing the hooks and fasteners.
5. Remove the cluster lids and cluster retaining screws.
6. Carefully withdraw the cluster from the instrument panel and disconnect the speedometer cable and electrical wiring from

the rear of the cluster. Make sure the wiring is labeled clearly to avoid confusion during installation.
7. Remove the cluster. Be careful not to damage the printed circuit.
8. Installation is the reverse of the removal procedure.

MAXIMA

NOTE: On 1989–91 Maxima, when removing the Head-Up Display (HUD) finisher, be careful not to scratch the HUD's reflective surface. To prevent this, cover the finisher and reflective surface with a protective covering.

1. Disconnect the negative battery cable.
2. Remove the instrument panel lower cover.
3. Remove the steering wheel and steering wheel covers.
4. Remove the cluster lids.
5. Genlty withdraw the combination meter assembly from the instrument pad and disconnect the speedometer cable (analog).
6. Disconnect the wiring and remove the cluster. Make sure the wiring is marked clearly to avoid confusion during installation.
7. Remove the cluster. Be careful not to damage the printed circuit.
8. Installation is the reverse of the removal procedure.

PULSAR, SENTRA AND STANZA

1. Disconnect the negative battery cable.
2. Remove the steering wheel and the steering column covers.
3. Remove the instrument cluster lid by removing its screws.
4. Remove the instrument cluster screws.
5. Gently withdraw the cluster from the instrument pad and disconnect all wiring and speedometer cable. Make sure the wires are marked clearly to avoid confusion during installation. Be careful not to damage the printed circuit.
6. Remove the cluster.
7. Installation is the reverse of removal.

Speedometer

NOTE: If equipped with a digital speedometer, the entire cluster assembly must be replaced if the speedometer is faulty.

Removal and Installation
ANALOG (NEEDLE TYPE) SPEEDOMETERS

1. Disconnect the negative battery cable.
2. Remove the cluster.

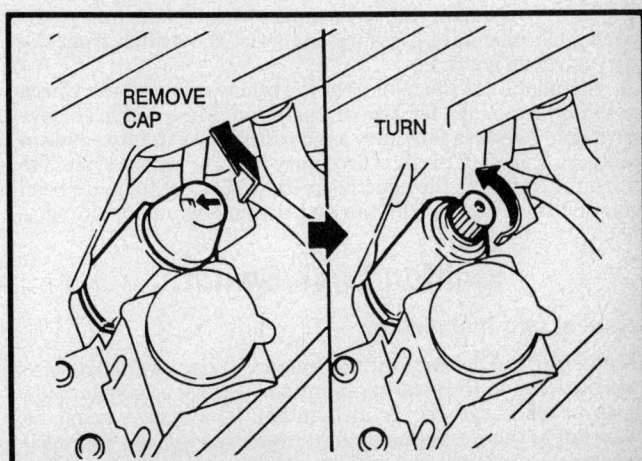

Manual operation of retractable headlights

3. Disconnect the speedometer cable and remove the speedometer fasteners.

4. Carefully remove the speedometer from the cluster. Be careful not to damage the printed circuit board.

5. Installation is the reverse of the removal procedure.

Concealed Headlights

— CAUTION —

Before attempting to manually operate the concealed (retractable) headlights, first disconnect the negative battery cable. Otherwise the headlights and motor shaft may suddenly move and injure hand and fingers.

Manual Operation

NOTE: If the headlights are frozen and inoperative, carefully melt the ice before attempting the manual operation procedure. Operation of a frozen headlight will drain the battery and may cause damage to the motor and operating linkages.

1. Switch the headlight and retractable headlight switches to the **OFF** position.

2. Disconnect the negative battery cable.

3. Remove the rubber cap from the motor shaft.

4. Manually turn the motor shaft in the counterclockwise position until the headlights are in the desired position (open or closed).

5. Install the motor shaft cap.

6. Connect the negative battery cable.

7. Check the head lights for proper operation.

Combination Switch

Removal and Installation

1. Disconnect the battery ground cable.

2. Remove the steering wheel. On 1989–91 Maxima with sonar suspension, remove the steering angle sensor from the steering column.

3. Remove the steering column covers.

NOTE: At this point, the individual switch assemblies can be removed without removing the combination switch base assembly. To service an individual switch/stalk assembly, disconnect the electrical lead and remove the 2 stalk-to-base mounting screws. If the switch base must be removed, proceed with the remainder of the removal procedure.

4. Disconnect the electrical plugs from the switch.

5. Remove the retaining screws, push down on the base of the switch with moderate pressure and twist the switch from the steering wheel shaft.

6. Installation is the reverse of the removal procedure. Check the switch functions for proper operation. Many vehicles have turn signal switches that have a tab which must fit into a hole in the steering shaft. This fit is necessary in order for the system to return the switch to the neutral position after the turn has been made. Be sure to align the tab and the hole when installing.

Ignition Lock/Switch

Removal and Installation

The steering lock/ignition switch/warning buzzer switch assembly is attached to the steering column by special screws or bolts whose heads shear off on installation. The screws must be drilled out to remove the assembly or removed with an appropriate tool.

1. Disconnect the negative battery cable.

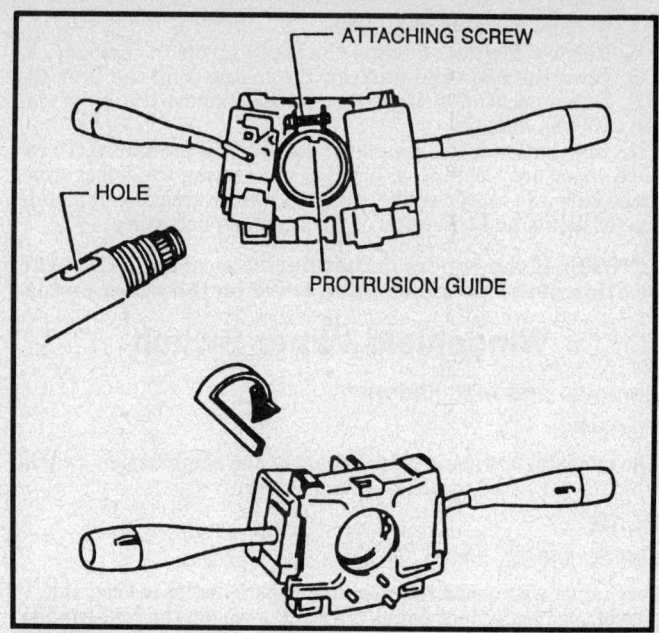

Combination switch removal, installation and alignment

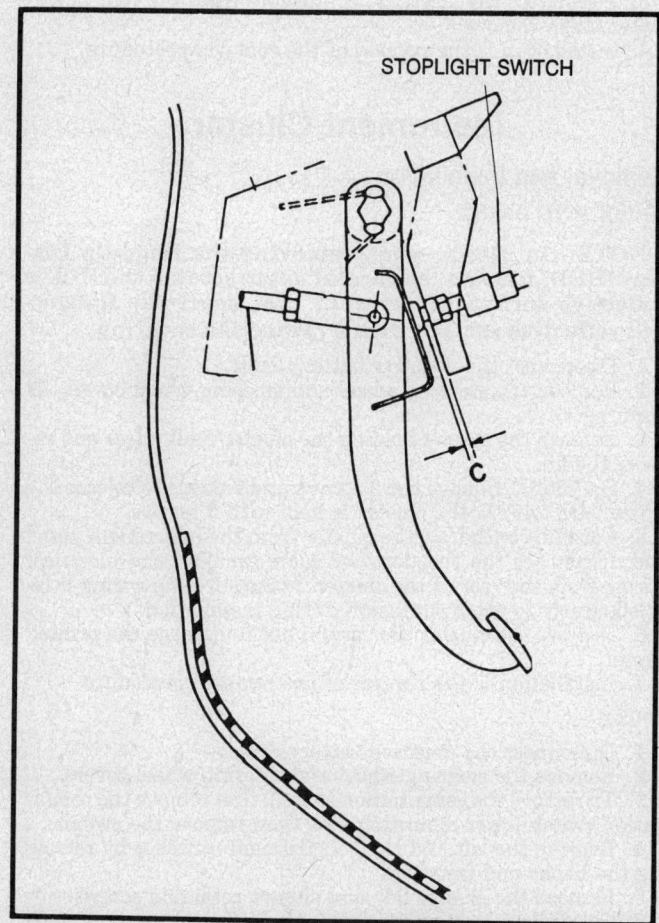

Stoplight switch clearance adjustment

2. Remove the steering wheel, steering column covers and combination switch.

3. Disconnect the switch wiring.

4. Lower the steering column, as required.

5. Break the self-shear screws with a drill or other appropriate tool.

6. Remove the steering lock from the column.

To install:

7. Install the steering lock onto the column with new self-shear bolts or screws. Tighten the bolts or screws until the heads shear off.

8. Raise and secure the steering column.

9. Install the combination switch, steering column covers and steering wheel.

10. Connect the negative battery cable.

Stoplight Switch

Adjustment

1. Before adjustment, check the clearance between the pedal stopper and the threaded end of the stoplight switch. The clearance should be 0.012–0.039 in. (0.3–1.0mm) for all vehicles.

2. If the clearance is not as specified, adjust by loosening the switch locknut and moving the switch in and out as required until the clearance is as specified.

3. Tighten the locknut.

4. Depress the brake pedal and have an assistant verify that the brake lights illuminate.

NOTE: If equipped with Automatic Speed Control Device (ASCD), the ASCD cancel switch must be adjusted with the stoplight switch.

Removal and Installation

1. Remove the floor mats.

2. Disconnect the multi-connector from the switch.

3. Note and record the amount of threads exposed on the switch.

4. Loosen the locknut and adjusting nuts and remove the switch from the mounting bracket.

5. Place the new switch in the mounting bracket.

6. Install and tighten the adjusting and locknuts so the same amount of threads is exposed as recorded in Step 3 or adjust the switch.

7. Connect the multi-connector and check that the brake lights illuminate when the brake pedal is depressed.

8. Replace the floor mats.

Clutch Switch

Adjustment

1. Before adjustment, check the clearance between the pedal stopper rubber and the threaded end of the clutch interlock switch with the clutch fully depressed. The clearance should be as follows:

 240SX—0.039–0.079 in. (1.0–2.0mm)
 300ZX:
  1987–89—0.059–0.138 in. (1.5–3.5mm)
  1990–91—0.039–0.188 in. (1.0–3.0mm)
 Maxima:
  1987–88—0.039–0.079 in. (1.0–2.0mm)
  1989–91—0.004–0.039 in. (0.1–1.0mm)
 Pulsar—0.004–0.039 in. (0.1–1.0mm)
 Sentra 1987–89—0.004–0.039 in. (0.1–1.0mm)
 Stanza:
  1987–88—0.039–0.079 in. (1.0–2.0mm)
  1989–91—0.039–0.079 in. (1.0–2.0mm)
 Stanza Wagon—0.059–0.138 in. (1.5–3.5mm)

2. If the clearance is not as specified, adjust by loosening the

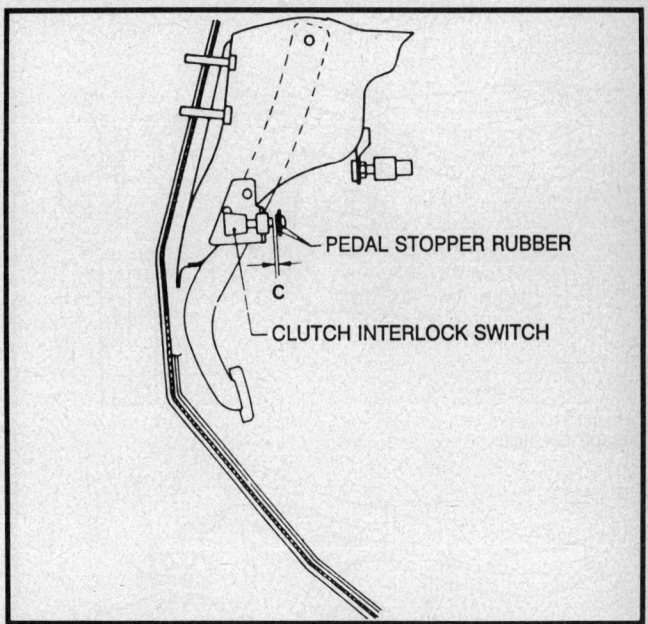

Clutch interlock switch clearance adjustment

switch locknut and moving the switch in and out as required until the clearance is as specified.

3. Tighten the locknut and make sure the vehicle won't start with the transmission or transaxle in any gear except **N**.

Removal and Installation

1. Remove the floor mats.

2. Disconnect the multi-connector from the switch.

3. Note and record the amount of threads exposed on the switch.

4. Loosen the locknut and adjusting nuts and remove the switch from the mounting bracket.

5. Place the new switch in the mounting bracket.

6. Install and tighten the adjusting and lock nuts so the same amount of threads is exposed as recorded in Step 3 or adjust the switch.

7. Connect the multi-connector.

8. Replace the floor mats.

Neutral Safety Switch

The switch unit is bolted to the left side of the transmission shift lever. The switch prevents the engine from being started in any position except **P** or **N**. It also controls the back-up lights.

Continuity Check

Hold the selector in the **N** position and move the manual control lever and equal amount in both directions to verify that current flow is almost the same in each direction. Current usually begins to flow when the manual control lever travels 1.5 degrees in either direction. Check for continuity in the **N**, **P** and **R** ranges.

 If the current flows are not close, adjust or replace the switch.

Adjustment

200SX AND 1987–89 300ZX

1. Shift the manual valve to the **N** position. In this position, the valve should be vertical.

2. Remove the machine screw from the rotor and loosen the hex head attaching bolts.

3. Insert a 0.079 in. (2mm) pin into the machine screw hole and move the switch until the pin falls into the hole.

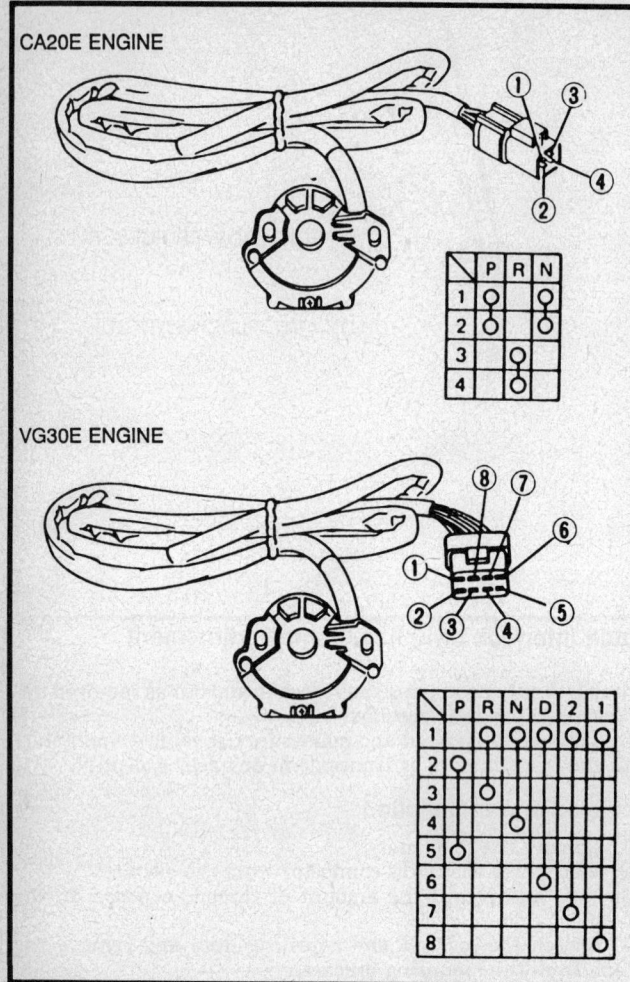

Checking neutral safety switch continuity—200SX and 1987–89 300ZX

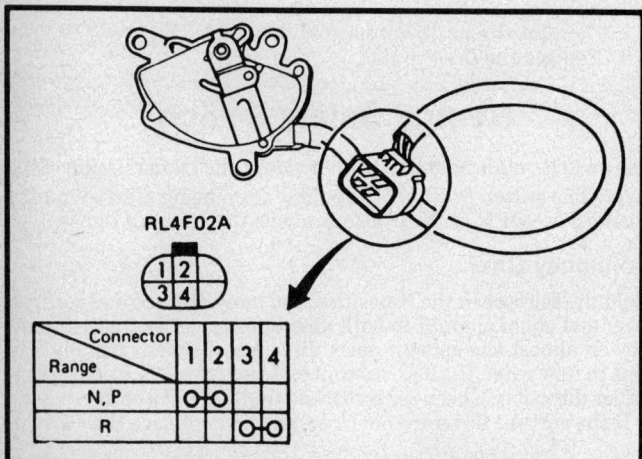

Checking neutral safety switch continuity—Pulsar, Sentra, 1987–89 Maxima and 1987–89 Stanza

4. Remove the pin and tighten the bolts equally.
5. Check for continuity in the **N**, **P** and **R** ranges.
6. With the brakes on, ensure that the engine will start only in **P** or **N**. Check that the back-up lights go on only in reverse.

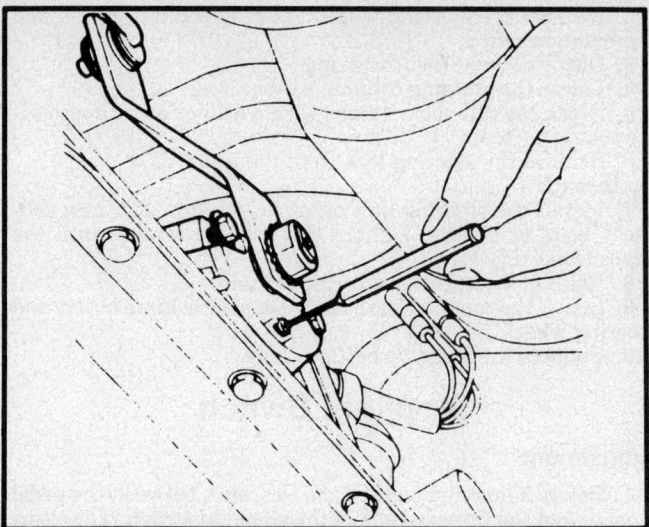

Neutral safety and back-up light switch adjustment—200SX and 1987–89 300ZX

240SX, 1990–91 300ZX, MAXIMA, PULSAR, SENTRA AND STANZA

1. Disconnect the manual control linkage from the manual shaft.
2. Set the manual shaft to the **N** position.
3. Loosen the inhibitor switch mounting screws enough to allow for movement of the switch.
4. Insert a 0.16 in. (4mm) diameter pin and move the switch until the pin falls through the locating holes in the inhibitor switch and manual shaft. Tighten the switch screws equally. On Pulsar, use a 0.1 in. (2.5mm) diameter pin.
5. Remove the pin and connect the manual control linkage to the shaft.
6. Check for continuity in the **N**, **P** and **R** ranges.
7. Make sure while holding the brakes on, that the engine will start only in **P** or **N**. Check that the back-up lights go on only in reverse.

Removal and Installation

1. On 1987–88 Stanza wagon, remove the battery, battery bracket, air cleaner and air flow meter. On 1987–88 Maxima, remove the battery, air cleaner and the air flow meter/air damper/solenoid valve assembly.
2. Disconnect the manual control shaft from the control lever.
3. Disconnect the switch harness connector.
4. Remove the switch attaching bolts and screws.
5. Remove the switch.

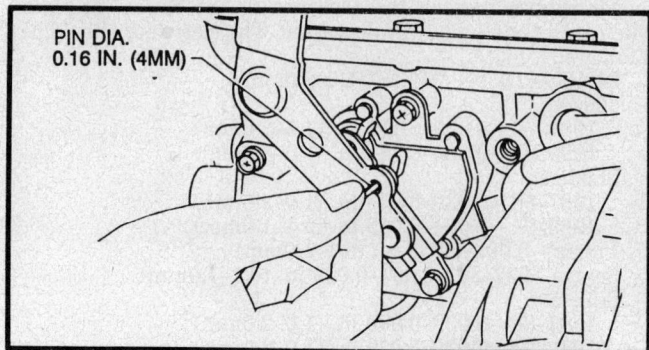

Inhibitor switch adjustment—Pulsar, Sentra and 1987–89 Stanza

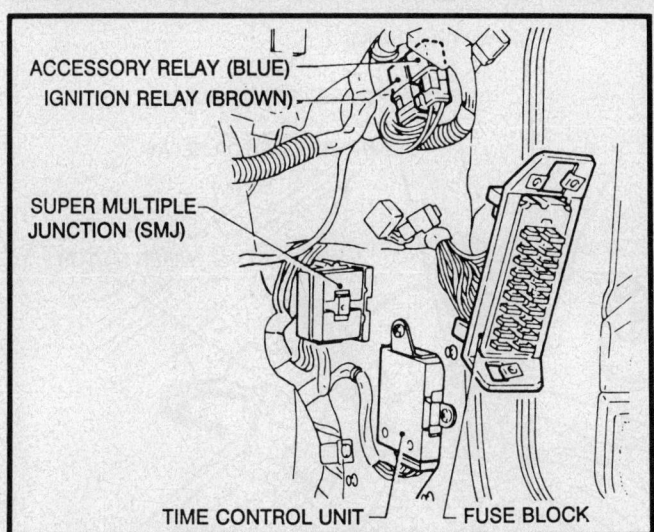

Fuse block, accessory relay, ignition relay and time control unit locations—200SX

6. Installation is the reverse of the removal procedure.
7. Adjust the switch and check for continuity.

Fuses, Circuit Breakers and Relays

Location

200SX

Fusible Link Holder—left side engine compartment to rear of battery; off negative battery cable.
Fuse Panel—extreme right side of dash behind glove box.

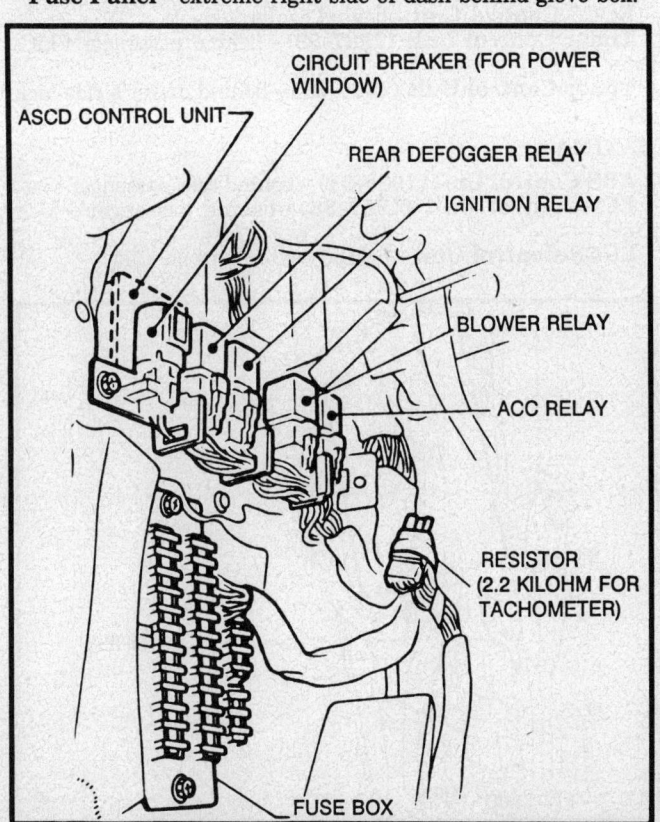

Relay box and fuse panel locations—300ZX

Circuit Breaker—left side of dash above stoplight switch; on top of combination flasher unit.
Fan Motor Relay (CA20E engines)—left side engine compartment to rear of fusible link holder.
Fan Motor Relay (VG30E engines)—left side engine compartment.
A/C Relay (VG30E engines only)—left side engine compartment to rear of fusible link holder.
Fuel Pump Relay—above right license lamp.
Ignition Relay—extreme right side of dash above fuse block

240SX

Fusible Links—left side engine compartment behind battery; in fuse and relay box.
Fuse Panels—(1) left side engine compartment behind battery and (2) under driver's side kick panel.
Fuel Pump Relay—left side engine compartment behind battery; in fuse and relay box.
A/C Relay—right side engine compartment in front of radiator; in relay box.
ECCS Relay—left side engine compartment behind battery; in fuse and relay box.
Circuit Breaker—behind driver's kick panel.

300ZX

Fusible links (1987–89)—left side engine compartment attached to left fender.
Fusible links (1990–91)—in front of battery off negative battery cable.
Relay Box (1987–89)—left side engine compartment; attached to left fender.
Relay and Fuse Box (1990–91)—right side engine compartment

MAXIMA

Fusible Link Holder (1987–88)—right side engine compartment rear of battery.
Fusible Link Holder (1989–91)—right side engine compartment; in fuse and relay box.

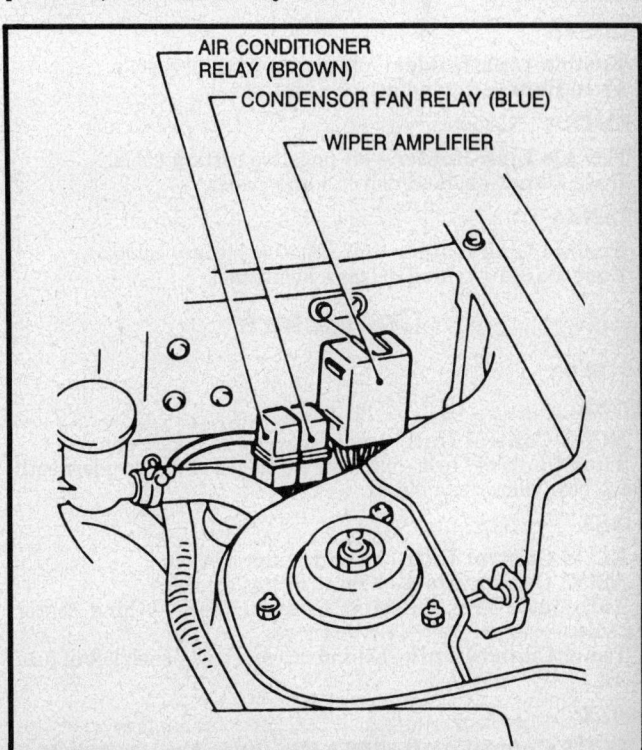

Accessory relay locations—Pulsar

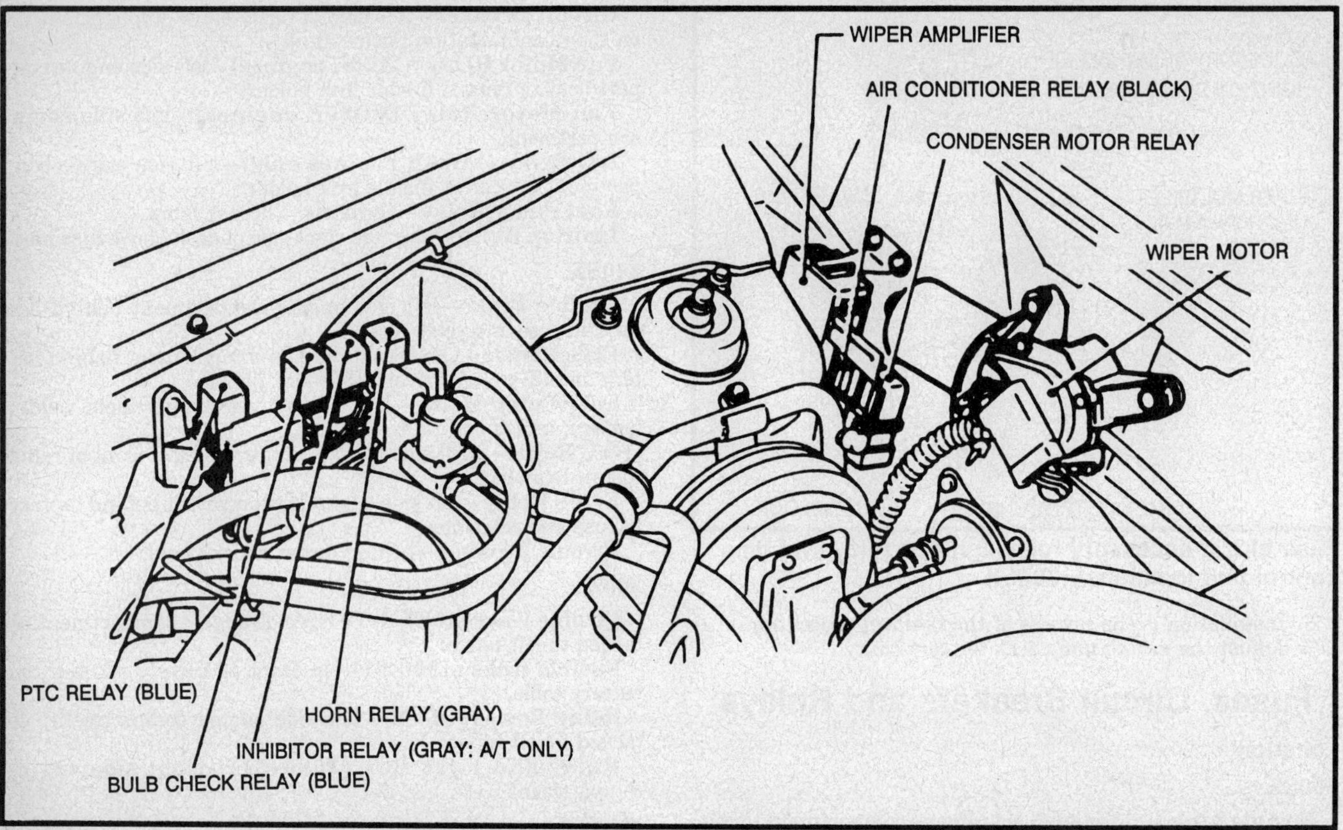

WIPER AMPLIFIER

AIR CONDITIONER RELAY (BLACK)

CONDENSER MOTOR RELAY

WIPER MOTOR

PTC RELAY (BLUE)

HORN RELAY (GRAY)

INHIBITOR RELAY (GRAY: A/T ONLY)

BULB CHECK RELAY (BLUE)

Accessory relay locations—1987–88 Sentra

Fuse panel—behind driver's kick panel.
Relay Box (1989–91)—right side engine compartment; in front of battery.

PULSAR

Fusible Link Holder—off negative battery cable.
Fuse Panel—behind driver's kick panel.

SENTRA

Fusible Link Holder—off negative battery cable.
Fuse Panel—behind driver's kick panel.

STANZA

Fusible Link Holder—off negative battery cable.
Fuse Panel—behind driver's kick panel.

Computers

Location

200SX

ECCS Control Unit—under driver's side kick panel.
Time Control Unit—extreme right side of dash underneath glove box; below fuse block.

240SX

ECCS Control Unit—behind center console.
ASCD Control Unit—behind center console.
Automatic Transmission Control Unit—behind center console.
Timer Control Unit—behind driver's kick panel; left of fuse block.

300ZX

ECCS Control Unit (1987–89)—behind passenger's kick panel.

ECCS Control Unit—behind center console.
Timer Control Unit (1987–89)—behind passenger's kick panel.
Timer Control Unit (1990–91)—behind driver's side kick panel.

MAXIMA

ABS Control Unit (1989–91)—behind rear passenger seat.
EFI Control Unit (1987–88)—behind passenger's kick panel.
ECCS Control Unit—behind center console.

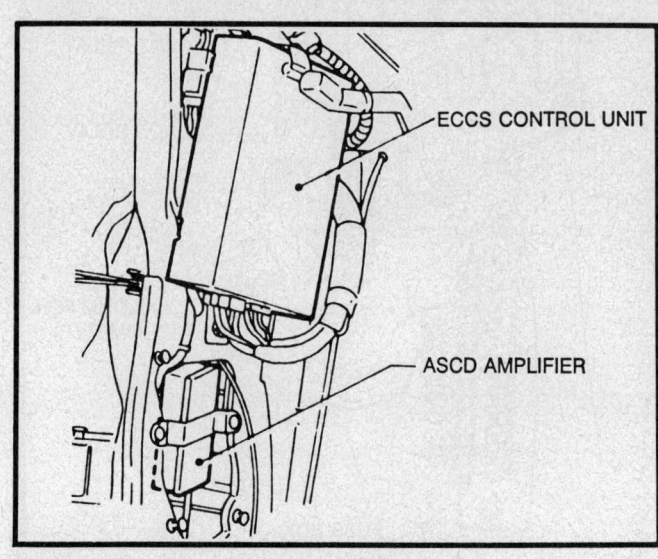

ECCS CONTROL UNIT

ASCD AMPLIFIER

ECCS control unit location—200SX

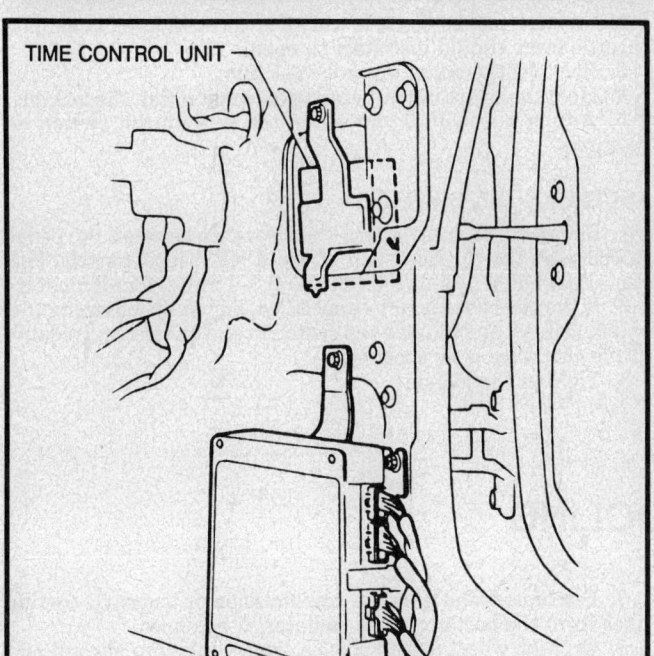

ECCS and timer control unit locations—1987-89 300ZX

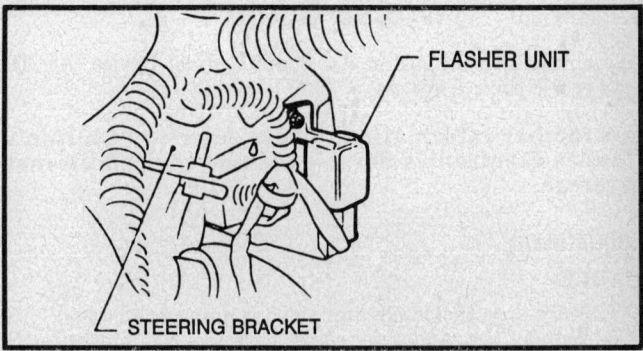

Flasher unit location—300ZX

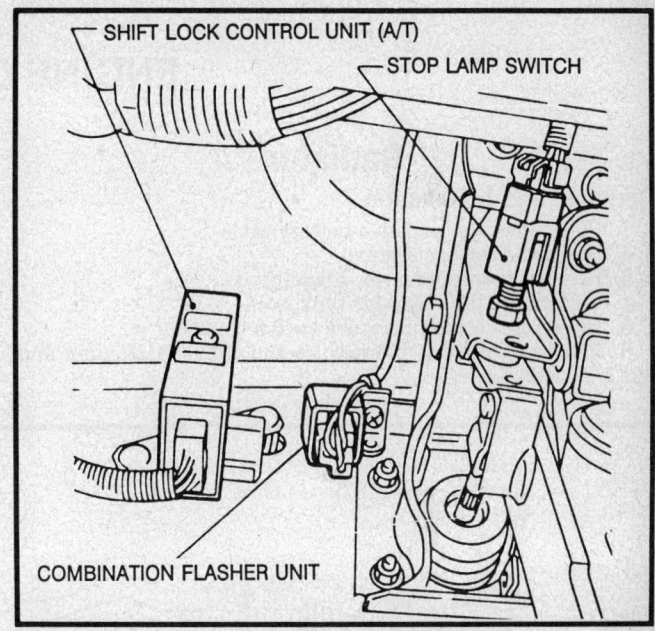

Flasher unit location—1989-91 Sentra

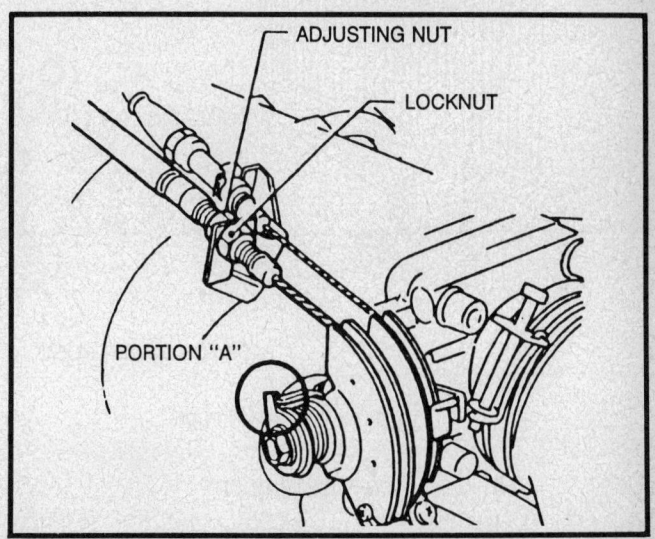

Typical Automatic Speed Control Device (ASCD) cable adjustment

Shock Absorber Control Unit (1988)—next to left rear speaker.
Sonar Suspension Control Unit (1989-91)—behind center console.

PULSAR

ECCS Control Unit—right side dash.
Air Bag Control Unit—under center console.

SENTRA

ECCS Control Unit (2WD)—between front seats.
ECCS Control Unit (4WD)—under left side of passenger seat.
Transfer Control Unit—extreme left side behind driver's kick panel.

STANZA

ECCS Control Unit—behind center console.
ASCD control unit—behind center console.

Flashers

Location

200SX—left side of dash above stoplight switch.
240SX—behind driver's kick panel.
300ZX—behind instrument cluster to right of the steering bracket.
Maxima—behind steering column next to stoplight switch.
Pulsar—behind driver's kick panel below stoplight switch.
Sentra—behind driver's kick panel below stoplight switch.
Stanza—behind driver's kick panel below stoplight switch

Cruise Control

All vehicles use the Automatic Speed Control Device (ASCD) type cruise control system.

For further information, please refer to "Chilton's Chassis Electronics Service Manual" for additional coverage.

Adjustment
CABLE
1. Make sure the accelerator cable is properly adjusted.
2. Without the accelerator cable depressed, tighten the Automatic Speed Control Device (ASCD) adjusting nut until the actuating lever makes contact with the throttle lever stop. The throttle lever should just start to open.
3. Back off the adjusting nut ½–1 turn.
4. Hold the adjusting nut stationary and tighten the locknut.
5. Adjust the ASCD cancel switch and clutch switch as required.

ASCD CANCEL SWITCH
1. Before adjustment, check the clearance between the pedal stopper and the threaded end of the ASCD cancel switch. The clearance should be 0.012–0.039 in. (0.3–1.0mm) for all models.
2. If the clearance is not as specified, adjust by loosening the switch locknut and moving the switch in and out as required until the clearance is as specified.
3. Tighten the locknut.

ENGINE COOLING

Radiator
Removal and Installation
1. Disconnect the negative battery cable.
2. Drain the cooling system.
3. Remove the undercover, if equipped.
4. Disconnect the reservoir tank hose.
5. Disconnect all temperature switch connectors.
6. Remove the front bumper on the 1987–88 Maxima and 1987–89 300ZX.
7. Disconnect and plug the transmission or transaxle cooling lines from the bottom of the radiator, if equipped.
8. On rear wheel drive vehicles, remove the fan shroud and position the shroud over the fan and clear of the radiator. On front wheel drive vehicles, discharge the air conditioning system, then unbolt and remove the condenser and radiator fan assembly from the radiator.
9. Disconnect the upper and lower hoses from the radiator.
10. Remove the radiator retaining bolts or the upper supports.
11. Lift the radiator off the mounts and out of the vehicle.

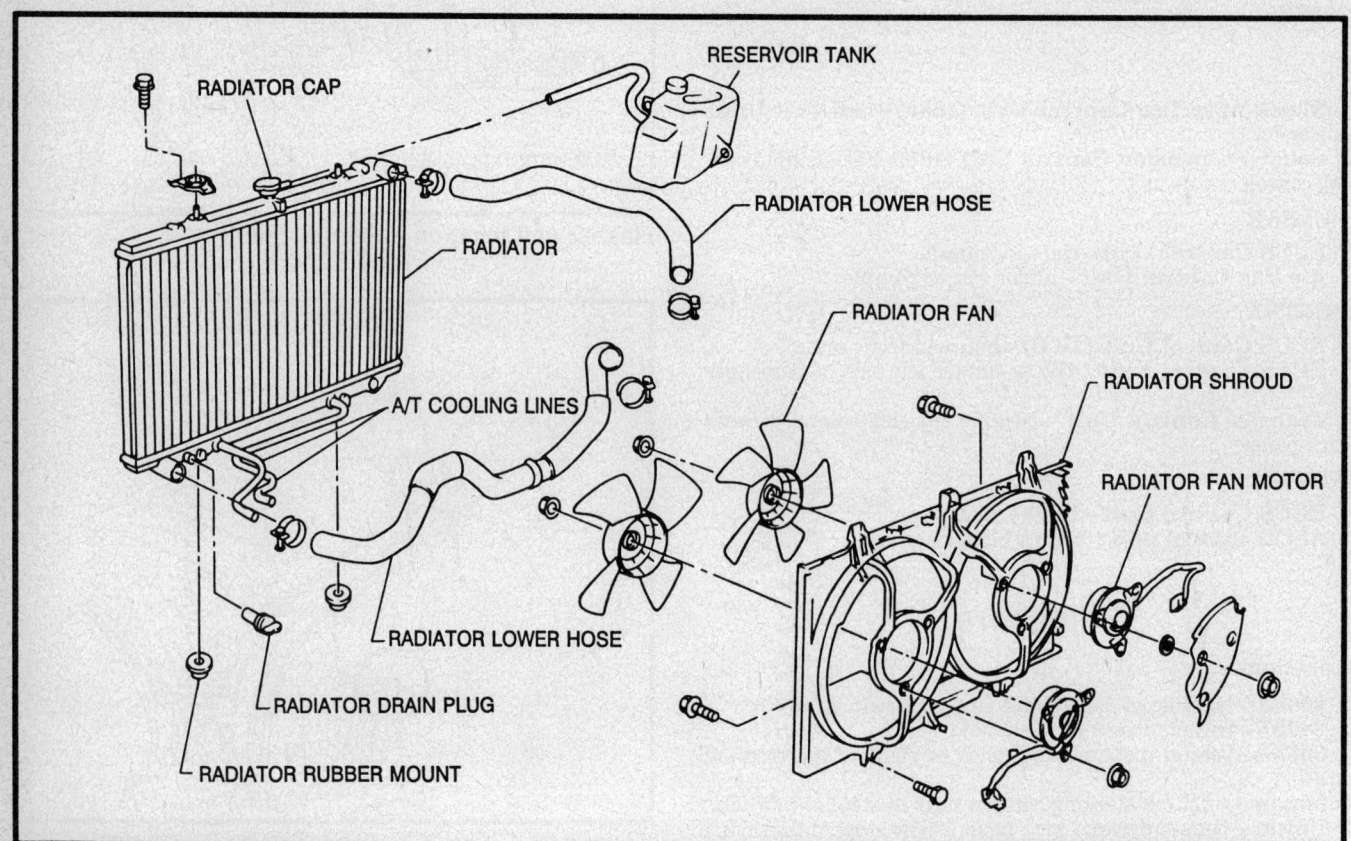

Typical radiator assembly

To install:

12. Lower the radiator onto the mounts and bolt in place.
13. Install the lower shroud, if removed.
14. Connect the upper and lower radiator hoses.
15. On rear wheel drive vehicles, install the fan shroud. On front wheel drive vehicles, install the condenser and radiator fan assembly.
16. Connect the transaxle or transmission cooling lines, if removed.
17. On 1987–88 Maxima and 1987–89 300ZX, install the front bumper.
18. Plug in the temperature switch connectors.
19. Connect the reservoir tank hose.
20. Fill the cooling system to the proper level.
21. Connect the negative battery cable.
22. Start the engine and check for leaks.

Electric Cooling Fan

Testing

MAXIMA

1. Warm up the engine to normal operating temperature, then shut it off.
2. Remove radiator fan relay No. 1.
3. Connect a jumper wire between terminals **3** and **5** of the relay.

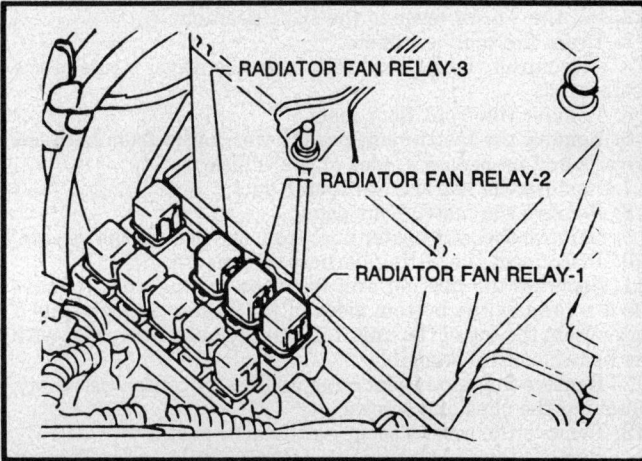

Radiator fan relay locations—Maxima

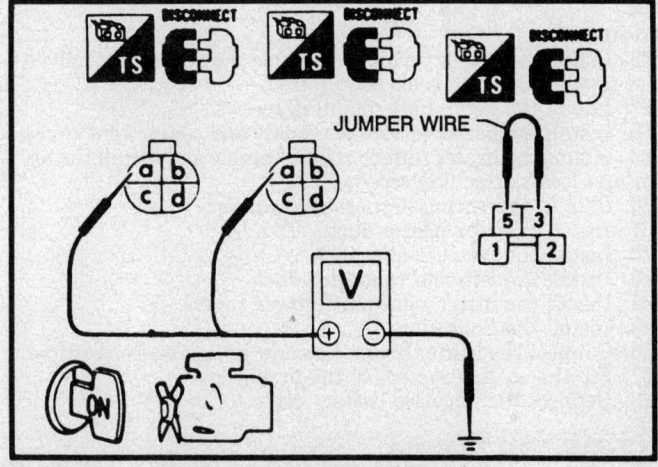

Checking radiator fan voltage—Maxima

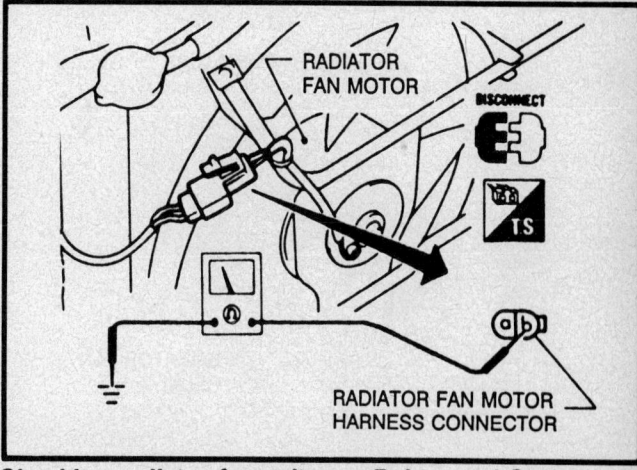

Checking radiator fan voltage—Pulsar and Sentra

4. Disconnect the cooling fan and condenser motor wiring harness connectors.
5. Turn the ignition switch to the **ON** position.
6. Check for voltage between terminal **A** of the fan motor harness connector and ground. Battery voltage should exist.
7. If battery voltage does not exist, check the ground circuit harness for continuity, check the radiator fan relay(s), inspect the harness connectors or replace the fan motor.

PULSAR AND SENTRA

1. Warm up the engine to normal operating temperature, then shut it off.
2. Disconnect the cooling fan motor wiring harness connector.
3. Turn the ignition switch to the **ON** position.
4. Check for voltage beteen terminal **A** of the fan motor harness connector and ground. Battery voltage should exist.
5. If battery voltage does not exist, check the ground circuit harness for continuity, check the radiator fan relays, or replace the fan motor.

STANZA

1. Warm up the engine to normal operating temperature, then shut it off.
2. Remove radiator fan relays No. 1 and 2.
3. Turn the ignition switch to the **ON** position.
4. Check for voltage beteen terminals **2** and **3** of the relays and ground. Battery voltage should exist.
5. If battery voltage does not exist, check the ground circuit

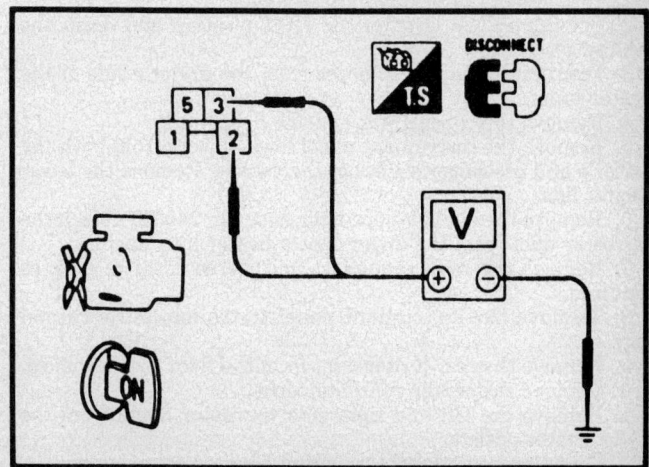

Checking radiator fan voltage—Stanza

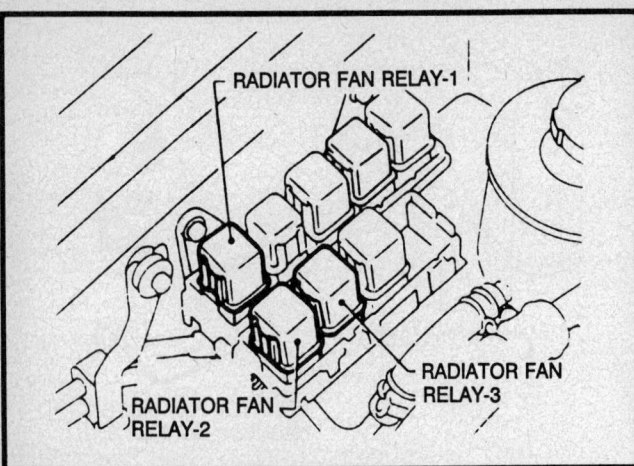

Radiator fan relay locations—Stanza

harness for continuity, check the radiator fan relay(s), inspect the harness connectors or replace the fan motor.

Removal and Installation

1. Disconnect the negative battery cable.
2. Unplug the condenser and radiator fan motor wiring harness connectors.
3. Remove the radiator shroud bolts.
4. Separate the shroud and cooling fan assembly from the radiator and remove.

To install:

5. Mount the radiator shroud and cooling fan assembly onto the radiator.
6. Install the radiator shroud bolts.
7. Plug in the radiator and condenser fan motor harness connectors.
8. Connect the negative battery cable.

Heater Core

For further information, please refer to "Chilton's Heating and Air Conditioning Manual" for additional coverage.

Removal and Installation

200SX, 240SX, 300ZX

1. Disconnect the negative battery cable.
2. Set the TEMP lever to the HOT position and drain the cooling system.
3. Disconnect the heater hoses from the driver's side of the heater unit.
4. Remove the console box and the floor mats.
5. Remove the instrument panel lower covers from both the driver's and passenger's sides of the vehicle. Remove the lower cluster lids.
6. Remove the left side ventilator duct. On 240SX, detach the defroster duct from the upper center heater unit opening.
7. Remove the radio, equalizer and stereo cassette deck as required.
8. Remove the instrument panel-to-transmission tunnel stay.
9. Remove the rear heater duct from the floor of the vehicle.
10. Remove the center ventilator duct.
11. Remove the left and right side ventilator ducts from the lower heater outlets.
12. Disconnect and label the wiring harness connections.
13. Separate the heating unit Remove the 2 screws at the bot-

tom sides of the heater unit and the 1 screw at the top of the unit and remove the unit together with the heater control assembly.
14. Separate the heater case halves and slide the core from the case.

To install:

15. Install the heater core and assemble the heater case halves. Use new gaskets and seals as required.
16. Mount the heater unit/control assembly and install the upper and lower attaching screws.
17. Plug in the wiring harness connectors.
18. Connect the left and right side ducts to the lower heater outlets.
19. Connect the center ventilator duct.
20. Connect the rear heater duct.
21. Attach the instrument panel-to-transmission stay.
22. Install the cassette deck, equalizer and radio.
23. On 240SX, connect the upper defroster duct to the upper center heater opening. Connect the left side ventilator duct.
24. Install the lower cluster lids and lower instrument panel covers.
25. Install the floor mats and console box.
26. Install the front seats. Torque the seat bolts to 32–41 ft. lbs. (43–55 Nm).
27. Connect the heater hoses. Use new grommets as required.
28. Fill the cooling system to the proper level.
29. Connect the negative battery cable.

MAXIMA

1. Disconnect the negative battery cable.
2. Set the TEMP lever to the HOT position.
3. Drain the cooling system.
4. Disconnect the heater hoses from the driver's side of the heater unit.
5. Remove the front floor mats.
6. Remove the instrument panel lower covers from both the driver's and passenger's sides of the vehicle.
7. Remove the left side ventilator duct.
8. Remove the instrument panel.
9. Remove the rear heater duct from the floor of the vehicle.
10. Disconnect the wiring harness connectors.
11. Separate the heating unit from the cooling unit. Remove the 2 screws at the bottom sides of the heater unit and the 1 screw from the top of the unit. Lift out the heater together with the heater control assembly.
12. Remove the center vent cover and heater control assembly, loosening the clips and screws.
13. Remove the screws securing the door shafts.
14. Remove the clips from the case and split the case. Remove the core.
15. Separate the heater case halves and slide the core from the case.

To install:

16. Install the heater core and assemble the heater case halves. Use new gaskets and seals as required.
17. Install the door shaft retaining screws.
18. Install the heater control assembly and center vent cover.
19. Mount the heater unit/control assembly and install the upper and lower attaching screws.
20. Plug in the wiring harness connectors.
21. Install the rear heater duct.
22. Install the instrument panel.
23. Install the left side ventilator duct.
24. Install the instrument panel lower covers.
25. Install the floor mats.
26. Connect the heater hoses. Use new grommets as required.
27. Fill the cooling system to the proper level.
28. Connect the negative battery cable.

PULSAR AND SENTRA

1. Disconnect the negative battery cable.

2. Set the TEMP lever to the maximum HOT position and drain the engine coolant.

3. Disconnect the heater hoses at the engine compartment.

4. Remove the instrument panel assembly.

5. Remove the heater control assembly.

6. If equipped with air conditioning, separate the heating unit from the cooling unit.

7. Remove the heater unit assembly.

8. Remove the case clips and split the case. Remove the core.

To install:

9. Install the heater core and assemble the heater case halves. Use new gaskets and seals as required. Always check the operation of the air mix door when re-attaching the heater case halves.

10. Mount the heater unit and connect it the cooling unit, if equipped.

11. Install the heater control assembly.

12. Install the instrument panel.

13. Connect the heater hoses. Use new grommets as required.

14. Fill and bleed the cooling system.

15. Connect the negative battery cable.

STANZA

1. Disconnect the negative battery cable.

2. Set the TEMP lever to the maximum HOT position and drain the engine coolant.

3. Disconnect the heater hoses at the engine compartment.

4. Remove the instrument panel assembly.

5. Remove the heater control assembly.

6. Remove pedal bracket mounting bolts, steering column mounting bolts, brake and clutch pedal cotter pins.

7. Move the pedal bracket and steering column to the left.

8. Disconnect the air mix door control cable and heater valve control lever, then remove the control lever.

9. Remove the core cover and remove the core.

To install:

10. Install the core and cover. Use new seals and gaskets as required.

11. Install the control and heater valve levers. Connect the air mix door control cable.

12. Move the steering column and brake pedal bracket to the right. Install the clutch and brake pedal cotter pins and steering column and brake pedal bolts.

13. Install the heater control assembly.

14. Install the instrument panel.

15. Connect the heater hoses to the core. Use new grommets as required.

16. Fill and bleed the cooling system.

17. Connect the negative battery cable.

Water Pump

Removal and Installation

4 CYLINDER ENGINE

1. Disconnect the negative battery cable.

2. Drain the coolant from the radiator and cylinder block.

3. Remove all the drive belts.

4. Unbolt the water pump pulley and the water pump attaching bolts.

5. Separate the water pump with the gasket, if installed, from the cylinder block.

6. Remove all gasket material or sealant from the water pump mating surfaces. On GA16i and KA24E engines, all sealant must be removed from the groove in the water pump surface also.

To install:

7. On GA16i and KA24E engines, apply a continuous bead of high temperature liquid gasket to the water pump housing mating surface. The housing must be attached to the cylinder block within 5 minutes after the sealant is applied. After the pump housing is bolted to the block, wait at least 30 minutes for the sealant to cure before starting the engine.

8. Position the water pump (and gasket) onto the block and install the attaching bolts.

9. Install the water pump pulley.

10. Install the drive belts and adjust the tension.

11. Fill the cooling system to the proper level.

12. Connect the negative battery cable.

6 CYLINDER ENGINE

1. Disconnect the negative battery cable and drain the coolant from the radiator and the left side drain cocks on the cylinder block. On 1989–91 Maxima and 1990–91 300ZX, there are 2 cylinder block drain plugs; one on the right side of the cylinder

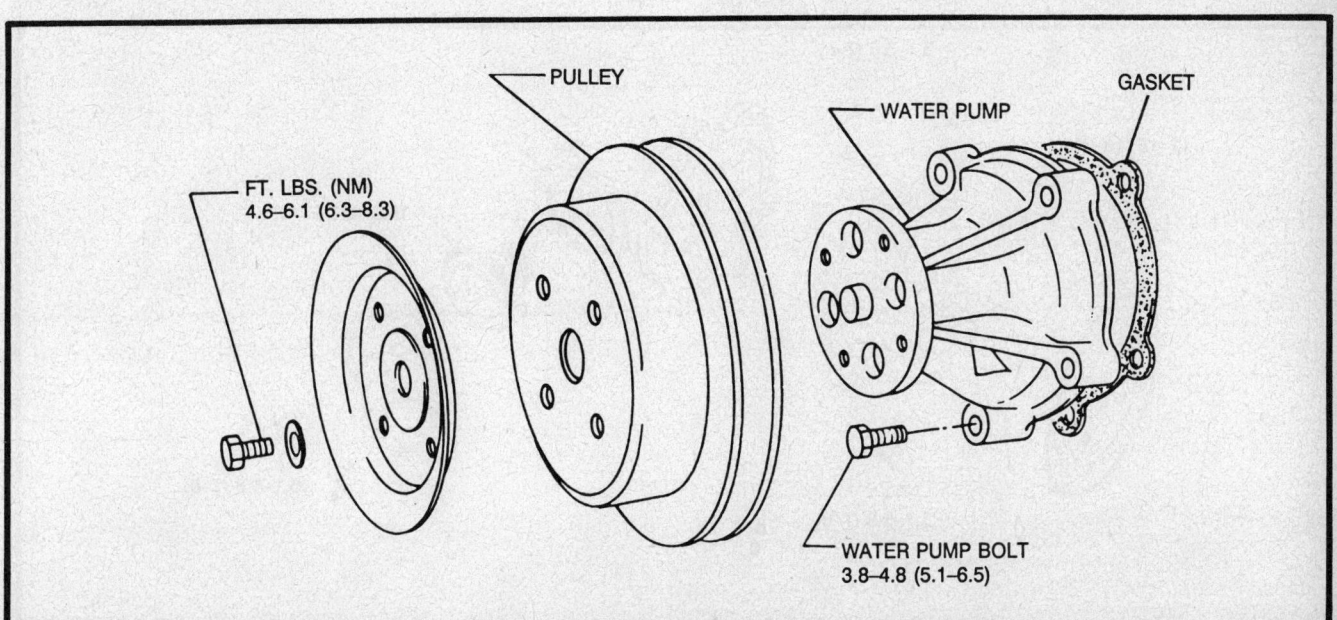

PULLEY

WATER PUMP

GASKET

FT. LBS. (NM)
4.6–6.1 (6.3–8.3)

WATER PUMP BOLT
3.8–4.8 (5.1–6.5)

Water pump assembly—E16I engine

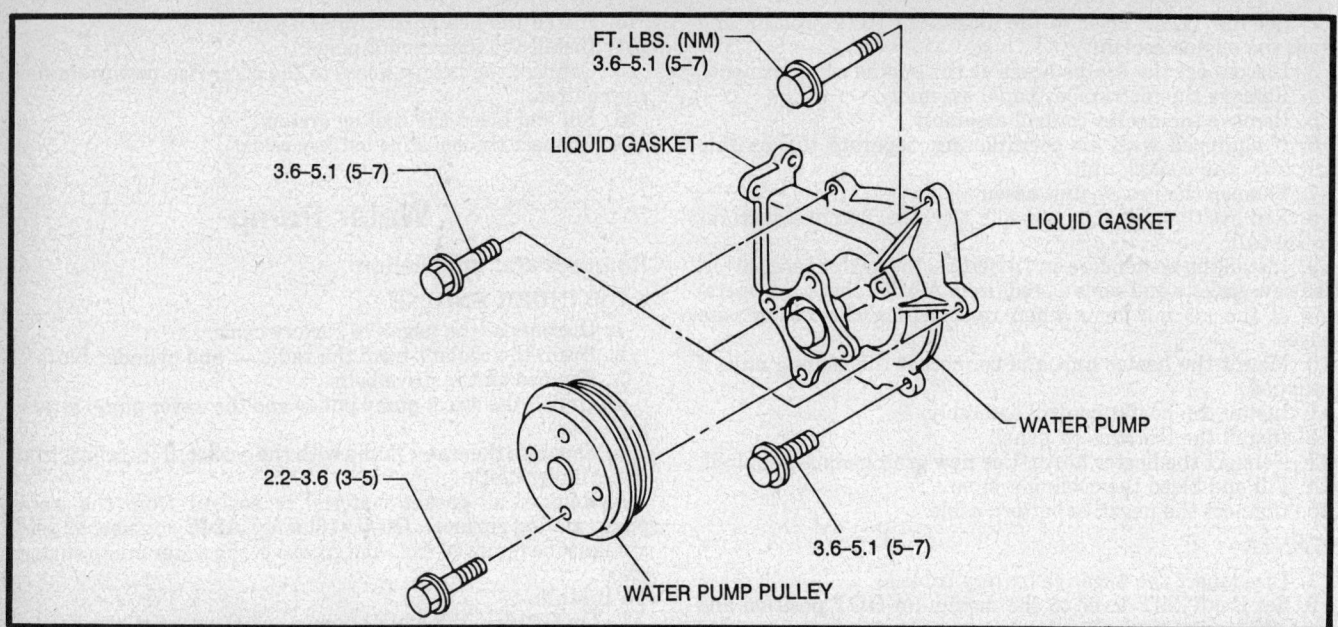

Water pump assembly—GA16i engine

block behind the right halfshaft boot and one on the left side of the block next to the oil level gauge.

2. On 1990–91 300ZX, remove the undercover and the radiator.

3. Remove the radiator shroud.

4. Remove the power steering, compressor and alternator drive belts.

5. Remove the cooling fan and coupling.

6. Disconnect the water pump hoses.

7. On 1990–91 300ZX, unbolt and remove the inlet and outlet pipes from the block.

8. Remove the water pump pulley, then the upper and lower timing covers.

NOTE: Be careful not to get coolant on the timing belt and to avoid deforming the timing cover, make sure there is enough clearance between the timing cover and the hose clamp.

9. Remove the water pump retaining bolts, note different lengths, and remove the pump.

10. Make sure the gasket sealing surfaces are clean and free of all the old gasket material.

To install:

11. Mount the water pump and gasket onto the cylinder block. Torque the retaining bolts to 12–15 ft. lbs. (16–21 Nm).

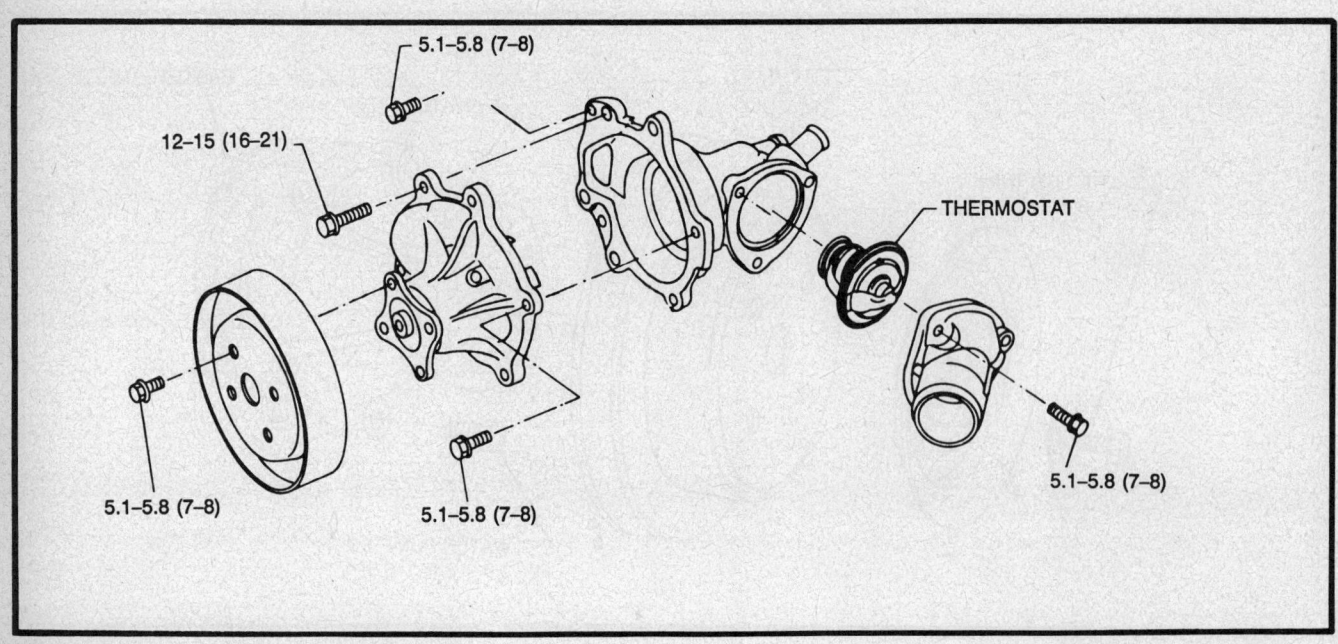

Water pump assembly—KA24E engine

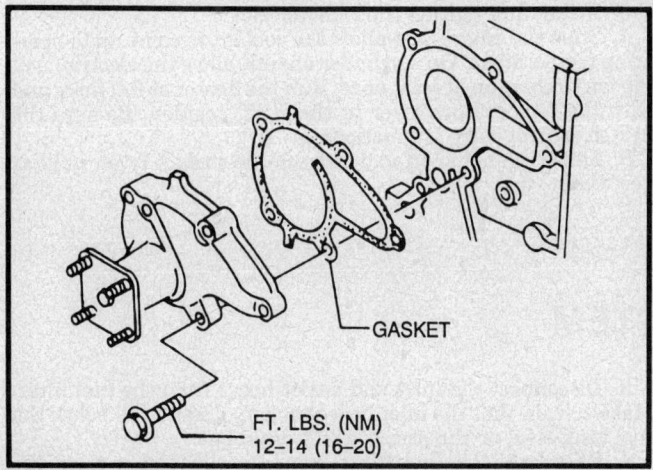

Water pump assembly—CA20E and CA18ET engines

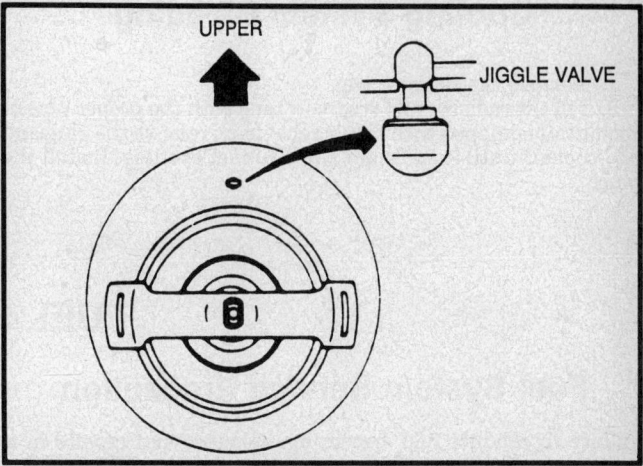

Always be sure the jiggle valve is facing upward when installing the thermostat

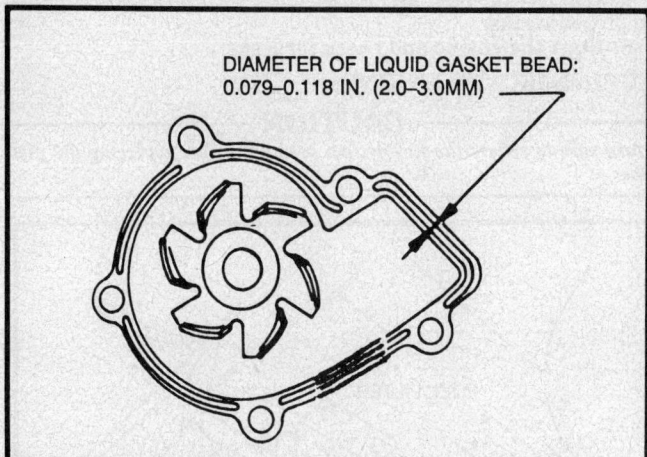

On GA16i and KA24E engines, apply a continuous bead oh high temperature sealant to the water pump housing mating surface

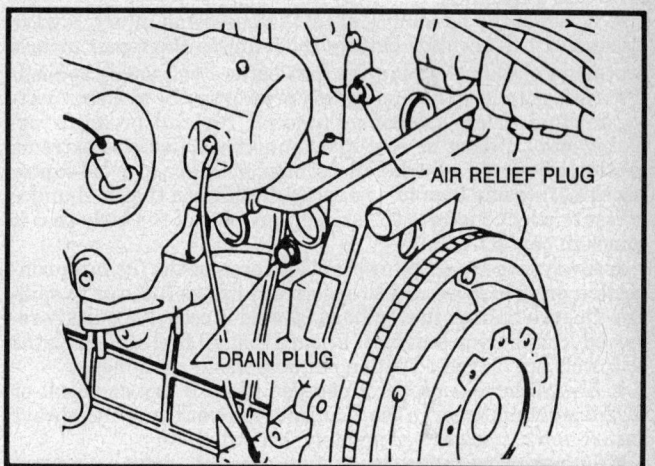

Typical air relief plug location for bleeding the cooling system

12. Install the upper and lower timing belt covers and crankshaft pulley.

13. On 1990–91 300ZX, install the inlet and outlet pipes and torque the nuts and bolts to 12–14 ft. lbs. (16–19 Nm).

14. Connect the water pump hoses.

15. Install the cooling fan and coupling.

16. Install and tension the drive belts.

17. Install the radiator shroud.

18. On 1990–91 300ZX, install the undercover and radiator.

19. Fill the cooling system and connect the negative battery cable.

Thermostat

Removal and Installation

1. Disconnect the negative battery cable and drain the coolant from the radiator and the left side drain cocks on the cylinder block. On 1989–91 Maxima and 1990–91 300ZX, there are 2 cylinder block drain plugs; one on the right side of the cylinder block behind the right halfshaft boot and one on the left side of the block next to the oil level gauge.

2. On 1990–91 300ZX, remove the undercover.

3. On GA16i engines, disconnect the water temperature switch connector from the thermostat housing.

4. Remove the upper radiator hose from the water outlet side

and remove the bolts securing the water outlet to the cylinder head.

5. On 200SX (V6) and 300ZX, remove the radiator shroud, drive belts for 1990–91 300ZX, cooling fan and coupling and water inlet pipe.

6. Remove the thermostat and clean off the old gasket or sealant from the mating surfaces.

To install:

7. Install the thertmostat with a new gasket. When installing the thermostat, be sure to install a new gasket or sealant and be sure the air bleed hole in the thermostat is facing the left side or upward on the engine. The jiggle valve must always face up. Also make sure the new thermostat to be installed is equipped with a air bleed hole. Some thermostats have the word TOP stamped next to the jiggle valve. Again, the word TOP and the jiggle valve must be facing up.

8. On 200SX (V6) and 300ZX, install the water inlet pipe, cooling fan and coupling, drive belts for 1990–91 300ZX and radiator shroud.

9. Install the water outlet and upper radiator hose.

10. On GA16i engines, connect the water temperature switch connector to the thermostat housing.

11. On 1990–91 300ZX, install the undercover.

12. Fill the cooling system and connect the negative battery cable.

Cooling System Bleeding

1. Remove the radiator cap.
2. Fill the radiator and reservoir tank with the proper type of coolant. If equipped with an air relief plug, remove the plug and add coolant until it spills out the air relief opening. Install the plug.

3. Install and tighten the radiator cap.
4. Start the engine and allow the coolant to come up to operating temperature. On 4 cylinder engine, allow the electric cooling fan to come on at least once. Run the heater at full force and with the temperature lever in the HOT position. Be sure the heater control valve is functioning.
5. Shut the engine off and recheck the coolant level, refill as necessary.

FUEL SYSTEM

Fuel System Service Precaution

Failure to conduct fuel system maintenance and repairs in a safe manner may result in serious personal injury. Maintenance and testing of the vehicle's fuel system components can be accomplished safely and effectively by adhering to the following rules and guidelines.

• To avoid the possibility of fire and personal injury, always disconnect the negative battery cable unless the repair or test procedure specifically requires that battery voltage be applied.
• Always relieve the fuel system pressure prior to disconnecting any fuel system component (injector, fuel rail, pressure regulator, etc.), fitting or fuel line connection. Exercise extreme caution whenever relieving fuel system pressure to avoid exposing skin, face and eyes to fuel spray. Be advised that fuel under pressure may penetrate the skin or any part of the body that it comes in contact with.
• Always place a shop towel or cloth around the fitting or connection prior to loosening to absorb any excess fuel due to spillage. Ensure that all fuel spillage (should it occur) is quickly removed from engine surfaces. Ensure that all fuel soaked cloths or towels are deposited into a suitable waste container.
• Always have a properly charged Class B dry chemical or CO2 fire extinguisher in the vicinity of the work area and always ensure work areas are adequately ventilated.
• Do not allow fuel spray or fuel vapors to come in contact with spark or open flame. Remember that smoking and fuel maintenance do not mix!
• Always use a backup wrench when loosening and tightening fuel line connection fittings. This will prevent unnecessary stress and torsion to fuel line piping. Always follow the proper torque specifications.
• Always replace worn fuel fitting O-rings with new ones. Do not substitute fuel hose or equivalent, where rigid fuel pipe is called for.
• Always use common sense.

Relieving Fuel System Pressure

1. Remove the fuel pump fuse from the fuse block, fuel pump relay or disconnect the harness connector at the tank while engine is running.
2. It should run and then stall when the fuel in the lines is exhausted. When the engine stops, crank the starter for about 3 seconds to make sure all pressure in the fuel lines is released.
3. Install the fuel pump fuse, relay or harness connector after repair is made.

Fuel Filter

Removal and Installation
CARBURETED ENGINE

1. Disconnect the negative battery cable.
2. Locate fuel filter on right-side of the engine compartment.

3. Disconnect the inlet and outlet hoses from the fuel filter. Make certain that the inlet hose (bottom) doesn't fall below the fuel tank level or the gasoline will drain out.
4. Withdraw the fuel filter from its clip and replace the assembly.
5. Connect the inlet and outlet lines; secure the hose clamps to prevent leaks.
6. Start the engine and check for leaks.

FUEL INJECTED ENGINE

— CAUTION —

Make sure to relieve the fuel system pressure before replacing the fuel filter.

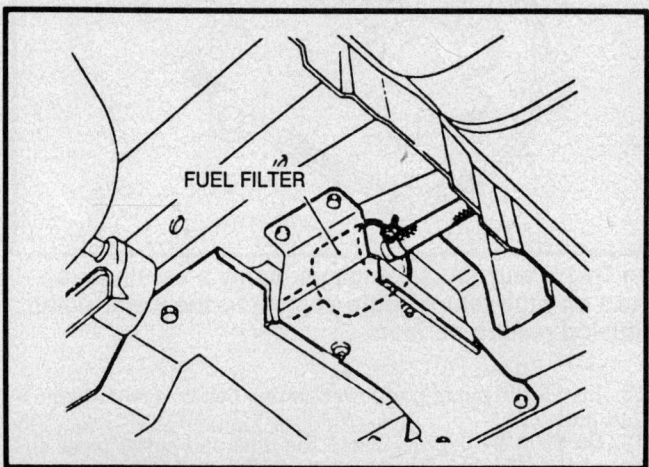

The fuel filter is found under the floor—Stanza wagons (4WD)

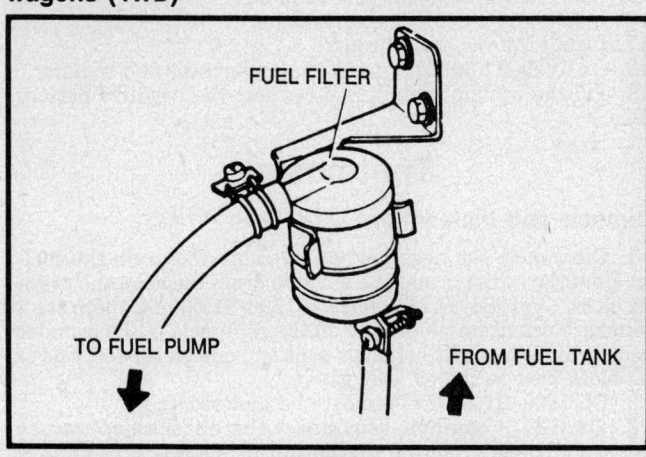

Typical fuel filters—all models

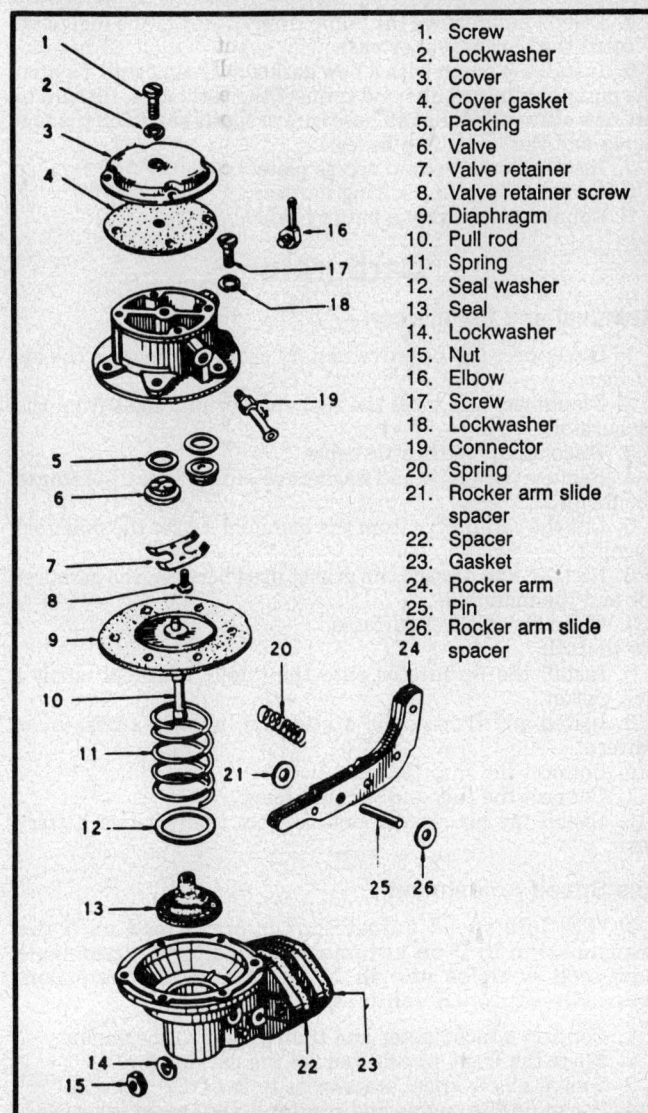

1. Screw
2. Lockwasher
3. Cover
4. Cover gasket
5. Packing
6. Valve
7. Valve retainer
8. Valve retainer screw
9. Diaphragm
10. Pull rod
11. Spring
12. Seal washer
13. Seal
14. Lockwasher
15. Nut
16. Elbow
17. Screw
18. Lockwasher
19. Connector
20. Spring
21. Rocker arm slide spacer
22. Spacer
23. Gasket
24. Rocker arm
25. Pin
26. Rocker arm slide spacer

Typical mechanical fuel pump

1. Relieve the fuel system pressure.
2. Disconnect the negative battery cable.
3. Loosen the fuel hose clamps and disconnect the hoses from the filter.

NOTE: On the Stanza 4WD wagon, the fuel filter is found in-line, under the floor, near the fuel pump.

4. Remove the bolt securing the filter to the bracket.
5. Remove the filter.
6. Install the new filter. Connect the fuel hoses and tighten the clamps.
8. Replace the fuel pump fuse, relay or connector.
9. Connect the negative battery cable.
10. Start the engine and check for leaks.

Mechanical Fuel Pump

The mechanical fuel pump is driven from the camshaft. It is bolted to the cylinder block on the right side of the engine.

Pressure Testing

1. Disconnect the negative battery cable.

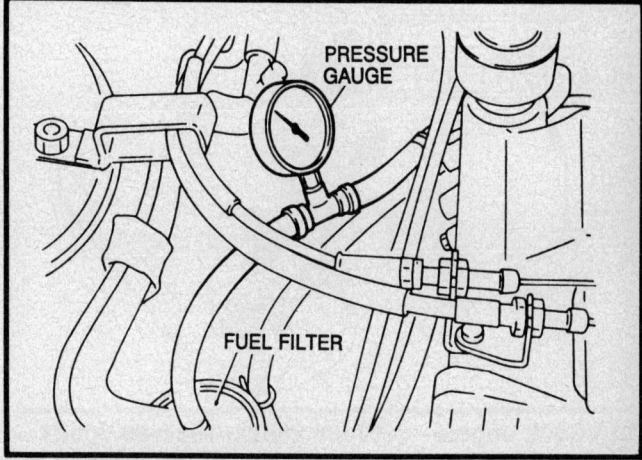

Checking fuel pump pressure—except GA16i engine

2. Attach an adapter and tee to the fuel pump outlet line and connect a pressure gauge of known calibration to the tee.
3. Connect the negative battery cable.
4. Start the engine and read the fuel pressure on the gauge. It should be 2.8–3.8 psi.

Removal and Installation

1. Disconnect the negative battery cable.
2. Disconnect the fuel inlet and outlet lines from the pump. Plug the ends to prevent fuel leakage.
3. Unbolt and separate the pump from the block.
4. Remove the gasket and discard it.
5. Clean the pump gasket mating surfaces.
6. Mount the pump and gasket onto the block. Install and tighten the mounting bolts.
7. Connect the fuel lines.
8. Connect the negative battery cable.

Electric Fuel Pump

Pressure Testing

EXCEPT PULSAR AND SENTRA WITH GA16I ENGINE

1. Relieve the fuel system pressure.
2. Remove the air duct, if required.
3. Connect a fuel pressure gauge between the fuel feed pipe and the fuel filter outlet.
4. Start the engine and read the fuel pressure. If the pressure is not as specified, replace the pump. If the pump output pressure is okay, go to Step 5 to check the pressure regulator.
5. Stop the engine and disconnect the fuel pressure regulator vacuum hose from the intake manifold.
6. Plug the intake manifold with a rubber cap.
7. On VG30E engines for 1987–88 200ZX, 1987–89 300ZX and 1987–89 Maxima, connect a jumper wire from terminal No. 108 of the ECU to a suitable body ground.
8. Connect a vacuum pump to the fuel pressure regulator.
9. On all except VG30E engines, start the engine and alternately increase and decrease the vacuum while watching the gauge. On VG30E engine, turn the ignition switch to the **ON** position without starting the engine. Fuel pressure should decrease as the vacuum is increased. If the pressure is incorrect, replace the pressure regulator. After replacement of the regulator, repeat the pressure test. If still incorrect, check the fuel lines for kinks or blockage, and replace the pump as necessary.

PULSAR AND SENTRA WITH GA16I ENGINE

1. Relieve the fuel system pressure.

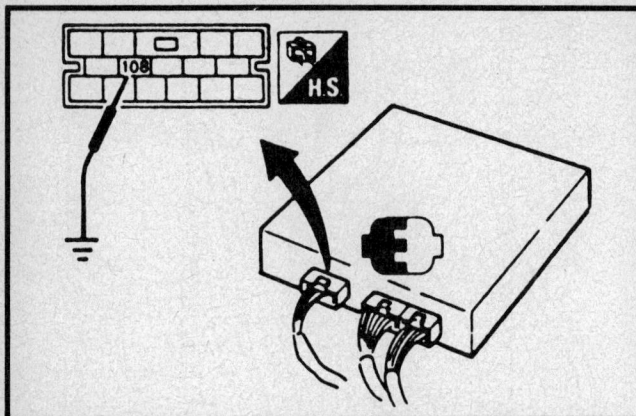

On VG30E engine—1987–88 200ZX, 1987–89 300ZX and 1987–89 Maxima—jump terminal 108 of the ECU to a body ground

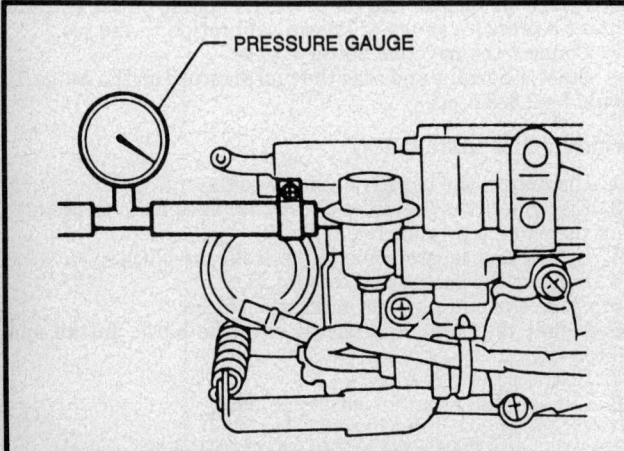

Checking fuel pump pressure—GA16i engine

2. Disconnect the fuel inlet hose from the electro-injection unit.

3. Connect a pressure gauge to the electro-injection unit inlet opening and connect the fuel inlet hose to the gauge.

4. Start the engine and check the fuel line and gauge connections for fuel leaks.

5. Read the fuel pressure. If the pressure is not as specified, replace the pump.

6. Release the fuel system pressure and disconnect the gauge.

7. Connect the fuel inlet hose to the electro-injection unit.

Removal and Installation

The fuel pump is located in the fuel tank on all models except the 2WD Stanza Wagon. On 2WD Stanza wagon the fuel pump is located in line to the fuel tank. In tank fuel pumps are accessible either by lifting up the rear seat or through an opening in the trunk compartment.

1. Relieve the pressure from the fuel system, then disconnect the negative battery cable.

2. Open the trunk, remove the mat and flip up the fuel pump access plate in the trunk floor. If there is no access plate in the luggage compartment, check under the rear seats.

3. On 2WD Stanza wagon, clamp the hose between the fuel tank and the fuel pump to prevent gas from spilling out of the tank. Disconnect and plug the fuel outlet hose and remove the pump from the mounting bracket.

4. Disconnect the inlet and outlet tubes from the fuel pump.

5. Unbolt and remove the pump from the top of the fuel tank. Discard the O-ring seal or gasket.

6. Install the pump with a new gasket or O-ring seal. Tighten the pump retaining bolts and connect the fuel hoses. Be sure to use new clamps and that all hoses are properly seated on the fuel pump and the fuel pump hoses.

7. Install the fuel pump access plate.

8. Connect the pump wiring harness.

9. Connect the negative battery cable.

Carburetor

Removal and Installation

1. Disconnect the negative battery cable and remove the air cleaner.

2. Disconnect and label the fuel and vacuum lines from the carburetor.

3. Disconnect the throttle cable.

4. Remove the 4 nuts and washers retaining the carburetor to the manifold.

5. Lift the carburetor from the manifold. Cover the manifold opening.

6. Remove and discard the gasket used between the carburetor and the manifold.

7. Clean the gaskset surfaces.

To install:

8. Install the carburetor onto the intake manifold using a new gasket.

9. Install and tighten the 4 attaching nuts in a criss-cross pattern.

10. Connect the throttle cable.

11. Connect the fuel and vacuum lines.

12. Install the air cleaner and connect the negative battery cable.

Idle Speed Adjustment

NOTE: Idle speed adjustment is performed with the transmission in D on automatic transmission/transaxle equipped vehicles and in N on manual transmission/transaxle equipped vehicles.

1. Connect a tachometer and timing light to the engine.

2. Block the front wheels and set the parking brake.

3. Switch all electrical accessories to the **OFF** position.

4. Warm up the engine and run for 2 minutes at idle speed.

5. Race the engine 2–3 times to 2000–3000 rpm and allow to idle.

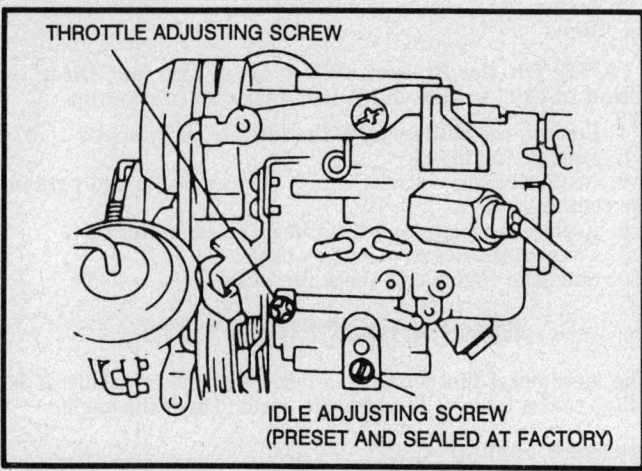

Idle speed adjusting screw on Sentra with carburetor

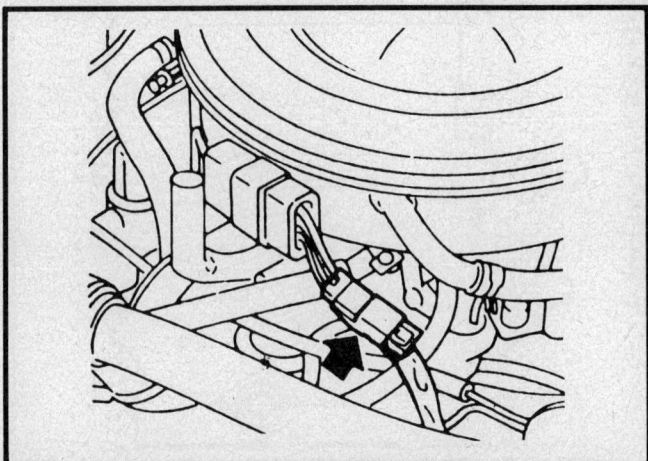

Air-fuel ratio solenoid harness connector

6. Check the ignition timing and adjust as necessary.
7. Place the transmission in **D** for automatic transmission/transaxle or **N** for manual transmission/transaxle and check the idle speed with the tachometer. If the radiator cooling fan comes on, wait unit it stops before checking the idle speed.
8. If the idle speed is not within specifications, adjust by turning the throttle adjusting screw on the carburetor.
9. Stop the engine and disconnect the test equipment.

Idle Mixture Adjustment

1. Connect a tachometer and timing light to the engine.
2. Block the front wheels and set the parking brake.
3. Switch all electrical accessories to the **OFF** position.
4. Warm up the engine and run for 2 minutes at idle speed.
5. Race the engine 2–3 times to 2000–3000 rpm and allow to idle.
6. Check the ignition timing and idle speed. Adjust as necessary.
7. Stop the engine and disconnect the air-fuel ratio solenoid harness connector. Disconnect the air induction hose from the air inlet pipe and cap the air pipe opening.
8. Start the engine and check the CO percentage using the proper equipment. For this check, the CO probe must be inserted at least 15.7 in. (400mm) into the tail pipe.
9. If the CO level is not within specifications, the idle mixture seal plug must be drilled out. To do this, remove the carburetor from the engine and continue with the remainder of this procedure.
10. Carefully drill a hole in the idle mixture seal plug and withdraw it from the plug hole using the proper tool.

NOTE: Do not drill to deep of the head of the idle mixture screw will be damaged. Do not scratch the link and shaft sliding surfaces. Make sure all metal shavings from the drilling are completely removed.

11. Mount the carburetor onto the engine.
12. Start the engine, check the idle speed and adjust the CO percentage by turning the idle mixture adjusting screw. If the CO level still cannot be brought into specifications, the carburetor must be overhauled or replaced.
13. Stop the engine and install a new seal plug.
14. Disconnect the test equipment.

FUEL LEVEL

All carburetors have a glass float chamber side cover marked

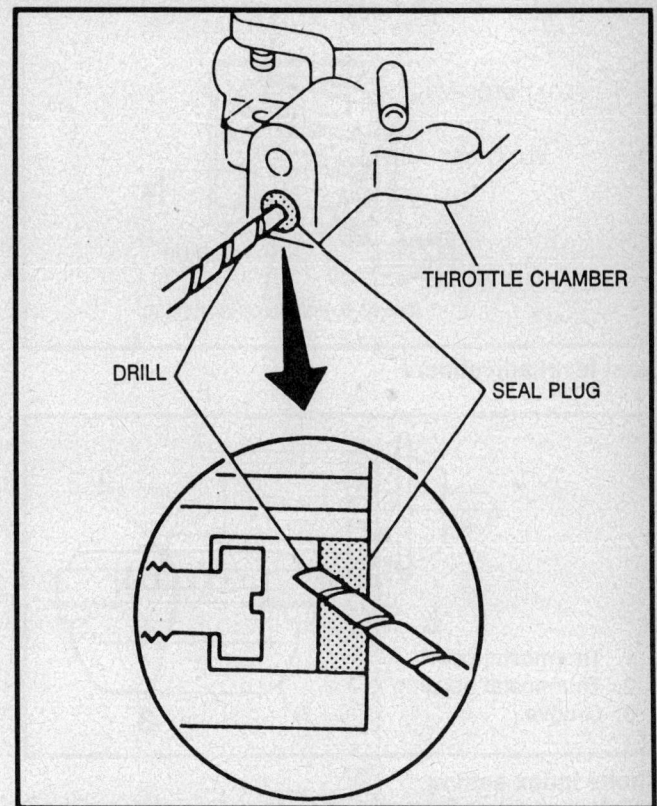

Drilling out the idle speed mixture seal plug

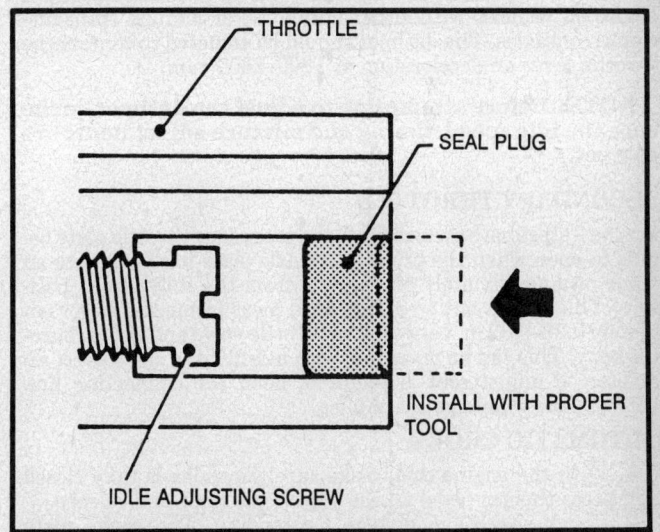

Idle mixture adjusting screw location

with a fuel level line; some have a small window in the side of the float chamber. Fuel level is adjusted by bending the float seat tab with the float cover removed and inverted, and the float fully raised.

THROTTLE LINKAGE

On all vehicles, make sure the throttle is wide open when the accelerator pedal is floored. Some vehicles have an adjustable accelerator pedal stop to prevent strain on the linkage.

DASHPOT

A dashpot is used on carburetors of vehicles with automatic

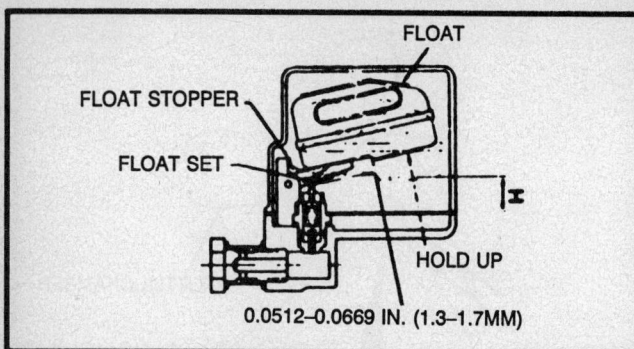

Float level adjustment

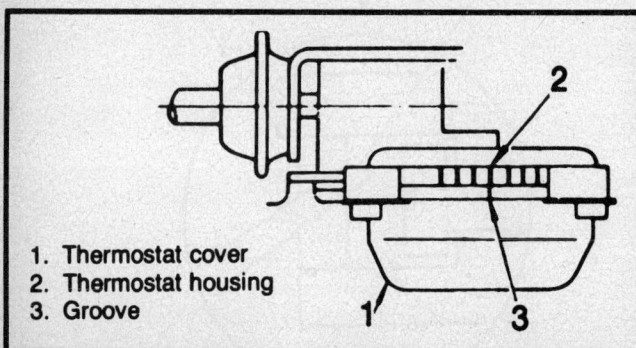

1. Thermostat cover
2. Thermostat housing
3. Groove

Choke index setting

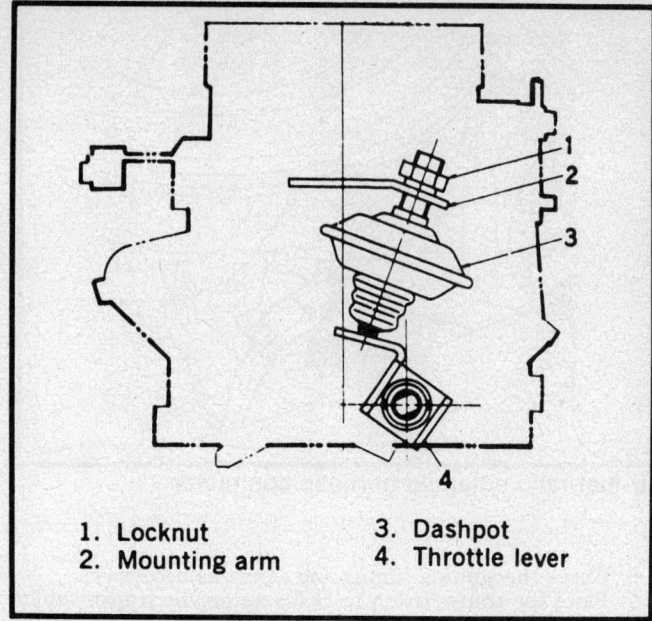

1. Locknut
2. Mounting arm
3. Dashpot
4. Throttle lever

View of the dashpot

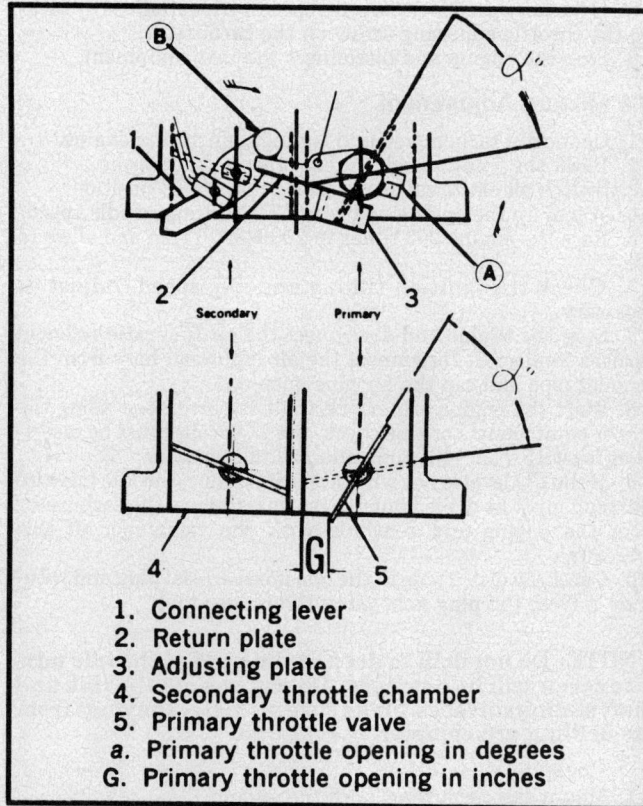

1. Connecting lever
2. Return plate
3. Adjusting plate
4. Secondary throttle chamber
5. Primary throttle valve
a. Primary throttle opening in degrees
G. Primary throttle opening in inches

Secondary throttle adjustment

transaxle as means of slowly closing the throttle valve to prevent stalling. It is also used in later years as an emission control device on vehicles with either automatic or manual transmissions/transaxles. The dashpot should be adjusted to contact the throttle lever on deceleration at 1800–2600 rpm.

NOTE: Before attempting to adjust the dashpot, make sure the idle speed, timing and mixture adjustments are correct.

SECONDARY THROTTLE

On the 2 stage carburetors used, the secondary throttle plate begins to open when the primary throttle plate has opened to an angle of approximately 50 degrees; from the fully closed position. This works out to a clearance measurement of approximately 0.28–0.32 in. between the throttle valve and the carburetor body. This can be measured with a drill bit of the correct diameter. If adjustment is required, bend the connecting link between the 2 linkage assemblies.

AUTOMATIC CHOKE

1. With the engine cold, make sure the choke is fully closed and press the gas pedal all the way to the floor and release.
2. Check the choke linkage for binding. The choke plate should be easily opened and closed with light finger pressure. If the choke sticks or binds, it can usually be freed with a liberal application of a carburetor cleaner made for the purpose. If not, the carburetor will have to be disassembled for repairs.
3. The choke is correctly adjusted when the index mark on the choke housing (notch) aligns with the center mark on the carburetor body. If the setting is incorrect, loosen the 3 screws clamping the choke body in place and rotate the choke cover left or right until the marks align. Tighten the screws carefully to avoid cracking the housing.

FAST IDLE

1. With the carburetor removed from the vehicle, place the upper side of the fast idle screw on the second step of the fast

idle cam and measure the clearance between the throttle valve and the wall of the throttle valve chamber at the center of the throttle valve. Check it against the following specifications:
California:
Manual Transaxle—0.0268–0.0039 in.
Automatic Transaxle—0.0378–0.0039 in.

Canada:
   Manual Transaxle—0.0268–0.0039 in.
   Automatic Transaxle—0.0378–0.0039 in.
2. Install the carburetor on the engine.
3. Start the engine and measure the fast idle rpm with the engine at operating temperature. The cam should be at the 2nd step. Idle speed for manual transaxles should be 1800–2600 rpm and 2100–2900 rpm for automatic transaxles.
4. To adjust the fast idle speed, turn the fast idle adjusting screw counterclockwise to increase the fast idle speed and clockwise to decrease the fast idle speed.

Fuel Injection

Idle Speed Adjustment

Before adjusting the idle speed, visually check the following items first: air cleaner for clogging, hoses and ducts for leaks, EGR valve for proper operation, all electrical connectors, gaskets and the throttle valve and throttle valve switch operation.

For further information, please refer to "Chilton's Electronic Engine Control's Manual" for additional coverage.

1987–89 STANZA AND 200SX (CA20E AND CA18ET ENGINES)

1. Connect a tachometer and timing light to the engine.
2. Turn all electrical accessories and air conditioner to the **OFF** position.
3. Warm up engine to normal operating temperature.
4. Run the engine at 2000 rpm for about 2 minutes without load.
5. Race the engine 2–3 times and allow to idle.
6. Check the idle speed.
7. If the idle speed is not within specifications, disconnect the Auxiliary Air Control (AAC) valve and throttle valve switch harness connectors.
8. Adjust the idle speed by turning the idle speed adjusting screw.
9. Connect the AAC and throttle valve switch connectors.
10. Check the timing and adjust as necessary.
11. Stop the engine and remove the test equipment.

240SX AND 1990 STANZA

1. Connect a tachometer and timing light to the engine.
2. Turn all electrical accessories and air conditioner to the **OFF** position.
3. Warm up engine to normal operating temperature.
4. Run the engine at 2000 rpm for about 2 minutes without load.
5. Race the engine 2–3 times and allow to idle.

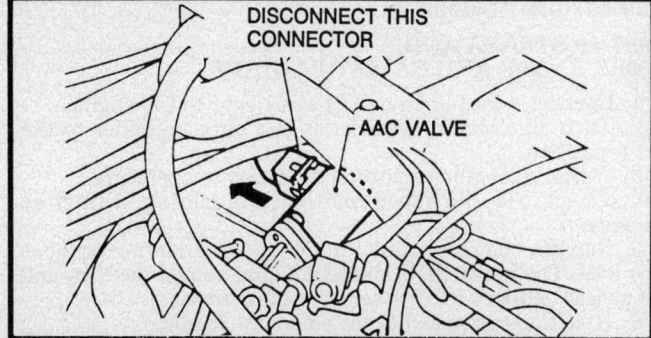

DISCONNECT THIS CONNECTOR

AAC VALVE

AAC valve connector—200SX with CA20E and CA18ET engines and 1987–89 Stanza

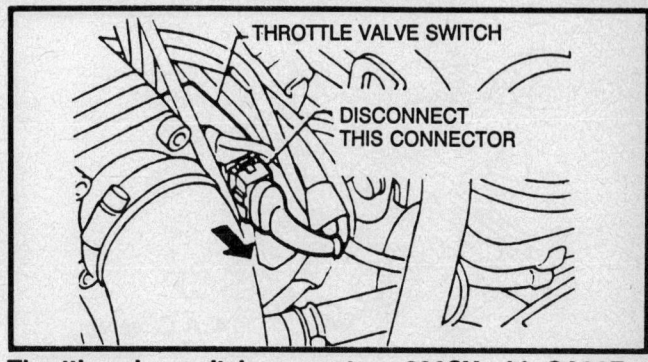

THROTTLE VALVE SWITCH

DISCONNECT THIS CONNECTOR

Throttle valve switch connector—200SX with CA20E and CA18ET engines and 1987–89 Stanza

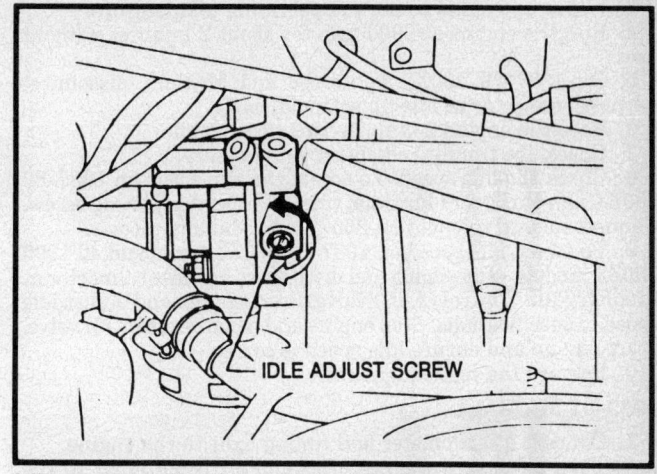

IDLE ADJUST SCREW

Idle speed adjusting screw—200SX with CA20E and CA18ET engines and 1987–89 Stanza

6. Check the idle speed in the **N** position for both manual and automatic transmission models.
7. To adjust the idle speed, first disconnect the throttle sensor harness connector.
8. Adjust the idle speed by turning the idle speed adjusting screw.
9. Stop the engine. Connect the throttle sensor harness connector.
10. Remove the test equipmemt.

300ZX AND 1987–88 MAXIMA

1. Connect a tachometer and timing light to the engine.
2. Turn all electrical accessories and air conditioner to the **OFF** position.

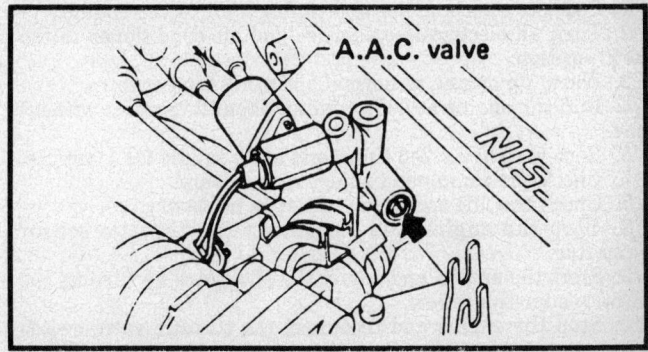

A.A.C. valve

AAC valve location on 1897–89 300ZX turbo engines

Idle speed adjusting screw—1989–91 Maxima

3. Warm up engine to normal operating temperature.

4. Run the engine at 2000 rpm for about 2 minutes without load.

5. On 1987–89 300ZX non-turbo and Maxima, disconnect harness connector at idle-up solenoid valve.

6. Race the engine 2–3 times and allow to idle.

7. Check the timing and adjust as necessary.

8. Check the idle speed. To adjust the idle speed on 1987–89 300ZX non-turbo and Maxima, turn idle speed adjusting screw. Connect idle-up solenoid on 300ZX and Maxima models.

9. To adjust idle speed on 1987–89 300ZX turbo and all 1990 300ZX models, stop engine and disconnect harness connector at Auxiliary Air Control (AAC) valve. Start engine and adjust idle speed to specifications. Stop engine and reconnect control valve. Start engine and ensure idle speed is correct.

10. Remove the test equipment.

1989–91 MAXIMA

1. Connect a tachometer and timing light to the engine.

2. Turn all electrical accessories and air conditioner to the **OFF** position.

3. Warm up engine to normal operating temperature.

4. Run the engine at 2000 rpm for about 2 minutes without load.

5. Race the engine 2–3 times and allow to idle for 1 minute.

6. Check the timing and adjust as necessary.

7. Check the idle speed in the **N** position for both manual and automatic transaxle models.

8. To adjust the idle speed, close the Auxiliary Air Control (AAC) valve by turning the diagnostic mode selector on the ECU fully clockwise.

9. Adjust the idle speed by turning the idle speed adjusting screw with transaxle in the **N** position.

10. Operate the AAC valve by turning the diagnostic mode selector on the ECU. fully conterclockwise.

11. Stop the engine and remove the test equipment.

PULSAR AND SENTRA

1. Connect a tachometer and timing light to the engine.

2. Turn all electrical accessories and air conditioner to the **OFF** position.

3. Warm up engine to normal operating temperature.

4. Run the engine at 2000 rpm for about 2 minutes without load.

5. Race the engine 2–3 times and allow to idle for 1 minute.

6. Check the timing and adjust as necessary.

7. Check the idle speed and adjust as necessary.

8. Stop the engine and disconnect the throttle sensor connector.

9. Start the engine and adjust the idle speed by turning the throttle adjusting screw.

10. Stop the engine and reconnect the throttle valve switch connector.

11. Remove the test equipment.

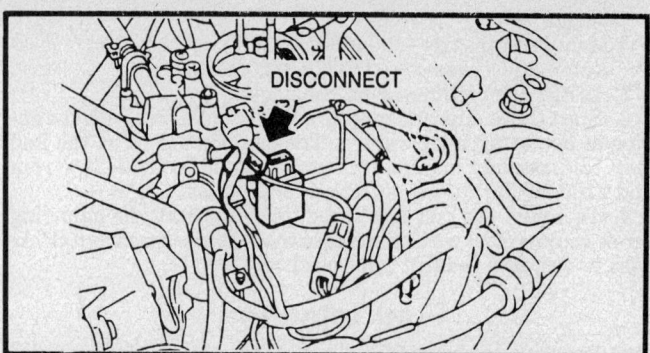

Throttle valve switch harness connector location— 1987–88 Pulsar and Sentra with E16i engine

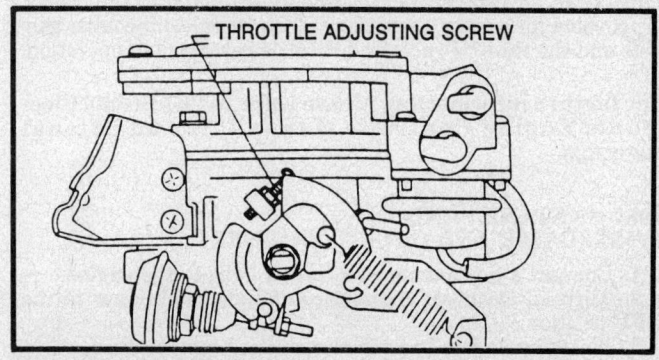

Throttle adjustment screw location—1987–88 Pulsar and Sentra with E16i engine

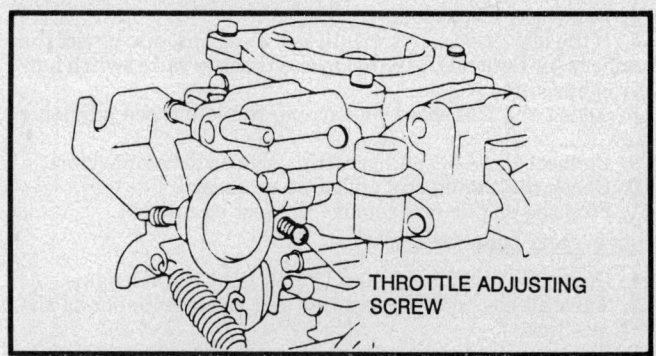

Throttle adjustment screw location—1989–91 Pulsar and Sentra with GA16i engine

Idle Mixture Adjustment

1987–89 STANZA AND 200SX (CA20E AND CA18ET ENGINES)

1. Connect a tachometer and timing light to the engine.

2. Turn all electrical accessories and air conditioner to the **OFF** position.

3. Warm up engine to normal operating temperature.

4. Check the idle speed and ignition timing. Adjust as necessary.

5. Run the engine at 2000 rpm for about 2 minutes without any load. The green ECU inspection light should flash on and off at least 9 times in 10 seconds at 2000 rpm.

6. Race the engine 2–3 times and allow to idle.

7. Set the ECU to the No. 2 diagnosis mode and disconnect the throttle valve switch connector. The red and green lights on the ECU should flash together. If they do, then the idle mixture

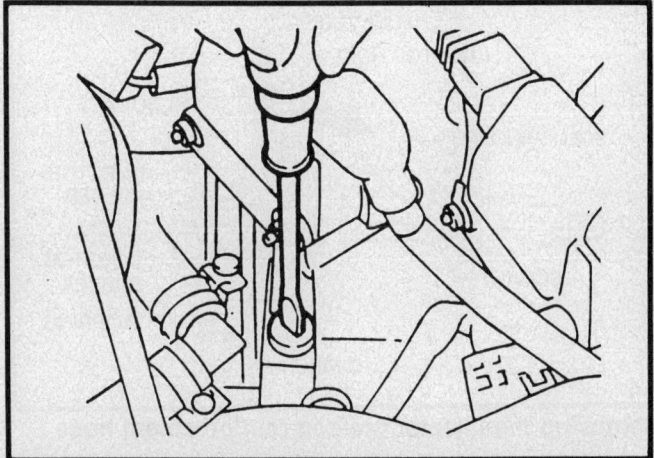

Adjusting idle mixture with variable resistor—200SX with CA20E and CA18ET engines and 1987–89 Stanza

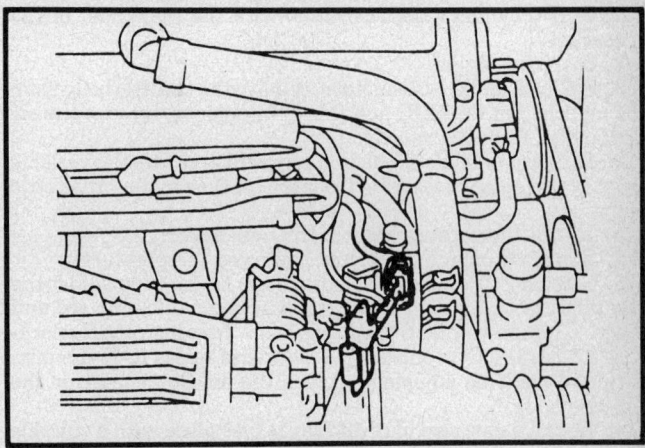

Connecting resistor to engine temperature sensor harness

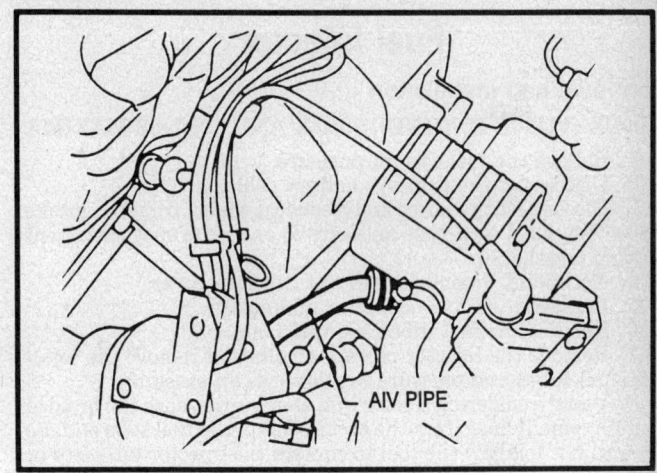

AIV pipe location on 240SX and 1990 Stanza

is correct and no further adjustment is required. If they don't, then continue with the remainder of the procedure.

8. Stop the engine and remove the air flow meter from the vehicle.

9. Drill a small hole in the seal plug which covers the variable resistor and remove the plug from the air flow meter.

10. Install the air flow meter.

11. Warm up engine to normal operating temperature.

12. Set the ECU to the No. 2 diagnosis mode, then adjust the idle mixture by turning the variable resistor until the red and green lights on the ECU flash together. If the mixture still can't be adjusted, replace the air flow meter.

13. Install a new seal plug and tap it into place with a suitable tool.

14. Connect the throttle valve switch connector and remove the test equipment.

200SX (VG30E ENGINE), 240SX, 300ZX, MAXIMA, AND 1990–91 STANZA

1. Connect a tachometer and timing light to the engine.

2. Turn all electrical accessories and air conditioner to the **OFF** position.

3. Warm up engine to normal operating temperature.

4. Check the idle speed and ignition timing. Adjust as necessary.

5. Run the engine at 2000 rpm for about 2 minutes without any load. The green ECU inspection lamp should flash on and off at least 5 times in 10 seconds at 2000 rpm.

6. Race the engine 2–3 times and allow to idle.

7. Set the ECU to the No. 2 diagnosis mode by turning the diagnostic mode selector screw on ECU fully counterclockwise. Disconnect the throttle valve switch connector. The red and green lights on the ECU should flash together. If they do, then the idle mixture is correct and no further adjustment is required. If they don't, then continue with the remainder of the procedure.

8. Stop the engine and disconnect the engine temperature sensor harness connector from the sensor. Connect a 2.5 kilo-ohm resistor across the terminals of the engine temperature harness connector. The sensor is located on the cylinder head.

9. On 240SX and 1990–91 Stanza, disconnect the AIV hose and plug the AIV pipe. On 1990–91 300ZX, disconnect the AIV control solenoid valve harness connector.

10. Start the engine and run for 5 minutes, then race the engine 2–3 times and allow to idle.

11. Check the CO content and make sure the engine runs smoothly. The idle mixture on these vehicles is controlled by the ECU, and is not adjustable. However, the following components should be checked before identifying the ECU as the source of the problem.

Exhaust gas sensor(s)
Exhaust gas sensor harness
Fuel pressure regulator
Air flow meter
Fuel injectors
Engine temperature sensor

12. Stop the engine. Remove the resistor from the engine temperature switch harness connector and plug in the connector. Connect the AIV hose.

13. Remove the test equipment.

PULSAR AND SENTRA

1. Connect a tachometer and timing light to the engine.

2. Turn all electrical accessories and air conditioner to the **OFF** position.

3. Warm up engine to normal operating temperature.

4. Check the idle speed and ignition timing. Adjust as necessary.

5. Run the engine at 2000 rpm for about 2 minutes without any load. The green ECU inspection lamp should flash on and off at least 5 times in 10 seconds at 2000 rpm.

6. Race the engine 2–3 times and allow to idle.

7. Set the ECU to the No. 2 diagnosis mode. The red and green lights on the ECU should flash together. If they do, then the idle mixture is correct and no further adjustment is re-

quired. If they don't then continue with the remainder of the procedure.

8. Stop the engine.

9. On E16i and GA16i engines, remove the throttle body from the vehicle. On CA16DE and CA18DE engines, remove the air flow meter from the vehicle.

10. Drill a small hole in the seal plug which covers the variable resistor and remove the plug from the air flow meter or throttle body.

11. Install the throttle body or air flow meter.

12. Warm up engine to normal operating temperature.

13. Set the ECU to the No. 2 diagnosis mode, then adjust the idle mixture by turning the variable resistor until the red and green lights on the ECU flash together. Turning counterclockwise lowers the CO content and clockwise raises it. If the mixture still can't be adjusted, replace the air flow meter or the throttle body.

14. Install a new seal plug and tap it into place with a suitable tool.

15. Remove the test equipment.

Fuel Injector

Removal and Installation

200SX (VG30E ENGINE), 300ZX AND 1987–88 MAXIMA

1. Relieve the fuel system pressure.
2. Disconnect the negative battery cable.
3. Disconnect the hoses and electrical wiring from the intake collector. Label each hose and wire to ensure proper placement during installation.
4. On 200SX, remove the intake collector cover.
5. Remove the intake collector and gasket.
6. Remove the fuel tube retaining bolts.
7. Remove the injector retaining bolts and remove the injector, fuel tubes and pressure regulator as an assembly.
8. Using a soldering iron or hot, sharp knife, slice the braided reinforcement hose from the socket end to the fuel tube end. Be careful not to allow the tool to contact the injector tail piece or the socket plastic connector. Pull the hose from the injector and repeat the procedure for the remaining injectors.

To install:

9. Clean the exterior of the injector tail piece and fuel tube end. Install new O-rings.
10. Wet the inside of the new fuel tube with clean fuel.
11. Push the end of the rubber hose and hose socket onto the injector tail piece and fuel tube end as far as it will go. Clamps are not required. Repeat the procedure for the remaining injectors.
12. Position and install the injector, fuel tube and pressure regulator assembly. Install the injector and fuel tube retaining bolts. Pressurize the fuel system and check for leaks at all fuel connections.
13. Install the intake collector.
14. On 200SX, install the intake collector cover and gasket. Position the gasket so the silicone rubber portion is facing down.
15. Connect all the hoses and electrical wiring to the intake collector.
16. Connect the negative battery cable.

1989–91 MAXIMA

1. Relieve the fuel system pressure.
2. Disconnect the negative battery cable.
3. Disconnect the automatic speed control device cable and accelerator cable from the intake manifold collector.
4. Disconnect the Auxiliary Air Control (AAC) valve, throttle sensor and idle switch connectors.
5. Disconnect the air cut valve water hose. Plug the end to prevent leakage.
6. Disconnect the PCV hoses.

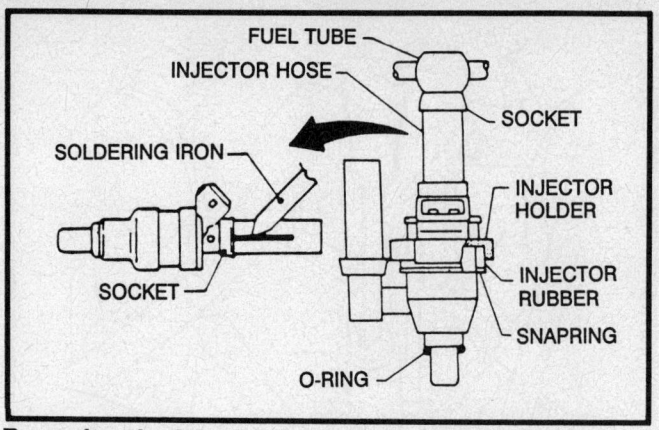

Removing the injector braided reinforcement hose

7. Disconnect the vacuum gallery, power valve actuator, master brake cylinder and EGR control valve vacuum hoses.
8. Loosen and disconnect the EGR flare tube.
9. Remove the upper manifold collector from the engine.
10. Disconnect the engine ground harness from the lower intake collector manifold and remove the manifold from the engine.
11. Disconnect pressure regulator vacuum hose, fuel supply and return tubes and injector electrical connectors.
12. Remove the fuel injector tube assembly.
13. Withdraw the injectors from the fuel tube.

To install:

14. Insert the fuel injector(s) into the fuel tubes with new O-rings.
15. Install the injector and fuel tube assembly.
16. Connect the injector electrical connectors, fuel supply and return tubes and pressure regulator vacuum hose. Pressurize the fuel system and check for leaks at all fuel connections.
17. Install the lower intake collector manifold and connect the engine ground harness.
18. Install the upper collector manifold.
19. Connect and tighten the EGR flare tube.
20. Connect the vacuum and PCV hoses, air cut valve water hose and electrical connectors.
21. Connect the accelerator cable and automatic speed control device cable to the intake manifold collector. Adjust the cables.
22. Connect the negative battery cable.

200SX (CA20E AND CA18ET ENGINES), 1987–89 STANZA AND PULSAR (CA18DE ENGINE)

1. Relieve the fuel system pressure.
2. Disconnect the negative battery cable.
3. Disconnect the ECU and ignition wires.
4. Disconnect the fuel supply and return hoses. Plug the hoses to prevent fuel leakage.
5. Disconnect the pressure regulator vacuum hose.
6. Remove the fuel tube retaining bolts.
7. Remove the injector retaining bolts and remove the injector, fuel tubes and pressure regulator as an assembly. Be careful not to smack the injectors or bend the fuel tube.
8. Using a soldering iron or hot, sharp knife, slice the braided reinforcement hose from the socket end to the fuel tube end. Be careful not to allow the tool to contact the injector tail piece or the socket plastic connector. Pull the hose from the injector and repeat the procedure for the remaining injectors.

To install:

9. Clean the exterior of the injector tail piece and fuel tube end. Install new O-rings.
10. Wet the inside of the new fuel tube with clean fuel.
11. Push the end of the rubber hose and hose socket onto the

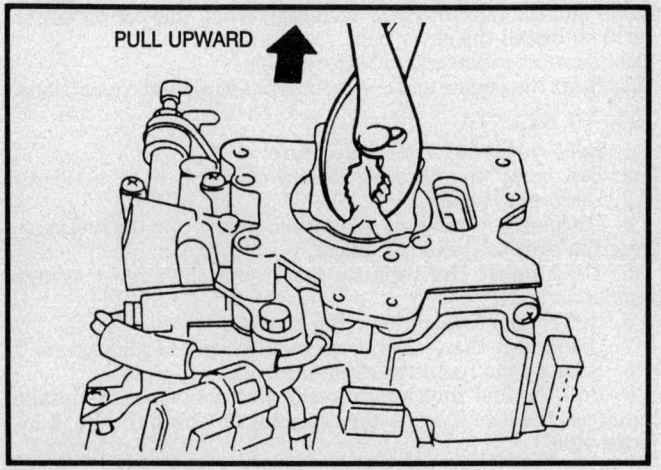

Injector removal on E16i and GA16i engines

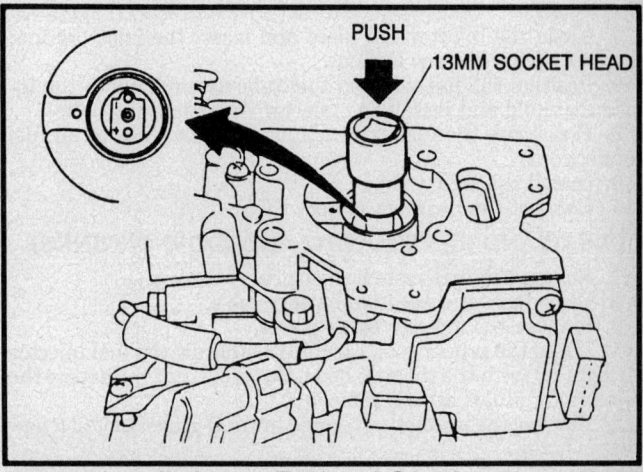

Injector installation on E16i and GA16i engines. Note injector terminal alignment

injector tail piece and fuel tube end as far as it will go. Clamps are not required. Repeat the procedure for the remaining injectors.

12. Position and install the injector, fuel tube and pressure regulator assembly. Install the injector and fuel tube retaining bolts. Pressurize the fuel system and check for leaks at all fuel connections.

13. Connect the pressure regulator vacuum hose.

14. Connect the fuel supply and return hoses.

15. Connect the ECU and ignition wires.

16. Connect the negative battery cable.

240SX

1. Relieve the fuel system pressure.
2. Disconnect the negative battery cable.
3. Remove the BPT valve.
4. Remove the fuel tube retaining bolts.
5. Remove the fuel tube and injector assembly from the intake manifold.
6. Withdraw the injectors from the fuel tube.

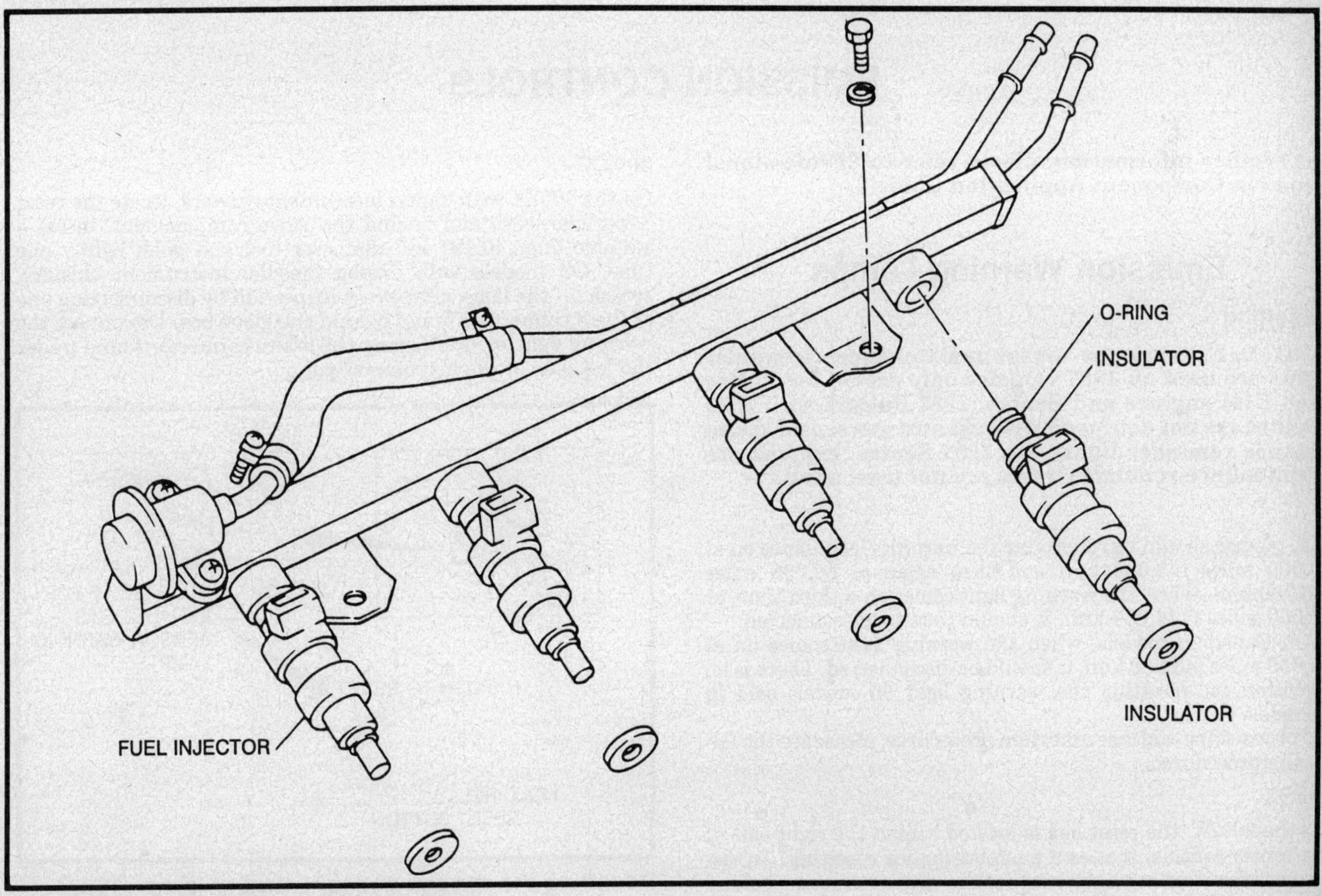

Fuel injector assembly—1990 Stanza

O-RING

INSULATOR

INSULATOR

FUEL INJECTOR

To install:

7. Clean the injector tail piece and insert the injectors into the fuel tube with new O-rings.

8. Position the injector and fuel tube assembly onto the intake manifold and install the injector tube retaining bolts.

9. Pressurize the fuel system and check for leaks at all fuel connections.

10. Install the BPT valve.

11. Connect the negative battery cable.

PULSAR AND SENTRA (E16I AND GA16I ENGINES)

1. Relieve the fuel system pressure.

2. Disconnect the negative battery cable.

3. Remove the injector cover plates.

4. Using the proper tool, carefully withdraw the fuel injector straight up from the throttle body. Be careful not to damage the injector terminals during removal.

5. Remove the injector upper and lower O-rings. Install a new lower O-ring.

To install:

6. Using a 13mm socket or suitable tool, carefully push the injector into the throttle body. Make sure the injector terminals are aligned properly. Be careful not to bend the injector terminals during installation.

7. Position the new upper injector O-ring and install it with a 19mm socket or other suitable tool.

8. Install the lower (white) injector cover plate. Do not over tighten the cover screws.

9. Install the injector cover without the rubber boot. Make sure the 2 O-rings (large and small) properly seated in the cover. Make sure there is a good connection between the injector ter-

minal and the injector cover terminal. When this connection is verified, install the cover boot.

10. Connect the negative battery cable.

11. Start the engine and check for leaks at all fuel connections.

1990-91 STANZA

1. Relieve the fuel system pressure.

2. Disconnect the negative battery cable.

3. Disconnect the air duct.

4. Disconnect the supply and return hoses from the fuel tube. Plug the ends to prevent leakage.

5. Disconnect the vacuum line from the fuel pressure regulator.

6. Detach the accelerator cable bracket.

7. Disconnect the fuel injector wiring harness connectors.

8. Remove the fuel tube retaining bolts.

9. Pull the fuel tube and injector assembly from the intake manifold. Remove the injector assembly out from the No. 4 injector side.

To install:

10. Remove the O-rings and insulators and install new ones.

11. Install the injector and fuel tube assembly into the intake manifold.

12. Install the injector tube retaining bolts.

13. Connect the injector wiring harness conectors.

14. Attach the accelerator cable bracket.

15. Connect the pressure regulator vacuum line.

16. Connect the fuel supply and return hoses.

17. Connect the air duct.

18. Connect the negative battery cable.

19. Start the engine and check for leaks at all fuel connections.

EMISSION CONTROLS

For further information, please refer to "Professional Emission Component Application Guide".

Emission Warning Lamps

Resetting

NOTE: Exhaust gas sensor maintenance remainder lights are used on 1987 vehicles only except for Pulsar with E16i engines and Sentra. 1987 Pulsars with E16i engines are not equipped with exhaust gas sensor maintenance reminder lights. On 1987 Sentra, exhaust gas maintenance reminder lights are not used at all.

U.S. models should be reset after the warning light comes on at 30,000 miles (43,000 km) and then again at 60,000 miles (96,000 km). When the warning light comes on a third time, at 90,000 miles (144,000 km), it should then be disconnected.

On Canadian models, when the warning light comes on at 30,000 miles (43,000 km), it should be disconnected. There is no provision for resetting the warning light on models sold in Canada.

For resetting and disconnection procedures, please see the following procedures:

200SX

On the 200ZX, the reset box is located behind the right side of the center console. It uses a push button for resetting. To disconnect the warning light, unplug the white connector behind the main fuse box.

300ZX

On the 300ZX with digital instrument clusters, locate the reset box underneath and behind the glove compartment, insert a suitable 5mm (0.197 in.) diameter tool and push lightly one time. On models with analog (needle) instrument clusters, switch off the lamp after every inspection by disconnecting one of the 3 connectors found behind the glove box. Disconnect the warning light by unplugging the white connector found under the left side of the instrument panel.

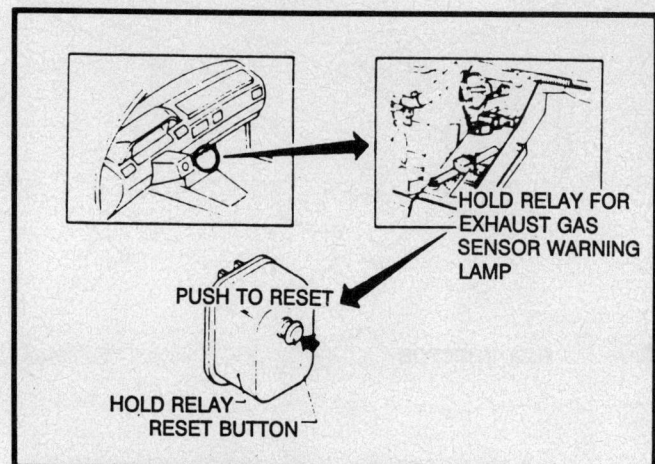

Resetting the oxygen sensor warning lamp—1987 200SX

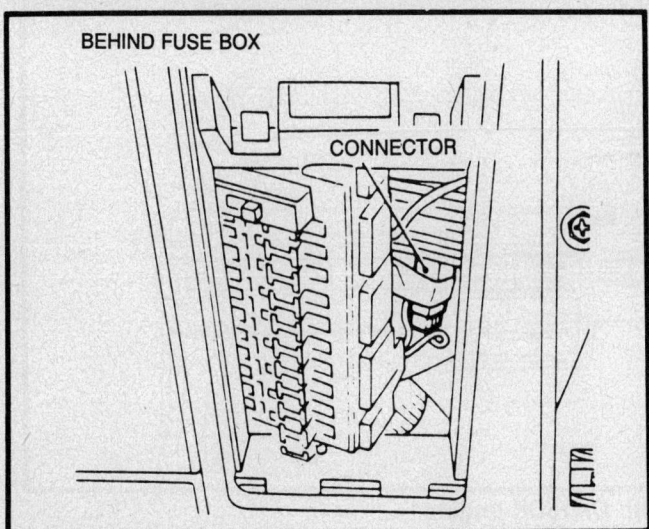

Disconnecting the oxygen sensor warning lamp connector—1987 200SX

Resetting the oxygen sensor warning lamp—1987 300ZX with analog (needle type) instrument cluster

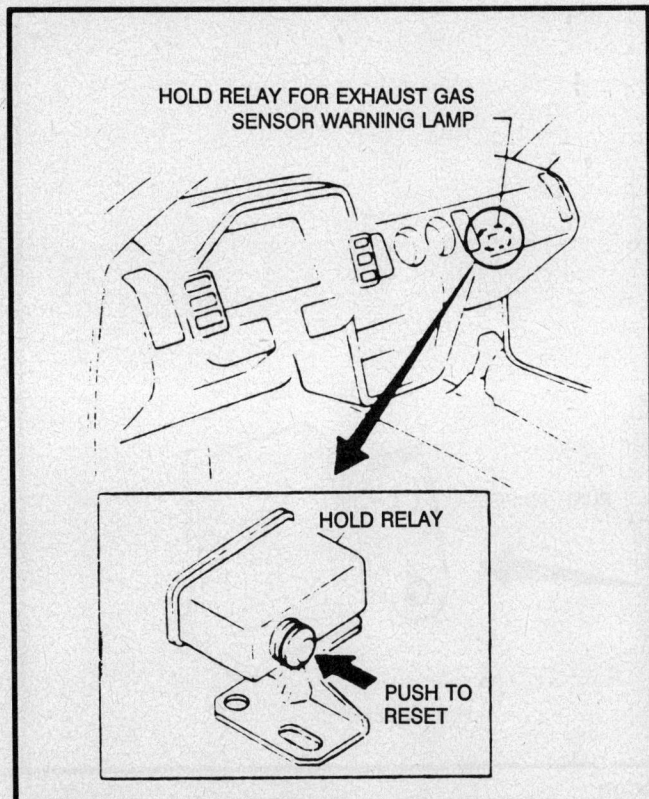

Resetting the oxygen sensor warning lamp—1987 300ZX with digital instrument cluster

MAXIMA

On the Maxima, reset the warning light by pressing the reset button on the small box found under the left side of the instrument panel. To disconnect the warning lamp, unplug the white connector behind and above the reset box. The oxygen sensor warning lamp is located near the right side kick panel.

PULSAR

On Pulsar, the reset box is located behind the left side kick pan-

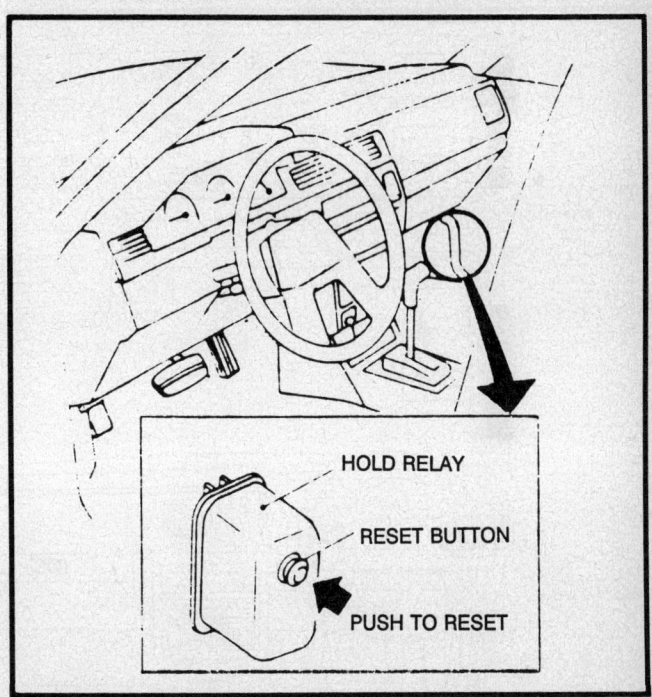

Resetting the oxygen sensor warning lamp—1987 Maxima

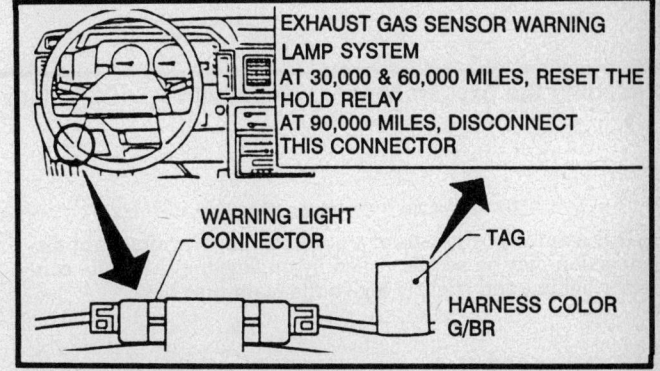

Disconnecting the oxygen sensor warning lamp connector—1987 Stanza sedan

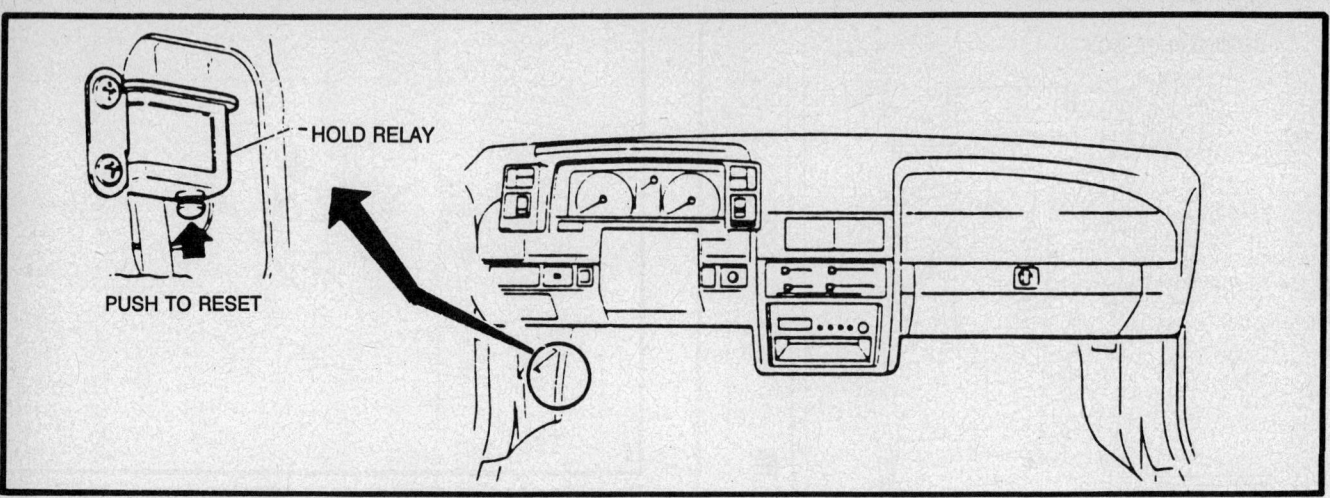

Resetting the oxygen sensor warning lamp—1987 Pulsar with CA16DE engine

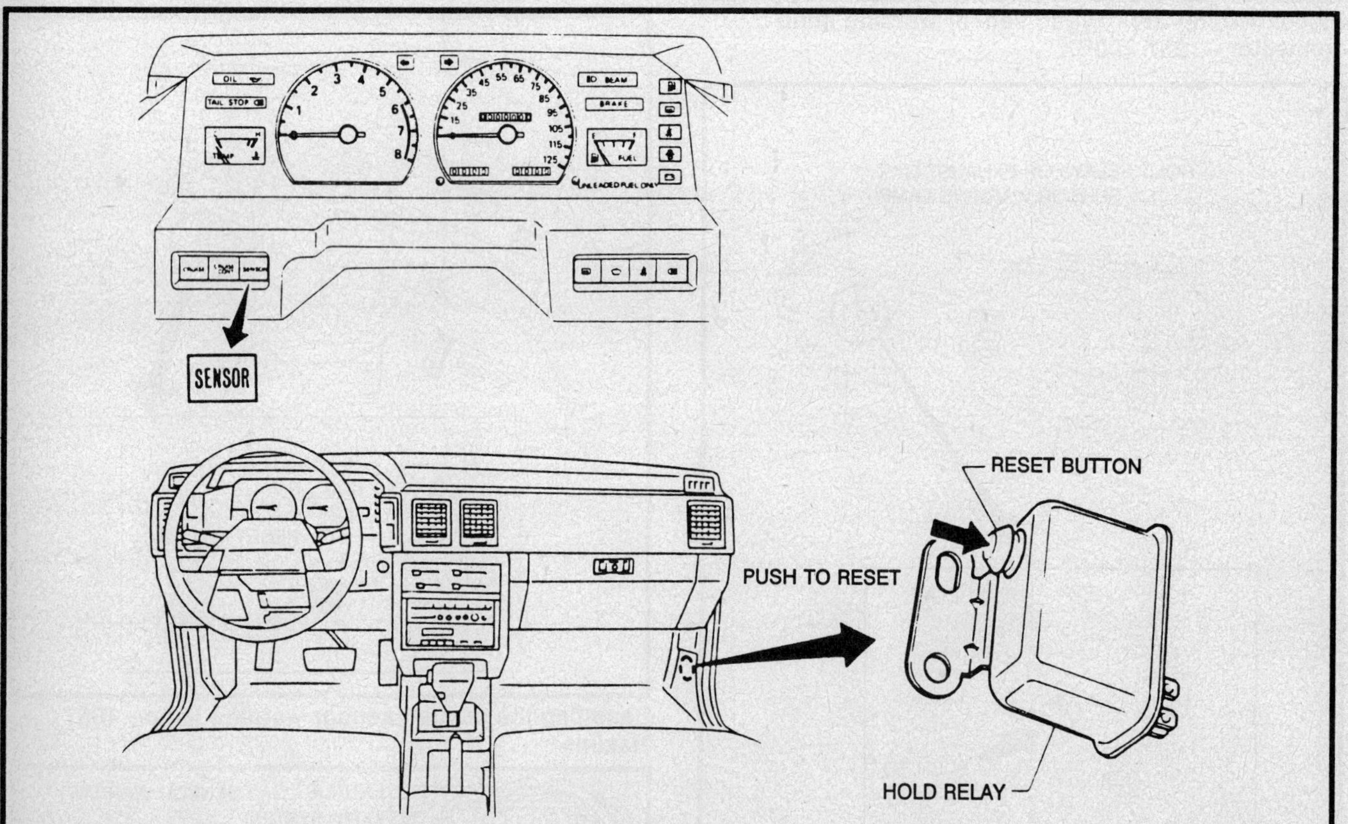

Resetting the oxygen sensor warning lamp—1987 Stanza sedan

el. It is actuated by means of a push button. Warning light disconnection may be accomplished by unplugging the white connector behind and slightly above the main fuse box.

NOTE: 1987 Pulsars with E16i engines are not equipped with exhaust gas sensor maintenance reminder lights.

STANZA

On the Stanza sedan, locate the reset box behind the right side kick panel and push the button one time.

On all Stanza wagons, the reset box is also under the passenger seat. A push button reset is used, similar to the sedan.

On all models, the warning light is disconnected by unplugging the white connector found behind the Electronic Control Unit, under the left side of the instrument panel.

ENGINE MECHANICAL

NOTE: Disconnecting the negative battery cable on some vehicles may interfere with the functions of the on board computer systems and may require the computer to undergo a relearning process, once the negative battery cable is reconnected.

Engine Assembly

Removal and Installation

200SX, 240SX AND 1987–89 300SX

1. Mark the hood hinge relationship and remove the hood.
2. Release the fuel system pressure and disconnect the negative battery cable.
3. Drain the cooling system and transmission fluid.
4. Remove the radiator after disconnecting the automatic transmission coolant tubes, if equipped.
5. Remove the air cleaner.
6. Remove the fan and pulley.
7. Disconnect or remove following:
    Water temperature gauge wire
    Oil pressure sending unit wire
    Ignition distributor primary wire
    Starter motor connections
    Fuel hose
    Alternator leads
    Heater hoses
    Throttle and choke connections
    Engine ground cable and all wiring harnesses
    Any interfering engine accessory

─────────────── **CAUTION** ───────────────

On vehicles with air conditioning, it is necessary to remove the compressor and the condenser from their mounts. Do not attempt to disconnect any of the air conditioner hoses.

8. Disconnect the power brake booster hose from the engine.
9. Remove the clutch operating cylinder and return spring, if equipped.
10. Disconnect the speedometer cable from the transmission. Disconnect the back up light switch and any other wiring or attachments to the transmission.

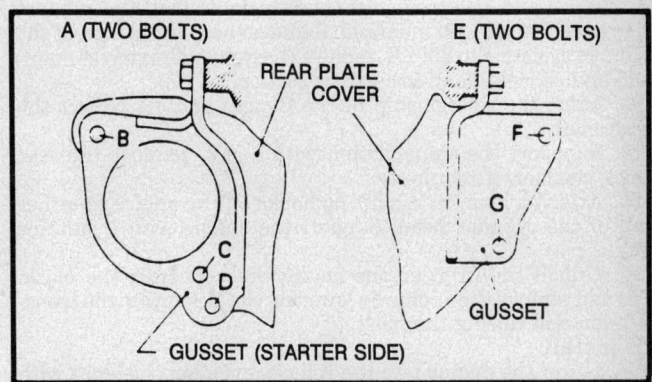

Torquing the 200SX (V6) engine gussets

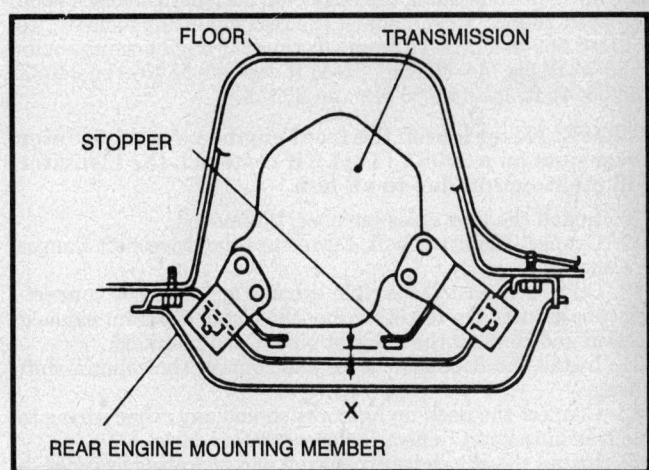

Adjust the rear mount stopper clearance (X) to 13mm ± 1.5mm — 200SX (4 cylinder) with automatic transmission

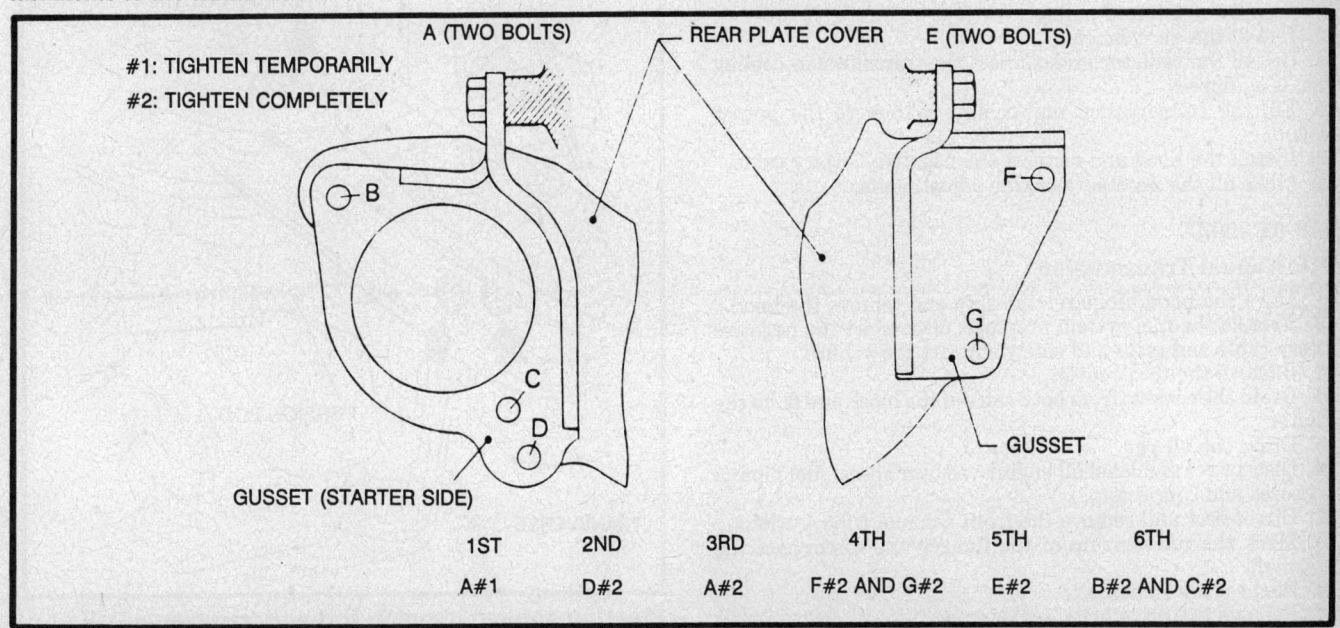

	1ST	2ND	3RD	4TH	5TH	6TH
	A#1	D#2	A#2	F#2 AND G#2	E#2	B#2 AND C#2

On 1987–89 300ZX, torque the engine gussets in 6 stages to 22–29 ft. lbs. (29–39 Nm)

11. Disconnect the column shift linkage. Remove the floor shift lever.

12. Raise and safely support the vehicle. Detach the exhaust pipe from the exhaust manifold. Remove the front section of the exhaust system. On 300ZX, remove the right side exhaust manifold and exhaust connecting tube section.

13. Mark the relationship of the flanges and disconnect the driveshaft.

14. Suppport the transmission with a jack. Remove the rear cross member, if required.

15. Attach a hoist to the lifting hooks on the engine at either end of the cylinder head. Support the engine with a suitable jack.

16. Unbolt the front engine mount brackets from the block. Tilt and remove the engine by lowering the jack under the transmission and raising the hoist.

To install:

17. Lower the engine into the vehicle and align the block with with the front mount brackets. On the 200SX (V6) and 300ZX, torque the engine gusset bolts in six stages to 22–29 ft. lbs. (29–39 Nm). When installing the engine on automatic transmission equipped 200SX (4 cyl.), adjust the rear mounting insulator to 0.451–0.569 in. (11.1–14.5mm). Torque the engine mount bolts to 33–43 ft. lbs. (44–59 Nm), 32–41 ft. lbs. (43–55 Nm) on 240SX and 33–44 ft. lbs. (45–60 Nm) on 300ZX.

NOTE: **Never loosen the front engine mount insulator cover nuts on a 200SX (4 cyl.); if removed, the insulator will malfunction due to oil loss.**

18. Install the rear cross member, if removed.

19. Connect the driveshaft. Make sure the driveshaft flanges are aligned properly.

20. On 300ZX, install the right exhaust manifold and connecting tube section. On the other models, install the front exhaust section and connect the exhaust pipe to the manifold.

21. Install the floor shift lever and connect the column shift linkage.

22. Connect the back-up light switch and any other wiring to the transmission. Connect the speedometer cable.

23. Install the clutch return spring and operating cylinder, if removed.

24. Connect the power brake booster hose to the engine.

25. Connect all engine hoses and electrical wires. Install any removed engine accessory.

26. Install the fan and pulley.

27. Install the air cleaner.

28. Install the radiator and connect the transmission cooling lines, if equipped.

29. Fill the transmission and cooling system to the proper levels.

30. Install the hood and connect the negative battery cable.

31. Make all the necessary engine adjustments.

1990–91 300ZX

With Manual Transmission

1. Mark the hood hinge relationship and remove the hood.

2. Release the fuel system pressure, disconnect the negative battery cable and raise and safely support the vehicle.

3. Remove the undercover.

4. Drain the coolant from both sides of the block and from the radiator.

5. Drain the oil pan.

6. Disconnect and label all engine vacuum hoses, fuel piping, harnesses and connectors.

7. Disconnect and remove the front exhaust tube sections.

8. Mark the relationship of the flanges and disconnect the driveshaft.

9. Remove the radiator.

10. Remove the drive belts.

11. Remove the cooling fan and coupling.

12. Remove the power steering pump, alternator, starter and clutch operating cylinder.

13. Discharge the air conditioning system and remove the compressor from the engine. Disconnect the air conditioning tube clamps.

14. Disconnect the steering column lower joint from the steering rack.

15. Remove the tension rod retaining bolts on both sides.

16. Loosen the transverse link bolts on both sides.

17. Support the rear suspension member using the proper equipment.

18. Install engine slingers to the block and connect a suitable lifting device to the slingers. Tension the lifting device slightly.

19. Remove the rear suspension member retaining bolts and center nut.

20. Remove the engine mount bracket bolts from both side and slowly lower the transmission jack. Lift the engine from the vehicle.

To install:

21. Lower the engine into the vehicle and slowly raise the transmission jack. Install the engine mount bracket bolts. Torque the bolts to 30–38 ft. lbs. (40–42 Nm).

22. Install the rear suspension bolts and center nut. Torque the bolts to 38–48 ft. lbs. (51–65 Nm) and the center nut to 26–33 ft. lbs. (35–45 Nm).

23. Remove the jack and disconnect the engine hoist.

24. Torque the transverse link bolts to 80–94 ft. lbs. (108–127 Nm).

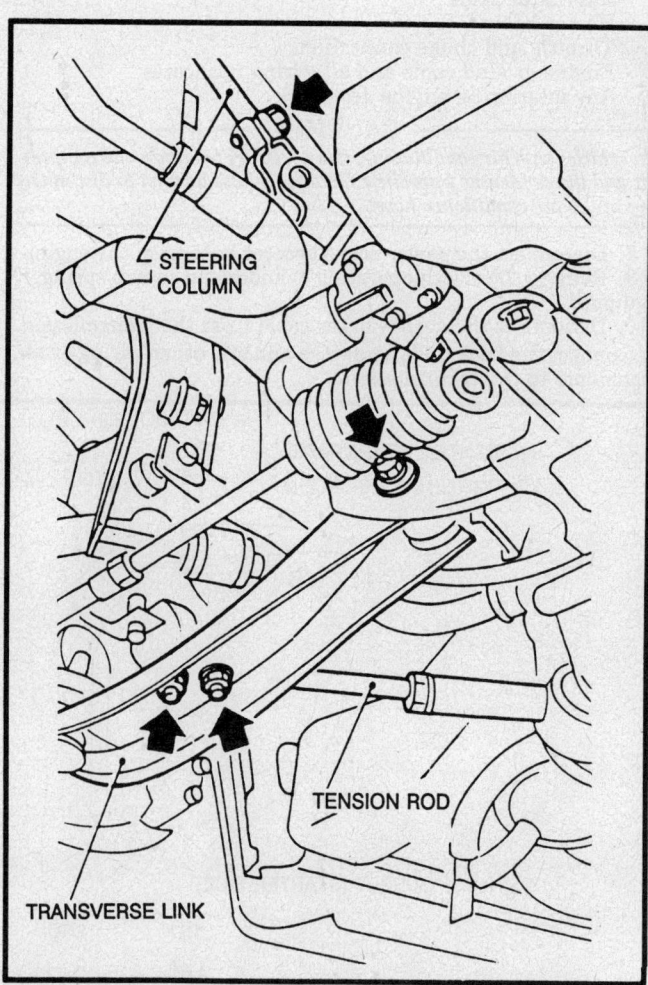

Steering column, tension rod and transverse link attachment points

25. Install the tension rod retaining bolts and torque them to 80–94 ft. lbs. (108–127 Nm).

26. Connect the steering column lower joint to the steering rack. Torque the lower joint bolt to 17–22 ft. lbs. (24–29 Nm).

27. Connect the air conditioning tube clamps and mount the air conditioning compressor on the engine.

28. Install the clutch operating cylinder, starter, alternator and power steering pump.

29. Install the cooling fan and coupling.

30. Install the drive belts.

31. Install the radiator.

32. Install the driveshaft. Make sure the flanges are aligned properly. On non-turbo models, torque the flange bolts to 29–33 ft. lbs. (39–45 Nm) and 40–47 ft. lbs. (54–64 Nm) on turbo-charged models.

33. Connect and install the front exhaust tube sections.

34. Connect the engine connectors, harnesses, fuel piping and vacuum hoses.

35. Install the undercover.

36. Fill the transmission and cooling system to the proper levels.

37. Install the hood and connect the negative battery cable.

38. Make all the necessary engine adjustments. Charge the air conditioning system.

With Automatic Transmission

1. Mark the hood hinge relationship and remove the hood.

2. Relieve the fuel system pressure, disconnect the negative battery cable and raise and support the vehicle safely.

3. Remove the undercover.

4. Drain the coolant from both sides of the block and from the radiator.

5. Drain the oil pan.

6. Disconnect and label all engine vacuum hoses, fuel piping, harnesses and connectors.

7. Disconnect and remove the front exhaust tube sections.

8. Mark the relationship of the flanges and disconnect the driveshaft.

9. Remove the radiator.

10. Remove the drive belts.

11. Remove the cooling fan and coupling.

12. Remove the power steering pump, alternator, starter and clutch operating cylinder.

13. Remove the transmission.

14. Connect an engine hoist to the engine lifting brackets and tension the hoist.

15. Remove the engine mount bracket bolts and slowly lift the engine from the vehicle.

To install:

16. Lower the engine into the vehicle and install the engine mount bracket bolts. Torque the bolts to 30–38 ft. lbs. (40–42 Nm).

17. Install the clutch operating cylinder, starter, alternator and power steering pump.

18. Install the cooling fan and coupling.

19. Install the drive belts.

20. Install the radiator.

21. Install the driveshaft. Make sure the flanges are aligned properly. On non-turbo models, torque the flange bolts to 29–33 ft. lbs. (39–45 Nm) and 40–47 ft. lbs. (54–64 Nm) on turbo-charged models.

22. Connect and install the front exhaust tube sections.

23. Connect the engine connectors, harnesses, fuel piping and vacuum hoses.

24. Install the undercover.

25. Fill the transmission and cooling system to the proper levels.

26. Install the hood and connect the negative battery cable.

27. Make all the necessary engine adjustments. Charge the air conditioning system.

MAXIMA, PULSAR, SENTRA AND STANZA

It is recommended that the engine and transaxle be removed as a unit. If need be, the units may be separated after removal.

NOTE: On the 1989–91 Sentra, the engine cannot be removed separately from the tranaxle. Remove the engine and the transaxle as a unit. If equipped with 4WD, remove the engine, transaxle and transfer case together.

1. Mark the hood hinge relationship and remove the hood.

2. Release the fuel system pressure, disconnect the negative battery cable and raise and support the vehicle safely.

3. Drain the cooling system and the oil pan.

4. Remove the air cleaner and disconnect the throttle cable.

5. Disconnect or remove the following:
   Drive belts
   Ignition wire from the coil to the distributor
   Ignition coil ground wire and the engine ground cable
   Block connector from the distributor
   Fusible links
   Engine harness connectors
   Fuel and fuel return hoses
   Upper and lower radiator hoses
   Heater inlet and outlet hoses
   Engine vacuum hoses
   Carbon canister hoses and the air pump air cleaner hose
   Any interfering engine accessory: power steering pump, air conditioning compressor or alternator
   Driveshaft from transfer for 4WD vehicles. Make sure to matchmark flanges

6. Remove the air pump air cleaner.

7. Remove the carbon canister.

8. Remove the auxiliary fan, washer tank, grille and radiator (with fan assembly).

9. Remove the clutch cylinder from the clutch housing for manual transaxles.

10. Remove both buffer rods without altering the length of the rods. Disconnect the speedometer cable.

11. Remove the spring pins from the transaxle gear selector rods.

12. Install engine slingers to the block and connect a suitable lifting device to the slingers. Do not tension the lifting device at this point.

13. Disconnect the exhaust pipe at both the manifold connection and the clamp holding the pipe to the engine.

14. On the Sentra, Pulsar and 1987–89 Stanza, remove the lower ball joint.

15. Drain the transaxle gear oil.

16. Disconnect the right and left side halfshafts from their side flanges and remove the bolt holding the radius link support.

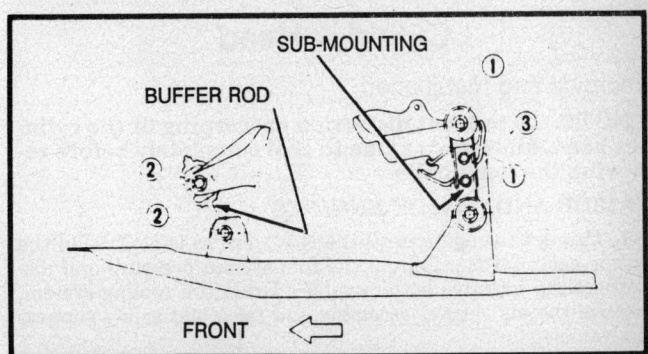

On 1987–88 Stanza wagon (2WD), tighten the buffer rod and sub-mounting bolts in the order shown

NOTE: When drawing out the halfshafts on the Sentra, Stanza and Pulsar, it is necessary to loosen the strut head bolts.

17. Lower the shifter and selector rods and remove the bolts from the motor mount brackets. Remove the nuts holding the front and rear motor mounts to the frame. On the Sentra, Stanza and Pulsar, disconnect the clutch and accelerator wires and remove the speedometer cable with its pinion from the transaxle.

18. Lift the engine/transaxle assembly up and away from the vehicle.

To install:

19. Lower the engine transaxle assembly into the vehicle. When lowering the engine onto the frame, make sure to keep it as level as possible.

20. Check the clearance between the frame and clutch housing and make sure the engine mount bolts are seated in the groove of the mounting bracket.

21. After installing the motor mounts, adjust and install the buffer rods. On the 1987–90 Pulsar with 16i and GA16i engines, 1989–91 Maxima and 1989–91 Sentra: front should be 3.50–3.58 in. (89–91mm), and the rear, 3.90–3.98 in. (99–101mm).

22. On the 1987–88 Stanza wagon (2WD), tighten the engine mount bolts first, then apply a load to the mounting insulators before tightening the buffer rod and sub-mounting bolts.

23. On the Sentra, Stanza and Pulsar, connect the clutch and accelerator wires and remove the speedometer cable with its pinion from the transaxle.

24. Raise the shifter and selector rods to their normal operating positions.

25. Connect the halfshafts.

26. On the Sentra, Pulsar and 1987–89 Stanza, connect the lower ball joint.

27. Connect the exhaust pipe to the manifold connection and the clamp holding the pipe to the engine.

28. Disconnect the lifting device and remove the engine slingers.

29. Insert the spring pins into the transaxle gear selector rods.

30. Connect the speedometer cable.

31. Mount the clutch cylinder onto the clutch housing.

32. Install the auxiliary fan, washer tank, grille and radiator (with fan assembly).

33. Install the carbon canister.

34. Install the air pump air cleaner.

35. Install or connect all hoses, belts, harnesses, connectors and components that were necessary to remove the engine.

36. Connect the throttle cable and install the air cleaner.

37. Fill the transaxle and cooling system to the proper levels.

38. Install the hood and connect the negative battery cable.

39. Make all the necessary engine adjustments. Charge the air conditioning system.

Cylinder Head

Removal and Installation

NOTE: To prevent distortion or warping of the cylinder head, allow the engine to cool completely before removing the head bolts.

CA16DE AND CA18DE ENGINES

1. Crank the engine until the No. 1 piston is at TDC of the compression stroke. Relieve the fuel system pressure and disconnect the negative battery cable. Drain the cooling system, remove the air cleaner assembly and raise and safely support the vehicle.

2. Loosen the alternator and remove all drive belts. Remove the alternator.

3. Disconnect the air duct at the throttle chamber.

4. Tag and disconnect all lines, electrical harnesses, hoses and wires which may interfere with cylinder head removal.

5. Remove the ornament cover.

6. Disconnect the oxygen sensor wire.

7. Remove the 2 exhaust heat shield covers.

8. Unbolt the exhaust manifold and wire the entire assembly aside.

9. Disconnect the EGR tube at the passage cover and then remove the passage cover and gasket.

10. Disconnect and remove the crank angle sensor from the upper front cover.

NOTE: Put an aligning mark on crank angle sensor and timing belt cover.

11. Remove the support stay from under the intake manifold assembly.

12. Unbolt the intake manifold and remove it along with the collector and throttle chamber.

13. Remove the fuel injectors as an assembly.

14. Remove the upper and lower front covers.

NOTE: Remove engine mount bracket but support engine under oil pan with wooden blocks.

15. Remove the timing belt and camshaft sprockets.

NOTE: When the timing belt has been removed, never rotate the crankshaft and camshaft separately because the valves will hit the top of the pistons.

16. Remove the camshaft cover.

17. Remove the breather separator.

18. Gradually loosen the cylinder head bolts in several stages, in the proper sequence.

19. Carefully remove the cylinder head from the block, pulling the head up evenly from both ends. If the head seems stuck, do not pry it off. Tap lightly around the lower perimeter of the head with a rubber mallet to help break the joint.

To install:

20. Thoroughly clean both the cylinder block and head mating surfaces. Avoid scratching either.

21. Lay the cylinder head gasket onto the block and lower the head onto the gasket.

22. When installing the bolts tighten the 2 center bolts temporarily to 15 ft. lbs. (20 Nm) and install the head bolts loosely. After the breather separator, camshaft cover, timing belt, camshaft sprockets and front cover have been installed, torque all the head bolts in the proper sequence as follows. Tighten all bolts to 22 ft. lbs. (29 Nm). Re-tighten all bolts to 76 ft. lbs. (103 Nm). Loosen all bolts completely and then re-tighten them once again to 22 ft. lbs. (29 Nm). Tighten all bolts to a final torque of 76 ft. lbs. (103 Nm) or 85–95 degrees if using an angle torque wrench.

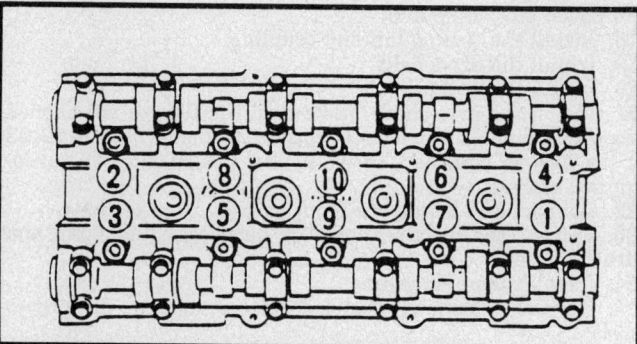

Cylinder head loosening sequence—CA16DE and CA18DE engines

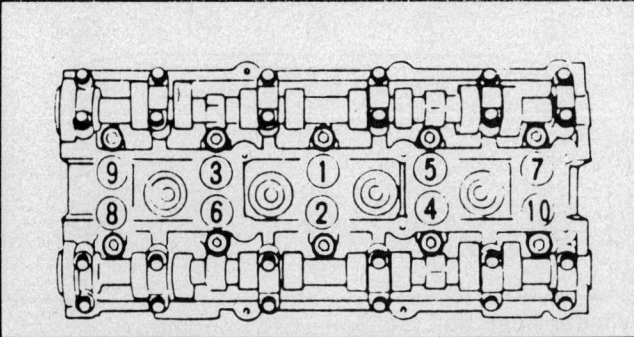

Cylinder head tightening sequence—CA16DE and CA18DE engines

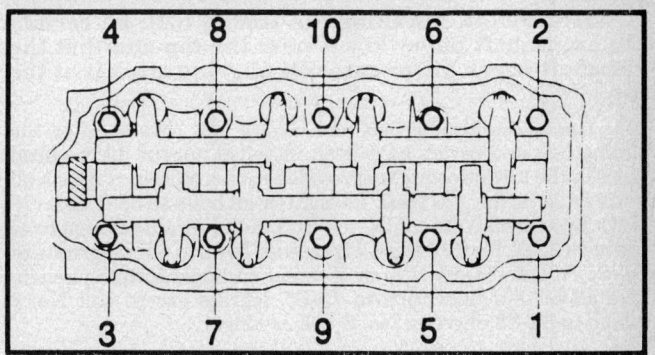

Cylinder head bolt loosening sequence—CA20E and CA18ET engines

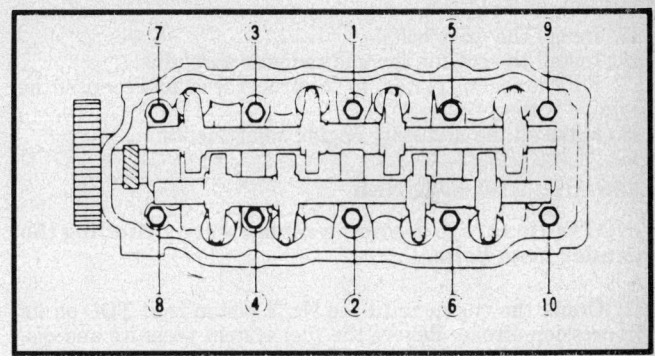

Cylinder head bolt tightening sequence—CA20E and CA18ET engines

NOTE: Newer models use cupped washers on the cylinder head bolts, always make sure the flat side of the washer is facing downward before tightening the cylinder head bolts.

23. Install the fuel injector assembly. Use new O-rings and insulators as required.
24. Install the intake manifold assembly and intake manifold stay.
25. Install the crank angle sensor. Make sure the sensor and upper front matchmarks are aligned properly.
26. Install the passage cover and gasket. Connect the EGR tube to the passage cover.
27. Install the exhaust manifold.
28. Install the exhaust manifold heat shield covers.
29. Install the ornament cover.
30. Connect all lines, electrical harnesses, hoses and wires.
31. Connect the air duct to the throttle chamber.
32. Install the alternator and drive belts.
33. Install the air cleaner assembly.
34. Fill the cooling system to the proper level and connect the negative battery cable.
35. Make all the necessary engine adjustments.

CA18ET AND CA20E ENGINES

1. Relieve the fuel system pressure, disconnect the negative battery cable and drain the cooling system.
2. Remove the air intake pipe.
3. Remove the cooling fan and radiator shroud.
4. Remove the alternator drive belt, power steering pump drive belt and the air conditioner compressor drive belt, if equipped.
5. Position the No. 1 cylinder at TDC of the compression stroke and remove the upper and lower timing belt covers.
6. Loosen the timing belt tensioner and return spring, then remove the timing belt.

NOTE: When the timing belt has been removed, do not rotate the crankshaft and the camshaft separately, because the valves will hit the tops of the pistons.

7. Remove the exhaust manifold.
8. Remove the camshaft pulley.
9. Remove the water pump pulley.
10. Remove the crankshaft pulley.
11. Remove the alternator adjusting bracket.
12. Remove the water pump.
13. Remove the oil pump.
14. Loosen the cylinder head bolts in sequence and in several steps.
15. Remove the cylinder head and manifolds as an assembly.
To install:
16. Clean the cylider head gasket surfaces.

17. Lay the cylinder head gasket onto the block and lower the head onto the gasket.
18. Install the cylinder head bolts. When installing the bolts, tighten the two center bolts temporarily to 15 ft. lbs. and install the head bolts loosely. They will be torqued after the timing belt and front cover are installed.
19. Install the oil pump.
20. Install the water pump.
21. Install the alternator adjusting bracket.
22. Install the crankshaft, water pump and camshaft pulleys.
23. Install the exhaust manifold.

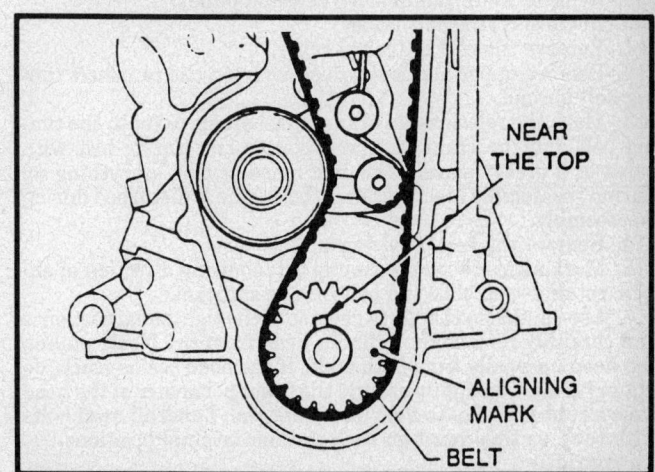

Make sure the crankshaft pulley key is near the top— C-Series engines

NOTE: Before installing the timing belt, be certain the crankshaft pulley key is near the top and that the camshaft knock pin or sprocket aligning mark is at the top.

24. Install the timing belt and timing belt covers. After the timing belt and covers have been installed, torque all the head bolts in the torque sequence provided in this section. Tighten all bolts to 22 ft. lbs. (29 Nm). Re-tighten all bolts to 58 ft. lbs. (78 Nm). Loosen all bolts completely and then re-tighten them once again to 22 ft. lbs. (29 Nm). Tighten all bolts to a final torque of 54–61 ft. lbs. (74–83 Nm) or if using an angle torque wrench, give all bolts a final turn to 75–80 degrees except bolt No. 8 which is 83–88 degrees. No. 8 bolt is longer.

NOTE: Newer models use cupped washers on the cylinder head bolts, always make sure that the flat side of the washer is facing downward before tightening the cylinder head bolts.

25. Install the drive belts.
26. Install the cooling fan and radiator shroud.
27. Fill the cooling system to the proper level and connect the negative battery cable.
28. Make all the necessary engine adjustments.

E16S AND E16I ENGINES

NOTE: Be sure to use new washers when installing the cylinder head bolts.

1. Crank the engine until the No. 1 piston is at TDC on its compression stroke. Relieve the fuel system pressure and disconnect the negative battery cable. Drain the cooling system and remove the air cleaner assembly.
2. Remove the alternator.
3. Remove the distributor, with all wires attached.
4. Remove the EAI pipe bracket and EGR tube at the right (EGR valve) side. Disconnect the same pipes on the front side of the manifold.
5. Remove the exhaust manifold cover and the exhaust manifold, taking note that the center manifold nut has a different diameter than the other nuts. Label this nut to ensure proper installation.
6. Remove the air conditioning compressor bracket and power steering pump bracket, if equipped.
7. Disconnect the carburetor throttle linkage, fuel line, and all vacuum and electrical connections.
8. Remove the intake manifold.
9. Remove water pump drive belt and pulley.
10. Remove crankshaft pulley.
11. Remove the rocker (valve) cover.
12. Remove upper and lower dust cover on the camshaft timing belt shroud.
13. Mark the relationship of the camshaft sprocket to the timing belt and the crankshaft sprocket to the timing belt with paint or a grease pencil. This will make setting everything up during reassembly much easier if the engine is disturbed during disassembly.
14. Remove the belt tensioner pulley.
15. Mark an arrow on the timing belt showing direction of engine rotation and slide the belt off the sprockets.
16. Loosen the head bolts in reverse of the tightening sequence and carefully remove the cylinder head from the block, pulling the head up evenly from both ends. If the head seems stuck, do not pry it off. Tap lightly around the lower perimeter of the head with a rubber mallet to help break the seal. Label all head bolts with tape, as they must go back in their original positions.
To install:
17. Thoroughly clean both the cylinder block and head mating surfaces. Avoid scratching either.
18. Turn the crankshaft and set the No. 1 cylinder at TDC on

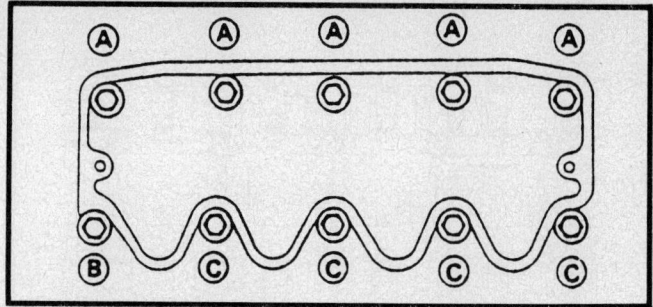

Cylinder head bolt location—E161 engine

its compression stroke. This causes the crankshaft timing sprocket mark to be aligned with the cylinder block cover mark.
19. Align the camshaft sprocket mark with the cylinder head cover mark. This causes the valves for No. 1 cylinder to position at TDC on the compression stroke.
20. Place a new gasket on the cylinder block.

NOTE: There are 3 different size head bolts used on the E16i engine. Bolt (A) is 3.74 in. (95mm), bolt (B) is 4.33 in. (110mm) and bolt (C) is 3.15 in. (80mm). Measure the length of each bolt prior to installation and make sure they are installed in their proper locations on the head.

21. Install the cylinder head on the block and tighten the bolts as follows:
   a. Tighten all bolts to 22 ft. lbs. (29 Nm), then retighten them all to 51 ft. lbs. (69 Nm).
   b. Loosen all bolts completely, and then retighten them again to 22 ft. lbs. (29 Nm).
   c. Tighten all bolts to a final torque of 51–54 ft. lbs. (69–74 Nm); or if an angle wrench is used, turn each bolt until they have achieved the specified number of degrees—bolts 1, 3, 6, 8

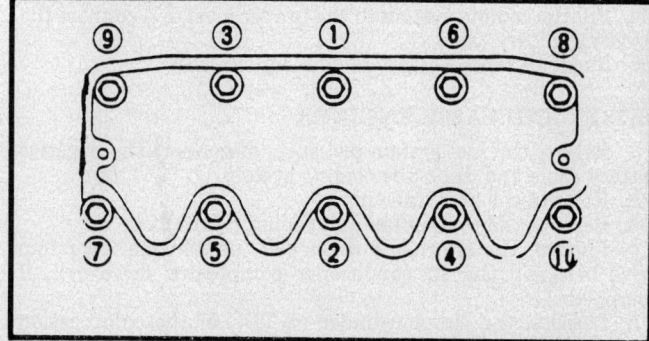

Cylinder head torque sequence—E-Series engine

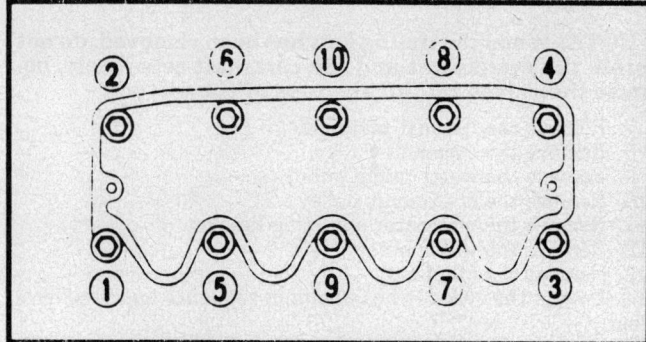

Loosen the cylinder head bolts, in stages, in the order shown—E-Series engine

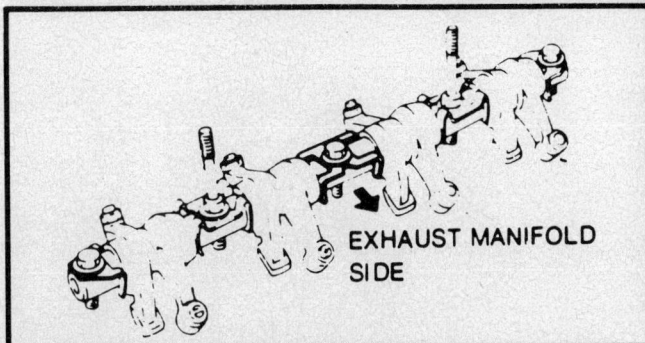

Make sure the cutout on the E-Series engine rocker shaft faces the exhaust manifold

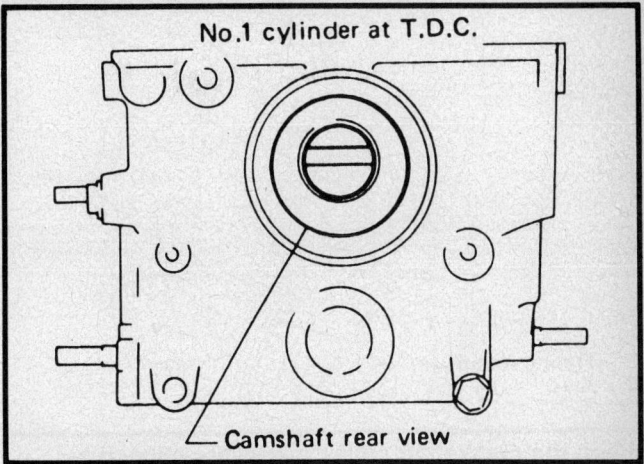

When camshaft is aligned as shown, the No. 1 piston is at TDC—GA161 engine

and 9: 45–50 degrees; bolt 7: 55–60 degrees and bolts 2, 4, 5 and 10: 40–45 degrees.

22. Install the timing belt.
23. Install the upper and lower dust covers on the camshaft timing belt shroud.
24. Install the rocker arm cover.
25. Install the crankshaft pulley, water pump pulley and drive belt.
26. Install the intake manifold.
27. Connect the carburetor throttle linkage, fuel line, and all vacuum and electrical connections.
28. Install the air conditioning compressor bracket and the power steering pump bracket, if equipped.
29. Install the exhaust manifold and exhaust manifold cover. Make sure the center manifold nut, which has a different diameter, is installed in the proper location.
30. Connect the EAI exhaust pipes and tubing.
31. Install the distributor and connect the spark plug wiring.
32. Install the alternator and air cleaner.
33. Fill the cooling system to the proper level and connect the negative battery cable.
34. Make all the necessary engine adjustments.

GA16I ENGINE

1. Disconnect the negative battery cable, drain the cooling system and relieve the fuel system pressure.
2. Disconnect the exhaust tube from the exhaust manifold.
3. Remove the intake manifold support bracket.
4. Remove the air cleaner assembly.
5. Disconnect the center wire from the distributor cap.
6. Remove the rocker arm cover.
7. Remove the distributor.
8. Remove the spark plugs.
9. Set the No. 1 cylinder at TDC of the compression stroke by rotating the engine until the cut out machined in the rear of the camshaft is horizontally aligned with the cylinder head.
10. Hold the camshaft sprocket stationary with the proper tool and loosen the sprocket bolt. Place highly visible and accurate paint or chalk alignment marks on the camshaft sprocket and the timing chain, then slide the sprocket from the camshaft and lift the timing chain from the sprocket. Remove the sprocket. The timing chain will not fall off the crankshaft sprocket unless the front cover is removed. This is due to the cast portion of the front cover located on the lower side of the crankshaft sprocket which acts a stopper mechanism. For this reason a chain stopper (wedge) is not required to remove the cylinder head.
11. Loosen the cylinder bolts in 2–3 stages to prevent warpage and cracking of the head. One of the cylinder head bolts is longer than the rest. Mark this bolt and make a note of its location.
12. Carefully remove the cylinder head from the block, pulling the head up evenly from both ends. If the head seems stuck, do not pry it off. Tap lightly around the lower perimeter of the head

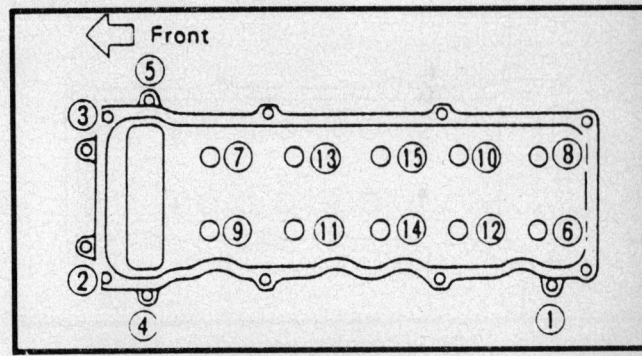

Loosen the cylinder head bolts in several stages in the order shown—GA161 engine

with a rubber mallet to help break the seal. The cylinder head and the intake and exhaust manifolds are removed together. Remove the cylinder head gasket.

To install:
13. Thoroughly clean both the cylinder block and head mating surfaces. Avoid scratching either.
14. Turn the crankshaft and set the No. 1 cylinder at TDC on its compression stroke. This is done by aligning the timing pointer with the appropriate timing mark on the pulley. To ensure that the No. 1 piston is at TDC, verify that the knock pin in the front of the camshaft is set at the top.
15. Place a new gasket on the block and lower the head onto the gasket.

NOTE: These engines use 2 different length cylinder head bolts. Bolt (1) is 5.24 in. (133mm) while bolts (2) thru (10) are 4.33 in. (110mm). Do not confuse the location of these bolts.

16. Coat the threads and the seating surface of the head bolts with clean engine oil and use a new set of washers. Install the cylinder head bolts in their proper locations and tighten as follows:
    a. Tighten all the bolts in sequence to 22 ft. lbs. (30 Nm).
    b. Tighten all bolts in sequence to 47 ft. lbs.(64 Nm).
    c. Loosen all bolts in reverse of the tightening sequence.
    d. Tighten all bolts again to 22 ft. lbs. (30 Nm).
    e. If an angle torque wrench is not available, torque the bolts in sequence to 43–51 ft. lbs. (58–59 Nm). If using an angle torque wrench for this step, tighten bolt (1) 80–85 degrees clockwise and bolts (6) thru (10) 60–65 degrees clockwise.

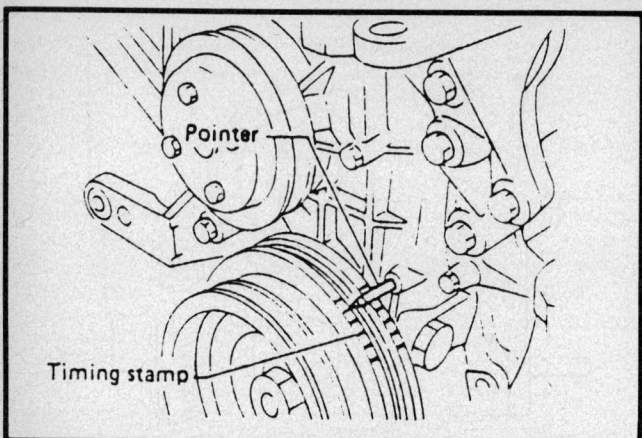

When the crankshaft pulley marks are aligned as shown, the No. 1 piston is at TDC

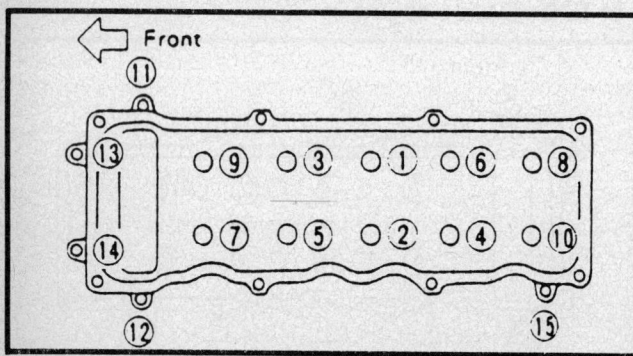

Cylinder head bolt tightening sequence—GA16i engine. Bolt (1) is the longest bolt

f. Finally, tighten bolts (11) thru (15) to 4.6– 6.1 ft. lbs. (6.3–8.3 Nm).

17. Place the timing chain on the camshaft sprocket using the alignment marks. Slide the sprocket and timing chain onto the camshaft and install the center bolt.

18. At this point, check the hydraulic valve lifters for proper operation pushing hard on each lifter hard with fingertip pressure. Make sure the rocker arm arm is not on the cam lobe when making this check. If the valve lifter moves more than 0.04 in. (1mm), air may be inside it.

19. Install the spark plugs.

20. Install the distributor.

21. Install the rocker arm cover.

22. Connect the center wire to the distributor cap.

23. Install the air cleaner assembly.

24. Install the intake manifold support bracket.

25. Fill the cooling system to the proper level and connect the negative battery cable.

26. Make all the necessary engine adjustments. If there was air in the lifters, bleed the air by running the engine at 1000 rpm for 10 minutes.

KA24E ENGINE

NOTE: After completing this procedure, allow the rocker cover to cylinder head rubber plugs to dry for 30 minutes before starting the engine. This will allow the liquid gasket sealer to cure properly.

1. Release the fuel system pressure.

2. Disconnect the negative battery cable and drain the cooling system.

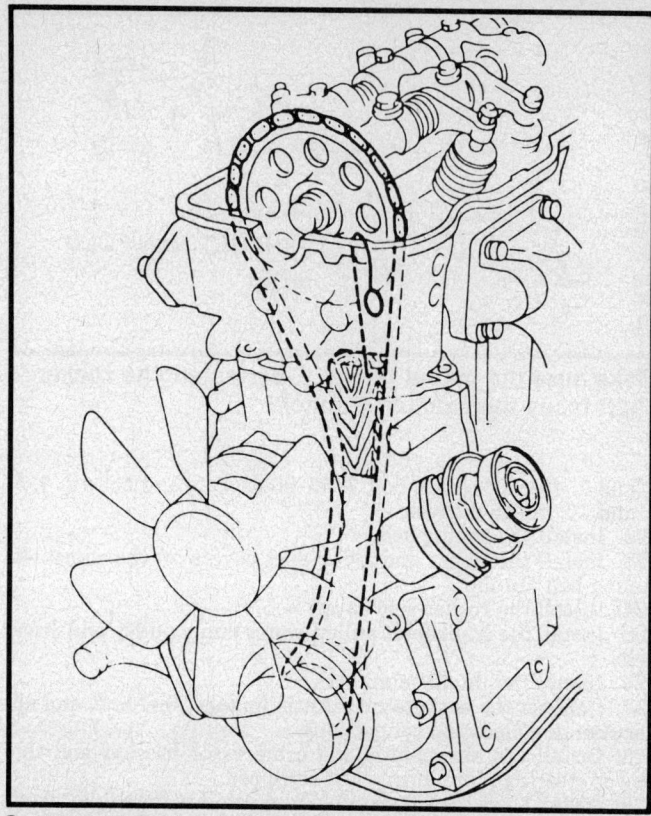

On KA24E engine, support the timing chain with a special tool when removing the cylinder head

3. On 240SX, remove the power steering drive belt, power steering pump, idler pulley and power steering brackets.

4. Tag and disconnect all the vacuum hoses, water hoses, fuel tubes and wiring harnesses necessary to gain access to cylinder head.

5. Disconnect the air induction hose from the collector assembly.

6. Detach the accelerator bracket. If necessary mark the position and remove the accelerator cable wire end from the throttle drum.

7. Unbolt the intake manifold collector from the intake manifold.

8. Remove the intake manifold.

9. Unplug the exhaust gas sensor and remove the exhaust cover and exhaust pipe at exhaust manifold connection. Remove the exhaust manifold from the cylinder head.

10. Remove the rocker cover. If cover sticks to the cylinder head, tap it with a rubber hammer. Be careful not to strike the rocker arms when removing the rocker arm cover.

NOTE: After removing the rocker cover matchmark the timing chain with the camshaft sprocket with paint or equivalent.

11. Set No. 1 cylinder piston at TDC on its compression stroke. The No. 1 will be at TDC when the timing pointer is aligned with the red timing mark on the crankshaft pulley.

12. Loosen the camshaft sprocket bolt. Do not turn engine when removing the bolt.

13. Support the timing chain with the proper tool.

14. Remove the camshaft sprocket.

15. Remove the front cover-to-cylinder head retaining bolts.

NOTE: The cylinder head bolts should be loosened in two or three steps in the correct order to prevent head warpage or cracking.

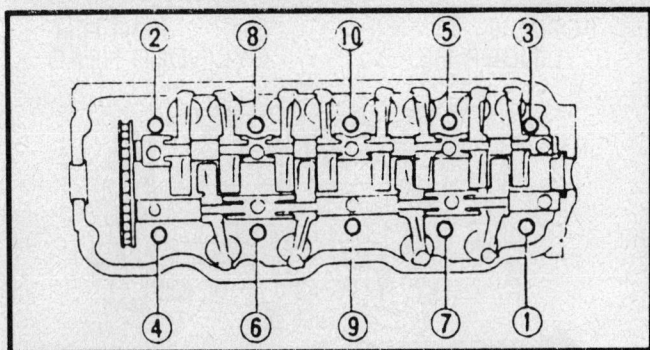

Cylinder head bolt loosening sequence—KA24E engine

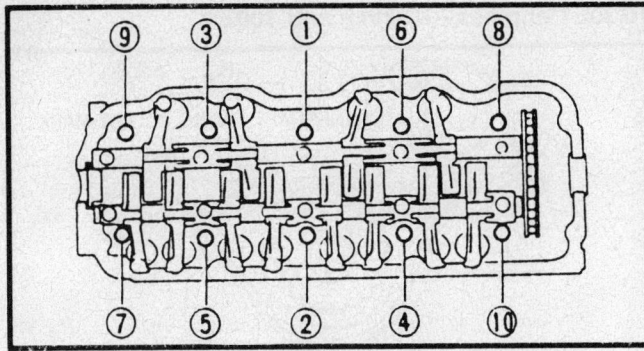

Cylinder head bolt tightening sequence—KA24E engine

When the camshaft knock pin is at the top, No. piston is at TDC—KA24E engine

16. Remove the cylinder head bolts in the correct sequence. Lift the cylinder head off the engine block. It may be necessary to tap the head lightly with a rubber mallet to loosen it.
To install:
17. Confirm that the No. 1 piston is at TDC on its compression stroke as follows: Align timing mark with the red (0 degree) mark on the crankshaft pulley. Make sure the distributor rotor head is set at No. 1 on the distributor cap. Confirm that the knock pin on the camshaft is set at the top position.
18. Install the cylinder head with a new gasket and torque the head bolts in numerical order using the following 5 step procedure:
   a. Torque all bolts to 22 ft. lbs. (29 Nm).

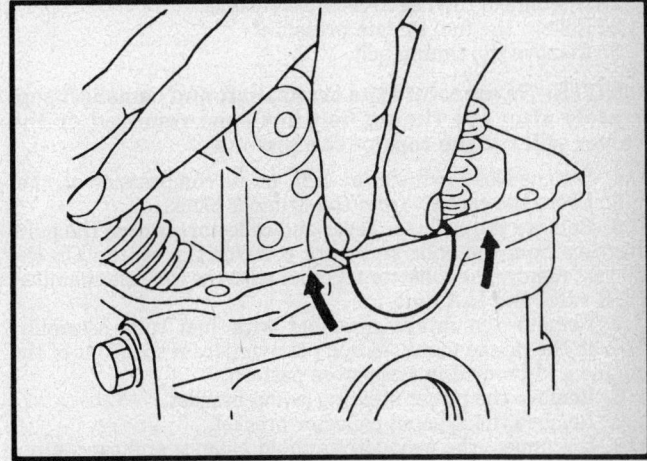

Rubber plug installation—KA24E engine

   b. Torque all bolts to 58 ft. lbs. (78 Nm).
   c. Loosen all bolts completely.
   d. Torque all bolts to 22 ft. lbs. (29 Nm).
   e. Torque all bolts to 54–61 ft. lbs. (74–83 Nm), or if an angle wrench is used, turn all bolts 80–85 degrees clockwise.

NOTE: Do not rotate crankshaft and camshaft separately, or valves will hit the tops of the pistons.

19. Remove the tool from the timing chain. Position the timing chain on the camshaft sprocket by aligning each matchmark. Install the camshaft sprocket to the camshaft.
20. Hold the camshaft sprocket stationary, and tighten the sprocket bolt to 87–116 ft. lbs. (118–157 Nm). Install front cover-to-cylinder head retaining bolts. Torque the 6mm bolts to 5–6 ft. lbs. (7–8 Nm) and the 8mm bolts to 12–15 ft. lbs. (16–21 Nm).
21. Install the intake manifold and collector assembly with new gaskets.
22. Install the exhaust manifold with new gaskets.
23. Apply liquid gasket to the rubber plugs and install the rubber plugs in the correct location in the cylinder head. The seating surface of the rubber plugs must be clean and dry. The rubber plugs should be installed within 5 minutes of the sealant application. After the sealant is applied and the rubber plugs are in place, rock the plugs back and forth a few times to distribute the sealant evenly. Wipe the excess sealant from the cylinder head with a clean rag.
24. Install the rocker cover with new gasket.
25. Attach the accelerator bracket and cable if removed.
26. Connect all the vacuum hoses, water hoses, fuel tubes and electrical connections that were removed to gain access to cylinder head.
27. Reconnect the air induction hose to collector assembly.
28. Install the spark plugs and spark plug wires in the correct location.
29. On 240SX, install the power steering brackets, idler pulley, and power steering pump.
30. Install the drive belts.
31. Fill the cooling system and connect the negative battery cable.
32. Make all the necessary engine adjustments.

VG30E AND VG30ET V6 ENGINES (200SX AND 1987–89 300ZX)

NOTE: On 1987 300ZX, the manufacturer recommends that the engine be removed before attempting to remove the cylinder head. On all models, a special hex head wrench ST10120000 (J24239-01) or equivalent will be needed to remove and install the cylinder head bolts.

1. Disconnect the negative battery cable.
2. Relieve the fuel system pressure.
3. Remove the timing belt.

NOTE: Never rotate the crankshaft and camshaft separately after the timing belt has been removed or the valves will hit the tops of the pistons.

4. Set the No. 1 cylinder at TDC on its compression stroke.
5. Drain the coolant from the cylinder block.
6. Remove the collector cover and collector. Loosen the bolts starting from the ends and work towards the center. On the 200SX, remove the collector together with the throttle chamber, EGR valve and IAA unit.
7. Remove the intake manifold with fuel tube assembly. Loosen the intake manifold bolts starting from the front of the engine and proceed in criss-cross pattern.
8. Remove the power steering pump bracket.
9. Remove the exhaust collector bracket.
10. Disconnect the exhaust manifold balance and connecting tubes.
11. Remove the bolts securing the camshaft pulleys and rear timing cover.
12. Discharge the air conditioning system system and remove the compressor and compressor bracket. Remove the rocker covers.
13. Loosen the cylinder head bolts in the proper sequence. Remove the cylinder head with the exhaust manifolds attached. It may be necessary to tap the head lightly with a rubber mallet to loosen it.

To install:

14. Make sure the No. 1 cylinder is set at TDC on its compression stroke as follows:

   a. Align the crankshaft timing mark with the mark on the oil pump housing.

   b. The knock pin in the front end of the camshaft should be facing upward.

NOTE: Do not rotate crankshaft and camshaft separately because valves will hit the tops of the pistons.

15. Position the cylinder head and gasket on the block and tighten the cylinder head bolts as follows using the proper sequence:

   a. Tighten all bolts to 22 ft. lbs. (29 Nm).

   b. Tighten all bolts to 43 ft. lbs. (59 Nm).

   c. Loosen all bolts completely.

   d. Tighten all bolts to 22 ft. lbs. (29 Nm).

   e. Tighten all bolts to 40–47 ft. lbs. (54–64 Nm) or if using an angle wrench, turn all bolts 60–65 degrees clockwise.

16. Tighten the rear timing belt cover.

17. Install the camshaft pulley and tighten to 58–65 ft. lbs. (79–88 Nm).

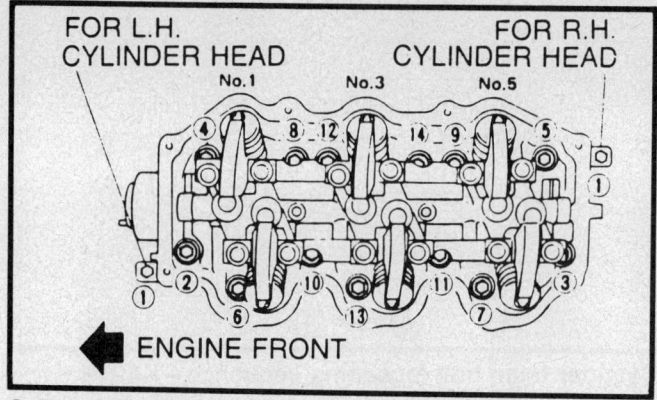

Cylinder head loosening sequence—VG30E and VG30ET engines—Maxima and 300ZX

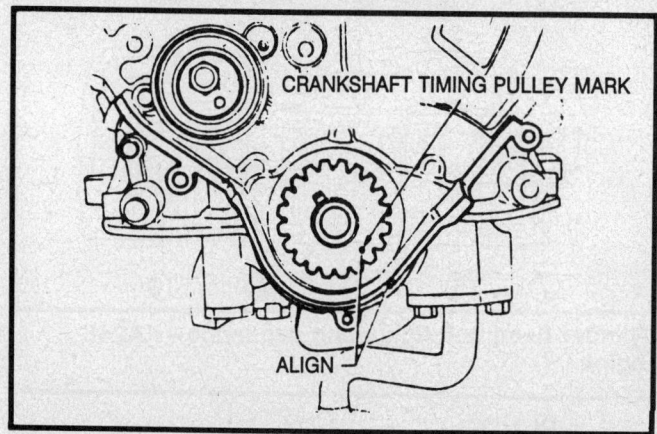

Aligning timing mark and mark on oil pump housing—V6 engine

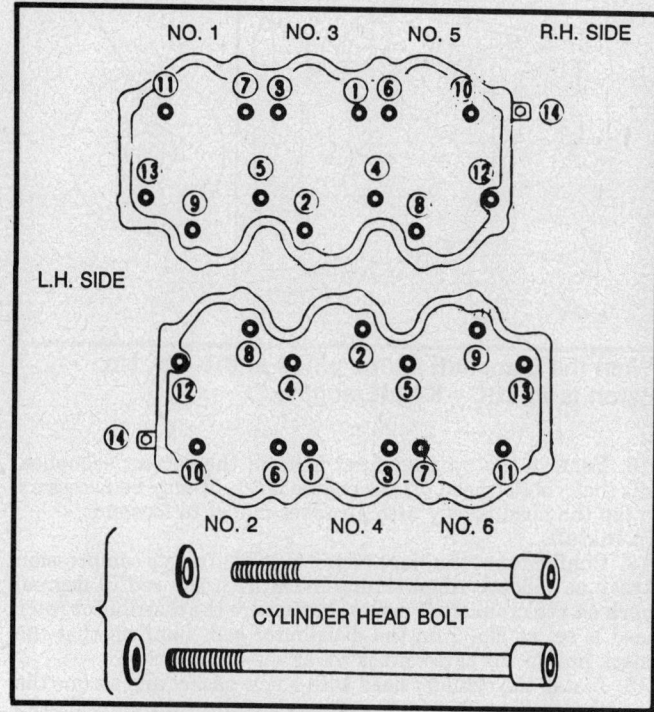

Cylinder head torque sequence—VG30E and VG30ET engines—Maxima and 300ZX

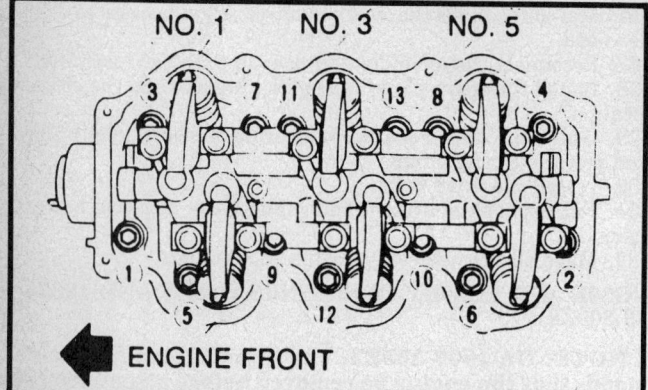

Cylinder head loosening sequence—VG30E engine—200SX

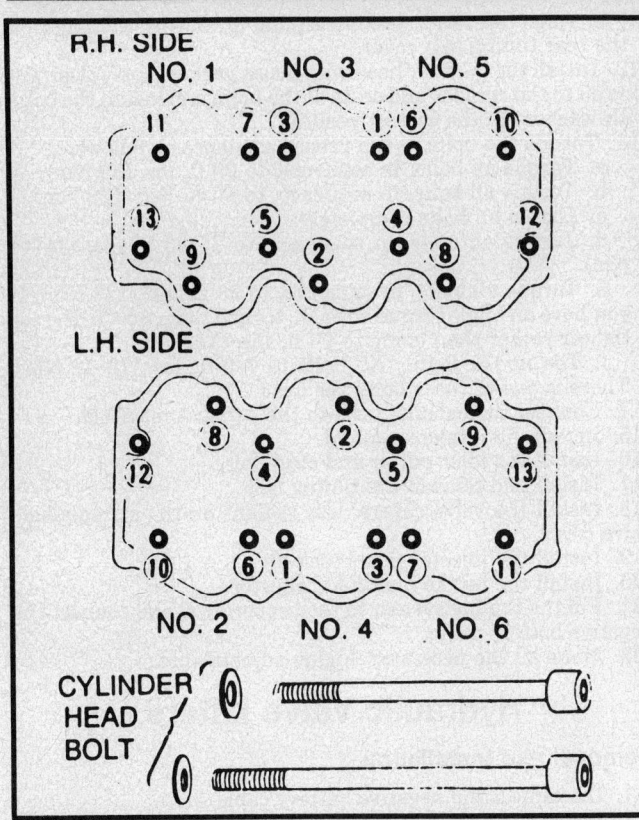

Cylinder head torque sequence—VG30E engine—200SX

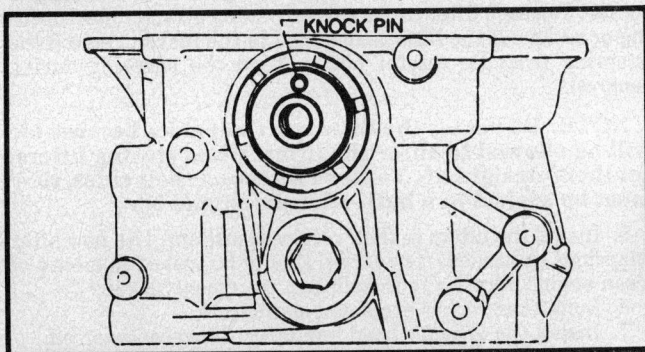

Knock pin of camshaft facing upward—V6 engine

NOTE: The right hand and left hand camshaft pulleys are different parts. Install them in the correct positions. The right hand pulley has an "R3" identification mark and the left hand pulley has an "L3".

18. Install the timing belt and adjust the tension.
19. Install the front upper and lower belt covers.
20. Install the rocker covers, compressor bracket and air conditioning compressor.
21. Install the intake manifold and fuel tube and tighten both the nuts and bolts as follows: first to 2–4 ft. lbs. (3–5 Nm), then to 17–20 ft. lbs. (24–27 Nm).
22. Connect the exhaust manifold balance and connecting tubes. Tighten the exhaust manifold connecting tube and tighten to 16–20 ft. lbs. (22–27 Nm).
23. Install the exhaust collector bracket.
24. Install the power steering pump bracket.
25. Install the intake manifold and fuel tube assembly. Make

sure to tighten the bolts in 2–3 stages using the proper torque sequence.
26. Install the collector and collector cover. When installing the collector cover, always use a new gasket. On the 200SX and 1988–89 300ZX, tighten the throttle chamber-to-collector bolts in two stages; 6.5–8 ft. lbs. (9–11 Nm) and then to 13–16 ft. lbs. (18–22 Nm).
27. Install and tension the drive belts.
28. Fill the cooling system to the proper level and connect the negative battery cable.
29. Make all the necessary engine adjustments. Charge the air conditioning system.

VG30E ENGINE (MAXIMA)

NOTE: A special hex head wrench ST10120000 (J24239-01) or equivalent will be needed to remove and install the cylinder head bolts.

1. Relieve the fuel system pressure and disconnect the negative batttery cable.
2. Drain the cooling system. On 1989–91 Maxima, there are 2 cylinder block drain plugs. The left side drain plug is located beside the oil level gauge and the right side drain plug is located behind the right hand halfshaft boot.
3. Remove the timing belt.

NOTE: Do not rotate either the crankshaft or camshaft from this point onward, or the valves could be bent by hitting the tops of the pistons.

4. Disconnect and tag all vacuum and water hoses connected to the intake collector.
5. On 1989–91 Maxima, remove the distributor, ignition wires and disconnect the accelerator and cruise control (ASCD) cables from the intake manifold collector.
6. Remove the collector cover and the collector from the intake manifold. On 1989–91 Maxima, there are upper and lower collector covers. Disconnect and tag all harness connectors and vacuum lines to gain access to the cover retaining bolts on these models.
7. Remove the intake manifold and fuel tube assembly. Loosen the intake manifold bolts starting from the front of the engine and proceed in criss-cross pattern towards the center.
8. Remove the exhaust collector bracket.
9. Remove the exhaust manifold covers.
10. Disconnect the exhaust manifold from the exhaust pipe.
11. Remove the camshaft pulleys and the rear timing cover securing bolts. Remove the rocker arm covers.
12. On 1989–91 Maxima, separate the air conditioning compressor and alternator from the their mounting brackets. Remove the mounting brackets. Do not disconnect the refrigerant lines from the compressor or serious injury will result.
13. Remove the cylinder head bolts in the correct sequence. Lift the cylinder head off the engine block with the exhaust manifolds attached. It may be necessary to tap the head lightly with a rubber mallet to loosen it.

To install:
14. Make sure the No. 1 cylinder is set at TDC on its compression stroke as follows:
   a. Align the crankshaft timing mark with the mark on the oil pump housing.
   b. The knock pin in the front end of the camshaft should be facing upward.

NOTE: Do not rotate crankshaft and camshaft separately because valves will hit piston head.

15. Install the cylinder head with a new gasket. Apply clean engine oil to the threads and seats of the bolts and install the bolts with washers in the correct position. Note that bolts 4, 5, 12, and 13 are 4.95 in. (127mm) long. The other bolts are 4.13 in. (106mm) long.

16. Torque the bolts in the proper sequence as follows:
    a. Torque all bolts, in sequence, to 22 ft. lbs. (29 Nm).
    b. Torque all bolts, in sequence, to 43 ft. lbs. (58 Nm).
    c. Loosen all bolts completely.
    d. Torque all bolts, in sequence, to 22 ft. lbs. (29 Nm).
    e. Torque all bolts, in sequence, to 40–47 ft. lbs. (54–64 Nm). If using an angle torque wrench, torque them 60–65 degrees tighter rather than going to 40–47 ft. lbs. (54–64 Nm).

17. On 1989–91 models, install the alternator and air conditioner compressor mounting brackets. Mount the compressor and alternator.

18. Install the rear timing cover bolts. Install the camshaft pulleys. Make sure the pulley marked R3 goes on the right and that marked L3 goes on the left. Align the timing marks if necessary and then install the timing belt and adjust the belt tension.

19. Connect the exhaust manifold to the exhaust pipe.
20. Install the exhaust manifold covers.
21. Install the exhaust collector bracket.
22. Install the intake manifold and fuel tube assembly.
23. Install the intake manifold collector cover.
24. On 1989–91 models, connect the accelerator and cruise control cables to the intake manifold and install the distributor and ignition wires.

25. Connect the vacuum and water hoses to the intake collector.
26. Install and tension the timing belt.
27. Fill the cooling system and connect the negative battery cable.
28. Make all the necessary engine adjustments.

VG30DE AND VG30DETT ENGINES

1. Relieve the fuel system pressure and disconnect the negative battery cable.
2. Drain the cooling system.
3. Remove the intake manifold collector.
4. Remove the injector pipe assembly.
5. Remove the valve covers.
6. Remove the timing belt.
7. Remove the idler pulley and idler pulley stud bolt.
8. Remove the intake manifold.
9. Disconnect the exhaust tube from the exhaust manifold.
10. Loosen the cylinder head bolts in 2–3 stages. Lift the cylinder head off the engine block wih the exhaust manifolds attached It may be necessary to tap the head lightly with a rubber mallet to loosen it.

To install:
11. Make sure the No. 1 cylinder is set at TDC on its compression stroke as follows:
    a. Align the crankshaft timing mark with the mark on the oil pump housing.

    b. Align camshaft sprocket timing mark with the mark on the rear timing belt cover.
12. Install the cylinder head with a new gasket. Apply clean engine oil to the threads and seats of the bolts and install the bolts with washers in the correct position.
13. Torque the bolts in the proper sequence as follows:
    a. Torque all bolts, in sequence, to 29 ft. lbs. (39 Nm).
    b. Torque all bolts, in sequence, to 90 ft. lbs. (123 Nm).
    c. Loosen all bolts completely.
    d. Torque all bolts, in sequence, to 25–33 ft. lbs. (34–44 Nm).
    e. Torque all bolts, in sequence, to 90 ft. lbs. (123 Nm). If you have an angle torque wrench, torque them 60–70 degrees tighter rather than going to 90 ft. lbs. (123 Nm).
    f. Torque the 6mm "X" bolts to 7–9 ft. lbs. (10–12 Nm). There is one of these bolts per head.
14. Connect the exhaust tube to the exhaust manifold.
15. Install the intake manifold.
16. Install the idler pulley and stud bolt.
17. Install and tension the timing belt.
18. Install the valve covers. Use sealant on the exhaust side valve cover.
19. Install the injector pipe assembly.
20. Install the intake manifold collector.
21. Fill the cooling system to the proper level and connect the negative battery cable.
22. Make all the necessary engine adjustments.

Hydraulic Valve Lifters

Removal and Installation

1. Disconnect the negative battery cable.
2. Remove the cylinder head, if required.
3. Remove the rocker arms and shafts.
4. Withdraw the lifters from the head or from the bore in the rocker. Tag each lifter to the corresponding cylinder head opening or rocker. If the lifter is installed in the rocker, remove the snapring first. Be careful not to bend the snapring during removal.

NOTE: Do not lay the lifters on their sides because air will be allowed to enter the lifter. When storing lifters, set them straight up. To store lifters on their sides, they must be soaked in a bath of clean engine oil.

5. Install the lifters in their original locations. Use new lifter snaprings as needed. New lifters should be soaked in a bath of clean engine oil prior to installation to remove the air.
6. Install the rocker arms and shafts.
7. Install the cylinder head and leave the valve cover off.
8. Check the lifters for proper operation by pushing hard on each lifter with fingertip pressure. If the valve lifter moves more than 0.04 in. (1mm), air may be inside it. Make sure the rocker arm is not on the cam lobe when making this check. If there was air in the lifters, bleed the air by running the engine at 1000 rpm for 10 minutes.

Valve Lash

Hydraulic valve lifters are used on all engines except on those models listed below. Engines with hydraulic lifters do not require periodic valve adjustment, because the lifter automatically compensates for any required adjustment. Hydraulic valve lifters are best maintained through regular, scheduled engine oil and filter changes.

Adjustment

STANZA WAGON, 200SX (CA18ET ENGINE) AND PULSAR AND SENTRA (E16S AND E16I ENGINES)

1. Run the engine until it reaches normal operating temperature and shut if off.

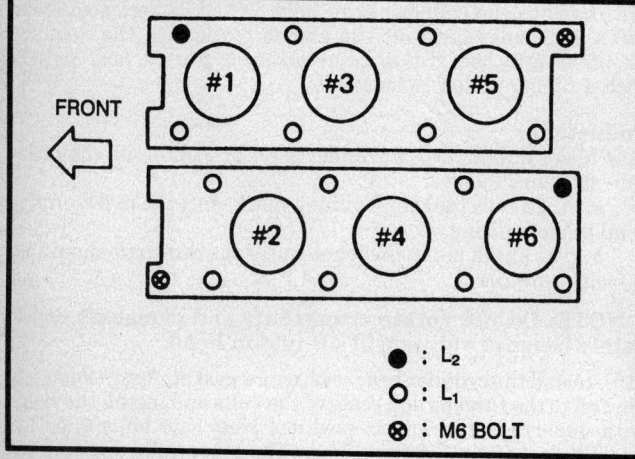

FRONT

● : L₂
○ : L₁
⊗ : M6 BOLT

Torque the 6mm "X" bolts to 7–9 ft. lbs. (10–12 Nm)

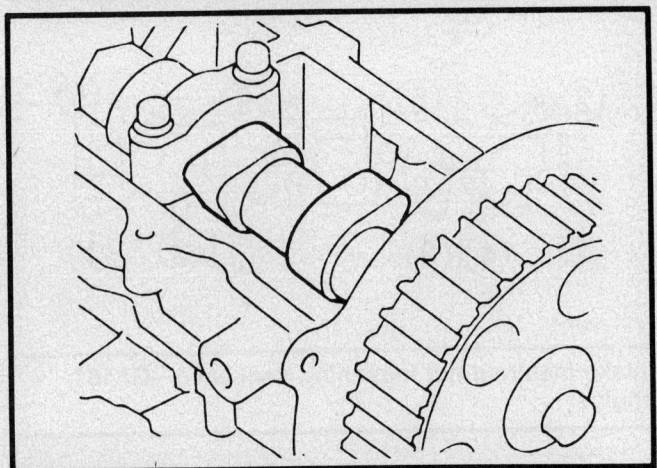
Position of No. 1 cylinder camshaft lobes at TDC

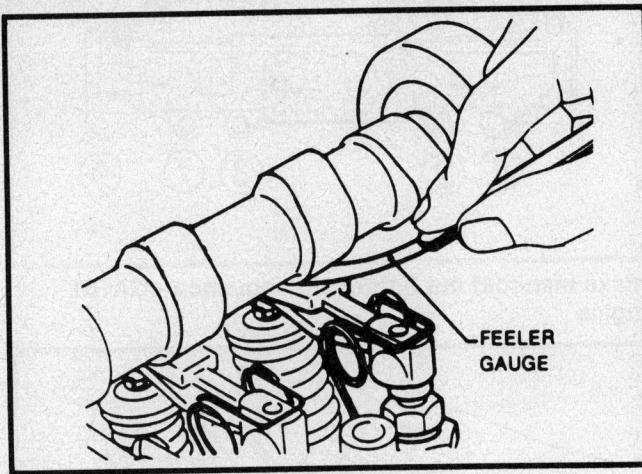
Checking lash with feeler gauge

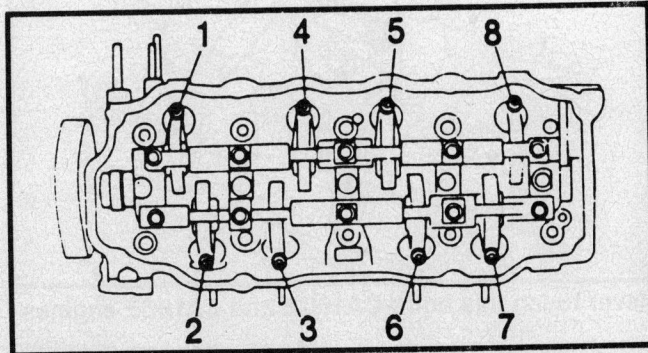
Valve adjustment sequence—200SX and Stanza wagon

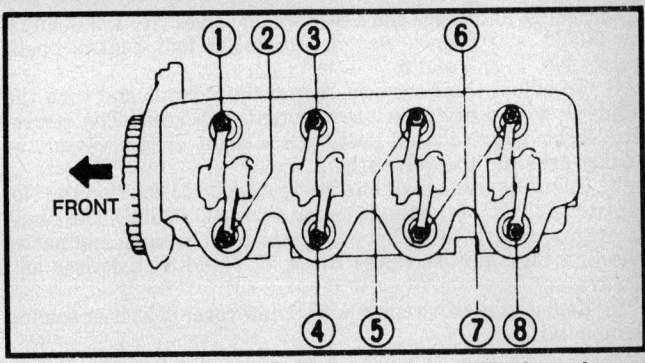
Valve adjustment sequence—E16S and E16i engines

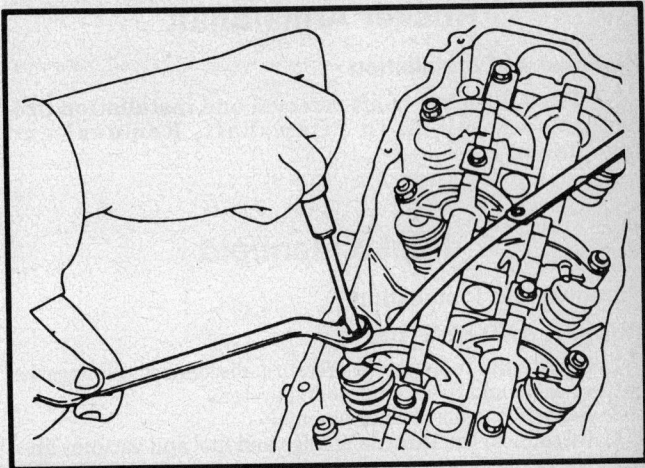
Adjusting the valves on 200SX and Stanza wagon

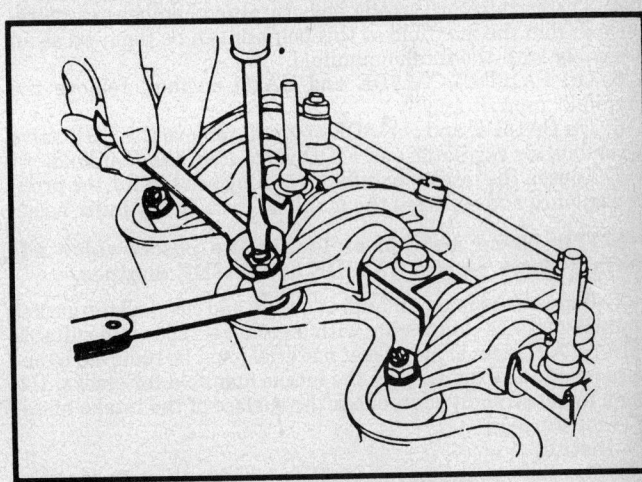
Adjusting the valves—E-Series engine

2. Remove the rocker cover.
3. Bring the No. 1 piston at TDC on the compression stroke. There are at least two ways to do it; you can bump the engine over with the starter or turn it over by using a wrench on the front pulley attaching bolt. The easiest way to find TDC is to turn the engine over slowly with a wrench, after first removing No. 1 plug, until the piston is at the top of its stroke and the TDC timing mark on the crankshaft pulley is in alignment with the timing mark pointer. At this point, the valves for No. 1 should be closed.

NOTE: Make sure both valves are closed with the valve springs up as high as they will go. An easy way to find the compression stroke is to remove the distributor cap and see toward which spark plug lead the rotor is pointing. If the rotor points to the No. 1 spark plug lead, the No. 1 cylinder is on its compression stroke. When the rotor points to the No. 2 spark plug lead, the No. 2 cylinder is on its compression stroke etc.

4. With No. 1 piston at TDC of the compression stroke, use a

feeler gauge and check the clearance on valves No. 1, 2, 4 and 6 on 200SX and Stanza wagon. On Pulsar and Sentra, check valves No. 1, 2, 3 and 6.

5. To adjust the clearance, loosen the locknut and turn the adjuster with a prybar while holding the locknut. The correct size feeler gauge should pass with a slight drag between the rocker arm and the valve stem.

6. Turn the crankshaft one full revolution to position the No. 4 piston at TDC of the compression stroke. On 200SX and Stanza wagon, adjust valves No. 3, 5, 7 and 8 in the same manner as the first four. Adjust valves No. 4, 5, 7 and 8 on Pulsar and Sentra.

7. Replace the valve cover with a new cover gasket or sealing compound.

Rocker Arms/Shaft

Removal and Installation

NOTE: All rocker shaft removal and installation procedures are given in "Camshaft, Removal and Installation".

Intake Manifold

Removal and Installation

PULSAR AND SENTRA

1. Relieve the fuel system pressure, disconnect the negative battery cable and drain the cooling system.
2. Remove the air cleaner assembly.
3. Disconnect the throttle linkage and fuel and vacuum lines from the carburetor—throttle body or throttle chamber on EFI engines.
4. The carburetor/throttle body/throttle chamber can be removed from the manifold at this point or can be removed as an assembly with the intake manifold.
5. On CA16DE, CA18DE and GA16i engines, remove the manifold support stay.
6. On CA16DE and CA18DE engines, remove the EGR valve assembly, air regulator and FICD valve from the manifold.
7. Loosen the intake manifold retaining bolts in the the proper sequence and separate the manifold from the cylinder head.

NOTE: Never tighten or loosen the power valve adjusting screw on the CA16DE or CA18DE engines.

8. Remove the intake manifold gasket and clean all the gasket contact surfaces thoroughly with a gasket scraper and suitable solvent. All traces of old gasket material must be removed to ensure proper sealing. Inspect the intake manifold for cracks. Using a metal straight edge, check the surface of the intake manifold for warpage.

To install:

9. Lay the new intake manifold gasket onto the cylinder head and position the intake manifold over the mounting studs and onto the gasket. Install the mounting nuts and torque them to specification in the proper sequence.
10. On CA16DE and CA18DE engines, install the EGR valve assembly, air regulator and FICD valve onto the manifold.
11. On CA16DE, CA18DE and GA16i engines, install the manifold support stay.
12. If removed, install the carburetor, throttle body or throttle chamber.
13. Connect the throttle linkage and fuel and vacuum lines.
14. Install the air cleaner.
15. Fill the cooling system to the proper level and connect the negative battery cable.
16. Make the necessary engine adjustments.

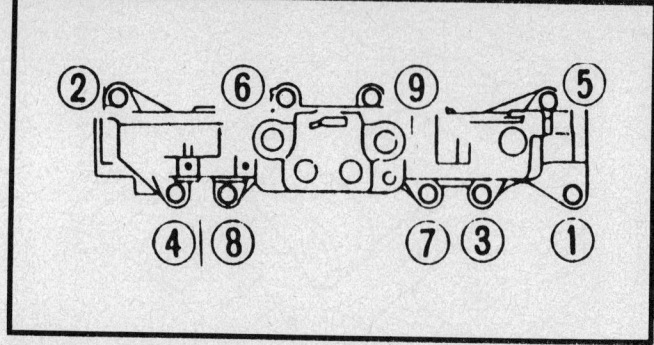

Intake manifold nut loosening sequence—GA161 engine

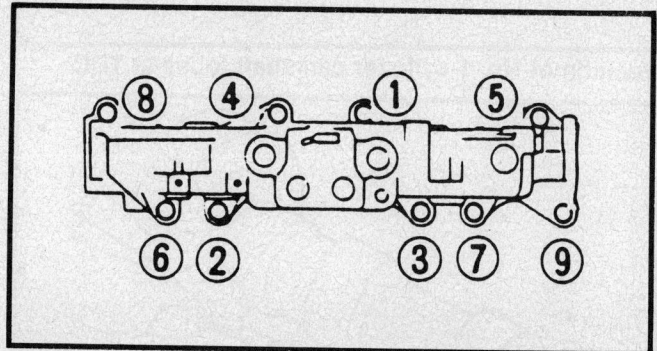

Intake manifold nut tightening sequence—GA161 engine

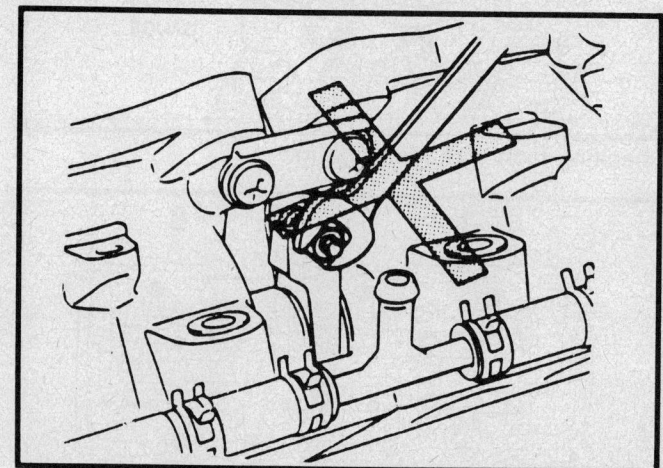

Never touch this bolt—CA16DE and CA18DE engines

200SX (4 CYLINDER) AND 1987–89 STANZA

1. Disconnnect the negative battery cable and drain the cooling system.
2. On the fuel injected engine, remove the air cleaner hoses. On the carbureted engine, remove the air cleaner.
3. Remove the radiator hoses from the manifold.
4. For the carbureted engine, disconnect the fuel, air and vacuum hoses from the carburetor. Remove the throttle linkage and remove the carburetor.
5. Remove the throttle cable and disconnect the fuel pipe and the fuel return line on fuel injected engines. Plug the fuel pipe to prevent spilling fuel.

6. Remove all remaining wires, tubes, the air cleaner bracket (carbureted engines) and the EGR and PCV tubes from the rear of the intake manifold. On carbureted engines, remove the air induction pipe. On fuel injected engines, remove the manifold supports.

7. Unbolt and remove the intake manifold. On fuel injected engines, remove the manifold with the fuel injectors/injection body, EGR valve, fuel pipes and associated running gear still attached.

8. Remove the intake manifold gasket and clean the gasket surfaces.

To install:

9. Install the intake manifold manifold with a new gasket.

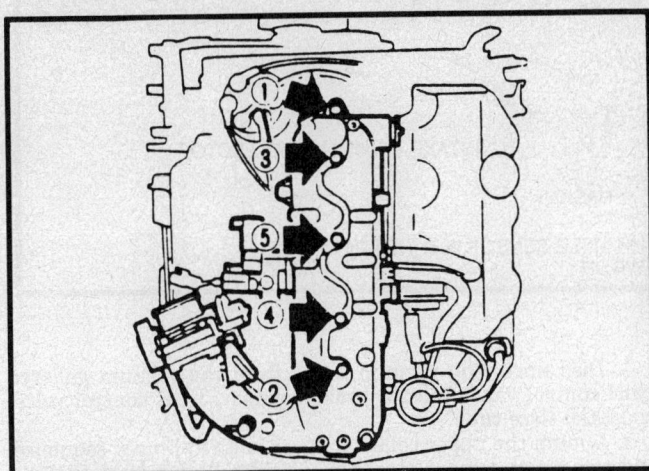

Intake manifold collector cover bolt removal sequence—200SX (V6), 1987–89 300ZX and 1987–88 Maxima

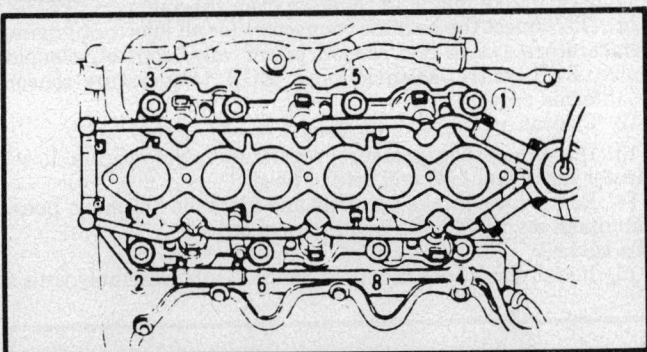

Intake manifold bolt torque sequence—200SX (V6), 1987–89 300ZX and 1987–88 Maxima

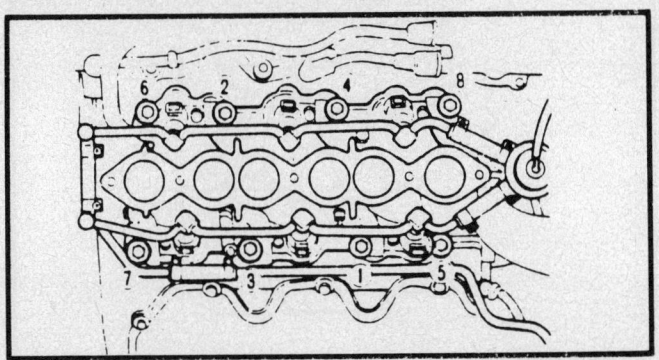

Intake manifold bolt removal sequence—200SX (V6), 1987–89 300ZX and 1987–88 Maxima

Tighten the intake manifold bolts in 2–3 stages.

10. On fuel injected engines, install the intake manifold supports. On carbureted engines, install the air induction pipe and connect the wires, tubes and hoses to the carburetor.

11. On fuel inejcted engines, connect the the fuel pipe, fuel return line and the throttle cable.

12. Install the carburetor, if equipped.

13. Connect the radiator hoses to the intake manifold.

14. Connect the air cleaner hoses (fuel injected) or install the air cleaner (carbureted).

15. Fill the cooling system and connect the negative battery cable.

200SX (V6), 1987–89 300ZX AND 1987–88 MAXIMA

1. Relieve the fuel system pressure, disconnect the negative battery cable and drain the cooling system.

2. Disconnect the valve cover-to-throttle chamber hose at the valve cover.

3. Disconnect the heater housing-to-water inlet tube at the water inlet.

4. Remove the bolt holding the water and fuel tubes to the head.

5. Remove the heater housing-to-thermostat housing tube.

6. Remove the intake collector cover and then remove the collector itself.

7. Disconnect the fuel line and remove the intake manifold bolts. Remove the intake manifold assembly, with the fuel tube assembly still attached, from the vehicle.

To install:

8. Install the intake manifold manifold with a new gasket. Tighten the intake manifold bolts in 2–3 stages in the proper sequence.

9. Connect the fuel line.

10. Install the intake manifold collector with a new gasket. Install the collector cover.

11. Connect the heater-to-thermostat housing tube.

12. Attach the water and fuel tubes to the cylinder head with the mounting bolt.

13. Connect the valve cover-to-throttle chamber hose.

14. Fill the cooling system to the proper level and connect the negative battery cable.

15. Make all the necessary engine adjustments.

1990–91 300ZX

1. Relieve the fuel system pressure, disconnect the negative battery cable and drain the cooling system.

2. Disconnect the air inlet hoses from both throttle chambers.

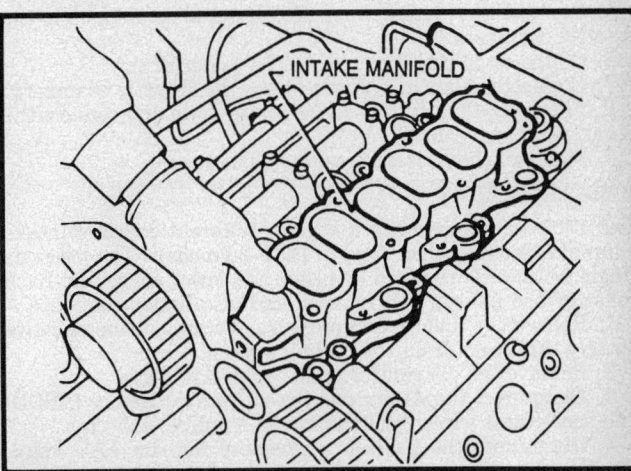

Intake manifold removal and installation—1990–91 300ZX

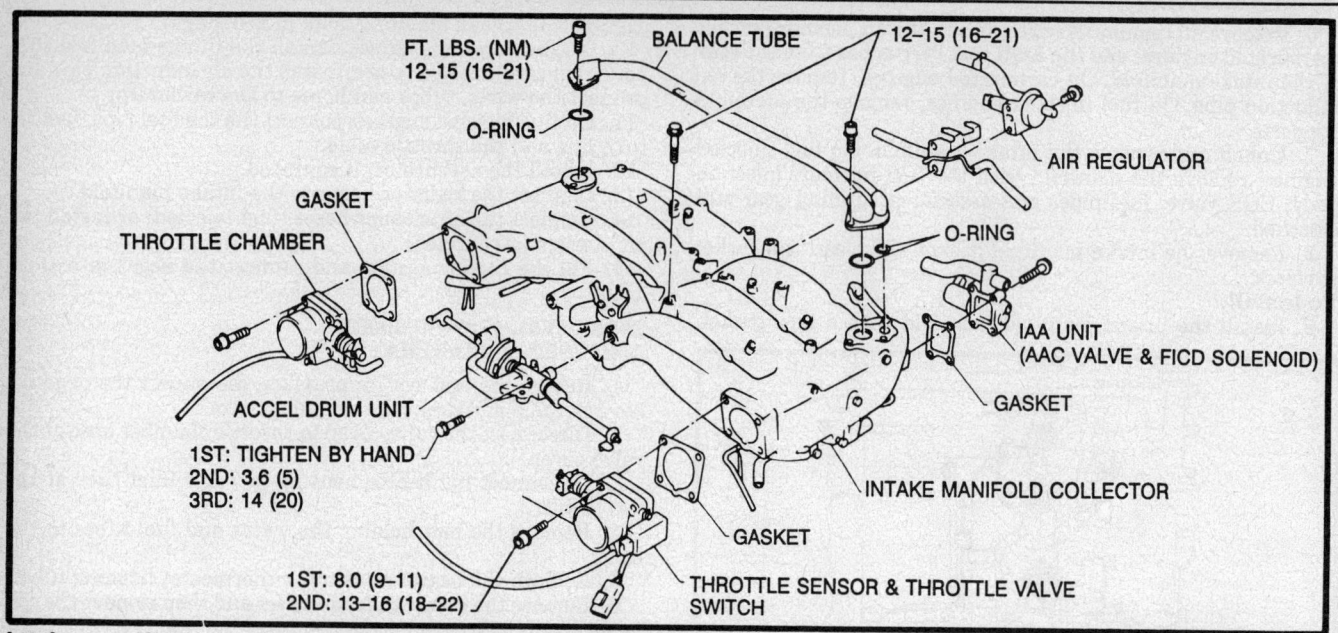

Intake manifold collector assembly—1990–91 300ZX

3. Disconnect the throttle cable from the accelerator drum located in the middle of the throttle chambers.

4. Disconnect the electrical connectors and vacuum lines from both throttle chambers.

5. Disconnect and tag the electrical wire connectors and vacuum lines from the intake manifold collector.

6. Unbolt and remove the intake manifold collector with the throttle chambers attached. Remove the collector gasket.

7. Disconnect the fuel supply and return lines from the injector assembly. Plug the lines to prevent leakage.

8. Remove the injector assembly from the intake manifold.

9. Remove the intake manifold and gaskets.

To install:

10. Install the intake manifold with a new gasket. Tighten the intake manifold bolts to specification.

11. Install the fuel injectors with new insulators and O-rings.

12. Connect the injector supply and return lines.

13. Install the intake manifold collector with a new gasket. Torque the collector bolts to 12–15 ft. lbs. (16–21 Nm).

14. Connect the vacuum lines and electrical connectors to the collector.

15. Connect the vacuum lines and electrical connectors to the throttle chambers.

16. Connect the throttle cable to the center drum.

17. Connect the air inlet hoses to the the throttle chambers.

18. Fill the cooling system to the proper level and connect the negative battery cable.

19. Make all the necessary engine adjustments.

1989–91 MAXIMA

The 1989–91 Maxima has a slightly different collector/intake manifold assembly than used in 1987–88 models. The previous single collector is replaced by upper and lower collectors. Each collector has its own bolt removal and installation sequence.

1. Relieve the fuel system pressure, disconnect the negative battery cable and drain the cooling system.

2. Remove the distributor and the ignition wires.

3. Disconnect the Automatic Speed Control Device (ASCD) and accelerator wires from the intake manifold collector.

4. Disconnect the harness connectors for the AAC valve, throttle sensor and idle switch.

5. Disconnect the air cut out valve water hose.

6. Disconnect the PCV valve hoses.

7. Disconnect the vacuum hoses from the vacuum gallery, swirl control valve, master brake cylinder, EGR control valve and EGR flare tube.

8. Loosen the upper collector cover bolts in proper sequence and remove the upper intake manifold collector from the engine. Remove the collector gasket.

9. Disconnect the engine ground harness.

10. Loosen the lower collector bolts, in sequence, and remove the lower intake manifold collector from the engine.

11. Disconnect the harness connectors for all injectors, engine temperature switch and sensor, power valve control solenoid valve, EGR control soleniod valve, EGR. temperature sensor (California only).

12. Disconnect the vacuum gallery hoses.

13. Disconnect the pressure regulator valve vacuum hose, heater hose, fuel feed and return hose.

14. Remove the intake manifold and fuel tube assembly. Loosen intake manifold bolts in numerical order.

To install:

15. Install the intake manifold and fuel tube assembly with a

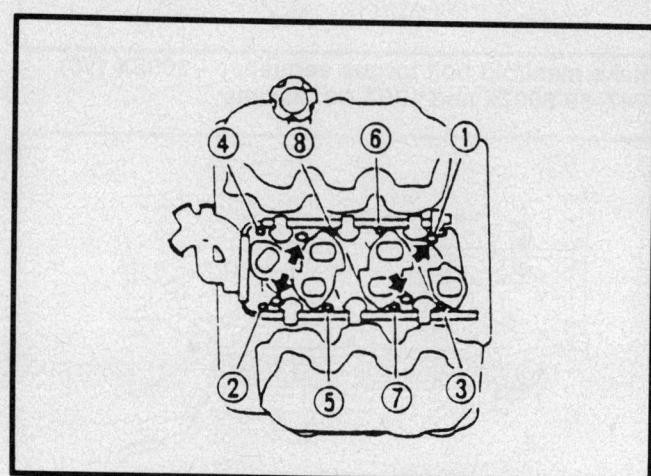

Intake manifold tightening sequence—1989–91 Maxima

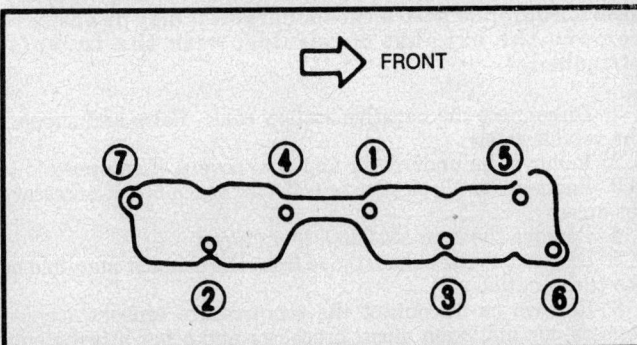

Intake manifold bolt torque sequence—240SX and 1990–91 Stanza

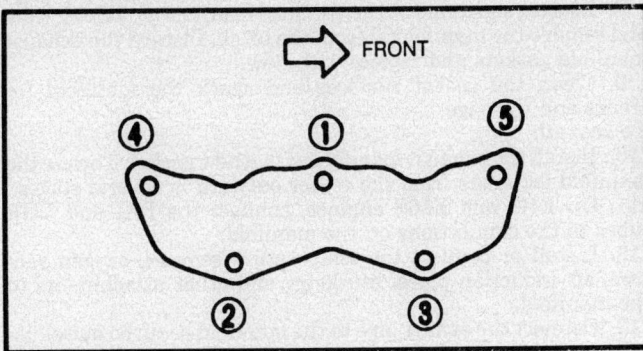

Intake manifold collector bolt torque sequence—240SX and 1990–91 Stanza

new gasket. Tighten the manifold bolts and nuts in 2–3 stages in sequence.

16. Connect the hoses and electrical wires to the intake manifold and fuel tube.

17. Install the upper and lower collector and collector cover with new gaskets. Tighten collector to intake manifold bolts in 2–3 stages by reversing the removal sequence.

18. Connect the vacuum lines, hoses, cables and brackets to the collector cover and collector assembly.

19. Install the distributor and ignition wires.

20. Fill the cooling system to the proper level and connect the negative battrey cable.

21. Make all the necessary engine adjustments.

240SX AND 1990–91 STANZA

1. Relieve the fuel system pressure, disconnect the negative battery cable and drain the cooling system.

2. Remove the air duct between the air flow meter and the throttle body.

3. Disconnect the throttle cable.

4. Disconnect the fuel supply and return lines from the fuel injector assembly. Plug the lines to prevent leakage.

5. Disconnect and tag the electrical connectors and the vacuum hoses to the throttle body and intake manifold/collector assembly.

6. Remove the spark plug wires.

7. Disconnect the EGR valve tube from the exhaust manifold.

8. Remove the intake manifold mounting brackets.

9. Unbolt the intake manifold collector/throttle body from the intake manifold or just remove the mounting bolts and separate the intake manifold from the cylinder head with the collector attached.

10. Using a putty knife, clean the gasket mounting surfaces. Check the intake manifold for cracks and warpage.

To install:

11. Install the intake manifold and gasket on the engine. Tighten the mounting bolts 12–15 ft. lbs. (16–20 Nm) from the center working to the end, in 2–3 stages. If the collector was separated from the intake manifold, torque the collector bolts to 12–15 ft. lbs. (16–20 Nm) from the center working to the end.

12. Install intake manifold mounting brackets.

13. Connect the EGR valve tube to the exhaust manifold.

14. Install the spark plug wires.

15. Connect the electrical connectors and the vacuum hoses to the throttle body and intake manifold/collector assembly.

16. Connect the fuel line(s) to the fuel injector assembly.

17. Connect the throttle cable.

18. Connect the air duct between the air flow meter and the throttle body.

19. Fill the cooling system to the proper level and connect the negative battery cable.

20. Make all the necessary engine adjustments.

Exhaust Manifold

Removal and Installation

NOTE: Removing the intake manifold first on many vehicles will provide better access to the exhaust manifold. If any fuel system components must be removed, make to relieve the fuel system pressure first. If the en-

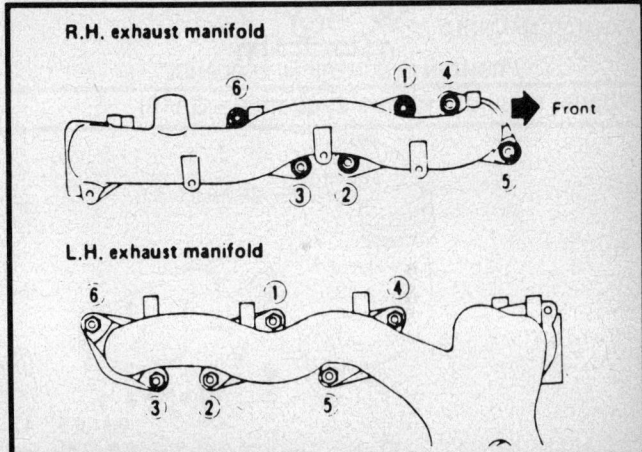

Exhaust manifold torque sequence—VG30E (200SX and 1987–89 Maxima)

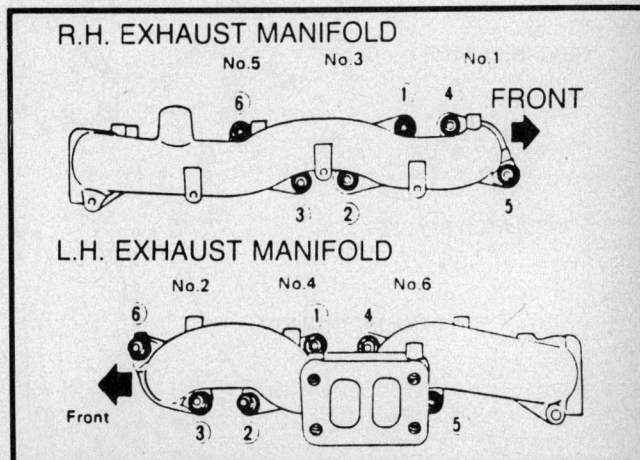

Exhaust manifold torque sequence—VG30E and VG30ET (1987–89 300ZX)

18-67

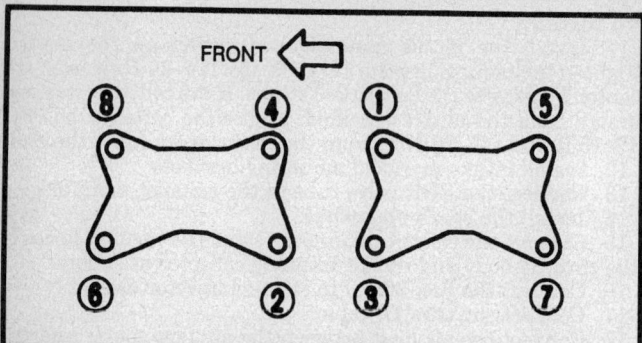

FRONT

Exhaust manifold torque sequence—240SX and 1990 Stanza

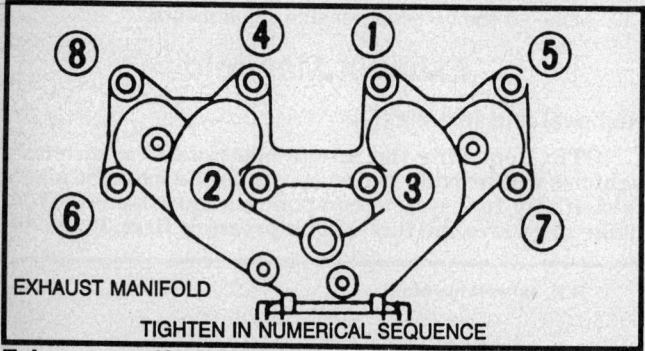

EXHAUST MANIFOLD

TIGHTEN IN NUMERICAL SEQUENCE

Exhaust manifold torque sequence—GA16i

gine is equipped with a turbocharger, it may be easier to remove the exhaust manifolds, with the turbo(s) atttached.

1. Disconnect the negative battery cable. Raise and support the vehicle safely.
2. Remove the undercover and dust covers, if equipped.
3. Remove the air cleaner or collector assembly, if necessary for access.
4. Remove the heat shield(s), if equipped.
5. Disconnect the exhaust pipe from the exhaust manifold or the turbo outlet.
6. Remove or disconnect the temperature sensors, oxygen sensors, air induction pipes, bracketry and other attachments from the manifold.
7. Disconnect the EAI and EGR tubes from their fittings on the E16i and E16S series engines.
8. Loosen and remove the exhaust manifold attaching nuts and remove the manifold(s) from the block. Discard the exhaust manifold gaskets and replace with new.
9. Clean the gasket surfaces and check the manifold for cracks and warpage.

To install:

10. Install the exhaust manifold with a new gasket. Torque the manifold fasteners from the center outward in several stages.
11. On E16i and E16S engines, connect the EAI and EGR tubes to the connections on the manifold.
12. Install or connect the temperature sensors, oxygen sensors, air induction pipes, bracketry and other attachments to the manifold.
13. Connect the exhust pipe to the manifold or turbo outlet using a new gasket.

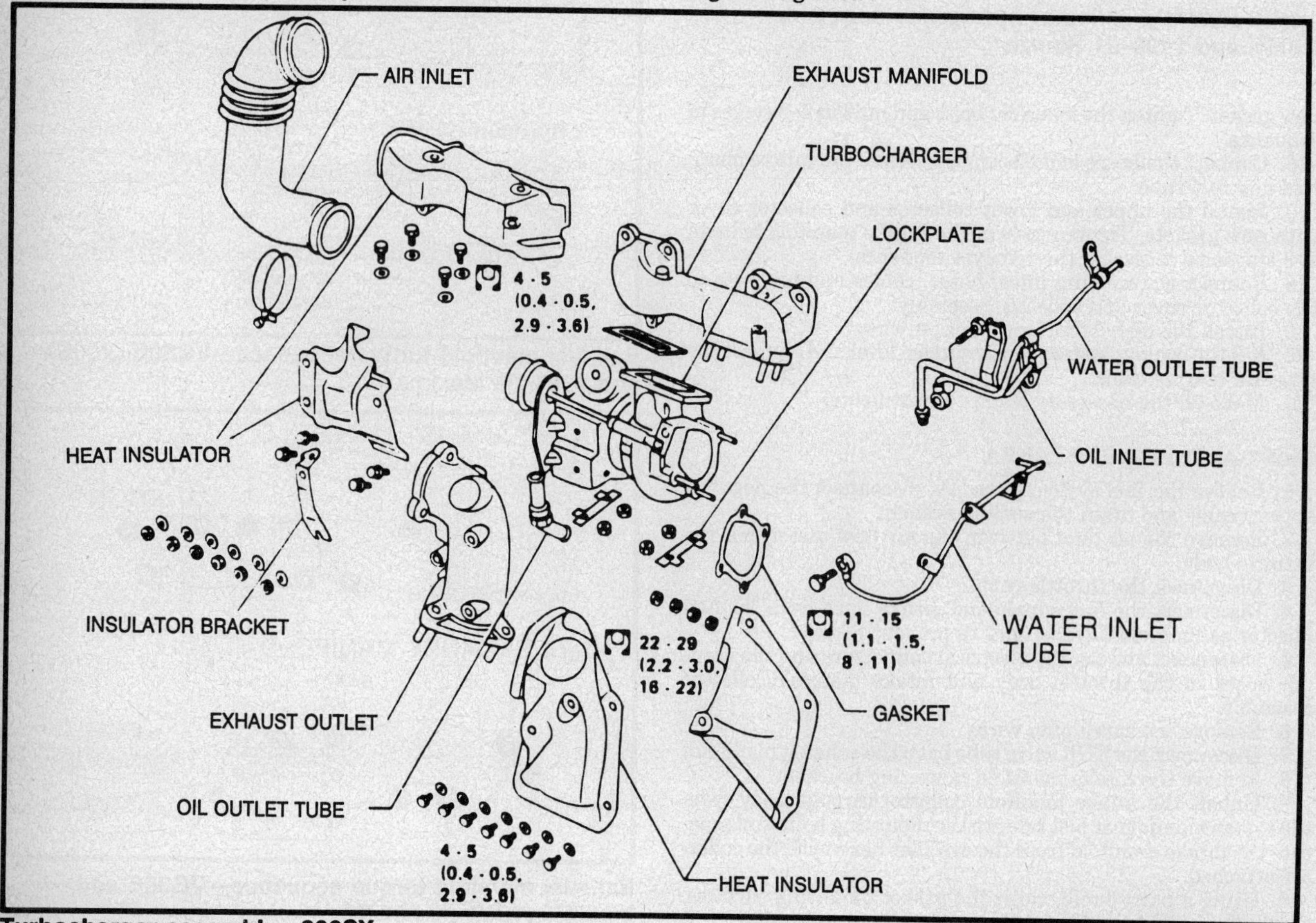

AIR INLET

EXHAUST MANIFOLD

TURBOCHARGER

LOCKPLATE

4 · 5
(0.4 - 0.5,
2.9 · 3.6)

WATER OUTLET TUBE

OIL INLET TUBE

HEAT INSULATOR

11 · 15
(1.1 · 1.5,
8 · 11)

WATER INLET TUBE

INSULATOR BRACKET

22 · 29
(2.2 · 3.0,
16 · 22)

GASKET

EXHAUST OUTLET

OIL OUTLET TUBE

4 · 5
(0.4 · 0.5,
2.9 · 3.6)

HEAT INSULATOR

Turbocharger assembly—200SX

14. Install the heat shields.
15. Install the air cleaner or collector assembly.
16. Install the undercovers and dust covers.
17. Connect the negative battery cable.

Turbocharger

Removal and Installation

NOTE: If the turbocharger is being replaced, always drain the crankcase and replace the oil and filter to ensure a clean oil supply. This is especially true in cases of complete turbo failure where there is the possibility of metal particles entering the engine's lubricating system and damaging the new turbocharger.

200SX TURBO

1. Disconnect the negative battery cable and drain the cooling system.
2. Remove the air duct and hoses, and the air intake pipe.
3. Disconnect the front exhaust pipe at the turbo exhaust outlet.
4. Remove the heat shield plates.
5. Disconnect and tag the oil supply tube and return hose. Plug the ends of the hoses to prevent leakage.
6. Disconnect the water inlet tube.
7. Unbolt and remove the turbocharger from the exhaust manifold.
To install:
8. Add 25cc of clean engine oil to the turbocharger oil passages before installing.
9. Mount the turbocharger onto the manifold using new gaskets. Torque the turbocharger outlet-to-housing bolts to 16–22 ft. lbs. (22–30 Nm).
10. Connect the water inlet tube. Use new metal crush washers on the banjo fitting.
11. Connect the oil supply and return tubes. Use new metal crush washers on the banjo fittings.
12. Install the heat shields.
13. Connect the exhaust pipe to turbo exhaust outlet.
14. Install the air intake pipe, air duct and hoses.
15. Fill the cooling system and connect the negative battery cable.
16. Disconnect the ignition coil wire and crank the engine for 20 seconds to ensure that oil reaches the center bearings of the turbo. Reconnect the coil and start the engine, letting it idle for 30 seconds to ensure the proper operation of the turbocharger.

1987–89 300ZX TURBO

1. Disconnect the negative battery cable.
2. Discharge the air conditioning system and remove the compressor and compressor mounting bracket.
3. Disconnect the exhaust front tube.
4. Disconnect the center cable.
5. Remove the heat insulator for the brake master cylinder.
6. Disconnect the air duct and hoses.
7. Disconnect the exhaust manifold connecting tube and remove the heat shield plate.
8. Disconnect the oil supply tube and return hose. Plug the ends of the hoses to prevent leakage.
9. Disconnect the water inlet line.
10. Remove the turbocharger from the exhaust manifold.
To install:
11. Add 25cc of clean engine oil to the turbocharger oil passages before installing.
12. Mount the turbocharger onto the manifold using new gaskets. Torque the turbocharger-to-manifold nuts to 33–40 ft. lbs. (45–54 Nm).
13. Connect the water inlet tube. Use new metal crush washers on the banjo fitting.
14. Connect the oil supply and return tubes. Use new metal crush washers on the banjo fittings.
15. Install the heat shield plate and connect the exhaust manifold tube.
16. Connect the air duct and hoses.
17. Install the brake master cylinder heat insulator.
18. Connect the center cable.
19. Connect the front exhaust tube.
20. Install the compressor bracket and mount the compressor.
21. Connect the negative battery cable and charge the air conditioning system.
22. Disconnect the coil and crank the engine for 20 seconds to ensure that oil reaches the center bearings. Connect the coil and start the engine, letting it idle for 30 seconds to ensure the proper operation of the turbocharger.

1990–91 300ZX TWIN TURBO

Right

1. Drain the cooling system and the oil pan.

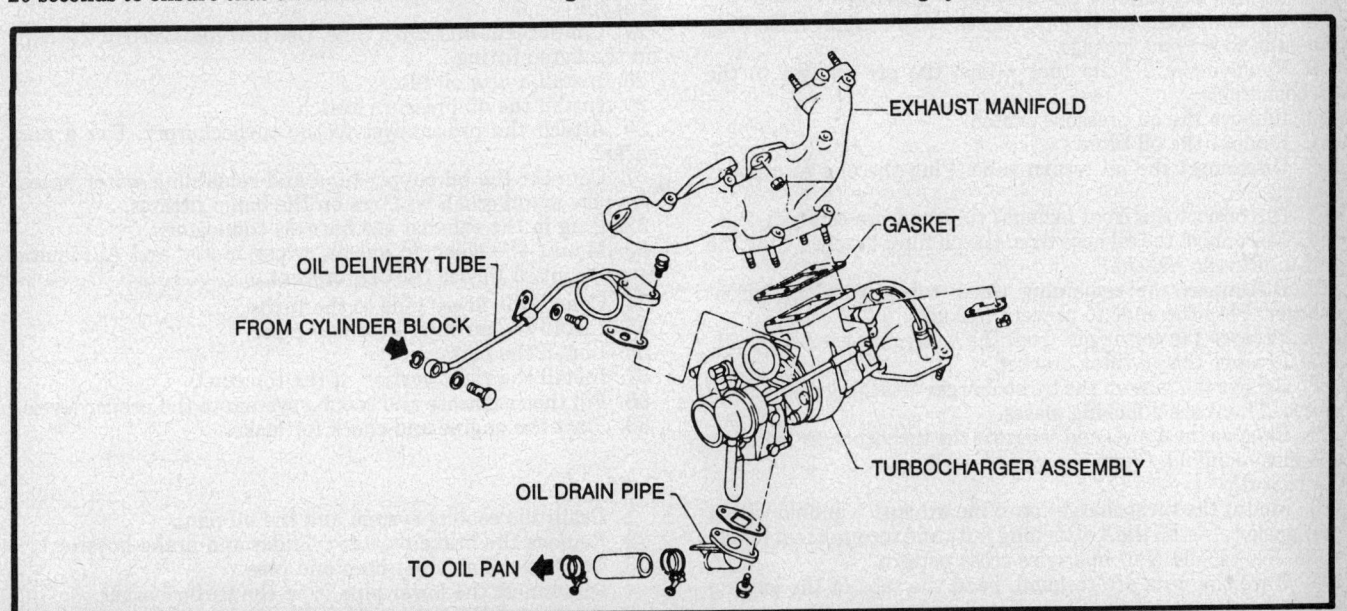

EXHAUST MANIFOLD

GASKET

OIL DELIVERY TUBE

FROM CYLINDER BLOCK

TURBOCHARGER ASSEMBLY

OIL DRAIN PIPE

TO OIL PAN ◀

Turbocharger assembly—1987–89 300ZX

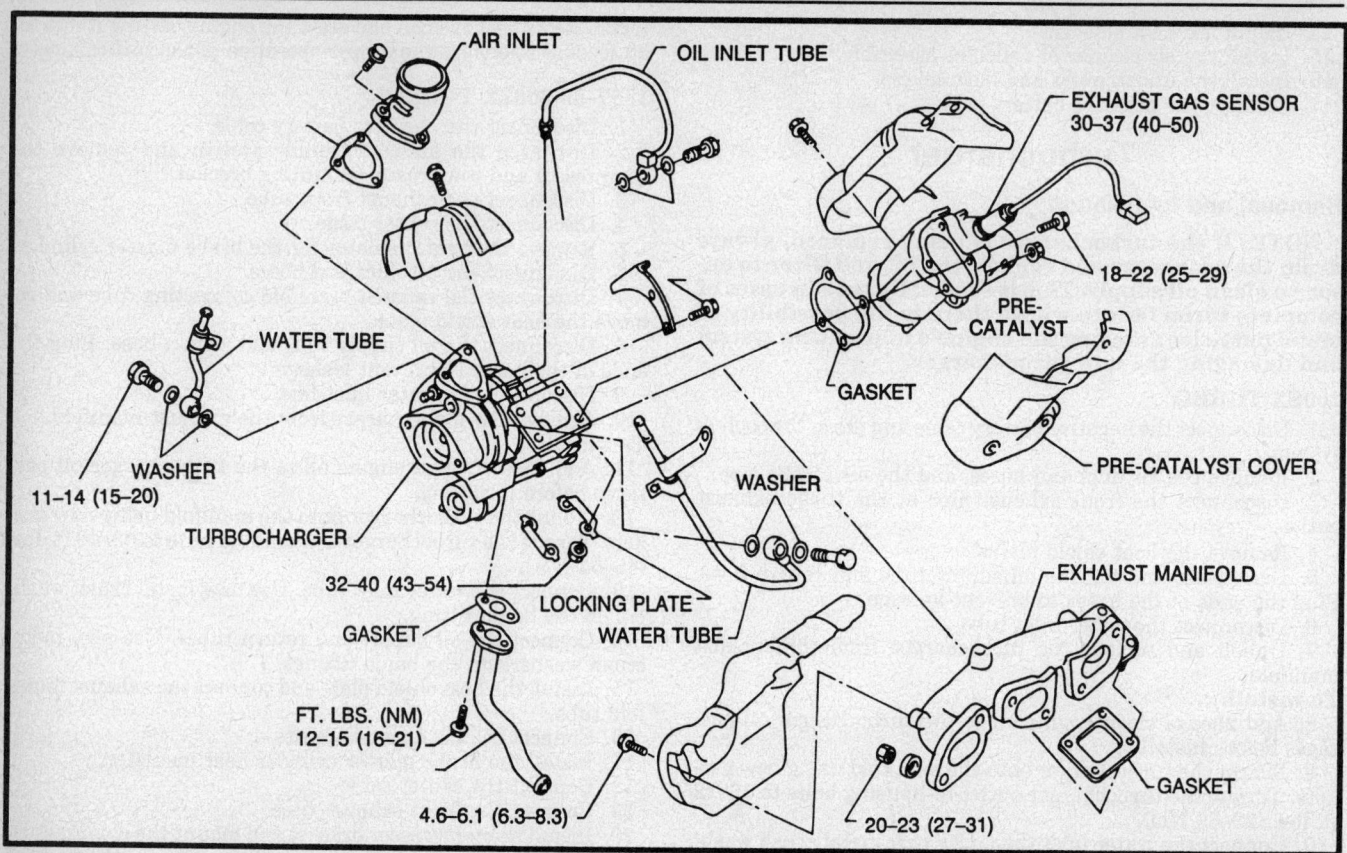

Right side turbocharger assembly—1990–91 300ZX

2. Remove the right portion of the cowl top.
3. Remove the battery.
4. Remove the air inlet hose and pipe.
5. Disconnect the lower pipe from the turbo.
6. Remove the Automatic Speed Control Device (ASCD) bracket with wiper motor and solenoid valves.
7. Unplug the exhaust gas harness connector.
8. Disconnect the turbo water hoses and oil supply tube. Plug the ends to prevent leakage.
9. Remove the 2 bolts that attach the pre-catalyst to the turbocharger.
10. Remove the oil pressure switch.
11. Remove the oil filter.
12. Disconnect the oil return tube. Plug the end to prevent leakage.
13. Disconnect the front exhaust tube and pre-catalyst.
14. Disconnect the oil hose from the oil filter bracket. Plug the end to prevent leakage.
15. Disconnect the remaining water tubes from the turbocharger. Plug the ends to prevent leakage.
16. Remove the cotter pin from the wastegate actuating rod.
17. Remove the oil filter bracket.
18. Relieve the tabs on the turbocharger attaching nut locking plates. There are 2 locking plates.
19. Remove the 4 nuts and separate the turbocharger from the exhaust manifold. Clean the gasket surfaces.
To install:
20. Mount the turbocharger onto the exhaust manifold with a new gasket. Install the 4 attaching nuts and torque them to 32–40 ft. lbs. (43–54 Nm) in a criss-cross pattern.
21. Once the nuts are torqued, bend the tabs of the locking plates firmly around the flats of each nut.
22. Install the oil filter bracket.

23. Connect the wastegate actuating rod and insert the cotter pin.
24. Connect the water tubes to the turbo. Use new metal crush washers on the banjo fittings.
25. Connect the oil hose to the oil filter bracket.
26. Connect the front exhaust tube and pre-catalyst. Use new gaskets.
27. Connect the oil return tube. Use new metal crush washers on the banjo fitting.
28. Install a new oil filter.
29. Install the oil pressure switch.
30. Attach the pre-catalyst to the turbocharger. Use a new gasket.
31. Connect the oil supply tube and remaining water hoses. Use new metal crush washers on the banjo fittings.
32. Plug in the exhaust gas harness connector.
33. Mount the solenoid valves, wiper motor and Automatic Speed Control Device (ASCD) bracket.
34. Conect the lower pipe to the turbo.
35. Install the air inlet hose and pipe.
36. Install the battery.
37. Install the right portion of the top cowl.
38. Fill the crankcase and cooling system to the proper levels.
39. Start the engine and check for leaks.

Left
1. Drain the cooling system and the oil pan.
2. Remove the brake master cylinder and brake booster.
3. Remove the air inlet hose and pipe.
4. Disconnect the lower pipe from the turbocharger.
5. Disconnect the water tubes. Plug the the tube ends to prevent leakage.

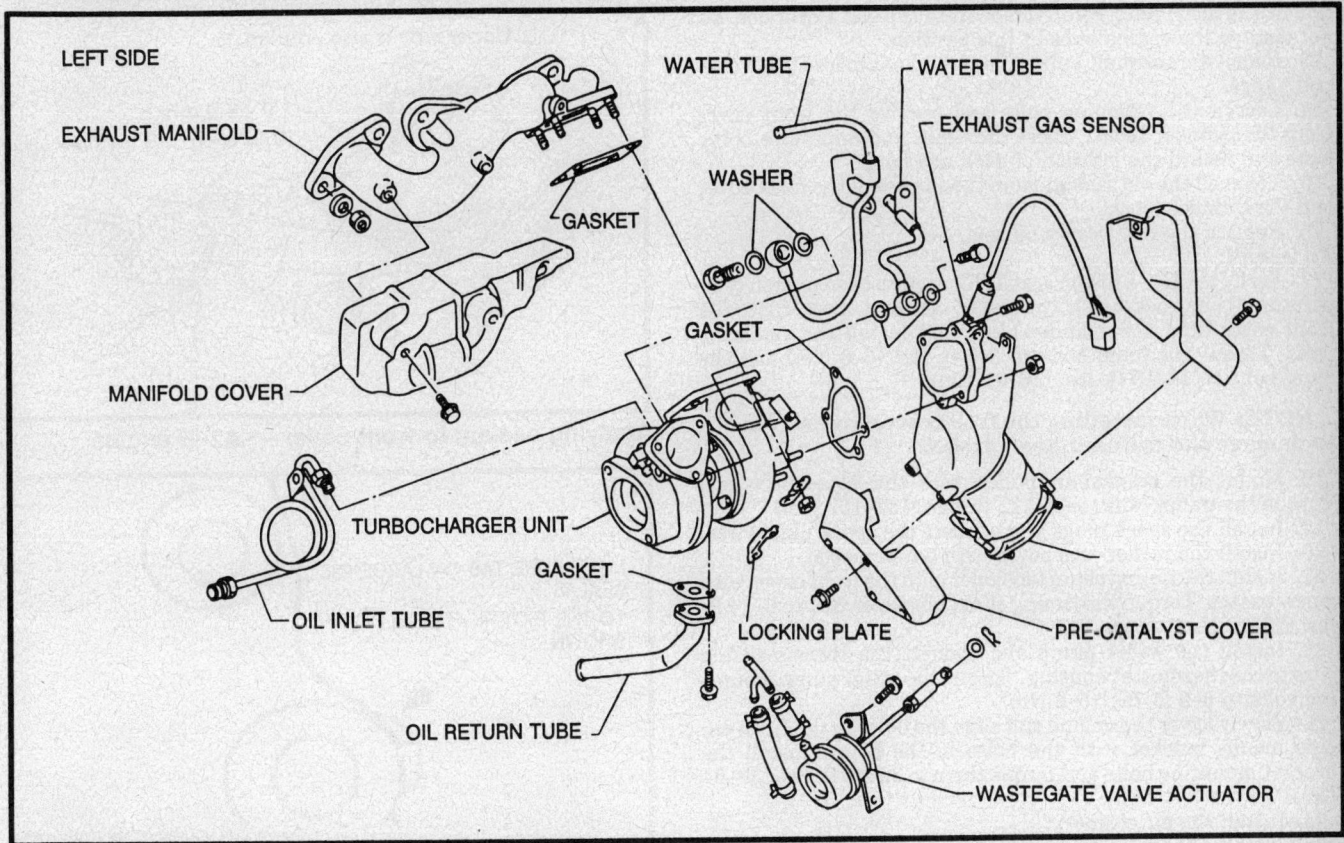

Left side turbocharger assembly—1990–91 300ZX

6. Remove the 2 bolts that attach the pre-catalyst to the turbocharger.

7. Remove the front exhaust tube and pre-catalyst.

8. Disconnect the steering column lower joint from the steering rack.

9. Disconnect the oil return tube and remaining water tubes. Plug the tube ends to prevent leakage.

10. Disconnect the EGR tube and remove the wastegate valve actuator bracket.

11. Remove the exhaust manifold cover.

12. Remove the exhaust manifold attaching nuts. Remove the turbocharger and exhaust manifold together as one unit. Release the tabs on the attaching nut locking plates. There are 2 locking plates. Remove the 4 nuts and separate the turbocharger from the exhaust manifold. Clean the gasket surfaces.

To install:

13. Mount the turbocharger onto the exhaust manifold with a new gasket. Install the 4 attaching nuts and torque them to 32–40 ft. lbs. (43–54 Nm) in a criss-cross pattern.

14. Once the nuts are torqued, bend the tabs of the locking plates firmly around the flats of each nut.

15. Install the exhaust manifold/turbocharger assembly with new gaskets. Torque the exhaust manifold nuts to 20–23 ft. lbs. (27–31 Nm).

16. Install the exhaust manifold cover.

17. Install the wastegate valve actuator bracket and connect the EGR tube.

18. Connect the water tubes and oil return tube. Use new metal crush gaskets on the banjo fittings.

19. Connect the steering column lower joint from the steering rack.

20. Install the front exhaust tube and pre-catalyst.

21. Attach the pre-catalyst to the turbocharger.

22. Connect the remaining water tubes.

23. Connnect the lower pipe to the turbocharger.

24. Install the air inlet hose and pipe.

25. Install the brake booster and master cylinder.

26. Fill the crankcase and cooling system to the proper levels.

27. Start the engine and check for leaks.

Timing Chain Front Cover

Removal and Installation

1989–91 PULSAR AND SENTRA (GA16I ENGINE)

1. Disconnect the negative battery cable.

2. Drain the cooling system.

3. Drain the crankcase and remove the oil pan.

4. Remove the power steering belt, if equipped.

5. Remove the air conditioning belt, if equipped.

6. Remove the alternator belt, alternator mounting bracket and alternator.

7. Remove the air cleaner.

8. Connect a suitable lifting device to the front side lifting bracket and tension the hoist to support the engine. Remove the front engine mounting bracket from the block and keep the hoist tensioned to support the weight of the engine.

9. Disconnect the thermo switch connector wire from the thermostat housing and remove the water pump.

10. Loosen the timing chain tensioner mounting bolt and remove the timing chain tensioner and gasket from the front cover.

11. Remove the rocker arm cover and cover gasket.

12. Remove the spark plugs and set the No. 1 piston to TDC of the compression stroke. When the No. 1 piston is at TDC the crankshaft and camshaft keyways will be in the 12 o'clock posi-

tion or the distributor rotor will point to the No. 1 cylinder. Do not disturb the engine once in this position.

13. Remove crankshaft pulley. Be careful not to lose the Woodruff® keys.

14. Loosen the retaining bolts and remove the front cover from the cylinder block. There are 6mm and 8mm size bolts. Note and record the location of each size bolt.

15. Clean all the old sealant from the surface of the front cover and the cylinder block.

16. Replace the front cover oil seal.

To install:

17. Verify the No. 1 piston is at TDC. Apply a bead of high temperature liquid gasket to both sides of the front cover. Place the front cover onto the cylinder block and install the retaining bolts. Torque the 6mm bolts to 5–6 ft. lbs. (6–8 Nm) and the 8mm bolts to 12–15 ft. lbs. (16–21 Nm).

NOTE: When installing the front cover, be careful not to damage the cylinder head gasket.

18. Mount the crankshaft pulley with the Woodruff® key. Torque the pulley bolt to 98–112 ft. lbs. (132–152 Nm).

19. Install the spark plugs and connect the spark plug wires.

20. Install the rocker arm cover with a new gasket.

21. Install the timing chain tensioner onto the front cover with a new gasket. Torque the timing chain tensioner bolt to 9–14 ft. lbs. (13–19 Nm).

22. Install the water pump and connect the thermo-switch wire to the thermostat housing. Torque the water pump mounting bolts to 5–6 ft. lbs. (6–8 Nm).

23. Slowly lower the engine and align the holes in the front engine mount bracket with the holes in the block. Install the bracket mounting bolts and torque them to 29–40 ft. lbs. (39–54 Nm).

24. Install the air cleaner.

25. Install the accessories and drive belts and adjust the tension.

26. Fill the crankcase and the cooling system to the proper levels.

27. Connect the negative battery cable.

240SX

1. Disconnect the negative battery cable.

2. Drain the cooling system and oil pan. To drain the cooling system, open the radiator drain cock and remove the engine block drain plug. The block plug is located on the left side of the block near the engine freeze plugs.

3. Remove the radiator shroud and the cooling fan.

4. Loosen the alternator drive belt adjusting screw and remove the drive belt.

5. Remove the power steering and air conditioning drive belts.

6. Remove the spark plugs and the distributor cap. Set the No. 1 piston to TDC of the compression stroke. Carefully re-

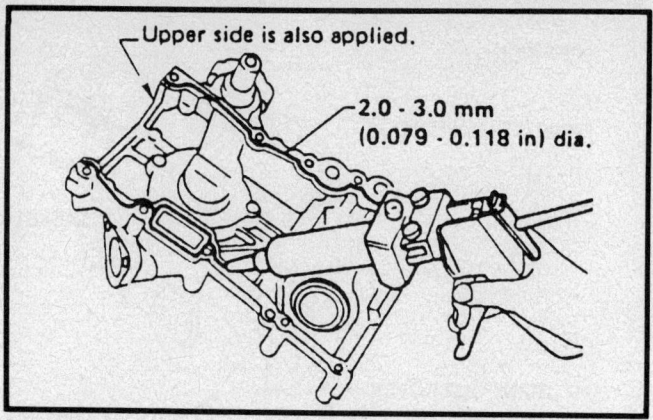

Applying sealant to front cover – KA24E engine

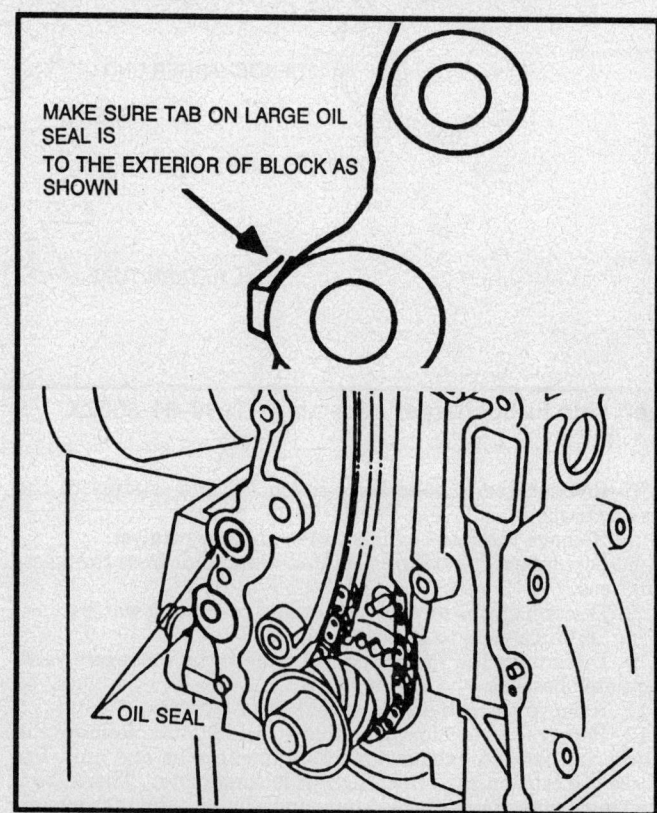

Cylinder block timing chain cover seals on KA24E engine. Make sure tab on larger seal is positioned as shown

move the the distributor. Before removal, scribe alignment marks in the timing cover and flat portion of the oil pump/distributor drive spindle. This alignment is critical and if not done properly, it could cause difficulty is aligning the distributor and setting the timing.

7. Remove the power steering pump, idler pulley and the power steering brackets.

8. Remove the air conditioning compressor idler pulley.

9. Remove the crankshaft pulley bolt and remove the crankshaft pulley with a 2 jawed puller.

10. Remove the oil pump attaching screws, and withdraw the pump and its drive spindle.

11. Remove the rocker arm cover.

12. Remove the oil pan.

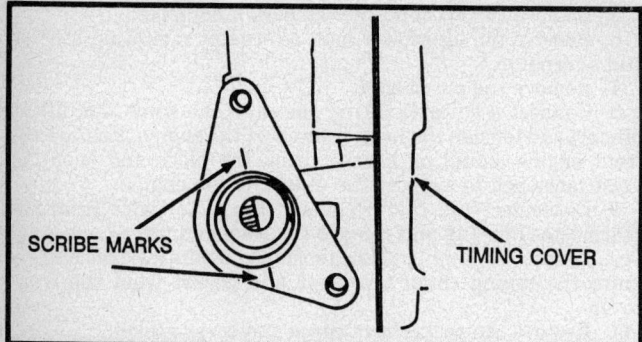

Aligning the timing cover and distributor/oil pump drive spindle – KA24E engine

13. Remove the bolts holding the front cover to the front of the cylinder block, the 4 bolts which retain the front of the oil pan to the bottom of the front cover, and the 4 bolts which are screwed down through the front of the cylinder head and into the top of the front cover. Carefully pry the front cover off the front of the engine. Clean all the old sealant from the surface of the front cover and the cylinder block.

14. Replace the crankshaft oil seal and the 2 timing chain cover oil seals in the block. These two seals should be installed in the block and not in the timing cover.

To install:

15. Verify the No. 1 piston is at TDC of the compression stroke. Apply a very thin bead of high temperature liquid gasket to both sides of the front cover and to where the cover mates with the cylinder head. Apply a light coating of grease to the crankshaft and timing cover oil seals and carefully bolt the front cover to the front of the engine.

NOTE: **When installing the front cover, be careful not to damage the cylinder head gasket or to disturb the position of the oil seals in the block. Make sure the tab on the larger block oil seal is pointing to the exterior of the block.**

16. Install new rubber plugs in the cylinder head.
17. Install the oil pan.
18. Install the rocker arm cover.
19. Before installing the oil pump, place the gasket over the shaft and make sure the mark on the drive spindle faces (aligned) with the oil pump hole. Install the oil pump and distributor driving spindle into the front cover with a new gasket.
20. Install the crankshaft pulley and bolt. Torque the pulley bolt to 87–116 ft. lbs. (118–157 Nm).
21. Install the distributor and the spark plugs.
22. Install the compressor idler pulley. Install power steering pump brackets, idler pulley and power steering pump. Install the drive belts and adjust the tension.
23. Install the radiator shroud and the cooling fan.
24. Refill the cooling system and crankcase to the proper levels.
25. Connect the negative battery cable.
26. Start the engine, set the ignition timing and check for leaks.

1990–91 STANZA

1. Disconnect the negative battery cable.
2. Raise the front of the vehicle and support safely.
3. Remove the right front wheel.
4. Remove the dust cover and undercover.
5. Drain the oil pan.
6. Set the No. 1 piston at TDC of the compression stroke.
7. Remove the alternator and air conditioning compressor drive belts.
8. Remove the alternator and adjusting bar.
9. Remove the oil separator.
10. Remove the power steering pump pulley, pump stay and mounting bracket.
11. Discharge the air conditioning system and remove the compressor and mounting bracket.
12. Remove the crankshaft pulley and oil pump drive boss.
13. Remove the oil pan.
14. Remove the oil strainer mounting bolt.
15. Remove the bolts that attach the front cover to the head and the block.
16. Remove the rocker cover.
17. Support the engine with a suitable lifting device.
18. Unbolt the right side engine mount bracket from the block and lower the engine.
19. Remove the front cover.
20. Clean all the old sealant from the surface of the front cover and the cylinder block.
21. Replace the crankshaft oil seal and the 2 timing chain cov-

er oil seals in the block. These two seals should be installed in the block and not in the timing cover.

To install:

22. Verify the No. 1 piston is at TDC. Apply a very thin bead of high temperature liquid gasket to both sides of the front cover and to where the cover mates with the cylinder head. Apply a light coating of grease to the crankshaft and timing cover oil seals and carefully mount the front cover to the front of the engine.

NOTE: **When installing the front cover, be careful not to damage the cylinder head gasket or to disturb the position of the oil seals in the block. Make sure the tab on the larger block oil seal is pointing to the exterior of the block.**

23. Install new rubber plugs in the cylinder head.
24. Raise the engine and install the right engine mount bracket bolts. Torque the bolts to 58–65 ft. lbs. (78–88 Nm).
25. Install the rocker arm cover.
26. Install the front cover bolts.
27. Install the oil strainer mounting bolt.
28. Install the oil pan.
29. Install the oil pump drive boss and the crankshaft pulley. Torque the pulley bolt to 87–116 ft. lbs. (118–157 Nm).
30. Install the air conditioning compressor bracket and mount the compressor.
31. Install the power steering bracket, pump stay and power steering pump.
32. Install the oil separator.
33. Install the dust cover and undercover.
34. Mount the right front wheel and lower the vehicle.
35. Fill the crankcase to the proper level and charge the air conditioning system.
36. Make all the necessary engine adjustments.

Replacement

1. Disconnect the negative battery cable.
2. Remove the crankshaft pulley.
3. Using a suitable tool, pry the oil seal from the front cover.

NOTE: **When removing the oil seal, be careful not the gouge or scratch the seal bore or crankshaft surfaces.**

4. Wipe the seal bore with a clean rag.
5. Lubricate the lip of the new seal with clean engine oil.
6. Install the seal into the front cover with a suitable seal installer.
7. Install the crankshaft pulley.
8. Connect the negative battery cable.

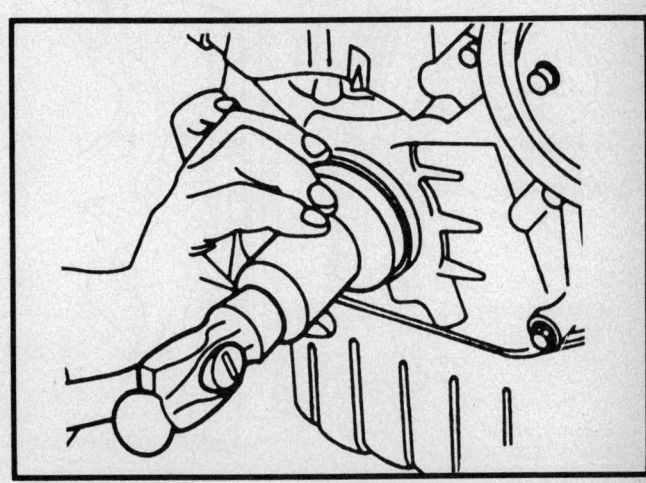

Timing chain front cover oil seal installation

Timing Chain and Sprockets

Removal and Installation

1989–91 PULSAR AND SENTRA (GA16I ENGINE)

1. Disconnect the negative battery cable.
2. Set the No. 1 piston at TDC of the compression stroke.
3. Remove the front cover.
4. If necessary, define the timing marks with chalk or paint to ensure proper alignment.
5. Hold the camshaft sprocket stationary with a spanner wrench or similar tool and remove the camshaft sprocket bolt.
6. Remove the chain guides.
7. Remove the camshaft sprocket.
8. Remove the oil pump spacer.
9. Remove the crankshaft sprocket and timing chain.

To install:

10. Verify that the No. 1 piston is at TDC of the compression stroke. The crankshaft keyways should be at the 12 o'clock position.
11. Install the camshaft sprocket, bolt and washer. The alignment mark must face towards the front. When installing the washer, place the non-chamfered side of the washer towards the face of camshaft sprocket. Tighten the bolt just enough to hold the sprocket in place.
12. Install the crankshaft sprocket making sure the alignment mark is facing the front.
13. Install the timing chain by aligning the silver links at the 12 o'clock and 6 o'clock positions on the chain with the timing

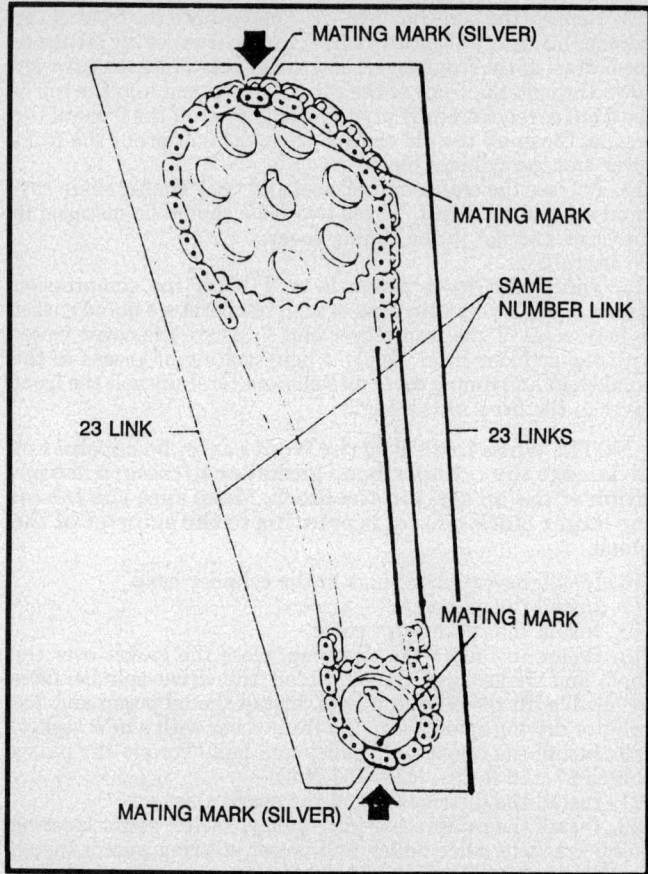

Timing chain and sprocket alignment marks—GA16I engine

marks on the crankshaft and camshaft sprockets. The number of links between the 2 silver links are the same for the left and the right sides of the chain, so either side of the chain may be used to align the sprocket timing marks.

14. Torque the camshaft sprocket bolt to 72–94 ft. lbs. (98–128 Nm) once the chain is in place and aligned.
15. Install the chain guides and tensioner. Use a new tensioner gasket and torque the tensioner and chain guide bolts to 9–14 ft. lbs. (13–19 Nm). When installing the chain guide, move the guide in the direction that applies tension to the chain.
16. Install the front cover.
17. Connect the negative battery cable.

240SX AND 1990–91 STANZA

1. Disconnect the negative battery cable.
2. Set the No. 1 piston at TDC of the compression stroke.
3. Remove the front cover.
4. If necessary, define the timing marks with chalk or paint to ensure proper alignment.
5. Hold the camshaft sprocket stationary with a spanner wrench or similar tool and remove the camshaft sprocket bolt.
6. Remove chain tensioner.
7. Remove the chain guides.
8. Remove the timing chain.
9. Remove the sprocket oil slinger, oil pump drive gear and crankshaft gear.

To install:

10. Install the crankshaft sprocket, oil pump drive gear and oil slinger onto the end of the crankshaft. Make sure the crankshaft sprocket timing marks face toward the front.
11. Install the camshaft sprocket, bolt and washer. The align-

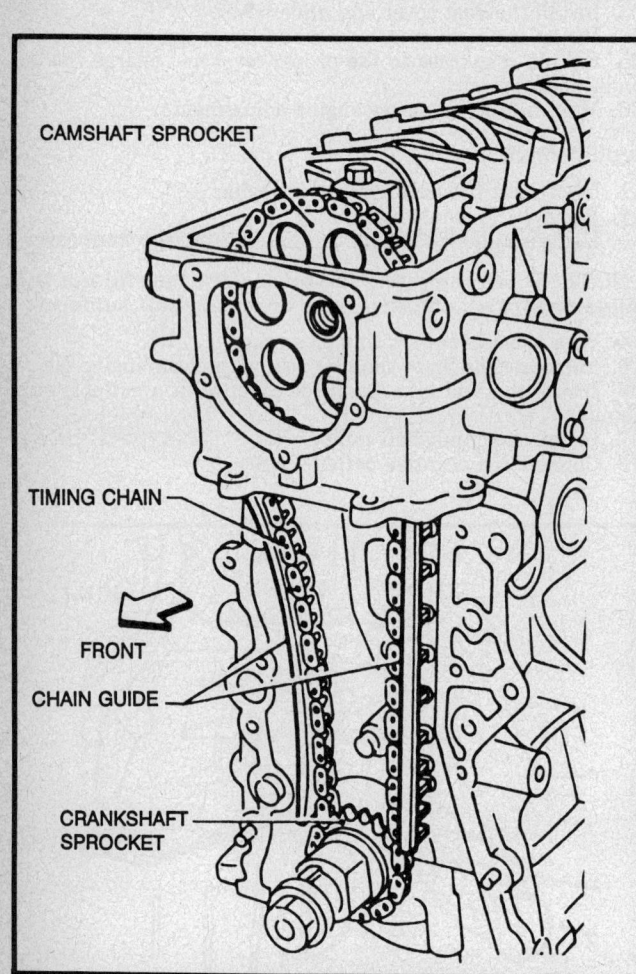

Timing chain assembly—GA16I engine

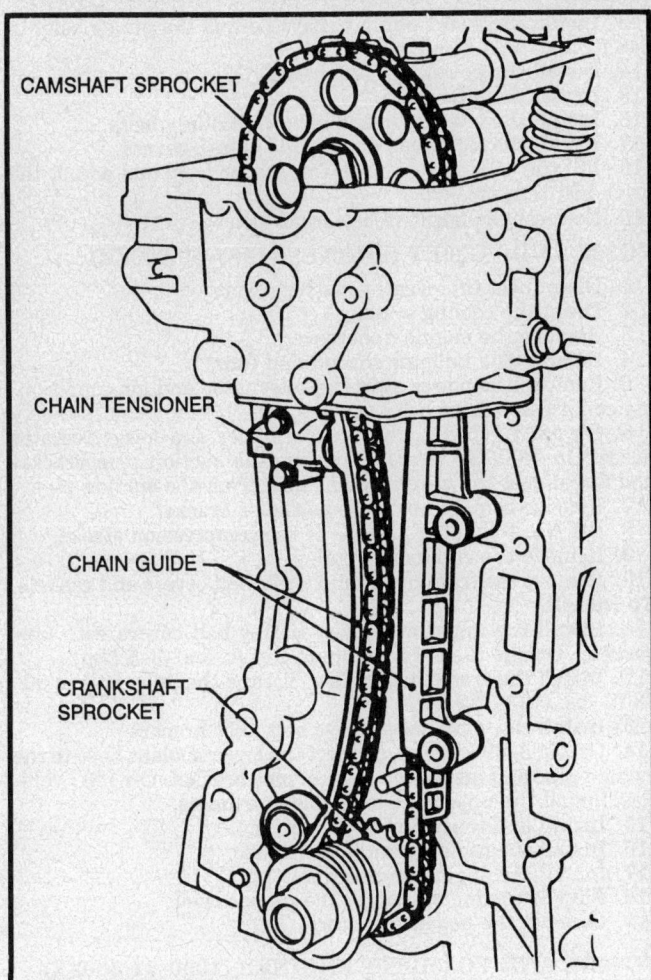

Timing chain assembly—KA24E engine

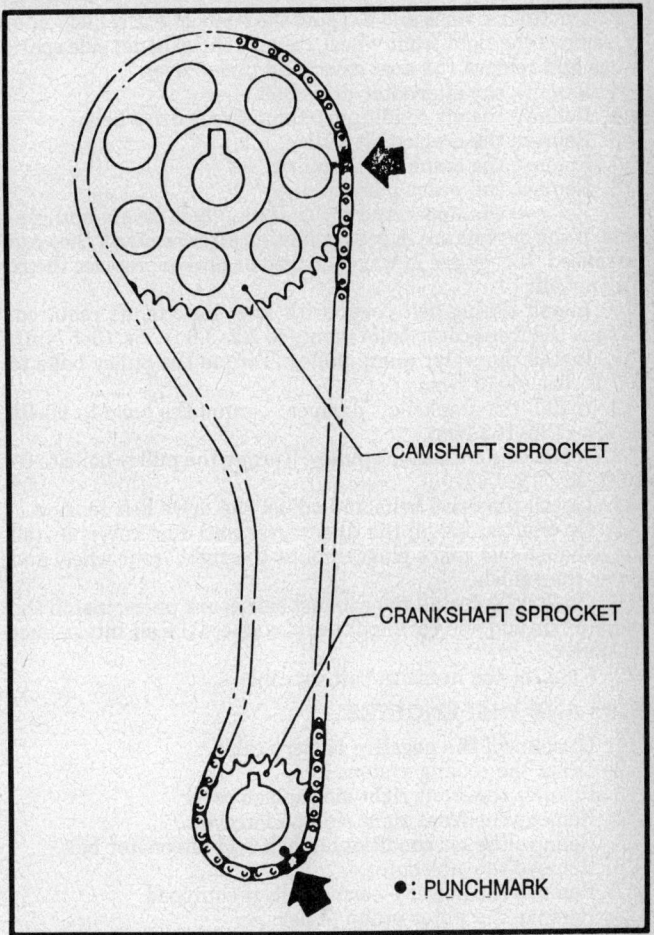

●: PUNCHMARK

Timing chain and sprocket alignment marks—KA24E engine

ment mark must face towards the front. Tighten the bolt just enough to hold the sprocket in place.

12. Verify that the No. 1 piston is at TDC of the compression stroke. The crankshaft keyways should be at the 12 o'clock position.

13. Install the timing chain by aligning the marks on the chain with the marks on the crankshaft and camshaft sprockets. Torque the camshaft sprocket bolt to 87–116 ft. lbs. (118–157 Nm) once the timing chain is in place and aligned.

14. Install the chain tensioner and chain guide.

15. Install the front cover.

16. Connect the negative battery cable.

Timing Belt Front Cover

Removal and Installation

CA16DE AND CA18DE ENGINES

1. Disconnect the negative battery cable.
2. Drain the cooling system.
3. Remove the upper radiator hose.
4. Remove the right side engine undercover.
5. Remove the power steering and air conditioning compressor drive belts.
6. Remove the water pump pulley.
7. Matchmark the crank angle sensor to the upper front cover and the remove it. Carefully position it aside.

8. Remove the upper front cover.

9. Align the timing marks on the camshaft pulley sprockets and then remove the crankshaft pulley.

NOTE: The crankshaft pulley may be reached by removing the side cover from inside the right hand wheel opening.

10. Remove the lower front cover.

To install:

11. Install the lower front cover with a new gasket.

12. Install the crankshaft pulley with its washer. Torque the pulley bolt to 105–112 ft. lbs. (145–152 Nm).

13. Install the crank angle sensor so the matchmarks made previously line up and tighten the bolts to 5.1–5.8 ft. lbs. (7–8 Nm).

14. Install the water pump pulley.

15. Install the power steering pump and air conditioning compressor drive belts. Adjust the belt tension.

16. Install the right side undercover.

17. Install the upper radiator hose.

18. Fill the cooling system to the proper level.

19. Connect the negative battery cable.

CA18ET AND CA20E ENGINES

1. Disconnect the negative battery cable.

2. On 200SX: disconnect the air intake duct (CA20E), remove the cooling fan and radiator shroud and remove the exhaust side spark plugs.

3. On Stanza: raise and support the front of the vehicle safely, remove the right front wheel, remove the exhaust side spark plugs and remove the dust cover and undercover.

4. Remove the alternator drive belt.

5. Remove the air conditioner compressor drive belt.

6. Remove the crankshaft pulley.

7. Remove the crankshaft damper.

8. Remove the water pump pulley.

9. Remove the upper and lower timing belt covers and gaskets. If the gaskets are in good condition after removal, they can be reused. If they are in way damaged or broken, replace them.

To install:

10. Install timing belt cover with new gaskets, as required. Torque the front cover bolts evenly to 2.2–3.6 ft. lbs. (3–5 Nm).

11. Install the water pump pulley. Torque the pulley bolts to 4–7 ft. lbs. (6–10 Nm).

12. Install the crankshaft damper. Torque the bolts to 90–98 ft. lbs. (123–132 Nm).

13. Install the crankshaft pulley. Torque the pulley bolts to 9–10 ft. lbs. 12–14 Nm).

14. Install the drive belts and adjust the drive belt tension.

15. On Stanza: install the undercover and dust cover, install the exhaust side spark plugs, mount the right front wheel and lower the vehicle.

16. On 200SX: install the exhaust side spark plugs, install the radiator shroud and cooling fan and connect the air intake duct (CA20E).

17. Connect the negative battery cable.

E16S AND E16I ENGINES

1. Disconnect the negative battery cable.

2. Drain the cooling system.

3. Remove the front right side splash cover.

4. Remove the front right side undercover.

5. Remove the air conditioning belt and alternator belt.

6. Remove the alternator.

7. Remove the power steering belt, if equipped.

8. Remove the water pump pulley.

9. Remove the crankshaft pulley.

NOTE: The crankshaft pulley is accessible after removing the side cover from the right side wheel house.

10. Loosen and remove the 8 Torx head bolts securing the timing covers and remove the upper and lower covers.

To install:

11. Install the upper and lower timing belt covers with new gaskets. Tighten the upper cover bolts to 4–5 ft. lbs. (7–8 Nm) and the lower cover bolts to 2–4 ft. lbs. (3–5 Nm).

12. Install the crankshaft pulley. Torque the pulley bolt to 80–94 ft. lbs. (108–127 Nm).

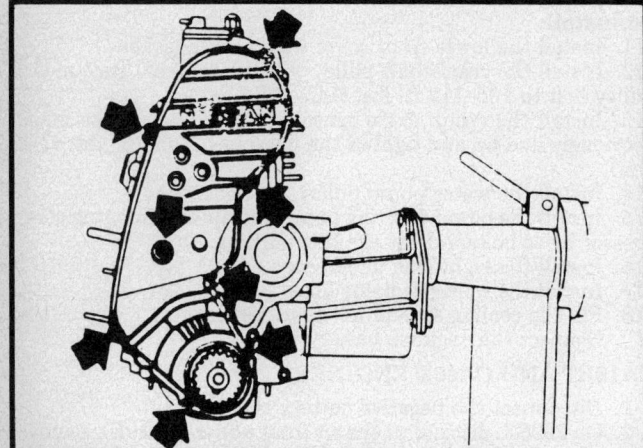

Front cover removal—E-Series engine

13. Install the water pump pulley. Torque the pulley bolts to 6–8 ft. lbs. (8–11 Nm).

14. Install the power steering belt.

15. Install the alternator.

16. Install the alternator and air conditioning belts.

17. Install the right side engine and splash covers.

18. Fill the cooling system to the proper level and adjust the drive belt tension.

19. Connect the negative battery cable.

VG30E AND VG30ET ENGINES (1987–89 300ZX)

1. Disconnect the negative battery cable.

2. Drain the cooling system.

3. Remove the engine undercovers.

4. Remove the radiator shroud and fan.

5. Remove the power steering, alternator and air conditioning compressor drive belts.

6. On 1987 vehicles, remove the upper and lower radiator hoses. On 1988–89 vehicles, remove the suction pipe bracket and disconnect the lower coolant hose from the suction pipe.

7. Remove compressor drive belt idler bracket.

8. Set No. 1 cylinder at TDC of the compression stroke.

9. Remove the crankshaft pulley.

10. Remove the front upper and lower belt covers and gaskets.

To install:

11. Install the upper and lower timing belt covers with new gaskets. Torque the covers bolts to 2–4 ft. lbs. (3–5 Nm).

12. Install the crankshaft pulley. Torque the pully bolt to 90–98 ft. lbs. (123–132 Nm).

13. Install the compressor drive belt idler bracket.

14. On 1988–89 vehicles, connect the lower coolant hose to the suction pipe and install the suction pipe bracket. On 1987 vehicles, install the upper and ower radiator hoses.

15. Install and tension the drive belts.

16. Install the radiator fan and shroud.

17. Install the engine undercovers.

18. Fill the cooling system to the proper level.

19. Connect the negative battery.

VG30DE AND VG30DETT ENGINES (1990–91 300ZX)

1. Disconnect the negative battery cable.

2. Remove the engine undercover.

3. Drain the cooling system.

4. Remove the radiator.

5. Remove the drive belts.

6. Remove the cooling fan and cooling fan coupling.

7. Remove the crankshaft pulley bolt.

8. Remove the starter and lock the flywheel ring gear using a suitable locking device. This is done to prevent the crankshaft gear from turning during removal and installation.

9. Remove the crankshaft pulley using a suitable puller.

10. Remove the water inlet and outlet housings.

11. Remove the timing belt covers and gaskets.

To install:

12. Install the timing belt covers with new gaskets. Torque the cover bolts to 2–4 ft. lbs. (3–5 Nm).

13. Install the water inlet and outlet housings with new gaskets.

14. Install the crankshaft pulley. Torque the pulley bolt to 159–174 ft. lbs. (21–235 Nm).

15. Remove the flywheel locking device and install the starter.

16. Install the cooling fan and cooling fan coupling.

17. Install and tension the drive belts.

18. Install the radiator.

19. Fill the cooling system to the proper level.

20. Connect the negative battery cable.

VG30E ENGINE (MAXIMA)

1. Disconnect the negative battery cable.

2. Raise and support the front of the vehicle safely.

3. Remove the engine undercovers.

4. Drain the cooling system.
5. Remove the right front wheel.
6. Remove the engine side cover.
7. On 1987–88 vehicles, remove the engine coolant reservoir tank, radiator hoses and the Automatic Speed Control Device (ASCD) actuator; remove the lower coolant hose support bracket and disconnect the lower hose from the suction pipe.
8. Remove the alternator, power steering and air conditioning compressor drive belts from the engine. When removing the power steering drive belt, loosen the idler pulley from the right side wheel housing.
9. On 1989–91 vehicles, remove the upper radiator and water inlet hoses; remove the water pump pulley.
10. Remove the idler bracket of the compressor drive belt.
11. Remove the crankshaft pulley with a suitable puller.
12. Remove the upper and lower timing belt covers and gaskets.

To install:

13. Install the upper and lower timing belt covers with new gaskets.
14. Install the crankshaft pulley. Torque the pulley bolt to 90–98 ft. lbs. (123–132 Nm).
15. Install the compressor drive belt idler bracket.
16. On 1989–91 vehicles, install the water pump pulley and torque the nuts to 12–15 ft. lbs. (16–21 Nm); install the upper radiator and water inlet hoses.
17. Install the drive belts.
18. On 1987–88 vehicles, connect the lower coolant hose to the suction pipe and install the hose support bracket; install the Automatic Speed Control Device (ASCD) actuator, radiator hoses and engine coolant reservoir tank.
19. Install the engine side cover.
20. Mount the front right wheel.
21. Install the engine undercovers.
22. Lower the vehicle.
23. Fill the cooling system and connect the negative battery cable.

Oil Seal Replacement

EXCEPT 300ZX

1. Disconnect the negative battery cable.
2. Remove the crankshaft pulley.
3. Using a suitable tool, pry the oil seal from the front cover.

NOTE: When removing the oil seal, be careful not the gouge or scratch the seal bore or crankshaft surfaces.

4. Wipe the seal bore with a clean rag.
5. Lubricate the lip of the new seal with clean engine oil.
6. Install the seal into the front cover with a suitable seal installer.
7. Install the crankshaft pulley.
8. Connect the negative battery cable.

300ZX

1. Disconnect the negative battery cable.
2. Remove the timing belt.
3. Remove the crankshaft sprocket.
4. Remove the oil pan and oil pump.
5. Using a suitable tool, pry the oil seal from the front cover.

NOTE: When removing the oil seal, be careful not the gouge or scratch the seal bore or crankshaft surface.

6. Wipe the seal bore with a clean rag.
7. Lubricate the lip of the new seal with clean engine oil.
8. Install the seal into the front cover with a suitable seal installer.
9. Install the oil pump and oil pan.
10. Install the crankshaft sprocket.
11. Install the timing belt.
12. Connect the negative battery cable.

Timing Belt and Tensioner

Removal and Installation

CA16DE AND CA18DE ENGINES

1. Disconnect the negative battery cable.
2. Drain the cooling system.
3. Remove the upper radiator hose.
4. Remove the right side engine undercover.
5. Loosen the power steering pump and the air conditioning compressor and then remove the drive belts.
6. Remove the water pump pulley.
7. Matchmark the crank angle sensor to the upper front cover and the remove it. Carefully position it aside.
8. Remove the water pump pulley.
9. Position a floor jack under the engine and raise it just enough to support the engine.
10. Remove the upper engine mount bracket at the right side of the upper front cover.
11. Remove the upper front cover.
12. Align the timing marks on the camshaft pulley sprockets and then remove the crankshaft pulley.

NOTE: The crankshaft pulley may be reached by removing the side cover from inside the right hand wheel opening.

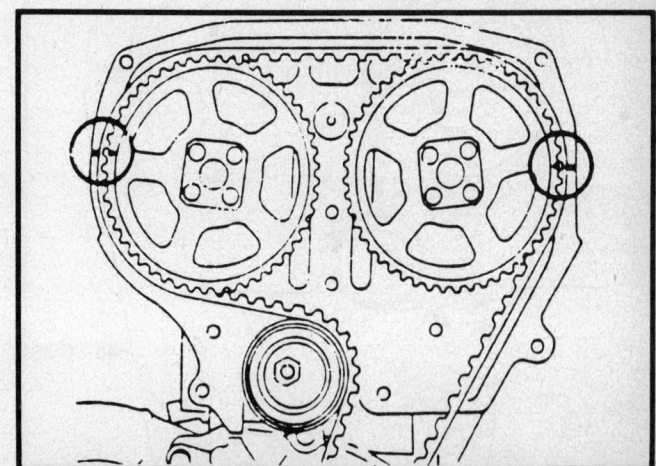

Camshaft timing pulley marks—CA16DE and CA18DE engines

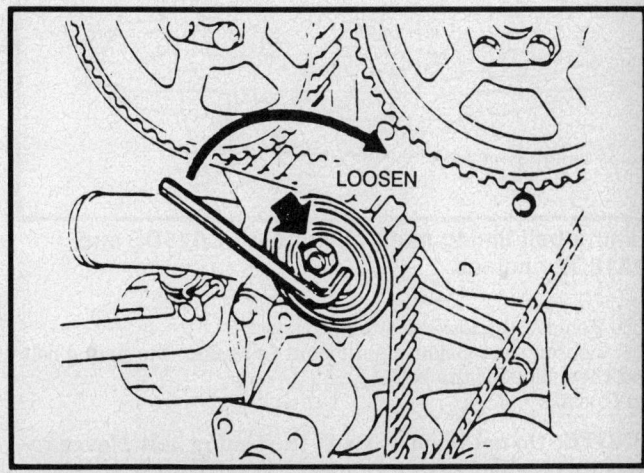

Loosen the tensioner pulley nut—CA16DE and CA18DE engines

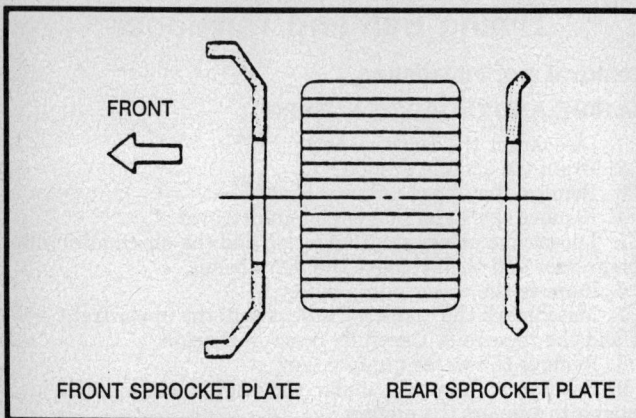

Crankshaft sprocket plate installation—CA16DE and CA18DE engines

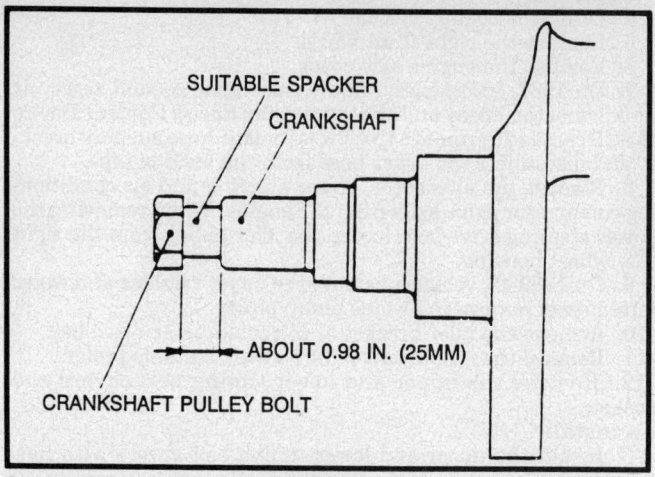

SUITABLE SPACKER
CRANKSHAFT
ABOUT 0.98 IN. (25MM)
CRANKSHAFT PULLEY BOLT

A spacer must be installed between the crankshaft and pulley bolt head before rotating the engine—CA16DE and CA18DE engines

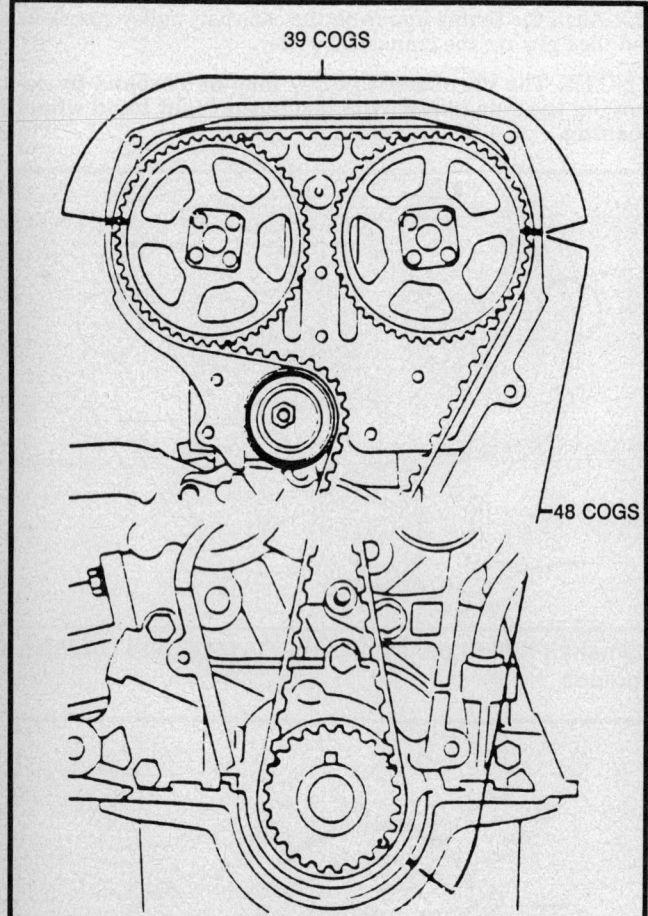

39 COGS

48 COGS

Timing belt timing mark alignment—CA16DE and CA18DE engines

13. Remove the lower front cover.
14. Loosen the tensioner pulley nut to slacken the timing belt and then slide off the belt.

To install:

NOTE: Do not bend or twist the timing belt. Never rotate the crankshaft and camshaft separately with the timing belt removed. Make sure the timing belt is free of any oil, water or debris.

15. Install the crankshaft sprocket with the sprocket plates.
16. Before installing the timing belt, ensure that the No. 1 piston is at TDC of the compression stroke. All sprocket timing marks should be aligned with the marks on the case.

NOTE: When the timing belt is on and in position, there should be 39 cogs between the timing mark on each of the camshaft sprocket and 48 cogs between the mark on the right camshaft sprocket and the mark on the crankshaft sprocket.

17. Loosen the timing belt tensioner pulley nut.
18. Temporarily install the crankshaft pulley bolt and then rotate the engine two complete revolutions.

NOTE: Fabricate and install a 0.98 in. (25mm) thick spacer between the end of the crankshaft and the head of the crankshaft pulley bolt to prevent bolt damage.

19. Tighten the tensioner pulley bolt to 16–22 ft. lbs. (22–29 Nm).
20. Install the upper and lower front covers with new gaskets.
21. Install the crankshaft pulley with its washer and tighten it to 105–112 ft. lbs. (145–152 Nm).
22. Install the engine mount bracket.
23. Install the water pump pulley. Install the crank angle sensor so the matchmarks made previously line up and tighten the bolts to 5.1–5.8 ft. lbs. (7–8 Nm).
24. Install the water pump pulley.
25. Installl the power steering pump and air conditioning compressor drive belts. Adjust the belt tension.
26. Install the right side undercover.
27. Install the upper radiator hose.
28. Fill the cooling system to the proper level.
29. Connect the negative battery cable.

CA18ET AND CA20E ENGINES

1. Disconnect the negative battery cable.
2. On 200SX, disconnect the air intake duct (CA20E); remove the cooling fan and radiator shroud; remove the exhaust side spark plugs.
3. On Stanza, raise and support the front of the vehicle safely. Remove the right front wheel. Remove the exhaust side spark plugs. Remove the dust cover and undercover.
4. Set the No. 1 piston at TDC of the compression stroke. The timing marks will all be aligned.
5. Remove the alternator drive belt.
6. Remove the air conditioner compressor drive belt.
7. Remove the crankshaft pulley.

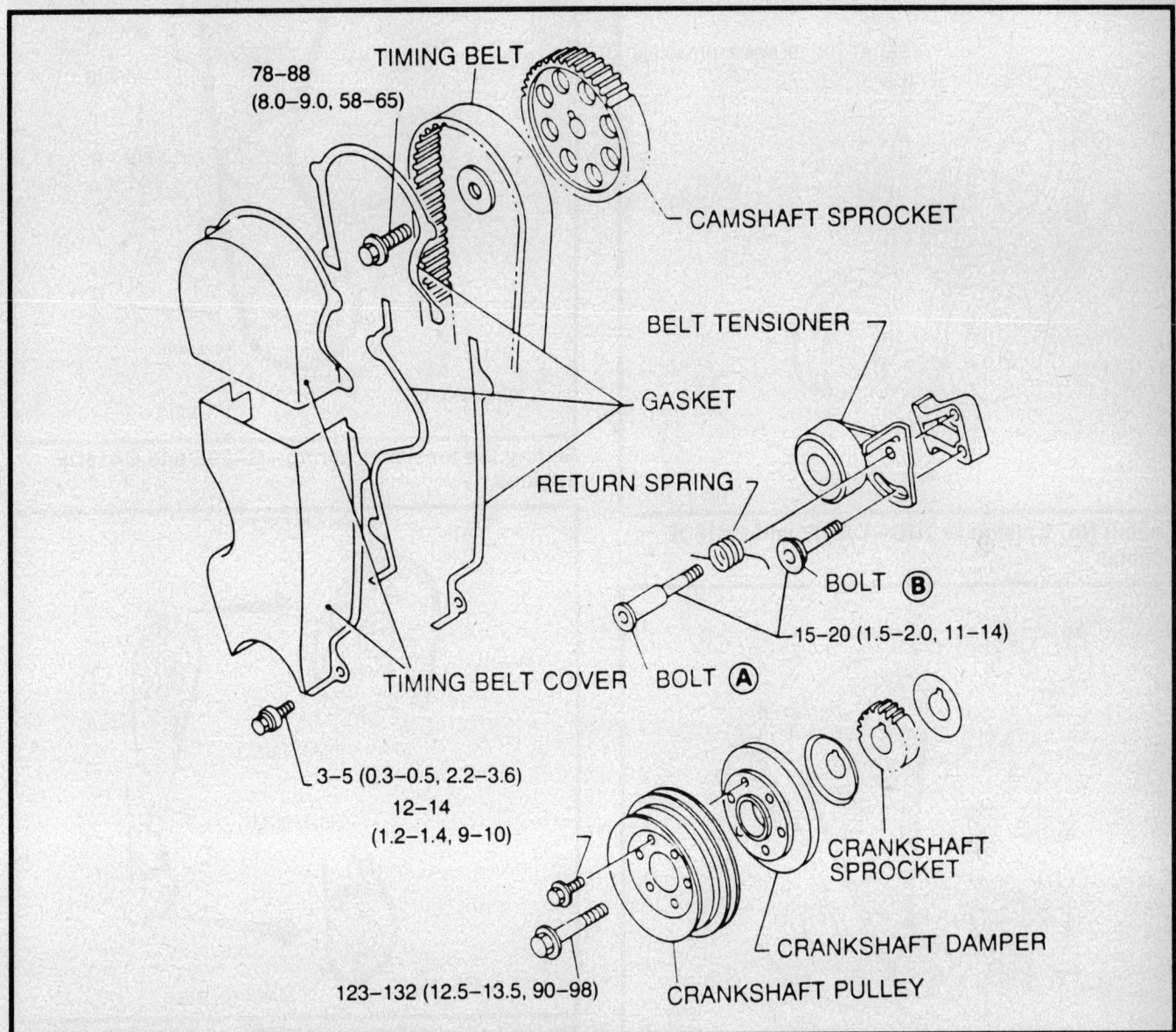

78–88
(8.0–9.0, 58–65)

TIMING BELT

CAMSHAFT SPROCKET

BELT TENSIONER

GASKET

RETURN SPRING

BOLT **B**

15–20 (1.5–2.0, 11–14)

TIMING BELT COVER BOLT **A**

3–5 (0.3–0.5, 2.2–3.6)

12–14
(1.2–1.4, 9–10)

CRANKSHAFT SPROCKET

CRANKSHAFT DAMPER

123–132 (12.5–13.5, 90–98) CRANKSHAFT PULLEY

Timng belt assembly—CA20E and CA18ET engines

8. Remove the crankshaft damper.
9. Remove the water pump pulley.
10. Remove the upper and lower timing belt covers and gaskets. If the gaskets are in good condition after removal, they can be reused; if they are in way damaged or broken, replace them.
11. Loosen the timing belt tensioner and return spring. Remove the timing belt.
12. Carefully inspect the condition of the timing belt. There should be no breaks or cracks anywhere on the belt. Be particularly careful when checking around the bottom of the cog teeth, where they the main belt; cracks often show up here first. Evidence of any wear or damage on the belt calls for replacement.
To install:
13. Check to make certain the No. 1 piston is still at TDC on the compression stroke.
14. Install the timing belt tensioner and return spring.

NOTE: If the coarse stud has been removed, apply Loctite® or another locking thread sealer to the stud threads prior to installation.

15. Make sure the tensioner mounting bolts are not securely tightened before installing the timing belt. The tensioner pulley should rotate smoothly.
16. Place the timing belt into position, aligning the lines on the belt with the punch marks on the camshaft and crankshaft pulleys. The arrow on the belt should be pointing toward the front belt covers.
17. Tighten the belt tensioner and assemble the spring. Hook one end of the spring around bolt **B** and then hook the other end over the tensioner bracket pawl. Rotate the crankshaft 2 complete revolutions clockwise, tighten bolt **B** and then bolt **A**.
18. Install timing belt cover with new gaskets, as required. Torque the front cover bolts evenly to 2.2–3.6 ft. lbs. (3–5 Nm).
19. Install the water pump pulley. Torque the pulley bolts to 4–7 ft. lbs. (6–10 Nm).
20. Install the crankshaft damper. Torque the bolts to 90–98 ft. lbs. (123–132 Nm).
21. Install the crankshaft pulley. Torque the pulley bolts to 9–10 ft. lbs. 12–14 Nm).
22. Install the drive belts and adjust the drive belt tension.

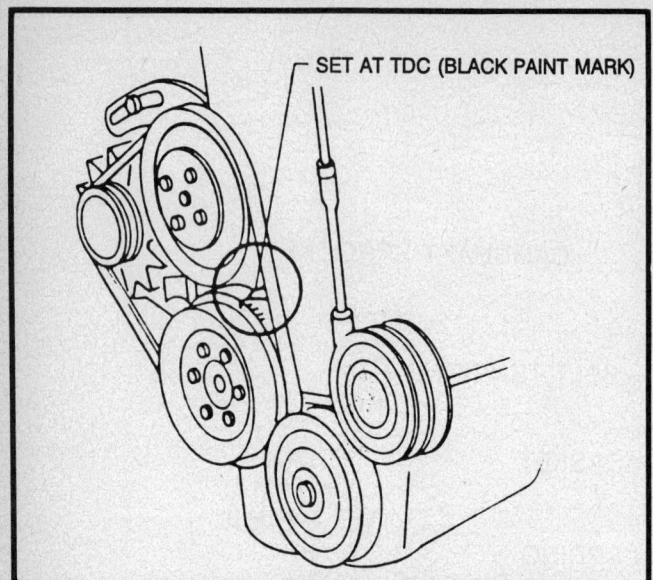

Setting No. 1 piston to TDC—CA20E and CA18DE engines

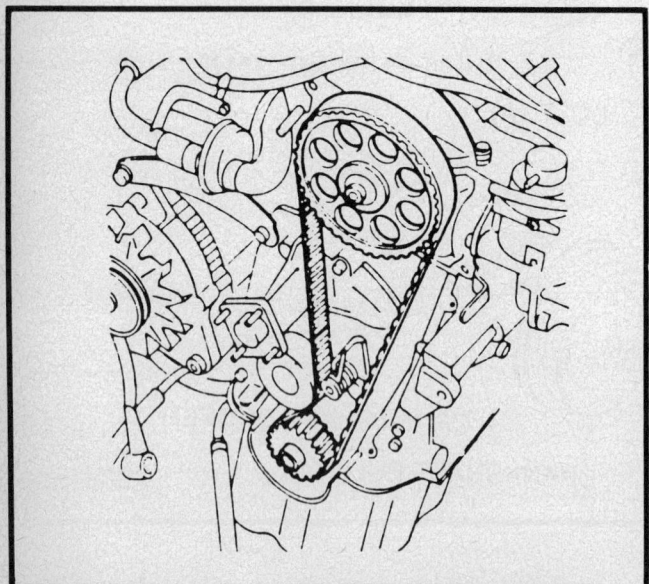

Timing belt with covers removed—CA20E and CA18DE engines

23. On Stanza, install the undercover and dust cover. Install the exhaust side spark plugs. Mount the right front wheel and lower the vehicle.
24. On 200SX, install the exhaust side spark plugs. Install the radiator shroud and cooling fan. Connect the air intake duct (CA20E).
25. Connect the negative battery cable.

E16S AND E16I ENGINES

1. Disconnect the negative battery cable.
2. Drain the cooling system.
3. Remove the front right side splash cover.
4. Remove the front right side undercover.
5. Remove the air conditioning belt and alternator belt.
6. Remove the power steering belt (if equipped).
7. Set the No. 1 piston to TDC of the compression stroke.

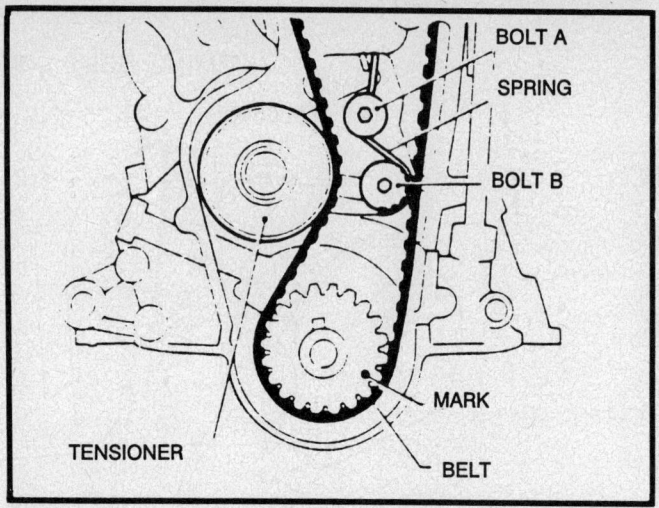

Setting the tensioner spring—CA20E and CA18DE engines

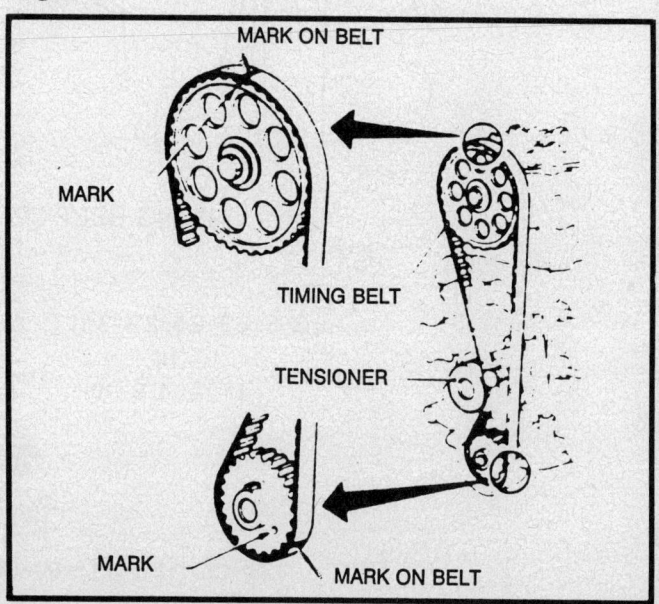

Timing belt installation—CA20E and CA18DE engines

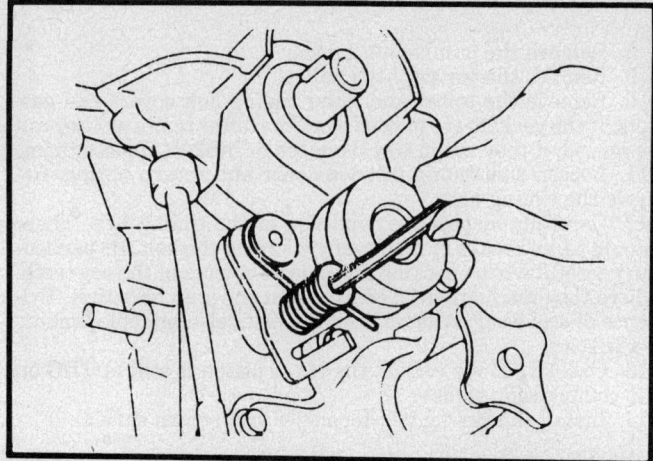

Installing the belt tensioner and return spring—CA20E and CA18DE engines

8. Remove the water pump pulley.
9. Remove the crankshaft pulley.

NOTE: The crankshaft pulley is accessible after removing the side cover from the right side wheel house.

10. Position a floor jack under the engine and raise it just enough to support the engine. Unbolt the right side engine mounting bracket from the block.
11. Loosen and remove the 8 Torx head bolts securing the timing covers and remove the upper and lower covers.
12. Mark the relationship of the camshaft sprocket to the timing belt and the crankshaft sprocket to the timing belt with paint or a grease pencil. This will make setting everything up during reassembly much easier if the engine is disturbed during disassembly.
13. Loosen the timing belt tensioner locknut and rotate the tensioner clockwise. Retighten the locknut.
14. Mark a rotational, direction arrow on the timing belt and then remove the belt.

NOTE: After removing the timing belt, do not rotate the crankshaft or camshaft separately or the valves will hit the pistons.

15. Remove the belt tensioner and its return spring.
To install:
16. Check that the timing marks on the camshaft sprocket and upper front cover and on the crankshaft sprocket and lower front cover are in alignment. This will ensure that the No. 1 piston is at TDC of its compression stroke.
17. Install the timing belt tensioner and return spring temporarily.
18. Rotate the tensioner about 70–80 degrees clockwise and then tighten the locknut.
19. Install the timing belt.
20. Loosen the tensioner locknut so the tensioner pushes on the timing belt and then turn the camshaft sprocket about 20 degrees clockwise (2 cogs).

NOTE: All spark plugs must be removed before turning the camshaft sprocket.

21. Prevent the the tensioner from spinning and tighten the locknut to 12–15 ft. lbs. (16–21 Nm).
22. Install the upper and lower timing belt covers with new gaskets. Tighten the upper cover bolts to 4–5 ft. lbs. (7–8 Nm) and the lower cover bolts to 2–4 ft. lbs. (3–5 Nm).
23. Attach the right side engine mounting bracket.
24. Install the crankshaft pulley. Torque the pulley bolt to 80–94 ft. lbs. (108–127 Nm).
25. Install the water pump pulley. Torque the pulley bolts to 6–8 ft. lbs. (8–11 Nm).
26. Install the power steering belt.
27. Install the alternator and air conditioning belts.
28. Install the right side engine and splash covers.
29. Fill the cooling system to the proper level and adjust the drive belt tension.
30. Connect the negative battery cable.

VG30E AND VG30ET ENGINES (1987 300ZX)

1. Disconnect the negative battery cable. Raise and support the vehicle safely.
2. Drain the cooling system.
3. Remove the engine undercovers.
4. Remove the radiator shroud and fan.
5. Remove the drive belts.
6. Remove the upper and lower radiator hoses.
7. Set the No. 1 cylinder at TDC on the compression stroke.
8. Remove the compressor drive belt idler bracket.
9. Remove the crankshaft pulley.
10. Remove the front upper and lower belt covers.
11. Using chalk or paint, mark the relationship of the timing

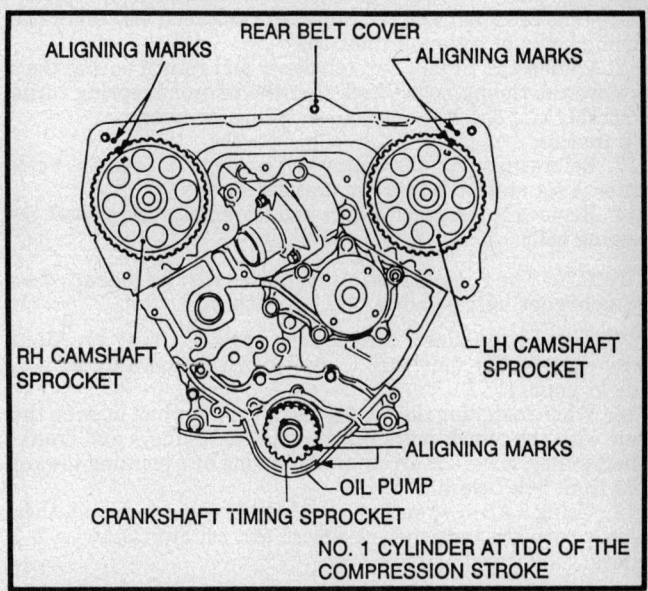

Camshaft and crankshaft pulley alignment marks— VG30E and VG30ET engines

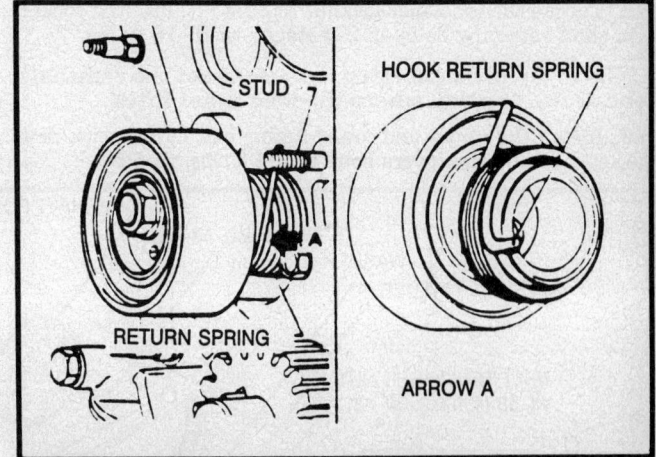

Tensioner and return spring installation—VG30E and VG30ET engines

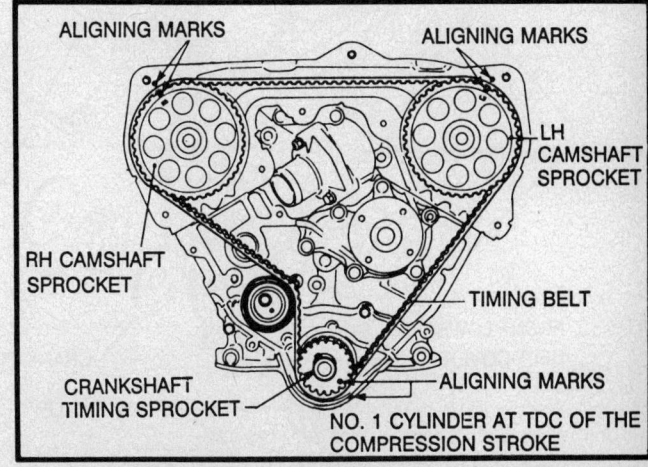

Timing belt installation and timing mark alignment— VG30E and VG30ET engines

belt to the camshaft and the camshaft sprockets; also mark the timing belt's direction of rotation.

12. Loosen the timing belt tensioner and return spring then remove the timing belt. Check that the tensioner spring turns smoothly and check the tensioner spring for wear.

To install:

13. Before installing the timing belt confirm that the No. 1 cylinder is set at TDC on its compression stroke.

14. Remove both rocker covers and loosen all rocker shaft retaining bolts.

NOTE: The rocker arm shaft bolts must be loosened so the correct belt tension can be obtained.

15. Install tensioner and return spring. Using an Allen wrench, turn the tensioner clockwise and temporarily tighten the locknut.

16. When installing the timing belt align the white lines on the belt with the punch mark on the camshaft pulleys and crankshaft pulley. Have the arrow on the timing belt pointing toward the front belt covers.

17. Using a Allen wrench, loosen the tensioner lock bolt, then slowly turn the tensioner clockwise and counterclockwise 2–3 times.

NOTE: If the coarse tensioner stud has been removed, be sure to apply locking sealer to the threads before installing it.

18. Torque the tensioner locknut to 32–43 ft. lbs., the rocker arm shaft retaining bolts, in 2–3 stages, to 13–16 ft. lbs.

NOTE: Before tightening, be sure to set the camshaft lobe at the position where the lobe is not lifted.

19. Install the upper and lower timing belt covers with new gaskets. Torque the covers bolts to 2–4 ft. lbs. (3–5 Nm).

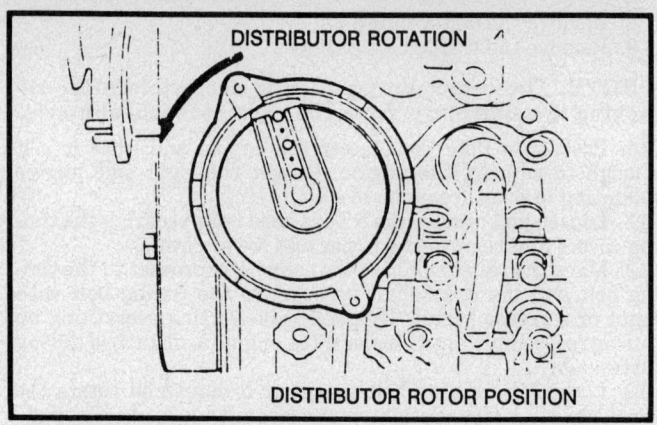

Distributor position when No. 1 piston is at TDC— VG30E and VG30ET engines

20. Install the crankshaft pulley. Torque the pulley bolt to 90–98 ft. lbs. (123–132 Nm).
21. Install the compressor drive belt idler bracket.
22. Install the upper and lower radiator hoses.
23. Install and tension the drive belts.
24. Install the radiator fan and shroud.
25. Install the engine undercovers.
26. Fill the cooling system to the proper level.
27. Connect the negative battery cable.

VG30E AND VG30ET ENGINES (1988–89 300ZX)

1. Disconnect the negative battery cable.
2. Drain the cooling system.
3. Remove the engine undercovers.

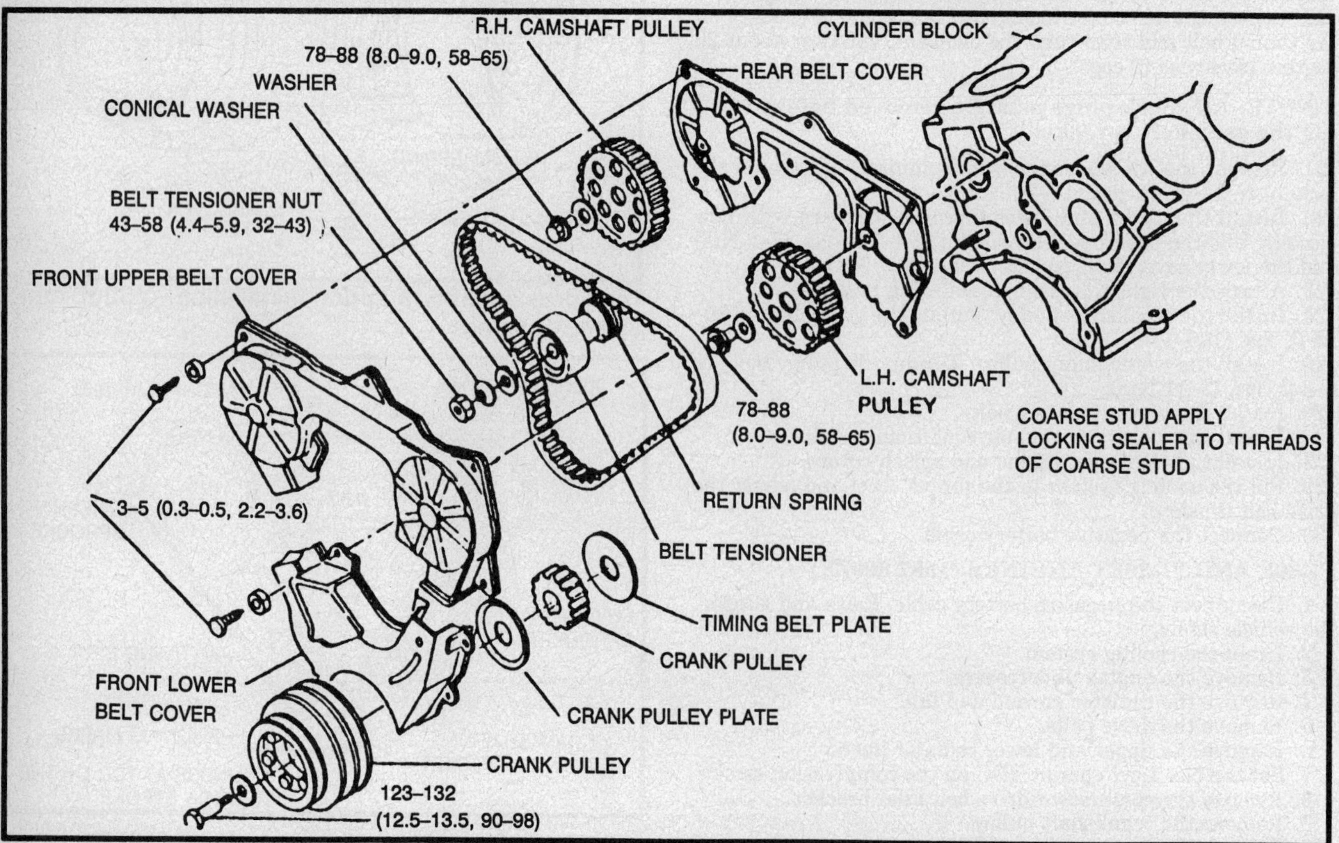

Timing belt assembly—VG30E and VG30ET engines

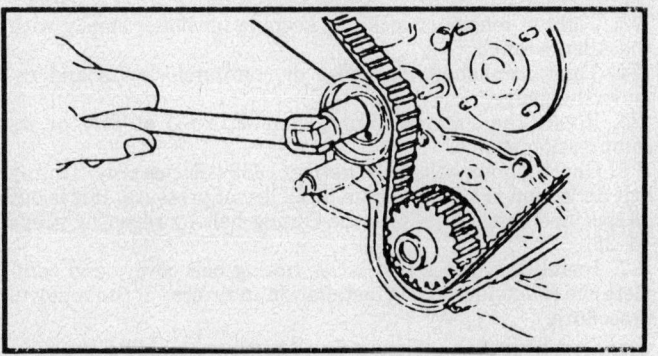

Loosening the timing belt tensioner—VG30E and VG30ET engines

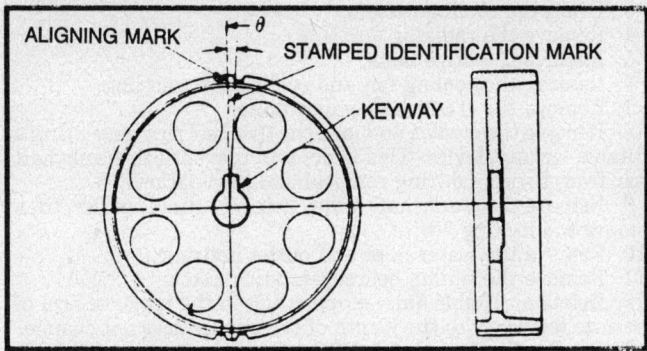

Camshaft pulley alignment marks—VG30E and VG30ET engines

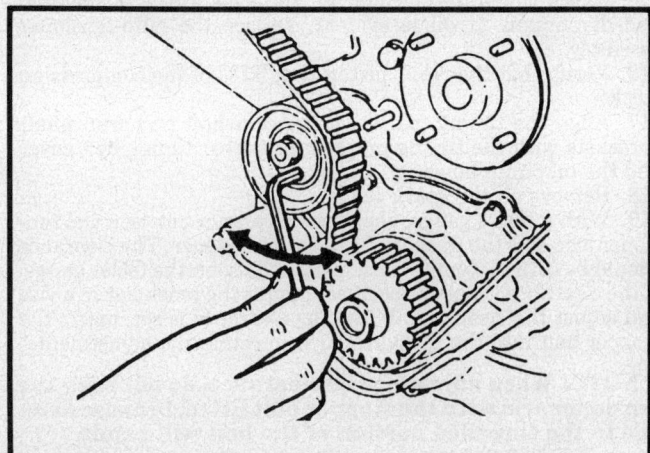

Tightening tensioner locknut—VG30E and VG30ET engines

4. Remove the radiator shroud and fan.
5. Remove the power steering, alternator and air conditioning compressor drive belts.
6. Remove the suction pipe bracket and disconnect the lower coolant hose from the suction pipe.
7. Remove the spark plugs.
8. Set No. 1 cylinder at TDC of the compression stroke.
9. Remove the compressor drive belt idler bracket.
10. Remove the crankshaft pulley.
11. Remove the front upper and lower belt covers and gaskets.
12. Using chalk or paint, mark the relationship of the timing belt to the camshaft and the camshaft sprockets. Also mark the timing belt's direction of rotation. Align the punch mark on the

left hand camshaft pulley with the mark on the upper rear timing belt cover. Align the punchmark on the crankshaft with the notch on the oil pump housing. Temporarily install the crankshaft pulley bolt to allow for crankshaft rotation.
13. Loosen the timing belt tensioner and return spring then remove the timing belt. Check that the tensioner spring turns smoothly and check the tensioner spring for wear.
To install:
14. Before installing the timing belt confirm that No. 1 cylinder is at TDC on its compression stroke. Install tensioner and tensioner spring. If stud is removed apply locking sealant to threads before installing.
15. Swing the tensioner fully clockwise with hexagon wrench and temporarily tighten locknut.
16. Point the arrow on the timing belt toward the front belt cover. Align the white lines on the timing belt with the punch marks on all 3 pulleys.

NOTE: There are 133 total timing belt teeth. If timing belt is installed correctly, there will be 40 teeth between left hand and right hand camshaft sprocket timing marks. There will be 43 teeth between left hand camshaft sprocket and crankshaft sprocket timing marks.

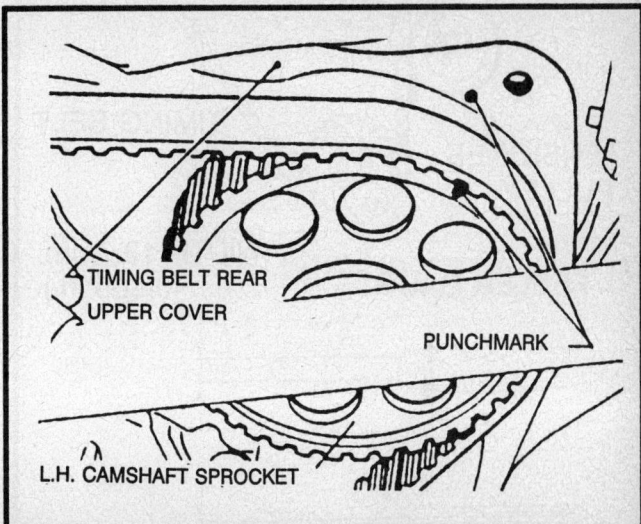

LH camshaft sprocket timing belt alignment marks—1988-91 VG30E and VG30ET engines

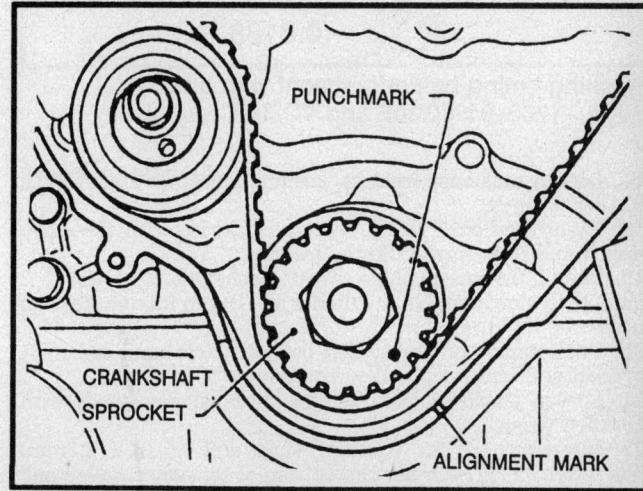

Crankshaft sprocket timing belt alignment marks—1988-91 VG30E and VG30ET engines

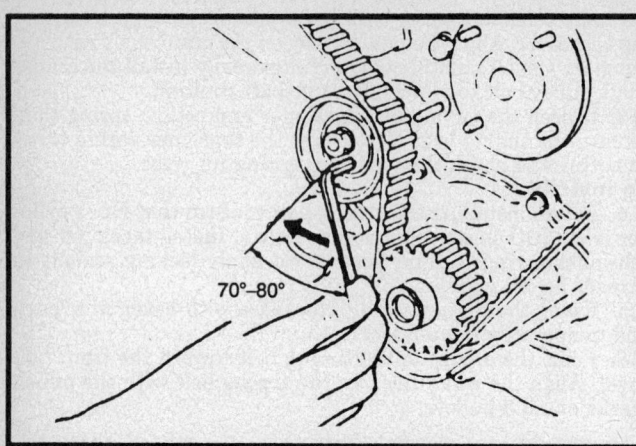

Swing the tensioner 70–80 degrees clockwise

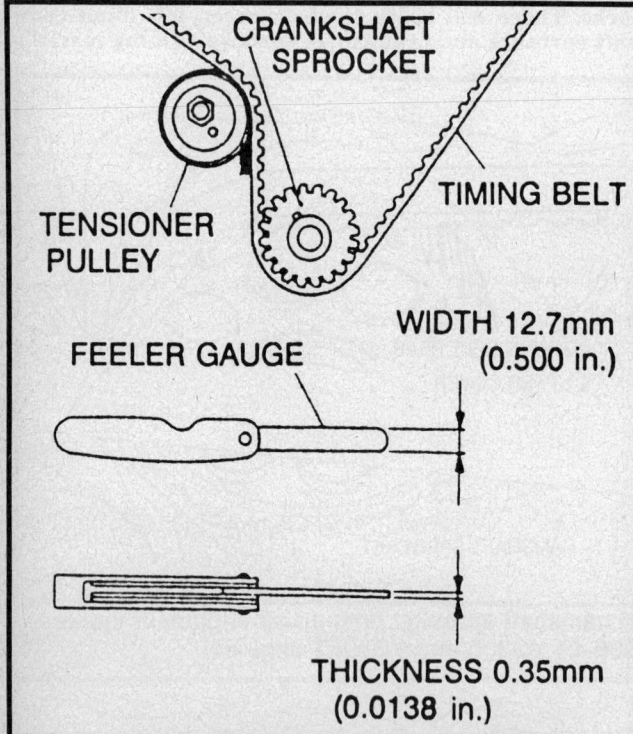

Checking timing belt adjustment with a feeler gauge—1988–91 VG30E and VG30ET engines

17. Loosen tensioner locknut, keeping tensioner steady with an Allen wrench.

18. Swing tensioner 70–80 degrees clockwise with the Allen wrench and temporarily tighten locknut.

19. Install the spark plugs. Turn crankshaft clockwise 2–3 times, then slowly set No. 1 cylinder at TDC on its compression stroke.

20. Push middle of timing belt between righthand camshaft sprocket and tensioner pulley with a force of 22 ft. lbs.

21. Loosen tensioner locknut, keeping tensioner steady with the Allen wrench.

22. Insert a 0.138 in. (0.35mm) thick and 0.5 in. (12.7mm) wide feeler gauge between the bottom of tensioner pulley and timing belt. Turn crankshaft clockwise and position gauge completely between tensioner pulley and timing belt. The timing belt will move about 2.5 teeth.

23. Tighten tensioner locknut, keeping tensioner steady with the Allen wrench.

24. Turn crankshaft clockwise or counterclockwise and remove the gauge.

25. Rotate the engine 3 times, then set No. 1 at TDC on its compression stroke.

26. Check timing belt deflection on 1988 vehicles only. Timing belt deflection is 13.0–14.5mm at 22 lbs. of pressure. If it is out of specified range, readjust the timing belt by repeatng Steps 14–25.

27. Install the upper and lower timing belt covers and complete the remainder of the installation in reverse of the removal procedure.

VG30DE AND VG30DETT ENGINES (1990–91 300ZX)

1. Disconnect the negative battery cable.
2. Remove the engine undercover.
3. Drain the cooling system.
4. Remove the radiator.
5. Remove the drive belts.
6. Remove the cooling fan and cooling fan coupling.
7. Remove the crankshaft pulley bolt.
8. Remove the starter and lock the flywheel ring gear using a suitable locking device. This is done to prevent the crankshaft gear from turning during removal and installation.
9. Remove the crankshaft pulley using a suitable puller, then remove the locking device.
10. Remove the water inlet and outlet housings.
11. Remove the timing belt covers and gaskets.
12. Install a suitable 6mm stopper bolt in the tenienr arm of the auto tensioner so the length of the pusher does not change.
13. Set the No. 1 piston at TDC of the compression stroke.
14. Remove the auto-tensioner and the timing belt.

To install:

15. Check the auto-tensioner for oil leaks in the pusher rod and diaphragm. If oil is evident, replace the auto-tensioner assembly.

16. Verify that the No. 1 piston is at TDC of the compression stroke.

17. Align the timing marks on the camshaft and crankshaft sprockets with the timing marks on the rear timing belt cover and the oil pump housing.

18. Remove all the spark plugs.

19. With a feeler gauge, check the clearance between the tensioner arm and the pusher of the auto-tensioner. The clearance should be 0.16 in. (4mm) with a slight drag on the feeler gauge. If the clearance is not as specified, mount the tensioner in a vise and adjust the clearance. When the clearance is set, insert the stopper bolt into the tensioner arm to retain the adjustment.

NOTE: When adjusting the clearance, do not push the tensioner arm with the stopper bolt fitted, because damage to the threaded portion of the bolt will result.

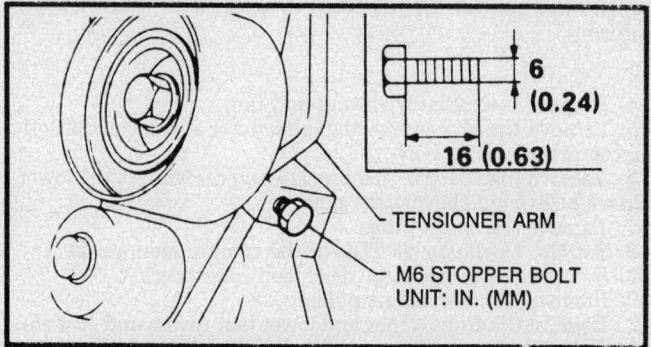

Installing suitable stopper bolt into auto-tensioner arm—VG30DE and VG30DETT engines

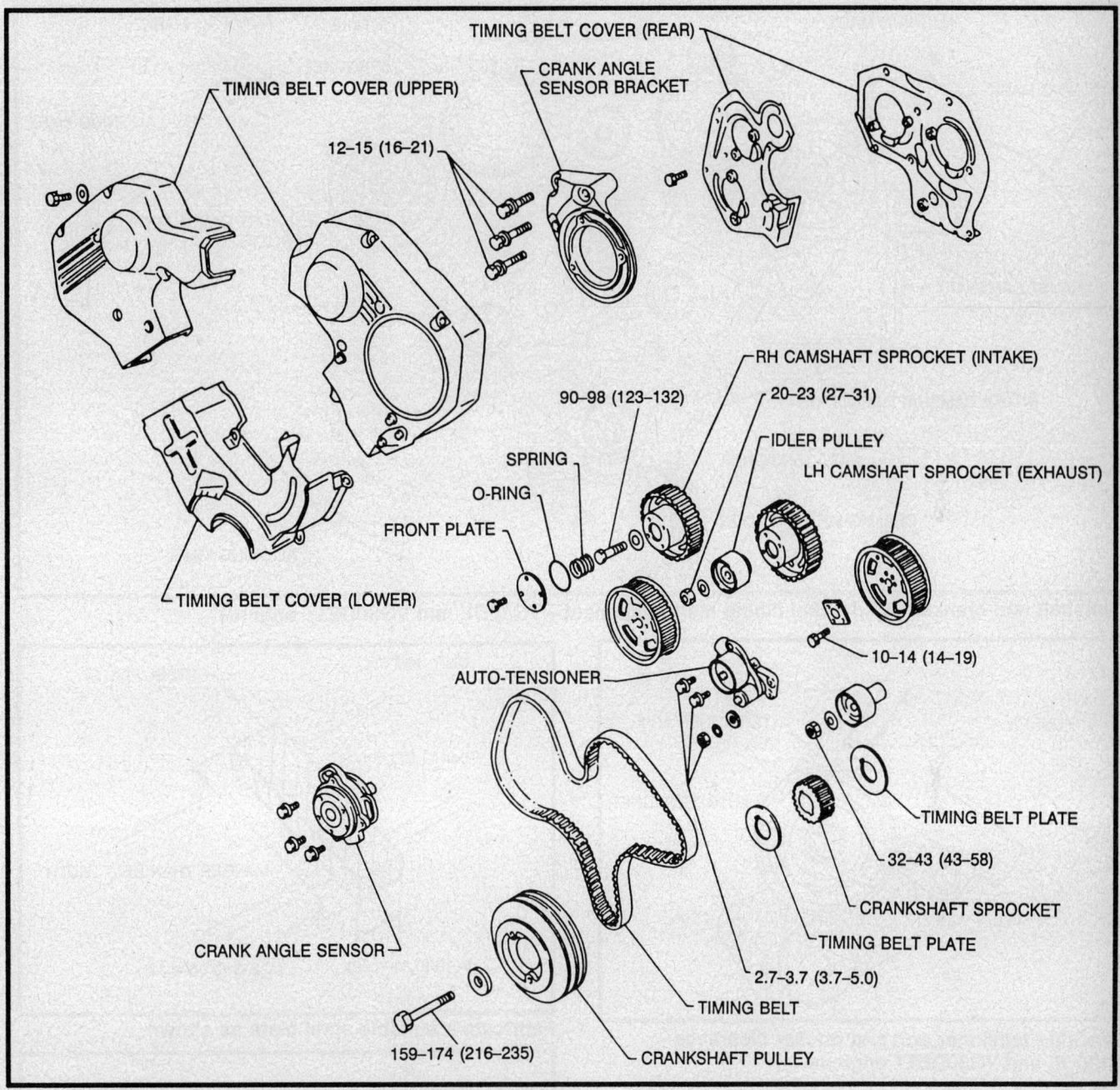

TIMING BELT COVER (REAR)

CRANK ANGLE SENSOR BRACKET

TIMING BELT COVER (UPPER)

12–15 (16–21)

90–98 (123–132)

SPRING

O-RING

FRONT PLATE

RH CAMSHAFT SPROCKET (INTAKE)

20–23 (27–31)

IDLER PULLEY

LH CAMSHAFT SPROCKET (EXHAUST)

TIMING BELT COVER (LOWER)

10–14 (14–19)

AUTO-TENSIONER

TIMING BELT PLATE

32–43 (43–58)

CRANKSHAFT SPROCKET

TIMING BELT PLATE

2.7–3.7 (3.7–5.0)

CRANK ANGLE SENSOR

TIMING BELT

159–174 (216–235)

CRANKSHAFT PULLEY

Timing belt assembly—VG30DE and VG30DETT engines

20. Mount the auto-tensioner and tighten nuts and bolts by hand.

21. Install the timing belt. Ensure the timing sprockets are free of oil and water. Do not bend or twist the timing belt. Align the white lines on the belt with the timing marks on the camshaft and crankshaft sprockets. Point the arrow on the belt towards the front.

22. Push the auto-tensioner slightly towards the timing belt to prevent the belt from slipping. At the same time, turn the crankshaft 10 degrees clockwise and torque the tensioner fasteners to 12–15 ft. lbs. (16–21 Nm).

NOTE: Do not push the tensioner too hard because it will create excessive tension on the belt.

23. Turn the crankshaft 120 degrees counterclockwise.

24. Turn the crankshaft clockwise and set the No. 1 piston at TDC of the compression stroke.

25. Back off on the auto-tensioner fasteners ½ turn.

26. Using push-pull gauge No. EG1486000 (J–38387) or equivalent, apply approximately 15.2–18.3 lbs. (67.7–81.4 N) of force to the tensioner.

27. Turn the crankshaft 120 degrees clockwise.

28. Turn the crankshaft counterclockwise and set the No. 1 piston at TDC of the compression stroke.

29. Fabricate a 0.35 in. (9mm) wide x 0.10 in. (2mm) deep steel plate. The length of the plate should be slightly longer than the width of the belt.

30. Set the steel plate at positions **A, B, C** and **D** of the timing

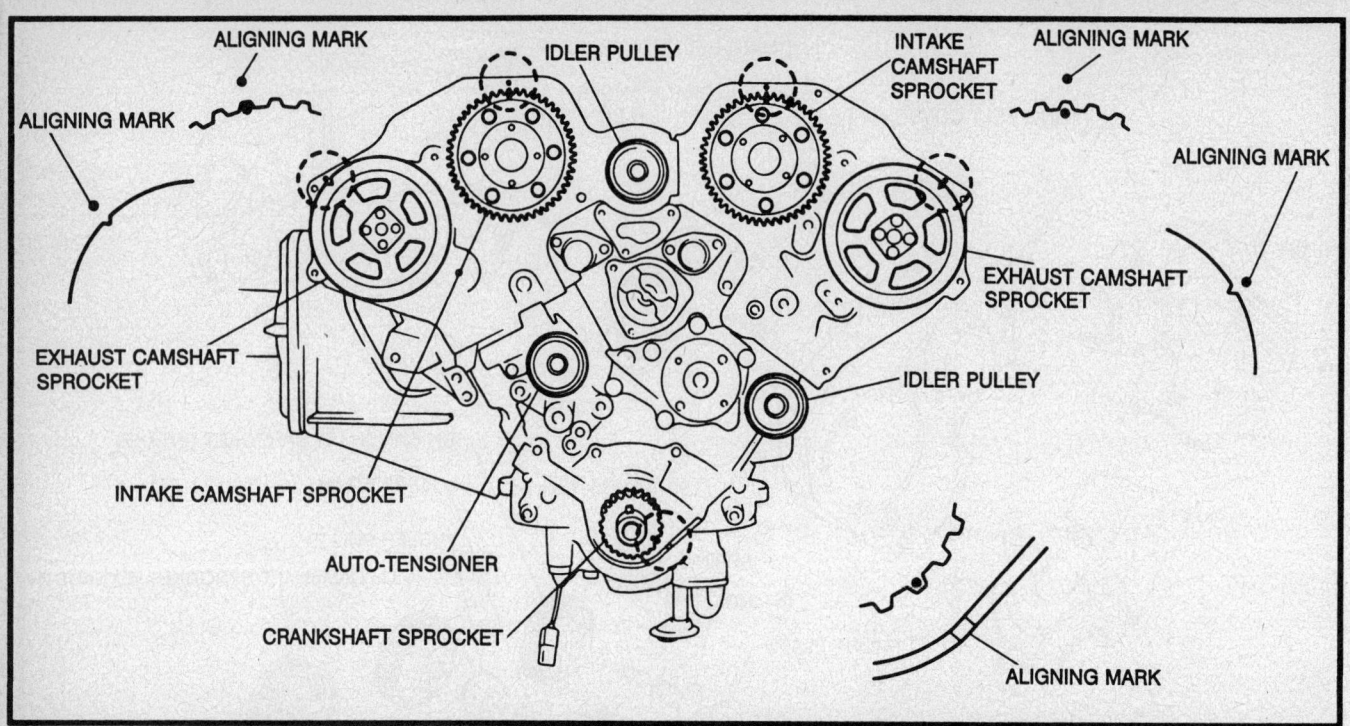

Camshaft and crankshaft sprocket timing mark alignment—VG30DE and VG30DETT engines

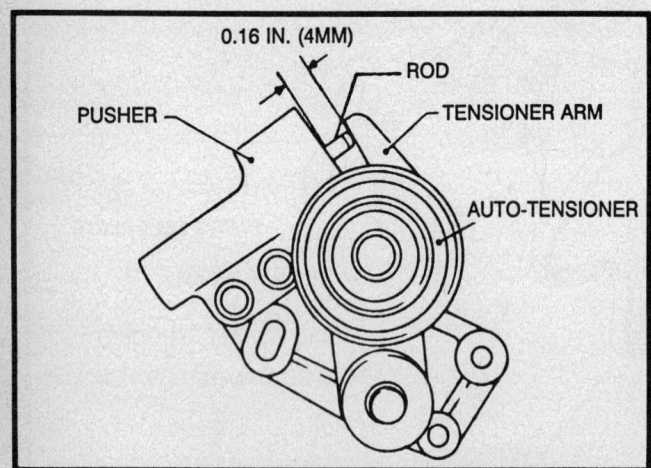

Checking tensioner arm and pusher clearance—VG30DE and VG30DETT engines

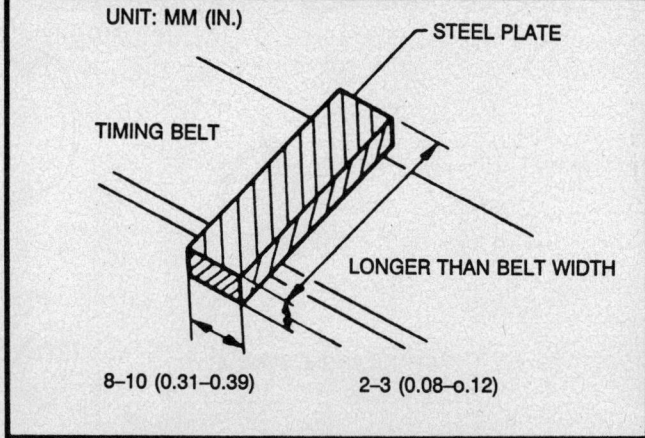

Fabricate a suitable steel plate as shown

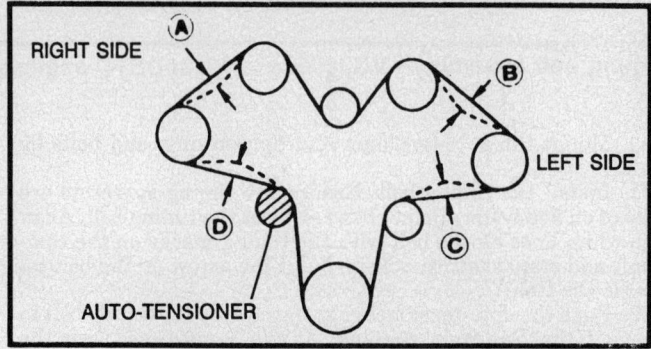

Set the steel plate at each position on the belt

belt mid-way between the pulleys as shown. Using the push-pull gauge or equivalent, apply approximately 11 lbs. (49 N) of force to the tensioner and check (and record) the belt deflection at each position with the steel plate in place. The timing belt deflection at each position should be 0.217–0.256 in. (5.5–6.5mm). Another means of determining the belt deflection is to add all deflection readings and divide them by 4. This average deflection should be 0.217–0.256 in. (5.5–6.5mm).

31. If the belt deflection is not as specified, repeat Steps 22–30 until the belt deflection is correct.

32. Once the belt is properly tensioned, torque the auto-tensioner fasteners to 12–15 ft. lbs. (16–21 Nm).

33. Remove the stopper bolt from the tensioner and wait 5 minutes. After 5 minutes, check the clearance between the tensioner arm and the pusher of the auto-tensioner. The clearance should remain at 0.138–0.205 in. (3.5–5.2mm).

34. Make sure the belt is installed and aligned properly on each pulley and timing sprocket. There must be no slippage or misalignment.

35. Install the timing belt covers with new gaskets. Torque the covers bolts to 2–4 ft. lbs. (3–5 Nm).

36. Install the water inlet and outlet housings with new gaskets.

37. Install the crankshaft pulley. Torque the pulley bolt to 159–174 ft. lbs. (21–235 Nm).

38. Remove the flywheel locking device and install the starter.

39. Install the cooling fan and cooling fan coupling.

40. Install and tension the drive belts.

41. Install the radiator.

42. Fill the cooling system to the proper level.

43. Connect the negative battery cable.

VG30E ENGINE (1987 MAXIMA)

1. Disconnect the negative battery cable.

2. Raise and support the front of the vehicle safely.

3. Remove the engine undercovers.

4. Drain the cooling system.

5. Remove the front right side wheel.

6. Remove the engine side cover.

7. Remove the engine coolant reservoir tank, radiator hoses and the Automatic Speed Control Device (ASCD).

8. Remove the alternator, power steering and air conditioning compressor drive belts from the engine. When removing the power steering drive belt, loosen the idler pulley from the right side wheel housing.

9. Remove the spark plugs and set the No. 1 piston to TDC of the compression stroke.

10. Remove the idler bracket of the compressor drive belt.

11. Remove the crankshaft pulley with a suitable puller.

12. Remove the upper and lower timing belt covers and gaskets.

13. Rotate the engine with a socket wrench on the crankshaft pulley bolt to align the 2 sets of timing marks. The marks are on the camshaft pulleys and rear belt covers.

14. Remove the rocker arm covers.

15. Loosen the rocker shaft securing bolts so rockers will no longer bear on the cam lobes.

16. Use a hex wrench to turn the belt tensioner clockwise and tighten the tensioner locknut just enough to hold the tensioner in position. Then, remove the timing belt.

To install:

17. Install the new timing belt, aligning the arrow on the timing belt forward. Align the white lines on the timing belt with the punch marks on all 3 pulleys.

18. Loosen the tensioner locknut to allow spring tension to tension the belt. Then, using the hex wrench, turn the tensioner first clockwise, then counterclockwise in 3 cycles. This will seat the belt. Now, torque the tensioner locknut to 32–43 ft. lbs. (44–58 Nm).

19. Tighten rocker shaft bolts alternately in 3 stages. Before tightening each pair of bolts, turn the engine over so the affected rocker will not touch its cam lobe. Final torque is 13–16 ft. lbs. (18–22 Nm). Install the rocker covers with new gaskets.

20. Install lower and upper timing belt covers.

21. Install the crankshaft pulley. Torque the pulley bolt to 90–98 ft. lbs. (123–132 Nm).

22. Install the compressor drive belt idler bracket.

23. Install the drive belts.

24. Connect the lower coolant hose to the suction pipe and install the hose support bracket; install the Automatic Speed Control Device (ASCD) actuator, radiator hoses and engine coolant reservoir tank.

25. Install the engine side cover.

26. Mount the front right wheel.

27. Install the engine undercovers.

28. Lower the vehicle.

29. Fill the cooling system and connect the negative battery cable.

VG30E ENGINES (1988–91 MAXIMA)

1. Disconnect the negative battery cable.

2. Raise and support the front of the vehicle safely.

3. Remove the engine undercovers.

4. Drain the cooling system.

5. Remove the front right side wheel.

6. Remove the engine side cover.

7. On 1988 vehicles, remove the engine coolant reservoir tank, radiator hoses and the Automatic Speed Control Device (ASCD) actuator; remove the lower coolant hose support bracket and disconnect the lower hose from the suction pipe.

8. Remove the alternator, power steering and air conditioning compressor drive belts from the engine. When removing the power steering drive belt, loosen the idler pulley from the right side wheel housing.

9. On 1989–91 vehicles, remove the upper radiator and water inlet hoses; remove the water pump pulley.

10. Remove the idler bracket of the compressor drive belt.

11. Remove the crankshaft pulley with a suitable puller.

12. Remove the upper and lower timing belt covers and gaskets.

13. Rotate the engine with a socket wrench on the crankshaft pulley bolt to align the punch mark on the left hand camshaft pulley with the mark on the upper rear timing belt cover; align the punchmark on the crankshaft with the notch on the oil pump housing; temporarily install the crankshaft pulley bolt to allow for crankshaft rotation.

14. Use a hex wrench to turn the belt tensioner clockwise and tighten the tensioner locknut just enough to hold the tensioner in position. Then, remove the timing belt.

To install:

15. Before installing the timing belt confirm that No. 1 cylinder is at TDC on its compression stroke. Install tensioner and tensioner spring. If stud is removed apply locking sealant to threads before installing.

16. Swing tensioner fully clockwise with hexagon wrench and temporarily tighten locknut.

17. Point the arrow on the timing belt toward the front belt cover. Align the white lines on the timing belt with the punch marks on all 3 pulleys.

NOTE: There are 133 total timing belt teeth. If timing belt is installed correctly there will be 40 teeth between left hand and right hand camshaft sprocket timing marks. There will be 43 teeth between left hand camshaft sprocket and crankshaft sprocket timing marks.

18. Loosen tensioner locknut, keeping tensioner steady with a hexagon wrench.

19. Swing tensioner 70–80 degrees clockwise with hexagon wrench and temporarily tighten locknut.

20. Turn crankshaft clockwise 2–3 times, then slowly set No. 1 cylinder at TDC of the compression stroke.

21. Push middle of timing belt between righthand camshaft sprocket and tensioner pulley with a force of 22 lbs.

22. Loosen tensioner locknut, keeping tensioner steady with a hexagon wrench.

23. Insert a 0.138 in. (0.35mm) thick and 0.5 in. (12.7mm) wide feeler gauge between the bottom of tensioner pulley and timing belt. Turn crankshaft clockwise and position gauge completely between tensioner pulley and timing belt. The timing belt will move about 2.5 teeth.

24. Tighten tensioner locknut, keeping tensioner steady with a hexagon wrench.

25. Turn crankshaft clockwise or counterclockwise and remove the gauge.

26. Rotate the engine 3 times, then set No. 1 at TDC on its compression stroke.

27. Install the upper and lower timing belt covers with new gaskets.

28. Install the crankshaft pulley. Torque the pulley bolt to 90–98 ft. lbs. (123–132 Nm).
29. Install the compressor drive belt idler bracket.
30. On 1989–91 vehicles, install the water pump pulley and torque the nuts to 12–15 ft. lbs. (16–21 Nm). Install the upper radiator and water inlet hoses.
31. Install the drive belts.
32. On 1988 vehicles, connect the lower coolant hose to the suction pipe and install the hose support bracket; install the Automatic Speed Control Device (ASCD) actuator, radiator hoses and engine coolant reservoir tank.
33. Install the engine side cover.
34. Mount the front right wheel.
35. Install the engine undercovers.
36. Lower the vehicle.
37. Fill the cooling system and connect the negative battery cable.

Timing Sprockets

Removal and Installation

1. Disconect the negative battery cable.
2. Set the No. 1 piston to TDC of the compression stroke.
3. Remove the timing belt covers.
4. Remove the timing belt.
5. Using a suitable spanner wrench and a socket wrench, remove the camshaft pulley bolt and washer.
   a. On CA16DE and CA18DE engines, the sprocket is held to the end of the cmashaft by a plate with 4 bolts.
   b. On E16S and E16i engines, the camshaft and jackshaft sprockets are held in place by a plate and 3 bolts. Pull the camshaft sprocket(s) from the camshaft(s). Be careful not to lose the Woodruff®key.
   c. On 1990–91 300ZX, remove the front plate, O-ring and spring from the right (intake) camshaft to gain access to the sprocket bolt.
   d. On 1990–91 300ZX, the left camshaft sprocket is held in place by plate and 4 bolts.
6. Using a suitable puller, remove the crankshaft gear and timing belt plates from the crankshaft. Be careful not to gouge or scratch the surface of the crankshaft when removing the gear.
7. Inspect the timing gear teeth for wear and replace as necessary.
To install:
8. Install the crankshaft gear with new Woodruff®keys.
9. Install the camshaft sprockets. Torque the sprocket bolts to 58–65 ft. lbs. (78–88 Nm) on CA20E, CA18ET, VG30E and VG30ET engines; 90–98 ft. lbs. (123–132 Nm) for right (intake) and 10–14 ft. lbs. (14–19 Nm) for the left (exhaust) on 1990–91 300ZX; 10–14 ft. lbs. (14–19 Nm) on CA16DE and CA18DE engines; 7–9 ft. lbs. (9–12 Nm) on E16S and E16i engines.

NOTE: On VG30E and VG30ET engines, the right hand and left hand camshaft pulleys are different. Install them in their correct positions. The right hand pulley has an R3 identification mark and the left hand pulley has an L3.

10. Install the timing belt.
11. Install the timing belt covers.
12. Connect the negative battery cable.

Camshaft

Removal and Installation
CA16DE AND CA18DE ENGINES

1. Disconnect the negative battery cable and relieve the fuel system pressure.

2. Drain the cooling system and remove the air cleaner assembly.
3. Crank the engine until the No. 1 piston is at TDC on its compression stroke.
4. Remove the drive belts.
5. Remove the alternator.
6. Disconect the air duct at the throttle chamber.
7. Tag and disconnect all lines, hoses and wires which may interfere with removal of the cylinder.
8. Remove the ornament cover.
9. Disconnect the oxygen sensor wire.
10. Remove the 2 exhaust heat shield covers.
11. Unbolt the exhaust manifold and wire the entire assembly aside to gain removal clearance for the cylinder head.
12. Disconnect the EGR tube at the passage cover and then remove the passage cover and its gasket.
13. Disconnect and remove the crank angle sensor from the upper front cover.

NOTE: Put an aligning mark on crank angle sensor and timing belt cover.

14. Remove the support stay from under the intake manifold assembly.
15. Unbolt the intake manifold and remove it along with the collector and throttle chamber.
16. Disconnect and remove the fuel injectors as an assembly.

NOTE: Upper and lower front timing belt cover must be removed. Support engine under oil pan with floor jack or equivalent then remove the upper engine mount bracket at the right side of the front cover.

17. Remove the timing belt.
18. Remove the camshaft cover and remove the cylinder head.
19. Remove the breather separater.
20. While holding the camshaft sprockets, remove the 4 mounting bolts and then remove the sprockets themselves.
21. Remove the timing belt tensioner pulley. Remove the rear timing belt cover.
22. Loosen the camshaft bearing caps in several stages, in the correct order. Remove the bearing caps, but be sure to keep them in order.
23. Remove the front oil seals and then lift out the camshafts.
24. Check the camshaft runout, endplay, wear and journal clearance.
To install:
25. Position the camshafts in the cylinder head so the knock pin on each is on the outboard side.

NOTE: The exhaust side camshaft has splines to accept the crank angle sensor.

26. Position the camshaft bearing caps and finger-tighten them. Each cap has an ID mark (E1, E2, I1, I2 etc.) and a directional arrow stamped into its top surface.
27. Coat the new oil seal with engine oil (on the lip) and install it on each camshaft end.
28. Tighten the camshaft bearing cap bolts to 7–9 ft. lbs. (9–12 Nm) in the order shown.
29. Install the cylinder head and cover.
30. Install the rear timing cover and tighten the 4 bolts to 5–6 ft. lbs. (7–8 Nm).
31. Install the timing belt tensioner and tighten it to 16–22 ft. lbs. (22–29 Nm).
32. Install the camshaft sprockets and tighten the bolts to 10–14 ft. lbs. (14–19 Nm) while holding the camshaft in place.
33. Install the cylinder head and related components.
34. Fill the cooling system to the proper level and connect the negative battery cable.

CA18ET AND CA20E ENGINES

1. Disconnect the negative battery cable and relieve the fuel system pressure.

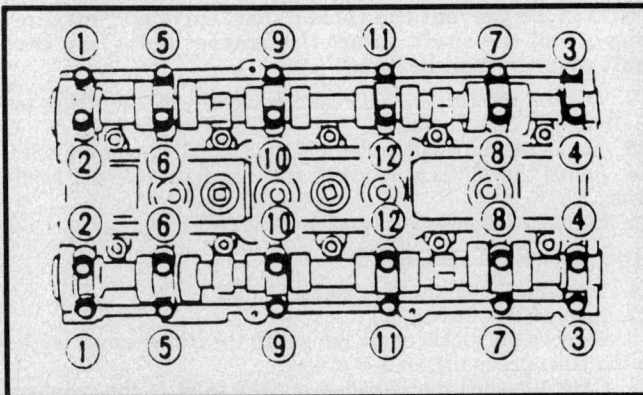

Loosen the camshaft bearing cap bolts in this order—CA16DE and CA18DE engines

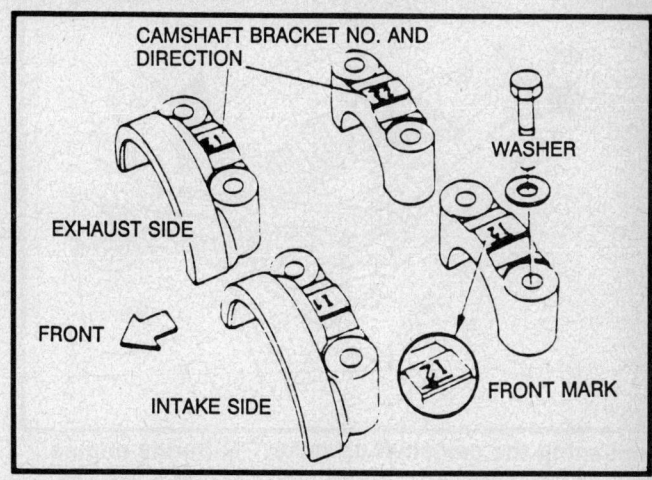

Camshaft bearing cap positioning—CA16DE and CA18DE engines

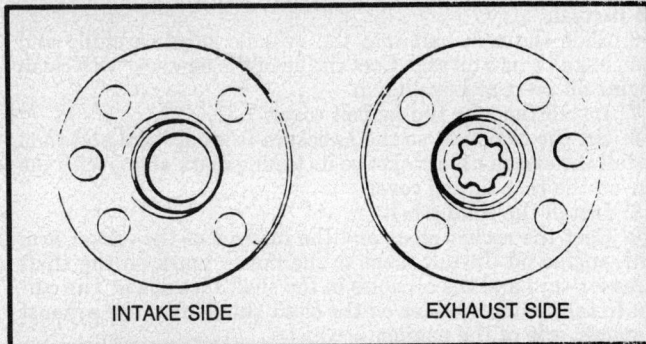

The exhaust side camshaft is splined—CA16DE and CA18DE engines

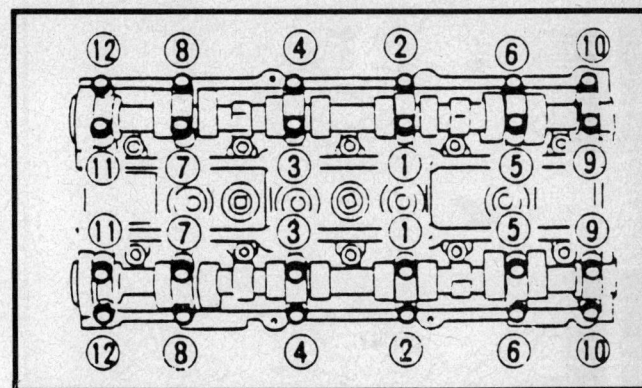

Tighten the camshaft bearing caps in this order—CA16DE and CA18DE engines

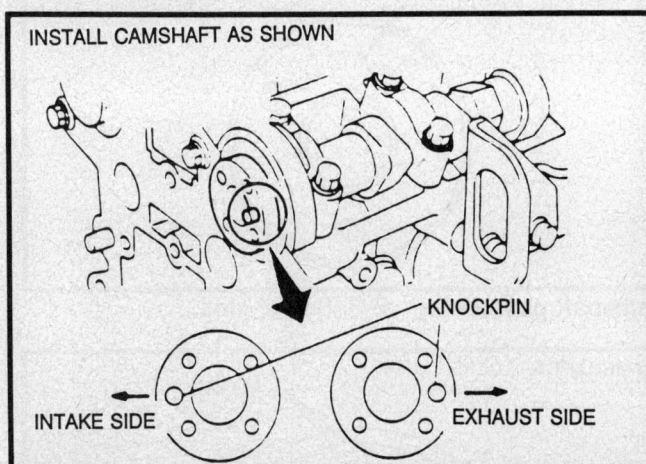

Install the camshaft as shown—CA16DE and CA18DE engines

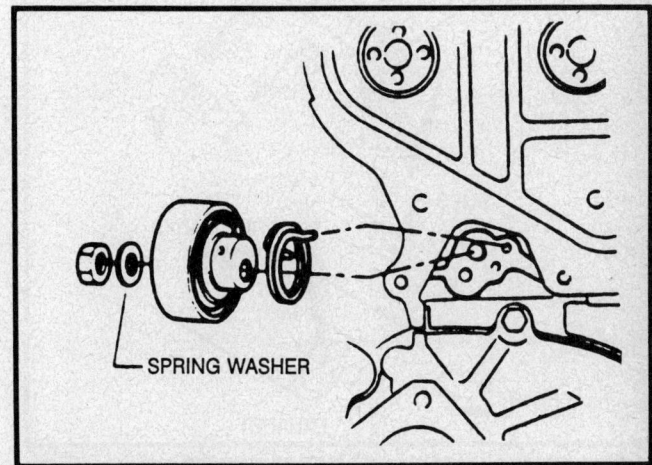

Timing belt tensioner installation—CA16DE and CA18DE engines

2. Set the No. 1 piston to TDC of the compression stroke.
3. Remove the timing belt.
4. Remove the valve rocker cover.
5. Fully loosen all rocker arm adjusting screws (the valve adjusting screws). Loosen the rocker shaft mounting bolts in 2–3 stages and then remove the rocker shafts as an assembly. Keep all components in the correct order for reassembly.
6. Hold the camshaft pulley and remove the pulley mounting bolt. Remove the pulley. Remove the camshaft thrust plate.
7. Carefully pry the camshaft oil seal out of the front of the cylinder head.

8. Slide the camshaft out the front of the cylinder head, taking extreme care not to score any of the journals.
To install:
9. Coat the camshaft with clean engine oil.
10. Carefully slide the camshaft into the cylinder head, coat the end with oil and install a new oil seal. Install the camshaft

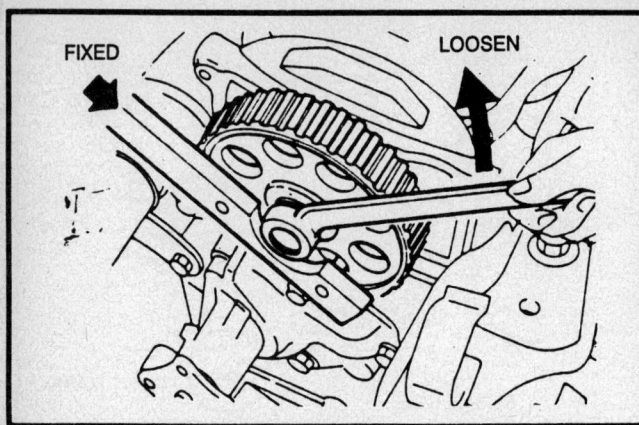

Loosening the camshaft sprocket—C-Series engine

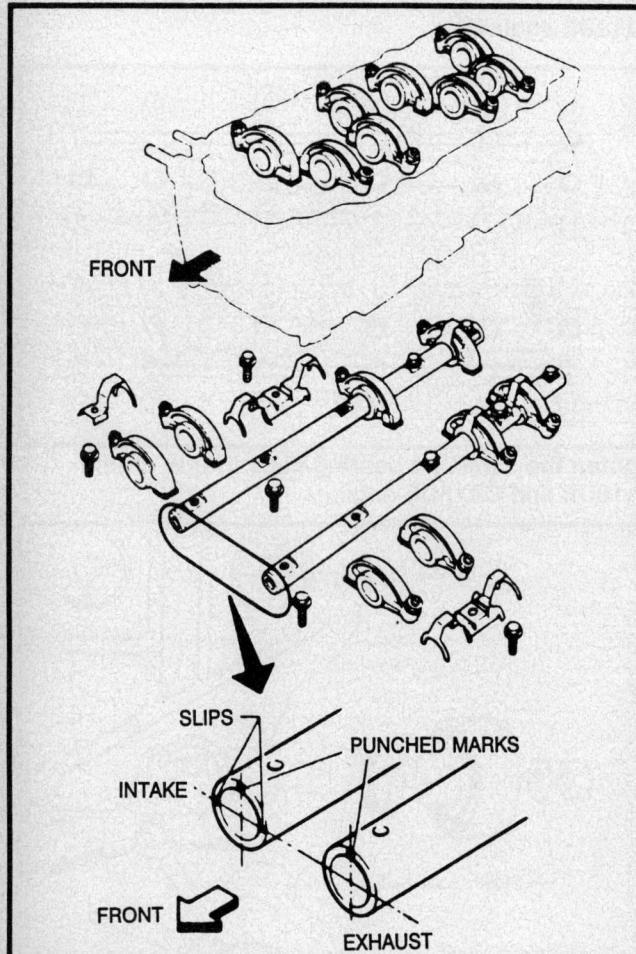

Rocker shaft assembly—C-Series engine

thrust plate and wedge the camshaft with a small wooden block inserted between one of the cams and the cylinder head. Torque the thrust plate bolt to 58–65 ft. lbs. (78–88 Nm). Remove the wooden block.

11. Lubricate the rocker shafts lightly with clean engine oil and install them, with the rocker arms, into the head. Both shafts have punch marks on their leading edges, while the intake shaft is also marked with 2 slits on its leading edge.

NOTE: To prevent the rocker shaft springs from slipping out of the shaft, insert the bracket bolts into the shaft prior to installation.

12. Tighten the rocker shaft bolts gradually, in 2–3 stages to 13–16 ft. lbs. (18–22 Nm).
13. Install the camshaft pulley and then install the timing belt.
14. Adjust the valves as required and install the cylinder head cover.
15. Connect the negative battery cable.

E16S AND E16I ENGINES

1. Disconnect the negative battery cable.
2. Remove the timing belt.
3. Remove the rocker shaft along with the rocker arms. Loosen the bolts gradually, in 2–3 stages.
4. Carefully slide the camshaft out the front of the cylinder head.
5. Check the camshaft runout, endplay, wear and journal clearance.

To install:

6. Slide the camshaft into the cylinder head carefully and then install a new oil seal. Coat the lip of the new seal with clean engine oil prior to installation.
7. Install the rear timing belt cover.
8. Set the camshaft so the knockpin faces upward and then install the camshaft sprocket so its timing mark aligns with the one on the rear timing cover.
9. Install the timing belt.
10. Coat the rocker shaft and the interior of the rocker arm with engine oil. Install them so the punch mark on the shaft faces forward and the oil holes in the shaft face down. The cutout in the center retainer on the shaft should face the exhaust manifold side of the engine.

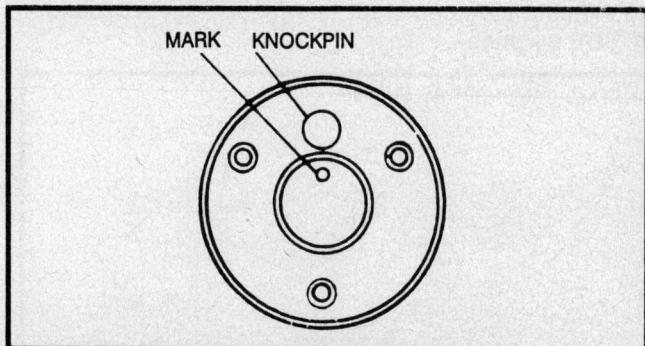

Camshaft positioning—E-Series engine

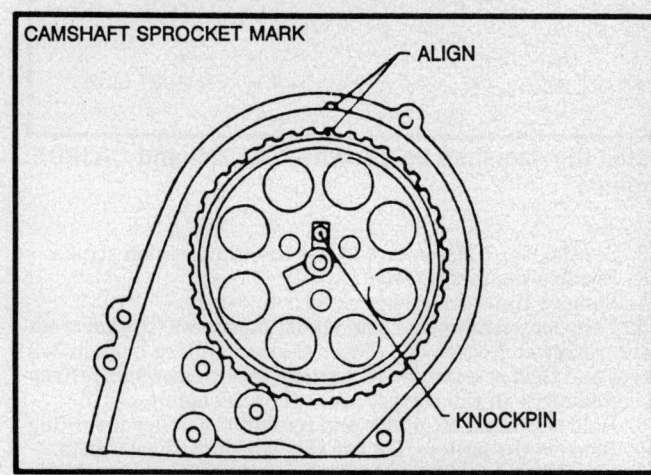

Camshaft sprocket alignment—E-Series engine

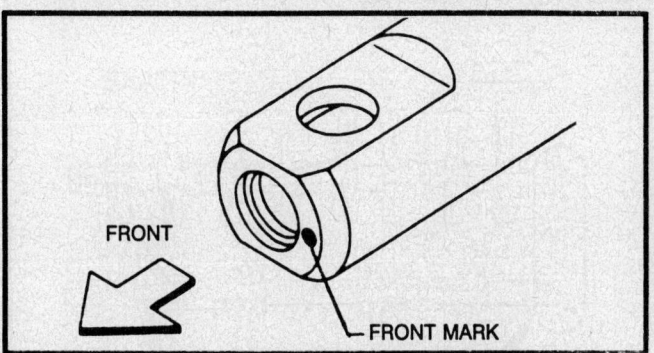

The punch mark on the rocker shaft should face forward—E-Series engine

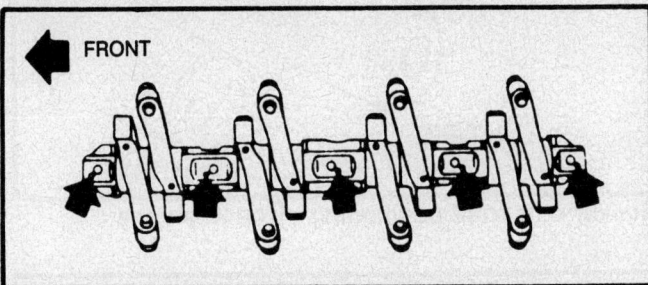

The oil holes must be facing down—E-Series engine

The center retainer cut-out should face the exhaust manifold—E-Series engine

11. Make sure the valve adjusting screws are loose and then tighten the shaft bolts to 13–15 ft. lbs. (18–21 Nm) in several stages, from the center out. The first and last mounting bolts should have a new bolt stopper installed.

12. Adjust the valves and connect the negative battery cable.

GA16I ENGINE

1. Disconnect the negative battery cable.
2. Remove the timing chain.
3. Remove the cylinder head with manifolds attached.
4. Remove the intake and exhaust manifolds from the cylinder head. Loosen the bolts in 2–3 stages in the proper sequence.
5. Loosen the rocker arm shaft bolts in 2–3 stages and lift the rocker arm/shaft assembly from the cylinder head. The rocker arm shaft is marked with an **F** to indicate that it faces towards the front of the engine. Place a similar mark on the cylinder head for your own reference.
6. Loosen the thrust plate retaining bolt.
7. Withdraw the camshaft and the thrust plate from the front of the cylinder head. The thrust plate is located to the camshaft with a key. Retain this key.

Rocker arm/shaft positioning and identification—GA16i engine

To install:

8. Clean all cylinder head, intake and exhaust manifold gasket surfaces. Lubricate the camshaft and rocker arm/shaft assemblies with a liberal coating of clean engine oil. Then, slide the camshaft and thrust plate into the front of the cylinder head. Don't forget to install the thrust plate key.

9. Install the rocker shafts and rocker arms making sure the **F** on the rocker shaft points toward the front of the engine. Install the rocker shaft retaining bolts, spring clips and washers. The center spring clip has a recess cut into one side. When in-

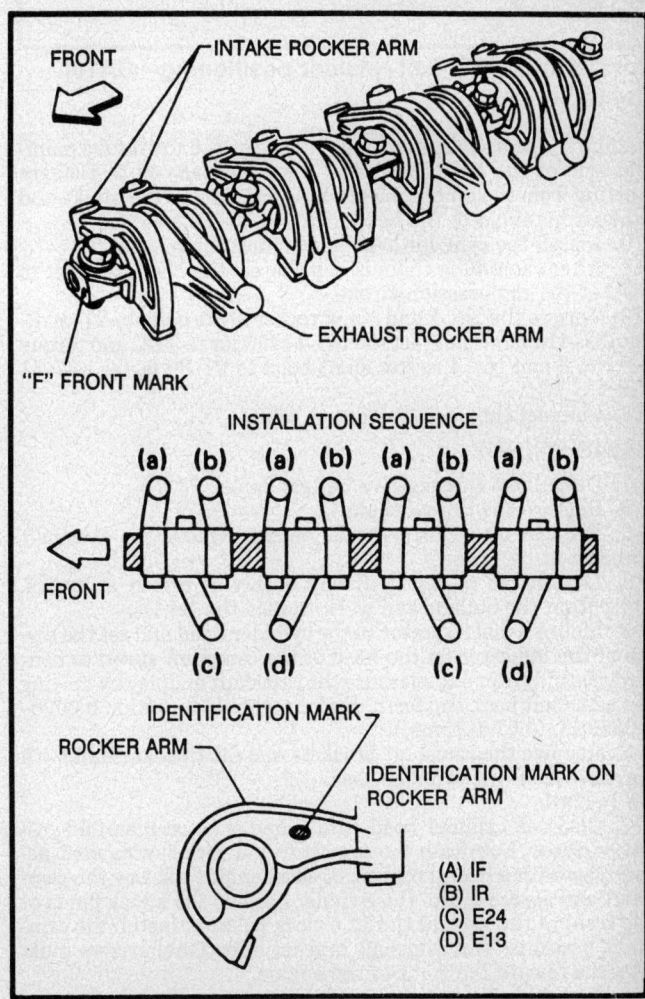

Rocker arm shaft identification—GA16i engine

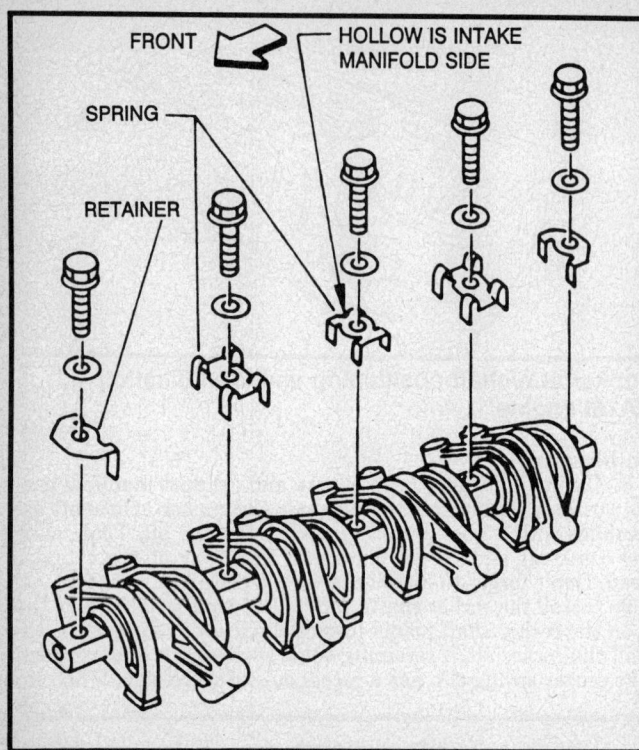

Rocker arm shaft bolt retainer positioning—GA16i engine

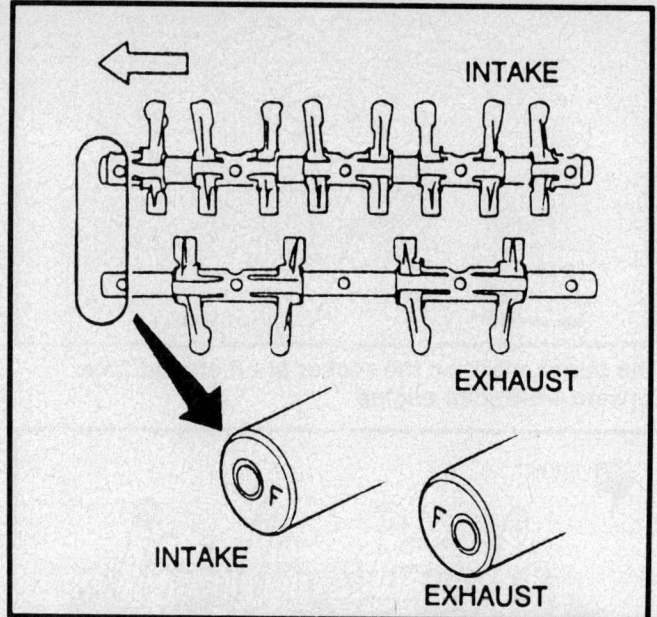

Rocker arm shaft positioning—KA24E engine

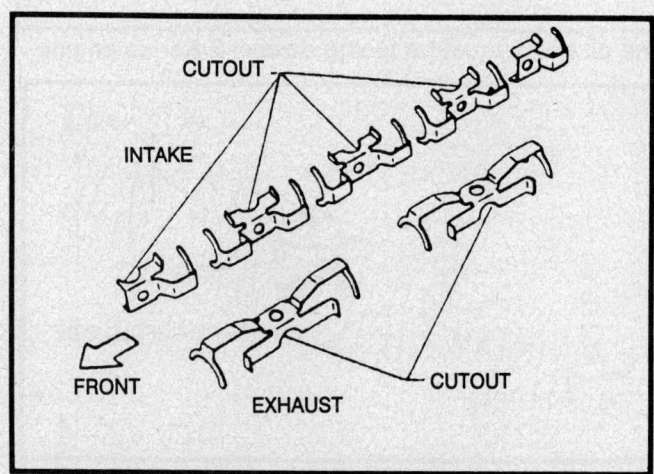

Spring clip installation—KA24E engine

stalling the center clip point this recess toward the intake manifold side of the head. Snug the bolts gradually in 2–3 stages starting from the center and working out. Attach the intake and exhaust manifold to the head with new gaskets.

10. Install the cylinder head and timing chain.

11. After the timing chain is in place, set the No. 1 cylinder to TDC of the compression stroke.

12. Torque the No. 1 and No. 2 rocker shaft bolts to 27–30 ft. lbs. (37–41 Nm). Then, set the No. 4 cylinder to TDC and torque the No. 3 and No. 4 rocker shaft bolts to 27–30 ft. lbs. (37–41 Nm).

13. Connect the negative battery cable.

KA24E ENGINE

1. Disconnect the negative battery cable.
2. Remove the timing chain.
3. Remove the cylinder head. Do not remove the camshaft sprocket at this time.
4. Loosen the rocker shaft bolt evenly in proper sequence. Start from the outside and work toward the center.
5. Mount a dial indicator to the cylinder head and set the stylus of the indicator on the head of the camshaft sprocket bolt. Zero the indicator and measure the camshaft endplay by moving the camshaft back and forth. Endplay should be within 0.0028–0.0059 in. (0.07–0.15mm).
6. Remove the camshaft brackets and lift the camshaft with sprocket from the cylinder head.

To install:

7. Clean all cylinder head, intake and exhaust manifold gasket surfaces. Lubricate the camshaft and rocker arm/shaft assemblies with a liberal coating of clean engine oil. Lay the camshaft and sprocket into the cylinder head so the knock pin is at the front of the head at the 12 o'clock position. Install the camshaft brackets. The camshaft bracket directional arrows must face the toward the front of the engine.

8. Install the rocker shaft and rocker arms. Both intake and exhaust rocker shafts are stamped with an **F** mark. This mark

Rocker shaft bolt LOOSENING sequence—KA24E engine. Tighten in reverse of loosening sequence

must face the front of the engine during installation. Install the rocker arm bolts and spring clips so the cut outs are facing as shown. Torque the rocker arm bolts in the proper sequence to 27–30 ft. lbs. (37–41 Nm).

9. Install the timing chain.

10. Install the cylinder head. Use new rubber plugs when installing the cylinder head.

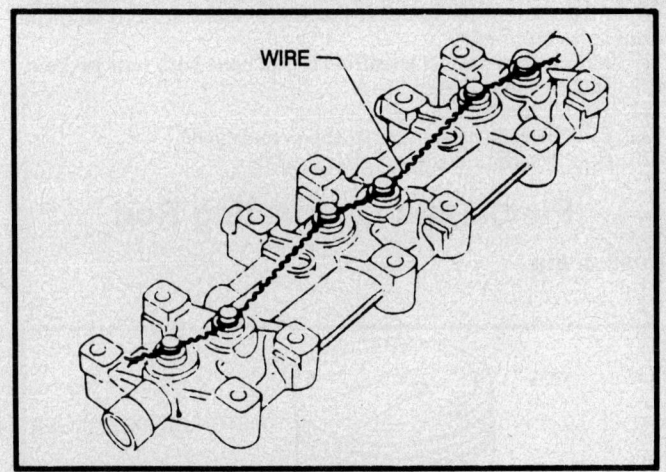

Holding the V6 valve lifters with a wire

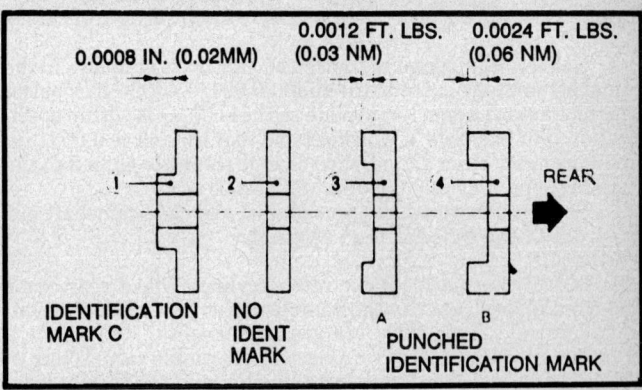

Select shim thickness so the camshaft thickness is within specs

11. Connect the negative battery cable.

VG30E AND VG30ET ENGINES

1. Disconnect the negative battery cable.
2. Drain the cooling system.
3. Remove the timing belt.
4. Remove the collector assembly.
5. Remove the intake manifold.
6. Remove the cylinder head.
7. Remove the rocker shafts with rocker arms. Bolts should be loosened in several steps in the proper sequence.
8. Remove hydraulic valve lifters and lifter guide. Hold hy-

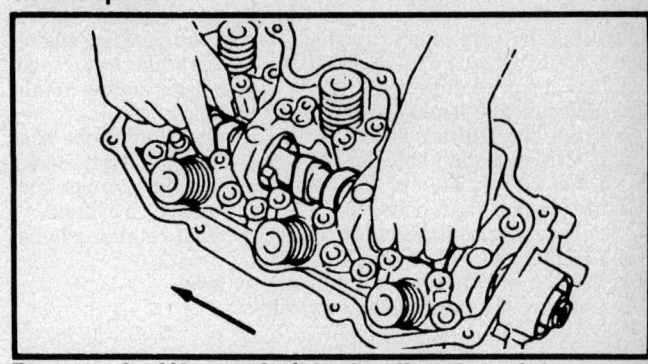

Remove the V6 camshaft in the direction of the arrow

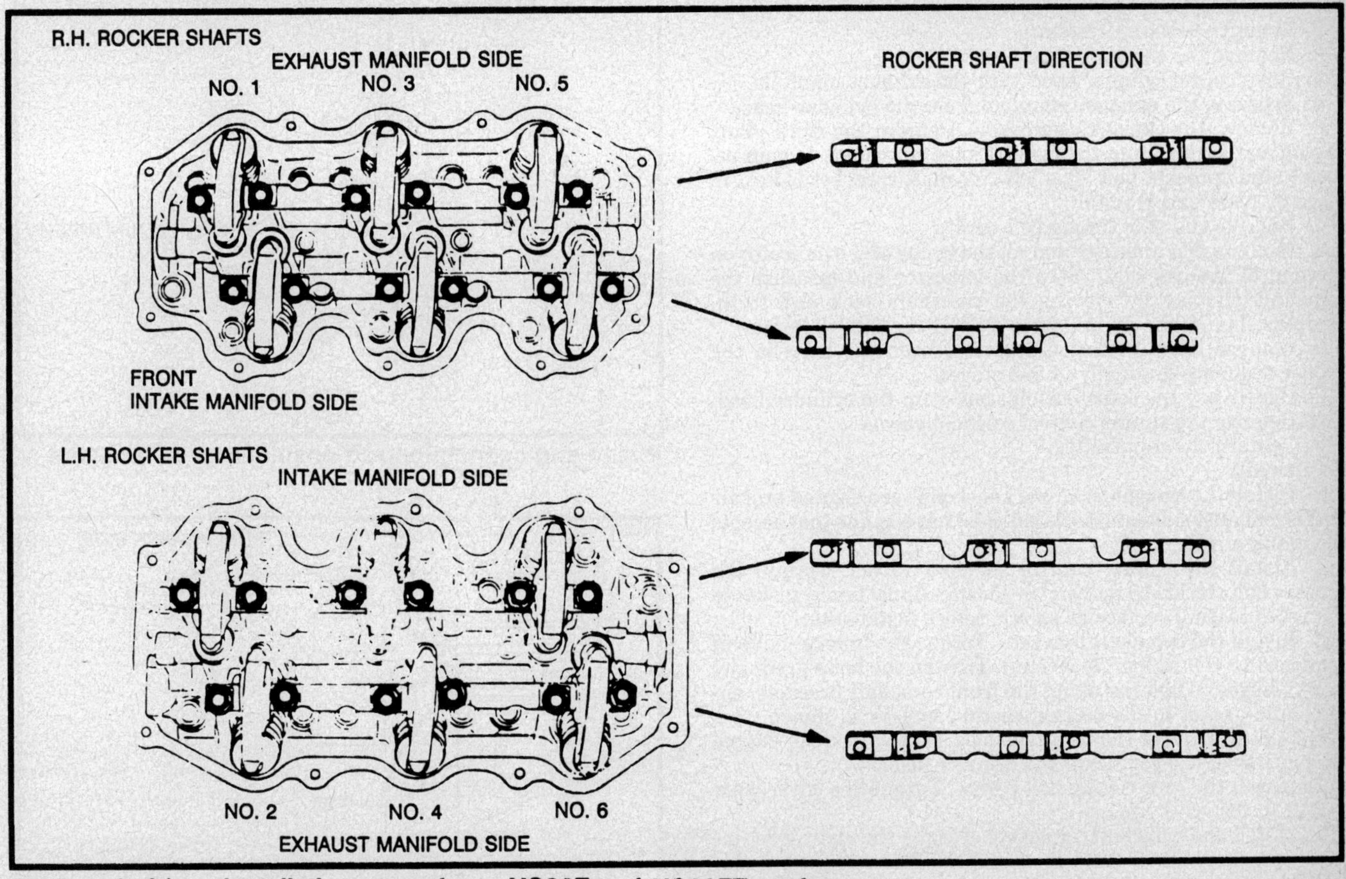

Rocker shaft/arm installation procedure—VG30E and VG30ET engines

draulic valve lifters with wire so they will not drop from lifter guide.

9. Using a dial gauge measure the camshaft endplay. If the camshaft endplay exceeds the limit (0.0012–0.0024 in.), select the thickness of a cam locate plate so the endplay is within specification. For example, if camshaft end play measures 0.0031 in. (0.08mm) with shim 2 used, then change shim 2 to shim 3 so the camshaft end play is 0.0020 in. (0.05mm).

10. Remove the camshaft front oil seal and slide camshaft out the front of the cylinder head assembly.

To install:

11. Install camshaft, locater plates, cylinder head rear cover and front oil seal. Set camshaft knock pin at 12 o'clock position. Install cylinder head with new gasket to engine.

12. Install valve lifter guide assembly. Assemble valve lifters in their original position. After installing them in the correct location remove the wire holding them in lifter guide.

13. Install rocker shafts in correct position with rocker arms. Tighten bolts in 2–3 stages to 13–16 ft. lbs. (18–22 Nm). Before tightening, be sure to set camshaft lobe at the position where lobe is not lifted or the valve closed. Set each cylinder 1 at a time or follow the procedure below. The cylinder head, intake manifold, collector and timing belt must be installed.

    a. Set No. 1 piston at TDC of the compression stroke and tighten rocker shaft bolts for No. 2, No. 4 and No. 6 cylinders.

    b. Set No. 4 piston at TDC of the compression stroke and tighten rocker shaft bolts for No. 1, No. 3 and No. 5 cylinders.

    c. Torque specification for the rocker shaft retaining bolts is 13–16 ft. lbs. (18–22 Nm).

14. Fill the cooling system to the proper level.

15. Connect the negative battery cable.

VG30DE AND VG30DETT ENGINES

1. Disconnect the negative battery cable.
2. Drain the cooling system.
3. Remove the the timing belt.
4. Remove the cylinder head with the exhaust manifold.
5. Separate the exhaust manifold from the cylinder head.
6. Remove the camshaft sprockets. Remove the front plate, O-ring and spring from the right (intake) camshaft to gain access to the sprocket bolt. The left camshaft sprocket is held in place by plate and 4 bolts.
7. Remove the rear timing belt cover.
8. Mount a dial indicator and set the stylus of the indicator on the end of the camshaft. Zero the indicator and measure the camshaft endplay by moving the camshaft back and forth. Endplay should be within 0.0012–0.0031 in. (0.03–0.08mm).
9. Remove the camshaft brackets. Loosen the bolts in the proper sequence gradually in 2–3 stages.
10. Gently pry the camshaft oil seals from the cylinder head.
11. Remove the timing control solenoid valves.
12. Remove the camshafts.

To install:

13. Install the camshafts so the knock pins are aligned properly. The exhaust side camshaft (left side) has a spline that accepts the crank angle sensor.

14. Install the timing control solenoid valves. Torque the bracket bolts to 12–18 ft. lbs. (16–25 Nm). Apply liquid gasket to the valve seating surface as shown before installation.

15. Install the camshaft brackets. Torque the bracket bolts in sequence to 7–9 ft. lbs. (9–12 Nm). Tighten the bolts gradually in 2–3 stages. When installing the front camshaft brackets, apply liquid gasket to the bracket seating surface as shown.

16. Coat the lips of the new camshaft seals with clean engine oil and install the seals into the cylinder head.

17. Install the rear timing belt covers. Torque the cover bolts to 5–6 ft. lbs. (6–8 Nm).

18. Install the camshaft sprockets. Torque the right side (intake) sprocket bolt 90–98 ft. lbs. (123–132 Nm) and the left side (exhaust) sprocket retainer bolts to 10–14 ft. lbs. (14–19 Nm).

When tightening the sprocket fasteners, make sure to hold the camshafts stationary.

19. Mount the exhaust manifold to the head with new gaskets.
20. Install the cylinder head.
21. Install the timing belt.
22. Fill the cooling system to the proper level.
23. Connect the negative battery cable.

Piston and Connecting Rod

Positioning

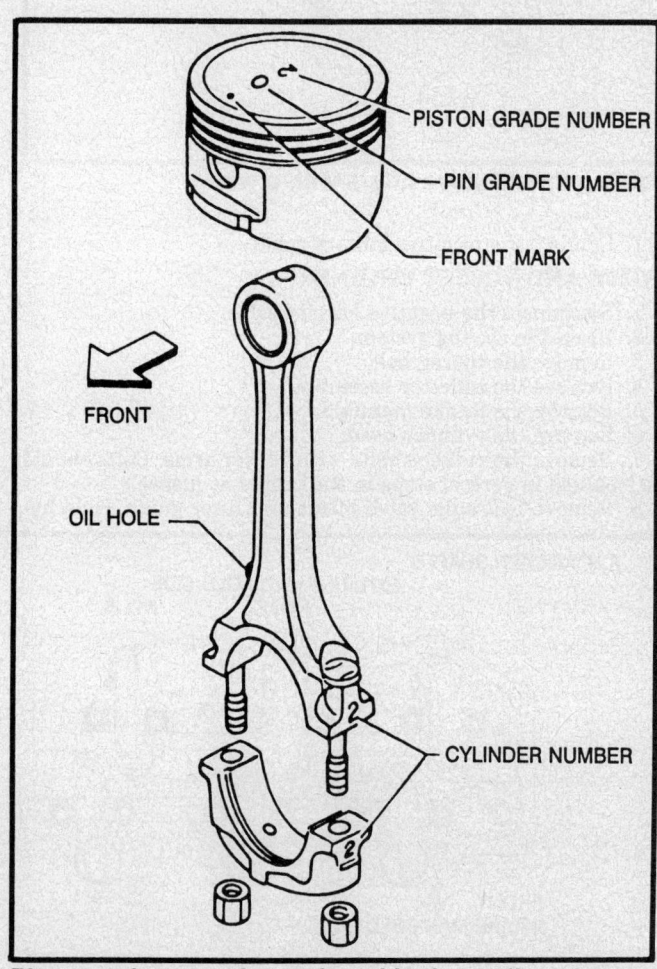

Piston and connection rod positioning—all engines

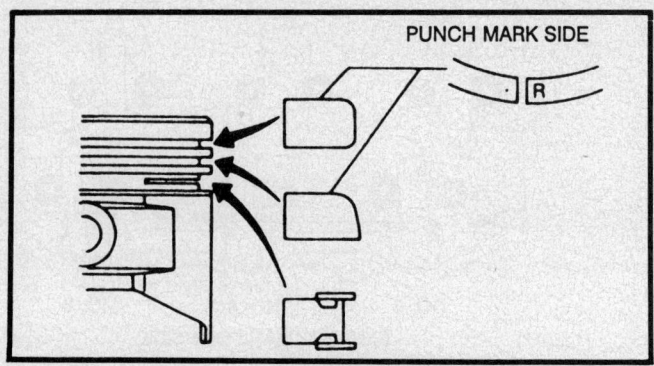

Piston ring installation—all engines

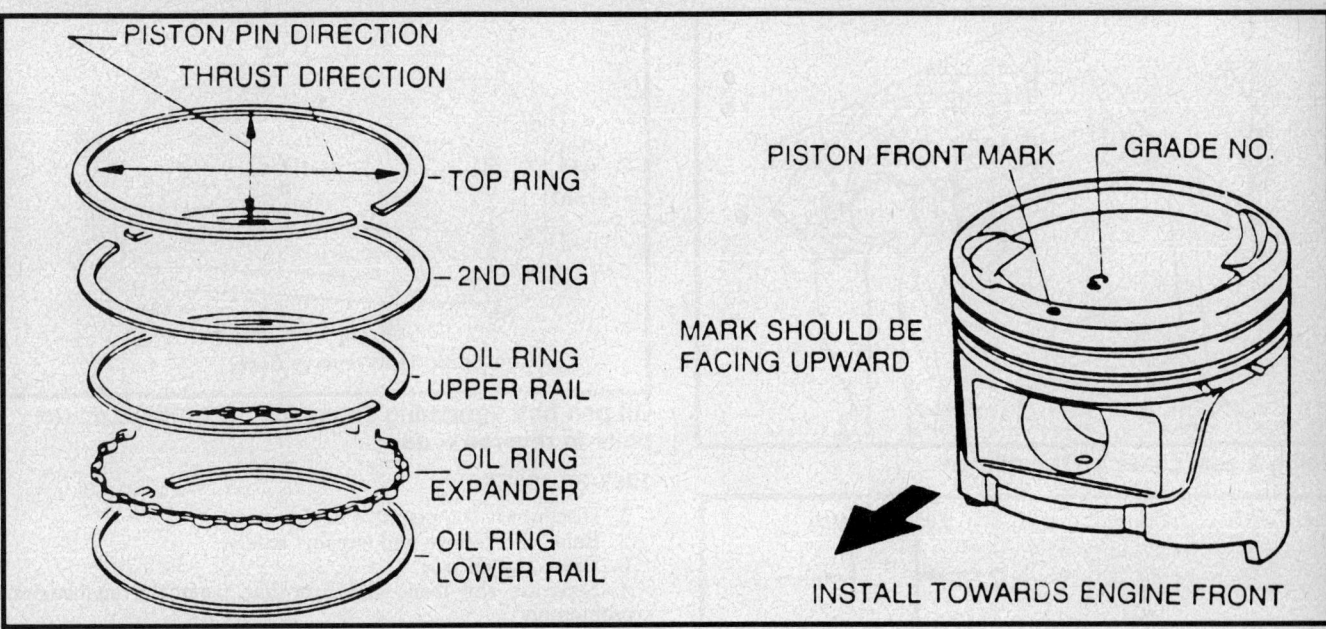

Piston ring identification and positioning—all engines

ENGINE LUBRICATION

Oil Pan

Removal and Installation

200SX

1. Disconnect the negative battery cable.
2. Raise the front of the vehicle and support safely.
3. Drain the oil pan.
4. Remove the power steering bracket from the suspension crossmember.
5. Separate the stabilizer bar from the transverse link.
6. Separate the tension rod from the transverse link.
7. Remove the front engine mounting insulator nuts.
8. Lift the engine.
9. Loosen the oil pan bolts in the proper sequence.
10. Remove the suspension crossmember bolts and remove the screws that secure the power steering oil tubes to the crossmember.
11. Lower the suspension crossmember until there is sufficient clearance to remove the oil pan.
12. Insert a seal cutter between the oil pan and the cylinder block.
13. Tapping the seal cutter with a hammer, slide the cutting tool around the entire edge of the oil pan. Do not drive the seal cutter into the oil pump or rear seal retainer portion or the aluminum mating surface will be deformed.
14. Lower the oil pan from the cylinder block and remove it from the front side of the engine.

To install:

15. Carefully scrape the old gasket material away from the pan and cylinder block mounting surfaces.
16. First apply sealant to the oil pump gasket and rear oil seal retainer gasket surfaces. Then, apply a continuous bead (3.5–4.5mm) of liquid gasket around the oil pan to the 4 corners of the cylinder block mounting surface. Wait 5 minutes and then install the pan. Tighten the oil pan bolts in sequence to 5–6 ft. lbs. (6–8 Nm).

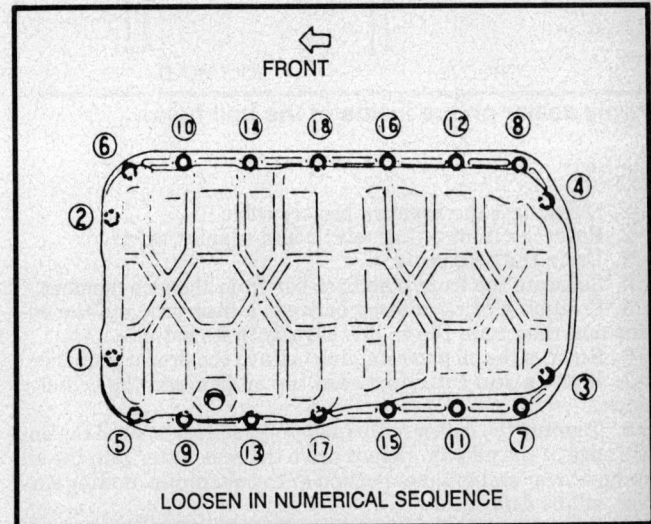

Oil pan bolt tightening sequence on 200SX. Loosen in reverse order

17. Raise the crossmember from the lowered position. Attach the power steering tubes and install the crossmember bolts.
18. Install the front engine mounting insulator nuts.
19. Connect the tension rod and stabilizer bar to the transverse link.
20. Attach the power steering bracket to the crossmember.
21. Lower the vehicle.
22. Fill the crankcase to the proper level.
23. Connect the negative battery cable. Start the engine and check for leaks.

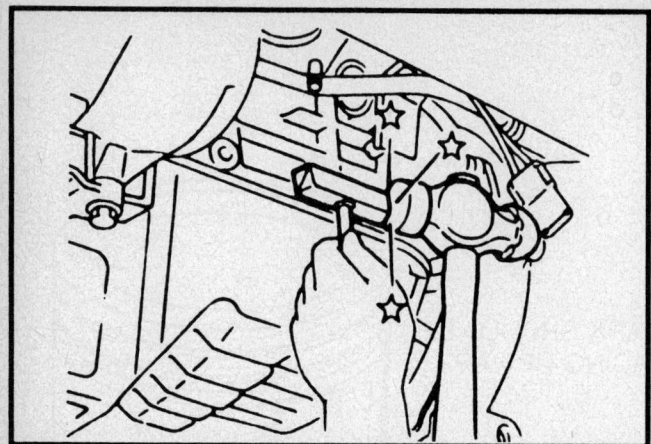

Using a seal cutter on the oil pan

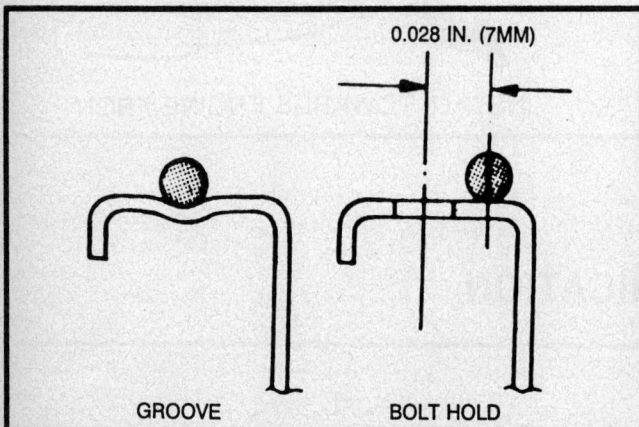

0.028 IN. (7MM)

GROOVE   BOLT HOLD

Apply sealer on the inside of the bolt holes

240SX

1. Disconnect the negative battery cable.
2. Raise the front of the vehicle and support safely.
3. Drain the oil pan.
4. Separate the front stabilizer bar from the side member.
5. Position a block of wood between a floor jack and the engine and then raise the engine slightly in its mounts.
6. Remove the oil pan retaining bolts in the proper sequence.
7. Insert a seal cutter between the oil pan and the cylinder block.
8. Tapping the cutter with a hammer, slide it around the entire edge of the oil pan. Do not drive the seal cutter into the oil pump or rear seal retainer portion or the aluminum mating surface will be deformed.
9. Lower the oil pan from the cylinder block and remove it from the front side of the engine.

To install:

10. To install, carefully scrape the old gasket material away from the pan and cylinder block mounting surfaces and then apply a continuous bead (3.5–4.5mm) of liquid gasket around the oil pan to the 4 corners of the cylinder block mounting surface. Wait 5 minutes and then install the pan.
11. Install the oil pan and tighten the mounting bolts from the inside, out, to 3.6–5.1 ft. lbs. (5–7 Nm). Wait 30 minutes before refilling the crankcase to allow for the sealant to cure properly.
12. Connect the front stabilizer to the side bar.
13. Lower the vehicle.
14. Fill the crankcase to the proper level.
15. Connect the negative battery cable. Start the engine and check for leaks.

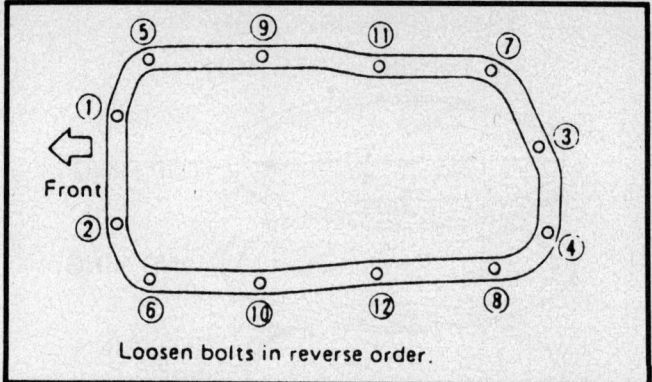

Front

Loosen bolts in reverse order.

Oil pan bolt tightening sequence on 240SX. Loosen bolts in reverse order

1987–89 300ZX

1. Disconnect the negative battery cable.
2. Raise the vehicle and support safely.
3. Drain the oil pan.
4. Separate the front stabilizer bar from the suspension crossmember.
5. Remove the steering column shaft from the gear housing.
6. Separate the tension rod retaining nuts from the transverse link.
7. Raise and support the engine.
8. Remove the rear plate cover from the transmission case.
9. Remove the oil pan retaining bolts in the proper sequence.
10. Remove the suspension crossmember retaining bolts.
11. Remove the strut mounting insulator retaining nuts.
12. Remove the screws retaining the refrigerant lines and power steering tubes to the suspension crossmember.
13. Lower the suspension crossmember.
14. Insert a seal cutter between the oil pan and the cylinder block.
15. Tapping the cutter with a hammer, slide it around the entire edge of the oil pan. Do not drive the seal cutter into the oil pump or rear seal retainer portion or the aluminum mating surface will be deformed.
16. Lower the oil pan from the cylinder block and remove it from the front rear of the engine.

To install:

17. Carefully scrape the old gasket material away from the pan and cylinder block mounting surfaces and then apply a continuous bead (3.5–4.5mm) of liquid gasket around the oil pan and to the 4 corners of the cylinder block mounting surface. Wait 5 minutes and then install the pan.
18. Install tighten the pan mounting bolts from the inside,

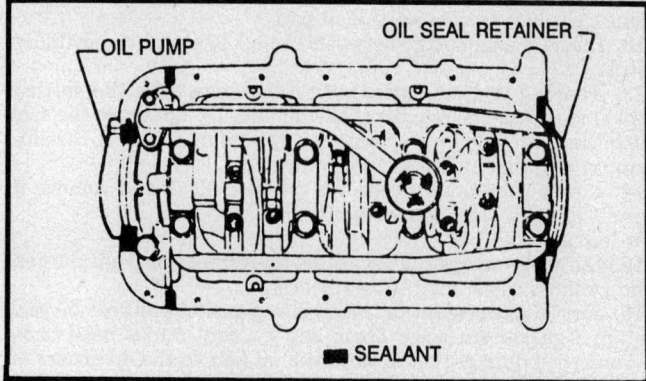

OIL PUMP   OIL SEAL RETAINER

SEALANT

Apply sealant to these areas before installing the oil pan gasket—V6 engine

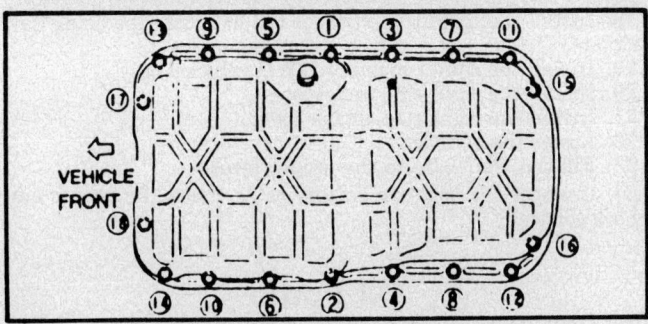

Oil pan bolt tightening sequence on Maxima and 1987–89 300ZX. Loosen bolts in reverse order

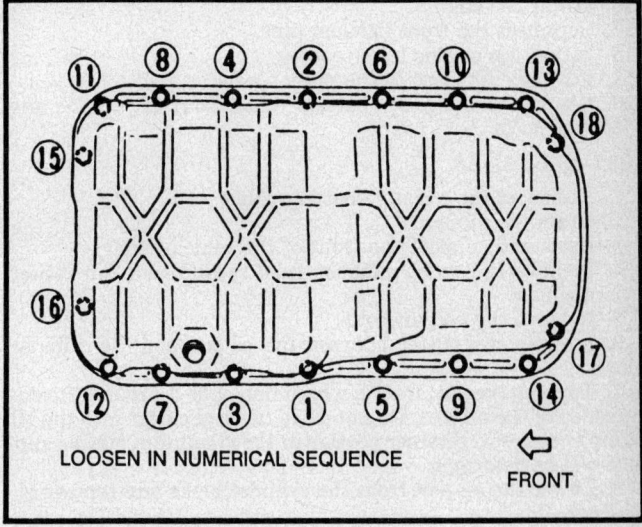

LOOSEN IN NUMERICAL SEQUENCE

FRONT

Oil pan bolt tightening sequence on 1990–91 300ZX. Loosen bolts in reverse order

out, to 5–6 ft. lbs. (7–8 Nm). Wait 30 minutes before refilling the crankcase to allow for the sealant to cure properly.

19. Raise the crossmember from the lowered postion and attach the power steering and refrigerant lines.
20. Install and tighten the strut mounting insulator nuts.
21. Install the crossmember bolts.
22. Install the rear cover plate to the transmission case.
23. Lower the engine.
24. Connect the tension rod to the transverse link.
25. Connect the steering column shaft to the gear housing.
26. Connnect the front stabilizer bar to the crossmember.
27. Lower the vehicle.
28. Fill the crankcase to the proper level.
29. Connect the negative battery cable. Start the engine and check for leaks.

1990–91 300ZX

1. Disconnect the negative battery cable.
2. Raise the front of the vehicle and support safely.
3. Remove the engine undercover.
4. Drain the oil pan.
5. Remove the oil filter and bracket.
6. Remove the rear engine gussets from both sides.
7. Disconnect the air conditioning tube clamps.
8. Disconnect the lower steering column joint from the steering rack.
9. Remove the tension rod and transverse link bolts from both sides.
10. Support the suspension member with a suitable transmission jack. Install engine lifting slingers, connect a lifting device to the slingers and lift the engine.
11. Remove the suspension member bolts and lower the suspension member.
12. Remove the engine mounting bolts from both sides and slowly lower the transmission jack.
13. Remove the oil pan bolts in the proper sequence.
14. Insert a seal cutter between the oil pan and the cylinder block.
15. Tapping the cutter with a hammer, slide it around the entire edge of the oil pan. Do not drive the seal cutter into the oil pump or rear seal retainer portion or the aluminum mating surface will be deformed.
16. Lower the oil pan from the cylinder block and remove it.
To install:
17. Carefully scrape the old gasket material away from the pan and cylinder block mounting surfaces and then apply a continuous bead (3.5–4.5mm) of liquid gasket around the oil pan and to the 4 corners of the cylinder block mounting surface. Wait 5 minutes and then install the pan.
18. Install tighten the pan mounting bolts from the inside, out, to 4–6 ft. lbs. (6–8 Nm). Wait 30 minutes before refilling the crankcase to allow for the sealant to cure properly.
19. Slowly raise the transmission jack, then install the engine mounting bolts.

20. Raise the suspension member and install the mounting bolts.
21. Lower the engine, disconnect the lifting device and remove the lifting slingers.
22. Install the tension rod and transverse link bolts.
23. Connect the lower steering column joint to the steering rack.
24. Install the air conditioning tube clamps.
25. Install the rear engine gussets.
26. Install the oil filter bracket with a new oil filter.
27. Install the engine undercover.
28. Lower the vehicle.
29. Fill the crankcase to the proper level.
30. Connect the negative battery cable. Start the engine and check for leaks.

MAXIMA

1. Disconnect the negative battery cable.
2. Raise the front of the vehicle and support safely.
3. Drain the oil pan.
4. Remove the engine lower covers.
5. Using a suitable jack and block of wood, support the engine in the area of the crank pulley.
6. Remove the engine mounting insulator fasteners.
7. Remove the center crossmember.
8. Remove the oil pan bolts in the proper sequence.
9. Insert a seal cutter between the oil pan and the cylinder block.
10. Tapping the cutter with a hammer, slide it around the entire edge of the oil pan. Do not drive the seal cutter into the oil pump or rear seal retainer portion or the aluminum mating surface will be deformed.
11. Lower the oil pan from the cylinder block and remove it.
To install:
12. Carefully scrape the old gasket material away from the pan and cylinder block mounting surfaces and then apply a thin continuous bead of liquid gasket around the oil pan and to the 4 corners of the cylinder block mounting surface. Do the same to the oil pan gasket; both upper and lower surfaces. Wait 5 minutes and then install the pan. Wait 30 minutes before refilling the crankcase to allow the sealant to cure properly.
13. Install the oil pan and tighten the mounting bolts from the inside, out, to 5–6 ft. lbs. (7–8 Nm) in the proper sequence.
14. Install the center crossmember assembly.
15. Install the engine mount insulator fasteners.

16. Lower the engine.
17. Connnect the front exhaust pipe.
18. Install the engine lower covers.
19. Fill the crankcase to the proper level.
20. Connect the negative battery cable. Start the engine and check for leaks.

1987–89 STANZA

1. Disconect the negative battery cable.
2. Drain the oil pan.
3. Raise and support the front of the vehicle safely.
4. Remove the front exhaust tube section and the center crossmember.
5. Remove the oil pan bolts.
6. Insert a seal cutter between the oil pan and the cylinder block.
7. Tapping the cutter with a hammer, slide it around the entire edge of the oil pan. Do not drive the seal cutter into the oil pump or rear seal retainer portion or the aluminum mating surface will be deformed.
8. Lower the oil pan from the cylinder block and remove it.

To install:

9. Carefully scrape the old gasket material away from the pan and cylinder block mounting surfaces and then apply a thin continuous bead of liquid gasket around the oil pan and to the 4 corners of the cylinder block mounting surface. Do the same to the oil pan gasket; both upper and lower surfaces. Wait 5 minutes and then install the pan. Wait 30 minutes before refilling the crankcase to allow the sealant to cure properly.
10. Install the oil pan and tighten the mounting bolts from the inside, out, to 4–5 ft. lbs. (5–7 Nm).
11. Install the center crossmember and front exhaust tube section.
12. Lower the vehicle.
13. Fill the crankcase to the proper level.
14. Connect the negative battery cable. Start the engine and check for leaks.

PULSAR, SENTRA AND 1990–91 STANZA

1. Disconnect the negative battery cable.
2. Raise the vehicle and support safely.
3. Drain the oil pan.
4. Remove the right side splash cover.
5. Remove the right side undercover.
6. Remove the center member (2WD vehicles only).
7. Remove the forward section of the exhaust pipe.
8. Remove the front buffer rod and its bracket (1987–88 models only).
9. Remove the engine gussets (1987–88 vehicles only).
10. Remove the oil pan bolts.
11. Insert a seal cutter between the oil pan and the cylinder block.
12. Tapping the cutter with a hammer, slide it around the entire edge of the oil pan. Do not drive the seal cutter into the oil pump or rear seal retainer portion or the aluminum mating surface will be deformed.
13. Lower the oil pan from the cylinder block and remove it.

To install:

14. Carefully scrape the old gasket material away from the pan and cylinder block mounting surfaces and then apply a thin continuous bead of liquid gasket around the oil pan and to the 4 corners of the cylinder block mounting surface. Do the same to the oil pan gasket; both upper and lower surfaces. Wait 5 minutes and then install the pan. Wait 30 minutes before refilling the crankcase to allow the sealant to cure properly.
15. Install the oil pan and tighten the mounting bolts from the inside, out, to 5–6 ft. lbs. (7–8 Nm).
16. Install the engine gussets (1987–88 vehicles only).
17. Install the front buffer rod and its bracket (1987–88 vehicles only).

18. Install the forward section of the exhaust pipe using new gaskets.
19. Install the center member (2WD vehicles only).
20. Install the right side undercover.
21. Install the right side splash cover.
22. Lower the vehicle.
23. Fill the crankcase to the proper level.
24. Connect the negative battery cable. Start the engine and check for leaks.

Oil Pump

Removal and Installation

CA16DE, CA18DE, CA18ET AND CA20E ENGINES

1. Disconnect the negative battery cable.
2. Drain the oil pan.
3. Remove all accessory drive belts.
4. Remove the alternator.
5. Remove the timing belt covers.
6. Remove the timing belt.
7. On 200SX and the Stanza wagon, unbolt the engine from its mounts and lift or jack the engine up from the unibody. On the Stanza (except wagon) and Pulsar, remove the center member from the body.
8. Remove the oil pan.
9. Remove the oil pump assembly along with the oil strainer. Remove the O-ring from the oil pump body and replace it.
10. Replace the front seal.

To install:

11. If installing a new or rebuilt oil pump, first pack the pump full of petroleum jelly to prevent the pump from cavitating when the engine is started. Apply RTV sealer to the front oil seal end of the pan prior to installation.
12. Install the pump and torque the oil pump mounting bolts to 8–12 ft. lbs. (12–16 Nm). Make sure the oil pump body O-ring is properly seated.
13. Install the oil pan.
14. On the Stanza (except wagon) and Pulsar, install the center member. On 200SX and the Stanza wagon, lower and remount the engine.
15. Install the timing belt.
16. Install the timing belt covers.
17. Install the alternator.
18. Install and tension the drive belts.
19. Fill the crankcase to the proper level.
20. Connect the negative battery cable. Start the engine and check for leaks.

E16S AND E16I ENGINES

1. Disconnect the negative battery cable.
2. Drain the oil pan.
3. Remove all accessory drive belts.
4. Remove the alternator.
5. Disconnect the oil pressure gauge harness.
6. Remove the oil filter.
7. Remove the oil pump and gasket.

To install:

8. If installing a new or rebuilt oil pump, first pack the pump full of petroleum jelly to prevent the pump from cavitating when the engine is started.
9. Mount the pump on the engine using a new gasket. Torque the pump mounting bolts to 7–9 ft. lbs. (10–12 Nm).
10. Install a new oil filter.
11. Connect the oil pressure gauge harness.
12. Install the alternator.
13. Install and tension the drive belts.
14. Fill the crankcase to the proper level.
15. Connect the negative battery cable. Start the engine and check for leaks.

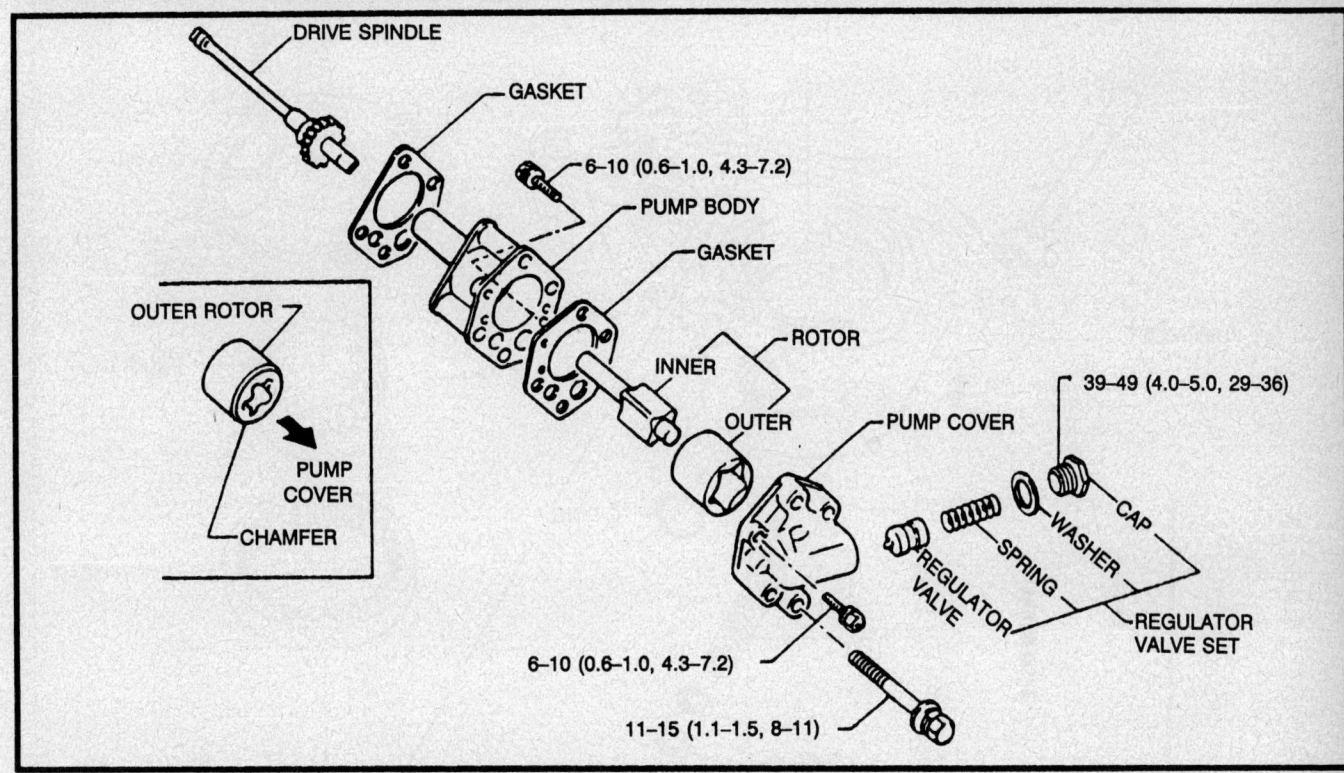

Align the punch mark on the drive spindle with the oil hole—240SX

GA16I ENGINES AND 1990 STANZA ENGINES

The oil pump used on the GA16i engine consists of an inner and outer gear located in the front cover. Removal of the front cover is necessary to gain access to the oil pump.

1. Disconnect the negative battery cable.
2. Remove the front cover with the strainer tube.
3. Loosen the oil pump cover retaining screw and mounting bolts and separate the oil pump cover from the front cover.
4. Remove the oil pump inner and outer gears.

To install:

5. Thoroughly clean the oil pump cover mating surfaces and the gear cavity.
6. Install the outer gear into the cavity.
7. Install the inner gear so the grooved side is facing up (towards the oil pump cover). Make sure the gears mesh properly and pack the pump cavity with petroleum jelly.
8. Install the oil pump cover. On GA16i engines, torque the retaining screws to 2.2–3.6 ft. lbs. (3–5 Nm) and the bolts to 3.6–5.1 ft. lbs. (5–7 Nm). On KA24E engines, torque the cover screws to 2.2–3.6 ft. lbs. (3–5 Nm) and the bolts to 12–15 ft. lbs. (16–21 Nm).
9. Install the front cover with a new seal.
10. Connect the negative battery cable. Start the engine and check for leaks.

KA24E ENGINE (240SX)

1. Disconnect the negative battery cable.
2. Drain the oil pan.
3. Turn the crankshaft so No. 1 piston is at TDC on its compression stroke.
4. Remove the distributor cap and mark the position of the distributor rotor in relation to the distributor base with a piece of chalk.
5. Remove the splash shield.
6. Remove the oil pump body with the drive spindle assembly.

To install:

7. To install, fill the pump housing with engine oil, align the punch mark on the spindle with the hole in the pump. No. 1 piston should be at TDC on its compression stroke.
8. With a new gasket and seal placed over the drive spindle, install the oil pump and drive spindle assembly. Make sure the tip of the drive spindle fits into the distributor shaft notch securely. The distributor rotor should be pointing to the matchmark made earlier.
9. Install the splash shield.
10. Install the distributor cap.
11. Fill the crankcase to the proper level.
12. Connect the negative battery cable. Start the engine and check for leaks. Check the ignition timing.

VG30E, VG30ET, VG30DE AND VG30DETT ENGINES

1. Disconnect the negative battery cable.
2. Remove the oil pan.
3. Remove the timing belt.
4. Remove the crankshaft timing sprocket using a suitable puller.
5. Remove the timing belt plate.

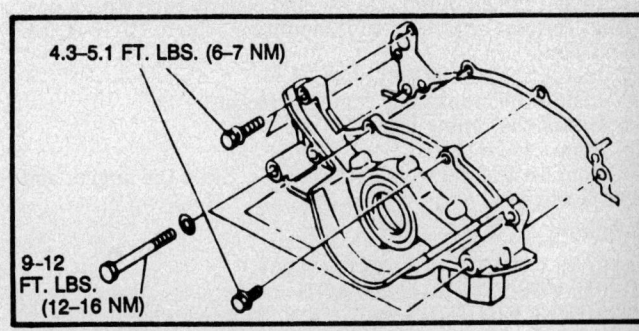

Oil Pump Installation—V6 engine

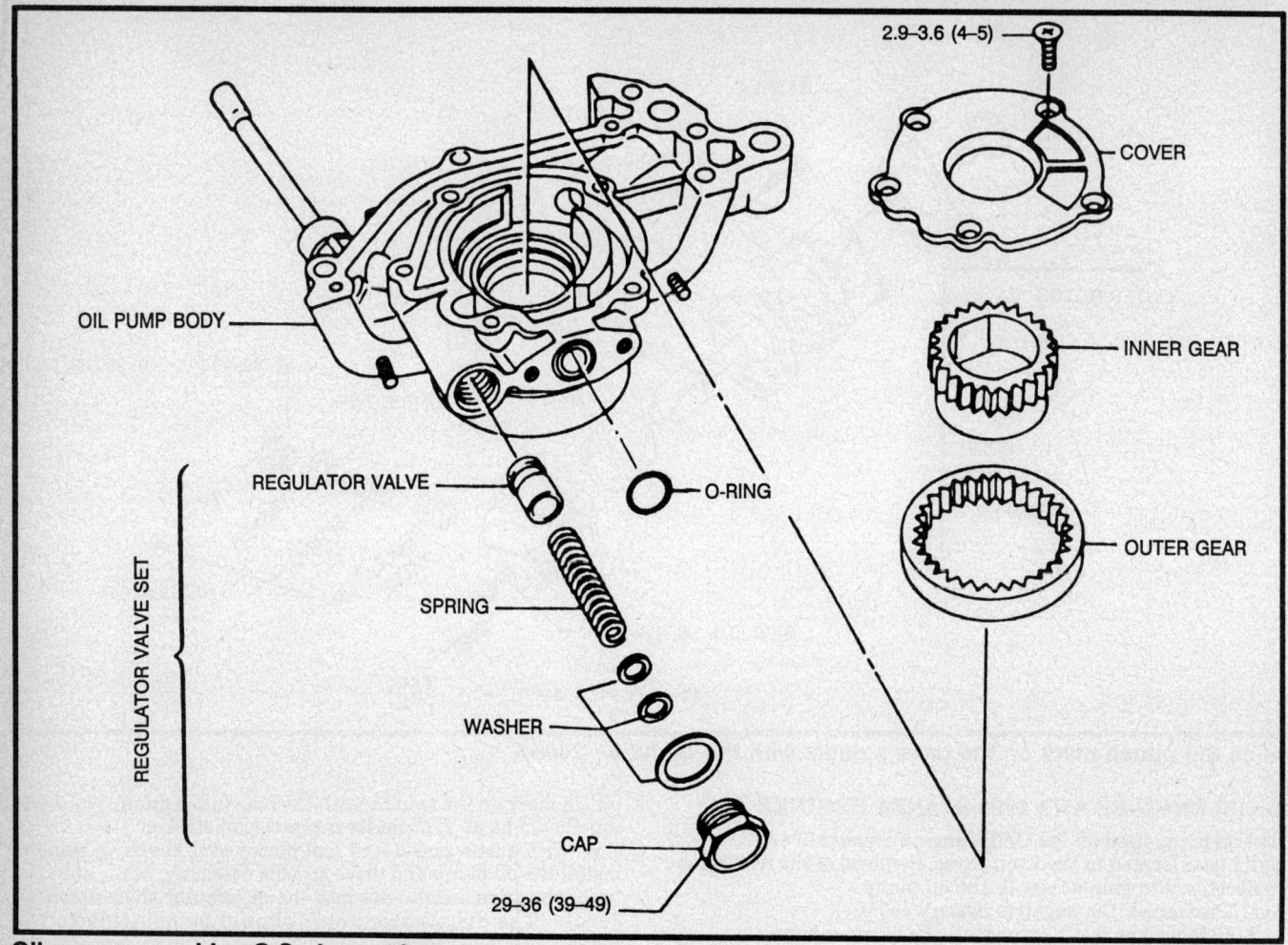

Oil pump assembly—C-Series engines

6. Remove the oil pump strainer and pick-up tube from the oil pump.

7. Remove the mounting bolts and remove the oil pump and gasket.

8. Replace the oil pump seal.

To install:

9. Before installing the oil pump, remove the front cover and pack the pump's cavity with petroleum jelly, then make sure the O-ring is fitted properly. Torque the front cover screws to 3–4 ft. lbs. (4–5 Nm).

10. Mount the oil pump with a new gasket. Torque the 8mm retaining bolts to 16–22 ft. lbs. (22–29 Nm) and the 6mm bolts to 5–6 ft. lbs. (6–8 Nm).

11. Install the oil pump strainer and pick-up tube with a new O-ring. Torque the pick-up tube mounting bolts to 12–15 ft. lbs. (16–21 Nm).

12. Install the timing belt plate.

13. Install the crankshaft timing sprocket.

14. Install the timing belt.

15. Install the oil pan.

16. Connect the negative battery cable. Start the engine and check for leaks.

Checking

CA16DE, CA18DE, CA18ET, CA20E, VG30E, VG30ET, VG30DE AND VG30DETT ENGINES

1. Remove the oil pump cover and gasket.

2. Disassemble the regulator valve components. Visually inspect all parts for wear and damage.

3. Make sure the regulator valve moves smoothly in the valve bore. Make sure the valve spring is sturdy.

4. Coat the regulator valve with clean engine oil and check that it falls into the valve bore by its own weight. Assemble the regulator valve components. Torque the valve cap to 29–36 ft. lbs. (39–49 Nm).

5. Inspect the oil pressure relief valve for movement, cracks and damage by pushing the ball in. If necessary, install a new valve by prying the old valve out and tapping the new valve in place.

6. Check the body-to-outer gear clearance. It should be 0.0043–0.0079 in. (0.11–0.20mm).

7. Check the inner gear-to-crescent clearance. It should be 0.0047–0.0091 in. (0.12–0.23mm).

8. Check the outer gear-to-crescent clearance. It should be 0.0083–0.0126 in. (0.21–0.32mm).

9. Check the body (housing)-to-inner gear clearance. It should be 0.0020–0.0035 in. (0.05–0.09mm).

10. Check the body (housing)-to-outer gear clearance. It should be 0.0020–0.0043 in. (0.05–0.11mm).

11. If any of the clearances exceed the specified limits, replace the gear set or the entire oil pump assembly.

12. Coat the inner and outer gears with clean engine oil prior to installation.

13. Install the oil pump cover with a new gasket. Tighten the cover screws to 3–4 ft. lbs. (4–5 Nm).

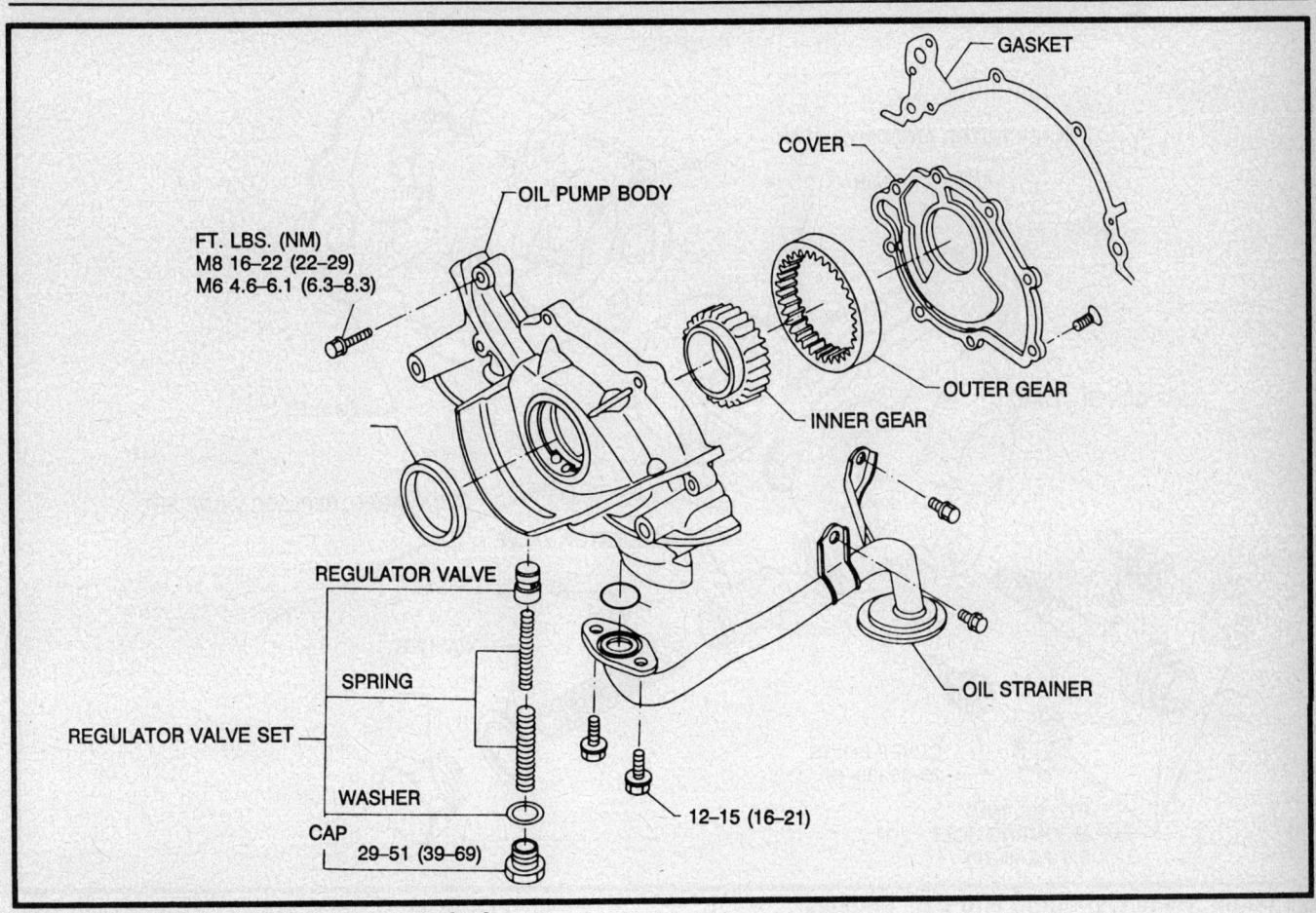

FT. LBS. (NM)
M8 16–22 (22–29)
M6 4.6–6.1 (6.3–8.3)

GASKET

COVER

OIL PUMP BODY

OUTER GEAR

INNER GEAR

REGULATOR VALVE

SPRING

REGULATOR VALVE SET

WASHER

CAP

29–51 (39–69)

12–15 (16–21)

OIL STRAINER

Oil pump assembly—V6 engines—typical

E16S, E16i AND KA24E (240SX) ENGINES

NOTE: Do not disassemble the inner rotor and drive gear.

1. Disassemble the regulator valve components. Visually inspect all parts for wear and damage.
2. Make sure the regulator valve moves smoothly in the valve bore. Make sure the valve spring is sturdy.
3. Coat the regulator valve with clean engine oil and check that it falls into the valve bore by its own weight. Assemble the regulator valve components. Torque the valve cap to 29–36 ft. lbs. (39–49 Nm).
4. Inspect the oil pressure relief valve for movement, cracks and damage by pushing the ball in. If necessary, install a new valve by prying the old valve out and tapping the new valve in place.
5. Check the rotor tip clearance. It should be less than 0.0047 in. (0.12mm).
6. Check the outer rotor-to-body clearance. It should be 0.0059–0.0083 in. (0.15–0.21mm).
7. With the pump body gasket installed, check the side clearance. It should be 0.0020–0.0047 in. (0.05–0.12mm) for E16S and E16i engines; and 0.0016–0.0031 in. (0.04–0.08mm) on KA24E engines.
8. If any of the clearances exceed the specified limits, replace the gear set or the entire oil pump assembly.
9. Coat the inner and outer gears with clean engine oil prior to installation.

GA16I AND KA24E (1990–91 STANZA) ENGINES

1. Remove the oil pump cover and gasket.
2. Disassemble the regulator valve components. Visually inspect all parts for wear and damage.
3. Make sure the regulator valve moves smoothly in the valve bore. Make sure the valve spring is sturdy.
4. Coat the regulator valve with clean engine oil and check that it falls into the valve bore by its own weight. Assemble the regulator valve components. Torque the valve cap to 29–36 ft. lbs. (39–49 Nm).
5. Inspect the oil pressure relief valve for movement, cracks and damage by pushing the ball in. If necessary, install a new valve by prying the old valve out and tapping the new valve in place.
6. Check the body-to-outer gear clearance. It should be 0.0043–0.0079 in. (0.11–0.20mm).
7. Check the inner gear-to-crescent clearance. It should be 0.0085–0.0129 in. (0.217–0.327mm).
8. Check the outer gear-to-crescent clearnce. It should be 0.0083–0.0126 in. (0.21–0.32mm).
9. Check the body-to-inner gear clearance. It should be 0.0020–0.0035 in. (0.05–0.09mm).
10. Check the body-to-outer gear clearance. It should be 0.0020–0.0043 in. (0.05–0.11mm).
11. On GA16i engines, check the clearance between the inner gear and the braised portion of the housing. It should be 0.0018–0.0036 in. (0.045–0.091mm). To do this, measure the diameter of the front cover seal opening with an inside micrometer, then measure the diameter of the inner gear race. Subtract the 2 readings to obtain the clearance.

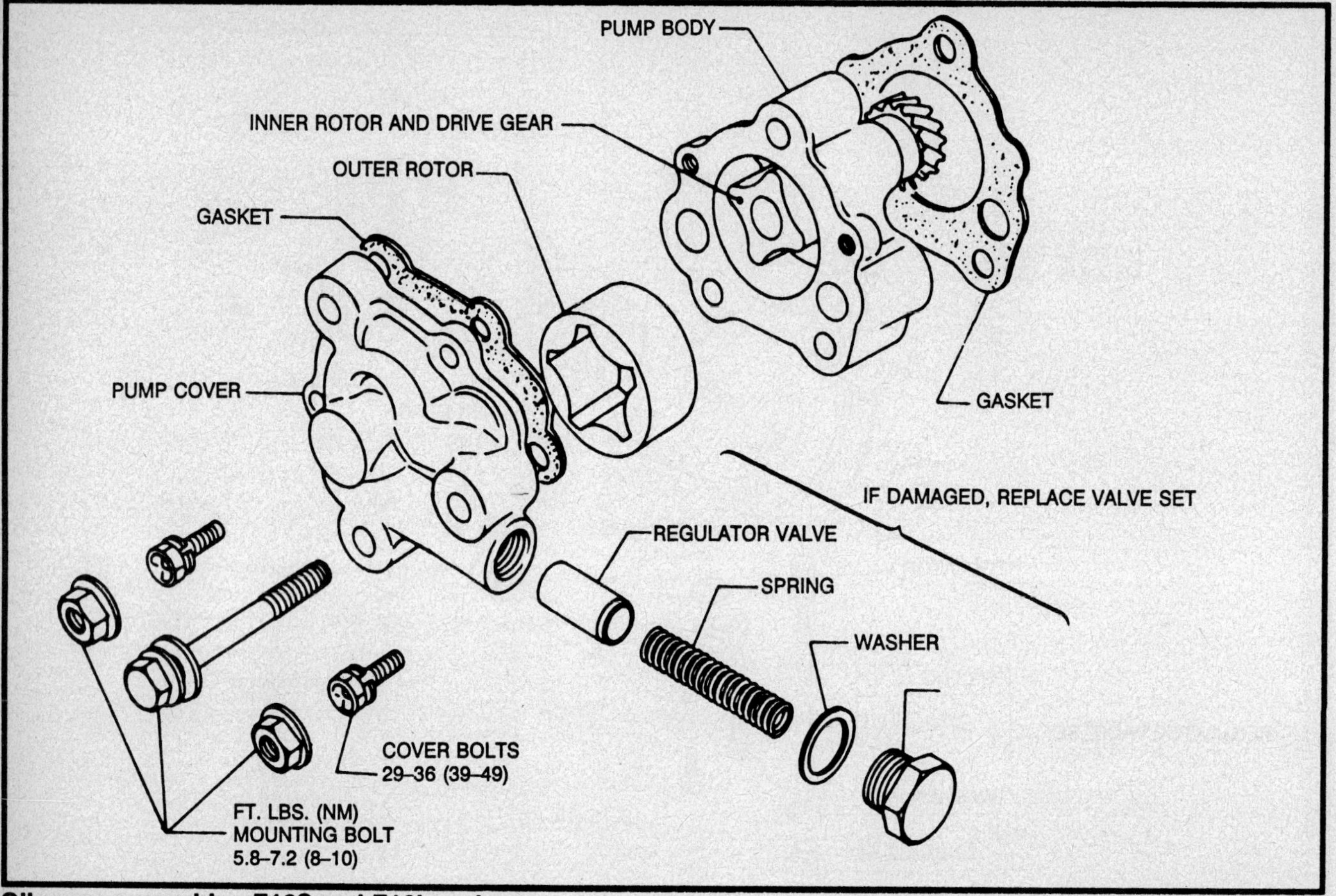

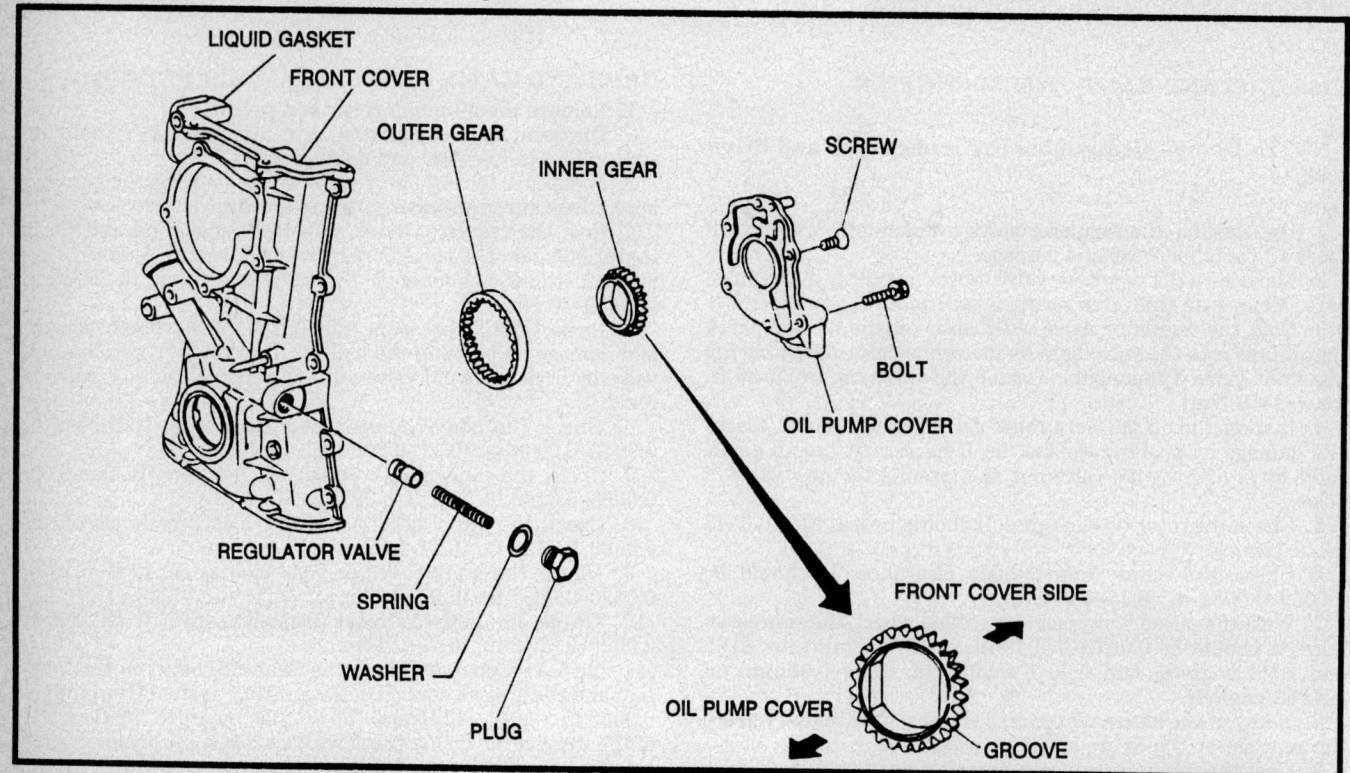

PUMP BODY

INNER ROTOR AND DRIVE GEAR

OUTER ROTOR

GASKET

PUMP COVER

GASKET

IF DAMAGED, REPLACE VALVE SET

REGULATOR VALVE

SPRING

WASHER

COVER BOLTS
29–36 (39–49)

FT. LBS. (NM)
MOUNTING BOLT
5.8–7.2 (8–10)

Oil pump assembly—E16S and E16i engines

LIQUID GASKET

FRONT COVER

OUTER GEAR

INNER GEAR

SCREW

BOLT

OIL PUMP COVER

REGULATOR VALVE

SPRING

WASHER

PLUG

FRONT COVER SIDE

OIL PUMP COVER

GROOVE

Oil pump assembly—GA16i engine

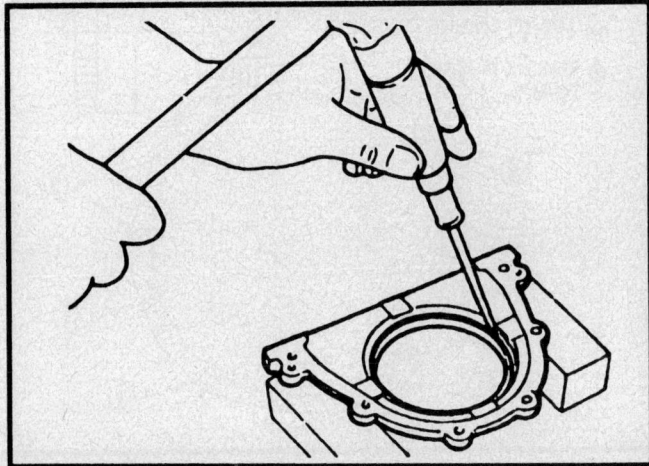

Rear seal removal

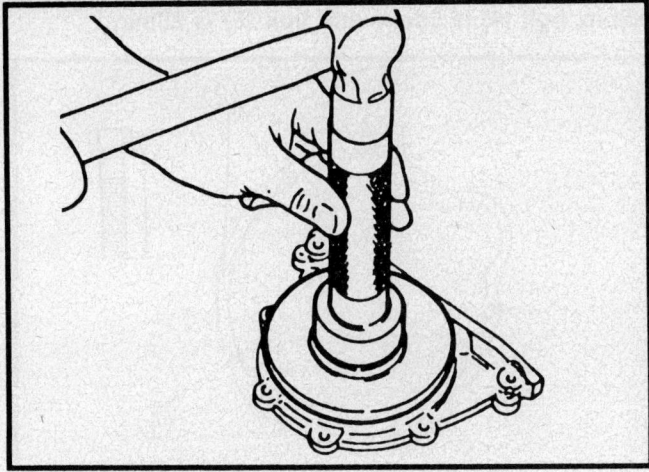

Rear seal installation

12. If any of the clearances exceed the specified limits, replace the gear set or the oil pump assembly.

13. Coat the inner and outer gears with clean engine oil prior to installation.

14. Install the oil pump cover. On GA16i engines, torque the retaining screws to 2.2–3.6 ft. lbs. (3–5 Nm) and the bolts to 3.6–

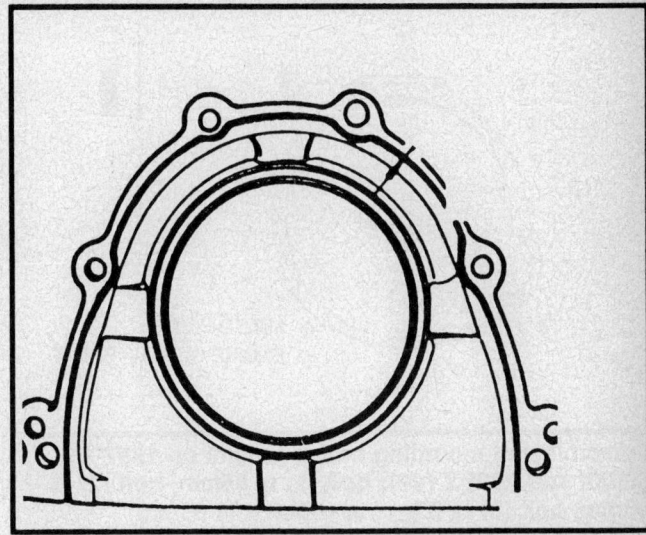

On GA16i and KA24E engines, apply a 0.08–0.12 in. (2–3mm) of liquid gasket to the rear oil seal retainer

5.1 ft. lbs. (5–7 Nm). On KA24E engines, torque the cover screws to 2.2–3.6 ft. lbs. (3–5 Nm) and the bolts to 12–15 ft. lbs. (16–21 Nm).

Rear Main Bearing Oil Seal

Removal and Installation

1. Remove the transmission or transaxle.
2. Remove the flywheel or drive plate.
3. Remove the rear oil seal retainer from the block.
4. Using a suitable prying tool, remove the oil seal from the retainer.
5. Thoroughly scrape the surface of the retainer to remove any traces of the existing sealant or gasket material.
6. Wipe the seal bore with a clean rag.
7. Apply clean engine oil to the new oil seal and carefully install it into the retainer using the proper seal installation tool.
8. Install the rear oil seal retainer into the engine, along with a new gasket. On GA16i and KA24E engines, apply a 0.08–0.12 in. (2–3mm) of liquid gasket to the rear oil seal retainer prior to installation. Torque the bolts to 3–6 ft. lbs. (4–8 Nm).
9. Install the flywheel or driveplate.
10. Install the transmission or transaxle.

MANUAL TRANSMISSION

For further information, please refer to "Professional Transmission Repair Manual" for additional coverage.

Transmission Assembly

Removal and Installation

200SX, 240SX AND 300ZX

1. Disconnect the negative battery cable.
2. Raise and support the vehicle safely.
3. On 1987–89 300ZX, remove the exhaust front tube, catalytic converter and exhaust manifold conecting tube. On 1990–91 300ZX, remove the exhaust tube section from the manifold and remove the support bracket from the transmission.

4. Unbolt the driveshaft at the rear and remove. If there is a center bearing, unbolt it from the crossmember. Seal the end of the transmission extension housing to prevent leakage.

5. Disconnect the speedometer drive cable from the transmission.

6. On 200SX, 1987–89 300ZX non-turbocharged and all 1990–91 300ZX, remove the shifter lever. On 1987–89 300ZX turbocharged, remove the shift knob and console boot finisher. On 240SX, disconnect the control rod front the shift lever.

NOTE: On the 1987–89 300ZX turbo, the shifter boot must not be removed from the shift lever.

7. Remove the clutch operating cylinder from the clutch housing.

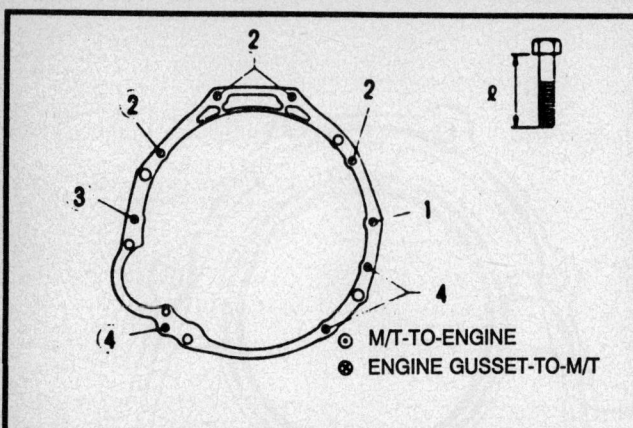

Transmission mounting bolt locations on 1987–89 300ZX and 200SX (V6); bolt (1) is 65mm, bolt (2) is 60mm, bolt (3) is 55mm and bolt 4 is 25mm

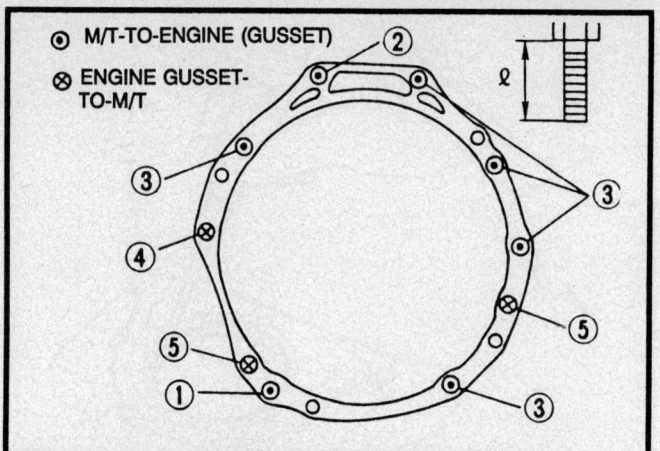

Transmission mounting bolt locations on 1990–91 300ZX; bolt (1) is 100mm, bolt (2) is 65mm, bolt (3) is 60mm, bolt (4) is 55mm and bolt (5) is 25mm

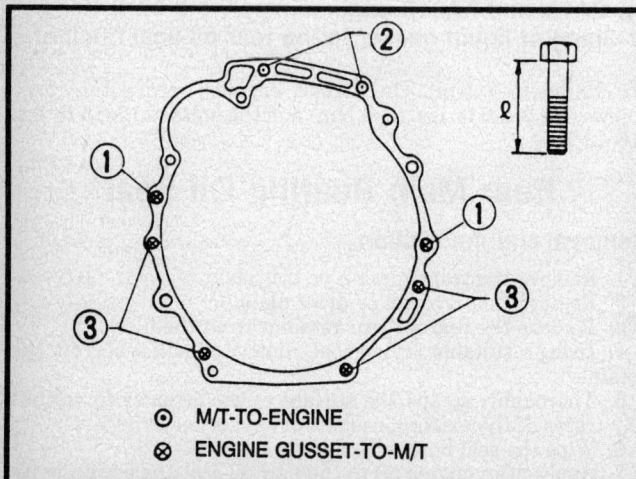

Transmission mounting bolt locations on 200SX (4 cylinder); bolt (1) is 75mm, bolt (2) is 65mm and bolt (3) is 25mm

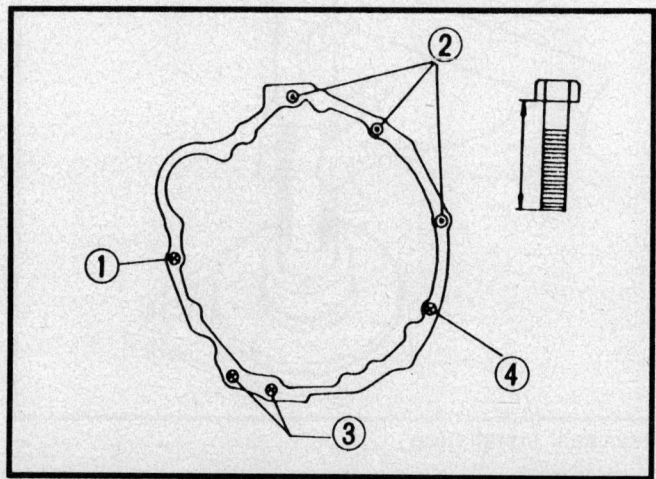

Transmission mounting bolt locations on 240SX; bolt (1) is 70mm, bolt (2) is 60mm, bolt (3) is 30mm and bolt (4) is 25mm

8. Support the engine with a large wood block and a jack under the oil pan. Do not place the jack under the oil pan drain plug.

9. Unbolt the transmission from the crossmember. Support the transmission with a jack and remove the crossmember.

10. Lower the rear of the engine to allow clearance.

11. Unplug the back-up light, neutral and overdrive switch connectors.

12. Unbolt the transmission. Lower and remove it to the rear.

NOTE: The transmission bolts are different lengths. Tagging the transmission-to-engine bolts upon removal will facilitate proper tightening during installation.

To install:

13. Raise the transmission onto the engine and install the mounting bolts. Torque the bolts as follows:

   a. 200SX with 4 cylinder engine—tighten bolts (1) and (2) to 29–36 ft. lbs. (39–49 Nm) and bolt (3) to 22–29 ft. lbs. (29–39 Nm).

   b. 200SX (V6) and 1987–89 300ZX—tighten the long mounting bolts (65mm and 60mm) to 29–36 ft. lbs. (39–49 Nm). Tighten the short bolts (55mm and 25mm) to 22–29 ft. lbs. (29–39 Nm).

   c. 240SX—tighten bolts (1), (2) and (4) to 29–36 ft. lbs. (39–49 Nm) and bolt (3) to 22–29 ft. lbs. (29–39 Nm)

   d. 1990–91 300ZX—tighten bolts (1), (2) and (3) to 29–36 ft. lbs. (39–49 Nm). Tighten bolts (4) and (5) to 22–29 ft. lbs. (29–39 Nm).

14. Plug in the back-up light, neutral and overdrive switch connectors.

15. Install the crossmember.

16. Install the clutch operating cylinder.

17. Install the shifter lever, shift knob and console boot finisher or control rod.

18. Connect the speedometer drive cable.

19. Install the driveshaft. Torque the flange bolts to 29–33 ft. lbs. (34–44 Nm) on all except 200SX turbocharged. On 200SX turbocharged, torque the flange bolts to 25–33 ft. lbs. (35–44 Nm). On 1990–91 300ZX, torque the center bearing bracket nuts to 19–29 ft. lbs. (25–39 Nm).

20. On 1990–91 300ZX, connect the exhaust tube section to the manifolds and attach the support bracket to the transmission. On 1987–89 300ZX, install the exhaust front tube, catalytic converter and exhaust manifold conecting tube.

21. Lower the vehicle and connect the negative battery cable.

MANUAL TRANSAXLE

For further information, please refer to "Professional Transmission Repair Manual" for additional coverage.

Transaxle Assembly

Removal and Installation

EXCEPT 1990–91 STANZA

1. Disconnect the negative battery cable.
2. Remove the battery and battery bracket.
3. Remove the air duct, air cleaner box and air flow meter.
4. Raise the front of the vehicle and support safely.
5. Drain the transaxle oil.
6. On Stanza wagon (4WD) and Sentra (4WD) vehicles, remove the transfer case.
7. Withdraw the halfshafts from the transaxle. On Stanza wagon (4WD), remove only the left halfshaft.

NOTE: When removing halfshafts, use care not to damage the lip of the oil seal. After shafts are removed, insert a steel bar or wooden dowel of suitable diameter to prevent the side gears from rotating and falling into the differential case.

8. On 1989–91 Maxima, remove the clutch operating cylinder from the transaxle.
9. Remove the wheel well protector(s).
10. Separate the control rod and support rod from the transaxle.
11. Remove the engine gusset securing bolt and the engine mounting.
12. Remove the clutch control cable from the operating lever.
13. Disconnect speedometer cable from the transaxle.
14. Disconnect the wires from the reverse (back-up), neutral and overdrive switches. On 1989–91 Maxima, disconnect the speed and position switch sensors from the transaxle also.
15. Support the engine by placing a jack under the oil pan, with a wooden block placed between the jack and pan for protection.
16. Support the transaxle with a hydraulic floor jack.
17. Remove the engine mounting securing bolts.

NOTE: Most of the transaxle mounting bolts are different lenghts. Tagging the bolts upon removal will facilitate proper tightening during installation.

18. Remove the bolts attaching the transaxle to the engine.
19. Using the hydraulic floor jack as a carrier, carefully lower the transaxle down and away from the engine.

To install:

20. Before installing, clean the mating surfaces on the engine rear plate and clutch housing. On 1988–91 Sentra (4WD) and Stanza wagon (4WD), apply sealant KP510–00150 or equivalent as shown.
21. Apply a light coat of a lithium-based grease to the spline parts of the clutch disc and the transaxle input shaft.
22. Raise the transaxle into place and bolt it to the engine. Install the engine mounts. Torque the transaxle mounting bolts as follows:

   a. 1987–88 Maxima—tighten bolts (1), (2) and (3) to 32–43 ft. lbs. (43–58 Nm). Tighten bolt (4) to 22–30 ft. lbs. (30–40 Nm) and bolt (5) to 12–15 ft. lbs. (16–21 Nm).

   b. 1989–91 Maxima—tighten bolt (1) to 12–15 ft. lbs. (16–21 Nm), bolt (2) to 22–30 ft. lbs. (30–40 Nm), bolts (3) and (4) to 32–43 ft. lbs. (43–58 Nm). Torque the front and rear gusset bolts to 22–30 ft. lbs. (30–40 Nm).

   c. 1987–88 Pulsar/Sentra (E16S and E16i)—tighten bolts (1) and (3) to 12–15 ft. lbs. (16–22 Nm). Tighten bolts (2) and (4) to 14–22 ft. lbs. (20–29 Nm). Bolts (3) and (4) are found on 1987 Pulsar and all Sentra.

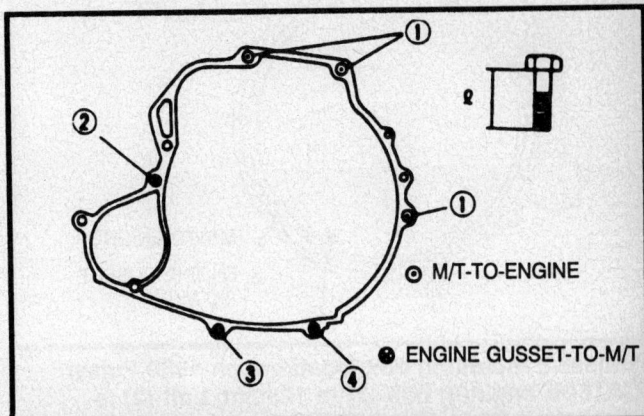

Transaxle mounting bolt locations on 1987–88 Maxima; bolt (1) is 65mm, bolt (2) is 55mm, bolt (3) is 60mm and bolts (4) and (5) are 25mm

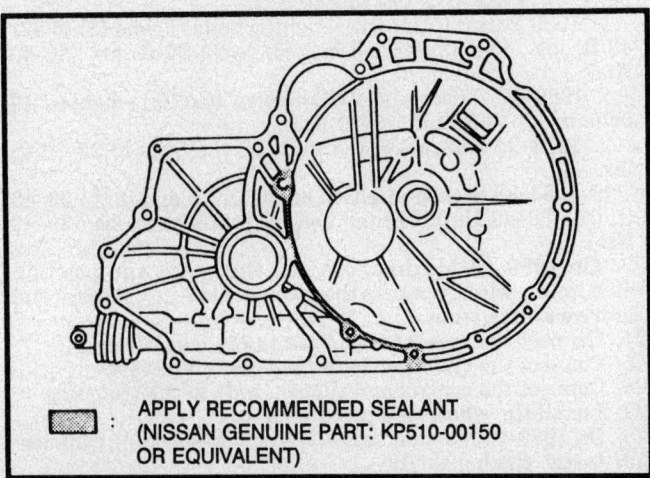

On 1988–91 Sentra (4WD) and Stanza wagon (4WD), apply sealant to the shaded area

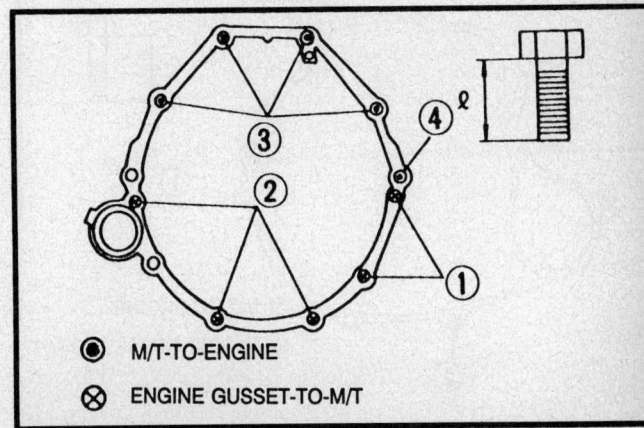

Transaxle mounting bolt locations on On 1989–91 Maxima; bolts (1) and (2) are 25mm, bolt (3) is 55mm and bolt (4) is 65mm

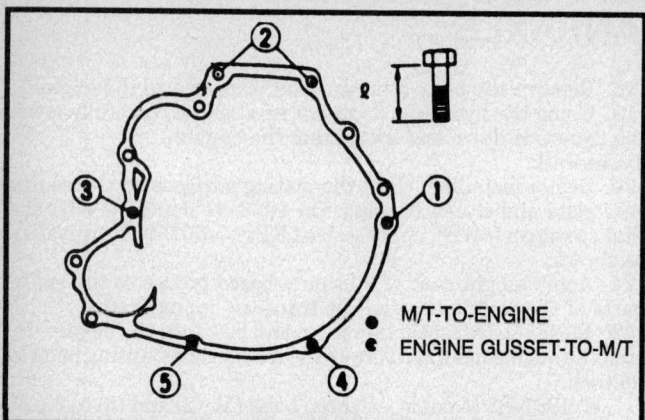

Transaxle mounting bolt locations on 1987 Pulsar with CA16DE engine; bolt (1) is 90mm, bolt (2) is 55mm, bolt (3) is 75mm, bolt (4) is 40mm, bolt (5) is 25mm

M/T-TO-ENGINE
ENGINE GUSSET-TO-M/T

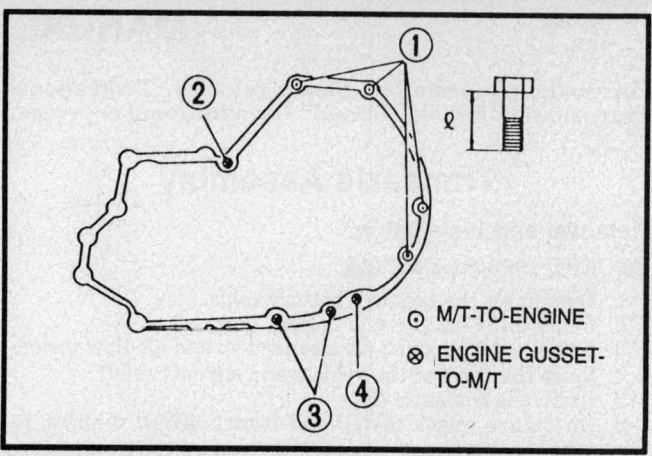

Transaxle mounting bolt locations on 1988–91 Sentra 4WD; bolt (1) is 70mm, bolt (2) is 40mm, bolt (3) is 20mm, bolt (4) is 55mm

M/T-TO-ENGINE
ENGINE GUSSET-TO-M/T

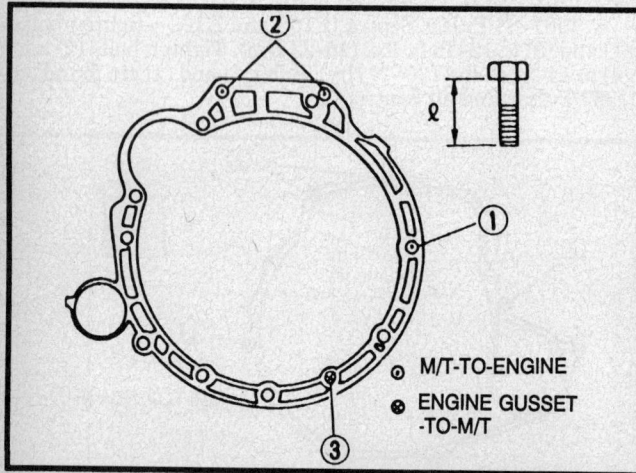

M/T-TO-ENGINE
ENGINE GUSSET-TO-M/T

Transaxle mounting bolt locations on 1989 Pulsar (CA18DE engine); bolt (1) is 125mm, bolt (2) is 65mm, bolt (3) is 45mm. Bolt (1) has a nut

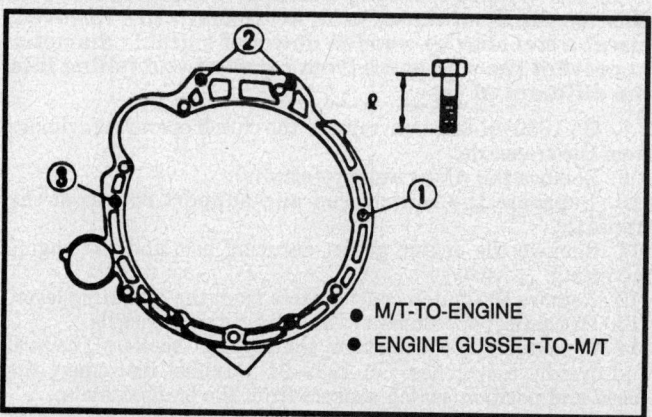

M/T-TO-ENGINE
ENGINE GUSSET-TO-M/T

On 1987–89 Stanza; bolt (1) is 120mm, bolt (2) is 65mm, bolt (3) is 70mm, bolt (4) is 25mm. Bolt (1) has a nut

d. 1987–88 Pulsar (CA16DE and CA18DE)—on CA16DE engines, tighten bolts (1), (2) and (3) to 22–30 ft. lbs. and bolts (4) and (5) to 12–15 ft. lbs. (16–21 Nm). On CA18DE engines, tighten bolts (1) and (2) to to 32–43 ft. lbs. (43–58 Nm) and bolts (3) to 22–30 ft. lbs. (30–40 Nm).

e. 1989 Pulsar (CA18DE)—tighten bolts (1) and (2) to 32–43 ft. lbs. (43–58 Nm) and bolt (3) to 22–30 ft. lbs. (30–40 Nm).

f. 1989–91 Pulsar and 2WD Sentra (GA16i)—tighten all bolts to 12–15 ft. lbs. (16–21 Nm).

g. 1988–91 Sentra 4WD—torque all the bolts to 22–30 ft. lbs.

h. 1987–89 Stanza—tighten bolts (1), (2) and (3) to 32–43 ft. lbs. (39–49 Nm). Tighten bolt (4) to 22–30 ft. lbs. (30–40 Nm).

23. On 1989–91 Maxima, connect the speed and position switch sensor wires. Connect the reverse (back-up), neutral and overdrive switch wires.

24. Connect the speedometer cable to the transaxle.

25. Connect the clutch cable to the operating lever.

26. Connect the control and support rods to the transaxle.

27. Install the wheel well protectors.

28. On 1989–91 Maxima, install the clutch operating cylinder.

29. Install the halfshafts.

30. On Stanza wagon (4WD) and Sentra (4WD) vehicles, install the transfer case.

31. Lower the vehicle.

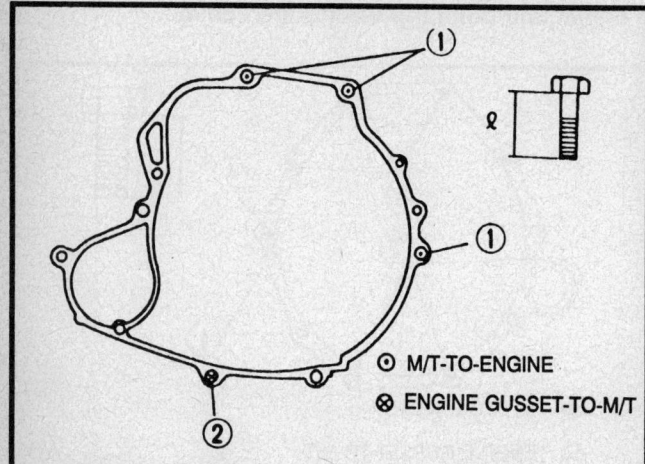

M/T-TO-ENGINE
ENGINE GUSSET-TO-M/T

Transaxle mounting bolt locations on 1989–91 Pulsar and 2WD Sentra (GA16i engine); bolt (1) is 70mm and bolt (2) is 25mm

32. Install the air duct, air cleaner box and air flow meter.
33. Install the battery and battery bracket.
34. Connect the negative battery cable.
35. Remove the filler plug and fill the transaxle to the proper level with fluid that meets API GL–4 specifications. Fill to the level of the plug hole. Apply a thread sealant to the threads of the filler plug and install the plug in the transaxle case.

1990–91 STANZA

1. Disconnect the negative battery cable.
2. Remove the battery and battery bracket.
3. Remove the air cleaner box with the air flow meter.
4. Remove the AIV unit.
5. Remove the clutch operating cylinder from the transaxle.
6. Remove the clutch hose clamp.
7. Raise and support the vehicle safely.
8. Disconnect the speedometer cable from the transaxle.
9. Disconnect the position switch and all electrical connectors from the transaxle. Tag each wire.
10. Remove the breather hose clamp from the transaxle.
11. Remove the starter.
12. Disconnect the shift control rod from the transaxle.
13. Drain the transaxle fluid.
14. Remove the front exhaust tube.
15. Withdraw the halfshafts from the transaxle.

NOTE: When removing halfshafts, use care not to damage the lip of the oil seal. After shafts are removed, insert a steel bar or wooden dowel of suitable diameter to prevent the side gears from rotating and falling into the differential case.

16. Support the engine by placing a jack under the oil pan, with a wooden block placed between the jack and pan for protection.
17. Support the transaxle with a suitable floor jack.
18. Remove the rear and left engine mounts.
19. Remove the bolts attaching the transaxle to the engine.

NOTE: The transaxle mounting bolts are different lengths. Tagging the bolts upon removal will facilitate proper tightening during installation.

20. Using the jack as a carrier, carefully lower the transaxle down and away from the vehicle.

NOTE: Be careful not to strike any adjacent parts or input shaft (the shaft protruding from the transaxle which fits into the clutch assembly) when removing the transaxle from the vehicle.

To install:
21. Before installing, clean the mating surfaces on the engine rear plate and clutch housing.

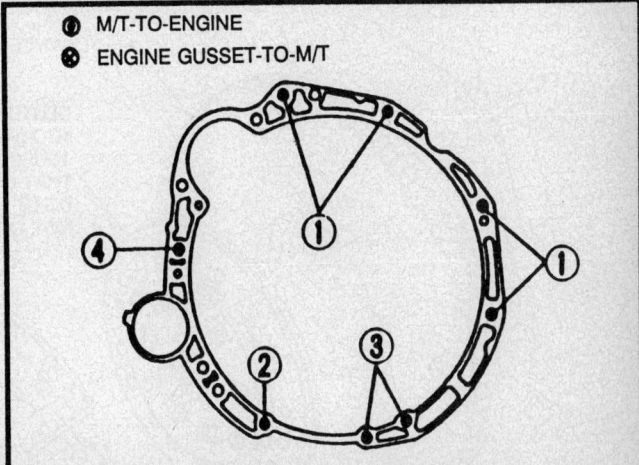

Transaxle mounting bolt locations on 1990–91 Stanza; bolt (1) is 45mm, bolt (2) is 25mm, bolt (3) is 30mm, bolt (4) is 40mm

22. Apply a light coat of a lithium-based grease to the spline parts of the clutch disc and the transaxle input shaft.
23. Raise the transaxle into place and install the mounting bolts. Tighten bolts (1) and (2) to 29–36 ft. lbs. (39–49 Nm). Tighten bolts (3) and (4) to 22–30 ft. lbs. (30–40 Nm).
24. Install the rear and left engine mounts.
25. Remove the transaxle and engine supports.
26. Install the halfshafts.
27. Install the front exhaust tube with new gaskets.
28. Connect the shift control rod.
29. Install the starter.
30. Connect the electrical and position switch wiring.
31. Connect the speedometer cable.
32. Lower the vehicle.
33. Install the clutch hose clamp.
34. Install the clutch operating cylinder.
35. Install the AIV unit.
36. Install the air cleaner box and air flow meter.
37. Install the battery bracket and battery.
38. Connect the negative battery cable.
39. Remove the filler plug and fill the transaxle to the proper level with fluid that meets API GL–4 specifications. Fill to the level of the plug hole. Apply a thread sealant to the threads of the filler plug and install the plug in the transaxle

CLUTCH

Clutch Assembly

Removal and Installation

1. Remove the transmission or transaxle.
2. Insert a clutch aligning bar or similar tool all the way into the clutch disc hub. This must be done so as to support the weight of the clutch disc during removal.
3. Mark the clutch assembly-to-flywheel relationship with paint or a center punch so the clutch assembly can be assembled in the same position from which it is removed.
4. Loosen the pressure plate bolts in criss-cross fashion, a

turn at a time to gradually relieve the spring pressure. Remove the bolts once the spring pressure is relieved.
5. Remove the pressure plate and clutch disc. Inspect the pressure plate or scoring for roughness, and reface or replace as necessary. Slight roughness can be smoothed with a fine emery cloth. Inspect the clutch disc for worn or oily facings, loose rivets and broken or loose springs, and replace.
6. Remove the release mechanism. On Pulsar and Sentra, the clutch lever is removed by aligning the lever retaining pins with the clutch cavity, then driving out the pins with a suitable pin punch. Inspect the release sleeve and lever contact surfaces for wear, rust or any other damage. Replace if necessary.

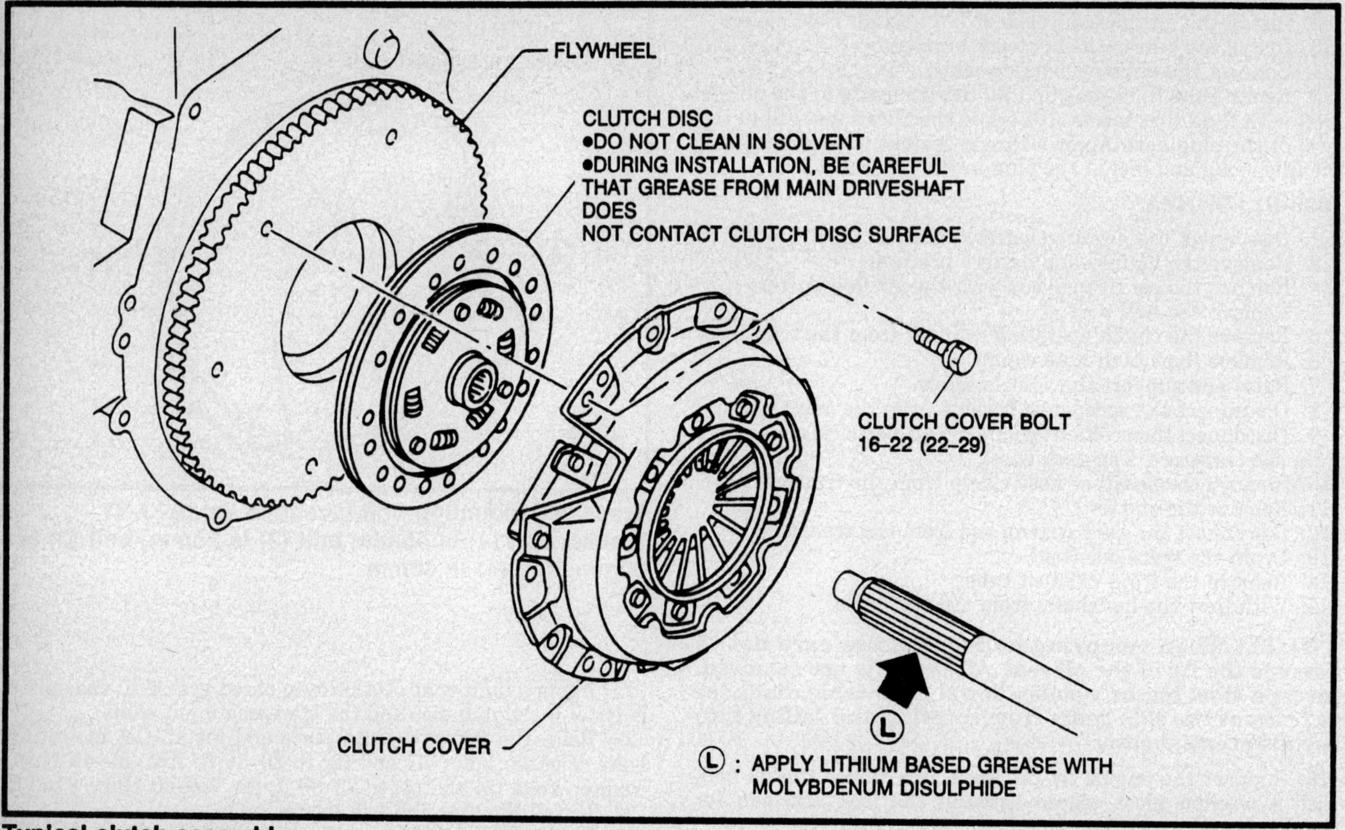

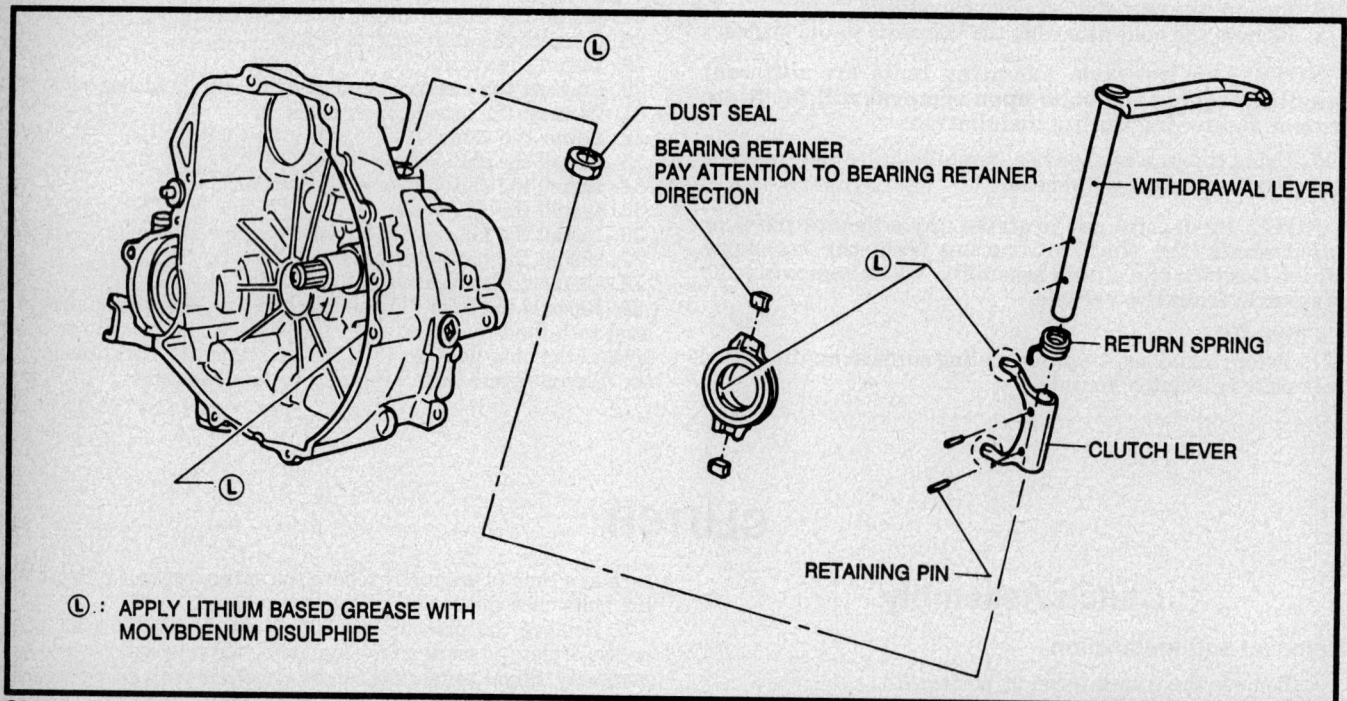

FLYWHEEL

CLUTCH DISC
●DO NOT CLEAN IN SOLVENT
●DURING INSTALLATION, BE CAREFUL
THAT GREASE FROM MAIN DRIVESHAFT
DOES
NOT CONTACT CLUTCH DISC SURFACE

CLUTCH COVER BOLT
16–22 (22–29)

CLUTCH COVER

Ⓛ : APPLY LITHIUM BASED GREASE WITH
MOLYBDENUM DISULPHIDE

Typical clutch assembly

DUST SEAL

BEARING RETAINER
PAY ATTENTION TO BEARING RETAINER
DIRECTION

WITHDRAWAL LEVER

RETURN SPRING

CLUTCH LEVER

RETAINING PIN

Ⓛ : APPLY LITHIUM BASED GREASE WITH
MOLYBDENUM DISULPHIDE

Clutch release mechanism—Pulsar and Sentra

7. Inspect the pressure plate for wear, scoring, etc., and reface or replace as necessary. Minor imperfections or discoloration may be removed with emery cloth.

8. Inspect the release bearing. The bearing should roll freely and quietly. It should not have any cracks, pitting or wear. Replace as necessary.

To install:

9. Apply multi-purpose grease to the bearing sleeve inside

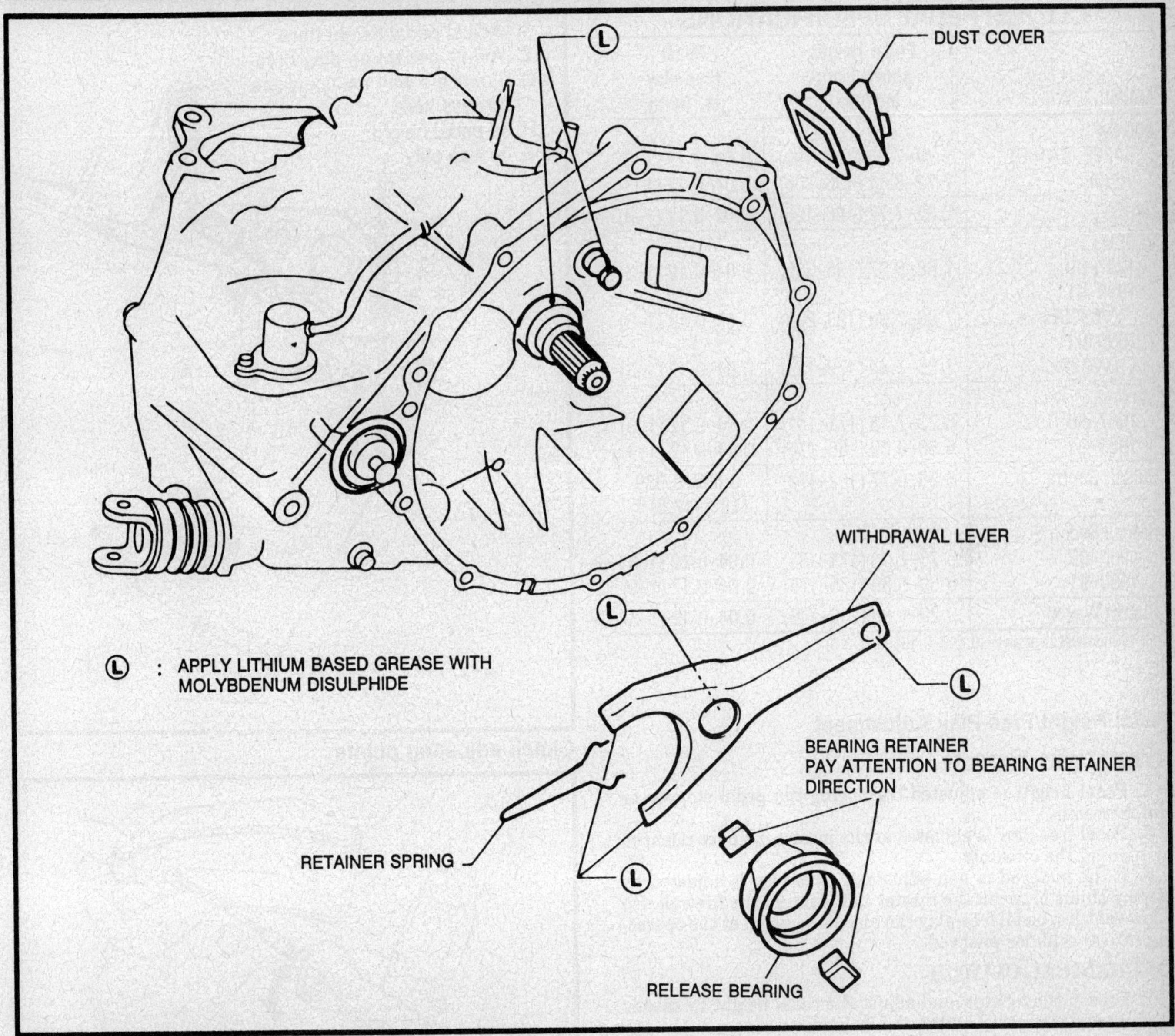

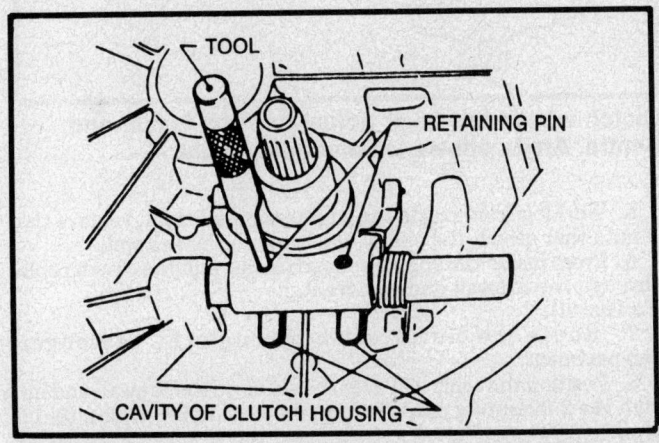

DUST COVER

WITHDRAWAL LEVER

Ⓛ : APPLY LITHIUM BASED GREASE WITH MOLYBDENUM DISULPHIDE

BEARING RETAINER
PAY ATTENTION TO BEARING RETAINER DIRECTION

RETAINER SPRING

RELEASE BEARING

Clutch release mechanism—except Pulsar and Sentra

TOOL

RETAINING PIN

CAVITY OF CLUTCH HOUSING

Clutch lever retaining pin removal—Pulsar and Sentra

groove, the contact point of the withdrawal lever and bearing sleeve, the contact surface of the lever ball pin and lever.

10. Apply a small amount of lithium based grease to the transmission splines.

11. Install the disc on the splines and slide it back and forth a few times. Remove the disc and remove any excess grease on the hub. Be sure no grease contacts the disc or pressure plate.

NOTE: Take special care to prevent any grease or oil from getting on the clutch facing. During assembly, keep all disc facings, flywheel and pressure plate clean and dry. Grease, oil or dirt on these parts will result in a slipping clutch when assembled.

12. Install the disc, aligning it with a splined dummy shaft.

13. Install the pressure plate and torque the bolts to 16–22 ft. lbs. (22–29 Nm) on all vehicles except 240SX, and 1990–91 300ZX. On 240SX and 1990–91 300ZX, torque the bolts to 25–33 ft. lbs. (34–44 Nm).

14. Remove the dummy shaft.

15. Install the transmission or transaxle.

CLUTCH PEDAL SPECIFICATIONS

Model	Pedal Height above Floor in. (mm)	Pedal Free-play in. (mm)
200 SX		
CA20E, CA18ET	7.44–7.83 (189–199)	0.04–0.12 (1–3)
V630E	7.72–8.11 (196–206)	0.04–0.12 (1–3)
240SX	7.32–7.72 (186–196)	0.04–0.12 (1–3)
300ZX		
1987–89	7.68–8.07 (195–205)	0.04–0.12 (1–3)
1990–91 (V630DE)	7.60–7.99 (193–203)	0.04–0.12 (1–3)
1990–91 (V632DETT)	7.05–7.44 (179–189)	0.04–0.12 (1–3)
Maxima		
1987–88	6.73–7.13 (171–181)	0.04–0.12 (1–3)
1989–91	6.50–6.89 (165–175)	0.04–0.12 (1–3)
Pulsar, Sentra	6.38–6.77 (162–172)	0.492–0.689 (12.5–17.5)①
Stanza Sedan		
1987–89	6.73–7.13 (171–181)	0.04–0.12 (1–3)
1990–91	6.50–6.89 (165–175)	0.04–0.12 (1–3)
Stanza Wagon	9.29–9.69 (236–246)	0.04–0.12 (1–3)

① Withdrawal lever play—0.098–0.138 (2.5–3.5)

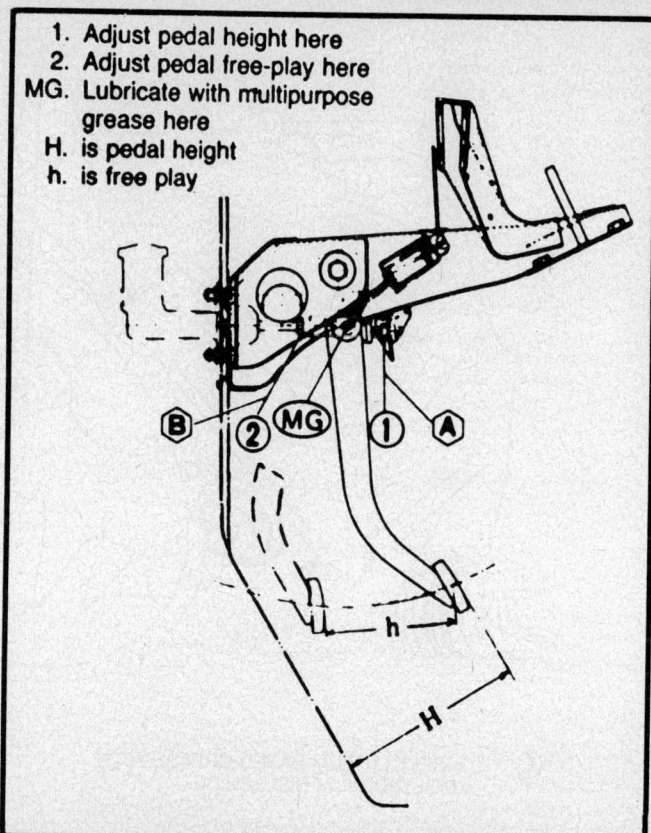

1. Adjust pedal height here
2. Adjust pedal free-play here
MG. Lubricate with multipurpose grease here
H. is pedal height
h. is free play

Clutch adjusting points

Pedal Height/Free-Play Adjustment

HYDRAULIC CLUTCH

1. Pedal height is adjusted by moving the pedal stopper or clutch switch.
2. Pedal free-play is adjusted at the master cylinder pushrod by turning the locknut.
3. If the pushrod is non-adjustable, free-play is adjusted by placing shims between the master cylinder and the firewall. On a few vehicles, pedal free-play can also be adjusted at the operating (slave) cylinder pushrod.

MECHANICAL CLUTCH

1. Loosen the locknut and adjust the pedal height by means of the pedal stopper. Tighten the locknut.
2. Push the withdrawal lever in by hand until resistance is felt. Adjust withdrawal lever play at the lever tip end with the locknuts. Withdrawal lever plat should be 0.0198–0.138 in. (2.5–3.5mm).
3. Depress and release the clutch pedal several times and then recheck the withdrawal lever play again. Readjust if necessary.
4. Measure the pedal free travel at the center of the pedal pad.

Clutch Cable

Removal and Installation

1. Disconnect the negative battery cable.
2. Remove the floor mats.
3. Working from inside the engine compartment, loosen the adjusting nuts and locknut and disconnect the clutch cable from the withdrawal lever.
4. Working from inside the vehicle, disconnect the clutch cable from the clutch pedal.

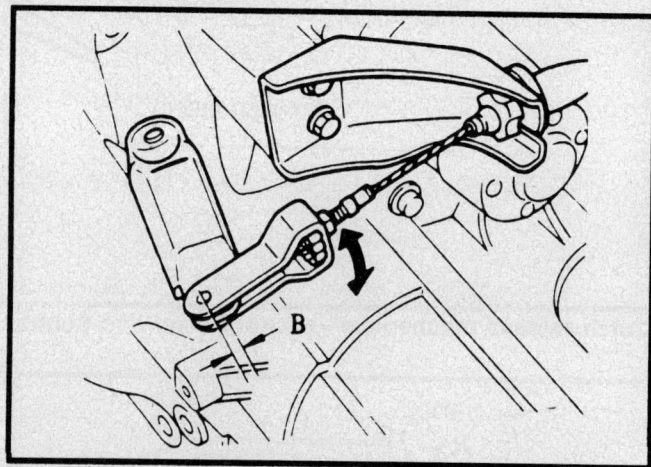

Clutch withdrawal lever adjustment on Pulsar and Sentra. Arrow shows locknut adjustment

5. Working from inside the engine compartment, remove the 2 nuts that attach the end of the cable to the fire wall.
6. From inside the engine compartment, pull the clutch cable through the firewall and remove it.

To install:

7. Route the clutch cable through the passenger compartment.
8. Position the cable end over the studs on the firewall and install the 2 mounting nuts. Torque the nuts to 6–8 ft. lbs. (9–11 Nm).
9. Connect the clutch cable to the clutch pedal.
10. Connect the clutch cable to the withdrawal lever.

11. Lubricate the pedal fulcrum pin and pivot points with lithium based grease.

12. Adjust the cable and the clutch switch.

13. Check the clutch for proper engagement.

14. Install the floor mats.

15. Connect the negative battery cable.

Clutch Master Cylinder

Removal and Installation

1. Disconnect the negative battery cable.

2. Disconnect the clutch pedal arm from the pushrod.

3. Disconnect the clutch hydraulic line from the master cylinder. Plug the end of line to prevent leakage.

4. Remove the nuts attaching the master cylinder and remove the master cylinder and pushrod toward the engine compartment side.

5. Install the master cylinder in the reverse order of removal.

6. Bleed the clutch hydraulic system and make all necessary clutch adjustments.

Clutch Slave Cylinder

Removal and Installation

1. Remove the slave cylinder attaching bolts and the pushrod from the shift fork.

2. Disconnect the flexible fluid hose from the slave cylinder and remove the unit form the vehicle. Plug the end of the hose.

3. Install the slave cylinder in the reverse order of removal and bleed the clutch hydraulic system.

Hydraulic Clutch System Bleeding

Bleeding is required to remove air trapped in the hydraulic system. This operation is necessary whenever the system has been leaking or opened for maintenance. The bleed screw is located on the clutch slave (operating) cylinder.

The 200SX, 240SX, 1987–89 300ZX and 1990–91 Stanza are also equipped with a clutch damper mechanism. The clutch damper is bled in exactly the same manner as the operating cylinder. It should be bled along with the operating cylinder.

1. Remove the bleed screw dust cap.

2. Attach a transparent vinyl tube to the bleed screw, immersing the free end in a clean container of clean brake fluid.

3. Fill the master cylinder with the proper fluid.

4. Open the bleed screw about ¾ turn.

5. Depress the clutch pedal quickly. Hold it down. Have an assistant tighten the bleed screw. Allow the pedal to return slowly.

6. Repeat Steps 2 and 5 until no more air bubbles are seen in the fluid container.

7. Remove the bleed tube. Replace the dust cap. Refill the master cylinder.

8. Bleed the clutch damper, if equipped.

AUTOMATIC TRANSMISSION

For further information, please refer to "Professional Transmission Repair Manual" for additional coverage.

Transmission Assembly

Removal and Installation

200SX, 240SX AND 300ZX

1. Disconnect the battery cable.

2. Remove the accelerator linkage.

3. Detach the shift linkage.

4. Disconnect the neutral safety switch and downshift solenoid wiring.

5. Remove the drain plug and drain the torque converter. If there is no converter drain plug, drain the transmission. If there is no transmission drain plug, remove the pan to drain. Replace the pan to keep out dirt.

6. Remove the front exhaust pipe.

7. Remove the vacuum tube and speedometer cable.

8. Disconnect the fluid cooler and charging tubes. Plug the tube ends to prevent leakage.

9. Lower the driveshaft and remove the starter.

10. Support the transmission with a jack under the oil pan. Support the engine also.

11. Remove the rear crossmember.

12. Mark the relationship between the torque converter and the driveplate. Remove the bolts holding the converter to the driveplate through the access hole at the front, under the engine by rotating the crankshaft. Unbolt the transmission from the engine and remove it.

NOTE: The transmission bolts are different lengths. Tag each bolt according to location to ensure proper installation. This is particularly important on the 240SX and 1990–91 300ZX.

13. Check the driveplate runout with a dial indictator. Runout must be no more than 0.020 in.

To install:

14. If the torque converter was removed from the engine for any reason, after it is installed, the distance from the face of the converter to the edge of the converter housing must be checked prior to installing the transmission. This is done to ensure proper installation of the torque converter. On 200SX and 1987–89 300ZX, the dimension should be 1.38 in. (35mm) or more. On

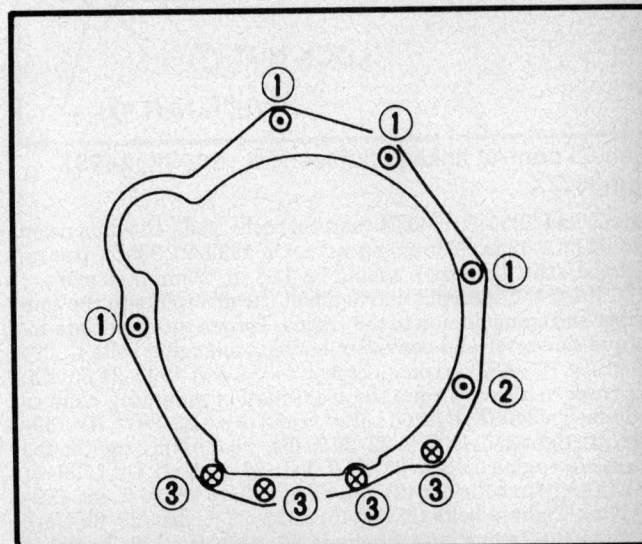

Transmission mounting bolt locations on 240SX; bolt (1) is 40mm, bolt (2) is 50mm, bolt (3) is 25mm and the gusset bolts are 20mm

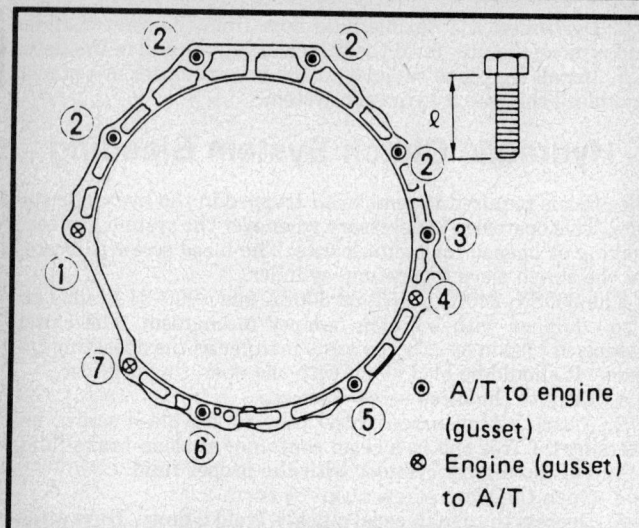

Transmission mounting bolt locations on 1990–91 300ZX (turbo and non-turbo)

- ⊙ A/T to engine (gusset)
- ⊗ Engine (gusset) to A/T

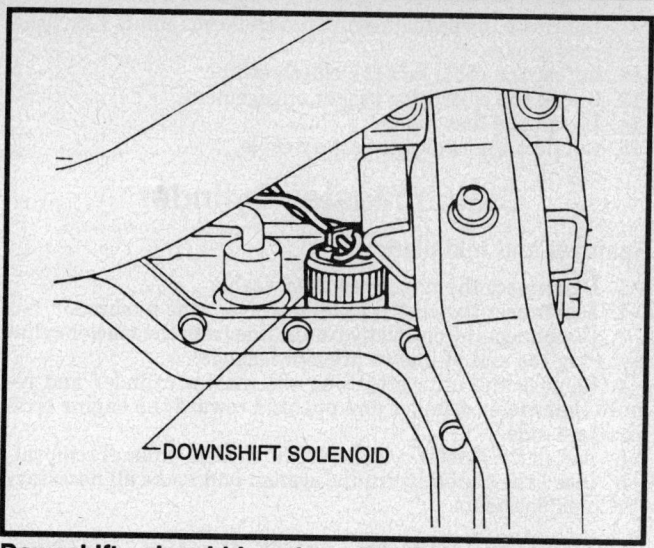

Downshift solenoid location—200SX and 1987–89 300ZX

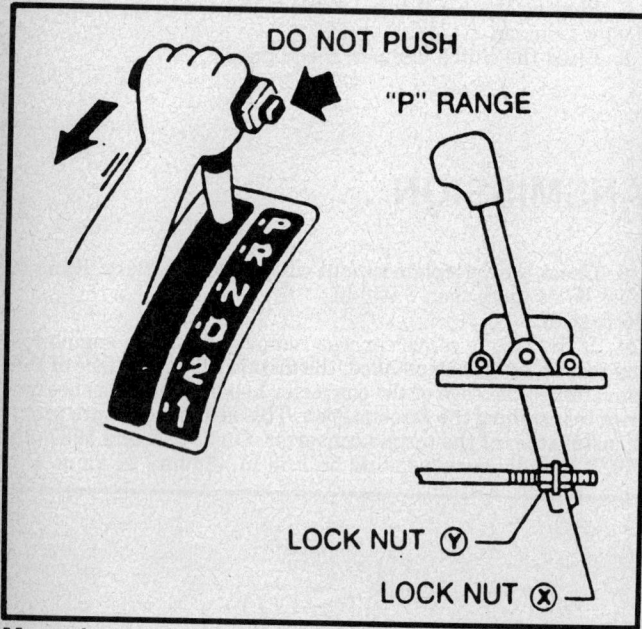

Manual control linkage adjustment—200SX, 240SX and 300ZX

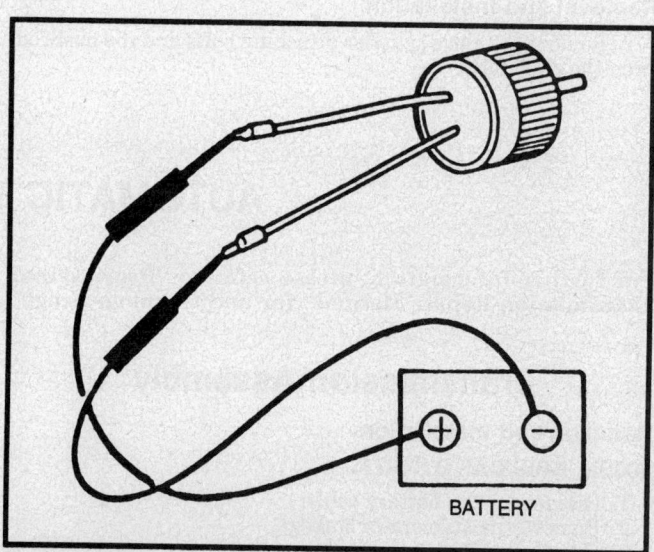

Check the downshift solenoid by applying battery voltage

240SX and 1990–91 300ZX (non-turbocharged), the dimension should be 1.02 in. (26mm) or more. On 1990–91 300ZX (turbocharged), the dimension should be 0.98 in. (25mm) or more.

15. Raise the transmission and bolt the driveplate to the converter and transmission to the engine. Torque the driveplate-to-torque converter and converter housing-to-engine bolts to 29–36 ft. lbs. (39–49 Nm) on all except 240SX and 1990–91 300ZX. On these vehicles, torque the transmission mounting bolts as follows: On 240SX, tighten bolts (1) and (2) to 29–36 ft. lbs. (39–49 Nm); tighten bolt (3) to 22–29 ft. lbs. (29–39 Nm); tighten the gusset-to-engine bolts to 22–29 ft. lbs. (29–39 Nm). On 1990–91 300ZX tighten bolts (1), (2), (3), (6) and (7) to 29–36 ft. lbs. (39–49 Nm). Tighten bolts (2) and (5) to 22–29 ft. lbs. (29–39 Nm). Tighten the engine gusset bolts to 22–29 ft. lbs. (29–39 Nm).

NOTE: After the converter is installed, rotate the crankshaft several times to make sure the transmission rotates freely and does not bind.

16. Install the rear crossmember.
17. Remove the engine and transmission supports.
18. Install the starter and connect the driveshaft. Torque the flange bolts to 29–33 ft. lbs. (34–44 Nm) on all except 200SX turbo and 1990–91 300ZX (turbo). On 200SX turbo, torque the flange bolts to 25–33 ft. lbs. (35–44 Nm). On 1990–91 300ZX (turbo), torque the flange bolts to 40–47 ft. lbs. (54–64 Nm).
19. Unplug, connect and tighten the fluid cooler tubes.
20. Connect the speedometer cable and the vacuum tube.
21. Connect the front exhaust pipe using new gaskets.
22. Connect the switch wiring to the transmission.
23. Connect the shift linkage.
24. Connect the negative battery cable, fill the transmission to the proper level and make any necessary adjustment.
25. Perform a road test and check the fluid level.

Shift Linkage Adjustment
200SX, 240SX AND 300SX
If the detents cannot be felt or the pointer indicator is improper-

ly aligned while shifting from the **P** range to range **1**, the linkage should be adjusted.

1. Place the shifter in the **P** position.
2. Loosen the locknuts.
3. Tighten the outer locknut **X** until it touches the trunnion, pulling the selector lever toward the **R** range side without pushing the button.
4. Back off the outer locknut **X** ¼–½ turns and then tighten the inner locknut **Y** to 5–11 ft. lbs. (8–15 Nm).
5. Move the selector lever from **P** to **1**. Make sure it moves smoothly.

NOTE: The 1988–91 300ZX has an automatic transmission interlock system. This interlock system prevents the transmission selector from being shifted from the P position unless the brake pedal is depressed.

Kickdown Switch Adjustment

When the accelerator pedal is depressed, a click can be heard just before the pedal bottoms out. If the click is not heard, loosen the locknut and extend the switch until the pedal lever makes contact with the switch and the switch clicks.

On 1990–91 300ZX, before adjusting the kickdown switch, make sure the accelerator cable is properly adjusted. Then, check the clearance between the stopper rubber and the threaded end of the switch with the accelerator cable fully depressed. The clearance should be 0.012–0.039 in. (0.3–1.0mm). If the clearance is not as specified, adjust by loosening the switch locknut and turning the switch in or out. Tighten the locknut and check the clearance again.

Downshift Solenoid Check

200SX AND 1987–89 300ZX

The solenoid is controlled by a downshift switch on the accelerator linkage inside the vehicle. To test the switch and solenoid operation, preform the following:

1. Turn the ignition to the **ON** position.
2. Push the accelerator all the way down to actuate the switch.
3. The solenoid should "click" when actuated. The solenoid is screwed into the outside of the case. If there is no click, check the switch, wiring, and solenoid.
4. To remove the solenoid, first drain 2–3 pints of fluid, then unscrew the unit.
5. Apply battery voltage to the switch and listen for the click. If no click is audible, replace the switch or repair the wiring.

AUTOMATIC TRANSAXLE

For further information, please refer to "Professional Transmission Repair Manual" for additional coverage.

Transaxle Assembly

Removal and Installation

1987–88 MAXIMA

NOTE: The engine/transaxle unit must be removed and installed as a unit. After removal, the transaxle may be separated from the engine.

1. Remove the transaxle/engine as an assembly.
2. Remove the transaxle-to-engine mounting bolts and then carefully draw out the rear plate.
3. Remove the bolts securing the torque converter to the driveplate.
4. Before removing the torque converter, use chalk or paint to matchmark at least 2 parts so they may be replaced in their original positions during installation. Remove the torque converter.
5. Check the driveplate runout with a dial indicator. Runout must be no more than 0.020 in.
6. If the torque converter was removed from the engine for any reason, after it is installed, the distance from the face of the converter to the edge of the converter housing must be checked prior to installing the transaxle. This is done to ensure proper installation of the torque converter. The dimension should be 0.709 in. (18mm) or more.
7. During installation of the transaxle/engine assembly, observe the following:
   a. When installing the torque converter to the driveplate, be certain the matchmarks made during removal are in alignment. Apply Loctite® or a similar sealing compound to the converter-to-driveplate bolts before installation.
   b. After the torque converter has been reinstalled, rotate the crankshaft a few times to ensure that the transaxle rotates freely, with no binding.
   c. Adjust the control cable and check the inhibitor switch.
   d. After installation of the engine/transaxle assembly into the vehicle, fill the transaxle and engine with the proper amounts of fluids, then road test the vehicle.

PULSAR, SENTRA, STANZA AND 1989–91 MAXIMA

1. Disconnect the negative battery cable.
2. Raise and support the vehicle safely.
3. Remove the left front tire.
4. Drain the transaxle fluid.
5. Remove the left side fender protector.
6. Remove the halfshafts.

NOTE: Be careful not to damage the oil seals when removing the halfshafts. After removing the halfshafts, install a suitable bar so the side gears will not rotate and fall into the differential case.

7. On Stanza wagon, disconnect and remove the forward exhaust pipe.
8. Disconnect the speedometer cable.
9. Disconnect the throttle wire from the carburetor throttle lever on carbureted vehicles.
10. Remove the control cable rear end from the unit and remove the oil level gauge tube.
11. Place a suitable jack under the transaxle and engine. Do not place the jack under the oil pan drain plug. Support the engine with wooden blocks placed between the engine and the center member.
12. Disconnect the oil cooler and charging tubes. Plug the tube ends to prevent leakage.
13. Remove the engine motor mount securing bolts, as required.
14. Remove the starter motor and disconnect all electrical wires from the transaxle.
15. Loosen and remove all but 3 of the bolts holding the transaxle to the engine. Leave the 3 bolts in to support the weight of the transaxle while removing the converter bolts.
16. Remove the driveplate or dust covers.
17. Remove the bolts holding the torque torque converter to the driveplate. Rotate the crankshaft to gain access to each bolt. Before separating the torque converter, place chalk marks on 2 parts for alignment purposes during installation.

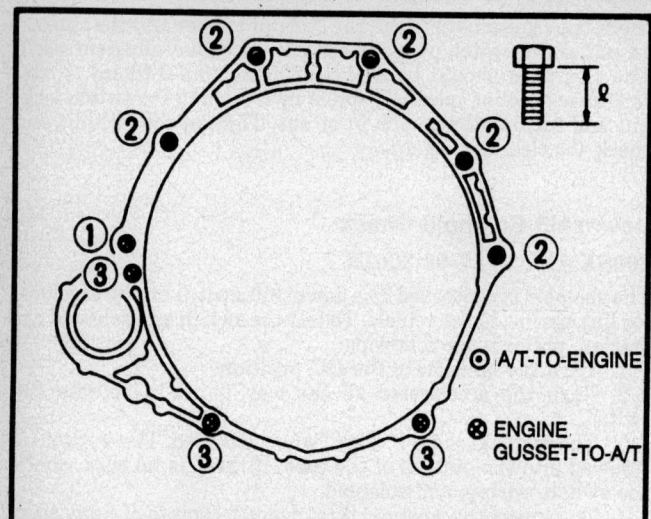

Transaxle mounting bolt locations on 1989–91 Maxima; bolt (1) is 60mm, bolt (2) is 45mm, bolt (3) is 25mm

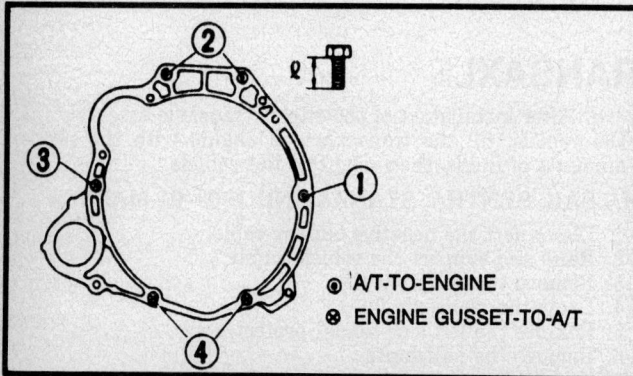

Transaxle mounting bolt locations on 1988–89 Stanza; bolt (1) is 85mm, bolt (2) is 50mm, bolt (3) is 70mm, bolt (4) is 25mm

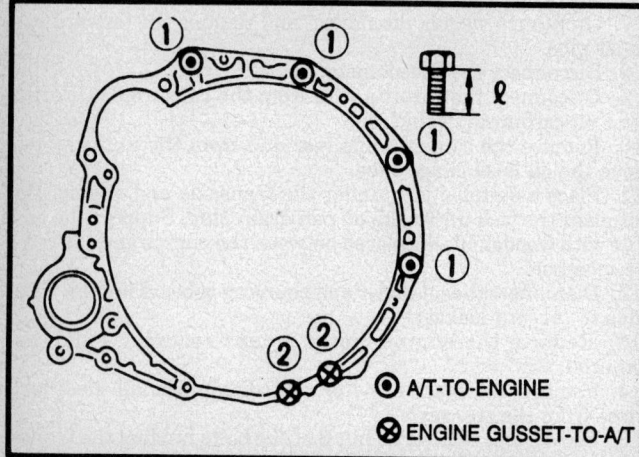

Transaxle mounting bolt locations on 1990–91 Stanza; bolt (1) is 45mm and bolt (2) is 20mm

NOTE: The transaxle bolts are different lengths. Tag each bolt according to location to ensure proper installation.

18. Remove the 3 temporary bolts. Move the jack gradually until the transaxle can be lowered and removed from the vehicle through the left side wheel housing.

19. Check the driveplate runout with a dial indictator. Runout must be no more than 0.020 in.

To install:

20. If the torque converter was removed from the engine for any reason, after it is installed, the distance from the face of the converter to the edge of the converter housing must be checked prior to installing the transaxle. This is done to ensure proper installation of the torque converter. On Maxima, the distance should be 0.71 in. (18mm) or more. On Pulsar with RL3F01A transaxles, it should be 0.831 in. (21mm) or more. On Pulsar with RL4F02A transaxles, it should be 0.748 in. (19mm) or more. On Stanza, it should be 0.75 in. (19mm) or more.

21. Raise the transaxle onto the engine and install the torque coverter-to-driveplate bolts. Torque the bolts to specification. Install 3 bolts to support the transaxle while tighten the converter bolts.

NOTE: After the converter is installed, rotate the crankshaft several times to make sure the transaxle rotates freely and does not bind.

22. Install the driveplate or dust covers.

23. Install the transaxle mounting bolts. On 1989–91 Maxima and 1988–91 Stanza, torque the bolts as follows: On 1989–91 Maxima, tighten bolts (1) and (3) to 22–30 ft. lbs. (30–40 Nm) and bolts (2) to 29–36 ft. lbs. (39–49 Nm). On 1988–89 Stanza, tighten bolts (1), (2) and (3) to 29–36 ft. lbs. Tighten bolts (4) to 22–30 ft. lbs. (30–40 Nm). On 1990–91 Stanza, tighten bolts (1) to 29–36 ft. lbs. (39–49 Nm) and bolts (2) to 22–30 ft. lbs. (30–40 Nm)

24. Connect the transaxle wiring and install the starter.

25. Install the engine mounts, if removed.

26. Connect the oil cooler and charging tubes.

27. Remove the engine and transaxle supports.

28. Install the oil level gauge tube and control cable rear end.

29. On carbureted vehicles, connect the throttle wire to the carburetor.

30. Connect the speedometer cable.

31. On Stanza wagon, install the front exhaust pipe using new gaskets.

32. Install the halfshafts.

33. Install the left side fender protector.

34. Mount the left front tire and lower the vehicle.

35. Fill the transaxle and engine with the proper amounts of fluids.

36. Adjust the control cable and throttle wire.

37. Check the inhibitor switch for proper operation.

38. Road test the vehicle.

Throttle Wire Adjustment

The throttle wire is adjusted by means of double nuts on the carburetor or throttle body.

NOTE: On 1989–91 Maxima and 1990–91 Stanza, there is no throttle wire adjustment.

EXCEPT 1990–91 PULSAR

1. Loosen the adjusting nuts.

2. With the throttle fully opened, turn the threaded shaft inward as far as it will go and then tighten the first nut against the bracket.

3. Back off the first nut ¾–1¼ turns on the 1987–88 Maxima; and 2¾–3¼ turns on the 1987–89 Stanza (including wagon) and then tighten the second nut against the bracket. On 1987–89 Pulsar back off the nut 2¾–3¼ turns (RL4F02A transaxles) and 1–1½ turns (RL3F01A transaxles) and tighten the nut.

4. Tighten both double nuts to 5.8–7.2 ft. lbs. (8–10 Nm). The throttle drum should be held securely in the full open position.

5. On 1987–89 Stanza and and 1987–88 Maxima vehicles,

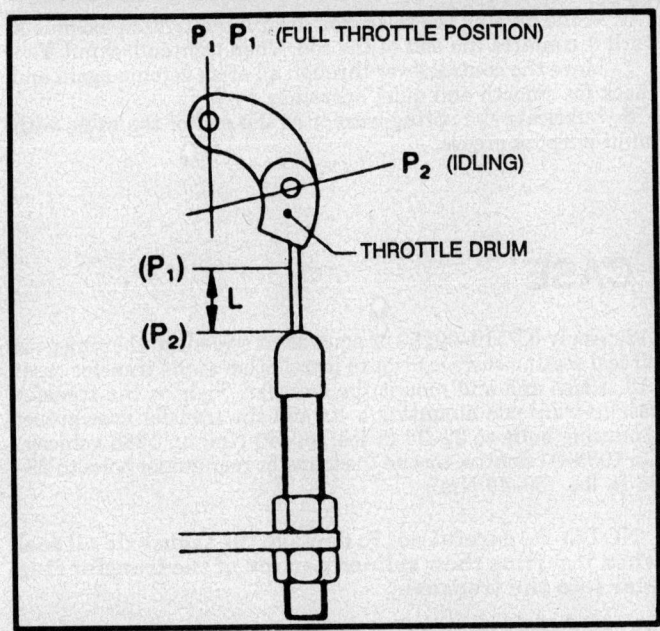

Throttle wire stroke—Sentra, 1987–89 Pulsar and 1987–88 Maxima

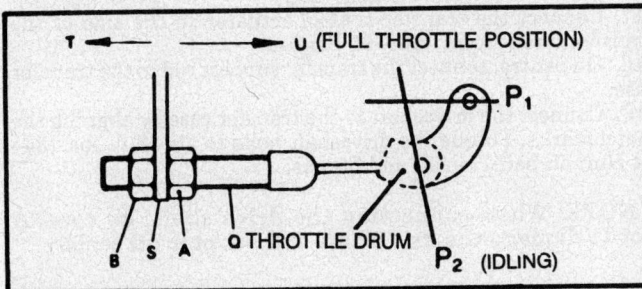

Throttle wire adjustment—Sentra, 1987–89 Pulsar and 1987–88 Maxima

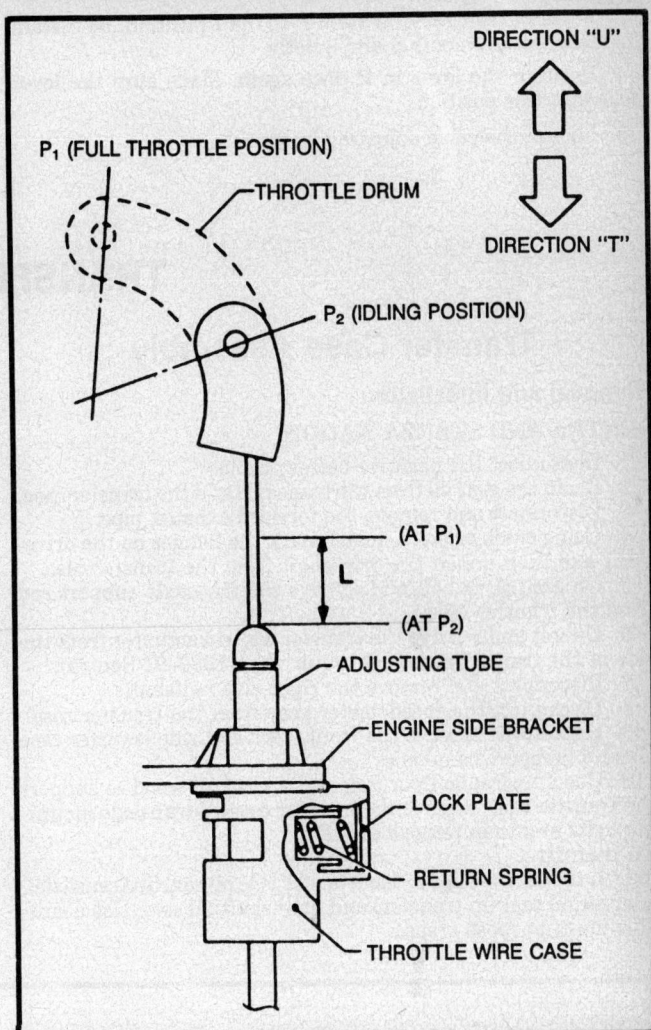

Throttle wire stroke adjustment—1990–91 Pulsar

check that the throttle wire stroke between full throttle and idling is 1.54–1.69 in. (39–43mm). On the 1987–90 Pulsar/Sentra it should be 1.079–1.236 in. (27.4–31.4mm).

1990–91 PULSAR

1. Remove the air cleaner cover.
2. While pressing on the lock plate, move the adjusting tube in the proper direction.
3. Return the lock plate to its original position.
4. Move the throttle drum from position P_1 to P_2 quickly.
5. Check that the throttle wire stroke (L) between full throttle and idling is 1.079–1.236 in. (27.4–31.4mm). Marking the throttle wire with paint dabs or a colored marker will help in measuring the throttle wire stroke.
6. Adjust the throttle wire stroke only if the throttle and accelerator wires are installed. After adjustment, make sure the parting line is straight.

Control Cable Adjustment

Move the selector from the **P** range through each gear to the **1** range. At each gear selection, the detent should be felt. If the detents cannot be felt or if the gear shift indicator pointer is not aligned properly, then the control, cable must be adjusted as follows:

1. Position the control lever (gear selector) in **P**.
2. Connect the control cable end to the lever in the transaxle unit and tighten the cable securing bolt.

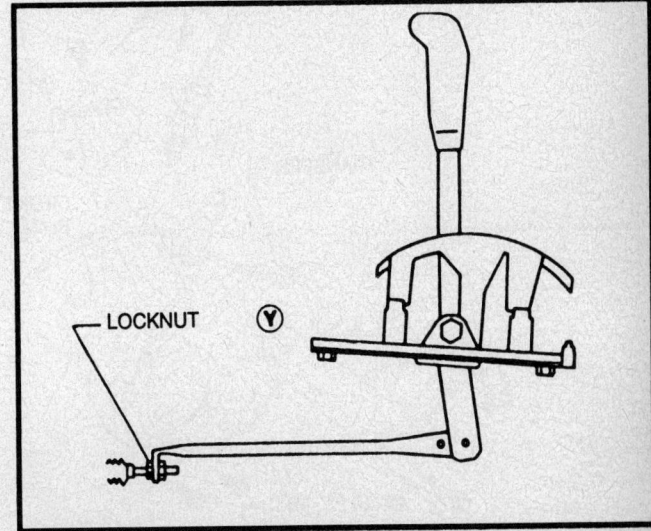

Automatic transaxle control cable adjustment—all vehicles

3. Move the control lever from **P** to the **1** position. Be certain the lever works smoothly and quietly.

4. Position the lever in **P** once again. Make sure the lever locks into this position.

5. Loosen the cable adjusting locknuts.

6. While holding the select rod horizontal, tighten locknut **X** until it contacts the end of the rod. Then tighten locknut **Y**.

7. Move the control lever through all of its detents again and check for smooth and quiet operation.

8. Lubricate the spring washer at the end of the cable with multi-purpose grease.

TRANSFER CASE

Transfer Case Assembly

Removal and Installation

SENTRA AND STANZA WAGON

1. Disconnect the negative battery cable.

2. Drain the gear oil from the transaxle and the transfer case.

3. Disconnect and remove the forward exhaust pipe.

4. Using chalk or paint, matchmark the flanges on the driveshaft and then unbolt the driveshaft from the transfer case.

5. On Sentra, unbolt and remove the transaxle support rod from the transfer case.

6. Unbolt and remove the transfer control actuator from the side of the transfer case (not required on 1989–91 Sentra).

7. Disconnect and remove the right side halfshaft.

8. Disconnect the speedometer gear from the transfer case.

9. Unbolt and remove the front, rear and side transfer case gussets (support members).

10. Use a hydraulic floor jack and a block of wood to support the transfer case, remove the transfer case-to-transaxle mounting bolts and then remove the case.

To install:

11. Lubricate the lips of the transfer side oil seal (in transaxle), adapter oil seal (in transfer) and driveshaft oil seal. Use a suitable multi-purpose grease.

12. Apply KP510–00150 or equivalent sealant to the ring gear oil seal seating surface prior to installation of the transfer case.

13. Raise and and mount the transfer. Tighten the transfer case-to-transaxle mounting bolts and the transfer case gusset mounting bolts to 22–30 ft. lbs. (30–40 Nm) on 1988 vehicles. On 1989–91 Sentra, torque the transfer rear gusset bolts to 29–36 ft. lbs. (39–49 Nm).

NOTE: Be careful not to damage the transaxle oil seal when inserting thew splined portion of the transfer ring gear into the transaxle.

14. Install the front, rear and side transfer case gussets.

15. Connect the speedometer cable.

16. Install the right side halfshaft.

17. Connect the transfer control actuator to the side of the transfer case (except 1989–91 Sentra).

18. On Sentra, connect the transfer support rod to the transfer case.

19. Connect the driveshaft to the transfer case by aligning the matchmarks. Torque the driveshaft bolts to 25–33 ft. lbs. (34–44 Nm) on both Sentra and Stanza.

NOTE: When connecting the drive shaft, be careful not to damage the driveshaft and adapter oil seals.

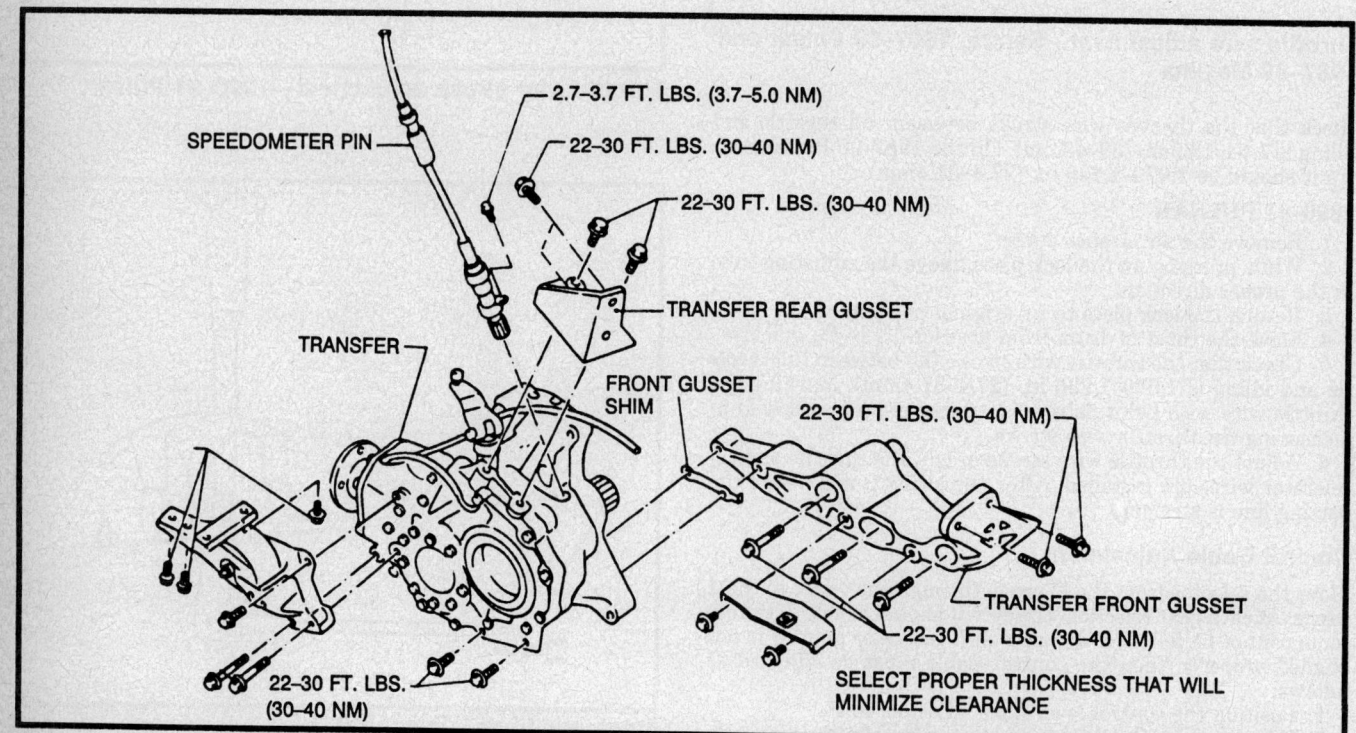

SPEEDOMETER PIN

2.7–3.7 FT. LBS. (3.7–5.0 NM)

22–30 FT. LBS. (30–40 NM)

22–30 FT. LBS. (30–40 NM)

TRANSFER REAR GUSSET

TRANSFER

FRONT GUSSET SHIM

22–30 FT. LBS. (30–40 NM)

TRANSFER FRONT GUSSET

22–30 FT. LBS. (30–40 NM)

22–30 FT. LBS. (30–40 NM)

SELECT PROPER THICKNESS THAT WILL MINIMIZE CLEARANCE

Transfer case removal—Stanza wagon 4WD—Sentra similar

20. Connect the forward exhaust pipe using new gaskets.
21. Fill the transfer case to the proper level with gear oil. The transfer case and the transaxle use different types and weights of lubricant.
22. Connect the negative battery cable.
23. Check the transfer case for proper operation.

DRIVE AXLE

Halfshaft

Removal and Installation

FRONT WHEEL DRIVE

This procedure applies to all 2WD drive vehicles and to the front halfshafts on 4WD vehicles. Removal and installation of the rear halfshafts on 4WD vehicles is described below.

NOTE: Installation of the halfshafts will require a special tool for the spline alignment of the halfshaft end and the transaxle case. Do not perform this procedure without access to this tool or suitable equivalent. The tool is J–34296, J–34297 or J–33904 depending on the vehicle.

1. Raise the vehicle and support safely.
2. Remove the wheel and tire assembly.

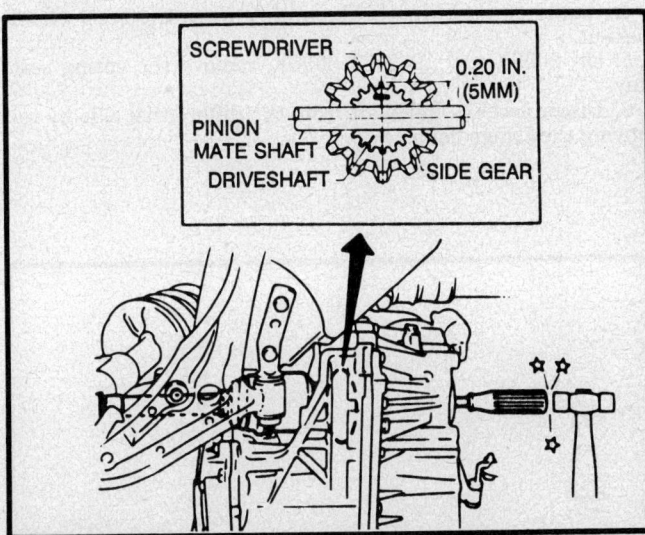

Left halfshaft removal on automatic transaxle vehicles—Maxima, Stanza and Stanza wagon

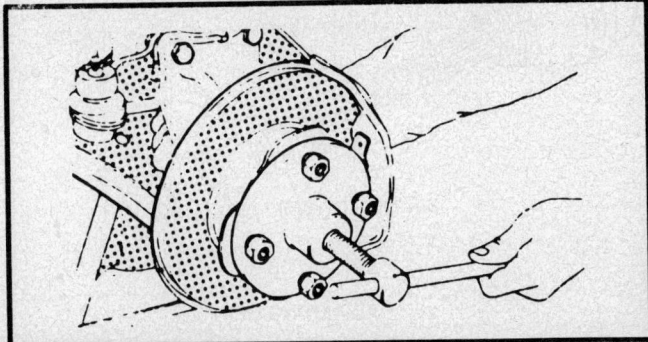

Removing halfshaft

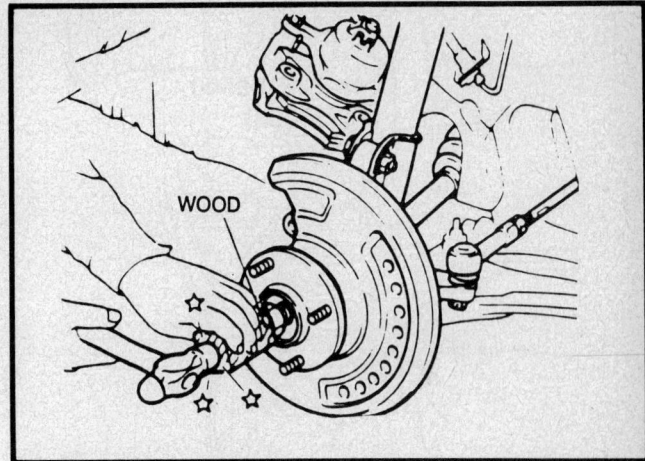

Separating the halfshaft from the steering knuckle

3. Withdraw the cotter pin from the castellated nut on the wheel hub.
4. Depress the brake pedal and remove the wheel bearing locknut.
5. Remove the brake caliper assembly without disconnecting the brake line. Support the caliper with wire.
6. Separate the halfshaft from the steering knuckle by tapping it with a block of wood and a mallet.
7. Remove the tie rod ball joint. Remove the 3 mounting nuts for the lower ball joint and then pull it down.

NOTE: Always use a new nut when replacing the tie rod ball joint.

8. Using a suitable tool, reach through the engine crossmember and carefully tap the right side inner CV-joint out of the transaxle case.
9. Using a block of wood and a suitable jack, support the engine under the oil pan.
10. Remove the support bearing bracket and bearing retainer bolts from the engine and then withdraw the right halfshaft (except Pulsar with E16i and GA16i and Sentra).
11. On vehicles with manual transaxles, carefully insert a small prybar between the left CV-joint inner flange and the transaxle case mounting surface and pry the halfshaft out of the case. Withdraw the shaft from the steering knuckle and remove it.
12. On vehicles with automatic transaxles, insert a dowel through the right side halfshaft hole and use a small mallet to tap the left halfshaft out of the transaxle case. Withdraw the shaft from the steering knuckle and remove it.

NOTE: Be careful not to damage the pinion mating shaft and the side gear while tapping the left halfshaft out of the transaxle case.

To install:

13. When installing the shafts into the transaxle, use a new oil seal and then install an alignment tool along the inner circumference of the oil seal.

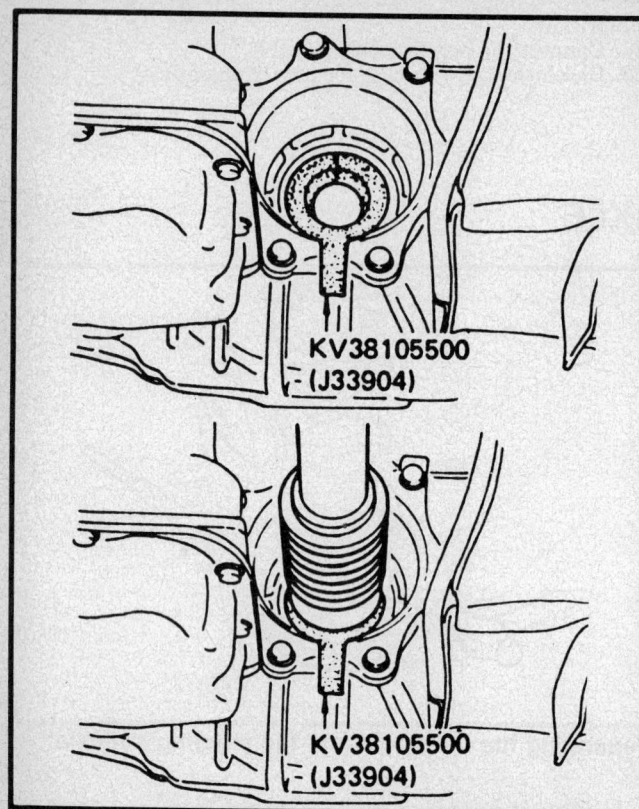

Halfshaft alignment tools used on front wheel drive vehicles

14. Insert the halfshaft into the transaxle, align the serrations and then remove the alignment tool.

15. Push the halfshaft, then press-fit the circular clip on the shaft into the clip groove on the side gear.

NOTE: After insertion, attempt to pull the flange out of the side joint to make sure the circular clip is properly seated in the side gear and will not come out.

16. Connect the tie rod end ball joint.
17. Insert the driveshaft into the steering knuckle.
18. Mount the brake caliper assembly.
19. Install the wheel bearing locknut. Torque the nut to 174–231 ft. lbs. (235–314 Nm) on Maxima and Stanza; 145–203 ft. lbs. (196–275 Nm) on 1987–89 Pulsar; 145–203 ft. lbs. (196–275 Nm) on Sentra and 1990–91 Pulsar. When tightening the nut, apply the brake pedal.
20. Install a new cotter pin into the wheel bearing locknut.
21. Mount the wheel and tire assembly.
22. Lower the vehicle.

REAR WHEEL DRIVE

Except Sentra (4WD) and Stanza Wagon (4WD)

NOTE: When removing the rear driveshafts, cover the CV-boots with cloth to prevent damage.

1. Raise and support the rear of the vehicle safely.
2. Remove the rear wheel and tire assembly.
3. Remove the adjusting cap and cotter pin from the wheel bearing locknut.
4. Apply the parking brake and remove the rear wheel locknut.
5. On 200SX and 1987–89 300ZX, remove the spring seat stay.
6. Disconnect the halfshaft from the differential side by removing the flange bolts.

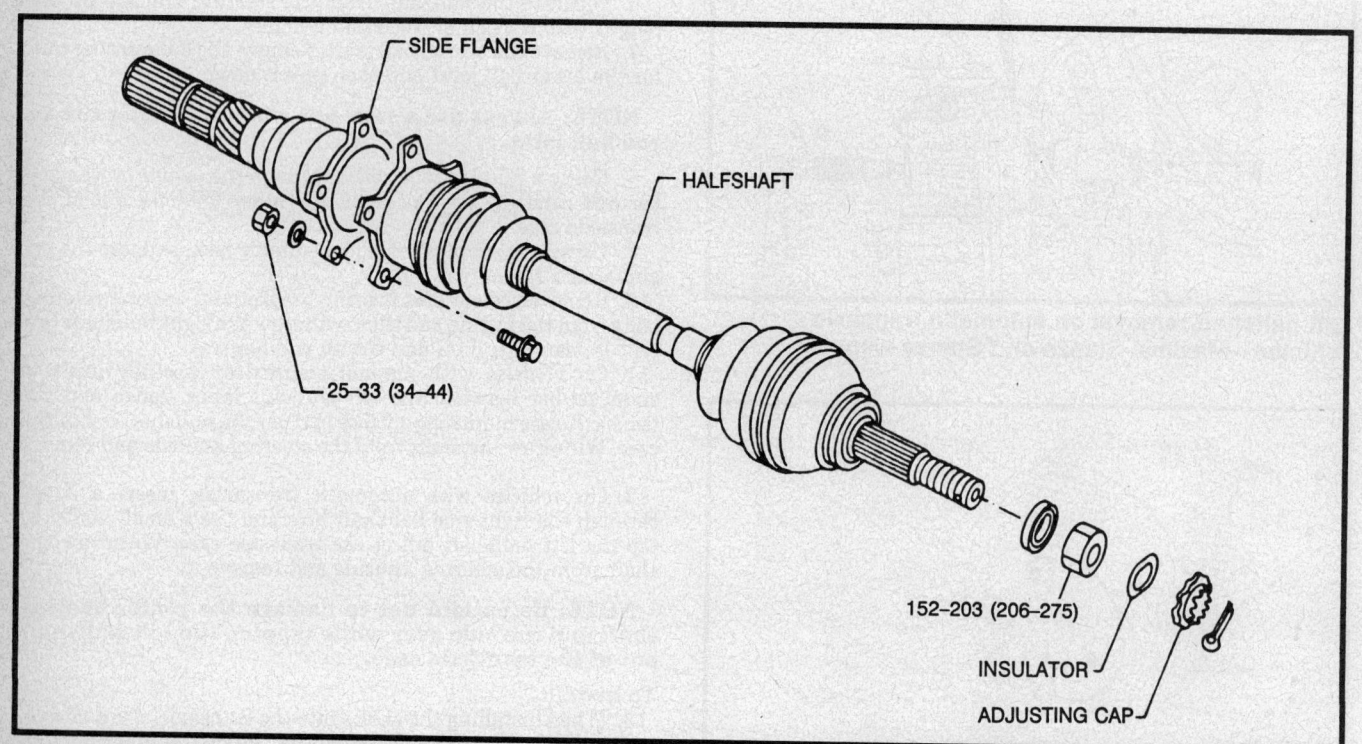

Typical rear halfshaft assembly on rear wheel drive vehicles (1990–91 300ZX shown)

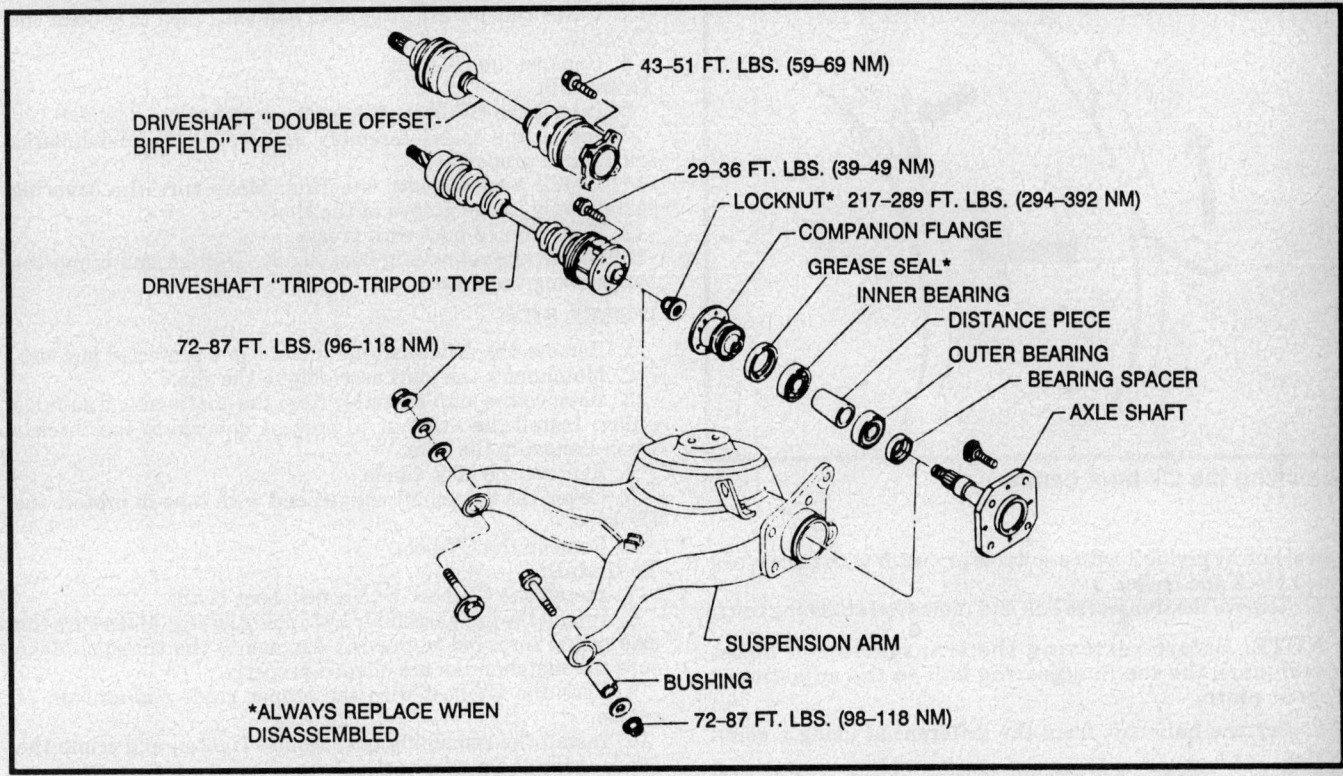

43–51 FT. LBS. (59–69 NM)

DRIVESHAFT "DOUBLE OFFSET-BIRFIELD" TYPE

29–36 FT. LBS. (39–49 NM)

LOCKNUT* 217–289 FT. LBS. (294–392 NM)

COMPANION FLANGE

GREASE SEAL*

INNER BEARING

DISTANCE PIECE

DRIVESHAFT "TRIPOD-TRIPOD" TYPE

OUTER BEARING

BEARING SPACER

72–87 FT. LBS. (96–118 NM)

AXLE SHAFT

SUSPENSION ARM

BUSHING

72–87 FT. LBS. (98–118 NM)

*ALWAYS REPLACE WHEN DISASSEMBLED

Exploded view of the rear axle shown with either the "Double Off-Set Birfield "type driveshaft or the "Tripod-Tripod" type driveshaft—models with IRS

7. Grasp the halfshaft at the center and extract if from the wheel hub by prying it with a suitable prybar or with the use of a wood block and mallet.

NOTE: To protect the threads of the shaft, temporarily install the locknut when loosening the shaft from the wheel hub.

To install:

8. Insert the shaft into the wheel hub and temporarily install the locknut.

NOTE: Take care not to damage the oil seal or either end of the halfshaft during installation.

9. Connect the halfshaft to the differential and install the flange bolts. On 240SX and 300ZX, torque the flange bolts to 25–33 ft. lbs. (34–44 Nm). On 200SX with CA18ET engines, torque the flange bolts to 20–27 ft. lbs. (27–37 Nm). On 200SX with CA20E and VG30E engines, torque the flange bolts to 29–36 ft. lbs. (39–49 Nm).

10. On 200SX and 1987–89 300ZX, install the spring seat stay.

11. Apply the parking brake and tighten the locknut. Torque the locknut to 152–210 ft. lbs. (206–284 Nm) on 200SX and 1987–89 300ZX; 174–231 ft. lbs. on 240SX and 154–203 ft. lbs. (206–275 Nm) on 1990–91 300ZX.

12. Install a new locknut cotter pin and install the adjusting cap.

13. Mount the rear wheel and tire assembly.

14. Lower the vehicle.

Sentra (4WD) and Stanza Wagon (4WD)

This procedure applies to removal and installation of the rear halfshafts only. Removal and installation of front halfshafts is described above.

NOTE: When removing the rear halfshafts, cover the CV-boots with cloth to prevent damage.

1. Raise and support the rear of the vehicle safely.

2. Remove the rear wheel and tire assembly.

3. Remove the adjusting cap, insulator and cotter pin from the wheel bearing locknut.

4. Apply the parking brake and remove the rear wheel locknut.

5. Disconnect the brake line. Use a brake line wrench or suitable equivalent. Plug the line to prevent leakage of brake fluid.

6. Disconnect the parking brake cable.

7. Grasp the halfshaft at the center and extract if from the

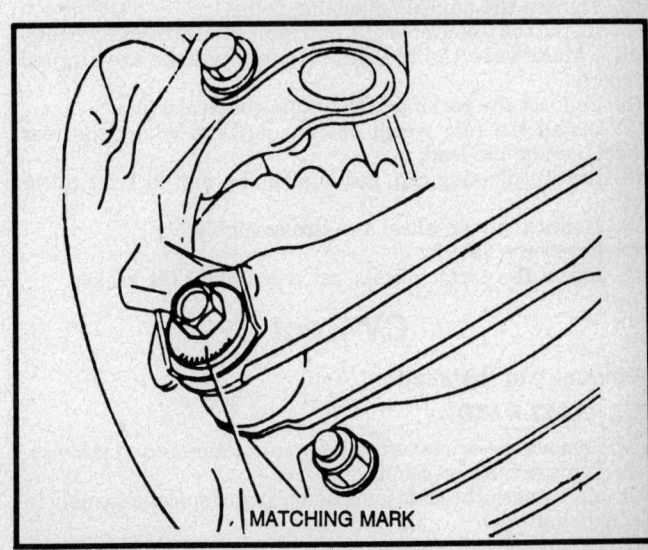

MATCHING MARK

Matchmark the toe adjustment bolt to the transverse link on the Stanza wagon (4 × 4)

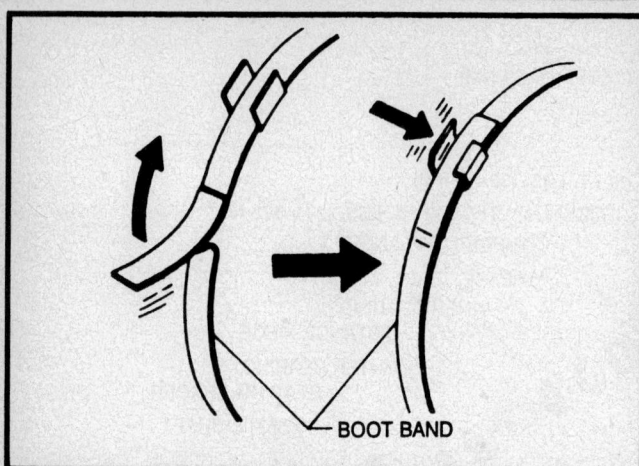

BOOT BAND

Installing the CV-boot bands

wheel hub by prying it with a suitable prybar or with the use of a wood block and mallet.

8. Remove the transverse link and radius rod attaching bolts.

NOTE: Before removing the transverse rod bolts, matchmark the toe-in adjusting bolt to the adjustment degree plate.

9. Pry the halfshaft from the differential using a small prybar.

10. Remove the knuckle attaching bolts and remove the wheel hub, baffle plate, knuckle and halfshaft as a unit. Be careful not to damage the differential drive gear oil seal during removal.

To install:

11. Mount the wheel hub, baffle plate, knuckle and driveshaft and temporarily install the wheel bearing locknut.

12. Insert the halfshaft into the transaxle and properly align the splines.

13. Push the halfshaft, then press-fit the circular clip on the shaft into the clip groove on the side gear.

NOTE: After insertion, attempt to pull the flange out of the side joint to make sure the circular clip is properly seated in the side gear and will not come out.

14. Tighten the knuckle attaching bolts.

15. Install the transverse link and radius rod attaching (fixing) bolts. Make sure the toe-in bolt matchmarks are aligned properly.

16. Connect the parking brake cable and brake line.

17. Install the rear wheel bearing nut and adjust the rear wheel bearing pre-load.

18. Install adjusting cap, insulator and a new locknut cotter pin.

19. Mount the rear wheel and tire assembly.

20. Lower the vehicle.

21. Adjust the parking brake cable and bleed the brakes.

CV-Boot

Removal and Installation

TRANSAXLE SIDE

1. Remove the driveshaft and mount in a protected jaw vise.

2. Remove the boot bands.

3. Matchmark the slide joint housing and spider assembly to the halfshaft.

4. Remove the slide joint housing from the halfshaft.

5. Remove the spider snapring.

6. Remove the spider assembly from the halfshaft.

7. Cover the driveshaft splined end with tape to protect the CV-boot.

8. Remove the CV-boot.

To install:

9. Install the CV-boot with a new boot band.

10. Install the spider assembly. Make sure the matchmarks are aligned properly.

11. Install a new spider snapring. Make sure the snapring seats evenly in the groove of the shaft.

12. Pack the CV-boot with grease.

13. Install the remaining boot bands. Tighten and crimp the bands using the proper tool.

WHEEL SIDE

1. Remove the driveshaft and mount in a protected jaw vise.

2. Matchmark the joint assembly to the shaft.

3. Remove the joint assembly from the shaft using a suitable puller. Install the axle nut to prevent damage to the threads when removing the joint.

4. Remove the boot bands.

5. Cover the driveshaft splined end with tape to protect the CV-boot.

6. Remove the CV-boot.

To install:

7. Install the CV-boot with a new boot band.

8. Install the joint assembly by tapping lightly. Make sure the axle nut is installed to prevent damage to the threads. Make sure the matchmarks are aligned properly.

9. Pack the CV-boot with the proper grade and amount of grease.

10. Install the remaining boot bands. Tighten and crimp the bands using the proper tool.

Driveshaft and U-Joints

Removal and Installation

200SX, 240SX AND 300ZX

1. Release the hand brake.

2. On 300ZX, remove the the front pipe and the heat shield plate.

3. Matchmark the flanges on the driveshaft and differential so the driveshaft can be reinstalled in its original orientation; this will help maintain drive line balance.

4. Unbolt the rear flange and the center bearing.

5. Withdraw the driveshaft from the transmission and pull the driveshaft down and back to remove.

6. Plug the transmission extension housing to prevent oil leakage.

To install:

7. Lubricate the sleeve yoke splines with clean engine oil prior to installation. Insert the driveshaft into the transmission and align the flange matchmarks.

8. Install the flange and the center bearing bolts.

9. On 200SX and 240SX, torque the center bearing support bracket bolts to 19–29 ft. lbs. (25–39 Nm). On 1990–91 300ZX, torque the center bearing bolts to 43–58 ft. lbs. (59–78 Nm).

10. On 200SX with CA20E and VG30E engines, torque the flange bolts to 29–33 ft. lbs. (39–44 Nm); 200SX with CA18ET engines torque to 25–33 ft. lbs. (34–44 Nm); 240SX and 1987–89 300ZX torque to 29–33 ft. lbs. (39–44 Nm). On 1990–91 300ZX turbo, torque the flange bolts to 47–54 ft. lbs. On 1990–91 300ZX non-turbo, torque the flange bolts to 29–33 ft. lbs. (39–44 Nm).

11. On 300ZX, install the the front pipe and the heat shield plate.

SENTRA (4WD) AND STANZA WAGON (4WD)

1. Mark the relationship of the driveshaft flange to the differential flange.

2. Unbolt the center bearing bracket.

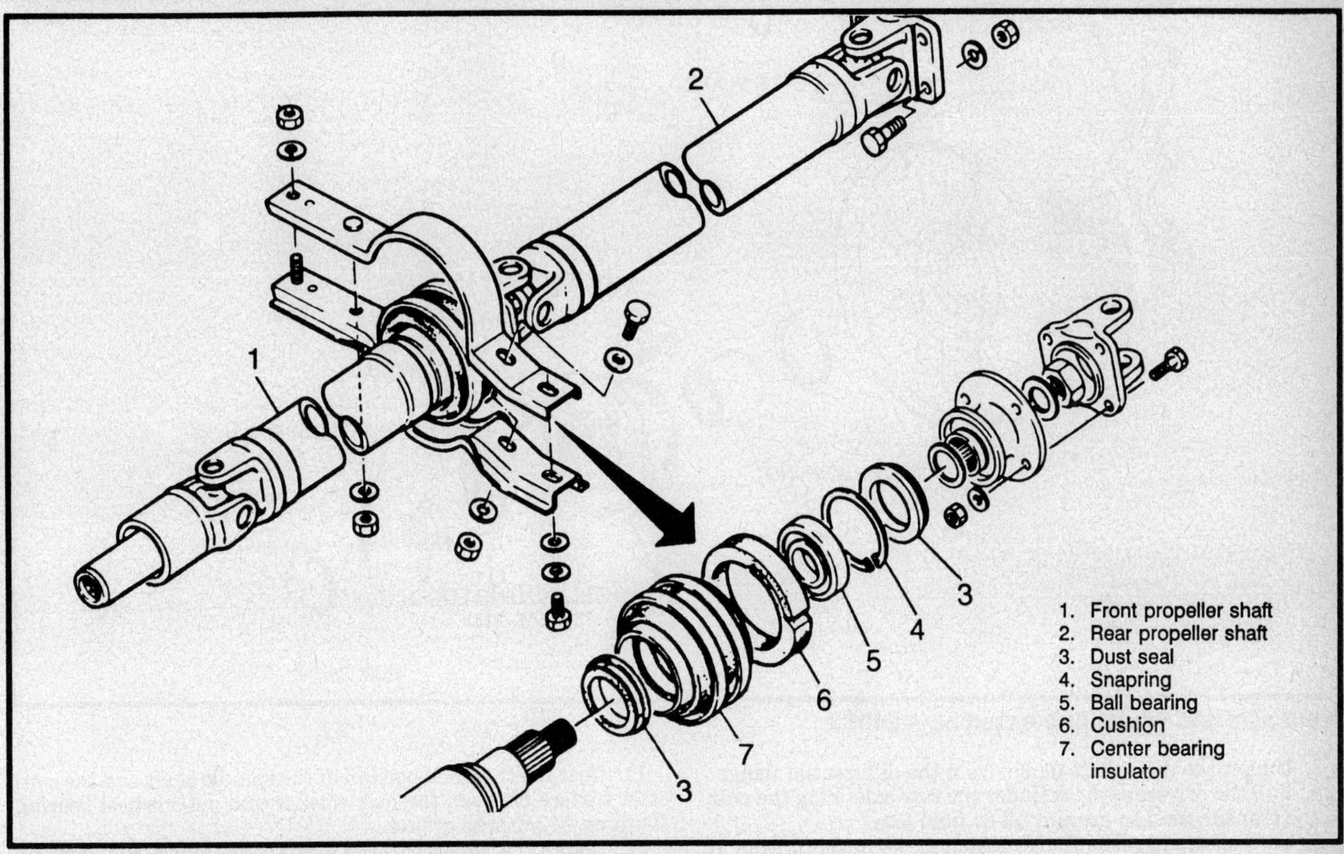

1. Front propeller shaft
2. Rear propeller shaft
3. Dust seal
4. Snapring
5. Ball bearing
6. Cushion
7. Center bearing insulator

Two piece driveshaft with center bearing and three U-points

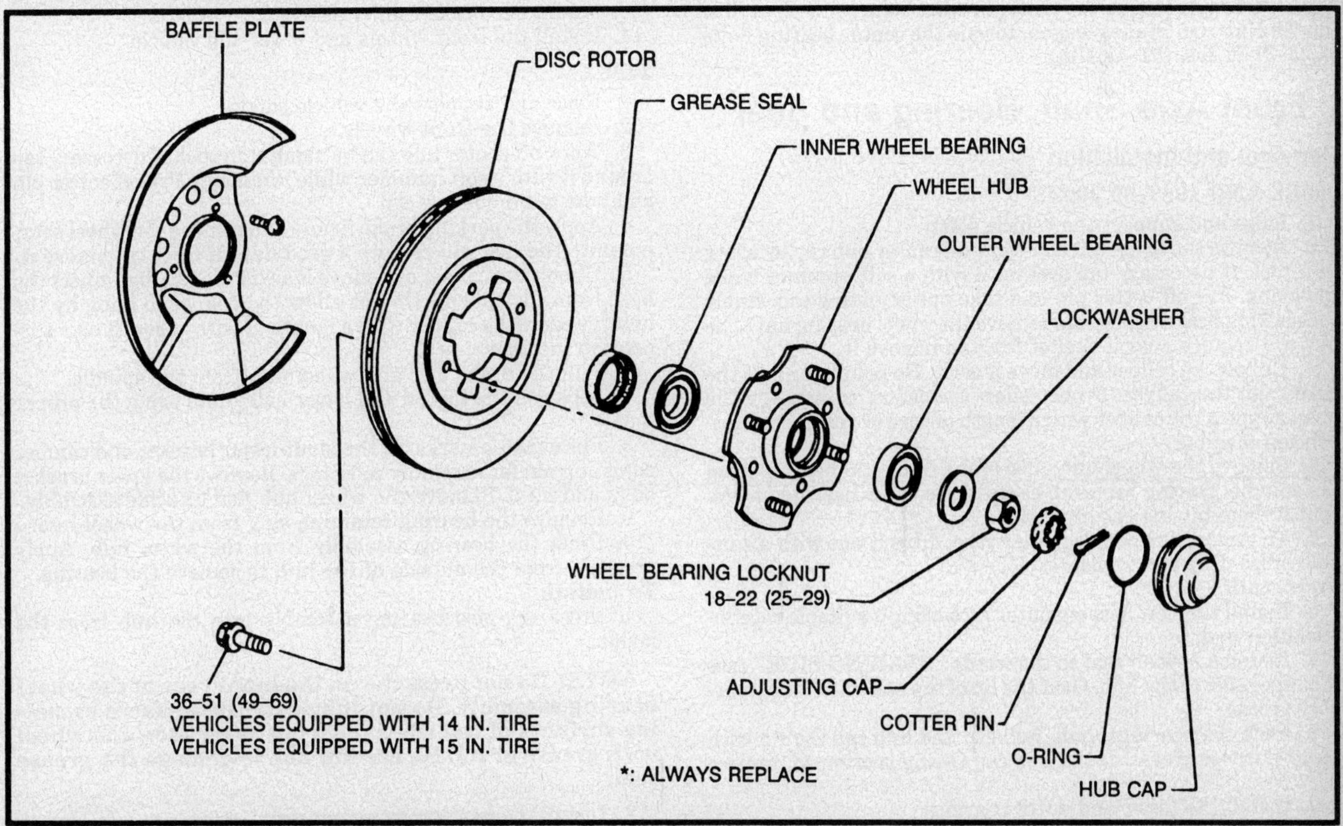

BAFFLE PLATE
DISC ROTOR
GREASE SEAL
INNER WHEEL BEARING
WHEEL HUB
OUTER WHEEL BEARING
LOCKWASHER
WHEEL BEARING LOCKNUT 18–22 (25–29)
ADJUSTING CAP
COTTER PIN
O-RING
HUB CAP

36–51 (49–69)
VEHICLES EQUIPPED WITH 14 IN. TIRE
VEHICLES EQUIPPED WITH 15 IN. TIRE

*: ALWAYS REPLACE

Front axle and wheel hub assembly—200SX

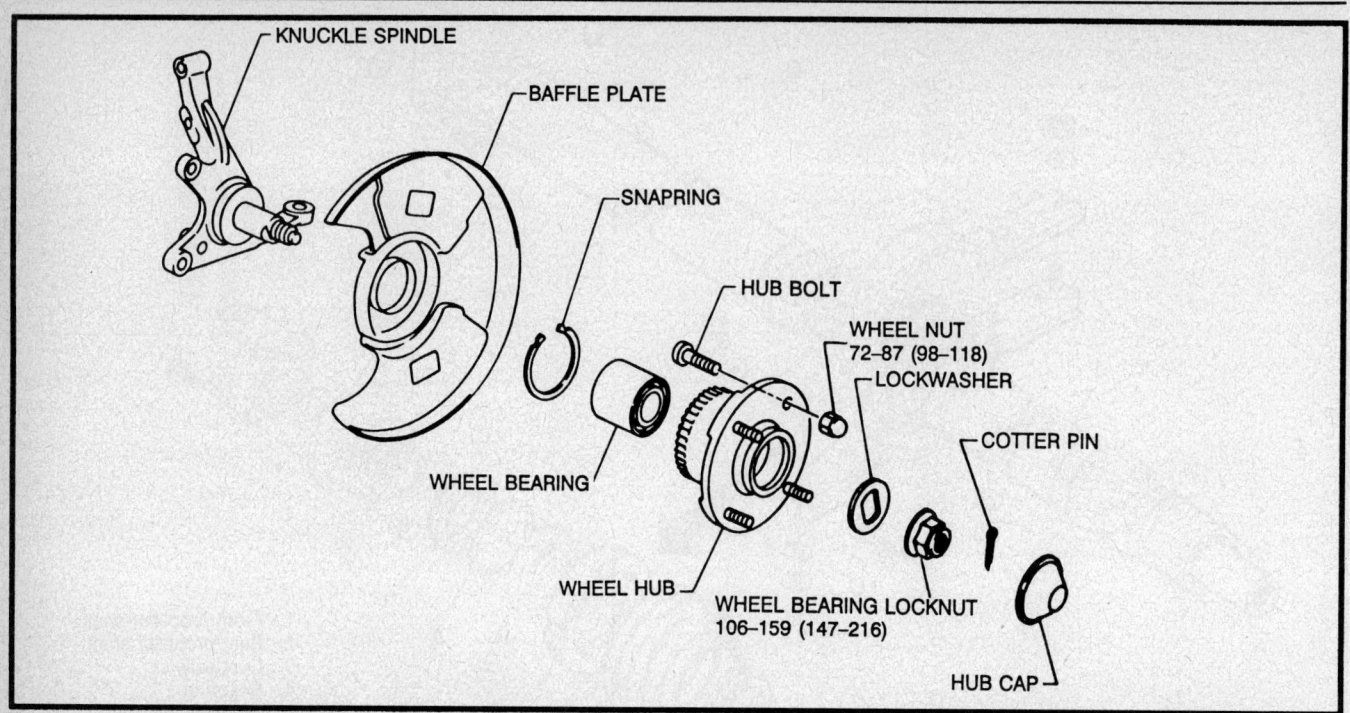

KNUCKLE SPINDLE
BAFFLE PLATE
SNAPRING
HUB BOLT
WHEEL NUT
72–87 (98–118)
LOCKWASHER
COTTER PIN
WHEEL BEARING
WHEEL HUB
WHEEL BEARING LOCKNUT
106–159 (147–216)
HUB CAP

Front axle and wheel hub assembly—240SX

3. Unbolt the driveshaft flange from the differential flange.
4. Pull the driveshaft back under the rear axle. Plug the rear of the transmission to prevent oil or fluid loss.
5. To install, align the flange matchmarks made in Step 1. Torque the front and rear flange bolts to 25–33 ft. lbs. (34–44 Nm). On Sentra torque the center bracket bolts to 19–29 ft. lbs. (25–39 Nm). On Stanza wagon, torque the center bearing bolts to 23–31 ft. lbs. (31–42 Nm).

Front Axle Shaft, Bearing and Seal

Removal and Installation

200SX AND 1987–89 300ZX

1. Raise and support the vehicle safely.
2. Remove the front wheels. Work off center hub cap by using thin tool. If necessary tap around it with a soft hammer while removing. Pry off cotter pin and take out adjusting cap. Apply the parking brake firmly and remove the wheel bearing nut. The nut will require a good deal of force to remove it.
3. Unbolt the caliper and move it aside. Do not disconnect the hose from the caliper. Do not allow the caliper to hang by the hose; support the caliper with a length of wire or rest it on a suspension member.
4. Remove the wheel hub, disc brake rotor and bearing from the spindle. During removal, capture the outer bearing to prevent it from hitting the ground.
5. To replace the bearing outer race, drive it out with a suitable brass drift and mallet.
To install:
6. Install the new bearing outer race using a suitable race installation tool.
7. Install a new oil seal so the words "BEARING SIDE" face the inner side of the hub. Coat the lip of the seal with multi-purpose grease.
8. Pack the bearings, hub, hub cap and hub cap O-ring with multi-purpose grease. If the hub cap O-ring is crimped, replace it.
9. Install the inner and outer bearings.
10. Install the wheel hub and rotor disc onto the spindle.

11. Coat the threaded portion of the spindle shaft and the contact surface between the lock washer and outer wheel bearing with multi-purpose grease.
12. Install the wheel bearing locknut and adjust the bearing pre-load. Use a new cotter pin.
13. Mount the brake caliper assembly.
14. Install the front wheels and lower the vehicle.

240SX

1. Raise and support the vehicle safely.
2. Remove the front wheels.
3. Work off center hub cap by using thin tool. If necessary tap around it with a soft hammer while removing. Pry off cotter pin and take out adjusting cap.
4. Apply the parking brake firmly and remove the wheel bearing nut. The nut will require a good deal of force to remove it.
5. Unbolt the caliper and move it aside. Do not disconnect the hose from the caliper. Do not allow the caliper to hang by the hose; support the caliper with a length of wire or rest it on a suspension member.
6. Pull the brake disc and wheel hub from the spindle.
7. Separate the tie rod and lower ball joints using the proper tool.
8. Place matchmarks on the strut lower bracket and camber adjusting pin for assembly reference. Remove the lower bracket bolts and nuts. Remove the wheel hub and knuckle assembly.
9. Remove the bearing retaining ring from the wheel hub.
10. Press the bearing assembly from the wheel hub. Apply pressure from the outside of the hub to remove the bearing.
To install:
11. Press the new bearing assembly into the hub from the inside.

NOTE: Do not press the on the inner race of the wheel bearing assembly. Do not lubricate the surfaces of mating surfaces of the wheel bearing outer race and wheel with grease or oil. Be careful not to damage the grease seal.

12. Install the bearing retaining ring.
13. Coat the lip of the grease seal with multi-purpose grease.

14. Manuever the wheel hub and axle assembly onto the lower mounting bracket and install the bracket bolts and nuts. Make sure the matchmarks on the bracket and the camber adjusting pin are aligned properly.

15. Connect the lower and tie rod ball joints.

16. Push the brake disc and wheel hub onto the spindle.

17. Install the brake caliper assembly.

18. Apply the parking brake and torque the wheel bearing locknut to 108–159 ft. lbs. (147–216 Nm). Mount a dial indicator so the stylus of the dial rests on the face of the hub and check the wheel bearing axial endplay by attempting to rock the wheel hub in and out. The endplay should be 0.0012 in. or less.

19. Install a new locknut cotter pin. Install the bearing hub cap after packing it with multi-purpose grease.

20. Mount the the front wheels and lower the vehicle.

1990-91 300ZX

1. Raise and support the vehicle safely.

2. Remove the front wheels.

3. Unbolt the caliper and move it aside. Do not disconnect the hose from the caliper. Do not allow the caliper to hang by the hose; support the caliper with a length of wire or rest it on a suspension member.

4. Separate the tie rod and lower ball joints using the proper tool.

NOTE: The steering knuckle is made of an aluminum alloy. Be careful no to strike it when removing the ball joints.

5. Remove the kin pin lower nut and remove the steering knuckle assembly.

6. Remove the hub cap, wheel bearing locknut, sensor rotor (with ABS) or washer (without ABS).

7. Remove the wheel hub with a suitable drift.

8. Remove the wheel bearing retaining ring.

9. Press the wheel bearing from the knuckle.

10. Drive out the wheel bearing inner race to the outside of the wheel hub.

11. Remove the grease seal and splash guard (baffle plate).

To install:

12. From the outside of the knuckle, press the new wheel bearing assembly into the knuckle.

NOTE: Do not press the on the inner race of the wheel bearing assembly. Do not lubricate the surfaces of mating surfaces of the wheel bearing outer race and wheel with grease or oil. Be careful not to damage the grease seal.

13. Install the bearing retaining ring. Make sure it seats evenly in the groove of the knuckle.

14. Coat the lip of the grease seal with multi-purpose grease and install.

15. Install the splash guard.

16. Press the wheel hub into the steering knuckle.

17. Install the washer (without ABS), sensor rotor (with ABS) and wheel bearing locknut. Torque the locknut to 152–210 ft. lbs. (206–284 Nm). Stake the locknut tabs using a small cold chisel.

18. Place the hub cap onto the knuckle and tap it into place using a rubber or plastic mallet. Once the cap is seated lightly into the knuckle, install the cap retaining bolts and torque to 8–12 ft. lbs. (11–16 Nm).

19. Mount the steering knuckle assembly and tighten the lower king pin nut.

20. Connect the tie rod and lower ball joints using the proper tool.

21. Install the brake caliper assembly.

22. Prior to checking the bearing pre-load, spin the wheel hub at least 10 revolutions in both directions to seat the bearing. Check the wheel bearing preload and axial end play as follows:

a. Pre-load—connect a spring scale of known calibration to a wheel hub bolt and measure the turning torque. If an NSK wheel bearing is used, the turning torque should be 1.3–8.4 lbs. (5.9–37.3 N). For NTN bearings, the turning torque should be 1.8–13.0 lbs. (7.8–57.9 N).

b. Axial endplay—mount a dial indicator so the stylus of the dial rests on the face of the hub and check the wheel bearing axial endplay by attempting to rock the wheel hub in and out. The endplay should be 0.0020 in. (0.05mm) or less.

23. Mount the front wheels and lower the vehicle.

Rear Axle Shaft, Bearings and Seal

Removal and Installation

200SX AND 1987-89 300ZX

1. Block the front wheels.

2. Raise and support the vehicle safely. Remove the front wheels.

3. Apply the parking brake firmly. This helps hold the stub axle while removing the axle nut. Also, hold the stub axle at the outside while removing the nut from the axle shaft side. The nut will require a good deal of force to remove, so be sure to hold the stub axle firmly. Discard the axle nut and replace with new.

4. On vehicles with rear disc brakes, unbolt the caliper and move it aside. Do not disconnect the hose from the caliper. Do not allow the caliper to hang by the hose; support the caliper with a length of wire or rest it on a suspension member.

5. Remove the brake disc on vehicles with rear disc brakes. Remove the brake drum on vehicles with drum brakes.

6. Remove the stub axle with a slide hammer and an adapter. The outer wheel bearing will come off with the stub axle.

7. Unbolt and remove the companion flange from the lower arm.

8. Remove and discard the grease seal and inner bearing from the lower arm using a drift made for the purpose or a length of pipe of the proper diameter. The outer bearing can be removed from the stub axle with a puller. If the grease seal or the bearings are removed, new parts must be used on assembly.

To install:

9. Clean all the parts to be reused in solvent.

10. Sealed-type bearings are used. When the new bearings are installed, the sealed side must face out. Install the sealed side of the outer bearing facing the wheel, and the sealed side of the inner bearing facing the differential.

11. Press the outer bearing onto the stub axle.

12. The bearing housing is stamped with an A, C or no mark. Select a spacer (distance piece) on the stub axle that matches the

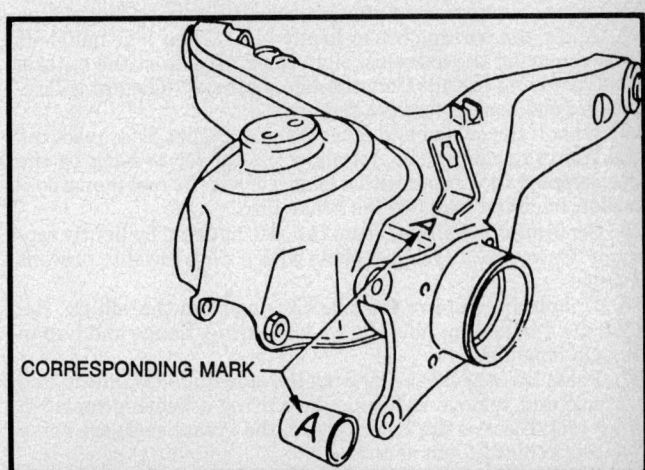

CORRESPONDING MARK

Match the bearing housing to the spacer with the proper letter

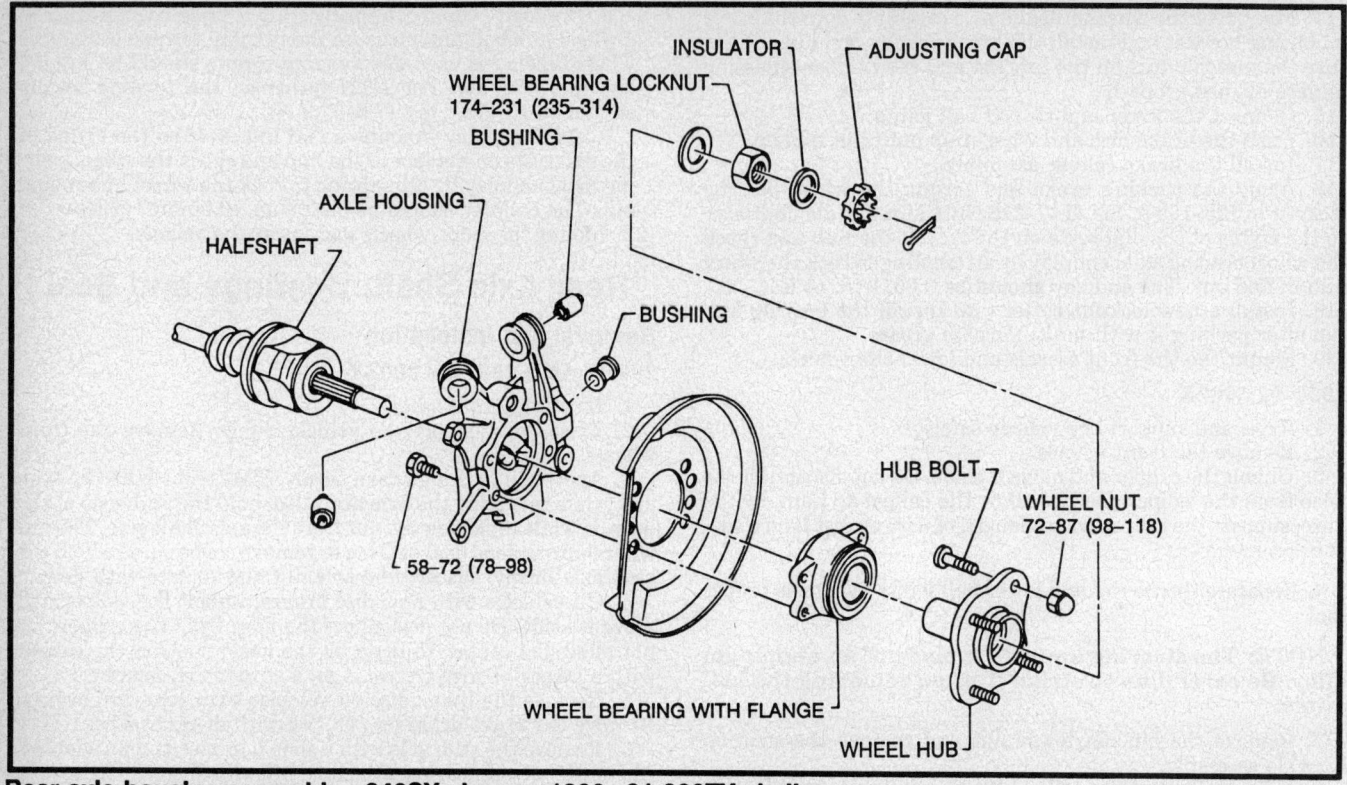

INSULATOR — ADJUSTING CAP

WHEEL BEARING LOCKNUT
174–231 (235–314)

BUSHING

AXLE HOUSING

HALFSHAFT

BUSHING

HUB BOLT

WHEEL NUT
72–87 (98–118)

58–72 (78–98)

WHEEL BEARING WITH FLANGE

WHEEL HUB

Rear axle housing assembly—240SX shown—1990–91 300ZX similar

letter stamped on the bearing housing except is there is no mark. Bearing housings with no mark always accept a B spacer.

13. Install the stub axle into the lower arm.

14. Install the new inner bearing into the lower arm with the stub axle in place. Install a new grease seal.

15. Install the companion flange onto the stub axle.

16. Install a new stub axle nut. Tighten to 152–210 ft. lbs. (206–284 Nm).

17. Install the brake disc or drum, and the caliper if removed.

18. Install the rear wheels and lower the vehicle.

240SX AND 1990–91 300ZX

1. Block the front wheels.

2. Raise and support the rear of the vehicle and remove the rear wheels. Remove the cotter pin, adjusting cap and insulator.

3. Apply the parking brake firmly to hold the rear halfshaft while removing the axle nut. Hold the stub axle at the outside while removing the nut from the axle shaft side. The nut will require a good deal of force to remove.

4. Unbolt the caliper and move it aside. Do not disconnect the hose from the caliper. Do not allow the caliper to hang by the hose; support the caliper with a length of wire or rest it on a suspension member. Remove the brake disc.

5. Separate the halfhaft from the axle housing by lightly tapping it. Cover the driveshaft boots with a shop towel to prevent damage.

6. Unbolt and remove the axle housing from the vehicle. Remove the 4 bolts that hold the wheel bearing, flange and hub to the axle housing.

7. Press the wheel bearing from the axle hub. Mount the hub in a vise and remove the inner race using a bearing replacer/puller tool. Discard the inner race. If the grease seals are being replaced, replace them as a set.

8. Clean all parts in a suitable solvent. Check the wheel hub and axle housing for cracks, preferably using the dye penetrant method. Check the wheel bearing seating surface for roughness,

seizure or other damage that may interfere with proper bearing function. Check the rubber bushing for wear.

To install:

9. Place the hub on a block of wood and seat the inner race using a suitable drift. Be careful not to damage the grease seals during installation of the inner race.

10. Press the bearing into the hub using a suitable drift.

11. Mount the axle housing. Torque the axle housing bolts to 58–72 ft. lbs. (78–98 Nm) on both the 240SX and 1990–91 300ZX.

12. Insert the halfshaft into the wheel hub. Lubricate the halfshaft splines prior to installation. Make sure the splines are aligned properly.

13. Install the caliper assembly.

14. Install the wheel bearing locknut. On 240SX, torque the nut to 174–231 ft. lbs. (235–314 Nm). On 1990–91 300ZX, torque the nut to 152–203 ft. lbs. (206–275 Nm). Install the insulator and fit adjusting cap. Install a new cotter pin.

15. On 1990–91 300ZX, check the axial endplay as follows before mounting the rear wheels: mount a dial indicator so the stylus of the dial rests on the face of the hub and check the wheel bearing axial endplay by attempting to rock the wheel hub in and out. The endplay should be 0.0020 in. (0.05mm) or less.

16. Mount the rear wheels and lower the vehicle.

Front Wheel Hub, Knuckle and Bearings

Removal and Installation

MAXIMA, PULSAR, SENTRA AND STANZA

1. Raise and support the vehicle safely.

2. Remove the front wheels.

3. Remove the brake rotor.

4. Remove the cotter pin, adjusting cap and insulator.

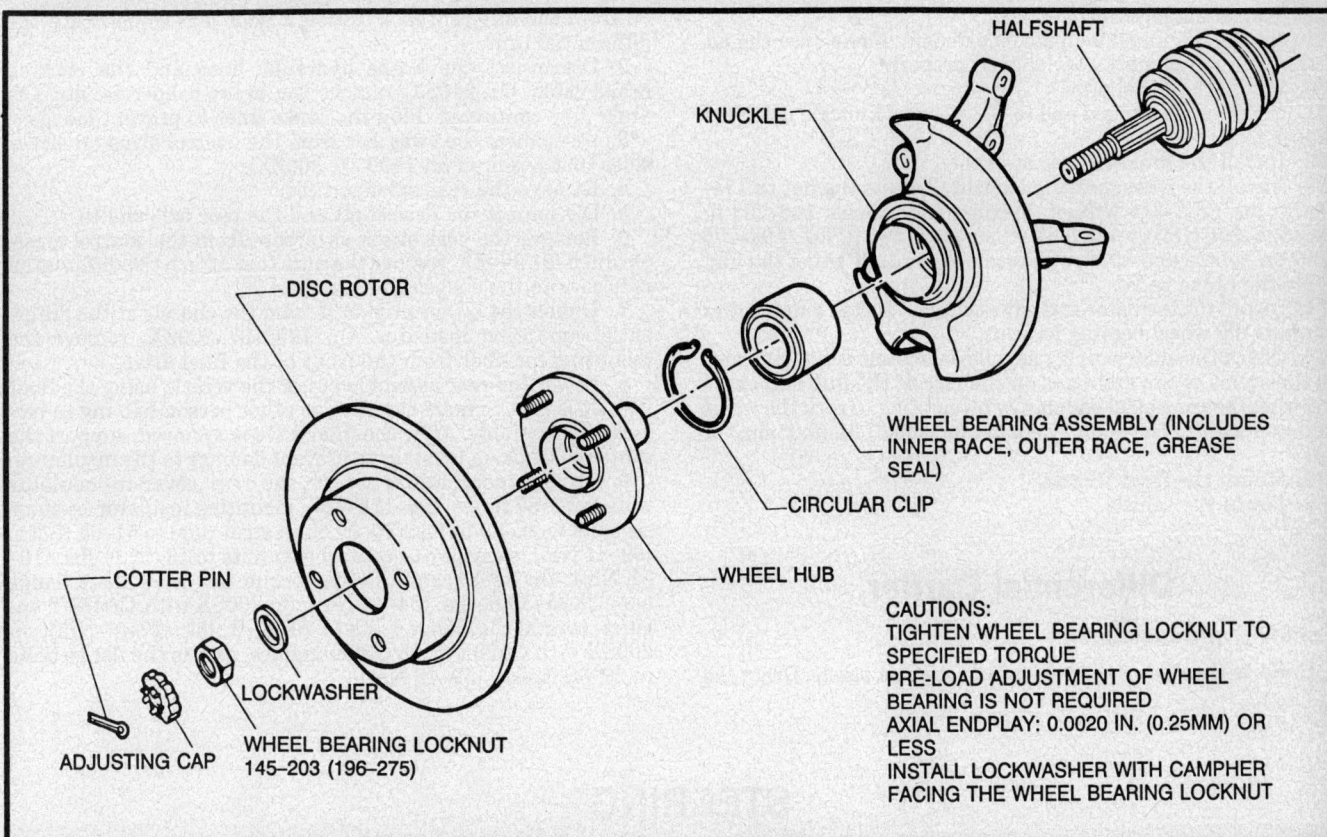

Front wheel hub, knuckle and bearing assembly— Pulsar and Sentra

5. Apply the parking brake firmly and remove the wheel bearing nut. The nut will require a good deal of force to remove it.

6. Unbolt the caliper and move it aside. Do not disconnect the hose from the caliper. Do not allow the caliper to hang by the hose; support the caliper with a length of wire or rest it on a suspension member.

7. Separate the tie rod end from the steering knuckle using the proper tool.

8. Disconnect the halfshaft from the transaxle using the proper tool or by tapping on it with a block of wood and a mallet.

NOTE: Cover the CV-boots with cloth to prevet damage when removing the halfshafts.

9. Remove the nuts and bolt that attach the knuckle to the strut. Make sure to place a visible matchmark on the adjusting pin and knuckle mounting bracket before removing these fasteners.

10. Remove the lower arm bolts.

11. On Pulsar and Sentra, loosen the lower ball joint nut and separate the knuckle from the lower ball joint stud using the proper tool.

12. Remove the knuckle and hub assembly.

13. Drive out the hub and outside inner race with a suitable tool.

14. Withdraw the outside inner race from the wheel hub.

15. On Maxima and Stanza, remove the outer and grease seals from the hub at this time, then press the outer race from the hub.

16. On Pulsar and Sentra, press the inside inner race from the hub. Set the race aside for use in removal of the wheel bearing.

17. Remove the wheel bearing retainer with the proper tool. On Maxima and Stanza, there are retainers on both sides of the hub. After both retainers are removed, the bearing can be pressed from the hub at this time.

18. On Pulsar and Sentra, place the inside inner race set aside in Step 16 on top of the wheel bearing and press the bearing out of the hub. Apply pressure to the inside of the knuckle to remove the bearing.

19. Clean all parts in a suitable solvent. Check the wheel hub and axle housing for cracks, preferably using the dye penetrant method. Check the wheel bearing seating surface for roughness, seizure or other damage that may interfere with proper bearing function.

To install:

20. On Maxima and Stanza, install the inner bearing retainer.

21. Press the new bearing into the knuckle by applying pressure to the outside of the knuckle. Do not exceed 3.3 tons of pressure.

NOTE: Do not press the on the inner race of the wheel bearing assembly. Do not lubricate the surfaces of mating surfaces of the wheel bearing outer race and wheel with grease or oil. Be careful not to damage the grease seal.

22. Install the remaining bearing retainer. Make sure it seats evenly in the groove of the knuckle.

23. Coat the lip of the seal with multi-purpose grease. On Maxima and Stanza, install the inner and outer grease seals. Make sure the lip of the seal(s) faces the inside of the hub.

24. Press the hub into the knuckle. Do not exceed 3.3 tons of pressure.

25. Clamp the knuckle portion in a vise and apply a pre-load of 3.5–5.0 tons to the outside (wheel bolt side) of the bearing with a suitable press. Spin the knuckle several turns in both directions and make sure the bearing spins freely and does not bind.

26. Mount the knuckle and hub assembly.

27. On Pulsar and Sentra, connect the lower ball joint to the knuckle.

28. Install the lower arm bolts.
29. Install the knuckle-to-strut fasteners. Make sure the adjusting pin matchmarks are aligned properly.
30. Install the halfshafts.
31. Connect the tire rod end to the steering knuckle using the proper tool.
32. Install the brake caliper assembly.
33. Install the wheel bearing locknut. Torque the nut to 174–231 ft. lbs. (235–314 Nm) on Maxima and Stanza; 145–203 ft. lbs. (196–275 Nm) on 1987–89 Pulsar; 145–203 ft. lbs. (196–275 Nm) on Sentra and 1990–91 Pulsar. When tightening the nut, apply the brake pedal.
34. Install the insulator and adjusting cap. Install a new cotter pin into the wheel bearing locknut.
35. Check the axial endplay as follows: mount a dial indicator so the stylus of the dial rests on the face of the hub and check the wheel bearing axial endplay by attempting to rock the wheel hub in and out. The endplay should be 0.0020 in. (0.05mm) or less.
36. Mount the front wheels.
37. Lower the vehicle.

Differential Carrier

Removal and Installation

1. Raise the rear of the vehicle and support safely. Drain the oil from the differential. Position a floor jack underneath the differential unit.
2. Disconnect the brake hydraulic lines and the parking brake cable. On 240SX, remove the brake caliper leaving the brake line connected. Plug the brake lines to prevent lakage.
3. Disconnect the sway bar from the control arms on either sides (not required on 1990–91 300ZX).
4. Remove the rear exhaust tube.
5. Disconnect the driveshaft and the rear axle shafts.
6. Remove the rear shock absorbers from the control arms. On 1990–91 300ZX, remove the nuts that attach the differential rear cove to the suspension member.
7. Unbolt the diffcrential unit from the chassis at the differential mounting insulator. On 1990–91 300ZX, remove the mounting member from the front of the final drive.
8. Lower the rear assembly out of the vehicle using the floor jack. It is best to have at least one other person helping to balance the assembly. After the final drive is removed, support the center suspension member to prevent damage to the insulators.
9. During installation, torque the rear cover-to-insulator nuts to 72–87 ft. lbs. (98–118 Nm); mounting insulator-to-chassis bolts to 22–29 ft. lbs. (30–39 Nm); strut nuts to 51–65 ft. lbs. (69–81 Nm); sway bar-to-control arm nuts to 12–15 ft. lbs. (16–21 Nm). On 240SX and 300ZX, torque the drive shaft flange bolts to 25–33 ft. lbs. (34–44 Nm); on 200SX with CA18ET engines, torque the flange bolts to 20–27 ft. lbs. (27–37 Nm); on 200SX with CA20E and VG30E engines, torque the flange bolts to 29–36 ft. lbs. (39–49 Nm).

STEERING

Steering Wheel

———————— CAUTION ————————
On vehicles equipped with an air bag, the negative battery cable must be disconnected, before working on the system. Failure to do so may result in deployment of the air bag and possible personal injury.

Removal and Installation

1. Position the wheels in the straight-ahead direction. The steering wheel should be right-side up and level.
2. Disconnect the negative battery cable.
3. Look at the back of the steering wheel. If there are countersunk screws in the back of the steering wheel spokes, remove the screws and pull off the horn pad. Some vehicles have a horn wire running from the pad to the steering wheel. Disconnect it.

NOTE: There are 3 other types of horn buttons or rings. The first simply pulls off. The second, which is usually a large, semi-triangular pad, must be pushed up, then pulled off. The third must be pushed in and turned clockwise.

4. Remove the rest of the horn switching mechanism, noting the relative location of the parts. Remove the mechanism only if it interferes with removal of the steering wheel.
5. Matchmark the top of the steering column shaft and the steering wheel flange.
6. Remove the attaching nut and remove the steering wheel with a puller.

NOTE: Do not strike the shaft with a hammer; which may cause the column to collapse.

To install:

7. Install the steering wheel by aligning the punch marks. Do not drive or hammer the wheel into place, or you may cause the collapsible steering column to collapse. Before installing the horn pad, apply multi-purpose grease to the surface of the cancel pin and horn contact slip ring.
8. Tighten the steering wheel nuts to 22–29 ft. lbs. (29–39 Nm).
9. Reinstall the horn button, pad, or ring.
10. Connect the negative battery cable.

Steering Column

Removal and Installation

1. Disconnect the negative battery cable.
2. Remove the steering wheel.
3. Remove the steering column covers.
4. Disconnect the combination switch and steering lock switch wiring.

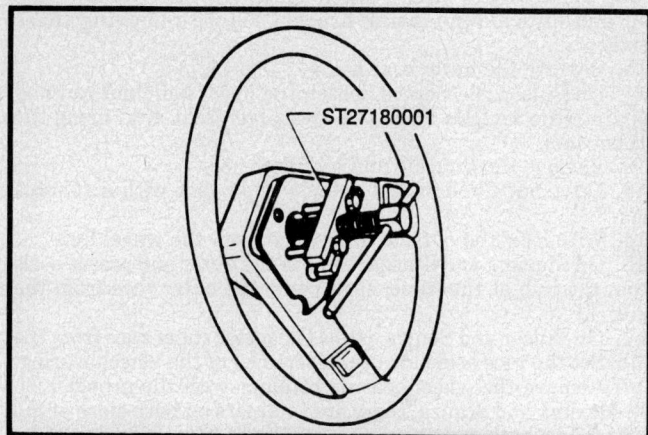

ST27180001

Use a puller to remove the steering wheel

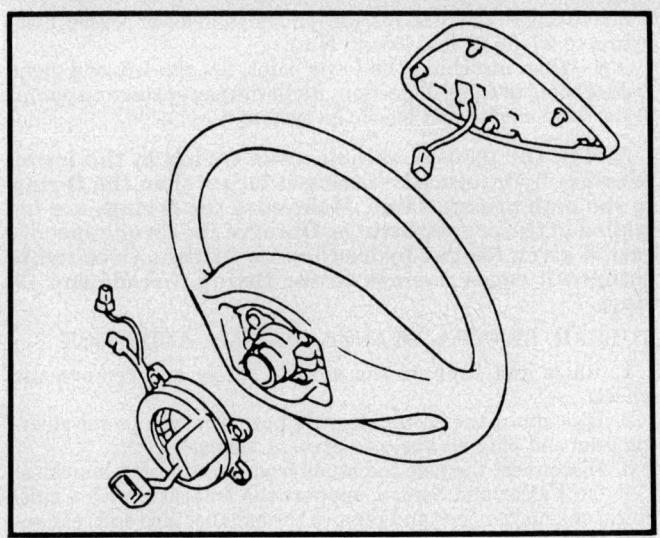

Steering wheel on 1989–91 Maxima with sonar suspension

5. Remove most of the steering column support bracket and clamp nuts and bolts. Leave a few of the fasteners loosely installed to support the column while disconnecting it from the steering gear.

6. Remove the bolt from the column lower joint.

7. Remove the temporarily installed column support bracket bolts and withdraw the column from the lower joint.

8. Withdraw the column spline shaft from the lower joint and remove the steering column. Be careful not to tear the column tube jacket insulator during removal.

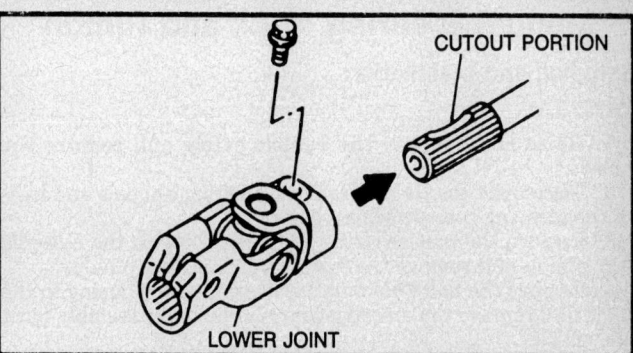

The cutout portion of the steering column spline shaft must perfectly aligned with the bolt

To install:

9. Insert the column spline shaft into the lower joint and install all column fasteners finger-tight.

10. Install the lower joint bolt. The cutout portion of the spline shaft must perfectly aligned with the bolt. Torque the bolt to 17–22 ft. lbs. (23–30 Nm). Tighten the steering bracket and clamp fasteners gradually. While tightening, make sure no stress is placed on the column.

11. Connect the combination switch and steering lock switch wiring.

12. Install the steering column covers.

13. Install the steering wheel.

14. Connect the negative battery cable.

15. After the installation is complete, turn the steering wheel from stop to stop and make sure it turns smoothly. The number of turns to the left and right stops must be equal.

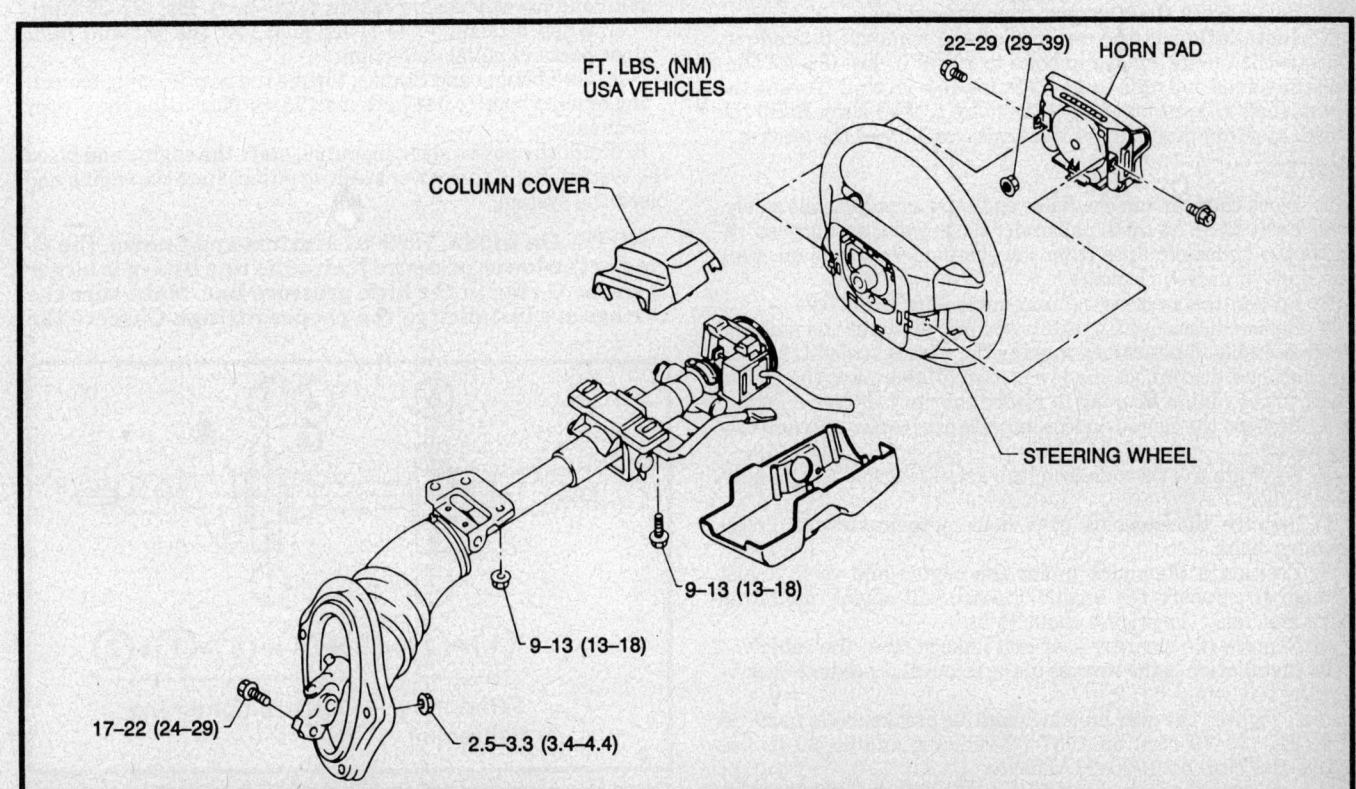

Steering column assembly—1990–91 Pulsar

Manual Steering Rack and Pinion

Removal and Installation

SENTRA

1. Raise and support the vehicle safely and remove the wheels.
2. Disconnect the tie rod from the steering knuckle and loosen the steering gear attaching bolts.
3. Remove the bolt securing the lower joint to the steering gear pinion and remove the lower joint from the pinion.
4. Remove the bolts holding the steering gear housing to the body, and remove the steering gear and linkage assembly from the vehicle.
5. Installation is the reverse order of the removal procedure. When fitting the lower U-joint, make sure the attaching bolt is aligned perfectly with the cut out in the splined end of the steering column shaft. Torque the steering gear mounting clamp bolts to 54–72 ft. lbs. (73–97 Nm). Torque the tie rod end nuts to 22–29 ft. lbs. (29–39 Nm).

Power Steering Rack and Pinion

Removal and Installation

200SX

1. Raise and support the vehicle safely.
2. Remove the air cleaner and remove the bolt securing the U-joint to the worm shaft.
3 Disconnect the hoses from the power steering gear and plug the hoses to prevent leakage.
4. Remove the pitman arm from the sector shaft using a suitable tool and remove the steering gear mounting bolts.
5. Remove the exhaust pipe mounting nut.
6. Disconnect the control cable or linkage for the transmission and position it aside.
7. Remove the steering gear from the vehicle.
8. Installation is the reverse of the removal procedure. Torque the mounting clamp bolts to 29–36 ft. lbs. (39–49 Nm) and the tie rod end nuts to 40–72 ft. lbs. (54–98 Nm). Torque the worm shaft U-joint bolt to 17–22 ft. lbs. (24–29 Nm). Refill the power steering pump, start the engine and bleed the system.

300ZX

1. Block the rear wheels. Raise and support the vehicle safely.
2. Position an oil catch pan under the power steering gear, remove the hydraulic lines from the gear and drain the oil. Plug the lines to prevent leakage.
3. Loosen the steering column lower joint shaft bolt.
4. Before disconnecting the lower ball joint set the steering gear assembly in neutral by making the wheels straight. Loosen the bolt and disconnect the lower joint. Matchmark the pinion shaft to the pinion housing to record the neutral gear position.
5. Remove the tie rod end-to-knuckle arm cotter pins and castle nuts.
6. Separate the tie rods from the knuckle arms using a suitable puller.
7. Remove the steering gear housing-to-suspension crossmember bolts.
8. Position a floor jack under the engine and raise it just enough to support the engine. Loosen the engine mounting bolts and raise the engine about ½ in.
9. Remove the steering gear and linkage from the vehicle.
10. Installation is the reverse of the removal procedure observing the following:
   a. Tighten the gear housing mouting bracket bolts to 29–36 ft. lbs. (39–49 Nm) on 1987–89 vehicles, and 65–80 ft. lbs. (88–108 Nm) on 1990–91 vehicles.
   b. Torque the tie rod end nuts to 22–29 ft. lbs. (29–39 Nm).
   c. On 1990–91 vehicles, torque the high pressure hydraulic

line fitting to 22–26 ft. lbs. (36–40 Nm) and lower pressure fitting to 27–30 ft. lbs. (36–40 Nm).
   d. When attaching the lower joint, set the left and right dust boots to equal deflection. Refill the power steering pump, start the engine and bleed the system.

NOTE: On 1990–91 vehicles, the O-ring in the lower pressure hydraulic line fitting is larger than the O-ring in the high pressure line. Make sure the O-rings are installed in the proper fittings. Observe the torque specification given for the hydraulic line fittings. Over-tightening will cause damage to the fitting threads and O-rings.

PULSAR, SENTRA, STANZA, MAXIMA AND 240SX

1. Raise and support the vehicle safely and remove the wheels.
2. Disconnect the power steering hose from the power steering gear and plug all hoses to prevent leakage.
3. Disconnect the side rod studs from the steering knuckles.
4. On Pulsar and Sentra, support the transaxle with a suitable transmission jack and remove the exhaust pipe and rear engine mounts.
5. On other vehicles, remove the lower joint assembly from the steering gear pinion. Before disconnecting the lower ball joint set the steering gear assembly in neutral by making the wheels straight. Loosen the bolt and disconnect the lower joint. Matchmark the pinion shaft to the pinion housing to record the neutral gear position.
6. Remove the steering gear and linkage assembly from the vehicle.
7. Installation is the reverse of the removal procedure observing the following:
   a. Make sure the pinion shaft and pinion housing are aligned properly.
   b. On 240SX, 1989–91 Maxima and Stanza vehicles, torque the high pressure hydraulic line fitting to 11–18 ft. lbs. (15–25 Nm) and lower pressure fitting to 20–29 ft. lbs. (27–39 Nm).
   c. When attaching the lower joint, set the left and right dust boots to equal deflection.
   d. On Maxima and Stanza, torque the gear housing mounting bracket bolts to 54–72 ft. lbs. (73–97 Nm) using the proper sequence.
8. Refill the power steering pump, start the engine and bleed the system. Refill the power steering pump, start the engine and bleed the system.

NOTE: On 240SX, 1989–91 Maxima and Stanza, the O-ring in the lower pressure hydraulic line fitting is larger than the O-ring in the high pressure line. Make sure the O-rings are installed in the proper fittings. Observe the

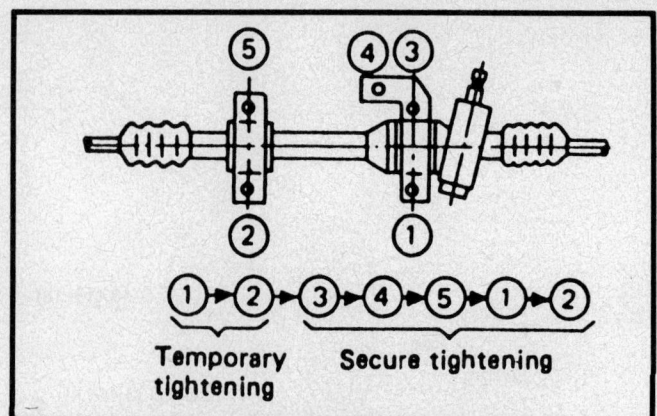

Gear housing mounting bracket bolt torque sequence – Stanza and Maxima

torque specification given for the hydraulic line fittings. Over-tightening will cause damage to the fitting threads and O-rings.

Power Steering Pump

Removal and Installation

1. On the 200SX, remove the air cleaner duct and air cleaner.
2. Loosen the idler pulley locknut and turn the adjusting nut counterclockwise, in order to remove the power steering belt.
3. Remove the drive belt on the air conditioning compressor, if so equipped.
4. Loosen the power steering hoses at the pump and remove the bolts holding the power steering pump to the bracket.
5. Disconnect and plug the power steering hoses and remove the pump from the vehicle.
6. Installation is the reverse of the removal procedure. Fill and bleed the power steering system.

Belt Adjustment

1. Loosen the tension adjustment and mounting bolts.
2. Move the pump toward or away from the engine so the belt deflects ¼–½ in. midway between the idler pulley and the pump pulley under moderate thumb pressure.
3. Tighten the bolts and recheck the tension adjustment.

System Bleeding

1. Check the level in the power steering pump reservoir. Add fluid as necessary to the proper level.
2. Safely raise and support the vehicle until the wheels are just off the ground.
3. With the engine running, quickly turn the steering wheel all the way to the left and all the way to the right 10 times.

4. Stop the engine and check to see if any more fluid is required in the pump reservoir. Add fluid as necessary.
5. If all the air cannot be bled from the system, repeat Steps 3–4 until all the air is removed from the system.

Tie Rod Ends

Removal and Installation

A ball joint remover tool or equivalent, is required for this operation.
1. Raise and support the vehicle safely.
2. Locate the faulty tie rod end. It will have a lot of play in it and the dust cover will probably be torn.
3. Remove the cotter key and nut from the tie rod stud. Note the position of the tie rod end in relation to the rest of the steering linkage.
4. Loosen the lock nut holding the tie rod to the rest of the steering linkage.
5. Free the tie rod ball joint from either the relay rod or steering knuckle by using a ball joint remover or equivalent tool.
6. Unscrew and remove the tie rod end, counting the number of turns it takes to completely free it.
7. Install the new tie rod end, turning it in exactly the same number of turns for removal. Make sure it is correctly positioned in relation to the rest of the steering linkage.
8. Fit the ball joint and nut. Torque the tie rod end to 22–29 ft. lbs. (29–39 Nm) on all vehicles except 200SX. On 200SX, torque the tie rod end nut to 40–72 ft. lbs. (54–98 Nm). Once the specified torque is reached, tighten further until the nut groove is aligned with the first pin hole. Install a new cotter pin.
9. Check and adjust the toe of the vehicle as needed.

BRAKES

Master Cylinder

Removal and Installation

1. Clean the outside of the cylinder thoroughly, particularly around the cap and fluid lines.
2. Disconnect the fluid lines and cap them to keep dirt out.
3. On vehicles with a fluid level gauge, disconnect the electrical connector.
4. Remove the clevis pin connecting the pushrod to the brake pedal arm inside the vehicle.
5. Unbolt the master cylinder from the firewall and remove along with gasket. If the pushrod is not adjustable, there will be shims between the cylinder and the firewall. These shims, or the adjustable pushrod, are used to adjust brake pedal free-play.
6. Installation of the master cylinder is the reverse of the removal procedure. Bleed the brakes.

Proportioning Valve

The proportioning valve is incorporated into the master cylinder. Consequently, removal and installation procedures are limited to replacement of the master cylinder unit as a whole.

Power Brake Booster

Removal and Installation

1. Remove the master cylinder.
2. Remove the vacuum hose at the power brake booster.
3. Remove the pushrod from the brake pedal.

4. From under the instrument panel, remove the cowl-to-booster nuts. Remove the brake booster.
5. Installation is in the reverse order of removal. Bleed the brake system.

Brake Calipers

Removal and Installation

1. Raise the vehicle and support safely.
2. Remove the front or rear wheels.
3. Disconnect the brake line from the caliper. Remove the metal gaskets from the brake hose fitting and discard them.
4. Disconnect the parking brake cable.
5. Remove the brake pads if they interfere with caliper removal.
6. Remove the brake caliper mounting bolts.
7. Remove the brake caliper assembly.
8. Installation is the reverse of the removal procedure. Torque the caliper bolts to 40–72 ft. lbs. (54–98 Nm). Use new brake hose fitting gaskets. Bleed the brake system and adjust the parking brake cable.

Front Disc Brake Pads

Removal and Installation

200SX AND MAXIMA

Type AD22V

AD22V type front disc brakes are used on 200SX with CA20E engines.

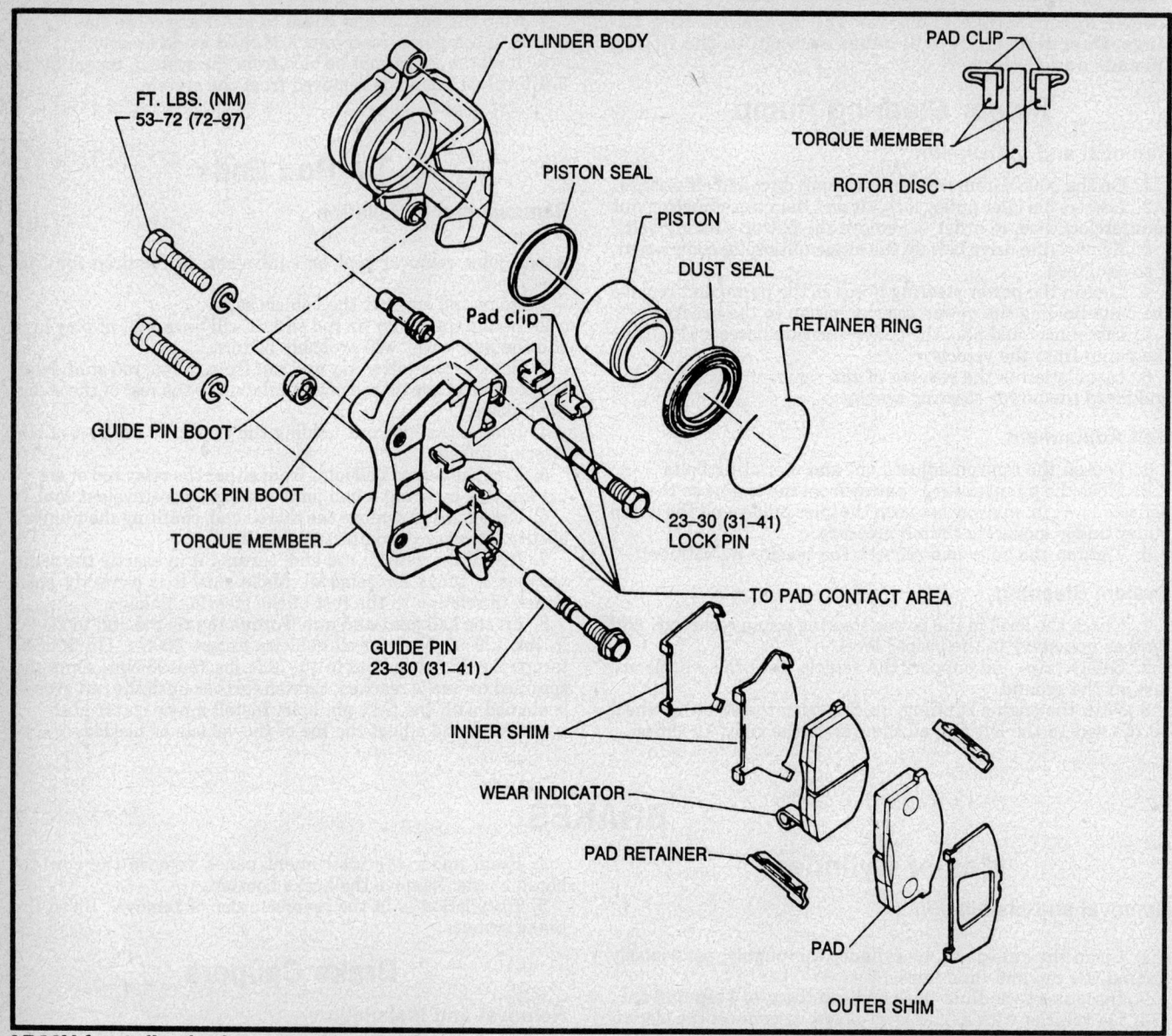

AD22V front disc brake assembly—200SX

1. Raise the vehicle and support safely.
2. Remove the front wheels.
3. Remove the lower caliper guide pin.
4. Rotate the brake caliper body upward.
5. Remove the brake pad retainer and the inner and outer pad shims.
6. Remove the brake pads.

NOTE: Do not depress the brake pedal when the caliper body is raised. The brake piston will be forced out of the caliper.

7. Clean the piston end of the caliper body and the pin bolt holes. Be careful not to get oil on the brake rotor.
8. Pull the caliper body to the outer side and install the inner brake pad.
9. Install the outer pad, shim and pad retainer.
10. Reposition the caliper body and then tighten the guide pin bolt to 23–30 ft. lbs. (31–41 Nm).
11. Apply the brakes a few times to seat the pads before driving out on the road.

Types CL25VB and CL28VB

CL28VB type front disc brakes are used on 200SX with VG30E engines and 1987–88 Maxima. CL25VB brake are used on 1989–91 Maxima.

1. Raise the vehicle and support safely.
2. Remove the front wheels.
3. Remove the pin (lower) bolt from the caliper.
4. Swing the caliper body upward on the upper bolt.
5. Remove the pad retainers and inner and outer shims.

NOTE: Do not depress the brake pedal when the cylinder body is in the raised position or the piston will pop out of the cylinder.

6. Check the level of fluid in the master cylinder. If the fluid is near the maximum level, use a clean syringe to remove fluid until the level is down well below the lip of the reservoir.
7. Use a large C-clamp or piston expansion tool to press the caliper piston back into the caliper, to allow room for the installation of the thicker new pads.

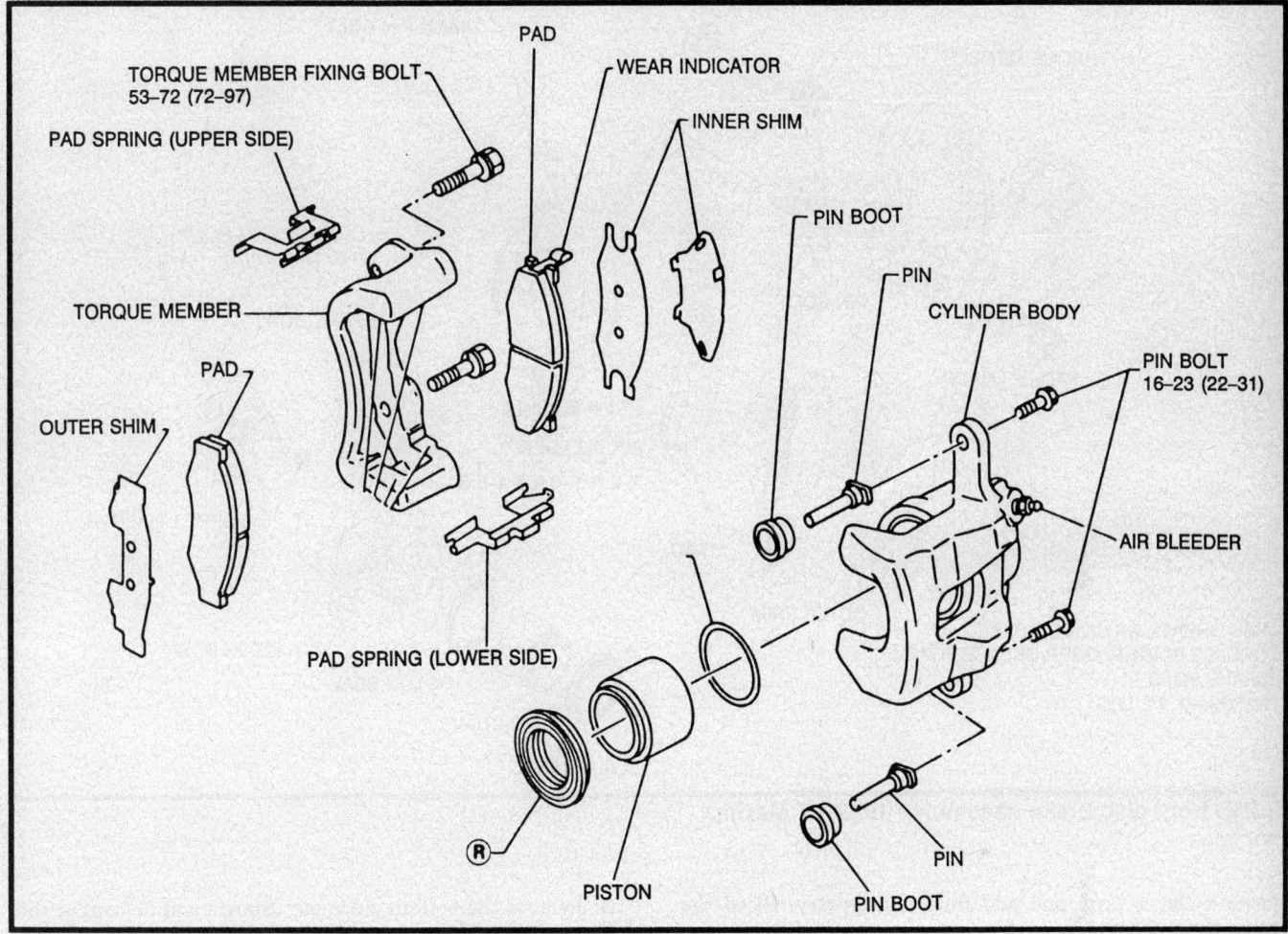

PAD
TORQUE MEMBER FIXING BOLT 53–72 (72–97)
WEAR INDICATOR
PAD SPRING (UPPER SIDE)
INNER SHIM
PIN BOOT
TORQUE MEMBER
PIN
CYLINDER BODY
PAD
OUTER SHIM
PIN BOLT 16–23 (22–31)
AIR BLEEDER
PAD SPRING (LOWER SIDE)
R
PISTON
PIN BOOT
PIN

CL28VB front brake disc assembly—200SX and 1987–89 300ZX (non-turbo)

8. Install the new pads, utilizing new shims, in reverse order. Torque the lower pin bolt to 16–23 ft. lbs. (22–31 Nm) on both types of brakes.

240SX

Types CL22VB and CL25VA

CL22VB type front disc brakes are used on vehicles without ABS and CL25VA type brake are used on vehicles with ABS.
1. Raise and support the vehicle safely.
2. Remove the front wheels.
3. Remove the pin (lower) bolt from the caliper.
4. Swing the caliper body upward on the upper bolt.
5. Remove the pad retainers and inner and outer shims.

NOTE: Do not depress the brake pedal when the cylinder body is in the raised position or the piston will pop out of the cylinder.

6. Check the level of fluid in the master cylinder. If the fluid is near the maximum level, use a clean syringe to remove fluid until the level is down well below the lip of the reservoir.
7. Use a large C-clamp or piston expansion tool to press the caliper piston back into the caliper, to allow room for the installation of the thicker new pads.
8. Install the new pads, utilizing new shims, in reverse order. Torque the lower and main pin bolts to 16–23 ft. lbs. (22–31 Nm) on both CL22VB and CL25VA type front disc brakes.

1987–89 300ZX

Types CL28VE and CL28VB

CL28VE type front disc brakes are used on turbocharged engines and CL28VB type brakes are used on non-turbocharged engines.
1. Raise and support the vehicle safely.
2. Remove the front wheels.
3. Remove the lower pin bolt which retains the caliper to the torque member.
4. Rotate the caliper up and aside, exposing the pads. Do not try to move the caliper sideways.
5. Remove the pad retainers, the inner and outer shims, then the pads.
6. To install, clean the piston end and pin bolts.
7. Install a new inner pad. Rotate the caliper back down into place, slightly open the bleeder screw, then using a long bar, lever the caliper to the outside to press the piston into place. Rotate the caliper back up and aside.
8. Lightly coat the sliding surfaces of the torque member with grease. Install a new outer pad with the inner and outer shims. Install the pad retainers; be careful not to install them upside down.
9. Rotate the caliper down and install the pin bolt. Tighten to 16-23 ft. lbs. (22-31 Nm).
10. Apply the brakes a few times to seat the pads. Check the

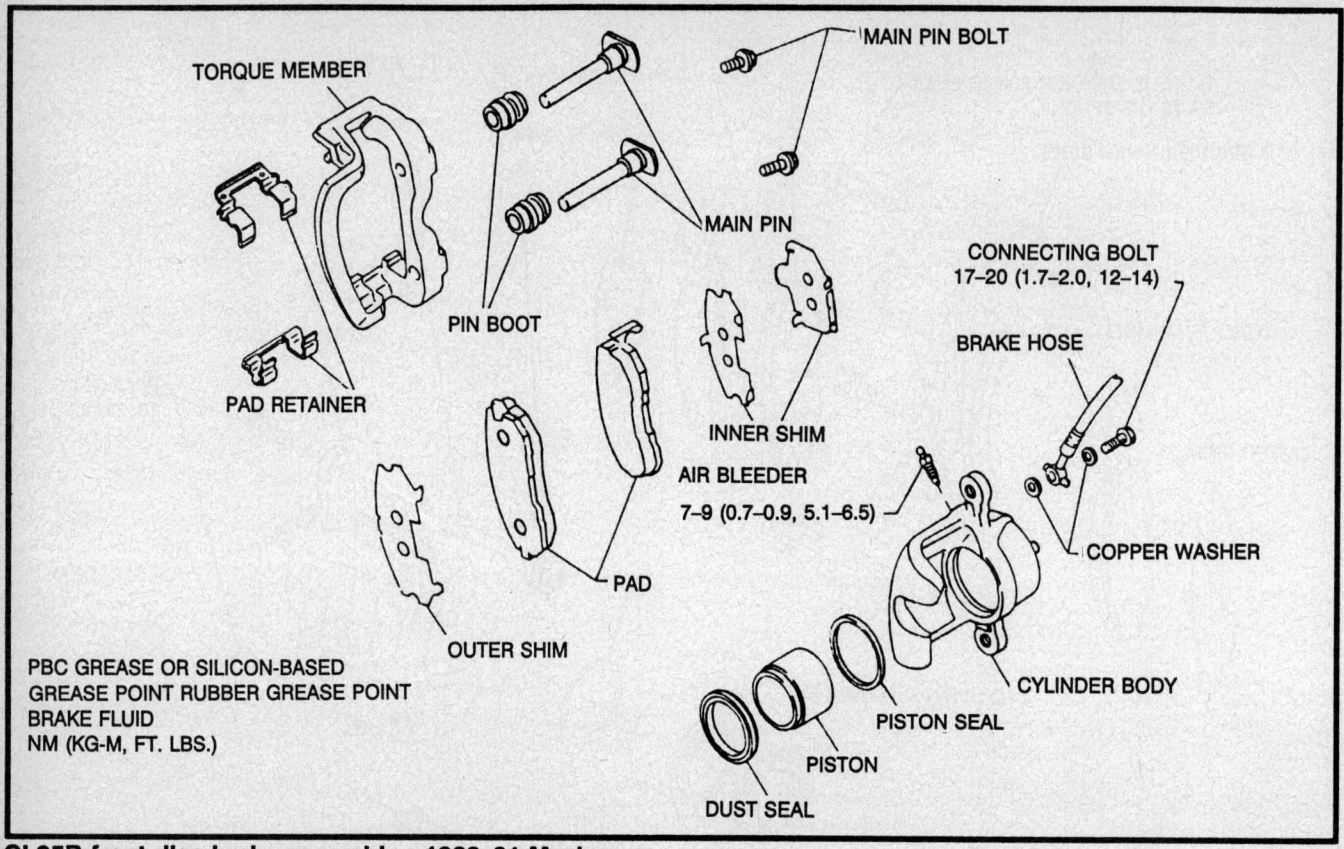

CL25B front disc brake assembly—1989–91 Maxima

master cylinder level and add fluid if necessary. Bleed the brakes if necessary.

1990–91 300ZX

Types OPZ25V and PZ25VA

OPZ25VA type front disc brakes are used on turbocharged engines. OPZ25V brakes are used on non-turbocharged engines.
1. Raise the vehicle and support safely.
2. Remove the front wheels.
3. Remove the clip from the pad pin and remove the pad pin.
4. Remove the cross spring.
5. Withdraw the outer pad and insert and temporarily insert it between the lower piston and the rotor.
6. Using a suitable tool, push the upper piston back and insert the new pad so it contacts the upper piston.
7. Withdraw the old pad.
8. Push the piston back with a suitable tool to prevent it from popping out.
9. Pull out the new pad and re-install it in the correct position.
10. Repeat steps 5–9 for the inner pad.
11. Install the cross spring, pad pin and pad clip.

PULSAR, SENTRA AND STANZA

Types AD18B, AD18V, CL18B, CL25VA and CL28VA

CL18B, AD18B and AD18V type front disc brakes are used on Pulsar and Sentra depending on engine application. CL28VA type brakes are used on 1987–89 Stanza and Stanza wagon. The 1990–91 Stanza uses CL25VA front disc brakes on both ABS equipped and non-ABS vehicles.
1. Raise the vehicle and support safely.
2. Remove the front wheels.

3. Remove the bottom guide pin (Stanza and Sentra) or the lock pin (Pulsar) from the caliper and swing the caliper cylinder body upward.
4. Remove the brake pad retainers and the pads.
5. Install the brake pads and caliper assembly.
6. Install the wheels and lower the vehicle.
7. Apply the brakes a few times to seat the pads. Check the master cylinder and add fluid if necessary. Bleed the brakes, if necessary.

Rear Disc Brake Pads

Removal and Installation

200SX, 240SX, MAXIMA AND 1990–91 STANZA WITH ABS

Types CL11H and CL9H

CL11H type rear disc brakes are used on 200SX with CA20E engines and on the 1988 Maxima. CL9H rear disc brake are used on 240SX and 1989–91 Maxima on both ABS equipped and non-ABS vehicles. CL9H rear disc brakes are also used on 1990–91 Stanza with ABS.
1. Raise and support the vehicle safely.
2. Remove the rear wheels.
3. Release the parking brake and remove the cable bracket bolt.
4. Remove the pin bolts and lift off the caliper body.
5. Pull out the pad springs and then remove the pads and shims.
6. Clean the piston end of the caliper body and the area around the pin holes. Be careful not to get oil on the rotor.
7. Using the proper tool, carefully turn the piston clockwise

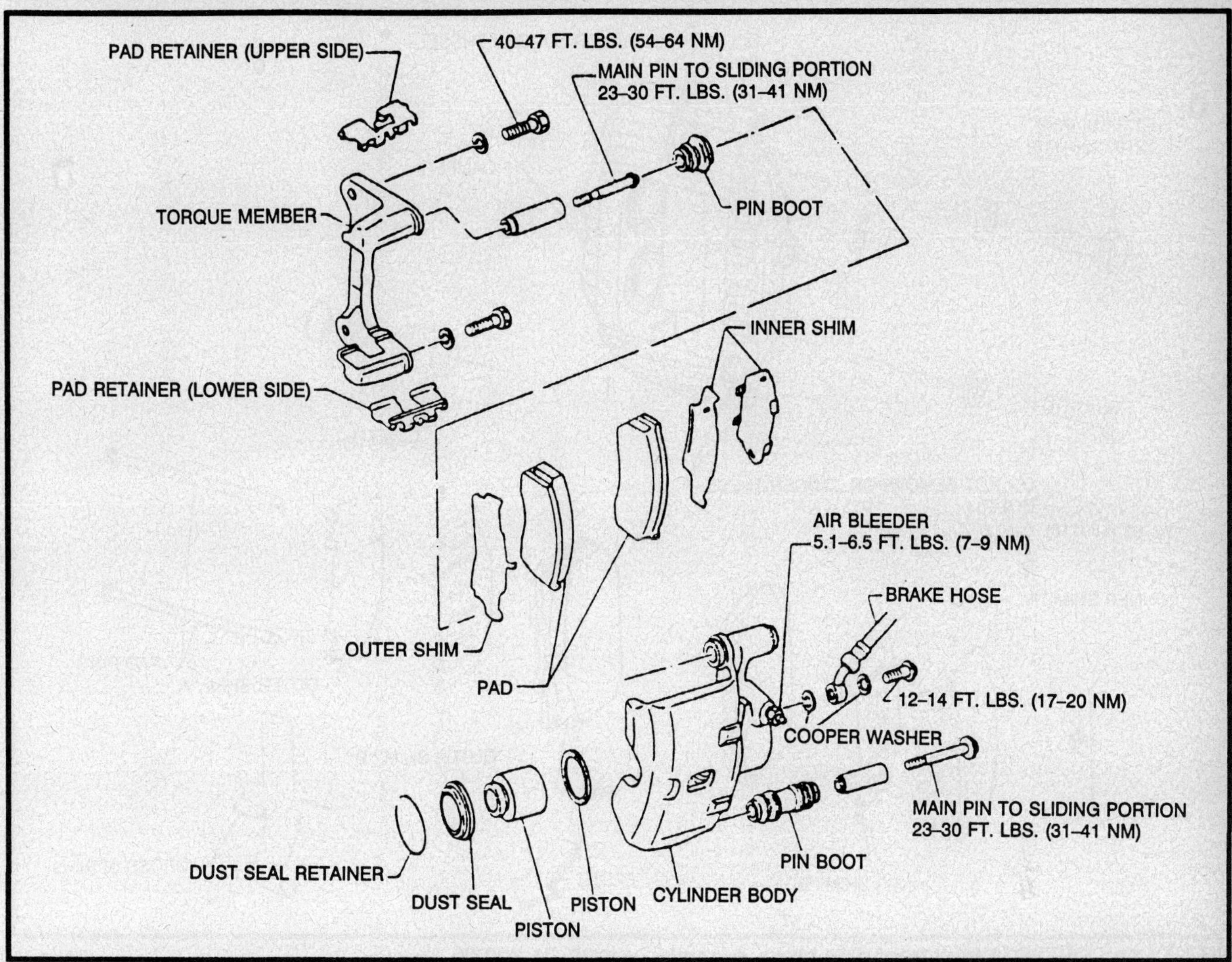

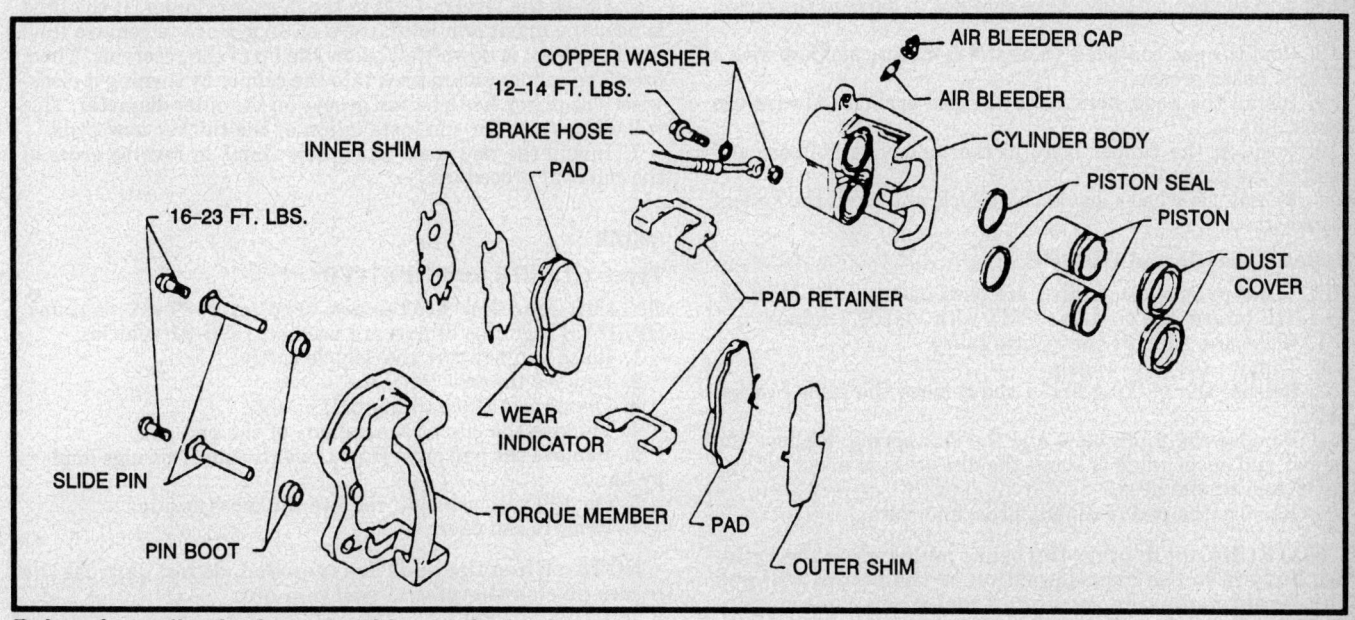

PAD RETAINER (UPPER SIDE)

40–47 FT. LBS. (54–64 NM)

MAIN PIN TO SLIDING PORTION
23–30 FT. LBS. (31–41 NM)

PIN BOOT

TORQUE MEMBER

INNER SHIM

PAD RETAINER (LOWER SIDE)

AIR BLEEDER
5.1–6.5 FT. LBS. (7–9 NM)

BRAKE HOSE

OUTER SHIM

12–14 FT. LBS. (17–20 NM)

PAD

COOPER WASHER

MAIN PIN TO SLIDING PORTION
23–30 FT. LBS. (31–41 NM)

DUST SEAL RETAINER

PIN BOOT

DUST SEAL   PISTON   CYLINDER BODY

PISTON

CL28VE front disc brake assembly—1987–89 300ZX (turbo)

COPPER WASHER
12–14 FT. LBS.

AIR BLEEDER CAP

AIR BLEEDER

BRAKE HOSE

CYLINDER BODY

INNER SHIM   PAD

PISTON SEAL

PISTON

16–23 FT. LBS.

DUST COVER

PAD RETAINER

WEAR
INDICATOR

SLIDE PIN

TORQUE MEMBER   PAD

PIN BOOT

OUTER SHIM

Pulsar front disc brake assembly—typical

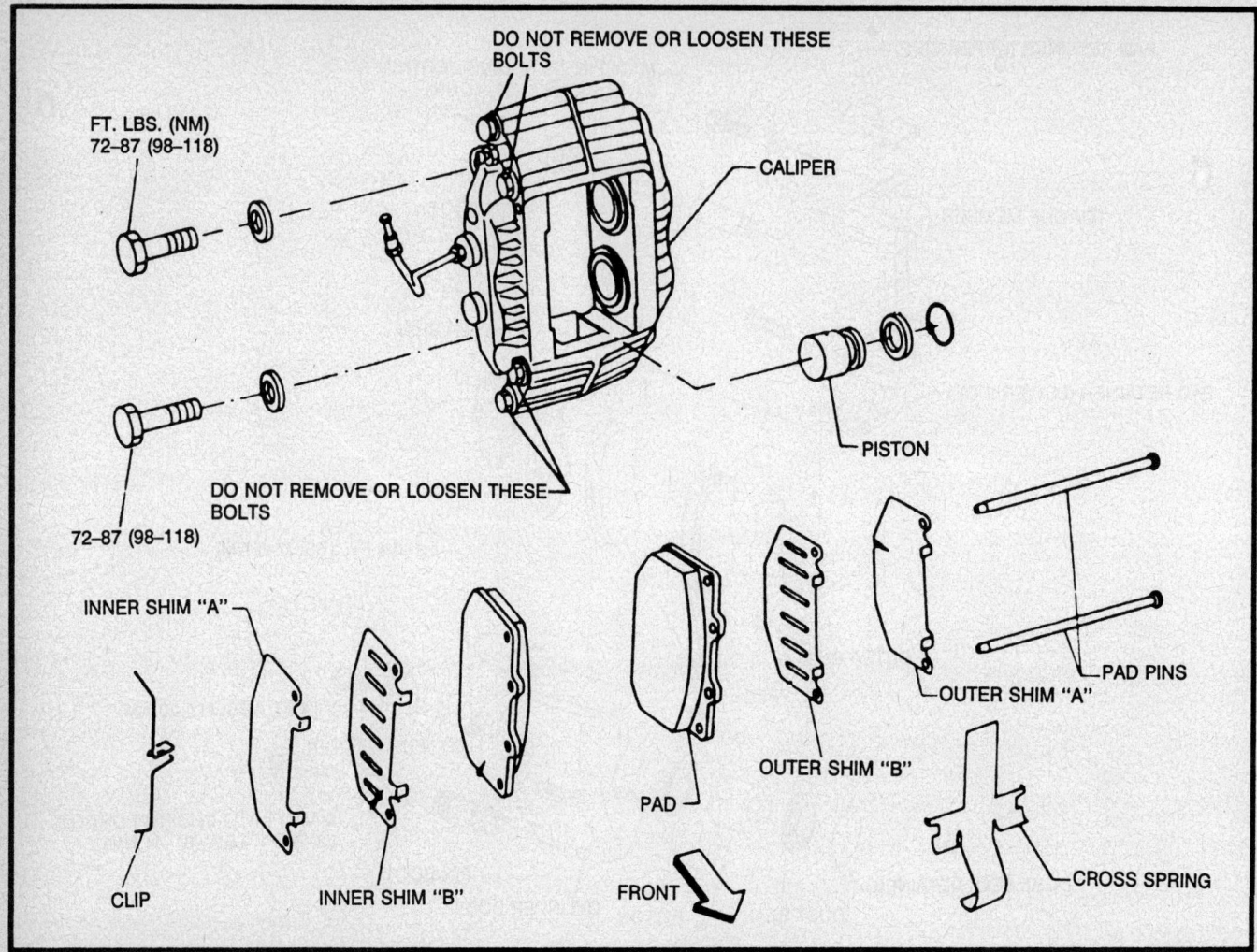

DO NOT REMOVE OR LOOSEN THESE BOLTS

FT. LBS. (NM) 72–87 (98–118)

CALIPER

DO NOT REMOVE OR LOOSEN THESE BOLTS

72–87 (98–118)

PISTON

INNER SHIM "A"

PAD PINS

OUTER SHIM "A"

OUTER SHIM "B"

PAD

CROSS SPRING

CLIP

INNER SHIM "B"

FRONT

OPZ25V and OPZ25VA type front disc brake assembly—1990–91 300ZX

back into the caliper body. Take care not to damage the piston boot.

8. Coat the pad contact area on the mounting support with a silicone based grease.

9. Install the pads, shims and the pad springs. Always use new shims.

10. Position the caliper body in the mounting support and tighten the pin bolts.

11. Mount the wheels, lower the vehicle and bleed the system if necessary.

Types CL11HB and CL14HB

CL11HB type rear disc brakes are used on the 1987 Maxima. CL14HB brakes are used on 200SX with VG30E engines.

1. Raise and support the vehicle safely.
2. Remove the rear wheels.
3. Release the parking brake and remove the cable bracket bolt.
4. Remove the 2 pin bolts and the lock spring. Remove the caliper and suspending it above the disc so as to avoid putting any strain on the hose.
5. Remove the pad retainers, pads, and shims.

NOTE: Do not depress the brake pedal when the cylinder body is in the raised position or the piston will pop out. Avoid damaging the piston seal when removing/installing the pads and retainers.

6. Check the level of fluid in the master cylinder. If the fluid is near the maximum level, use a clean syringe to remove fluid until the level is down well below the lip of the reservoir. Then, press the caliper piston back into the caliper by turning it clockwise. The piston has a helical groove on the outer diameter. This will allow room for the installation of the thicker new pads.

7. Install the new pads using new shims in reverse order of the removal procedure.

300ZX

Types CL14HB and OPZ11VB

CL14HB rear disc brakes are used on 1987–89 vehicles. OPZ11VB rear disc brakes are used on 1990–91 vehicles.

1. Raise and support the vehicle safely.
2. Remove the rear wheels.
3. Disconnect the parking brake cable.
4. Remove the clip at the outside of the pad pins.
5. Remove the pad pins. Hold the anti-squeal springs in place by hand.
6. On 1990–91 vehicles, remove the cross spring.
7. Remove the pads.

NOTE: When the pads are removed, do not depress the brake or else the piston will pop out.

8. Clean the end of the piston with clean brake fluid. Lightly

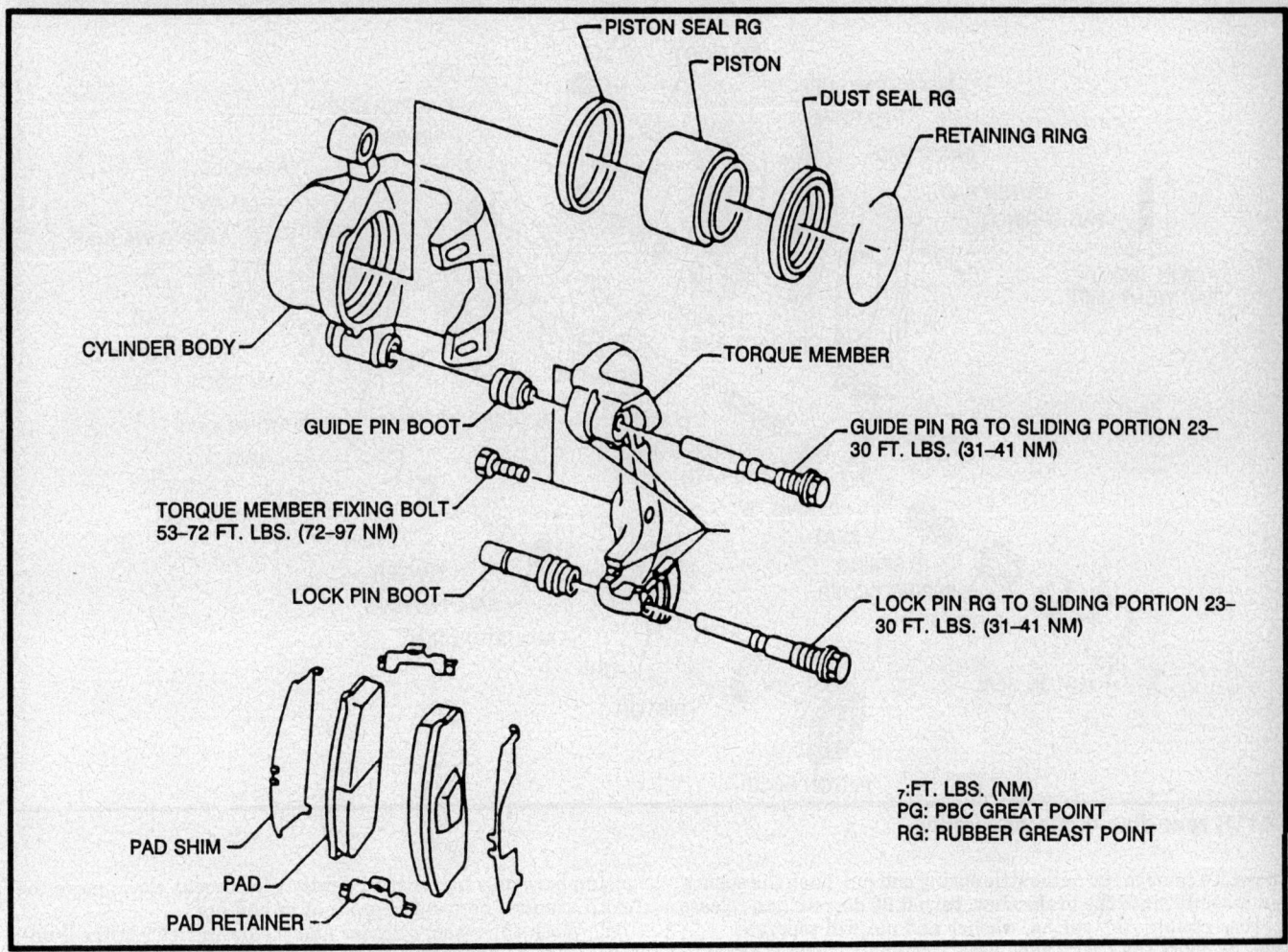

PISTON SEAL RG
PISTON
DUST SEAL RG
RETAINING RING
CYLINDER BODY
TORQUE MEMBER
GUIDE PIN BOOT
GUIDE PIN RG TO SLIDING PORTION 23–30 FT. LBS. (31–41 NM)
TORQUE MEMBER FIXING BOLT 53–72 FT. LBS. (72–97 NM)
LOCK PIN BOOT
LOCK PIN RG TO SLIDING PORTION 23–30 FT. LBS. (31–41 NM)

7:FT. LBS. (NM)
PG: PBC GREAT POINT
RG: RUBBER GREAST POINT

PAD SHIM
PAD
PAD RETAINER

Stanza front disc brake assembly—typical

coat the caliper-to-pad, the yoke-to-pad, the retaining pin-to-pad and the retaining pin-to-bracket surfaces with brake grease.

9. Push in on the piston while at the same time turning it clockwise into the bore. Then, with a lever between the rotor and yoke, push the yoke over until there is clearance to install the pads, equally.

10. Install the cross spring (1990–91 vehicles) shims, the pads, the anti-squeal springs and the pins. Install the clip. Note that the inner pad has a tab which must fit into the piston notch. Make sure the piston notch is centered to allow for proper pad installation.

11. Apply the brakes a few times to center the pads. Check the master cylinder fluid level and add fluid, if necessary.

Brake Rotor

Removal and Installation

1. Safely raise and support the vehicle.
2. Remove the front or rear wheels.
3. Remove the front or rear caliper assembly and suspend it with a piece of wire. Leave the brake hose connected.

NOTE: Do not allow the caliper to hang by the brake hose unsupported.

4. As required, pry off the grease cap, then remove the cotter pin, adjusting cap, insulator and wheel bearing locknut.

5. Remove the hub/rotor assembly.
6. Installation is the reverse of the removal procedure.

Brake Drums

Removal and Installation

1. Raise and support the vehicle safely.
2. Remove the rear wheels.
3. Release the parking brake lever fully.
4. If required, remove the wheel bearing grase cap, cotter pin and locknut.
5. Remove the brake drum. On some vehicles, there are 2 threaded service holes in each drum which accept 8mm bolts. If the drums are hard to remove, insert the bolts into the service holes and screw them in to force the drum away from the axle.
6. Installation is the reverse of the removal procedure.

Brake Shoes

Removal and Installation

PULSAR, SENTRA AND STANZA

1. Raise and support the vehicle safely.
2. Remove the rear wheels and the drums.
3. Release the parking brake lever.
4. Remove the anti-rattle spring and the pin from the brake

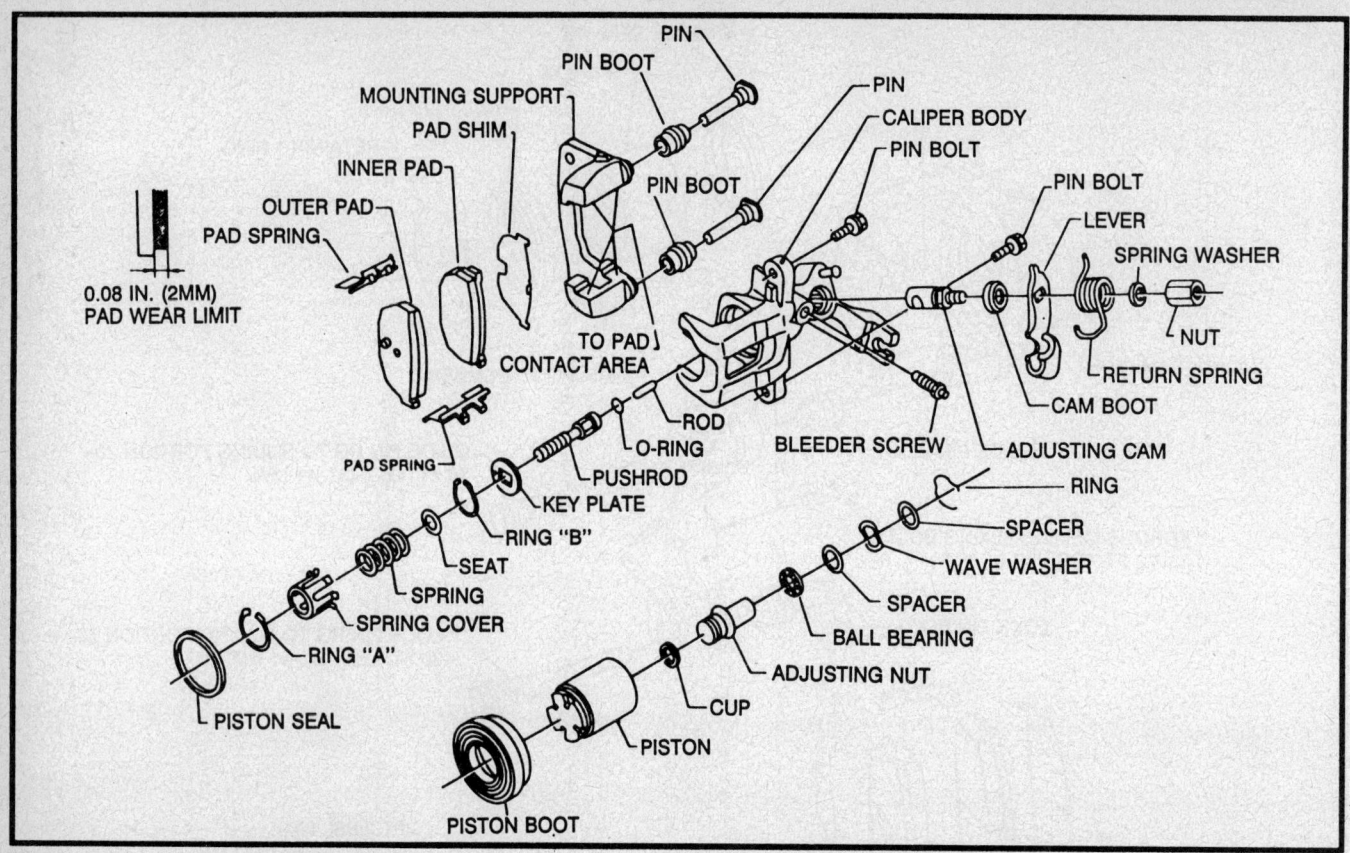

CL11H rear disc brake assembly

shoes. To remove the anti-rattle spring and pin, push the spring/pin assembly into the brake shoe, turn it 90 degrees and release it; the retainer cap, spring, washer and pin will separate.

5. Support the brake shoe assembly and remove the return springs and brake shoes.

NOTE: If the brake shoes are difficult to remove, loosen the brake adjusters. Use a C-clamp or heavy rubber band around the cylinder to prevent the piston from popping out.

6. Clean the backing plate and check the wheel cylinder for leaks.

7. Lubricate the backing plate pads and the screw adjusters with lithium base grease.

8. Install the brake shoes and springs.

9. Install the drum assembly.

10. Adjust brakes and bleed the system if necessary.

Wheel Cylinder

Removal and Installation

1. Raise and support the vehicle safely.

2. Remove the tire and wheel assembly.

3. Remove the brake drum and brake shoes.

4. Disconnect the hydraulic line from the wheel cylinder. Plug the line to prevent leakage.

5. Remove the wheel cylinder from the brake backing plate.

6. Remove the dust boot and take out the piston. Discard the piston cup. The dust boot can be reused although it is best to replace it.

7. Wash all of the components in clean brake fluid.

8. Inspect the piston and piston bore. Replace any components that are severely corroded, scored or worn. The piston and

piston bore may be polished lightly with crocus cloth; move the cloth around the piston bore, not in and out.

9. Wash the wheel cylinder and piston in clean brake fluid.

10. Coat all new components to be installed with clean brake fluid.

11. Assemble the cylinder and install it on the backing plate. Connect the hydraulic line.

12. Install the brake shoes and brake drum.

13. Install the wheel and tire assembly.

14. Lower the vehicle.

15. Bleed the brake system.

Parking Brake Cable

Adjustment

1. Pull up the hand brake lever, counting the number of notches for full engagement. Full engagement should be:

200SX: 7–8 notches
240SX: 6–8 notches
300ZX
    1987–89: 8–10 notches

    1990–91: 8–10 notches
Maxima
    1987–88: 11–13 notches
    1989–91: 8–11 notches
Pulsar: 7–11 notches
Sentra
    1987–88: 11–13 notches
    1989–91: 7–11 notches
Stanza sedan
    1987–88: 11–13 notches
    1989–91: 11–13 notches

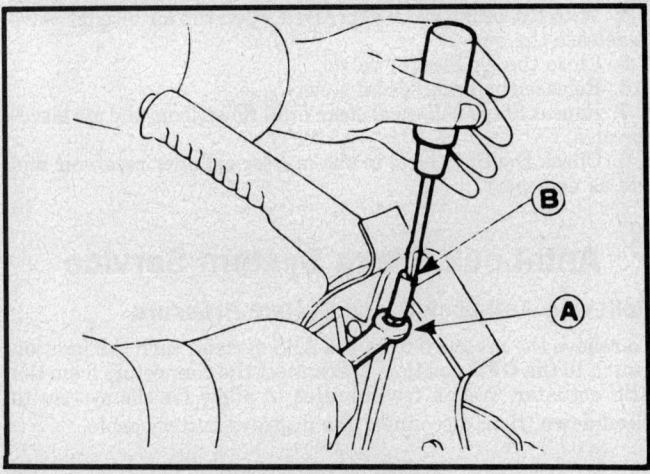

Typical parking brake adjustment

Stanza wagon
    2WD: 11–17 notches
    4WD: 8–9 notches

2. Release the parking brake.

3. Except on 200SX, adjust the lever stroke by loosening the locknut and tightening the adjusting nut to reduce the number of notches necessary for engagement. Tighten the locknut. The locknut and adjuster can be found inside the handbrake assembly, in the passenger compartment. Some vehicles just have an adjusting nut. Access to the locknut is gained by removing the parking brake console or through an access hole in the console itself. On 200SX, the lever stroke is adjusted by turning the equalizer under the vehicle.

4. Check the adjustment and repeat as necessary.

5. After adjustment, check to see that the rear brake levers, at the calipers, return to their full off positions when the lever is released, and that the rear cables are not slack when the lever is released.

6. To adjust the parking brake light, bend the light switch plate down so the light comes on when the lever is engaged 1–2 notches.

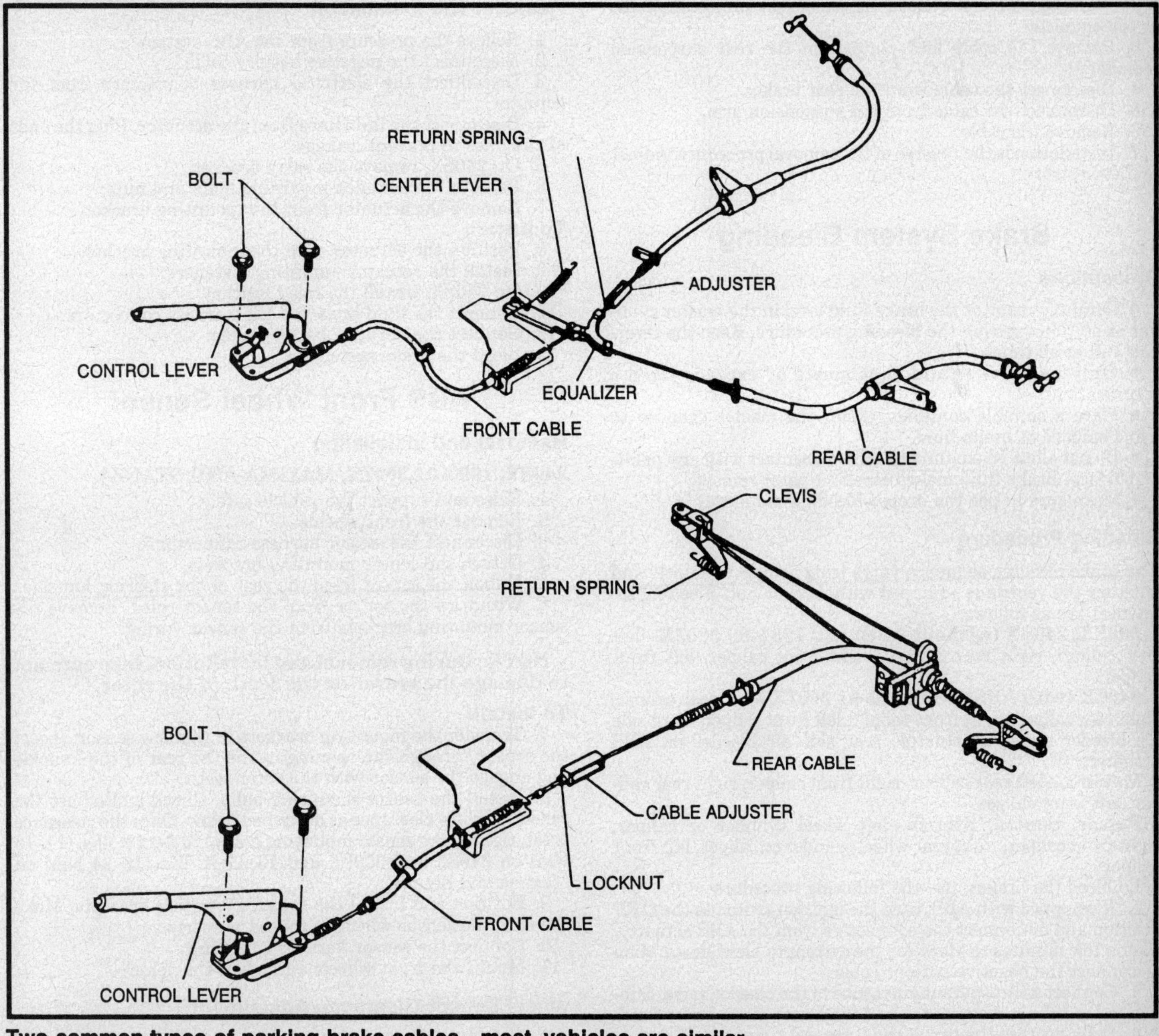

Two common types of parking brake cables—most vehicles are similar

Removal and Installation

FRONT CABLE

1. Remove the parking brake console box.
2. Remove the heat insulator, if equipped.
3. Remove the front passenger seat, if required.
4. Disconnect the warning lamp switch plate connector.
5. Unbolt the lever from the floor.
6. Working from under the vehicle, remove the locknut, adjusting nut and equalizer.
7. Pull the front cable out through the compartment and remove it from the vehicle.

NOTE: On some vehicles it may be necessary to separate the front cable from the lever by breaking the pin.

8. Installation is the reverse of the removal procedure. Adjust the lever stroke.

REAR CABLE

1. Back off on the adjusting nut or equalizer to loosen the cable tension.
2. Working from underneath the vehicle, disconnect the cable at the equalizer.
3. Remove the cable lock plate from the rear suspension member.
4. Disconnect the cable from the rear brakes.
5. Disconnect the cable from the suspension arm.
6. Remove the cable.
7. Installation is the reverse of the removal procedure. Adjust the lever stroke.

Brake System Bleeding

Precautions

• Carefully monitor the brake fluid level in the master cylinder at all times during the bleeding procedure. Keep the reservoir full at all times.
• Only use brake fluid that meets or exceeds DOT 3 specifications.
• Place a suitable container under the master cylinder to avoid spillage of brake fluid.
• Do not allow brake fluid to come in contact with any painted surface. Brake fluid makes excellent paint remover.
• Make sure to use the proper bleeding sequence.

Bleeding Procedure

The brake bleeding sequence varys from vehicle to vehicle and whether the vehicle is equipped with ABS or not. Bleeding sequences are as follows:

200SX, 240SX (without ABS) and 1987–89 300ZX—left rear caliper, right rear caliper, right front caliper, left front caliper.

240SX (with ABS) and 1990–91 300ZX—left rear caliper, right rear caliper, right front caliper, left front caliper, front side air bleeder on ABS actuator, rear side air bleeder on ABS actuator

Maxima—left rear caliper, right front caliper, right rear caliper, left front caliper

Pulsar, Sentra, Stanza—left wheel cylinder or caliper, right front caliper, right rear wheel cylinder or caliper, left front caliper

To bleed the brakes, use the following procedure:
1. If equipped with ABS, turn the ignition switch to the **OFF** position and disconnect the connectors from the ABS actuator. Wait a few minutes to allow for the system to bleed down, then disconnect the negative battery cable.
2. Connect a transparent vinyl tube to the bleeder valve. Submerge the tube in a container half filled with clean brake fluid.
3. Fully depress the brake pedal several times.

4. With the brake pedal depressed, open the air bleeder valve to release the air.
5. Close the air bleeder valve.
6. Release the brake pedal slowly.
7. Repeat Steps 3–6 until clear fluid flows from the air bleeder valve.
8. Check the fluid level in the master cylinder reservoir and add as necessary.

Anti-Lock Brake System Service

Relieving Anti-Lock Brake System Pressure

To relieve the pressure from the ABS system, turn the ignition switch to the **OFF** position. Disconnect the connectors from the ABS actuator. Wait a few minutes to allow for the system to bleed down, then disconnect the negative battery cable.

ABS Actuator

Removal and Installation

1. Relieve the pressure from the ABS system.
2. Disconnect the negative battery cable.
3. Disconnect the electrical harness connectors from the actuator.
4. Disconnect the fluid lines from the actuator. Plug the ends of the lines to prevent leakage.
5. On 240SX, remove the relay bracket.
6. Remove the actuator mounting bolts and nuts.
7. Remove the actuator from the mounting bracket.
To install:
8. Position the actuator onto the mounting bracket.
9. Install the actuator mounting fasteners.
10. On 240SX, install the relay bracket.
11. Connect the fluid lines and the harness connectors.
12. Connect the negative battery cable.
13. Bleed the brake system.

ABS Front Wheel Sensor

Removal and Installation

240SX, 1990–91 300ZX, MAXIMA AND STANZA

1. Raise and support the vehicle safely.
2. Remove the front wheels.
3. Disconnect the sensor harness connector.
4. Detach the sensor mounting brackets.
5. Unbolt the sensor from the rear of the steering knuckle.
6. Withdraw the sensor from the sensor rotor. Remove the sensor mounting brackets from the sensor wiring.

NOTE: During removal and installation, take care not to damage the sensor or the teeth of the rotor.

To install:
7. Transfer the mounting brackets to the new sensor. Insert the sensor through the opening in the the rear of the knuckle and engage the sensor with the rotor teeth.
8. Install the sensor mounting bolts. Check and adjust the sensor-to-rotor clearance as described below. Once the clearance is set, tighten the sensor mounting bolt(s) to 8–12 ft. lbs. (11–16 Nm) on 240SX and 300ZX and 13–17 ft. lbs. (18–24 Nm) on Maxima and Stanza.
9. Position and install the sensor mounting brackets. Make the sure the sensor wiring is routed properly.
10. Connect the sensor harness connector.
11. Mount the front wheels and lower the vehicle.

Wheel Sensor Clearance Adjustment

1. Install the sensor.

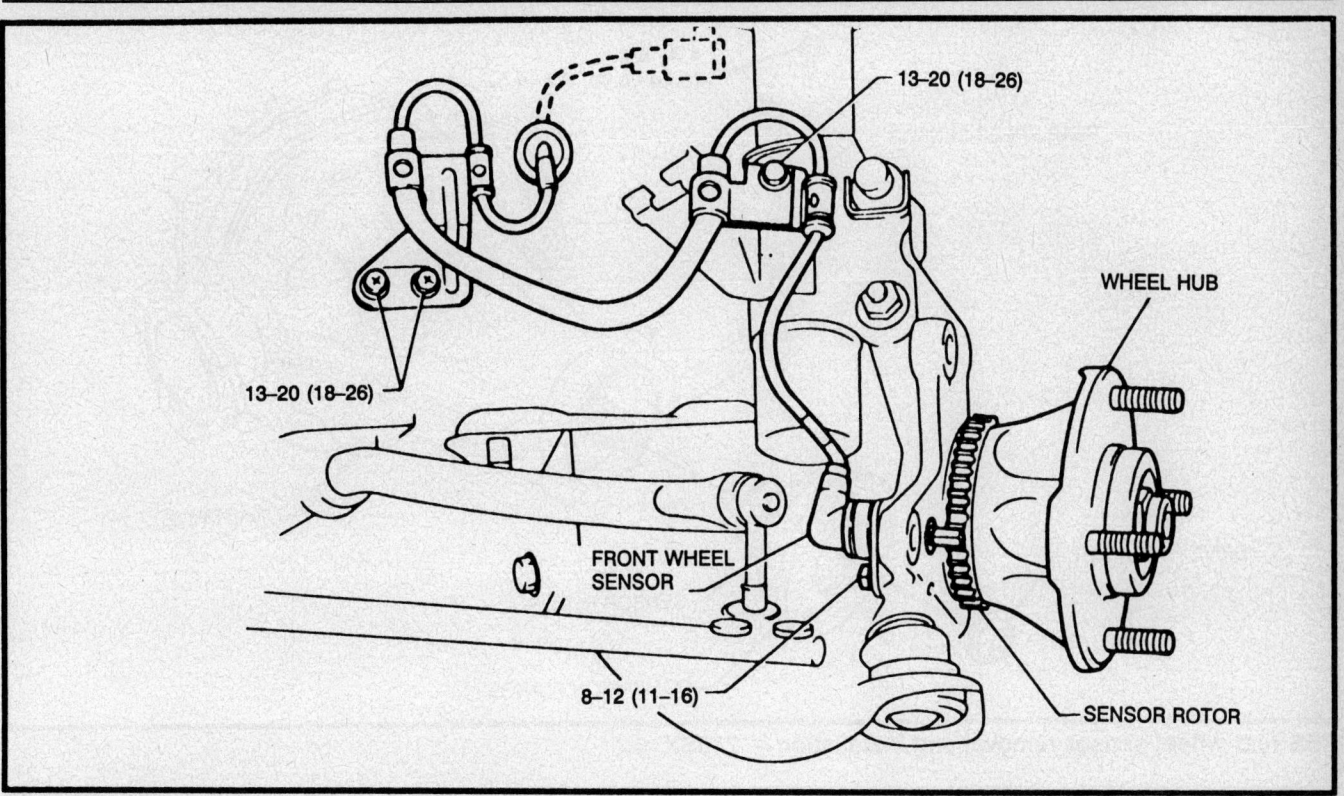

13-20 (18-26)

WHEEL HUB

13-20 (18-26)

FRONT WHEEL
SENSOR

8-12 (11-16)

SENSOR ROTOR

ABS front wheel sensor removal and installation— 240SX

2. Check the clearance between the edge of the sensor and rotor teeth using a feeler gauge. Clearances should be as follows:

a. On 240SX, front wheel sensor clearance should be 0.0108–0.0295 in. (0.275–0.75mm).

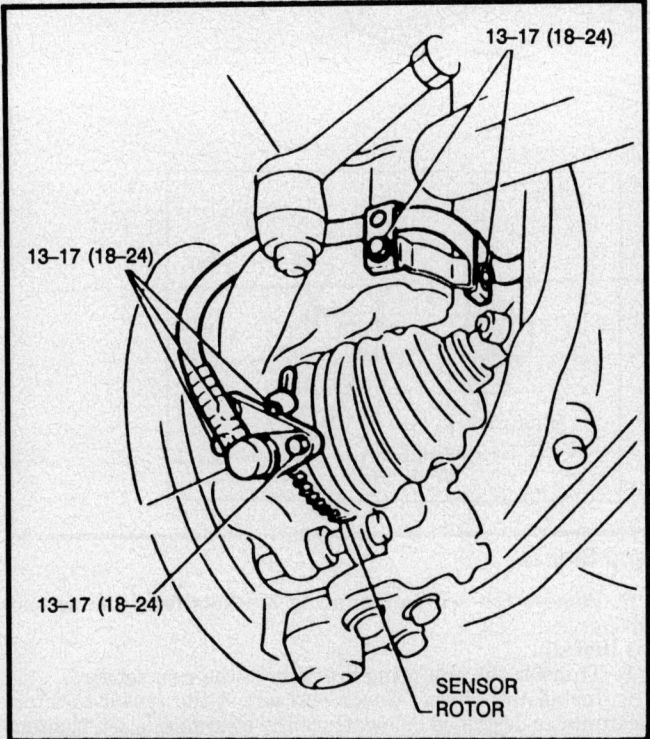

13-17 (18-24)

13-17 (18-24)

13-17 (18-24)

SENSOR
ROTOR

ABS front wheel sensor removal and installation— Maxima and Stanza

b. On 300ZX, front wheel sensor clearance should be 0.0087–0.0280 in. (0.22–0.71mm).

c. On Maxima and Stanza, the clearance should be 0.008–0.039 in. (0.2–1.0mm).

3. To adjust the clearance, loosen the sensor mounting bolt(s) and move the sensor back and forth until the clearance is as specified.

4. Once the clearance is set, tighten the sensor mounting bolt(s) to 8–12 ft. lbs. (11–16 Nm) on 240SX and 300ZX and 13–17 ft. lbs. (18–24 Nm) on Maxima and Stanza.

ABS Rear Wheel Sensor

Removal and Installation

240SX, 1990–91 300ZX, MAXIMA AND STANZA

1. Raise and support the vehicle safely.

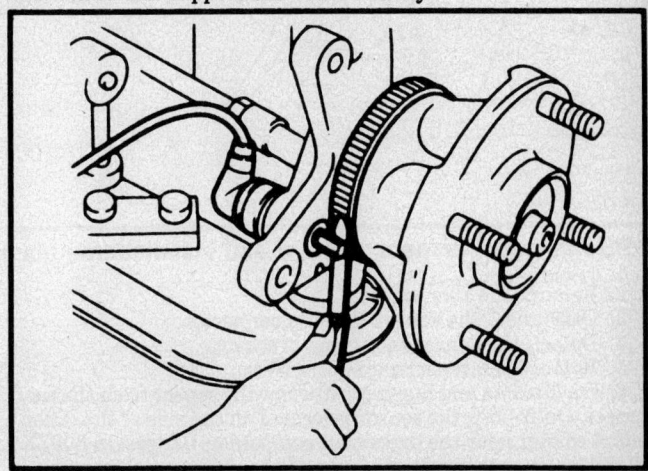

Checking front wheel sensor-to-rotor clearance

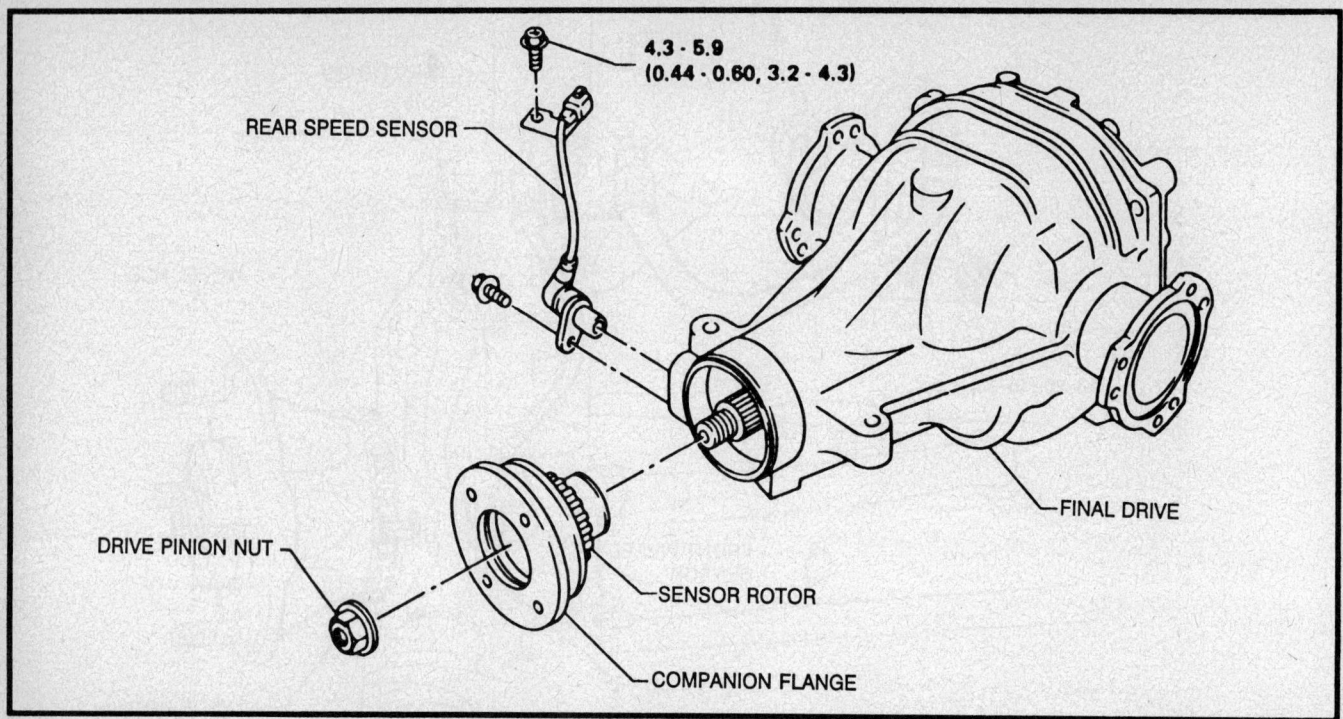

4.3 - 5.9
(0.44 - 0.60, 3.2 - 4.3)

REAR SPEED SENSOR

FINAL DRIVE

DRIVE PINION NUT

SENSOR ROTOR

COMPANION FLANGE

ABS rear wheel sensor removal and Installation— 240SX

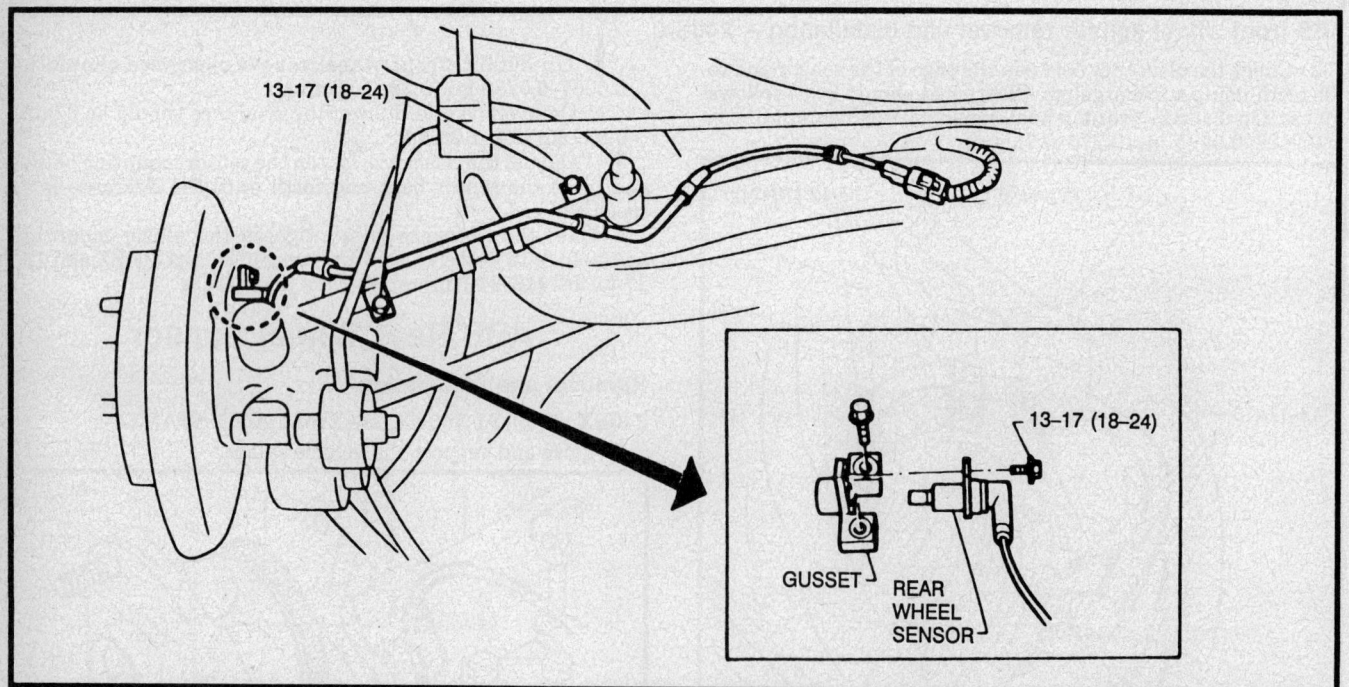

13–17 (18–24)

13–17 (18–24)

GUSSET

REAR WHEEL SENSOR

ABS rear wheel sensor removal and Installation— Maxima and Stanza

2. Remove the rear wheels.
3. Disconnect the sensor harness connector.
4. Detach the sensor mounting brackets.
5. Remove the sensor mounting bolts.
6. On Maxima and Stanza, withdraw the sensor from the rear gusset. On 240SX, the sensor is located on the side of the differential carrier near the driveshaft companion flange. On 300ZX, there are 2 sensors on the side of the differential near each halfshaft.

7. Remove the sensor mounting brackets from the sensor wiring.
To install:
8. Transfer the mounting brackets to the new sensor.
9. Install the sensor. Check and adjust the sensor-to-rotor clearance as described below. Once the clearance is set, tighten the sensor mounting bolt(s) to to 13–20 ft. lbs. (18–26 Nm).
10. Install the sensor mounting brackets. Make the sure the sensor wiring is routed properly.

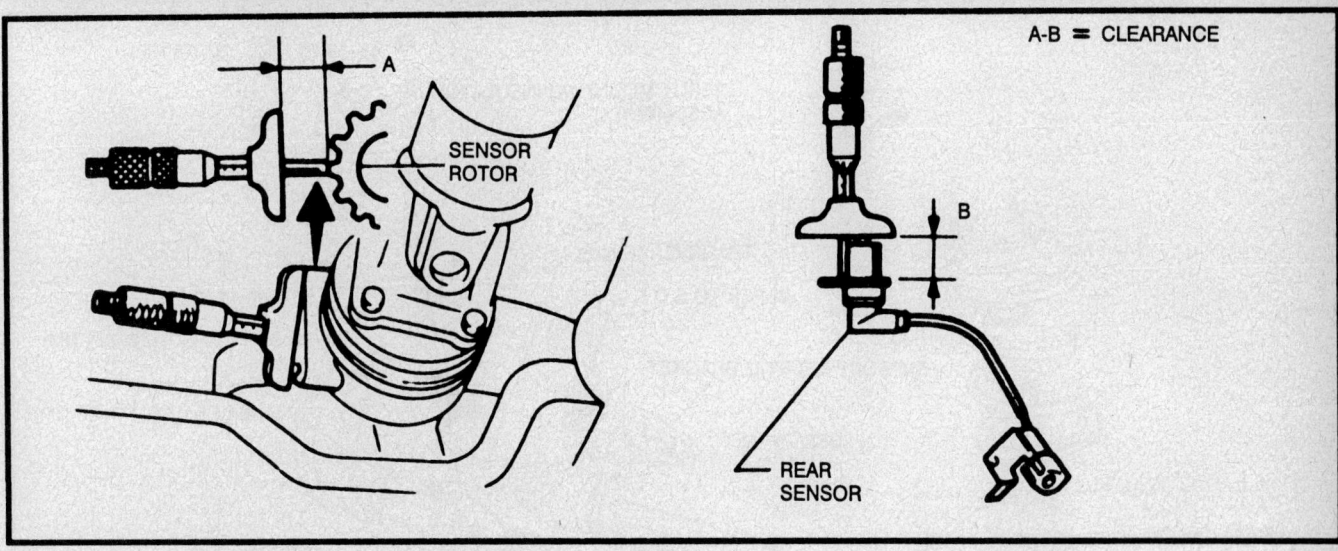

A-B = CLEARANCE

Checking rear wheel sensor-to-rotor clearance on 240SX

11. Connect the sensor harness connector.
12. Mount the rear wheels and lower the vehicle.

Wheel Sensor Clearance Adjustment

1. Install the rear wheel sensor.
2. Check the clearance between the edge of the sensor and rotor teeth using a feeler gauge. Clearances should be as follows:
   a. On 240SX, rear wheel sensor clearance should 0.0138–0.0246 in. (0.035–0.625mm).
   b. On 300ZX, rear wheel sensor clearance should be 0.0024–0.0366 in. (0.06–0.93mm).
   c. On Maxima and Stanza, the clearance should be 0.008–0.039 in. (0.2–1.0mm).
3. To adjust the clearance, loosen the sensor mounting bolt(s) and move the sensor back and forth until the clearance is as specified.
4. Once the clearance is set, tighten the sensor mounting bolt(s) to to 13–20 ft. lbs. (18–26 Nm).

FRONT SUSPENSION

MacPherson Strut

Removal and Installation

1. Raise and support the vehicle safely.
2. Remove the front wheels.
3. Disconnect and plug the brake line if it interferes with removal of the strut.
4. Disconnect the tension rod and stabilizer bar from the transverse link.
5. Unbolt the steering arm from the lower end of the strut.
6. Support the bottom of the strut with a jack or equivalent. On 240SX, place matchmarks on the strut lower bracket and camber adjusting pin for assembly reference.
7. Open the hood and remove the nuts holding the top of the strut. On 300ZX and Maxima equipped with adjustable or sonar suspension shocks, disconnect the electrical lead from the actuating unit.
8. Lower the jack slowly and cautiously until the strut assembly can be removed.
9. During installation, observing the following:
   a. The self locking nuts holding the top of the strut must be replaced.
   c. On 240SX, make sure the matchmarks on the bracket and the camber adjusting pin are aligned properly.
   d. On 1989–91 Maxima with sonar suspension, before installing the actuator ensure the output shaft on the inside of the actuating unit is aligned with the shock absorber control rod. If this is not done, the actuator will be damaged.

Tension Rod And Stabilizer Bar

Removal and Installation
200SX, 240SX AND 300SX

1. Raise and support the vehicle safely.
2. Remove the tension rod-to-frame lock nuts.
3. Remove the 2 mounting bolts at the transverse link, lower control arm, and then slide out the tension rod.
4. On 240SX, to remove the tension rod, remove the bolt and nut that holds the rod to the tension rod bracket (through the bushing), then swing the rod upward and remove the tranverse link bolts, nuts, bushings and washers. If the bushings are worn replace them.
5. Unbolt the stabilizer bar at each transverse link or connecting rod. On 240SX, engage the flats of stabilizer bar connecting rod with a wrench to keep the rod from moving when removing the nuts.
6. Remove the 4 stabilizer bar bracket bolts, and remove the stabilizer bar.
7. During installation observe the following:
   a. Tighten the stabilizer bar-to-transverse link bolts to 12–16 ft. lbs. (16–22 Nm) and 34–38 ft. lbs. (46–52 Nm) on 240SX.
   b. Tighten the stabilizer bar bracket bolts to 22–29 ft. lbs. (29–39 Nm) and 29–36 ft. lbs. (39–49 Nm) on 240SX.
   c. Tighten the tension rod-to-transverse link nuts to 31–43 ft. lbs. (42–59 Nm). On 240SX, torque the plain nuts to 65–80 ft. lbs. (88–108 Nm) and the nuts with bushings and washers

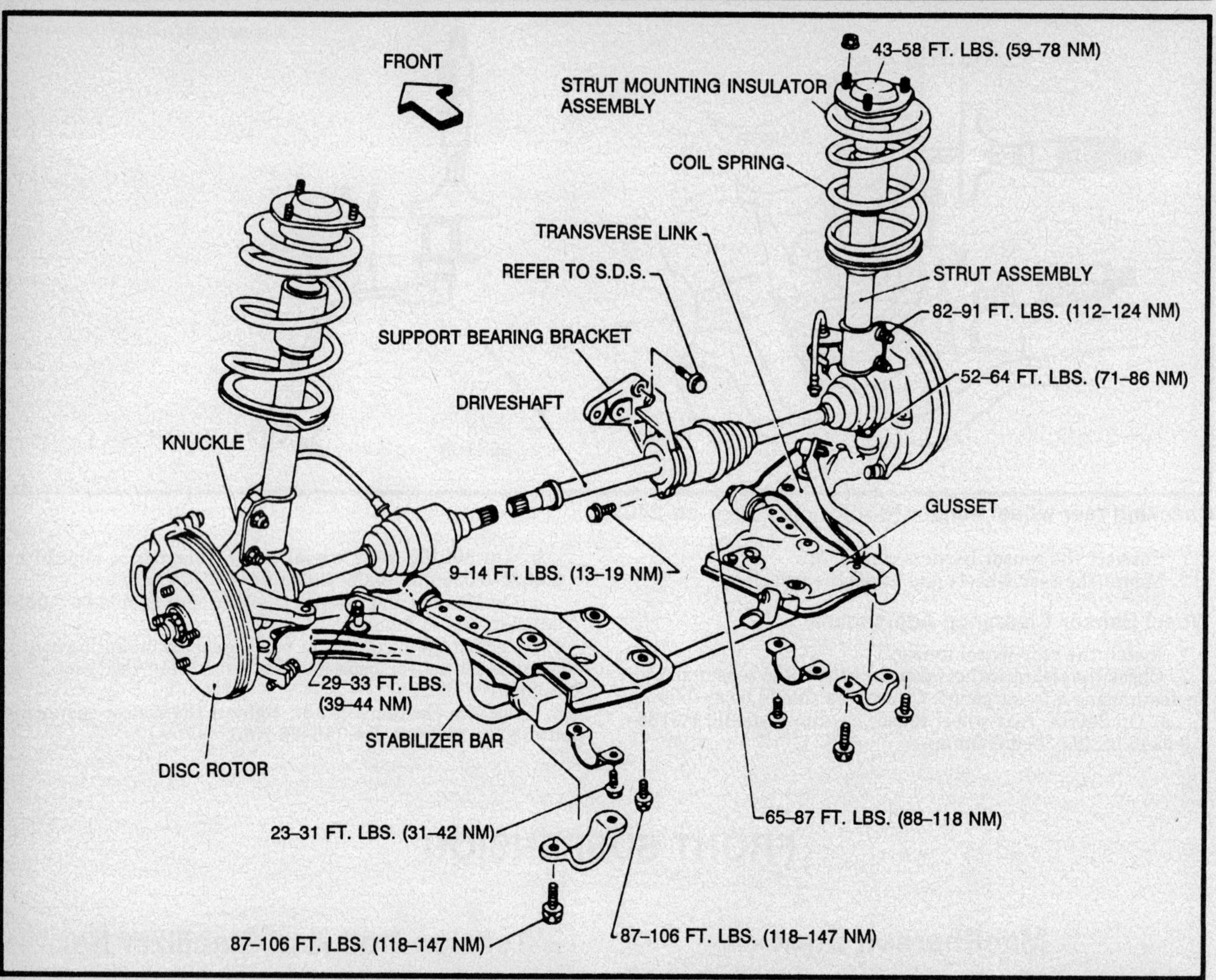

FRONT

43–58 FT. LBS. (59–78 NM)

STRUT MOUNTING INSULATOR ASSEMBLY

COIL SPRING

TRANSVERSE LINK

REFER TO S.D.S.

STRUT ASSEMBLY

82–91 FT. LBS. (112–124 NM)

SUPPORT BEARING BRACKET

52–64 FT. LBS. (71–86 NM)

DRIVESHAFT

KNUCKLE

GUSSET

9–14 FT. LBS. (13–19 NM)

29–33 FT. LBS. (39–44 NM)

STABILIZER BAR

DISC ROTOR

65–87 FT. LBS. (88–118 NM)

23–31 FT. LBS. (31–42 NM)

87–106 FT. LBS. (118–147 NM)

87–106 FT. LBS. (118–147 NM)

Strut-type front suspension—front wheel drive models

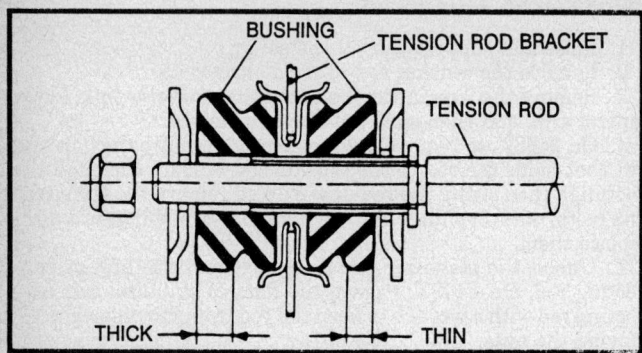

BUSHING — TENSION ROD BRACKET

TENSION ROD

THICK — THIN

Tension rod bushing positioning—rear wheel drive models

to 14–22 ft. lbs. (20–29 Nm). Make sure to hold the connecting rod stationary.

d. Tighten the tension rod-to-frame nut (bushing end) to 33–40 ft. lbs. (44–54 Nm). Always use a new locknut when reconnecting the tension rod to the frame.

e. Be certain the tension rod bushings are installed properly. Make sure the stabilizer bar ball joint socket is properly positioned.

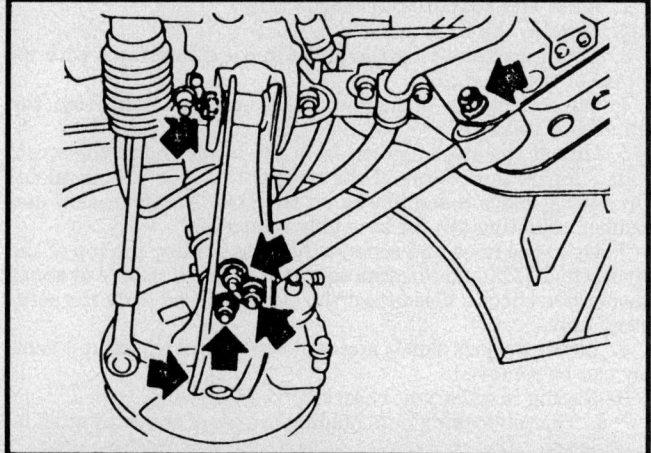

Tension rod and stabilizer bar attaching points—240SX

NOTE: Never tighten any bolts or nuts to their final torque unless the vehicle is resting, unsupported, on the wheels.

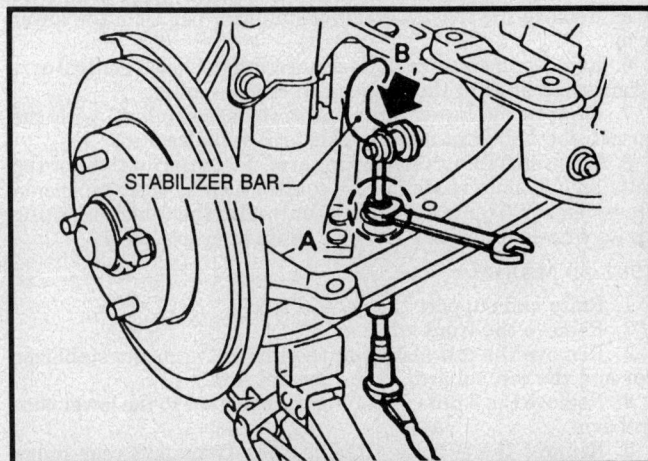

Hold the stabilizer connecting rod with a wrench when removing and installing the mounting nuts

PULSAR, SENTRA, STANZA WAGON AND 1989-91 MAXIMA

1. Raise and support the vehicle safely. Disconnect the parking brake cable at the equalizer on the Stanza wagon.
2. On the Stanza wagon (4WD), remove the mounting nuts for the transaxle support rod and the transaxle control rod.
3. Disconnect the front exhaust pipe at the manifold and position it aside (not required on Maxima).
4. On the Stanza wagon (4WD), matchmark the flanges and then separate the driveshaft from the transfer case.
5. Remove the stabilizer bar-to-transverse link (lower, control arm) mounting bolts. Engage the flats of stabilizer bar connecting rod with a wrench to keep the rod from moving when removing (and installing) the bolts.
6. Matchmark the stabilizer bar to the mounting clamps.

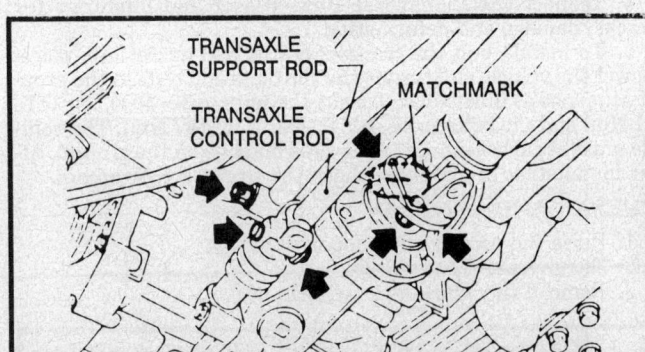

Removing the stabilizer bar—4WD Stanza wagon

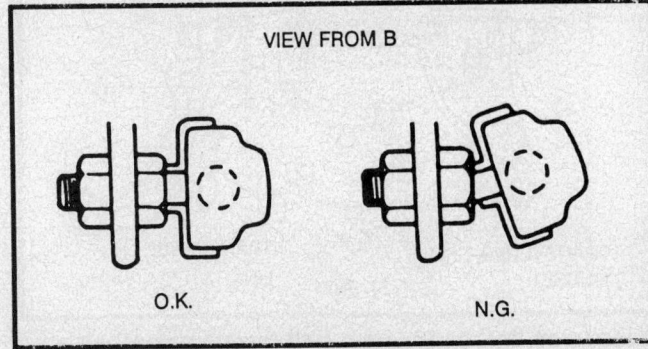

Ball joint socket positioning

7. Remove the stabilizer bar mounting clamp bolts and then pull the bar out, around the link and exhaust pipe.
8. Installation is the reverse of the removal procedure. Never tighten the mounting bolts unless the vehicle is resting on the ground with normal weight upon the wheels. On Pulsar and Sentra, be sure the stabilizer bar ball joint socket is properly positioned.

Lower Ball Joints

Inspection
DIAL INDICATOR METHOD
1. Raise and support the vehicle safely.
2. Clamp a dial indicator to the transverse link and place the tip of the dial on the lower edge of the brake caliper.
3. Zero the indicator.
4. Make sure the front wheels are straight ahead and the brake pedal is fully depressed.
5. Insert a long prybar between the transverse link and the inner rim of the wheel.
6. Push down and release the prybar and observe the reading (deflection) on the dial indicator. Take several readings and use the maximum dial indicator deflection as the ball joint vertical endplay. Make sure to 0 the indicator after each reading. If the reading is not within specifications, replace the transverse link or the ball joint. Ball joint vertical endplay specifications are as follows:

200SX and 240SX—0 in. (0mm)
300ZX
  1987-89—0.098 in. (2.5mm) or less
  1990-91—0 in. (0mm)
Maxima
  1987—0.004-0.039 in. (0.1-1.0mm)
  1988—0.098 in. (2.5mm) or less
  1989-91—0 in. (0mm)
Pulsar
  1987—0.028 in. (0.7mm) or less
  1988—0.098 in. (2.5mm) or less
  1989-91—0 in. (0mm)
Sentra
  1987—0.028 in. (0.7mm) or less
  1988-91—0 in. (0mm)
Stanza
  1987-89—0.004-0.039 in. (0.1-1.0mm)
  1990-91—0 in. (0mm)
Stanza wagon—0.098 in. (2.5mm) or less

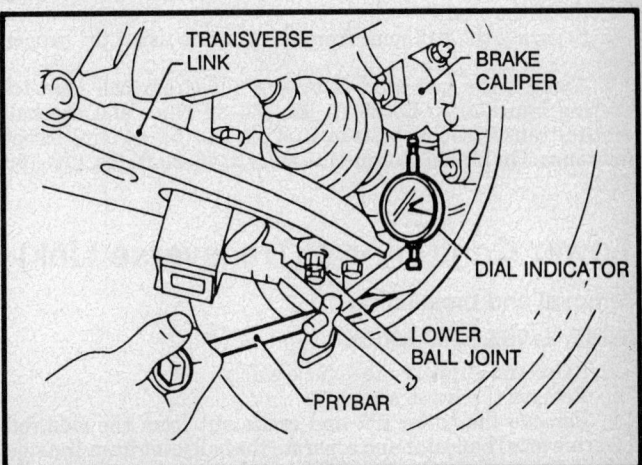

Measuring ball joint vertical endplay with a dial indicator

VISUAL APPROXIMATION METHOD

The lower ball joint should be replaced when play becomes excessive. An effective way to visually approximate ball joint verticle endplay without the use of a dial indicator is to preform the following:

1. Raise and safely support the vehicle until the wheel is clear of the ground. Do not place the jack under the ball joint; it must be unloaded.
2. Place a long prybar under the tire and move the wheel up and down. Keep one hand on top of the tire while doing this.
3. If ¼ in. or more of play exists at the top of the tire, the ball joint should be replaced. Be sure the wheel bearings are properly adjusted before making this measurement. A double check can be made; while the tire is being moved up and down, observe the ball joint. If play is seen, replace the ball joint.

Removal and Installation
REAR WHEEL DRIVE

On 200SX and 1987–89 300SX, there is a plugged hole in the bottom of the joint for installation of a grease fitting. The ball joint should be greased every 30,000 miles.

NOTE: The transverse link (lower control arm) must be removed and then the ball joint must be pressed out.

1. Raise and support the vehicle safely.
2. Remove the front wheels.
3. Separate the knuckle arm from the tie rod using the proper tool.
4. Separate the knuckle arm from the strut.
5. Remove the stabilizer bar and tension rod.
6. Remove the transverse link and knuckle arm.
7. Separate the knuckle arm from the ball joint with a suitable press.
8. Replace the transverse link/ball joint assembly.
9. Installation is the reverse of the removal procedure.

FRONT WHEEL DRIVE

1. Raise and support the vehicle safely.
2. Remove the front wheels.
3. Remove the wheel bearing locknut.
4. Separate the tie rod end ball joint from the steering knuckle with a ball joint remover, being careful not to damage the ball joint dust cover if the ball joint is to be used again.
5. On 1989–91 Maxima and 1990–91 Stanza, loosen, but do not remove the strut upper nuts.
6. Remove the nut that attaches the ball joint to the transverse link.
7. Separate the halfshaft from the knuckle by lightly taping the end of the shaft.
6. Separate the ball joint from the knuckle using the proper tool.
7. Tighten the ball stud attaching nut (from ball joint-to-steering knuckle) to 22–29 ft. lbs. (30–39 Nm), and the ball joint-to-transverse link bolts to 40–47 ft. lbs. (54–64 Nm) except on Stanza. On Stanza, torque the bolts to 56–80 ft. lbs. (76–108 Nm).

Lower Control Arm (Transverse Link)

Removal and Installation
200SX, 240SX AND 300ZX

1. Raise and support the vehicle safely.
2. Remove the front wheels.
3. Remove the cotter pin and castle nut from the side rod (steering arm) ball joint and separate the ball joint from the side rod using the proper tool.
4. Separate the steering knuckle arm from the MacPherson strut.

5. Remove the tension rod and stabilizer bar from the lower arm.
6. Remove the nuts or bolts connecting the lower control arm (transverse link) to the suspension crossmember.
7. Remove the lower control arm (transverse link) with the suspension ball joint and knuckle arm still attached.
8. When installing the control arm, temporarily tighten the nuts and/or bolts securing the control arm to the suspension crossmember. Tighten them fully only after the vehicle is sitting on its wheels. Lubricate the ball joints after assembly.

1987–89 MAXIMA

1. Raise and support the vehicle safely.
2. Remove the front wheels.
3. Remove the nut fastening the link between the stabilizer bar and the control arm to the control arm.
4. Remove the 3 nuts fastening the ball joint to the lower control arm.
5. Remove the 2 bolts attaching the front and rear hinge joints of the control arm to the body.
6. Remove the control arm.
7. Installation is the reverse of the removal procedure. Tighten all bolts and nuts until they are snug enough to support the weight of the vehicle, but not quite fully tightened. Lower the vehicle so it rests on the ground. Tighten the forward bolts attaching the hinge joint to the body to 65–87 ft. lbs. (88–118 Nm). Tighten the rear hinge joint bolts to 87–108 ft. lbs. (118–147 Nm) and the ball joint mounting nuts to 56–80 ft. lbs. (76–108 Nm). Check the front end alignment.

1989–91 MAXIMA AND 1990–91 STANZA

1. Raise the vehicle and support it safely.
2. Unbolt and remove the stabilizer bar. The bar is removed by unfastening the clamp bolts and the bolts that hold the bar to the transverse link gusset plate. When removing the clamps, note the relationship between the clamp and paint mark on the bar.
3. Unbolt and remove the transverse link and gusset.
4. Inspect the transverse link, gusset and bushings for cracks, damage and deformation.
5. To install, bolt the transverse link and gusset into place. Lower the vehicle and torque the the bolts and nuts in the proper sequence as illustrated. Torque the nuts to 30–35 ft. lbs. (41–51 Nm) and the bolts to 87–108 ft. lbs. (118–147 Nm). The vehicle must at curb weight and the tires must be on the ground. After installation is complete, check the front end alignment.

PULSAR AND SENTRA

1. Raise the vehicle and support it safely.
2. Remove the front wheels.
3. Remove the wheel bearing locknut.

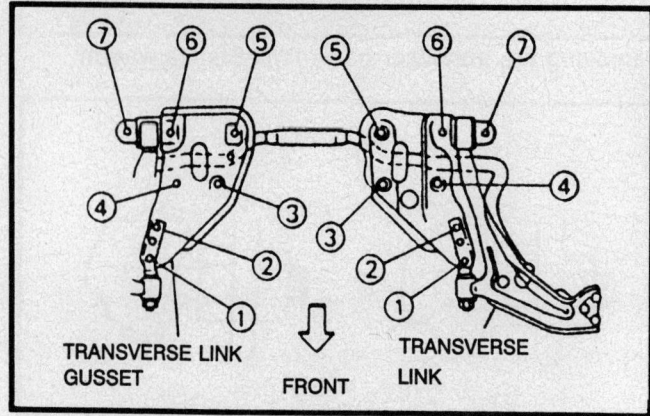

Transverse link and gusset bolt torque sequence— 1989–91 Maxima and 1990–91 Stanza

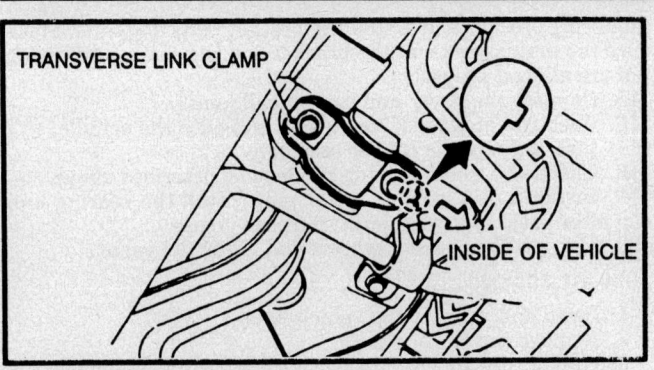

Transverse link clamp positioning—Pulsar and Sentra

4. Remove the tie rod ball joint with a suitable puller.

5. Remove the lower strut-to-knuckle mounting bolts and separate the strut from the knuckle.

6. Separate the outer end of the halfshaft from the steering knuckle by carefully tapping it with a rubber mallet. Be sure to cover the CV-joints with a shop rag.

7. Using a suitable ball joint removal tool, separate the lower ball joint stud from the steering knuckle.

8. Unbolt and remove the transverse link and ball joint as an assembly.

9. Installation is the reverse of the removal procedure. Make sure the tab on the transverse link clamp is pointing in the proper direction. Final tightening of all bolts should take place with the weight of the vehicle on the wheels. Check wheel alignment.

1987–89 STANZA

NOTE: Always use new nuts when installing the ball joint to the control arm.

1. Raise the vehicle and support it safely.
2. Remove the front wheels.
3. Remove the lower ball joint bolts from the control arm.

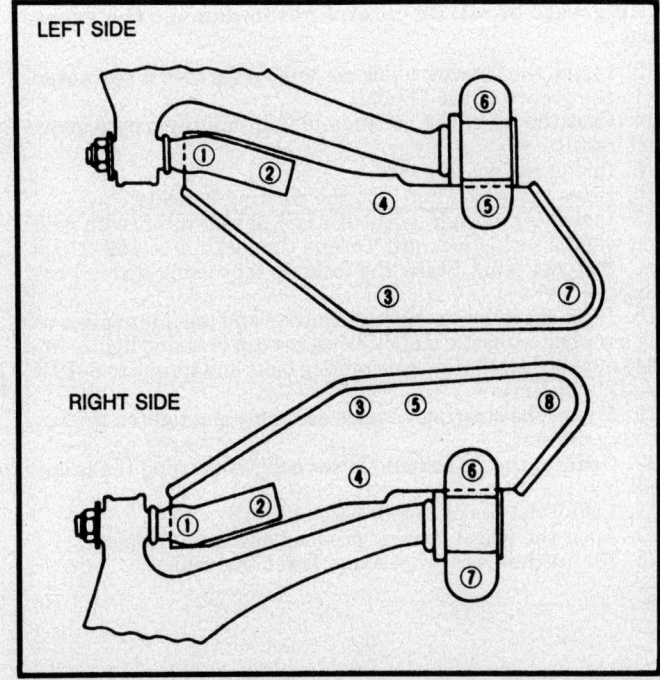

Transverse link gusset bolt torque sequence—Stanza wagon

NOTE: If equipped with a stabilizer bar, disconnect it at the control arm.

4. Remove the control arm-to-body bolts.
5. Remove the gusset.
6. Remove the control arm.
7. Installation is the reverse of the removal procedure using the following torque specifications: gusset-to-body bolts to 87–108 ft. lbs. (118–147 Nm); control arm securing nut to 87–108 ft. lbs. (118–147 Nm) and lower ball joint-to-control arm nuts to 56–80 ft. lbs. (76–108 Nm). When installing the link, tighten the nut securing the link spindle to the gusset. Final tightening should be made with the weight of the vehicle on the wheels.

NOTE: On the Stanza wagon, make sure to torque the gusset bolts in the proper sequence.

Front Wheel Bearings

Adjustment

200SX AND 1987–89 300ZX

1. Raise and support the vehicle safely.
2. Remove the front wheels.
3. While rotating the brake disc, torque wheel bearing lock nut to 18–22 ft. lbs.
4. Loosen locknut approximately 60 degrees on all vehicles. Install adjusting cap and align groove of nut with hole in spindle. If alignment cannot be obtained, change position of adjusting cap. Also, if alignment cannot be obtained, loosen locknut slightly but not more than 15 degrees.
5. Install the front wheels and lower the vehicle.

240SX

There is no procedure for torquing the front wheel bearings due to the design of the bearing. Once the final torque is applied to the wheel bearing axle nut and the axial play is checked, no further adjustment is either necessary or possible.

Check the torque of the wheel bearing locknut. This value is 108–159 ft. lbs. (147–216 Nm). Then, mount a dial indicator to the face of the hub and check the axial play. It should not exceed 0.0012 in. (0.03mm). If the axial play is not as specified, replace the wheel bearing.

1990–91 300ZX

1. Raise the vehicle and suppport safely.
2. Remove the front wheels.
3. Prior to checking the bearing pre-load, spin the wheel hub at least 10 revolutions in both directions to seat the bearing.
4. To check the pre-load: connect a spring scale of known calibration to a wheel hub bolt and measure the turning torque. If an NSK wheel bearing is used, the turning torque should be 1.3–8.4 lbs. (5.9–37.3 N). For NTN bearings, the turning torque should be 1.8–13.0 lbs. (7.8–57.9 N).
5. To check the axial endplay: mount a dial indicator so the stylus of the dial rests on the face of the hub and check the wheel bearing axial endplay by attempting to rock the wheel hub in and out. The endplay should be 0.0020 in. (0.05mm) or less.
6. Mount the front wheels and lower the vehicle.

Removal and Installation

200SX AND 1987–89 300ZX

1. Raise and support the vehicle safely.
2. Remove the front wheels. Work off center hub cap by using thin tool. If necessary tap around it with a soft hammer while removing. Pry off cotter pin and take out adjusting cap. Apply

the parking brake firmly and remove the wheel bearing nut. The nut will require a good deal of force to remove it.

3. Unbolt the caliper and move it aside. Do not disconnect the hose from the caliper. Do not allow the caliper to hang by the hose; support the caliper with a length of wire or rest it on a suspension member.

4. Remove the wheel hub, disc brake rotor and bearing from the spindle. During removal, capture the outer bearing to prevent it from hitting the ground.

5. To replace the bearing outer race, drive it out with a suitable brass drift and mallet.

To install:

6. Install the new bearing outer race using a suitable race installation tool.

7. Install a new oil seal so the words "BEARING SIDE" face the inner side of the hub. Coat the lip of the seal with multi-purpose grease.

8. Pack the bearings, hub, hub cap and hub cap O-ring with multi-purpose grease. If the hub cap O-ring is crimped, replace it.

9. Install the inner and outer bearings.

10. Install the wheel hub and rotor disc onto the spindle.

11. Coat the threaded portion of the spindle shaft and the contact surface between the lockwasher and outer wheel bearing with multi-purpose grease.

12. Install the wheel bearing locknut and adjust the bearing pre-load as described above. Use a new cotter pin.

13. Mount the brake caliper assembly.

14. Install the front wheels and lower the vehicle.

240SX

1. Raise and support the vehicle safely.

2. Remove the front wheels.

3. Work off center hub cap by using a suitable thin tool. If necessary tap around it with a soft hammer while removing. Pry off cotter pin and take out adjusting cap.

4. Apply the parking brake firmly and remove the wheel bearing nut. The nut will require a good deal of force to remove it.

5. Unbolt the caliper and move it aside. Do not disconnect the hose from the caliper. Do not allow the caliper to hang by the hose; support the caliper with a length of wire or rest it on a suspension member.

6. Pull the brake disc and wheel hub from the spindle.

7. Separate the tie rod and lower ball joints using the proper tool.

8. Place matchmarks on the strut lower bracket and camber adjusting pin for assembly reference. Remove the lower bracket bolts and nuts. Remove the wheel hub and knuckle assembly.

9. Remove the bearing retaining ring from the wheel hub.

10. Press the bearing assembly from the wheel hub. Apply pressure from the outside of the hub to remove the bearing.

To install:

11. Press the new bearing assembly into the hub from the inside.

NOTE: Do not press the on the inner race of the wheel bearing assembly. Do not lubricate the surfaces of mating surfaces of the wheel bearing outer race and wheel with grease or oil. Be careful not to damage the grease seal.

12. Install the bearing retaining ring.

13. Coat the lip of the grease seal with multi-purpose grease.

14. Manuever the wheel hub and axle assembly onto the lower

mounting bracket and install the bracket bolts and nuts. Make sure the matchmarks on the bracket and the camber adjusting pin are aligned properly.

15. Connect the lower and tie rod ball joints.

16. Push the brake disc and wheel hub onto the spindle.

17. Install the brake caliper assembly.

18. Check the wheel bearing pre-load as described above.

19. Install a new locknut cotter pin. Install the bearing hub cap after packing it with multi-purpose grease.

20. Mount the the front wheels and lower the vehicle.

1990–91 300ZX

1. Raise and support the vehicle safely.

2. Remove the front wheels.

3. Unbolt the caliper and move it aside. Do not disconnect the hose from the caliper. Do not allow the caliper to hang by the hose; support the caliper with a length of wire or rest it on a suspension member.

4. Separate the tie rod and lower ball joints using the proper tool.

NOTE: The steering knuckle is made of an aluminum alloy. Be careful no to strike it when removing the ball joints.

5. Remove the kinpin lower nut and remove the steering knuckle assembly.

6. Remove the hub cap, wheel bearing locknut, sensor rotor (with ABS) or washer (without ABS).

7. Remove the wheel hub with a suitable drift.

8. Remove the wheel bearing retaining ring.

9. Press the wheel bearing from the knuckle.

10. Drive out the wheel bearing inner race to the ouside of the wheel hub.

11. Remove the grease seal and splash guard (baffle plate).

To install:

12. From the outside of the knuckle, press the new wheel bearing assembly into the knuckle.

NOTE: Do not press the on the inner race of the wheel bearing assembly. Do not lubricate the surfaces of mating surfaces of the wheel bearing outer race and wheel with grease or oil. Be careful not to damage the grease seal.

13. Install the bearing retaining ring. Make sure it seats evenly in the groove of the knuckle.

14. Coat the lip of the grease seal with multi-purpose grease and install.

15. Install the spash guard.

16. Press the wheel hub into the steering knuckle.

17. Install the washer (without ABS), sensor rotor (with ABS) and wheel bearing locknut. Torque the locknut to 152–210 ft. lbs. (206–284 Nm). Stake the locknut tabs using a small cold chisel.

18. Place the hub cap onto the knuckle and tap it into place using a rubber or plastic mallet. Once the cap is seated lightly into the knuckle, install the cap retaining bolts and torque to 8–12 ft. lbs. (11–16 Nm).

19. Mount the steering knuckle assembly and tighten the lower king pin nut.

20. Connect the tie rod and lower ball joints using the proper tool.

21. Install the brake caliper assembly.

22. Ajust the wheel bearing pre-load and axial endplay.

23. Mount the front wheels and lower the vehicle.

REAR SUSPENSION

Shock Absorbers

Removal and Installation

200SX AND STANZA WAGON (2WD)

1. Open the trunk and remove the cover panel, if necessary, to expose the shock mounts. Pry off the mount covers, if equipped.
2. Remove the 2 nuts holding the top of the shock absorber.
3. Unbolt the bottom of the shock absorber.
4. Remove the shock absorber.
5. Installation is the reverse of removal. Final tightening of the lower end of the shock absorber should be performed with the wheels on the ground in the unladen position.

1987–89 300ZX

With Adjustable Shocks

1. Open the hatch and remove the luggage side trim.
2. Disconnect the sub-harness connector from the top of the shock.
3. Remove the 2 upper retaining nuts.
4. Remove the lower thru-bolt.
5. Remove the shock absorber.
6. Installation is the reverse of the removal procedure. Final tightening of the shock absorber upper and lower end should be performed with the wheels on the ground in the unladen position. Torque the bottom bolt to 43–58 ft. lbs. (59–78 Nm) and top nuts to 23–31 ft. lbs. (31–42 Nm)

Without Adjustable Shocks

1. Open the hatch and remove the luggage side trim.
2. Remove the 2 upper retaining nuts.
3. Remove the lower thru-bolt.
4. Remove the shock absorber.
5. Installation is the reverse of the removal procedure. Final tightening of the shock absorber upper and lower end should be performed with the wheels on the ground in the unladen position. Torque the bottom bolt to 43–58 ft. lbs. (59–78 Nm) and the 2 top nuts to 23–31 ft. lbs. (31–42 Nm).

MacPherson Strut

Removal and Installation

240SX AND 1990–91 300ZX

1. Block the front wheels.
2. Raise and support the vehicle safely.

NOTE: The vehicle should be far enough off the ground so the rear spring does not support any weight.

3. Working inside the luggage compartment, turn and remove the caps above the strut mounts. Remove the strut mounting nuts.
4. Remove the mounting bolt for the strut at the lower arm (transverse link) and then lift out the strut.
5. Installation is in the reverse order of removal. Install the upper end first and secure with the nuts snugged down but not fully tightened. Attach the lower end of the strut to the transverse link and the tighten the upper nuts to 12–14 ft. lbs. (16–19 Nm). Tighten the lower mounting bolt to 65–80 ft. lbs. (88–108 Nm).

PULSAR AND SENTRA (2WD)

1. Raise and support the rear of the vehicle safely.
2. Remove the rear wheels.
3. Disconnect the brake tube and parking brake cable.
4. If necessary, remove the brake assembly and wheel bearing.

5. Disconnect the parallel links and radius rod from the strut or knuckle.
6. Support the strut with a jackstand.
7. Remove the strut upper end nuts and then remove the strut from the vehicle.
8. Installation is the reverse of the removal procedure. Tighten the radius rod-to-knuckle nuts to 43–61 ft. lbs. (59–83 Nm), the strut-to-knuckle and parallel link-to-knuckle bolts to 72–87 ft. lbs. (98–118 Nm) and the strut-to-body nuts to 18–22 ft. lbs. (25–29 Nm).

SENTRA (4WD) AND STANZA WAGON (4WD)

1. Block the front wheels.
2. Raise and support the vehicle safely.
3. Position a suitable floor jack under the transverse link on the side of the strut to be removed. Raise it just enough to support the strut.
4. Open the rear of the vehicle and remove the 3 nuts that attach the top of the strut to the body.
5. Remove the rear wheels.
6. Remove the brake line from its bracket and position it aside. Do not disconnect the brake line.
7. Remove the 2 lower strut-to-knuckle mounting bolts.
8. Carefully lower the floor jack and remove the strut.
9. Installation is the reverse order of removal. Final tightening of the strut mounting bolts should take place with the wheels on the ground and the vehicle unladen. Tighten the upper strut-to-body nuts to 33–40 ft. lbs. (45–60 Nm). Tighten the lower strut-to-knuckle bolts to 111–120 ft. lbs. (151–163 Nm).

1987–88 MAXIMA AND 1987–89 STANZA

Right Strut

1. Unclip the rear brake line at the strut. Do not disconnect it.
2. Remove the radius rod mounting bolt, radius rod mounting bracket.
3. Remove the 2 parallel link mounting bolts.
4. Remove the rear seat and parcel shelf.
5. On Maxima with adjustable suspension, disconnect the sub-harness connector and the connector from the cap. Grasp the cap connector from both sides during removal to avoid damage. This connector is very sensitive.
6. Position a suitable floor jack under the strut and raise it just enough to support the strut.

NOTE: Do not support the strut at the parallel links or the radius rods.

7. Remove the 3 upper strut mounting nuts and then lift out the strut and rear axle assembly.
8. Installation is the reverse of the removal procedure. Tighten all bolts sufficiently to safely support the vehicle and then lower the vehicle to the ground so it rests on its own weight. Tighten the upper strut mounting nuts to 23–31 ft. lbs. (31–42 Nm); the radius rod bracket bolts to 43–58 ft. lbs. (59–78 Nm) and the parallel link mounting bolts to 65–87 ft. lbs. (88–118 Nm).

Left Strut

1. Unclip the rear brake line at the strut. Do not disconnect it.
2. Remove the radius rod mounting bolt.
3. Remove the stabilizer bar connecting bracket.
4. Remove the suspension crossmember mounting nuts.
5. Remove the strut upper mounting nuts.
6. Remove the left suspension assembly and the crossmember.
7. Installation is the reverse of the removal procedure. Tighten all bolts sufficiently to safely support the vehicle and then

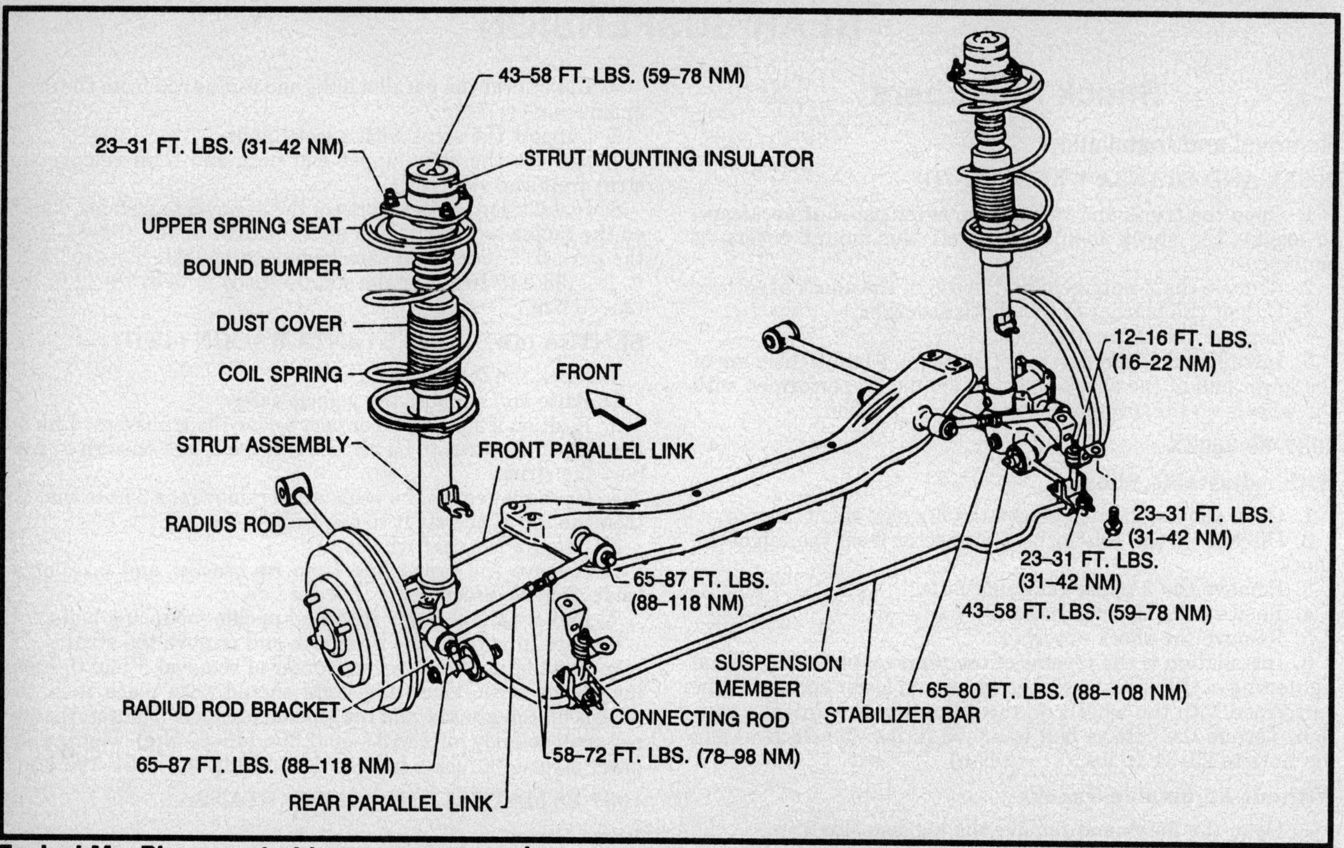

43–58 FT. LBS. (59–78 NM)

23–31 FT. LBS. (31–42 NM)

STRUT MOUNTING INSULATOR

UPPER SPRING SEAT

BOUND BUMPER

DUST COVER

COIL SPRING

FRONT

STRUT ASSEMBLY

FRONT PARALLEL LINK

RADIUS ROD

12–16 FT. LBS. (16–22 NM)

23–31 FT. LBS. (31–42 NM)

23–31 FT. LBS. (31–42 NM)

43–58 FT. LBS. (59–78 NM)

65–87 FT. LBS. (88–118 NM)

SUSPENSION MEMBER

65–80 FT. LBS. (88–108 NM)

RADIUD ROD BRACKET

CONNECTING ROD

STABILIZER BAR

65–87 FT. LBS. (88–118 NM)

58–72 FT. LBS. (78–98 NM)

REAR PARALLEL LINK

Typical MacPherson strut-type rear suspension— front wheel drive models

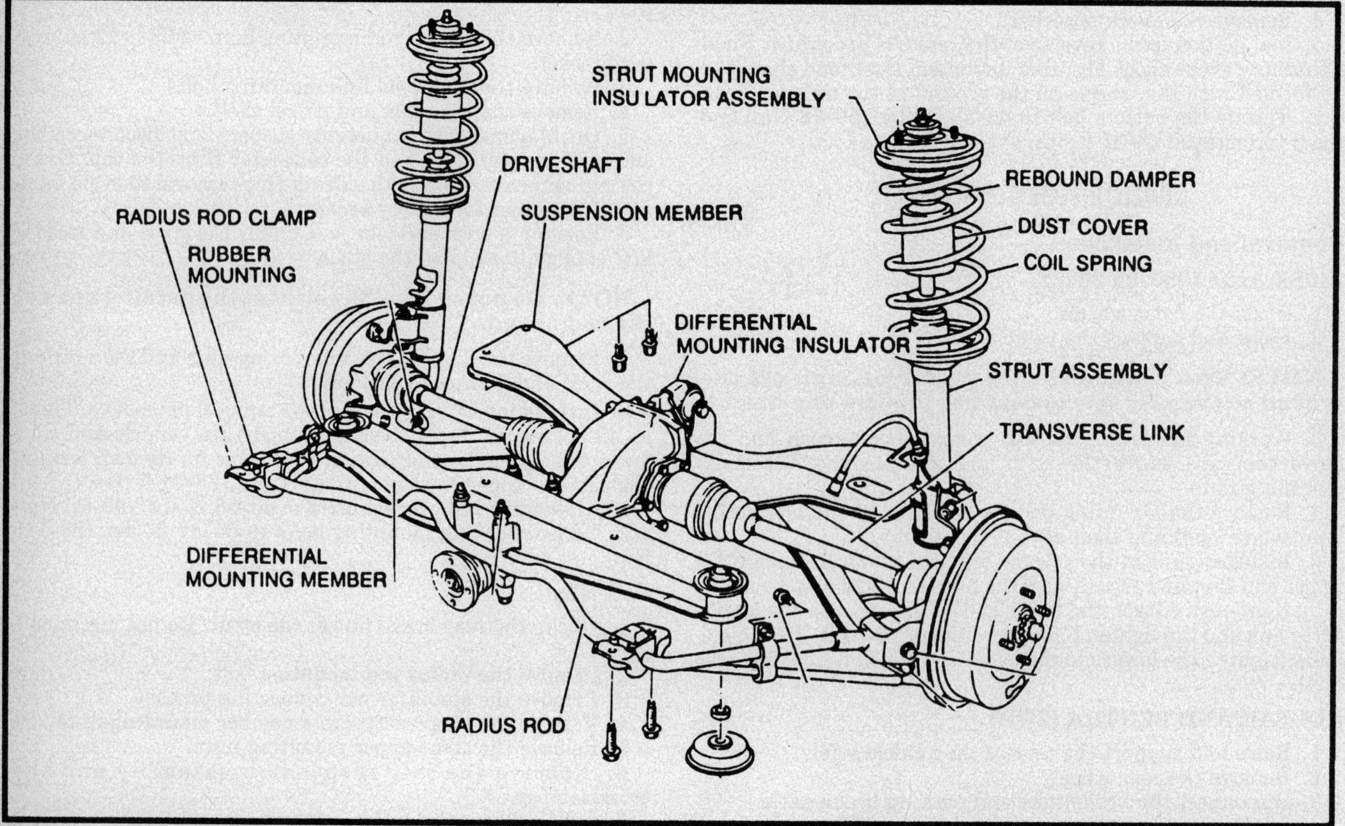

STRUT MOUNTING INSULATOR ASSEMBLY

DRIVESHAFT

RADIUS ROD CLAMP

SUSPENSION MEMBER

RUBBER MOUNTING

REBOUND DAMPER

DUST COVER

COIL SPRING

DIFFERENTIAL MOUNTING INSULATOR

STRUT ASSEMBLY

TRANSVERSE LINK

DIFFERENTIAL MOUNTING MEMBER

RADIUS ROD

MacPherson strut rear suspension—Stanza wagon (4WD)

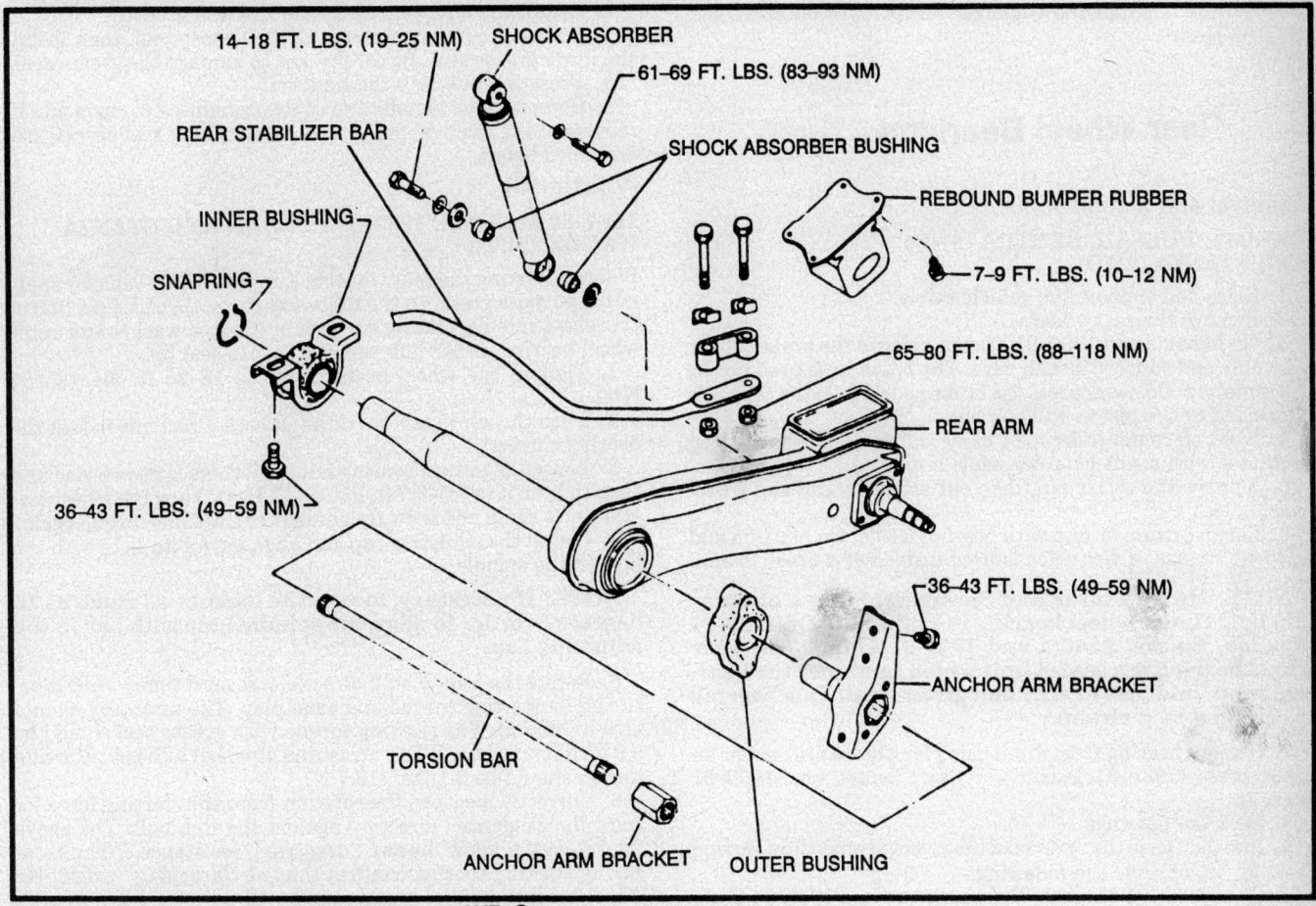

14–18 FT. LBS. (19–25 NM)
SHOCK ABSORBER
61–69 FT. LBS. (83–93 NM)
REAR STABILIZER BAR
SHOCK ABSORBER BUSHING
INNER BUSHING
REBOUND BUMPER RUBBER
SNAPRING
7–9 FT. LBS. (10–12 NM)
65–80 FT. LBS. (88–118 NM)
REAR ARM
36–43 FT. LBS. (49–59 NM)
36–43 FT. LBS. (49–59 NM)
ANCHOR ARM BRACKET
TORSION BAR
ANCHOR ARM BRACKET
OUTER BUSHING

Typical torsion bar rear suspension—2WD Stanza wagon

lower the vehicle to the ground so it rests on its own weight. Tighten the upper strut mounting nuts to 23–31 ft. lbs. (31–42 Nm); the radius rod bracket bolts to 43–58 ft. lbs. (59–78 Nm) and the parallel link mounting bolts to 65–87 ft. lbs. (88–118 Nm).

1989–91 MAXIMA AND 1990–91 STANZA

1. Unclip the rear brake line at the strut. Do not disconnect it.
2. Disconnect the parking brake at the equalizer.
3. Remove the parallel link mounting bolts, radius rod mounting bolts, stabilizer mounting bolts, stabilizer connecting brackets and paking brake cable mounting bracket bolts.
4. Remove the rear seat and parcel shelf.
5. Remove the 3 upper strut mounting nuts and then lift out the strut.
6. Installation is the reverse of the removal procedure. Tighten all bolts sufficiently to safely support the vehicle and then lower the vehicle to the ground so it rests on its own weight. Tighten the upper strut mounting nuts to 31–40 ft. lbs. (42–54 Nm); parallel link mounting bolts to 65–87 ft. lbs. (88–118 Nm); connecting rod bracket nuts to 30–35 ft. lbs. (41–47 Nm); stabilizer bar mounting bolts to 43–58 ft. lbs. (59–78 Nm) and radius rod mounting bolts to 65–87 ft. lbs. (88–118 Nm).

Coil Springs

——— CAUTION ———

Coil springs are under considerable tension and can exert enough force to cause bodily injury. Exercise extreme caution when working with them.

Removal and Installation

200SX AND 1987–89 300ZX

This suspension is similar to the IRS MacPherson strut type, except this type utilizes separate coil springs and shock absorbers, instead of strut units.

1. Compress the coil spring with a suitable spring compressor.
2. Raise the vehicle and support safely.
3. Compress the coil spring until it is of sufficient length to be removed. Remove the spring.
4. When installing the spring, be sure the upper and lower spring seat rubbers are not twisted and have not slipped off when installing the coil spring.

STANZA WAGON (2WD)

1. Raise the vehicle and support safely.
2. Remove the rear wheels.
3. Release the parking brake.
4. Remove the inner hub cap, the cotter pin and the wheel bearing locknut. Remove the brake drum.
5. Disconnect and plug the hydraulic brake line.
6. Disconnect the parking brake cable.
7. Remove the 4 brake backing plate mounting bolts and then slide the backing plate along with the inner wheel bearing off of the rear axle.
8. Disconnect the rear stabilizer bar.
9. Unbolt the anchor arm bracket and then remove the inner bushing bracket mounting bolts. Remove the torsion bar.
10. Installation is in the reverse order of removal. Tighten the inner bushing and anchor arm mounting bolts to 36–43 ft. lbs.

(49–59 Nm). Tighten the stabilizer bar bolts to 65–80 ft. lbs. (88–108 Nm).

Rear Wheel Bearings

Removal and Installation
MAXIMA, PULSAR, SENTRA (2WD) AND STANZA (2WD)

1. Raise and support the vehicle safely.
2. Remove the rear wheels.
3. On Maxima and 1990–91 Stanza, remove the brake caliper assembly and support it with wire. The brake hose need not be disconnected. Do not depress the brake pedal while the caliper is supported or the piston will pop out.
4. Work off center hub cap by using thin tool. If necessary tap around it with a soft hammer while removing.
5. Remove the cotter pin, take out adjusting cap and wheel bearing lock nut.
6. Remove drum or disc with bearing inside. On Maxima and 1990–91 Stanza, a disc rotor is used instead of a brake drum.

NOTE: On all Pulsar and Sentra vehicles, a circular clip holds inner wheel bearing in brake hub. On 1989–91 Maxima, Pulsar, Sentra and 1990–91 Stanza, the rear wheel bearing is a sealed unit which combines the bearing, inner and outer races and grease seal. This bearing is retained by a circlip.

7. Remove bearing from drum using long brass drift pin or an arbor press (1989–91 Maxima, Pulsar, Sentra and 1990–91 Stanza).
8. Pack the bearings.
9. Installation is the reverse of the removal procedire: During installation, observe the following:
   a. On 1989–91 Maxima, Pulsar, Sentra and 1990–91 Stanza, the bearing must be pressed into the brake drum or brake disc.
   b. Do not press the inner race of the bearing; do not coat the wheel bearing and outer hub mating surfaces with oil or grease and do not damage the grease seal.
   c. Adjust wheel bearings as desribed below.

SENTRA (4WD) AND STANZA (4WD)

1. Raise and support the vehicle safely.
2. Remove wheel bearing locknut while depressing brake pedal.
3. Disconnect brake hydraulic line and parking brake cable.
4. Separate halfshaft from knuckle by slightly tapping it with suitable tool. Cover axle boots with waste cloth so as not to damage them when removing halfshaft.
5. Remove all knuckle retaining bolts and nuts. Make a matchmark before removing adjusting pin.
6. Separate the hub from the knuckle using a suitable tool.
7. Drive out the inner (outside) race using a suitable press.
8. Remove the outer grease seal.
9. Drive the inner race (inside) from the hub. The inner grease seal will be removed with it.
10. Remove inner and outer circular clips.
11. Remove the bearings.
12. Drive out the outer race using a suitable tool.
To install:
13. Install the inner circlip in the knuckle groove.
14. Press in the new outer race from the outside of the knuckle.

NOTE: Do not apply grease the wheel bearing outer race and knuckle surfaces.

15. Pack the bearings and the grease seal lip with grease.

16. Install the outer circlip in the knuckle groove.
17. Install the inner races uisng the proper tool, then install the inner grease seal. Be careful not to damage the grease seal.
18. Press the hub into the knuckle.
19. Complete the installation of the remaining components in reverse of the removal procedure. Adjust the wheel bearings as described below.

Adjustment
1987–88 MAXIMA, 1987–88 PULSAR AND STANZA WAGON (2WD)

Before adjusting the rear wheel bearings on these vehicles apply multi-purpose grease to the following parts: threaded portion of the wheel spindle, mating surfaces of the lock washer and outer wheel bearing, inner hub cap and grease seal lip.

1. Tighten the wheel bearing nut to 18–25 ft. lbs. (25–34 Nm).
2. Turn the wheel several times in both directions to seat the bearing correctly.
3. Loosen the wheel bearing nut until there is no pre-load and then tighten it to 6.5–8.7 ft. lbs. (9–12 Nm). Turn the wheel several times again and then retighten it to the same torque again.
4. Install the adjusting cap and align any of its slots with the hole in the spindle.

NOTE: If necessary, loosen the locknut as much as 15 degrees in order to align the spindle hole with one in the adjusting cap.

5. Rotate the hub in both directions several times while measuring its starting torque and axial play. The axial play should be 0 in. (0mm). The starting torque with grease seal should be 6.9 inch lbs. or less. When measured at wheel hub bolt, starting torque should be 3.1 lbs. (13.7 N).
6. Correctly measure the rotation from the starting force toward the tangential direction against the hub bolt. The above figures do not allow for any "dragging" resistance. When measuring starting torque, confirm that no "dragging" exists. No wheel bearing axial play can exist at all.
7. Spread the cotter pin and install the inner hub cap.

1989–91 MAXIMA, SENTRA AND 1990–91 STANZA

Due to a bearing change on these models, there is no procedure for torquing the rear wheel bearings. Once the final torque is applied to the wheel bearing axle nut and the axial play is checked, no further adjustment is either necessary or possible.

Check the torque of the wheel bearing locknut. This value is 137–188 ft. lbs. (137–188 Nm) on Maxima, Pulsar, Sentra (2WD) and 1990–91 Stanza. On Sentra (4WD), the torque value is 174–231 ft. lbs. (235–314 Nm). Rotate the hub and make sure the bearing turn smoothly and quietly. Then, mount a dial indicator to the face of the hub and check the axial play. It should not exceed 0.0020 in. (0.05mm). If the axial play is not as specified, replace the wheel bearing.

Rear Axle Assembly

Removal and Installation

1. Raise and support the vehicle safely.
2. Remove the rear wheels.
3. Disconnect the brake line and parking brake cable.
4. Work off center hub cap by using thin tool. If necessary tap around it with a soft hammer while removing.
5. Remove the cotter pin, take out adjusting cap and wheel bearing lock nut.
6. Remove drum and wheel hub assembly.
7. Unbolt and remove the knuckle/ spindle assembly.
8. Installation is the reverse of the removal procedure. Adjust the rear wheel bearings and bleed the brakes.

SPECIFICATIONS

ENGINE IDENTIFICATION

Year	Model	Engine Displacement cu. in. (cc/liter)	Engine Series Identification	No. of Cylinders	Engine Type
1987	505	128 (2100/2.1)	N9TEA①	4	OHC
		128 (2100/2.1)	N9TE①	4	OHC
		134 (2200/2.2)	ZDJL	4	OHC
		171 (2800/2.8)	ZN3J	6	OHC
1988	505	128 (2100/2.1)	N9TEA①	4	OHC
		128 (2100/2.1)	N9TE①	4	OHC
		134 (2200/2.2)	ZDJL	4	OHC
		171 (2800/2.8)	ZN3J	6	OHC
1989	405	116 (1900/1.9)	XU9J2	4	OHC
		116 (1900/1.9)	XU9J4	4	DOHC②
	505	128 (2100/2.1)	N9TEA①	4	OHC
		134 (2200/2.2)	ZDJL	4	OHC
		171 (2800/2.8)	ZN3J	6	OHC
1990–91	405	116 (1900/1.9)	XU9J2	4	OHC
		116 (1900/1.9)	XU9J4	4	DOHC②
	505	128 (2100/2.1)	N9TEA①	4	OHC
		134 (2200/2.2)	ZDJL	4	OHC

① Turbocharged engine
② 16 valve engine

GENERAL ENGINE SPECIFICATIONS

Year	Model	Engine Displacement cu. in. (cc)	Fuel System Type	Net Horsepower @ rpm	Net Torque @ rpm (ft. lbs.)	Bore × Stroke (in.)	Compression Ratio	Oil Pressure @ rpm
1987	505	128/2100	F.I.	180 @ 5000①	210 @ 2500	3.61 × 3.21	7.5:1	—
	505	134/2200	F.I.	120 @ 5000	131 @ 3500	3.46 × 3.5	8.8:1	—
	505	171/2800	F.I.	145 @ 5000	176 @ 2800	3.58 × 2.87	9.5:1	—
1988	505	128/2100	F.I.	180 @ 5000①	210 @ 2500	3.61 × 3.21	7.5:1	—
	505	134/2200	F.I.	120 @ 5000	131 @ 3500	3.46 × 3.5	8.8:1	—
	505	171/2800	F.I.	145 @ 5000	176 @ 2800	3.58 × 2.87	9.5:1	—
1989	405	116/1900②	F.I.	110 @ 5200	120 @ 4250	3.27 × 3.46	8.4:1	—
	405	116/1900③	F.I.	150 @ 6400	128 @ 5000	3.27 × 3.46	9.5:1	—
	505	128/2100	F.I.	180 @ 5000①	210 @ 2500	3.61 × 3.21	7.5:1	—
	505	134/2200	F.I.	120 @ 5000	131 @ 3500	3.46 × 3.5	8.8:1	—
	505	171/2800	F.I.	145 @ 5000	176 @ 2800	3.58 × 2.87	9.5:1	—
1990–91	405	116/1900②	F.I.	110 @ 5200	120 @ 4250	3.27 × 3.46	8.4:1	—
	405	116/1900③	F.I.	150 @ 6400	128 @ 5000	3.27 × 3.46	9.5:1	—
	505	128/2100	F.I.	180 @ 5000①	210 @ 2500	3.61 × 3.21	7.5:1	—
	505	134/2200	F.I.	120 @ 5000	131 @ 3500	3.46 × 3.5	8.8:1	—

① Wagons—160 @ 5000 rpm
② Except 16 valve engine
③ 16 valve engine

GASOLINE ENGINE TUNE-UP SPECIFICATIONS

Year	Model	Engine Displacement cu. in. (cc)	Spark Plugs Type	Spark Plugs Gap (in.)	Ignition Timing (deg.) MT	Ignition Timing (deg.) AT	Compression Pressure (psi)	Fuel Pump (psi)	Idle Speed (rpm) MT	Idle Speed (rpm) AT	Valve Clearance In.	Valve Clearance Ex.
1987	505	128/2100	WR7DS	0.035	10	10	—	34–37	960	1010	0.008	0.012
	505	134/2200	HR6DS	0.028	10	10	—	32–38	900–950	900–950	0.004	0.010
	505	171/2800	HR6DC	—	—	—	—	32–38	750–800	750–800	0.004	0.010
1988	505	128/2100	WR7DS	0.035	10	10	—	34–37	900	950	0.008	0.012
	505	134/2200	HR6DS	0.028	10	10	—	32–38	900–950	900–950	0.004	0.010
	505	171/2800	HR6DC	—	—	—	—	32–38	750–800	750–800	0.004	0.010
1989	405	116/1900 ①	FL42LS	0.031	—	—	—	42	800–900	800–900	0.007	0.015
	405	116/1900 ②	FL62LS3	0.047	—	—	—	42	830–930	830–930	—	—
	505	128/2100	WR7DS	0.035	10	10	—	34–37	960	1010	0.008	0.012
	505	134/2200	HR6DS	0.028	10	10	—	32–38	900–950	900–950	0.004	0.010
	505	171/2800	HR6DC	—	—	—	—	32–38	750–800	750–800	0.004	0.010
1990	405	116/1900 ①	FL42LS	0.031	—	—	—	42	800–900	800–900	0.007	0.015
1991		SEE UNDERHOOD SPECIFICATIONS										

① Except 16 valve engine
② 16 valve engine

FIRING ORDERS

NOTE: To avoid confusion, always replace spark plug wires one at a time.

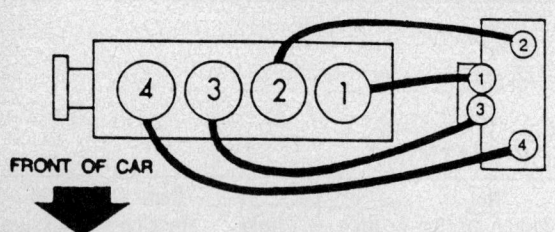

XU9J2 (1.9L), XUJ94 (1.9L) and ZDJL (2.2L) Engines
Engine Firing Order: 1–3–4–2
Distributor Rotation: Counterclockwise

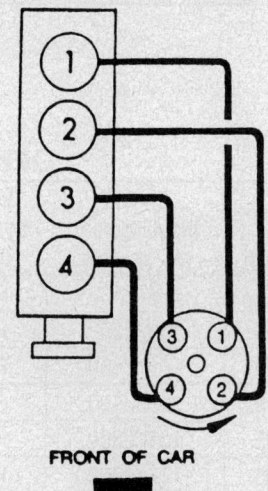

N9TE (2.1L) and N9TEA (2.1L) Engines
Engine Firing Order: 1–3–4–2
Distributor Rotation: Counterclockwise

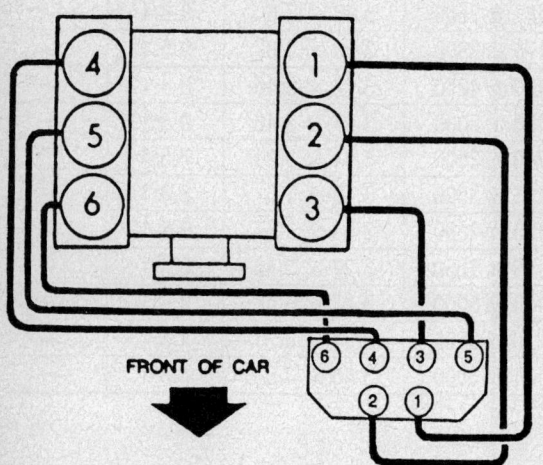

ZN3J (2.8L) Engine
Engine Firing Order: 1–5–3–4–6–2
Distributor Rotation: Counterclockwise

CAPACITIES

Year	Model	Engine Displacement cu. in. (cc)	Engine Crankcase with Filter	Engine Crankcase without Filter	Transmission (pts.) 4-Spd	Transmission (pts.) 5-Spd	Transmission (pts.) Auto.	Drive Axle (pts.)	Fuel Tank (gal.)	Cooling System (qts.)
1987	505	128/2100	5.3	5.0	—	3	15.8	3.3	18	10
	505	134/2200	5.8	5.5	—	3	15.8	3.3	18	7.9
	505	171/2800	6.9	6.6	—	3	15.8	3.3	18	10
1988	505	128/2100	5.3	5.0	—	3	15.8	3.3	18	10
	505	134/2200	5.8	5.5	—	3	15.8	3.3	18	7.9
	505	171/2800	6.9	6.6	—	3	15.8	3.3	18	10
1989	405	116/1900①	5.3	4.8	—	4.2	13.2	—	17.2	7.0
	405	116/1900②	5.6	5.3	—	4.2	—	—	17.2	7.6
	505	128/2100	5.3	5.0	—	3	15.8	3.3	18	10
	505	134/2200	5.8	5.5	—	3	15.8	3.3	18	7.9
	505	171/2800	6.9	6.6	—	3	15.8	3.3	18	10
1990–91	405	116/1900①	5.3	4.8	—	4.2	13.2	—	17.2	7.0
	405	116/1900②	5.6	5.3	—	4.2	—	—	17.2	7.6
	505	128/2100	5.3	5.0	—	3	15.8	3.3	18	10
	505	134/2200	5.8	5.5	—	3	15.8	3.3	18	10

① Except 16 valve engine
② 16 valve engine

CRANKSHAFT AND CONNECTING ROD SPECIFICATIONS

All measurements are given in inches.

Year	Engine Displacement cu. in. (cc)	Crankshaft Main Brg. Journal Dia.	Crankshaft Main Brg. Oil Clearance	Crankshaft Shaft End-play	Crankshaft Thrust on No.	Connecting Rod Journal Diameter	Connecting Rod Oil Clearance	Connecting Rod Side Clearance
1987	128/2100	2.2427	—	0.003–0.010	3	2.0456–2.0459	—	—
	134/2200	1.1811	—	0.005–0.011	2	2.2163–2.2171	—	—
	171/2800	2.7583	—	0.002–0.010	2	2.3622–2.3625	—	—
1988	128/2100	2.2427	—	0.003–0.010	3	2.0456–2.0459	—	—
	134/2200	1.1811	—	0.005–0.011	2	2.2163–2.2171	—	—
	171/2800	2.7583	—	0.002–0.010	2	2.3622–2.3625	—	—
1989	116/1900①	2.3622	—	0.002–0.010	3	1.9685	—	—
	116/1900②	2.3622	—	0.002–0.010	3	1.9685	—	—
	128/2100	2.2427	—	0.003–0.010	3	2.0456–2.0459	—	—
	134/2200	1.1811	—	0.005–0.011	2	2.2163–2.2171	—	—
	171/2800	2.7583	—	0.002–0.010	2	2.3622–2.3625	—	—

CRANKSHAFT AND CONNECTING ROD SPECIFICATIONS
All measurements are given in inches.

Year	Engine Displacement cu. in. (cc)	Crankshaft Main Brg. Journal Dia.	Crankshaft Main Brg. Oil Clearance	Crankshaft Shaft End-play	Crankshaft Thrust on No.	Connecting Rod Journal Diameter	Connecting Rod Oil Clearance	Connecting Rod Side Clearance
1990-91	116/1900 ①	2.3622	—	0.002–0.010	3	1.9685	—	—
	116/1900 ②	2.3622	—	0.002–0.010	3	1.9685	—	—
	128/2100	2.2427	—	0.003–0.010	3	2.0456–2.0459	—	—
	134/2200	1.1811	—	0.005–0.011	2	2.2163–2.2171	—	—

① Except 16 valve engine
② 16 valve engine

VALVE SPECIFICATIONS

Year	Engine Displacement cu. in. (cc)	Seat Angle (deg.)	Face Angle (deg.)	Spring Test Pressure (lbs.)	Spring Installed Height (in.)	Stem-to-Guide Clearance (in.) Intake	Stem-to-Guide Clearance (in.) Exhaust	Stem Diameter (in.) Intake	Stem Diameter (in.) Exhaust
1987	128/2100	45	45	—	2.059	—	—	0.3539	0.3529
	134/2200	①	①	②	③	—	—	0.3149	0.3149
	171/2800	45	45	④	⑤	—	—	—	—
1988	128/2100	45	45	—	2.059	—	—	0.3539	0.3529
	134/2200	①	①	②	③	—	—	0.3149	0.3149
	171/2800	45	45	④	⑤	—	—	—	—
1989	116/1900 ⑥	45	45	⑦	⑧	—	—	0.3141	0.3141
	116/1900 ⑨	45	45	⑩	⑪	—	—	0.2748	0.2748
	128/2100	45	45	—	2.059	—	—	0.3539	0.3529
	134/2200	①	①	②	③	—	—	0.3149	0.3149
	171/2800	45	45	④	⑤	—	—	—	—
1990-91	116/1900 ⑥	45	45	⑦	⑧	—	—	0.3141	0.3141
	116/1900 ⑨	45	45	⑩	⑪	—	—	0.2748	0.2748
	128/2100	45	45	—	2.059	—	—	0.3539	0.3529
	134/2200	①	①	②	③	—	—	0.3149	0.3149

① Intake 30°, ad exhaust 45°
② Outer spring 64 ft. lbs.
   Inner spring 155 ft. lbs.
③ Outer spring 1.55 inch
   Inner spring 1.17 inch
④ Outer spring 55 ft. lbs.
   Inner spring 145 ft. lbs.
⑤ Outer spring 1.5748 inch
   Inner spring 1.1811 inch
⑥ Except 16 valve engine
⑦ Outer spring 90 ft. lbs.
   Inner spring 194 ft. lbs.
⑧ Outer spring 1.6732 inch
   Inner spring 1.2204 inch
⑨ 16 valve engine
⑩ Outer spring 88 ft. lbs.
   Inner spring 181 ft. lbs.
⑪ Outer spring 1.5275 inch
   Inner spring 1.1653 inch

TORQUE SPECIFICATIONS
All readings in ft. lbs.

Year	Engine Displacement cu. in. (cc)	Cylinder Head Bolts	Main Bearing Bolts	Rod Bearing Bolts	Crankshaft Pulley Bolts	Flywheel Bolts	Manifold Intake	Manifold Exhaust	Spark Plugs
1987	128/2100	①	80	48	98	58	11	15	22
	134/2200	②	68	48	95	46	—	—	—
	171/2800	③	22④	35	129	33	—	—	—

TORQUE SPECIFICATIONS
All readings in ft. lbs.

Year	Engine Displacement cu. in. (cc)	Cylinder Head Bolts	Main Bearing Bolts	Rod Bearing Bolts	Crankshaft Pulley Bolts	Flywheel Bolts	Manifold Intake	Manifold Exhaust	Spark Plugs
1988	128/2100	①	80	48	98	58	11	15	22
	134/2200	②	68	48	95	46	—	—	—
	171/2800	③	22④	35	129	33	—	—	—
1989	116/1900⑤	⑥	41	⑦	81	81	15	15	—
	116/1900⑧	⑥	41	⑦	18	37	15	7	—
	128/2100	①	80	48	98	58	—	—	—
	134/2200	②	68	48	95	46	—	—	—
	171/2800	③	22④	35	129	33	—	—	—
1990-91	116/1900⑤	⑥	41	⑦	81	81	15	15	—
	116/1900⑧	⑥	41	⑦	18	37	15	7	—
	128/2100	①	80	48	98	58	—	—	—
	134/2200	②	68	48	95	46	—	—	—

① Pretorque to 37 ft. lbs., final torque to 62 ft. lbs.
② Pretorque to 37 ft. lbs., torque to 58 ft. lbs., then loosen bolt by 1/4 turn and final torque of 69 ft. lbs.
③ Pretorque to 44 ft. lbs., loosen and retorque to 15 ft. lbs., then turn an additional 105 degrees using an angle torque wrench
④ Torque an additional 75 degrees using an angle torque wrench
⑤ Except 16 valve engine
⑥ Pretorque to 44 ft. lbs., loosen and retorque to 15 ft. lbs., then turn an additional 300 degrees using an angle torque wrench
⑦ Pretorque to 30 ft. lbs., loosen and torque to 15 ft. lbs. and turn an additional 70 degrees using an angle torque wrench
⑧ 16 valve engine

BRAKE SPECIFICATIONS
All measurements in inches unless noted

Year	Model	Lug Nut Torque (ft. lbs.)	Master Cylinder Bore	Brake Disc Minimum Thickness	Brake Disc Maximum Runout	Standard Brake Drum Diameter	Minimum Lining Thickness Front	Minimum Lining Thickness Rear
1987	505	—	—	0.4429①	0.002	—	—	—
1988	505	—	—	0.4429①	0.002	—	—	—
1989	405	62	0.8110	0.7283②	0.002	—	—	—
	505	—	—	0.4429①	0.002	—	—	—
1990-91	405	62	0.8110	0.7283②	0.002	—	—	—
	505	—	—	0.4429①	0.002	—	—	—

① Rear Disc, 0.4330.
② Rear Disc, 0.3149.

WHEEL ALIGNMENT

Year	Model	Caster Range (deg.)	Caster Preferred Setting (deg.)	Camber Range (deg.)	Camber Preferred Setting (deg.)	Toe-in (in.)	Steering Axis Inclination (deg.)
1987	505①	1¹/₂N–2¹/₂P	2P	1⁷/₁₆N–⁷/₁₆N②	¹⁵/₁₆N②	⁵/₃₂②	9⁷/₁₆
	505③	2³/₁₆N–3³/₁₆P	2¹¹/₁₆P	1¹/₂N–¹/₂N④	1N⑤	³/₈⑥	9¹/₂
	505⑦	2¹/₂N–3¹/₂P	3P	1¹³/₁₆N–¹³/₁₆N④	1⁵/₁₆N⑤	¹/₄⑥	12⁹/₁₆
	505⑧	2³/₁₆N–3³/₁₆P	2¹¹/₁₆P	1¹/₄N–¹/₄N④⑨	³/₄N⑤⑨	¹/₄⑥⑨	9¹/₂
	505⑩	2¹/₂N–3¹/₂P	3P	1¹³/₁₆N–¹³/₁₆N④⑨	1⁵/₁₆N⑤⑨	¹/₄⑥⑨	12⁹/₁₆

WHEEL ALIGNMENT

Year	Model	Caster Range (deg.)	Caster Preferred Setting (deg.)	Camber Range (deg.)	Camber Preferred Setting (deg.)	Toe-in (in.)	Steering Axis Inclination (deg.)
1988	505①	1¹/₂N–2¹/₂P	2P	1⁷/₁₆N–⁷/₁₆N②	¹⁵/₁₆N②	⁵/₃₂②	9⁷/₁₆
	505③	2³/₁₆N–3³/₁₆P	2¹¹/₁₆P	1¹/₂N–¹/₂N④	1N⑤	³/₈⑥	9¹/₂
	505⑦	2¹/₂N–3¹/₂P	3P	1¹³/₁₆N–¹³/₁₆N④	1⁵/₁₆N⑤	¹/₄⑥	12⁹/₁₆
	505⑧	2³/₁₆N–3³/₁₆P	2¹¹/₁₆P	1¹/₄N–¹/₄N④⑨	³/₄N⑤⑨	¹/₄⑥⑨	9¹/₂
	505⑩	2¹/₂N–3¹/₂P	3P	1¹³/₁₆N–¹³/₁₆N④⑨	1⁵/₁₆N⑤⑨	¹/₄⑥⑨	12⁹/₁₆
1989	405⑪	1¹/₂N–2¹/₂P	2P	⁵/₁₆N–¹¹/₁₆P⑫	³/₁₆P⑬	¹/₈⑭	10²⁷/₃₂
1990–91	405⑪	1¹/₂N–2¹/₂P	2P	⁵/₁₆N–¹¹/₁₆P⑫	³/₁₆P⑬	¹/₈⑭	10²⁷/₃₂
	405⑮	2¹/₁₆N–3¹/₁₆P	2⁹/₁₆P	¹³/₃₂N–¹⁹/₃₂P⑫	³/₃₂P⑬	¹/₈⑯	10⁵/₁₆
	505⑦	2¹/₂N–3¹/₂P	3P	1¹³/₁₆N–¹³/₁₆N④	1⁵/₁₆N⑤	¹/₄⑥	12⁹/₁₆
	505⑧	2³/₁₆N–3³/₁₆P	2¹¹/₁₆P	1¹/₄N–¹/₄N④⑨	³/₄N⑤⑨	¹/₄⑥⑨	9¹/₂

① Wagon
② Rear, 0
③ Vehicles equipped with 2.1 Turbocharged engines, except with ABS
④ Rear, All models, 1¹/₂N–¹/₂N
⑤ Rear, All models, 1N
⑥ Rear, All models, ¹/₄
⑦ Vehicles equipped with 2.1 Turbocharged engine, with ABS
⑧ Vehicles equipped with 2.2L engine
⑨ Wagon Rear, 0
⑩ Vehicles equipped with 2.8L engine
⑪ Except 16 valve engine
⑫ Rear, 1²⁷/₃₂N–²⁷/₃₂N
⑬ Rear, 1¹¹/₃₂N
⑭ Rear, ¹/₆₄
⑮ 16 valve engine
⑯ Rear, ¹/₁₆

ENGINE ELECTRICAL

NOTE: Disconnecting the negative battery cable on some vehicles may interfere with the functions of the on board computer systems and may require the computer to undergo a relearning process, once the negative battery cable is reconnected.

Distributor

Removal

1. Rotate the crankshaft to bring the No. 1 cylinder to TDC on its compression stroke. Disconnect the battery negative cable.

2. Remove the distributor cap, leaving the spark plug wires connected and disconnect the vacuum lines from the distributor.

3. Scribe alignment marks between the distributor body and the engine, then mark the position of the rotor to the distributor body.

4. Remove the distributor hold-down bolt and/or clamp and the distributor from the vehicle. Note the position of the slot in the distributor driveshaft.

Installation

TIMING NOT DISTURBED

1. Install the distributor into the engine so the rotor is aligned with the matchmark on the housing and the housing is aligned with the matchmark on the engine. Ensure that the distributor is fully seated and the distributor shaft fully seated.

2. Install the hold-down bolts.

3. Connect the distributor electrical connectors and vacuum lines.

4. Install the distributor cap and spark plug wires.

5. Connect the battery negative cable and adjust the timing, if necessary.

TIMING DISTURBED

1. Position the engine so the No. 1 cylinder is at TDC of its compression stroke and the timing marks on the crankshaft pulley align.

2. Install the distributor in the engine so the rotor is aligned with the No. 1 ignition wire on the distributor cap and the housing is aligned with the matchmark on the engine. Ensure that the distributor is fully seated.

3. Install the distributor hold-down bolts.

4. Connect the distributor electrical connectors and vacuum lines.

5. Install the distributor cap and wires.

6. Connect the battery negative cable and adjust the timing.

Ignition Timing

Adjustment

1. Start and allow engine to reach normal operating temperature.

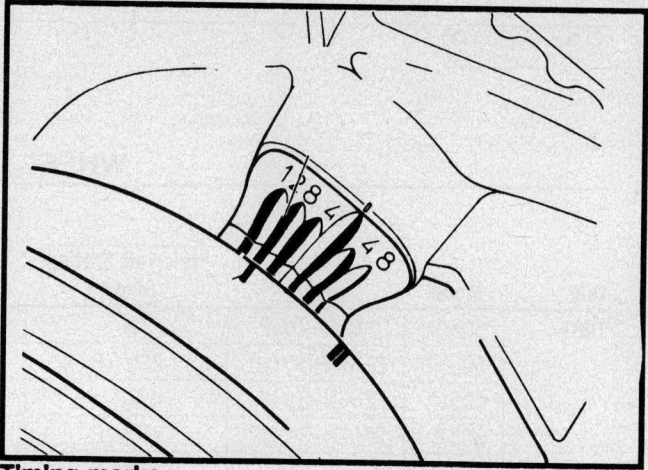

Timing marks

2. Connect a timing light to the No. 1 cylinder high tension lead. A scope may also be connected using the diagnostic plug. Install tachometer to engine.

3. With the mircoswitch closed, check to ensure that the idle speed is 900 rpm. If specification obtained is not as indicated, adjust the idle speed using the air bleed screw on the throttle housing.

4. Check the ignition timing. Ignition timing should be 10 degrees BTDC at 900 rpm.

5. If ignition timing is not within specification, loosen the distributor hold-down bolt and turn the distributor until the TDC notch on the crankshaft pulley is aligned with the 10 degree mark on the timing plate. Tighten the distributor hold-down bolt.

Alternator

Precautions

Several precautions must be observed with alternator equipped vehicles to avoid damage to the unit.

● If the battery is removed for any reason, make sure it is reconnected with the correct polarity. Reversing the battery connections may result in damage to the one-way rectifiers.

● When utilizing a booster battery as a starting aid, always connect the positive to positive terminals and the negative terminal from the booster battery to a good engine ground on the vehicle being started.

● Never use a fast charger as a booster to start vehicles.

● Disconnect the battery cables when charging the battery with a fast charger.

● Never attempt to polarize the alternator.

● Do not use test lamps of more than 12 volts when checking diode continuity.

● Do not short across or ground any of the alternator terminals.

● The polarity of the battery, alternator and regulator must be matched and considered before making any electrical connections within the system.

● Never separate the alternator on an open circuit. Make sure all connections within the circuit are clean and tight.

● Disconnect the battery ground terminal when performing any service on electrical components.

● Disconnect the battery if arc welding is to be done on the vehicle.

Belt Tension Adjustment

The belt tension is adjusted by moving the alternator within the range of the slotted bracket. Belt tension should be adjusted every 12 months and/or 10,000 miles. Push in on the belt about midway between the crankshaft pulley and the driven component. If the belt deflects more than $9/16$ in., adjustment is required.

1. Loosen the adjustment nut and bolt on the alternator bracket. Slightly loosen pivot bolt.

2. Using a suitable prybar, push the alternator outward to increase tension, and/or inward to reduce tension. Tighten the adjusting nut/bolt and the pivot bolt.

3. Recheck the drive belt tension and readjust, if necessary.

Removal and Installation

1. Disconnect the battery negative cable.

2. Remove the alternator adjusting nut and bolt and the pivot bolt.

3. Remove the belt from the pulley and disconnect the electrical connectors from the alternator.

4. Remove the alternator from the vehicle.

5. Reverse procedure to install. Connect the battery negative cable.

Starter

Removal and Installation

1. Disconnect the battery negative cable.

2. Raise and safely support the vehicle, if necessary.

3. Disconnect the electrical connectors from the starter.

4. Remove the starter mounting bolts and the starter from the vehicle.

5. Reverse procedure to install. Connect the battery negative cable.

CHASSIS ELECTRICAL

Heater Blower Motor

Removal and Installation

405

1. Disconnect the battery negative cable.

2. Working under the dashboard, unclip the wires from the blower motor and disconnect the electrical connectors.

3. Remove the blower motor attaching screws and the blower motor from the vehicle.

4. Reverse procedure to install. Connect the battery negative cable.

505

Without Air Conditioning

1. Disconnect the battery negative cable.

2. Unclip the right side front brake line from the firewall.

3. Remove the heater sound proofing.

4. Carefully remove the the corrugated section of the duct from the blower motor housing.

NOTE: Do not remove the corrugated duct from the firewall.

5. Disconnect the electrical connectors from the blower motor and remove the securing clips from the blower motor housing.

6. Remove the blower motor from the vehicle.

7. Reverse procedure to install. Connect the battery negative cable.

With Air Conditioning

1. Disconnect the battery negative cable.

2. Remove sound proofing shield.

3. Remove the auxiliary air device.

4. Remove the nipple from the upper right corner of the shield and the first clip along the lower edge.

5. Remove the clips and the blower motor-to-evaporator duct.

6. Remove the 7 clips from the blower motor housing, disconnect the electrical connectors and remove the blower motor from the vehicle.

7. Reverse procedure to install. Connect the battery negative cable.

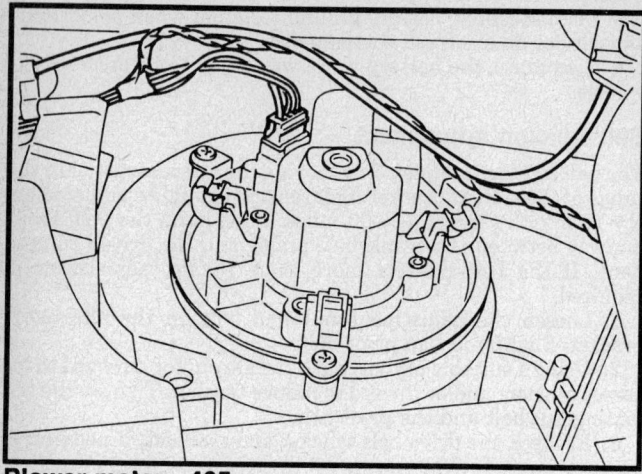

Blower motor—405

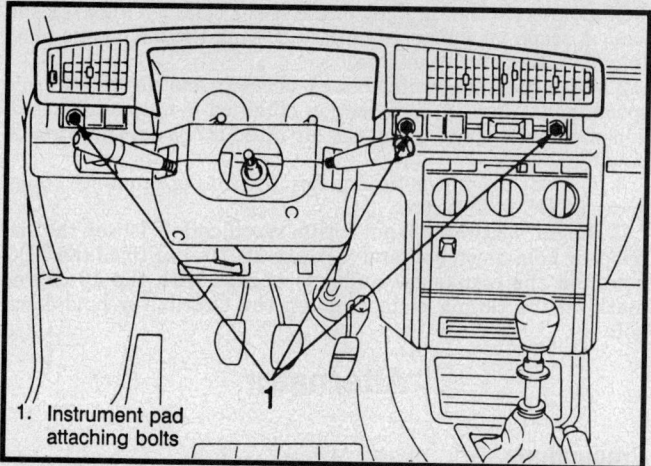

1. Instrument pad attaching bolts

Instrument panel pad attaching bolt locations—405

Windshield Wiper Motor

Removal and Installation

1. Disconnect the battery negative cable.
2. Disconnect the wiper motor linkage.
3. Disconnect the electrical connectors from the wiper motor.
4. Remove the wiper motor attaching screws and the wiper motor from the vehicle.
5. Reverse procedure to install. Connect the battery negative cable.

Instrument Cluster

Removal and Installation

405

1. Disconnect the battery negative cable.
2. Remove steering wheel.
3. Tilt steering column to its lowest level and remove the steering column upper and lower covers.
4. Remove 3 instrument panel pad attaching bolts and the instrument panel pad from the vehicle.
5. Remove the 5 screws attaching the center panel and remove the center panel from the vehicle.
6. Remove the instrument cluster filler strip.
7. Remove the instrument cluster attaching screws and tilt cluster outwards. Disconnect the electrical connectors and speedometer cable. Remove instrument cluster from vehicle.
8. Reverse procedure to install. Connect the battery negative cable.

505

1. Disconnect the battery negative cable.
2. Remove the steering wheel. Tilt steering column to its lowest level.
3. Press the 2 release clip on the instrument cluster. Tilt cluster outward.
4. Disconnect the electrical connectors and the speedometer cable.
5. Remove the instrument cluster from the vehicle.
6. Reverse procedure to install. Connect the battery negative cable.

Combination Switch

Removal and Installation

1. Disconnect the battery negative cable.
2. Remove the steering wheel.

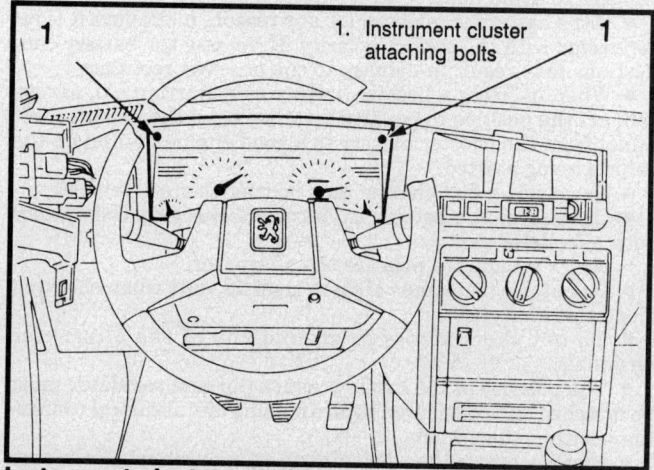

1. Instrument cluster attaching bolts

Instrument cluster attaching screws location—405

3. On 505 models, remove the upper and lower steering column covers.
4. On 405 models, remove the lower steering column cover.
5. Remove the combination switch attaching screws and disconnect the electrical connectors.
6. Remove the combination switch from the vehicle.
7. Reverse procedure to install. Connect the battery negative cable.

Stoplight Switch

Removal and Installation

405

1. Disconnect the battery negative cable.
2. Disconnect the electrical connector from the switch.
3. Pull the switch out from its mounting bracket.
4. Reverse procedure to install. Connect the battery negative cable.

505

1. Disconnect the battery negative cable.
2. Disconnect the switch electrical connector and remove the switch locknut.
3. Remove the stoplight switch from the vehicle.
4. Reverse procedure to install. Ensure that a 0.059 in. (1.5mm) clearance is obtained between the switch and the brake pedal. Connect the battery negative cable.

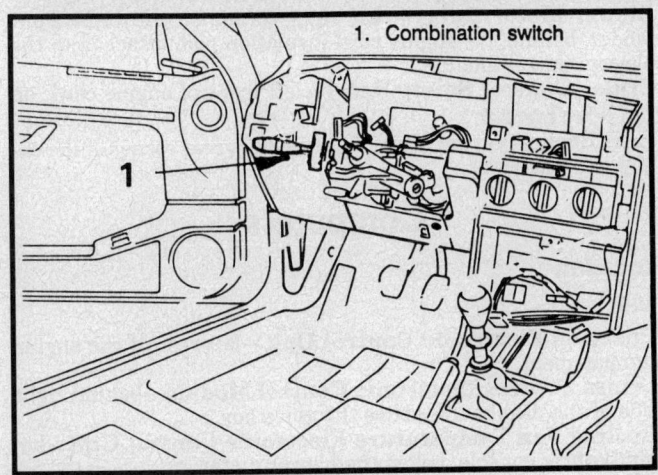

Combination switch

Fuses and Relays

Location

FUSE BLOCK

405 — located on the left side of the dashboard.

505 — located in the left rear corner of the engine compartment.

RELAYS

405

Cooling Fan Low Speed Relay — front of the engine compartment, on the right side of the radiator shroud.

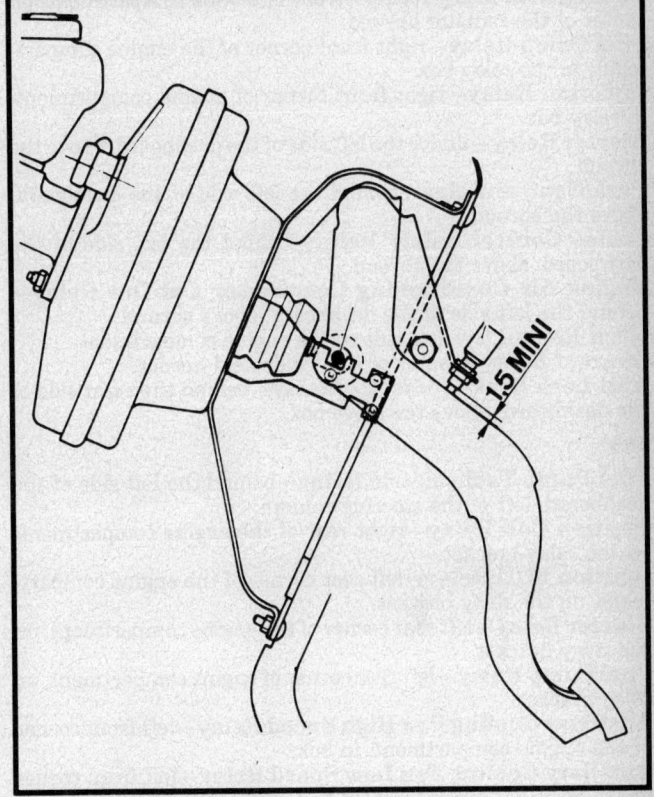

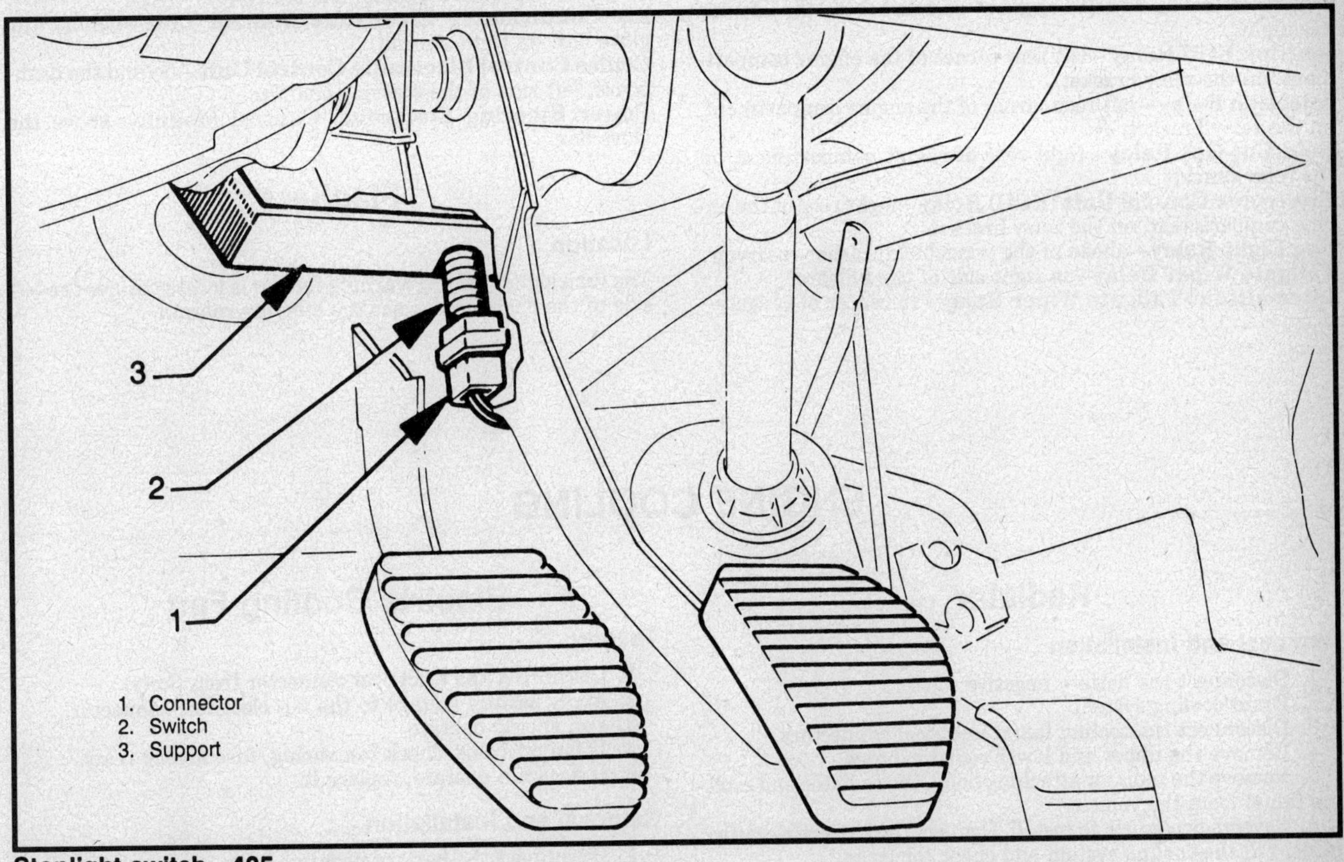

Stoplight switch—505

1. Connector
2. Switch
3. Support

Stoplight switch—405

Cooling Fan Main Relay—front of engine compartment, on center of the radiator shroud.
Fuel Pump Relay—right front corner of the engine compartment, in the relay box.
Injection Relay—right front corner of engine compartment, in relay box.
Starter Relay—under the left side of the dashboard, above the shroud.
Park/Neutral Relay—behind the left side of the dashboard, above the shroud.
Cruise Control Safety Relay—behind the left side of the dashboard, above the shroud.
Engine Air Conditioning Compressor Cut-Out Relay—behind the left side of the dashboard, above shroud.
Horn Relay—rear left side of the engine compartment.
Sunroof Relay—center of the windshield header.
Anti-Lock Brake Indicator Relay—behind the right side of the dashboard, above the glove box.

505

Fuel Pump Tachymetric Relay—behind the left side of the dashboard, left of the steering column.
Ignition Coil Relay—right rear of the engine compartment, on the relay bracket.
Ignition ECU Relay—left rear corner of the engine compartment, on the relay bracket.
Starter Relay—left rear corner of the engine compartment, on the relay bracket
Fuel Pump Relay—left rear corner of engine compartment, on relay bracket.
Auxiliary Cooling Fan High Speed Relay—left front corner of the engine compartment, in box.
Auxiliary Cooling Fan Low Speed Relay—left front corner of the engine compartment, in box.
Auxiliary Cooling Fan Relay, models with automatic transmission and N9TE engine—in box, behind the left side headlight.
Ignition ECU Relay—left rear corner of the engine compartment, on the relay bracket.
Injection Relay—left rear corner of the engine compartment, on the relay bracket.
Cold Cut-Out Relay—right rear of engine compartment, on the relay bracket.
Electronic Control Unit (ECU) Relay—right rear of the engine compartment, on the relay bracket.
Fog Light Relay—ahead of the windshield washer reservoir.
Tailgate Wiper Relay—in right side of the tailgate.
Intermittent Tailgate Wiper Relay—in center of tailgate.

Blower Motor Relay—rear right corner on the right front fender, behind the engine cowl insulation pad, attached to the blower control module.
Cruise Control Safety Relay—left front of engine cowl, on the relay bracket.
Anti-Brake System Main Relay—right rear corner of the engine compartment.

Computers

Location

405

Injection Electronic Control Unit—left rear of the engine compartment.
Cruise Control Electronic Control Module—behind right side of the dashboard, above the glove box.
Cooling Fan Temperature Electronic Control Unit—behind center console, below the blower motor.
Climate Control Electronic Control Unit—behind the right side of the dashboard, above the glove box.
Passengers Seatbelt Electronic Control Unit—below the front passengers seat.
Drivers Seatbelt Electronic Control Unit—below the drivers seat.
Anti-Brake System Electronic Control Unit—left rear of the engine compartment.

505

Electronic Control Module—in front of the right shock tower, in the engine compartment.
Injection Electronic Control Module—behind the glove box.
Ignition Electronic Control Unit—right front of the passengers compartment, under the footrest.
Air Conditioning Electronic Control Unit—behind the glove box, on right shroud.
Cruise Control Electronic Control Unit—behind the dashboard, left side of the steering column.
Power Steering Electronic Control Module—above the glove box.

Flashers

Location

The turn signal/hazard warning flasher is located under the left side of the dashboard, near the steering column.

ENGINE COOLING

Radiator

Removal and Installation

1. Disconnect the battery negative cable.
2. Drain cooling system.
3. Disconnect the cooling fan(s) electrical connectors.
4. Remove the upper and lower radiator hoses.
5. Remove the radiator attaching bolts, the radiator and cooling fan(s) from the vehicle.
6. Reverse procedure to install. Connect the battery negative cable. Fill the cooling system and check for leaks.

Electric Cooling Fan

Testing

1. Disconnect the electrical connector from fan(s).
2. Apply battery voltage to the fan electrical connector.
3. Fan should operate.
4. If fan operates, check fan wiring, fuse and/or relay.
5. If does not operate, replace it.

Removal and Installation

1. Disconnect the battery negative cable.

2. Drain cooling system
3. Remove the radiator.
4. Remove the cooling fan(s) attaching bolts and the cooling fan(s) from the vehicle.
5. Reverse procedure to install. Fill cooling system and check for leaks. Connect the battery negative cable.

Heater Core

For further information, please refer to "Chilton's Heating and Air Conditioning Manual" for additional coverage.

Removal and Installation

405

1. Disconnect the battery negative cable.
2. Drain the cooling system.
3. Disconnect the fuse block and relay electrical connectors from under the steering column.
4. Disconnect the dashboard right and left side harness electrical connectors and the ground connector at the right side kick panel.
5. Remove the dashboard attaching bolts and lift dashboard outward. Disconnect the speedometer cable and all electrical connectors and remove the dashboard from the vehicle.
6. Remove the blower motor air inlet cover and the bolt attaching the heater/air conditioning assembly.
7. Disconnect the heater pipes and the 2 air ducts. Place a container under the heater pipes.
8. Remove the screws attaching the heater/air conditioning assembly to the floor.
9. Remove the blower motor and the 2 heater core attaching bolts. Remove the heater core from the vehicle.
10. Reverse procedure to install. Fill cooling system and check for leaks. Connect the battery negative cable.

505

1. Disconnect the battery negative cable.
2. Drain the cooling system.
3. Remove the glove box assembly.
4. Remove the steering column lower cover and the lower dashboard trim panel.
5. Disconnect the heater valve cables and the heater hoses.
6. Remove the heater core attaching bolt and the heater core from the vehicle.
7. Reverse procedure to install. Fill cooling system and connect the battery negative cable. Check system for leaks.

Cooling System Bleeding

EXCEPT 2.8L ENGINE

1. Start and allow engine to reach normal operating temperature. Cooling fan(s) should operate.
2. Stop engine.

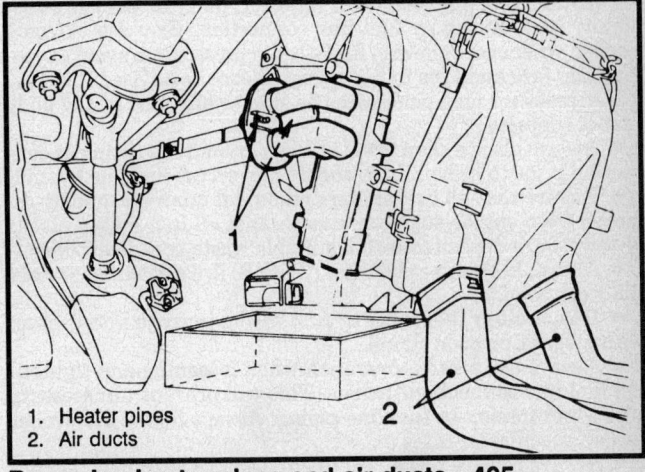

1. Heater pipes
2. Air ducts

Removing heater pipes and air ducts—405

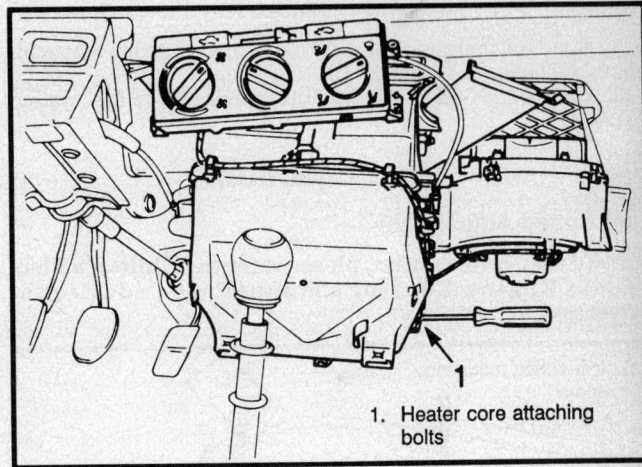

1. Heater core attaching bolts

Heater core attaching screws—405

3. Remove pressure cap and fill radiator with coolant while the engine is warm.
4. Install pressure cap.

2.8L ENGINE

1. Open the bleed screw located on the top of the radiator, near the upper radiator hose.
2. Remove the coolant level sensor from the radiator.
3. Fill the radiator with coolant through the expansion jar, until coolant comes out through the filler neck.
4. Install the coolant level sensor. Ensure that the sensor is installed properly.
5. Close the bleed screw when the coolant comes out steadily.

FUEL SYSTEM

Fuel System Service Precautions

Safety is the most important factor when performing not only fuel system maintenance but any type of maintenance. Failure to conduct maintenance and repairs in a safe manner may result in serious personal injury or death. Maintenance and testing of the vehicle's fuel system components can be accomplished safely and effectively by adhering to the following rules and guidelines.

• To avoid the possibility of fire and personal injury, always disconnect the negative battery cable unless the repair or test procedure requires that battery voltage be applied.

• Always relieve the fuel system pressure prior to disconnecting any fuel system component (injector, fuel rail, pressure regulator, etc.), fitting or fuel line connection. Exercise extreme caution whenever relieving fuel system pressure to avoid exposing skin, face and eyes to fuel spray. Please be advised that fuel under pressure may penetrate the skin or any part of the body that it contacts.

● Always place a shop towel or cloth around the fitting or connection prior to loosening to absorb any excess fuel due to spillage. Ensure that all fuel spillage (should it occur) is quickly removed from engine surfaces. Ensure that all fuel soaked cloths or towels are deposited into a suitable waste container.

● Always keep a dry chemical (Class B) fire extinguisher near the work area.

● Do not allow fuel spray or fuel vapors to come into contact with a spark or open flame.

● Always use a backup wrench when loosening and tightening fuel line connection fittings. This will prevent unnecessary stress and torsion to fuel line piping. Always follow the proper torque specifications.

● Always replace worn fuel fitting O-rings with new. Do not substitute fuel hose or equivalent where fuel pipe is installed.

Relieving Fuel System Pressure

1. Wrap the fuel supply line fitting with a rag to prevent spillage of fuel over the engine.
2. Loosen the fuel supply line fitting release the fuel system pressure.

Fuel Injection

Idle Speed Adjustment

For further information, please refer to "Chilton's Electronic Engine Control's Manual" for additional coverage.

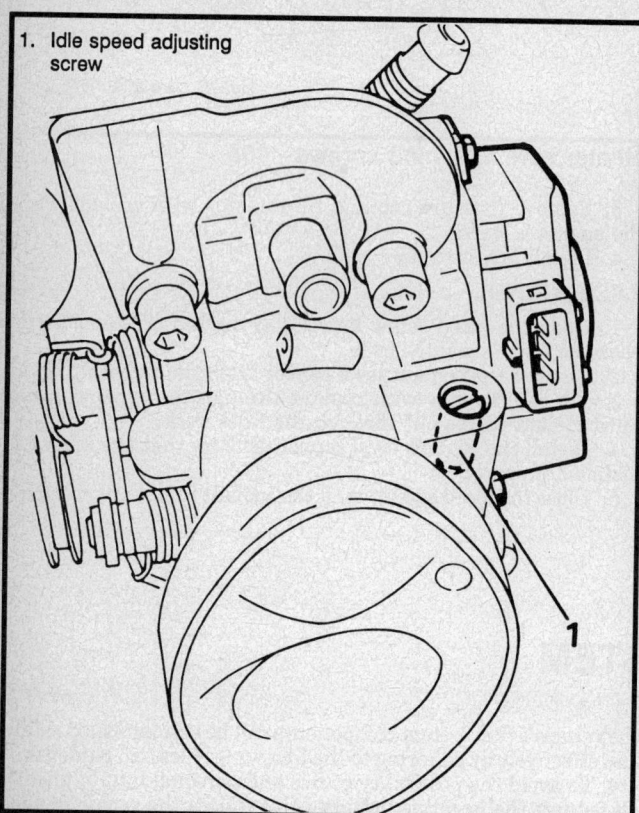

1. Idle speed adjusting screw

Adjusting idle speed—1.9L engine, except DOHC engine

EXCEPT 1.9L DOHC ENGINE

1. Start and allow engine to reach normal operating temperature.
2. Check that the throttle flap is operating properly.
3. Check that the throttle switch is adjusted properly.
4. Check that the cooling fan and air conditioning compressor are released.
5. Place transmission in **P** or **N** position.
6. Connect a suitable tachometer onto the engine. Check the idle speed.
7. Idle speed should be 800–900 rpm. If not, adjust the idle speed by turning the adjusting screw.

1.9L DOHC ENGINE

The idle speed on this engine is not adjustable. It is controlled by the electrovalve. The idle speed should be 830–930 rpm.

2.1L ENGINE

1. Start and allow engine to reach normal operating temperature.
2. Ensure that the throttle flap is operating properly.
3. Ensure that all accessories are in the OFF position.
4. Connect a suitable tachometer on to the engine. Check idle speed. Idle speed should be as follows:
   a. Manual transmission—900–950 rpm.
   b. Automatic transmission—950–1000 rpm.
5. If necessary, adjust the idle speed by turning the idle adjusting screw.

2.2L ENGINE

1. Start and allow engine to reach normal operating temperature.
2. Ensure that the throttle flap is operating properly.
3. Ensure that the throttle switch is adjusted correctly.
4. Connect a suitable tachometer onto the engine. Check idle speed.
5. Idle speed should be 900 rpm. If not, adjust the idle speed by turning the air screw.

2.8L ENGINE

The idle speed on this engine is programmed into the ECU. However, it is still necessary to preset the idle. Once the idle is preset, never readjust the idle screw.

1. Start and allow engine to reach normal operating temperature.

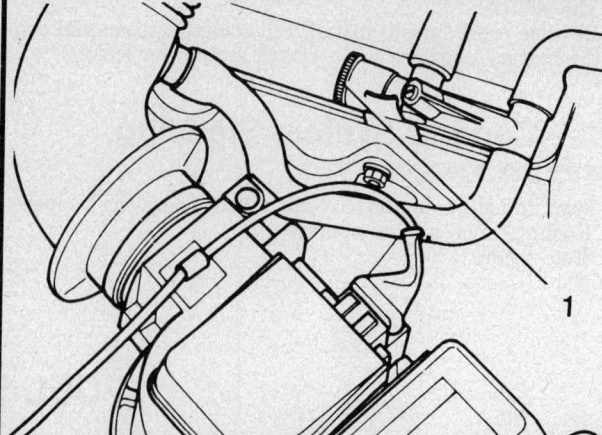

1. Idle speed screw

Adjusting idle speed—2.2L engine

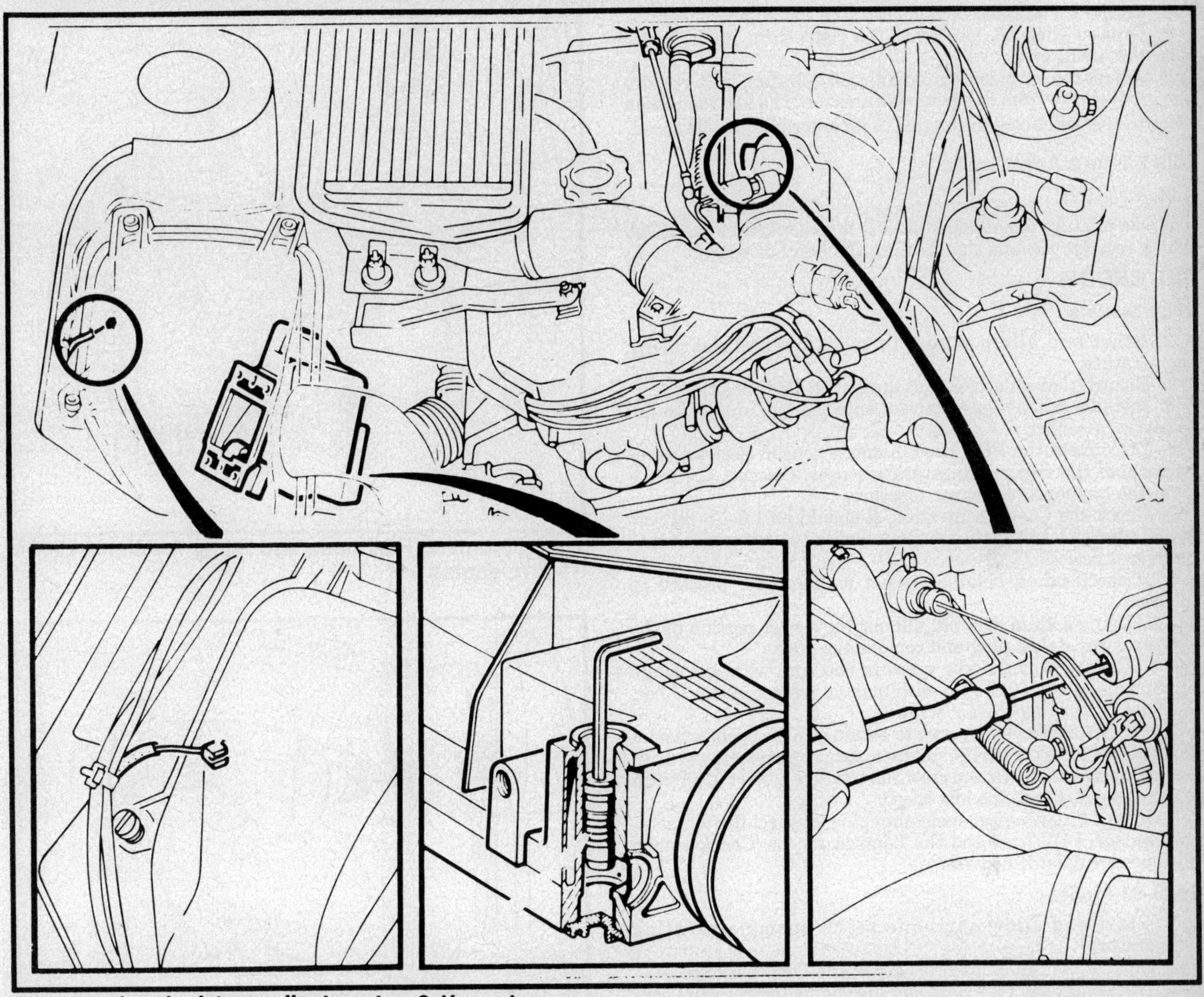

Idle speed and mixture adjustments—2.1L engine

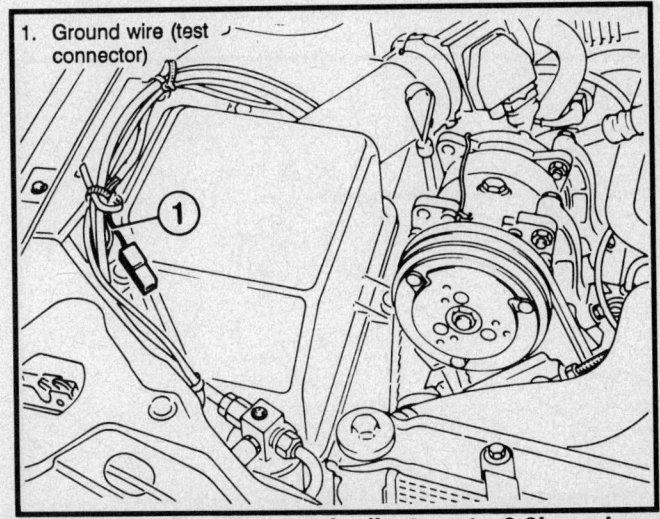

1. Ground wire (test connector)

Ground wire for idle speed adjustment—2.8L engine

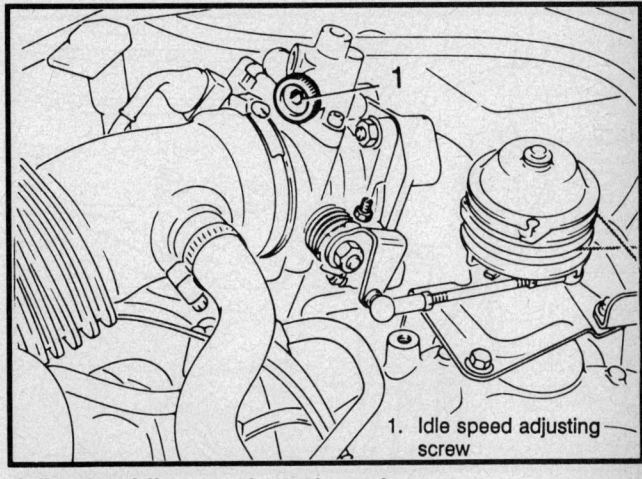

1. Idle speed adjusting screw

Adjusting idle speed—2.8L engine

2. Connect a suitable tachometer onto the engine.

3. Ground wire 12, located at the right front inner fender near the air filter.

4. Adjust the air bleed screw to obtain 700 rpm, then remove the ground wire from the ground connector. The idle regulation electrovalve will bring the engine to its programmed idle speed.

Idle Mixture Adjustment

1.9L ENGINE

The idle mixture is not adjustable. It is controlled by the ECU, which receives various signals from the Lambda sensor.

2.1L ENGINE

1987 Models

1. Start and allow engine to reach normal operating temperature.

2. Ensure that all accessories are in the **OFF** position.

3. Install an exhaust gas analyzer onto the tap, located on the catalytic converter.

4. Disconnect the PCV hose, Lambda sensor electrical connector and the engine temperature sensor. Connect the wires from the temperature sensor together.

5. Check the CO concentration, it should be 1.0-1.6 percent at 960 rpm with automatic transmission or 1010 rpm with manual transmission.

6. If specification obtained is not as indicated, proceed as follows:

   a. Using a 4mm drill bit, dill out the center portion of the tamper resistance plug and remove the plug.

   b. Ensure that the idle speed is 960 rpm with automatic transmission or 1010 rpm with manual transmission. If not, adjust by turning the air screw.

   c. Turn the richness screw to obtain a CO concentration of 1.3 percent. To enrich the mixture, turn the screw inward. To lean out the mixture, unscrew the mixture screw. After each adjustment, check the idle speed.

7. Install a new tamper resistance plug, connect the temperature sensor, PCV hose and the Lambda sensor. Check engine idle speed. Adjust if necessary.

1988-91 Models

1. Start and allow engine to reach normal operating temperature.

2. Ensure that all accessories are in the **OFF** position.

3. Disconnect the PCV hose and the engine temperature sensor electrical connector. Connect the wires from the temperature sensor together.

4. Install a voltmeter to wire No. 22 on the test connector, located on the right front inner fender, near the air filter.

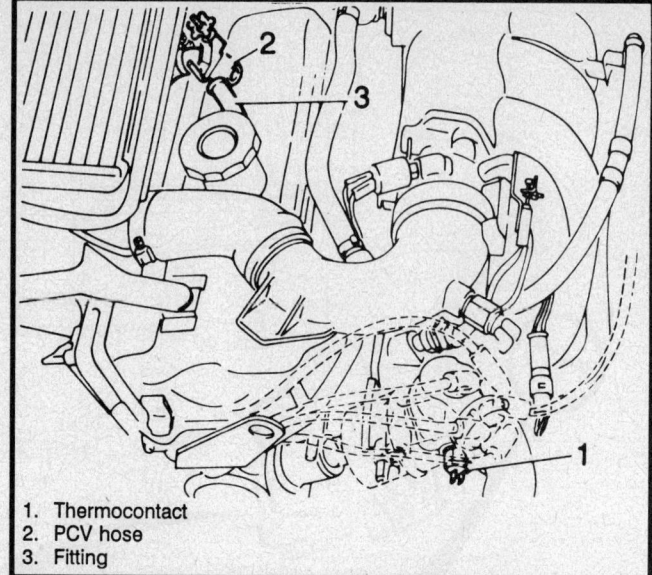

1. Thermocontact
2. PCV hose
3. Fitting

Thermocontact, PCV hose and fitting location—1988–91 2.1L engine

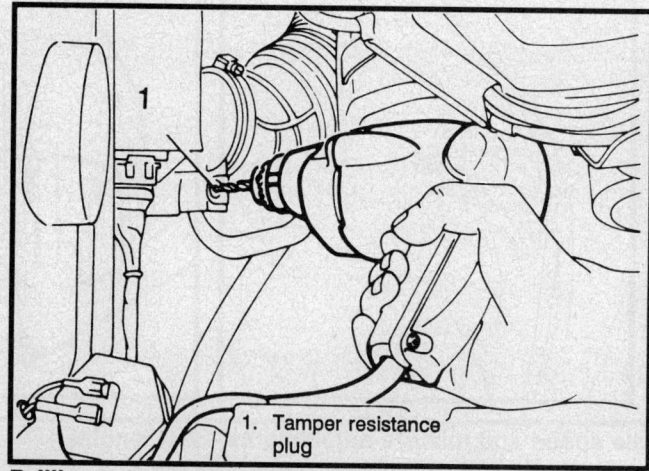

1. Tamper resistance plug

Drilling out tamper resistance plug—1987–91 2.1L engine

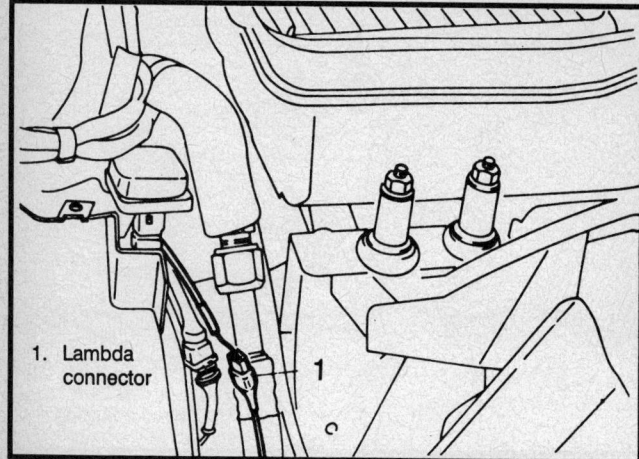

1. Lambda connector

Lambda sensor connector—1987 2.1L engine

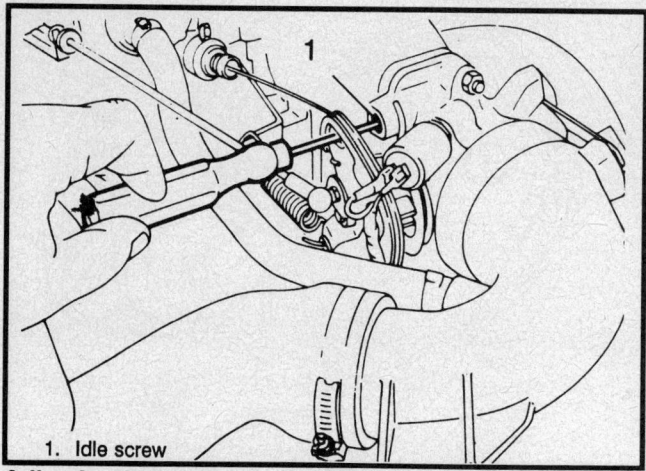

1. Idle screw

Adjusting idle speed—1987–91 2.1L engine

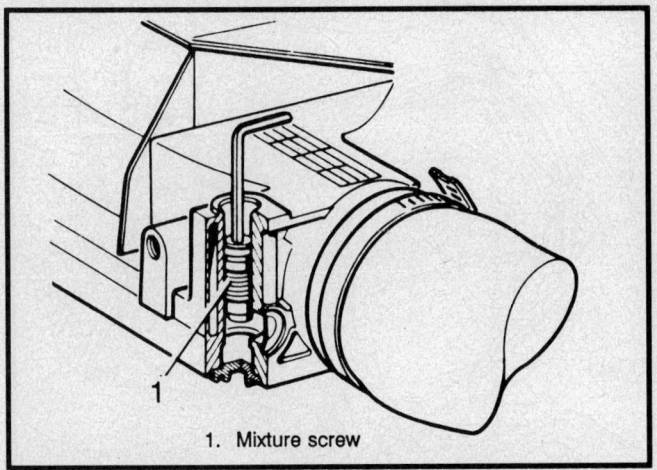

1. Mixture screw

Adjusting mixture—1987–91 2.1L and 2.2L engines

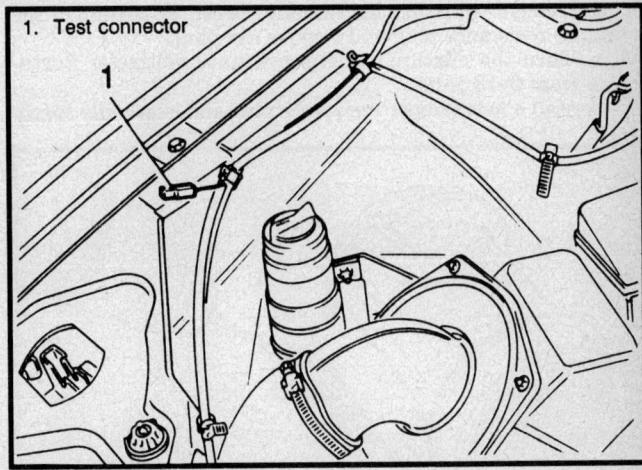

1. Test connector

Test connector location—2.2L engine

5. Measure voltage. Voltmeter should read 7.0–7.4 volts at 900 rpm with automatic transmission or 950 rpm with manual transmission.

6. If specifications obtained is not as indicated, proceed as follows:

  a. Using a 4mm drill bit, dill out the center portion of the tamper resistance plug and remove the plug.

  b. Ensure that the idle speed is 900 rpm with automatic transmission or 950 rpm with manual transmission. If not, adjust by turning the air screw.

  c. Turn the richness screw to obtain a 7.2 volts. To reduce the voltage, enrichening the mixture, turn the screw inward. To increase the voltage, leaning out the mixture, unscrew the mixture screw. After each adjustment, check the idle speed.

7. Install a new tamper resistance plug, connect the engine temperature sensor electrical connectror and the PCV hose. Check the idle speed and adjust, if necessary.

2.2L ENGINE

1. Start and allow engine to reach normal operating temperature.

2. Install a voltmeter to wire No. 22 on the test connector, located on the right front inner fender, near the air filter.

3. Measure voltage. Voltmeter should read 6.5–7.5 volts at 900–950 rpm.

4. If specifications obtained is not as indicated, proceed as follows:

  a. Using a 4mm drill bit, dill out the center portion of the tamper resistance plug and remove the plug.

  b. Ensure that the idle speed is 900–950 rpm.

  c. Turn the richness screw to obtain a 7.0 volts. To reduce the voltage, enrichening the mixture, turn the screw inward. To increase the voltage, leaning out the mixture, unscrew the mixture screw. After each adjustment, check the idle speed.

5. Install a new tamper resistance plug. Check the idle speed and adjust, if necessary.

2.8L ENGINE

1. Start and allow the engine to reach normal operating temperature.

2. Check idle speed. Ensure that the idle speed is 750–800 rpm.

3. Install a voltmeter to wire No. 22 on the test connector, located on the right front inner fender, near the air filter.

3. Measure voltage. Voltmeter should fluctuate from 0–13 volts indicating correct mixture.

4. If specifications obtained is not as indicated, proceed as follows:

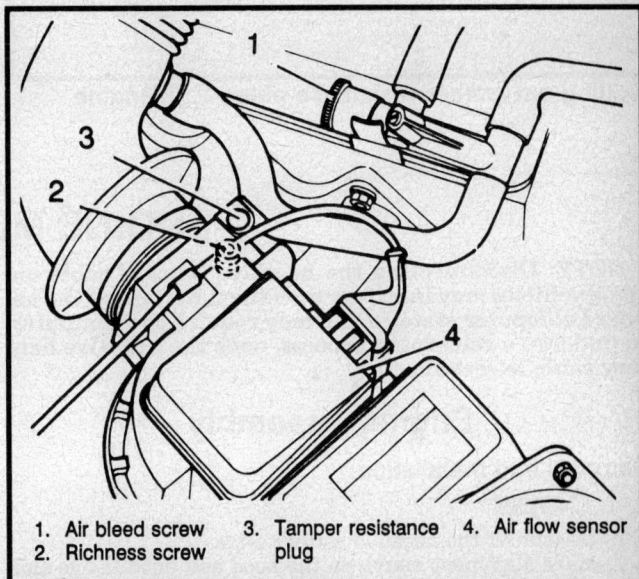

1. Air bleed screw
2. Richness screw
3. Tamper resistance plug
4. Air flow sensor

Air bleed screw, mixture screw, airflow sensor and tamper resistance plug location—2.2L engine

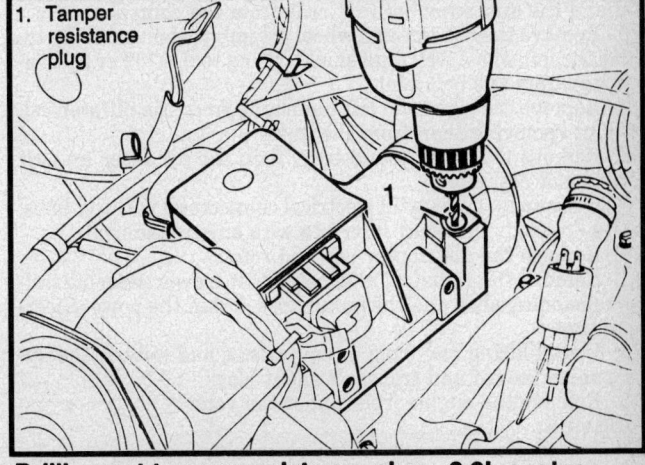

1. Tamper resistance plug

Drilling out tamper resistance plug—2.2L engine

a. Using a 4mm drill bit, dill out the center portion of the tamper resistance plug and remove the plug.

b. Turn the mixture adjust screw until voltmeter fluctuates from 0–13 volts.

5. Install a new tamper resistance plug and check idle speed.

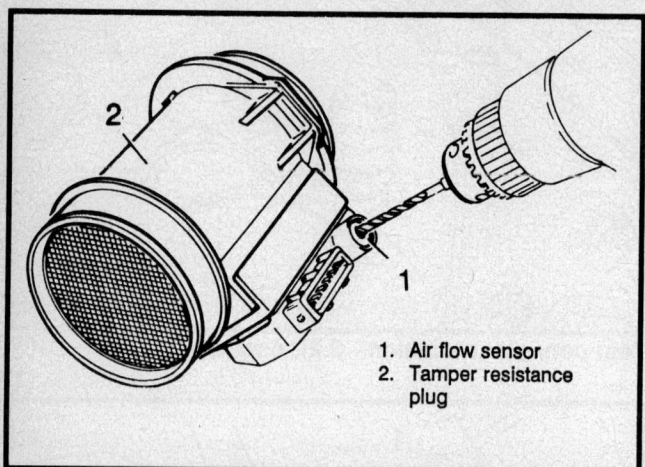

1. Air flow sensor
2. Tamper resistance plug

Drilling out tamper resistance plug—2.8L engine

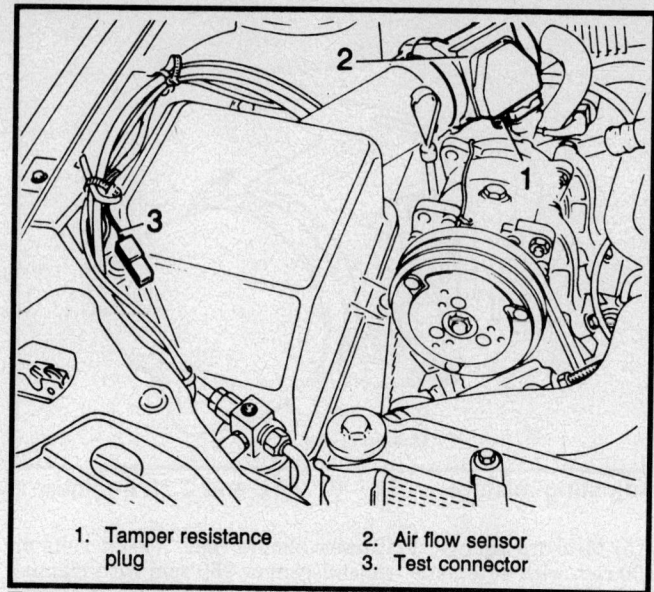

1. Tamper resistance plug
2. Air flow sensor
3. Test connector

Tamper resistance plug, air flow sensor and test connector location—2.8L engine

ENGINE MECHANICAL

NOTE: Disconnecting the negative battery cable on some vehicles may interfere with the functions of the on board computer systems and may require the computer to undergo a relearning process, once the negative battery cable is reconnected.

Engine Assembly

Removal and Installation

1.9L ENGINE

1. Disconnect the negative battery cable.
2. Make alignment marks on the hood and hood flange and remove the hood.
3. Drain the cooling system and the engine oil.
4. Remove the lower engine mount junction bracket attaching nut and through bolt.
5. Disconnect the front header pipe from the exhaust manifold and the anti-sway bar link rods from the control arm.
6. Remove the left tire and wheel assembly, then partially remove the left wheel well mud shield. Using tool .0709 or equivalent, separate the ball joint.
7. Remove the right and left halfshafts from the differential, without removing then from the hubs.
8. Remove the battery and tray, then the air filter and air flow sensor assembly.
9. Disconnect and tag all electrical connectors, vacuum lines, cables and rods that may interfere with engine removal.
10. Remove the distributor cap and rotor.
11. Remove the radiator, alternator belt, power steering pulley, tensioning slide and the pump hose. Drain the power steering pump.
12. Install lifting bar .0102 or equivalent, and remove the upper engine mount and transaxle silent block.
13. Remove the engine from under the vehicle.

To install:

14. Installation is reverse of the removal procedure.
15. Install engine, transaxle silent block and the upper right engine mount. Torque the upper right engine mount to 33 ft. lbs.
16. Install the slide tensioner, the power steering pulley and belt. Torque pulley bolts to 6 ft. lbs.
17. Install radiator, hoses and cooler lines.
18. Connect all electrical connectors, vacuum lines, cables and rod that were disconnected during removal.
19. Install distributor, relay housing, if removed, air filter and air flow sensor assembly, battery tray and battery.
20. Install the front header pipe to the exhaust manifold.
21. Install the halfshafts into the differential.
22. Install the lower engine mount nut and through bolt. Torque bolt to 26 ft. lbs.
23. Install the lower engine mount junction bracket. Torque the bracket bolt to 33 ft. lbs.
24. Install ball joints. Torque ball joint nut to 22 ft. lbs.
25. Install anti-sway link rods to the control arms. Torque bolts to 48 ft. lbs.
26. Refill transaxle with engine oil, power steering pump reservoir and the cooling system. Bleed cooling and power steering systems.
27. Install hood. Start engine and check for leaks.

2.1L ENGINE

1. Disconnect the negative battery cable.
2. Make alignment marks on the hood and hinges and remove the hood.
3. Drain the cooling system and the engine oil.
4. Remove the power steering attaching bolts and the power steering pump. Plug all openings.
5. Remove the air conditioning compressor attaching bolts and position the compressor aside. It is not necessary to disconnect the air conditioning lines.
6. Disconnect and tag all electrical connectors and vacuum lines that will interfere with engine removal.
7. Install a suitable engine lifting device onto the engine. Remove the cruise control servo and the auxiliary air device connector.

8. Remove the turbocharger-to-front header attaching bolts and the disconnect the header from the turbocharger.

9. Remove the TDC sensor from the transmission reinforcement bracket.

10. Remove the 3 reinforcement bracket attaching bolts and the 5 upper bellhousing bolts. Do not remove the 2 lower bolts.

11. Remove the right and left engine mount attaching bolts. Carefully lift the engine until the front header pipe contacts the floor board.

12. Install a support under the engine. Remove the the 2 remaining bolts on the reinforcement bracket and the 2 lower bellhousing attaching bolts.

13. Remove the engine.

To install:

14. Before installing the engine, the turbocharger should be lubricated as follows:

    a. Remove the heat shield and the flange.

    b. Using engine oil, fill the oil passage of the turbocharger.

    c. Reinstall the flange, using a new O-ring.

15. Install engine and bellhousing attaching bolts. Torque bolts to 26 ft. lbs.

16. Install the reinforcement bracket and bolts. Torque bolts to 40 ft. lbs. Ensure that the TDC sensor harness retaining clip is in its proper position.

17. Install the air conditioning compressor.

18. Install the power steering pump. Torque bolts to 22 ft. lbs.

19. Connect all electrical connectors and vacuum hoses that was disconnected during removal.

20. Install the TDC sensor.

21. Fill cooling system and engine oil.

22. Install hood and connect the negative battery cable. Start engine and check for leaks.

2.2L ENGINE

1. Disconnect the negative battery cable.

2. Make alignment marks on the hood flange and hood, then remove the hood.

3. Drain the cooling system and engine oil.

4. Remove the battery.

5. Remove the upper and lower radiator hoses, then the radiator attaching bolts and the radiator.

6. Remove the air filter and disconnect the air flow sensor electrical connector.

7. Disconnect all electrical connectors and vacuum hoses that may interfere with engine removal.

8. Remove the power steering pump attaching bolts and position pump aside. It is not necessary to disconnect the hydraulic lines.

9. Remove the air conditioning compressor attaching bolts and position compressor aside. It it not necessary to disconnect the lines from the compressor.

10. Remove the starter motor attaching bolts, disconnect electrical connectors and remove the starter motor.

11. Raise and safely support the vehicle. Disconnect the steering column shaft and carefully lower the crossmember using the bolts.

12. On Sedan models equipped with automatic transmission, remove the bellhousing inspection plate with the TDC. Do not alter the TDC sensor position.

13. On Station Wagon models equipped with automatic transmission, remove the TDC sensor attaching bolts and the TDC sensor.

14. If equipped with a manual transmission, remove the bellhousing inspection plate with the TDC sensor. Do not alter the TDC sensor position. Lock ring gear using clamp .0144B or equivalent. Remove the 4 converter attaching bolts. Remove the ring gear locking clamp and lock converter using tool .0318 or equivalent.

15. On all models, disconnect the exhaust system.

16. Install engine lifting tool .0102X or equivalent. Remove the 4 upper bellhousing attaching bolts.

17. Remove the right and left engine mount bolts from the crossmember. Lift the engine carefully until the transmission contacts the floorboard.

18. Support the trransmission using tool .0125 or its equivalent and remove the 2 lower bellhousing attaching bolts.

19. Remove the engine.

To install:

20. Install the engine into the vehicle. Torque the following bolts:

    a. Engine-to-transmission—37 ft. lbs.

    b. Engine-to-crossmember—26 ft. lbs.

    c. Crossmember-to-body—31 ft. lbs.

    d. Steering column clamp—19 ft. lbs.

    e. Oil cooler lines on radiator—20 ft. lbs.

21. Remove the torque converter retaining clamp. Install the converter attaching bolts and torque to 44 ft. lbs.

22. Install the TDC sensor.

24. Connect all electrical connectors and vacuum lines that were disconnected during removal.

25. Install the power steering pump and torque bolts to 24 ft. lbs.

26. Install air conditioning compressor and torque bolts to 22 ft. lbs.

27. Refill the cooling system and check engine oil. Check transmission fluid level and the power steering fluid level.

28. Connect the negative battery cable and install the hood. Start the engine and check for leaks.

2.8L ENGINE

1. Disconnect the negative battery cable.

2. Scribe alignment marks on the hood and hood flanges, then remove the hood.

3. Drain the engine oil and the cooling system.

4. Remove the battery, expansion jar and its bracket.

5. Disconnect the ground cable from the cylinder head and disconnect the electrical connectors from the power supply cables.

6. Remove the power steering reservoir attaching bolts and position aside. It is not necessary to disconnect the power steering lines.

7. If equipped with manual transmission, disconnect the oil cooler lines from the radiator.

8. Remove the fan, fan shroud, radiator upper/lower hoses, air filter and air flow sensor assembly.

9. Remove the air conditioning compressor attaching bolts and position compressor aside. It is not necessary to disconnect the lines from the compressor.

10. Disconnect the harness electrical connectors.

11. Remove the idle electronic regulation electrovalve, located on the right bank valve cover.

12. Remove the air intake pre-heat system assembly.

13. Remove the power steering pump attaching bolts and position pump aside. It is not necessary to disconnect the power steering lines.

14. Disconnect the accelerator control cable. If equipped with a manual transmission, disconnect the kickdown cable. It is not necessary to disconnect the cruise control cable.

15. Disconnect and tag the fuel feed, injector ramp return and vacuum to the cruise control hoses.

16. Disconnect the climate control coolant hoses, located at the front of the right cylinder head.

17. Disconnect the ignition sensor electrical connector, located at the rear of the left cylinder head.

18. Disconnect the steering column shaft at the coupling. Lower the front crossmember slightly using special bolts .1511c or equivalent.

19. Remove the 2 right header pipe attaching nuts and the 2 starter motor bolts without removing the starter.

20. Remove the left header pipe attaching nuts and the 2 bellhousing inspection plates.

19-19

21. If equipped with a manual transmission, lock the flywheel using tool .0134Q and remove the 4 torque converter attaching bolts. Remove the flywheel tool .0134Q and install clamp .0318 to hold the torque converter in place.

22. Remove the 2 upper transmission-to-engine attaching bolts and the transmission dip stick tube attaching bolt.

23. Remove the 2 engine mount-to-crossmember attaching nuts and using engine lifting tool .0135 ZZ or equivalent, lift engine carefully until the engine contacts the floor pan.

24. Install support brace .0125 and pad 0.0155 under the transmission. Remove the 2 lower transmission attaching bolts and lift engine from vehicle.

To install:

25. Install the engine in the reverse order of the removal procedure, torquing the following bolts:
   a. Engine-to-transmission—37 ft. lbs.
   b. Header pipe—26 ft. lbs.
   c. Engine mount-to-crossmember—26 ft. lbs.
   d. Starter motor—15 ft. lbs.

26. Remove the torque converter clamp .0318 and install flywheel lock tool .0134.

27. Coat the 4 torque converter attaching bolts with Loctite. Install the 4 bolts and torque to 44 ft. lbs.

28. Install the bellhousing inspection plates.

29. Install the front crossmember and torque mounting bolts to 31 ft. lbs.

30. Connect the steering column shaft to the coupling and torque bolt to 18 ft. lbs.

31. Connect all the body harness electrical connectors.

32. Connect the heater hoses to the front of the right cylinder head and to the rear of the left cylinder head.

33. Connect the ignition sensor electrical connector.

34. Connect the fuel supply, fuel return and the vacuum to cruise control hoses.

35. Connect the accelerator cable to the center groove of the throttle drum.

36. Connect the kickdown cable onto the lower groove of the throttle drum, if equipped.

37. Install the air conditioning compressor and torque mounting bolts to 18 ft. lbs.

38. Install the power steering pump and its reservoir.

39. Install the radiator, fan shroud, fan and the remaining engine accessories.

40. Refill engine and cooling system.

41. Install battery and connect the negative cable.

42. Install the hood. Start engine and check for leaks.

Cylinder Head

Removal and Installation

1.9L ENGINE EXCEPT DOHC ENGINE

1. Disconnect the negative battery cable.
2. Drain cooling system.
3. Remove the air filter and air flow sensor assembly.
4. Remove timing belt.
5. Remove the lower engine mount nut and through bolt.
6. Disconnect the front header pipe from the exhaust manifold.
7. Remove the injector distribution pipe attaching bolts and position aside.
8. Disconnect and tag all electrical connectors, vacuum lines and cables that may interfere with the cylinder head removal.
9. Remove the dipstick tube attaching bolt and position dipstick tube aside.
10. Remove the intake manifold attaching nuts and bolts from the engine block and the bellhousing.
11. Remove the upper right engine mount nut and the camshaft cover.
12. Using a suitable lifting device, lift engine slightly and re-

move the 2 remaining engine mount bolts.

13. Loosen the cylinder head attaching bolts in sequential order. Remove the cylinder head bolts and the cylinder head.

To install:

14. Install the cylinder head and a new gasket onto the engine block.

15. Coat the cylinder head bolts with Molykote G Rapid Plus grease No. 9732.05 and install bolts.

16. Pre-torque bolts, in sequential order, to 44 ft. lbs., then loosen bolts completely. Retorque bolts, in sequential order, to 15 ft. lbs. Using Angle Torque tool J-36384, torque bolts in sequential order an additional 300 degrees.

17. Install timing belt.

18. Raise engine slightly and install the 2 engine mount bolts. Torque bolts to 33 ft. lbs.

19. Install the engine mount nut and torque nut to 33 ft. lbs.

20. Reverse the removal procedure to continue installation. Bleed the cooling system and check engine oil level. Adjust valves. Start engine and check for leaks.

1.9L DOHC ENGINE

1. Disconnect the battery cables and remove the battery and tray.
2. Drain cooling system and remove the air filter/air flow sensor assembly.
3. Remove the upper timing belt guard and the timing belt.
4. Disconnect and tag all electrical connectors, vacuum lines and cables that may interfere with the cylinder head removal.
5. Remove the ignition coil attaching bolt and position coil aside.
6. Remove the intake manifold bracket bolt and the oil dipstick nut.
7. Remove the intake manifold attaching nuts and bolts. Separate the manifold from the cylinder head. Place a piece of cardboard against the radiator.
8. Disconnect any cables or electrical connectors that may interfere with manifold removal and remove the intake manifold.
9. Disconnect the exhaust pipe. Remove the cam cover attaching bolts and the cam cover with its gasket.
10. Remove timing belt.
11. Remove the cylinder head bolts in sequential order.
12. Move the timing belt cover away from the water pump.
13. Remove the oil pipe and the cylinder head.

To install:

14. Install the cylinder head onto the engine using a new gasket. Coat head bolts with Molykote grease.

15. Pretorque bolts, in sequential order, to 44 ft. lbs. Loosen bolts, then torque bolts to 15 ft. lbs. and using an Angle Torque wrench, turn bolts an additional 300 degrees.

16. Install timing belt.

17. Install intake manifold with new gasket, oil pipe and cam cover with gasket.

18. Connect all cables, connectors and lines that were disconnected during removal.

19. Fill and bleed cooling system. Start engine and check for leaks.

2.1L ENGINE

1. Disconnect the negative battery cable.
2. Riase and safely support the vehicle.
3. Drain the cooling system.
4. Disconnect the Lambda sensor electrical connector. Remove the front exhaust pipe attaching bolts and disconnect the front exhaust header pipe from the manifold.
5. Remove intercooler, if equipped.
6. Remove the 3 lower turbocharger attaching bolts.
7. Remove the air conditioning compressor attaching bolts and position compressor aside. It is not necessary to disconnect the compressor lines.
8. Remove the air conditioning compressor mount attaching bolts and remove the mount from the engine.

9. Disconnect the turbocharger lubrication line. Remove the access plug for the hydraulic chain tensioner adjustment.

10. Insert a suitable tool into the access plug hole and push in shaft against its stop. Rotate the shaft to its right. Shaft should then protrude outward.

11. Remove the distributor cap and wires. Disconnect the electrical connectors and vacuum lines to the distributor.

12. Remove the hose from the thermostat housing.

13. Remove the common manifold attaching bolts and move manifold aside.

14. Remove the valve cover attaching bolts and the valve cover.

15. Bring the No. 4 cylinder to TDC on its compression stroke. The TDC notch on the crankshaft pulley should align with the "0" notch on the timing chain housing. The camshaft pulley alignment mark should also align with the mark on the cylinder head.

16. Remove the distributor hold-down bolt and the distributor.

17. Remove the upper timing chain housing attaching bolts and the upper timing chain housing.

18. Remove the camshaft sprocket attaching bolts. Bring the timing chain over the camshaft pinion 1 row at a time. The chain may be turned all around the camshaft pinion; there are no timing reference marks on it.

19. Install timing chain retainers .0934 R and remove the cylinder head from the engine.

To install:

20. Check cylinder head warpage. Warpage must not exceed 0.004 in. (0.10mm).

21. Install a new head gasket onto the engine and a new O-ring seal on the turbocharger inlet flange.

22. Ensure that the TDC notch on the crankshaft pulley is aligned with the "0" notch on the timing chain housing.

23. Install the cylinder head onto the engine.

24. Install the camshaft sprocket. Ensure that the reference mark on the camshaft sprocket aligns with the mark on the cylinder head. Torque the camshaft attaching bolts to 11 ft. lbs.

25. Coat the cylinder head bolts with oil. Pre-torque bolts to 37 ft. lbs., in sequential order. Then, final torque of 62 ft. lbs., in sequential order.

26. Adjust timing chain tension by loosening the tensioner upper bolt and pushing the pad against the chain as far as possible, then tighten the tensioner bolt.

27. Adjust the valves.

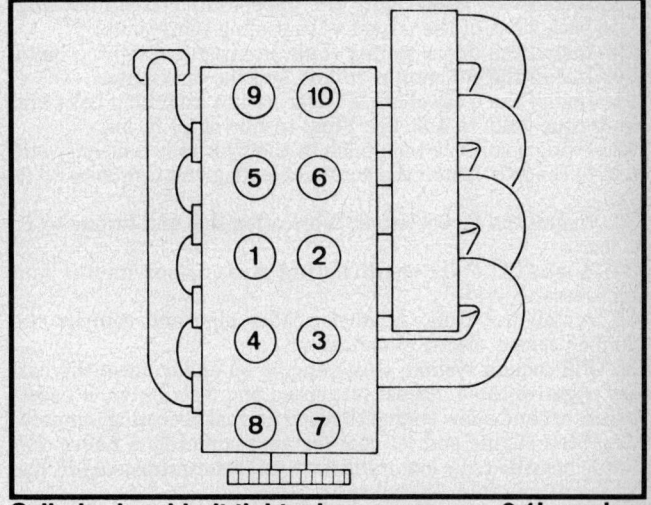
Cylinder head bolt tightening sequence—2.1L engine

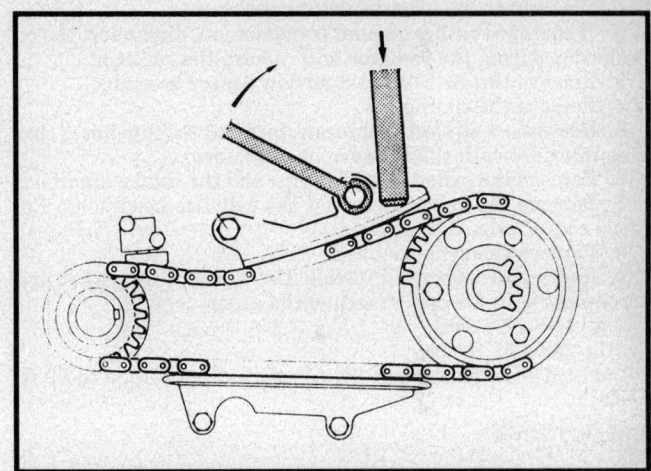
Adjusting timing chain tension—2.1L engine

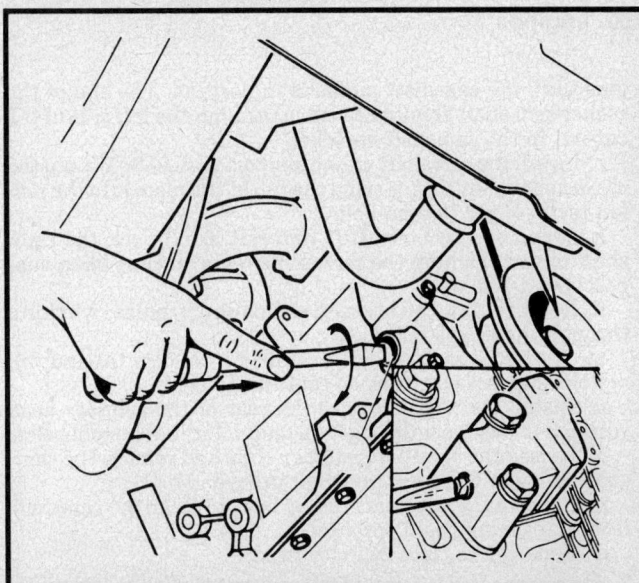
Locking hydraulic chain tensioner—2.1L engine

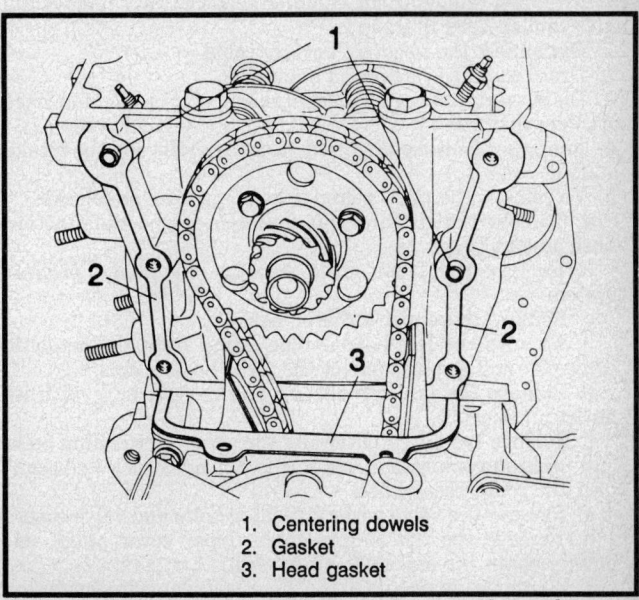
1. Centering dowels
2. Gasket
3. Head gasket

Checking centering dowels position—2.1L engine

28. Install new gasket onto the upper timing chain housing. Coat both sides of the gasket with sealing compound.

29. Install the upper timing chain housing and tighten bolts.

30. Install the common manifold and the distributor.

31. Install the turbocharger lower mount attaching bolts and pre-torque bolts to 4 ft. lbs. Final torque of 26 ft. lbs.

32. Using a suitable tool, push in the hydraulic tensioner and turn to the left. Install the access hole plug and torque to 26 ft. lbs.

33. Install the turbocharger lubrication line and torque to 19 ft. lbs.

34. Install the air conditioning compressor mount and compressor.

35. Install the front exhaust header pipe and connect the Lambda sensor electrical connector.

36. Fill cooling system, check engine oil and connect the battery negative cable. Adjust idle speed and distributor, if necessary. Start and allow engine to reach normal operating temperature. Stop engine and let cool for approximately 6 hours. Retorque head bolts by loosening first and retorquing to 62 ft. lbs. in sequential order. Install valve cover.

2.2L ENGINE

1. Disconnect the negative battery cable.

2. If equipped with a manual transmission, disconnect the oil cooler lines from the radiator and remove the radiator.

3. Remove the air filter and airflow sensor assembly.

4. Remove the timing belt.

5. Disconnect all electrical connectors and vacuum hoses that may interfere with the cylinder head removal.

6. Remove the exhaust header pipe and the intake manifold.

7. Remove the valve cover and the cylinder head bolts. Remove rocker arm, if necessary.

8. Remove the cylinder head.

9. Reverse procedure to install. Use a new head gasket and torque bolts, in 3 steps, in sequential order:
   a. 1st—36 ft. lbs.
   b. 2nd—58 ft. lbs.
   c. 3rd—Loosening bolt by a ¼ turn, then torque to 69 ft. lbs.

2.8L ENGINE

The engine, is equipped with 2 counterweights located at each end of the right cylinder head. The counterweights are driven by the camshaft and are timed in relation to the paint marks on the pinions. When removing the cylinder heads, always remove the right cylinder head first.

1. Disconnect the negative battery cable.

2. Drain cooling system and engine oil.

3. Disconnect and tag all electrical connectors, vacuum lines and cables that may interfere with the cylinder head(s) removal.

4. Remove the intake manifold attaching bolts and the intake manifold.

5. To remove the right cylinder head, proceed as follows:
   a. Remove the air filter, air flow sensor and the junction hose assembly.
   b. Remove the front grille and the air intake preheat system.
   c. Remove the upper radiator hose.
   d. Remove the left header pipe clamp from the catalytic converter and the disconnect the right header pipe.
   e. Remove the fan, fan shroud and coolant hose with its outlet junction.
   f. Remove the air conditioning compressor attaching bolts and position compressor aside. It is not necessary to disconnect the compressor lines.
   g. Remove the valve cover attaching bolts and valve cover.
   h. Remove the the timing chain upper cover plugs and bolts. Loosen the camshaft pinion bolt.
   i. Rotate the engine until the No. 6 cylinder cylinder rocker arms are in the rocking position. Continue to rotate the en-

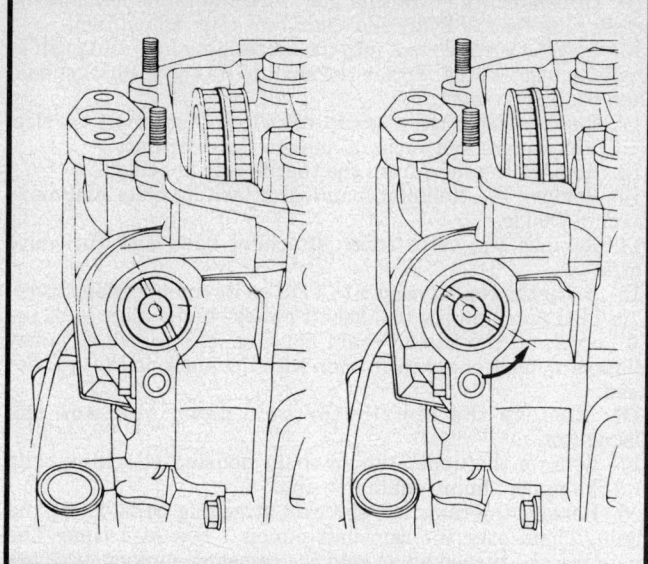

Installing distributor drive—2.1L engine

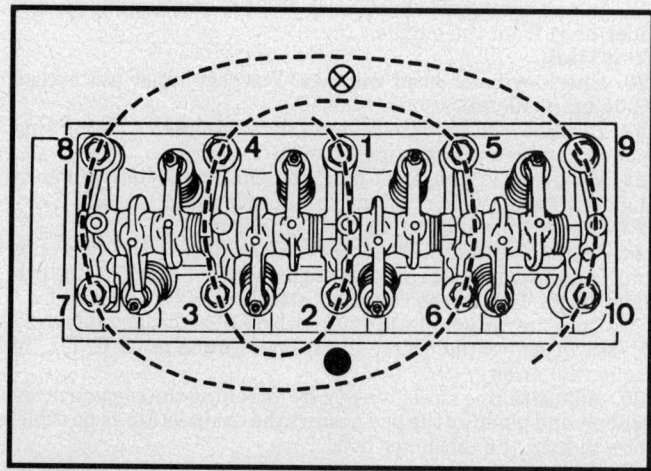

Cylinder head bolt tightening sequence—1.9L and 2.2L engines

gine until the camshaft pinion is in position. The end of the rocker arm shaft should be visible through the left side of the cut-out in the camshaft sprocket.

   j. Install the camshaft pinion support tool .0134 W onto the timing chain housing, placing the tab of the plate into the pinion teeth. Hand tighten bolts.
   k. Using special bolt .0134 and nut .0143, lock the camshaft pinion. Tighten the remaining bolts on the pinion support tool .0134 W.
   l. Remove the counterweight support bolts, working through the access holes.
   m. Using 2 suitable tools, installed into slots (a) and (b), pry the support out from its centering dowel.
   n. Install tool .0134 X onto the rear of the cylinder head with pin (c) between the 2 gear's teeth. Tighten he tool bolts.
   o. Loosen the camshaft retainer bolts and remove the camshaft retainer from the camshaft groove.
   p. Remove the camshaft center bolt, to clear the camshaft from the timing chain sprocket.
   q. Remove the right cylinder head.

6. To remove the left cylinder head, proceed as follows:
   a. Remove battery.

b. Remove the expansion jar and its mounting bracket.

c. Remove the ground bolt from the head and disconnect the left header pipe.

d. Remove the power pump reservoir attaching bolts and position reservoir aside.

e. Remove the valve cover attaching bolts and the valve cover.

f. Rotate the engine clockwise until the valves of the No. 2 cylinder are in its rocking position. Rotate the engine again 1 complete revolution until the camshaft sprocket is in position.

g. Remove the distributor cap, wires and the rotor.

h. Remove the 5 upper timing sprocket cover attaching bolt.

i. Remove the coolant hose and its fitting.

j. Install camshaft sprocket support .0134 N onto the timing chain housing. Install bolts hand tight.

k. Using special bolt .0134 N2 and nut .0143 N3, lock the camshaft. Tighten the sprocket support .0134 N bolts.

l. Remove the cylinder head attaching bolts. Pull bolts up as far as possible, and wrap a rubber band around the bolts to retain them in this position.

m. Loosen the camshaft retainer clamps bolt and pull the clamp away from the camshaft groove.

n. Using a suitable prybar, move the camshaft away from the sprocket.

o. Remove the cylinder head.

To install:

7. Install a 3mm pin in locations (a) and (b).

8. Install the centering dowels on the engine block butted against the pins, to avoid overdriving of the centering dowls.

9. Install a new gaskets onto the block.

10. Install head(s). Tighten the camshaft bolt to seat the camshaft sprocket.

11. Install camshaft retainer and torque bolt to 9.5 ft. lbs.

12. Lubricate the head bolts with oil and install bolts into cylinder head. Pretorque bolts, in sequential order, to 44 ft. lbs. Then, completely loosen 1 bolt at a time and retorque bolts, in sequential order, to 15 ft. lbs. Using a suitable angle torque wrench, torque bolts, in sequential order, an additional 105 degrees.

13. To complete installation on the right cylinder head, proceed as follows:

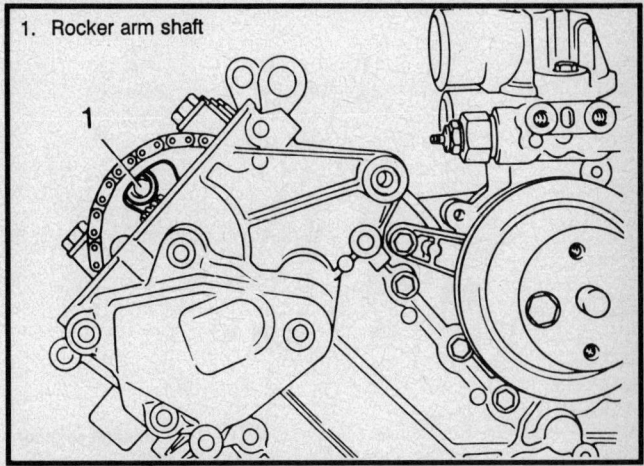

1. Rocker arm shaft

Removing right cylinder head, positioning camshaft pinion—2.8L engine

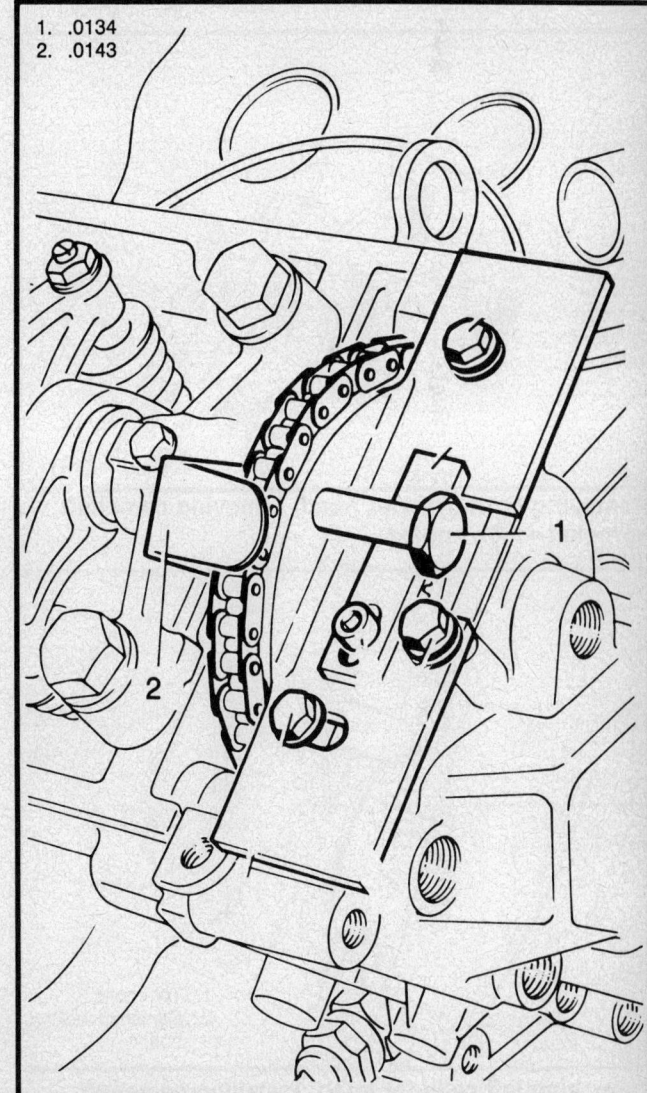

1. .0134
2. .0143

Removing right cylinder head, installing camshaft pinion support—2.8L engine

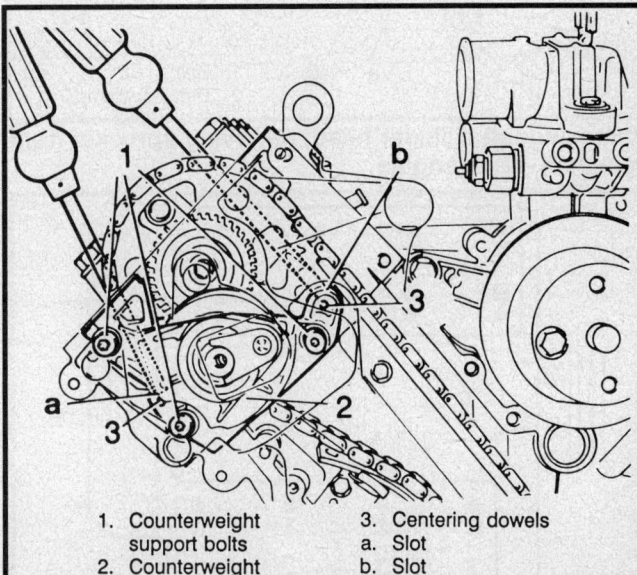

1. Counterweight support bolts
2. Counterweight
3. Centering dowels
a. Slot
b. Slot

Removing right cylinder head, removing counterweight support—2.8L engine

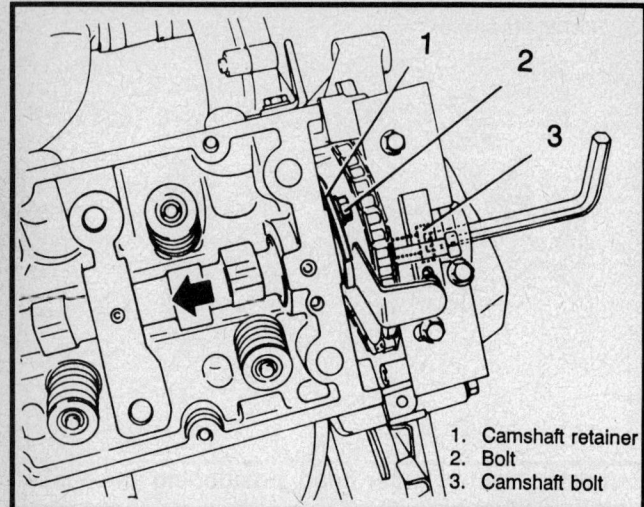

1. Camshaft retainer
2. Bolt
3. Camshaft bolt

Removing right cylinder head, removing camshaft retainer and camshaft sprocket bolt—2.8L engine

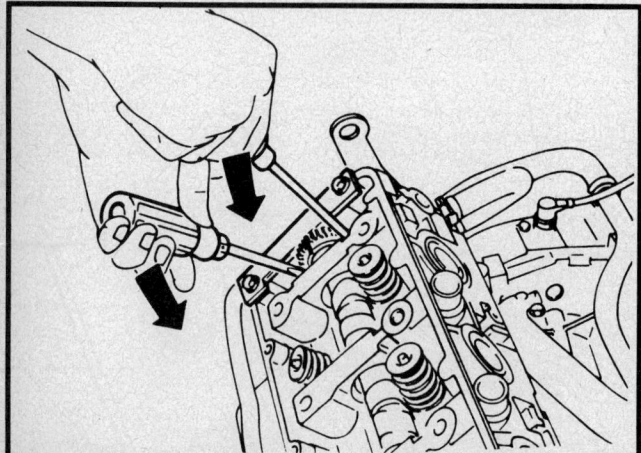

Removing right cylinder head; removing camshaft sprocket—2.8L engine

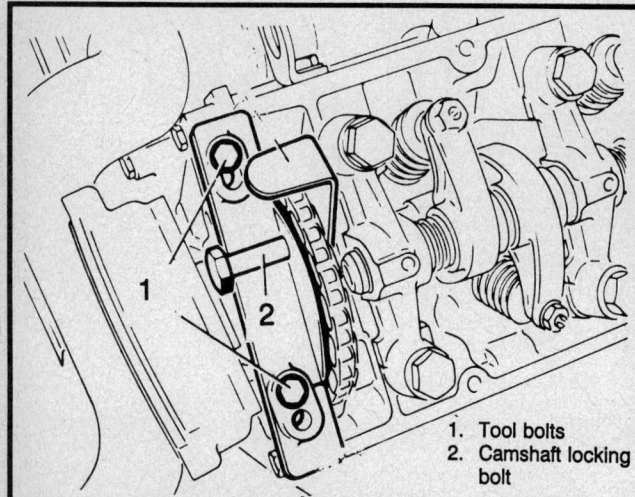

1. Tool bolts
2. Camshaft locking bolt

Removing left cylinder head; installing camshaft sprocket support onto the timing chain housing—2.8L engine

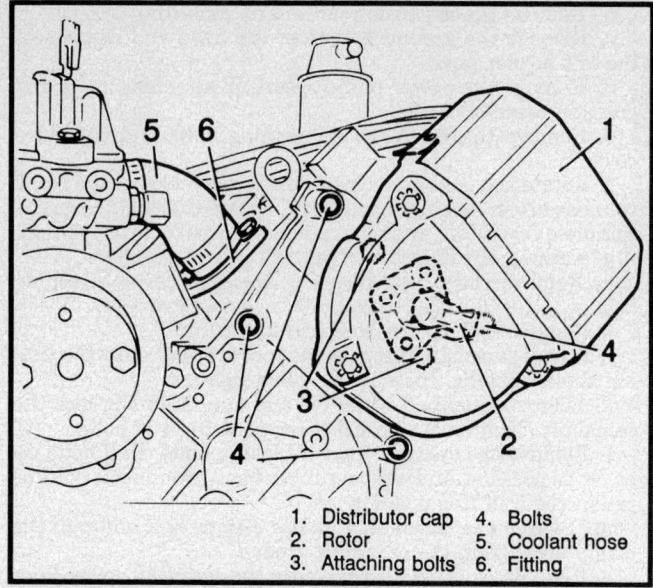

1. Distributor cap
2. Rotor
3. Attaching bolts
4. Bolts
5. Coolant hose
6. Fitting

Removing left cylinder head; removing distributor cap, rotor, cover, coolant hose and fitting—2.8L engine

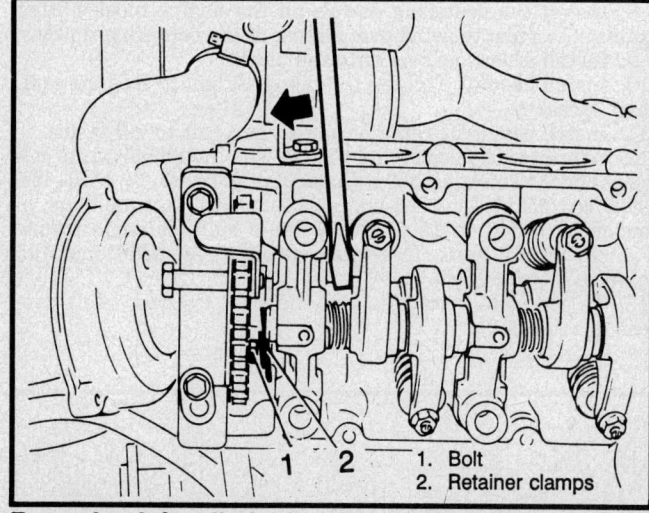

1. Bolt
2. Retainer clamps

Removing left cylinder head; removing sprocket from camshaft—2.8L engine

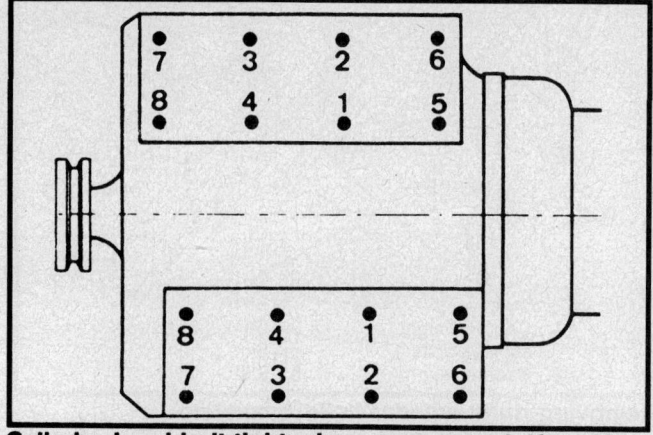

Cylinder head bolt tightening sequence—2.8L engine

a. Install the counterweight support through the access holes. Torque bolts to 9 ft. lbs.

b. Remove the service tools from the front and rear of the cylinder head.

c. Torque the camshaft pinion bolt to 59 ft. lbs.

d. Install the remainig bolts and the plugs into the upper timing chain cover housing. Coat plugs with Loctite before installing.

14. To complete installation of the left cylinder head, proceed as follows:

a. Remove the service tool from the front of the cylinder head.

b. Torque the camshaft pinion bolt to 59 ft. lbs.

c. Install bolts, rotor and distributor cap.

15. Adjust valves. Reinstall the remaining components in the reverse order of the removal procedure.

16. Start engine and run for approximately 12 minutes at 2000 rpm. Allow the engine to cool for 2 hours. In sequential order, torque 1 bolt at a time an additional 45 degrees. Check and adjust valves, if necessary.

Valve Lash

Adjustment

1. Remove the distributor cap and wires.
2. Remove the valve cover.
3. Using a feeler gauge, adjust valves to to the following specifications:

a. 2.1L turbocharged engine—intake valves, 0.008 in. (0.20mm) and exhaust valves to 0.012 in. (0.030mm).

b. 2.2L and 2.8L engines—intake valves, 0.004 in. (0.10mm) and exhaust valves to 0.010 in. (0.25mm).

c. 1.9L except DOHC engine—intake valves, 0.008 in. (0.20mm) and exhaust valves to 0.016 in. (0.40mm). If clearance obtained is incorrect, adjust by calculating the size of the correct shim needed using the shim chart.

Valve adjustment—2.2L engine

Valve adjustment—2.1L engine

Valve clearance specification in mm «J»

● Intake : 0,20
⊗ Exhaust : 0,40
  Tolerance : ± 0,05

Full open valve		To check or adjust			
⊗	1	●	3	⊗	4
⊗	3	●	4	⊗	2
⊗	4	●	2	⊗	1
⊗	2	●	1	⊗	3

Column	A Valve Too Tight	B Clearance Too Loose	C Using Base Shims
Clearance specification	0,20	0,20	0,20
Base shim	–	–	2,25
Clearance measured	0,10	0,35	0,45
Difference	– 0,10	+0,15	+0,25
«e» original shim	2,35	2,95	2,25
Difference	– 0,10	+0,15	+0,25
Shim to be installed	2,25	3,10	2,50
Clearance obtained	0,20	0,20	0,20

Valve adjustment and shim chart—1.9L engine except DOHC engine

LEFT BANK :   ADJUSTMENT ON ONE BANK AT A TIME

VALVES IN ROCKING POSITION		VALVES TO BE ADJUSTED	
● 1	⊗ 1	● 3	⊗ 2
● 2	⊗ 2	● 1	⊗ 3
● 3	⊗ 3	● 2	⊗ 1

Valve adjustment, left bank—2.8L engine

RIGHT BANK :

VALVES IN ROCKING POSITION		VALVES TO BE ADJUSTED	
● 4	⊗ 4	● 6	⊗ 5
● 5	⊗ 5	● 4	⊗ 6
● 6	⊗ 6	● 5	⊗ 4

Valve adjustment, right bank—2.8L engine

Turbocharger

Removal and Installation

1. Disconnect the negative battery cable.
2. Raise and safely support the vehicle.
3. Remove the air filter/air flow sensor assembly and the rubber junction to the turbocharger.
4. Remove the air intake pipe assembly.
5. If equipped with intercooler, drain the cooling system and remove intercooler.
6. Remove the turbocharger cooling lines and the lubrication feed pipe attaching screws.
7. Remove the lubrication feed pipe and clamp, mounted on the exhaust manifold. Position the lubrication feed pipe away from the turbocharger.
8. Cap the oil feed inlet hole and the air outlet on the turbocharger to prevent the entry of dirt or dust.

9. Disconnect the Lambda sensor electrical connector and remove the front exhaust header pipe.
10. Using a 6mm allen wrench, remove the lower turbocharger mount.

NOTE: If removal of the engine mount for additional clearance, ensure that the engine is properly supported. Do not support the engine on the oil pan.

11. Remove the exhaust manifold attaching nuts, then the turbocharger and exhaust manifold assembly.
12. Separate the turbocharger from the exhaust manifold.
To install:
13. Using a new gasket, install the turbocharger onto the exhaust manifold. Torque the 4 nuts to 47 ft. lbs.
14. Install the turbocharger exhaust manifold assembly. Torque the nuts to 18 ft. lbs. Ensure to install the flame rings and the O-ring on the lower turbocharger mount. Do not install the nut that holds the turbocharger lubrication pipe clamp.
15. Install the turbocharger lower mount. Pretorque bolts to 4 ft. lbs. and final torque to 25 ft. lbs.
16. Before installing the lubrication pipe, add the specified oil through the inlet hole, then install the lubrication pipe. Tighten the 2 flange screws and nut on the exhaust manifold for the lubricating pipe clamp.
17. Ensure that the cooling system is filled and bled.
18. Disconnect the connector from the distributor and crank the engine for approximately 30 seconds to prime the turbocharger oil system.
19. Reconnect the distributor connector and start engine. Wait approximately 30 seconds before raising the idle or accelerating.

Timing Belt and Tensioner

Adjustment

1.9L EXCEPT DOHC AND 2.2L ENGINES

1. Loosen the 2 spring tensioner attaching bolts.
2. The belt is then automatically tensioned by the tensioner spring.
3. Torque the spring tensioner atttaching bolts to 18 ft. lbs. on 2.2L and 12 ft. lbs. on 1.9L engine.

Removal and Installation

2.2L ENGINE

1. Disconnect the negative battery cable.
2. Drain the cooling system.
3. Renmove the radiator shroud and the radiator.
4. Remove the alternator, thermostat housing and the auxiliary air device.
5. Remove the crankshaft pulley. If equipped with manual transmission, engage 5th gear and apply the hand brake. If equipped with automatic transmission, remove the bellhousing inspection plate with the TDC sensor. Do not alter the TDC sensor position.
6. Lock the flywheel using clamp .0144B or equivalent.
7. Remove camshaft pulley and cover, then remove the clamp .0144B from the flywheel.
8. Reinstall the pulley bolt and rotate the crankshaft the position the camshaft sprocket so reference or rectangular hole is positioned 45 degrees above horizontal on the right side of the engine.
9. Remove the timing belt tensioner attaching bolts and remove the tensioner and timing belt.
To install:
10. Install the timing belt tensioner. Check that clearance between tensioner support plate and bolt is 0.0039–0.0059 in. If not adjust by using bolt (6). Coat bolt threads with Loctite.
11. Ensure that the crankshaft sprocket is in position (a) and install rocker compressor tool .0144A and tighten nuts until the camshaft rotates freely.

12. Position the intermediate shaft (b) as shown. The distributor rotor finger must be perpendicular to the engine axis, if not, turn the intermediate shaft once or twice.

13. Position the camshaft (c) approximately 45 degrees as shown.

14. Install the timing belt with the belt references aligned with the timing marks on the sprockets. Center belt on the sprockets and the tensioner.

15. Loosen the tensioner bolts. The belt is automatically tensioned by the spring. Torque the tensioner attaching bolts to 19 ft. lbs.

16. Install the timing belt cover.

17. Install the crankshaft pulley, ensuring that the 2 split pins are in position.

18. Reverse removal procedure to install remaining components. Refill cooling system.

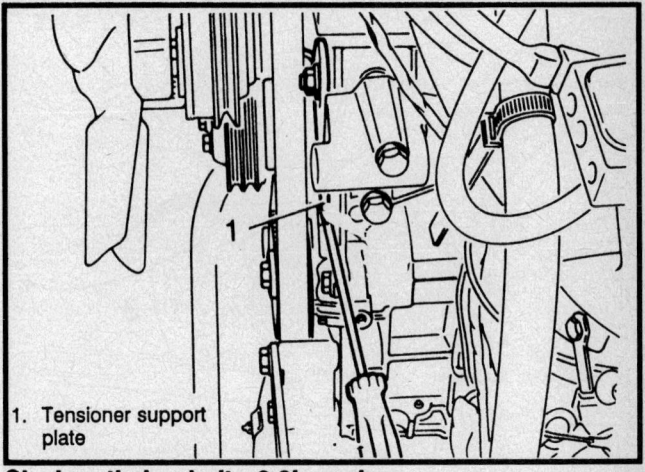

1. Tensioner support plate

Slacken timing belt—2.2L engine

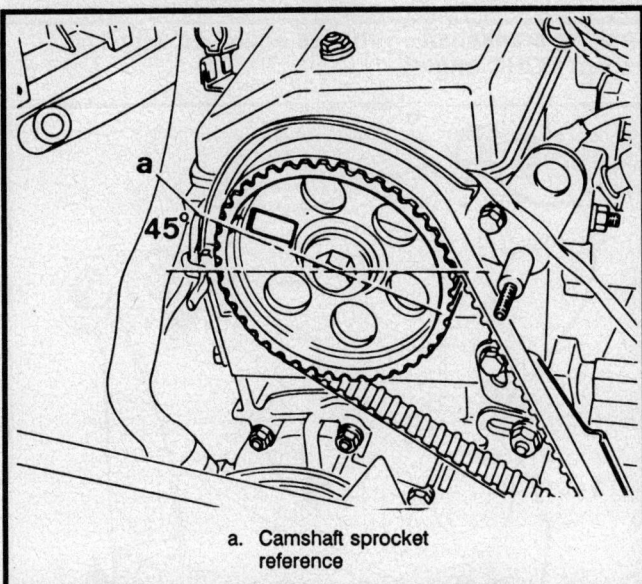

a. Camshaft sprocket reference

Positioning camshaft sprocket—2.2L engine

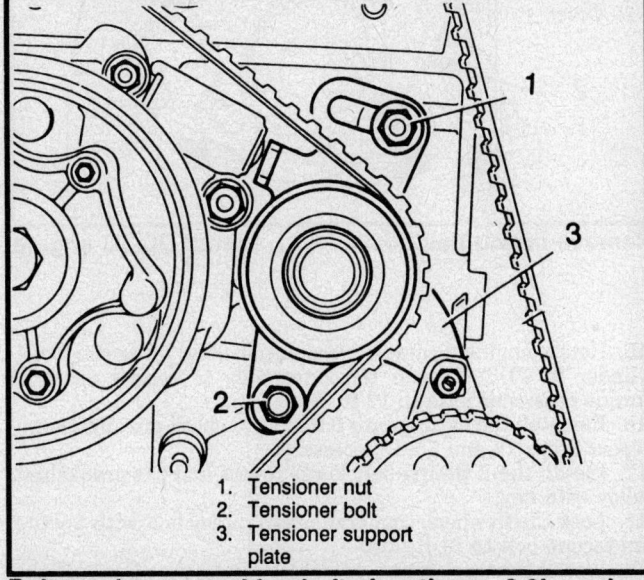

1. Tensioner nut
2. Tensioner bolt
3. Tensioner support plate

Belt tensioner attaching bolts locations—2.2L engine

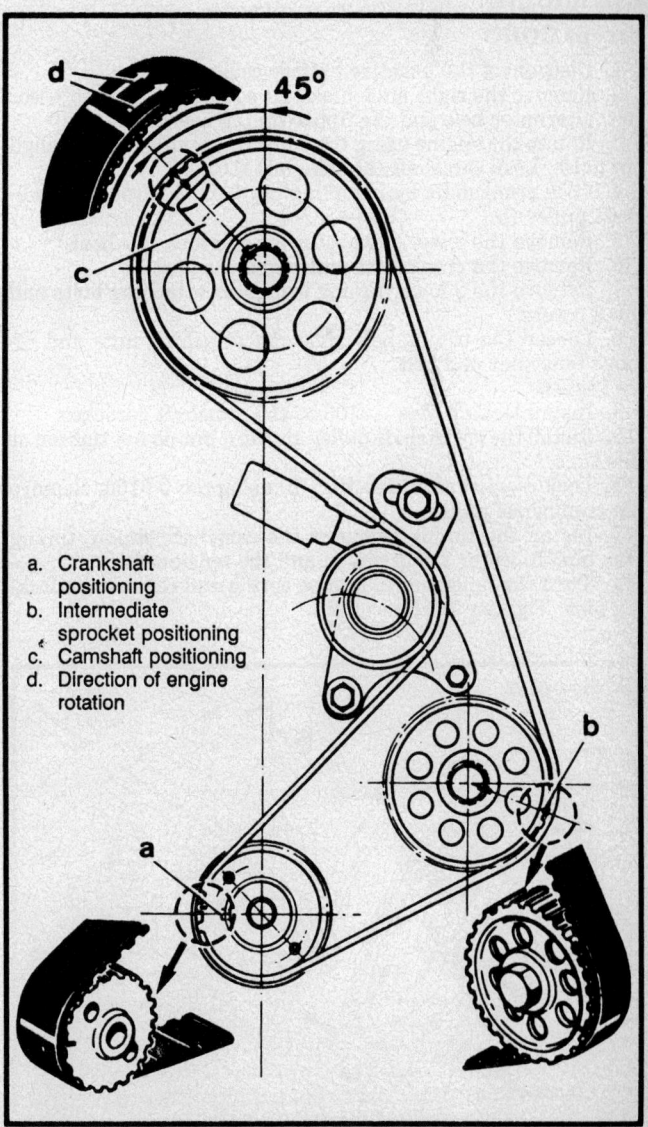

a. Crankshaft positioning
b. Intermediate sprocket positioning
c. Camshaft positioning
d. Direction of engine rotation

Timing belt installation—2.2L engine

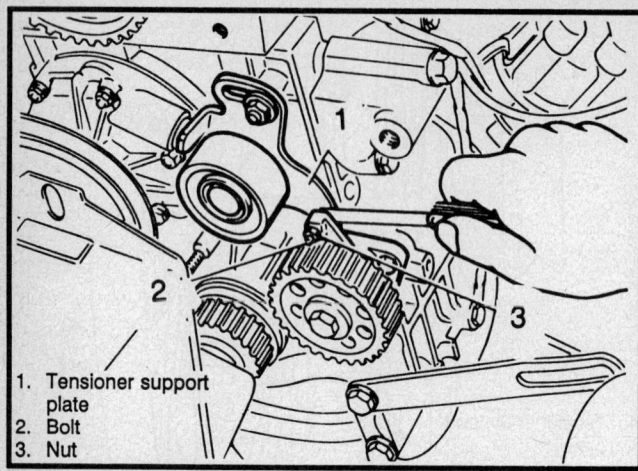

1. Tensioner support plate
2. Bolt
3. Nut

Checking clearance between tensioner support plate—2.2L engine

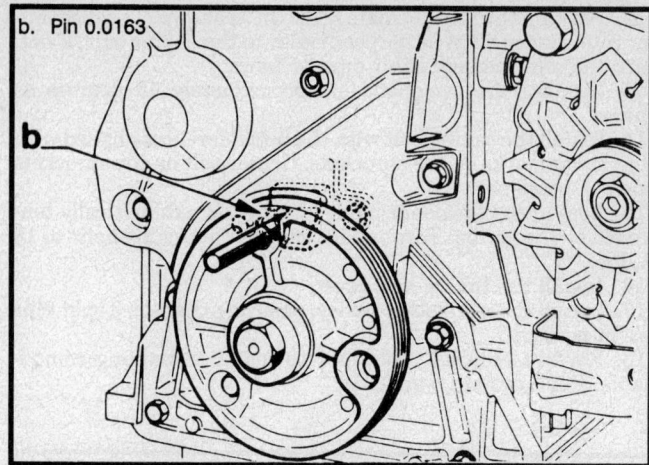

b. Pin 0.0163

Locking crankshaft—vehicles equipped with 1.9L except DOHC engine

1.9L ENGINE

Except DOHC

1. Disconnect the negative battery cable.
2. Remove the right mudshield, air conditioning compressor belt, alternator belt and the upper timing belt cover.
3. Rotate the engine using the crankshaft pulley bolt to align pin holes. Lock camshaft (a) using pin 0.0163.
4. Lock crankshaft by installing pin 0.0163 through crankshaft pulley (b).
5. Remove the lower flywheel cover and lock flywheel.
6. Remove the crankshaft pulley and the pins.
7. Remove the 2 lower timing belt cover attaching bolts and the 2 covers.
8. Loosen the timing belt tensioner attaching nuts and remove tensioner and belt.

To install:

9. Install locking pins 0.0163 to the camshaft sprocket.
10. Install the crankshaft pulley and key, but do not tighten at this time.
11. Lock crankshaft at location (b) using pin 0.0163. Remove the crankshaft pulley.
13. Install the timing belt over the camshaft pinion, timing gear pinion, water pump pinion and the tensioners.
14. Turn the tensioner to release spring and remove the locking pins. Tighten tensioner nuts.

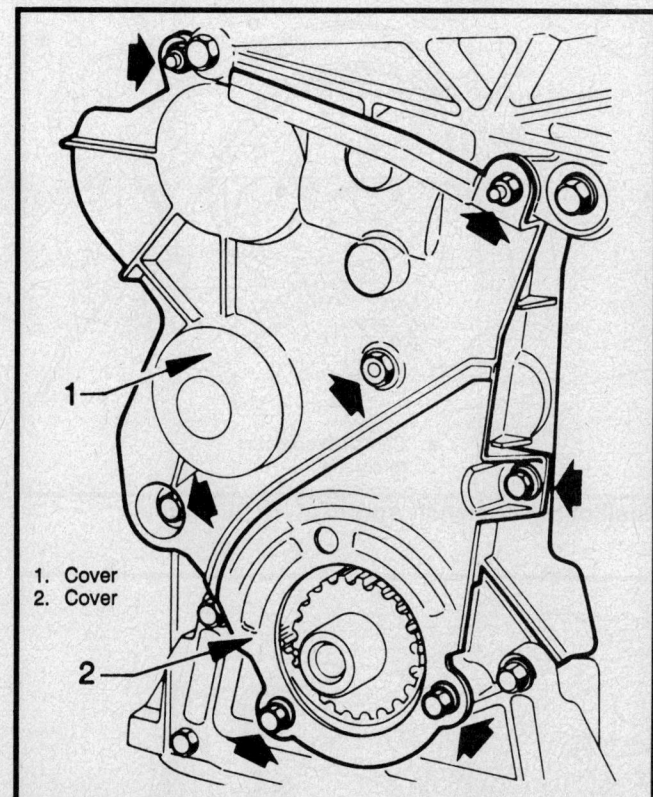

1. Cover
2. Cover

Remove timing belt cover—1.9L except DOHC engine

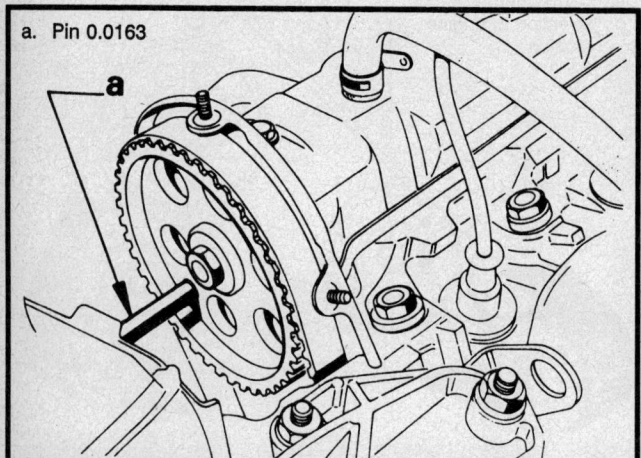

a. Pin 0.0163

Locking camshaft—1.9L except DOHC engine

15. Rotate engine 2 complete revolutions and bring the No. 1 cylinder to TDC. Loosen tensioner nuts to release tension. Torque tensioner nuts to 12 ft. lbs.
16. Reinstall the locking pins 0.0163 and check pin alignment. Repeat Steps 14 and 15, if necessary.
17. Install the 2 timing belt lower covers and the crankshaft pulley with key.
18. Lock the flywheel, coat crankshaft pulley bolt with Loctite and torque bolt to 81 ft. lbs.
19. Install flywheel cover, mudshield and belts. Connect the negative battery cable.

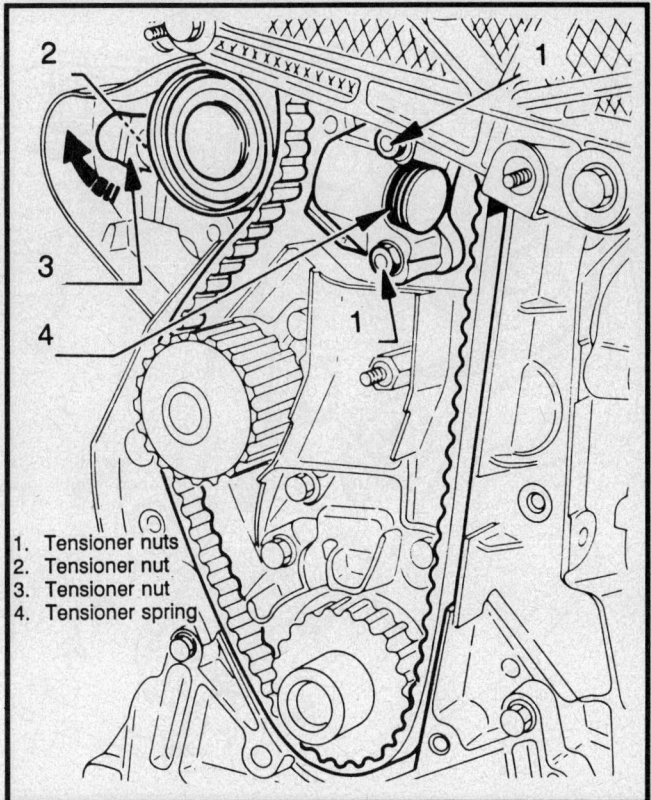

Removing timing belt tensioners—1.9L engine except DOHC engine

1. Tensioner nuts
2. Tensioner nut
3. Tensioner nut
4. Tensioner spring

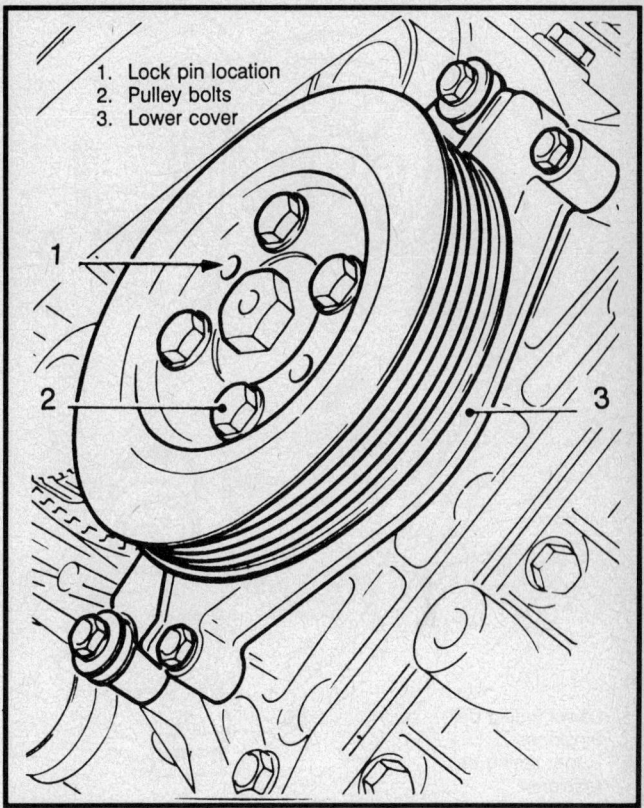

Crankshaft pulley locking pin location—1.9L DOHC engine

1. Lock pin location
2. Pulley bolts
3. Lower cover

DOHC

1. Disconnect the negative battery cable.
2. Raise and safely support the vehicle.
3. Remove the air conditioning compressor attaching bolts and position compressor aside.
4. Remove the alternator belt and the alternator.
5. Support the engine.
6. Remove the upper engine mount bolt and the timing belt cover attaching bolts.
7. Tilt engine as far as possible and remove the upper timing belt cover.
8. Remove the lower flywheel cover and lock flywheel using tool J 36358.
9. Remove the right mudshield and the crankshaft pulley.
10. Remove the lower cover and the flywheel locking tool.
11. Rotate the engine using the crankshaft pulley bolt to bring it to its pin locking position. Lock crankshaft at (b) using pin .0153 G.
12. Lock the camshaft sprockets at location (c) and (d) using pins .0153 M.
13. Remove the tensioner bolts and the tensioners and timing belt from the vehicle.

To install:

14. Install the tensioners. Lock the crankshaft with pin .0153 G.
15. Install the timing belt over the camshaft sprockets, lower tensioner, crankshaft pinion, water pump sprocket and the upper tensioner.
16. Tilt engine as far as possible and position the belt tensioner tool on section (a) of the belt. Lock in position.
17. Rotate the tensioner No. 5 one complete turn, then counterclockwise until 15 SEEM units is reached. Tighten tensioner to 18 ft. lbs.
18. Rotate tensioner No. 7 counterclockwise until 25 SEEM

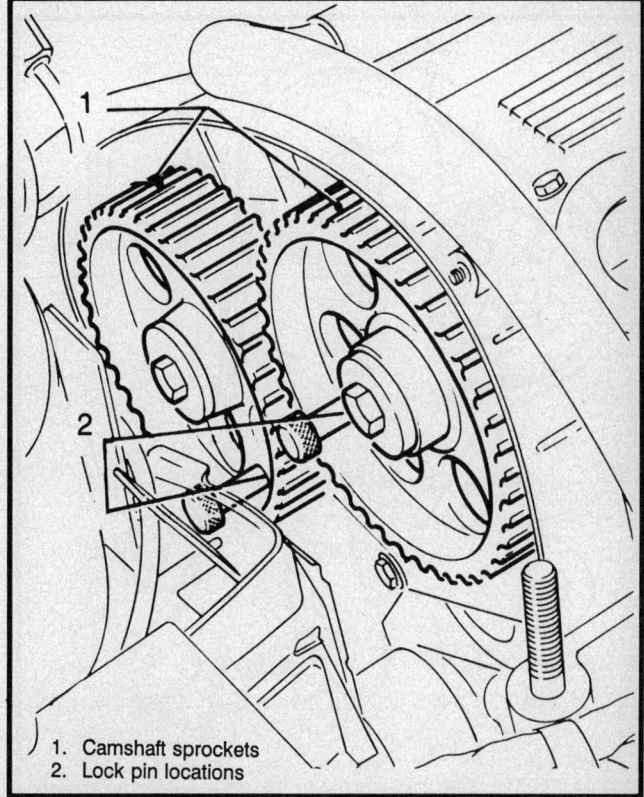

Camshaft sprocket locking pin location—1.9L DOHC engine

1. Camshaft sprockets
2. Lock pin locations

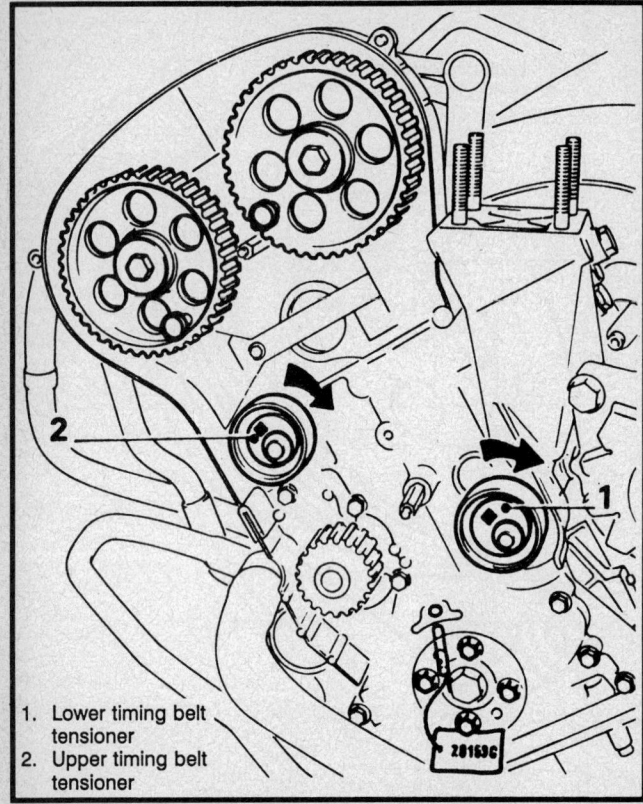

1. Lower timing belt tensioner
2. Upper timing belt tensioner

Timing belt tensioners—1.9L DOHC engine

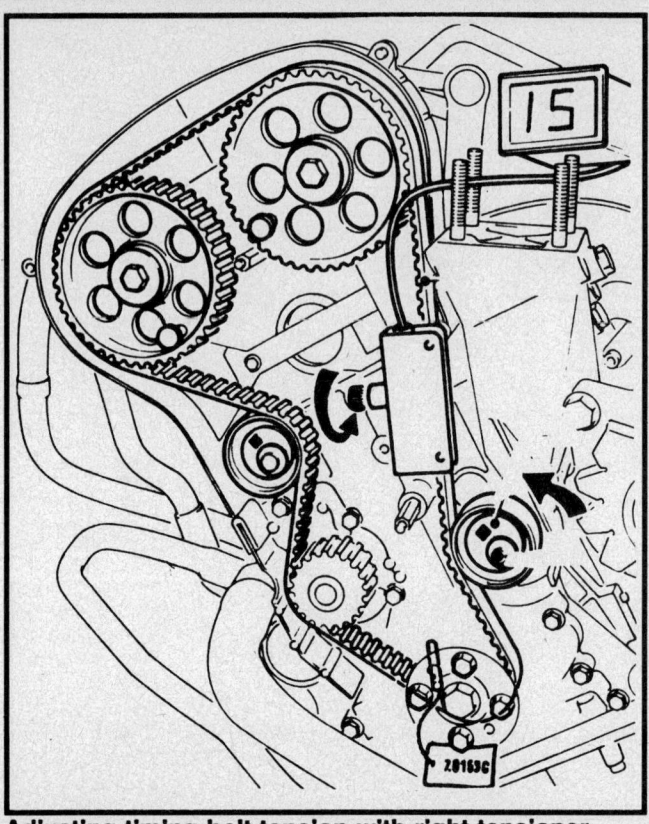

Adjusting timing belt tension with right tensioner—1.9L DOHC engine

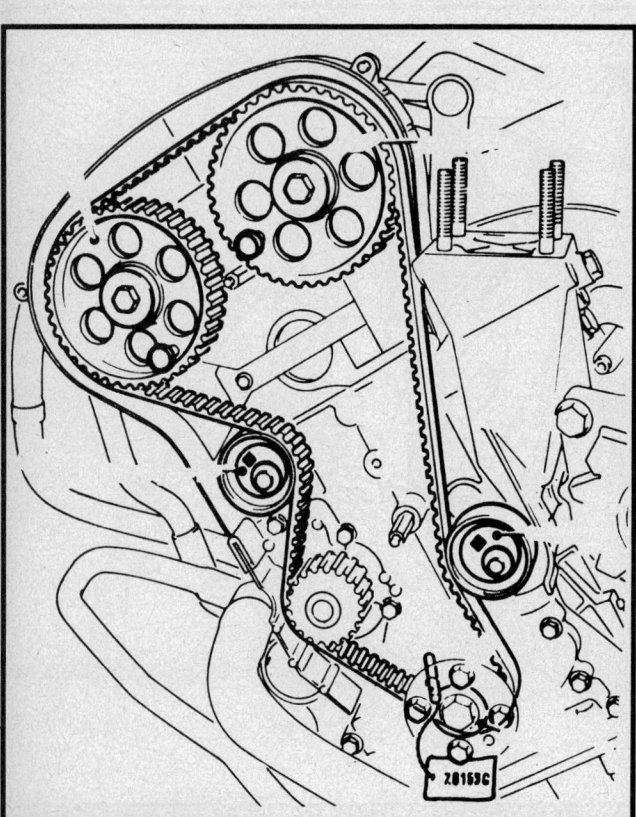

Timing belt installation—1.9L DOHC valve engine

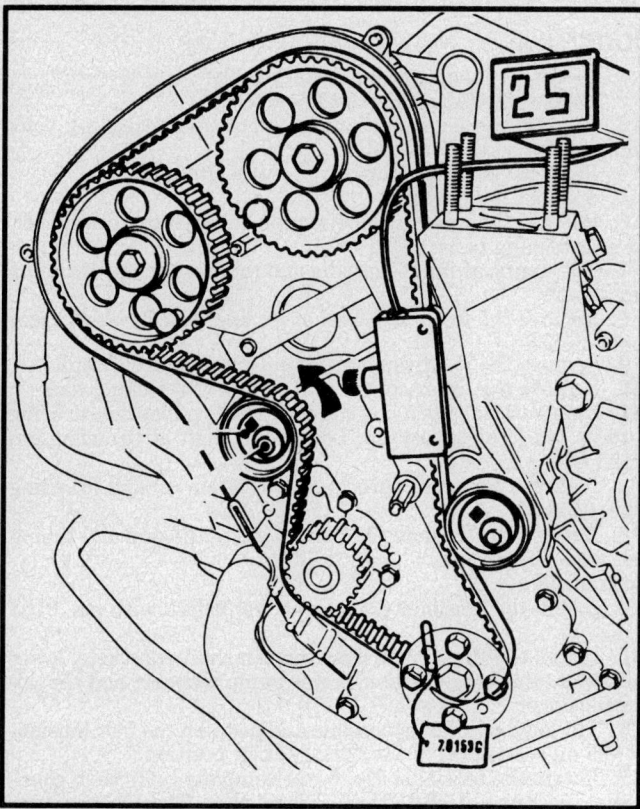

Adjusting timing belt tension with left tensioner—1.9L DOHC engine

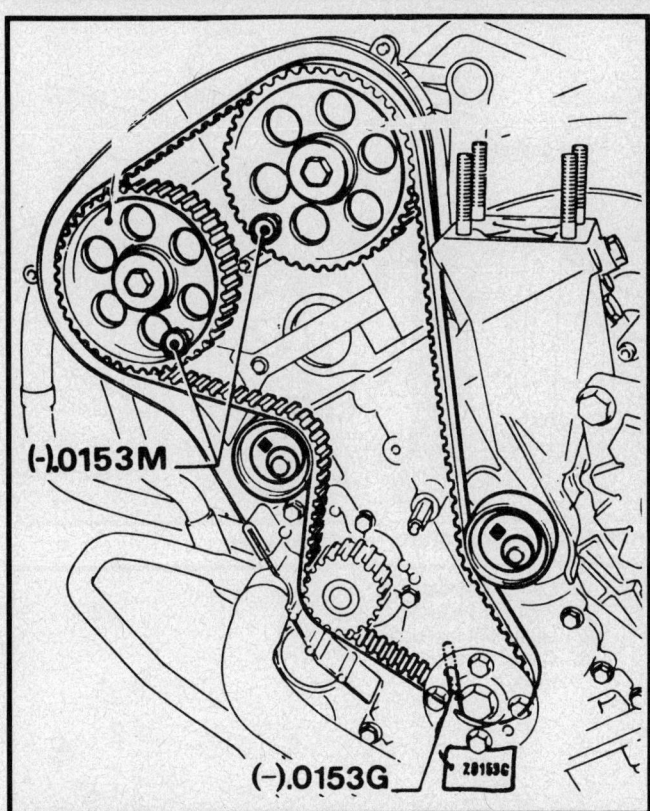

Ensuring that locking pin holes align—1.9L DOHC engine

10. Release timing chain tension by pushing in shaft all the way and turning to the right.
11. Remove the chain tensioner, fixed pads, camshaft sprocket, crankshaft sprocket and the timing chain.
To install:
12. Ensure that the Woodruff® key is in its position and install the crankshaft sprocket with double row of teeth toward the block.
13. Run timing chain through the head gasket and fit to end of camshaft and onto the crankshaft sprocket.
14. Install the camshaft sprocket with the inset facing the camshaft flange. Ensure that the punch mark on the camshaft sprocket is aligned with the mark on the cylinder head.
15. Install chain guide pads. Press adjustable pad against chain to tension the opposite strand of chain. Ensure that alignment marks are still aligned.
16. Install the chain tensioner. Press in shaft and turn counterclockwise to tension the tensioner.
17. Reverse removal procedure to install remaining components. Connect the negative battery cable.

units is obtained. Torque tensioner bolt to 18 ft. lbs.
19. Remove the locking pins and rotate the engine 2 complete revolutions. Lock the crankshaft using pin .0153 G.
20. Position the belt tension tool on the belt. Tool should read 40–50 SEEM units. If not, repeat Steps 17 and 18. Remove the locking pin.
21. Install the lower cover and the crankshaft pulley. Torque the bolts to 18 ft. lbs.
22. Install the upper timing belt cover and engine mount nuts. Torque nuts to 33 ft. lbs.
23. Install the alternator and belt.
24. Install the air conditioning compressor and the mud shield. Connect the negative battery cable.

Timing Chain and Sprockets

Removal and Installation

2.1L TURBOCHARGED ENGINE

1. Disconnect the negative battery cable.
2. Remove the engine, if necessary.
3. Remove the air conditioning compressor mount and the turbocharger assembly.
4. Remove the distributor, alternator, power steering pump and the intake manifold. Disconnect all connectors, cables and vacuum hoses that may interfere with timing chain and sprocket removal.
5. Remove the water pump and crankshaft pulley.
6. Remove valve cover and the upper part of the timing chain cover.
7. Remove oil sending unit and the oil pan.
8. Remove the power steering pump bracket and the timing chain cover.
9. Remove the oil pump and drive chain.

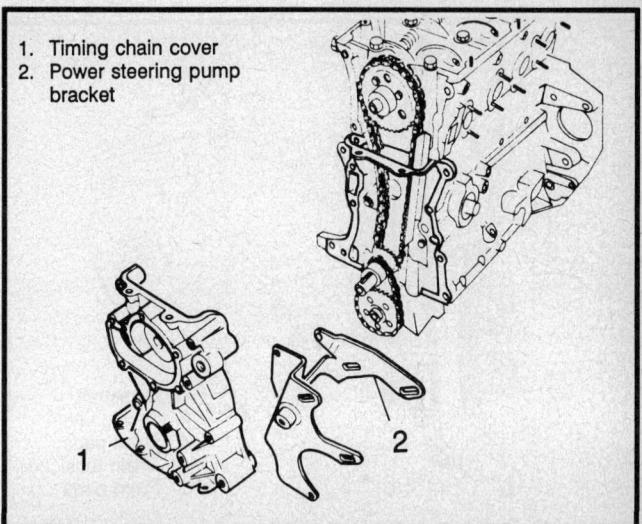

1. Timing chain cover
2. Power steering pump bracket

Removing timing chain cover and power steering pump bracket—2.1L engine

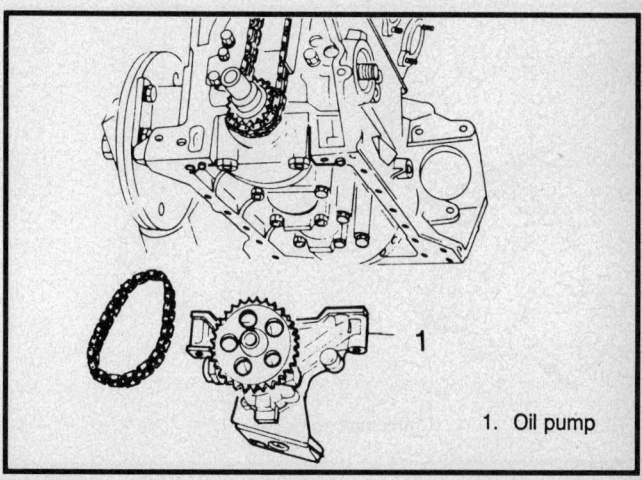

1. Oil pump

Removing oil pump and drive chain—vehicles 2.1L engine

19-31

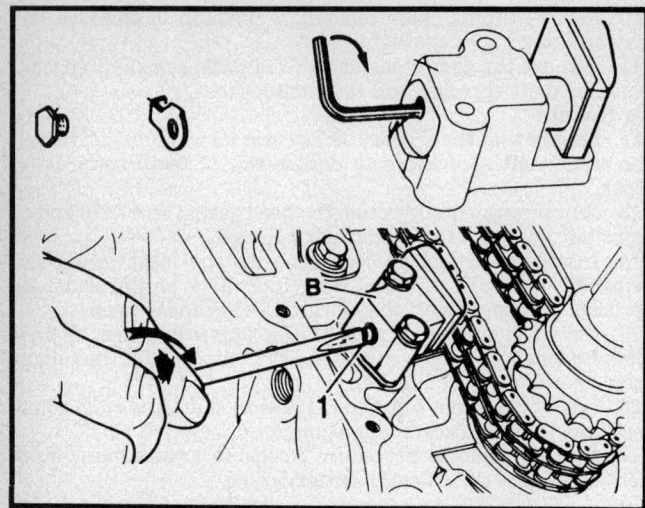

Relieving timing chain tension—2.1L engine

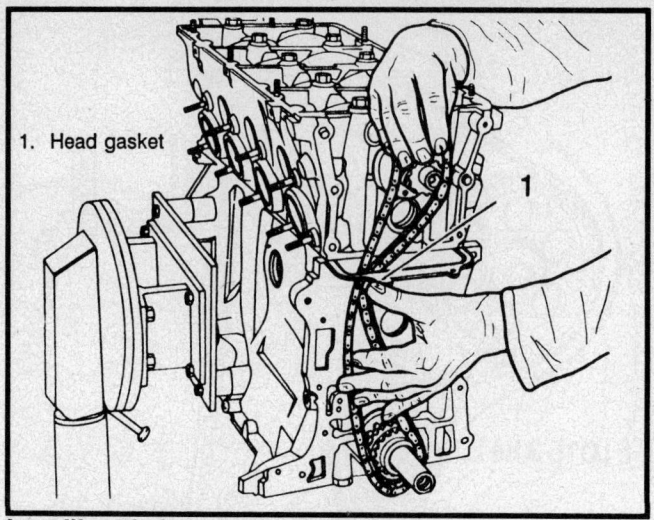

1. Head gasket

Installing timing chain—2.1L engine

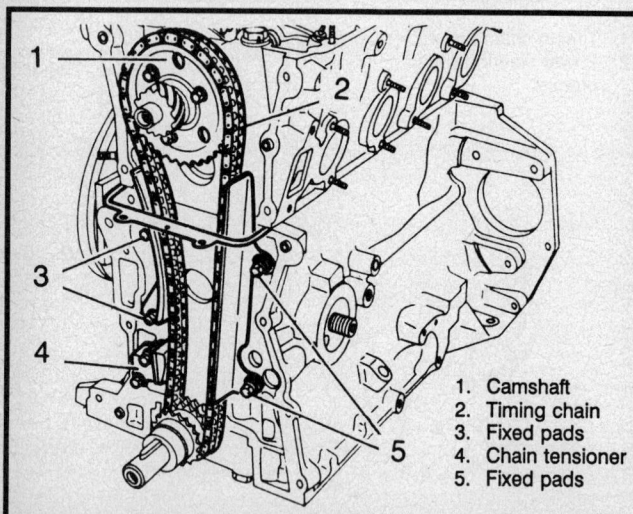

1. Camshaft
2. Timing chain
3. Fixed pads
4. Chain tensioner
5. Fixed pads

Removing chain tensioner, pads camshaft sprocket and timing chain—2.1L engine

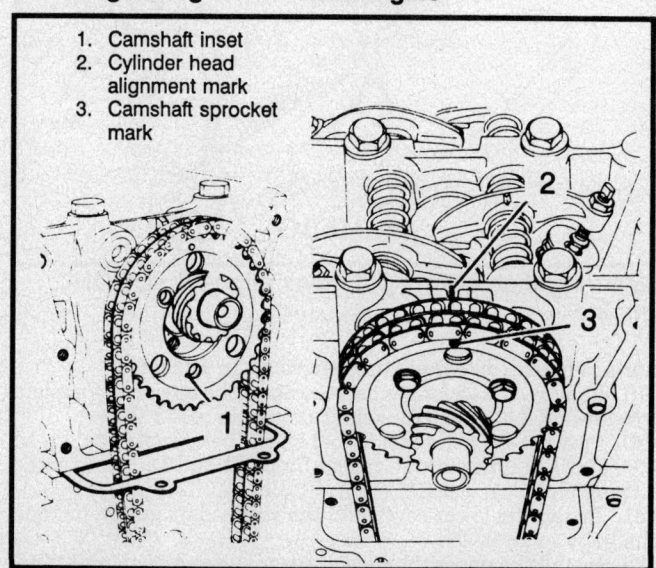

1. Camshaft inset
2. Cylinder head alignment mark
3. Camshaft sprocket mark

Aligning camshaft sprocket with cylinder head—2.1L engine

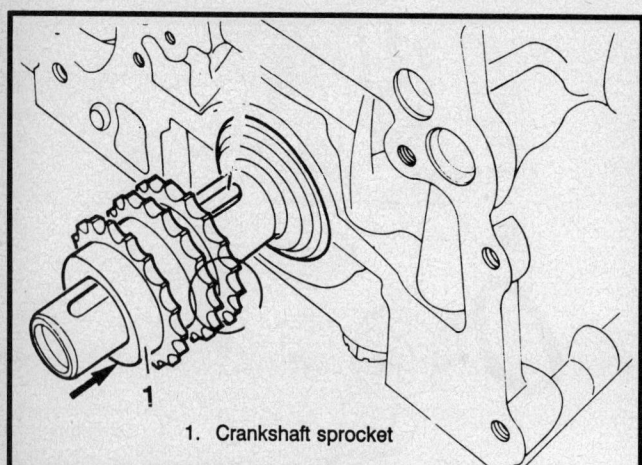

1. Crankshaft sprocket

Crankshaft sprocket removal and installation—2.1L engine

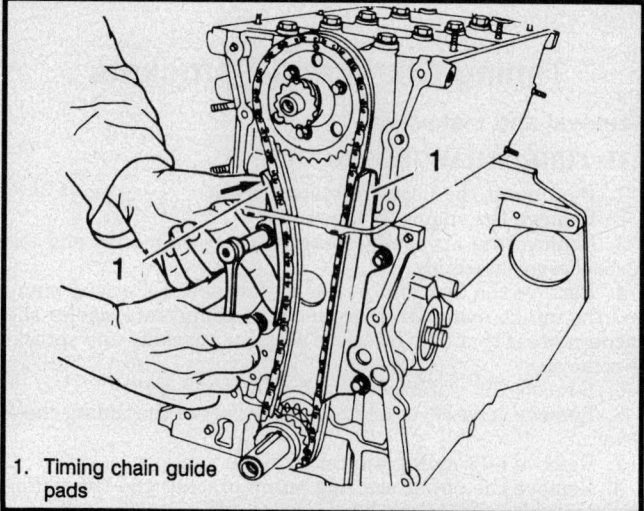

1. Timing chain guide pads

Installing timing chain pads—2.1L engine

Piston and Connecting Rod

Positioning

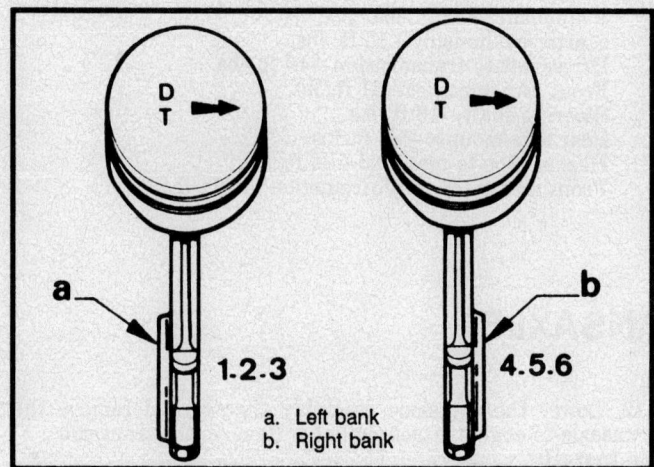

a. Left bank
b. Right bank

Piston and connecting rod—2.8L engine

Piston and connecting rod—1.9L, 2.1L and 2.2L engines

MANUAL TRANSMISSION

For further information, please refer to "Professional Transmission Repair Manual" for additional coverage.

Transmission Assembly

Removal and Installation

505

1. Disconnect the negative battery cable.
2. Scribe alignment marks on the hood and hood hinges and remove the hood.

3. Remove the fan shroud attaching bolts and the fan shroud.
4. Remove the front header pipe attaching bolts and disconnect the Lambda sensor electrical connector.
5. Remove the exhaust system heat shield and the front seat track floor brace attaching bolts.
6. Remove the rear tailpipe bracket attaching bolts.
7. Remove the rear axle mount attaching bolts.
8. Make alignment marks on the steering column shaft and strap and and remove the steering column shaft attaching bolts.
9. Remove 1 crossmember bolt at a time and install service

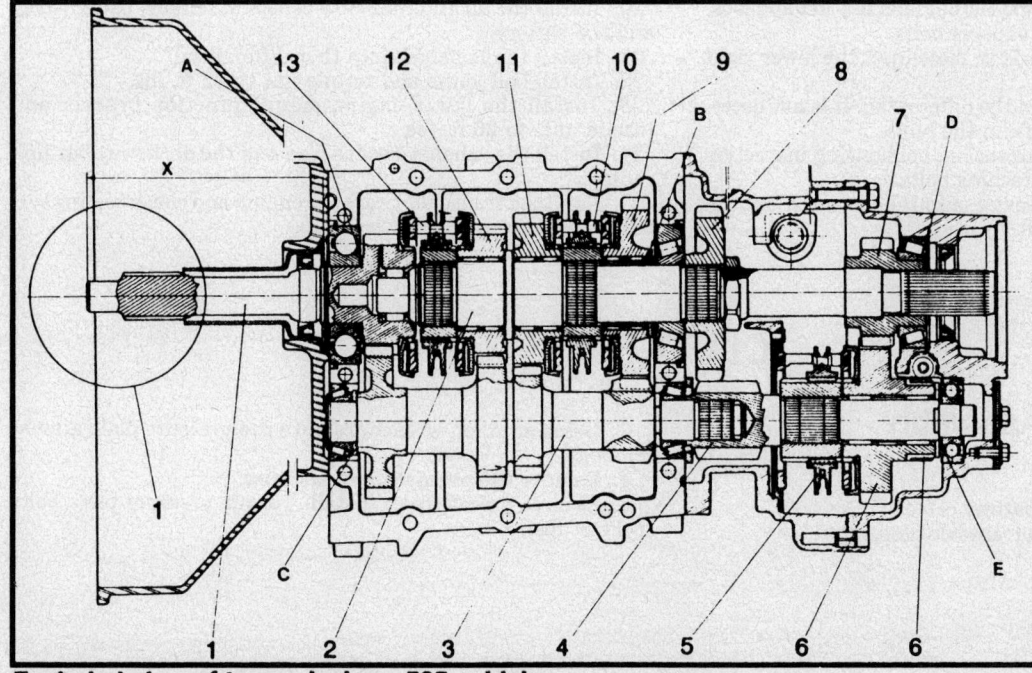

I - Gearbox identification
X = 138 mm
1 - Input shaft
2 - Main shaft
3 - Intermediate shaft
4 - 5 th/reverse intermediate shaft
5 - 5th/reverse synchroniser
6 - 5 th drive gear
6' - Speedometer driving gear
7 - 5th driven gear
8 - Reverse driven gear
9 - 1st driven gear
10 - 1st/2nd synchroniser
11 - 2nd driven gear
12 - 3rd driven gear
13 - 3rd/4th synchroniser
Adjusting shims :
A - 4 th speed synchro cone position
B - 2nd speed synchro cone position
C - Intermediate shaft taper roller bearing pre-load
D - Main shaft taper roller bearing pre-load
E - 5th/reverse intermediate shaft end float

Exploded view of transmission—505 vehicles

bolt 8.1511 C in its place. Remove the remaining bolts on the crossmember.

10. Place a suitable transmission jack under the transmsision and disconnect the driveshaft from the transmission.

11. Remove the attaching nut for the gear selector rod and disconnect the shifting link rod, selector link rod, back-up light switch electrical connector and the speedometer cable.

12. Remove the slave cylinder circlip and the flexible hose bracket.

13. Remove the bellhousing attachiing bolts and the starter motor bolts and remove the transmission.

To install:

14. Installation is the reverse of the removal procedure. Light-ly coat the input shaft splines with Molykotte 321 or its equivalent.

15. Ensure that the throwout bearing is properly installed.

16. Torque the following nuts and bolts:
Bellhousing—41 ft. lbs.
Starter/bellhousing—15 ft. lbs.
Driveshaft-to-transmsision—40 ft. lbs.
Front crossmember—31 ft. lbs.
Steering shaft—13 ft. lbs.
Rear axle mounts—28 ft. lbs.
Header pipe-to-manifold—26 ft. lbs.
Front seat track reinforcements—13 ft. lbs.

MANUAL TRANSAXLE

Transaxle Assembly

Removal and Installation

405

1. Disconnect the cables from the battery and remove the battery and tray.

2. Remove the air filter and air flow sensor assembly.

3. Disconnect all electrical connectors, cables and link rods that may interfere with transaxle removal.

4. Drain transaxle fluid.

5. If equipped with 1.9L DOHC engine, proceed as follows:
   a. Remove the radiator. Rap cardboard around the condenser to protect it from damage.
   b. Remove the power steering pump attaching bolts and position pump aside. It is not necessary to disconnect the hoses.
   c. Remove the power steering pump bracket attaching bolts and the bracket.

6. Remove the RPM sensor and disconnect the anti-sway bar link from the A-frame.

7. Remove the lower engine mount junction bracket and loosen the right halfshaft bearing support bolts.

8. Using tool .0709 or equivalent, disconnect the lower right ball joint.

9. Remove the halfshaft from the differential. It is not necessary to remove the halfshafts from the hubs.

10. Remove the differential extension, bellhousing inspection plate and the starter motor attaching bolts.

11. Install a suitable lifting device onto the transaxle and remove the silent block and shaft.

12. Lower the transaxle assembly slightly and remove the transaxle-to-engine attaching bolts. Remove the transaxle.

To install:

13. Coat the input splines, throwout bearing and throwout bearing forks with Molykote BR2 or equivalent.

14. Install new Nylstop nuts and differential side carrier seals. Pack the seal ridges with grease.

15. Install the transaxle to the engine and lift engine/transaxle assembly to the horizontal position and remove the lifting device.

16. Install the silent block shaft with washer. Coat shaft with Loctite.

17. Install the silent block, starter motor and differential extension.

18. Install the bellhousing inspection plate and connect all electrical connectors, cables and link rods that were disconnect during removal.

19. On models equipped with the 1.9L DOHC engine, proceed as follows:
   a. Install the power steering pump bracket and the pump.
   b. Install the radiator and remove the cardboard from the condenser.

20. Install the air filter/air flow sensor assembly, battery tray and the battery.

21. Install the halfshaft into ther differential.

22. Install ball joints and torque nut to 22 ft. lbs.

23. Install the lower engine mount junction bracket and torque nuts to 26 ft. lbs.

24. Install the exhaust header pipe and the anti-sway bar link rods.

25. Refill the transaxle. Start the engine and check cooling system and the transaxle for leaks.

CLUTCH

Clutch Assembly

Removal and Installation

1. Disconnect the negative battery cable.
2. Remove the transmission/transaxle assembly.
3. Using an Allen wrench, remove the pressure plate attaching bolts.
4. Remove the presure plate and disc.
5. Reverse procedure to install. Torque pressure plate bolts to 11 ft. lbs.

AUTOMATIC TRANSMISSION

For further information, please refer to "Professional Transmission Repair Manual" for additional coverage.

Transmission Assembly

Removal and Installation

505

1. Disconnect the negative battery cable.
2. Remove the air duct between the fuel metering distributor and the throttle body.
3. Remove the upper and lower radiator attaching bolts and the fan shroud. Place a piece of cardboard between the fan and the radiator.
4. Disconnect the kickdown control cable from the throttle body.
5. Disconnect the front exhaust pipe from the transmission bracket, tail pipe from the differential bracket, exhaust pipe from the exhaust manifold and the rear muffler support from the driveshaft bracket.
6. Remove the 2 differential side attaching bolts.
7. Support the driveshaft tube on the rear crossmember.
8. Disconnect the steering coupling flange.
9. Install 1 bolt at each end of the crossmember using service bolt 8.1511 C.
10. Remove the crossmember 2 remaining bolts and lower the crossmember approximately 2 inches by unscrewing the service bolts.
11. Drain transmission and disconnect the cooler lines.
12. Remove the starter attaching bolt and transmission dipstick tube.

13. Remove the bellhousing cover plate attaching bolts and the bellhousing cover plate.
14. Remove the 4 torque converter attaching bolts and lock the flywheel ring gear using lock 8.0144B or 8.0110 J. Secure the torque converter.
15. Place a jack under the transmission and remove the 4 bolts attaching the driveshaft to the transmission.
16. Separate the engine and transmission approximately 1 inch and install reatiner plate 8.0403 SZ.
17. Pull the driveshaft tube and differential assembly rearward, to allow the assembly to rest on the crossmember.
18. Disconnect the shift linkage, transmission switch electrical connector and the speedometer cable.
19. Lower the jack slowly, to tilt the transmission as far down as possible.
20. Using a suitable engine lifting device, raise the front of the engine to pivot it as far rearward, as the engine mount will allow.
21. Remove the bellhousing attaching bolts and the transmission.

To install:

22. Using a transmission jack, install transmission into position.
23. Install tool 8.0315A to hold converter into position.
24. Install the bellhousing bolts, starter and cover plate, dipstick tube and the kickdown cable. Torque the starter bolts to 20 ft. lbs.
25. Install the torque converter attaching bolts and torque bolts to 40 ft. lbs.
26. Remove the converter retainer and install the transmission ventilation grille.

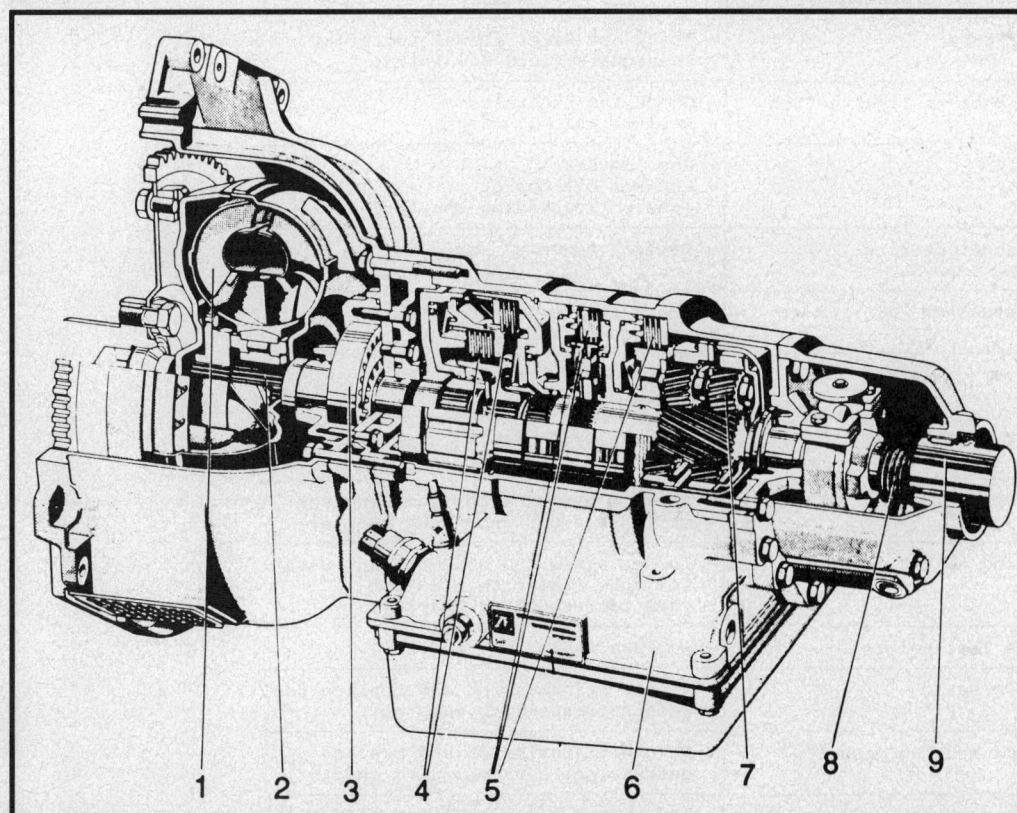

1 - Torque convertor
2 - Input shaft
3 - Oil pump
4 - Clutches (**A** and **B**)
5 - Brakes (**C'**, **C** and **D**)
6 - Hydraulic block
7 - Epicyclic train
8 - Speedometer drive worm
9 - Output shaft

Exploded view of automatic transmission

27. Install tools 8.0144 B or 8.0110 J to lock the flywheel and torque bolts to 21 ft. lbs.
28. Install the driveshaft tube to the transmission and torque bolts to 40 ft. lbs.
29. Install the remaining components by reversing the removal procedure. Refill cooling system and transmission. Start engine and check for leaks.

Shift Linkage Adjustment

1. Install a 0.197 in. (5mm) spacer against the accelerator pedal stop, then depress accelerator pedal against stop in the full throttle position.
2. Open the throttle fully and connect the cable to the throttle lever.
3. Pull lightly on the cable and install a lock pin in position to ensure that the least amount of play between the pin and the manifold.
4. With the throttle in the idle position, tighten the control cable to obtain a maximum of 0.020 in. (0.5mm) play between the sleeve and the cable housing. Lock the cable on the throttle lever.

AUTOMATIC TRANSAXLE

For further information, please refer to "Professional Transmission Repair Manual" for additional coverage.

Transaxle Assembly

Removal and Installation
405
1. Remove the battery and the battery tray.

2. Remove the air filter/air flow sensor assembly and duct.
3. Disconnect and tag all electrical connectors, pipes, hoses and cables from the transaxle.
4. Drain the transaxle and disconnect the anti-sway bar link rods from the lower control arms.
5. Raise and safely support the vehicle and using tool .07094, remove the lower ball joints from the lower control arm.
6. Remove the halfshafts, converter housing, inspection plates, torque converter attaching bolts, dipstick tube nut and the starter motor attaching bolts.

AUTOMATIC TRANSAXLE TROUBLESHOOTING CHART

AREAS OF POSSIBLE LEAKS	REMEDY
Breather tube	- Check the level (level too high) - Inadequate fluid (emulsion)
Neutral/Back-up light switch	- Check the tightness - Replace the "O" ring
Oil cooler	- Replace seals - Replace oil cooler (see corresponding chapter)
Output shaft bearing retaining screws	- Replace seals
Oil sump gasket	- Check sump bolts for tightness - Replace gasket
Side cover gasket	- Check bolts for tightness - Replace gasket
Selector shaft seal	- Replace seal (see corresponding chapter)
Kick-down cable base fitting	- Replace O-ring after removing the cable (see corresponding chapter)
Brake band adjusting screw	- Loosen screw and coat threads with silicone sealer then adjust (see corresponding chapter)
Pressure test points	- Replace seals
Converter seal	- Remove transmission and replace seal (see corresponding chapter)
Converter housing gasket	- Remove transmission and replace gasket (see corresponding chapter)
Torque converter	- Remove transmission and replace torque converter

AUTOMATIC TRANSAXLE TROUBLESHOOTING CHART (CONT.)

For each defect, depending upon the position of the selector lever, proceed by elimination in the order indicated, i.e. 1, then 2, 3, 4....

SYMPTOM

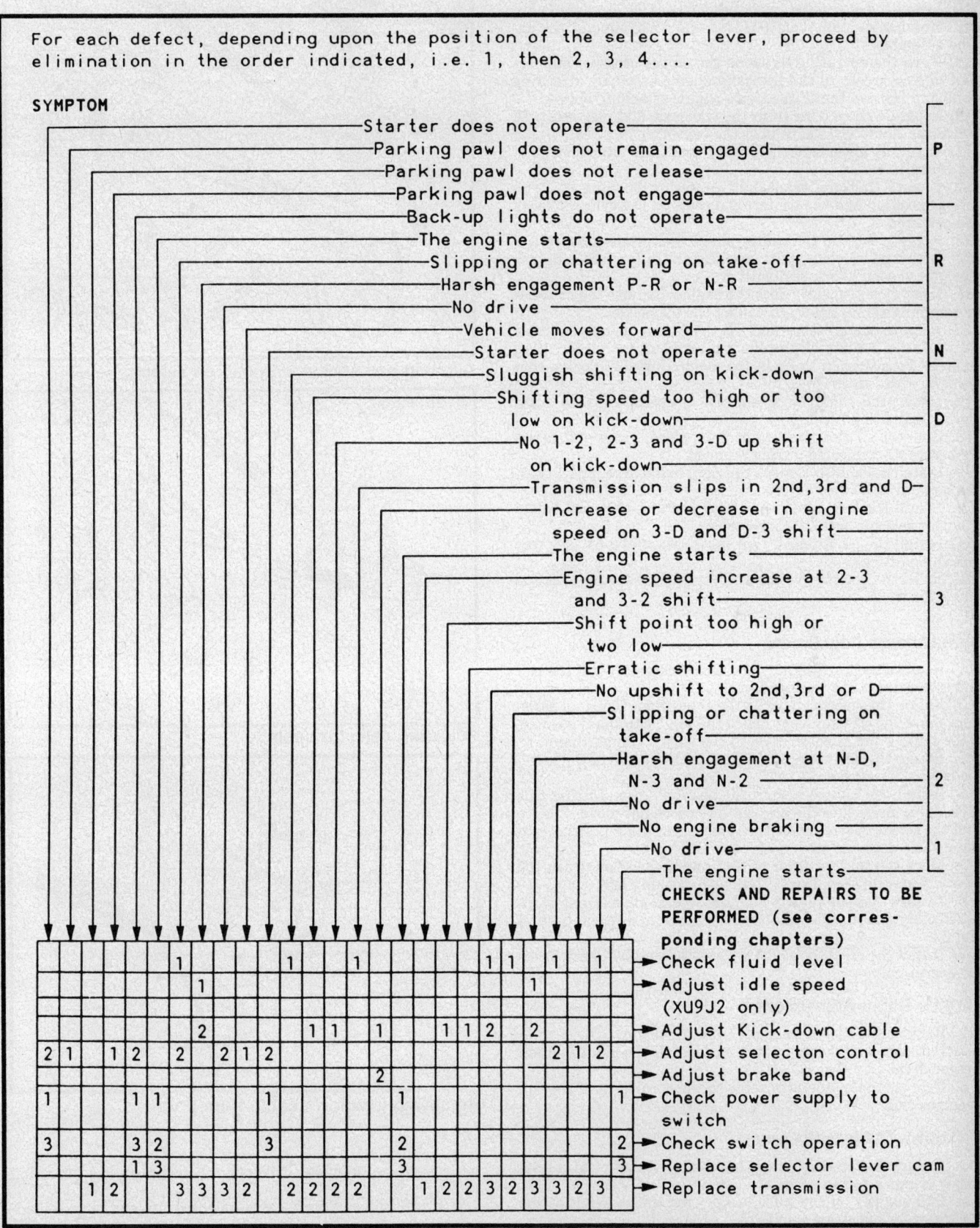

Selector	Symptom
P	Starter does not operate
P	Parking pawl does not remain engaged
P	Parking pawl does not release
P	Parking pawl does not engage
R	Back-up lights do not operate
R	The engine starts
R	Slipping or chattering on take-off
R	Harsh engagement P-R or N-R
R	No drive
N	Vehicle moves forward
N	Starter does not operate
D	Sluggish shifting on kick-down
D	Shifting speed too high or too low on kick-down
D	No 1-2, 2-3 and 3-D up shift on kick-down
D	Transmission slips in 2nd, 3rd and D
D	Increase or decrease in engine speed on 3-D and D-3 shift
D	The engine starts
3	Engine speed increase at 2-3 and 3-2 shift
3	Shift point too high or two low
3	Erratic shifting
3	No upshift to 2nd, 3rd or D
2	Slipping or chattering on take-off
2	Harsh engagement at N-D, N-3 and N-2
2	No drive
1	No engine braking
1	No drive
1	The engine starts

CHECKS AND REPAIRS TO BE PERFORMED (see corresponding chapters)

- ► Check fluid level
- ► Adjust idle speed (XU9J2 only)
- ► Adjust Kick-down cable
- ► Adjust selection control
- ► Adjust brake band
- ► Check power supply to switch
- ► Check switch operation
- ► Replace selector lever cam
- ► Replace transmission

7. Using a suitable lifting device, raise engine slightly and remove the silent block and its shaft.

8. Lower the engine/transaxle assembly as far as possible. Install crossbar support tools .0911 A1 and A2 to support the engine assembly.

9. Turn the operating screw on the on the crossbar support tool to gain access to the transaxle/engine assembly attaching bolts and remove the transaxle-to-engine attaching bolts.

10. Separate the engine from the transaxle and install torque converter clamp 0315A, to hold the converter in place.

11. Carefully lower and remove the transaxle assembly.

To install:

12. Ensure that the crankshaft centering bushing is in its proper position and the centering dowels on the cylinder block are centered.

13. Apply grease on the center pin of the torque converter.

14. Install new Nylstop nuts, washers and differential side carrier grease seals. Pack seal with grease.

15. Install the transaxle onto the engine. Remove the converter retaining clamp before installing the transaxle.

16. Remove the crossbar and tilt the engine using a suitable lifting device and install the silent block shaft with its limiting washer. Torque bolts to 30 ft. lbs. Before installing bolts, coat threads with Loctite.

17. Install the silent block and the transaxle dipstick tube. Torque bolts to 33 ft. lbs.

18. Connect all electrical connectors, pipes, hoses and cables that were disconnected during removal.

19. Install halfshafts. Torque the right halfshaft support bearing bolts to 13 ft. lbs.

20. Install the ball joints, anti-sway bar link rods and adjust the gear selector and kickdown cables.

21. Install the air filter/air flow meter assembly, battery tray and the battery.

22. Refill the cooling system and transaxle. Start engine and check for leaks.

Shift Linkage Adjustment

1. Remove the air filter/air flow sensor assembly and the ball and socket from the selector lever.

2. Rotate the selector lever to the **P** position. Using an assistant, move the selector lever inside the vehicle to the **P** position while pulling the selector cable in the engine compartment.

3. Rotate the ball socket to align it with the ball of the selector lever.

4. Install the ball socket on the selector lever. During this procedure, make sure the selector lever does not move. Ensure that the selector lever inside the vehicle is in the **P** position and the vehicle does not move.

5. Move the selector lever to the Reverse position. Push the lever against its stop. Do not touch the locking bar.

6. Ensure that the vehicle can be moved. If adjustment is unsatisfactory, loosen the ball socket by 1 turn and repeat Steps 4 and 5.

7. Install the air filter/air flow sensor assembly. Check selector operation.

Throttle Cable Adjustment

1. Remove the kickdown cable from the drum.

2. Pull the cable housing stop and install the clip to obtain clearance (a).

3. Depress the accelerator cable so the throttle is in the full open position.

Kickdown Cable Adjustment

1. Ensure that the cable stops are correctly positioned and securely crimped to the cable.

2. Pull slightly on the cable, until a resistance is felt at the begining of the kickdown cable. A 1.5354 in. (39mm) clearance,

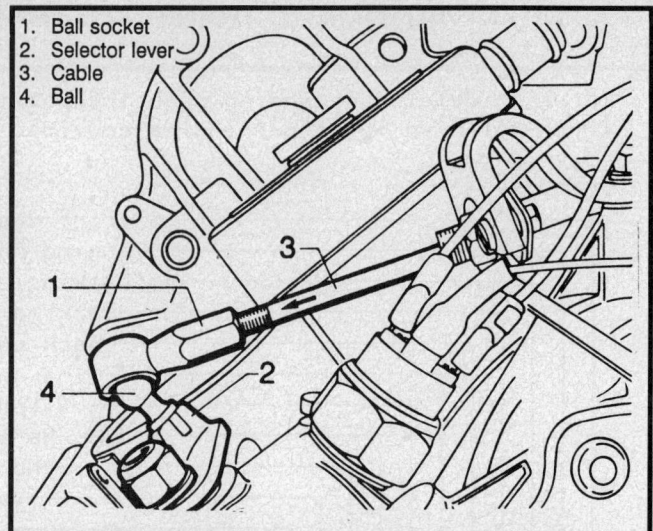

1. Ball socket
2. Selector lever
3. Cable
4. Ball

Aligning ball socket with ball on selector lever

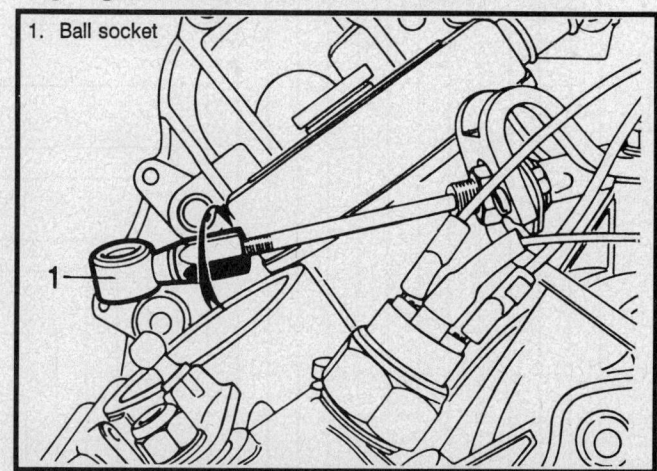

1. Ball socket

Adjusting selector cable

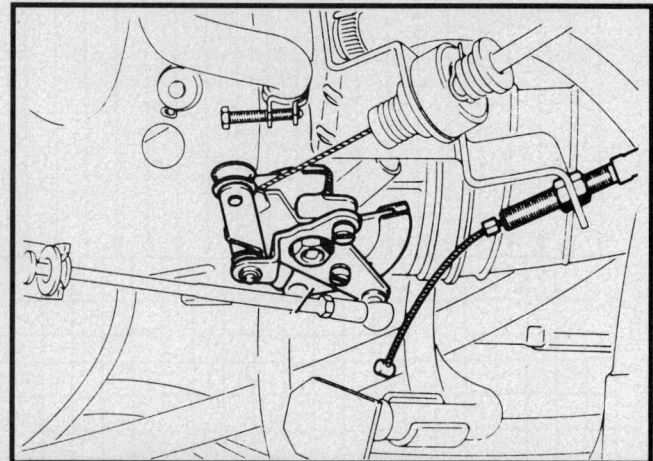

Removing kickdown cable from drum

(x), should be obtained between the stop and the adjusting screw.

3. Install the kickdown cable on the drum and turn the adjusting nuts to obtain a clearance of 0.0196 in. (0.5mm) at (b).

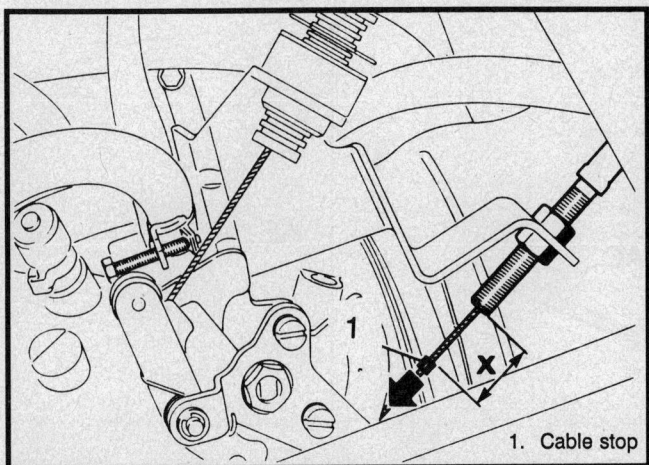

1. Cable stop

Adjusting kickdown cable, positioning cable stops with cable disconnected

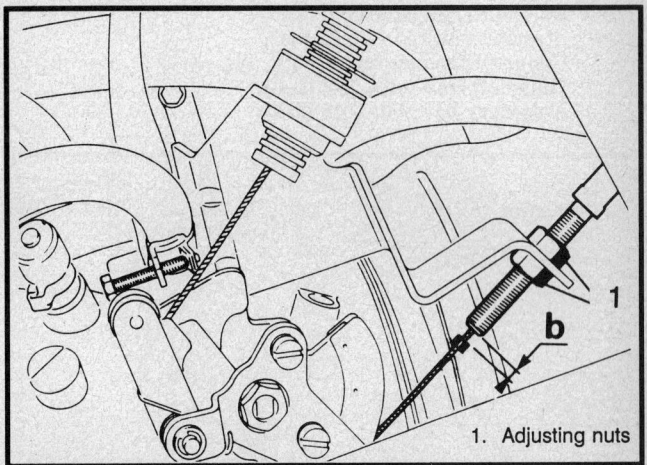

1. Adjusting nuts

Adjusting kickdown cable, positioning cable stops with cable connected

DRIVE AXLE

Halfshaft

Removal and Installation

405

1. With the vehicle on the ground, remove the anti-sway bar attaching bolt. Raise and safely support the vehicle.
2. Remove the front tire and wheel assembly. Drain the transaxle.
3. Remove the pin and cage nut from the spindle. Using tool .0606 AY, remove the halfshaft attaching nut.
4. Remove the lower ball joint attaching nut and the lower ball joint. If equipped with anti-lock brakes, remove the wheel sensors.
5. Working on the right side, loosen the 2 nuts on the bearing housing and rotate a ½ turn to disengage the offset head from the bearing housing.
6. Turn the steering wheel all the way to the left and remove the steering knuckle to disengage the halshaft from the hub.
7. Remove the halfshaft from the differential and slide it through the support bearing.
8. Rotate the steering wheel all the way to the right and remove the steering knuckle to disengage the halshaft from the hub.
9. Remove the halfshafts from the differential. Do not move the vehicle after the halshafts have been removed.
To install:
10. Using tools .0317 G on left side and .0317 S on the right side, install new oil seals into the differential. Fill seal lips with grease.
11. Install the protector on the inner end of the halfshaft bearing before installing the right halfshaft.
12. Reverse the remainder of the removal procedure to install, noting the following:
   a. Remove the protectors after installing halfshaft bearing bolts.
   b. If equipped with anti-brakes, install and adjust speed sensors.
   c. Install new Nylstop nuts on the right halfshaft bearing bolts. Torque bolts to 13 ft. lbs. Install a new halshaft retaining nut and torque to 195 ft. lbs.

   d. Install the anti-sway bar and torque attaching nuts to 22 ft. lbs.
   e. Install ball joints and torque ball joints to 43 ft. lbs.
   f. Fill the transaxle with fluid. Start engine and check for leaks.

Steering Knuckle, Hub and Bearings

Removal and Installation

405

1. Raise and safely support the vehicle.
2. Remove the tire and wheel assembly, lockpin and cover. Using tool .0606 AY, remove the halfshaft hub nut.
3. Turn steering wheel all the way to the right and install retaining cables .0903 AF. Use two 6mm bolts to hold the lower end of the cables from slipping out of bottom slot.
4. Remove the caliper and position aside. Do not disconnect the brake line.
5. Remove the anti-sway control rod bolts (3,5) and the wheel sensors, if equipped with ABS.
6. Remove the ball joints and the steering knuckle clamp attaching nut. Install removal tool .0903 AE and turn a ¼ turn.
7. Lower the steering knuckle and separate it from the strut. Remove the steering knuckle.
8. Remove the steering knuckle bearing retainer ring using a suitable prybar.
9. Using a suitable extractor tool, remove the bearing inner race.
10. Using the bearing race removed, drive out the bearing.
To install:
11. Reverse removal procedure to install, noting the following:
   a. Lubricate the bearing housing before installing bearing into hub.
   b. Use new Nylstop nuts.
   c. Install wheel sensors and adjust, if equipped with ABS.
   d. The shock absorber body must seat. If not, loosen the nut and the shock assembly will seat itself.
   e. Remove the retaining cables .0903 AF.
   f. Torque the following:
   Steering knuckle clamp nut—41 ft. lbs.

Ball joint—22 ft. lbs.
Steering link rod—26 ft. lbs.
Caliper attaching nuts—74 ft. lbs.
Halfshaft hub nut—195 ft. lbs.
Anti-sway bar bolts—48 ft. lbs.

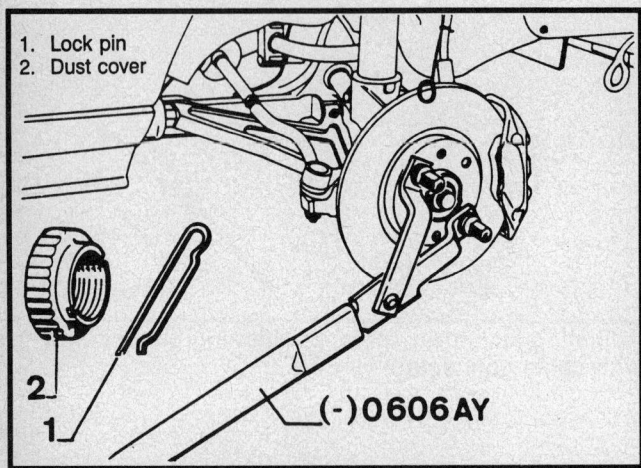

1. Lock pin
2. Dust cover

(-)0606AY

Removing the halfshaft hub nut—405

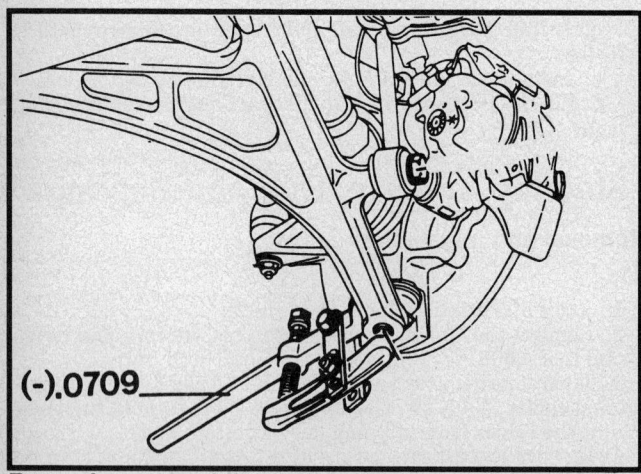

(-).0709

Removing control link bolt and ball joint bolt—405

Differential Carrier

Removal and Installation

505

1. Raise and safely support the vehicle.
2. Remove the left rear tire and wheel assembly.
3. Remove the anti-squeal brake pad spring, retaining fork and the pads.
4. Disconnect the brake hose retaining clip, located on the rear arm.
5. Remove the brake caliper attaching bolts and position caliper aside. It is not necessary to disconnect the brake lines.

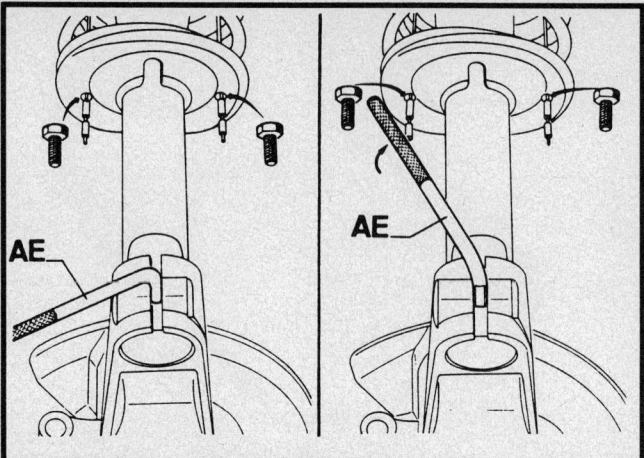

Installing spreader wrench—405

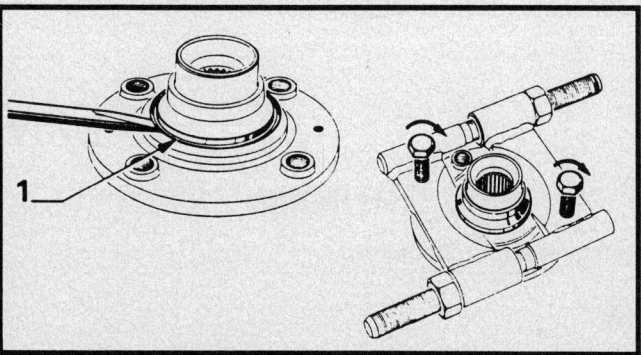

Hub bearing removal—405

6. Remove the screws attaching the disc to the hub. Mark relationship of disc-to-hub. Remove the disc.
7. Remove the Allen screw attaching the hub carrier to the rear arm.
8. Remove the thrust plate and bolts.
9. Drain differential and remove the brake compensator lever and springs.
10. Remove the 4 nuts attaching the torque tube to the differential.
11. Remove the 2 Allen screws attaching the differential to the suspension crossmember.
12. Remove the differential by pulling towards the rear of the vehicle and to the left.
To install:
13. Using a suitable jack, raise the differential into position and install the right halfshaft into the differential.
14. Install the torque tube to the differential and torque the 4 attaching nuts to 44 ft. lbs.
15. Install the 2 Allen screws attaching the differential to the suspension crossmember. Torque screws to 27 ft. lbs.
16. Install the brake disc to the hub. Make sure alignment marks align. Torque attaching bolts to 37 ft. lbs.
17. Reverse remaining procedure to install.

STEERING

Steering Wheel

Removal and Installation

1. Disconnect the negative battery cable.
2. Remove the steering column covers.
3. Remove the horn pad.
4. Remove the steering wheel attaching bolt and using a suitable puller, remove the steering wheel.
5. Reverse procedure to install.

Power Steering Rack

Removal and Installation

1. Raise and safely support the vehicle.
2. Drain system.
3. Disconnect the hydraulic line from the distribution valve.
4. Remove the power steering ram heat shield from the assembly.
5. Remove the protective cap and bolt from the rack assembly, if equipped.
6. Remove the steering column shaft clamp bolt and the tie-rod end nuts.
7. Using ball joint extractor .0709 or equivalent, remove the ball joints.
8. Remove the steering rack assembly attaching bolts and pivot the rack on itself.
9. Move the rack assembly towards the right and remove the rack assembly.

To install:

10. Reverse procedure to install, noting the following:
   a. Use Nylstop nuts on the ball joints and torque the nuts to 26 ft. lbs.
   b. Torque the 2 steering rack assembly attaching bolts to 30 ft. lbs.
   c. Torque the steering column shaft coupling bolts to 15 ft. lbs.
   d. Torque the hydraulic line to the distribution valve to 18 ft. lbs.
11. Refill and bleed the system. Check steering operation.

Power Steering Pump

Removal and Installation

405

1. Disconnect the negative battery cable and drain the power steering system.
2. If equipped with 1.9L DOHC engine, proceed as follows:
   a. Remove the battery and the battery tray.
   b. Remove the power steering hose.
   c. Remove the hydraulic line from the pump.
   d. Remove the pump assembly attaching bolts and the pump assembly with its intermediate support bracket.
   e. Remove the support bracket from the pump.
3. On models except 1.9L DOHC engine, proceed as follows:
   a. Remove the alternator belt.
   b. Remove the power steering pump pulley attaching bolts and the pulley.
   c. Remove the tensioner slide and disconnect the hose from the pump.
   d. Remove the hydraulic line from the pump.
4. Reverse procedure to install. Bleed system and check fluid level.

System Bleeding

1. Start engine and run at idle.

2. Bleed the air from the system by turning the steering wheel several times in each direction, from left-to-right.
3. Top the reservoir as soon as the fluid level drops.
4. Repeat Steps 2 and 3, as necessary.

Tie Rod Ends

Removal and Installation

1. Raise and safely support the vehicle.
2. Loosen nut and install extractor 8.0908 D. Continue to loosen nut to push out ball joint.
3. Using a suitable prybar, slide back steering rack boot.
4. Using spanner wrench 8.0707 or equivalent, loosen the ball joint casing from the steering box end.
5. Remove the track bar, then the tie-rod from the track bar.
6. Reverse procedure to install. Torque the ball joint casing at the steering rack to 37 ft. lbs., ball joint nut to 25.5 ft. lbs. and the track bar locknuts to 32. ft. lbs.

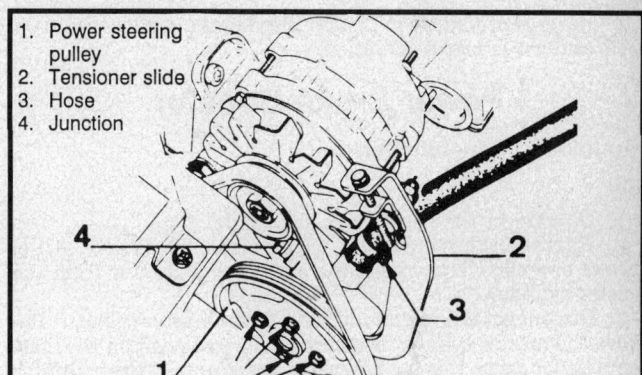

1. Power steering pulley
2. Tensioner slide
3. Hose
4. Junction

Removing power steering pump—405 vehicles equipped with 1.9L engine except DOHC

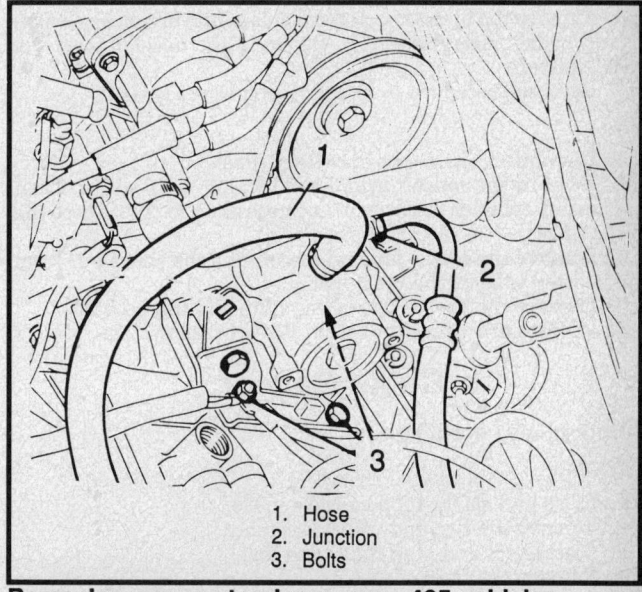

1. Hose
2. Junction
3. Bolts

Removing power steering pump—405 vehicles equipped with 1.9L DOHC engine

BRAKES

Master Cylinder

Removal and Installation

405

1. Disconnect the negative battery cable.
2. Remove the windshield wiper arms.
3. Remove the air intake grille attaching screws and the air intake grille, screws and clips.
4. Disconnect the electrical connector from the master cylinder.
5. Disconnect the vacuum hose and the hydraulic line. Remove the master cylinder attaching nuts and the master cylinder.
6. Reverse procedure to install. Bleed brake system. Start vehicle and check brake operation.

505

1. Disconnect the battery neagtive cable.
2. Disconnect the hydraulic brake lines.
3. Remove the master cylinder attaching bolts and the master cylinder.
4. Reverse procedure to install. Bleed brake system. Start vehicle and check brake operation.

Power Brake Booster

Removal and Installation

405

1. Disconnect the negative battery cable.
2. Remove the windshield wiper arms, air intake grille, screws and clips. Disconnect the electrical connector from the master cylinder.
3. Disconnect the vacuum hose from the master cylinder. Remove the master cylinder attaching bolts and position the master cylinder aside. It is not necessary to disconnect the hydraulic lines.
4. Disconnect the clutch cable from the brake pedal by unclipping the plastic clip.
5. Disconnet the electrical connector from the stoplight switch.
6. Remove the brake booster attaching nuts and brake booster and pedal cluster assembly. Separate the booster from the pedal cluster.
7. Reverse procedure to install. Bleed brake system.

505

1. Disconnect the negative battery cable.
2. Remove the master cylinder attaching nuts and position the master cylinder aside. It is not necessary to disconnect the brake lines or the vacuum hose.
3. Remove the cotter pin and disconnect the clevis pin from the booster yoke at the brake pedal.
4. Remove the booster attaching nuts and the booster.
5. Reverse procedure to install. Bleed brake system.

Brake Caliper

Removal and Installation

FRONT

1. Raise and safely support the vehicle.
2. Remove the tire and wheel assembly.
3. Disconnect and plug the brake line.
4. Remove the brake pads.
5. Disconnect the brake pad wear indicator connector.
6. Disconnect the flexible brake hose.

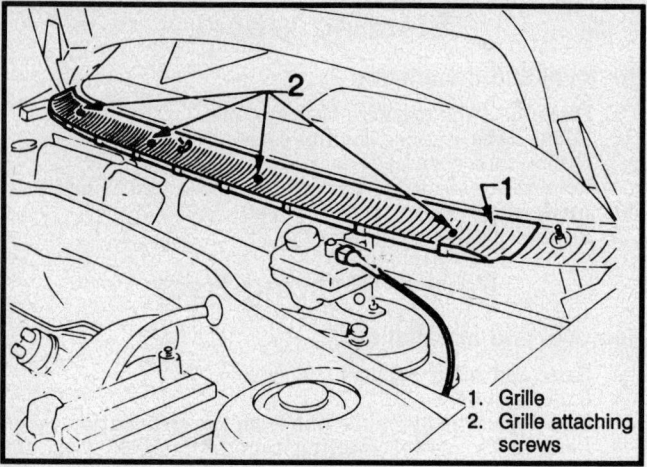

1. Grille
2. Grille attaching screws

Removing the air intake grill—405

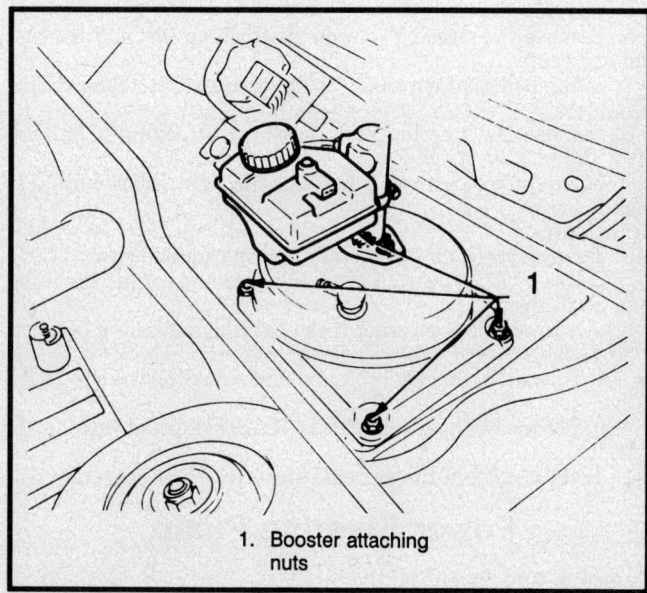

1. Booster attaching nuts

Removing master cylinder—405

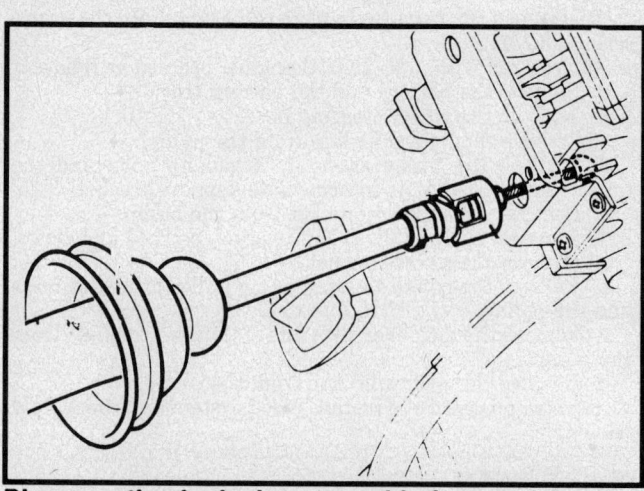

Disconnecting brake booster cable from pedal—405

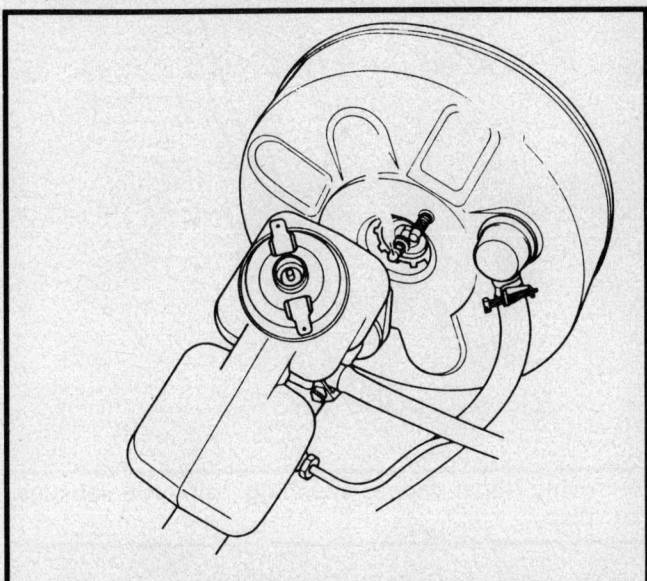

Removing master cylinder from brake booster—505

7. Remove the caliper attaching bolts and remove the caliper.

To install:
8. Coat the caliper attaching bolts with Loctite.
9. Install caliper and torque bolts to 26 ft. lbs.
10. Install flexible brake hose, brake line and pad indicator connector.
11. Install tire and wheel assembly. Bleed brake system.

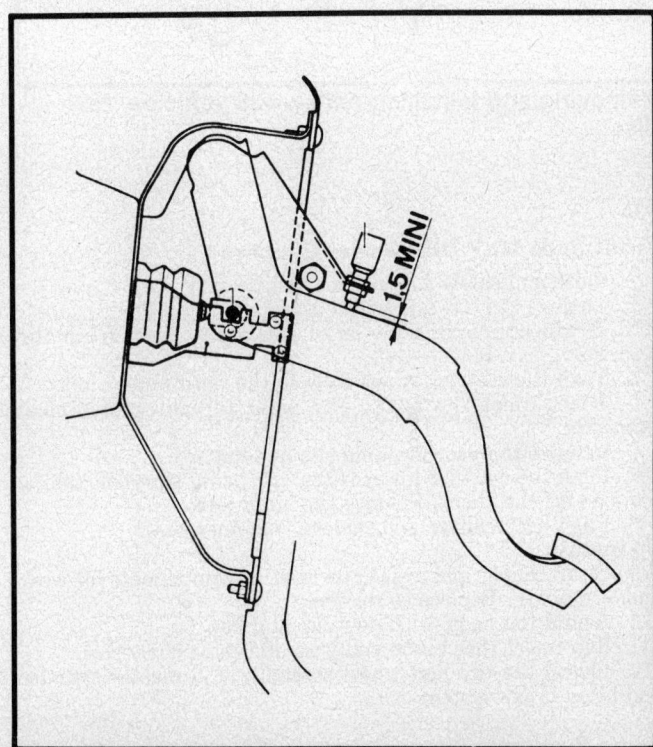

Removing the booster rod from brake pedal support—505

REAR
1. Raise and safely support the vehicle.
2. Remove the tire and wheel assembly.
3. Remove pads and disconnect the brake line. Plug all openings.
4. Remove the brake hose and plug the caliper.
5. Remove the guide bolt and disconnect the brake cable from the caliper.
6. Remove the caliper attaching bolts and the caliper.

To install:
7. Install the caliper using the upper mounting bolt first. Coat lower bolt with Loctite and install.
8. Connect the brake line, hose and install the pads. Torque caliper attaching bolts to 26 ft. lbs.
9. Connect the brake cable, install tire and wheel assembly and bleed brake system.

Disc Brake Pads

Removal and Installation

405
Front
1. Raise and safely support the vehicle.
2. Remove the tire and wheel assembly.
3. Drain approximately ⅔ of the brake fluid from the master cylinder.
4. Disconnect the brake wear indicator wire and remove the lower caliper attaching bolt.

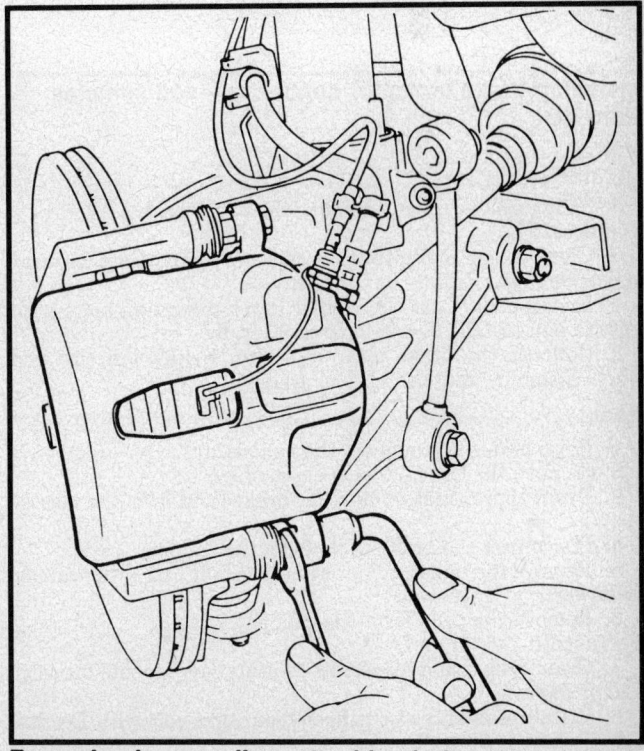

Removing lower caliper attaching bolt—405 vehicles, front disc

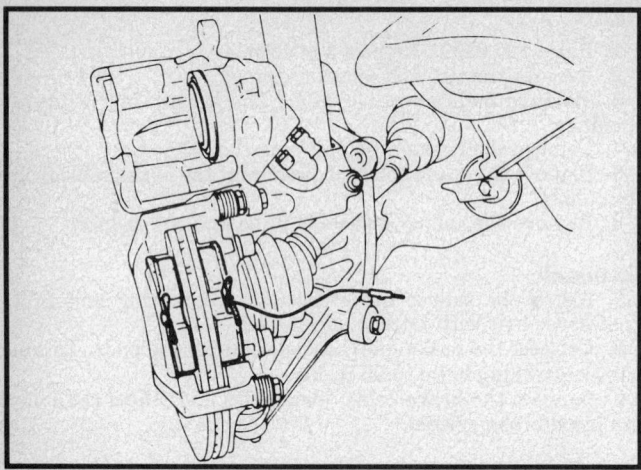

Removing and installing brake pads—405 vehicles, front disc

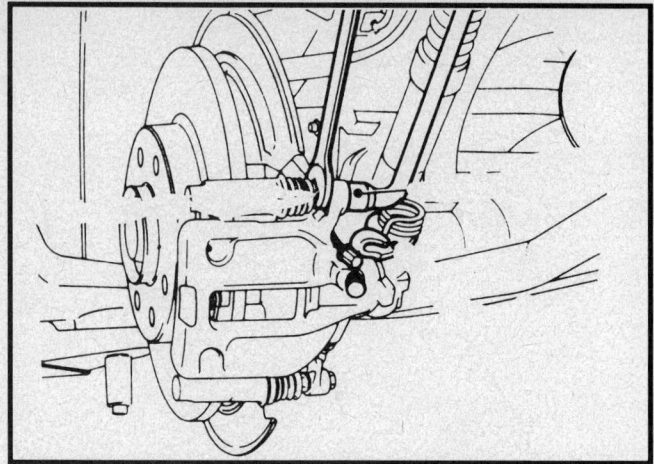

Removing upper caliper attaching bolt—405 vehicles, rear disc

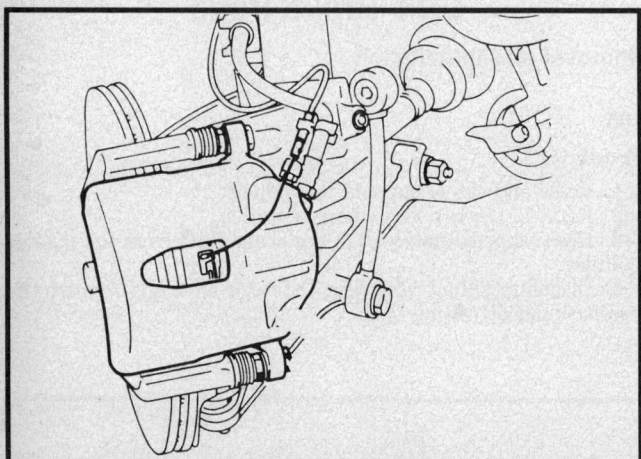

Installing brake indicator connector—405 vehicles, front disc

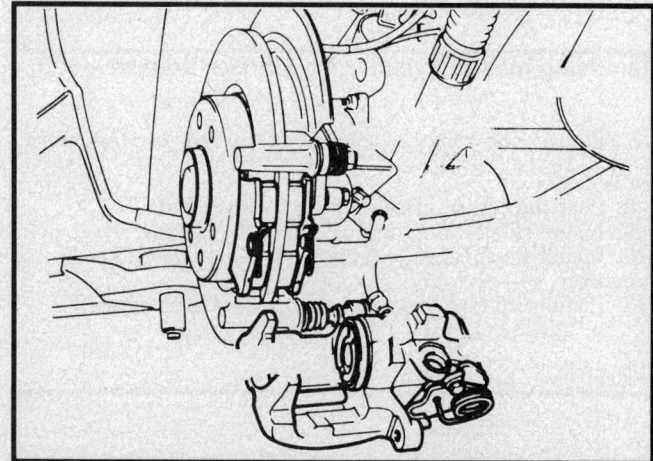

Removing and installing pads—405 vehicles, rear disc

5. Swing caliper up and remove the brake pads.

To install:

6. Clean caliper and inspect its relating components for wear and/or damage. Replace as necessary.

7. Install pads. Coat the caliper lower mounting bolts with Loctite and install. Torque bolt to 26 ft. lbs.

8. Connect the brake wear indicator, install the tire and wheel assembly and bleed brake system.

Rear

1. Raise and safely support the vehicle.
2. Remove the tire and wheel assembly.
3. Drain approximately ⅔ of the brake fluid from the master cylinder.
4. Disconnect the brake cable from the caliper.
5. Remove the upper caliper attaching bolt and swing caliper downward.
6. Remove the pads form the caliper.

To install:

7. Clean caliper and inspect its relating components for wear and/or damage.

8. Install pads and coat caliper mounting bolt with Loctite. Torque bolt to 26 ft. lbs.

9. Connect the brake cable, install the tire and wheel assembly and bleed the brake system.

505

Front Pads With DBA Series Calipers

1. Raise and safely support the vehicle.
2. Remove the tire and wheel assembly.
3. Drain approximately ⅔ of the brake fluid from the reservoir.
4. Turn the steering wheel fully to the right and/or left.
5. Disconnect the brake pad wear indicator electrical connector.
6. Remove the pad retaining clip and key.
7. Push the cylinder towards the disc using a prybar, taking the load off the shock. Remove the outer pad.
8. Push back caliper and remove the inner pad.

To install:

9. Clean caliper and inspect its relating components for wear and/or damage. Replace as necessay.

10. Install the pads, with new clip and key.

11. Reconnect ther brake pad wear indicator connector.

12. Install the tire and wheel assembly. Fill master cylinder and bleed brake system.

Front Pads with Teves Caliper

1. Raise and safely support the vehicle.
2. Remove the tire and wheel assembly.

3. Drain approximately ⅔ of the brake fluid from the fluid reservoir.

4. Remove the retaining clip, pad pins and retaining springs.

5. Disconnect the brake pad wear indicating electrical connector.

6. Lift caliper up and remove the inner pad. Push caliper outward, towards outside of vehicle, and remove the outer pad.

7. Reverse procedure to install. Bleed brake system.

Rear Pads With Girling Series Calipers

1. Raise and safely support the vehicle.
2. Remove the tire and wheel assembly.
3. Disconnect the brake pad wear indicator electrical connector.
4. Remove the brake pad safely clip and retaining spring.
5. Remove the brake pad retaining fork, fork spring and the pads.
6. Reverse procedure to install. Fill brake reservoir and bleed brake system.

Brake Rotor

Removal and Installation

1. Raise and safely support the vehicle.
2. Remove the tire and wheel assembly.
3. If removing the font rotors, the front hub must be removed.
4. If removing the rear rotor, the stub axle/halfshaft must be removed.
5. Remove the rotor to hub and/or stub axle attaching bolts and remove the rotor.
6. Reverse procedure to install. Torque the rotor attaching bolts to 27 ft. lbs.

Brake Drums

Removal and Installation

1. Raise and safely support the vehicle.
2. Remove the tire and wheel assembly.
3. Loosen the brake cable locknuts and unscrew the adjusting nuts.
4. Remove the backing plate plug and insert a prybar through plug opening to release the brake shoes. Reinstall plug.
5. Remove the drum.
6. Reverse procedure to install. Adjust brake cable.

Brake Shoes

Removal and Installation

GIRLING SHOES

1. Raise and safely support the vehicle.
2. Remove the tire and wheel assembly.
3. Remove drum.
4. Using a prybar, unhook the lower shoe return spring.
5. Using a prybar, unhook the upper shoe return spring.
6. Using a suitable tool, expand the shoes outward as far as possible and remove the adjuster spring and its spring, spacer cup and the pushrod.
7. Remove the shoe retaining springs and the shoes. Disconnect the brake cable from the trailing shoe.
8. Reverse procedure to install. Adjust brakes.

DBA SHOES 1ST TYPE

1. Raise and safely support the vehicle.
2. Remove the tire and wheel assembly.
3. Remove drum.
4. Using a suitable prybar, unhook the lower shoe return spring.

5. Check the automatic adjuster lever link clearance. Clearance should be 0.035–0.043 in. (0.9–1.1mm). If not, replace parts as necessary.

6. Using a prybar, remove the upper return spring.

7. Remove the shoe hold-down spring, move the leading shoe outward and disconnect the link rod from the adjuster lever. Remove shoe assembly.

8. Disconnect the brake cable, remove the shoe hold-down spring and remove the trailing shoe.

9. Reverse procedure to install. Transfer serviceable components to the replacement brake shoes. Adjust brakes, if necessary.

DBA SHOES 2ND TYPE

1. Raise and safely support the vehicle.
2. Remove the tire and wheel assembly.
3. Remove drum.

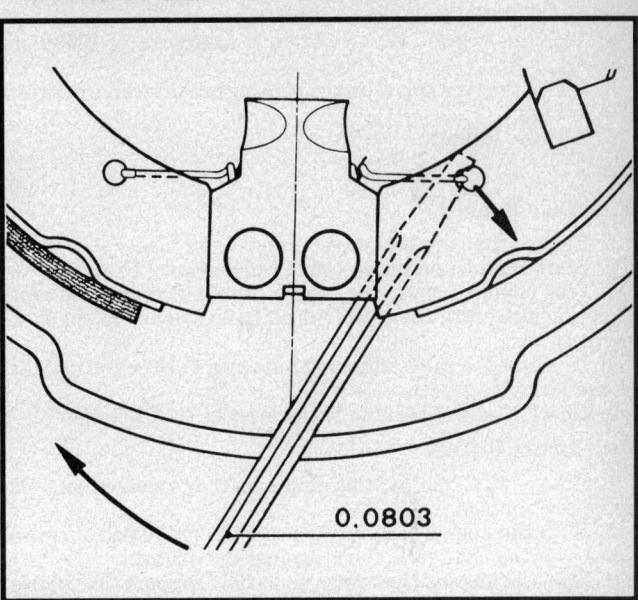

Unhooking lower return spring—vehicles equipped with Girling shoes

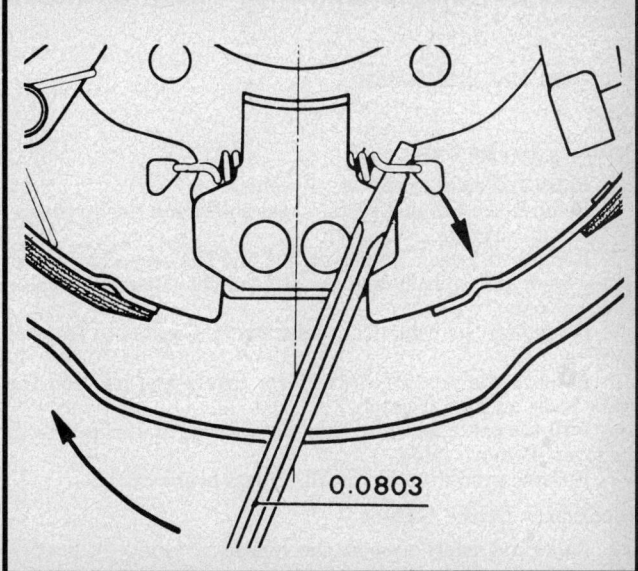

Unhooking lower return spring—vehicles equipped with DBA 1st type shoes

4. Using a prybar, unhook the lower shoe return spring, then the upper return spring.

5. Remove the shoe hold-down springs and the leading shoe. Disconnect the brake cable and remove the trailing shoe with its link rod.

6. Reverse procedure to install. Transfer serviceable components to the replacement shoes. Adjust brakes, if necessary.

Parking Brake Cable

Adjustment

405

1. Ensure that the parking brake lever is released and the system bleed.
2. Pump the brake pedal several times.
3. Loosen locknut (1) and turn locknut (2) to obtain a clearance of 0.078 in. (2mm) at each lever.
4. Tighten locknut (2) to obtain a clearance of 0.590 in. (15mm) at X.
5. Check that the travel on the parking brake lever is between 7–9 notches.
6. Tighten locknut.

505

With Disc Brakes

1. Ensure that the brake system has been bled.
2. Start engine and pump brake pedal several times.
3. Stop engine. Loosen the cable locknuts. Screw in the cable adjusting nuts until the levers lift off their nylon stop, on backing plate.
4. Unscrew the cable adjusting nuts by a ½ turn and retighten the locknut.
5. Check that the parking brake lever is 7–13 notches.

With Drum Brakes

1. Ensure that the parking brake lever is released and the brake system bled.
2. With the engine running, depress the brake pedal several times to bring the brake shoes against the drums.
3. Stop the engine, then raise and safely support the vehicle.
4. Loosen the cable locknuts and turn the adjusting nut until the brake shoes are touching the drum.
5. Unscrew the adjusting nut by ½ turn and check the parking brake lever travel is between 4–7 notches. Tighten the locknuts.

Removal and Installation

405

Primary Brake Cable

1. Raise and safely support the vehicle.
2. Remove the exhaust system heat shield and unclip the cable from its support.
3. Remove the cable adjusting nut and the secondary brake cables from the splitter and its attachment. Disengage cable from splitter.
4. Disengage the cable from its support. Located in front of muffler.
5. Remove the parking brake lever covers and position the brake lever on its 5th notch.
6. Pull the cable forward, then downward, to unclip it from the lever. Remove cable.
7. Reverse procedure to install. Adjust brake cable.

Secondary Brake Cables

1. Raise and safely support the vehicle.
2. Ensure that the parking brake lever is released.
3. Remove the cable adjusting nuts, then the secondary cables from splitter and its attachment.

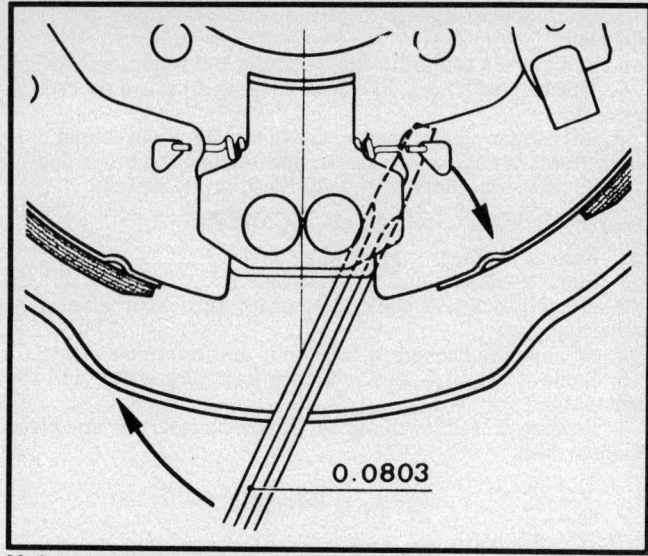

0.0803

Unhooking lower return spring—vehicles equipped with DBA 2nd type shoes

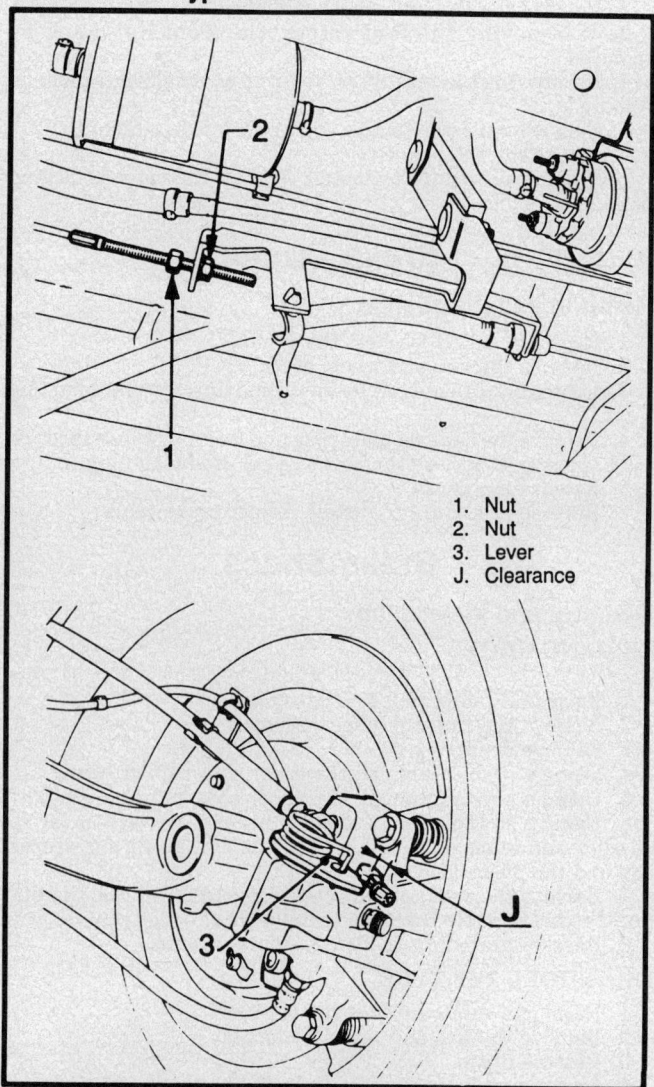

1. Nut
2. Nut
3. Lever
J. Clearance

Adjusting parking brake cable—405

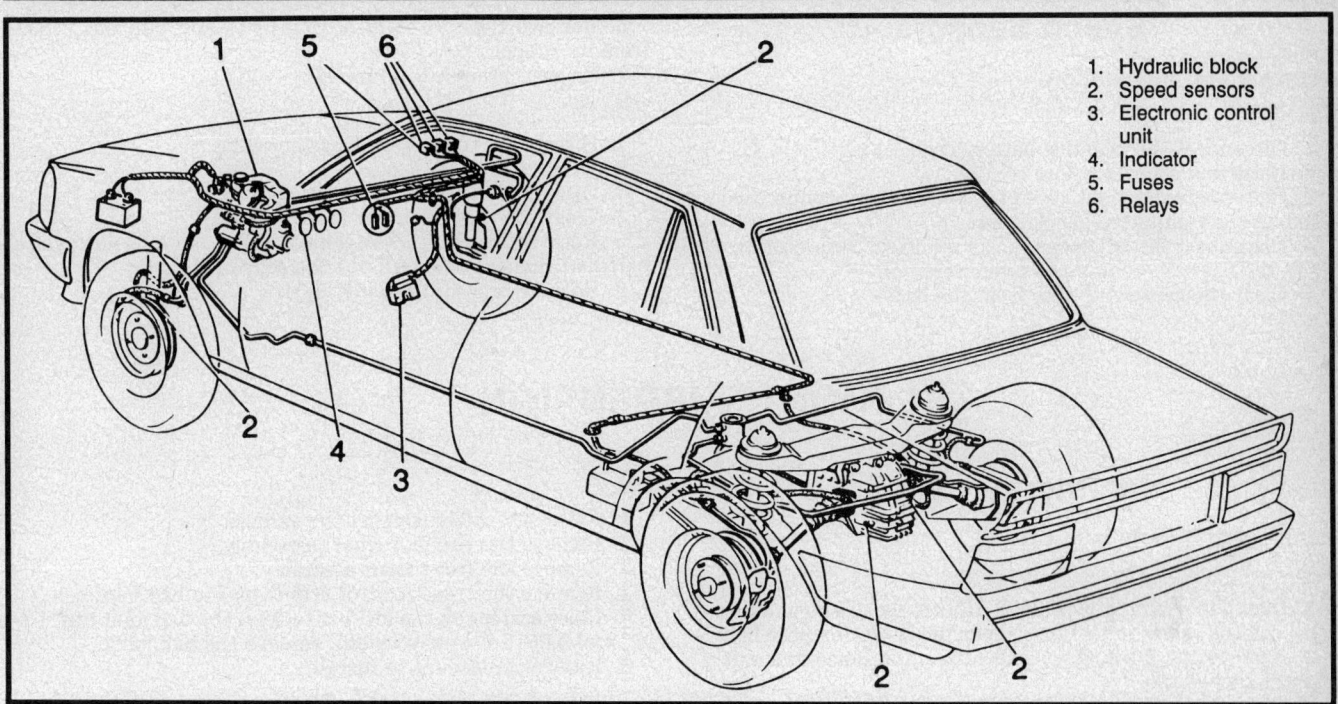

1. Hydraulic block
2. Speed sensors
3. Electronic control unit
4. Indicator
5. Fuses
6. Relays

Anti-Lock brake system schematic layout—typical, 505 shown

4. Remove each cable from its lever on the caliper. Remove the cables.
5. Reverse procedure to install. Adjust brakes.

Anti-Lock Brake System Service

Precaution

Failure to observe the following precautions may result in system damage.

● Before performing electric arc welding on the vehicle, disconnect the Electronic Brake Control Module (EBCM) and the hydraulic modulator connectors.

● When performing painting work on the vehicle, do not expose the Electronic Brake Control Module (EBCM) to temperatures in excess of 185°F (85°C) for longer than 2 hrs. The system may be exposed to temperatures up to 200°F (95°C) for less than 15 min.

● Never disconnect or connect the Electronic Brake Control Module (EBCM) or hydraulic modulator connectors with the ignition switch ON.

● Never disassemble any component of the Anti-Lock Brake System (ABS) which is designated non-servicable; the component must be replaced as an assembly.

● When filling the master cylinder, always use Delco Supreme 11 brake fluid or equivalent, which meets DOT-3 specifications; petroleum base fluid will destroy the rubber parts.

Relieving Anti-Lock Brake System Pressure

1. Disconnect the negative battery cable.
2. Ensure that the ignition switch is in the **OFF** position.
3. Relieve the pressure in the system by depressing the brake pedal approximately 25 times, until hard.

Hydraulic Block

Removal and Installation

1. Disconnect the negative battery cable.
2. Disconnect and tag all the electrical connectors from the hydraulic block.

3. Drain approximately ⅔ of the brake fluid from the reservoir.
4. Place a suitable container under the hydraulic lines and disconnect the brake lines.
5. Remove the coil and ignition module support bracket.
6. Remove the panel under dash, disconnect the brake pedal securing pin and remove the hydraulic block attaching nuts.
7. Remove hydraulic block.
8. Reverse procedure to install. Torque front brake lines to 11 ft. lbs. and the rear lines to 13 ft. lbs. Fill the brake reservoir and bleed system.

Brake Electronic Control Unit

Removal and Installation

1. Disocnnect the negative battery cable.
2. Remove the front passenger's footrest.
3. Remove the electrical connector retaining screw and disconnect the connector from the control unit.
4. Remove the control unit attaching screws and the control unit.
5. Reverse procedure to install.

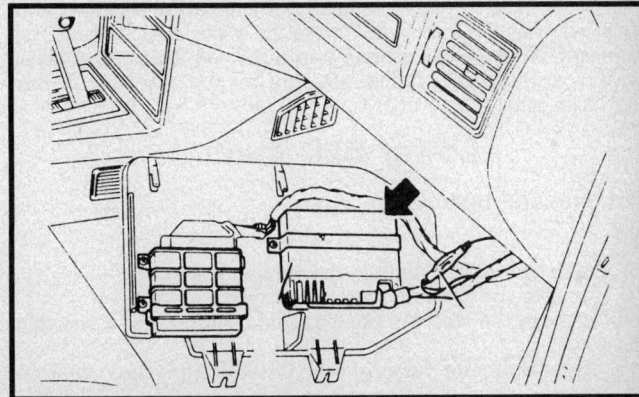

Brake ECU location—505

Speed Sensors

Removal and Installation

FRONT

1. Disconnect the negative battery cable.
2. Raise and safely support vehicle.
3. Disconnect the right speed sensor electrical connector located on the right strut shock tower.
4. Disconnect the left speed sensor electrical connector located on the firewall, behind the brake reservoir.
5. Clear the sensor harness from the body.

6. Remove the sensor attaching bolts and pull out sensor from its support.
7. Reverse procedure to install.

REAR

1. Disconnect the negative battery cable.
2. Remove the rear seat.
3. Disconnect the sensor electrical connectors.
4. Clear the harness away from the body.
5. Remove the sensor attaching bolt from the differential halfshaft housing and pull out the sensor.
6. Reverse procedure to install.

FRONT SUSPENSION

MacPherson Strut

Removal and Installation

405

1. Install retaining cables .0903 AF through the strut assembly. Lock the cables in the lower housing using two 6mm bolts.
2. Remove the 2 top strut attaching nuts. Raise and safely support the vehicle.
3. Remove the tire and wheel assembly.
4. Remove the control link rod bolt and the strut housing nut and bolt.
5. Secure the steering knuckle to the subframe with wire to prevent the halfshaft from slipping out of the transaxle.
6. Install spreader wrench .0903 AE or equivalent into the steering knuckle strut housing. Turn wrench to spread knuckle and remove the strut assembly.
7. Reverse procedure to install. Torque the 2 upper strut nuts to 11 ft. lbs., lower strut attaching nut to 41 ft. lbs. and the control link rod nut to 48 ft. lbs.

505

1. Raise and safely support the vehicle.
2. Remove the tire and wheel assembly.
3. Remove the brake caliper without disconnecting the brake line. Position caliper aside.
4. Remove the rear control arm nut ad through bolt.
5. Remove the sway bar link rod bolt and the front control arm attaching bolt. Clear the rear control arm away from the crossmember and the front control arm.
6. Support the wheel hub.
7. Remove the 3 upper strut assembly attaching bolts and remove the strut assembly.
8. Reverse procedure to install. Coat caliper attaching bolts with Loctite and torque bolts to 61 ft. lbs. with Teves caliper and 94 ft. lbs. with DBA caliper. Torque the upper 3 strut attaching bolts to 7 ft. lbs., Rear control arm nut to 33 ft. lbs., stabilizer bar link rod nuts to 33 ft. lbs., steering link rod nuts to 26 ft. lbs. and front control arm nuts to 33 ft. lbs.

Lower Ball Joints

Removal and Installation

405

1. Raise and safely support the vehicle.
2. Remove the tire and wheel assembly.
3. Remove the steering knuckle and position into a suitable vice.
4. Using ball joint removal tool .0615 or equivalent, remove the ball joint from the steering knuckle.
5. Reverse procedure to install.

505

1. Raise and safely support the vehicle.
2. Remove the tire and wheel assembly.
3. Remove the front strut assembly.
4. Remove the track control arm from the ball joint.
5. Raise and break the locking tabs on the ball joint nut. Using tool 8.0616 F or equivalent, remove the ball joint.
6. Reverse procedure to install.

Lower Control Arms

Removal and Installation

405

1. Raise and safely support the vehicle.
2. Remove the tire and wheel assembly.
3. Remove bolt attaching the control link rod to the lower control arm.
4. Remove the ball joint nut and extract the ball joint using tool .0709 or equivalent.
6. Remove the front lower control arm attaching bolt.
7. Remove the 2 rear lower control arm attaching bolts. Loosen the subframe bolt approximately 10mm.
8. Remove the control arm.
9. Reverse procedure to install. Torque the following:
   Subframe bolt—66 ft. lbs.
   Two rear control arm attaching nuts—33 ft. lbs.
   Front control arm attaching bolt—55 ft. lbs.
   Control link rod-to-control arm bolt—48 ft. lbs.
   Ball joint nut to 22 ft. lbs.

Front Wheel Bearings

Removal and Installation

505

1. Raise and safely support the vehicle.
2. Remove the tire and wheel assembly.
3. Remove the brake caliper and position aside using wire. Do not disconnect the brake hose.
4. Remove the hub dust cap and nut, then the hub assembly, taking care not to drop and/or damage the outer bearing.
5. If the inner bearing on the spindle is seized, remove the bearing using a puller.
6. Mark the position of the rotor and remove the bolts. Separate the rotor from the hub.
To install:
7. Clean and inspect bearings. Replace as necessary.
8. Pack bearings using suitable grease.
9. Assemble the hub and rotor, aligning the matching marks made during removal. Apply Loctite onto the the bolts and torque bolts to 27 ft. lbs.

10. Install the bearings into the hub and press a new seal into the rear of hub.

11. Install hub assembly. Reverse the remaining removal procedure to complete installation.

REAR SUSPENSION

Shock Absorbers

Removal and Installation

405

1. Raise and safely support the vehicle.
2. Remove the upper and lower shock attaching nuts.
3. Remove the shock and washer.
4. Reverse procedure to install. Torque the Nylstop nuts to 81 ft. lbs.

505

1. Working from inside the trunk, remove the shock tower nut, washer and rubber bushing.
2. Raise and safely support the vehicle.
3. Remove the lower shock attaching nut and through bolt, then remove the shock through the control arm.
4. Reverse procedure to install. Torque the upper tower nut to 9 ft. lbs. and the lower shock nut to 48 ft. lbs.

Coil Spring

Removal and Installation

1. Raise and safely support the vehicle, under the rear suspension arm.
2. Remove the tire and wheel assembly.
3. Unclip the brake hose from the control arm and disconnect the brake line from the flexible hose junction.
4. If equipped with drum brakes, proceed as follows:
    a. Remove the drum, brake line to wheel cylinder and disconnect the brake cable from its lever.
    b. Remove the plastic clips that retain the cable to the control arm.
    c. Using a suitable drift, knock out the cable end retainer from the anchor plate.
    d. Remove the stub axle, hub and driveshaft assembly attaching bolts and remove assembly.
5. If equipped with disc brakes, proceed as follows:
    a. Remove the pads.
    b. Disconnect the parking brake cable.
    c. Remove the caliper and position aside.
    d. Remove the driveshaft, stub axle and hub assembly attaching bolts and remove the assembly.
6. Remove the shock absorber attaching bolt.
7. Remove the control arm link-to-control rod attaching bolt. Then reinstall the bolt to prevent parts from falling into the suspension arm.
8. Remove the the 2 front control arm nuts, then the through bolts.
9. Lower the jack slowly and remove the spring.
10. Reverse procedure to install.

Rear Control Arms

Removal and Installation

1. Raise and safely support the vehicle, under the rear suspension arm.
2. Remove the tire and wheel assembly.

3. Unclip the brake hose from the control arm and disconnect the brake line from the flexible hose junction.
4. If equipped with drum brakes, proceed as follows:
    a. Remove the drum, brake line to wheel cylinder and disconnect the brake cable from its lever.
    b. Remove the plastic clips that retain the cable to the control arm.
    c. Using a suitable drift, knock out the cable end retainer from the anchor plate.
    d. Remove the stub axle, hub and driveshaft assembly attaching bolts and remove assembly.
5. If equipped with disc brakes, procced as follows:
    a. Remove the pads.
    b. Disconnect the parking brake cable.
    c. Remove the caliper and position aside.
    d. Remove the driveshaft, stub axle and hub assembly attaching bolts and remove the assembly.
6. Remove the shock absorber attaching bolt.
7. Remove the control arm link-to-control rod attaching bolt. Then reinstall the bolt to prevent parts from falling into the suspension arm.
8. Remove the the 2 front control arm nuts, then the through bolts.
9. Lower the jack slowly and remove the spring.
10. Support the control arm in a horizontal position, then remove 1 through bolt and install pin 8.0906 J or equivalent.
11. Remove the other through bolt, then the pin and remove the control arm.

To install:

12. If equipped with disc brakes, insert the brake cable into the control arm.
13. Grease the unthreaded portion of the through bolts and install bolts.
14. Install spring, with the rubber cup facing upwards.
15. Using a suitable jack, push control arm into place until the shock absorber points align. Then install the shock through bolt and the control arm link-to-control arm atttaching bolt. Torque link bolt to 9 ft. lbs.
16. If equipped with disc brakes, proceed as follows:
    a. Install the hub/driveshaft assembly onto vehicle. Torque the attaching bolts to 36.5 ft. lbs.
    b. Install the caliper and pads onto the rotor. Torque the caliper attaching bolts to 31 ft. lbs.
17. If equipped with drum brakes, proceed as follows:
    a. Install the hub/driveshaft assembly onto the vehicle. Torque the attaching bolts to 36.5 ft. lbs.
    b. Connect the brake cable and secure cable to the control arm using new plastic clips.
    c. Reconnect the brake line to the wheel cylinder, hose to the control arm. Secure brake line to control arm.
    d. Install the drum and bleed brake system.
18. Reverse removal procedure to complete installation. Torque the control arm through bolts to 40 ft. lbs. and shock absorber attaching bolt to 47 ft. lbs.

Rear Wheel Bearings

Removal and Installation

The hub/wheel bearing is a factory assembled unit, therfore, if replacement is necessary, they must be replaced as an assembly.

1. Raise and safely support the vehicle.

2. Remove the tire and wheel assembly.

3. Remove the wheel speed sensor, if equipped.

4. Disconnect the brake cable from the caliper.

5. Remove the caliper attaching bolts and position caliper aside.

6. Remove the rotor, the dust cap and the hub shaft attaching nut.

7. Using a suitable puller and adapter .0317 or equivalent, remove the hub/bearing assembly.

8. Remove the inner race, washer and the seal.

To install:

9. Install new seal on shaft.

10. Using tool .0530 E or equivalent, install new bearing race onto the spindle.

11. Install the hub and bearing assembly onto shaft.

12. Install new washer and nut. Torque the nut to 203 ft. lbs.

13. Install dust cap, wheel speed sensor, if equipped, rotor and caliper. Coat the caliper attaching bolts with Loctite and torque to 41 ft. lbs.

14. Reconnect the brake cable and install the tire and wheel assembly.

Rear Axle Assembly

Removal and Installation

1. Disconnect the negative battery cable.

2. Raise and safely support the vehicle.

3. Remove the tire and wheel assembly.

4. Drain the fuel tank and remove any under carriage protection that may interfere with axle removal.

5. Remove the fuel filler pipe and the exhaust system heat shield.

6. Remove the parking brake cable.

7. Unscrew the 2 rear fuel tank attaching bolts but do not remove them.

8. Disconnect and plug the brake line from the left side.

9. Disconnect the hydraulic lines from the brake compensator.

10. If equipped with ABS, remove the wheel speed sensors electrical connectors and clear from the parking brake cables.

11. Using a suitable jack, support the crossmember tube.

12. Using torque driver .0530 G or equivalent, remove the 6 rear axle assemble attaching bolts.

13 Carefully lower jack to ensure that the suspension assembly clears the filler neck and remove the axle assembly.

To install:

14. Reverse the removal procedure to install, noting the following:

a. Ensure not to damage the fuel tank filler neck when installing the rear axle assembly.

b. Torque the rear axle assembly attaching bolts to 41 ft. lbs.

c. Bleed the brake system.

d. If equipped with ABS, reinstall the wheel speed sensors and ensure to clamp the wheel speed sensor lead to the parking brake lever.

SERIAL NUMBER IDENTIFICATION

Vehicle Identification Plate

The chassis number is located on the left (driver) side windshield post and is visible from the outside of the vehicle. On the 911 and 911 Turbo, the chassis number is also found in the luggage compartment under the rug and on the identification plate near the front hood lock catch. On all other vehicles, the VIN plate is in the engine compartment near the battery.

Engine Number

On all vehicles, except the 911 and 911 Turbo, the engine serial number is stamped on the left of the crankcase near the clutch housing. On the 911 and 911 Turbo, the engine number is located on the right side of the crankcase adjacent to the blower.

Transaxle Number

The manual transaxle number is usually stamped in a cross reinforcement rib in the rear area of the transaxle case. The automatic transaxle number is usually stamped in an intermediate plate between the transaxle case and final drive case. Either way, the numbers should be visible from under the vehicle.

9 2 8
8 2 0
0001-9500
SERIES NUMBER
BODY TYPE (O:COUPE)
ENGINE TYPE
MODEL YEAR
TYPE

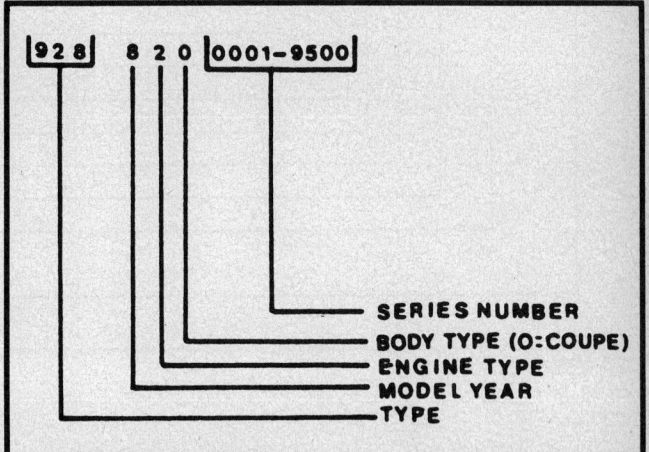

928 VIN Indentification

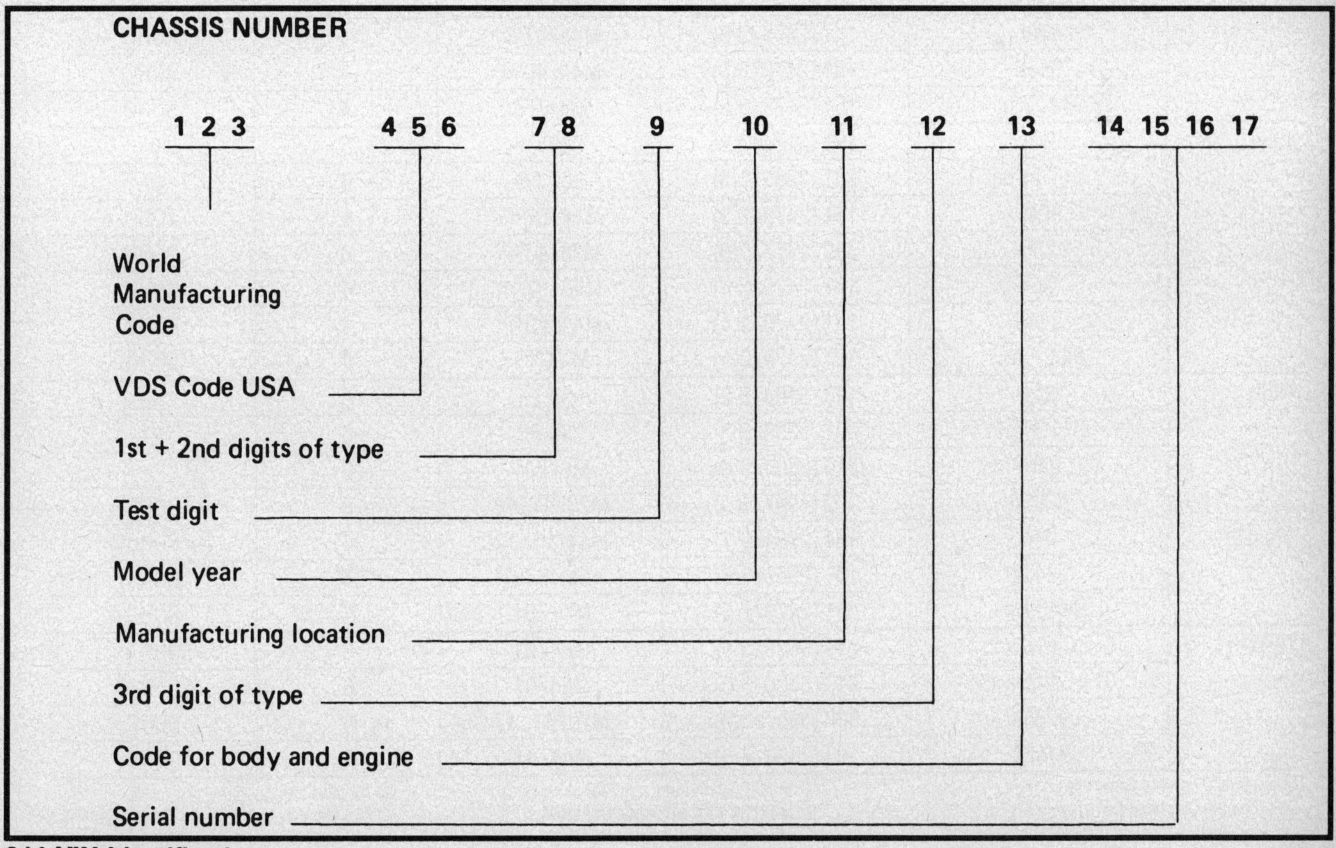

CHASSIS NUMBER
1 2 3
4 5 6
7 8
9
10
11
12
13
14 15 16 17
World Manufacturing Code
VDS Code USA
1st + 2nd digits of type
Test digit
Model year
Manufacturing location
3rd digit of type
Code for body and engine
Serial number

911 VIN Identification

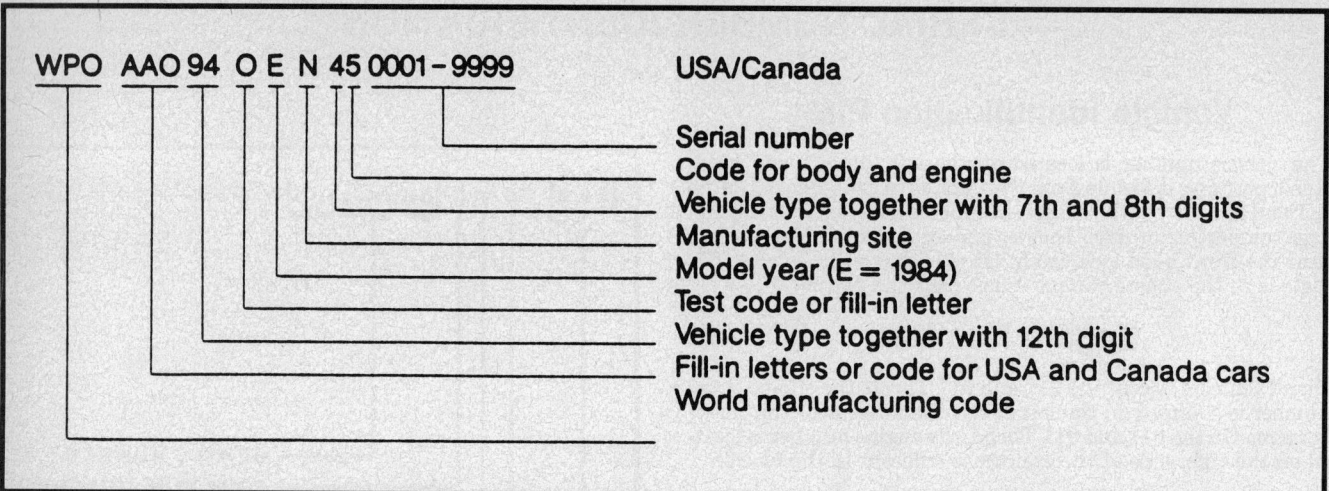

| WPO | AAO | 94 | O | E | N | 45 | 0001 – 9999 | USA/Canada |

Serial number
Code for body and engine
Vehicle type together with 7th and 8th digits
Manufacturing site
Model year (E = 1984)
Test code or fill-in letter
Vehicle type together with 12th digit
Fill-in letters or code for USA and Canada cars
World manufacturing code

944 VIN Identification

ENGINE IDENTIFICATION

Year	Model	Engine Displacement cu. in. (cc/liter)	Engine Series Identification	No. of Cylinders	Engine Type
1987	911	193 (3164/3.2)	930.21	6	①
	911 Turbo	201 (3299/3.3)	930.68	6	①
	924S	151 (2479/2.5)	M44/07 ⑤	4	SOHC
	928S4	302 (4957/5.0)	M28/43 ④	8	DOHC
	944	151 (2479/2.5)	M44/07 ⑤	4	SOHC
	944S	151 (2479/2.5)	M44/40 ⑥	4	DOHC
	944 Turbo	151 (2479/2.5)	M44/51	4	SOHC
1988	911	193 (3164/3.2)	930.21	6	①
	911 Turbo	201 (3299/3.3)	930.68	6	①
	924S	151 (2479/2.5)	M44/07 ⑤	4	SOHC
	928S4	302 (4957/5.0)	M28/43 ④	8	DOHC
	944	151 (2479/2.5)	M44/07 ⑤	4	SOHC
	944S	151 (2479/2.5)	M44/40 ⑥	4	DOHC
	944 Turbo	151 (2479/2.5)	M44/51	4	SOHC
1989	911	193 (3164/3.2)	930.25	6	①
	911 Turbo	201 (3299/3.3)	930.68	6	①
	911 Carrera 4	219 (3600/3.6)	M64/01	6	①
	928S4	302 (4957/5.0)	M28/41, 42	8	DOHC
	944	164 (2681/2.7)	M44/11, 12	4	SOHC
	944S2	181 (2969/3.0)	M44/41	4	DOHC
	944 Turbo	151 (2479/2.5)	M44/51	4	SOHC
1990–91	911 Carrera 2 ⑦	219 (3600/3.6)	M64/01	6	SOHC ①
	911 Carrera 4 ⑧	219 (3600/3.6)	M64/01	6	SOHC ①
	928S4	302 (4957/5.0)	M28/41, 42	8	DOHC
	944S2	183 (2990/3.0)	M44/41	4	DOHC

DOHC Dual Overhead Camshaft
SOHC Single Overhead Camshaft
① Air cooled, 6 cylinder, horizontally opposed, rear-mounted

② M28/20 with automatic transaxle
③ M44/04 with automatic transaxle
④ M28/44 with automatic transaxle
⑤ M44/08 with automatic transaxle

⑥ 16 valve engine
⑦ Includes Carrera 2 Coupe, Targa, Cabriolet
⑧ Includes Carrera 4 Coupe, Targa, Cabriolet

GENERAL ENGINE SPECIFICATIONS

Year	Model	Engine Displacement cu. in. (cc)	Fuel System Type	Net Horsepower @ rpm	Net Torque @ rpm (ft. lbs.)	Bore × Stroke (in.)	Compression Ratio	Oil Pressure @ rpm
1987	911	193 (3164)	DME	214 @ 5900	195 @ 4800	3.74 × 2.93	9.5:1	50 @ 5000
	911 Turbo	201 (3299)	KE	282 @ 5500	278 @ 4000	3.82 × 2.93	7.0:1	60 @ 5500
	924S	151 (2479)	DME	147 @ 5800	140 @ 3000	3.94 × 3.11	9.7:1	50–70 @ 5500
	928S4	302 (4957)	LH	316 @ 6000	317 @ 3000	3.94 × 3.11	10.0:1	70 @ 5500
	944	151 (2479)	DME	147 @ 5800	144 @ 3000	3.94 × 3.11	9.7:1	50–70 @ 5500
	944S	151 (2479)	DME	188 @ 6000	170 @ 4300	3.94 × 3.11	10.9:1	50–70 @ 5500
	944 Turbo	151 (2479)	DME	220 @ 5800	243 @ 3500	3.94 × 3.11	8.0:1	50–70 @ 5500
1988	911	193 (2164)	DME	214 @ 5900	195 @ 4800	3.74 × 2.93	9.5:1	50 @ 5000
	911 Turbo	201 (3299)	KE	282 @ 5500	278 @ 4000	3.82 × 2.93	7.0:1	60 @ 5500
	924S	219 (3600)	DME	147 @ 5800	140 @ 3000	3.94 × 3.11	9.7:1	50–70 @ 5500
	928S4	302 (4957)	LH	316 @ 6000	317 @ 3000	3.94 × 3.11	10.0:1	70 @ 5500
	944	164 (2681)	DME	147 @ 5800	144 @ 3000	3.94 × 3.11	9.7:1	50–70 @ 5500
	944S	181 (2969)	DME	188 @ 6000	170 @ 4300	3.94 × 3.11	10.9:1	50–70 @ 5500
	944 Turbo	151 (2479)	DME	220 @ 5800	243 @ 3500	3.94 × 3.11	8.0:1	50–70 @ 5500
1989	911	193 (2164)	DME	214 @ 5900	195 @ 4500	3.74 × 2.93	9.5:1	66 @ 5000
	911 Turbo	201 (3299)	KE	282 @ 5500	288 @ 4000	3.82 × 2.93	7.0:1	66 @ 5500
	911 Carrera 4	219 (3600)	DME	247 @ 6100	247 @ 4800	3.94 × 3.01	11.3:1	74 @ 5000
	928S4	302 (4957)	LH	316 @ 6000	317 @ 3000	3.94 × 3.11	10.0:1	74 @ 4000
	944	164 (2681)	DME	162 @ 5800	166 @ 4200	4.09 × 3.11	10.9:1	52 @ 6000
	944S2	181 (2969)	DME	208 @ 5800	207 @ 4100	4.09 × 3.11	10.9:1	52 @ 6000
	944 Turbo	151 (2479)	DME	247 @ 6000	258 @ 4000	3.94 × 3.11	8.0:1	52 @ 6000
1990–91	911 Carrera 2	219 (3600)	DME	247 @ 6100	228 @ 4800	3.94 × 3.01	11.3:1	73 @ 5000
	911 Carrera 4	219 (3600)	DME	247 @ 6100	228 @ 4800	3.94 × 3.01	11.3:1	73 @ 5000
	928S4	302 (4957)	LH	326① @ 6200	317 @ 4100	3.94 × 3.11	10.0:1	74 @ 4000
	944S2	183 (2990)	DME	208 @ 5800	207 @ 4100	4.09 × 3.46	10.9:1	58 @ 5000

DME Digital Motor Electronic Fuel Injection
KE   Bosch Electronic CIS Fuel Injection
LH   Bosch Air Flow Controlled Fuel Injection
① 326 w/MT
   316 w/AT

TUNE-UP SPECIFICATIONS

Year	Model	Engine Displacement cu. in. (cc)	Spark Plugs Type	Gap (in.)	Ignition Timing (deg @ rpm)	Compression Pressure (psi)	Fuel Pump (psi)	Idle Speed (rpm)	Valve Clearance In.	Valve Clearance Ex.
1987	911	193 (3164)	WR7DC	.028	26B @ 4000	①	34–40	780–820	0.004	0.004
	911 Turbo	201 (3299)	W3DP	.028	26B @ 4000	①	34–40	850–950	0.004	0.004
	924S	151 (2479)	WR7DC	.028	5B @ 840	①	34–40	800–880	Hyd.	Hyd.
	928S4	302 (4957)	WR7DC	.028	NA	①	NA	800–880	Hyd.	Hyd.
	944	151 (2479)	WR7DC	.028	10B @ 850	①	34–40	800–880	Hyd.	Hyd.
	944S	151 (2479)	WR7DC	.028	NA	①	34–40	800–880	Hyd.	Hyd.
	944 Turbo	151 (2479)	WR6DC	.028	5B @ 840	①	34–40	800–880	Hyd.	Hyd.
1988	911	193 (2164)	WR7DC	.028	26B @ 4000	①	34–40	780–820	0.004	0.004
	911 Turbo	201 (3299)	W3DP	.028	26B @ 4000	①	34–40	850–950	0.004	0.004
	924S	219 (3600)	WR7DC	.028	5B @ 840	①	34–40	800–880	Hyd.	Hyd.
	928S4	302 (4957)	WR7DC	.028	10° ± 2 BTDC②	①	NA	800–880	Hyd.	Hyd.

TUNE-UP SPECIFICATIONS

Year	Model	Engine Displacement cu. in. (cc)	Spark Plugs Type	Gap (in.)	Ignition Timing (deg @ rpm)	Compression Pressure (psi)	Fuel Pump (psi)	Idle Speed (rpm)	Valve Clearance In.	Valve Clearance Ex.
1988	944	164 (2681)	WR7DC	.028	10B @ 850	①	34–40	800–880	Hyd.	Hyd.
	944S	181 (2969)	WR7DC	.028	10°±3 BTDC③	①	NA	800–880	Hyd.	Hyd.
	944 Turbo	151 (2479)	WR6DS	.028	5B @ 840	①	34–40	800–880	Hyd.	Hyd.
1989	911	193 (2164)	WR7DC	.028	0°±3 BTDC②	①	34–40	880±20	0.004	0.004
	911 Turbo	201 (3299)	W3DP0	.028	26B @ 4000	①	NA	900±50	0.004	0.004
	911 Carrera 4	219 (3600)	FR5DTC	.031	0°±3	①	53–59	880±40	0.004	0.004
	928S4	302 (4957)	WR7DC	.028	10°±2 BTDC②	①	56	675±25	Hyd.	Hyd.
	944	164 (2681)	WR7DC	.028	5°±3 BTDC②	①	53–59	840±40	Hyd.	Hyd.
	944S2	181 (2969)	WR5DC	.028	10°±3	①	NA	840±40	Hyd.	Hyd.
	944 Turbo	151 (2479)	WR7DC	.028	5°±3 BTDC②	①	34–40	840±40③	Hyd.	Hyd.
1990–91	911 Carrera 2	219 (3600)	FR5DTC④	.031	0°±3°	①	48–50	880±90②	0.004	0.004
	911 Carrera 4	219 (3600)	FR5DTC④	.031	0°±3°	①	48–50	880±40②	0.004	0.004
	928S4	302 (4957)	WR7DC④	.028	10°±2°BTDC②	①	56	675±25②	Hyd.	Hyd.
	944S2	183 (2990)	WR5DC④	.028	10°±3°	①	48⑤	840±40②	Hyd.	Hyd.

NOTE: The Underhood Specifications sticker often reflects tune-up specifications changes made in production. Sticker Figures must be used if they disagree with those in this chart

B Before Top Dead Center
BTDC Before Top Dead Center
NA Not available at time of publication
① All cylinders should be within 22 psi of the highest reading
② Checking only, not adjustable
③ With idle stabilization system disconnected
④ Bosch number
⑤ At Idle

FIRING ORDERS

NOTE: To avoid confusion, always replace spark plug wires one at a time.

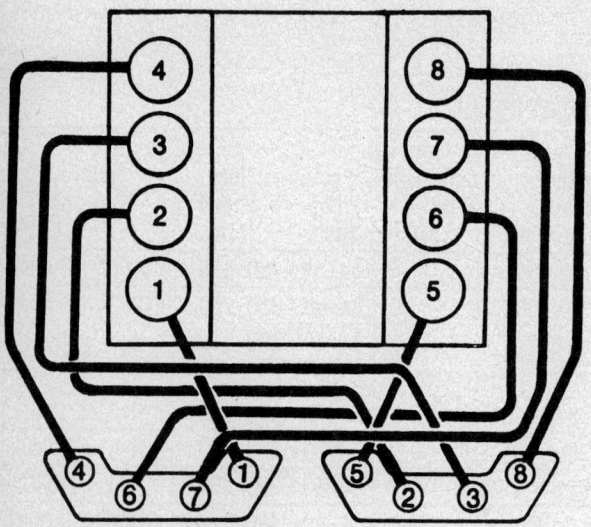

928 S4 vehicle
Engine Firing Order: 1–3–7–2–6–5–4–8
Distributorless Ignition System

FRONT
928 and 928S Models

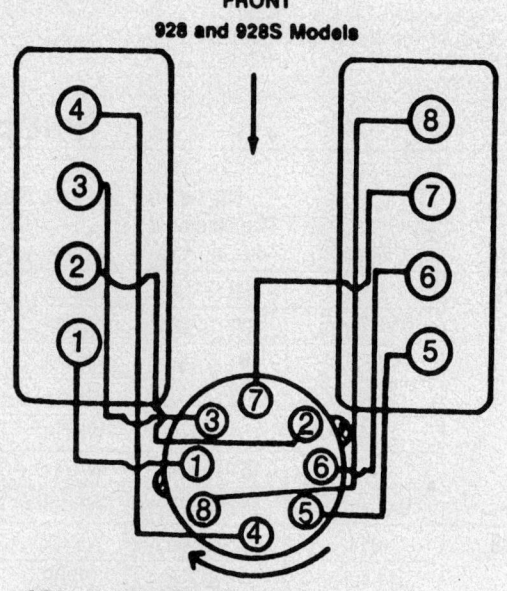

928 and 928S vehicles
Engine Firing Order: 1–3–7–2–6–5–4–8
Distributor Rotation: Clockwise

FIRING ORDERS

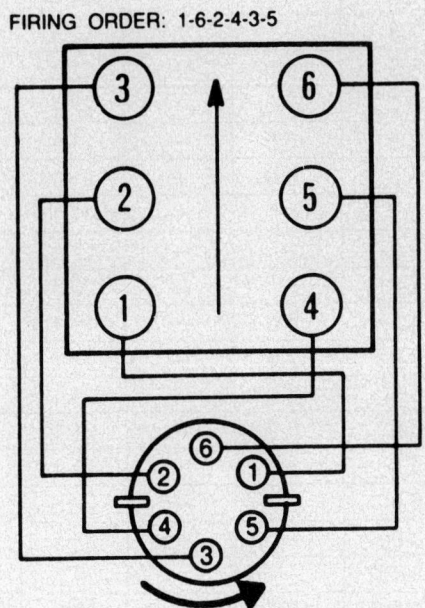

FIRING ORDER: 1-6-2-4-3-5

911, 911SC and 911 Turbo vehicles
Engine Firing Order: 1–6–2–4–3–5
Distributor Rotation: Counterclockwise

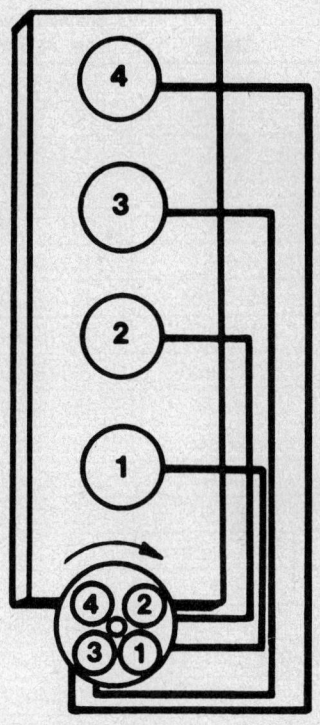

924S and 944 vehicles
Engine Firing Order: 1–3–4–2
Distributor rotation: Clockwise

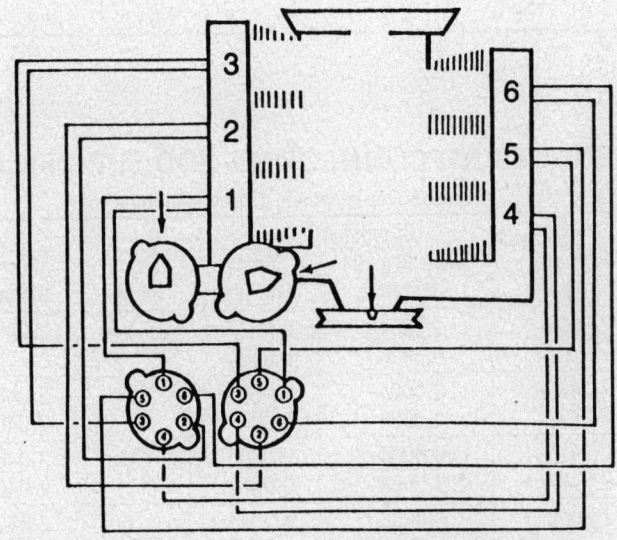

911 Carrera 4 with Dual Ignition
Engine Firing Order: 1–6–2–4–3–5
Distributor Rotation: Clockwise

CAPACITIES

Year	Model	Engine Displacement cu. in. (cc)	Engine Crankcase (qts.) with Filter	Engine Crankcase (qts.) without Filter	Transaxle (pts.) Manual	Transaxle (pts.) Auto.	Drive Axle (pts.)	Fuel Tank (gal.)	Cooling System (qts.)
1987	911	193 (3164)	10.6	—	6.6	—	—	22.5	—
	911 Turbo	201 (3299)	10.6	—	7.8	—	—	22.5	—
	924S	151 (2479)	6.4	—	5.5	6.0	—	17.4	9.0
	928S4	302 (4957)	8.5	8.0	8.0	17.0	—	22.7	17.0
	944	151 (2479)	6.4	—	5.5	6.0	—	21.1	8.5
	944S	151 (2479)	6.4	—	5.5	6.0	—	21.1	8.5
	944 Turbo	151 (2479)	6.9	—	5.5	—	—	21.1	9.0
1988	911	193 (3164)	10.6	—	6.6	—	—	22.5	—
	911 Turbo	201 (3299)	10.6	—	7.8	—	—	22.5	—
	924S	151 (2479)	6.4	—	5.5	6.0	—	17.4	9.0
	928S4	302 (4957)	8.5	8.0	8.0	17.0	—	22.7	17.0
	944	151 (2479)	6.4	—	5.5	6.0	—	21.1	8.5
	944S	151 (2479)	6.4	—	5.5	6.0	—	21.1	8.5
	944 Turbo	151 (2479)	6.9	—	5.5	—	—	21.1	9.0
1989	911	193 (2164)	14.0	—	6.0	—	—	22.5	—
	911 Turbo	201 (3299)	14.0	—	8.0	—	—	22.5	—
	911 Carrera 4	219 (3600)	12.0	—	8.0①	—	—	20.3	—
	928S4	302 (4957)	8.0	—	8.2	16.0	—	22.7	16.5
	944	164 (2681)	5.8	—	3.6	8.4	—	21.1	7.2
	944S2	181 (2969)	5.8	—	3.6	8.4	—	21.1	7.2
	944 Turbo	151 (2479)	7.2	—	4.1	—	—	21.1	9.0
1990–91	911 Carrera 2	219 (3600)	12.2	—	7.2	—	—	20.3	—
	911 Carrera 4	219 (3600)	12.2	—	7.2①	—	—	20.3	—
	928S4	302 (4957)	8.0	—	8.2	16.0	—	22.7	16.9
	944S2	183 (2990)	6.9	—	3.6	8.4	—	21.1	8.2

① Front final drive 2.3 pts.

CRANKSHAFT AND CONNECTING ROD SPECIFICATIONS

All measurements are given in inches

Year	Engine Displacement cu. in. (cc)	Crankshaft Main Brg. Journal Dia.	Crankshaft Main Brg. Oil Clearance	Crankshaft Shaft End-play	Crankshaft Thrust on No.	Connecting Rod Journal Diameter	Connecting Rod Oil Clearance	Connecting Rod Side Clearance
1987	151 (2479)	2.8000	0.0004–0.0028	0.0044–0.0124	3	2.0800	0.0008–0.0028	—
	193 (3164)	2.2429–2.2437	0.0004–0.0028	0.0004–0.0077	1	2.0461–2.0468	0.0012–0.0035	0.0079–0.0158
	201 (3299)	2.2429–2.2437	0.0004–0.0028	0.0004–0.0077	1	2.0461–2.0468	0.0012–0.0035	0.0079–0.0158
	302 (4957)	2.8000	0.0008–0.0039	0.0044–0.0124	3	2.0800	0.0008–0.0028	—
1988	151 (2479)	2.8000	0.0004–0.0028	0.0044–0.0124	3	2.0800	0.0008–0.0028	—
	193 (3164)	2.2429–2.2437	0.0004–0.0028	0.0004–0.0077	1	2.0461–2.0468	0.0012–0.0035	0.0079–0.0158

CRANKSHAFT AND CONNECTING ROD SPECIFICATIONS

All measurements are given in inches

| Year | Engine Displacement cu. in. (cc) | Crankshaft | | | | Connecting Rod | | |
		Main Brg. Journal Dia.	Main Brg. Oil Clearance	Shaft End-play	Thrust on No.	Journal Diameter	Oil Clearance	Side Clearance
1988	201 (3299)	2.2429–2.2437	0.0004–0.0028	0.0004–0.0077	1	2.0461–2.0468	0.0012–0.0035	0.0079–0.0158
	302 (4957)	2.8000	0.0008–0.0039	0.0044–0.0124	3	2.0800	0.0008–0.0028	—
1989	151 (2479)	2.8000	0.0004–0.0028	0.0044–0.0124	3	2.0800	0.0008–0.0028	—
	193 (3164)	2.2429–2.2437	0.0004–0.0028	0.0004–0.0077	1	2.0461–2.0468	0.0012–0.0035	0.0079–0.0158
	201 (3299)	2.2429–2.2437	0.0004–0.0028	0.0004–0.0077	1	2.0461–2.0468	0.0012–0.0035	0.0079–0.0158
	302 (4957)	2.8000	0.0008–0.0039	0.0044–0.0124	3	2.0800	0.0008–0.0028	—
1990–91	183 (2990)	2.7547–2.7555	0.0007–0.0038	0.0039–0.0157	3	2.0460–2.0468	0.0013–0.0036	—
	219 (3600)	2.3610–2.3618	0.0004–0.0028	0.0004–0.0077	1	2.1642–2.1649	0.0012–0.0035	0.0079–0.0158
	302 (4957)	2.7547–2.7555	0.0007–0.0038	0.0043–0.0122	3	2.0460–2.0468	0.0007–0.0027	—

VALVE SPECIFICATIONS

| Year | Engine Displacement cu. in. (cc) | Seat Angle (deg.) | Face Angle (deg.) | Spring Test Pressure (lbs.) | Spring Installed Height (in.) | Stem-to-Guide Clearance (in.) | | Stem Diameter (in.) | |
						Intake	Exhaust	Intake	Exhaust
1987	193 (3164)	45	45	176.4 @ 1.21 ①	1.3779 ②	0.030–0.057	0.050–0.077④	0.353	0.352
	201 (3299)	45	45	176.4 @ 1.21 ①	1.3779 ②	0.030–0.057	0.050–0.077④	0.353	0.352
	302 (4957)	45	45	—	—	0.020	0.020④	0.352	0.352
	151 (2479)	45	45	—	—	0.032	0.032④	0.352	0.352
1988	193 (3164)	45	45	176.4 @ 1.21 ①	1.3779 ②	0.030–0.057	0.050–0.077④	0.353	0.352
	201 (3299)	45	45	176.4 @ 1.21 ①	1.3779 ②	0.030–0.057	0.050–0.077④	0.353	0.352
	302 (4957)	45	45	—	—	0.020	0.020④	0.352	0.352
	151 (2479)	45	45	—	—	0.032	0.032④	0.352	0.352
1989	193 (3164)	45	45	176.4 @ 1.21 ①	1.3779 ②	0.030–0.057	0.050–0.077④	0.353	0.352
	201 (3299)	45	45	176.4 @ 1.21 ①	1.3779 ②	0.030–0.057	0.050–0.077④	0.353	0.352
	302 (4957)	45	45	—	—	0.020	0.020④	0.352	0.352
	151 (2479)	45	45	—	—	0.032	0.032④	0.352	0.352

VALVE SPECIFICATIONS

Year	Engine Displacement cu. in. (cc)	Seat Angle (deg.)	Face Angle (deg.)	Spring Test Pressure (lbs.)	Spring Installed Height (in.)	Stem-to-Guide Clearance (in.)		Stem Diameter (in.)	
						Intake	Exhaust	Intake	Exhaust
1990–91	183 (2990)	45	45	—	1.6141 ③	0.0012–0.0018–⑤	0.0020–0.0026⑤	0.3531	0.3523
	219 (3600)	45	45	—	—	0.0016–0.0022⑤	0.0024–0.0030⑤	0.3527	0.3519
	302 (4957)	45	45	—	1.6141	0.0012–0.0018⑤	0.0020–0.0026⑤	0.2744	0.2732

① 165.3 @ 1.25 for exhaust valve
② 1.3976 in. for exhaust
③ 1.5748 in. for exhaust
④ With the valve in the guide, with the valve stem flush with the end of the valve guide, measure the rock (side play) with a dial indicator on the side of the valve head.
⑤ Measure guide I.D., valve stem O.D., and subtract for clearance.

PISTON AND RING SPECIFICATIONS

All measurements are given in inches

Year	Engine Displacement cu. in. (cc)	Piston Clearance	Ring Gap			Ring Side Clearance		
			Top Compression	Bottom Compression	Oil Control	Top Compression	Bottom Compression	Oil Control
1987	193 (3164)	0.0060	0.004–0.008	0.004–0.008	0.006–0.012	0.003–0.004	0.002–0.003	0.001–0.002
	201 (3299)	0.0060	0.004–0.008	0.004–0.008	0.006–0.012	0.003–0.004	0.002–0.003	0.001–0.002
	302 (4957)	0.0031	0.008–0.018	0.008–0.018	0.015–0.055	0.002–0.003	0.002–0.003	0.001–0.005
	151 (2479)	0.0031	0.008–0.018	0.008–0.018	0.015–0.055	0.002–0.003	0.002–0.003	0.001–0.005
1988	193 (3164)	0.0060	0.004–0.008	0.004–0.008	0.006–0.012	0.003–0.004	0.002–0.003	0.001–0.002
	201 (3299)	0.0060	0.004–0.008	0.004–0.008	0.006–0.012	0.003–0.004	0.002–0.003	0.001–0.002
	302 (4957)	0.0031	0.008–0.018	0.008–0.018	0.015–0.055	0.002–0.003	0.002–0.003	0.001–0.005
	151 (2479)	0.0031	0.008–0.018	0.008–0.018	0.015–0.055	0.002–0.003	0.002–0.003	0.001–0.005
1989	193 (3164)	0.0060	0.004–0.008	0.004–0.008	0.006–0.012	0.003–0.004	0.002–0.003	0.001–0.002
	201 (3299)	0.0060	0.004–0.008	0.004–0.008	0.006–0.012	0.003–0.004	0.002–0.003	0.001–0.002
	302 (4957)	0.0031	0.008–0.018	0.008–0.018	0.015–0.055	0.002–0.003	0.002–0.003	0:001–0.005
	151 (2479)	0.0031	0.008–0.018	0.008–0.018	0.015–0.055	0.002–0.003	0.002–0.003	0.001–0.005
1990–91	183 (2990)	0.0003–0.0012①	0.0078–0.0157	0.0078–0.0157	0.0118–0.0236	0.0015–0.0028	0.0011–0.0024	0.0007–0.0021
	219 (3600)	0.0009–0.0016	0.0078–0.0157	0.0078–0.0157	0.0118–0.0236	0.0027–0.0040	0.0015–0.0028	0.0007–0.0020
	302 (4957)	0.0009–0.0018①	0.0078–0.0157	0.0078–0.0157	0.0078–0.0574	0.0023–0.0040	0.0015–0.0028	0.0005–0.0049

① Wear limit 0.0031 in.

TORQUE SPECIFICATIONS

All readings in ft. lbs.

Year	Engine Displacement cu. in. (cc)	Cylinder Head Bolts	Main Bearing Bolts	Rod Bearing Bolts	Crankshaft Pulley Bolts	Flywheel Bolts	Manifold Intake	Manifold Exhaust	Spark Plugs
1987	151 (2479)	⑦	⑧	55.3	155 ⑪	65	15	15	18–22
	193 (3164)	24	25	36	58	65	18	14–17	18–22
	201 (3299)	24	25	36	58	65	18	14–17	18–22
	302 (4957)	⑨	⑩	54	213	65	17	15	18–22
1988	151 (2479)	⑦ ⑥	⑤	55.3	155 ⑪	65	15	15	18–22
	193 (3164)	③ ④	25	①	58 ②	65	18	14–17	18–22
	201 (3299)	③ ④	25	①	58 ②	65	18	14–17	18–22
	302 (4957)	⑨	⑩	54	213	65	17	15	18–22
1989	151 (2479)	⑦ ⑥	⑤	55.3	155 ⑪	65	15	15	18–22
	193 (3164)	③ ④	25	①	58 ②	65	18	14–17	18–22
	201 (3299)	③ ④	25	①	58 ②	65	18	14–17	18–22
	302 (4957)	⑨	⑩	54	213	65	17	15	18–22
1990–91	183 (2990)	⑬	⑤	54	145 ⑪	65	14	15	18–22
	219 (3600)	③	⑫	⑨	173	66	15	15	18–22
	302 (4957)	⑭	⑮	55	215	65	11	14–17	18–22

① Step 1—14 ft. lbs.
  Step 2—Turn additional 90° ± 2°
② If equipped with air conditioning—123
③ Step 1—11 ft. lbs.
  Step 2—Turn additional 90° ± 2°
④ Apply a thin coat of Optimoly HT
⑤ M12 bolts
   Step 1—14 ft. lbs.
   Step 2—29 ft. lbs.
   Step 3—54 ft. lbs.
  M10 bolts
   Step 1—14 ft. lbs.
   Step 2—36 ft. lbs.
  M6 bolts
   Step 1—6 ft. lbs.
  M8 bolts
   Step 1—14 ft. lbs.
⑥ Dip studs in engine oil
⑦ Tighten in 3 steps (in order each time)
  1st—14 ft. lbs.

2nd—36 ft. lbs.
3rd—65 ft. lbs.
30 minutes later, loosen each bolt 1/4 turn then
repeat the tightening sequence.
⑧ M10 bolts
   Step 1—14.5 ft. lbs.
   Step 2—33.5 ft. lbs.
  M12 bolts
   Step 1—14.5 ft. lbs.
   Step 2—30.0 ft. lbs.
   Step 3—48 ft. lbs.
⑨ Step 1—14 ft. lbs.
  Step 2—turn additional 90°
  Step 3—turn additional 90°
⑩ M12 bolts
   Step 1—14 ft. lbs.
   Step 2—29 ft. lbs.
   Step 3—54 + 3.6 ft. lbs.
  M10 bolts
   Step 1—14 ft. lbs.

   Step 2—36 + 3.6 ft. lbs.
⑪ Gear wheel to crankshaft
⑫ Crankcase Studs M10—29 ft. lbs.
  Nuts or Bolts M8—17 ft. lbs.
⑬ Step 1—14 ft. lbs.
  Step 2—36 ft. lbs.
  Step 3—65 ft. lbs.
⑭ With hexbolts, see ⑨
  With studs:
   Step 1—14 ft. lbs.
   Step 2—turn additional 90°
   Step 3—turn additional 90°
   Step 4—turn additional 90°
⑮ M12 bolts
   Step 1—22 ft. lbs.
   Step 2—40 ft. lbs.
   Step 3—55 ft. lbs.
  M10 bolts
   Step 1—15 ft. lbs.
   Step 2—37 ft. lbs.

BRAKE SPECIFICATIONS

All measurements in inches unless noted

Year	Model	Lug Nut Torque (ft. lbs.)	Master Cylinder Bore	Brake Disc Minimum Thickness	Brake Disc Maximum Runout	Maximum Brake Drum Diameter	Maximum Lining Thickness Front	Maximum Lining Thickness Rear
1987	911	94	0.813	0.890	0.004	—	0.080	0.080
	911 Turbo	94	0.937	⑥	0.004	—	0.080	0.080
	924S	94	0.940	0.807 ⑦	0.004	—	0.080	0.080
	928S4	94	0.950	1.228	0.004	—	0.080	0.080
	944	94	0.940	0.807 ⑦	0.004	—	0.080	0.080
1988	911	94	0.813	0.890	0.004	—	0.080	0.080
	911 Turbo	94	0.937	⑥	0.004	—	0.080	0.080
	924S	94	0.940	0.807 ⑦	0.004	—	0.080	0.080
	928S4	94	0.950	1.228	0.004	—	0.080	0.080

BRAKE SPECIFICATIONS
All measurements in inches unless noted

Year	Model	Lug Nut Torque (ft. lbs.)	Master Cylinder Bore	Brake Disc Minimum Thickness	Brake Disc Maximum Runout	Maximum Brake Drum Diameter	Maximum Lining Thickness Front	Maximum Lining Thickness Rear
1988	944	94	0.940	0.807⑦	0.004	—	0.080	0.080
	944S	94	0.940	0.807⑦	0.004	—	0.080	0.080
	944 Turbo	94	0.940	0.807⑦	0.004	—	0.080	0.080
1989	911	94	0.810	0.940	0.004	—	0.080	0.080
	911 Turbo	94	0.940	1.260②	0.004	—	0.080	0.080
	911 Carrera 4	94	0.940	1.100④	0.004	—	0.080	0.080
	928S4	94	0.940	1.260⑤	0.004	—	0.080	0.080
	944	94	0.940	0.810⑥	0.004	—	0.080	0.080
	944S2	94	0.940	0.810⑥	0.004	—	0.080	0.080
	944 Turbo	94	0.940	1.260⑤	0.004	—	0.080	0.080
1990-91	911 Carrera 2	94	0.940	1.100④	0.004	—	0.080	0.080
	911 Carrera 4	94	0.940	1.100④	0.004	—	0.080	0.080
	928S4	94	0.940	1.260⑤	0.004	—	0.080	0.080
	944S2	94	0.940	0.810⑥	0.004	—	0.080	0.080

① Front—0.752 Rear—0.732
② Rear—1.100
③ Rear—0.732
④ Rear—0.950
⑤ Rear—0.940
⑥ Front—1.205 Rear—0.790
⑦ Rear—0.788

WHEEL ALIGNMENT

Year	Model	Caster Range (deg.)	Caster Preferred Setting (deg.)	Camber Range (deg.)	Camber Preferred Setting (deg.)	Toe-in (in.)	Steering Axis Inclination (deg.)
1987	911	$5^{11}/_{16}$P–$6^{5}/_{16}$P	$6^{1}/_{16}$P	$3/_{16}$P–$5/_{16}$P	$1/_4$P①	$1/_4$	—
	924S	$2^{1}/_4$P–3P	$2^{1}/_2$P	$1/_{16}$N–$9/_{16}$N	$5/_{16}$P	$1/_{16}$–$1/_8$	—
	928	3P–4P	$3^{1}/_2$P	$11/_{16}$N–$5/_{16}$N	$1/_2$N	$3/_{32}$–$5/_{32}$	—
	944	$2^{1}/_4$P–3P	$2^{1}/_2$P	$1/_{16}$N–$9/_{16}$N	$5/_{16}$P	$1/_{16}$–$1/_8$	—
1988	911	$5^{13}/_{16}$P–$6^{5}/_{16}$P	$6^{1}/_{16}$P	$3/_{16}$P	0	$1/_8$	—
	911 Turbo	$5^{13}/_{16}$P–$6^{5}/_{16}$P	$6^{1}/_{16}$P	$3/_{16}$P	0	$1/_8$	—
	924S	$2^{1}/_4$P–3P	$2^{1}/_2$P	$9/_{16}$N–$1/_{16}$N	$5/_{16}$N	$5/_{64}$	—
	928S4	3P–4P	$3^{1}/_2$P	$11/_{16}$N–$5/_{16}$N	$1/_2$N	$5/_{32}$	—
	944	$2^{1}/_4$P–3P	$2^{1}/_2$P	$9/_{16}$N–$1/_{16}$N	$5/_{16}$N	$5/_{64}$	—
	944S	$2^{1}/_4$P–3P	$2^{1}/_2$P	$9/_{16}$N–$1/_{16}$N	$5/_{16}$N	$5/_{64}$	—
	944 Turbo	$2^{1}/_4$P–3P	$2^{1}/_2$P	$9/_{16}$N–$1/_{16}$N	$5/_{16}$N	$5/_{64}$	—
1989	911	$5^{13}/_{16}$P–$6^{5}/_{16}$P	$6^{1}/_{16}$P	$3/_{16}$P	0	$1/_8$	—
	911 Turbo	$5^{13}/_{16}$P–$6^{5}/_{16}$P	$6^{1}/_{16}$P	$3/_{16}$P	0	$1/_8$	—
	928S4	3P–4P	$3^{1}/_2$P	$11/_{16}$N–$5/_{16}$N	$1/_2$N	$5/_{32}$	—
	944	$2^{1}/_4$P–3P	$2^{1}/_2$P	$9/_{16}$N–$1/_{16}$N	$5/_{16}$N	$5/_{64}$	—
	944S2	$2^{1}/_4$P–3P	$2^{1}/_2$P	$9/_{16}$N–$1/_{16}$N	$5/_{16}$N	$5/_{64}$	—
	944 Turbo	$2^{1}/_4$P–3P	$2^{1}/_2$P	$9/_{16}$N–$1/_{16}$N	$5/_{16}$N	$5/_{64}$	—
1990-91	911 Carrera 2	$5^{13}/_{16}$P–$6^{5}/_{16}$P	$6^{1}/_{16}$P	$3/_{16}$N–$3/_{16}$P	0	$11/_{64}$	—
	911 Carrera 4	$3^{13}/_{16}$P–$4^{7}/_{16}$P	$4^{3}/_{16}$P	$3/_{16}$N–$3/_{16}$P	0	$1/_4$	—
	928S4	3P–4P	$3^{1}/_2$P	$11/_{16}$N–$5/_{16}$N	$1/_2$N	$1/_8$	—
	944S2	$2^{1}/_4$P–3P	$2^{1}/_2$P	$9/_{16}$N–$1/_{16}$N	$-5/_{16}$	$5/_{64}$	—

① 911 Turbo—$1/_2$P

ENGINE ELECTRICAL

NOTE: Disconnecting the negative battery cable on some vehicles may interfere with the functions of the on board computer systems and may require the computer to undergo a relearning process, once the negative battery cable is reconnected.

Distributor

Removal and Installation

911, 911 TURBO AND 911 CARRERA 4

1. Disconnect the negative battery cable.
2. Set cylinder No. 1 at TDC.
3. Remove the heated air intake duct.
4. Take the ignition leads from the holders, if necessary.

NOTE: Some variants of the 911 engine such as that used in the Carrera 4 have dual ignition. Dual spark plugs per cylinder are used to reduce the spark travel and knocking. The ignition timing is about 6 degrees later than other engines because of the shorter spark travel. A double distributor is used.

5. Remove the distributor cap(s) and position aside.
6. Mark the direction of the rotor(s) in relationship to the body of the distributor.

NOTE: Some engines have a scribe mark indicating the correct rotor position for No. 1 cylinder. On these engines it will be more convenient to turn the engine so the rotor points to this mark before removing the distributor.

7. Detach the distributor leads. Remove the vacuum line, if used.

To install:

8. Loosen and remove the retaining nut from the base of the distributor. Pull the distributor straight out of the engine. Check and, if necessary, replace the sealing ring on the distributor housing.
9. Insert the distributor into the engine. Swivel the rotor back and forth to engage the distributor and crankshaft gears. If the engine has been turned while the distributor was out, bring the No. 1 cylinder to TDC before installing the distributor.
10. Check and adjust the ignition timing as necessary.

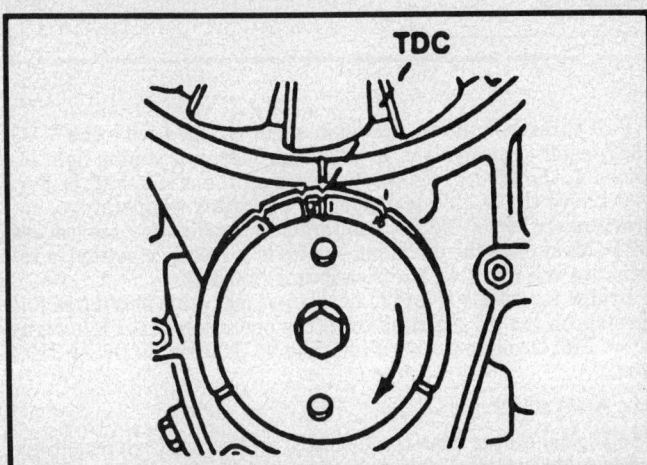

Timing marks on 911 vehicle

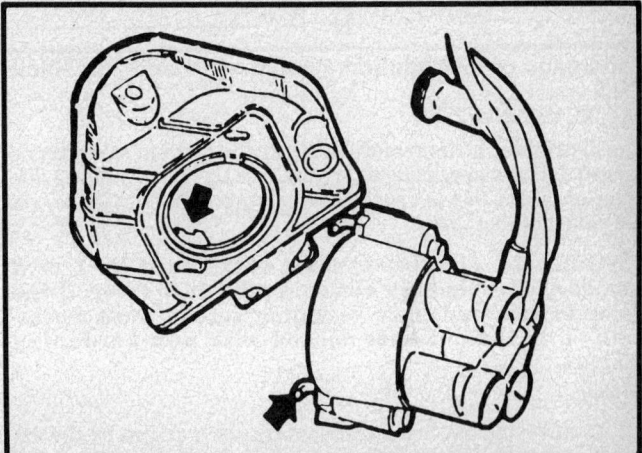

Distributor cap and distributor cap mount of the 944. Note how the distributor cap screw clips are to engage (arrows)

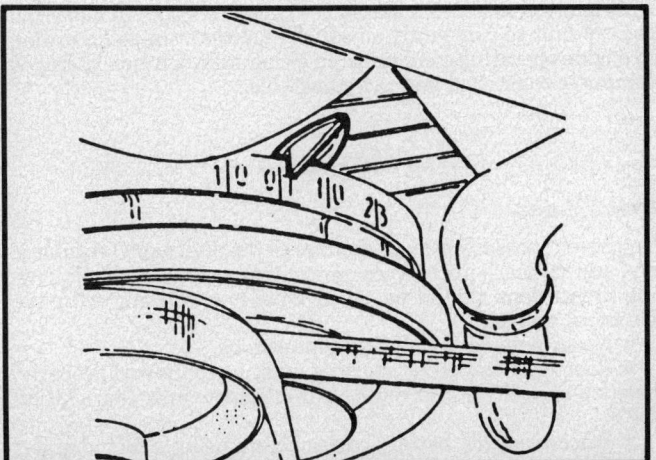

Timing marks on the 928 and 928S are located on the vibration damper at the front of the engine

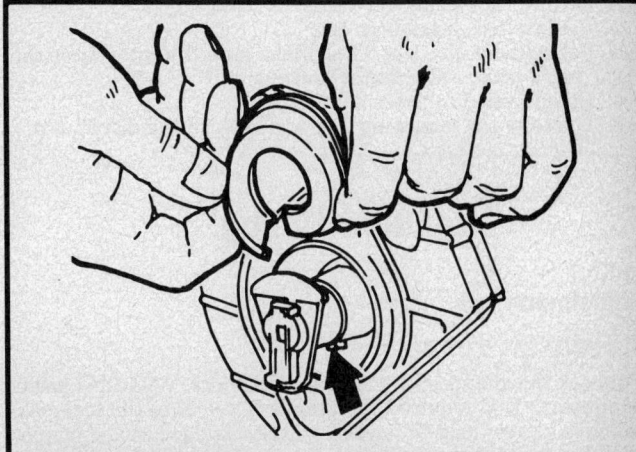

On the 944, the distributor rotor is held to the shaft by a screw (arrow)

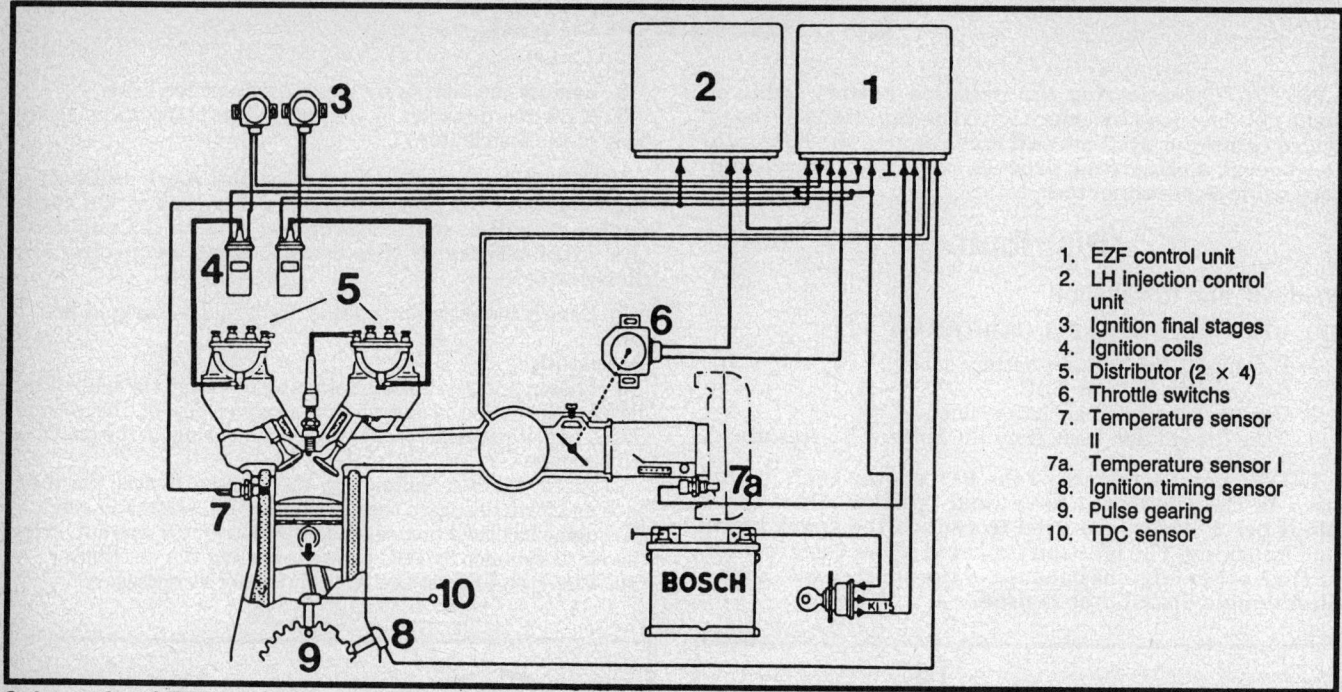

Schematic of EZF Ignition system used on 928 vehicle

1. EZF control unit
2. LH injection control unit
3. Ignition final stages
4. Ignition coils
5. Distributor (2 × 4)
6. Throttle switchs
7. Temperature sensor II
7a. Temperature sensor I
8. Ignition timing sensor
9. Pulse gearing
10. TDC sensor

944, 924S AND 928S

The distributor is not removable. Only the cap and rotor can be removed. Noise appearing to originate in the vicinity of the distributor on the 944 is usually due to a worn Woodruff® key on the camshaft sprocket.

NOTE: The distributor rotor is retained by 1 or 3 screws accessible after removing the dust cover. If the rotor is removed, new retaining screws must be installed or the old ones coated with non-hardening sealant.

928S4

All 32-valve engines use 2 distributors, each driven by the exhaust camshaft for the cylinder bank it controls and mounted on the front of the engine. The distributor caps are retained by 3 screws, as is the rotor. The rotor can only be installed 1 way.

928

1. Disconnect the battery negative cable.
2. Remove the distributor cap.
3. Set cylinder No. 1 at TDC. Make sure the rotor faces the No. 1 mark on the distributor housing.
4. Detach vacuum hoses and wires.
5. Unscrew the mounting bolt and remove the distributor

Ignition Timing

Adjustment

911 AND 911 TURBO

To check the idle speed, a Porsche special tool (VAG 1367 tester or equivalent) is required. Terminals **B** and **C** of the test jack, which is located next to the coil must be bridged with a jumper wire in order to bypass the idle regulator. Timing is then checked in the normal manner. At 800 rpm, ignition timing should be 3 degrees ATDC.

Full throttle ignition timing is again checked with the VAG 1367 tester or equivalent, or with a stroboscopic timing light directed at the 25 degrees timing mark on the crankshaft pulley. Make sure the engine is at normal operating temperature, approximately 194°F (90°C), and that all electrical accessories are **OFF**. Make sure the distributor rotor is correctly installed in relation to the mark on the distributor housing.

Bridge terminals **B** and **C** of the test jack; this simulates full throttle on the control unit and stops operation of the idle regulator. Full throttle timing should be 25 degrees BTDC at 3800 rpm.

944 AND 924S

The Digital Motor Electronic (DME) ignition system is self-adjusting. No periodic ignition timing adjustments are necessary or possible.

928S AND 928S4

The EZF ignition system used on 928S is self-adjusting. The EZK ignition system on 928S4 uses knock sensors to allow the control unit to constantly adjust the ignition timing according to engine operating conditions. In either case, ignition timing is computer-controlled and not adjustable.

Alternator

Precautions

To prevent possibly serious damage to the alternator, regulator and any on-board microprocessor control computers, the following precautions should be taken whenever working with the electrical system.
- Never reverse the battery connections.
- Booster batteries for starting must be connected properly: positive-to-positive and negative-to-negative with the ignition **OFF**.
- Disconnect the battery cables before using a fast charger; the charger has a tendency to force current through the diodes in the opposite directions for which they were designed. This burns out the diodes.

● Never use a fast charger as a booster for starting the vehicle.

● Never disconnect the voltage regulator while the engine is running.

● Avoid long soldering times when replacing diodes or transistors. Prolonged heat is damaging to AC generators.

● Do not use test lamps of more than 12 volts for checking diode continuity.

● Do not short across or ground any of the terminal on the AC generator.

● The polarity of the battery, generator, and regulator must be matched and considered before making any electrical connections within the system.

● Never operate the alternator on an open circuit and make sure all connections within the circuit are clean and tight.

● Disconnect the battery terminals when performing any service on the electrical system. This will eliminate the possibility of accidental reversal of polarity.

● Disconnect the battery ground cable if arc welding is to be done on any part of the vehicle.

Belt Tension Adjustment

911 AND 911 TURBO

A correctly tightened belt can be deflected ½–¾ in. by light hand pressure. If the tension is not within specifications, follow the steps below to adjust or replace the belt.

1. Disconnect the negative battery cable. Remove the pulley nut.
2. Remove the outside half of the pulley.
3. Remove the adjustment spacers to increase belt tension. Add spacers to decrease belt tension.
4. When the correct spacer grouping is achieved, install the belt, pulley half, spacers, and nut.
5. Tighten the nut to 29 ft. lbs. (39 Nm).

NOTE: If spacers have been removed, install the extra spacers on the outside of the pulley so they won't become lost or misplaced.

6. Recheck the belt tension after about 60 miles of driving.

NOTE: On the 911 Carrera 4, the cooling blower and alternator are driven independently of one another. The small V-belt pulley is for the alternator, the large V-belt pulley is for the cooling blower. It has a belt monitor. A faulty or broken drive belt turns on an instrument panel warning light.

Removal and Installation

911 AND 911 TURBO

The alternator is located in the blower housing.

1. Disconnect the negative battery cable.
2. Remove the air cleaner assembly.
3. Remove the upper shroud retaining bolts.
4. Hold the alternator pulley and remove the pulley nut.
5. Remove the drive belt.
6. Remove the blower housing strap retaining bolts.
7. Pull the assembly towards the rear until there is enough clearance to disconnect the wiring.
8. Remove the alternator.
9. Install the alternator in the reverse order of removal. Be sure the blower housing is seated on the dowel in the crankcase.
10. Tighten the pulley nut to 29 ft. lbs. (39 Nm).

EXCEPT 911 AND 911 TURBO

1. Disconnect the negative battery cable.
2. Raise the vehicle and support it safely.
3. Remove the engine splash shield and the alternator cooling vent cover and tube.
4. Loosen the belt tension lock bolt, move the alternator inward and remove the belt from the pulley.

Alternator pulley nut removal

Alternator removal

Fan belt pulley adjustment spacers

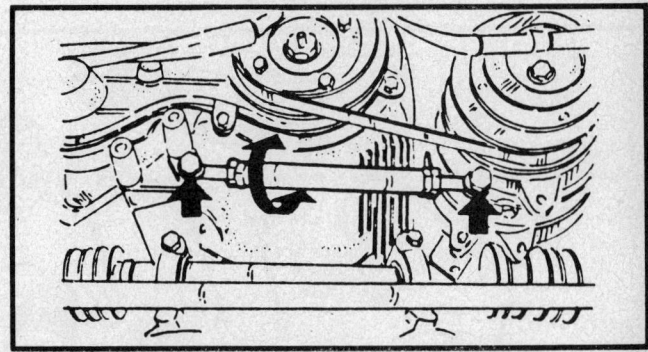
To loosen the alternator and air conditioning compressor drive belt of the 944: Loosen the tensioner end bolts (outer arrow); loosen the locknuts; then turn the tensioner tube (circular arrow) as required. When tightening the belt, the end bolts are to be tightened last.

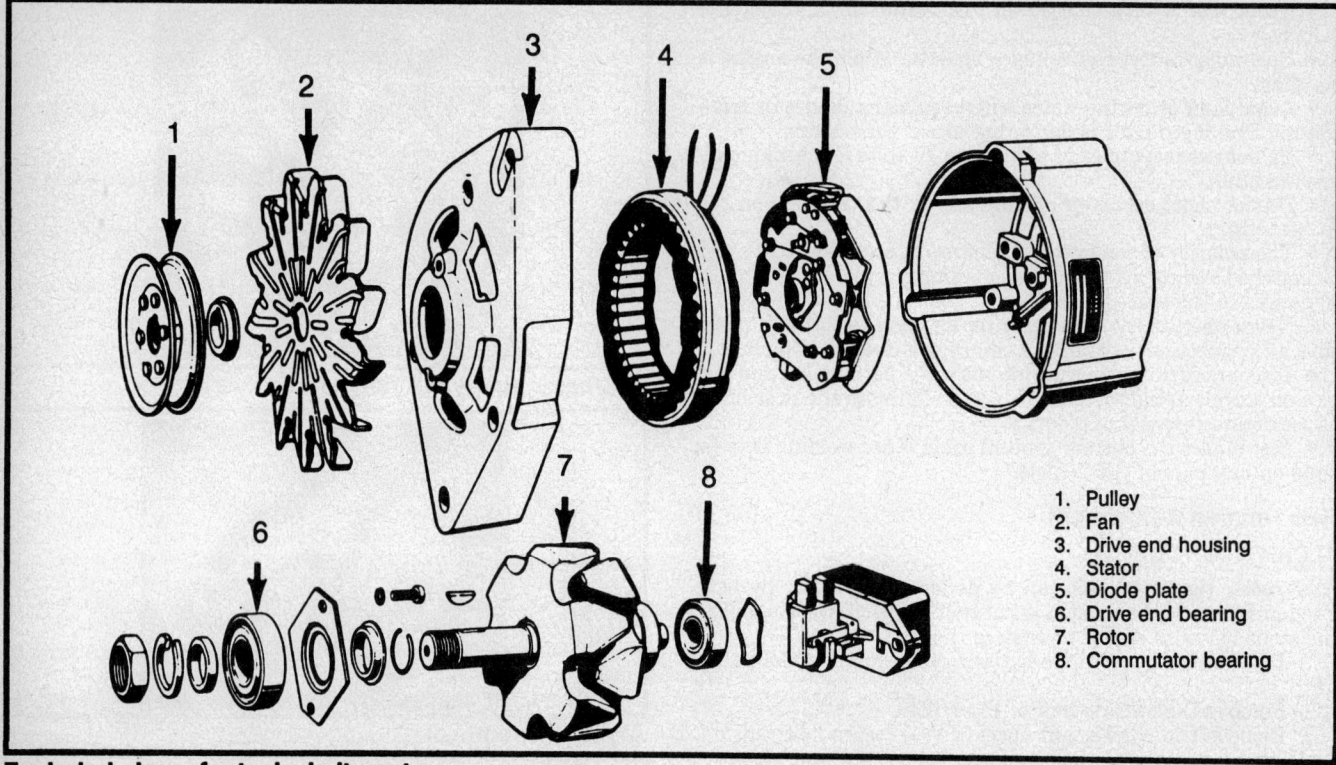

1. Pulley
2. Fan
3. Drive end housing
4. Stator
5. Diode plate
6. Drive end bearing
7. Rotor
8. Commutator bearing

Exploded view of a typical alternator

NOTE: On the 924S and 944, first loosen the end bolts of the tensioner, then loosen the locknuts of the tensioner and rotate the tensioner tube as necessary.

5. Remove the wire connections from the rear of the alternator.

6. Remove the alternator pivot bolt and remove the alternator from the engine.

7. Installation is the reverse of removal.

Voltage Regulator

Removal and Installation
911 AND 911 TURBO

1. Disconnect the battery ground cable.

2. Disconnect the wiring from the regulator.

3. Remove the mounting screws and remove the regulator.

4. Install the regulator. Do not over tighten the screws.

EXCEPT 911 AND 911 TURBO

The voltage regulator is bolted to the rear of the alternator. Remove the alternator before attempting to remove the voltage regulator.

Starter

Removal and Installation
911 AND 911 TURBO

1. Disconnect the negative battery cable.

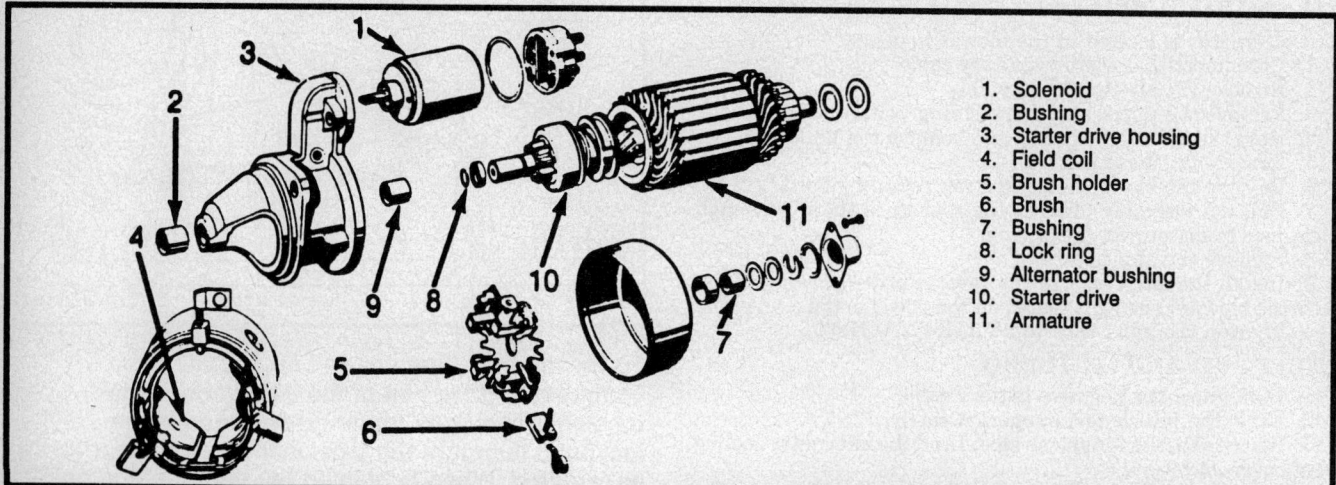

1. Solenoid
2. Bushing
3. Starter drive housing
4. Field coil
5. Brush holder
6. Brush
7. Bushing
8. Lock ring
9. Alternator bushing
10. Starter drive
11. Armature

Exploded view of the starter

2. Raise and support the vehicle safely.

3. Tag and remove the starter electrical connections.

4. Loosen the retaining bolts while supporting the starter, then remove the bolts and pull out the starter.

5. Install the starter in the reverse order of the removal procedure. Make sure the terminal connections are correctly installed, clean and tight.

6. Lower the vehicle. Connect the battery ground cable.

EXCEPT 911 AND 911 TURBO

1. Disconnect the negative battery cable.

2. Raise and support the vehicle safely.

3. Disconnect the 2 small wires form the starter solenoid. One wire connects to the ignition coil and the second to the ignition switch through the wiring harness.

4. Disconnect the large cable, which is the positive battery cable, from the solenoid.

5. Remove the 2 starter retaining bolts.

6. Pull the starter straight out and to the front, then lower it from the vehicle.

7. Installation is the reverse of removal.

CHASSIS ELECTRICAL

Heater Blower Motor

Removal and Installation

911 AND 911 TURBO

1. Disconnect the battery cable.

2. Fold back the luggage compartment mat.

3. Unscrew the cover, remove the screen and bracket and remove the air hoses.

4. Disconnect the control cable and unclip the sleeve.

5. On vehicles with air conditioning, remove the air distributor.

6. Disconnect the electrical plug. Loosen the fastening screws.

7. Disconnect the water drain hose and remove the blower motor.

To install:

8. Installation is the reverse of the removal procedure. Make sure all clamps and fasteners are secure.

9. Connect the electrical wiring.

10. Install the cover and mat. Reconnect the battery cable.

EXCEPT 911

The heater core and blower are contained in the heater assembly which is removed and disassembled to service either component. The heater heater assembly is located under the center of the instrument panel. What follows is a general procedure.

1. Disconnect the negative battery cable.

2. Drain the cooling system.

3. Disconnect the 2 hoses from the heater core connections at the firewall.

4. Unplug the heater electrical connector.

5. Detach the center console and the right side of the instrument panel.

6. Remove the heater control knobs from the instrument panel.

7. Remove the 2 retaining screws and remove the controls from the instrument panel.

8. Disconnect the heater control cables.

9. Using a suitable tool, pry the retaining clip off the heater housing. Detach the both hoses.

10. Remove the heater-to-instrument panel mounting screws and lower the heater.

11. Pull out the 2 pins and remove the heater top cover. Pry the retaining clips off and separate the 2 heater halves.

12. Remove the heater core and/or blower.

13. Installation is the reverse of removal. Refill the cooling system.

Windshield Wiper Switch

Removal and Installation

911 AND 911 TURBO

The combination turn signal, headlight dimmer, and flasher switch is located in the steering column housing. The wiper/washer switch removal and installation procedure is identical.

1. Disconnect the negative battery cable. Remove the steering wheel.

2. Reach under the instrument panel and disconnect all wiring to the switch.

3. Remove the 2 horn contact ring screws, disconnect the wire, and remove the ring.

4. Remove the 2 upper housing retaining nuts. Pull the entire assembly off the column, leading the switch wires through the hole in the housing.

5. Remove the 3 retaining screws and remove the switch.

6. Reverse the removal steps to reinstall the switch.

EXCEPT 911 AND 911 TURBO

1. Disconnect the negative battery cable.

2. Remove the steering wheel.

3. Disconnect the wire harness connector at the switch.

4. Remove the 4 screws holding the switch to the steering column and remove the switch.

5. Install in reverse of the removal procedure. Do not over tighten the mounting screws.

Instrument Cluster

Removal and Installation

911 AND 911 TURBO

The gauges are mounted in individual rubber rings.

1. Disconnect the negative battery cable. Pry the gauge out until it can be grasped firmly, then pull it from the instrument panel.

2. Disconnect the wiring and/or cable and remove the gauge.

3. At installation, connect the wiring or cable and position the gauge in its opening.

4. Align the gauge and then push it into place.

EXCEPT 911 AND 911 TURBO

1. Disconnect the negative battery cable.

2. Remove the steering wheel.

3. Remove the steering column switch, if necessary for working clearance.

4. Remove the instrument cover mounting screws.

5. Remove the rear window wiper and defogger switch, if necessary for clearance.

6. Pull the instrument cluster forward, then disconnect the multipin connector(s) at the rear of the instrument cluster.

7. Lift the instrument cluster carefully and tilt it to the rear. Unscrew the mounting bolt and remove the instrument cluster.

Combination Switch

Removal and Installation

911 AND 911 TURBO

The combination turn signal, headlight dimmer, and flasher switch is located in the steering column housing. The headlight switch removal and installation procedure is identical.

1. Disconnect the negative battery cable. Remove the steering wheel.

2. Reach under the instrument panel and disconnect all wiring to the switch.

3. Remove the 2 horn contact ring screws, disconnect the wire, and remove the ring.

4. Remove the 2 upper housing retaining nuts. Pull the entire assembly off the column, leading the switch wires through the hole in the housing.

5. Remove the 3 retaining screws and remove the switch.

6. Reverse the removal steps to reinstall the switch.

EXCEPT 911 AND 911 TURBO

1. Disconnect the negative battery cable.

2. Remove the steering wheel.

3. Disconnect the wire harness connector at the switch.

4. Remove the 4 screws holding the switch to the steering column and remove the switch.

5. Install in reverse of the removal procedure. Do not over tighten the mounting screws.

Ignition Lock and Switch

Removal and Installation

911 AND 911 TURBO

1. Disconnect the negative battery cable and remove the ignition switch cover.

2. Drill out the 2 shear bolts which retain the switch.

3. Remove the steering lock and spacer.

4. Disconnect the wire harness connector and remove the switch.

5. Install the new ignition switch/steering lock into position on the steering column.

6. Insert the protective plate.

7. Install and evenly tighten the new shear bolts until the heads break off.

8. Install the ignition switch cover and connect the negative battery cable.

EXCEPT 911 AND 911 TURBO

1. Disconnect the negative battery cable.

2. Remove steering wheel as previously described.

3. Drill out the casing tube shear bolts, then disconnect the wire harness connectors and pull the column and casing from the vehicle.

4. Remove the pinch bolt holding the switch housing to the column.

5. Remove the retaining screw and pull the ignition switch from the rear of the casing.

6. Depress the lock cylinder retainer using a suitable tool and remove the lock cylinder.

7. Installation is the reverse of removal. Make sure the wheels are straight-ahead and steering wheel is centered when installing. Tighten the shear bolts until the heads break off.

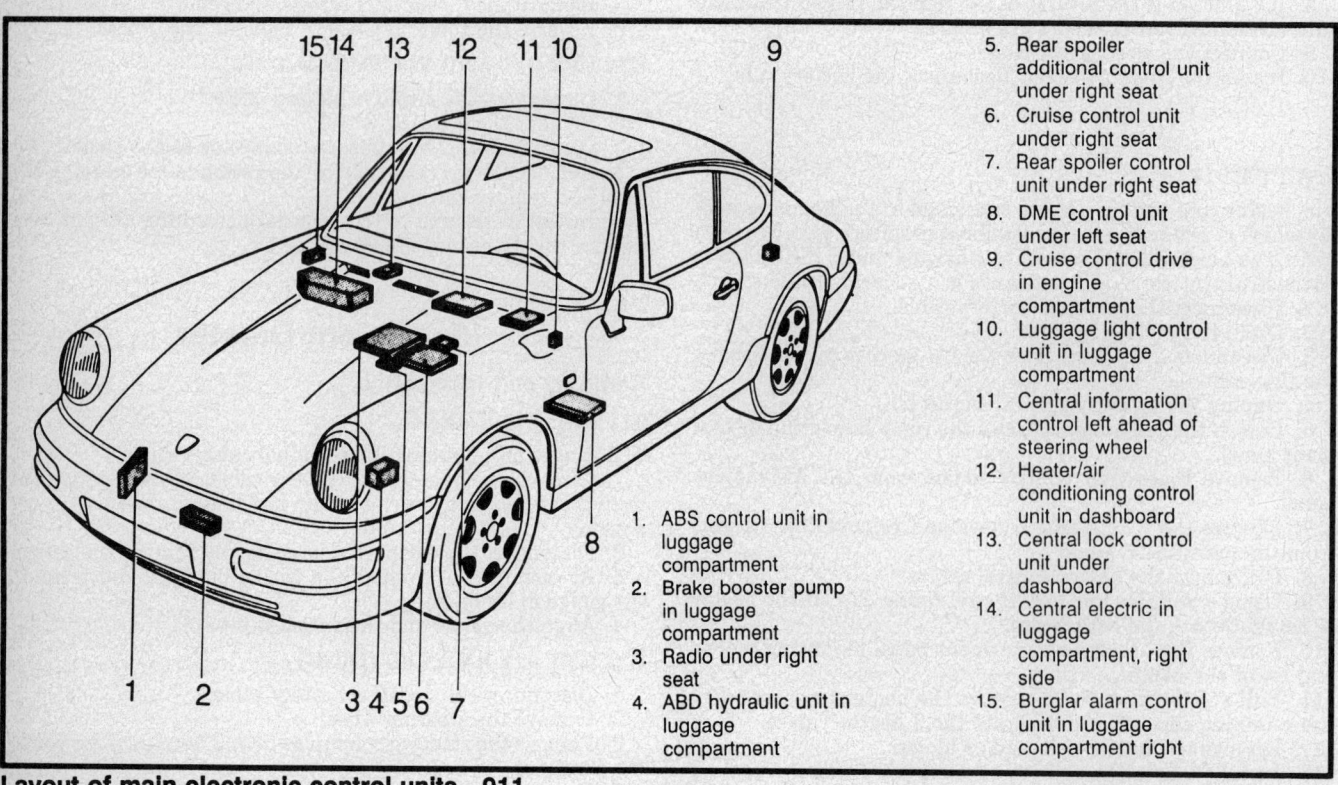

1. ABS control unit in luggage compartment
2. Brake booster pump in luggage compartment
3. Radio under right seat
4. ABD hydraulic unit in luggage compartment
5. Rear spoiler additional control unit under right seat
6. Cruise control unit under right seat
7. Rear spoiler control unit under right seat
8. DME control unit under left seat
9. Cruise control drive in engine compartment
10. Luggage light control unit in luggage compartment
11. Central information control left ahead of steering wheel
12. Heater/air conditioning control unit in dashboard
13. Central lock control unit under dashboard
14. Central electric in luggage compartment, right side
15. Burglar alarm control unit in luggage compartment right

Layout of main electronic control units—911

Stoplight Switch

Removal and Installation

1. Disconnect the negative battery cable. Remove the under dash trim panel, if equipped.
2. Disconnect the electrical connector from the switch assembly.
3. Remove the switch from the vehicle.
4. Installation is the reverse of the removal procedure.

Neutral Safety Switch

Adjustment

The neutral safety switch prevents the engine from being started in any position except **P** and **N**. To test it, set the parking brake firmly and apply the brakes, then position the gear selector lever in every position of its quadrant and attempt to start the engine. If the engine starts in any position besides **P** or **N**, the neutral safety switch is out of adjustment. To adjust it, remove the selector gate for the selector lever, loosen the neutral safety switch mounting bolts and adjust its position, then retighten the bolts and repeat the test.

On the 928, the neutral safety switch is mounted on the side of the transaxle. To adjust it, first loosen the switch mounting bolts, then insert a locating pin made from 4mm diameter welding wire or similar 4mm bar stock, through the lug and into the locating bore in the switch housing. Tighten the mounting bolts to 7 ft. lbs. (10 Nm) and remove the locating pin.

Fuses, Circuit Breakers and Relays

Location

On the 911 and 911 Turbo, the fuse box is located in the left front of the luggage compartment.

The fuse panel on the 924S and 944 is located under the dashboard on the driver's side of the vehicle. The relays are arranged above the fuses. On some vehicles, an additional line of fuses is located above the main fuse/relay panel.

The fuse panel on the 928, 928S and 928S4 is located beneath a hinged panel at the front of the passenger's floor area. Pull back the carpet to expose the cover. The relays are arranged below the fuse line.

On all vehicles, fuse amperage ratings and applications are given in the owner's manual.

ENGINE COOLING

Radiator

Removal and Installation

EXCEPT 911

1. Disconnect the negative battery cable. Allow system to cool, then remove cap on expansion tank. Remove air cleaner with air flow sensor. Remove the splash guard. Drain the cooling system.
2. Locate the wiring to the radiator mounted temperature switch and disconnect the plug. Remove the electric cooling fan. Two electric fans are installed in vehicles with air conditioning. In addition, vehicles with automatic transaxle have ATF coolers built into the radiator.
3. Remove the radiator hoses. Disconnect and plug any ATF cooler lines attached to the radiator.
4. Disconnect the expansion tank, if necessary for clearance and move it aside.
5. Unbolt the radiator and remove it from the vehicle from below.
6. Installation is the reverse of the removal procedure. Make sure the radiator fits properly in the rubber mounts. Put the radiator on the bottom mounts first, then press forward, making sure the rubber seal between the top of the radiator and the lock carrier is not damaged.
7. Add coolant and bleed system.

Water Pump

Removal and Installation

1. Be sure the engine is cold. Disconnect the negative battery cable. drain the cooling system.
2. Rotate the engine to TDC, with the No. 1 piston on the firing stroke and the distributor rotor pointing to the No. 1 terminal of the distributor cap.
3. On the 924S and 944, remove the timing belt cover assembly. On the 928, remove the upper right and left timing belt covers and remove the fan and bracket.
4. When removing the cooling fan, be sure to keep it in an upright position if it is a viscous coupling cooling fan.
5. Loosen and remove the toothed drive belt from the water pump pulley.
6. Remove the bolts and water pump from the engine block.
7. Using a new gasket, install the water pump in the reverse order of removal.

Thermostat

Removal and Installation

The thermostat is located in a remote housing that also contains the temperature switches and sensors including the cold-start switch.

1. Be sure the engine is cold. Disconnect the negative battery cable. Drain the cooling system.
2. Remove the 6mm bolts from the thermostat cover. Remove the cover and pull out the thermostat. Note that the O-ring seal should be replaced.
3. Clean the mating surfaces and install the new thermostat with a new seal.
4. Refill and bleed the cooling system.

Cooling System Bleeding

1. Set the heater to the full hot position and run engine briefly.
2. Remove the vent plug on the radiator hose.
3. Fill the cooling system with the recommended amount of coolant.
4. Start the engine and run it for about a minute at fast idle.
5. Replace the vent plug when no more air bubbles appear at the plug opening.

FUEL SYSTEM

Fuel System Service Precautions

Safety is the most important factor when performing not only fuel system maintenance but any type of maintenance. Failure to conduct maintenance and repairs in a safe manner may result in serious personal injury or death. Maintenance and testing of the vehicle's fuel system components can be accomplished safely and effectively by adhering to the following rules and guidelines.

• To avoid the possibility of fire and personal injury, always disconnect the negative battery cable unless the repair or test procedure requires that battery voltage be applied.

• Always relieve the fuel system pressure prior to disconnecting any fuel system component (injector, fuel rail, pressure regulator, etc.), fitting or fuel line connection. Exercise extreme caution whenever relieving fuel system pressure to avoid exposing skin, face and eyes to fuel spray. Please be advised that fuel under pressure may penetrate the skin or any part of the body that it contacts.

• Always place a shop towel or cloth around the fitting or connection prior to loosening to absorb any excess fuel due to spillage. Ensure that all fuel spillage (should it occur) is quickly removed from engine surfaces. Ensure that all fuel soaked cloths or towels are deposited into a suitable waste container.

• Always keep a dry chemical (Class B) fire extinguisher near the work area.

• Do not allow fuel spray or fuel vapors to come into contact with a spark or open flame.

• Always use a backup wrench when loosening and tightening fuel line connection fittings. This will prevent unnecessary stress and torsion to fuel line piping. Always follow the proper torque specifications.

• Always replace worn fuel fitting O-rings with new. Do not substitute fuel hose or equivalent, where fuel pipe is installed.

Relieving Fuel System Pressure

1. Be sure the engine is cold.
2. Disconnect the electrical lead from the fuel pump. Remove the fuel pump fuse from its mounting.
3. Run the engine until it stalls. Crank the engine several times.
4. Install the fuel pump fuse. Connect the fuel pump electrical connector.
5. Disconnect the negative battery cable.
6. Carefully crack the fuel line, using the proper tools. If any fuel is remaining in the system, do not allow it to spray all over.

Fuel Filter

Removal and Installation
911 AND 911 TURBO

The fuel filter is located in the fuel line, mounted near the tank. Replacement involves depressurizing the fuel system and disconnecting the line fittings from the filter canister. Install a new fuel filter and tighten the fittings using a backup wrench on the nuts to avoid twisting the fuel line.

924S, 944, 944S AND 944 TURBO

On the 924S and 944, the fuel filter is located at the right rear of the vehicle above the axle halfshaft.

1. Relieve the fuel system pressure. Disconnect the negative battery cable. Raise and support the vehicle safely.
2. Place a shop rag under the filter. Using a line wrench, unscrew both line connections from the filter.
3. Loosen the filter clamp and remove the filter.
4. Install the replacement filter in the line and tighten both fittings. Tighten the filter clamp, if equipped.

928, 928S AND 928S4

The fuel filter and fuel accumulator on the 928 is located behind a cover, in front of the right rear wheel well. On the 928S and 928S4, remove the shield under the gas tank. Disconnect the fuel lines, remove the filter and install in reverse order.

Electric Fuel Pump

Pressure Testing

No adjustments may be made to the fuel pump. If the pump is not functioning properly, it must be discarded and replaced. To check the function of the fuel pump, the pump should be connected to a pressure gauge. Be careful not to switch the electrical leads. If the pump fails to pump its normal capacity or it cannot pump that capacity at its specified rate of current consumption, it must be replaced.

A pressure tester such as P 378 or equivalent, is necessary to check the fuel pressure. The pressure gauge is attached the fuel distributor test connection after first relieving the fuel system pressure. Make sure the sealing ball does not fall out when taking off the capped nut. Start the engine and measure the fuel pressure at idle. The fuel pressure should be approximately 28 psi (2 bar) at idle.

─────────────── CAUTION ───────────────

Relieve fuel system pressure before attempting to disconnect any fuel lines. Take precautions to avoid the risk of fire while working on the fuel system and cap all line openings to prevent contamination of the fuel system by dirt.

Removal and Installation
911 AND 911 TURBO

The 911 Turbo is equipped with 2 electric pumps. One is mounted at the front crossmember, near the fuel tank; the second at the rear, near the engine. The fuel pumps are located at the front near the tank.

1. Relieve the fuel system pressure. Disconnect the negative battery cable. Raise and support the vehicle.
2. Remove the cap nuts. Withdraw the pump with its mounting bracket.
3. Loosen the hose clamp and remove the pump from its bracket.
4. Loosen the hose clamps and remove the fuel lines from the pump.
5. Install the pump in the reverse of the removal procedure. Coat both electrical terminals with grease and make sure the rubber boot is firmly seated.

Fuel filter on the 944. Loosen the line fittings first (outer arrows) then the filter mounting clamp (inner arrow) to remove the filter

924S, 944, 944S AND 944 TURBO

The vehicles are equipped with a fuel pump located near the fuel tank behind the right rear wheel. Replacement involves simply depressurizing the fuel system and disconnecting the fuel lines and electrical connector from the pump. Remove the fuel pump and its mounting bracket as an assembly and separate them on the workbench.

928, 928S AND 928S4

A single fuel pump is located with the fuel filter on a mutual mounting bracket, under a plastic hood on top of the fuel tank.
1. Relieve the fuel system pressure. Disconnect the negative battery cable.
2. Raise and support the vehicle safely. Expose the fuel pump.
3. Pinch shut the hose running from the fuel tank to the fuel pump with a suitable clamp.
4. Disconnect the pump wiring, disconnect both fittings from the pump, loosen its retaining strap and remove the pump. Some fuel will be present in the lines. Have a container ready to catch it.
5. Install a new pump in the reverse order of pump removal.

Fuel Injection

Idle Speed Adjsutment

911 TURBO
(CIS FUEL INJECTION SYSTEM)

1. Install the exhaust pickup line on to the test connection of the catalytic converter.
2. Connect the CO tester according to the manufacturers instructions.
3. Disconnect the plug for the oxygen sensor, located on the left side of the engine compartment.

NOTE: Make sure the oil tank cap and seal are installed properly before checking or adjusting the idle speed. Air leaks can cause false readings when performing the adjusting procedure.

4. Turn the control screw on the throttle housing until the proper idle rpm is obtained.
5. Check the CO level using a suitable emissions analyzer. Correct the CO level as required.
6. If adjustment is necessary, remove the plug from the mixture control unit, which is located between the fuel distributor unit and the venturi, then insert the CO adjusting tool.
7. Do not force the tool down while making the adjustments or the engine will stall. Turn the adjusting screw very slowly, as the slightest turn will change the CO reading radically.
8. Remove the adjusting tool. Accelerate the engine. Allow

the engine to return to idle and recheck both the idle speed and the CO level.
9. Once all adjustments are complete, disconnect the test equipment and plug all connections as required.

911

NOTE: Idle adjustment on these vehicles can only be performed using a CO analyzer. For accurate adjustments, the procedure must be closely followed.

1. Run the engine up to normal operating temperature. Engine oil temperature must be approximately 194°F (90°C). Intake air temperature must be 59–95°F.
2. Disconnect the oxygen sensor.
3. Connect the CO analyzer in front of the catalytic converter. Check the CO content percentage at idle. Content in the exhaust gas should be 0.6–1.0 percent.
4. Reconnect the oxygen sensor.
5. Bridge terminals **B** and **C** on the test connection jack located to the rear of the coil on the driver's side engine compartment wall to bypass the idle stabilizer.
6. Check the idle speed (rpm) and adjust,if necessary. Idle speed should be 800 rpm. Adjustments are made with the throttle housing adjustment screw.
7. Remove the bridge from the test jack. Recheck the CO percent content and idle rpm. Remove the CO analyzer probe and close the catalytic converter connection.

EXCEPT 911 AND 911 TURBO

Idle speed is electronically controlled on these vehicles. No adjustment is possible.

Fuel Injector

Removal and Installation

1. Relieve fuel system pressure and disconnect the negative battery negative cable.
2. Remove the electrical connector from the injector.
3. Most vehicles use a metal retaining band or sleeve to retain the fuel hose to the distribution line or fuel rail. Cut this sleeve off with metal snips.
4. Remove the fuel hose end from the injector. In some cases, metal clips retaining the fuel rail may need to be removed and the fuel rail pulled aside.
5. Remove the injector hold-down plate. On some vehicles it may be possible to remove all of the injectors on the fuel rail at one time. Pull the fuel injector from its bore.
To install:
6. Installation is the reverse of the removal process. Use new seals. Lubricate with fuel or silicone grease. Push the injector into its bore. Install retaining clamps.
7. Connect battery cable. Test run and check for leaks.

EMISSION CONTROLS

For further information, please refer to "Professional Emission Component Application Guide".

Emission Warning Lamps

Resetting

The vehicles are equipped with an oxygen sensor. The **OXS** light will come on at 30,000 miles on all vehicles except the 928S with LH Jetronic fuel injection and the 944. When this light comes on it is time to replace the sensor. The 928S and the 944

do not have a reminder light but it is recommended that the sensor be replaced after 60,000 miles.

911 AND 911 TURBO

1. Disconnect the negative battery cable. The sensor plug is located on the left side of the engine compartment, just below the ignition coil.
2. Disconnect the electrical wire at the plug and push the grommet and plug through the grommet hole.
3. Raise and support the vehicle safely. Remove the left rear tire and wheel assembly.
4. Remove the exhaust shield. Pull the safety plug from the

sensor. Remove the sensor from its mounting.

5. Installation is the reverse of the removal procedure. Be sure to coat the sensor with the proper anti-seize compound. Use care not to get any of the anti-seize compound in the sensor slot.

928, 928S AND 928S4

1. Disconnect the negative battery cable. The sensor wire connector is located inside the vehicle behind the lower section of the foot support on the passenger side.
2. Disconnect the electrical wire at the plug and push the grommet and plug through the grommet hole.
3. Raise and support the vehicle safely.
4. Remove the sensor from its mounting.
5. Installation is the reverse of the removal procedure. Be sure to coat the sensor with the proper anti-seize compound. Use care not to get any of the anti-seize compound in the sensor slot.

944, 944 TURBO AND 944S2

1. Disconnect the negative battery cable. Raise and support the vehicle safely.
2. Locate the sensor in the exhaust pipe. Disconnect the electrical connector. Pull the plug from the sensor.
3. Remove the sensor from its mounting.
4. Installation is the reverse of the removal procedure. Be sure to coat the sensor with the proper anti-seize compound. Use care not to get any of the anti-seize compound in the sensor slot.

ENGINE MECHANICAL

NOTE: Disconnecting the negative battery cable on some vehicles may interfere with the functions of the on-board computer systems and may require the computer to undergo a relearning process, once the negative battery cable is reconnected.

Engine Assembly

Removal and Installation

911 AND 911 TURBO

All 911 engines are removed and installed from below the vehicle, with the transaxle attached. The recommended method for removal is to raise the rear of the vehicle high enough for working clearance and then support it safely.

1. Disconnect the negative battery cable.
2. Open the engine compartment lid and detach the hot air ducts from the air gates and exhaust manifold heat exchangers.
3. Detach the 2 heater control cables. Disconnect the brake booster vacuum line.
4. Remove the hot air ducts from the T-union between the air cleaners and then remove the T-union from the blower housing.
5. Remove the tops of the air cleaners. If equipped with air conditioning, remove the compressor and position it aside.
6. Tag for identification and then remove the electrical cables from the generator and blower housing.
7. Tag for identification and then remove the wires from the ignition coil, oil temperature and pressure sending units.
8. Carefully relieve the fuel system pressure, then remove the fuel line from the fuel pump and detach its clip from the engine shield.
9. Raise and support the vehicle safely. Drain the engine oil. drain the transaxle fluid.
10. Remove the Allen bolts retaining the halfshaft flange to the transaxle. Free the halfshafts from the transaxle and drop them aside.

NOTE: On later vehicles, be sure to properly suspend the left halfshaft to avoid damage to the transaxle cooling line coil

11. On 911, unbolt the clutch release cylinder. Move the assembly aside with the lines connected. Do not depress the clutch pedal with the release cylinder unbolted.
12. Remove the starter electrical leads. Disconnect the clutch cable from the control lever, if equipped. Remove the ground strap. Detach the back-up light lead.
13. Remove the rear stabilizer, if equipped. Disconnect the electronic speedometer sensor and rubber plug, as required.
14. Disconnect the throttle linkage from the cross shaft at the transaxle. Remove the cover in the center of the rear floor.
15. Detach the rubber shift lever cover from the flange on the body and pull it forward on the control lever.
16. Remove the safety wire from the square-headed joint. Loosen the screw and slide the shift rod off its base.
17. Position the jack, including a flat support plate, under the engine/transaxle. The jack should be under the point of balance of the powertrain.
18. Raise the jack a slight amount. Remove the body mounting bolts on either side of the engine compartment.
19. Remove the body mounting bolts from the short transaxle crossmember. The engine is removed with this crossmember attached.
20. Very carefully lower the engine.

Rear engine-to-body mounts in 911 vehicles

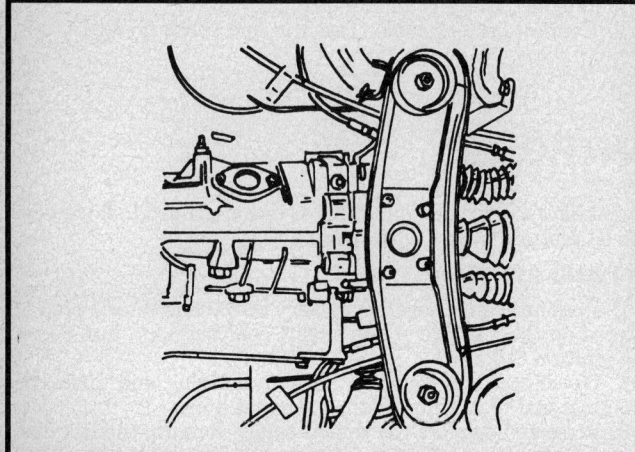

Transaxle crossmember mounting on 911 vehicles

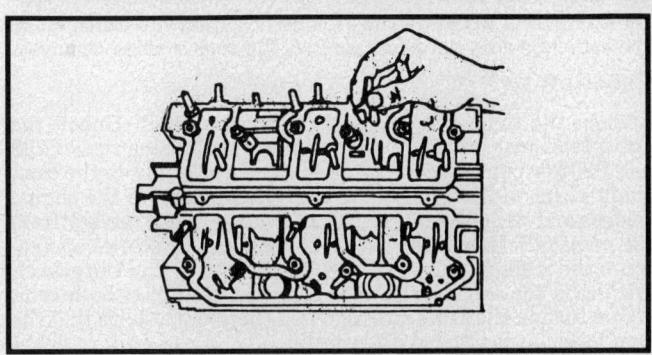

Rocker arm removal on 911 vehicles

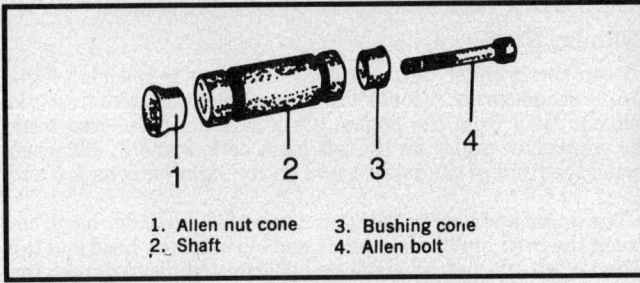

1. Allen nut cone   3. Bushing cone
2. Shaft   4. Allen bolt

Typical 911 rocker arm shaft assembly

21. Roll the engine/transaxle out from under the vehicle. Remove the starter. Release the throw-out fork tension by disconnecting the return spring if used. After releasing throw-out bearing tension, it is necessary to slide the throw-out fork past the bearing. To do this, insert a suitable tool in the opening in the transaxle and turn the bearing 90 degrees. Slide the fork past the bearing. The transaxle may now be separated from the engine.

22. Remove the engine-to-transaxle bolts and nuts. Carefully pull the transaxle away from the engine. Be sure the full weight of the transaxle is supported, so as not to damage the pilot bushing, throwout bearing, clutch disc or pressure plate.

23. Which ever component being repaired or rebuilt may now be moved to a suitable workbench, dolly or engine stand.

To install:

24. Installation is the reverse of the removal process. Before reinstalling the transaxle, fill the pilot bushing in the gland nut with a small amount of graphite grease, no more than $\frac{1}{10}$ oz. (3cc).

25. Lightly grease the transaxle input shaft splines, starter shaft bushing, and the starter and flywheel gear teeth.

26. Carefully attach the transaxle to the engine. Remember the transaxle input shaft will be passing through the throw-out bearing, pressure plate, clutch disc, and pilot bushing, so give ample support during the attachment procedure.

NOTE: If the clutch disc splines and the input shaft splines don't align, turn the crankshaft pulley until the input shaft engages the clutch.

27. Push the transaxle into position so the mounting flanges are flush. Align the bottom holes and install the bolts. Install the top bolts, and then tighten all of the remaining bolts evenly.

28. The engine/transaxle is installed by following the removal steps in reverse order.

29. After the engine is installed, check the clutch adjustment. Refill the engine and transaxle with the correct lubricant. Lower the vehicle.

30. Start the engine and check for leaks.

Rocker Shafts

Removal and Installation

Each rocker arm has an individual shaft on this single overhead camshaft engine. One or all of the shafts and rocker arms may be removed with the engine in the chassis.

1. Disconnect the negative battery cable. Remove the hot air ducts between the fan and the heat exchanger assembly.

2. Remove the camshaft housing cover nuts and spring washers. Remove the covers. Scribe the rocker arms being removed so they can be returned to the same position.

3. Unscrew the Allen bolt in the rocker shaft. Push the shaft from its bore and remove it along with the rocker arm.

NOTE: If the rocker arm is under pressure, the shaft cannot be removed. Turn the crankshaft until the rocker rests on the heel of the cam lobe.

4. Check the rocker arm and shaft for excessive wear or damage. Replace any suspect part.

NOTE: End rockers are installed with the Allen screw heads facing towards cylinders No. 2 and No. 5 respectively.

5. Place the rocker arm on its shaft.

6. The rocker arm shaft should be centered in its bore so each groove is recessed 0.059 in. (1.15mm).

   a. Insert a 0.06 in. feeler gauge in the groove on a side of the shaft. Push the shaft in until the feeler gauge is held tight against the edge.

   b. Carefully remove the gauge and push the shaft in approximately 0.06 in. more, using the feeler gauge to judge the distance.

7. Tighten the Allen bolt to 13 ft. lbs. (17.5 Nm).

8. Install the camshaft cover.

Exhaust Manifold Heat Exchanger

Removal and Installation

1. Disconnect the negative battery cable. Raise and support the vehicle safely.

2. Remove the muffler. Detach and remove the connecting hose from the heat exchanger to the heater valve chamber.

3. Detach the heater hose from the heat exchanger. Remove the 3 sunken bolts from the bottom of the heat exchanger.

4. Remove the 6 cylinder head-to-heat exchanger nuts Remove the heat exchanger.

5. Examine the heat exchanger for damaged flanges or cracks. Replace it, if necessary.

6. Install the heat exchanger in the reverse order of removal. Use new flange gaskets and tighten the retaining nuts and bolts alternately.

Engine

Disassembly and Assembly

NOTE: Further component removal and installation requires engine removal and disassembly. Follow steps of engine disassembly and then assembly for the part being replaced.

1. Remove the engine/transaxle from the vehicle. Separate the 2 assemblies and position the engine in a suitable holding fixture.

2. Remove the muffler and heat exchanger.

3. Remove the rear engine cover plate.

4. Remove the intake distributor and intake pipe with the injection valves.

5. Remove the distributor and the front engine cover plate.

6. Remove the cooling blower impeller, then remove the cooling blower housing with the alternator attached.

7. Remove the engine mount.

8. Remove the front and rear cylinder jackets with the warm air guides.

9. Remove the oil cooler, oil filter, and oil pump.

10. Remove the cylinder head covers. Remove the rocker arm shafts with the protective tubes, pushrods and lifters.

11. Removal of the cylinder heads involves removing the overhead camshafts. All 3 cylinder heads on each bank can be removed as a unit complete with the camshaft and rockers or each cylinder head can be removed individually. For access to the cylinder heads and valves, the camshaft housing must be disassembled and removed.

Rockers

Scribe a mark on the rockers for later installation. Remove the 5mm Allen retaining screws in the rocker shafts, holding the cone-nut that is released on the other end of the shaft. Push out

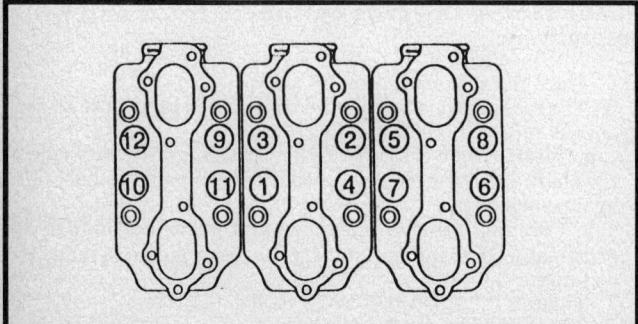

Cylinder head torque sequence on 911 vehicles

the shafts and lift away the rockers. Position the camshaft so the cam lobe does not press against the rocker being removed.

Camshaft

Remove the timing chain cover at each camshaft. Unbolt the chain tensioner and the intermediate wheel, using tools P202 and P203 or equivalent. Withdraw the dowel pin from the camshaft wheel with tool P212 or equivalent. Remove the sliding wedges and withdraw the wheel and flange. Take the key from the camshaft, then unscrew the 3 sealing ring screws and remove the sealing ring together with the O-ring and the gasket. Withdraw the camshaft toward the rear. Note that both camshafts turn in the same direction and therefore require that the cam lobes be positioned differently.

Cam Housing

Unscrew the hex nuts and the 3 Allen screws to lift off the camshaft housing. Each housing fits either cylinder bank.

Cylinder Head

Loosen the cylinder head securing nuts in the reverse of the torque sequence using tool P119 or equivalent, then remove the cylinder head from the engine. Cylinders are numbered from the crankshaft pulley on the left bank as 1, 2 and 3, left when facing the front of the vehicle, and on the right bank as 4, 5 and 6.

The upper and lower sealing surfaces of the cylinder head, between the head and the camshaft and between the head and the cylinder, should not be machined. Permitted distortion at the cylinder sealing surface must not exceed 0.0059 in. (0.15mm). Examine the mating surfaces to ensure that they are in good condition.

NOTE: If a cylinder head stud is broken above the threads, a new Dilavar cylinder head stud should be installed. Grind the broken stud flat, then center punch it in the center. Using a ¼ in. carbide-tipped drill bit chucked into a drill press, drill approximately 15mm

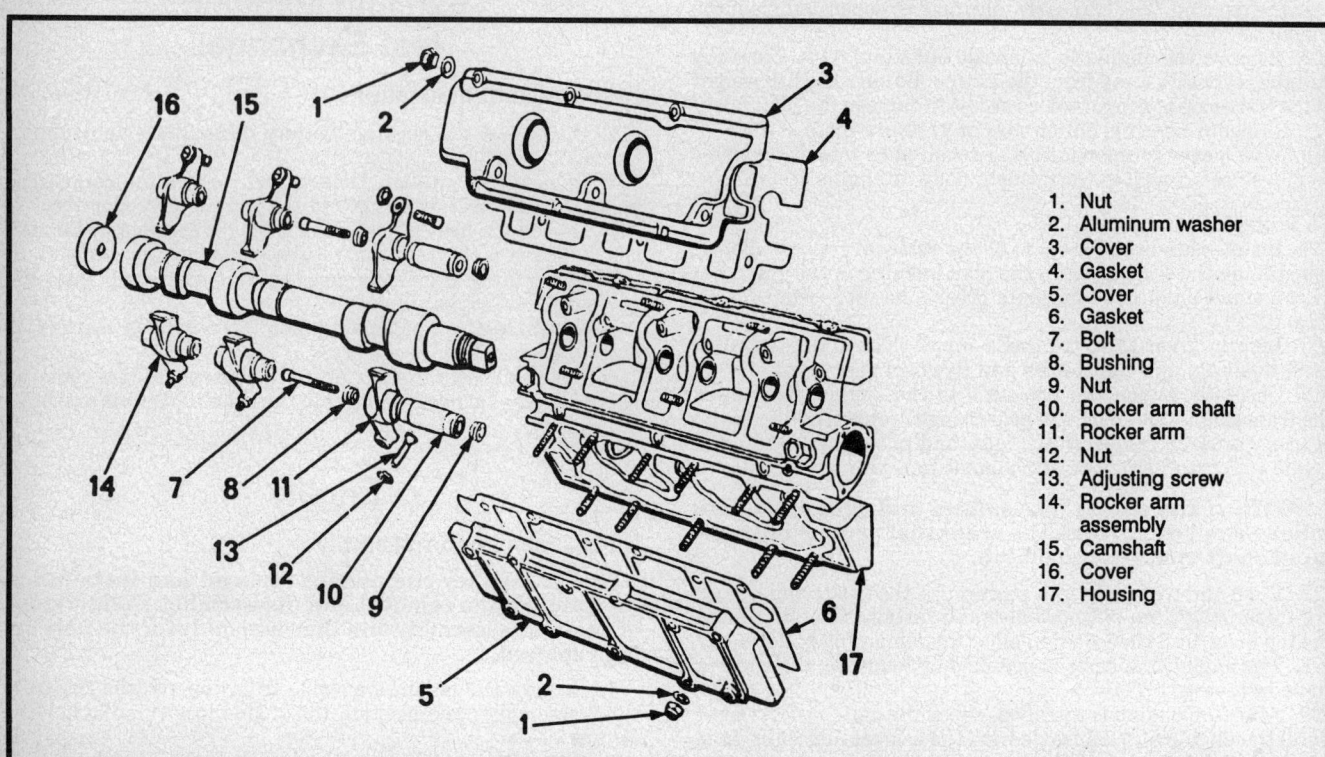

1. Nut
2. Aluminum washer
3. Cover
4. Gasket
5. Cover
6. Gasket
7. Bolt
8. Bushing
9. Nut
10. Rocker arm shaft
11. Rocker arm
12. Nut
13. Adjusting screw
14. Rocker arm assembly
15. Camshaft
16. Cover
17. Housing

Exploded view of 911 camshaft housing assembly

into the stud. Drive a No. 3 screw extractor approximately 10mm into the bore. Heat the case evenly in an oven or with a torch to 392°F (200°C) to loosen the grip of the Loctite. Turn out the broken stud, retap the threads in the crankcase and install a new Dilavar stud 928 101 921 00 or equivalent.

When installing the cylinder heads, use new cylinder head gaskets with the perforations set towards the cylinder. Carefully position each head, insert the washers and tighten the hex nuts lightly.

The camshaft housing is sealed to the cylinder heads only with sealing compound. Assemble the camshaft housing and oil return pipes on the cylinder heads but only hand-tighten.

Porsche suggests that at this point in reassembly, the cylinder head be torqued down first and then the camshaft housing. Some mechanics prefer to torque the camshaft housing first for more accurate tensioning. Either way, the camshaft must be checked frequently for free turning. If tightening 1 side binds the crankshaft, tightening the opposite side must free it again. If not, the housing must be loosened, and tightening steps must be made in a different sequence.

Tighten the cylinder head to specification. Tighten the camshaft housing to 15–18 ft. lbs. (20–24 Nm).

Valve Timing Adjustment

Turn the crankshaft until the **Z1** mark on the pulley is aligned accurately with the joint of the crankcase or the stripe on the blower housing. Position both camshafts with punch marks or code **903** facing upward. The basic engine setting for No. 1 cylinder at TDC and No. 4 cylinder is given by aligning the **Z1** mark on the pulley to the joint and punch marks on the camshafts face up.

In the above mentioned position a bore in the sprocket will be aligned with a bore in the sprocket flange. Insert the dowel pin in the bores. Screw the bolts for the sprockets, finger-tight. In case one of the camshafts has been moved, take a dowel pin from the camshaft in the basic setting position so it cannot turn.

To fine adjust the components, Check and adjust the valve clearance. Cylinders No. 1 and No. 4 must be adjusted properly to obtain the proper timing.

To perform the left camshaft adjustment, install a dial indicator gauge on the stud of the camshaft case. Set the gauge to 0 with an approximate preload of 10mm on the spring retainer of the closed intake valve on the No. 1 cylinder. Turn the crankshaft a complete turn in the clockwise direction from **Z1** while observing the dial gauge. The proper reading should be 1.1–1.4mm. Unscrew and remove the mounting bolt on the left chain sprocket. Using a puller tool remove the dowel pin. Rotate the crankshaft until the **Z1** mark is properly aligned. Install the dowel pin and screw the bolt in finger-tight. Rotate the crankshaft 2 complete revolutions clockwise and recheck the adjustment. Tighten the bolt on the left camshaft to a final torque of 87 ft. lbs. (120 Nm).

To perform the right camshaft adjustment, install a dial indicator gauge on the stud of the camshaft case. Set the gauge to 0 with an approximate preload of 10mm on the spring retainer of the closed intake valve on the No. 4 cylinder. Turn the crankshaft a complete turn in the clockwise direction from **Z1** while observing the dial gauge. The proper reading should be 1.1–1.4mm. Unscrew and remove the mounting bolt on the left chain sprocket. Using a puller tool remove the dowel pin. Rotate the crankshaft until the **Z1** mark is properly aligned. Install the dowel pin and screw the bolt in finger-tight. Rotate the crankshaft 2 complete revolutions clockwise and recheck the adjustment. Tighten the bolt on the left camshaft to a final torque of 87 ft. lbs. (120 Nm).

Lower Assembly

Remove the cylinder heads, cylinders and pistons. Remove the clutch and flywheel. Disassemble the crankcase, being careful not to score any of the mating surfaces by trying to pry the halves apart. Remove the camshaft and crankshaft with the connecting rods.

Assembly is the reverse of disassembly, noting the following procedures:

1. Check the riveting of the camshaft gear and the camshaft. Check the camshaft for out-of-true using V-blocks. The maximum allowable wear is 0.0016 in. Check the endplay of the guide bearing which should be 0.0016–0.0051 in.

2. The oil holes in the crankshaft bearing journals and bearings should have no sharp edges. Carefully remove any metallic, foreign substances before installing the crankshaft and connecting rods.

3. Install the camshaft and gear so the tooth marked with **0** is located between the 2 teeth of the crankshaft gear which are

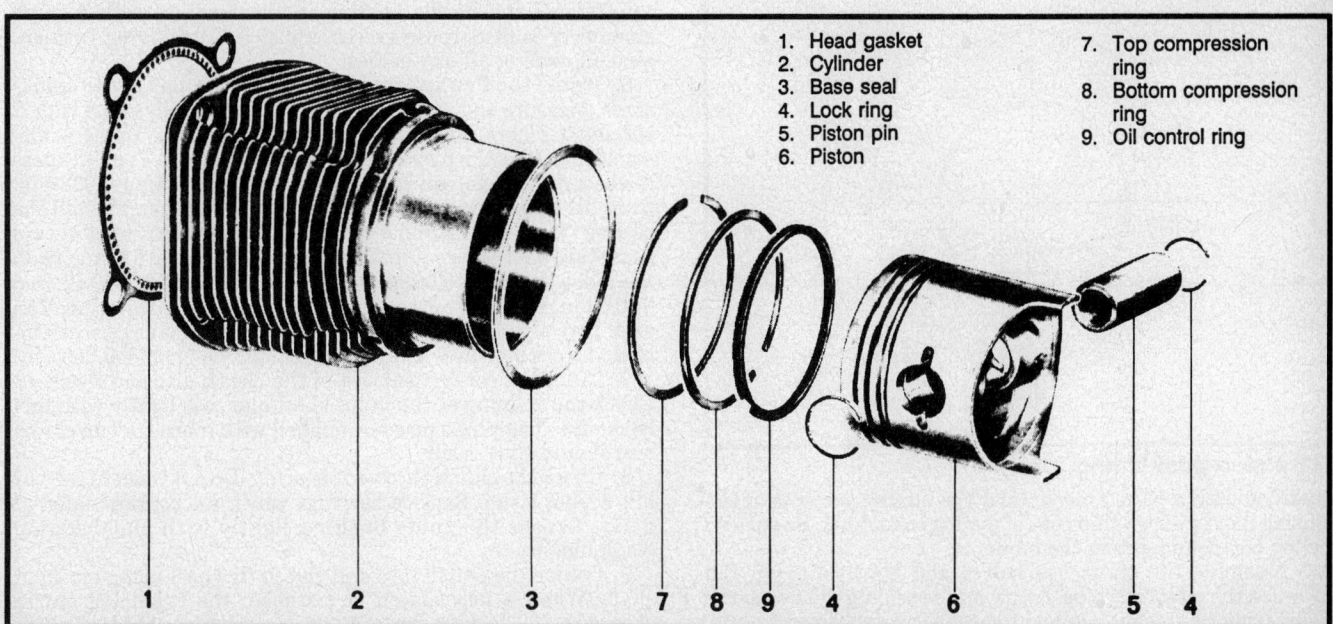

1. Head gasket
2. Cylinder
3. Base seal
4. Lock ring
5. Piston pin
6. Piston
7. Top compression ring
8. Bottom compression ring
9. Oil control ring

911 cylinder and piston assembly

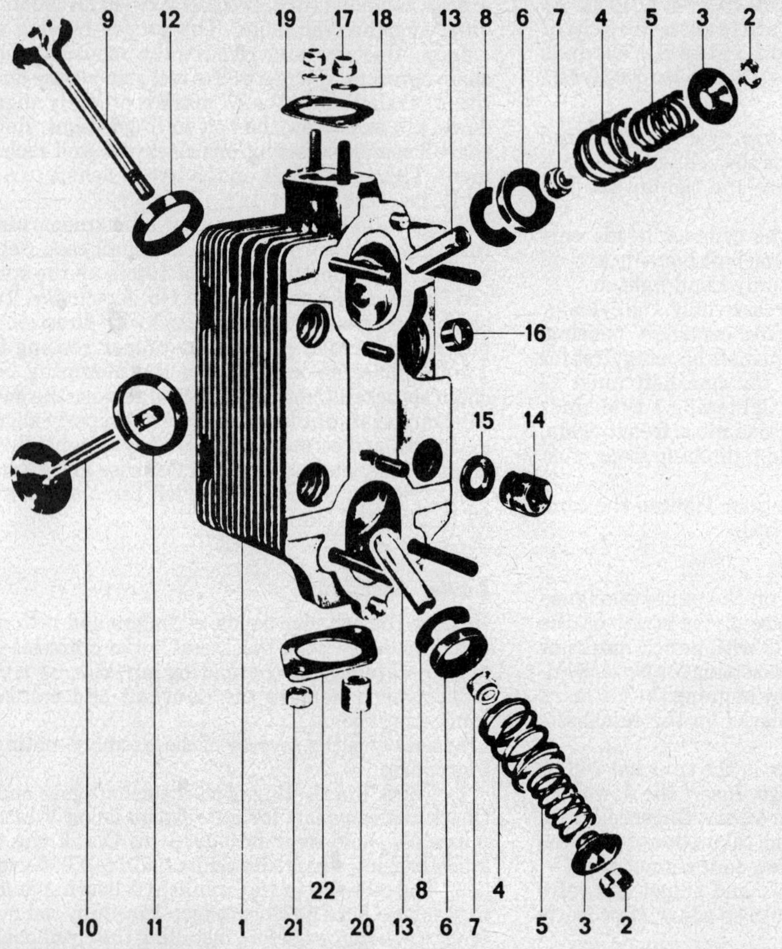

1. Cylinder head
2. Keys
3. Valve spring retainer
4. Outer valve spring
5. Inner valve spring
6. Spring seat
7. Valve seal
8. Washer
9. Exhaust valve
10. Intake valve
11. Intake valve seat
12. Exhaust valve seat
13. Valve guide
14. Retaining nut
15. Washer
16. Threaded insert
17. Nut
18. Washer
19. Intake seal
20. Nut
21. Nut
22. Exhaust seal

911 cylinder head components

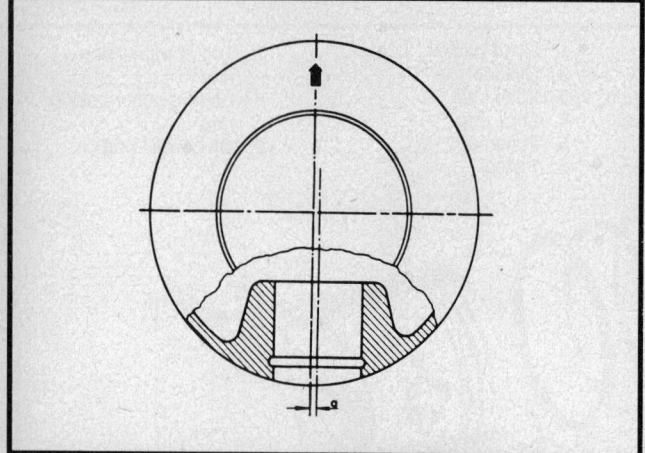

911 piston positioning

identified with a punch mark. Coat the mating surfaces of the housing halves with a thin coat of sealing compound. Be sure no sealing compound enters the oil ducts.

4. Assemble the crankcase halves and lightly tighten the screw for the oil intake pipe. Screw on the sealing nuts with the sealing ring on the outside and tighten to the specified torque. Rotate the crankshaft to ensure free rotation.

5. Grease the needle bearing in the flywheel with a small amount of multipurpose grease. Moisten the felt ring with engine oil, wiping off any excess.

6. Install the flywheel and adjust the axial play of the crankshaft. Measure the axial play by installing the flywheel with 2 spacing washers but without the sealing rings. Using a dial gauge, measure the play by rotating the flywheel. The thickness of the third spacer can be computed by subtracting 0.0039 in. from the measured result. Remove the flywheel and install the sealing ring, felt ring and 3 spacers. Three spacers must always be installed for the required thickness. Spacers are available in the following sizes: 0.0094, 0.0118, 0.0126, 0.0134, 0.0142, and 0.0150 in. Each spacer is marked for proper identification. The axial play of the crankshaft, measured with the engine assembled and the flywheel screwed on, should be 0.0028–0.0051 in.

7. Clean the contact surface of the clutch disc and flywheel. Check the splining of the input shaft and coat lightly with molybdenum disulphide powder, applied with a brush. The clutch disc should slide easily.

8. Check the clutch throwout bearing. Do not wash in solvent but wipe it clean. Replace bearings which are contaminated or noisy. Grease the guide bushing lightly with molybdenum disulphide paste.

9. Center the clutch disc and clutch flywheel using an input shaft. When a new clutch is installed, the balancing marks should be 180 degrees apart. A white paint stripe on the outside edge of the flywheel indicates the heavy side, and a white paint

stripe indicates the heavy side of the clutch. Tighten the bolts to 14.5 ft. lbs. (20 Nm).

10. Clean all pistons and check for wear. Check the marking of the pistons according to the following designations:

a. The letter head next to the arrow is the index of the spare parts number.

b. The punched-in arrow indicates that the piston must be installed with the arrow facing the flywheel.

c. The color dot (blue, pink or green) indicates the paired size of the piston.

d. A statement of weight class (+ or −) is punched in or printed. The weight class is indicated by a color dot; brown equals (−) weight and grey equals (+) weight.

e. Number indicates the piston size in mm.

11. Fit the compression and oil scraper rings. The designation **TOP** should face up.

12. Insert the locking rings of pistons 1 and 2 on the side facing the flywheel. The locking rings of pistons 3 and 4 should be fitted on the impeller side.

13. Install the piston pin. The piston pin may slide in easily by hand, which is normal. Should the pin not fit easily, heat the piston to approximately 176°F and slide in the piston pin without bottoming the pin on the locking ring. Seat the second locking ring. Lubricate the piston and piston pin.

14. Compress the piston rings using a suitable tool, then lubricate the cylinder bore and fit the cylinder bore to the crankcase with the sealing ring. The studs of the crankcase may not touch the cooling fins of the cylinder.

15. Check the cylinder head for cracks and the spark plug threads for damage. Replace the sealing ring and the cylinder head. Pre-tighten the cylinder head nuts slightly, then tighten in sequence to the specified torque.

16. Replace the baffle plate. Coat the lifters with clean engine oil and install them. Slide the protective tubes with the new sealing rings up to the stop, taking care not to damage the sealing rings. Slide the bearing pieces on the rocker arm shafts so the slots face downward and the broken edges outward when settling on the studs. The clip which secures the protective tubes should enter the slots of the bearing pieces and rest against the bottom edges of the protective tubes.

17. Lubricate the gear wheel and driveshaft and insert into the oil pump housing. Install the oil pump cover with the lubricated rubber sealing ring. Check the gear wheels for proper running. Install the oil pump, with a new seal, into the crankcase. The journal of the driveshaft should be in alignment with the slot in the camshaft gear. Center the oil pump by rotating the crankshaft two revolutions and then tightening the nuts.

18. Clean the sealing surface on the flange for the oil filter. Lubricate the rubber seal slightly and screw the filter in until the filter is seated. Tighten the oil filter.

19. Install the oil cooler after checking for leaks and tightening all welded seats.

20. Install the front and rear cylinder jackets and warm air guides. Replace the engine mount.

21. Install the cooling blower housing with the alternator and adjust the V-belt tension. Replace the cooling blower impeller and the front engine cover plate.

22. Install the ignition distributor. Bring cylinder No. 1 to TDC on the compression stroke. The black notch should be in alignment with the reference mark. The center offset slot in the head of the ignition distributor driveshaft should be at an angle of approximately 12 degrees in relation to the longitudinal axis of the engine. Turn the distributor rotor to the mark for cylinder No. 1 on the distributor housing. Insert the ignition distributor.

23. Replace the oil filler neck with the oil vent.

24. Replace the intake distributor with the intake pipes and injection valves.

25. Mount the rear engine cover plate, then replace the exhaust muffler and heat exchanger.

26. Mate the engine to the transaxle. Install the assembly in the vehicle.

27. Fill the engine with oil.

ENGINE MECHANICAL

Engine

Removal and Installation

924S AND 944

NOTE: If equipped with a turbocharger, some components may have to be removed during engine removal.

1. Disconnect the battery cables. Raise the vehicle and support it safely.

2. Support the engine using the proper equipment. If using a jack under the engine, be careful not to damage the aluminum oil pan. Use a wooden block between the jack and pan.

3. Remove the splash panel. Remove the windshield washer tank and bracket and place it behind the right headlight.

4. If equipped, disconnect the clutch cable. Remove the bottom clutch adjustment locknut and detach the cable from the lever.

5. Remove the access plate from the bottom of the clutch housing.

6. Have an assistant turn the engine with the crankshaft pulley. Remove the pressure plate bolts gradually until all pressure is released.

7. Remove the exhaust pipe flange bolts.

8. Remove the bracket at the rear of the transaxle.

9. Remove the entire exhaust system.

10. Remove the backup light switch from the transaxle.

11. Disconnect the axle halfshafts at the transaxle and let them hang down aside.

NOTE: If the vehicle is going to be moved with the engine removed, wire the halfshafts up so they don't become damaged.

12. Remove the clutch housing-to-engine bolts. If equipped

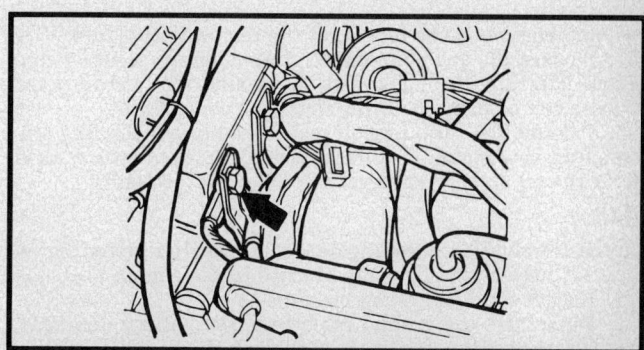

A loose or disconnected engine ground strap could cause damage to the DME electronic control unit.

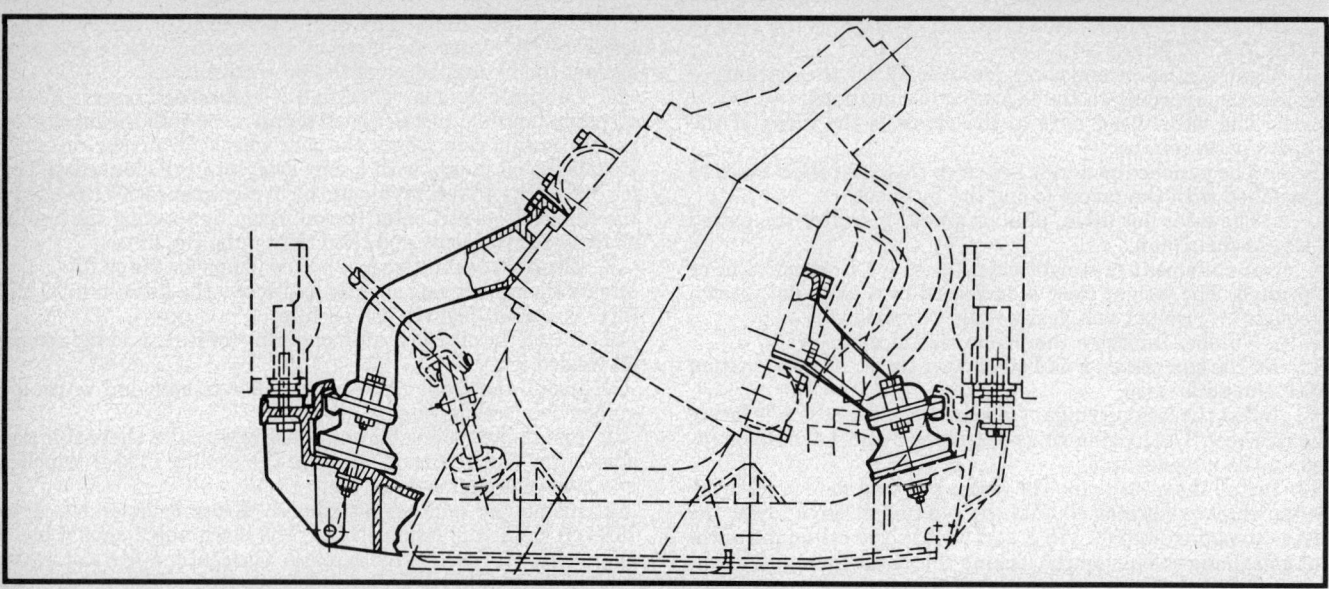

The 944 engine mounts are hydraulically dampened. Antifreeze flows though a small hole in a plate between 2 chambers when the mount is under stress, not unlike the action of a hydraulic shock absorber.

with a clutch slave cylinder, remove it from its mounting and position it aside.

13. Place a wooden block under the front tunnel reinforcement to support the transaxle tube.

14. Remove the transaxle mounting bolts and slide the transaxle toward the rear. Lower the vehicle.

15. Remove the air cleaner. Disconnect the brake booster vacuum line.

16. Relieve the fuel system pressure, then disconnect and plug the fuel line.

17. Disconnect the accelerator cable.

18. Drain the cooling system. If equipped, disconnect and plug the transaxle cooler lines.

19. Disconnect the radiator hoses. Remove the electric cooling fan.

20. Remove the hood. Detach the air conditioning compressor and place it aside. Do not disconnect the refrigerant lines.

21. Remove the radiator and expansion tank. Disconnect the heater hoses from the engine.

22. Disconnect the starter wiring.

23. Attach the engine lift chains to the engine. Disconnect the steering at the rack universal joint.

24. Disconnect the 2 side mounts on the engine block. Remove the lift side mount from the vehicle.

25. Remove the engine from the vehicle.

To install:

26. Installation is the reverse of the removal procedure.

27. Be sure the engine-to-frame ground wire is securely connected. Starting the engine with the ground wire disconnected or loose can damage the DME electronic control unit.

28. Fill and bleed the cooling system and power steering system. Run the engine to normal operating temperature, then check the oil and coolant level and top off, if necessary.

944S

On the 16 valve 944S, the engine is removed from below the vehicle with the clutch housing attached to the engine.

1. Relieve the fuel system pressure.

2. Disconnect the ground cable from the battery and body, then disconnect the positive (+) cable from the battery. Take the cables apart and slide both cables with rubber grommets through the firewall. Remove the cable retainers.

3. Raise the vehicle and support it safely. Remove the front wheels.

4. Remove the cover plate in the footwell on the right (passenger) side. Unscrew the carrier for the DME control unit and disconnect the control unit plugs.

5. Loosen the fuel return hose clamp and pull off the hose. Disconnect the fuel feed hose using a backup wrench to hold the fitting while loosening the connection.

6. Disconnect the cable on the cruise control servo motor and disconnect the electrical connectors at the fuel injectors.

7. Loosen the ventilation hose for the toothed belt cover on the air filter lower section at the rear. Loosen and remove the complete filter system. Remove the air flow sensor.

8. Loosen the distributor cap and rotor and remove them. Mark the position of the rotor for installation reference.

9. Remove the oil filter and automatic transaxle fluid supply tank.

10. Remove the throttle operating cable with deflection roller and bracket assembly. Disconnect the oxygen sensor plug connector, then loosen and remove the hose clamps on the intake distributor and brake booster.

11. Loosen the cable retainers from the bulkhead, then disconnect the electrical connectors after tagging them for installation. Remove the vacuum hose from the tank ventilation valve.

12. Remove the engine splash guard.

13. Drain the cooling system and disconnect the venting hose for the alternator.

14. Disconnect and remove the coolant hose on the radiator at the bottom right.

15. Disconnect the electrical connections to the fan motors. Disconnect the fan motor brackets from the radiator and remove from below.

16. Disconnect and remove the coolant and vent hose on the radiator at the top left. Disconnect the harness connector at the temperature switch on the radiator. Disconnect and remove the coolant hose from the expansion tank.

17. Loosen the radiator mounting and remove the radiator from below.

18. Suspend the engine by its front transporting bracket to hold the engine in its installed position. Make sure the suspension tool is correctly seated and supporting the engine securely.

19. Loosen the air conditioning compressor drive belt tension-

er and remove the belt. Disconnect the compressor mounting bolts and wire it aside with the refrigerant lines connected. Do not let the compressor hang by the refrigerant lines.

20. Disconnect and remove the stabilizer with holders on the body and control arms. Disconnect the right and left tie rods.

21. Disconnect the hose between the transaxle cooler and steering.

22. Disconnect the power steering pump, remove the spacer sleeve from the front and wire the pump to the steering gear. Do not let the pump hang by the power steering lines.

23. Disconnect the both control arms on the front axle crossmember and rear mount, then remove from the front.

24. Disconnect the universal joint on the steering gear and upper hydraulic engine mounts on the engine supports. Remove the front axle crossmember with steering gear and power steering pump from below.

25. Tag and disconnect the starter wire connectors and remove the starter.

26. Remove the clutch slave cylinder from the clutch housing with the line connected. Loosen and remove the holder for the fluid line on the clutch housing upper section.

27. Loosen the exhaust assembly at the flange of the exhaust manifold and at the exhaust test line. Disconnect the oxygen sensor.

28. Disconnect the flange behind the catalytic converter and suspension and remove the assembly.

29. Remove the upper transaxle/clutch housing mounting bolts.

30. Disconnect the coolant hoses for the heater above the exhaust manifold and on the cylinder head.

31. Attach a lifting device to the engine and tighten it to support the full weight. Note that since the engine is removed from below, rig a hoist that is tall enough to allow the body to be raised, and will allow the engine to be lowered onto a dolly.

CAUTION

Make sure the engine is securely supported by the lifting device before proceeding. Serious injury and damage could result.

32. Remove the lower transaxle/clutch housing mounting bolts.

33. Pull the engine forward and press the rubber sleeve from the firewall and into the engine compartment. Remove the wire harness carefully from the front passenger footwell.

NOTE: Remember that the connector end of the wire harness plugs into a computer which is very sensitive to damage or contamination on the connections. Keep the plug clean and handle it carefully during service.

34. Disconnect the engine from the central tube or shaft and carefully lower the engine onto a dolly. Lower slowly while watching for snags or obstructions and make sure it is securely supported on the dolly before disconnecting the hoist. Roll the engine from beneath the vehicle and continue service as required.

To install:

35. Installation is the reverse of removal. When installing the engine, note the following:

a. Guide the DME wire harness connector through the firewall carefully and connect it securely. Make sure the connectors are free from grease, dirt or damage before installing the connector onto the computer in the front passenger footwell.

b. Install but do not tighten the transaxle/clutch housing bolts. Tighten the mounting bolts to final torque only after the installation of the hydraulic engine mounts on the front axle crossmember. Torque the mounting bolts to 31 ft. lbs. (42 Nm).

c. When installing control arms, pressing down slightly on the sleeves in the rubber/metal mounts makes installation easier.

Pins for the TDC sensor must face down as shown when removing the engine on 928 vehicle

d. A steel washer 4mm thick is located at each of the bolted connections between the right (passenger) side engine support and the hydraulic mount. Make sure they are installed properly.

e. Make sure the radiator fits correctly into its rubber mounts.

36. Torque all bolts to specifications as follows:

a. Stabilizer-to-aluminum control arm—18 ft. lbs. (25 Nm)

b. Tie rod-to-steering knuckle—15–22 ft. lbs. (20–30 Nm)

c. Steering universal joint—22 ft. lbs. (30 Nm)

d. Control arm-to-crossmember—48 ft. lbs. (65 Nm)

e. Crossmember-to-body—63 ft. lbs. (85 Nm)

37. Fill and bleed the cooling system and power steering system. Run the engine to normal operating temperature, then check the oil and coolant level and top off, if necessary.

928, 928S AND 928S4

1. Disconnect the battery ground cable. Vehicles are equipped with an engine control computer located on the right (passenger side) kick panel. When removing the engine, carefully disconnect the main harness connector from the computer and feed the wire through the firewall and into the engine compartment. Use care when handling the connector end of the harness to protect it from contamination or damage during service.

2. Relieve the fuel system pressure. Remove the engine compartment crossbrace.

NOTE: The vehicle must be on its wheels when the crossbrace is removed or replaced.

3. Disconnect wiring and hoses to the under side of the hood, loosen hood bolts and supports, and remove the hood.

4. Remove the air intake hoses and the air cleaner assembly.

5. Raise and safely support the vehicle.

6. Remove the bottom splash pan and drain the coolant from the radiator.

7. Drain the engine block of coolant by removing the drain plugs on the right and left sides of the crankcase.

8. Drain the engine oil.

9. Remove the lower body brace.

10. Disconnect the exhaust pipe flanges at the exhaust manifolds and the right and left side heat shields. Disconnect the secondary air injection lines.

11. Disconnect the body ground cable from the engine.

12. Remove the clutch slave cylinder at the clutch housing. Do not disconnect the hydraulic line.

13. Tag and disconnect the starter wires, then remove the starter along with the clutch housing cover. Remove the starter wires from the clamps on the steering crossmember.

14. Disconnect the clutch release lever at the ball pin by depressing the release lever in the direction of the clutch.

15. On automatic transaxle equipped vehicles, remove both transaxle mount bolts. Remove the vacuum hose for the automatic transaxle at the cylinder head, along with its clamp.

16. Remove the bolts from the clamping sleeve on the driveshaft and slide the sleeve rearward on the central shaft.

NOTE: On the 928S, the TDC sensor pins on the flywheel must be at the bottom, facing toward the ground, to prevent damage during engine removal.

17. Unscrew the throwout bearing sleeve mounting bolts and push the sleeve toward the clutch.
18. Disconnect the both engine shock absorber at the control arms and remove with the right and left upper shock mounts.
19. On vehicles with air conditioning:
   a. Disconnect the temperature switch wires on the radiator.
   b. Disconnect the power lead to the compressor.
   c. Loosen the compressor, remove the compressor from the mounting brackets. Do not remove the hoses.
   d. Suspend the compressor from the frame with a wire.
20. Remove the air pump filter housing and disconnect the alternator cooling hose.
21. Remove the lower fan shroud from the radiator, remove the cooling hoses and the oil cooler line from the radiator bottom.
22. By lifting the engine a side at a time, remove the engine mounts and carefully set the engine on the front crossmember.
23. On manual transaxle equipped vehicles, remove the clutch housing to engine bolts and lower the vehicle to the ground.
24. Remove the upper coolant hose and the vent from the radiator and thermostat housing.
25. Remove the upper oil cooler line form the upper part of the radiator.
26. Loosen the top mounting of the radiator and remove the assembly carefully.
27. Remove the heater hoses and electrical connections from the engine. Tag all electrical connections for identification before removal.
28. Pull off the ignition leads on the both sides of the distributor cap. Disconnect both ignition coils and lay them aside. Disconnect the ground wire in front of the right ignition coil on the body.
29. Relieve the fuel system pressure, then disconnect the fuel feed and return lines. Use a backup wrench on the fuel fittings to avoid twisting the line connections.

CAUTION

Fuel pressure must be relieved before attempting to disconnect any fuel lines. Take precautions to avoid the risk of fire.

---

30. Disconnect the oil hoses on the power steering supply tank, drain the oil, then remove the tank.
31. Disconnect the vacuum hoses to the EZF control unit and brake booster. Remove the hose from the fuel vapor canister to the charging valve.
32. Disconnect the throttle, cruise control and automatic transaxle cables by either removing the holder and clamp or at the ball connectors on the linkage bracket. Tag each cable ball to identify its position for assembly.

NOTE: On air conditioned vehicles, cover the condenser with a wood board to prevent damage during engine removal.

33. Remove the central fuse/relay cover and disconnect the plugs for the oxygen sensor, sensor heating and ignition control unit. Disconnect the multipin connectors from the fuel injection and ignition computers at the right kick panel in the passenger compartment. Push the grommet and wire harness through into the engine compartment and carefully remove the connectors.

NOTE: Remember that each multi-pin connector end of the wire harness plugs into a computer which is very sensitive to damage or contamination on the connec-

tions. Keep the plugs clean and handle them carefully during service.

34. Attach a lifting cable to the lifting device and to the engine. Raise the assembly slightly and remove the engine block-to-clutch housing upper mounting bolts. Disconnect the both engine mount bolts at the bottom.
35. Pull the engine forward and remove the short driveshaft with the guide tube.
36. Lift the engine carefully while tilting forward and slowly remove it from the engine compartment. As soon as clearance permits, disconnect and remove the pressure hose from the power steering pump after marking its installed position for installation reference. Remove the engine slowly and watch for snagged wires, linkage, etc. during removal.

To install:
37. Installation is the reverse of removal. Refill all fluids, then start the engine and allow it to reach normal operating temperature while checking for leaks.

Cylinder Head

Removal and Installation

928, 928S AND 928S4

NOTE: The cylinder heads can be removed with the engine in the vehicle. 928S and 928S4 engines are equipped with dual distributors driven off the exhaust camshafts. The cylinder head and camshaft case are a component and the cylinder heads are identical for right and left sides but the head gaskets are not. The following is a general procedure for all engines.

1. Disconnect the negative battery cable. Drain the cooling system.
2. Remove the upper timing belt cover assembly. On engines with dual distributors, remove the distributor caps to allow removal of the timing belt cover.
3. Remove the upper coolant hoses and heater hoses from the thermostat housing area.
4. Remove the air intake tube and the air cleaner assembly.
5. Relieve fuel system pressure, then tag and remove all con-

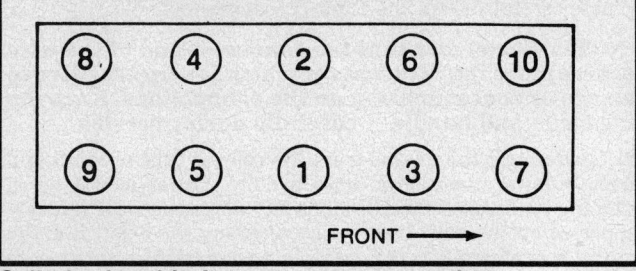

Cylinder head bolt torque sequence—944

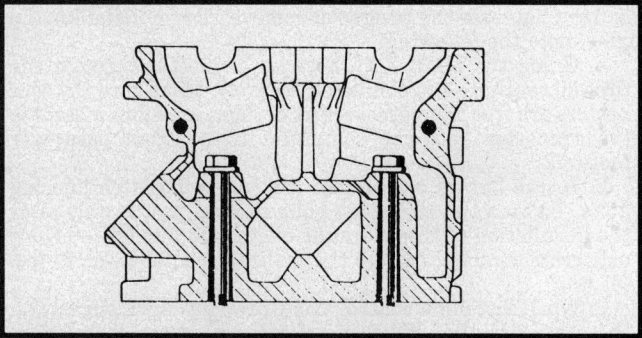

Cylinder head bolt location—928

necting linkages, wires and hoses from the intake manifold and fuel injection system.

6. Rotate the engine to TDC and make certain all timing marks are aligned.

7. Remove the intake manifold and fuel injection system from the cylinder head and engine block.

8. From the lower right side of the engine block, loosen the timing belt tensioner bolt and remove the timing belt from the sprockets. Accessory drive belts may have to either loosened or removed.

9. Remove the camshaft covers to expose the head retaining bolts.

10. Remove the exhaust manifold from the cylinder head.

11. Remove the inner right and left belt housing, as necessary.

12. Remove the cylinder head nuts and washers or bolts, by starting from the center and alternating toward each end. If in doubt, simply reverse the tightening sequence to remove the head retainers.

13. Remove the cylinder head from the engine block studs, being careful not to mark or scratch the cylinder head sealing surface.

NOTE: Because of the use of aluminum, do not allow the antifreeze coolant mixture to enter the cylinders. Severe engine damage could result after engine start-up.

14. Remove the head gasket from the studs and clean both the head and the block.

To install:

15. Installation is the reverse of removal. During the installation, attention should be given to the following:

a. Both cylinder head gaskets are different. TOP/OBEN faces up and the arrow faces forward.

b. Turn both camshafts until the notches on the sprockets align with the marks on the camshaft housing. Be sure the crankshaft pulley is at TDC on the compression stroke. Install the toothed belt and the belt tensioner.

c. If leaks occur between the cylinder head and block install a new cylinder head gasket.

16. Tighten the cylinder head bolts in the proper sequence and to the correct torque specification.

924S, 944 AND 944S

NOTE: The cylinder head can be removed with the engine in the vehicle. On 944S 16 valve engine, the cylinder head and camshaft housing are an assembly but the removal procedures are basically the same.

1. Disconnect the negative battery cable. Relieve the fuel system pressure. Remove the cap from the coolant expansion tank.

2. Remove the engine splash guard. Remove the radiator drain plug and allow the coolant to drain into a clean container.

3. Remove the drive belts for the power steering pump, alter-

nator and air conditioning compressor from the front of the engine.

4. Remove the timing belt cover.

5. Rotate the engine as necessary to position the No. 1 piston on TDC compression. Align the TDC marks of both the camshaft sprocket and the flywheel.

6. Remove the distributor cap. Unscrew the distributor arm and remove the plastic cap.

7. Remove the distributor cap mount.

8. Release the tension of the camshaft drive belt and pull the belt off of the camshaft sprocket.

9. Remove the 2 rear drive belt cover mounting bolts.

10. Disconnect and cap the fuel lines.

11. Remove the plastic cover from the fuel collection tube. Tag and disconnect the wiring connectors from the fuel injectors and lay the wiring harness aside.

12. On all vehicles, except the 944S, remove the aluminum plugs from the camshaft housing and detach the coolant line from the camshaft housing. Remove the camshaft housing from the cylinder head. On the 944S, remove the camshaft cover.

NOTE: When removing the camshaft housing, use care to keep the hydraulic valve tappets in place.

13. Remove the air cleaner assembly. Remove the bolt of the air intake brace.

14. Remove the intake manifold by disconnecting the following items:

a. Oil dipstick tube bracket
b. Brake booster hose
c. Intake manifold hose
d. Accelerator cable retaining clamp.

15. Remove the intake manifold bolts and the manifold.

16. Remove the bolts from the exhaust manifold/converter pipe flange.

17. Remove the hose clamp from the heater regulating valve and the 2 screws from the valve neck.

18. Remove the cylinder head mounting bolts in the reverse order of the installation torque sequence.

19. Remove the cylinder head. Clean all gasket mating surfaces carefully. The cylinder head gasket for the 944 Turbo has a partially recessed silicone bead on both sides and the word **TURBO** stamped in the top surface for identification.

To install:

20. Installation is the reverse of the removal procedure. After installing the head, tighten the mounting bolts, in sequence, to the correct torque specifications. Torque the camshaft housing mounting bolts to 14 ft. lbs. (19 Nm) and the aluminum plugs to 29 ft. lbs. (39 Nm). Install and adjust the camshaft drive (timing) belt. Adjust the power steering pump, alternator and air conditioning compressor drive belt tension.

Intake Manifold

Removal and Installation

924S AND 944

The intake manifold consists of a cast aluminum assembly with equal length air intake tubes that bolt directly to the cylinder head. The throttle valve assembly bolts to a single flange.

1. Disconnect the negative battery cable.

2. Remove the air cleaner assembly, air intake ducts and filter. On the 944 turbo, remove both charging air guide pipes.

3. Relieve fuel system pressure, then disconnect the fuel feed and return lines. Disconnect the vacuum hoses on the pressure regulator and damper.

4. Disconnect the cable to the cruise control motor, if equipped, along with the throttle and transaxle linkage.

5. Disconnect the spark plug wires and remove the distributor cap. Disconnect the fuel collection pipe with the fuel injec-

Check that the scribe mark on the flywheel is aligned with the TDC mark on the clutch housing

tors and ignition leads on the intake manifold and camshaft housing.

6. Remove the fuel collection pipe with fuel injectors and ignition leads from the intake manifold assembly carefully and lay them aside.

7. Tag and disconnect any vacuum lines or hoses attached to the intake manifold. Disconnect the air flow sensor wire harness connector.

8. Remove the mounting nuts and lift off the intake manifold with the throttle housing as a unit. Continue disassembly on a workbench and transfer components to the replacement manifold, if necessary. Cover the air intake ports during service procedures to prevent the entry of dirt or debris.

9. Installation is the reverse of removal. Tighten the mounting bolts to specification.

928, 928S AND 928S4

The intake manifold assembly consists of a series of equal length pipes, attached by hose clamps and short rubber sleeves to the air cleaner plenum and bolted to the cylinder head.

1. Disconnect the negative battery cable.

2. Remove the air cleaner assembly, air intake ducts and filter. Disconnect the mass air flow sensor, if necessary to gain working clearance.

3. Depressurize the fuel system, then disconnect the fuel feed and return lines. Disconnect the vacuum hoses on the pressure regulator and damper.

4. Disconnect the cable to the cruise control motor, if equipped, along with the throttle and transaxle linkage at the bracket, if necessary. Tag the linkage for identification during installation.

5. Tag and disconnect all vacuum lines and wire connectors as necessary to allow removal of the manifold assembly.

6. Remove the mounting bolts from the intake manifold tubes at the cylinder head and remove the manifold with the fuel injectors attached. It may be easier of the early engines to remove the injectors before disconnecting the manifold.

7. Installation is the reverse of removal procedures. Torque all manifold mounting bolts to specification.

Exhaust Manifold

Removal and Installation

EXCEPT 944 TURBO

NOTE: Always use new gaskets when installing the exhaust manifold.

1. Disconnect the negative battery cable.
2. Disconnect the EGR line from the exhaust manifold.
3. If equipped, remove the air pump connections.
4. Disconnect the exhaust pipe(s) from the manifold(s) at the flange.
5. Remove the retaining nuts and remove the manifold(s).
6. Clean the cylinder heads(s) and manifold mating surfaces.
7. Using new gaskets, install the exhaust manifold(s). On the 928, the filler seals are placed in grooves on the exhaust ports for sealing between the cylinder head and exhaust manifold.
8. Tighten the nuts to 15 ft. lbs. (20 Nm). Work from the inside out.
9. Install the remaining components in the reverse order of remove. Use a new manifold flange gasket, as required.

944 TURBO

1. Disconnect the negative battery cable.
2. Depressurize the fuel system, then disconnect the fuel hoses from the pressure regulator and the pressure chamber. Tie the fuel hoses back aside.
3. Release the pressure from the coolant tank by loosening the radiator cap. Loosen and remove the coolant hoses on the

connecting pipe near the water pump. Cap all hoses with a suitable plug to prevent coolant loss during service.

4. Remove the coolant connecting pipe bolts and position the pipe over the cam housing.

5. To remove the exhaust manifolds, remove some of the mounting studs; both manifolds must be removed together. Remove both exhaust manifold studs from cylinders 1 and 3, and the front stud from cylinders 2 and 4.

6. Working from above, remove the 2–3 manifold first, then remove the 1–4 manifold.

7. Installation is the reverse of removal procedure. Torque all manifold nuts and bolts to 15 ft. lbs. (20 Nm).

Turbocharger

Removal and Installation

944 TURBO

1. Disconnect the negative battery cable.
2. Loosen the air cleaner upper section and remove it together with the air intake duct and filter cartridge.
3. Remove both charging air guide pipes.
4. Relieve fuel system pressure, then disconnect the fuel feed and return lines and lay them aside aside.

――――――――― **CAUTION** ―――――――――
Always relieve fuel system pressure before disconnecting any fuel lines. Take precautions to avoid the risk of fire.
――――――――――――――――――――――――――――

5. Tag and disconnect the vacuum hoses from the pressure regulator and damper. Disconnect the cable on the cruise control motor.

6. Disconnect the spark plug cables and remove the distributor cap.

7. Disconnect the fuel collection pipe with the fuel injectors and ignition leads on the intake manifold and camshaft housing.

8. Remove the fuel collection pipe with the fuel injectors attached from the intake manifold carefully and place the assembly aside. Do not allow grease or dirt to contaminate the ends of the injectors during service.

9. Disconnect the throttle cable, then tag and disconnect any remaining vacuum hoses on the intake manifold. Remove the intake manifold assembly with the throttle housing and cover the intake ports on the cylinder head to prevent the entry of dirt or debris during service.

10. Disconnect and remove the guide tube with the oil dipstick and the deflection plate for the master cylinder.

11. Remove the engine splash guard. Drain the cooling system, then loosen and pull off the air hose alternator venting.

12. Disconnect the flange between the turbocharger and the exhaust assembly.

13. Disconnect the exhaust flange on the turbine housing. Disconnect the coolant lines and oil pressure line on the turbocharger.

14. Loosen and remove the intake air cowl between the air flow sensor and turbocharger compressor housing. Disconnect the pressure hose to the charging air cooler (intercooler) and remove the turbocharger assembly from the vehicle.

15. Installation is the reverse of removal. Note the following:
   a. Always use new seals.
   b. Make sure the seal fits correctly on the left engine port.
   c. Insert the seals for the exhaust flanges after coating them with grease to prevent their falling out when installing the turbocharger assembly.
   d. Replace the locknuts for the exhaust flanges and tighten the M8 bolt of the exhaust flange only after installation of all bolts for the exhaust flanges and turbocharger.

Timing Chain and Sprockets

Removal and Installation

911

Replacement cam drive chains are continuous, riveted chain. Segmented chains are also available from Porsche. These make it possible to replace timing chains without removing and dismantling the engine. Do not fit segmented chains simultaneously but one after the other as the chains are made to run in different directions. However, Porsche suggests using the continuous, riveted chains when reconditioning an engine.

1. Disconnect the battery negative cable.
2. Remove the spark plugs to make it easier to turn the crankshaft.
3. Set the engine to TDC on No. 1 cylinder.
4. Remove the chain tensioner, sprocket carrier, guide rails and camshaft sprocket.
5. Grind through both bolts of a link in the chain and remove the link only. Leave the chain in place for now. Make sure no grinding dust gets into the engine.

To install:

6. Attach the new chain with the connecting link to the end of the old chain. Make sure the new chain is attached to the proper end of the old chain—the end that will be pulled into the engine as the crankshaft is rotated.
7. Turn the camshaft until the center mark or 930 mark points to approximately 45 degrees outwards. No valves should be completely opened when the camshaft is in this position.
8. Turn the crankshaft slowly in the proper direction of rotation, keeping the chain tensioned.

NOTE: When turning the crankshaft make sure the valves do not contact the piston top. Work slowly and carefully. If any pressure is felt, move the crankshaft backward immediately and adjust the camshaft accordingly.

9. Turn the crankshaft until the connecting pin can be inserted on the other end of the new chain.
10. Remove the old chain and connect the new, drawn-in chain with the connecting pin.

NOTE: Insert the connecting pin from the front or housing side. Don't forget to add the spacers. Insert the spring fastener with the closed end pointing in the direction of rotation.

11. Install the guide rails, sprocket carrier and camshaft sprocket. Adjust valve timing.

Rough Timing Adjustment

911

1. Turn the crankshaft until mark **Z1** on the pulley is aligned accurately with the joint of the crankcase or stripe on the blower housing.
2. Set both camshafts with punch marks or Code 930 facing upwards. Basic engine setting is when cylinder No. 1 is at TDC, cylinder 4 is at overlap and crankshaft pulley mark **Z1** is aligned to the crankcase joint and punch marks or code 930 stamping on camshafts face up.
3. In this position, a hole in the cam sprocket should be precisely aligned with a hole in the sprocket flange or housing, behind the sprocket. Insert a suitable alignment pin in these accurately aligned holes.
4. Apply a thin coat of Optimoly HT or equivalent, on the threads of the bolts for the sprockets and install them finger tight.
5. If one of the camshafts is out of position, take the alignment pin from the alignment hole in the camshaft sprocket so it cannot turn during adjustment. Correct the camshaft, return-

ing it to the basic setting position—punch mark or stamping 930 facing up. A special tool is available to turn the sprocket. Remove the sprocket mounting bolt and dowel pin and turn the cranksaft back to **Z1** on pulley, aligned to the crankcase joint.

Fine Adjustment

911

Left Camshaft Adjustment—Cylinder 1

1. Check the valve clearance or adjust to 0.10mm. Precise valve clearance of intake valves in cylinders 1 and 4 is sufficient for adjustment of timing.
2. Set up a dial indicator on top of the camshaft case. Set gauge to 0 with approximately 10mm of preload. Set the indicator tip on the valve spring retainer of closed cylinder No. 1 intake valve.
3. Turn the crankshaft slowly clockwise from **Z1** or TDC approximately 1 turn while observing the dial gauge. Turn far enough that the mean value of the adjusting tolerance is reached.

Adjusting range is 1.1–1.4mm
Ideal value—1.25mm

4. Unscrew and remove the mounting bolt on the left chain sprocket and pull out the dowel pin. Turn the crankshaft until mark **Z1** on the pulley is aligned accurately with the joint of the crankcase or the stripe mark on the blower housing.
5. Install the dowel pin again and screw on the bolt finger tight. Keep the sprocket from turning as the bolt is snugged down.

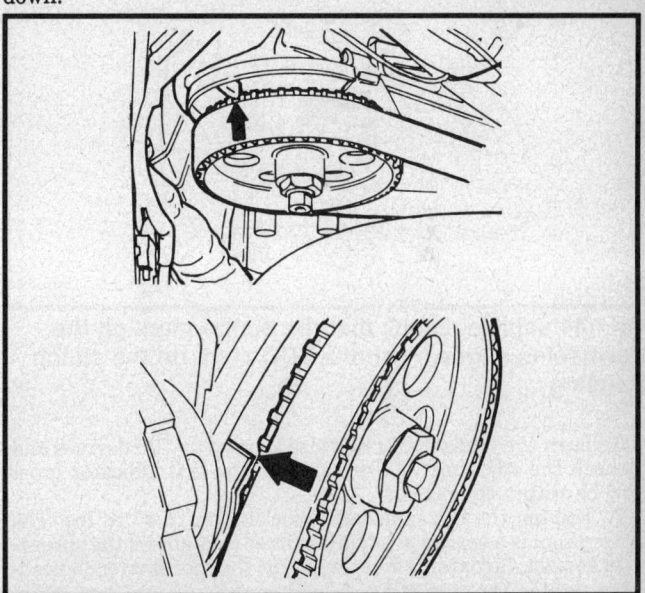

When the 928, 928S engine is at TDC on No. 1 cylinder, the camshaft sprocket marks (arrow) will align with the marks on the housing

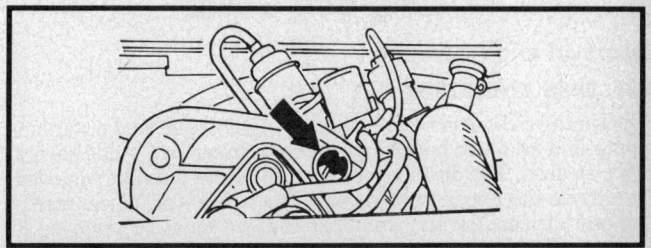

On 944 vehicle, the TDC mark on the camshaft sprocket will align with the cast mark as shown

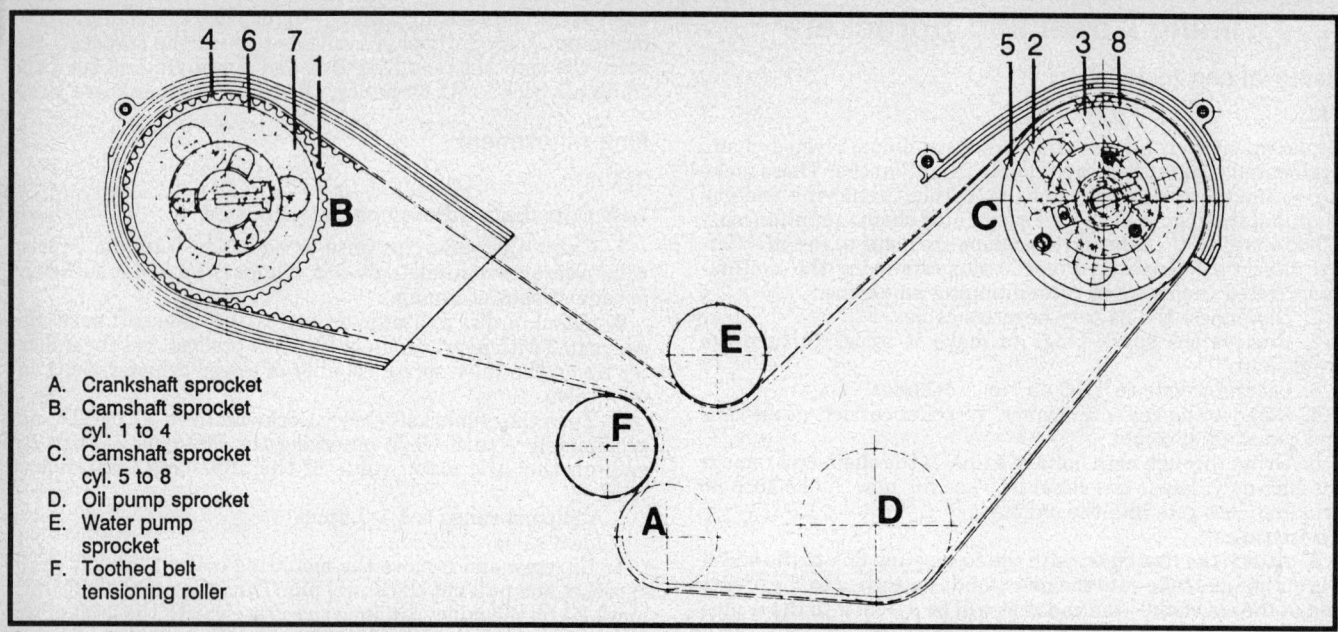

A. Crankshaft sprocket
B. Camshaft sprocket cyl. 1 to 4
C. Camshaft sprocket cyl. 5 to 8
D. Oil pump sprocket
E. Water pump sprocket
F. Toothed belt tensioning roller

Camshaft belt routing—928 vehicle

On 944 vehicle, check that the scribe mark on the flywheel is aligned with the TDC mark on the clutch housing

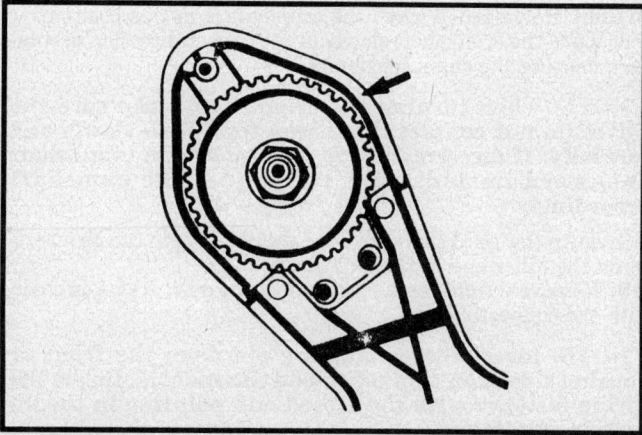

On 944 vehicle, align the camshaft sprocket and rear timing belt cover as shown before installing the timing belt

6. Turn the crankshaft clockwise 2 turns or 720 degrees and recheck the adjustment. The value on the dial indicator must now be within tolerance.

7. Tighten the left camshaft sprocket bolt to 87 ft. lbs. The factory tool is a special pin-type spanner that allows the sprocket to be held. It contains an opening for the socket wrench needed to tighten the sprocket bolt.

8. Turn the crankshaft to cylinder No. 4 TDC. Repeat the adjusting procedures on No. 4

Timing Belt Cover

Removal and Installation

928, 928S AND 928S4

The timing cover consists of an outer right upper, and outer left upper and an outer bottom cover. Both inner belt guide covers are also used. The distributor caps and rotors must be removed to remove the upper front covers. The alternator, power steering and air conditioning compressor belts must be removed if the entire timing belt cover is being removed. Disconnect the intake air ducts and air flow sensor, if necessary, to gain working clearance.

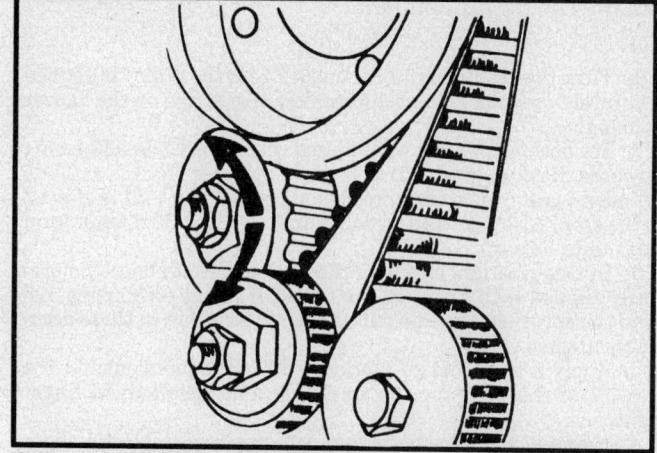

Adjust the timing belt tensioner and turn the large hex nut as required to loosen or tighten the belt

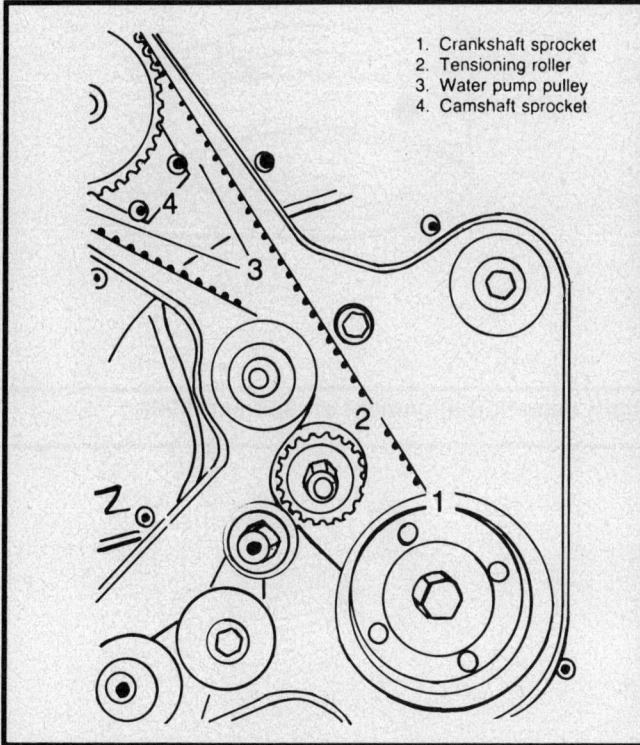

1. Crankshaft sprocket
2. Tensioning roller
3. Water pump pulley
4. Camshaft sprocket

Install the timing belt on each sprocket in numerical order

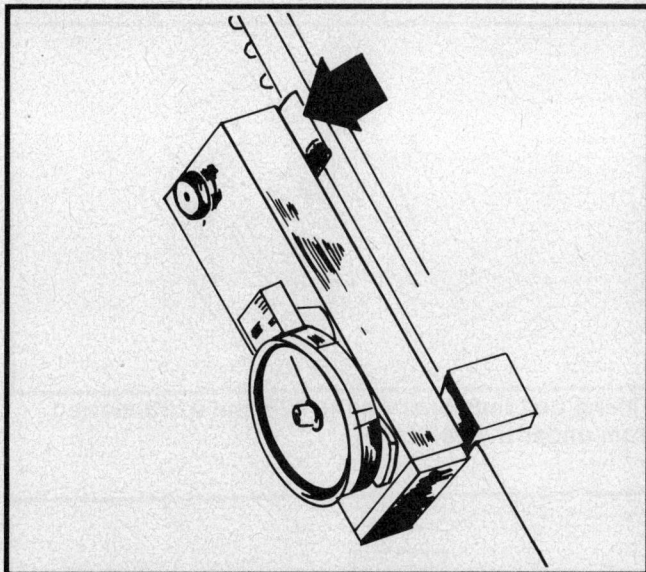

Special timing belt tension tool shown installed on the 944 timing belt. Note that the tool is installed in the same manner on the balance shaft drive belt. Measuring needle (arrow) is pushed in when setting up the tool

924S AND 944

NOTE: On the 944 Turbo, the intercooler assembly and air charge pipes will have to be removed to gain working clearance when removing the timing belt cover.

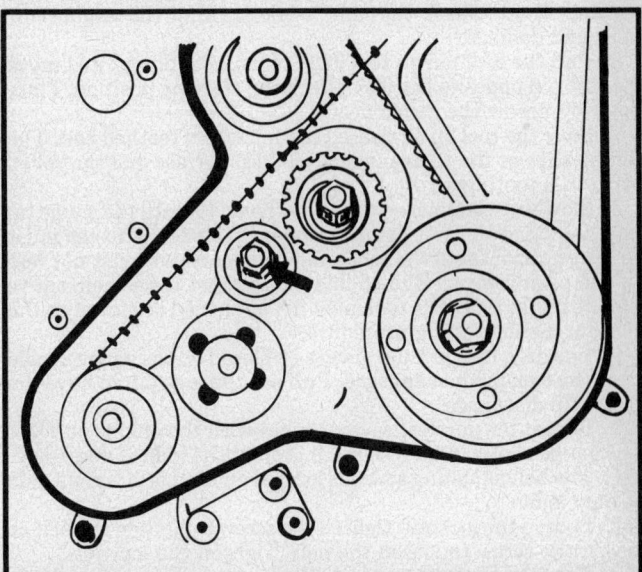

During removal of the balance shaft drive belt the pulley should be adjusted so that it does not touch the belt

1. Disconnect the negative battery cable.
2. Loosen the alternator and compressor drive belt tensioner and remove the belt. Remove the power steering drive belt, if equipped.
3. Remove the distributor cap and rotor.
4. Remove the cover retaining bolts and lift off the timing belt cover.
5. Installation is the reverse of the removal procedure.

Timing Belt

Checking Tension

NOTE: A special tension gauge tool 9201 or equivalent, is recommended to check the tension of the camshaft and balance shaft drive belts. All belt tension checks and adjustments should be performed on a cold engine only.

928S AND 928S4

NOTE: These vehicles incorporate a cam belt tension warning light in the instrument cluster. The warning light will illuminate when the belt tension is insufficient.

1. Disconnect the negative battery cable. Remove the air guide hoses.
2. Remove the air guide retaining screws and the air guide from the top of the radiator.
3. Remove the distributor caps and the toothed belt cover upper section on the right side. Unscrew and push the toothed belt cover on the left side forward.
4. Turn the engine in the normal direction of rotation until No. 1 cylinder is at TDC on the compression stroke. Never turn the engine counterclockwise. Marks on the camshaft and flange bearing must be aligned in this position.
5. Turn the engine 2 more turns until the TDC mark is

reached again. Check the bolt, while turning the engine, for wear and damage.

6. Pull the lock pin on tool 9201 or equivalent, out and move the test pin opposite the lock pin to the starting position. Place the drag needle the gauge needle.

7. Slide the tool on a released section of the toothed belt. The sliding shoe of the tool on a smooth belt surface and the rolled fitted in a tooth gap.

8. Slowly press down on the tester housing until the gauge tip engages. Read the test gauge without tension, the tester must be kept horizontal to the toothed belt. The tester must not rest on the plastic cover. The sliding shoes must have their entire surface on the belt. The tool must not be turned or moved on the belt during the testing procedure.

9. The drag needle must always be placed on the gauge needle after the lock pin had engaged. Pull out the lock pin to have the gauge tip disengage.

10. Repeat tension test several times with the engine at TDC. The gauge should read 5.0 ± 0.3. Adjust the belt, if necessary.

11. The belt adjusting screw is located on the bottom right side of the engine.

12. Loosen the locknut, tighten the screw to tighten the belt or loosen the screw to loosen the belt. Tighten the locknut.

13. Turn the engine 2 complete turns and recheck belt tension.

944S

1. Be sure the engine is cold. Disconnect the negative battery cable.

2. Remove the complete air filter housing. Remove the air hose from the top of the cam belt housing.

3. Remove the cable holder from the top of the cam belt housing.

4. Remove the top camshaft drive belt housing retaining bolts. Remove the housing assembly.

5. Remove the high tension wire on the distributor cap, coming from the coil.

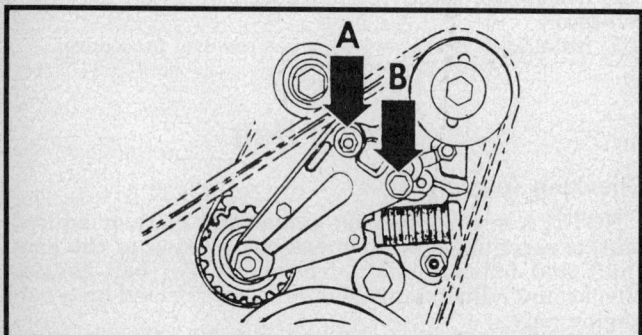

Loosen bolts A and B to adjust the timing belt tension

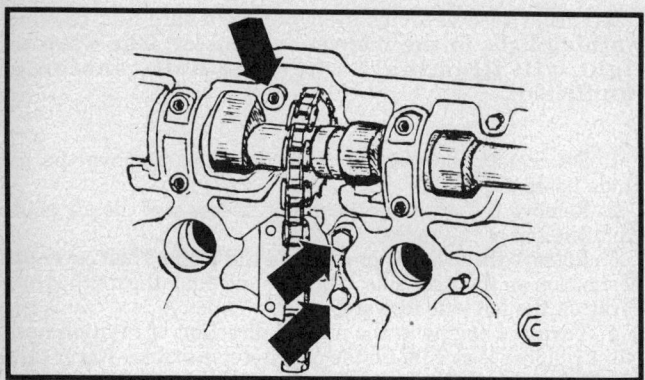

Hydraulic chain tensioner used on 928, 928S4 and 944

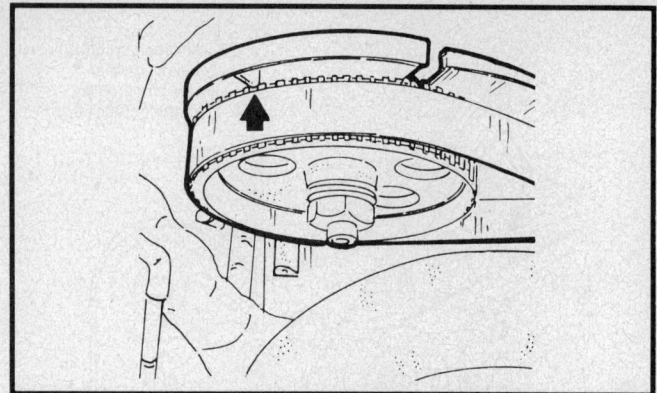

Right camshaft alignment on 928 and 928S

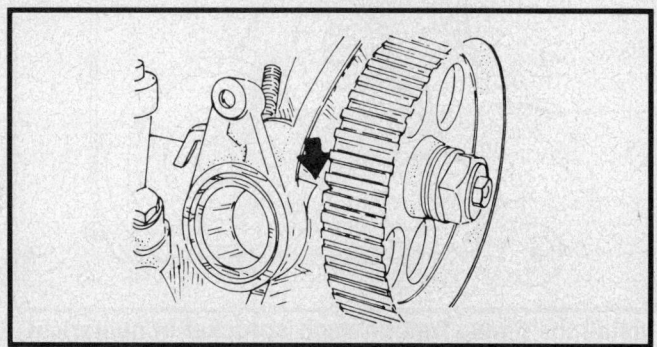

Left camshaft alignment of the 928

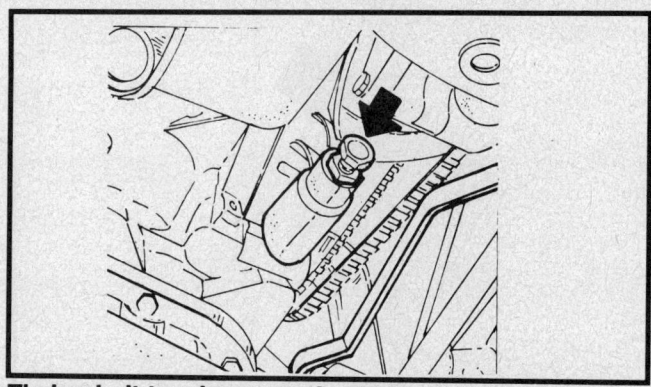

Timing belt tensioner on the 928 and 928S viewed from under the vehicle

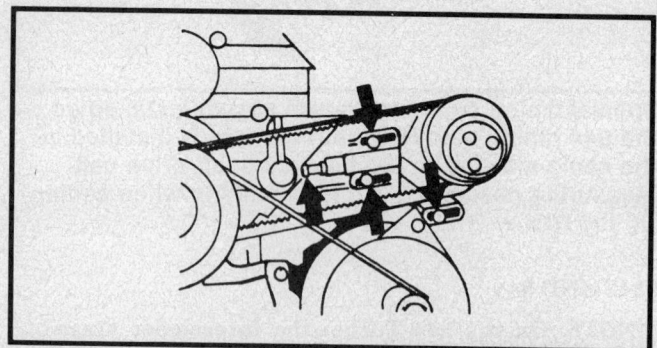

On 928S and 928S4 loosen the bolts (arrows) to remove the drive belts

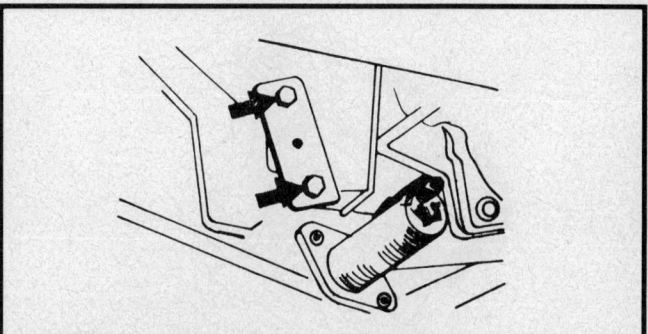

On 928S and 928S4 mount the special tool as shown to hold the crankshaft in position

6. Remove the top metal drive belt cover together with the installed distributor cap and position it to the rear.

7. Position the engine at TDC on the compression stroke. Check the condition of the belt while slowly turning the crankshaft clockwise until the TDC mark on No. 1 cylinder on the camshaft drive sprocket is aligned with the mark on the rear toothed belt cover.

8. Raise and support the vehicle safely. Check the TDC marking on the flywheel bell housing. Lower the vehicle.

9. To adjust the camshaft belt, loosen the tensioner nut and the tensioner bolt. Press the belt twice with a thumb against the bell housing between the camshaft sprocket and the water pump pulley.

10. Torque the nut and bolt to 14 ft. lbs. (20Nm). Reinstall the removed components.

924S, 944 AND 944 TURBO

Balance Shafts Drive Belt

1. Remove the splash guard under the engine.
2. Remove the alternator and the compressor belt.
3. Remove the upper and lower belt covers.
4. Release the tension from the belt. There are 2 methods to release the tension. If equipped with guide rollers without a slot, turn the eccentric to release the tension from the belt. If equipped with a locking nut on the guide roller (with slot), loosen the locknut and slide the roller away from the belt.
5. Remove the plug from the distributor cap mount.
6. Turn the crankshaft in the direction of normal rotation until the TDC mark on the camshaft sprocket aligns with the cast mark.
7. Check to be sure the scribe mark on the flywheel is visible through the clutch housing and opposite the TDC mark.
8. Check that the balance shaft marks are aligned with the marks on the rear belt cover.
9. Special tool 9201 or equivalent, is recommended to check the belt tension. Pull out the lockpin and let the gauge slide drop. Zero the gauge and slide it onto the belt. Push up on the measuring slide until the lockpin engages. Pull out the lockpin and let the gauge slide drop. Zero the gauge and slide it onto the belt. Push up on the measuring slide until the lockpin engages. Pull out the lockpin and remove the gauge. Read the measured value. If the guide rollers have no slot, the gauge should read 4.0–4.6 lbs. for a new belt or 3.7–4.3 lbs. for a used belt. If the guide roller has a slot, the gauge should read 2.4–3.0 lbs. for new and used belts. If necessary, adjust the tension.

Camshaft Belt

1. Remove the splash guard, belt covers and alternator compressor belt.
2. Turn the crankshaft in the direction of normal rotation and check the condition of the drive belt. If damaged or worn, it should be replaced.

3. Remove the plug from the distributor cap mount.

4. Turn the crankshaft in the direction of normal rotation until the TDC mark on the camshaft sprocket is aligned with the cast mark on the mounting for the distributor cap.

5. Be sure the TDC mark on the flywheel and clutch housing are aligned.

6. Turn the crankshaft counterclockwise approximately 10 degrees; 1½ teeth on the camshaft sprocket. This step is mandatory. If it is not performed, the tension measurement may be incorrect and engine damage could result.

7. Prepare the gauge to take the reading. Pull the lockpin from tool 9201 or equivalent, and listen for the gauge slide to drop. Zero the gauge and slide it onto the belt. Push up on the measuring slide until the lockpin engages. Pull the lockpin out and read the gauge. It should read 2.4–3.0 lbs. for used belts or 3.7–4.3 lbs. for new belts.

8. As required, adjust the belt tension.

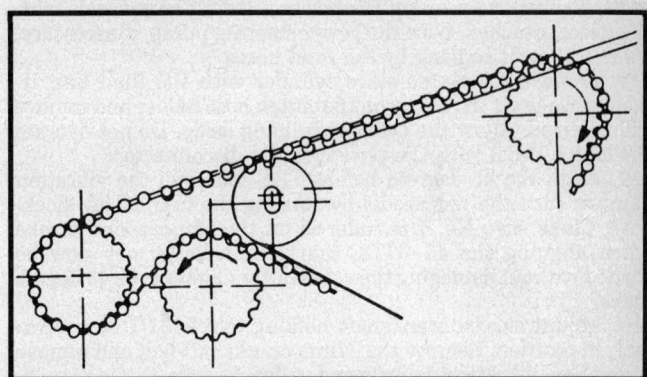

Maintain 0.002–0.004 in. clearance between the guide roller and the lower balance shaft on 924S and 944 vehicles

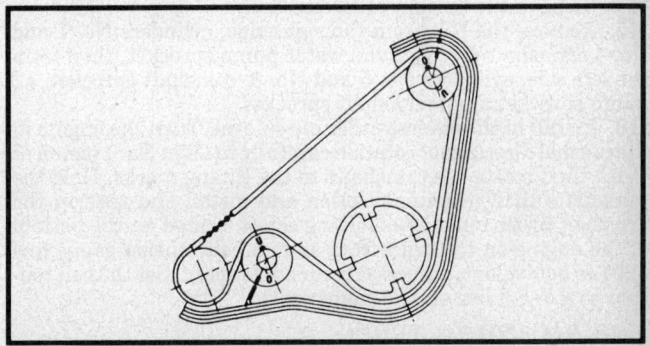

Prior to removing or installing the balance shaft drive belt, the balance shaft sprocket marks should be aligned with the marks on the rear cover as shown

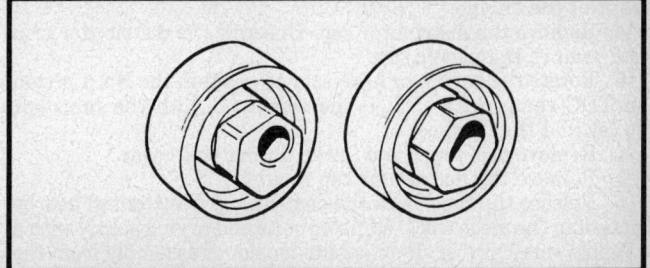

Old style eccentric tensioner (without slot) is on the left; newer style eccentric tensioner (with slot) is on the right

Removal and Installation

928S AND 928S4

1. Disconnect the negative battery cable. Remove the air cleaner intake hoses.
2. Remove the air guide from the top of the radiator.
3. Loosen and remove all drive belts. Tag and disconnect the cables from the throttle, cruise control and automatic transaxle.
4. Remove the fan assembly from the engine after disconnecting all wires and cables. If equipped with a viscous fan coupling, do not lay the fan flat or the fluid will leak out. Once the fluid is gone, the fan must be replaced.
5. Remove the distributor caps and wires. Remove the distributor rotors. Disconnect the wiring connectors for the air conditioning compressor and belt tension indicator.
6. Remove the mounting screws for the upper belt cover on both sides and remove the upper right side cover.
7. Remove and position the power steering pump aside with the hoses attached. Wire the power steering pump, if necessary. Do not allow it to hang by the fluid hoses.
8. Remove the clutch slave cylinder with the fluid line attached. Take off the clamp on the clutch hose holder and remove the pushrod. Allow the cylinder to hang aside. Do not operate the clutch pedal with the slave cylinder disconnected.
9. Align the 45 degrees before TDC mark on the vibration damper with the red needle by turning the crankshaft clockwise. Make sure No. 1 cylinder is on the compression stroke when aligning the 45 BTDC mark. Camshafts may now be turned without damaging the valves after aligning the 45 degree mark.
10. Mount special crankshaft holding tool 9161/1 or equivalent, in position. Remove the 27mm crankshaft bolt and remove the pulley, vibration damper and collar.
11. Remove the guide tube for the engine oil dipstick. Remove the alternator and mounting brackets.
12. Remove the center belt cover and left upper cover.
13. Loosen the toothed belt tension with the adjuster screw.
14. Remove the tension roller assembly.
15. Remove the belt from the right side, cylinders No. 1 and No. 4, camshaft sprocket and water pump sprocket, then from the left side, cylinders No. 5 and No. 8, camshaft sprocket, oil pump sprocket and crankshaft sprocket.
16. Install in the reverse order of removal. Turn the engine in the normal direction of rotation carefully to align No. 1 piston at TDC, then rotate the camshafts to the timing marks. Hold the camshafts firmly in this position and install and tension the drivebelt by turning the adjusting screw located on the bottom of the engine on the right front side. A belt tension gauge tool 9201 or equivalent, is necessary for adjustment. Set the belt tension to 4.7–5.3 lbs. on the gauge scale.

924S, 944 AND 944 TURBO

1. Disconnect the negative battery cable.
2. Remove the engine splash guard.
3. Remove the drive belt for the power steering pump, if equipped, alternator and air conditioning compressor from the front of the engine.
4. Remove the distributor cap. Unscrew the distributor arm and remove the plastic cap.
5. Rotate the engine as necessary to position the No. 1 piston on TDC compression. Align the marks on both the camshaft pulley and the flywheel.
6. Remove the upper and lower timing belt cover.
7. Remove the distributor cap mount.
8. Release the tension of the camshaft drive (timing) belt by loosening the mechanical adjuster bolts and prying gently with a suitable small prybar. Remove the tensioner assembly from the crankcase upper section and carefully remove the camshaft belt from the sprockets.
9. Install the new belt in reverse sequence. Install the mechanical tensioner and allow it to tension the drive belt by

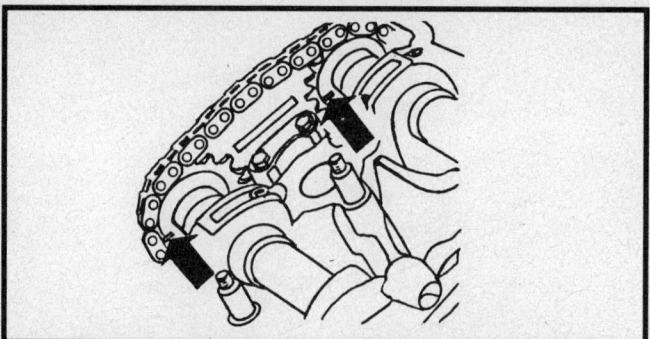

Correct alignment of early version camshaft marks. The marks should face the exhaust side of the cylinder head as shown

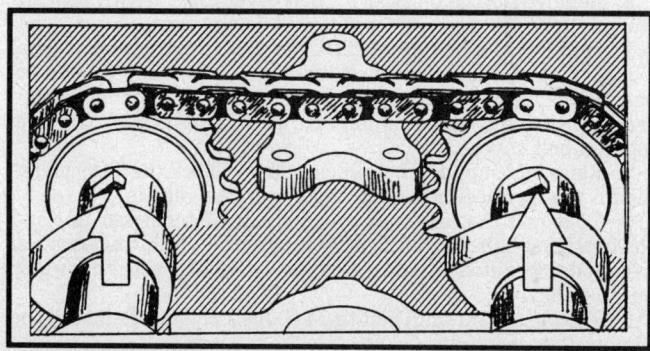

Correct alignment of late version camshaft marks with the bright links on the camshaft chain

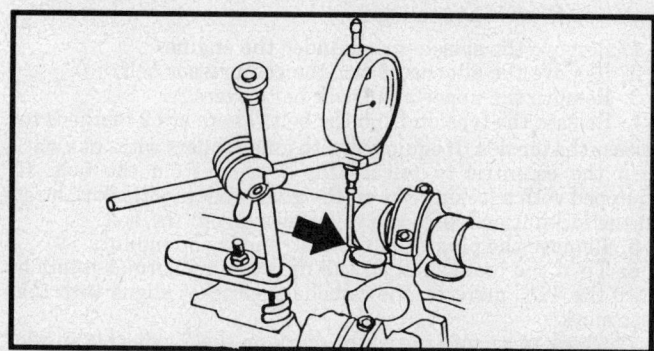

Installing the camshaft timing equipment on 928, 944

spring tension alone. Do not attempt to increase the belt tension by prying on the mechanical adjuster. Tighten the tensioner bolts to 15 ft. lbs. (20 Nm). Rotate the engine 2 times in the normal direction of rotation and check the timing mark alignment before completing the installation procedure.

944S

1. Be sure the engine is cold. Disconnect the negative battery cable.
2. Remove the complete air filter housing. Remove the air hose from the top of the cam belt housing.
3. Remove the cable holder from the top of the cam belt housing.
4. Remove the top camshaft drive belt housing retaining bolts. Remove the housing assembly.
5. Remove the high tension wire on the distributor cap, coming from the coil.
6. Remove the top metal drive belt cover together with the installed distributor cap and position it to the rear.

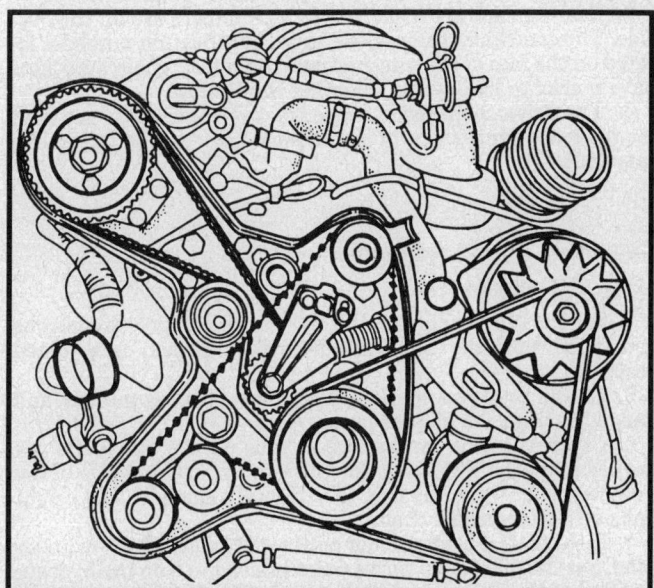

Timing belt configuration on 944S

7. Raise and support the vehicle safely. Remove the lower engine protection cover. Loosen the adjusting rod for the servo pump and remove the belt.

8. Loosen the adjusting rod for the alternator and air conditioning compressor. Remove the drive belt.

9. Remove the bottom belt cover. Do not loosen or remove the pulley pack on the crankshaft. Position the engine at TDC on the compression stroke.

10. Loosen the nut on the balance shaft tensioning wheel about 1 turn. To counter hold the component use tool 9200. Matchmark the belt for reinstallation.

11. Remove the balance shaft belt. Lower the vehicle.

12. Loosen the camshaft drive belt. Slide the belt from the camshaft gear.

13. Remove the idle roller on the oil pump bolt. Remove both nuts on the belt guide rail. Pull off the guide rail. Remove the nuts on the tensioner. Remove the complete unit.

NOTE: For easier belt removal, bring the tensioner into the center of the adjusting area of the tensioner assembly.

14. Remove the camshaft drive belt. Raise and support the vehicle safely, as the belt must be reinstalled from under the vehicle.

To install:

15. To install the new belt, slip it over the pulley pack by starting at the bottom right side. Push the belt over the balance shaft drive gear. As required, push the cam cover back to gain clearance.

16. Once installed, check the crankshaft TDC on the flywheel housing. If necessary, bring the engine to TDC by turning the crankshaft slightly to the right or left. Do not rotate the engine more than 20 degrees either way.

17. Lower the vehicle. Reinstall the belt tensioner and torque the retaining bolts to 14 ft. lbs.

18. Move the tensioner to the fully off position. Slip the new cam belt onto the camshaft drive gear. Do not move the camshaft.

19. Reinstall the idler roller onto the oil pump. Torque the retaining bolt to 33 ft. lbs.

20. Reinstall the belt rail. Be sure to use new nuts and torque them to 8 ft. lbs. Raise and support the vehicle safely.

21. Rotate the engine 2 revolutions and bring it back to TDC on the compression stroke. Lower the vehicle.

22. Check to be sure the crank and the camshaft are in proper alignment. Readjust the cam belt, by loosening the bolt and nut on the tensioner. Torque them to 20 ft. lbs.

23. Raise and support the vehicle safely. Reinstall the balance shaft drive belt and assure correct position of the balance shaft. Loosen the idler pulley. Adjust the idler pulley using special tool 9207 or equivalent, to a preload of 1mm. Torque the bolt to 33 ft. lbs.

24. Reinstall the lower balance shaft drive gear bolt and washers. Torque the retaining bolt to 33 ft. lbs.

25. Continue the installation in the reverse order of the removal procedure.

Camshaft Coupler and Chain Tensioner

Removal and Installation

928S, 928S4 AND 944S

NOTE: The intake camshaft is chain-driven off of the exhaust camshaft. This chain is tightened by a hydraulic chain tensioner which maintains the proper chain tension automatically. No adjustment is necessary but note that the tensioners are different for right and left sides on the 928S and 928S4.

1. With the vehicle on the ground and full weight on the wheels, remove the cross strut.

2. Remove the air intake hoses and complete air cleaner assembly.

3. Loosen the hose clamps on the intake air distributor and vacuum line. Pull off and lay the suction pump aside. Remove the intake air distributor.

4. Remove the lifting bracket from the left rear of the engine.

5. Twist and pull the spark plug wires from the plug. Remove the plug wires form the valve cover clips and remove the valve cover(s).

NOTE: Take note when removing valve cover retaining bolts, some are equipped with a seal. These bolts must be returned to their original positions.

6. Remove the hollow union bolt and check valve from the cylinder head. A seal is used under the bolt head. Remove the chain tensioner.

7. The chain tensioner piston is under spring pressure. Compress the tensioner piston when removing and secure with suitable binding wire.

8. Install tensioner in reverse order. To apply tensioner to chain on Nos. 1–4 cylinders, push tensioner chain up; Nos. 5–8 cylinders, push tensioner chain down. Tighten the chain tensioner bolts to 6 ft. lbs. (8 Nm) after installation. No further adjustment is necessary.

Balance Shaft Drive Belt

Removal and Installation

924S, 944, 944 TURBO AND 944S

1. Disconnect the negative battery cable.
2. Remove the engine splash guard.
3. Remove the alternator and air conditioning drive belt.
4. Remove the camshaft drive (timing) belt cover.
5. Loosen the balance shaft idler pulley so the pulley does not touch the balance shaft drive belt.
6. Rotate the crankshaft clockwise as necessary to position the No. 1 cylinder at TDC on the compression stroke.

NOTE: At this point, the marks on the balance shaft sprockets should be aligned with the marks on the rear belt cover.

7. Turn the tensioner nut counterclockwise to loosen the balance shaft drive belt. Carefully remove the old belt from the sprocket.

NOTE: There are 2 types of tensioners used. The older type (without a slot) is an eccentric that is turned to adjust tension. The newer type (with a slot) is held in place by a locknut and slides away from the belt to release tension. Do not move any sprocket while the belt is removed or while installing the new belt.

8. Carefully route the new belt around the sprocket, making sure the color coded tooth of the belt faces away from the sprockets.

9. Adjust the belt tension in the same manner as the camshaft drive (timing) belt. Turn the tensioner nut (same as used during Step 7) to tighten the belt to the proper value (2.4–3.0 dial reading). On guide rollers with no slot, loosen the locknut and turn the eccentric clockwise to tighten or counterclockwise to loosen. Tighten the locknut to 33 ft. lbs. (44 Nm).

10. On rollers with a slot, adjust the idler pulley so there is 0.5mm clearance between the pulley and the portion of the belt below the pulley. Tighten the pulley nut in this position. The remaining components are installed in the reverse order of removal.

NOTE: If the correct clearance cannot be obtained, rotate the pulley 180 degrees and repeat Step 10. A special clearance gauge tool 9207 or equivalent, is available to aid in the adjustment.

Timing Sprockets

Removal and Installation

The camshaft and crankshaft sprockets are located by keys on their respective shafts and each is retained by a single bolt. To remove either or both of the sprockets, first remove the timing belt cover and belt and then use the following procedure.

NOTE: If equipped, don't remove the 4 bolts which retain the outer belt pulley to the timing belt sprocket.

1. Remove the center bolt.
2. Gently pry the sprocket off the shaft. If the sprocket is stubborn, use a gear puller. Don't hammer on the sprocket.
3. Remove the sprocket and the key.
4. Install the sprocket in the reverse order of removal.
5. Tighten the center bolt on the crankshaft sprocket to 58 ft. lbs. (79 Nm); tighten the camshaft sprocket retaining bolt to 33 ft. lbs. (45 Nm).

NOTE: The 944 is equipped with polygon head bolts instead of the Allen head bolts. These should be torqued to 48 ft. lbs. (65 Nm).

6. Install the timing belt. Check valve timing and belt tension, then install the cover.

Camshaft

Removal and Installation

928S, 928S4 AND 944S

The camshaft housing and cylinder head are a complete unit on these vehicles. Refer to the "Cylinder Head Removal and Installation" procedures and remove the camshaft housing covers, timing belt and camshaft sprocket.

1. Remove the hydraulic chain tensioner, the camshaft bearing caps and lift out both camshafts together with the timing chain.
2. Camshaft bearing caps are numbered from 1–8. Check that the bearing cap positions and cylinder head numbers are correct when installing.

3. Bearing caps are installed so the numbers are on the outside. The camshafts themselves have identification numbers located on the face of the camshaft and the timing chain sprockets have marks to help when adjusting the timing.

4. The drive chain has 2 copper-plated links which are used for the basic adjustment of the exhaust camshaft to the intake camshaft.

Camshaft Timing Adjustment

928S AND 928S4

1. Set the No. 1 cylinder at TDC on the compression stroke and make sure the camshaft drive belt tension is adjusted properly.

2. Check that the marks on the camshaft sprockets and flange bearings are aligned properly.

3. Check that the marks or cast tabs on the camshafts are aligned properly. The marks should face the exhaust side of the cylinder head, while the cast tabs should align with the bright links on the camshaft chain.

4. Install a dial gauge holder with a dial gauge on the cylinder head. Set the dial gauge with a 5mm preload to 0 on the hydraulic lifter of No. 6 cylinder intake valve. The dial gauge must be perpendicular to the intake valve.

5. Slowy move the crankshaft in the normal direction of rotation (clockwise) past TDC while observing the reading on the dial gauge. Continue turning until the dial indicates 2.0 ± 0.1mm lift. The 20 degrees ATDC mark should now be aligned with the pointer on the drive belt cover. If it is, then the valve timing is correct and no adjustment is necessary.

NOTE: Make all measurements using metric specifications when checking or adjusting valve timing, and make all steps and adjustments as smoothly and accurately as possible. If the engine is rotated a little past 2mm lift when setting up the measurement, continue around in the normal direction of rotation and begin at Step 1 again. Never rotate the engine counterclockwise to align any timing marks; always rotate the engine clockwise. All timing degree specifications and timing mark alignments are on the No. 1 cylinder compression stroke, either approaching or leaving TDC.

6. If the alignment of the pointer and the 20 degrees ATDC mark is not correct, remove the ignition rotor and install 3 additional M5 × 15 bolts into the camshaft sprocket to prevent the camshaft and sprocket from turning while loosening the sprocket bolts.

7. Turn the crankshaft clockwise until the dial gauge reads 2.0 ± 0.01mm, then loosen the sprocket bolts.

8. Turn the crankshaft to 20 degrees ATDC, cylinder No. 1 compression stroke, then retorque the camshaft mounting bolt to 47 ft. lbs. (65 Nm). Hold the sprocket securely with the bolts as before.

9. Remove the M5 × 15 bolts from the sprocket and recheck the camshaft timing on cylinder bank 1–4 by rotating the engine clockwise to TDC on cylinder No. 6 (not No. 1).

10. Install the dial gauge on the hydraulic lifter for the intake valve of No. 1 cylinder. The dial gauge must be perpendicular to the intake valve.

11. Slowly rotate the crankshaft clockwise away from TDC/No. 6 and observe the reading on the dial gauge. Continue turning until the dial indicates 1.6 ± 0.1mm lift. The 20 degrees ATDC mark should now be aligned with the pointer on the drive belt cover.

12. If the alignment of the pointer and the 20 degrees ATDC mark is not correct, repeat the timing procedure from Step 1.

13. When installing the cylinder head cover, additional sealing is required. Apply a small bead of silicone Silastic 730 RTV seal-

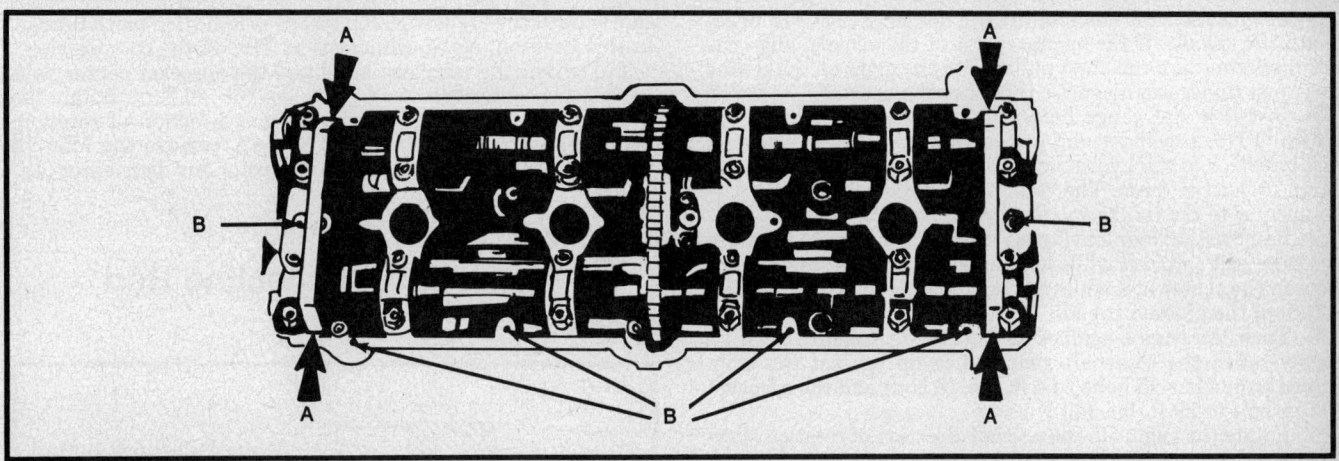

On 928S4 vehicles, apply silicone sealer at the arrows (A) and the spacers at the cover bolt holes indicated (B) TDC/compression on 944S vehicles

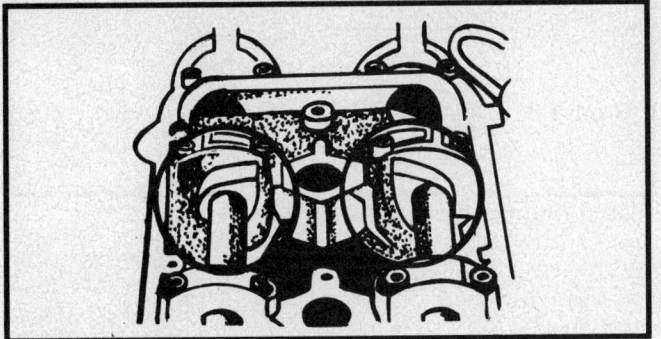

Correct cam lobe alignment for No. 1 cylinder at 944S vehicles

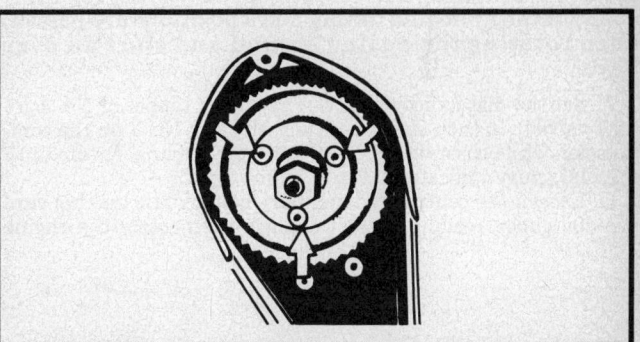

Install 3 M5 x 15 bolts as shown to hold the sprocket in place

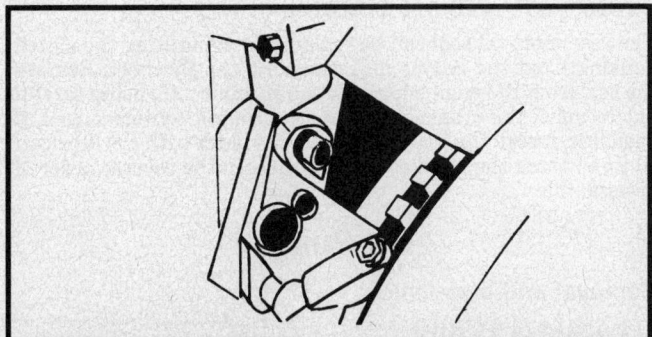

TDC mark alignment on the crankshaft pulley for on 944 vehicles

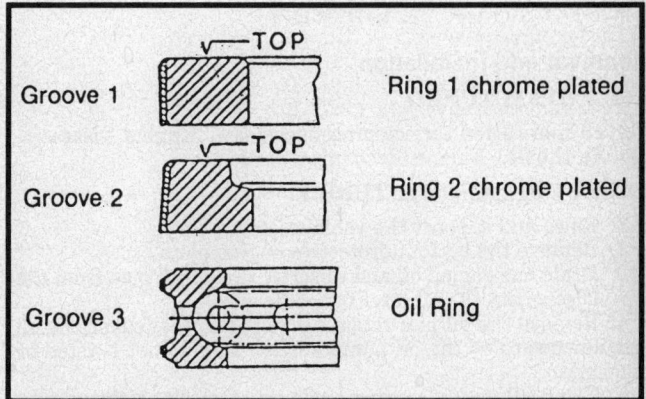

Piston ring positioning—typical

er (or equivalent) in the area where end camshaft bearing caps meet the head cover mating surface. Avoid using excessive amounts of the sealer and torque the head cover bolts to 7 ft. lbs. (10 Nm). On 928S4 engines, 12 spacers are used between the guide washers and the mounting bolt heads. These spacers should only be added to the 4 mounting bolts along the bottom (exhaust side) of the cover and the 2 mounting bolts, 1 centered at each end of the cover.

944S

1. Rotate the engine in the normal direction of rotation to set No. 1 cylinder at TDC of the compression. Check the cam belt tension adjustment.

2. Remove the distributor cap and make sure the rotor is pointing straight-up. Check that the cam lobes for No. 1 cylinder are leaning in toward each another with the noses at approximately 10–2 o'clock. The notch on the flywheel should also be

aligned with the TDC notch in the bell housing, visible from beneath the vehicle. If the engine is out of the vehicle, align the **OT** marks on the crankshaft pulley with the mark on the engine case, just under the magnetic timing probe bracket.

3. Install a dial gauge holder and indicator on the piston crown of No. 1 cylinder and preload to 3mm. Install a second dial indicator to the hydraulic tappet of No. 1 intake valve and again preload to 3mm. The second dial indicator must be perpendicular to the intake valve.

4. Remove the rotor and install three M5 × 15 bolts to secure the camshaft sprocket while loosening the sprocket center bolt. Loosen the center bolt while counter holding to prevent engine rotation, then loosen the M5 × 15 bolts.

5. Turn the engine against its normal direction of rotation slowly, until the camshaft gear comes up against the stop. Tighten the M5 × 15 bolts to 4 ft. lbs. (6 Nm) and the sprocket center bolt to 29 ft. lbs. (40 Nm).

6. Rotate the engine in the normal direction of rotation slowly, until the highest piston stroke position is indicated by the dial gauge.

NOTE: Do not rotate the engine against the normal direction of rotation in an attempt to correct for overshoot. If the indicated timing mark positions are passed, keep rotating the engine around and start all over again.

7. Set the dial indicator on the hydraulic tappet of No. 1 intake valve to 0, then slowly rotate past TDC, No. 1 on the compression while observing the dial indicator reading. Rotate until the dial gauge indicates 1.4 ± 0.1mm.

8. Loosen the central and auxiliary bolts, while making sure the dial gauge reading doesn't change, then rotate the engine slowly until the highest piston stroke is indicated on the gauge. In this position, No. 4 cylinder is at TDC of the compression.

9. Tighten the auxiliary bolts and the sprocket center bolt. Torque the center bolt to 48–52 ft. lbs. (65–70 Nm). Rotate the crankshaft 2 more times in the normal direction of rotation, then recheck the adjustment. If correct, remove the M5 × 15 bolts from the sprocket and install the rotor and distributor cap.

Piston and Connecting Rod

Positioning

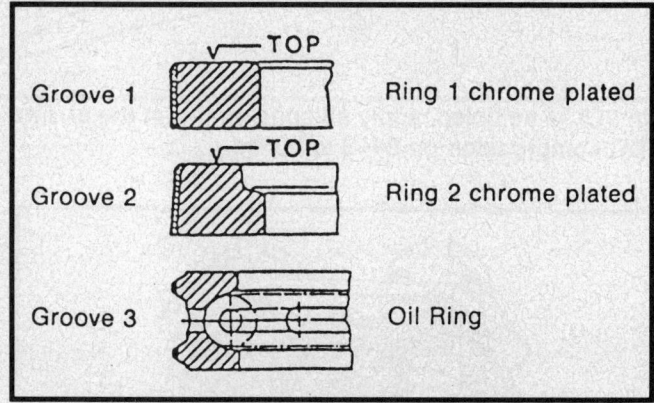

Piston ring positioning—944, typical

ENGINE LUBRICATION

Oil Pan

Removal and Installation

911 AND 911 TURBO

For all lubrication service procedures, see "Engine Disassembly" in the 911 Engine Mechanical section.

EXCEPT 911 AND 911 TURBO

1. Raise and support the vehicle safely.
2. Remove the bottom protective engine plate.
3. Drain the engine oil and unscrew the oil fill pipe from the pan. Disconnect the oil level indicator wire.
4. Remove the oil pan retaining bolts and maneuver the oil pan downward so the oil pump suction tube is not twisted or damaged.
5. Clean all gasket mating surfaces carefully. Using a new gasket, install the oil pan in the reverse order of removal.

Rear Main Bearing Oil Seal

Replacement

911 AND 911 TURBO

For all lubrication service procedures, see "Engine Disassembly" in the 911 Engine Mechanical section.

EXCEPT 911 AND 911 TURBO

The rear main oil seal can be replaced by separating the clutch housing from the engine and removing the flywheel. Remove the seal from the engine block with a suitable tool, being careful not to mark the crankshaft surface. Using a centering tool, if available, install the seal into the engine block with the lubricated lip towards the crankshaft. Assemble in the reverse order of disassembly.

Oil Pump

Removal and Installation

911 AND 911 TURBO

For all lubrication service procedures, see "Engine Disassembly" in the 911 Engine Mechanical section.

EXCEPT 911 AND 911 TURBO

The oil pump is located on the front of the engine block and is driven by the toothed timing belt.

1. Remove the timing belt.
2. Remove the oil pump sprocket and the oil pump retaining bolts.
3. Remove the oil pump from the engine block.
4. Installation is the reverse of removal. Install a new O-ring seal on the pump body.

NOTE: An oil pump shaft seal is used and can be replaced after removal of the sprocket and Woodruff® key.

MANUAL TRANSAXLE

Removal and Installation

911 AND 911 TURBO

The engine and transaxle are removed as a unit, then serviced separately out of the vehicle. Transaxle separation is covered under the "Engine Removal" procedure in the 911 Engine Mechanical section.

924S AND 944

1. Disconnect the negative battery cable. Raise and support the vehicle safely.
2. Remove the entire exhaust system from behind the catalytic converter.
3. Disconnect the wires from the backup light switch.
4. Remove the reinforcement strut at the front of the transaxle to facilitate work procedures.
5. Engage 4th gear for 4 speed transaxle or 5th gear for 5 speed transaxle. Remove the rubber cap from the front transaxle cover. Position the socket head screw for removal by turning a rear wheel (hold the other wheel). Unscrew the screw from the coupling using a long reach extension and a 6 mm socket. Keep the transaxle in the proper gear.
6. Detach the axle halfshafts from the transaxle and suspend them on wire to prevent damage.
7. Remove the self-locking nuts from the transaxle mounts (the rubber/metal mounts).
8. Position a jack under the transaxle and secure the transaxle to it using a strap.
9. Unscrew the bolts from the rubber/metal mounts, lift the transaxle slightly with he jack and remove the mounts. Do not lift the unit too far, as the brake line for the left rear wheel may be damaged.
10. Disconnect the shift linkage.
11. Remove the bolts between the driveshaft tube and the transaxle. Remove or disconnect any other interfering components, then carefully remove the transaxle unit, moving rearward and down.
12. Installation is the reverse of removal.

928, 928S AND 928S4

1. Remove the nuts from the spring strut bolts extending into the trunk compartment.
2. Remove the battery and loosen the rear wheel lugnuts.
3. Place the transaxle in 5th gear.
4. Raise the vehicle and remove the rubber plug from underneath the front of the transaxle. Looking into the hole, position the coupling bolt head between the drive and input shafts, so it can be removed.

NOTE: During removal of the bolt, do not allow the shaft to turn and jam the socket or bolt in the transaxle housing.

5. Place the transaxle in **N**, remove the rear wheels and remove the brake calipers. Wire the calipers to the frame; do not allow them to hang from their brake hoses.
6. Remove the exhaust system from the catalytic converter rearward.
7. Remove the exhaust heat shield and the battery box.
8. Disconnect the backup light switch wires and loosen the pulse transmitter for the speedometer. Remove the wires form the clip.
9. Move the dust cover from the shift rod coupling and remove the locking set screw. Remove the shift rod from the main rod.
10. Disconnect the halfshafts at the transaxle end. Suspend the axles from the crossmember.
11. Disconnect the stabilizer bar at the lower control arm.
12. Support the transaxle assembly from the stabilizer bar with the use of a strap, chain or heavy wire.
13. Remove the transaxle to rear axle crossmember bolts and the bolts between the rear axle crossmember and frame.
14. Mark the position of the rear axle crossmember and place a jack under member. Remove the bolts and tilt the rear axle so

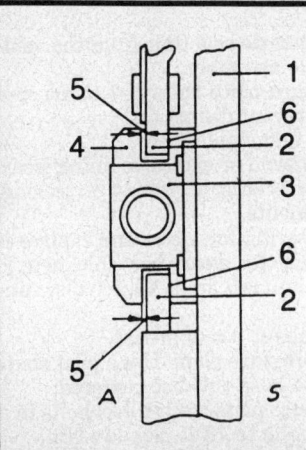

1. Intermediate ring
2. Intermediate plate
3. Stop bracket
4. Stop
5. Distance 0.7 to 1.0mm
6. Position of intermediate plate
A. Release bearing side
B. Flywheel side

To prevent clutch drag on the 928, move the 3 clutch stop brackets toward the pressure plate until the correct gap at point 5 is obtained

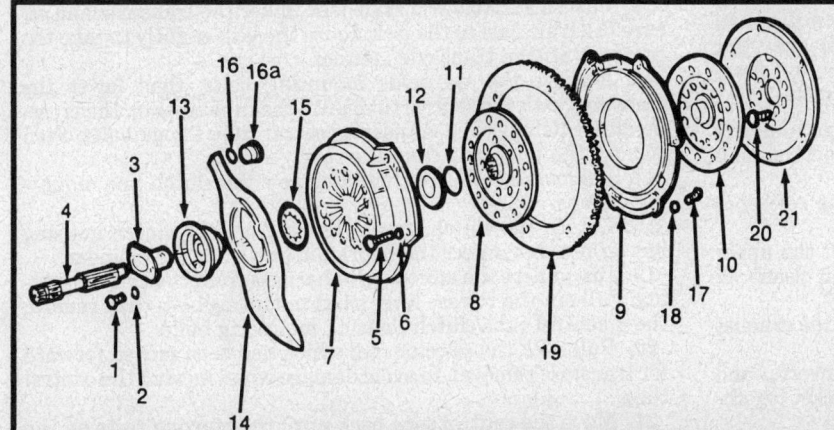

1. Bolt	12. Thrust washer
2. Washer	13. Release bearing
3. Guide sleeve	14. Release lever
4. Driveshaft	15. Preload washer
5. Bolt	16. Snap-ring
6. Wahser	16A. Ball socket bushing
7. Pressure plate	17. Bolt
8. Clutch disc (spring loaded)	18. Washer
9. Intermediate plate	19. Starter ring
10. Clutch disc (not spring loaded)	20. Bolt
11. Snap-ring	21. Flywheel with centering collar

Diameter centered clutch assembly on 928 and 928S

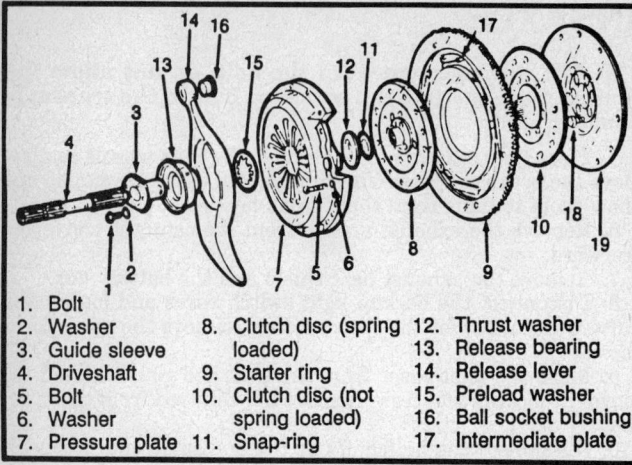

1. Bolt
2. Washer
3. Guide sleeve
4. Driveshaft
5. Bolt
6. Washer
7. Pressure plate
8. Clutch disc (spring loaded)
9. Starter ring
10. Clutch disc (not spring loaded)
11. Snap-ring
12. Thrust washer
13. Release bearing
14. Release lever
15. Preload washer
16. Ball socket bushing
17. Intermediate plate

Dowel pin centered clutch assembly on 928 and 928S

the spring struts and control arms do not twist. Support the rear axle in the tilted position to keep the weight off the lower control arm link pins.

15. Place under the transaxle assembly and remove the bolts between the driveshaft tube and the transaxle. Remove the holding strap, pull the unit rearward and lower.

16. Installation is the reverse of removal.

911 AND 911 TURBO

1. Position the shift lever in the **N** detent. Remove the rear tunnel cover in front of the rear seat.

2. Pull the rubber dust cover forward on the shift rod.

3. Loosen the clamp bolt on the shift rod.

4. Move the transaxle selector shaft all the way to its left stop, keeping it in **N**.

5. With the transaxle still in **N**, move the gearshift rod to the right to its stop.

6. Tighten the clamp bolt to 18 ft. lbs. (24 Nm).

7. Test the shift lever. Play should be the same in all gears in all directions.

CLUTCH

Removal and Installation

911 AND 911 TURBO

1. Remove the engine and transaxle as a unit from the vehicle. Separate the engine/transaxle assembly.

2. Gradually loosen the pressure plate bolts 1–2 turns at a time in a crisscross pattern to prevent distortion.

3. Remove the pressure plate and clutch disc.

4. Check the clutch disc for uneven or excessive lining wear. Examine the pressure plate for cracking, scorching or scoring. Replace any questionable components.

5. Check the clutch release bearing for wear, and replace if necessary. Measure the clutch disc for wear; new thickness is 8.1mm, and the maximum wear limit is 6.3mm. Clutch disc run-out (maximum) is 0.6mm.

6. Fill the pilot bearing with about 2cc of grease.

7. Install the clutch disc and pressure plate. Use a pilot shaft or an old transaxle input shaft to keep the disc centered.

8. Gradually tighten the pressure plate-to-flywheel bolts in a criss-cross pattern. Torque the bolts to 18 ft. lbs. (24 Nm).

9. Install the throwout bearing.

10. Install the transaxle on the engine and install the engine/transaxle assembly.

924S AND 944

NOTE: The flywheel sensing components used in these vehicles for the digital ignition system are very delicate and easily damaged. Exercise care when handling, removing and installing these components.

1. Disconnect the negative battery cable and the ground wire from the body to the clutch housing. Raise and support the vehicle safely.

2. Remove the socket head bolts and remove the reference mark sensor and speed sensor from the bracket.

3. Disconnect the wire harness for the starter at the upper mounting point. It may be necessary to remove the air cleaner to gain access.

4. Disconnect the oxygen sensor wire and remove the exhaust assembly at the manifold.

5. Remove the heat shield above the catalytic converter and the splash shield. Remove the rear exhaust pipe bracket together with the bracket bolted on the central tube.

6. Pull back the dust cover, then remove the lockwire on the clamp bolt of the selector linkage and remove the bolt.

7. Lift and fold down the dust cover and sleeve on the shift lever. Remove the shift lever boot retainer and remove the shift knob.

8. Remove the circlip on the shift lever, then pull off the selector rod and washer on the bolt of the shift lever.

9. Remove the insulator above the shift lever console, then remove the shift lever after first marking its location. Press down on the insulation sheet and push the selector rod forward about 12 in. (300mm).

10. Remove the 2 upper mounting bolts on the clutch housing.

11. Remove the end cap on the central tube housing. Push back the protective tube for the selector rod far enough to allow the rod to be moved outside of the housing. This is done by inserting a suitable tool through the assembly opening in the central tube housing and prying open the retainer on the protective tube.

12. Disconnect and remove the clamping sleeve bolts through the assembly openings, then push the clamping sleeve toward the transaxle.

13. Disconnect the halfshafts from the transaxle and wire them in a horizontal position. Do not let the shafts hang down.

14. Disconnect the backup light switch connector. Pull off the plug on the speedometer drive.

15. Place a suitable transaxle jack under the transaxle and secure the transaxle to the jack. Raise the jack slightly to take the pressure off the transaxle mounts.

16. Remove the transaxle mounting bolts, then lower the transaxle with the central tube until the tube rests on the crossmember. Remove the transaxle/central tube flange bolts, then remove the transaxle from the rear.

17. Remove the starter, then unscrew the clutch line mounting clamps.

18. Detach the clutch slave cylinder from the clutch housing but do not disconnect the hydraulic line from the cylinder.

19. Disconnect the starter wire harness from the clutch housing. Pull out the release lever shaft mounting bolt, then remove the 4 central tube/clutch housing mounting bolts.

20. Pull back the selector rod, which had been moved forward for transaxle removal, to avoid damage when moving the central tube.

21. Move the central tube back until the housing rests on the transaxle carrier. Make sure the brake lines are not damaged by the tube.

NOTE: If the central tube cannot be moved from the clutch housing without applying force, hold the engine tight with the transport eye mounted on the camshaft housing with special tool VW 10–222 or equivalent. If this is the case, the engine has excessive inclination at the rear. Check the engine mounts.

22. Remove the guard on the clutch housing and the right support.

23. Remove the 2 lower mounting bolts on the clutch housing after removing the engine mount nuts and pushing the engine to the right. Move out the guard and clutch housing with the release lever as an assembly.

24. Disconnect the clutch assembly from the flywheel and remove it.

To install:

25. Check the flywheel, starter ring gear, pilot bearing in the flywheel, crankshaft seal, release bearing, guide sleeve, release lever, pressure plate and clutch disc for wear or damage. Replace parts as necessary.

26. Coat the guide sleeve with multi-purpose grease, then apply a light coat to the spline of the driveshaft and the area of the pilot bearing/flywheel. Lubricate the release lever pivot, ball socket and needle bearings with white grease.

27. Make sure the clutch disc and flywheel are clean and free from grease, then install the clutch disc. Use a suitable clutch alignment tool to center the clutch disc and install the mounting bolts. Tighten the clutch disc bolts in a crisscross pattern evenly to 18 ft. lbs. (25 Nm).

28. Continue installation in reverse of the removal procedures.

When installing the clutch housing assembly, make sure the flywheel reference bolts are facing down to avoid damage during installation.

29. Tighten the central tube mounting bolts after the engine and transaxle mounting bolts have been tightened. Torque the clutch housing to engine bolts to 54 ft. lbs (75 Nm), the central tube flange to clutch housing bolts to 30 ft. lbs. (42 Nm), and the driveshaft to transaxle input shaft clamp bolt to 58 ft. lbs. (80 Nm).

928, 928S AND 928S4

1. Disconnect the negative battery cable.
2. Raise and support the vehicle safely.
3. Remove the lower body brace.
4. Remove the clutch slave cylinder and keep hydraulic lines attached.
5. Remove the starter and clutch housing cover as a unit and attach to the stabilizer bar with a wire. Remove the catalytic converter.
6. Remove the coupling screws and push the coupler rearward on the driveshaft.
7. Remove the release bearing sleeve bolts and move the sleeve towards the flywheel.
8. Matchmark the clutch components and loosen all pressure plate mounting bolts evenly until all the pressure is removed from the plate.
9. Remove the mounting bolts and press down on the release lever (towards the flywheel) and disconnect the release lever at the ball stud.

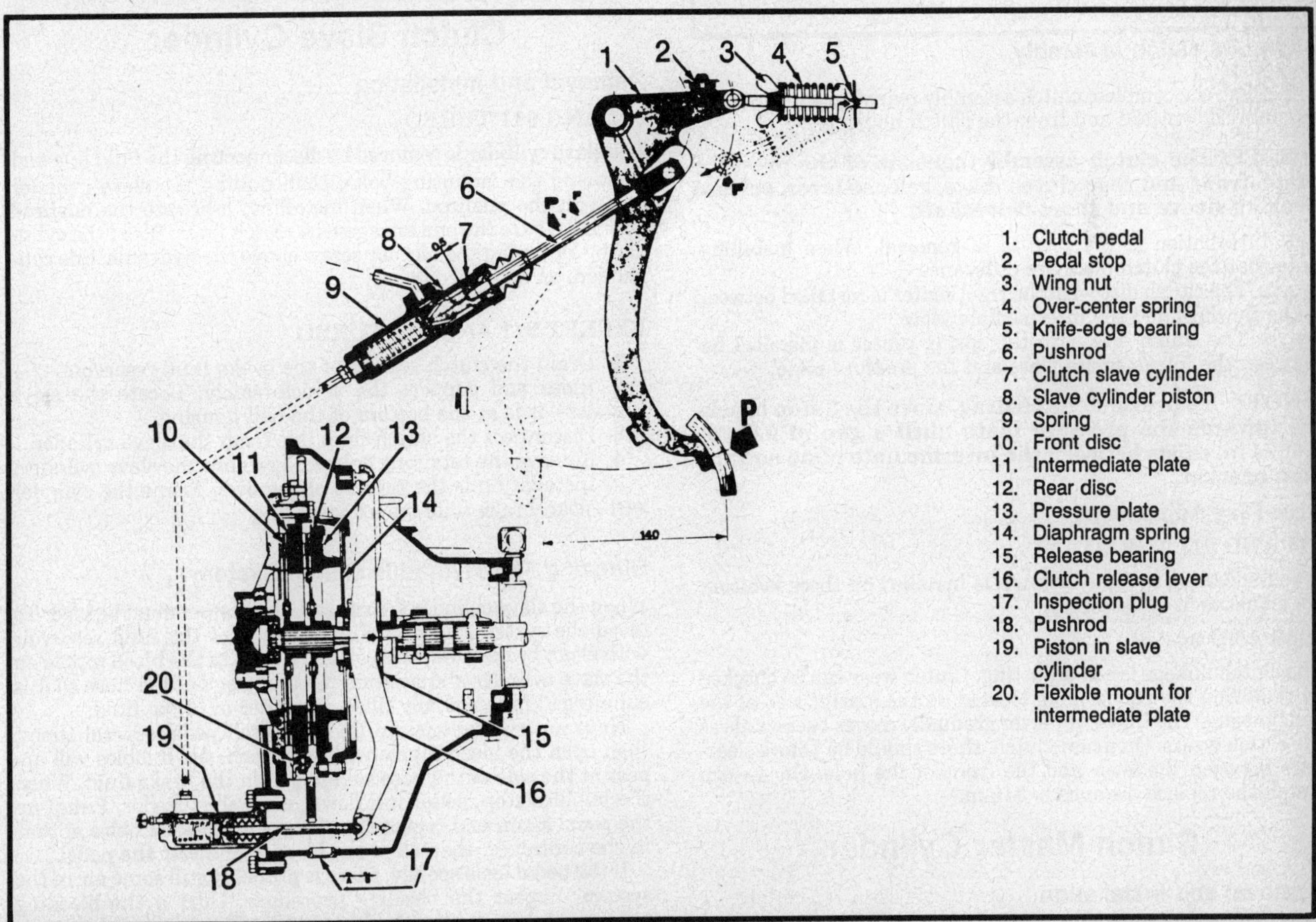

1. Clutch pedal
2. Pedal stop
3. Wing nut
4. Over-center spring
5. Knife-edge bearing
6. Pushrod
7. Clutch slave cylinder
8. Slave cylinder piston
9. Spring
10. Front disc
11. Intermediate plate
12. Rear disc
13. Pressure plate
14. Diaphragm spring
15. Release bearing
16. Clutch release lever
17. Inspection plug
18. Pushrod
19. Piston in slave cylinder
20. Flexible mount for intermediate plate

Hydraulic clutch actuation system on the 928 and 928S. Clutch wear can be checked after removing the rubber plug (17).

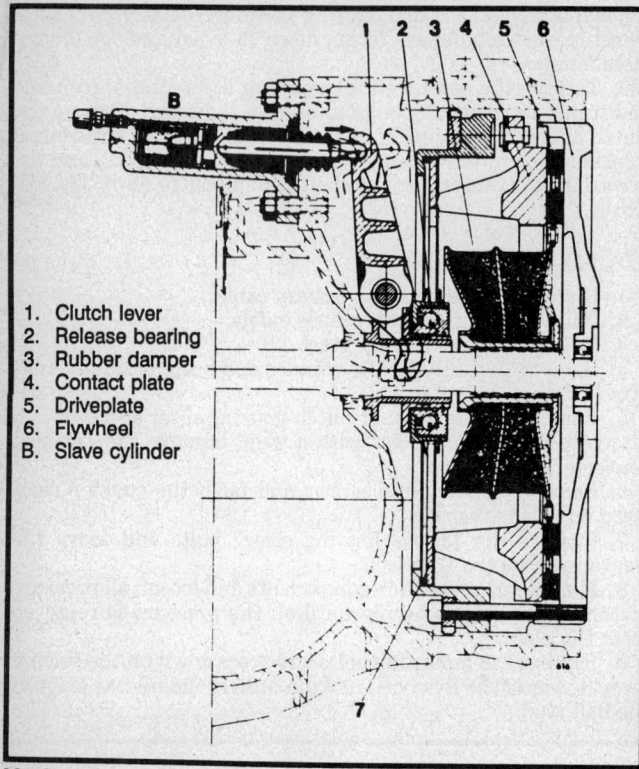

1. Clutch lever
2. Release bearing
3. Rubber damper
4. Contact plate
5. Driveplate
6. Flywheel
B. Slave cylinder

Hydraulic clutch assembly

10. Push the complete clutch assembly rearward and move the assembly downward and from the clutch housing.

NOTE: The clutch assembly consists of the pressure plate, front and rear clutch discs, release lever, release bearing sleeve and short driveshaft.

11. Installation is the reverse of removal. When installing, note that the clutch discs are different:
   a. The clutch disc with the rigid center is installed between the flywheel and the intermediate plate.
   b. The clutch disc with the spring center is installed between the intermediate plate and the pressure plate.

NOTE: To prevent clutch drag, move the 3 stop brackets towards the pressure plate until a gap of 0.0275–0.0394 in. exists between the intermediate plate and the stop bracket.

Free-Play Adjustment

911 AND 911 TURBO

A self-adjusting hydraulic clutch is installed on these vehicles. No adjustment is necessary.

924S AND 944

The clutch linkage is self-adjusting. Clutch wear can be checked by removing the rubber plug located on the starter side of the bell housing. The throw out lever gradually moves backwards as the clutch wears. On a new clutch, there should be 18mm clearance between the lever and the front of the hole. On a worn clutch the replace distance is 34mm.

Clutch Master Cylinder

Removal and Installation

911 AND 911 TURBO

The hydraulic clutch receives its fluid from the brake fluid tank to master cylinder, where it passes through the line to the slave cylinder mounted on the transaxle case. The master cylinder is attached to the pedal bracket assembly.

EXCEPT 911 AND 911 TURBO

The clutch master cylinder is located beside the brake master cylinder in the engine compartment and shares the brake master cylinder's fluid reservoir. Access is limited and, depending on the year and options, several other components may have to be relocated before the clutch master cylinder can be removed.

1. Drain the clutch section of the fluid reservoir. Remove and plug the line leading to the clutch master cylinder from the brake master cylinder fluid reservoir.

NOTE: Be very careful not to let any brake fluid drip onto painted surfaces, as it will permanently discolor them.

2. From inside the vehicle, disconnect the clutch master cylinder pushrod.
3. Disconnect the fluid tube which runs to the clutch slave cylinder from the master cylinder and plug it. Before loosening the tube's fitting, wrap a rag around it so brake fluid is not spilled.
4. Disconnect and remove the master cylinder from the vehicle.
5. Installation is the reverse of removal. Bleed the system at the slave cylinder.

Clutch Slave Cylinder

Removal and Installation

911 AND 911 TURBO

The slave cylinder is removed by disconnecting the fluid line and removing the mounting bolts, then pulling the slave cylinder out with the pushrod. When installing, lubricate the pushrod and make sure the end engages the clutch lever. Bleed the cylinder by loosening the bleeder screw above the hydraulic line connection, as described below.

EXCEPT 911 AND 911 TURBO

1. Drain the clutch section of the brake fluid reservoir.
2. Raise and support the vehicle safely. Locate the slave cylinder—it is at the bottom of the bell housing.
3. Disconnect the clutch fluid line form the slave cylinder.
4. Remove the retaining bolts and remove the slave cylinder.
5. Installation is the reverse of removal. Prime the cylinder with clean brake fluid before installing.

Bleeding The Hydraulic Clutch System

When the slave cylinder is installed, the system must be bled. To bleed the system, fill the clutch portion of the fluid reservoir with clean brake fluid, then attach a hose to the bleed nipple on the slave cylinder and position the other end of the hose so it is submerged in a partially filled container of brake fluid.

Have an assistant pump up the clutch pedal several times, then open the bleed nipple with a wrench. Air bubbles will appear at the side of the hose submerged in the brake fluid. When the bubbles stop, pedal still down, close the bleeder. Pump up the pedal again and repeat the process until no bubbles appear in the container, then close the bleeder and test the pedal.

If the pedal feels spongy, there is probably still some air in the system. Repeat the bleeding procedure. During the bleeding process, make sure the fluid in the clutch section of the reservoir does not completely disappear or air will enter the system again.

AUTOMATIC TRANSAXLE

Removal and Installation

1. Disconnect the negative battery cable.
2. Disconnect the battery ground strap from the body.
3. Disconnect the multi-pin plugs in the spare tire well and pull the wires out from below.
4. Remove the upper and lower air cleaner housings. Remove the upper air guide section.
5. Disconnect the control cable on the throttle housing. Disconnect the oxygen sensor wire on the fuse panel and pull it out from below.
6. Remove the engine air guide. Raise and safely support the vehicle.
7. Remove the complete exhaust system with all of the heat shields.
8. Remove the starter and suspend it aside.
9. Place a suitable drain pan under the transaxle and drain the fluid. Remove the fluid reservoir.
10. Disconnect the halfshafts from the rear of the transaxle and suspend them on a piece of wire.
11. Remove the transaxle crossmember suspension mounting bolts. Support the transaxle on the stabilizer bar, using support tool 9164 or equivalent.
12. Mark the position of the toe eccentric and the rear axle crossmember for reinstallation purposes. Remove the rear axle crossmember. Remove the clamp bolt from the central tube.
13. Disconnect the selector lever cable on the transaxle lever, unscrew the cable holder and sleeve.
14. Remove the fluid cooler and return lines. Plug the openings.
15. Pull off the vacuum modulator hose. Disconnect the pressure cable on the transaxle and pull the guide out carefully.
16. Place a universal transaxle jack or equivalent, under the transaxle and tighten the retaining strap.
17. Remove the front and rear transaxle reinforcement plates. Lift the transaxle slightly and remove the support tool from the stabilizer.
18. Lower transaxle far enough to so central tube mounting bolts and control cable bolt can be removed.
19. After removing the central tube-to-transaxle bolts, reposition the central tube in the installed position and loosely install the mounting plate. Place a block of wood under the central tube to keep it in position.
20. Slowly lower the transaxle assembly, pulling back on it as it comes out. Remove the transaxle from under the vehicle.

To install:

21. Before installation, coat the splines of the central shaft with an appropriate lubricant.
22. With the transaxle on a suitable lifting device, slowly raise it into an installed position under the vehicle. While raising it slide it onto the central shaft.
23. Install and lightly tighten the central shaft bolts. Lift the transaxle slightly and remove the block of wood and the support from the central shaft.
24. Lower the transaxle slightly and install the remaining central shaft bolts. Tighten all central shaft bolts to 87 ft. lbs. (120 Nm).
25. Mount the guide tube for the control cable on the converter housing. Tighten it to 6 ft. lbs.
26. Push the wiring harness up through the spare tire well.
27. Lift the transaxle up slightly and install the holding tool 9164 or equivalent, to the stabilizer bar.
28. Install the rear axle mount and tighten all bolts. Lift the transaxle and remove the holding tool.
29. Install the transaxle crossmember and bolts, tighten all bolts to 85 ft. lbs.
30. Adjust the transaxle suspension using the following procedure:
   a. Install the transaxle crossmember mounting bolts loosely.
   b. Lift the transaxle in the middle of the case far enough so there is a gap between both transaxle mounts and the crossmember. Measure this gap on both sides and take up the difference with shims.
   c. Lower the transaxle and tighten the bolts to 85 ft. lbs.
   d. Check the clearance on the transaxle stops after tightening the bolts, there should be at least 1mm clearance between the case stop and the transaxle.
31. Check the selector lever adjustment and the throttle cable adjustment.
32. Reconnect the halfshafts and lower the vehicle.
33. Road test the vehicle and check all gearshift operations.

Shift Linkage Adjustment

1. Raise and support the vehicle safely.
2. Move the selector lever into the **P** position.
3. Loosen the clamping bolt at the transaxle lever.
4. Pull the transaxle lever against the stop.
5. Tighten the clamping bolt with the lever in this position.

NOTE: When tightening the clamping bolt, make sure the cable does not twist and that the transaxle lever does not bend. The in-vehicle selector lever must not touch the selector gate in either the P or the 1 positions.

6. Apply the brakes while running the engine at idle and move the selector lever form **P** to **R**, then from **N** to **D**. In each case the gear should engage within a second after the selector is moved. The clearance between the selector and the front of the selector gate in **P** should be the same as the clearance between the selector and the back of the gate in 1st gear.

Throttle Cable Adjustment

1. Screw in the cable sleeve mounting nut on the transaxle bracket completely and tighten.
2. Loosen the bolts on the roller holder bracket, push the roller holder in its slot forward, as seen from the driving direction, as far as possible and tighten the bolts.
3. Completely loosen the short cable at the firewall and the long cable on the roller holder.
4. Turn the roller so the operating lever faces forward at an angle of 29 degrees; in this position the opening for the cable locator will face the reinforcement rib of the holder.
5. Hold the roller in this position and mount the throttle valve pushrod without tension on the rod.
6. Place the cable around the roller in the correct position and adjust the long cable sleeve until the cable locator just rests in the opening without tension.
7. Adjust the cable going to the accelerator pedal so it does not have tension at the adjuster. When the cable has been adjusted correctly, the accelerator pedal will be in its neutral position, the throttle valve will be closed and the lever on the transaxle will be on its bottom stop.
8. To check the full throttle position adjustment, depress the accelerator pedal to the first noticable pressure point and check whether the throttle valve is fully open.
9. To check the kickdown adjustment, depress the pedal past the full throttle pressure point until it comes against its stop and check to make sure the roller has lifted off the operating lever by about ¼ in. In this position the lever on the transaxle should be resting on the final stop or at most about 1 degree away.

DRIVE AXLE

Halfshaft

Removal and Installation

911 AND 911 TURBO

1. Raise the vehicle and support it safely.
2. Remove the wheels. Remove the brake caliper and disc.
3. Raise the trailing arm with a hydraulic jack.
4. Remove the lower shock absorber mounting.
5. Install a fixture similar to tool to hold the hub.
6. Remove the cotter pin and, using a long ratchet handle extension, remove the hub nut.
7. Remove the Allen bolts at the axle driveshaft/transaxle flange.
8. Use a flat chisel to pry the flanges apart. Don't damage the flanges when separating them.
9. Check the axle driveshaft joints for excessive play and replace them if necessary.
10. Use a new gasket on the transaxle flange. Ensure that the flanges are clean and free from burrs.
11. Pack the joints with a moly type grease.
12. Install the axle driveshaft using a reverse of the removal procedure.
13. Tighten the flange bolts to 60 ft. lbs. (81.5 Nm). The hollow side of the lock washer should face the spacer slot.
14. Using a long extension handle wrench, tighten the castellated nut to 217–253 ft. lbs. (295–344 Nm) and install a new cotter pin.
15. Tighten the shock absorber bolt to 54 ft. lbs. (73 Nm).
16. Install the brake caliper and disc.
17. Install the wheels and lower the vehicle.

EXCEPT 911 AND 911 TURBO

1. Raise the vehicle and support it safely.
2. Remove the 6 star bolts on the inside joint at the transaxle.
3. Remove the 6 bolts at the stub axle. Use a wide, flat bladed prybar to pry the flanges apart.
4. Drop the axle driveshaft down and out on the 924 and 944. On the 928, remove the axle from the upper left side of the hub assembly.
5. Pack the constant velocity joints with grease before installation.
6. Installation is the reverse of removal. Tighten the bolts to 30 ft. lbs. (41 Nm).

Front Axle Final Drive

Removal and Installation

911 CARRERA 4

1. Raise and safely support vehicle using vehicle jacking points.
2. Remove the floor panel from the pedal assembly.
3. Remove both universal joint clamping screws between the steering gear and steering shaft and pull the joint upwards.
4. Remove the front and middle floor panels.
5. Remove the retaining clamp from the power steering lines.
6. Unclip the power steering lines from holder.
7. Remove the transaxle mount center screw.
8. Remove the screws from the front axle crossmembers and side members and drop the front axle.
9. Remove the stabilizer.
10. Remove the driveshaft at the flange from the front axle final drive.
11. Remove the Allen-head screw from the front central-shaft clamping sleeve and slide the clamping sleeve along the central shaft to the rear.
12. Undo the upper fastening screws for the central tube by pressing the central pipe (driveshaft tube) aside with a suitable tool. Do not damage lines.
13. Remove the central pipe fastening screws and free the linkage from the tube.

To install:

14. Installation is the reverse of the removal process with the following points noted. Install front final drive assembly. Locate the rubber seal in the forward end of the driveshaft tube. This seal should be replaced. Lube with glycerine.
15. Make sure all lines are connected properly. Check oil level in all gear boxes.
16. Align front end.

CV-Boot

Removal and Installation

1. Remove the halfshaft from the vehicle.
2. The inboard or transaxle end of the halfshaft has a metal closing cover over the end of the inboard CV-joint. Tap this cover off with a soft metal drift pin. Note that it was originally installed with sealer.
3. Locate and remove the circlip inside the joint.
4. Slide the CV-joint dust boot forward along the halfshaft to

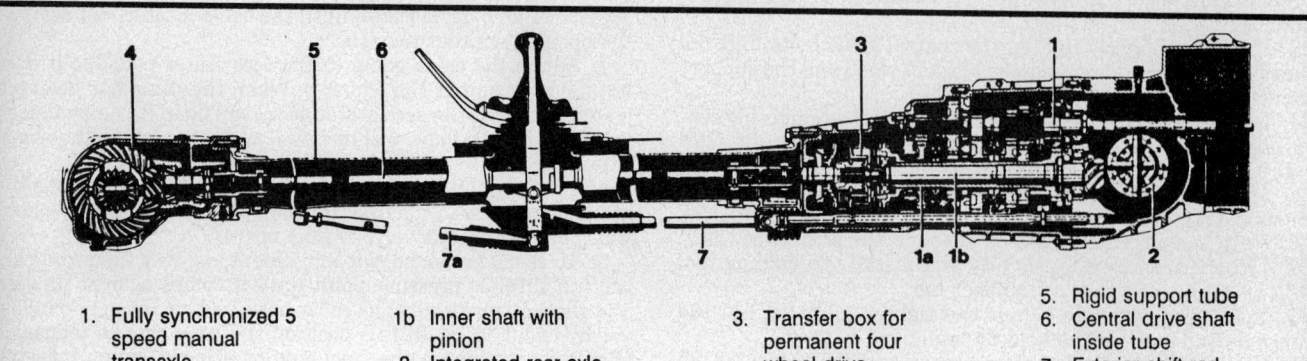

1. Fully synchronized 5 speed manual transaxle
1a Hollow output shaft
1b Inner shaft with pinion
2. Integrated rear axle differential (transaxle)
3. Transfer box for permanent four wheel drive
4. Front axle differential
5. Rigid support tube
6. Central drive shaft inside tube
7. Exterior shift rod
7a Connecting rod

Drivetrain layout of 911 Carrera 4 all-wheel drive

make room for setting up the halfshaft in a press with suitable adapters to press off the inboard joint. After removing the joint, remove the boot retainer rings and both boots can now be removed.

To install:

5. Installation is the reverse of the removal process. Slide the boots onto the shaft.

6. Press the inboard CV-joint onto the shaft. Use a new circlip. Pack the joints with the proper grease. The special grease is to be packed into the joint part only. Do not put any grease into the dust boot.

7. To grease the friction-welded or outboard wheel end joint, force the special grease through the metal cap in between the cap opening and the halfshaft into the joint. Do not remove the cap.

8. Place the halfshaft on a flat surface so the shaft will be straight. Install new clamp rings on the boots. Coat the sealing surfaces of the closing cover and making sure the bolt holes are aligned, tap the cover gently into place on the inboard CV-joint.

9. Install the halfshaft into the vehicle.

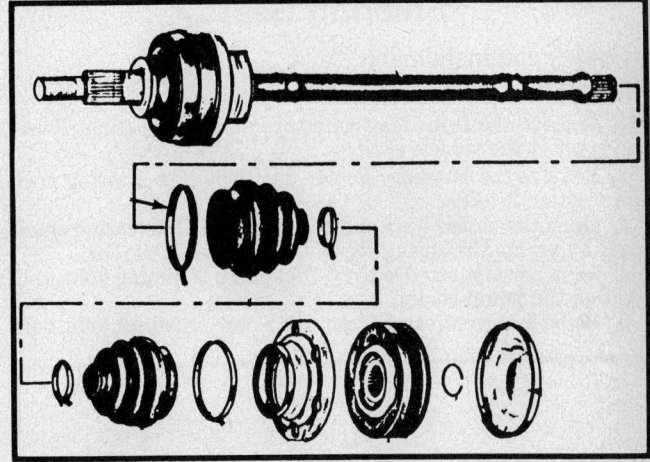

Halfshaft—911 Carrera, typical

STEERING

Steering Wheel

— CAUTION —

On vehicles equipped with an air bag, the negative battery cable must be disconnected, before working on the vehicle. Failure to do so may result in deployment of the air bag and possible personal injury. Note that some Porsche vehicles may also be equipped with an airbag on the passenger side.

The Porsche airbag system is monitored continuously by a diagnostic unit in the control unit. Any fault which may occur is indicated by the word **AIRBAG** in the instrument cluster.

When the ignition is switched on, the airbag annunciator remains lit for approximately 5 seconds before going out. When the engine is started the annunciator lights up for another 5 seconds. Any further response of the light indicates a defect in the system. The fault can be output to the light, the flashes corresponding to trouble codes.

Removal and Installation

911 AND 911 TURBO

1. Disconnect the negative battery cable. Place the wheels in a straight-ahead position.

2. If equipped with an airbag, remove the screws from behind the steering wheel. Take apart the plug connector and remove the air bag. Store upholstered side up. On non-airbag vehicles, twist the center cover to the left and remove it.

3. Remove the horn contact pin.

4. Remove the steering wheel nut.

5. Mark the steering wheel and the shaft so it can be reinstalled in the same position.

6. Remove the steering wheel, using the proper tool. Catch the bearing support ring and spring.

7. Install the spring and bearing support ring on the wheel hub.

8. Lightly grease the horn contact ring.

9. Install the wheel. Make sure to align the match marks before removal.

10. Tighten the steering wheel nut to 58 ft. lbs. (79 Nm).

11. Reinstall the airbag, if equipped. Twist the center cover back on to the right to snap it into place.

EXCEPT 911 AND 911 TURBO

1. Disconnect the negative battery cable.

2. If equipped with an airbag, remove the screws from behind the steering wheel. Take apart the plug connector and remove the air bag. Store upholstered side up. Remove horn pad and straighten the front wheels.

3. If necessary, disconnect the horn wiring. Matchmark the steering wheel to the steering shaft.

4. Remove retaining nut and washer.

5. Use a suitable steering wheel puller to remove the wheel. Do not strike the steering wheel.

6. Installation is the reverse of removal. Align the matchmarks on the wheel and shaft. Make sure the wheels are straight-ahead and steering wheel is centered, then torque steering wheel nut to 33–36 ft. lbs. (45–49 Nm).

7. Reinstall airbag, if equipped.

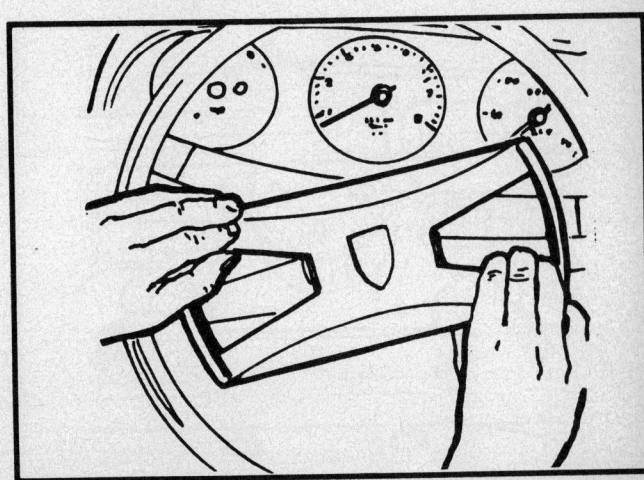

Steering wheel center cover removal on 911 models

Steering Gear

Removal and Installation

911 AND 911 TURBO

1. Remove the front luggage compartment carpeting. Raise and support the vehicle safely.
2. Remove the auxiliary heater duct from the steering post and position it aside.
3. Open the access door and the intermediate steering shaft cover by prying the spring clips off with a small prybar.
4. As necessary, remove the 3 fuel pump retaining bolts and position the pump aside.
5. Remove the cotter pin from the lower universal joint bolt

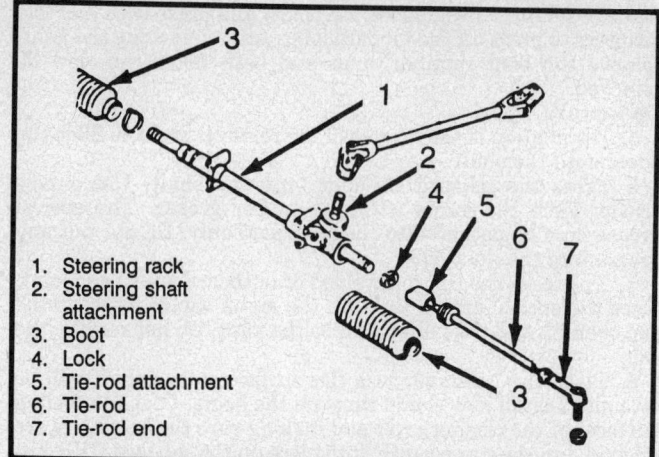

1. Steering rack
2. Steering shaft attachment
3. Boot
4. Lock
5. Tie-rod attachment
6. Tie-rod
7. Tie-rod end

Steering rack on the 924, 924 Turbo and 944

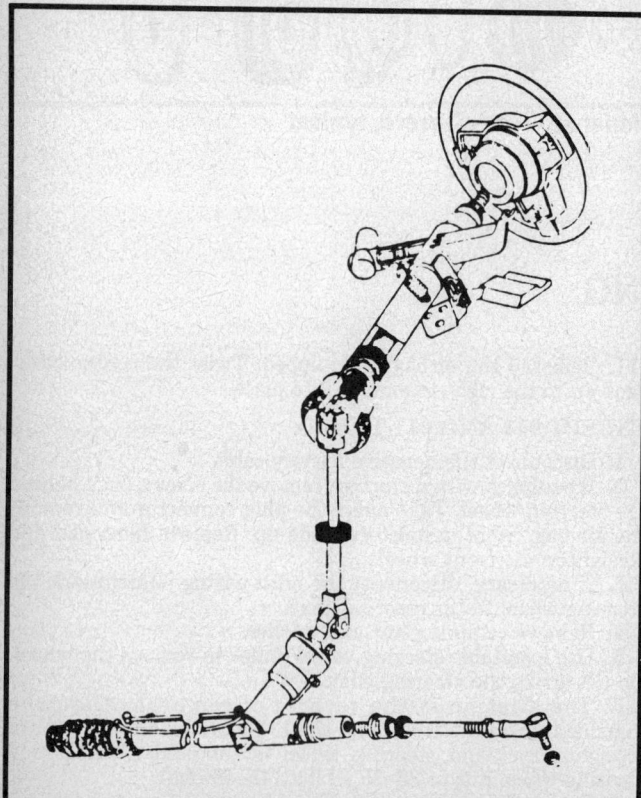

Steering column and gear used on the 928 and 928S

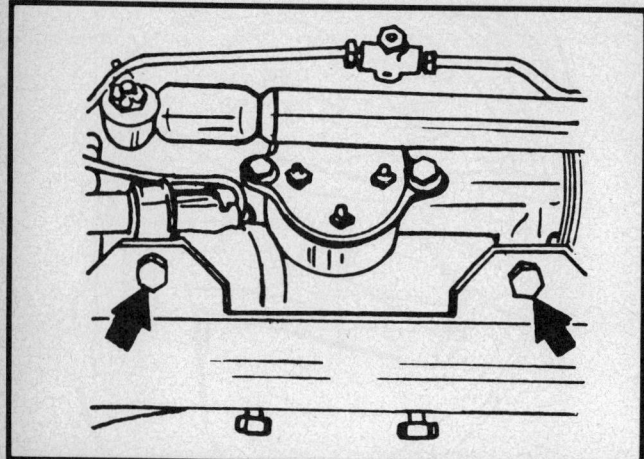

Rack and pinion retaining bolts on 911 models

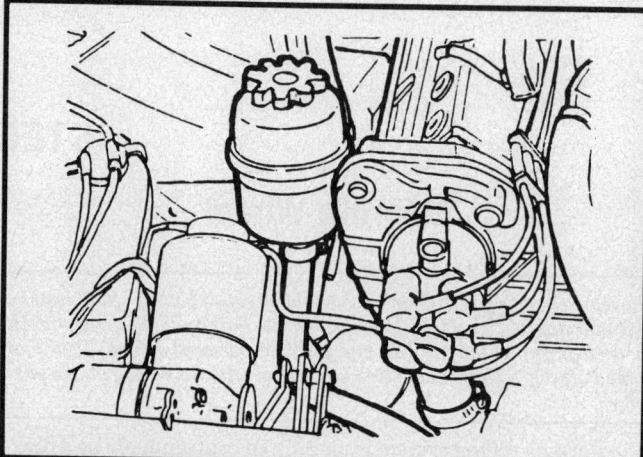

The 944 power steering reservoir is located on the inner wheel well under the hood

and loosen the castellated nut. Pull the universal joint off the steering shaft.

6. Remove the Allen bolts from the steering shaft bushing bracket. Remove the bracket and pull the bushing and dust cover.
7. Loosen and remove the steering coupling bolts.
8. Remove the retaining bolts and remove the bottom shield.
9. Remove the cotter pins and nuts, and then pull the tie rod ends from the suspension struts with a suitable puller.
10. Remove the 2 rack and pinion housing retaining bolts.
11. Remove the right side crossmember brace.
12. Pull the steering assembly out the right side of the vehicle.
13. Remove the retaining bolts from the tie rod yokes.
14. Installation is the reverse of the removal procedure.
15. Tighten the yoke bolts to 34 ft. lbs. (46 Nm).
16. Make sure the crossmember brace mounts without binding. Tighten the nuts to 47 ft. lbs. (64 Nm) and the bolts to 34 ft. lbs. (46 Nm).
17. Install the steering housing bolts with new lockwashers and tighten to 34 ft. lbs. (46 Nm).
18. Tighten the tie rod end nuts to 33 ft. lbs. (45 Nm) and install new cotter pins.
19. Tighten the steering bushing bracket Allen bolts to 18 ft. lbs. (24 Nm).
20. Install new washers on the steering coupling bolts and tighten them to 18 ft. lbs. (24 Nm).
21. Lower the vehicle.

EXCEPT 911 AND 911 TURBO

1. Raise the vehicle and support it safely. Remove the front wheels and splash shield.

2. Remove the stabilizer by disconnecting the stabilizer mounts on the control arms and stabilizer suspension on the side members.

3. Disconnect the ground wire on the front axle crossmember. Remove the bolt connecting gear box to steering column driveshaft.

4. Disconnect and press out the tie rod ends from the steering knuckles. Disconnect the power steering fluid lines at the pump, if equipped, and cap the ends to prevent contamination by dirt during service.

5. Remove the 4 mounting bolts and remove the steering gear and tie rods from the vehicle.

6. Remove the tie rods from the steering gear on a workbench, if necessary.

7. To install, reverse the above. Center steering gear with tool 9116 or equivalent. Be sure both tie rod lengths are equal 68–68.5mm. Tighten tie rod counter nuts to 29 ft. lbs. (39 Nm) and gear box to driveshaft bolt to 23 ft. lbs. (31 Nm). If equipped with power steering, tighten the fluid line connections to 14 ft. lbs. (20 Nm) and bleed the system.

Power Steering Pump

Removal and Installation

944

1. Disconnect the negative battery cable. Remove the lower engine splash shield.

2. Disconnect the fluid lines on the power steering pump. Catch the escaping fluid in a suitable container and discard. Do not reuse power steering fluid.

3. Unscrew the connecting rod on the power steering pump and nut, then turn the connecting rod down.

4. Remove the mounting bolts from the pump housing and remove the drive belt.

5. Raise the power steering pump in its bracket and remove the spacer from below.

6. Lower the power steering pump from the vehicle.

7. Installation is the reverse of removal. Tighten the power steering pressure hose fitting at the pump to 22 ft. lbs. (30 Nm). Adjust the pump drive belt tension and bleed the power steering system.

928 AND 928S

1. Disconnect the intake hose to the air cleaner on the left side, then drain the hydraulic fluid from the reservoir into a suitable container and discard. Do not reuse power steering fluid.

2. Remove the engine splash shield.

3. Loosen the front mounting bolts on the power steering pump slightly, then remove the rear bolt from the pump.

4. Remove the drive belt from the power steering pump pulley.

5. Remove the left upper section of the drive belt cover to facilitate removal procedures.

6. Disconnect the pressure and suction hoses from the pump. Cap the hose ends to prevent contamination by dirt during service procedure.

7. Remove the front mounting bolts and lower the power steering pump from the vehicle.

8. Installation is the reverse of removal. Make sure the power steering hoses are not routed close to the exhaust manifold or hose failure will occur. Tighten the pump hose connections to 43 ft. lbs. (60 Nm). Adjust the drive belt tension and bleed the power steering system.

Belt Adjustment

The power steering pump drive belt is properly adjusted if the belt can be moved about 10mm at a point midway between the pulleys.

Some vehicles such as the 911 Carrera 4 use a pump driven by a toothed belt. This belt cannot be adjusted.

System Bleeding

1. Fill the power steering reservoir with fluid, then start and immediately stop the engine several times to allow the system to fill with fluid. The level in the reservoir will drop very quickly, so fluid must be added frequently during this step to keep the fluid at the maximum level mark on the reservoir. Do not let the reservoir run dry.

2. When the reservoir fluid level stops dropping, start the engine and allow it to idle.

3. Turn the steering wheel from lock-to-lock quickly to bleed the air from the system. Do not apply pressure on the wheel at each lock or hold the wheel in the lock position to avoid building up unnecessary pressure.

4. Watch the oil level during this procedure and keep adding

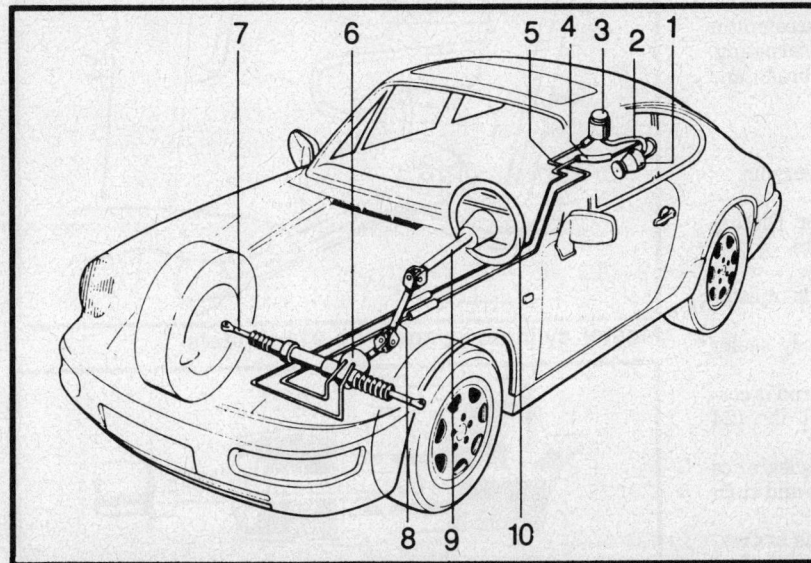

1. Power steering pump
2. Intake pipe
3. Supply tank
4. Pressure pipe
5. Return pipe
6. Rack and pinion steering gear
7. Tie rod
8. Steering intermediate shaft
9. Steering outer tube
10. Steering wheel

Major components 911 power steering system

Disconnecting the steering coupling on 911 models

oil until the level stops dropping. The fluid level should remain constant at the full mark on the reservoir tank and no air bubbles should rise in the hydraulic fluid while turning the steering wheel.

5. Stop the engine and observe the fluid level in the reservoir. It should not rise more than 10mm. If the fluid level between a running and stopped engine deviates more than 10mm, there is still air trapped in the hydraulic system. Repeat the procedure. After all air is bled from the system, recheck the fluid level in the reservoir and top off as necessary.

Tie Rod Ends

Removal and Installation

1. Raise and support the vehicle safely. Loosen the self-lock-

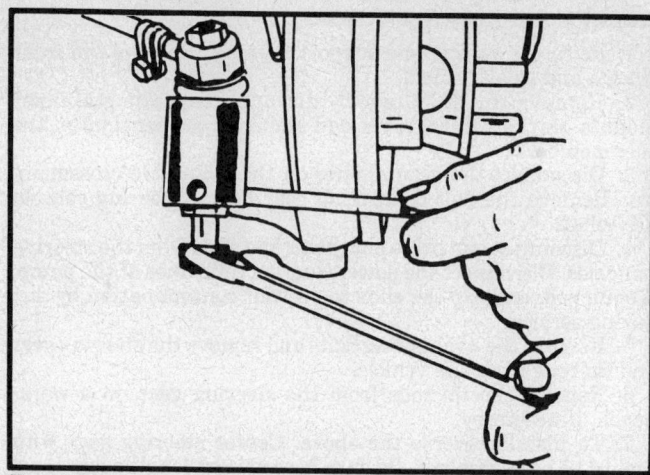

Removing the tie-rod ends on 911 models

ing nut which connects the tie rod to the steering knuckle. Mark the tie rod position on the threads of the steering rack rod, then loosen the jam nut.

2. Remove the self-locking nut and discard. Using a ball joint separator tool, remove the tie rod end from the steering knuckle. Unscrew the tie rod end from the steering rack, counting how many complete turns it takes to remove it.

3. Install a new tie rod end in reverse order of removal, threading the new tie rod end the same number of turns as counted in Step 2, then tighten the jam nut. Tighten the new tie rod self-locking nut to 47 ft. lbs. (65 Nm). Check the front wheel alignment.

BRAKES

Master Cylinder

Removal and Installation

911 AND 911 TURBO

1. Disconnect the negative battery cable. Pull the accelerator back and from its pushrod. Pull back the driver's side carpeting.
2. Unscrew the floorboard retainer(s) under the brake and clutch pedals.
3. Remove the master cylinder dust cover.
4. Raise the vehicle and support it safely.
5. Siphon and discard the brake fluid from the reservoir.
6. Unbolt the front splash shield.
7. Remove the brake lines from the master cylinder. Disconnect the brake failure warning light sending unit wire.
8. Remove the 2 master cylinder mounting nuts.
9. Disconnect the reservoir lines and remove the master cylinder.
10. Before installing the master cylinder, apply body sealer around the mounting flange.
11. Install the cylinder, making sure the piston pushrod is correctly positioned. Torque the mounting nuts to 18 ft. lbs. (24 Nm).
12. The piston pushrod should have 0.04 in. (1mm) clearance between it and the piston. Loosen the piston rod nut and turn the rod to adjust the clearance.
13. Refill the system with new brake fluid. Bleed the brakes.
14. Tighten the splash shield large bolts to 34 ft. lbs. (46 Nm) and the smaller bolts to 18 ft. lbs. (24 Nm).

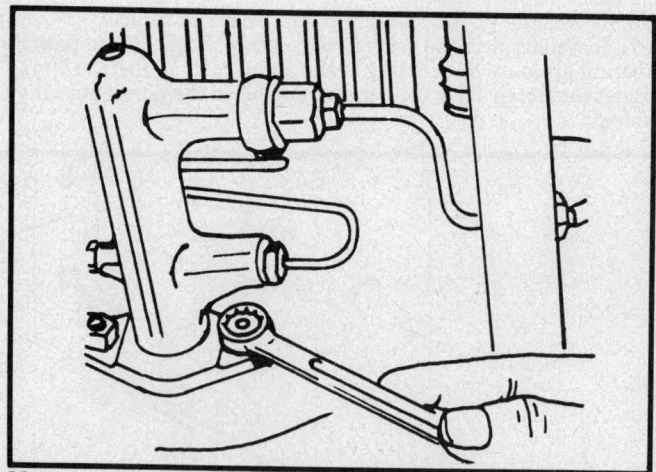

Master cylinder removal on 911 models

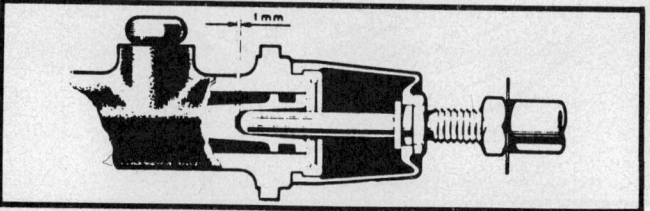

Correct piston pushrod clearance on 911 models

15. Test the brake failure warning light for proper operation as follows:

    a. Switch on the ignition. The handbrake warning light will go on. If it doesn't, replace the bulb.

    b. Start the engine. While depressing the brake pedal, have an assistant open a bleeder valve on 1 of the wheels to simulate a brake failure. The light should go on.

    c. When the valve is closed, the light should go out.

    d. Repeat the test on the other brake circuit.

16. If the light fails to light during 1 of the tests, check the circuit failure sender which screws into the master cylinder.

EXCEPT 911 AND 911 TURBO

1. Disconnect the negative battery cable.
2. Disconnect and plug the brake lines.
3. Disconnect the electrical plug from the sending unit for the brake failure switch.
4. Remove the 2 master cylinder mounting nuts.
5. Lift the master cylinder and reservoir from the engine compartment being careful not to spill any fluid on the fender. Discard the brake fluid. Do not depress the brake pedal while the master cylinder is removed.
6. Position the master cylinder and reservoir assembly onto the studs for the booster and tighten the nuts to 10 ft. lbs. (13 Nm).
7. Remove the plugs and connect the brake lines.
8. Bleed the brake system.

Power Brake Booster

Removal and Installation

911 AND 911 TURBO

1. Disconnect the negative battery cable. Remove the lock pin for the master cylinder operating rod.
2. Remove the mounting bolts for the brake master cylinder, located inside on the luggage compartment floor plate.
3. Siphon the fluid from the brake reservoir, being careful not to spill any brake fluid on painted surfaces. Discard the fluid.
4. Disconnect the stop light switch, vacuum hose and remove the brake fluid lines.
5. Remove the upper bolt for the brace and the nuts for the booster base.
6. Remove the brake booster and master cylinder as an assembly. The brace and operating rod do not have to be disconnected at the pedal assembly to remove the brake booster.
7. Installation is the reverse of removal. Torque the booster base nuts and master cylinder bolt to 18 ft. lbs. (25 Nm). Torque the support rod bolt to 25 ft. lbs. (35 Nm). Bleed the brake system.

924S AND 944

1. Disconnect the negative battery cable. Pull the brake fluid reservoir from the master cylinder and drain the brake fluid into a suitable container. Discard the fluid and do not allow it to spill on any painted surfaces.
2. Disconnect the brake lines from the master cylinder, then remove the master cylinder.
3. Disconnect the vacuum hose to the check valve on the booster and remove the oil dipstick.
4. Carefully pry off the fuel line holding clip on the mounting bolt.
5. Remove the lockpin for the pushrod on the brake pedal.
6. Remove the mounting nuts for the brake booster/adapter assembly. The mounting nuts are accessible after disconnecting the throttle cable and pulling down the insulation sheet in the footwell.
7. Remove the brake booster from above in the engine compartment.
8. Installation is the reverse of removal. Tighten the booster

and master cylinder mounting nuts to 15 ft. lbs. (21 Nm). Bleed the brake system.

928, 928S AND 928S4

1. Disconnect the battery negative cable.
2. Remove the brake master cylinder.
3. Depress the brake pedal and secure the pushrod for the master cylinder with a suitable hose clamp.
4. Adjust the connector to limit the amount of protrusion of the pushrod from the booster, then depress the brake pedal again and adjust the position of the hose clamp. Remove the connector.
5. Remove the cover, then remove the brake booster mounting nuts. If applicable, remove the right front brake line from the holder and push it toward the engine carefully.
6. Route the hose for the clutch master cylinder and the wire harness connectors so they will not interfere with removal.
7. Remove the brake booster. The air cleaner lower section may have to be removed to allow clearance for the booster assembly.
8. Installation is the reverse of removal. Replace the gasket between the booster and firewall. Tighten the booster and master cylinder mounting nuts to 17 ft. lbs. (23 Nm). Bleed the brake system.

NOTE: Some vehicles with Anti-Lock Braking System (ABS) may use a hydraulic booster that receives its pressure from the ABS hydraulic control unit. The booster is a small unit that bolts directly to the master cylinder. The brake master cylinder circuits and the ABS hydraulic system are completely separate of the booster circuit.

Disc Brake Pads

Removal and Installation

1. Disconnect the negative battery cable. Raise and support the vehicle safely.
2. Remove the tire and wheel assembly.
3. Remove the caliper retaining bolts or clips. Remove the disc brake pads.
4. Position the caliper aside, do not allow it hang for any extended period of time.
5. Installation is the reverse of the removal procedure.
6. If equipped, after replacing the brake pads with power brakes the brake warning light will come on. To reset the light, disconnect the negative battery cable for 1 minute.
7. On the 944 Turbo, the silencers for the 4 piston front calipers must be replaced when new disc pads are installed.

Parking Brake Cable

Adjustment

911 AND 911 TURBO

1. Raise the vehicle and support it safely. Remove the wheels.
2. Release the handbrake lever.
3. Push the brake pads away from the disc so it can be turned by hand.
4. Loosen the cable adjusting nuts to release tension.
5. Insert a suitable tool into the disc access hole and rotate the handbrake star wheel until the disc can no longer be turned by hand.
6. Repeat this operation on the other side.
7. Readjust the cable nuts to take up the slack.
8. Pull up the center tunnel cover and handbrake lever boot at the rear. By looking through the 2 inspection holes, see if the cable equalizer is exactly perpendicular to the vehicles centerline.
9. If the equalizer positioning is off, correct it by loosening or

tightening the cable adjusting nuts. Tighten the locknuts after the adjustment is correct.

10. Back off each brake star wheel by 4–5 teeth until the disc can be turned by hand.

11. Check the handbrake lever clearance. There should be a slight clearance at the lever. The handbrake should be set when the lever is pulled up.

12. After completing the handbrake adjustment, depress the brake pedal several times to reposition the rear caliper pistons. Check the fluid level in the reservoir and add, if necessary.

EXCEPT 911 AND 911 TURBO

1. Raise the vehicle and remove the rear wheels.

2. Release the parking brake lever and move the disc brake pads so the rotor can be easily moved.

3. Loosen the cable adjusting nuts so no tension exists on the cable.

4. Insert a suitable tool through the hole in the brake rotor and turn the brake adjuster until the rotor cannot be moved.

5. Turn the adjuster in the opposite direction just until the rotor is free to rotate.

6. Pull the brake lever up 2 notches and adjust the cable so the rotors can just be turned.

NOTE: At 4 notches of the lever, the rotors should be tight and unable to turn.

7. Release the handbrake and make sure the rotors turn freely. Install the wheels and lower the vehicle.

Removal and Installation

911 AND 911 TURBO

1. Raise the vehicle and support it safely. Remove the wheels.

2. Remove the center tunnel cover and handbrake lever boot.

3. Remove the heater control knob.

4. Remove the handbrake support housing bolts.

5. Unscrew the heater control lever nut. Remove the cup spring, discs, and the lever.

6. Slightly raise the handbrake support housing. Snap off the retaining clip and pull out the cable equalizing stud.

7. Disconnect the handbrake light switch wire.

8. Remove the handbrake support housing.

9. Detach the cables from the cable equalizer.

10. Remove the rear brake calipers.

11. Remove the rear brake discs and spacer rings.

12. Remove the cotter pin, castellated nut and disc from each cable. Pull the cable toward the center of the vehicle.

13. Pull the cables out from the center tunnel in the passenger compartment.

14. Lubricate the replacement cables with multi-purpose grease and then feed them into the tube.

15. Place a washer between the spacer sleeve and the brake expander. Place another washer under the castellated nut.

16. Tighten the nut until a new cotter pin can be inserted. Make sure the brake expander is correctly seated.

17. Install the brake disc and calipers.

18. Connect the handbrake light wire to the switch.

19. Insert the heater control lever into the handbrake support housing.

20. Install and clip the equalizer stud. Ensure that the handbrake cables are correctly seated.

21. Torque the handbrake support housing bolts to 18 ft. lbs. (24 Nm).

22. Install a friction disc, the heater control lever, another friction disc, pressure disc, cup spring, and the nut.

23. Tighten the nut so the lever doesn't slip back when the heater is on full, and yet isn't too tight to operate.

24. Bleed the brakes.

25. Check the handbrake adjustment.

26. Install the wheels and lower the vehicle.

EXCEPT 911 AND 911 TURBO

The parking brake cable is attached to the handbrake lever by 2 nuts, 1 of which serves as a locknut for the adjusting nut. To remove the cable, remove both the locknut and adjusting nut and feed the cable rearward. Disconnect the parking brake cable at the rear wheels, then install the new cable and feed it back forward to the handbrake lever. Adjust the parking brake cable.

Anti-Lock Brake System Service

The 3 channel ABS system used by Porsche is manufactured by Bosch. The system uses a separate sensor for each wheel. A

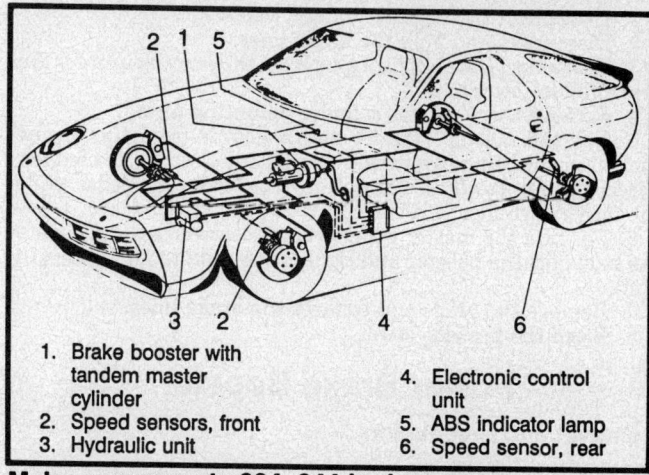

1. Brake booster with tandem master cylinder
2. Speed sensors, front
3. Hydraulic unit
4. Electronic control unit
5. ABS indicator lamp
6. Speed sensor, rear

Major components 924, 944 brake system

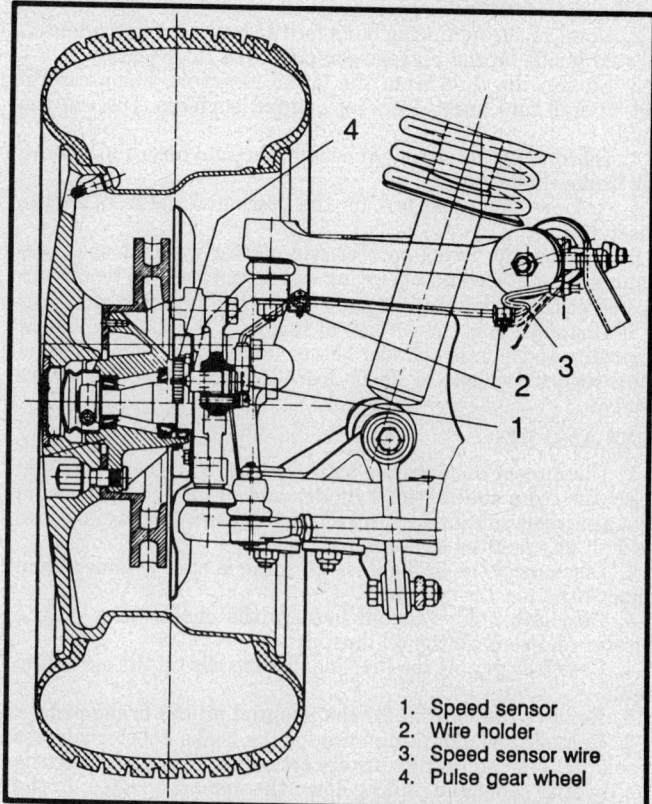

1. Speed sensor
2. Wire holder
3. Speed sensor wire
4. Pulse gear wheel

Front axle assembly 944 with ABS. The pulse gear wheel has 90 teeth and is pressed on the front wheel hub.

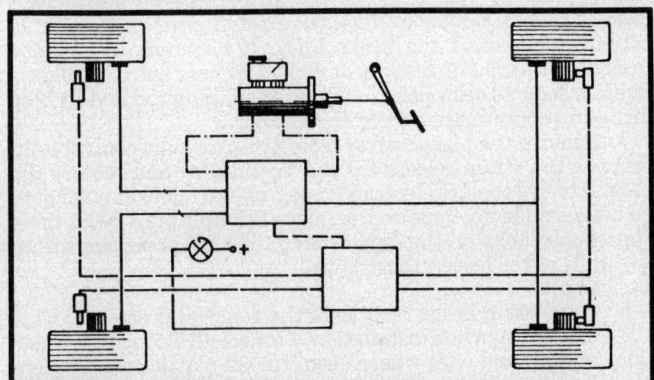

Schematic 928S ABS brake system components

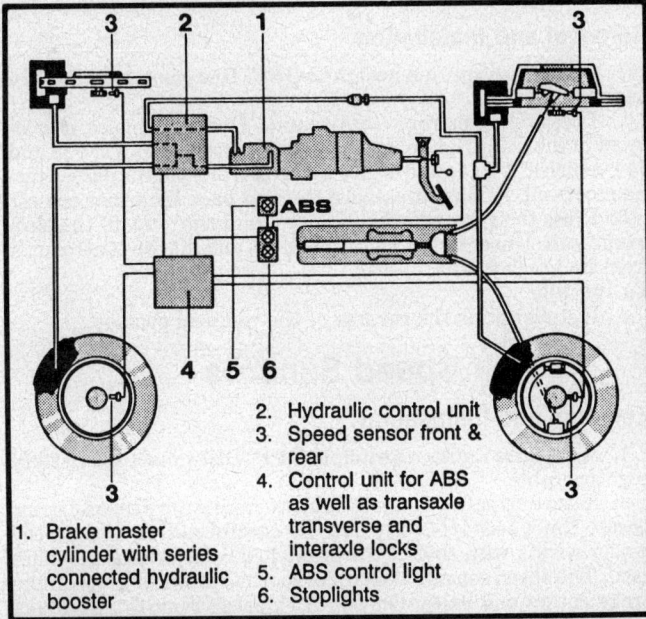

2. Hydraulic control unit
3. Speed sensor front & rear
4. Control unit for ABS as well as transaxle transverse and interaxle locks
5. ABS control light
6. Stoplights

1. Brake master cylinder with series connected hydraulic booster

Schematic 911 ABS brake system components

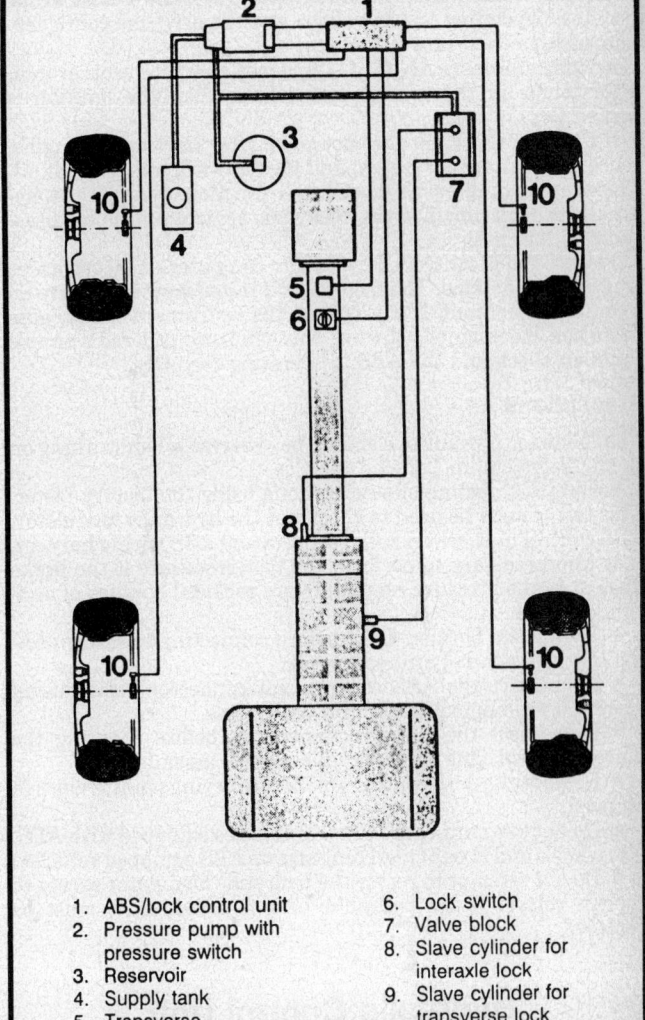

1. ABS/lock control unit
2. Pressure pump with pressure switch
3. Reservoir
4. Supply tank
5. Transverse acceleration sensor
6. Lock switch
7. Valve block
8. Slave cylinder for interaxle lock
9. Slave cylinder for transverse lock
10. Wheel speed sensor

Four wheel drive control layout—911 Carrera 4

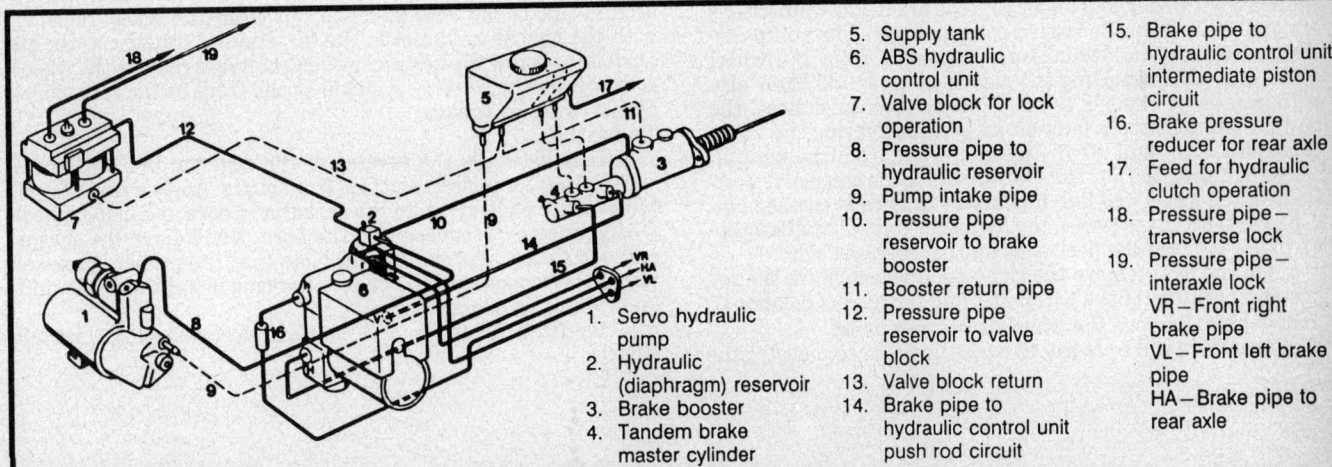

5. Supply tank
6. ABS hydraulic control unit
7. Valve block for lock operation
8. Pressure pipe to hydraulic reservoir
9. Pump intake pipe
10. Pressure pipe reservoir to brake booster
11. Booster return pipe
12. Pressure pipe reservoir to valve block
13. Valve block return
14. Brake pipe to hydraulic control unit push rod circuit

15. Brake pipe to hydraulic control unit intermediate piston circuit
16. Brake pressure reducer for rear axle
17. Feed for hydraulic clutch operation
18. Pressure pipe— transverse lock
19. Pressure pipe— interaxle lock
VR—Front right brake pipe
VL—Front left brake pipe
HA—Brake pipe to rear axle

1. Servo hydraulic pump
2. Hydraulic (diaphragm) reservoir
3. Brake booster
4. Tandem brake master cylinder

Layout 911 ABS brake system and line identification

front/rear braking circuit split is used. Differences exist in the systems, depending on the vehicle and the driveline configuration such as 2WD or 4WD.

An indicator lamp **ANTILOCK** comes on with the other indicator lamps in the instrument cluster when the ignition is turned **ON**.

If the indicator lamp does not go on after starting the engine, there is a fault in the system and the ABS will switch itself off. The regular brake system will still function. Neither the hydraulic control unit nor the electronic control unit is be disassembled for repair.

The system is controlled by its own computer. It incorporates diagnostic functions. The factory ABS tester must be used to do a complete checkout. If the light on the instrument cluster goes out when the engine is started, this can be considered a simple function check and the ABS is operating correctly.

Precautions

The following precautions should be observed when working on the ABS system on Porsche vehicles.

• Electrical testing should be done using the factory tester. This tester must be used to check out the hydraulic modulator, ABS control unit, wheel speed sensors and ABS wiring harness. It is also necessary to perform the test procedure if the brake lines or brake pressure regulators are replaced because of accident damage.

• Switch the ignition **OFF** before connecting or disconnecting the ABS control unit connector.

• Disconnect the ABS control unit connector before using electrical welding equipment on the vehicle.

• Disconnect the battery connections before charging the battery or replacing the hydraulic control assembly.

• Remove the ABS control unit before drying paint repairs in an oven.

• Do not use mini-spare tires on vehicles equipped with ABS. Use wheels and tires of matching size on ABS equipped vehicles.

• Do not attempt to repair the hydraulic modulator except to replace relays. If the hydraulic unit is defective, it must be replaced.

Hydraulic Control Unit

Removal and Installation

1. Make sure ignition switch is **OFF**. Disconnect the battery negative cable.
2. Locate the hydraulic control unit.
   a. On the 928S, it is located on a bracket in an opening of the left front wheel house wall, and the brake line connections are accessible from the engine compartment. The pump motor and electric connections are accessible from the wheel house side after removing the plastic cover. It will likely also be necessary to remove the left intake air cleaner hose, the power steering supply tank on its bracket, leaving the hoses connected. Also pull off the ignition leads from the ignition coil and remove the left front wheel. Mark the respective positions of the wheel and hub for correct balance at reassembly.
   b. On the 911 Carrera 4, the hydraulic control unit is located in the luggage compartment on the left-hand side.
   c. On the 944, remove the right-hand wheel. Mark the respective positions of the wheel and hub for correct balance at reassembly. Remove the wheel-arch inner panel.
3. Since there will be at least 6 brake line connections, tag the

location of each since they must be reinstalled in their proper locations. Disconnect the brake lines. If necessary, unclip the brake lines from any holders or clips. Use care not to damage a line. As soon as each line is disconnected, plug the end to keep dirt and contamination from the system.

4. Remove the plastic cover from the hydraulic control unit. Remove the strain release for the 12-pin plug and remove the plug. Remove the ABS hydraulic control unit. This unit is not to be disassembled or repaired. Replace the unit only. Note the 4 star shaped bolts on the unit. Due to the high pressures within the unit, never loosen these bolts.

To install:

5. Installation is the reverse of the removal process.
6. Check brake line installation, connect all electrical connections and ground wire where used. Install plastic covers where required.
7. Bleed the brake system. The bleeding procedure for ABS equipped vehicles is the same as that for non-ABS vehicles.

Electronic Control Unit

Removal and Installation

1. Make sure ignition switch is **OFF**. Disconnect the battery negative cable.
2. Locate the electronic control unit. On 911 vehicles, it is located in the front right of the luggage compartment. On 928 and 944 vehicles, it is located either in the driver's side or passenger-side footwell. In this case, move the seat back for easier access.
3. Press the spring-loaded lock and pull the plug off the electronic unit. Unscrew the mounting nuts and lift the control unit from its bracket.

To install:

4. Installation is the reverse of the removal process.

Speed Sensors

Removal and Installation

1. Make sure ignition switch is **OFF**. Disconnect the battery negative cable.
2. Raise and safely support vehicle. Remove wheel and tires. Locate the wheel speed sensors. Be careful not to confuse the sensor wiring with that of the brake pad wear indicator, where used. The speed sensors read off of toothed impulse rings on the brake rotors and axles. On 928 S vehicles, remove the intake hose from the air cleaner. Disconnect the plug for the sensor wire, under the hood on the 928. On 944 vehicles, disconnect the cable from the spring strut.
3. On 928 vehicles, remove the front exhaust shield for easier access. Unclip the wire and pull out from the wheel housing with the rubber grommet in the direction of the wheel. On all models, unscrew the hex socket-head bolt and remove the wheel sensor from the steering knuckle on the front or the rear wheel carrier the rear brakes.

To install:

4. Installation is the reverse of the removal process. Make sure the sensor is clean and free from burrs. Apply a thin coat of Molycoat or equivalent, to the sensor and bore and using a new O-ring, insert the sensor into the bore. Don't force the sensor and don't over tighten the bolt. Note that the proper space between the sensor tip and the impulse ring is built into the unit and cannot be adjusted.
5. Reinstall all wires and connect electrical plugs. Install wheels.

FRONT SUSPENSION

Shock Absorbers

Removal and Installation

911 AND 911 TURBO

1. Raise the vehicle and support it safely. Remove the wheels.
2. Remove the brake line from the clip on the suspension strut. A small amount of brake fluid will run out of the line, plug it so dirt cannot enter the system.
3. Unscrew the retaining bolts and remove the caliper.
4. Using a soft mallet, tap the hub cap to loosen it.
5. Pry the hubcap off with a small prybar.
6. Loosen the Allen screw in the wheel bearing clamp. Unscrew the clamp nut and remove the nut and washer.
7. Remove the wheel hub along with the brake disc and wheel bearing.
8. Remove the backing plate retaining bolts and remove the plate.
9. Withdraw the cotter pin from the castellated nut on the tie rod end and remove the nut. Using a suitable puller, remove the tie rod joint from the strut.
10. Remove the control arm-to-strut ball joint retaining bolt and pull the ball joint from the strut by pulling down on the lower control arm.

NOTE: The torsion bar adjusting screw will have to be loosened and the adjusting arm removed.

11. Remove the keeper for the nut on the top of the strut. Unscrew the nut and remove it, the keeper plate, and washer.
12. Remove the strut from the bottom. It will be necessary to loosen and pull the side of the luggage compartment out for clearance.
13. Check the shock absorber strut for excessive free travel and leaking. Replace the shock absorber if necessary.

To install:

14. Install the strut in a reverse order of the removal.
15. Tighten the top nut to 58 ft. lbs. (79 Nm). Use a new keeper plate and ensure that the peg on the plate is pointing up.
16. Tighten the ball joint nut to 47 ft. lbs. (64 Nm).

NOTE: Remember to install the washer between the ball joint seal and strut.

17. Install the torsion bar adjusting lever.
18. Tighten the tie rod nut to 33 ft. lbs. (45 Nm) and install a new cotter pin.
19. Torque the backing plate bolts to 18 ft. lbs. (24 Nm).
20. Install and adjust the wheel bearings.
21. Tighten the caliper retaining bolts to 50 ft. lbs. (68 Nm).
22. Refill the master cylinder, as required. Bleed the brakes.
23. Install the wheels and lower the vehicle.
24. Check the front wheel alignment.

MacPherson Strut

Removal and Installation

924, 924S AND 944

1. Raise the vehicle and support it safely.
2. Remove the brake line from the bracket on the strut.

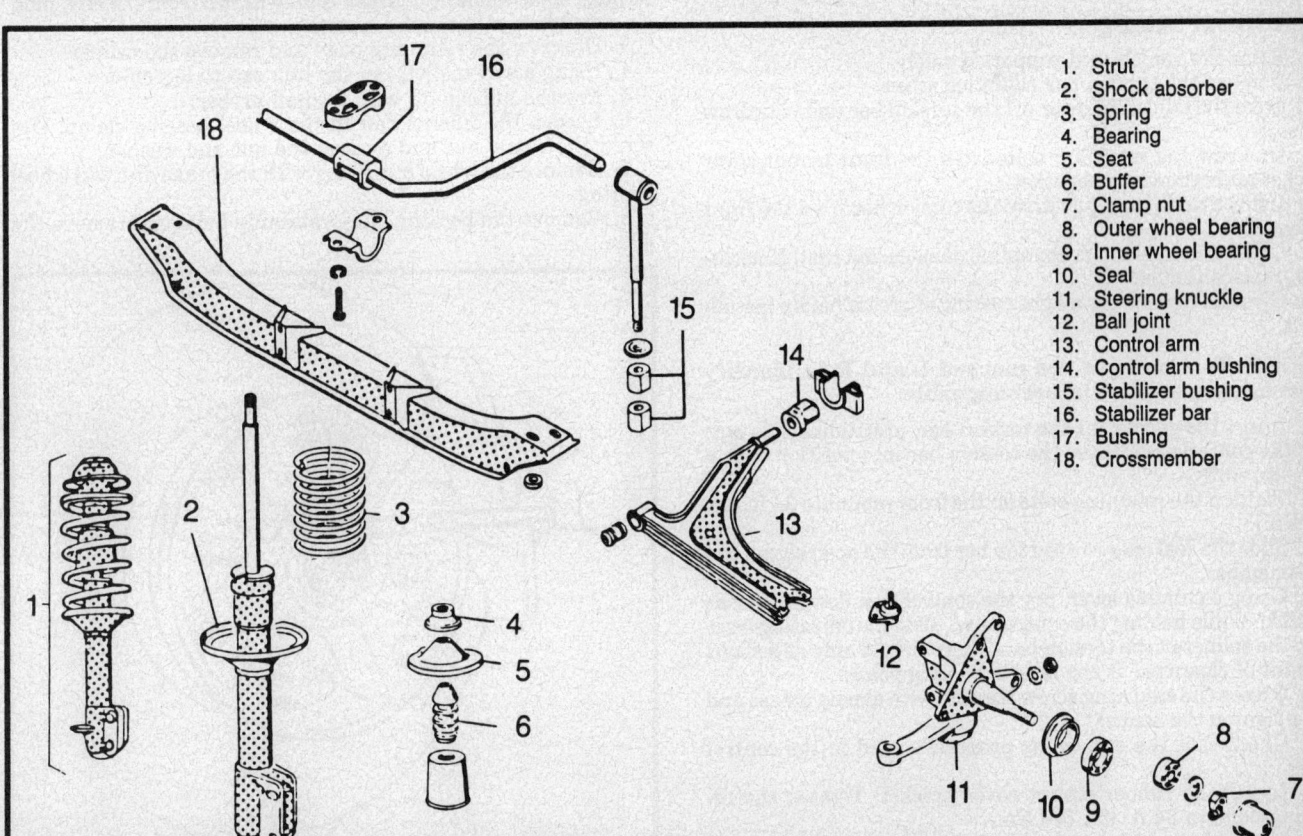

1. Strut
2. Shock absorber
3. Spring
4. Bearing
5. Seat
6. Buffer
7. Clamp nut
8. Outer wheel bearing
9. Inner wheel bearing
10. Seal
11. Steering knuckle
12. Ball joint
13. Control arm
14. Control arm bushing
15. Stabilizer bushing
16. Stabilizer bar
17. Bushing
18. Crossmember

Typical front suspension and related components

3. Remove the 2 through bolts that retain the strut to the steering knuckle.

4. Remove the 4 retaining nuts from the inner fender in the engine compartment.

5. Pry the lower control arm down and remove the strut from the vehicle.

6. To replace either the spring or shock absorber, place the strut in a spring compressor and remove the large retaining nut at the top.

7. Installation is the reverse of removal.

—— CAUTION ——
Any attempt to remove the retaining nut without a suitable spring compressor can result in serious injury.

8. Check and adjust the front end alignment.

928, 928S AND 928S4

1. Remove the self-locking nuts on the upper strut mount, located on the inner fender panel.

2. Raise and support the vehicle safely. Remove the front wheel. Remove the flange locknut and press the upper ball joint from the spindle carrier.

3. Remove the inner pivot shaft nuts from the upper control arm.

4. Remove the strut mounting bolts and remove the strut and upper arm as an assembly.

Torsion Bars

Removal and Installation

911 AND 911 TURBO

1. Raise the vehicle and support it safely.
2. Remove the torsion bar adjusting screw.
3. Take the adjusting lever off the torsion bar and withdraw the seal.
4. Unscrew the retaining bolts from the front mount cover bracket and remove the bracket.
5. Using a drift, carefully drive the torsion bar from the front of the arm.
6. Check the torsion bar for spline damage and rust. If necessary, replace the bar.
7. Give the torsion bar a light coating of grease before installing it.

NOTE: Torsion bars are marked L and R to identify them as they are not interchangeable.

8. Insert the end cap of the torsion bar, protruding side out, into the control arm. Drive the torsion bar into position with a drift, carefully.
9. Tighten the retaining bolts on the front mount to 34 ft. lbs. (46 Nm).
10. Slide the seal onto the torsion bar from the open side of the crossmember.
11. Using a suitable lever, pry the control arm down as far as possible. While holding the control arm, slide the adjusting lever onto the splines of the torsion bar. There should only be a slight amount of clearance at the lever adjusting point.
12. Grease the adjusting screw threads with a moly grease and hand tighten the screw.
13. Check that the end cap is properly seated in the control arm.
14. Install the rubber mount cover bracket. Tighten the retaining bolts to 34 ft. lbs. (46 Nm).
15. Lower the vehicle.
16. Check the front wheel alignment.

Stabilizer Bar

Removal and Installation

911 AND 911 TURBO

1. Raise and support the vehicle safely.
2. Loosen the stabilizer clamp bolts and pry the lever ends off their mounts.
3. Remove the stabilizer bar along with the levers.
4. Check the rubber bushings for deterioration and, if necessary, replace them. Lubricate the bushings with glycerine or some other rubber preservative. Do not use oil or grease for lubrication.
5. Install the stabilizer bar in a reverse order of the removal.
6. The square end of the stabilizer should protrude slightly above the clamp. Tighten the clamp nuts to 18 ft. lbs. (24 Nm).

Ball Joint

Inspection

With the front wheels in the straight-ahead position, insert a suitable prybar between the control arm and wheel rim. Insert a vernier caliper between the upper edge of the control arm and lower edge of the steering knuckle mounting bolt and measure the distance. Press down on the prybar to lever out the play, then check the distance again with the caliper. The wear limit is 1.5mm.

Removal and Installation

911 AND 911 TURBO

1. Raise the vehicle and support it safely. Remove the wheels.
2. Remove the brake line from the clip on the suspension strut. A small amount of brake fluid will run from the line, plug it so dirt cannot enter the system.
3. Unscrew the retaining bolts and remove the caliper.
4. Using a soft mallet, tap the hub cap to loosen it.
5. Pry the hubcap off with a small prybar.
6. Loosen the Allen screw in the wheel bearing clamp. Unscrew the clamp nut and remove the nut and washer.
7. Remove the wheel hub along with the brake disc and wheel bearing.
8. Remove the backing plate retaining bolts and remove the plate.

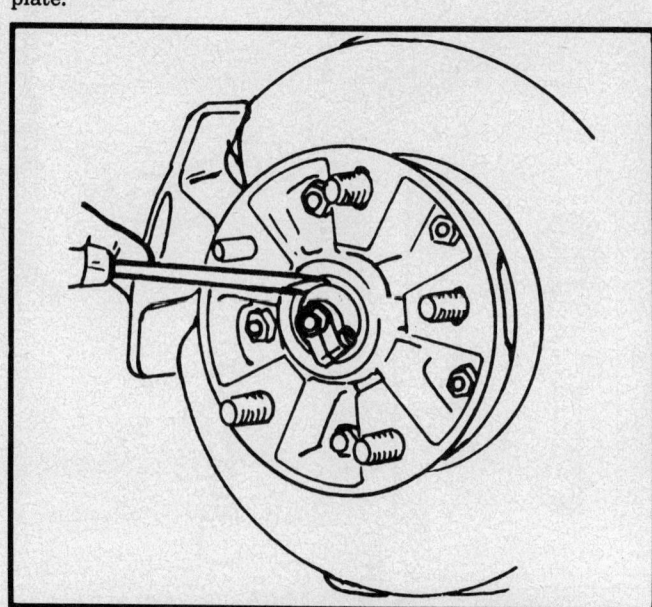

Checking wheel bearing play on 911 vehicles

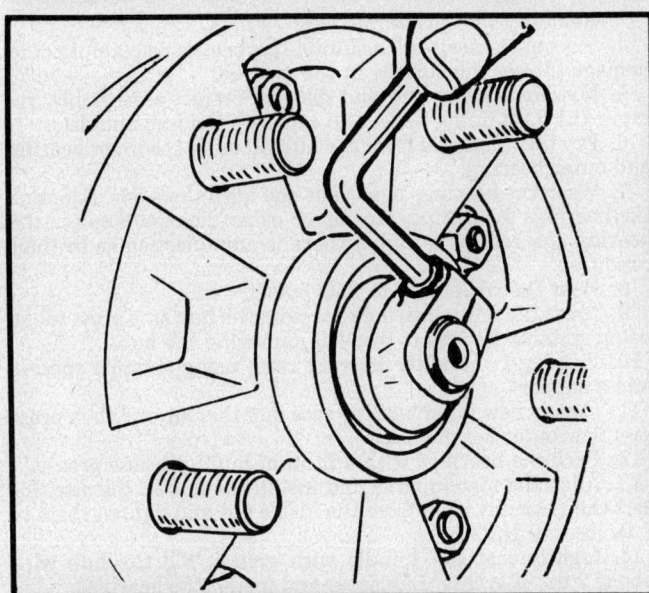

Final tightening of the wheel clamp nut on 911 vehicles. Check the play again before installing the hub cap

9. Withdraw the cotter pin from the castellated nut on the tie rod end and remove the nut. Using a suitable puller, remove the tie rod joint from the strut.

10. Remove the control arm-to-strut ball joint retaining bolt and pull the ball joint from the strut by pulling down on the lower control arm.

NOTE: The torsion bar adjusting screw will have to be loosened and the adjusting arm removed.

11. Installation is the reverse of the removal procedure.

924S AND 944

1. Raise and support the vehicle safely. Remove the lower control arm.
2. Drill out the the rivets retaining the ball joint to the control arm.
3. Install the replacement ball joint using the bolts and nuts supplied in the kit.
4. Reinstall the control arm and align the front wheels.

928, 928S AND 928S4

NOTE: The front wheels must be realigned after the suspension work is done.

The upper ball joint is replaced as a unit with the upper arm assembly.

Lower Control Arm

Removal and Installation

924S AND 944

1. Raise the vehicle and support it safely.
2. Remove the bolts at the front that retain the control arm to the suspension crossmember.
3. Detach the stabilizer bar from the control arm.
4. Remove the 2 bolts that retain the control arm bracket at the rear.
5. Remove the ball joint pinch bolt at the steering knuckle.
6. Pry the control arm down and remove it from the vehicle.
7. Installation is the reverse of removal. Caster must be reset after the control arm has been removed.

928, 928S AND 928S4

NOTE: The front wheels must be aligned upon completion of the installation.

1. Raise and support the vehicle safely, then remove the wheel.
2. Mark the alignment eccentrics on the lower arm for approximate installation location, if the ball joint is to be removed.
3. Remove the strut bottom link bracket and stabilizer link bolt.
4. Remove the lower ball joint stud nut and press the stud from the spindle. Move the spindle and upper arm upward and block it to gain working clearance.
5. Remove the bolts from the tie-down bracket and control arm bracket. Lower the control arm from the vehicle.
6. The lower ball joint can be replaced, if necessary, while the lower arm is out of the vehicle.
7. Installation is the reverse of removal.

Front Wheel Bearings

Adjustment

911 AND 911 TURBO

Check and adjust the front wheel bearings after the vehicle has not been run for a few hours. The bearings will be cold then. The front wheel bearings are correctly adjusted when the thrust washer can be moved slightly sideways under light pressure from a small prybar but no bearing play is evident when the wheel hub is shaken axially.

1. Raise the vehicle and support it safely. Remove the wheels. Turn the hub several times to seat the bearings.
2. Pry the hub cap off and perform the above check.
3. If the bearings require an adjustment, loosen the Allen screw and turn the clamp nut in or out, as necessary.
4. Tighten the clamp nut Allen screw to 11 ft. lbs. (15 Nm) without altering the adjusted position of the clamp nut.
5. Double check the adjustment and readjust, if necessary.
6. Give the clamp nut and thrust washer a light coating of lithium grease. Tap the hub cap into place with a plastic or rubber mallet.
7. Install the wheels and lower the vehicle.

EXCEPT 911 AND 911 TURBO

The front wheel bearings are correctly adjusted when the thrust washer can be moved slightly sideways under light pressure but no bearing play is evident when the wheel hub is shaken axially.

1. Raise the vehicle and support it safely. Remove the tire and wheel assemblies.
2. Pry the hub cap off and perform the above check. Don't press against the hub.
3. If the bearings require an adjustment, loosen the Allen screw and turn the clamp nut. Proper adjustment is achieved when the flat washer can just be moved by finger pressure on a suitable tool.
4. Tighten the clamp nut Allen screw to 11 ft. lbs. (15 Nm) without altering the adjusted position of the clamp nut.

Removal and Installation

911 AND 911 TURBO

NOTE: The inner bearing, seal, and outer bearing may be removed and lubricated once the hub/disc assembly is removed from the vehicle. If after cleaning, the bearings are noticeably worn or damaged they should be replaced along with their races. If the bearings are satisfactory, skip the race removal steps.

1. Remove the brake disc/hub assembly.
2. Matchmark the hub and disc for correct reassembly, remove the 5 retaining bolts, and separate the hub and disc.

3. Pry the inner seal out of the hub. Remove the inner bearing and outer bearing.

4. Wash the bearings in solvent and blow them dry. Examine the bearings for pitting, scoring or other damage. Replace the bearing and race as a unit if there is any question as to their condition.

5. Heat the wheel hub to 250–300°F.

6. Press the inner bearing race from the hub on a press table, using suitable spacers to prevent damaging the hub.

7. Press out the outer bearing race, using suitable spacers and a support the assembly.

To install:

8. Press a new inner bearing race into the hub and then press in a new outer bearing race.

9. Pack the bearings with a lithium multi-purpose grease.

10. Align the matchmarks and install the hub in the disc. Insert the assembly bolts from the inside out and tighten them to 17 ft. lbs. (23 Nm).

11. Lightly coat the spindle with grease. Fill the hub with about 2 oz of grease. Lubricate and install the bearings.

12. Grease the sealing edges of a new inner oil seal and carefully tap it into place. The oil seal must be flush with the hub.

13. Install the hub/disc assembly on the vehicle.

14. Adjust the wheel bearings.

EXCEPT 911 AND 911 TURBO

1. Raise and support the vehicle safely.

2. Remove the front wheels.

3. Remove the bearing hub cap.

4. Pry out the seal with a suitable prybar, being careful not to damage the sealing surface in the process.

5. Matchmark the hub and disc for correct reassembly, remove the 5 retaining bolts, and separate the hub and disc.

6. Pry the inner seal from the hub. Remove the inner bearing and outer bearing.

7. Wash the bearings in solvent and blow them dry. Examine the bearings for pitting, scoring or other damage. Replace the bearing and race as a unit if there is any question as to their condition.

8. Heat the wheel hub to 250–300°F.

9. Press the inner bearing race from the hub on a press table, using suitable spacers to prevent damaging the hub.

10. Press out the outer bearing race, using suitable spacers and a support.

11. Press a new inner bearing race into the hub and then press in a new outer bearing race.

12. Pack the bearings with a lithium multi-purpose grease.

13. Align the matchmarks and install the hub in the disc. Insert the assembly bolts from the inside out and tighten them to 7 ft. lbs. (10 Nm).

14. Lightly coat the spindle with grease. Fill the hub with about 2 oz. of grease. Lubricate and install the bearings.

15. Grease the sealing edges of a new inner oil seal and carefully tap it into place. The oil seal must be flush with the hub.

16. Install the hub/disc assembly on the vehicle.

17. Adjust the wheel bearings.

REAR SUSPENSION

Shock Absorbers

Removal and Installation

911 AND 911 TURBO

1. Open the engine compartment lid and remove the rubber cover from the top of the shock absorber.

2. Raise and support the vehicle safely.

3. Hold the shock absorber shaft and remove the nut.

4. On the bottom, remove the retaining nut and bolt.

5. Remove the shock absorber.

6. If the shock exhibits excessive free travel or is leaking, replace it.

7. Install the shock up through the body and screw the nut on hand-tight.

8. Align the shock absorber eye with the hole in the trailing arm and install the nut and bolt.

9. Tighten the top nut and install the rubber cover.

10. Tighten the bottom retaining bolt to 54 ft. lbs. (73 Nm).

Top rear shock absorber mount on 911 vehicles

924S AND 944

1. This procedure is performed with the weight of the vehicle resting on the rear wheels. Raise and support the vehicle safely.

2. Remove the bottom shock retaining bolt and nut.

3. Remove the top bolt.

4. Remove the shock absorber.

5. Install the replacement shock in the reverse order of removal. Tighten the retaining bolts to 50 ft. lbs. (68 Nm).

MacPherson Struts

Removal and Installation

928, 928S AND 928S4

1. Remove the locking nuts form the spring strut, located within the trunk area.

2. Raise the vehicle, support safely and remove the wheel.

3. Remove the front nut on the outer pivot pin rod and remove the pivot rod from the rubber bushings.

4. Disconnect the stabilizer bar link from the lower control arm.

5. Remove the spring strut form the vehicle.

6. Installation is the reverse of removal.

NOTE: The spring can be removed from the shock unit with the use of a spring clamping tool. An adjusting nut and sleeve is used to control the vehicle rear height.

Torsion Bars

Removal and Installation

911 AND 911 TURBO

1. Raise and support the vehicle safely.

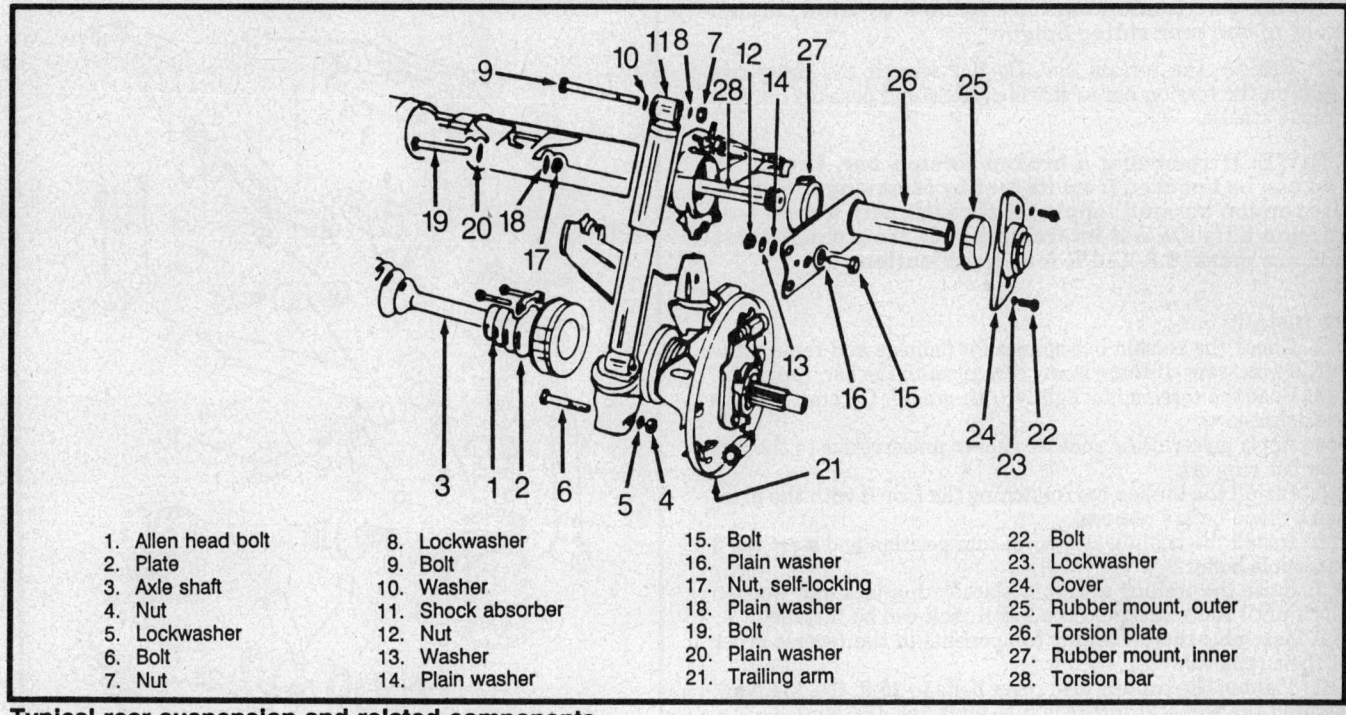

1. Allen head bolt	8. Lockwasher	15. Bolt	22. Bolt
2. Plate	9. Bolt	16. Plain washer	23. Lockwasher
3. Axle shaft	10. Washer	17. Nut, self-locking	24. Cover
4. Nut	11. Shock absorber	18. Plain washer	25. Rubber mount, outer
5. Lockwasher	12. Nut	19. Bolt	26. Torsion plate
6. Bolt	13. Washer	20. Plain washer	27. Rubber mount, inner
7. Nut	14. Plain washer	21. Trailing arm	28. Torsion bar

Typical rear suspension and related components

2. Remove the wheel on the side where the torsion bar is being removed.

3. A fixture is necessary to hold the trailing arm while it is raised and lowered. The special tool for this purpose is P 289 or equivalent.

4. Using a hydraulic jack under the holding fixture, raise the trailing arm.

5. Remove the lower shock absorber bolt.

6. Remove the trailing arm retaining bolts. Remove the toe and chamber adjusting bolts.

7. Remove the 4 retaining bolts from the trailing arm cover. Withdraw the spacer.

8. Using 2 small prybars, pry off the trailing arm cover.

9. Remove the holding fixture.

10. Knock out the round body plug and remove the trailing arm.

11. Paint a reference mark on the torsion bar support, matching the location of the L or R side identification letter, so the torsion bar may be installed in the same position.

NOTE: The torsion bars are splined to allow adjustment of the rear riding height.

12. Remove the torsion bar. Do not scratch the protective

911 Carrera 4

paint on the torsion bar or it will corrode and possible develop fatigue cracks.

NOTE: If removing a broken torsion bar, the inner end can be knocked from its seat by removing the opposite torsion bar and tapping through with a steel rod. Torsion bars are not interchangeable from side-to-side and are marked L and R for identification.

13. Check the torsion bar splines for damage and replace if necessary. If any corrosion is present on the bar, replace it.

14. Coat the torsion bar lightly with a multipurpose grease. Carefully grease the splines.

15. Apply glycerine or another rubber preservative to the torsion bar support.

16. Install the torsion bar, matching the L or R with the paint mark made before removal.

17. Install the trailing arm cover into position and start the 3 accessible bolts.

18. Raise the trailing arm into place with the holding fixture or special tool P 289, until the spacer and the 4th bolt can be installed.

19. Assemble the remaining components in a reverse order of their removal.

20. Tighten the trailing arm cover bolts to 34 ft. lbs. (46 Nm). Tighten the trailing arm retaining bolts to 65 ft. lbs. (88 Nm).

21. Tighten the camber adjusting bolt to 43 ft. lbs. (58 Nm) and the toe-in adjusting bolt to 36 ft. lbs. (49 Nm). Tighten the shock absorber bolt to 45 ft. lbs. (61 Nm).

22. Adjust the rear wheel camber and toe-in.

924S AND 944

NOTE: This procedure requires that the rear wheel camber and toe-in be checked and adjusted as the final step.

1. Raise and support the vehicle safely.

2. Remove the wheel on the side where the torsion bar is being removed.

3. Using a hydraulic jack and a block of wood with a slot cut in it, raise the trailing arm.

4. Remove the lower strut bolt.

5. Remove the trailing arm retaining bolts, then remove the toe and camber adjusting bolts.

6. Remove the 4 retaining bolts from the trailing arm cover.

7. Pry off the trailing arm cover.

8. Lower the jack.

9. Remove the round body plug and remove the trailing arm.

10. Paint a reference mark on the torsion bar support, matching the location of the L or R side identification letter, so the torsion bar may be installed in the same position.

NOTE: The torsion bars are splined to allow adjustment of the rear riding height.

11. Remove the torsion bar. Do not scratch the protective paint on the torsion bar or it will corrode and possibly develop fatigue cracks.

NOTE: If removing a broken torsion bar, the inner end can be knocked from its seat by removing the opposite torsion bar and tapping it through with a steel bar. Torsion bars are not interchangeable from side to side and are marked L and R for identification.

To install:

12. Check the torsion bar splines for damage and replace the bar, if necessary. If there is any corrosion on the bar, replace it.
13. Coat the torsion bar lightly with grease. Carefully grease the splines.
14. Apply glycerine or another rubber preservative to the torsion bar support.
15. Install the torsion bar, matching the L or R with the paint mark made before removal.
16. Install the trailing arm cover into position and start the 3 accessible bolts.
17. Raise the trailing arm into place with a jack and wooden block until the spacer and the fourth bolt can be installed.
18. Assemble the remaining components in the reverse order of their removal.
19. Tighten the trailing arm cover bolts to 25 ft. lbs. (34 Nm). Tighten the shock absorber bolt to 50 ft. lbs. (68 Nm).
20. Adjust rear wheel camber and toe in.

Upper Control Arm

Removal and Installation

928, 928S AND 928S4

1. Raise and support the vehicle safely. Remove the rear wheels and support the lower arm assembly with a jack.
2. Loosen and remove the inner and outer bolts from the upper arm ends.
3. Remove the upper arm from the rear crossmember and from the rear flexible mount. The bushings are replaceable.
4. Installation is the reverse of removal.

Lower Control Arm

Removal and Installation

928, 928S AND 928S4

1. Raise and support the vehicle safely. Remove the rear wheels.
2. Support the hub assembly and the spring strut with a hydraulic jack.
3. Remove the outer pivot pins nuts and washers. Disconnect the stabilizer bar link.
4. Remove the inner pivot bolts from the hub assembly and the spring strut. The bushings are replaceable.
5. Installation is the reverse of removal.

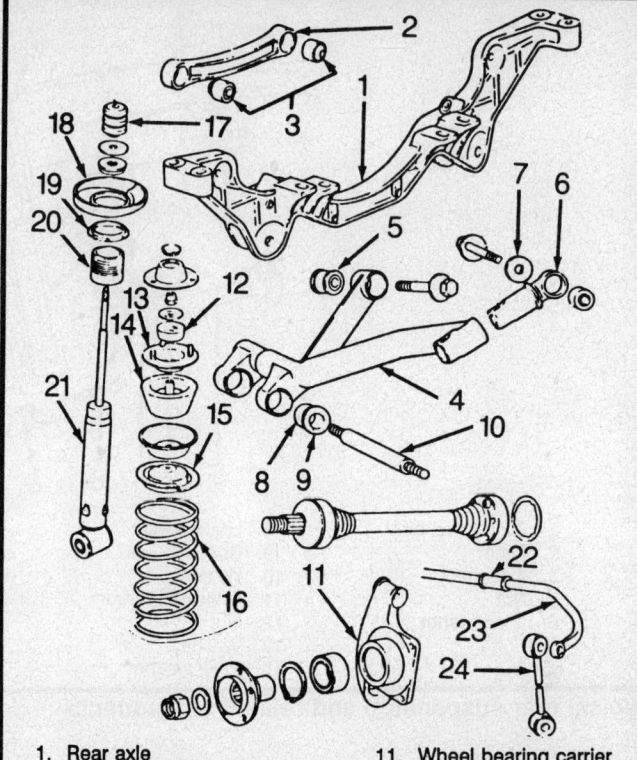

1. Rear axle crossmember	11. Wheel bearing carrier
2. Upper strut	12. Upper shock mount
3. Upper strut bushings	13. Shock mount retainer
4. Lower control arm	14. Lower shock mount
5. Lower control arm inner bushing	15. Upper spring mount
6. Lower control arm rocker	16. Coil spring
7. Lower control eccentric	17. Shock bumper
8. Lower control arm outer bushing	18. Lower spring seat
9. Cone washer	19. Suspension height adjuster
10. Pivot pin	20. Flange
	21. Shock absorber
	22. Stabilizer bar mount
	23. Stabilizer bar
	24. Link

Exploded view of the 928 and 928S rear suspension

Stabilizer

Removal and Installation

911 AND 911 TURBO

1. Raise and support the vehicle safely.
2. Using a large prybar, pry the upper eyes of the stabilizer bar off the studs in the trailing arm.
3. Remove the body mounting brackets.
4. Remove the stabilizer.
5. Check the rubber bushings for wear or damage and, if necessary, replace them.
6. Installation is the reverse of removal.

SERIAL NUMBER IDENTIFICATION

Vehicle Identification Plate

900 SERIES

The vehicle serial number is located in 2 places; it is stamped on a plate at the lower left corner of the windshield or is punched in the vehicle body under the left side of the rear seat cushion.

The vehicle serial number is located on the right side of the rear cross beam in the luggage compartment.

9000 SERIES

These vehicles have the chassis number plate located on the inner right fender panel and the left fire wall area of the engine compartment. The chassis number is also punched in the vehicle body, left of the right rear light, behind the panel in the luggage compartment.

Engine Number

The engine identification number is stamped on a plate which is secured to the upper portion of the engine directly forward of the fuel injection unit.

SPECIFICATIONS

ENGINE IDENTIFICATION

Year	Model	Engine Displacement cu. in. (cc/liter)	Engine Series Identification	No. of Cylinders	Engine Type
1987	900	121 (1985/2.0)	B201	4	SOHC 8-Valve
	900	121 (1985/2.0)	B202 (Turbo)	4	DOHC 16-Valve
	900	121 (1985/2.0)	B202	4	DOHC 16-Valve
	9000	121 (1985/2.0)	B202 (Turbo)	4	DOHC 16-Valve
1988	900	121 (1985/2.0)	B201	4	SOCH 8-Valve
	900	121 (1985/2.0)	B202 (Turbo)	4	DOHC 16-Valve
	900	121 (1985/2.0)	B202	4	DOHC 16-Valve
	9000	121 (1985/2.0)	B202 (Turbo)	4	DOHC 16-Valve
1989	900	121 (1985/2.0)	B202 (Turbo)	4	DOHC 16-Valve
	900	121 (1985/2.0)	B202	4	DOHC 16-Valve
	9000	121 (1985/2.0)	B202 (Turbo)	4	DOHC 16-Valve
1990-91	900	121 (1985/2.0)	B202 (Turbo)	4	DOHC 16-Valve
	900	121 (1985/2.0)	B202	4	DOHC 16-Valve
	9000	121 (1985/2.0)	B202 (Turbo)	4	DOHC 16-Valve

SOHC Single Overhead Camshaft
DOHC Double Overhead Camshaft

GENERAL ENGINE SPECIFICATIONS

Year	Model	Engine Displacement cu. in. (cc)	Fuel System Type	Net Horsepower @ rpm	Net Torque @ rpm (ft. lbs.)	Bore × Stroke (in.)	Compression Ratio	Oil Pressure @ rpm
1987	900	121 (1985)	Fuel Injection	110 @ 5250	119 @ 3500	3.543 × 3.071	9.25:1	64–71 ①
	900S	121 (1985)	Fuel Injection	125 @ 5500	123 @ 3000	3.543 × 3.071	10.1:1	51–74 ①
	900 Turbo	121 (1985)	Fuel Injection	160 @ 5500 ②	188 @ 3000 ③	3.543 × 3.071	9.0:1	64–71 ①
	9000	121 (1985)	Fuel Injection	160 @ 5500	188 @ 3000	3.543 × 3.071	9.0:1	64–71 ①
	9000S	121 (1985)	Fuel Injection	125 @ 5500	125 @ 3000	3.543 × 3.071	10.0:1	51–74 ①

GENERAL ENGINE SPECIFICATIONS

Year	Model	Engine Displacement cu. in. (cc)	Fuel System Type	Net Horsepower @ rpm	Net Torque @ rpm (ft. lbs.)	Bore × Stroke (in.)	Compression Ratio	Oil Pressure @ rpm
1988	900	121 (1985)	Fuel Injection	110 @ 5250	119 @ 3500	3.543 × 3.071	9.25:1	64–71 ①
	900S	121 (1985)	Fuel Injection	125 @ 5500	123 @ 3000	3.543 × 3.071	10.1:1	51–74 ①
	900 Turbo	121 (1985)	Fuel Injection	160 @ 5500 ②	188 @ 3000 ③	3.543 × 3.071	9.0:1	64–71 ①
	9000	121 (1985)	Fuel Injection	160 @ 5500	188 @ 3000	3.543 × 3.071	9.0:1	64–71 ①
	9000S	121 (1985)	Fuel Injection	125 @ 5500	125 @ 3000	3.543 × 3.071	10.0:1	51–74 ①
1989	900	121 (1985)	Fuel Injection	125 @ 5500	123 @ 3000	3.543 × 3.071	10.1:1	51–74 ①
	900S	121 (1985)	Fuel Injection	125 @ 5500	123 @ 3000	3.543 × 3.071	10.1:1	51–74 ①
	900 Turbo	121 (1985)	Fuel Injection	160 @ 5500 ②	188 @ 3000 ③	3.543 × 3.071	9.0:1	64–71 ①
	9000	121 (1985)	Fuel Injection	160 @ 5500	188 @ 3000	3.543 × 3.071	9.0:1	64–71 ①
	9000S	121 (1985)	Fuel Injection	125 @ 5500	125 @ 3000	3.543 × 3.071	10.0:1	51–74 ①
1990–91	900	121 (1985)	Fuel Injection	125 @ 5500	123 @ 3000	3.543 × 3.071	10.1:1	51–74 ①
	900S	121 (1985)	Fuel Injection	125 @ 5500	123 @ 3000	3.543 × 3.071	10.1:1	51–74 ①
	900 Turbo	121 (1985)	Fuel Injection	160 @ 5500 ②	188 @ 3000 ③	3.543 × 3.071	9.0:1	64–71 ①
	9000	121 (1985)	Fuel Injection	160 @ 5500	188 @ 3000	3.543 × 3.071	9.0:1	64–71 ①
	9000S	121 (1985)	Fuel Injection	125 @ 5500	125 @ 3000	3.543 × 3.071	10.0:1	51–74 ①

① at 2000 rpm
② SPG option—165 @ 5500
③ SPG option—195 @ 3000

ENGINE TUNE-UP SPECIFICATIONS

Year	Model	Engine Displacement cu. in. (cc)	Spark Plugs Type	Spark Plugs Gap (in.)	Ignition Timing (deg.) MT	Ignition Timing (deg.) AT	Compression Pressure (psi)	Fuel Pump (psi)	Idle Speed (rpm) MT	Idle Speed (rpm) AT	Valve Clearance In.	Valve Clearance Ex.
1987	900 ⑧	121 (1985)	①	0.024–0.028	④	④	NA	⑦	875	875	.008–.010	.016–.018
	900	121 (1985)	③	0.024–0.028	⑥	⑥	NA	⑦	875	875	Hyd.	Hyd.
	900 Turbo	121 (1985)	②	0.024–0.028	⑤	⑤	NA	⑦	875	875	Hyd.	Hyd.
	9000	121 (1985)	②	0.024–0.028	⑤	⑤	NA	⑦	875	875	Hyd.	Hyd.

ENGINE TUNE-UP SPECIFICATIONS

Year	Model	Engine Displacement cu. in. (cc)	Spark Plugs Type	Spark Plugs Gap (in.)	Ignition Timing (deg.) MT	Ignition Timing (deg.) AT	Compression Pressure (psi)	Fuel Pump (psi)	Idle Speed (rpm) MT	Idle Speed (rpm) AT	Valve Clearance In.	Valve Clearance Ex.
1988	900 ⑧	121 (1985)	①	0.024–0.028	④	④	NA	⑦	875	875	.008–.010	.016–.018
	900	121 (1985)	③	0.024–0.028	⑥	⑥	NA	⑦	875	875	Hyd.	Hyd.
	900 Turbo	121 (1985)	②	0.024–0.028	⑤	⑤	NA	⑦	875	875	Hyd.	Hyd.
	9000	121 (1985)	②	0.024–0.028	⑤	⑤	NA	⑦	875	875	Hyd.	Hyd.
1989	900	121 (1985)	⑨	0.024–0.028	⑥	⑥	NA	⑦	875	875	Hyd.	Hyd.
	900 Turbo	121 (1985)	②	0.024–0.028	⑤	⑤	NA	⑦	875	875	Hyd.	Hyd.
	9000	121 (1985)	②	0.024–0.028	⑤	⑤	NA	⑦	875	875	Hyd.	Hyd.
1990	900	121 (1985)	⑨	0.024–0.028	⑥	⑥	NA	⑦	875	875	Hyd.	Hyd.
	900 Turbo	121 (1985)	②	0.024–0.028	⑤	⑤	NA	⑦	875	875	Hyd.	Hyd.
	9000	121 (1985)	⑨	0.024–0.028	⑥	⑥	NA	⑦	875	875	Hyd.	Hyd.
	9000 Turbo	121 (1985)	⑩	0.024–0.028	⑤	⑤	NA	⑦	875	875	Hyd.	Hyd.
1991			SEE UNDERHOOD SPECIFICATION STICKER									

DOHC—Double Overhead Camshaft
① BP6ES, W7DC, N9Y, N9YC, BP7ES
② BCP7EV
③ BCP6ES, C9YC, F7DC
④ 20° @ 2000 rpm
18° @ 2000 rpm Canada with manual transmission
23° @ 2000 rpm Canada with automatic transmission

⑤ 16° BTDC @ 850 rpm
⑥ 14° @ 850 rpm
⑦ Fuel injected engines—Fuel line pressure before the control pressure regulator is 66.9–69.7 (setting valve), and 48.5–54.0 psi (warm engine) after the control pressure regulator (located in fuel distributor).

⑧ SOHC—Single Overhead Camshaft
⑨ BCP5ES
⑩ BCPR7ES

FIRING ORDERS

NOTE: To avoid confusion, always replace spark plug wires one at a time.

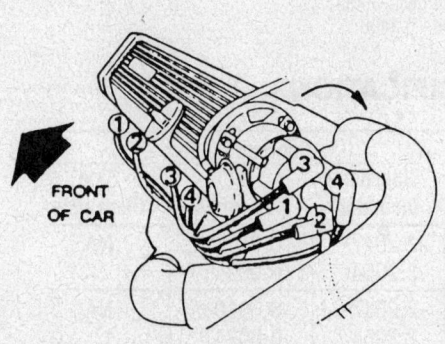

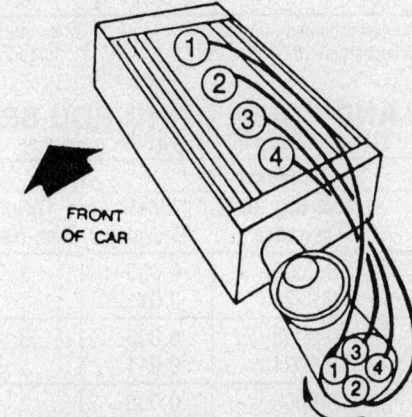

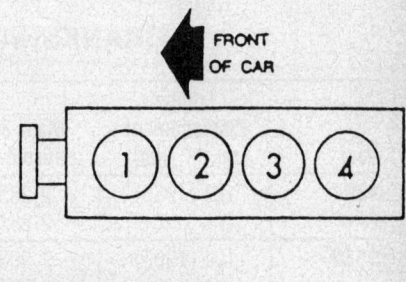

B201 (8-Valve) Engine
Engine Firing Order: 1–3–4–2
Distributor Rotation: Clockwise

B202 (16-Valve) Engine
Engine Firing Order: 1–3–4–2
Distributor Rotation: Clockwise

B202 (16-Valve) Engine
Engine Firing Order: 1–3–4–2
Distributorless Ignition System

CAPACITIES

Year	Model	Engine Displacement cu. in. (cc)	Engine Crankcase (qts.) with Filter	Engine Crankcase (qts.) without Filter	Transmission (pts.) 4-Spd	Transmission (pts.) 5-Spd	Transmission (pts.) Auto.	Drive Axle (pts.)	Fuel Tank (gal.)	Cooling System (qts.)
1987	900 ①	121 (1985)	4.0	3.5	5.2	6.4	17	2.6②	18.0	10.5
	900 Turbo	121 (1985)	4.5	4.0	5.2	6.4	17	2.6②	18.0	10.5
	900	121 (1985)	4.0	3.5	5.2	6.4	17	2.6②	18.0	10.5
	9000	121 (1985)	4.5	4.0	5.2	6.4	17	2.6②	18.0	10.5
1988	900 ①	121 (1985)	4.0	3.5	5.2	6.4	17	2.6②	18.0	10.5
	900 Turbo	121 (1985)	4.5	4.0	5.2	6.4	17	2.6②	18.0	10.5
	900	121 (1985)	4.0	3.5	5.2	6.4	17	2.6②	18.0	10.5
	9000	121 (1985)	4.5	4.0	5.2	6.4	17	2.6②	18.0	10.5
1989	900 Turbo	121 (1985)	4.5	4.0	5.2	6.4	17	2.6②	18.0	10.5
	900	121 (1985)	4.0	3.5	5.2	6.4	17	2.6②	18.0	10.5
	9000	121 (1985)	4.5	4.0	5.2	6.4	17	2.6②	18.0	10.5
1990–91	900 Turbo	121 (1985)	4.5	4.0	5.2	6.4	17	2.6②	18.0	10.5
	900	121 (1985)	4.0	3.5	5.2	6.4	17	2.6②	18.0	10.5
	9000	121 (1985)	4.5	4.0	5.2	6.4	17	2.6②	18.0	10.5

① SOHC—Single Overhead Camshaft   ② 3.0 for Borg Warner Type 37

CAMSHAFT SPECIFICATIONS

Year	Engine Displacement cu. in. (cc)	Journal Diameter 1	Journal Diameter 2	Journal Diameter 3	Journal Diameter 4	Journal Diameter 5	Lobe Lift In.	Lobe Lift Ex.	Bearing Clearance	Camshaft End Play
1987	121 (1985)①	1.1394	1.1394	1.1394	1.1394	1.1394	0.425	0.433	NA	0.0031–0.0098
	121 (1985)	1.1387–1.1392	1.1387–1.1392	1.1387–1.1392	1.1387–1.1392	1.1387–1.1392	②	③	NA	0.0031–0.0138
1988	121 (1985)①	1.1394	1.1394	1.1394	1.1394	1.1394	0.425	0.433	NA	0.0031–0.0098
	121 (1985)	1.1387–1.1392	1.1387–1.1392	1.1387–1.1392	1.1387–1.1392	1.1387–1.1392	②	③	NA	0.0031–0.0138
1989	121 (1985)③	1.1387–1.1392	1.1387–1.1392	1.1387–1.1392	1.1387–1.1392	1.1387–1.1392	③	③	NA	0.0031–0.0138
1990–91	121 (1985)	1.1387–1.1392	1.1387–1.1392	1.1387–1.1392	1.1387–1.1392	1.1387–1.1392	②	③	NA	0.0031–0.0138

① SOHC—Single Overhead Camshaft   ② Non-turbocharged—0.425 Turbocharged—0.3406/0.2618   ③ Non-turbocharged—0.433 Turbocharged—0.3406

CRANKSHAFT AND CONNECTING ROD SPECIFICATIONS
All measurements are given in inches.

Year	Engine Displacement cu. in. (cc)	Crankshaft Main Brg. Journal Dia.	Crankshaft Main Brg. Oil Clearance	Crankshaft Shaft End-play	Crankshaft Thrust on No.	Connecting Rod Journal Diameter	Connecting Rod Oil Clearance	Connecting Rod Side Clearance
1987	121 (1985)	2.283–2.284	0.0008–0.0024	0.003–0.011	3	2.2047–2.2054	0.0010–0.0024	NA
1988	121 (1985)	2.283–2.284	0.0008–0.0024	0.003–0.011	3	2.2047–2.2054	0.0010–0.0024	NA
1989	121 (1985)	2.283–2.284	0.0008–0.0024	0.003–0.011	3	2.2047–2.2054	0.0010–0.0024	NA
1990–91	121 (1985)	2.283–2.284	0.0008–0.0024	0.003–0.011	3	2.2047–2.2054	0.0010–0.0024	NA

NA Not available at time of publication

VALVE SPECIFICATIONS

Year	Engine Displacement cu. in. (cc)	Seat Angle (deg.)	Face Angle (deg.)	Spring Test Pressure (lbs.)	Spring Installed Height (in.)	Stem-to-Guide Clearance (in.)		Stem Diameter (in.)	
						Intake	Exhaust	Intake	Exhaust
1987	121 (1985) ①	45	44.5	178–198 @ 1.16	1.56	0.020	0.020	0.3134–0.3139	0.3132–0.3142
	121 (1985)	45	44.5	133–145 @ 1.18	1.45	0.020	0.020	0.2740–0.2746	0.2738–0.2748
1988	121 (1985) ①	45	44.5	178–198 @ 1.16	1.56	0.020	0.020	0.3134–0.3139	0.3132–0.3142
	121 (1985)	45	44.5	133–145 @ 1.18	1.45	0.020	0.020	0.2740–0.2746	0.2738–0.2748
1989	121 (1985)	45	44.5	133–145 @ 1.18	1.45	0.020	0.020	0.2740–0.2746	0.2738–0.2748
1990–91	121 (1985)	45	44.5	133–145 @ 1.18	1.45	0.020	0.020	0.2740–0.2746	0.2738–0.2748

① SOHC—Single Overhead Camshaft

PISTON AND RING SPECIFICATIONS

All measurements are given in inches.

Year	Engine Displacement cu. in. (cc)	Piston Clearance	Ring Gap			Ring Side Clearance		
			Top Compression	Bottom Compression	Oil Control	Top Compression	Bottom Compression	Oil Control
1987	121 (1985) ①	.0009–.0020	0.014–0.022	0.012–0.018	0.015–0.055	0.002–0.003	0.002–0.003	NA
	121 (1985)	.0009–.0020	0.013–0.021	0.011–0.017	0.014–0.055	0.002–0.003	0.002–0.003	NA
1988	121 (1985) ①	.0009–.0020	0.014–0.022	0.012–0.018	0.015–0.055	0.002–0.003	0.002–0.003	NA
	121 (1985)	.0009–.0020	0.013–0.021	0.011–0.017	0.014–0.055	0.002–0.003	0.002–0.003	NA
1989	121 (1985)	.0009–.0020	0.013–0.021	0.011–0.017	0.014–0.055	0.002–0.003	0.002–0.003	NA
1990–91	121 (1985)	.0009–.0020	0.013–0.021	0.011–0.017	0.014–0.055	0.002–0.003	0.002–0.003	NA

① SOHC—Single Overhead Camshaft
NA Not available at time of publication

TORQUE SPECIFICATIONS

All readings in ft. lbs.

Year	Engine Displacement cu. in. (cc)	Cylinder Head Bolts	Main Bearing Bolts	Rod Bearing Bolts	Crankshaft Pulley Bolts	Flywheel Bolts	Manifold		Spark Plugs
							Intake	Exhaust	
1987	121 (1985)	① ②	40	80	140	43	13	18	18–21
1988	121 (1985)	① ②	40	80	140	43	13	18	18–21
1989	121 (1985)	① ②	40	80	140	43	13	18	18–21
1990–91	121 (1985)	① ②	40	80	140	43	13	18	18–21

① 1987–89
1st stage—43 ft. lbs.
2nd stage—72 ft. lbs.—run engine to warm. Allow 30 minutes cool time—Retighten to 72 ft. lbs.
1987–91: Tighten each bolt another ¼ (90 degrees) of a turn.

② Turbo 16-Valve
1st stage—45 ft. lbs.
2nd stage—67 ft. lbs. Engine to normal operating temp. Allow to cool for 30 minutes.

3rd stage—Tighten another 90 degrees turn (¼ turn). Retorque after 1200 miles or after engine reaches normal operating temperature.

BRAKE SPECIFICATIONS

All measurements in inches unless noted.

Year	Model	Lug Nut Torque (ft. lbs.)	Master Cylinder Bore	Brake Disc Minimum Thickness	Brake Disc Maximum Runout	Standard Brake Drum Diameter	Minimum Lining Thickness Front	Minimum Lining Thickness Rear
1987	900	65–80	NA	0.461①	—	—	—	—
	9000	76–90	NA	0.787②	0.768③	—	0.039	0.039
1988	900	65–80	NA	0.461①	—	—	—	—
	9000	76–90	NA	0.787②	0.768③	—	0.039	0.039
1989	900	65–80	NA	0.461①	—	—	—	—
	9000	76–90	NA	0.787②	0.768③	—	0.039	0.039
1990–91	900	65–80	NA	0.461①	—	—	—	—
	9000	76–90	NA	0.787②	0.768③	—	0.039	0.039

NA—Not available at time of publication
① 0.374 Rear
② 0.295 Rear
③ 0.276 Rear

WHEEL ALIGNMENT

Year	Model	Caster Range (deg.)	Caster Preferred Setting (deg.)	Camber Range (deg.)	Camber Preferred Setting (deg.)	Toe-in (in.)	Steering Axis Inclination (deg.)
1987	900	$1^1/_2$–$2^1/_2$①	2①	0–1	$^1/_2$	$^5/_{64}$	NA
	9000	$1^1/_8$–$2^1/_8$	$1^5/_8$	$1^1/_8$N–$^1/_8$N	$^5/_8$N	$^1/_{16}$	NA
1988	900	$1^1/_2$–$2^1/_2$①	2①	0–1	$^1/_2$	$^5/_{64}$	NA
	9000	$1^1/_8$–$2^1/_8$	$1^5/_8$	$1^1/_8$N–$^1/_8$N	$^5/_8$N	$^1/_{16}$	NA
1989	900	$1^1/_2$–$2^1/_2$①	2①	0–1	$^1/_2$	$^5/_{64}$	NA
	9000	$1^1/_8$–$2^1/_8$	$1^5/_8$	$1^1/_8$N–$^1/_8$N	$^5/_8$N	$^1/_{16}$	NA
1990–91	900	$1^1/_2$–$2^1/_2$①	2①	0–1	$^1/_2$	$^5/_{64}$	NA
	9000	$1^1/_8$–$2^1/_8$	$1^5/_8$	$1^1/_8$N–$^1/_8$N	$^5/_8$N	$^1/_{16}$	NA

NA—Not available at time of publication
① Manual Steering $^1/_2$–$1^1/_2$
N Negative

ENGINE ELECTRICAL

NOTE: Disconnecting the negative battery cable on some vehicles may interfere with the functions of the on board computer systems and may require the computer to undergo a relearning process, once the negative battery cable is reconnected.

Distributor

Removal and Installation

1. Disconnect the negative battery cable. Remove the distributor cap after marking the location of the No. 1 spark plug wire on the distributor housing. No. 1 cylinder is at the rear of the engine.
2. Disconnect the primary wire and Hall transducer connector from the distributor and hose from the vacuum advance unit.

Distributor assembly location

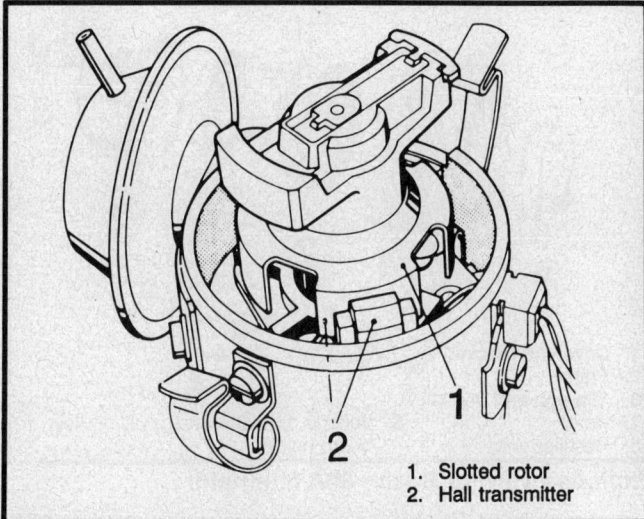

1. Slotted rotor
2. Hall transmitter

Distributor assembly with Hall effect pick up

3. Crank the engine until the flywheel marking is at TDC (0 degrees) and the distributor rotor is pointing to the indicating or reference mark on the distributor housing for the No. 1 cylinder.

4. Matchmark the distributor housing to the valve cover housing. Remove the distributor retaining bolts and pull the distributor forward from the end of the valve cover housing. Note the position of the distributor drive lugs. Do not rotate the engine crankshaft when the distributor is removed from the engine.

5. Installation is the reverse of the removal procedure. Be sure to align the distributor rotor to the No. 1 spark plug wire reference mark on the distributor housing, while aligning the matchmarks on the valve cover housing and distributor housing.

Ignition Timing

Adjustment

Ignition timing is set in the conventional manner, using the marks that are located on the flywheel. However, the engine is also equipped for checking the timing using an ignition service (ISI) instrument.

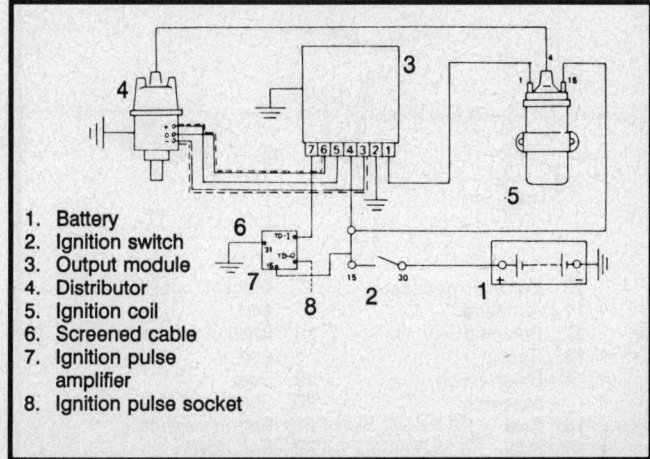

1. Battery
2. Ignition switch
3. Output module
4. Distributor
5. Ignition coil
6. Screened cable
7. Ignition pulse amplifier
8. Ignition pulse socket

Electronic ignition system components—9000 Series

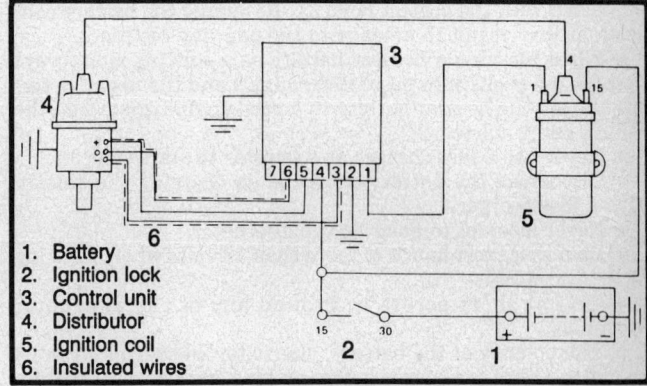

1. Battery
2. Ignition lock
3. Control unit
4. Distributor
5. Ignition coil
6. Insulated wires

Electronic ignition system schematic—8 valve engine

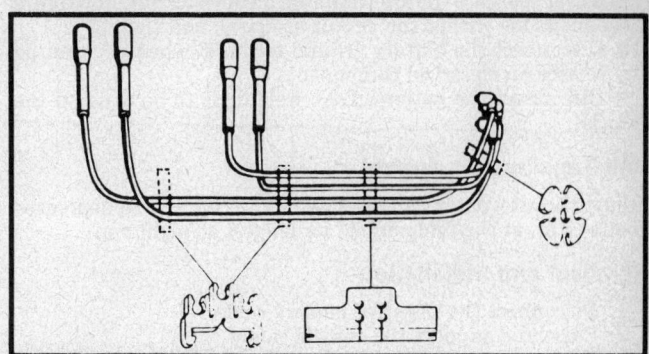

Secondary wiring routing—8 valve engine

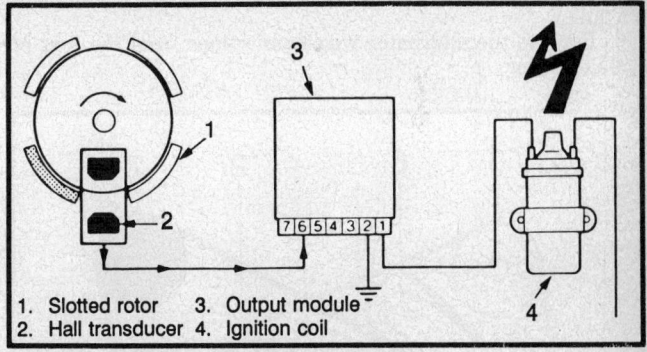

1. Slotted rotor
2. Hall transducer
3. Output module
4. Ignition coil

Output module—16 valve engine

The equipment in the vehicle comprises a pin in the engine flywheel and a service socket in the clutch cover. The ignition service instrument is connected to the clutch cover by means of a special connector and the plug lead No. 1 cylinder by means of a terminal. The ignition service instrument is also connected to the ignition service socket at the fuse box and by means of an impulse transmitter at the plug lead for No. 1 cylinder.

The Saab ignition service instrument consists of a tachometer, cam angle meter, stroboscope lamp and switch for operating the starter.

Alternator

Precautions

Several precautions must be observed with alternator equipped vehicles to avoid damage to the unit.

• If the battery is removed for any reason, make sure it is reconnected with the correct polarity. Reversing the battery connections may result in damage to the one-way rectifiers.

• When utilizing a booster battery as a starting aid, always connect the positive to positive terminals and the negative terminal from the booster battery to a good engine ground on the vehicle being started.

• Never use a fast charger as a booster to start vehicles.

• Disconnect the battery cables when charging the battery with a fast charger.

• Never attempt to polarize the alternator.

• Do not use test lamps of more than 12 volts when checking diode continuity.

• Do not short across or ground any of the alternator terminals.

• The polarity of the battery, alternator and regulator must be matched and considered before making any electrical connections within the system.

• Never separate the alternator on an open circuit. Make sure all connections within the circuit are clean and tight.

• Disconnect the battery ground terminal when performing any service on electrical components.

• Disconnect the battery if arc welding is to be done on the vehicle.

Belt Tension Adjustment

Adjust the alternator belt tension so the belt can be depressed about ½ in. at the midpoint of its longest straight run.

Removal and Installation

1. Disconnect the negative battery cable.
2. Raise and support the vehicle safely.
3. Remove the right front wheel assembly.
4. Remove the inner fender panel from the right fender.
5. Loosen the alternator belt and remove it from the alternator pulley.
6. Remove the alternator wire connections from the rear of the alternator.

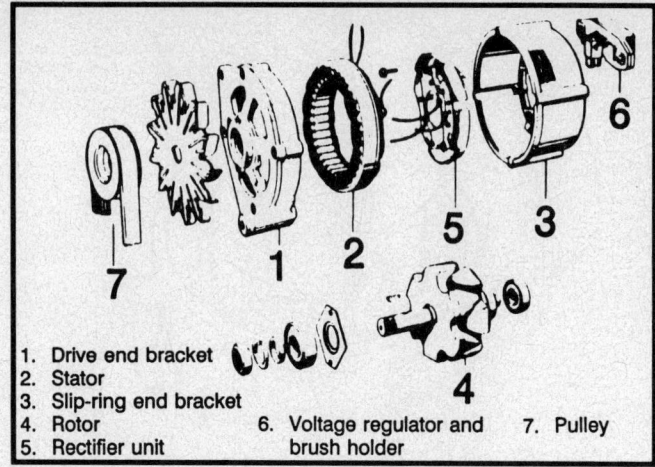

1. Drive end bracket
2. Stator
3. Slip-ring end bracket
4. Rotor
5. Rectifier unit
6. Voltage regulator and brush holder
7. Pulley

Exploded view of Bosch 80A alternator

7. Loosen the 2 securing bolts for the alternator.
8. Using a prybar, push the alternator to the left, pull the alternator forward and remove it from the vehicle.
9. Installation is the reverse of the removal procedure.

Starter

Removal and Installation
EXCEPT TURBOCHARGED ENGINE

1. Disconnect the negative battery cable.
2. Remove the flywheel cover. Remove the gearbox dipstick, if equipped with manual transmission.

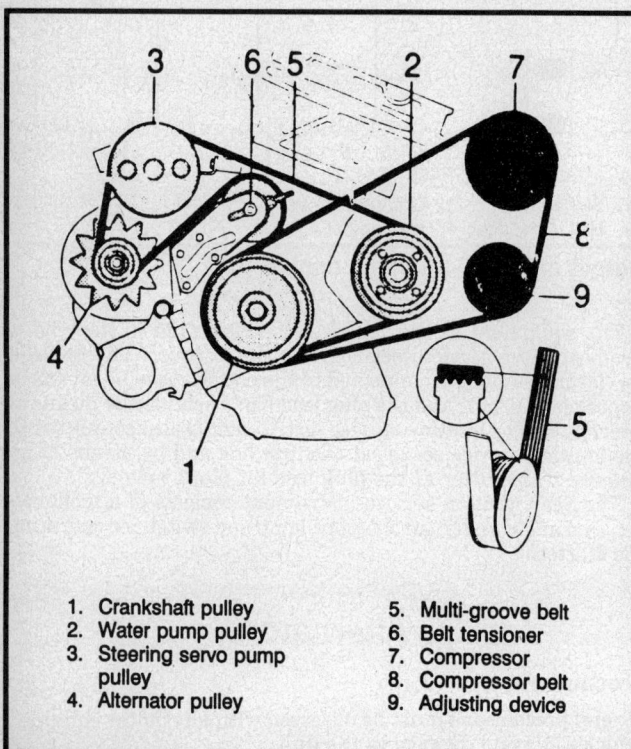

1. Crankshaft pulley
2. Water pump pulley
3. Steering servo pump pulley
4. Alternator pulley
5. Multi-groove belt
6. Belt tensioner
7. Compressor
8. Compressor belt
9. Adjusting device

Serpentine drive belt routing

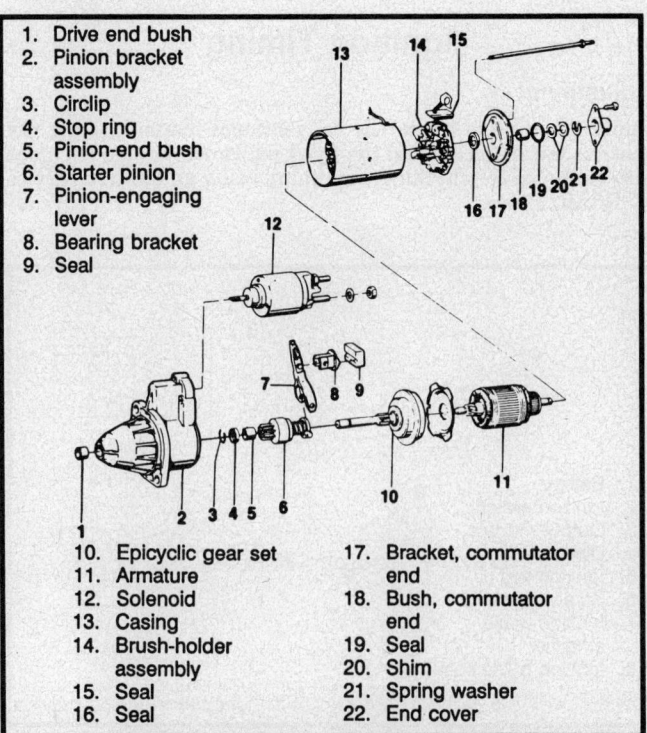

1. Drive end bush
2. Pinion bracket assembly
3. Circlip
4. Stop ring
5. Pinion-end bush
6. Starter pinion
7. Pinion-engaging lever
8. Bearing bracket
9. Seal
10. Epicyclic gear set
11. Armature
12. Solenoid
13. Casing
14. Brush-holder assembly
15. Seal
16. Seal
17. Bracket, commutator end
18. Bush, commutator end
19. Seal
20. Shim
21. Spring washer
22. End cover

Exploded view of starter assembly—typical

3. Remove the starter motor heat shield and the rear mounting bolts.

4. Disconnect the starter motor wires. Remove the front mounting bolts.

5. Remove the starter from the vehicle.

6. Installation is the reverse of removal.

TURBOCHARGED ENGINE

1. Disconnect the negative battery cable. Remove the battery and the battery tray.

2. Remove the turbocharger suction pipe, preheater hose and the flywheel cover.

3. Remove the gearbox dipstick, if equipped with manual transmission. Remove the bracket and bolts between the turbocharger and the gearbox.

4. Disconnect the starter motor wires.

5. Loosen the oil return pipe on the turbocharger enough to allow it to be bent slightly.

6. Remove the starter motor heat shield and the rear mounting bolts.

7. Remove the front starter mounting bolts.

8. Remove the starter from the vehicle. The starter will have to be tilted downward and then lifted out forward.

9. Installation is the reverse the removal procedure. Be sure to use a new gasket on the oil return pipe connecting flange on the turbocharger.

CHASSIS ELECTRICAL

CAUTION

On vehicles equipped with an air bag, the negative battery cable must be disconnected, before working on the system. Failure to do so may result in deployment of the air bag and possible personal injury.

Heater Blower Motor

Removal and Installation

WITHOUT AIR CONDITIONING

900 Series

1. Disconnect the negative battery cable.

2. Remove the switch panel and the upper section of the instrument panel.

3. Disconnect the electrical leads to the fan motor.

4. Remove the retaining screws for the right defroster valve housing.

5. Remove the fan retaining screws. Remove the fan from its housing.

6. The installation is in the reverse of the removal procedure.

9000 Series

1. Disconnect the negative battery cable.

2. Remove the cover from the windshield wipers.

3. Remove the fresh air filter assembly.

4. Unplug the connectors for the fan motor and fan resistors.

5. Disconnect the temperature control cable.

6. Release the clips on either side of the fan body and turn the body diagonally upwards.

7. Remove the screws in the center of the casing, release the clips and remove the grille from the discharge duct.

8. Separate the fan casing. Remove the screw securing the fan motor.

9. Lift the cover for the lead and withdraw the motor complete with impeller.

10. Installation is the reverse of the removal procedure.

WITH AIR CONDITIONING

900 Series

1. Disconnect the negative battery cable.

2. Remove the switch panel and the upper section of the instrument panel.

3. Disconnect the electrical leads to the fan motor.

4. Remove the retaining screws for the right defroster valve housing.

5. Remove the fan retaining screws. Remove the fan from its housing.

6. The installation is in the reverse of the removal procedure.

9000 Series

1. Disconnect the negative battery cable. Remove the hood assembly.

2. Disconnect the wiper arms. Remove the covers on the evaporator and wiper motor. Unplug the connector for the fan control unit on vehicles with automatic climate control.

3. Remove the false fire wall panel.

4. Remove the plastic drainage tube moulding below the windshield moulding.

5. Remove the securing bolts the electronic ignition control unit and position it aside.

6. Remove the clip and unplug the connectors. Remove the complete wiper assembly.

7. Remove the rubber lead through panel for the coolant hoses. Drain cooling system. Disconnect the quick release couplings for the coolant hoses at the heat exchanger.

8. Remove the throttle dash pot assembly.

9. Remove the vacuum pump retaining screws. Position the pump aside.

10. Remove the evaporator body retaining screws and the clips for the refrigerant hoses.

11. Remove the lock washer and disconnect the cable for the temperature valve.

12. Carefully lift the evaporator and remove the clips on either side of the fan. Remove the complete fan assembly by twisting the fan diagonally upwards.

13. Remove the screw in the center of the casing. Release the clips and the grille at the discharge duct.

14. Separate the fan housing and undo the securing screw for the fan motor.

15. Lift the cover upward and withdraw the motor complete with the impeller.

16. To install the fan motor assembly, reverse the removal procedure. Be careful not to separate the connector for the radiator fan control when installing the false fire wall panel.

Windshield Wiper Motor

Removal and Installation

900 SERIES

1. Disconnect the negative battery cable. Remove the wiper arms from the vehicle. Remove the rubber grommets.

2. Remove the 4 mounting screws. Disconnect the electrical lead. Remove the wiper unit from the vehicle.

3. Separate the wiper motor from the wiper assembly.

4. Installation is the reverse of the removal procedure.

9000 SERIES

1. Disconnect the negative battery cable.

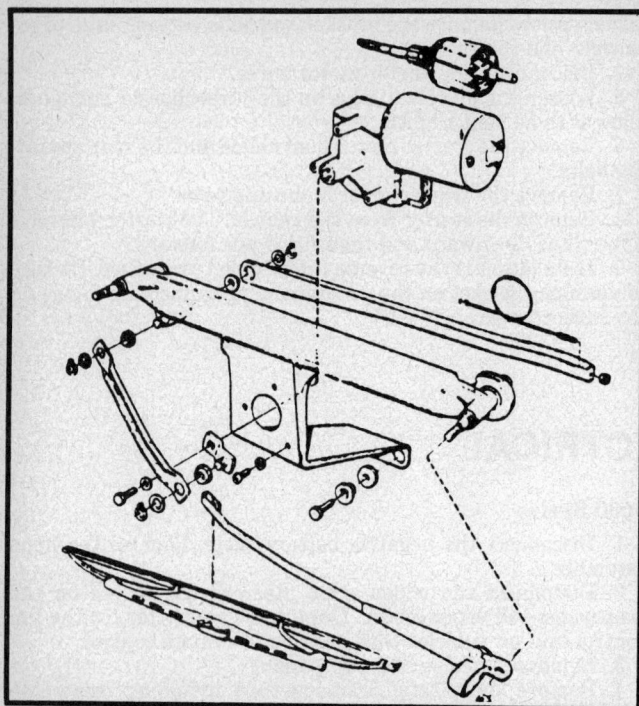

Windshield wiper and motor assembly

2. Raise the covers on the wiper arms, remove the retaining nuts and lift the arms off.

3. Remove the rubber grommets from the spindles and remove the 4 bulkhead panel bolts.

4. Lift the bulkhead panel from the vehicle.

5. Disconnect the electrical connector from the wiper motor.

6. Remove the spindle nuts and remove the 4 retaining bolts for the wiper motor bracket.

7. Push downward and pull forward on the pushrod for the left wiper.

8. Lift out the wiper motor assembly complete with the bracket and the pushrod linkage.

9. Installation is the reverse of the removal procedure.

Windshield Wiper Switch

Removal and Installation

1. Disconnect the negative battery cable.

2. Pull the steering wheel as far forward as it will go. Remove the cover from under the steering column assembly.

3. Disconnect the electrical connector from the switch assembly.

4. Remove the switch retaining screws. Remove the switch from the vehicle.

5. Installation is the reverse of the removal procedure.

Instrument Cluster

Removal and Installation

900 SERIES

1. Disconnect the negative battery cable. Remove the steering wheel.

2. Remove the 4 screws in the switch panel and tilt the panel back.

3. Remove the left speaker/defroster grille. Pull apart the instrument panel connectors. Disconnect the speedometer cable.

4. Remove the instrument panel retaining screws. Carefully remove the unit from the vehicle.

5. Installation is the reverse of the removal procedure.

9000 SERIES

1. Disconnect the negative battery cable.

2. Remove the speaker grilles on either side of the panel.

3. Unscrew the top section of the instrument panel, which is retained by 7 screws including 1 in the glove box.

4. Lift off the top instrument panel section.

5. Remove the air duct from the opening in the top.

6. Disconnect the speedometer cable, the vacuum hoses to the turbo pressure gauge and unplug all connectors to the display panel.

7. Remove the 2 screws of the instrument display panel.

8. Withdraw the instrument cluster through the top of the instrument panel.

9. Installation is the reverse of the removal procedure. Be sure the air duct fitting is tight when reassembling the duct tubing.

Headlight Switch

Removal and Installation

1. Disconnect the negative battery cable.

2. Pull the switch from its mounting on the instrument panel assembly.

3. Disconnect the electrical connectors from the switch.

4. Remove the switch from the vehicle.

5. Installation is the reverse of the removal procedure.

Combination Switch

Removal and Installation

1. Disconnect the negative battery cable.

2. Remove the steering wheel.

3. Remove the cover under the bearing support.

4. Remove the combination switch retaining bolts and electrical connections.

5. Remove the switch from the vehicle.

6. Installation is the reverse of the removal procedure.

Ignition Switch

Removal and Installation

900 SERIES

1. Disconnect the negative battery cable.

2. Remove the center console.

3. Disconnect the electrical connections from the switch.

4. Remove the assembly from the vehicle.

5. Installation is the reverse of removal.

9000 SERIES

1. Disconnect the negative battery cable.

2. Remove the steering wheel assembly.

3. Remove the cover panels from the wiper/washer and direction indicator switches.

4. Remove the upper section of the instrument panel. Remove the instrument cluster assembly.

5. Remove the clip securing the wiring loom and flexible ducts to the steering column.

6. Unplug the connector for the wipers, direction signals and leads for the horn switch and ignition switch.

7. Remove the pinch bolt in the upper joint, loosen the other bolts and withdraw the universal joint from the splines on the steering column shaft.

8. Remove the steering column wheel adjustment assembly by tapping out the roll pin and removing the nut and washer. Withdraw the shaft from the clamp and lift the upper section of the steering wheel adjustment assembly. Remove the 3 socket head bolts and lift off the holder for the directional indicator unit.

9. Remove the upper section of the steering column, removing the rubber bushing completely from the housing.

10. Remove the shake-proof washer. Remove the column bearing.

11. With the switch support out remove the socket head screws and remove the ignition switch.

12. To remove the cylinder, turn the ignition key to position **1**, press in on the locking tab and withdraw the cylinder.

13. Installation is the reverse of the removal procedure.

Stoplight Switch

Removal and Installation

1. Disconnect the negative battery cable.
2. Remove the necessary trim and padding to gain access to the switch assembly.
3. Disconnect the electrical connections from the switch assembly.
4. Remove the switch from its mounting.
5. Installation is the reverse of the removal procedure.

Neutral Safety Switch

Adjustment

1. Disconnect the wires from the switch. The wide terminals are for back-up lights and the narrow ones are for the starter motor.

2. Loosen the locknut and unscrew the switch 2 turns.

3. With the selector in **D**, connect a test light between the narrow terminals. The light should light up.

4. Screw in the switch until the light goes out. Mark that position on both the transmission and the switch.

5. Move the test light, the wide terminals and screw switch in until the light goes out again. Count the number between the lights going out.

6. Turn the switch to a point halfway between the 2 lights-out points.

7. Secure the locknut to 4–6 ft. lbs. torque. If the safety switch is locked too tight, it may be damaged.

Fuses, Circuit Breakers and Relays

Location

The fuse panel is located under the hood of the vehicle. It is on the left side for the 900 series vehicles. The fuse panel for the 9000 series vehicles is located and accessed through an access panel in the glove compartment.

ENGINE COOLING

Radiator

Removal and Installation

1. Disconnect the negative battery cable. Drain the radiator. As required, remove the radiator grille. As required disconnect and plug the transmission lines.

2. Disconnect the hoses from the radiator. Disconnect the electrical leads to the radiator fan and the auxiliary fan, if equipped.

3. Disconnect the electrical lead to the thermal switch and solenoid valve. Remove the ignition coil and solenoid valve from the bracket. Remove the oil cooler.

4. Remove the 2 bolts from the upper radiator support Lift the radiator out of the vehicle by pulling the top of the radiator slightly backwards.

5. Installation is the reverse of the removal procedure.

Heater Core

For further information, please refer to "Chilton's Heating and Air Conditioning Manual" for additional coverage.

Removal and Installation
900 SERIES

1. Disconnect the negative battery cable. Remove the dash panel under the switches on the steering column and the lower section of the instrument panel.

2. Remove the air diffuser and retaining screws.

3. Remove the left defroster and speaker grille.

4. Remove the control rod from between the coolant shut off valve and the control rod by sliding the rod as far forward as it will go to free it from the knob, then pull it rearward to free it from the shut off valve.

NOTE: The plastic joint at the control knob is accessible from underneath once the switches below the heater controls have been moved backward.

5. Remove the lower section of the heater housing.

6. Drain the coolant and disconnect the hoses. Plug the ends of the hoses to prevent coolant from leaking into the compartment.

7. Separate the heater core from the housing and guide it backward and downward. It will be necessary to disconnect the brake pedal return spring and depress the brake pedal slightly.

8. The water valve and the heater core can be separated after their removal. Do not kink or break the capillary tube.

9. Installation is the reverse of the removal procedure.

9000 SERIES

1. Disconnect the negative battery cable. Remove the hood assembly.

2. Disconnect the wiper arms. Remove the covers on the evaporator and wiper motor. Unplug the connector for the fan control unit on vehicles with automatic climate control.

3. Remove the false fire wall panel. Drain the radiator.

4. Remove the plastic drainage tube moulding below the windshield moulding.

5. Remove the securing bolts the electronic ignition control unit and position it aside.

6. Remove the clip and unplug the connectors. Remove the complete wiper assembly.

7. Remove the rubber lead through panel for the coolant hoses. Drain cooling system. Disconnect the quick release couplings for the coolant hoses at the heat exchanger.

8. Remove the throttle dash pot assembly.

9. Remove the vacuum pump retaining screws. Position the pump aside.

10. Remove the evaporator body retaining screws and the clips for the refrigerant hoses.

11. Remove the lock washer and disconnect the cable for the temperature valve.

12. Carefully lift the evaporator and remove the clips on either side of the fan. Remove the complete fan assembly by twisting the fan diagonally upwards.

13. Remove the screw in the center of the casing. Release the clips and the grille at the discharge duct.

14. Separate the fan housing and undo the securing screw for the fan motor.

15. Lift the cover upward and withdraw the motor complete with the impeller.

16. Release the retaining clips and disconnect the hoses from the heater core.

17. Pull the heater core from the engine side of the fire wall.

18. To install, position new O-rings and connect the heater hoses. Complete the assembly in the reverse order of the removal procedure.

Water Pump

Removal and Installation

8 VALVE ENGINE

1. Disconnect the negative battery cable. Drain the cooling system.

2. Remove the necessary components in order to gain access to the water pump assembly.

3. Remove the drive belts. Remove the water pump pulley.

4. Remove the water pump retaining bolts. Remove the water pump from the engine.

5. Installation is the reverse of the removal procedure.

16 VALVE ENGINE

1. Disconnect the negative battery cable. Raise and support the vehicle safely.

2. Remove the right front wheel assembly. Remove the front section of the inner fender panel.

3. Drain the engine coolant. Loosen the drive belts. Remove the water pump pulley and the belt tensioning pulley.

4. Remove the clips holding the oil lines at the oil cooler. Remove the clips securing the water pipe to the engine block. Disconnect the coolant hoses from the water pump.

5. Remove the bolt securing the water pump to the bracket. Remove the water pump.

6. Installation is the reverse of the removal procedure.

Thermostat

Removal and Installation

Thermostats on both the 8 valve and 16 valve engines are located in housings on the fronts of the cylinder heads, facing their respective radiators. The housings are cast elbows, which are unbolted from the heads in order to gain access to the thermostats. When installing the new thermostat, always install with the spring facing down. Use sealing compound on the joining surfaces of the elbow and head.

FUEL SYSTEM

Fuel System Service Precautions

Safety is the most important factor when performing not only fuel system maintenance but any type of maintenance. Failure to conduct maintenance and repairs in a safe manner may result in serious personal injury or death. Maintenance and testing of the vehicle's fuel system components can be accomplished safely and effectively by adhering to the following rules and guidelines.

• To avoid the possibility of fire and personal injury, always disconnect the negative battery cable unless the repair or test procedure requires that battery voltage be applied.

• Always relieve the fuel system pressure prior to disconnecting any fuel system component (injector, fuel rail, pressure regulator, etc.), fitting or fuel line connection. Exercise extreme caution whenever relieving fuel system pressure to avoid exposing skin, face and eyes to fuel spray. Please be advised that fuel under pressure may penetrate the skin or any part of the body that it contacts.

• Always place a shop towel or cloth around the fitting or connection prior to loosening to absorb any excess fuel due to spillage. Ensure that all fuel spillage (should it occur) is quickly removed from engine surfaces. Ensure that all fuel soaked cloths or towels are deposited into a suitable waste container.

• Always keep a dry chemical (Class B) fire extinguisher near the work area.

• Do not allow fuel spray or fuel vapors to come into contact with a spark or open flame.

• Always use a backup wrench when loosening and tightening fuel line connection fittings. This will prevent unnecessary stress and torsion to fuel line piping. Always follow the proper torque specifications.

• Always replace worn fuel fitting O-rings with new. Do not substitute fuel hose or equivalent where fuel pipe is installed.

Relieving Fuel System Pressure

1. Remove the luggage compartment floor and the panel over the fuel pump and unplug the connector for the leads to the pump.

2. Disconnect the delivery line from the fuel pump.

3. Open the glove compartment and the hinged cover for the fuse panel.

4. Remove fuses 14 and 22 and connect a jumper lead between the terminals and across switch 8393886 to provide power to the pump. Make sure the switch is OFF.

5. Start the pump by moving the switch to ON.

6. The pressure is released through the discharge outlet on the pump.

Fuel Filter

Removal and Installation

1. Disconnect the electrical connectors at the fuel pump. Remove the fuel pump fuse.

2. Crank the engine until fuel is exhausted from the system. Disconnect the negative battery cable.

3. Carefully remove the fuel filter fittings, using the proper wrench and covering it with a shop towel.

4. Remove the fuel filter assembly from the vehicle.

5. Installation is the reverse of the removal procedure. The filter is installed with arrows pointing in direction of flow.

Electric Fuel Pump

Pressure Testing

VOLTAGE CHECK

1. Remove the round cover plate from the top of the fuel pump.

2. Measure the voltage between the positive and negative terminals when the fuel pump is operating.

3. The lowest permissible voltage is 11.5 volts.

CAPACITY CHECK

NOTE: Be sure the fuel filter is not clogged and that the battery is fully charged.

1. Disconnect the return fuel pipe from the fuel distributor.

2. Connect the test pipe to the fuel distributor and place the other end in a suitable container.

3. On vehicles with the safety switch on the air flow sensor, remove the switch connector from the air flow sensor.

4. On vehicles with the fuel pump relay and the pulse sensor, remove the pump relay. Connect a jumper lead between terminals 30 and 87 on 900 series vehicles.

5. Switch on the ignition and allow the pump to run for 30 seconds. Measure the quantity of fuel. The proper specification should be 900cc/30 seconds. This should be measured in the return line.

Removal and Installation

NOTE: All vehicles are equipped with a plastic gas tank. Care should be exercised when removing the fuel pump from the plastic gas tank.

1. Disconnect the electrical connectors at the fuel pump. Remove the fuel pump fuse.

2. Crank the engine until fuel is exhausted from the system. Disconnect the negative battery cable.

3. Remove the rear floor panel in the luggage compartment. Remove the valve cover from above the fuel pump.

4. Disconnect the electrical connections from the fuel pump.

5. Carefully disconnect the fuel lines from the fuel pump. Be sure to use the proper wrench and cover it with a shop towel while removing the connections.

6. Remove the fuel pump mounting clamp. Lift the fuel pump from the tank assembly.

7. Installation is the reverse of the removal procedure.

Fuel Injection

For further information, please refer to "Chilton's Electronic Engine Control's Manual" for additional coverage.

Idle Speed and Mixture Adjustment

8 VALVE ENGINE

1. Run the engine until it reaches operating temperature.

2. Adjust the idle speed to 825–925 rpm.

3. If not equipped with a catalytic converter, remove the pulse/air hose and plug the air intake to the non-return valves. Connect the CO meter sensor to the exhaust pipe.

4. Remove the oxygen sensor wire.

5. If equipped with a catalytic converter, remove and plug the front exhaust pipe and connect the CO meter sensor to the pipe with the aid of a connecting piece. Remove the oxygen sensor wire.

6. Read and adjust the idle speed and CO valve as required. Before each reading, increase the engine speed and allow it to return to idle. Wait 30 seconds before taking the next CO reading.

7. Adjust the idle speed by turning the idle adjusting screw on the throttle valve housing.

8. Adjust the CO by turning the adjusting screw located on the fuel distributor clockwise for a richer mixture and counterclockwise for a leaner mixture. These adjustments affect each other, therefore these adjustments should be carried out in steps.

9. On catalyst equipped vehicles, connect the oxygen sensor wire and remove the CO meter probe from the front exhaust pipe connection. Install the plug in the front exhaust pipe. Insert the probe at the rear of the tailpipe. The CO meter reading should be less than 0.3 percent with the engine at idle, and the engine and converter at normal operating temperature.

16 VALVE ENGINE

1. Start the engine and allow it to run until it reaches normal operating temperature.

2. Connect a tachometer to the engine.

3. Ground the green/red lead of the single pole test socket on the right wheel housing to close the idling control valve. Use a jumper lead to do the grounding.

4. Set the idling speed to 775–825 rpm.

5. Disconnect the jumper lead from the test socket. Check that the engine speed changes and then settles down at 775–925 rpm.

6. CO value at simulated full load conditions should be 4.0–6.0 percent. Refer to underhood specifications label.

NOTE: Be careful not to confuse the connector for the throttle switch with that of the idling control valve, as this will destroy the electronic control unit!

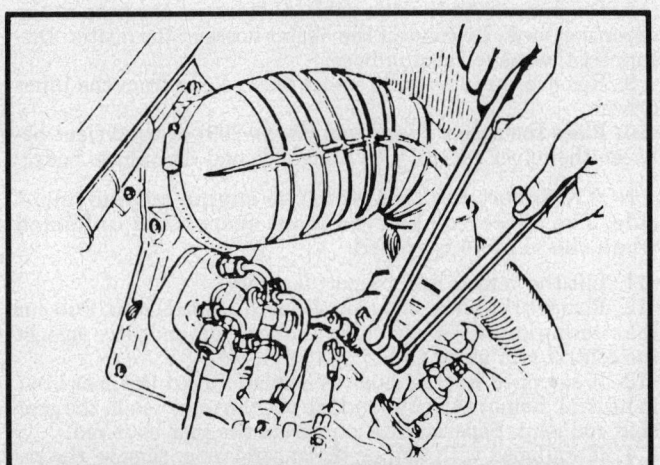

CIS Injection idle speed adjustment

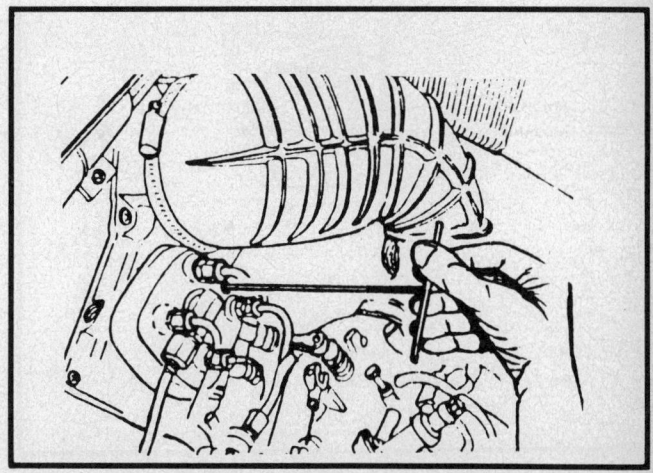

CIS Injection CO value adjustment

EMISSION CONTROLS

For further information, please refer to "Professional Emission Component Application Guide".

Emission Warning Lamps

Resetting

On all vehicles except the Turbo, the **EXH** maintenance light on the dash comes on every 30,000 miles. The oxygen sensor should be changed at this time. On the Turbo vehicles, the **EXH** maintenance light is not used and the oxygen sensor is replaced every 60,000 miles.

To reset the mileage counter for the **EXH** light, press the reset button on the counter unit. The unit is located at the flasher relay under the instrument panel.

ENGINE MECHANICAL

NOTE: Disconnecting the negative battery cable on some vehicles may interfere with the functions of the on board computer systems and may require the computer to undergo a relearning process, once the negative battery cable is reconnected.

Engine Assembly

Removal and Installation

900 SERIES

8 Valve Engine

NOTE: The engine and transmission should be removed as a unit.

1. Disconnect the negative battery cable. Drain the radiator.
2. Disconnect the windshield washer hose, unbolt the hood hinge links and remove the hood from the vehicle.

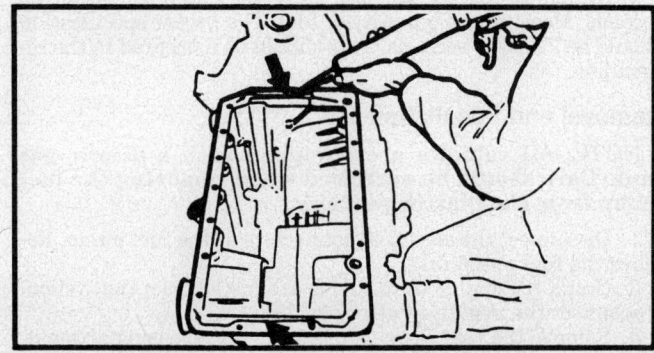

Sealer should only be applied to the grooves at each end of the steel engine-to-transaxle gasket

3. If equipped with power steering, disconnect the lines at the servo pump.
4. Disconnect the positive battery lead at the starter. Remove the radiator hoses. Remove the engine ground wire. Disconnect the temperature transmitter cable. Remove the coil.
5. Disconnect the cable harness from the clutch cover. If equipped with manual transmission, disconnect the hydraulic line from the clutch slave cylinder and plug the lines.
6. Disconnect the CI system electrical connections from the warm up regulator, thermo-time switch cold start valve and the auxiliary air valve. On catalytic converter equipped vehicles, also disconnect the oxygen sensor and the throttle switch cables.
7. Disconnect the oil pressure transmitter cable. Loosen the fuel line connections at the fuel distributor. Remove the air filter along with the mixture control unit.
8. Disconnect the throttle cable. Disconnect the hose at the expansion tank. Disconnect the heater hoses at the heater. Disconnect the brake vacuum hose.
9. Remove the clips and remove the bellows from the inner drivers.
10. Place the spacer (Saab tool 83–93–209) or equivalent between the upper control arm underside and the vehicle body.

NOTE: Insert the tool from the engine compartment side. The spacer makes the front suspension unloaded when the vehicle is raised.

11. Lift the vehicle and support it safely.
12. Remove the lower end piece from the control arm. Pull out the steering knuckle assembly and support the end piece against the control arm outer end.
13. If equipped with manual transmission, put the gear lever in neutral. Remove the nut and tap out the taper pin in the gear shift rod joint. Separate the joint from the gear shift rod.
14. If equipped with automatic transmission, remove the retaining screw from the gear selector cable at the transmission. Withdraw the cable with the gear selector rod in its extreme for-

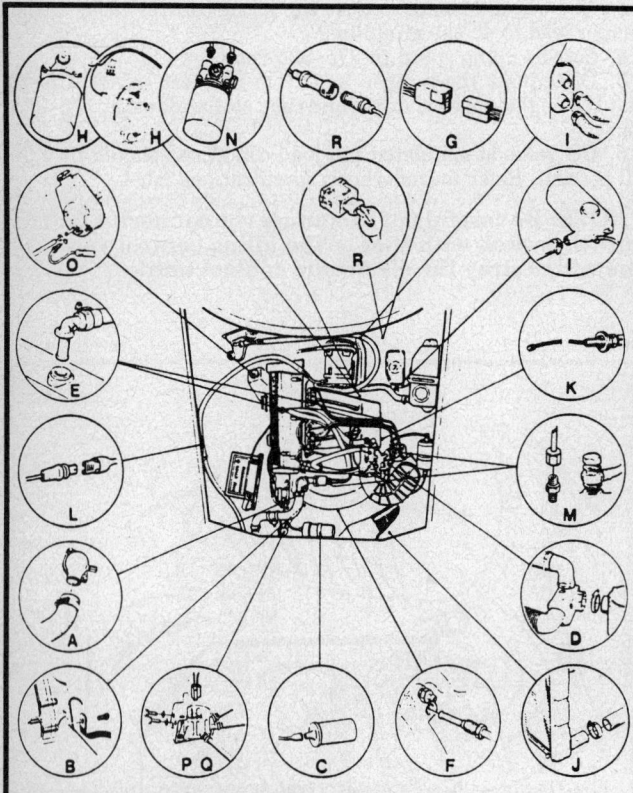

Disconnect these points before removing the engine—8 valve engines

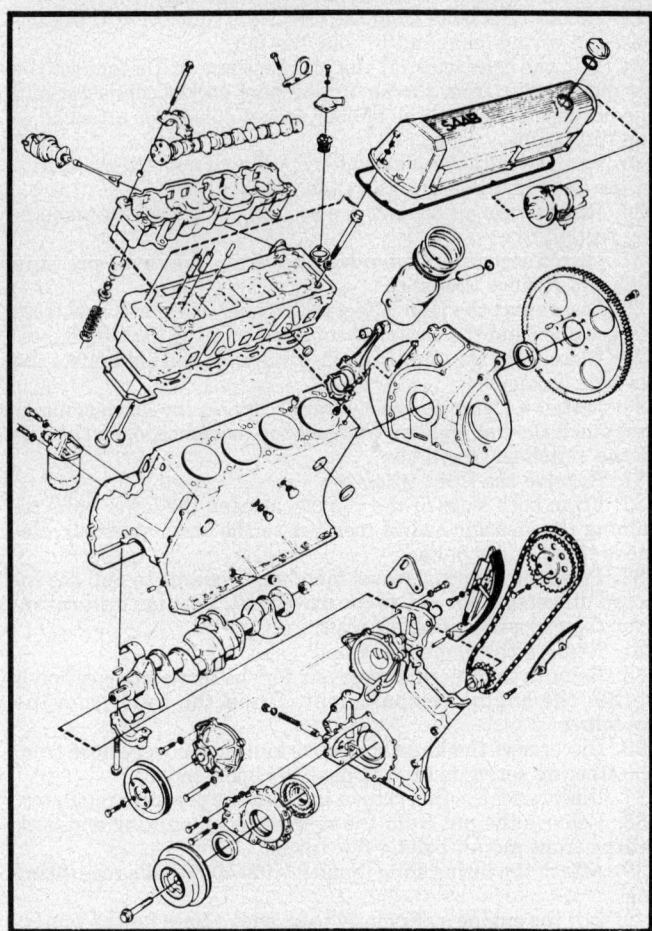

Eight valve engine and related components

ward position **P**. Slide back the spring loaded sleeve on the gear shift rod and unhook the end of the cable.

15. Separate the exhaust pipe from the exhaust manifold. Disconnect the speedometer cable from the transmission.

16. Remove the rear engine mounting bolts. Slacken the front engine mounting nut so the mounting can be lifted out of the bracket.

17. Attach the hoist to the 2 lugs on the engine and raise the assembly slightly. Move the assembly to one side and free the 2 U-joints.

18. Carefully remove the unit from the vehicle.

19. Installation is the reverse of removal. Upon installation properly seal the transaxle to engine assembly.

16 Valve Engine

NOTE: The engine and transaxle assembly are removed together.

1. Remove the hood, after scribing lines around the mounting bolt positions to aid later refitting.

2. Install Saab special tool 83–93–209 under the upper control arm on the right side.

3. Disconnect and remove the battery.

4. Drain the engine coolant.

5. Slacken the wheel nuts on the right front wheel.

6. Raise and safely support the vehicle.

7. Put the transmission selector into **R**.

8. Under the vehicle, remove the taper pin from the gearshift rod joint.

9. Disconnect the speedometer cable.

10. Remove the bolt securing the exhaust pipe to the clamp bracket on the transaxle.

11. Loosen the clips around the rubber boots on the CV-joints and slide the boots clear, this operation can also be done from above.

12. On the right side of the vehicle, remove the front wheel.

13. Separate the end piece from the lower control arm.

14. Separate the universal joint and position the knuckle in front of the driver. Support the end piece against the outer end of the control arm.

15. Disconnect the positive lead from the battery and free it from the clips holding it to the body. Disconnect the ground cable from the transaxle.

16. Disconnect the starter motor leads.

17. Unbolt the exhaust pipe from the exhaust manifold.

18. Disconnect the pressure pipe from the steering servo pump and have a plug handy to prevent oil escaping from the pipe. Take care not to drip oil onto the engine mounting and control arm rubbers.

19. From the left side of the vehicle, disconnect the cooling system hoses at the following connections, the heat exchanger valve, the expansion tank, the bottom of the radiator and the thermostat housing.

20. Disconnect the left fuel injection system cable harness as follows, at the air mass meter sensor, at the throttle switch, at the A.I.C. actuator, at the injectors, at the the NTC resistor (thermostatic switch) and at the ground points on the front lifting lug. Use the proper tool to release the tension in the springs on the terminal blocks.

21. Disconnect the block and plug connector (ground lead). Disconnect the lead at the alternator and the green/white cable to the positive terminal on the regulator. Disconnect the ground (black) cable. Disconnect the black cable from the oil pressure switch. Disconnect the cable for the A.I.C. actuator. Disconnect the yellow/white cable from the temperature transmitter. Disconnect the gray cable from the knock detector. Release the cable harness from the clip on the fuel injection manifold, from the rear of the engine and from the coolant hose between the engine and the expansion tank.

22. Withdraw the loose cables and guide the harness unit out of the engine compartment. Place it on top of the power distribution unit.

23. Remove the adjusting bolt in the alternator bracket, remove the drive belts and lift off the alternator.

24. Disconnect the brake servo hose from the intake manifold. Disconnect the throttle cable and sheath.

25. Remove the air conditioner compressor and bracket from the block. Place them on the filter housing for the heater system. Secure the alternator so it will not drop or become damaged.

26. Disconnect the fuel lines at their connections at the front of the fuel injection manifold and on the fuel pressure regulator.

27. Remove the coil.

28. Disconnect the turbo pressure line from the turbo compressor and the intercooler/throttle housing.

29. Remove the auxiliary fan.

30. Remove the air mass meter together with the suction pipe for the turbo unit. Disconnect the hoses at the solenoid valve and the crankcase ventilation at the suction pipe.

31. Disconnect the cables from the Hall transmitter and coil in the distributor. Free the Hall transmitter cable from the clips on the clutch cover.

32. Disconnect the solenoid valve hoses from the connections on the turbo unit and charging pressure regulator.

33. Disconnect the hydraulic hose from the clutch slave cylinder. Plug the hose to stop fluid from escaping.

34. Remove the engine mounting bolts.

35. Attach suitable lifting equipment to the engine lifting hooks. Raise the engine until the left, inner CV-joint can be separated.

36. Raise the engine to enable the hoses on the oil cooler to be disconnected.

37. Disconnect the hose to the power steering pump and drain the oil in the system.

NOTE: When lifting the engine out of the vehicle, keep it close to the fire wall to prevent the radiator and solenoid valve from being damaged by the front engine mounting.

38. Before installation, check that the inner CV-joint boots are packed with the correct grease.

39. Suspend the engine from the lifting gear. Adjust the lifting gear so the front engine mounting is slightly lower than the rear mounting.

40. Lower the engine into the engine compartment until the hoses to the oil cooler and servo pump can be connected.

41. Guide the engine into position, attending to the following items in order, the front engine mounting, left inner CV-joint and right inner CV-joint. Lower the engine until it rests on the rear engine mountings and install the mounting bolts. Unhook the lifting gear and unbolt the lifting lug from the water pump.

42. Reverse the remaining removal steps for installation.

9000 SERIES

NOTE: The engine and transaxle assembly are removed together.

1. Raise the vehicle and support it safely.
2. Drain the cooling system. Remove the battery.
3. Remove the thru-bolt for the expansion tank, disconnect the tank from the suction and remove the overflow hoses from the radiator.
4. Disconnect the upper radiator hose.
5. Loosen the drive belt for the compressor by loosening the locknut, and loosening the adjusting nut under the locknut.
6. Disconnect the upper connection on the oil cooler, loosen the pipe clip on the radiator and slide the pipe down behind the radiator.
7. Unplug the connector to the electromagnetic clutch on the compressor and loosen the compressor mounting complete with the belt tensioner.
8. Place a protective cloth over the radiator member and rest the compressor on the radiator member. Secure the compressor to the radiator member.
9. Remove the turbo pressure pipe, situated between the turbo unit and the intercooler.
10. Disconnect the Lambda probe connector leads and disconnect them from the clips.
11. From the engine compartment, unbolt the flange joint between the exhaust pipe and the exhaust manifold. Push the exhaust pipe to one side and unhook the rubber hangers from the exhaust system. Disconnect the bottom coolant hose from the water pump.
12. From under the vehicle, remove the bottom retaining bolt for the radiator fan.
13. Disconnect the speedometer drive from the gearbox.
14. Select the 4th gear and separate the rubber joint in the gear selector linkage.
15. Remove the clips on the rubber gaiters over the inboard universal joints and slide the gaiters off the drive axles.
16. Disconnect the electrical leads from the alternator and the starter motor. Unplug the connector for the oil pressure switch.
17. Remove the clips and remove the top radiator hose.
18. Disconnect the top radiator at the cylinder head.
19. Unscrew the junction block from the battery shelf. Remove the clamp for the fuel filter.
20. Remove the battery shelf from the compartment.
21. Disconnect the high tension lead from the ignition coil at the distributor cap.
22. Remove the solenoid valve from the bracket on the radiator and unplug the electrical connections.

23. Remove the bolts from the top of the radiator fan. Disconnect the wiring loam and lift out the fan.

24. Pull the connector off the air mass meter. Disconnect the air mass meter from the air intake duct socket connector and the air cleaner. Leave the rubber socket connector attached to the turbo unit.

25. Remove the air intake duct by pulling it out of the aperture in the wing and twisting the ends inwards.

26. Remove the air cleaner top section first, then the remaining section.

27. Disconnect the relief valve hose from the turbo pressure pipe and remove the pipe.

28. Disconnect the Hall Effect transducer, the earth lead from the gear box and the electrical connector for the back-up lights.

29. Disconnect the end of the throttle cable and disconnect the throttle linkage.

30. Install a clamp to the hydraulic line to the slave cylinder and pinch the line tightly. With proper wrenches, open the line to the clutch slave cylinder.

31. Remove the front wheels.

32. From both sides of the vehicle, slacken the lower bolts retaining the steering swivel member to the strut assembly. Remove the 2 upper bolts.

33. Pivot the steering swivel member outwards to pull the inboard universal joint out of the driveshaft. Position dust covers over the exposed driveshaft cups.

34. Remove the engine stay bolt.

35. Remove the steering reservoir for the servo and position it within the engine compartment. Drain the fluid from the container.

36. Disconnect the large bore hose and the delivery hose from the steering servo pump and plug the open ends.

37. Disconnect the fuel return lie from the pressure regulator.

38. Remove the nut from the rear engine mounting and back off the front mount bolts a few turns.

39. Attach the lifting sling (Saab 83–92–409) to the rear lifting lug.

40. Lift the engine sufficiently to provide access for the removal of the components located between the engine and the fire wall.

41. Disconnect the vacuum hoses from the inlet manifold.

42. Remove the coolant hoses running between the heat exchanger and the water pump pipe.

43. Separate the coupling between the fuel pipe and the fuel injection manifold. Do not allow the fuel to spill or collect.

44. Cut the clips securing the wiring looms to the oil pipe, water pipe, inlet manifold steady bar and the oil supply pipe.

45. Unclip the wiring loom to the fuel injection manifold.

46. Disconnect the grounding connections and the electrical connectors from the wiring harness.

47. Unbolt the air cooled oil cooler and place it on top of the engine. The 2 lower bolts need only be loosened.

48. Carefully remove the engine from the vehicle, taking care not to damage the radiator.

49. Installation is the reverse of the removal procedure. Fill the engine with coolant, oil and power steering fluid. Test engine operation.

Cylinder Head

Removal and Installation

900 SERIES

8 Valve Engine

1. Disconnect the negative battery cable. Drain the radiator.
2. Remove the rubber bellows from between the air flow sensor and the throttle valve housing and disconnect the throttle cable from the throttle valve housing.
3. Disconnect the cable from the temperature transmitter.

Remove the vacuum hose of the power brake booster from the intake manifold.

4. Disconnect the fuel lines from the fuel distributor to the injection valves. Tape the ends of the lines to prevent dirt from entering the system. Remove the bracket from the throttle valve housing mounting.

5. Remove the hose clamps at the connections to the thermostat housing, water pump and intake manifold.

6. Unbolt the exhaust pipe from the exhaust manifold.

7. Remove the distributor cap and ignition wires. Rotate the engine until cylinders No. 1 and No. 4 are at TDC. This must be done due to the design of the distributor driving dog which only allows the valve cover/distributor assembly to be removed with the engine in this position. Remove the valve cover.

8. Remove the camshaft sprocket bolts. Keep the chain on the sprocket and place sprocket/chain assembly between chain guide and tensioner. A center bolt is not used on the sprocket.

9. Remove the 2 bolts from the timing cover under the front of the head.

10. Remove the cylinder head bolts.

11. Raise the vehicle and support it safely. Place a support under the rear end of the engine. Remove the engine mounting bolt in the cylinder head.

12. Remove the screws in the transmission cover. Remove the cylinder head from the vehicle.

13. Installation is the reverse of the removal procedure. Be sure to use a new cylinder head gasket. Torque the bolts first to 44 ft. lbs. and then to 70 ft. lbs.

14. Make sure the markings on the camshaft and the bearing cap are aligned with one another.

15. Check that the flywheel mark is in line with the mark on the cylinder block and that the engine is set on No. 1 cylinder.

16. Install the 2 screws in the timing cover on the front of the cylinder head. Install the timing chain and sprocket as follows. Remove the tension from the chain tensioner with special tool 83-93-357 or equivalent. Hook the tool into the catch of the tensioner and pull upwards. Place the timing sprocket on the camshaft so the mark on the sprocket and the screw holes coincide. If necessary, move the chain to position. Install the 3 retaining bolts in the sprocket and camshaft. If the distributor is mounted to the valve cover, the rotor should be facing the line on the edge of the distributor housing.

Alignment of cam gear to camshaft

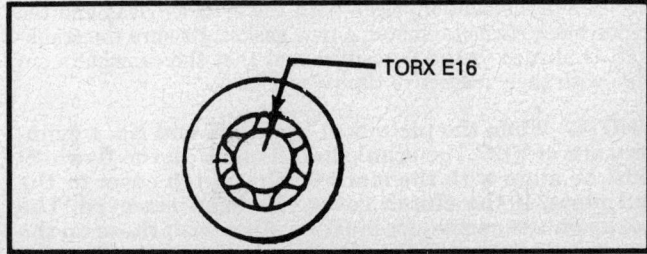
Top view of Torx head cylinder head bolts

Alignment of marks on camshaft bearing caps

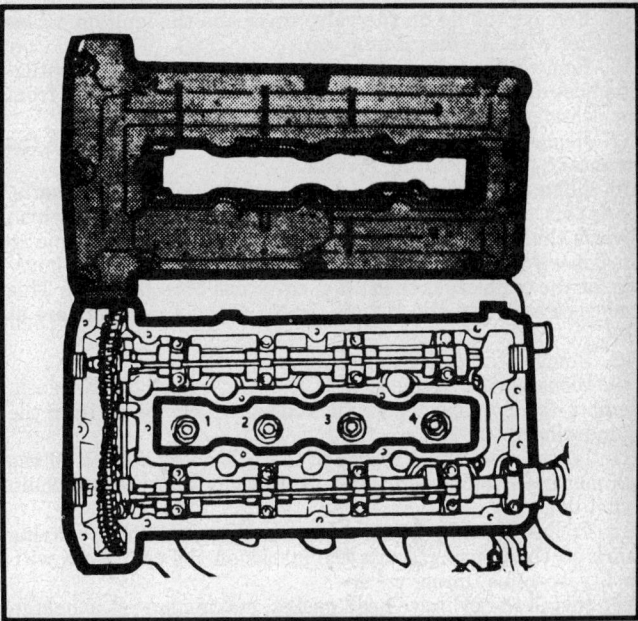
Top view of 16 valve cylinder head

16 Valve Engine

1. Remove the hood after scribing reference marks next to the mounting bolts, to aid later installation.
2. Remove the battery.
3. Drain the coolant from the radiator and cylinder block.
4. Remove the exhaust manifold and turbo unit.
5. Remove the tensioning pulley and drive belt for the air conditioner compressor.
6. Slacken the securing bolts for the steering pump bracket, remove the drive belt and push the pump aside.
7. Undo the wiring harness clips on the cylinder head.
8. Remove the 2 bolts in the timing cover, which are screwed into the cylinder head from underneath.
9. Remove the bolts in the right-hand engine mounting which are screwed into the cylinder head, together with the spacer sleeves.
10. Disconnect the hose between the thermostat housing and the radiator at the thermostat housing.
11. Remove the fuel pressure regulator and disconnect the ground leads for the fuel injection system.
12. Remove the AIC actuator. Remove the bracket for the air conditioning compressor from the cylinder head.
13. Remove the intake manifold complete with injectors and injection manifold.
14. Disconnect the lead from the temperature transmitter.

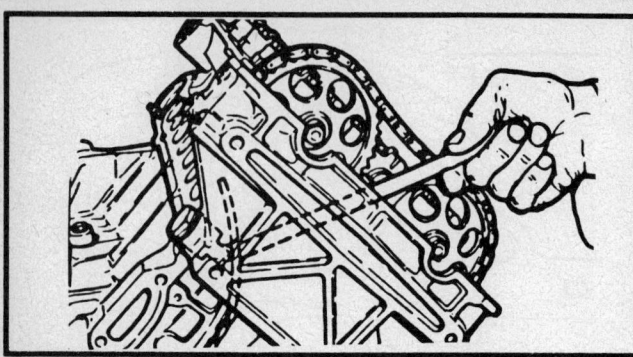

Releasing chain tensioner — 16 valve engine

15. Remove the lid on the valve cover and the ignition cables together with the distributor cap.

16. Remove the valve cover. Disconnect the crankcase ventilation hose and remove the semi-circular rubber plug halves from the cylinder head.

17. Remove the air conditioning compressor and put it on the air intake for the heating system.

18. Align the timing marks on the crankshaft and camshafts. To do this, remove the cover on the transaxle bell housing which reveals the timing marks on the flywheel. Turn the engine so the **0** mark on the flywheel is aligned with the mark on the housing, or the endplate if the clutch cover has been removed. This makes certain that the pistons for No. 1 and 4 cylinders are at TDC.

19. Remove the cam chain tensioner.

20. Block up the engine to lift the cylinder head off the block. Remove the cylinder head bolts and siphon off the oil from the cylinder head.

21. Install a guide pin in one of the bolt holes and lift off the cylinder head, making sure the pivoting guide for the cam chain is not damaged.

22. To install, align the **0** mark on the flywheel with the timing mark on the housing. Align the marks on the camshafts with their respective timing marks.

23. Install the cylinder head gasket, making sure it is held in position by the guide sleeves in the cylinder head flange.

24. Install the guide pin (Saab special tool 83–92–128 or equivalent) and position the timing chain and pivoting guide.

25. Carefully install the cylinder head. Use the guide pin as a pivot for the head, which must be turned slightly to enable it to pass the pivoting guide. Thereafter, alignment will be determined by the guide sleeves.

26. Install the cylinder head bolts and tighten them in 3 stages. Stage 1, torque to 45 ft. lbs. evenly. Stage 2, torque to 63 ft. lbs. evenly. Stage 3, another 90 degrees (¼ turn). Retighten the bolts after the engine has reached normal operating temperature. Remember to install the 2 M8 sized bolts in the underside of the cylinder head.

27. Install the camshaft sprockets, fitting the sprocket for the exhaust cam first. Make sure the chain between the crankshaft sprocket and the camshaft sprocket is kept tight. Next install the intake cam sprocket. Keep the chain tight between the sprockets.

28. Lightly tighten the center bolts securing the camshaft sprockets. Adjust the chain tensioner and install it under tension. Tighten the bolt.

29. Release the tensioner by pressing the pivoting guide firmly against it. Thereafter, press the pivoting guide against the chain to put a basic tension on the chain.

30. Depress the pivoting guide to check that the tensioner is working. Rotate the crankshaft 2 complete turns clockwise, viewed from the transmission end. Check that the earlier settings of the crankshaft and camshaft timings have not changed. Tighten the cam sprocket bolts to 49 ft. lbs.

31. Continue the installation in the reverse order of the removal procedure.

9000 SERIES

1. Disconnect the negative battery cable. Raise and support the vehicle safely.

2. Remove the right front wheel assembly and the inner fender panel.

3. Drain the coolant. Remove the radiator expansion tank. Disconnect the steering servo reservoir and set aside. Leave the hoses attached.

4. Loosen the compressor drive belt and remove the belt.

5. Disconnect the electrical leads from the air compressor.

6. Unbolt the compressor from its mounting bracket. Disconnect the top pipe connecting on the air cooled oil cooler and push the pipe to one side. Rest the compressor on the radiator crossmember. Unbolt the compressor mounting bracket and remove it.

7. Unbolt the front exhaust pipe flange and unhook the rubber hangers.

8. Remove the steady bar for the turbo unit and the oil return pipe.

9. Disconnect the hose from the intercooler at the turbo unit. Disconnect the oil supply pipe from the turbo.

10. Disconnect the hose between the air mass meter and the turbo unit. Disconnect the coolant hose from the thermostat housing and the hose from the cylinder head.

11. Disconnect the oil supply hose or pipe so as not to obstruct the removal of the exhaust manifold. If necessary, remove the clip holding the pipe to the cylinder head and slave cylinder.

12. Unbolt and lift off the exhaust manifold complete with the turbo unit, pushing the oil supply pipe aside at the same time.

13. Disconnect the lead to the temperature transducer.

14. Remove the engine stay bracket from its attachment point on the wing.

15. Remove and remove the bolt securing the engine stay bracket to the cylinder head. Remove the intake manifold from the cylinder head.

16. Disconnect the breather hose for the crankcase ventilation from the camshaft cover.

17. Disconnect the vacuum hose and the Hall Effect transducer lead from the distributor and remove the distributor cap complete with the high tension leads.

18. Unscrew and remove the spark plug inspection plate and the clips for the high tension leads.

19. Remove the camshaft cover.

20. Align the crankshaft with the **0** timing mark and check that the camshaft timing marks also coincide. Remove the camshaft sprockets.

21. Remove the camshaft tensioner. Remove the 2 cylinder head bolts adjacent to the timing cover, which is accessible from below.

22. Disconnect the starter motor lead from the clip on the thermostat housing.

23. Remove the Torx® type cylinder head bolts.

24. Install a guide pin in the drilled hole in the right top corner of the cylinder head. Make sure the timing chain is positioned such that the pivoting chain guide will not obstruct the cylinder head and carefully lift the cylinder head from the engine block.

25. Before installation, clean both the cylinder head and the engine block surfaces. Install a new gasket. Be sure the crankshaft is aligned in the **0** position and that the camshafts are align with their respective timing marks.

NOTE: When the pistons of the No. 1 and No. 4 cylinders are at TDC, the crankshaft 0 mark on the flywheel must be align with the mark on the clutch cover or the end plate, if the clutch cover has been removed. The marks on the camshafts must be align with those on the cam bearing caps. This indicates the exhaust valves for No. 1 and No. 4 cylinders are closed.

26. Install a guide pin in the drilled hole in the top of the right corner of the cylinder head and lower the cylinder head carefully into position on the engine block. Locate the cylinder head on the guide sleeves.

27. Install the cylinder head bolts, tightening them in the correct sequence to the specified torque.

Stage 1–Torque to 44 ft. lbs.
Stage 2–Torque to 67 ft. lbs.
Stage 3–Run the engine to normal operating temperature and allow the engine to cool for 30 minutes.
Stage 4–Slacken the bolts and retighten each bolt to 66 ft. lbs.
Stage 5–Tighten by turning the bolts through a further 90 degrees (¼ turn).

28. Position the inlet valve camshaft sprocket, followed by the exhaust valve camshaft sprocket. Be sure the chain is correctly positioned between the guides. Tighten the sprocket center bolts to 48 ft. lbs.

29. Install the timing chain tensioner. Advance the tensioner before installing it. Release the tensioner and rotate the crankshaft 2 revolutions. Make sure the camshaft and flywheel timing marks are correctly aligned.

30. Install the both halves of the split seal and the camshaft cover. Install the bolt at the distributor end and the middle bolt at the other end first. Tighten the bolts to 16 ft. lbs.

31. Check that the timing marks for the distributor rotor are aligned, Install the distributor cap and connect the lead for the Hall Effect transducer. Connect all vacuum hoses.

32. Connect the high tension leads to the spark plugs. Secure the leads in the clips. Install the inspection plate and tighten the retaining screws.

33. Install the clip securing the starter motor lead to the thermostat housing.

34. Install a new gasket on the inlet manifold and install the manifold in place. Install the top securing bolts first and then install the lower bolts, using an extension bar.

35. Install the bolt for the engine stay bracket to the cylinder head and position the stay bracket in place. Install a new gasket onto the exhaust manifold and position the exhaust manifold to the cylinder head.

36. Install the oil supply pipe. Install the clip and the slave cylinder bolt. Install the oil return line and the steady bar for the turbo unit.

37. Connect the hose between the turbo unit and the intercooler. Connect the cooler hose to the thermostat housing and the hose to the cylinder head.

38. Install the air mass meter socket connector into the turbo unit and tighten the clip. Connect the hose between the intercooler and the turbo unit.

39. Install and tighten the nuts securing the front section of the exhaust pipe to the turbo compressor. Bolt the air conditioing compressor mounting bracket onto the cylinder head and engine block.

40. Install the air conditioning compressor. Leave the coolant hose in the bracket when installing the compressor.

41. Connect the electrical leads and make sure the lead is clear of the compressor pulley. Install the steering servo reservoir. Install the coolant expansion tank and tighten the hose clip.

42. Connect the top pipe to the air cooled oil cooler and secure the cooler to the radiator. Install the overflow line between the expansion tank and the radiator.

43. Install the compressor belt, adjust the tension and tighten the belt tensioner bolt. Install the inner right wheel arch, and install the wheel.

44. Lower the vehicle and tighten the wheel. Connect the negative battery cable and fill the cooling system with coolant. Start the engine and test the engine operation.

Valve Lash

Adjustment

All vehicles equipped with a turbocharged engine require no normal valve adjustment as they are equipped with hydraulic tappets.

1. Remove the valve cover. The pistons of cylinders No's 1 and 4 must be at TDC before distributor and valve cover can be removed.

2. Using an special Saab tool 8392185 or equivalent, rotate the crankshaft as necessary to position the high point of the camshaft lobe 180 degrees away from the valve depressor face, base circle of the cam lobe must contact the valve depressor, on the valve which the clearance is to be checked.

NOTE: The special crankshaft turning wrench fits the center screw of the crankshaft belt pulley at the dash panel.

3. Check the maximum and minimum clearances using a feeler gauge. The minimum feeler gauge should slip in, but the maximum feeler gauge should not.

4. Measure and record the clearance of all the valves in the same manner. Adjust the clearance of any valves that are not within specification.

5. To adjust the valves, remove the camshaft, tappets and adjusting pallets (shims) of any valves that need to be adjusted.

6. Using a micrometer, measure and record the thickness of the pallet (shim). This thickness plus the valve clearance adds up to the total distance between the valve and the cam.

7. The choice of the adjusting pallet (shim) is determined by the measured total distance between the valve depressor (tappet) and the cam, less the specified valve clearance for an intake or exhaust valve as the case may be.

8. Insert the new adjusting pallet (shim) an the valve depressor (tappet) and reinstall the camshaft.

9. Repeat the measurement procedure to insure that the clearances are correct.

10. Install the valve cover using a new valve cover gasket.

Intake Manifold

Removal and Installation
8 VALVE ENGINE

1. Disconnect the negative battey cable. Disconnect all hoses, wires and connectors that would inhibit the intake manifold from being removed.

2. It may be necessary to remove the distributor cap and the ignition wires to gain clearance. Remove the throttle valve housing.

3. Remove the intake manifold retaining bolts. Remove the intake manifold from the engine.

4. Installation is the reverse of the removal procedure. Be sure the proper gasket is used. A coolant leakage could occur if the wrong one is used.

16 VALVE ENGINE

1. Disconnect the negative battery cable. Disconnect all hoses, wires and connectors that would inhibit the intake manifold being removed.

2. Remove the turbo pressure pipe, the lubricating oil pressure pipe and the return oil pipe.

3. Remove the intake manifold retaining bolts. Remove the intake manifold along with the injection manifold, injectors and the AIC regulator.

4. Installation is the reverse of the removal procedure. Be sure the proper gasket is used. A coolant leak could occur if the wrong one is used.

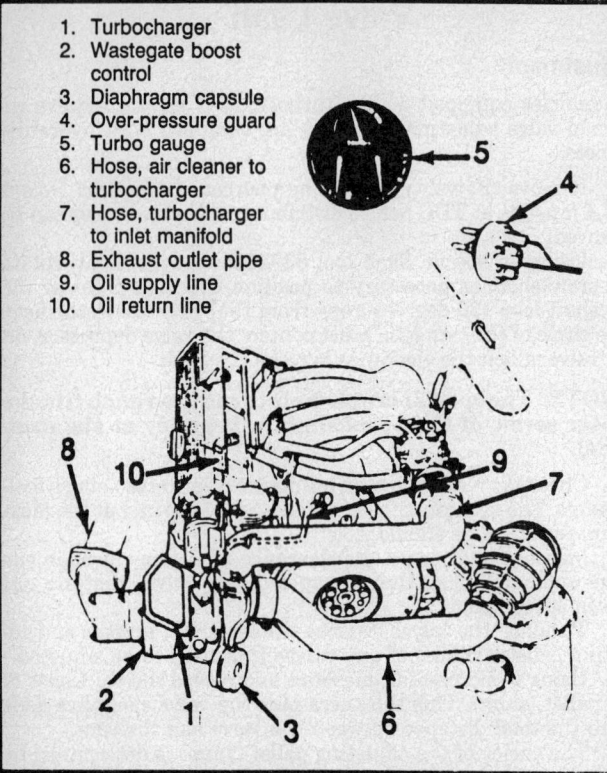

1. Turbocharger
2. Wastegate boost control
3. Diaphragm capsule
4. Over-pressure guard
5. Turbo gauge
6. Hose, air cleaner to turbocharger
7. Hose, turbocharger to inlet manifold
8. Exhaust outlet pipe
9. Oil supply line
10. Oil return line

8 valve engine turbocharger assembly

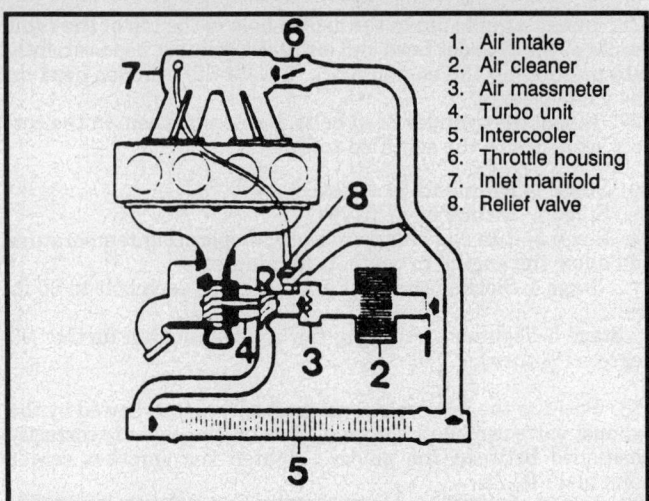

1. Air intake
2. Air cleaner
3. Air massmeter
4. Turbo unit
5. Intercooler
6. Throttle housing
7. Inlet manifold
8. Relief valve

16 valve engine turbocharger assembly

Exhaust Manifold

Removal and Installation

1. Disconnect the negative battery cable. Disconnect all necessary hoses, wires, and connectors that would inhibit the exhaust manifold from being removed.
2. Unbolt the exhaust pipe at the connecting flange.
3. If equipped with a heat shield, remove it.
4. Remove the exhaust manifold bolts. Remove the exhaust manifold from the vehicle.
5. Installation is the reverse of removal.

Turbocharger

Removal and Installation

900 SERIES

1. Disconnect the negative battery cable. Remove the charge pressure regulator and block off the exhaust pipe. Remove the battery as required. Remove the tension on compressor belt.
2. Disconnect the hose between the compressor and the throttle housing.
3. Disconnect the oil supply line and the oil return line at the turbo unit.
4. Remove the retaining bolts securing the turbo to the exhaust manifold. Remove the turbo unit from the vehicle. Plug the holes in the turbo unit to prevent dirt from entering.
5. Installation is the reverse of the removal procedure.
6. Fill the lubricating inflow of the turbo unit with engine oil before connecting the oil return line at the turbo.
7. Crank the engine for about 30 seconds with terminal 15 on the ignition coil disconnected. This will fill the lubricating system of the turbo before the engine is started.

9000 SERIES

1. Disconnect the negative battery cable. Release the tension on the compressor belt by slackening the belt tensioner.
2. Disconnect the top pipe coupling on the air cooled oil cooler and disconnect the clips securing the pipe to the radiator.
3. Remove the compressor mounting bolts. Insert a sheet of metal to protect the oil cooler and lift the compressor towards the expansion tank.
4. Remove the solenoid valve from its mounting on the radiator and disconnect the electrical leads.
5. Disconnect the electrical leads at the radiator fan. Unbolt and remove the fan.
6. Unplug the electrical connectors for the air mass meter. Disconnect the toggle fasteners securing the air mass meter to the air cleaner cover and pull the rubber socket connector off the turbo unit.
7. Disconnect the turbo pressure pipe from the compressor.
8. Remove the oil pipe to the turbo unit. Unbolt the clutch slave cylinder and remove the clip securing the oil pipe to the cylinder head. Disconnect the oil pipe banjo coupling from the block and undo the clip on the inlet manifold.
9. Disconnect the exhaust pipe from the turbo compressor.
10. Disconnect the front rubber hangers for the exhaust pipe.
11. Remove the steady bar bracket between the sump and the compressor. Remove the securing bolts and loosen the oil return lines. Cap the aperture to prevent washers or nuts from the exhaust manifold dropping inside during the removal.
12. Remove the nuts securing the exhaust manifold to the cylinder head.
13. Lift the exhaust manifold from the cylinder head, along with the turbo unit.
14. Should further disassembly be necessary, complete as required.
15. To install, position the turbo unit to the exhaust manifold and tighten the retaining nuts. Install the new locknuts with the locking flange turned inwards.
16. Install a new gasket over the studs for the exhaust manifold and install the manifold/turbo unit to the cylinder head assembly. Tighten the nuts to 30 ft. lbs.
17. Install the clip holding the turbo oil supply pipe to the inlet manifold. Connect and tighten the banjo coupling to the engine block. Make sure the copper washers are in good condition. Secure the pipe to the turbo unit.
18. Install the return oil pipe and the steady bar bracket between the turbo unit and the crankcase. Connect the rubber hangers for the front exhaust hanger.

19. Bolt the exhaust pipe to the turbo compressor. Use new locking nuts with the locking flanges turned outward. Tighten to 19 ft. lbs.

20. Install the turbo pressure pipe to the compressor and assemble the air mass meter and rubber socket connector between the air cleaner body and the inlet side of the turbo compressor.

21. Assemble the fan and solenoid valve, securing the electrical leads into their clips. Connect the return hose to the solenoid valve. Insert a piece of metal to protect the oil cooler and install the air conditioning compressor.

22. Reconnect the oil pipe to the oil cooler and secure the pipe clip to the radiator. Install the compressor belt and tighten it to specification.

Timing Chain Front Cover

Removal and Installation

1. Disconnect the negative battery cable.
2. Drain the engine oil and the coolant.
3. Remove the camshaft cover retaining bolts and lift off the cover.
4. Remove the bracket for the steering servo pump, complete with the pump and alternator.
5. Remove the chain tensioner.
6. Secure the flywheel and loosen the crankshaft pulley nut and remove the pulley.
7. Remove the belt tensioner and the water pump pipe.
8. Remove the oil pipes and the water pump pulley.
9. Remove the oil pump.
10. Remove the bolts and lift off the timing cover.
11. Install in the reverse order of removal.

Front Cover Oil Seal

Replacement

8 VALVE ENGINE

1. Disconnect the negative battery cable. Remove the alternator belt. If equipped with power steering or air conditioning, remove the required belts.
2. Remove the clutch cover (torque converter cover) and lock the crankshaft using Saab tool 83–92–987 or equivalent by locking the tool to the ring gear.
3. From under the vehicle, remove the pulley retaining bolt using Saab tool 83–92–961 or equivalent. Remove the pulley from the vehicle.
4. Pull off the old seal ring using a suitable tool.
5. Installation is the reverse of removal. Torque the retaining bolt to 137 ft. lbs.

16 VALVE ENGINE

1. Disconnect the negative battery cable. Raise and support the vehicle safely.
2. Remove the right front wheel and tire assembly. remove the inner front fender panel.
3. Loosen and remove the drive belts.
4. Remove the retaining bolt for the crankshaft pulley.
5. Remove the crankshaft pulley.
6. Using a prybar, carefully remove the oil seal without marring the crankshaft stub end.
7. Install a new, oiled seal, using an appropriate seal installer.
8. Install the pulley and tighten the retaining bolt to 134 ft. lbs. (180 Nm).
9. Tighten the drive belts, using a belt tension gauge. (New belt–180 lbs.; Used belt–120 lbs.)
10. Install the forward section of the inner fender panel.
11. Replace the front wheel and lower the vehicle.

Timing Chain and Sprockets

Removal and Installation

8 VALVE ENGINE

1. Disconnect the negative battery cable. Remove the engine from the vehicle.
2. Remove the distributor cap and ignition wires. Rotate the engine until cylinders No. 1 and No. 4 are at TDC. This must be done due to the design of the distributor driving dog which only allows the valve cover/distributor assembly to be removed with the engine in this position.
3. Remove the valve cover assembly. Remove the sprocket from the camshaft and rest it on the chain tensioner and the chain guide.
4. Remove the cylinder head. Remove the crankshaft pulley and oil pump assembly. Remove the water pump and pulley assembly.
5. Remove the timing chain cover. Remove the timing chain and chain wheel from the engine. Remove the chain tensioner, if required.

NOTE: Engines beginning with engine No. E57340, are equipped with a new cam chain tensioner that requires a different release procedure. The new tensioner is also a direct replacement for the old style unit and

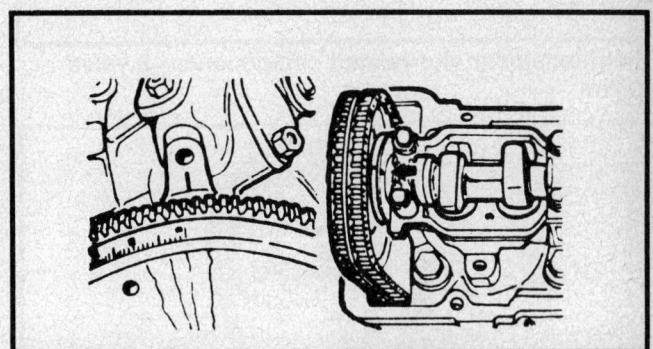

Timing mark location–8 valve engine

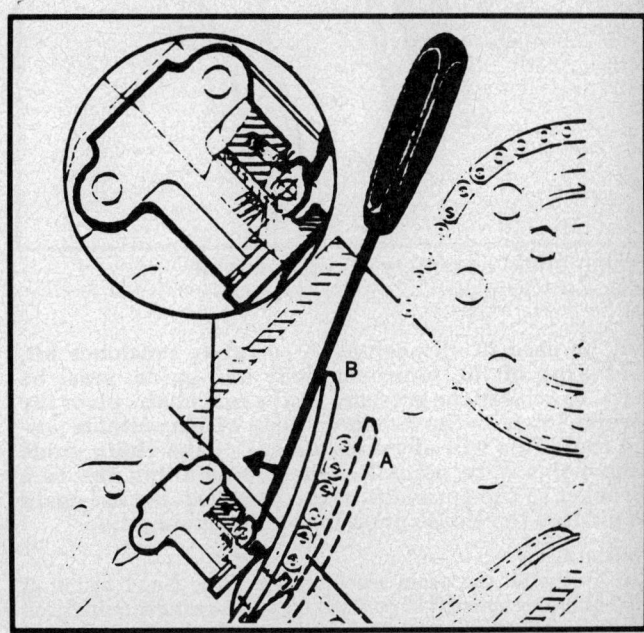

Releasing cam chain tensioner–8 valve engine

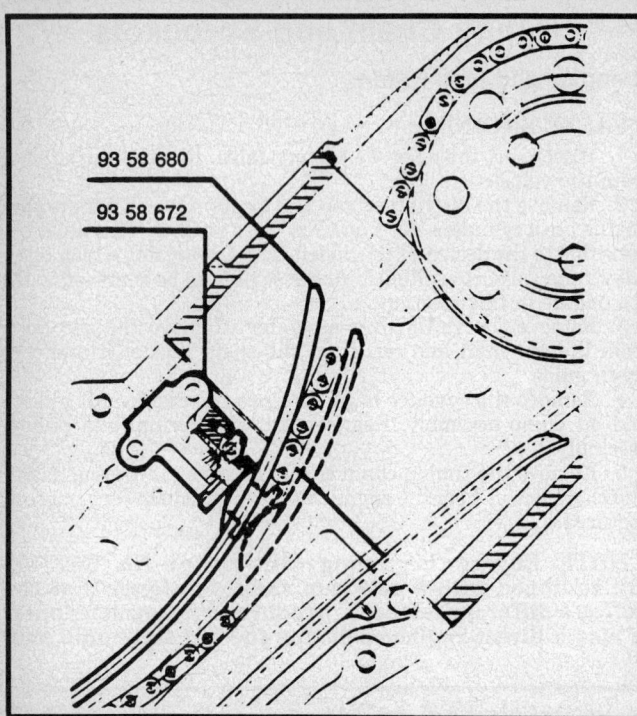

93 58 680

93 58 672

Chain tensioner and related components—8 valve engine

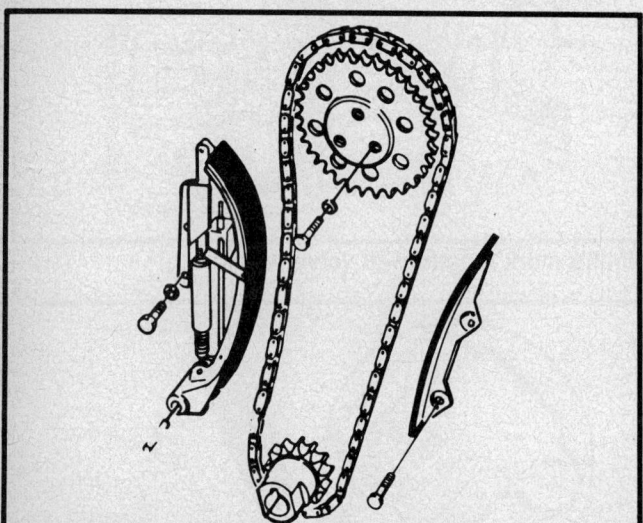

Timing chain assembly—8 valve engine

may be used in all engines. A complete tensioner kit, consisting of the tensioner body and guide, must be used. To release the pressure on the cam chain, pivot the reverse latch on the tensioner body with a suitable prying tool. This will allow movement of the chain guide from point A to point B. When reinstalling the cam sprocket to the camshaft, the reverse latch must again be pivoted to release pressure on the chain guide.

To install:

6. To install the chain assembly, have the No. 1 piston at TDC and the camshaft in position for No. 1 cylinder firing position to be in its firing mode, before the cylinder head is installed.

7. Do not rotate either the camshaft or the crankshaft with-

out the chain in place. Damage to the valves or pistons can occur, after the cylinder head is installed.

8. Replace the chain tensioner, if removed.

9. Place the camshaft sprocket to the chain and suspend it from the crankshaft sprocket. Position the chain between the chain guide and the tensioner.

10. Install the timing chain cover assembly while pulling up the chain to avoid being caught under the cover.

11. Install the water pump assembly and install the cylinder head. Torque the head bolts to specification.

12. Using the tensioner release tool, disengage the tensioner and install the cam sprocket and chain to the camshaft. Align the marks on the sprocket and the camshaft bearing.

13. Install the sprocket retaining bolts. Release the tensioner assembly. Install the oil pump assembly, seal and pulley.

14. Continue the installation as required. Do not use an early type inlet manifold gasket as coolant leakage could occur within the engine.

16 VALVE ENGINE

1. Disconnect the negative battery cable. Remove the engine from the vehicle.

2. Remove the lid on the valve cover and remove the ignition wires. Remove the valve cover.

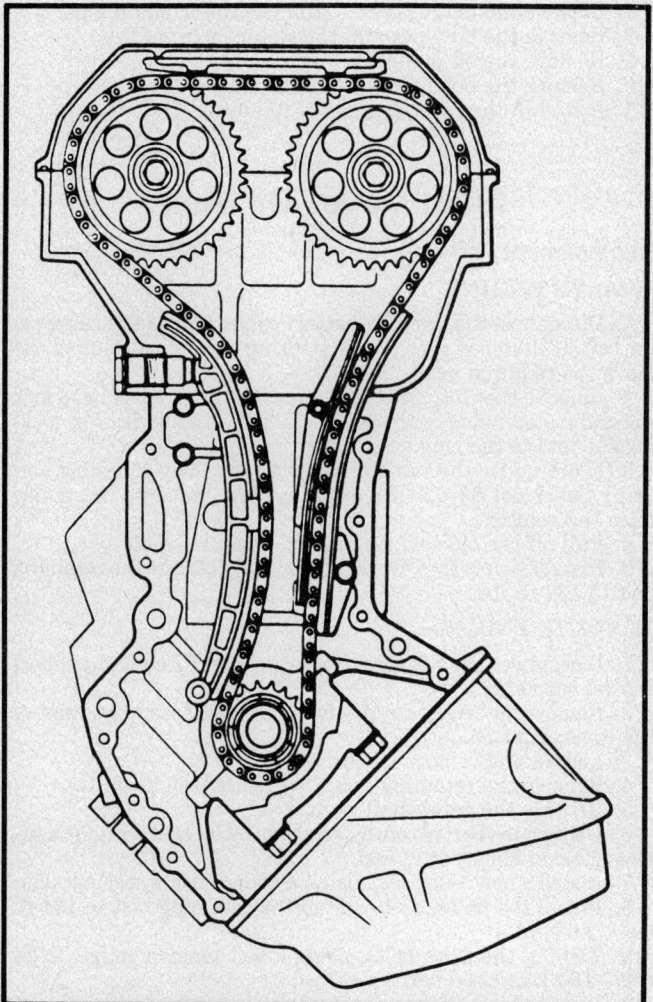

Timing mark location—16 valve engine

Crankshaft locking procedure

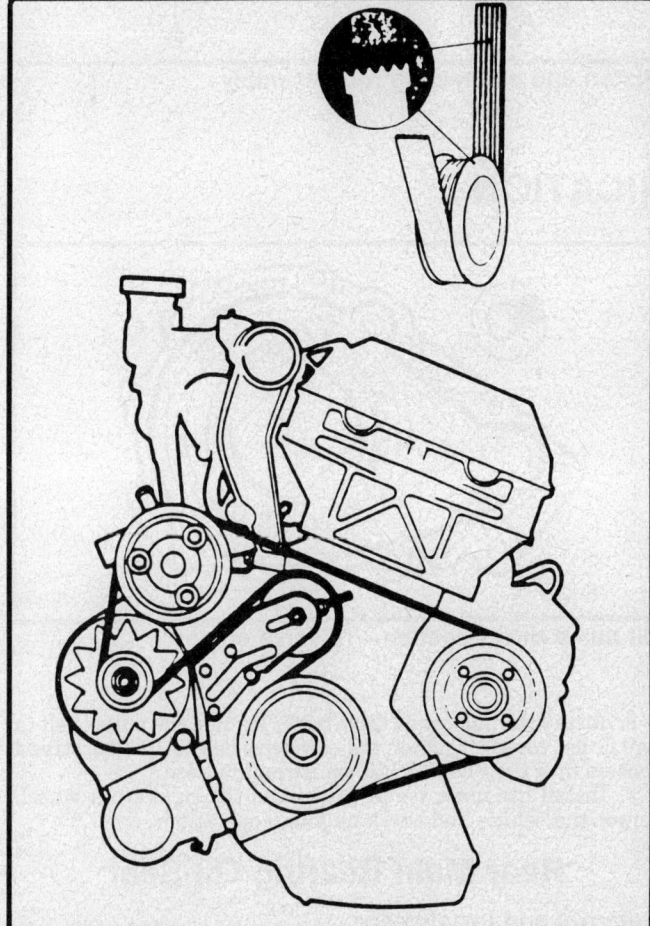
Serpentine drive belt adjustment

3. Position the crankshaft for TDC, with the **0** mark on the flywheel align with the timing mark on the transaxle end plate. These marks must be aligned before the timing chain is removed.

4. Remove the crankshaft pulley using a puller. Remove the water pump, located behind the crankshaft pulley. Remove the timing cover, 2 bolts of which are screwed into the underside of the cylinder head.

5. The cam chain and crankshaft timing sprocket should now both be visible. From above, release the timing chain tensioner

by pressing the pivoting guide firmly against it. Remove the chain tensioner.

6. Using a special tool to hold the camshafts, remove the center bolts securing the camshaft sprockets. Throughout this procedure, keep the camshafts in their basic correct setting. If they are rotated out of position at any stage, especially without their sprockets and chain, the valves can be damaged.

7. Disconnect the timing chain from the sprockets and remove the chain, clearing it from the crankshaft sprockets.

To install:

8. To install the timing chain, place the chain around the crankshaft sprocket. Run the chain up through the opening in the cylinder head if not already done. Install the chain and sprocket on the exhaust cam first. Make sure the chain is taut between the crankshaft and camshaft sprockets. Install the bolts but do not tighten.

9. Install the chain and sprocket to the intake cam. Keep the chain taut between the cam sprockets while it is being installed. Install the bolts but do not tighten. Make sure the chain is seated in the guide tensioner grooves.

10. Tension the chain tensioner by fully depressing the piston and then rotating it to the locked position.

11. Install the chain tensioner with the piston under tension. Make sure the copper gasket is in good condition and that the sealing surface is clean and free from burrs.

12. Trigger the chain tensioner by pressing the pivoting chain guide against it, thereafter, press the pivoting guide against the chain to give the chain its basic tension. Check that the chain tensioner maintains tension on the chain when the pressure on the chain guide is released and that the basic setting stop for the tensioner holds the chain guide tight against the chain. A limited amount of play will be present until the hydraulic pressure takes over once the engine is running.

13. Check the setting by rotating the crankshaft 2 complete turns in its normal direction of rotation around to the timing mark. The basic setting of the cams should remain unaltered.

14. Lock the exhaust cam by using a wrench on the cast hex bolt and torque the sprocket bolt to 48 ft. lbs. Repeat this on the intake cam.

15. Complete the procedure on the intake cam sprocket. When loosening or torquing the sprocket center bolts, hold the cam still using a wrench installed over the flats on the camshaft. The accuracy of the timing chain adjustment will depend on the condition of the chain.

Camshaft

Removal and Installation
8 VALVE ENGINE

1. Disconnect the negative battery cable. Remove the distributor cap and ignition wires. Rotate the engine until cylinders No. 1 and No. 4 are at TDC. This must be done due to the design of the distributor driving dog which only allows the valve cover/distributor assembly to be removed with the engine in this position.

2. Remove the valve cover assembly.

3. Be sure both the crankshaft and camshaft are at the No. 1 cylinder firing mode and the indexing lines still are aligned.

4. Remove the camshaft sprocket, keeping the chain on the sprocket. Place the sprocket between the chain guide and tensioner.

5. Remove the camshaft bearing caps and lift the camshaft from the bearing assembly housing. The bearing assembly housing can then be removed, if necessary.

6. Installation is the reverse of the removal procedure. Be sure the timing marks are aligned.

16 VALVE ENGINE

1. Disconnect the negative battery cable. Remove the engine from the vehicle.

2. Remove the lid on the valve cover. Disconnect the spark plug wires and vacuum hose from the distributor and remove the distributor cap.

3. Remove the valve cover and position the crankshaft for TDC. The **0** mark on the flywheel should align with the timing mark on the bell housing end plate.

4. Remove the distributor. Remove the oil pipe.

5. Remove the center bolts securing the camshaft sprockets. Use a proper holding tool to hold the camshafts from rotating. Always keep the camshafts in their correct basic setting. If the setting of the crankshaft or camshafts is altered at this stage the valves can be damaged.

6. Remove the camshaft timing chain tensioner. Remove the camshaft sprockets.

7. Remove the camshaft bearing caps. Keep them in correct order for later reassembly. Lift out the camshafts.

8. Installation is the reverse the removal procedure. When installing, the bearing caps marked 1–5 belong to the intake cam, while those marked 6–10 go with the exhaust cam. Torque the bearing cap bolts to 11 ft. lbs.

Piston and Connecting Rod

Positioning

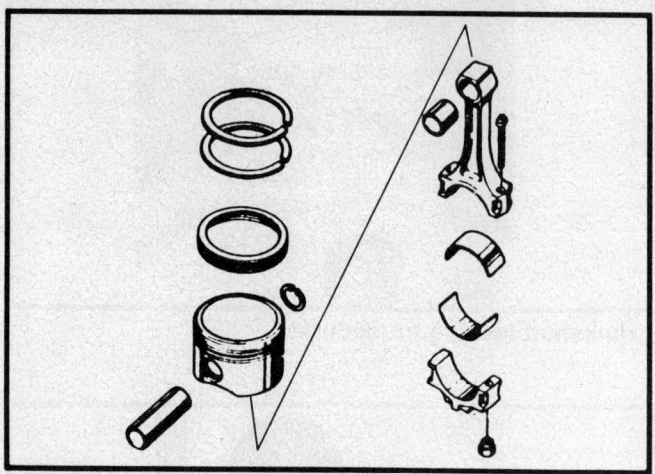

Piston and connecting rod assembly

ENGINE LUBRICATION

Oil Pump

Removal and Installation

8 VALVE ENGINE

The oil pump is a gear type pump and is driven by the crankshaft. It is positioned between the timing cover and crankshaft pulley. The pump assembly can be removed with the engine in the vehicle.

1. Disconnect the negative battery cable. Remove the crankshaft pulley.

2. Lock the crankshaft in place by using a flywheel locking bracket.

3. Remove the oil pump retaining bolts. Remove the oil pump from the timing cover.

To install:

4. Before installation, prime the pump assembly and be sure the mark on the outer gear is visible.

5. Install a new gasket and install the pump and the timing cover. Complete the assembly as required.

6. Before starting the engine, remove the oil filter base and fill the passage way on the pressure side with oil. Replace the filter base.

16 VALVE ENGINE

1. Raise the vehicle and support it safely.

2. Remove the right front wheel and the front inner fender panel section.

3. Loosen and remove the multi-groove belt. Loosen the compressor drive belt.

4. Remove the crankshaft pulley. It may be necessary to hold the crankshaft while removing the pulley bolt.

5. Remove the oil pump cover retaining bolts. Remove the oil pump.

To install:

6. Before installing the pump, install a new O-ring seal.

7. Install the pump to the engine and install the retaining bolts.

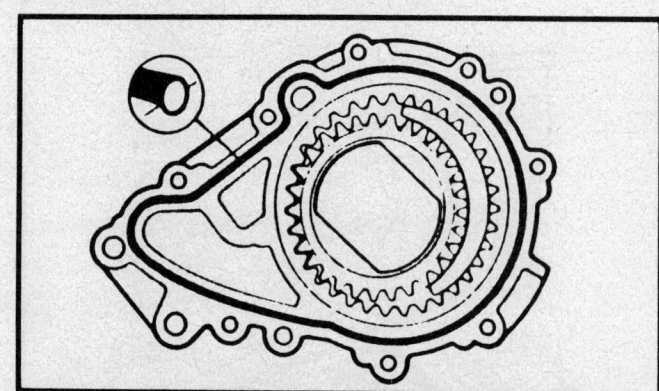

Oil pump cross-section—16 valve engine

8. Install the pulley and drive belts. Tighten the pulley bolt to 140 ft. lbs. torque. Tighten the new drive belt to 180 lbs. strand tension or a used belt to 120 lbs. strand tension.

9. Install the inner fender panel and the right front wheel. Lower the vehicle and check oil pump operation.

Rear Main Bearing Oil Seal

Removal and Installation

This seal is otherwise known as the crankshaft seal at the flywheel end. The seal can be changed with the engine in the vehicle, but the clutch and flywheel must first be removed.

1. Remove the clutch and the flywheel from the vehicle.

2. Remove the old seal ring using the proper tool.

3. Install the new seal with the spring ring turned inwards toward the crankshaft using the proper seal installation tool.

4. Continue the installation in the reverse order of the removal.

MANUAL TRANSAXLE

For further information, please refer to "Professional Transmission Repair Manual" for additional coverage.

Transaxle Assembly

Removal and Installation

900 SERIES

1. Remove the engine and transaxle from the vehicle as an assembly.
2. Position the engine and transaxle assembly in a suitable holding fixture. Drain the engine oil.
3. Remove the clutch shaft using a slide hammer and special tool 87-90-529.
4. Remove the slave cylinder retaining bolts. Remove the bolts retaining the transaxle assembly to the engine.
5. Carefully separate the engine from the transaxle.

9000 SERIES

1. Disconnect the negative battery cable. Remove the battery. Raise and support the vehicle safely.
2. Remove the air intake duct for the air cleaner from the fender. Remove the washer fluid reservoir and disconnect the positive lead from the washer terminal block.
3. Remove the fuel filter, the terminal block and the battery tray.
4. Remove the electrical connector from the air mass meter and remove the air mass meter carefully.
5. Remove the intake dust cover for the air cleaner.
6. Disconnect the Hall transmitter lead at the distributor.
7. Remove the cover and the filter element from the air cleaner.
8. Remove the air cleaner body.
9. Remove the turbo pressure pipe.
10. Disconnect the battery ground cable and the back-up light switch leads from the gear box assembly.

11. Install a clamp onto the hose in the slave cylinder line and pinch the hose together. Separate the pressure line between the pipe and the hose.
12. Remove the left engine mount and attach the engine to an engine lifting beam, or its equivalent.
13. Be sure the lifting beam or its equivalent is properly secured and seated.
14. Remove the left front wheel assembly and the inner fender panel.
15. Separate the suspension arm from the ball joint on the left side.
16. Disconnect the speedometer cable. Do not allow the drive gear to fall into the gear box.
17. Separate the 2 halves of the selector rod joint and remove the clip from the dust cover on the intermediate driveshaft.
18. Unbolt the support bar from the inlet manifold. Unbolt the starter motor from the gear box and push the support bar aside. Allow the starter motor to hang, but support it to prevent undue strain on the electrical wires.
19. Leave 1 of the bolts in position in the top of the flange between the engine and the gear box. Remove the other bolts and install the locating dowels, if available.
20. Loosen the 2 subframe pivot mountings and remove the 4 securing bolts.
21. Unbolt the front attachment point for the subframe. Unbolt the 4 subframe mounting bolts.
22. Remove the bolts securing the lower attaching point for the wheel arch bracket and let the subframe hang from the anti-roll bar.
23. Remove the clip securing the rubber boot on the inboard universal joint. Withdraw the driveshaft and install protective covers to the open ends of the boot and drive cup.
24. Attach a lifting sling to the transaxle and remove the remaining bolt. Carefully remove the transaxle assembly from the vehicle.
25. Installation is the reverse of the removal procedure.

CLUTCH

Clutch Assembly

Removal and Installation

900 SERIES

1. Disconnect the negative battery cable. Remove the clutch housing cover.
2. Install the spacer (Saab part 83-90-023) between the clutch fork and the diaphragm spring. Keep the clutch pedal depressed when the ring is being installed.
3. Unhook the spring clip and remove the cover located in front of the clutch shaft. Remove the clutch shaft plastic propeller.
4. Remove the clutch shaft by means of an M8 bolt installed in the shaft end and Saab tool 83-93-175. Withdraw the shaft as far as possible.
5. Remove the clutch slave cylinder retaining bolts.
6. Remove the clutch retaining bolts and remove the clutch, clutch disc and the slave cylinder complete with the clutch release bearing. Be sure the slave cylinder sleeve is not damaged by the clutch during the removal procedure.
7. Installation is the reverse of the removal procedure.

Pressure plate and related components

9000 SERIES

1. Disconnect the negative battery cable. Remove the transaxle assembly.

2. Install a flywheel locking tool, if available and remove the clutch assembly from the flywheel.

3 To install the clutch assembly, use a centering arbor type tool or an appropriate input shaft to center the clutch plate to the flywheel.

4. Tighten the pressure plate bolts to 10.4–19.4 ft. lbs. Remove the flywheel lock, if used.

5. Slide the transaxle assembly over the locating dowels, engaging the transaxle input shaft into the clutch plate splines.

6. Secure the transaxle to the engine with the necessary attaching bolts. Remove the lifting sling from the transaxle.

7. Continue the installation in the reverse order of the removal procedure.

Pedal Height/Free-Play Adjustment

1. Remove the inspection hole cover and look through the inspection hole.

2. When the distance between the plastic sleeve front edge and the front edge of the turned surface is less than 2.0mm the clutch disc must be replaced.

Clutch Master Cylinder

Removal and Installation

1. Disconnect the negative battery cable. Remove the clamp holding the pipe from the cylinder at the body and remove the pipe at the cylinder.

2. Remove the left screen under the instrument panel.

3. Remove the pin holding the pushrod to the clutch pedal.

4. Remove the bolts inside the dash panel. Remove the clutch cylinder from inside the engine compartment.

5. Remove the hose from the fluid container and hang it aside so the fluid does not come out.

6. Installation is the reverse of the removal procedure.

Clutch Slave Cylinder

Removal and Installation
900 SERIES

1. Disconnect the negative battery cable.

2. Remove the clutch assembly.

3. Remove the clutch release bearing together with the clutch slave cylinder.

4. Installation is the reverse of the removal procedure.

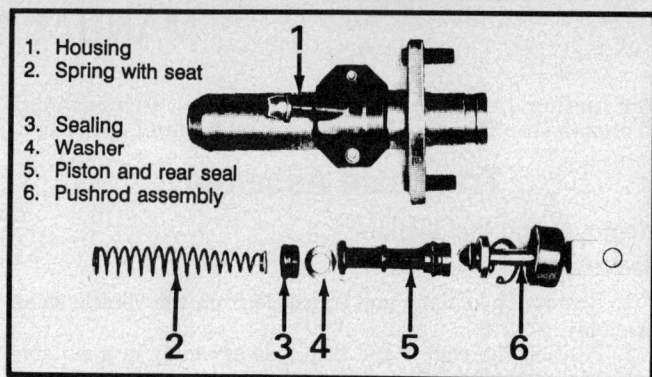

1. Housing
2. Spring with seat
3. Sealing
4. Washer
5. Piston and rear seal
6. Pushrod assembly

Exploded view of clutch master cylinder

9000 SERIES

1. Disconnect the negative battery cable.

2. Remove the transaxle from the vehicle.

3. Remove the clutch release bearing. Disconnect the pressure pipe. Remove the bleed nipple.

4. Remove the retaining bolts that hold the slave cylinder in place.

5. Remove the clutch slave cylinder.

6. Installation is the reverse of the removal procedure.

Hydraulic Clutch System Bleeding

1. Connect a hose to the slave cylinder bleeder valve. Place the other end of the hose in a suitable jar partially filled with brake fluid.

2. Fill the master cylinder with brake fluid.

3. Open the bleeder valve on the slave cylinder a ½ turn.

4. Place a cooling system tester gauge over the opening of the master cylinder.

5. Pump the tester until all air has been expelled from the system.

6. Close the slave cylinder bleeder valve.

7. Check that all air has been removed from the system by depressing the clutch pedal.

AUTOMATIC TRANSAXLE

For further information, please refer to "Professional Transmission Repair Manual" for additional coverage.

Transaxle Assembly

Removal and Installation
900 SERIES

NOTE: The engine and transaxle must be removed as an assembly. Removal of the engine by itself is not recommended.

1. Disconnect both battery cables. Drain the engine coolant.

2. Disconnect the windshield washer hose. Mark the engine hood hinges. Remove engine hood retaining bolts then hood assembly.

3. Disconnect and remove the following items:

   a. Disconnect all electrical connections from the starter motor.

   b. Disconnect the upper radiator hose.

   c. Disconnect all ground leads.

   d. Disconnect the temperature sending unit electrical connection.

   e. Remove the ignition coil.

   f. Disconnect the lower radiator hose.

   g. Remove the air cleaner, air intake, preheater hose, crank case ventilation hose and intake hose.

   h. Disconnect and plug the end of the fuel lines.

   i. Disconnect the choke cable and the throttle cable.

   j. Disconnect the hoses to the expansion tank.

   k. Disconnect the oil pressure sending unit electrical connection.

l. Disconnect the alternator wiring harness.

m. Disconnect the heater hoses and the brake servo vacuum hoses.

4. On fuel injected vehicles, disconnect the electric wiring and fuel connections to the fuel injection system. Disconnect the flow meter and air cleaner with electrical connections.

5. If equipped with the APC system, disconnect the wiring to the solenoid valve. Remove the solenoid valve and the electrical connector to the knock sensor.

6. Remove the boot clips and rubber boots from the inner axle shafts.

7. Place special spacer tool 8393209 or equivalent between the underside of the upper frame and the vehicle body from the wheel housing side. The spacer tool relives the front suspension of load when the vehicle is raised.

8. Remove the lower end piece from the frame. Remove the steering knuckle package and support the end piece against the outer end of the frame.

9. Remove the gear selector cable retaining screw at the gearbox. Pull out the cable with the gear selector rod to its outer or **P** position. Move back the spring loaded sleeve on the gear selector rod and unhook the cable end piece.

10. Remove the exhaust pipe from the exhaust manifold.

11. Disconnect the speedometer cable from the transaxle.

12. Remove the rear engine mounting bolts.

13. Using a suitable lifting tool slightly raise the engine transaxle assembly. Move the unit slightly to the side and remove the 2 universal joints.

14. Lift the engine transaxle assembly out of the vehicle. If equipped with power assisted steering, disconnect and plug the 2 hydraulic lines at the servo pump.

15. At this point of the procedure separate the engine from the automatic transaxle.

16. Clean the outside of the engine and automatic transaxle and drain the oil out of the engine.

17. Remove the cover over the flywheel ring gear. On turbocharged vehicles remove the turbocharger support.

18. Remove the starter motor if necessary.

19. Disconnect the throttle cable at the throttle housing.

20. Remove all retaining bolts between the engine and transaxle and disconnect the hydraulic hoses from the oil cooler.

21. Remove the retaining bolts securing the ring gear to the torque converter.

22. Turn the flexplate, so the plate angles will be horizontal. Lift the engine carefully off the transaxle.

23. Install the torque converter support special tool 8790255 or equivalent.

24. Position the transaxle assembly on suitable workstand or holding fixture.

To install:

25. Before installing the transaxle to the engine make sure the mating surfaces are thoroughly clean.

26. Check that there are no cracks in the flexplate, of the engine particularly on a turbocharged engine.

27. Remove the torque converter support. Apply anti-corrosion grease to the center pin of the torque converter and the center of the flexplate. Make sure the 2 guide sleeves are installed into the gearcase.

28. Install a new sheet metal gasket to the joint face of the gearcase. Apply Bostik silicone compound part 2680 or equivalent, into the grooves in the gasket. Install the transaxle to the engine.

29. Position the flexplate so the sheetmetal angles are horizontal.

30. Take care not to damage the torque converter when lowering the engine onto the transaxle.

31. Apply thread sealing compound and tighten all retaining bolts.

32. Align the torque converter with the flexplate then gradually tighten the retaining bolts to 25–30 ft. lbs. (33–39 Nm).

33. Install the starter motor. Connect the throttle cable to the throttle housing.

34. On turbocharged vehicles install the support for the turbocharger. Install the cover over the ring gear.

35. Refill the engine with the correct amount of engine oil.

36. Pack the inner universal joins and rubber boots with a suitable grease.

37. Install new gaskets to the exhaust manifold flanges. Install new clamps on the inner axle shafts.

38. Position the engine transaxle assembly so the front mounting will engage in its bracket slightly before the rear mountings.

39. Lower the engine transaxle assembly into the vehicle. Guide the front mounting into the bracket and lower the rear of the engine transaxle assembly to approximately 2 inches (50–60mm) above the mountings.

40. Position the engine to the side, guide the left universal joint into position and then move the engine to the left.

41. Carefully lower the engine transaxle assembly and guide it onto the engine mountings, at the same time aligning the right universal joint with its axle shaft.

42. Align the exhaust system flanges. Check that the gaskets are correctly installed.

43. Install the right end piece to the frame. Check that the right universal joint is aligned with the axle shaft.

44. Install the bolts into the rear engine mountings and tighten all of the engine mountings and bolt together the exhaust flanges.

45. Reconnect the speedometer cable.

46. Reconnect the cable to the gear selector rod and bolt the cable end piece to the transaxle casing. Make sure gear selector operates properly.

47. Install the boot clamps to the inner universal joints. Remove the special spacer tool 8393209.

48. Connect and install the following items:

a. Connect all electrical connections to the starter motor.

b. Connect the upper radiator hose.

c. Connect all ground leads.

d. Connect the temperature sending unit electrical connection.

e. Install the ignition coil.

f. Connect the lower radiator hose.

g. Install the air cleaner, air intake, preheater hose, crank case ventilation hose and intake hose.

h. Connect the fuel lines.

i. Connect the choke cable and the throttle cable.

j. Connect the hoses to the expansion tank.

k. Connect the oil pressure sending unit electrical connection.

l. Connect the alternator wiring harness.

m. Connect the heater hoses and the brake servo vacuum hoses.

49. On fuel injected vehicles, connect the electric wiring and fuel connections to the fuel injection system. Reconnect the flow meter and air cleaner electrical connections.

NOTE: On fuel injected engines make sure there is at least ½ in. (10mm) of clearance at the bottom of the throttle control assembly.

50. If equipped with the APC system, reconnect the wiring to the solenoid valve. Install the solenoid valve and the electrical connector to the knocking sensor.

51. Refill the coolant and bleed the cooling system through the bleeder nipple on the thermostat housing. If equipped with power assisted steering, connect the hydraulic lines to the servo pump.

52. Reconnect both battery cables. Refill the transaxle assembly with the correct amount of specified fluid.

53. Install the engine hood in the marked position and connect the windshield washer hose.

54. Road test the vehicle in all driving ranges for proper operation.

9000 SERIES

1. Disconnect the battery cables and remove the battery.
2. Remove the windshield washer fluid reservoir. Plug the outlet to keep the fluid from running out.
3. Open the terminal box and disconnect the cables.

NOTE: When removing the fuel filter, wrap a rag around the line to prevent fuel from spraying out. Use proper caution when working with the fuel system.

4. Release the fuel filter clamp and remove the filter. Remove the battery cable.
5. Disconnect the wiring from the air mass meter and remove the meter.
6. Disconnect the hose from the transaxle and the bypass hose from the turbocharger delivery pipe. Remove the delivery pipe.
7. Disconnect the throttle cable form the throttle housing.
8. Disconnect the gear selector lever cable from the selector lever. Do not separate the ball joint on the cable.
9. Disconnect the inlet hose from the oil cooler on top of the transaxle. Disconnect the selector lever from the transaxle.
10. Remove the return line from the oil cooler. Place a drain pan under the transaxle to collect the oil.
11. Remove the clamp retaining the turbocharger oil supply line to the transaxle, if equipped.
12. Disconnect the speedometer cable from the transaxle. Remove the top retaining bolt for the starter motor.
13. Disconnect the starter motor stay from the intake manifold. Disconnect the top end of the starter stay from the wheel housing.
14. Place engine support yoke 83–93–977 or equivalent, in position on the wheel housing to support the engine when the transaxle has been removed.
15. Raise and safely support the vehicle. Remove the left front wheel and remove the inner fender liner.
16. Remove the starter motor and suspend it aside. Remove the bolts retaining the torque converter to the driveplate.
17. Remove the bolts retaining the ball joint to the suspension arm. Remove the anti-roll bar mounting nut from the suspension arm. Remove the 2 bolts retaining the anti-roll bar bearing.
18. Remove the front engine mount bolt.
19. Split the sub-frame at the front and slightly open the joint. Remove the 2 bolts at the rear of the sub-frame, 1 of the bolts retains the steering gear.
20. Remove the bolts for the rear sub-frame joint and remove the 2 bolts in the front corner. Lower the sub-frame from the vehicle.
21. Remove the clamps from both the left and right CV-joints, separate the joints. Allow the driveshafts to hang down.
22. Position a suitable lifting device under the transaxle and lower it from the vehicle.

To install:

23. Install a suitable converter holding device to prevent the converter from falling out during installation. With the transaxle on a suitable lifting device, raise it into position under the vehicle.
24. Guide the transaxle into position aligning the converter pin as a guide. Install 1 bolt to retain the assembly.
25. Reattach the driveshafts and install the clamps over the CV-boots.

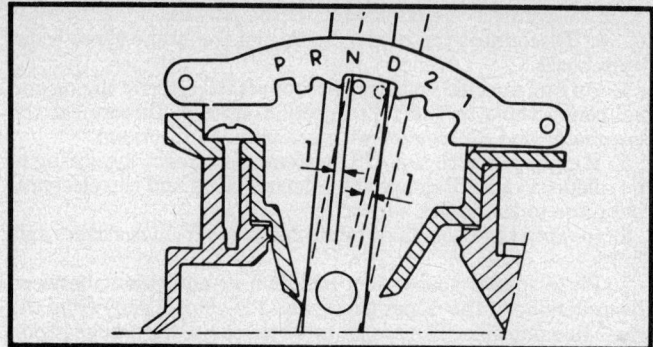

Manual linkage clearance, equal in "N" and "D"

26. Install the transaxle mounting bolt through the engine mount.
27. Raise the sub-frame assembly into position. Make sure the engine mount is in position.
28. Install all sub-frame bolts and the engine mount bolt.
29. Install the anti-roll bar and bearing into the suspension arm. Install all of the suspension arm bolts.
30. Install the torque converter-to-driveplate bolts. Use Loctite® 242 on the bolts.
31. Install the starter and stay. Lower the vehicle.
32. Remove the engine support tool. Install the upper starter mount bolts. Connect the speedometer cable.
33. Install the turbocharger oil pipe to the engine block.
34. Reconnect the selector lever cable. The selector should be in the **N** detent. Adjust the selector as needed.
35. Reconnect the oil cooler hose to the transaxle oil cooler.
36. Reconnect the turbocharger delivery pipe. Install the air mass meter.
37. Install the battery tray. Install the fuel filter.
38. Attach the battery cable to the battery tray. Reconnect the cables to the terminal box.
39. Install the windshield washer fluid bottle and connect the electrical leads.
40. Install the battery and reconnect the cables.
41. Raise and safely support the vehicle.
42. Install the inner fender cover. Install the wheel and tire assembly.
43. Lower the vehicle, refill the fluid in the transaxle.
44. Road test the vehicle and check the operation of the transaxle. Adjust the throttle linkage as needed. Check the fluid level.

Shift Linkage Adjustment

1. Remove the gear selector lever cover.
2. Slack off the gear selector lever housing nuts with tool 83–91–23 or equivalent.
3. Lift the gear selector lever housing and turn it so the adjustment nuts of the cable will be reachable.
4. Adjust the cable longer or shorter to bring the **N** and **D** clearance to specification.
5. Assemble the gear selector housing and check the clearance in **N** and **D**.
6. The proper setting of the selector cable can be accomplished by adding or removing shims at the transmission case end of the cable. A maximum of 3 shims may be used.

DRIVE AXLE

Halfshaft

Removal and Installation

900 SERIES

NOTE: The entire front axle assembly must be removed in order to remove the halfshaft from the vehicle.

1. Disconnect the negative battery cable. Remove the upper shock absorber bolt.
2. Raise the vehicle and support it safely. Remove the wheel and tire assembly.
3. Remove the brake housing and position it on the wheel housing to avoid damage to the brake hose. Remove the brake disc and parking brake assembly along with the cable.
4. Remove the large clamp from the rubber bellows on the inner universal joint. To separate the inner universal joint, install the cover (Saab part 7323736) in the rubber bellows to stop the needle bearings from falling out and to keep dirt from entering. Install the protective cap (Saab part 7838469) on the inner driver.
5. Disconnect the tie rod from the steering arm using the proper tool. Remove the nut on the upper ball joint. Remove the bolts from the lower control arm bracket.
6. Remove the halfshaft through the wheel housing and remove the entire front axle assembly.
7. If the differential bearing cap is to be removed, remove the retaining bolts and remove the cap and the inner drive using the proper removal tools.
8. Installation is the reverse of the removal procedure.

9000 SERIES

1. Disconnect the negative battery cable. Remove the hubcap and loosen the center axle nut. Raise and support the vehicle safely.
2. Remove the inner fender panel for working access.
3. Unbolt the MacPherson strut from the steering swivel member and detach the flexible brake hose from the clip on the strut.
4. Loosen the clip on the rubber boot on the inboard universal joint.
5. Separate the 2 halves of the joint. Install protective covers over the rubber boot and the drive axle.
6. Remove the hub center nut and withdraw the driveshaft from the steering swivel member.
7. Installation is the reverse of the removal procedure.
8. Torque the bolts securing the strut to the steering swivel to 56–75 ft. lbs.
9. Tighten the hub center nut to 195–208 ft. lbs.

Front Wheel Hub, Knuckle and Bearings

Removal and Installation

900 SERIES

NOTE: The entire front axle assembly must be removed from the vehicle when removing the wheel bearings.

1. Disconnect the negative battery cable. Remove the upper bolt of the shock absorber.
2. Raise the vehicle and support it safely. Remove the tire and wheel assembly.

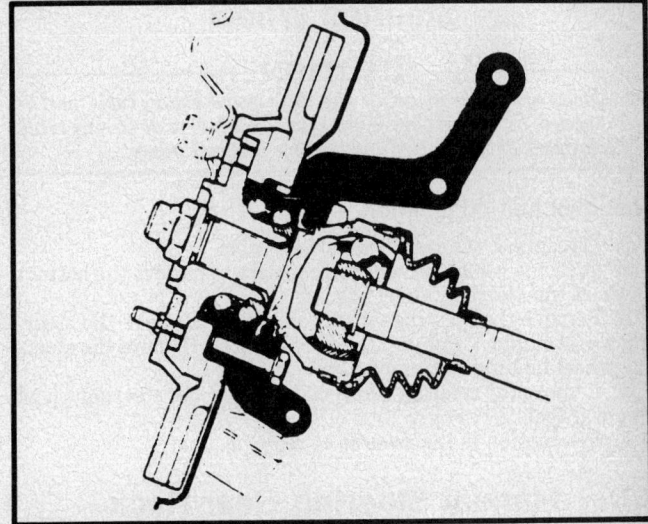

Front axle assembly—9000 Series

3. Remove the brake housing and position it by the wheel housing to avoid damage to the brake hose. Remove the brake disc and parking brake assembly with the cable.
4. Remove the large clamp from the rubber bellows on the inner universal joint. To separate the inner universal joint, install the cover (SAAB part 7323736) in the rubber bellows to stop the needle bearing from falling out and to keep dirt from entering. Install the protective cap (SAAB part 7838469) on the inner drive.
5. Disconnect the tie rod from the steering arm using the proper tool. Remove the nut on the upper ball joint. Remove the bolts from the lower control arm bracket.
6. Remove the driveshaft through the wheel housing and remove the entire front axle assembly.
7. Place the steering knuckle housing in a press and press out the driveshaft.
8. Remove the lockring and press out the bearing using a suitable drift.
9. Installation is the reverse of the removal procedure.

9000 SERIES

The front wheel bearing are double row angular contact bearings which are permanently lubricated and maintenance free. The bearings cannot be replaced individually. To remove the hub proceed as follows:

1. Loosen the hub center nut and the wheel bolts.
2. Raise the vehicle and support it safely.
3. Remove the tire and wheel assembly. Remove the hub center nut and thrust washer.
4. Remove the flexible brake hose from its support clip.
5. Unbolt the caliper and rest it upon the suspension arm.
6. Unscrew the locating stud for the disc and remove it from the hub.
7. Push in on the driveshaft. Remove the 4 bolts securing the hub to the steering swivel member.
8. Lift the hub and disc back plate from the suspension assembly. Renew the bearings or replace the hub.
9. The installation of the hub is in the reverse of the removal procedure.
10. Tighten the hub securing bolts to 40–43 ft. lbs., and the center hub nut to 195–208 ft. lbs.

STEERING

Steering Wheel

— CAUTION —

On vehicles equipped with an air bag, the negative battery cable must be disconnected, before working on the system. Failure to do so may result in deployment of the air bag and possible personal injury.

Removal and Installation

1. Disconnect the negative battery cable.
2. On some vehicles it will be necessary to remove the bottom cover of the steering wheel bearing.
3. Remove the steering wheel safety pad. Remove the steering wheel emblem. Remove the horn contact. Remove the steering wheel holding nut and washer.
4. Remove the steering wheel using the proper steering wheel removal tool.
5. Installation is the reverse of removal.

Manual Steering Gear/Rack

Adjustment

RADIAL PLAY

1. Install the plunger without the spring and screw on the cap without the gasket by hand until it butts against the plunger. Do not use a wrench, as the cap will become damaged.
2. Measure the clearance between the cap and the housing with a feeler gauge.
3. Add 0.002–0.006 in. to the measured clearance to allow for the play to be left between the plunger and cap after assembly. Measure the thickness of the gasket and shims with a micrometer. Shims are available in thickness of 0.005 in., 0.0075 in., 0.010 in., 0.015 in. and 0.020 in.

Removal and Installation

900 SERIES

1. Disconnect the negative battery cable. Remove the left screen under the instrument panel and loosen the rubber bellows at the body lead through for the steering gear intermediate shaft, if required.
2. Raise and support the vehicle safely. Remove the bolt holding the joint to the steering gear pinion or intermediate shaft.
3. Loosen the steering column tube from the body and separate the steering column joint from the pinion. Position the steering column so the wiring harness is not damaged.
4. Remove both tire and wheel assemblies. Remove the tie rod ends at the steering arms with the proper removal tool. Remove the 2 steering gear clamps.
5. Move the rack to the right as far as possible. Lift the steering gear to the right so the tie rod can be bent down in the opening of the engine compartment floor.
6. Pull the rack to the left and lift the steering gear down through the opening in the engine compartment floor.
7. Installation is the reverse of the removal procedure.

Power Steering Gear

Adjustment

RADIAL PLAY

900 Series

1. Screw in the adjusting screw all the way until the resistance of the twisting steering gear is felt.
2. Back off the adjusting screw ½ turn.
3. Check that the steering gear can be turned from lock to lock in both directions without jamming.
4. Tighten the locknut with a torque of 50–60 ft. lbs.

9000 Series

1. Turn the adjusting screw completely in.
2. Back off the adjusting screw approximately 40–60 ft. lbs.
3. Tighten the locknut to 47–54 ft. lbs. (65–75 Nm).

Removal and Installation

900 SERIES

1. Disconnect the negative battery cable. Remove the left screen under the instrument panel and loosen the rubber bellows at the body lead through for the steering gear intermediate shaft, if required. Disconnect and plug the power steering fluid lines.
2. Raise and support the vehicle safely. Remove the bolt holding the joint to the steering gear pinion or intermediate shaft.
3. Loosen the steering column tube from the body and separate the steering column joint from the pinion. Position the steering column so the wiring harness is not damaged.
4. Remove both tire and wheel assemblies. Remove the tie rod ends at the steering arms with the proper removal tool. Remove the 2 steering gear clamps.

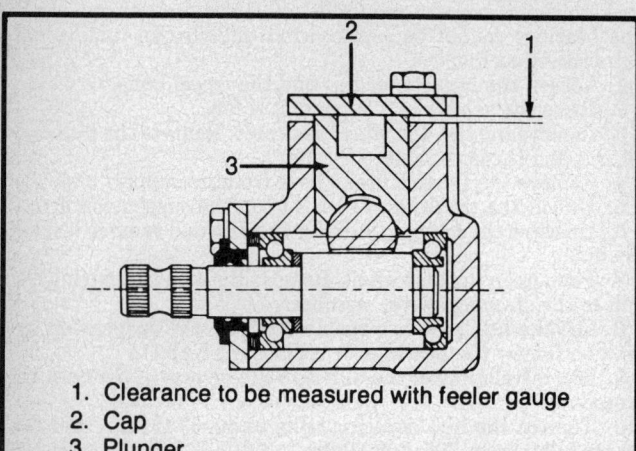

1. Clearance to be measured with feeler gauge
2. Cap
3. Plunger

Radial-play adjustment

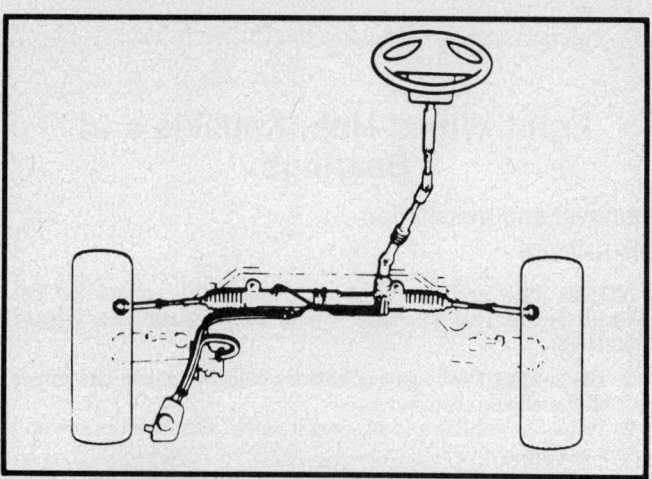

Power steering assembly—9000 Series

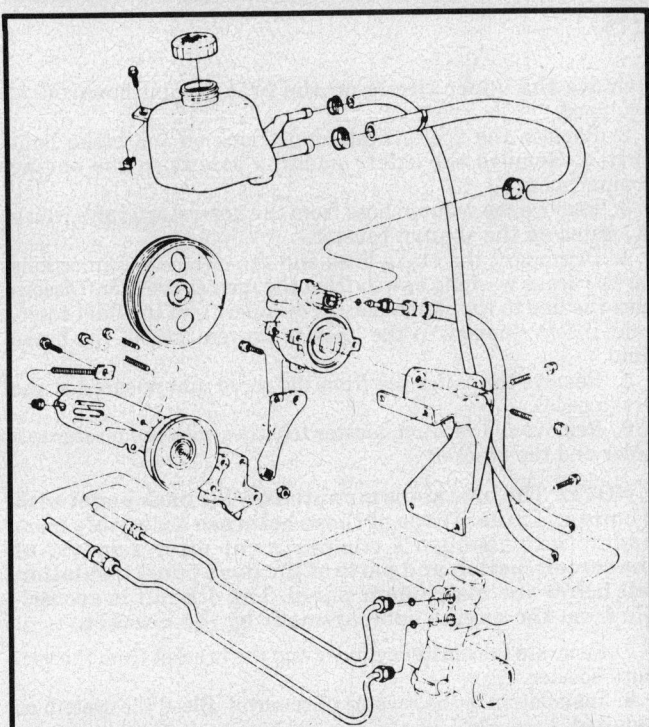

Power steering system and related components— 9000 Series

5. Move the rack to the right as far as possible. Lift the steering gear to the right so the tie rod can be bent down in the opening of the engine compartment floor.

6. Pull the rack to the left and lift the steering gear down through the opening in the engine compartment floor.

7. Installation is the reverse of the removal procedure.

9000 SERIES

1. Disconnect the negative battery cable. Remove the padding from under the instrument panel and the trim on the left side of the center tunnel, as required. Fold back the carpet where the steering column passes through the fire wall. Remove the rubber boot from the intermediate shaft.

2. Remove the pinch bolt in the lower clamp, loosen the bolt in the upper clamp and remove the intermediate shaft.

3. Remove the cover panel from the fire wall. Take care not to damage the gasket, seal and plastic bushing.

4. Raise and support the vehicle safely. Remove both tire and wheel assemblies.

5. Remove the rear section of the inner fender panel under the left fender.

6. Separate the left and right tie rod ends from the steering arms.

7. Drain the power steering fluid from the pump reservoir.

8. Disconnect the hoses from the pump and reservoir. Plug the openings to prevent fluid from leaking out and dirt from entering.

9. Remove the retaining bolts from the rack and pinion assembly.

10. Remove the vertical brace between the engine subframe and the body.

11. Lift out the rack and pinion unit through the left fender inner panel opening. Do not damage the rubber boots or brake hose.

12. Installation is the reverse of the removal procedure. Fill the reservoir and bleed the system by allowing the engine to run at idle.

Power Steering Pump

Removal and Installation
900 SERIES

1. Disconnect the negative battery cable. Drain the fluid from the power steering pump.

2. Drain the coolant from the drain cock on the engine block and disconnect the hose from between the expansion tank and the water pump.

3. Disconnect the power steering pump hoses. Grip the hexagonal nipple on the pump when removing the delivery line.

4. Unbolt the pump unit from the bracket and the engine mounting. Remove the power steering belt. Remove the pump complete with its mounting.

5. Installation is the reverse of the removal procedure.

9000 SERIES

1. Disconnect the negative battery cable. Remove the fluid from the pump reservoir.

2. Raise and support the vehicle safely. Remove the right front wheel and the right inner fender panel.

3. Remove the drive belt. Remove the bracket for the engine oil filler pipe. Remove the engine stay bracket. Disconnect the hoses from the pump. Plug the openings.

4. Remove the pump retaining bolts. Remove the pump. Note that 1 bolt is located behind the pump pulley and is accessible only through the aperature in the pulley.

5. Installation is the reverse of the removal procedure.

Belt Adjustment
900 SERIES

Tighten the belt so when pressure is applied to the belt at a given point the distance between both belt pulleys is 5–10mm.

9000 SERIES

1. After the belt has been installed, a strand tension gauge must be used to tighten the belt properly.

2. A new belt must be tightened to 170–200 lbs. or 735–865 N.

3. A used belt must be tightened to 110–130 lbs. or 490–580 N.

System Bleeding

1. Fill the power steering pump with the proper fluid.

2. Start the engine and top off the level of fluid to 0.4 in. above the bottom of the filter.

3. Turn the steering wheel from left to right several times to expel air from the system.

4. Refill the pump as needed.

5. Allow the engine to operate at idle.

Tie Rod Ends

Removal and Installation

1. Disconnect the negative battery cable. Raise and support the vehicle safely.

2. Remove the tire and wheel assembly. Remove the nut.

3. Disconnect the ball joint bolt from the steering arm using the proper removal tool. Do not knock the ball joint bolt out, as this could cause damage to the ball joint and other related parts.

4. Back off the nut that locks the end assembly to the tie rod.

5. Unscrew the end assembly from the tie rod.

6. Installation is the reverse of the removal procedure. Check and adjust the toe-in as required.

BRAKES

Master Cylinder

Removal and Installation

1. Disconnect the negative battery cable. Disconnect the electrical connection to the brake warning switch.
2. Disconnect the hose from the clutch master cylinder to the fluid reservoir. Insert a plastic stopper in the nipple of the reservoir.
3. Disconnect the brake lines to the master cylinder.
4. Remove the nuts that hold the master cylinder to the power brake booster. Remove the master cylinder from the vehicle.
5. Installation is the reverse of removal. Bleed the system as required.

Power Brake Booster

Removal and Installation

1. Disconnect the negative battery cable. Remove the steering column bearing cover, ash tray and safety padding screw.

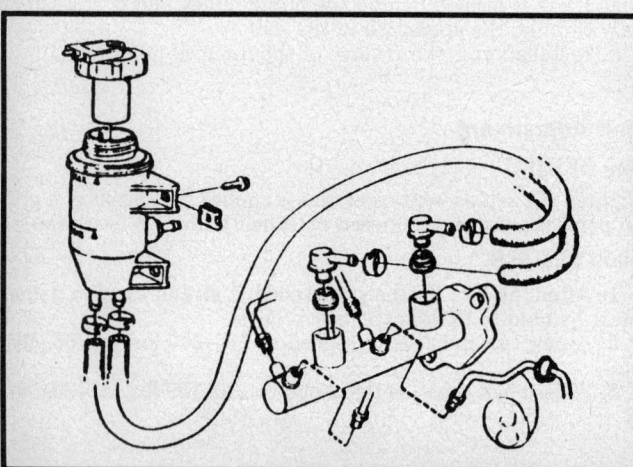

Brake master cylinder and related components—9000 Series

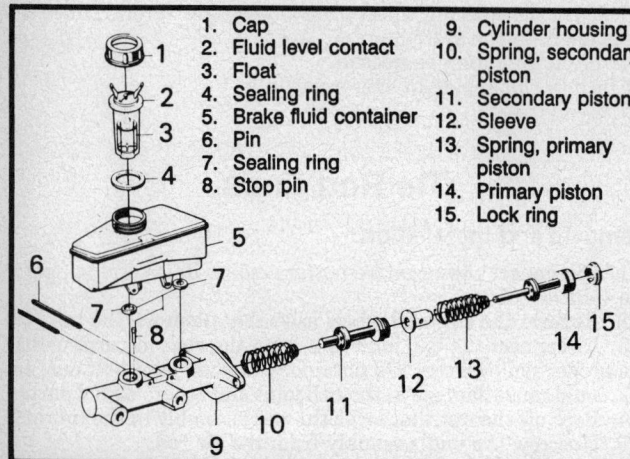

1. Cap	9. Cylinder housing
2. Fluid level contact	10. Spring, secondary piston
3. Float	
4. Sealing ring	11. Secondary piston
5. Brake fluid container	12. Sleeve
6. Pin	13. Spring, primary piston
7. Sealing ring	
8. Stop pin	14. Primary piston
	15. Lock ring

Typical brake master cylinder

Remove the upper circlip on the brake pedal pushrod, if equipped.
2. Remove the 2 electrical connections on the brake light switch. Remove the safety padding screws in the engine compartment.
3. Remove the vacuum hose from the non-return valve which is located on the vacuum booster.
4. Disconnect the brake lines and the electrical connections for the brake warning switch from the master cylinder. Disconnect the line to the clutch master cylinder from the fluid reservoir. Insert stoppers in the lines to prevent loss of the brake fluid.
5. Remove the cotter pin from the servo unit pushrod at the brake pedal.
6. Remove the vacuum booster together with the master cylinder and the bracket.

NOTE: The bracket is mounted on the dash panel with 4 bolts and nuts. Three of these bolts are accessible from under the passenger's compartment after removal of the screen section and parts of the dash panel insulation felt below the instrument panel. The 4th nut is accessible from the engine compartment by the bracket.

7. Separate the master cylinder and the bracket from the vacuum booster.
8. Installation is the reverse of removal. Bleed the system as required.

Disc Brake Pads

Removal and Installation

900 SERIES

Front

1. Raise and support the vehicle and support it safely. Remove the wheel.
2. Clean the brake housing.
3. Rotate the brake disc so 1 of the recesses in the edge of the disc aligns with the brake pads.
4. Remove the damper spring, pin retaining clip and pad retaining pin. If the pad retaining pin is dificult to remove, use a tapping-out tool 83 90 270 and removal tool 89 96 175.
5. Withdraw the brake pads, if the pads are seating firmly, use pad extractor No. 89 95 771.

To install:

6. Siphon a sufficient quantity of brake fluid from the master cylinder reservoir to prevent the brake fluid from overflowing the master cylinder when installing new pads. This is necessary as the piston must be forced into the cylinder bore to provide sufficient clearance to install the pads.
7. Inspect the caliper and piston assembly for breaks, cracks or other damage. Overhaul or replace the caliper as necessary.
8. Push the piston next to the rotor back into the cylinder bore until the end of the piston is flush with the boot retaining ring. Rotate the piston using tool 89 96 043, while simultaneously pushing the piston back into the cylinder. The automatic handbrake is reset this way.

— **CAUTION** —

If the piston is pushed further than this, the seal will be damaged and the caliper assembly will have to be overhauled.

NOTE: Check that the position of the piston has not displaced the dust cover and the yoke moves easily in the groove on the brake housing.

9. Fit the new brake pads together with the pad retaining pin, pin retaining clip and damper spring.

10. Check the adjustment of the handbrake cable. Check the distance between the lever and the yoke. The clearance should be 0.019 in. (0.5mm) maximum, on both sides. If adjustment is required, make it on the adjustment nut on the handbrake lever.

NOTE: Note that the cable cross over, which implies that the right adjusting nut should be used to adjust the left brake mechanism and vice-versa.

11. Refill the master cylinder with fresh brake fluid.

12. With the engine switched off, pump the brake pedal repeatedly until the foot brake starts to operate.

13. Pull the handbrake lever up 5 notches. Continue to pump the brake pedal until the handbrake operates after having been pulled up a further 24 notches.

14. Install the tire and wheel assembly. Pump the brake pedal several times to bring the pads into adjustment. Road test the vehicle. If a firm pedal cannot be obtained, bleed the brakes.

Rear

1. Raise the vehicle and support it with safely. Remove the wheel.

2. Clean the brake housing.

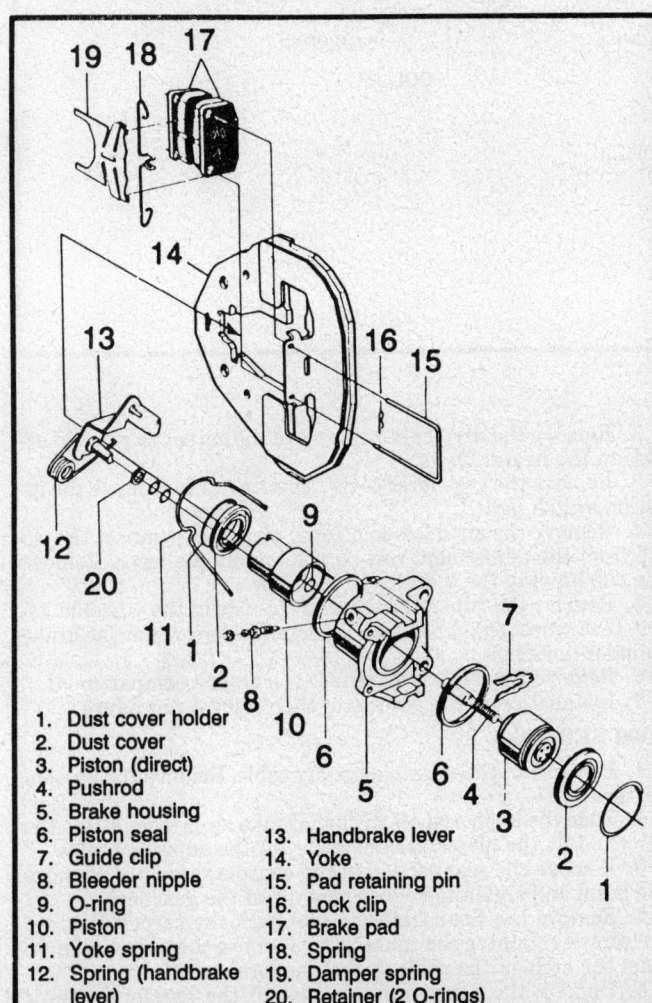

1. Dust cover holder
2. Dust cover
3. Piston (direct)
4. Pushrod
5. Brake housing
6. Piston seal
7. Guide clip
8. Bleeder nipple
9. O-ring
10. Piston
11. Yoke spring
12. Spring (handbrake lever)
13. Handbrake lever
14. Yoke
15. Pad retaining pin
16. Lock clip
17. Brake pad
18. Spring
19. Damper spring
20. Retainer (2 O-rings)

Exploded view of the front brake caliper

3. Tap out the brake pad retaining pins using a 0.11 in. (2.5mm) drift. Save the retaining spring.

4. Withdraw the brake pads. If they are difficult to remove, use extractor tool 89 95 771.

To install:

5. Siphon a sufficient quantity of brake fluid from the master cylinder reservoir to prevent the brake fluid from overflowing the master cylinder when installing new pads. This is necessary as the piston must be forced into the cylinder bore to provide sufficient clearance to install the pads.

6. Inspect the caliper and piston assembly for breaks, cracks or other damage. Overhaul or replace the caliper as necessary. Check that the dust cover retainer is properly in position and the cover is in good condition.

7. Push the piston back into the cylinder bore just enough to allow clearance for installation of the new pads.

8. Fit the pad retaining pins and the pin retaining clip.

9. Refill the master cylinder to the correct level with the proper brake fluid.

10. Replace the wheel and lower the vehicle. Pump the brake pedal several times to bring the pads into correct adjustment. Road test the vehicle.

NOTE: If a firm pedal cannot be obtained, the system will require bleeding.

9000 SERIES

Front

1. Raise and support the vehicle and support it safely. Remove the wheel.

2. Remove the lower guide pin bolt.

3. Pivot the caliper upwards and remove the pads.

4. Check that the guide pins slide freely and the dust covers are in good condition.

5. Clean the abutment surfaces between the pads and the carrier.

To install:

6. Fit the new pads and pivot the hydraulic body back to its normal position.

7. Refit and tighten the bolt in the lower guide pin.

8. Install the wheel and lower the vehicle.

9. Pump the brake pedal to move the pads to their operating positions.

Rear

1. Raise the vehicle and support it with safely. Remove the wheel.

2. Release the handbrake and remove the retaining spring.

3. Slide the handbrake cable out of the slot of the lever.

4. Remove the dust caps and then use a 7mm Allen key, hexagon bit adapter, to remove the guide pins.

5. Lift off the hydraulic body and remove the pads.

To install:

6. Remove the screw plug from the handbrake adjusting screw and screw the piston into the hydraulic body by means of the adjusting screw.

7. Place the new pads into position.

8. Replace the hydraulic body and install the guide pins complete with dust caps.

9. Install the retaining spring for the handbrake lever.

10. Screw the adjusting screw fully home and then back it off approximately ¼–½ turn. Check that the brake disc is running freely and refit the plug.

11. Install the handbrake cable to the lever and check with a feeler gauge, that the clearance between the lever and the stop is 0.02–0.06 in. (0.5–1.5mm) Adjust as necessary by means of the adjusting screw at the handbrake lever inside the vehicle.

12. Replace the wheel and lower the vehicle.

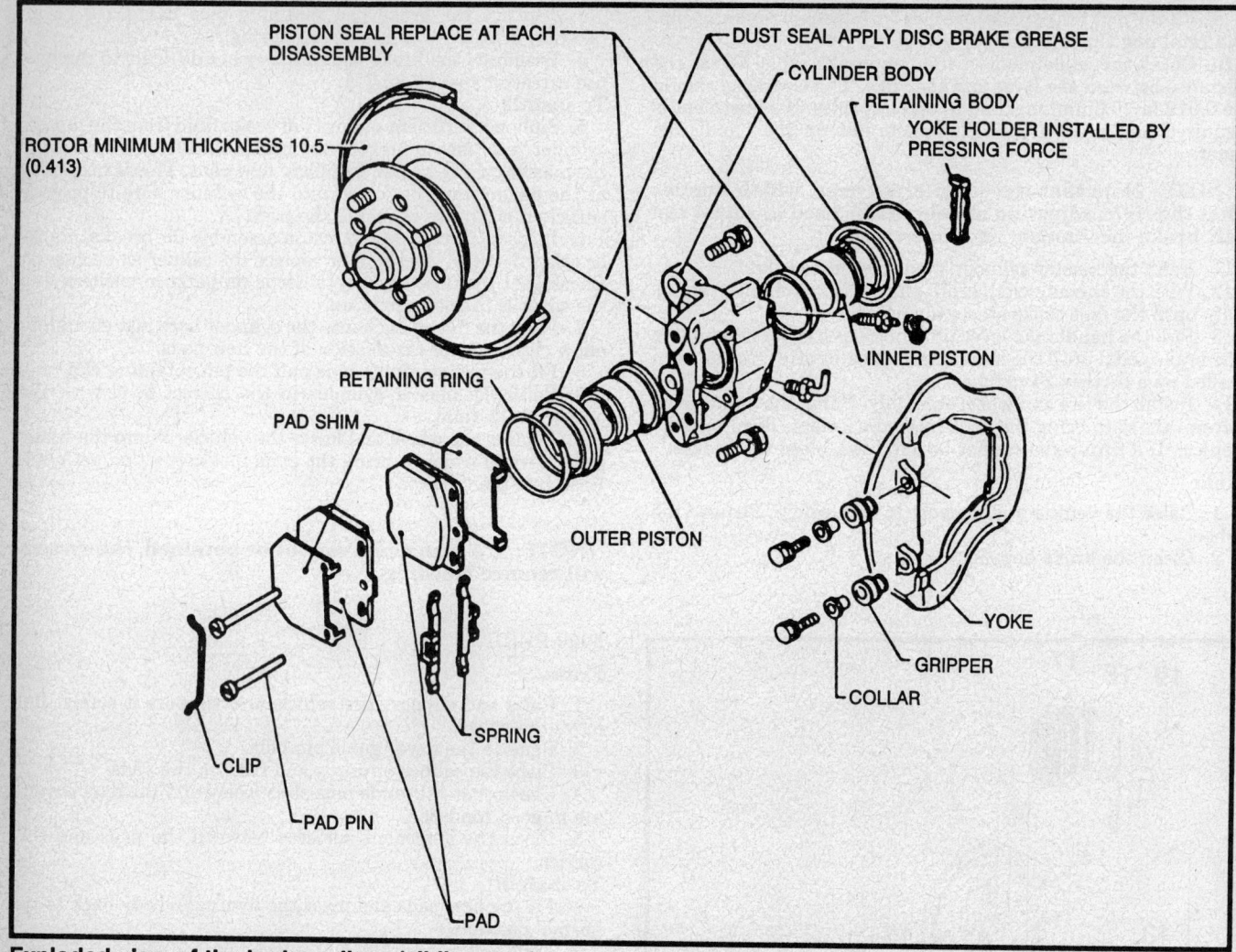

PISTON SEAL REPLACE AT EACH DISASSEMBLY

DUST SEAL APPLY DISC BRAKE GREASE

CYLINDER BODY

RETAINING BODY

YOKE HOLDER INSTALLED BY PRESSING FORCE

ROTOR MINIMUM THICKNESS 10.5 (0.413)

RETAINING RING

PAD SHIM

INNER PISTON

OUTER PISTON

YOKE

GRIPPER

COLLAR

CLIP

PAD PIN

SPRING

PAD

Exploded view of the brake caliper (sliding type)

Parking Brake Cable

Adjustment

900 SERIES

Check the adjustment of the handbrake cable. Check the distance between the handbrake lever and the yoke: the clearance should be a maximum 0.019 in. and should be equal on both sides. Adjust as necessary using the adjustment nut on the handbrake lever.

Note that the cables cross over therefore, the right adjustment nut should be used to adjust the left brake mechanism and vice-versa.

9000 SERIES

The parking brake is self adjusting on the rear calipers, however if necessary, check with a feeler gauge, that the clearance between the lever and the stop is 0.02–0.06 in. (0.5–1.5mm) Adjust as necessary by means of the adjusting screw at the handbrake lever inside the vehicle.

Removal and Installation

900 SERIES

1. Disconnect the negative battery cable.

2. Remove the drivers seat. Remove the carpet to provide access to the heater ducts.

3. Remove the gear lever cover. Be sure not to damage the ignition switch light.

4. Remove the air ducts and cover plates. Disconnect the cable from the adjustment nut on the handbrake lever. Remove the clip holding the 2 cables to the floor.

5. Remove the rubber bushing in the side of the wheel housing. Disconnect the cable from the handbrake lever at the brake cylinder housing.

6. Remove the cable from under the engine compartment.

7. Installation is the reverse of the removal procedure.

9000 SERIES

1. Disconnect the negative battery cable. Remove the passenger seat.

2. Slide the bush seal off the handbrake lever from inside the vehicle. Lift the plastic locking plate off the adjusting nuts.

3. Remove the rear section of the console assembly. Remove the bezel and slide the rubber boot off of the gear lever.

4. Remove the floor trim and fold back the carpet. Remove the screws retaining the cable cover. Remove the adjusting nuts from the ends of the cable at the handbrake.

5. Unhook the cable from the slot in the handbrake lever which is located on the caliper. Remove the boot and withdraw the cable.

6. Unscrew the cable lead through the bracket and the spring link.

7. Remove the cable from the vehicle.
8. Installation is the reverse of the removal procedure.

FRONT SUSPENSION

Shock Absorbers

Removal and Installation

900 SERIES

1. Disconnect the negative battery cable. Remove the upper shock absorber nut.
2. Raise the vehicle and support it safely. Remove the tire and wheel assembly.
3. Remove the shock absorber retaining bolts. Remove the shock from the vehicle. Save all washers and rubber parts.
4. Installation is the reverse of removal.

MacPherson Strut

Removal and Installation

9000 SERIES

1. Disconnect the negative battery cable. Raise and support the vehicle safely. Remove the front tire and wheel assembly.
2. Remove the front brake hose from the retaining clip on the strut assembly.
3. Unbolt the strut from the steering swivel arm.
4. Remove the 3 retaining bolts from the top of the strut.
5. Remove the strut from the vehicle.
6. Installation is the reverse of the removal procedure.

Coil Springs

Removal and Installation

900 SERIES

1. Disconnect the negative battery cable. Remove the upper shock absorber retaining nuts.
2. Raise and support the vehicle safely. Remove the tire and wheel assembly.
3. Install a spring compression tool or equivalent, engaging the upper shanks directly in the spring at the second free turn from the top of the lower shanks around the spring caps. These alignment shanks are located on the last turn of the spring with the color coded cup right beside the end of the coil.
4. Compress the spring at the top end, approximately 1½ in. If the upper spring attachment of the steel cone is left behind in the wheel housing, remove it.
5. Remove the spring and the steel cone from the vehicle.
6. Installation is the reverse of removal.

Ball Joints

Removal and Installation

1. Disconnect the negative battery cable. Raise and support the vehicle safely. Remove the tire and wheel assembly.

1. Upper control arm
2. Lower spring support
3. Coil spring
4. Rubber buffer
5. Shock absorber

Front suspension assembly

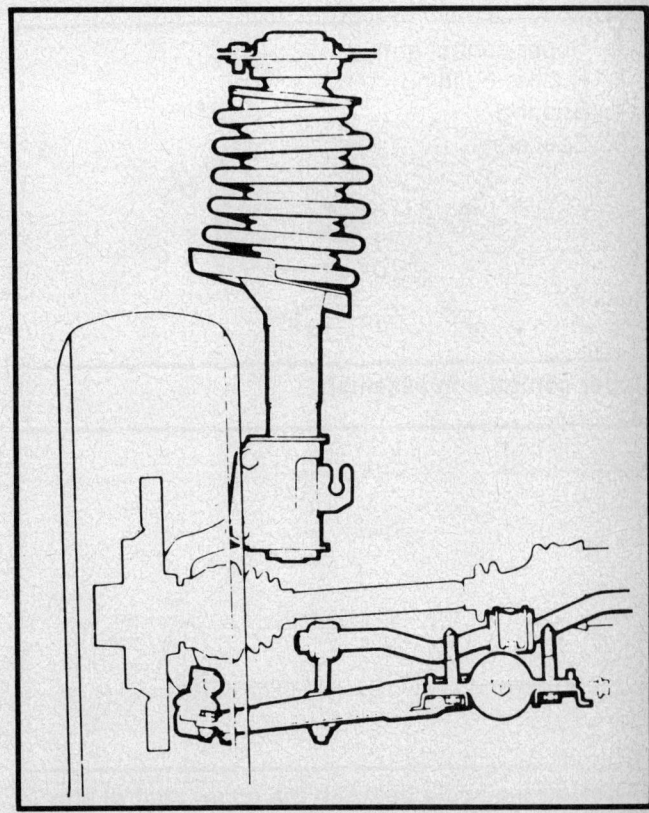

Front suspension assembly—9000 Series

2. Remove the brake housing and position it aside so the brake hose will not be damaged.

3. Remove the nut that holds the ball joint ball bolt to the steering knuckle housing. Remove the bolt using the proper removal tool.

4. Remove the ball joint from the control arm assembly.

5. Installation is the reverse of removal.

Upper Control Arms

Removal and Installation

900 SERIES

NOTE: To remove the left upper control arm, the engine must first be removed from the vehicle.

1. Raise the vehicle and support it safely.

2. Remove the tire and wheel assembly. Remove the shock absorber. Compress the coil spring, using a spring compression tool.

3. Remove the 2 bolts attaching the upper ball joint and lower spring seat to the upper control arm.

4. Remove the bolts from both upper control arm bearing brackets.

5. Remove the coil spring from the vehicle.

6. Remove the control arm and bearings from the vehicle. Save the spacers under the bearings and record the number of spacers used under each bearing.

7. Remove both of the bearing nuts. Now the bearings and bushings can be removed from the control arm.

8. Installation is the reverse of the removal procedure. When installing the bearings to the control arm, the angle between the control arm and the bearing should be 50–54 degrees when both nuts are tightened.

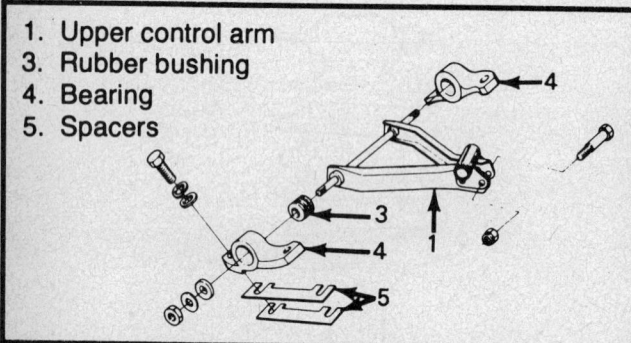

1. Upper control arm
3. Rubber bushing
4. Bearing
5. Spacers

Upper control arm assembly

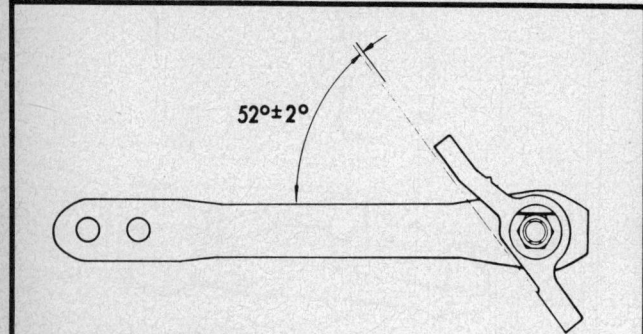

52°±2°

Checking the angle between the upper control arm and bearing

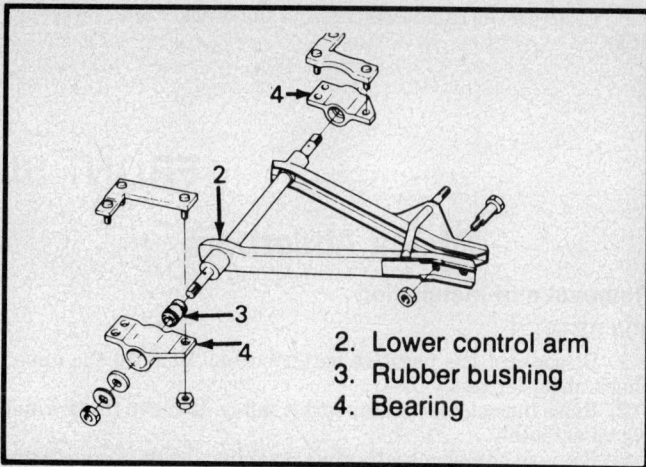

2. Lower control arm
3. Rubber bushing
4. Bearing

Lower control arm bushings—9000 Series

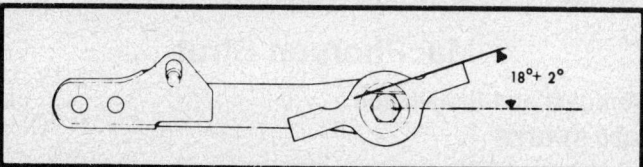

18°± 2°

Checking the angle between the lower control arm and bearing

Lower Control Arms

Removal and Installation
900 SERIES

1. Disconnect the negative battery cable. Raise the vehicle and support it safely. Remove the tire and wheel assembly.

2. Disconnect the lower end of the shock absorber.

3. Remove the 2 bolts that attach the ball joint to the control arm.

4. Remove the lower control arm attaching bolts from under the engine compartment floor.

5. Remove the control arm and its attaching brackets from the vehicle.

6. Remove the control arm bearing nuts and remove the bearings from the control arm.

7. Installation is the reverse of the removal procedure. When

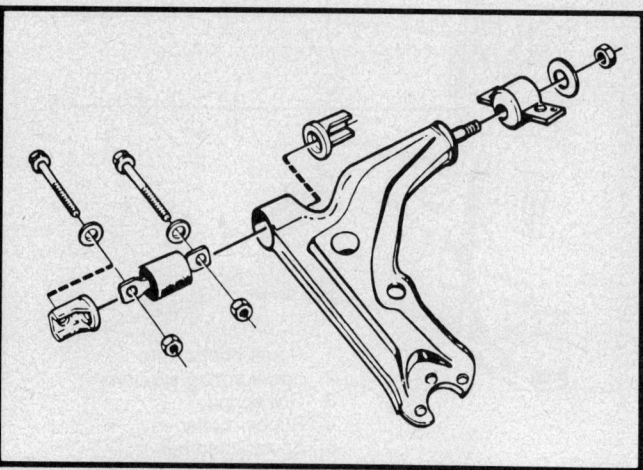

Lower control arm bushings—9000 Series

installing the bearings to the control arm., the angle between the control arm and the bearing should be 16–20 degrees when both nuts are tightened.

9000 SERIES

1. Disconnect the negative battery cable. Raise the vehicle and support it safely. Remove the tire and wheel assembly.
2. Remove the bolts securing the suspension arm to the ball joint.
3. Remove the nut from the bolt securing the suspension arm to the anti-roll bar link. Remove the upper securing bolt for the link.
4. Press down on the suspension arm and withdraw the anti-roll bar link.

5. Remove the nuts at the front of the suspension arm from the bolts securing the arm to the frame.
6. Remove the rear bolts securing the reinforcement member to the frame.
7. Remove the bolts securing the control arm rear pivot to the frame. Remove the control arm.
8. To install the arm, reverse the removal procedure, leaving the nuts for the bushings in the suspension arm rear pivot loose.

9. After the arm is installed and the remaining bolts in place, tighten the rear pivot bolts.
10. Check the wheel alignment and adjust as required, after the vehicle has been allowed to settle by bouncing or driving.

REAR SUSPENSION

Shock Absorbers

Removal and Installation

1. Disconnect the negative battery cable. Raise the vehicle and support it safely.
2. Place a suitable jackstand under the rear axle to prevent it from dropping and stretching the brake lines.
3. Position a jack at the rear of the spring link. Remove the shock absorber retaining nuts.
4. Remove the bolts in the spring link mounting on the rear axle—anti-roll bar on the 9000 series.
5. Lower the spring link so the shock absorber can be removed from the vehicle.
6. Installation is the reverse of removal.

Coil Springs

Removal and Installation

1. Disconnect the negative battery cable. Raise and support the vehicle safely.

2. Remove the tire and wheel assembly. Position a jack under the spring link and disconnect the lower end of the shock absorber.
3. From under the vehicle, remove the 2 locknuts that secure the front spring link bearing to the body of the vehicle.
4. Position a jackstand under the rear axle to prevent the brake lines from being damaged by the weight of the rear axle.
5. Lower the spring link so the spring can be removed from the vehicle together with the upper spring support and the rubber spacer at the lower spring seating which is retained by the spring tension.
6. Installation is the reverse of the removal procedure.

Rear Wheel Bearings

Removal and Installation

900 SERIES

1. Slide the hub onto the stub axle and install the washer locknut.

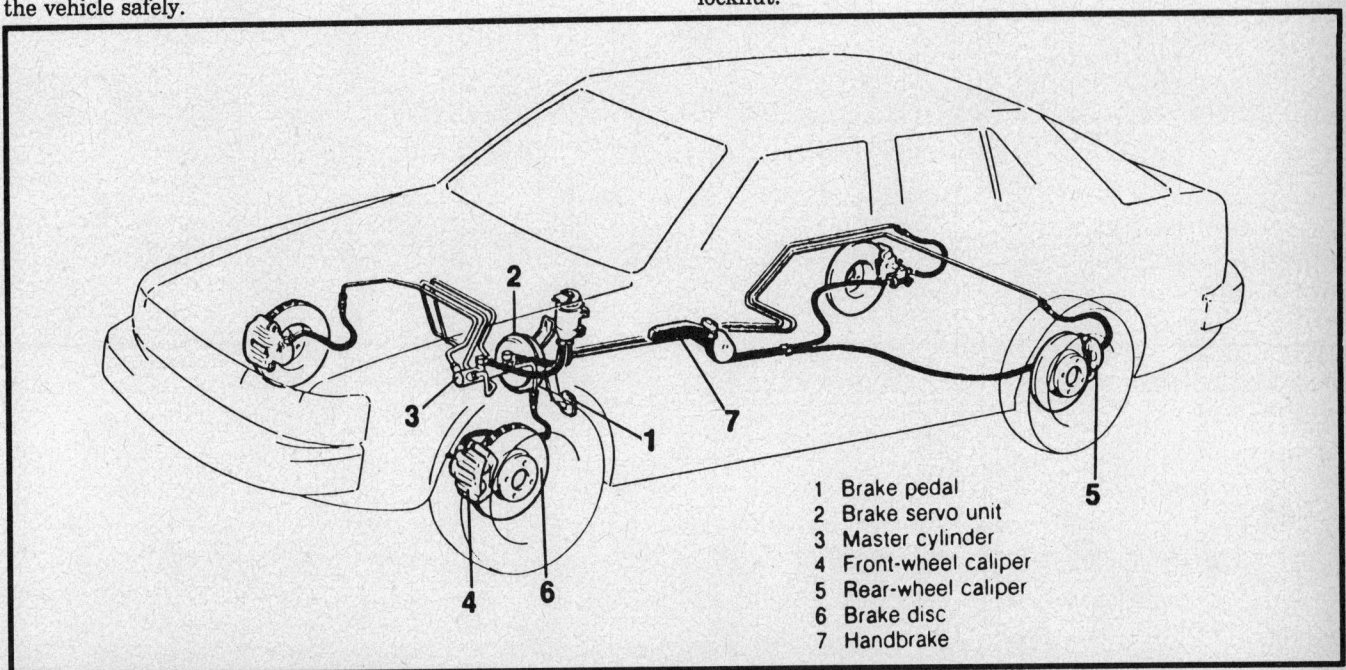

1 Brake pedal
2 Brake servo unit
3 Master cylinder
4 Front-wheel caliper
5 Rear-wheel caliper
6 Brake disc
7 Handbrake

Brake components—9000 Series

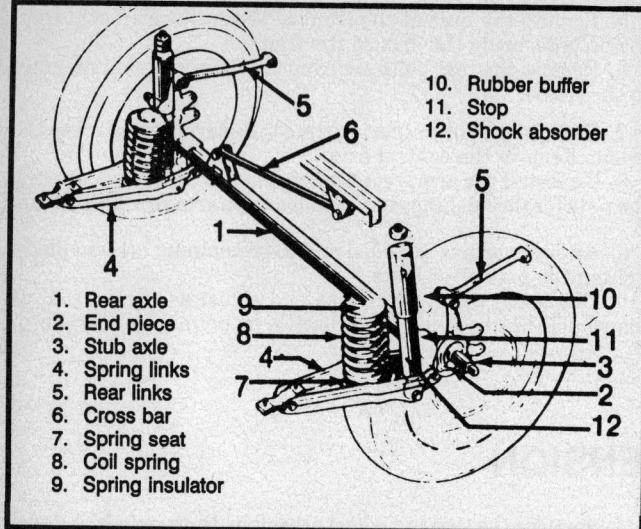

10. Rubber buffer
11. Stop
12. Shock absorber

1. Rear axle
2. End piece
3. Stub axle
4. Spring links
5. Rear links
6. Cross bar
7. Spring seat
8. Coil spring
9. Spring insulator

Rear suspension assembly

2. Tighten the locknut to a torque of 210 ft. lbs. (300 Nm). If the part of the nut collar that had previously been staked aligns with the locking groove, install a new nut.

3. Stake the nut collar into the locking groove.
4. Complete the assembly by installing the dust cap and install the brake disc, brake housing, wheel and wheel nuts.

9000 SERIES

The wheel bearings are not press fitted on the outboard driveshaft or stub axle, but are incorporated in the hub. The wheel bearings are double row, angular contact bearings which are permanently lubricated and maintenance free. The bearings cannot be replaced individually.

1. Disconnect the negative battery cable. Raise the vehicle and support it safely.
2. Remove the tire and wheel assembly.
3. Remove the brake caliper and disc back plate. Support the disc caliper on the rear axle. Remove the brake disc.
4. Remove the dust cap from the hub center nut. Remove the center nut and thrust washer. Pull the hub from the axle.
5. Upon installation of the hub, install the thrust washer and the nut.
6. Tighten the center nut to a torque of 195–208 ft. lbs.
7. Lock the nut by using drift to punch the flange of the nut in the stub axle thread. Install the dust cap, the disc brake components, the wheel and lower the vehicle.

SERIAL NUMBER IDENTIFICATION

Vehicle Identification Plate

The vehicle identification plate is located on the bulkhead in the engine compartment.

Vehicle Identification Plate is located on a plate attached to the bulkhead panel in the engine compartment

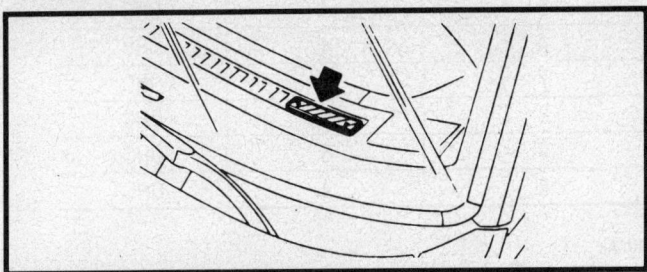

Vehicle Identification Number is located on the left side of the dash

Engine Number

The engine serial number is stamped on the front right side of the crankcase, on all engines except the 1200cc engine. On the

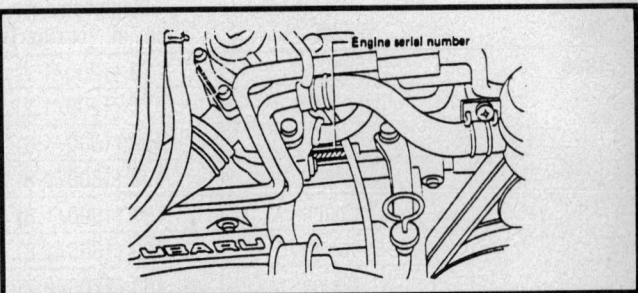

The engine number is stamped on the front right-side of the crankcase—except 1200cc engine

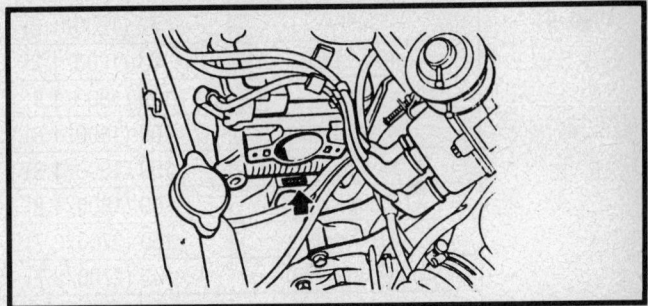

The engine number is stamped on the rear-side of the engine, below the cylinder head—1200cc engine

1200cc engine, the serial number is stamped at the right rear side of the engine below the cylinder head.

Vehicle Identification Number

The Vehicle Identification Number (VIN) is stamped on a plate located on the top of the dashboard on the drivers side and is visible through the windshield.

ENGINE IDENTIFICATION

Year	Model	Engine Displacement cu. in. (cc/liter)	Engine Series Identification	No. of Cylinders	Engine Type
1987	Justy	73 (1200/1.2)	7	3	OHC
	Justy 4WD	73 (1200/1.2)	8	3	OHC
	STD	109 (1800/1.8)	4	4	OHC
	STD 4WD	109 (1800/1.8)	5 ①	4	OHC
	XT Coupe	109 (1800/1.8)	4	4	OHC
	XT Coupe 4WD	109 (1800/1.8)	7	4	OHC
1988	Justy	73 (1200/1.2)	7	3	OHC
	Justy 4WD	73 (1200/1.2)	8	3	OHC
	STD	109 (1800/1.8)	4	4	OHC
	STD 4WD	109 (1800/1.8)	5 ①	4	OHC
	XT Coupe	109 (1800/1.8)	4	4	OHC
	XT Coupe 4WD	109 (1800/1.8)	7	4	OHC
	XT Coupe	163 (2700/2.7)	8	6	OHC
	XT Coupe 4WD	163 (2700/2.7)	9	6	OHC

ENGINE IDENTIFICATION

Year	Model	Engine Displacement cu. in. (cc/liter)	Engine Series Identification	No. of Cylinders	Engine Type
1989	Justy	73 (1200/1.2)	7	3	OHC
	Justy 4WD	73 (1200/1.2)	8	3	OHC
	STD	109 (1800/1.8)	4	4	OHC
	STD 4WD	109 (1800/1.8)	5②	4	OHC
	XT Coupe	109 (1800/1.8)	4	4	OHC
	XT Coupe 4WD	109 (1800/1.8)	7①	4	OHC
	XT Coupe	163 (2700/2.7)	8	6	OHC
	XT Coupe 4WD	163 (2700/2.7)	9①	6	OHC
	Legacy	135 (2200/2.2)	6	4	OHC
1990–91	Justy	73 (1200/1.2)	7	3	OHC
	Justy 4WD	73 (1200/1.2)	8	3	OHC
	Loyale	109 (1800/1.8)	4	4	OHC
	Loyale 4WD	109 (1800/1.8)	5	4	OHC
	XT Coupe	109 (1800/1.8)	4	4	OHC
	XT Coupe 4WD	109 (1800/1.8)	7	4	OHC
	XT Coupe	160 (2700/2.7)	8	6	OHC
	XT Coupe 4WD	163 (2700/2.7)	9	6	OHC
	Legacy	135 (2200/2.2)	6	4	OHC

NOTE: STD designates—4 door sedan
Station wagon
Touring wagon
3 door wagon

① Air Suspension
② Without Air Suspension; Code 7 with Air Suspension

GENERAL ENGINE SPECIFICATIONS

Year	Engine	Engine Displacement cu. in. (cc)	Fuel System Type	Net Horsepower @ rpm	Net Torque @ rpm (ft. lbs.)	Bore × Stroke (in.)	Compression Ratio	Oil Pressure @ 2000 rpm
1987	3 cyl (OHC)	73 (1200)	EFC Carb.	66 @ 5200	70 @ 3200	3.07 × 3.27	9.0:1	35–40
	4 cyl (OHC)	109 (1800)	Carb.	82 @ 4800	92 @ 2400	3.62 × 2.64	9.0:1	57–64
	4 cyl (OHC)	109 (1800)	SPFI	90 @ 5600	101 @ 2800	3.62 × 2.64	9.5:1	57–64
	4 cyl (OHC)	109 (1800)	MPFI	94 @ 5200	101 @ 2800	3.62 × 2.64	9.0:1	57–64
	4 cyl (OHC)	109 (1800)	MPFI Turbo	110 @ 4800	134 @ 2400	3.62 × 2.64	7.7:1	57–64
1988	3 cyl (OHC)	73 (1200)	EFC Carb.	66 @ 5200	70 @ 3200	3.07 × 3.27	9.0:1	35–40
	4 cyl (OHC)	109 (1800)	SPFI	84 @ 5200	137 @ 2800	3.62 × 2.64	9.5:1	57–64
	4 cyl (OHC)	109 (1800)	MPFI Turbo	115 @ 5200	181 @ 2800	3.62 × 2.64	7.7:1	57–64
	6 cyl (OHC)	163 (2700)	MPFI	NA	NA	3.62 × 2.64	9.5:1	57–64
1989	3 cyl (OHC)	73 (1200)	EFC Carb.	66 @ 5200	70 @ 3200	3.07 × 3.27	9.1:1	35–40
	4 cyl (OHC)	109 (1800)	EEM-SPFI	90 @ 5200	101 @ 2800	3.62 × 2.64	9.5:1	57–64
	4 cyl (OHC)	109 (1800)	EEM-MPFI Turbo	115 @ 5200	134 @ 2800	3.62 × 2.64	7.7:1	57–64
	4 cyl (OHC)	109 (1800)	EFC Carb. ①	73 @ 4400	94 @ 2400	3.62 × 2.64	8.7:1	57–64
	4 cyl (OHC)	109 (1800)	EEM MPFI ②	97 @ 5200	103 @ 3200	3.62 × 2.64	9.5:1	57–64
	4 cyl (OHC)	135 (2200)	EEM-MPFI	130 @ 5600	137 @ 2400	3.82 × 2.95	9.5:1	③
	6 cyl (OHC)	163 (2700)	EEM-MPFI	145 @ 5200	156 @ 4000	3.62 × 2.64	9.5:1	57–64

GENERAL ENGINE SPECIFICATIONS

Year	Engine	Engine Displacement cu. in. (cc)	Fuel System Type	Net Horsepower @ rpm	Net Torque @ rpm (ft. lbs.)	Bore × Stroke (in.)	Compression Ratio	Oil Pressure @ 2000 rpm
1990-91	3 cyl (OHC)	73 (1200)	EFC Carb.	66 @ 5200	70 @ 3200	3.07 × 3.27	9.1:1	35–40
	4 cyl (OHC)	109 (1800)	EEM-SPFI	90 @ 5200	101 @ 2800	3.62 × 2.64	9.5:1	57–64
	4 cyl (OHC)	109 (1800)	EEM-MPFI Turbo	115 @ 5200	134 @ 2800	3.62 × 2.64	7.7:1	57–64
	4 cyl (OHC)	109 (1800)	EEM MPFI ②	97 @ 5200	103 @ 3200	3.62 × 2.64	9.5:1	57–64
	4 cyl (OHC)	135 (2200)	EEM-MPFI	130 @ 5600	137 @ 2400	3.82 × 2.95	9.5:1	③
	6 cyl (OHC)	163 (2700)	EEM-MPFI	145 @ 5200	156 @ 4000	3.62 × 2.64	9.5:1	57–64

EEM Electronic Engine Managemnet
EFC Electronic Fuel Control
MPFI Multi-point Fuel Injection

SPFI Single-point Fuel Injection
① GL Hatchback
② XT

③ 14 psi 600 rpm
43 psi @ 5000 rpm

ENGINE TUNE-UP SPECIFICATIONS

Year	Model	Engine Displacement cu. in. (cc)	Spark Plugs Type	Gap (in.)	Ignition Timing (deg.) MT	AT	Compression Pressure (psi)	Fuel Pump (psi)	Idle Speed (rpm) MT	AT	Valve Clearance In.	Ex.
1987	Justy	73 (1200)	BPR6ES-11	0.040	5B	—	160	1.3–2.0	750–850	—	.0051–.0067	.0091–.0100
	STD	109 (1800)	BPR6ES-11	0.040	20B	20B	168	①	600–800	700–900	Hyd.	Hyd.
	XT Coupe	109 (1800)	BPR6ES-11	0.040	20	20	168	61–71	600–800	700–900	Hyd.	Hyd.
1988	Justy	73 (1200)	BPR6ES-11	0.040	5B	—	160	1.3–2.0	750–850	—	.0051–.0067	.0091–.0106
	STD	109 (1800)	BPR6ES-11	0.040	20B	20B	168	61–71 ④	600–800	700–900	Hyd.	Hyd.
	XT Coupe	109 (1800)	BPR6ES-11	0.040	20B	20B	168	61–71	600–800	700–900	Hyd.	Hyd.
	XT-6 Coupe	163 (2700)	BPR6ES-11	0.040	20	20B	168	61–71	600–850	700–850	Hyd.	Hyd.
1989	Justy	73 (1200)	BPR6ES-11	0.040	5B	5B	160	1.3–2.0	750–850 ②	800–900 ③	.0057–.0067	.0091–.0106
	STD	109 (1800)	BPR6ES-11	0.040	20B	20B	168	61–71 ④	600–800	700–900	Hyd.	Hyd.
	XT Coupe	109 (1800)	BPR6ES-11	0.040	20B	20B	168	61–71	600–800	700–900	Hyd.	Hyd.
	XT-6 Coupe	163 (2700)	BPR6ES-11	0.040	20B	20B	168	61–71	600–800	700–900	Hyd.	Hyd.
	Legacy	135 (2200)	BKR6E-11	0.040	20B	20B	168	36	600–800	700–800	Hyd.	Hyd.
1990	Justy	73 (1200)	BPR6ES-11	0.040	5B	5B	160	1.3–2.0	750–850 ②	800–900 ③	.0057–.0067	.0091–.0106
	Loyale	109 (1800)	BPR6ES-11	0.040	20B	20B	168 ⑤	61–71 ④	600–800	700–900	Hyd.	Hyd.
	XT Coupe	109 (1800)	BPR6ES-11	0.040	20B	20B	168	61–71	600–800	700–900	Hyd.	Hyd.

ENGINE TUNE-UP SPECIFICATIONS

Year	Model	Engine Displacement cu. in. (cc)	Spark Plugs Type	Gap (in.)	Ignition Timing (deg.) MT	AT	Compression Pressure (psi)	Fuel Pump (psi)	Idle Speed (rpm) MT	AT	Valve Clearance In.	Ex.
1990	XT-6 Coupe	163 (2700)	BPR6ES-11	0.040	20B	20B	168	61–71	600–800	700–900	Hyd.	Hyd.
	Legacy	135 (2200)	BKR6E-11	0.040	20B	20B	168	36	600–800	700–800	Hyd.	Hyd.
1991		SEE UNDERHOOD SPECIFICATIONS STICKER										

B BTDC
① Carb.—2.6-3.3   ② Idle-up system on—850–950   ④ SPFI—36–50
   MPFI—61-71   ③ Idle-up system on—900–1000   ⑤ MPFI Turbo—145
   SPFI—36–50

FIRING ORDERS

NOTE: To avoid confusion, always replace the spark plug wires one at a time.

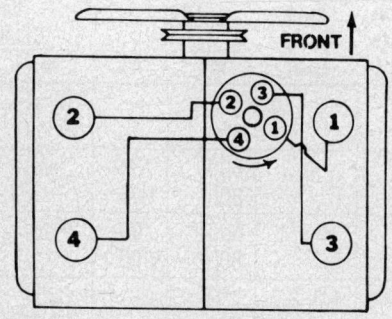

1600cc and 1800cc Engines
Engine Firing Order: 1–3–2–4
Distributor Rotation: Counterclockwise

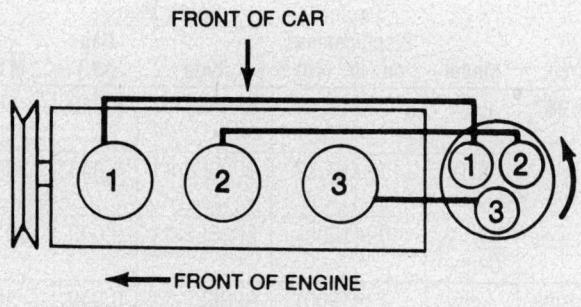

1200cc Engine
Engine Firing Order: 1–3–2
Distributor Rotation: Counterclockwise

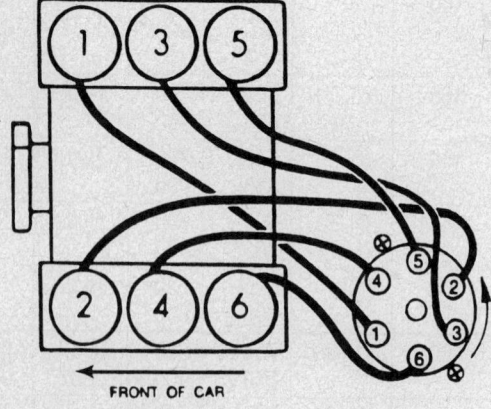

2700cc Engine
Engine Firing Order: 1–6–3–2–5–4
Distributor Rotation: Counterclockwise

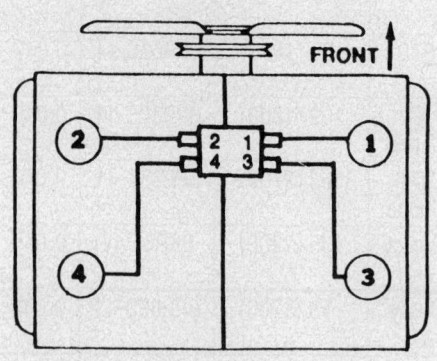

2200cc Engine
Engine Firing Order: 1–3–2–4
Distributorless Ignition System

CAPACITIES

Year	Model	Engine Displacement cu. in. (cc)	Engine Crankcase (qts.) with Filter	Engine Crankcase (qts.) without Filter	Transmission (pts.) 4-spd	Transmission (pts.) 5-Spd	Transmission (pts.) Auto.	Drive Axle (pts.)	Fuel Tank (gal.)	Cooling System (qts.)
1987	Justy	73 (1200)	3.0	2.0	—	4.8④	—	1.6	9.2	4.5
	STD	109 (1800)	4.2	3.2	—	6.0	10–13②	1.6	15.9	5.8
	XT Coupe	109 (1800)	4.2	3.2	—	5.4①	18	1.6	15.9	5.8
1988	Justy	73 (1200)	3.0	2.0	—	4.8④	—	1.6	9.2	4.5
	STD	109 (1800)	4.2	3.2	—	6.0	10–13②	1.6	15.9	5.8
	XT Coupe	109 (1800)	4.2	3.2	—	5.4④	20	1.6	15.9	5.8
	XT Coupe	160 (2700)	4.2	3.2	—	5.4④	20	1.6	15.9	7.4
1989	Justy	73 (1200)	3.0	2.0	—	4.8④	6.6–7.2	1.6	9.2	4.9
	STD	109 (1800)	4.2	3.2	—	④	14	2.6	15.9	5.8
	XT Coupe	109 (1800)	4.2	3.2	—	5.4④	19.6	3.0	15.9	5.8
	XT-6 Coupe	163 (2700)	5.3	4.2	—	7.4	19.6③	3.0	15.9	7.4
	Legacy	135 (2200)	4.8	4.3	—	7.0⑤	18.2	3.0	15.9	6.3
1990–91	Justy	73 (1200)	3.0	2.0	—	4.8④	6.6–7.2	1.6	9.2	4.9
	Loyale	109 (1800)	4.2	3.2	—	④	14	2.6	15.9	5.8
	XT Coupe	109 (1800)	4.2	3.2	—	5.4④	19.6	3.0	15.9	5.8
	XT-6 Coupe	163 (2700)	5.3	4.2	—	7.4	19.6③	3.0	15.9	7.4
	Legacy	135 (2200)	4.8	4.3	—	7.0⑤	18.2	3.0	15.9	6.3

① 4WD—11.9
② Differential—2.6
③ 4WD—29 pts.
④ 4WD—7 pts.
⑤ 4WD—7.4 pts.

CAMSHAFT SPECIFICATIONS

All measurements given in inches.

Year	Engine Displacement cu. in. (cc)	Journal Diameter 1	Journal Diameter 2	Journal Diameter 3	Journal Diameter 4	Journal Diameter 5	Lobe Lift In.	Lobe Lift Ex.	Bearing Clearance	Camshaft End Play
1987	73 (1200)	—	—	—	—	—	1.4520–1.4528	1.4520–1.4528	—	0.0012–0.0150
	109 (1800)	1.4946–1.4953	1.9080–1.9087	1.8883–1.8890	①	—	1.5650–1.5689	1.5650–1.5689	0.0008–0.0021	0.0012–0.0102
1988	73 (1200)	—	—	—	—	—	1.4520–1.4528	1.4520–1.4528	—	0.0012–0.0150
	109 (1800)	1.4946–1.4953	1.9080–1.9087	1.8883–1.8890	①	—	1.5650–1.5689	1.5650–1.5689	0.0008–0.0021	0.0012–0.0102
	163 (2700)	1.4946–1.4953	1.9080–1.9087	1.8883–1.8890	1.8687–1.8693	①	1.5606–1.5646	1.5606–1.5646	0.0008–0.0021	0.0012–0.0102
1989	73 (1200)	—	—	—	—	—	1.4520–1.4528	1.4520–1.4528	—	0.0012–0.0150
	109 (1800)	1.4946–1.4953	1.9080–1.9087	1.8883–1.8890	①	—	1.5650–1.5689	1.5650–1.5689	0.0008–0.0021	0.0012–0.0102
	135 (2200)	②	③	④			1.2752–1.2791	1.2752–1.2791	0.0022–0.0035	0.0012–0.0102

CAMSHAFT SPECIFICATIONS

All measurements given in inches.

| Year | Engine Displacement cu. in. (cc) | Journal Diameter | | | | | Lobe Lift | | Bearing Clearance | Camshaft End Play |
		1	2	3	4	5	In.	Ex.		
1989	163 (2700)	1.4946–1.4953	1.9080–1.9087	1.8883–1.8890	1.8687–1.8693	①	1.5606–1.5646	1.5606–1.5646	0.0028	0.0012–0.0102
1990-91	73 (1200)	—	—	—	—	—	1.4520–1.4528	1.4520–1.4528	—	0.0012–0.0150
	109 (1800)	1.4946–1.4953	1.9080–1.9087	1.8883–1.8890	①	—	1.5650–1.5689	1.5650–1.5689	0.0008–0.0021	0.0012–0.0102
	135 (2200)	②	③	④	—	—	1.2752–1.2791	1.2752–1.2791	0.0022–0.0035	0.0012–0.0102
	163 (2700)	1.4946–1.4953	1.9080–1.9087	1.8883–1.8890	1.8687–1.8693	①	1.5606–1.5646	1.5606–1.5646	0.0028	0.0012–0.0102

① Camshaft distributor LH journal: 1.5340–1.5346 in.
② RH front and LH rear—1.2573–1.2579 in.
③ RH and LH center—1.4738–1.4744 in.
④ RH rear and LH front—1.4935–1.4941 in.

CRANKSHAFT AND CONNECTING ROD SPECIFICATIONS

All measurements are given in inches.

| Year | Engine Displacement cu. in. (cc) | Crankshaft | | | | Connecting Rod | | |
		Main Brg. Journal Dia.	Main Brg. Oil Clearance	Shaft End-play	Thrust on No.	Journal Diameter	Oil Clearance	Side Clearance
1987	73 (1200)	1.6525–1.6529	0.0006–0.0018	0.0031–0.0070	4	1.6531–1.6535	0.0008–0.0021	0.0028–0.0118
	109 (1800)	①	②	0.0004–0.0037	2	1.7715–1.7720	0.0004–0.0021	0.0028–0.0130
1988	73 (1200)	1.6525–1.6529	0.0006–0.0018	0.0031–0.0070	4	1.6531–1.6535	0.0008–0.0021	0.0028–0.0118
	109 (1800)	①	②	0.0004–0.0037	2	1.7715–1.7720	0.0004–0.0021	0.0028–0.0130
	163 (2700)	③	④	0.0004–0.0037	3	1.7715–1.7720	0.0004–0.0028	0.0028–0.0130
1989	73 (1200)	1.6525–1.6529	0.0006–0.0018	0.0031–0.0070	4	1.6531–1.6535	0.0008–0.0021	0.0028–0.0118
	109 (1800)	①	②	0.0004–0.0037	2	1.7715–1.7720	0.0004–0.0021	0.0028–0.0130
	135 (2200)	2.3616–2.3622	0.0004–0.0012	0.0012–0.0045	3	2.0466–2.0472	0.0005–0.0015	0.0028–0.0130
	163 (2700)	③	④	0.0004–0.0037	3	1.7715–1.7720	0.0004–0.0028	0.0028–0.0130
1990-91	73 (1200)	1.6525–1.6529	0.0006–0.0018	0.0031–0.0070	4	1.6531–1.6535	0.0008–0.0021	0.0028–0.0118
	109 (1800)	①	②	0.0004–0.0037	2	1.7715–1.7720	0.0004–0.0021	0.0028–0.0130
	135 (2200)	2.3616–2.3622	0.0004–0.0012	0.0012–0.0045	3	2.0466–2.0472	0.0005–0.0015	0.0028–0.0130
	163 (2700)	③	④	0.0004–0.0037	3	1.7715–1.7720	0.0004–0.0028	0.0028–0.0130

① Front—2.1637–2.1642
Center—2.1635–2.1642
Rear—2.1636–2.1642
② Front and Rear—0.0001–0.0014
Center—0.0003–0.0011
③ Front—2.1637–2.1642
Center Both—2.1635–2.1642
Rear—2.1636–2.1642
④ Front and Rear—0.0001–0.0014
Center Both—0.0003–0.0011

VALVE SPECIFICATIONS

Year	Engine Displacement cu. in. (cc)	Seat Angle (deg.)	Face Angle (deg.)	Spring Test Pressure (lbs.)①	Spring Installed Height (in.)①	Stem-to-Guide Clearance (in.)		Stem Diameter (in.)	
						Intake	Exhaust	Intake	Exhaust
1987	73 (1200)	45	45	⑤	125	0.0008–0.0020	0.0016–0.0028	0.2742–0.2748	0.2734–0.2740
	109 (1800)	45	45	45.2–51.8 @ 1.121②	1.12⑪	0.0014–0.0026	0.0016–0.0028	0.2736–0.2742	0.2734–0.2740
1988	73 (1200)	45	45	⑤	125	0.0008–0.0020	0.0016–0.0028	0.2742–0.2748	0.2734–0.2740
	109 (1800)	45	45	45.2–51.8 @ 1.122④	—	0.0014–0.0026	0.0016–0.0028	0.2736–0.2742	0.2734–0.2740
	163 (2700)	45	45	45.2–51.8 @ 1.122③	—	0.0014–0.0026	0.0016–0.0028	0.2736–0.2742	0.2734–0.2740
1989	73 (1200)	45	45	⑤	125	0.0008–0.0020	0.0016–0.0028	0.2742–0.2748	0.2734–0.2740
	109 (1800)	45	45	45.2–51.8 @ 1.122④	—	0.0014–0.0026	0.0016–0.0028	0.2736–0.2742	0.2734–0.2740
	135 (2200)	45	45	⑥	—	0.0014–0.0024	0.0016–0.0026	0.2343–0.2348	0.2341–0.2346
	163 (2700)	45	45	45.2–51.8 @ 1.122③	—	0.0014–0.0026	0.0016–0.0028	0.2736–0.2742	0.2734–0.2740
1990–91	73 (1200)	45	45	⑤	125	0.0008–0.0020	0.0016–0.0028	0.2742–0.2748	0.2734–0.2740
	109 (1800)	45	45	45.2–51.8 @ 1.122④	—	0.0014–0.0026	0.0016–0.0028	0.2736–0.2742	0.2734–0.2740
	135 (2200)	45	45	⑥	—	0.0014–0.0024	0.0016–0.0026	0.2343–0.2348	0.2341–0.2346
	163 (2700)	45	45	45.2–51.8 @ 1.122③	—	0.0014–0.0026	0.0016–0.0028	0.2736–0.2742	0.2734–0.2740

① All values are for inner spring
② Outer spring—112–127 @ 1.201
③ Outer spring—100.5–115.5 @ 1.240
④ Outer spring—112.9–129.7 @ 1.240
⑤ Spring—112.8–129.8 @ 1.248
⑥ 1.457 in. @ 34.0–39.0 lbs.
1.154 in. @ 92.2–106.1 lbs.

PISTON AND RING SPECIFICATIONS

All measurements are given in inches.

Year	Engine Displacement cu. in. (cc)	Piston Clearance	Ring Gap			Ring Side Clearance		
			Top Compression	Bottom Compression	Oil Control	Top Compression	Bottom Compression	Oil Control
1987	73 (1200)	0.0015–0.0024	0.0079–0.0138	0.0079–0.0138	0.0120–0.0350 ①	0.0014–0.0030	0.0010–0.0026	Snug
	109 (1800)	0.0004–0.0016	0.0079–0.0138	0.0079–0.0138	0.0120–0.0350 ①	0.0016–0.0031	0.0012–0.0028	Snug
1988	73 (1200)	0.0015–0.0024	0.0079–0.0138	0.0079–0.0138	0.0120–0.0350 ①	0.0014–0.0030	0.0010–0.0026	Snug
	109 (1800)	0.0004–0.0016	0.0079–0.0138	0.0079–0.0138	0.0120–0.0350 ①	0.0016–0.0031	0.0012–0.0028	Snug
	163 (2700)	0.0006–0.0014	0.0079–0.0138	0.0079–0.0138	0.0120–0.0350 ①	0.0016–0.0031	0.0012–0.0028	Snug

PISTON AND RING SPECIFICATIONS
All measurements are given in inches.

Year	Engine Displacement cu. in. (cc)	Piston Clearance	Ring Gap			Ring Side Clearance		
			Top Compression	Bottom Compression	Oil Control	Top Compression	Bottom Compression	Oil Control
1989	73 (1200)	0.0015–0.0028	0.0079–0.0138	0.0079–0.0138	0.0120–0.0350 ①	0.0014–0.0030	0.0010–0.0026	Snug
	109 (1800)	0.0006–0.0012 ②	0.0079–0.0138	0.0079–0.0138	0.0120–0.0350 ①	0.0016–0.0031	0.0012–0.0028	Snug
	132 (2200)	0.0004–0.0012	0.0079–0.0138	0.0079–0.0138	0.0076–0.0276 ①	0.0016–0.0031	0.0012–0.0028	Snug
	163 (2700)	0.0006–0.0014	0.0079–0.0138	0.0079–0.0138	0.0120–0.0350 ①	0.0016–0.0031	0.0012–0.0028	Snug
1990–91	73 (1200)	0.0015–0.0028	0.0079–0.0138	0.0079–0.0138	0.0120–0.0350 ①	0.0014–0.0030	0.0010–0.0026	Snug
	109 (1800)	0.0006–0.0012 ②	0.0079–0.0138	0.0079–0.0138	0.0120–0.0350 ①	0.0016–0.0031	0.0012–0.0028	Snug
	132 (2200)	0.0004–0.0012	0.0079–0.0138	0.0079–0.0138	0.0076–0.0276 ①	0.0016–0.0031	0.0012–0.0028	Snug
	163 (2700)	0.0006–0.0014	0.0079–0.0138	0.0079–0.0138	0.0120–0.0350 ①	0.0016–0.0031	0.0012–0.0028	Snug

① For rails only
② Non-turbo; 0.0004–0.0012 for turbo models

TORQUE SPECIFICATIONS
All readings in ft. lbs.

Year	Engine Displacement cu. in. (cc)	Cylinder Head Bolts	Main Bearing Bolts	Rod Bearing Bolts	Crankshaft Pulley Bolts	Flywheel Bolts	Manifold		Spark Plugs
							Intake	Exhaust	
1987	73 (1200)	51–56 ②	30–35	29–33	47–54	65–71	14–22	14–22	13–15
	109 (1800)	44–50	30–35	29–31	66–79	51–55	13–16	19–22	13–15
1988	73 (1200)	51–57 ②	30–35	29–33	47–54	65–71	14–22	14–22	13–17
	109 (1800)	44–50	30–35	29–31	66–79	51–55	13–16	19–22	13–17
	163 (2700)	44–50	30–35	29–31	66–79	51–55	13–16	19–22	13–17
1989	73 (1200)	51–57 ②	30–35	29–33	58–72	65–71 ③	14–22	14–22	13–17
	109 (1800)	47 ①	29–35	29–31	66–79	51–55	13–16	19–22	13–17
	132 (2200)	④	⑤	32–34	66–79	58–62	NA	19–26	14–22
	163 (2700)	47 ⑥	29–35	29–31	66–79	51–55	13–16	19–22	13–17
1990–91	73 (1200)	51–56 ②	30–35	29–33	58–72	65–71 ③	14–22	14–22	13–17
	109 (1800)	47 ①	29–35	29–31	66–79	51–55	13–16	19–22	13–17
	132 (2200)	④	⑤	32–34	66–79	58–62	NA	19–26	14–22
	163 (2700)	47 ⑥	29–35	29–31	66–79	51–55	13–16	19–22	13–17

NA Not available
① 1st step—22 ft. lbs.
2nd step—43 ft. lbs.
3rd step—47 ft. lbs.
② 1st step—29 ft. lbs.
2nd step—54 ft. lbs.

3rd step—back off 90 degrees or more in reverse of tightening sequence
4th step—54 ft. lbs.
③ ECVT—54–61 ft. lbs.
④ 1st step—51 ft. lbs.
2nd step—back off bolts by 180 degrees

3rd step—25 ft. lbs. (bolts 1 & 2)
4th step—14 ft. lbs. (bolts 3–6)
5th step—Tighten all bolts 80–90 degrees in sequence
6th step—Retighten all bolts 80–90 degrees in sequence; not to exceed 180 degrees in 5th and 6th step

⑤ See text
⑥ 1st step—29 ft. lbs.
2nd step—47 ft. lbs.
3rd step—back off 90 degrees or more in reverse of tightening sequence
4th step—44–50 ft. lbs.

BRAKE SPECIFICATIONS
All measurements in inches unless noted.

Year	Model	Lug Nut Torque (ft. lbs.)	Master Cylinder Bore	Brake Disc Minimum Thickness	Brake Disc Maximum Runout	Standard Brake Drum Diameter	Minimum Lining Thickness Front	Minimum Lining Thickness Rear
1987	Justy	58–72	⑤	⑧	0.0060	7.09⑩	0.295①	0.067⑦
	STD	58–72	0.8125	0.630③	0.0040	7.09⑩	0.295①	0.259②
	XT Coupe	58–72	0.8125	0.630③	0.0040	7.09⑩	0.295①	0.259②
1988	Justy	58–72	⑤	⑧	0.0060	7.09⑩	0.295①	0.067⑦
	STD	58–72	0.8125	0.630	0.0040	7.09⑩	0.295①	0.259B
	XT Coupe	58–72	0.8125	0.787③	0.0040	7.09⑩	0.295①	0.259④
1989	Justy	58–72	⑤	0.610⑧	0.0060	7.09⑩	0.295①	0.067⑦
	STD	58–72	⑨	0.630③	0.0040	7.09⑩	0.295	0.059②
	XT Coupe	58–72	⑨	0.630⑪	0.0040	7.09⑩	0.295	0.059② ④
	Legacy	58–72	⑬	0.870③ ⑫	0.0039	⑥	0.295	0.256
1990–91	Justy	58–72	⑤	0.610⑧	0.0060	7.09⑩	0.295①	0.067⑦
	Loyale	58–72	⑨	0.630③	0.0040	7.09⑩	0.295	0.059②
	XT Coupe	58–72	⑨	0.630⑪	0.0040	7.09⑩	0.295	0.059② ④
	Legacy	58–72	⑬	0.870③ ⑫	0.0039	⑥	0.295	0.256

① Justy GL—0.315 in. (includes metal backing)
② Rear disc brake including metal backing
③ Rear disc brake—0.335 in. service limit 0.390 in standard
④ XT Coupe with 2700cc engine. Rear disc brake including metal backing—0.315
⑤ Small diuameter—7/8 in. Large diameter—1 in.
⑥ Not applicable
⑦ Standard—0.173 in.
⑧ Standard—0.709 in.
⑨ Small diuameter—13/16 in. Large diameter—1 in.
⑩ Service limit—7.17 in.
⑪ XT-6—0.787 in.
⑫ Standard thickness—0.940
⑬ L, LS models—1 in. LX models—1¹/₁₆ in.

WHEEL ALIGNMENT

Year	Model	Caster Range (deg.)	Caster Preferred Setting (deg.)	Camber Range (deg.)	Camber Preferred Setting (deg.)	Toe-in (in.)	Steering Axis Inclination (deg.)
1987	2WD XT Coupe	3⁵/₁₆P–4¹³/₁₆P	4¹/₁₆P	³/₄N–³/₄P	0	¹/₈–¹/₈	NA
	4WD XT Coupe	2⁵/₈P–4¹/₈P	3³/₈P	¹/₁₆N–1³/₈P	⁵/₈P	³/₆₄–¹/₈	NA
	2WD Sedan	1³/₄P–3¹/₄P	2¹/₂P	0–1¹/₂P	³/₄P	¹³/₆₄–³/₆₄①	NA
	4WD Sedan with Air Sup.	1⁷/₁₆P–2¹⁵/₁₆P	2³/₁₆P	⁷/₁₆P–1¹⁵/₁₆P	1¹³/₁₆P	⁵/₆₄–⁵/₁₆①	NA
	4WD Sedan without Air Sup.	1¹/₁₆P–2⁹/₁₆P	1¹³/₁₆P	¹⁵/₁₆P–2⁷/₁₆P	1¹¹/₁₆P	⁵/₆₄–⁵/₁₆①	NA
	2WD SW	1⁵/₁₆P–2¹³/₁₆P	2¹/₁₆P	¹/₄P–1³/₄P	1⑯	¹³/₆₄–³/₆₄①	NA
	4WD SW with Air Sup.	1⁷/₁₆P–2¹⁵/₁₆P	2³/₁₆P	⁷/₁₆P–1¹⁵/₁₆P	1¹³/₁₆P	⁵/₆₄–⁵/₁₅①	NA
	4WD SW without Air Sup.	1³/₁₆P–2⁵/₁₆P	1⁹/₁₆P	¹⁵/₁₆P–2⁷/₁₆P	1³/₄P	⁵/₆₄–⁵/₁₆①	NA
	Justy	1¹/₂P–3¹/₂P	2¹/₂P	⁵/₁₆N–1¹¹/₁₆P	¹¹/₁₆P	³/₃₂–¹/₂①	NA
1988	2WD XT Coupe	3¹⁵/₁₆P–4¹³/₁₆P	4¹/₁₆P	³/₄N–³/₄P	0	¹/₈–¹/₈	NA
	4WD XT Coupe (4 cylinder)	2⁵/₈P–4¹/₈P	3³/₈P	¹/₁₆N–1³/₈P	⁵/₈P	³/₆₄–¹/₈	NA
	4WD XT Coupe (6 cylinder)	2³/₄P–4¹/₄P	3¹/₂P	¹/₁₆P–1⁹/₁₆P	1³/₁₆P	³/₆₄–¹³/₆₄	NA
	2WD Sedan	1³/₄P–3¹/₄P	2¹/₂P	0–1¹/₂P	³/₄P	¹³/₆₄–³/₆₄①	NA

WHEEL ALIGNMENT

Year	Model	Caster Range (deg.)	Caster Preferred Setting (deg.)	Camber Range (deg.)	Camber Preferred Setting (deg.)	Toe-in (in.)	Steering Axis Inclination (deg.)
1988	4WD Sedan with Air Sup.	$1^{7}/_{16}$P–$2^{15}/_{16}$P	$2^{3}/_{16}$P	$^{7}/_{16}$P–$1^{15}/_{16}$P	$1^{13}/_{16}$P	$^{5}/_{64}$–$^{5}/_{16}$①	NA
	4WD Sedan without Air Sup.	$1^{1}/_{16}$P–$2^{9}/_{16}$P	$1^{13}/_{16}$P	$^{15}/_{16}$P–$2^{7}/_{16}$P	$1^{11}/_{16}$P	$^{5}/_{64}$–$^{5}/_{16}$①	NA
	2WD SW	$1^{5}/_{16}$P–$2^{13}/_{16}$P	$2^{1}/_{16}$P	$^{1}/_{4}$P–$1^{3}/_{4}$P	1P	$^{13}/_{64}$–$^{3}/_{64}$	NA
	4WD SW with Air Sup.	$1^{7}/_{16}$P–$2^{15}/_{16}$P	$2^{3}/_{16}$P	$^{7}/_{16}$P–$1^{15}/_{16}$P	$1^{13}/_{16}$P	$^{5}/_{64}$–$^{5}/_{15}$①	NA
	4WD SW	$^{13}/_{16}$P–$2^{5}/_{16}$P	$1^{9}/_{16}$P	$^{15}/_{16}$P–$2^{7}/_{16}$P	$1^{3}/_{4}$P	$^{5}/_{64}$–$^{5}/_{16}$	NA
	Justy	$1^{1}/_{2}$P–$3^{1}/_{2}$P	$2^{1}/_{2}$P	$^{5}/_{16}$N–$1^{11}/_{16}$P	$^{11}/_{16}$P	$^{3}/_{32}$–$^{1}/_{2}$①	NA
1989	2WD XT Coupe	$3^{15}/_{16}$P–$4^{13}/_{16}$P	$4^{1}/_{16}$P	$^{3}/_{4}$N–$^{3}/_{4}$P	0	$^{1}/_{8}$–$^{1}/_{8}$①	NA
	4WD XT Coupe (4 cylinder)	$2^{5}/_{8}$P–$4^{1}/_{8}$P	$3^{3}/_{8}$P	$^{1}/_{16}$N–$1^{3}/_{8}$P	$^{5}/_{8}$P	$^{3}/_{8}$① –$^{1}/_{8}$①	NA
	4WD XT Coupe (6 cylinder)	$2^{3}/_{4}$P–$4^{1}/_{4}$P	$3^{1}/_{2}$P	$^{1}/_{16}$P–$1^{9}/_{16}$P	$^{13}/_{16}$P	$^{3}/_{8}$① –$^{1}/_{8}$①	NA
	2WD Sedan	$1^{3}/_{4}$P–$3^{1}/_{4}$P	$2^{1}/_{2}$P	0–$1^{1}/_{2}$P	$^{3}/_{4}$P	$^{1}/_{4}$–$^{1}/_{16}$①	NA
	4WD Sedan with Air Sup.	$1^{7}/_{16}$P–$2^{15}/_{16}$P	$2^{3}/_{16}$P	$^{7}/_{16}$P–$1^{15}/_{16}$P	$1^{13}/_{16}$P	$^{1}/_{16}$① –$^{3}/_{16}$①	NA
	4WD Sedan without Air Sup.	$1^{1}/_{16}$P–$2^{9}/_{16}$P	$1^{13}/_{16}$P	$^{15}/_{16}$P–$2^{7}/_{16}$P	$1^{11}/_{16}$P	$^{1}/_{16}$① –$^{3}/_{16}$①	NA
	2WD SW	$1^{5}/_{16}$P–$2^{13}/_{16}$P	$2^{1}/_{16}$P	$^{1}/_{4}$P–$1^{3}/_{4}$P	1P	$^{1}/_{16}$① –$^{3}/_{16}$①	NA
	4WD SW with Air Sup.	$1^{7}/_{16}$P–$2^{15}/_{16}$P	$2^{3}/_{16}$P	$^{7}/_{16}$P–$1^{15}/_{16}$P	$1^{13}/_{16}$P	$^{1}/_{16}$① –$^{3}/_{16}$①	NA
	4WD SW	$^{13}/_{16}$P–$2^{5}/_{16}$P	$1^{9}/_{16}$P	$^{15}/_{16}$P–$2^{7}/_{16}$P	$1^{3}/_{4}$P	$^{1}/_{16}$① –$^{3}/_{16}$①	NA
	Justy	$1^{1}/_{2}$P–$3^{1}/_{2}$P	$2^{1}/_{2}$P	$^{5}/_{16}$N–$1^{11}/_{16}$P	$^{11}/_{16}$P	$^{5}/_{16}$–$^{1}/_{16}$①	NA
	Legacy FWD Sedan	$2^{1}/_{16}$P–$4^{1}/_{16}$P	$3^{1}/_{16}$P	$^{3}/_{4}$N–$^{1}/_{4}$P	$^{1}/_{4}$N	$^{1}/_{16}$–$^{1}/_{16}$①	NA
	Legacy FWD Wagon	$1^{13}/_{16}$P–$3^{13}/_{16}$P	$2^{13}/_{16}$P	$^{3}/_{4}$N–$^{1}/_{4}$P	$^{1}/_{4}$N	$^{1}/_{16}$–$^{1}/_{16}$①	NA
	Legacy 4WD Sedan	2P–4P	3P	$^{1}/_{2}$N–$^{1}/_{2}$P	0	$^{1}/_{16}$–$^{1}/_{16}$①	NA
	Legacy With Air Sup.	2P–4P	3P	$^{1}/_{2}$N–$^{1}/_{2}$P	0	$^{1}/_{16}$–$^{1}/_{16}$①	NA
1990–91	2WD XT Coupe	$3^{15}/_{16}$P–$4^{13}/_{16}$P	$4^{1}/_{16}$P	$^{3}/_{4}$N–$^{3}/_{4}$P	0	$^{1}/_{8}$–$^{1}/_{8}$①	NA
	4WD XT Coupe (4 cylinder)	$2^{5}/_{8}$P–$4^{1}/_{8}$P	$3^{3}/_{8}$P	$^{1}/_{16}$N–$1^{3}/_{8}$P	$^{5}/_{8}$P	$^{3}/_{8}$① –$^{1}/_{8}$①	NA
	4WD XT Coupe (6 cylinder)	$2^{3}/_{4}$P–$4^{1}/_{4}$P	$3^{1}/_{2}$P	$^{1}/_{16}$P–$1^{9}/_{16}$P	$^{13}/_{16}$P	$^{3}/_{8}$① –$^{1}/_{8}$①	NA
	2WD Loyale Sedan	$1^{3}/_{4}$P–$3^{1}/_{4}$P	$2^{1}/_{2}$P	0–$1^{1}/_{2}$P	$^{3}/_{4}$P	$^{1}/_{4}$–$^{1}/_{16}$①	NA
	4WD Loyale Sedan without Air Sup.	$1^{1}/_{16}$P–$2^{9}/_{16}$P	$1^{13}/_{16}$P	$^{15}/_{16}$P–$2^{7}/_{16}$P	$1^{11}/_{16}$P	$^{1}/_{16}$① –$^{3}/_{16}$①	NA
	2WD Loyale SW	$1^{5}/_{16}$P–$2^{13}/_{16}$P	$2^{1}/_{16}$P	$^{1}/_{4}$P–$1^{3}/_{4}$P	1P	$^{1}/_{16}$① –$^{3}/_{16}$①	NA
	4WD Loyale SW	$^{13}/_{16}$P–$2^{5}/_{16}$P	$1^{9}/_{16}$P	$^{15}/_{16}$P–$2^{7}/_{16}$P	$1^{3}/_{4}$P	$^{1}/_{16}$① –$^{3}/_{16}$①	NA
	Justy	$1^{1}/_{2}$P–$3^{1}/_{2}$P	$2^{1}/_{2}$P	$^{5}/_{16}$N–$1^{11}/_{16}$P	$^{11}/_{16}$P	$^{5}/_{16}$–$^{1}/_{16}$①	NA
	Legacy FWD Sedan	$2^{1}/_{16}$P–$4^{1}/_{16}$P	$3^{1}/_{16}$P	$^{3}/_{4}$N–$^{1}/_{4}$P	$^{1}/_{4}$N	$^{1}/_{16}$–$^{1}/_{16}$①	NA
	Legacy FWD Wagon	$1^{13}/_{16}$P–$3^{13}/_{16}$P	$2^{13}/_{16}$P	$^{3}/_{4}$N–$^{1}/_{4}$P	$^{1}/_{4}$N	$^{1}/_{16}$–$^{1}/_{16}$①	NA

WHEEL ALIGNMENT

Year	Model	Caster		Camber		Toe-in (in.)	Steering Axis Inclination (deg.)
		Range (deg.)	Preferred Setting (deg.)	Range (deg.)	Preferred Setting (deg.)		
1990-91	Legacy 4WD Sedan	2P-4P	3P	1/2N-1/2P	0	1/16-1/16 ①	NA
	Legacy With Air Sup.	2P-4P	3P	1/2N-1/2P	0	1/16-1/16 ①	NA
	Legacy 4WD Wagon	1³/₄P-3³/₄P	2³/₄P	1/2N-1/2P	0	1/16-1/16 ①	NA

Air Sup. Air suspension
SW Station Wagon
P Positive
N Negative
① Toe out

ENGINE ELECTRICAL

NOTE: Disconnecting the negative battery cable on some vehicles may interfere with the functions of the on board computer systems and may require the computer to undergo a relearning process, once the negative battery cable is reconnected.

Distributor

NOTE: The 1800cc and 2700cc engines with both the SPFI and MPFI systems use a LED and photodiode pulse pick-up in the distributor for cylinder and crankshaft location determination, for use in the electronic ignition system. The ignition circuits operates in the same basic manner as the standard electronic distributors used on the remaining engines.

Removal and Installation

UNDISTURBED ENGINE

1. Disconnect the negative battery cable. Remove the air cleaner assembly. If equipped, label and disconnect the hose from the distributor.
2. Disconnect the primary wire from the coil. If equipped with a breakerless ignition, disconnect the distributor electrical wiring connector from the vehicle wiring harness.
3. Disconnect the distributor cap retaining clamps or remove the screws and the cap from the distributor. Position the cap and ignition wires aside.

NOTE: If necessary to remove the ignition wires from the cap to provide room to remove the distributor, be sure to label the wires and the cap terminals for easy and accurate reinstallation.

4. Position the engine at TDC with No. 1 cylinder on the compression stroke or using chalk, mark the distributor rotor to distributor housing and the distributor housing to engine relationships.
5. Remove the distributor to engine hold-down bolt.
6. Remove the distributor from the engine, taking care not to damage or lose the O-ring.

NOTE: Do not disturb the engine while the distributor is removed. If the engine cranked or rotated while the distributor is removed, the engine will have to be retimed.

To install:
7. Position the distributor in the block, make sure the O-ring is in place, align the distributor rotor to housing marks and the distributor housing to engine marks.

NOTE: If equipped with an octane selector, install and tighten the hold-down bolt finger-tight.

8. To complete the installation, reverse the removal procedures. Recheck the ignition timing.

DISTURBED ENGINE

1. Disconnect the negative battery cable. Remove the air cleaner assembly. If equipped, label and disconnect the hose from the distributor.
2. Disconnect the primary wire from the coil. If equipped with a breakerless ignition, disconnect the distributor electrical wiring connector from the vehicle wiring harness.
3. Disconnect the distributor cap retaining clamps or remove the screws and the cap from the distributor. Position the cap and ignition wires aside.

NOTE: If necessary to remove the ignition wires from the cap to provide room to remove the distributor, be sure to label the wires and the cap terminals for easy and accurate reinstallation.

4. Remove the distributor to engine hold-down bolt.
5. Remove the distributor from the engine, taking care not to damage or lose the O-ring.

To install:
6. If equipped, remove the plastic dust cover from the timing port on the flywheel housing.
7. Remove the No. 1 spark plug. Use a wrench on the crankshaft pulley bolt and place the transmission in the N position and slowly rotate the engine until the TDC 0 degree mark on the flywheel aligns with the pointer.
8. If Step 7 is impractical for any reason, the following method can be used to get the No. 1 piston on TDC. Remove the 2 bolts that hold the right valve cover and remove the cover to expose the valves on No. 1 cylinder. Rotate the engine so the valves in No. 1 cylinder are closed and the TDC 0 degree mark on the flywheel aligns with the pointer.
9. Align the small depression on the distributor drive pinion with the mark on the distributor housing; this will align the rotor with the No. 1 spark plug terminal on the distributor cap.

NOTE: If equipped with an octane selector, set the pointer midway between the A and R. Make sure the O-ring is located in the proper position.

10. Align the distributor housing to engine matchmarks and install the distributor into the engine. Make sure the drive is engaged. Install the hold-down bolt finger-tight. Using a timing light, perform the ignition timing procedures.

11. To complete the installation, remove the timing light and reverse the removal procedures.

Distributorless Ignition

Removal and Installation

IGNITION COIL

2200cc Engine

1. Disconnect the battery negative terminal.
2. Remove the intake manifold cover.
3. Disconnect the wires from the ignition coil.
4. Remove the ignition coil.
5. To install, reverse the installation procedure.

Ignition Timing

Adjustment

JUSTY

1. Connect test mode connectors (2 pin type, Green in color), located beneath the left side of the instrument panel.
2. Allow the engine to reach operating temperature. Adjust the idle speed to specification. Connect a timing light, according to manufacturer's instructions.
3. Start the engine and check the ignition timing. If timing is not within specification, loosen the distributor hold-down bolt.
4. Rotate the distributor until the correct timing specification is reached. Tighten the distributor hold-down bolt.
5. Disconnect the test mode connector.

XT COUPE AND LEGACY

1. Allow the engine to reach operating temperature. Adjust the idle speed to specification. Connect a timing light, according to manufacturers instructions.
2. Be sure the idle contact of the throttle sensor is in the engaged position. Connect the test mode connectors together, located in the trunk area for both the 1800cc and 2700cc engines, using the MPFI system. The connectors will be found near of each other.

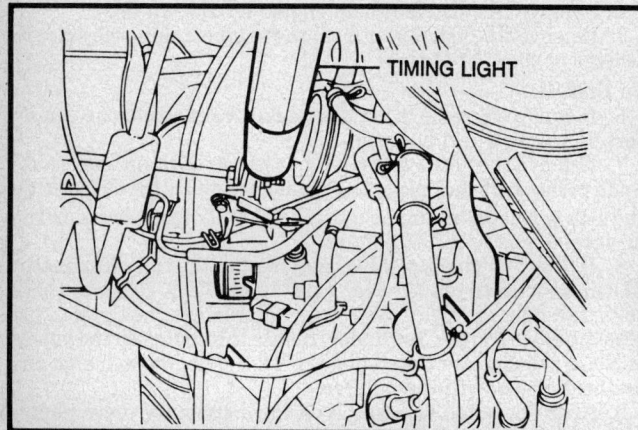

Timing mark location—except XT Coupe

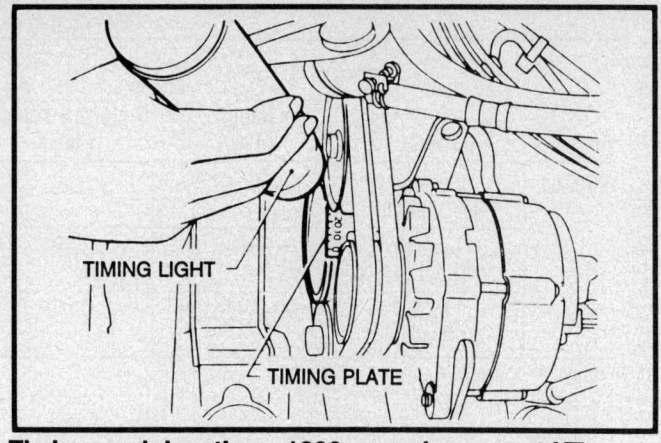

Timing mark location—1800cc engine except XT Coupe

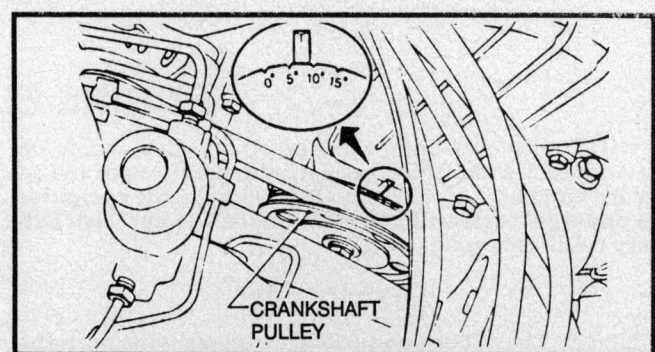

Timing mark location—1200cc engine

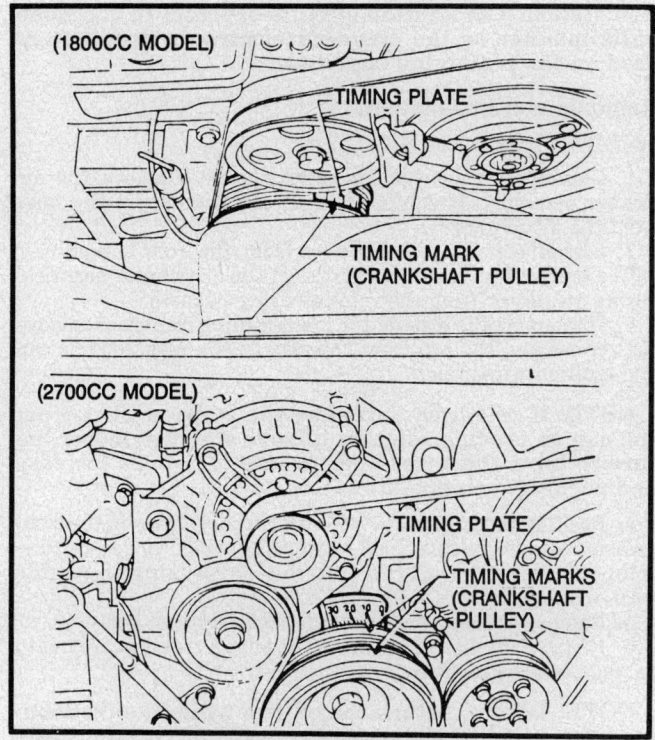

Timing mark locations—XT coupe equipped 1800cc and 2700cc engines

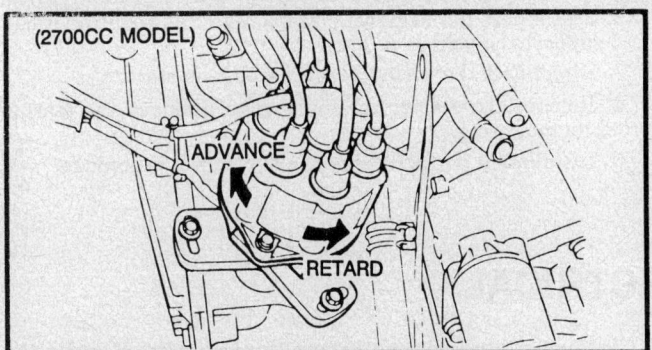

Distributor movement to change basic timing—2700cc engine

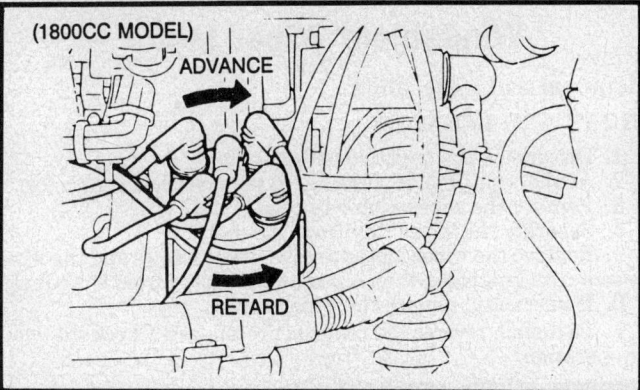

Distributor movement to change basic timing—1800cc engine

NOTE: The check engine warning light will come on; this does not indicate there is a problem. The ignition timing must not be adjusted and cannot be checked while the idle switch is disengaged or the test mode connectors disconnected.

3. If timing is not within specification, loosen the distributor hold-down bolt.

4. Rotate the distributor until the correct timing specification is reached. Tighten the distributor hold-down bolt.

EXCEPT JUSTY, XT COUPE AND LEGACY

1. Allow the engine to reach operating temperature. Adjust the idle speed to specification. Connect a timing light, according to manufacturer's instructions.

2. If the engine is equipped with a carburetor, disconnect and plug the distributor vacuum line.

3. Be sure the idle switch is in the engaged position. Connect the test mode connectors, located under the left side of the dash for the MPFI system or on the left side of the engine compartment for the SPFI system. The connectors will be located side-by-side.

NOTE: The check engine warning light will come on; this does not indicate that there is a problem. The ignition timing must not be adjusted and cannot be checked while the idle switch is inoperative or the test mode connectors disconnected.

4. If timing is not within specification, loosen the distributor hold-down bolt.

5. Rotate the distributor until the correct timing specification is reached. Tighten the distributor hold-down bolt.

NOTE: There is no timing procedures available for the 2200cc (2.2L), SOHC, 4 valve engine, since the ignition system is distributorless and is operated from crankshaft and camshaft sensors, using the "waste type" spark system.

Alternator

Precautions

Observing these precautions will ensure safe handling of the electrical system components and will avoid damage to the vehicle's electrical system.

• Be absolutely sure of the polarity of a booster battery before making connections. Connect the cables positive to positive and negative to negative. If jump starting, connect the positive cables first and the last connection to a ground on the body of the booster vehicle, so arcing cannot ignite the hydrogen gas that may have accumulated near the battery. Even a momentary connection of a booster battery with polarity reserved may damage the alternator diodes.

• Disconnect both vehicle battery cables before attempting to charge the battery.

• Never ground the alternator output or battery terminal. Be cautious when using metal tools around a battery to avoid creating a short circuit between the terminals.

• Never run an alternator without a load unless the field circuit is disconnected.

• Never attempt to polarize an alternator.

• Never disconnect any electrical components with the ignition switch turned **ON**.

Belt Tension Adjustment

1. To adjust the belt tension, first loosen the alternator to bracket adjusting bolt.

2. Lift up on the alternator to increase the tension on the belt. When it takes moderate thumb pressure to move the longest span of belt ½ in., the tension adjustment is correct.

3. Tighten the adjusting bolt so the alternator will not move in the adjusting bracket.

Removal and Installation

1. Disconnect the negative battery cable.

2. Label and disconnect the wiring from the alternator. Remove the necessary components in order to gain access to the alternator retaining bolts.

3. Remove the alternator retaining bolts.

4. Remove the drive belt. Remove the alternator from the vehicle.

5. Installation is the reverse of the removal procedure.

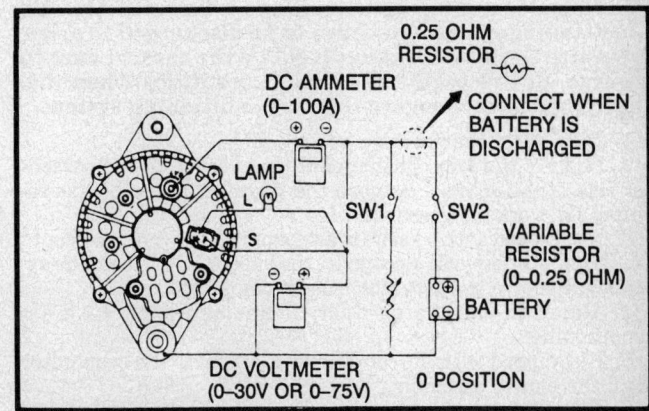

Test procedure for alternator

Starter

Removal and Installation

1. Remove the spare tire from the engine compartment, as required.

2. Disconnect the negative battery cable. As required, raise and support the vehicle safely.

3. Disconnect the wiring harness from the starter.

4. Remove the starter retaining bolts. Remove the starter from its mounting.

5. Installation is the reverse of the removal procedure.

CHASSIS ELECTRICAL

Blower Motor

Removal and Installation
JUSTY

1. Disconnect the negative battery cable.
2. Remove the coupler that connects the instrument panel harness to the blower motor.
3. Remove the coupler that connects the resistor to the instrument panel harness.
4. Detach the blower assembly. Remove the screws retaining the blower motor to the blower assembly.
5. Remove the motor assembly. Remove the nut retaining the fan to the motor assembly.
6. Installation is the reverse of the removal procedure.

XT COUPE AND LEGACY

NOTE: Depending upon working clearance the air conditioning system may have to be discharged in order to service the blower motor. If this is the case, be sure to observe all the required safety precautions when discharging and recharging the air conditioning system.

1. Disconnect the negative battery cable.
2. Remove the lower instrument panel cover on the passenger side of the vehicle.
3. Remove the glove box assembly, as required for working clearance.
4. Remove the heater duct, if not equipped with air conditioning.
5. If equipped with air conditioning, separate the evaporator from the blower assembly.
6. Disconnect the blower motor harness and the resistor electrical harness connector.
7. Remove the blower motor retaining bolts. Remove the blower motor assembly from its mounting.
8. Installation is the reverse of the removal procedure.

EXCEPT JUSTY, XT COUPE AND LEGACY

NOTE: Depending upon working clearance the air conditioning system may have to be discharged in order to service the blower motor. If this is the case, be sure to observe all the required safety precautions when discharging and recharging the air conditioning system.

1. Disconnect the negative battery cable.
2. Remove the lower instrument panel cover on the passenger side of the vehicle. Remove the glove box assembly, as required for working clearance.
3. If equipped with a vacuum actuator, set the control lever to the **CIRC** position and disconnect the vacuum hose from the assembly. Remove the actuator from its mounting.
4. Remove the heater duct, if not equipped with air conditioning.
5. If equipped with air conditioning, separate the evaporator from the blower assembly.
6. Disconnect the blower motor harness and the resistor electrical harness connector.

7. Remove the blower motor retaining bolts. Remove the blower motor assembly from its mounting. As required, separate the fan from the blower motor.
8. Installation is the reverse of the removal procedure.

Windshield Wiper Motor

Removal and Installation
JUSTY AND LEGACY

1. Disconnect the negative battery cable.
2. At the wiper motor, disconnect the electrical connector.
3. Remove the wiper motor to cowl bolts.
4. Separate the wiper link from the motor.
5. Remove the wiper motor to cowl panel screws and the wiper motor to link bolts, then separate the motor from the panel.
6. If necessary, replace the wiper motor.
7. To install, reverse the removal procedures. Check the wiper operation.

EXCEPT JUSTY AND LEGACY

1. Disconnect the negative battery cable.
2. Remove the wiper blades from the wiper arms by pulling the retaining lever up and sliding the blade away from the arm.
3. Slide the covering boot up the wiper arm.
4. Remove the wiper arms to linkage nuts and the arms.
5. Disconnect the electrical wiring connectors from the wiper motor.
6. Remove the cowl to body screws and the cowl from the vehicle.
7. Find or fabricate a ring which has the same diameter as the outer diameter of the plastic joint that retains the linkage to the wiper motor. Force the ring down over the joint to force the 4 plastic retaining jaws inward, then disconnect and remove the linkage.
8. Remove the wiper motor to firewall bolts and the motor.
9. To install, reverse the removal procedures. Install the wiper arms after the ignition switch has been ON for a few seconds to put the linkage in Park position.

Windshield Wiper Switch

Removal and Installation

1. Disconnect the negative battery terminal from the battery.
2. Remove the necessary dash to chassis screws in order to gain access to the wiper switch retaining screws.
3. Remove the windshield wiper switch to dash screws.
4. Remove the wiper switch.
5. Installation is the reverse of the removal procedure.

Instrument Cluster

Removal and Installation
JUSTY

1. Disconnect the negative battery cable. Remove the steering wheel.

2. Remove the defroster duct assembly.

3. Disconnect the heater control cable from the inside/outside air selector rod at the heater unit.

4. Disconnect the speedometer cable. Disconnect the electrical harness connectors.

5. Remove the covers for the instrument cluster retaining bolts.

6. Remove the instrument cluster retaining bolts. Remove the instrument cluster from its mounting.

7. Installation is the reverse of the removal procedure.

XT COUPE AND LEGACY

1. Disconnect the negative battery cable. Remove the lower cover on the driver's side. Remove the side ventilation duct.

2. Open the fuse box lid. Remove the fuse box to instrument panel screws and the fuse box.

3. Remove the lower cover on the passenger's side. Using a medium prybar, pry the upper cover, at 3 points, from the instrument panel.

4. Remove the console. Remove the steering column assembly, the combination meter and the control wing as a unit.

5. Disconnect the electrical harness connectors from the radio and other necessary components.

6. Remove the instrument panel to chassis bolts and the instrument panel from the vehicle.

7. Installation is the reverse of the removal procedure.

EXCEPT JUSTY, XT COUPE AND LEGACY

1. Disconnect the negative battery cable.

2. Remove the bolts securing the steering column and pull it down.

3. Disconnect the electrical wiring connectors, then remove the cluster visor screws and the visor, except on GL and GLF.

4. On the GL and GLF, remove the center ventilator control lever by pulling it. Remove the 3 screws accessible through the ventilator grille to the right of the cluster and the 1 screw accessible through the grille on the left. Remove the visor.

5. On the station wagon 4WD GL, remove the turn signal light switch.

6. Remove the cluster retaining screws, then pull the cluster out far enough to disconnect the speedometer cable and electrical connectors from behind, then remove the cluster assembly from the vehicle.

7. Installation is the reverse of the removal procedure.

Headlight Switch

Removal and Installation
EXCEPT JUSTY

The headlight switch is a part of a lighting switch assembly, installed on a control wing at the left side of the steering wheel.

1. Disconnect the negative battery cable.

2. Remove the lower steering column upper and lower cover screws. Remove the upper and lower covers from the column.

3. Remove the steering wheel center cover, the steering wheel to shaft nut and the steering wheel from the steering column.

4. Disconnect the electrical harness to steering column clip and band.

5. Remove the combination switch to steering column screws and the switch assembly from the steering wheel.

6. Remove the left control wing to steering column bolts and the left control wing from the steering column.

7. Remove the control wing case screws and separate the cases from each other. This will provide access to the headlight switch.

8. To replace the headlight switch knob, perform the following procedure.

    a. Using a pin rod, lightly push the pawl, inside the switch knob, inward and pull the knob outward. When removing the switch knob, be careful not to damage the switch brush.

    b. To install the knob onto the switch, place the knob on the switch, place a finger on the back side of the switch and squeeze the knob onto the switch.

9. If necessary, replace the headlight switch.

10. Installation is the reverse of the removal procedure. When reassembling the control wing cases, be careful not to get the electrical harness caught between the cases.

JUSTY

The headlight switch is a part of a gang switch located on the left side of the instrument panel

1. Disconnect the negative battery cable.

2. Remove the lower instrument panel cover and disconnect the electrical connectors.

3. Remove the upper instrument cluster glass screw and pull outward on the glass.

4. From the rear of the instrument panel cover, remove the lighting switch to panel screw and the lighting switch assembly from the cover.

5. Installation is the reverse of the removal procedure.

Combination Switch

Removal and Installation

1. Disconnect the negative battery cable. Remove the lower cover to instrument panel screws and the lower cover.

2. Remove the covers to steering column screws and the upper and lower column covers.

3. Remove the steering wheel cover and the nut. Using a steering wheel puller tool, remove the steering wheel from the steering column.

4. Remove the electrical harness to steering column clip and band fitting, then disconnect the electrical connectors.

5. Remove the combination switch to control wing bracket screws. Remove the switch assembly from its mounting.

6. Installation is the reverse of the removal procedure.

Ignition Switch

Removal and Installation

NOTE: The ignition switch is mounted to the steering column using shear bolts. These bolts are constructed so the heads shear off when the bolt is torqued.

1. Disconnect the negative battery cable. Remove the steering wheel.

2. Remove the upper and lower steering column covers from the steering column.

3. Remove the hazard knob.

4. Drill a pilot hole into the shear bolts, then using a screw extractor, remove the screws from the steering column.

5. Remove the ignition switch from the steering column.

6. Installation is the reverse of the removal procedure. Be sure to use new shear bolts to install the ignition switch.

Stoplight Switch

Removal and Installation

The stoplight switch is located on the brake pedal bracket, under the instrument panel. The switch is held in place by 2 locknuts which all the proper adjustment to be accomplished. To replace the switch, the wiring is disconnected, the locknuts are loosened and the switch removed.

After installation, the travel to operate the switch plunger is 0.071−0.130 in.

Neutral Safety Switch

Adjustment

This switch is mounted on the transaxle shift lever shaft, bolted to the transaxle. It also operates the back-up lights.
1. Remove the shift lever shaft nut.
2. Remove the shift lever from the shaft.
3. Make sure the slot in the shaft is vertical, **N** position.
4. Remove the switch mounting bolts but leave the switch in place.
5. Remove the setscrew from the lower face of the switch.
6. Insert a 0.059 in. drill bit through the set screw hole. Turn the switch slightly so the bit passes through into the back part of the switch.
7. Bolt the switch down.
8. Remove the drill bit and replace the set screw.
9. Install the lever and tighten the shaft nut.
10. Make sure the engine can start only in **P** or **N** and that the back-up lights turn functioning in **R**. Adjust the shift linkage, if necessary.

Fuse Box

Location

The fuse box is located under the left side of the instrument panel. The amperage for each fuse is stamped on the fuse box cover.

If equipped with 4WD, a fuse holder is located near the ignition coil. For servicing purposes, to change 4WD to FWD, insert a 15A fuse into the FWD fuse holder. The FWD pilot light, on the instrument panel, will turn illuminate to indicate the vehicle is set in the FWD mode.

On the Justy, a main fuse is located in the engine compartment, next to the brake master cylinder. All current, except for the starter, will flow through this fuse. When replacing the main fuse, be aware of the amperage rating, a 30A (pink) or a 60A (yellow).

ENGINE COOLING

Radiator

Removal and Installation

JUSTY

1. Disconnect the negative battery cable. Drain the cooling system.
2. Disconnect the radiator fan electrical connection. Remove the upper and lower radiator hoses.
3. Remove the radiator mounting bolts. Remove the radiator from the vehicle.
4. Installation is the reverse of the removal procedure.

XT COUPE

1800cc and 2700cc Engines

1. Disconnect the negative battery cable. Drain the cooling system.
2. Remove the radiator hoses. Disconnect and plug the automatic transaxle lines, if equipped.
3. Disconnect the main wire harness at the thermo-switch. Disconnect the fan electrical connection.
4. Disconnect the electrical wire from the secondary fan motor. Remove the upper and lower bolts retaining the shrouds to the radiator assembly.
5. Remove the shroud assembly along with the fan motor.
6. Remove the radiator mounting bolts. Remove the radiator from the vehicle.
7. Installation is the reverse of the removal procedure.

LEGACY

2200cc Engine

1. Disconnect the battery cables and remove the battery from the vehicle.
2. Drain the engine coolant and disconnect the radiator hoses at the engine.
3. Remove the V-belt cover.
4. Remove the reservoir overflow tank and hose.
5. Disconnect the radiator and air conditioning fan electrical wiring connectors.
6. Remove the radiator brackets at the top radiator support panel. Move the radiator sightly to the left.

7. Disconnect the automatic transaxle cooler lines from the radiator. Allow the fluid to drain into a container.
8. Lift the radiator/fan assemblies up and from the vehicle.

To install:
9. Attach radiator mounting cushions to the pins on the lower side of the radiator.
10. Fit the cushions on the lower side of the radiator, into holes on the body side and install the radiator with inlet and outlet hoses attached.
11. Install the radiator brackets and tighten the attaching bolts.
12. Connect the electrical wiring, the inlet and outlet hoses, install the reservoir tank and overflow hose.
13. Install the V-belt and tighten. Install the battery and connect the cables.
14. Remove the air vent plug on the radiator. Install the coolant into the radiator.
15. Operate the engine and correct the coolant level as required. Open the air vent plug as required to remove air from system.

─────────── **CAUTION** ───────────
Allow engine/coolant to cool before opening pressure cap or removing air vent plug. Excessive coolant temperature can cause personal injury should coolant blow-off occur.

EXCEPT JUSTY, XT COUPE AND LEGACY

1800cc Engine

1. Disconnect the negative battery cable. Drain the cooling system.
2. Remove the radiator hoses. Disconnect and plug the automatic transaxle lines, if equipped.
3. Disconnect the main wire harness at the thermo-switch. Disconnect the fan electrical connection.
4. Disconnect the electrical wire from the secondary fan motor. Remove the upper and lower bolts retaining the shrouds to the radiator assembly.
5. Remove the shroud assembly along with the fan motor.
6. Remove the radiator mounting bolts. Remove the radiator from the vehicle.
7. Installation is the reverse of the removal procedure.

Heater Core

Removal and Installation

JUSTY

1. Disconnect the negative battery cable. Drain the cooling system.
2. Disconnect the heater hoses from the heater core assembly.
3. Pull off the right and left defroster ducts from the defroster nozzles. Pull the ducts from the heater unit.
4. Disconnect the electrical wires from the fan switch and the blower motor.
5. Disconnect the air mix cable from the heater unit. Disconnect the mode cable from the heater unit.
6. Remove the bolts that retain the heater unit to the instrument panel.
7. As required, for working clearance remove the glove box door assembly.
8. Disconnect the inside/outside air control cable from the blower assembly.
9. Remove the instrument panel assembly.
10. Remove the heater unit retaining bolts. Remove the heater unit from the vehicle.
11. Remove the heater core cushion. Loosen the heater core holder and than remove it. Pull the heater core from its mounting and remove it from the heater case.
12. Installation is the reverse of the removal procedure.

XT COUPE AND LEGACY

NOTE: Depending upon working clearance the air conditioning system may have to be discharged in order to service the blower motor. If this is the case, be sure to observe all the required safety precautions when discharging and recharging the air conditioning system.

1. Disconnect the negative battery cable. Drain the cooling system.
2. Disconnect the heater hoses from the heater core assembly.
3. Remove the instrument panel assembly.
4. Disconnect the electrical harness connector from the blower motor assembly. Disconnect the temperature control cable.
5. Remove the heater unit retaining bolts. Remove the heater unit from the vehicle.
6. Remove the heater core retaining connectors. Remove the heater core from its mounting.
7. Installation is the reverse of the removal procedure.

EXCEPT JUSTY, XT COUPE AND LEGACY

NOTE: Depending upon working clearance the air conditioning system may have to be discharged in order to service the blower motor. If this is the case, be sure to observe all the required safety precautions when discharging and recharging the air conditioning system.

1. Disconnect the negative battery cable. Drain the cooling system.
2. Disconnect the heater hoses from the heater core assembly.
3. Remove the instrument panel assembly. Remove the console assembly.
4. Disconnect the electrical harness connector from the blower motor assembly. Disconnect the temperature control cable.
5. Remove the heater unit retaining bolts. Remove the heater unit from the vehicle.
6. Remove the heater core retaining connectors. Remove the heater core from its mounting.
7. Installation is the reverse of the removal procedure.

Water Pump

Removal and Installation

JUSTY

1. Disconnect the negative battery cable. Drain the engine oil. Drain the cooling system.
2. Remove the oil dipstick, dipstick guide and guide sealing.
3. Remove the alternator. Remove the timing belt.
4. Raise and support the vehicle safely. Remove the oil pan. Lower the vehicle.
5. Remove the water pump cover. Remove the water pump impeller. When removing the impeller, lock the balance shaft using the proper tool.
6. Remove the crankcase cover retaining bolts. Remove the crankcase cover along with the remaining water pump assembly.
7. Installation is the reverse of the removal procedure. Be sure to use new gaskets or RTV sealant, as required.

XT COUPE

1800cc Engine

1. Disconnect the negative battery cable. Drain the cooling system.
2. Disconnect the radiator hose and bypass hose from the water pump.
3. Loosen the pulley nuts. Loosen the alternator mounting bolts. Remove the drive belt.
4. Remove the timing belt cover. Remove the water pump retaining bolts. Remove the water pump from the engine.
5. Installation is the reverse of the removal procedure. Be sure to use a new gasket or RTV sealant, as required.

2700cc Engine

1. Disconnect the negative battery cable. Drain the cooling system.
2. Disconnect the radiator hose, bypass hose and air vent hose from the water pump.
3. Loosen the pulley nuts. Loosen the belt tensioner pulley locking nut. Remove the drive belt.
4. Remove the timing belt cover. Remove the water pump retaining bolts. Remove the water pump from the engine.
5. Installation is the reverse of the removal procedure. Be sure to use a new gasket or RTV sealant, as required.

LEGACY

2200cc Engine

1. Disconnect the negative cable from the battery.
2. Drain the cooling system.
3. Disconnect the lower radiator hose.
4. Disconnect the electrical connectors and remove the radiator fan motor assembly.
5. Remove the V-belts as necessary.
6. Remove the timing belt covers and the timing belt.
7. Remove the tensioner adjuster and the cam angle sensor.
8. Remove the left camshaft pulley.
9. Remove the left rear timing belt cover.
10. Remove the tensioner bracket.
11. Disconnect the radiator and heater hoses from the water pump assembly.
12. Remove the water pump assembly.
13. Inspect the water pump and replace, as required.
14. After the water pump is in place, complete the assembly of the components in the reverse of their removal.
15. Fill the cooling system and correct the level as required, during and after the warm-up.

─────── **CAUTION** ───────

Allow engine/coolant to cool before opening pressure cap or removing air vent plug. Excessive coolant temperature can cause personal injury should coolant blow-off occurs.

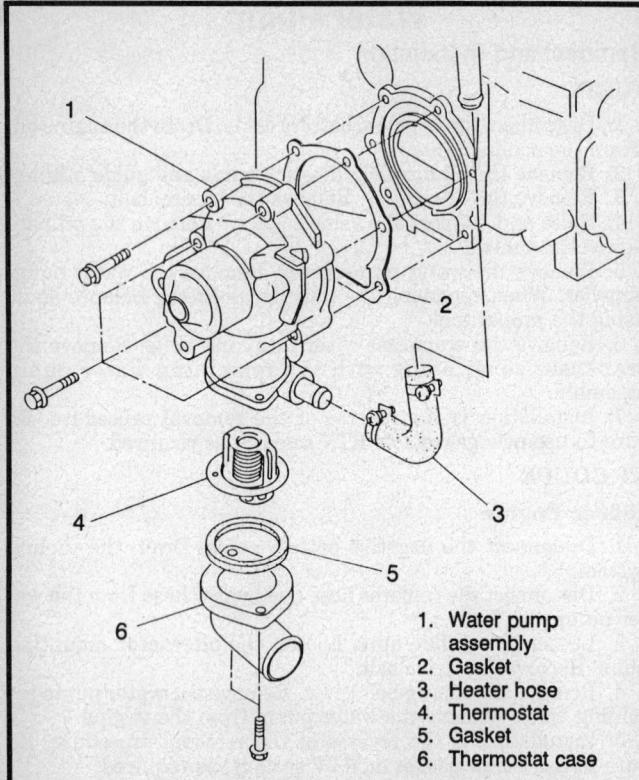

Water pump servicing—2200cc engine

1. Water pump assembly
2. Gasket
3. Heater hose
4. Thermostat
5. Gasket
6. Thermostat case

EXCEPT JUSTY, XT COUPE AND LEGACY

1800cc Engine

1. Disconnect the negative battery cable. Drain the cooling system.
2. Disconnect the radiator hose and bypass hose from the water pump.
3. Loosen the pulley nuts. Loosen the alternator mounting bolts. Remove the drive belt.
4. Remove the timing belt cover. Remove the water pump retaining bolts. Remove the water pump from the engine.

5. Installation is the reverse of the removal procedure. Be sure to use a new gasket or RTV sealant, as required.

Thermostat

Removal and Installation
JUSTY

1. Disconnect the negative battery cable. Drain the cooling system.
2. Remove the thermostat housing retaining bolts. Remove the thermostat housing and cover assembly.
3. Remove the thermostat from the intake manifold.
4. Installation is the reverse of the removal procedure. Be sure to use a new gasket or RTV sealant, as required.

XT COUPE

1800cc and 2700cc Engines

1. Disconnect the negative battery cable. Drain the cooling system.
2. Remove the thermostat housing retaining bolts. Remove the thermostat housing and cover assembly.
3. Remove the thermostat from the intake manifold.
4. Installation is the reverse of the removal procedure. Be sure to use a new gasket or RTV sealant, as required.

LEGACY

2200cc Engine

NOTE: The thermostat housing is bolted to the lower front of the water pump assembly. The manufacturer has not published a procedure for thermostat replacement. The thermostat may have to be replace from under the vehicle or the removal of necessary components in order to remove it from the top of the vehicle.

EXCEPT JUSTY, XT COUPE AND LEGACY

1800cc Engine

1. Disconnect the negative battery cable. Drain the cooling system.
2. Remove the thermostat housing retaining bolts. Remove the thermostat housing and cover assembly.
3. Remove the thermostat from the intake manifold.
4. Installation is the reverse of the removal procedure. Be sure to use a new gasket or RTV sealant, as required.

FUEL SYSTEM

Relieving Fuel System Pressure
FUEL INJECTED VEHICLES

1. Disconnect the electrical wiring connector from the fuel pump.
2. Start the engine. Once the engine has stopped, crank the engine for more than 5 seconds. If the engine starts, let the engine run until it stops.
3. Turn the ignition switch OFF.
4. Reconnect the electrical wiring connector of the fuel pump.

Fuel Filter

Removal and Installation
JUSTY

1. Carefully relieve the fuel pump pressure. As required, raise and support the vehicle safely.

2. Remove the flange bolts and remove the lower fuel pump bracket assembly.
3. Disconnect and plug the fuel lines at the fuel filter.
4. Remove the fuel filter retaining bolts. Remove the fuel filter assembly from its mounting.
5. Installation is the reverse of the removal procedure.

XT COUPE AND LEGACY

The fuel filter is located inside the engine compartment on the left fender assembly.

1. Properly relieve the fuel system pressure.
2. Disconnect the fuel lines from the fuel filter.
3. Pull the fuel filter from the bracket and remove it from the vehicle.
4. Installation is the reverse of the removal procedure. Start the engine and check for leaks.

EXCEPT JUSTY, XT COUPE AND LEGACY

Carbureted Engine

1. Disconnect the negative battery cable.
2. Raise and support the vehicle safely.
3. Disconnect the fuel hoses from the fuel filter.
4. Pull the fuel filter from the bracket and remove it from the vehicle.
5. Installation is the reverse of the removal procedure.

Fuel Injected Engine

The fuel filter is located inside the engine compartment on the left fender assembly.

1. Properly relieve the fuel system pressure.
2. Disconnect the fuel lines from the fuel filter.
3. Pull the fuel filter from the bracket and remove it from the vehicle.
4. Installation is the reverse of the removal procedure. Start the engine and check for leaks.

Electric Fuel Pump

Pressure Testing

1. Raise and support the vehicle safely.
2. Using a fuel pressure gauge, connect into the fuel line.
3. Turn the ignition switch to the **ON** position. Observe the fuel pressure, it should be:
   - 2.6–3.3 psi for carburetor equipped vehicle.
   - 61–71 psi for MPFI equipped vehicle.
   - 36–50 psi for SPFI equipped vehicle.
4. If the fuel pump does not meet specification, replace it.
5. After testing, disconnect the pressure gauge and reconnect the fuel line.

Removal and Installation

JUSTY

1. Carefully relieve the fuel pump pressure. As required, raise and support the vehicle safely.
2. Remove the flange bolts and remove the lower fuel pump bracket assembly.
3. Disconnect and plug the fuel lines at the fuel pump assembly. Disconnect the fuel pump electrical connector.
4. Remove the fuel pump assembly retaining bolts. Remove the fuel pump assembly from its mounting.
5. Installation is the reverse of the removal procedure.

XT COUPE AND LEGACY

1. Relieve the fuel system pressure.
2. Raise and support the vehicle safely. Devise a clamp for the thicker hose leading to the pump and clamp it off a few inches from the nipple on the pump. This will prevent the fuel from running from the tank while the pump is disconnected.
3. Being careful not to bend the hose sharply, loosen the hose clamp and disconnect the large hose leading into the pump. Do the same with the outlet from the damper.
4. Remove the pump bracket to chassis retaining bolts. Remove the fuel pump and pump damper assembly.
5. Installation is the reverse of the removal procedure.

EXCEPT JUSTY, XT COUPE AND LEGACY

Carbureted Engine

1. Carefully relieve the fuel pump pressure. As required, raise and support the vehicle safely.
2. Remove the flange bolts and remove the lower fuel pump bracket assembly.
3. Disconnect and plug the fuel lines at the fuel pump assembly. Disconnect the fuel pump electrical connector.
4. Remove the fuel pump assembly retaining bolts. Remove the fuel pump assembly from its mounting.

5. Installation is the reverse of the removal procedure.

Fuel Injected Engine

1. Properly relieve the fuel system pressure.
2. Raise and support the vehicle safely. Devise a clamp for the thicker hose leading to the pump and clamp it off a few inches from the nipple on the pump. This will prevent the fuel from running from the tank while the pump is disconnected.
3. Being careful not to bend the hose sharply, loosen the hose clamp and disconnect the large hose leading into the pump. Do the same with the outlet from the damper.
4. Remove the pump bracket to chassis retaining bolts. Remove the fuel pump and pump damper assembly.
5. Installation is the reverse of the removal procedure.

Carburetor

Removal and Installation

JUSTY

1. Disconnect the negative battery cable. Remove the air cleaner assembly.
2. Disconnect the fuel line. Disconnect the return and vent line hoses.
3. Disconnect the main diaphragm, distributor vacuum line and canister vent hose.
4. Disconnect the idle solenoid valve wires and hoses. Disconnect the harness electrical connector.
5. Disconnect the primary and secondary air bleed hoses. Disconnect the accelerator cable from the throttle lever.
6. Remove the carburetor retaining bolts. remove the carburetor from its mounting. Discard the gasket.
7. Installation is the reverse of the removal procedure. Be sure to use a new base gasket.

EXCEPT JUSTY AND XT COUPE

1. Disconnect the negative battery cable. Remove the air cleaner assembly.
2. Disconnect the fuel line. Disconnect the return and vent line hoses.
3. Disconnect the carburetor vent hose for the ECC system. Disconnect the remaining required vacuum hoses.
4. Disconnect the EGR tube, if equipped. Disconnect the distributor vacuum hose.
5. If equipped with an Hitachi carburetor, disconnect the ignition retard, if applicable. Disconnect the vacuum hoses from the solenoid valves, the main diaphragm on high altitude carburetors and the secondary main air bleed. Disconnect the duty solenoid valve connector, if equipped.
6. Disconnect the electrical harness connectors and the accelerator cable from the throttle lever.
7. Drain the radiator, to a level below the water heated throttle bore.
8. Remove the carburetor to intake manifold nuts. Remove the carburetor from the vehicle.
9. Installation is the reverse of the removal procedure.

Primary/Secondary Throttle Linkage Adjustment

1. With the carburetor removed from the engine, operate the linkage so the connecting rod contacts the groove on the end of the secondary actuating lever.
2. Measure the clearance between the lower end of the primary throttle valve and it's bore. It should be:
   - Except Justy—0.27 in.
   - Justy—0.26 in.
3. Adjust the clearance by bending the connecting rod.
4. Check that the linkage operates smoothly.

Float and Fuel Level Adjustment

If equipped with a sight glass on the carburetor float bowl, the

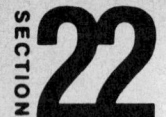
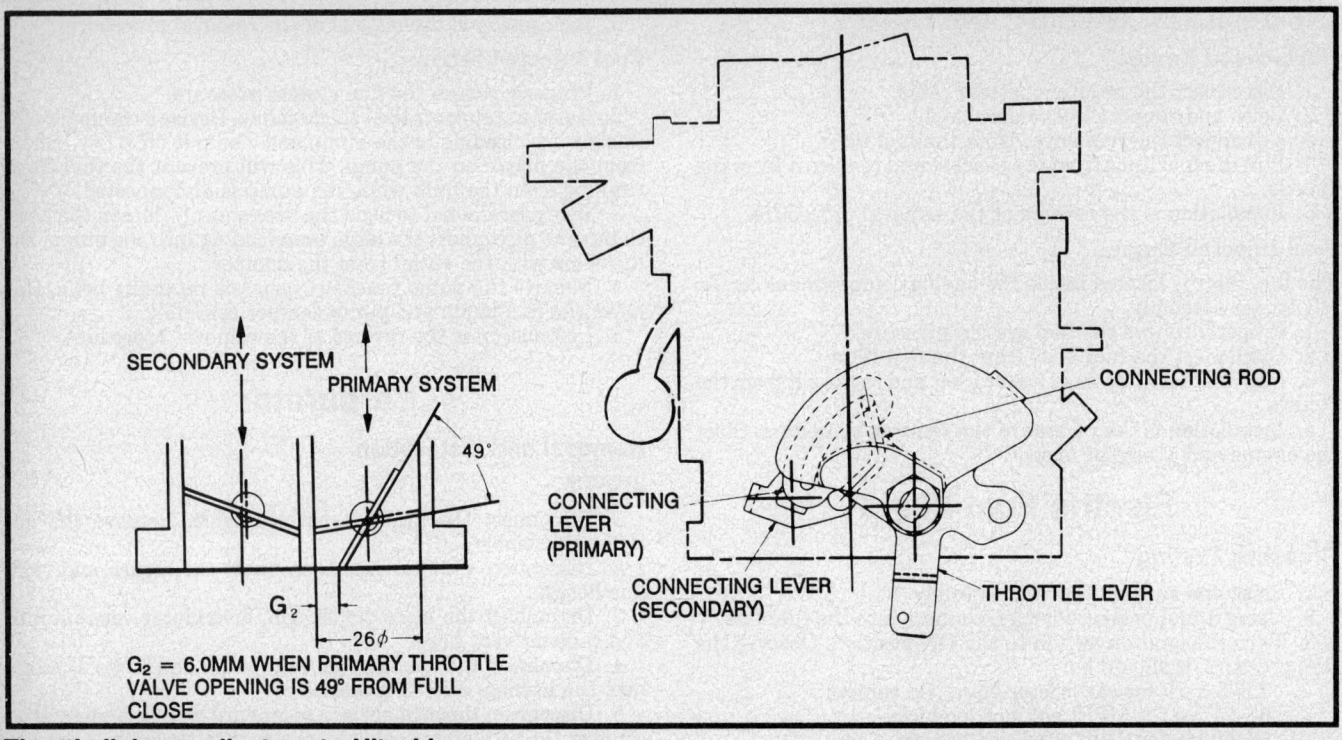

SECONDARY SYSTEM

PRIMARY SYSTEM

49°

G_2

26φ

G_2 = 6.0MM WHEN PRIMARY THROTTLE VALVE OPENING IS 49° FROM FULL CLOSE

CONNECTING ROD

CONNECTING LEVER (PRIMARY)

CONNECTING LEVER (SECONDARY)

THROTTLE LEVER

Throttle linkage adjustment—Hitachi

fuel should be within $\frac{1}{16}$ in. with the dot on the glass when the engine is running. The float level may be adjusted with the carburetor installed on the engine:

1. Disconnect the accelerator pump actuating rod from the pump lever.
2. Remove the throttle return spring.
3. Disconnect the choke cable from the choke lever, and remove it from the spring hanger.
4. Remove the spring hanger, the choke bellcrank and the remaining air horn retaining screws.
5. Lift the air horn slightly, disconnect the choke connecting rod and remove the air horn.
6. Invert the air horn, and measure the distance between the surface of the air horn and the float.
7. Bend the float arm until the clearance is approximately:
   Except Justy—0.453–0.492 in.
   Justy—0.437 in.
8. Invert the air horn to it's installed position and measure the distance between the float arm and the needle valve stem. This dimension should be 0.059–0.075 in.
9. The dimension is adjusted by bending the float stops.

Fast Idle Adjustment

NOTE: Before adjusting the fast idle make sure the idle speed and mixture have been adjusted properly."

1. Remove the carburetor from the intake manifold.
2. With the choke plate fully closed, operate the fast idle cam and the linkage to position the primary throttle valve to it's slightly open position.

NOTE: In this position, the top of the cam adjusting lever rests on the highest (first) step of the fast idle cam; this angle is called the fast idle opening angle, suitable for cold weather starting.

3. Using a carburetor plug gauge set or drill bit, measure the G1 clearance; the clearance between the lower edge of the primary throttle valve and its bore. To adjust the valve opening, adjust the fast idle screw.

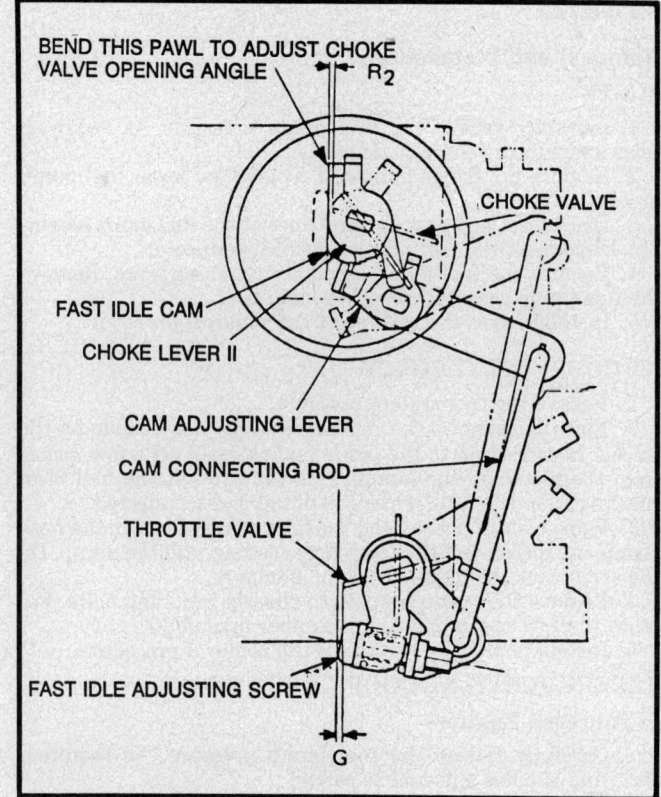

BEND THIS PAWL TO ADJUST CHOKE VALVE OPENING ANGLE

R_2

CHOKE VALVE

FAST IDLE CAM

CHOKE LEVER II

CAM ADJUSTING LEVER

CAM CONNECTING ROD

THROTTLE VALVE

FAST IDLE ADJUSTING SCREW

G

Fast idle adjustment—Hitachi

4. To install, reverse the removal procedures. Start the engine and check the carburetor performance.

Idle Speed Adjustment

JUSTY

1. Run the engine until normal operating temperature is reached.
2. Check and adjust the ignition timing, as required. Position the gear selector lever in the N detent.
3. Install a tachometer to the engine according to manufacturers instructions.
4. Be sure all electrical accessories are turned OFF. Be sure the idle up system is in the disengaged position.
5. If not equipped with air conditioning, adjust the idle speed with the idle up system off, using the throttle adjusting screw. Adjust the idle speed with the idle up system on using the idle up adjusting screw. Be sure the headlights are on.
6. If equipped with air conditioning, adjust the idle speed with the idle up system off and the FICD for the air conditioning system off, using the throttle adjusting screw. Adjust the idle speed using the air conditioning idle up adjusting screw with the air conditioning on. Adjust the idle speed with the idle up system on and the air conditioning on using the idle up adjusting screw. Be sure the headlights are on.

XT COUPE

1. Run the engine until normal operating temperature is reached.
2. Check and adjust the ignition timing, as required. Position the gear selector lever in the neutral detent for manual transaxle and in P for automatic transaxle.
3. Install a tachometer to the engine according to manufacturer's instructions.
4. Be sure the auxiliary air valve is completely closed.
5. Adjust the idle speed to specification by using the idle adjusting screw, which is located on the throttle body assembly.

EXCEPT JUSTY AND XT COUPE

1. Operate the engine and allow it to reach normal operating temperature.

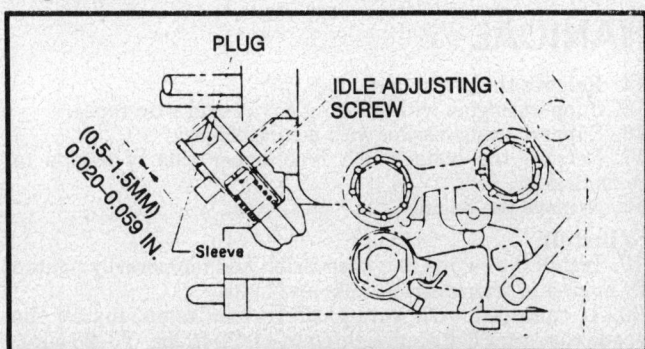

View of the idle mixture screw and plug—carburetor models

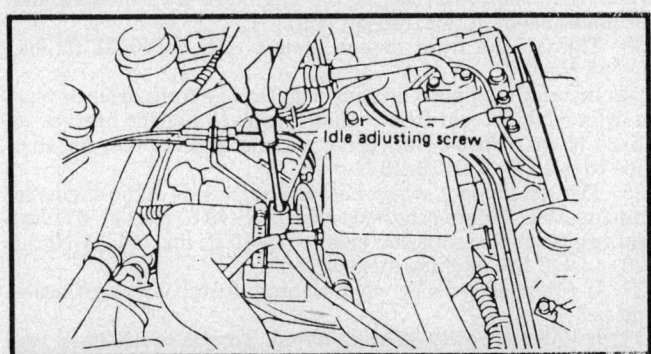

Idle speed adjustment point—1800cc engine with FI

2. Stop the engine and connect a tachometer in accordance with the manufacturer's instructions.
3. Perform the following, as necessary:
   a. If equipped with air injection system, disconnect the air hoses from the air distribution manifolds, plug the hoses and the manifold openings.
   b. If equipped with a distributor vacuum retard unit, disconnect and plug the hose that runs to the distributor.
   c. If equipped with a secondary air cleaner or purge valve hose, disconnect and plug the hose to the engine.
4. Remove the air cleaner assembly.
5. Check and adjust the idle speed to specification by turning the throttle adjusting screw.

Idle Mixture Adjustment

1. Remove the carburetor from the engine and position it in a suitable holding fixture. Using a drill, make a hole through the idle mixture screw plug, then pry the plug from the carburetor.
2. Reinstall the carburetor on the engine. Start the engine and allow it to reach normal operating temperature.
3. Disconnect and plug the air suction valve to air cleaner hose.
4. Disconnect and plug the idle compensator to intake manifold hose, plug both openings.
5. Without the secondary air, inspect the idle speed and the CO percent. Using the throttle adjusting screw and the idle mixture adjusting screw, adjust the idle speed to specification. Adjust the CO percent, specification should be 1.0–2.0 percent (without secondary air) or 0–0.4 percent (with secondary air).

Fuel Injection

Idle Speed Adjustment

1. Run the engine until normal operating temperature is reached.
2. Check and adjust the ignition timing, as required. Position the gear selector lever in the neutral detent for manual transaxle and in P for automatic transaxle.
3. Install a tachometer to the engine according to manufacturer's instructions.
4. Be sure the auxiliary air valve is completely closed.
5. Adjust the idle speed to specification by using the idle adjusting screw, which is located on the throttle body assembly.

Idle Mixture Adjustment

Idle mixture adjustment cannot be accomplished, if equipped with SPFI or MPFI fuel injection systems.

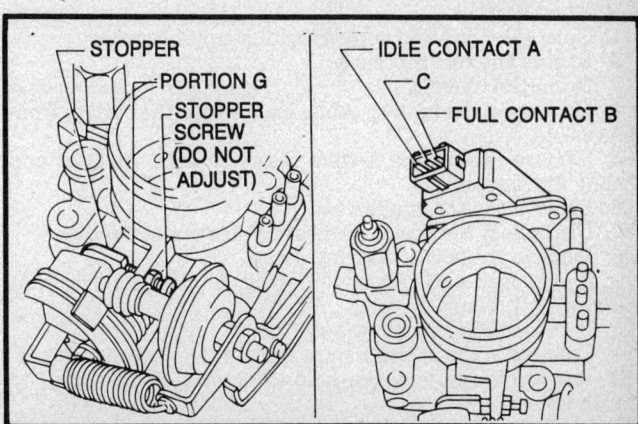

Fuel injection adjustment terminals

Fuel Injector

Removal and Installation

SPFI ENGINE

1. Disconnect the negative battery cable.
2. Remove the injector cap and gasket.
3. Hold the injector using pliers, then pull out the injector from the throttle body.
4. Remove the injector and O-ring from the throttle body.
5. To install, reverse the removal procedure.

MPFI ENGINE

1. Relieve the fuel pressure by disconnecting the fuel pump connector, starting the engine and allow the engine to run until it stalls. After stalling, crank the starter for approximately 5 seconds and turn ignition switch OFF.
2. Remove the spark plug caps.
3. Disconnect the connector from the fuel injector.
4. Remove the fuel injector cover.
5. Remove the injector while turning.

NOTE: Do not attempt to pry the injectors with a prybar or similar tool. Do not pinch the injector pin with pliers. Be careful not to damage the O-ring. If the injector is difficult to remove by hand, remove the injector and fuel pipe as a unit and push the injector out from the back side.

6. To install, reverse the removal procedure.

EMISSION CONTROLS

For further information, please refer to "Professional Emission Component Application Guide".

Emission Warning Lamps

Resetting

Some 1987 vehicles are equipped with an EGR light that illuminates when the vehicle attains 60,000 miles (96,000 km). In order to reset the light for an other 60,000 mile increment, the following procedure must be done:

1. Remove the lower instrument panel cover, exposing the fuel panel.
2. Directly behind or along the side of the fuse panel, a blue 2 piece connector will be noted. Disconnect the 2 blue connectors.
3. Near the blue connectors will be a green connector that is not connected to any other wire.
4. Connect the green connector into the matching blue connector, thus resetting the emission light and recycling the system for another 60,000 mile increment.
5. Be sure the indicator light is out and reinstall the lower instrument panel cover.

ENGINE MECHANICAL

NOTE: Disconnect the negative battery cable on some vehicles may interfere with the functions on the on board computer systems and may require the computer to undergo a relearning process, once the negative battery cable is reconnected

Engine Assembly

Removal and Installation

LEGACY

2200cc Engine

1. Open the hood and support with a suitable prop.
2. Relieve the fuel pressure.
3. Drain the coolant.
4. Disconnect the battery cables and remove the battery from the vehicle.
5. Remove the cooling system reservoir tank, radiator and cooling fan assembly.
6. Remove the air intake duct.
7. Disconnect the hoses, harness connectors and cables.
8. Remove the power steering pump.
9. If equipped with air conditioning; discharge refrigerant and remove pressure lines.
10. Remove the exhaust system.
11. Disconnect the engine mount from the front crossmember.
12. Remove the nuts which hold lower side of the engine to transmission.
13. If equipped with automatic transmission, disconnect the driveplate from the torque converter.
14. Remove the pitching stopper rod.
15. Support engine with a lifting device and wire ropes.
16. Support transmission with a suitable jack.
17. Remove the bolts which hold upper side of engine to transmission.
18. Remove the engine.

To install:
19. Install the engine to transmission and temporarily tighten the engine to transmission nuts and bolts.
20. If equipped with automatic transmission, install the torque converter bolts and tighten to 17–20 ft. lbs. (23–26 Nm).
21. Remove the jack and hoist.
22. Raise the vehicle and support safely. Tighten the nuts which hold the lower side of the engine to transmission and torque to 34–61 ft. lbs. (46–54 Nm).
23. Tighten the front engine mount nuts to 40–61 ft. lbs. (54–83 Nm).
24. Install the exhaust system. Tighten the front exhaust pipe to cylinder head and front exhaust pipe to hanger bracket to 18–25 ft. lbs. (25–34 Nm), front exhaust pipe to rear exhaust pipe to 9–17 ft. lbs. (13–23 Nm).
25. Tighten the nuts which hold the upper side of the engine to transmission. Tighten the body side to 35–49 ft. lbs. (47–67 Nm) and engine or transmission side to 33–40 ft. lbs. (44–54 Nm).
26. Install the pitching stopper rod.
27. If equipped with air conditioning, install pressure hoses and belt.
28. Install the power steering pump. Torque to 22–36 ft. lbs. (29–49 Nm).
29. Connect all cables, hoses and harness connectors.

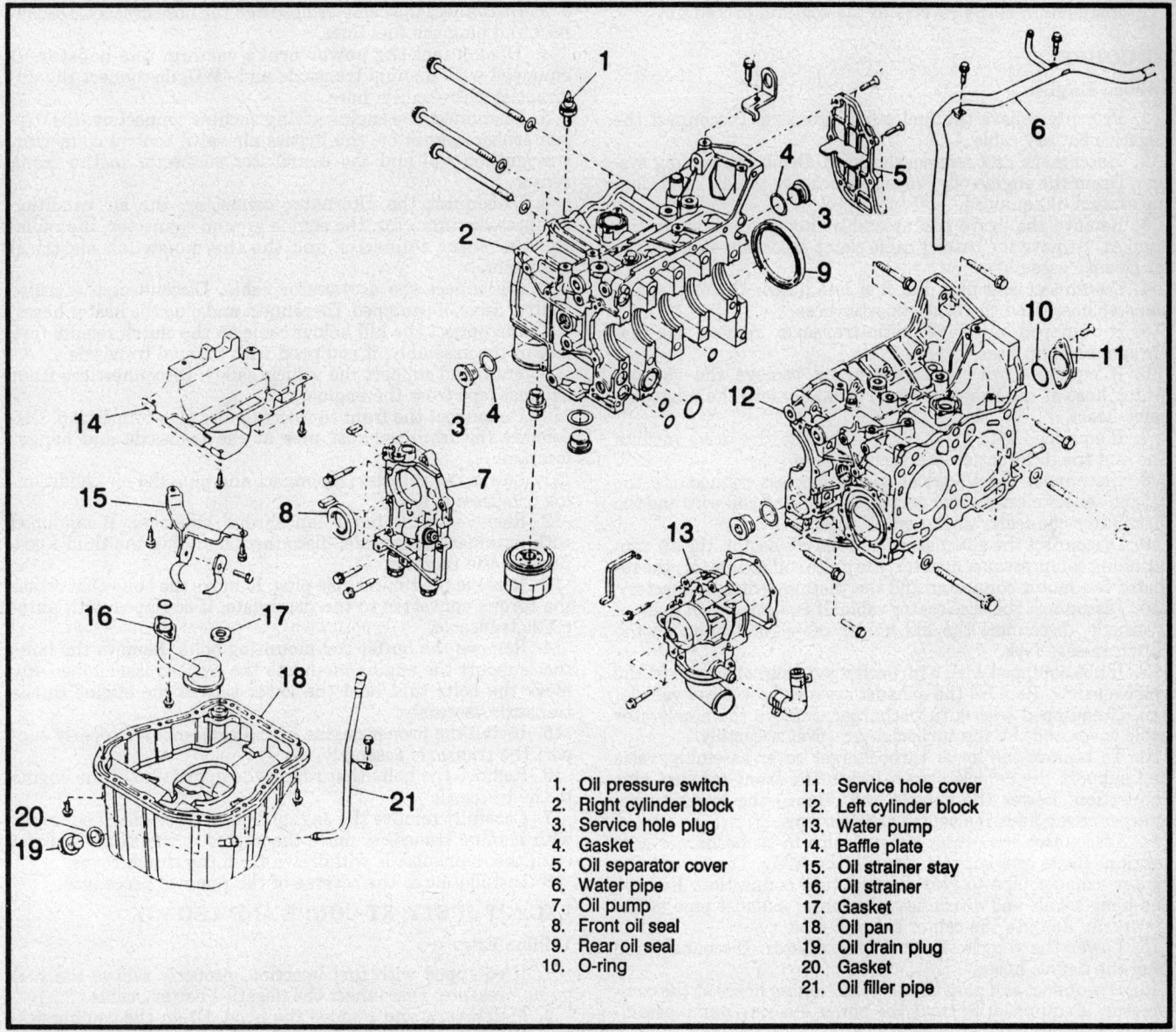

1. Oil pressure switch	11. Service hole cover
2. Right cylinder block	12. Left cylinder block
3. Service hole plug	13. Water pump
4. Gasket	14. Baffle plate
5. Oil separator cover	15. Oil strainer stay
6. Water pipe	16. Oil strainer
7. Oil pump	17. Gasket
8. Front oil seal	18. Oil pan
9. Rear oil seal	19. Oil drain plug
10. O-ring	20. Gasket
	21. Oil filler pipe

Cylinder block assembly and components—2200cc engine

30. Install the air intake duct.
31. Install the cooling system.
32. Fill the cooling system with coolant.
33. Install the battery and connect the battery cables.
34. Check and correct the coolant and oil level.
35. If equipped with air conditioning, recharge the system with refrigerant.

JUSTY

NOTE: The engine and transaxle are removed as an assembly.

1. Disconnect the negative battery cable. Matchmark and remove the hood.
2. Drain the cooling system. Drain the engine oil. Drain the transaxle fluid.
3. Remove the front bumper and grille assembly.
4. Disconnect the radiator hoses. Remove the radiator retaining bolts. Remove the radiator from the vehicle.

5. Remove the air cleaner assembly. Disconnect the accelerator linkage. Disconnect the clutch cable, if equipped with manual transaxle.
6. Disconnect the heater hoses from the heater unit. Disconnect the brake booster hose. Disconnect the speedometer cable from the transaxle.
7. If equipped with 4WD, disconnect the hoses for the assembly. Disconnect any other required hoses and vacuum lines necessary to remove the engine.
8. Raise and support the vehicle safely. Disconnect the exhaust pipes from the their mounting. Disconnect the gearshift rod from the transaxle.
9. Matchmark and remove the driveshaft. Properly support the engine and transaxle assembly. Remove the center member and crossmember assembly.
10. Remove the engine mount retaining bolts. Lower the vehicle.
11. Using the proper lifting equipment, carefully remove the engine and transaxle assembly from the vehicle.

12. Installation is the reverse of the removal procedure.

XT COUPE

1800cc Engine

1. Properly relieve the fuel pump pressure. Disconnect the negative battery cable.

2. Matchmark and remove the hood. Drain the cooling system. Drain the engine oil. Properly discharge the air conditioning system, if equipped.

3. Remove the spare tire assembly. Remove the spare tire support. Remove the battery cable clamp assembly. Remove the air cleaner assembly.

4. Disconnect and plug the fuel line hoses. Disconnect the canister hoses and the brake booster hose.

5. If equipped with automatic transaxle, remove the diaphragm vacuum hose.

6. If equipped with a turbocharger, remove the vacuum switch hose at the heater vacuum tank. Remove the wastegate valve hoses.

7. If equipped with 4WD, remove the selective drive vacuum line and the differential lock vacuum hose.

8. Disconnect the electrical wiring harness connectors, the oxygen sensor electrical connector, the ignition coil wire and the distributor connector at the crank sensor.

9. Disconnect the alternator electrical connector, the air conditioning compressor connector, the pulse coil connector, the radiator fan motor connector and the thermo-switch connector.

10. Disconnect the accelerator cable. If equipped with manual transaxle, disconnect the hill holder cable connection on the clutch release fork.

11. If not equipped with a turbocharger, raise and support the vehicle safely. Remove the exhaust system. Lower the vehicle.

12. If equipped with a turbocharger, remove the accelerator cable cover and the top turbocharger cover assembly.

13. To remove the lower turbocharger cover assembly, raise and support the vehicle safely, loosen the front exhaust pipe connection. Lower the vehicle and remove the lower turbocharger cover from the center exhaust pipe.

14. Disconnect the center exhaust pipe to turbocharger connection. Raise and support the vehicle safely. Disconnect the center exhaust pipe to rear exhaust pipe connection. Remove the hanger bolt and disconnect the center exhaust pipe at the transaxle. Remove the center exhaust pipe.

15. Lower the vehicle. Remove the radiator. Disconnect and plug the heater hoses.

16. Disconnect and plug the air conditioning hoses at the compressor, if equipped. Remove the power steering pump assembly, if equipped.

17. Remove the engine pitching stopper rod. Remove the timing cover plate. Remove the retaining bolts that hold the torque converter to the driveplate, if equipped with automatic transaxle.

18. Properly support the engine and the transaxle assemblies, using the proper equipment.

19. Remove the bolts which hold the engine mount to the front crossmember. Remove the bolts which hold the lower side of the engine to the transaxle.

20. Properly install the proper engine lifting equipment to the engine. Remove the bolts that retain the upper side of the engine to the transaxle.

21. Carefully remove the engine from the vehicle. If equipped with manual transaxle, move the engine horizontally until the mainshaft is withdrawn from the clutch cover.

22. Installation is the reverse of the removal procedure.

2700cc Engine

1. Properly relieve the fuel system pressure. Disconnect the negative battery cable. Matchmark and remove the hood.

2. Properly discharge the air conditioning system, if equipped. Drain the engine oil. Drain the cooling system.

3. Disconnect the canister hose and the hose bracket. Disconnect and plug the fuel lines.

4. Disconnect the power brake vacuum line booster. If equipped with manual transaxle and 4WD, disconnect the differential lock vacuum hose.

5. Disconnect the engine wiring harness connectors, the oxygen sensor connector, the bypass air valve control connector, the ignition coil and the distributor connector to the crank sensor.

6. Disconnect the alternator connector, the air condition compressor connector, the engine ground connector, the radiator fan motor connector and the thermo-switch electrical connector.

7. Disconnect the accelerator cable. Disconnect the cruise control cable, if equipped. Disconnect and plug the heater hoses.

8. Disconnect the hill holder cable on the clutch release fork side of the assembly, if equipped with manual transaxle.

9. Raise and support the vehicle safely. Disconnect the front exhaust pipe from the engine.

10. Disconnect the front to rear exhaust pipe connection. Disconnect the front exhaust pipe at the transaxle and hanger locations.

11. Lower the vehicle. Disconnect and plug the air conditioning compressor hoses.

12. Remove the radiator fan shroud assembly. If equipped with automatic transaxle, disconnect and plug the fluid lines. Remove the radiator.

13. Remove the timing hole plug. Remove the bolts that retain the torque converter to the driveplate, if equipped with automatic transaxle.

14. Remove the buffer rod mounting bolts. Remove the bolts that support the engine mount to the front crossmember. Remove the bolts that hold the lower side of the engine to the transaxle assembly.

15. Install the proper engine lifting equipment. Properly support the transaxle assembly.

16. Remove the bolts that retain the upper side of the engine to the transaxle

17. Carefully remove the engine from the vehicle. If equipped with manual transaxle, move the engine in the axial direction until the mainshaft is withdrawn from the clutch cover.

18. Installation is the reverse of the removal procedure.

EXCEPT JUSTY, XT COUPE AND LEGACY

1800cc Engine

1. If equipped with fuel injection, properly relieve the fuel pump pressure. Disconnect the negative battery cable.

2. Matchmark and remove the hood. Drain the cooling system. Drain the engine oil. Properly discharge the air conditioning system, if equipped.

3. Remove the spare tire assembly. Remove the spare tire support. Remove the battery cable clamp assembly. Remove the air cleaner assembly.

4. Disconnect and plug the fuel line hoses. Disconnect the canister hoses and the brake booster hose.

5. If equipped with automatic transaxle, remove the diaphragm vacuum hose.

6. If equipped with a turbocharger, remove the vacuum switch hose at the heater vacuum tank. Remove the wastegate valve hoses.

7. If equipped with 4WD, remove the selective drive vacuum line and the differential lock vacuum hose.

8. Disconnect the electrical wiring harness connectors, the oxygen sensor electrical connector, the ignition coil wire and the distributor connector at the crank sensor.

9. Disconnect the alternator electrical connector, the air conditioning compressor connector, the pulse coil connector, the radiator fan motor connector and the thermo-switch connector.

10. Disconnect the accelerator cable. If equipped with manual transaxle, disconnect the hill holder cable connection on the clutch release fork.

11. If not equipped with a turbocharger, raise and support the vehicle safely. Remove the exhaust system. Lower the vehicle.

12. If equipped with a turbocharger, remove the accelerator cable cover and the top turbocharger cover assembly.

13. To remove the lower turbocharger cover assembly, raise and support the vehicle safely, loosen the front exhaust pipe connection. Lower the vehicle and remove the lower turbocharger cover from the center exhaust pipe.

14. Disconnect the center exhaust pipe to turbocharger connection. Raise and support the vehicle safely. Disconnect the center exhaust pipe to rear exhaust pipe connection. Remove the hanger bolt and disconnect the center exhaust pipe at the transaxle. Remove the center exhaust pipe.

15. Lower the vehicle. Remove the radiator. Disconnect and plug the heater hoses.

16. Disconnect and plug the air conditioning hoses at the compressor, if equipped. Remove the power steering pump assembly, if equipped.

17. Remove the pitching stopper rod. Remove the timing cover plate. Remove the retaining bolts that hold the torque converter to the driveplate, if equipped with automatic transaxle.

18. Properly support the engine and the transaxle assemblies, using the proper equipment.

19. Remove the bolts which hold the engine mount to the front crossmember. Remove the bolts which hold the lower side of the engine to the transaxle.

20. Properly install the proper engine lifting equipment to the engine. Remove the bolts that retain the upper side of the engine to the transaxle.

21. Carefully remove the engine from the vehicle. If equipped with manual transaxle, move the engine horizontally until the mainshaft is withdrawn from the clutch cover.

22. Installation is the reverse of the removal procedure.

Cylinder Head

Removal and Installation

JUSTY

1. Disconnect the negative battery cable. Drain the cooling system.

2. Remove the air cleaner assembly. Remove the drive belts. Remove the spark plug wires.

3. Position the engine at TDC with No. 1 cylinder on the compression stroke. Matchmark and remove the distributor assembly.

4. Remove the crankshaft pulley, using pulley removal tool 499205500 or equivalent. Remove the outer front timing belt cover.

5. Loosen the tensioner bolt and position it in the direction that loosens the belt. Tighten the tensioner bolt in that position.

6. Remove the camshaft driveplate. Mark the timing belt, in the direction of rotation, for reinstallation and than remove it from the engine.

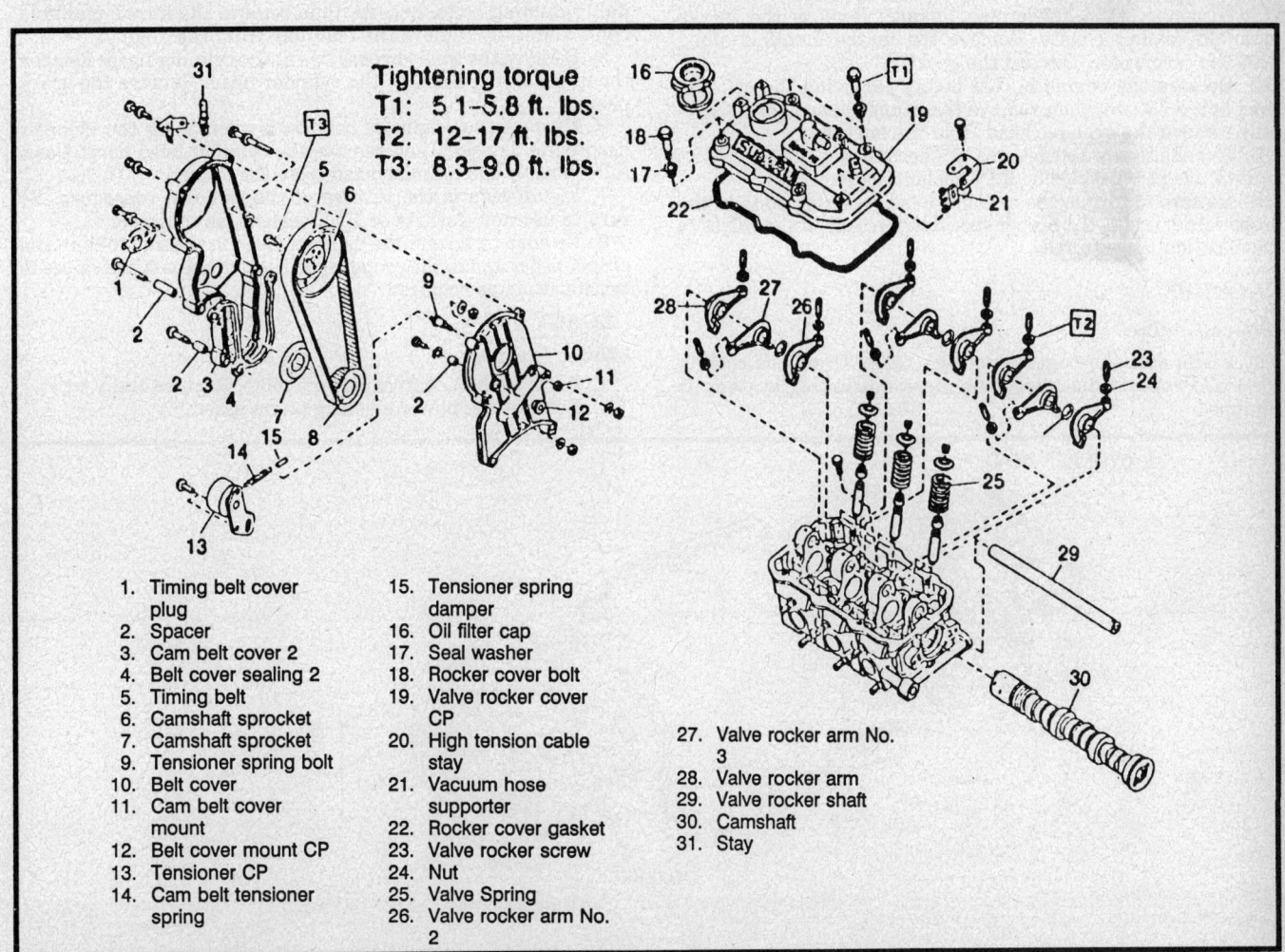

Tightening torque
T1: 5 1–5.8 ft. lbs.
T2: 12–17 ft. lbs.
T3: 8.3–9.0 ft. lbs.

1. Timing belt cover plug
2. Spacer
3. Cam belt cover 2
4. Belt cover sealing 2
5. Timing belt
6. Camshaft sprocket
7. Camshaft sprocket
9. Tensioner spring bolt
10. Belt cover
11. Cam belt cover mount
12. Belt cover mount CP
13. Tensioner CP
14. Cam belt tensioner spring
15. Tensioner spring damper
16. Oil filter cap
17. Seal washer
18. Rocker cover bolt
19. Valve rocker cover CP
20. High tension cable stay
21. Vacuum hose supporter
22. Rocker cover gasket
23. Valve rocker screw
24. Nut
25. Valve Spring
26. Valve rocker arm No. 2
27. Valve rocker arm No. 3
28. Valve rocker arm
29. Valve rocker shaft
30. Camshaft
31. Stay

Cylinder head and related components—1200cc engine

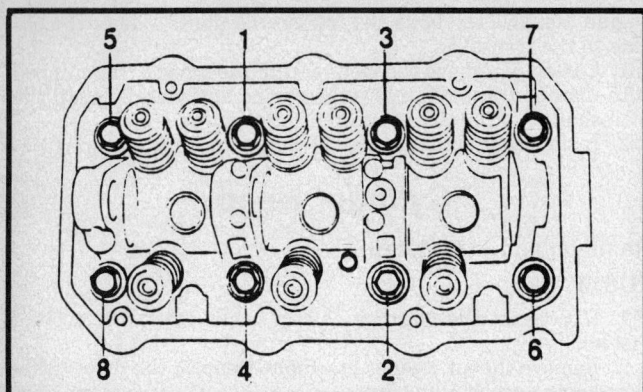

Cylinder head bolt torque sequence—1200cc engine

7. Remove the tensioner and spring. Remove the camshaft pulley, using pulley removal tool 499205500 or equivalent. Remove the inner belt cover and cover mount.

8. Remove the PCV hose from the rocker arm cover. Remove the rocker arm cover retaining bolts. Remove the rocker arm cover from the engine. Remove the rocker arm assembly.

9. Remove the exhaust manifold retaining bolts. Remove the exhaust manifold from the engine. Discard the gasket.

10. Disconnect all required electrical wiring and vacuum lines. Remove the air suction valve and pipe, if equipped.

11. Disconnect the accelerator linkage. Remove the intake manifold retaining bolts. Remove the intake manifold along with the carburetor. Discard the gasket.

12. Be sure the engine is cold before removing the cylinder head bolts. Loosen, than remove the cylinder head bolts. Carefully remove the cylinder head from the engine.

13. Installation is the reverse of the removal procedure. Be sure to use new gaskets or RTV sealant, as required.

14. Be sure to torque the cylinder head retaining bolts in the proper order and to the proper specification. Adjust the valves to specification, as required.

XT COUPE

1800cc Engine

1. Disconnect the negative battery cable. Drain the cooling system. Properly discharge the air conditioning system, if equipped.

2. Remove the timing belt assemblies. Remove the camshaft assemblies.

3. On non air conditioning equipped vehicles, remove the bolt attaching the alternator bracket to the cylinder head and the bolt retaining the adjusting bar to the cylinder head.

4. Be sure the engine is cold before removing the intake manifold retaining bolts. Loosen, then remove the intake manifold bolts. Carefully remove the manifold from the engine.

5. Remove the water bypass line at the cylinder head. Remove the spark plugs.

6. Be sure the engine is cold before removing the cylinder head bolts. Loosen, then remove the cylinder head bolts. Carefully remove the cylinder head from the engine.

7. Installation is the reverse of the removal procedure. Be sure to use new gaskets or RTV sealant, as required.

8. Be sure to torque the cylinder head retaining bolts in the proper order and to the proper specification. Adjust the valves to specification, as required.

2700cc Engine

1. Disconnect the negative battery cable. Drain the cooling system. Properly discharge the air conditioning system, if equipped.

2. Remove the timing belt assemblies. Remove the camshaft assemblies.

3. Remove the alternator. Remove the air conditioning compressor.

4. Be sure the engine is cold before removing the intake manifold retaining bolts. Loosen, than remove the intake manifold bolts. Carefully remove the manifold from the engine.

5. Remove the water bypass line at the cylinder head. Remove the alternator bracket at the cylinder head. Remove the spark plugs.

6. Be sure the engine is cold before removing the cylinder head bolts. Loosen, than remove the cylinder head bolts. Carefully remove the cylinder head from the engine.

7. Installation is the reverse of the removal procedure. Be sure to use new gaskets or RTV sealant, as required.

8. Be sure to torque the cylinder head retaining bolts in the proper order and to the proper specification. Adjust the valves to specification, as required.

LEGACY

2200cc Engine

1. Remove the negative battery cable. Remove the V-belt.
2. Remove the power steering pump assembly.

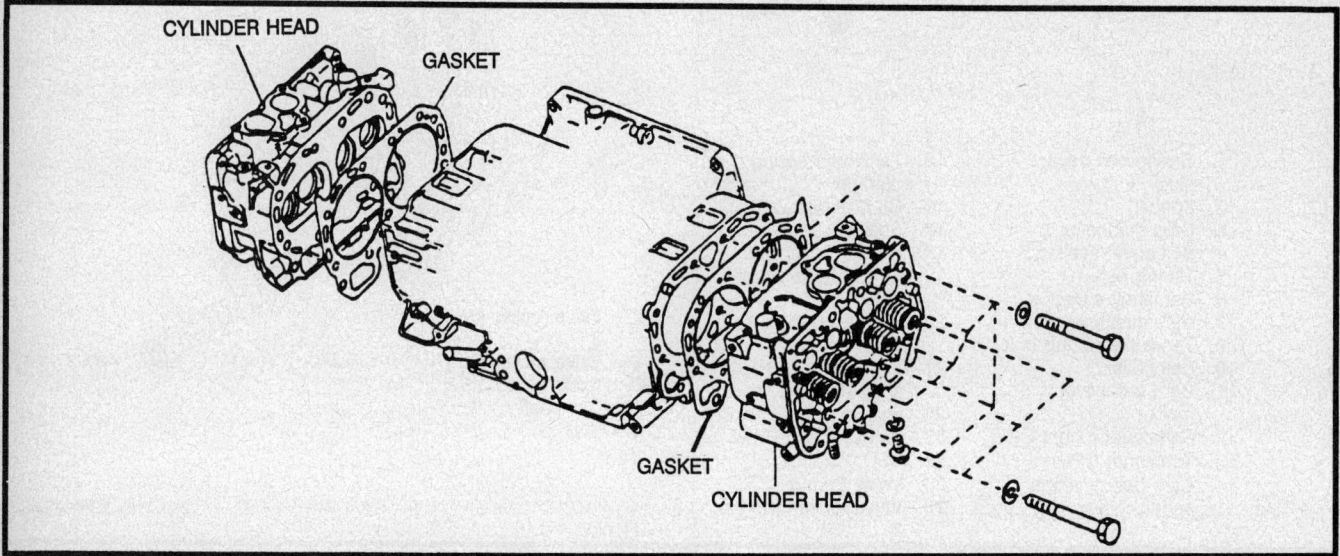

Cylinder head and related components—1800cc engine

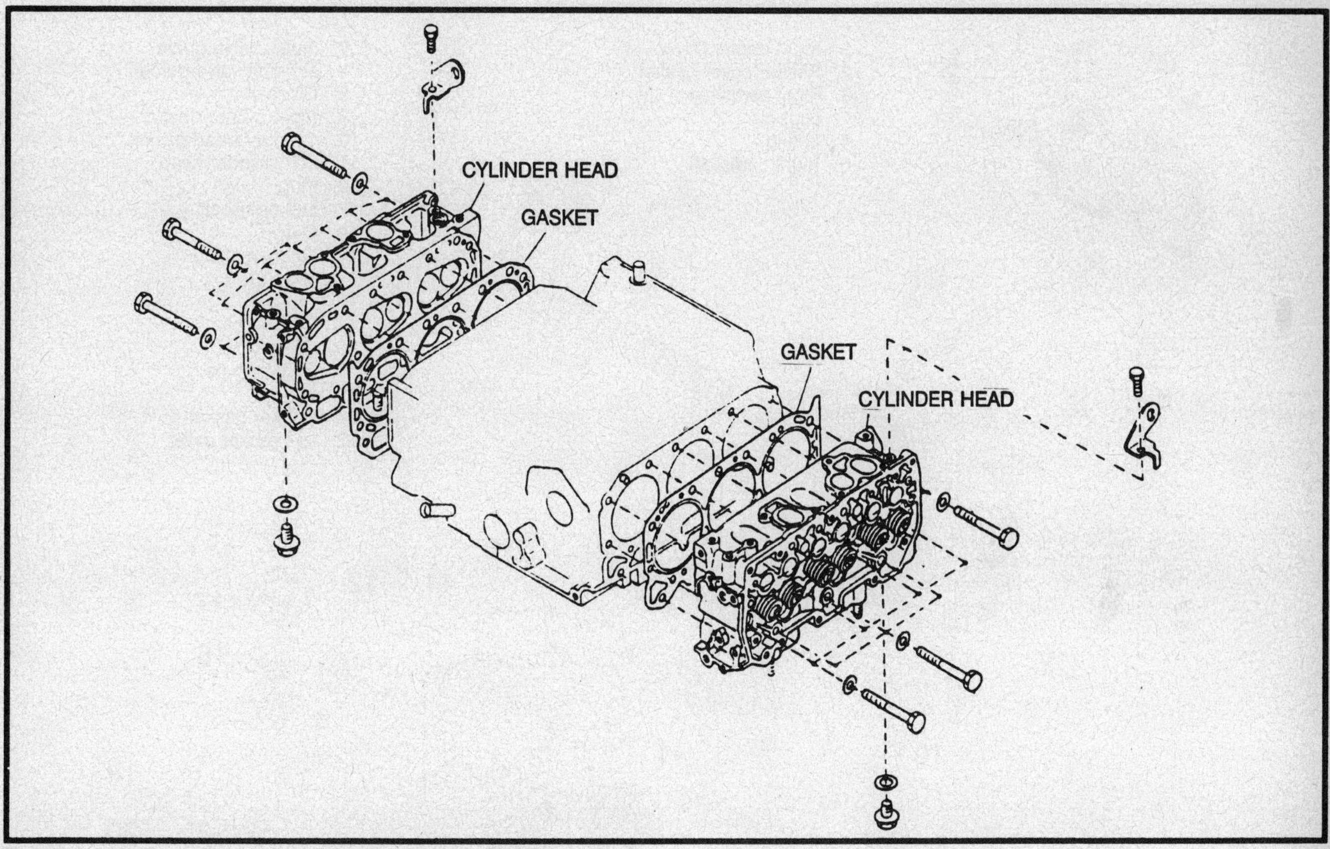

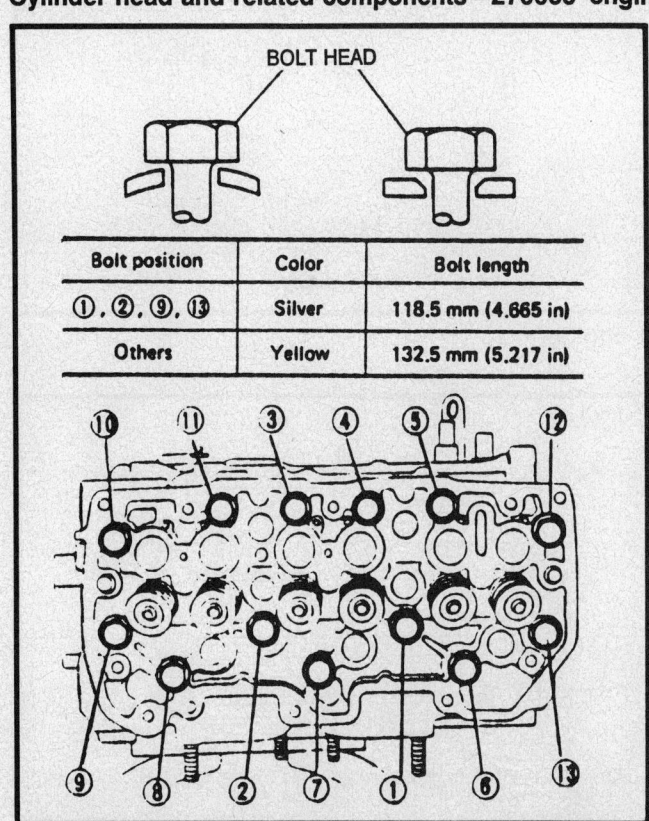

Cylinder head and related components—2700cc engine

BOLT HEAD

Bolt position	Color	Bolt length
①, ②, ⑨, ⑬	Silver	118.5 mm (4.665 in)
Others	Yellow	132.5 mm (5.217 in)

Cylinder head bolt torque sequence—2700cc engine

3. Remove the alternator and its bracket.

4. Remove the intake manifold cover and disconnect the PCV hose.

5. Disconnect the spark plug wire connectors and remove the connector from the bracket attaching bolt.

6. Remove the crankshaft and cam angle sensors. Remove the oil pressure switch connector.

7. Remove the knock sensor and the PCV blow-by hose.

8. Remove the intake manifold and gasket. Remove the water pipe.

9. Remove the timing belt, camshaft sprocket and related components.

10. Remove the left hand dipstick tube attaching bolt.

11. Remove the cylinder head bolts in sequence, leaving 2 top (1 and 3) loosely in block to keep cylinder head from falling.

12. If necessary, tap cylinder head with a plastic hammer to loosen from cylinder block.

13. Remove the retaining bolts and separate the cylinder head from the engine block.

14. Remove the cylinder head gasket.

To install:

15. Using new cylinder head gaskets, install the head and gasket on the engine block.

16. Apply a coating of engine oil to the cylinder head bolts and washers.

17. Tighten all cylinder head bolts to 51 ft. lbs. (69 Nm) torque in sequence.

18. Back off all bolts 180 degrees.

19. Retighten No. 1 and No. 2 bolts in sequence to 25 ft. lbs. (34 Nm).

20. Retighten bolts No. 3, 4, 5 and 6 to 14 ft. lbs. (20 Nm).

21. Tighten all bolts an additional 80–90 degrees in sequence. Do not tighten over 90 degrees.

22. Further tighten all bolts an additional 80–90 degrees in sequence.

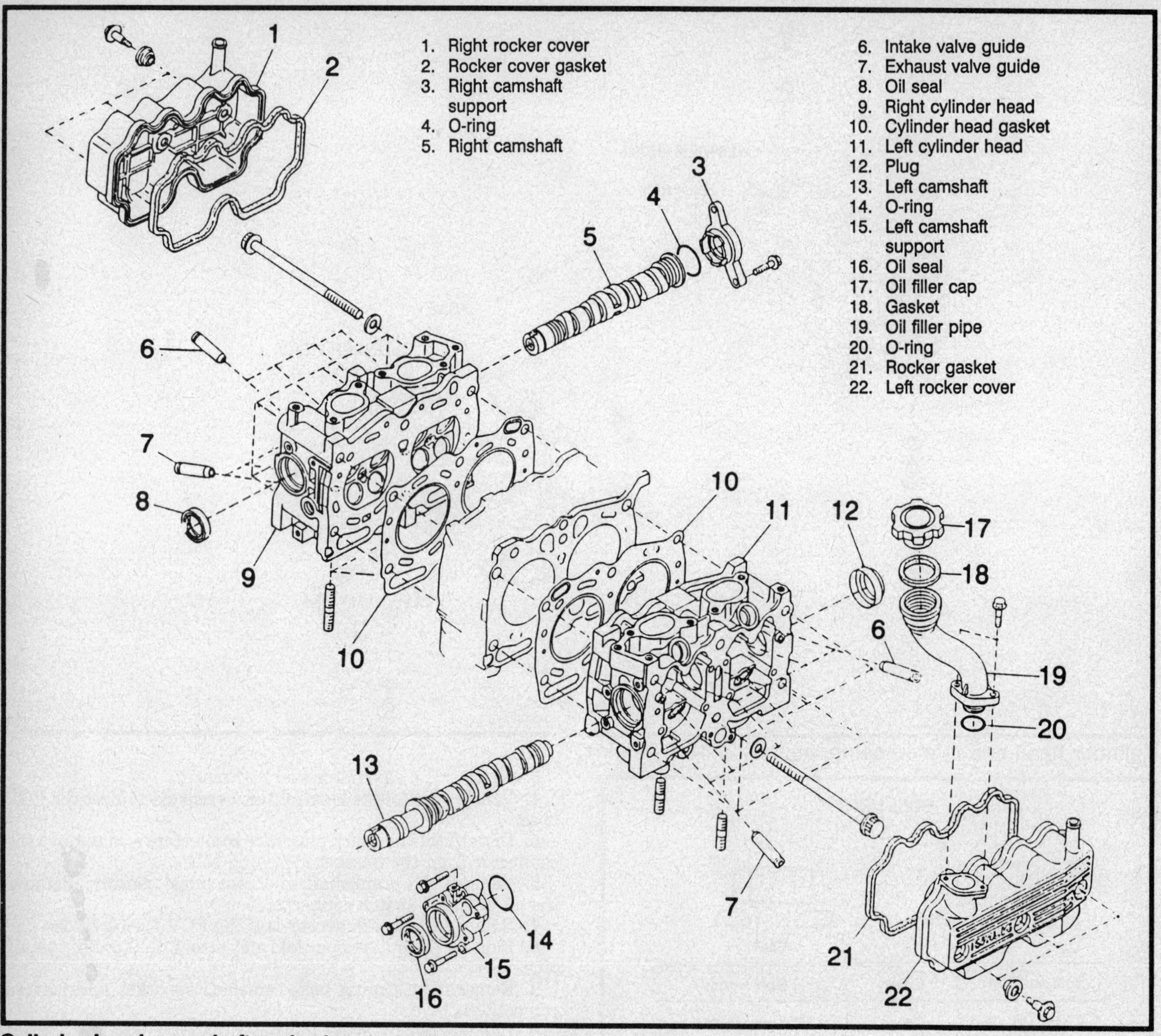

1. Right rocker cover
2. Rocker cover gasket
3. Right camshaft support
4. O-ring
5. Right camshaft
6. Intake valve guide
7. Exhaust valve guide
8. Oil seal
9. Right cylinder head
10. Cylinder head gasket
11. Left cylinder head
12. Plug
13. Left camshaft
14. O-ring
15. Left camshaft support
16. Oil seal
17. Oil filler cap
18. Gasket
19. Oil filler pipe
20. O-ring
21. Rocker gasket
22. Left rocker cover

Cylinder head, camshaft and related components— 2200cc engine

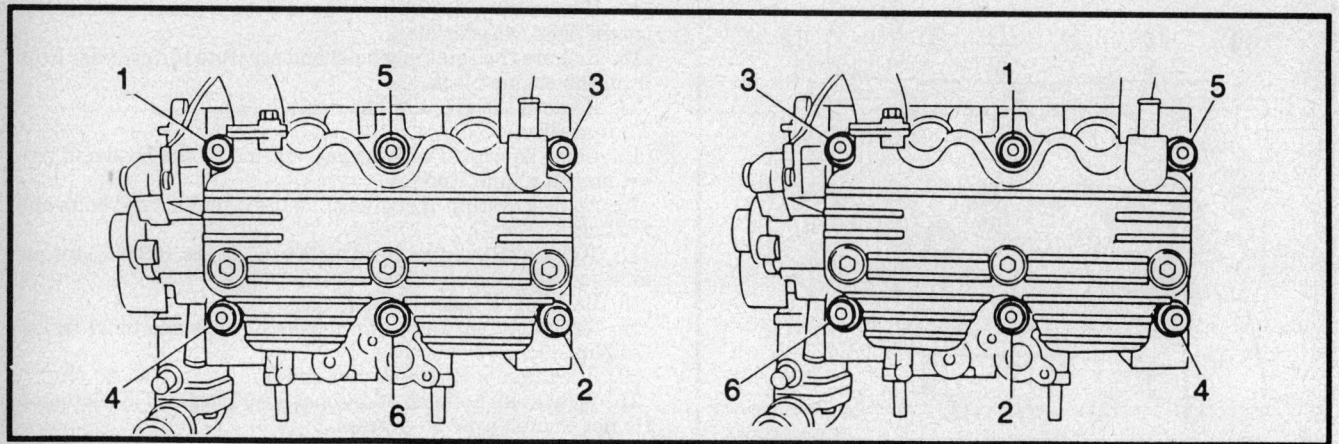

Cylinder head bolts removal and installation sequence—2200cc engine

NOTE: The total retightening range must not exceed 180 degrees maximum.

23. Complete the assembly in the reverse of the removal procedure.

EXCEPT JUSTY, XT COUPE AND LEGACY

1800cc Engine

1. Disconnect the negative battery cable. Drain the cooling system. Properly discharge the air conditioning system, if equipped.
2. Remove the timing belt assemblies. Remove the camshaft assemblies.
3. On non air conditioning equipped vehicles, remove the bolt attaching the alternator bracket to the cylinder head and the bolt retaining the adjusting bar to the cylinder head.
4. Be sure the engine is cold before removing the intake manifold retaining bolts. Loosen, than remove the intake manifold bolts. Carefully remove the manifold from the engine.

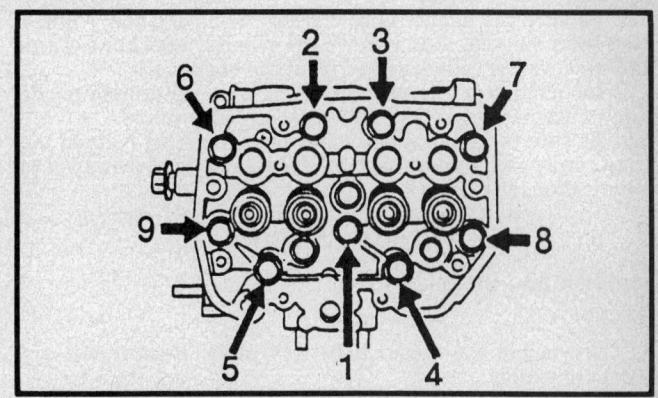

Cylinder head bolt torque sequence—1800cc engine

5. Remove the water bypass line at the cylinder head. Remove the spark plugs.

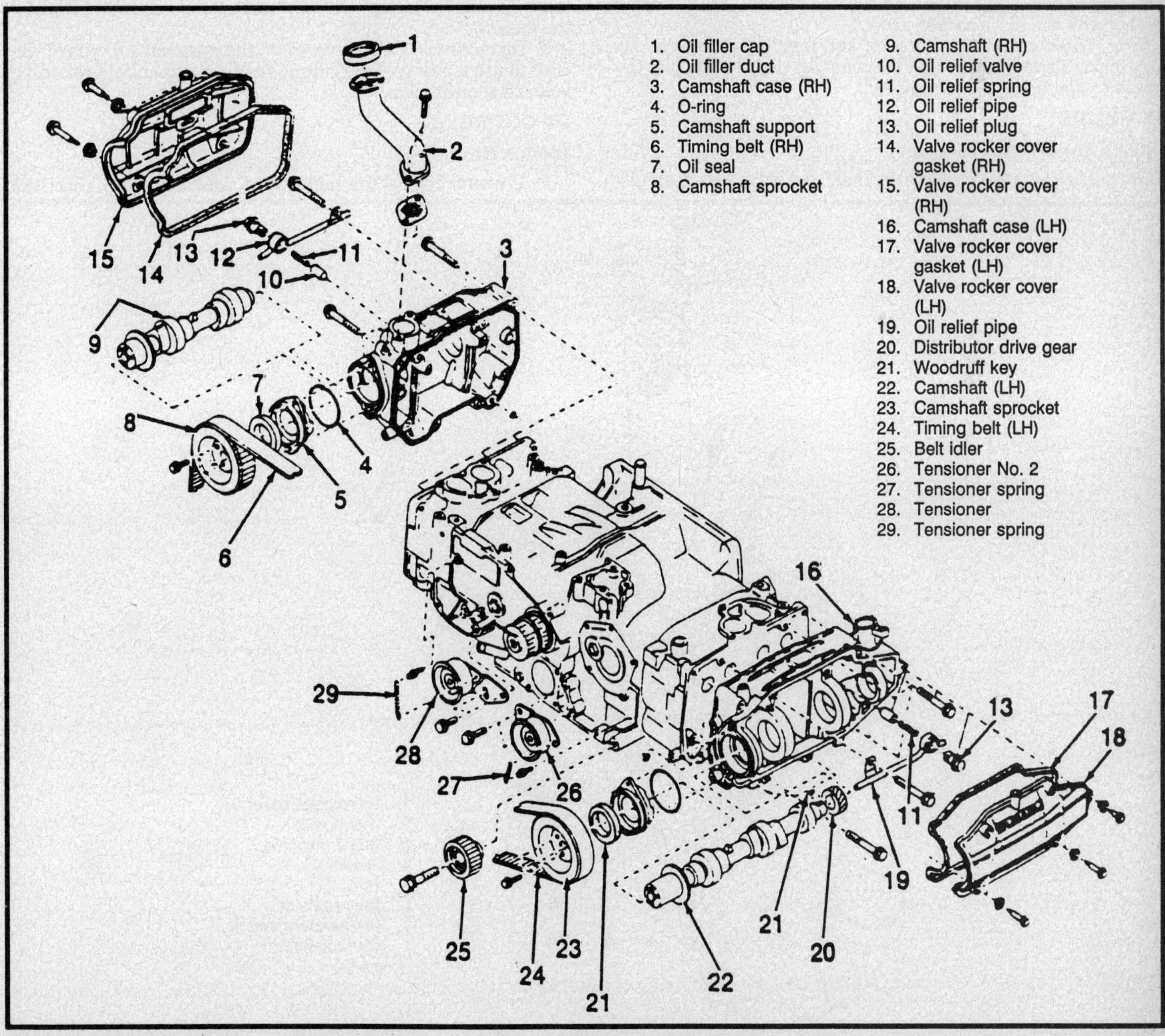

1. Oil filler cap	9. Camshaft (RH)
2. Oil filler duct	10. Oil relief valve
3. Camshaft case (RH)	11. Oil relief spring
4. O-ring	12. Oil relief pipe
5. Camshaft support	13. Oil relief plug
6. Timing belt (RH)	14. Valve rocker cover gasket (RH)
7. Oil seal	15. Valve rocker cover (RH)
8. Camshaft sprocket	16. Camshaft case (LH)
	17. Valve rocker cover gasket (LH)
	18. Valve rocker cover (LH)
	19. Oil relief pipe
	20. Distributor drive gear
	21. Woodruff key
	22. Camshaft (LH)
	23. Camshaft sprocket
	24. Timing belt (LH)
	25. Belt idler
	26. Tensioner No. 2
	27. Tensioner spring
	28. Tensioner
	29. Tensioner spring

Cylinder head assembly—1800cc engine

6. Be sure the engine is cold before removing the cylinder head bolts. Loosen, than remove the cylinder head bolts. Carefully remove the cylinder head from the engine.

7. Installation is the reverse of the removal procedure. Be sure to use new gaskets or RTV sealant, as required.

8. Be sure to torque the cylinder head retaining bolts in the proper order and to the proper specification. Adjust the valves to specification, as required.

Rocker Shafts
Removal and Installation
JUSTY

1. Disconnect the negative battery cable. Remove the air cleaner assembly.

2. Remove the valve cover retaining bolts. Remove the valve cover from the engine.

3. Using the valve clearance adjuster tool 498767000 or equivalent, loosen the valve rocker nut and screw.

4. Remove the bolt from the valve rocker shaft journal. Pull the rocker shaft out from the cylinder head. Remove the spring washer and the valve rocker arms.

5. Installation is the reverse of the removal procedure. Be sure to use a new gasket or RTV sealant, as required. Adjust the valves to specification, as required.

XT COUPE
1800cc and 2700cc Engines

Neither engine uses a rocker arm shaft, the valve rocker simply floats between the valve stem and the hydraulic lifter, the center of the valve rocker rides against the camshaft.

EXCEPT JUSTY AND XT COUPE
1800cc Engine

This engine does not use a rocker arm shaft, the valve rocker simply floats between the valve stem and the hydraulic lifter, the center of the valve rocker rides against the camshaft.

Intake Manifold
Removal and Installation
JUSTY

1. Disconnect the negative battery cable. Drain the cooling system. Remove the air cleaner assembly.

2. Disconnect the accelerator cable. Disconnect the required vacuum lines. Remove the upper radiator hose.

3. Remove the necessary components in order to gain access to the intake manifold retaining bolts.

4. Remove the intake manifold retaining bolts. Remove the intake manifold along with the carburetor assembly. Discard the gasket.

5. Installation is the reverse of the removal procedure. Be sure to use a new gasket. Torque the intake manifold retaining bolts to specification.

XT COUPE
1800cc Engine

1. Properly relieve the fuel system pressure. Disconnect the

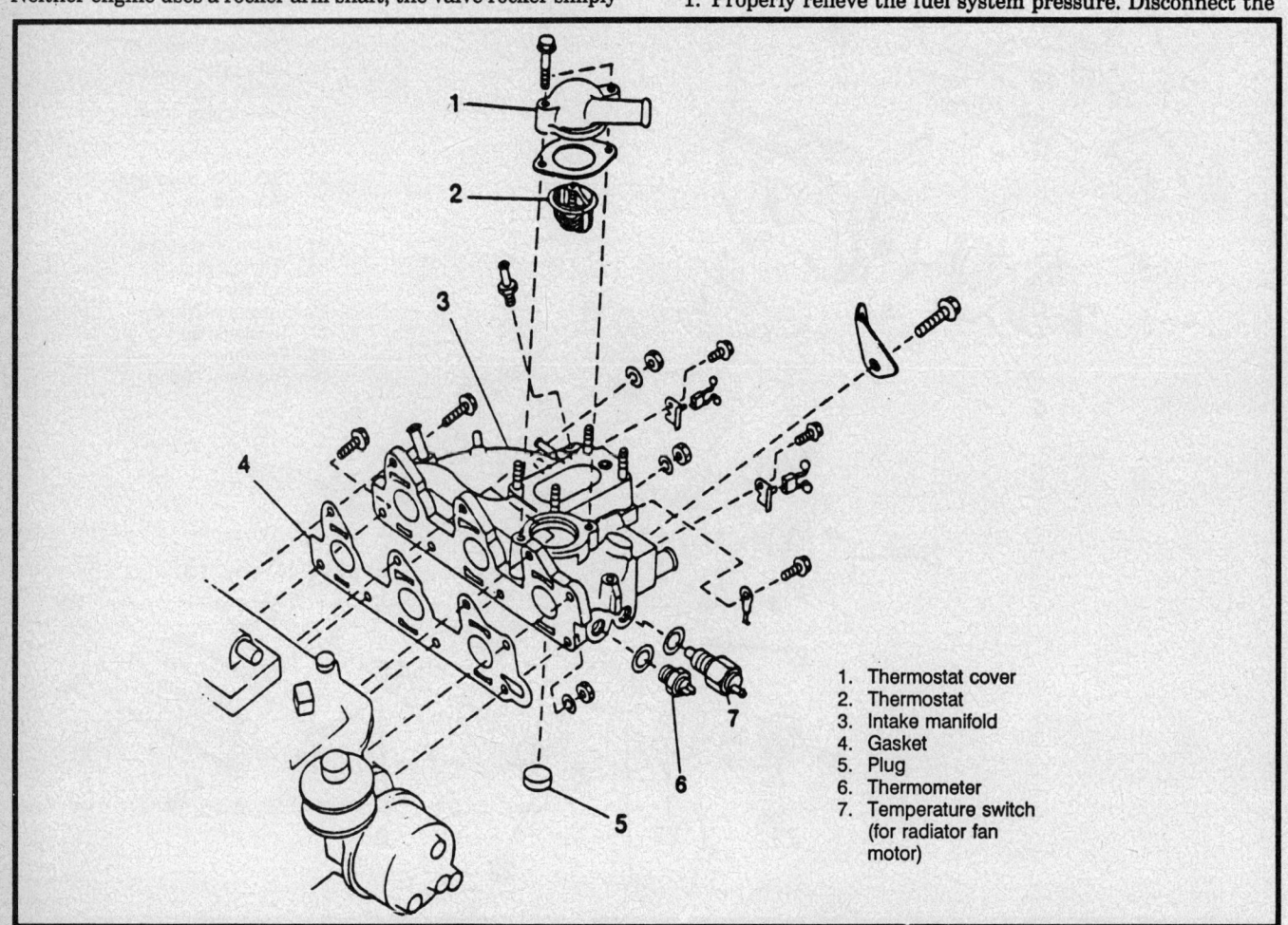

1. Thermostat cover
2. Thermostat
3. Intake manifold
4. Gasket
5. Plug
6. Thermometer
7. Temperature switch (for radiator fan motor)

Intake manifold assembly—1200cc engine

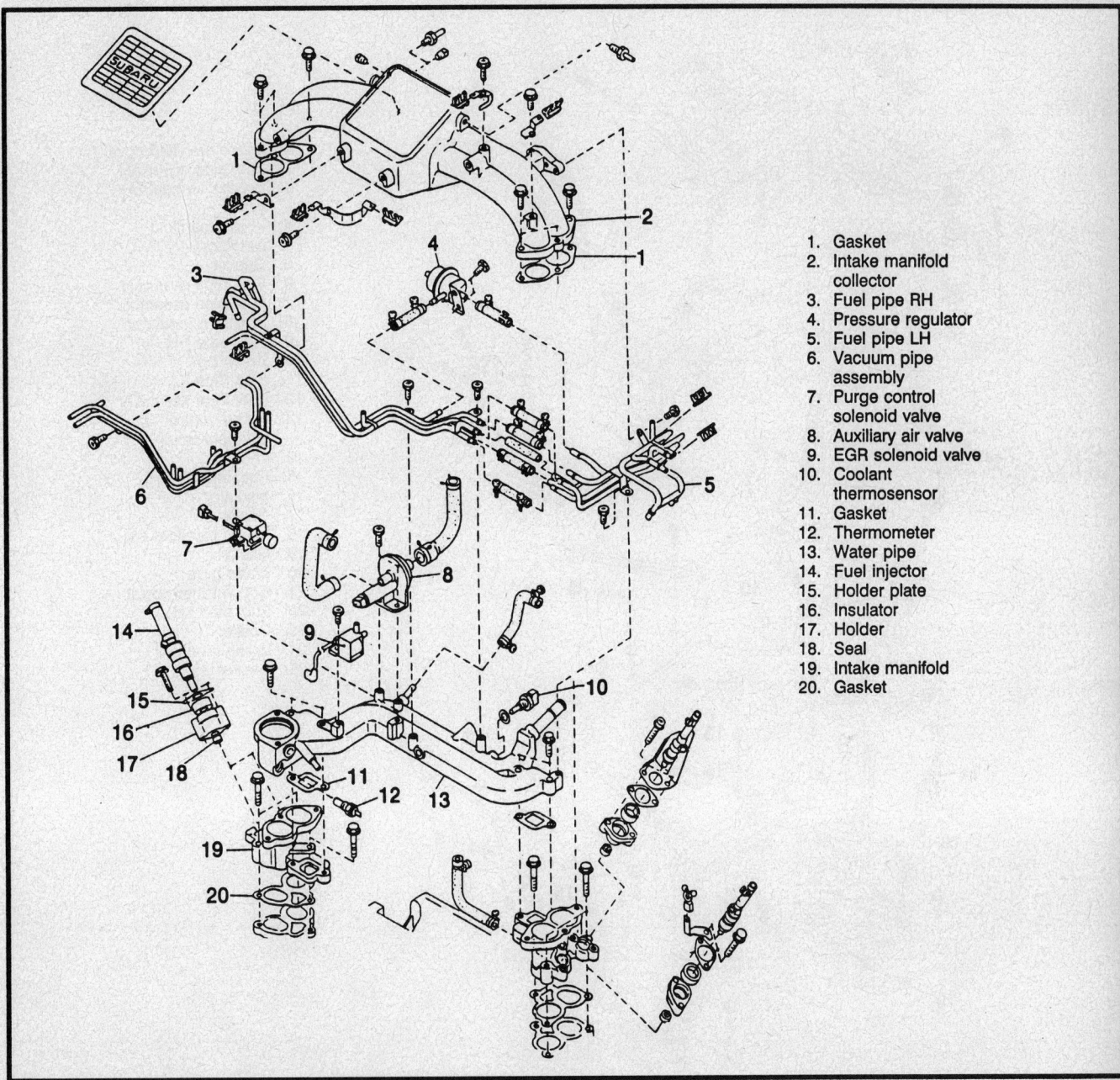

1. Gasket
2. Intake manifold collector
3. Fuel pipe RH
4. Pressure regulator
5. Fuel pipe LH
6. Vacuum pipe assembly
7. Purge control solenoid valve
8. Auxiliary air valve
9. EGR solenoid valve
10. Coolant thermosensor
11. Gasket
12. Thermometer
13. Water pipe
14. Fuel injector
15. Holder plate
16. Insulator
17. Holder
18. Seal
19. Intake manifold
20. Gasket

Intake manifold assembly—1800cc engine with MPFI

negative battery cable. Drain the cooling system. Remove the air cleaner assembly.

2. Remove the fuel pipe covers. Remove the fuel pipe assemblies.

3. Disconnect the required electrical connectors and vacuum hoses.

4. Remove the purge control solenoid valve. Remove the water pipe assembly.

5. Remove the necessary components in order to gain access to the intake manifold collector retaining bolts.

6. Remove the intake manifold collector retaining bolts. Remove the intake manifold collector from the engine. Discard the gaskets.

7. As required, remove the fuel injectors from their bores. Remove the intake manifold retaining bolts. Remove the intake manifold from the engine. Discard the gaskets.

8. Installation is the reverse of the removal procedure. Be sure to torque the retaining bolts to specification.

2700cc Engine

1. Properly relieve the fuel system pressure. Disconnect the negative battery cable. Drain the cooling system. Remove the air cleaner assembly.

2. Remove the fuel pipe covers. Remove the fuel pipe assemblies.

3. Disconnect the required electrical connectors and vacuum hoses.

4. Remove the purge control solenoid valve. Remove the water pipe assembly.

5. Remove the necessary components in order to gain access to the intake manifold collector retaining bolts.

6. Remove the intake manifold collector retaining bolts. Re-

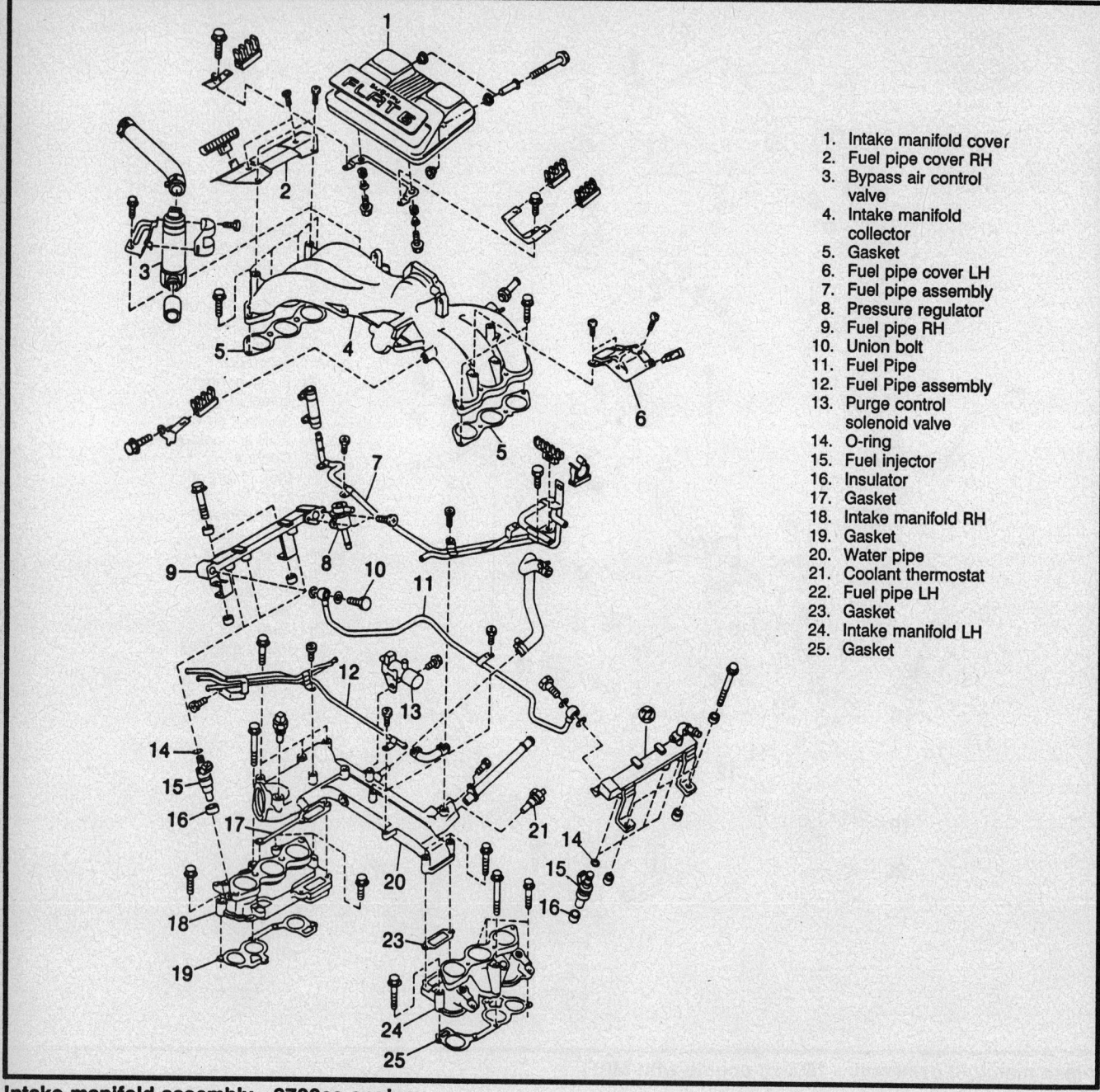

1. Intake manifold cover
2. Fuel pipe cover RH
3. Bypass air control valve
4. Intake manifold collector
5. Gasket
6. Fuel pipe cover LH
7. Fuel pipe assembly
8. Pressure regulator
9. Fuel pipe RH
10. Union bolt
11. Fuel Pipe
12. Fuel Pipe assembly
13. Purge control solenoid valve
14. O-ring
15. Fuel injector
16. Insulator
17. Gasket
18. Intake manifold RH
19. Gasket
20. Water pipe
21. Coolant thermostat
22. Fuel pipe LH
23. Gasket
24. Intake manifold LH
25. Gasket

Intake manifold assembly—2700cc engine

move the intake manifold collector from the engine. Discard the gaskets.

7. As required, remove the fuel injectors from their bores. Remove the intake manifold retaining bolts. Remove the intake manifold from the engine. Discard the gaskets.

8. Installation is the reverse of the removal procedure. Be sure to torque the retaining bolts to specification.

LEGACY

2200cc Engine

1. Remove the negative battery cable. Remove the V-belt.

2. Remove the power steering pump assembly.
3. Remove the alternator and its bracket.
4. Remove the intake manifold cover and disconnect the PCV hose.
5. Disconnect the spark plug wire connectors and remove the connector from the bracket attaching bolt.
6. Remove the crankshaft and cam angle sensors. Remove the oil pressure switch connector.
7. Remove the knock sensor and the PCV blow-by hose.
8. Remove the intake manifold and gasket. Remove the water pipe.
9. To install, reverse the removal procedure, using new gasket.

EXCEPT JUSTY, XT COUPE AND LEGACY

1800cc Engine

1. If equipped with fuel injection, properly relieve the fuel system pressure. Disconnect the negative battery cable. Remove the spare tire from the engine compartment.

2. Disconnect the emission control system hoses, remove the mounting bracket screws and withdraw the air cleaner assembly.

3. If equipped with a turbocharger or a fuel injection system, loosen the hose clamps and remove the air intake duct.

4. Drain the cooling system. Remove the water hoses from the thermostat housing. Disconnect the thermo-switch connector.

5. If equipped with a distributor vacuum control valve, disconnect the hoses and electrical leads from it.

6. Disconnect the automatic choke to voltage regulator wire at the connector, the EGR solenoid wiring, if equipped and the EGR pipe.

7. Disconnect the throttle cable from it's bracket. If equipped with a carburetor, disconnect the fuel line.

8. If equipped with a turbocharger or fuel injection system, disconnect the hose clamps, pull off hoses and remove the fuel pressure regulator assembly.

9. If equipped with and MPFI system, remove the fuel injectors from the intake manifold.

10. Remove the intake manifold to cylinder head bolts. Remove the intake manifold assembly from the engine. The air cleaner brackets will come off as the unit is unbolted. Make sure to note locations of these brackets and remove them.

11. Installation is the reverse of the removal procedure. Be sure to use new gaskets or RTV sealant, as required.

Exhaust Manifold

Removal and Installation

JUSTY

1. Disconnect the negative battery cable. Remove the air cleaner assembly.

2. Raise and support the vehicle safely. Disconnect the exhaust manifold from the exhaust pipe. Lower the vehicle.

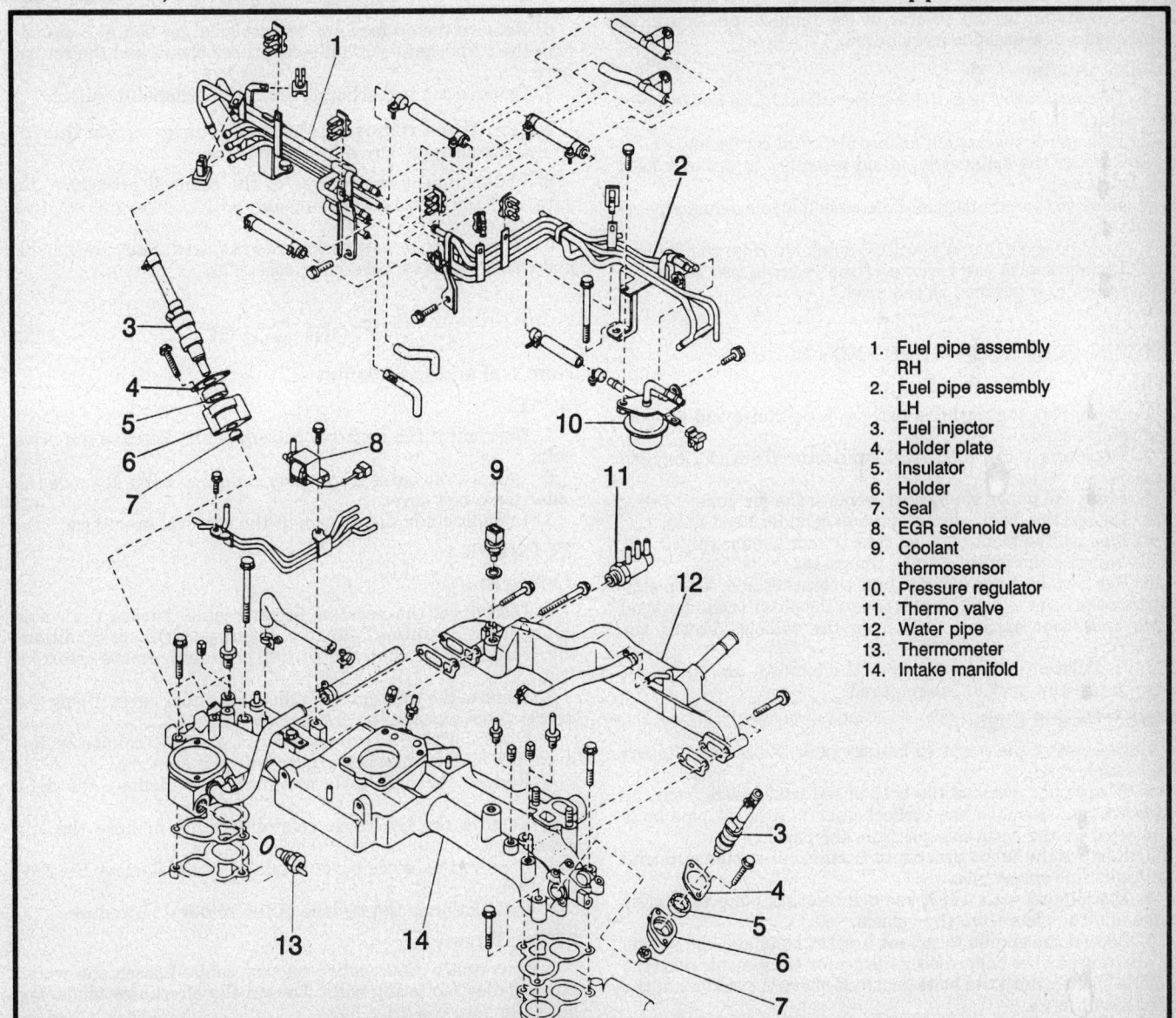

1. Fuel pipe assembly RH
2. Fuel pipe assembly LH
3. Fuel injector
4. Holder plate
5. Insulator
6. Holder
7. Seal
8. EGR solenoid valve
9. Coolant thermosensor
10. Pressure regulator
11. Thermo valve
12. Water pipe
13. Thermometer
14. Intake manifold

Intake manifold assembly—1800cc engine with TBI

3. Disconnect the oxygen sensor electrical connector. Remove the exhaust manifold cover plate assembly.

4. Remove the exhaust manifold retaining bolts. Remove the exhaust manifold from the engine. Discard the gasket.

5. Installation is the reverse of the removal procedure. Be sure to use a new gasket. Torque the exhaust manifold retaining bolts to specification.

XT COUPE AND LEGACY

1800cc Engine

1. Disconnect the negative battery cable. Raise and support the vehicle safely.

2. Disconnect the oxygen sensor electrical connector.

3. Remove the exhaust manifold assembly to cylinder head retaining bolts.

4. Remove the exhaust manifold assembly to exhaust pipe retaining bolts.

5. If equipped with a turbocharger, remove the exhaust pipe to turbocharger assembly. Remove the turbocharger plate and gasket.

6. Remove the exhaust manifold assembly from the vehicle.

7. Installation is the reverse of the removal procedure. Be sure to use new gaskets, as required.

2700cc Engine

1. Disconnect the negative battery cable. Raise and support the vehicle safely.

2. Disconnect the oxygen sensor electrical connector.

3. Remove the exhaust manifold assembly to cylinder head retaining bolts.

4. Remove the exhaust manifold assembly to exhaust pipe retaining bolts.

5. Remove the exhaust manifold assembly from the vehicle.

6. Installation is the reverse of the removal procedure. Be sure to use new gaskets, as required.

EXCEPT JUSTY, XT COUPE AND LEGACY

Without Turbocharged Engine

1. Disconnect the negative battery cable. Raise and support the vehicle safely.

2. Disconnect the electrical connector from the oxygen sensor.

3. From the upper shell cover, remove the air duct.

4. Loosen the front exhaust pipe to cylinder head nuts.

5. Remove the front exhaust pipe to rear exhaust pipe nuts, then separate the pipes, discard the gasket.

6. Remove the front exhaust pipe to bracket bolt. While supporting the front exhaust pipe, remove the pipe to cylinder head nuts and front exhaust pipe from the vehicle; discard the gaskets.

7. Installation is the reverse of the removal procedure. Be sure to use new gaskets, as required.

Turbocharged Engine

1. Disconnect the negative battery cable. Raise and support the vehicle safely.

2. If equipped, remove the both sheetmetal covers from the turbocharger. Remove the turbocharger to exhaust pipe bolts and separate the turbocharger from the pipe.

3. Remove the turbo bracket to front exhaust pipe nuts and the right side splash pan.

4. If equipped with 4WD, remove the skid plate to chassis bolts and the plate from the vehicle.

5. Loosen the engine to mount bracket bolts and the engine to pitching stopper bolts. Using the proper equipment, raise the engine slightly until the bolts protrude above the surface of the crossmember.

6. Disconnect the front exhaust pipe to cylinder head bolts and separate the exhaust pipe from its mounting. If equipped

with a power steering, be careful not to damage the power steering hoses.

7. Installation is the reverse of the removal procedure. Be sure to use new gaskets, as required.

Turbocharger

Removal and Installation

1800CC ENGINE

1. Disconnect the negative battery cable. Drain the cooling system. Remove the air cleaner.

2. Disconnect the airflow meter to turbocharger inlet clamp, then remove the air intake duct. Cover the airflow meter and turbocharger openings.

3. Loosen the turbocharger to air outlet hose clamp and the throttle body inlet to air inlet hose clamp. Remove the turbocharger to throttle body hose. Plug all of the openings.

4. Remove the turbocharger to center exhaust pipe nuts and the front exhaust pipe to turbocharger nuts.

5. Disconnect and plug the coolant lines.

6. Remove the oil feed line to turbocharger bolt and disconnect the turbocharger to oil return hose clamp and the return hose.

7. Remove the turbocharger from the exhaust manifold.

NOTE: When removing the turbocharger from the vehicle, disconnect the oil return hose.

8. Installation is the reverse of the removal procedure. Be sure to fill the turbocharger assembly with clean engine oil prior to installation.

9. Be sure to use new gaskets, as required. Start the engine and check for leaks, correct as necessary.

Front Cover

Removal and Installation

JUSTY

1. Disconnect the negative battery cable. Remove the drive belts.

2. Remove the outer front cover retaining bolts. Remove the outer front belt cover.

3. Installation is the reverse of the removal procedure.

XT COUPE

1800cc Engine

1. Disconnect the negative battery cable. Loosen the water pump pulley mounting bolts. If not equipped with air conditioning, loosen the alternator mounting bolts and remove the drive belt.

2. Remove the water pump pulley and pulley cover. Using the proper tools, remove the crankshaft pulley.

3. Disconnect the oil pressure switch electrical connector. Remove the oil level dipstick gauge and tube assembly.

4. Remove the right cover retaining bolts. Remove the right cover.

5. Remove the left cover retaining bolts. Remove the left cover.

6. Remove the center cover retaining bolts. Remove the center cover.

7. Installation is the reverse of the removal procedure.

2700cc Engine

1. Disconnect the negative battery cable. Loosen the water pump pulley mounting bolts. Loosen the alternator mounting bolts. Remove the drive belts.

2. Remove the water pump pulley. Using the proper tools, remove the crankshaft pulley.

3. Disconnect the oil pressure switch electrical connector. Remove the oil level dipstick gauge and tube assembly.

4. Remove the right cover retaining bolts. Remove the right cover.

5. Remove the left cover retaining bolts. Remove the left cover.

6. Remove the center cover retaining bolts. Remove the center cover.

7. Installation is the reverse of the removal procedure.

LEGACY

1. Disconnect the negative battery cable.

2. Remove the V-belt.

3. Remove the crankshaft pulley bolt. Use a tool to lock the crankshaft. Remove the crankshaft pulley

4. Remove the left cover retaining bolts. Remove the left cover.

5. Remove the right cover retaining bolts. Remove the right cover.

6. Remove the center cover retaining bolts. Remove the center cover.

7. Installation is the reverse of the removal procedure.

EXCEPT JUSTY, XT COUPE AND LEGACY

1. Disconnect the negative battery cable. Loosen the water pump pulley mounting bolts. If not equipped with air conditioning, loosen the alternator mounting bolts and remove the drive belt.

2. Remove the water pump pulley and pulley cover. Using the proper tools, remove the crankshaft pulley.

3. Disconnect the oil pressure switch electrical connector. Remove the oil level dipstick gauge and tube assembly.

4. Remove the right cover retaining bolts. Remove the right cover.

5. Remove the left cover retaining bolts. Remove the left cover.

6. Remove the center cover retaining bolts. Remove the center cover.

7. Installation is the reverse of the removal procedure.

Front Oil Seal Replacement

1. Remove the timing belt cover assembly.

2. On the 1800cc engine, slide both the No. 1 and No. 2 crankshaft sprockets from the crankshaft. On the 1200cc engine, slide crankshaft sprocket from the crankshaft. When removing the crankshaft sprockets, be sure to remove the Woodruff® key from the crankshaft.

3. Using a small prybar, pry the front oil seal from the crankcase.

4. To install, use a new oil seal lubricated with engine oil and drive it into the crankcase until it seats. When installing the new oil seal, be careful not to cut the sealing lips.

5. To complete the installation, reverse the removal procedures.

Timing Belt and Tensioner

Removal and Installation

JUSTY

1. Disconnect the negative battery cable. Remove the alternator drive belt. Loosen the crankshaft pulley bolts but do not remove.

NOTE: An access hole is provided in the wheelhouse panel to loosen and then remove the crankshaft pulley bolts.

2. Position the crankshaft with No. 3 cylinder at TDC.

3. Remove the crankshaft bolts and pulley, using pulley removal tool 499205500 or equivalent. Remove the outer front timing belt cover.

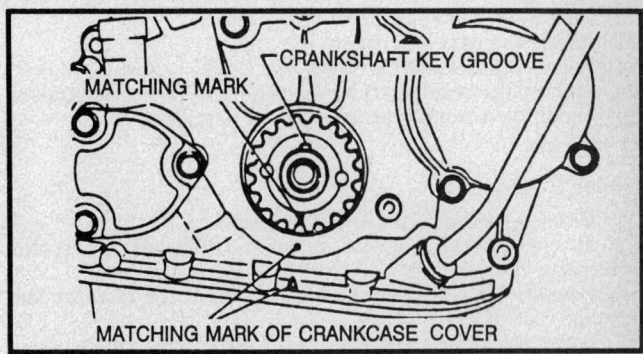

Crankshaft gear alignment—1200cc engine

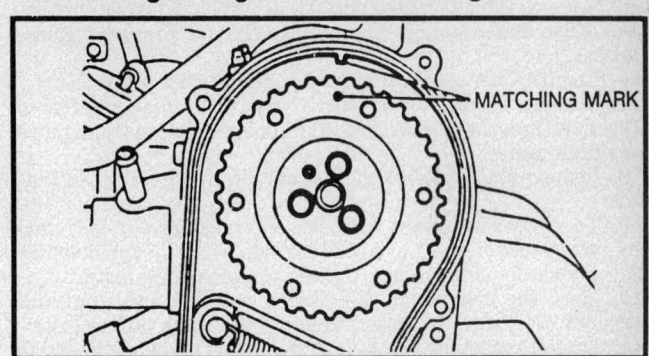

Camshaft gear alignment—1200cc engine

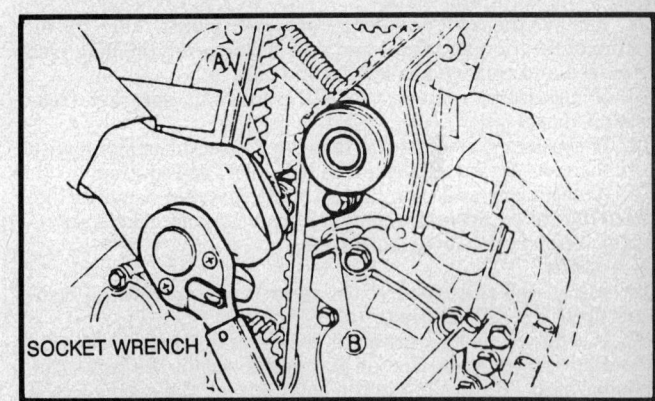

Timing belt tension adjustment—1200cc engine

4. Loosen the tensioner bolt and position it in the direction that loosens the belt. Tighten the tensioner bolt in that position.

5. Remove the camshaft drive pulley plate. Mark the timing belt, if to be used again, in the direction of rotation for reinstallation. Remove the belt from the sprockets.

6. If necessary, remove the tensioner and spring. Remove the camshaft pulley, using pulley removal tool 499205500 or equivalent. Remove the inner belt cover and cover mount only as required.

To install:

7. When installing the timing belt, rotate and align the matchmark of the camshaft driven pulley 0.120 in. diameter hole with the matchmark of the cam belt side cover.

8. Align the matchmark of the crankshaft drive pulley with the matchmark of the crankshaft cover. Install the camshaft drive belt.

9. Loosen the tensioner bolt ½ turn.

10. Tighten the tensioner bolt below the adjusting wheel first. Tighten the other bolt. Check to be sure all sprocket and housing matching marks are in agreement.

11. Install the camshaft drive pulley plate.
12. Install the cam belt cover.
13. Install the crankshaft pulley and bolts.
14. Tighten the crankshaft bolts to 58–72 ft. lbs. and complete any remaining assembly procedures, as required.

XT COUPE

1800cc Engine

1. Disconnect the negative battery cable.
2. Raise the vehicle and support safely. Remove the underpans.
3. Remove the bolts from the underside of the radiator fan shroud.
4. Lower the vehicle and remove the fan shroud bolts and the shroud. Disconnect the fan motor connector.
5. Remove the alternator and the drive belt. Remove the dipstick tube and dipstick. Disconnect the oil pressure gauge harness.
6. Remove the water pump pulley and the air intake boot.
7. Attach a stopper tool to the flywheel or torque converter to prevent it from turning. With the crankshaft stationary, remove the crank pulley.
8. Remove the front left, right and center belt covers, in that order.
9. To remove the right belt, loosen tensioner No. 1 (right) mounting bolts on the No. 1 cylinder side. With the tensioner in the fully slackened position, tighten the mounting bolts.
10. Mark the belt in the direction of rotation and front and rear indicator, if to be reused. Remove the right timing belt.
11. Loosen tensioner No. 2 (left) mounting bolts on the No. 2 cylinder side. With the tensioner in the fully slackened position, tighten the mounting bolts.
12. Remove the right crankshaft sprocket (front). Mark the direction of rotation and front and rear indicator on the belt, if to be reused and remove the left timing belt.
13. If necessary, remove the left crankshaft sprocket (rear without dowel pin).
14. If necessary, remove the tensioner assemblies along with the tensioner spring. Remove the belt idler, as required.
15. If necessary and using a camshaft sprocket removal tool 499207000 or equivalent, remove the camshaft sprockets. As required, remove the inner belt covers.

To install:

16. Install the belt cover seals, as required. Install the camshaft sprockets, if removed.
17. If removed, install the right tensioner and attach the tensioner spring to the tensioner and position it to the right side cylinder block. Hand tighten the bolts. Attach the spring to the assembly and tighten the top bolt. Loosen it ½ turn. Push down on the tensioner until it stops, hand tighten the lower bolt.
18. To install the left tensioner, if removed, attach the tensioner spring to the tensioner and position it to the left side cylinder block. Hand tighten the bolts. Attach the spring to the assembly and tighten the top bolt. Loosen it ½ turn. Raise the tensioner until it stops, hand tighten the lower bolt.
19. Install the belt idler to the cylinder block. Install the crankshaft sprockets. Temporarily install the crankshaft pulley.
20. To install the left timing belt, align the center of the 3 lines on the flywheel with the timing mark on the flywheel housing.
21. Align the timing mark on the camshaft sprocket with the notch in the belt cover.
22. Install the timing belt to the crankshaft sprocket (No. 2), the oil pump sprocket, belt idler pulley and the camshaft sprocket, in that order to prevent downward slackening of the belt.

NOTE: The No. 2 crankshaft sprocket is identified as the sprocket without a dowel pin.

23. Loosen the tensioner and ensure smooth movement for belt tension adjustment.
24. Using belt tension wrench tool 499437000 of equivalent, apply 33–55 lbs. of tension to the left camshaft sprocket in the counterclockwise direction.
25. While applying torque, tighten the lower tensioner retaining bolt 12–14 ft. lbs. Tighten the upper tensioner retaining bolt 12–14 ft. lbs. Be sure the timing marks remain in alignment.
26. To install the right belt, rotate the crankshaft one full turn clockwise from the position where the left timing belt was installed. Align the center of the 3 lines on the flywheel with the timing mark on the flywheel housing.
27. Align the timing mark on the camshaft sprocket with the notch in the belt cover. Install the right timing belt over the crankshaft sprocket (with dowel pin) and camshaft sprocket.
28. Using belt tension wrench tool 499437000 or equivalent, apply 33–55 lbs. of tension to the right camshaft sprocket in the counterclockwise direction. While applying torque, tighten the lower tensioner retaining bolt 12–14 ft. lbs. Tighten the upper tensioner retaining bolt 12–14 ft. lbs. Be certain the timing marks remain in alignment.
29. Remove the crankshaft pulley and install the necessary seals, if not in place and install the front center cover to the engine block.
30. Install the left and right belt covers.
31. Install the crankshaft pulley and while holding the crankshaft stationary, tighten the bolt to 66–79 ft. lbs.
32. Complete the assembly of the water pump pulley, the oil dipstick tube, the alternator drive belt and the radiator shroud. Complete any other Step that is needed to complete this procedure.

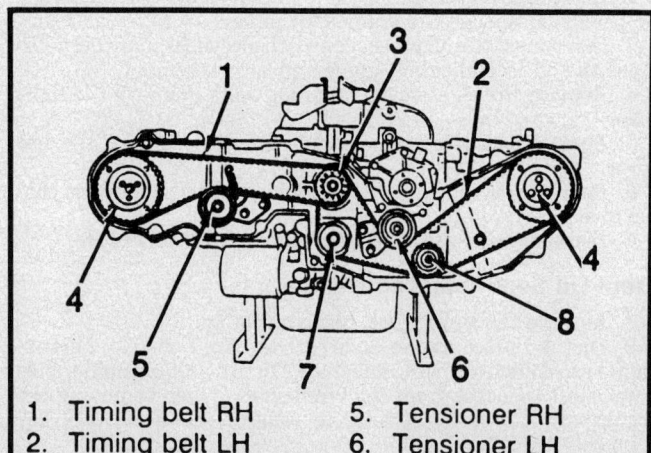

1. Timing belt RH
2. Timing belt LH
3. Crankshaft sprocket
4. Camshaft sprocket
5. Tensioner RH
6. Tensioner LH
7. Oil pump sprocket
8. Idler

Timing belt configuration-1800cc and 2700cc engines

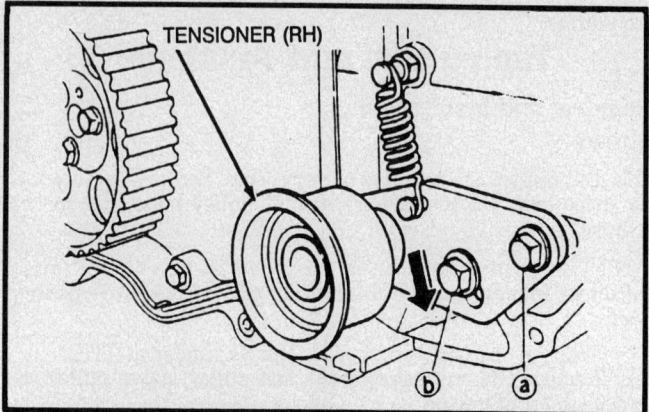

TENSIONER (RH)

Timing belt tension adjustment—2700cc engine

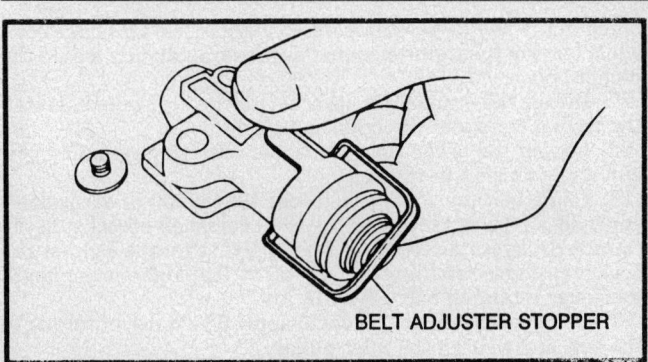

Installation of belt adjuster stopper clip—2700cc engine

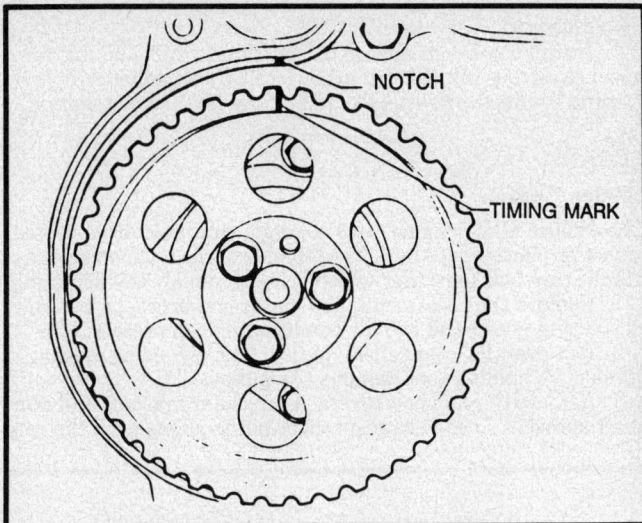

Camshaft gear alignment—2700cc engine

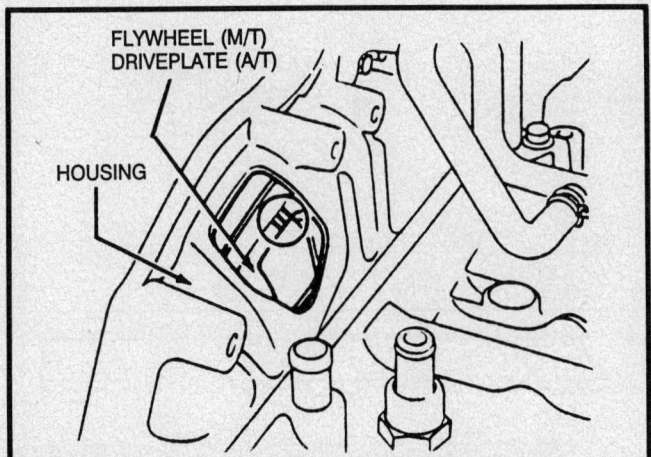

Flywheel timing mark alignment—2700cc engine

2700cc Engine

1. Disconnect the negative battery cable. Loosen the V-belt tensioner locknut fully counterclockwise.

2. Loosen 2 alternator mounting bolts. Loosen water pump pulley mounting bolts. Remove the water pump pulley.

3. Lock the crankshaft and remove the crankshaft pulley.

4. Remove the right, left and center belt covers. To remove the right belt, loosen the tensioner mounting bolts on the No. 1

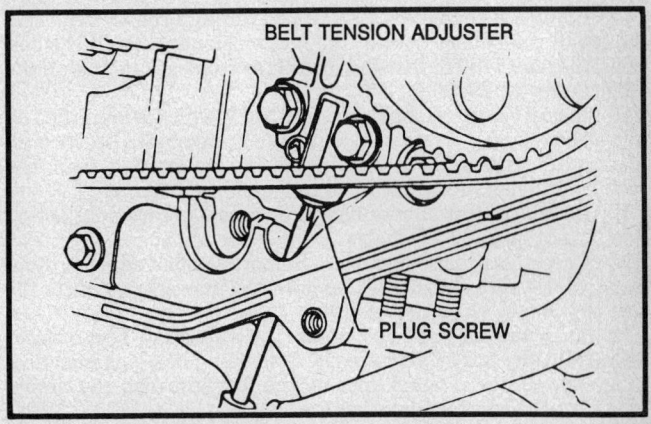

Removing the plug screw from the belt tension adjuster—2700cc engine

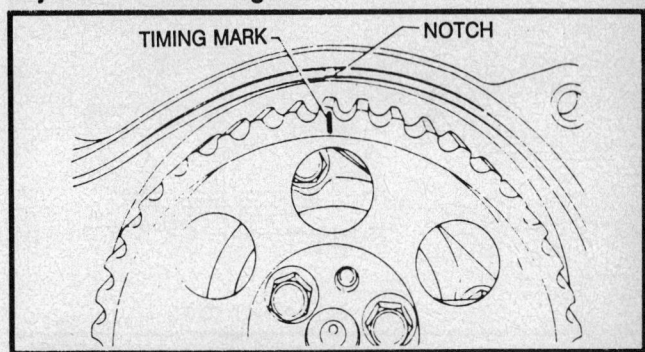

Alignment of left cam sprocket timing mark to notch in belt cover—2700cc engine

cylinder. With the tensioner in the fully slackened position, tighten the mounting bolts.

5. Mark the belt in the direction of rotation. Remove the right timing belt.

6. If necessary, remove the right tensioner assembly. Remove the crankshaft sprocket.

7. To remove the left belt, remove the idler pulley. Remove the rubber plug. Remove the plug screw from the belt tension adjuster lower side.

8. Position a tool into the hole in the bottom of the belt tension adjuster. Turn the screw clockwise to loosen the belt tension.

9. Install belt adjuster stopper tool 13082AA000. Remove the left belt tensioner assembly.

10. Mark the belt in the direction of rotation. Remove the left timing belt.

11. If necessary, remove the crankshaft sprocket and the idler pulley. Remove the belt tensioner assembly. Reinstall the plug screw in its mounting.

12. As required, remove the inner belt covers. As required, check the belt tensioners and replace, as necessary.

To install:

13. Align the center of the 3 lines on the flywheel with the timing mark on the flywheel housing. Install the camshaft sprockets, if removed and align the timing mark on the camshaft sprocket with the notch in the belt cover.

14. Install the hydraulic belt tensioner assembly. Remove the plug screw from the tensioner lower side. Install a prybar into the hole in the bottom of the tensioner and turn the screw clockwise to compress the rubber boot. Install the belt adjuster stopper tool.

NOTE: The clip furnished as a spare part can be used in place of the belt adjuster stopper tool.

15. Using a syringe type tool, add oil through the air vent hole on top of the rubber boot of the belt tensioner. Install the belt tensioner to 17–20 ft. lbs. and install the rubber plug. Install the idler pulley to 29–35 ft. lbs..

16. Install the crankshaft sprocket No. 2, which is identified by the absence of a dowel pin, onto the crankshaft. Be sure all marks are in alignment and install the timing belt from the crankshaft side. Be careful not to loosen the belt.

17. Install the left tensioner and be sure its movement is correct. Tighten to 29–35 ft. lbs.

18. Check for proper operation. Remove the belt adjuster stopper tool. Be sure the end of the left tensioner arm contacts the top of the belt tensioner adjuster.

19. To install the right belt, rotate the crankshaft 1 turn clockwise from the position where the left timing belt was installed. Align the center of the 3 lines on the flywheel with the timing mark on the flywheel housing.

20. Align the timing mark on the camshaft sprocket with the notch in the belt cover. Temporarily tighten the tensioner bolts while moving the right tensioner downward. Slightly loosen the higher bolt.

21. Install the crankshaft sprocket to the crankshaft. Install the timing belt from the crankshaft side.

22. Loosen the lower right tensioner assembly retaining bolt and apply tension to the belt.

23. Using belt tension wrench tool 499437100 or equivalent, apply 33–55 lbs. of tension to the right camshaft sprocket in the counterclockwise direction. While applying torque tighten the lower tensioner retaining bolt 17–20 ft. lbs. Tighten the upper tensioner retaining bolt 17–20 ft. lbs.

24. Using a belt tension wrench, apply 33–55 lbs. of torque to the belt and tighten the idler pulley.

25. Install the crankshaft pulley and tighten to 66–79 ft. lbs. Install the oil dipstick, if removed.

26. Install the water pipe, the water pump pulley, the center, right and left covers, the air conditioning compressor and install the alternator.

27. Install the V-belt and adjust tension to 143–166 lbs. for a new belt or 99–143 lbs. for a used belt. Lock adjuster bolt by turning counterclockwise. Complete any further installation.

LEGACY

2200cc Engine

The 2200cc OHC engine uses a single cam belt drive system with a serpentine type belt. The left side of the engine uses a hydraulic cam belt tensioner which is continuously self adjusting.

1. Remove the accessories, alternator and brackets, the power steering pump and the air conditioning compressor.

2. Remove the crankshaft pulley bolt by using a special crankshaft holding tool. Remove the pulley.

3. Remove the cam belt covers. Align the crankshaft and camshaft sprocket so each cam sprocket notch aligns with the cam

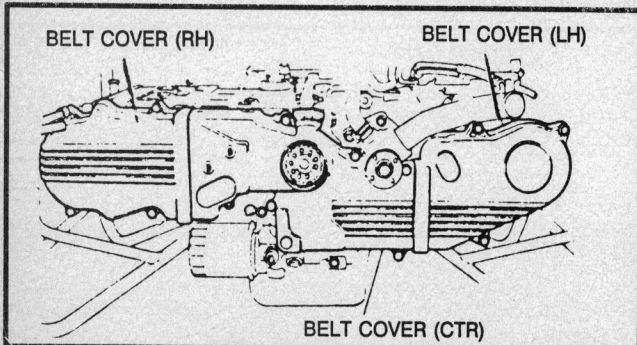

Left, center and right belt covers—typical of 1800cc, 2200cc and 2700cc engines

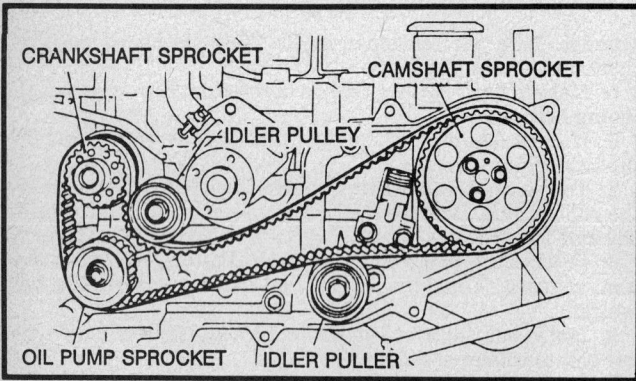

Installation of left timing belt—2700cc engine

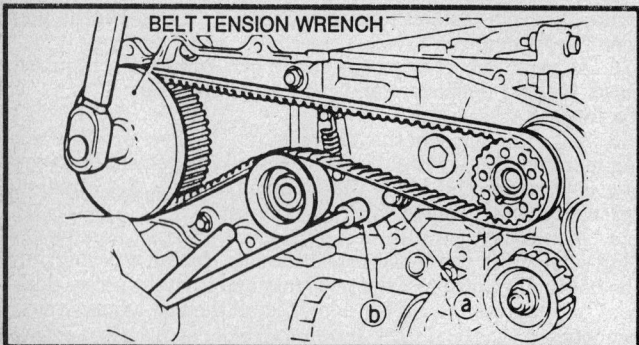

Adjustment of right timing belt tension with belt tension wrench—2700cc engine

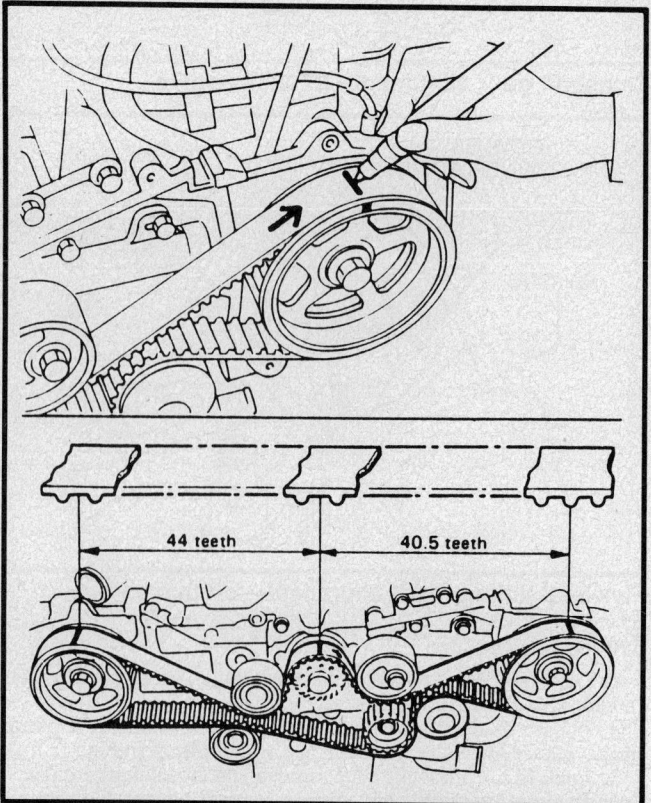

Mark the timing belt for easy reference on installation

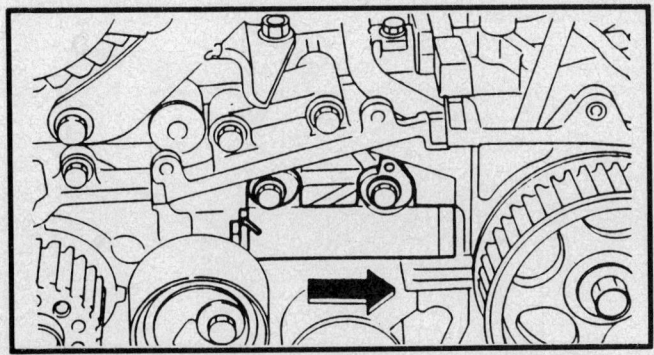

Temporarily move the tension adjuster aside with snugged bolts—2200cc engine

After belt installation, move the tension adjuster all the way to the right and tighten bolts—2200cc engine

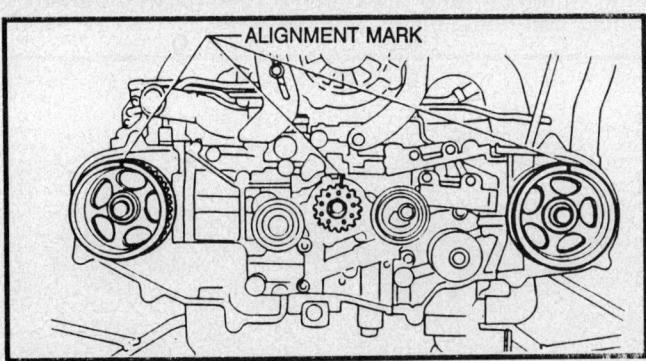

Alignment marks—2200cc engine

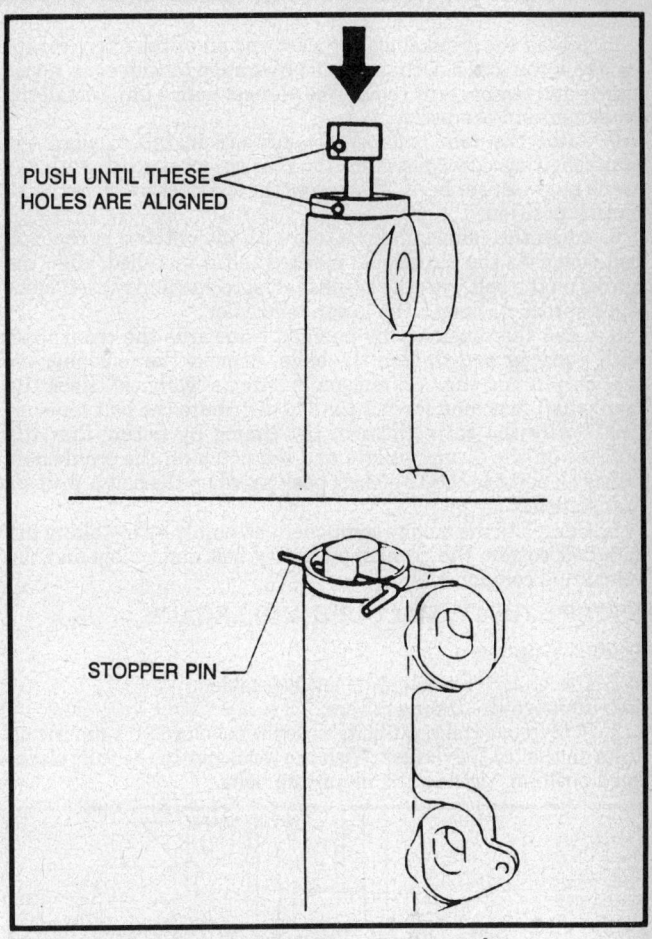

PUSH UNTIL THESE HOLES ARE ALIGNED

STOPPER PIN

Timing belt tensioner adjuster stopper pin installation—2200cc engine

cover notches. Align the crankshaft sprocket top tooth notch, located at the rear of the tooth, with the notch on the crank angle sensor boss. Mark the 3 alignment points as well as the direction of the cam belt.

4. Loosen the tensioner adjusting bolts and remove the bottom 3 idlers, the cam belt and the cam belt tensioner. The cam sprockets can then be removed with a modified camshaft sprocket wrench tool.

5. If the sprockets are removed, note the reference sensor at the rear of the left cam sprocket.

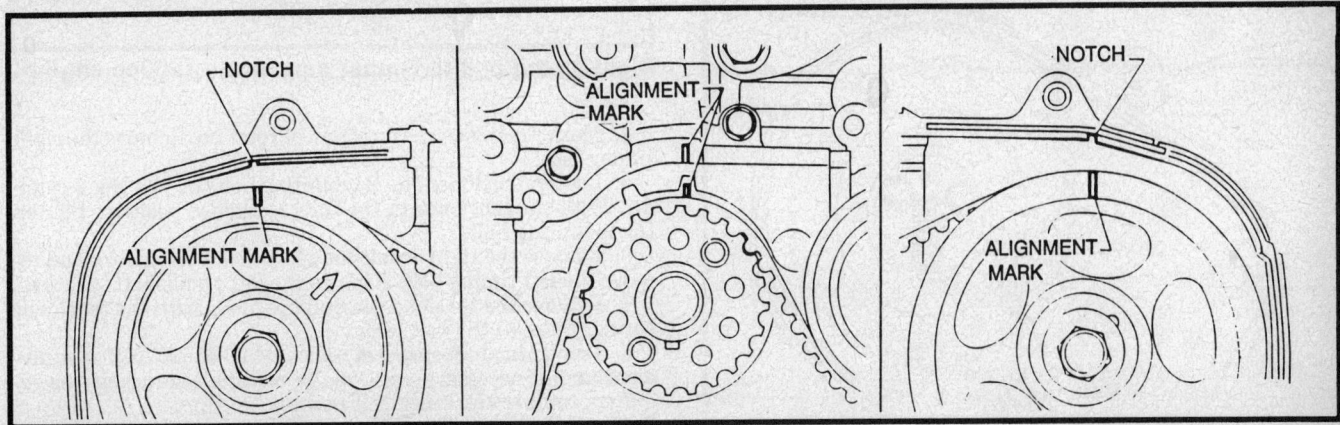

Matching alignment marks—2200cc engine

To install:

6. Install the crankshaft sprocket and all of the idlers except for the lower right. Compress the hydraulic tensioner in a vise slowly and temporarily secure the plunger with a pin. Install the tensioner and the pulley.

7. After the cam belt components are installed, align the crankshaft sprocket notch on the rear sprocket tooth with the crank angle sensor boss. This places the sprocket notch in the 12 o'clock position.

8. Align the camshaft sprockets with the notches in the cam belt cover. As the directional marked belt is installed, align the marks on the belt with the crankshaft sprocket and the left camshaft sprocket. Install the lower right idler.

9. Load the tensioner by pushing it towards the crankshaft with a prybar and tighten the bolts. Remove the tensioner retention pin and the belt tension is automatically set. Rock the crankshaft back and forth 1 time to distribute the belt tension.

10. Verify the correctness of the timing by noting that the notches on the 2 cam pulleys and the notch on the crankshaft pulley all point to the 12 o'clock position when the belt is properly installed.

11. Complete the engine component assembly by installing the cam belt covers, the crankshaft pulley bolt and pulley and the remaining components.

EXCEPT JUSTY, XT COUPE AND LEGACY

1800cc Engine

1. Disconnect the negative battery cable.
2. Remove the timing covers.
3. To remove the right belt, loosen tensioner No. 1 mounting bolts on the No. 1 cylinder. With the tensioner in the fully slackened position, tighten the mounting bolts.

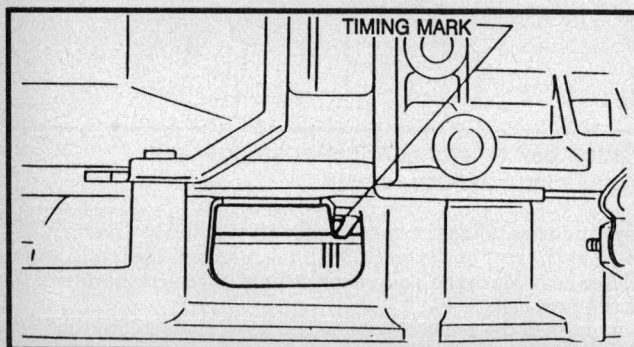

Flywheel alignment marks for timing belt servicing— 1800cc engine

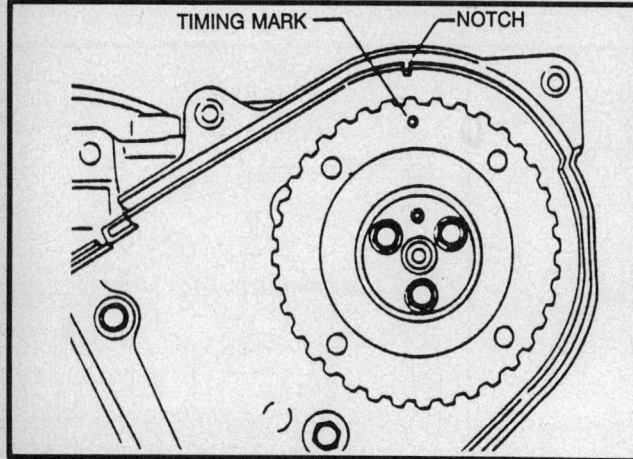

Left camshaft gear alignment—1800cc engine

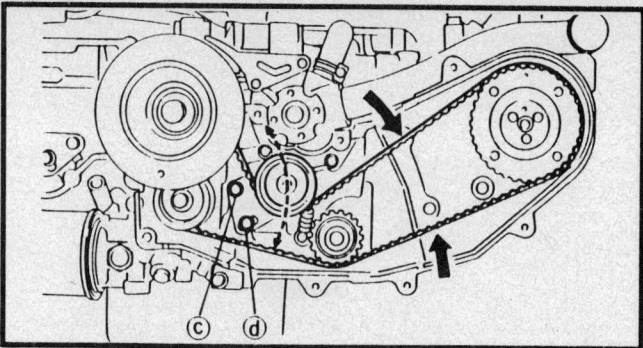

Left timing belt tensioner servicing—1800cc engine

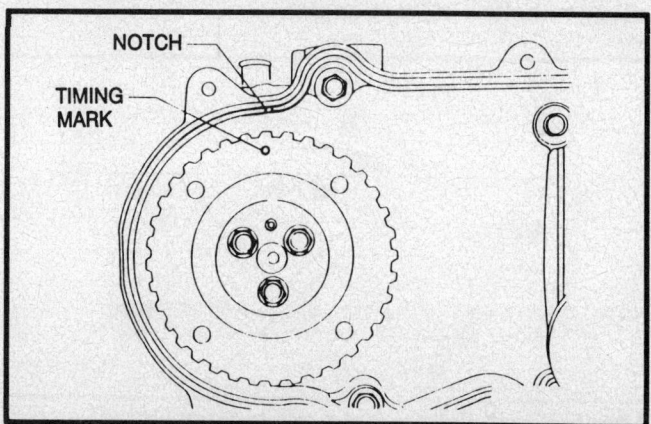

Right camshaft gear alignment—1800cc engine— after turning engine 1 complete rotation with the left timing belt installed

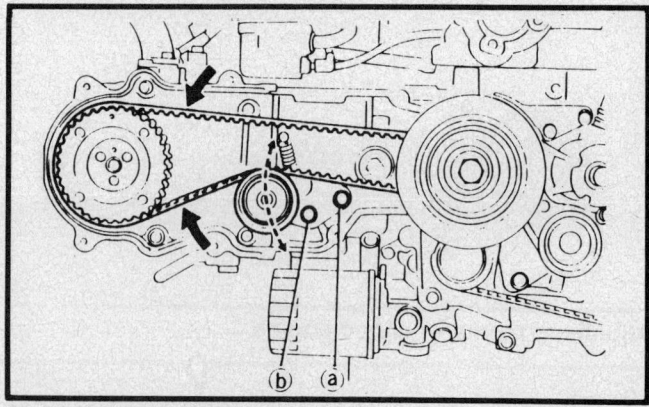

Right timing belt tensioner servicing—1800cc engine

4. Mark the belt in the direction of rotation. Remove the right timing belt.

5. Loosen tensioner No. 2 mounting bolts on the No. 2 cylinder. With the tensioner in the fully slackened position, tighten the mounting bolts.

6. Remove the right crankshaft sprocket. Matchmark and remove the left timing belt. Remove the left crankshaft sprocket.

7. Remove the tensioner assemblies along with the tensioner spring. Remove the belt idler.

8. Using camshaft sprocket removal tool 499207000 or equivalent and, if necessary, remove the camshaft sprockets. As required, remove the inner belt covers.

To install:

9. Install the camshaft sprockets, if removed.

10. To install the right tensioner, attach the tensioner spring to the tensioner and position it to the right side cylinder block. Hand tighten the bolts. Attach the spring to the assembly and tighten the top bolt. Loosen it ½ turn. Push down on the tensioner until it stops, hand tighten the lower bolt.

11. To install the left tensioner, attach the tensioner spring to the tensioner and position it to the left side cylinder block. Hand tighten the bolts. Attach the spring to the assembly and tighten the top bolt. Loosen it ½ turn. Raise the tensioner until it stops, hand tighten the lower bolt.

12. Install the belt idler to the cylinder block. Install the crankshaft sprockets. Temporarily install the crankshaft pulley.

13. To install the left timing belt, align the center of the 3 lines on the flywheel with the timing mark on the flywheel housing. Align the timing mark on the camshaft sprocket with the notch in the belt cover. Install the timing belt to the No. 2 crankshaft gear (without dowel pin), oil pump gear and the belt idler, in that order.

14. Using belt tension wrench tool 499437000 or equivalent, apply 33–55 lbs. of tension to the left camshaft sprocket in the counterclockwise direction. While applying torque, tighten the lower tensioner retaining bolt 12–14 ft. lbs. Tighten the upper tensioner retaining bolt 12–14 ft. lbs.

15. To install the right belt, rotate the crankshaft 1 turn clockwise from the position where the left timing belt was installed. Align the center of the 3 lines on the flywheel with the timing mark on the flywheel housing.

16. Align the timing mark on the camshaft sprocket with the notch in the belt cover. Install the right timing belt.

17. Using belt tension wrench tool 499437000, apply 33–55 lbs. of tension to the right camshaft sprocket in the counterclockwise direction. While applying torque tighten the lower tensioner retaining bolt 12–14 ft. lbs. Tighten the upper tensioner retaining bolt 12–14 ft. lbs.

18. Install the crankshaft pulley. Continue the installation of the removed components.

Camshaft

Removal and Installation

JUSTY

1. Disconnect the negative battery cable. Drain the radiator, as required. Remove the air cleaner assembly. Remove the drive belts. Properly discharge the air condition system, as required.

2. Remove the tensioner and spring. Remove the camshaft pulley, using pulley removal tool 499205500 or equivalent. Remove the inner belt cover and cover mount.

3. Remove the PCV hose from the rocker arm cover. Remove the rocker arm cover retaining bolts. Remove the rocker arm cover from the engine. Remove the rocker arm assembly.

4. As required, remove the radiator, air conditioning condenser and grille work in order to remove the camshaft from the cylinder head.

5. Carefully withdraw the camshaft from the cylinder head.

6. Installation is the reverse of the removal procedure. Before installing the camshaft be sure to coat it with clean engine oil.

7. Be sure to use new gaskets or RTV sealant, as required. Adjust the valves to specification, as required.

XT COUPE

1800cc Engine

1. Disconnect the negative battery cable. Drain the cooling system.

2. Remove the timing covers. Matchmark and remove the timing belt.

3. Remove the distributor. Remove the water pipe assembly.

4. Remove the valve cover retaining bolts. Remove the valve covers.

5. Remove the camshaft case, camshaft support and camshaft assembly as a complete unit. When removing the camshaft case, the valve rockers may come off their mounting.

6. As required, remove the lash adjusters from the cylinder head. Be sure to keep the adjusters and the rockers in the proper order for reinstallation.

7. Remove the camshaft support from the camshaft case. Carefully remove the camshaft from its mounting.

To install:

8. Installation is the reverse of the removal procedure. Be sure to coat the camshaft assembly with clean engine oil prior to installation.

9. When installing the camshaft case to the cylinder head, use sealing compound 1207B or equivalent. Torque the retaining bolts 17–20 ft. lbs.

10. Adjust the valves, as required. Be sure to use new gaskets or RTV sealant, as required.

2700cc Engine

1. Disconnect the negative battery cable. Drain the cooling system.

2. Remove the timing covers. Matchmark and remove the timing belt.

3. Remove the distributor. Remove the water pipe assembly.

4. Remove the valve cover retaining bolts. Remove the valve covers.

5. Remove the camshaft case, camshaft support and camshaft assembly as a complete unit. When removing the camshaft case the valve rockers may come off their mounting.

6. As required, remove the lash adjusters from the cylinder head. Be sure to keep the adjusters and the rockers in the proper order for reinstallation.

7. Remove the camshaft support from the camshaft case. Carefully remove the camshaft from its mounting.

To install:

8. Installation is the reverse of the removal procedure. Be sure to coat the camshaft assembly with clean engine oil prior to installation.

9. When installing the camshaft case to the cylinder head using sealing compound 1207B or equivalent. Torque the retaining bolts 17–20 ft. lbs.

10. Adjust the valves, as required. Be sure to use new gaskets or RTV sealant, as required.

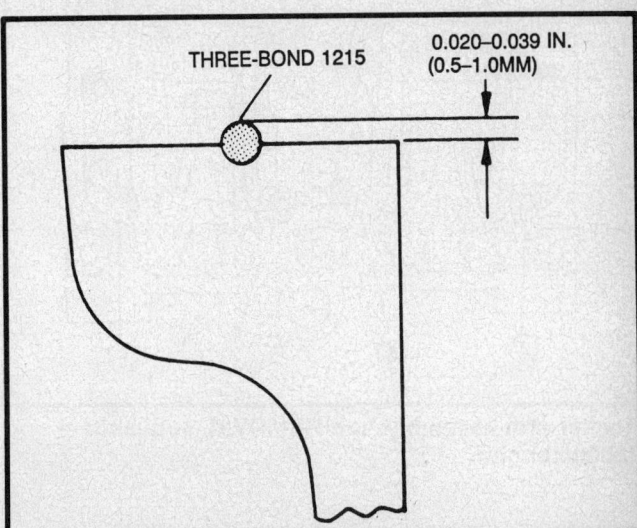

THREE-BOND 1215

0.020–0.039 IN. (0.5–1.0MM)

Camshaft case to cylinder head installation—1800cc engine

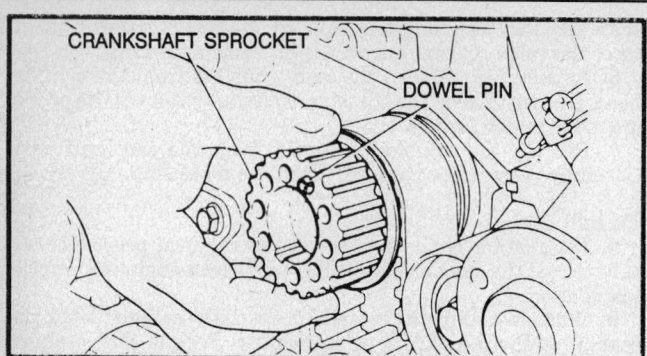

Installation of No. 1 (outer) crankshaft sprocket with dowel pin—2700cc engine

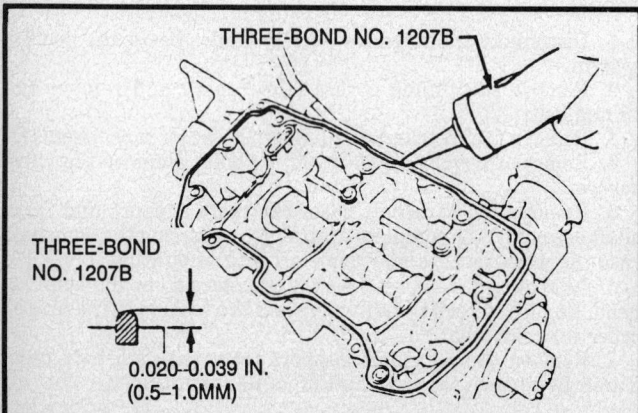

Camshaft case to cylinder head installation—2700cc engine

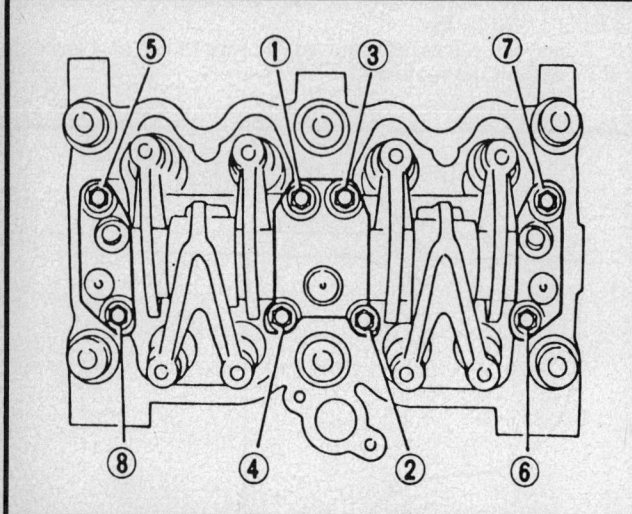

Rocker arm assembly bolt REMOVAL sequence— 2200cc engine

LEGACY

2200cc Engine

NOTE: It is assumed that engine has been removed from the vehicle.

1. Remove the timing belt covers, the timing belt, camshaft sprockets and other components necessary to expose the camshaft.
2. Remove the valve covers. Remove the rocker arm assembly bolts in sequence.
3. To remove the left camshaft, perform the following procedures:
    a. Remove the cam angle sensor.
    b. Remove the oil dipstick tube attaching bolt.
    c. Remove the camshaft support on the left side.
    d. Remove the O-ring.
    e. Remove the camshaft and seal(rear) from the left side.
4. To remove the right camshaft, perform the following procedures:
    a. Remove the camshaft support on the right side.
    b. Remove the O-ring.
    c. Remove the camshaft and seal (rear) from the right side. Remove the oil seal from the camshaft support.

To install:

5. To install the left camshaft, perform the following procedures:
    a. Lubricate the camshaft journals, install the oil seal (rear) and install the camshaft into the cylinder head.
    b. Install the O-ring into the camshaft support and install the support.
    c. Install oil seal into the camshaft support.
    d. Install the bolt into the dipstick tube and install the camshaft sensor.
6. To install the right camshaft, perform the following procedures:
    a. Lubricate the camshaft journals and install the right camshaft.
    b. Install the O-ring into the camshaft support and install the support.
    c. Install a new oil seal in the rear of the cylinder head.
7. To complete assembly, perform the following procedures:
    a. Install the rocker arm assemblies and torque bolts to 9 ft. lbs., in proper sequence.
    b. Install the camshaft sprockets and related components. Install the timing belt and complete the assembly of covers.

EXCEPT JUSTY, XT COUPE AND LEGACY

1800cc Engine

1. Disconnect the negative battery cable. Drain the cooling system.
2. Remove the timing covers. Matchmark and remove the timing belt.
3. Remove the distributor. Remove the water pipe assembly.
4. Remove the valve cover retaining bolts. Remove the valve covers.
5. Remove the camshaft case, camshaft support and camshaft assembly as a complete unit. When removing the camshaft case the valve rockers may come off their mounting.
6. As required, remove the lash adjusters from the cylinder head. Be sure to keep the adjusters and the rockers in the proper order for reinstallation.
7. Remove the camshaft support from the camshaft case. Carefully remove the camshaft from its mounting.

To install:

8. Installation is the reverse of the removal procedure. Be

sure to coat the camshaft assembly with clean engine oil prior to installation.

9. When installing the camshaft case to the cylinder head using sealing compound 1207B or equivalent. Torque the retaining bolts 17–20 ft. lbs.

10. Adjust the valves, as required. Be sure to use new gaskets or RTV sealant, as required.

Piston and Connecting Rod

Positioning

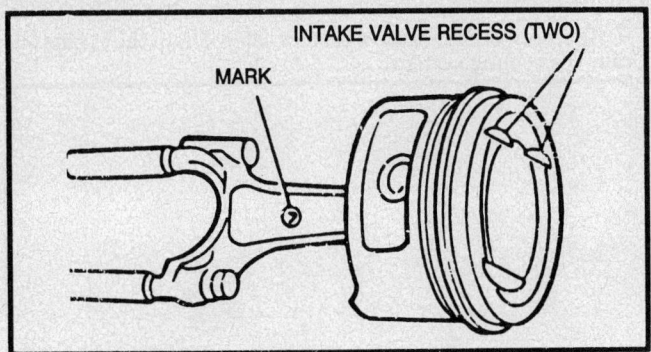

Piston identification—1800cc and 2700cc engines— typical of 2200cc engine

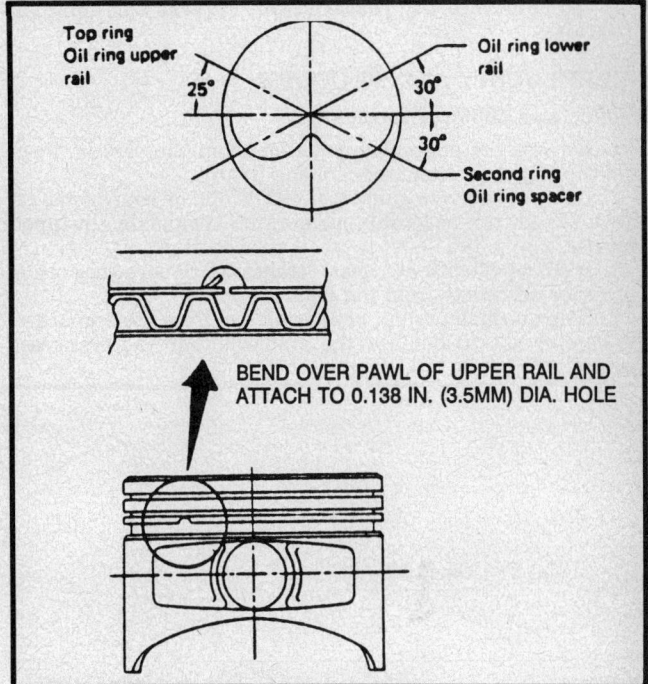

Piston identification—1200cc engine

ENGINE LUBRICATION

Oil Pan

Removal and Installation

1. Disconnect the negative battery cable. Drain the engine oil.
2. Raise and support the vehicle safely.
3. Remove the required components in order to gain access to the oil pan retaining bolts.
4. Remove the oil pan retaining bolts. Remove the oil pan from the engine.
5. Installation is the reverse of the removal procedure. Be sure to use new gaskets or RTV sealant, as required.

Rear Main Bearing Oil Seal

Removal and Installation

JUSTY

1200cc Engine

1. Remove the engine from the vehicle and position it in a suitable holding fixture.
2. Remove the clutch assembly and the flywheel from the crankshaft.
3. Using a small prybar, pry the rear oil seal from the crankcase. Be careful not to damage the crankshaft or the crankcase housing.

To install:

4. To install, use a new oil seal, lubricate the seal with engine oil.
5. Using the crankshaft rear oil seal guide tool 498725600 or equivalent, and the rear oil seal press tool 498725500 or equivalent, drive the new oil seal into the housing until it seats.
6. To complete the installation, reverse the removal procedures.

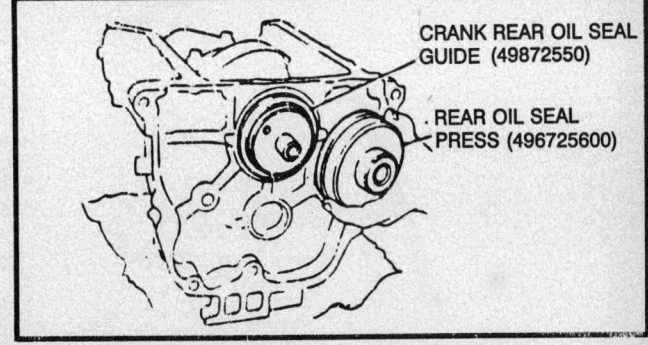

Rear main seal installation—1200cc engine

XT COUPE

1800cc and 2700cc Engines

1. Remove the engine from the vehicle. Position the engine in a suitable holding fixture.
2. Using clutch disc guide tool 499747000 or equivalent, remove the clutch assembly on manual transaxle equipped vehicles.
3. If equipped with automatic transaxle, remove the torque converter driveplate from the crankshaft.
4. Using a small prybar, pry the oil seal from the crankcase. Be careful not to damage the crankshaft or the crankcase housing.

To install:

5. Using a new rear oil seal, coat the seal lips with grease and the housing with engine oil.
6. Using rear oil seal installation tool 499587000 or equivalent, drive the new oil seal into the crankcase until it seats.

7. To complete the installation, reverse the removal procedures

EXCEPT JUSTY AND XT COUPE

1800cc and 2200cc Engines

1. Remove the engine/transmission from the vehicle. Position the engine in a suitable holding fixture.

2. Using clutch disc guide tool 499747000 or equivalent, remove the clutch assembly on manual transaxle equipped vehicles.

3. If equipped with automatic transaxle, remove the torque converter driveplate from the crankshaft.

4. Using a small prybar, pry the oil seal from the crankcase. Be careful not to damage the crankshaft or the crankcase housing.

To install:

5. Using a new rear oil seal, coat the seal lips with grease and the housing with engine oil.

6. Using rear oil seal installation tool 499587000 or equivalent, drive the new oil seal into the crankcase until it seats.

7. To complete the installation, reverse the removal procedures.

Oil Pump

Removal and Installation

JUSTY

1200cc Engine

1. Disconnect the negative battery cable. Drain the engine oil. Drain the cooling system.

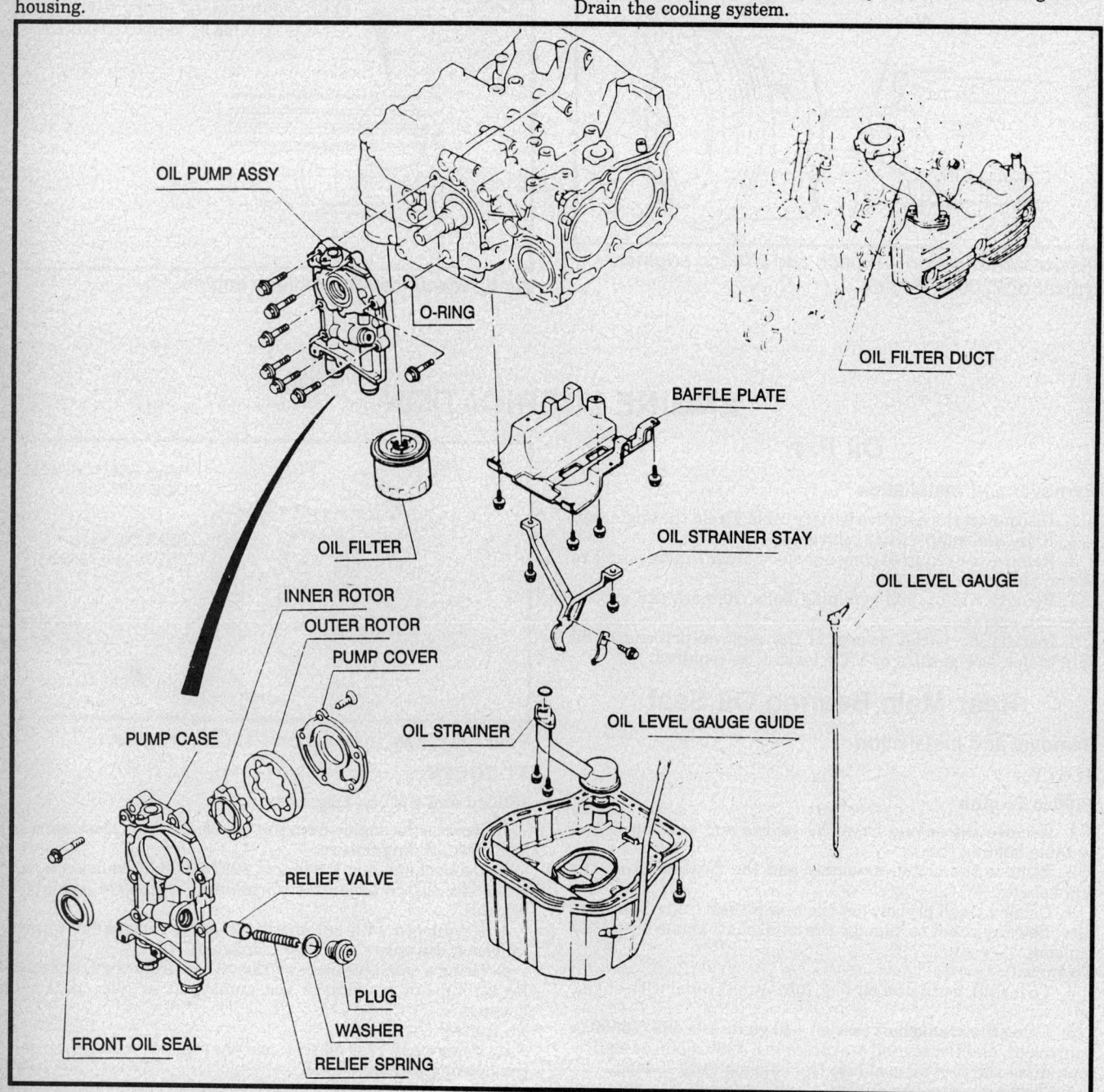

Oil pump servicing—2200cc engine

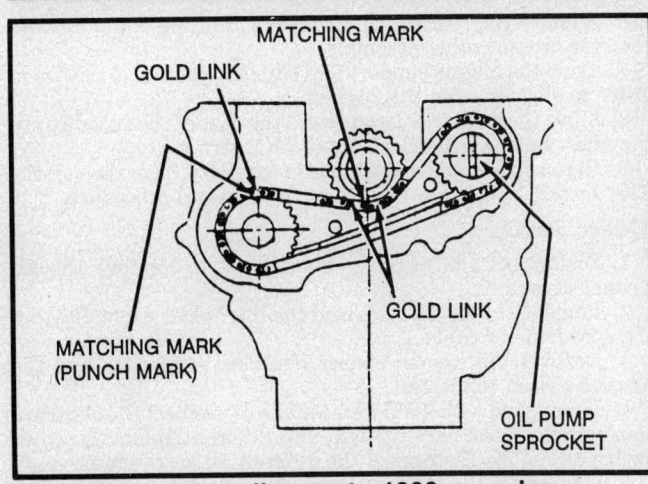

Oil pump sprocket alignment—1200cc engine

2. Remove the oil dipstick, dipstick guide and guide sealing.

3. Remove the alternator. Remove the timing belt.

4. Raise and support the vehicle safely. Remove the oil pan. Lower the vehicle.

5. Remove the water pump cover. Remove the water pump impeller. When removing the impeller, lock the balance shaft using the proper tool.

6. Remove the crankcase cover retaining bolts. Remove the crankcase cover along with the oil pump assembly.

7. Installation is the reverse of the removal procedure. Be sure to use new gaskets or RTV sealant, as required.

XT COUPE

1800cc and 2700cc Engines

1. Disconnect the negative battery cable. Drain the engine oil.

2. Remove the timing belts. Before removing the camshaft drive belts, loosen the oil pump pulley mounting nut.

3. Remove the oil pump retaining bolts. Remove the oil pump along with the oil filter.

4. Remove the oil pump outer rotor from the cylinder block. Remove the oil filter from the oil pump.

5. Installation is the reverse of the removal procedure.

EXCEPT JUSTY AND XT COUPE

1800cc Engine

1. Disconnect the negative battery cable. Drain the engine oil.

2. Remove the timing belts. Before removing the camshaft drive belts, loosen the oil pump pulley mounting nut.

3. Remove the oil pump retaining bolts. Remove the oil pump along with the oil filter.

4. Remove the oil pump outer rotor from the cylinder block. Remove the oil filter from the oil pump.

5. Installation is the reverse of the removal procedure.

2200cc Engine

NOTE: It is assumed the engine is from the vehicle.

1. Drain the engine oil.

2. Drain remaining coolant from engine.

3. Remove all belt covers, drive belts and other necessary components.

4. Remove the belt tensioner bracket.

5. Remove the water pump.

6. Remove the oil pump.

7. The oil pump can be disassembled. However, scribe alignment marks on the inner and outer rotors for ease of assembly.

8. The oil pump is installed with a new front seal and the gears lubricated with engine oil.

9. Use new O-ring and gaskets where necessary. Complete the assembly.

MANUAL TRANSAXLE

Removal and Installation
JUSTY

1. Disconnect the negative battery cable. Remove the air cleaner assembly. Raise and support the vehicle safely.

2. Disconnect the electrical wiring connectors from the starter. Remove the starter to transaxle bolts and the starter from the vehicle.

3. From the transaxle, disconnect the speedometer cable, the back-up light switch connector and the ground cable. If equipped with 4WD, remove the activation hoses from the actuator.

4. Disconnect the electrical connector between the ignition coil and the distributor.

5. Disconnect the clutch cable and the bracket from the transaxle. In place of the clutch cable bracket, install the lifting hook.

6. Removing the pitching stopper and brackets between the transaxle and chassis.

7. Install engine supporter tool 921540000 or equivalent.

8. Install the vertical hoist to T000100 transaxle lifting hook and raise the transaxle slightly.

9. From under the vehicle, remove the under covers.

10. Disconnect the rear exhaust pipe from the front exhaust pipe and the vehicle.

11. Remove the center crossmember to engine/transaxle assembly bolts.

12. Using a pin punch and a hammer, drive out the axle shaft to driveshaft spring pin. Discard the spring pin and separate the axle shaft.

13. Remove the transaxle mounting bracket.

14. Disconnect the gearshift rod and stay from the transaxle.

15. Properly support the engine assembly. Remove the transaxle to engine bolts.

16. Using the vertical hoist, lift the transaxle from the vehicle.

17. Installation is the reverse of the removal procedure. Be sure to use new spring pins.

XT COUPE AND LEGACY

1800cc Engine

1. Disconnect the negative battery cable. Remove the air cleaner assembly.

2. If equipped with a turbocharger, remove the center exhaust pipe from its mounting on the transaxle.

3. Raise and support the vehicle safely. Disconnect the front exhaust pipe from the engine.

4. If equipped with 4WD, disconnect the rear exhaust pipe from the muffler.

5. Remove the clutch cable and the hill holder cable, if equipped.

6. Disconnect the speedometer cable from the transaxle.

7. Disconnect the electrical harness connectors from the neutral start switch and the back-up light switch.

8. If equipped with 4WD disconnect the transaxle electrical harness. This harness consists of the back-up light switch and the indicator light or switch for the 4WD mechanism.

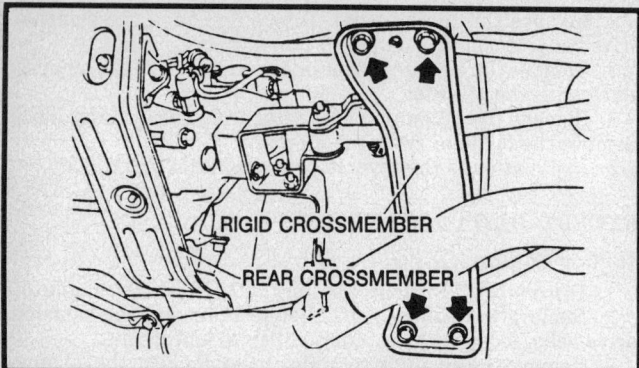

View of the rigid and rear crossmembers—XT Coupe

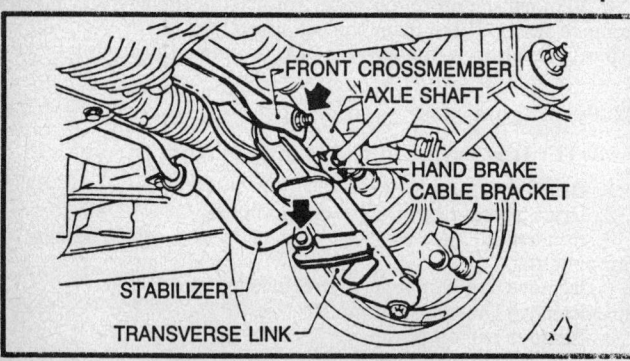

View of the front suspension assembly—XT Coupe

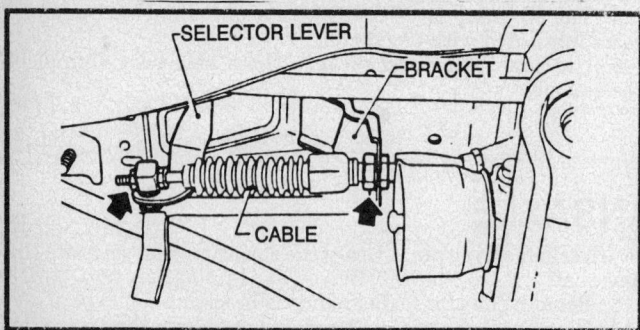

View of the selector cable and the selector cable bracket—XT Coupe

9. If equipped with 4WD, disconnect the vacuum hose and the differential lock vacuum hose, as necessary.

10. Remove the starter to transaxle bolts. Remove the starter from the transaxle. Lower the vehicle.

11. Remove the pitching stopper rod to engine bracket bolt, the rod and the engine bracket from the engine. Using the engine support bracket tool 927010000 or equivalent, install it to the engine hanger. Using the engine support assembly tool 927000000 or equivalent, install it to the support bracket.

12. On the right side of the vehicle that secures the transverse link to the stabilizer. Remove the lower bolt and separate the link from the stabilizer.

13. Remove the right brake cable bracket from the transverse link. Remove the bolt retaining the link to the crossmember on each side.

14. Lower the transverse link. Using tool 398791700 or equivalent, remove the spring pin and separate the axle shaft from the driveshaft on each side of the assembly by pushing the rear of the tire outward.

15. Remove the engine to transaxle mounting bolts. Position the proper transaxle jack under the transaxle assembly.

16. Remove the rear cushion rubber mounting bolts. Remove the rear crossmember assembly.

17. Turn the engine support tool adjuster counterclockwise in order to slightly raise the engine.

18. Move the transaxle jack toward the rear of the vehicle until the mainshaft is withdrawn from the clutch cover.

19. Carefully remove the transaxle assembly from the vehicle.

20. Installation is the reverse of the removal procedure.

2700cc Engine

1. Disconnect the negative battery cable. Remove the air cleaner assembly.

2. Remove the clutch cable and the hill holder cable. Remove the speedometer cable.

3. Remove the oxygen sensor electrical connector and the neutral switch connector.

4. If equipped with 4WD, remove the disconnect the electrical connections at the back up light and differential lock indicator switch assembly. Disconnect the differential lock vacuum hose.

5. Disconnect the starter electrical connections. Remove the starter retaining bolts. Remove the starter from the transaxle case.

6. Remove the air intake boot. Disconnect the pitching stopper rod from its mounting bracket. Remove the right side engine to transmission mounting bolt.

7. Install engine support bracket 927160000 and engine support tool 927150000 or their equivalents. Remove the buffer rod from the engine and body side bracket.

NOTE: Before attaching the special engine support tools, connect the adjuster to the buffer rod assembly on the right side of the engine.

8. Raise and support the vehicle safely.

9. Disconnect the exhaust pipes at the exhaust manifold flange. Remove the exhaust system up to the rear exhaust pipe assembly.

10. If equipped with 4WD, matchmark and remove the driveshaft. Remove the complete gear shift assembly.

11. Loosen the upper bolt and nut from the plate that secures the transverse link to the stabilizer. Remove the lower bolt and separate the link from the stabilizer.

12. Remove the right brake cable bracket from the transverse link. Remove the bolt retaining the link to the crossmember on each side.

13. Lower the transverse link. Using tool 398791700 or equivalent, remove the spring pin and separate the axle shaft from the driveshaft on each side of the assembly by pushing the rear of the tire outward.

14. Remove the engine to transaxle mounting bolts. Position the proper transaxle jack under the transaxle assembly.

15. Remove the rear cushion rubber mounting bolts. Remove the rear crossmember assembly.

16. Turn the engine support tool adjuster counterclockwise in order to slightly raise the engine.

17. Move the transaxle jack toward the rear of the vehicle until the mainshaft is withdrawn from the clutch cover.

18. Carefully remove the transaxle assembly from the vehicle.

19. Installation is the reverse of the removal procedure.

EXCEPT JUSTY, XT COUPE AND LEGACY

1. Disconnect the negative battery cable. Remove the engine/transaxle ground strap and starter.

2. Remove the starter retaining bolts. Disconnect the starter electrical connectors.

3. Remove the starter from the vehicle.

4. If equipped with a turbocharger, remove the center pipe assembly.

5. From the right side, remove the transaxle assembly to chassis support bolt and loosen the lower nuts.

6. Raise and support the vehicle safely.

Separating the axle shaft from the driveshaft

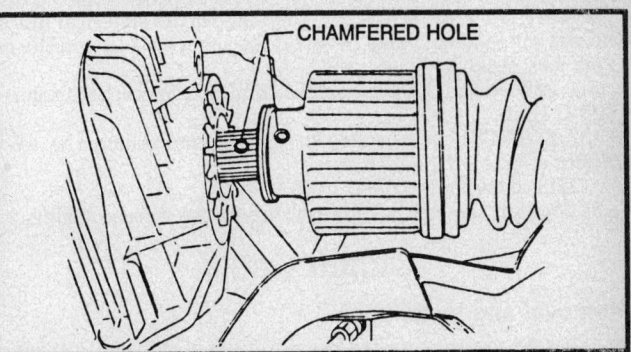

CHAMFERED HOLE

Aligning the chamfered holes of the axle shaft with the driveshaft

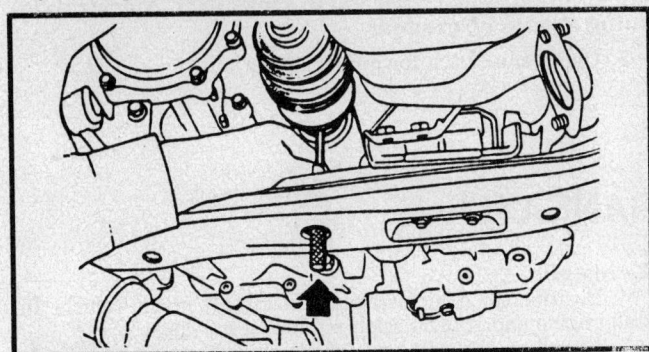

Removing the spring pin from the axle shaft—Justy

7. If not equipped with a turbocharger, remove the exhaust pipe to cylinder head nuts, the exhaust pipe to rear pipe bolts, the exhaust pipe to hanger bracket and the front exhaust pipe from the vehicle.

8. If equipped with 4WD, disconnect the rear exhaust pipe from the muffler. Disconnect the driveshaft from the rear of the transaxle.

9. Remove the retaining spring, the CP rod and stay from the transaxle. Loosen the stabilizer to transverse link nuts and bolts, on the lower side of the plate.

10. Loosen the upper bolt and nut from the plate that secures the transverse link to the stabilizer. Remove the lower bolt and separate the link from the stabilizer.

11. Remove the right brake cable bracket from the transverse link. Remove the bolt retaining the link to the crossmember on each side.

12. Lower the transverse link. Using tool 398791700 or equivalent, remove the spring pin and separate the axle shaft from the driveshaft on each side of the assembly by pushing the rear of the tire outward.

13. Remove the engine to transaxle mounting bolts. Position the proper transaxle jack under the transaxle assembly.

14. Remove the rear cushion rubber mounting bolts. Remove the rear crossmember assembly.

15. Turn the engine support tool adjuster counterclockwise in order to slightly raise the engine.

16. Move the transaxle jack toward the rear of the vehicle until the mainshaft is withdrawn from the clutch cover.

17. Carefully remove the transaxle assembly from the vehicle.

18. Installation is the reverse of the removal procedure.

CLUTCH

Removal and Installation

1. Remove the transaxle from the vehicle.

2. Gradually loosen the pressure plate to flywheel assembly bolts. Loosen the bolts 1 turn at a time, working around the pressure plate.

3. Remove the clutch plate and the disc from the vehicle.

4. Inspect the parts for wear or damage and replace any parts, as necessary.

5. Installation is the reverse of the removal procedure.

6. Use clutch disc guide tool 499747000 or equivalent, to align the clutch on the non-turbocharged 1800cc and 2700cc engines. Use tool 499747100 or equivalent, to align the clutch on the turbocharged 1800cc engine. Use tool 499745500 or equivalent, to align the clutch on the 1200cc engine.

7. When installing the clutch pressure plate assembly, make sure the marks on the flywheel and the clutch pressure plate assembly are at least 120 degrees apart. This is for purposes of balance. Also, make sure the clutch disc is installed properly, noting the **FRONT** and **REAR** markings.

Free-Play Adjustment

1. Remove the clutch release fork return spring.

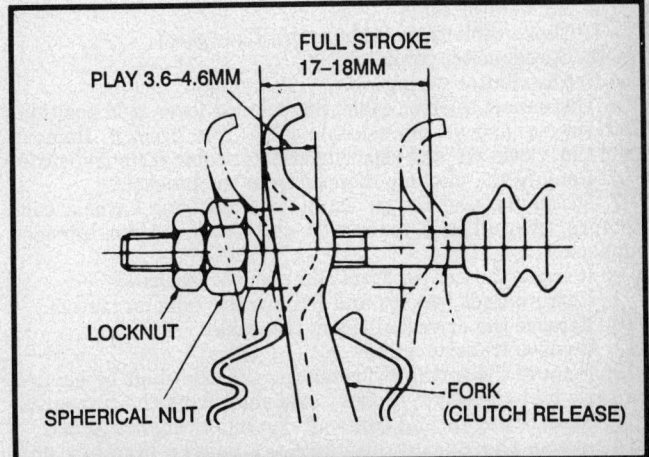

PLAY 3.6–4.6MM

FULL STROKE 17–18MM

LOCKNUT

SPHERICAL NUT

FORK (CLUTCH RELEASE)

Clutch linkage free-play adjustment at the release fork

2. Loosen the cable locknut, then adjust the spherical nut so there is the following play between the spherical nut and the release fork seat.

1800cc and 2700cc engines, 2WD except turbocharger—0.08–0.12 in.

2WD/4WD turbocharged, 1800cc engine and the 4WD 2700cc engine—0.12–0.16 in.

1200cc engine—0.08–0.16 in.

3. Tighten the locknut and reconnect the release spring.

Clutch Cable

Removal and Installation

The clutch cable is connected to the clutch pedal at 1 end and to the clutch release lever at the other end. The cable conduit is retained by a bolt and clamp on a bracket mounted on the flywheel housing.

1. If necessary, raise and support the vehicle safely.

2. Disconnect both ends of the cable and the conduit, then remove the assembly from under the vehicle.

3. Using engine oil, lubricate the clutch cable. If the cable is defective, replace it.

4. Installation is the reverse the removal procedure.

Cable Adjustment

The clutch cable can be adjusted at the cable bracket where the cable is attached to the side of the transaxle housing.

1. Remove the circlip and clamp.

2. Slide the cable end in the direction desired and then replace the circlip and clamp into the nearest gutters on the cable end.

NOTE: The cable should not be stretched out straight nor should it have right angle kinks in it. Any straightening should be gradual.

3. Check the clutch for proper operation.

AUTOMATIC TRANSAXLE

Transaxle

Removal and Installation

JUSTY

With ECVT Transaxle

NOTE: When removing and installing ECVT transaxle, always remove and install the engine and transaxle as an assembly.

1. Disconnect the negative battery cable. Drain the coolant by removing drain plug from radiator.

2. Remove the grille. Disconnect hoses and electric wiring from radiator and remove the radiator.

3. Remove front hood release cable and remove radiator upper support member. Disconnect horn and remove the air cleaner assembly.

4. Disconnect the following hoses and cables:
   a. Hoses from carburetor
   b. Hoses from the heater unit
   c. Hose for brake booster
   d. Clutch cable
   e. Accelerator cable
   f. Choke cable from carburetor, if equipped
   g. Speedometer cable
   h. Distributor wiring

5. Disconnect selector cable. Set selector lever at **N** position. Remove clip and detach selector cable from bracket. Remove snap pin, clevis pin and separate selector cable from transaxle.

6. Remove the pitching stopper from the bracket.

7. Disconnect the starter cable, engine wiring harness connectors, ground lead terminals and brush holder harness connector.

8. Remove the hanger from the rear of transaxle.

9. Remove under covers and remove the exhaust system.

10. Remove the driveshaft from transaxle.

11. Remove transverse link.

12. Remove the spring pin retaining the axle shaft by using a suitable tool and separate front axle shaft from the transaxle.

13. Remove engine and transmission mounting brackets.

14. Raise the engine and remove center member and crossmember.

15. Lift up the engine/transaxle assembly carefully and remove it from the vehicle.

To install:

16. Position the engine/transaxle assembly in the vehicle. Install engine and transmission mounting brackets.

17. Install center member and crossmember.

18. Install the axle shaft to transaxle with new spring pin.

19. Install gearshift rod and stay to transaxle.

20. Install the exhaust system. Connect driveshaft to transaxle.

21. Install transverse link and under covers to the vehicle.

22. Reconnect the pitching stopper to bracket.

23. Reconnect the following hoses and cables:
   a. Hoses to carburetor
   b. Hoses to the heater unit
   c. Hose to brake booster
   d. Clutch cable to transaxle
   e. Accelerator cable
   f. Choke cable from carburetor, if equipped
   g. Speedometer cable
   h. Distributor wiring

24. Reconnect the starter cable, engine wiring harness connectors, ground lead terminals and brush holder harness connector. Install the air cleaner assembly.

25. Install radiator upper member and connect hood release cable to lock assembly. Reconnect the horn.

26. Install the radiator and connect hoses and electric wiring. Attach grille to the vehicle.

27. Refill the coolant. Reconnect the battery cable.

28. Check all fluid levels. Road test vehicles for proper operation in all driving ranges.

XT COUPE

1800cc Engine

1. Disconnect the negative battery cable. Remove the air cleaner assembly.

2. If equipped with a turbocharger, refer to the turbocharger removal procedure and remove the center exhaust pipe from its mounting on the transaxle.

3. Raise and support the vehicle safely. Disconnect the front exhaust pipe from the engine.

4. Disconnect the oxygen sensor electrical harness. If equipped with 4WD, disconnect the rear exhaust pipe from the muffler.

5. Disconnect the speedometer cable from the transaxle. Dis-

connect the electrical harness connectors from the neutral start switch and the back-up light switch.

6. If equipped with 4WD, disconnect the transaxle electrical harness.

7. This harness consists of the back-up light switch and the indicator light or switch for the 4WD mechanism.

8. If equipped with 4WD, disconnect the vacuum hose.

9. Remove the air breather to pitching stopper clip band.

10. Remove the starter to transaxle bolts. Remove the starter from the transaxle. Lower the vehicle.

11. Remove the timing hole plug. Remove the torque converter retaining bolts.

12. Remove the pitching stopper rod to engine bracket bolt, the rod and the engine bracket from the engine. Using the engine support bracket tool 927010000 or equivalent, install it to the engine hanger. Using the engine support assembly tool 927000000 or equivalent, install it to the support bracket.

13. On the right side of the vehicle, remove the engine to transaxle bolt.

14. Raise and support the vehicle safely. Disconnect and plug the transaxle fluid lines.

15. If equipped with 4WD, remove the rear driveshaft center bearing assembly to chassis bolts and the driveshaft to rear differential flange bolts, then remove the driveshaft from the vehicle.

16. Remove the CP stay to transaxle bolt, the spring and the CP rod to transaxle bolt. Remove the selector lever assembly.

17. Loosen the upper bolt and nut from the plate that secures the transverse link to the stabilizer. Remove the lower bolt and separate the link from the stabilizer.

18. Remove the right brake cable bracket from the transverse link. Remove the bolt retaining the link to the crossmember on each side.

19. Lower the transverse link. Using tool 398791700 or equivalent, remove the spring pin and separate the axle shaft from the driveshaft on each side of the assembly by pushing the rear of the tire outward.

20. Remove the engine to transaxle mounting bolts. Position the proper transaxle jack under the transaxle assembly.

21. Remove the rear cushion rubber mounting bolts. Remove the rear crossmember assembly.

22. Turn the engine support tool adjuster counterclockwise in order to slightly raise the engine.

23. Move the torque converter and transaxle unit away from the engine. Carefully remove the transaxle assembly from the vehicle.

24. The installation of the assembly is the reverse of the removal procedure.

2700cc Engine

1. Disconnect the negative battery cable. Remove the air cleaner assembly.

2. Remove the speedometer cable. If equipped with 4WD, remove the speed sensor connector.

3. Remove the oxygen sensor electrical connector and the neutral switch connector. Remove the transmission electrical harness connector.

4. Disconnect the starter electrical connections. Remove the starter retaining bolts. Remove the starter from the transaxle case.

5. Remove the air intake boot. Remove the timing hole plug. Remove the torque converter retaining bolts.

6. Disconnect the pitching stopper rod from its mounting bracket. Remove the right side engine to transmission mounting bolt.

7. Install engine support bracket 927160000 and engine support tool 927150000 or their equivalents. Remove the buffer rod from the engine and body side bracket.

NOTE: Before attaching the special engine support tools, connect the adjuster to the buffer rod assembly on the right side of the engine.

8. Raise and support the vehicle safely. Disconnect and plug the transaxle fluid lines.

9. Disconnect the exhaust pipes at the exhaust manifold flange. Remove the exhaust system up to the rear exhaust pipe assembly.

10. If equipped with 4WD, matchmark and remove the driveshaft. Remove the complete gear shift assembly.

11. Loosen the upper bolt and nut from the plate that secures the transverse link to the stabilizer. Remove the lower bolt and separate the link from the stabilizer.

12. Remove the right brake cable bracket from the transverse link. Remove the bolt retaining the link to the crossmember on each side.

13. Lower the transverse link. Using tool 398791700 or equivalent, remove the spring pin and separate the axle shaft from the driveshaft on each side of the assembly by pushing the rear of the tire outward.

14. Remove the engine to transaxle mounting bolts. Position the proper transaxle jack under the transaxle assembly.

15. Remove the rear cushion rubber mounting bolts. Remove the rear crossmember assembly.

16. Turn the engine support tool adjuster counterclockwise in order to slightly raise the engine.

17. Move the torque converter and transaxle unit away from the engine. Carefully remove the transaxle assembly from the vehicle.

18. Installation is the reverse of the removal procedure.

1800 SEDAN/STATION WAGON, LOYALE AND XT COUPE

2WD and 4WD Non-Electronic 3 and 4 Speed Transaxles

1. Disconnect the negative battery cable.

2. Remove clamp from spare tire supporter and remove the spare tire.

NOTE: Use care when removing spare tire assembly from the vehicle.

3. Remove spare tire supporter and battery clamp.

4. Remove speedometer cable and retaining clip. Before disconnecting speedometer cable, remove front exhaust pipe on 4 speed automatic transaxle.

5. Disconnect the following electrical harness connections on the 3 speed automatic transaxle:
   a. Oxygen sensor connector
   b. ATF temperature switch connector
   c. Kickdown solenoid valve connector
   d. 4WD solenoid valve connector on 4WD equipped vehicles

6. Disconnect the following electrical harness connections on the 4 speed automatic transaxle:
   a. Oxygen sensor connector
   b. Transaxle harness connector
   c. Inhibitor switch connector
   d. Revolution sensor connector on 4WD equipped vehicles

7. Disconnect the diaphragm vacuum hose on 3 speed automatic transaxle and 4WD vacuum hose on 4WD equipped vehicles.

8. Remove clip band which secures air breather hose to pitching stopper.

9. Remove the pitching stopper rod. Remove the starter.

10. Remove timing hole inspection plug and remove the 4 bolts which hold torque converter to driveplate.

11. Support the engine assembly with special engine support tool 926610000 or equivalent.

12. Remove engine to transaxle mounting nut and bolt on the right side.

13. Remove the exhaust system.

NOTE: Apply a penetrating oil or equivalent to all exhaust retaining nuts in advance to facilitate removal.

14. On turbocharged vehicles, remove accelerator cable cover and upper and lower turbocharger covers. Remove the center exhaust pipe at turbocharger location and at rear exhaust pipe. Remove any exhaust brackets or hangers that attach to the transaxle, as necessary.

15. On non-turbocharged vehicles, disconnect front exhaust pipe from the engine and from the rear exhaust pipe. Remove any exhaust brackets or hangers that attach to the transaxle as necessary.

16. Drain all transaxle fluid from the oil pan.

17. Remove the driveshaft on 4WD vehicles. Plug the opening at the rear of extension housing to prevent oil from flowing out.

18. Disconnect the linkage rod for a 3 speed or cable for a 4 speed. from the select lever.

19. Remove stabilizer from transverse link by loosening (not removing) nut and bolt on the lower side of plate.

20. Remove parking brake cable bracket from transverse link and bolt holding transverse link to crossmember on each side. Lower the transverse link.

21. Remove spring pin and separate axle shaft from transaxle on each side.

NOTE: Use a suitable tool to remove spring pin. Discard old spring pin and always install a new pin.

22. Disconnect the axle shaft from transaxle on each side. Be sure to remove axle shaft from transaxle by pushing the rear of tire outward.

23. Remove engine to transaxle mounting nuts.

24. Disconnect oil cooler hoses and oil supply pipe. Be careful not to damage the oil supply pipe O-ring.

25. Place transmission jack or equivalent under transaxle. Always support transaxle case with a transmission jack.

NOTE: Do not place jack under oil pan otherwise oil pan may be damaged.

26. Remove rear cushion rubber mounting nuts and rear crossmember. Move torque converter and transaxle as a unit away from the engine. Remove the transaxle.

To install:

27. Install transaxle to engine and temporarily tighten engine to transaxle mounting nuts.

28. Install rear crossmember to rear cushion rubber mounts. Align rear cushion guide with rear crossmember guide hole and tighten nuts.

29. Install rear crossmember to chassis. Be careful not to damage threads. Torque rear crossmember bolts to 39–49 ft. lbs.

30. Tighten engine to transaxle nuts on the lower side to 34–40 ft. lbs. Remove transmission jack from the vehicle.

31. Install axle shaft to transaxle and install spring pin into place.

NOTE: Always use new spring pin. Be sure to align the axle shaft and shaft from the transaxle at chamfered holes and engage shaft splines correctly.

32. Install transverse link temporarily to front crossmember by using bolt and self-locking nut. Do not complete final torque at this point.

33. Install stabilizer temporarily to transverse link. Install parking brake cable bracket to transverse link.

34. Connect the linkage rod for a 3 speed or cable for a 4 speed to the select lever. Make sure the lever operates smoothly all across the operating range.

35. Install propeller shaft on 4WD vehicles. Torque propeller shaft to rear differential retaining bolts to 13–20 ft. lbs. and center bearing location retaining bolts to 25–33 ft. lbs.

36. Connect oil cooler hoses and oil supply pipe. Lower vehicle to floor.

37. Tighten transverse link to front crossmember mounting bolts and transverse link to stabilizer mounting bolts with the tires placed on the ground when the vehicle is not loaded. Tight-

ening torque for transverse link to front crossmember (self-locking nuts) 43–51 ft. lbs. and transverse link to stabilizer 14–22 ft. lbs.

38. Tighten engine to transaxle nuts on the upper side to 34–40 ft. lbs.

39. Raise vehicle and safely support. Install exhaust system.

NOTE: Before installing exhaust system, connect speedometer cable on 4 speed vehicles.

40. On turbocharged vehicles, install the center exhaust pipe at turbocharger location and at rear exhaust pipe. Install any exhaust brackets or hangers that attach to the transaxle as necessary. Install upper and lower turbocharger covers and accelerator cable cover.

41. On non-turbocharged vehicles, connect front exhaust pipe to the engine and rear exhaust pipe. Install any exhaust brackets or hangers that attach to the transaxle as necessary.

42. Remove the special engine support tool. Install and tighten torque converter to driveplate mounting bolts to 17–20 ft. lbs.

43. Install timing hole inspection plug.

44. Install starter.

45. Install pitching stopper. Be sure to tighten the bolt for the body side first and then the 1 for engine or transaxle side. Tightening torque for chassis side is 27–49 ft. lbs. and for engine or transmission side is 33–40 ft. lbs.

46. Reconnect the following electrical harness connections on the 3 speed automatic transaxle:
   a. Oxygen sensor connector
   b. ATF temperature switch connector
   c. Kickdown solenoid valve connector
   d. 4WD solenoid valve connector on 4WD equipped vehicles

47. Reconnect the following electrical harness connections on the 4 speed automatic transaxle:
   a. Oxygen sensor connector
   b. Transaxle harness connector
   c. Inhibitor switch connector
   d. Revolution sensor connector on 4WD equipped vehicles

48. Reconnect the diaphragm vacuum hose on 3 speed automatic transaxle and 4WD vacuum hose on 4WD equipped vehicles.

49. Secure air breather hose to pitching stopper with a clip band.

50. Reconnect the speedometer cable. Manually tighten cable nut all the way and then turn it approximately 30 degrees more with a tool.

51. Connect the battery ground cable. Refill and check transaxle oil level.

52. Install spare tire supporter and battery clamp. Install spare tire.

53. Road test vehicle for proper operation across all operating ranges.

XT COUPE AND 1990 LEGACY

4 Speed Electronic Transaxle

1. Disconnect the negative battery cable.

2. Remove speedometer cable or electronic wiring connector from speed sensor.

3. Disconnect the following electrical harness connections on the automatic transaxle:
   a. Oxygen sensor connector
   b. Transaxle harness connector
   c. Inhibitor switch connector
   d. Revolution sensor connector on 4WD equipped vehicles
   e. Crankshaft and camshaft angle sensor connector on Legacy vehicles
   f. Knock sensor connectors and transaxle ground terminal on Legacy vehicles

4. Remove clip band which secures air breather hose to pitching stopper.

5. Remove the starter and air intake boot.

6. Remove timing hole inspection plug and remove the 4 bolts which hold torque converter to driveplate.

7. Disconnect pitching stopper rod from bracket.

8. Remove engine to transaxle mounting nut and bolt on the right side.

9. Remove the buffer rod from the vehicle. Support the engine assembly with special engine support tool or equivalent.

10. Remove the exhaust system. Remove exhaust brackets or hangers that attach to the transaxle, as necessary.

11. Matchmark and remove the driveshaft on 4WD vehicles. Plug the opening at the rear of extension housing to prevent oil from flowing out.

12. Disconnect the gear shift cable from the transaxle select lever.

13. Remove stabilizer from transverse link.

14. Remove parking brake cable bracket from transverse link and bolt holding transverse link to crossmember on each side. Lower the transverse link.

15. Remove spring pin and separate axle shaft from transaxle on each side.

NOTE: Use a suitable tool to remove spring pin. Discard old spring pin and always install a new pin.

16. Disconnect the axle shaft from transaxle on each side. Be sure to remove axle shaft from transaxle by pushing the rear of tire outward.

17. Remove engine to transaxle mounting nuts.

18. Disconnect oil cooler hoses.

19. Place transmission jack or equivalent, under transaxle. Always support transaxle case with a transmission jack.

NOTE: Do not place jack under oil pan otherwise oil pan may be damaged.

20. Remove rear cushion rubber mounting nuts and rear crossmember.

21. Move torque converter and transaxle as a unit away from the engine. Remove the transaxle.

To Install:

22. Install transaxle to engine and temporarily tighten engine to transaxle mounting nuts.

23. Install rear crossmember to rear cushion rubber mounts. Align rear cushion guide with rear crossmember guide hole and tighten nuts.

24. Install rear crossmember to chassis; be careful not to damage threads. Torque rear crossmember bolts to 39–49 ft. lbs.

25. Tighten engine to transaxle retaining nuts to 34–40 ft. lbs. Remove transmission jack from the vehicle.

26. Remove the engine support tool and install buffer rod.

27. Install axle shaft to transaxle and install spring pin into place.

NOTE: Always use new spring pin. Be sure to align the axle shaft and shaft from the transaxle at chamfered holes and install shaft splines correctly.

28. Install transverse link temporarily to front crossmember by using bolt and self locking nut. Do not complete final torque at this point.

29. Install stabilizer temporarily to transverse link. Install parking brake cable bracket to transverse link.

30. Lower vehicle to floor. Tighten transverse link to front crossmember mounting bolts and transverse link to stabilizer mounting bolts with the tires placed on the ground when the vehicle is not loaded. Tightening torque for transverse link to front crossmember (self locking nuts) 43–51 ft. lbs. and transverse link to stabilizer 14–22 ft. lbs.

31. Raise and safely support the vehicle. Reconnect the gear shift cable to the select lever. Make sure the lever operates smoothly all across the operating range.

32. Install propeller shaft on 4WD vehicles. Torque propeller shaft to rear differential retaining bolts to 17–24 ft. lbs. and center bearing location retaining bolts to 25–33 ft. lbs.

33. Connect oil cooler hoses.

34. Tighten engine to transaxle bolts to 34–40 ft. lbs.

35. Install starter.

36. Install pitching stopper. Be sure to tighten the bolt for the body side first and then the 1 for engine or transaxle side. Tightening torque for chassis side is 27–49 ft. lbs. and for engine or transaxle side is 33–40 ft. lbs.

37. Install and tighten torque converter to driveplate mounting bolts to 17–20 ft. lbs.

38. Install timing hole inspection plug, air intake boot and air breather hose to pitching stopper.

39. Reconnect the following electrical harness connections on the automatic transaxle:

    a. Oxygen sensor connector

    b. Transaxle harness connector

    c. Inhibitor switch connector

    d. Revolution sensor connector on 4WD equipped vehicles

    e. Crankshaft and camshaft angle sensor connector on Legacy

    f. Knock sensor connectors and transaxle ground terminal on Legacy

40. Reconnect the speedometer cable. Manually tighten cable nut all the way and then turn it approximately 30 degrees more with a tool.

41. Install exhaust system and exhaust brackets or hangers that attach to the transaxle, as necessary.

42. Connect the battery ground cable. Refill and check transaxle oil level.

43. Road test vehicle for proper operation across all operating ranges.

Pan Removal

1. Raise and support the vehicle safely.

2. Position a drain pan under the transaxle, remove the drain plug and drain the transaxle.

3. Remove the oil pan to transaxle bolts and lower the oil pan from the transaxle.

4. Installation is the reverse of the removal procedure. Be sure to use a new gasket or RTV sealant, as required.

Filter Service

1. Remove the transaxle oil pan.

2. Remove the oil stainer to transaxle bolt and the oil strainer from the transaxle.

3. Installation is the reverse of the removal procedure. Be sure to use a new gasket or RTV sealant, as required.

Shift Linkage Adjustment

1. Loosen the clamp nuts on the shifting rod at the bottom of the shift lever on the transaxle.

2. Place the selector lever in N and hold it forward against the detent.

3. Check that the transaxle shift lever is in the N position by pulling it all the way back into P and then pushing it forward 2 positions.

4. Tighten the clamp nuts.

Kickdown Solenoid Adjustment

If used, an audible click should be heard from the solenoid on the right side of the transaxle, when the accelerator pedal is pushed down all the way with the engine off and the ignition switch in the ON position. The switch is operated by the upper part of the accelerator lever inside the vehicle. The position of the switch can be varied to give quicker or slower kickdown response.

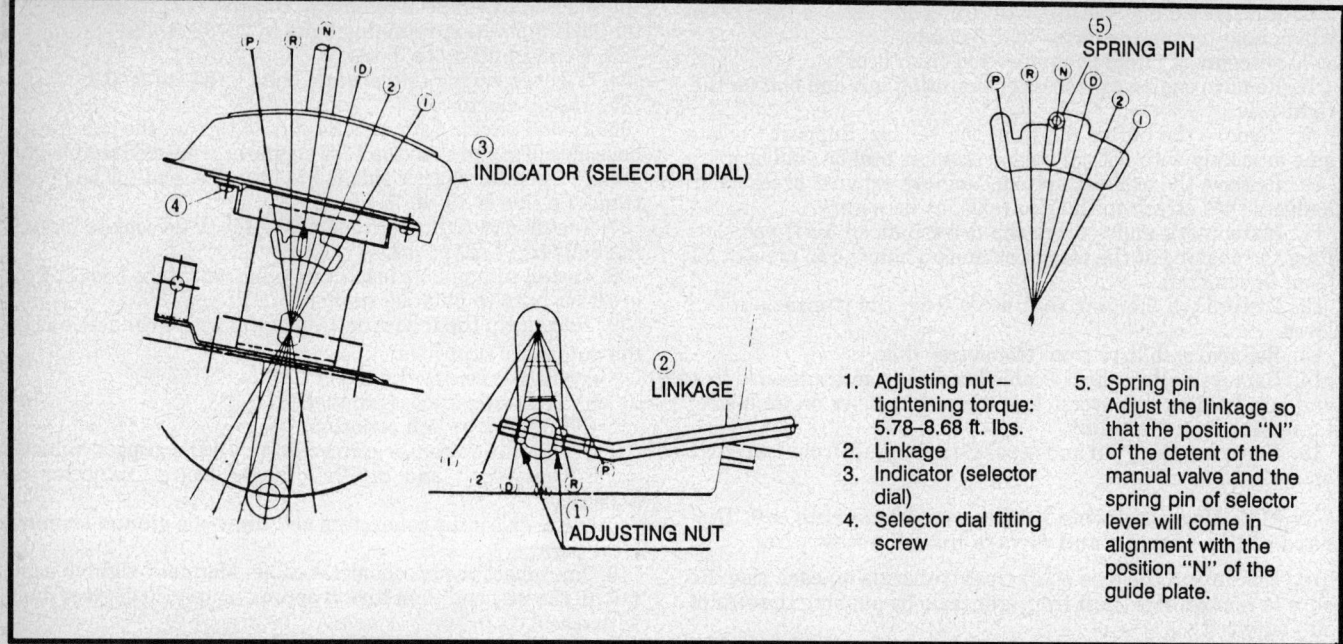

1. Adjusting nut— tightening torque: 5.78–8.68 ft. lbs.
2. Linkage
3. Indicator (selector dial)
4. Selector dial fitting screw
5. Spring pin
   Adjust the linkage so that the position "N" of the detent of the manual valve and the spring pin of selector lever will come in alignment with the position "N" of the guide plate.

Details for automatic shift linkage adjustment

Brake Band Adjustment
EXCEPT 1988–90 VEHICLES

1. Raise and support the vehicle safely.
2. Locate the adjusting screw above the pan on the left side of the transaxle.
3. Loosen the locknut.
4. Torque the adjusting screw to 6.5 ft. lbs., then turn it back exactly 2 full turns.
5. Tighten the locknut.

NOTE: Following the above procedure will adjust the transaxle brake band to the factory specified setting.

6. If any of the following conditions are detected, the adjusting screw can be moved ¼ turn in either direction after Step 4. Turn the adjusting screw ¼ turn clockwise if the transaxle jolts when shifting from 1st to 2nd, engine speed abruptly rises from 2nd to 3rd, or shift delays in kickdown from 3rd to 2nd.

7. Turn the adjusting screw ¼ turn counterclockwise if the transaxle slips between 1st and 2nd speeds or there is a braking action between the 2nd and 3rd shift.

1988–90 VEHICLES

If both 2nd and 4th gears are possible, but the engine rpm increases considerably when shifting up from 2nd to 3rd, it is attributed to excessive clearance between the reverse clutch drum and the brake band. Tighten the adjusting screw by turning it clockwise to correct this condition.

If both 2nd and 4th gear is possible but a shift delay is present at kickdown from 3rd to 2nd, it is attributed to excessive clearance between the reverse clutch drum and the brake band. Tighten the adjusting screw by turning it clockwise to correct this condition.

TRANSFER CASE

Removal and Installation

1. Disconnect the negative battery cable.
2. Raise and support the vehicle safely.
3. Remove the transaxle assembly from the vehicle.
4. Position the assembly in a suitable holding fixture.
5. Disassemble the transfer case from the transaxle.
6. Installation is the reverse of the removal procedure.

DRIVE AXLE

Halfshaft

Removal and Installation
JUSTY

1. Raise and support the vehicle safely. Remove the tire and wheel assembly.
2. Remove the disc brake assembly. Remove the dust cover, cotter pin, castle nut, conical spring. Remove the center piece, using the proper tools.
3. Pull the hub and disc assembly from the halfshaft. Remove the disc cover from the housing.
4. Drive out the spring pin connecting the halfshaft to the differential, using the proper tool.
5. Remove the cotter pin and the castle nut from the tie rod end ball joint.

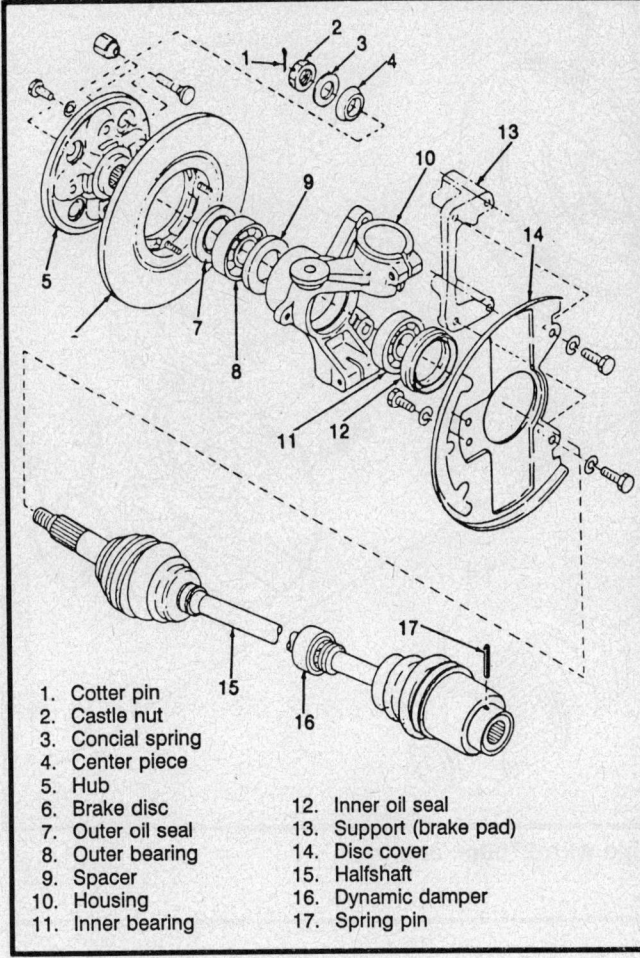

1. Cotter pin
2. Castle nut
3. Concial spring
4. Center piece
5. Hub
6. Brake disc
7. Outer oil seal
8. Outer bearing
9. Spacer
10. Housing
11. Inner bearing
12. Inner oil seal
13. Support (brake pad)
14. Disc cover
15. Halfshaft
16. Dynamic damper
17. Spring pin

Front halfshaft assembly and related components—Justy

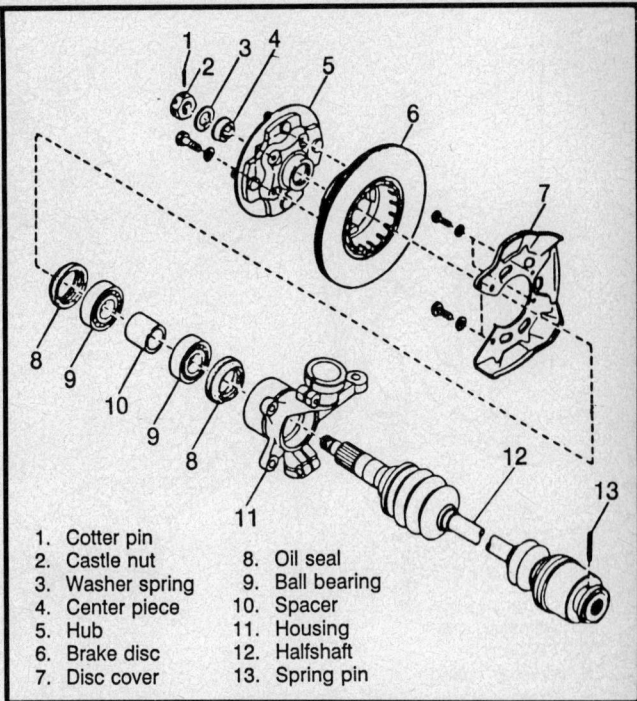

1. Cotter pin
2. Castle nut
3. Washer spring
4. Center piece
5. Hub
6. Brake disc
7. Disc cover
8. Oil seal
9. Ball bearing
10. Spacer
11. Housing
12. Halfshaft
13. Spring pin

Front halfshaft assembly and related components— except Justy and XT Coupe with 2700cc engine

6. Remove the tie rod end ball joint from the knuckle arm, using the proper puller.

7. Remove the bolt that retains the housing to the strut. Carefully push down the housing in order to remove it from the strut.

8. Remove the ball joint of the transverse link from the housing. Remove the housing and the halfshaft assembly as a complete unit.

9. Separate the housing from the halfshaft, using removal tools 922493000 and 921122000 or their equivalents.

10. Installation is the reverse of the removal procedure.

EXCEPT JUSTY

1. Release the parking brake. Raise and support the vehicle safely. Remove the tire and wheel assembly.

2. Pull out the parking brake cable outer clip from the caliper. Disconnect the parking brake cable end from the caliper lever.

3. Drive out the double offset joint spring pin, using the proper tools.

4. Loosen the 2 retaining bolts and remove the disc brake assembly from the housing. Remove the 2 bolts that connect the housing and the damper strut.

5. Remove the dust cover, cotter pin. Disconnect the tie rod end ball joint from the housing knuckle arm, using the proper puller tool.

6. Remove the halfshaft from the differential spindle along with the housing assembly.

7. Remove the housing from the halfshaft, using tool 926470000 or equivalent.

8. Installation is the reverse of the removal procedure.

Driveshaft

Removal and Installation

4WD

1. Raise and support the vehicle safely.
2. Remove the driveshaft flange to rear differential flange bolts.
3. Position a drain pan under the rear of the transaxle. Remove the driveshaft from the vehicle.

NOTE: If equipped with a center bearing, remove the center bearing to chassis bolts and lower the assembly from the vehicle.

4. Installation is the reverse of the removal procedure.

Rear Axle Shafts

Removal and Installation

JUSTY

2WD

1. Raise and support the vehicle safely. Remove the tire and wheel assembly.

2. Remove the dust cap. Straighten the locking washer edge. Remove the nut, lock washer and washer.

3. Remove the brake drum. Be sure not to drop the outer bearing.

4. Remove the brake line bracket from the spindle housing.

5. Loosen the bolts and remove the brake assembly. Suspend the assembly aside with wire.

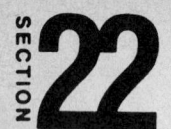

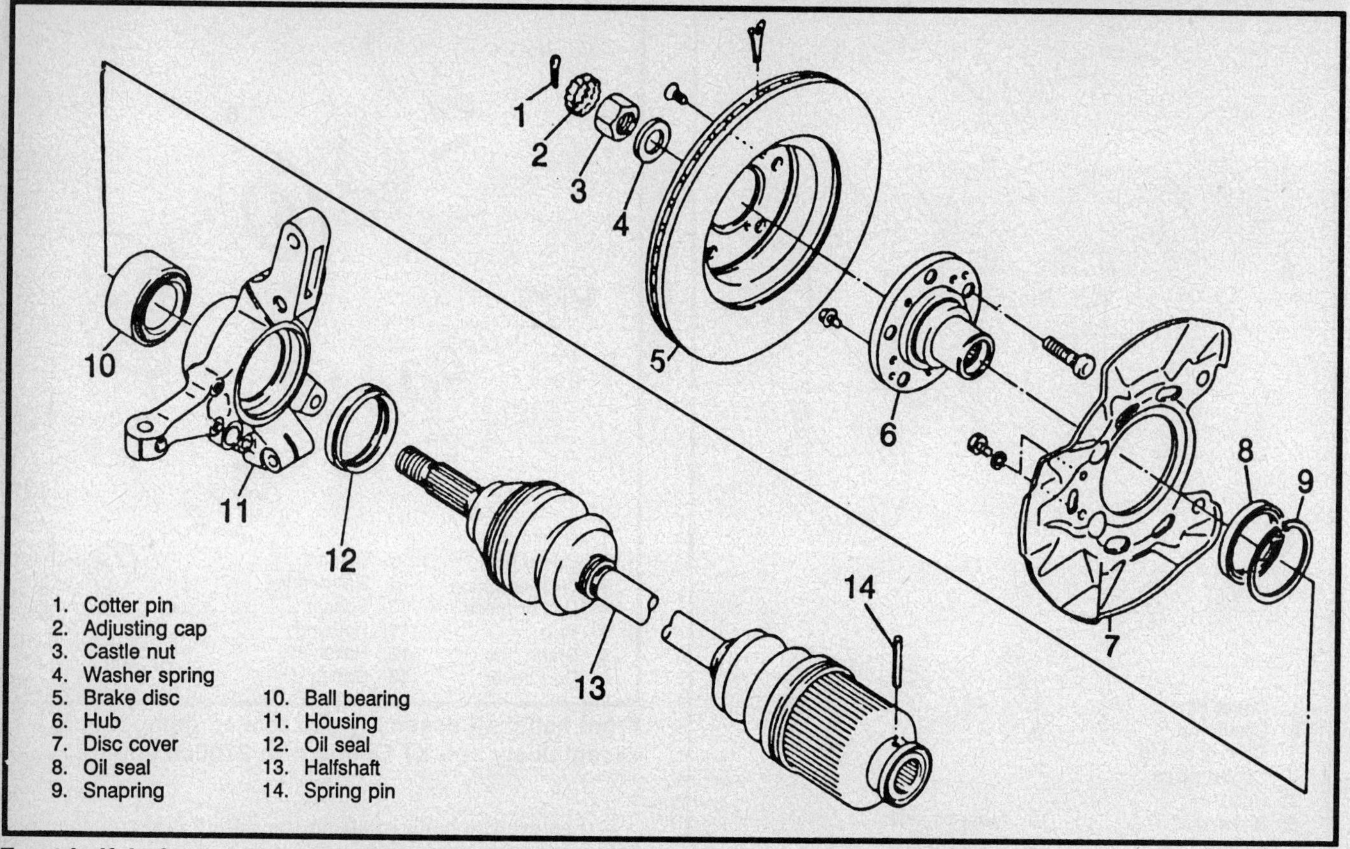

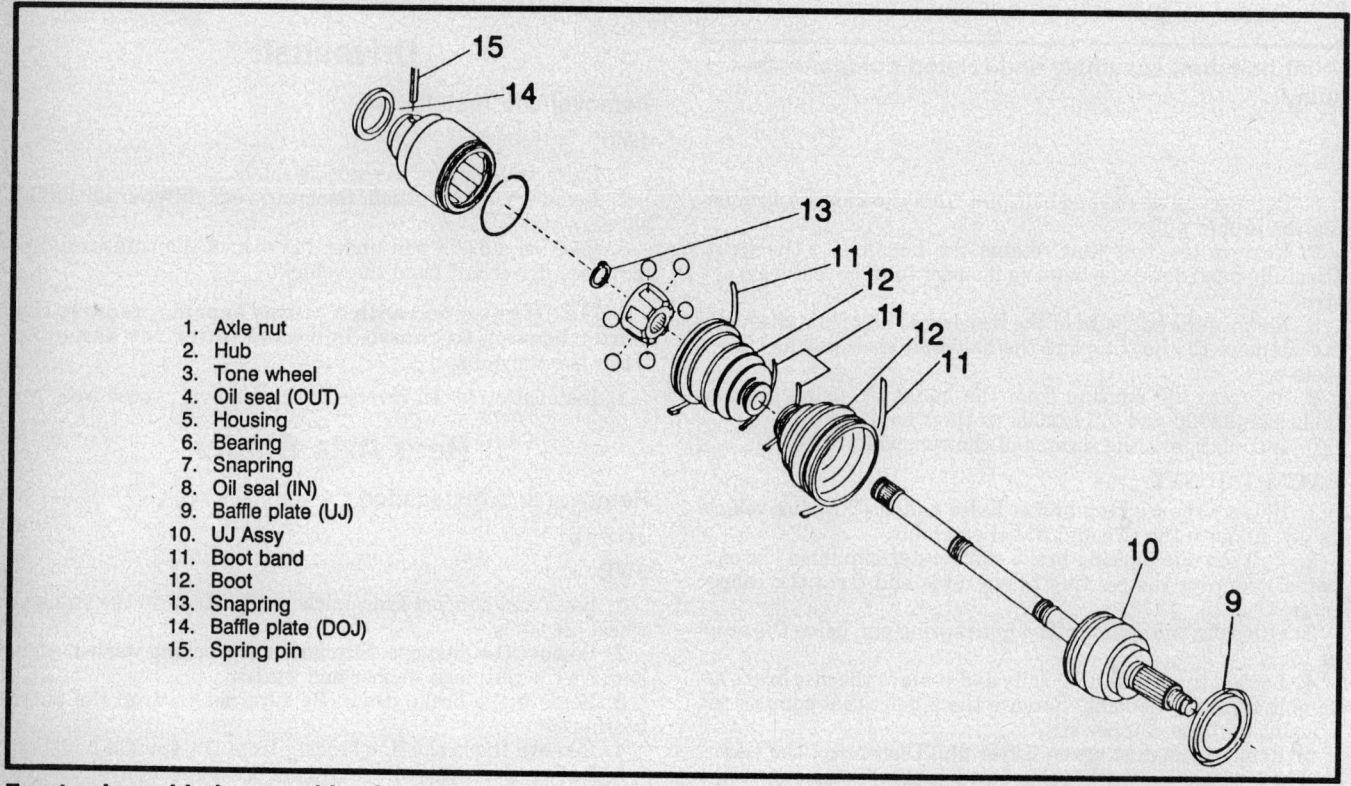

1
2
3
4
5
6
7
8
9
10
11
12
13
14
1. Cotter pin
2. Adjusting cap
3. Castle nut
4. Washer spring
5. Brake disc
6. Hub
7. Disc cover
8. Oil seal
9. Snapring
10. Ball bearing
11. Housing
12. Oil seal
13. Halfshaft
14. Spring pin

Front halfshaft assembly and related components— XT Coupe with 2700cc engine

15
14
13
11
12
11
12
11
10
9
1. Axle nut
2. Hub
3. Tone wheel
4. Oil seal (OUT)
5. Housing
6. Bearing
7. Snapring
8. Oil seal (IN)
9. Baffle plate (UJ)
10. UJ Assy
11. Boot band
12. Boot
13. Snapring
14. Baffle plate (DOJ)
15. Spring pin

Front axle and hub assembly—Legacy

6. Remove the bracket assembly.

7. Remove the brake assembly. Suspend the assembly aside with wire.

8. Using the proper tools, drive out the spring pin connecting the halfshaft assembly to the differential.

9. Remove the strut, lower link and trailing link. Pull the housing along with the halfshaft from its mounting.

10. Separate the housing from the halfshaft, using removal tools 922493000 and 921122000 or their equivalent.

11. Installation is the reverse of the removal procedure. After tightening the rear axle halfshaft to axle housing nut, tighten the axle shaft nut 30 degrees further.

LEGACY

2WD

1. Disconnect the negative battery cable.

2. Raise the vehicle and support safely.

3. Remove the wheels and unlock the axle nut. Remove the axle nut.

4. Loosen the parking brake adjuster. Remove the disc brake assembly from the backing plate and suspend it with a wire from the strut.

5. Remove the disc brake rotor from the hub and disconnect the end of the parking brake cable.

6. Remove the bolts that retain the lateral link, trailing link and the strut to the rear spindle.

7. Remove the rear spindle, backing plate and hub as a unit.

8. The installation is the reverse of the removal procedure. Use the following torque values during installation.

a. Rear spindle to strut assembly — 98–119 ft. lbs.
b. Rear spindle assembly to trailing link — 72–94 ft. lbs.
c. Rear spindle to lateral link — 87–116 ft. lbs.
d. Disc brake assembly to backing plate — 34–43 ft. lbs.
e. Axle nut — 123–152 ft. lbs.
f. Wheel nuts — 58–72 ft. lbs.

4WD

1. Disconnect the negative battery cable.

2. Raise the vehicle and support safely. Remove the wheel assemblies.

3. Unlock axle nut and remove from axle.

4. Loosen the parking brake adjuster.

5. Remove the disc brake assembly and suspend it on a wire from the body or strut.

6. Remove the disc rotor from the hub and disconnect the end of the parking brake cable.

7. Remove the speed senor from the backing plate, if equipped with Automatic Brake System (ABS).

8. Remove the bolts that secure the lateral link assembly and the trailing link assembly to the rear housing. Discard the self-locking nuts and replace with new nuts.

9. Remove the spring pin that secures the rear differential spindle to the inner CV-joint.

10. Remove the inner CV-joint and shaft from the differential spindle.

11. Disengage the rear drive shaft from the rear hub and remove the shaft.

12. When installing the shaft, reverse the removal procedures with the following additions:

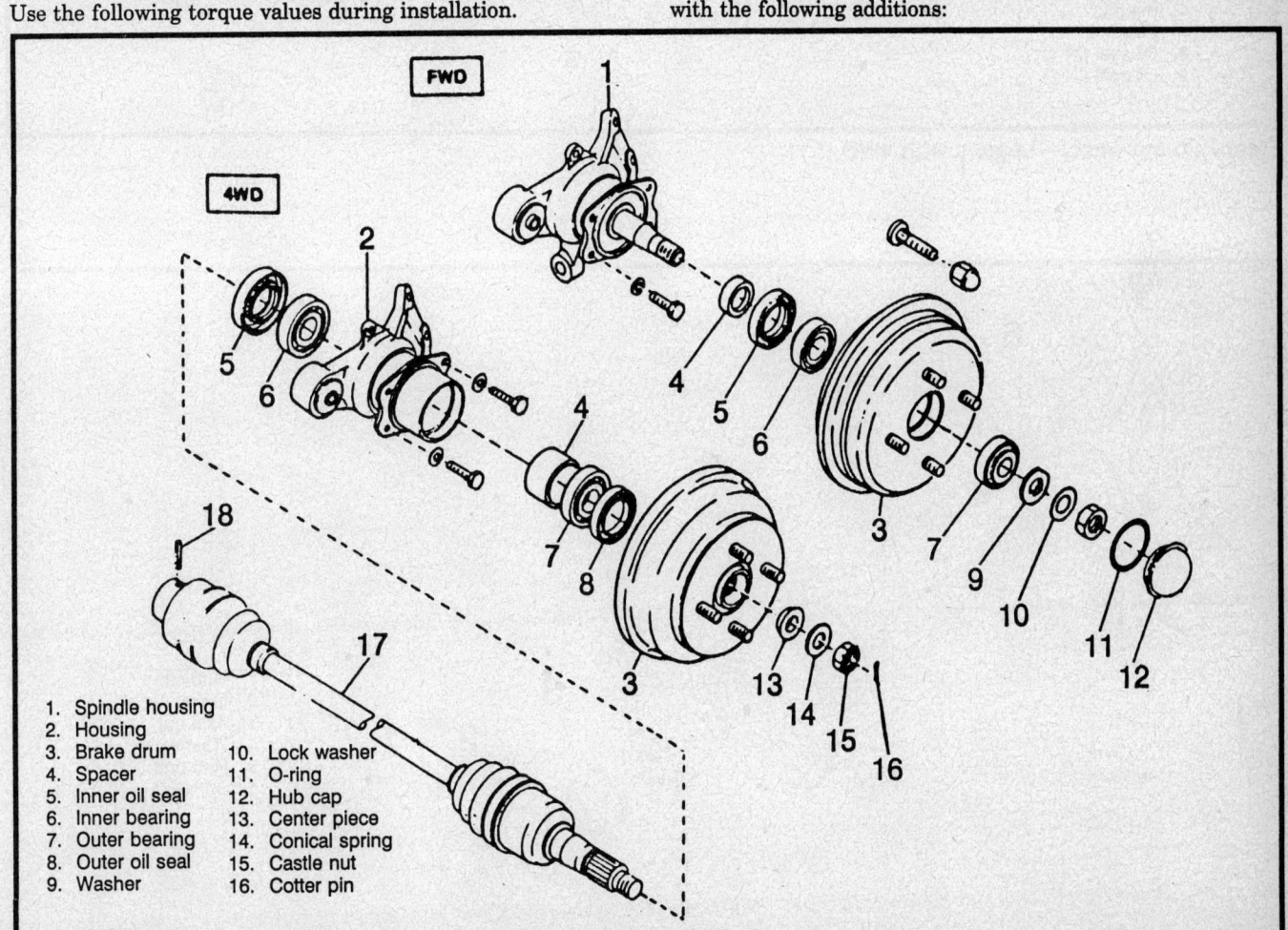

1. Spindle housing
2. Housing
3. Brake drum
4. Spacer
5. Inner oil seal
6. Inner bearing
7. Outer bearing
8. Outer oil seal
9. Washer
10. Lock washer
11. O-ring
12. Hub cap
13. Center piece
14. Conical spring
15. Castle nut
16. Cotter pin

Rear axle assembly — Justy

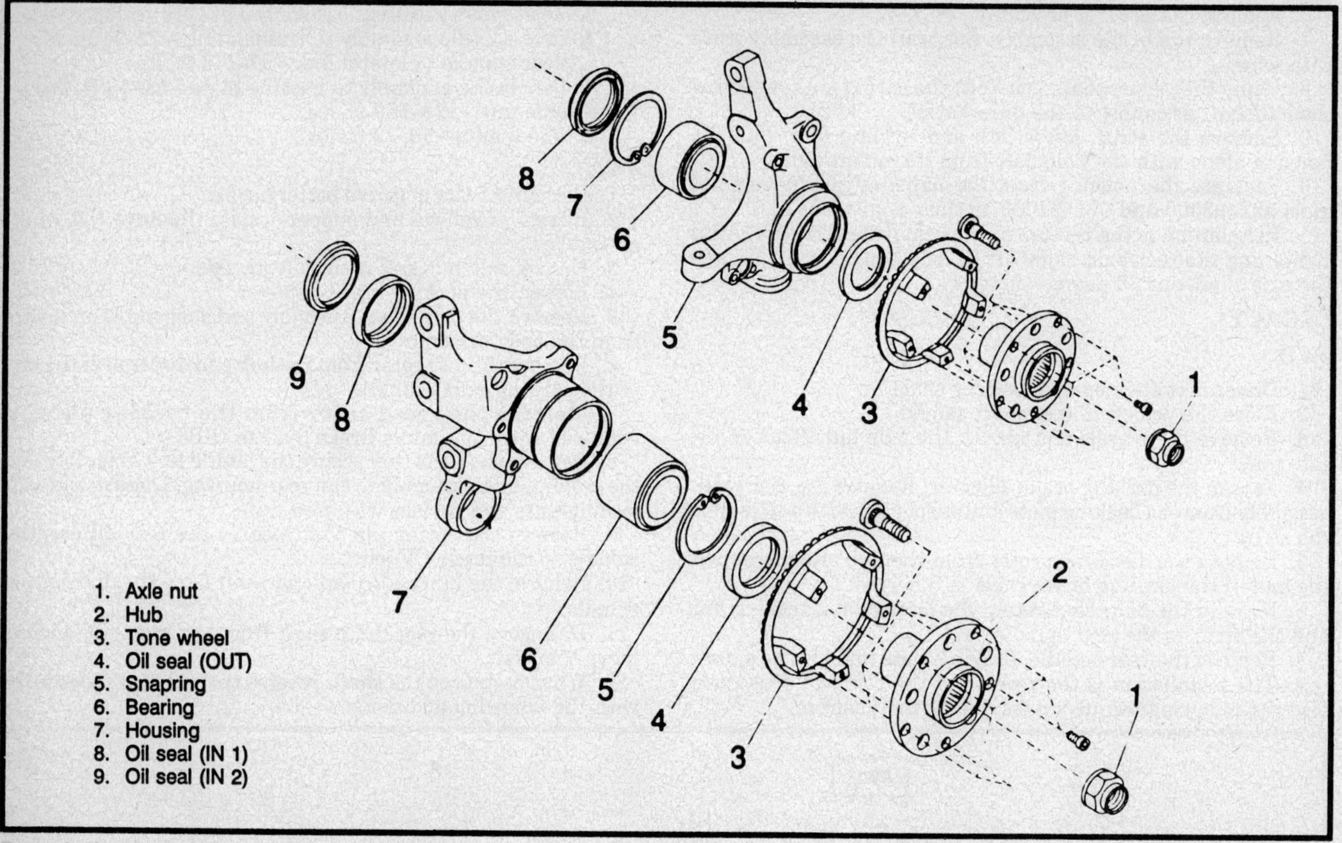

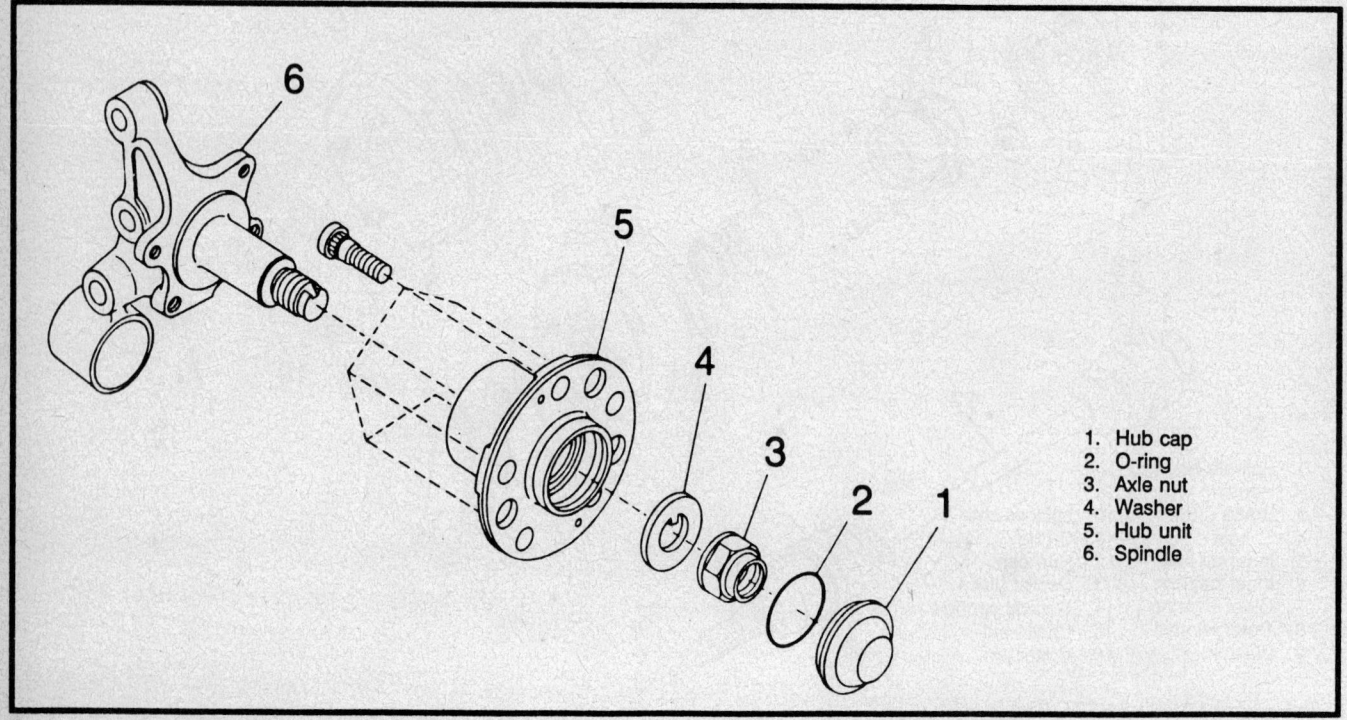

1
2
3
4
5
6
7
8
9
1. Axle nut
2. Hub
3. Tone wheel
4. Oil seal (OUT)
5. Snapring
6. Bearing
7. Housing
8. Oil seal (IN 1)
9. Oil seal (IN 2)

Rear hub assembly—Legacy with 4WD

1
2
3
4
5
6
1. Hub cap
2. O-ring
3. Axle nut
4. Washer
5. Hub unit
6. Spindle

Rear axle/hub assembly—Legacy with FWD

a. Use new seals.

b. Using a new axle nut, pull the axle shaft through the hub splines.

c. Install the axle shaft onto the differential spindle and install the spring pin into place.

d. Using new nuts on the trailing link, tighten to 72–94 ft. lbs.

e. Torque disc brake assembly to the rear housing assembly bolts/nuts to 34–43 ft. lbs.

f. Torque the axle nut to 123–152 ft. lbs.

g. Wheel nut torque to 58–72 ft. lbs.

EXCEPT JUSTY AND LEGACY

2WD

1. Raise and support the vehicle safely. Remove the tire and wheel assembly.

2. Remove the dust cap. Straighten the lock washer. Remove the nut, lock washer and washer.

3. Remove the brake drum. Be sure not to drop the outer bearing.

4. Remove the brake line bracket from the spindle housing.

5. Loosen the bolts and remove the brake assembly. Suspend the assembly aside with wire.

6. Remove the damper strut, lower link and trailing link.

7. Remove the spindle assembly retaining bolts. Remove the spindle from its mounting.

8. Installation is the reverse of the removal procedure.

4WD

1. Firmly apply the parking brake.

2. Remove the rear wheel cap and the cotter pin, then loosen the castle nut.

3. Disconnect the shock absorber from the inner arm.

4. Loosen the crossmember outer bushing lock bolts. Remove the inner trailing arm to chassis bolt and the inner arm.

5. Raise and support the vehicle safely. Remove the rear wheel assemblies.

6. Using a 0.24 in. (6mm) diameter steel rod or a pin punch, drive the inner/outer spring pins from the double offset joints.

7. With the trailing arm fully lowered, remove the ball joint from the trailing arm spindle and the inner double offset joint and the differential spindle.

8. Remove the castle nut and the brake drum or rear wheel caliper If equipped, remove the brake caliper and properly position it aside. Do not disconnect the brake hose from the caliper.

9. Disconnect and plug the brake hose from the inner arm bracket.

10. If equipped with rear brake drums, remove the brake assembly from the trailing arm.

11. Disconnect the inner arm from the outer arm and remove the inner arm from the vehicle.

12. Secure the inner arm in a vise, then using a hammer and a punch, straighten the staked portion of the ring nut or remove the cotter pin from the castled nut. Using the wrench tool 925550000 or equivalent, remove the ring nut.

13. Using a plastic hammer on the outside of the spindle, drive it inward to remove it.

14. Clean, inspect and replace the necessary parts.

To install:

15. Using an arbor press and a piece of 1.38 in. (35mm) dia. pipe, insert the spindle from the inside and press the outer bearing's inner race from outside.

16. Using the wrench tool 925550000 or equivalent, torque the axle shaft ring nut to 127–163 ft. lbs. Using a punch and a hammer, stake the ring nut, facing the ring nut groove or install a new cotter pin in the castled nut.

17. To complete the installation, use new spring pins and reverse the removal procedures. Torque the backing plate to axle housing bolts to 34–43 ft. lbs., the axle spindle to axle housing nut to 145 ft. lbs. and the shock absorber to inner arm bolt to 65–87 ft. lbs. Bleed the brake system.

18. After tightening the rear axle halfshaft to axle housing nut, tighten the axle shaft nut 30 degrees further to align cotter pin holes as required. Be careful not to install the double offset joint and the constant velocity joint oppositely.

Front Wheel Hub, Knuckle and Bearing

Removal and Installation

1. Remove the negative battery cable. Apply the parking brake.

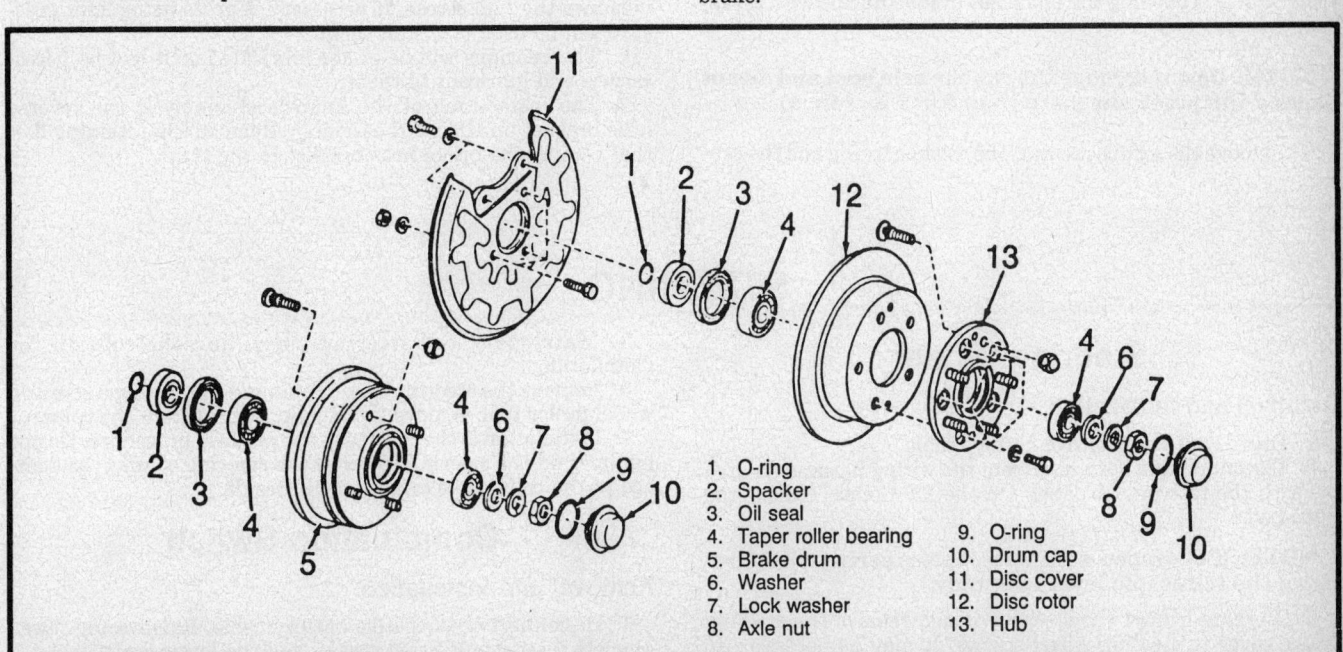

1. O-ring
2. Spacer
3. Oil seal
4. Taper roller bearing
5. Brake drum
6. Washer
7. Lock washer
8. Axle nut
9. O-ring
10. Drum cap
11. Disc cover
12. Disc rotor
13. Hub

Rear axle assembly—XT Coupe with 2700cc engine and 2WD

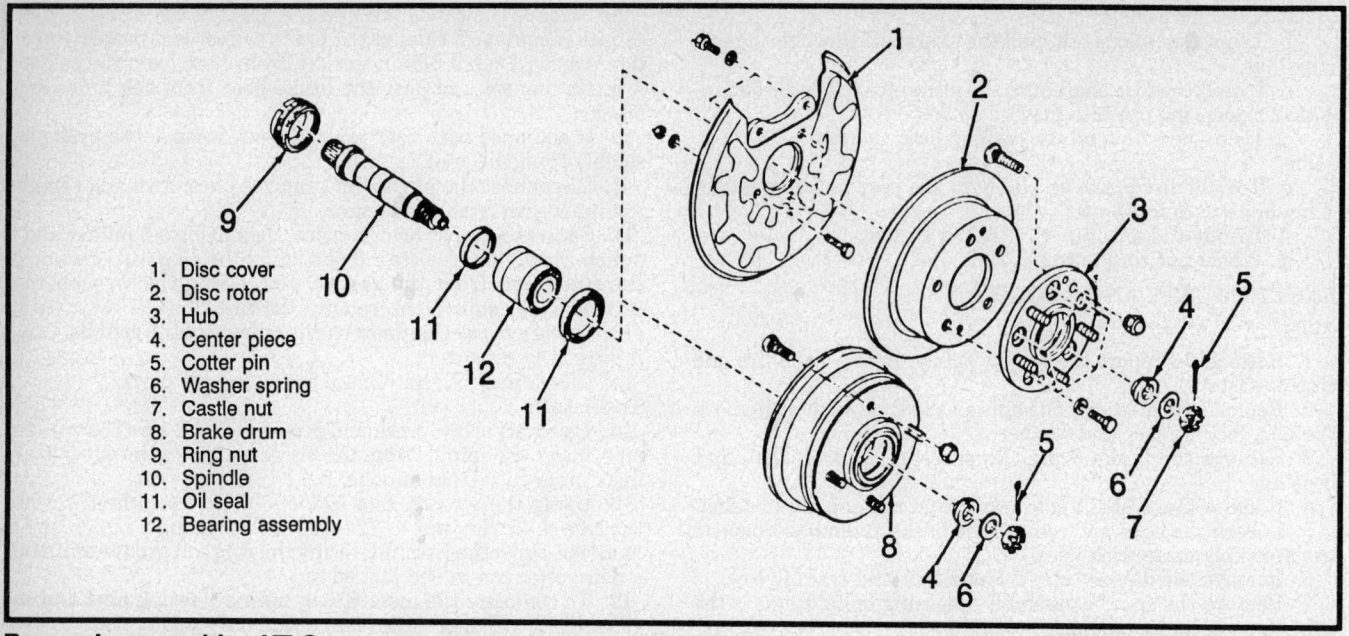

1. Disc cover
2. Disc rotor
3. Hub
4. Center piece
5. Cotter pin
6. Washer spring
7. Castle nut
8. Brake drum
9. Ring nut
10. Spindle
11. Oil seal
12. Bearing assembly

Rear axle assembly—XT Coupe with 2700cc engine and 4WD

2. Remove the axle cap and the cotter pin. Loosen the axle nut and the wheel lugs.

3. Raise and safely support the vehicle. Remove the wheel assemblies as required.

4. Release the parking brake. Pull out the parking brake outer clip from the caliper lever. Disconnect the parking brake cable.

5. Loosen and remove the 2 caliper retaining bolts. Remove the caliper and support from the body with wire.

6. Remove the 2 bolts retaining the damper strut to the knuckle.

7. Disconnect the tie rod end from the knuckle arm.

8. Disconnect the strut from the knuckle by removing the pinch bolt and opening the pinch slit in the knuckle with an appropriate pry tool.

NOTE: Do not damage the rubber axle boot and do not expand the pinch slit more than 0.016 in. (4mm).

9. Remove the axle castle nut, the washer spring and the center piece on the axle shaft and remove the hub and disc assembly.

10 Remove the disc cover from the knuckle.

11. Install a puller to the knuckle assembly and force the knuckle from the axle shaft.

12. Disengage the transverse link ball joint from the knuckle and remove the knuckle assembly.

13. Should the inner, outer bearings or seals remain on the axle, remove them with a puller.

14. To remove the bearings from the knuckle hub, use a drift and hammer to tap them from the hub recess.

To install:

15. The drift and hammer should be used to install the bearings into the hub recess. If necessary, a press using light pressure can be used to install them.

16. The bearings will be either lubricated or it will be necessary to add lubricant to them.

17. The installation of the knuckle assembly is the reverse hose bracket on the strut assembly. Remove the retaining bolt that retains the brake hose bracket to the strut.

STEERING

Steering Wheel

Removal and Installation

1. Disconnect the negative battery cable.

2. Disconnect the horn lead from the wiring harness, located beneath the instrument panel. On the XT Coupe, remove the horn pad.

NOTE: If equipped with telescopic steering wheel, remove the telescopic lever assembly.

3. Working behind the steering wheel, remove the steering wheel cover to steering wheel screws. It may be necessary to lower the column from the dash by removing the screws.

4. Lift the crash pad assembly from the front of the wheel.

5. Matchmark the steering wheel and the column for installation.

6. Remove the steering wheel retaining nut. Using a steering wheel puller tool, remove the steering wheel from the column.

7. Installation is the reverse of the removal procedure. Do not hammer on the steering wheel or the steering column, as damage to the collapsible column could result.

Combination Switch

Removal and Installation

1. Disconnect the negative battery cable. Remove the lower cover to instrument panel screws and the lower cover.

2. Remove the covers to steering column screws and the upper and lower column covers.

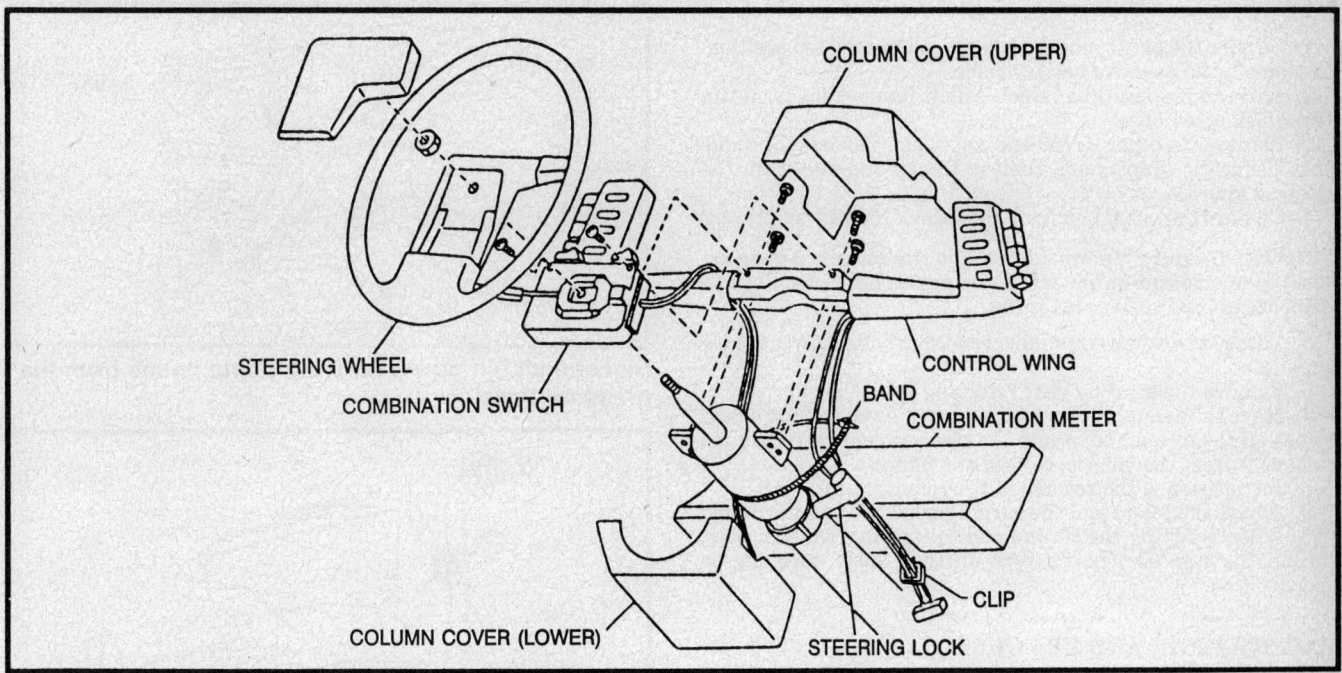

Typical steering wheel and related components

3. Remove the steering wheel cover and the nut. Using a steering wheel puller tool, remove the steering wheel from the steering column.

4. Remove the electrical harness to steering column clip and band fitting, then disconnect the electrical connectors.

5. Remove the combination switch to control wing bracket screws. Remove the switch assembly from its mounting.

6. Installation is the reverse of the removal procedure.

Ignition Switch

Removal and Installation

NOTE: The ignition switch is mounted to the steering column using shear bolts. These bolts are constructed so the heads shear off when the bolt is torqued.

1. Disconnect the negative battery cable. Remove the steering wheel.

2. Remove the upper and lower steering column covers from the steering column.

3. Remove the hazard knob.

4. Drill a pilot hole into the shear bolts, then using a screw extractor, remove the screws from the steering column.

5. Remove the ignition switch from the steering column.

6. Installation is the reverse of the removal procedure. Be sure to use new shear bolts to install the ignition switch.

Manual Steering Gear

Removal and Installation

JUSTY

1. Disconnect the negative battery cable. Raise and support the vehicle safely. Remove the front tire and wheel assemblies.

2. Disconnect the universal joint coupling bolts. Remove the dust seal.

3. Using the proper tools, disconnect the tie rod ends from the knuckle arms.

4. Remove the steering gear retaining bolts. Lower the assembly and pull the pinion from the dust seal toward the engine compartment.

5. Remove the steering gear from the vehicle.

6. Installation is the reverse of the removal procedure.

7. Adjust the toe-in and the turning angles to specifications.

8. When torquing the tie rod end to steering knuckle nuts, torque the nut 45 degrees turn further, after torquing to specification.

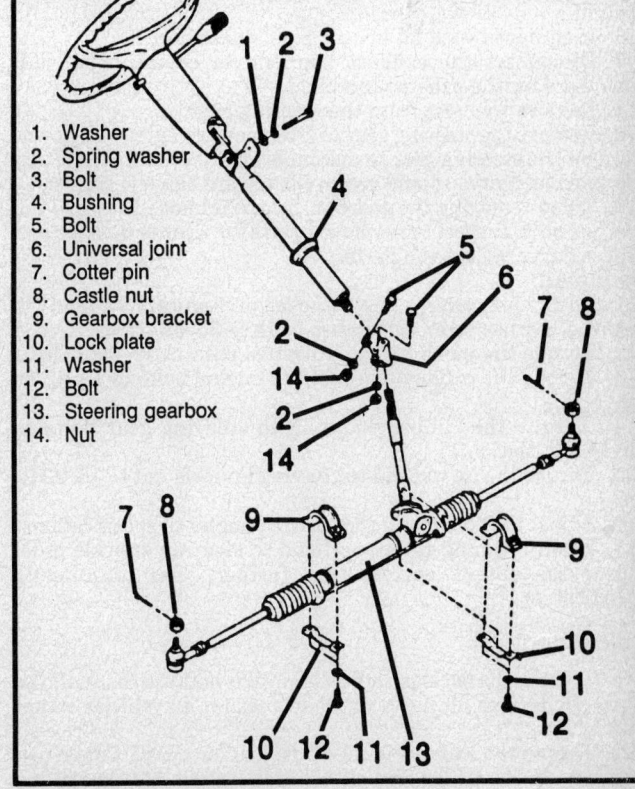

1. Washer
2. Spring washer
3. Bolt
4. Bushing
5. Bolt
6. Universal joint
7. Cotter pin
8. Castle nut
9. Gearbox bracket
10. Lock plate
11. Washer
12. Bolt
13. Steering gearbox
14. Nut

Typical steering system

XT COUPE

1. Be sure the parking brake lever is in the released position. Disconnect the negative battery cable.

2. Raise and support the vehicle safely. Remove the front tire and wheel assemblies.

3. Remove the outer tie rod end cotter pin. Remove the castle nut. Using the proper tool, remove the tie rod end from the steering knuckle.

4. Remove the pinch bolt from the torque rod universal joint.

NOTE: Do not attempt to remove the steering gear assembly or crossmember with the pinch bolt installed to the torque rod universal joint.

5. Loosen the exhaust manifold retaining bolts. Lower the exhaust pipe.

6. Remove the steering gear retaining bolts.

7. Move the assembly toward the pinion. As the pinion shafts comes off the torque rod, rotate the steering gear rearward and remove it from the vehicle, toward the pinion.

8. Installation is the reverse of the removal procedure.

9. Adjust the toe-in and the turning angles to specifications.

10. When torquing the tie rod end to steering knuckle nuts, torque the nut 60 degrees turn further, after torquing to specification.

EXCEPT JUSTY AND XT COUPE

1. Disconnect the negative battery cable.

2. Raise and support the vehicle safely. Remove the front tire and wheel assemblies.

3. Remove the tie rod end cotter pin and loosen the castle nut. Using a ball joint puller, separate the tie rod ends from the housing knuckle arm.

4. If necessary, disconnect the handbrake cable hanger from the tie rod.

5. Remove the pinch bolt from the torque rod universal joint. Disconnect the pinion with the gearbox from the steering column.

6. If equipped with an hot air pipe, disconnect it.

7. Disconnect the exhaust manifold to engine bolts, pull downward on the exhaust manifold.

8. Remove the boot from the steering gear.

9. Remove the steering gear to crossmember bolts, pull downward on the steering gear to disconnect the pinion flange. Turn the gearbox rearward and remove it toward the left side.

10. When removing the gearbox, be careful not to damage the gearbox boot. Inspect the removed parts for wear or damage and if necessary, replace the parts.

To install:

11. To install, reverse the removal procedures. Torque the steering gearbox to crossmember bolts to 35–52 ft. lbs.

12. Torque the pinch bolt to universal joint to 15–20 ft. lbs.

13. Torque the exhaust manifold to engine bolts to 19–22 ft. lbs.

14. Torque the rubber coupling to steering gear bolts to 10–14.5 ft. lbs.

15. Torque the tie rod end to steering knuckle nut to 18–22 ft. lbs.

16. Adjust the toe-in and the turning angles to specifications.

17. When torquing the tie rod end to steering knuckle nuts, torque the nut 60 degrees turn further, after torquing to specification.

Adjustment

1. Tighten the backlash adjuster until it bottoms, back off the screw 15 degrees for Justy or 25 degrees for all vehicles except Justy.

2. Torque the locknut to 22–36 ft. lbs. for all XT Coupe and Justy or 36–47 ft. lbs. for all vehicles, except XT Coupe and Justy.

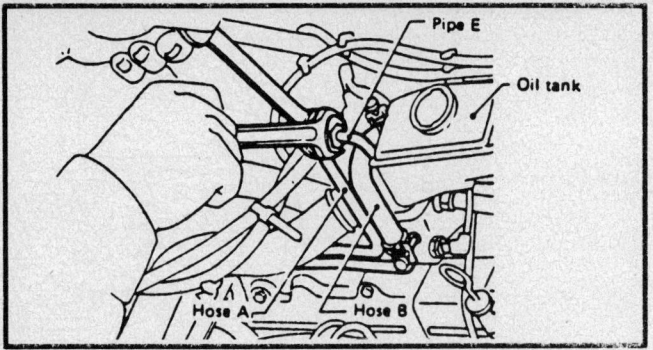

Disconnect the power steering pump hoses from the pressure lines

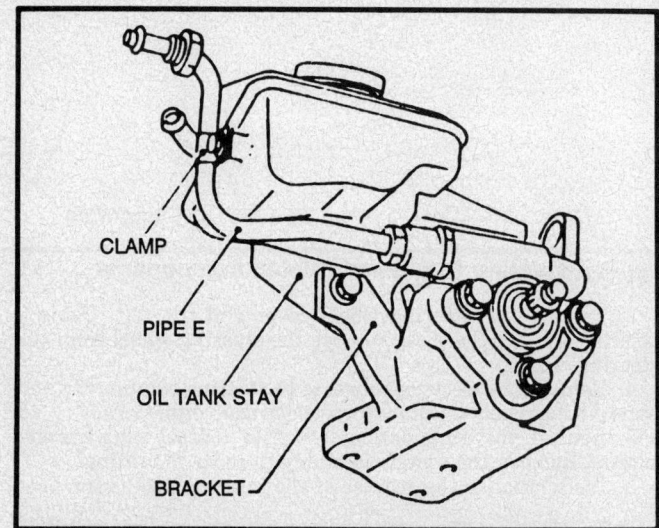

View of the power steering pump with reservoir attached

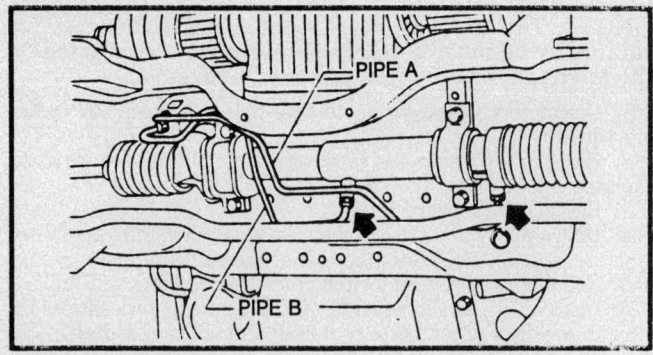

Remove the pressure lines to drain the power steering fluid

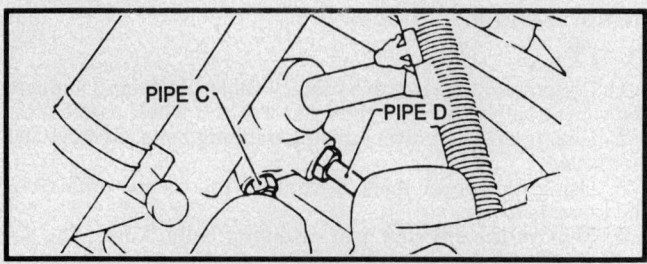

View of the power steering gear pressure lines

3. A clearance of 0.0025 in. is provided between the screw tip and the sleeve plate for Justy.

4. A clearance of 0.004 in. for all vehicles except Justy, is provided between the screw tip and the sleeve plate.

Power Steering Gear

Removal and Installation

1. Disconnect the negative battery cable. Remove the spare tire. If equipped with a turbocharger, remove the spare tire support.

2. If necessary, disconnect the thermo-sensor connector.

3. Raise and support the vehicle safely. Remove the front tire and wheel assemblies.

4. Disconnect the electrical connector from the oxygen sensor. Remove the front exhaust pipe assembly. If equipped with an air stove, remove it.

5. Remove the tie rod end cotter pin and loosen the castle nut. Using a ball joint puller, separate the tie rod ends from the steering knuckle arm.

6. As required, remove the jack up plate and the clamp.

7. From the power steering gear, remove the center pressure pipe, connect a vinyl hose to the pipe and joint, then turn the steering wheel to discharge the fluid into a container.

NOTE: When discharging the power steering fluid, turn the steering wheel fully, left and right. Be sure to disconnect the other pipe and drain the fluid in the same manner.

8. Make alignment marks on the steering shaft universal joint assembly to power steering unit and the steering shaft to universal joint assembly. Remove the lower and upper universal joint to shaft bolts. Lift the universal joint assembly upward and secure it aside.

9. From the control valve of the gearbox assembly, remove the power steering **C** and **D** pressure pipes. Remove pipe **D** first and pipe **C** second.

10. From the control valve of the gearbox assembly, remove the power steering **A** and **B** pressure pipes. Remove pipe **A** first and pipe **B** second.

11. Remove the power steering gearbox to crossmember assembly bolts. Remove the gearbox assembly from the vehicle.

12. Installation is the reverse of the removal procedure. When installing the universal joint assembly, be sure to align the matchmarks.

13. Torque the power steering gearbox to crossmember bolts to 35–52 ft. lbs.

14. Torque the power steering pressure pipes 7–12 ft. lbs., the universal joint assembly to power steering gearbox bolts 16–19 ft. lbs. and the universal joint assembly to steering shaft bolts 16–19 ft. lbs.

15. Torque the tie rod end to steering knuckle nut 18–22 ft. lbs. After torquing this nut, turn it 60 degrees further.

16. Torque the wheel lug nuts to specification. Refill and bleed the power steering system. Check and adjust the toe-in and the steering angle.

Adjustment

Tighten the backlash adjuster until it bottoms, back off the screw 30 degrees and torque the locknut to 22–36 ft. lbs., 0.0049 in. should be provided between the screw tip and the sleeve plate.

Power Steering Pump

Removal and Installation

1. Disconnect the negative battery cable.

2. Using a siphon, drain the power steering fluid from the reservoir.

3. Loosen, but do not remove the power steering pump pulley nut. Loosen the pulley drive belts.

4. Remove the power steering pump pulley nut and the pulley.

5. Disconnect and plug the **A** pressure hose from the **E** pipe. Disconnect the **B** pressure hose from the oil tank.

6. When disconnecting the **A** hose, use wrenches to prevent the **E** pipe from twisting.

7. Remove the **E** hose to reservoir clamp. Loosen the reservoir to bracket bolt, then remove the **A** and **B** bolts on the upper part of the reservoir, this will allow the fluid to run out.

NOTE: To minimize the fluid loss from the reservoir, remove both bolts while the reservoir is pressed against the oil pump, then quickly remove the reservoir. It is a good idea to remove the pump and the reservoir as a unit, then separate the reservoir from the pump on a bench.

8. Remove the power steering pump to bracket bolts. Remove the pump from the vehicle.

9. Installation is the reverse of the removal procedure; be sure to use new O-rings.

10. Torque the power steering pump to bracket bolts to 22–36 ft. lbs.

11. Torque the reservoir stay to bracket bolts to 14–17 ft. lbs.

12. Torque the reservoir to pump bolts to 14–22 ft. lbs.

13. Torque the pulley nut to pump nut to 31–46 ft. lbs.

14. Refill the power steering reservoir. Bleed the power steering system.

Drive Belt Adjustment

1. Using a pair of adjustable jawed pliers, with a piece of rag between the jaws, remove the idler cover cap by turning and pulling.

2. Turn the adjusting bolt until the correct belt tension is obtained. If removing the belt, loosen the adjusting bolt until the drive belt can be removed.

3. After a new belt is installed and the correct tension obtained, replace the idler cap cover by pushing in and turning.

System Bleeding

1. Be sure the power steering reservoir is filled with fluid. Raise and support the vehicle safely.

2. With the engine running, turn the steering wheel back and forth, from lock to lock, until the air is removed from the fluid.

3. Lower the vehicle, recheck the reservoir fluid level and correct, as required.

Tie Rod Ends

Removal and Installation

1. Raise and support the vehicle safely.

2. Remove the front tire and wheel assemblies.

3. Remove the cotter pin and castle nut from the tie rod end stud.

4. Using a ball joint puller, separate the tie rod end from the steering knuckle.

5. Installation is the reverse of the removal procedure. Torque the castle nut to 18–22 ft. lbs.

BRAKES

Master Cylinder

Removal and Installation

1. Disconnect the negative battery cable. Disconnect and plug the brake lines at the master cylinder.
2. It is advised to thoroughly drain the fluid from the master cylinder before performing any removal procedures.
3. If equipped with fluid level indicator, disconnect the electrical harness connector from the master cylinder.
4. Remove the master cylinder to power brake booster retaining nuts. Remove the master cylinder from its mounting.
5. Installation is the reverse of the removal procedure. As required, bleed the brake system.

Proportioning Valve

The proportioning valve is attached to a bracket and is located directly under the master cylinder. It's purpose is to provide even braking pressure to all of the wheels.

Removal and Installation

1. Disconnect the negative battery cable. Disconnect and plug the brake tubes from the proportioning valve. If equipped with an electrical connector, disconnect it.
2. Remove the proportioning valve to bracket bolts. Remove the valve from the vehicle.
3. Installation is the reverse of the removal procedure. As required, bleed the brake system.

Power Brake Booster

Removal and Installation

1. Disconnect the negative battery cable. Disconnect the vacuum hose from the power brake booster. If equipped, disconnect the connector for the brake fluid level indicator.
2. Remove the master cylinder from the brake booster. Depending upon the vehicle, it may not be necessary to completely remove the master cylinder. It may be possible to remove the retaining bolts and position the assembly aside.
3. Remove the brake pedal pushrod to power booster spring pin and clevis pin, then disconnect the pushrod from the brake pedal.
4. From under the dash, remove the power booster to firewall bolts.
5. Remove the brake booster assembly from the vehicle.
6. Installation is the reverse of the removal procedure. Bleed the brake system, as required.

Disc Brake Pads

Removal and Installation
FRONT

1. Raise and support the vehicle safely. Remove the wheel assemblies.
2. Release the parking brake and disconnect the cable from the caliper lever.
3. Remove the lock pin bolts from the lower front of the caliper.
4. Rotate the caliper on the support, swinging it upward and aside.
5. Remove the brake disc pads, noting the position of the shim pads and pad clips.
To install:
6. Inspect the brake rotor, calipers and retaining components. Correct as necessary.

7. Remove a small portion of brake fluid from the master cylinder reservoir. With an appropriate tool, turn the caliper piston clockwise into the cylinder bore and align the notches. Be sure the boot is not twisted or pinched.

NOTE: Do not force the piston straight into the caliper bore. The piston is mounted on a threaded spindle which will bend under pressure.

8. Install the new pads into the calipers, being sure all shims and clips are in their original positions.
9. Swing the calipers down into position and install the lock pin bolts.
10. Reconnect the parking brake cable and fill the master cylinder reservoir.
11. Install the wheel assembly. Bleed the brakes as required and lower the vehicle. Road test the vehicle.

REAR

1. Raise and safely support the vehicle. Remove the wheel assemblies.
2. Disconnect the brake pad lining wear indicator, if equipped. Remove any anti-rattle springs or clips, if equipped.
3. Pull the caliper away from the center of the vehicle to push piston into caliper bore. Remove the caliper guide pins and remove the caliper from the rotor. Hang the caliper from the body with a support wire.
4. Slide the disc pads from the caliper, noting any shims or shields behind the pad.

NOTE: If equipped with parking brake, use a suitable tool to rotate the piston back into the caliper bore. If not equipped with parking brake, the piston can be pushed straight back into the bore.

5. Push the piston into the caliper bore. To install the pads, position any shims or shields in place and reverse the removal procedure.

Brake Shoes

Removal and Installation

1. Raise and safely support the vehicle. Remove the rear wheels.
2. Remove the brake drums.
3. Remove the adjusting wedge spring and the upper and lower return springs.
4. Remove the hold-down springs.
5. Lift the brake shoes from the backing plate and disconnect the parking brake, if equipped.
6. Disconnect the rear shoe from the push bar.
7. Clamp the push bar in a vise and remove the tension spring and adjusting wedge.
8. The installation is the reverse of the removal procedure.
9. Center the brake shoes on the backing plate, making sure the adjusting wedge is fully released before installing the drum.
10. Install the drums and the wheel assemblies.
11. Apply the brakes several times to automatically adjust the shoes. If necessary, bleed the brake system to obtain proper brake operation.
12. Road test the vehicle as required.

Wheel Cylinder

Removal and Installation

1. Raise and support the vehicle safely. Remove the wheel and tire assembly.
2. Remove the brake drum and the brake shoes from the backing plate.

3. Disconnect and plug the brake line at the back of the wheel cylinder.

4. Remove the wheel cylinder to backing plate bolts. Remove the wheel cylinder from the backing plate.

5. Installation is the reverse of the removal procedure. Be sure to bleed the brake system, as required.

Parking Brake Cable

Adjustment

1. Pull the parking brake lever up forcefully. Release it and repeat several times.

2. It should take the specified number of notches to apply the parking brake.
Except Justy—3–5 notches
Justy—6 notches

3. Loosen the locknut on the turnbuckle and adjust the length of the cable, so the parking brake is applied within specification.

4. Tighten the locknut and recheck operation of the parking brake lever.

Removal and Installation
JUSTY

1. Set the parking brake lever.

2. Remove the hub cap, the cotter pin, the castle nut and the wheel lug nuts.

3. Raise and support the vehicle safely. Release the brake lever.

4. Remove the wheel assemblies and the brake drums.

5. Disassemble the equalizer joint to separate the parking brake cable from the rod.

6. Remove the exhaust cover to vehicle bolts and the cover.

7. Remove the cable clamps and the hangers.

8. Disconnect the parking brake cable from the parking brake lever.

9. Disconnect the parking brake cable from the backing plate of the rear brake assemblies.

10. Installation is the reverse of the removal procedure. Torque the mounting clamps and hanger bolts to 9–17 ft. lbs. and the exhaust cover to body bolts to 4–7 ft. lbs. Adjust the parking brakes.

EXCEPT JUSTY

1. Raise and support the vehicle safely. Remove the front wheels.

2. Remove the parking brake cover and loosen the locknut. Loosen the parking brake adjuster until the tension is almost released, then, disconnect the inner cable ends from the equalizer.

3. Remove the clips that fasten the cable grommets in place where the cable passes through the body.

4. Pull the parking brake cable clamp from the caliper and disconnect the end of the cable.

5. Remove the cable to transverse link bracket bolts and the bracket.

6. Remove the cable to crossmember bracket bolt and the bracket.

7. Detach the cable rear crossmember guide and pull the cable from the passenger compartment.

8. Installation is the reverse of the removal procedure. Make sure the cable passes through the guide inside the driveshaft tunnel. Adjust the parking brakes.

FRONT SUSPENSION

MacPherson Strut

Removal and Installation

JUSTY

1. Disconnect the negative battery cable. Remove the bolts that retain the strut assembly to the body.

2. Raise and support the vehicle safely. Remove the tire and wheel assembly.

3. Remove the brake hose from the brake hose bracket on the strut assembly. Remove the retaining bolt that retains the brake hose bracket to the strut.

4. Properly support the hub and disc assembly. Remove the retaining bolt from the strut to the housing.

5. Fit the proper tool into the housing slit and pull the strut assembly from the housing.

6. Remove the strut from the vehicle.

7. Installation is the reverse of the removal procedure.

EXCEPT JUSTY

1. Disconnect the negative battery cable. If equipped with air suspension, remove the cover and the air line assembly.

2. Remove the bolts that retain the strut assembly to the body.

3. Raise and support the vehicle safely. Remove the tire and wheel assembly.

4. Disconnect the brake hose from the caliper body. Pull the brake hose retaining clip and remove the brake hose from the damper strut bracket.

5. Remove the bolt that retains the damper strut to the housing. Remove the bolt that retains the damper strut bracket to the housing.

6. Pull the strut assembly from the housing gradually and carefully, with the housing assembly in the downward position.

7. Remove the strut assembly from the vehicle.

8. Installation is the reverse of the removal procedure. As required, bleed the brake system.

Ball Joints

Inspection

1. Raise and support the vehicle safely.

2. Using a prybar, position it under the wheel, then pry upward on the wheel several times. If more than 0.012 in. (3mm) of movement is noticed at the ball joint it should be replaced.

3. Inspect the dust seal, if damaged it should be replaced.

Removal and Installation

1. Raise and support the vehicle safely. Remove the tire and wheel assembly.

2. Properly support the lower control arm assembly. Remove the cotter pin and castle nut from the ball joint.

3. Disconnect the ball joint from the lower control arm assembly.

4. Remove the bolt retaining the ball joint to the housing. Remove the ball joint from the housing.

5. Installation is the reverse of the removal procedure.

Lower Control Arm

Removal and Installation
JUSTY

1. Raise and support the vehicle safely. Remove the tire and wheel assembly.
2. Properly support the lower control arm. Remove the bolt that retains the lower control arm to the crossmember.
3. Remove the bolt coupling housing to ball joint retaining bolt. Using the proper tool, insert it into the slit and pull the ball joint from the housing.
4. Remove the lower control arm from the vehicle.
5. Installation is the reverse of the removal procedure.

EXCEPT JUSTY

1. Raise and support the vehicle safely. Remove the tire and wheel assembly.
2. As required, remove the parking brake cable from the lower control arm assembly.
3. Remove the bolt that retains the stabilizer assembly to the lower control arm.
4. Remove the front exhaust pipe, as necessary to gain working clearance.
5. Properly support the lower control arm assembly. Remove the ball joint from its mounting.
6. Remove the lower control arm to crossmember retaining bolt. Remove the lower control arm from the vehicle.
7. Installation is the reverse of the removal procedure.

REAR SUSPENSION

Shock Absorbers

Removal and Installation

1. Raise and support the vehicle safely. Remove the tire and wheel assembly.
2. Properly support the rear axle assembly. Loosen the upper shock absorber to chassis nuts.
3. Remove the washer and the bushing, being sure to note their correct assembly sequence for installation.
4. Remove the shock absorber to trailing arm retaining bolt. Remove the shock absorber from its mounting.
5. Installation is the reverse of the removal procedure. Be sure to properly install the washers.
6. Do not fully tighten the upper mounting nuts until the lower shock nut has been installed with the washer and the pin shoulder contracting each other.

MacPherson Strut

Removal and Installation
JUSTY

1. Raise and support the vehicle safely. Remove the tire and wheel assembly. Properly support the rear axle assembly.
2. From the upper portion of the strut mount, remove the trim cover.
3. Remove the strut to body retaining nut. Push the lower arm downward, and remove the coil spring.
4. Remove the strut to axle housing bolts. Remove the strut from the vehicle.
5. Installation is the reverse of the removal procedure.

EXCEPT JUSTY

1. Raise and support the vehicle safely. Remove the tire and wheel assembly.
2. If equipped with air suspension, remove the cover and disconnect the air line.
3. Properly support the rear axle assembly. Remove the upper strut retaining bolts.
4. Remove the lower strut retaining bolts.
5. Remove the strut assembly from the vehicle.
6. Installation is the reverse of the removal procedure.

Springs

Removal and Installation
JUSTY

1. Raise and support the vehicle safely. Remove the tire and wheel assembly. Properly support the rear axle assembly.
2. From the upper portion of the strut mount, remove the trim cover.
3. Remove the strut to body retaining nut. Push the lower arm downward, and remove the coil spring.
4. Installation is the reverse of the removal procedure.

Rear Control Arms

Removal and Installation
JUSTY

1. Raise and support the vehicle safely. Remove the tire and wheel assembly.
2. Properly support the rear axle assembly. Remove the coil spring assembly.
3. Remove the control arm to crossmember bolt. Separate the control arm from the crossmember.
4. Remove the control arm to axle housing bolt Separate the control arm from the axle housing.
5. Remove the assembly from the vehicle.
6. Installation is the reverse of the removal procedure.

LEGACY
Trailing Link

1. Loosen the rear wheel lugs, raise and safely support the vehicle and remove the wheel assemblies.
2. Remove the rear parking brake clamps and the ABS sensors, as required.
3. Remove the bolts retaining the trailing link to the body.
4. Remove the bolts retaining the trailing link to the rear housing.
5. Remove the trailing link from the vehicle.
6. To install the trailing link, place in position and install the bolts at each end.
7. Torque the bolts to 72–94 ft. lbs.
8. Complete the assembly.

Lateral Link

1. Remove the stabilizer from the lateral link.
2. Remove the parking brake cable and the ABS sensor clamp from the trailing link, as required.
3. Loosen the bolts that secure the trailing link to the bracket and remove the bolts that retain the trailing link to the rear housing.
4. If equipped with 4WD, remove the Double Offset Joint (DOJ) pin and axle shaft to provide working space.
5. Remove the front lateral link from the rear crossmember.
6. Temporarily install front lateral link to the rear crossmember and remove the rear lateral link from the crossmember.

7. To install the link, reverse the removal procedure. Torque the bolts to the following specifications:
   a. 4WD – 61–83 ft. lbs.
   b. FWD – 87–116 ft. lbs.

EXCEPT JUSTY AND LEGACY

1. Raise and support the vehicle safely. Remove the tire and wheel assembly.
2. Properly support the rear axle assembly.
3. Remove the strut to lower control arm bolt and separate the strut from the lower control arm.
4. If equipped with 4WD, use a 0.24 in. (6mm) pin punch and drive the spring pins from the halfshaft to axle shaft and the halfshaft to differential assembly. While pushing downward on the inner arm, separate the halfshaft from the axle shaft. Pull the halfshaft from the differential and position it aside.
5. Disconnect and plug the brake hose from the brake line at the lower control arm.
6. Remove the outer arm to lower control arm bolts, then separate the lower control arm from the outer arm. Properly support the inner arm.
7. Remove the inner arm to crossmember bolt. Remove the lower control arm from the vehicle.
8. Installation is the reverse of the removal procedure.
9. If equipped with 4WD, use new spring pins. As required, bleed the brake system.

Rear Wheel Bearings

Adjustment

2WD

1. Raise and support the vehicle safely. Remove the rear wheel assembly.
2. Temporarily tighten the axle nut to 36 ft. lbs. on all vehicles except Justy or to 29 ft. lbs. for Justy.
3. Turn the drum or disc back and forth several times to ensure that bearings are properly seated.
4. Turn the nut backwards $1/8$–$1/10$ turn in order to obtain the correct starting force.
5. Using a spring gauge at 90 degrees to the wheel lug, check the rotating force. Specifications should be 1.9–3.2 lbs. for all vehicles except Justy or for Justy are 3.1–4.4 lbs.
6. After the adjustment is completed, bend the lock washer. After installing a new O-ring to the grease cap, install the cap.

Removal and Installation

1. Raise and support the vehicle safely. Remove the rear tire and wheel assembly.
2. If equipped with rear disc brakes, remove the caliper and properly support it.
3. Using a small prybar, remove the rear wheel grease cap.
4. Using a hammer and a punch, flatten the lock washer and loosen the axle nut. Remove the lock washer and the thrust plate. When removing the drum or disc, be careful not to drop the inner race from the outer bearing.

NOTE: If the brake drum on the Justy is difficult to remove, use wheel puller tool 9224930000 or equivalent, to remove the brake drum.

5. Using a gear puller, remove the spacer and the inner race of the inner bearing.
6. Using a brass drift and a hammer, drive the outer race of the inner bearing from the drum or disc.
7. Using a brass drift and a hammer, drive the outer race of the outer bearing from the drum or disc.
8. Clean and inspect the parts for damage, replace defective parts, if necessary.
9. Using bearing installation tool 925220000 or equivalent, for all vehicles except Justy or tool 922111000 or equivalent, for Justy, press the outer race of the inner bearing into the drum or disc until it seats against the shoulder.
10. When pressing the bearing, be sure not to exceed the load to the bearing, so as not to damage it.
11. Apply a small amount of grease to the oil seal lips, then install the oil seal until it is flush with the drum or disc.
12. Using bearing installation tool 921130000 or equivalent, for all vehicles except Justy or tool 922111000 or equivalent, for Justy, press the outer race of the outer bearing into the drum or disc until it seats against the shoulder.
13. Apply approximately $1/8$ oz. of wheel bearing grease to the inner and the outer bearings. Fill the disc or drum hub with 1 oz. of wheel bearing grease.
14. Install a new spacer O-ring, the spacer and the inner race of the inner bearing onto the trailing arm spindle.
15. When installing the spacer, be sure to face the stepped surface toward the bearing. Use a new thrust plate and lock washer.
16. To complete the installation, reverse the removal procedure. Adjust the wheel bearing.

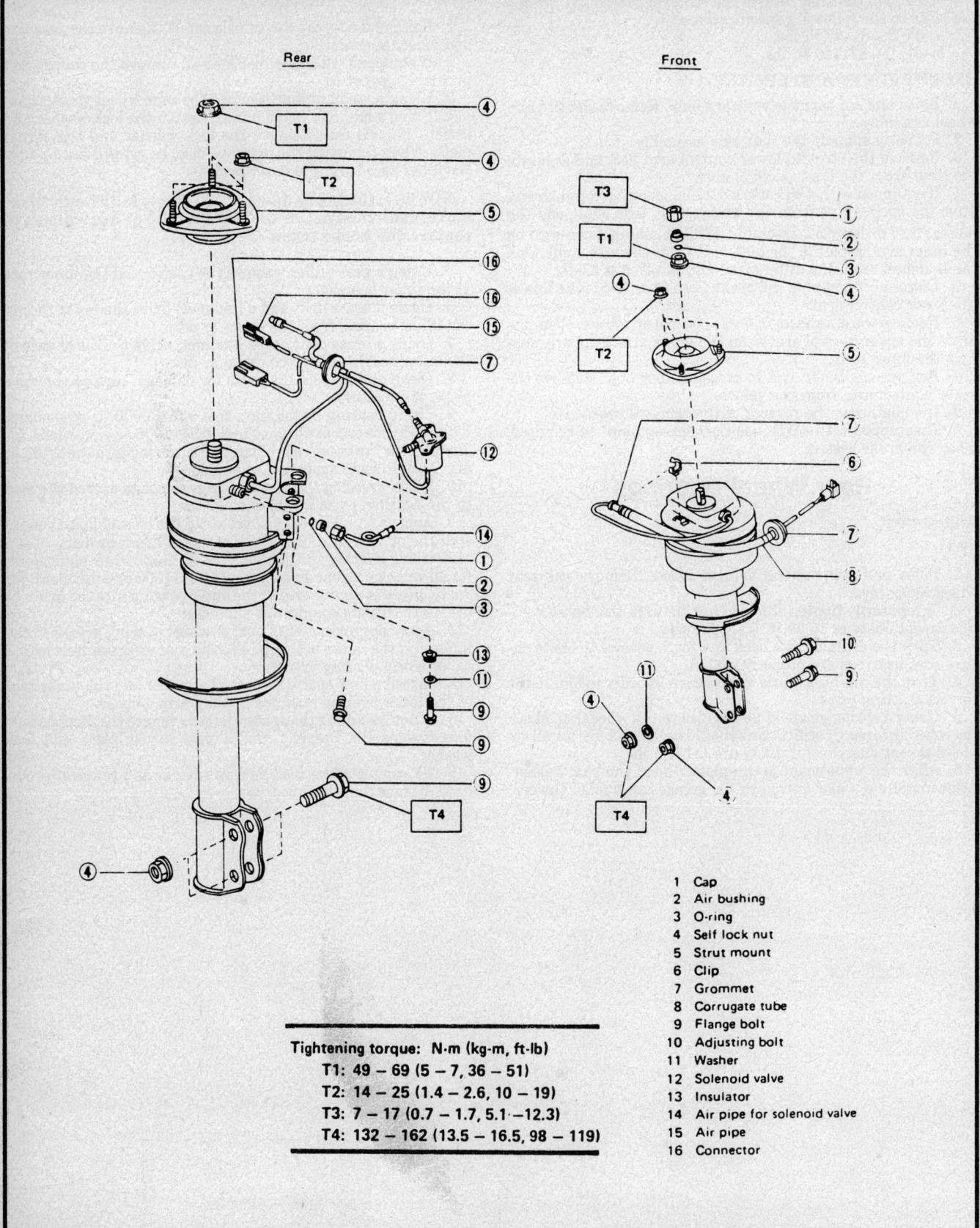

Rear

Front

Tightening torque: N·m (kg-m, ft-lb)
T1: 49 — 69 (5 — 7, 36 — 51)
T2: 14 — 25 (1.4 — 2.6, 10 — 19)
T3: 7 — 17 (0.7 — 1.7, 5.1 — 12.3)
T4: 132 — 162 (13.5 — 16.5, 98 — 119)

1   Cap
2   Air bushing
3   O-ring
4   Self lock nut
5   Strut mount
6   Clip
7   Grommet
8   Corrugate tube
9   Flange bolt
10 Adjusting bolt
11 Washer
12 Solenoid valve
13 Insulator
14 Air pipe for solenoid valve
15 Air pipe
16 Connector

Exploded view of the air suspension system — Legacy

SERIAL NUMBER IDENTIFICATION

Vehicle Identification Plate

All vehicles have the Vehicle Identification Number (VIN) stamped on a plate which is attached to the left side of the instrument panel. This plate is visible through the windshield.

The serial number consists of a series identification number followed by a 6-digit production number.

Engine Number

Basically, Toyota uses 5 types of engines:
A-Series
  3A-C
  4A-LC
  4A-F, 4A-FE
4A-GE
  4A-GEC, 4A-GELC
E-Series
  3E, 3E-E

M-Series
  5M-GE, 7M-GE, 7M-GTE
S-Series
  3S-FE, 3S-GE, 3S-GTE, 5S-FE
Z-Series
  2VZ-FE

Engines within each series are similar, as the cylinder block designs are the same. Variances within each series may be due to ignition types, displacements and cylinder head design.

Serial numbers of the engines may be found on the following locations:

A-Series engines—stamped vertically on the left side rear of the engine block.

E-Series engines—stamped on the left side rear of the engine block.

M-Series engines—stamped horizontally on the passenger side of the engine block, behind the alternator.

S-Series engines—the serial number can be found on the rear left side of the block, under the thermostat housing.

Z-Sseries engines—stamped on the front, right (passenger) side of the cylinder block.

SPECIFICATIONS

ENGINE IDENTIFICATION

Year	Model	Engine Displacement cu. in. (cc/liter)	Engine Series Identification	No. of Cylinders	Engine Type
1987	Tercel	88.6 (1452/1.4)	3A-C	4	SOHC
		88.9 (1456/1.5)	3E	4	SOHC
	Corolla	97.0 (1587/1.6)	4A-LC	4	SOHC
		97.0 (1587/1.6)	4A-GEC, 4A-GELC	4	DOHC
	Camry	121.9 (1998/2.0)	3S-FE	4	DOHC
	Celica	121.9 (1998/2.0)	3S-FE, 3S-GE	4	DOHC
	Supra	180.3 (2954/3.0)	7M-GE	6	DOHC
		180.3 (2954/3.0)	7M-GTE	6	DOHC, TURBO
	MR2	97.0 (1587/1.6)	4A-GELC	4	DOHC
	Cressida	168.4 (2759/2.8)	5M-GE	6	DOHC
1988	Tercel	88.6 (1452/1.4)	3A-C	4	SOHC
		88.9 (1456/1.5)	3E	4	SOHC
	Corolla	97.0 (1587/1.6)	4A-LC	4	SOHC
		97.0 (1587/1.6)	4A-GEC, 4A-GELC	4	DOHC
		97.0 (1587/1.6)	4A-F	4	DOHC
	Camry	121.9 (1998/2.0)	3S-FE	4	DOHC
	Celica	121.9 (1998/2.0)	3S-FE, 3S-GE	4	DOHC
		121.9 (1998/2.0)	3S-GTE	4	DOHC, TURBO
	Supra	180.3 (2954/3.0)	7M-GE	6	DOHC
		180.3 (2954/3.0)	7M-GTE	6	DOHC, TURBO
	MR2	97.0 (1587/1.6)	4A-GELC	4	DOHC
		97.0 (1587/1.6)	4A-GZE	4	DOHC, SUPER
	Cressida	168.4 (2759/2.8)	5M-GE	6	DOHC

ENGINE IDENTIFICATION

Year	Model	Engine Displacement cu. in. (cc/liter)	Engine Series Identification	No. of Cylinders	Engine Type
1989	Tercel	88.9 (1457/1.5)	3E	4	SOHC
	Corolla	97.0 (1587/1.6)	4A-GE	4	DOHC
		97.0 (1587/1.6)	4A-F, 4A-FE	4	DOHC
	Camry	121.9 (1998/2.0)	3S-FE	4	DOHC
		153.0 (2058/2.5)	2VZ-FE	6	DOHC
	Celica	121.9 (1998/2.0)	3S-FE, 3S-GE	4	DOHC
		121.9 (1998/2.0)	3S-GTE	4	DOHC, TURBO
	Supra	180.3 (2954/3.0)	7M-GE	6	DOHC
		180.3 (2954/3.0)	7M-GTE	6	DOHC, TURBO
	MR2	97.0 (1587/1.6)	4A-GELC	4	DOHC
		97.0 (1587/1.6)	4A-GZE	4	DOHC, SUPER
	Cressida	180.3 (2954/3.0)	7M-GE	6	DOHC
1990–91	Tercel	88.9 (1457/1.5)	3E	4	SOHC
		88.9 (1457/1.5)	3F-E	4	SOHC
	Corolla	97.0 (1587/1.6)	4A-FE	4	DOHC
		97.0 (1587/1.6)	4A-GE	4	DOHC
	Camry	121.9 (1998/2.0)	3S-FE	4	DOHC
		153.0 (2058/2.5)	2VZ-FE	6	DOHC
	Celica	97.0 (1587/1.6)	4A-FE	4	DOHC
		121.9 (1998/2.0)	3S-GTE	4	DOHC, TURBO
		132.0 (2164/2.2)	5S-FE	4	DOHC
	Supra	180.3 (2954/3.0)	7M-GE	6	DOHC
		180.3 (2954/3.0)	7M-GTE	6	DOHC, TURBO
	MR2	121.9 (1998/2.0)	3S-GTE	4	DOHC, TURBO
		132.0 (2164/2.2)	5S-FE	4	DOHC
	Cressida	180.3 (2954/3.0)	7M-GE	6	DOHC

OHV Overhead Valves
SOHC Single Overhead Camshaft
DOHC Dougle Overhead Camshaft
TURBO Turbocharged
SUPER Supercharged

GENERAL ENGINE SPECIFICATIONS

Year	Model	Engine Displacement cu. in. (cc)	Fuel System Type	Net Horsepower @ rpm	Net Torque @ rpm (ft. lbs.)	Bore × Stroke (in.)	Compression Ratio	Oil Pressure ①
1987	Tercel	88.6 (1452)	2 bbl	62 @ 4800	76 @ 2800	3.05 × 3.03	9.0.1	4.3
		88.9 (1456)	2 bbl	78 @ 6000	87 @ 4000	2.87 × 3.43	9.3:1	4.3
	Corolla	97.0 (1587)	2 bbl	74 @ 5200	86 @ 2800	3.19 × 3.03	9.0:1	4.3
		97.0 (1587)	EFI	112 @ 6600②	97 @ 4800	3.19 × 3.03	9.4:1	4.3
	Camry	121.9 (1998)	EFI	115 @ 5200	124 @ 4400	3.39 × 3.39	9.3:1	4.3
	Celica	3S-FE 121.9 (1998)	EFI	115 @ 5200	124 @ 4400	3.39 × 3.39	9.3:1	4.3
		3S-GE 121.9 (1998)	EFI	135 @ 6000	125 @ 4800	3.39 × 3.39	9.2:1	4.3
	Supra	7M-GE 180.3 (2954)	EFI	200 @ 6000	185 @ 4800	3.27 × 3.58	9.2:1	4.3
		7M-GTE 180.3 (2954)	EFI	230 @ 5600	246 @ 4000	3.27 × 3.58	8.4:1	4.3
	MR2	97.0 (1587)	EFI	112 @ 6600	97 @ 4800	3.19 × 3.03	9.4:1	4.3
	Cressida	168.4 (2759)	EFI	156 @ 5200	165 @ 4400	3.27 × 3.35	9.2:1	4.3

GENERAL ENGINE SPECIFICATIONS

Year	Model	Engine Displacement cu. in. (cc)	Fuel System Type	Net Horsepower @ rpm	Net Torque @ rpm (ft. lbs.)	Bore × Stroke (in.)	Compression Ratio	Oil Pressure ①
1988	Tercel	88.6 (1452)	2 bbl	62 @ 4800	76 @ 2800	3.05 × 3.03	9.0:1	4.3
		88.9 (1456)	2 bbl	78 @ 6000	87 @ 4000	2.87 × 3.43	9.3:1	4.3
	Corolla	4A-LC 97.0 (1587)	2 bbl	74 @ 5200	86 @ 2800	3.19 × 3.03	9.0:1	4.3
		4A-F 97.0 (1587)	2 bbl	90 @ 6000	95 @ 3600	3.19 × 3.03	9.5:1	4.3
		97.0 (1587)	EFI	116 @ 6600③	110 @ 4800④	3.19 × 3.03	9.4:1	4.3
	Camry	121.9 (1998)	EFI	115 @ 5200	124 @ 4400	3.39 × 3.39	9.3:1	4.3
	Celica	3S-FE 121.9 (1998)	EFI	115 @ 5200	124 @ 4400	3.39 × 3.39	9.3:1	4.3
		3S-GE 121.9 (1998)	EFI	135 @ 6000	125 @ 4800	3.39 × 3.39	9.2:1	4.3
		3S-GTE 121.9 (1998)	EFI	190 @ 6000	190 @ 3200	3.39 × 3.39	8.5:1	4.3
	Supra	7M-GE 180.3 (2954)	EFI	200 @ 6000	185 @ 4800	3.27 × 3.58	9.2:1	4.3
		7M-GTE 180.3 (2954)	EFI	230 @ 5600	246 @ 4000	3.27 × 3.58	8.4:1	4.3
	MR2	4A-GELC 97.0 (1587)	EFI	112 @ 6600	100 @ 4800	3.19 × 3.03	9.4:1	4.3
		4A-GZE 97.0 (1587)	EFI	145 @ 6400	140 @ 4000	3.19 × 3.03	8.0:1	4.3
	Cressida	168.4 (2759)	EFI	156 @ 5200	165 @ 4400	3.27 × 3.35	9.2:1	4.3
1989	Tercel	88.6 (1452)	2 bbl	78 @ 6000	87 @ 4000	2.87 × 3.43	9.3:1	4.3
	Corolla	4A-FE 97.0 (1587)	EFI	100 @ 5600	101 @ 4400	3.19 × 3.03	9.5:1	4.3
		4A-F 97.0 (1587)	2 bbl	90 @ 6000	95 @ 3600	3.20 × 3.00	9.5:1	4.3
		97.0 (1587)	EFI	116 @ 6600	100 @ 4800	3.19 × 3.03	9.4:1	4.3
	Camry	121.9 (1998)	EFI	115 @ 5200	124 @ 4400	3.39 × 3.39	9.3:1	4.3
		153.0 (2507)	EFI	153 @ 5600	155 @ 4400	3.44 × 2.74	9.0:1	4.3
	Celica	3S-FE 121.9 (1998)	EFI	115 @ 5200	124 @ 4400	3.39 × 3.39	9.3:1	4.3
		3S-GE 121.9 (1998)	EFI	135 @ 6000	125 @ 4800	3.39 × 3.39	9.2:1	4.3
		3S-GTE 121.9 (1998)	EFI	190 @ 6000	190 @ 3200	3.39 × 3.39	8.5:1	4.3
	Supra	7M-GE 180.3 (2954)	EFI	200 @ 6000	188 @ 3600	3.27 × 3.58	9.2:1	4.3
		7M-GTE 180.3 (2954)	EFI	232 @ 5600	254 @ 3200	3.27 × 3.58	8.4:1	4.3
	MR2	4A-GELC 97.0 (1587)	EFI	115 @ 6600	100 @ 4800	3.19 × 3.03	9.4:1	4.3
		4A-GZE 97.0 (1587)	EFI	145 @ 6400	140 @ 4000	3.19 × 3.03	8.0:1	4.3
	Cressida	180.3 (2954)	EFI	190 @ 5600	185 @ 4400	3.27 × 3.58	9.2:1	4.3

GENERAL ENGINE SPECIFICATIONS

Year	Model	Engine Displacement cu. in. (cc)	Fuel System Type	Net Horsepower @ rpm	Net Torque @ rpm (ft. lbs.)	Bore × Stroke (in.)	Compression Ratio	Oil Pressure ①
1990–91	Tercel	3E 88.9 (1457)	1 bbl	78 @ 6000	87 @ 4000	2.87 × 3.43	9.3:1	4.3
		3E-E 88.9 (1457)	EFI	82 @ 5200	89 @ 4400	2.87 × 3.43	9.3:1	4.3
	Corolla	4A-FE 97.0 (1587)	EFI	102 @ 5800	101 @ 4800	3.19 × 3.03	9.5:1	4.3
		4A-GE 97.0 (1587)	EFI	130 @ 6800	102 @ 5800	3.19 × 3.03	9.5:1	4.3
	Camry	3S-FE 121.9 (1998)	EFI	115 @ 5200	124 @ 4400	3.39 × 3.39	9.3:1	4.3
		2VZ-FE 153.0 (2508)	EFI	156 @ 5600	160 @ 4400	3.44 × 2.74	9.0:1	4.3
	Celica	4A-FE 97.0 (1587)	EFI	103 @ 6000 ⑤	102 @ 3200 ⑥ ⑦	3.19 × 3.03	9.5:1	4.3
		5S-GTE 121.9 (1998)	EFI	200 @ 6000	200 @ 3200	3.39 × 3.39	9.5:1	4.3
		3S-FE 132.0 (2164)	EFI	130 @ 5400	140 @ 4400	3.43 × 3.58	9.5:1	4.3
	Supra	7M-GE 180.3 (2954)	EFI	200 @ 6000	188 @ 3600	3.27 × 3.58	9.2:1	4.3
		7M-GTE 180.3 (2954)	EFI	232 @ 5600	254 @ 3200	3.27 × 3.58	8.4:1	4.3
	MR2	3S-GTE 121.9 (1998)	EFI	200 @ 6000	200 @ 3200	3.39 × 3.39	9.5:1	4.3
		5S-FE 132.0 (2164)	EFI	130 @ 5400	140 @ 4400	3.43 × 3.58	9.5:1	4.3
	Cressida	180.3 (2954)	EFI	190 @ 5600	185 @ 4400	3.27 × 3.35	9.2:1	4.3

EFI Electronic Fuel Injection
① At Idle
② FX-16: 108 @ 6600
③ FX-16: 110 @ 6600
④ FX-16: 98 @ 4800
⑤ California: 102 @ 5800
⑥ California: 101 @ 4800

GASOLINE ENGINE TUNE-UP SPECIFICATIONS

Year	Model	Engine Displacement cu. in. (cc)	Spark Plugs Type	Gap (in.)	Ignition Timing (deg.) MT	Ignition Timing (deg.) AT	Compression Pressure (psi)	Fuel Pump (psi)	Idle Speed (rpm) MT	Idle Speed (rpm) AT	Valve Clearance In.	Valve Clearance Ex.
1987	Tercel	88.6 (1452)	BPR5EY-11 ①	0.043	5B	5B	178	2.6–3.5	650	900	0.008	0.012
		88.9 (1456)	BPR5EY-11	0.043	3B	3B	184	2.6–3.5	650	900	0.008	0.008
	Corolla	4A-LC 97.0 (1587)	BPR5EY-11	0.043	5B	5B	178	2.5–3.5	700	850	0.008	0.012
		4A-GE 97.0 (1587)	BCPR5EP-11	0.043	10B	10B	179	33–38	800	800	0.008	0.010
	Camry	121.9 (1998)	BCPR5EY-11	0.043	10B	10B	178	38–44	700	750	0.009	0.013
	Celica	3S-FE 121.9 (1998)	BCPR5EY-11	0.043	10B	10B	178	38–44	700	700	0.009	0.013
		3S-GE 121.9 (1998)	BCPR5EP-11	0.043	10B	10B	178	33–38	750	750	0.008	0.010

GASOLINE ENGINE TUNE-UP SPECIFICATIONS

Year	Model	Engine Displacement cu. in. (cc)	Spark Plugs Type	Gap (in.)	Ignition Timing (deg.) MT	AT	Compression Pressure (psi)	Fuel Pump (psi)	Idle Speed (rpm) MT	AT	Valve Clearance In.	Ex.
1987	Supra	7M-GE 180.3 (2954)	BCPR5EP-11	0.043	10B	10B	156	33–40	700	600	0.008	0.010
		7M-GTE 180.3 (2954)	BCPR6EP-N8	0.031	10B	10B	142	33–40	650	650	0.008	0.010
	MR2	97.0 (1587)	BCPR5EP-11	0.043	10B	10B	179	33–38	800	—	0.008	0.010
	Cressida	168.4 (2759)	BPR5EP-11	0.043	—	10B	164	35–38	—	650	Hyd.	Hyd.
1988	Tercel	88.6 (1452)	BPR5EY-11 ①	0.043	5B	5B	178	2.6–3.5	650	900	0.008	0.012
		88.9 (1456)	BPR5EY-11	0.043	3B	3B	184	2.6–3.5	650	900	0.008	0.008
	Corolla	4A-LC 97.0 (1587)	BPR5EY-11	0.043	5B	5B	163	2.5–3.5	650	750	0.008	0.012
		4A-F 97.0 (1587)	BPR5EY-11	0.043	5B	5B	191	2.5–3.5	650	750	0.008	0.010
		4A-GE 97.0 (1587)	BCPR5EP-11	0.043	10B	10B	179	33–38	800	800	0.008	0.010
	Camry	121.9 (1998)	BCPR5EY-11	0.043	10B	10B	178	38–44	700	750	0.009	0.013
	Celica	3S-FE 121.9 (1998)	BCPR5EY-11	0.043	10B	10B	178	38–44	650	650	0.009	0.013
		3S-GE 121.9 (1998)	BCPR5EP-11	0.043	10B	10B	178	33–38	750	750	0.008	0.010
		3S-GTE 121.9 (1998)	BCPR5EP-8	0.031	10B	—	178	33–38	750	—	0.008	0.010
	Supra	7M-GE 180.3 (2954)	BCPR5EP-11	0.043	10B	10B	156	33–40	700	700	0.008	0.010
		7M-GTE 180.3 (2954)	BCPR6EP-N8	0.031	10B	10B	142	33–40	650	650	0.008	0.010
	MR2	4A-GE 97.0 (1587)	BCPR5EP-11	0.043	10B	10B	179	38–44	800	800	0.008	0.010
		4A-GZE 97.0 (1587)	BCPR6EP-11	0.043	10B	10B	156	33–38	800	800	0.008	0.010
	Cressida	168.4 (2759)	BPR5EP-11	0.043	—	10B	164	35–38	—	650	Hyd.	Hyd.
1989	Tercel	88.9 (1456)	BPR5EY-11	0.043	3B	3B	184	2.6–3.5	700	900	0.008	0.008
	Corolla	4A-FE 97.0 (1587)	BCPR5EY	0.031	10B	10B	191	38–44	800	800	0.008	0.010
		4A-F 97.0 (1587)	BCPR5EY-11	0.043	5B	5B	191	2.5–3.5	650	750	0.008	0.010
		4A-GE 97.0 (1587)	BCPR5EP-11	0.043	10B	10B	179	33–44	800	800	0.008	0.010
	Camry	121.9 (1998)	BCPR5EY-11	0.043	10B	10B	178	38–44	700	700	0.009	0.013
		153.0 (2507)	BCPR6E-11	0.043	10B	10B	142	38–44	700	700	0.007	0.013
	Celica	3S-FE 121.9 (1998)	BCPR5EY-11	0.043	10B	10B	178	38–44	700	700	0.009	0.013
		3S-GE 121.9 (1998)	BCPR5EP-11	0.043	10B	10B	178	33–38	750	750	0.008	0.010
		3S-GTE 121.9 (1998)	BCPR5EP-8	0.031	10B	—	178	33–38	750	—	0.008	0.010

GASOLINE ENGINE TUNE-UP SPECIFICATIONS

Year	Model	Engine Displacement cu. in. (cc)	Spark Plugs Type	Gap (in.)	Ignition Timing (deg.) MT	AT	Compression Pressure (psi)	Fuel Pump (psi)	Idle Speed (rpm) MT	AT	Valve Clearance In.	Ex.
1989	Supra	7M-GE 180.3 (2954)	BCPR5EP-11	0.043	10B	10B	156	38–44	700	700	0.008	0.010
		7M-GTE 180.3 (2954)	BCPR6EP-N8	0.031	10B	10B	142	33–40	650	650	0.008	0.010
	MR2	4A-GE 97.0 (1587)	BCPR5EP-11	0.043	10B	10B	179	38–44	800	800	0.008	0.010
		4A-GZE 97.0 (1587)	BCPR6EP-11	0.043	10B	10B	156	33–38	800	800	0.008	0.010
	Cressida	180.3 (2954)	BCPR5EP-11	0.043	—	10B	156	38–44	—	700	0.008	0.010
1990	Tercel	3E 88.9 (1457)	5PR5EY-11	0.043	3B	3B	184	2.6–3.5	700	900	0.008	0.008
		3E-E 88.9 (1457)	5PR5EY-11	0.043	10B	10B	184	38–44	800	800	0.008	0.008
	Corolla	4A-FE 97.0 (1587)	BCPR5EY	0.031	10B	10B	190	38–44	②	②	0.006–0.010	0.008–0.012
		4A-CE 97.0 (1587)	BCPR5EY	0.031	10B	10B	190	38–44	800	800	0.006–0.010	0.008–0.012
	Camry	3S-FE 121.9 (1998)	BCPR5EY-11	0.043	10B	10B	178	38–44	650–750	650–750	0.007–0.011	0.011–0.015
		2VZ-FE 153.0 (2508)	BCPR6E-11	0.043	10B	10B	178	38–44	650–750	650–750	0.005–0.009	0.011–0.015
	Celica	4A-FE 97.0 (1587)	BCPR5EY	0.031	10B	10B	191	38–44	800	800	0.006–0.010	0.008–0.012
		3S-GTE 121.9 (1998)	BCPR5EP-8	0.031	10B	—	178	38–44	750	—	0.006–0.010	0.008–0.012
		5S-FE 132.0 (2164)	BPR5EYA-11	0.043	10B	10B	178	38–44	650–750 ③	650–750 ④	0.007–0.011	0.011–0.015
	Supra	7M-GE 180.3 (2954)	BCPR5EP-11	0.043	10B	10B	156	38–44	700	700	0.006–0.010	0.008–0.012
		7M-GTE 180.3 (2954)	BCPR6EP-N8	0.031	10B	10B	142	33–40	650	650	0.006–0.010	0.006–0.010
	MR2	3S-GTE 121.9 (1998)	BKR6EP-8	0.031	10B	10B	164	33–38	750–850	—	0.006–0.010	0.008–0.012
		5S-FE 132.0 (2164)	BKR5EYA-11	0.043	10B	10B	142	38–44	700–800 ⑤	650–750 ④	0.007–0.011	0.011–0.015
	Cressida	180.3 (2954)	BCPR5EP-11	0.043	—	10B	156	38–44	—	700	0.006–0.010	0.008–0.012
1991			SEE UNDERHOOD SPECIFICATIONS STICKER									

NOTE: The Underhood Specifications sticker often reflects tune-up specification changes made in production. Sticker figures must be used if they disagree with those in this chart.
MT Manual transmission
AT Automatic transmissino
NA Not adjustable
A After Top Dead Center
B Before Top Dead Center
Hyd. Hydraulic valve lash adjusters
① Can. wagon w/MT: BPR5EY; 0.031 in.
② 2WD: 700
  4WD: 800
③ Canada: 750–850
④ Canada: 700–800
⑤ Canada: 800–900

FIRING ORDERS

NOTE: To avoid confusion, always replace spark plug wires one at a time.

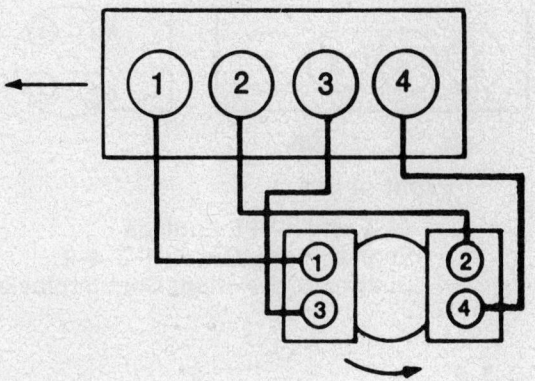

3A-C and 4A-F Engines
Engine Firing Order: 1–3–4–2
Distributor Rotation: Counterclockwise

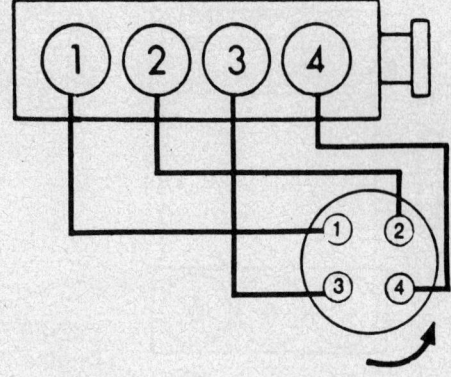

3E and 3E-E Engines
Engine Firing Order: 1–3–4–2
Distributor Rotation: Counterclockwise

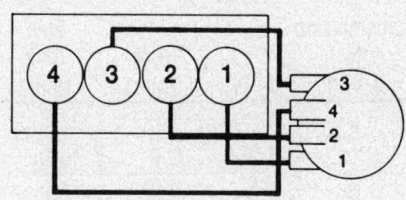

3S-FE, 3S-GE, 3S-GTE and 5S-FE Engines
Engine Firing Order: 1–3–4–2
Distributor Rotation: Counterclockwise

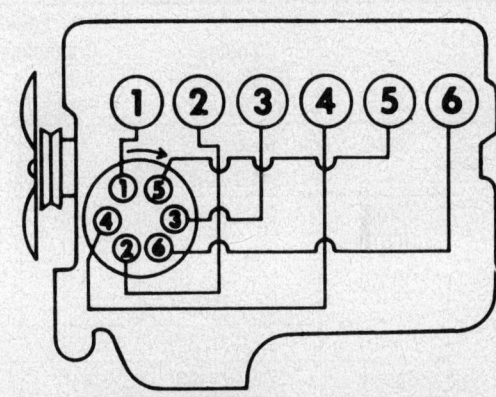

5M-GE Engine
Engine Firing Order: 1–5–3–6–2–4
Distributor Rotation: Clockwise

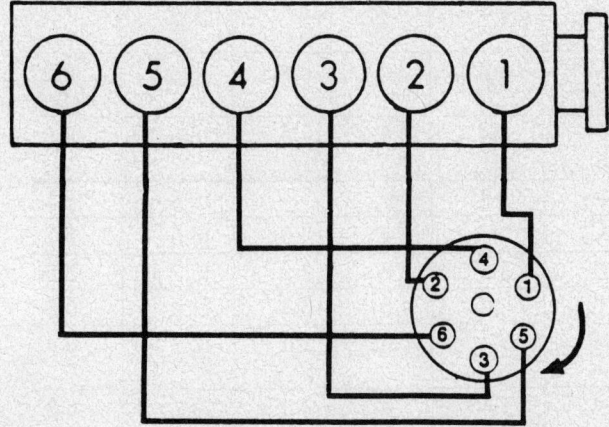

7M-GE Engine
Engine Firing Order: 1–5–3–6–2–4
Distributor Rotation: Clockwise

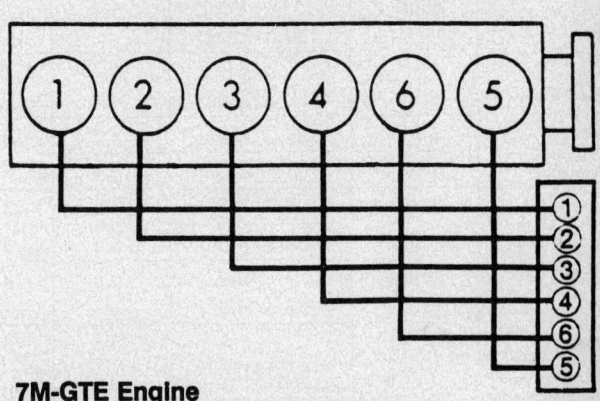

7M-GTE Engine
Engine Firing Order: 1–5–3–6–2–4
Distributorless Ignition System

FIRING ORDERS

NOTE: To avoid confusion, always replace spark plug wires one at a time.

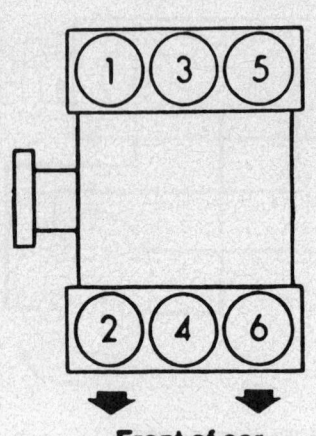
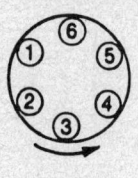

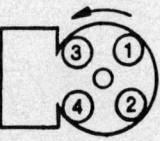

4A-F and 4A-FE Engines
Engine Firing Order: 1–3–4–2
Distributor Rotation: Counterclockwise

2VZ-FE Engine
Engine Firing Order: 1–2–3–4–5–6
Distributor Rotation: Counterclockwise

Front of car

CAPACITIES

Year	Model	Engine Displacement cu. in. (cc)	Engine Crankcase (qts.) with Filter	Engine Crankcase (qts.) without Filter	Transmission (pts.) 4-spd	Transmission (pts.) 5-Spd	Transmission (pts.) Auto.	Drive Axle (pts.)	Fuel Tank (gal.)	Cooling System (qts.)
1987	Tercel	88.6 (1452)	3.5	3.2	7.2①	7.2①	4.6②	2.0	13.2	5.6
		88.9 (1456)	3.4	3.1	5.0	5.0	5.2	3.0	11.9	4.9
	Corolla (RWD)	97.0 (1587)	3.5	3.2	3.6	3.6	5.0	2.2	13.2	④
	(RWD)	4A-GE 97.0 (1587)	3.9	3.5	3.6	3.6	5.0	2.8	13.2	④
	(FWD)	97.0 (1587)	3.5	3.2	5.4	5.4	5.0	3.0	13.2③	6.3
	Camry	121.9 (1998)	4.1	3.9	5.4	5.4	5.2	3.4	15.9	6.8
	Celica	3S-FE 121.9 (1998)	4.1	3.9	5.4	5.4	4.2	3.4	15.9	6.8
		3S-GE 121.9 (1998)	4.1	3.9	5.4	5.4	5.0	3.4	15.9	7.4
	Supra	7M-GE 180.3 (2954)	4.7	3.9	—	5.0	3.4	2.8	18.5	8.6
		7M-GTE 180.3 (2954)	4.7	3.9	—	6.4	3.4	2.8	18.5	8.6
	MR2	97.0 (1587)	3.9	3.5	—	4.8	—	—	10.8	13.6
	Cressida	168.4 (2759)	5.4	4.9	—	—	3.4	2.6⑤	18.5	8.7
1988	Tercel	88.6 (1452)	3.5	3.2	8.2	8.2	8.8	2.2	13.2	5.6
		88.9 (1456)	3.4	3.1	5.0	5.0	4.6	3.0	11.9	5.3
	Corolla	4A-LC 97.0 (1587)	3.5	3.2	5.4	5.4	⑥	3.0	13.2⑦	6.4
		4A-F 97.0 (1587)	3.3	3.2	5.4	5.4	⑥	3.0	13.2	6.3
		4A-GE 97.0 (1587)	3.9	3.5	5.4	5.4	⑥	3.0	13.2	6.3
	Camry	121.9 (1998)	4.1	3.9	5.4	5.4	5.2	3.4⑦	15.9	6.8

CAPACITIES

Year	Model	Engine Displacement cu. in. (cc)	Engine Crankcase (qts.) with Filter	without Filter	Transmission (pts.) 4-spd	5-Spd	Auto.	Drive Axle (pts.)	Fuel Tank (gal.)	Cooling System (qts.)
1988	Celica	3S-FE 121.9 (1998)	4.1	3.9	5.4	5.4	5.2	3.4	15.9	6.8
		3S-GE 121.9 (1998)	4.1	3.9	5.4	5.4	5.2	3.4	15.9	7.4
		3S-GTE 121.9 (1998)	3.8	3.6	—	10.2	—	—	15.9	8.5
	Supra	7M-GE 180.3 (2954)	4.4	4.1	—	5.0	3.4	2.8	18.5	8.6
		7M-GTE 180.3 (2954)	4.4	4.1	—	6.4	3.4	2.8	18.5	8.7
	MR2	97.0 (1587)	3.5	3.2	—	⑧	6.6	—	10.8	⑨
	Cressida	168.4 (2759)	5.2	4.9	—	—	3.4	2.6	18.5	8.7
1989	Tercel	88.9 (1456)	3.4	3.1	5.0	5.0	4.6	3.0	11.9	5.5
	Corolla	4A-F, 4A-FE 97.0 (1587)	3.4	3.2	5.4	5.4	⑥	3.0	13.2	5.9
		4A-GE 97.0 (1587)	3.9	3.6	5.4	5.4	⑥	3.0	13.2	6.3
	Camry	121.9 (1998)	4.1	3.9	—	5.4 ⑨	5.2	3.4 ⑦	15.9	6.8
		153.0 (2507)	4.1	3.9	—	—	5.2	2.2	15.9	9.0
	Celica	3S-FE 121.9 (1998)	4.1	3.9	—	5.4	5.2	3.4	15.9	6.6
		3S-GE 121.9 (1998)	4.1	3.8	—	5.4	5.2	3.4	15.9	6.4
		3S-GTE 121.9 (1998)	3.8	3.5	—	10.2	—	2.4	15.9	6.8
	Supra	7M-GE 180.3 (2954)	4.7	4.3	—	5.0	3.4	2.8	18.5	8.6
		7M-GTE 180.3 (2954)	4.9	4.5	—	6.4	3.4	2.8	18.5	8.7
	MR2	97.0 (1587)	3.5	3.2	—	⑧	6.6	—	10.8	13.6
	Cressida	180.3 (2954)	4.7	4.3	—	—	3.4	—	18.5	8.8
1990-91	Tercel	3E 88.9 (1457)	3.4	3.1	—	5.0	4.6	—	11.9	⑩
		3E-E 88.9 (1457)	3.4	3.1	—	5.0	4.6	—	11.9	5.9
	Corolla	4A-FE 97.0 (1587)	3.3	3.2	—	⑪	⑫	⑬	13.2	⑭
		4A-GE 97.0 (1587)	3.4	3.6	—	⑪	⑫	⑬	13.2	⑭
	Camry	3S-FE 121.9 (1998)	4.1	3.9	—	⑮	⑯	⑰	15.9	⑱
		2VZ-FE 132.0 (2508)	4.1	3.9	—	⑮	⑯	⑰	15.9	10.0
	Celica	4A-FE 97.0 (1587)	3.3	3.1	—	5.4	7.0	—	15.9	㉑
		3S-GTE 121.9 (1998)	3.8	3.5	—	10.2	—	2.4	15.9	6.8
		5S-FE 132.0 (2164)	⑲	⑳	—	5.4	7.0	—	15.9	㉒

CAPACITIES

Year	Model	Engine Displacement cu. in. (cc)	Engine Crankcase (qts.) with Filter	without Filter	Transmission (pts.) 4-spd	5-Spd	Auto.	Drive Axle (pts.)	Fuel Tank (gal.)	Cooling System (qts.)
1990–91	Supra	7M-GE 180.3 (2954)	4.7	4.3	—	5.0	3.4	1.8	18.5	8.6
		7M-GTE 180.3 (2954)	4.7	4.3	—	6.4	3.4	2.8	18.5	8.7
	MR2	3S-GTE 121.9 (1998)	4.1	3.8	—	5.4	7.0	—	10.8	14.4
		5S-FE 132.0 (2164)	4.4	4.0	—	8.8	7.0	—	10.8	13.7
	Cressida	180.3 (2954)	4.3	4.7	—	—	3.4	—	18.5	8.8

① 4wd: 8.2
② 4wd: 8.8
③ Station wagon: 12.4
④ 1987: FWD—6.3; RWD MT—5.9, AT—5.8
⑤ Station wagon: 3.0
⑥ A240E, A241H: 6.6
   A131L: 5.2
⑦ 4wd rear diff.: 2.4
⑧ C52: 5.4; E51: 8.8
⑨ 42d: 10.4
⑩ M/T: 5.5
   M/T (EL31L-NGKB5A) 5.3
   A/T: 5.4
⑪ C50, C52: 5.4
   All-trac (E5SFS, ES7F5): 10.6

⑫ AL131L: 5.2
   A240L: 6.6
   A241H: 6.6
⑬ Transfer (A241H A/T only): 3.0
   Rear differential: 2.4
⑭ M/T (except AE29L-ACMXRR): 5.9
   M/T (AE29L-ACMXKK): 6.6
   A/T: 6.4
⑮ S51: 5.4
   ES6FS: 10.6
   ES2: 8.8
⑯ A140L, A140E, A540E: 5.2
   A540H: 7.0

⑰ Differential
   SV21 A/T: 3.4
   VZV21 A/T: 2.1
   Transfer (A540H only): 1.48
⑱ M/T: 6.8
   A/T (2WD): 6.7
   A/T (4WD): 7.2
⑲ w/oil cooler: 4.4
   w/out oil cooler: 4.3
⑳ w/oil cooler: 4.0
   w/out oil cooler: 3.9
㉑ M/T: 5.5
   A/T: 5.8
㉒ M/T: 6.6
   A/T: 6.4

CAMSHAFT SPECIFICATIONS
All measurements given in inches.

Year	Engine Displacement cu. in. (cc)	Journal Diameter 1	2	3	4	5	6	7	Bearing Clearance	Camshaft End Play
1987	3A-C 88.6 (1452)	1.1015–1.1022	1.1015–1.1022	0.1015–1.1022	0.1015–1.1022	—	—	—	0.0015–0.0029	0.0031–0.0071
	3E 88.9 (1456)	1.0622–1.0628	1.0622–1.0628	1.0622–1.0628	1.0622–1.0628	—	—	—	0.0015–0.0029	0.0031–0.0071
	4A-LC 97.0 (1587)	1.1015–1.1022	1.1015–1.1022	0.1015–1.1022	0.1015–1.1022	—	—	—	0.0015–0.0029	0.0031–0.0071
	4A-GEC, 4A-GELC 97.0 (1587)	1.0610–1.0616	1.0610–1.0616	1.0610–1.0616	1.0610–1.0616	—	—	—	0.0014–0.0028	0.0031–0.0075
	3S-FE 121.9 (1998)	1.0614–1.0620	1.0614–1.0620	1.0614–1.0620	1.0614–1.0620	—	—	—	0.0010–0.0024	0.0018–0.0039
	3S-GE 121.9 (1998)	1.0614–1.0620	1.0614–1.0620	1.0614–1.0620	1.0614–1.0620	—	—	—	0.0010–0.0024	0.0047–0.0079
	5M-GE 168.4 (2759)	1.4944–1.4951	1.6913–1.6919	1.7110–1.7116	1.7307–1.7313	1.7504–1.7510	1.7700–1.7707	1.7897–1.7904	0.0010–0.0026	0.0028–0.0098
	7M-GE, 7M-GTE 180.3 (2954)	1.0610–1.0616	1.0586–1.0620	1.0586–1.0620	1.0586–1.0620	1.0586–1.0620	1.0586–1.0620	1.0586–1.0620	0.0010–0.0037 ①	0.0031–0.0075
1988	3A-C 88.6 (1452)	1.1015–1.1022	1.1015–1.1022	0.1015–1.1022	0.1015–1.1022	—	—	—	0.0015–0.0029	0.0031–0.0071
	3E 88.9 (1456)	1.0622–1.0628	1.0622–1.0628	1.0622–1.0628	1.0622–1.0628	—	—	—	0.0015–0.0029	0.0031–0.0071
	4A-F 97.0 (1587)	0.9035–0.9041 ③	0.9035–0.9041	0.9035–0.9041	0.9035–0.9041	—	—	—	0.0015–0.0028	②

CAMSHAFT SPECIFICATIONS

All measurements given in inches.

Year	Engine Displacement cu. in. (cc)	Journal Diameter							Bearing Clearance	Camshaft End Play
		1	2	3	4	5	6	7		
1988	4A-LC 97.0 (1587)	1.1015– 1.1022	1.1015– 1.1022	0.1015– 1.1022	0.1015– 1.1022	—	—	—	0.0015– 0.0029	0.0031– 0.0071
	4A-GZE, 4A-GEC, 4A-GELC 97.0 (1587)	1.0610– 1.0616	1.0610– 1.0616	1.0610– 1.0616	1.0610– 1.0616	—	—	—	0.0014– 0.0028	0.0031– 0.0075
	3S-FE 121.9 (1998)	1.0614– 1.0620	1.0614– 1.0620	1.0614– 1.0620	1.0614– 1.0620	—	—	—	0.0010– 0.0024	0.0018– 0.0039
	3S-GE, 3S-GTE 121.9 (1998)	1.0614– 1.0620	1.0614– 1.0620	1.0614– 1.0620	1.0614– 1.0620	—	—	—	0.0010– 0.0024	0.0047– 0.0079 ④
	5M-GE 168.4 (2759)	1.4944– 1.4951	1.6913– 1.6919	1.7110– 1.7116	1.7307– 1.7313	1.7504– 1.7510	1.7700– 1.7707	1.7897– 1.7904	0.0010– 0.0026	0.0028– 0.0098
	7M-GE, 7M-GTE 180.3 (2954)	1.0610– 1.0616	1.0586– 1.0620	1.0586– 1.0620	1.0586– 1.0620	1.0586– 1.0620	1.0586– 1.0620	1.0586– 1.0620	0.0010– 0.0037 ①	0.0031– 0.0075
1989	3E 88.9 (1456)	1.0622– 1.0628	1.0622– 1.0628	1.0622– 1.0628	1.0622– 1.0628	—	—	—	0.0015– 0.0029	0.0031– 0.0071
	4A-F, 4A-FE 97.0 (1587)	0.9035– 0.9041 ③	0.9035– 0.9041	0.9035– 0.9041	0.9035– 0.9041	—	—	—	0.0015– 0.0028	②
	4A-GZE, 4A-GEC, 4A-GELC 97.0 (1587)	1.0610– 1.0616	1.0610– 1.0616	1.0610– 1.0616	1.0610– 1.0616	—	—	—	0.0014– 0.0028	0.0031– 0.0075
	3S-FE 121.9 (1998)	1.0614– 1.0620	1.0614– 1.0620	1.0614– 1.0620	1.0614– 1.0620	—	—	—	0.0010– 0.0024	0.0018– 0.0039
	3S-GE, 3S-GTE 121.9 (1998)	1.0614– 1.0620	1.0614– 1.0620	1.0614– 1.0620	1.0614– 1.0620	—	—	—	0.0010– 0.0024	0.0047– 0.0114
	2VZ-FE 153.0 (2507)	1.0610– 1.0616	1.0610– 1.0616	1.0610– 1.0616	1.0610– 1.0616	1.0610– 1.0616	—	—	0.0014– 0.0028	0.0012– 0.0031
	7M-GE, 7M-GTE 180.3 (2954)	1.0610– 1.0616	1.0586– 1.0620	1.0586– 1.0620	1.0586– 1.0620	1.0586– 1.0620	1.0586– 1.0620	1.0586– 1.0620	0.0010– 0.0037 ①	0.0031– 0.0075
1990–91	3E, 3E-E 88.9 (1457)	1.0622– 1.0628	1.0622– 1.0628	1.0622– 1.0628	1.0622– 1.0628	—	—	—	0.0015– 0.0029	0.0031– 0.0071
	4A-FE 97.0 (1587)	0.9035– 0.9041 ③	0.9035– 0.9041	0.9035– 0.9041	0.9035– 0.9041	—	—	—	0.0014– 0.0028	②
	4A-GE 97.0 (1587)	1.0610– 1.0616	1.0610– 1.0616	1.0610– 1.0616	1.0610– 1.0616	—	—	—	0.0014– 0.0028	0.0031– 0.0075
	3S-FE 121.9 (1998)	1.0614– 1.0620	1.0614– 1.0620	1.0614– 1.0620	1.0614– 1.0620	—	—	—	0.0010– 0.0024	⑤
	3S-GTE 121.9 (1998)	1.0614– 1.0620	1.0614– 1.0620	1.0614– 1.0620	1.0614– 1.0620	—	—	—	0.0010– 0.0024	0.0047– 0.0114
	5S-FE 132.0 (2164)	1.0614– 1.0620	1.0614– 1.0620	1.0614– 1.0620	1.0614– 1.0620	—	—	—	0.0010– 0.0024	⑤
	2VZ-FE 153.0 (2507)	1.0610– 1.0616	1.0610– 1.0616	1.0610– 1.0616	1.0610– 1.0616	1.0610– 1.0616	—	—	0.0014– 0.0028	0.0012– 0.0031
	7M-GE, 7M-GTE 180.3 (2954)	1.0610– 1.0616	1.0586– 1.0620	1.0586– 1.0620	1.0586– 1.0620	1.0586– 1.0620	1.0586– 1.0620	1.0586– 1.0620	0.0010– 0.0037 ①	0.0031– 0.0075

① No. 1: 0.0014–0.0028
② Intake: 0.0012–0.0033
   Exhaust: 0.0014–0.0035
③ Exhaust No. 1: 0.9822–0.9829
④ 35-GTE: 0.0039–0.0094
⑤ Intake: 0.0018–0.0039
   Exhaust: 0.0012–0.0033

CRANKSHAFT AND CONNECTING ROD SPECIFICATIONS

All measurements are given in inches.

Year	Engine Displacement cu. in. (cc)	Crankshaft				Connecting Rod		
		Main Brg. Journal Dia.	Main Brg. Oil Clearance	Shaft End-play	Thrust on No.	Journal Diameter	Oil Clearance	Side Clearance
1987	3A-C 88.6 (1452)	1.8891–1.8898	0.0006–0.0013	0.0008–0.0087	3	1.5742–1.5748	0.0008–0.0020	0.0059–0.0098
	3E 88.9 (1456)	1.9683–1.9685	0.0006–0.0014	0.0008–0.0087	3	1.8110–1.8113	0.0006–0.0019	0.0059–0.0138
	3S-FE, 3S-GE 121.9 (1998)	2.1648–2.1653	0.0007–0.0015①	0.0008–0.0087	3	1.8892–1.8898	0.0009–0.0022	0.0063–0.0123
	4A-LC 97.0 (1587)	1.8891–1.8898	0.0006–0.0013	0.0008–0.0087	3	1.5742–1.5748	0.0008–0.0020	0.0059–0.0098
	4A-GEC, 4A-GELC 97.0 (1587)	1.8891–1.8898	0.0005–0.0015	0.0008–0.0087	3	1.5742–1.5748	0.0008–0.0020	0.0059–0.0098
	5M-GE 168.4 (2759)	2.3625–2.3627	0.0012–0.0048	0.0020–0.0098	4	2.1659–2.1663	0.0008–0.0021	0.0063–0.0117
	7M-GE, 7M-GTE 180.3 (2954)	2.3625–2.3627	0.0012–0.0022	0.0020–0.0098	4	2.1659–2.1663	0.0012–0.0019	0.0063–0.0117
1988	3A-C 88.6 (1452)	1.8891–1.8898	0.0006–0.0013	0.0008–0.0087	3	1.5742–1.5748	0.0008–0.0020	0.0059–0.0098
	3E 88.9 (1456)	1.9683–1.9685	0.0006–0.0014	0.0008–0.0087	3	1.8110–1.8113	0.0006–0.0019	0.0059–0.0138
	3S-FE, 3S-GE, 3S-GTE 121.9 (1998)	2.1648–2.1653	0.0007–0.0015①	0.0008–0.0087	3	1.8892–1.8898	0.0009–1.0022	0.0063–0.0123
	4A-F, 4A-LC 97.0 (1587)	1.8891–1.8898	0.0006–0.0013	0.0008–0.0087	3	1.5742–1.5748	0.0008–0.0020	0.0059–0.0098
	4A-GEC, 4A-GELC 97.0 (1587)	1.8891–1.8898	0.0005–0.0015	0.0008–0.0087	3	1.5742–1.5748	0.0008–0.0020	0.0059–0.0098
	4A-GZE 97.0 (1587)	1.8891–1.8898	0.0006–0.0013	0.0008–0.0087	3	1.6529–1.6535	0.0008–0.0020	0.0059–0.0098
	5M-GE 168.4 (2759)	2.3625–2.3627	0.0012–0.0048	0.0020–0.0098	4	2.1659–2.1663	0.0008–0.0021	0.0063–0.0117
	7M-GE, 7M-GTE 180.3 (2954)	2.3625–2.3627	0.0012–0.0048	0.0020–0.0098	4	2.1659–2.1663	0.0008–0.0021	0.0063–0.0117
1989	3E 88.9 (1456)	1.9683–1.9685	0.0006–0.0014	0.0008–0.0087	3	1.8110–1.8113	0.0006–0.0019	0.0059–0.0138
	3S-FE, 3S-GE, 3S-GTE 121.9 (1998)	2.1649–2.1655	0.0006–0.0013①	0.0008–0.0087	3	1.8892–1.8898	0.0009–0.0022	0.0063–0.0123
	4A-F, 4A-FE 97.0 (1587)	1.8891–1.8898	0.0006–0.0013	0.0008–0.0087	3	1.5742–1.5748	0.0008–0.0020	0.0059–0.0098
	4A-GEC, 4A-GELC 97.0 (1587)	1.8891–1.8898	0.0006–0.0013	0.0008–0.0087	3	1.6529–1.6535	0.0008–0.0020	0.0059–0.0098
	4A-GZE 97.0 (1587)	1.8891–1.8898	0.0006–0.0013	0.0008–0.0087	3	1.6529–1.6535	0.0008–0.0020	0.0059–0.0098
	2VZ-FE 153.0 (2507)	2.5191–2.5197	0.0011–0.0022	0.0008–0.0087	3	1.8892–1.8898	0.0011–0.0026	0.0059–0.0130
	7M-GE, 7M-GTE 180.3 (2954)	2.3625–2.3627	0.0012–0.0019	0.0020–0.0098	4	2.1659–2.1663	0.0008–0.0021	0.0063–0.0117

CRANKSHAFT AND CONNECTING ROD SPECIFICATIONS

All measurements are given in inches.

| Year | Engine Displacement cu. in. (cc) | Crankshaft | | | | Connecting Rod | | |
		Main Brg. Journal Dia.	Main Brg. Oil Clearance	Shaft End-play	Thrust on No.	Journal Diameter	Oil Clearance	Side Clearance
1990–91	3E, 3E-E 88.9 (1457)	1.9683–1.9685	0.0006–0.0014	0.0008–0.0087	3	1.8110–1.8113	0.0006–0.0019	0.0059–0.0138
	4A-FE 97.0 (1587)	1.8891–1.8898	0.0006–0.0013	0.0008–0.0087	3	1.5742–1.5748	0.0008–0.0020	0.0059–0.0098
	4A-GE 97.0 (1587)	1.8891–1.8898	0.0006–0.0013	0.0008–0.0087	3	1.6529–1.6535	0.0008–0.0020	0.0059–0.0098
	3S-FE 121.9 (1998)	2.1649–2.1655	0.0010–0.0017	0.0008–0.0087	3	1.8892–1.8898	0.0009–0.0022	0.0063–0.0123
	3S-GTE 121.9 (1998)	2.1653–2.1655	0.0006–0.0013①	0.0008–0.0087	3	1.8892–1.8898	0.0009–0.0022	0.0063–0.0123
	5S-FE 132.0 (2164)	2.1653–2.1655	0.0006–0.0013①	0.0008–0.0087	3	1.8892–1.8898	0.0009–0.0022	0.0063–0.0123
	2VZ-FE 153.0 (2507)	2.5191–2.5197	0.0011–0.0022	0.0008–0.0087	3	1.8892–1.8898	0.0011–0.0026	0.0059–0.0123
	7M-GE, 7M-GTE 180.3 (2954)	2.3625–2.3627	0.0012–0.0019	0.0020–0.0098	4	2.0470–2.0474	0.0008–0.0021	0.0063–0.0117

① No. 3: 0.0012–0.0022 (1987)
 No. 3: 0.0011–0.0019 (1988)
 No. 3: 0.0010–0.0017 (1989–91)

VALVE SPECIFICATIONS

| Year | Engine Displacement cu. in. (cc) | Seat Angle (deg.) | Face Angle (deg.) | Spring Test Pressure (lbs.) | Spring Installed Height (in.) | Stem-to-Guide Clearance (in.) | | Stem Diameter (in.) | |
						Intake	Exhaust	Intake	Exhaust
1987	3A-C 88.6 (1452)	45	44.5	52.0	1.520	0.0010–0.0024	0.0012–0.0026	0.2744–0.2750	0.2742–0.2748
	3E 88.9 (1456)	45	44.5	35.1	1.384	0.0010–0.0024	0.0012–0.0026	0.2350–0.2356	0.2348–0.2354
	3S-FE 121.9 (1998)	45.5	44.5	39.6	1.366	0.0010–0.0024	0.0012–0.0026	0.2350–0.2356	0.2348–0.2354
	3S-GE 121.9 (1998)	45.5	44.5	38.6	1.366	0.0010–0.0023	0.0012–0.0025	0.2346–0.2352	0.2344–0.2350
	4A-LC 97.0 (1587)	45	44.5	52.0	1.520	0.0010–0.0024	0.0012–0.0026	0.2744–0.2750	0.2742–0.2748
	4A-GEC, 4A-GELC 97.0 (1587)	45	44.5	35.9	1.366	0.0010–0.0024	0.0012–0.0026	0.2350–0.2356	0.2348–0.2354
	5M-GE 168.4 (2759)	45	44.5	①	②	0.0010–0.0024	0.0012–0.0026	0.3138–0.3144	0.3136–0.3142
	7M-GE, 7M-GTE 180.3 (2954)	45	44.5	35.0	1.378	0.0010–0.0024	0.0012–0.0026	0.2350–0.2356	0.2348–0.2354
1988	3A-C 88.6 (1452)	45	44.5	52.0	1.520	0.0010–0.0024	0.0012–0.0026	0.2744–0.2750	0.2742–0.2748
	3E 88.9 (1456)	45	44.5	35.1	1.384	0.0010–0.0024	0.0012–0.0026	0.2350–0.2356	0.2348–0.2354
	3S-FE 121.9 (1998)	45.5	44.5	39.6	1.366	0.0010–0.0024	0.0012–0.0026	0.2350–0.2356	0.2348–0.2354
	3S-GE, 3S-GTE 121.9 (1998)	45.5	44.5	38.6③	1.366	0.0010–0.0023	0.0012–0.0025	0.2346–0.2352	0.2344–0.2350

VALVE SPECIFICATIONS

Year	Engine Displacement cu. in. (cc)	Seat Angle (deg.)	Face Angle (deg.)	Spring Test Pressure (lbs.)	Spring Installed Height (in.)	Stem-to-Guide Clearance (in.)		Stem Diameter (in.)	
						Intake	Exhaust	Intake	Exhaust
1988	4A-F 97.0 (1587)	45	44.5	34.8	1.366	0.0010–0.0024	0.0012–0.0026	0.2350–0.2356	0.2348–0.2354
	4A-LC 97.0 (1587)	45	44.5	52.0	1.520	0.0010–0.0024	0.0012–0.0026	0.2744–0.2750	0.2742–0.2748
	4A-GEC, 4A-GELC 4A-GZE 97.0 (1587)	45	44.5	35.9	1.366	0.0010–0.0024	0.0012–0.0026	0.2350–0.2356	0.2348–0.2354
	5M-GE 168.4 (2759)	45	44.5	①	②	0.0010–0.0024	0.0012–0.0026	0.3138–0.3144	0.3136–0.3142
	7M-GE, 7M-GTE 180.3 (2954)	45	44.5	35.0	1.378	0.0010–0.0024	0.0012–0.0026	0.2350–0.2356	0.2348–0.2354
1989	3E 88.9 (1456)	45	44.5	35.1	1.384	0.0010–0.0024	0.0012–0.0026	0.2350–0.2356	0.2348–0.2354
	3S-FE 121.9 (1998)	45.5	44.5	39.6	1.366	0.0010–0.0024	0.0012–0.0026	0.2350–0.2356	0.2348–0.2354
	3S-GE, 3S-GTE 121.9 (1998)	45.5	44.5	38.6 ③	1.366	0.0010–0.0023	0.0012–0.0025	0.2346–0.2352	0.2344–0.2350
	4A-F, 4A-FE 97.0 (1587)	45	44.5	34.8	1.366	0.0010–0.0024	0.0012–0.0026	0.2350–0.2356	0.2348–0.2354
	4A-GEC, 4A-GZE 97.0 (1587)	45	44.5	34.7	1.366	0.0010–0.0024	0.0012–0.0026	0.2350–0.2356	0.2348–0.2354
	2VZ-FE 153.0 (2507)	45	44.5	41.0–47.2	1.331	0.0010–0.0024	0.0012–0.0026	0.2350–0.2356	0.2348–0.2354
	7M-GE, 7M-GTE 180.3 (2954)	45	44.5	35.0	1.378	0.0010–0.0024	0.0012–0.0026	0.2350–0.2356	0.2348–0.2354
1990-91	3E, 3E-E 88.9 (1457)	45	45.5	35.1	1.3842	0.0010–0.0024	0.0012–0.0026	0.2350–0.2356	0.2348–0.2354
	4A-FE 97.0 (1587)	45	45.5	34.8	1.366	0.0010–0.0024	0.0012–0.0026	0.2350–0.2356	0.2348–0.2354
	4A-GE 97.0 (1587)	45	45.5	35.9	1.366	0.0010–0.0024	0.0012–0.0026	0.2350–0.2356	0.2348–0.2354
	3S-FE 121.9 (1998)	45	45.5	42.5	1.366	0.0010–0.0024	0.0012–0.0026	0.2350–0.2356	0.2348–0.2354
	3S-GTE 121.9 (1998)	45	45.5	53.1	1.354	0.0010–0.0023	0.0012–0.0025	0.2346–0.2352	0.2344–0.2350
	5S-FE 132.0 (2164)	45	45.5	42.5	1.366	0.0010–0.0024	0.0012–0.0026	0.2350–0.2356	0.2356–0.2354
	2VZ-FE 153.0 (2507)	45	45.5	47.2	1.331	0.0010–0.0024	0.0012–0.0026	0.2350–0.2356	0.2348–0.2354
	7M-GE, 7M-GTE 180.3 (2954)	45	45.5	35	1.378	0.0010–0.0024	0.0012–0.0026	0.2350–0.2356	0.2348–0.2354

① Intake: 76.5–84.4; Exhaust: 73.4–80.9
② Intake: 1.575; Exhaust: 1.693
③ 3S-GTE: 44.1

PISTON AND RING SPECIFICATIONS

All measurements are given in inches.

Year	Engine Displacement cu. in. (cc)	Piston Clearance	Ring Gap			Ring Side Clearance		Oil Control
			Top Compression	Bottom Compression	Oil Control	Top Compression	Bottom Compression	
1987	3A-C 88.6 (1452)	0.0039–0.0047	0.0079–0.0185	0.0079–0.0204	0.0118–0.0402	0.0016–0.0031	0.0012–0.0028	Snug
	3E 88.9 (1456)	0.0028–0.0035	0.0102–0.0142	0.0118–0.0177	0.0059–0.0157	0.0016–0.0031	0.0012–0.0028	Snug
	3S-FE 121.9 (1998)	0.0018–0.0026	0.0106–0.0193	0.0106–0.0197	0.0079–0.0323	0.0012–0.0028	0.0012–0.0028	Snug
	3S-GE 121.9 (1998)	0.0012–0.0020	0.0130–0.0213	0.0079–0.0173	0.0079–0.0350	0.0012–0.0028	0.0008–0.0024	Snug
	4A-LC 97.0 (1587)	0.0035–0.0043	0.0098–0.0138	0.0059–0.0165	0.0078–0.0276	0.0016–0.0031	0.0012–0.0028	Snug
	4A-GEC, 4A-GELC 97.0 (1587)	0.0039–0.0047	0.0098–0.0138	0.0078–0.0118	0.0078–0.0276	0.0016–0.0031	0.0012–0.0028	Snug
	5M-GE 168.4 (2759)	0.0024–0.0031	0.0091–0.0150	0.0098–0.0209	0.0040–0.0201	0.0012–0.0028	0.0008–0.0024	Snug
	7M-GE 180.3 (2954)	0.0024–0.0031	0.0091–0.0150	0.0098–0.0209	0.0039–0.0201	0.0012–0.0028	0.0008–0.0024	Snug
	7M-GTE 180.3 (2954)	0.0028–0.0035	0.0114–0.0173	0.0098–0.0209	0.0039–0.0220	0.0012–0.0028	0.0008–0.0024	Snug
1988	3A-C 88.6 (1452)	0.0039–0.0047	0.0079–0.0185	0.0079–0.0204	0.0118–0.0402	0.0016–0.0031	0.0012–0.0028	Snug
	3E 88.9 (1456)	0.0028–0.0035	0.0102–0.0142	0.0118–0.0177	0.0059–0.0157	0.0016–0.0031	0.0012–0.0028	Snug
	3S-FE 121.9 (1998)	0.0018–0.0026	0.0106–0.0205	0.0106–0.0209	0.0079–0.0323	0.0018–0.0028	0.0018–0.0028	Snug
	3S-GE 121.9 (1998)	0.0012–0.0020	0.0130–0.0264	0.0177–0.0323	0.0079–0.0283	0.0012–0.0028	0.0008–0.0024	Snug
	3S-GTE 121.9 (1998)	0.0012–0.0020	0.0130–0.0224	0.0177–0.0272	0.0079–0.0244	0.0015–0.0031	0.0012–0.0028	Snug
	4A-F 97.0 (1587)	0.0024–0.0031	0.0098–0.0138	0.0059–0.0118	0.0039–0.0236	0.0016–0.0031	0.0012–0.0028	Snug
	4A-LC 97.0 (1587)	0.0035–0.0043	0.0098–0.0138	0.0059–0.0165	0.0078–0.0276	0.0016–0.0031	0.0012–0.0028	Snug
	4A-GEC, 4A-GELC, 4A-GZE 97.0 (1587)	0.0039–0.0047①	0.0098–0.0185	0.0078–0.0118	②	0.0016–0.0031	0.0012–0.0028	Snug
	5M-GE 168.4 (2759)	0.0024–0.0031	0.0091–0.0150	0.0098–0.0209	0.0040–0.0201	0.0012–0.0028	0.0008–0.0024	Snug
	7M-GE 180.3 (2954)	0.0020–0.0028	0.0091–0.0150	0.0098–0.0209	0.0039–0.0157	0.0012–0.0028	0.0008–0.0024	Snug
	7M-GTE 180.3 (2954)	0.0028–0.0035	0.0114–0.0173	0.0098–0.0209	0.0039–0.0173	0.0012–0.0028	0.0008–0.0024	Snug
1989	3E 88.9 (1456)	0.0028–0.0035	0.0102–0.0142	0.0118–0.0177	0.0059–0.0157	0.0016–0.0031	0.0012–0.0028	Snug
	3S-FE 121.9 (1998)	0.0018–0.0026	0.0106–0.0197	0.0106–0.0201	0.0079–0.0217	0.0012–0.0028	0.0012–0.0028	Snug
	3S-GE 121.9 (1998)	0.0012–0.0020	0.0130–0.0217	0.0177–0.0276	0.0079–0.0236	0.0012–0.0028	0.0008–0.0024	Snug
	3S-GTE 121.9 (1998)	0.0012–0.0020	0.0130–0.0217	0.0177–0.0264	0.0079–0.0236	0.0015–0.0031	0.0012–0.0028	Snug

PISTON AND RING SPECIFICATIONS

All measurements are given in inches.

Year	Engine Displacement cu. in. (cc)	Piston Clearance	Ring Gap Top Compression	Ring Gap Bottom Compression	Ring Gap Oil Control	Ring Side Clearance Top Compression	Ring Side Clearance Bottom Compression	Ring Side Clearance Oil Control
1989	4A-F 97.0 (1587)	0.0024–0.0031	0.0098–0.0138	0.0059–0.0118	0.0039–0.0236	0.0016–0.0031	0.0012–0.0028	Snug
	4A-FE 97.0 (1587)	0.0024–0.0031	0.0098–0.0138	0.0059–0.0118	0.0039–0.0236	0.0020–0.0031	0.0012–0.0028	Snug
	4A-GEC, 4A-GELC, 4A-GZE 97.0 (1587)	0.0039–0.0047 ①	0.0098–0.0185	0.0079–0.0165	②	0.0016–0.0031	0.0012–0.0028	Snug
	2VZ-FE 153.0 (2507)	0.0018–0.0026	0.0118–0.0205	0.0138–0.0236	0.0079–0.0217	0.0004–0.0031	0.0012–0.0028	Snug
	7M-GE 180.3 (2954)	0.0020–0.0028 ③	0.0091–0.0150	0.0098–0.0209	0.0039–0.0157	0.0012–0.0028	0.0008–0.0024	Snug
	7M-GTE 180.3 (2954)	0.0028–0.0035	0.0114–0.0173	0.0098–0.0209	0.0039–0.0173	0.0012–0.0028	0.0008–0.0024	Snug
1990–91	3E, 3E-E 88.9 (1457)	0.0028–0.0035	0.0102–0.0189	0.0118–0.0224	0.0059–0.0205	0.0016–0.0031	0.0012–0.0028	Snug
	4A-FE 97.0 (1587)	0.0024–0.0031	0.0098–0.0177	0.0059–0.0157	0.0039–0.0276	0.0016–0.0031	0.0012–0.0028	Snug
	4A-GE 97.0 (1587)	0.0039–0.0047	0.0098–0.0185	0.0079–0.0165	0.0059–0.0205	0.0012–0.0031	0.0012–0.0028	Snug
	3S-FE 121.9 (1998)	0.0018–0.0026	0.0118–0.0205	0.0138–0.0236	0.0079–0.0217	0.0004–0.0031	0.0012–0.0028	Snug
	3S-GTE 121.9 (1998)	0.0028–0.0035	0.0130–0.0217	0.0177–0.0264	0.0079–0.0236	0.0016–0.0031	0.0012–0.0028	Snug
	5S-FE 132.0 (2164)	0.0031–0.0039	0.0106–0.0197	0.0138–0.0234	0.0079–0.0217	0.0012–0.0028	0.0012–0.0028	Snug
	2VZ-FE 153.0 (2507)	0.0018–0.0026	0.0118–0.0205	0.0138–0.0236	0.0079–0.0217	0.0004–0.0031	0.0012–0.0028	Snug
	7M-GE 180.3 (2954)	0.0031–0.0039	0.0091–0.0150	0.0098–0.0209	0.0039–0.0157	0.0012–0.0028	0.0008–0.0024	Snug
	7M-GTE 180.3 (2954)	0.0028–0.0035	0.0114–0.0173	0.0098–0.0209	0.0039–0.0173	0.0008–0.0024	0.0008–0.0024	Snug

① 4A-GZE: 0.0047–0.0055
② Code T: 0.0059–0.0205
   Code R: 0.0118–0.0402
③ 1990 Supra: 0.0031–0.0039

TORQUE SPECIFICATIONS

All readings in ft. lbs.

Year	Engine Displacement cu. in. (cc)	Cylinder Head Bolts	Main Bearing Bolts	Rod Bearing Bolts	Crankshaft Pulley Bolts	Flywheel Bolts	Manifold Intake	Manifold Exhaust	Spark Plugs
1987	3A-C 88.6 (1452)	40–47	40–47	34–39	80–94	55–61	15–21	15–21	16–20
	3E 88.9 (1456)	④	40–47	27–31	105–117	60–70	11–17	33–42	11–15
	3S-FE 121.9 (1998)	45–50	40–45	33–38	78–82	70–75	11–17	27–33	11–15
	3S-GE 121.9 (1998)	38–42	40–45	44–50	78–82	①	12–16	30–34	11–15
	4A-LC 97.0 (1587)	40–47	40–47	32–40	80–94	55–61	15–21	15–21	16–20
	4A-GEC, 4A-GELC 97.0 (1587)	40–47	40–47	32–40	100–110	50–58	15–21	15–21	11–15
	5M-GE 168.4 (2759)	55–61	72–78	31–34	185–205	51–57	11–15	26–32	11–15
	7M-GE, 7M-GTE 180.2 (2954)	55–61	72–78	45–49	185–205	51–57	11–15	26–32	11–15
1988	3A-C 88.6 (1452)	40–47	40–47	34–39	80–94	55–61	15–21	15–21	16–20
	3E 88.9 (1456)	②	40–47	27–31	105–117	60–70	11–17	33–42	11–15
	3S-FE 121.9 (1998)	45–50	40–45	33–38	78–82	70–75	11–17	27–33	11–15
	3S-GE, 3S-GTE 121.9 (1998)	38–42	40–45	44–50	78–82	①	12–16	30–34 ③	11–15
	4A-F 97.0 (1587)	40–47	40–47	32–40	80–94	55–61	11–17	15–21	11–15
	4A-LC 97.0 (1587)	40–47	40–47	32–40	80–94	55–61	15–21	15–21	16–20
	4A-GEC, 4A-GELC 4A-GZE 97.0 (1587)	④	40–47	32–40	100–110	50–58	15–21	27–31	11–15
	5M-GE 168.4 (2759)	55–61	72–78	31–34	185–205	51–57	11–15	26–32	11–15
	7M-GE, 7M-GTE 180.2 (2954)	55–61	72–78	45–49	185–205	51–57	11–15	26–32	11–15
1989	3E 88.9 (1456)	②	40–47	27–31	105–117	60–70	11–17	33–42	11–15
	3S-FE 121.9 (1998)	45–50	40–45	33–38	78–82	70–75	11–17	27–33	11–15
	3S-GE, 3S-GTE 121.9 (1998)	38–42	40–45	44–50	78–82	①	12–16	30–34	11–15
	4A-F, 4A-FE 97.0 (1587)	40–47	40–47	32–40	80–94	55–61	11–17	15–21	11–15
	4A-GEC, 4A-GELC 4A-GZE 97.0 (1587)	②	40–47	④	95–105	50–58	18–22	27–31	11–15
	2VZ-FE 153.0 (2507)	②	43–47	16–20	176–186	58–64	11–15	26–32	11–15
	7M-GE, 7M-GTE 180.2 (2954)	55–61	72–78	45–49	185–205	51–57	11–15	26–32	11–15

TORQUE SPECIFICATIONS

All readings in ft. lbs.

Year	Engine Displacement cu. in. (cc)	Cylinder Head Bolts	Main Bearing Bolts	Rod Bearing Bolts	Crankshaft Pulley Bolts	Flywheel Bolts	Manifold Intake	Manifold Exhaust	Spark Plugs
1990–91	3E, 3E-E 88.9 (1457)	②	42	29	112	88	14	38	13
	4A-FE 97.0 (1587)	44	44	36	87	58	14	18	13
	4A-GE 97.0 (1587)	④	44	29	101	54	9	29	13
	3S-FE 121.9 (1998)	②	43	36	80	⑤	14	36	13
	3S-GTE 121.9 (1998)	⑥	43	49	80	80	14	38	13
	5S-FE 132.0 (2164)	⑥	43	⑦	80	⑤	14	36	13
	2VZ-FE 153.0 (2507)	②	⑧	⑨	181	61	13	13	13
	7M-GE, 7M-GTE 180.3 (2954)	58	75	47	195	54	13	29	13

① New: 65; Used: 63
② See text
③ 3S-GTE: 38
④ 29 ft. lbs. and an additional 90° turn
⑤ M/T: 65
 A/T: 61
⑥ 36 ft. lbs. and an additional 90° turn
⑦ 18 ft. lbs. and an additional 90° turn
⑧ 45 ft. lbs. and an additional 90° turn

BRAKE SPECIFICATIONS

All measurements in inches unless noted.

Year	Model	Lug Nut Torque (ft. lbs.)	Master Cylinder Bore	Brake Disc Minimum Thickness	Brake Disc Maximum Runout	Standard Brake Drum Diameter	Minimum Lining Thickness Front	Minimum Lining Thickness Rear
1987	Tercel	65–86	①	0.394	0.006	7.126②	0.040	0.040
	Corolla	65–86	①	⑥	0.006	9.079⑤	0.040	0.040
	Camry	65–86	①	0.827	0.006	9.079	0.040	0.040
	Celica	65–86	①	0.827⑧	0.006	7.913	0.040	0.040
	Supra	65–86	①	0.827④	0.006	—	0.040	0.040
	MR2	65–86	①	0.827③	0.006	—	0.040	0.040
	Cressida	65–86	①	0.827⑦	0.006	9.079	0.040	0.040
1988	Tercel	65–86	①	0.394	0.006	7.126②	0.040	0.040
	Corolla	65–86	①	⑥	0.006	7.874	0.040	0.040
	Camry	65–86	①	0.945⑨	0.003	9.079	0.040	0.040
	Celica	65–86	①	0.827⑧	0.006	7.913	0.040	0.040
	Supra	65–86	①	0.827④	0.005	—	0.040	0.040
	MR2	65–86	①	0.827③	0.006	—	0.040	0.040
	Cressida	65–86	①	0.827④	0.006	—	0.040	0.040

BRAKE SPECIFICATIONS
All measurements in inches unless noted.

Year	Model	Lug Nut Torque (ft. lbs.)	Master Cylinder Bore	Brake Disc Minimum Thickness	Brake Disc Maximum Runout	Standard Brake Drum Diameter	Minimum Lining Thickness Front	Minimum Lining Thickness Rear
1989	Tercel	65–86	①	0.394	0.006	7.087②	0.040	0.040
	Corolla	65–86	①	⑥	0.004	7.874	0.040	0.040
	Camry	65–86	①	0.945⑨	0.003⑩	7.874	0.040	0.040
	Celica	65–86	①	0.827⑧	0.003	7.874	0.040	0.040
	Supra	65–86	①	0.827④	0.005	—	0.040	0.040
	MR2	65–86	①	0.827③	0.006	—	0.040	0.040
	Cressida	65–86	①	0.827④	0.003⑩	—	0.040	0.040
1990–91	Tercel	65–86	①	0.394	0.0059	7.087	0.394	0.039
	Corolla	65–86	①	⑪	⑫	7.874	0.039	0.039
	Camry	65–86	①	⑬	⑭	7.874	0.039	0.039
	Celica	65–86	①	⑮	⑭	7.874	0.039	0.039
	Supra	65–86	①	0.827⑧	0.005	—	0.039	0.039
	MR2	65–86	①	⑯	⑰	—	0.039	0.039
	Cressida	65–86	①	⑱	⑲	—	0.039	0.039

① Not specified by the manufacturer
② Wagon & 4wd: 7.913
③ Rear disc: 0.354
④ Rear disc: 0.669
⑤ FWD: 7.874
⑥ 1987 FWD (exc. FX16): 0.492
  1988–89 FWD & FX16: 0.669
  1987 RWD: 0.669
  1987 Rear disc: 0.315
  1988–89 Rear disc: 0.354
⑦ Rear disc: 1987—0.354

⑧ ABS or 4wd: 0.945
⑨ 4wd rear disc: 0.354
⑩ Rear disc: 0.006
⑪ Front:
  4A-FE—0.669
  4A-GE—0.827
  Rear: 0.315
⑫ Front disc: 0.0035
  Rear disc: 0.0039
⑬ Front: 0.945
  Rear: 0.354

⑭ Front: 0.0028
  Rear: 0.0059
⑮ Front: 0.787
  Rear: 0.354
⑯ Front: 0.945
  Rear: 0.591
⑰ Front: 0.0028
  Rear: 0.0039
⑱ Front: 0.827
  Rear: 0.669
⑲ Front: 0.0028
  Rear: 0.0052

WHEEL ALIGNMENT

Year	Model	Caster Range (deg.)	Caster Preferred Setting (deg.)	Camber Range (deg.)	Camber Preferred Setting (deg.)	Toe-in (in.)	Steering Axis Inclination (deg.)
1987	Tercel (Sedan)	⑭	⑮	3/4N–3/4P	0	0.08 out–0.08 in	12 1/2
	(Wagon)	①	②	3/4N–3/4P	0P	0.12 out–0.04 in	12 1/2
	(4WD)	1 1/16P–3 3/16P	2 1/4P	3/16N–1 5/16P	9/6P	0.12 out–0.04 in.	12
	Corolla (RWD)	⑫	⑬	1/2N–1P	1/4P	0.04 out–0.12 in	9
	(FWD)	1/8P–1 5/8P	7/8P	1N–1/2P	1/4N	0.04 out–0.12 in	12 1/2
	Camry (Sedan)	15/16P–2 7/16P	1 11/16P	3/16N–1 5/16P	9/16P	0.04 out–0.12 in	12 3/4
	(Wagon)	1/4P–1 3/4P	1P	1/4N–1 1/4P	1/2P	0.04 out–0.12 in	13
	Celica	7/16P–1 15/16P	1 3/16P	15/16N–9/16P	3/16N	0.08 out–0.08 in	13 1/2
	Supra	6 3/4P–8 1/4P	7 1/2P	13/16N–1 11/16P	1/16N	0.08 out–0.08 in	11
	MR2	4 15/16P–5 13/16P	5 1/16P	1/2N–1P	1/4P	0–0.08	12
	Cressida (Sedan)	4 1/16P–5 9/16P	4 13/16P	5/16N–1 3/16P	7/16P	0–0.16	10 1/2
	(Wagon)	3 1/2P–5P	4 1/4P	5/16N–1 3/16P	7/16P	0–0.16	10 1/2

WHEEL ALIGNMENT

Year	Model	Caster Range (deg.)	Caster Preferred Setting (deg.)	Camber Range (deg.)	Camber Preferred Setting (deg.)	Toe-in (in.)	Steering Axis Inclination (deg.)
1988	Tercel (Sedan)	③	⑨	3/4N–3/4P	0	0.08 out–0.08 in	11 1/2
	(Wagon)	1 11/16P–3 3/16P	2 1/4P	3/16N–1 5/16P	9/16P	0.12 out–0.04 in	12
	Corolla (FX/FX16)	1/8P–1 5/8P	7/8P	1N–1/2P	1/4N	0.04 out–0.12 in	12 1/2
	(4A-F)	⑤	⑥	15/16N–9/16P	3/16N	0–0.08	12 11/16
	(4A-GE)	9/16P–2 1/16P	1 5/16P	1N–1/2P	1/4N	0–0.08	12 13/16
	Camry (Sedan)	15/16P–2 7/16P	1 11/16P	3/16N–1 5/16P	9/16P	0.04 out–0.12 in	12 3/4
	(Wagon)	1/4P–1 3/4P	1P	1/4N–1 1/4P	1/2P	0.04 out–0.12 in	13
	Celica	7/16P–1 15/16P	1 3/16P	15/16N–9/16P	3/16N	0.08 out–0.08 in	13 1/2
	Supra	6 3/4P–8 1/4P	7 1/2P	13/16N–1 1/16P	1/16N	0.08 out–0.08 in	11
	MR2	4 15/16P–5 13/16P	5 1/16P	1/2N–1P	1/4P	0–0.08	12
	Cressida	4 1/16P–5 9/16P	4 13/16P	5/16N–1 3/16P	7/16P	0–0.16	10 1/2
1989	Tercel	③	④	3/4N–3/4P	0	0.08 out–0.08 in	11 1/2
	Corolla	③	⑥	15/16N–9/16P	3/16N	0–0.08	12 11/16
	(4A-GE)	9/16P–2 1/16P	1 5/16P	1N–1/2P	1/4N	0–0.08	12 13/16
	Camry (Sedan)	15/16P–2 7/16P	1 11/16P	3/16N–1 5/16P	9/16P	0.04 out–0.12 in	12 3/4
	(Wagon)	1/4P–1 3/4P	1P	1/4N–1 1/4P	1/2P	0.04 out–0.12 in	13
	Celica	7/16P–1 15/16P	1 3/16P	15/16N–9/16P	3/16N	0.08 out–0.08 in	13 1/2
	Supra	6 3/4P–8 1/4P	7 1/2P	13/16N–1 1/16P	1/16N	0.08 out–0.08 in	11
	MR2	4 15/16P–5 13/16P	5 1/16P	1/2N–1P	1/4P	0–0.08	12 1/16
	Cressida	4 1/16P–5 9/16P	4 13/16P	5/16N–1 3/16P	7/16P	0–0.16	10 1/2
1990-91	Tercel	③	④	3/4N–3/4P	0	0.08 out–0.08 in	11 1/2
	Corolla	9/16P–2 1/16P	1 5/16P	1N–1/2P	1/4N	0–5/32	12 13/16
	(4WD)	3/4P–1 3/4P	1 1/4P	5/16N–1 1/16P	3/16P	0–5/32	12
	Camry (Sedan)	1 3/16P–2 3/16P	1 11/16P	1/16N–1 1/16P	9/16P	0.04 out–0.04 in	12 3/4
	(Wagon)	1/2P–1 1/2P	1P	0–1P	1/2P	0.04 out–0.04 in.	12 13/16
	Celica	1/4P–1 3/4P	1P	15/16N–9/16P	3/16N	1/16–1/8	14 3/16
	Supra	7 3/16P–8 3/16P	7 11/16P	11/16N–5/16P	3/16N	3/64 out–3/64 in	10 15/16
	MR2	2P–13 1/4P	2 3/4P	1 13/32N–13/32N	1N	0.04 out–0.04 in	13
	Cressida	6 9/16P–8 1/16P	7 5/16P	0–1P	1/2P	3/32–1/4	13 3/16

① Man. Str.: 1/16N–1 1/3P
　Pwr. Str.: 1 1/4P–3P
② Man. Str.: 2/3P
　Pwr. Str.: 2 1/4P
③ Man. Str.: 1/4P–1 3/4P
　Pwr. Str.: 1 3/4–3 1/4P
④ Man. Str.: 1P
　Pwr. Str.: 2 1/2P
⑤ Exc. Coupe: 9/16P–2 1/16P
　Coupe: 3/4P–2 1/4P
⑥ Exc. Coupe: 1 5/16P
　Coupe: 1 1/2P

ENGINE ELECTRICAL

--- **CAUTION** ---

If equipped with an air bag, wait 20 seconds or longer after disconnecting the negative battery cable before attempting to remove or service any electrical component. The air bag control system is equipped with a back-up power source that remains charged for a minimum of 20 seconds after the negative battery cable is disconnected. Attempting to remove or service an electrical component without allowing the time interval to elapse may result in deployment of the air bag and possible personal injury.

NOTE: **Disconnecting the negative battery cable on some vehicles may interfere with the functions of the on board computer systems and may require the computer to undergo a relearning process, once the negative battery cable is reconnected.**

Distributor

Removal

5M-GE ENGINE (1987–88 CRESSIDA)

1. Disconnect the negative battery cable.
2. Disconnect the cables from the spark plugs, after marking the wiring order.
3. Disconnect the high tension cable from the coil.
4. Remove the primary wire and the vacuum line from the distributor.
5. Remove the distributor cap.
6. Matchmark the distributor housing and the engine block and the rotor to the distributor housing; this will aid in correct positioning of the distributor during installation.
7. Remove the clamp from the distributor.
8. Withdraw the distributor from the block.

EXCEPT 5M-GE ENGINE

1. Disconnect the negative battery cable.

--- **CAUTION** ---

If equipped with an air bag, wait 20 seconds or longer after disconnecting the negative battery cable before attempting to remove the distributor. The air bag control system is equipped with a back-up power source that remains charged for a minimum of 20 seconds after the negative battery cable is disconnected. Attempting to remove the distributor without allowing the time interval to elapse may result in deployment of the air bag and possible personal injury.

2. Disconnect the electrical leads and spark plug wires from the distributor.
3. Remove the water-proof cover, if installed.
4. On the Supra, with the 7M-GE engine, remove the oil filler cap and rotate the crankshaft clockwise until the nose of the camshaft is visible through the hole. Turn the crankshaft counterclockwise 120 degrees. Now, turn it clockwise 10–40 degrees until the TDC marks on the front cover and the crankshaft pulley are aligned.
5. Remove the intercooler on the 3S-GTE engine.
6. Matchmark the distributor housing and the engine block and the rotor to the distributor housing; this will aid in correct positioning of the distributor during installation.
7. Remove the hold-down bolts and pull the distributor from the engine.

Installation

TIMING NOT DISTURBED

5M-GE Engine (1987–88 Cressida)

1. Insert the distributor in the block and align the matchmarks.

2. Engage the distributor drive with the oil pump driveshaft; make sure the gear teeth mesh properly.
3. Install the distributor clamp, cap, high tension wire, primary wire and vacuum line.
4. Install the wires on the spark plugs.
5. Start the engine. Check the timing and adjust, as necessary.

Except 5M-GE Engine

1. Install a new distributor housing O-ring. Apply a thin coat of clean engine oil to the new O-ring before installation.
2. Insert the distributor in the block and align the matchmarks on the housing and the rotor made during removal.
3. Install the distributor hold-down bolts.
4. On 3S-GTE engine, install the intercooler.
4. Install the water-proof cover, if removed.
5. Connect the electrical leads and spark plug wires to the distributor.
6. Connect the negative battery cable.
7. Set the timing.

TIMING DISTURBED

5M-GE Engine (1987–88 Cressida)

1. Determine Top Dead Center (TDC) of the No. 1 cylinder's compression stroke by removing the spark plug from the No. 1 cylinder and placing a finger or a compression gauge over the spark plug hole. Crank the engine until compression pressure starts to build up. Continue cranking the engine until the timing marks indicate TDC or 0 degrees.
2. Remove the oil filler cap. Looking into the camshaft housing with the aid of a flashlight, check to make sure the match hole on the second (No. 2) journal of the camshaft housing is aligned with the hole in the No. 2 journal of the camshaft. If the holes are not aligned, rotate the camshaft 1 full turn.
3. Install a new O-ring on the distributor cap shaft; make sure the distributor cap is still removed at this time. Align the matchmark on the distributor drive gear with that of the distributor housing.
4. Insert the distributor into the camshaft housing, align the center of the mounting flange with the bolt hole in the side of the housing.
5. Align the rotor tooth in the distributor with the pickup coil. Temporarily install the distributor pinch bolt. Install the distributor cap and install the oil filler cap.

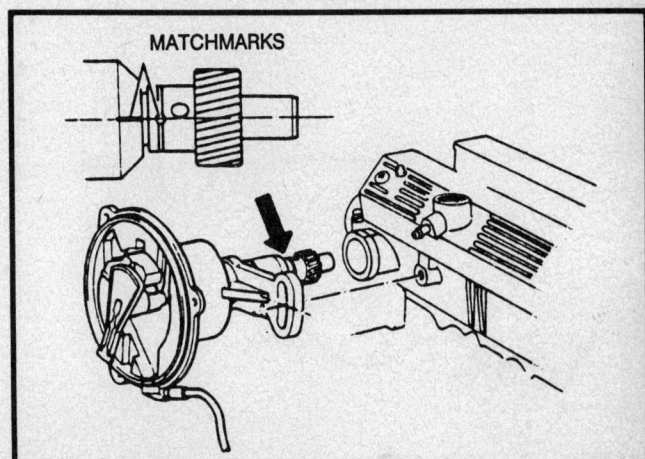

MATCHMARKS

Align the matchmarks on the distributor gear and housing—5M-GE engine

6. Connect the cables to the spark plugs in the proper order by using the marks made during removal. Install the high tension wire on the coil.

7. Start the engine. Adjust the ignition timing.

Except 5M-GE Engine

1. Set the engine at TDC of the No. 1 cylinder's firing stroke. This can be accomplished by removing the No. 1 spark plug and turning the engine by hand with a finger over the spark plug hole. As No. 1 is coming up on its firing stroke, pressure will be felt. Make sure the timing marks are set as follows:

a. On 4A-GE, 4A-GEC and 4A-GELC, align the groove on the crankshaft pulley with the 0 mark on the No. 1 timing cover.

b. For all, except the Supra (7M-GE), 1989–91 Cressida, MR2, Corolla (4A-GE) and Camry, coat the spiral gear and governor shaft tip with clean engine oil. Align the protrusion on the distributor housing with the pin on the spiral gear drill mark side. Insert the distributor and align the center of the flange with the bolt hole on the cylinder head. Tighten the bolts.

c. On the Supra (7M-GE) and 1989–91 Cressida, align the drilled mark on the driven gear with the groove on the distributor housing. Insert the distributor and align the stationary flange center with bolt hole in the head. Tighten the bolts.

d. On Celica and Camry, turn the crankshaft clockwise until the slot in the forward end of the No. 1 camshaft (front of vehicle) is positioned in the vertical position. Lightly coat a new O-ring with the engine oil and slide it into position. Align the drilled mark or cutout, on the coupling with the notch of the shaft housing. Insert the distributor into the cylinder head so the center of the flange is aligned with the bolt hole on the cylinder head.

e. On the MR2, except 5S-FE, and the Corolla GTS with 4A-GE, install a new O-ring. Align the drilled mark on the distributor driven gear with the cavity of the housing. On MR2 with 5S-FE, turn the crankshaft clockwise until the slot in the forward end of the No. 1 camshaft, front of vehicle, is positioned in the vertical position. Then, align the cutout portion of the coupling with the groove in the housing. Insert the distributor and align the center of the flange with the bolt hole on the cylinder head. Tighten the hold-down bolts.

f. On the Corolla (4A-F, 4A-FE), install a new O-ring. Align the protrusion on the distributor housing with the groove of the coupling side. On the 4A-FE, align the center of the flange

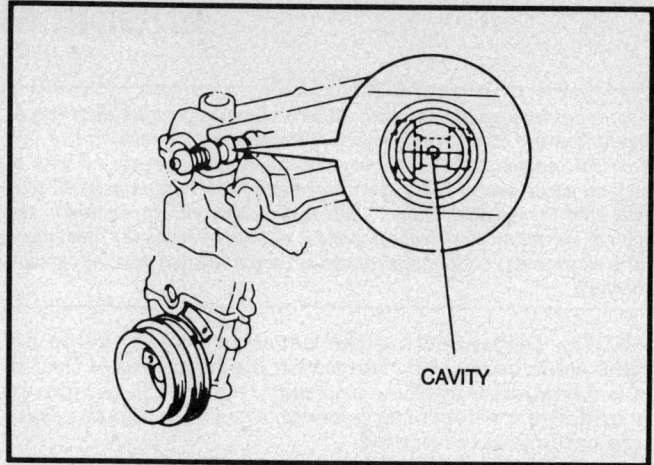

Setting the No. 1 cylinder to TDC of the compression stroke—4A-GE engine

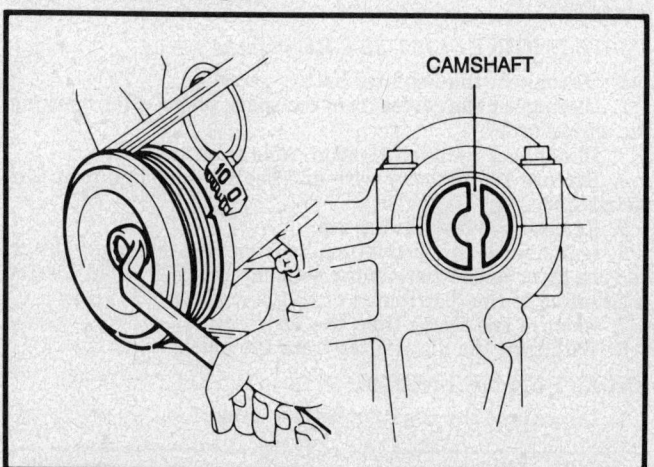

CAMSHAFT

Positioning the No. 1 camshaft—3S-FE, 3S-GE and 3S-GTE engines

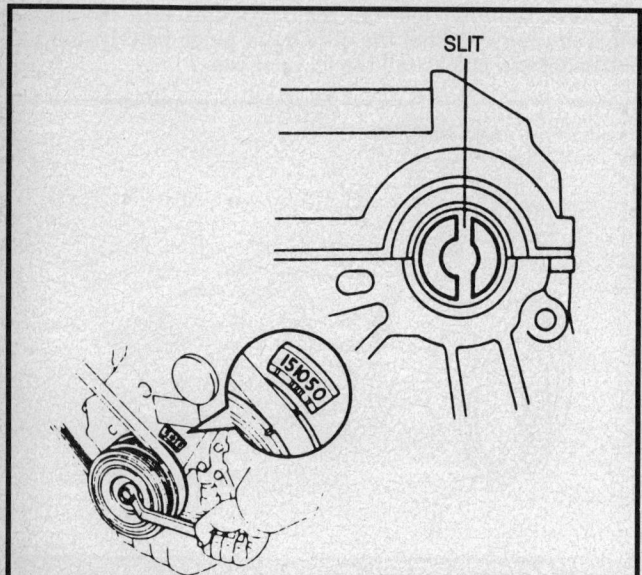

SLIT

Positioning the No. 1 camshaft—5S-FE engine

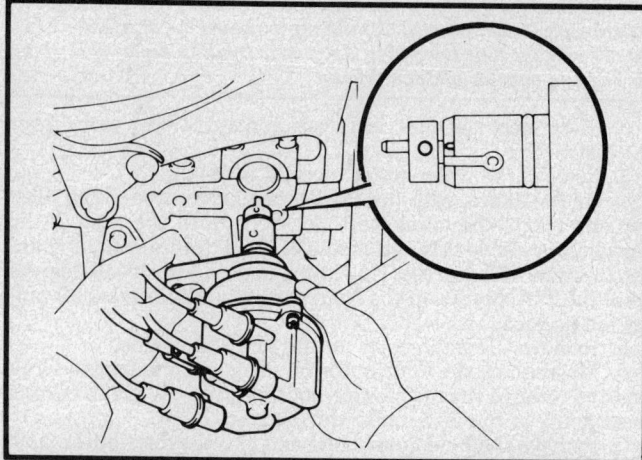

Distributor alignment—3S-FE and 3S-GE engines

with the bolt hole on the cylinder head. Tighten the hold-down bolts.

g. On Camry with 2VZ-FE, align the cut-out marks of the coupling and the housing and then insert the distributor so the line on the housing and the cut-out on the distributor attachment cap are aligned. Tighten the hold-down bolts.

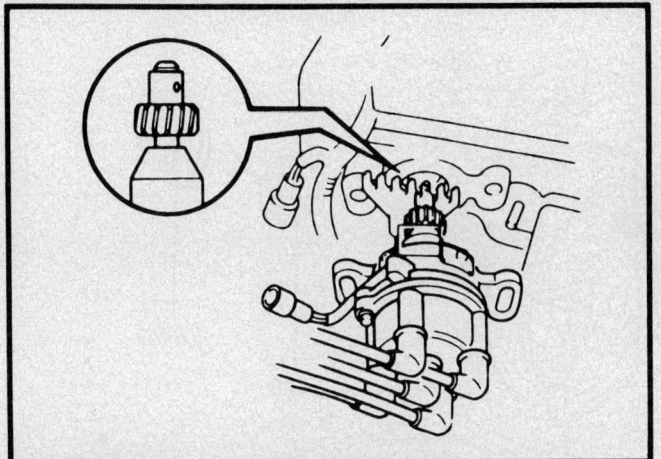

Align the drilled mark on the drive gear with the cavity of the housing—4A-GE engine

Position the camshaft slit as shown—4A-F engine

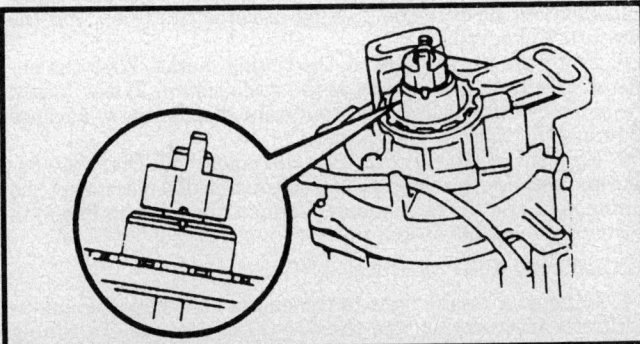

Align the marks on the coupling and the housing—2VZ-FE engine

2. Connect the spark plug wires; check the idle speed and the ignition timing.

Distributorless Ignition

Removal and Installation

CAMSHAFT POSITION SENSOR

Supra (7M-GTE)

1. Disconnect the negative battery cable.
2. Disconnect the cam position sensor connector.
3. Remove the oil filler cap.
4. Look into the oil filler opening with a flashlight and rotate

Distributor Installation—2VZ-FE engine

the crankshaft clockwise until the the nose of the cam can be seen.

5. Once the nose of the cam comes into view, rotate the crankshaft approximately 120 degrees counterclockwise.

6. Turn the crankshaft approximately 10–40 degrees clockwise until the TDC mark on the timing belt cover is aligned with the TDC mark on the crankshaft pulley; the engine is now at TDC. Don't move it from this position.

7. Remove the No. 4 air cleaner pipe with the No. 1 and No. 2 air cleaner hoses.

8. Disconnect the 3 air hoses and the PCV hose.

9. Disconnect the air flow meter connector.

10. Disconnect the power steering idle up air hose.

11. Remove the air flow meter mounting bolt and attendant hose clamps. Remove the No. 7 air cleaner hose, air flow meter and air cleaner cap as a unit.

12. Unbolt and remove the power steering reservoir tank. Leave the hoses connected and move the tank aside.

13. Remove the cam position sensor hold-down bolt.

14. Withdraw the cam postion sensor from the cylinder head.

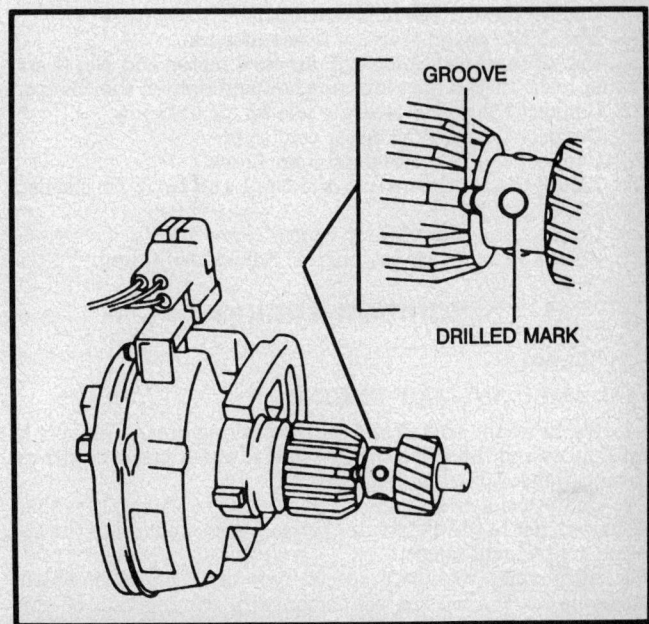

Align the mark on the gear with the groove in the housing—7M-GTE engine

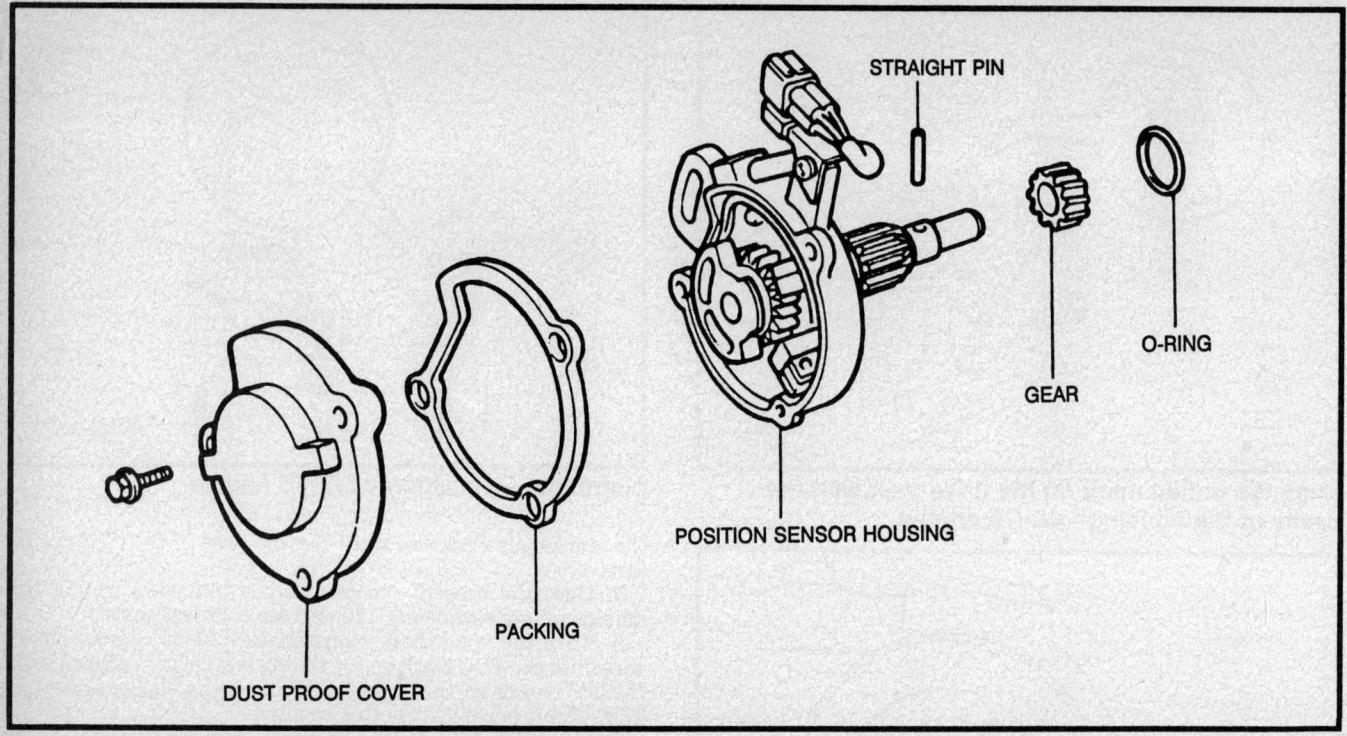

STRAIGHT PIN

O-RING

GEAR

POSITION SENSOR HOUSING

PACKING

DUST PROOF COVER

Cam position sensor exploded view — 7M-GTE engine

15. Remove the cam postion sensor O-ring. Discard the O-ring and replace with new.

To install:

16. Install a new O-ring.

17. Align the drilled mark on the driven gear with the groove of the housing.

18. Insert the cam position sensor into the cylinder head so the center of the sensor flange is aligned with the bolt hole in the head.

19. Lightly tighten the hold-down bolt.

20. Install the power steering reservoir tank.

21. Install the air cleaner cap, air flow meter and No. 7 air cleaner hose. Install the mounting bolt and tighten the clamps.

22. Connect the power steering idle up air hose.

23. Connect the air flow meter connector.

24. Connect the PCV hose and 3 air hoses.

25. Install the air cleaner pip and No. 1 and No. 2 air cleaner hoses.

26. Connect the cam position sensor connector.

27. Start and warm up the engine. Adjust the timing.

Ignition Timing

Adjustment

3A-C, 4A-LC AND 4A-F ENGINE

1. Warm up the engine and set the parking brake. Connect a tachometer and check the engine speed to make sure it is within specifications. Adjust as required.

2. Connect the dwell meter or tachometer to the negative side of the coil, not to the distributor primary lead, damage to the ignition control will result.

3. All engines require a special type of tachometer which hooks up to the service connector wire coming out of the distributor.

4. Connect a timing light to the engine, as outlined in the instructions supplied by the manufacturer of the light.

5. Disconnect and plug the vacuum line from the distributor vacuum unit. If a vacuum advance/retard distributor is used, disconnect and plug both vacuum lines from the distributor.

6. Allow the engine to run at the specified idle speed with the gear shift in **N** for a manual transmission or **D** for an automatic transmission. Be sure the parking brake is firmly set and the wheels are chocked.

7. Point the timing light at the timing marks. With the engine at idle, timing should be at the specification. If not, loosen the pinch bolt at the base and rotate the distributor to advance or retard the timing, as required.

8. Stop the engine and tighten the pinch bolt. Start the engine and recheck the timing. Stop the engine and disconnect the timing light and the tachometer. Connect the vacuum line(s) to the vacuum and advance unit.

EXCEPT 3E AND 3E-E ENGINE

1. Connect a timing light to the engine following the manufacturer's instructions. On the 7M-GTE, connect the timing light pick-up to the No. 6 spark plug wire.

2. The engines require a special type of tachometer which hooks up to the service connector wire coming from the distributor.

3. Start the engine and run it at idle. Remove the rubber cap from the check connector or open the lid; short the connector at terminals **T** and E_1 on 1988 California vehicles. On all 1989–91 vehicles, with the 4A-GE, 4A-FE, 3S-FE, 3S-GTE, 5S-FE, 2VZ-FE and 7M-GE, short the TE_1 and E_1 terminals.

4. Loosen the distributor pinch bolt so the distributor can be turned. Aim the timing light at the marks on the crankshaft pulley and slowly turn the distributor until the timing mark is aligned. Tighten the distributor pinch bolt. Unshort the connector.

NOTE: The 7M-GTE utilizes a cam position sensor in place of a distributor. Turn this the same as a distributor.

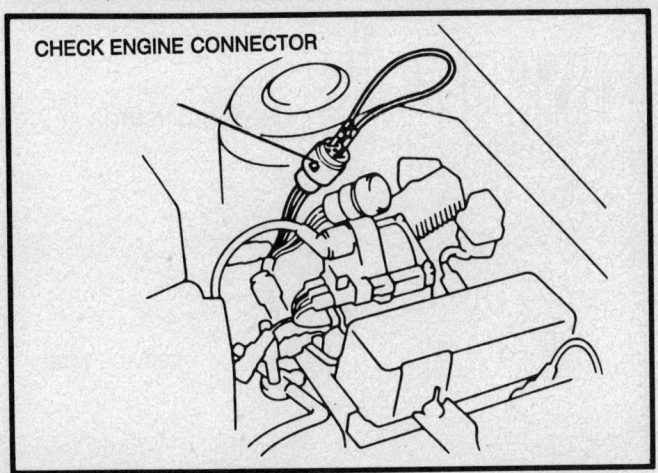

Shorting the test connector—5M-GE (Supra) engine

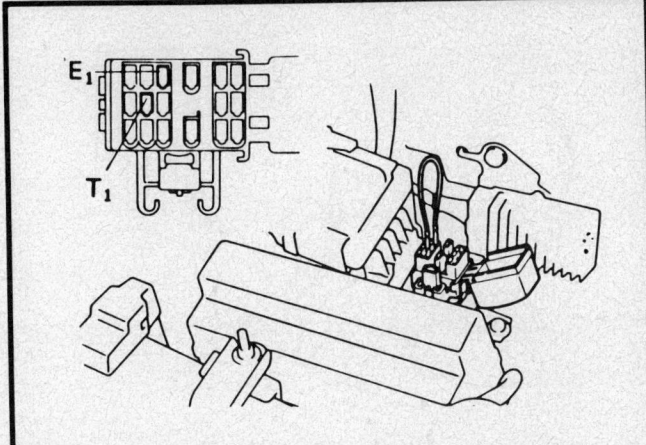

Shorting the test connector—5M-GE (Cressida) engine

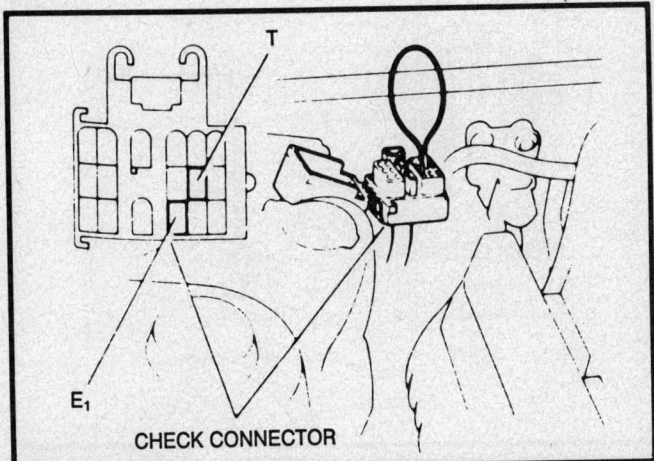

Shorting the test connector—4A-GEC, 4A-GELC and 4A-GZE engines

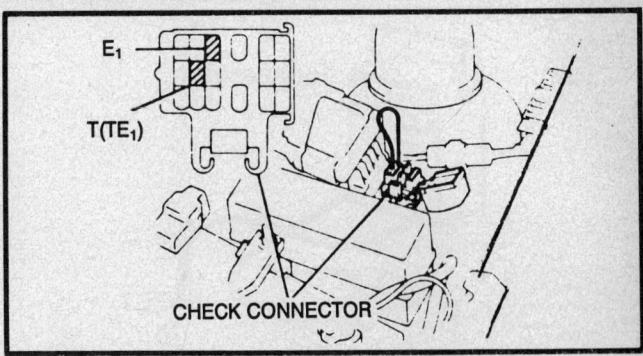

Shorting the test connector—7M-GE (Supra) engine

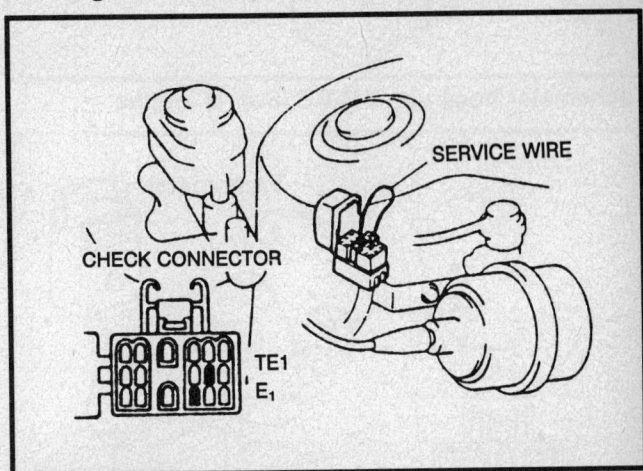

Shorting the test connector—7M-GE engine (Cressida)

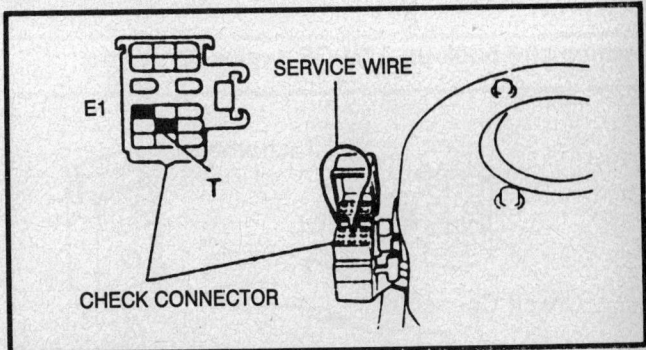

Shorting the test connector—4A-FE engine

3E ENGINE

1. Remove the cap. Using the proper tachometer, connect the test probe of the tachometer to the service probe connector at the Integrated Ignition Assembly (IIA).

2. Disconnect the vacuum hose from the IIA sub-diaphragm and plug it.

3. With the engine idling and the electric fan off, check the timing.

4. Loosen the hold-down bolt and adjust the timing, as required.

5. Retighten the hold-down bolt and recheck the ignition timing.

3E-E ENGINE

1. Warm up the engine to normal operating temperature.

2. Connect a tachometer and timing light to the engine. The tachometer may be connected either to the service connector of the distributor or to the **IG** terminal of the check connector.

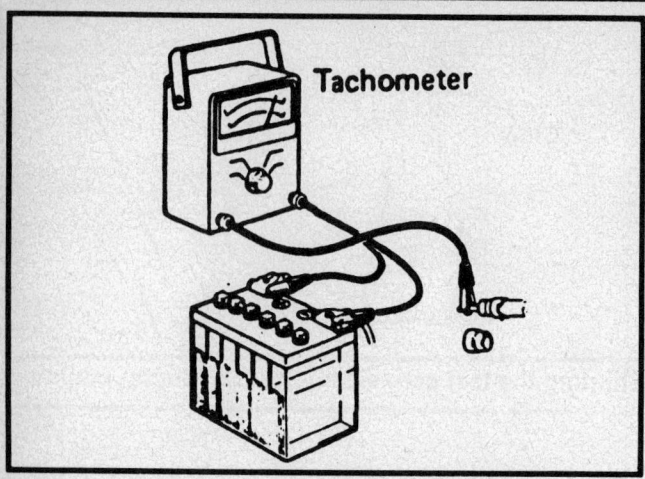

Tachometer hook-up—5M-GE (Supra) engine

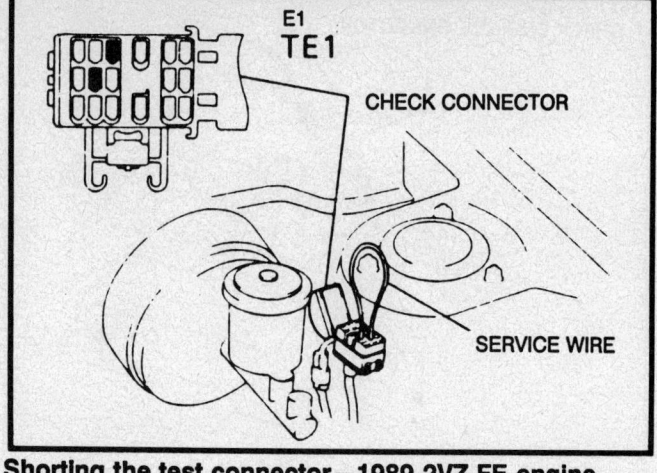

Shorting the test connector—1989 2VZ-FE engine

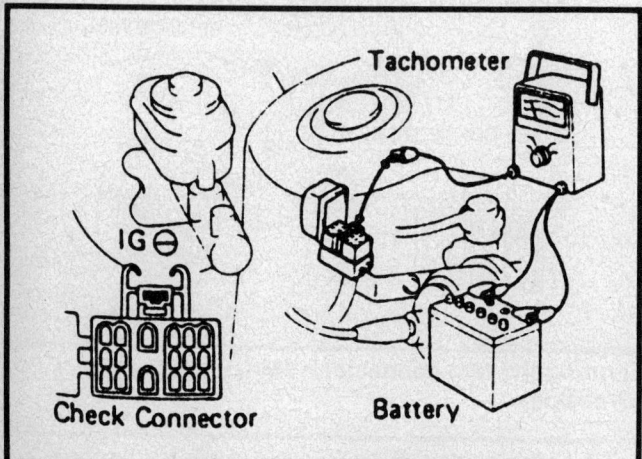

Tachometer hook-up—7M-GE engine (Cressida)

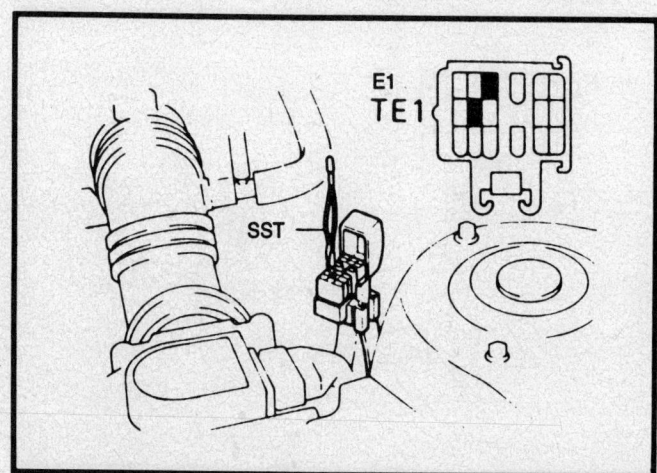

Shorting the test connector—1990–91 2VZ-FE engine

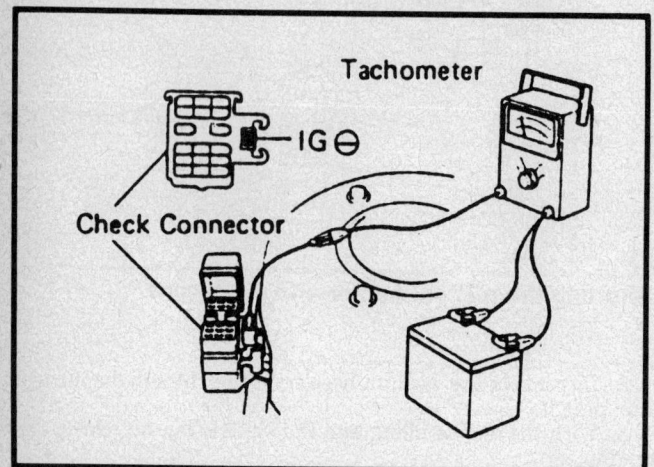

Tachometer hook-up—4A-FE engine

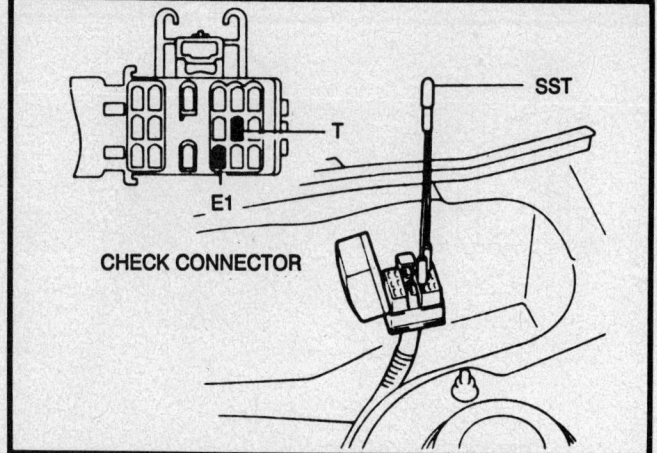

Shorting the test connector—3E-E engine

NOTE: The engines require a special type of tachometer which hooks up to the service connector wire coming from the distributor.

3. Open the lid on the check connector and short the connector at terminals T and E$_1$.

4. Loosen the distributor pinch bolt so the distributor can be turned. Aim the timing light at the marks on the crankshaft pulley and slowly turn the distributor until the timing mark is aligned. Tighten the distributor pinch bolt. Unshort the connector.

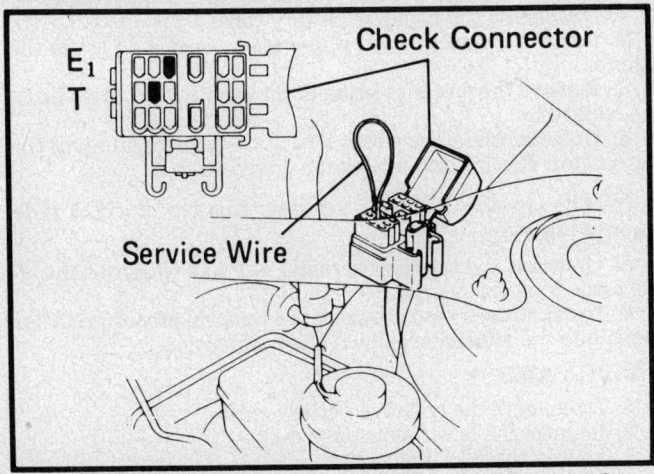

Shorting the test connector—3S-FE, 3S-GE and 3S-GTE engines

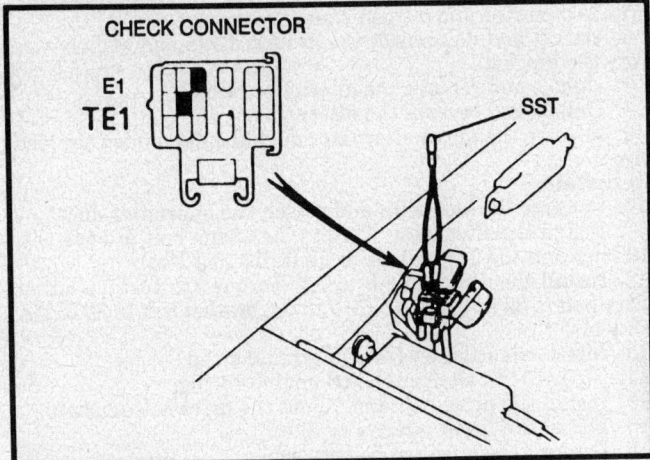

Shorting the test connector—5S-FE engine

Tachometer hook-up—5M-GE (Cressida) (Supra) and 7M-GTE engines

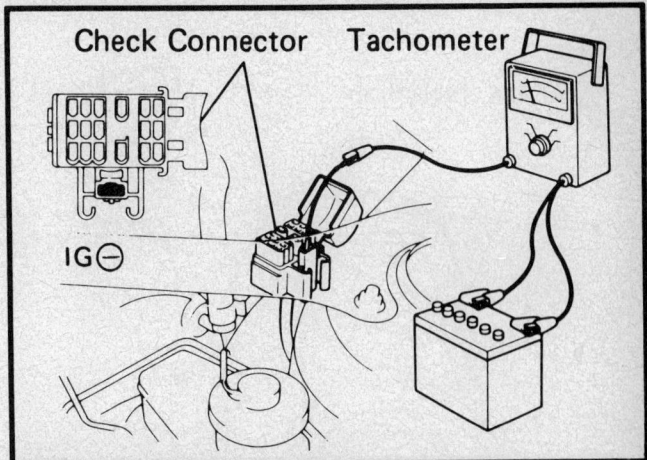

Tachometer hook-up—2VZ-FE, 3S-GE, 3S-GTE and 1989–91 4A-GE (Corolla) engines

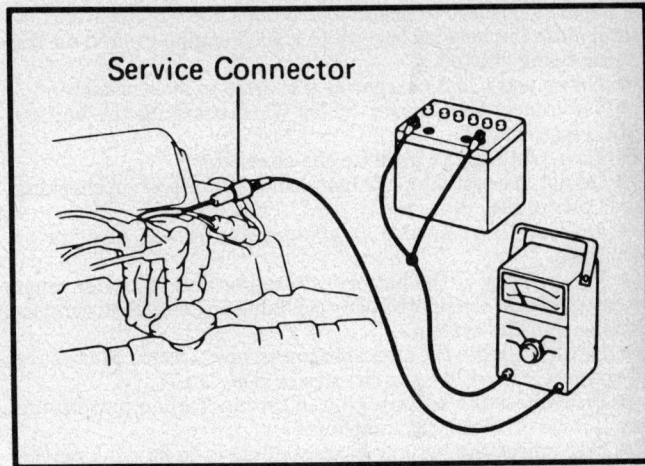

Tachometer hook-up—3E, 4A-C, 4A-F, 4A-LC (1987–88 3A-C similar)

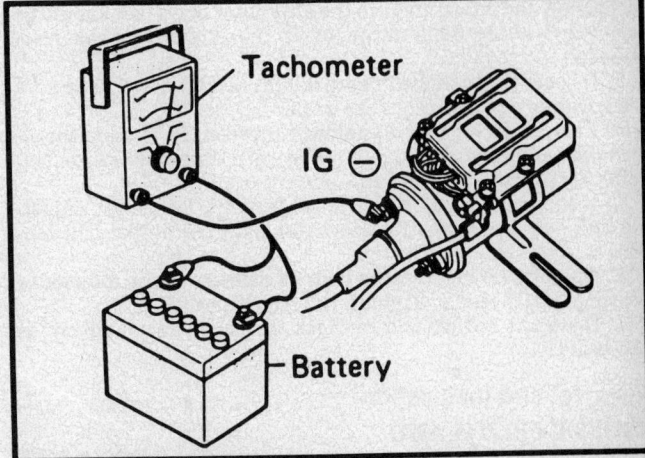

Tachomter hook-up—4A-GE (except 1989–91 Corolla) and 4A-GZE engines

Alternator

Precautions

Several precautions must be observed with alternator equipped vehicles to avoid damage to the unit.

• If the battery is removed for any reason, make sure it is reconnected with the correct polarity. Reversing the battery connections may result in damage to the one-way rectifiers.

• When utilizing a booster battery as a starting aid, always

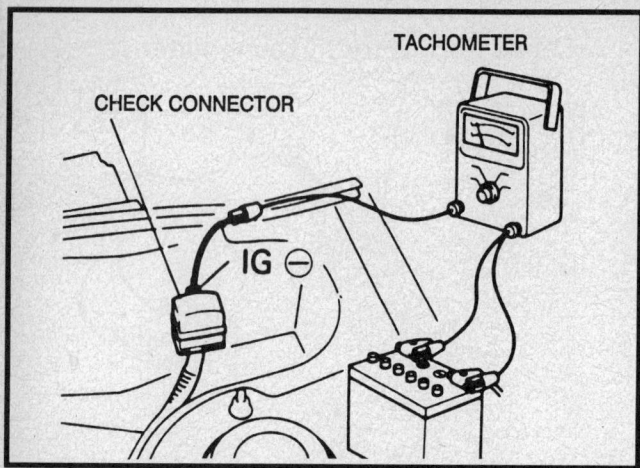

Tachometer hook-ups—3E-E engine

connect the positive to positive terminals and the negative terminal from the booster battery to a good engine ground on the vehicle being started.

- Never use a fast charger as a booster to start vehicles.
- Disconnect the battery cables when charging the battery with a fast charger.
- Never attempt to polarize the alternator.
- Do not use test lamps of more than 12 volts when checking diode continuity.
- Do not short across or ground any of the alternator terminals.
- The polarity of the battery, alternator and regulator must be matched and considered before making any electrical connections within the system.
- Never separate the alternator on an open circuit. Make sure all connections within the circuit are clean and tight.
- Disconnect the battery ground terminal when performing any service on electrical components.
- Disconnect the battery if arc welding is to be done on the vehicle.

Belt Tension Adjustment

Inspection and adjustment to the alternator drive belt should be performed every 3000 miles or if the alternator has been removed.

1. Inspect the drive belt to see if it is cracked or worn; be sure it's surfaces are free of grease or oil.
2. Push down on the belt halfway between the fan and the alternator pulleys or crankshaft pulley with thumb pressure; belt deflection should be ⅜–½ in.
3. If the belt tension requires adjustment, loosen the adjusting link bolt and move the alternator until the proper belt tension is obtained.
4. Do not over-tighten the belt, as damage to the alternator bearings could result. Tighten the adjusting link bolt.
5. Drive the vehicle and re-check the belt tension; adjust, as necessary.

Removal and Installation
EXCEPT CELICA AWD

NOTE: On some vehicles, the alternator is mounted very low on the engine. On these vehicles it may be necessary to remove the gravel shield and work from under the vehicle in order to gain access to the alternator.

1. Disconnect the negative battery cable.
2. Remove the air cleaner, if necessary, to gain access to the alternator.
3. Remove the power steering or air conditioning drive belts, as required.
4. Unfasten the bolts which attach the adjusting link to the alternator. Remove the alternator drive belt.

NOTE: On the 2VZ-FE, remove the No. 2 right side mounting stay.

5. Unfasten and tag the alternator bolt and withdraw the alternator from it's bracket.
6. Installation is the reverse of the removal procedure. After installing the alternator, adjust the belt tension.

CELICA AWD

1. Disconnect the negative battery cable.
2. Remove the lower alternator duct.
3. Loosen the idler pulley bolt.
4. Loosen the adjusting bolt and remove the drive belt.
5. Disconnect the alternator connectors, alternator lead wire, air conditioning compressor connector, water temperature switch connector and oxygen sensor connector.
6. Unbolt and disconnect the ground strap and engine wire from the brackets.
7. Unbolt and remove the alternator bracket.
8. Unbolt and remove the alternator.
9. Remove the upper alternator duct and disconnect the lead wire.

To install:
10. Connect the lead wire and attach the alternator duct.
11. Install the alternator. Torque the 12mm bolt to 14 ft. lbs. (19 Nm) and the 14mm bolt to 38 ft. lbs. (52 Nm).
12. Install the alternator bracket. Torque the turbine outlet elbow bolt to 32 ft. lbs. (43 Nm) and the bracket bolt to 39 ft. lbs. (29 Nm).
13. Install the engine wire and ground strap.
14. Connect the alternator and engine wiring.
15. Install the drive belt and adjust the drive belt tension.
16. Install the lower alternator duct.
17. Connect the negative battery cable.

Starter

Removal and Installation

1. Disconnect the negative battery cable. Disconnect the cable which runs from the starter to the battery, at the battery end.
2. Remove the air cleaner assembly, if necessary, to gain access to the starter.
3. If equipped with an automatic transmission/transaxle, it may be necessary to disconnect the throttle linkage connecting rod or the transmission/tranasaxle oil filler tube.
4. On the 3S-GE, disconnect the exhaust pipe at the manifold. On the Camry with 2VZ-FE, remove the ignitor bracket. On 1990–91 Celica with 3S-GTE, remove the engine compartment relay box and the battery. On 1990–91 Celica with 4A-FE, remove the lower suspension crossmember and the air cleaner cap. On 1990–91 Celica with 5S-FE, cruise control and ABS, remove the engine compartment relay box and the cruise control actuator. On 1990–91 Corolla with 4A-GE, remove both engine undercovers, front exhaust pipe and electric cooling fan.
5. Disconnect all of the wiring at the starter. Remove the starter retaining bolts. Remove the starter from the vehicle.
6. Installation is the reverse of the removal procedure.

CHASSIS ELECTRICAL

—————————— **CAUTION** ——————————

On vehicles equipped with an air bag, the negative battery cable must be disconnected, before working on the system. Failure to do so may result in deployment of the air bag and possible personal injury.

Heater Blower Motor

NOTE: On most vehicles, the air conditioner assembly is integral with the heater assembly (including the blower motor) and therefore the blower motor removal may differ from the procedures detailed below. In some case it may be necessary to remove the air conditioning-heater housing and assembly to remove the blower motor. Due to the lack of information available at the time of this publication, a general blower motor removal and installation procedure is outlined. The removal steps can be altered, as required.

Removal and Installation
CELICA AND SUPRA

1. Disconnect the negative battery cable.
2. Working from under the instrument panel, unfasten the defroster hoses from the heater box.
3. Unplug the multi-connector.
4. Loosen the mounting screws and withdraw the blower assembly.
5. Installation is the reverse of the removal procedure.
6. Check the blower for proper operation at all speeds.

CRESSIDA

1. Disconnect the negative battery cable.
2. Remove the instrument panel undercover and cowl side trim panel.
3. Remove the air duct and the glove box.
4. Disconnect the heater control cable from the blower motor and remove the blower duct.
5. Disconnect the heater relay from the heater relay electrical connector.
6. Remove the retaining screws from the blower motor assembly. Remove the assembly from the vehicle.
7. Remove the blower motor from the blower motor assembly.
8. Installation is the reverse order of the removal procedure.
9. Check the blower for proper operation at all speeds.

COROLLA AND TERCEL

1. Disconnect the negative battery cable.
2. Remove the under tray, if equipped.
3. Remove the blower duct and air duct. Before removing the air duct, remember to remove the 2 attaching clamps.
4. Remove the glove box and the heater control cable.
5. Disconnect the electrical connector on the blower motor.
6. Remove the blower motor retaining bolts and remove the blower motor.
7. Installation is the reverse of the removal procedure.
8. Check the blower for proper operation at all speeds.

CAMRY AND MR2

1. Disconnect the negative battery cable.
2. Remove the 3 screws attaching the retainer.
3. Remove the glove box. Remove the duct between the blower motor assembly and the heater assembly.
4. Disconnect the blower motor wire connector at the blower motor case.
5. Disconnect the air source selector control cable at the blower motor assembly.

6. Loosen the nuts and bolts attaching the blower motor to the blower case, remove the blower motor from the vehicle.
7. Installation is the reverse of the removal procedure.
8. Check the blower for proper operation at all speeds.

Front Windshield Wiper Motor

Removal and Installation
TERCEL AND COROLLA

1. Disconnect the negative battery terminal.
2. Remove the wiper arm.
3. Insert a small prybar between the linkage and the motor. Pry up to separate the linkage from the motor.
4. Disconnect the electrical connector from the motor.
5. Remove the mounting bolts and remove the motor.
6. Installation is the reverse of the removal procedure.

CELICA, SUPRA, CAMRY AND CRESSIDA

1. Remove the access hole cover.
2. Separate the wiper and motor by prying gently with a small prybar.
3. Remove the left and right cowl ventilators.
4. Remove the wiper arms and the linkage mounting nuts. Push the linkage pivot ports into the ventilators.
5. Loosen the wiper link connectors at their ends and with the linkage from the cowl ventilator.
6. Start the wiper motor and turn the ignition key to the **OFF** when the crank is a position best suited for removal of the motor.

NOTE: The wiper motor is difficult to remove when it is in the parked position. If the motor is turned off at the wiper switch, it will automatically return to this position.

7. Unplug the wiper motor connector.
8. Loosen the motor mounting bolts and withdraw the motor.
9. Installation is the reverse of the removal procedure. Be sure to install the wiper motor with it in the park position by connecting the multi-connector and operating the wiper control switch. Assemble the crank.

MR2

1. With the wiper arms in the up position and the wiper switch on **LOW**, turn the ignition switch to the **OFF** postion.
2. Disconnect the negative battery cable. Disconnect the wiper motor electrical connector, then remove the light retractor relay from the wiper bracket.
3. Remove the wiper motor set bolts. Manually lower the wiper arms, then connect the wiper link hook to the dash panel service hole.
4. Disconnect the wiper motor link. Remove the wiper motor attaching bolts then remove the wiper motor.
5. Installation is the reverse order of the removal procedure.

Rear Wiper Motor

Removal and Installation

1. Disconnect the negative battery cable.
2. Remove the wiper arm and rear door trim cover.
3. Disconnect the wiper motor wire connector.
4. Remove the wiper motor bracket attaching bolts and the wiper motor along with the bracket.
5. Installation is the reverse of the removal procedure.

Instrument Cluster

Removal and Installation

CRESSIDA

1. Disconnect the negative battery cable.
2. Remove the cluster finish panel.
3. Loosen the instrument cluster retaining screws and tilt the panel forward.
4. Detach the speedometer cable and wiring connectors.
5. Remove the entire cluster assembly.
6. Remove the instruments from the panel as required.
7. Installation is the reverse of the removal proecedure.

TERCEL AND COROLLA

1. Disconnect the negative battery cable.
2. Remove the steering column cover.

NOTE: Be careful not to damage the collapsible steering column mechanism.

3. On Tercel, remove the heater control knob and the center instrument cluster finish panel.
4. Remove the switches and hole cover from the cluster hood.
5. Remove the cluster hood.
6. Remove the cluster attaching screws and pull the unit forward.
7. Disconnect the speedometer and any other electrical connections that are necessary.
8. Remove the instruments from the panel as required.
9. Installation is the reverse of the removal proecedure.

CAMRY, CELICA AND SUPRA

1. Disconnect the negative battery cable.
2. Remove the fuse box cover from under the left side of the instrument panel.
3. Remove the heater control knobs.
4. Carefully pry off the heater control panel.
5. Remove the cluster hood.
6. Unscrew the cluster finish panel retaining screws and pull out the bottom of the panel.
7. Unplug the electrical connectors and disconnect the speedometer cable.
8. Remove the instrument cluster.
9. Remove the instruments from the panel as required.
10. Installation is the reverse of the removal proecedure.

MR2

1. Disconnect the negative battery cable.
2. Remove the steering column covers.
3. Pull the rheostat knob from the cluster finish panel and remove the nut from the rheostat. Remove the cluster finish panel and disconnnect the rheostat multi-connector.
4. Remove the cluster hood.
5. Remove the cluster attaching screws and pull the unit forward.
6. Disconnect the speedometer and any other electrical connections that are necessary.
7. Remove the instruments from the panel as required.
8. Installation is the reverse of the removal proecedure.

Concealed Headlights

——— CAUTION ———

Before attempting to manually operate the concealed (retractable) headlights, first pull the fuse or disconnnect the negative battery cable. Otherwise the headlights and motor shaft may suddenly move and catch hand and fingers. When opening and closing retractable headlights, make sure nobody is near them, otherwise personal injury may result.

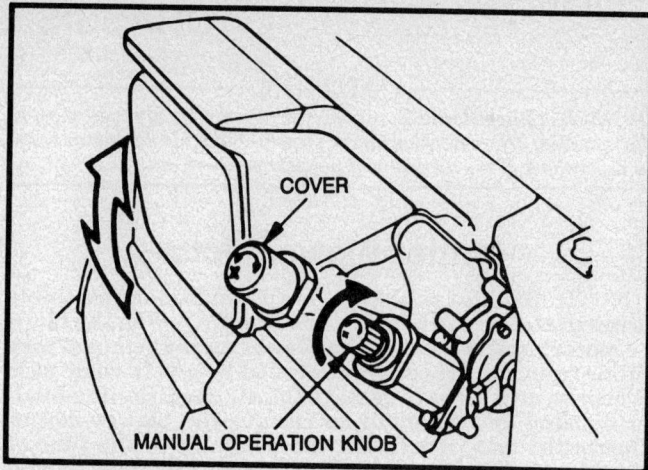

Manual operation of concealed headlights

Manual Operation

NOTE: If the headlights are frozen and inoperative, carefully melt the ice before attempting the manual operation procedure. Operation of a frozen headlight will drain the battery and may cause damage to the motor and operating linkages.

1. Switch the headlight and retractable headlight switches to the **OFF** position.
2. Pull the retractable headlight fuse or disconnect the negative battery cable.
3. Remove the rubber cap from the manual operation knob.
4. Manually turn the knob clockwise until the headlights are in the desired position (open or closed).
5. Install the rubber cap.
6. Install the fuse.
7. Make sure the lights work properly.

Combination Switch

Removal and Installation

1. Disconnect the negative battery cable.
2. Remove the steering column garnish.
3. Remove the upper and lower steering column covers.
4. Remove the steering wheel.
5. Trace the switch wiring harness to the multi-connector. Push in the lock levers and pull apart the connectors.

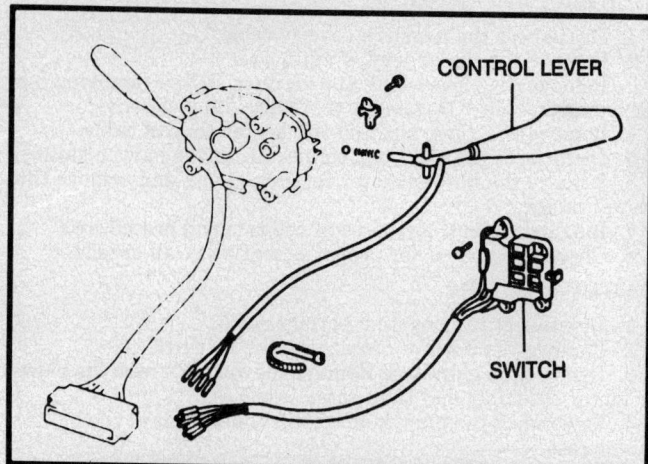

Typical headlight control lever and switch assembly

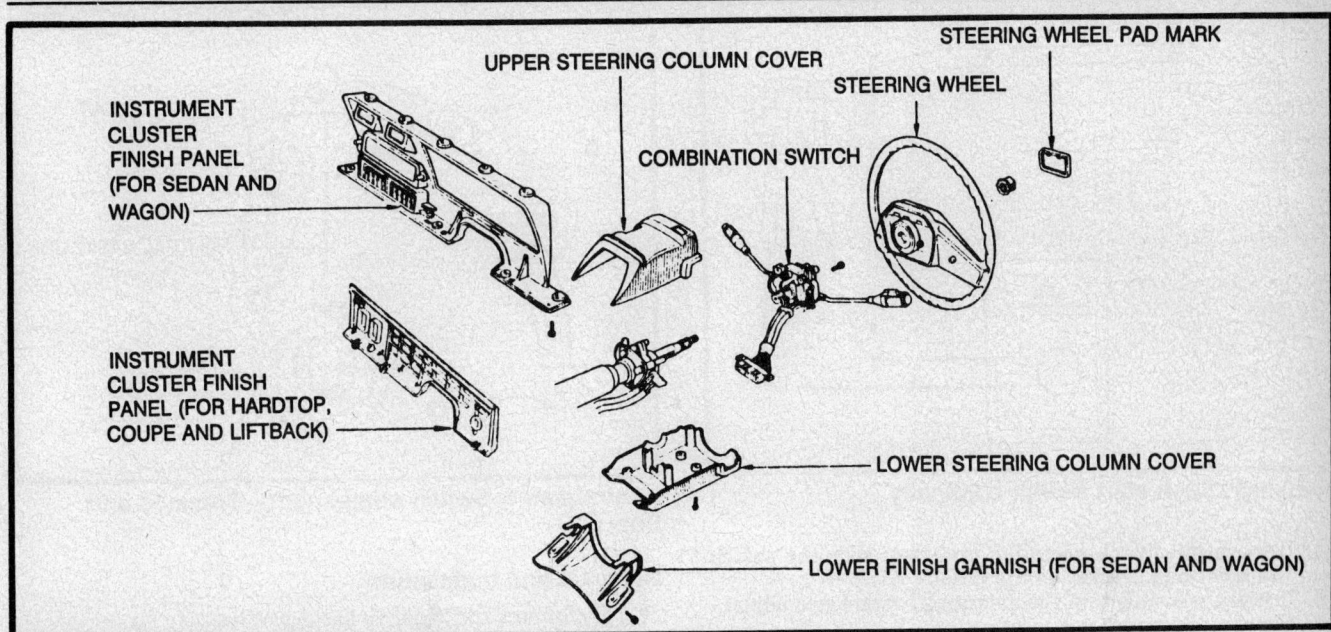

STEERING WHEEL PAD MARK

UPPER STEERING COLUMN COVER

STEERING WHEEL

INSTRUMENT CLUSTER FINISH PANEL (FOR SEDAN AND WAGON)

COMBINATION SWITCH

INSTRUMENT CLUSTER FINISH PANEL (FOR HARDTOP, COUPE AND LIFTBACK)

LOWER STEERING COLUMN COVER

LOWER FINISH GARNISH (FOR SEDAN AND WAGON)

Typical combination switch mounting

6. If equipped with electronic modulated suspension (TEMS), remove the steering sensor. On air bag equipped vehicles, disconnect the sprial cable connectors, remove the spiral cable housing attaching screws and slide the cable assembly from the front of the combination switch.

7. Unscrew the mounting screws and slide the combination switch from the steering column.

8. Installation is the reverse of the removal procedure. Check all switch functions for proper operation.

Ignition Lock/Switch

Removal and Installation

1. Disconnect the negative battery cable.
2. Unfasten the ignition switch connector under the instrument panel.
3. Remove the screws which secure the upper and lower halves of the steering column cover.
4. Turn the lock cylinder to the **ACC** position with the ignition key.

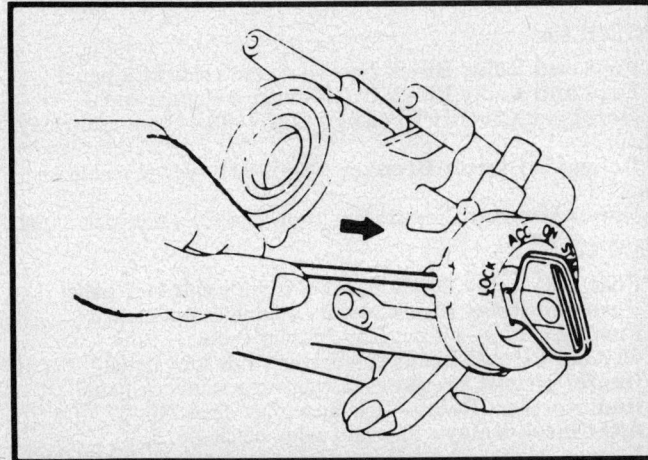

Ignition lock/switch removal

5. Push the lock cylinder stop in with a small, round object (cotter pin, punch, etc.).

NOTE: On some vehicles, it may be necessary to remove the steering wheel and combination switch first.

6. Withdraw the lock cylinder from the lock housing while depressing the stop tab.
7. To remove the ignition switch, unfasten its securing screws and withdraw the switch from the lock housing.
To install:
8. Align the locking cam with the hole in the ignition switch and insert the switch into the lock housing.
9. Secure the switch with its screw(s).
10. Make sure both the lock cylinder and column lock are in the **ACC** position. Slide the cylinder into the lock housing until the stop tab engages the hole in the lock.
11. Install the steering column covers.
12. Connect the ignition switch connector.
13. Connect the negative battery cable.

Stoplight Switch

Adjustment

1. Remove the instrument lower finish panel and the air duct if required to gain access to the stoplight switch.
2. Disconnect the stoplight switch connector.
3. Loosen the switch locknut.
4. Turn the stoplight switch until the end of the switch lightly contacts the pedal stopper.
5. Hold the switch and tighten the locknut.
6. Connect the switch connector.
7. Depress the brake pedal and verify that the brake lights illuminate.
8. Install the air duct and the lower finish panel, if removed.

Removal and Installation

1. Disconnect the negative battery cable.
2. Remove the instrument lower finish panel and the air duct if required to gain access to the stoplight switch.
3. Disconnect the stoplight switch connector.

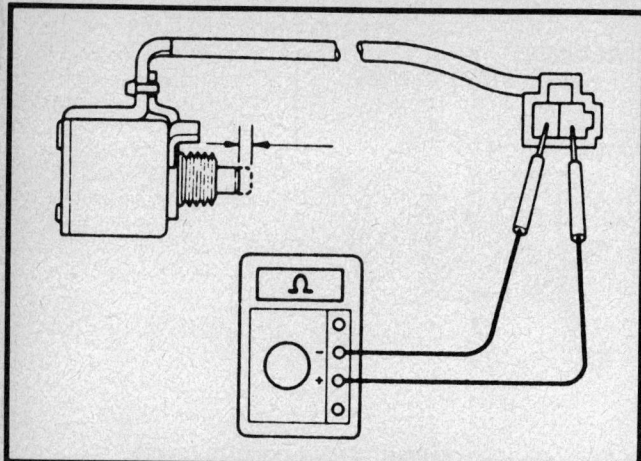

Checking clutch start switch continuity

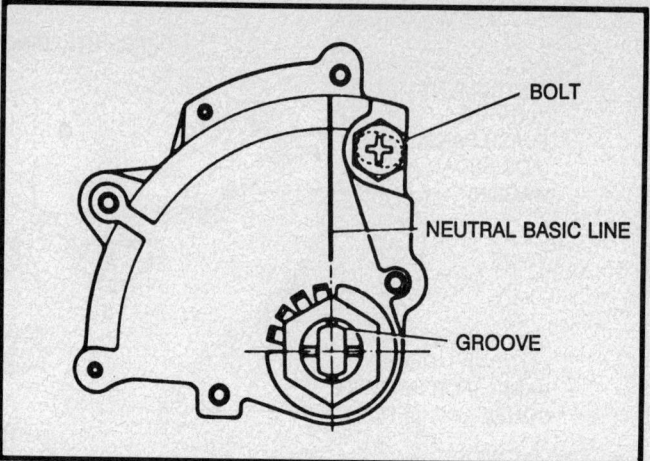

Neutral safety switch adjustment—Cressida and Supra

4. Remove the switch mounting nut, then slide the switch from the mounting bracket on the pedal.
5. Install the switch into the mounting bracket and adjust.
6. Connect the switch connector.
7. Depress the brake pedal and verify that the brake lights illuminate.
8. Install the air duct and the lower finish panel, if removed.

Clutch Switch

Adjustment

1. Attempt to start the engine when the clutch pedal is released. The engine should not start.
2. Depress the clutch pedal fully and attempt to start the engine. The engine should start.
3. If the engine does not start, depress the clutch pedal fully. With the clutch pedal depressed, loosen the switch locknut.
4. Use the adjusting nut to turn the switch until the tip of the switch contacts the clutch pedal stop.
5. Tighten the locknut and attempt to start the engine. Readjust as necessary.
6. If the switch cannot be adjusted, check the switch continuity with a suitable ohmmeter. There should be continuity between the switch terminals when the switch is on (tip pushed in) and no continuity when the switch is off (tip released). If the continuity is not as specified, replace the switch.

Removal and Installation

1. Disconnect the negative battery cable.
2. Disconnect the switch connector.
3. Remove the switch adjusting nut.
4. Withdraw the switch from the mounting bracket.
5. Installation is the reverse of the removal procedure. Adjust the switch.

Neutral Safety Switch

The shift lever is adjusted properly if the engine will not start in any position other than **N** or **P**.

Adjustment

1. Loosen the neutral start switch bolt. Position the selector in the N position.
2. Align the switch shaft groove with the neutral base line which is located on the switch.
3. Tighten the bolt to 48 inch lbs. (5.4 Nm). on all vehicles except Tercel wagon. On the Tercel wagon, tighten to 9 ft. lbs. (13 Nm).

Removal and Installation

1. Disconnect the negative battery cable.
2. Unplug the switch wiring connectors.
3. Disconnect the transmission control cable from the manual shift lever.
4. Remove the manual shift lever.
5. Pry the C-washer from the manual shaft nut. Discard the washer and replace with new.
6. Remove the manual shaft nut and washer.
7. Remove the manual shaft lever packing (1990–91 Celica with A241E transaxle).
8. Remove the retaining bolts and withdraw the switch from the tranaxle case.
9. Installation is the reverse of the removal procedure. Adjust the switch.

Fuses, Circuit Breakers and Relays

Location

TERCEL

Fuse and Relay Block No. 1—driver's side kick panel
Fuse and Relay Block No. 2—engine compartment
Defogger Circuit Breaker—fuse and relay block No. 1
Radiator Fan Relay—fuse and relay block No. 2
A/C Clutch Relay—fuse and relay block No. 2
A/C Cut Relay (USA 3E-E and Canada only)—fuse and relay block No. 1

COROLLA

Fuse and Relay Block No. 1—driver's side kick panel
Fuse and Relay Block No. 2—engine compartment
Defogger Circuit Breaker (1987–88)—fuse and relay block No. 1
Defogger Circuit Breaker (1989–91)—driver's side kick panel
Power Window Circuit Breaker—driver's side kick panel

CAMRY

Fuse and Relay Block No. 1—driver's side kick panel
Fuse and Relay Block No. 2—engine compartment
Fusible Links—off negative battery cable
30 Amp Circuit breaker—driver's side kick panel
Heater circuit breaker—passenger's side kick panel
Radiator Fan Relay—fuse and relay block No. 2
A/C Clutch Relay—fuse and relay block No. 2
Blower, Heater and Horn Relays—passenger's side kick panel

CELICA

Fuse and Relay Block No. 1—driver's side kick panel
Fuse and Relay Block No. 2—engine compartment
Fuse and Relay Block No. 4—passenger's side kick panel
Fuse and Relay Block No. 5—engine compartment
Fusible Links—off negative battery cable

SUPRA

Fuse Block No. 1 and Relay Block No. 5—driver's side kick panel
Junction Block No. 2—engine compartment
Relay Block No. 4—passenger's side kick panel
Fusible Links—off negative battery cable

MR2

Fuse and Relay Block No. 1—driver's side kick panel
Fuse and Relay Block No. 2—behind driver's seat
Fuse and Relay Block No. 5—engine compartment
Fusible Links—off negative battery cable

CRESSIDA

Fuse and Relay Block No. 1—driver's side kick panel
Fuse and Relay Block No. 2—engine compartment
Fuse and Relay Block No. 4—passenger's side kick panel
Fusible Links—off negative battery cable

Computers

Location

On Tercel, Corolla, Camry and Celica, the ECU is located be-hind the center console. On Supra, the ECU is located behind the glove box. On MR2, the ECU is located behind the rear seat. On Cressida, the ECU is located in the glove box.

On Tercel, the cruise control computer is located behind center console. On Corolla, Camry and Cressida, the cruise control computer is located on the driver's side kick panel. On Supra, the cruise control computer is located under the dash on the driver's side. On MR2, the cruise control computer is located behind the driver's seat.

On Cressida with seat position memory, the power seat computer is located under the driver's seat.

Flashers

Location

On Tercel, the turn signal/hazard flasher (USA only) is located on the under the driver's side dash left of the steering column.

On Corolla, Camry and and 1987–89 MR2, the turn signal/hazard flasher is located on the driver's side kick panel.

On Celica, 1889–91 Cressida and 1990–91 MR2, the turn signal/hazard flasher is located in fuse and relay block No. 1 which is on the driver's side kick panel. On 1987–88 Cressida, the turn signal/hazard flasher is located under the dash on the left side of the steering column.

On Supra, the turn signal/hazard flasher is located in relay block No. 5 which is on the driver's side kick panel.

ENGINE COOLING

Radiator

Removal and Installation

1. Disconnect the negative battery cable.
2. Drain the cooling system.
3. On 1990–91 MR2, remove the front under covers.
4. Remove the radiator hoses.
5. If equipped with an automatic transmission or transaxle, disconnect and plug the oil cooler lines.
6. Remove the ignition coil, ignitor and bracket assembly on the 2VZ-FE.
7. Remove the hood lock from the radiator upper support, as required. It may be necessary to remove the grille in order to gain access to the hood lock/radiator support assembly.
8. Remove the fan shroud, as required. If equipped with an electric fan (2 on the MR2), disconnect the wiring harness and thermo-switch connectors.
9. Disconnect the overflow hose from the thermal expansion tank and remove the tank from its bracket.
10. Unbolt and remove the radiator upper support.
11. Remove the radiator retaining bolts. Raise the radiator and cooling fan(s) from the lower supports and remove from vehicle.

To install:
12. Lower the radiator and cooling fan(s) onto the lower supports and install the retaining bolts.
13. Install the radiator upper support.
14. Mount the thermal expansion tank and connect the overflow hose.
15. Connect the cooling fan wiring harnesses and thermo-switch connectors. Install the fan shroud, if removed.
16. Install the hood lock and grille, if removed.

17. On 2VZ-FE, install the ignition coil, igniter and bracket assembly.
18. If equipped automatic transmission or transaxle, connect the oil cooler lines.
19. Install the radiator hoses.
20. On 1990–91 MR2, install the front under covers.
21. Fill the cooling system to the proper level.
22. Connect the negative battery cable. Start the engine and check for leaks.

Electric Cooling Fan

Testing

1. Disconnect the cooling fan motor connector.
2. Apply battery voltage to the fan motor connector terminals and check that the fan operates smoothy.
3. If the fan does not rotate, check the cooling fan relay, fan motor, engine main relay and fuse, temperature switches or for short circuits in the sensor and relay wiring.

Removal and Installation

1. Disconnect the negative battery cable.
2. Drain the cooling system.
3. Remove the radiator cover, if equipped.
4. Disconnect the reservoir overflow hose from the radiator neck.
5. Disconnect the upper hose from the radiator.
6. Remove the relay box if it interferes with cooling fan removal.
7. Disconnect the fan motor wiring.
8. Remove the cooling fan bolts and remove the cooling fan.
9. Installation is the reverse of the removal procedure.

Heater Core

For further information, please refer to "Chilton's Heating and Air Conditioning Manual" for additional coverage.

NOTE: On some vehicles, the air conditioning assembly is integral with the heater assembly (including the heater core) and therefore the heater core removal may differ from the procedures detailed below. In some case it may be necessary to remove the air conditioning/heater housing and assembly to remove the heater core. Due to the lack of information available at the time of this publication, a general heater core removal and installation procedure is outlined for each vehicle. The removal steps can be altered as required.

Removal and Installation

TERCEL

1. Disconnect the negative battery terminal.
2. Drain the radiator.
3. Remove the ash tray and retainer.
4. Remove the rear heater duct (optional).
5. Remove the left and right side defroster ducts.
6. Remove the under tray (optional).
7. Remove the glove box.
8. Remove the main air duct.
9. Disconnect the radio and remove it.
10. Disconnect the heater control cables and remove them. Mark each cable with the control lever that it connects to.
11. Disconnect the heater hoses.
12. Remove the front and rear air ducts.
13. Disconnect the electrical connectors and vacuum hoses going to the heater unit.
14. Remove the heater bolts and remove the heater. Slide the heater to the right side of vehicle to remove it.
15. Remove the heater core.
16. Installation is the reverse of the removal procedure. Fill the cooling system to the proper level. Operate the heater and check for leaks.

COROLLA

1. Disconnect the negative battery cable.
2. Drain the cooling system.
3. Remove the gear shift knob and console as necessary.
4. Tag and disconnect the vacuum hoses from heater housing assembly.
5. Remove the under tray or package tray from the right side of the vehicle.
6. Release the two clamps and remove the blower duct from the right side of the heater housing.
7. Remove any interfering air ducts.
8. Disconnect the 2 water (heater) hoses from the rear of the heater housing.
9. Tag and disconnect all wires and cables leading from the heater housing and position them aside.
10. Remove all mounting bolts and then remove the heater housing carefully toward the rear of the vehicle.
11. Remove the heater housing assembly from the vehicle. Remove any retaining brackets or hardware that may retain the heater core to the heater housing. Grasp the heater core by the end plate and carefully pull it out of the heater housing.
12. Install the heater core into the heater housing, make sure to clean heater housing of all dirt, leaves, etc. before heater core installation.
13. Installation is the reverse of the removal procedure. Fill the cooling system to the proper level. Operate the heater and check for leaks.

CAMRY

1. Drain the cooling system.
2. Remove the console, if equipped, by removing the shift knob (manual), wiring connector, and console attaching screws.
3. Remove the carpeting from the tunnel.
4. If necessary, remove the cigarette lighter and ash tray.
5. Remove the package tray, if it makes access to the heater core difficult.
6. Remove the bottom cover/intake assembly screws and withdraw the assembly.
7. Remove the cover from the water valve.
8. Remove the water valve.
9. Remove the hose clamps and remove the hoses from the core.
10. Remove the heater core.
11. Installation is the reverse of the removal procedure. Fill the cooling system to the proper level. Operate the heater and check for leaks.

CRESSIDA

1. Disconnect the negative battery cable.
2. Drain the cooling system.
3. Remove the hood release and the fuel lid release levers.
4. Remove the left instrument panel undercover and lower center pad. Remove the finish plate, then remove the radio assembly.
5. Remove the heater control knobs, heater control panel and ashtray.
6. Remove the right side instrument panel undercover, glove box door and glove box.
7. Remove the front pillar garnish, cluster finish panel and instrument cluster gauge assembly.
8. Remove the safety pad and side defroster hose. Remove the heater assembly air ducts.
9. Remove the lower pad reinforcement and remove the front seats. Remove the center console assembly and the cowl side trim panel.
10. Remove the scuff plate, then position the floor carpeting aside. Remove the rear heater duct, if equipped, and heater control assembly.
11. Disconnect the heater hoses from the heater core assembly, remove the heater core grommet.
12. Remove the blower motor duct, center duct and instrument panel brace. Remove the heater core assembly from the vehicle.
13. Remove the nuts securing the heater core to the heater core assembly and remove the heater core.
14. Installation is the reverse of the removal procedure. Fill the cooling system to the proper level. Operate the heater and check for leaks.

COROLLA

1. Disconnect the negative battery cable.
2. Drain the cooling system.
3. Remove the center console, scuff plate and front seats.
4. Position the floor carpet aside and remove the heater duct, if equipped.
5. Remove the under tray, glove box and blower duct.
6. On the Corolla station wagon and sedan vehicles, remove the following components:
    a. Remove the heater control knobs and lens. Remove the cluster lower center panel finish, ashtray and heater control assembly.
    b. Remove the instrument cluster finish panel, radio and air ducts.
7. On the Corolla coupe and liftback vehicles, remove the following components:
    a. The instrument cluster finish panel, instrument cluster, radio trim panel and radio.
    b. Ashtray, heater control knobs, heater control panel, heater control assembly and air duct.

8. Disconnect the heater hoses from the heater core assembly and remove the heater hose grommet.

9. Remove the heater core assembly retaining screws and remove the heater core assembly from the vehicle.

10. Remove the heater core from the heater core assembly.

11. Installation is the reverse of the removal procedure. Fill the cooling system to the proper level. Operate the heater and check for leaks.

MR2

1. Disconnect the negative battery cable.
2. Drain the cooling system.
3. Disconnect the heater hose at the engine compartment.
4. Remove the clips retaining the lower part of the heater unit case, then remove the lower part of the case.
5. Using a suitable tool, carefully pry open the lower part of the heater unit case.
6. Remove the heater core assembly from the heater unit case.
7. Installation is the reverse of the removal procedure. Fill the cooling system to the proper level. Operate the heater and check for leaks.

Water Pump

Removal and Installation

1. Disconnect the negative battery cable.
2. Drain the cooling system.
2. Remove the fan shroud retaining bolts and remove the fan shroud, if equipped. Loosen and remove all drive belts.
3. Remove all necessary components in order to gain access to the water pump retaining bolts.
4. On some vehicles, it will be necessary to remove the timing covers. On the 1987–91 Camry and 1990–91 MR2 and 1990–91 Celica (5S-FE), remove the timing belt and pulleys.
5. As required, remove the complete air cleaner assembly.
6. Remove all hoses from the water pump assembly.
7. Remove the water pump retaining bolts. Remove the water pump (and fan) assembly.
8. Installation is the reverse of the removal procedure. Always use a new gasket, O-ring or sealant between the pump body and its mounting. Check for leaks after installation is completed.

Thermostat

Removal and Installation

1. Disconnect the negative battery cable. Drain the cooling system.
2. Remove the upper radiator or water inlet hose from the thermostat housing.
3. Disconnect the electrical wire from the thermo-switch on the thermostat housing, if equipped.
4. Remove the thermostat housing retaining bolts. Remove the thermostat housing from the engine.
5. Remove the thermostat.
6. Installation is the reverse of the removal procedure. Be sure to use a new thermostat gasket. Be sure the thermostat is installed with the spring pointing down and the jiggle valve up. On the 3S-FE, 5S-FE, 4A-FE (type A thermostat) and 3S-GTE engines, align the jiggle valve with the protrusion on the thermostat housing. The jiggle valve may be aligned within 5–10 degrees on either side of the protrusion. On the 2VZ-FE and 4A-FE (type B thermostat), align the jiggle valve with the upper stud bolt in the housing.

Cooling System Bleeding

1. Fill the radiator with the proper type of coolant.

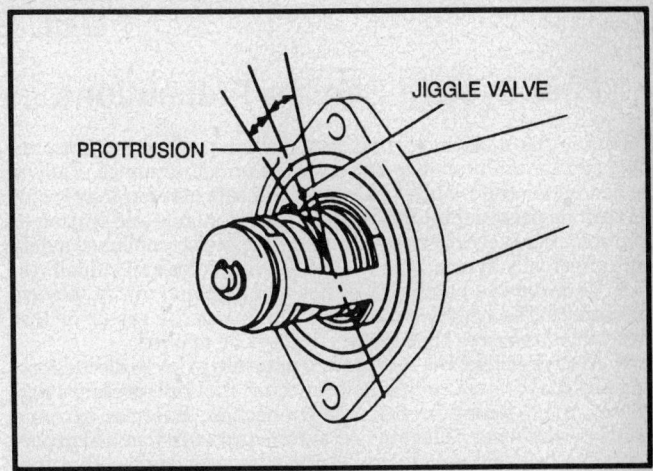

Thermostat jiggle valve alignment

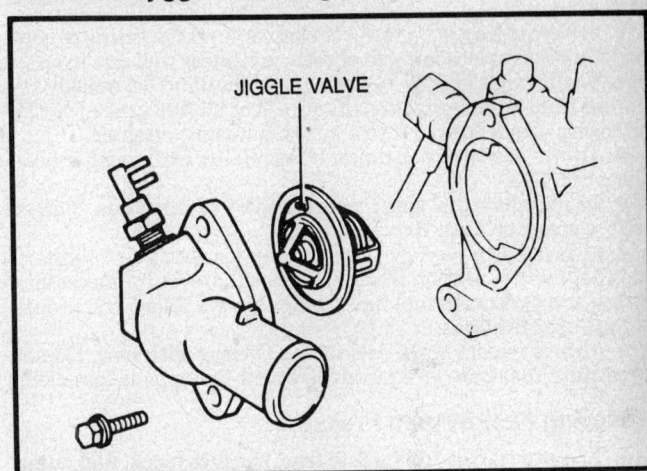

Typical thermostat assembly

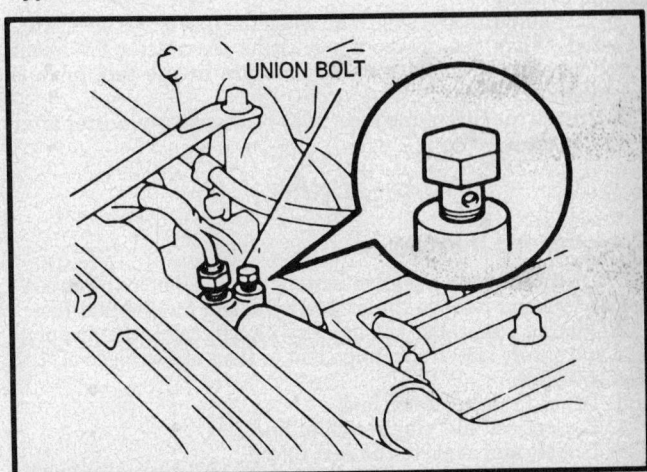

Cooling system air relief location—2VZ-FE engine

2. With the radiator cap off, start the engine and allow it to run and reach normal operating temperature.

3. Run the heater at full force and with the temperature lever in the hot position. Be sure the heater control valve is functioning.

4. Shut the engine off and recheck the coolant level, refill as necessary. On 2VZ-FE engine, release the air from the cooling system by backing off on air relief union bolt about 4–5 turns.

FUEL SYSTEM

Fuel System Service Precautions

Safety is the most important factor when performing not only fuel system maintenance but any type of maintenance. Failure to conduct maintenance and repairs in a safe manner may result in serious personal injury or death. Maintenance and testing of the vehicle's fuel system components can be accomplished safely and effectively by adhering to the following rules and guidelines.

• To avoid the possibility of fire and personal injury, always disconnect the negative battery cable unless the repair or test procedure requires that battery voltage be applied.

• Always relieve the fuel system pressure prior to disconnecting any fuel system component (injector, fuel rail, pressure regulator, etc.), fitting or fuel line connection. Exercise extreme caution whenever relieving fuel system pressure to avoid exposing skin, face and eyes to fuel spray. Please be advised that fuel under pressure may penetrate the skin or any part of the body that it contacts.

• Always place a shop towel or cloth around the fitting or connection prior to loosening to absorb any excess fuel due to spillage. Ensure that all fuel spillage (should it occur) is quickly removed from engine surfaces. Ensure that all fuel soaked cloths or towels are deposited into a suitable waste container.

• Always keep a dry chemical (Class B) fire extinguisher near the work area.

• Do not allow fuel spray or fuel vapors to come into contact with a spark or open flame.

• Always use a backup wrench when loosening and tightening fuel line connection fittings. This will prevent unnecessary stress and torsion to fuel line piping. Always follow the proper torque specifications.

• Always replace worn fuel fitting O-rings with new. Do not substitute fuel hose or equivalent where fuel pipe is installed.

Relieving Fuel System Pressure

1. Remove the fuel pump fuse from the fuse block, fuel pump relay or disconnect the harness connector at the tank while engine is running.

2. It should run and then stall when the fuel in the lines is exhausted. When the engine stops, crank the starter for about three seconds to make sure all pressure in the fuel lines is released.

3. Install the fuel pump fuse, relay or harness connector after repair is made.

Fuel Filter

Removal and Installation

1. Disconnect the negative battery cable. Unbolt the retaining screws and remove the protective shield for the fuel filter.

2. Place a pan under the delivery pipe to catch the dripping fuel and slowly loosen the union bolt or flare nut to bleed off the fuel pressure.

3. Drain the remaining fuel.

4. Disconnect and plug the inlet line.

5. Unbolt and remove the fuel filter.

NOTE: When tightening the fuel line bolts to the fuel filter, use a torque wrench. The tightening torque is very important, as under or over tightening may cause fuel leakage. Insure that there is no fuel line interference and that there is sufficient clearance between it and any other parts.

6. Coat the flare nut, union nut and bolt threads with engine oil.

7. Hand tighten the inlet line to the fuel filter.

8. Install the fuel filter and then tighten the inlet bolt to 22 ft. lbs. (30 Nm).

9. Reconnect the delivery pipe using new gaskets and then tighten the union bolt to 22 ft. lbs. (30 Nm).

10. Run the engine for a few minutes and check for any fuel leaks.

11. Install the protective shield.

Mechanical Fuel Pump

The 3E, 3A-C, 4A-C and 4A-F engines use a mechanical type fuel pump. It is located on the right rear of the cylinder head.

Pressure Testing

1. Remove the line which runs from the fuel pump to the carburetor.

2. Attach a pressure gauge to the outlet side of the pump.

3. Run the engine and check the pressure.

4. Check the pressure against the specifications.

5. If the pressure is below the specifications replace the pump.

6. Reconnect the carburetor line.

Removal and Installation

1. Disconnect and plug the fuel lines to the pump.

2. Remove the nuts which hold the pump to the cylinder head.

3. Remove the pump assembly.

4. Installation is the reverse of removal. Always use a new gasket when installing a fuel pump.

Electric Fuel Pump

Pressure Testing

―――――――――― CAUTION ――――――――――
Do not operate the fuel pump unless it is immersed in gasoline and connected to its resistor.

1. Turn the ignition switch to the **ON** position, but don't start the engine.

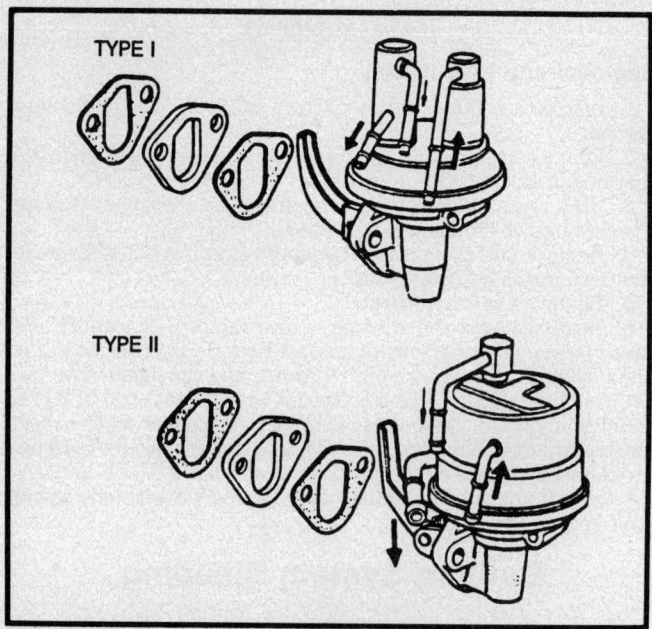

Typical mechanical fuel pump styles

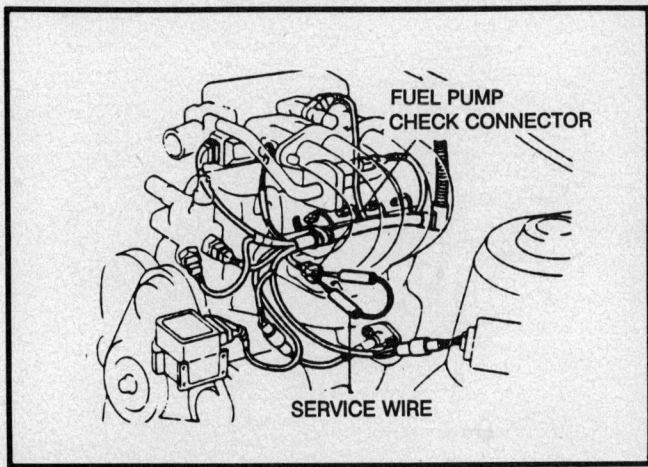

Shorting the fuel pump check connector—typical

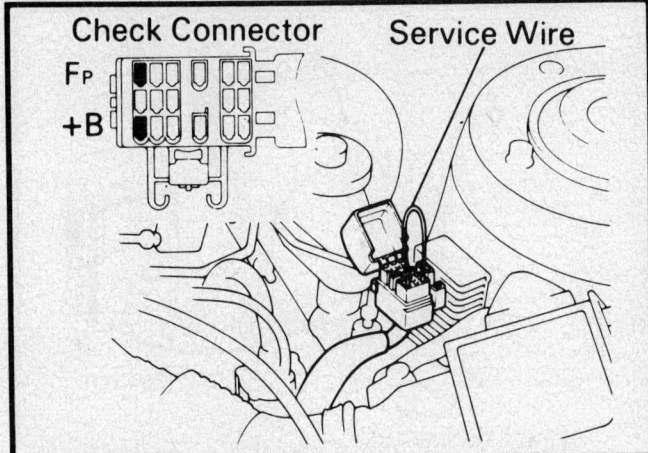

Shorting the fuel pump check connector (3S-GE shown, check connector terminals are in same location for all engines)

2. Remove the rubber cap from the fuel pump check connector and short terminals **Fp** and **+B** with a jumper wire.

NOTE: The check connector on all engines is in a small plastic box with a flip-up lid; it is found near the strut tower or battery. The box is roughly the same size and shape for every engine and terminals Fp and +B are always in the same location.

3. Check that there is pressure in the hose to the cold start injector. On 4A-FE and 4A-GE engines, check for pressure at the regulator fuel return hose. On 2VZ-FE, 3S-FE, 5S-FE, 3S-GE 4A-GE and 3S-GTE engines, check for pressure at the fuel filter hose.

NOTE: At this time, fuel return noise from the pressure regulator should be audible.

4. If no pressure can be felt in the line, check the fuses and all other related electrical connections. If everything is alright, the fuel pump will probably require replacement.

5. Remove the jumper wire, reinstall the rubber cap and turn off the ignition switch.

Removal and Installation

The fuel pump is mounted inside the fuel tank on all vehicles. On all vehicles except 1990 Celica (non-turbocharged) removal

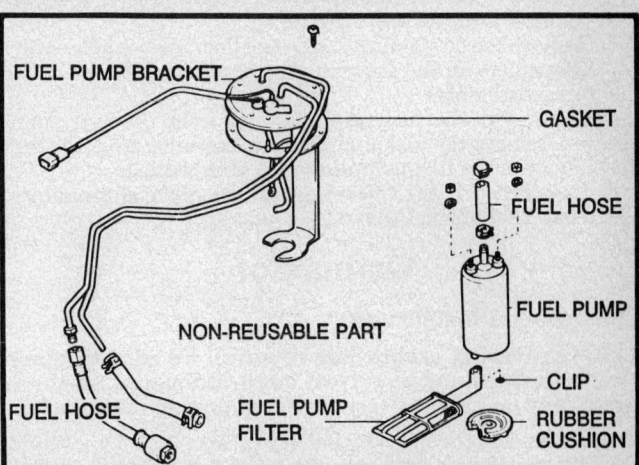

Typical fuel pump assembly—except 1990–91 Celica non-turbo

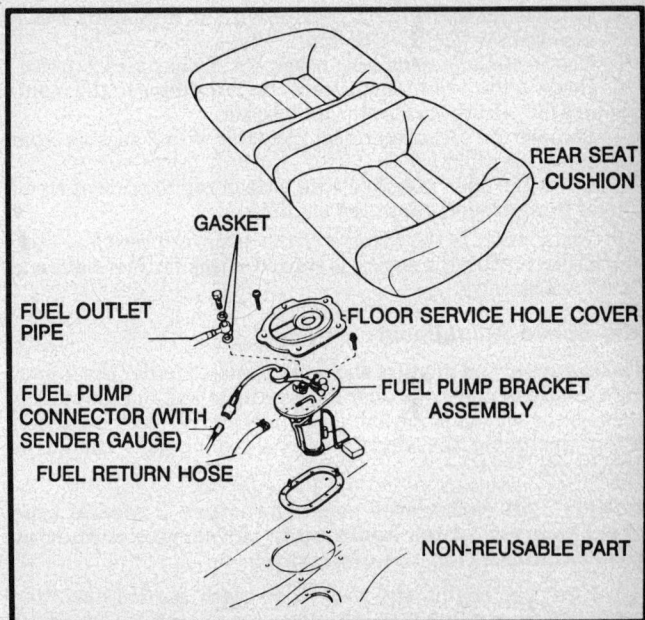

Fuel pump assembly—1990–91 Celica non-turbo

of the fuel tank is necessary to remove the fuel pump. On 1990–91 Celica non-turbocharged, access to the pump is gained by removing the rear seat cushion.

EXCEPT 1990–91 CELICA NON-TURBOCHARGED

1. Disconnect the negative battery cable.
2. Drain the fuel from the tank and then remove the fuel tank.
3. Remove the bolts and then pull the fuel pump bracket up and out of the fuel tank.
4. Remove the mounting nuts then tag and disconnect the wires at the fuel pump.
5. Pull the fuel pump out of the lower side of the bracket. Disconnect the pump from the fuel hose.
6. Remove the rubber cushion and the clip. Disconnect the fuel pump filter from the pump.
7. Installation is in the reverse order of removal procedure. Use a new fuel bracket gasket.

1990–91 CELICA NON-TURBOCHARGED

1. Disconnect the negative battery cable.

2. Remove the rear seat cushion.

3. Remove the 5 retaining screws and floor service hole cover.

4. Disconnect all the electrical fuel pump connections at the fuel pump assembly.

5. Disconnect the fuel pipe and hose from the fuel pump bracket. Remove the fuel pump bracket assembly from the fuel tank. Remove the fuel pump from the fuel bracket.

6. Installation is the the reverse of the removal procedure. Use a new fuel bracket gasket.

Carburetor

Removal and Installation

NOTE: During carburetor removal, be sure to mark all hoses, lines and electrical connectors, etc., so these items may be properly reconnected during installation.

1. Disconnect the negative battery cable.

2. Remove the air cleaner housing and disconnect all air hoses from the air cleaner base.

3. Disconnect the fuel line, choke pipe, and distributor vacuum line.

4. Remove the accelerator linkage. With an automatic transaxle, also remove the throttle rod.

5. Disconnect any remaining hoses, etc., from the carburetor.

6. Remove the 4 nuts that secure the carburetor to the manifold and lift off the carburetor and gasket.

7. Remove the carburetor heat insulator with 2 gaskets from the intake manifold.

8. Cover the open manifold with a clean rag to prevent small objects from dropping into the engine.

9. Installation is the reverse of the removal procedure. Use new gaskets. After the engine is started, check for fuel leaks and float level settings.

Idle Speed Adjustment

The idle speed and mixture should be adjusted under the following conditions: the air cleaner must be installed, the choke fully opened, the transmission should be in **N** and all electrical accessories (including the electric engine cooling fan) should be turned off.

NOTE: All carbureted engines require a special type of tachometer which hooks up to the service connector wire coming out of the distributor.

1. Start the engine and allow it to reach normal operating temperature.

2. Check the float setting; the fuel level should be just about

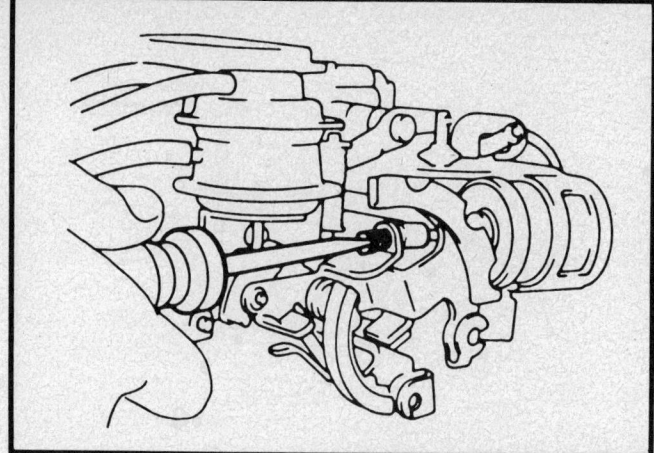

Idle speed adjusting screw—Tercel with carburetor

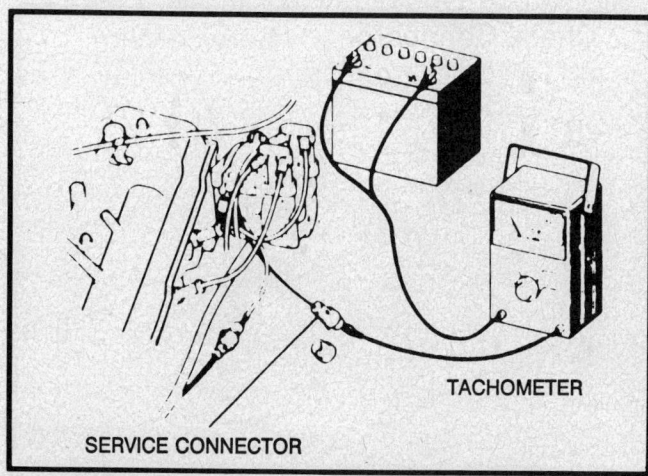

Tachometer hook-up—Corolla and Tercel with carburetor

even with the spot on the sight glass. If the fuel level is too high or low, adjust the float level.

3. Stop the engine.

4. Remove the rubber cap from the IIA service connector the comes out of the distributor and connect the positive terminal of the tachometer to the connector.

5. Start the engine and check the idle speed.

6. If the idle speed is not within specifications, turn the idle speed adjusting screw until the idle speed is correct.

7. Stop the engine and disconnect the tachometer.

Idle Mixture Adjustment

MIXTURE PLUG REMOVAL

To conform with Federal regulations, the mixture adjusting screw is plugged at the factory to prevent tampering with the adjustment. Normally, this plug should not be removed. When troubleshooting a rough idle, check all other possible causes before removing the plug and adjusting the idle mixture.

NOTE: Depending on the age of the vehicle, the idle mixture plug may have been removed already. This is determined by looking down into the mixture screw bore with an inspection mirror. If the head of the mixture adjusting screw can be seen, then the mixture plug has been drilled out and removal of carburetor is not necessary to adjust the idle mixture.

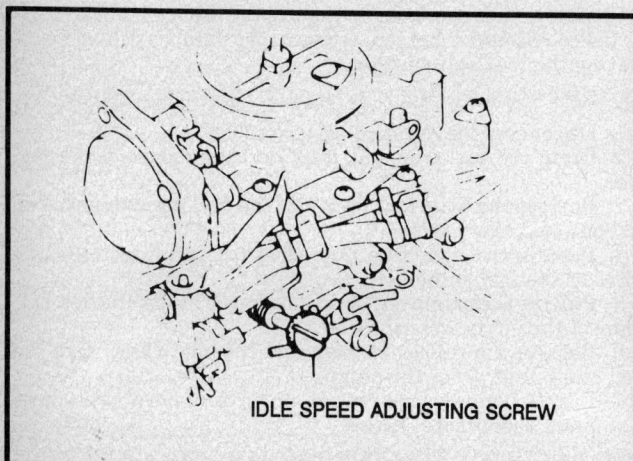

IDLE SPEED ADJUSTING SCREW

Idle speed adjusting screw—Corolla with carburetor

1. Remove the carburetor from the engine, if required.
2. Plug each carburetor vacuum port to prevent entry of shavings when drilling.
3. Mark the center of the plug with a punch.
4. Drill a 0.256 in. (6.5mm) hole in the center of the plug. Drill carefully and slowly to avoid drilling into the screw, since there is only 0.04 in. (1mm) clearance between the plug and the screw. The drill may force the plug off.
5. Lightly seat the mixture screw by inserting a flat blade tool into the drilled hole and turning the screw clockwise. Be careful not to tighten the screw or damage to the needle tip may result.
6. If the plug is still in place, use a 0.295 in. (7.5mm) drill bit to force the plug out of the hole.
7. Remove the mixture adjusting screw and inspect it for damage. If the tapered needle portion is damaged or scored, replace the mixture adjusting screw.
8. Fully seat the mixture adjusting screw lightly once again, then back it out the following number of turns:
    Tercel—3½ turns counterclockwise.
    Tercel AWD wagon (Canada vehicles)—2½ turns counterclockwise.
    Corolla (USA vehicles)—3¼ turns counterclockwise.
    Corolla (Canada vehicles)—2½ turns counterclockwise.
9. Install the carburetor and continue the idle speed and mixture adjustments.

Idle Mixture Adjustment

1. Remove the idle mixture plug, as required.
2. Connect a tachometer to the engine.
3. All adjustments should be made with the engine at normal operating temperature under the following conditions:
    a. Air cleaner installed.
    b. Choke fully open.
    c. All accessories switched off.
    d. All vacuum lines connected.
    e. Ignition timing set to specifications.
    f. Transmission in **N**.
4. Start the engine and allow it to reach normal operating temperature.
5. Turn the idle mixture screw to obtain the maximum idle speed, then use the idle speed screw to adjust the idle as follows:
    Corolla—700 rpm.
    Tercel with manual transaxles—750 rpm.
    Tercel with automatic transaxles—900 rpm.
6. Continue going back and forth until the idle speed doesn't rise when the mixture screw is adjusted.

NOTE: The cooling fan should be off for all adjustments.

7. Adjust the idle speed down as follows by turning in the idle mixture screw. This is the lean drop method of adjustment.
    Corolla with manual transaxle—650 rpm.
    Corolla with automatic transaxle—750 rpm.
    Tercel with manual transaxle—700 rpm.
    Tercel with automatic transaxle—900 rpm.
8. Adjust the idle speed to specifications by turning the idle speed adjusting screw.
9. Once the idle speed is adjusted, install a new tamper-proof plug over the mixture adjusting screw.

Service Adjustments

FLOAT LEVEL

Float level adjustments are unnecessary, if equipped with a carburetor sight glass, if the fuel level falls within the lines or aligns with the dot when the engine is running.

There are 2 float level adjustments which may be made on the carburetors. One is with the air horn inverted, so the float is in a fully raised position; the other is with the air horn in an upright position, so the float falls to the bottom of its travel.

The float level can be measured with a special carburetor float level gauge, which comes with a rebuilding kit or with a standard wire gauge.

NOTE: Gap specifications are also given so a float level gauge may be fabricated.

Adjust the float level by bending the tabs on the float levers, either upper or lower, as required. Float level adjustment specifications are as follows:

3A-C and 4A-F engines—the distance between the float tip and the air horn should be 0.283 in. (7.2mm). The distance between the needle valve plunger and the float tab should be 0.0657–0.0783 in. (2mm).

3E engine—the distance between the float tip and the air horn should be 0.169 in. (4.3mm). The distance between the needle valve plunger and the float tab should be 0.039 in. (1mm).

FAST IDLE

1. Apply the emergency brake and block the wheels.
2. Start the engine and let it run until it reaches normal operating temperature.
3. Connect a suitable tachometer to the engine and check the curb idle speed and adjust as necessary.
4. Stop the engine and remove the air cleaner.
5. Plug the air suction hose (on California and Canada vehicles) to prevent leakage of the exhaust gas and plug the air suction valve hose (California vehicles) and plug the hot idle compensator hose to prevent rough idling.
6. Disconnect the hose from the thermostatic vacuum switching valve (TVSV) **M** port (second from the top) and plug the **M** port. This will shut off the choke opener and the EGR system.
7. Set the fast idle cam, by holding the throttle slightly open and pushing the choke valve closed as the throttle valve is released.
8. Start the engine, but do not depress the accelerator pedal. Set the fast idle speed by turning the fast idle adjustment screw. The fast idle speed should be 3000 rpm (3E with automatic transaxle: 2800 rpm).
9. After setting the fast idle speed check the curb idle speed.

AUTOMATIC CHOKE

NOTE: The automatic choke should be adjusted with the carburetor installed and the engine running.

1. Check to see that the choke valve will close from fully opened when the coil housing is turned counterclockwise.
2. Align the mark on the coil housing with the center line on the thermostat case. In this position, the choke valve should be fully closed when the ambient temperature is 77°F.
3. If necessary, adjust the mixture by turning the coil housing. If the mixture is too rich, rotate the housing clockwise; of too lean, rotate the housing counterclockwise.

NOTE: Each graduation on the thermostat case is equivalent to 9°F.

MANUAL CHOKE

1. Close the choke by turning the choke shaft lever.
2. Check the 1st throttle valve opening angle with the tool supplied in the rebuild kit.
3. Adjust by turning the fast idle adjusting screw.

CHOKE BREAK

4A-F Engine Only

1. Push the rod which comes out of the upper (choke break) diaphragm so the choke valve opens.
2. Measure the choke valve opening angle. It should be 38 degrees.
3. Adjust the angle, if necessary, by bending the relief lever link.

Initial Idle Screw Adjustment

When assembling the carburetor, turn the idle mixture screw the number of turns specified below. After the carburetor is installed, perform the appropriate idle/speed mixture adjustment.

3A-C, 4A-C Engine—3¼ turns from seating (1987–88, U.S.); 2½ turns from seating (1987, Canada).

4A-F Engine—3¼ turns from seating.

3E Engine—turn the idle mixture adjusting screw in until the head of the screw is 0.0138 in. (3.5mm) below the lower surface of the carburetor.

NOTE: Seat the idle mixture screw lightly; over tightening will damage the tip of the screw.

Fuel Injection

For further information, please refer to "Chilton's Electronic Engine Control's Manual" for additional coverage.

Idle Speed Adjustment

Idle speed adjustment is performed under the following conditions:

Engine at normal operating temperature.
Air cleaner installed.
Air pipes and hoses of the air induction and EGR systems properly connected.
All vacuum lines and electrical wires connected and plugged in properly.
All electrical accessories in the **OFF** position.
Transaxle in the **N** position.

SUPRA, 1989–91 CRESSIDA, CAMRY (2VZ-FE ENGINE) AND 1990 CELICA (3S-GTE ENGINE)

Idle speed is controlled by the Electronic Control Unit (ECU) and is not adjustable.

1987–88 CRESSIDA

1. Connect a tachometer and timing light to the engine.
2. Start the engine and warm up to normal operating temperature.
3. Check the ignition timing. Adjust as necessary.
4. Check the idle speed.
5. If the idle speed is not within specifications, adjust by turning the idle speed adjusting screw on the throttle body.
6. Stop the engine and disconnect the tachometer.

TERCEL

1. Run the engine until it reaches normal operating temperature. The cooling fan must not be running during the idle speed adjustment.
2. Connect a tachometer to the engine.

NOTE: Do not allow the tachometer or coil terminals to be grounded. This will damage the injection system.

3. On 3E-E engine, disconnect the idle up Vacuum Switching Valve (VSV) connector.
4. Run the engine at 2500 rpm for 2 minutes.
5. Adjust the idle speed by turning the idle speed adjusting screw.
6. On 3E-E engine, connect the idle up Vacuum Switching Valve (VSV) connector.
7. Disconnect the tachometer.

COROLLA

1. Run the engine until it reaches normal operating temperature. The cooling fan must not be running during the idle speed adjustment.

2. Connect a tachometer to the engine.

NOTE: Do not allow the tachometer or coil terminals to be grounded. This will damage the injection system.

3. Run the engine at 2500 rpm for 2 minutes.
4. On 1990 vehicles, short the check connector at terminals TE_1 and E_1 using a suitable jumper wire.
5. Adjust the idle speed by turning the idle speed adjusting screw.
6. On 1990–91 vehicles, remove the jumper wire from the connector terminals.
7. Disconnect the tachometer.

CAMRY AND 1987–88 CELICA (3S-FE ENGINE)

1. Run the engine until it reaches normal operating temperature. The cooling fan must not be running during the idle speed adjustment.
2. Connect a tachometer to the engine.

NOTE: Do not allow the tachometer or coil terminals to be grounded. This will damage the injection system.

3. On 1987–88 Camry, short the check connector at terminals **T** and E_1 using a suitable jumper wire. On 1989–91 Camry, short the check connector at terminals TE_1 and E_1. On Celica, short the check connector at terminals TE_1 (California) or **T** (except California) and E_1.
4. Run the engine at 1000–3000 rpm for 5 seconds and return the engine to idle.
5. Adjust the idle speed by turning the idle speed adjusting screw.
6. Remove the jumper wire from the connector terminals.
7. Disconnect the tachometer.

1987–89 CELICA (3S-GE ENGINE)

1. Run the engine until it reaches normal operating temperature. The cooling fan must not be running during the idle speed adjustment.
2. Connect a tachometer to the engine.

NOTE: Do not allow the tachometer or coil terminals to be grounded. This will damage the injection system.

3. Run the engine at 2500 rpm for 2 minutes.
4. Pinch the No. 1 air intake chamber vacuum hose.
5. Adjust the idle speed by turning the idle speed adjusting screw.
6. Release the No. 1 vacuum hose.
7. Disconnect the tachometer.

1990–91 MR2 (5S-FE ENGINE) AND 1990–91 CELICA (4A-FE AND 5S-FE ENGINE)

1. Run the engine until it reaches normal operating temperature. The cooling fan must not be running during the idle speed adjustment.
2. Connect a tachometer to the engine.

NOTE: Do not allow the tachometer or coil terminals to be grounded. This will damage the injection system.

3. On 4A-FE engine, run the engine at 2500 rpm for 2 minutes. On 5S-FE engine, run the engine at 1000–3000 rpm for 5 seconds. Allow the engine to return to idle.
4. Short the check connector at terminals TE_1 and E_1 using a suitable jumper wire.
5. Adjust the idle speed by turning the idle speed adjusting screw.
6. Remove the jumper wire from the connector terminals.
7. Disconnect the tachometer.

MR2 (4A-GE ENGINE)

1. Run the engine until it reaches normal operating tempera-

ture. The cooling fan must not be running during the idle speed adjustment.

2. Connect a tachometer to the engine.

NOTE: Do not allow the tachometer or coil terminals to be grounded. This will damage the injection system.

3. Run the engine at 2500 rpm for 2 minutes.

4. Adjust the idle speed by turning the idle speed adjusting screw.

5. Disconnect the tachometer.

MR2 (4A-GZE ENGINE)

1. Run the engine until it reaches normal operating temperature. The cooling fan must not be running during the idle speed adjustment.

2. Connect a tachometer to the engine.

NOTE: Do not allow the tachometer or coil terminals to be grounded. This will damage the injection system.

3. Short the check connector at terminals T and E_1 using a suitable jumper wire.

4. Adjust the idle speed by turning the idle speed adjusting screw.

5. Remove the jumper wire from the connector terminals.

6. Disconnect the tachometer.

Idle Mixture Adjustment

On all fuel injected engines, the idle mixture is controlled by the Electronic Control Unit (ECU) and is not adjustable.

Fuel Injector

Removal and Installation

TERCEL

1. Relieve the fuel system pressure.
2. Disconnect the negative battery cable.
3. Disconnect and tag the PCV and vacuum hoses.
4. Remove the air intake connnector.
5. Disconnect the accelerator and throttle cables.
6. Disconnect the vacuum sensing hose.
7. Remove the 2 bolts remove the dashpot and link bracket. Disconnect the spring from the dashpot and throttle linkage.
8. Remove the pulsation damper and disconnect the fuel inlet hose from it.
9. Remove the clamp and disconnect the fuel return hose.
10. Remove the cold start injector pipe.
11. Disconnect the injector harness connectors.
12. Remove the 2 bolts attaching the fuel delivery pipe to the cylinder head.
13. Pull the delivery pipe and fuel injectors from the cylinder head.

NOTE: Whe removing the delivery pipe, be careful not to drop the injectors.

14. Remove the injectors from the delivery pipe.
15. Remove the 4 spacers and insulators from the cylinder head. Remove the grommets and O-rings from the injectors. Discard these components and replace with new.
To install:
16. Install new injector grommets and O-rings. Coat the O-rings with clean fuel prior to installation. Make sure the O-ring seats properly in the injector groove. If not, the O-ring will become pinched.
17. Install new spacers and insulators into the cylinder head. Install the injectors into the delivery pipe using a moderate back and forth twisting motion.
18. Mount the injector and delivery pipe assembly onto the cylinder head.

19. Install the delivery pipe retaining bolts and torque them to 14 ft. lbs. (19 Nm). After the bolts are tight, attempt to twist each injector back and forth a small amount by hand. The injectors should rotate smoothly. If not, the injector O-ring are probably not installed properly. Replace the O-rings as required.
20. Connect the injector harness connectors.
21. Install the cold start inejctor pipe.
22. Connect the fuel return hose to the delivery pipe.
23. Connect the fuel inlet hose to the delivery pipe using new gaskets. Install the pulsation damper and torque to 22 ft. lbs. (29 Nm).
24. Connect the spring to the throttle linkage and dashpot. Install the dashpot and link bracket.
25. Connect the vacuum sensing hose.
26. Connect the throttle and accelerator cables.
27. Install the air intake connector.
28. Connect the PCV hoses.
29. Connect the negative battery cable.
30. Start the engine and check for fuel leaks.

COROLLA AND 1987–89 MR2

1. Relieve the fuel system pressure.
2. Disconnect the negative battery cable. On MR2 with 4A-GZE engine, remove the throttle body.
3. Disconnect and tag the vacuum and PCV hoses. On MR2 with 4A-GZE engine, loosen the air outlet duct and remove the throttle cable bracket.
4. Disconnect the fuel return hose from the pressure regulator. On MR2 with 4A-GZE engine, remove the fuel pressure regulator.
5. Disconnect the injector harness connectors.
6. Remove the cold start injector pipe.
7. Disconnect the fuel inlet pipe.
8. Remove the delivery pipe bolts and remove the delivery pipe and fuel injectors from the cylinder head.

NOTE: When removing the delivery pipe, be careful not to drop the injectors.

9. On Corrola and MR2 with 4A-GE engine, remove the 2 spacers and 2 insulators from the cylinder head. On MR2 with 4A-GZE engine, there are 3 spacers and 4 insulators.
10. Remove the injectors from the delivery pipe. Remove the O-rings and grommets from the injectors and discard them.
To install:
11. Install new injector grommets and O-rings. Coat the O-rings with clean fuel prior to installation. Make sure the O-ring seats properly in the injector groove. If not, the O-ring will become pinched.
12. Install new spacers and insulators into the cylinder head.
13. Install the injectors into the delivery pipe using a moderate back and forth twisting motion.
14. Mount the injector and delivery pipe assembly onto the cylinder head.
15. Install the delivery pipe retaining bolts and torque them to 11–13 ft. lbs. (15–17 Nm). After the bolts are tight, attempt to twist each injector back and forth a small amount. The injectors should rotate smoothly. If not, the injector O-ring are probably not installed properly. Replace the O-ring(s) as required.
16. Connnect the fuel inlet pipe using new gaskets. Torque the union bolt to 22 ft. lbs. (29 Nm).
17. Install the cold start injector pipe.
18. Connect the injector harness connectors.
19. Connect the fuel return hose to the fuel pressure regulator.
20. Connect the vacuum and PCV hoses.
21. Connect the negative battery cable.
22. Start the engine and check for leaks.

CAMRY AND CELICA (3S-FE ENGINE)

1. Relieve the fuel system pressure and disconnect the negative battery cable

2. Remove the cold start injector pipe.

3. Disconnect the vacuum sensing hose from the fuel pressure regulator.

4. Disconnect the injector harness connectors.

5. Disconnect the hose from fuel return pipe.

6. Remove the fuel pressure pulsation damper.

7. Remove the 2 bolts and the delivery pipe together with the 2 injectors attached.

NOTE: When removing the delivery pipe, be careful not to drop the injectors.

8. Remove the 4 insulators and the 2 spacers from the cylinder head. Pull out the four injectors from the delivery pipe.

To install:

9. Insert 4 new insulators and 2 spacers into the injector holes in the cylinder head.

10. Install the grommet and a new O-ring to the delivery pipe end of each injector.

11. Apply a thin coat of fuel to the O-ring on each injector and then press them into the delivery pipe.

12. Install the injectors together with the delivery pipe into the cylinder head. Tighten the 2 mounting bolts to 9 ft. lbs. (13 Nm). After the bolts are tight, attempt to twist each injector back and forth a small amount. The injectors should rotate smoothly. If not, the injector O-ring are probably not installed properly. Replace the O-ring(s) as required.

13. Install the fuel pressure pulsation damper with 2 new gaskets on the union bolt.

14. Connect the hose to the fuel return pipe.

15. Connect the injector harness connectors.

16. Connect the vacuum sensing hose to the fuel pressure regulator.

17. Install the cold start injector pipe.

18. Connect the negative battery cable.

19. Start the engine and check for leaks.

CAMRY (2VZ-FE ENGINE)

1. Relieve the fuel system pressure.

2. Disconnect the negative battery cable.

3. Drain the cooling system.

4. If equipped with automatic transaxle, disconnect the throttle cable from the bracket and throttle body.

5. Remove the air cleaner cap, air flow meter and air cleaner flexible hose.

6. Disconnect and tag all interfering vacuum hoses and electrical wiring harness connectors.

7. Remove the right engine mounting stay.

8. Disconnect the cold start injector connector.

9. Disconnect the cold start injector tube.

10. Disconnect the EGR pipe.

11. Remove the engine hanger and air intake chamber stay.

12. Remove the air intake chamber.

13. Disconnect harness connectors from the tops of the injectors.

14. Disconnect the wiring harness clamps from the left delivery pipe.

15. Disconnect the fuel hoses from the pressure regulator, fuel filter and delivery pipes.

16. Unbolt and pull the left and right delivery pipes with fuel injectors from the intake manifold.

NOTE: When removing the delivery pipes, be careful not to drop the injectors.

17. Remove the injectors from the delivery pipes.

18. Remove the 6 insulator and 4 spacers from the injector openings.

To install:

19. Insert 6 new insulators and 4 spacers into the injector openings in the intake manifold.

20. Install the grommet and a new O-ring to the delivery pipe end of each injector.

21. Apply a thin coat of fuel to the O-ring on each injector and then press them into the delivery pipe.

22. Mount the injectors together with the delivery pipes onto the intake manifold. Tighten the mounting bolts to 9 ft. lbs. (13 Nm). After the bolts are tight, attempt to twist each injector back and forth a small amount. The injectors should rotate smoothly. If not, the injector O-ring are probably not installed properly. Replace the O-ring(s) as required.

23. Connect the fuel hoses to the pressure regulator, fuel filter and delivery pipes. Use new gaskets on union bolt connections.

24. Connect the wiring harness clamps to the left delivery pipe.

25. Connect the harness connectors to the tops of the injectors.

26. Install the air intake chamber. Torque the mounting nuts to 32 ft. lbs. (43 Nm).

27. Install the air intake chamber stay and engine hanger.

28. Connect the EGR pipe and torque the pipe union nut to 58 ft. lbs. (78 Nm).

29. Connect the cold start injector tube and plug in the connector.

30. Install the right engine mounting stay.

31. Connect all vacuum hoses and electrical wiring harness connectors.

32. Install the air cleaner cap, air flow meter and air cleaner flexible hose.

33. If equipped with automatic transaxle, connect the throttle cable to the cable bracket and throttle body.

34. Fill the cooling system and connect the negative battery cable.

35. Start the engine and check for leaks.

CELICA (3S-GE ENGINE)

1. Disconnect the negative battery cable.

2. Relieve the fuel system pressure.

3. Drain the cooling system.

4. Disconnect the throttle cable and the accelerator cable from the throttle linkage.

5. Disconnect the ignition coil connector and the high tension cord, then remove the suspension upper brace.

6. Disconnect the air cleaner hose.

7. Remove the ignitor.

8. Remove the throttle body.

9. Remove the No. 2 engine hanger and the No. 2 intake manifold stay.

10. Loosen the union nut of the EGR pipe.

11. Remove the cold start injector pipe.

12. Remove the EGR modulator.

13. Tag and disconnect all hoses and wires which interfere with injector removal.

14. Raise and support the vehicle safely.

15. Remove the suspension lower crossmember.

16. Disconnect the exhaust pipe.

17. Remove the No. 1 and the No. 3 intake manifold stays.

18. Disconnect the ground strap.

19. Remove the intake manifold.

20. Remove the 3 bolts and the delivery pipe with the injectors.

NOTE: When removing the delivery pipes, be careful not to drop the injectors.

21. Remove the injectors from the delivery pipes.

22. Remove the insulators and spacers from the injector openings.

To install:

23. Insert new insulators and spacers into the injector openings in the intake manifold.

24. Install the grommet and a new O-ring to the delivery pipe end of each injector.

25. Apply a thin coat of fuel to the O-ring on each injector and then press them into the delivery pipe.

26. Mount the injectors together with the delivery pipes onto the intake manifold. Tighten the mounting bolts to 9 ft. lbs. (13 Nm). After the bolts are tight, attempt to twist each injector back and forth a small amount. The injectors should rotate smoothly. If not, the injector O-ring are probably not installed properly. Replace the O-ring(s) as required.

27. Installation of the remaining components is the reverse of the removal procedure. Fill the cooling system. Start the engine and check for fuel leaks.

CELICA (3S-GTE ENGINE)

1. Relieve the fuel system pressure and disconnect the negative battery cable.
2. Remove the throttle body.
3. Remove the fuel pressure regulator.
4. Remove the EGR vacuum modulator
5. Disconnect the electrical connections from fuel injectors.
6. Remove the pulsation damper. Disconnect fuel inlet hose from the delivery pipe.
7. Disconnect the fuel return hose from the return pipe.
8. Remove the delivery pipe and fuel injectors and related components (insulators, spacers, O-ring and grommet).

NOTE: When removing the delivery pipes, be careful not to drop the injectors.

9. Remove the injectors from the delivery pipes.
10. Remove the insulators and spacers from the injector openings.
To install:
11. Insert new insulators and spacers into the injector openings in the intake manifold.
12. Install the grommet and a new O-ring to the delivery pipe end of each injector.
13. Apply a thin coat of fuel to the O-ring on each injector and then press them into the delivery pipe.
14. Mount the injectors together with the delivery pipes onto the intake manifold. Tighten the mounting bolts to 9 ft. lbs. (13 Nm). After the bolts are tight, attempt to twist each injector back and forth a small amount. The injectors should rotate smoothly. If not, the injector O-ring are probably not installed properly. Replace the O-ring(s) as required.
15. Installation of the remaining components is the reverse of the removal procedure. Start the engine and check for fuel leaks.

MR2 (3S-GTE ENGINE)

1. Relieve the fuel system pressure.
2. Disconnect the negative battery cable.
3. Remove the throttle body.
4. Remove the left engine hood side panel.
5. Remove the air cleaner.
6. Remove the charcoal canister.
7. Remove the EGR vacuum switching valve, vacuum modulator, EGR valve and pipe.
8. Remove the cold start injector pipe and cold start injector.
9. Remove the Idle Speed Control (ISC) water bypass hoses and air hoses.
10. Disconnect the vaccum sensing hose from the vacuum sensing pipe on the injector cover.
11. Disconnect the harness connectors from the tops of the injectors.
12. Disconnect the 2 wire clamps from the mounting bolts on the No. 2 timing cover. Disconnect the 2 wire clamps from the wire brackets on the intake manifold.
13. Disconnect the fuel inlet hose from the fuel filter.
14. Disconnect the fuel return hose from the fuel pressure regulator.
15. Remove the bolt that attaches the fuel inlet hose to the water outlet.

16. Remove the 3 bolts holding the delivery pipe to the cylinder head.
17. Disconnect the fuel inlet hose from the delivery pipe.
18. Remove the delivery pipe and fuel injectors and related components (4 insulators, 3 spacers and injector O-ring and grommets).

NOTE: When removing the delivery pipes, be careful not to drop the injectors.

19. Disconnect the vacuum sensing hose from the pressure regulator and remove the cover plate from the delivery pipe. Remove the injectors from the delivery pipe using the proper tool.
To install:
20. Insert 4 new insulators and 3 spacers into the injector openings.
21. Install the grommet and a new O-ring to the delivery pipe end of each injector.
22. Apply a thin coat of fuel to the O-ring on each injector and then press them into the delivery pipe. Make sure the injector connectors are positioned correctly.
23. Mount the injectors together with the delivery pipes. Tighten the mounting bolts to 14 ft. lbs. (19 Nm).
24. Installation of the remaining components is the reverse of the removal procedure. The injector harness connectors are color coded. The No. 1 and No. 3 injector connectors are brown and the No. 2 and No. 4 connectors are grey. Start the engine and check for fuel leaks.

CELICA AND MR2 (5S-FE ENGINE)

1. Disconnect the negative battery cable.
2. Remove the throttle body.
3. On MR2, remove the engine hood side panels, air cleaner and cruise control actuator.
4. Remove the cold start injector pipe.
5. On Celica, remove the fuel pressure regulator. On MR2, disconnect the brake booster vacuum hose from the intake manifold.
6. Disconnect necessary engine wiring and remove the left and right accelerator brackets.
7. Disconnect the electrical connectors from fuel injectors.
8. Disconnect wire retaining clamps from the No. 2 timing belt cover and and intake manifold as necessary to gain access for removal/installation of fuel injectors.
9. Disconnect the fuel return hose from the return pipe.
10. Remove the delivery pipe and fuel injectors and related components (insulators, spacers, O-ring and grommet).

NOTE: When removing the delivery pipes, be careful not to drop the injectors.

11. Remove injectors from the delivery pipe.
To install:
12. Insert new insulators and spacers into the injector openings in the intake manifold.
13. Install the grommet and a new O-ring to the delivery pipe end of each injector.
14. Apply a thin coat of fuel to the O-ring on each injector and then press them into the delivery pipe.
15. Mount the injectors together with the delivery pipes onto the intake manifold. Tighten the mounting bolts to 9 ft. lbs. (13 Nm). After the bolts are tight, attempt to twist each injector back and forth a small amount. The injectors should rotate smoothly. If not, the injector O-ring are probably not installed properly. Replace the O-ring(s) as required.
16. Installation of the remaining components is the reverse of the removal procedure. Start the engine and check for leaks.

SUPRA

1. Relieve the fuel system pressure.
2. Disconnect the negative battery cable.
3. Drain the cooling system.

4. Tag and disconnect all hoses and wires which interfere with injector removal.

5. Disconnect accelerator connecting rod.

6. On 7M-GE engine, remove the air intake connector. On 7M-GTE engine, remove the throttle body.

7. Remove the ISC valve and gasket.

8. Disconnect the injector connectors.

9. Disconnect the cold start injector tube from the delivery pipe.

10. Remove the pulsation damper and the 2 gaskets.

11. Remove the union bolts and 2 gaskets from the fuel return pipe support.

12. Remove the clamp bolts from the No. 1 fuel pipe and Vacuum Switching Valve (VSV).

13. Remove the union bolts and 2 gaskets from the pressure regulator.

14. Disconnect the fuel hose from the No. 2 fuel pipe.

15. Remove the clamp bolt and the return fuel pipe.

16. Loosen the locknut and remove the pressure regulator.

17. Remove the 3 bolts, and then remove the delivery pipe with the injectors.

NOTE: When removing the delivery pipe, be careful not to drop the injectors.

18. Remove the 6 insulators and the 3 spacers from the cylinder head, then pull out the injectors from the delivery pipe.
To install:

19. Before installing, apply a thin coat of gasoline to the O-ring on each injector and then press them into the delivery pipe.

20. Insert 6 new insulators into the injector hole of the cylinder head.

21. Install the black rings on the upper portion of each of the 3 spacers, then install the spacers on the delivery pipe mounting hole of the cylinder head.

22. Install the 3 spacers and bolts and torque to 13 ft. lbs. (After the bolts are tight, attempt to twist each injector back and forth a small amount. The injectors should rotate smoothly. If not, the injector O-ring are probably not installed properly. Replace the O-ring(s) as required.

23. Fully loosen the locknut of the pressure regulator. Push the pressure regulator completely into the delivery pipe by hand, then turn the regulator counterclockwise until the outlet faces outward in the correct position. Torque the locknut to 18 ft. lbs. (24 Nm).

24. Install the No. 2 fuel pipe and clamp bolt.

25. Connect the fuel hose.

26. Install the union bolt and 2 new gaskets to the pressure regulator and torque the union bolt to 18 ft. lbs. (24 Nm).

27. Install the No. 1 fuel pipe, Vacuum Switching Valve (VSV) and clamp bolt.

28. Install the union bolt and 2 new gaskets to the support pipe and torque the union bolts to 22 ft. lbs. (30 Nm).

29. Install the pulsation damper and 2 new gaskets and torque to 29 ft. lbs. (39 Nm).

30. Connect the injector connectors.

31. Install the Idle Speed Control (ISC) valve with a new gasket and torque to 9 ft. lbs. (13 Nm).

32. Install the throttle body or the air intake connector.

33. Connect the accelerator connecting rod.

34. Connect all vacuum hoses and electrical wires.

35. Refill the cooling system and connect the negative battery cable.

36. Start the engine and check for leaks.

CRESSIDA (5M-GE ENGINE)

1. Disconnect the negative battery cable.

2. Relieve the fuel system pressure.

3. Remove the air intake chamber.

4. Remove the distributor.

5. Remove the fuel pipe.

6. Unplug the wiring connectors from the tops of the fuel injectors and remove the 2 plastic clamps that hold the wiring harness to the fuel delivery pipe.

7. Unscrew the 4 mounting bolts and remove the delivery pipe with the injectors attached. Do not remove the injector cover.

NOTE: When removing the delivery pipe, be careful not to drop the injectors.

8. Pull the injectors out of the delivery pipe.
To install:

9. Insert 6 new insulators into the injector holes on the intake manifold.

10. Install the grommet and a new O-ring to the delivery pipe end of each injector.

11. Apply a thin coat of gasoline to the O-ring on each injector and then press them into the delivery pipe.

12. Install the injectors together with the delivery pipe in the intake manifold. Tighten the mounting bolts to 13 ft. lbs. (17 Nm). After the bolts are tight, attempt to twist each injector back and forth a small amount. The injectors should rotate smoothly. If not, the injector O-ring are probably not installed properly. Replace the O-ring(s) as required.

13. Secure the injector wiring harness to the delivery pipe with the plastic clamps. Connect the harness connectors to the tops of the injectors.

14. Install the fuel pipe, distributor and air intake chamber.

15. Connect the negative battery cable.

16. Start the engine and check for leaks.

CRESSIDA (7M-GE ENGINE)

1. Disconnect the negative battery cable and drain the cooling system.

2. Relieve the fuel system pressure.

3. Remove the throttle body.

4. Remove the Idle Speed Control (ISC) valve.

5. Disconnect the injector harness connectors.

6. Disconnect the cold start inejctor from the delivery pipe.

7. Disconnect the EGR Vacuum Switching Valve (VSV) connector.

8. Remove the union bolt and 2 gaskets from the delivery pipe and fuel filter.

9. Remove the clamp bolt and remove the No. 1 fuel pipe with the vacuum switching valve.

10. Disconnect the No. 3 PCV hose.

11. Disconnect the vacuum sensing hose.

12. Disconnect the fuel hose from the No. 2 fuel pipe.

13. Remove the union bolt and 2 gaskets from the pressure regulator.

14. Remove the clamp bolts and remove the No. 2 fuel pipe.

15. Loosen the locknut and remove the fuel pressure regulator.

16. Remove the delivery pipe attaching bolts. Remove the delivery pipe with the 6 fuel injectors.

17. Remove the 6 insulators and 3 spacers from the cylinder head.

18. Remove the injectors from the delivery pipe.
To install:

19. Install new injector grommets and O-rings. Coat the O-rings with clean fuel prior to installation. Make sure the O-ring seats properly in the injector groove. If not, the O-ring will become pinched.

20. Install new insulators into the cylinder head. Install the black rings on the upper portion of each spacer. Then, install the spacers into the mounting holes in the head.

21. Install the injectors into the delivery pipe using a moderate back and forth twisting motion.

22. Mount the injector and delivery pipe assembly onto the cylinder head. Make sure the injector connectors are facing up.

23. Install the delivery pipe retaining bolts and torque them to 13 ft. lbs. (18 Nm). After the bolts are tight, attempt to twist

each injector back and forth a small amount by hand. The injectors should rotate smoothly. If not, the injector O-ring are probably not installed properly. Replace the O-rings as required.

24. Install the fuel pipes and pressure regulator.
25. Connect the vacuum hoses and injector harness connectors. Install the Idle Speed Control (ISC) valve and throttle body.
26. Fill the cooling system to the proper level and connect the negative battery cable.
27. Start the engine and check for leaks.

ENGINE MECHANICAL

NOTE: Disconnecting the negative battery cable on some vehicles may interfere with the functions of the on board computer systems and may require the computer to undergo a relearning process, once the negative battery cable is reconnected.

Engine Assembly

Removal and Installation

2VZ-FE ENGINE

1. Disconnect the negative battery cable.
2. Remove the battery.
3. Drain the cooling system and engine oil.
4. Remove the hood.
5. Remove the ignition coil, igniter and bracket assembly.
6. Remove the radiator.
7. Remove the and coolant reservoir tank.
8. If equipped with automatic transaxle, disconnect the throttle cable from the throttle body.
9. If equipped with cruise control, remove the cruise control actuator and vacuum pump.
10. Remove the air cleaner assembly.
11. If equipped with manual transaxle, remove the clutch release cylinder. Position it aside with the hydraulic line still attached.
12. Disconnect the speedometer and transaxle control cables.
13. Remove the alternator and the belt adjusting bar.
14. Remove the air conditioning compressor and position it aside. Do not disconnect the refrigerant lines.
15. Disconnect the 2 water bypass hoses and fuel lines.
16. Tag and disconnect the brake booster, air conditioning control valve and charcoal canister vacuum hoses.
17. Tag and dsiconnect any additional wires and lines which may interfere with engine removal.
18. Raise and support the vehicle safely.
19. Remove the engine under covers.
20. Remove the lower suspension crossmember.
21. Remove the halfshafts.
22. Remove the power steering pump and position it aside without disconnecting the hydraulic lines.
23. Remove the front exhaust pipe.
24. Remove the engine mounting centermember.
25. Remove the front, center and rear engine mount insulator and bracket assemblies.
26. Lower the vehicle. Remove the glove box and then tag and disconnect the 3 ECU connectors, the circuit opening, cowl wire and instrument wire connectors. Pull the main engine harness out through the firewall.
27. Remove the power steering reservoir tank and position it aside without disconnecting the hydraulic lines.
28. Remove the 2 right side engine mounting stays. Remove the left side engine mounting stay.
29. Connect a suitable lifting device to the 2 engine hangers. If with ABS, remove the clamp bolts for the power steering oil cooler pipes. Remove the right and left engine mount insulators and their brackets. Slowly remove the engine/transaxle assembly as a unit.
30. Installation is the reverse of the removal procedure.

3A-C ENGINE

1. Disconnect the negative battery cable.
2. Remove the battery and battery carrier.
3. Remove the hood.
4. Drain the cooling system.
5. Disconnect and plug the transaxle fluid lines, if equipped with automatic transaxle.
6. Remove the radiator.
7. Remove the windshield washer tank.
8. Disconnect the heater hoses.
9. If equipped with air conditioning, remove the condenser fan assembly.
10. If equipped with power steering, remove the power steering pump and position it aside. Plug the lines to prevent fluid leakage.
11. If equipped with air conditioning, remove the air conditioning compressor and position it aside. Leave the refrigerant lines connected.
12. Disconnect and tag the engine ground strap, the oxygen sensor wire, the distributor connector, the ground strap from the dash panel, the oil pressure switch wire, the coolant fan wire, the water temperature gauge wire, the back-up light switch and neutral safety switch wires.
13. Disconnect the accelerator cable. If equipped with automatic transaxle, disconnect the accelerator cable.
14. Disconnect and plug the fuel line hoses. Disconnect and tag all vacuum hoses.
15. Disconnect the air suction filter from the cylinder block.
16. Remove the transaxle upper mount bolts.
17. Raise and support the vehicle safely.
18. Remove the front exhaust pipe.
19. Remove the oil cooler lines, if equipped.
20. If equipped with manual transaxle, disconnect the clutch release cable.
21. Remove the stiffener plates.
22. Disconnect the engine mounting absorber.
23. Remove the engine mount bolts.
24. Remove the torque converter cover and torque converter bolts.
25. Position a lifting device under the transaxle assembly. Remove the lower transaxle retaining bolts. As required, remove the starter.
26. Properly support the engine/transaxle assembly. Connect a suitable lifting device to the engine lifting hooks. Carefully remove the engine from the vehicle.
27. Installation is the reverse of the removal procedure. During installation, observe the following torque specifications:
   a. On manual transaxles, torque the flywheel bolts to 58 ft. lbs. (78 Nm).
   b. On automatic transaxles, torque the driveplate bolts to 47 ft. lbs. (64 Nm).
   c. Engine mount nuts to 29 ft. lbs. (39 Nm).
   d. Stiffener plate bolts to 29 ft. lbs. (34 Nm).
   e. 14mm upper and lower transaxle mount bolts to 29 ft. lbs. (39 Nm); 17mm upper and lower transaxle bolts to 43 ft. lbs. (39 Nm).

3E AND 3E-E ENGINE

1. Disconnect the negative battery cable.

2. Remove the battery.

3. Remove the hood.

4. Remove the engine under covers.

5. Drain the cooling system.

6. If equipped with automatic transaxle, disconnect and plug the transaxle fluid lines.

7. Remove the radiator.

8. Remove the windshield washer tank.

9. Disconnect the heater hoses. On 3E-E engine, disconnect the PCV hoses and remove the air cleaner assembly with the air intake collector.

10. If equipped with cruise control, disconnect and remove the actuator assembly. Disconnect the accelerator cable.

11. If equipped with automatic transaxle, disconnect the accelerator cable.

12. Disconnect and plug the fuel line hoses.

13. Remove the charcoal canister assembly.

14. Disconnect the brake booster hose.

15. Disconnect the transaxle control cables.

16. Disconnect the speedometer cable.

17. If equipped with automatic transaxle, remove the clutch release cylinder and the selecting bell crank.

18. Disconnect the engine ground strap, the oxygen sensor wire, the oil pressure switch wire, the coolant fan wire, the water temperature gauge wire, the back-up light switch and neutral safety switch wires. Tag all wires.

19. Disconnect and tag all vacuum hoses.

20. Disconnect the wiring harness from the intake manifold. Remove the intake manifold ground strap. Disconnect the Cold Mixture Heater (CMH) connector, the alternator electrical connector, starter electrical wires and all other wires necessary to remove the engine.

21. Remove the Vacuum Switching Valve (VSV).

22. If equipped with power steering, remove the power steering pump and position it aside.

23. If equipped with air conditioning, remove the air conditioning compressor and position it aside. Leave the refrigerant lines connected.

24. Disconnect the exhaust pipe at the manifold.

25. Remove the halfshafts.

26. Support the engine/transaxle assembly properly.

27. Connect a suitable lifting device to the engine lifting hooks.

28. If equipped with manual transaxle, remove the rear mounting thru-bolt and the rear mounting assembly. If equipped with automatic transaxle, remove the front mounting thru-bolt and front mounting assembly.

29. Remove the right and left side mounting bolts and brackets.

30. Carefully lift the engine assembly out of the vehicle.

31. Installation is the reverse of the removal procedure. During installation, observe the following torque specifications:

    a. On manual transaxles, torque the flywheel bolts to 65 ft. lbs. (88 Nm).

    b. On automatic transaxles, torque the driveplate bolts to 13 ft. lbs. (18 Nm).

    c. Left bracket and mounting insulator bolts to 35 ft. lbs. (48 Nm).

    d. Right mounting insulator and front through bolts to 47 ft. lbs. (64 Nm); rear mounting insulator-to-body bolts to 54 ft. lbs. (73 Nm).

    e. If equipped with automatic transaxle, torque the rear mounting insulator bolts to 43 ft. lbs. (58 Nm).

3S-FE ENGINE

Camry (2WD)

1. Disconnect the negative battery cable.

2. Remove the hood.

3. Drain the cooling system.

4. Remove the igniter and bracket assembly.

5. Tag and disconnect all vacuum hoses, electrical wires and cables that are necessary to remove the engine.

6. Remove the radiator and coolant reservoir tank.

7. If equipped with automatic transaxle, disconnect the throttle cable and bracket from the throttle body.

8. Disconnect the accelerator cable from the throttle body.

9. If equipped with cruise control, remove the cruise control actuator and bracket.

10. Disconnect the ground wire from the alternator upper bracket.

11. Remove the air cleaner assembly, air flow meter and air cleaner hose.

12. Remove the heater hoses.

13. Disconnect and plug the fuel lines.

14. Disconnect the speedometer cable.

15. If equipped with manual transaxle, remove the clutch release cylinder and tube bracket. Do not disconnect the tube from the bracket.

16. Disconnect the transaxle control cable.

17. If equipped with air conditioning, remove the air conditioning compressor and position it aside. Do not disconnect the refrigerant lines.

18. If equipped with power steering, remove the power steering pump and position it aside. Do not disconnect the lines.

19. Raise and support the vehicle safely.

20. Drain the engine oil.

21. Remove the engine under covers.

22. Remove the suspension lower crossmember.

23. Remove the halfshafts.

24. Disconnect the exhaust pipe from the catalytic converter.

25. Disconnect the engine mounting center crossmember member.

26. Lower the vehicle.

27. Tag and disconnect the ECU electrical connectors.

28. Connect a suitable lifting device to the engine. Raise the engine slightly and remove the engine retaining brackets and bolts.

29. Carefully remove the engine/transaxle assembly from the vehicle.

NOTE: Be careful not to hit the power steering gear housing or the neutral safety switch.

30. Installation is the reverse of the removal procedure.

Camry (AWD)

1. Disconnect the negative battery cable.

2. Drain the cooling system.

3. Remove the hood.

4. Disconnect the accelerator cable from the throttle body.

5. Remove the radiator and the coolant reservoir tank.

6. Disconnect the heater hoses.

7. Disconnect the inlet hose at the fuel filter. Disconnect the return hose at the fuel return pipe.

8. Disconnect and remove the cruise control actuator.

9. Remove the air cleaner assembly.

10. Remove the clutch slave cylinder and hose bracket without disconnecting the hydraulic line. Position the assembly aside.

11. Disconnect the speedometer cable and the transaxle control cables.

12. If equipped with air conditioning, disconnect and remove the compressor with the refrigerant lines still attached. Move the compressor aside.

13. Tag and disconnect all wires, connecters and vacuum lines necessary to remove engine.

14. Raise and support the vehicle safely.

15. Drain the engine oil and remove the engine under covers.

16. Remove the lower suspension crossmember and the halfshafts.

17. Disconnect and remove the driveshaft.

18. Remove the power steering pump with the hydraulic lines still attached and position it aside.

19. Remove the front exhaust pipe.

20. Remove the engine mounting centermember and the stabilizer bar. Lower the vehicle.

21. Tag and disconnect the ECU connectors and pull them out through the firewall.

22. Remove the power steering pump reservoir tank.

23. Connect a suitable lifting device to the eyelets on the engine.

24. Remove the right side engine mount stay and then remove the insulator and bracket.

25. Remove the left side engine mount insulator and bracket.

26. Remove the engine and transaxle as an assembly.

NOTE: Be careful not to hit the power steering gear housing or the neutral safety switch.

27. Installation is the reverse of the removal procedure. During installation, observe the following torque specifications:

   a. Right and left engine mount bracket bolts and nuts to 38 ft. lbs. (52 Nm).

   b. Right side engine mount stay bolt and nut to 54 ft. lbs. (73 Nm).

   c. Engine mounting centermember: member-to-body bolts—29 ft. lbs. (39 Nm); member-to-other bolts—38 ft. lbs. (52 Nm)

   d. Lower crossmember bolts: outer—153 ft. lbs. (206 Nm); inner—29 ft. lbs. (39 Nm).

Celica

1. Disconnect the negative battery cable.

2. Remove the battery.

3. Remove the hood.

4. Drain the cooling system.

5. Tag and disconnect all vacuum hoses, electrical wires and cables that are necessary to remove the engine.

6. Disconnect the ignition coil connector and high tension wire from the coil.

7. Remove the suspension upper brace.

8. Remove the radiator.

9. Remove the coolant reservoir tank.

10. If equipped with automatic transaxle, disconnect the throttle cable and bracket from the throttle body.

11. Disconnect the accelerator cable from the throttle body.

12. If equipped with cruise control, remove the cruise control actuator and bracket.

13. Remove the oxygen sensor.

14. Remove the air cleaner assembly, air flow meter, air cleaner hose and air cleaner bracket.

15. Remove the igniter.

16. Remove the heater hoses.

17. Disconnect and plug the fuel lines.

18. Disconnect the speedometer cable.

19. If equipped with manual transaxle, remove the clutch release cylinder and tube bracket. Do not disconnect the tube from the bracket.

20. Disconnect the transaxle control cable.

21. Remove the air conditioning compressor and position it aside. Do not disconnect the refrigerant lines.

22. Raise and support the vehicle safely.

23. Drain the engine oil and transaxle fluid.

24. Remove the right under cover.

25. Remove the power steering pump and position it aside. Do not disconnect the lines.

26. Remove the suspension lower crossmember.

27. Remove the halfshafts.

28. Disconnect the exhaust pipe from the catalytic converter.

29. Remove the engine rear mounting bolt. Lower the vehicle.

30. Disconnect the ECU electrical connectors.

31. Remove the power steering pump reservoir mounting bolts.

32. Connect a suitable lifting device to the engine. Raise the engine slightly and remove the engine retaining brackets and bolts.

33. Carefully remove the engine/transaxle assembly from the vehicle. Be careful not to hit the power steering gear housing or the neutral safety switch.

34. Installation is the reverse of the removal procedure.

3S-GE ENGINE

1. Disconnect the negative battery cable.

2. Remove the battery.

3. Remove the hood.

4. Drain the cooling system.

5. Tag and disconnect the connector high tension lead at the ignition coil.

6. Remove the 4 bolts and 2 nuts securing the upper suspension brace. Remove the brace.

7. If equipped with automatic transaxle, disconnect the throttle cable and its bracket at the throttle body.

8. If equipped with manual transaxle, disconnect the throttle cable from the throttle body.

9. Remove the coolant overflow tank.

10. Remove the cruise control actuator and its bracket.

11. Remove the oxygen sensor.

12. Tag and disconnect the cooling fan leads at the radiator.

13. Disconnect the heater hoses.

14. If equipped with automatic transaxle, disconnect the fluid cooler lines.

15. Remove the radiator and the 2 supports.

16. Remove the air cleaner assembly and bracket.

17. Remove the igniter.

18. Tag, disconnect and plug the fuel hoses at the filter and fuel return pipe.

19. Disconnect the speedometer cable.

20. If equipped with manual transaxle, disconnect the transaxle control cable at the shift and selector levers. If equipped with automatic transaxle, disconnect the cable at the swivel and at the bracket and then remove it.

21. Unbolt the air conditioning compressor and position it aside with the refrigerant lines still attached.

22. Tag and disconnect any remaining wires or electrical leads. Tag and disconnect any remaining vacuum hoses.

23. Raise and support the vehicle safely.

24. Drain the engine oil.

25. Remove the right side engine under cover.

26. Remove the lower suspension crossmember.

27. Remove both halfshafts.

28. Unbolt the power steering pump. Disconnect the 2 vacuum hoses and remove the drive belt. Position the pump aside with the hydraulic lines still connected to it.

29. Disconnect the exhaust pipe at the manifold.

30. Remove the rear engine mount bolt. Lower the vehicle and then remove the front engine mount bolts.

31. Remove the power steering pump reservoir and position it aside.

32. Connect a suitable lifting device to the engine lifting hooks. Take up the engine's weight with the hoist and remove the right and left engine mounts.

33. Slowly and carefully, remove the engine and transaxle assembly. Be careful not to hit the power steering gear housing or the neutral safety switch.

34. Installation is the reverse of the removal procedure.

3S-GTE ENGINE

Celica (2WD)

1. Disconnect the negative battery cable.

2. Remove the battery.

3. Drain the coolant from the engine and turbocharger intercooler.

4. Remove the hood.

5. Disconnect the accelerator cable at the throttle body.

6. Remove the radiator.

7. Disconnect the heater and intercooler hoses.

8. Disconnect the fuel inlet line at the fuel filter and the return line at the return pipe.

9. Remove the cruise control actuator and bracket.

10. Remove the air cleaner assembly.

11. Remove the clutch release cylinder and bracket without disconnecting the hydraulic line. Move it aside.

12. Disconnect the speedometer and transaxle control cables.

13. Remove the alternator.

14. Remove the air conditioning compressor and position it aside. Do not disconnect the refrigerant lines.

15. Tag and disconnect any wires, cables, hoses, connectors and vacuum lines which might interfere with engine removal.

16. Raise and support the vehicle safely.

17. Drain the engine oil and remove the under covers.

18. Remove the lower suspension crossmember.

19. Remove the front halfshafts and the driveshaft.

20. Remove the power steering pump and bracket without disconnecting the hydraulic lines. Position the power steering pump aside.

21. Disconnect the front exhaust pipe at the manifold and tailpipe and remove it.

22. Remove the engine mounting centermember and lower the vehicle.

23. Unplug the 3 ECU connectors, remove the 2 screws and pull the connectors out through the firewall.

24. Remove the power steering pump reservoir tank.

25. Connect a suitable lifting device to the lifting brackets on the engine. Remove the 2 bolts holding the right engine mount insulator to the mounting bracket. Remove the 4 bolts holding the left engine mount insulator to the mounting bracket and then lower the engine out of the vehicle.

26. Installation is the reverse of the removal procedure. During installation, observe the following torque specifications:

    a. Torque the right and left engine mount bracket bolts to 38 ft. lbs. (52 Nm).

    b. When installing the engine mounting centermember, tighten the outer bolts to 29 ft. lbs. (39 Nm), tighten the inner bolts to 38 ft. lbs. (52 Nm).

    c. Tighten the front exhaust pipe bolts to 46 ft. lbs. (62 Nm).

    d. When installing the lower suspension crossmember, tighten the outer bolts to 154 ft. lbs. (208 Nm), tighten the inner bolts to 29 ft. lbs. (39 Nm).

Celica (AWD)

1. Disconnect the negative battery cable.

2. Remove the hood.

3. Raise and support the vehicle safely.

4. Remove the engine under covers.

5. Drain the cooling system, engine oil and transaxle fluid.

6. Remove the air cleaner assembly.

7. Disconnect the accelerator cable from the throttle body.

8. Remove the relay box from the battery. Disconnect the wires and connectors from the box.

9. Remove the air conditioning relay box from its mounting bracket.

10. Remove the injector solenoid resistor and fuel pump resistor from the engine compartment.

11. Remove the radiator and coolant overflow tank.

12. If equipped with cruise control, disconnect the wiring and remove the cruise control actuator.

13. Remove the wiper arms and outside windshield moulding. Then, remove the upper brace which is retained by 4 nuts and 2 bolts. The brace connects from the struts to the firewall.

14. Remove the ignition coil.

15. From inside the engine compartment, tag and disconnect all electrical wiring and vacuum hoses necessary to remove the engine.

16. Remove the engine wire bracket.

17. Remove the charcoal canister.

18. Disconnect the heater hoses.

19. Disconnect the speedometer cable from the transaxle.

20. Disconnect and plug the fuel hoses.

21. Remove the starter.

22. Remove the clutch release cylinder without disconnecting the hydraulic tube. Move the unit aside.

23. Disconnect the control cables from the transaxle.

24. Remove the turbocharger pressure sensor and air conditioning Air Switching Valve (ASV) from inside the engine compartment.

25. From the passenger compartment, unplug the connectors from the ECU, air conditioning amplifier and cowl wires. Pull the wiring harnesses through the firewall.

26. Remove the suspesnion lower crossmember.

27. Remove the front halfshafts and the driveshaft.

28. Remove the power steering pump and bracket without disconnecting the hydraulic lines. Position the pump aside.

29. Disconnect the front exhaust pipe at the manifold and tailpipe and remove it.

30. Remove the engine mounting centermember and lower the vehicle. Unplug the 3 TCCS ECU connectors, remove the 2 screws and pull the connectors out through the firewall.

31. Remove the power steering pump reservoir tank.

32. Connect a suitable lifting device to the lifting brackets on the engine.

33. Remove the 2 bolts holding the right engine mount insulator to the mounting bracket. Remove the 4 bolts holding the left engine mount insulator to the mounting bracket.

34. Slowly and carefully, remove the engine and transaxle assembly for the top of the vehicle.

35. Installation is the reverse of the removal procedure. During installation, observe the following torque specifications:

    a. Torque the left mounting bracket-to-transaxle case bolts to 38 ft. lbs. (52 Nm).

    b. Torque the left mounting insulator through bolt to 47 ft. lbs. (63 Nm) and 4 hex head bolts to 64 ft. lbs. (87 Nm).

    c. Torque the right mounting insulator nuts to 38 ft. lbs. (52 Nm) and the thru bolt to 64 ft. lbs. (87 Nm).

    d. Torque the front and rear bolts to 57 ft. lbs. (77 Nm).

    e. Torque the front and rear engine mounting through bolts to 64 ft. lbs. (87 Nm).

    f. Torque the lower crossmember nuts and bolts to 112 ft. lbs. (152 Nm).

    g. Torque the suspension upper brace nuts to 47 ft. lbs. (64 Nm) and bolts to 15 ft. lbs. (21 Nm).

1990–91 MR2

1. Disconnect the negative battery cable.

2. Remove the hood.

3. Raise and support the vehicle safely.

4. Remove the engine under covers.

5. Drain the cooling system, engine oil and transaxle fluid.

6. Remove the suspension upper brace that criss-crosses from the struts to the firewall.

7. Remove the air cleaner assembly.

8. Remove both air connector tubes.

9. Disconnect the accelerator cable from the throttle body.

10. If equipped with cruise control, disconnect the wiring and remove the cruise control actuator and accelerator linkage assemblies.

11. Disconnect the brake booster vacuum hose.

12. Disconnect the ground strap connector.

13. Remove the check connector and turbocharger pressure sensor.

14. Remove the injector solenoid resistor, fuel pump relay, fuel pump resistor and the air conditioning vacuum switching valve.

15. Disconnect the filler and overflow hoses from the water filler connection. Remove the water filler from the engine.

16. Remove the engine relay box. Disconnect the wires and connectors from the box.

17. Remove the ignition coil and igniter.

18. From inside the luggage compartment, disconnect the wiring harnesses for the ECU, starter relay, cooling fan and engine wires.

19. Disconnect the starter wiring.

20. Disconnect the radiator hose from the water inlet.

21. Disconnect and plug the fuel inlet and return hoses.

22. Disconnect the radiator hoses from the water outlet housing.

23. Disconnect the heater hoses.

24. Disconnect the control cables from the transaxle.

25. Remove the tailpipe and front exhaust pipe.

26. Remove the engine compartment cooling fan.

27. Remove the idler pulley bracket and unbolt the air conditioning compressor. Move the compressor aside. Leave the refrigerant lines connected.

28. Remove the intercooler.

29. Remove the rear engine mounting insulator.

30. Disconnect the speedometer cable from the transaxle.

31. Disconnect the stabilizer link from the shock absorber.

32. Remove the wire clamp bolt and remove the ABS speed sensor.

33. Remove the lower suspension arms.

34. Remove the driveshafts.

35. Remove the 4 bolts and remove the lower crossmember.

36. Remove the front engine mounting insulator.

37. Remove the nut and bolt attaching the clutch release cylinder to the transaxle. Remove the mounting bracket bolts and remove the clutch release cylinder without disconnecting the hydraulic tube.

38. Remove the right and left engine mounting stays.

39. Remove the lateral control rod and air cleaner case bracket.

40. Connect a suitable lifting device to the engine hanger brackets. Tension the lifting device to support the weight of the engine, then remove the left and right mounting insulator fasteners; 2 bolts and 3 nuts for each insulator.

41. Carefully lower then raise the engine from the vehicle.

42. Installation is the reverse of the removal procedure.

1987 4A-LC ENGINE

1. Disconnect the negative battery cable.

2. Drain the cooling system, transmission, and engine oil.

3. Disconnect the battery-to-starter cable at the positive battery terminal.

4. Remove the hood supports from the body. Remove the hood. Do not remove the supports from the hood.

5. Unfasten the headlight bezel retaining screws and remove the bezels.

6. Remove the 5 radiator grille attachment screws and remove the grille.

7. Remove the hood lock assembly after detaching the release cable.

8. Unfasten the nuts from the horn retainers and disconnect the wiring. Remove the horn assembly.

9. Remove the upper and lower radiator hoses.

10. If equipped with with automatic transmission, disconnect the lines from the oil cooler.

11. Remove the radiator.

12. Remove the heater and bypass hoses from the engine.

13. Remove the heater control cable from the water valve.

14. Remove the wiring from the coolant temperature and oil pressure sending units.

15. Remove the air cleaner assembly.

16. Unfasten the accelerator torque rod from the carburetor.

17. If equipped with automatic transmission, disconnect the transmission linkage.

18. Remove the emission control system hoses and wiring, as necessary.

19. Remove the clutch hydraulic line support bracket.

20. Disconnect the high tension and primary wires from the coil. Remove the spark plug wires.

21. Detach the right front engine mount.

22. Remove the fuel line at the pump.

23. Detach the down pipe from the exhaust manifold.

24. Detach the left front engine mount.

25. Disconnect all of the wiring harness multi-connectors necessary to remove the engine.

26. If equipped with manual transmission, remove the shift lever boot and the shift lever cap boot.

27. Unfasten the 4 gear selector cap retaining screws and remove the gasket and withdraw the gear selector lever assembly from the top of the transmission. On 5 speed transmissions, the floor console must be removed first.

28. Raise and support the vehicle safely.

29. If equipped with automatic transmission, disconnect the gear selector control rod.

30. Detach the exhaust pipe support bracket.

31. Disconnect the driveshaft from the rear of the transmission.

32. Disconnect the speedometer cable from the transmission.

33. Disconnect the wiring from the back-up light switch and the neutral safety switch, if equipped.

34. Detach the clutch release cylinder assembly, complete with hydraulic lines. Do not disconnect the lines.

35. Unbolt the rear support member mounting insulators.

36. Support the transmission properly and detach the rear support member retaining bolts. Remove the support member.

37. Install lifting hooks on the engine lifting brackets. Connect a suitable device to the engine. Remove the jack from under the transmission.

38. Raise the engine and move it toward the front of the vehicle. Use care to avoid damaging the components which remain on the vehicle.

39. Installation is the reverse of the removal procedure.

1988 4A-LC ENGINE

1. Disconnect the negative battery cable.

2. Remove the battery.

3. Remove the hood.

4. Drain the cooling system and the oil.

5. Remove the air cleaner hose and air cleaner.

6. Remove the coolant reservoir tank, radiator and fan shroud.

7. Disconnect the actuator, accelerator and throttle cables at the carburetor.

8. Tag and disconnect all wires, hoses and lines which might interfere with engine removal.

9. Disconnect the fuel lines at the fuel pump.

10. Remove the heater hoses.

11. Remove the power steering pump and air conditioning compressor and position them aside. Do not disconnect the hydraulic or refrigerant lines.

12. Disconnect the speedometer cable at the transaxle.

13. Remove the clutch release cylinder without disconnecting the hydraulic line and position it aside.

14. Disconnect the shift control cable and then raise the vehicle and support it with safety stands.

15. Disconnect the exhaust pipe at the manifold.

16. Disconnect the front and rear engine mounts at the centermember. Remove the centermember.

17. Disconnect the halfshafts at the transaxle and lower the vehicle.

18. Connect a suitable lifting device to the lift brackets on the engine.

19. Remove the right engine mount thru-bolt. Remove the left engine mount and bracket.

20. Lift the engine out of the vehicle.

21. Installation is the reverse of the removal procedure. During installation, observe the following torque specifications:

a. Tighten the engine mount centermember to 29 ft. lbs. (39 Nm).

b. Tighten the front and rear engine mounts to 29 ft. lbs. (39 Nm).

c. Tighten the exhaust pipe-to-manifold bolts to 46 ft. lbs. (62 Nm).

4A-F ENGINE

1. Disconnect the negative battery cable.
2. Remove the battery.
3. Remove the hood.
4. Remove the engine under covers.
5. Drain the cooling system, engine oil and transaxle oil.
6. Remove the air cleaner and air cleaner flexible hose.
7. Remove the coolant reservoir tank, radiator and cooling fan.
8. If equipped with automatic transaxle, disconnect the accelerator and throttle cables at the carburetor.
9. Disconnect all electrical wires and vacuum lines necessary to remove the engine.
10. Disconnect the fuel lines at the fuel pump. Plug the lines.
11. Disconnect the heater hoses at the water inlet housing.
12. Remove the power steering pump and set it aside with the hydraulic lines still attached.
13. Remove the air conditioning compressor and set it aside with the refrigerant lines still attached.
14. Disconnect the speedometer cable from the transaxle.
15. If equipped with manual transaxle, remove the clutch release cylinder and position it aside with the hydraulic lines still attached.
16. Disconnect the shift control cables.
17. Raise and support the vehicle safely.
18. Remove the 2 nuts from the flange and then disconnect the exhaust pipe at the manifold.
19. Disconnect the halfshafts at the transaxle.
20. Remove the 2 hole covers and then remove the front, center and rear engine mounts from the centermember. Remove the 5 bolts and insulators and remove the centermember.
21. Connect a suitable lifting device to the lifting brackets on the engine.
22. Remove the 3 bolts and mounting stay. Remove the bolt, 2 nuts and the thru-bolt and pull out the right side engine mount. Remove the 2 bolts and the left mounting stay. Remove the 3 bolts and disconnect the left engine mount bracket from the transaxle.
23. Lift the engine/transaxle assembly out of the vehicle.
24. Installation is the reverse of the removal procedure. During installation, observe the following torque specifications:

a. Torque the right engine mount insulator bolt to 47 ft. lbs. (64 Nm); tighten the nut to 38 ft. lbs. (52 Nm). Align the insulator with the bracket on the body and tighten the bolt to 64 ft. lbs. (87 Nm).

b. Align the left engine mount insulator bracket with the transaxle bracket and tighten the bolt to 35 ft. lbs. (48 Nm).

c. Install the right mounting stay and tighten the 3 bolts to 31 ft. lbs. (42 Nm). Install the left stay and tighten the 2 bolts to 15 ft. lbs. (21 Nm).

d. Install the engine centermember and tighten the 5 bolts to 45 ft. lbs. (61 Nm).

e. Install the front and rear engine mounts and bolts. Align the bolts holes in the brackets with the centermember and tighten the front mount bolts to 35 ft. lbs. (48 Nm); tighten the center and rear mounts to 38 ft. lbs. (52 Nm). Install the 2 hole covers and tighten the rear mounting bolt to 58 ft. lbs. (78 Nm).

4A-FE ENGINE

Corolla

1. Disconnect the negative battery cable.
2. Remove the battery.

3. Remove the hood.
4. Remove the engine under covers.
5. Drain the cooling system, engine and transaxle oil.
6. Remove the air cleaner and air cleaner flexible hose.
7. Remove the coolant reservoir tank, radiator and cooling fan.
8. If equipped with automatic transaxle, disconnect the accelerator and throttle cables.
9. If equipped with cruise control, remove the cruise control actuator.
10. Disconnect the No. 2 junction block, the ground strap connector and the ground strap.
11. Disconnect the check, vacuum sensor and oxygen sensor connectors. Disconnect the air conditioning compressor wire.
12. Disconnect the vacuum hoses at the brake booster, power steering pump, vacuum sensor, charcoal canister and vacuum switch.
13. Disconnect the fuel lines at the fuel pump.
14. Disconnect the heater hoses at the water inlet housing.
15. Remove the power steering pump and set it aside with the hydraulic lines still attached.
16. Remove the air conditioning compressor and set it aside with the refrigerant lines still attached.
17. Disconnect the speedometer cable at the transaxle.
18. If equipped with manual transaxle, remove the clutch release cylinder and position it aside with the hydraulic lines still attached.
19. Disconnect the shift control cables.
20. Raise and support the vehicle safely.
21. Disconnect the oil cooler lines and the exhaust pipe (at the manifold).
22. Disconnect the halfshafts and the driveshaft at the transaxle.
23. Connect a suitable lifting device to the lifting brackets on the engine and raise it just enough to relieve pressure on the mounts.
24. Pull out the hole covers and remove the 5 bolts on the front and rear engine mounts. Remove the mounts from the center crossmember. Remove the 4 center crossmember bolts and the 8 bolts from the sub-frame. Remove the front and rear mounting bolts and then remove the member.
25. Remove the engine mount stay and the mount.
26. Remove the air cleaner bracket. Disconnect the left side mounting bracket from the transaxle bracket and then lift out the engine/transaxle assembly slowly and carefully.
27. Installation is the reverse of the removal procedure. During installation, observe the following torque specifications:

a. Torque the right engine mount insulator bolt and nuts to 38 ft. lbs. (52 Nm). Align the insulator with the bracket on the body and tighten the bolt to 64 ft. lbs. (87 Nm).

b. Align the left engine mount insulator bracket with the transaxle bracket and tighten the bolt to 35 ft. lbs. (48 Nm).

c. Install the left stay and tighten the 2 bolts to 15 ft. lbs. (21 Nm).

d. Install the engine centermember and tighten the 5 bolts to 45 ft. lbs. (61 Nm).

e. Install the front and rear engine mounts and bolts. Align the bolts holes in the brackets with the centermember and tighten the front mount bolts to 35 ft. lbs. (48 Nm); tighten the center and rear mounts to 42 ft. lbs. (57 Nm). Install the 8 sub-frame bolts and tighten the lower arm bolt to 152 ft. lbs. (206 Nm) and the rear bolt to 94 ft. lbs. (127 Nm).

1990–91 Celica

1. Disconnect the negative battery cable.
2. Remove the battery.
3. Raise the vehicle and support safely.
4. Remove the engine under covers.
5. Drain the cooling system and engine oil.
6. Remove the air cleaner assembly along with its hose and any attachments.

7. Disconnect the accelerator and throttle cables at the bracket.

8. Remove the lower cover from the relay box. Disconnect the fusible link cassette and connectors. Remove the engine relay box.

9. Remove the air conditioning relay box from the bracket.

10. Remove the coolant reservoir tank, radiator and cooling fan.

11. Disconnect the check connector, vacuum sensor connector and ground strap from the left front fender apron. Remove the engine wiring bracket. Disconnect the noise filter assembly.

12. Remove the charcoal canister.

13. Disconnect the heater hose from the water inlet.

14. Disconnect the speedometer cable at the transaxle.

15. Disconnect the fuel hose.

16. If equipped with manual transaxle, remove the clutch release cylinder and position it aside with the hydraulic lines still attached.

17. Disconnect the shift control cables from the transaxle.

18. Tag and disconnect all vacuum hoses and electrical wires neccesary to remove the engine.

19. Remove the suspension lower crossmember.

20. Disconnect the oxygen sensor connector.

21. Remove the front exhaust pipe assembly.

22. If equipped with automatic transaxle, disconnect control cable from engine mounting centermember.

23. Remove the front halfshafts.

24. Unbolt the air conditioning compressor and wire it aside with the refrigerant lines still attached.

25. Remove the power steering pump assembly without disconnecting the hydraulic lines.

26. Connect a suitable lifting device to the engine lifting brackets. Tension the lifting device slightly to take the pressure off the mounts.

27. Remove the engine mounting centermember.

28. Remove the front engine mounting insulator and bracket.

29. Remove the rear mounting insulator and bracket.

30. Disconnect the ground wire from the fender apron. Remove the ground strap from the transaxle.

31. Remove the right and left engine mounting stay.

32. Slowly and carefully, remove the engine and transaxle assembly from the top of the vehicle.

NOTE: Be careful not to hit the power steering gear housing or the neutral safety switch.

33. Installation is the reverse of the removal procedure. During installation, observe the following torque specifications:

   a. Torque the left mounting bracket-to-transaxle case bolts to 38 ft. lbs. (52 Nm).

   b. Torque the left mounting insulator-to-bracket bolts to 35 ft. lbs. (48 Nm) and the thru bolt to 64 ft. lbs. (87 Nm).

   c. Torque the right engine stay bolts to 31 ft. lbs. and the left engine stay bolts to 15 ft. lbs. (21 Nm).

   d. Torque the front and rear engine mounting bracket and insulator fasteners to 57 ft. lbs. (77 Nm).

   e. Torque the engine centermember bolts to 38 ft. lbs. (52 Nm) and the centermember-to-insulator bolts to 47 ft. lbs. (64 Nm).

   f. Torque the front and rear engine mounting through bolts to 64 ft. lbs. (87 Nm).

4A-GEC AND 4A-GELC ENGINE

1. Disconnect the negative battery cable.

2. Remove the battery.

3. Remove the air cleaner assembly.

4. Drain the cooling system and engine oil.

5. Remove the fuel tank protectors and the engine under cover.

6. Disconnect the accelerator cable.

7. If equipped with cruise control, disconnect the cruise control at the cable actuator. If equipped with automatic transaxle, disconnect the throttle cable.

8. Disconnect the heater hoses at the water inlet housing on the rear of the cylinder head cover. Disconnect the radiator hose and the air bleeder hose at the water inlet housing.

9. Disconnect and plug the fuel line at the fuel filter. Disconnect the fuel return hose. Tag and disconnect the vacuum hose at the charcoal canister.

10. Tag and disconnect the engine ground strap and the main wiring harness connector at the engine. Disconnect the back-up light switch connector as required.

11. Disconnect the speedometer cable.

12. Remove the transaxle gravel shield.

13. Remove the ground strap from the water inlet housing.

14. Remove the radiator overflow tank.

15. Remove the air conditioning and alternator drive belts. Remove the alternator.

16. Disconnect the radiator hose at the water outlet housing.

17. Tag and disconnect the 2 connectors at the igniter, the noise filter connector, the cooling fan electrical connector, the cylinder head ground strap, the air condition compressor connector and the high tension leads at the ignition coil.

18. Remove the rear luggage compartment trim.

19. Tag and disconnect the circuit opening relay connector, the ball connections at the electronic control unit and the electrical lead for the cooling fan computer.

20. Pull the main wiring harness out and through the engine compartment.

21. Remove the mounting bolts and remove the air conditioning compressor. Position it aside without disconnecting the refrigerant lines.

22. If equipped with a manual transaxle, disconnect the control cables from the outer shift lever and gear shift selector lever. If equipped with automatic transaxle, disconnect the control cable at the gear shift lever.

23. If equipped with a manual transaxle, remove the control cable bracket on the transaxle. Remove the clutch release cylinder.

24. Disconnect the engine oil cooler lines, if equipped. Disconnect the automatic transaxle fluid lines if equipped.

25. Remove the exhaust pipe assembly. Remove the oxygen sensor at the exhaust manifold.

26. If equipped with automatic transaxle, remove the mounting bolts and remove the stiffener plate at the transaxle. Remove the flywheel shield.

27. Remove the right halfshaft. Disconnect the left halfshaft from the side gear shaft and position it aside.

28. Remove the front and rear engine mount bolts. Place a block of wood on an hydraulic floor jack and carefully position the jack under the engine. Raise the jack just enough to ease the engine's weight on the mounts. Remove the right and left engine mounts.

29. Make sure there are no remaining wires or hoses connected to the engine and then slowly and carefully raise the vehicle while lowering the jack supporting the engine/transaxle assembly.

30. Installation is the reverse of the removal procedure. During installation, please observe the floowing torque specifications:

   a. Torque the right engine mount insulator bolt and nuts to 38 ft. lbs. (52 Nm). Align the insulator with the bracket on the body and tighten the bolt to 64 ft. lbs. (87 Nm).

   b. Align the left engine mount insulator bracket with the transaxle bracket and tighten the bolt to 35 ft. lbs. (48 Nm).

   c. Install the left stay and tighten the 2 bolts to 15 ft. lbs. (21 Nm).

   d. Install the engine centermember and tighten the 5 bolts to 45 ft. lbs. (61 Nm).

   e. Install the front, center and rear engine mounts and bolts. Align the bolts holes in the brackets with the centermember and tighten the front mount bolts to 35 ft. lbs.

(48 Nm); tighten the center mounts to 38 ft. lbs. (52 Nm); and the rear mount bolts to 42 ft. lbs. (57 Nm).

f. Bounce the engine several times to unload the front and rear mounts, for automatic transmission only, and then tighten the rear bolt to 64 ft. lbs. (87 Nm). Install the front bolt and tighten it to 64 ft. lbs. (87 Nm).

4A-GZE ENGINE

1. Disconnect the negative battery cable.
2. Raise and support the vehicle safely.
3. Remove the fuel tank protectors and the engine under cover.
4. Drain the cooling system and engine oil.
5. Remove the supercharger intercooler.
6. Remove the battery.
7. Disconnect the air conditioning idle-up, charcoal canister and cruise control vacuum hoses. Disconnect the air bleeder hose at the water inlet housing.
8. If equipped with automatic transmission, disconnect the throttle cable.
9. Disconnect the cruise control cable, the heater hoses and radiator hose.
10. Disconnect the fuel inlet and return lines.
11. Disconnect the speedometer cable and the brake booster vacuum line.
12. Remove the radiator reservoir tank. Disconnect the radiator hose at the water outlet housing.
13. Tag and disconnect any remaining hoses, wires or lines which may interfere with engine removal.
14. Remove the 5 clip fasteners and pull out the rear luggage compartment trim. Disconnect the connectors and pull the wiring harness through the engine compartment.
15. Remove the air conditioning compressor and position it aside with the refrigerant lines still connected.
16. Disconnect the shifter control cables.
17. Remove the clutch release cylinder and bracket and position it aside with the hydraulic lines still attached.
18. Disconnect the coolant lines at the engine and transmission oil coolers.
19. Remove the front exhaust pipe.
20. Remove the rear halfshafts.
21. Remove the front and rear engine mount insulators. Lower the engine slightly and then remove the right and left engine mounts. Carefully support the engine and raise the vehicle, over the engine.
22. Installation is the reverse of the removal procedure. During installation, observe the following torque specifications:

a. When installing the rear engine mount insulator, tighten the 10mm bolts to 38 ft. lbs. (52 Nm); tighten the 12mm bolts to 58 ft. lbs. (78 Nm).

b. Install the front engine mount insulator to the body and tighten the inner bolt to 38 ft. lbs. (52 Nm), tighten the outer bolts to 54 ft. lbs. (73 Nm).

c. Connect the mounting bracket to the insulator and install the thru-bolt. Bounce the engine several times and tighten the thru-bolt to 58 ft. lbs. (78 Nm).

5M-GE ENGINE

1. Disconnect the negative battery cable.
2. Remove the battery.
3. Remove the hood.
4. Remove the air cleaner assembly.
5. Remove the fan shroud.
6. Drain the cooling system.
7. Disconnect the upper and lower radiator hoses.
8. If equipped with automatic transmission, disconnect and plug the oil lines from the oil cooler.
9. Detach the hose which runs to the thermal expansion tank and remove the expansion tank from its mounting bracket.
10. Remove the radiator.

11. If equipped with automatic transmission, remove the throttle cable bracket from the cylinder head. Remove the accelerator and actuator cable bracket from the cylinder head.
12. Tag and disconnect the cylinder head ground cable, the oxygen sensor wire, the oil pressure sending unit, alternator wires, the high tension coil wire, the water temperature sending, the thermo-switch wires, the starter wires, the ECT connectors, the solenoid resistor wire connector and the knock sensor wire.
13. Tag and disconnect the brake booster vacuum hose from the air intake chamber, along with the EGR valve vacuum hose. Disconnect the actuator vacuum hose from the air intake chamber, if equipped with cruise control. Disconnect the heater bypass hoses from the engine.
14. Remove the glove box, and remove the ECU computer module. Disconnect the 3 connectors, and pull out the EFI wiring harness from the engine compartment side of the firewall.
15. Remove the 4 shroud and 4 fluid coupling screws, and the shroud and coupling as a unit.
16. Remove the engine undercover protector.
17. Disconnect the coolant reservoir hose. Remove the radiator and the coolant expansion tank.
18. Remove the air conditioning compressor drive belt, and remove the compressor mounting bolts. Without disconnecting the refrigerant hoses, lay the compressor aside and secure it.
19. Disconnect the power steering pump drive belt and remove the pump stay. Unbolt the pump and lay it aside without disconnecting the fluid hoses.
20. Remove the engine mounting bolts from each side of the engine. Remove the engine ground cable.
21. If equipped with manual transmission, remove the shift lever from the inside of the vehicle.
22. Raise and support the vehicle safely.
23. Drain the engine oil.
24. Disconnect the exhaust pipe from the exhaust manifold. Remove the exhaust pipe clamp from the transmission housing.
25. If equipped with manual transmission, remove the clutch slave cylinder.
26. Disconnect the speedometer cable at the transmission.
27. If equipped with automatic transmission, disconnect the shift linkage from the shift lever. If equipped with manual transmission, disconnect the wire from the back-up light switch.
28. Remove the stiffener plate from the ground cable.
29. Disconnect and plug the fuel line from the fuel filter and the return hose from the fuel hose support.
30. Remove the 2 bolts from the top and bottom of the steering universal, and remove the sliding yoke.
31. Disconnect the tie rod ends. Disconnect the pressure line mounting bolts from the front crossmember.
32. Remove the intermediate shaft from the driveshaft.
33. Position a jack under the transmission, with a wooden block between the 2 to prevent damage to the transmission case. Place a wooden block between the cowl panel and the cylinder head rear end to prevent damage to the heater hoses.
34. Unbolt the engine rear support member from the frame, along with the ground cable.
35. Make sure all wiring is disconnected, all hoses disconnected, and everything clear of the engine and transmission. Connect a suitable lifting device to the lift brackets on the engine, and carefully lift the engine and transmission up and out of the vehicle.
36. Installation is the reverse of the removal procedure.

5S-FE ENGINE

1990–91 Celica

1. Disconnect the negative battery cable.
2. Remove the battery.
3. Remove the hood.
4. Raise the vehicle and support safely.

5. Remove the engine under covers.

6. Drain the cooling system and engine oil.

7. Remove the air cleaner assembly along with hoses and any attachments.

8. Disconnect the accelerator and throttle cables at the bracket.

9. Remove the lower cover from the relay box. Disconnect the fusible link cassette and connectors. Remove the engine relay box.

10. Remove the air conditioning relay box from the bracket.

11. Remove the cruise control actuator assembly.

12. Remove the coolant reservoir tank, radiator and cooling fan.

13. Remove the 2 wiper arms and outside lower winshield moulding. Remove the suspension upper brace where it attaches to the struts and the firewall.

14. Remove the ignition coil assembly. Disconnect the check connector, igniter connector, vacuum sensor connector and ground strap from the left front fender apron. Remove the engine wiring bracket. Disconnect the noise filter assembly.

15. Remove the charcoal canister.

16. Disconnect the heater hose from the water inlet.

17. Disconnect the speedometer cable.

18. Disconnect the fuel hose.

19. If equipped with a manual transaxle, remove the clutch release cylinder and position it aside with the hydraulic lines still attached.

20. Disconnect the shift control cables from the transaxle.

21. Tag and disconnect the vacuum sensor hose from the gas filter on the air intake chamber, brake booster vacuum hose and air conditioning vacuum hoses on air intake chamber.

22. Disconnect 2 cowl wire connectors and engine wire clamp from engine fender apron.

23. Tag and disconnect: engine ECU connector, cowl wire connectors and air conditioning amplifier connector.

24. Remove the suspension lower crossmember.

25. Disconnect the oxygen sensor connector.

26. Remove all necessary brackets and retaining bolts.

27. Remove the front exhaust pipe assembly.

28. If equipped with automatic transaxle, disconnect control cable from engine mounting centermember. Remove the front halfshafts.

29. Unbolt the air conditioning compressor and then wire it aside with the refrigerant lines still attached.

30. Remove the power steering pump assembly without disconnecting the hydraulic lines.

31. Connect a suitable lifting device to the engine lifting brackets.

32. Remove the engine mounting centermember.

33. Remove the front engine mounting insulator and bracket.

34. Remove the rear mounting insulator and bracket.

35. Disconnect the ground wire from the fender apron. Remove the ground strap from the transaxle.

36. Remove the right and left engine mounting stay.

37. Slowly and carefully, remove the engine and transaxle assembly from the top of the vehicle.

NOTE: Be careful not to hit the power steering gear housing or the neutral safety switch.

38. Installation is the reverse of the removal procedure. During installation, observe the following torque specifications:

　a. Torque the left mounting bracket-to-transaxle case bolts to 38 ft. lbs. (52 Nm).

　b. Torque the left mounting insulator-to-bracket bolts to 35 ft. lbs. (48 Nm) and the thru bolt to 64 ft. lbs. (87 Nm).

　c. Torque the right engine stay bolts to 31 ft. lbs. and the left engine stay bolts to 15 ft. lbs. (21 Nm).

　d. Torque the front and rear engine mounting bracket and insulator fasteners to 57 ft. lbs. (77 Nm).

　e. Torque the engine centermember bolts to 38 ft. lbs. (52

Nm) and the centermember-to-insulator bolts to 47 ft. lbs. (64 Nm).

　f. Torque the front and rear engine mounting through bolts to 64 ft. lbs. (87 Nm).

1990–91 MR2

1. Disconnect the negative battery cable.

2. Remove the hood and engine side panels.

3. Raise and support the vehicle safely.

4. Remove the engine under covers.

5. Drain the cooling system, engine oil and transaxle fluid.

6. Remove the suspension upper brace that criss-crosses from the struts to the firewall.

7. Remove the air cleaner assembly.

8. Disconnect the accelerator cable from the throttle body.

9. If equipped with cruise control, disconnect the wiring and remove the cruise control actuator and accelerator linkage assemblies.

10. Disconnect the brake booster vacuum hose.

11. Disconnect the ground strap connector.

12. Remove the check connector and vacuum sensor.

13. Remove the the air conditioning vacuum switching valve.

14. Disconnect the filler and overflow hoses from the water filler connection. Remove the water filler from the engine.

15. Remove the engine relay box. Disconnect the wires and connectors from the box.

16. Remove the ignition coil and igniter.

17. From inside the luggage compartment, disconnect the wiring harnesses for the ECU, starter relay, cooling fan and engine wires.

18. Disconnect the starter wiring.

19. Disconnect the radiator hose from the water inlet.

20. Disconnect and plug the fuel inlet and return hoses.

21. Disconnect the radiator hoses from the water outlet housing.

22. Disconnect the heater hoses.

23. Disconnect the control cables from the transaxle.

24. If equipped with automatic transaxle, disconnect and plug the oil cooler hoses.

25. Remove the front exhaust pipe.

26. Remove the driveshafts.

27. Remove the idler pulley bracket and unbolt the air conditioning compressor. Move the compressor aside. Leave the refrigerant lines connected.

28. Remove the front and rear engine mounting insulator.

29. Disconnect the speedometer cable from the transaxle.

30. If equipped with manual transaxle, remove the nut and bolt attaching the clutch release cylinder to the transaxle. Remove the mounting bracket bolts and remove the clutch release cylinder without disconnecting the hydraulic tube. If equipped with automatic transaxle, unbolt and remove the control cable bracket from the transaxle.

31. Remove the rear engine mounting bracket.

32. Remove the right and left engine mounting stays.

33. If equipped with manual transaxle, remove the lateral control rod and air cleaner case bracket. If equipped with automatic transaxle, unbolt the air cleaner case bracket, disconnect the charcoal canister tube and the ground strap from the transaxle.

34. Connect a suitable lifting device to the engine hanger brackets. Tension the lifting device to support the weight of the engine, then remove the left and right mounting insulator fasteners.

35. Carefully lower then raise the engine from the vehicle.

36. Installation is the reverse of the removal procedure.

7M-GE AND 7M-GTE ENGINE

Supra

1. Disconnect the negative battery cable.

2. Remove the hood.

3. Rasie and support the vehicle safely.

4. Remove the engine under cover.

5. Drain the cooling system and engine oil.

6. Remove the radiator.

7. On 7M-GE, remove the air cleaner assembly. On 7M-GTE, remove the No. 4 air cleaner pipe along with the No. 1 and 2 air cleaner hose.

8. Remove the No. 7 air cleaner hose with the air flow meter and air cleaner cap.

9. Remove the air conditioning belt. Remove the alternator drive belt, water pump pulley and fan assembly. Remove the power steering belt.

10. Disconnect the brake booster hose, the heater valve hose, the cruise control hose and the charcoal canister hose.

11. Remove the heater hoses.

12. Tag and disconnect all electrical wire and vacuum hoses necessary to remove the engine.

13. If equipped with cruise control, disconnect the cruise control cable.

14. Disconnect the accelerator cable.

15. If equipped with automtic transmission, disconnect the throttle cable.

16. Remove the air conditioning compressor. Position the unit aside. Do not disonnect the refrigerant lines.

17. On the 7M-GTE, remove the No. 6 air cleaner hose and the upper radiator outlet hose.

18. Remove the power steering pump. Position the unit aside; do not disonnect the hydraulic lines.

19. If equipped with manual transmission, remove the shift lever.

20. Disconnect the ground strap from the fuel hose clamp. On the 7M-GTE, remove the engine mounting absorber.

21. Disconnect and plug the fuel lines.

22. Raise the vehicle and support safely.

23. Remove the exhaust pipe.

24. Remove the driveshaft.

25. Disconnect the speedometer cable.

26. If equipped with automatic transmission, remove the shift linkage. If equipped with manual transmission, remove the clutch release cylinder.

27. Properly support the engine and transmission assembly. Remove the No. 1 front crossmember. Remove the engine retaining mounts.

28. Position a piece of wood between the engine firewall and the rear of the cylinder head to prevent damage to the heater hose.

29. Make sure there are no remaining wires or hoses connected to the engine and then slowly and carefully remove the engine and transmission from the vehicle.

30. Installation is the reverse of the removal procedure.

Cressida

1. Disconnect the negative battery cable.

2. Drain the cooling system.

3. Remove the hood.

4. Remove the battery and tray.

5. Disconnect the accelerator, throttle and cruise control cables.

6. Remove the air cleaner assembly complete with the air flow meter, hoses and connector pipe.

7. Tag and disconnect all electrical wires and vacuum hoses necessary to remove the engine.

8. Remove the radiator.

9. Remove the drive belt and unbolt the air conditioning compressor. Position it aside and suspend it with wire. Do not disconnect the refrigerant lines.

10. Unbolt the power steering pump. Position it aside and suspend it with wire. Do not disconnect the hydraulic lines.

11. Remove the windshield washer fluid reservoir.

12. Remove the glove box and disconnect the 6 connectors from the main wiring harnerss and then pull the main wiring harness through the firewall and into the engine compartment.

13. Disconnect the heater hoses.

14. Raise the vehicle and support it safely.

15. Remove the engine under cover and drain the oil.

16. Disconnect the exhaust pipe at the manifold.

17. Disconnect the driveshaft at the transmission flange and position it aside.

18. Disconnect the speedometer cable and the transmission linkage.

19. Disconnect the starter lead and the ground lines at the stiffener plate and left side engine mount.

20. Disconnect and plug the fuel lines.

21. Remove the front wheels and then disconnect the power steering rack. Leave the hydraulic lines attached and lay the rack aside.

22. Loosen the 8 bolts and the ground strap and then remove the rear engine support.

23. Lower the vehicle and remove the 4 engine mount-to-suspension bolts. Attach an engine hoist to the 2 engine hangers and then slowly and carefully lift the engine out of the vehicle.

24. Installation is the reverse of the removal procedure.

Cylinder Head

Removal and Installation

2VZ-FE ENGINE

1. Disconnect the negative battery cable and drain the cooling system.

2. Disconnect the throttle cable at the throttle body. If equipped with cruise control, remove the cruise control actuator and vacuum pump.

3. Remove the air cleaner hose.

4. Raise the vehicle and support safely. Remove the engine undercovers.

5. Remove the lower suspension crossmember and the front exhaust pipe.

6. Remove the alternator. Remove the ISC valve.

7. Remove the throttle body, EGR pipe, EGR valve and vacuum modulator.

8. Remove the vacuum pipe and the distributor.

9. Remove the exhaust crossover pipe. Disconnect the cold start injector and then remove the injector tube.

10. Tag and disconnect all hoses leading to the air intake chamber and then remove the chamber.

11. Remove the fuel delivery pipes and the injectors.

12. Disconnect the water temperature sensor and remove the upper radiator hose. Remove the water outlet. Remove the water bypass outlet.

13. Loosen the 2 bolts and remove the cylinder head rear plate.

14. Remove the intake and exhaust manifolds.

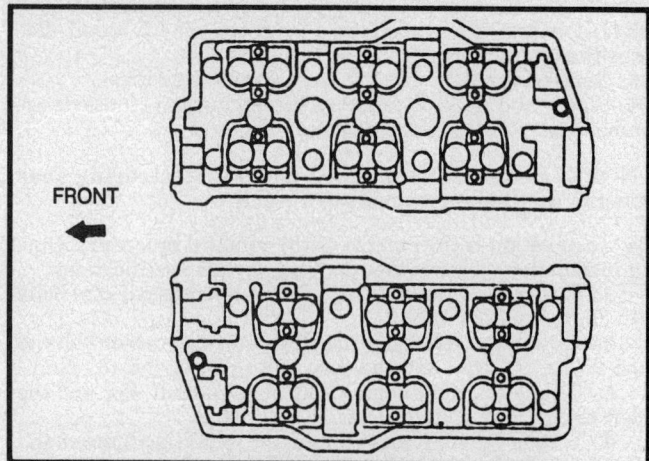

FRONT

Remove the 2 hex head bolts—2VZ-FE engine

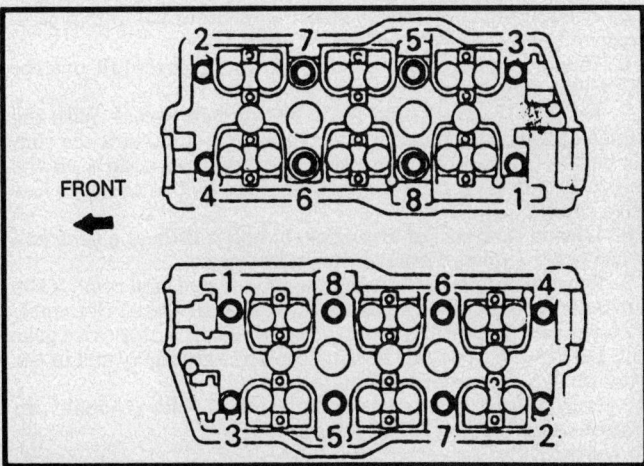

Cylinder head bolt loosening sequence—2VZ-FE engine

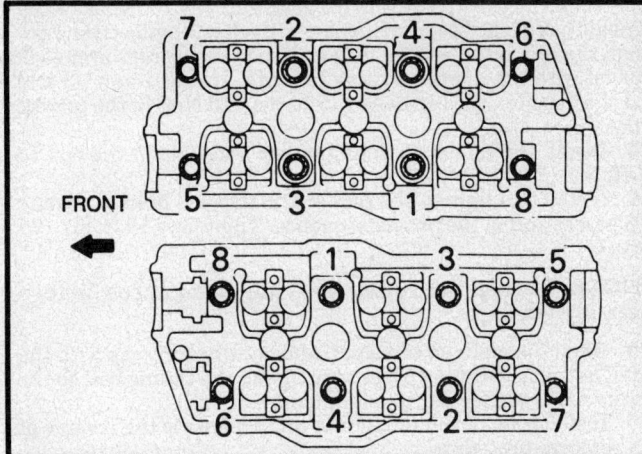

Cylinder head bolt tightening sequence—2VZ-FE engine

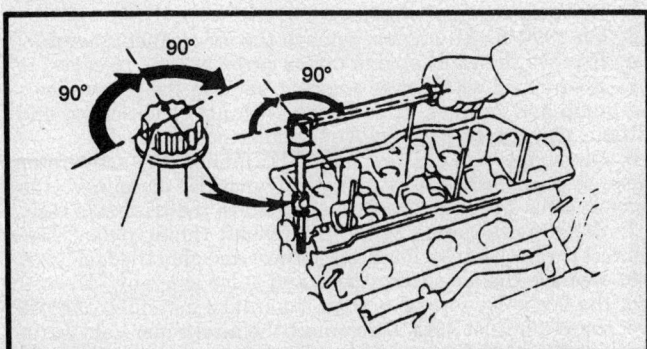

Angle torquing the cylinder head bolts—2VZ-FE engine

15. Remove the timing belt, camshaft pulleys and the No. 2 idler pulley.

16. Remove the No. 3 timing belt cover.

17. Remove the cylinder head covers and then remove the camshafts.

18. Remove the 2 hex head cylinder head bolts. Loosen and remove the remaining cylinder head bolts, in several stages, in the proper sequence. Remove the cylinder heads from the block.

To install:

19. Install new cylinder head gaskets on the block and then position the cylinder heads.

20. Torque the clinder head bolts as follows:

a. Install the regular (12-sided) cylinder head bolts and tighten them to 25 ft. lbs. (34 Nm) in the the proper sequence.

b. Mark the front of each bolt with a dab of paint and then tighten each bolt, in order, an additional 90 degrees (the dab of paint will be at the 3 o'clock position.

c. Retighten all bolts, in sequence, an additional 90 degrees so the paint dab is now at 6 o'clock.

d. Coat the threads of the 2 hex head bolts with engine oil and install them. Tighten each bolt to 13 ft. lbs. (18 Nm).

21. Installation of the remaining components is in the reverse order of removal.

3A-C, 4A-C AND 4A-LC ENGINES

Except 1987–88 Corolla FX

1. Disconnect the negative battery cable. Remove the exhaust pipe from the manifold. Drain the cooling system.

2. Remove the air cleaner. Tag and disconnect all hoses necessary to remove the cylinder head.

3. Remove all linkages from the carburetor. Disconnect and plug the fuel lines at the cylinder head and manifold.

4. Remove the fuel pump, carburetor and intake manifold.

5. Remove the cylinder head cover. Note the position of the spark plug wires and remove them. Remove the spark plugs.

6. Set the No. 1 cylinder to TDC of its compression stroke. This is accomplished by removing the No. 1 spark plug, placing finger over the hole and then turning the crankshaft pulley until pressure is exerted against finger.

7. Remove the crankshaft pulley with the proper tool. Remove the water pump pulley. Remove the top and bottom timing cover.

8. Matchmark the camshaft pulley and timing belt for reassembly. Loosen the belt tensioner. Remove the water pump.

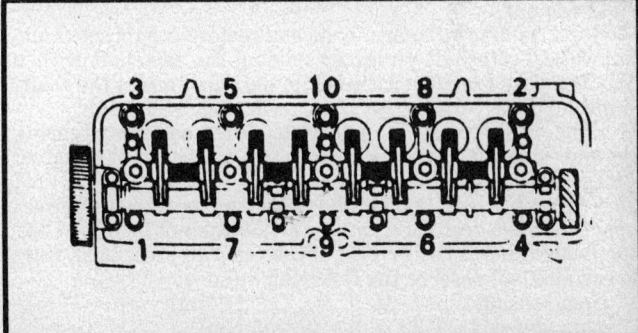

Cylinder head bolt loosening sequence—3A-C, 4A-C and 4A-LC engines

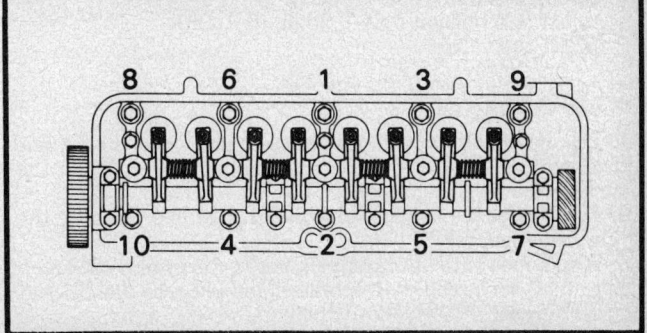

Cylinder head bolt tightening sequence—3A-C, 4A-C and 4A-LC engines

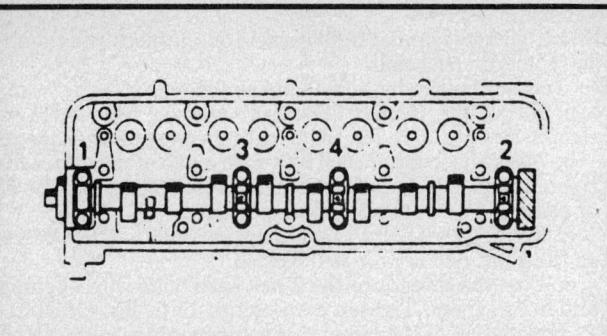

Camshaft bearing cap loosening sequence—3A-C, 4A-C and 4A-LC engines

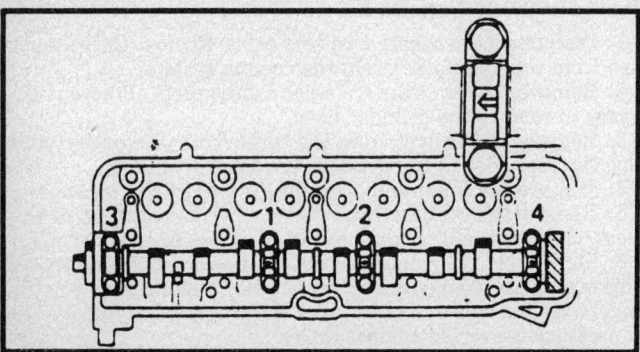

Camshaft bearing cap tightening sequence—3A-C, 4A-C and 4A-LC engines

9. Remove the timing belt. Do not bend, twist, or turn the belt inside out.

10. Remove the rocker arm bolts and remove the rocker arms. Remove the camshaft pulley by holding the camshaft with a suitable tool and removing the belt in the pulley end of the shaft. Do not hold the cam on the lobes, as damage will result.

11. Remove the camshaft seal. Remove the camshaft bearing caps and set them down in the order they appear on the engine. Remove the camshaft.

12. Loosen the head bolts in the reverse order of the torque sequence. Lift the head directly up. Do not attempt to slide it off.

13. Installation is the reverse of the removal procedure. During installation, observe the following torques:

Cam bearing caps 8–10 ft. lbs. (11–14 Nm).
Cam sprocket 29–39 ft. lbs. (39–53 Nm).
Crankshaft pulley 55–61 ft. lbs. (75–83 Nm)
Manifold bolts 15–21 ft. lbs. (20–29 Nm).
Rocker arm bolts 17–19 ft. lbs. (23–26 Nm).
Timing gear idler bolt 22–32 ft. lbs. (30–44 Nm).
Adjust belt tension 0.24–0.28 in. (6–7mm).
Adjust the valves.

1987–88 Corolla FX

1. Disconnect the negative battery cable. Raise the vehicle and support safely. Remove the engine under cover. Drain the cooling system and engine oil.

2. Disconnect the exhaust pipe at the manifold. Remove the air cleaner assembly.

3. If equipped with automatic transaxle, disconnect the accelerator and throttle cables. Disconnect and plug the fuel lines at the fuel pump.

4. Disconnect the water hose and remove the water outlet housing. Disconnect the water hoses at the cylinder head. Disconnect the water pump pulley.

5. If equipped with power steering, remove the pump stay. Remove the distributor and spark plugs.

6. Remove the cylinder head cover and gasket. Lift out the half circle plug.

7. Remove the No. 1 and No. 2 timing belt covers. With the engine at TDC of the compression stroke, matchmark the timing belt to the camshaft timing pulley and then slide it off the pulley. Be sure to secure the bottom of the belt so as not to lose valve timing.

8. Loosen each rocker arm support bolt a little at a time and in the order shown. Remove the rocker arms.

9. Secure the camshaft, using the proper tool, and remove the camshaft timing pulley. Measure the camshaft thrust clearance. With the camshaft still secure, loosen the distributor drive gear bolt. With the camshaft secure, loosen the camshaft bearing cap bolts gradually and in the order shown. Remove the camshaft.

10. Loosen and remove the cylinder head bolts gradually, in several stages. Remove the cylinder head.

To install:

11. Position the cylinder head on the block with a new gasket and tighten the head bolts in several stages, in the order shown, to a final torque of 43 ft. lbs. (59 Nm).

12. Install the distributor drive gear and plate washer to the camshaft, coat the bearing journals with clean engine oil and position the cam into the head. Position the bearing caps over each journal with the arrow pointing forward. Install a new oil seal and then tighten the cap bolts to 9 ft. lbs. (13 Nm) in the correct order.

13. Install the camshaft timing pulley and tighten the bolt to 34 ft. lbs. (47 Nm).

14. Install and tighten the rocker arm support bolts gradually in 3 passes and in the proper sequence. Tighten to 18 ft. lbs. (25 Nm).

NOTE: Loosen the rocker arm adjusting screw before installation.

15. Align the mark on the No. 1 camshaft bearing cap with the small hole in the timing pulley and install the timing belt so the marks made earlier are in alignment.

16. Installation of the remaining components is the reverse of the removal procedure.

3E ENGINE

1. Disconnect the negative battery cable.

2. Drain the cooling system.

3. On 1990–91 3E engine, remove the air cleaner assembly.

4. Remove the right engine under cover.

5. If equipped with power steering, remove the power steering pump and bracket. If equipped with air conditioning and without power steering, remove the idler pulley bracket.

6. Disconnect the radiator hoses. Disconnect the accelerator cable. If equipped with automatic transaxle, disconnect the throttle cable from the bracket mounted on the transaxle case.

7. Remove the timing belt and camshaft timing pulley. Disconnect the heater inlet hose. Disconnect and plug the fuel lines.

8. Remove the air suction hose and valve assembly. Disconnect the brake booster hose from the intake manifold. Disconnect the water inlet hose. Disconnect the intake manifold water hose from the intake manifold.

9. Tag and disconnect all electrical wires, vacuum lines and cables that will interfere with cylinder head removal.

10. Remove the EVAP, VSV and the No. 2 cold enrichment breaker valves. Disconnect the water bypass hoses from the carburetor. Remove the valve cover.

11. Disconnect the exhaust pipe. Remove the intake manifold stay and ground strap. Remove the wire harness clamp bolt from the intake manifold.

12. Measure the cylinder head camshaft thrust clearance using a dial indicator gauge. Standard clearance should be 0.0031–0.071 in. Maximum clearance should be 0.0098 in. If not within specification replace defective parts as required.

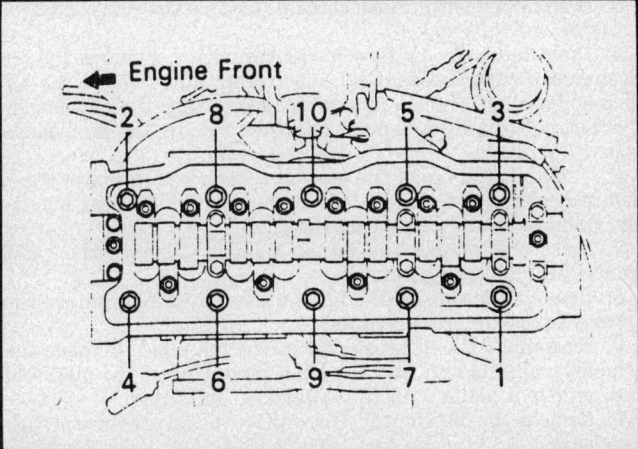

Cylinder head bolt loosening sequence—3E and 3E-E engines

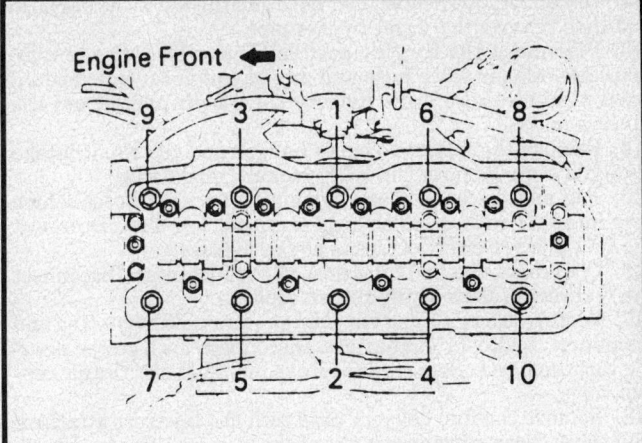

Cylinder head bolt tightening sequence—3E and 3E-E engines

13. Loosen then remove the cylinder head bolts in 3 phases and in the proper sequence. Remove the cylinder head from the engine.

14. Installation is the reverse of the removal procedure. During installation, use a new head gasket. Torque the cylinder head bolts as follows:

a. Tighten the cylinder head bolts in sequence to 22 ft. lbs. (29 Nm).

b. Tighten the bolts is sequence again to 36 ft. lbs. (49 Nm).

c. Retighten each bolt an additional 90 degree turn.

3E-E ENGINE

1. Disconnect the negative battery cable.
2. Remove the right engine under cover.
3. Drain the cooling system.
4. Disconnect the accelerator and throttle cables.
5. Remove the PCV hoses.
6. Remove the air cleaner and air intake collector assembly.
7. If equipped with power steering, remove the power steering pump and bracket. If equipped with air conditioning and without power steering remove the idler pulley bracket.
8. Remove the pulsation damper; disconnect the fuel inlet and return hoses from the dleivery pipe. Plug the hoses to prevent fuel leakage.
9. Disconnect the radiator hoses.
10. Disconnect the heater and water inlet hoses.

11. From the water inlet pipe, disconnect the water bypass hose that connects to the auxiliary air valve.

12. Tag and disconnect all electrical wire and vacuum hoses that interfere with removal of the cylinder head.

13. Remove the exhaust pipe stay and disconnect the exhaust pipe from the manifold.

14. Remove the intake manifold stay.

15. Remove the timing belt and the camshaft timing pulley.

16. Remove the valve cover.

17. Loosen then remove the cylinder head bolts in 3 phases and in the proper sequence. Remove the cylinder head from the engine.

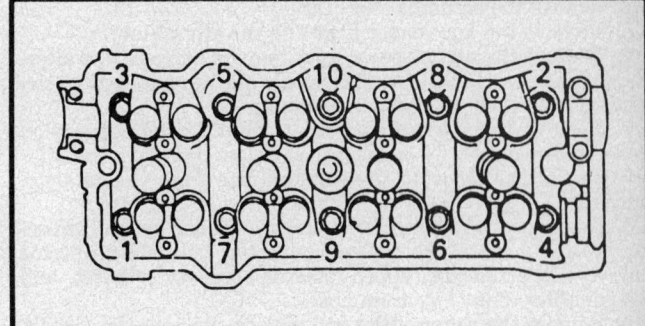

Cylinder head bolt loosening sequence—3S-FE engines

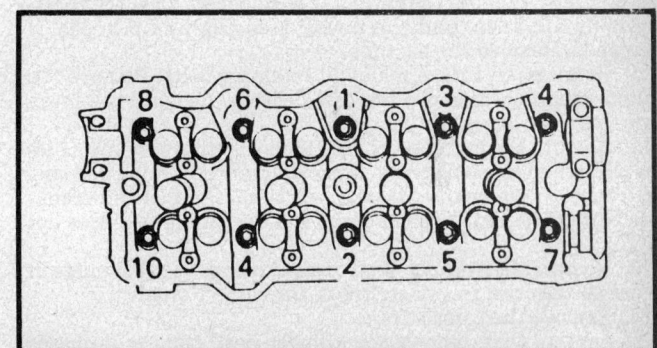

Cylinder head bolt torquing sequence—3S-FE engines

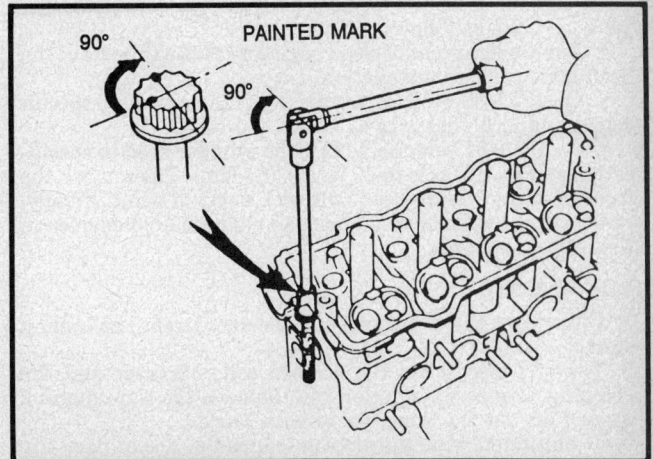

On 1990–91 3S-FE engine, torque the cylinder head bolts an additional 90 degrees in sequence.

18. Installation is the reverse of the removal procedure. Torque the cylinder head bolts as follows:

    a. Tighten the cylinder head bolts in sequence to 22 ft. lbs. (29 Nm).

    b. Tighten the bolts is sequence again to 36 ft. lbs. (49 Nm).

    c. Retighten each bolt an additional 90 degree turn each.

3S-FE ENGINE

1. Disconnect the negative battery cable.
2. Drain the cooling system.
3. If equipped with automatic transaxle, disconnect the throttle cable and bracket from the throttle body.
4. Disconnect the accelerator cable and bracket from the throttle body and intake chamber. If equipped with cruise control, remove the actuator and bracket.
5. Remove the air cleaner hose and the alternator.
6. Remove the oil pressure gauge, engine hangers and alternator upper bracket. Raise the vehicle and support safely. Remove the right wheel and tire assembly.
7. Remove the right under cover. Remove the suspension lower crossmember. Disconnect the exhaust pipe from the catalytic converter. Separate the exhaust pipe from the catalytic converter.
8. Disconnect the water temperature sender gauge connector, water temperature sensor connector, cold start injector time switch connector, upper radiator hose, water hoses, and the emission control vacuum hoses.
9. Remove the water outlet and gaskets. Remove the distributor. Remove the water bypass pipe. Remove the EGR valve and modulator.
10. Remove the throttle body assembly. Remove the cold start injector pipe. Remove the air intake chamber air hose, the throttle body air hose, and the power steering pump hoses, if equipped. Remove the air tube.
11. Remove the intake manifold retaining bolts. Remove the intake manifold. Remove the fuel delivery pipe and the injectors. Remove the spark plugs.
12. Remove the camshaft timing pulley. Remove the No. 1 idler pulley and tension spring. Remove the No. 3 timing belt cover. Properly support the timing belt so meshing of the crankshaft timing pulley does not occur and the timing belt does not shift.
13. Remove the cylinder head cover. Arrange the grommets in order so they can be reinstalled in the correct order.
14. Remove the camshafts.
15. Loosen, then remove the cylinder head bolts in 3 phases and in the proper sequence. Remove the cylinder head from the engine.
16. Installation is the reverse of the removal procedure. During installation, use a new cylinder head gasket. Torque the cylinder head bolts as follows:

    a. Apply a light coat of clean engine oil to the threads of the head bolts prior to installation.

    b. On 1987–89 vehicles, torque the cylinder head to specification and in 3 phases to 47 ft. lbs. (64 Nm).

    c. On 1990–91 vehicles, torque the cylinder head to specification and in 3 phases to 47 ft. lbs. (64 Nm). Then, mark the front of each cylinder head bolt with a dab of paint. Finally, re-torque the cylinder head bolts an additional 90 degrees in the proper sequence.

3S-GE ENGINE

1. Disconnect the negative battery cable. Drain the cooling system.
2. Tag and disconnect the ignition coil connector and the spark plug wire at the ignition coil. Remove the 4 nuts and 2 bolts and lift out the upper suspension brace.
3. If equipped with automatic transaxle, disconnect the throttle cable with its bracket from the throttle body. Disconnect the accelerator cable from the throttle body. Remove the radiator overflow tank.

4. If equipped with cruise control, remove the cruise control actuator and its bracket.
5. Disconnect the air flow meter connector. Remove the air cleaner cap clips. Loosen the hose clamp and remove the air cleaner hose and the air flow meter along with the air cleaner top. Lift out the filter element and then remove the air cleaner case.
6. Tag and disconnect the oxygen sensor lead. Remove the 4 mounting bolts and remove the exhaust manifold heat insulator. Remove the alternator and bracket.
7. Raise the vehicle and support safely. Remove the right front wheel and tire assembly.
8. Remove the right side engine under cover and remove the lower suspension crossmember.
9. Disconnect the exhaust pipe at the manifold. Remove the exhaust manifold stay and the EGR pipe. Unbolt the manifold and remove it along with the lower heat insulator.
10. Remove the distributor. Disconnect the oil pressure switch connector.
11. Tag and disconnect all electrical leads and vacuum hoses at the water outlet. Remove the upper radiator hoses, the heater outlet hose and the water bypass hose. Remove the water outlet.
12. Disconnect the heater inlet hose and the water bypass hose and then remove the water bypass pipe.
13. Disconnect the throttle position sensor lead, the ventilation hose, the air valve hose and any emission control vacuum hoses at the throttle body. Remove the 4 bolts and lift out the throttle body.
14. Remove the forward engine hanger and the No. 2 intake manifold stay. Remove the EGR vacuum modulator.
15. Tag and disconnect any remaining vacuum hoses which may interfere with cylinder head removal. Tag and disconnect the fuel injector electrical leads at the injector.
16. Disconnect the fuel inlet hose at the fuel filter. Disconnect the fuel return hose at the return pipe.
17. Remove the No. 1 and No. 3 intake manifold stays. Tag and disconnect the 2 VSV connectors. Disconnect the 2 power steering vacuum hoses. Remove the intake manifold and the air control valve.
18. Remove the fuel delivery pipe with the injectors attached. Pull the 4 injector insulators out of the injector holes in the cylinder head.
19. Remove the cylinder head cover. Remove the spark plugs. Remove the No. 1 engine hanger.
20. Remove the power steering reservoir and position it aside with the hydraulic lines still attached.
21. Remove the camshaft timing pulleys. Remove the No. 1 idler pulley and tension spring.
22. Remove the bolt holding the No. 2 and No. 3 timing covers. Remove the 4 mounting bolts and remove the No. 3 timing cover.
23. Loosen and remove the camshaft bearing caps, in several stages, and in the proper sequence. Lift out the camshafts and the oil seal. When removing the camshaft bearing caps, keep them in the proper order.
24. Loosen and remove the cylinder head bolts, in several stages, and in the proper sequence. Remove the cylinder head.

To install:

25. Position the cylinder head onto the cylinder block with a new gasket. Lightly coat the cylinder head bolts with engine oil, install them into the head and tighten them in several passes, in the proper sequence, to 40 ft. lbs. (53 Nm).
26. Position the camshafts into the cylinder head so the No. 1 cam lobes are facing outward.
27. Apply silicone sealant to the outer edge of the mating surface on the No. 1 bearing cap only. Position the bearing caps over each journal with the arrows pointing forward and in numerical order from the front to the rear.
28. Lightly coat the cap bolt threads with engine oil. Tighten them in several stages, and in the proper sequence, to 14 ft. lbs. (19 Nm).

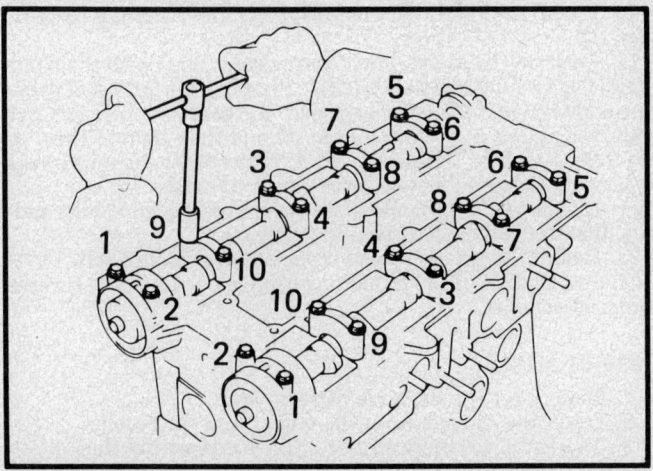

Remove the camshaft bearing caps in the order—3S-GE and 3S-GTE engines

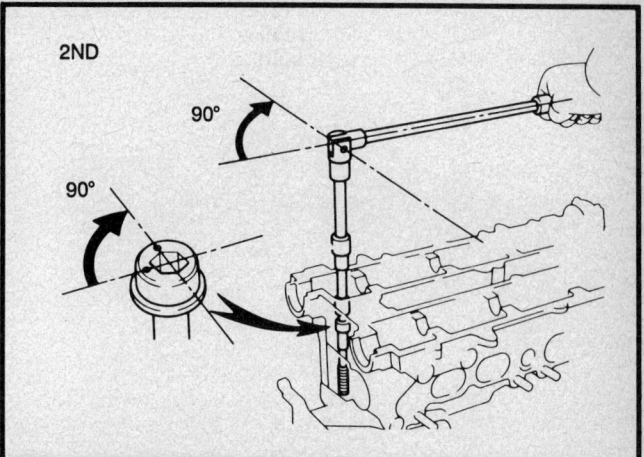

Mark the head bolts prior to angle-torquing—3S-GE and 3S-GTE engines

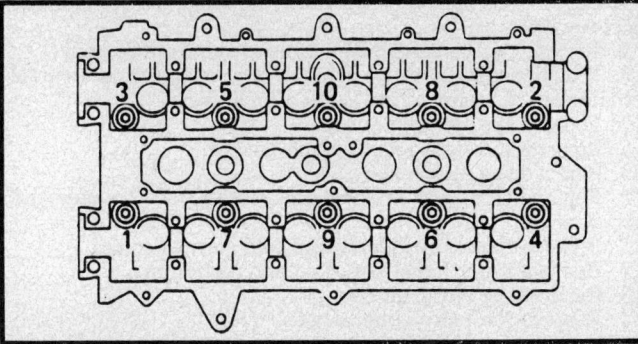

Cylinder head bolt loosening sequence—3S-GE and 3S-GTE engines

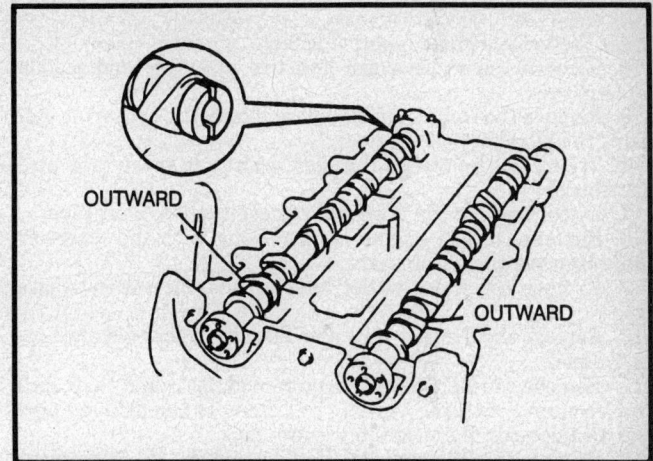

Camshaft positioning—3S-GE and 3S-GTE engines

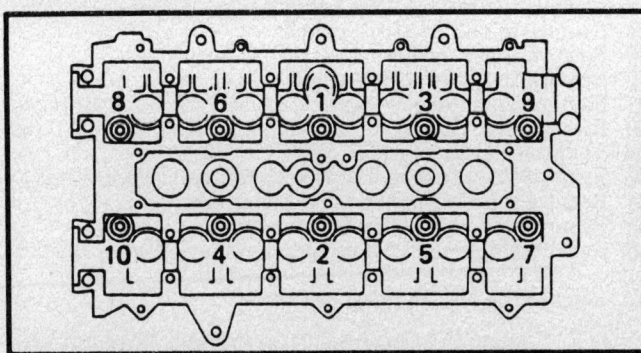

Cylinder head bolt tightening sequence—3S-GE and 3S-GTE engines

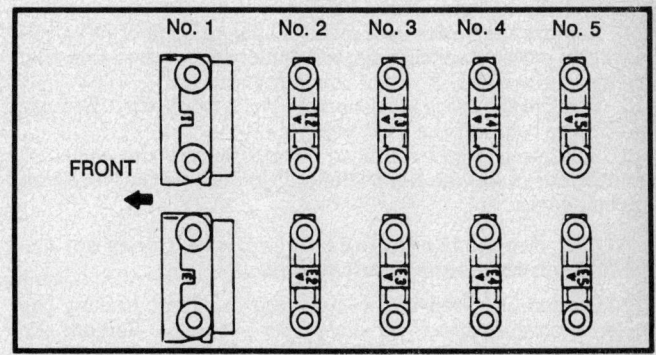

Camshaft bearing cap positioning—3S-GE and 3S-GTE engines

29. Check the camshaft thrust clearance. Coat the inside of a new oil seal with grease and carefully tap it onto the camshaft with a suitable drift. Install the No. 3 timing belt cover.

30. Connect the idler pulley tension spring to the pulley and the pin on the cylinder head. Install the idler pulley onto the pivot pin, force it to the left as far as it will go and tighten it. Make sure the tension spring is not out of the groove in the pin. Install the camshaft timing pulleys and the timing belt.

31. Installation of the remaining components is in the reverse order of removal. Tighten the lower suspension crossmember end bolts to 154 ft. lbs. (209 Nm) and the center bolt to 29 ft. lbs. (39 Nm). Tighten the upper suspension brace bolts to 15 ft. lbs. (20 Nm) and the nuts to 47 ft. lbs. (64 Nm). Refill the engine with coolant. Check the idle speed and ignition timing.

3S-GTE ENGINE

Celica

1. Disconnect the negative battery cable. Drain the coolant from the engine and intercooler.

2. Remove the upper suspension brace that runs between the strut towers. Disconnect the accelerator cable at the throttle body. Remove the radiator reservoir tank.

3. Remove the air cleaner assembly. Remove the alternator.

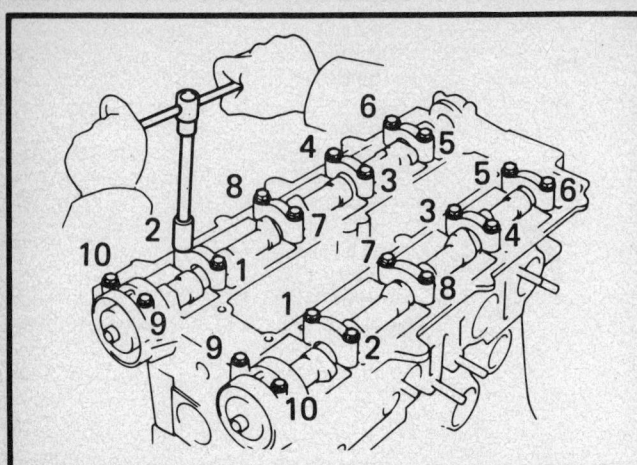

Tighten the bearing cap bolts in this order—3S-GE and 3S-GTE engines

Raise the vehicle and support it safely.

4. Remove the right wheel and tire assembly and engine undercovers.

5. Remove the front exhaust pipe and catalytic converter. Remove the alternator brackets.

6. Remove the turbocharger, exhaust manifold and distributor.

7. Disconnect the air hose and remove the No. 2 air pipe.

8. Remove the left engine hanger along with the reservoir tank. Remove the oil pressure switch.

9. Remove the water outlet housing and the water bypass pipe.

10. Remove the throttle body and disconnect the cold start injector lead.

11. Remove the EGR valve, vacuum modulator and EGR control Vacuum Swithcing Valve (VSV). Remove the delivery pipe and all injectors. Remove the vacuum pipe.

12. Remove the intake manifold stays and the No. 1 air pipe.

13. Disconnect the vacuum hose and remove the fuel pressure VSV. Remove the T-VIS Vacuum Switching (VSV), vacuum tank and the turbo pressure VSV.

14. Remove the intake manifold with the air control valve. Remove the power steering reservoir tank without disconnecting the hydraulic hoses. Position the pump aside.

15. Remove the spark plugs and the No. 2 front cover. Remove the timing belt and the PCV pipe.

16. Remove the cylinder head cover. Remove the camshaft timing pulleys and the No. 1 idler pulley. Remove the No. 3 timing belt cover.

NOTE: Secure the timing belt so the belt does not unmesh from the cranskahsft pulley.

17. Gradually loosen and remove the camshaft bearing cap bolts, in several passes, in the proper sequence. Remove the bearing caps, oil seals and lift out the camshafts.

18. Remove the right rear engine hanger. Remove the cylinder head bolts, in several stages, in the sequence and lift off the cylinder head.

To install:

19. Position the cylinder head and a new gasket on the block and torque the bolts as follows:

   a. Coat the head bolts with engine oil and tighten them in several passes, in sequence, to 40 ft. lbs. (54 Nm).

   b. Mark the front of each bolt with a dab of paint.

   c. Retighten the bolts an additional 90 degrees turn. The paint dabs should now all be at a 90 degree angle to the front of the head.

20. Install the right rear engine hanger and tighten it to 14 ft. lbs. (19 Nm).

21. Position the camshafts in the cylinder head with the No. 1 lobes facing outward. Coat the No. 1 bearing cap with seal packing and then install all the caps over the bearing journals. Coat the bearing cap bolts with engine oil and then tighten them to 14 ft. lbs. (19 Nm) in several stages, in the order shown. Grease 2 new oil seals and install them into the camshafts.

22. Install the No. 3 timing belt cover and the No. 1 idler pulley. Install the camshaft timing pulleys.

23. Install the cylinder head cover and the timing belt.

24. Installation of the remaining components is in the reverse order of removal.

1990-91 MR2

1. Disconnect the negative battery cable.

2. Drain the coolant from the engine and intercooler.

3. Tag and disconnect all hoses, lines and wiring that interfere with removal of the turbocharger, exhaust manifold, intake manifold and cylinder head.

4. Remove the engine hood side panels.

4. Remove the upper suspension brace that runs between the strut towers.

5. Disconnect the accelerator cable at the throttle body.

6. If equipped with cruise control, remove the cruise control actuator and disconnect the accelerator linkage.

7. Remove the air cleaner cap.

8. Remove the right front engine hanger.

9. Remove the intercooler.

10. Remove the front exhaust pipe, catalalytic conveter and turbocharger.

11. Remove the throttle body and cold start injector.

12. Remove the exhaust manifold and distibutor.

13. Remove the No. 2 air tube.

14. Remove the left engine hanger.

15. Remove the EGR vacuum modulator and Vacuum Switching Valve (VSV).

16. Remove the vacuum pipe, EGR valve and EGR pipe.

17. Remove the water outlet and housing.

18. Remove the oil pressure switch.

19. Remove the oil cooler.

20. Remove the water bypass pipe.

21. Remove the intake manifold stays and the No. 1 air pipe.

22. Remove the T-VIS Vacuum Switching (VSV), vacuum tank and the turbocharger pressure VSV.

23. Remove the intake manifold with the air control valve.

24. Remove the delivery pipe and fuel injectors.

25. Remove the cylinder head cover.

26. Remove the camshaft timing pulleys and the No. 1 idler pulley.

27. Remove the No. 3 timing belt cover.

NOTE: Secure the timing belt so the belt does not unmesh from the cranskahsft pulley.

28. Gradually loosen and remove the camshaft bearing cap bolts in several passes, in the proper sequence. Remove the bearing caps, oil seals and lift out the camshafts.

29. Remove the cylinder head bolts in several stages, in the the proper sequence and lift off the cylinder head from the alignment dowels on the block.

To install:

30. Position the cylinder head and a new gasket on the block.

31. Torque the cylinder head bolts as follows:

   a. Coat the head bolts with engine oil and tighten them in several passes, in sequence to 36 ft. lbs. (49 Nm).

   b. Mark the front of each bolt with a dab of paint.

   c. Retighten the bolts an additional 90 degrees turn. The paint dabs should now all be at a 90 degree angle to the front of the head.

32. Position the camshafts in the cylinder head with the No. 1

lobes facing outward. Coat the No. 1 bearing cap with seal packing and then install all the caps over the bearing journals. Coat the bearing cap bolts with engine oil and then tighten them to 14 ft. lbs. (19 Nm) in several stages, in the order shown. Grease 2 new oil seals and install them into the camshafts.

33. Check and adjust the valve clearance, as necessary.

34. Install the No. 3 timing belt cover, No. 1 idler pulley and camshaft timing pulleys.

35. Install the cylinder head cover with 2 new gaskets and 12 new bolt seal washers. Torque the cover bolts to 21 inch lbs. (2.5 Nm).

36. Installation of the remaining components is the reverse of the removal procedure.

4A-F ENGINE

1. Disconnect the negative battery cable. Drain the cooling system.

2. Remove the engine undercover and then disconnect the exhaust pipe at the manifold.

3. Remove the air cleaner and hoses. If equipped with automatic transaxle, disconnect the accelerator and throttle cables at the bracket.

4. Tag and disconnect all wires, lines and hoses that may interfere with removal of the exhaust manifold, intake manifold and cylinder head.

5. Disconnect the fuel lines at the fuel pump. Disconnect the heater hoses at the engine.

6. Disconnect the water hose and the bypass hose at the rear of the cylinder head. Remove the 2 bolts and pull off the water outlet pipe.

7. Remove the 2 mounting bolts and lift out the exhaust manifold stay. Remove the upper manifold insulator and then remove the exhaust manifold.

8. Remove the distributor.

9. Disconnect the 2 water hoses at the water inlet (front of head) and then remove the inlet housing.

10. Remove the fuel pump.

11. Disconnect the PCV and water hoses at the intake manifold. Remove the manifold stay and then remove the intake manifold and wire clamp.

12. Remove the drive belts and the power steering pump support.

13. Remove the spark plugs and the cylinder head cover.

14. Remove the No. 3 and No. 2 front covers. Turn the crankshaft pulley and align its groove with the 0 mark on the No. 1 front cover. Check that the camshaft pulley hole aligns with the mark on the No. 1 camshaft bearing cap (exhaust side).

15. Remove the plug from the No. 1 front cover and matchmark the timing belt to the camshaft pulley. Loosen the idler pulley mounting bolt and push the pulley to the left as far as it will go; tighten the bolt. Slide the timing belt off the camshaft pulley and support it so it won't fall into the case.

16. Remove the camshaft pulley and check the camshaft thrust clearance. Remove the camshafts.

17. Gradually loosen the cylinder head mounting bolts in several passes, in the sequence. Remove the cylinder head.

To install:

18. Position the cylinder head on the block with a new gasket. Lightly coat the cylinder head bolts with engine oil and then install them. Tighten the bolts in 3 stages, in the proper sequence. On the final pass, torque the bolt to 44 ft. lbs. (60 Nm).

19. Position the camshafts into the cylinder head. Position the bearing caps over each journal with the arrows pointing forward.

20. Tighten each bearing cap a little at a time and in the reverse of the removal sequence. Tighten to 9 ft. lbs. (13 Nm) Recheck the camshaft endplay.

21. Install the camshaft timing pulleys making sure the camshaft knock pins and the matchmarks are in alignment. Lock each camshaft and tighten the pulley bolts to 43 ft. lbs. (59 Nm).

22. Align the matchmarks made during removal and then install the timing belt on the camshaft pulley. Loosen the idler pulley set bolt. Make sure the timing belt meshing at the crankshaft pulley does not shift.

23. Rotate the crankshaft clockwise 2 revolutions from TDC to TDC. Make sure each pulley aligns with the marks made previously. If the marks are not in alignment, the valve timing is wrong. Shift the timing belt meshing slightly and then repeat Steps 21–23.

24. Tighten the set bolt on the timing belt idler pulley to 27 ft. lbs. (37 Nm). Measure the timing belt deflection at the top span between the 2 camshaft pulleys. It should deflect no more than 0.16 in. at 4.4 lbs. of pressure. If deflection is greater, readjust by using the idler pulley.

25. Installation of the remaining components is the reverse of the removal procedure.

4A-FE ENGINE

Corolla

1. Disconnect the negative battery cable at the battery. Drain the cooling system.

2. Remove the engine undercover and then disconnect the exhaust pipe at the manifold.

3. Remove the air cleaner and hoses; disconnect the intake air temperature sensor. Disconnect the accelerator and throttle cables at the bracket on vehicles with automatic transaxle.

4. Remove the cruise control actuator cable.

5. Tag and disconnect all wires, lines and hoses that may interfere with exhaust manifold, intake manifold and cylinder head removal.

6. Disconnect the fuel lines at the fuel pump. Disconnect the heater hoses at the engine.

7. Disconnect the water hose and the bypass hose at the rear of the cylinder head. Remove the 2 bolts and pull off the water outlet pipe.

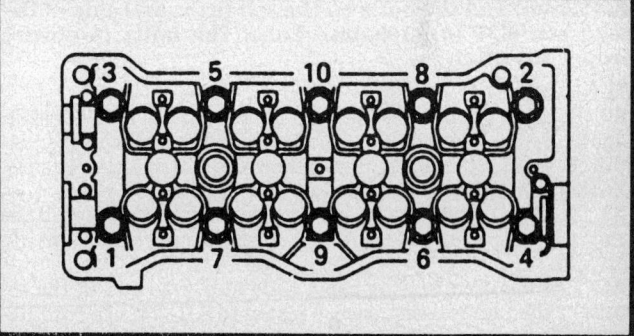

Cylinder head bolt loosening sequence—4A-F and 4A-FE engines (Corolla and Celica)

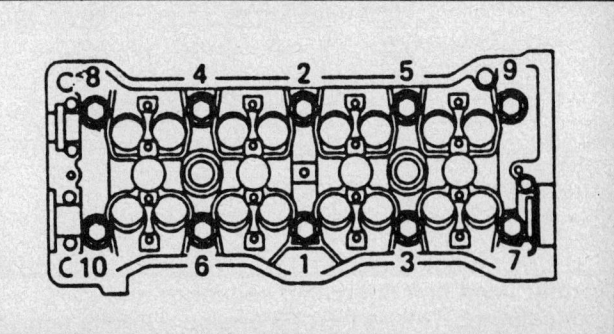

Cylinder head bolt tightening sequence—4A-F and 4A-FE engines (Corolla)

8. Remove the 2 mounting bolts and lift out the exhaust manifold stay. Remove the upper manifold insulator and then remove the exhaust manifold.

9. Remove the distributor.

10. Disconnect the 2 water hoses at the water inlet (front of head) and then remove the inlet housing.

11. Disconnect the PCV, fuel return and vacuum sensing hoses.

12. Remove the fuel inlet pipe and the cold start injector pipe. Disconnect the 4 vacuum hoses and then remove the EGR vacuum modulator.

13. Remove the fuel delivery pipe along with the injectors, spacers and insulators.

14. Unbolt the engine wire cover at the intake manifold and then disconnect the wire at the cylinder head.

15. Remove the intake manifold.

16. Remove the drive belts and then remove the water pump.

17. Remove the spark plugs, cylinder head cover and semi-circular plug.

18. Remove the No. 3 and No. 2 front covers. Turn the crankshaft pulley and align its groove with the 0 mark on the No. 1 front cover. Check that the camshaft pulley hole aligns with the mark on the No. 1 camshaft bearing cap (exhaust side). If not, rotate the crankshaft 360 degrees until the marks are aligned.

19. Remove the plug from the No. 1 front cover and matchmark the timing belt to the camshaft pulley. Loosen the idler pulley mounting bolt and push the pulley to the left as far as it will go; tighten the bolt. Slide the timing belt off the camshaft pulley and support it so it won't fall into the case.

20. Remove the camshaft pulley and check the camshaft thrust clearance. Remove the camshafts.

21. Gradually loosen the cylinder head mounting bolts in several passes, in the the proper sequence. Remove the cylinder head.

NOTE: On 1990–91 vehicles, the cylinder head bolts on the right (intake) side of the cylinder head are 3.54 in. (90mm) and the bolts on the left (exhaust) side of the head are 4.25 in. (108mm). Label the bolts to ensure proper installation.

To install:

22. Position the cylinder head on the block with a new gasket. Lightly coat the cylinder head bolts with engine oil and then install them. Tighten the bolts in 3 stages, in the proper sequence. On the final pass, torque the bolt to 44 ft. lbs. (60 Nm).

23. Position the camshafts into the cylinder head. Position the bearing caps over each journal with the arrows pointing forward.

24. Tighten each bearing cap a little at a time and in the reverse of the removal sequence. Tighten to 9 ft. lbs. (13 Nm) Recheck the camshaft endplay.

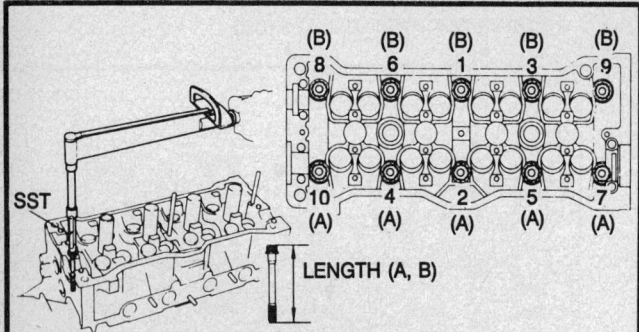

Cylinder head bolt tightening sequence and positioning on 1990–91 4A-FE engine (Corolla and Celica). The "A" bolts are 3.54 in. (90mm) and the "B" bolts are 4.25 in. (108mm)

25. Install the camshaft timing pulleys making sure the camshaft knock pins and the matchmarks are in alignment. Lock each camshaft and tighten the pulley bolts to 43 ft. lbs. (59 Nm).

26. Align the matchmarks made during removal and then install the timing belt on the camshaft pulley. Loosen the idler pulley set bolt. Make sure the timing belt meshing at the crankshaft pulley does not shift.

27. Rotate the crankshaft clockwise 2 revolutions from TDC to TDC. Make sure each pulley aligns with the marks made previously. If the marks are not in alignment, the valve timing is wrong. Shift the timing belt meshing slightly and then repeat Steps 4–6.

28. Tighten the set bolt on the timing belt idler pulley to 27 ft. lbs. (37 Nm). Measure the timing belt deflection at the top span between the 2 camshaft pulleys. It should deflect no more than 0.24 in. (6mm) at 4.4 lbs. of pressure. If deflection is greater, readjust by using the idler pulley.

29. Installation of the remaining components is the reverse of the removal procedure.

1990–91 Celica

1. Disconnect the negative battery cable. Drain the cooling system.

2. If equipped with automatic transaxle, disconnect the throttle cable and bracket from the throttle body.

3. Disconnect the accelerator cable and bracket from the throttle body.

4. Remove the air cleaner cap and hose.

5. Remove the engine under covers. Remove the suspension lower crossmember.

6. Disconnect all lines, hoses and electrical wires that interfere with exhaust manifold, intake manifold and cylinder head removal.

7. Disconnect the front exhaust pipe, distributor and exhaust manifold.

8. Remove the water outlet and gaskets. Remove the water inlet and inlet housing.

9. Unbolt and remove the power steering pump without disconnecting hoses.

10. Remove the throttle body, cold start injector pipe, cold start injector, delivery pipe and fuel injectors.

11. Remove the Air Control Valve (ACV) assembly. Disconnect engine wiring from the timing belt cover and from the intake manifold.

12. Remove the vacuum pipe, EGR vacuum modulator and EGR Vacuum Switching Valve (VSV) assembly.

13. Remove the EGR valve and gasket. Remove the water inlet pipe and fuel return hose from the fuel filter.

14. Remove the intake manifold with retaining manifold stay (bracket).

15. Remove the valve cover.

16. Remove the camshaft timing pulley, No. 1 idler pulley and tension spring and No. 3 timing belt cover. Properly support the timing belt so meshing of the crankshaft timing pulley does not occur and the timing belt does not shift.

17. Remove the fan belt adjusting bar, engine hangers and power steering drive belt adjusting strut or bracket.

18. Remove the camshafts. Make sure to uniformly loosen and remove bearing cap bolts in several phases and in the proper sequence when removing the camshafts.

19. Loosen then remove the cylinder head bolts in three phases and in the proper sequence. Remove the cylinder head from the engine.

NOTE: The cylinder head bolts on the right (intake) side of the cylinder head are 3.54 in. (90mm) and the bolts on the left (exhaust) side of the head are 4.25 in. (108mm). Label the bolts to ensure proper installation.

To install:

20. Install the cylinder head on the cylinder head block. Place the cylinder head in position on the cylinder head gasket.

21. Apply a light coat of clean engine oil to the threads of the head bolts before installation. Tighten the bolts in 3 stages, in the proper sequence. On the final pass, torque the bolt to 44 ft. lbs. (60 Nm).

22. Installation of the camshafts and remaining components is the reverse of the removal procedure.

4A-GE, 4A-GEC AND 4A-GELC ENGINES

1. Disconnect the negative battery cable. Remove the engine undercover. Drain the cooling system and engine oil.

2. Loosen the clamp and then disconnect the No. 1 air cleaner hose from the throttle body. Disconnect the actuator and accelerator cables from the bracket on the throttle body.

3. If equipped with power steering, Remove the power steering pump and its bracket. Position the pump aside with the hydraulic lines connected.

4. Loosen the water pump pulley set nuts. Remove the drive belt adjusting bolt and then remove the belt. Remove the set nuts and then remove the fluid coupling along with the fan and the water pump pulley.

5. Disconnect the upper radiator hose at the water outlet on the cylinder head. Disconnect the 2 heater hoses at the water bypass pipe and the cylinder head rear plate.

6. Remove the distributor. Remove the cold start injector pipe and the PCV hose from the cylinder head.

7. Remove the pulsation damper from the delivery pipe. Disconnect the fuel return hose from the pressure regulator.

8. Tag and disconnect all vacuum hoses which may interfere with cylinder head remvoval. Remove the wiring harness and the vacuum pipe from the No. 3 timing cover. Tag and disconnect all wires which might interfere with exhaust manifold, intake manifold and cylinder head removal.

9. Disconnect the exhaust bracket from the exhaust pipe. Disconnect the exhaust manifold from the exhaust pipe.

10. Remove the vacuum tank and the VCV valve. Remove the exhaust manifold.

11. Remove the 2 mounting bolts and remove the water outlet housing from the cylinder head with the No. 1 bypass pipe and gasket. Pull the No. 1 bypass pipe out of the housing.

12. Remove the fuel delivery pipe along with the fuel injectors.

13. Remove the intake manifold stay. Remove the intake manifold along with the air control valve.

14. Remove the cylinder head covers and their gaskets. Remove the spark plugs. Remove the No. 1 and No. 2 timing belt covers and their gaskets.

15. Rotate the crankshaft pulley until its groove is in alignment with the 0 mark on the No. 1 timing belt cover. Check that the valve lifters on the No. 1 cylinder are loose. If not, rotate the crankshaft 1 complete revolution (360 degrees).

16. Place matchmarks on the timing belt and 2 timing pulleys. Loosen the idler pulley bolts and move the pulley to the left as far as it will go and then retighten the bolt.

17. Remove the timing belt from the camshaft pulleys. When removing the timing belt, support the belt so the meshing of the crankshaft timing pulley and the timing belt does not shift. Never drop anything inside the timing case cover. Be sure the timing belt does not come in contact with dust or oil.

18. Lock the camshafts and remove the timing pulleys. Remove the No. 4 timing belt cover.

19. Using a dial indicator, measure the endplay of each camshaft. If not within specification, replace the thrust bearing.

20. Loosen each camshaft bearing cap bolt a little at a time and in the sequence shown. Remove the bearing caps, camshaft and oil seal.

21. Loosen the cylinder head bolts gradually in 3 stages, and in the proper order using the proper tool.

22. Remove the cylinder head.

NOTE: On 1990–91 engines, the cylinder head bolts on the right (intake) side of the cylinder head are 3.54 in. (90mm) and the bolts on the left (exhaust) side of the head are 4.25 in. (108mm). Label the bolts to ensure proper installation.

To install:

23. Position the cylinder head on the block with a new gasket. Lightly coat the cylinder head bolts with engine oil and then install the short head bolts on the intake side and the long ones on the exhaust side. Tighten the bolts in 3 stages, in the proper sequence. On the final pass, torque the bolt to 43 ft. lbs.

24. On 1988–91 engines, coat the head bolts with engine oil and tighten them in several passes, in the sequence shown to 22 ft. lbs. (29 Nm). Mark the front of each bolt with a dab of paint and then retighten the bolts a further 90 degree turn. The paint dabs should now all be at a 90 degree angle to the front of the head. Retighten the bolts one more time a further 90 degree turn. The paint dabs should now all be pointing toward the rear of the head.

25. Position the camshafts into the cylinder head. Position the bearing caps over each journal with the arrows pointing forward.

26. Tighten each bearing cap a little at a time and in the reverse of the removal sequence. Tighten to 9 ft. lbs. (13 Nm). Recheck the camshaft endplay.

27. Drive the camshaft oil seals onto the end of the camshafts using a suitable seal installer. Be careful not to install the oil seals crooked. Install the No. 4 timing belt cover.

28. Install the camshaft timing pulleys making sure the camshaft knock pins and the matchmarks are in alignment. Lock each camshaft and tighten the pulley bolts to 34 ft. lbs. (47 Nm).

29. Align the matchmarks made during removal and then install the timing belt on the camshaft pulley. Loosen the idler pulley

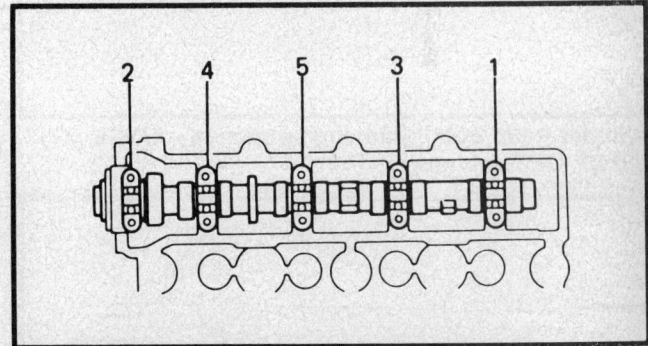

Loosen the camshaft bearing cap bolts in this order—4A-GE (all) and 4A-GZE engines

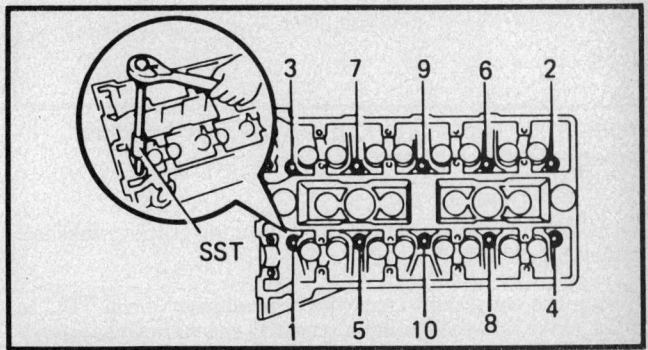

Cylinder head bolt loosening sequence—4A-GE and 4A-GZE engines

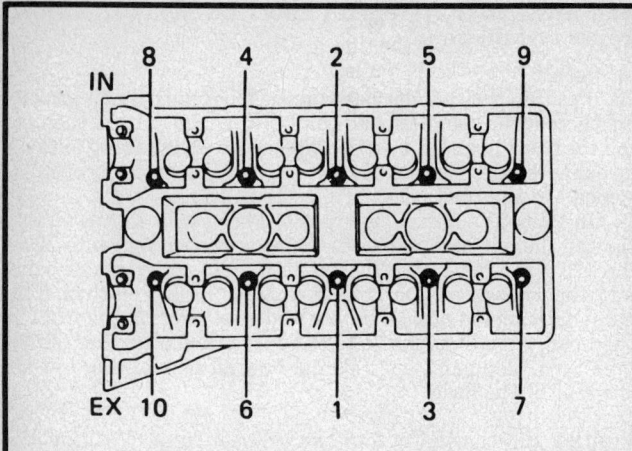

Cylinder head bolt tightening sequence—4A-GE and 4A-GZE engines

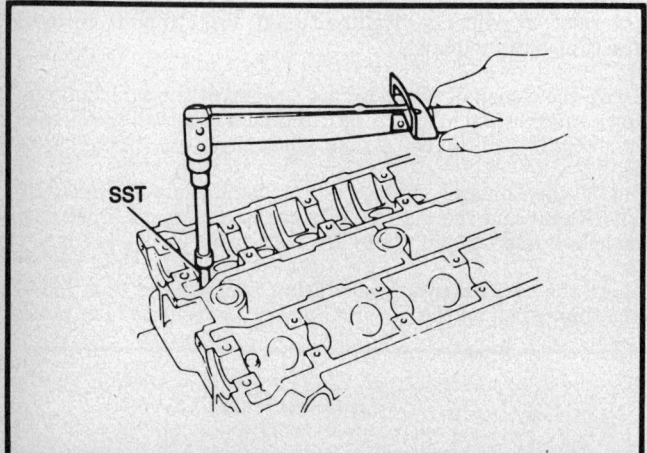

Cylinder head bolt tightening sequence—4A-GE (all) and 4A-GZE engines

Position the camshafts into the cylinder head as shown—4A-GE (all) and 4A-GZE engines

set bolt. Make sure the timing belt meshing at the crankshaft pulley does not shift.

30.
Rotate the crankshaft clockwise 2 revolutions from TDC to TDC. Make sure each pulley aligns with the marks made previously. If the marks are not in alignment, the valve timing is wrong. Shift the timing belt meshing slightly and then repeat Steps 28–30.

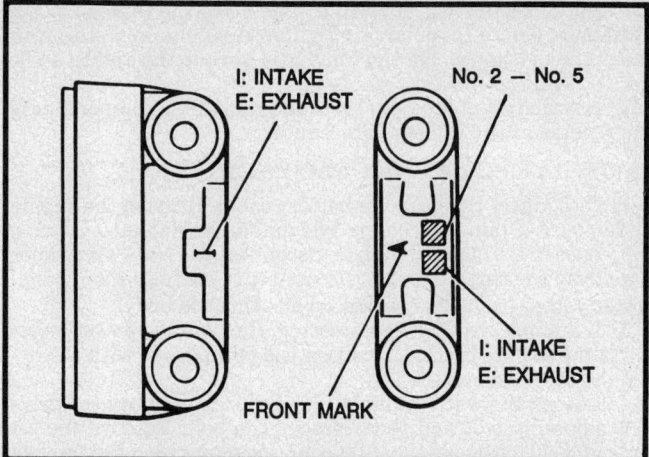

Camshaft bearing cap positioning (the arrows must always point forward)—4A-GE (all) and 4A-GZE engines

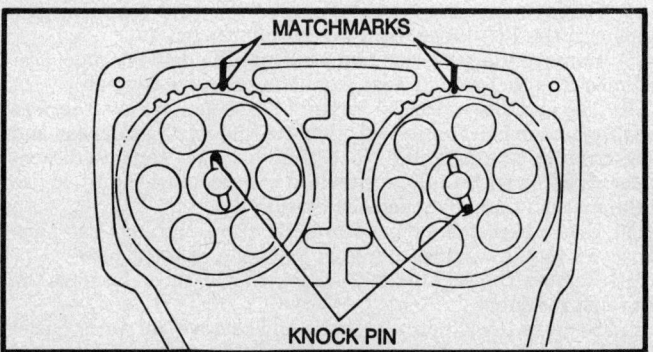

Align the camshaft knockpin with the camshaft timing pulley—4A-GE (all) and 4A-GZE engines

31.
Tighten the set bolt on the timing belt idler pulley to 27 ft. lbs. (37 Nm). Measure the timing belt deflection at the top span between the 2 camshaft pulleys. It should deflect no more than 0.16 in. at 4.4 lbs. of pressure. If deflection is greater, readjust by using the idler pulley.

32.
Installation of the remaining components is in the reverse order of removal.

4A-GZE ENGINE

1. Disconnect the negative battery cable. Remove the hood and engine undercovers.
2. Drain the engine coolant and remove the intercooler. Remove the battery.
3. Disconnect the air bleeder hose at the water inlet housing. Disconnect the cruise control vacuum hose and the throttle cable.
4. Remove the air flow meter with the No. 3 air cleaner hose. Disconnect the accelerator cable.
5. Remove the accelerator link and disconnect the air conditioning idle-up vacuum hoses.
6. Disconnect the heater hose at the rear of the cylinder head. Disconnect the brake booster vacuum hose and remove the radiator reservoir tank. Disconnect the No. 1 radiator hose at the water outlet housing.
7. Tag and disconnect any remaining hoses, wires or connections which may interfere with exhaust manifold, intake manifold and cylinder head removal.

8. Remove all drive belts and then remove the water pump pulley. Remove the supercharger.

9. Remove the No. 2 air outlet duct and the No. 3 fuel pipe. Remove the No. 1 vacuum transmitting pipe.

10. Disconnect the No. 2 fuel hose and remove the cylinder head rear cover.

11. Remove the fuel delivery pipe and the fuel injectors.

12. Remove the water outlet with the bypass pipe. Remove the EGR valve with the pipe still attached.

13. Remove the intake manifold. Remove the front exhaust pipe.

14. Remove the air conditioning compressor and bracket. Remove the distributor and alternator with its bracket.

15. Remove the exhaust manifold.

16. Rotate the crankshaft pulley until its groove is in alignment with the **0** mark on the No. 1 timing belt cover. Check that the valve lifters on the No. 1 cylinder are loose. If not, rotate the crankshaft 1 complete revolution (360 degrees).

17. Place matchmarks on the timing belt and 2 timing pulleys. Loosen the idler pulley bolts and move the pulley to the left as far as it will go and then retighten the bolt.

18. Remove the timing belt from the camshaft pulleys. When removing the timing belt, support the belt so the meshing of the crankshaft timing pulley and the timing belt does not shift. Never drop anything inside the timing case cover. Be sure the timing belt does not come in contact with dust or oil.

19. Lock the camshafts and remove the timing pulleys. Remove the No. 4 timing belt cover.

20. Using a dial indicator, measure the endplay of each camshaft. If not within specification, replace the thrust bearing.

21. Loosen each camshaft bearing cap bolt a little at a time and in the sequence shown. Remove the bearing caps, camshaft and oil seal.

22. Loosen the cylinder head bolts gradually in 3 stages, and in the proper order, using the proper tool.

23. Remove the cylinder head from the vehicle.

To install:

24. Position the cylinder head on the block with a new gasket.

25. Torque the cylinder head bolts as follows:

   a. Lightly coat the cylinder head bolts with engine oil and then install the short head bolts on the intake side and the long ones on the exhaust side.

   b. Tighten them in several passes, in the proper sequence to 22 ft. lbs. (29 Nm).

   c. Mark the front of each bolt with a dab of paint and then retighten the bolts a further 90 degree turn. The paint dabs should now all be at a 90 degree angle to the front of the head.

   d. Retighten the bolts one more time a further 90 degree turn. The paint dabs should now all be pointing toward the rear of the head.

26. Position the camshafts into the cylinder head. Position the bearing caps over each journal with the arrows pointing forward.

27. Tighten each bearing cap a little at a time and in the reverse of the removal sequence. Tighten to 9 ft. lbs. (13 Nm). Recheck the camshaft endplay.

28. Drive the camshaft oil seals onto the end of the camshafts using a suitable seal installer. Be careful not to install the oil seals crooked. Install the No. 4 timing belt cover.

29. Install the camshaft timing pulleys making sure the camshaft knock pins and the matchmarks are in alignment. Lock each camshaft and tighten the pulley bolts to 34 ft. lbs. (47 Nm).

30. Align the matchmarks made during removal and then install the timing belt on the camshaft pulley. Loosen the idler pulley set bolt. Make sure the timing belt meshing at the crankshaft pulley does not shift.

31. Rotate the crankshaft clockwise 2 revolutions from TDC to TDC. Make sure each pulley aligns with the marks made previously. If the marks are not in alignment, the valve timing is wrong. Shift the timing belt meshing slightly and then repeat Steps 28–30.

32. Tighten the set bolt on the timing belt idler pulley to 27 ft. lbs. (37 Nm). Measure the timing belt deflection at the top span between the 2 camshaft pulleys. It should deflect no more than 0.16 in. (4mm). at 4.4 lbs. of pressure. If deflection is greater, readjust by using the idler pulley.

33. Installation of the remaining components is the reverse of the removal procedure.

5M-GE ENGINE

1. Disconnect the negative battery cable. Drain the cooling system.

2. Disconnect the exhaust pipe from the exhaust manifold.

3. Remove the throttle cable bracket from the cylinder head if equipped with automatic transmission, and remove the accelerator and actuator cable bracket.

4. Tag and disconnect the ground cable, oxygen sensor wire, high tension coil wire, distributor connector, solenoid resistor wire connector and thermo- switch wire, if equipped with automatic transmission.

5. Tag and disconnect the brake booster vacuum hose, EGR valve vacuum hose, fuel hose from the intake manifold and actuator vacuum hose, if equipped with cruise control.

6. Disconnect the upper radiator hose from the thermostat housing, and disconnect the 2 heater hoses.

7. Disconnect the No. 1 air hose from the air intake connector. Remove the 2 clamp bolts, loosen the throttle body hose clamp and remove the air intake connector and the connector pipe.

8. Tag and disconnect all emission control hoses from the throttle body and air intake chamber, the 2 PCV hoses from the cam cover and the fuel hose from the fuel hose support.

9. Remove the air intake chamber stay and the vacuum pipe and ground cable. Remove the bolt that attaches the spark plug wire clip, leaving the wires attached to the clip. Remove the distributor from the cylinder head with the cap and wires attached, by removing the distributor holding bolt.

10. Tag and disconnect the cold start injector wire and disconnect the cold start injector fuel hose from the delivery pipe.

11. Loosen the nut of the EGR pipe, remove the 5 bolts and 2 nuts and remove the air intake chamber and gasket.

12. Remove the glove box and remove the ECU module. Disconnect the 3 connectors and pull the EFI (fuel injection) wire harness out through the engine side of the firewall.

13. Remove the pulsation damper and the No. 1 fuel pipe. Remove the water outlet housing by first loosening the clamp and disconnecting the water bypass hose.

14. Remove the intake manifold.

15. Disconnect the power steering pump drive belt and remove

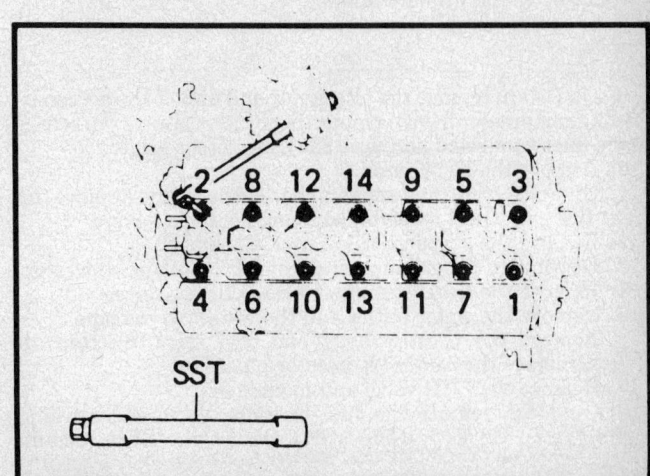

Cylinder head bolt loosening sequence—5M-GE engine

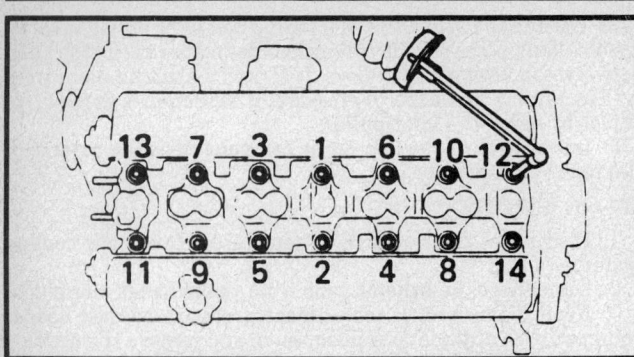

Cylinder head bolt tightening sequence—5M-GE engine

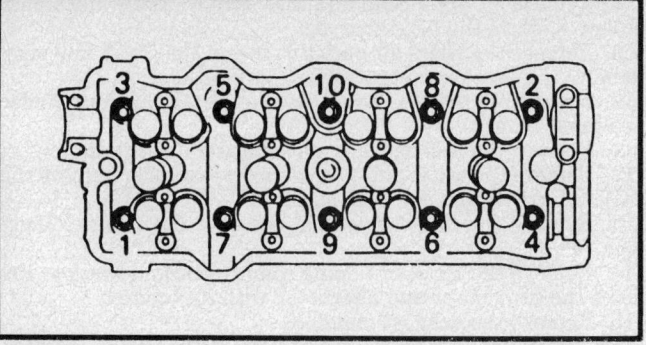

Cylinder head bolt loosening sequence—5S-FE engine

the power steering pump without disconnecting the fluid hoses. Position the pump aside.

16. Disconnect the oxygen sensor connector and remove the exhaust manifold.

17. Remove the timing belt and camshaft timing gears. Remove the timing belt cover stay, and remove the oil pressure regulator and gasket. Remove the No. 2 timing belt cover and gasket.

18. Tag and disconnect any other wires, linkage and/or hoses still attached to the cylinder head or may interfere with its removal.

19. Carefully remove the 14 head bolts gradually in 2–3 passes and in the proper sequence.

20. Carefully lift the cylinder head from the dowels on the cylinder block and remove it.

21. Installation is the reverse of the removal procedure. Torque the cylinder head bolts, in several stages, to 58 ft. lbs. (78 Nm).

5S-FE ENGINE

1. Disconnect the negative battery cable. Drain the cooling system.

2. Tag and disconnect all lines, hoses and electrical wires that interfere with exhaust manifold, intake manifold and cylinder head removal.

3. MR2, remove the engine under covers, engine hood side panels and the brace that runs across the struts.

4. If equipped with automatic transaxle, disconnect the throttle cable and bracket from the throttle body.

5. Disconnect the accelerator cable and bracket from the throttle body and intake chamber.

6. If equipped with cruise control, remove the actuator and bracket.

8. Remove the air cleaner cap.

9. On Celica, remove the alternator and unbolt the air conditioning compressor from its mounting bracket. Leave the refrigerant lines connected and wire the compressor aside.

10. Remove the distributor.

11. On Celica, raise and support the vehicle safely. Remove the right tire and wheel assembly and engine under covers.

12. Remove the suspension lower crossmember.

13. Disconnect the exhaust pipe from the catalytic converter.

14. Remove the exhaust pipe and catalytic converter.

15. Remove the water outlet and the water bypass pipe.

16. Remove the throttle body and cold start injector. On Celica, remove the cold start injector pipe.

17. Remove the EGR valve and modulator.

18. On MR2, remove the fuel pressure Vacuum Switching Valve (VSV). On Celica and MR2, remove the EGR vacuum switching valve.

19. Remove the air intake chamber air hose, the throttle body air hose, and the power steering pump hoses, if equipped. On Celica, remove the air tube.

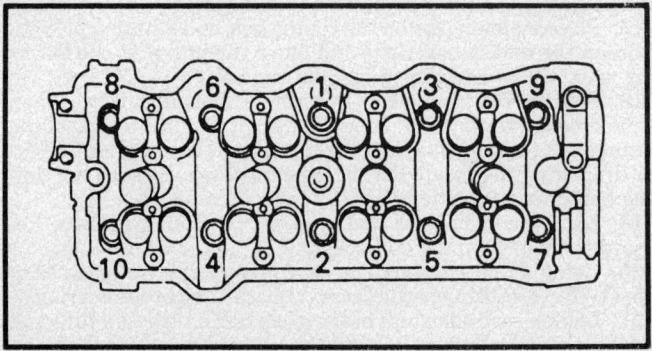

Exploded view of the cylinder head—3E-E engine

20. Remove the intake manifold.

21. Remove the fuel delivery pipe and the injectors.

22. Remove the camshaft timing pulley, No. 1 idler pulley and tension spring and No. 3 timing belt cover. Properly support the timing belt so meshing of the crankshaft timing pulley does not occur and the timing belt does not shift.

23. Remove the engine hangers and oil pressure switch. On Celica, remove the alternator bracket.

24. Remove the valve cover.

25. Remove the camshafts.

26. Loosen then remove the cylinder head bolts in 3 phases and in the proper sequence. Remove the cylinder head from the engine.

To install:

27. Install the cylinder head on the cylinder head block. Place the cylinder head in position on the cylinder head gasket.

28. Torque the cylinder head bolts as follows:

   a. Apply a light coat of clean engine oil to the threads of the head bolts before installation.

   b. Tighten the bolts in several passes, in the proper sequence to 36 ft. lbs. (49 Nm).

   c. Mark the front of each bolt with a dab of paint.

   d. Retighten the bolts a further 90 degree turn. The paint dabs should now all be at a 90 degree angle to the front of the head.

29. Installation of the remaining components is the reverse of the removal precedure.

7M-GE AND 7M-GTE ENGINE

1. Disconnect the negative battery cable. Drain the cooling system.

2. Disconnect the exhaust pipe from the exhaust manifold. Disconnect the cruise control cable, if equipped.

3. Disconnect the accelerator cable. Disconnect the throttle cable, if equipped with automatic transmission. Disconnect the engine ground strap.

4. On the 7M-GE, remove the No. 1 air cleaner hose along with the intake air pipe assembly. On the 7M-GTE, remove the No. 4 air cleaner pipe along with the No. 1 and No. 2 air cleaner hose.

5. Disconnect the cruise control vacuum hose, the charcoal canister hose and the brake booster hose.

6. Remove the radiator and heater inlet hoses. Remove the alternator.

7. On the 7M-GTE, remove the power steering reservoir tank. On the 7M-GTE, remove the cam position sensor.

8. Remove the air intake chamber with the connector. Remove the PCV pipe. Disconnect and tag all lines, hoses and electrical wires that interfere with exhaust manifold, intake manifold and cylinder head removal.

9. Remove the EGR pipe mounting bolts. Remove the manifold stay retaining bolts. On the 7M-GE, remove the throttle body bracket. On the 7M-GTE, remove the ISC pipe.

10. Remove the air intake connector mounting bolt (7M-GTE). On the 7M-GE, remove the cold start injector tube. On the 7M-GTE, disconnect the cold start injector. Disconnect the EGR vacuum modulator from the bracket.

11. Disconnect the engine wire from the clamps of the intake chamber. Remove the nuts and bolts, vacuum pipes and intake chamber with the connector and gasket.

12. On the 7M-GTE, remove the ignition coil and bracket.

13. Remove the pulsation damper, the VSV and the No. 1 fuel pipe. Remove the No. 2 and No. 3 fuel pipes. On the 7M-GTE, remove the auxiliary air pipe.

14. On the 7M-GE, remove the high tension wires and the distributor. Remove the oil dipstick. On the 7M-GTE, remove the turbocharger assembly.

15. Remove the exhaust manifold. Remove the water outlet housing. Remove the cylinder head covers. Remove the spark plugs.

16. Remove the timing belt and the camshaft timing pulleys. Remove the cylinder head retaining bolts gradually and in the

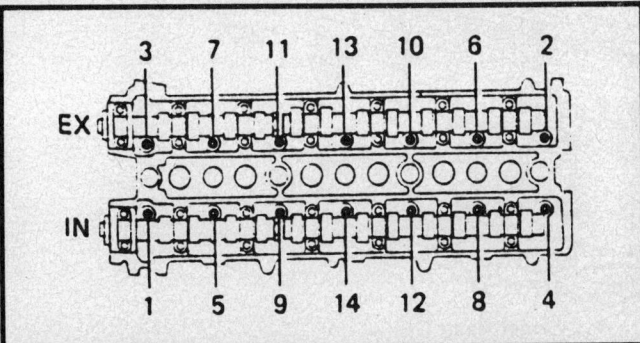

Cylinder head bolt loosening sequence—7M-GE and 7M-GTE engines

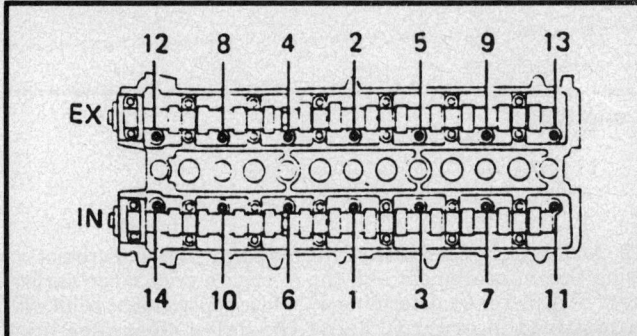

Cylinder head bolt tightening sequence—7M-GE and 7M-GTE engines

proper sequence. carefully remove the cylinder head from the engine. As the cylinder head is lifted, separate the No. 5 water bypass line from its union.

17. Installation is the reverse of the removal procedure.

18. Be sure to use a new gasket and install it in the proper direction. Torque the cylinder head bolts to specification and in the proper sequence.

Valve Lifters

Removal and Installation

1. Disconnect the negative battery cable.
2. Drain the cooling system.
3. Remove the valve cover(s).
4. Remove the camshafts.
5. Remove the valve lifters and shims from the cylinder head.
5. Label each lifter and shim with the respective cylinder head bore.
6. Inspect the lifters and shims for excesive wear. Replace worn lifters and shims as required.

To install:
7. Install the lifters and shims into the cylinder head. Make sure the lifter can be rotated freely by hand.
8. Install the camshafts.
9. Install the valve cover(s) using new gaskets and sealant, as required.
10. Fill the cooling system to the proper level.
11. Connect the negative battery cable.

Valve Lash

Adjustment

2VZ-FE ENGINE

1. Remove the air intake chamber and the cylinder head covers.

2. Use a wrench and turn the crankshaft until the notch in the pulley aligns with the timing mark **0** of the No. 1 timing belt cover. This will insure that No. 1 piston is at TDC of the compression stroke.

NOTE: Check that the valve lifters on the No. 1 (intake) cylinder are loose and those on No. 1 cylinder (exhaust)are tight. If not, turn the crankshaft 1 complete revolution (360 degrees) and then re-align the marks.

3. Using a flat feeler gauge measure the clearance between the camshaft lobe and the valve lifter on the first set of valves shown. This measurement should correspond to specification.

NOTE: If the measurement is within specifications, go on to the next step. If not, record the measurement taken for each individual valve.

4. Turn the crankshaft ⅔ revolution (240 degrees).
5. Measure the clearance of the second set of valves shown.

NOTE: If the measurement is within specifications, go on to the next step. If not, record the measurement taken for each individual valve.

6. Turn the crankshaft ⅔ revolution (240 degrees).
7. Measure the clearance of the third set of valves shown.

NOTE: If the measurement for this set of valves (and also the previous ones) is within specifications, go no further, the procedure is finished. If not, record the measurements and then proceed to Step 8.

8. Turn the crankshaft to position the intake camshaft lobe of the cylinder to be adjusted, upward.

23-69

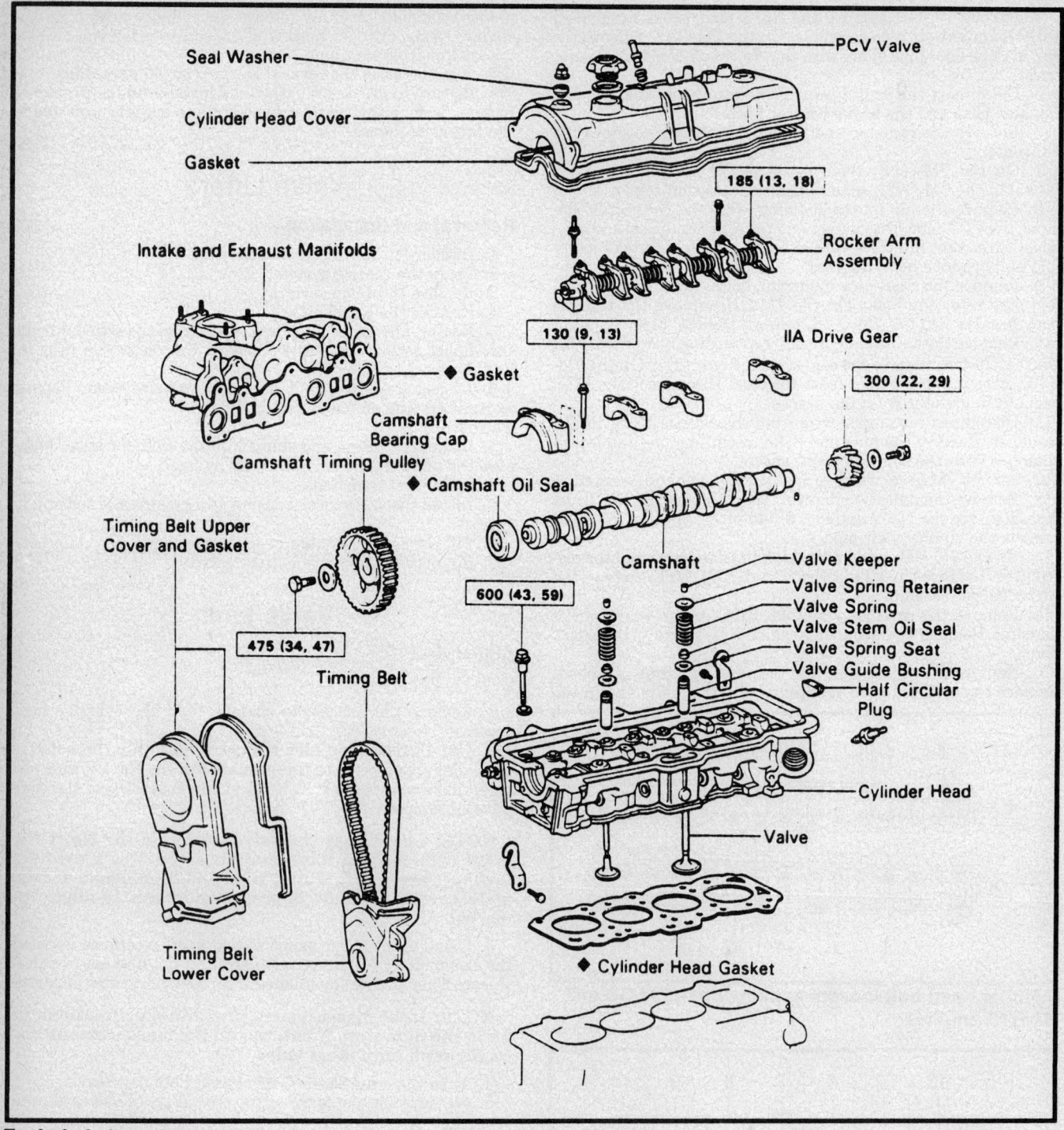

Seal Washer

Cylinder Head Cover

Gasket

PCV Valve

185 (13, 18)

Rocker Arm Assembly

Intake and Exhaust Manifolds

130 (9, 13)

◆ Gasket

Camshaft Bearing Cap

Camshaft Timing Pulley

◆ Camshaft Oil Seal

Camshaft

IIA Drive Gear

300 (22, 29)

Timing Belt Upper Cover and Gasket

475 (34, 47)

Timing Belt

600 (43, 59)

Valve Keeper
Valve Spring Retainer
Valve Spring
Valve Stem Oil Seal
Valve Spring Seat
Valve Guide Bushing
Half Circular Plug

Cylinder Head

Valve

Timing Belt Lower Cover

◆ Cylinder Head Gasket

Exploded view of the cylinder head—3A-C, 4A-C and 4A-LC engines

9. Using a suitable tool, turn the valve lifter so the notch is easily accessible; it should be toward the spark plug.

10. Install tool 09248–55010 or equivalent, between the 2 camshafts lobes and then turn the handle so the tool presses down the valve lifter evenly.

11. Using a suitable tool and a magnet, remove the valve shims.

12. Measure the thickness of the old shim with a micrometer. Using this measurement and the clearance ones made earlier (from Step 3, 5 or 7), determine what size replacement shim will be required in order to bring the valve clearance into specification.

NOTE: Replacement shims are available in 17 sizes, in

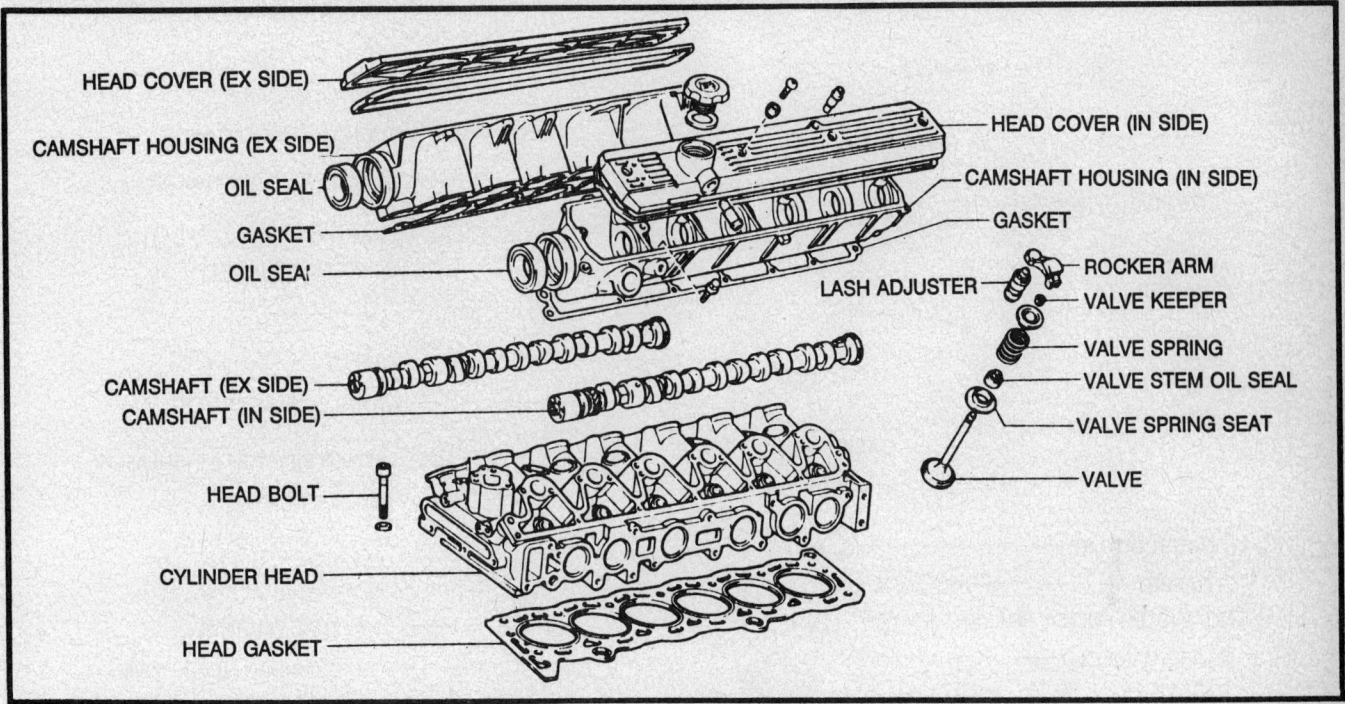

HEAD COVER (EX SIDE)
CAMSHAFT HOUSING (EX SIDE)
OIL SEAL
GASKET
OIL SEAL
CAMSHAFT (EX SIDE)
CAMSHAFT (IN SIDE)
HEAD BOLT
CYLINDER HEAD
HEAD GASKET

HEAD COVER (IN SIDE)
CAMSHAFT HOUSING (IN SIDE)
GASKET
LASH ADJUSTER
ROCKER ARM
VALVE KEEPER
VALVE SPRING
VALVE STEM OIL SEAL
VALVE SPRING SEAT
VALVE

Exploded view of the cylinder head—3A-C, 4A-C and 4A-LC engines

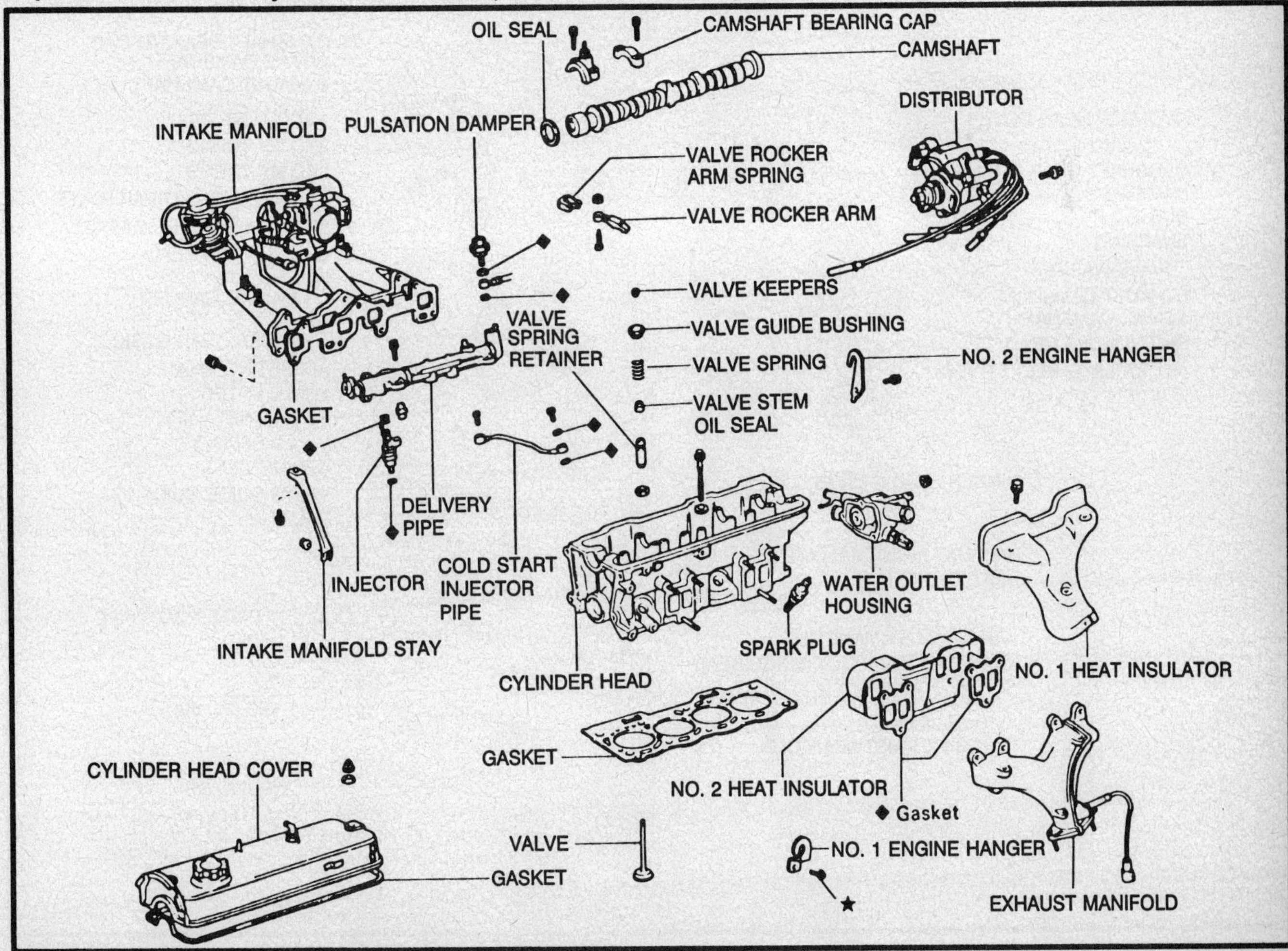

OIL SEAL
CAMSHAFT BEARING CAP
CAMSHAFT
INTAKE MANIFOLD
PULSATION DAMPER
DISTRIBUTOR
VALVE ROCKER ARM SPRING
VALVE ROCKER ARM
VALVE KEEPERS
VALVE GUIDE BUSHING
VALVE SPRING
NO. 2 ENGINE HANGER
VALVE STEM OIL SEAL
VALVE SPRING RETAINER
GASKET
DELIVERY PIPE
COLD START INJECTOR PIPE
INJECTOR
INTAKE MANIFOLD STAY
WATER OUTLET HOUSING
SPARK PLUG
CYLINDER HEAD
GASKET
NO. 1 HEAT INSULATOR
NO. 2 HEAT INSULATOR
◆ Gasket
NO. 1 ENGINE HANGER
CYLINDER HEAD COVER
VALVE
GASKET
GASKET
EXHAUST MANIFOLD

Cylinder head bolt tightening sequence—5S-FE engine

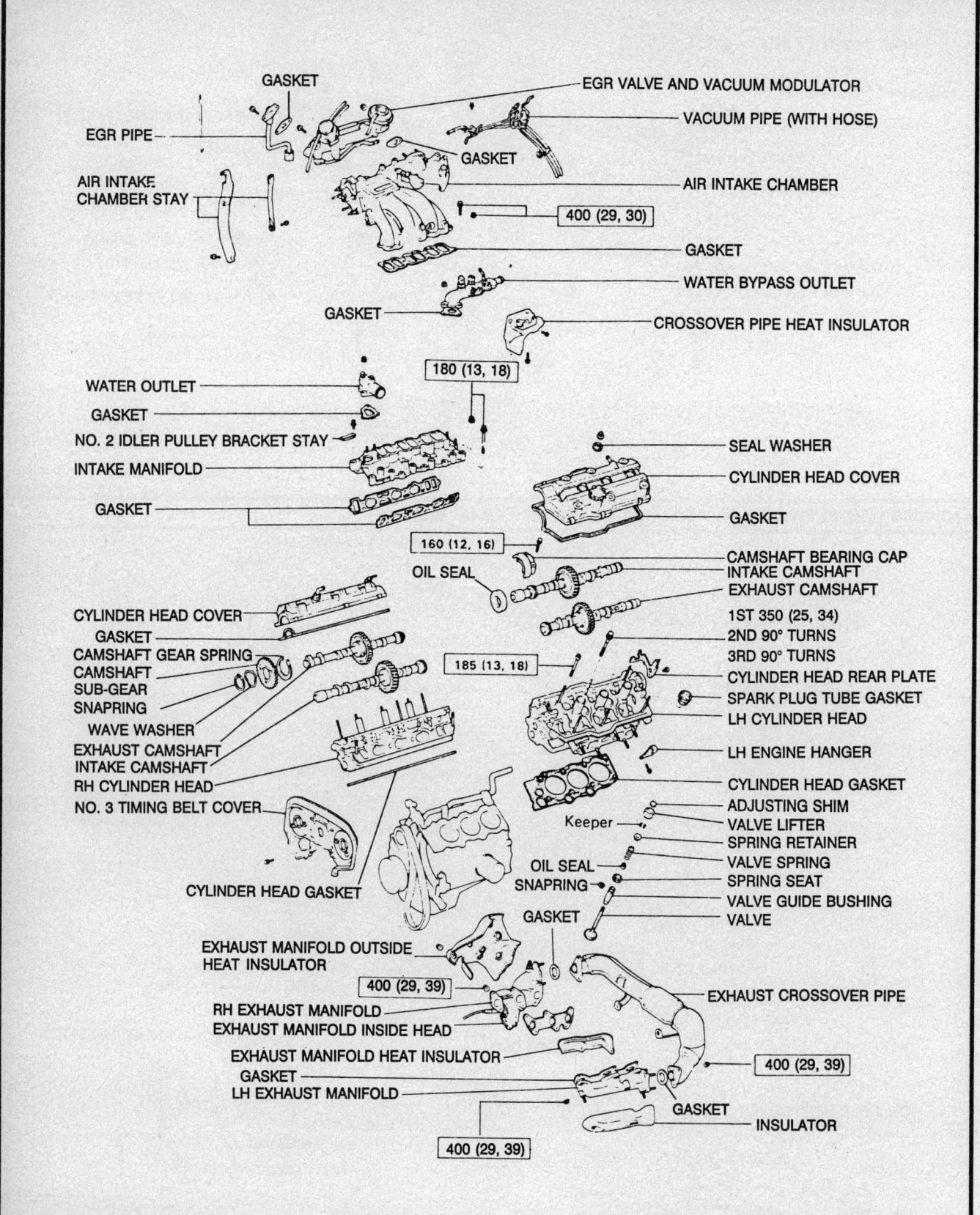

GASKET

EGR VALVE AND VACUUM MODULATOR

EGR PIPE

VACUUM PIPE (WITH HOSE)

AIR INTAKE CHAMBER STAY

GASKET

AIR INTAKE CHAMBER

400 (29, 30)

GASKET

WATER BYPASS OUTLET

GASKET

CROSSOVER PIPE HEAT INSULATOR

180 (13, 18)

WATER OUTLET

GASKET

SEAL WASHER

NO. 2 IDLER PULLEY BRACKET STAY

CYLINDER HEAD COVER

INTAKE MANIFOLD

GASKET

GASKET

160 (12, 16)

CAMSHAFT BEARING CAP

OIL SEAL

INTAKE CAMSHAFT

EXHAUST CAMSHAFT

CYLINDER HEAD COVER

1ST 350 (25, 34)

GASKET

2ND 90° TURNS

CAMSHAFT GEAR SPRING

3RD 90° TURNS

CAMSHAFT SUB-GEAR

185 (13, 18)

CYLINDER HEAD REAR PLATE

SNAPRING

SPARK PLUG TUBE GASKET

WAVE WASHER

LH CYLINDER HEAD

EXHAUST CAMSHAFT

LH ENGINE HANGER

INTAKE CAMSHAFT

RH CYLINDER HEAD

CYLINDER HEAD GASKET

NO. 3 TIMING BELT COVER

Keeper

ADJUSTING SHIM

VALVE LIFTER

SPRING RETAINER

OIL SEAL

VALVE SPRING

CYLINDER HEAD GASKET

SNAPRING

SPRING SEAT

VALVE GUIDE BUSHING

GASKET

VALVE

EXHAUST MANIFOLD OUTSIDE HEAT INSULATOR

400 (29, 39)

RH EXHAUST MANIFOLD

EXHAUST CROSSOVER PIPE

EXHAUST MANIFOLD INSIDE HEAD

400 (29, 39)

EXHAUST MANIFOLD HEAT INSULATOR

GASKET

LH EXHAUST MANIFOLD

GASKET

INSULATOR

400 (29, 39)

Exploded view of the cylinder head—2VZ-FE engine

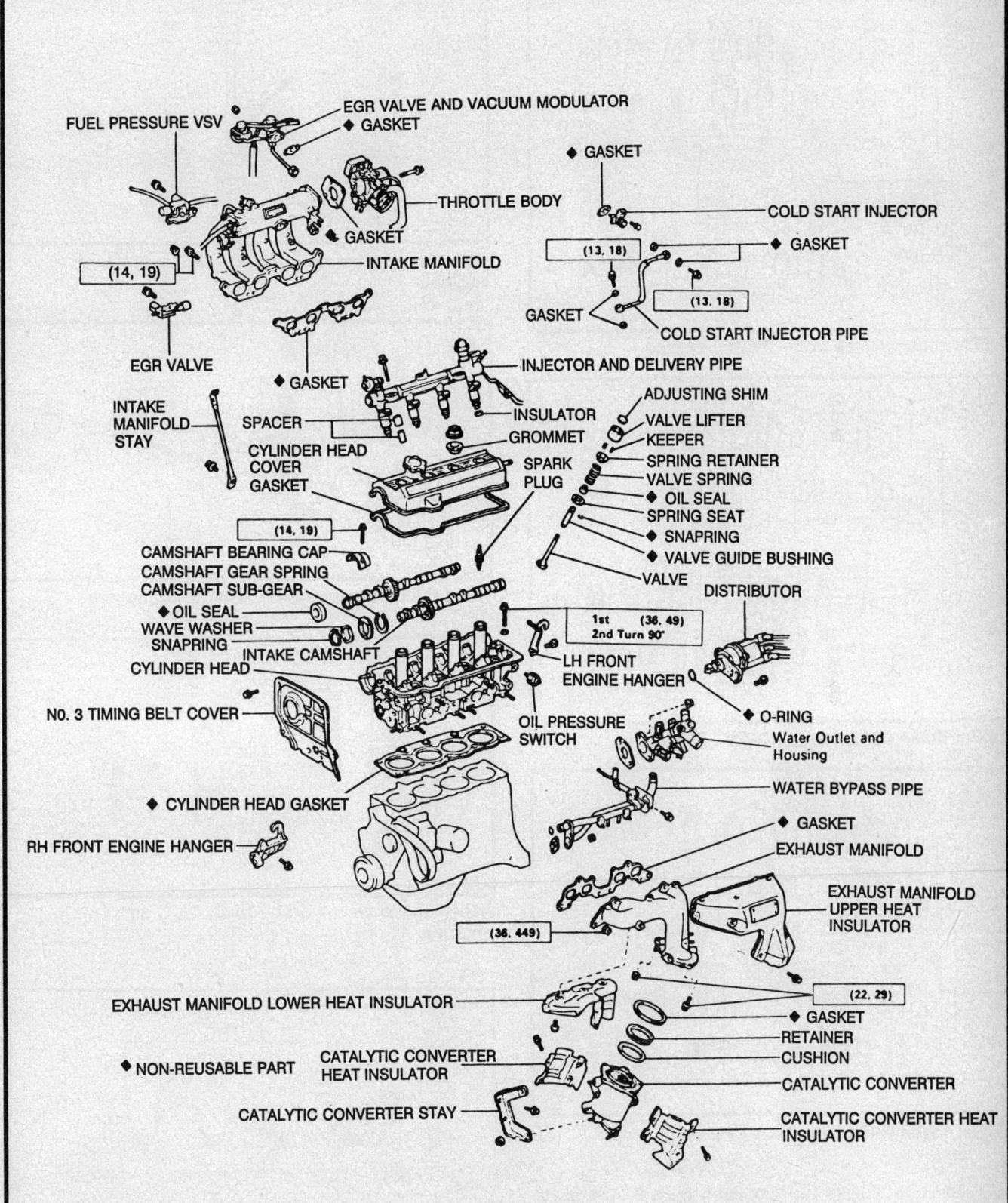

Exploded view of the cylinder head—5S-FE engine

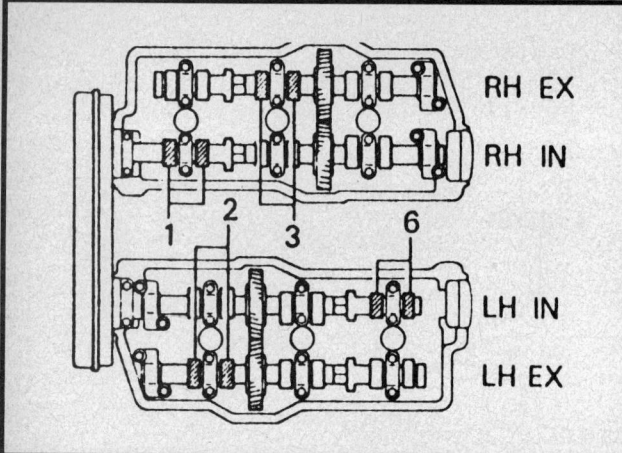

Adjust these valves first—2VZ-FE engine

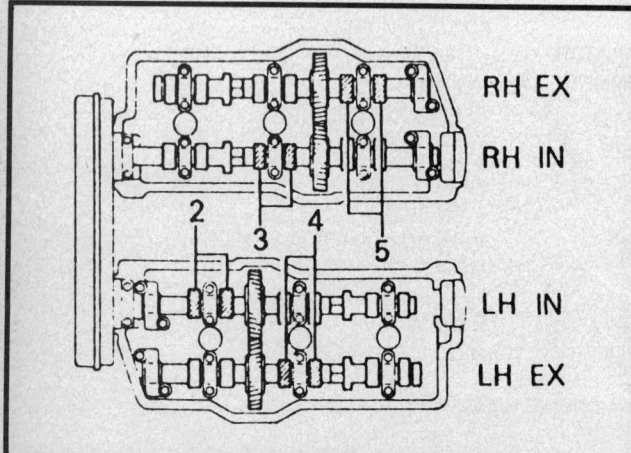

Adjust these valves second—2VZ-FE engine

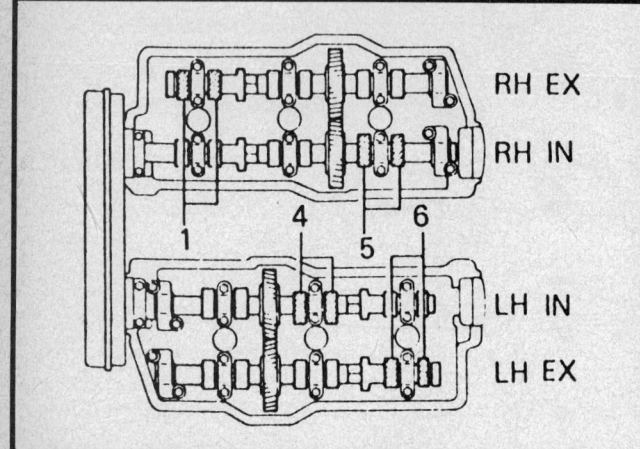

Adjust these valves third—2VZ-FE engine

increments of 0.0020 in. (0.05mm), from 0.0984 in. to 0.1299 in. (2.50mm to 3.300mm)

13. Install the new shim, remove the special tool and then recheck the valve clearances.

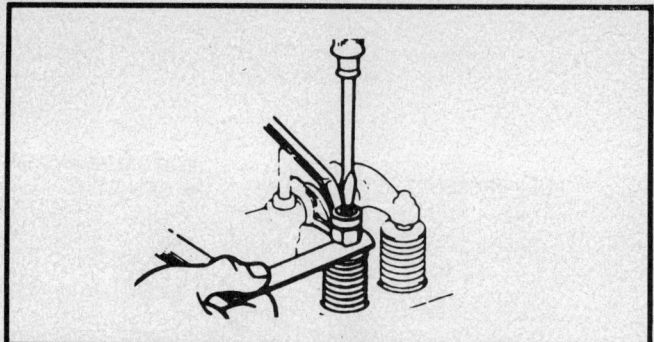

Valve lash adjustment—3A-C, 4A-C and 4A-LC engines

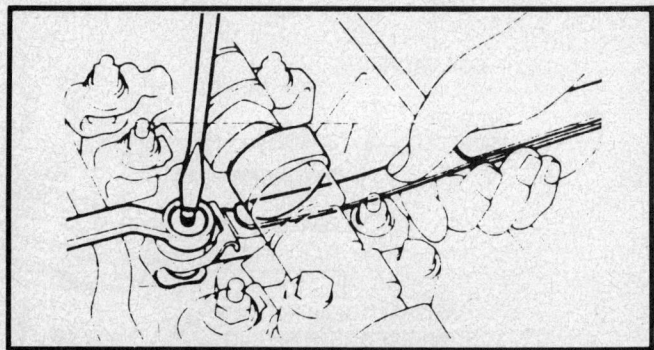

Valve lash adjustment—3E and 3E-E engines

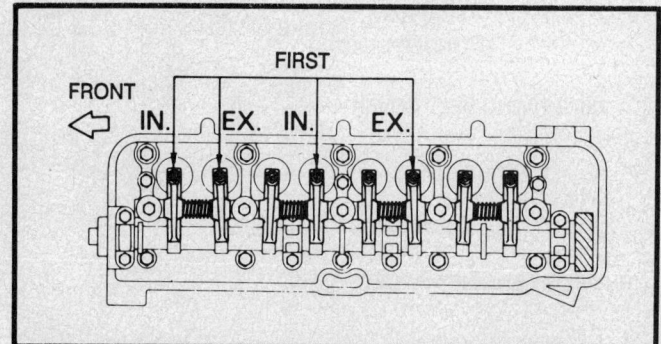

Adjust these valves first—3A-C, 4A-C and 4A-LC engines

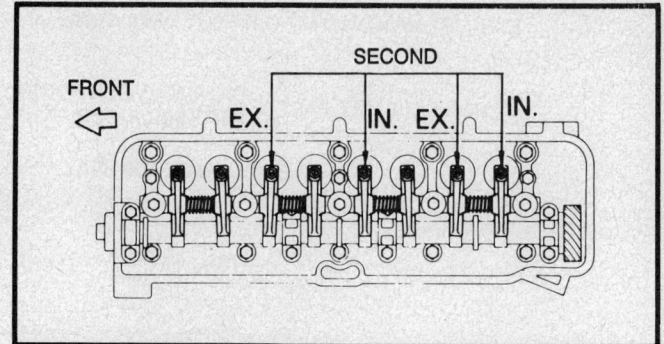

Adjust these valves second—3A-C, 4A-C and 4A-LC engines

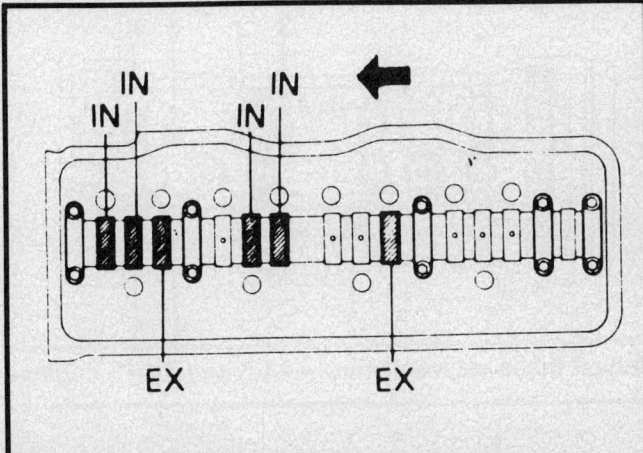

Adjust these valves first—3E and 3E-E engines

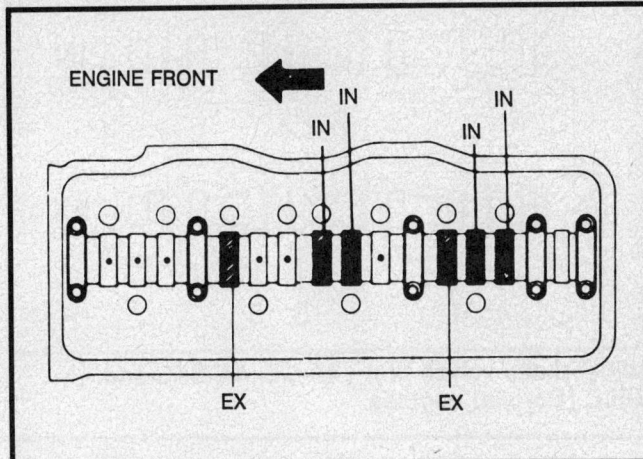

Adjust these valves second—3E and 3E-E engines

3A-C, 3E, 3E-E AND 4A-C ENGINES

1. Start the engine and run it until it reaches normal operating temperature.

2. Stop the engine. Remove the air cleaner assembly and the cylinder head cover.

3. Turn the crankshaft until the point or notch on the pulley aligns with the **0** or **T** mark on the timing scale. This will set the engine to TDC of the compression stroke.

NOTE: Check that the rocker arms on the No. 1 cylinder are loose. If not, turn the crankshaft one complete revolution (360 degrees).

4. Retighten the cylinder head bolts to specifications. Also, retighten the valve rocker support bolts to the proper specifications.

5. Using a flat feeler gauge, check the clearance between the bottom of the rocker arm; top for 3E and 3E-E engines, and the top of the valve stem; bottom of cam lobe for 3E and 3E-E engines.

6. If the clearance is not within specification, the valves will require adjustment. Loosen the locknut on the end of the rocker arm and, still holding the nut with an open end wrench, turn the adjustments screw to achieve the correct clearance.

7. Once the correct valve clearance is achieved, keep the adjustment screw from turning with a suitable tool and then tighten the locknut. Recheck the valve clearances.

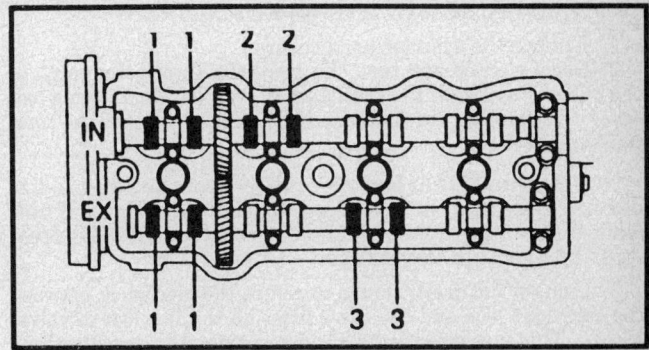

Adjust these valves first—3S-FE engine

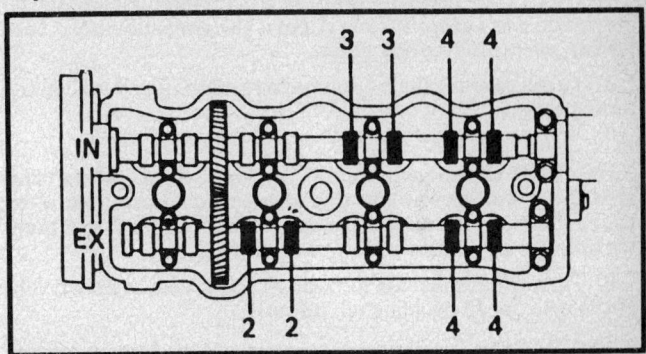

Adjust these valves second—3S-FE engine

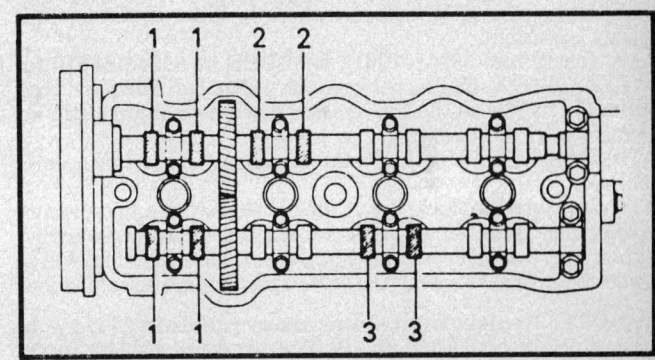

Adjust these valves first—3S-GE, 3S-GTE and 5S-FE engines

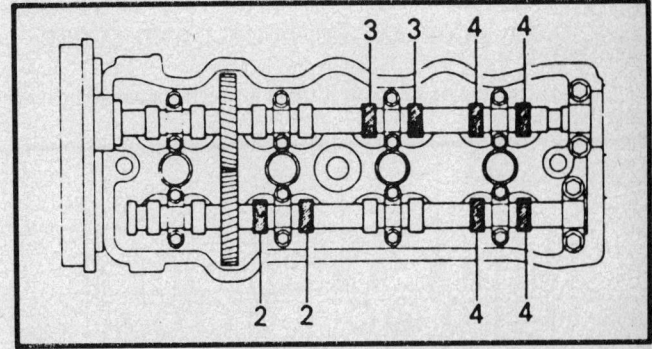

Adjust these valves second—3S-GE, 3S-GTE and 5S-FE engines

8. Turn the engine 1 complete revolution (360 degrees) and adjust the remaining valves.

9. Use a new gasket and then install the cylinder head cover. Install the air cleaner assembly.

3S-FE, 3S-GE, 3S-GTE AND 5S-FE ENGINES

1. Remove the cylinder head covers.
2. Use a wrench and turn the crankshaft until the notch in the pulley aligns with the timing mark **0** of the No. 1 timing belt cover. This will insure that No. 1 piston is at TDC of the compression stroke.

NOTE: Check that the valve lifters on the No. 1 cylinder are loose and those on No. 4 cylinder are tight. If not, turn the crankshaft 1 complete revolution (360 degrees) and then realign the marks.

3. Using a flat feeler gauge measure the clearance between the camshaft lobe and the valve lifter on the first set of valves shown. This measurement should correspond to specification.

NOTE: If the measurement is within specifications, go on to the next step. If not, record the measurement taken for each individual valve.

4. Turn the crankshaft 1 complete revolution and realign the timing marks.
5. Measure the clearance of the second set of valves.

NOTE: If the measurement for this set of valves (and also the previous one) is within specifications, go no further, the procedure is finished. If not, record the measurements and then proceed to Step 6.

6. Turn the crankshaft to position the intake camshaft lobe of the cylinder to be adjusted, upward.

NOTE: Both intake and exhaust valve clearance may be adjusted at the same time, if required.

7. Using a suitable tool, turn the valve lifter so the notch is easily accessible.
8. Install tool 09248–70012 for 3S-GE or 09248–55010 for 3S-FE, 3S-GTE, 5S-FE, between the 2 camshaft lobes and then turn the handle so the tool presses down both (intake and exhaust) valve lifters evenly.
9. Using a suitable tool and a magnet, remove the valve shims.
10. Measure the thickness of the old shim with a micrometer. Using this measurement and the clearance ones made earlier (from Step 3 or 5), determine what size replacement shim will be required in order to bring the valve clearance into specification.

NOTE: Replacement shims are available in 27 sizes, in increments of 0.0020 in. (0.05mm), from 0.0787 in. to 0.1299 in. (2.00mm to 3.3mm).

11. Install the new shim, remove the special tool and then recheck the valve clearances.

4A-F, 4A-FE, 4A-GE, 4A-GEC, 4A-GELC AND 4A-GZE ENGINES

1. Start the engine and run it until it reaches normal operating temperature.

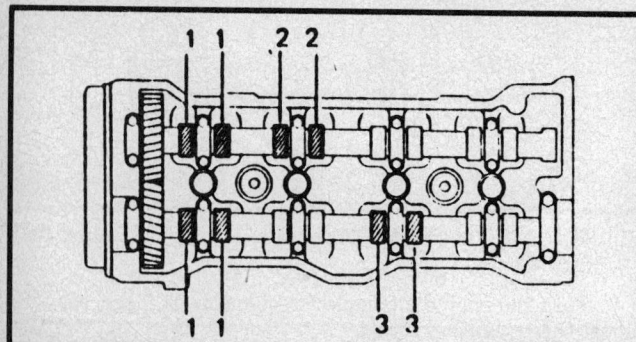

Adjust these valves first—4A-F and 4A-FE engines

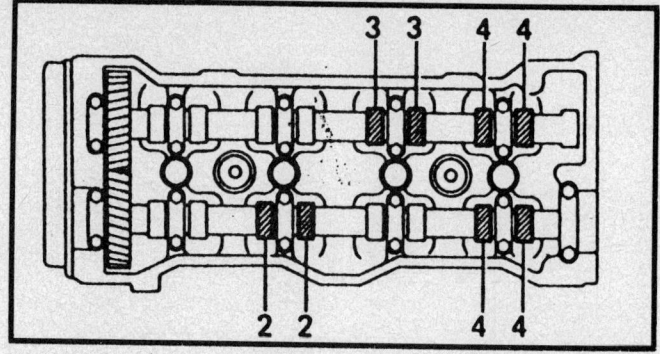

Adjust these valves second—4A-F and 4A-FE engines

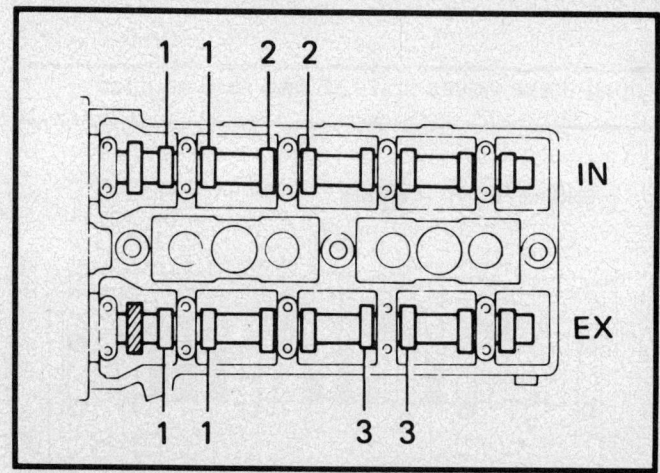

Adjust these valves first—4A-GE, 4A-GEC and 4A-GELC (Corolla) engines

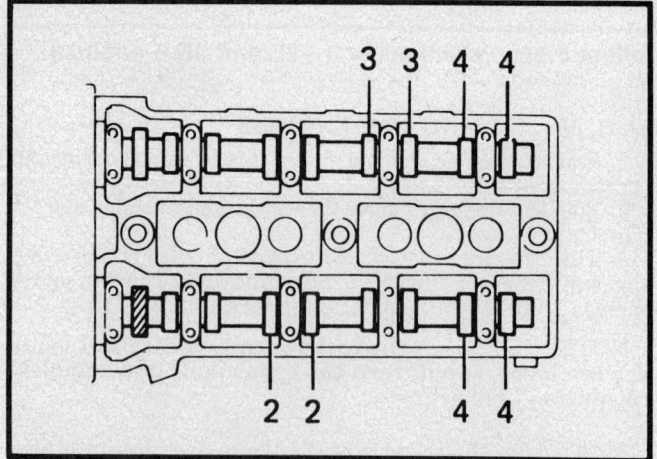

Adjust these valves second—4A-GE, 4A-GEC and 4A-GELC (Corolla) engines

2. Stop the engine. Remove the air cleaner assembly and the valve cover.
3. Use a wrench and turn the crankshaft until the notch in the pulley aligns with the timing pointer in the front cover. This will insure that engine is at TDC.

NOTE: Check that the valve lifters on the No. 1 cylinder are loose and those on No. 4 cylinder are tight. If not, turn the crankshaft one complete revolution (360 degrees) and then re-align the marks.

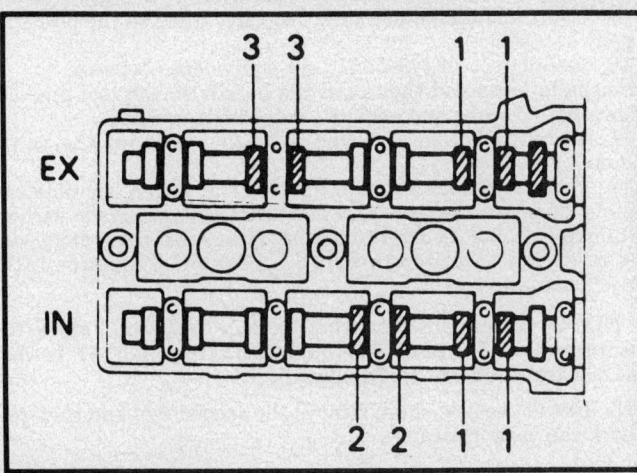

Adjust these valves first—4A-GE, 4A-GELC and 4A-GZE (MR2) engines

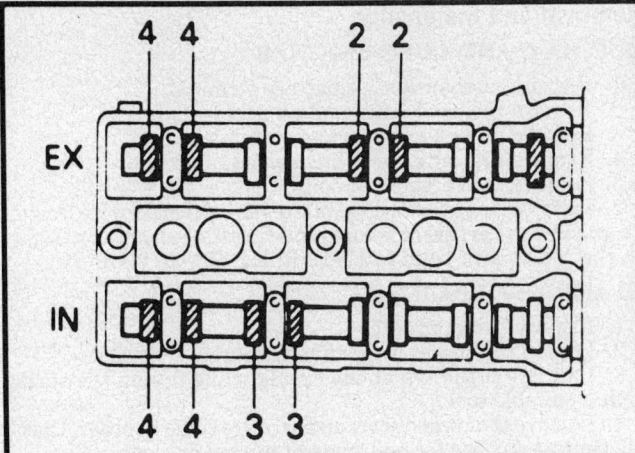

Adjust these valves second—4A-GE, 4A-GELC and 4A-GZE (MR2) engines

4. Using a flat feeler gauge measure the clearance between the camshaft lobe and the valve lifter. Check the first set of valves shown.

NOTE: If the measurement is within specifications, go on to the next step. If not, record the measurement taken for each individual valve.

5. Turn the crankshaft 1 complete revolution and realign the timing marks. Measure the clearance of the second set of valves shown.

NOTE: If the measurement for this set of valves (and also the previous one) is within specification, go no further, the procedure is finished. If not, record the measurements and then proceed to Step 6.

6. Turn the crankshaft to position the intake camshaft lobe of the cylinder to be adjusted, upward. Both intake and exhaust valve clearance may be adjusted at the same time, if required.

7. Using a suitable tool, turn the valve lifter so the notch is easily accessible.

8. Install tool 09248–70011 for 4A-GE or 09248–55010 4A-F, 4A-FE, 4A-GEC, 4A-GELC, 4A-GZE or equivalent, between the 2 camshafts lobes and then turn the handle so the tool presses down both (intake and exhaust) valve lifters evenly. On the 4A-GE, the tool will work on only one valve lifter at a time.

NOTE: On the 4A-FE, 4A-GEC, 4A-GELC and 4A-GZE, position the notch toward the spark plug before pressing down the valve lifter.

9. Using a suitable tool and a magnet, remove the valve shims.

10. Measure the thickness of the old shim with a micrometer. Using this measurement and the clearance of ones made earlier, determine what size replacement shim will be required in order to bring the valve clearance into specification.

11. Install the new shim, remove the special tool and then re-check the valve clearance.

5M-GE ENGINE

These engine is equipped with hydraulic lash adjusters in the valve train. The adjusters maintain a 0 clearance between the rocker arm and valve stem, no adjustment is possible or necessary.

7M-GE AND 7M-GTE ENGINES

1. Remove the cylinder head covers.

2. Use a wrench and turn the crankshaft until the notch in the pulley aligns with the timing mark **0** of the No. 1 timing belt cover. This will insure that engine is at TDC.

NOTE: Check that the valve lifters on the No. 1 cylinder are loose and those on No. 6 cylinder are tight. If not, turn the crankshaft 1 complete revolution (360 degrees) and then realign the marks.

3. Using a flat feeler gauge measure the clearance between the camshaft lobe and the valve lifter. This measurement should correspond to specification. Check the first set of valves shown.

NOTE: If the measurement is within specifications, go on to the next step. If not, record the measurement taken for each individual valve.

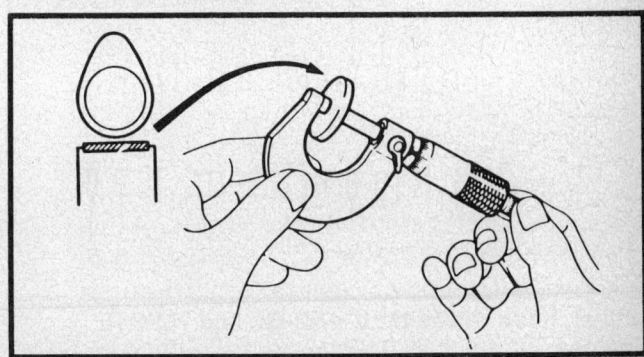

Measuring the shim size (thickness)

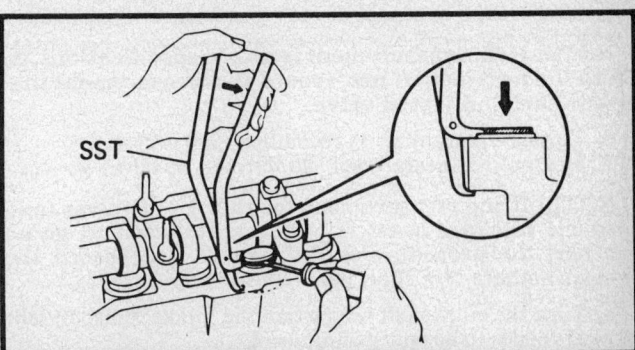

Depressing the valve lifter to remove the shim—3S-GE and 4A-GE engines

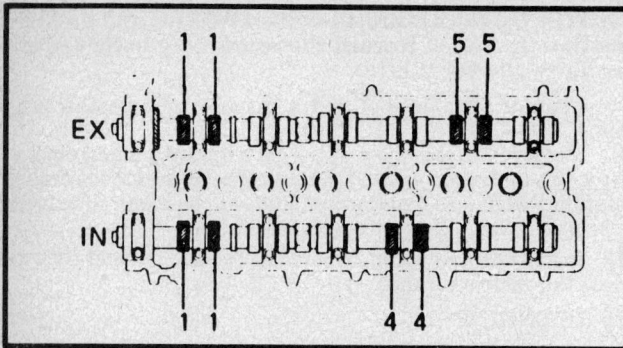

Adjust these valves first—7M-GE and 7M-GTE engines

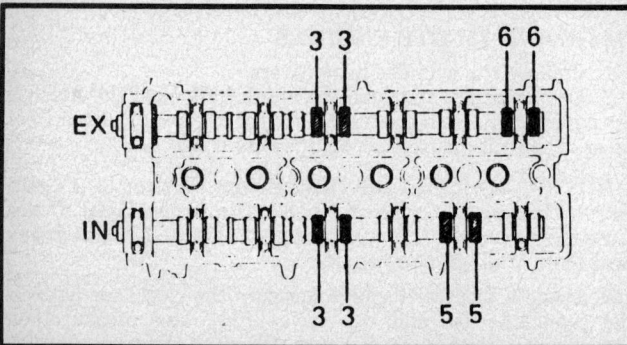

Adjust these valves second—7M-GE and 7M-GTE engines

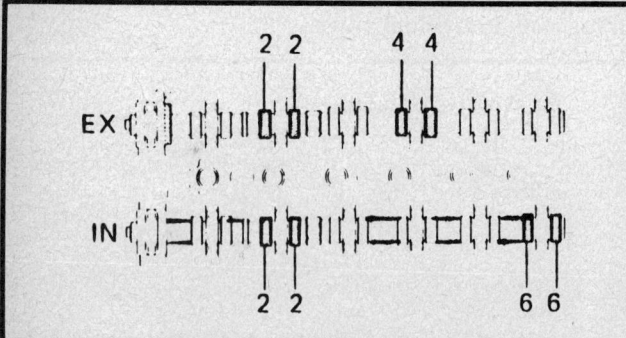

Adjust these valves third—7M-GE and 7M-GTE engines

4. Turn the crankshaft ⅔ revolution (240 degrees).
5. Measure the clearance of the second set of valves shown.

NOTE: If the measurement is within specifications, go on to the next step. If not, record the measurement taken for each individual valve.

6. Turn the crankshaft ⅔ revolution (240 degrees).
7. Measure the clearance of the third set of valves shown.

NOTE: If the measurement for this set of valves (and also the previous ones) is within specifications, go no further, the procedure is finished. If not, record the measurements and then proceed to Step 8.

8. Turn the crankshaft to position the intake camshaft lobe of the cylinder to be adjusted, upward.

NOTE: Both intake and exhaust valve clearance may be adjusted at the same time, if required.

9. Using a suitable tool, turn the valve lifter so the notch is easily accessible.
10. Install tool 09248-55010 or equivalent, between the 2 camshafts lobes and then turn the handle so the tool presses down both (intake and exhaust) valve lifters evenly.
11. Using a suitable tool and a magnet, remove the valve shims.
12. Measure the thickness of the old shim with a micrometer. Using this measurement and the clearance ones made earlier (from Step 3, 5 or 7), determine what size replacement shim will be required in order to bring the valve clearance into specification.

NOTE: Replacement shims are available in 17 sizes, in increments of 0.0020 in. (0.05mm), from 0.0787 in. to 0.1299 in. (2.00mm to 3.300mm).

13. Install the new shim, remove the special tool and then re-check the valve clearance.

Rocker Arms/Shafts

Removal and Installation

3A-C, 4A-C AND 4A-LC ENGINES

1. Disconnect the negative battery terminal.
2. Remove the air cleaner and all necessary hoses.
3. Remove all linkage from the carburetor.
4. Remove the valve cover and gasket.
5. Remove the rocker arm bolts.
6. Installation is the reverse of the removal procedure. Install a new valve cover gasket before replacing the valve cover. Tighten the rocker arm bolts to 17–19 ft. lbs. (23–26 Nm).

3E AND 3E-E ENGINES

1. Remove the camshaft.
2. Loosen the rocker arm adjusting screw locknuts.
3. Pull up on the top of the spring while prying the spring with a suitable tool.
4. Remove the rocker arms and arrange them in order. Check the contact surface for any signs of pitting or wear.
5. Check that the adjusting screw is as shown and install a new spring to the rocker arm.
6. Press the bottom lip of the spring until it fits into the groove on the rocker arm pivot.

NOTE: Put the valve adjusting screw in the rocker arm pivot.

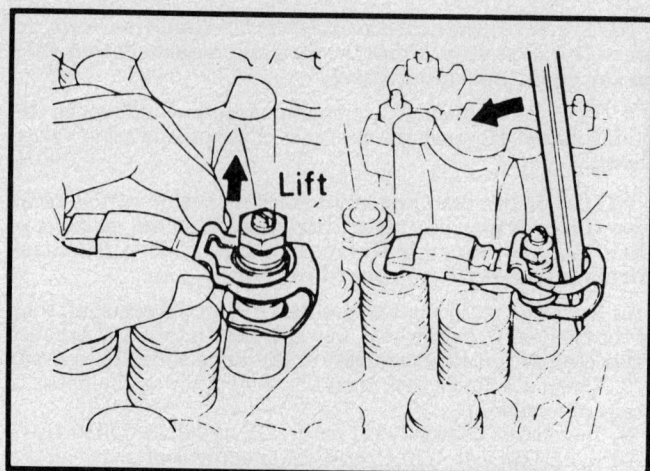

Rocker arm spring clip removal—3E and 3E-E engines

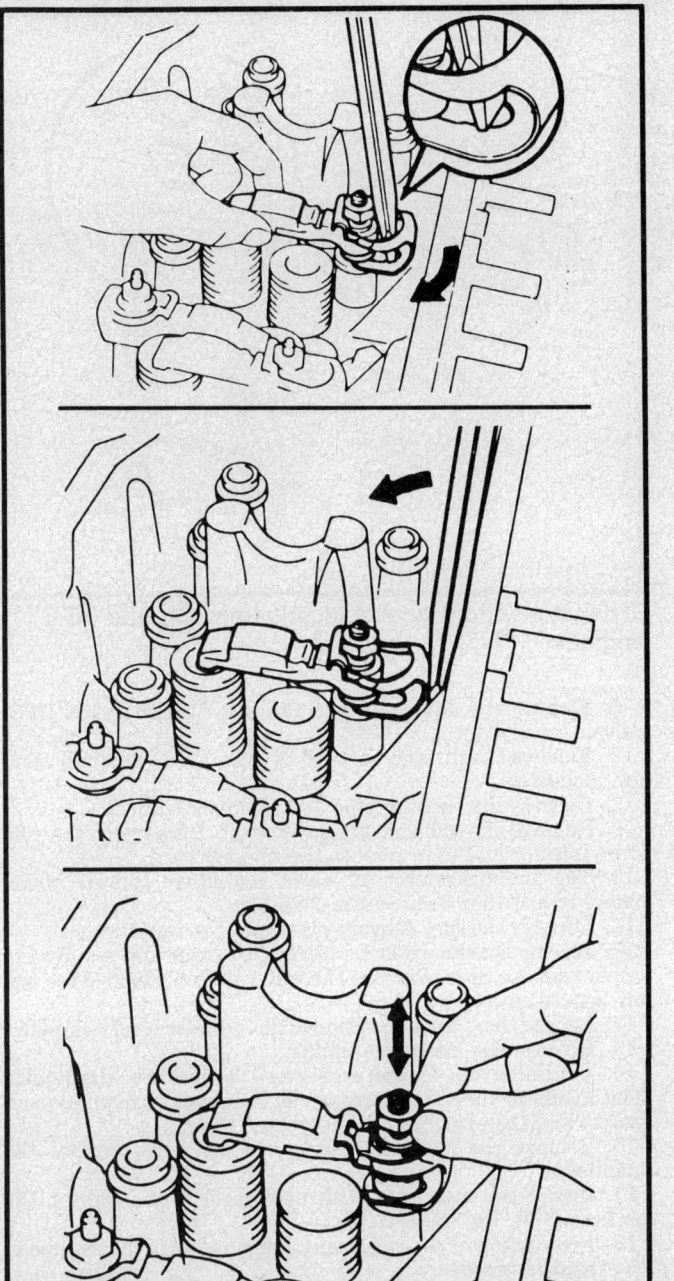

Rocker arm spring clip installation—3E and 3E-E engines

7. Pry the rocker spring clip onto the pivot. Pull the rocker arm up and down to check that there is spring tension and that the rocker does not rattle.

ALL OTHER ENGINES

All other engines do not utilize rocker arms shafts. The valves are activated directly by the camshaft.

Intake Manifold

Removal and Installation

2VZ-FE ENGINE

1. Disconnect the negative battery cable and drain the cooling system.

2. Disconnect the throttle cable at the throttle body. If equipped, remove the cruise control actuator and vacuum pump.

3. Remove the air cleaner hose.

4. Raise the vehicle and suppport safely. Remove the engine undercovers.

5. Remove the lower suspension crossmember and the front exhaust pipe.

6. Remove the alternator. Remove the ISC valve.

7. Remove the throttle body. Remove the EGR pipe, valve and vacuum modulator.

8. Remove the vacuum pipe and the distributor.

9. Remove the exhaust crossover pipe. Disconnect the cold start injector and then remove the injector tube.

10. Tag and disconnect all hoses leading to the air intake chamber and then remove the chamber.

11. Remove the fuel delivery pipes and the injectors.

12. Disconnect the water temperature sensor and remove the upper radiator hose. Remove the water outlet. Remove the water bypass outlet.

13. Loosen the 2 bolts and remove the cylinder head rear plate.

14. Remove the No. 2 idler pulley bracket stay.

15. Remove the 8 bolts and 4 nuts and lift out the intake manifold with its 2 gaskets.

16. Use 2 new gaskets when installing the manifold and tighten the bolts, from the center outward, to 13 ft. lbs. (18 Nm).

17. Installation of the remaining components is the reverse of the removal procedure.

3E AND 3E-E ENGINES

1. Disconnect the negative battery cable. Drain the coolant. Remove the air cleaner assembly.

2. Tag and disconnect all wires, hoses or cables that interfere with intake manifold removal.

3. Remove the necessary components in order to gain access to the intake manifold retaining bolts.

4. Remove the carburetor from the throttle body.

5. Disconnect the intake manifold water hoses.

6. Remove the intake manifold retaining bolts. Remove the intake manifold from the vehicle.

6. Installation is the reverse of the removal procedure. Use new gaskets, as required. Tighten to 14 ft. lbs. (19 Nm).

3S-FE AND 5S-FE ENGINES

1. Disconnect the negative battery cable. Drain the cooling system. Remove the air cleaner assembly.

2. Tag and disconnect all wires, hoses or cables that interfere with intake manifold removal.

3. Remove the necessary components in order to gain access to the intake manifold retaining bolts.

4. Remove the throttle body and cold start injector pipe.

5. Remove the air tube assembly. If equipped with power steering, remove the hoses before removing the air tube assembly.

6. Remove the intake manifold retaining bolts. Remove the intake manifold from the vehicle.

7. Installation is the reverse of the removal procedure. Use new gaskets, as required. Tighten the intake manifold mounting bolts to 14 ft. lbs. (19 Nm). Tighten the 12mm manifold stay bolt to 14 ft. lbs. (19 Nm); tighten the 14mm bolts to 31 ft. lbs. (42 Nm).

3S-GE AND 3S-GTE ENGINES

1. Disconnect the negative battery cable. Drain the cooling system. Remove the air cleaner assembly.

2. Tag and disconnect all wires, hoses or cables that interfere with intake manifold removal.

3. Remove the necessary components in order to gain access to the intake manifold retaining bolts.

4. Remove the intake manifold retaining bolts and nuts. Remove the intake manifold from the vehicle.

5. Installation is in the reverse of the removal procedure. Use new gaskets, as required. Torque the bolts and nuts to 14 ft. lbs. (19 Nm).

4A-F, 4A-FE, 4A-GE, 4A-GEC, 4A-GELC & 4A-GZE ENGINES

1. Disconnect the negative battery cable. Drain the coolant. Remove the air cleaner assembly.
2. Tag wires, hoses or cables in the way of manifold removal.
3. Remove the necessary components in order to gain access to the intake manifold retaining bolts.
4. Remove the intake manifold retaining bolts. Remove the intake manifold from the vehicle.
5. Installation is the reverse of the removal procedure. Use new gaskets, as required.

5M-GE ENGINE

1. Disconnect the negative battery cable. Drain the engine coolant.
2. Tag and disconnect all wires, hoses or cables that interfere with intake manifold removal.
3. Remove the air intake chamber.
4. Disconnect and move the wiring away from the fuel delivery and injector pipe.
5. Remove the fuel injector and delivery pipe.
6. Remove the fuel pressure regulator, which is mounted on the center of the intake manifold.
7. Disconnect the radiator hoses, heater hoses, and vacuum lines from the intake manifold.
8. Remove the distributor cap and position it aside.
9. Remove the intake manifold retaining bolts. Remove the intake manifold and gasket from the engine.
10. Installation is the reverse of the removal procedure. Use new gaskets, as required. Torque the manifold fasteners to 10–15 ft. lbs. (13.6–20 Nm)

7M-GE AND 7M-GTE ENGINES

1. Disconnect the negative battery cable. Drain the cooling system.
2. Remove the air cleaner assembly.
3. Tag and disconnect all wires, hoses or cables that interfere with intake manifold removal.
4. Remove the necessary components in order to gain access to the intake manifold retaining bolts.
5. Remove the air intake connector along with the air intake chamber assembly.
6. Remove the fuel delivery pipe with the injectors still attached.
7. Remove the intake manifold retaining bolts. Remove the intake manifold from the vehicle.
8. Installation is the reverse of the removal procedure. Use new gaskets, as required. Tighten the bolts from the inside to the outside, to 13 ft. lbs. (18 Nm).

Exhaust Manifold

Removal and Installation

2VZ-FE ENGINE

1. Disconnect the negative battery cable and drain the cooling system.
2. Disconnect the throttle cable at the throttle body. If equipped with cruise control, remove the cruise control actuator and vacuum pump.
3. Remove the air cleaner hose.
4. Raise the vehicle and suppport safely. Remove the engine undercovers.
5. Remove the lower suspension crossmember and the front exhaust pipe.

Exhaust manifold gasket installation—3E and 3E-E engines

6. Remove the alternator and the Idle Speed Control (ISC) valve.
7. Remove the throttle body, EGR pipe, EGR valve and vacuum modulator.
8. Remove the vacuum pipe and the distributor.
9. Remove the exhaust crossover pipe. Disconnect the cold start injector and then remove the injector tube.
10. Tag and disconnect all hoses leading to the air intake chamber and then remove the chamber.
11. Remove the fuel delivery pipes and the injectors.
12. Disconnect the water temperature sensor and remove the upper radiator hose. Remove the water outlet. Remove the water bypass outlet.
13. Loosen the 2 bolts and remove the cylinder head rear plate.
14. Remove the intake manifold.
15. Disconnect the oxygen sensor and then remove the outside heat insulator for the righ manifold. Remove the manifold and gasket and then remove the inner heat shield.
16. Remove the left side heat shield and then remove the manifold.
17. Install the manifolds with new gaskets and tighten the bolts to 29 ft. lbs. (39 Nm).
18. Installation of the remaining components is the reverse of the removal procedure.

3E AND 3E-E ENGINES

1. Disconnect the negative battery cable. Remove the exhaust manifold heat insulator shield assembly.
2. Remove the necessary components in order to gain access to the exhaust manifold retaining bolts.
3. Disconnect the exhaust manifold bolts at the exhaust pipe. Disconnect the oxygen sensor electrical wire. It may be necessary to raise and support the vehicle safely before removing these bolts.
4. Remove the exhaust manifold retaining bolts. Remove the exhaust manifold from the vehicle.
5. Installation is the reverse of the removal procedure. During installation, the **E** mark on the gasket must face outward. Tighten the exhaust manifold retainng bolts to 38 ft. lbs. (51 Nm).

3S-FE AND 5S-FE ENGINES

1. Disconnect the negative battery cable.

2. Raise and support the vehicle safely.

3. Remove the exhaust manifold heat insulator shield assembly.

4. Remove the necessary components in order to gain access to the exhaust manifold retaining bolts.

5. Disconnect the exhaust manifold bolts at the exhaust pipe or catalytic converter. It may be necessary to raise and support the vehicle safely before removing these bolts.

6. Remove the exhaust manifold retaining bolts. Remove the exhaust manifold from the vehicle. On 5S-FE engine, the exhaust manifold and catalytic converter are removed as one unit.

7. Installation is the reverse of the removal procedure. Be sure to use new gaskets. On 5S-FE, the **R** mark should be toward the rear. On 3S-FE, tighten the exhaust manifold bolts to 31 ft. lbs. (41 Nm). On 5S-FE, torque the exhaust manifold retaining bolts to 36 ft. lbs. (49 Nm).

5M-GE, 3S-GE, 3S-GTE, 4A-F, 4A-FE, 4A-GE, 4A-GEC, 4A-GELC AND 4A-GZE ENGINES

1. Disconnect the negative battery cable. Raise the vehicle and support safely. Remove the right gravel shield from under the vehicle.

2. Remove the throttle body and turbocharger.

3. Remove the exhaust pipe support stay. Unbolt the exhaust pipe from the exhaust manifold flange.

4. Disconnect the oxygen sensor connector. On the 3S-GE and 4A-F, remove the upper heat insulator.

5. Remove the manifold retaining nuts. Remove the exhaust manifold from the vehicle.

6. Installation is the reverse of the removal procedure. Use a new gasket, as required. Torque all nuts evenly to the specified torque.

7M-GE AND 7M-GTE ENGINES

1. Disconnect the negative battery cable. Remove the exhaust manifold heat insulator shield assembly, if equipped.

2. Remove the necessary components in order to gain access to the exhaust manifold retaining bolts.

3. Disconnect the exhaust manifold bolts at the exhaust pipe. It may be necessary to raise and support the vehicle safely before removing these bolts.

4. On 7M-GTE, remove the turbocharger.

5. Remove the exhaust manifold retaining bolts. Remove the exhaust manifold from the vehicle.

6. Installation is the reverse of the removal procedure. Be sure to use new gaskets. Tighten the nuts from the inside to the outside, to 29 ft. lbs. (39 Nm).

Combination Manifold

Removal and Installation

3A-C, 4A-C AND 4A-LC ENGINES

1. Disconnect the negative battery cable.
2. Remove the air cleaner and all necessary hoses.
3. Remove all the carburetor linkages.
4. Remove the carburetor.
5. Remove the intake/exhaust manifold pipe.
6. Remove the intake/exhaust manifold.
7. Installation is the reverse of the removal procedure. Tighten the manifold bolts to 15–21 ft. lbs. (20–29 Nm).

Supercharger

Removal and Installation

4A-GZE ENGINE

1. Disconnect the negative cable at the battery. Drain the cooling system and remove the radiator reservoir tank.

2. Remove the Vacuum Switching Valve (VSV) and the intercooler.

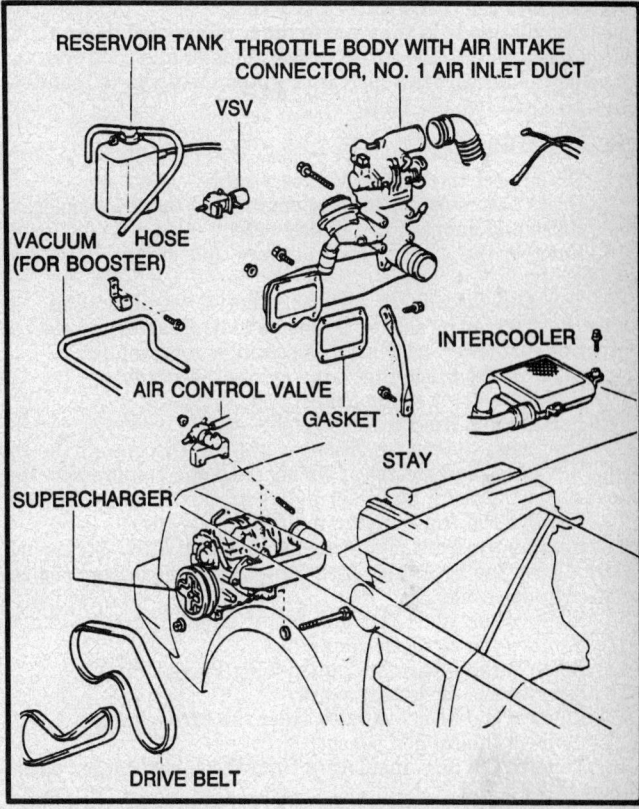

Supercharger and related components

3. Remove the air flow meter with the No. 3 air cleaner hose. Disconnect the accelerator cable (rod) and throttle cable.

4. Disconnect the PCV, brake booster, ACV, air conditioning idle-up and emission control vacuum hoses.

5. Remove the No. 1 intake air connector pipe and its air hose.

6. Loosen the idler pulley locknut and adjusting bolt and remove the supercharger drive belt.

7. Disconnect the No. 2 and 3 water bypass hoses. Loosen the air hose clamp.

8. Remove the air inlet duct stay. Remove the throttle body.

9. Disconnect the ACV and supercharger connectors and the 2 ACV hoses. Remove the 2 nuts and the ACV. Remove the pivot bolt and nut, remove the 2 stud bolts and then rotate the assembly so the hub is facing upward; remove the supercharger.

10. Installation is the reverse of the removal procedure. Tighten the 2 stud bolts to 25 ft. lbs. (34 Nm).

Turbocharger

Removal and Installation

3S-GTE ENGINE

Celica

1. Disconnect the negative battery cable. Drain the coolant from the engine and intercooler.

2. Remove the air cleaner assembly.

3. Remove the catalytic converter and the oxygen sensor.

3. Disconnect the 2 intercooler water lines and the reservoir tank line. Loosen the clamps, disconnect the air hose and remove the intercooler.

4. Remove the alternator duct and the No. 2 alternator bracket.

5. Remove the turbocharger heat insulator and the turbocharger outlet elbow. Remove the turbocharger stay.

6. Remove the turbocharger.

7. Installation is in the reverse order of removal. Pour about 20cc of new oil into the turbocharger oil inlet and then spin the impeller to lubricate the bearing. Tighten the turbo-to-manifold bolts to 47 ft. lbs. (64 Nm).

1990–91 MR2

1. Disconnect the negative battery cable.
2. Drain the coolant from the engine and the intercooler.
3. Raise and support the vehicle safely.
4. Remove the engine under covers and engine hood side panels.
5. Tag and disconnect all water hoses, vacuum lines, air tubes, engine control cables, transaxle control cables and electrical wires that interfere with turbocharger removal.
6. Remove the brace that runs across the struts.
7. Remove the air cleaner assembly.
8. Remove the front exhaust pipe.
9. Discharge the air conditioning system. Disconnect the refrigerant hoses and electrical wiring from the compressor. Remove the compressor and idler pulley bracket from the engine.
10. Remove the front engine mounting insulator.
11. Remove the front mounting bracket and clutch release cylinder. Leave the hydraulic lines connected and position the release cylinder aside.
12. Remove the engine cooling fan.
13. Remove the catalytic converter.
14. Remove the Vacuum Transmitting Valve (VTV).
15. Remove the air bypass valve.
16. Remove the heat insulator from the turbocharger.
17. Remove the oxygen sensor.
18. Remove the heat insulators from the turbocharger outlet elbow.
19. Disconnect the oil hose from the turbocharger oil pipe.
20. Remove the turbocharger mounting stay.
21. Unbolt and remove the turbocharger oil pipe from the block.
22. Remove the 4 nuts and separate the turbocharger and gasket from the exhaust manifold.

To install:

23. Clean the turbocharger and exhaust manifold gasket surfaces.
24. Prior to installing the turbocharger, pour approximately 1.2 cu. in. (20cc) of new oil into the oil inlet and then turn the impeller wheel by hand a few times inorder to lubricate the bearing.
25. Install a new gasket onto the exhaust manifold.
26. Mount the turbocharger onto the gasket and install the 4 nuts. Torque the nuts in a criss-cross pattern to 47 ft. lbs. (64 Nm).
27. Installation of the remaining components is the reverse of the removal procedure. Torque the oil pipe union bolt to the block to 38 ft. lbs. (51 Nm); stay-to-turbocharger bolts to 51 ft. lbs.; stay-to-block bolts to 43 ft. lbs. (59 Nm) and oxygen sensor to 33 ft. lbs. (44 Nm).

7M-GTE ENGINE

1. Disconnect the negative battery cable and drain the cooling system.
2. Remove the No. 4 air cleaner pipe with the No. 1 and No. 2 air cleaner hoses still attached.
3. Disconnect the 3 air hoses, the PCV hose and the electrical lead at the air flow meter. Disconnect the power steering idle-up air hose and then remove the No. 7 air cleaner hose with the air flow meter and cap still attached.
4. Disconnect the oxygen sensor and remove the turbocharger heat insulator.
5. Remove the oil dipstick guide.
6. Remove the No. 1 air cleaner pipe with the No. 6 air cleaner hose.
7. Disconnect the front exhaust pipe.

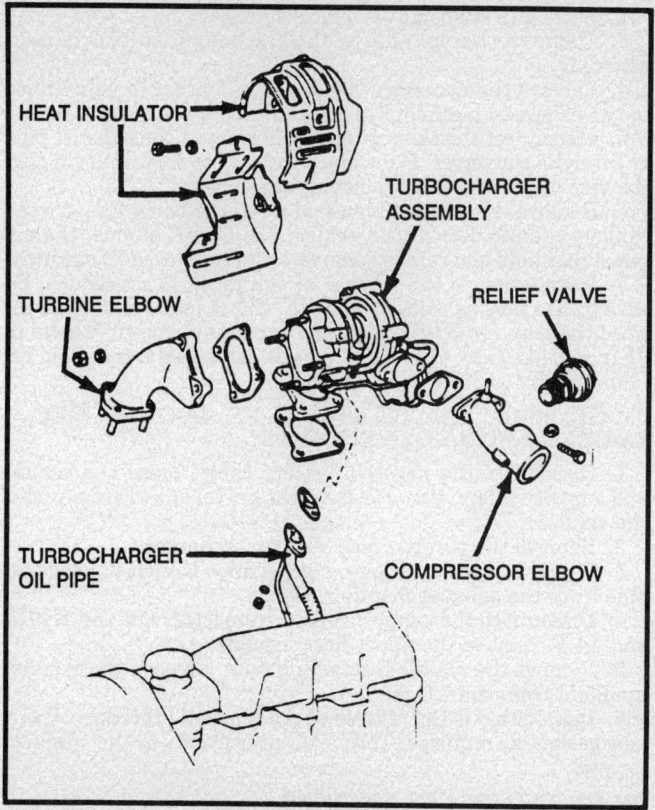

Typical turbocharger assembly

8. Remove the mounting nuts and union bolt for the turbocharger oil line. Remove the turbocharger stay.
9. Remove the No. 2 turbocharger stay. Disconnect the No. 1 turbocharger water hose at the water outlet housing. Disconnect the union pipe.
10. Remove the turbocharger and its gasket.
11. Prior to installing the turbocharger, pour approximately 1.2 cu. in. (20cc) of new oil into the oil inlet and then turn the impeller wheel by hand a few times in order to lubricate the bearing.
12. Position a new gasket with the protrusion pointing toward the rear and then install the turbocharger unit. Tighten the mounting bolts to 33 ft. lbs. (44 Nm). Tighten the union bolt to 25 ft. lbs. (34 Nm) and the nut to 9 ft. lbs. (13 Nm). The remainder of the installation is in the reverse order of removal.

Timing Belt Front Cover

Removal and Installation

3A-C, 4A-LC AND 4A-C ENGINES

1. Disconnect the negative battery cable.
2. Remove all drive belts.
3. Bring the No. 1 cylinder to TDC on the compression stroke.
4. Remove the crankshaft pulley with a suitable puller.
5. Remove the water pump pulley.
6. Remove the upper and lower timing case covers.
7. Installation is the reverse of removal. Tighten the timing belt cover to 5–8 ft. lbs. (7–11 Nm).

3E AND 3S-FE ENGINES

1. Disconnect the negative battery cable.
2. On 3E and 3E-E engines, remove the air cleaner assembly. On 3E-E engine, disconnect the accelerator and throttle cables.

3. Remove all drive belts.

4. On the 3S-FE engine remove the alternator, alternator bracket and right engine mounting stay (2WD). If equipped with cruise control remove the actuator and bracket assembly.

5. Raise and support the vehicle safely.

6. Remove the right tire and wheel assembly. Remove the right side engine under cover. Remove the right side engine mount insulator.

7. On the 3E and 3E-E engines, remove the cylinder head cover.

8. Set the No. 1 piston to TDC of the compression stroke and remove the crankshaft pulley using the proper tools.

9. Remove the engine front cover retaining bolts. Remove both front covers from the engine.

10. Installation is the reverse of the removal procedure. Use new cover seals. On 3E and 3E-E engines, torque the crankshaft pulley bolt to 112 ft. lbs. (154 Nm). On 3S-FE engine, torque the crankshaft pulley bolt to 80 ft. lbs. (108 Nm).

7M-GE AND 7M-GTE ENGINES

1. Disconnect the negative battery cable.
2. Drain the cooling system.
3. Remove the radiator and water outlet.
4. Remove the spark plugs, drive belts and alternator.
5. Remove the upper timing belt cover and seal.
6. Set the No. 1 piston to TDC of the compression stroke.
7. Remove the timing belt from the camshaft sprockets.
8. Remove the crankshaft pulley using the proper tool.
9. Remove the lower timing belt cover and seal.
10. Installation is the reverse of the removal procedure. Use new cover seals. Torque the crankshaft pulley bolt to 195 ft. lbs. (265 Nm).

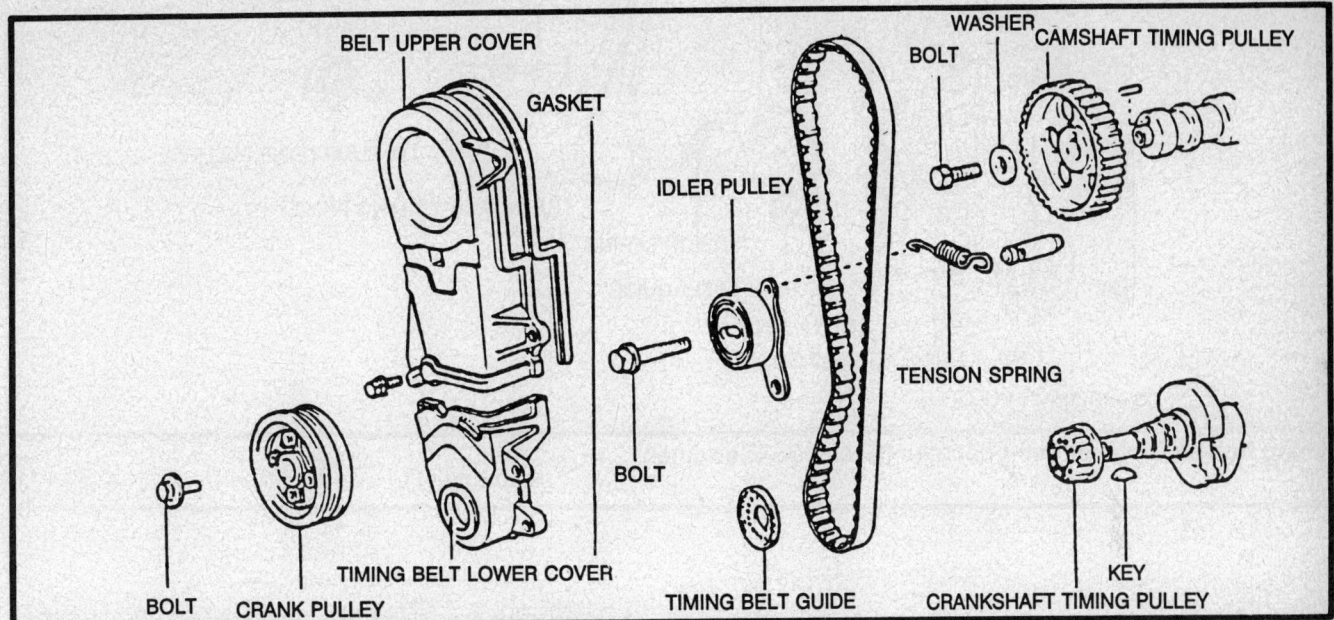

Timing belt and related components—3A-C engine

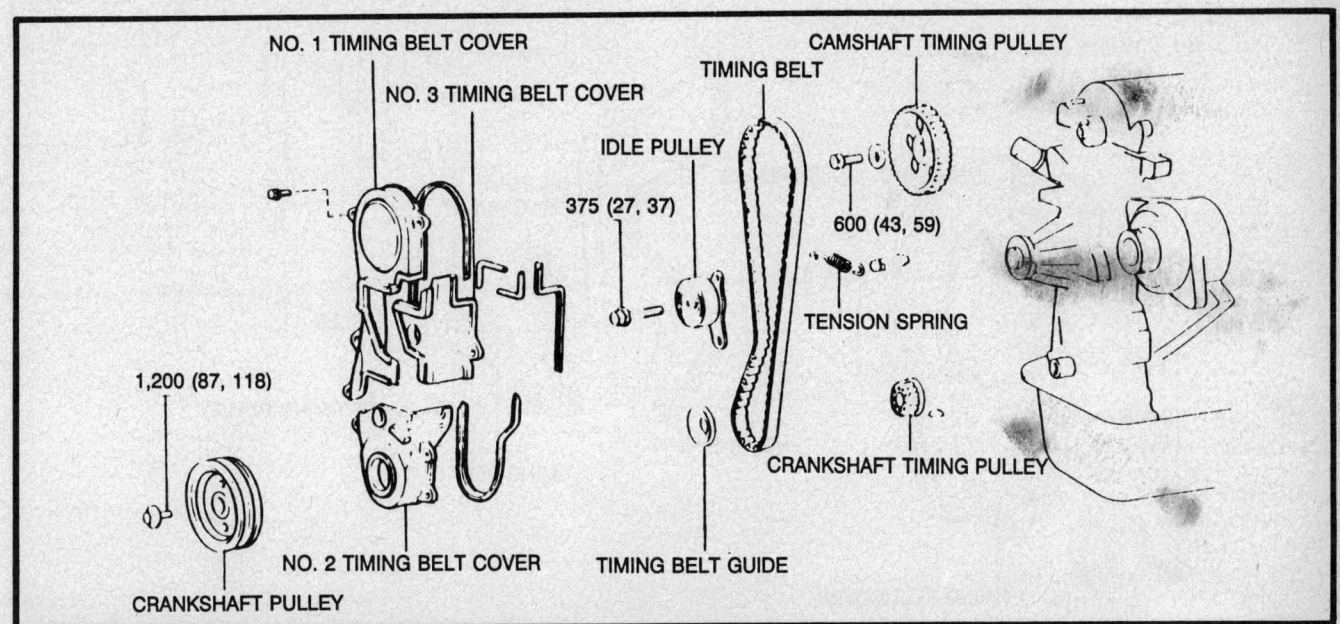

Timing belt and related components—4A-C and 4A- LC engines

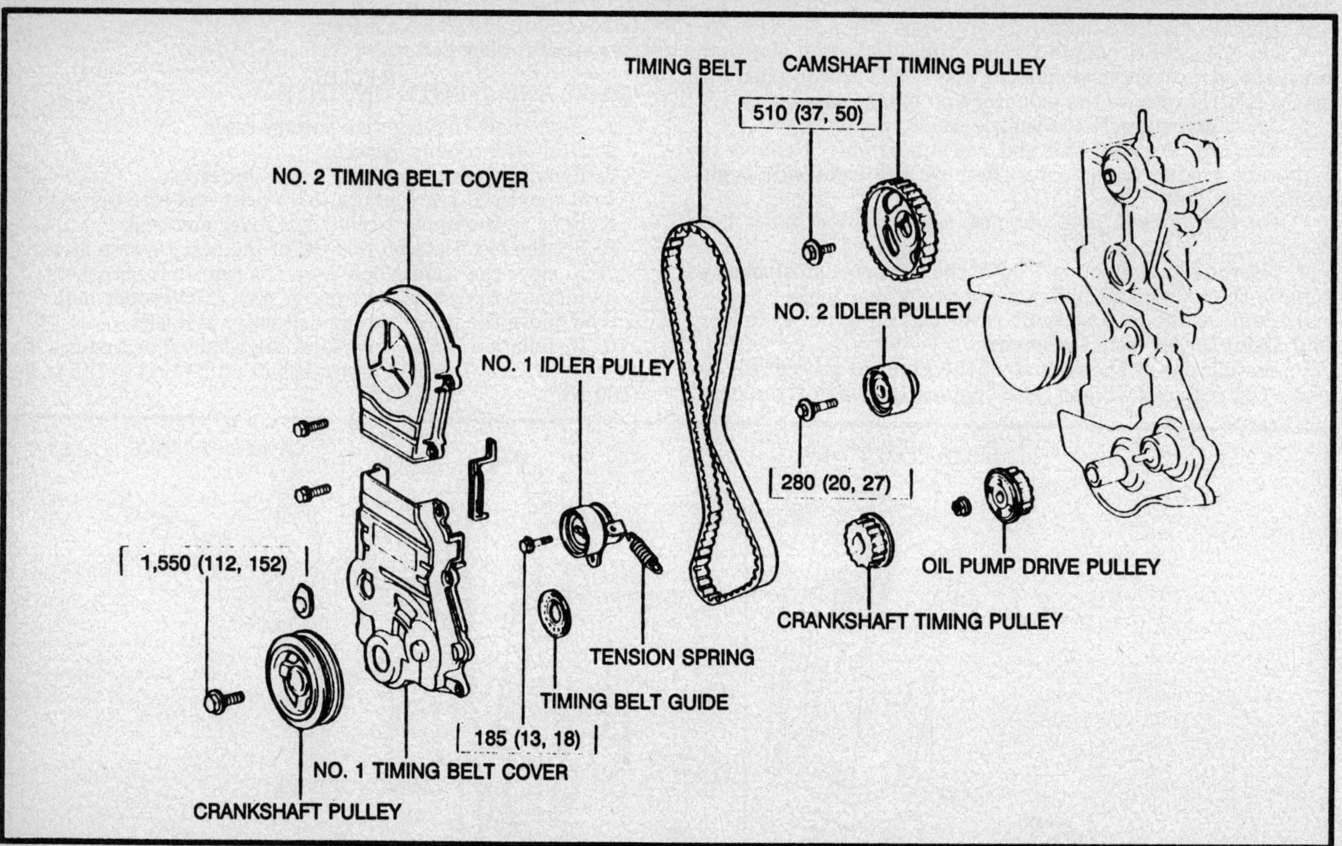

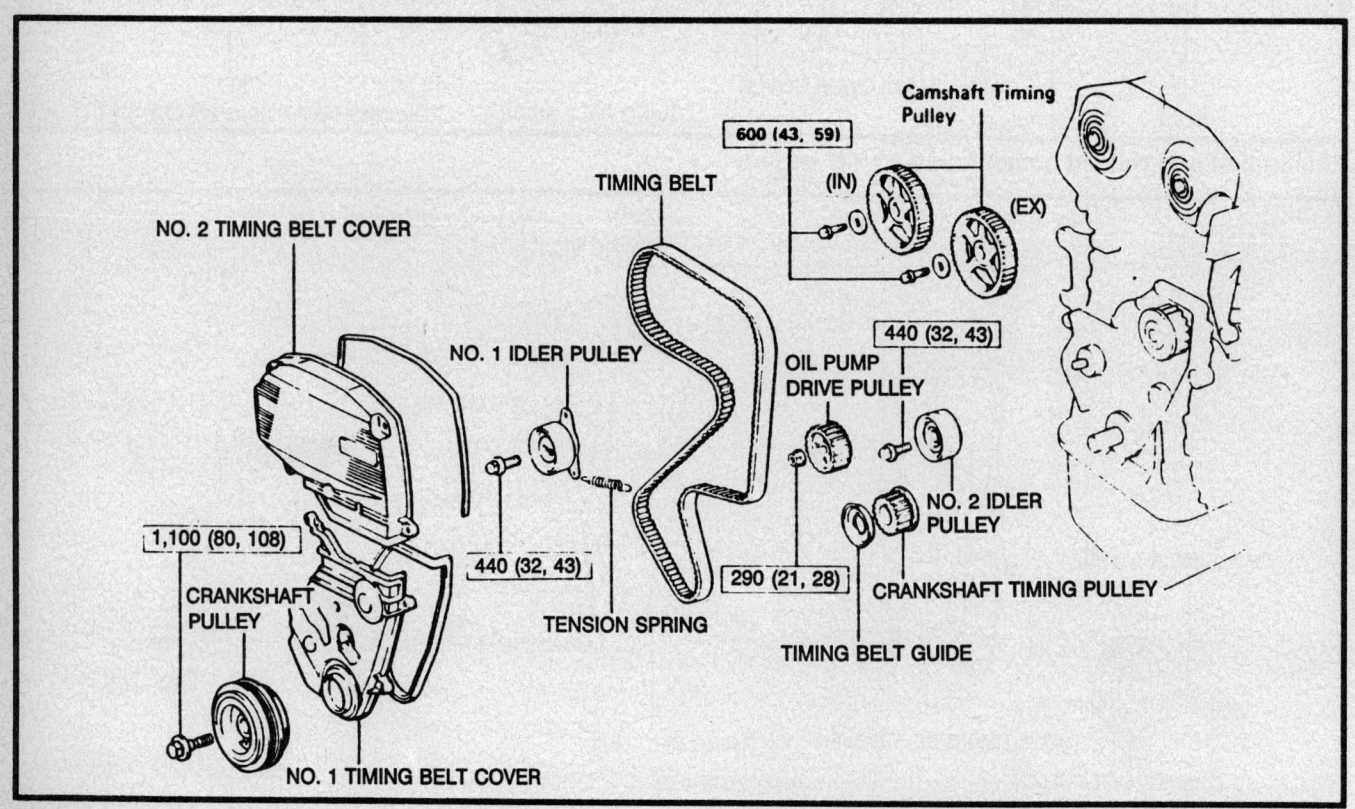

Timing belt and related components—3E and 3E-E engines

TIMING BELT

CAMSHAFT TIMING PULLEY

510 (37, 50)

NO. 2 TIMING BELT COVER

NO. 2 IDLER PULLEY

NO. 1 IDLER PULLEY

280 (20, 27)

1,550 (112, 152)

OIL PUMP DRIVE PULLEY

TENSION SPRING

CRANKSHAFT TIMING PULLEY

TIMING BELT GUIDE

185 (13, 18)

NO. 1 TIMING BELT COVER

CRANKSHAFT PULLEY

Timing belt and related components—3S-GE and 3S-GTE engines

TIMING BELT

Camshaft Timing Pulley

600 (43, 59)

(IN)   (EX)

NO. 2 TIMING BELT COVER

NO. 1 IDLER PULLEY

OIL PUMP DRIVE PULLEY

440 (32, 43)

1,100 (80, 108)

440 (32, 43)

NO. 2 IDLER PULLEY

290 (21, 28)

CRANKSHAFT TIMING PULLEY

CRANKSHAFT PULLEY

TENSION SPRING

TIMING BELT GUIDE

NO. 1 TIMING BELT COVER

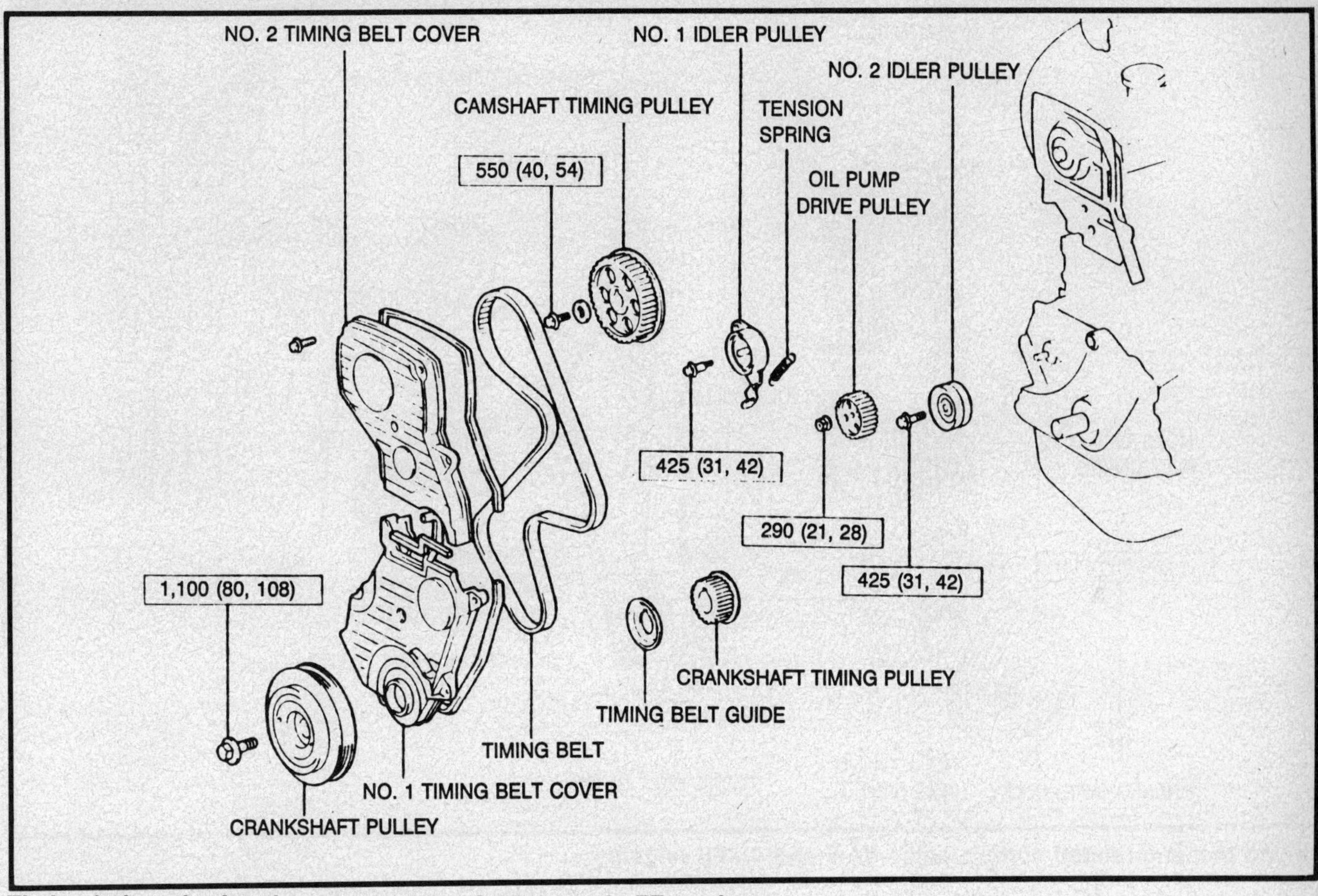

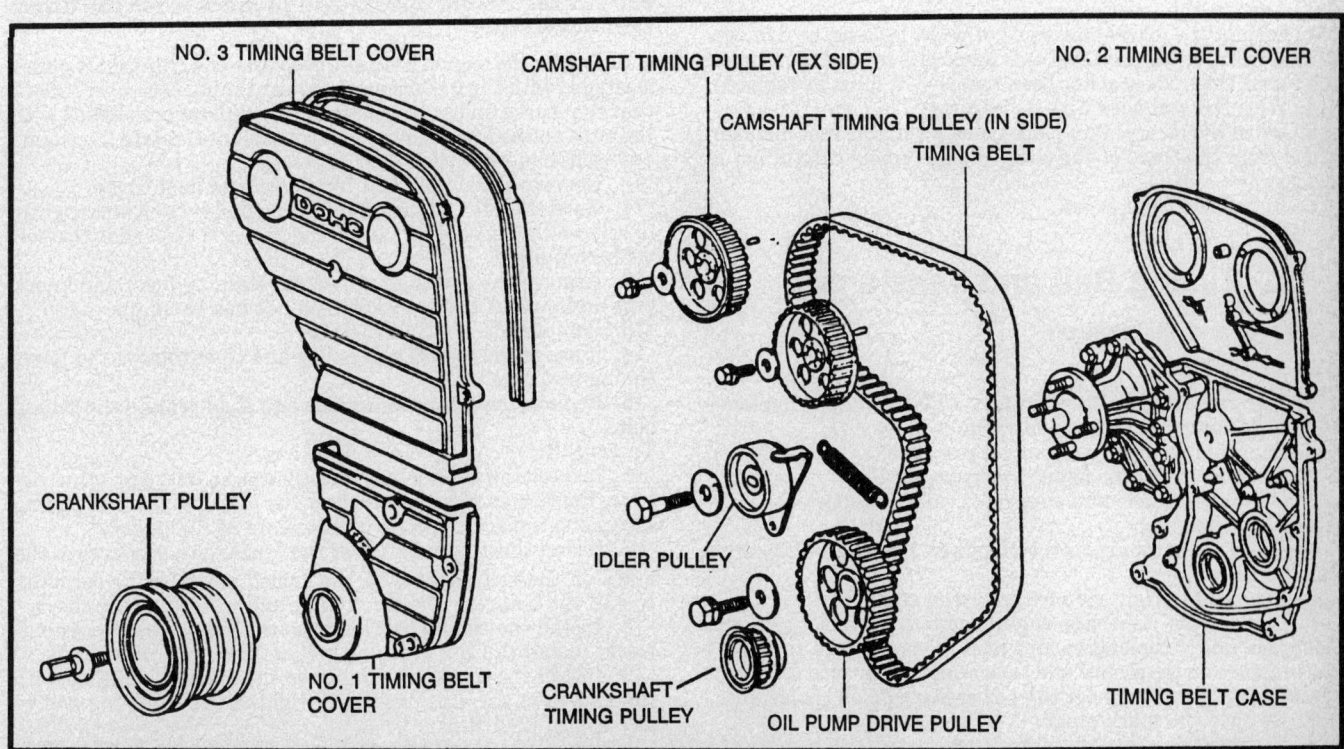

NO. 2 TIMING BELT COVER

CAMSHAFT TIMING PULLEY

550 (40, 54)

NO. 1 IDLER PULLEY

TENSION SPRING

NO. 2 IDLER PULLEY

OIL PUMP DRIVE PULLEY

425 (31, 42)

290 (21, 28)

425 (31, 42)

1,100 (80, 108)

CRANKSHAFT TIMING PULLEY

TIMING BELT GUIDE

TIMING BELT

NO. 1 TIMING BELT COVER

CRANKSHAFT PULLEY

Timing belt and related components—3S-FE and 5S-FE engines

NO. 3 TIMING BELT COVER

CAMSHAFT TIMING PULLEY (EX SIDE)

NO. 2 TIMING BELT COVER

CAMSHAFT TIMING PULLEY (IN SIDE)

TIMING BELT

CRANKSHAFT PULLEY

IDLER PULLEY

NO. 1 TIMING BELT COVER

CRANKSHAFT TIMING PULLEY

OIL PUMP DRIVE PULLEY

TIMING BELT CASE

Timing belt and related components—5M-GE, 7M-GE and 7M-GTE engines

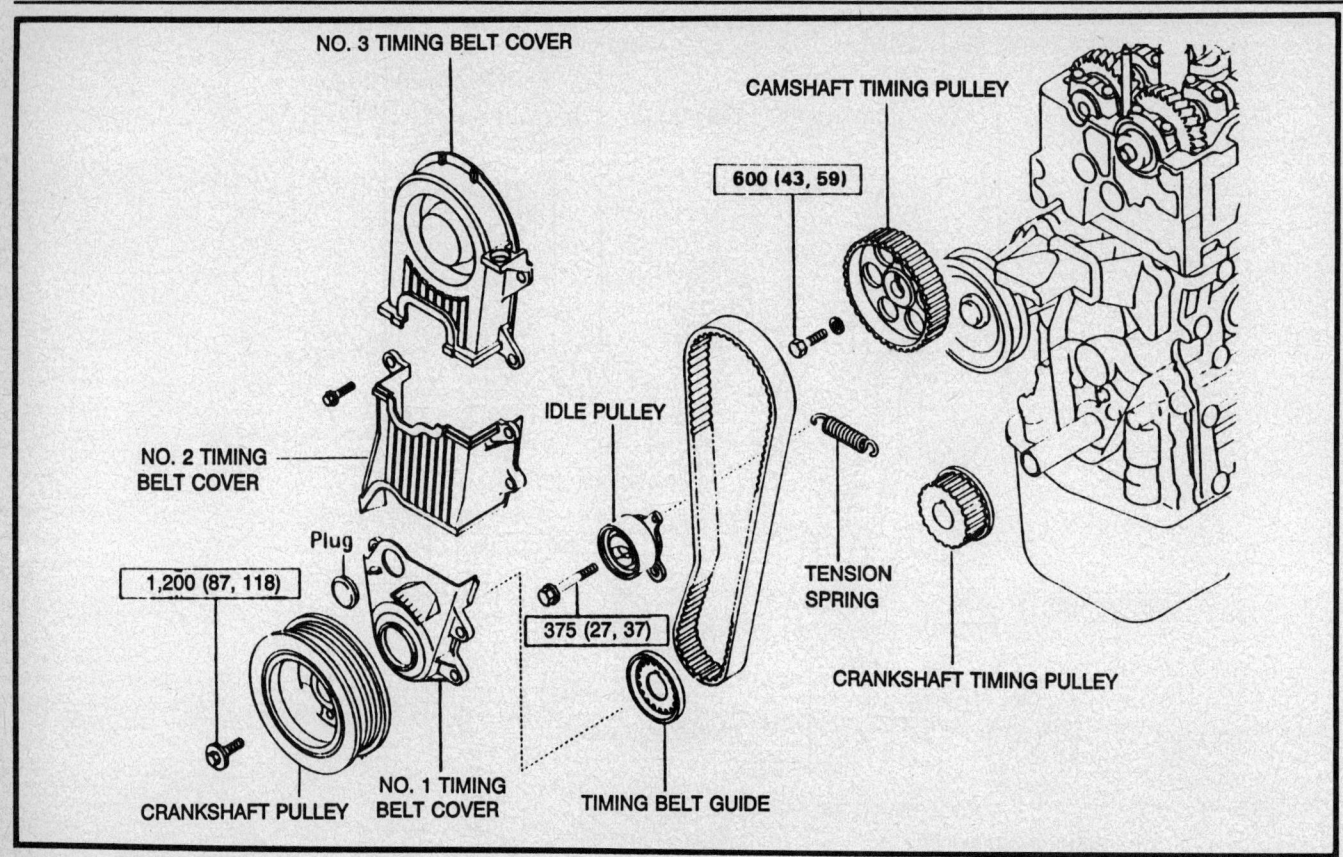

NO. 3 TIMING BELT COVER

CAMSHAFT TIMING PULLEY

600 (43, 59)

NO. 2 TIMING BELT COVER

IDLE PULLEY

TENSION SPRING

Plug

1,200 (87, 118)

375 (27, 37)

CRANKSHAFT TIMING PULLEY

CRANKSHAFT PULLEY

NO. 1 TIMING BELT COVER

TIMING BELT GUIDE

Timing belt and related components—4A-F and 4A-FE engines

Oil Seal Replacement

1. Remove the front cover.
2. Inspect the oil seal for signs of wear, leakage, or damage.
3. If worn, pry the old seal out. Remove it toward the front of the cover. Once the seal has been removed, it must be replaced.
4. Wipe the seal bore with a clean rag.
5. Drive the oil seal into place using a suitable seal installer. Work from the front of the cover. Be extremely careful not to damage the seal.
6. Install the front cover.

Timing Belt and Tensioner

Removal and Installation

2VZ-FE ENGINE

1. Disconnect the negative battery cable. If equipped, remove the cruise control actuator and vacuum pump.
2. Remove the power steering oil reservoir tank and position it aside without disconnecting the hydraulic lines.
3. Raise the vehicle and support it safely. Remove the right wheel and tire assembly.
4. Remove the alternator and power steering pump drive belts.
5. Remove the right side fender apron seal.
6. Remove the right side engine mounting stays, position a floor jack under the engine and raise it just enough to release the pressure on the mount and then remove it. If with ABS, first remove the clamp bolts for the power steering oil cooler lines.
7. Remove the spark plugs.
8. Remove the upper timing belt cover and then remove the right side engine mounting bracket.

NOTE: **If re-using the old timing belt, matchmark it to each of the timing pulleys and to mark it for the direction of rotation.**

9. Rotate the engine until the groove in the crankshaft pulley is aligned with the **0** mark on the lower timing belt cover. Check that the marks on the camshaft timing pulleys are aligned with the ones on the inner timing belt cover; if not, rotate the engine one complete revolution (360 degrees).
10. Remove the timing belt tensioner and dust cover.
11. Turn the left side camshaft timing pulley clockwise slightly to release the tension on the timing belt and then slide the belt off both pulleys.
12. Remove the camshaft sprocket retaining bolts and knock pins and pull off the sprockets. Do not mix them up.
13. Remove the No. 2 idler pulley.
14. Remove the crankshaft pulley and then remove the lower timing belt cover.
15. Remove the timing belt guide and then remove the timing belt.

To install:

16. Inspect the timing belt for any cracks, tears or other defects. Replace as required. Inspect the idler pulleys and timing sprockets; replace defective components as necessary.
17. Install the timing belt over the crankshaft sprocket so the mark on the belt aligns with the drilled mark on the sprocket. Install the belt over the No. 1 idler and water pump pulleys.
18. Install the timing belt guide so the cupped side faces outward. Install the No. 1 timing belt cover with a new gasket.
19. Install the crankshaft pulley so the set key is aligned with the groove in the shaft and then tighten the retaining bolt to 181 ft. lbs. (245 Nm).
20. Install the No. 2 idler pulley and tighten the bolt to 29 ft. lbs. (39 Nm). Check the pulley for smooth operation.

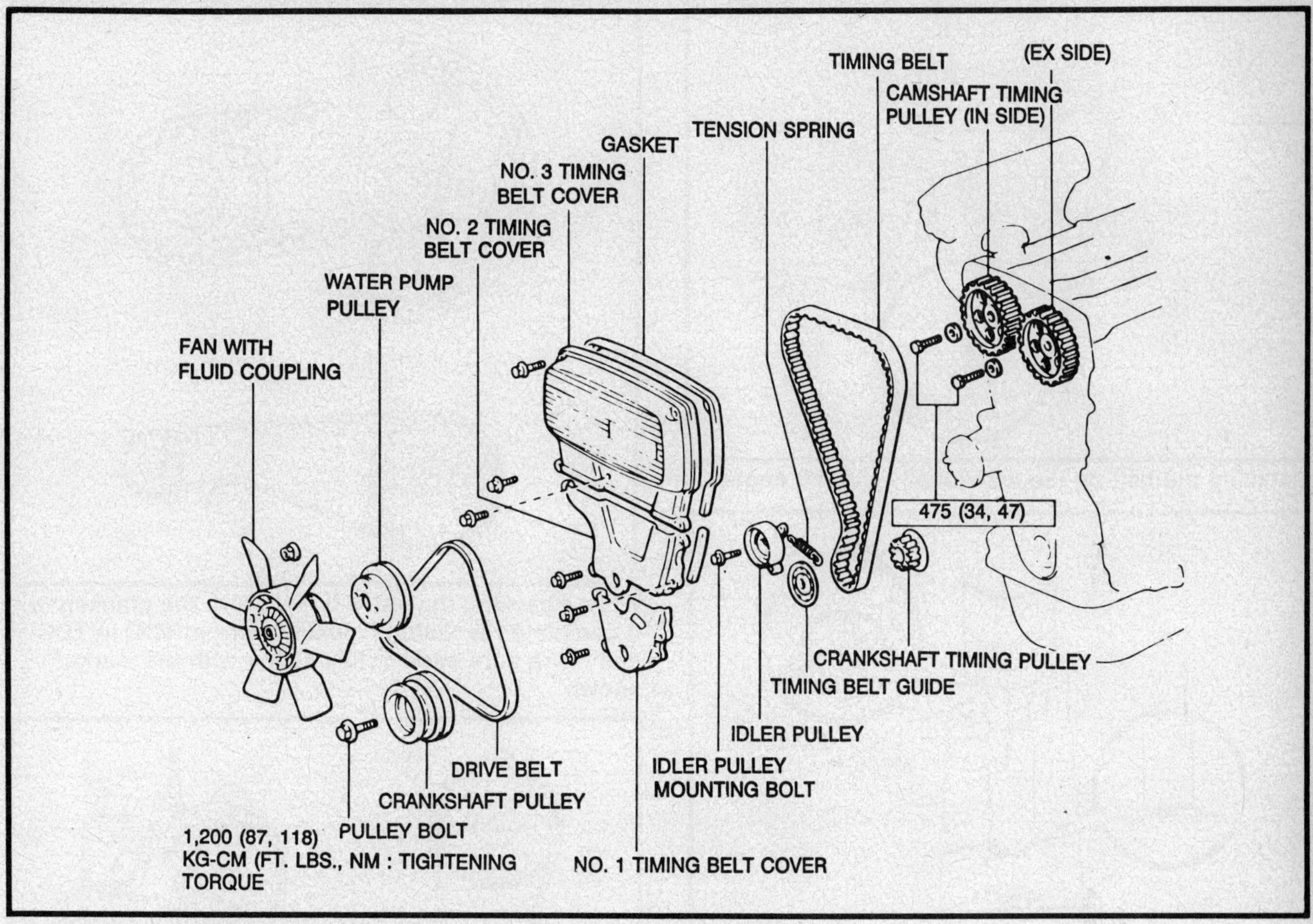

FAN WITH FLUID COUPLING

WATER PUMP PULLEY

NO. 2 TIMING BELT COVER

NO. 3 TIMING BELT COVER

GASKET

TENSION SPRING

TIMING BELT

(EX SIDE)

CAMSHAFT TIMING PULLEY (IN SIDE)

475 (34, 47)

CRANKSHAFT TIMING PULLEY

TIMING BELT GUIDE

IDLER PULLEY

IDLER PULLEY MOUNTING BOLT

NO. 1 TIMING BELT COVER

DRIVE BELT

CRANKSHAFT PULLEY

PULLEY BOLT

1,200 (87, 118) KG-CM (FT. LBS., NM : TIGHTENING TORQUE

Timing belt and related components—4A-GE and 4A- GZE engines

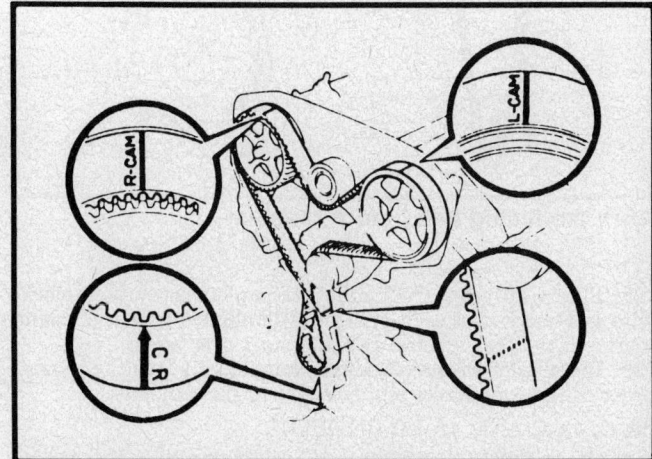

There should be installation marks on the timing belt—2VZ-FE engine

Check that the marks on the sprockets and the No. 3 cover are aligned--2VZ-FE engine

21. Install the left camshaft sprocket, flange side out, so the camshaft knock pin hole aligns with the groove in the sprocket. Install the knock pin and tighten the sprocket bolt to 80 ft. lbs. (108 Nm).

22. Set the No. 1 piston to TDC of the compression stroke again. Rotate the right camshaft until the knock pin hole is aligned with the timing mark on the No. 3 timing belt cover. Ro-

tate the left camshaft sprocket until the timing mark on the sprocket is aligned with the one on the No. 3 cover.

23. Check that the mark on the timing belt aligns with the edge of the No. 1 timing belt cover. Rotate the left camshaft sprocket clockwise slightly so the mark on the timing belt will align with the timing mark on the sprocket, slide the belt over the sprocket and then align the mark on the sprocket with the one on the No. 3 belt cover. Check for tension between the crankshaft and camshaft sprockets.

24. Align the mark on the timing belt with the timing mark on the right camshaft sprocket.

25. Hang the belt over the sprocket, flange side inward, and

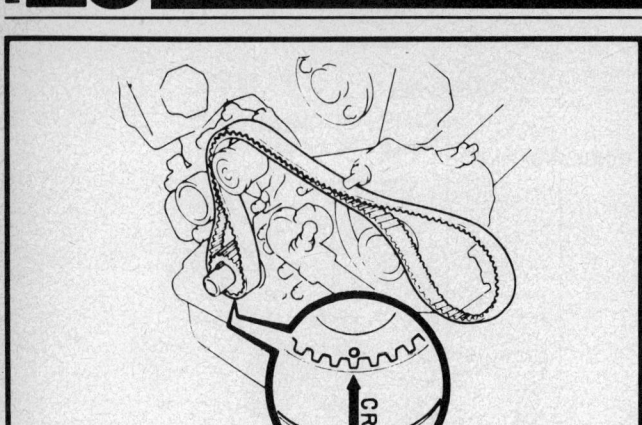

Installing the belt on the crankshaft—2VZ-FE engine

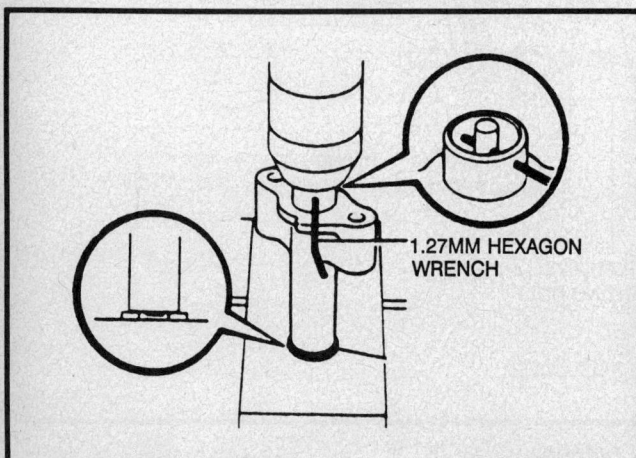

Set the timing belt tensioner—2VZ-FE engine

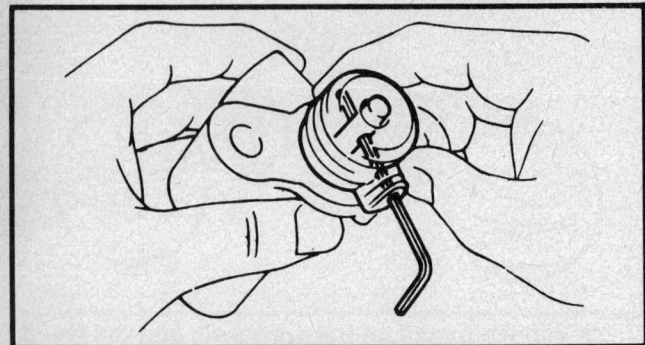

Install the hex wrench—2VZ-FE engine

then align the marks on the sprocket with the one on the No. 3 timing belt cover.

26. Slide the sprocket onto the camshaft so the knock pin hole and groove align. Install the knock pin and then tighten the retaining bolt to 80 ft. lbs. (108 Nm).

27. Install a plate washer between the timing belt tensioner and the cylinder block and then slowly press in the pushrod. When the holes in the pushrod and the housing align, insert a 1.27mm Allen wrench to retain the pushrod and then release the pressure. Install the tensioner and tighten the mounting bolts to 20 ft. lbs. (26 Nm); remove the Allen wrench.

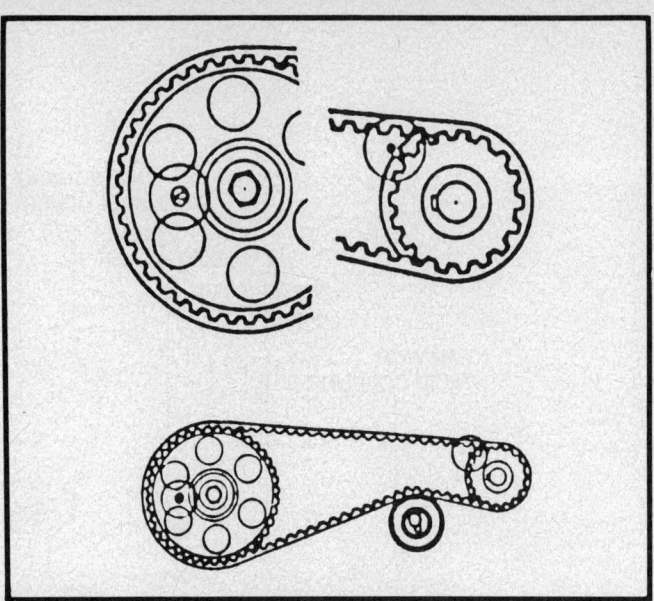

When checking the valve timing, turn the crankshaft 2 complete revolutions clockwise from TDC to TDC and make sure each pulley aligns with the marks shown

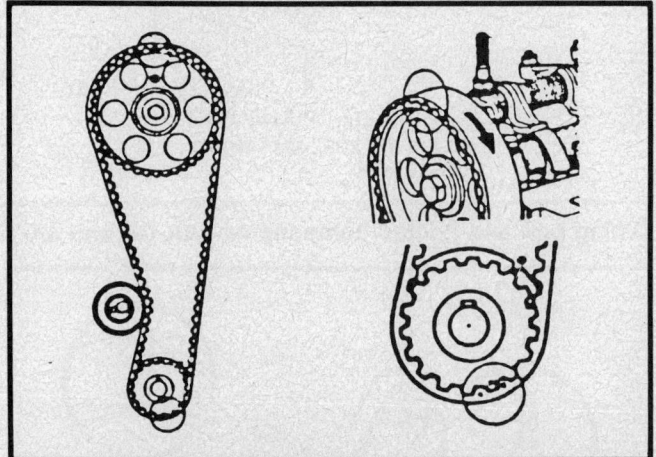

Mark the timing belt before removal

28. Rotate the crankshaft pulley 2 complete revolutions clockwise and check that each pulley is still aligned with the timing marks. If not, remove the belt and start over again.

29. Installation of the remaining components is in the reverse order of removal. Make all necessary engine adjustments.

3A-C, 4A-C AND 4A-LC ENGINES

1. Remove the timing belt upper and lower covers.

2. If the timing belt is to be reused, mark an arrow in the direction of engine revolution on its surface. Matchmark the belt to the pulleys at the proper locations.

3. Loosen the idler pulley bolt, push it to the left as far as it will go and then temporarily tighten it.

4. Remove the timing belt, idler pulley bolt, idler pulley and the return spring Do not bend, twist, or turn the belt inside out. Do not allow grease or water to come in contact with it.

5. Inspect the timing belt for cracks, missing teeth or overall wear. Replace as necessary. Install the return spring and idler pulley.

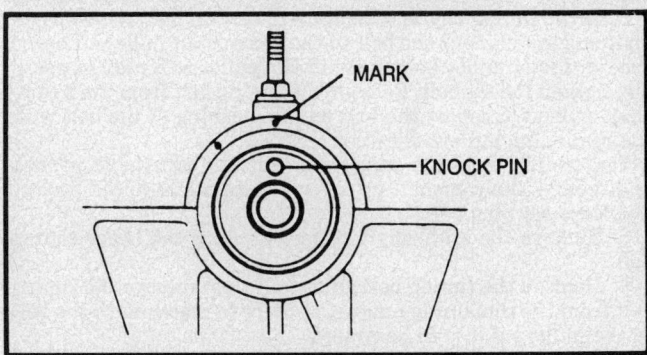

Camshaft alignment—3E and 3E-E engines

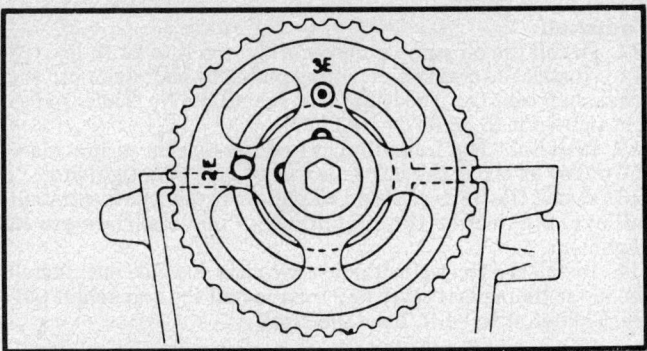

Timing sprocket installation—3E and 3E-E engines

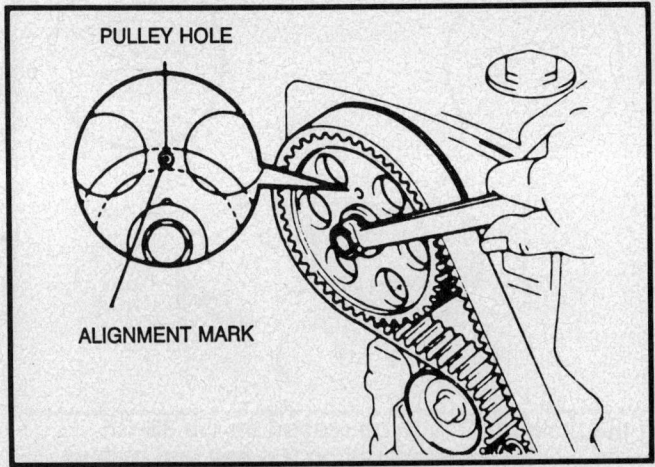

Timing sprocket alignment—3E and 3E-E engines

6. Install the timing belt. Align the marks made earlier, if reusing the old belt.

7. Adjust the idler pulley so the belt deflection is 0.24–0.28 in. (6–7mm) at 4.5 lbs. of pressure. Check the valve timing.

8. Installation of the remaining components is in the reverse order of removal.

3E AND 3E-E ENGINES

1. Disconnect the negative battery cable. Remove the right side engine under cover. On 3E-E engine, disconnect the accelerator and throttle cables.

2. Remove the drive belts, alternator and alternator bracket. Remove the air cleaner and air intake collector (3E-E) assemblies and spark plugs.

3. Raise the engine and remove the right side engine mounting insulator assembly.

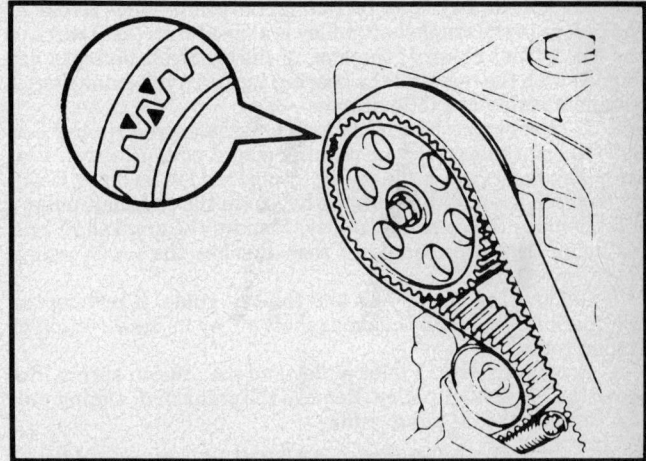

Timing belt alignment—3E and 3E-E engines

4. Remove the cylinder head cover. Set the engine to TDC on the compression stroke. Remove the crankshaft pulley using the proper removal tool.

5. Remove both timing belt covers. Remove the timing belt guide. Remove the timing belt and the No. 1 idler pulley. If using the old belt matchmark it in the direction of engine rotation. Matchmark the pulleys.

6. Remove the tension spring. Remove the No. 2 idler pulley. Remove the crankshaft pulley, camshaft pulley and oil pump pulley using the proper tools.

To install:

7. Inspect the belt for defects. Replace as required. Inspect the idler pulleys and springs. Replace defective components as required.

8. Align and install the oil pump pulley. Torque the retaining bolt to 20 ft. lbs. (26 Nm).

9. To install the camshaft timing pulley, align the camshaft knock pin with the No. 1 bearing cap mark. Align the knock pin hole on the 3E mark side with the camshaft knock pin hole. Torque the retaining bolt to 37 ft. lbs. (50 Nm).

10. Install the crankshaft timing pulley and align the TDC marks on the oil pump body and the crankshaft timing pulley. Install the No. 1 idler pulley. Pry the idler pulley toward the left as far as it will go and temporarily tighten the retaining bolt.

11. Install the No. 2 idler pulley and torque the retaining bolt to 20 ft. lbs. (27 Nm). Install the timing belt. If reusing the old belt align it with the marks made during the removal procedure.

12. Inspect the valve timing and the belt tension by loosening the No. 1 idler pulley set bolt. Temporarily install the crankshaft pulley bolt and turn the crankshaft 2 complete revolutions in the clockwise direction.

13. Check that each pulley aligns with the proper markings. Torque the No. 1 idler pulley bolt to 13 ft. lbs. (18 Nm). Check for proper belt tension. Install the belt guide.

14. Install the timing belt covers. Align and install the crankshaft pulley. Torque the retaining bolt to 112 ft. lbs. (152 Nm).

15. Installation of the remaining components is the reverse of the removal procedure.

3S-FE AND 5S-FE ENGINES

1. Disconnect the negative battery cable. Raise and support the vehicle safely. Remove the right tire and wheel assembly.

2. If equipped, remove the cruise control actuator and bracket. Remove the drive belts.

3. Remove the alternator and alternator bracket and right engine mounting stay. Raise the engine enough to remove the right side engine mounting insulator and brackets.

4. Remove the spark plugs. Remove the upper timing cover.

Position the No. 1 cylinder to TDC on the compression stroke so the groove in the crankshaft pulley is aligned with the **0** mark in the No. 1 front cover. If the hole in the camshaft pulley is not aligned with the mark on the bearing cap, turn the crankshaft 1 complete revolution (360 degrees).

5. If reusing the belt place matchmarks on the timing belt and the camshaft pulley. Loosen the mount bolt of the No. 1 idler pulley and position the pulley toward the left as far as it will go. Tighten the bolt. Remove the belt from the camshaft pulley.

6. Remove the camshaft pulley. Remove the crankshaft pulley using the proper removal tool. Remove the lower timing cover.

7. Remove the timing belt and the belt guide. If reusing the belt mark the belt and the crankshaft pulley in the direction of engine rotation.

8. Remove the No. 1 idler pulley and the tension spring. Remove the No. 2 idler pulley. Remove the crankshaft timing pulley. Remove the oil pump pulley.

To install:

9. Inspect the belt for defects. Replace as required. Inspect the idler pulleys and springs. Replace defective components as required.

10. Align the cutouts of the oil pump pulley and shaft. Install the oil pump pulley and torque the retaining nut to 21 ft. lbs. (28 Nm).

11. To install the crankshaft pulley, align the pulley set key with the key groove of the pulley and slide it in position. Install the No. 2 idler pulley and torque the bolt to 31 ft. lbs. (42 Nm). Be sure the pulley moves freely.

12. Temporarily install the No. 1 idler pulley and tension spring. Pry the pulley toward the left as far as it will go. Tighten the bolt.

13. Temporarily install the timing belt. If reusing the old belt align the marks made during removal. Install the timing belt guide.

14. Install the No. 1 timing belt cover. Install the crankshaft pulley and tighten the bolt to 80 ft. lbs. (108 Nm).

15. Install the camshaft pulley by aligning the camshaft knock pin with the knock pin groove in the pulley. Install the washer and torque the retaining bolt to 40 ft. lbs. (54 Nm).

16. With the engine set at TDC on the compression stroke install the timing belt. If reusing the belt align with the marks made during the removal procedure.

17. Once the belt is installed be sure there is tension between the crankshaft pulley, water pump pulley and camshaft pulley. Loosen the No. 1 idler pulley mount bolt ½ turn. Turn the crankshaft pulley 2 revolutions from TDC to TDC, in the clockwise direction. Torque the No. 1 idler pulley mount bolt to 31 ft. lbs. (42 Nm).

18. Installation the remaining components is the reverse of the removal procedure.

3S-GE AND 3S-GTE ENGINES

Celica (2WD)

1. Disconnect the negative battery cable. Raise the vehicle and support safely. Remove the right front tire and wheel assembly. Remove the right side fender liner.

2. Remove the windshield washer and radiator reservoir tanks. Remove the cruise control actuator, if equipped.

3. Remove the power steering belt. Remove the power steering pump and position it aside with the hydraulic lines still attached.

4. Remove the alternator and support bracket. Remove the upper timing belt cover.

5. Set the No. 1 piston to TDC of the compression stroke by aligning the groove on the crankshaft pulley with the **0** mark on the lower timing belt cover. Check that the matchmarks on the 2 camshaft timing pulleys and the rear timing belt cover are aligned, if not, turn the crankshaft 1 complete revolution clockwise (360 degrees).

6. If the timing belt is to be reused, draw a directional arrow on it and matchmark the belt to the 2 camshaft pulleys. Loosen the No. 1 idler pulley bolt and shift the pulley as far left as possible; tighten the set bolt. Remove the timing belt from the 2 camshaft pulleys. Support the belt so the meshing of the belt with the remaining pulleys does not shift.

7. Carefully hold the camshafts with an adjustable wrench and remove the camshaft pulley set bolts. Remove the pulleys and their set pins.

8. Remove the crankshaft pulley. Remove the lower timing belt.

9. Remove the timing belt guide and then remove the timing belt from the remaining pulleys. Be sure to matchmark the belt to the pulleys if it is to be reused.

10. Remove the No. 1 idler pulley and the tension spring. Remove the No. 2 idler pulley, the crankshaft timing pulley and the oil pump pulley.

To install:

11. Install the oil pump pulley and tighten it to 21 ft. lbs. (28 Nm). Install the crankshaft timing pulley by sliding it onto the crankshaft over the Woodruff® key. Install the No. 2 idler pulley and tighten it to 32 ft. lbs. (43 Nm).

12. Install the No. 1 idler pulley and the tension spring. Move the pulley as far to the left as it will go and then tighten it.

13. Install the timing belt on all pulleys except the 2 camshaft pulleys. Make sure the matchmarks made earlier are in alignment.

14. Install the timing belt guide with the cup side out. Install the lower timing belt cover and then install the crankshaft pulley. Tighten it to 80 ft. lbs. (108 Nm).

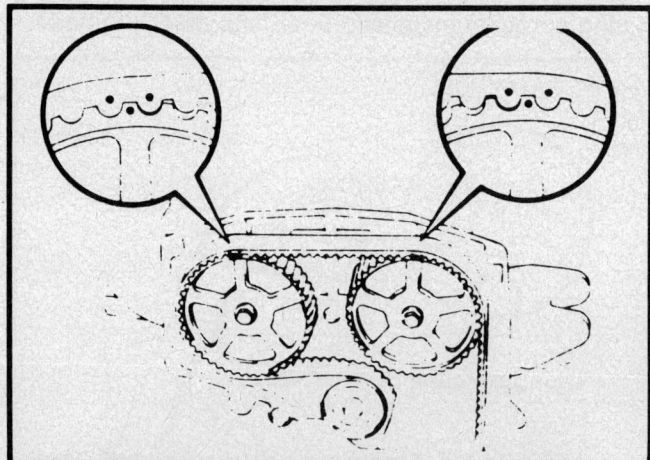

If the timing belt is to be reused on the 3S-GE engine, place matchmarks on the belt and pulleys

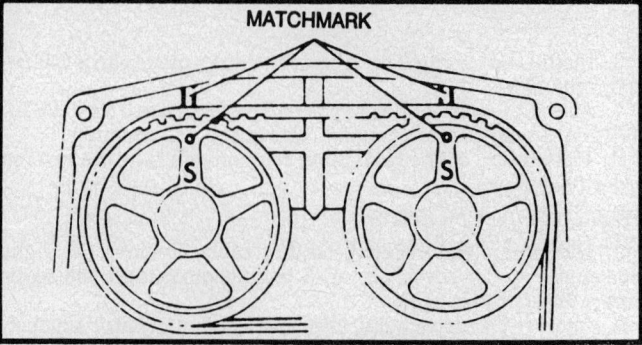

Align the matchmarks on the camshaft timing pulleys with those on the rear timing belt cover—3S-GE engine

Hold the camshaft with an adjustable wrench when removing the camshaft timing pulley—3S-GE engine

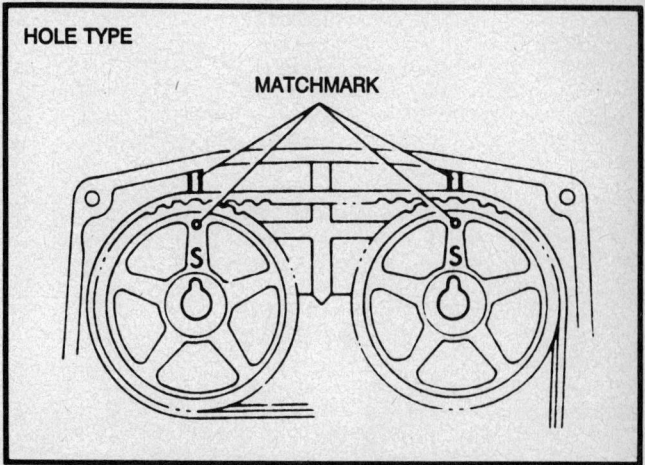

Align the camshaft knock pin with the hole in the camshaft timing pulley—3S-GE engine (1 hole type pulley only)

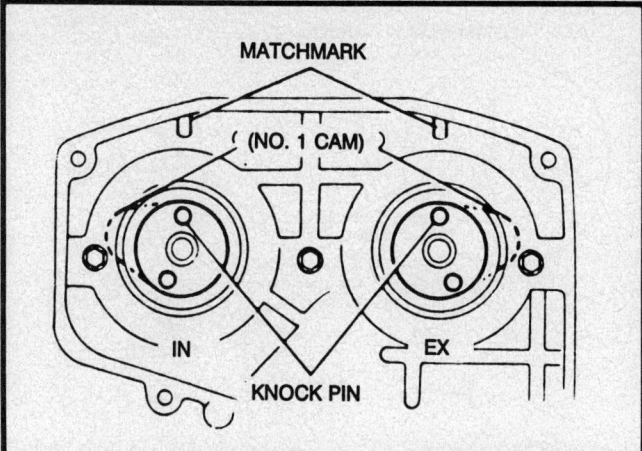

Turn the camshaft so the knock pins align with the matchmark on the rear timing cover and the No. 1 lobes are facing outward—3S-GA engine (2 hole type)

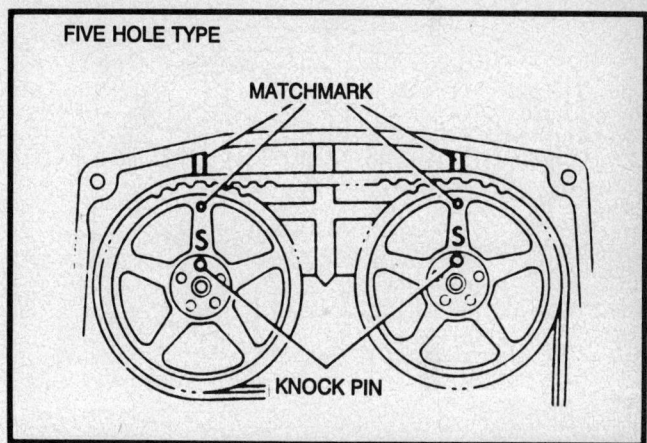

Insert the knock pin into whichever camshaft timing pulley and camshaft holes are aligned—3S-GE engine (5 hole type pulley only)

NOTE: There are 2 types of camshafts, one with 2 holes on the timing pulley contact surface and one with 5 holes on the timing pulley contact surface. All replacement camshaft have 5 holes.

2 Hole: Using a wrench, turn the camshafts so the camshaft knock pin aligns with the matchmark on the rear timing belt cover. And the No. 1 cam lobe is pointing outward.

5 Hole: Using a wrench, turn the camshaft so the knock pin aligns with the notch in the No. 1 camshaft bearing cap.

17. Hang the timing belt on the 2 camshaft timing pulleys. Align all matchmarks made during removal. The **S** mark on the pulley should face outward.

NOTE: There are 2 types of camshaft pulleys. One has 5 holes on the camshaft contact surface and one has 1 hole on the contact surface. All replacement pulleys have 5 holes.

18. Align the timing pulley matchmark with the rear timing belt cover matchmark and install the pulleys with the belt.

NOTE: On 1 hole pulleys, match the camshaft knock pin with the camshaft pulley hole. On 5 hole pulleys, insert the knock pin into whichever pulley and camshaft holes are aligned.

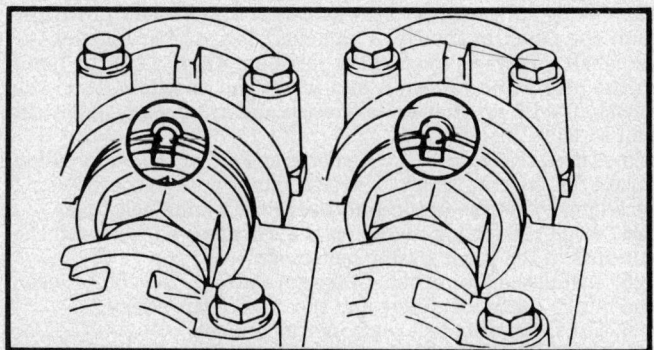

Align the knock pin and the No. 1 bearing cap mark—3S-GE engine (5 hole type)

15. Check that the No. 1 cylinder is at TDC of the compression stroke for the crankshaft. The crankshaft pulley groove should be aligned with the **0** mark on the lower timing belt cover.

16. Check that the No. 1 cylinder is at TDC of the compression stroke for the camshaft.

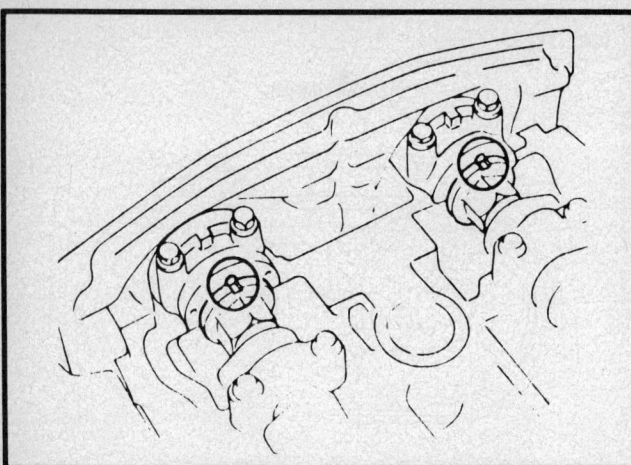

Aligning the camshaft grooves with the drilled marks in the No. 1 camshaft bearing caps—3S-GTE engine

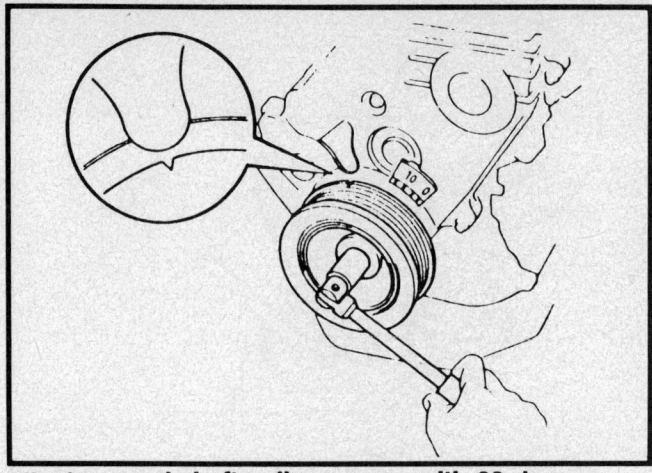

Aligning crankshaft pulley groove with 60 degree ATDC mark on the timing belt cover

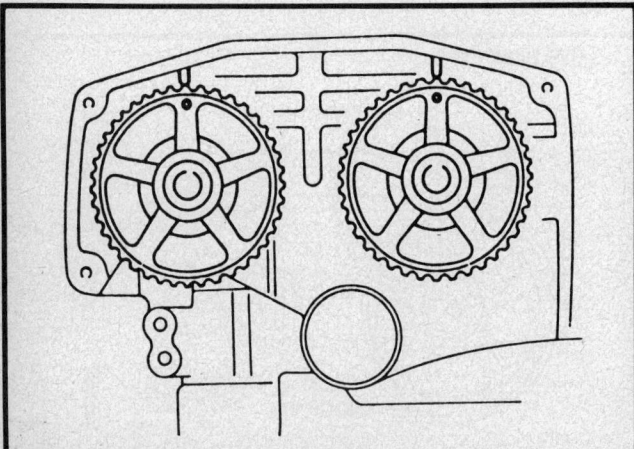

Aligning the camshaft and timing belt cover marks— 3S-GTE engine

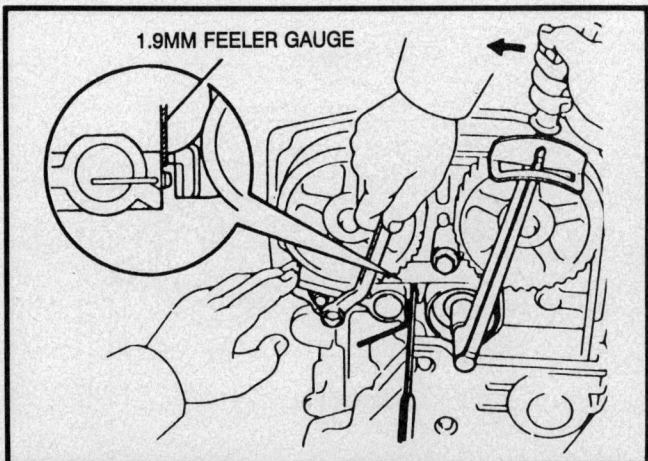

Checking the clearance between the tensioner body and the No. 1 idler puller stopper

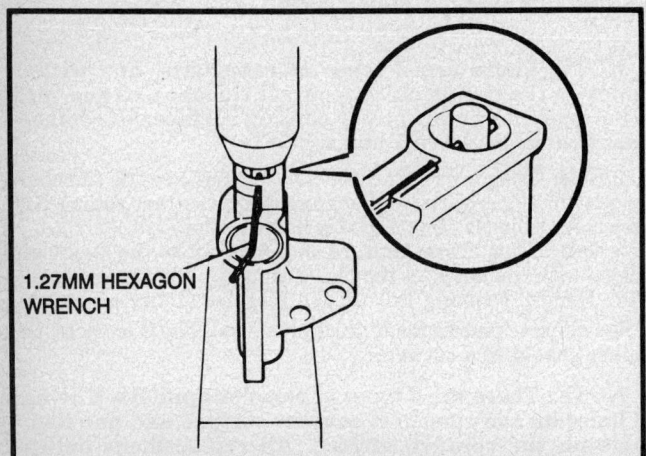

1.27MM HEXAGON WRENCH

Setting the timing belt tensioner—3S-GTE engine

19. Hold the camshaft with an adjustable wrench and tighten the pulley set bolt to 43 ft. lbs. (59 Nm).

20. Loosen the No. 1 idler pulley set bolt just enough to move the pad earlier are in alignment.

21. Install the timing belt guide with the cup side out. Install

the lower timing belt cover and then install the crankshaft pulley. Tighten it to 80 ft. lbs. (108 Nm).

22. Using a wrench, turn the camshaft so the knock pin aligns with the notch in the No. 1 camshaft bearing cap. Install the camshaft pulleys so the **S** mark faces up. Then, align the holes in the pulley and camshaft and insert the knockpin. Hold the camshaft with an adjustable wrench and tighten the pulley set bolt to 43 ft. lbs. (59 Nm).

23. Check that the No. 1 cylinder is at TDC of the compression stroke for the crankshaft. The crankshaft pulley groove should be aligned with the **0** mark on the lower timing belt cover.

24. Align the timing marks on the camshaft pulleys with the cut-outs in the inner timing belt cover.

25. Install the timing belt. Make sure there is tension between the intake camshaft pulley and the crankshaft pulley.

26. Set the timing belt tensioner as follows:

    a. Mount the tensioner in a vise and align the holes in the tensioner pushrod with the holes in the housing.

    b. Using a press, slowly press the pushrod into the housing until the holes are exaclty aligned.

    c. Insert a 1.27 mm hex wrench through the holes to retain the position of the pushrod.

    d. Release the press.

27. Using a torque wrench, turn the No. 1 idler pulley bolt counterclockwise to 13 ft. lbs. (18 Nm), then temporarily install the timing belt tensioner with the 2 mounting bolts.

28. Slowly turn the crankshaft pulley $^5/_6$ turn and align the groove in the pulley with the 60 degrees ATDC mark on the timing belt cover. Always turn the crankshaft in the clockwise direction.

29. Insert a 0.75 in. (1.90mm) feeler gauge between the tensioner body and the No. 1 idler pulley stopper.

30. Using a suitable torque wrench, turn the No. 1 idler pulley bolt counterclockwise to 13 ft. lbs. (18 Nm). Push on the tensioner and torque the tensioner retaining bolts to 15 ft. lbs. (21 Nm).

31. Remove the 1.27mm hex wrench from the tensioner.

32. Slowly turn the crankshaft pulley in the clockwise direction $^5/_6$ turn and align the groove in the pullley with the 60 degrees ATDC mark on the timing belt cover. Always turn the crankshaft in the clockwise direction.

33. Turn the No. 1 idler pulley bolt to 18 ft. lbs. (25 Nm).

34. Using a feeler gauge, check the clearance between the tensioner body and the No. 1 idler pulley stop. The clearance should be 0.071–0.087 in. (1.8–2.2mm). If the clearance is not as specified, remove the tensioner and reinstall it.

35. Installation of the remaining components is the reverse of the removal procedure.

4A-F AND 4A-FE ENGINES

1. Raise and support the vehicle safely. Remove the right wheel and undercover. Remove the air cleaner.

2. Remove the drive belts. Remove the power steering pump and the air conditioning compressor, with brackets, and position them aside. Leave the hydraulic and refrigerant lines connected.

3. Remove the spark plugs and the cylinder head cover. Rotate the crankshaft pulley so the **0** mark is in alignment with the groove in the No. 1 front cover. Check that the lifters on the No. 1 cylinder are loose; if not, turn the crankshaft 1 complete revolution (360 degrees).

4. Position a floor jack under the engine and remove the right side engine mounting insulator.

5. Remove the water pump and crankshaft pulleys. The crankshaft pulley will require a 2-armed puller.

6. Loosen the 9 bolts and remove the No. 1, No. 2 and No. 3 front covers. Remove the timing belt guide.

7. Loosen the bolt on the idler pulley, push it to the left as far as it will go and then retighten it. If reusing the timing belt, draw an arrow on it in the direction of engine revolution (clockwise) and then matchmark the belt to the pulleys.

8. Remove the timing belt. Remove the idler pulley bolt, the pulley and the tension spring.

9. Remove the crankshaft timing pulley.

10. Lock the camshaft and remove the camshaft timing pulleys.

To install:

11. Install the camshaft timing pulley so it aligns with the knockpin on the exhaust camshaft. Tighten the pulley to 34 ft. lbs. (47 Nm)—1988; 43 ft. lbs. (59 Nm)—1989–91. Align the mark on the No. 1 camshaft bearing cap with the center of the small hole in the pulley.

12. Install the crankshaft timing pulley so the marks on the pulley and the oil pump body are in alignment.

13. Install the idler pulley and its tension spring, move it to the left as far as it will go and tighten it temporarily.

14. Align the matchmarks made during removal and then install the timing belt on the camshaft pulley. Loosen the idler pulley set bolt. Make sure the timing belt meshing at the crankshaft pulley does not shift.

15. Rotate the crankshaft clockwise 2 revolutions from TDC to TDC. Make sure each pulley aligns with the marks made previously. If the marks are not in alignment, the valve timing is wrong. Shift the timing belt meshing slightly and then repeat Steps 14–15.

16. Tighten the set bolt on the timing belt idler pulley to 27 ft. lbs. (37 Nm). Measure the timing belt deflection at the top span

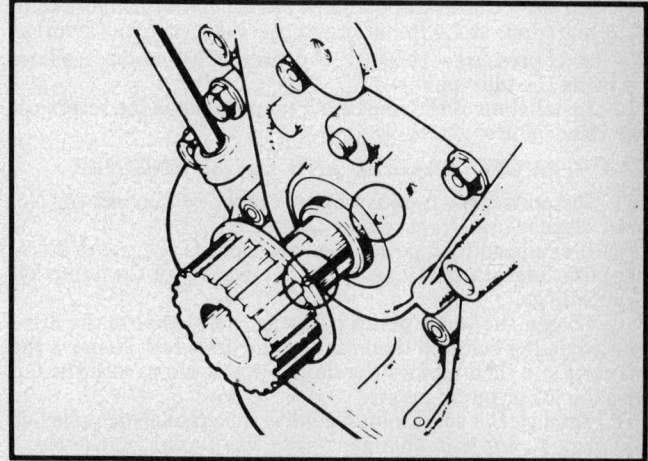

When installing the crankshaft pulley, make sure the TDC marks on the oil pump body and the pulley are in alignment—4A-GE engine

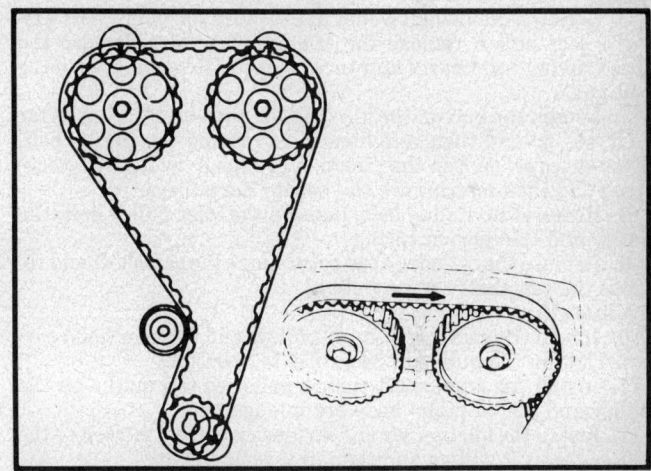

If the timing belt is to be reused, draw a directional arrow and matchmark the belt to the pulleys as shown—4A-GE engine

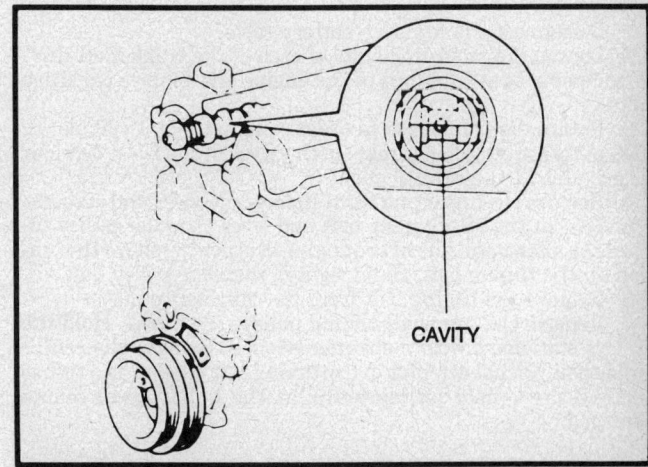

When setting the No. 1 cylinder at TDC on the 4A-GE engine, remove the oil filler cap and check that the cavity in the camshaft is visible

CAVITY

between the 2 camshaft pulleys. It should deflect no more than 0.16 in. (4mm) at 4.4 lbs. of pressure—1988; 0.24 in. (7mm) at 4.4 lbs. of pressure—1989–91. If deflection is greater, readjust by using the idler pulley.

17. Installation of the remaining components is the reverse of the removal procedure.

4A-GE, 4A-GEC, 4A-GELC AND 4A-GZE ENGINES

1. Disconnect the negative battery cable. Disconnect the No. 2 air cleaner hose from the air cleaner.

2. If equipped with power steering, remove the power steering pump and position it aside. Do not disconnect the pump hydraulic lines.

3. Loosen the water pump pulley set nuts, remove the drive belt adjusting bolt and then remove the drive belt. Remove the set nuts and then remove the fluid coupling along with the fan and the water pump pulley.

4. Remove the spark plugs. Rotate the crankshaft pulley so the groove on it is in alignment with the **0** mark on the No. 1 timing belt cover. Remove the oil filler cap and check that the cavity in the camshaft is visible. If not, turn the camshaft 1 complete revolution (360 degrees).

5. On the MR2 and 1988–91 Corolla, remove the right side engine mount insulator.

6. Lock the crankshaft pulley and remove the pulley bolt. Using a gear puller, remove the crankshaft pulley. Remove the three timing belt covers and their gaskets. Remove the timing belt guide.

7. Loosen the bolt on the idler pulley, push it to the left as far as it will go and then retighten it. If reusing the timing belt, draw an arrow on it in the direction of engine revolution (clockwise) and then matchmark the belt to the pulleys.

8. Remove the timing belt. Remove the idler pulley bolt, the pulley and the tension spring.

9. Remove the cylinder head covers, lock the camshaft and remove the camshaft timing pulleys.

To install:

10. Install the camshaft timing pulleys and cylinder head covers. Tighten the pulley to 34 ft. lbs. (47 Nm).

11. Install the crankshaft timing pulley so the marks on the pulley and the oil pump body are in alignment.

12. Install the idler pulley and its tension spring, move it to the left as far as it will go and tighten it temporarily.

13. Install the timing belt. If the old one is being used, align all the marks made during removal.

14. Installation of the remaining components is the reverse order of the removal procedure.

5M-GE ENGINE

1. Disconnect the negative battery cable.

2. Loosen the mounting bolts of each of the crankshaft-driven components at the front of the engine and remove the drive belts.

3. Rotate the crankshaft in order to set the No. 1 cylinder to TDC of its compression stroke (both valves of the No. 1 cylinder closed, and TDC marks aligned).

4. Remove the upper and front timing belt cover and gaskets.

5. Loosen the idler pulley bolt and lever the idler pulley toward the alternator side of the engine in order to relieve the tension on the timing belt. Hand tighten the idler pulley bolt.

6. Remove the timing belt from the camshaft pulleys.

7. Remove the camshaft timing pulleys as follows. Hold the pulleys stationary with a spanner wrench. Remove the center pulley bolt. Do not attempt to use timing belt tension as a tool to remove the center pulley bolts, as the belt could become damaged.

NOTE: Do not interchange the intake and exhaust timing pulleys, as they differ for use with each camshaft.

8. Remove the center crankshaft pulley bolt. Using a puller, remove the crankshaft pulley.

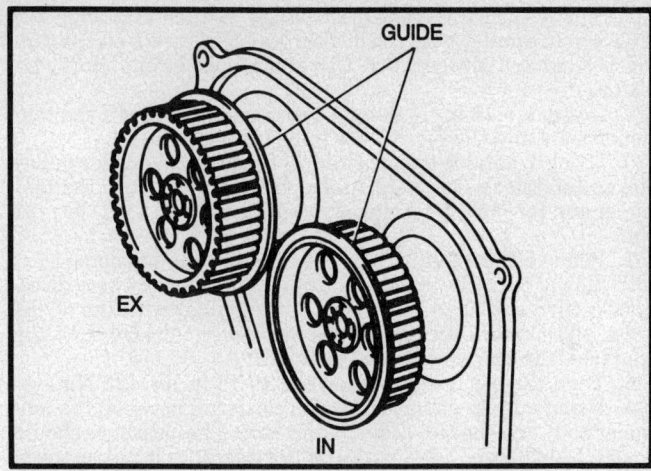

5M-GE engine—When installing the camshaft sprockets, be sure that the guides are positioned as shown. (IN—Intake camshaft sprocket; EX—exhaust camshaft sprocket)

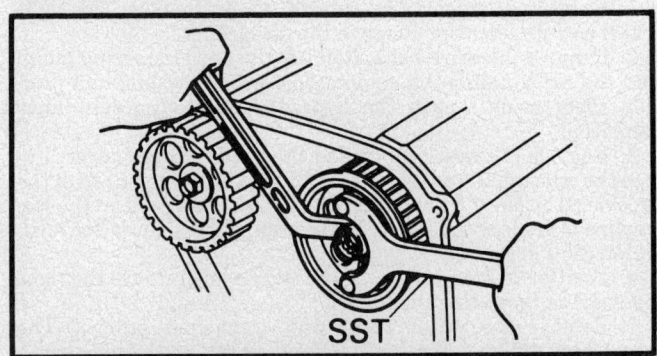

5M-GE engine—Use a spanner wrench 9SST, as shown, to hold the camshaft sprocket while loosening the camshaft sprocket bolt. Do not attempt to use belt tension to hole the sprocket in place while removing the camshaft sprocket bolt

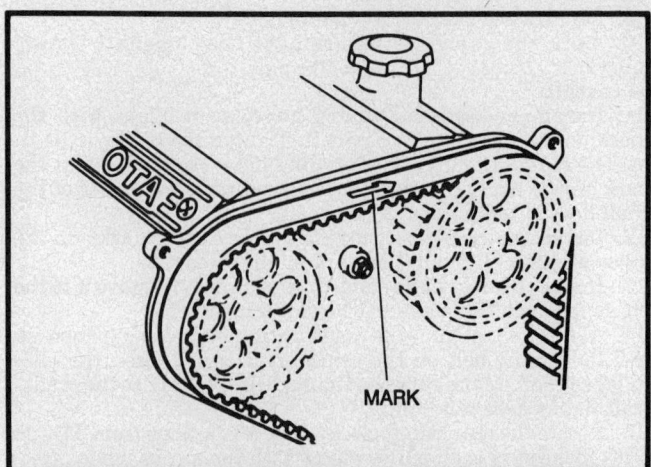

5M-GE engine—Paint a mark on the timing belt prior to belt removal to indicate the belts direction of normal rotation. Point the mark in the same direction if the belt is to be reinstalled

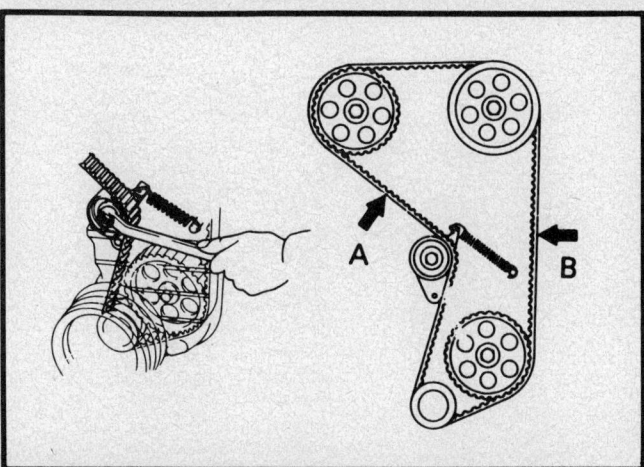

5M-GE engine—When adjusting the timing belt tension, be sure the tension at "A" is the same as that at "B"

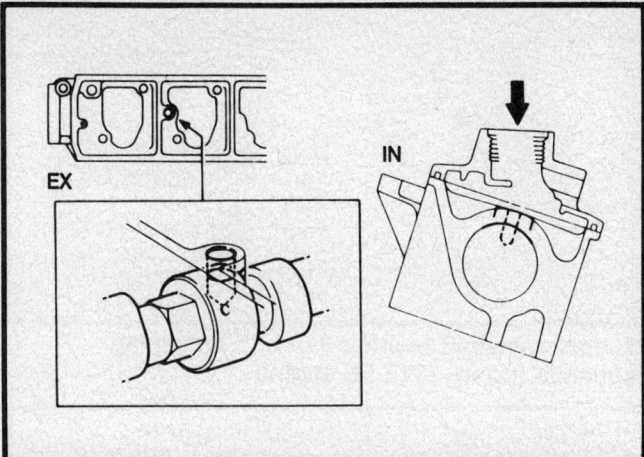

5M-GE engine—Proper alignment of the camshaft matchmarks with the match holes of the camshaft housings (IN—intake; EX—exhaust)

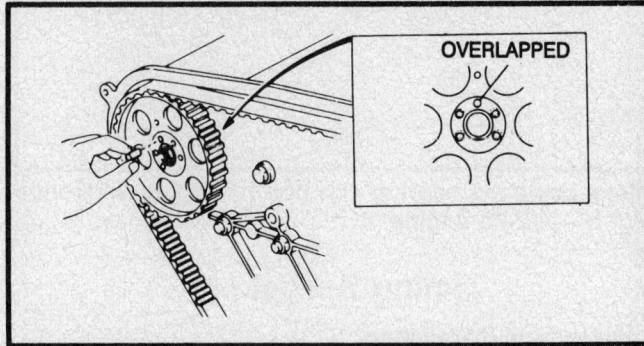

5M-GE engine—Locating the overlapped holes of the camshaft and the camshaft sprocket. Install the match pin into the aligned set of holes (typical of either the intake or exhaust camshaft)

9. Using chalk or crayon, mark the timing belt to indicate its direction of rotation. This mark must face the same direction during installation of the belt.

10. Remove the lower timing belt cover, then the belt.

11. If damaged, the crankshaft pulley can be removed using a puller; the oil pump driveshaft pulley can be removed in the same manner as the camshaft pulleys.

12. Inspect the timing belt for damage, such as cuts, cracks, missing teeth, abrasions, nicks, etc. If the belt teeth are damaged, check that the camshafts rotate freely and correct as necessary.

13. Should damage be evident on the belt face, check the idler pulley belt surface for damage. If damage is present on one side of the belt only, check the belt guide and the alignment of each pulley. If the belt teeth are excessively worn, check the timing belt cover gasket for damage and/or proper installation.

14. Check the idler pulley for damage and smoothness of rotation. Also check the free length of the tension spring, which should be 2.8 in. (71mm), measured between the inside of each end "clip". Replace the spring if the length exceeds this limit.
To install:
15. Install the crankshaft and oil pump driveshaft if these items were removed previously. Torque the oil pump driveshaft center pulley bolt to 16 ft. lbs. (22 Nm). The crankshaft pulley must be evenly driven into place.

16. Install the idler pulley and the tension spring. Lever the pulley towards the alternator side of the engine and tighten the bolt.

17. Check the mark made during Step 9 of removal and temporarily install the timing belt on the crankshaft pulley. The mark must face in the same direction as it did originally.

18. Install the lower timing belt cover. Install the crankshaft pulley and torque the center pulley bolt to 98–119 ft. lbs. (1987); 195 ft. lbs. (1988).

19. Remove the oil filter cap of the intake camshaft cover, and the complete camshaft cover on the exhaust side.

20. Check that the match holes of both No. 2 camshaft journals are visible through the camshaft housing match holes. If necessary, temporarily install the camshaft pulley and guide pin, and rotate the camshaft(s) until the holes are aligned.

21. Install the timing pulleys. Note that the belt guide of the exhaust camshaft pulley should be positioned towards the engine; the belt guide of the intake camshaft pulley should be positioned away from the engine. Do not yet install the pulley retaining bolts.

22. Align the following marks. Each camshaft pulley mark must be aligned with its respective mark on the rear, upper timing belt cover. Align the crankshaft pulley notch with the TDC (0) mark of the timing tab.

NOTE: The No. 1 cylinder must be positioned at TDC on its compression stroke.

23. Install the timing belt.

24. Loosen the idler pulley bolt and tension the timing belt. The timing belt tension must be the same between the exhaust camshaft pulley and the crankshaft pulley, as it is between the intake camshaft pulley and the oil pump driveshaft pulley.

25. There are 5 pin holes on each camshaft and each timing pulley. On the exhaust side: Install the match pin into the one hole of the pulley which is aligned with one of the camshaft pin holes. Repeat this on the intake side. Only one of the holes of each side should be aligned to allow insertion of the match pins.

26. Using a spanner wrench to hold the camshaft pulleys, install and tighten the camshaft pulley bolts. These bolts should be torqued to 51 ft. lbs. (69 Nm).

27. Install the exhaust camshaft cover, using a new gasket. Install the oil filler cap. Install the timing belt cover and gasket.

28. Install and adjust the drive belts at the front of the engine. Reconnect the battery cable.

7M-GE AND 7M-GTE ENGINES

1. Disconnect the negative battery cable. Drain the cooling system. Remove the radiator. Remove the water outlet.

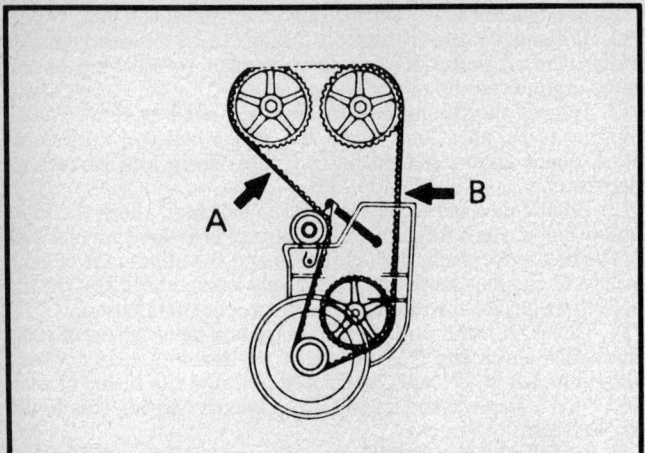

7M-GE and 7M-GTE engines timing belt tension check

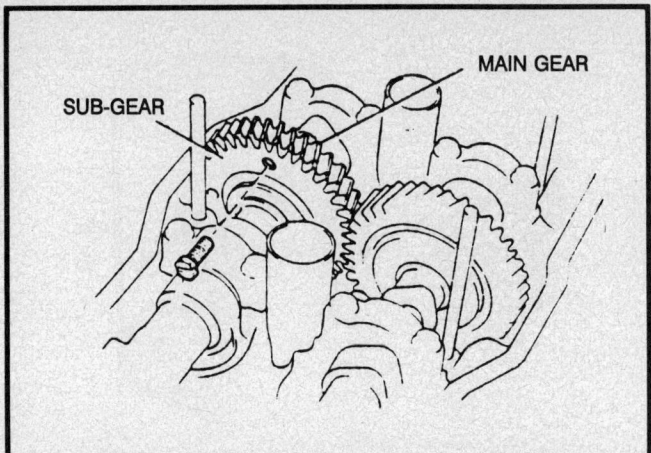

Install a service bolt in the exhaust camshaft sub-gear (right)—2VZ-FE engine

2. Remove the spark plugs. Remove the drive belts. Remove the No. 3 timing belt cover.

3. Position the engine at TDC on the compression stroke. Remove the timing belt from the camshaft sprockets. If reusing the belt, matchmark the belt and the sprockets in the direction of engine rotation.

4. Remove the camshaft pulleys. Remove the crankshaft pulley using the proper removal tools. Remove the power steering air pipe, if equipped.

5. If equipped with air conditioning remove the compressor and position it aside. Do not disconnect the refrigerant lines.

6. Remove the No. 1 timing belt cover. Remove the timing belt. Remove the idler pulley and the tension spring. Remove the oil pump drive pulley.

To install:

7. Inspect the belt for defects. Replace as required. Inspect the idler pulleys and springs. Replace defective components as required.

8. Install the oil pump drive pulley and retaining bolt. Tighten the bolt to 16 ft. lbs. (22 Nm).

9. Install the crankshaft timing pulley. Temporarily install the idler pulley and tension spring. Tighten the assembly to 36 ft. lbs. (49 Nm). Pry the idler pulley toward the left as far as it will go and temporarily tighten the bolt.

10. Temporarily install the timing belt. If reusing the old belt install it using the marks made during the removal procedure. Install the No. 1 timing belt cover.

11. If equipped with air conditioning, install the compressor assembly. If equipped, install the power steering air pipe.

12. Align the set key with the key groove and install the crankshaft pulley and torque the retaining bolt to 195 ft. lbs. (265 Nm).

13. Install the camshaft timing pulleys. Torque the retaining bolts to 36 ft. lbs. (49 Nm).

14. Loosen the idler pulley bolt. Install the timing belt to the INTAKE side and the EXHAUST side. Tighten the idler pulley bolt to 36 ft. lbs. (49 Nm).

15. Make sure the timing belt tension **A** is equal to the timing belt tension **B**. If not adjust the idler pulley. Turn the engine 2 complete revolutions in the clockwise direction and check to see that everything is aligned properly.

16. Turn both the intake and exhaust camshaft pulleys inward at the same time to loosen the timing belt between the 2 sprockets. Belt deflection should be 4.4–6.6 lbs. If not adjust the idler pulley.

17. Installation of the remaining components is in reverse order of removal.

Exhaust camshaft bearing cap bolt loosening sequence (right)—2VZ-FE engine

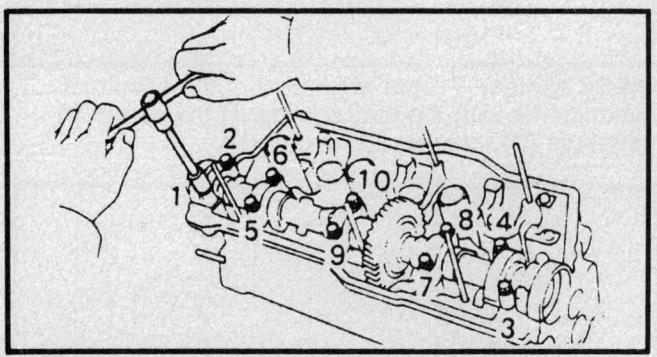

Intake camshaft bearing cap bolt loosening sequence (right)—2VZ-Fe engine

Timing Sprockets

Removal and Installation
Timing sprocket/pulley removal and installation procedures are detailed within the individual Timing Belt sections.

Camshaft

Removal and Installation
2VZ-FE ENGINE

NOTE: Due to a nominal thrust clearance, the cam-

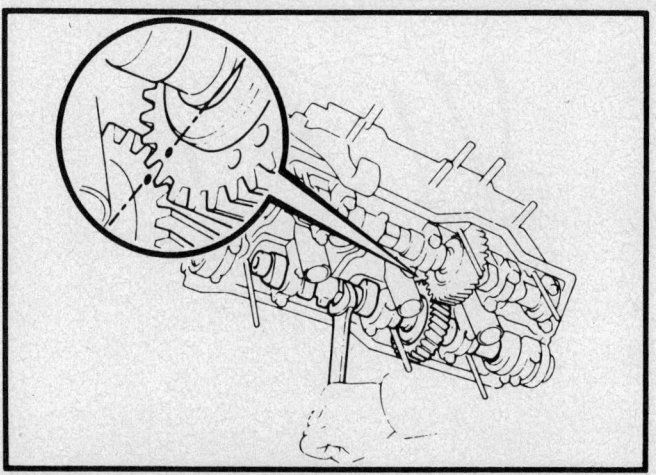

Align the single mark on the exhaust camshaft (left)—2VZ-FE engine

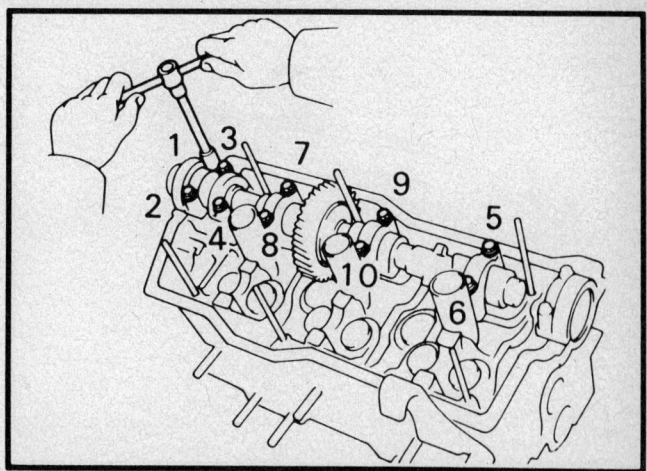

Intake camshaft bearing cap bolt loosening sequence (left)—2VZ-FE engine

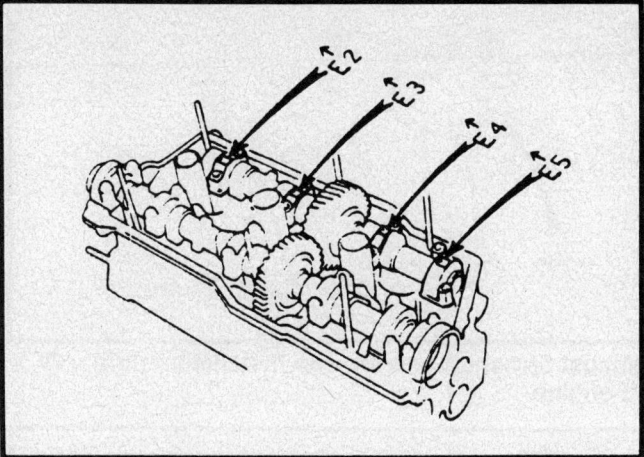

Exhaust camshaft bearing cap installation (right)— 2VZ-FE engine

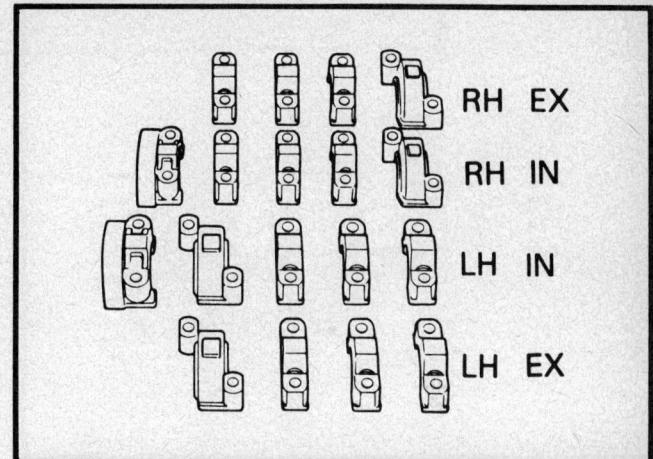

Camshaft bearing cap identification—2VZ-FE engine

shafts must be held absolutely level during removal. If not, the section of the cylinder head receiving the thrust may crack or be damaged, thus causing the camshaft to break.

1. Remove the cylinder head(s).
2. Rotate the exhaust camshaft in the right cylinder head until the 2 pointed marks on the camshaft drive and driven gears are aligned.
3. Secure the exhaust camshaft sub-gear to the driven gear with bolt. This is important as it will eliminate the torsional spring force of the sub-gear.
4. Loosen the bearing cap bolts in the proper sequence and then remove the 4 bearing caps and the right side exhaust camshaft.
5. Loosen the bearing cap bolts in the proper sequence and then remove the 5 bearing caps and the right side intake camshaft.

NOTE: Be sure to arrange all the bearing caps in their proper order.

6. Rotate the exhaust camshaft in the left cylinder head until the pointed mark on the camshaft drive and driven gears are aligned.

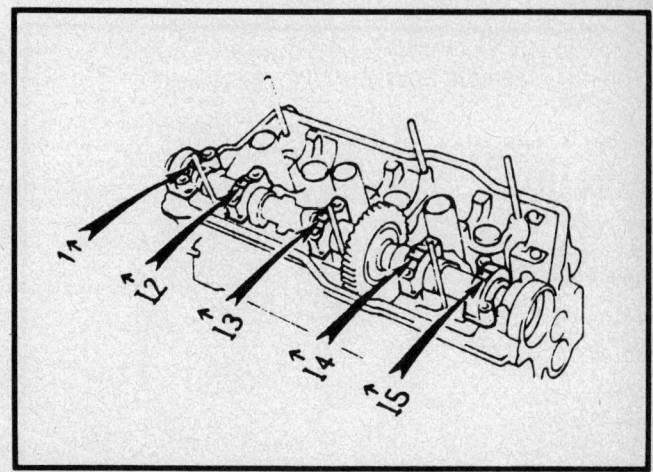

Intake camshaft bearing cap installation (right)—2VZ-FE engine

7. Secure the exhaust camshaft sub-gear to the driven gear with bolt. This is important as it will eliminate the torsional spring force of the sub-gear.

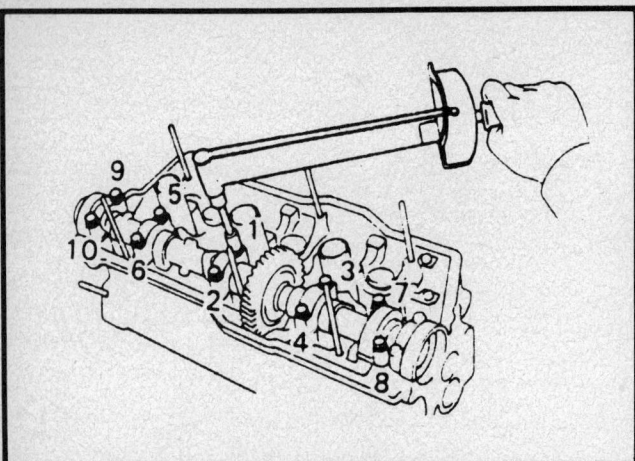

Intake camshaft bearing cap bolt tightening sequence (right)—2VZ-FE engine

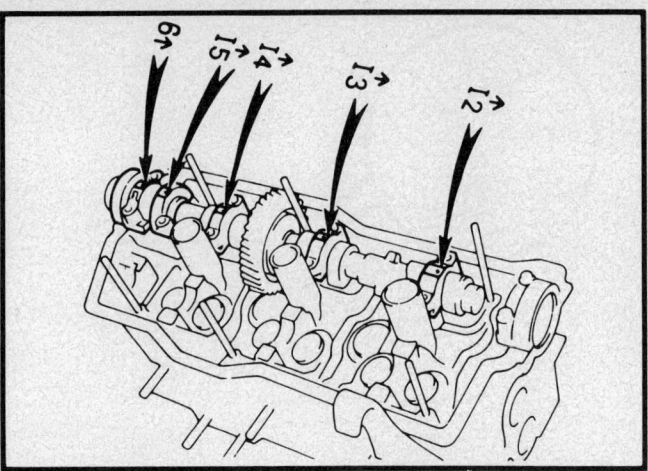

Intake camshaft bearing cap installation (left)—2VZ-FE engine

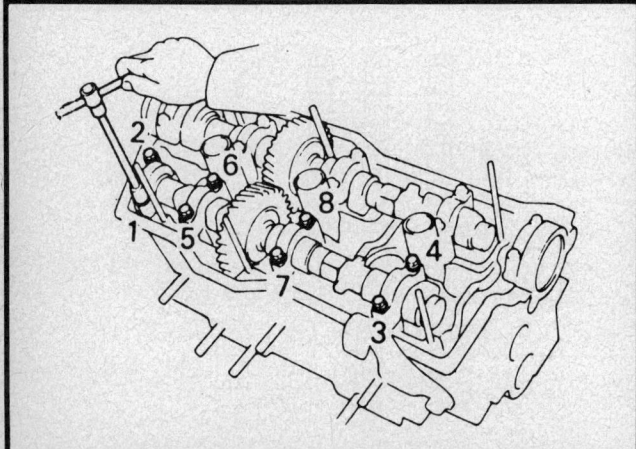

Exhaust camshaft bearing cap bolt loosening sequence (left)—2VZ-FE engine

Exhaust camshaft bearing cap installation (left)—2VZ-FE engine

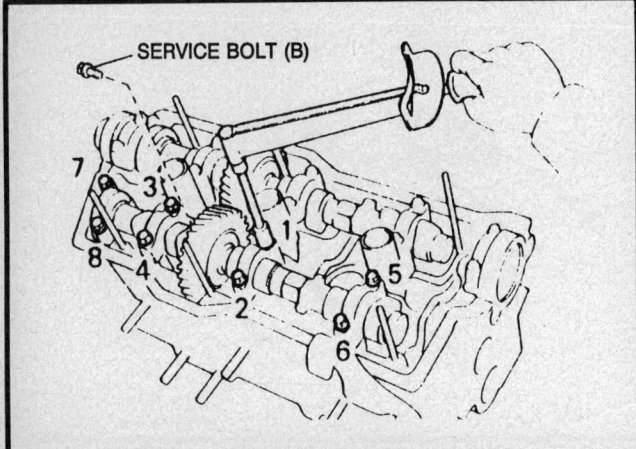

Exhaust camshaft bearing cap bolt tightening sequence (right)—2VZ-FE engine

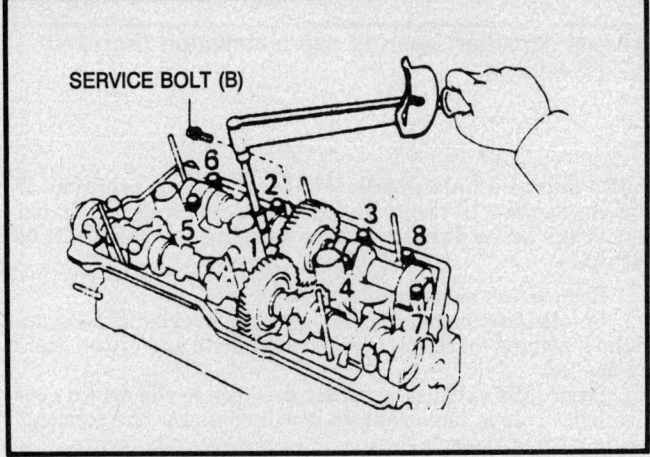

Exhaust camshaft bearing cap bolt tightening sequence (left)—2VZ-FE engine

8. Loosen the bearing cap bolts in the proper sequence and then remove the 4 bearing caps and the left side exhaust camshaft.

9. Loosen the bearing cap bolts in the proper sequence and then remove the 5 bearing caps and the left side intake camshaft.

NOTE: Be sure to arrange all the bearing caps in their proper order.

To install:
10. Coat the thrust portion of the right side intake camshaft

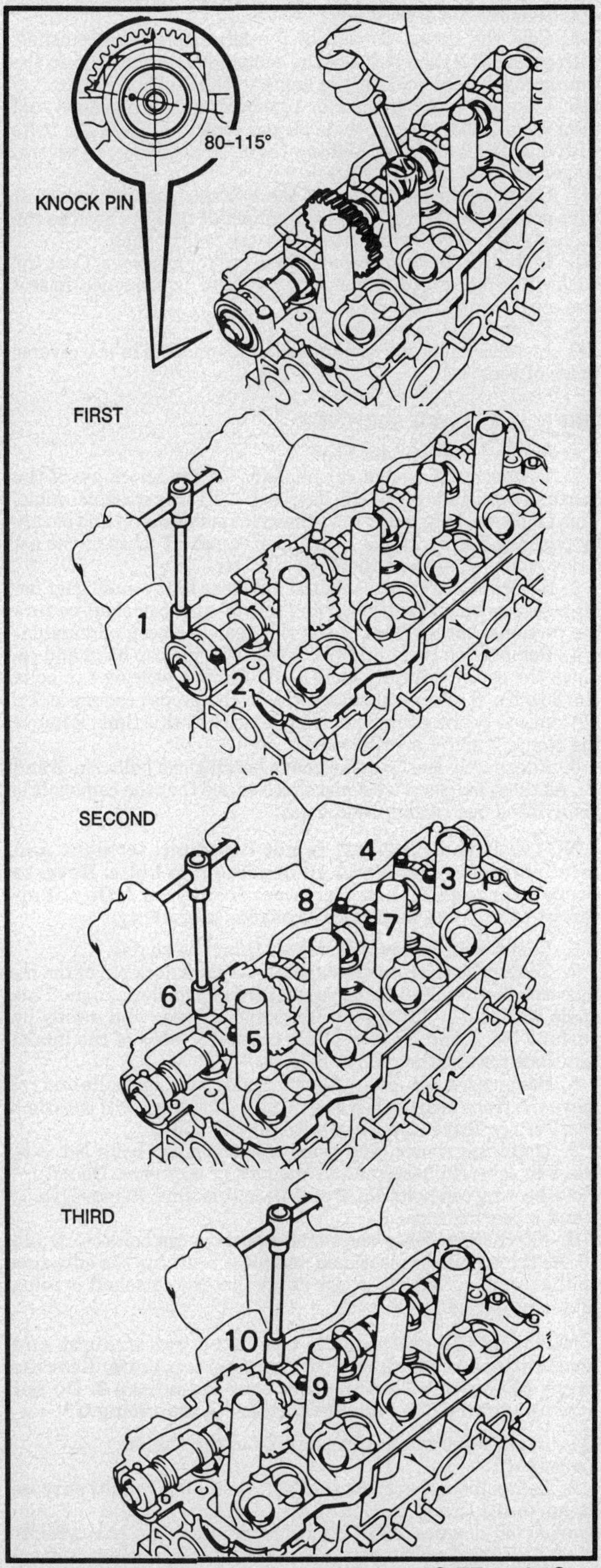

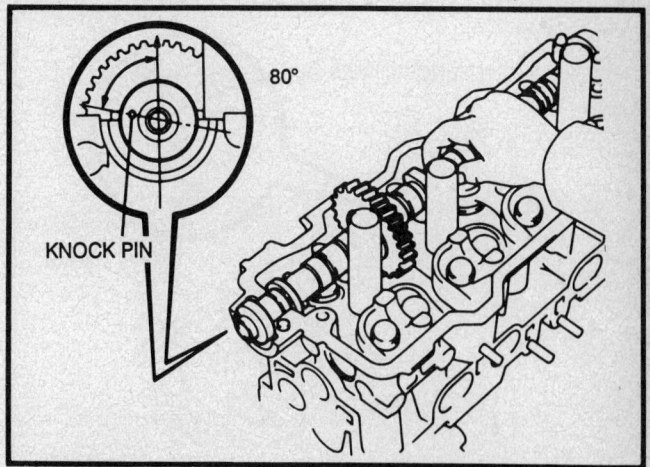

Installing the intake camshaft—3S-FE and 5S-FE engines

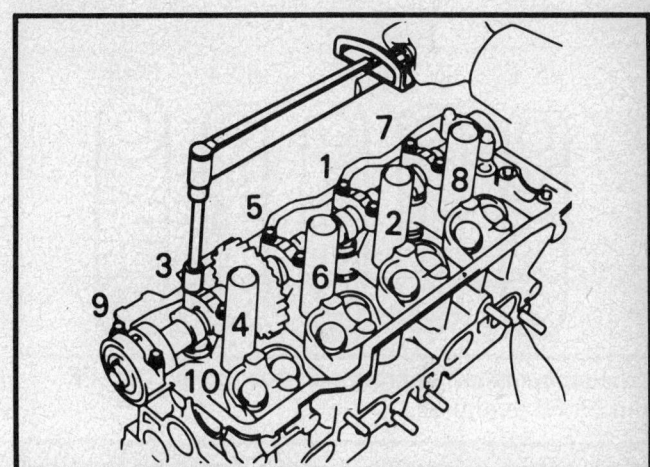

Intake camshaft bearing bolt tightening sequence— 3S-FE and 5S-FE engines

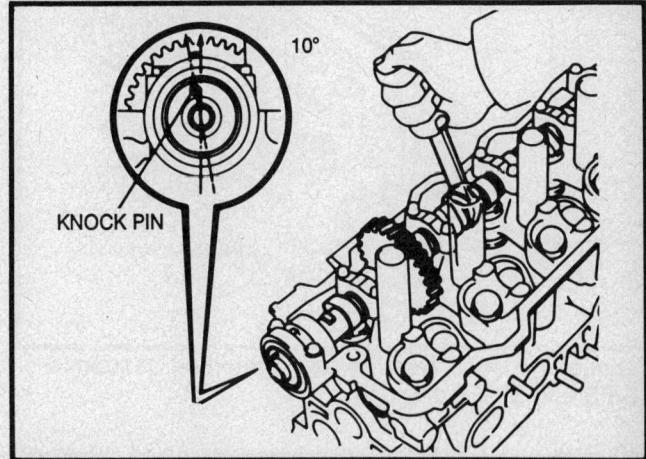

Exhaust camshaft installation—3S-FE and 5S-FE engines

Intake camshaft removal procedure—3S-FE and 5S-FE engines

with suitable grease and then position the camshaft into the head so the 2 timing marks are at a 90 degree angle to the head.

11. Coat the edges of the No. 1 bearing cap with sealant and then install all 5 caps in their proper locations. Coat the bolts

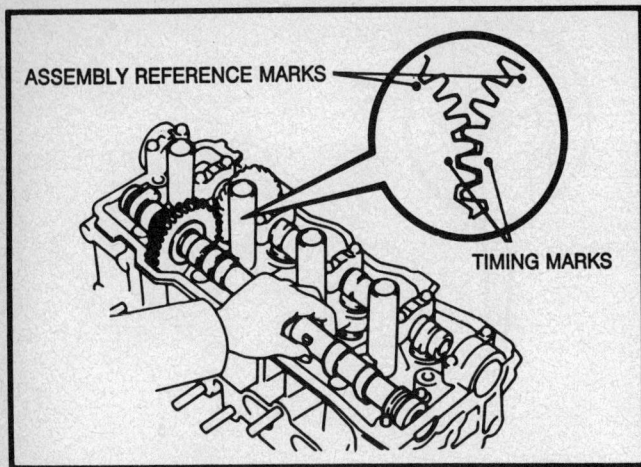

Intake and exhaust camshaft engagement—3S-FE and 5S-FE engines

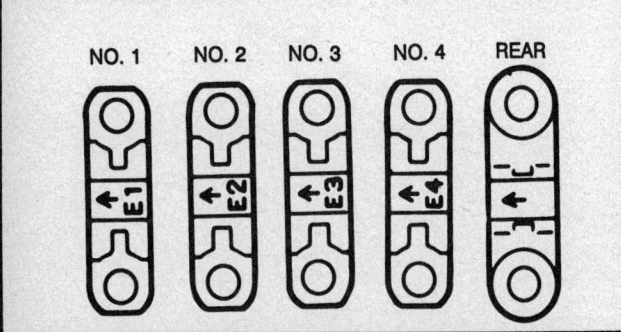

Exhaust camshaft bearing cap positioning—3S-FE and 5S-FE engines

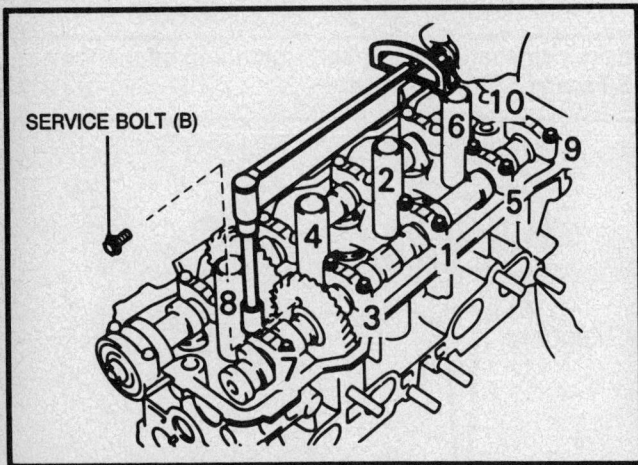

Exhaust camshaft bearing bolt tightening sequence—3S-FE and 5S-FE engines

with engine oil and then tighten them, in sequence, in several stages, to 12 ft. lbs. (16 Nm).

12. Coat the thrust portion of the right side exhaust camshaft with grease and then position the camshaft into the head so the 2 timing marks align with those on the intake shaft.

13. Install all 4 bearing caps in their proper locations. Coat the bolts with engine oil and then tighten them, in sequence, in several stages, to 12 ft. lbs. (16 Nm).

14. Remove the service bolt.

15. Coat the thrust portion of the left side intake camshaft with grease and then position the camshaft into the head so the timing mark is at a 90 degree angle to the head.

16. Coat the edges of the No. 1 bearing cap with sealant and then install all 5 caps in their proper locations. Coat the bolts with engine oil and then tighten them, in sequence, in several stages, to 12 ft. lbs. (16 Nm).

17. Coat the thrust portion of the left side exhaust camshaft with grease and then position the camshaft into the head so the timing mark aligns with the one on the intake shaft.

18. Install all 4 bearing caps in their proper locations. Coat the bolts with engine oil and then tighten them, in sequence, in several stages, to 12 ft. lbs. (16 Nm).

19. Remove the service bolt.

20. Installation of the remaining components is in the reverse order of removal.

3S-FE AND 5S-FE ENGINES

1. Remove the cylinder head.

2. To remove the exhaust camshaft, set the knock pin of the exhaust camshaft at 10–45 degree BTDC of camshaft angle. This angle will help to lift the exhaust camshaft level and evenly by pushing No. 2 and No. 4 cylinder camshaft lobes of the exhaust camshaft toward their valve lifters.

3. Secure the exhaust camshaft sub-gear to the main gear using a service bolt. When removing the exhaust camshaft be sure the torsional spring force of the sub-gear has been eliminated.

4. Remove the No. 1 and No. 2 rear bearing cap bolts and remove the cap. Uniformly loosen and remove bearing cap bolts No. 3 to No. 8 in several passes and in the proper sequence. Do not remove bearing cap bolts No. 9 and 10 at this time. Remove the No. 1, 2 and 4 bearing caps.

5. Alternately loosen and remove bearing cap bolts No. 9 and 10. As these bolts are loosened check to see that the camshaft is being lifted out straight and level.

NOTE: If the camshaft is not lifted out straight and level retighten No. 9 and 10 bearing cap bolts. Reverse Steps 4 through 1, than start over from Step 3. Do not attempt to pry the camshaft from its mounting.

6. Remove the exhaust camshaft from the engine.

7. To remove the intake camshaft, set the knock pin of the intake camshaft at 80–115 degrees BTDC of camshaft angle. This angle will help to lift the intake camshaft level and evenly by pushing No. 1 and No. 3 cylinder camshaft lobes of the intake camshaft toward their valve lifters.

8. Remove the No. 1 and No. 2 front bearing cap bolts and remove the front bearing cap and oil seal. If the cap will not come apart easily, leave it in place without the bolts.

9. Uniformly loosen and remove bearing cap bolts No. 3 to No. 8 in several phases and in the proper sequence. Do not remove bearing cap bolts No. 9 and 10 at this time. Remove No. 1, 3 and 4 bearing caps.

10. Alternately loosen and remove bearing cap bolts No. 9 and 10. As these bolts are loosened and after breaking the adhesion on the front bearing cap, check to see that the camshaft is being lifted out straight and level.

NOTE: If the camshaft is not lifted out straight and level retighten No. 9 and 10 bearing cap bolts. Reverse Steps 10 through 7, than start over from Step 8. Do not attempt to pry the camshaft from its mounting.

11. Remove the intake camshaft from the engine.

To install:

12. Before installing the intake camshaft, apply multi purpose grease to the thrust portion of the camshaft. Position the camshaft at 80 degrees BTDC of camshaft angle on the cylinder head. Apply seal packing kit 08826–00080 or equivalent, and apply it to the front bearing cap. Coat the bearing cap bolts with

clean engine oil. Uniformly and in several phases tighten the camshaft bearing caps to 14 ft. lbs. (19 Nm).

13. To install the exhaust camshaft, set the knock pin of the camshaft at 10 degrees BTDC of camshaft angle. Apply multi-purpose grease to the thrust portion of the camshaft. Position the exhaust camshaft gear with the intake camshaft gear so the timing marks are in alignment with one another. Be sure to use the proper alignment marks on the gears. Do not use the assembly reference marks.

14. Turn the intake camshaft clockwise or counterclockwise little by little until the exhaust camshaft sits in the bearing journals evenly without rocking the camshaft on the bearing journals.

15. Coat the bearing cap bolts with clean engine oil. Uniformly and in several phases tighten the camshaft bearing caps to 14 ft. lbs. (19 Nm). Remove the service bolt from the assembly.

16. Installation of the remaining components is the reverse of the removal procedure.

4A-F AND 4A-FE ENGINES

1. Disconnect the negative battery cable. Drain the cooling system.
2. Remove the spark plugs and the cylinder head cover.
3. Remove the No. 3 and No. 2 front covers. Turn the crankshaft pulley and align its groove with the **0** mark on the No. 1 front cover. Check that the camshaft pulley hole aligns with the mark on the No. 1 camshaft bearing cap (exhaust side).
4. Remove the plug from the No. 1 front cover and matchmark the timing belt to the camshaft pulley. Loosen the idler pulley mounting bolt and push the pulley to the left as far as it will go; tighten the bolt. Slide the timing belt off the camshaft pulley and support it so it won't fall into the case.
5. Remove the camshaft pulley and check the camshaft thrust clearance. Remove the camshafts.

NOTE: Due to the relatively small amount of camshaft thrust clearance, the camshaft must be held level during removal. If the camshaft is not level on removal, the portion of the head receiving the thrust may crack or be damaged.

6. Set the service bolt hole on the intake camshaft gear (the one not attached to the timing pulley) at the 12 o'clock position so the Nos. 1 and 3 cylinder camshaft lobed can push their lifters evenly. Loosen the No. 1 bearing caps on each camshaft a little at a time and remove them.
7. Secure the intake camshaft sub-gear to the main gear with a service bolt to eliminate any torsional spring force. Loosen the remaining bearing caps a little at a time, in the proper sequence

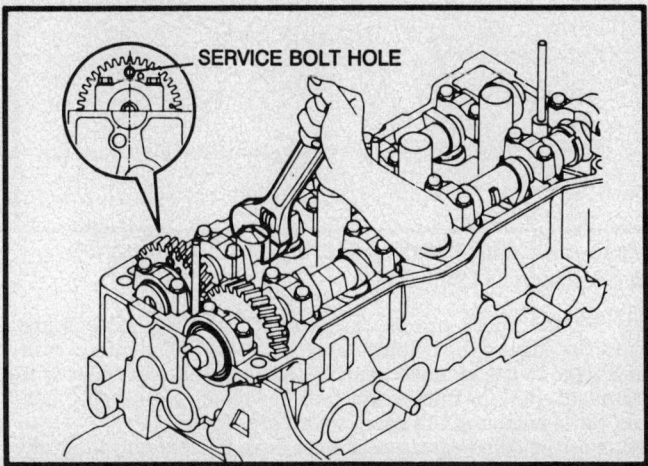

Service bolt hole positioning (intake camshaft) — 4A-F and 4A-FE engines

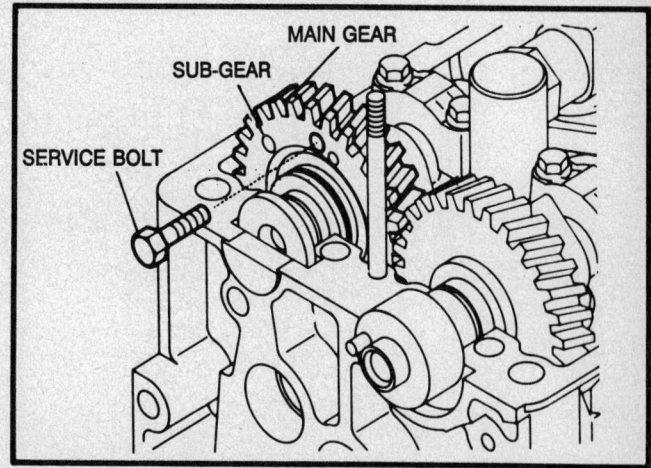

Installing the service bolt in the intake camshaft — 4A-F and 4A-FE engines

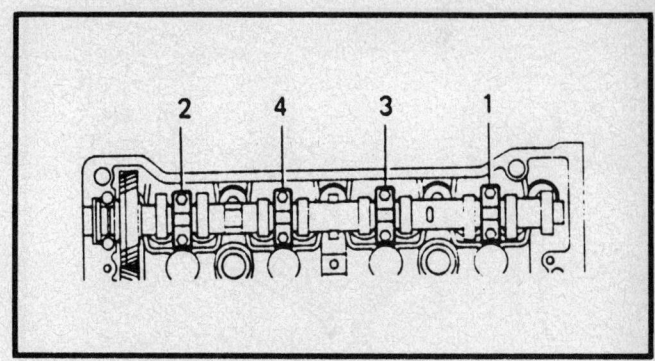

Camshaft bearing cap bolt loosening sequence — 4A-F and 4A-FE engines (1987–89)

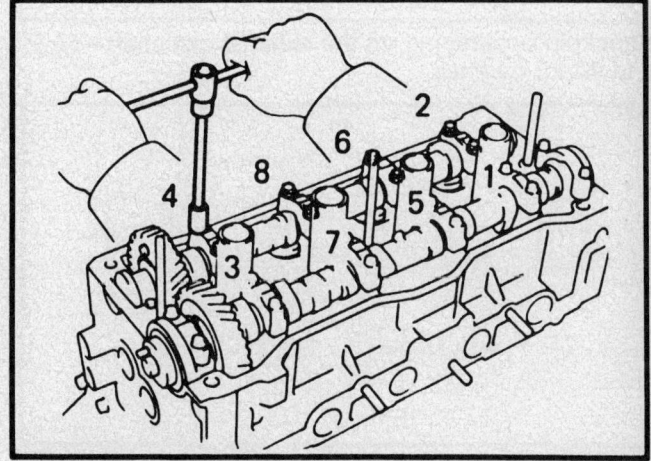

Intake camshaft bearing cap loosening sequence — 4A-FE engine (1990–91)

and remove the intake camshaft. If the camshaft cannot be lifted out straight and level, retighten the bolts in the No. 3 bearing cap and loosen them a little at a time with the gear pulled up.

8. Turn the exhaust camshaft approximately 105 degrees so the knock pin is about 5 minutes before the 6:30 o'clock position. Loosen the remaining bearing caps a little at a time, in the proper sequence and remove the exhaust camshaft. If the camshaft cannot be lifted out straight and level, retighten the bolts

Exhaust camshaft bearing cap loosening sequence—4A-FE engine (1990–91)

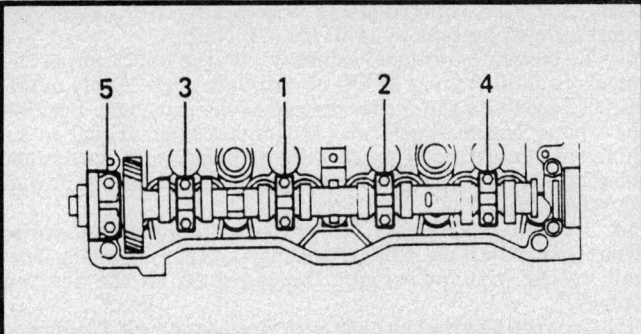

Camshaft bearing cap bolt tightening sequence—4A-F and 4A-FE engines (1987–89)

Knockpin positioning on the exhaust camshaft—4A-F and 4A-FE engines

Exhaust camshaft bearing cap tightening sequence—4A-FE engine (1990–91)

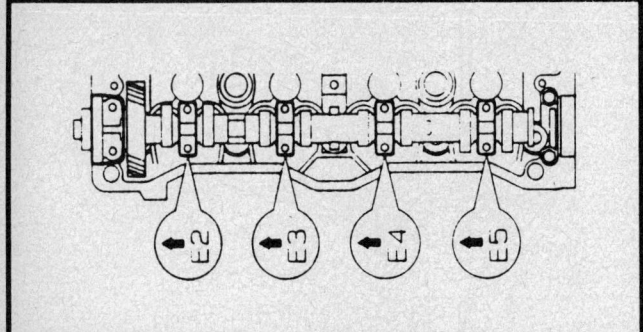

Exhaust camshaft bearing cap positioning—4A-F and 4A-FE engines

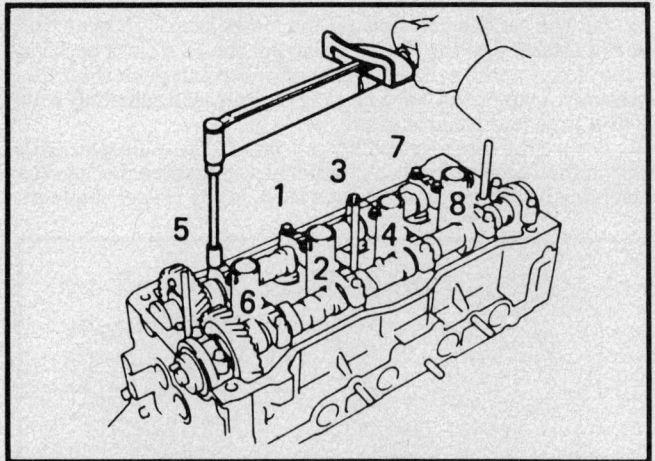

Intake camshaft bearing cap tightening sequence—4A-FE engine (1990–91)

in the No. 3 bearing cap and loosen them a little at a time with the gear pulled up.

To install:

9. Position the exhaust camshaft into the cylinder head as it was removed. Position the bearing caps over each journal so the arrows point forward and then tighten the bolts gradually, in the proper sequence to 9 ft. lbs. (13 Nm).

10. Coat the lip of a new oil seal with MP grease and drive it into the camshaft.

11. Set the knock pin on the exhaust camshaft so it is just above the edge of the cylinder head and engage the intake camshaft gear to the exhaust gear so the mark on each gear is in alignment. Roll the intake camshaft down onto the bearing journals while engaging the gears with each other.

12. Position the bearing caps over each journal on the intake camshaft so the arrows point forward and then tighten the bolts gradually, in the proper sequence to 9 ft. lbs. (13 Nm).

13. Remove the service bolt and install the No. 1 intake bear-

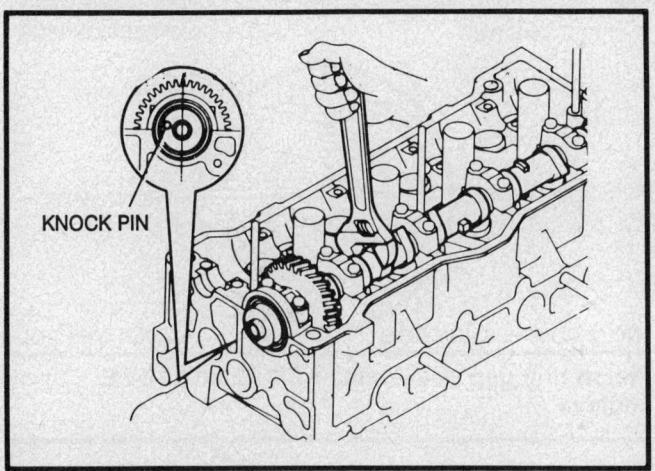

Turn the exhaust camshaft until the knockpin is here—4A-F and 4A-FE engines

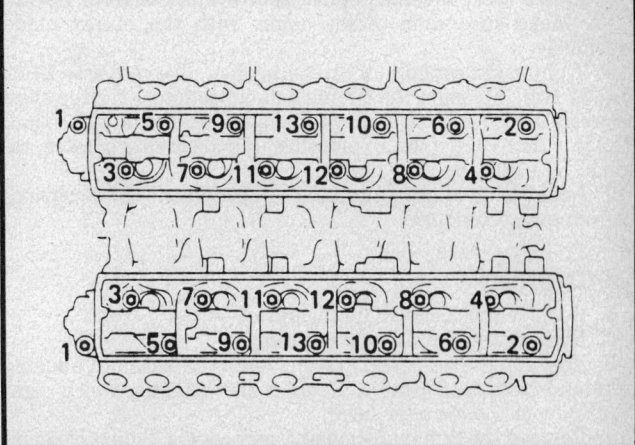

5M-FE engine camshaft housing bolt removal sequence. Loosen bolts gradually on three passes

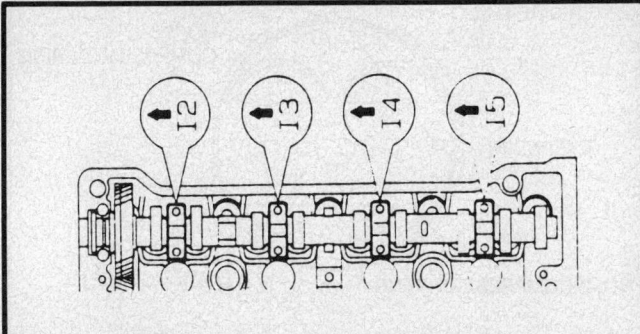

Intake camshaft bearing cap positioning—4A-F and 4A-FE engines

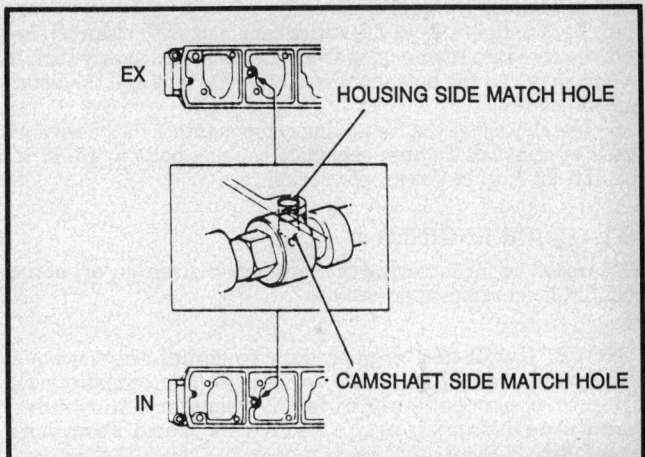

5M-GE engine camshaft housing torque sequence

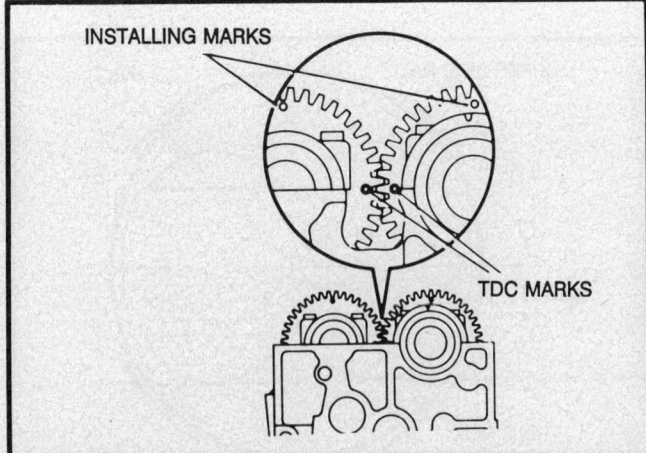

Rotate the camshaft one revolution from TDC to TDC and check that the marks are lined up—4A-F and 4A-FE engines

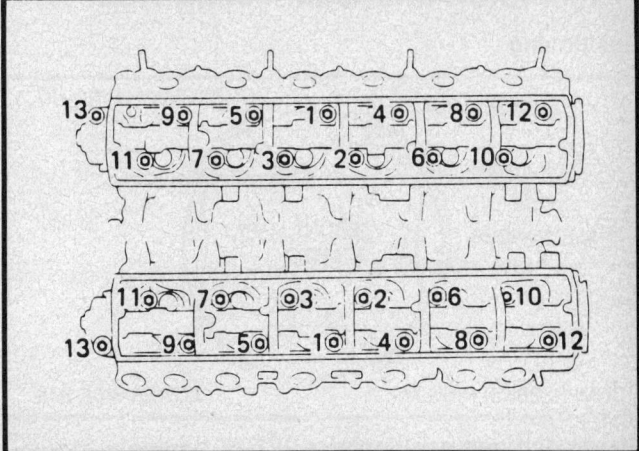

Before installing the camshaft housings, align the match hole on each No. 2 cam journal with the hole in the housing

ing cap. If it does not fit properly, pry the camshaft gear backwards until it does. Tighten the bolts to 9 ft. lbs. (13 Nm).

14. Rotate the camshafts 1 revolution (360 degrees) from TDC to TDC and check that the marks on the 2 gears are still aligned.

15. Install the camshaft timing pulley making sure the camshaft knock pins and the matchmarks are in alignment. Lock each camshaft and tighten the pulley bolts to 43 ft. lbs. (59 Nm).

16. Align the matchmarks made during removal and then install the timing belt on the camshaft pulley. Loosen the idler pulley set bolt. Make sure the timing belt meshing at the crankshaft pulley does not shift.

17. Rotate the crankshaft clockwise 2 revolutions from TDC to TDC. Make sure each pulley aligns with the marks made previously.

18. Tighten the set bolt on the timing belt idler pulley to 27 ft. lbs. (37 Nm). Measure the timing belt deflection at the top span between the 2 camshaft pulleys. It should deflect no more than 0.24 in. (7mm) at 4.4 lbs. of pressure. If deflection is greater, re-adjust by using the idler pulley.

19. Installation of the remaining components is the reverse of the removal procedure.

5M-GE ENGINE

1. Remove the 2 camshaft covers.

2. Remove the timing belt assembly.

3. Followin the sequence shown, loosen the camshaft housing nuts and bolts in 3 passes. Remove the housings (with camshafts) from the cylinder head.

4. Remove the camshaft housing rear covers. Squirt clean oil down around the cam journals in the housing, to lubricate the lobes, oil seals and bearings as the cam is removed. Begin to pull the camshaft out of the back of the housing slowly, turning and pulling. Remove the cam completely.

5. To install, lubricate the entire camshaft with clean oil. Insert the cam into the housing from the back, and slowly turn it and push it into the housing. Install new O-rings and the housing end covers.

6. Installation of the remaining components is in the reverse order of removal. Tighten camshaft housing bolts to 15–17 ft. lbs. (20–23 Nm) in the proper sequence.

ALL OTHER ENGINES

The procedure for removing the camshaft is given as part of the cylinder head removal procedure.

NOTE: It will not be necessary to completely remove the cylinder head in order to remove the camshaft(s). Therefore, proceed only as far as necessary, to remove the camshaft, with the cylinder head removal procedure.

Piston and Connecting Rod

Positioning

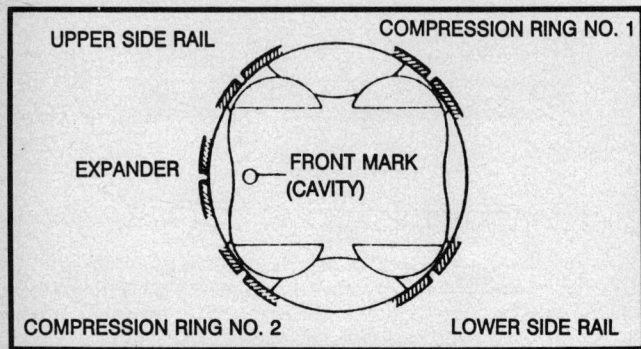

Piston ring gap positioning—2VZ-FE engine

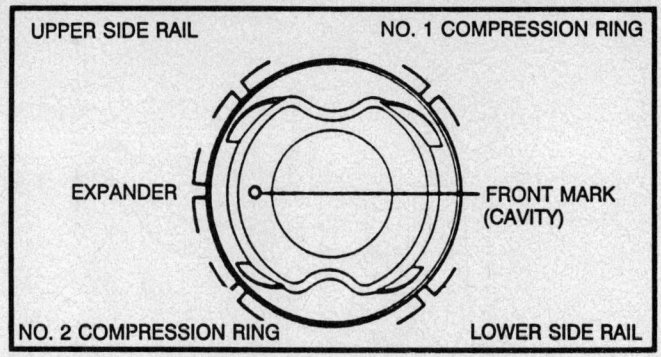

Piston ring gap positioning—3S-FE and 5S-FE engines

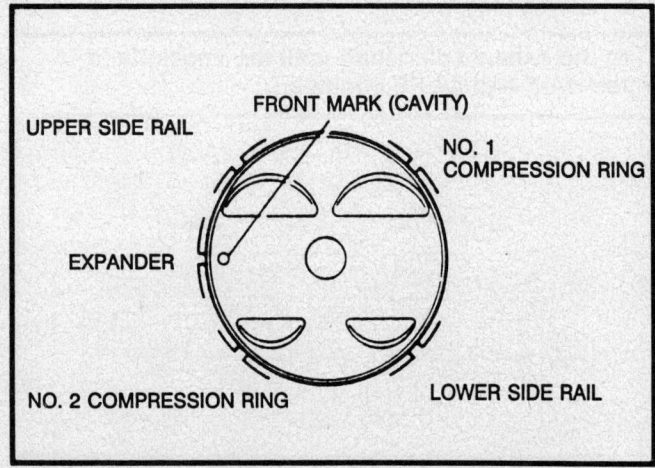

Piston ring gap positioning—3S-GE and 3S-GTE engines

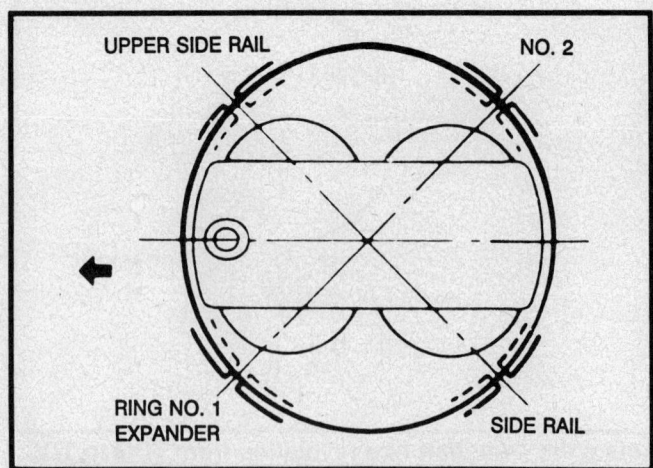

Piston ring gap positioning—4A-F, 4A-FE and 4A-GE (all) engines

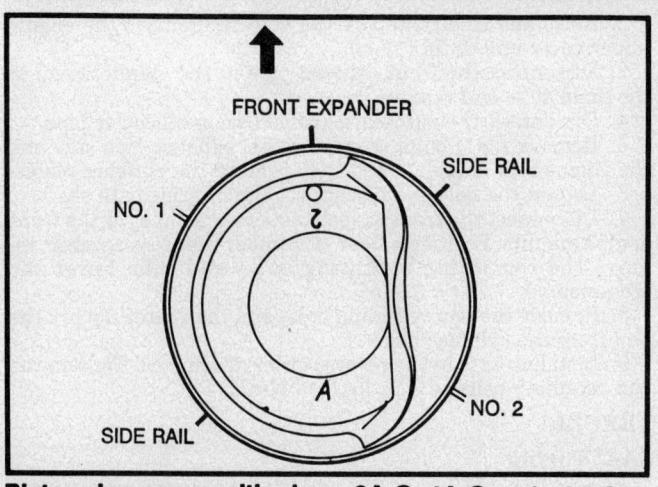

Piston ring gap positioning—3A-C, 4A-C and 4A-LC engines

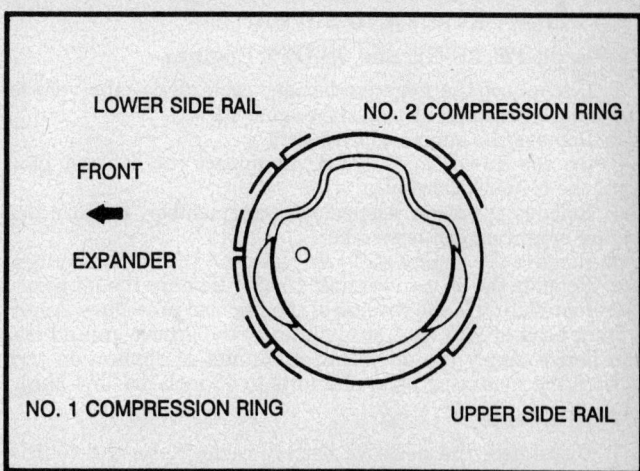

Piston ring gap positioning—3E and 3E-E engines

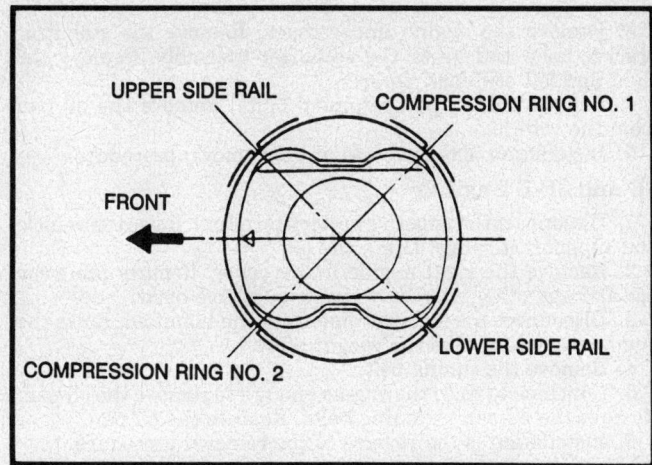

Piston ring gap positioning—5M-GE engine

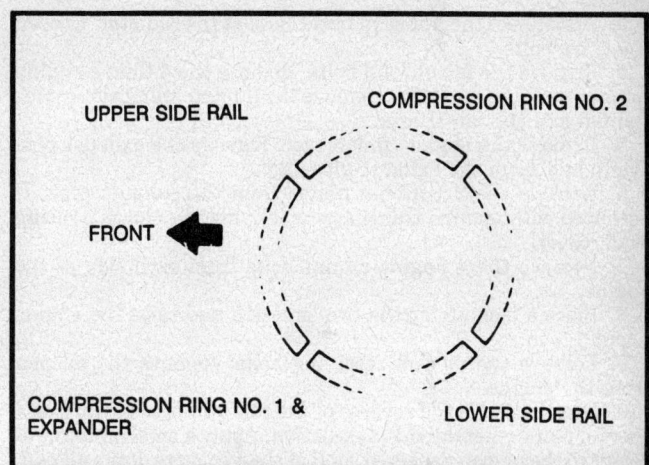

Piston ring gap positioning—4A-GZE engine

ENGINE LUBRICATION

Oil Pan

Removal and Installation

COROLLA

1. Disconnect the negative battery cable. Raise and support the vehicle safely. Drain the oil.
2. Remove the splash shield from under the engine.
3. Place a jack under the transmission to support it.
4. Remove the bolts which secure the engine rear supporting crossmember to the chassis. On the 4A-GE, remove the center mounting and stiffener plate.
5. Raise the jack under the transmission, slightly.
6. Remove the front exhaust pipe.
7. Remove the oil pan retaining bolts. Remove the oil pan from the vehicle. If the oil pan does not come out easily, it may be necessary to unbolt the rear engine mounts from the crossmember.

8. Installation is the reverse of the removal procedure. Tighten the oil pan bolts to 43 inch lbs. (4.9 Nm).

CAMRY

1. Disconnect the negative battery cable. Raise the vehicle and support it safely. Drain the oil.
2. Remove the engine undercover. Remove the dipstick.
3. On the 3S-FE, disconnect the exhaust pipe. Remove the suspension lower crossmember. Remove the engine mounting centermember. Remove the front engine mount insulator and bracket; 2VZ-FE only. Remove the stiffener plate.
4. Remove the oil pan retaining bolts. Remove the oil pan.
5. Installation is the reverse of the removal procedure. Clean the gasket mating surfaces. Always use a new pan gasket. Some engines were assembled using RTV gasket material in place of a conventional gasket. In that case, apply a thin (5mm) bead of RTV material to the groove around the pan mating surface. Assemble the pan within 15 minutes. Torque pan bolts to 48 inch lbs. (5.4 Nm). On the 2VZ-FE, tighten the pan bolts to 52 inch lbs. (5.9 Nm).

CRESSIDA, CELICA AND SUPRA

3S-FE, 5S-FE, 3S-GE and 3S-GTE Engines

1. Disconnect the negative battery cable. Raise the vehicle and support it safely. Drain the engine oil.

2. Remove the engine undercovers.

3. On the 3S-GE and 5S-FE, disconnect the exhaust pipe from the exhaust manifold.

4. Remove the lower suspension crossmember. Remove the engine mounting centermember.

5. Remove the engine stiffener plate and the oil level gauge.

6. Remove the oil pan retaining bolts. Remove the oil pan.

7. Installation is the reverse of the removal procedure. Apply a 5mm bead of RTV gasket material to the groove around the pan flange. Apply the oil within 3 minutes of application and tighten the mounting bolts and nuts to 48 inch lbs. (5.4 Nm).

5M-GE Engine

1. Disconnect the negative battery cable. Raise the vehicle and support it safely. Drain the oil and cooling system.

2. Remove the air cleaner assembly. Mark any disconnected lines and/or hoses for easy reassembly. Remove the oil level gauge.

3. Disconnect the upper radiator hose at the radiator. Loosen the drive belts.

4. Remove the fan shroud bolts. Remove the 4 fluid coupling flange attaching nuts, then remove the fluid coupling along with the fan and the fan shroud.

5. Remove the engine undercover. Remove the exhaust pipe clamp bolt from the exhaust pipe stay.

6. Remove the 2 stiffener plates from the exhaust pipe. If equipped with manual transmission, remove the clutch housing undercover.

7. Remove the 4 engine mount bolts from each side of the engine.

8. Place a jack under the transmission and raise the engine about 1¾ in.

9. Remove the oil pan retaining bolts. Remove the oil pan from the engine.

10. Installation is the reverse of the removal procedure. Use a new oil pan gasket during installation. Apply a small amount of sealer to the oil pan gasket at each of the 4 corners of the oil pan. Torque the oil pan fasteners to 57–82 inch lbs. (8–11 Nm).

SUPRA

7M-GE and 7M-GTE Engines

1. Disconnect the negative battery cable. Remove the hood.

2. Raise the vehicle and support it safely. Remove the engine under cover. Drain the engine oil.

3. If equipped with automatic transmission, remove the fluid cooler hose clamp.

4. Remove the No. 1 front suspension crossmember. Remove the front exhaust pipe bracket and stiffener plates.

5. On the 7M-GTE disconnect the engine oil cooler hose from the engine oil pan.

6. Remove the brake hose brackets and clips. Disconnect the intermediate shaft. Disconnect the stabilizer bar links from the lower control arms.

7. Properly support the engine assembly. Remove the engine mounting bolts. Remove the TEMS actuator assembly.

8. Remove the shock absorbers from the body. Disconnect the front suspension member.

9. Remove the oil pan retaining bolts. Remove the oil pan from the engine.

10. Installation is the reverse of the removal procedure. Tighten the mounting bolts to 9 ft. lbs. (13 Nm).

CRESSIDA

7M-GE Engine

1. Disconnect the negative battery cable and drain the cooling system.

2. Raise and safely support the vehicle. Remove the engine under cover and drain the oil.

3. Disconnect the front exhaust pipe at the manifold and at the main tube and remove it.

4. Disconnect the automatic transmission oil cooler pipe.

5. Remove the 9 bolts, ground strap, exhaust pipe stay and the engine rear end plate and then remove the stiffener plates.

6. Loosen the bolt and disconnect the intermediate shaft.

7. Disconnect the front suspension crossmember at the front engine mounts. Position a floor jack under the crossmember, remove the remaining mounting bolts and then lower the crossmember.

8. Remove the pan retaining bolts and then carefully pry the pan from the cylinder block.

9. Installation is in the reverse order of removal. Tighten the pan retaining bolts to 9 ft. lbs. (13 Nm).

TERCEL

3A-C Engine

1. Disconnect the negative battery cable. Drain the cooling system. Remove the radiator.

2. Raise the vehicle and support it safely. Drain the engine oil.

3. Remove the engine under cover. Remove the stabilizer bracket bolts and lower the stabilizer assembly. Remove the right and left stiffener plates.

4. Remove the oil pan retaining bolts. Remove the oil pan from the vehicle.

5. Installation is the reverse of the removal procedure.

3E and 3E-E Engines

1. Disconnect the negative battery terminal. Raise the vehicle and suppport it safely. Drain the oil.

2. Remove the right engine under cover. Remove the sway bar and any other necessary steering linkage parts.

3. Disconnect the exhaust pipe from the manifold. Raise the engine enough to take the weight off it.

4. Remove the timing belt.

5. Continue to raise the engine enough to remove the oil pan. Remove the oil pan retaining bolts. Remove the oil pan.

6. Installation is the reverse of the removal procedure.

MR2

4A-GELC and 4A-GZE Engines

1. Disconnect the negative battery cable. Raise and support the vehicle safely. Drain the engine oil.

2. Remove the exhaust manifold pipe. Remove the timing belt. Remove the crankshaft timing pulley.

3. Support the weight of the engine with a floor jack and then remove the right side engine mount.

4. Remove the oil pan retaining bolts. Remove the oil pan..

5. Installation is in the reverse order of removal. Apply a 5mm bead of RTV gasket material to the groove around the pan flange. Apply the oil pan within 3 minutes of application and tighten the mounting bolts and nuts to 43 inch lbs. (6 Nm).

3S-GTE and 5S-FE Engines

1. Disconnect the negative battery cable.

2. Drain the engine oil and remove the engine under covers.

3. Remove the right engine hood side panel.

4. Remove the brace that runs across the struts.

5. If equipped with cruise control, remove the cruise control actuator assembly and disconnect the accelerator linkage.

6. Remove the front exhaust pipe.

7. On 3S-GTE with air conditioning, unbolt the compressor and move it aside. Leave the refrigerant lines connected. On 5S-FE, remove the air conditioner idler pulley.

8. On 3S-GTE, remove the catalytic converter and the intercooler.

9. Remove the stiffener plate.

10. On 3S-GTE, disconnect the turbocharger outlet hose where it connects to the oil pan.

11. Remove the dipstick.

12. Remove the oil pan 17 bolts and 2 nuts that attach the oil pan to the block.

13. Insert a suitable seal cutting tool between the oil pan and the block. Work the tool around the pan to break the sealant. Remove the oil pan.

14. Installation is the reverse of the removal procedure. Scrape the oil pan and block surfaces to remove the oil sealant. Apply a 5mm bead of RTV gasket material to the groove around the pan flange. Apply the oil pan within 5 minutes of application and tighten the mounting bolts and nuts to 43 inch lbs. (6 Nm).

Oil Pump

Removal and Installation

2VZ-FE, 3E, 3E-E AND 3S-FE ENGINES

1. Remove the oil pan. Remove the oil strainer. On the 3E, remove the dipstick.

2. Raise the engine using a chain hoist. Remove the timing belt and pulleys.

3. On the 2VZ-FE, remove the alternator and the air conditioning compressor and bracket. Do not disconnect the refrigerant lines.

4. Remove the oil pump from the engine.

5. Installation is the reverse of the removal procedure.

3A-C, 3S-GE, 3S-GTE (EXCEPT MR2), 4A-F AND 4A-GE ENGINES

1. Remove the fan shroud. Raise and support the vehicle safely.

2. Drain the oil. On the Tercel, drain the coolant and remove the radiator.

3. Remove the oil pan and the oil strainer. Remove the oil pan baffle plate on the 4A-GE. Remove the crankshaft pulley and the timing belt. Remove the oil dipstick guide and then the dipstick.

4. Remove the mounting bolts and then use a rubber mallet to carefully tap the oil pump body from the cylinder block.

5. To install, position a new gasket on the cylinder block.

6. Position the oil pump on the block so the teeth on the pump drive gear are engaged with the teeth of the crankshaft gear.

7. Installation of the remaining components is the reverse of the removal procedure.

3S-GTE (1990–91 MR2) AND 5S-FE (1990–91 CELICA AND MR2) ENGINES

1. Disconnect the negative battery cable.

2. Drain the engine oil.

3. Remove the oil pan.

4. Remove the oil pump strainer and baffle plate.

5. Connect a suitable lifting device to the engine and raise the engine a small amount.

6. Remove the timing belt.

7. Remove the No. 2 idler pulley, crankshaft timing pulley and oil pump pulley.

8. Remove the oil pump retaining bolts.

9. Remove the oil pump and gasket by carefully tapping on the outside of the oil pump body. Discard the gasket.

NOTE: One of the oil pump bolts is longer than the rest. Make sure this bolt is identified so it may be installed in the original location.

10. Installation is the reverse of he removal procedure. Use a new oil pump gasket. On 3S-GTE, torque the oil pump bolts to 69 inch lbs. (8 Nm). On 5S-FE, torque the bolts to 82 inch lbs. (9.3 Nm).

ALL OTHER ENGINES

1. Remove the oil pan.

2. Unbolt the oil pump retaining bolts. Remove the oil pump from the engine.

3. Installation is the reverse of the removal procedure.

Checking

1. Remove the oil pump cover.

2. Remove the oil pump cover O-ring.

3. Using a feeler gauge, check the clearance bewteen the drive rotor and the oil pump body. The clearance should be 0.0039–0.0063 in. (0.1–0.16mm) and should not exceed 0.0079 in. (0.2mm). If the clearance exceeds the maximum specification, replace the rotors as a set or replace the entire oil pump assembly.

4. Using a feeler gauge, check the clearance between the drive and driven rotors. The clearance should be 0.0016–0.0063 in. (0.040–0.160mm) and should not 0.0079 in. (0.2mm) maximum. If the clearance exceeds the maximum specification, replace the rotors as a set or replace the entire oil pump assembly.

5. Inspect the relief valve for proper operation.

6. Replace the oil pump and front crankshaft seals.

7. Install a new O-ring into the groove in the oil pump body.

8. Install the oil pump cover and torque the cover retaining screws to 78 inch lbs. (9 Nm).

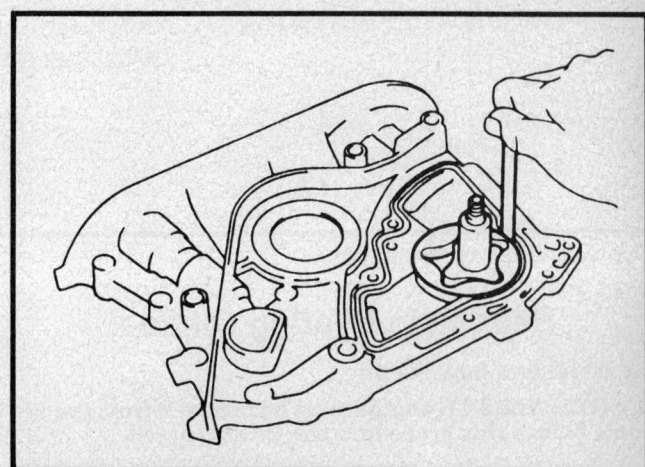

Checking rotor-to-body clearance

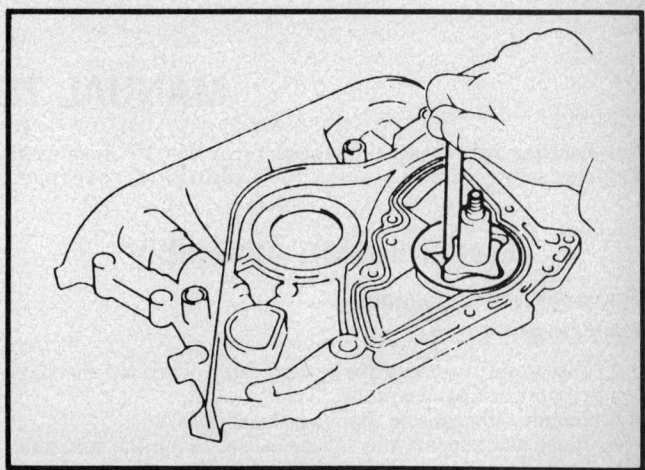

Checking rotor tip clearance.

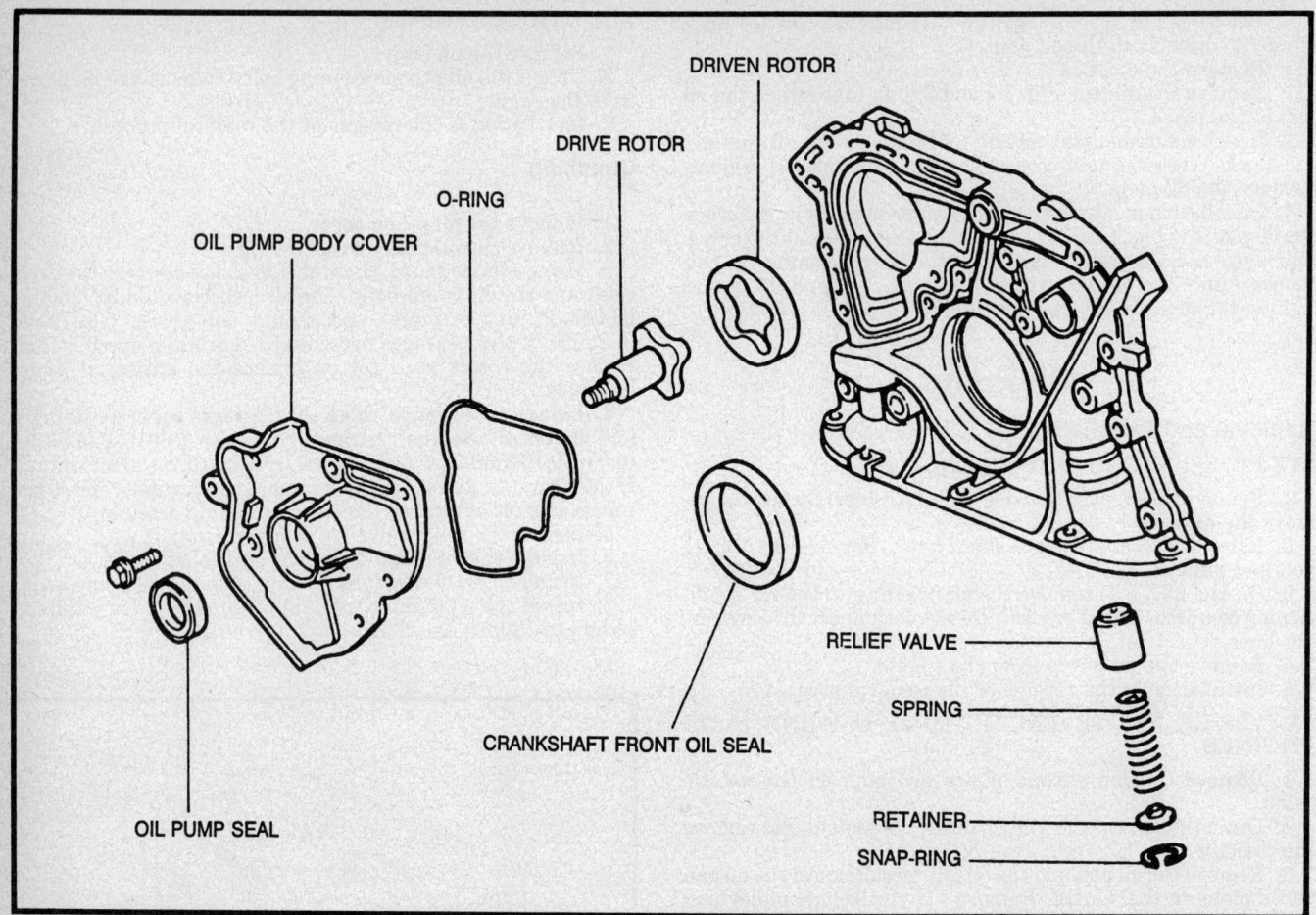

Typical oil pump assembly

Rear Main Bearing Oil Seal

Removal and Installation

NOTE: The 3A-C engine must be removed from the vehicle before this procedure can be attempted.

1. Remove the transmission or transaxle.
2. Remove the clutch cover assembly and flywheel.
3. Remove the oil seal retaining plate, complete with the oil seal.
4. Using a suitable tool pry the old seal from the retaining plate. Be careful not to damage the plate.
5. Install the new seal, carefully, by using a block of wood to drift it into place. Do not damage the seal as a leak will result.
6. Lubricate the lips of the seal with multipurpose grease. Installation is the reverse of removal.

MANUAL TRANSMISSION

For further information, please refer to "Professional Transmission Repair Manual" for additional coverage.

Transmission Assembly

Removal and Installation

1987 COROLLA

1. Disconnect the negative battery cable. Turn the distributor to gain working clearance.
2. Remove the console. Remove the shift lever.
3. Raise and support the vehicle safely. Drain the transmission fluid. Remove the front exhaust pipe.
4. Disconnect the driveshaft flange from the flange on the differential. Remove the center support bearing and the heat insulator assembly. Remove the driveshaft.
5. Disconnect the speedometer cable. Disconnect the back-up light switch electrical connector.
6. Remove the clutch release cylinder. Remove the starter.
7. Support the engine and the transmission using the proper equipment. Remove the rear crossmember.
8. Remove the stiffener plate. Remove the transmission to engine retaining bolts. Carefully remove the transmission from the vehicle.
9. Installation is the reverse of the removal procedure.

1987 CRESSIDA

NOTE: Manual transmissions are not available in 1988-90 Cressidas.

1. Disconnect the negative battery cable. Drain the radiator and remove the upper radiator hose.

2. Remove the console. Remove the shift lever assembly.

3. Raise and support the vehicle safely. Drain the transmission fluid.

4. If equipped with power steering, remove the steering gear housing. It may be possible to remove the gear and properly suspend it aside without disconnecting the fluid lines.

5. Remove the driveshaft. Disconnect the exhaust pipe from the tailpipe. Remove the clamp from the transmission case.

6. Disconnect the speedometer cable. Disconnect the back-up light switch electrical connector.

7. Remove the clutch release cylinder. Remove the starter.

8. Support the engine and the transmission using the proper equipment. remove the rear crossmember assembly.

9. Remove the transmission-to-engine retaining bolts. Carefully lower the transmission to the floor.

10. Installation is the reverse of the removal procedure.

SUPRA

1. Disconnect the negative battery cable. Remove the center console trim panel. Remove the shift lever.

2. Raise and support the vehicle safely. Drain the transmission fluid. Remove the driveshaft.

3. Disconnect the front exhaust pipe from the tailpipe. Remove the front exhaust pipe.

4. Disconnect the speedometer cable. Disconnect the back-up light switch electrical connector. If equipped with ABS, disconnect the rear speed sensor electrical connector.

5. Remove the clutch release cylinder. Remove the starter assembly.

6. Support the engine and the transmission using the proper equipment. Remove the transmission support crossmember.

7. Remove the transmission mounting bolts. Remove the flywheel housing bolts. Carefully, move the transmission rearward, down, and out of the vehicle.

NOTE: On turbocharged vehicles, it will be necessary to remove the transmission with the clutch cover and disc. To do this pull the release fork through the left clutch housing hole and then remove the assembly.

8. Installation is the reverse of the removal procedure. Tighten the mounting bolts to 29 ft. lbs. (39 Nm).

Linkage Adjustment

Manual transmission linkage adjustments are neither possible or necessary.

MANUAL TRANSAXLE

For further information, please refer to "Professional Transmission Repair Manual" for additional coverage.

Transaxle Assembly

Removal and Installation

TERCEL

Sedan (2WD)

1. Disconnect the negative battery cable. If equipped with cruise control remove the battery and cruise control actuator with mounting bracket.

2. Remove the clutch release cylinder and tube clamp. Disconnect the back-up light switch electrical connector.

3. Disconnect the transaxle shift control cables. Remove the selecting bellcrank along with the bracket from the transaxle case. Remove the upper transaxle-to-engine retaining bolts.

4. Raise the vehicle and support it safely. Remove the under covers. Drain the transaxle fluid. Disconnect the speedometer cable.

5. Disconnect both halfshafts. Remove the engine rear mounting brackets. Remove the starter assembly.

6. Support the engine and transaxle assembly using the proper equipment. Disconnect the left engine mounting.

7. Remove the remaining engine-to-transaxle retaining bolts. Carefully remove the transaxle assembly from the vehicle.

8. Installation is the reverse of the removal procedure. Tighten the transaxle-to-engine bolts to 47 ft. lbs. (64 Nm)—A; 34 ft. lbs. (46 Nm)—B; and 65 inch lbs. (7.4 Nm)—C. Tighten the front engine mount bracket bolts to 43 ft. lbs. (58 Nm). Tighten the rear engine mount bracket bolts to 21 ft. lbs. (28 Nm). Tighten the left engine mount bolts to 35 ft. lbs. (48 Nm) and the front and rear mount bolts to 47 ft. lbs. (64 Nm).

1987 Wagon (2WD)

1. Disconnect the negative battery cable. Remove the air cleaner assembly. Remove the upper transaxle-to-engine retaining bolts.

2. Remove both halfshaft assemblies.

3. Raise and support the vehicle safely. Drain the transaxle fluid. Disconnect the clutch cable.

4. On some vehicles, it will be necessary to remove the catalytic converter air inlet pipe. Remove the front exhaust pipe.

5. Disconnect the selector rod. Disconnect the shift lever housing rod. Disconnect the speedometer cable.

6. Disconnect the back-up light switch electrical connector. Remove the right side stiffener plate.

7. Support the engine and transaxle assembly using the proper equipment. Remove the rear crossmember. Remove the remaining engine-to-transaxle retaining bolts.

8. Carefully remove the transaxle from the vehicle.

9. Installation is the reverse of the removal procedure. Tighten the 14mm transaxle-to-engine bolts to 29 ft. lbs. (39 Nm) and the 17mm bolts to 43 ft. lbs. (59 Nm). Tighten the rear support member bolts to 70 ft. lbs. (95 Nm) and the right stiffener plate bolts to 29 ft. lbs. (39 Nm).

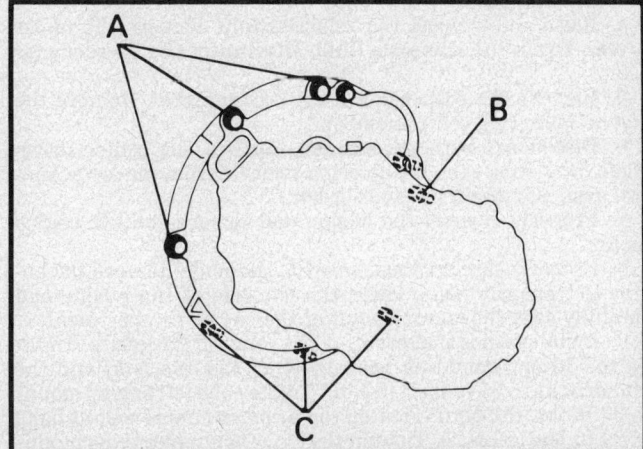

Manual transaxle mounting bolt locations on Tercel (2WD)

1987–88 Wagon (AWD)

1. Disconnect the negative battery cable. Remove the air cleaner assembly.

2. Remove the console. Remove the shift lever assembly. Remove the upper engine-to-transaxle retaining bolts.

3. Raise and support the vehicle safely. Drain the transaxle fluid. Remove both halfshafts.

4. On some vehicles, it will be necessary to remove the catalytic converter air inlet pipe. Remove the front exhaust pipe.

5. Disconnect the selector rod from the rear drive shift link lever. Disconnect the speedometer cable. Remove the right stiffener plate.

6. Disconnect the back-up light switch electrical connector. Disconnect the AWD and the low gear indicator switch electrical connectors.

7. Support the engine and the transaxle using the proper equipment. Remove the remaining transaxle-to-engine retaining bolts. Remove the rear crossmember assembly.

NOTE: Properly position a piece of wood between the engine and the firewall so the assembly will not make contact with the power brake booster when it is removed.

8. Carefully remove the transaxle assembly from the vehicle.

9. Installation is the reverse of the removal procedure. Tighten the 14mm transaxle-to-engine bolts to 29 ft. lbs. (39 Nm) and the 17mm bolts to 43 ft. lbs. (59 Nm). Tighten the rear support member bolts to 70 ft. lbs. (95 Nm) and the right stiffener plate bolts to 29 ft. lbs. (39 Nm).

COROLLA

2WD (Except C52 Transaxle)

1. Disconnect the negative battery cable. Remove the air cleaner assembly.

2. Disconnect the back-up light switch electrical connector. Remove the speedometer cable. Disconnect the transmission control cables.

3. Raise the vehicle and support safely. Remove the water inlet from the transaxle. Remove the clutch release cylinder.

4. Remove the under cover. Remove the front and rear mounting. Remove the engine mounting centermember.

5. Disconnect the halfshaft from the transaxle. Disconnect the steering knuckle from the lower control arm. Pull the steering knuckle outward and remove the left halfshaft.

6. Remove the starter. Disconnect the ground strap. Remove the No. 2 engine rear plate.

7. Support the engine and the transaxle using the proper equipment. Remove the left engine mounting.

8. Remove the engine-to-transaxle retaining bolts. Carefully remove the transaxle assembly from the vehicle.

9. Installation is the reverse of the removal procedure. Tighten the 12mm engine-to-transaxle bolts to 47 ft. lbs. (64 Nm) and the 10mm bolts to 34 ft. lbs. (46 Nm). Tighten the left engine mount bolts to 38 ft. lbs. (52 Nm). Tighten the front and rear engine mount bolts and the engine mounting centermember bolts to 29 ft. lbs. (39 Nm).

2WD (C52 Transaxle)

1. Disconnect the negative battery cable. Drain the radiator. Remove the air cleaner assembly. Remove the engine cooling fan assembly.

2. Disconnect the oxygen sensor electrical connector and the back-up light switch connector.

3. Remove the clutch release cylinder. It may be possible to leave the fluid lines attached to the cylinder.

4. Disconnect the water inlet from the transaxle. Disconnect the transaxle control cables. Disconnect the speedometer cable. Disconnect the ground cable.

5. Remove the starter. Remove the engine under covers. Remove the front exhaust pipe.

6. Disconnect the front and rear engine mountings. Remove the engine mounting centermember.

7. Remove the left front wheel. Loosen the 6 nuts while depressing the brake pedal. Disconnect the halfshaft from the side gear shaft. Disconnect the lower ball joint from the lower control arm. Pull the shock absorber outward. Remove the halfshaft.

8. Support the engine and the transaxle assembly using the proper equipment. Remove the No. 2 engine rear plate. Remove the left engine mounting.

9. Remove the transaxle retaining bolts. Carefully remove the transaxle assembly from the vehicle.

10. Installation is the reverse of the removal procedure. Tighten the 12mm engine-to-transaxle bolts to 47 ft. lbs. (64 Nm) and the 10mm bolts to 34 ft. lbs. (46 Nm). Tighten the left engine mount bolts to 38 ft. lbs. (52 Nm). Tighten the front and rear engine mount bolts and the engine mounting centermember bolts to 29 ft. lbs. (39 Nm).

AWD

1. Remove the engine and transaxle as an assembly.

2. Remove the rear end plate.

3. Disconnect the vacuum lines and then remove the transfer case vacuum actuator.

4. Remove the right and center transfer case stiffener plates.

5. Pull the transaxle out slowly until there is approximately 2.36–3.15 in. (60–80mm) clearance between the transaxle and the engine.

6. Turn the output shaft in a clockwise direction and then remove the transaxle.

7. Install the transaxle assembly to the engine and tighten the 10mm bolts to 34 ft. lbs. (46 Nm). Tighten the 12mm bolts to 47 ft. lbs. (64 Nm).

8. Tighten the 8mm stiffener plate bolts to 14 ft. lbs. (20 Nm) and the 10mm bolts to 27 ft. lbs. (37 Nm).

9. Tighten the rear end plate mounting bolts to 17 ft. lbs. (23 Nm).

10. Install the engine/transaxle assembly.

CAMRY

2WD

1. Disconnect the negative battery cable. Remove the clutch release cylinder and tube clamp. Remove the clutch tube bracket.

2. Disconnect the control cables. Disconnect the back-up light switch electrical connector. Remove the ground strap.

3. Remove the starter assembly. Remove the transaxle upper mounting bolts.

4. Raise and support the vehicle safely. Remove the under covers. Drain the transaxle fluid. Disconnect the speedometer cable.

5. Remove the suspension lower crossmember. Remove the engine mounting centermember.

6. Disconnect both driveshafts. Remove the center driveshaft. Disconnect the left steering knuckle from the lower control arm. Remove the stabilizer bar.

7. Properly support the engine and remove the left engine mount.

8. Properly support the transaxle assembly. Remove the engine-to-transaxle bolts, lower the left side of the engine and carefully ease the transaxle out of the engine compartment.

9. Installation is the reverse of the removal procedure. Tighten the 12mm mounting bolts to 47 ft. lbs. (64 Nm) and the 10mm bolts to 34 ft. lbs. (46 Nm). Tighten the left engine mount to 38 ft. lbs. (52 Nm). Tighten the 4 center engine mount bolts to 29 ft. lbs. (39 Nm). Tighten the front and rear engine mount bolts to 32 ft. lbs. (43 Nm). Tighten the lower crossmember bolts to 153 ft. lbs. (207 Nm)–4 outer bolts; and, 29 ft. lbs. (39 Nm)–2 inner bolts.

AWD

1. Remove the engine/transaxle assembly.
2. Remove the transfer case stiffener plate and the exhaust pipe front brake.
3. Remove the left stiffener plate and the front engine mount.
4. Remove the left engine mount bracket and then separate the transaxle from the engine.
5. Installation is in the reverse order of removal. Tighten the 12mm transaxle-to-engine mounting bolts to 47 ft. lbs. (64 Nm) and the 10mm bolts to 34 ft. lbs. (46 Nm).

CELICA

2WD

1. Disconnect the negative battery cable. On some vehicles, it may be necessary to remove the battery. Remove the air cleaner assembly.
2. Remove the clutch tube bracket. Disconnect the back-up light switch at the transaxle. Disconnect the speedometer and the engine ground strap.
3. Disconnect the transaxle control cable and position them aside.
4. Unbolt the clutch release cylinder. It may be possible to position it aside with the hydraulic line still attached.
5. Remove the upper transaxle retaining bolts. Raise the vehicle and support safely. Remove the engine undercover. Drain the transaxle fluid.
6. Disconnect the exhaust pipe from the manifold. Remove the lower suspension crossmember. Remove the starter assembly.
7. Properly support the engine and transaxle assembly. Remove the front and rear transaxle mounts. Remove the center engine mount.
8. Disconnect both halfshafts at the transaxle. Unbolt the steering knuckle from the suspension arm and pull it outward. Remove the left halfshaft.
9. On some vehicles, remove the No. 2 rear engine plate. With the engine properly supported remove the left engine mount.
10. Remove the engine-to-transaxle bolts, lower the left side of the engine and carefully ease the transaxle out of the engine compartment.
11. Installation is the reverse of the removal procedure. Tighten the 12mm engine-to-transaxle bolts to 47 ft. lbs. (64 Nm) and the 10mm bolts to 34 ft. lbs. (46 Nm). Tighten the left engine mount bolts to 38 ft. lbs. (52 Nm) Tighten the centermember bolts and the front and rear engine mount bolts to 29 ft. lbs. (39 Nm).

AWD

1. Remove the engine and transaxle assembly.
2. Separate the transaxle from the engine.
3. Installation is in the reverse order of removal. Tighten the 12mm engine-to-transaxle bolts to 47 ft. lbs. (64 Nm) and the 10mm bolts to 34 ft. lbs. (46 Nm). Tighten the left engine mount bolts to 38 ft. lbs. (52 Nm) Tighten the centermember bolts and the front and rear engine mount bolts to 29 ft. lbs. (39 Nm).

MR2

1. Disconnect the negative battery cable. Drain the radiator. Raise and suport the vehicle safely. Drain the transaxle fluid.
2. Disconnect the back-up light switch and the speedometer cable at the transaxle. On 4A-GZE engine, remove the intercooler.
3. Loosen the mounting bolts and remove the water inlet from the transaxle.
4. Remove the engine undercover. Remove the fuel tank protector.
5. Disconnect the transaxle control cables at the transaxle and position them aside.
6. Remove the water hose clamp from the control cable bracket and then remove the No. 2 control cable bracket.
7. Remove the main control cable bracket and the clutch release cylinder. Position these components aside.
8. Disconnect the exhaust pipe from the manifold, remove the pipe bracket from the chassis and then remove the exhaust pipe assembly from the bracket.
9. Remove the transaxle protector. Disconnect the halfshaft from the side gear shaft. Remove the starter assembly.
10. Remove the No. 2 engine rear plate. Remove the front and rear engine mounts from the body.
11. Properly support the engine and remove the left engine mount.
12. Properly support the transaxle assembly. Remove the engine-to-transaxle bolts, lower the left side of the engine and carefully ease the transaxle out of the engine compartment.
13. Remove the side gear shaft from the transaxle.
14. Installation is the reverse of the removal procedure. Tighten the 12mm engine-to-transaxle bolts to 47 ft. lbs. (64 Nm) and the 10mm bolts to 34 ft. lbs. (46 Nm). On 1987–89 vehicles, tighten the left and rear engine mounts to 38 ft. lbs. (52 Nm). On 1990–91 vehicles, tighten the front engine mounting bracket thru-bolt to 71 ft. lbs. (96 Nm) and the rear engine mounting thru-bolt to 64 ft. lbs. (87 Nm).

Linkage Adjustment

Manual transmission linkage adjustments are neither possible or necessary.

CLUTCH

Clutch Assembly

Removal and Installation

1. Disconnect the negative battery cable.
2. Remove the transmission or transaxle assembly from the vehicle.

NOTE: On some 1987–90 Supra's, the clutch assembly is removed along with the transmission. On the 1989–91 Corolla (AWD) and the 1988–91 Camry and Celica AWD, the engine and transaxle are removed from the vehicle as an assembly.

3. Matcmark the cluch cover to the flywheel.
4. Remove the clutch pressure plate retaining bolts small amounts in a criss-cross pattern to relieve the clutch disc spring tension.
5. Remove the clutch cover.
6. Remove the clutch disc.
7. Remove the retaining clip and withdraw the release bearing.
8. remove the relase fork and boot assembly.

To install:

9. Using a suitable clutch disc alignment tool, install the clutch disc onto the flywheel.

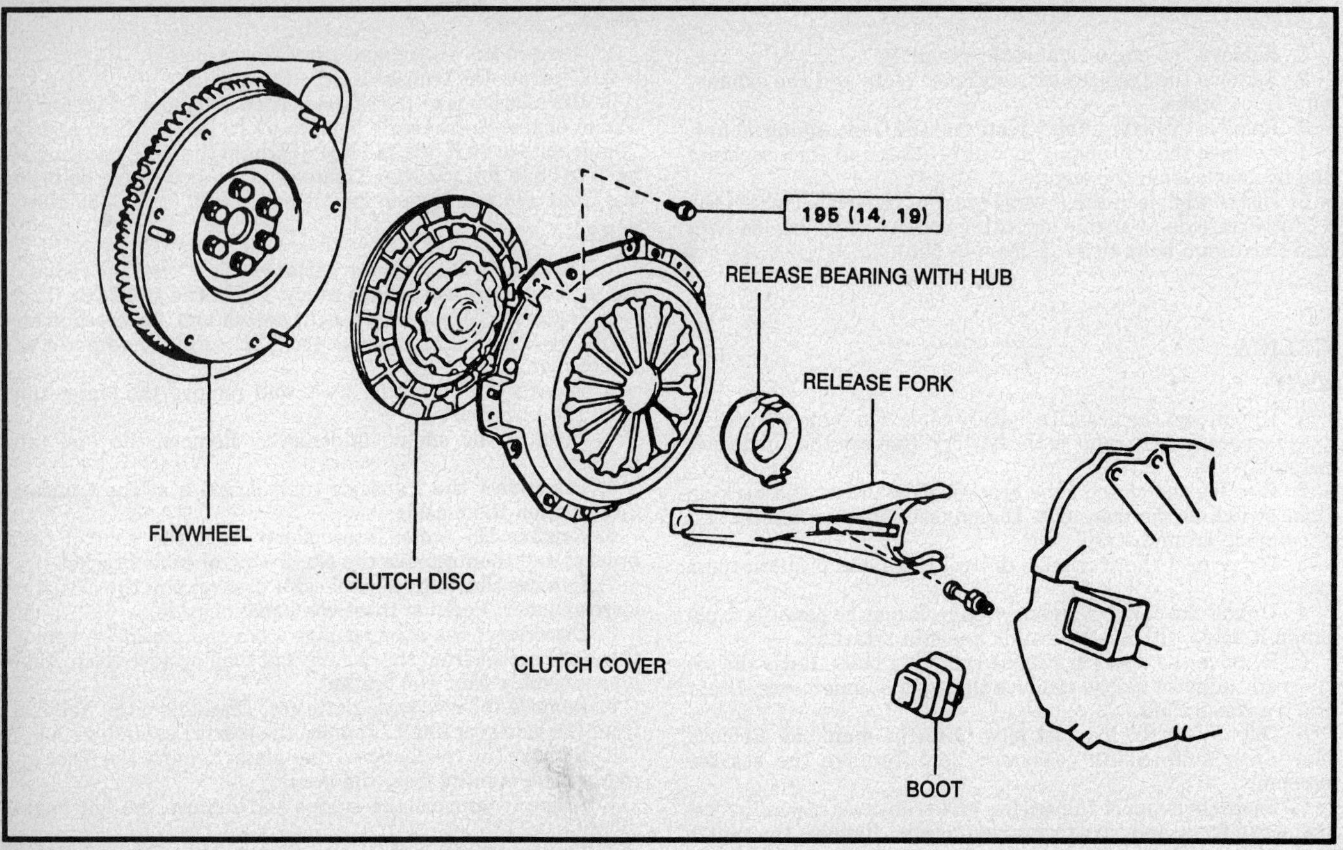

195 (14, 19)

RELEASE BEARING WITH HUB

RELEASE FORK

FLYWHEEL

CLUTCH DISC

CLUTCH COVER

BOOT

Typical clutch assembly

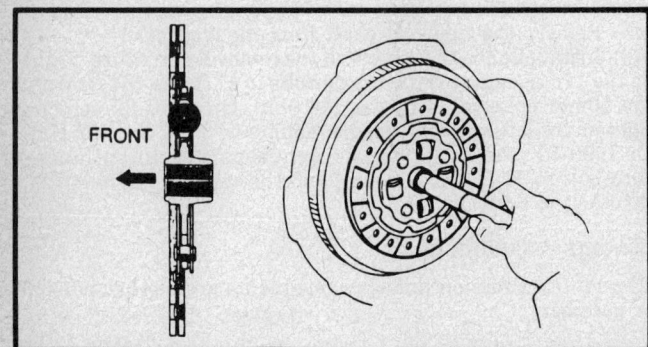

FRONT

Use a clutch pilot tool to center the clutch disc on the flywheel

10. Position the clutch cover onto the flywheel and align the matchmarks.
11. Install the clutch cover retainig bolts. Torque the bolts in a criss-cross pattern to 14 ft. lbs. (19 Nm).
12. Lubricate the release fork pivot and contact points, release bearing, bearing hub and input shaft spline surfaces with a suitable molybdenum disulphide lithium based or multi-purpose grease.
13. Install the boot, relase fork, hub and bearing assemblies.
14. Install the transmission or transaxle.

Pedal Height/Free-Play Adjustment
EXCEPT 1987–88 TERCEL WAGON

1. Adjust the clearance between the master cylinder piston and the pushrod to specification by loosening the pushrod lock-

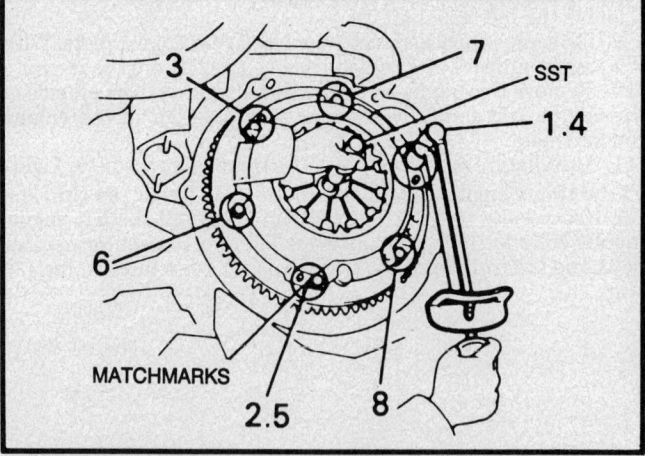

3   7   SST

1.4

6

MATCHMARKS

2.5   8

Tighten the clutch cover retaining bolts in a criss-cross pattern

nut and rotating the pushrod while depressing the clutch pedal lightly.
2. Tighten the locknut when finished the adjustment.
3. Adjust the release cylinder free-play by loosening the release cylinder pushrod locknut and rotating the pushrod until proper specification is obtained.
4. Measure the clutch pedal free-play after performing the adjustments. If it fails to fall within specification, repeat the procedure. Pedal free-play specifications are as follows:
   1987 Tercel—0.08–0.98 in. (2–28mm)
   1988–91 Tercel—0.2–0.59 in. (5–15mm)

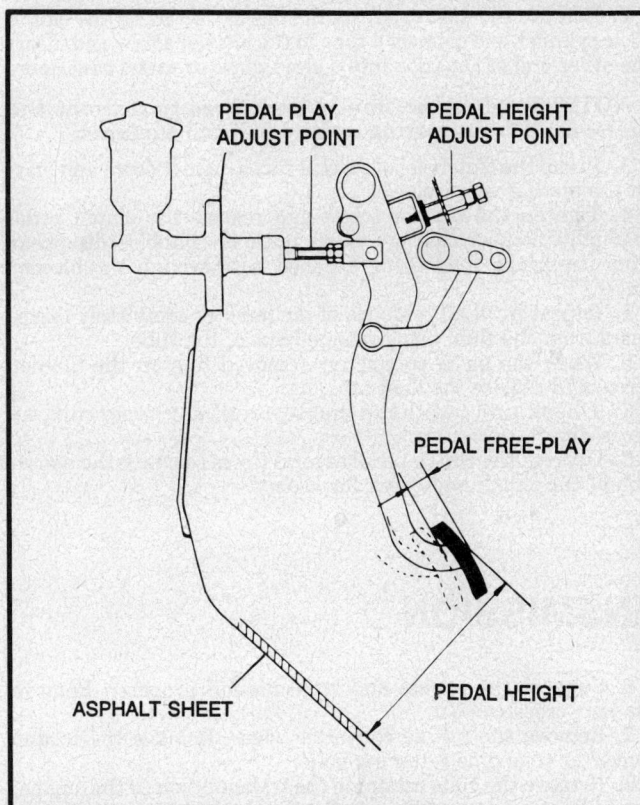

PEDAL PLAY ADJUST POINT

PEDAL HEIGHT ADJUST POINT

PEDAL FREE-PLAY

ASPHALT SHEET

PEDAL HEIGHT

Typical clutch pedal adjustment points

1987 Corolla (RWD W/4A-LC)—0.51–0.91 in. (13–23mm)
1987 Corolla (RWD W/4A-GE)—0.2–0.59 in. (5–15mm)
1987 Corolla (FWD)—0.28–0.67 in. (7–17mm)
1988–91 Corolla—0.2–0.59 in. (5–15mm)
Celica—0.2–0.59 in. (5–15mm)
Supra—0.2–0.59 in. (5–15mm)
1987 Cressida—0.2–0.59 in. (5–15mm)
MR2—0.2–0.59 in. (5–15mm).

1987–88 TERCEL WAGON

1. Depress the clutch pedal several times.
2. Depress the clutch pedal until resistance is felt. Free-play should be within specification.
3. Check the clutch release sector pawl. Six notches should remain between the pawl and the end of the sector. If less than 6 notches, replace the clutch disc. If the clutch disc has been replaced, the pawl should be 3–10 notches.
4. To obtain either the used or new position on the Starlet, change the position of the E-ring.

Clutch Cable

Removal and Installation

1987–88 TERCEL WAGON

1. Disconnect the negative battery cable.
2. Disconnect the sector tension spring from the clutch pedal.
3. Disconnect the clutch release cable from the release fork lever.
4. Turn the release sector toward the front side and disconnect the release cable from the release sector. Remove the release cable.
5. Installation is the reverse of the removal procedure.

Clutch Master Cylinder

Removal and Installation

REAR WHEEL DRIVE VEHICLES

1. Disconnect the negative battery cable. Remove the pushrod clevis pin and clip.

NOTE: On some vehicles, it will be necessary to remove the under dash panel in order to gain access to the pushrod clevis pin.

2. Disconnect the fluid line.
3. Unbolts and remove the clutch master cylinder.
4. Installation is the reverse of the removal procedure. Bleed the system.

FRONT WHEEL DRIVE VEHICLES

1. Disconnect the negative battery cable.
2. On the Tercel, remove the reservoir tank from the clutch master cylinder.
3. On Celica with 3S-GTE engine, remove the brace that runs across the struts. On the MR-2, remove the spare tire guard and luggage compartment trim cover.
4. Remove the ABS control relay, if equipped.
5. Remove the pushrod clevis pin and clip.

NOTE: On some vehicles it will be necessary to remove the under dash panel in order to gain access to the pushrod clevis pin.

6. On the 1988–91 Corolla (4A-GE) remove the brake booster.
7. Disconnect the fluid line and plug the end of the line to prevent leakage.
8. Unbolt and remove the clutch master cylinder.
9. Installation is the reverse of the removal procedure. Bleed the system.

Clutch Slave Cylinder

Removal and Installation

EXCEPT 1990–91 MR2

1. Disconnect the negative battery cable. Raise and support the vehicle safely.
2. Remove the gravel shield, if equipped.
3. Disconnect the fluid line.
4. Remove the slave cylinder retaining bolts.
5. Remove the clutch slave cylinder from the vehicle.
6. Installation is the reverse of the removal procedure. Bleed the system.

1990–91 MR2

1. Disconnect the negative battery cable.
2. Raise and support the vehicle safely.
3. Remove the engine under cover.
4. Disconnect the control cables from the transaxle.
5. Disconnect the fluid line.
6. Support the engine and transaxle.
7. From the engine side, remove the engine front mounting bracket bolts.
8. Unbolt and remove the clutch slave cylinder.
9. Installation is the reverse of the removal procedure. Bleed the system.

Hydraulic Clutch System Bleeding

1. Check and fill the clutch fluid reservoir to the specified level as necessary. During the bleeding process, continue to check and replenish the reservoir to prevent the fluid level from getting lower than ½ the specified level.

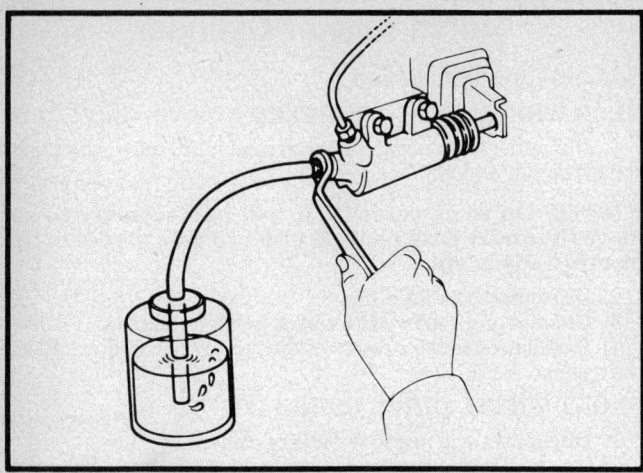

Bleeding the clutch hydraulic system

2. Remove the dust cap from the bleeder screw on the clutch slave cylinder and connect a tube to the bleeder screw and insert the other end of the tube into a clean glass or metal container.

NOTE: Take precautionary measures to prevent the brake fluid from getting on any painted surfaces.

3. Pump the clutch pedal several times, hold it down and loosen the bleeder screw slowly.

4. Tighten the bleeder screw and release the clutch pedal gradually. Repeat this operation until air bubbles disappear from the brake fluid being expelled out through the bleeder screw.

5. Repeat until all evidence of air bubbles completely disappears from the fluid being pumped out of the tube.

6. When the air is completely removed tighten the bleeder screw and replace the dust cap.

7. Check and refill the master cylinder reservoir, as necessary.

8. Depress the clutch pedal several times to check the operation of the clutch and check for leaks.

AUTOMATIC TRANSMISSION

For further information, please refer to "Professional Transmission Repair Manual" for additional coverage.

Transmission Assembly

Removal and Installation

COROLLA

1. Disconnect the negative battery cable.

2. Remove the air cleaner assembly. Disconnect the transmission throttle cable. Disconnect the starter assembly electrical connections.

3. Raise the vehicle and support it safely. Drain the transmission fluid. Remove the driveshaft.

4. Remove the exhaust pipe clamp. Disconnect the exhaust pipe from the exhaust manifold.

5. Disconnect the manual shift linkage. Disconnect the oil cooler lines. Remove the starter.

6. Support the engine and transmission using the proper equipment. Remove the rear crossmember.

7. Disconnect the speedometer cable. Disconnect all necessary electrical wiring from the transmission.

8. Remove the torque converter cover. Remove the torque converter-to-engine retaining bolts.

9. Remove the bolts retaining the transmission to the engine. carefully remove the transmission from the vehicle.

10. Installation is the reverse of the removal procedure.

CRESSIDA

1. Disconnect the negative battery cable. Drain the radiator and remove the upper radiator hose. Remove the air cleaner assembly. Disconnect the transmission throttle cable.

2. Raise the vehicle and support it safely. Drain the transmission fluid. Remove the driveshaft along with the center bearing.

3. Remove the exhaust pipe together with the catalytic converter. Disconnect the manual shift linkage. Remove the speedometer cable.

4. Disconnect the oil cooler lines. As necessary, remove the transmission oil filler tube. As required, remove the starter assembly. Remove the speedometer cable.

5. Remove both stiffener plates and the catalytic converter cover from the transmission housing and cylinder block.

6. Support the engine and transmission properly. Remove the rear crossmember.

7. Remove the torque converter cover. Remove the torque converter-to-engine retaining bolts.

8. Remove the bolts retaining the transmission to the engine. carefully remove the transmission from the vehicle.

9. Installation is the reverse of the removal procedure. Tighten the transmission housing bolts to 47 ft. lbs. (64 Nm). Tighten the torque converter bolts to 20 ft. lbs. (27 Nm).

SUPRA

1. Disconnect the negative battery cable. Remove the air cleaner assembly. Disconnect the transmission throttle cable.

2. Raise the vehicle and support it safely. Drain the transmission fluid. Disconnect the electrical connectors for the neutral safety switch and back-up lights.

3. Remove the intermediate driveshaft along with the center bearing. Disconnect the exhaust pipe from the tail pipe.

4. Disconnect the transmission oil cooler lines. Plug the lines

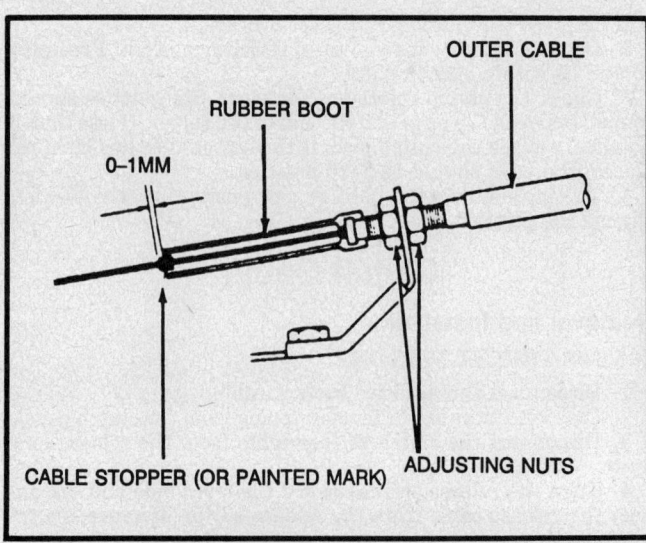

Throttle cable adjustment

to prevent leakage. Disconnect the manual shift linkage and speedometer cable.

5. Remove the exhaust pipe bracket and torque converter cover.

6. Remove both stiffener brackets.

7. Support the engine and transmission using the proper equipment. Remove the rear crossmember.

8. Remove the engine under cover. Remove the torque converter-to-engine retaining bolts. Remove the starter.

9. Remove the bolts retaining the transmission to the engine. carefully remove the transmission from the vehicle.

10. Installation is the reverse of the removal procedure. Adjust the throttle cable and fill the transmission to the proper level.

Shift Linkage Adjustment
COROLLA

1. Loosen the nut on the shift linkage.
2. Push the selector lever all the way to the rear of the vehicle.
3. Return the lever 2 notches to the **N** shift position.
4. While holding the selector lever slightly toward the **R** shift position tighten the connecting rod nut.

CRESSIDA AND SUPRA

1. Loosen the nut on the shift linkage. Push the selector lever all the way to the rear of the vehicle.
2. Return the lever 2 notches to the **N** shift position.
3. While holding the selector lever slightly toward the **R** shift position, tighten the connecting rod nut.

Throttle Linkage Adjustment

1. Remove the air cleaner.
2. Confirm that the accelerator linkage opens the throttle fully. Adjust the linkage as necessary.
3. Peel the rubber dust boot back from the throttle cable.
4. Loosen the adjustment nuts on the throttle cable bracket (cylinder head cover) just enough to allow cable housing movement.
5. Have an assistant depress the accelerator pedal fully.
6. Adjust the cable housing so the gap between its end and the cable stop collar is 0.04 in. (1mm).
7. Tighten the adjustment nuts. Make sure the adjustment hasn't changed. Install the dust boot and the air cleaner.

AUTOMATIC TRANSAXLE

For further information, please refer to "Professional Transmission Repair Manual" for additional coverage.

Transaxle Assembly

Removal and Installation

TERCEL

1. Disconnect the negative battery cable. Drain the radiator and remove the upper radiator hose, as required. Remove the air cleaner assembly.
2. Raise the vehicle and support it safely. Remove both halfshafts. Drain the fluid from the transaxle and differential, if equipped.
3. Remove the torque converter cover. Remove the bolts that retain the torque converter to the crankshaft. Remove the exhaust pipe. Remove the shift lever rod.
4. Remove the speedometer cable and back-up light connector. If equipped with AWD, remove the electrical solenoid connector. Disconnect and remove all throttle linkage.
5. Remove the fluid lines from the transaxle. Remove the starter assembly, as required. On AWD vehicles, remove the rear driveshaft.
6. Support the engine and transaxle using a suitable jack. Remove the rear crossmember.
7. Remove the transaxle-to-engine retaining bolts. Seperate the transaxle from the engine and carefully remove it from the vehicle.
8. Installation is the reverse of the removal procedure. Tighten the transmission-to-engine bolts to 47 ft. lbs. (64 Nm). Tighten the left engine mount bracket bolts to 32 ft. lbs. (43 Nm). Tighten the rear engine mount bracket bolts to 43 ft. lbs. (58 Nm). Tighten the torque converter mounting bolts to 13 ft. lbs. (18 Nm).

COROLLA

1. Disconnect the negative battery cable. Remove the air cleaner.
2. Disconnect the neutral start switch. Disconnect the speedometer cable.

3. Disconnect the shift control cable and throttle linkage.
4. Disconnect the oil cooler hose. Plug the end of the hose to prevent leakage.
5. Drain the radiator and remove the water inlet pipe.
6. Raise and support the vehicle safely. Drain the transaxle fluid. As required remove the exhaust front pipe.
7. Remove the engine undercover. Remove the front and rear transaxle mounts.
8. Support the engine and transaxle using the proper equipment. Remove the engine center support member.
9. Remove the halfshafts. Remove the starter assembly. Remove the steering knuckles, as required.
10. Remove the flywheel cover plate. Remove the torque converter bolts.
11. Remove the left engine mount. Remove the transaxle-to-engine bolts. Slowly and carefully back the transaxle away from the engine. Lower the assembly to the floor.
12. Installation is the reverse of the removal procedure. When installing the A241H vehicle transaxle on AWD vehicles, be sure the mode selector lever is positioned in the **FREE** mode and attach the lock bolt.

CAMRY

1. Disconnect the negative battery cable. Remove the air flow meter and the air cleaner assembly.
2. Disconnect the transaxle wire connector. Disconnect the neutral safety switch electrical connector.
3. Disconnect the transaxle ground strap. Disconnect the throttle cable from the throttle linkage.
4. Remove the transaxle case protector. Disconnect the speedometer cable and control cable.
5. Disconnect the oil cooler hoses. Remove the upper starter retaining bolts, as required remove the starter assembly. Remove the upper transaxle housing bolts. Remove the engine rear mount insulator bracket set bolt.
6. Raise and support the vehicle safely. Drain the transaxle fluid.
7. Remove the left front fender apron seal. Disconnect both driveshafts.
8. Remove the suspension lower crossmember assembly. Remove the center driveshaft.

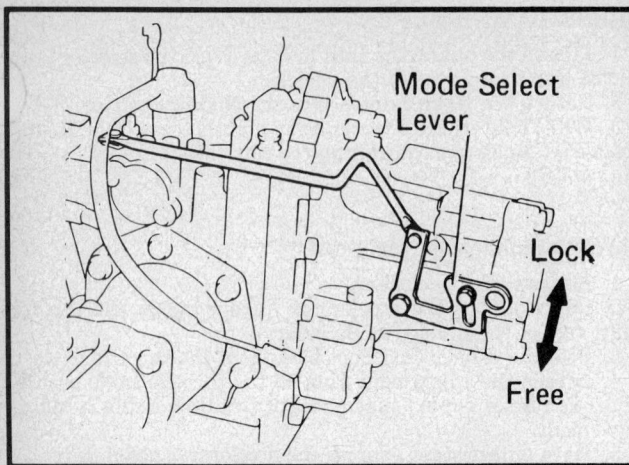

Setting the mode selector—Corolla w/A241H

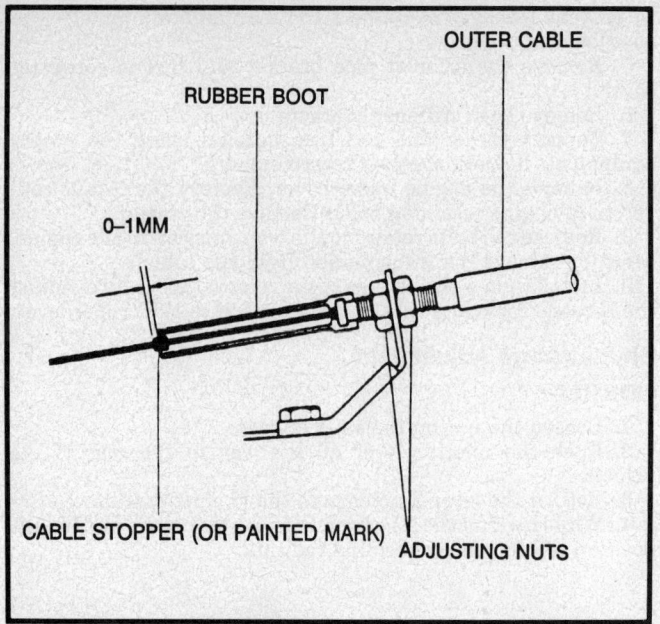

Throttle cable adjustment

9. Remove the engine mounting center crossmember. Remove the stabilizer bar. Remove the left steering knuckle from the lower control arm.

10. Remove the torque converter cover. Remove the torque converter retaining bolts.

11. Properly support the engine and transaxle assembly. Remove the rear engine mounting bolts. Remove the remaining transaxle to engine retaining bolts.

12. Carefully remove the transaxle assembly from the vehicle.

13. Installation is the reverse of the removal procedure. Tighten the 12mm transaxle housing bolts to 47 ft. lbs. (64 Nm); tighten the 10mm bolts to 34 ft. lbs. (46 Nm). Tighten the rear engine mount set bolts to 38 ft. lbs. (52 Nm). Tighten the torque converter mounting bolts to 20 ft. lbs. (27 Nm).

CELICA

1. Disconnect the negative battery cable. Remove the air flow meter and the air cleaner hose.

2. Disconnect the speedometer cable. Remove the starter assembly electrical connections. Disconnect the throttle cable from the throttle linkage and bracket.

3. Disconnect the ground strap. Remove the starter retaining bolts and as required remove the starter assembly.

4. Remove the upper transaxle housing retaining bolts. Remove the engine rear mount insulator bracket retaining bolt.

5. Raise and support the vehicle safely. Drain the transaxle fluid. Remove the engine under covers.

6. Remove the lower suspension crossmember. Disconnect the front and rear mounting components. Remove the engine mounting centermember.

7. Remove the left halfshaft. Disconnect the right halfshaft.

8. Disconnect the exhaust pipe from the manifold. Remove the stiffener plate. Disconnect the control cable.

9. Disconnect the oil cooler hoses. Remove the torque converter cover. Remove the torque converter retaining bolts.

10. Support the engine and transaxle assembly, using the proper equipment. Remove the transaxle-to-engine retaining bolts. Disconnect the front and rear transmission mount bolts.

11. Carefully lower the transaxle assembly to the floor.

12. Installation is the reverse of the removal procedure. Tighten the 12mm engine-to-transaxle bolts to 47 ft. lbs. (64 Nm) and the 10mm bolts to 34 ft. lbs. (46 Nm). Tighten the torque converter bolts to 20 ft. lbs. (27 Nm).

MR2

1. Disconnect the negative battery cable. Remove the air flow meter and the air cleaner hose.

2. Remove the intercooler on the 4A-GZE.

3. Remove the water inlet set bolts. Disconnect the ground strap. Remove the transaxle mounting set bolt.

4. Disconnect the speedometer cable at the transaxle. Disconnect the throttle cable from the throttle linkage and the bracket.

5. Raise and support the vehicle safely. Drain the transaxle fluid. Remove the left tire.

6. Remove the transaxle gravel shield. Disconnect the speedometer cable at the transaxle assembly.

7. Disconnect the oil cooler lines at the transaxle. Remove the transaxle control cable clip and retainer and then disconnect the cable from the bracket. Remove the bracket.

8. Remove the starter assembly. Disconnect the exhaust pipe at the manifold. Remove the pipe.

9. Disconnect the stiffner plate. Remove the rear engine end plate. Remove the torque converter cover. Remove the torque converter retaining bolts.

10. Disconnect both the right and left halfshafts from their side gear shafts. Depress and hold the brake pedal while removing the halfshaft retaining nuts. Properly position the halfshaft aside.

11. Disconnect the suspension arm from the rear axle carrier, using the proper tools. Disconnect the rear axle carrier from the lower control arm.

12. Disconnect the halfshaft from the side gear shaft. Properly position the driveshaft aside.

13. Support the engine and transaxle assembly, using the proper equipment. Remove the transaxle-to-engine retaining bolts. Disconnect the front and rear transmission mount bolts.

14. Carefully lower the transaxle assembly to the floor.

15. Installation is the reverse of the removal procedure. Tighten the transmission-to-engine bolts to 47 ft. lbs. (64 Nm). Torque the torque converter bolts to 20 ft. lbs. (27 Nm).

Shift Linkage Adjustment
TERCEL
Sedan

1. Loosen the swivel nut on the selector lever.

2. Push the lever fully toward the right side of the vehicle.

3. Return the lever 2 notches to the **N** position.

4. Set the shift lever in the **N** position.

5. While holding the selector lever slightly toward the **R** shift position tighten the swivel nut to 48 inch lbs. (5.4 Nm).

Wagon

1. Push the selector lever all the way to the rear of the vehicle.
2. Return the lever 2 notches to the **N** shift position.
3. Set the selector lever in the **N** position.
4. While holding the selector lever slightly toward the **R** shift position tighten the connecting rod nut.

COROLLA, CAMRY, MR2 AND CELICA

1. Loosen the swivel nut on the selector lever.
2. Push the lever fully toward the right side of the vehicle.
3. Return the lever 2 notches to the **N** position.
4. Set the selector lever in the **N** position.

5. While holding the selector lever slightly toward the **R** shift position tighten the swivel nut to 48 inch lbs. (5.4 Nm).

Throttle Linkage Adjustment

1. Remove the air cleaner.
2. Confirm that the accelerator linkage opens the throttle fully. Adjust the linkage as necessary.
3. Peel the rubber dust boot back from the throttle cable.
4. Loosen the adjustment nuts on the throttle cable bracket (cylinder head cover) just enough to allow cable housing movement.
5. Have an assistant depress the accelerator pedal fully.
6. Adjust the cable housing so the distance between its end and the cable stop collar is 0.04 in.
7. Tighten the adjustment nuts. Make sure the adjustment hasn't changed. Install the dust boot and the air cleaner.

TRANSFER CASE

Transfer Case Assembly

Removal and Installation
CAMRY (AWD) AND CELICA (AWD)

1. Remove the engine/transaxle assembly.
2. Separate the transaxle from the engine.

3. Remove the 3 bolts and 5 nuts and separate the transfer case from the transaxle. Use a rubber mallet to get the 2 separated.
4. Installation is in the reverse order of removal. Remove any packing material from the transfer case mating surface. Be careful not to get any oil on it. Tighten the mounting bolts and nuts to 51 ft. lbs. (69 Nm).

DRIVE AXLE

Halfshaft

Removal and Installation
TERCEL

1. Raise the vehicle and support it safely.
2. Remove the cotter pin and locknut cap.
3. Have an assistant step on the brake pedal and at the same time, loosen the bearing locknut.
4. Remove the brake caliper and position it aside. Remove the brake disc.
5. Remove the cotter pin and nut from the tie rod end. Using a suitable puller, disconnect the tie rod end from the steering knuckle.
6. Matchmark the lower strut mounting bracket where it attaches to the steering knuckle, remove the mounting bolts and then disconnect the steering knuckle from the strut bracket.
7. Using a suitable puller, pull the axle hub off the outer halfshaft end.
8. Remove the stiffener plate from the left side of the transaxle assembly.
9. Using the proper tool, tap the halfshaft out of the transaxle casing.

NOTE: Be sure to cover the halfshaft input opening.

10. Installation is in the reverse order of removal. During installation, observe the following:
   a. Coat the oil seal in the transaxle input opening with MP grease before inserting the halfshaft.
   b. On 1987 vehicles, tighten the steering knuckle-to-strut bolts to 105 ft. lbs. On 1988–91 vehicles, torque the bolts to 166 ft.
   c. Tighten the tie rod end nut to 36 ft. lbs. (49 Nm).

   d. Tighten the bearing locknut to 137 ft. lbs. (186 Nm).
   e. Tighten the stiffner plate bolts to 29 ft. lbs. (39 Nm).
   f. Check the front wheel alignment.

COROLLA FX/FX16
1987 COROLLA (4A-C)
1987–88 COROLLA (4A-GE)

1. Raise and support the vehicle safely.
2. Remove the cotter pin, locknut cap and locknut from the hub.
3. Remove the engine under cover. Remove the 6 nuts attaching the halfshaft (front driveshaft) to the transaxle (differential side gear).
4. Remove the brake caliper from the steering knuckle and support it aside with wire. Remove the rotor disc.
5. Disconnect the steering knuckle from the lower arm by removing the bolt and 2 nuts, then disconnect the lower arm from the steering knuckle.
6. Using a suitable puller, pull the axle hub from the halfshaft. Be sure to cover the dust boot with a shop rag to prevent damage to the the boot.
7. Installation is the reverse of the removal procedure. During installation, observe the following:
   a. Torque the steering knuckle to 47–64 ft. lbs. (64 Nm) on 1987–88 FX and 105 ft. lbs. (142 Nm) on 1987–88 sedan and wagon.
   b. Torque the caliper bolts to 65 ft. lbs. (88 Nm).
   c. Torque the bearing nut to 137 ft. lbs. (186 Nm).
   d. Torque the halfshaft nuts to 27 ft. lbs. (36 Nm).

1988–91 COROLLA (EXCEPT 1988 4A-GE)

1. Raise and safely support the vehicle.
2. Remove the cotter pin and locknut cap.

3. Have an assistant step on the brake pedal and at the same time, loosen the bearing locknut.

4. Remove the engine undercovers and then drain the gear oil or fluid.

5. Remove the cotter pin and nut from the tie rod end. Using a suitable puller, disconnect the tie rod end from the steering knuckle.

6. Remove the mounting bolts and then disconnect the steering knuckle from the lower control arm.

7. Use a rubber mallet and drive the outer end of the shaft out of the axle hub.

8. Using the proper tools, tap or pry the halfshaft out of the transaxle casing.

NOTE: Be sure to cover the halfshaft input opening.

9. Installation is in the reverse order of removal. During installation, observe the following:

    a. Coat the oil seal in the transaxle input hole with MP grease before inserting the halfshaft.

    b. Tighten the steering knuckle-to-lower arm bolts to 105 ft. lbs. (142 Nm).

    c. Tighten the tie rod end nut to 36 ft. lbs. (49 Nm).

    d. Tighten the bearing locknut to 137 ft. lbs. (186 Nm).

    e. Check that there is 0.08–0.12 in. (2–3mm) axial play on each shaft.

    f. Check the front wheel alignment.

1987–89 CELICA (2WD)

1. Raise and safely support the vehicle.
2. Remove the wheels.
3. Remove the cotter pin, cap and locknut from the hub.
4. Remove the engine under covers.
5. Drain the transmission fluid or the differential fluid on the GTS.
6. Remove the transaxle gravel shield on the GTS.
7. Loosen the six nuts attaching the inner end of the halfshaft to transaxle (all except Celica GTS).

NOTE: Wrap the exposed end of the halfshaft in an old shop cloth to prevent damage to it.

8. Remove the cotter pin from the tie end rod and then press the tie rod out of the steering knuckle. Remove the bolt and 2 nuts and disconnect the steering knuckle from the lower arm control.

9. On all but the GTS, use a 2-armed gear puller or equivalent, and press the halfshaft out of the steering knuckle.

10. On the GTS, mark a spot somewhere on the left halfshaft and measure the distance between the spot and the transaxle case. Using the proper tool, pull the halfshaft out of the transaxle.

11. On the GTS, use a 2-armed puller and press the outer end of the right halfshaft out of the steering knuckle. Use a pair of pliers to remove the snap-ring at the inner end and pull the halfshaft out of the center driveshaft.

12. On all but the GT-S, remove the snap-ring on the center shaft with a pair of pliers and then pull the center shaft out of the transaxle case.

To install:

13. When installing the center driveshaft on ST and GT vehicles, coat the transaxle oil seal with grease, insert the halfshaft through the bearing bracket and secure it with a new snap-ring.

14. Repeat Step 13 when installing the inner end of the right halfshaft on the GTS.

15. On the right halfshaft of the GTS, use a new snap-ring, coat the transaxle oil seal with grease and then press the inner end of the shaft into the differential housing. Check that the measurement made in Step 10 is the same. Check that there is 0.08–0.11 in. (2–3mm) of axial play. Check also that the halfshaft will not come out by trying to pull it back by hand.

16. Press the outer end of each halfshaft into the steering knuckle on the GTS.

17. On the ST and GT, press the outer end of the halfshafts into the steering knuckle and then finger-tighten the nuts on the inner end.

18. Connect the steering knuckle to the lower control arm and tighten the bolts to 94 ft. lbs. (127 Nm).

19. Connect the tie rod end to the steering knuckle and tighten the nut to 36 ft. lbs. (49 Nm). Install a new cotter pin.

20. Tighten the hub locknut to 137 ft. lbs. (186 Nm) while depressing the brake pedal. Install the cap and use a new cotter pin.

21. On the ST and GT, tighten the 6 nuts on the inner halfshaft ends to 27 ft. lbs. (36 Nm) while depressing the brake pedal.

22. Install the transaxle gravel shield on the GTS.

23. Fill the transaxle with gear oil or fluid.

24. Install the engine under cover.

1990 CELICA (2WD)

NOTE: The hub bearing can be damaged if it is subjected to the vehicle weight such as moving the vehicle when the driveshaft is removed. If with ABS, after disconnecting driveshaft, work carefully so as not damage the sensor rotor serrations on the driveshaft.

1. Raise and safely support the vehicle. Remove the wheels.
2. Remove the cotter pin, cap and locknut (loosen locknut while depressing brake pedal) from the hub.
3. Remove the engine under covers.
4. Drain the transaxle fluid.
5. Remove the brake caliper and rotor disc.
6. Disconnect the tie rod end (remove cotter pin and nut) from the steering knuckle.
7. Disconnect steering knuckle from the lower arm.
8. Remove the driveshaft from the steering knuckle using a suitable puller. Cover the driveshaft boot with shop cloth or equivalent to protect it from damage.
9. Remove the left side driveshaft using the proper tool.
10. Remove the the right side driveshaft. On the 5S-FE engine, remove the 2 bolts of the center bearing bracket and pull out the driveshaft with center bearing case and center driveshaft. On the 4A-FE engine, use a suitable brass punch tap out the right side driveshaft.

To install:

11. Install the left side driveshaft. Apply grease to the transaxle oil seal lip. Position the new snap-ring opening side facing downward using brass punch, tap driveshaft in until it makes contact with the pinion shaft. Install the outboard joint side of the driveshaft to the axle hub.

12. Install right side driveshaft on the 5S-FE engine using the following procedure:

    a. Apply grease to the transaxle oil seal lip.

    b. Insert the center driveshaft with the right side to the transaxle through the bearing bracket. When inserting the driveshaft, insert so the straight pin on the center bearing case aligns with the hole on the bearing bracket.

    c. Install retaining bolts and torque to 47 ft. lbs. (64 Nm).

    d. Install the outboard joint side of the driveshaft to the axle hub.

13. Install right side driveshaft on the 4A-FE engine using the following procedure:

    a. Apply grease to the transaxle oil seal lip.

    b. Position the new snap-ring opening side facing downward using brass punch, tap driveshaft in until it makes contact with the pinion shaft.

    c. Install the outboard joint side of the driveshaft to the axle hub.

14. Check that the driveshaft will not come out by trying to pull it by hand.

15. Connect the steering knuckle to the lower control arm and tighten the bolts to 94 ft. lbs. (128 Nm).

16. Connect the tie rod end to the steering knuckle and tighten the nut to 36 ft. lbs. (49 Nm). Install a new cotter pin.

17. Install all necessary brake components. Tighten the hub locknut to 137 ft. lbs. (186 Nm) while depressing the brake pedal. Install the cap and use a new cotter pin.

18. Fill the transaxle to the proper level. Install the engine under cover. Check front wheel alignment.

CELICA (AWD)

Front

NOTE: **The hub bearing can be damaged if it is subjected to the vehicle weight such as moving the vehicle when the driveshaft is removed. On 1990–91 vehicles with ABS, after disconnecting driveshaft work carefully so as not damage the sensor rotor serrations on the driveshaft.**

1. Raise and support the vehicle safely.
2. Remove the wheels.
3. Remove the cotter pin, cap and locknut from the hub.
4. Remove the transaxle gravel shield, if with manual transmission. Remove the engine under cover and front fender apron seal.
5. Remove the cotter pin and nut from the tie rod end and then disconnect it from the steering knuckle.
6. Remove the bolt and 2 nuts and disconnect the steering knuckle from the lower control arm.
7. Loosen the 6 nuts attaching the inner end of the halfshaft to the transaxle side gear shaft.
8. Grasp the halfshaft and push the axle carrier outward until the shaft can be removed from the side gear shaft.

NOTE: **Wrap the exposed end of the halfshaft in an old shop cloth to prevent damage to it.**

9. Use a rubber mallet and tap the outer end of the shaft from the axle hub.
To install:
10. Press the outer end of the halfshaft into the axle hub, position the inner end and install the 6 nuts finger-tight.
11. Connect the tie rod end to the steering knuckle and tighten the nut to 36 ft. lbs. (49 Nm). Install a new cotter pin. If the cotter pin holes do not align, tighten the nut until they align. Never loosen it.
12. Connect the steering knuckle to the lower control arm and tighten to 94 ft. lbs. (127 Nm).
13. Tighten the 6 inner shaft mounting nuts to 48 ft. lbs. (65 Nm). Measure the distance between the right and left side shafts; it must be less then 27.75 in. (704.7mm).
14. With the brake pedal depressed, install the bearing locknut and tighten it to 137 ft. lbs. (186 Nm). Install the cap and a new cotter pin.
15. Install the wheels and lower the vehicle.

Rear

1. Raise and safely support the vehicle. Remove the wheels.
2. Remove the cotter pin, locknut cap and bearing nut.
3. Scribe matchmarks on the inner joint tulip and the side gear shaft flange. Loosen and remove the 4 nuts.
4. Disconnect the inner end of the shaft by puching it upward and then pull the outer end from the axle carrier. Remove the halfshaft.
To install:
5. Position the halfshaft into the axle carrier and pull the inner end down until the matchmarks are aligned.
6. Connect the halfshaft to the side gear shaft and tighten the nuts to 51 ft. lbs. (69 Nm).
7. Install the bearing nut and tighten it to 137 ft. lbs. (186 Nm) with the brake pedal depressed. Install the cap and a new cotter pin.
8. Install the wheels and lower the vehicle.

CAMRY (2WD)

1987–88

1. Raise and support the vehicle safely.
2. Remove the wheels.
3. Remove the cotter pin, cap and locknut from the hub.
4. Remove the transaxle gravel shield, if with manual transaxle. Remove the engine under cover and front fender apron seal.
5. Loosen the 6 nuts attaching the inner end of the halfshaft to the transaxle or center shaft.

NOTE: **Wrap the exposed end of the halfshaft in an old shop cloth to prevent damage to it.**

6. Remove the brake caliper with the hydraulic line still attached, position it aside and suspend it with a wire. Remove the rotor.
7. Remove the 2 bolts attaching the ball joint to the steering knuckle. Pull the lower control arm down while pulling the strut outward; this will disconnect the inner end of the halfshaft from the transaxle.
8. Using a 2-armed puller, or the like, press the outer end of the halfshaft from the steering knuckle and then remove the halfshaft.
9. Drain the transaxle fluid, remove the snap-ring with pliers and pull the shaft out of the transaxle case.
To install:
10. When installing the center driveshaft, coat the transaxle oil seal with grease, insert the driveshaft through the bearing bracket and secure it with a new snap-ring.
11. Press the outer end of the halfshaft into the steering knuckle, position the inner end and install the 6 nuts finger-tight.
12. Reconnect the ball joint to the steering knuckle, if disconnected, and tighten the bolts to 94 ft. lbs. (127 Nm).
13. Install the rotor and brake caliper. Tighten the caliper-to-knuckle bolts to 65 ft. lbs. (88 Nm).
14. Tighten the wheel bearing locknut to 137 ft. lbs. (186 Nm) while depressing the brake pedal. Install the locknut cap and use a new cotter pin.
15. Tighten the 6 inner end nuts to 27 ft. lbs. (36 Nm) while depressing the brake pedal.
16. Install the transaxle gravel shield, if equipped.
17. Fill the transaxle to the proper level.

1989–91

1. Raise and support the vehicle safely.
2. Remove the front wheels.
3. Remove the cotter pin, cap and locknut from the hub.
4. Remove the engine under covers.
5. Drain the transmission fluid or the differential fluid on the wagon.
6. Remove the transaxle gravel shield on the wagon.
7. Loosen the 6 nuts attaching the inner end of the halfshaft to transaxle, all except wagon.

NOTE: **Wrap the exposed end of the halfshaft in an old shop cloth to prevent damage to it.**

8. Remove the cotter pin from the tie end rod and then press the tie rod out of the steering knuckle. Remove the bolt and 2 nuts and disconnect the steering knuckle from the lower arm control.
9. On all except 4 cylinder wagon, use a 2-armed gear puller or equivalent, and press the halfshaft out of the steering knuckle.
10. On the 4 cylinder wagon, mark a spot somewhere on the left halfshaft and measure the distance between the spot and the transaxle case. Using the proper tool, pull the halfshaft out of the transaxle.
11. On the 4 cylinder wagon, use a 2-armed puller and press

the outer end of the right halfshaft out of the steering knuckle. Remove the snap-ring at the inner end and pull the halfshaft out of the center driveshaft.

12. On all except the 4 cylinder wagon, remove the snap-ring on the center shaft and pull the center shaft out of the transaxle case.

To install:

13. When installing the center driveshaft on sedan and V6 vehicles, coat the transaxle oil seal with grease, insert the halfshaft through the bearing bracket and secure it with a new snap-ring.

14. Repeat Step 13 when installing the inner end of the right halfshaft on the 4 cylinder wagon.

15. On the right halfshaft of the 4 cylinder wagon, use a new snap-ring, coat the transaxle oil seal with grease and then press the inner end of the shaft into the differential housing. Check that the measurement made in Step 10 is the same. Check that there is 0.08–0.12 in. (2–3mm) of axial play. Check also that the halfshaft will not come out by trying to pull it by hand.

16. Press the outer end of each halfshaft into the steering knuckle on the 4 cylinder wagon.

17. On all except the 4 cylinder wagon, press the outer end of the halfshafts into the steering knuckle and then finger-tighten the nuts on the inner end.

18. Connect the steering knuckle to the lower control arm and tighten the bolts to 83 ft. lbs. (113 Nm).

19. Connect the tie rod end to the steering knuckle and tighten the nut to 36 ft. lbs. (49 Nm). Install a new cotter pin.

20. Tighten the hub locknut to 137 ft. lbs. (186 Nm) while depressing the brake pedal. Install the cap and use a new cotter pin.

21. On all except the 4 cylinder wagon, tighten the 6 nuts on the inner halfshaft ends to 27 ft. lbs. (36 Nm) while depressing the brake pedal.

22. Install the transaxle gravel shield on the wagon.

23. Fill the transaxle with gear oil or fluid.

24. Install the engine under cover.

CAMRY (AWD)

Front—1988

1. Raise and safely support the vehicle.
2. Remove the wheels.
3. Remove the cotter pin, cap and locknut from the hub.
4. Remove the transaxle gravel shield. Remove the engine under cover and front fender apron seal.
5. Remove the cotter pin and nut from the tie rod end and then disconnect it from the steering knuckle.
6. Remove the bolt and 2 nuts and disconnect the steering knuckle from the lower control arm.
7. Loosen the 6 nuts attaching the inner end of the halfshaft to the transaxle side gear shaft.
8. Grasp the halfshaft and push the axle carrier outward until the shaft can be removed from the side gear shaft.

NOTE: Wrap the exposed end of the halfshaft in an old shop cloth to prevent damage to it.

9. Use a rubber mallet and tap the outer end of the shaft from the axle hub.

To install:

10. Press the outer end of the halfshaft into the axle hub, position the inner end and install the 6 nuts finger-tight.
11. Connect the tie rod end to the steering knuckle and tighten the nut to 36 ft. lbs. (49 Nm). Install a new cotter pin. If the cotter pin holes do not align, tighten the nut until they align. Never loosen it.
12. Connect the steering knuckle to the lower control arm and tighten to 94 ft. lbs. (127 Nm).
13. Tighten the 6 inner shaft mounting nuts to 48 ft. lbs. (65 Nm). Measure the distance between the right and left side shafts; it must be less then 27.75 in. (704.7mm).

14. With the brake pedal depressed, install the bearing locknut and tighten it to 137 ft. lbs. (186 Nm). Install the cap and a new cotter pin.

15. Install the wheels and lower the vehicle.

Front—1989–91

1. Raise and support the vehicle safely.
2. Remove the wheels.
3. Remove the cotter pin, cap and locknut from the hub.
4. Remove the engine undercovers.
5. Disconnect the tie rod end from the steering knuckle.
6. Disconnect the lower control arm at the steering knuckle and pull it down and aside.
7. Use a plastic hammer and carefully tap the outer end of the halfshaft until it frees itself from the axle hub.
8. Cover the outer boot with a rag and then remove the inner end of the halfshaft from the transaxle. Use the proper tools.

To install:

9. Coat the lip of the oil seal with grease and then carefully drive the inner end of the shaft into the transaxle until it makes contact with the pinion shaft.

NOTE: Be careful not to damage the boots when installing the halfshafts; also, position the boot snap-ring so the opening is facing downward.

10. Put the outer end of each shaft into the axle hub, being careful not to damage the boots.
11. Check that there is 0.08–0.12 in. (2–3mm) of axial play. Check also that the halfshaft will not come out by hand.
12. Connect the lower control arm to the steering arm and tighten the bolt to 83 ft. lbs. (113 Nm).
13. Connect the tie rod to the steering knuckle and tighten the nut to 36 ft. lbs. (49 Nm). Use a new cotter pin to secure it.
14. Install the axle bearing locknut and tighten it to 137 ft. lbs. (186 Nm) while stepping on the brake pedal. Install the locknut cap and then a new cotter pin.
15. Fill the transaxle with gear oil or fluid, install the undercovers and wheels. Lower the vehicle and check the front end alignment.

Rear—1988–91

1. Raise and support the vehicle safely. Remove the wheels.
2. Remove the cotter pin, locknut cap and bearing nut.
3. Scribe matchmarks on the inner joint tulip and the side gear shaft flange. Loosen and remove the 4 nuts.
4. Disconnect the inner end of the shaft by puching it upward and then pull the outer end from the axle carrier. Remove the halfshaft.
5. Position the halfshaft into the axle carrier and pull the inner end down until the matchmarks are aligned.
6. Connect the halfshaft to the side gear shaft and tighten the nuts to 51 ft. lbs. (69 Nm).
7. Install the bearing nut and tighten it to 137 ft. lbs. (186 Nm) with the brake pedal depressed. Install the cap and a new cotter pin.
8. Install the wheels and lower the vehicle.

MR2

NOTE: On 1990–91 vehicles with ABS, after disconnecting driveshaft, work carefully so as not damage the sensor rotor serrations on the driveshaft.

1. Raise and support the vehicle safely.
2. Remove the wheels.
3. Remove the cotter pin, cap and locknut from the hub.
4. Remove the transaxle gravel shield.
5. Loosen the 6 nuts attaching the inner end of the halfshaft to transaxle.

NOTE: Wrap the exposed end of the halfshaft in an old shop cloth to prevent damage to it.

6. If equipped with automatic transaxle, remove the 2 bolts holding the ball joint to the rear axle carrier and disconnect the lower arm from the rear axle carrier.

7. Also, if equipped with automatic transaxle, remove the cotter pin and nut using the proper tool. Disconnect the suspension arm from the rear axle carrier.

8. While holding the halfshaft, knock the outer end of the wheel hub assembly. Remove the halfshaft.

To install:

9. Press the outer end of the halfshaft into the wheel hub assembly.

10. Position the inner end of the halfshaft and install the 6 nuts finger-tight.

11. Install the transaxle gravel shield.

12. Tighten the wheel bearing locknut to 137 ft. lbs. (186 Nm) while depressing the brake pedal. Install the locknut cap and use a new cotter pin.

13. Tighten the 6 inner end nuts to 27 ft. lbs. (36 Nm) while depressing the brake pedal. Torque the suspension arm nut to 36 ft. lbs. (49 Nm) and the lower arm to rear axle carrier to 83 ft. lbs. (113 Nm).

14. Fill the transaxle to the proper level.

1987–88 CRESSIDA

1. Raise and support the vehicle safely.

2. Place matchmarks on the halfshaft and flanges.

3. Remove the 4 nuts retaining the halfshaft to the differential and disconnect the halfshaft from the differential.

4. Remove the 4 nuts retaining the halfshaft to the axle shaft and disconnect the halfshaft from the axleshaft. Remove the halfshaft from the under the vehicle.

5. Installation is the reverse order of the removal procedure. Be sure to align the matchmarks on the halfshaft and torque the retaining nuts to 51 ft. lbs. (69 Nm).

SUPRA AND 1989–91 CRESSIDA

1. Raise and support the vehicle safely. Remove the rear wheels.

2. Using a suitable jack, raise the No. 2 suspension arm until

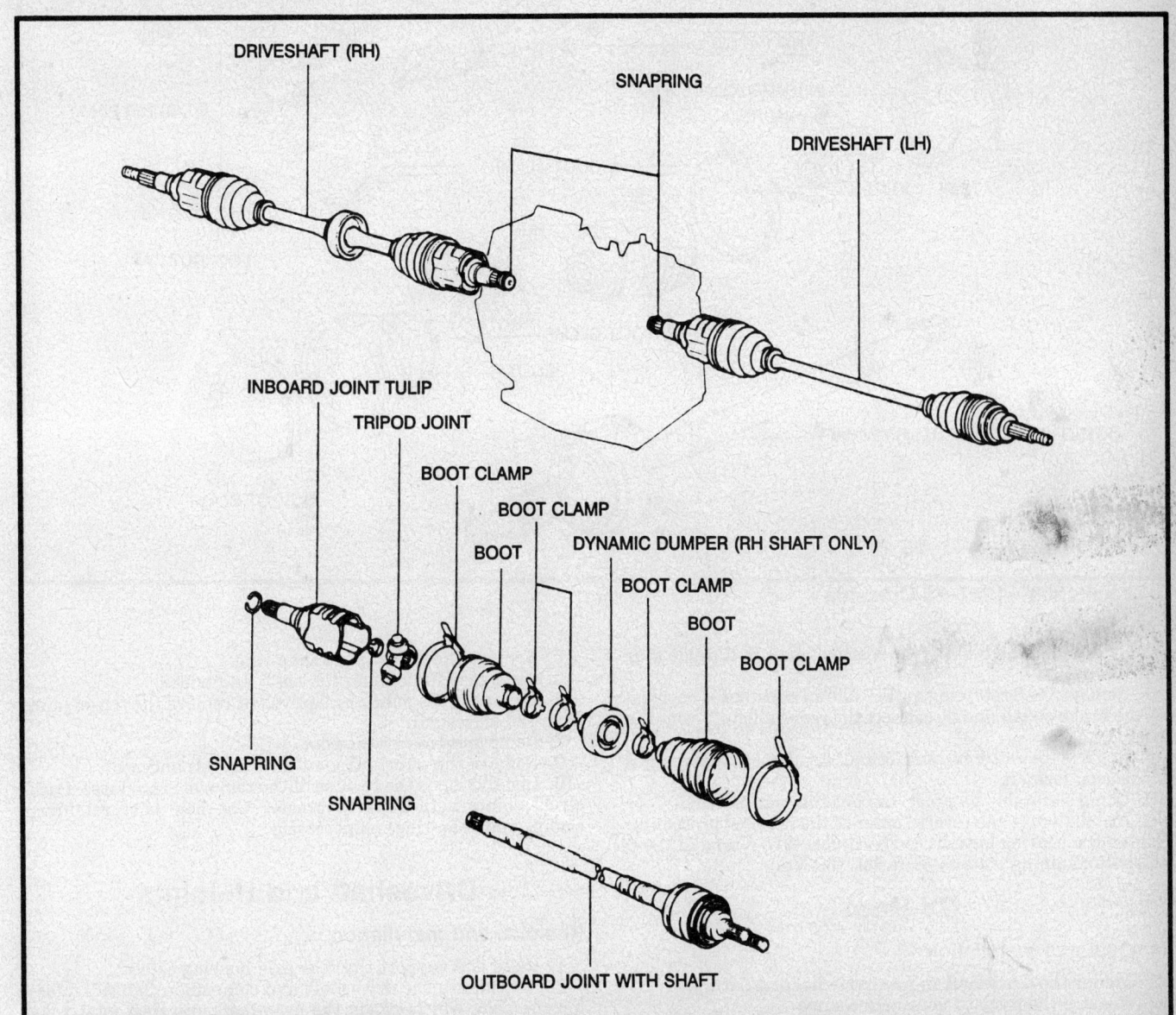

Front halfshaft—Tercel

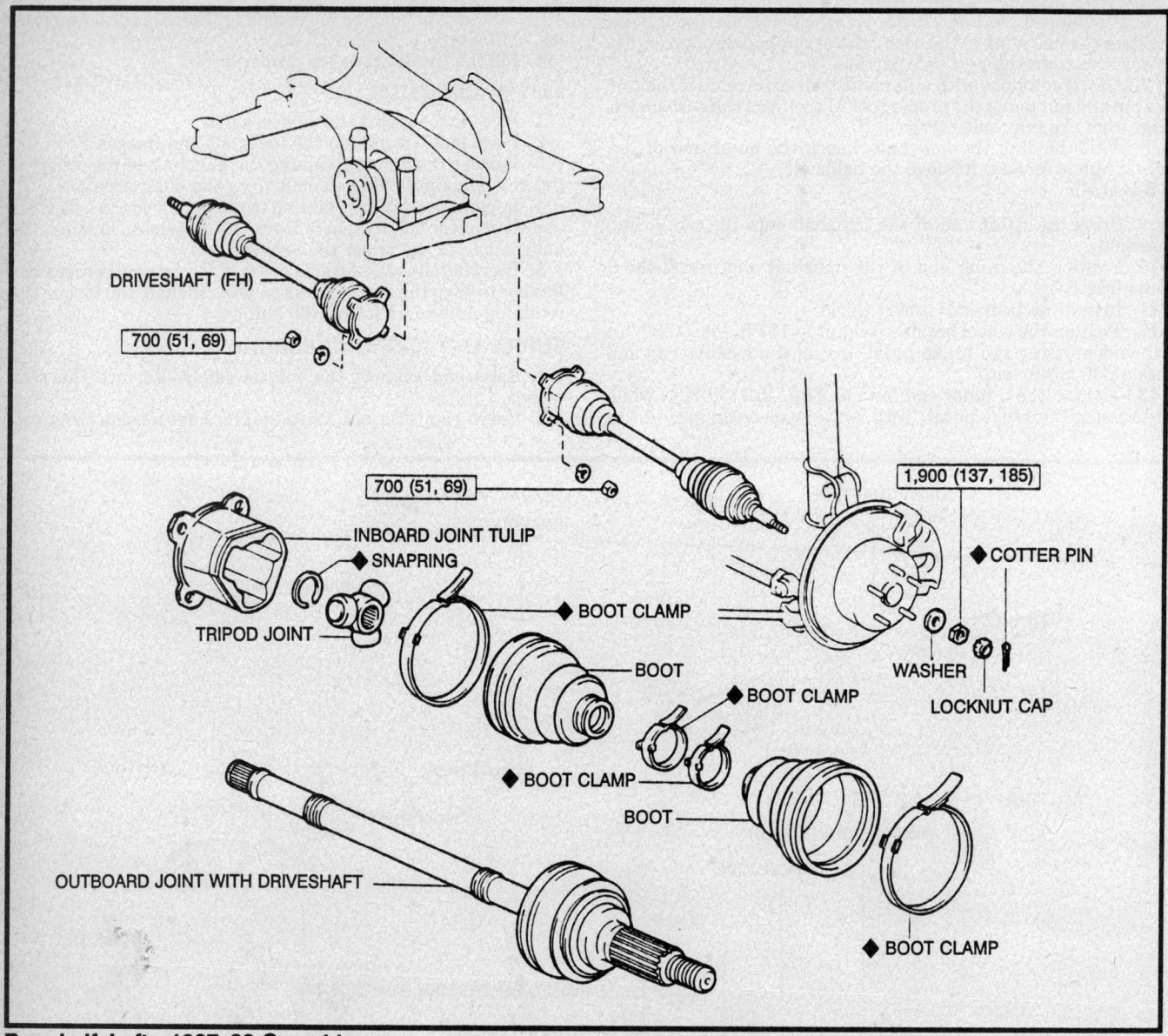

DRIVESHAFT (FH)

700 (51, 69)

700 (51, 69)

1,900 (137, 185)

INBOARD JOINT TULIP
◆ SNAPRING
TRIPOD JOINT
◆ BOOT CLAMP
BOOT
◆ BOOT CLAMP
◆ BOOT CLAMP
BOOT
◆ BOOT CLAMP
OUTBOARD JOINT WITH DRIVESHAFT
◆ COTTER PIN
WASHER
LOCKNUT CAP

Rear halfshaft—1987–88 Cressida

it is horizontal. Matchmarks the rear halfshaft to the side gear shaft flange.

3. Remove the 6 retaining nuts (while an assistant is depressing the brake pedal) and disconnect the rear halfshaft from the differential.

4. Remove the cotter pin and locknut cap. Loosen and remove the bearing locknut.

5. Using a suitable hammer, tap out the rear halfshaft.

6. Installation is the reverse order of the removal procedure. Tighten the bearing locknut to 203 ft. lbs. (275 Nm) and the 6 halfshaft retaining bolts to 51 ft. lbs. (69 Nm).

CV-Boot

Removal and Installation

1. Mount the driveshaft in a suitable holding fixture.
2. Remove the inboard joint boot clamps.
3. Place matchmarks on the inboard joint tulip and tripod.
4. Remove the inboard joint tulip from the driveshaft.

5. Remove the tripod joint snap-ring.
6. Place matchmarks on the shaft and tripod.
7. Using a brass punch or equivalent remove the tripod joint from the driveshaft.
8. Remove inboard joint boot.
9. Remove the outboard joint boot clamps and boot.
10. Installation is the reverse of the removal procedures. Pack all CV-joints with suitable grease. Use new boot retaining clamps and snap-rings as necessary.

Driveshaft and U-Joints

Removal and Installation

1. Raise and support the rear axle housing safely.
2. Matchmark the driveshaft and companion flange. Unfasten the bolts which attach the driveshaft universal joint yoke flange to the mounting flange on the differential drive pinion.
3. If equipped with 3 universal joints, perform the following:

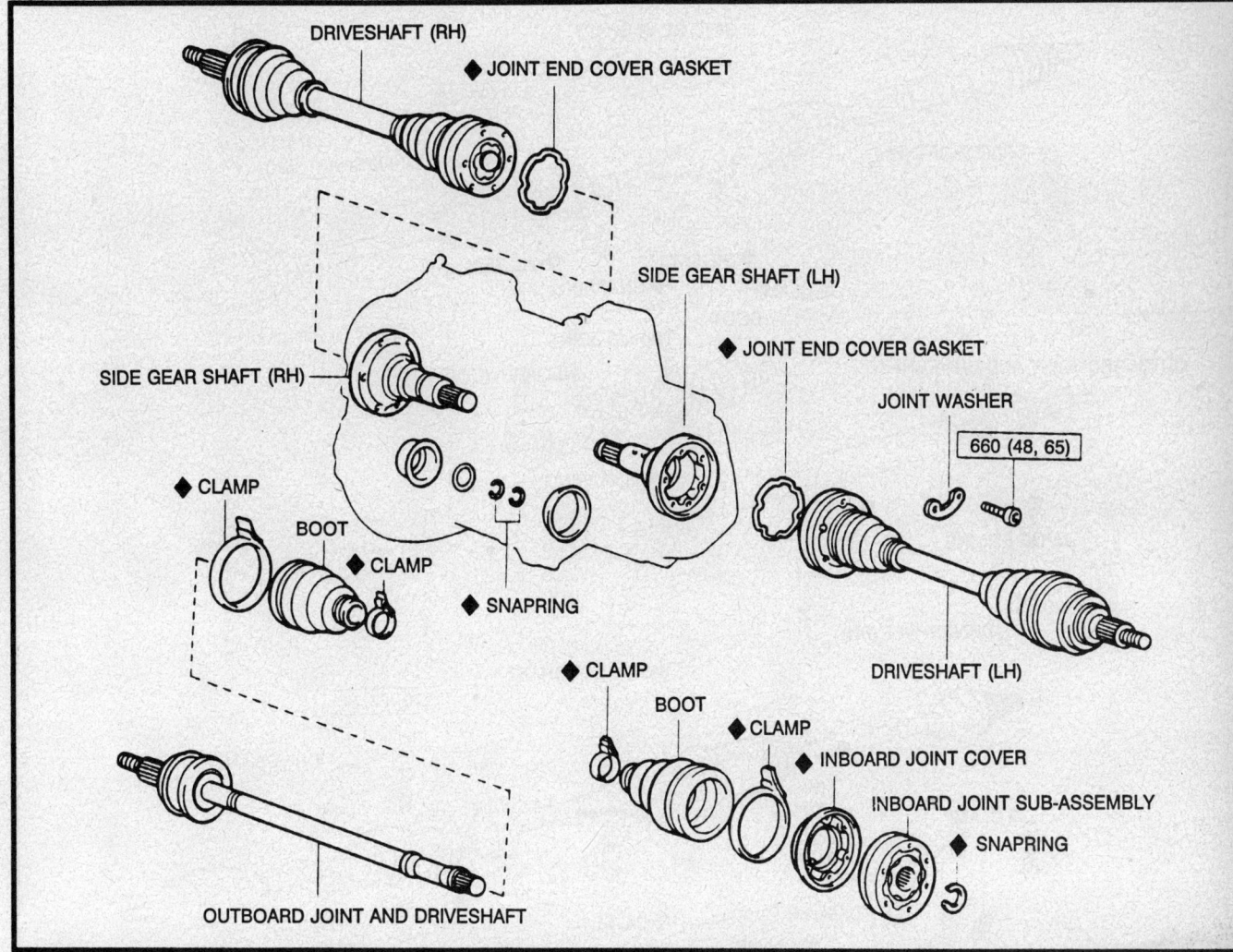

Front halfshaft—Celica All-Trac (4WD) and 1988 Camry All-Trac (4WD)

a. Remove the driveshaft sub-assembly from the U-joint sleeve yoke.

b. Remove the center support bearing from its bracket.

4. Remove the driveshaft end from the transmission.

5. Plug the transmission opening to keep the transmission oil from running out.

NOTE: On 1987 Supra, the exhaust pipe assembly must be removed in order to remove the driveshaft assembly.

6. Remove the driveshaft.

To install:

7. Apply multipurpose grease on the section of the U-joint sleeve which is to be inserted into the transmission.

8. Insert the driveshaft sleeve into the transmission.

NOTE: Be careful not to damage any of the seals.

9. If equipped with 3 U-joints and center bearings, perform the following:

a. Adjust the center bearing clearance with no load placed on the drive line components; the top of the rubber center cushion should be 0.04 in. (1mm) behind the center of the elongated bolt hole.

b. Install the center bearing assembly. Use the same number of washers on the center bearing brackets as were removed.

c. Matchmark the arrow marks on the driveshaft and grease fittings.

10. Align the matchmarks. Secure the U-joint flange to the differential pinion flange with the mounting bolts.

NOTE: Be sure the bolts are of the same type as those removed and that they are tightened securely.

11. Remove the axle housing supports and lower the vehicle.

12. Tighten the center bearing-to-bracket bolts to 30 ft. lbs. (40 Nm) on 1987–88 Cressida, 27 ft. lbs. (37 Nm) on 1989–91 Cressida or 36 ft. lbs. (49 Nm) on Supra. Tighten the flange bolts to 31 ft. lbs. (42 Nm) on 1987–88 Cressida or 54 ft. lbs. (74 Nm) on Supra and 1989–91 Cressida.

1988–91 CAMRY (AWD), 1988–91 CELICA (AWD), 1989–91 COROLLA (AWD), 1987–88 TERCEL WAGON (AWD)

1. Matchmark the front driveshaft flange and the front center bearing flange. Remove the 4 bolts, washers and nuts and disconnect the rear end of the front driveshaft from the front center bearing flange. Pull the shaft out of the transfer case and remove it. Plug the transfer case to prevent leakage.

2. Depress the brake pedal and loosen the cross groove set bolts ½ turn. These bolts are at the front edge of the rear driveshaft; rear edge of the rear center bearing.

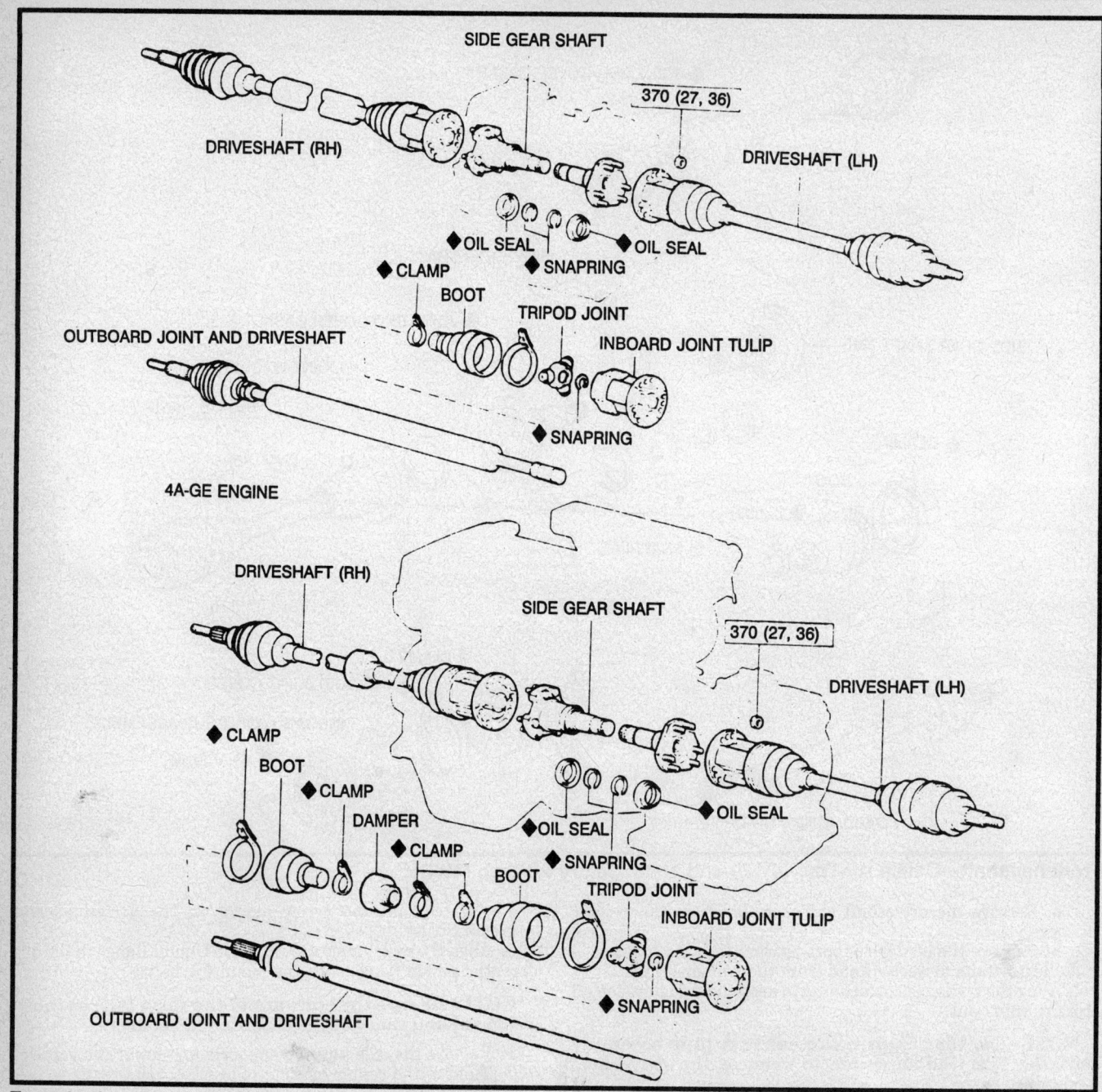

SIDE GEAR SHAFT

370 (27, 36)

DRIVESHAFT (RH)

DRIVESHAFT (LH)

◆ OIL SEAL   OIL SEAL

◆ CLAMP   ◆ SNAPRING

BOOT

TRIPOD JOINT

INBOARD JOINT TULIP

OUTBOARD JOINT AND DRIVESHAFT

◆ SNAPRING

4A-GE ENGINE

DRIVESHAFT (RH)

SIDE GEAR SHAFT

370 (27, 36)

DRIVESHAFT (LH)

◆ CLAMP

BOOT

◆ CLAMP

DAMPER

◆ CLAMP

OIL SEAL   ◆ OIL SEAL

SNAPRING

BOOT

TRIPOD JOINT

INBOARD JOINT TULIP

◆ SNAPRING

OUTBOARD JOINT AND DRIVESHAFT

Front halfshafts—Corolla FX

3. Matchmark the rear flange of the rear driveshaft to the differential pinion flange and then disconnect them.

4. Remove the 2 mounting bolts from the front and rear center bearings and then remove the 2 center bearings, intermediate shaft and rear driveshaft as an assembly.

5. Matchmark the universal joint and the rear center bearing flange, remove the bolts and separate the rear driveshaft from the rear center bearing.

6. Pull the front and rear center bearings from the intermediate shaft.

To install:

7. Install the 2 center bearings onto the intermediate shaft ends and then temporarily install the assembly.

8. Align the matchmarks and connect the rear driveshaft to

the differential. Tighten the bolts to 54 ft. lbs. (74 Nm); 27 ft. lbs. (37 Nm) on the Corolla.

9. Press the front driveshaft yoke into the transfer case, align the matchmarks at the rear of the shaft with those on the front center bearing flange and tighten the bolts to 54 ft. lbs. (74 Nm); 27 ft. lbs. (37 Nm) on the Corolla.

10. With the front edge of the rear driveshaft in position, depress the brake pedal and tighten the cross groove joint set bolts to 20 ft. lbs. (27 Nm) on all except 1989–91 Celica. On 1989–91 Celica, torque the bolts to 48 ft. lbs. (65 Nm).

11. With the vehicle in an unladen condition, adjust the distance between the rear edge of the boot cover and the rear driveshaft to 2.58–2.78 in. (65.5–70.5mm) on all except 1989–91 Celica. On 1989–91 Celica adjust the distance to 2.85–3.05 in. (72.5–77.5mm).

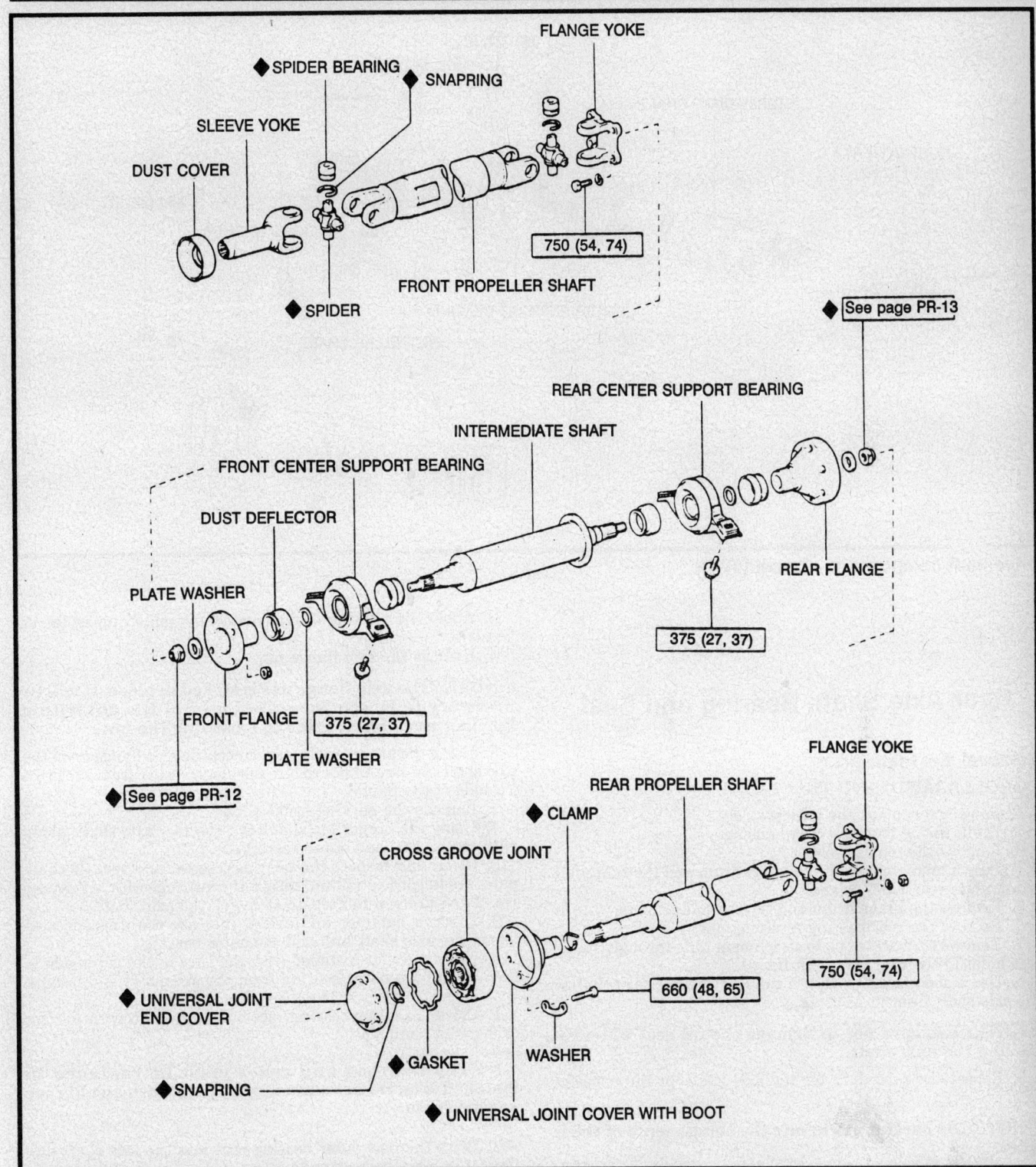

Driveshaft components—Camry/Celica All-Trac (4WD) and Corolla (4WD)

12. With the vehicle in an unladen condition, adjust the distance between the rear side of the center bearing housing and the rear side of the cushion to 0.45–0.53 in. (11.5–13.5mm).

13. Tighten the center bearing mounting bolts to 27 ft. lbs. (37 Nm). Make sure the center line of the bracket is at right angles to the shaft axial direction.

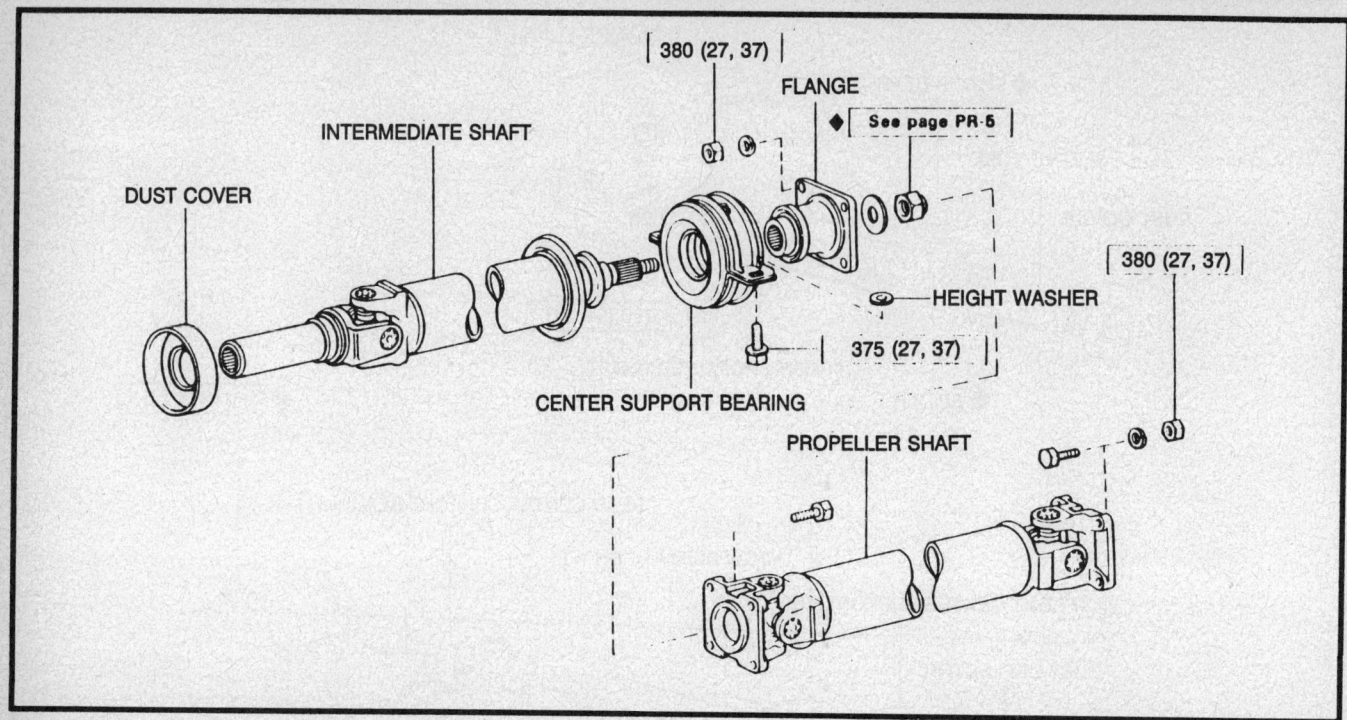

Driveshaft components—Tercel (4WD)

Rear Axle Shaft, Bearing and Seal

Removal and Installation

COROLLA (AWD) AND TERCEL (AWD)

1. Raise and support the vehicle safely.
2. Drain the oil from the axle housing.
3. Remove the rear wheels.
4. Punch matchmarks on the brake drum and the axle shaft to maintain rotational balance.
5. Remove the brake drum and related components.
6. Remove the rear bearing retaining nut.
7. Remove the backing plate attachment nuts through the access holes in the rear axle shaft flange.
8. Use a slide hammer with a suitable adapter to withdraw the axle shaft from its housing.

NOTE: Use care not to damage the oil seal when removing the axle shaft.

9. Repeat the procedure for the axle shaft on the opposite side.

NOTE: Be careful not to mix the components of the 2 sides.

10. Installation is performed in the reverse order of removal. Coat the lips of the rear housing oil seal with multipurpose grease prior to installation of the rear axle shaft. Always use new nuts, as they are the self-locking type.

1987–88 CRESSIDA

1. Raise and safely support the vehicle.
2. Disconnect the halfshaft from the axle flange and lower the halfshaft aside.

3. Apply the parking brake completely; pulled up as far as possible.
4. Remove the axle flange nut.

NOTE: The axle flange nut is staked in place. It will be necessary to loosen the staked part of the nut with a hammer and chisel, prior to loosening the nut.

5. Using the proper tools, disconnect the axle flange from the axle shaft. Be careful not to lose the plate washer from the bearing side of the flange.
6. Remove the parking brake shoes.
7. Using the proper tools, pull out the rear axle shaft, along with the oil seal and outer bearing.
8. Clean and inspect the bearings, races, and seal. If these parts are in good condition, repack the bearings with MP grease No. 2 and proceed to Step 15 to install the axle shaft.
9. Using a hammer and chisel, increase the clearance between the axle shaft hub and the outer bearing.
10. Using a puller installed with the jaws in the gap made in Step 9, pull the outer bearing from the axle shaft and remove the oil seal.
11. Drive the outer bearing race out of the hub with a brass drift and a hammer.

NOTE: Bearing and races must be replaced in matched sets. Do not use a new bearing with an old race or vice-versa.

12. Drive the new outer bearing race into the axle shaft hub until it is completely seated.

NOTE: The inner bearing race is replaced in the same manner as Steps 11 and 12.

13. Repack and install both bearings into the hub, being careful not to mis the bearings. The bearings should be packed with No. 2 multi-purpose grease.

14. Drive the seals into place. The inner seal should be driven to a depth of 1.22 in.; the outer to 0.217 in.

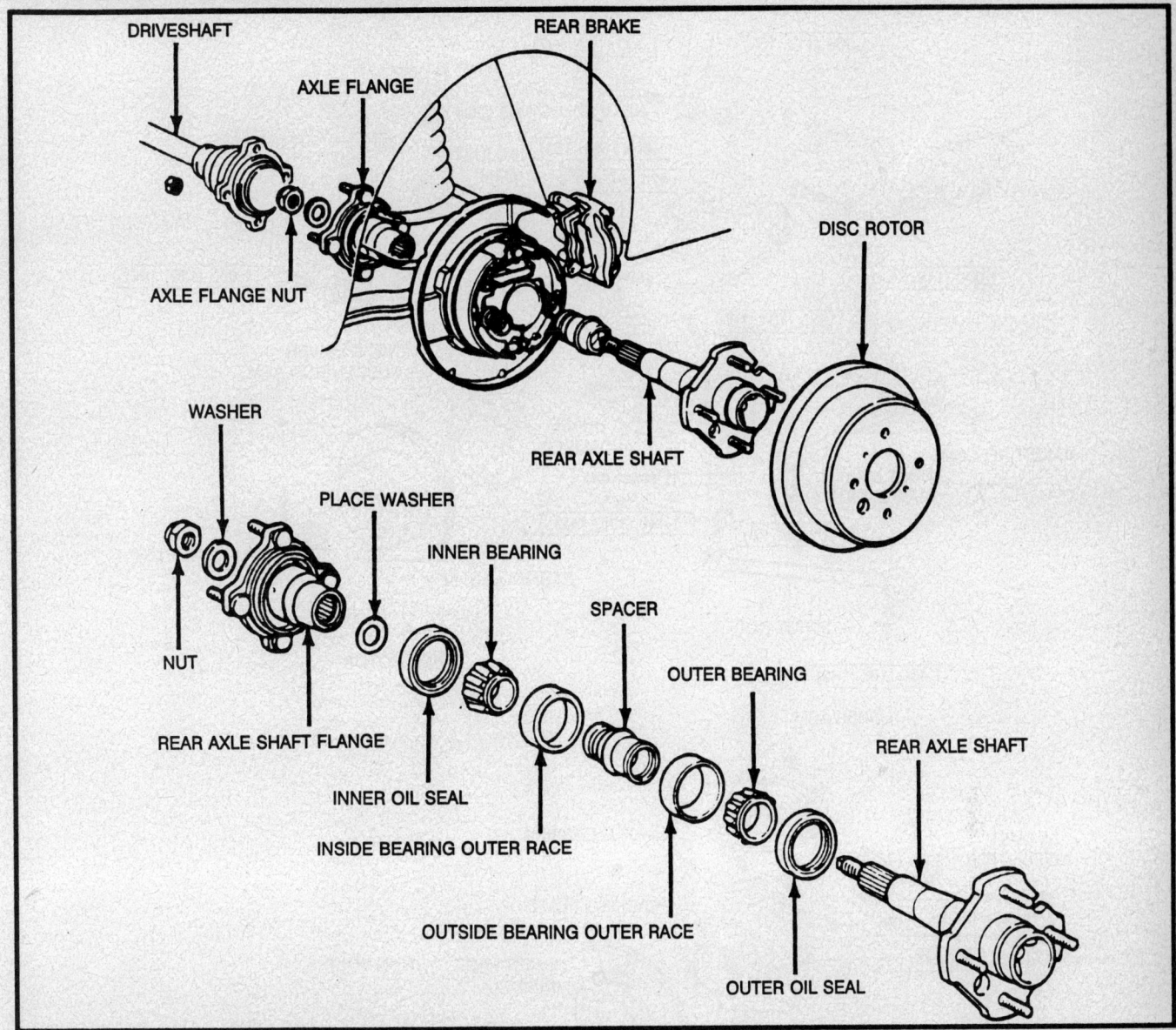

Rear axle shafts—1987–88 Cressida

To install:

15. Apply a thin coat of grease to the axle shaft flange. Install the rear axle shaft into the housing and install the flange with the plate washer.

16. Using the proper tools, draw the axle shaft into the flange.

17. Install a new axle shaft flange nut. Torque the nut to 22–36 ft. lbs. (30–49 Nm). There should be no horizontal play evident at the axle shaft.

18. Turn the axle shaft back and forth and retorque the nut to 58 ft. lbs. (78 Nm).

19. Using a torque wrench, check the amount of torque required to turn the axle shaft. The correct rotational torque is 0.9–3.5 inch lbs.

NOTE: The shaft should be turned at a rate of 6 seconds per turn to attain a true rotational torque reading.

20. If the rotational torque is less than specified, tighten the nut 5–10 degrees at a time until the proper rotational torque is reached. Do not tighten the nut to more than 145 ft. lbs. (196 Nm).

21. If the rotational torque is greater than specified, replace the bearing spacer and repeat Steps 18–20, if necessary.

22. After the proper rotational torque is reached, restake the nut into position.

23. Install the parking brake shoes.

24. Connect the axle driveshaft to the flange and torque the nuts to 51 ft. lbs. (69 Nm).

NOTE: If the maximum torque is exceeded while retightening the nut, replace the bearing spacer and repeat Steps 18–20. Do not back off the axle shaft nut to reduce the rotational torque.

25. Install the rear wheel and lower the vehicle.

SUPRA AND 1989–91 CRESSIDA

1. Raise and support the vehicle safely.

2. Remove the rear wheel and tire assembly. Remove the disc brake caliper from the rear axle carrier and suspend it with wire. Remove the rotor disc.

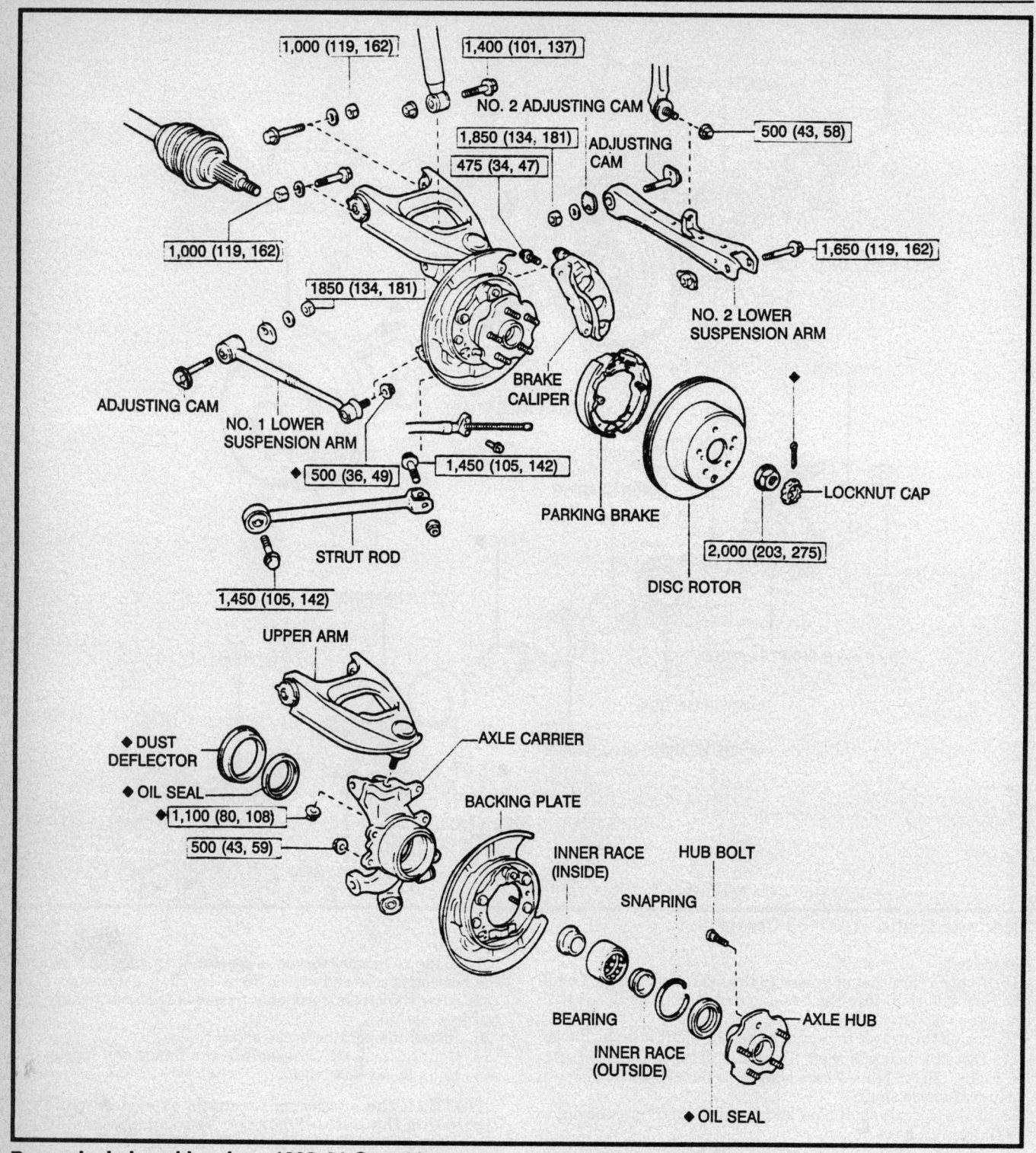

1,000 (119, 162)

1,400 (101, 137)

NO. 2 ADJUSTING CAM

1,850 (134, 181)

475 (34, 47)

ADJUSTING CAM

500 (43, 58)

1,000 (119, 162)

1850 (134, 181)

1,650 (119, 162)

NO. 2 LOWER SUSPENSION ARM

ADJUSTING CAM

NO. 1 LOWER SUSPENSION ARM

BRAKE CALIPER

◆ 500 (36, 49)

1,450 (105, 142)

PARKING BRAKE

LOCKNUT CAP

STRUT ROD

1,450 (105, 142)

2,000 (203, 275)

DISC ROTOR

UPPER ARM

◆ DUST DEFLECTOR

AXLE CARRIER

◆ OIL SEAL

BACKING PLATE

◆ 1,100 (80, 108)

500 (43, 59)

INNER RACE (INSIDE)

HUB BOLT

SNAPRING

BEARING

AXLE HUB

INNER RACE (OUTSIDE)

◆ OIL SEAL

Rear axle, hub and bearing—1988–91 Cressida

3. Remove the rear driveshaft. Disconnect the parking brake cable assembly.

4. Remove the bolt and nut attaching the carrier to the No. 1 suspension arm. Using the proper tool, separate the No. 1 suspension arm from the axle carrier.

5. Remove the bolt and nut attaching the carrier to the No. 2 suspension arm.

6. Disconnect the strut rod from the axle carrier. Disconnect the strut assembly from the axle carrier.

7. Disconnect the upper arm from the body and remove the axle hub assembly. Remove the upper arm mounting nut and remove the upper arm from the axle carrier.

8. Separate the backing plate and axle carrier. Using a suitable puller, remove the upper arm from the axle carrier.

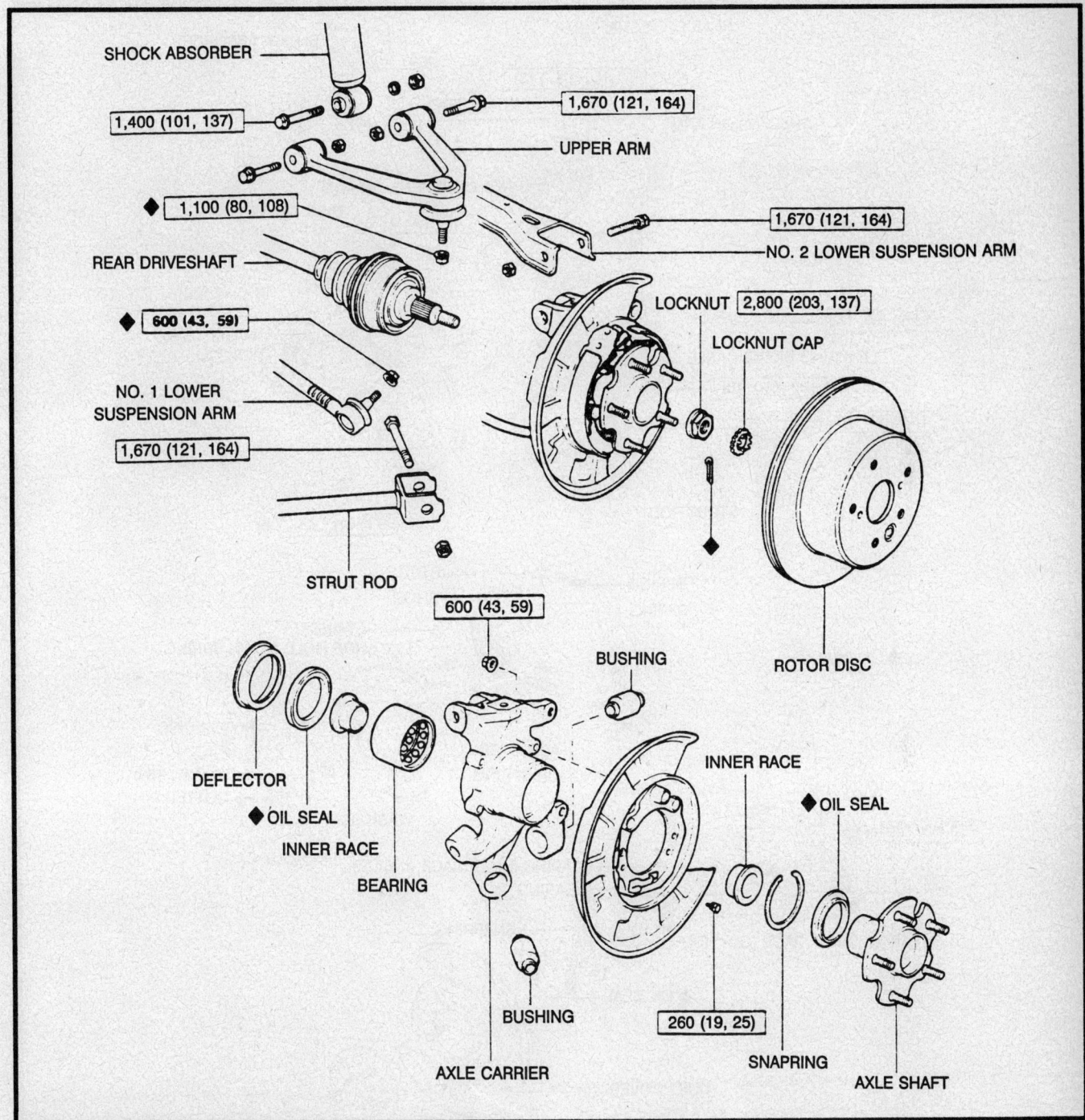

SHOCK ABSORBER

1,400 (101, 137)

1,670 (121, 164)

UPPER ARM

1,100 (80, 108)

1,670 (121, 164)

NO. 2 LOWER SUSPENSION ARM

REAR DRIVESHAFT

600 (43, 59)

LOCKNUT 2,800 (203, 137)

LOCKNUT CAP

NO. 1 LOWER SUSPENSION ARM

1,670 (121, 164)

STRUT ROD

600 (43, 59)

BUSHING

ROTOR DISC

DEFLECTOR

OIL SEAL

INNER RACE

BEARING

INNER RACE

OIL SEAL

BUSHING

AXLE CARRIER

260 (19, 25)

SNAPRING

AXLE SHAFT

Rear axle hub and carrier—Supra

9. Remove the dust deflector from the axle hub. Using a suitable puller remove the inner oil seal. Remove the hole snap-ring.

10. Using a suitable press, press out the bearing outer race from the axle carrier. Be sure to always replace the bearing as an assembly.

11. Remove the bearing inner race (inside) and 2 bearings from the bearing outer race.

To install:

12. Installation is the reverse order of the removal procedure. Observe the following torques:

Backing plate to axle carrier nuts—43 ft. lbs. (58 Nm).

Backing plate to axle carrier bolts—19 ft. lbs. (26 Nm).

No. 1 suspension arm nut—43 ft. lbs. (59 Nm)—Supra. 36 ft. lbs. (49 Nm)—Cressida.

Upper arm mounting nut—80 ft. lbs. (108 Nm).

Strut assembly nut—101 ft. lbs. (137 Nm).

Upper arm to body bolt—121 ft. lbs. (164 Nm) for Supra or 119 ft. lbs. (162 Nm) for Cressida.

No. 2 suspension arm to axle carrier—121 ft. lbs. (164 Nm) for Supra or 119 ft. lbs. (162 Nm) for Cressida.

Strut rod to axle carrier—121 ft. lbs. (164 Nm) for Supra. 105 ft. lbs. or (142 Nm) for Cressida.

Disc brake caliper bolts—34 ft. lbs. (47 Nm).

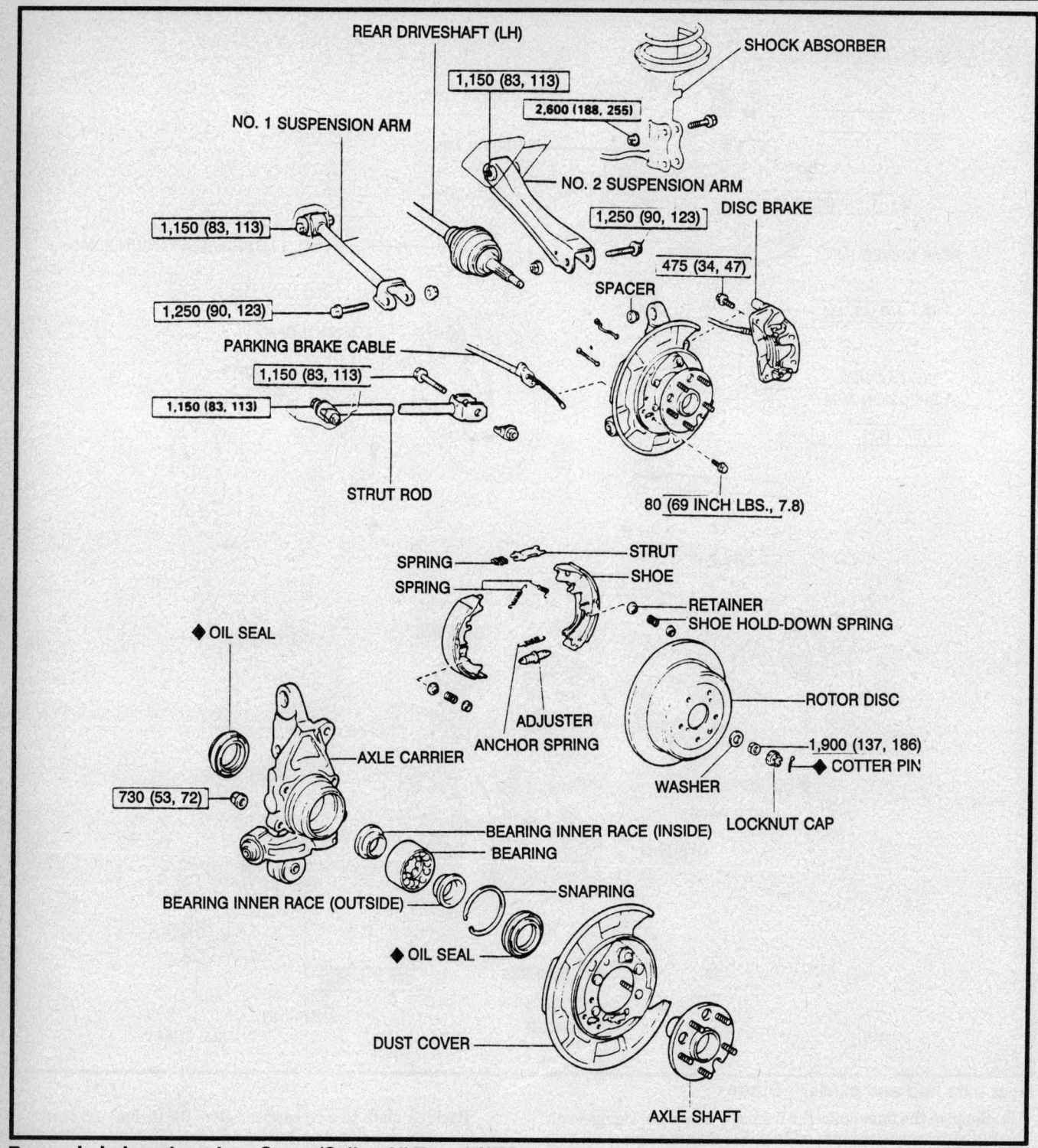

REAR DRIVESHAFT (LH)

1,150 (83, 113)

2,600 (188, 255)

SHOCK ABSORBER

NO. 1 SUSPENSION ARM

NO. 2 SUSPENSION ARM

DISC BRAKE

1,150 (83, 113)

1,250 (90, 123)

475 (34, 47)

SPACER

1,250 (90, 123)

PARKING BRAKE CABLE

1,150 (83, 113)

1,150 (83, 113)

STRUT ROD

80 (69 INCH LBS., 7.8)

SPRING — STRUT

SPRING — SHOE

RETAINER
SHOE HOLD-DOWN SPRING

◆ OIL SEAL

ROTOR DISC

ADJUSTER
ANCHOR SPRING

1,900 (137, 186)

◆ COTTER PIN

AXLE CARRIER

WASHER

LOCKNUT CAP

730 (53, 72)

BEARING INNER RACE (INSIDE)

BEARING

SNAPRING

BEARING INNER RACE (OUTSIDE)

◆ OIL SEAL

DUST COVER

AXLE SHAFT

Rear axle hub and carrier—Camry/Celica All-Trac (4WD)

1988–91 CAMRY (AWD) AND CELICA (AWD)

1. Raise the vehicle and support it safely.
2. Remove the rear wheel. Remove the disc brake caliper from the rear axle carrier and suspend it with wire. Remove the rotor disc.
3. Remove the rear halfshaft. Disconnect the parking brake cable assembly and remove the cable.

4. Remove the 2 axle carrier set nuts and the 2 bolts and then remove the camber adjusting cam.
5. Disconnect the strut rod at the axle carrier. Disconnect the No. 1 and No. 2 suspension arms at the axle carrier. Remove the axle carrier and hub.
6. Press the axle shaft out of the axle hub.
7. Using a 2-armed puller, remove the bearing inner race (outside) from the axle shaft. Remove the dust cover.

8. Remove the inner and outer oil seal from the axle carrier. Remove the hole snap-ring.

9. Using a suitable press, press out the bearing.

To install:

10. Installation is in the reverse order of removal. Please observe the following notes:

Tighten the axle carrier-to-shock bolts to 188 ft. lbs. (255 Nm).

Tighten the brake caliper mounting bolts to 34 ft. lbs. (47 Nm).

With the parking brake engaged, tighten the bearing locknut to 137 ft. lbs. (186 Nm).

With the wheels resting on the ground, tighten the strut rod bolt to 83 ft. lbs. (113 Nm); tighten the 2 suspension arms to 90 ft. lbs. (123 Nm).

Check the rear wheel alignment.

MR2

1. Raise and support the vehicle safely.

2. Remove the rear wheel and tire assembly. Remove the cotter pin, bearing locknut cap and bearing locknut.

3. Disconnect the parking brake cable. Remove the disc brake caliper from the rear axle carrier and suspend it with wire. Remove the rotor disc.

4. Disconnect the rear axle carrier from the lower arm. Remove the cotter pin and nut from the suspension arm. If

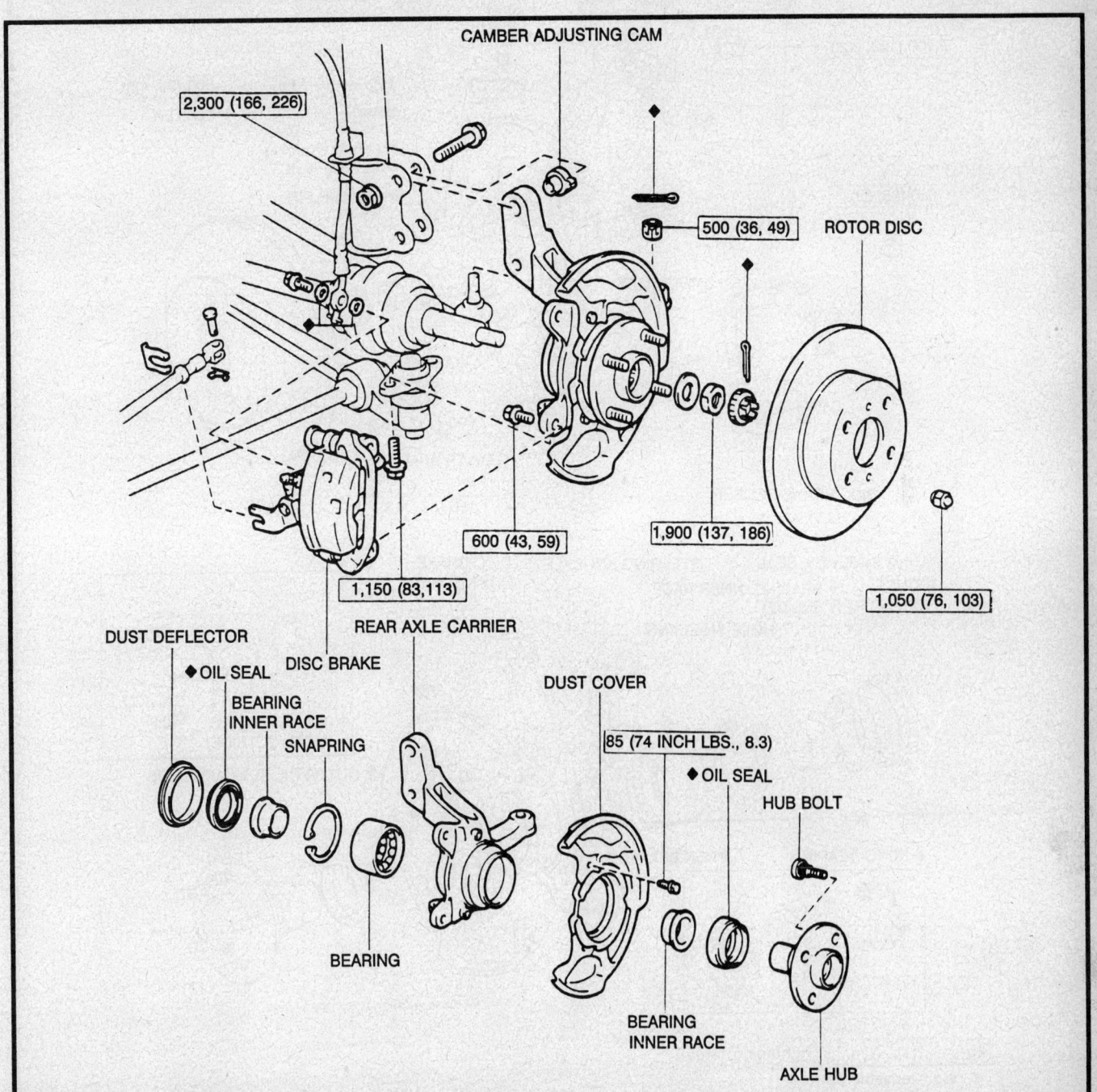

Rear axle hub and carrier—MR2

equipped with ABS, remove the speed sensor from the axle carrier.

5. Using a suitable tool separate the suspension arm from the rear axle carrier.

6. Place matchmarks on the strut lower bracket and camber adjusting cam.

7. Remove the 2 axle carrier set nuts and 2 bolts with the camber adjusting cam. Remove the rear axle carrier and axle hub.

8. Remove the dust deflector from the axle hub. Using a suitable puller remove the inner oil seal. Remove the hole snap-ring.

9. Remove the 3 bolts holding the disc brake dust cover to the rear axle carrier. Using a suitable puller remove the axle hub from the rear axle carrier.

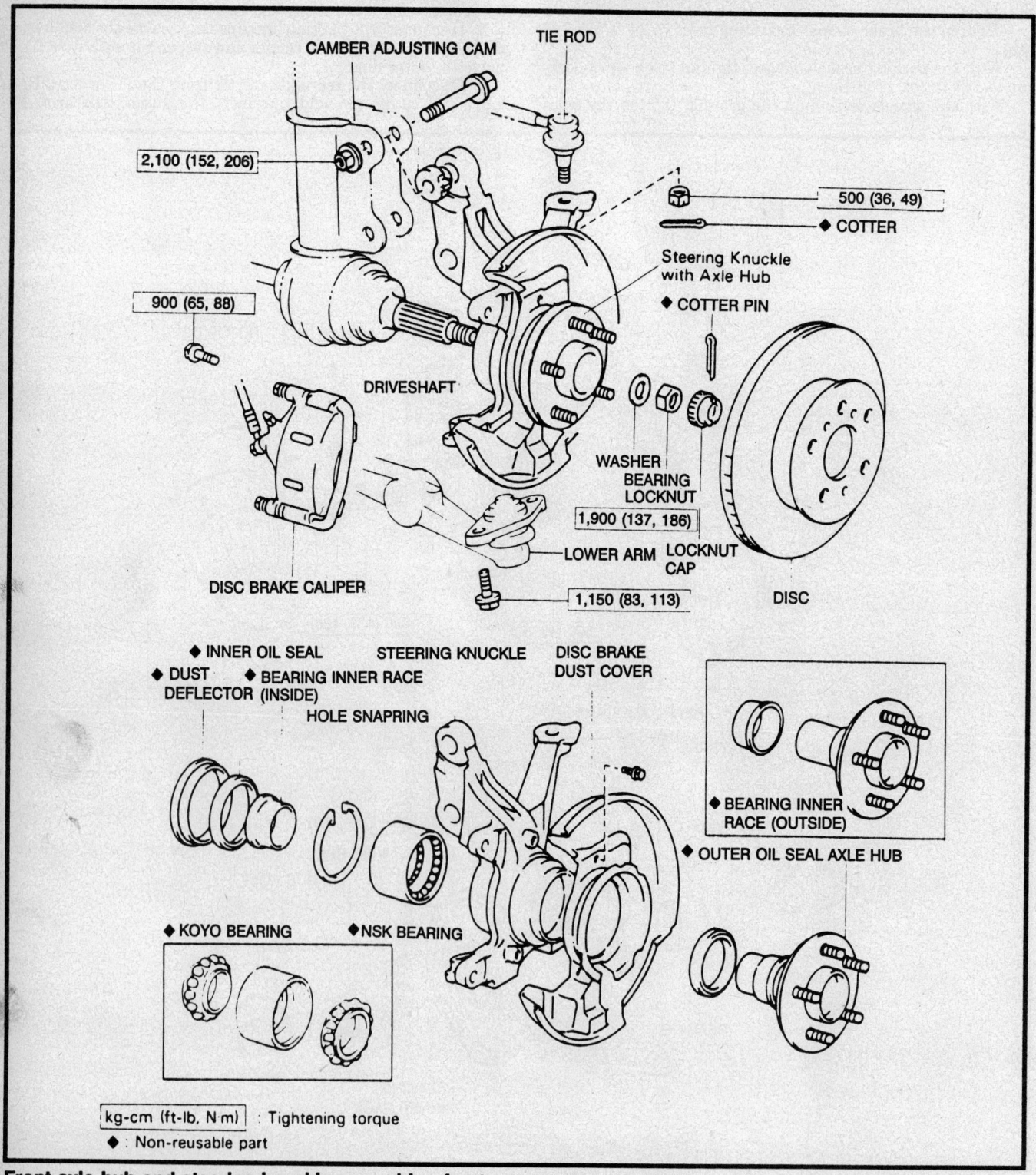

CAMBER ADJUSTING CAM   TIE ROD

2,100 (152, 206)

500 (36, 49)

◆ COTTER

Steering Knuckle with Axle Hub

◆ COTTER PIN

900 (65, 88)

DRIVESHAFT

WASHER
BEARING
LOCKNUT

1,900 (137, 186)

LOWER ARM   LOCKNUT CAP

DISC BRAKE CALIPER

1,150 (83, 113)

DISC

◆ INNER OIL SEAL   STEERING KNUCKLE   DISC BRAKE DUST COVER

◆ DUST DEFLECTOR   ◆ BEARING INNER RACE (INSIDE)

HOLE SNAPRING

◆ BEARING INNER RACE (OUTSIDE)

◆ OUTER OIL SEAL AXLE HUB

◆ KOYO BEARING   ◆ NSK BEARING

kg-cm (ft-lb, N·m) : Tightening torque

◆ : Non-reusable part

Front axle hub and steering knuckle assembly—front wheel drive models

10. Remove the bearing inner (inside) race. Using a suitable puller remove the bearing inner race (outside) from the rear axle hub.

11. Using a suitable puller remove the outer oil seal.

12. Remove the hub bearing by first placing the removed inner race (outside) in the bearing and using a suitable press, press out the bearing. Be sure to always replace the bearing as an assembly.

To install:

13. Installation is the reverse order of the removal procedure. During installation, observe the following torque specifications:

Two camber adjusting cam set bolts—166 ft. lbs. (226 Nm).

Suspension arm nut—36 ft. lbs. (49 Nm).

Rear axle carrier to the lower arm—59 ft. lbs. (1988–91: 83 ft. lbs.).

Brake caliper—43 ft. lbs. (59 Nm).

Bearing locknut—137 ft. lbs. (186 Nm) all except 3S-GTE engine. On 3S-GTE engine torque the rear wheel bearing locknut to 217 ft. lbs. (294 Nm).

If equipped with ABS, torque the wheel sensor bolt to 74 inch lbs. (8.3 Nm).

Front Wheel Hub, Knuckle and Bearings

Removal and Installation

FRONT WHEEL DRIVE VEHICLES ONLY

1. Raise and support the vehicle safely. Remove the front wheels.

2. Remove the cotter pin from the bearing locknut cap and then remove the cap.

3. Depress the brake pedal and loosen the bearing locknut.

4. Remove the brake caliper mounting nuts, position the caliper aside with the hydraulic line still attached and suspend it with a wire.

5. Remove the brake disc.

6. Remove the cotter pin and nut from the tie rod end and then, using a tie rod end removal tool, remove the tie rod.

7. Place matchmarks on the shock absorber lower mounting bracket and the camber adjustment cam, remove the bolts and separate the steering knuckle from the strut.

8. Remove the 2 ball joint attaching nuts and disconnect the lower control arm from the steering knuckle.

9. Carefully grasp the axle hub and knuckle assembly and pull it out from the halfshaft using the proper tool.

NOTE: Cover the halfshaft boot with a shop rag to protect it from any damage.

10. Clamp the steering knuckle in a vise and remove the dust deflector. Remove the nut holding the steering knuckle to the ball joint. Press the ball joint out of the steering knuckle.

11. Remove the dust deflector from the hub.

12. Pry out the bearing inner oil seal and then remove the hole snap-ring.

13. Remove the 3 bolts attaching the steering knuckle to the disc brake dust cover.

14. Remove the axle hub from the steering knuckle using the proper tool.

15. Remove the bearing inner race (inside).

16. Remove the bearing inner race (outside).

17. Remove the oil seal from the knuckle.

18. Position an old bearing inner race (outside) on the bearing and then use a hammer and a drift to carefully knock the bearing out of the knuckle.

To install:

19. Press a new bearing into the steering knuckle.

20. Using a suitable oil seal installation tool, drive a new oil seal into the knuckle.

21. Install the disc brake dust cover onto the knuckle using liquid sealant.

22. Apply grease between the oil seal lip, oil seal and the bearing and then press the axle hub into the steering knuckle.

23. Install a new hole snap-ring into the knuckle.

24. Press a new oil seal onto the knuckle and coat the contact surface of the seal and the halfshaft with grease. Press a new dust deflector into the knuckle.

25. Position the ball joint on the steering knuckle and tighten the nut to 14 ft. lbs. (20 Nm). Remove the nut, install a new one and tighten it to 82 ft. lbs. (111 Nm). On 1987–88 Camry and Corolla torque the nut to 94 ft. lbs. (127 Nm).

26. Connect the knuckle assembly to the lower strut bracket. Insert the mounting bolts from the rear and make sure the matchmarks made earlier are in alignment. Tighten the nuts as follows:

105 ft. lbs. (142 Nm) on 1987–88 Celica and 1987 Tercel.

188 ft. lbs. (255 Nm) on 1989–91 Celica.

166 ft. lbs. (226 Nm) on 1987–88 Camry and 1988–91 Tercel.

224 ft. lbs. (304 Nm) on 1989–91 Camry.

194 ft. lbs (263 Nm) on Corolla sedan and wagon.

27. Connect the tie rod end to the knuckle, tighten the nut to 36 ft. lbs. (49 Nm) and install a new cotter pin.

28. Connect the ball joint to the lower control arm and tighten the bolt to 47 ft. lbs. (64 Nm) except on the following vehicles:

1987–88 Camry—67 ft. lbs. (91 Nm).

1989–91 Camry—90 ft. lbs. (123 Nm).

1988–91 Celica—94 ft. lbs. (122 Nm).

1988–91 Tercel—59 ft. lbs. (80 Nm).

Corolla sedan and wagon—105 ft. lbs. (142 Nm).

29. Install the brake disc and the caliper. Tighten the caliper mounting bolts to 65 ft. lbs. (88 Nm) on all vehicles excpet Camry and 1988–91 Celica. On Camry torque the caliper mounting bolts to 86 ft. lbs. (117 Nm). On 1988–91 Celica, torque the caliper mountng bolts to 70 ft. lbs. (95 Nm).

30. Install the bearing locknut while having someone depress the brake pedal. Tighten it to 137 ft. lbs. (186 Nm). Install the adjusting nut cap and insert a new cotter pin.

31. Check the front end alignment.

STEERING

Steering Wheel

——— CAUTION ———

On vehicles equipped with an air bag, the negative battery cable must be disconnected, before working on the system. Failure to do so may result in deployment of the air bag and possible personal injury.

Removal and Installation

1. Position the front wheels straight ahead.

2. Unfasten the horn and turn signal multi-connector(s) at the base of the steering column shroud.

3. I equipped with a 3 spoked wheel, loosen the trim pad retaining screws from the back side of the steering wheel. The 2 spoke steering wheel is removed on the same manner as the

three spoke, except that the trim pad should be pried off with a small prybar. Remove the pad by lifting it toward the top of the wheel.

4. Lift the trim pad and horn button assembly from the wheel.

5. Remove the steering wheel hub retaining nut.

6. Scribe matchmarks on the hub and shaft to aid in correct installation.

7. Use a suitable puller to remove the steering wheel.

─────────── CAUTION ───────────

Do not attempt to remove or install the steering wheel by hammering on it. Damage to the energy-absorbing steering column could result.

8. Installation is the reverse of removal. Tighten the wheel retaining nut to 25 ft. lbs. (34 Nm).

Steering Column

Removal and Installation

1. Disconnect the negative battery cable.

2. If equipped, remove the universal joint at the steering gear and at the main shaft of the steering column assembly.

3. If equipped, disconnect upper universal joint from the intermediate shaft.

4. Remove the steering wheel.

5. Remove the instrument lower finish panels, air ducts and column covers.

6. Disconnect all electrical connections for ignition switch and combination switch. Remove the combination switch, as necessary.

7. Loosen column hole cover clamp bolt. Remove the support mounting bolt. Remove the 4 column tube mounting bolts. Pull out steering column. On some vehicles, remove the bolts from the column hole cover plate and remove 2 column bracket mounting nuts. Turn the steering column assembly clockwise and remove it from the vehicle, as necessary.

To install:

8. Place the the steering column assembly in the installed position. Tighten all necessary mounting nuts (torque evenly). Install and tighten all column cover bolts. Tighten column hole cover clamp bolt, as necessary.

9. Install combination switch. Reconnect all electrical connectors.

10. Install instrument lower finish panels, air duct and column covers.

11. Install or connect the universal joint. Insure that the retaining bolts are installed through both shaft grooves.

12. Install steering wheel and connect the negative battery cable.

Manual and Power Steering Rack

Removal and Installation

COROLLA (RWD)

1. Raise and support the vehicle safely. Remove the front wheels. Remove the bolt attaching the coupling yoke (U-joint) to the steering worm.

2. Disconnect the relay rod from the pitman arm. Disconnect the cotter pin and nut holding the knuckle arm to the tie rod.

3. If equipped with power steering, remove the front exhaust pipe, disconnect and plug the hydraulic lines and wire them aside.

4. Remove the gear housing bracket set bolts and remove the steering gear housing down and to the left.

5. Install in reverse of removal. Torque the housing-to-frame bolts to 25–36 ft. lbs. (34–49 Nm); the coupling yoke bolt to 26 ft. lbs. (35 Nm) and the relay rod to 36–50 ft. lbs. (49–68 Nm).

CRESSIDA

1. Raise and support the vehicle safely and remove the front wheels. Place matchmarks on the coupling and steering column shaft. Disconnect the solenoid connectors.

2. Disconnect the Pitman arm from the relay rod using a tie rod puller on the Pitman arm set nut. Disconnect the tie rod ends from the steering knuckles.

3. Remove the steering damper, if equipped.

4. Disconnect the steering gearbox at the coupling. Unbolt the gearbox from the chassis and remove. Remove the grommets from the gear housing.

5. Installation is in the reverse order of removal, with the exception of first aligning the matchmarks and connecting the steering shaft to the coupling before bolting the gearbox into the vehicle permanently. Tighten the steering damper bolts to 20 ft. lbs. (26 Nm). Tighten the tie rod ends to 43 ft. lbs. (59 Nm). Tighten the mounting bracket bolts to 56 ft. lbs. (76 Nm).

COROLLA (FWD), CAMRY AND SUPRA

1. Raise and support the vehicle safely. Remove the front wheels. Open the hood. Remove the 2 set bolts, and remove the sliding yoke from between the steering rack housing and the steering column shaft. On Supra, unbolt and remove the intermediate shaft (rack housing side first).

2. Remove the cotter pin and nut holding the knuckle arm to the tie rod end. Using a tie rod puller, disconnect the tie rod end from the knuckle arm.

3. On Corolla and Camry with power steering, remove the lower crossmember, remove the engine under cover, center engine mount member and the rear engine mount.

4. On Supra with turbocharger, remove the No. 1 air intake connector with No. 2 air hose.

5. Disconnect the power steering lines, if equipped. Remove the steering gear housing brackets. Slide the gear housing to the right side and then to the left side to remove the housing.

6. Installation is the reverse of removal. Torque the rack housing mounting bolts to 29–39 ft. lbs. (39–53 Nm) on the Celica and Supra; 43 ft. lbs. (58 Nm) on the Corolla and Camry, and the tie rod set nuts to 37–50 ft. lbs. (50–68 Nm) on Celica and Supra; 36 ft. lbs. (49 Nm) on the the Corolla and Camry. Use a new cotter pin. On Supras, install the intermediate shaft column side first, then rack side. On Corollas with power steering, tighten the rear engine mount bolts to 29 ft. lbs. (39 Nm) On Camry tighten the rear engine mounting bolts to 38 ft. lbs. (52 Nm). Tighten the center mounting member to 29 ft. lbs. (39 Nm). On power steering-equipped vehicles, bleed the power steering system and check for fluid leaks. Adjust toe-in on all vehicles.

CELICA

1. Raise and support the vehicle safely. Remove the front wheels.

2. Remove the both engine under covers.

3. Remove the 2 bolts that connect the steering column U-joint to the rack and then disconnect the column from the rack.

4. Remove the cotter pin and nut and then using a tie rod end removal tool, disconnect the tie rod end from the steering knuckle.

5. Remove the lower suspension crossmember.

6. Remove the mounting bolts and remove the center engine mount member.

7. Disconnect the exhaust pipe from the manifold. Position it aside.

8. Tag and disconnect the 2 hydraulic lines. Position them aside and suspend on a wire.

9. Remove the rear engine mount bracket.

10. Remove the mounting bolts and brackets and lower steering rack from the vehicle.

To install:

11. Position the rack assembly, install the grommets and

brackets and then tighten the 2 bolts and 2 nuts to 43 ft. lbs. (59 Nm).

12. Install the rear engine mount bracket and tighten the 2 bolts to 38 ft. lbs. (52 Nm).

13. Connect the hydraulic lines and tighten the union nuts to 29 ft. lbs. (39 Nm).

14. Connect the exhaust pipe to the manifold.

15. Install the center engine mount member and tighten the bolts to 29 ft. lbs. (39 Nm).

16. Install the lower crossmember and tighten the 5 outer bolts to 154 ft. lbs. (208 Nm). Tighten the center bolts to 29 ft. lbs.

17. Installation of the remaining components is in the reverse order of removal. Tighten the tie rod end nuts to 36 ft. lbs. (49 Nm) and use a new cotter pin. Tighten the steering column U-joint bolts to 26 ft. lbs. (35 Nm). Fill the power steering pump to the proper level, bleed the system and check the wheel alignment.

MR2 AND TERCEL

1. Rasie and support the vehicle safely.

2. Remove the front wheels and the engine under cover.

3. Place matchmarks on the main shaft, joint yoke and pinion shaft. Remove the intermediate shaft from the worm gear shaft.

4. If equipped with power steering, disconnect the 2 hydraulic lines. Position them aside and suspend on a wire.

5. Remove both tie rod ends.

6. Remove the lower suspension crossmember. Remove the center floor crossmember.

7. Remove the rack housing bracket mounting bolts and brackets.

NOTE: **Be careful not to damage the rubber boots.**

8. Remove the steering linkage.

9. Installation is the reverse of the removal procedure. Fill the power steering pump to the proper level and bleed the system. Check the wheel alignment.

Power Steering Pump

Removal and Installation

TERCEL, COROLLA, CAMRY, CELICA, 1987–89 MR2 AND 1987–88 CRESSIDA

1. Raise and support the vehicle safely. Remove the fan shroud.

2. On Camry and Celica, remove the right front wheel and the engine under cover. Remove the lower suspension crossmember.

3. Unfasten the nut from the center of the pump pulley. Disconnect the vacuum hose from the air control valve, if equipped.

NOTE: **Use the drive belt as a brake to keep the pulley from rotating.**

4. Withdraw the drive belt. On some vehicles, it may be necessary to remove the pulley in order to remove the drive belt.

5. If equipped with an idler pulley and on the Corolla FX, push on the drive belt to hold the pulley in place and remove the pulley set nut. Loosen the idler pulley set nut and adjusting bolt. Remove the drive belt and loosen the drive pulley to remove the Woodruff® key.

6. Remove the pulley and the Woodruff® key from the pump shaft.

7. Detach and plug the intake and outlet hoses from the pump reservoir.

NOTE: **Tie the hose ends up high so the fluid cannot flow out of them. Drain or plug the pump to prevent fluid leakage.**

8. Remove the bolt from the rear mounting brace.

9. Remove the front bracket bolts and withdraw the pump.

To install:

10. Tighten the pump pulley mounting bolt to 25–39 ft. lbs. (34–53 Nm).

11. Tighten the 5 outer mounting bolts on the lower crossmember to 154 ft. lbs. (209 Nm). On Celica, tighten the center bolt to 29 ft. lbs. (39 Nm).

12. Adjust the pump drive belt tension. The belt should deflect 0.13–0.93 in. under thumb pressure applied midway between the air pump and the power steering pump.

13. Fill the reservoir with Dexron® II automatic transmission fluid. Bleed the air from the system.

SUPRA AND 1989–91 CRESSIDA

7M-GE

1. Raise and support the vehicle safely. Drain the fluid from the reservoir tank.

2. Disconnect the air hose from the air control tank. Disconnect the return hose from the reservoir tank.

3. Remove the engine under cover. Disconnect and plug the pressure hose from the power steering pump.

4. Holding the power steering pump pulley, remove the pulley set nut. Remove the drive belt adjusting nut.

5. Remove the power steering pump set bolt. Remove the drive belt, pulley and Woodruff® key.

6. Disconnect the oil cooler hose bracket from the power steering pump. Remove the drive belt adjust bolt and remove the power steering set bolt and power steering pump.

7. Installation is the reverse order of the removal procedure. Be sure to bleed the system upon completion of the installation procedure.

7M-GTE

1. Raise and support the vehicle safely. Drain the fluid from the reservoir tank.

2. Remove the No. 1 and No. 2 air hoses with the No. 4 air cleaner pipe.

3. Disconnect the connector from the air flow meter. Remove the air flow meter installation bolt. Loosen the 5 clamps and disconnect the air hoses, release the 3 clips on the air cleaner case. Loosen the No. 7 air hose clamp and remove the No. 7 air cleaner hose with the air flow meter.

4. Remove the oil reservoir tank with bracket. Disconnect the 2 air hoses from the air control valve on the power steering pump.

5. Remove the adjusting strut. Remove the engine under cover.

6. Holding the power steering pump pulley, remove the pulley set nut. Remove the drive belt adjusting nut.

7. Remove the power steering pump set bolt. Remove the drive belt, pulley and Woodruff® key.

8. Disconnect and plug the pressure hose from the power steering pump.

9. Remove the power steering set bolt and power steering pump.

10. Installation is the reverse order of the removal procedure. Be sure to bleed the system upon completion of the installation procedure.

1990–91 MR2

The power steering pump is not driven by a conventional drive belt. Instead the pump is driven by an electric motor. The pump and motor are combined as one unit. Removal and installation is as follows:

1. Disconnect the negative battery cable.

2. Raise and support the vehicle safely.

3. Remove the front luggage under cover.

4. Remove the pump shield and rear stay.

5. Disconnect the hydraulic lines from the pump. Plug the lines to prevent the loss of power steering fluid.

6. Disconnect the electrical wires from the top of the motor.

7. Remove the pump mounting bolts, bushings and spacers. Check the bushings for cracks and deformation. Replace as necessary.

8. Remove the pump and motor assembly.

To install:

9. Position the pump and install the mounting bolts, bushings and spacers. Torque the bolts to 19 ft. lbs. (25 Nm).

10. Connect the electrical wires to the top of the motor.

11. Connect the hydraulic lines.

12. Install the rear stay and pump shield.

13. Install the front luggage under cover.

14. Lower the vehicle and connect the negative battery cable.

15. Fill the power steering reservoir to the proper level and bleed the system.

Belt Adjustment

1. Inspect the power steering drive belt to see that it is not cracked or worn. Be sure its surfaces are free of grease or oil.

2. Push down on the belt halfway between the fan and the alternator pulleys (or crankshaft pulley) with thumb pressure. Belt deflection should be ⅜–½ in. (10–13mm).

3. If the belt tension requires adjustment, loosen the adjusting link bolt and move the power steering pump until the proper belt tension is obtained.

4. Do not over-tighten the belt, as damage to the power steering pump bearings could result. Tighten the adjusting link bolt.

5. Drive the vehicle and re-check the belt tension. Adjust as necessary.

System Bleeding

1. Raise and support the vehicle safely.

2. Fill the pump reservoir with the proper fluid.

3. Rotate the steering wheel from lock-to-lock several times. Add fluid if necessary.

4. With the steering wheel turned fully to one lock, crank the starter while watching the fluid level in the reservoir.

NOTE: Do not start the engine. Operate the starter with a remote starter switch or have an assistant do it from inside the vehicle. Do not run the starter for prolonged periods.

5. Repeat Step 4 with the steering wheel turned to the opposite lock.

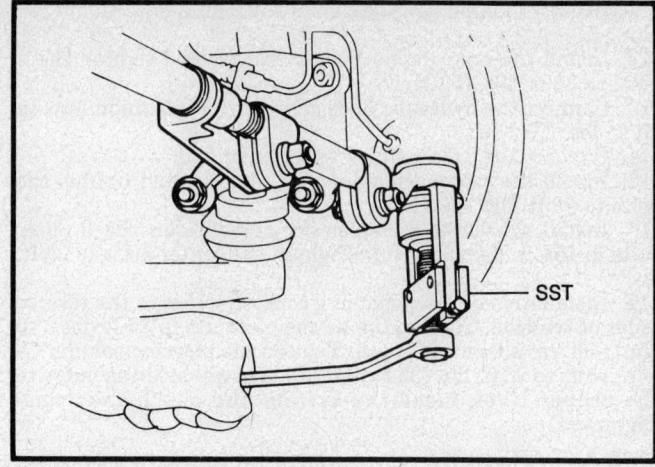

Typical tie rod end removal

6. Start the engine. With the engine idling, turn the steering wheel from lock-to-lock several times.

7. Lower the front of the vehicle and repeat Step 6.

8. Center the wheel at the midpoint of its travel. Stop the engine.

9. The fluid level should not have risen more than 0.2 in. (5mm). If it does, repeat Step 7.

10. Check for fluid leakage.

Tie Rod Ends

Removal and Installation

1. Scribe alignment marks on the tie rod and rack end.

2. Working at the steering knuckle arm, pull out the cotter pin and then remove the castellated nut.

3. Using a tie rod end puller, disconnect the tie rod from the steering knuckle arm.

4. Repeat the first 2 steps on the other end of the tie rod (where it attaches to the relay rod or steering rack).

To install:

5. Align the alignment marks on the tie rod and rack end.

6. Install the tie rod end.

7. Tighten the tie rod end nuts to 36 ft. lbs. (49 Nm).

BRAKES

Master Cylinder

Removal and Installation

1. Disconnect the level warning switch connector.

2. Remove the fluid in the master cyclinder with a suitable syringe.

3. On MR2, remove the luggage compartment.

4. Disconnect the hydraulic lines from the master cylinder. Plug the ends of the lines to prevent loss of fluid.

5. Detach the hydraulic fluid pressure differential switch wiring connectors.

6. Loosen the master cylinder reservoir mounting nuts.

7. Unfasten the nuts and remove the master cylinder assembly from the power brake unit.

8. Before tightening the master cylinder mounting nuts or bolts, screw the hydraulic line into the cylinder body a few turns.

9. After installation is completed, bleed the master cylinder and the brake system.

Proportioning Valve

A proportioning valve is used to reduce the hydraulic pressure to the rear brakes because of weight transfer during high speed stops. This helps to keep the rear brakes from locking up by improving front to rear brake balance.

Removal and Installation

1. Disconnect the brake lines from the valve unions.

2. Remove the valve mounting bolt, if used, and remove the valve.

NOTE: If the proportioning valve is defective, it must be replaced as an assembly; it cannot be rebuilt.

3. Installation is the reverse of removal. Bleed the brake system after it is completed.

Power Brake Booster

Removal and Installation

1. Remove the master cylinder. Disconnect the vacuum hose from the brake booster.
2. Remove the instrument lower finish panel, as required.
3. On the MR2, remove the wheel guard, instrument lower finish panel and air duct.
4. Remove the brake pedal return spring.
5. Remove clip and clevis pin.
6. Remove the brake booster nuts and clevis pin.
7. Pull out the brake booster and gasket.
8. Installation is the reverse order of the removal procedure. Bleed the brake system.

Brake Caliper

Removal and Installation

1. Raise and support the vehicle safely.
2. Remove the front or rear wheels.
3. Disconnect the brake hose from the caliper. Plug the end of the hose to prevent loss of fluid.
4. Remove the bolts that attach the caliper to the torque plate.
5. Lift up and remove the caliper assembly.
6. Installation is the reverse of the removal procedure. Torque the caliper bolts to 20–27 ft. lbs. (27–41 Nm) on front disc brakes and 14 ft. lbs. (20 Nm) for rear disc brakes. Fill and bleed the system.

Disc Brake Pads

Removal and Installation

MR2 – REAR, CRESSIDA – FRONT AND REAR, 1988–91 CELICA (AWD) – FRONT, 1987 COROLLA (RWD) – FRONT AND REAR

1. Raise and support the vehicle safely.
2. Remove the wheels.
3. Siphon a sufficient quantity of brake fluid from the master cylinder reservoir to prevent any brake fluid from overflowing the master cylinder when removing or installing new pads. This is necessary as the piston must be forced into the caliper bore to provide sufficient clearance when installing the pads.
4. Grasp the caliper from behind and carefully pull it to seat the piston in its bore.
5. On 1987 Corolla RWD with rear discs, remove the parking brake cable clip, cotter pin and hole pin and then disconnect the cable from the parking brake cable bracket.
6. Loosen and remove the lower caliper slide pin (mounting bolt).
7. Swivel the caliper upward and aside, exposing the brake pads. Do not disconnect the brake line.
8. Slide out the old brake pads along with any anti-squeal shims, anti-rattle springs, pad wear indicators, pad guide plates and pad support plates. Take great care to note the position of all assorted pad hardware.
9. Check the brake disc (rotor) for thickness and run-out. Inspect the caliper and piston assembly for breaks, cracks, fluid seepage or other damage. Overhaul or replace as necessary.

To install:

10. Install the pad support plates, anti-rattle springs or guide plates into the torque plate.

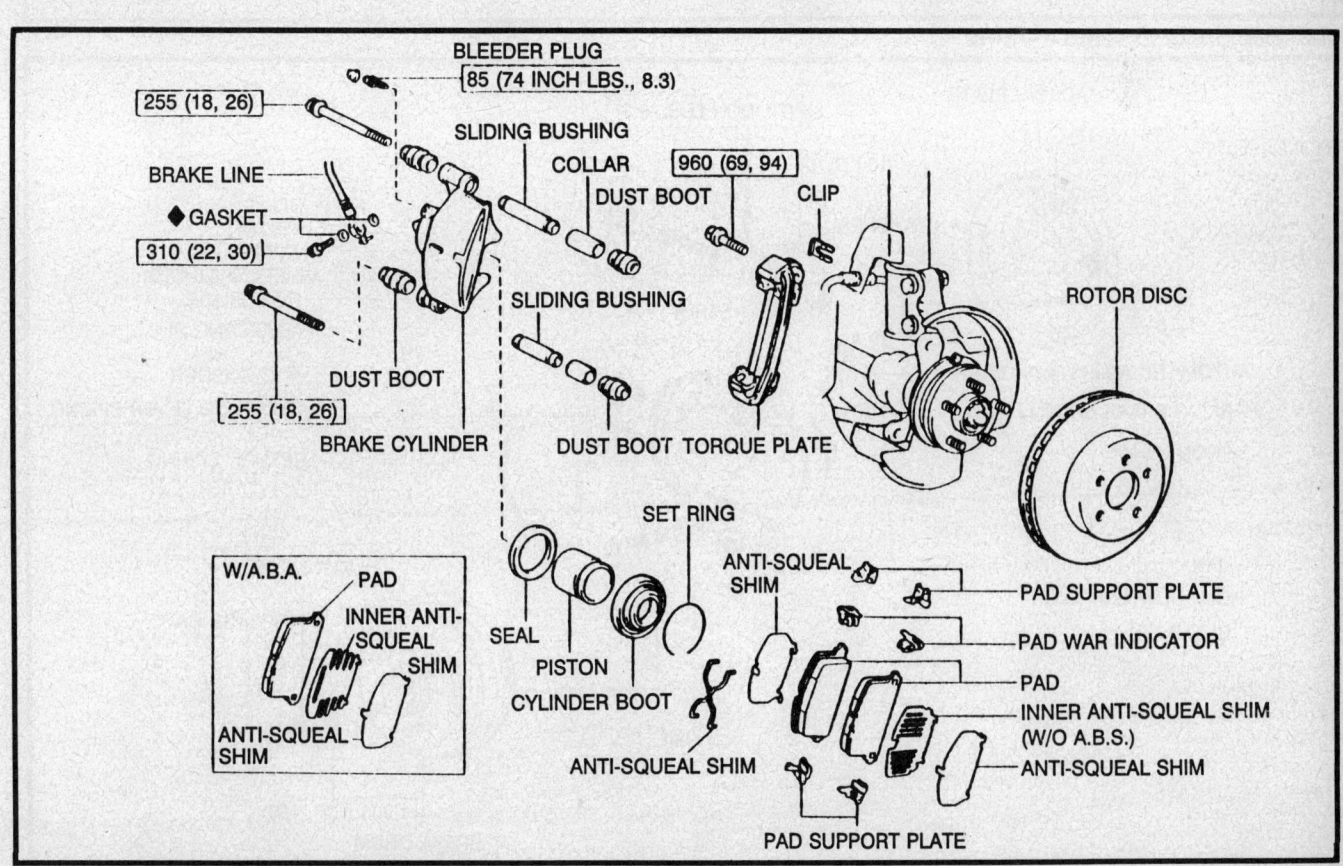

Front disc brake assembly—Celica 2WD

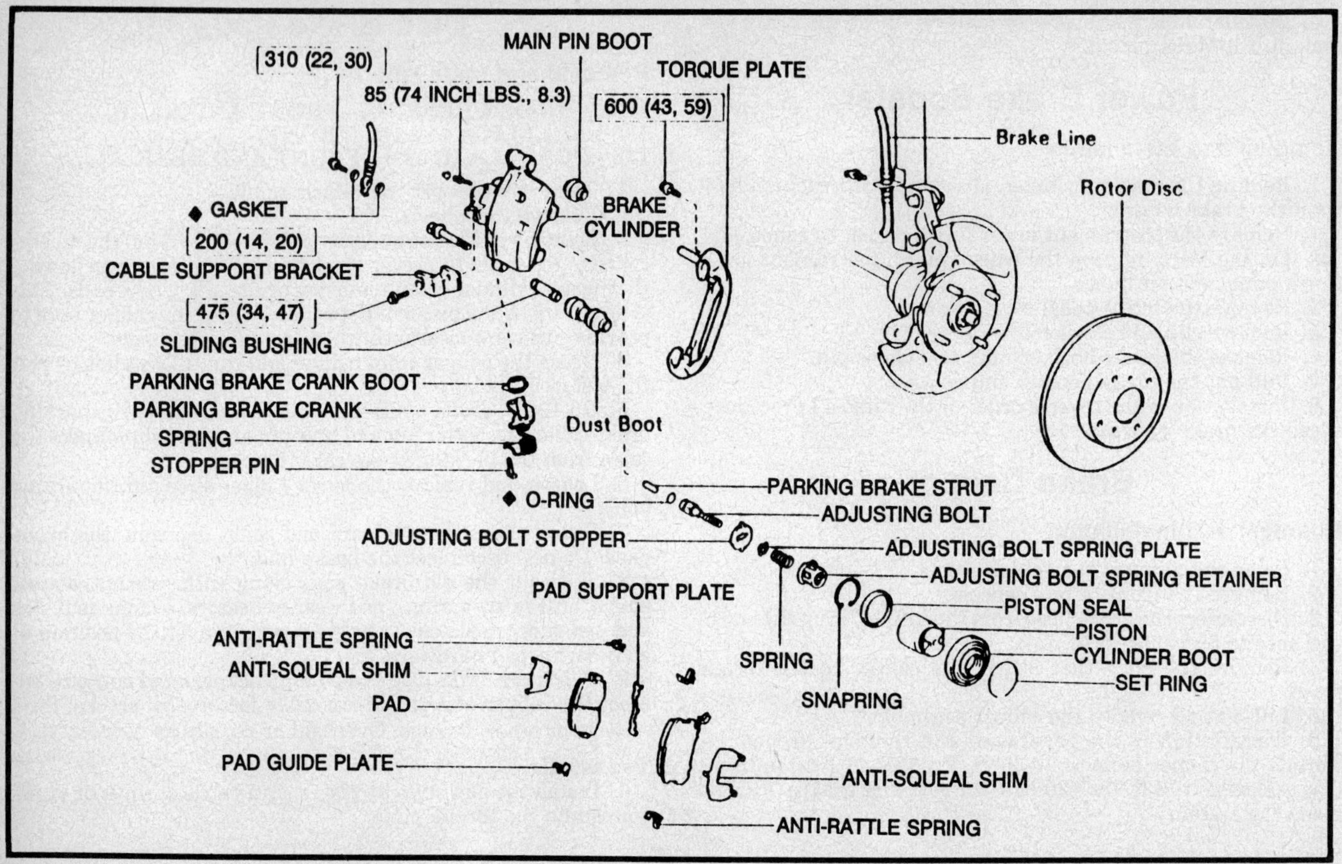

MAIN PIN BOOT

[310 (22, 30)]

TORQUE PLATE

85 (74 INCH LBS., 8.3)

[600 (43, 59)]

Brake Line

Rotor Disc

◆ GASKET

BRAKE CYLINDER

[200 (14, 20)]

CABLE SUPPORT BRACKET

[475 (34, 47)]

SLIDING BUSHING

PARKING BRAKE CRANK BOOT

PARKING BRAKE CRANK

SPRING

STOPPER PIN

Dust Boot

◆ O-RING

PARKING BRAKE STRUT

ADJUSTING BOLT

ADJUSTING BOLT STOPPER

ADJUSTING BOLT SPRING PLATE

ADJUSTING BOLT SPRING RETAINER

PAD SUPPORT PLATE

PISTON SEAL

ANTI-RATTLE SPRING

PISTON

ANTI-SQUEAL SHIM

SPRING

CYLINDER BOOT

PAD

SNAPRING

SET RING

PAD GUIDE PLATE

ANTI-SQUEAL SHIM

ANTI-RATTLE SPRING

Rear disc brake assembly—MR2

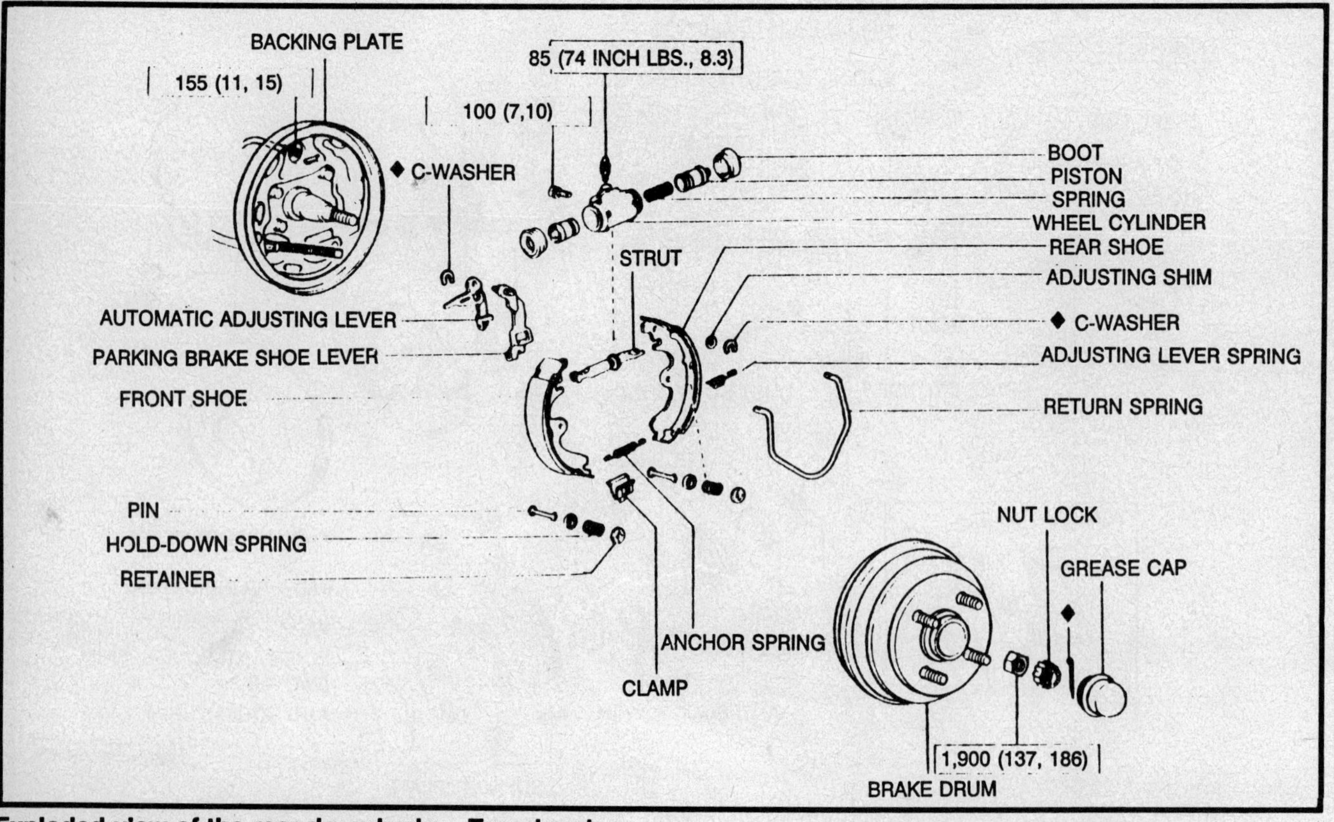

BACKING PLATE

85 (74 INCH LBS., 8.3)

| 155 (11, 15) |

| 100 (7,10) |

◆ C-WASHER

BOOT

PISTON

SPRING

WHEEL CYLINDER

REAR SHOE

ADJUSTING SHIM

STRUT

◆ C-WASHER

AUTOMATIC ADJUSTING LEVER

ADJUSTING LEVER SPRING

PARKING BRAKE SHOE LEVER

FRONT SHOE

RETURN SPRING

PIN

NUT LOCK

HOLD-DOWN SPRING

GREASE CAP

RETAINER

ANCHOR SPRING

CLAMP

| 1,900 (137, 186) |

BRAKE DRUM

Exploded view of the rear drum brake—Tercel sedan

11. Install the pad wear indicators onto the pad.

12. Install the anti-squeal shims on the outside of each pad and then install the pad assemblies into the torque plate.

13. Swivel the caliper back down over the pads. If it won't fit, use a C-clamp or hammer handle and carefully force the piston into its bore.

14. On the MR2 rear disc, turn the piston clockwise while pushing it in until it locks in place. Fit the protrusion on the inner pad into the groove in the piston stopper and then install the caliper. Be careful not to pinch the boot.

15. Install and tighten the lower slide pin or mounting bolt.

16. Install the parking brake cable on the Corolla with rear discs and then adjust the automatic adjuster by pulling and releasing the parking brake lever several times.

17. Install the wheel and lower the vehicle. Check the brake fluid level. Adjust the parking brake on rear disc brake vehicles.

MR2 – FRONT, TERCEL – FRONT
CAMRY – FRONT AND REAR
SUPRA – FRONT AND REAR
1988-91 CELICA (AWD) – REAR
CELICA (2WD) – FRONT AND REAR
COROLLA (FWD) – FRONT AND REAR

1. Raise and support the vehicle safely.

2. Remove the wheels.

3. Siphon a sufficient quantity of brake fluid from the master cylinder reservoir to prevent any brake fluid from overflowing the master cylinder when removing or installing new pads. This is necessary as the piston must be forced into the caliper bore to provide sufficient clearance when installing the pads.

4. Grasp the caliper from behind and carefully pull it to seat the piston in its bore.

5. Loosen and remove the 2 caliper mounting pins (bolts) and then remove the caliper assembly. Position it aside. Do not disconnect the brake line.

6. Slide out the old brake pads along with any anti-squeal shims, springs, pad wear indicators and pad support plates. Make sure to note the position of all assorted pad hardware.

To install:

7. Check the brake disc (rotor) for thickness and run-out. Inspect the caliper and piston assembly for breaks, cracks, fluid seepage or other damage. Overhaul or replace as necessary.

8. Install the pad support plates into the torque plate.

9. Install the pad wear indicators onto the pads. Be sure the arrow on the indicator plate is pointing in the direction of rotation.

10. Install the anti-squeal shims on the outside of each pad and then install the pad assemblies into the torque plate.

11. Position the caliper back down over the pads. If it won't fit, use a C-clamp or hammer handle and carefully force the piston into its bore.

12. Install and tighten the caliper mounting bolts.

13. Install the wheels and lower the vehicle. Check the brake fluid level.

Brake Rotor

Removal and Installation

1. Raise and support the vehicle safely.

2. Remove the wheels.

3. Temporarily attach 2 lug nuts onto the rotor disc.

4. Unbolt the torque plate from the steering knuckle.

5. Remove the lug nuts and pull the rotor from the wheel hub.

6. Installation is the reverse of the removal procedure.

Brake Drums

Removal and Installation

1. Raise and support the vehicle safely.

2. Remove the wheels.

3. Remove the brake drum. Tap the drum lightly with a rubber mallet in order to free it. If the brake drum cannot be removed easily, insert a small prybar through the hole in the backing plate and hold the automatic adjuster lever away from the adjusting bolt. Using another prybar, relieve the brake shoe tension by rotating the adjusting bolt (star wheel) in a clockwise direction. If the drum still will not come off, use a puller; but, first make sure the parking brake is released.

4. Installation is the reverse of the removal procedure.

Brake Shoes

Removal and Installation

TERCEL SEDAN, COROLLA (RWD)
1987-88 CRESSIDA

1. Raise and support the vehicle safely. Remove the wheels.

2. Remove the brake drums.

NOTE: Do not depress the brake pedal once the brake drum has been removed.

3. Carefully unhook the tension spring from the leading (front) brake shoe. On the Tercel, its a return spring; also remove the clamp.

4. Press the hold-down spring retainer in and turn the pin.

5. Remove the hold-down spring, retainers and the pin. Pull out the brake shoe and unhook the anchor spring from the lower edge.

6. Remove the hold-down spring from the trailing (rear) shoe. Pull the shoe out with the adjuster strut, automatic adjuster assembly and springs attached and disconnect the parking brake cable. Remove the tension/return and anchor springs from the rear shoe.

7. Remove the adjusting strut. Unhook the adjusting lever spring from the rear shoe and then remove the automatic adjuster assembly by popping out the C-clip.

To install:

8. Inspect the shoes for signs of unusual wear or scoring.

9. Check the wheel cylinder for any sign of fluid seepage or frozen pistons.

10. Clean and inspect the brake backing plate and all other components. Check that the brake drum inner diameter is within specified limits. Lubricate the backing plate bosses and the anchor plate.

11. Mount the automatic adjuster assembly onto a new rear brake shoe. Make sure the C-clip fits properly. Connect the adjusting strut and install the spring.

12. Connect the parking brake cable to the rear shoe and then position the shoe so the lower end rides in the anchor plate and the upper end is against the boot in the wheel cylinder. Install the pin and the hold-down spring. Press the retainer down over the pin and rotate the pin so the crimped edge is held by the retainer. Install the anchor spring between the front and rear shoes and then stretch the spring enough so the front shoe will fit as the rear did in Step 10. Install the hold-down spring, pin and retainer. Stretch the tension/return spring between the 2 shoes and connect it so it rides freely. Don't forget the return spring clamp on the Tercel.

13. Check that the automatic adjuster is operating properly; the adjusting bolt should turn when the parking brake lever, in the brake assembly, not in the vehicle!, is moved. Adjust the strut as short as possible and then install the brake drum. Set and release the parking brake several times.

14. Install the wheel and lower the vehicle. Check the level of brake fluid in the master cylinder.

CAMRY, CELICA, TERCEL WAGON AND COROLLA (FWD)

1. Raise and support the vehicle safely. Remove the wheels.

2. Remove the brake drums.

NOTE: Do not depress the brake pedal once the brake drum has been removed!

3. Carefully unhook the return spring from the leading (front) brake shoe. Grasp the hold-down spring pin with pliers and turn it until its in line with the slot in the hold-down spring. Remove the hold-down spring and the pin. Pull out the brake shoe and unhook the anchor spring from the lower edge.

4. Remove the hold-down spring from the trailing (rear) shoe. Pull the shoe out with the adjuster strut, automatic adjuster assembly and springs attached and disconnect the parking brake cable. Unhook the return spring and then remove the adjusting strut. Remove the anchor spring.

5. Remove the adjusting strut. Unhook the adjusting lever spring from the rear shoe and then remove the automatic adjuster assembly by popping out the C-clip.

To install:

6. Inspect the shoes for signs of unusual wear or scoring.

7. Check the wheel cylinder for any sign of fluid seepage or frozen pistons.

8. Clean and inspect the brake backing plate and all other components. Check that the brake drum inner diameter is within specified limits. Lubricate the backing plate bosses and the anchor plate.

9. Mount the automatic adjuster assembly onto a new rear brake shoe. Make sure the C-clip fits properly. Connect the adjusting strut/return spring and then install the adjusting spring.

10. Connect the parking brake cable to the rear shoe and then position the shoe so the lower end rides in the anchor plate and the upper end is against the boot in the wheel cylinder. Install the pin and the hold-down spring. Rotate the pin so the crimped edge is held by the retainer.

11. Install the anchor spring between the front and rear shoes and then stretch the spring enough so the front shoe will fit as the rear did in Step 10. Install the hold-down spring and pin. Connect the return spring/adjusting strut between the 2 shoes and connect it so it rides freely.

12. Check that the automatic adjuster is operating properly; the adjusting bolt should turn when the parking brake lever (in the brake assembly, not in the vehicle!) is moved. Adjust the strut as short as possible and then install the brake drum. Set and release the parking brake several times.

13. Install the wheel and lower the vehicle. Check the level of brake fluid in the master cylinder.

Wheel Cylinder

Removal and Installation

1. Plug the master cylinder inlet to prevent hydraulic fluid from leaking.

2. Remove the brake drums and shoes.

3. Working from behind the backing plate, disconnect the hydraulic line from the wheel cylinder.

4. Unfasten the screws retaining the wheel cylinder and withdraw the cylinder.

To install:

5. Installation is performed in the reverse order of removal. However, once the hydraulic line has been disconnected from the wheel cylinder, the union seat must be replaced. To replace the seat, proceed in the following manner:

   a. Use a screw extractor with a diameter of 0.1 in. or equivalent, having reverse threads, to remove the union seat from the wheel cylinder.

   b. Drive in the new union seat with a $5/16$ in. bar, used as a drift.

   c. Bleed the brake system after completing wheel cylinder, brake shoe and drum installation.

Parking Brake Cable

Adjustment

1. Slowly pull the parking brake lever upward, without depressing the button on the end of it, while counting the number of notches required until the parking brake is applied.

NOTE: Two "clicks" are equal to 1 notch.

2. Check the number of notches against the following specifications.

   Tercel (2WD)—5–8 clicks.
   1988–91 Tercel (2WD)—7–9 clicks.
   1987–88 Tercel (AWD)—6–8 clicks.
   1987 Celica—5–8 clicks.
   1988–90 Celica—4–7 clicks.
   1987 Corolla RWD (rear drum brakes)—5–8 clicks.
   1987 Corolla RWD (rear disc brakes)—6–9 clicks.
   1987–90 Corolla FWD—4–7 clicks (FX16 and vehicles w/ rear disc—5–8).
   MR2—5–8 clicks.
   Cressida—5–8 clicks.
   Camry—5–8 clicks.

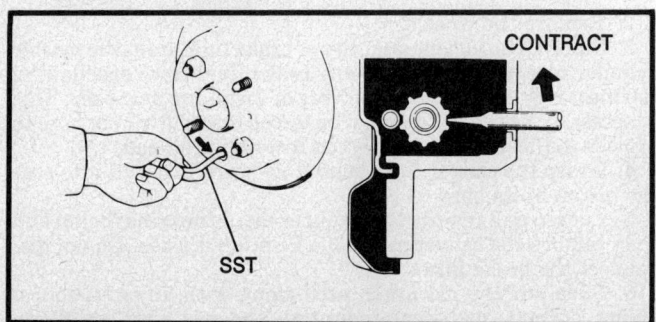

Parking brake adjustment—models with rear disc brakes; the arrow indicates the direction for loosening the parking brake shoes

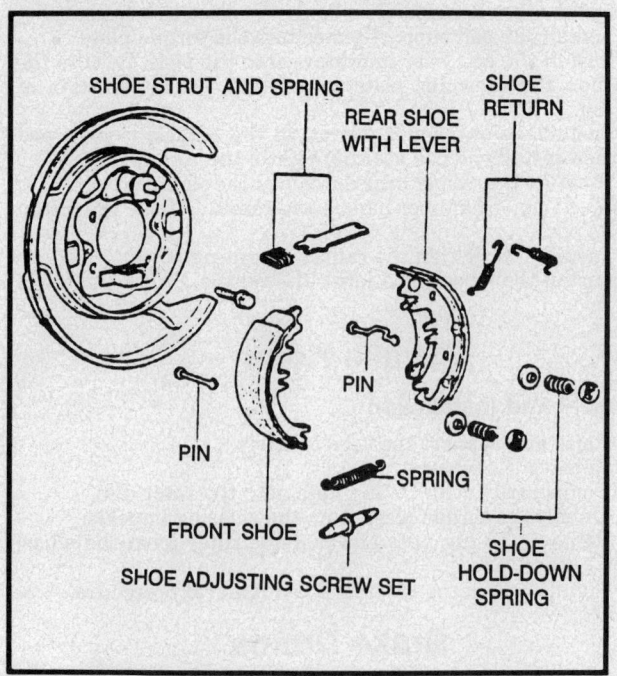

Exploded view of the parking brake on models with rear disc brakes

Supra—5–8 clicks.

3. If the brake system requires adjustment, loosen the cable adjusting nut cap which is located at the rear of the parking brake lever.

NOTE: On some vehicles, the adjustment and lock nuts are located under the vehicle, beneath the lever assembly.

4. Take up the slack in the parking brake cable by rotating the adjusting nut with another open end wrench.
 a. If the number of notches is less than specified, turn the nut counterclockwise.
 b. If the number of notches is more than specified, turn the nut clockwise.
5. Tighten the adjusting cap, using care not to disturb the setting of the adjusting nut.
6. Check the rotation of the rear wheels to be sure the brakes are not dragging.

Brake System Bleeding

MASTER CYLINDER

1. Check the fluid level in the master cylinder. Add fluid as necesary.
2. Disconnect the brake tubes from the master cylinder.
3. Slowly depress the brake pedal and hold it.
4. Close off the outlet opening on the master cylinder with finger pressure and release the brake pedal.
5. Repeat Steps 3 and 4 several times to bleed all the air from the master cylinder.

BRAKE LINES

1. Connect a vinyl tube the to the bleeder screw on the brake cylinder and submerge the other end of the tube in a transparent container half filled with clean brake fluid.
2. Pump the brake pedal several times and loosen the bleeder screw with the pedal held down.
3. When brake fluid stops coming out of the tube, tighten the bleeder screw and release the brake pedal.
4. Repeat Steps 2 and 3 until no air bubbles can be seen in the container.
5. Repeat the procedure for each wheel.
6. Check the level in the master cylinder. Add fluid as necessary.

Anti-Lock Brake Actuator

Removal and Installation

1. Remove the brake fluid from the master cylinder with a syringe.

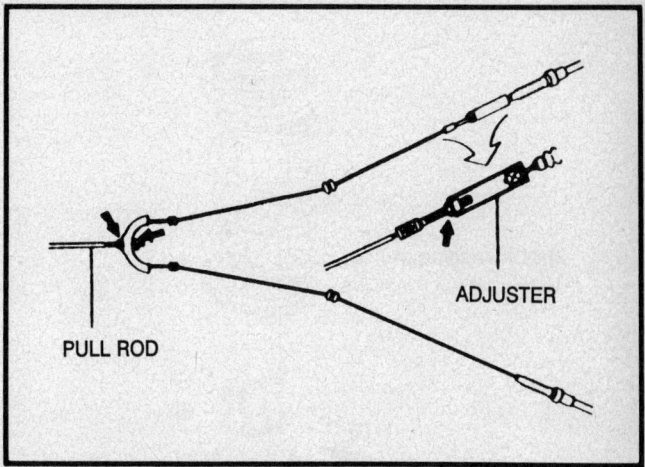

Parking brake adjustment—Cressida

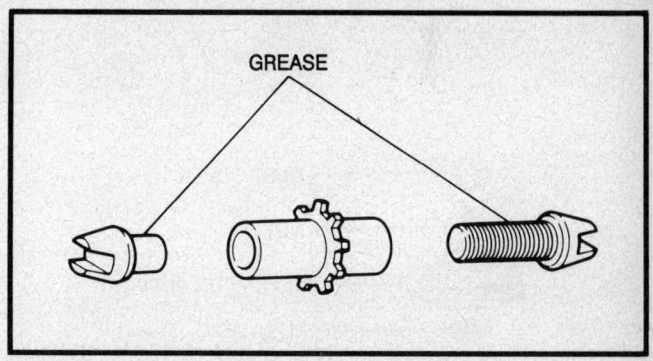

Before assembly, lubricate the adjuster parts as indicated—models with rear disc brakes

2. Remove the plastic cover from the actuator.
2. Disconnect the hydraulic lines from the actuator. Plug the lines to prevent loss of fluid.
4. Disconnect the electrical connectors from the actuator.
5. Remove the actuator from the bracket.
6. Installation is the reverse of the removal procedure. Fill and bleed the system.

FRONT SUSPENSION

MacPherson Strut

Removal and Installation

1. Remove the hubcap and loosen the lug nuts.
2. Raise and support the vehicle safely.

NOTE: Do not support the weight of the vehicle on the suspension arm; the arm will deform under its weight.

3. Unfasten the lug nuts and remove the wheel.
4. Remove the union bolt and 2 washers and disconnect the front brake line from the disc brake caliper. Remove the clip from the brake hose and pull off the brake hose from the brake hose bracket.
5. Remove the caliper and wire it aside. Matchmark on the strut lower bracket and camber adjust cam, if equipped. Remove the 2 bolts and nuts which attach the strut lower end to the steering knuckle lower arm.
6. Disconnect and remove the TEMS actuator from the top of the strut on late Cressida and Supra.
7. Unbolt the upper control arm where it attaches to the body on 1987–89 Supra.
8. Remove the 3 nuts (4 nuts on the FX vehicles) which secure the upper strut mounting plate to the top of the wheel arch.

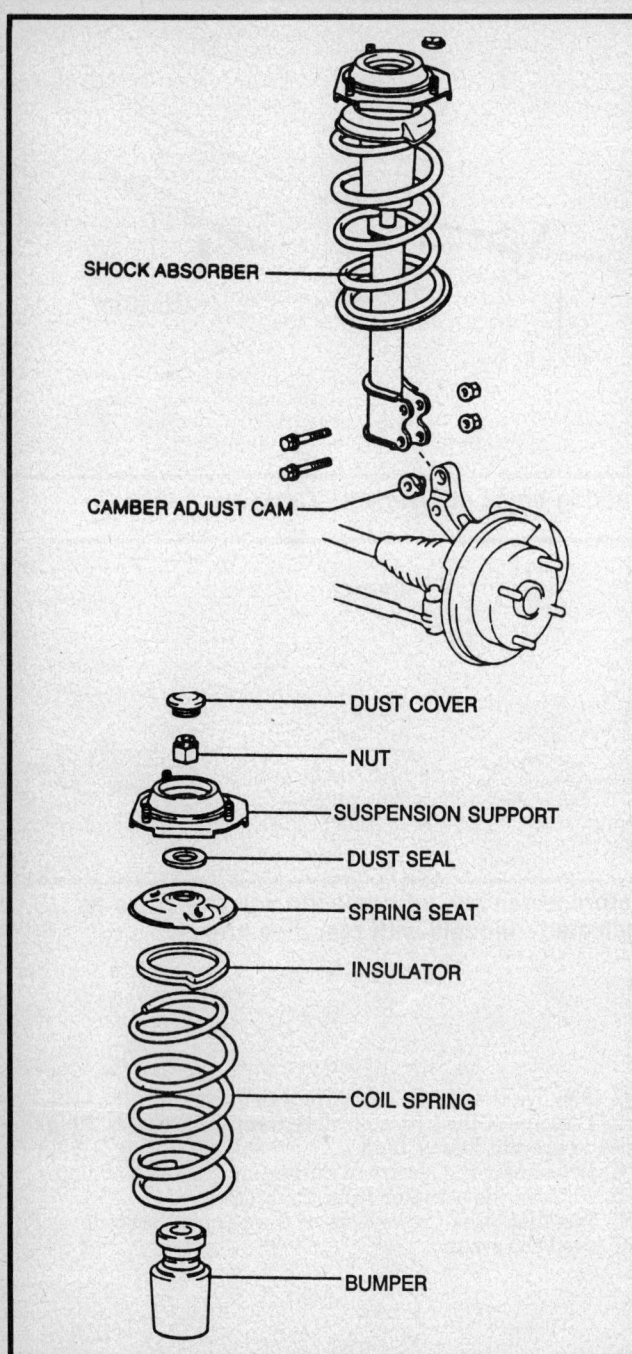

SHOCK ABSORBER

CAMBER ADJUST CAM

DUST COVER

NUT

SUSPENSION SUPPORT

DUST SEAL

SPRING SEAT

INSULATOR

COIL SPRING

BUMPER

Strut used on all front wheel drive cars

NOTE: Press down on the suspension lower arm, in order to remove the strut assembly. This must be done to clear the collars on the steering knuckle arm bolt holes when removing the shock/spring assembly.

To install:

9. Align the hole in the upper suspension support with the shock absorber piston or end, so they fit properly.

10. Always use a new nut and nylon washer on the shock absorber piston rod end when securing it to the upper suspension support. Torque the nut to 29–40 ft. lbs. (39–54 Nm).

NOTE: Do not use an impact wrench to tighten the nut.

11. Coat the suspension support bearing with multipurpose grease prior to installation. Pack the space in the upper support with multipurpose grease, also, after installation.

12. Tighten the suspension support-to-wheel arch bolts to the following specifications:

> Corolla RWD — 11–16 ft. lbs. (11–22 Nm).
> Corolla FWD (1987–90) — 29 ft. lbs. (39 Nm).
> Celica — 47 ft. lbs. (64 Nm).
> Camry — 47 ft. lbs. (64 Nm).
> Supra — 26 ft. lbs. (35 Nm).
> 1987–88 Cressida — 25–29 ft. lbs. (34–39 Nm).
> 1989–91 Cressida — 32 ft. lbs. (43 Nm).
> 1987 Tercel — 11–15 ft. lbs. (11–20 Nm).
> 1988–90 Tercel — 20–25 ft. lbs. (27–34 Nm).
> 1987–89 MR2 — 21–25 ft. lbs. (28–34 Nm).
> 1990–91 MR2 — 29 ft. lbs. (39 Nm).

13. Tighten the shock absorber-to-steering knuckle arm bolts to the following specifications:

> Corolla (RWD) — 50–65 ft. lbs. (68–88 Nm).
> Corolla (FWD) — 1988–91 sedan and wagon 194 ft. lbs. (263 Nm).
> 1987 Tercel — 105 ft. lbs. (143 Nm).
> 1988–91 Tercel Sedan — 166 ft. lbs. (226 Nm).
> 1987–88 MR2 — 105 ft. lbs. (143 Nm).
> 1989 MR2 — 119 ft. lbs. (162 Nm).
> 1990–91 MR2 — 188 ft. lbs. (255 Nm).
> Supra — 106 ft. lbs. (144 Nm).
> 1987–88 Celica FWD — 152 ft. lbs.
> 1989–91 Celica FWD — 188 ft. lbs. (255 Nm).
> Cressida — 80 ft. lbs.
> 1987–88 Camry — 166 ft. lbs. (226 Nm).
> 1989–91 Camry — 224 ft. lbs. (304 Nm).
> All others — 65 ft. lbs. (88 Nm).

14. Adjust the front wheel bearing preload.
15. Bleed the brake system.

Upper Ball Joints

Inspection

Disconnect the ball joint from the steering knuckle and check free-play by hand. Replace the ball joint, if it is noticeably loose.

Removal and Installation

NOTE: If equipped with both upper and lower ball joints—if both are to be removed, always remove the lower one first.

SUPRA

The ball joint is an integral component of the upper control arm. Ball joint replacement requires that the entire arm assembly be replaced. Please refer to Upper Control Arm.

Lower Control Arm/Ball Joints

Inspection

COROLLA (RWD) AND CRESSIDA

Raise the front end and position a piece of wood under the wheel and lower the vehicle until there is an ½ load on the strut. Check the front wheel play. Replace the lower ball joint if the play at the wheel rim exceeds 0.1 in. (2.54mm) vertical motion or 0.25 in. (6mm) horizontal motion. Be sure the dust covers are not torn and that they are securely glued to the ball joints.

NOTE: Do not raise the control arm on Corolla or Cressida vehicles; damage to the arm will result.

TERCEL, CAMRY, COROLLA (FWD), CELICA, SUPRA AND MR2

1. Raise the vehicle and place wooden blocks under the front wheels. The block height should be 7.09–7.87 in. (180–200 Nm).

2. Use jack stands for additional safety.

3. Make sure the front wheels are in a straight forward position.

4. Check the wheels.

5. Lower the jack until there is approximately half a load on the front springs.

6. Move the lower control arm up and down to check that there is no ball joint play.

Removal and Installation

NOTE: If equipped with both upper and lower ball joints, if both ball joints are to be removed, always remove the lower and then the upper ball joint.

COROLLA (RWD)

The ball joint and control arm cannot be separated from each other. If one fails, then both must be replaced as an assembly, in the following manner:

1. Remove the stabilizer bar securing bolts.

2. Unfasten the torque strut mounting bolts.

3. Remove the control arm mounting bolt and detach the arm from the front suspension member. .

4. Remove the steering knuckle arm from the control arm with a ball joint puller.

5. Inspect the suspension components, which were removed for wear or damage. Replace any parts, as required.

6. Installation is the reverse of the removal procedure. During installation, please observe the following:

a. When installing the control arm on the suspension member, tighten the bolts partially at first.

b. Complete the assembly procedure and lower the vehicle to the ground.

c. Bounce the front of the vehicle several times. Allow the suspension to settle, then tighten the lower control arm bolts to 51–65 ft. lbs. (69–88 Nm).

d. Lubricate the ball joint.

e. Check the front end alignment.

CELICA

1. Raise and support the vehicle safely. Remove the wheels.

2. Disconnect the lower control arm from the steering knuckle.

3. Remove the nut and disconnect the stabilizer bar from the control arm.

4. On all but the left-side control arm, if with automatic transmissions, remove the control arm front set nut and washer. Remove the rear bracket bolts and then remove the arm.

5. On the left arm, if with automatic transmissions, remove the control arm front set nut and washer. Remove the 4 bolts and 2 nuts that attach the lower suspension crossmember to the frame and remove the crossmember. Remove the bolt and nut and lift out the lower arm with the lower arm shaft.

To install:

6. On all but the left-side control arm, if with automatic transmissions, install the lower control arm shaft washer with the tapered side toward the body. Install the lower arm with the bracket and then temporarily install the washer and nut to the lower arm shaft and bracket bolts.

7. On the left-side arm, if with automatic transmissions, position the washer on the lower arm shaft and then install them to the lower arm. Temporarily install the washer and nut to the shaft with the tapered side toward the body. Install the lower arm with the shaft to the body and temporarily install the rear brackets. Install the bolt and nut to the lower arm shaft and tighten them to 154 ft. lbs. (208 Nm). Install the crossmember to the body and tighten the 4 bolts to 154 ft. lbs. (208 Nm). Tighten the 2 nuts to 29 ft. lbs. (39 Nm).

8. Connect the lower arm to the steering knuckle and tighten the bolt and 2 nuts to 94 ft. lbs. (127 Nm).

9. Connect the stabilizer bar to the control arm and tighten the nut to 26 ft. lbs. (35 Nm).

10. Install the wheel, lower the vehicle and bounce it several times to set the suspension.

11. Tighten the front set nut to 156 ft. lbs. (212 Nm). Tighten the rear bracket bolts to 72 ft. lbs. (98 Nm).

MR2

1. Raise the vehicle and support it safely. Remove the wheel.

2. Remove the cotter pin and castle nut and then press the lower arm out of the ball joint.

3. Press the ball joint out of the steering knuckle.

4. Remove the 2 nuts and disconnect the strut bar from the control arm.

5. Remove the lower control arm-to-body bolt and remove the arm.

To install:

6. When installing the lower arm, position it in the strut bar and tighten the nuts finger-tight. Do the same thing with the arm-to-body bolt.

7. Connect the control arm to the ball joint and tighten the castle nut to 58 ft. lbs. (78 Nm). Install a new cotter pin.

8. Tighten the strut bar-to-arm bolts to 83 ft. lbs. (113 Nm).

9. Install the tires, lower the vehicle and bounce it several times to set the suspension.

10. Tighten the control arm-to-body bolt to 94 ft. lbs. (127 Nm) on 1987–89 vehicles and 87 ft. lbs. (118 Nm) on 1990–91 vehicles. Check the wheel alignment.

CRESSIDA

1. Raise and support the vehicle safely. Remove the wheels.

2. Remove the 2 knuckle arm-to-strut bolts, pull down on the control arm and disconnect it and the knuckle arm from the strut.

3. Remove the cotter pin and nut and press the tie rod off the knuckle arm.

4. Remove the nut attaching the stabilizer bar to the control arm and disconnect the bar.

5. Remove the 2 nuts and then disconnect the strut bar from the control arm.

6. Disconnect the control arm from the crossmember and remove it and the rack boot protector as an assembly.

7. Remove the cotter pin and nut and then press the knuckle arm off the control arm.

To install:

8. Press the knuckle arm into the control arm and then install the assembly into the crossmember.

9. Connect the stabilizer bar to the control arm and tighten the nut to 13 ft. lbs. (18 Nm).

10. Connect the strut bar to the control arm and tighten the nuts to 48 ft. lbs. (60 Nm) for 1987, 54 ft. lbs. (73 Nm) for 1988 or 76 ft. lbs. (103 Nm) for 1989–91.

11. Connect the knuckle arm to the strut housing and tighten the bolts to 72 ft. lbs. (98 Nm) for 1987 or 80 ft. lbs. (108 Nm) for 1988–91.

12. Install the wheel and lower the vehicle. Bounce the vehicle several times to set the suspension and then tighten the control arm-to-body bolt to 80 ft. lbs. (108 Nm) for 1987–88 or 121 ft. lbs. (164 Nm) for 1989–91.

13. Check the front wheel alignment.

SUPRA

NOTE: This procedure is for ball joint removal only. To remove the lower control arm, please refer to the Lower Control Arm procedure.

1. Raise and support the vehicle safely.

2. Remove the wheels.

3. Remove the steering knuckle and then remove the upper control arm.

4. Remove the lower ball joint mounting nuts and the bolt. Remove the attachment plate.

5. Remove the lower ball joint.

6. Installation is in the reverse order of removal. Tighten the ball joint mounting bolt and nuts to 94 ft. lbs. (127 Nm).

TERCEL

1. Raise and support the vehicle safely. Remove the wheels.

2. Remove the 2 bolts attaching the ball joint to the steering knuckle.

3. Remove the stabilizer bar nut, retainer and cushion.

4. Raise the opposite wheel until the body of the vehicle just lifts off the supports.

5. Loosen the lower control arm mounting bolt, wiggle the arm back and forth and then remove the bolt. Disconnect the lower control arm from the stabilizer bar.

NOTE: When removing the lower control arm, be careful not to lose the caster adjustment spacer.

6. Carefully mount the lower control arm in a vise and then, using a ball joint removal tool, disconnect the ball joint from the arm.

To install:

7. Tighten the ball joint-to-control arm nut to 51–65 ft. lbs. (69–88 Nm) and use a new cotter pin.

8. Tighten the steering knuckle-to-control arm bolts to 59 ft. lbs. (80 Nm).

9. Before tightening the stabilizer bar nuts, mount the wheels and lower the vehicle. Bounce the vehicle several times to settle the suspension and then tighten the stabilizer bolts to 66–90 ft. lbs. (90–122 Nm).

10. Tighten the arm-to-body bolts to 83 ft. lbs.

11. Check the front end alignment.

COROLLA (FWD)

1. On all vehicles, except the left side on those with automatic transaxle, perform the following:

   a. Remove the bolt and 2 nuts attaching the ball joint to the lower arm and disconnect the lower arm from the steering knuckle.

   b. On 4A-F and 4A-FE, remove the nut holding the stabilizer bar to the lower arm and disconnect the bar from the arm.

   c. On 4A-GE, remove the lower nut on the stabilizer bar link and disconnect the link from the arm.

   d. Remove the rear bracket bolts and nut. Remove the lower arm front mounting bolt.

   e. Remove the rear bracket and the stabilizer bar bracket and lift out the lower control arm.

2. To remove the left control arm, if with automatic transaxle, perform the following:

   a. Disconnect the arm at the steering knuckle.

   b. Disconnect the stabilizer bar at the lower arm.

   c. Remove the lower arm rear brackets. Move the stabilizer bar toward the rear and remove the bracket.

   d. Remove the 6 bolts and 2 nuts and remove the suspension crossmember with the lower arm.

   e. Remove the lower arm from the crossmember.

To install:

3. To install the left control arm, if with automatic transaxle, install the lower arm on the crossmember and install the assembly to the body.

4. On all others, install the lower arm to the body, move the stabilizer bar into position and install the front mounting bolt. Install the stabilizer bar and rear brackets.

5. Connect the lower arm to the steering knuckle and tighten the bolts to 105 ft. lbs. (142 Nm).

6. On 4A-F, connect the stabilizer bar to the lower arm and tighten the nut to 13 ft. lbs. (18 Nm).

7. On 4A-GE, connect the stabilizer bar link to the lower arm and tighten the nut to 26 ft. lbs. (35 Nm).

8. Lower the vehicle and bounce it several times to stabilize the suspension. Tighten the lower arm front bolt to 174 ft. lbs. (235 Nm) for 1987–88 or 152 ft. lbs. (206 Nm) for 1989–91. Tighten the rear bracket bolts to 94 ft. lbs. (127 Nm) on the lower arm side, 37 ft. lbs. (50 Nm) on the stabilizer bar side and tighten the small bolt and nut to 14 ft. lbs. (19 Nm).

9. Check the front end alignment.

CAMRY

1. Raise and support the vehicle safely. Remove the wheels.

2. Remove the 2 bolts attaching the ball joint to the steering knuckle.

3. Remove the stabilizer bar nut, retainer and cushion.

4. Remove the nut attaching the lower arm shaft to the lower arm.

5. Remove the lower suspension crossmember (2 bolts and 4 nuts).

6. Remove the lower control arm and lower arm shaft as an assembly.

7. Grip the lower arm assembly in a vise and remove the ball joint cotter pin and retaining nut. With a ball joint removal tool, pull the ball joint out of the control arm.

To install:

8. Position the ball joint in the lower arm and tighten the nut to 67 ft. lbs. (91 Nm) for 1987–88 or 90 ft. lbs. (123 Nm) for 1989–91. Install a new cotter pin.

9. Install the lower arm to the stabilizer bar and then install the lower arm shaft to the body. Install the lower arm nut and retainer. Screw on a new stabilizer bar end nut and retainer.

10. Conect the ball joint to the steering knuckle and tighten the bolts to 94 ft. lbs. (127 Nm) for 1987–88 or 83 ft. lbs. (113 Nm) for 1989–91.

11. Install the suspension lower crossmember. Tighten the inner bolts to 32 ft. lbs. (43 Nm) and the outer ones to 153 ft. lbs. (207 Nm).

12. Install the wheels and lower the vehicle. Bounce it several times to set the suspension.

13. Tighten the stabilizer bar end nut and the lower arm shaft-to-lower arm bolt to 156 ft. lbs. (212 Nm).

Upper Control Arm

Removal and Installation

1987–90 SUPRA

1. Raise and support the vehicle safely. Remove the wheels.

2. Unclip the brake hose bracket at the steering knuckle, remove the retaining nut and press the upper arm out of the knuckle.

3. Remove the upper mounting bolt and nut and lift out the upper control arm.

4. Connect the upper arm to the body. Connect the arm to the steering knuckle.

5. Install the wheels and lower the vehicle. Bounce it several times to set the suspension and then tighten the arm-to-knuckle nut to 80 ft. lbs. (108 Nm). Tighten the arm-to-body bolt to 121 ft. lbs. (164 Nm).

Lower Control Arms

Removal and Installation

COROLLA (RWD)

1. Raise and support the vehicle safely.

2. Remove the wheel.

3. Disconnect the steering knuckle from the control arm.

4. Disconnect the tie rod, stabilizer bar and strut bar from the control arm.

5. Remove the control arm mounting bolts, and remove the arm.

6. Install in reverse of above. Tighten, but do not torque fasteners until vehicle is on the ground.

7. Lower vehicle to ground, rock it from side-to-side several times and torque control arm mounting bolts to 51–65 ft. lbs., stabilizer bar to 16 ft. lbs., strut bar to 40 ft. lbs. and shock absorber to 65 ft. lbs.

SUPRA

1. Raise and support the vehicle safely. Remove the wheels.
2. Disconnect the stabilizer bar link from the lower control arm. Remove the locknut and press the ball joint out of the steering knuckle.
3. Disconnect the lower control arm at the strut. Matchmark the front and rear adjusting cams to the body. Remove the nuts and cams and then remove the lower arm.
4. Unbolt the ball joint from the control arm.

To install:

5. Install the ball joint to the arm and tighten the nuts to 94 ft. lbs. (127 Nm).
6. Position the lower control arm and install the adjusting cams and nuts finger-tight.
7. Connect the ball joint to the steering knuckle and tighten a conventional nut to 14 ft. lbs. (20 Nm). Install a locknut on top of the other and tighten it to 107 ft. lbs. (145 Nm).
8. Tighten the arm-to-strut bolt to 106 ft. lbs. (143 Nm). Tighten the stabilizer bar link nut to 47 ft. lbs. (64 Nm).
9. Install the wheels and lower the vehicle. Bounce the vehicle several times to set the suspension. Align the matchmarks on the adjusting cams and the body and tighten them to 177 ft. lbs. (240 Nm). Check the front alignment.

Front Wheel Bearings

Adjustment

1. With the front hub/disc assembly installed, tighten the castellated nut to 19–23 ft. lbs. (26–31 Nm).

2. Rotate the disc back and forth, 2–3 times, to allow the bearing to seat properly.
3. Loosen the castellated nut until it is only finger-tight.
4. Tighten the nut firmly, using a box wrench.
5. Measure the bearing preload with a spring scale attached to a wheel mounting stud. Check it against the specifications.
6. Install the cotter pin.

NOTE: If the hole does not align with the nut (or cap) holes, tighten the nut slightly until it does.

7. Finish installing the brake components and the wheel.

Removal and Installation

1. Remove the disc/hub assembly.
2. If either the disc or the entire hub assembly is to be replaced, unbolt the hub from the disc.

NOTE: If only the bearings are to be replaced, do not separate the disc and hub.

3. Using a brass rod as a drift, tap the inner bearings cone out. Remove the oil seal and the inner bearings.

NOTE: Throw the old oil seal away.

4. Drive out the inner bearing cup.
5. Drive out the outer bearing cup. Inspect the bearings and the hub for signs of wear or damage. Replace components, as necessary.

To install:

6. Install the inner bearing cup an then the outer bearing cup, by driving them into place.

NOTE: Use care not to cock the bearing cups in the hub.

7. Pack the bearings, hub inner well and grease cap with multipurpose grease.
8. Install the inner bearing into the hub.
9. Carefully install a new oil seal with a soft drift.
10. Install the hub on the spindle. Be sure to install all of the washers and nuts which were removed.
11. Adjust the bearing preload.
12. Install the caliper assembly and the wheel.

REAR SUSPENSION

Shock Absorbers

Removal and Installation
COROLLA (RWD) AND 1989–91 COROLLA (AWD)

1. Raise and support the vehicle safely. Support the rear axle.
2. Unfasten the upper shock absorber retaining nuts. It may be necessary to hold the shock absorber shaft with a suitable tool while removing the top retaining nut.

NOTE: Always remove and install the shock absorbers one at a time. Do not allow the rear axle to hang in place as this may cause undue damage.

3. Remove the lower shock retaining nut where it attaches to the rear axle housing.
4. Remove the shock absorber.
5. Inspect the shock for wear, leaks or other signs of damage.

6. Installation is in the reverse order of removal. Durng installation, observe the following:
   a. Tighten the upper retaining nuts to 18 ft. lbs. (25 Nm).
   b. Tighten the lower retaining nuts to 27 ft. lbs. (37 Nm).

1987–88 CRESSIDA

1. Raise and support the differential housing and the suspension control arms safely.
2. Remove the brake hose clips. Disconnect the stabilizer bar end.
3. Disconnect the halfshaft at the CV-joint on the wheel side.
4. With a jackstand under the suspension control arm, unbolt the shock absorber at its lower end. Using a prybar to keep the shaft from turning, remove the nut holding the shock absorber to its upper mounting. If with TEMS, disconnect the actuator and remove it. Remove the shock.
5. Installation is in the reverse order of removal. Torque the halfshaft nuts to 44–57 ft. lbs. (60–78 Nm), the upper shock mounting nut to 14–22 ft. lbs. (19–30 Nm) and the lower shock mounting nut to 22–32 ft. lbs. (30–44 Nm).

MacPherson Strut

Removal and Installation

TERCEL

1. Working inside the vehicle, remove the shock absorber cover and package tray bracket.

2. Raise the rear of the vehicle and support it with jackstands. Remove the wheel.

3. Disconnect the brake line from the wheel cylinder, if necessary. Disconnect the brake line from the flexible hose at the mounting bracket on the strut tube. Disconnect the flexible hose from the strut.

4. Loosen the nut holding the suspension support to the shock absorber; do not remove the nut.

5. Remove the bolts and nuts mounting on the strut on the axle carrier and then disconnect the strut.

6. Remove the 3 upper strut mounting nuts and carefully remove the strut assembly.

To install:

7. Installation is in the reverse order of removal. During installation, observe the following:

    a. Tighten the upper strut retaining nuts to 17 ft. lbs on 1987 vehicles and 23 ft. lbs. (31 Nm) on 1988–91 vehicles.

    b. Tighten the lower strut-to-axle carrier bolts to 105 ft. lbs. (143 Nm) on 1987 vehicles.

    c. Tighten the nut holding the suspension support to the shock absorber to 36 ft. lbs. (49 Nm) on 1987 vehicles.

    d. Tighten the strut-to-axle beam nut to 47 ft. lbs. (64 Nm) on 1988–91 vehicles.

    e. Bleed the brakes.

CAMRY AND COROLLA (2WD)

1. On the 4-door sedan, remove the package tray and vent duct.

2. On the hatchback, remove the speaker grilles.

3. Disconnect the brake line from the wheel cylinder.

4. Remove the brake line from the brake hose.

5. Disconnect the brake hose from its bracket on the strut.

6. Remove the strut suspension support cover. Loosen, but

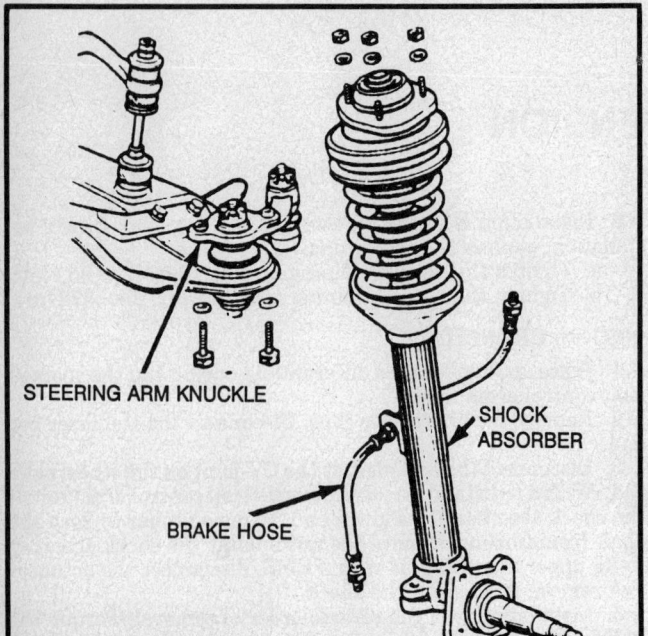

STEERING ARM KNUCKLE

SHOCK ABSORBER

BRAKE HOSE

Strut used on all rear wheel drive cars

do not remove, the nut holding the suspension support to the strut.

7. Unbolt the strut from the rear arm and or axle carrier.

8. Unbolt the strut from the body.

To install:

9. Installation is the reverse of removal. During installation, please observe the following:

    a. Tighten the strut-to-body bolts to 23 ft. lbs. (31 Nm) on 1987–88 Camry or 29 ft. lbs. (39 Nm) on 1987–89 Corolla sedan/wagon and 1989–91 Camry).

    b. Tighten the strut-to-axle carrier bolts 166 ft. lbs. on 1987–91 Camry and 105 ft. lbs. (143 Nm) on Corolla.

    c. Tighten the the suspension support-to-strut nut to 36 ft. lbs. (49 Nm).

    d. Refill and bleed the brake system.

CELICA (FWD)

1. Raise and support the vehicle safely. Position an hydraulic jack under the rear hub assembly; raise it just enough to support the assembly.

2. On the liftback, remove the rear speaker grilles.

3. On the coupe, remove the suspension service hole cover.

4. On the ST and GT vehicles, disconnect and plug the brake line at the backing plate. Remove the clip and E-ring and then disconnect the brake hose and tube from the strut housing.

5. On the GTS, remove the union bolts and gaskets and disconnect the brake line from the brake cylinder. Remove the clip and E-ring from the strut and then disconnect the brake hose from the strut housing.

6. Loosen, but do not remove, the nut attaching the suspension support to the strut.

7. Disconnect the stabilizer bar at the lower end of the strut housing.

8. Disconnect the strut at the axle carrier.

9. Remove the 3 strut-to-body bolts and then remove the strut.

To install:

10. Tighten the upper strut-to-body nuts to 23 ft. lbs. (31 Nm).

11. Tighten the lower strut-to-carrier bolts to 119 ft. lbs. (162 Nm).

12. Connect the stabilizer bar to the strut and tighten the bolts to 26 ft. lbs. (35 Nm).

13. Tighten the strut holding nut to 36 ft. lbs. (49 Nm). Install the dust cover onto the suspension support.

14. Reconnect the brake line and hose. Bleed the system, lower the vehicle and check the rear wheel alignment.

MR2

1. Raise and support the vehicle safely. Position a hydraulic floor jack under the rear hub assembly; raise it just enough to support the assembly.

2. Remove the union bolts and gaskets and disconnect the brake line from the brake cylinder. Remove the clip and E-ring from the strut and then disconnect the brake hose from the strut housing.

3. Matchmark the lower strut bracket and the camber adjusting cam, remove the 2 axle carrier bolts and the adjusting cam and disconnect the strut from the carrier.

4. Remove the engine hood side panel.

5. Remove the 3 upper strut-to-body nuts and then remove the strut.

To install:

6. Position the strut and tighten the upper mounting nuts to 23 ft. lbs. (31 Nm).

7. Install the engine hood side panel.

8. Connect the axle carrier to the lower strut bracket. Insert the mounting bolts from the rear and align the matchmarks made in Step 3. Tighten the nuts to 105 ft. lbs. (142 Nm) on 1987–88 vehicles and 166 ft. lbs. (226 Nm) on 1989–91 vehicles.

9. Connect the brake line, bleed the system and check rear wheel alignment.

SUPRA AND 1989–91 CRESSIDA

1. Raise and support the vehicle safely. Remove the wheels.
2. Remove the speaker grill and interior quarter panel trim, if equipped with TEMS.
3. Disconnect the strut from the axle carrier.
4. Remove the strut cap. Remove the Toyota Electronic Modulated Suspension (TEMS) actuator.
5. Remove the 3 strut mounting nuts from the body and remove the strut assembly.
6. Mount the strut assembly in a vise. Using a spring compressor, compress the coil spring.
7. Remove the strut suspension support nut. Remove the strut suspension support, remove the coil spring and bumper.

To install:

8. Mount the strut in a vise. Using a spring compressor, compress the coil spring.
9. Install the bumper to the strut, align the coil spring end with the lower seat hollow and install the coil spring.
10. Align the strut suspension support hole and piston rod and install it. Align the suspension support with the strut lower bushing.
11. Install the strut suspension support nut and torque it to 20 ft. lbs. (27 Nm).Connect the strut assembly with the 3 retaining nuts and torque them to 10 ft. lbs. (14 Nm).
12. Connect the strut assembly to the axle carrier and torque it to 101 ft. lbs. (137 Nm).
13. Install the TEMS actuator and strut cap. Install the quarter panel trim panel and speaker grille.

Coil Springs

Removal and Installation

1. Loosen the rear wheel lug nuts.
2. Raise and support the rear axle housing and frame safely.
3. Remove the lug nuts and wheel.
4. If equipped, disconnect the rear stabilizer bar from the axle housing or suspension arm on 1987–89 Supra and 1987–88 Cressida. Remove the bolt holding the stabilizer bar bushing to the rear axle housing.
5. Unfasten the lower shock absorber end. On the Corolla RWD, Corolla FWD (AWD) and Tercel AWD, disconnect the lateral control rod from the axle.

NOTE: On Supra and 1987–88 Cressida with IRS suspension, remove the rear halfshafts.

6. Slowly lower the jack under the rear axle housing until the axle is at the bottom of its travel.
7. Withdraw the coil spring, complete with its insulator.
8. Inspect the coil spring and insulator for wear, cracks or weakness; replace either or both, as necessary.
9. Installation is the reverse of the removal procedure.

Lower Control Arms

Removal and Installation

MR2

1. Raise and support the vehicle safely. Remove the wheels.
2. Remove the cotter pin and retaining nut from the bottom of the ball joint stem. Using a ball joint removal tool, press the ball joint out of the control arm.
3. Remove the strut rod nut and retainer from the lower control arm.
4. Remove the bolt holding the lower control arm to the body. Remove the cushion and then disconnect the lower arm from the strut rod. Remove the lower control arm.
5. Connect the lower arm to the strut rod. Install the strut rod nut, cushion and retainer.

6. Connect the lower arm to the body and install the retaining nut fingertight.
7. Connect the lower control arm to the ball joint and tighten the retaining nut to 67 ft. lbs. (91 Nm). Install a new cotter pin.

NOTE: If the holes do not align when installing the new cotter pin, tighten the nut until they are aligned. Do not loosen the nut!

8. Install the wheel and lower the vehicle. Tighten the strut rod nut to 86 ft. lbs. (117 Nm) and the arm-to-body bolt to 94 ft. lbs. (127 Nm).

SUPRA AND 1989–91 CRESSIDA

1. Raise and support the vehicle safely. Remove the wheels.
2. Remove the halfshaft.
3. Remove the nut and disconnect the No. 1 lower arm from the axle carrier. Matchmark the adjusting cam to the body, remove the cam and bolt and then lift out the No. 1 arm.
4. Remove the bolt and nut and disconnect the No. 2 lower arm from the axle carrier. Matchmark the adjusting cam to the body, remove the cam and bolt and then lift out the No. 2 arm.

To install:

5. Position the No. 2 arm and install the adjusting cam and bolt so the matchmarks are in alignment. Connect the arm to the axle carrier.
6. Position the No. 1 arm and install the adjusting cam and bolt so the matchmarks are in alignment. Connect the arm to the axle carrier. Use a new nut and tighten it to 43 ft. lbs. (59 Nm).
7. Install the halfshaft.
8. Install the wheels and lower the vehicle. Bounce it several times to set the suspension and then tighten the body-to-arm bolts and nuts to 136 ft. lbs. (184 Nm) on Supra or 134 ft. lbs. (181 Nm) on Cressida. Tighten the No. 2 arm-to-carrier bolt to 121 ft. lbs. (164 Nm) on Supra or 119 ft. lbs. (162 Nm) — Cressida. Tighten the No. 1 arm-to-carrier nut to 36 ft. lbs. (49 Nm).
9. Check the rear wheel alignment.

Upper Control Arm

Removal and Installation

SUPRA AND 1989–91 CRESSIDA

1. Raise and support the rear of the vehicle safely. Remove the wheels.
2. Unbolt the brake caliper and suspend aside. Remove the halfshaft.
3. Disconnect the parking brake cable at the equalizer. Remove the 2 cable brackets from the body and then pull the cable through the suspension member.
4. Disconnect the 2 lower arms and the strut rod at the axle carrier. Disconnect the lower strut mount.
5. Disconnect the upper arm at the body and remove the axle hub assembly.
6. Remove the upper arm mounting nut. Remove the backing plate mounting nuts and separate the plate from the carrier. Press the upper arm out of the axle carrier.

To install:

7. Connect the upper arm to the body.
8. Connect the axle hub assembly to the arm with a new nut.
9. Connect the No. 1 lower control arm with a new nut and tighten it to 43 ft. lbs. (59 Nm) on Supra and 36 ft. lbs. (49 Nm) on Cressida. Connect the No. 2 lower arm and the strut rod.
10. Tighten the upper arm mounting nut to 80 ft. lbs. (108 Nm). Tighten the strut to 101 ft. lbs. (137 Nm).
11. Reconnect the parking brake cable and install the halfshaft. Install the brake caliper and tighten the bolts to 34 ft. lbs. (47 Nm).
12. Install the wheels and lower the vehicle. Bounce it several times to set the suspension and then tighten the upper arm-to-

body bolt, the No. 2 lower arm-to-carrier and the strut rod to 121 ft. lbs. (164 Nm) on Supra and 119 ft. lbs. (162 Nm) on Cressida.

Upper And Lower Control Arms

Removal and Installation

**TERCEL WAGON (AWD)
AND 1989–91 COROLLA (AWD)**

1. Raise and support the vehicle safely. Remove the wheels and support the rear axle safely.
2. Remove the upper control arm-to-body bolt. Remove the upper arm-to-axle bolt and lift out the upper control arm.
3. Remove the lower control arm-to-body bolt. Remove the lower arm-to-axle bolt and lift out the lower control arm.
To install:
4. Install the upper control arm with the nuts and bolts just snugged down.
5. Install the lower control arm with the nuts and bolts just snugged down.
6. Install the wheels, remove the safety stands and floor jack and then lower the vehicle.
7. Bounce the vehicle several times to stabilize the suspension and then raise the axle housing until the body is free.
8. Tighten all bolts to 83 ft. lbs. (113 Nm) on the Tercel and 72 ft. lbs. (98 Nm) on the Corolla.

Rear Wheel Bearings

Removal and Installation

TERCEL SEDAN

1. Raise and support the vehicle safely.
2. Remove the rear wheels.
3. Remove the brake drums.
4. Remove the locknut cap and cotter pin. Pry off the locknut and then remove the locknut itself.
5. Pull off the axle hub along with the outer wheel bearing and thrust washer.
6. Pry the inner bearing oil seal out of the brake drum and then remove the inner bearing.
7. Using a brass drift and hammer, drive out the bearing races.
To install:
8. Press new outer bearing races into the axle hub and fill it and the bearing cap with grease.
9. Pack the bearing with grease.
10. Position the inner bearing into the hub and then drive in a new oil seal. Coat the seal with grease.
11. Position the axle hub/brake drum onto the axle shaft. Install the outer bearing, fill the hole with grease and position the thrust washer. Install the bearing locknut and tighten it to 22 ft. lbs. (29 Nm).
12. Spin the axle hub several times to snug down the bearing and then loosen the bearing locknut until it can be turned by hand.

NOTE: There must be absolutely no brake drag at this time.

13. Retighten the bearing locknut until there is a bearing pre-load of 0.9–2.2 lbs. (3.2–9.8 N) while turning the wheel.

14. Install the locknut lock, a new cotter pin and the cap. If the cotter pin hole does not align properly, align the holes by tightening the nut.
15. Lower the vehicle.

**CAMRY (2WD), CELICA (2WD)
COROLLA (2WD) AND TERCEL
WAGON (2WD)**

1. Raise and support the vehicle safely.
2. Remove the rear wheel and tire assembly.
3. Remove the brake drum. On the Corolla FX, remove the disc brake caliper from the axle carrier and suspend it with a wire.
4. Disconnect and plug the brake line at the backing plate.
5. Remove the 4 axle hub-to-carrier bolts and slide off the hub and brake assembly. Remove the O-ring from the backing plate.
6. Remove the bolt and nut attaching the carrier to the strut rod.
7. Remove the bolt and nut attaching the carrier to the No. 1 suspension arm.
8. Remove the bolt and nut attaching the carrier to the No. 2 suspension arm.
9. Unbolt the carrier from the rear strut tube and remove the carrier.
10. Using a hammer and cold chisel, loosen the staked part of the hub nut and remove the nut.
11. Using a 2-armed puller or the like, press the axle shaft from the hub.
12. Remove the bearing inner race (inside).
13. Using a 2-armed puller again, pull off the bearing inner race (outside) over the bearing and then press it out of the hub.
To install:
14. Position a new bearing inner race (outside) on the bearing and then press a new oil seal into the hub. Coat the lip of the seal with grease.
15. Position a new bearing inner race (inside) on the bearing and then press the inner race with the hub onto the axle shaft.
16. Install the nut and tighten it to 90 ft. lbs. (123 Nm). Stake the nut with a brass drift.
17. Position the axle carrier on the strut tube and tighten the nuts to 119 ft. lbs. (162 Nm), 105 ft. lbs. (142 Nm) on Corolla FX and Corolla sedan and wagon; 166 ft. lbs. (226 Nm) on Camry.
18. Install the bolt and nut attaching the carrier to the No. 2 suspension arm; finger-tighten it only.

NOTE: Make sure the lip of the nut is in the hole on the arm.

19. Repeat Step 5 for the No. 1 suspension arm.

NOTE: Make sure the lip of the nut is in the hole on the arm.

20. Install the strut rod-to-carrier bolt so the lip of the nut is in the groove on the bracket.
21. Install a new O-ring onto the axle carrier. Install the axle hub and brake backing plate. Tighten the 4 bolts to 59 ft. lbs. (80 Nm).
22. Reconnect the brake line, install the brake drum and then bleed the brakes.
23. Lower the vehicle and bounce it a few times to set the rear suspension.
24. Tighten the suspension arm bolts and the strut rod bolt to 64 ft. lbs. (87 Nm). On the Camry and Celica, tighten the strut rod mounting bolts to 83 ft. lbs. (113 Nm) and the suspension arm bolts to 134 ft. lbs. (181 Nm).

SERIAL NUMBER IDENTIFICATION

Vehicle Identification Plate

All vehicles have an identification plate bearing the chassis number on the top of the dash board at the driver's side. This plate is easily visible through the windshield and aids in rapid identification. Since each vehicle has a different VIN code, consult the vehicle owner's manual for a detailed explaination of how to interpret the information it provides.

Engine Number

The diesel engine number with it's 2 letter code is stamped on

the block between the injection pump and the vacuum pump. On other vehicles, the engine code/number is stamped on the block just below the cylinder head, near the No. 2 or No. 3 spark plug.

Vehicle Identification Lable

This label provides engine and transaxle codes, paint, interior and option codes.

SPECIFICATIONS

ENGINE IDENTIFICATION

Year	Model	Engine Displacement cu. in. (cc/liter)	Engine Series Identification	No. of Cylinders	Engine Type
1987	Jetta	109 (1780/1.8)	RV	4	SOHC
	Jetta GL	109 (1780/1.8)	PF	4	SOHC
	Jetta GLI 16V	109 (1780/1.8)	PL	4	DOHC
	Quantum GL5	136 (2226/2.2)	KX	5	SOHC
	Quantum Syncro	136 (2226/2.2)	JT	5	SOHC
	Scirocco-16V	109 (1780/1.8)	PL	4	DOHC
	Cabriolet	109 (1780/1.8)	JH	4	SOHC
	Golf/GL	109 (1780/1.8)	RV	4	SOHC
	Golf/GT	109 (1780/1.8)	PF	4	SOHC
	Golf GTI 16V	109 (1780/1.8)	PL	4	DOHC
	Fox/GL	109 (1780/1.8)	UM	4	SOHC
1988	Jetta	109 (1780/1.8)	RV	4	SOHC
	Jetta GL	109 (1780/1.8)	PF	4	SOHC
	Jetta GLI 16V	109 (1780/1.8)	PL	4	DOHC
	Jetta Carat	109 (1780/1.8)	PF	4	DOHC
	Quantum GL5	136 (2226/2.2)	KX	5	SOHC
	Quantum Syncro	136 (2226/2.2)	JT	5	SOHC
	Scirocco-16V	109 (1780/1.8)	PL	4	DOHC
	Cabriolet	109 (1780/1.8)	JH	4	SOHC
	Golf/GL	109 (1780/1.8)	RV	4	SOHC
	Golf/GT	109 (1780/1.8)	PF	4	SOHC
	Golf GTI 16V	109 (1780/1.8)	PL	4	DOHC
	Fox/GL	109 (1780/1.8)	UM	4	SOHC
1989	Jetta	109 (1780/1.8)	RV	4	SOHC
	Jetta Diesel	97.0 (1588/1.6)	ME	4	Water cooled in-line Diesel
	Jetta GL	109 (1780/1.8)	PF	4	SOHC
	Jetta GLI 16V	109 (1780/1.8)	PL	4	DOHC
	Jetta Carat	109 (1780/1.8)	PF	4	DOHC

ENGINE IDENTIFICATION

Year	Model	Engine Displacement cu. in. (cc/liter)	Engine Series Identification	No. of Cylinders	Engine Type
1989	Quantum GL5	136 (2226/2.2)	KX	5	SOHC
	Quantum Syncro	136 (2226/2.2)	JT	5	SOHC
	Scirocco-16V	109 (1780/1.8)	PL	4	DOHC
	Cabriolet	109 (1780/1.8)	JH	4	SOHC
	Golf/GL	109 (1780/1.8)	RV	4	SOHC
	Golf/GT	109 (1780/1.8)	PF	4	SOHC
	Golf GTI 16V	109 (1780/1.8)	PL	4	DOHC
	Fox/GL	109 (1780/1.8)	UM	4	SOHC
1990–91	Jetta GL	109 (1780/1.8)	RV	4	SOHC
	Jetta GLI 16V	121 (1984/2.0)	9A	4	DOHC
	Jetta Carat	109 (1780/1.8)	PF	4	DOHC
	Jetta Diesel	97 (1588/1.6)	ME	4	Water cooled in-line Diesel
	Golf/GL	109 (1780/1.8)	RV	4	SOHC
	Golf GTI	109 (1780/1.8)	PF	4	SOHC
	Golf GTI 16V	121 (1984/2.0)	9A	4	DOHC
	Cabriolet	109 (1780/1.8)	JH	4	SOHC
	Fox	109 (1780/1.8)	UM, JN	4	SOHC
	Passat, GL	121 (1984/2.0)	9A	4	DOHC
	Corrado	109 (1780/1.8)	PG	4	SOHC G-Charger

GENERAL ENGINE SPECIFICATIONS

Year	Model	Engine Displacement cu. in. (cc)	Fuel System Type	Net Horsepower @ rpm	Net Torque @ rpm (ft. lbs.)	Bore × Stroke (in.)	Compression Ratio	Oil Pressure @ rpm
1987	Jetta	109 (1780)	Digifant II	100 @ 5400	107 @ 3400	3.19 × 3.40	10.0:1	28 @ 2000
	Jetta GL	109 (1780)	Digifant II	105 @ 5400	110 @ 3400	3.19 × 3.40	10.0:1	28 @ 2000
	Jetta GLI 16V	109 (1780)	CIS-E Fuel Inj.	123 @ 5800	120 @ 4250	3.19 × 3.40	10.0:1	28 @ 2000
	Quantum GL5	136 (2226)	CIS-E Fuel Inj.	110 @ 5500	122 @ 2400	3.19 × 3.40	8.5:1	28 @ 2000
	Quantum Syncro	136 (2226)	CIS-E Fuel Inj.	115 @ 5500	126 @ 3000	3.19 × 3.40	8.5:1	28 @ 2000
	Scirocco 16V	109 (1780)	CIS-E Fuel Inj.	123 @ 5800	120 @ 4250	3.19 × 3.40	10.0:1	28 @ 2000
	Cabriolet	109 (1780)	CIS-E Fuel Inj.	90 @ 5500	100 @ 3000	3.19 × 3.40	9.0:1	28 @ 2000
	Golf GL	109 (1780)	Digifant II	100 @ 5400	107 @ 3400	3.19 × 3.40	10.0:1	28 @ 2000
	Golf GT	109 (1780)	Digifant II	105 @ 5400	110 @ 3400	3.19 × 3.40	10.0:1	28 @ 2000
	Golf GTI 16V	109 (1780)	CIS-E Fuel Inj.	123 @ 5800	120 @ 4250	3.19 × 3.40	10.0:1	28 @ 2000
	Fox/GL	109 (1780)	CIS-E Fuel Inj.	81 @ 5500	93 @ 3250	3.19 × 3.40	9.0:1	28 @ 2000
1988	Jetta	109 (1780)	Digifant II	100 @ 5400	107 @ 3400	3.19 × 3.40	10.0:1	28 @ 2000
	Jetta GL	109 (1780)	Digifant II	105 @ 5400	110 @ 3400	3.19 × 3.40	10.0:1	28 @ 2000
	Jetta GLI 16V	109 (1780)	CIS-E Fuel Inj.	123 @ 5800	120 @ 4250	3.19 × 3.40	10.0:1	28 @ 2000
	Jetta Carat	109 (1780)	Digifant II	105 @ 5400	110 @ 3400	3.19 × 3.40	10.0:1	28 @ 2000
	Quantum GL5	136 (2226)	CIS-E Fuel Inj.	110 @ 5500	122 @ 2400	3.19 × 3.40	8.5:1	28 @ 2000
	Quantum Syncro	136 (2226)	CIS-E Fuel Inj.	115 @ 5500	126 @ 3000	3.19 × 3.40	8.5:1	28 @ 2000
	Scirocco 16V	109 (1780)	CIS-E Fuel Inj.	123 @ 5800	120 @ 4250	3.19 × 3.40	10.0:1	28 @ 2000
	Cabriolet	109 (1780)	CIS-E Fuel Inj.	90 @ 5500	100 @ 3000	3.19 × 3.40	9.0:1	28 @ 2000
	Golf GL	109 (1780)	Digifant II	100 @ 5400	107 @ 3400	3.19 × 3.40	10.0:1	28 @ 2000

GENERAL ENGINE SPECIFICATIONS

Year	Model	Engine Displacement cu. in. (cc)	Fuel System Type	Net Horsepower @ rpm	Net Torque @ rpm (ft. lbs.)	Bore × Stroke (in.)	Compression Ratio	Oil Pressure @ rpm
1988	Golf GT	109 (1780)	Digifant II	105 @ 5400	110 @ 3400	3.19 × 3.40	10.0:1	28 @ 2000
	Golf GTI 16V	109 (1780)	CIS-E Fuel Inj.	123 @ 5800	120 @ 4250	3.19 × 3.40	10.0:1	28 @ 2000
	Fox/GL	109 (1780)	CIS-E Fuel Inj.	81 @ 5500	93 @ 3250	3.19 × 3.40	9.0:1	28 @ 2000
1989	Jetta	109 (1780)	Digifant II	100 @ 5400	107 @ 3400	3.19 × 3.40	10.0:1	28 @ 2000
	Jetta (Diesel)	97.0 (1588)	Fuel Inj.	52 @ 4800	72 @ 2000	3.01 × 3.40	23.0:1	28 @ 2000
	Jetta GL	109 (1780)	Digifant II	105 @ 5400	110 @ 3400	3.19 × 3.40	10.0:1	28 @ 2000
	Jetta GLI 16V	109 (1780)	CIS-E Fuel Inj.	123 @ 5800	120 @ 4250	3.19 × 3.40	10.0:1	28 @ 2000
	Jetta Carat	109 (1780)	Digifant II	105 @ 5400	110 @ 3400	3.19 × 3.40	10.0:1	28 @ 2000
	Quantum GL5	136 (2226)	CIS-E Fuel Inj.	110 @ 5500	122 @ 2400	3.19 × 3.40	8.5:1	28 @ 2000
	Quantum Syncro	136 (2226)	CIS-E Fuel Inj.	115 @ 5500	126 @ 3000	3.19 × 3.40	8.5:1	28 @ 2000
	Scirocco 16V	109 (1780)	CIS-E Fuel Inj.	123 @ 5800	120 @ 4250	3.19 × 3.40	10.0:1	28 @ 2000
	Cabriolet	109 (1780)	CIS-E Fuel Inj.	90 @ 5500	100 @ 3000	3.19 × 3.40	9.0:1	28 @ 2000
	Golf GL	109 (1780)	Digifant II	100 @ 5400	107 @ 3400	3.19 × 3.40	10.0:1	28 @ 2000
	Golf GT	109 (1780)	Digifant II	105 @ 5400	110 @ 3400	3.19 × 3.40	10.0:1	28 @ 2000
	Golf GTI 16V	109 (1780)	CIS-E Fuel Inj.	123 @ 5800	120 @ 4250	3.19 × 3.40	10.0:1	28 @ 2000
	Fox/GL	109 (1780)	CIS-E Fuel Inj.	81 @ 5500	93 @ 3250	3.19 × 3.40	9.0:1	28 @ 2000
1990-91	Jetta GL	109 (1780)	Digifant II	105 @ 5400	110 @ 3400	3.19 × 3.40	10.0:1	28 @ 2000
	Jetta GLI 16V	121 (1984)	CIS-E Fuel Inj.	134 @ 5800	133 @ 4400	3.25 × 3.65	10.8:1	28 @ 2000
	Jetta Carat	109 (1780)	Digifant II	105 @ 5400	110 @ 3400	3.19 × 3.40	10.0:1	28 @ 2000
	Jetta (Diesel)	97.0 (1588)	Fuel Inj.	52 @ 4800	71 @ 2000	3.01 × 3.40	23.0:1	28 @ 2000
	Cabriolet	109 (1780)	CIS-E Fuel Inj.	94 @ 5400	100 @ 3000	3.19 × 3.40	10.0:1	28 @ 2000
	Golf GL	109 (1780)	Digifant II	100 @ 5400	107 @ 3400	3.19 × 3.40	10.0:1	28 @ 2000
	GTI	109 (1780)	Digifant II	105 @ 5400	110 @ 3400	3.19 × 3.40	10.0:1	28 @ 2000
	GTI 16V	121 (1984)	CIS-E Fuel Inj.	134 @ 5800	133 @ 4400	3.25 × 3.65	10.8:1	28 @ 2000
	Fox/GL	109 (1780)	CIS-E Fuel Inj.	81 @ 5500	93 @ 3250	3.19 × 3.40	9.0:1	28 @ 2000
	Passat GL	121 (1984)	CIS-E Fuel Inj.	134 @ 5800	133 @ 4400	3.25 × 3.65	10.8:1	28 @ 2000
	Corrado	109 (1780)	Digifant II	158 @ 5600	166 @ 4000	3.19 × 3.40	8.0:1	28 @ 2000

GASOLINE ENGINE TUNE-UP SPECIFICATIONS

Year	Model	Engine Displacement cu. in. (cc)	Spark Plugs Type	Gap (in.)	Ignition Timing (deg.) MT	AT	Compression Pressure (psi)	Fuel Pump (psi)	Idle Speed (rpm) MT	AT	Valve Clearance In. ②	Ex. ②
1987	Jetta	109 (1780)	WR7DS	0.024–0.032	6 BTDC @ Idle	6 BTDC @ Idle	131–174 ①	NA	800–900	800–900	Hyd.	Hyd.
	Jetta GL	109 (1780)	W7DTC	0.027–0.035	6 BTDC @ Idle	6 BTDC @ Idle	131–174	NA	800–900	800–900	Hyd.	Hyd.
	Jetta GLI 16V	109 (1780)	F6DTC	0.027–0.035	6 BTDC @ Idle	6 BTDC @ Idle	145–189	NA	800–900	800–900	Hyd.	Hyd.
	Quantum GL5	136 (2226)	WR7DS	0.027–0.035	6 BTDC @ Idle	3 ATDC @ Idle	131–174	NA	750–850	750–850	Hyd.	Hyd.
	Quantum Syncro	136 (2226)	WR7DS	0.027–0.035	6 BTDC @ Idle	3 ATDC @ Idle	131–174	NA	750–850	750–850	Hyd.	Hyd.
	Scirocco 16V	109 (1780)	F6DTC	0.027–0.035	6 BTDC @ Idle	—	145–189	NA	800–900	800–900	Hyd.	Hyd.

GASOLINE ENGINE TUNE-UP SPECIFICATIONS

Year	Model	Engine Displacement cu. in. (cc)	Spark Plugs Type	Gap (in.)	Ignition Timing (deg.) MT	AT	Compression Pressure (psi)	Fuel Pump (psi)	Idle Speed (rpm) MT	AT	Valve Clearance In. [2]	Ex. [2]
1987	Cabriolet	109 (1780)	W7DTC	0.027–0.035	6 BTDC @ Idle	6 BTDC @ Idle	131–174	NA	850–1000	850–1000	Hyd.	Hyd.
	Golf GL	109 (1780)	WR7DS	0.024–0.032	6 BTDC @ Idle	6 BTDC @ Idle	131–174	NA	800–900	800–900	Hyd.	Hyd.
	Golf GT	109 (1780)	W7DTC	0.027–0.035	6 BTDC @ Idle	6 BTDC @ Idle	131–174	NA	800–900	800–900	Hyd.	Hyd.
	Golf GTI 16V	109 (1780)	F6DTC	0.027–0.035	6 BTDC @ Idle	—	145–189	NA	800–900	800–900	Hyd.	Hyd.
	Fox/GL	109 (1780)	W7DTC	0.027–0.035	6 BTDC @ Idle	6 BTDC @ Idle	131–174	NA	800–1000	800–1000	Hyd.	Hyd.
1988	Jetta	109 (1780)	WR7DS	0.024–0.032	6 BTDC @ Idle	6 BTDC @ Idle	131–174 [1]	NA	800–900	800–900	Hyd.	Hyd.
	Jetta GL	109 (1780)	W7DTC	0.027–0.035	6 BTDC @ Idle	6 BTDC @ Idle	131–174 [1]	NA	800–900	800–900	Hyd.	Hyd.
	Jetta GLI 16V	109 (1780)	F6DTC	0.027–0.035	6 BTDC @ Idle	6 BTDC @ Idle	145–189	NA	800–900	800–900	Hyd.	Hyd.
	Jetta Carat	109 (1780)	W7DTC	0.027–0.035	6 BTDC @ Idle	6 BTDC @ Idle	131–174	NA	800–900	800–900	Hyd.	Hyd.
	Quantum GL5	136 (2226)	WR7DS	0.027–0.035	6 BTDC @ Idle	3 ATDC @ Idle	131–174	NA	750–850	750–850	Hyd.	Hyd.
	Quantum Syncro	136 (2226)	WR7DS	0.027–0.035	6 BTDC @ Idle	3 ATDC @ Idle	131–174	NA	750–850	750–850	Hyd.	Hyd.
	Scirocco 16V	109 (1780)	F6DTC	0.027–0.035	6 BTDC @ Idle	—	145–189	NA	800–900	800–900	Hyd.	Hyd.
	Cabriolet	109 (1780)	W7DTC	0.027–0.035	6 BTDC @ Idle	6 BTDC @ Idle	131–174	NA	850–1000	850–1000	Hyd.	Hyd.
	Golf GL	109 (1780)	WR7DS	0.024–0.032	6 BTDC @ Idle	6 BTDC @ Idle	131–174	NA	800–900	800–900	Hyd.	Hyd.
	Golf GT	109 (1780)	W7DTC	0.027–0.035	6 BTDC @ Idle	6 BTDC @ Idle	131–174	NA	800–900	800–900	Hyd.	Hyd.
	Golf GTI 16V	109 (1780)	F6DTC	0.027–0.035	6 BTDC @ Idle	—	145–189	NA	800–900	800–900	Hyd.	Hyd.
	Fox/GL	109 (1780)	W7DTC	0.027–0.035	6 BTDC @ Idle	6 BTDC @ Idle	131–174	NA	800–1000	800–1000	Hyd.	Hyd.
1989	Jetta	109 (1780)	WR7DS	0.024–0.032	6 BTDC @ Idle	6 BTDC @ Idle	131–174 [1]	NA	800–900	800–900	Hyd.	Hyd.
	Jetta GL	109 (1780)	W7DTC	0.027–0.035	6 BTDC @ Idle	6 BTDC @ Idle	131–174	NA	800–900	800–900	Hyd.	Hyd.
	Jetta GLI 16V	109 (1780)	F6DTC	0.027–0.035	6 BTDC @ Idle	6 BTDC @ Idle	145–189	NA	800–900	800–900	Hyd.	Hyd.
	Jetta Carat	109 (1780)	W7DTC	0.027–0.035	6 BTDC @ Idle	6 BTDC @ Idle	131–174	NA	800–900	800–900	Hyd.	Hyd.
	Quantum GL5	136 (2226)	WR7DS	0.027–0.035	6 BTDC @ Idle	3 ATDC @ Idle	131–174	NA	750–850	750–850	Hyd.	Hyd.
	Quantum Syncro	136 (2226)	WR7DS	0.027–0.035	6 BTDC @ Idle	3 ATDC @ Idle	131–174	NA	750–850	750–850	Hyd.	Hyd.
	Scirocco 16V	109 (1780)	F6DTC	0.027–0.035	6 BTDC @ Idle	6 BTDC @ Idle	145–189	NA	800–900	800–900	Hyd.	Hyd.

GASOLINE ENGINE TUNE-UP SPECIFICATIONS

Year	Model	Engine Displacement cu. in. (cc)	Spark Plugs Type	Gap (in.)	Ignition Timing (deg.) MT	AT	Compression Pressure (psi)	Fuel Pump (psi)	Idle Speed (rpm) MT	AT	Valve Clearance In.②	Ex.②
1989	Cabriolet	109 (1780)	W7DTC	0.027–0.035	6 BTDC @ Idle	6 BTDC @ Idle	131–174	NA	850–1000	850–1000	Hyd.	Hyd.
	Golf GL	109 (1780)	WR7DS	0.024–0.032	6 BTDC @ Idle	6 BTDC @ Idle	131–174	NA	800–900	800–900	Hyd.	Hyd.
	Golf GT	109 (1780)	W7DTC	0.027–0.035	6 BTDC @ Idle	6 BTDC @ Idle	131–174	NA	800–900	800–900	Hyd.	Hyd.
	Golf GTI 16V	109 (1780)	F6DTC	0.027–0.035	6 BTDC @ Idle	—	145–189	NA	800–900	800–900	Hyd.	Hyd.
	Fox/GL	109 (1780)	W7DTC	0.027–0.035	6 BTDC @ Idle	6 BTDC @ Idle	131–174	NA	800–1000	800–1000	Hyd.	Hyd.
1990–91	Jetta GL	109 (1780)	W7DTC	0.024–0.032	6 BTDC @ Idle	6 BTDC @ Idle	145–189 ①	NA	800–900	800–1000	Hyd.	Hyd.
	Jetta GLI 16V	121 (1984)	F6DSR ①	0.024–0.032	6 BTDC @ Idle	—	NA	NA	800–900	—	Hyd.	Hyd.
	Jetta Carat	109 (1780)	W7DCO	0.024–0.032	6 BTDC @ Idle	6 BTDC @ Idle	145–189	NA	800–900	800–1000	Hyd.	Hyd.
	Golf GL	109 (1780)	W7DCO	0.024–0.032	6 BTDC @ Idle	6 BTDC @ Idle	145–189	NA	800–900	800–1000	Hyd.	Hyd.
	Golf GTI	109 (1780)	W7DCO	0.024–0.032	6 BTDC @ Idle	—	145–189	NA	800–900	—	Hyd.	Hyd.
	Golf GTI 16V	121 (1984)	F6DSR ①	0.027–0.035	6 BTDC @ Idle	—	NA	NA	800–900	—	Hyd.	Hyd.
	Fox	109 (1780)	W7RDS	0.024–0.032	6 BTDC @ Idle	6 BTDC @ Idle	131–174	NA	800–1000	800–1000	Hyd.	Hyd.
	Cabriolet	109 (1780)	W7DCO	0.024–0.032	6 BTDC @ Idle	6 BTDC @ Idle	145–189	NA	800–1000	800–1000	Hyd.	Hyd.
	Passat	121 (1984)	F6DSR ①	0.028–0.032	6 BTDC @ Idle	6 BTDC @ Idle	NA	NA	800–900	800–1000	Hyd.	Hyd.
	Corrado	109 (1780)	W6DPO	0.028–0.031	6 BTDC @ Idle	—	116–174	NA	800–900	—	Hyd.	Hyd.

DIESEL ENGINE TUNE-UP SPECIFICATIONS

Year	Engine Displacement cu. in. (cc)	Valve Clearance ① Intake (in.)	Exhaust (in.)	Intake Valve Opens (deg.)	Injection Pump Setting (deg.)	Injection Nozzle Pressure (psi) New	Used	Idle Speed (rpm)	Cranking Compression Pressure (psi)
1989	97.0 (1588)	0.008–0.012	0.016–0.020	N.A.	Align Marks	1885③	1706③	800–850②④	406 minimum
1990–91	97.0 (1588)	0.008–0.012	0.016–0.020	N.A.	Align Marks	1885③	1706③	800–850②④	406 minimum

N.A. Not Available
① Warm clearance given.
    Cold clearance:
       Intake—0.006–0.010
       Exhaust—0.014–0.018

② Volkswagen has lowered the idle speed on early models to this specification. Valve clearance need not be adjusted unless it varies more than 0.002 in. from specification.

③ Turbo diesel—
    New—2306
    Used—2139
④ Turbo diesel—900–1000

FIRING ORDERS

NOTE: To avoid confusion, always replace spark plug wires one at a time.

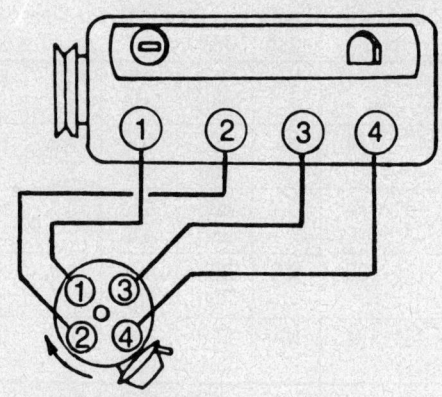

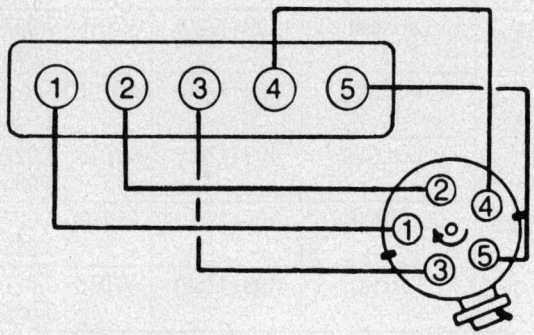

4 Cylinder Engines
Engine Firing Order: 1–3–4–2
Distributor Rotation: Counterclockwise

5 Cylinder Engine
Engine Firing Order: 1–2–4–5–3
Distributor Rotation: Counterclockwise

CAPACITIES

Year	Model	Engine Displacement cu. in. (cc)	Engine Crankcase with Filter	without Filter	Transmission (pts.) 4-Spd	5-Spd	Auto.	Drive Axle (pts.)	Fuel Tank (gals.)	Cooling System (qts.)
1987	Jetta	109 (1780)	4.3	3.8	—	4.2	6.4	—	14.5	7.3
	Jetta GL	109 (1780)	4.3	3.8	—	4.2	6.4	—	14.5	7.3
	Jetta GLI 16V	109 (1780)	4.3	3.8	—	4.2	6.4	—	14.5	7.3
	Quantum GL5	136 (2226)	4.0	3.8	—	4.2	6.4	—	15.8	8.5
	Quantum Syncro	136 (2226)	4.0	3.5	—	5.0	6.4	1.2	18.5	8.5
	Scirocco 16V	109 (1780)	4.3	3.8	—	4.2	6.4	—	13.8	5.1
	Cabriolet	109 (1780)	4.3	3.8	—	4.2	6.4	—	13.8	5.1
	Golf GL	109 (1780)	4.3	3.8	—	4.2	6.4	—	14.5	7.3
	Golf GT	109 (1780)	4.3	3.8	—	4.2	6.4	—	14.5	7.3
	Golf GTI 16V	109 (1780)	4.3	3.8	—	4.2	6.4	—	14.5	7.3
	Fox/GL	109 (1780)	3.7	3.2	3.6	—	—	—	12.4	6.9
1988	Jetta	109 (1780)	4.3	3.8	—	4.2	6.4	—	14.5	7.3
	Jetta GL	109 (1780)	4.3	3.8	—	4.2	6.4	—	14.5	7.3
	Jetta GLI 16V	109 (1780)	4.3	3.8	—	4.2	6.4	—	14.5	7.3
	Jetta Carat	109 (1780)	4.3	3.8	—	4.2	6.4	—	14.5	7.3
	Quantum GL5	136 (2226)	4.0	3.8	—	4.2	6.4	—	15.8	8.5
	Quantum Syncro	136 (2226)	4.0	3.5	—	5.0	6.4	1.2	18.5	8.5
	Scirocco 16V	109 (1780)	4.3	3.8	—	4.2	6.4	—	13.8	5.1
	Cabriolet	109 (1780)	4.3	3.8	—	4.2	6.4	—	13.8	5.1
	Golf GL	109 (1780)	4.3	3.8	—	4.2	6.4	—	14.5	7.3
	Golf GT	109 (1780)	4.3	3.8	—	4.2	6.4	—	14.5	7.3
	Golf GTI 16V	109 (1780)	4.3	3.8	—	4.2	6.4	—	14.5	7.3
	Fox/GL	109 (1780)	3.7	3.2	3.6	—	—	—	12.4	6.9

CAPACITIES

Year	Model	Engine Displacement cu. in. (cc)	Engine Crankcase with Filter	Engine Crankcase without Filter	Transmission (pts.) 4-Spd	Transmission (pts.) 5-Spd	Transmission (pts.) Auto.	Drive Axle (pts.)	Fuel Tank (gals.)	Cooling System (qts.)
1989	Jetta	109 (1780)	4.3	3.8	—	4.2	6.4	—	14.5	7.3
	Jetta (Diesel)	97.0 (1588)	4.8	4.3	—	4.2	6.4	—	13.7	7.3
	Jetta GL	109 (1780)	4.3	3.8	—	4.2	6.4	—	14.5	7.3
	Jetta GLI 16V	109 (1780)	4.3	3.8	—	4.2	6.4	—	14.5	7.3
	Jetta Carat	109 (1780)	4.3	3.8	—	4.2	6.4	—	14.5	7.3
	Quantum GL5	136 (2226)	4.0	3.8	—	4.2	6.4	—	15.8	8.5
	Quantum Syncro	136 (2226)	4.0	3.5	—	5.0	6.4	1.2	18.5	8.5
	Scirocco 16V	109 (1780)	4.3	3.8	—	4.2	6.4	—	13.8	5.1
	Cabriolet	109 (1780)	4.3	3.8	—	4.2	6.4	—	13.8	5.1
	Golf GL	109 (1780)	4.3	3.8	—	4.2	6.4	—	14.5	7.3
	Golf GT	109 (1780)	4.3	3.8	—	4.2	6.4	—	14.5	7.3
	Golf GTI 16V	109 (1780)	4.3	3.8	—	4.2	6.4	—	14.5	7.3
	Fox/GL	109 (1780)	3.7	3.2	3.6	—	—	—	12.4	6.9
1990–91	Jetta	109 (1780)	4.3	3.8	—	4.2	6.4	—	14.5	7.3
	Jetta (Diesel)	97.0 (1588)	4.3	3.8	—	4.2	6.4	—	13.7	7.3
	Jetta GLI 16V	121 (1984)	4.3	3.8	—	4.2	—	—	14.5	7.3
	Jetta Carat	109 (1780)	4.3	3.8	—	4.2	6.4	—	14.5	7.3
	Cabriolet	109 (1780)	4.3	3.8	—	4.2	6.4	—	13.8	5.1
	Golf GL	109 (1780)	4.3	3.8	—	4.2	6.4	—	14.5	7.3
	Golf GTI	109 (1780)	4.3	3.8	—	4.2	—	—	14.5	7.3
	Golf GTI 16V	121 (1984)	4.3	3.8	—	4.2	—	—	14.5	7.3
	Fox	109 (1780)	3.7	3.2	3.6	4.2	—	—	12.4	6.4①
	Passat	121 (1984)	4.3	3.8	—	4.2	6	—	18.5	7.3
	Corrado	109 (1780)	4.3	3.8	—	4.2	—	—	14.5	7.3

① With A/C, 6.9 qts.

CRANKSHAFT AND CONNECTING ROD SPECIFICATIONS

All measurements are given in inches.

Year	Engine Displacement cu. in. (cc)	Crankshaft Main Brg. Journal Dia.	Crankshaft Main Brg. Oil Clearance	Crankshaft Shaft End-play	Crankshaft Thrust on No.	Connecting Rod Journal Diameter	Connecting Rod Oil Clearance	Connecting Rod Side Clearance
1987	109.0 (1780)	2.126	0.001–0.003	0.003–0.007	3	1.881	0.0049 ①	0.015①
	136.0 (2226)	2.282	0.001–0.003	0.003–0.007	3	1.881	0.0006–0.002	0.015①
1988	109.0 (1780)	2.126	0.001–0.003	0.003–0.007	3	1.881	0.0049 ①	0.015①
	136.0 (2226)	2.282	0.001–0.003	0.003–0.007	3	1.881	0.0006–0.002	0.015①
1989	97.0 (1588)	2.126	0.001–0.003	0.003–0.007	3	1.881	0.0049 ①	0.015①
	109.0 (1780)	2.126	0.001–0.003	0.003–0.007	3	1.881	0.0049 ①	0.015①
	136.0 (2226)	2.282	0.001–0.003	0.003–0.007	3	1.881	0.0006–0.002	0.015①

CRANKSHAFT AND CONNECTING ROD SPECIFICATIONS

All measurements are given in inches.

Year	Engine Displacement cu. in. (cc)	Crankshaft Main Brg. Journal Dia.	Crankshaft Main Brg. Oil Clearance	Crankshaft Shaft End-play	Crankshaft Thrust on No.	Connecting Rod Journal Diameter	Connecting Rod Oil Clearance	Connecting Rod Side Clearance
1990–91	97.0 (1588)	2.126	0.001–0.003	0.003–0.007	3	1.881	0.0049 ①	0.015 ①
	109.0 (1780)	2.126	0.001–0.003	0.003–0.007	3	1.881	0.0049 ①	0.015 ①
	121.0 (1984)	2.126	0.001–0.003	0.003–0.007	3	1.881	0.0049 ①	0.015 ①

NOTE: Main and connecting rod bearings are available in 3 undersizes.
① Wear limit
② Bearings marked with blue dot. Bearing marked with red dot—2.3988–2.3991.

VALVE SPECIFICATIONS

Year	Engine Displacement cu. in. (cc)	Seat Angle (deg.)	Face Angle (deg.)	Spring Test Pressure (lbs.)	Spring Installed Height (in.)	Stem-to-Guide Clearance (in.) Intake	Stem-to-Guide Clearance (in.) Exhaust	Stem Diameter (in.) Intake	Stem Diameter (in.) Exhaust
1987	109.0 (1780)	45	45	NA	NA	0.039 ① max	0.051 ① max	0.3140	0.3130
	136.0 (2226)	45	45	NA	NA	0.039 ① max	0.051 ① max	0.3140	0.3130
1988	109.0 (1780)	45	45	NA	NA	0.039 ① max	0.051 ① max	0.3140	0.3130
	136.0 (2226)	45	45	NA	NA	0.039 ① max	0.051 ① max	0.3140	0.3130
1989	97.0 Diesel (1588)	45	45	96–106 @ 0.92	NA	0.051 ① max	0.051 ① max	0.3140	0.3130
	109.0 (1780)	45	45	NA	NA	0.039 ① max	0.051 ① max	0.3140	0.3130
	136.0 (2226)	45	45	NA	NA	0.039 ① max	0.051 ① max	0.3140	0.3130
1990–91	97.0 (1588)	45	45	96–106 @ 0.92	NA	0.051 ① max	0.051 ① max	0.3140	0.3130
	109.0 (1780)	45	45	NA	NA	0.039 ① max	0.051 ① max	0.3140	0.3130
	121.0 (1984)	45	45	NA	NA	0.039 ① max	0.051 ① max	0.3140	0.3130

NOTE: Exhaust valves must be ground by hand
NA Not available
① Measure at valve face end, stem flush with cam end of guide opening.

PISTON AND RING SPECIFICATIONS

All measurements are given in inches.

Year	Engine Displacement cu. in. (cc)	Piston Clearance	Ring Gap Top Compression	Ring Gap Bottom Compression	Ring Gap Oil Control	Ring Side Clearance Top Compression	Ring Side Clearance Bottom Compression	Ring Side Clearance Oil Control
1987	109.0 (1780)	0.001–0.003	0.0120–0.0180	0.0120–0.0180	0.0120–0.0180	0.0008–0.0020	0.0008–0.0020	0.0008–0.0020
	136.0 (2226)	0.0011	0.0100–0.0200	0.0100–0.0200	0.0100–0.0200	0.0008–0.0030	0.0008–0.0030	0.0008–0.0030

PISTON AND RING SPECIFICATIONS

All measurements are given in inches.

Year	Engine Displacement cu. in. (cc)	Piston Clearance	Ring Gap			Ring Side Clearance		
			Top Compression	Bottom Compression	Oil Control	Top Compression	Bottom Compression	Oil Control
1988	109.0 (1780)	0.0010–0.0030	0.0120–0.0180	0.0120–0.0180	0.0120–0.0180	0.0008–0.0020	0.0008–0.0020	0.0008–0.0020
	136.0 (2226)	0.0011	0.0100–0.0200	0.0100–0.0200	0.0100–0.0200	0.0008–0.0030	0.0008–0.0030	0.0008–0.0030
1989	97.0 (1588)	0.001–0.003	0.0120–0.0200	0.0120–0.0200	0.0100–0.0180	0.0020–0.0040	0.0020–0.0030	0.0010–0.0020
	109.0 (1780)	0.0010–0.0030	0.0120–0.0180	0.0120–0.0180	0.0120–0.0180	0.0008–0.0020	0.0008–0.0020	0.0008–0.0020
	136.0 (2226)	0.0011	0.0100–0.0200	0.0100–0.0200	0.0100–0.0200	0.0008–0.0030	0.0008–0.0030	0.0008–0.0030
1990–91	97.0 (1588)	0.0010–0.0030	0.0120–0.0180	0.0120–0.0180	0.0100–0.0180	0.0020–0.0040	0.0020–0.0030	0.0010–0.0020
	109.0 (1780) (Exc. Corrado)	0.0010–0.0030	0.0120–0.0180	0.0120–0.0180	0.0120–0.0180	0.0008–0.0020	0.0008–0.0020	0.0008–0.0020
	109.0 (1780) (Corrado)	0.0010–0.0020	0.0060–0.0140	0.0600–0.0140	0.0100–0.0200	0.0010–0.0030	0.0010–0.0030	0.0010–0.0020
	121.0 (1984)	0.0010–0.0200	0.0070–0.0150	0.0070–0.0150	0.0090–0.0190	0.0008–0.0027	0.0008–0.0027	0.0008–0.0020

TORQUE SPECIFICATIONS

All readings in ft. lbs.

Year	Engine Displacement cu. in. (cc)	Cylinder Head Bolts	Main Bearing Bolts	Rod Bearing Bolts ①	Crankshaft Pulley Bolts	Flywheel Bolts	Manifold		Spark Plugs
							Intake	Exhaust	
1987	109.0 (1780)	②	47	33③	145④	14⑥	18	18	14
	136.0 (2226)	②	47	33③	253	14	18	18	14
1988	109.0 (1780)	②	47	33③	145④	14⑥	18	18	14
	136.0 (2226)	②	47	33③	253	14	18	18	14
1989	97.0 Diesel (1588)	① ②	47	33③	130	14	18	18	14
	109.0 (1780)	②	47	33③	145④	14⑥	18	18	14
	136.0 (2226)	②	47	33③	253	14	18	18	14
1990–91	97.0 Diesel (1588)	① ②	47	33③	253	14	18	18	14
	109.0 (1780) (Exc. Corrado)	②	47	22③	④	14⑥	18	18	14
	109.0 (1780)	②	47	22① ⑤	④	72	11	18	14
	121.0 (1984)	②	47	22③	④	74	15	18	14

① Always use new bolts.
② With 12 points (polygon) head bolts
Torque in 4 steps:
  1st step—29 ft./lbs.
  2nd step—43 ft./lbs.
  3rd step—additional 1/4 turn (180 degrees) further in one movement (two 90 degree turns are permissible)

Note tightening sequence
Do not retorque at 1000 miles
With 6 point (hex) head bolts
Torque in steps to 54 ft. lbs. with engine cold, when engine is warmed up, torque to 61 ft. lbs. Head bolts must be retorqued after 1000 miles.

③ Stretch bolts: 22 ft. lbs. plus 1/4 (90 degree) turn.
④ Engine UM up to JN707651
133 ft. lbs.
From Engine JN707652
66 ft. lbs. plus 1/2 turn (180°)
⑤ Stretch Bolts: 22 ft. lbs. plus 1/2 (180°) turn.
⑥ Auto. trans., 72 ft. lbs.

BRAKE SPECIFICATIONS
All measurements in inches unless noted.

Year	Model	Lug Nut Torque (ft. lbs.)	Master Cylinder Bore	Brake Disc Minimum Thickness	Brake Disc Maximum Runout	Maximum Brake Drum Diameter	Minimum Lining Thickness Front	Minimum Lining Thickness Rear
1987	Jetta	81	0.820	0.393② ④	0.002	7.087	0.276	0.098③
	Quantum	81	0.820	0.410①	0.002	7.080	0.250	0.098
	Scirocco	81	0.820	0.410①	0.002	7.080	0.250	0.098
	GTI	81	0.820	0.393② ④	0.002	7.087	0.276	0.098③
	GLI	81	0.820	0.393② ④	0.002	7.087	0.276	0.098③
	Golf	81	0.820	0.393② ④	0.002	7.087	0.276	0.098③
	Fox/GL	81	0.820	0.393	0.002	7.087	0.276	0.098③
1988	Jetta	81	0.820	0.393② ④	0.002	7.100	0.276	0.098③
	Quantum	81	0.820	0.410② ④	0.002	7.900	0.276	0.098③
	Scirocco	81	0.820	0.410② ④	0.002	—	0.276	③
	Cabriolet	81	0.820	0.393② ④	0.002	7.100	0.276	0.098③
	Golf	81	0.820	0.393② ④	0.002	7.100	0.276	0.098③
	Fox/GL	81	0.820	0.393	0.002	7.100	0.276	0.098③
1989	Jetta	81	0.820	0.393② ④	0.002	7.900	0.276	0.098③
	Quantum	81	0.820	0.410② ④	0.002	7.900	0.276	0.098③
	Scirocco	81	0.820	0.410② ④	0.002	—	0.276	③
	Cabriolet	81	0.820	0.393② ④	0.002	7.100	0.276	0.098
	Golf	81	0.820	0.393② ④	0.002	7.100	0.276	0.098③
	Fox/GL	81	0.820	0.393	0.002	7.100	0.276	0.098
1990	Jetta	81	0.809	0.393② ④	0.002	7.087	0.276	0.098
	Jetta ABS	81	0.874	0.787④	0.001	—	0.276	0.276
	Golf	81	0.809	0.393② ④	0.002	7.087	0.276	0.098
	Fox	81	0.809	0.393	0.002	7.087⑤	0.276	0.098
	Passat	81	0.874①	0.708④	0.001	—	0.276	0.276
	Corrado	81	0.874①	0.787④	0.001	—	0.276	0.276

NOTE: Minimum lining thickness is as recommended by manufacturer. Due to variations in state inspection regulations, the minimum thickness may be different than that recommended by the manufacturer.
① Non ABS; NA
② Vented discs; 0.708
③ Disc brake: 0.276
④ Rear disc brake: 0.315
⑤ Wagon; 7.913

WHEEL ALIGNMENT

Year	Model	Caster① Range (deg.)	Caster① Preferred Setting (deg.)	Camber Range (deg.)	Camber Preferred Setting (deg.)	Toe-in (in.)	Steering Axis Inclination (deg.)
1987	Jetta GL	±30′	1°30′	±20′	−30′	0°±10′	NA
	Jetta GLI	±30′	1°35′	±20′	−35′	0°±10′	NA
	Jetta GLI 16V	±30′	1°35′	±20′	−40′	0°±10′	NA
	Quantum	±30′	+30′ ②	±30′	−40′	+10′±10′	NA
	Quantum Syncro	±20′	1°	±30′	−20′	+12′±5′	NA
	Scirocco 16V	±30′	1°50′	±30′	+20′	−5′ to −30′	NA
	Cabriolet	±30′	1°50′	±30′	+20′	−5′ to −30′	NA

WHEEL ALIGNMENT

Year	Model	Caster ① Range (deg.)	Caster ① Preferred Setting (deg.)	Camber Range (deg.)	Camber Preferred Setting (deg.)	Toe-in (in.)	Steering Axis Inclination (deg.)
	Golf GL	±30′	1°30′	±20′	−30′	0° to ±10′	NA
	Golf GTI	±30′	1°35′	±20′	−35′	0° to ±10′	NA
	Golf GTI 16V	±30′	1°35′	±20′	−40′	0° to ±10′	NA
	Fox	±20′	2°	±20′	−30′	−20′ to 0°	NA
	Fox Wagon	±20′	1°45′	±20′	−30′	−20′ to 0°	NA
1988	Jetta GL	±30′	1°30′	±20′	−30′	0°±10′	NA
	Jetta GLI	±30′	1°35′	±20′	−35′	0°±10′	NA
	Jetta GLI 16V	±30′	1°35′	±20′	−40′	0°±10′	NA
	Quantum	±30′	+30′ ②	±30′	−40′	+10′±10′	NA
	Quantum Syncro	±20′	1°	±30′	−20′	+12′±5′	NA
	Scirocco 16V	±30′	1°50′	±30′	+20′	−5′ to −30′	NA
	Cabriolet	±30′	1°50′	±30′	+20′	−5′ to −30′	NA
	Golf GL	±30′	1°30′	±20′	−30′	0° to ±10′	NA
	Golf GTI	±30′	1°35′	±20′	−35′	0° to ±10′	NA
	Golf GTI 16V	±30′	1°35′	±20′	−40′	0° to ±10′	NA
	Fox	±20′	2°	±20′	−30′	−20′ to 0°	NA
	Fox Wagon	±20′	1°45′	±20′	−30′	−20′ to 0°	NA
1989	Jetta GL	±30′	1°30′	±20′	−30′	0°±10′	NA
	Jetta GLI	±30′	1°35′	±20′	−35′	0°±10′	NA
	Jetta GLI 16V	±30′	1°35′	±20′	−40′	0°±10′	NA
	Quantum	±30′	+30′ ②	±30′	−40′	+10′±10′	NA
	Quantum Syncro	±20′	1°	±30′	−20′	+12′±5′	NA
	Scirocco 16V	±30′	1°50′	±30′	+20′	−5′ to −30′	NA
	Cabriolet	±30′	1°50′	±30′	+20′	−5′ to −30′	NA
	Golf GL	±30′	1°30′	±20′	−30′	0° to ±10′	NA
	Golf GTI	±30′	1°35′	±20′	−35′	0° to ±10′	NA
	Golf GTI 16V	±30′	1°35′	±20′	−40′	0° to ±10′	NA
	Fox	±20′	2°	±20′	−30′	−20′ to 0°	NA
	Fox Wagon	±20′	1°45′	±20′	−30′	−20′ to 0°	NA
1990-91	Jetta GL	±30′	1°30′	±20′	−30′	0°±10′	NA
	Jetta GLI 16V	±30′	1°35′	±20′	−40′	0°±10′	NA
	Scirocco 16V	±30′	1°50′	±30′	+20′	−5′ to −30′	NA
	Cabriolet	±30′	1°50′	±30′	+20′	−5′ to −30′	NA
	Golf GL	±30′	1°30′	±20′	−30′	0° to ±10′	NA
	Golf GTI	±30′	1°35′	±20′	−35′	0° to ±10′	NA
	Golf GTI 16V	±30′	1°35′	±20′	−40′	0° to ±10′	NA
	Fox	±20′	2°	±20′	−30′	−20′ to 0°	NA
	Fox Wagon	±20′	1°45′	±20′	−30′	−20′ to 0°	NA
	Passat	±30′	+1°40′	±20′	−1°20′	0°±10′	NA
	Corrado	±30′	+1°35′	±20′	−35′	0°±10′	NA

① Not adjustable
② With link rod stabilizer bar: +55′ to +1°55′

ENGINE ELECTRICAL

NOTE: Disconnecting the negative battery cable on some vehicles may interfere with the functions of the on board computer systems and may require the computer to undergo a relearning process, once the negative battery cable is reconnected.

Distributor

Removal and Installation

1. Disconnect the vacuum hoses, coil high tension wire and the connector plug at the distributor.
2. Unsnap the cap retainer clips, and remove the cap and static shield as a unit.
3. At the front crankshaft pulley bolt, turn the engine to Top Dead Center (TDC) on No. 1 cylinder. Make a chalk or paint mark where the rotor points to the rim of the distributor; some vehicles already have a notch there. Also matchmark the distributor to the engine block or head.
4. Remove the bolt and distributor clamp and lift the distributor straight out.

NOTE: On some vehicles, the distributor engages it's drive with an offset slot and is easy to reinstall in the reverse order of removal even if the drive has been disturbed, especially on the 16 valve engine.

5. If the engine has been disturbed with the distributor removed, turn the engine to TDC on cylinder No. 1 and align the timing marks.
6. With the rotor on the distributor, align the rotor with the matchmark for No. 1 spark plug wire and insert the distributor into it's mounting hole. Turn the rotor slightly back and forth while gently pushing in on the distributor to make sure the drive engages with the matchmarks aligned.
7. If the drive does not engage, remove the distributor and, with a suitable tool, turn the oil pump drive so it is parallel with the crankshaft and try again.
8. With the distributor installed, align the matchmarks and reinstall the hold-down clamp and bolt, connector plug, cap and static shield, and high tension wire.
9. Check and adjust the ignition timing.

Ignition Timing

Adjustment

NOTE: The manufacturer recommends timing, idle speed and CO value all be adjusted together.

1. Run the engine to normal operating temperature, stop engine and connect a tachometer and timing light according to manufacturer's instructions.
2. If equipped, disconnect both plugs from the idle stabilizer and plug them together. On engines with Digifant engine management systems, with the ignition ON, engine not running, verify that the idle stabilizer valve hums or buzzes. Do not disconnect any vacuum lines from the distributor.
3. Start the engine, on vehicles with Digifant engine management systems, disconnect the blue coolant temperature sensor plug. Turn off all electrical equipment and set the idle speed to 800–950 rpm.
4. Remove the timing mark cover from the top of the bell housing at the flywheel end of the engine and with the engine running, shine the timing light at the marks on the flywheel. If adjustment is required, loosen the distributor clamp bolt and rotate the distributor as needed to align the correct timing marks.
5. Stop the engine and reconnect plugs.

Alternator

Precautions

• Before doing any work on any electrical system, always STOP the engine and disconnect the battery cables. Also disconnect the battery and ABS control unit, if equipped, if any electric welding is to be done on the vehicle.
• Electronic parts and systems that can be easily and permanently damaged through careless use of electric welding, charging, soldering or test equipment. Carefully follow manufacturer's instructions when using such equipment.
• If equipped with electronically theft-protected radios, record the security code from the owner before disconnecting the battery.

Belt Tension Adjustment

EXCEPT CORRADO

1. Loosen both upper alternator bracket bolts.
2. Loosen the lower alternator pivot bolt. This is a long bolt with a 6mm socket head which should be accessible with the proper tool without removing the timing belt shield.
3. Do not use a prybar to tighten the belt. It is easy to gain enough tension pulling the alternator by hand against the belt. Some vehicles have a toothed rack for setting belt tension.
4. Proper belt tension is attained when moderate finger pressure deflects the belt midway between the pulleys about 0.200 in. (5mm).
5. Securely tighten the mounting bolts.

CORRADO

The vehicle is equipped with a serpentine ribbed belt which drives the alternator, G-Charger and air conditioner. On vehicles without air, this belt drives the water pump instead. Belt tension is maintained with a spring loaded belt tension damper and idler pulley. Before installing the damper onto it's mounting bolts, it must be compressed 5 times to evacuate air, using VW tool 3191 or equivalent.

Removal and Installation

EXCEPT CORRADO

The alternator and voltage regulator are all in the same housing but the regulator can be removed separately. The brushes are on the regulator and should project no less than 0.200 in. (5mm) from the regulator. If the brushes are smaller, replace the regulator.

1. Disconnect the battery cables.

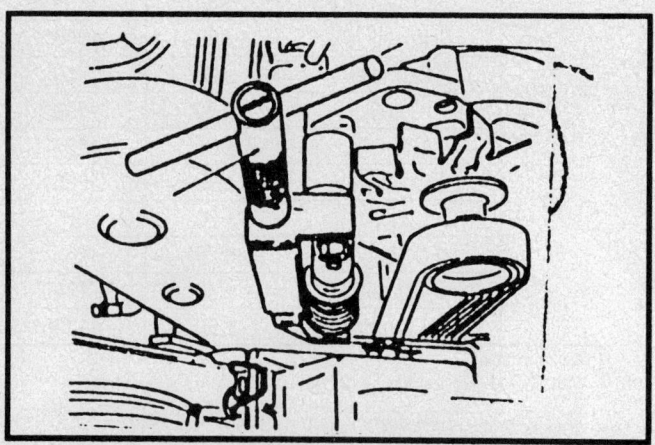

Belt tensioner compressing tool installed

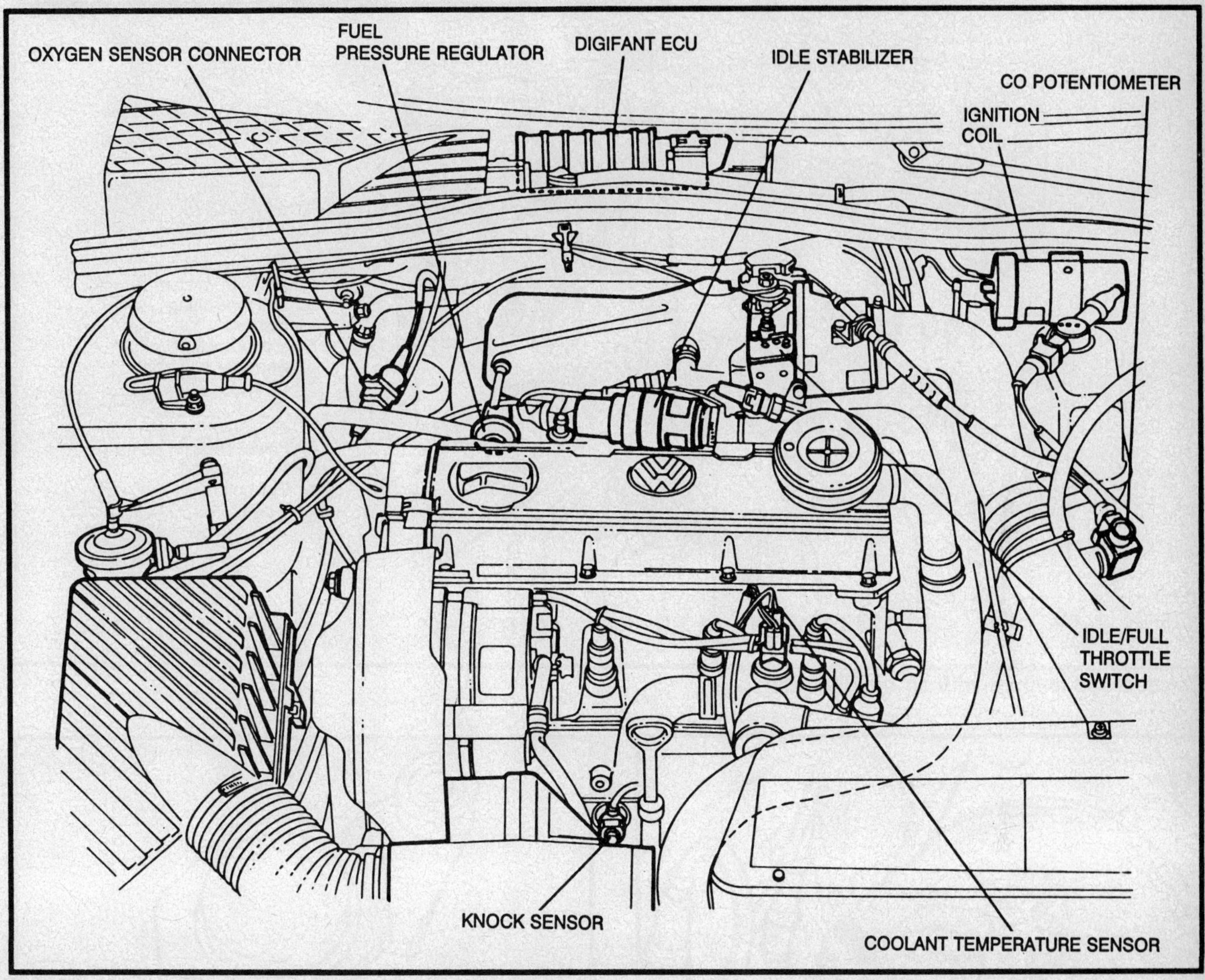

OXYGEN SENSOR CONNECTOR

FUEL PRESSURE REGULATOR

DIGIFANT ECU

IDLE STABILIZER

CO POTENTIOMETER

IGNITION COIL

IDLE/FULL THROTTLE SWITCH

KNOCK SENSOR

COOLANT TEMPERATURE SENSOR

Digifant Engine Management System—Corrado shown

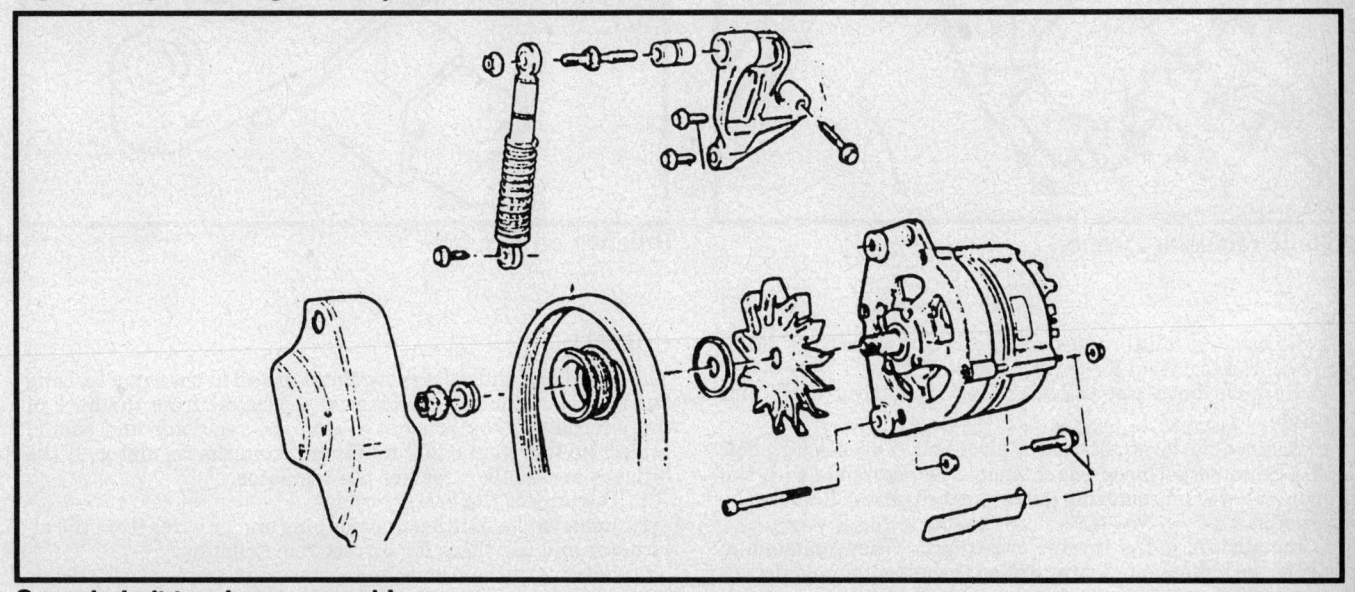

Corrado belt tensioner assembly

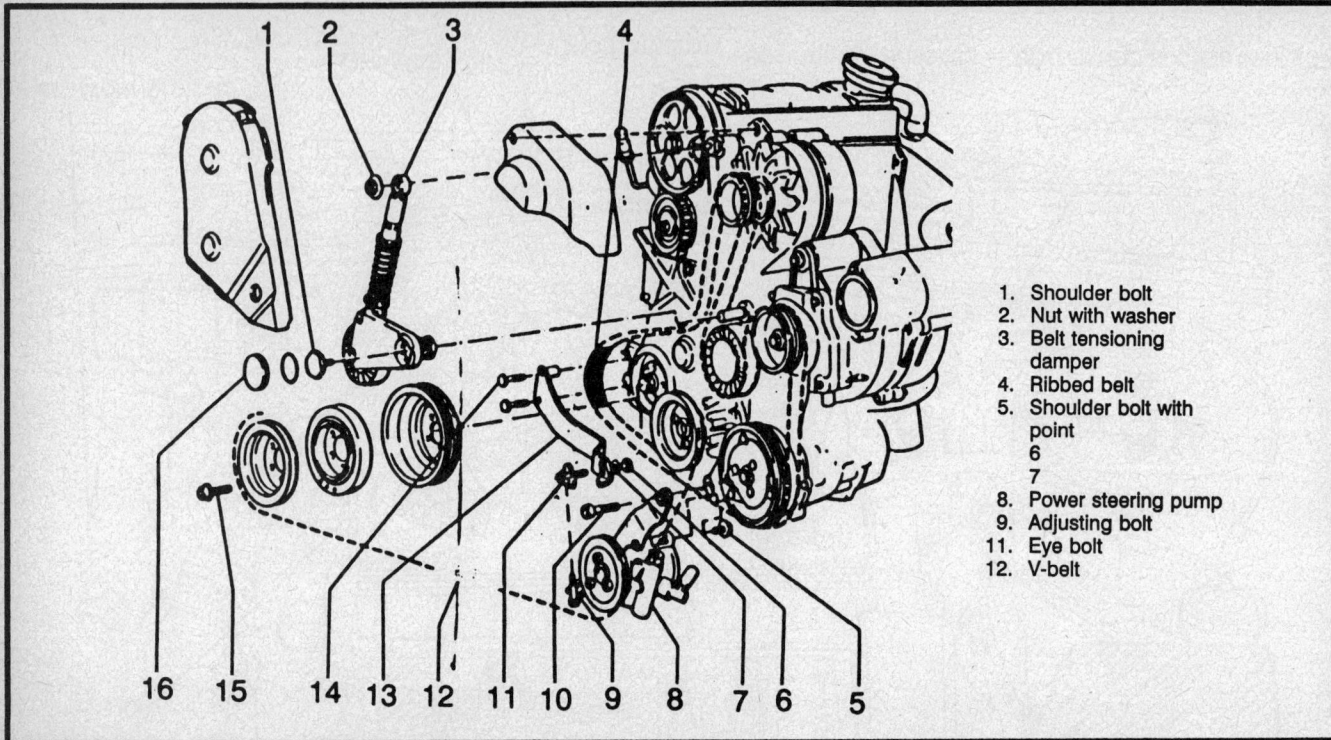

1. Shoulder bolt
2. Nut with washer
3. Belt tensioning damper
4. Ribbed belt
5. Shoulder bolt with point
6
7
8. Power steering pump
9. Adjusting bolt
11. Eye bolt
12. V-belt

Corrado belt layout—with air conditioning

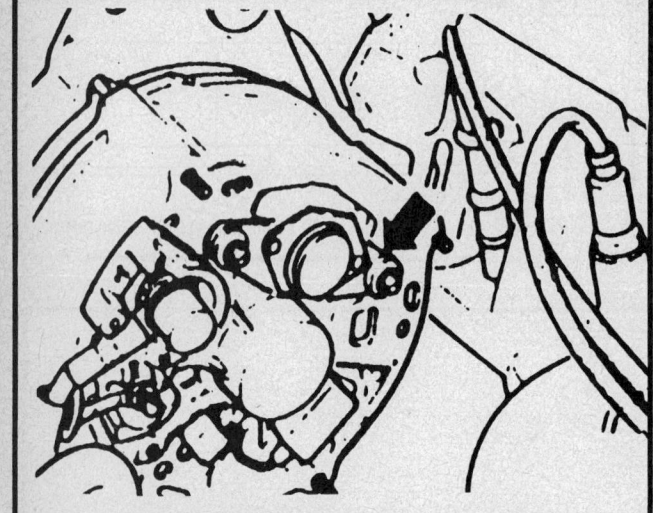

Voltage regulator location

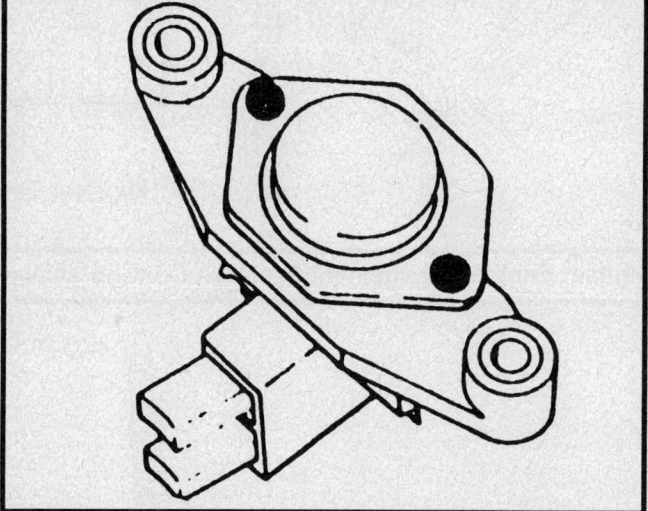

Brushes on regulator

2. Remove the multi-connector plug and/or wires from the alternator and tag them for correct reinstallation.

3. Remove both upper alternator mounting bolts and bracket.

4. Remove the lower alternator pivot bolt. This is a long bolt with a 6mm socket head which should be accessible with the proper tool without removing the timing belt shield. Remove the alternator.

5. Installation is the reverse of removal. When reinstalling the belt, with moderate finger pressure the belt should deflect about 0.200 in. (5mm).

CORRADO
The alternator and voltage regulator are all in the same housing but the regulator can be removed separately from the back of the alternator. The brushes are on the regulator and should project no less than 0.200 in. (5mm) from the regulator. If the brushes are smaller, replace the regulator.

1. Disconnect the battery cables.
2. Remove the multi-connector plug and/or wires from the alternator and tag them for correct reinstallation.
3. Remove the belt cover and install the clamping tool 3191 or equivalent, to collapse the automatic belt tensioner.

Engine support tool in place

4. Carefully remove the tensioner mounting bolts and tensioner and remove the alternator pivot bolt to lift the alternator from the vehicle.

5. Installation is the reverse of removal.

Starter

Removal and Installation
BOSCH STARTERS

NOTE: On some engines, the same bolts hold an en- gine mount and the starter. On some vehicles, the starter bolts also hold the engine and transaxle together. Support the weight of the engine when removing the starter.

1. Disconnect the battery ground cable.
2. Raise and safely support the vehicle.
3. Support the weight of the engine with tool 10–222 or equivalent. Don't lift the enginep, just take the weight off the motor mounts. Be careful not to bend the oil pan.
4. Tag and disconnect the wires from the starter.
5. Remove the starter retaining nuts and bolts.
6. Remove starter mounting bolts and remove the starter.
7. Installation is the reverse of removal.

MITSUBISHI STARTERS

1. Disconnect the battery ground cable.
2. Raise and safely support the vehicle.
3. Support the weight of the engine with tool 10–222 or equivalent. Don't lift the engine, just take the weight off the motor mounts. Be careful not to bend the oil pan.
4. Remove the engine/transaxle cover plate.
5. Unbolt and remove the starter side motor mount and carrier.
6. Disconnect and mark the starter wiring.
7. Remove starter mounting bolts and the starter.
8. Installation is the reverse of removal.

Diesel Glow Plugs

Removal and Installation

1. Remove the busbar connecting the glow plugs and determine which plugs need replacement.
2. Remove the defective plugs.

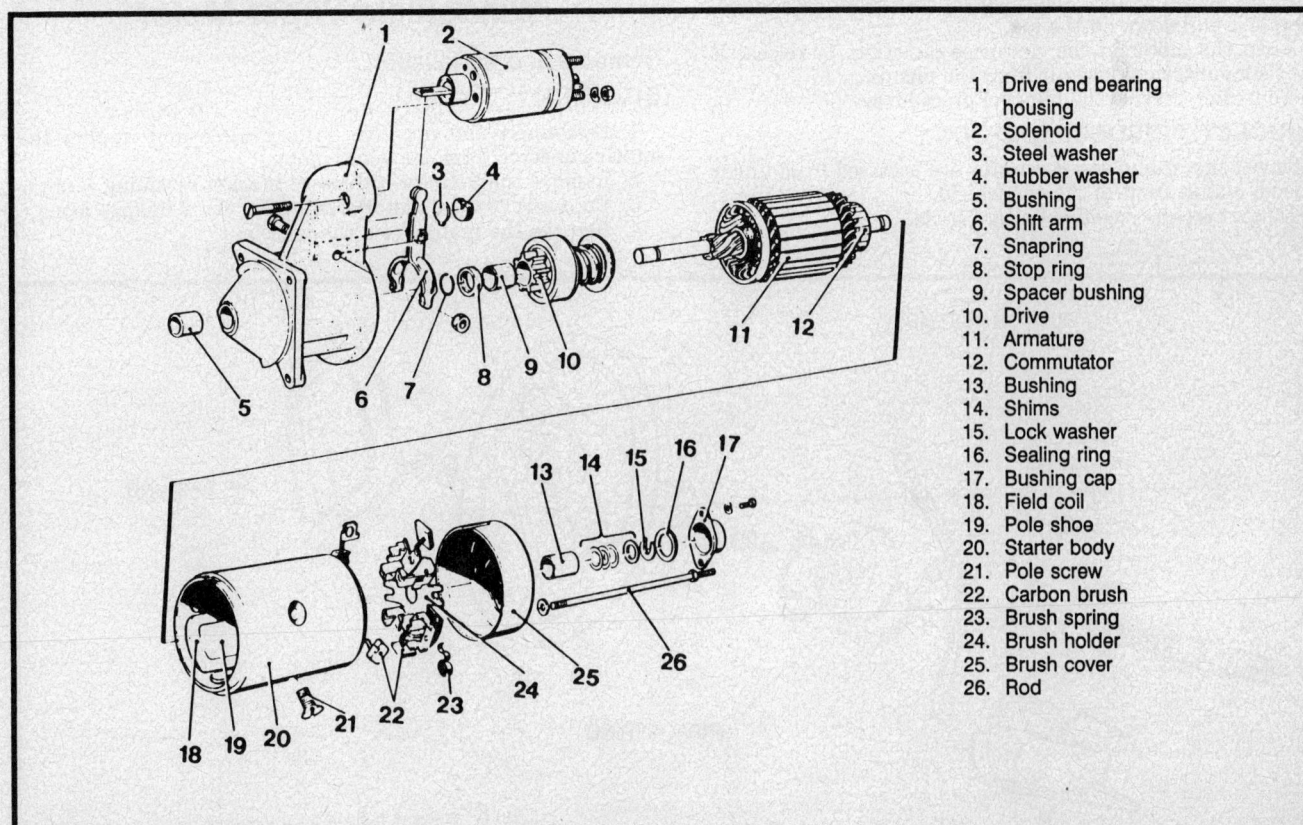

1. Drive end bearing housing
2. Solenoid
3. Steel washer
4. Rubber washer
5. Bushing
6. Shift arm
7. Snapring
8. Stop ring
9. Spacer bushing
10. Drive
11. Armature
12. Commutator
13. Bushing
14. Shims
15. Lock washer
16. Sealing ring
17. Bushing cap
18. Field coil
19. Pole shoe
20. Starter body
21. Pole screw
22. Carbon brush
23. Brush spring
24. Brush holder
25. Brush cover
26. Rod

Typical Bosch starter

3. When installing new plugs, torque to 22 ft. lbs.

NOTE: Diesel glow plugs have an air gap much like a spark plug to prevent overheating of the plug. Over-torquing the glow plug will close the gap and cause the plug to burn out.

Glow Plug System Check

1. Disconnect the engine temperature sensor.
2. Connect a test light between No. 4 cylinder glow plug and ground. The glow plugs are connected by a flat, coated busbar, located near the bottom of the cylinder head.

3. Turn the ignition key **ON**; the test light should light, then go out after 10–30 seconds.
4. If not, possible problems include a blown fuse, lack of power to or from the glow plug relay (check wiring) or the relay itself.

Testing

1. Remove the wire and busbar from the glow plugs.
2. Connect a test light to the battery positive terminal.
3. Touch the test light probe to each glow plug in turn. If the test light lights, the plug is good. If the light does not light, replace the glow plug(s).

CHASSIS ELECTRICAL

— CAUTION —

If equipped with an air bag, the negative battery cable must be disconnected, before working on the system. Failure to do so may result in deployment of the air bag and possible personal injury.

Heater Blower Motor

Removal and Installation

GOLF, JETTA, CORRADO, PASSAT

The blower motor is located behind the glove box and it may be easier to remove the glove box to gain access to the motor. The series resistor is mounted on the motor.

1. Disconnect the wires at the blower motor.
2. At the blower motor flange near the cowl, disengage the retaining lug; pull down on the lug.
3. Turn the motor in the clockwise direction, to release it from it's mount, then lower it from the plenum.
4. To install, reverse the removal procedures.

CABRIOLET, SCIROCCO AND FOX

The blower motor and series resistor are accessed from under the hood, just in front of the windshield.

1. Disconnect the negative battery cable.

2. Remove the clips and gasket holding the water deflector in place and remove the deflector.
3. To remove the plastic cover that is now visible, some vehicles have fasteners which are accessed from both under the hood and under the dash. If after removing all screws, bolts or clips visible from above, the cover still won't lift off, check under the dash for more screws.
4. On vehicles with air conditioning, disconnect the linkage for the air distribution flaps. Then remove the remaining plastic cover.
5. The blower and series resistor are now accessible. Remove the motor.
6. Installation is the reverse of removal. Be sure the seal around the motor is properly reinstalled.

Windshield Wiper Motor

Removal and Installation

QUANTUM

1. Disconnect the negative battery cable and unplug the multi-connector from the wiper motor.
2. Remove the 3 motor-to-linkage bracket retaining screws.
3. Carefully pry the motor crank from the 2 linkage arms.
4. Remove the motor from the vehicle.

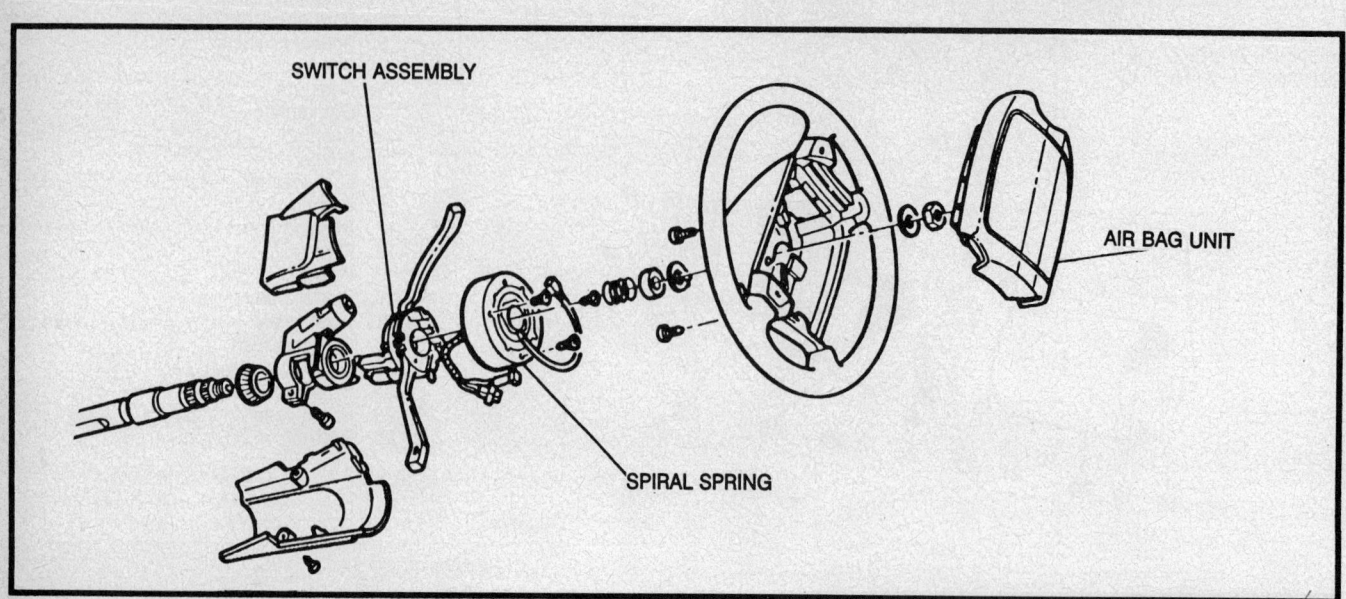

SWITCH ASSEMBLY

AIR BAG UNIT

SPIRAL SPRING

Steering column assembly with air bag

5. Install the motor in the reverse order of removal. The crank arm should be at a right angle to the motor.

EXCEPT QUANTUM

When removing the wiper motor, leave the mounting frame in place. If possible, do not remove the wiper drive crank from the motor shaft.

1. Disconnect the negative battery cable and unplug the multi-connector from the wiper motor.

2. Disconnect the crank arm from the wiper arm assembly.

3. Remove the retaining nut and the crank arm from the wiper motor shaft.

4. Remove the motor mounting bolts and the motor from the vehicle.

5. To install, run the motor, turn it off and disconnect the power after the motor stops; it will stop in the park position.

6. Install the motor.

7. To complete the installation, connect the crank arm to the wiper assembly and reverse the removal procedures.

Windshield Wiper/Washer Switch

Removal and Installation

— CAUTION —

If equipped with an air bag, the negative battery cable must be disconnected for 20 minutes before working on the system. Failure to do so may result in deployment of the air bag and possible personal injury.

1. Disconnect the negative battery cable and remove the steering wheel.

2. Remove the screws securing the steering column covers and remove the covers.

3. Remove the 3 retaining screws and remove the combination switch.

4. Remove the windshield wiper/washer switch and carefully disconnect the wires.

5. Installation is the reverse of the removal procedure.

Instrument Cluster

Removal and Installation
QUANTUM

— CAUTION —

If equipped with an air bag, the negative battery cable must be disconnected for 20 minutes before working on the system. Failure to do so may result in deployment of the air bag and possible personal injury.

1. Disconnect the negative battery cable.

2. Carefully pry off switch trim below instrument cluster.

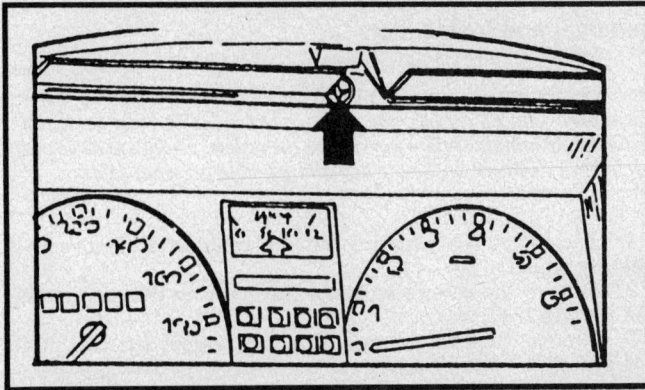

Tip down cluster panel, revealing phillips screw

Instrument cluster removal—Scirocco—Quantum similar

3. Pull heater control knobs off and press out heater control plate.

4. Remove 2 Phillips head screws holding heater control trim to panel.

5. Remove the 7 Phillips screws around perimeter of instrument cluster.

6. Disconnect all wiring to switches and warning lights. Remove all trim panels.

7. Start to pull down on the instrument cluster and remove the screws at the top of the cluster.

8. Tip out the top of the instrument cluster.

9. Remove the speedometer cable by twisting the tabs of the plastic fixture around the end of the cable.

10. Disconnect the multi-point connector and remove instrument cluster.

11. To install, reverse the removal procedures.

GOLF, FOX, GTI, JETTA, SCIROCCO AND CABRIOLET

1. Disconnect the negative battery cable and pull off the temperature control knobs and levers, except Scirocco.

2. Unclip the heater control trim plate, separate the electrical connectors and remove the plate, except Scirocco.

3. Remove the retaining screws and the instrument panel trim plate.

4. Remove the retaining screws and pull out the instrument panel.

5. Squeeze the clips on the speedometer cable head and remove the cable from the instrument cluster.

6. Disconnect all of the vacuum hose and the electrical connections.

7. To install, reverse the removal procedures.

CORRADO AND PASSAT

— CAUTION —

If equipped with an air bag, the negative battery cable must be disconnected for 20 minutes before working on the system. Failure to do so may result in deployment of the air bag and possible personal injury.

1. Disconnect negative battery cable.

2. Remove the horn button cover, starting at the bottom and the steering wheel.

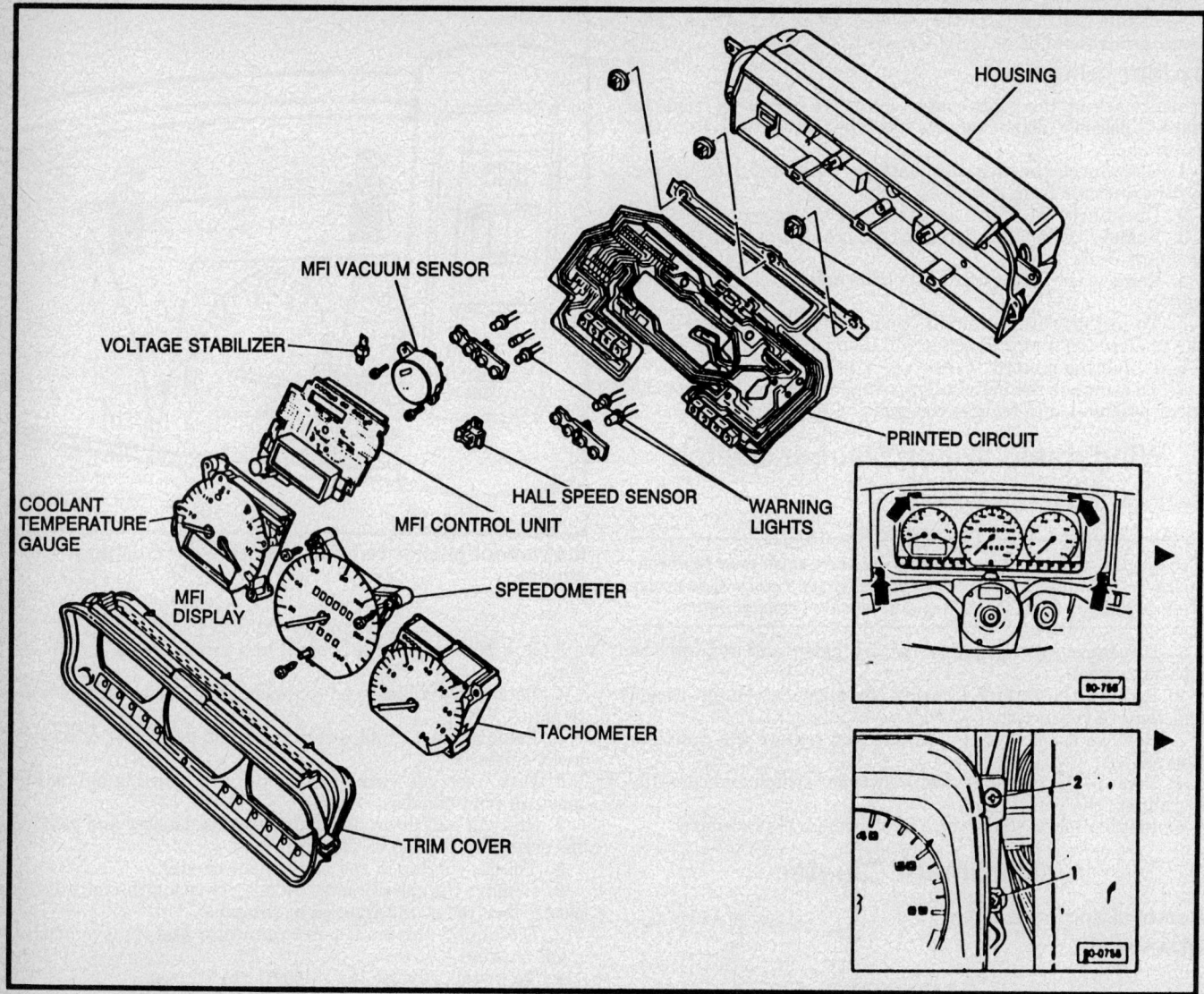

Instrument cluster assembly

3. Remove the screw trim caps, trim screws and cluster trim.

4. Unscrew the trip odometer reset button.

5. Remove the cover screws (1) and cover, then remove the cluster screws (2) and cluster.

6. Carefully disconnect the vacuum line, speedometer drive cable and multi-point connector.

7. Installation is the reverse of removal.

Headlight Switch

Removal and Installation

1. To remove, disconnect the battery.

2. Carefully pry on one side of the switch, then the other, to walk the switch from it's position; be careful not to damage the dash padding.

3. To reinstall, reconnect the wires and push the switch back into it's position.

Combination Switch

Removal and Installation

— **CAUTION** —

If equipped with an air bag, the negative battery cable must be disconnected for 20 minutes before working on the system. Failure to do so may result in deployment of the air bag and possible personal injury.

1. Disconnect the negative battery cable and remove the steering wheel.

2. Remove the screws securing the steering column covers and remove the covers.

3. Remove the 3 retaining screws and remove the combination switch.

4. Carefully disconnect the wires.

5. Installation is the reverse of removal.

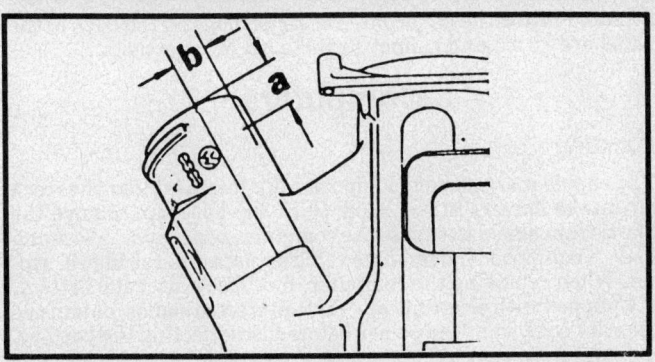

Dimension A 0.470 in. (12mm)—dimension B 0.390 in. (10mm)

Ignition Lock/Switch

Removal and Installation

1. Disconnect the negative battery cable and remove steering wheel.
2. Remove bottom switch cover, turn signal and wiper switches.
3. Some vehicles have a locking ring and spring below the switches. To remove, place a thin tube or pipe over the splines and push lightly against the spring. Remove the locking ring with snapring pliers and allow the spring to push the locking ring and spacer up. Lift out the remaining parts.
4. Unplug the ignition switch, remove the socket-head screw and remove the entire lock and support ring housing.
5. To remove the lock cylinder, carefully drill a ⅛ in. hole into the housing at the spot indicated, insert a key into the lock and remove the key and cylinder.

Clutch Switch

Adjustment

On vehicles with cruise control, the system is deactivated when the clutch pedal is pushed by a vacuum switch connected to the clutch linkage. There is no adjustment or repair possible. If the switch malfunctions, it must be replaced.

Neutral Safety Switch

Adjustment

Neutral safety switches, in all vehicles, are at the shifter inside the vehicle. Adjustment is accomplished by moving the switch on the slots so the starter will operate only in **P** or **N**.

All newer vehicles have an automatic shift lock that prevents the shifter from moving out of **P** or **N** with the engine running unless the brake pedal is pushed. If the vehicle speed is over 3 mph, the locking system will not activate. There is also a 1 second delay when shifting into **N**.

With the ignition **ON** and the shifter in **P** or **N**, a solenoid is activated and a blocking piece prevents the locking pin from moving when the shifter button is pushed. When the brake pedal is pushed, the solenoid is deactivated and the spring loaded blocking piece moves away, allowing the shifter button to be pushed in.

1. Put the shifter in **P**.
2. With the cable screw loose at the gear lever shaft, move the shaft into the park detent.
3. Rock the vehicle to make sure the transaxle is really in park and tighten the shift lever screw to 18 ft. lbs. (25 Nm).

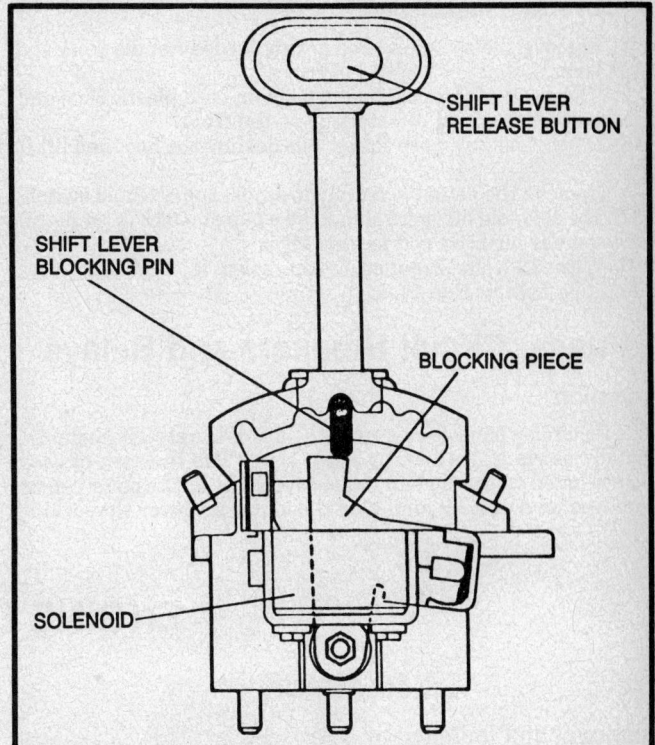

Automatic shift lock activated

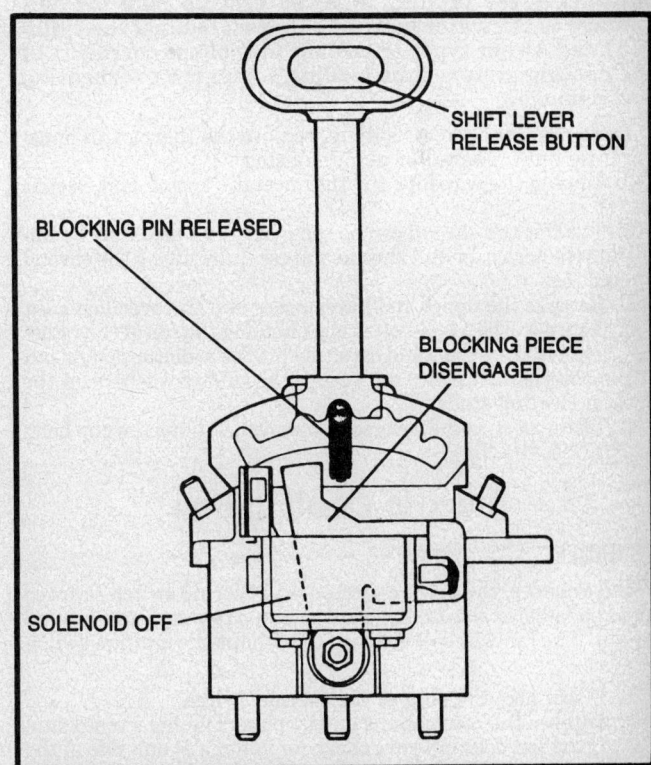

Automatic shift lock released

4. With the solenoid off, the distance between the blocking piece and the pin should be 0.012 in. (0.3mm). If the system does not work properly, the solenoid can be moved on it's slots to adjust this dimension.

Removal and Installation

1. Remove the set screw and spring loaded handle from the shift lever.
2. The cover of the shift boot is held on with plastic clips and can be carefully pried off, starting at the front.
3. If necessary, remove the screws holding the boot and lift it aside.
4. Remove the detent assembly to adjust the solenoid switch. With the solenoid off there should be a gap of 0.012 in. (0.3mm) between the pushrod and locking lever.
5. With 12 volts supplied to the solenoid, the shift lever should be held in **P** or **N**.

Fuses, Circuit Breakers and Relays

Location

The fuse/relay panel is located to the left of the steering column, usually above a small swing down shelf. The function of each fuse is listed on the shelf or panel cover. The entire panel can be removed as a unit by removing the single screw or the locking clips and lifting the panel out. The large plugs on the back of the panel are keyed and cannot be installed incorrectly.

Computers

Location

The engine management computers are located under the fresh air intake louvers in the hood. With the hood up, remove the plastic rain shield to expose the computer, wiper gear, idle stabilizer, if equipped, and on some vehicles, access to the blower motor. When removing the computer, first disconnect the battery. If equipped with electronically theft-protected radios, obtain the security code from the owner before disconnecting the battery.

Flashers

Location

The flasher is always on the relay assembly but its location varies from year-to-year, even on the same vehicle. It is always one of the corner locations.

ENGINE COOLING

Radiator

Removal and Installation

NOTE: When replacing coolant/antifreeze, only a phosphate-free product must be used to help prevent damage to the water jacket sealing surfaces of the cylinder head. Other types of coolant may cause corrosion of the cooling system thus leading to engine overheating and damage.

1. To drain the cooling system, remove the thermostat housing from under the water pump housing.
2. Unplug the wires for the thermostatic switch and electric fan(s).
3. The fan and shroud can be removed as an assembly by unbolting the top cover and shroud and carefully lifting the shroud up and out.
4. Remove the upper and lower hoses and the overflow hose.
5. There will be 1 or 2 bolted clips holding the top of the radiator. Remove these clips and carefully lift the radiator up and out of the vehicle. Be careful not to lose the rubber washers on the bottom locating studs.
6. Installation is the reverse of removal. Torque the clip bolts to 7 ft. lbs. (10 Nm).

Electric Cooling Fan

Testing

On all vehicles, the fan is operated by a thermo switch screwed into the radiator side tank, which turns on to complete a ground circuit. The fan will operate with or without the ignition switch ON.

1. Disconnect the plug at the thermo switch.
2. Jumper the connections on the plug. The fan should run.
3. If the fan does not run, check for voltage at one side of the plug. If there is power there, the problem is either in the wiring between the plug and the fan or the fan itself.
4. If the fan does run during the test but not with a coolant temperature of 200°F (98°C), replace the switch.
5. The fan and shroud can be removed as an assembly by unbolting the top cover and shroud and carefully lifting the shroud up and out.

Heater Core

Removal and Installation

The heater core is contained in the fresh air housing located in the center of the dashboard. On air conditioned vehicles, the evaporator is also located in the heater box. On Quantum, the evaporator is located under the hood separate from the heater box.

EXCEPT FOX, GOLF AND JETTA

1. Disconnect the negative battery cable.
2. Drain the cooling system or clamp the heater hoses.
3. Remove the heater hoses at the firewall and plug the core fittings.
4. Inside the vehicle remove the center console side panels and/or any ducting that may be in the way. Locate the heater core cover on the side of the case and remove the retaining clips and the cover.
5. The heater core can now be slid from the case.
6. To install, insert the heater core into the case. Install the heater core cover, making sure the gasket on the cover is properly fitted.
7. Connect the heater hoses at the fire wall. Fill the cooling system.

FOX, GOLF AND JETTA

1. On these vehicles, the entire heater assembly must be removed. Disconnect the negative battery cable.
2. Drain the engine coolant or clamp the heater hoses.
3. Disconnect the heater hoses at the firewall and plug the core fittings.
4. Inside the vehicle, remove the knee bar for Golf and Jetta, shifter handle and boot, the center console and the temperature controls from the dash.
5. Remove the left and right air distribution ducts.
6. In the engine compartment, remove the cowl cover and remove the air distribution housing cover.
7. Inside the vehicle, remove the lower housing retaining clips and remove the housing.

NOTE: If equipped with air conditioning the heater box also contains the air conditioning system evaporator mounted in the lower housing cover. When removing

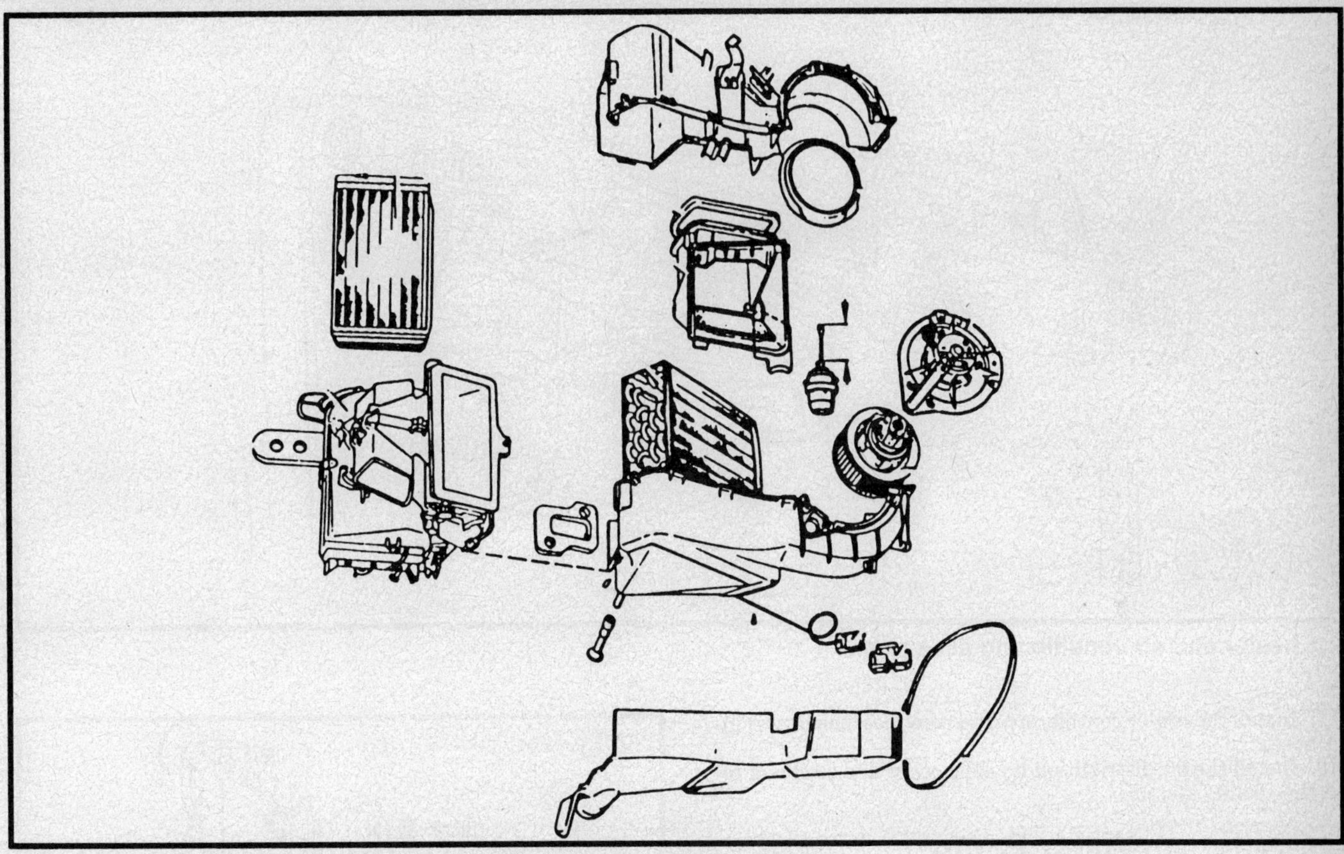

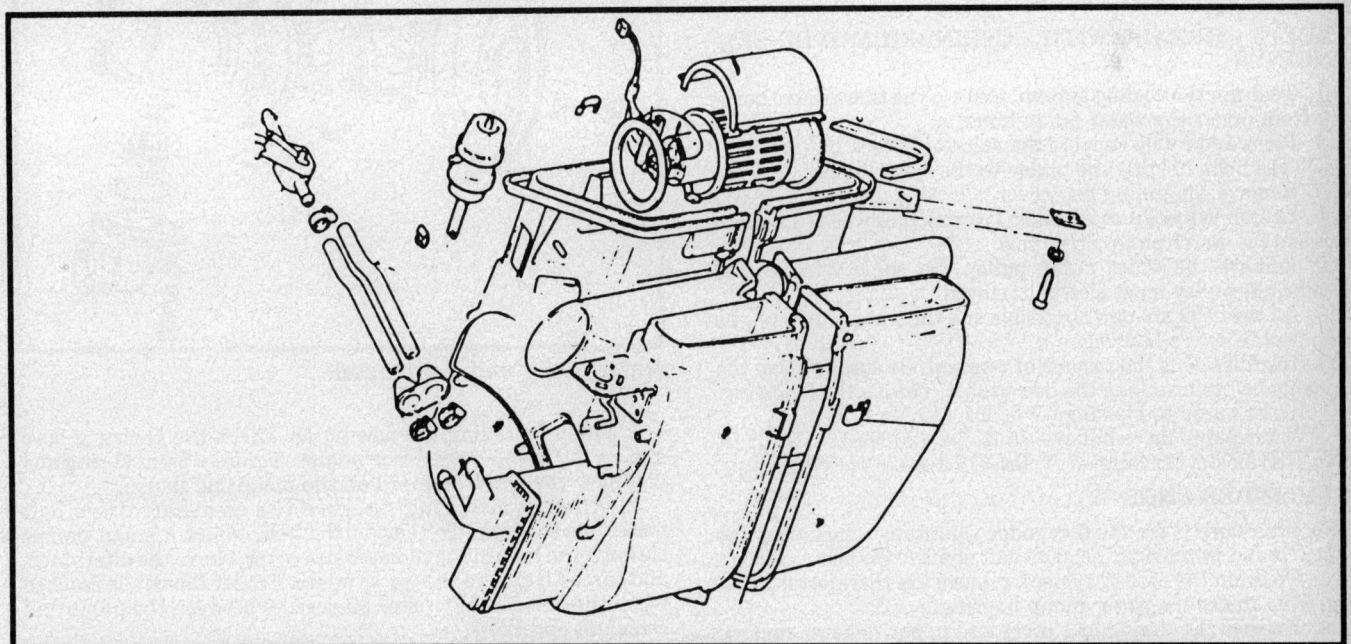

Passat and Corrado—heater and air conditioning assembly

Scirocco and Cabriolet—heater and air conditioning assembly

the lower cover, lay the cover and evaporater aside without removing the refrigerant lines.

8. Remove the bolts retaining the heater case and remove the case.

9. Remove the clips holding the case together and split the case, the heater core can now be removed.

To install:

10. To install, insert the heater core into the case and reassemble the case.

11. Install the case into the vehicle. Attach the lower heater case cover to the heater case. Install the air distribution ducts and the control cables.

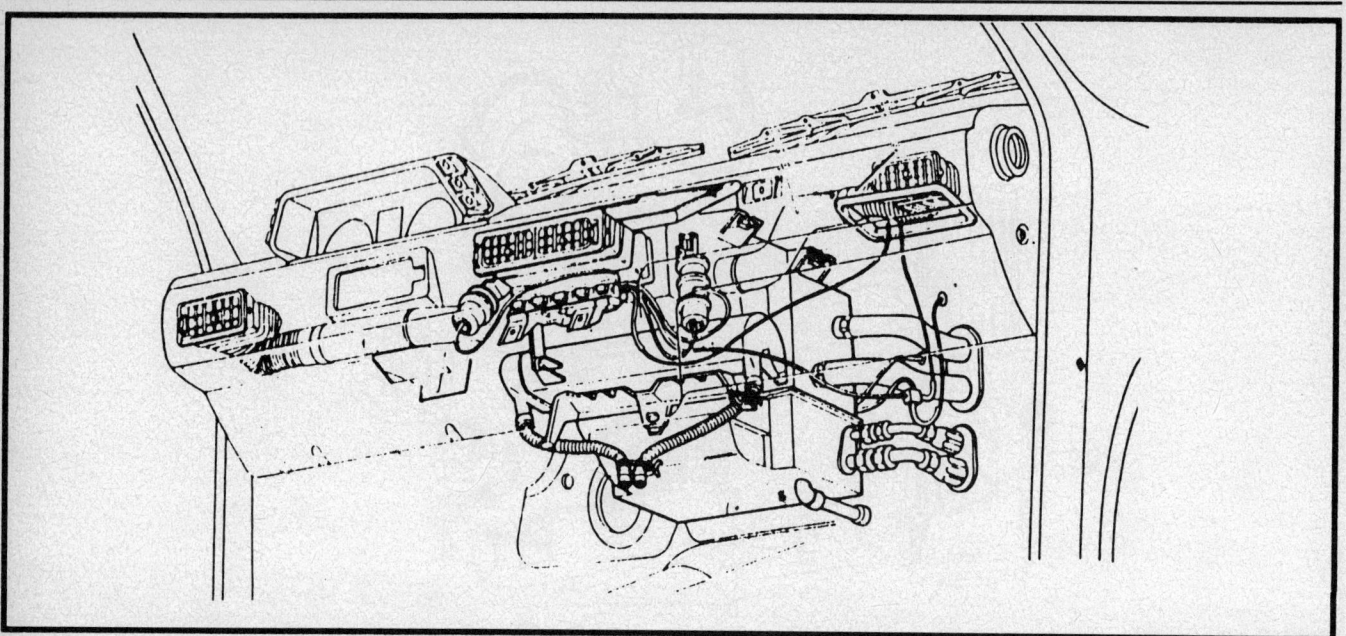

Fox heater and air conditioning assembly

12. Install the center console, etc. and reconnect the heater inlet hoses.

13. Install the air distribution housing cover and cowl and refill the cooling system.

Water Pump

Removal and Installation

EXCEPT CORRADO WITH 5 CYLINDER AND DIESEL ENGINES

1. To drain the cooling system, remove the thermostat housing from under the water pump housing.

2. Raise and safely support the vehicle. Loosen but don't remove the bolts holding the pulley to the water pump.

3. Remove the timing belt cover.

4. Loosen the alternator and/or steering pump as required to remove the water pump drive belt.

5. Remove the water pump pulley. On some vehicles, the crankshaft pulley must also be removed.

6. All the bolts are now accessible and the water pump can be removed from it's housing.

7. Installation is the reverse of removal. Be sure to clean the housing before installing the new gasket. Torque the following:

    Water pump-to-housing—7 ft. lbs. (10 Nm).
    Water pump drive pulley—15 ft. lbs. (20 Nm).
    Thermostat housing—7 ft. lbs. (10 Nm).

5 CYLINDER ENGINE

This procedure is for the 5 cylinder Quantum, which uses the water pump to tension the camshaft shaft drive belt.

1. To drain the cooling system, remove the thermostat housing from under the water pump housing.

2. Remove the timing belt cover and upper radiator cover.

3. Turn the crankshaft to place the engine on TDC; align the flywheel with the mark on the clutch housing. Use a crayon or paint to matchmark the timing belt to the camshaft sprocket and crankshaft sprocket.

4. Loosen the water pump to relieve the tension on the timing belt and remove the belt.

5. All the bolts are now accessible and the water pump can be removed from it's housing.

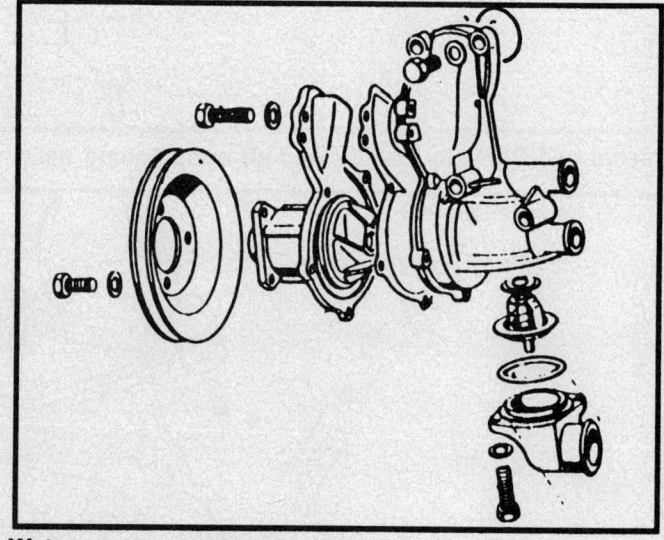

Water pump and thermostat

6. When installing the new pump, check the O-ring groove size on the pump body. Some pumps require a 5mm O-ring and will have the No. 5 stamped on the mounting flange.

7. When reinstalling, be sure the camshaft drive belt matchmarks align. To tension the belt, insert a small prybar through the hole in the radiator side cover, above the alternator, and carefully pry on the water pump. Proper tension is reached when the belt can be twisted 90 degrees between the pump and camshaft sprockets.

8. Observe the following torques:

    Water pump mounting bolts—15 ft. lbs. (20 Nm).
    Thermostat housing bolts—7 ft. lbs. (10 Nm).
    Water pump pulley bolts—18 ft. lbs. (25 Nm).

CORRADO

Without Air Conditioning

The water pump is driven by the same belt that drives the alter-

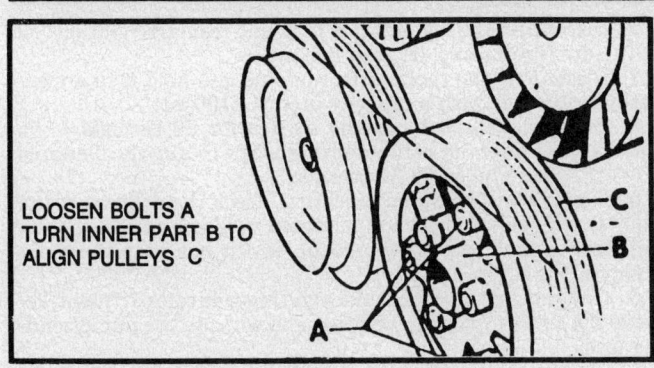

LOOSEN BOLTS A
TURN INNER PART B TO
ALIGN PULLEYS C

Water pump pulley alignment

nator and G-charger. Vehicles with air conditioning, drive the water and steering pumps on the same V-belt.

1. To drain the cooling system, remove the thermostat housing from under the water pump housing.

2. Loosen the water pump pulley bolts but don't remove the pulley yet.

3. Install the belt tensioner holding tool VW3191 or equivalent, to compress the tensioner and loosen the belt.

4. Loosen the power steering pump and remove it's drive belt.

5. With the water pump pulley removed, the pump bolts are now accessible. Remove the pump.

To install:

6. When installing the new pump, be sure to clean the housing before installing the new gasket.

7. The water pump and crank shaft pulleys must be aligned. Loosen the outer section bolts and turn the outer section relative to the inner section until the 2 pulleys are aligned; water pump pulley moves in and out.

8. Remove the tensioner tool and complete the reassembly. Torque the following:
> Water pump mounting bolts—7 ft. lbs. (10 Nm).
> Thermostat housing bolts—7 ft. lbs. (10 Nm).
> Water pump pulley bolts—18 ft. lbs. (25 Nm).

With Air Conditioning

1. To drain the cooling system, remove the thermostat housing from under the water pump housing.

2. Raise and safely support the vehicle.

3. Working under the vehicle, loosen but don't remove the bolts holding the pulley to the water pump.

4. Loosen the power steering pump and remove the drive belt.

5. Remove the water pump pulley and remove the pump.

6. Installation is the reverse of removal. Be sure to clean the pump housing before installing the new gasket. Torque the following:
> Water pump-to-housing—7 ft. lbs. (10 Nm).
> Water pump drive pulley—15 ft. lbs. (20 Nm).
> Thermostat housing—7 ft. lbs. (10 Nm).
> Steering pump bolts—18 ft. lbs. (25 Nm).

DIESEL ENGINE

On some engines, the belt tension is adjusted with shims between the outer and inner halves of the pulley. On others, the alternator swivels to adjust belt tension.

1. To drain the cooling system, remove the thermostat housing from under the water pump housing.

2. Raise and safely support the vehicle.

3. Working under the vehicle, loosen but don't remove the bolts holding the pulley to the water pump.

4. On vehicles with a movable alternator, loosen the alternator and remove the drive belt.

5. Remove the water pump pulley and remove the pump.

6. Installation is the reverse of removal. Be sure to clean the pump housing before installing the new gasket. Torque the following:
> Water pump-to-housing—7 ft. lbs. (10 Nm).
> Water pump drive pulley—15 ft. lbs. (20 Nm).
> Thermostat housing—7 ft. lbs. (10 Nm).
> Alternator mounting bolts—18 ft. lbs. (25 Nm).

Thermostat

Removal and Installation

The thermostat is the lowest point in the cooling system and is on the bottom of the water pump housing. Removing the thermostat is the only way to completely drain the coolant.

1. With a catch pan under the vehicle, loosen the bolts on the thermostat housing.

2. Remove the cap from the overflow bottle and allow the coolant to drain completely.

3. When the coolant is drained, remove the housing and clean both mating surfaces.

4. When installing, the thermostat spring goes up into the water pump housing and the new O-ring goes onto the thermostat. Torque the bolts to 7 ft. lbs. (10 Nm).

5. Refill the cooling system and check for leaks.

GASOLINE FUEL SYSTEM

Fuel System Service Precautions

Safety is the most important factor when performing not only fuel system maintenance but any type of maintenance. Failure to conduct maintenance and repairs in a safe manner may result in serious personal injury or death. Maintenance and testing of the vehicle's fuel system components can be accomplished safely and effectively by adhering to the following rules and guidelines.

• To avoid the possibility of fire and personal injury, always disconnect the negative battery cable unless the repair or test procedure requires that battery voltage be applied.

• Always relieve the fuel system pressure prior to disconnecting any fuel system component (injector, fuel rail, pressure regulator, etc.), fitting or fuel line connection. Exercise extreme caution whenever relieving fuel system pressure to avoid exposing skin, face and eyes to fuel spray. Please be advised that fuel under pressure may penetrate the skin or any part of the body that it contacts.

• Always place a shop towel or cloth around the fitting or connection prior to loosening to absorb any excess fuel due to spillage. Ensure that all fuel spillage (should it occur) is quickly removed from engine surfaces. Ensure that all fuel soaked cloths or towels are deposited into a suitable waste container.

• Always keep a dry chemical (Class B) fire extinguisher near the work area.

• Do not allow fuel spray or fuel vapors to come into contact with a spark or open flame.

• Always use a backup wrench when loosening and tighten-

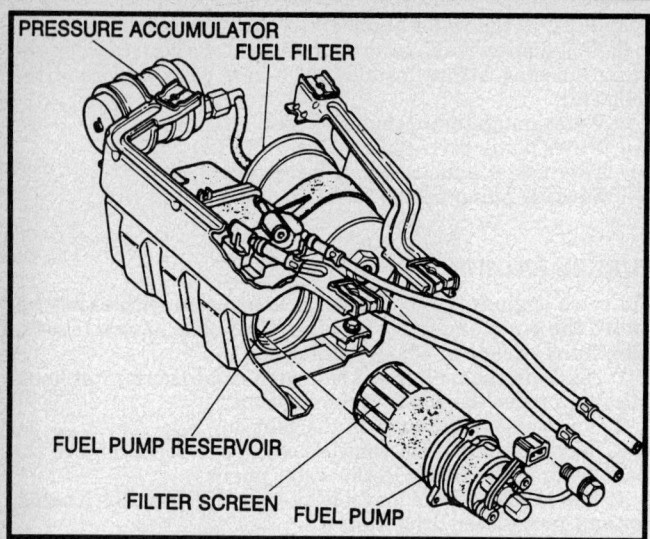

Fuel pump assembly

ing fuel line connection fittings. This will prevent unnecessary stress and torsion to fuel line piping. Always follow the proper torque specifications.

• Always replace worn fuel fitting O-rings with new. Do not substitute fuel hose or equivalent, where fuel pipe is installed.

Relieving Fuel System Pressure

On CIS systems, fuel pressure can be vented at the cold start injector line, either at the fuel distributor end or the injector end. Lay a rag over the fitting and use a socket or line wrench to crack the fitting.

On Digifant systems, pressure can be vented at the fuel pump run-on switch right in front of the throttle body. Lay a rag over the switch and loosen the clamp.

Fuel Filter

Removal and Installation

The fuel filter is a lifetime filter and only needs to be changed in the event of contamination. It is mounted under the vehicle, near the rear axle. It is in assembly with the pump, accumulator and reservoir, but can usually be removed seperately.
1. Disconnect the negative battery cable.
2. Raise and safely support the vehicle.
3. Relieve the fuel system pressure.

--- CAUTION ---
When relieving the pressure in the fuel system, place a container under the filter to catch the excess fuel.

4. Remove the fuel lines, the mounting bracket nut and the filter.
5. Installation is the reverse of removal. Be sure to use the new sealing rings and torque the fuel lines to the filter to 14 ft. lbs. (20 Nm).

Electric Fuel Pump

Testing
FUEL PUMP DELIVERY

NOTE: **Before testing the fuel pump, the battery must be fully charged and the fuel tank at least ¼ full.**

1. Check the condition of the fuel filter.

2. Disconnect the high tension terminal from the ignition coil at the distributor and securely ground it.
3. Disconnect the fuel return fuel line and hold it in a measuring container with a capacity of 1 qt. (1000cc).
4. Have an assistant run the starter for 30 seconds while watching the quantity of fuel delivered. The minimum allowable flow is $\frac{9}{10}$ qt. (760cc) in 30 seconds.
5. If the flow is below specification, check the delivery of the fuel transfer pump, which is mounted with the gauge sending unit in the tank, except Quantum, which has only the main pump in the tank.
6. Under the rear seat or under the luggage compartment, remove the cover to expose the hoses and wires to the pump/sending unit.
7. Disconnect the output hose and plug it, install a temporary fuel line and put the other end into the measuring container.
8. Have an assistant operate the starter for 10 seconds and measure the fuel delivered. The specification is about 10 oz. (300cc).
9. If the transfer pump is good, check for a dirty fuel filter, blocked lines or blocked fuel tank strainer, if equipped. If all of these are in good condition, replace the main pump.

Removal and Installation

NOTE: **The fuel pump is located under the vehicle in front of the rear axle or in front of the tank on the right side.**

1. Disconnect the negative battery cable.
2. Raise and safely support the vehicle.
3. Disconnect the electrical connector.
4. Relieve the fuel system pressure.
5. Remove the mounting bolts and the fuel pump.
6. Installation is the reverse of removal. Be sure to use new sealing rings and/or gaskets.

Transfer Pump

Removal and Installation

1. Disconnect the negative battery cable.
2. Under the rear seat or in the rear of the vehicle, pull back the carpet and remove the access plate from the floor (3 screws).
3. Disconnect the electrical connector from the sending unit.
4. Remove the fuel hoses from the sending unit.
5. Unscrew the cap and carefully lift the sending unit from the fuel tank. Note the direction of the float in the tank.
6. Remove the transfer pump from the sending unit.
7. Installation is the reverse of removal. Be sure the float points the same way and use a new O-ring at the sending unit.

Fuel Injection

For further information, please refer to "Chilton's Electronic Engine Control's Manual" for additional coverage.

Idle Speed Adjustment

NOTE: **The manufacturer states that timing, idle speed and CO value must all be adjusted together.**

1. Run the engine to normal operating temperature, stop engine and connect a tachometer and timing light according to manufacturer's instructions.
2. If equipped, disconnect both plugs from the idle stabilizer and plug them together. On engines with Digifant engine management systems, with the ignitionON, engine not running, verify that the idle stabilizer valve hums or buzzes. Do not disconnect any vacuum lines from the distributor.

Engine Code		% CO Value
PF		0.3–1.1
RV		0.3–1.1
9A		0.2–1.2
UM		0.3–1.2
JN		0.3–1.2
PG		0.3–1.1
JH	Checking	0.3–3.0
	Setting	0.8–1.2

Carbon dioxide rating chart

3. Start the engine; on vehicles with Digifant engine management systems, disconnect the blue coolant temperature sensor plug. Turn off all electrical equipment and set the idle speed to 800–950 rpm.

4. Remove the timing mark cover from the top of the bell housing and with the engine running, shine the timing light at the marks on the flywheel. If adjustment is required, loosen the distributor clamp bolt and rotate the distributor as needed to correctly align the timing marks.

5. Stop the engine and reconnect plugs.

Idle Mixture Adjustment

NOTE: Air/fuel mixture is set at the factory and controlled by an Electronic Control Unit (ECU). If the measured value is out of specification, look for other problems such as a vacuum leak, bad sensor, loose connection, etc. and correct any faults before adjusting. It is recommended that mixture be set 1st, then idle speed.

1. With engine at normal operating temperature, stop engine and connect a tachometer and timing light.

2. On vehicles with CIS engine management systems, find the auxiliary air regulator, usually near the intake manifold, and clamp either the inlet or outlet hose. Disconnect the crank case breather hose(s) and move it so only fresh air can enter. Disconnect the vacuum line from the charcoal canister, except Corrado, making sure the T, which has a 0.059 in. (1.5mm) restrictor, is still connected to the intake manifold; there is no T on 16 valve engine.

3. Insert the probe (leak-tight) into the CO test point under the hood, a metal tube with a blue cap. On engines with Digifant engine management systems, turn the ignition ON and check for a hum or buzz at the idle stabilizer valve to confirm operation.

4. Start the engine. If any fuel injection lines have been disconnected, rev the engine to 3000 rpm, 2–3 times to clear any air from the system. Turn OFF all electrical equipment and on vehicles with Digifant engine management systems, disconnect the blue coolant temperature sensor plug.

5. With correct ignition timing, set CO first, then idle speed. On Digifant systems, adjust CO with the CO adjustment potentiometer to the value specified. On CIS systems, CO is adjusted through the hole between the fuel distributor and the sensor plate boot.

NOTE: To adjust CO, it is necessary to remove a tamper-proof plug. Dealership technicians must obtain factory authorization to break this seal, so be sure it really is necessary before making CO adjustments.

6. Idle speed is set with the idle speed adjustment screw on the throttle body; do not adjust the throttle stop screw on top of

CO adjustment—CIS Systems

Idle speed adjustment—CIS Systems

the throttle body. On some Digifant engine management systems, idle speed is controlled by the ECU and no adjustment is available.

Fuel Injector

Removal and Installation

CIS SYSTEMS

1. Relieve the pressure from the system.

2. Using a fuel injector removal tool, pry the injectors up out of the head.

3. Hold the fuel line fitting with a line wrench and unscrew the injector.

4. Installation is the reverse of removal. Lightly lubricate the rubber rings.

AFC SYSTEMS

The electric injectors are held in place by the rail and cannot be removed seperately.

1. Disconnect the negative battery cable.

2. Relieve the pressure from the fuel system.

3. Dismount the idle stabilizer valve and lay it aside.

4. Remove the intake manifold supports and cylinder head cover.

5. Unplug the wiring harness end connector and pry wiring guide away from the fuel distributor retainers.

6. Remove the fuel distributor retaining bolts and remove the rail, wiring guide and injectors as an assembly.

7. Installation is the reverse of removal.

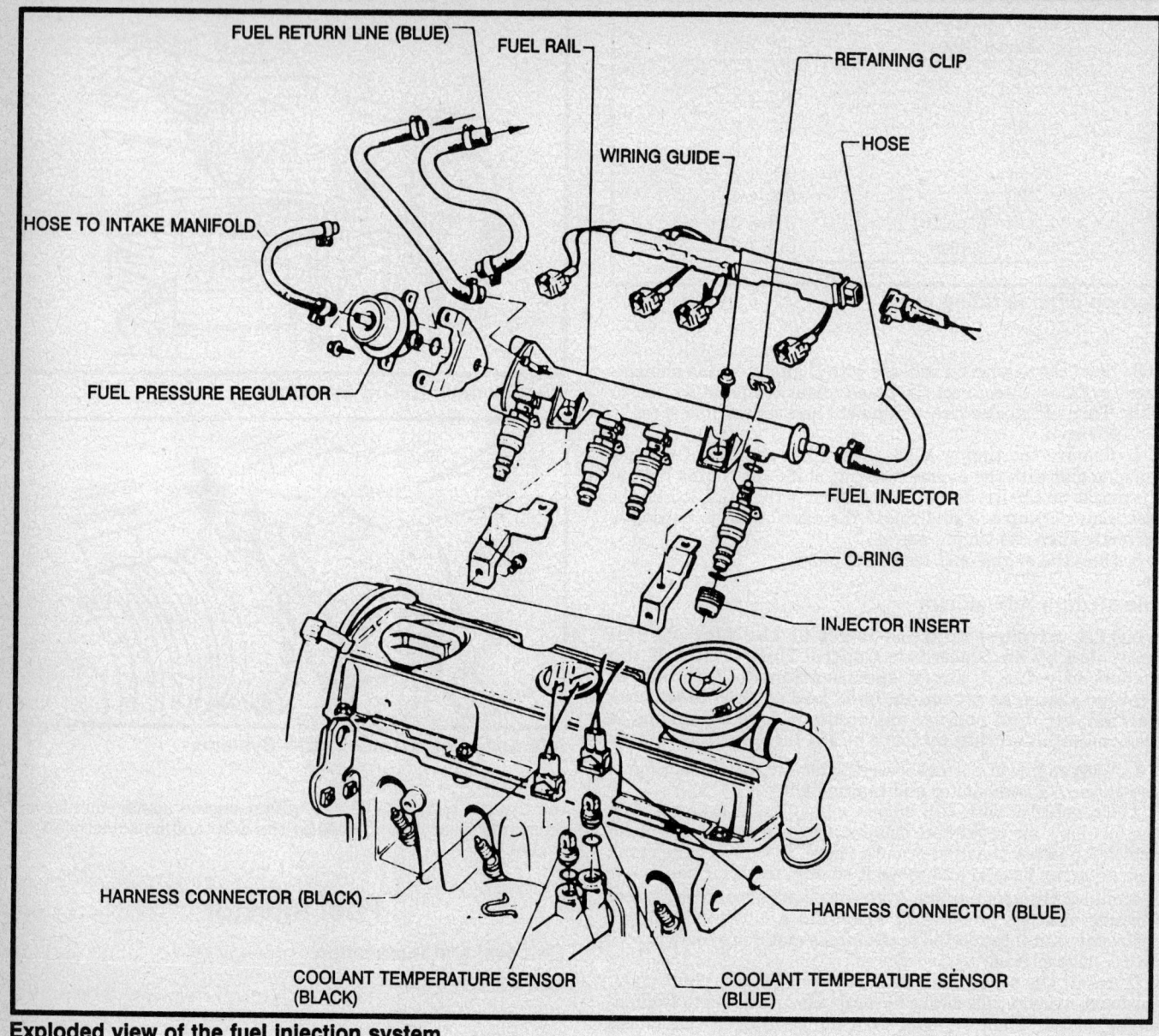

FUEL RETURN LINE (BLUE)

FUEL RAIL

RETAINING CLIP

WIRING GUIDE

HOSE

HOSE TO INTAKE MANIFOLD

FUEL PRESSURE REGULATOR

FUEL INJECTOR

O-RING

INJECTOR INSERT

HARNESS CONNECTOR (BLACK)

HARNESS CONNECTOR (BLUE)

COOLANT TEMPERATURE SENSOR (BLACK)

COOLANT TEMPERATURE SENSOR (BLUE)

Exploded view of the fuel injection system

DIESEL FUEL SYSTEM

Fuel System Service Precautions

Safety is the most important factor when performing not only fuel system maintenance but any type of maintenance. Failure to conduct maintenance and repairs in a safe manner may result in serious personal injury or death. Maintenance and testing of the vehicle's fuel system components can be accomplished safely and effectively by adhering to the following rules and guidelines.

• To avoid the possibility of fire and personal injury, always disconnect the negative battery cable unless the repair or test procedure requires that battery voltage be applied.

• Always relieve the fuel system pressure prior to disconnecting any fuel system component (injector, fuel rail, pressure reg-

ulator, etc.), fitting or fuel line connection. Exercise extreme caution whenever relieving fuel system pressure to avoid exposing skin, face and eyes to fuel spray. Please be advised that fuel under pressure may penetrate the skin or any part of the body that it contacts.

• Always place a shop towel or cloth around the fitting or connection prior to loosening to absorb any excess fuel due to spillage. Ensure that all fuel spillage (should it occur) is quickly removed from engine surfaces. Ensure that all fuel soaked cloths or towels are deposited into a suitable waste container.

• Always keep a dry chemical (Class B) fire extinguisher near the work area.

• Do not allow fuel spray or fuel vapors to come into contact with a spark or open flame.

• Always use a backup wrench when loosening and tightening fuel line connection fittings. This will prevent unnecessary stress and torsion to fuel line piping. Always follow the proper torque specifications.

• Always replace worn fuel fitting O-rings with new. Do not substitute fuel hose or equivalent, where fuel pipe is installed.

• Clean all fittings before opening them and maintain a dust free work area while the system is open.

Fuel Filter

Replacement

1. The fuel filter is located in the engine compartment near the fuel injection pump. Using clamps, pinch off the fuel lines at the fuel filter.
2. Remove the fuel lines from the filter.
3. Loosen the mounting clamp or screws and lift the filter assembly straight up.

NOTE: When installing a new filter, partly fill it with diesel fuel.

4. Installation is the reverse of removal. Make sure the flow direction is correct. Torque the filter assembly to mount nuts to 18 ft. lbs. (25 Nm). Start the engine, accelerate it a few times, to clear the air bubbles, and check for fuel leaks.

Draining Water

AT THE FILTER

1. Disconnect the negative battery cable.
2. Remove the fuel return line from the injection pump to provide room to open the vent screw on the fuel filter flange.
3. Remove the 2 filter assembly mounting nuts and lift the filter from the mount.

NOTE: When draining the water from the fuel filter, place a container under the filter to catch the water and the excess fuel.

4. Loosen the drain plug on the bottom of the filter and drain the fuel into a container, until it runs free of water.
5. Tighten the drain plug.
6. To install, reverse the removal procedures. Torque the filter assembly mounting nuts to 18 ft. lbs. (25 Nm). Start the engine, accelerate it a few times, to clear the air bubbles, and check for leaks.

AT THE WATER SEPARATOR

The optional water separator is located in front of the fuel tank under the right side of the vehicle; it's purpose is to filter the water from the fuel. When the water level in the separator reaches a certain point, a sensor turns on the glow plug indicator light, causing it to blink continuously.

1. Raise and safely support the vehicle.
2. At the separator, connect a hose from the separator drain to a catch pan.
3. Open the drain valve (3 turns) and remove the water until a steady stream of fuel flows from the separator, then close the valve.

Diesel Injection Pump

Removal and Installation

1. Disconnect the negative battery cable and remove the air cleaner, cylinder head cover and timing belt cover.
2. Turn the engine to TDC of No. 1 cylinder and remove the camshaft drive belt and sprocket. Insert a setting bar into the

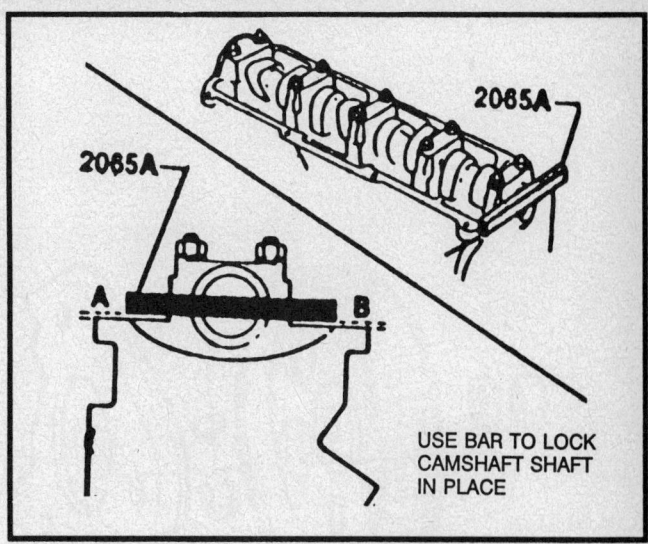

Camshaft holding bar

slot on the front of the camshaft, VW tool 2065A or equivalent, to hold the camshaft in place.

3. Loosen the pump sprocket nut but don't remove it yet. Install a puller on the sprocket and apply moderate tension.
4. Rap the puller bolt with light hammer taps until the sprocket jumps off the tapered shaft, then remove the puller and sprocket. Be careful not to lose the Woodruff® key.
5. Hold the delivery valves with a wrench and using a line wrench, remove the injection lines from the pump. Do not bend or distort these lines. If necessary, remove the lines from the injectors also and set them aside as an assembly.
6. Disconnect the control cables, fuel solenoid wire, supply and return lines.
7. Remove the pump mounting bolts and lift the pump from the vehicle.

To install:

8. When reinstalling, align the marks on the top of the mounting plate and the pump and torque the mounting bolts to 18 ft. lbs. (25 Nm).
9. Install the Woodruff® key and sprocket and torque the nut to 33 ft. lbs. (45 Nm).
10. When reinstalling the supply and return lines, be sure the fitting marked OUT is used for the return line. This fitting has an orifice and must be in the correct place.
11. Turn the pump sprocket so the mark alignes with the mark on the side of the mounting plate and insert a pin through the hole in the sprocket to hold it in place.
12. Install the camshaft drive sprocket and belt and set the belt tension. Tension the drive belt by turning the tensioner pulley clockwise until belt flex of ½ in. (13mm) is established between the camshaft and the pump sprockets. Remove the pin.
13. Turn the engine through 2 full turns and return to TDC of No. 1 cylinder and recheck the belt tension. Set the injection timing and reinstall the lines and control cables.

Diesel Injection Timing

Adjustment

1. Turn the engine to TDC of No. 1 cylinder.
2. Be sure the cold start control is pushed in all the way and the pump lever is on the low idle stop.
3. Remove the center plug on the pump head and install the adapter tool VW-2066 or equivalent, and a dial indicator. Preload the dial indicator to 2.5mm.

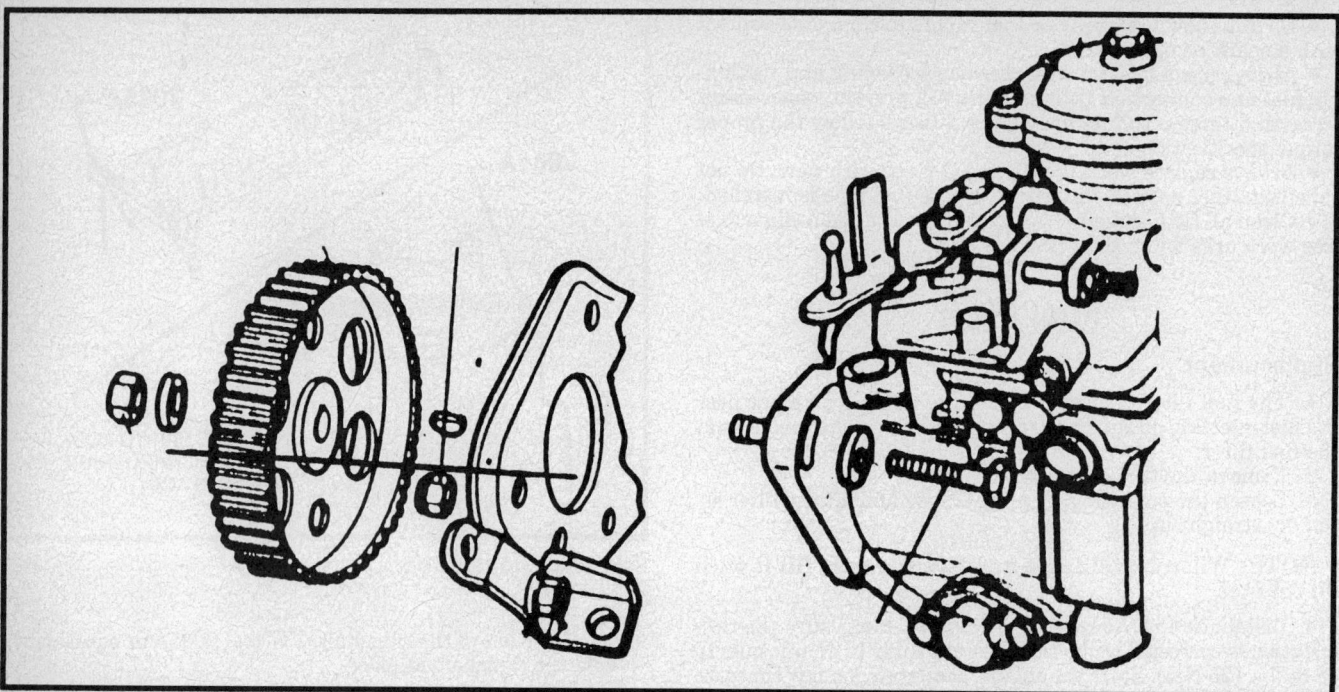

Diesel pump

4. Slowly turn the engine counterclockwise until the dial gauge stops moving, then zero the dial indicator.

5. Turn the engine clockwise until the TDC mark on the flywheel aligns with the pointer on the bell housing.

6. The dial indicator should read 0.83–0.97mm for non-turbocharged engines or 0.95–1.05mm for turbocharged engines.

7. If adjustment is required, remove the timing belt cover and loosen the pump mounting bolts without turning the engine.

8. Turn the pump body to attain the correct setting: non-turbocharged setting is 0.90mm or turbocharged setting is 1.00mm.

9. Torque the mounting bolts to 18 ft. lbs. (25 Nm) and turn the engine backwards about 1 turn. Turn the engine forwards to TDC of No. 1 cylinder and recheck the dial indicator.

10. When the correct setting is reached on the dial indicator, reinstall the belt cover and the center plug on the pump, with a new copper gasket.

Idle Speed Adjustment

Diesel engines have both an idle speed and a maximum speed adjustment. The maximum speed adjustment is a high-idle speed that prevents the engine from over-revving. No increase in power is available through this adjustment. The adjusters are located side by side on top of the injection pump. The screw closest to the engine is the low-idle adjustment, the outer screw is the high-idle adjustment.

1. If the vehicle has no tachometer, connect a suitable diesel engine tachometer as per the manufacturer's instructions.

2. Run the engine to normal operating temperature.

3. Make sure the cold start knob is pushed in all the way.

4. Loosen the locknut and set the low idle to 950 rpm.

5. When tightening the locknut, apply a thread sealer to prevent the screw from vibrating loose.

6. Advance the control lever (throttle) to full speed. The high

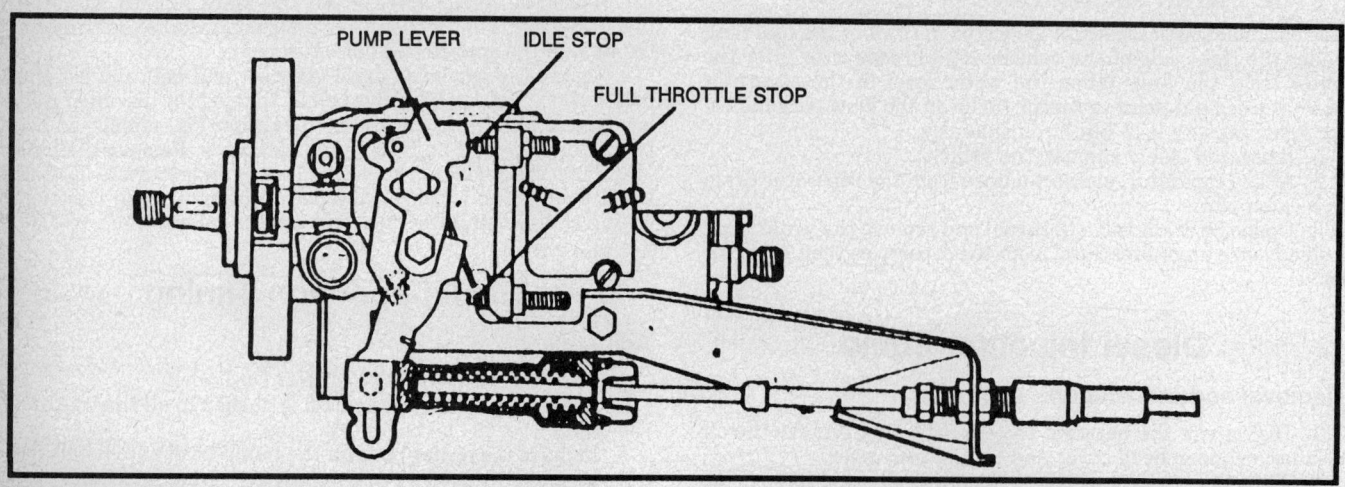

Non-turbocharged diesel pump—idle adjustment

idle speed is 5300–5400 rpm for non-turbo engines or 5050–5100 rpm for turbo engines. Adjust as needed and secure the locknut with sealer.

Fuel Injector

Removal and Installation

Faulty injectors can be located by loosening each pipe union one at a time with the engine at a fast idle. If the engine speed remains constant after loosening a pipe union, that injector is faulty.

1. Remove the lines from all the injectors using a line wrench.
2. Carefully remove the injectors using a clean socket.
3. With a magnet or small pick, remove the heat shields from the injector holes and disgard them. New heat shields must be installed.

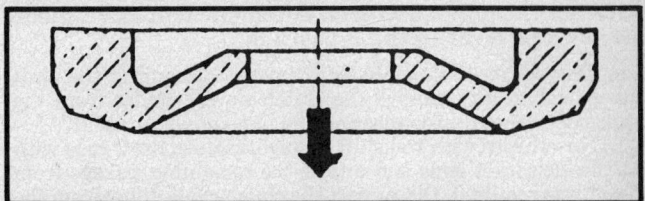

Injector heat shield, arrow towards head

4. Install the new heat shield and torque the injectors to 51 ft. lbs. (70 Nm). Torque the pipe unions to 18 ft. lbs. (25 Nm). Do not over torque the pipe unions or the flares will be flattened and a leak could result.

EMISSION CONTROLS

For further information, please refer to "Professional Emission Component Application Guide".

Emission Warning Lamps

Resetting

When the OXS warning light on the dash comes on, it is time to replace the oxygen sensor. Under the hood, near the wiper motor, is a black box with the speedometer cable connected to it. This is the mileage counter for the oxygen sensor that turns on the warning light. To reset the counter, find the white button on the box and push it in with a pen, listening (feeling) for the click.

Oxygen sensor light reset button

GASOLINE ENGINE MECHANICAL

NOTE: Disconnecting the negative battery cable on some vehicles may interfere with the functions of the on board computer systems and may require the computer to undergo a relearning process, once the negative battery cable is reconnected.

Engine Assembly

Removal and Installation
EXCEPT FOX AND QUANTUM

NOTE: The engine and transmission assembly is lifted up from the vehicle.

—————— CAUTION ——————
Use care when disconnecting the fuel lines. Fuel under pressure may still be in the lines and, if sprayed, may cause fire or personal injury.

1. Disconnect the battery cables and remove the battery.
2. Open the fuel filler cap to relieve tank pressure and then relieve the fuel system pressure.
3. Remove the air intake duct between the fuel distributor and the throttle body. On Corrado, remove the air tubing from the G-charger and the intercooler. At the throttle body, pull back the accelerator cable clip and disconnect the cable from the ball. Loosen the accelerator cable locknut and remove the cable from the cylinder head cover.

4. Remove the radiator cap. Turn the heater temperature control valve to fully open. Place a pan under the thermostat housing, remove the thermostat flange and drain the coolant.
5. Remove the upper radiator and heater hoses from the engine. Remove the electrical connector from the radiator fan motor and switch. Remove the radiator mounting nuts or bolts, the upper radiator clips and lift out the radiator and fan shroud as an assembly.
6. At the front of the vehicle, remove the apron, the trim and the grille. Disconnect the headlight electrical connectors and the hood release cable from the hood latch assembly.
7. Begin disconnecting electrical connections and vacuum lines, carefully labeling each one. Don't forget ground connections that are screwed to the body.

NOTE: If equipped with power steering, remove pump and reservoir and set them aside; do not disconnect the fluid lines. If equipped with air conditioning, remove the compressor and set it aside without disconnecting the lines.

8. On CIS fuel systems, much of the system can be removed as a unit without disconnecting fuel lines. Remove the injectors from their holes and protect them with caps. Remove the cold start injector and warm-up regulator, if equipped, and disconnect the fuel supply and return lines from the fuel distributor.
9. Unsnap the clips holding the air cleaner housing together and lift the fuel distributor/air sensor assembly from the vehicle with all the other fuel lines attached.

NOTE: If equipped with an automatic transaxle, place the selector lever in the P position.

10. On vehicles with cable shift linkage, disconnect the shift linkage cables and remove the clutch slave cylinder from the transaxle without disconnecting the line and set it aside.

11. On vehicles with rod shift linkage, remove the 2 rods with the plastic socket ends and unbolt the remaining linkage from the case as required. Disconnect the clutch cable, lift it from the case and set it aside.

12. Disconnect the electrical connectors from the starter, the back-up light switch and the ground cable from the transaxle. Remove the speedometer cable from the transaxle and plug the hole in the case.

13. On vehicles with automatic transmission, disconnect the cable from the actuating lever and remove it from the bracket.

14. Attach an engine sling tool VW-2024A or equivalent, to the engine and attach the sling to a suitable lifting device. On 16 valve engine, remove the idle stabilizer valve and the upper intake manifold to attach the sling.

15. Remove the spring clamps holding the exhaust pipe to the manifold and lower the pipe.

NOTE :Special tools are required for removing and installing the exhaust pipe spring clips; VW3140/1 and /2 or equivalent. This is a set of wedges for spreading the spring clips that hold the pipe to the manifold. The installed spring clip has considerable tension and could cause damage or injury if not properly removed.

16. Unbolt the halfshafts from the flanges and hang them from the body with wire.

17. Make sure everything is disconnected and unbolt the mounts. Remove the starter first and the front mount with it.

18. With all mounts unbolted, slightly lower the engine/transaxle assembly and tilt it towards the transaxle side. Then carefully lift the assembly from the vehicle.

To install:

19. Installation is the reverse of removal. Check the adjustment of clutch and shift linkages.

20. Torque the following components:
Driveshaft flange-to-transaxle bolts—33 ft. lbs. (45 Nm).
Starter bolts—33 ft. lbs. (45 Nm).
Transaxle to body mount—33 ft. lbs. (41 Nm) for 10mm bolts or 54 ft. lbs. (73 Nm) for 12mm bolts.
Power steering bolts—14 ft. lbs. (19 Nm).
Thermostat flange bolts—7 ft. lbs. (9 Nm).

QUANTUM

4 Cylinder Engine

NOTE: The engine is lifted from the vehicle without the transaxle.

1. Disconnect the negative battery cable.

2. Set the heater control to full open, remove the radiator cap and drain the cooling system. Remove the radiator hoses from the engine.

3. Remove the power steering pump mounting bolts, the drive belt and move the pump aside, leaving the hoses attached.

4. Disconnect the electrical connectors from the thermo-time switch, the alternator and the control pressure regulator.

5. Disconnect the distributor vacuum hoses from the distributor.

6. Remove the control pressure regulator bolts and move the regulator aside, with the fuel lines attached.

7. Disconnect the radiator fan wires. Remove the radiator bolts and the radiator assembly, with the air duct.

8. Remove the clip on the clutch cable and disconnect the cable.

9. Remove the left engine mount nut.

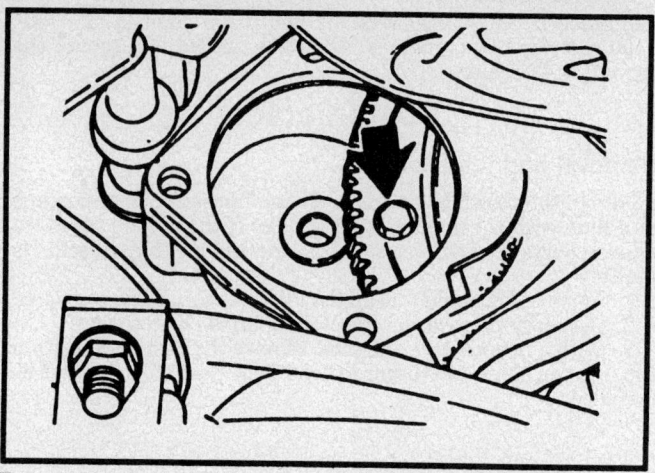

Removing flywheel bolts on automatic transaxle

10. Disconnect the coolant temperature sender wire from the engine, oxygen sensor thermo-switch, the Hall sending unit wire and the coil wire from the distributor.

11. Disconnect the electrical connectors from the auxiliary air regulator, the cold start and the frequency valves.

12. Remove the emissions canister hose from the air duct.

13. Remove the preheater hose and the cold start valve; leave the fuel line attached.

14. Disconnect the distributor vacuum hose from the intake manifold. Remove the accelerator cable, the crankcase breather hose and the brake booster hose.

— **CAUTION** —

Use care when disconnecting the fuel lines. Fuel under pressure may still be in the lines and, if sprayed, may cause fire or personal injury.

15. Remove the fuel injectors, protect them with caps, the fuel distributor, leave the lines attached, and move them aside.

16. If equipped with air conditioning, remove the following components:
   a. Throttle body housing
   b. Auxiliary air regulator
   c. Horn bracket
   d. Ccrankcase pulley nuts
   e. Ccompressor drive belt
   f. Ccompressor bracket bolts
   g. Ccompressor and condenser
   h. Place and secure the compressor and the condenser aside.

17. Remove the right engine mount nuts.

18. Remove the exhaust pipe at the manifold.

19. Remove the starter wiring and the starter. Remove the lower engine-to-transaxle bolts and the flywheel cover plate.

20. If equipped with an automatic transaxle, remove the torque converter to flywheel bolts. Attach the engine support tool VW 785/1B or equivalent, to the transaxle and support it.

21. Loosen the nuts on the outer half of the damper pulley and remove the drive belt.

22. Remove the air conditioner compressor bracket mounting bolts and move the compressor aside, with the lines attached.

23. Attach the engine sling US-1105 or equivalent, to the engine, support it with a vertical hoist and lift the engine slightly, then remove the right engine mount.

24. Remove the upper engine to transaxle bolts, separate the engine from the transaxle. Lift and turn the engine to remove it from the vehicle.

NOTE: If equipped with an automatic transaxle, secure the torque converter to keep it from falling out.

To install:

25. To install, reverse the removal procedures. Torque the following components:

Transaxle-to-engine bolts – 40 ft. lbs. (54 Nm).
Engine mount bolts – 25 ft. lbs. (34 Nm).
Exhaust pipe-to-exhaust manifold – 18 ft. lbs. (24 Nm).
Starter bolts – 14 ft. lbs. (19 Nm).
Torque converter-to-drive plate bolts – 22 ft. lbs. (30 Nm).
Support bolts – 18 ft. lbs. (24 Nm).
Power steering pump bolts – 14 ft. lbs. (19 Nm).
A/C compressor lower bolts – 18 ft. lbs. (24 Nm) and the upper bolts – 22 ft. lbs. (30 Nm).

5 Cylinder Engine

NOTE: The engine is lifted out of the vehicle without the transaxle.

1. Disconnect the negative battery cable.
2. Move the heater control valve to fully open and remove the radiator cap.
3. At the power steering pump, remove the drive belt cover, the drive belt, the mounting bolts and the pump. Move the pump aside with the hoses connected.
4. Remove the grille and the radiator cover.
5. Remove the lower radiator hose and drain the coolant.
6. Remove the front bumper with the energy absorber.
7. Remove the vacuum hoses from the intake manifold, the upper radiator hose, the radiator hose from the thermostat housing and the heater hose, drain the remaining coolant.
8. Disconnect the electrical connectors from the oil pressure switch, the control pressure regulator and the thermo-time switches.
9. Remove the cylinder head cover ground wire.
10. Remove the control pressure regulator, leave the lines attached, and, on the linkage rod near it, the ball joint circlip, disconnect it at the pushrod.
11. Remove the alternator drive belt, the bracket bolts and the alternator assembly.
12. Remove the air duct and the front engine stop.
13. Disconnect the electrical connectors from the cold start valve, the frequency valve and the throttle switch. Disconnect the electrical leads at the idle stabilizer valve, the Hall sender at the distributor and the oxygen sensor.
14. Remove the accelerator cable circlip and disconnect the cable rod from the throttle body.
15. Remove the distributor cap, the cold start valve and the vacuum hose from the thermo valve.
16. Remove the fuel injection cooling hose.
17. Remove the fuel injectors from the intake manifold; leave the fuel lines connected.

NOTE: When removing the fuel injectors and the cold start valve, place caps on the ends to protect them from damage.

18. Remove the air filter housing bolts and the filter.
19. Remove the heater hoses and, if equipped with an automatic transmission, disconnect the oil cooler hoses. Remove the exhaust pipe bracket from the engine and transaxle assembly.

NOTE: If equipped with air conditioning, remove the drive belt, the electrical connector at the compressor, the compressor bracket to engine bolts and the compressor assembly. Move it aside and support it. Do not support the compressor with the pressure hoses.

20. Attach the supporting tool 2084 or equivalent, to the crankshaft pulley to keep the engine from turning and remove the crankshaft bolt.
21. Of the 4 crankshaft pulley bolts, remove 2 and loosen 2. To loosen the pulley, tap lightly on the remaining bolts. Remove the bolts and the pulley.

NOTE: When removing the pulley from the crankshaft, leave the drive belt sprocket attached to the crankshaft.

22. Remove the front engine mount and the subframe-to-body bolts. Remove the exhaust pipe from the exhaust manifold and the support bracket.
23. Disconnect the starter cables and remove the starter.
24. Working through the starter hole, remove the torque converter to flywheel bolts. Unhook the shift rod clip and disconnect the rod.
25. Remove the rubber plugs from the left side frame member. Using the support tool VW 785/1 or equivalent, connect it to the transaxle and to the frame member, then adjust to make contact with the transaxle. This tool is to hold the transaxle in place while the engine is out of the vehicle.
26. Remove the upper engine-to-transaxle bolts; leave 1 bolt in place.
27. Attach the engine support tool US 1105 and the lift tool 9019 or equivalent, to the engine.

NOTE: If equipped with an automatic transmission, secure the torque converter before removing the engine from the transaxle.

28. Remove the remaining engine-to-transmisssion bolts and engine mount bolts and lift the engine, while prying the engine apart from the transmission. Remove the engine from the vehicle by twisting the front slightly to the left and lift straight out.

To install:

29. To install, reverse the removal procedures. Torque the following components:

Transaxle-to-engine bolts – 22 ft. lbs. (30 Nm) for 8mm bolts, 32 ft. lbs. (43 Nm) for 10mm bolts or 43 ft. lbs. (58 Nm) for 12mm bolts.
Engine mount bolts – 32 ft. lbs. (43 Nm).
Exhaust pipe-to-manifold bolts – 22 ft. lbs. (30 Nm).
Subframe-to-body bolts – 28 ft. lbs. (35 Nm), plus ¼ turn.
Torque converter-to-flywheel bolts – 22 ft. lbs. (30 Nm).
Front engine stop bolts – 32 ft. lbs. (43 Nm).
Damper pulley center bolt – 331 ft. lbs. (450 Nm).
Crankshaft pulley bolts – 14 ft. lbs. (19 Nm).
Power steering pump bolts – 14 ft. lbs. (19 Nm).

30. Adjust the belt tension and refill the cooling system.

NOTE: When installing the crankshaft pulley, align the matchmark on the sprocket with the mark on the pulley. When installing the crankshaft bolt, coat the threads with Loctite® thread sealer or equivalent. If only the engine was removed, torque the engine mount bolts with the engine running at idle. This will help minimize vibration.

FOX

NOTE: The engine is lifted from the vehicle without the transaxle.

--- **CAUTION** ---

Do not disconnect or loosen any refrigerant hose connections during engine removal, if equipped with air conditioning.

---

1. Disconnect the battery ground cable and remove the battery.
2. Open the heating valve and the cap on the coolant expansion tank. Drain the coolant by removing the bottom hose. Disconnect the electrical connector from the radiator cooling fan.
3. Remove the radiator and fan as an assembly.
4. If equipped with air conditioning, remove the compressor and condenser and place them aside without disconnecting any refrigerant lines.
5. Detach and label all the electrical wires and vacuum lines connecting the engine to the body.

6. Much of the fuel system can be removed as a unit without disconnecting fuel lines. Remove the injectors from their holes and protect them with caps. Remove the cold start injector and warm-up regulator, if equipped, disconnect the throttle cable and remove the air duct. Lay these aside without disconnecting the fuel lines.

7. Disconnect the speedometer cable from the transaxle and plug the hole. Detach the clutch cable.

8. Loosen the charcoal filter clamp and move the filter to the rear of the engine compartment.

9. Remove the upper engine-to-transaxle bolts.

10. Remove the left and right engine mounting nuts.

11. Remove the front engine stop and the starter.

12. Remove the clutch cover and the 2 lower engine-to-transaxle bolts.

13. Disconnect the exhaust pipe from the manifold at the flange. Then remove the bolt from the exhaust pipe support and remove the exhaust pipe from the manifold.

14. Install transaxle support bar VW-758/1 or equivalent, with slight preload. This is to hold the transmission in place while the engine is out.

15. Install sling US-1105 or equivalent, on the engine lifting eyes, located on the left side of the cylinder head.

16. Lift the engine until its weight is taken off the engine mounts.

17. Adjust the support bar to contact the transaxle.

18. Separate the engine and transaxle.

19. Carefully lift the engine out of the engine compartment so as not to damage the transaxle main shaft, clutch and body.

To install:

20. To install: Lubricate the clutch release bearing and transaxle main shaft splines with MOS_2 grease or equivalent; do not lubricate the guide sleeve or the clutch release bearing.

21. Carefully guide the engine into the vehicle and attach to the transaxle while keeping weight off the motor mounts.

22. Remove the transaxle support bar and lower the engine onto the engine mounts.

23. The remainder of the installation is the reverse of the removal procedure. Torque the engine mounts and subframe bolts with the engine running at idle speed. This will minimize vibration.

24. Torque the following:

Cold start valve, the radiator mount bolts and the engine-to-transaxle cover plate bolts—7 ft. lbs. (10 Nm).

Engine-to-transaxle bolts—42 ft. lbs. (55 Nm).

Engine mount bolts—30 ft. lbs. (40 Nm).

Engine stop-to-body block and exhaust pipe support bolts—18 ft. lbs. (25 Nm).

Exhaust pipe-to-manifold bolts—22 ft. lbs. (30 Nm).

Starter bolts—18 ft. lbs. (25 Nm).

Engine Mounts

Removal and Installation

Earlier vehicles have all rubber, not hydraulic mounts. These mounts are replaceable with the same type but they must be pressed in and out.

1. With the engine properly supported from above using 10-222 or equivalent, remove the mount carrier.

2. Note the position of the mount in the carrier before pressing the old mount out. The large air gap is always at the top.

3. Reinstall the carrier and mount and center the mount in the bracket on the frame while tightening the bolts.

Engine Alignment

If the complaint is excessive engine vibration, before removing mounts, an engine alignment procedure may cure the problem. Loosen all the bolts that go into the rubber mounts themselves. With the vehicle safely supported, shake the engine/transaxle as a unit to settle it in the mounts. Retorque all mounting bolts, starting at the rear and working forward. This procedure helps to minimize vibration.

Cylinder Head

Removal and Installation

CAUTION

Do not disconnect or loosen any refrigerant hose connections during cylinder head removal.

1. Disconnect the battery ground cable.

2. Drain the cooling system.

3. Disconnect the throttle cable and remove the air duct and the throttle body assembly. On 16 valve engine, leave the throttle body on and remove the upper half of the intake manifold.

4. On CIS systems, without disconnecting fuel lines, remove the injectors and the cold start valve and cap them.

5. On AFC systems, the injectors and fuel rail assembly may be left on the head. Disconnect the fuel supply and return lines and the wiring connector for the injectors.

6. Disconnect the radiator and heater hoses.

7. Disconnect and label the vacuum and PCV lines.

8. Remove the auxiliary air regulator from the intake manifold, if equipped.

9. Disconnect and label all electrical lines and remove the spark plugs.

10. Separate the exhaust manifold from the exhaust pipe.

NOTE: Special tools are required for removing and installing the exhaust pipe spring clips; VW3140/1 and /2. This is a set of wedges for spreading the spring clips that hold the pipe to the manifold. The installed spring clip has considerable tension and could cause damage or injury if not properly removed. See the section on exhaust manifold removal.

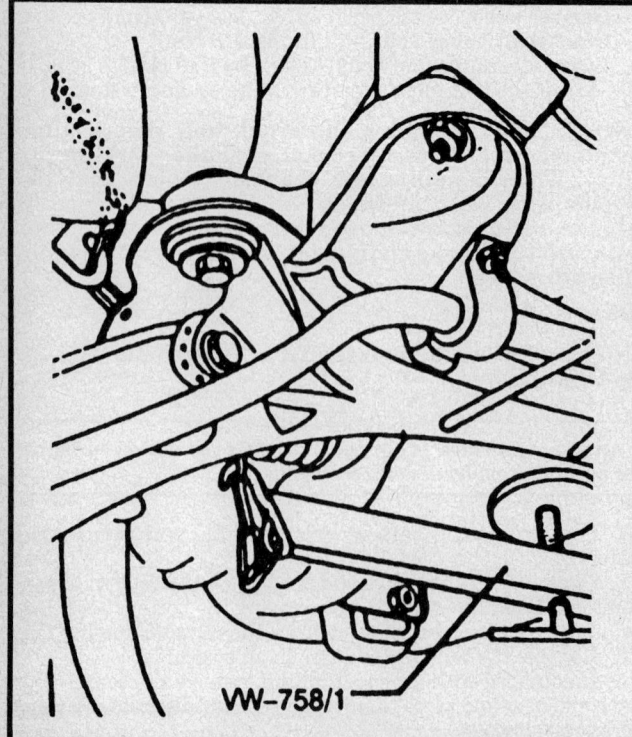

VW-758/1

Transaxle support tool Installed

11. Remove the EGR line from the exhaust manifold, if equipped.

12. Remove the accessory drive belts and any accessory that is bolted to the head. On Corrado, a special clamping tool (3191) is required to remove the spring loaded belt tensioner.

13. Turn the engine to TDC of No. 1 cylinder, if possible, and remove the cylinder head cover, timing belt cover and belt.

14. Loosen the cylinder head bolts in the reverse of the tightening sequence.

15. Remove the bolts and lift the head straight off.

To install:

16. Before reinstalling the head, check the flatness of the head and block in both width and length, then diagonally from each corner.

17. Install the new cylinder head gasket with the word TOP or OBEN facing upward; do not use any sealing compound.

18. Carefully lower the head on and install bolts No. 10 and 8 first. These holes are smaller and will properly locate the gasket and cylinder head.

19. Install the remaining bolts. Torque the bolts in sequence in 3 steps: 29 ft. lbs. (39 Nm), 44 ft. lbs. (60 Nm) and an additional ½ turn. Two quarter turns are allowed.

20. To complete the installation, reverse the removal procedures. Be sure to change the oil and filter.

Valve Lash

Most vehicles now have hydraulic valve lifters and require no adjustment. On these vehicles there will be a sticker under the hood indicating hydraulic lifters. The overhead camshaft acts directly on the valves through bucket-type camshaft followers which fit over the springs and valves. On solid lifters, adjustment is made with an adjusting disc (shim) which fits into the camshaft follower. Different thickness discs result in changes in valve clearance.

NOTE: VW recommends that 2 special tools (VM 546) and the special pliers (VW 208) or equivalent, be used to remove and install the adjustment discs. One is a prybar to compress the valve springs and the other a pair of special pliers to remove the disc. Care must be taken not to gouge the camshaft lobes. The camshaft follower has 2 slots which permit the disc to be lifted out.

1. Valve clearance is checked with the engine moderately warm; coolant temperature should be about 95°F (35°C). Remove the accelerator linkage and the upper drive belt cover. On diesel engine, remove the air cleaner and any hoses or lines as needed.

2. Remove the cylinder head cover. Valve clearance is checked in the firing order 1–3–4–2 for the 4 cylinder and 1–2–4–5–3 for the 5 cylinder engine, with the piston of the cylinder being checked at TDC of the compression stroke. Both valves will be closed at this position and the camshaft lobes will be pointing straight up.

3. Turn the crankshaft pulley bolt with a socket wrench to position the camshaft for checking.

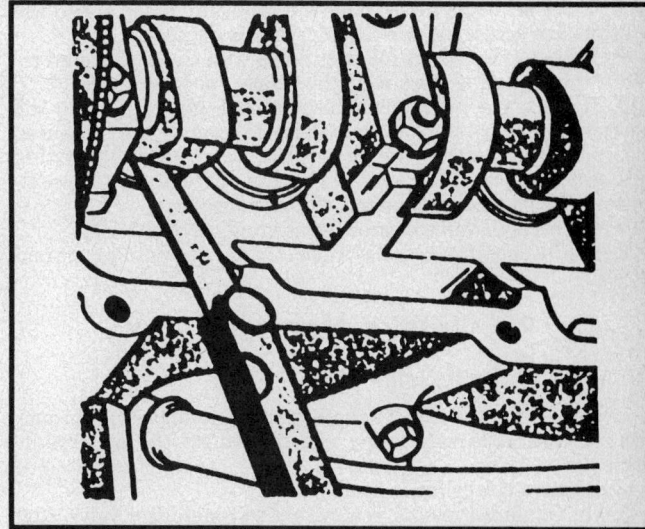
Checking valve lash

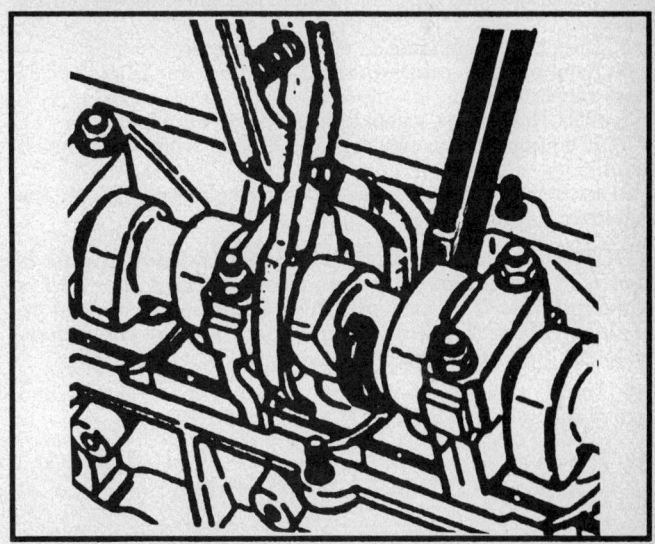
Changing adjustment shim

NOTE: Do not turn the camshaft by the camshaft sprocket mounting bolt, this will stretch the drive belt. When turning the crankshaft pulley bolt, turn it clockwise only.

4. With the No. 1 piston at TDC of the compression stroke, determine the clearance with a feeler gauge. Intake clearance should be 0.008–0.012 in. (0.2–0.3mm); exhaust clearance should be 0.016–0.020 in. (0.4–0.5mm).

5. Check the other cylinders in the firing order, turning the crankshaft to bring each particular piston to the top of the compression stroke. Record the individual clearances.

6. If measured clearance is within tolerance levels of 0.002 in., it is not necessary to replace the adjusting discs.

7. If adjustment is necessary, the discs will have to be removed and replaced with thicker or thinner ones which will yield the correct clearance. Discs are available in 0.002 in. increments from 0.12–0.17 in.

NOTE: The thickness of the adjusting discs is etched on 1 side. When installing, the marks must face the camshaft followers. Discs can be reused if they are not worn or damaged.

Head bolt torque sequence—4 cylinder engine

8. To remove the discs, turn the camshaft followers so the grooves are accessible when the prybar is depressed.

9. Press the camshaft follower down with the prybar and remove the adjusting discs with the proper tool.

10. Replace the adjustment discs as necessary to bring the clearance within the 0.002 in. tolerance level. If the measured clearance is larger than the given tolerance, remove the existing disc and insert a thicker one to bring the clearance up to specification. If it is smaller, insert a thinner one.

11. Recheck all valve clearances after adjustment.

12. Install the valve cover. Connect the accelerator linkage and hoses.

Intake Manifold

Removal and Installation

1. Disconnect the negative battery cable. Remove the air duct from the throttle valve body and disconnect the accelerator cable.

2. Remove the cylinder head cover.

3. On Digifant systems, remove the idle stabilizer valve, fuel pump pressure switch and the fuel injector wiring harness.

4. Disconnect and label the vacuum and the emission control hoses.

5. Disconnect and label all electrical linnes.

6. Remove the injectors and disconnect the line from the cold start valve.

7. On CIS systems, remove the auxiliary air regulator.

8. If equipped, disconnect the EGR line from the exhaust manifold.

9. Loosen and remove the retaining bolts and lift off the manifold.

NOTE: The intake manifold on the 16 valve engine is removed in 2 halves (upper and lower). The upper half is removed first. The gasket between the halves should be replaced if the manifold is separated. Torque the upper-to-lower bolts to 15 ft. lbs.

10. Installation is the reverse of removal. Use new gaskets and torque the manifold bolts to 18 ft. lbs. (25 Nm).

Exhaust Manifold

Removal and Installation

NOTE: Special tools are required for removing and installing the exhaust pipe; VW3140/1 and /2. This is a set of wedges for spreading the spring clips that hold the pipe to the manifold. The installed spring clip has considerable tension and could cause damage or injury if not properly removed.

1. Disconnent the negative battery cable and remove any heat shields that may be in the way.

2. Remove the emissions sample tap and, if equipped, disconnect the EGR tube from the exhaust manifold.

3. Expand the spring clamp by pushing the exhaust pipe to one side and insert the starter wedge into the clamp all the way up to the shoulder.

4. Push the pipe to the other side and install another wedge in the opposite clamp. Continue to work the pipe side to side while pushing the wedges into the clamps until the clamps are spread far enough to lift off easily.

--- **CAUTION** ---

The removed spring clamps with wedges in them are very highly loaded and, if miss handled, could fly apart with enough force to cause serious injury. Store the removed clamps in a closed box where they won't be disturbed.

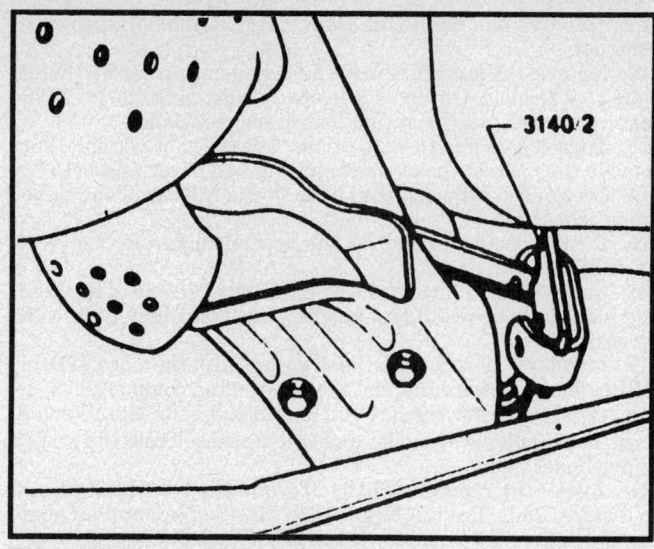

Exhaust pipe clamp removal tools

5. Remove the manifold locking nuts and lift the manifold off the head.

6. Installation is the reverse of removal. Use new gaskets and locking nuts and torque to 18 ft. lbs. (25 Nm).

Supercharger

Removal and Installation

The Corrado has a supercharger with an intercooler for supply-

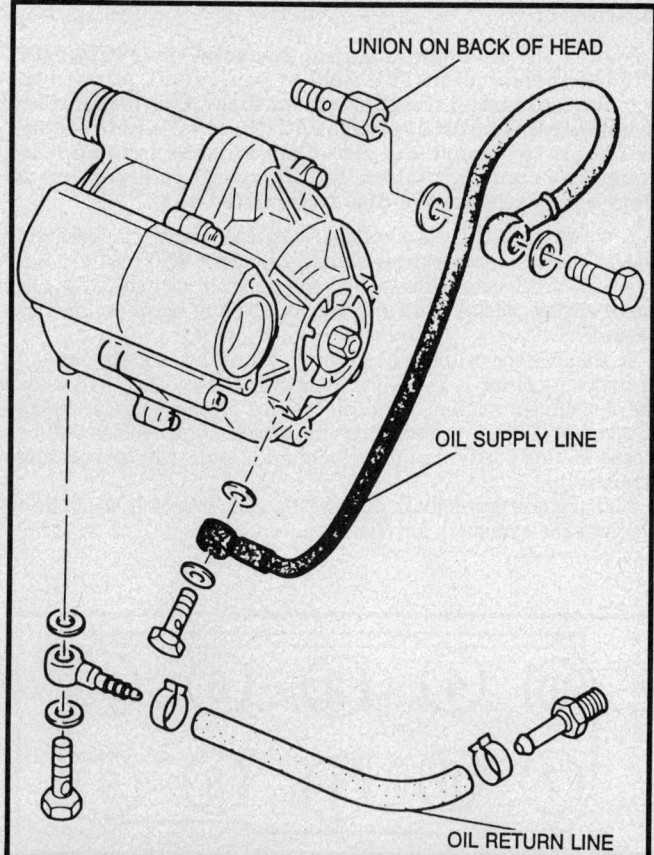

UNION ON BACK OF HEAD

OIL SUPPLY LINE

OIL RETURN LINE

G-charger oil lines

ing up to 11.6 psi (0.8 BAR) of boost and is belt driven. The belt is the same serpentine ribbed belt used to drive the other engine accessories and it's removal requires a special tool VW3191 or equivalent, clamping tool. This unit can be replaced but not repaired.

1. Install tool 3191 and compress the belt tensioner. Remove the belt from the G-charger pulley.

2. Remove the connector hose and silencer from the outlet side of the G-charger and remove the 2 upper inlet hoses.

3. Remove the front and rear mounting bolts and carefully lift the G-charger onto the top of the engine.

4. Allow the oil to drain back into the engine for a few minutes, then remove the oil lines and take the G-charger out of the vehicle.

5. Installation is the reverse of removal. Start the fittings for the oil lines but don't tighten them until the unit is bolted in place. Be sure to use new sealing rings. Torque the following:

    G-charger mounting bolts – 18 ft. lbs. (25 Nm).
    Mounting bracket-to-engine bolt – 33 ft. lbs. (45 Nm).
    Oil line fittings – 11 ft. lbs. (15 Nm).

Timing Belt Front Cover

Removal and Installation

1. Disconnect the negative battery cable.

2. The accessory drive belts must be removed. On Corrado, this requires special tool 3191 to compress the spring loaded belt tensioner.

3. To remove the crankshaft accessory drive pulley, hold the center crank sprocket bolt with a socket and loosen the pulley bolts.

4. The cover is now accessible. It comes off in 2 pieces, remove the upper half first. Take note of any special spacers or other hardware.

5. Installation is the reverse of removal.

Front Oil Seal Replacement

EXCEPT 5 CYLINDER ENGINE

1. Remove the timing belt cover and the timing belt.

2. Remove the crankshaft sprocket.

3. Using a small prybar, pry the seal from the carrier or use the seal extractor tool VW-10-219 or equivalent, to pull out the seal.

NOTE: When removing the seal, be careful not to damage the carrier.

4. To install, lubricate the new seal lips, use the seal installation tool VW-10-203 or equivalent, to press the new seal into the carrier and reverse the removal procedures. Torque the crankshaft pulley bolt to 133 ft. lbs. (180 Nm) for 12mm or 66 ft. lbs. (90 Nm) plus ½ turn for all 12 sided bolts. Check and/or adjust the timing.

5 CYLINDER ENGINE

1. Remove the timing belt cover and remove the timing belt.

2. Remove the crankshaft sprocket.

3. Install the hex head bolt of the seal removal tool VW-3083 or equivalent, into the seal extractor guide VW-2085.

4. Attach the tools to the oil seal and pull the seal from the carrier.

5. To install, slide the sleeve of the installation tool VW-3083 onto the crankshaft journal, lubricate the seal and slide it over the sleeve. Install the thrust sleeve against the oil seal and press it in until seated.

6. To complete the installation procedures, reverse the removal procedures. Torque the crankshaft pulley bolt to 258 ft. lbs. (350 Nm). Check and/or adjust the timing.

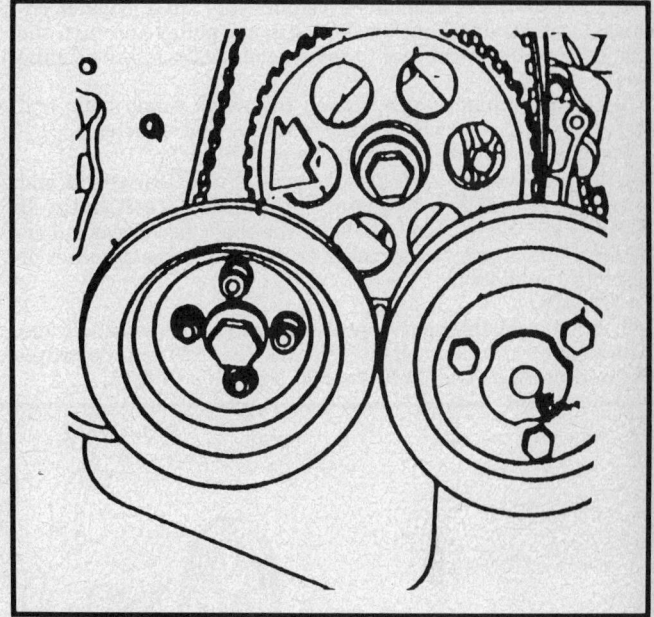

Timing marks

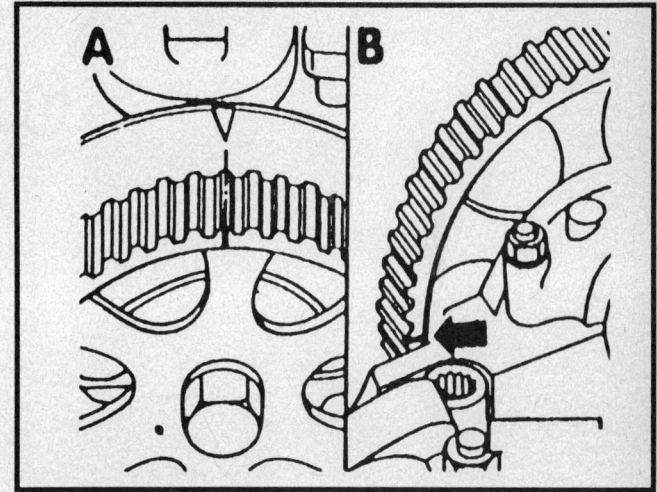

A: 16 valve B: 8 valve

Timing Belt and Sprockets

Removal and Installation

NOTE: Do not turn the engine or camshaft with the camshaft drive belt removed. The pistons will contact the valves and cause internal engine damage.

1. Remove the accessory drive belts, crankshaft pulley and the timing belt cover(s). On Corrado this requires special tool 3191 for compressing the spring loaded belt tensioner.

2. Temperarily reinstall the crankshaft pulley and turn the engine to TDC of No. 1 cylinder, use timing marks on flywheel. The mark on camshaft sprocket should be aligned with the mark on the rear drive belt cover, if equipped, or the edge of the cylinder head.

3. On 8 valve engine, the notch on the crankshaft pulley should align with the dot on the intermediate shaft sprocket. The distributor rotor, remove distributor cap, should be pointing toward the mark on the rim of the distributor housing.

4. Remove the crankshaft drive pulley(s). On 4 cylinder engines, loosen the locknut on the tensioner pulley and turn the tensioner counterclockwise to relieve the tension on the timing belt.

5. On 5 cylinder engine, loosen the water pump bolts and turn the pump clockwise to relieve timing belt tension.

6. Slide the timing belt from the pulleys.

7. To remove the sprockets, remove the retaining bolt and gently pry or tap the sprocket off the shaft with a soft mallet. If the sprocket will not easily slide off the shaft, use a gear puller. Do not hammer on the sprocket or damage to the sprocket or bearings could occur.

To install:

8. When reinstalling the sprockets, torque the camshaft and intermediate sprocket bolts to 48 ft. lbs. (65 Nm) and the crankshaft sprocket bolt to 66 ft. lbs. (90 Nm) plus ½ turn.

9. Install the new timing belt and retension the belt so it can be twisted 90 degrees at the middle of it's longest section, between the camshaft and intermediate sprockets.

10. Recheck the alignment of the marks and, if correct, turn the engine 2 full revolutions and return to TDC of No. 1 cylinder. Recheck belt tension and timing marks. Readjust as required. Torque the tensioner nut to 33 ft. lbs. (45 Nm).

11. Reinstall the belt cover and accessory drive belts and run the engine.

Camshaft

Removal and Installation

8 VALVE ENGINE

1. Disconnect the negative battery cable. Remove the timing

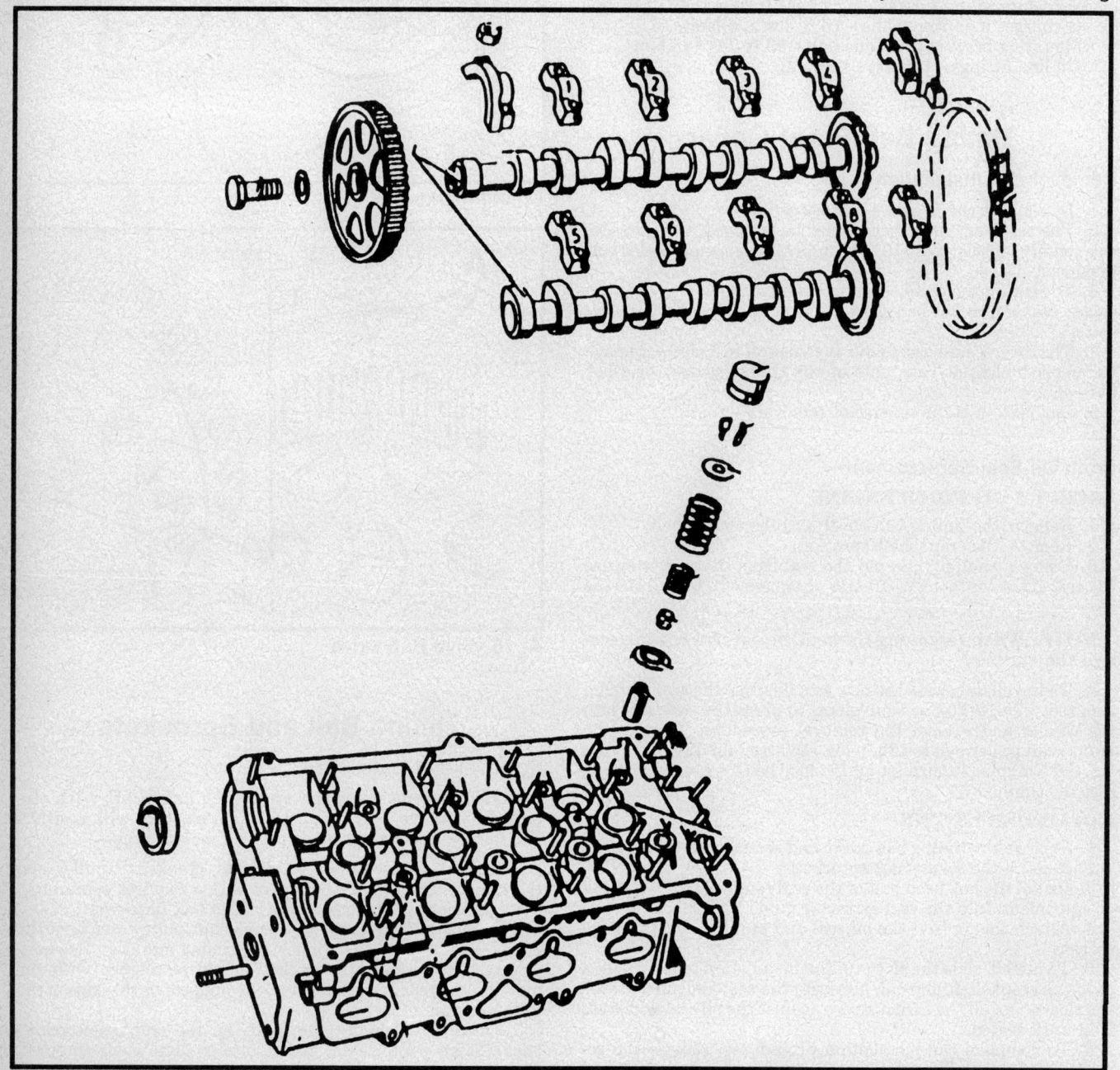

16 valve engine—numbered bearing caps

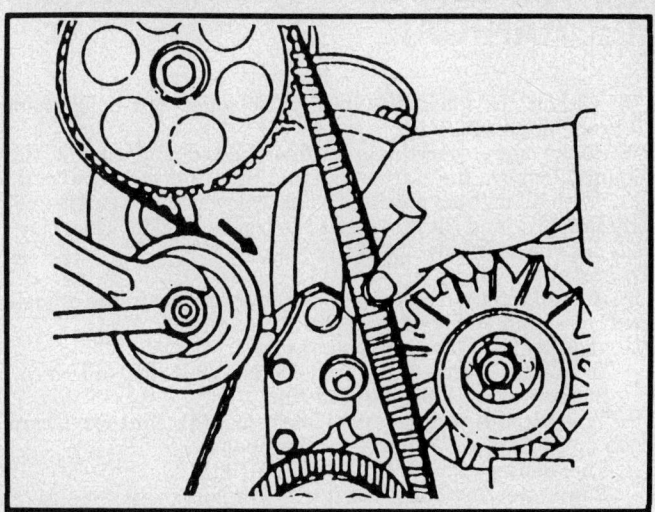

Checking belt tension

belt cover(s), the timing belt, camshaft sprocket and camshaft (valve) cover.

2. Number the bearing caps from front to back. Scribe an arrow facing front. The caps are offset and must be installed correctly. Factory numbers on the caps are not always on the same side.

3. Remove the front and rear bearing caps. Loosen the remaining bearing cap nuts diagonally, in several steps, starting from the outside caps near the ends of the head and working toward the center.

4. Remove the bearing caps and the camshaft.

5. Install a new oil seal and end plug in the cylinder head. Lightly coat the camshaft bearing journals and lobes with a film of assembly lube or heavy engine oil. Install the bearing caps in the reverse order of removal. Tighten the cap nuts diagonally and in several steps until they are torqued to 14 ft. lbs.

6. Install the drive sprocket and timing belt. On solid lifters, check valve clearance and adjust, if necessary. Install remaining parts in reverse order of removal.

7. On engines with hydraulic lifters, wait at least ½ hour after installing camshaft shaft before starting the engine to allow the lifters to leak down. Observe the following torques:

Camshaft shaft endplay—0.006 in. (0.15mm).
Bearing cap bolts—15 ft. lbs. (20 Nm).
Camshaft sprocket bolt—58 ft. lbs. (80 Nm).

16 VALVE ENGINE

1. Remove the timing belt cover.

2. Remove the upper intake manifold and cylinder head cover.

3. Turn the engine to TDC on cylinder No. 1, then slacken and remove the timing belt and camshaft sprocket.

16 valve engine—camshaft shaft alignment

4. With a felt marker only, matchmark the timing chain to the camshafts for reinstallation.

5. Remove the camshaft chain.

6. On the intake camshaft, remove bearing caps No. 5 and 7 and the chain end cap. Then loosen bearing caps No. 6 and 8 alternately and diagonally.

7. On the exhaust camshaft, remove bearing caps No. 1 and 3 and the end caps. Then loosen bearing caps No. 2 and 4 alternately and diagonally.

8. Remove the remaining bearing cap bolts and remove the camshaft.

9. Install the camshaft drive chain so the marks on the chain sprockets are matched at the base of the cylinder head, directly across from each other.

NOTE: When installing the bearing caps, make sure the notch points towards the intake side of the head.

10. On the intake camshaft, install and torque bearing caps No. 6 and 8 alternately and diagonally.

11. Install and torque the remaining bearing caps.

12. On the exhaust camshaft, torque bearing caps No. 2 and 4 alternately and diagonally.

13. Install and torque the remaining bearing caps.

14. Install the drive sprocket and timing belt. On solid lifters, check valve clearance and adjust if necessary. Install remaining parts in reverse order of removal. On engines with hydraulic lifters, wait at least ½ hour after installing camshaft shafts before starting the engine to allow the lifters to leak down.

Camshaft shaft end play—0.006 in. (0.15mm).
Bearing cap bolts—11 ft. lbs. (15 Nm).
camshaft shaft sprocket bolt—48 ft. lbs. (65 Nm).

Piston and Connecting Rod

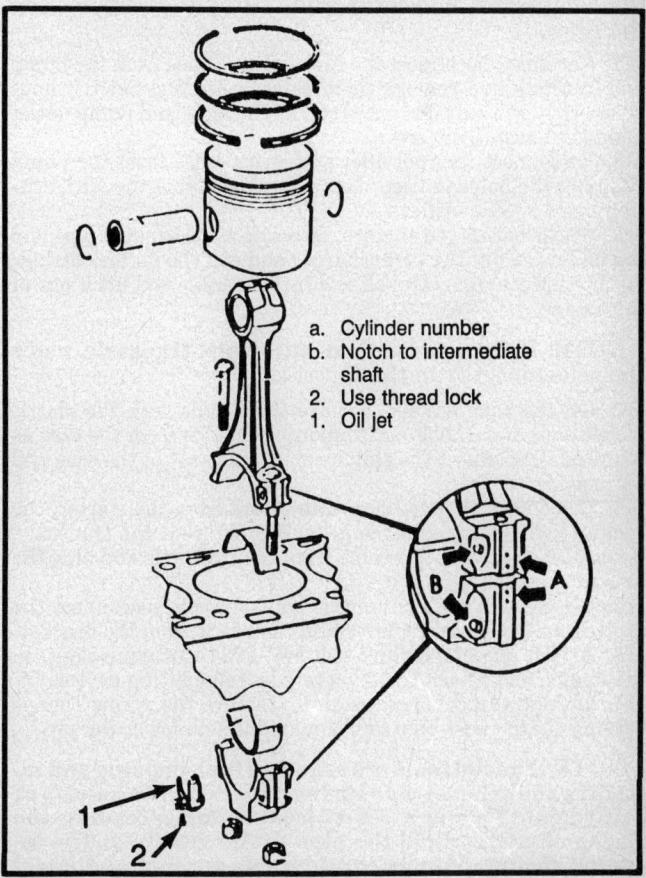

a. Cylinder number
b. Notch to intermediate shaft
2. Use thread lock
1. Oil jet

Piston and rod positioning

DIESEL ENGINE MECHANICAL

Engine Assembly

Removal and Installation

NOTE: **The engine and transmission are lifted from the vehicle as an assembly.**

--- CAUTION ---

Use care when disconnecting the fuel lines. Fuel under pressure may still be in the lines and, if sprayed, may cause fire or personal injury.

1. Disconnect the battery cables and remove the battery.
2. Open the fuel filler cap to relieve tank pressure and then relieve the fuel system pressure.
3. Remove the air filter and disconnect the accelerator cable from the injection pump and set it aside.
4. Remove the radiator cap. Turn the heater temperature control valve to fully pen. Place a pan under the thermostat housing, remove the thermostat flange and drain the coolant.
5. Remove the upper radiator and heater hoses from the engine. Remove the electrical connector from the radiator fan motor and switch. Remove the radiator mounting nuts or bolts, the upper radiator clips and lift out the radiator and fan shroud as an assembly.
6. Begin disconnecting electrical connections and vacuum lines, carefully labeling each one. Don't forget ground connections that are screwed to the body.

NOTE: **If equipped with power steering, remove pump and reservoir and set them aside. Do not disconnect the fluid lines. If equipped with air conditioning, remove the compressor and set it aside without disconnecting the lines.**

7. Carefully disconnect the fuel delivery lines from the pump and injectors and remove them as an assembly. Set the lines where they will stay clean and cap the injector and pump outlet fittings to keep them clean.
8. Disconnect the fuel inlet and outlet lines from the pump and plug the holes to keep the pump clean. Note the outlet fitting has a special orifice.
9. On turbocharged engines, disconnect the exhaust pipe and the oil lines from the turbocharger and cap the oil line fittings on the turbocharger. Unbolt the turbocharger and lift it out of the engine.

NOTE: **If equipped with an automatic transaxle, place the selector lever in the P position.**

10. On the shift linkage, remove the 2 rods with the plastic socket ends and unbolt the remaining linkage from the case as required. Disconnect the clutch cable, lift it out of the case and set it aside.
11. Disconnect the electrical connectors from the starter, the backup light switch and the ground cable from the transaxle. Remove the speedometer cable from the transaxle and plug the hole in the case.
12. On vehicles with automatic transmission, disconnect the cable from the actuating lever and remove it from the bracket.
13. Attach an engine sling tool VW-2024A or equivalent, to the engine and attach the sling to a suitable lifting device.
14. On non turbocharged engines, remove the spring clamps holding the exhaust pipe to the manifold and lower the pipe.

NOTE :**Special tools are required for removing and installing the exhaust pipe spring clips; VW3140/1 and /2 or equivalent. This is a set of wedges for spreading the spring clips that hold the pipe to the manifold. The installed spring clip has considerable tension and could cause damage or injury if not properly removed.**

15. Unbolt the halfshafts from the flanges and hang them from the body with wire.
16. Make sure everything is disconnected and unbolt the mounts. Remove the starter first and the front mount with it.
17. With all mounts unbolted, slightly lower the engine/transaxle assembly and tilt it towards the transaxle side. Then carefully lift the assembly out of the vehicle.
To install:
18. Installation is the reverse of removal. Check the adjustment of clutch and shift linkages.
19. Torque the following components:
Driveshaft flange-to-transaxle bolts—33 ft. lbs. (45 Nm).
Starter bolts—33 ft. lbs. (45 Nm).
Transaxle to body mount—33 ft. lbs. (41 Nm) for 10mm bolts or 54 ft. lbs. (73 Nm) for 12mm bolts.
Fuel delivery lines—18 ft. lbs. (24 Nm).
Power steering bolts—14 ft. lbs. (19 Nm).
Thermostat flange bolts—7 ft. lbs. (9 Nm).

Engine Alignment

After reinstalling all the mounts and mounting bolts, loosen all the bolts that go into the rubber mounts themselves. With the vehicle safely supported, shake the engine/transaxle as a unit to settle it in the mounts. Retorque all mounting bolts, starting at the rear and working foreward. This procedure helps to minimize vibration.

Cylinder Head

Removal and Installation

NOTE: **The cylinder head bolts on all Diesel vehicles are stretch bolts and cannot be reused.**

1. Disconnect the battery ground cable.
2. Remove the thermostat and drain the cooling system.
3. Remove the fuel lines from the injectors and the pump as an assembly. Put the lines where they'll stay clean and protect the injector and pump fittings with caps.
4. Disconnect the radiator and heater hoses.
5. Disconnect all vacuum and electrical connections and carefully label for installation.
6. On turbocharged vehicles, unbolt the exhaust pipe and oil lines from the turbocharger and remove the turbocharger.
7. On non-turbocharged vehicles, remove the air cleaner and disconnect the exhaust pipe from the manifold.

NOTE: **Special tools are required for removing and installing the exhaust pipe spring clips; VW3140/1 and /2 or equivalent. This is a set of wedges for spreading the spring clips that hold the pipe to the manifold. The installed spring clip has considerable tension and could cause damage or injury if not properly removed.**

8. Remove the cylinder head cover and camshaft drive belt cover.
9. Turn the engine to TDC of No. 1 cylinder, if possible, and remove the camshaft drive belt.
10. Remove the head bolts in the reverse order of installation sequence and lift the head out of the vehicle.
To install:
11. On these engines, the pistons actually project above the deck of the block. If the crank shaft and pistons are not to be removed, examine the old head gasket to see how many notches are on the edge near the oil return hole, between No. 2 and 3 cylinders. Replace the gasket with the same thickness.
12. If the pistons were removed, the piston height (pop up) must be measured to select the proper head gasket. Use a dial indicator or caliper to obtain the measurement.

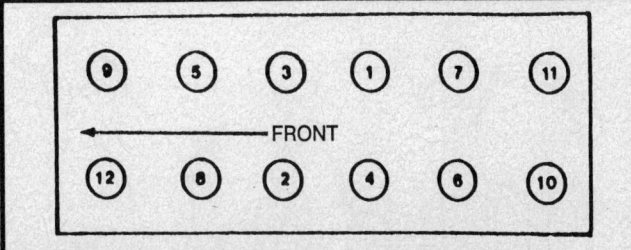

Head bolt torque sequence—5 cylinder engine

13. Install the new cylinder head gasket with the word TOP or OBEN facing upward. Do not use any sealing compound.

14. Turn the crankshaft to TDC of No. 1 cylinder, then back about ¼ turn to bring all pistons about even.

15. Carefully lower the head on and install new bolts No. 10 and 8 first. These holes are smaller and will properly locate the gasket and cylinder head.

16. Install the remaining bolts and torque in the proper sequence in 3 steps: 29 ft. lbs. (40 Nm), 44 ft. lbs. (60 Nm), then a full ½ turn more. Two quarter turns are allowed.

17. Installation of the remaining parts is the reverse of removal, be sure to change the oil and filter. Install the camshaft drive belt and set injection timing.

18. After the engine is assembled and running, warm it up until the oil is 50°C, check oil temp gauge in vehicle, turn the engine OFF and turn each head bolt, in sequence, an additional ¼ turn in 1 movement.

Valve Lash

Adjustment

Most vehicles have hydraulic valve lifters and require no adjustment. On these vehicles there will be a sticker under the hood indicating hydraulic lifters. The overhead camshaft acts directly on the valves through bucket-type camshaft followers which fit over the springs and valves. On solid lifters, adjustment is made with an adjusting disc (shim) which fits into the camshaft follower. Different thickness discs result in changes in valve clearance.

NOTE: The manufacturer recommends that 2 special tools VM 546 and the special pliers VW 208 or equivalent, be used to remove and install the adjustment discs. One is a prybar to compress the valve springs and the other a pair of special pliers to remove the disc. Care must be taken not to gouge the camshaftshaft lobes. The camshaft follower has 2 slots which permit the disc to be lifted out.

1. Valve clearance is checked with the engine moderately warm; coolant temperature should be about 95°F (35°C). Remove the air cleaner and any hoses, lines or cables as needed.

2. Remove the cylinder head cover. Valve clearance is checked in the firing order 1–3–4–2, with the piston of the cylinder being checked at TDC of the compression stroke. Both valves will be closed at this position and the camshaft lobes will be pointing straight up.

3. Turn the crankshaft pulley bolt with a socket wrench to position the camshaft for checking.

NOTE: Do not turn the camshaft by the camshaft sprocket mounting bolt, this will stretch the drive belt. When turning the crankshaft pulley bolt, turn it clockwise only.

4. With the No. 1 piston at TDC of the compression stroke, determine the clearance with a feeler gauge. Intake clearance should be 0.008–0.012 in. (0.2–0.3mm); exhaust clearance should be 0.016–0.020 in. (0.4–0.5mm).

5. Check the other cylinders in the firing order, turning the crankshaft to bring each particular piston to the top of the compression stroke. Record the individual clearances.

6. If measured clearance is within tolerance levels of 0.002 in., it is not necessary to replace the adjusting discs.

7. If adjustment is necessary, the discs will have to be removed and replaced with thicker or thinner ones which will yield the correct clearance. Discs are available in 0.002 in. increments from 0.12–0.17 in.

NOTE: The thickness of the adjusting discs is etched on 1 side. When installing, the marks must face the camshaft followers. Discs can be reused if they are not worn or damaged.

8. To remove the discs, turn the camshaft followers so the grooves are accessible when the prybar is depressed.

9. Press the camshaft follower down with the prybar and remove the adjusting discs with the proper tool.

NOTE: Do not press the camshaft follower down with that piston at TDC. The valves will contact the piston and may damage the engine. Turn the engine ¼ turn past TDC and press the tappet down.

10. Replace the adjustment discs as necessary to bring the clearance within the 0.002 in. tolerance level. If the measured clearance is larger than the given tolerance, remove the existing disc and insert a thicker one to bring the clearance up to specification. If it is smaller, insert a thinner one.

11. Recheck all valve clearances after adjustment.

12. Install the valve cover. Connect the accelerator linkage and hoses.

Exhaust Manifold

Removal and Installation

NOTE: Special tools are required for removing and installing the exhaust pipe; VW3140/1 and /2 or equivalent. This is a set of wedges for spreading the spring clips that hold the pipe to the manifold. The installed spring clip has considerable tension and could cause damage or injury if not properly removed.

1. Disconnent the negative battery cable and remove any heat shields that may be in the way.

2. On turbocharged engines, unbolt the exhaust pipe from the turbocharger outlet.

3. On non-turbocharged engines, expand the spring clamp by pushing the exhaust pipe to one side and insert the starter wedge into the clamp all the way up to the shoulder.

4. Push the pipe to the other side and install another wedge in the opposite clamp. Continue to work the pipe side to side while pushing the wedges into the clamps until the clamps are spread far enough to lift off easily.

——————— **CAUTION** ———————

The removed spring clamps with wedges in them are very highly loaded and, if miss handled, could fly apart with enough force to cause serious injury. Store the removed clamps in a closed box where they won't be disturbed.

5. On turbocharged engines, remove the turbocharger oil lines and the turbocharger.

6. Remove the manifold locking nuts and lift the manifold off the head.

7. Installation is the reverse of removal. Use new gaskets and locking nuts and torque to 18 ft. lbs. (25 Nm).

Turbocharger

Removal and Installation

1. Disconnect the negative battery cable.

2. Remove the exhaust connection from the turbocharger outlet.

3. Clean the oil supply fitting on the top of the turbocharger and remove the supply line and bracket.

4. Remove the inlet air hose.

5. Under the vehicle, remove the oil return line and the turbocharger mounting bracket.

6. Still underneath, remove the turbo-to-manifold bolts and lift the turbocharger out from the top.

7. Installation is the reverse of removal. Before installing the oil supply line, fill the connection on the turbocharger with engine oil. Torque the following:

Turbocharger-to-exhaust manifold—33 ft. lbs. (45 Nm).
Mounting bracket nuts—18 ft. lbs. (25 Nm).
Turbocharger outlet nuts—18 ft. lbs. (25 Nm).
Oil return line—22 ft. lbs. (30 Nm).

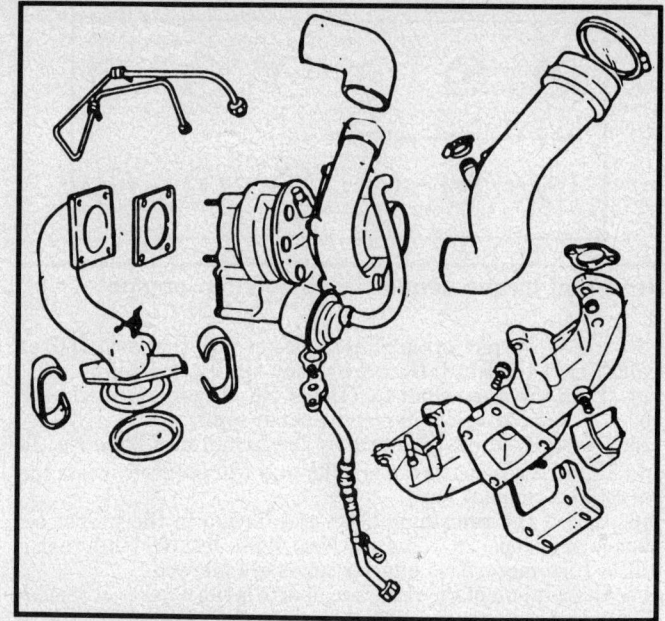

Diesel turbocharger

ENGINE LUBRICATION

Oil Pan

Removal and Installation
EXCEPT QUANTUM AND FOX

The oil pan can be removed with the engine in the vehicle, however on the Quantum and Fox, the engine must be raised off it's mounts.

1. Raise and safely support the vehicle and drain the oil.

2. Loosen and remove the bolts retaining the oil pan.

3. Lower the pan from the engine.

4. Make sure the gasket surface is flat and install the pan and new gasket.

5. Torque the retaining bolts in a criss-cross pattern to 14 ft. lbs. (20 Nm). Do not over torque.

6. Refill the engine with oil. Start the engine and check for leaks.

QUANTUM

1. Raise and safely support the vehicle and drain the oil.

2. Support and slightly raise the engine from overhead with a suitable lifting device.

3. Gradually loosen the engine crossmember mounting bolts. Remove the left and right side engine mounts.

4. Carefully lower the crossmember from the vehicle.

5. Remove the oil pan retaining bolts and lower the pan from the vehicle.

To install:

6. Make sure the gasket surface is flat and install the pan and new gasket.

7. Torque the retaining bolts in a crosswise pattern to 14 ft. lbs. (20 Nm) on 4 cylinder engines or 5 cylinder pan bolts to 7 ft. lbs. (10 Nm).

8. Raise the crossmember. Torque the crossmember bolts to 42 ft. lbs. (57 Nm) and the engine mounting bolts to 32 ft. lbs. (43 Nm).

9. Refill the engine with oil. Start the engine and check for leaks.

Oil Pump

Removal and Installation
4 CYLINDER ENGINE

1. Raise and safely support the vehicle and remove the oil pan.

2. Remove the 2 mounting bolts and lower the pump from the engine.

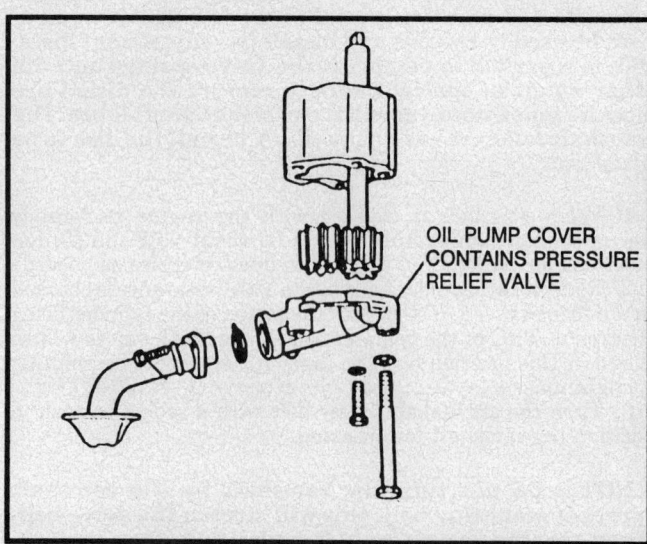

OIL PUMP COVER CONTAINS PRESSURE RELIEF VALVE

4 cylinder oil pump

3. Remove the bottom cover and disassemble the pump. The pressure relief valve is in the bottom cover.

4. Clean and inspect all parts for ware and replace as needed.

5. After reassembling the pump, prime it with oil and install in the reverse order of removal.

6. Observe the following torques:
Oil pump bottom cover bolts—7 ft. lbs. (10 Nm).
Oil pump suction foot bolts—7 ft. lbs. (10 Nm).
Oil pump retainting bolts—15 ft. lbs. (20 Nm).

5 CYLINDER ENGINE

On these vehicles, the oil pump is on the front of the engine, behind the front crankshaft sprocket. However it is still necessary to remove the oil pan.

1. Remove the accessory drive belts and the steering pump. Lay the pump aside without disconnecting the lines.

2. Remove the timing belt cover and the upper radiator cover and turn the engine to TDC of No. 1 cylinder. Check to see that the mark on the camshaft drive sprocket alignes with the top edge of the head.

3. Loosen the water pump bolts and pry the pump to loosen the camshaft drive belt.

4. Remove the drive belt sprocket from the crankshaft; do not turn the engine with the camshaft drive belt removed. The pistons may contact the valves and cause engine damage.

5. Remove the oil dip stick and drain the crankcase.

6. Support and slightly raise the engine with a suitable lifting device.

7. Gradually loosen the engine crossmember mounting bolts. Remove the left and right side engine mounts.

8. Carefully lower the crossmember from the vehicle.

9. Remove the oil pan and the oil pickup tube.

10. Remove the oil pump from the front of the engine.

11. When disassembling the pump, note the mark on the gears faces the rear end cover of the pump.

12. Clean all parts and check the pump for wear or damage, replace parts as necessary. The gears can be replaced as a set and the rear cover should be replaced if it's scored.

13. Reassemble the pump and pack it with petroleum jelly.

14. Installation is the reverse of removal. Torque the following:
Oil pump cover and pickup tube—7 ft. lbs. (10 Nm).
Oil pump mounting bolts—15 ft. lbs. (20 Nm).
Oil pan—7 ft. lbs. (10 Nm).
Crossmember bolts—42 ft. lbs. (57 Nm).

Motor mount bolts—32 ft. lbs. (43 Nm).
Front crankshaft sprocket—258 ft. lbs. (350 Nm).

Rear Main Bearing Oil Seal

Removal and Installation

The rear main oil seal is located in a housing on the rear of the cylinder block. To replace the seal on all vehicles it is necessary to remove the transaxle and flywheel.

1. Remove the transaxle and flywheel.

2. Using a small prybar tool VW-2086 on 5 cylinder engine, VW-10-221 on 4 cylinder engine or equivalent, pry the old seal out of the support ring.

3. Remove the seal.

4. To install, lightly oil the new seal and press it into place using tool VW-2003/2A or equivalent, to start the seal and tool VW-2003/1 or equivalent, to seat the seal. Be careful not to damage the seal or score the crankshaft.

5. Install the flywheel and transaxle.

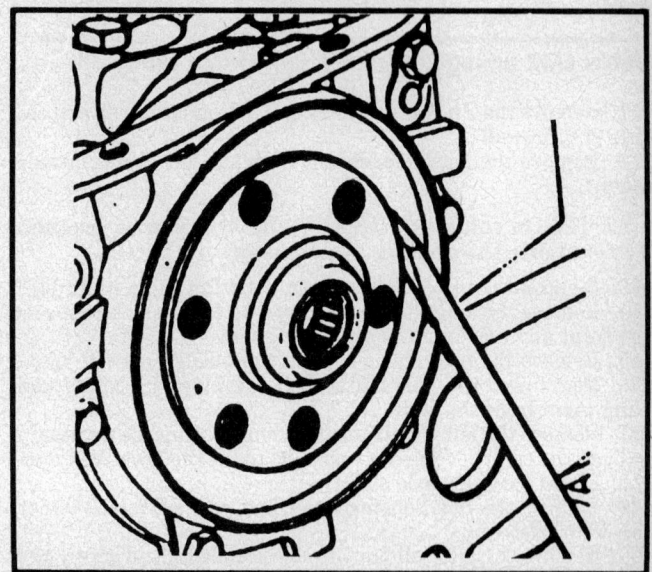

Rear main oil seal removal

MANUAL TRANSAXLE

For further information, please refer to "Professional Transmission Repair Manual" for additional coverage.

Transaxle Assembly

Removal and Installation

PASSAT AND CORRADO

NOTE: If equipped with electronically theft-protected radios, obtain the security code before disconnecting the battery.

1. Disconnect the negative battery cable.

2. On Corrado, remove the intercooler tubing.

3. Disconnect the backup light switch connector and the speedometer cable from the transaxle, plug the speedometer cable hole.

4. Remove the clutch slave cylinder without disconnecting the hydraulic line. Hang the cylinder from the body with wire.

5. On cable shift linkage, remove backup light switch bracket and disconnect the cable from the relay lever but remove the gearshift lever with the cable still attached. Remove the cable support and set the cables aside.

6. If necessary, remove the intake hose from the air flow sensor.

7. Remove the upper transaxle-to-engine bolts.

8. Raise and safely support the vehicle and remove the front wheels. Connect the engine sling tool VW-10-222A or equivalent, to the loop in the cylinder head and just take the weight of the engine off the mounts. On 16 valve engine, the idle stbilizer valve must be removed to attach the tool. Do not try to support the engine from below.

9. Remove the drain plug and drain the oil from the transaxle. Dispose of the oil properly.

10. Remove the starter and front mount.

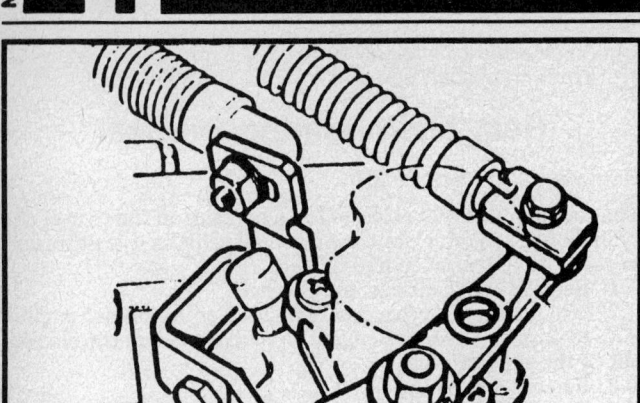

Cable shift linkage at transaxle—switch removed

11. Remove the 3 bolts from the right side mount, between engine and firewall.

12. Remove the large center bolt from the left side transaxle mount.

NOTE: On vehicles with ABS, this bolt can be reached by removing the cooling system overflow bottle.

13. Remove the radiator fan shroud and fan as an assembly.

14. Remove the long transaxle support bracket which connects the front and rear mounts on the left side.

15. Remove the heat shield for the right side inner CV-joint.

16. Disconnect the halfshafts from the inner CV-joints and hang them from the body.

17. Remove the left rear transaxle mount. It may be necessary to push the engine/transaxle rearward to get the lower bolt out.

18. Lower the transaxle slightly.

19. Remove the bell housing cover and position a jack under the transaxle.

20. Remove the last bell housing-to-block bolts and gently pry the transaxle away from the engine. Lower it carefully from the vehicle.

To install:

21. To install, coat the input shaft and shift levers lightly with Moly lube and reverse the removal procedures.

22. Torque the following components:
Engine-to-transaxle bolts—59 ft. lbs. (80 Nm).
Starter bolts—44 ft. lbs. (60 Nm).
Halfshaft-to-flange—33 ft. lbs. (45 Nm).

JETTA AND GOLF

NOTE: If equipped with electronically theft-protected radios, obtain the security code before disconnecting the battery.

1. Disconnect the negative battery cable.

2. Disconnect the backup light switch connector and the speedometer cable from the transaxle; plug the speedometer cable hole.

3. Remove the upper engine-to-transaxle bolts.

4. Remove the 3 right side engine mount bolts, between engine and firewall.

5. To disconnect the shift linkage, pry open the ball joint ends and remove the shift and relay shaft rods.

6. Remove the center bolt from the left transaxle mount.

7. Raise and safely support the vehicle and remove the front wheels. Connect the engine sling tool VW-10-222A or equivalent, to the loop in the cylinder head and just take the weight of

the engine off the mounts. On 16 valve engine, the idle stabilizer valve must be removed to attach the tool. Do not try to support the engine from below.

8. Remove the drain plug and drain the oil from the transaxle. Dispose of the oil properly.

9. Remove the left inner fender liner.

10. Disconnect the halfshafts from the inner CV-joints and hang them from the body.

11. Remove the clutch cover plate and the small plate behind the right halfshaft flange.

12. Remove the starter and front engine mount.

13. Disconnect the clutch cable and remove it from the transaxle housing.

14. Remove the remaining transmission mount bolts and mounts.

15. Place a jack under the transmission and remove the last bolts holding it to the engine. Carefully pry the transaxle away from the engine and lower it from the vehicle.

16. To install, coat the input shaft and shift levers lightly with Moly lube and reverse the removal procedures.

17. Torque the following components:
Engine-to-transaxle bolts—55 ft. lbs. (75 Nm).
Starter bolts—44 ft. lbs. (60 Nm).
Halfshaft-to-flange—33 ft. lbs. (45 Nm).
Transaxle bracket-to-rear mount—44 ft. lbs. (60 Nm).
Front rubber mount—36 ft. lbs. (50 Nm).

SCIROCCO AND CABRIOLET

NOTE: If equipped with electronically theft-protected radios, obtain the security code before disconnecting the battery.

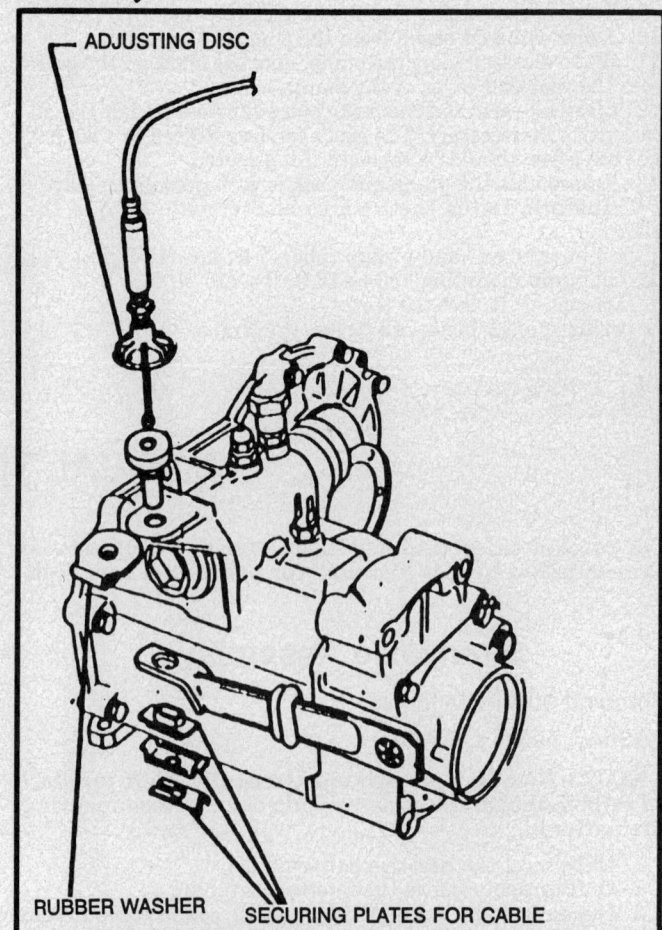

ADJUSTING DISC

RUBBER WASHER   SECURING PLATES FOR CABLE

Clutch cable attachment

1. Disconnect the negative battery cable.

2. Disconnect the backup light switch connector and the speedometer cable from the transaxle, plug the speedometer cable hole.

3. Turn the engine to align the timing marks to TDC.

4. To disconnect the shift linkage, pry open the ball joint ends and remove both selector rods. Remove the pin, disconnect the relay rod and put the pin back in the hole on the rod for safe keeping.

5. Raise and safely support the vehicle and remove the front wheels. Connect the engine sling tool VW–10–222A or equivalent, to the loop in the cylinder head and just take the weight of the engine off the mounts. On 16 valve engine, the idle stbilizer valve must be removed to attach the tool. Do not try to support the engine from below.

6. Remove the drain plug and drain the oil from the transaxle. Dispose of the oil properly.

7. Detach the clutch cable from the linkage and remove it from the transmission case.

8. Remove the starter and front engine mount.

9. Remove the small cover behind the right halfshaft flange and remove the clutch cover plate.

10. Disconnect the halfshafts from the flanges and hang them up with wire.

11. Remove the long center bolt from the left side transaxle mount.

12. Remove the entire rear mount assembly from the body and differential housing.

13. Lower the engine hoist enough to let the left mount free of the body and remove the mount from the transaxle.

14. Place a transaxle support jack under the transaxle, remove all the transaxle-to-engine bolts and carefully pry the transaxle away from the engine. Lower the transaxle from under the vehicle.

15. To install, coat the input shaft and shift levers lightly with Moly lube and reverse the removal procedures.

16. Torque the following components:
Engine-to-transaxle bolts—55 ft. lbs. (75 Nm).
Starter bolts—44 ft. lbs. (60 Nm).
Halfshaft-to-flange—33 ft. lbs. (45 Nm).
Transaxle rubber mounts—44 ft. lbs. (60 Nm).
Adjust the clutch free-play.

FOX

NOTE: If equipped with electronically theft-protected radios, obtain the security code before disconnecting the battery.

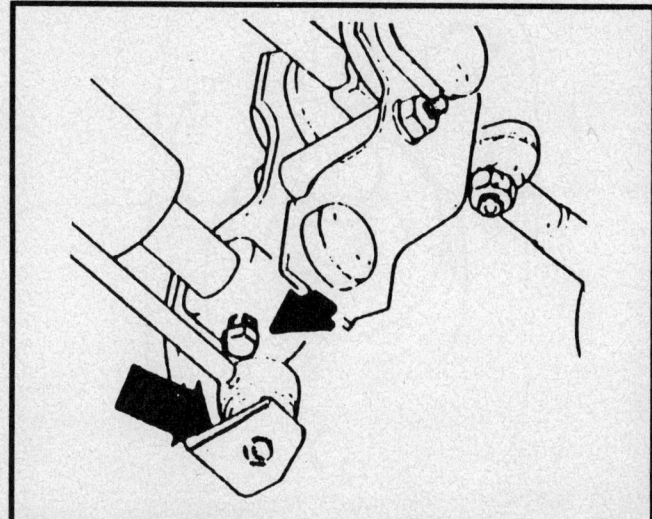

Fox and Quantum control rod joint

1. Raise and safely support the vehicle and remove the front wheels.

2. Remove the drain plug and drain the oil from the transaxle. Dispose of the oil properly.

3. Disconnect the battery ground cable.

4. Disconnect the clutch cable.

5. Disconnect the exhaust pipe from the manifold.

6. Disconnect the speedometer cable and backup light switch.

7. Remove the bolt on the shift linkage, pry the control rod joint off and push the shift linkage coupling off the transaxle.

8. Detach the halfshafts from the transaxle.

9. Remove the starter and clutch cover plate.

10. Remove the exhaust pipe bracket from the transaxle and remove the pipe at the catalyst.

11. Support the transaxle with a jack.

12. Remove the engine-to-transmission bolts.

13. Remove the transaxle crossmember and front mount bolts.

14. Carefully pry the transaxle away from the engine and lower it from the vehicle.

15. Installation is the reverse of removal. Finger tighten the mounting bolts and when the mounts are aligned and free of tension, tighten them.

16. Torque the following components:
Engine-to-transaxle bolts—40 ft. lbs. (55 Nm).
Halfshaft bolts—30 ft. lbs. (40 Nm).
Subframe-to-body—48 ft. lbs. (65 Nm).
Rubber mount-to-body—81 ft. lbs. (110 Nm).
Starter bolts—33 ft. lbs. (45 Nm).

On vehicles with the rubber core left side transaxle mount, the rubber core must be centered in its housing.

QUANTUM

4 Cylinder Engine

NOTE: If equipped with electronically theft-protected radios, obtain the security code before disconnecting the battery.

1. Raise and safely support the vehicle and remove the front wheels.

2. Remove the drain plug and drain the oil from the transaxle. Dispose of the oil properly.

3. Disconnect the battery ground strap.

4. Disconnect the exhaust pipe from the manifold and remove the front muffler and exhaust pipe.

5. Unhook the clutch cable.

6. Disconnect the speedometer cable and the backup light wiring.

7. Remove the front engine stop (rubber bumper).

8. Unbolt both halfshafts at the transaxle.

9. Remove the clutch cover on the bottom of transaxle case.

10. Remove the starter bolt.

11. Remove the bolt on the shift linkage, pry the control rod joint off and push the shift linkage coupling off the transaxle.

12. Place a jack under the transmission and lift slightly.

13. Remove the transaxle support bolts and transaxle rubber mounts.

14. Remove the transaxle-to-engine bolts and carefully pry the transmission away from the engine.

15. Lower the transaxle from the vehicle.

16. Installation is the reverse of removal. Finger tighten the mounting bolts and when the mounts are aligned and free of tension, tighten them.

17. Torque the following components:
Transaxle-to-engine bolts—40 ft. lbs. (54 Nm).
Halfshaft-to-drive flange bolts—30 ft. lbs. (40 Nm).
Transaxle-to-mount bolts—18 ft. lbs. (24 Nm).
Transaxle mount-to-body bolts—81 ft. lbs. (110 Nm).
Subframe to body—48 ft. lbs. (65 Nm).

5 Cylinder Engine

NOTE: If equipped with electronically theft-protected radios, obtain the security code before disconnecting the battery.

1. Remove the battery ground strap.
2. Remove the 2 upper transmission-to-engine bolts.
3. Connect the engine sling tool VW–10–222A or equivalent, to the loop in the cylinder head and just take the weight of the engine off the mounts.
4. Raise and safely support the vehicle and remove the front wheels.
5. Remove the drain plug and drain the oil from the transaxle. Dispose of the oil properly.
6. On vehicles with cable clutch, unhook the cable and remove it from the housing.
7. On vehicles with hydraulic clutch, take the clip off the slave cylinder, drive out the roll pin and set the cylinder aside without opening the hydraulic line.
8. Remove the front exhaust pipe, bracket and heat shield.
9. Disconnect the backup light wires.
10. Remove the bolt on the shift linkage, pry the control rod joint off and push the shift linkage coupling off the transaxle.
11. Remove the clutch cover, starter and lower transaxle-to-engine bolts.
12. Place a jack under the transmission and remove the mounts.
13. Gently pry the transaxle away from the engine and lower it from the vehicle.
14. Installation is the reverse of removal. Finger tighten the mounting bolts and when the mounts are aligned and free of tension, tighten them.
15. Torque the following components:
   Transaxle-to-engine bolts—40 ft. lbs. (54 Nm).
   Halfshaft-to-drive flange bolts—33 ft. lbs. (45 Nm) for M8 bolts or 59 ft. lbs. (80 Nm) for M10 bolts.
   Transaxle-to-mounting bracket—29 ft. lbs. (40 Nm).
   Rubber mount-to-body bolts—81 ft. lbs. (110 Nm).
   Subframe-to-body—52 ft. lbs. (70 Nm).

QUANTUM SYNCRO

NOTE: If equipped with electronically theft-protected radios, obtain the security code before disconnecting the battery.

1. Raise and safely support the vehicle and remove the front wheels.
2. Remove the drain plug and drain the oil from the transaxle. Dispose of the oil properly.
3. Disconnect the battery ground strap.
4. Remove the front muffler and exhaust header.
5. Disconnect the tie rod coupling from the steering rack.
6. Disconnect the speedometer cable.

7. Remove the locking pin and clutch slave cylinder without opening the hydraulic line.
8. Remove the bolt on the shift linkage, pry the control rod joint off and push the shift linkage coupling off the transaxle.
9. Connect the engine sling tool VW–10–222A or equivalent, to the loop in the cylinder head and just take the weight of the engine off the mounts.
10. Disconnect the driveshaft to the rear drive.
11. Disconnect the wiring for the backup lights and differential lock and the vacuum lines from the servo.
12. Remove the starter and clutch cover plate.
13. Remove the right side transmission mount and disconnect the halfshaft.
14. Place a jack under the transmission and disconnect the left side mount and halfshaft.
15. Remove the front engine stop (rubber bumper) and the remaining engine-to-transaxle bolts.
16. Carefully pry the transaxle away from the engine and lower it from the vehicle.
17. Installation is the reverse of removal. Finger tighten the mounting bolts and when the mounts are aligned and free of tension, tighten them.
18. Torque the following components:
   Transaxle-to-engine bolts—43 ft. lbs. (60 Nm).
   Halfshaft-to-drive flange bolts—33 ft. lbs. (45 Nm).
   Rear driveshaft bolts—40 ft. lbs. (55 Nm).
   Transaxle-to-mount bolts—29 ft. lbs. (40 Nm).
   Transaxle mount-to-subframe bolts—32 ft. lbs. (45 Nm).
   Tie rod coupling bolts—29 ft. lbs. (40 Nm).
   Exhaust pipe flange—18 ft. lbs. (25 Nm).

Shift Linkage Adjustment

QUANTUM

This procedure requires special tool VW–3057 or equivalent.
1. Place the lever in neutral.
2. Raise and safely support the vehicle and loosen the clamp nut.
3. Inside the vehicle, remove the gear lever knob and the shift boot. It is not necessary to remove the console. Align the centering holes of the lever housing and the lever bearing housing.

Engine support

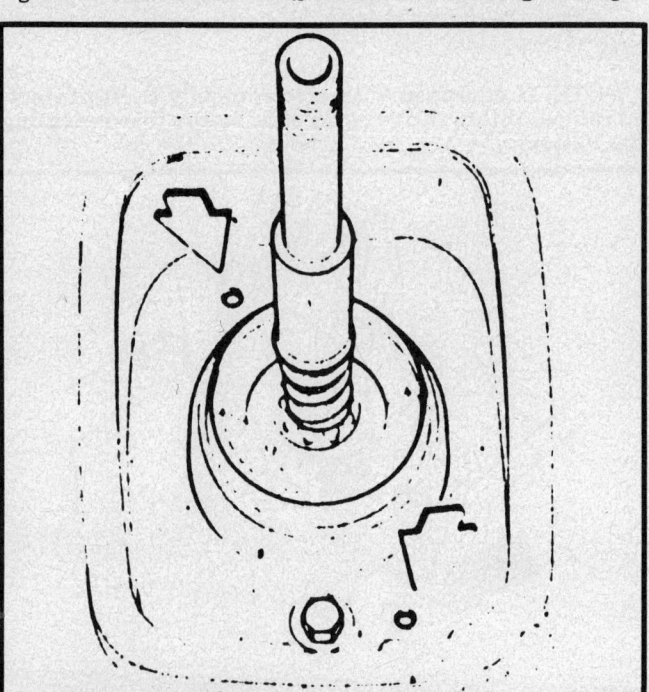

Align holes in shift plate

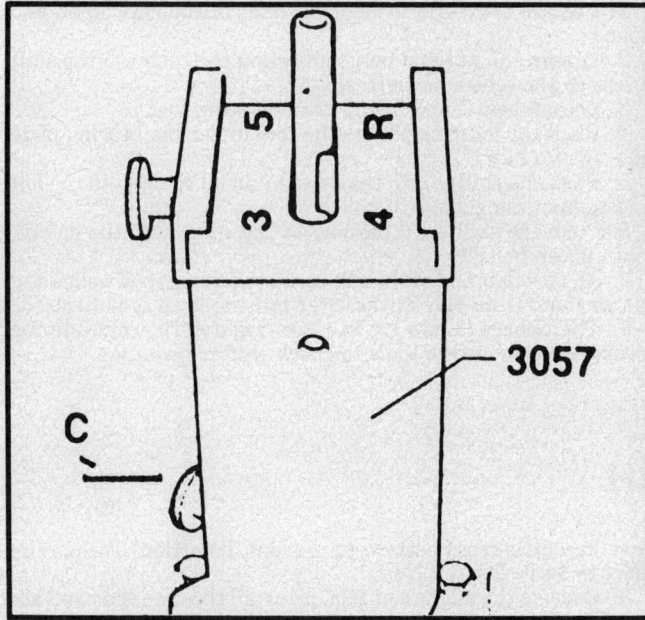

Shifter alignment tool in place

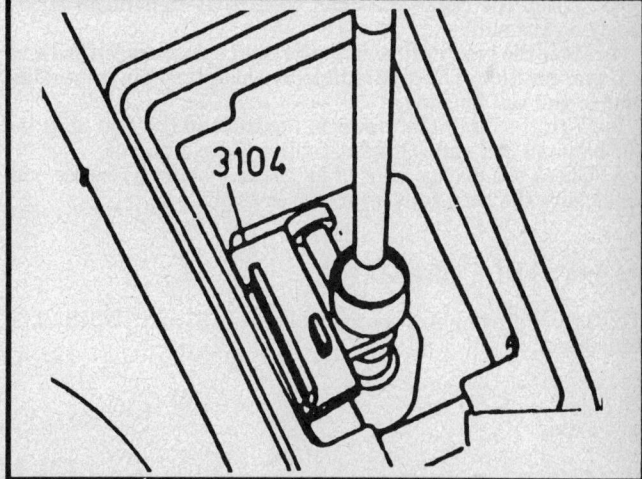

Golf and Jetta shifter adjusting tool

4. Install the tool with the locating pin toward the front. Push the lever to the left side of the tool cut-out. Tighten the lower knurled knob to secure the tool.

5. Move the top slide of the tool to the left stop and tighten the upper knurled knob.

6. Push the shift lever to the right side of the cutout. Align the shift rod and shift finger under the vehicle and tighten the clamp nut. Remove the tool.

7. Place the lever in first. Press the lever to the left side against the stop. Release the lever; it should spring back ¼–½ in. If not, move the lever housing slightly sideways to correct. Check that all gears can be engaged easily, particularly reverse.

SCIROCCO AND CABRIOLET

1. Remove the shifter knob and boot.

2. Align the holes of the lever housing plate with the holes of the lever bearing plate. Check shifter operation.

3. If further adjustment is required, working under the vehicle remove the boot and loosen the shift rod clamp so the shifter moves easily on the rod.

4. Center the shift finger (fore and aft) in the lockout plate and move the shifter so the finger is disengaged from the lock out by ⁹⁄₁₆ in. (15mm).

5. Tighten the rod clamp to 14 ft. lbs. (20 Nm) and check shifter operation. If operation is spongy or binding, readjust the lock out finger to ½ in. (13mm).

GOLF AND JETTA

This procedure requires special tool VW 3104 or equivalent.

1. Put the transaxle in neutral.

2. Under the vehicle, loosen the clamp on the shifter rod so the shifter moves freely on the rod.

3. Remove the shifter knob and the boot.

4. Position the gauge alignment tool VW–3104 on the shifting mechanism, lock it in place.

5. Align the shift rod with the selector lever and torque the clamp to 19 ft. lbs. (26 Nm). The shifter linkage must not be under load during the adjustment.

6. Check shifter operation.

FOX

1. Shift into neutral.

2. Remove the gear shift lever knob and shift boot.

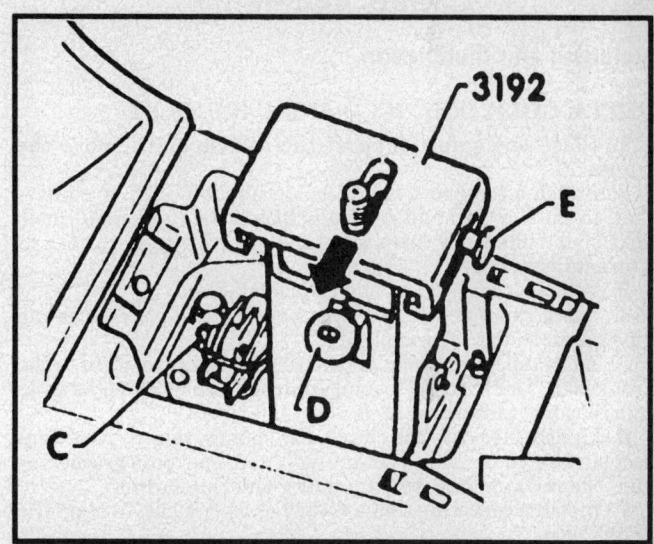

Passat and Corrado shifter adjustment

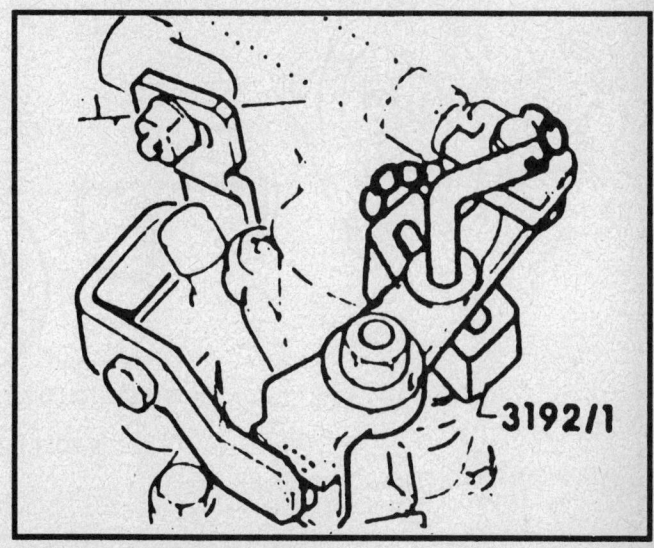

Adjusting wedge in place

3. Loosen the clamp nuts and check that shift finger slides freely on the shift rod.

4. Move the gear shift lever to the right side, between 3rd and 4th gear position. The gear shift lever should remain perpendicular to the ball housing.

5. With the inner shift lever in neutral and the gear shift lever between 3rd and 4th gear, tighten the clamp nut.

6. Check the engagement of all gears, including reverse and make sure the gear shift lever moves freely.

PASSAT AND CORRADO

This procedure requires special tools VW 3193 and VW3192/1 or equivalent.

1. Put the transaxle in neutral, remove the shift knob and boot.

2. Loosen the nut and bolt connecting the cables to the shift levers so the cables move freely.

3. Loosen bolt C and install the adjusting tool.

4. Pivot the locating pin for the tool under the bearing plate and tighten nut D.

5. Push the shifter into the detent and all the way to the left and tighten the slide with bolt E.

5. Push the shifter all the way to the right, into the detent, and tighten bolt C.

6. At the other end of the cables, install the special wedge and pin so there is no play in the lever but the lever is not raised.

7. The linkage is now set in place. Tighten the cables to the levers and remove the tools to check shifter operation.

CLUTCH

Clutch Assembly

Removal and Installation

JETTA, GOLF, SCIROCCO AND CABRIOLET

1. Raise and safely support the vehicle and remove the transaxle.

2. Attach a toothed flywheel holder tool VW–558 or equivalent, to the flywheel and gradually loosen the flywheel-to-pressure plate bolts a few turns at a time in a criss-cross pattern to prevent distortion.

3. Remove the flywheel and the clutch disc.

4. Use a small prybar to remove the release plate retaining ring. Remove the release plate.

5. To install, use new bolts to attach the pressure plate to the crankshaft. Use a thread locking compound and torque the bolts in a diagonal pattern to 72 ft. lbs. (100 Nm).

6. Lightly lubricate the clutch disc splines, release plate contact surface and pushrod socket with multi-purpose grease. Install the release plate, retaining ring and clutch disc.

7. Install a centering tool VW–547 or equivalent, to align the clutch disc.

8. Install the flywheel, tightening the bolts 1–2 turns at a time in a criss-cross pattern to prevent distortion. Torque the bolts to 14 ft. lbs. (20 Nm).

9. Remove the alignment tool, reinstall the transaxle and adjust the clutch cable.

FOX, QUANTUM, PASSAT AND CORRADO

1. Raise and safely support the vehicle and remove the transaxle.

2. Matchmark the flywheel and pressure plate if the pressure plate is going to be reused.

3. Gradually loosen the pressure plate bolts 1–2 turns at a time in a criss-cross pattern to prevent distortion.

4. Remove the pressure plate and disc.

5. Check the clutch disc for uneven or excessive lining wear. Examine the pressure plate for cracking, scorching or scoring. Replace any questionable components.

6. Install the clutch disc and pressure plate with the springs on the disc towards the plate. Use an alignment tool to keep the clutch disc centered.

7. Gradually tighten the pressure plate-to-flywheel bolts in a criss-cross pattern. Tighten the bolts to 18 ft. lbs.

8. Install the throwout bearing.

9. Install the transaxle.

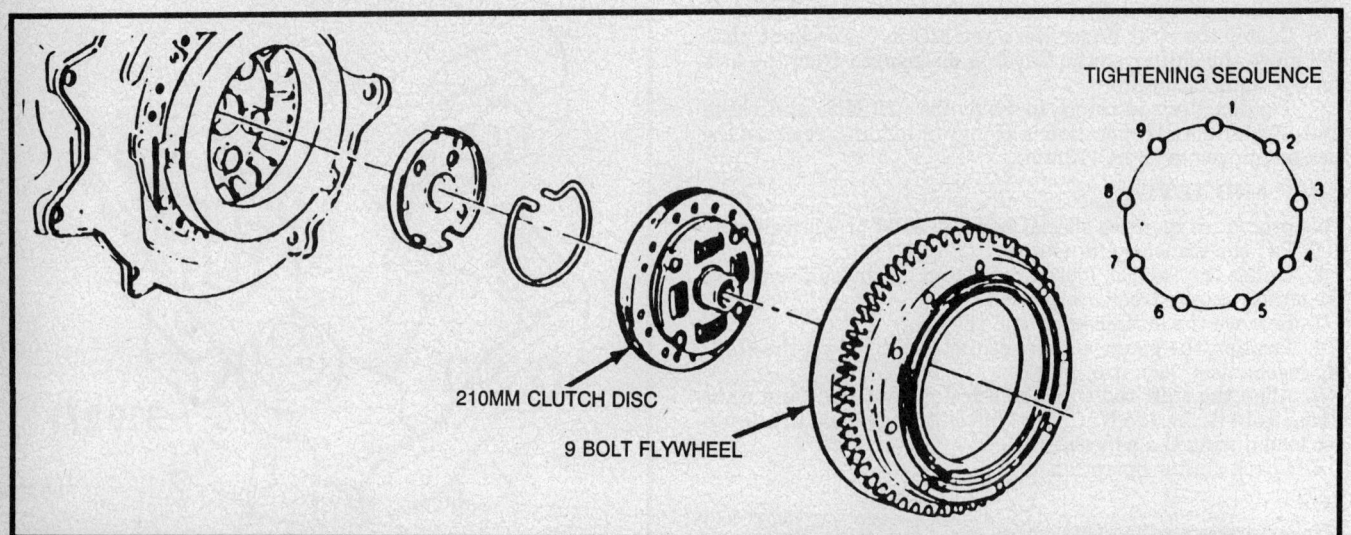

TIGHTENING SEQUENCE

210MM CLUTCH DISC

9 BOLT FLYWHEEL

Clutch assembly on Golf, Jetta, Scirocco and Cabriolet

Pedal Height/Free-Play Adjustment

HYDRAULIC CLUTCH

If equipped with hydraulic clutch linkage, the slave cylinder has a bleeder screw to purge air from the system. The clutch pedal linkage rod is adjustable to maintain proper pedal height; 10mm above brake pedal.

ADJUSTABLE CABLE

NOTE: On cable clutches, there is a special tool US5043 or equivalent, which can be used to determine proper adjustment, however proper adjustment can be accomplished without it.

1. Depress the clutch pedal several times.
2. Pull the cable adjusting sleeve up at the transaxle until resistance is felt and insert the gauge or measure the clearance.
3. Loosen the locknut and turn the adjusting sleeve until there is no free play at the gauge. Without the gauge, this distance should be 0.472 in. (12mm).
4. Tighten the locknut and operate the pedal several times. Recheck the adjustment.

SELF-ADJUSTING CABLES

1. If the cable is being reinstalled, compress the spring and hold the cable in place on the transaxle. A 2nd person is required to attach the cable to the clutch lever.
2. If a new cable is being installed, there is a strap holding the spring in place. Remove the strap after the cable is in place.
3. Operate the pedal several times to adjust the cable.

Removal and Installation

EXCEPT SELF-ADJUSTING

1. Loosen the adjustment.
2. Disengage the cable at the lever arm, noting the placement of the parts.

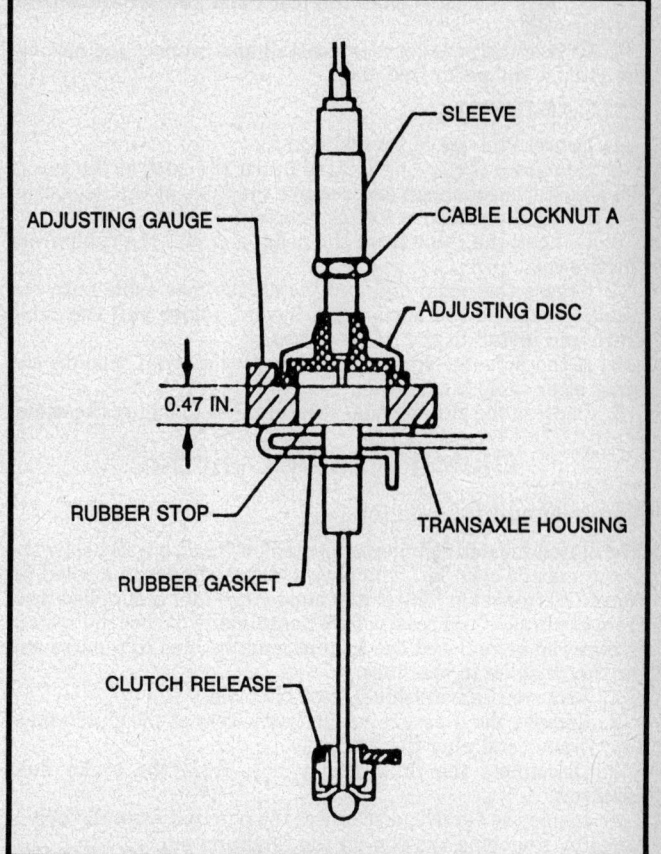

Clutch adjstment on cable clutch

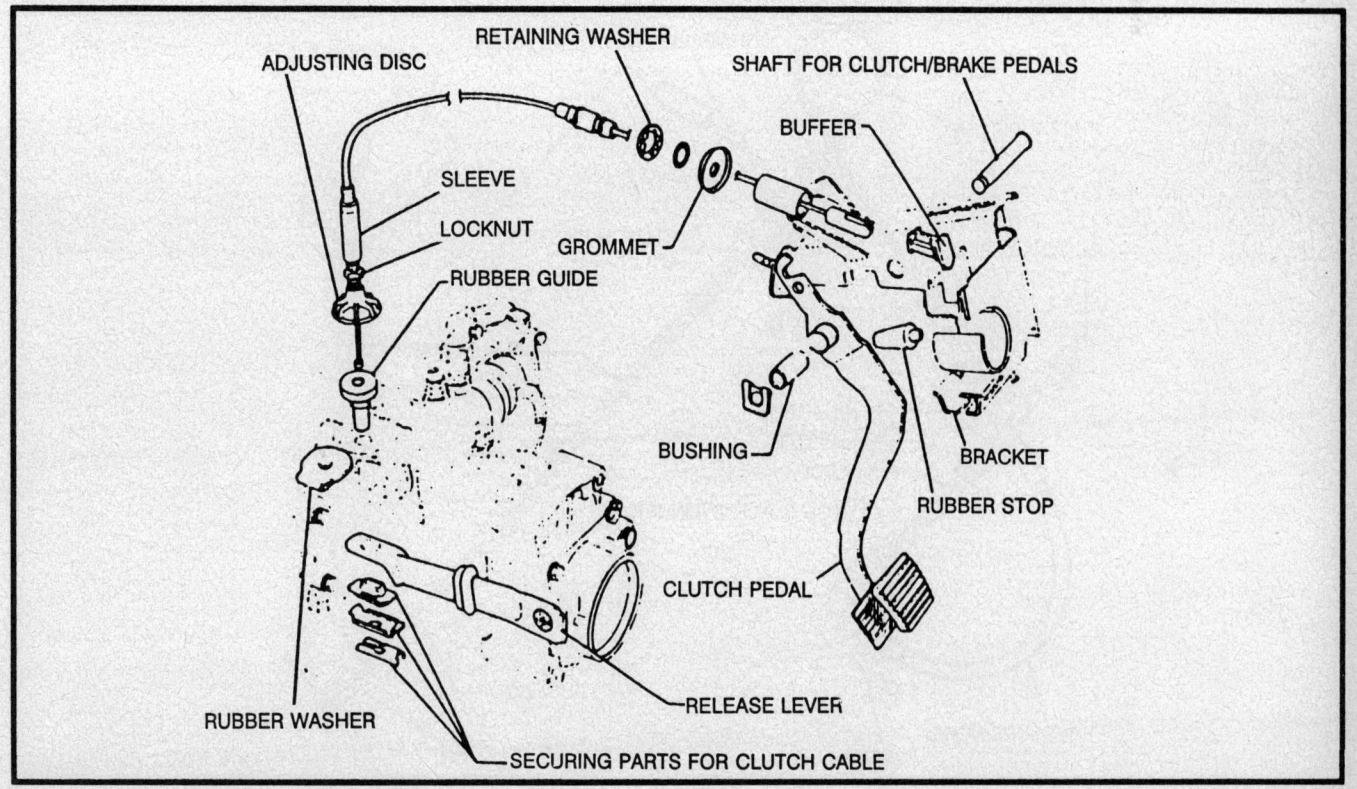

Clutch pedal and cable assembly

3. Unhook the cable from the pedal and pull the cable from the firewall.

4. Grease the pedal end and install and connect the new cable. Adjust the pedal free-play.

SELF-ADJUSTING

1. Depress the pedal several times.

2. Compress the spring located under the boot at the top of the adjuster mechanism and remove the cable at the release lever, noting the placement of the parts.

3. Unhook the cable from the pedal and pull the cable from the firewall.

4. Grease the pedal end and install the new cable onto the pedal. Compress the spring and have a helper pull the cable down and install to the release lever.

5. If the adjuster spring is retained by a strap, remove the strap after cable installation.

6. Depress the clutch pedal several times to adjust the cable.

Clutch Master Cylinder

Removal and Installation

The clutch master cylinder is located on the fire wall below the brake master cylinder. The clutch slave cylinder is located on top of the transaxle. The clutch master cylinder is supplied fluid from the brake fluid reservoir. Whenever any part of the system is removed or replaced the system must be bled to remove any air that may be in the lines.

1. Remove the windshield washer bottle.

2. Remove the pressure line from the rear of the clutch master cylinder and plug the fitting.

3. Disconnect the fluid supply hose from the brake fluid reservoir.

4. Inside the vehicle, disconnect the pushrod from the clutch pedal by removing the clip on the retaining pin.

5. Remove the 2 mounting nuts and remove the cylinder from the vehicle.

To install:

6. To install, insert the pushrod through the firewall, install new nuts and torque to 5 ft. lbs. (7 Nm). Pin the rod to the pedal and install the clip.

7. Install the supply line to the brake master cylinder and install the pressure line to the rear of the clutch master cylinder.

8. Fill the brake reservoir and bleed the clutch system.

Clutch Slave Cylinder

Removal and Installation

1. Raise and safely support the vehicle.

2. Disconnect and plug the pressure line to the slave cylinder.

3. Remove the slave cylinder by removing the spring pin and clip from the transaxle.

4. To install, align the slave cylinder on the transaxle housing and insert the spring pin and clip. Then bolt up the cylinder.

5. Connect the pressure line and lower the vehicle.

6. Fill the brake reservoir and bleed the system.

Hydraulic Clutch System Bleeding

1. The clutch and brakes share the same reservoir. Clean all dirt and grease from the cap to make sure no foreign subtances enter the system.

2. Remove the cap and diaphragm and fill the reservoir to the top with the approved DOT brake fluid. Fully loosen the bleed screw which is in the slave cylinder body next to the inlet connection.

3. At this point bubbles of air will appear at the bleed screw outlet. When the slave cylinder is full and a steady stream of fluid comes out of the slave cylinder bleeder, tighten the bleed screw.

4. Refill the reservoir and cap it. Exert a light load of about 20 lbs. to the slave cylinder piston by pushing the release lever towards the cylinder and loosen the bleed screw. Maintain a con-

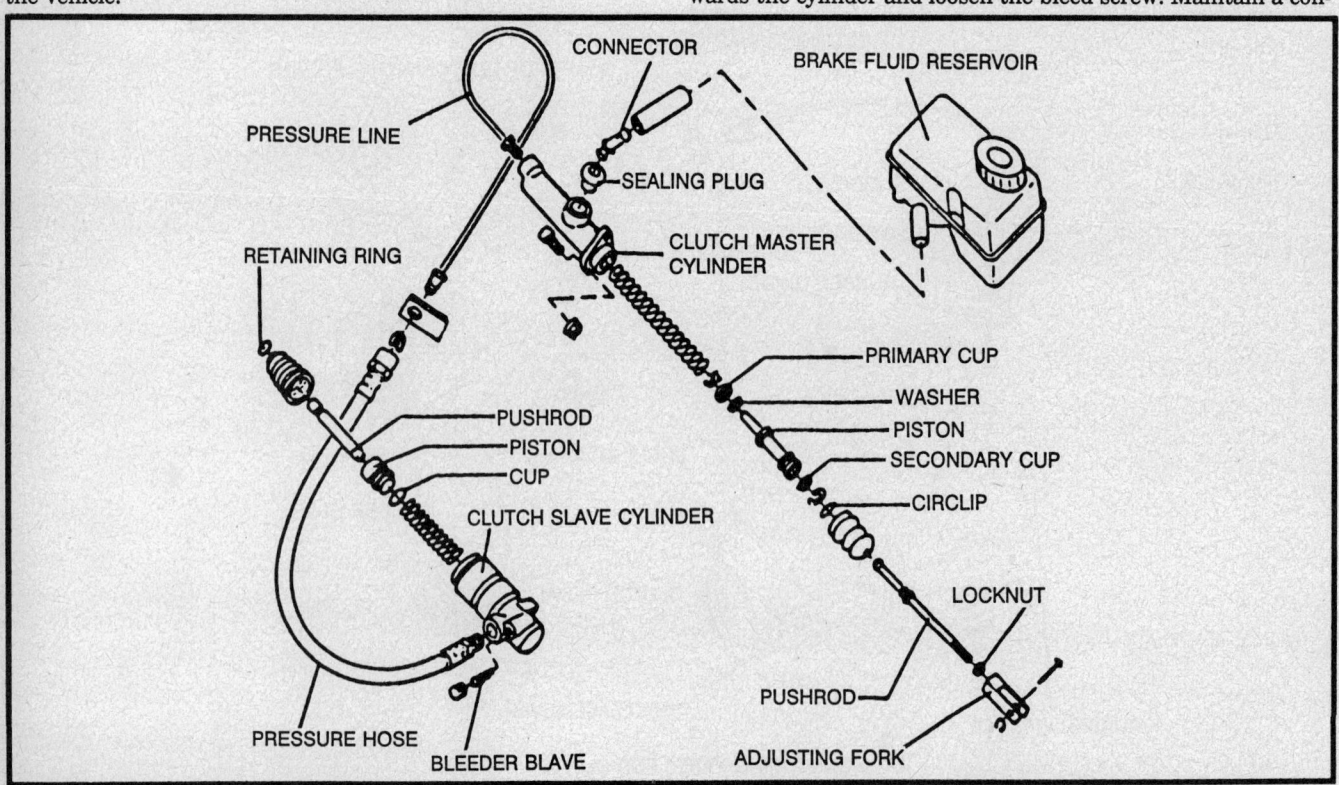

Hydraulic clutch components

stant light load, fluid and any air that is left will be expelled through the bleed port. Tighten the bleed screw when a steady flow of fluid and no air is being expelled.

5. Fill the reservoir fluid level back to normal capacity and if necessary repeat Step 4.

6. Exert a light load to the release lever but do not open the bleeder screw as the piston in the slave cylinder will move slowly

down the bore. Repeat this operation 2–3 times, the fluid movement will force any air left in the system into the reservoir. The hydraulic system should now be fully bled.

7. Check the the operation of the clutch hydraulic system and repeat this procedure, if necessary. Check the pushrod travel at the slave cylinder to insure the minimum travel 0.57 in. (15mm).

AUTOMATIC TRANSAXLE

For further information, please refer to "Professional Transmission Repair Manual" for additional coverage.

Transaxle Assembly

Removal and Installation

PASSAT

1. If equipped with electronically theft-protected radios, obtain the security code before disconnecting the battery.

2. Disconnect the battery and the speedometer drive and plug the hole in the transaxle.

3. Remove the upper engine-to-transaxle bolts.

4. Raise and safely support the vehicle and remove the front wheels. Connect the engine sling tool VW-10–222A or equivalent, to the cylinder head and just take the weight of the engine off the mounts. On 16 valve engine, the idle stabilizer valve must be removed to attach the tool. Do not try to support the engine from below.

5. Put the shifter in park and disconnect the shift cable and all of the electrical connections.

6. Clamp and remove the hoses at the transaxle cooler.

7. Remove the starter and the engine's left and right mounts.

8. Remove the skid plate and disconnect the halfshafts from the drive flanges. Hang them from the body with wire.

9. Remove the torque converter plate and turn the engine as needed to remove the torque converter-to-flywheel bolts.

10. Remove the remaining transmission mounts and lower the hoist slightly.

11. Support the transaxle with a jack and remove the remaining engine-to-transaxle bolts. Be careful to secure the torque converter so it does not fall out of the transaxle.

12. Carefully lower the transaxle out of the vehicle.

13. Installation is the reverse of removal, using the following torque values:

    M12 Bolts—59 ft. lbs. (80 Nm).
    M10 Bolts—44 ft. lbs. (60 Nm).
    Torque converter bolts—44 ft. lbs. (60 Nm).
    Left side bracket-to-transaxle—18 ft. lbs. (25 Nm).
    Bracket to mount—44 ft. lbs. (60 Nm).
    Halfshaft bolts—33 ft. lbs. (45 Nm).

GOLF, JETTA, SCIROCCO AND CABRIOLET

1. If equipped with electronically theft-protected radios, obtain the security code before disconnecting the battery.

2. Disconnect the battery and the speedometer drive and plug the hole in the transaxle.

3. On Golf and Jetta, with the vehicle on the ground, remove the front axle nuts.

4. Raise and safely support the vehicle and remove the front wheels. Connect the engine sling tool VW-10–222A or equivalent, to the cylinder head and just take the weight of the engine off the mounts. On 16 valve engine, the idle stabilizer valve must be removed to attach the tool. Do not try to support the engine from below.

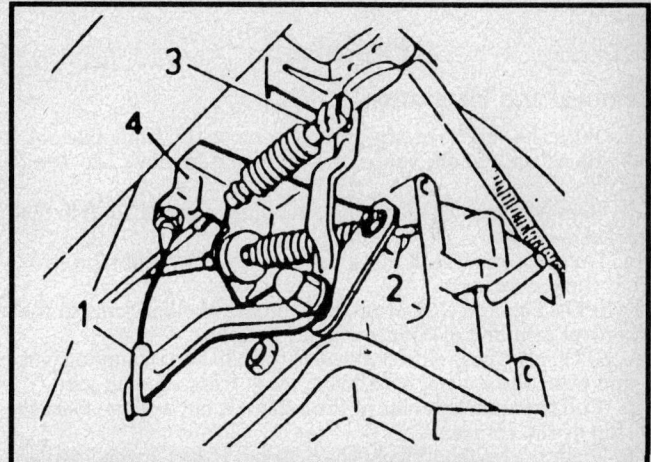

Remove No. 4—leave 1, 2 and 3 attached

5. Remove the driver's side rear transaxle mount and support bracket.

6. On Golf and Jetta, remove the front mount bolts from the transaxle and from the body and remove the mount as a complete assembly.

7. Remove the selector and accelerator cables from the transaxle lever but leave them attached to the bracket. Remove the bracket assembly to save the adjustment.

8. Unbolt the halfshafts from the drive flanges. On Golf and Jetta, the shafts must be removed, which may require separating the ball joints from the wheel bearing housing to gain the necessary clearance. Remove the ball joint clamping bolt.

9. Remove the heat shield and brackets and remove the starter. On Scirocco and Cabriolet, the front mount comes off with the starter.

10. Turn the engine as needed to remove the torque converter-to-flywheel bolts.

11. Remove the remaining transmission mounts and, on Golf and Jetta, the subframe bolts and allow the subframe to hang free.

12. Support the transaxle with a jack and remove the remaining engine-to-transaxle bolts. Be careful to secure the torque converter so it does not fall out of the transaxle.

13. Carefully lower the transaxle from the vehicle.

To install:

14. When reinstalling, take extra care to make sure the torque converter is fully seated on the pump shaft splines. The converter should be recessed into the bell housing and turn by hand. Keep checking that it still turns while drawing the engine and transaxle together with the bolts.

15. Installation is the reverse of removal, using the following torque values:

    Transaxle to engine—55 ft. lbs. (75 Nm).
    Torque converter bolts—26 ft. lbs. (35 Nm).

Halfshaft to flange—33 ft. lbs. (45 Nm).
Ball joint clamping bolts—37 ft. lbs. (50 Nm).

Shift/Throttle Linkage Adjustment

1. With the engine warm, gear selector in **P**, loosen the adjusting nut and disconnect the accelerator pedal cable from the transaxle.
2. On the intake plenum, loosen the nuts on the cable bracket and move the sleeve away from the throttle to take up any play.

The throttle must remain closed.
3. Turn the nut on the throttle side of the bracket up to the bracket and tighten the other nut against the bracket. Be sure the throttle is still against it's stop.
4. Reconnect the cable to the transmission and have an assistant push the gas pedal to the floor.
5. Push the transaxle lever against the stop and turn the adjusting nut to remove all slack from the cable. Tighten the locknut, release the pedal and push it again to check adjustment.

DRIVE AXLE

Halfshaft

Removal and Installation

1. With the vehicle on the ground, remove the front axle nut.
2. Raise and safely support vehicle and remove the front wheels.
3. Remove the socket head bolts retaining the halfshaft to the transaxle flange.
4. On some vehicles, it may be necessary to seperate the strut from the control arm.
    a. On Fox and Quamtum, matchmark the ball joint to the control arm and disconnect the strut there.
    b. On all other vehicles, remove the ball joint clamping bolt and push the control arm down, away from the ball joint.
5. Pull the transaxle side of the halfshaft out and up, place it on top of the transaxle.
6. Push the halfshaft from the bearing. Use of a wheel puller may be required.
7. Before reinstalling, apply a thread locking compound to the outer ¼ in. of the spline.
8. Installation is the reverse of removal. Always use a new center axle nut. If suspension was disconnected, check front end alignment.
9. Torque the inner axle bolts to 25–33 ft. lbs. (34–45 Nm). The center axle nut should be tightened to 175 ft. lbs. (240 Nm) on Fox and Quantum and Scirocco/Cabriolet or 195 ft. lbs. (265 Nm) on Golf, Jetta, Passat and Corrado.

Driveshaft and U-Joints

Removal and Installation

The Quantum Syncro has a driveshaft connecting the transaxle to the rear differential. A special tool, VW3139 or equivalent, is used as a retainer to keep the shaft from flexing and overloading the center U-joint and bearing. Use of this tool or a suitable substitute is required for proper alignment during installation. No parts are available for repairs, the shaft must be replaced as a unit.

When installing the driveshaft mounted in the retaining tool, the distance from the center bearing bracket to the body must be no more than 0.120 in. (3mm). Shims are available for adjusting this dimension.

Front Wheel Hub, Knuckle and Bearing

Removal and Installation

FOX AND QUANTUM

The strut must be removed but no spring compressor is needed. The hub and bearing are pressed into the strut and the bearing cannot be reused once the hub has been removed.

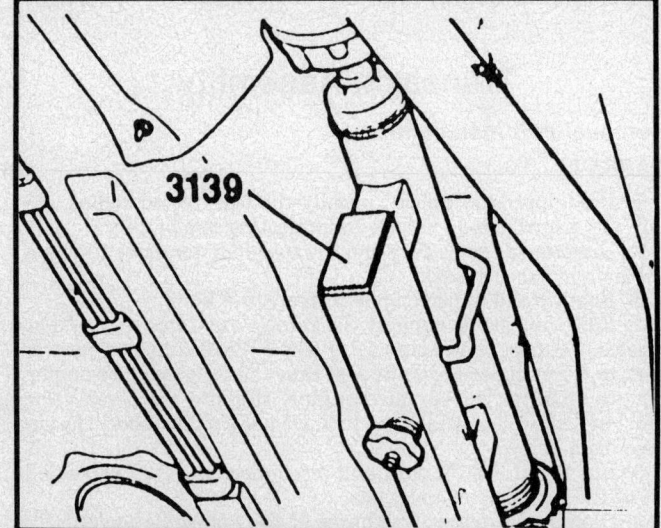

Driveshaft support tool in place

1. With the vehicle on the ground, remove the front axle nut.
2. Raise and safely support the vehicle and remove the wheels.
3. Remove the brake caliper from the strut and hang from the body it with wire. Detach the brake line from the strut and remove the caliper carrier and rotor.
4. At the tie rod end, remove the cotter pin, back off the castellated nut and remove the end from the strut with a puller.
5. Loosen the stabilizer bar bushings and detach the end from the strut being removed.
6. Remove the ball joint clamp bolt and ball joint from the strut.
7. On some vehicles, the halfshaft spline is secured into the hub with thread sealer. The best way to remove it is to push it out with a wheel puller. Do not use heat, this will ruin the bearing. Pull the strut away from the halfshaft.
8. The strut is now hanging from the fender. Remove the upper strut-to-fender retaining nut and lower the strut assembly down and from the vehicle.

EXCEPT FOX AND QUANTUM

1. With the vehicle on the ground, remove the front axle nut.
2. Raise and safely support the vehicle and remove the front wheels.
3. Detatch the brake line from the strut and remove the caliper. Hang it from the body with wire.
4. Remove the caliper carrier and brake rotor.
5. Remove the cotter pin and nut and press out the tie rod end. A small puller is required.

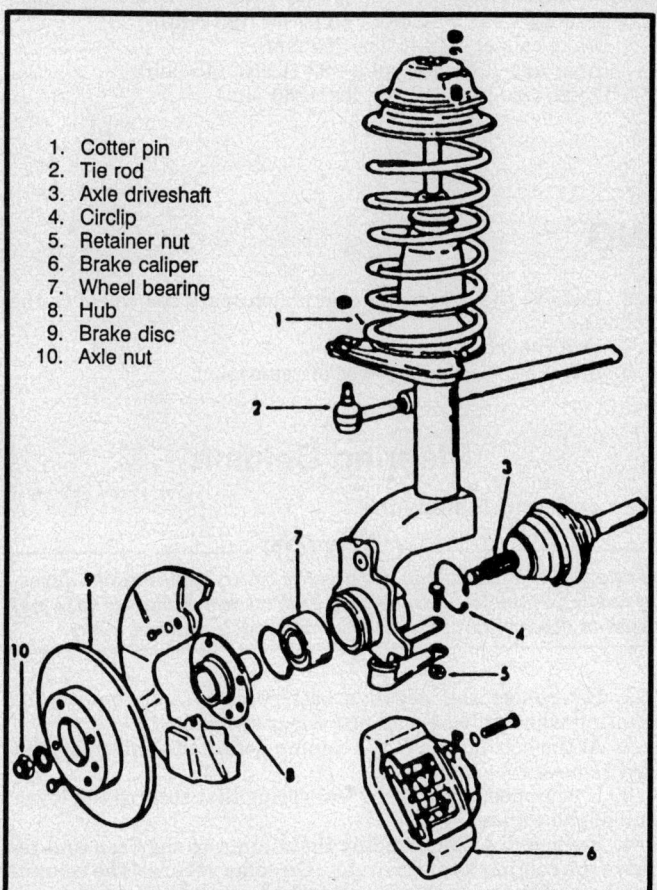

1. Cotter pin
2. Tie rod
3. Axle driveshaft
4. Circlip
5. Retainer nut
6. Brake caliper
7. Wheel bearing
8. Hub
9. Brake disc
10. Axle nut

Front suspension components—Fox and Quantum

Camber adjusting washers; mark carefully

6. Remove the ball joint clamp bolt and push the control arm down to disengage the ball joint.

7. Front wheel camber is set with eccentric washers on the bolts holding the bearing housing to the strut. Clean and mark the position of these washers so they can be reinstalled in the same position.

8. Remove the bolts and take the bearing housing off the strut.

9. To remove the hub, place a set of parallel rail blocks on an arbor press and place the strut assembly on top of the tools with the hub facing down.

10. Stack tools VW–295A, VW–420 and VW–412 or equivalents in order on top of the hub and press it out.

11. If the inner bearing race stayed on the hub, clamp the hub in a vise and use a bearing puller to remove it.

12. On the strut, remove the splash shield and internal snaprings from the bearing housing.

13. With the strut in the same pressing position, stack tools VW–519, VW–432 and VW–409 or equivalent, in order on the outer race of the bearing and press it out.

14. Clean the bearing housing and hub with a wire brush and inspect all parts. Replace parts that have been discolored from heat.

15. The new bearing is pressed in from the hub side. Install the snaphing and support the bearing housing on the press.

16. Using VW–511 or equivalent, the old bearing, press the new bearing into the housing up against the snapring. Make sure the press tool contacts only the outer race of the bearing.

17. Install the outer snapring and splash shield.

18. Support the inner race on the press with VW–519 or equivalent, and press the hub into the bearing.

19. Spin the hub by hand. The grease in the new bearing will be stiff but noise or roughness indicates damage to the bearing during installation.

20. To complete the installation, reverse the removal procedures. Always use a new axle nut.

21. Torque the following components:
Ball joint clamping bolt—37 ft. lbs. (50 Nm).
Tie rod end—26 ft. lbs. (35 Nm).
Brake caliper carrier—52 ft. lbs. (50 Nm).
Axle nut—175 ft. lbs. (237 Nm)—Scirocco, Cabriolet, Fox and Quantum.
Axle nut—195 ft. lbs. (265 Nm)—Passat, Corrado, Golf and Jetta.

Rear Axle Shafts/Stub Axles

Removal and Installation

EXCEPT QUANTUM SYNCRO

1. Raise and safely support the vehicle and remove the rear wheels.

2. On drum brakes, insert a small pry tool through one of the wheel bolt holes and push the adjusting wedge up. On disc brakes, remove the caliper and carrier. Hang the caliper from the spring with wire.

3. Remove the grease cap, cotter pin, locknut, adjusting nut, thrust washer, wheel bearing and brake drum or disc.

4. On drum brakes, disconnect and plug the brake line.

5. Remove the brake backing plate, with the brakes attached, and the stub axle.

6. When reinstalling the wheel bearing nut, the thrust washer must still move with a small pry tool. Don't forget to bleed the drum brakes.

7. Torque the following:
Stub axle/Back plate on Golf and Jetta—52 ft. lbs. (70 Nm).
Stub axle/Back plate on all others—44 ft. lbs. (60 Nm).
Disc brake caliper—48 ft. lbs. (65 Nm).

QUANTUM SYNCRO

The Quantum Syncro is a 4WD vehicle with similar bearing installations both front and rear. To remove the rear bearing, the control arm must be removed.

1. With the vehicle on the ground, loosen the axle nut.

2. Raise and safely support the vehicle and remove the wheels.

3. Remove the bolts retaining the axle shaft to the differential and slide the axle shaft from the vehicle.

4. Remove the disc brake caliper and support aside, do not hang it by the brake lines.

5. Unbolt the stabilizer bar from the control arm.

6. Remove the lower shock mount bolt and the control arm mounting bolts and lower the arm from the vehicle.

7. The bearing and hub can now be pressed out using the same procedure as the front bearing.

8. Installation is the reverse of removal.
9. Torque the following:
Control arm bolts—88 ft. lbs. (120 Nm).
Lower shock mount—48 ft. lbs. (65 Nm).

Stabilizer bar brackets—18 ft. lbs. (25 Nm).
Brake caliper—48 ft. lbs. (65 Nm).
Inner axle CV-joint bolts—33 ft. lbs. (45 Nm).
Outer axle nut—170 ft. lbs. (230 Nm).

STEERING

Steering Wheel

CAUTION

If equipped with an air bag, the negative battery cable must be disconnected for 20 minutes before working on the system. Failure to do so may result in deployment of the air bag and possible personal injury. An air bag is an explosive device. Handle with extreme caution. Read and follow these safety precautions.

Precautions

- Always disconnect the battery before beginning work on the air bag system and wait 20 minutes for the capacitor to discharge. The system is still considered armed while the capacitor is charged. Use of a computer memory saver will keep the capacitor charged.
- Air bag components must not be repaired or opened. Always use new parts.
- Always place a removed air bag unit with the horn pad facing up.
- Do not leave a removed air bag unit unattended. Reinstall into vehicle as soon as possible.
- The unit must not be exposed to grease, fluids, or cleaning agents.
- The unit must not be exposed to temperatures above 194°F (90°C) at any time. Even the heat of a soldering iron can damage or ignite the charge.
- Any testing on the air bag system must be done with the air bag installed in the vehicle. Use only Volkswagen test equipment and procedure specified with that equipment's instruction manual.
- Storage and transport of air bags is subject to rules governing explosive
devices and should be done only in the original package.
- Failure to follow these safety precautions may result in personal injury through accidental firing of the air bag, or through failure of the air bag in an accident.

Removal and Installation
WITH AIR BAG

1. Disconnect battery, wait 20 minutes.
2. Remove the Torx® head screws at the back of the steering wheel.
3. Carefully detach the airbag unit from the wheel and disconnect the wire at the center.
4. Place unit in a safe place, horn pad up.
5. Point front wheels straight ahead, remove ignition key to lock steering column and remove the nut and spring washer.
6. Mark the position of the wheel to the spindle and pull the wheel straight off.
7. Installation is the reverse of removal. Torque the steering wheel nut to 30 ft. lbs. (40 Nm). When installing the air bag, use new Torx screws and tighten to 7.5 ft. lbs. (10 Nm.). Do not over torque or air bag malfunction could result.

WITHOUT AIR BAG

1. Remove the horn pad.
2. Remove the ignition key and turn the wheel until it locks.

3. Remove the center nut and match mark the wheel to the splines.
4. Pull the wheel straight off.
5. Installation is the reverse of removal.

Steering Column

Removal and Installation

CAUTION

If equipped with an air bag, the negative battery cable must be disconnected for 20 minutes before working on the system. Failure to do so may result in deployment of the air bag and possible personal injury.

1. Disconnect the negative battery cable and remove the steering wheel, turn signal and wiper switches.
2. At the bottom end of the column, locate the universal joint and remove the clamp bolt.
3. If equipped, pry out the leaf spring that secures the lower end of the column.
4. Remove the bolts holding the column to the dash and remove the column as an assembly. On some vehicles, the column is attached to the dash with shear bolts with heads that break off at a specific torque. Removing these bolts is similar to removing broken studs. If a drill is being used, be carefull not to damage the threads in the dash. These bolts are torqued to only 18 ft. lbs. (25 Nm).
5. Installation is the reverse of removal.

NOTE: Adjustable height steering columns are not repairable and must be replaced as a unit.

Manual Steering Rack

Adjustment

On some vehicles, there is a rack and pinion free-play adjustment screw and locknut, however this is not always accessible with the rack installed in the vehicle. Loosen the locknut and adjust the screw to allow smooth, non-binding movement of the rack.

Removal and Installation

1. Raise and safely support the vehicle.
2. Remove both front wheels and disengage both tie rod ends.
3. At the steering column, remove the boot clamp, push the boot towards the body and remove the clamp bolt from the universal joint.
4. Remove the rack mounting nuts and remove the rack from it's mounts.
5. At this point on some vehicles, the rack cannot be removed from the body. Support the engine/transmission and remove the subframe bolts or the rear transaxle mount and bracket to allow the rack to move towards the rear.
6. Installation is the reverse of removal. Torque the subframe bolts to 96 ft. lbs. (130 Nm).

Power Steering Rack

Adjustment

On some vehicles, there is a rack and pinion free-play adjustment screw and locknut, however this is not always accessible with the rack installed in the vehicle. Loosen the locknut and adjust the screw to allow smooth, non-binding movement of the rack.

Removal and Installation

1. Raise and safely support the vehicle.
2. Remove both front wheels and disengage both tie rod ends.
3. Remove the low pressure (sucton) hose from the pump and drain the system into a catch pan. Properly discard fluid.
4. At the steering column, remove the boot clamp, push the boot towards the body and remove the clamp bolt from the universal joint.
5. On Scirocco and Cabriolet, remove the exhaust manifold and shift linkage bracket.
6. Remove the rack mounting nuts and remove the rack from it's mounts.
7. At this point on some vehicles, the rack cannot be removed from the body. Support the engine/transaxle and remove the subframe bolts to allow the rack to move towards the rear. On Scirocco and Cabriolet, remove the transmission mount and bracket.
8. Disconnect the power steering lines and remove the rack.
9. Installation is reverse of removal. Torque the subframe bolts to 96 ft. lbs. (130 Nm). Don't forget to refill and bleed the system using the correct steering fluid.

Power Steering Pump

Removal and Installation

1. Remove the suction hose and the pressure line from the pump, drain the fluid a the catch pan. Properly discard the fluid.
2. Loosen the tensioning bolt at the front of the tensioning bracket and remove the drive belt from the pump's drive pulley.
3. Remove the pump's mounting bolts and lift the pump from the vehicle.

4. To install, reverse the removal procedures. Torque the mounting bolts to 15 ft. lbs. (20 Nm). Tension the drive belt. Fill the reservoir with approved power steering fluid and bleed the system.

Belt Adjustment

To tension the drive belt, adjust the tensioner bolt, so the belt will flex ½ in. under light thumb pressure.

System Bleeding

1. With the wheels turned all the way to the left, add power steering fluid to the **COLD** mark on the fluid level indicator.
2. Start the engine and run at fast idle momentarily, shut engine off and recheck fluid level. If necessary add fluid to to bring level to the **COLD** mark.
3. Start the engine and bleed the system by turning the wheels from side to side without hitting the stops.

NOTE: Fluid with air in it has a light tan or red appearance.

4. Return the wheels to the center position and keep the engine running for 2–3 minutes.
5. Road test the vehicle and recheck the fluid level making sure it is at the **HOT** mark.

Tie Rod Ends

Removal and Installation

1. Raise and safely support the vehicle and remove the front wheels.
2. Remove the cotter pin and nut and press out the tie rod end. A small puller is required.
3. Hold the tie rod with a small pipe wrench or locking pliers and loosen the locking nut.
4. Back the nut away from the rod end far enough to mark the threads at the rod end with a crayon or chaulk, then unscrew the end off of the rod.
5. When installing the new tie rod end, screw it onto the rod up to the mark on the threads. When tightening the locknut, hold the tie rod end and tighten the nut securely against it.

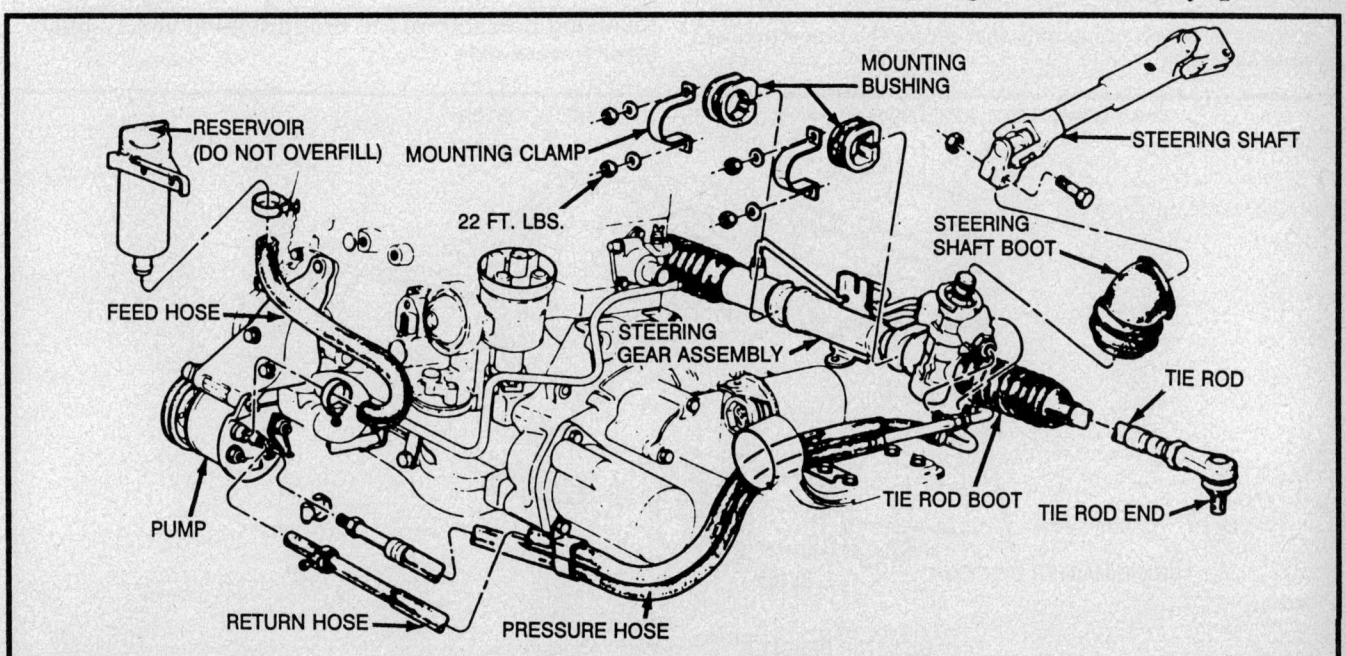

Power steering assembly

6. Reinstall the tie rod end into the steering knuckle, torque the nut to 22 ft. lbs. (30 Nm) and install a cotter pin.

7. With the wheels on, put the vehicle back on the ground and roll it back and forth to settle the suspension. Then check toe adjustment

NOTE: On some vehicles, only the right tie rod is adjustable.

BRAKES

Master Cylinder

Removal and Installation
WITHOUT ABS

1. Disconnect and plug the brake lines.
2. Disconnect the electrical plug from the sending unit for the low fluid switch.
3. Remove the 2 master cylinder mounting nuts.
4. Lift the master cylinder and reservoir from the engine compartment.

—————————— CAUTION ——————————
Do not depress the brake pedal while any component is removed. System damage or personal injury may result.
————————————————————————

5. Remove the reservoir. The reservoir is held into the master cylinder by a press fit into rubber sealing plugs and can easily be pulled off. To reinstall, moisted the plugs with brake fluid and press it on.
6. To install, position the master cylinder and reservoir assembly onto the mounting studs on the booster and install the washers and nuts. Tighten the nuts to 15 ft. lbs. (20 Nm).
7. Remove the plugs and connect the brake lines.
8. Bleed the entire brake system.

Proportioning Valve

Removal and Installation

1. Raise and safely support the vehicle.
2. Using a line wrench, loosen the lines to the proportioning valve.
3. Remove the retaining nuts that secure the proportioning valve to the frame.

4. Installation is the reverse of removal.
5. Bleed the brake system.

Power Brake Booster

Removal and Installation

1. Remove the master cylinder from in front of the booster.
2. In the driver's compartment, remove the clevis pin on the end of the booster pushrod by unclipping it and pulling it from the clevis.
3. On the gasoline engine vehicles, remove the vacuum line running from the booster to intake manifold. On diesel engine, the line connects to a vacuum pump located where the distributor on a gasoline engine would be. Remove the line.
4. Unbolt the booster; remove the 2 nuts from inside the driver's compartment or the 4 nuts holding the booster to its bracket. Remove the booster.

Relieving pressure at the proportioning valve—push lever toward axle

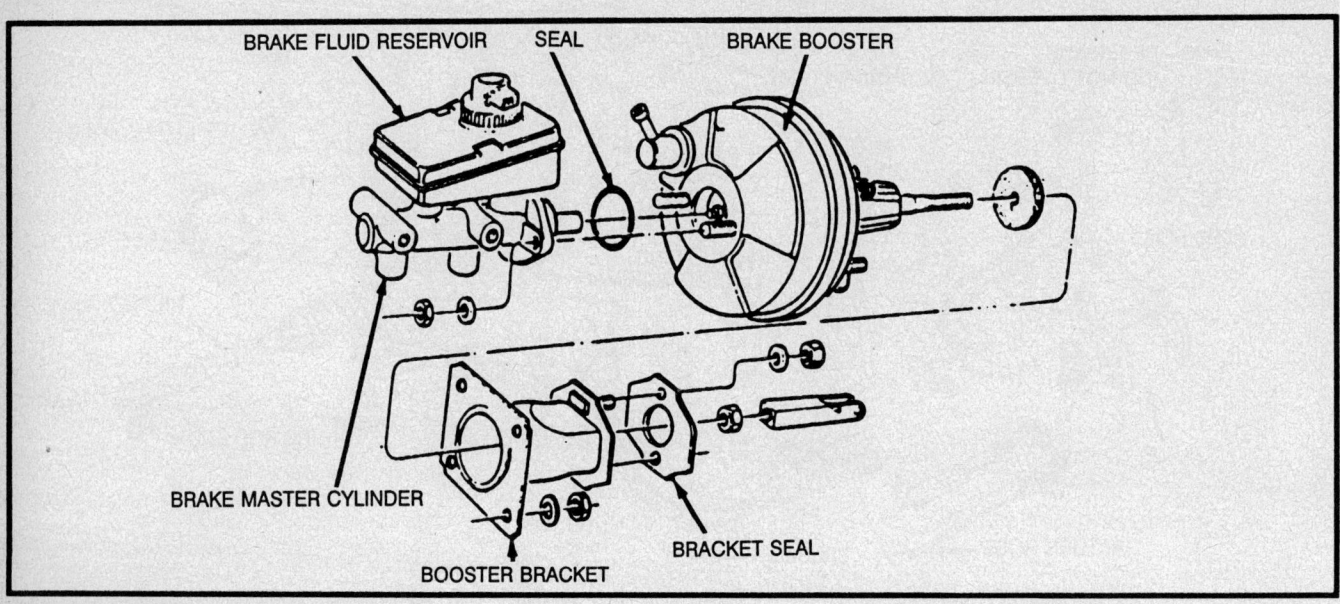

Master clyinder vond brake boos¡er

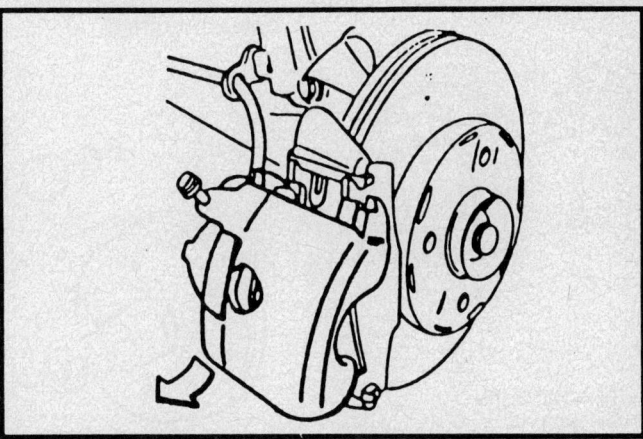

Caliper removal

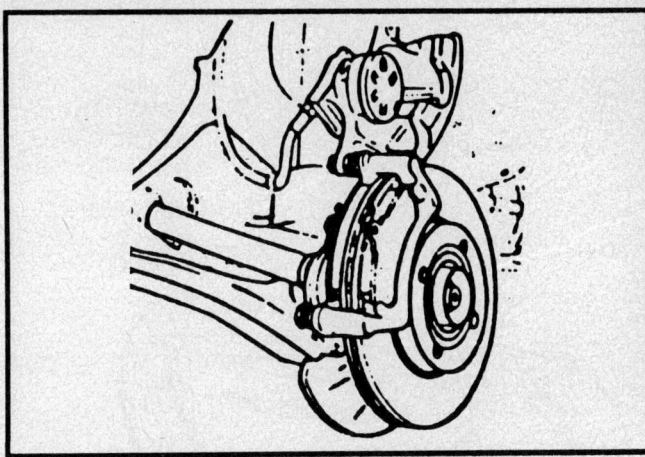

Girling caliper positioned for pad removal

Collapsing the caliper piston

5. The brake booster cannot be repaired and must be replaced as a unit.
6. Installation is the reverse of removal.
7. Install the master cylinder and bleed the system.

Disc Brake Caliper and Pads

Removal and Installation

1. Raise and safely support the vehicle and remove the front wheels.
2. Remove a sufficient quantity of brake fluid from the master cylinder reservoir to prevent it from over flowing when installng the pads. This is necessary as the caliper piston must be forced into the cylinder bore to provide sufficient clearance to install new pads.
3. Remove the lower caliper mounting bolt while holding the guide pin. Push the caliper up and swing it out from the bottom.
4. Note the position of the anti-rattle springs. Remove the pads from the pad carrier and note the position of the short and long pad. Remove any anti-squeek shims or heat shields behind the pads and note their positions.

To install:

5. Install the anti-rattle hardware and then the pads in their proper positions.
6. Using a suitable tool, push the caliper piston into the bore.
7. Install any pad shims.
8. Swing the caliper down and tighten the caliper mounting bolts to 26 ft. lbs.
9. Refill the master cylinder with fresh brake fluid.
10. Install the wheels and then pump the brake pedal several times to bring the pads into adjustment. Road test the vehicle.

Brake Rotor

Removal and Installation

FRONT DISC BRAKES

1. Raise and safely support vehicle and remove the wheel.
2. With the wheel removed, the rotor is held in place only with a countersunk screw threaded into the hub.
3. Remove the brake caliper, pads, pad carrier and rotor.
4. When reinstalling, torque the carrier bolts to 53 ft. lbs. (70 Nm). Before installing the rotor screw, lightly coat the threads with an anti-seize lubricant.
5. Reinstall the brake pads and caliper and pump the brake pedal several times to bring the pads into adjustment. Road test the vehicle.

REAR DISC BRAKES

1. Raise and safely support the vehicle and remove the wheels.
2. Remove a sufficient quantity of brake fluid from the master cylinder reservoir to prevent it from over flowing when installng the pads. This is necessary as the caliper piston must be forced into the cylinder bore to provide sufficient clearance to install new pads.
3. Remove the parking brake cable clip from the caliper. Remove the parking brake cable.
4. Remove the upper mounting bolt from the brake caliper.
5. Swing the housing downward and remove the brake pads.
6. Check the rotor for scoring and resurface or replace as necessary. Check the caliper for fluid leaks or cracked boots. If any damage is found, the caliper will require overhauling or replacement.

To install:

NOTE: **When replacing brake pads, always replace both pads on both sides of the vehicle. Mixed pads will cause uneven braking.**

7. Retract the piston into the housing by rotating the piston clockwise using a 12mm Allen wrench.
8. Carefully clean the anchor plate and install the new brake pads onto the pad carrier.
9. Install the caliper to pad carrier using a new self locking bolt and torque to 26 ft. lbs.
10. Fasten the hand brake cable to the caliper. It may be necessary to back off the adjustment nuts at the hand brake handle.
11. Fill the reservoir with brake fluid and pump the brake pedal about 40 times with the engine off to set the piston. Setting the piston with the power assist could cause the piston to jam.
12. Check the parking brake operation, adjust the cable, if necessary.
13. Road test the vehicle.

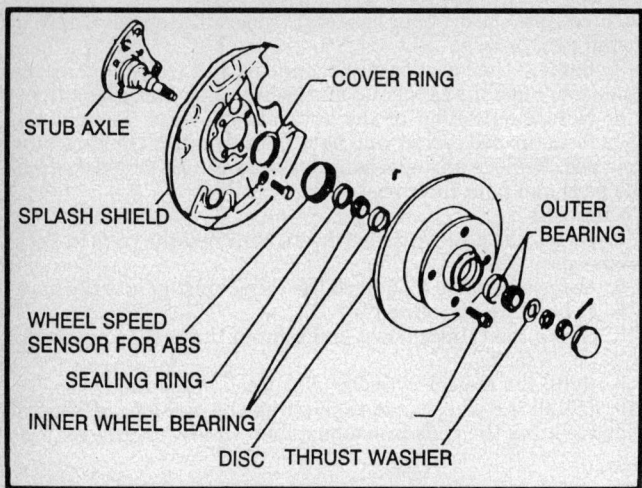

Rear wheel bearing assembly on disc brake

Brake Drums

Removal and Installation

1. Raise and safely support vehicle and remove the rear wheels.
2. Insert a small pry tool through a wheel bolt hole and push up on the adjusting wedge to slacken the rear brake adjustment.
3. Remove the grease cap, cotter pin, locking ring, axle nut and thrust washer. Carefully remove the bearing and put all these parts where they will stay clean.
4. Carefully remove the drum.
5. Before installing, if any brake dust has fallen onto the axle, wipe off all the axle grease and put new high temperature bearing grease on. Installation is reverse of removal.

NOTE: When tightening the axle nut, the thrust washer must still be movable with a small pry tool. Spin the drum and check the axle nut and thrust washer again.

6. When installing the locking ring, keep trying different positions of the ring on the nut until the cotter pin goes into the hole. Don't turn the nut to align the locking ring with the hole in the axle. Use a new cotter pin. Install the grease cap with a rubber hammer.

Brake Shoes

Removal and Installation

1. Raise and safely support the vehicle and remove the rear wheels.
2. Remove the rear brake drum.
3. Remove the spring retainers by holding the pin behind the back plate, push in on the retainer and turn it ¼ turn.
4. Remove the shoes from the back plate by pulling first 1 shoe, then the other against the upper spring and from it's wheel cylinder slot. Detach the parking brake cable from the brake lever. The entire shoe assembly should now be free of the vehicle.
5. Carefully note the position of each spring, as spring shapes and positions have varied from vehicle to vehicle and year to year.
6. Clamp the pushrod in a vice and begin removing the springs, starting with the lower return spring, adjusting wedge spring, upper return spring and then the tensioning spring and adjusting wedge.
7. On most vehicles, the parking brake lever must be removed from the old shoes and reused. When new parts are pur-

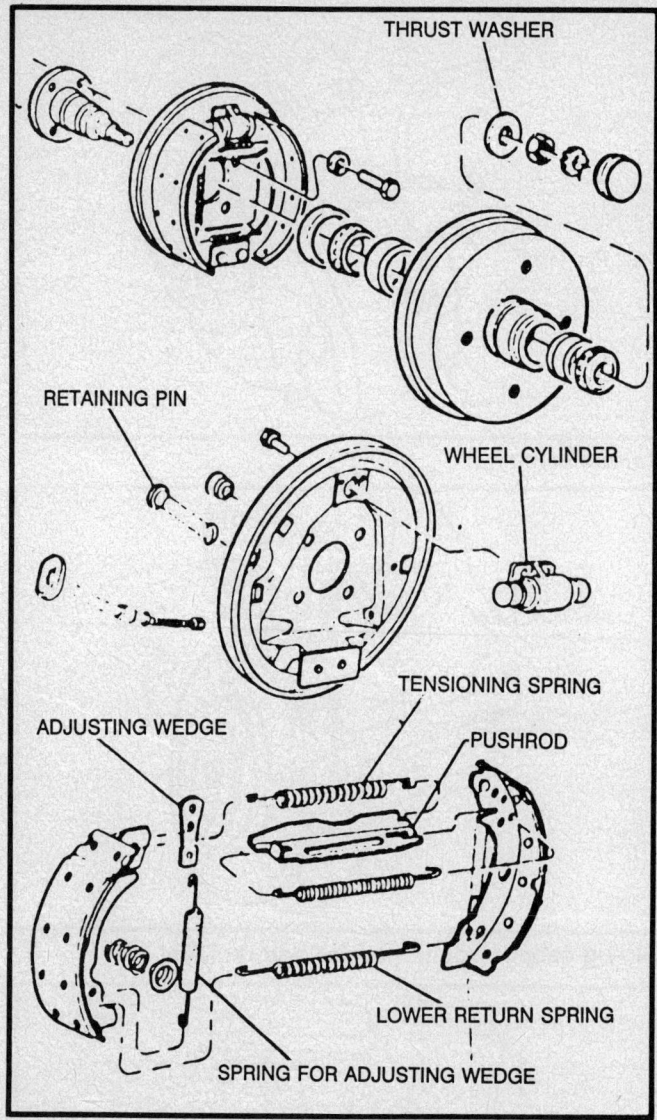

Rear wheel bearing and brake assembly on drum brake

chased, don't forget the clip that holds the parking brake lever pin in place.

To install:

8. Check the wheel cylinder for frozen pistons or leaks. If any defects are found replace the wheel cylinder.
9. Inspect the springs. If the springs are damaged or show signs of overheating they should be replaced. Indications of overheated springs are discoloration and distortion.
10. Inspect the brake drum and recondition or replace, as necessary.
11. Clean and lubricate all contact points on the backing plate with a suitable brake lubricant.
12. With the front brake shoe in a vise, attach the pushrod and tensioning spring.
13. Insert the adjusting wedge between the front shoe and pushrod so its lug is pointing toward the backing plate.
14. Remove the parking brake lever from the old shoe and attach it onto the new rear brake shoe.
15. Put the rear brake shoe and parking brake lever assembly onto the pushrod and hook up the spring.

16. Connect the parking brake cable to the lever and place the whole assembly onto the backing plate.
17. Install the hold-down springs.
18. Install the upper and lower return springs.
19. Install the adjusting wedge spring.
20. Center the brake shoes on the backing plate making sure the adjusting wedge is fully released (all the way up) before installing the drum.
21. Install the drum and wheel assembly.
22. Apply the brake pedal a few times to bring the brake shoe into adjustment.
23. If the wheel clyinder was replaced, bleed the system.
24. Road test the vehicle.

Wheel Cylinder

Removal and Installation

1. Raise and safely support the vehicle and remove the wheel, drum and brake shoes.
2. Loosen the brake line on the rear of the cylinder but do not pull the line away from the cylinder or it may bend.
3. Remove the bolts and lockwashers that attach the wheel cylinder to the backing plate and remove the cylinder.
4. Position the new wheel cylinder on the backing plate and install the cylinder attaching bolts and lockwashers. Torque to 6 ft. lbs. (8 Nm).
5. Attach the brake line.
6. Install the brakes and bleed the system.
7. Road test the vehicle.

Disc Parking Brake

Adjustment

1. Let the parking brake lever all the way down.
2. At the brake handle, loosen the locknuts and turn the adjusting nuts until the lever on the calipers just lifts from the stop. The lift should be no more than ¼ in. (1mm).
3. Operate the brake handle a few times, put the handle down and make sure both rear wheels still turn freely.

Lever moved off stop (arrow) no more than ¼ in. (1.0mm)

4. Retighten the locknuts at the handle.

Drum Parking Brake

Adjustment

Fox and Quantum parking brake adjustment is made at the cable compensator, which is attached to the lever under the vehicle. On all other vehicles, the cable end nuts are in front of or behind the hand brake lever. Adjustment is performed at the cable end nuts.

REAR DRUM BRAKES

1. Raise and safely support the vehicle.
2. Apply the parking brake so the lever is on the 2nd notch.
3. The Fox and Quantum adjustment is made directly under the passenger compartment, under a heat shield.
4. Tighten the compensator nut or adjusting nuts until both rear wheels can not be turned by hand.
5. Release the parking brake lever and check that both wheels can be easily turned.
6. Lubricate the Fox and Quantum compensator with chassis grease and reinstall the heat shield.

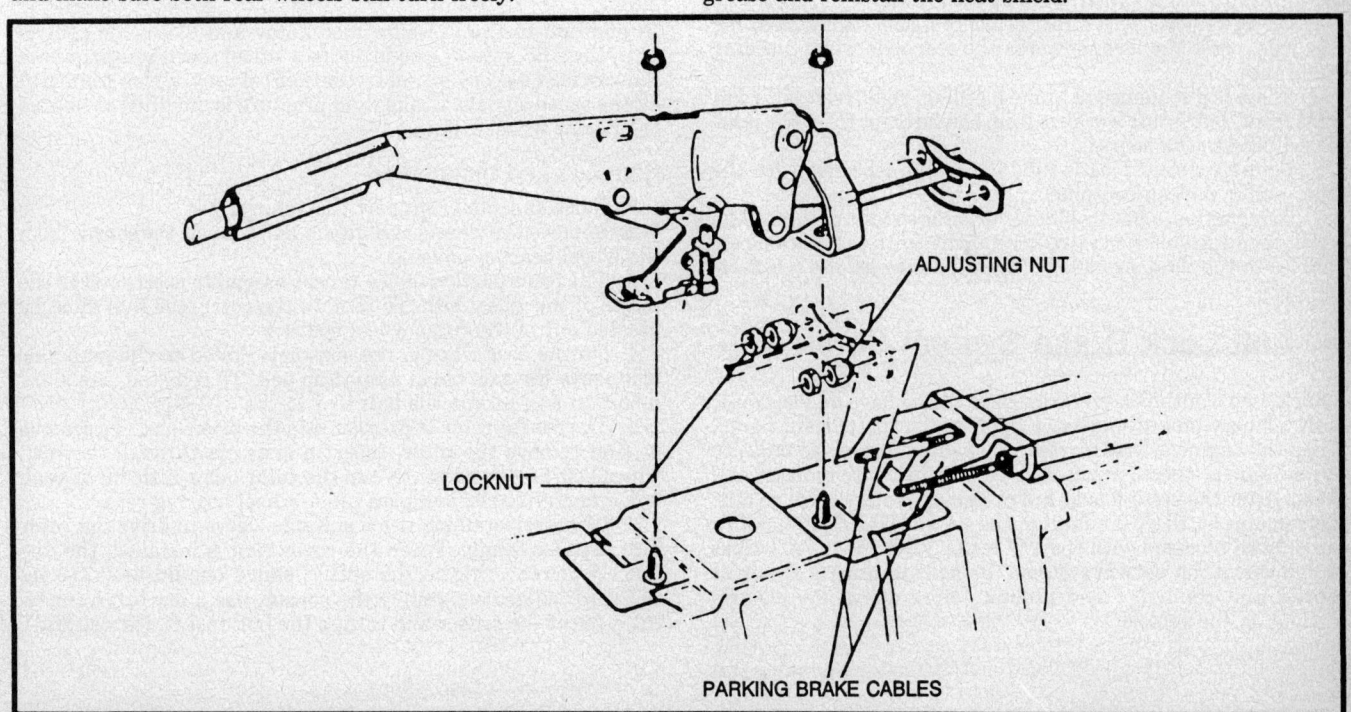

Parking brake adjusters—Corrado shown

Removal and Installation

REAR DRUM BRAKES

1. Block the front wheels and release the hand brake.
2. Raise and safely support the rear of the vehicle.
3. Remove the rear brake shoes.
4. Remove the brake cable assembly from the back plates.
5. On Fox and Quantum, unhook the cable from the compensator.
6. On all others, remove the cable adjusting nut(s) and detach the cable guides from the floor pan.
7. Pull the cables out from under the vehicle.
8. Installation is the reverse of removal. Adjust the brakes and parking brake and road test the vehicle.

REAR DISC BRAKES

1. Raise and safely support the vehicle.
2. Release the parking brake. It may be necessary to unscrew the adjusting nuts to provide slack in the brake cable.
3. At each rear wheel brake caliper, remove the spring clip retaining the parking brake cable to the caliper.
4. Lift the cable from the caliper mount and disengage it from the parking brake lever.
5. Installation is the reverse of removal. Adjust the parking brake.

Brake System Bleeding

WITHOUT ABS

NOTE: Use only new DOT 4 brake fluid in all Volkswagen vehicles. Do not use silicone (DOT 5) fluid. Even the smallest traces can cause severe corrosion to the hydraulic system. All brake fluids are corrosive to paint.

1. On vehicles with power brakes, bleed brakes with the engine off and booster vacuum discharged; pump the pedal with the bleeders closed about 20 times until the pedal effort gets stiff.
2. Fill the fluid reservoir.
3. On Quantum Syncro, there is a pressure regulator valve at the master cylinder which must be bled first.
4. On all vehicles with a rear brake pressure regulator at the rear axle, press the lever towards the rear axle when bleeding the brakes.
5. There is a sequence to brake bleeding: right rear, left rear, right front, left front: working from the farthest from the master cylinder to the nearest.
6. Connect a clear plastic tube to the bleeder valve with the other end in a clean container.
7. Using either a power bleeder or an assistant pumping the pedal, open each bleeder valve in sequence until there are no air bubbles in the fluid stream. Be careful not to let the reservoir run out.

Anti-Lock Brake System Service

Vehicles with anti-lock brake systems (ABS) have an electronic fault memory and an indicator light on the instrument panel. When the engine is first started, the light will go on to indicate the system is pressurizing and performing a self diagnostic check. After the system is at full pressure, the light will go out. If it remains lit, there is a fault in the system. The fault memory can only be accessed with the VW tester VAG 1551, VAG 1598 or equivalent, on earlier systems. Be sure to unplug the ABS control unit connector and ground before doing any electric welding on the vehicle.

--- CAUTION ---

The ABS modulator assembly is capable of self pressurizing to more than 3000 psi. Serious injury may result if the brake service is attempted without disabling and depressurizing the system.

Relieving Anti-Lock Brake System Pressure

With the ignition off, pump the brake pedal 25–35 times to depressurize the system. The system will recharge itself via the electric pump as soon as the ignition is turned on. Disconnect the battery to prevent unintended pressurization.

Modulator Assembly

Removal and Installation

1. Switch OFF ignition and depress the brake pedal 25–35 times to depressurize the modulator assembly, master cylinder. Disconnect the battery to prevent unintended pressurization.
2. Inside the vehicle, under the left rear seat for Passat, behind the left kick panel for Corrado or near the right tail light for Golf and Jetta, locate and disconnect the ABS control unit and the ground connection.
3. Remove the brake fluid from the reservoir with a suction pump.
4. Disconnect the brake lines from the modulator assembly and protect it's connections from contamination with suitable plugs.
5. Working inside the vehicle, remove the left shelf under the dash to gain access to the brake pedal linkage. Remove the clevis bolt and disconnect the pedal.
6. Remove the locknuts and remove the pressure modulator.
7. Installation is the reverse of removal. Use new locknuts and torque to 18 ft. lbs. (25 Nm). Refill the reservoir with new brake fluid and bleed the system.

Wheel Sensor

In addition to the pressure modulator and electronic control unit, the ABS system also includes a wheel speed sensor. These sensors feed a speed signal to the control unit, which compares all the speed signals. Brake fluid pressure is modified as needed to prevent wheel lockup.

Removal and Installation

1. Raise and safely support the vehicle.
2. Remove the wheels and unbolt and remove the sensor from the wheel bearing housing.
3. The rotor portion of the sensor assembly is screwed to the inside of the wheel hub. To remove the rotor, the hub must be pressed out of the front wheel bearing.
4. On the rear wheels, the sensor is bolted to the stub axle just above the axle beam mounting pad. To reinstall, use a dry lubricant and torque the bolt to 7 ft. lbs. (10 Nm).
5. The sensor rotor is pressed into the brake disc. To remove it, first remove the rotor. Insert a drift pin through the road wheel bolt holes and gently tap the rotor out a little bit at each hole, much like removing an inner wheel bearing race.
6. When reinstalling, use a suitable sleeve to drive the rotor into the disc evenly. When the cover ring is installed, the distance from the ring to the splash shield should be 0.375 in. (9.5mm). When reinstalling the sensor, use a dry lubricant on the sides of the sensor and torque the bolt to 7 ft. lbs. (10 Nm).

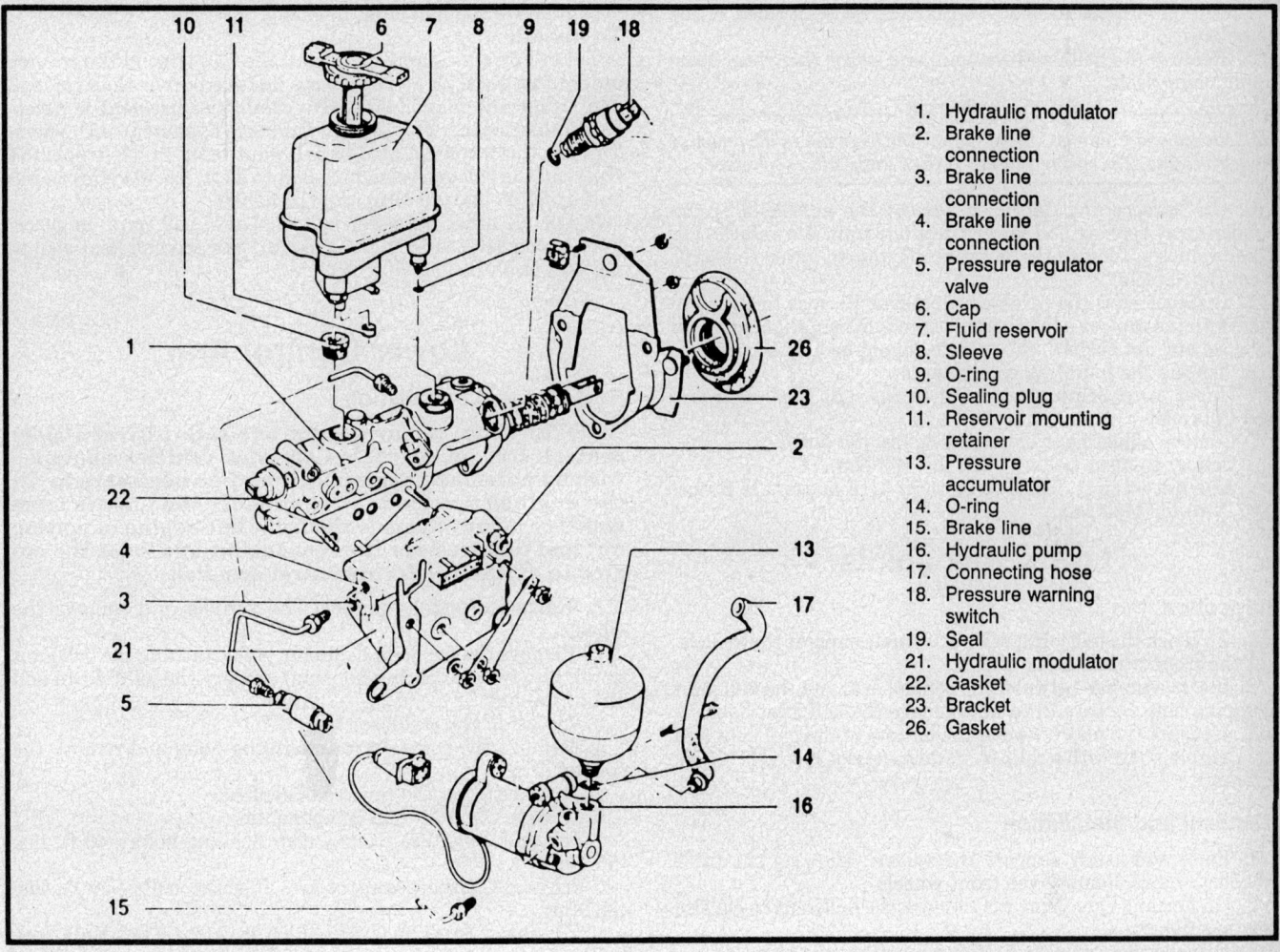

1. Hydraulic modulator
2. Brake line connection
3. Brake line connection
4. Brake line connection
5. Pressure regulator valve
6. Cap
7. Fluid reservoir
8. Sleeve
9. O-ring
10. Sealing plug
11. Reservoir mounting retainer
13. Pressure accumulator
14. O-ring
15. Brake line
16. Hydraulic pump
17. Connecting hose
18. Pressure warning switch
19. Seal
21. Hydraulic modulator
22. Gasket
23. Bracket
26. Gasket

ABS brake modulator assembly

FRONT SUSPENSION

MacPherson Strut

Removal and Installation

FOX AND QUANTUM

1. With the vehicle on the ground, remove the front axle nut. Loosen the wheel bolts.

2. Raise and safely support the vehicle and remove the wheels.

3. Remove the brake caliper from the strut and hang from the body it with wire. Detach the brake line from the strut and remove the rotor.

4. At the tie rod end, remove the cotter pin, back off the castellated nut and remove the end from the strut with a puller.

5. Loosen the stabilizer bar bushings and detach the end from the strut being removed.

6. Remove the ball joint clamp bolt and ball joint from the strut.

7. On some vehicles, the halfshaft spline is secured in the hub with thread sealer. The best way to remove it is to push it out with a wheel puller. Do not use heat, this will ruin the bearing. Pull the strut away from the halfshaft.

8. Remove the upper strut-to-fender retaining nut and lower the strut assembly down and out of the vehicle.

9. Installation is the reverse of removal.

10. Apply fresh thread sealer to the outer end of clean axle splines.

11. Torque the following components:

Axle nut—145 ft. lbs. (196 Nm) for M18 nut or 175 ft. lbs. (237 Nm) for M20 nut.

Ball joint-to-strut nut to 25 ft. lbs. (34 Nm) for M8 nut or 36 ft. lbs. (49 Nm) for M10 nut.

Caliper-to-strut bolts—44 ft. lbs. (60 Nm).

Stabilizer-to-control arm bolts—7 ft. lbs. (9 Nm).

EXCEPT FOX AND QUANTUM

1. With the vehicle on the ground, remove the front axle nut. Loosen the wheel bolts.

2. Raise and safely support the vehicle. Remove the wheels.

3. Detach the brake line from the strut and remove the caliper. Hang it from the body with wire.

4. Front wheel camber is set with eccentric washers on the bolts holding the bearing housing to the strut. Clean and mark

the position of these washers so they can be reinstalled in the same position.

5. Remove the bolts and washers and swing the wheel bearing housing aside.

——————————— CAUTION ———————————

On Scirocco and Cabriolet, do not remove the large nut in the center of the top bearing. The spring will be released while still compressed.

6. On Scirocco and Cabriolet, remove the nuts holding the rubber strut bearing and lower the strut from the vehicle. On other vehicles, remove the large center nut to lower the strut from the vehicle.

7. Installation is the reverse of removal. Be sure to align the marks on the camber adjustment washers. Wheel alignment will be close but not correct, the vehicle should be aligned.

8. Torque the following components:

Upper strut bearing nuts — 14 ft. lbs. (20 Nm) — Scirocco and Cabriolet.

Camber adjustment bolts — 58 ft. lbs. (80 Nm).

Caliper-to-strut bolts — 44 ft. lbs. (60 Nm).

Axle nut — 145 ft. lbs. (196 Nm) for M18 nut or 175 ft. lbs. (237 Nm) for M20 nut.

Lower Ball Joints

Inspection

1. To check the ball joint, raise and safely support the vehicle. Let the front wheels hang free.

2. Insert a prybar between the control arm and the ball joint clamping bolt. Be careful to not damage the ball joint boot.

3. Measure the play between the bottom of the ball joint and the clamping bolt with a caliper. Total must not exceed 0.100 in. (2.5mm).

Removal and Installation

1. Raise and safely support the vehicle, allowing the front wheels to hang. Remove the front wheels.

2. On Fox and Quantum, matchmark the ball joint-to-control arm position.

3. Remove the clamping bolt and nut from the hub.

4. Pry the lower control arm and ball joint down and from the strut.

5. Remove the ball joint-to-lower control arm retaining nuts and bolts or drill out the rivets with a ¼ in. (6mm) drill.

6. Remove the ball joint assembly.

To install:

7. On Fox and Quantum, install the ball joint in the reverse order of removal. If no parts were installed other than the ball joint, align the matchmarks. No camber adjustment is necessary if this is done. Pull the ball joint into alignment with pliers. Tighten the 2 control arm-to-ball joint bolts to 47 ft. lbs. (64 Nm) and the ball joint clamping bolt to 25 ft. lbs. (34 Nm) on M8 bolt or 36 ft. lbs. (49 Nm) on M10 bolt.

8. On all other vehicles, bolt the new ball joint in place. Torque the bolts to 18 ft. lbs. (25 Nm) and the ball joint clamping bolt to 37 ft. lbs. (50 Nm).

Lower Control Arm

Removal and Installation

NOTE: **When removing the left side (driver's side) control arm on Scirocco/Cabriolet vehicles equipped with an automatic transaxle, it may be necessary to lift the engine/transaxle. First support the engine from above or below. Remove the front left engine mounting nut and bolt, remove the rear mount and raise the engine to expose the front control arm bolt.**

1. Raise and safely support the vehicle and remove the wheels.

2. Remove the ball joint clamping bolt attaching the ball joint to the hub (wheel bearing housing) and pry the joint down and out of the hub.

3. Unfasten the stabilizer bar.

4. Remove the control arm mounting bolts and remove the control arm.

5. Installation is the reverse of removal.

6. Torque the following components:

Fox and Quantum control arm bushing bolts — 40 ft. lbs. (55 Nm).

Scirocco/Cabriolet control arm bushing bolts — 50 ft. lbs. (68 Nm).

All others: front bushing bolts — 96 ft. lbs. (130 Nm), rear bolts — 59 ft. lbs. (80 Nm).

Stabilizer bar link rods — 18 ft. lbs. (25 Nm).

Stabilizer bar bushing clamp bolts — 32 ft. lbs. (43 Nm).

Ball joint clamping bolt — 25 ft. lbs. (34 Nm) for M8 nut or 36 ft. lbs. (48 Nm) for M10 nut.

REAR SUSPENSION

Shock Absorbers

Removal and Installation

NOTE: **Do not remove both suspension struts at the same time as this will overload the axle beam bushings and brake lines.**

1. Working inside the vehicle, remove the cap from the top shock mount and note the way the washers and bushings stack up.

2. Unscrew the strut from the body.

3. Slowly lift the vehicle until the wheels are slightly off the ground.

4. Unbolt the strut from the axle.

5. Take the strut out of the lower mounting. Press the wheel down slightly when removing the strut.

6. Guide the strut out carefully between the wheel and the wheel housing. Do not damage the paint on the spring or wheel housing.

7. Installation is the reverse of removal. Torque the strut-to-body to 26 ft. lbs. (35 Nm) and the strut-to-axle to 52 ft. lbs. (70 Nm).

Rear Control Arms

Removal and Installation

QUANTUM SYNCRO

The Quantum Syncro is a 4WD vehicle with similar bearing installations both front and rear. To remove the rear bearing, the control arm must be removed.

1. With the vehicle on the ground, loosen the axle nut.

2. Raise and safely support the vehicle and remove the wheels.

3. Remove the bolts retaining the axle shaft to the differential and slide the axle shaft from the vehicle.

4. Remove the disc brake caliper and support aside, do not hang it by the brake lines.

5. Unbolt the stabilizer bar from the control arm.

6. Remove the lower shock mount bolt and the control arm mounting bolts and lower the arm from the vehicle.

7. The bearing and hub can now be pressed out using the same procedure as the front bearing.

8. Installation is the reverse of removal.

9. Torque the following:

Control arm bolts—88 ft. lbs. (120 Nm).
Lower shock mount—48 ft. lbs. (65 Nm).
Stabilizer bar brackets—18 ft. lbs. (25 Nm).
Brake caliper—48 ft. lbs. (65 Nm).
Inner axle CV-joint bolts—33 ft. lbs. (45 Nm).
Outer axle nut—170 ft. lbs. (230 Nm).

Rear Wheel Bearings

Removal and Installation

1. Raise and safely support the vehicle and remove the rear wheels.

2. On drum brakes, insert a small pry tool through a wheel bolt hole and push up on the adjusting wedge to slacken the rear brake adjustment.

3. On disc brakes, remove the caliper.

4. Remove the grease cap, cotter pin, locking ring, axle nut and thrust washer. Carefully remove the bearing and put all these parts where they will stay clean.

5. Before installing, pack the bearing. If any brake dust has fallen onto the axle, wipe off all the axle grease and put on new high temperature bearing grease.

6. Installation is reverse of removal.

Adjustment

1. When adjusting the bearing nut, the thrust washer must still be movable with light effort with a small pry tool.

2. When installing the locking ring, keep trying different positions of the ring on the nut until the cotter pin goes into the hole. Don't turn the nut to align the locking ring with the hole in the axle. Use a new cotter pin. Install the grease cap with a rubber hammer.

Rear Axle Assembly

Removal and Installation

EXCEPT SYNCRO

1. Raise and safely support the vehicle and remove the rear wheels.

2. Remove the rear brake caliper or drum.

3. Disconnect the brake line and remove the caliper or back plate (with brakes attached) from the vehicle.

4. Disconnect the other end of the brake line and unclip the brake line and parking brake cable from the axle. Unhook the brake pressure regulator spring from the bracket.

5. Support one side of the axle beam so it does not fall and remove the lower shock mount bolts from both sides.

6. Unless that is the part being repaired, avoid removing the axle bushing brackets. Removing these will mean aligning the rear bushings upon reassembly.

7. Remove the bolt from the center of each bushing and lower the axle from the vehicle.

8. When reinstalling, torque the bushing bolts with the vehicle on the ground to properly align the bushings. Torque the right side first, then pry the left side bushing slightly towards the center of the vehicle and torque the left side.

9. Torque the following:

Passat and Quantum axle bushing bolts—52 ft. lbs. (70 Nm).
All other axle bushing bolts—44 ft. lbs. (60 Nm).
Passat lower shock bolt—77 ft. lbs. (105 Nm).
Golf/Jetta and Corrado shock mount—52 ft. lbs. (70 Nm).
Scirocco/Cabriolet shock mount—32 ft. lbs. (45 Nm).
Fox/Quantum shock mount—52 ft. lbs. (70 Nm).

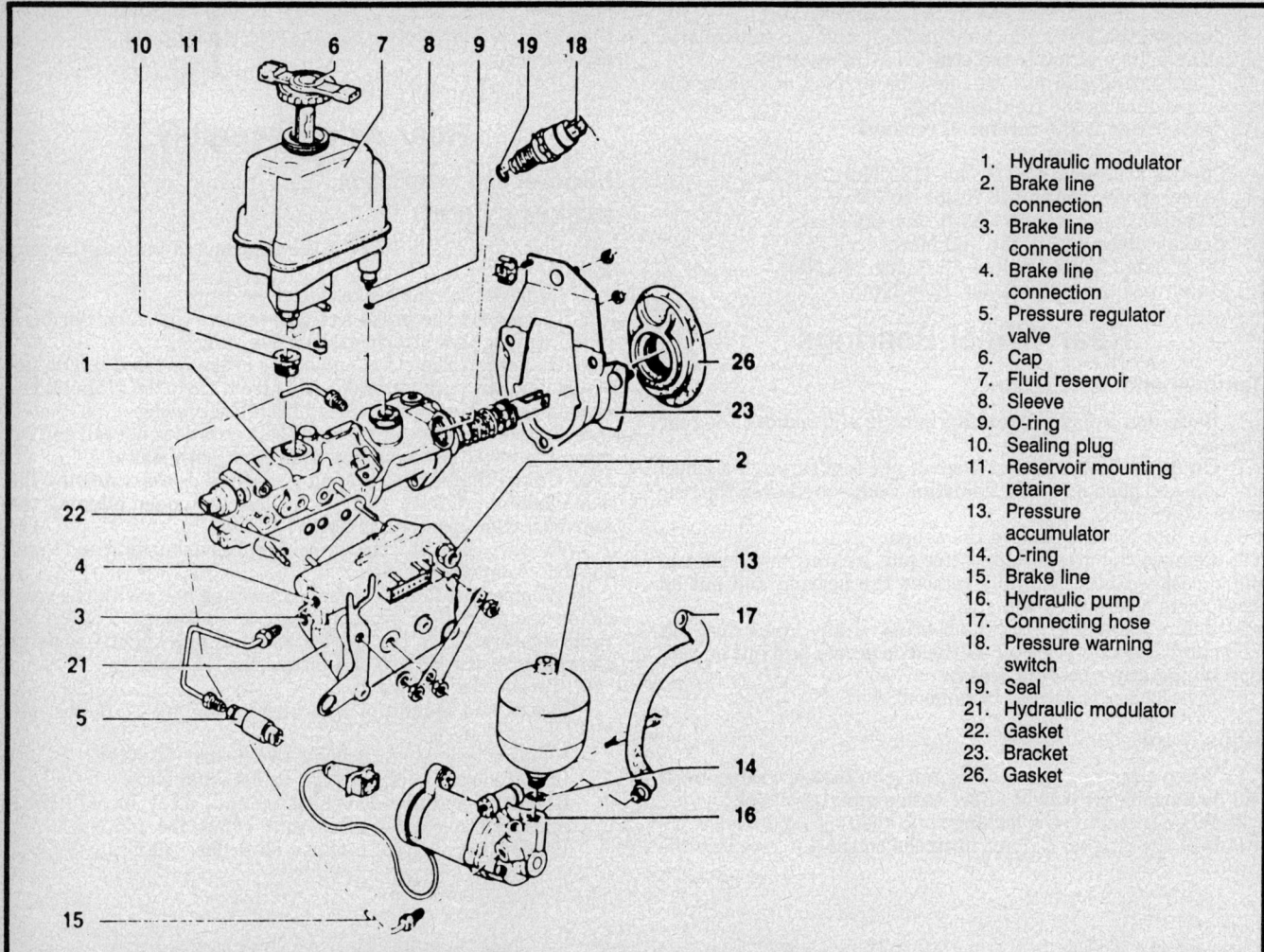

1. Hydraulic modulator
2. Brake line connection
3. Brake line connection
4. Brake line connection
5. Pressure regulator valve
6. Cap
7. Fluid reservoir
8. Sleeve
9. O-ring
10. Sealing plug
11. Reservoir mounting retainer
13. Pressure accumulator
14. O-ring
15. Brake line
16. Hydraulic pump
17. Connecting hose
18. Pressure warning switch
19. Seal
21. Hydraulic modulator
22. Gasket
23. Bracket
26. Gasket

Exploded view of the ABS modulator assembly

SERIAL NUMBER IDENTIFICATION

Vehicle Identification Plate

The VIN plate on these vehicles is located on the top left surface of the dash and is also stamped on the right door pillar. Emission control information is on a label located on the left shock tower under the hood. There is also a model plate on the right shock tower that includes the VIN number, engine type, emission equipment, vehicle weights and color codes.

Engine Number

The engine type designation, part number and serial number are given on the left side of the block. The last figures of the part number are stamped on a tab and are followed by the serial number stamped on the block.

Transmission Number

The transmission type designation, serial number and part number appear on a metal plate riveted to the underside of the transmission. The final drive reduction ratio, part number and serial number are found on a metal plate riveted to the left side of the differential.

B28F engine number locations

B234F engine identification location

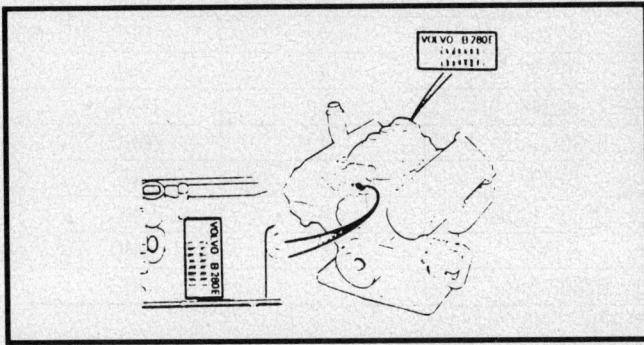

B280F engine identification location

LAST THREE DIGITS OF ENGINE IDENTIFICATION NUMBER PRINTED ON LABEL ON TIMING BELT COVER

B21 series engine number locations

SPECIFICATIONS

ENGINE IDENTIFICATION

Year	Model	Engine Displacement cu. in. (cc/liter)	Engine Series Identification	No. of Cylinders	Engine Type
1987	240 DL	140 (2320/2.3)	B230F	4	OHC
	240 GL	140 (2320/2.3)	B230F	4	OHC
	740 GL	140 (2320/2.3)	B230F	4	OHC
	740 GLE	140 (2320/2.3)	B230F	4	OHC
	740 Turbo	140 (2320/2.3)	B230F-Turbo	4	OHC
	760 GLE	174 (2849/2.9)	B280F	6	OHC
	760 Turbo	140 (2320/2.3)	B230F-Turbo	4	OHC
	780	174 (2849/2.9)	B280F	6	OHC

ENGINE IDENTIFICATION

Year	Model	Engine Displacement cu. in. (cc/liter)	Engine Series Identification	No. of Cylinders	Engine Type
1988	240 DL	140 (2320/2.3)	B230F	4	OHC
	240 GL	140 (2320/2.3)	B230F	4	OHC
	740 GL	140 (2320/2.3)	B230F	4	OHC
	740 GLE	140 (2320/2.3)	B230F	4	OHC
	740 Turbo	140 (2320/2.3)	B230F-Turbo	4	OHC
	760 GLE	174 (2849/2.9)	B280F	6	OHC
	760 Turbo	140 (2320/2.3)	B230F-Turbo	4	OHC
	780	174 (2849/2.9)	B280F	6	OHC
1989	240 DL	140 (2320/2.3)	B230F	4	OHC
	240 GL	140 (2320/2.3)	B230F	4	OHC
	740 GL	140 (2320/2.3)	B230F	4	OHC
	740 GLE	140 (2320/2.3)	B234F	4	DOHC
	740 Turbo	140 (2320/2.3)	B230F-Turbo	4	OHC
	760 GLE	174 (2849/2.9)	B280F	6	OHC
	760 Turbo	140 (2320/2.3)	B230F-Turbo	4	OHC
	780	174 (2849/2.9)	B280F	6	OHC
1990–91	240 DL	140 (2320/2.3)	B230F	4	OHC
	240 GL	140 (2320/2.3)	B230F	4	OHC
	740 GL	140 (2320/2.3)	B230F	4	OHC
	740 GLE	140 (2320/2.3)	B234F	4	DOHC
	740 Turbo	140 (2320/2.3)	B230F-Turbo	4	OHC
	760 GLE	174 (2849/2.9)	B280F	6	OHC
	760 Turbo	140 (2320/2.3)	B230F-Turbo	4	OHC
	780	174 (2849/2.9)	B280F	6	OHC
	780 Turbo	140 (2320/2.3)	B230F-Turbo	4	OHC

GENERAL ENGINE SPECIFICATIONS

Year	Model	Engine Displacement cu. in. (cc)	Fuel System Type	Net Horsepower @ rpm	Net Torque @ rpm (ft. lbs.)	Bore × Stroke (in.)	Compression Ratio	Oil Pressure @ rpm
1987	240 DL	140 (2320) B230F	LH	114 @ 5400	136 @ 2750	3.78 × 3.15	9.8:1	35–85 @ 2000
	240 GL	140 (2320) B230F	LH	114 @ 5400	136 @ 2750	3.78 × 3.15	9.8:1	35–85 @ 2000
	740 GL	140 (2320) B230F	LH	114 @ 5400	136 @ 2750	3.78 × 3.15	9.8:1	35–85 @ 2000
	740 GLE	140 (2320) B230F	LH	114 @ 5400	136 @ 2750	3.78 × 3.15	9.8:1	35–85 @ 2000
	740 Turbo	140 (2320) B230F-Turbo	LH	160 @ 5300	187 @ 2900	3.78 × 3.15	8.7:1	35–85 @ 2000
	760 GLE	174 (2849) B280F	LH	146 @ 5100	173 @ 3750	3.58 × 2.86	9.5:1	57 @ 3000
	760 Turbo	140 (2320) B230F-Turbo	LH	160 @ 5300	187 @ 2900	3.78 × 3.15	8.7:1	35–85 @ 2000
	780	174 (2849) B280F	LH	146 @ 5100	173 @ 3750	3.58 × 2.86	9.5:1	57 @ 3000

GENERAL ENGINE SPECIFICATIONS

Year	Model	Engine Displacement cu. in. (cc)	Fuel System Type	Net Horsepower @ rpm	Net Torque @ rpm (ft. lbs.)	Bore × Stroke (in.)	Compression Ratio	Oil Pressure @ rpm
1988	240 DL	140 (2320) B230F	LH	114 @ 5400	136 @ 2750	3.78 × 3.15	9.8:1	35–85 @ 2000
	240 GL	140 (2320) B230F	LH	114 @ 5400	136 @ 2750	3.78 × 3.15	9.8:1	35–85 @ 2000
	740 GL	140 (2320) B230F	LH	114 @ 5400	136 @ 2750	3.78 × 3.15	9.8:1	35–85 @ 2000
	740 GLE	140 (2320) B230F	LH	114 @ 5400	136 @ 2750	3.78 × 3.15	9.8:1	35–85 @ 2000
	740 Turbo	140 (2320) B230F-Turbo	LH	160 @ 5300	187 @ 2900	3.78 × 3.15	8.7:1	35–85 @ 2000
	760 GLE	174 (2849) B280F	LH	146 @ 5100	173 @ 3750	3.58 × 2.86	9.5:1	57 @ 3000
	760 Turbo	140 (2320) B230F-Turbo	LH	160 @ 5300	187 @ 2900	3.78 × 3.15	8.7:1	35–85 @ 2000
	780	174 (2849) B280F	LH	146 @ 5100	173 @ 3750	3.58 × 2.86	9.5:1	57 @ 3000
1989	240 DL	140 (2320) B230F	LH	114 @ 5400	136 @ 2750	3.78 × 3.15	9.8:1	35–85 @ 2000
	240 GL	140 (2320) B230F	LH	114 @ 5400	136 @ 2750	3.78 × 3.15	9.8:1	35–85 @ 2000
	740 GL	140 (2320) B230F	LH	114 @ 5400	136 @ 2750	3.78 × 3.15	9.8:1	35–85 @ 2000
	740 GLE	140 (2320) B234F	LH	153 @ 5700	150 @ 4450	3.78 × 3.15	10.0:1	73 @ 3000
	740 Turbo	140 (2320) B230F-Turbo	LH	160 @ 5300	187 @ 2900	3.78 × 3.15	8.7:1	35–85 @ 2000
	760 GLE	174 (2849) B280F	LH	146 @ 5100	173 @ 3750	3.58 × 2.86	9.5:1	57 @ 3000
	760 Turbo	140 (2320) B230F-Turbo	LH	160 @ 5300	187 @ 2900	3.78 × 3.15	8.7:1	35–85 @ 2000
	780	174 (2849) B280F	LH	146 @ 5100	173 @ 3750	3.58 × 2.86	9.5:1	57 @ 3000
	780 Turbo	140 (2320) B230F-Turbo	LH	175 @ 5300	187 @ 2900	3.78 × 3.15	8.7:1	35–85 @ 2000
1990–91	240 DL	140 (2320) B230F	LH	114 @ 5400	136 @ 2750	3.78 × 3.15	9.8:1	35–85 @ 2000
	240 GL	140 (2320) B230F	LH	114 @ 5400	136 @ 2750	3.78 × 3.15	9.8:1	35–85 @ 2000
	740 GL	140 (2320) B230F	LH	114 @ 5400	136 @ 2750	3.78 × 3.15	9.8:1	35–85 @ 2000
	740 GLE	140 (2320) B234F	LH	153 @ 5700	150 @ 4450	3.78 × 3.15	10.0:1	73 @ 3000
	740 Turbo	140 (2320) B230F-Turbo	LH	160 @ 5300	187 @ 2900	3.78 × 3.15	8.7:1	35–85 @ 2000
	760 GLE	174 (2849) B280F	LH	146 @ 5100	173 @ 3750	3.58 × 2.86	9.5:1	57 @ 3000
	760 Turbo	140 (2320) B230F-Turbo	LH	160 @ 5300	187 @ 2900	3.78 × 3.15	8.7:1	35–85 @ 2000

GENERAL ENGINE SPECIFICATIONS

Year	Model	Engine Displacement cu. in. (cc)	Fuel System Type	Net Horsepower @ rpm	Net Torque @ rpm (ft. lbs.)	Bore × Stroke (in.)	Com-pression Ratio	Oil Pressure @ rpm
1990-91	780	174 (2849) B280F	LH	146 @ 5100	173 @ 3750	3.58 × 2.86	9.5:1	57 @ 3000
	780 Turbo	140 (2320) B230F-Turbo	LH	175 @ 5300	187 @ 2900	3.78 × 3.15	8.7:1	35–85 @ 2000

CIS Continuous Injection System
DFI Diesel Fuel Injection
LH LH-Jetronic Injection
① Canada only
② Station Wagon
③ California only
④ With manual transmission
⑤ With automatic transmission

ENGINE TUNE-UP SPECIFICATIONS

Year	Model	Engine Displacement cu. in. (cc)	Spark Plugs Type	Spark Plugs Gap (in.)	Ignition Timing ③ (deg.) MT	Ignition Timing ③ (deg.) AT	Com-pression Pressure (psi)	Fuel Pump (psi)	Idle Speed (rpm) MT	Idle Speed (rpm) AT	Valve Clearance In.	Valve Clearance Ex.
1987	240 DL	140 (2320) B230F	WR7DC	0.030	12B ④	12B ④	NA	36	750	750	0.014–0.016	0.014–0.016
	240 GL	140 (2320) B230F	WR7DC	0.030	12B ④	12B ④	NA	36	750	750	0.014–0.016	0.014–0.016
	740 GL	140 (2320) B230F	WR7DC	0.030	12B ④	12B ④	NA	36	750	750	0.014–0.016	0.014–0.016
	740 GLE	140 (2320) B230F	WR7DC	0.030	12B ④	12B ④	NA	36	750	750	0.014–0.016	0.014–0.016
	740 Turbo	140 (2320) B230F-Turbo	WR7DC	0.026	12B ④	12B ④	NA	43	750	750	0.014–0.016	0.014–0.016
	760 GLE	174 (2849) B280F	HR6DC	0.026	16B ④	16B ④	NA	35	750	750	0.004–0.006	0.010–0.012
	760 Turbo	140 (2320) B230F-Turbo	WR7DC	0.026	12B ④	12B ④	NA	43	750	750	0.014–0.016	0.014–0.016
	780	174 (2849) B280F	HR6DC	0.026	16B ④	16B ④	NA	35	750	750	0.004–0.006	0.010–0.012
1988	240 DL	140 (2320) B230F	WR7DC	0.030	12B ④	12B ④	NA	36	750	750	0.014–0.016	0.014–0.016
	240 GL	140 (2320) B230F	WR7DC	0.030	12B ④	12B ④	NA	36	750	750	0.014–0.016	0.014–0.016
	740 GL	140 (2320) B230F	WR7DC	0.030	12B ④	12B ④	NA	36	750	750	0.014–0.016	0.014–0.016
	740 GLE	140 (2320) B230F	WR7DC	0.030	12B ④	12B ④	NA	36	750	750	0.014–0.016	0.014–0.016
	740 Turbo	140 (2320) B230F-Turbo	WR7DC	0.026	12B ④	12B ④	NA	43	750	750	0.014–0.016	0.014–0.016
	760 GLE	174 (2849) B280F	HR6DC	0.026	16B ④	16B ④	NA	35	750	750	0.004–0.006	0.010–0.012
	760 Turbo	140 (2320) B230F-Turbo	WR7DC	0.026	12B ④	12B ④	NA	43	750	750	0.014–0.016	0.014–0.016
	780	174 (2849) B280F	HR6DC	0.026	16B ④	16B ④	NA	35	750	750	0.004–0.006	0.010–0.012

ENGINE TUNE-UP SPECIFICATIONS

Year	Model	Engine Displacement cu. in. (cc)	Spark Plugs Type	Gap (in.)	Ignition Timing ③ (deg.) MT	AT	Compression Pressure (psi)	Fuel Pump (psi)	Idle Speed (rpm) MT	AT	Valve Clearance In.	Ex.
1989	240 DL	140 (2320) B230F	WR7DC	0.030	12B ④	12B ④	NA	36	750	750	0.014–0.016	0.014–0.016
	240 GL	140 (2320) B230F	WR7DC	0.030	12B ④	12B ④	NA	36	750	750	0.014–0.016	0.014–0.016
	740 GL	140 (2320) B230F	WR7DC	0.030	12B ④	12B ④	NA	36	750	750	0.014–0.016	0.014–0.016
	740 GLE	140 (2320) B234F	WR7DC	0.030	15B ⑧	15B ⑧	NA	36	850	850	Hyd.	Hyd.
	740 Turbo	140 (2320) B230F-Turbo	WR7DC	0.026	12B ④	12B ④	NA	43	750	750	0.014–0.016	0.014–0.016
	760 GLE	174 (2849) B280F	HR6DC	0.026	16B ④	16B ④	NA	35	750	750	0.004–0.006	0.010–0.012
	760 Turbo	140 (2320) B230F-Turbo	WR7DC	0.026	12B ④	12B ④	NA	43	750	750	0.014–0.016	0.014–0.016
	780	174 (2849) B280F	HR6DC	0.026	16B ④	16B ④	NA	35	750	750	0.004–0.006	0.010–0.012
	780 Turbo	140 (2320) B230F-Turbo	WR7DC	0.026	12B ④	12B ④	NA	43	750	750	0.014–0.016	0.014–0.016
1990	240 DL	140 (2320) B230F	WR7DC	0.030	12B ④	12B ④	NA	36	750	750	0.014–0.016	0.014–0.016
	240 GL	140 (2320) B230F	WR7DC	0.030	12B ④	12B ④	NA	36	750	750	0.014–0.016	0.014–0.016
	740 GL	140 (2320) B230F	WR7DC	0.030	12B ④	12B ④	NA	36	750	750	0.014–0.016	0.014–0.016
	740 GLE	140 (2320) B234F	WR7DC	0.030	15B ⑧	15B ⑧	NA	36	850	850	Hyd.	Hyd.
	740 Turbo	140 (2320) B230F-Turbo	WR7DC	0.026	12B ④	12B ④	NA	43	750	750	0.014–0.016	0.014–0.016
	760 GLE	174 (2849) B280F	HR6DC	0.026	16B ④	16B ④	NA	35	750	750	0.004–0.006	0.010–0.012
	760 Turbo	140 (2320) B230F-Turbo	WR7DC	0.026	12B ④	12B ④	NA	43	750	750	0.014–0.016	0.014–0.016
	780	174 (2849) B280F	HR6DC	0.026	16B ④	16B ④	NA	35	750	˙750	0.004–0.006	0.010–0.012
	780 Turbo	140 (2320) B230F-Turbo	WR7DC	0.026	12B ④	12B ④	NA	43	750	750	0.014–0.016	0.014–0.016
1991	ALL	SEE UNDERHOOD SPECIFICATIONS STICKER										

NOTE: Some models are equipped with the Constant Idle Speed system (CIS) and cannot be adjusted.
Hyd. Hydraulic
① Canada only
② Station Wagon
③ Vacuum advance disconnected, A/C turned off
④ @ 750 rpm
⑤ @ 900 rpm
⑥ @ 800 rpm
⑦ @ 2500 rpm
⑧ @ 850 rpm

FIRING ORDERS

NOTE: To avoid confusion, always replace spark plug wires one at a time.

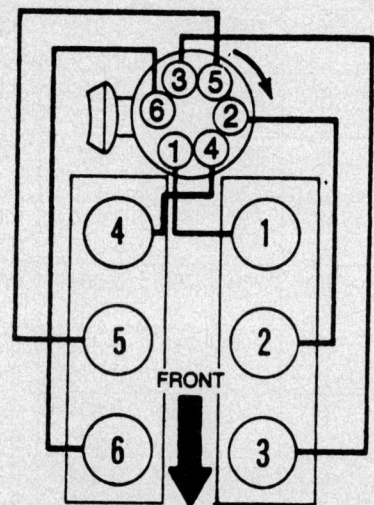

B28 Engine
Engine Firing Order: 1–6–3–5–2–4
Distributor Rotation: Clockwise

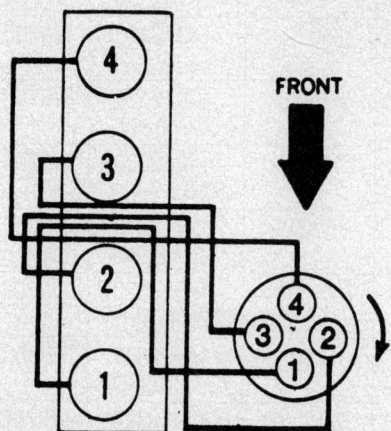

B23, B230 and B234 Engines
Engine Firing Order: 1–3–4–2
Distributor Rotation: Clockwise

CAPACITIES

Year	Model	Engine Displacement cu. in. (cc)	Engine Crankcase (qts.) ③ with Filter	without Filter	Transmission (pts) 4-Spd	5-Spd	Auto.	Drive Axle (pts.)	Fuel Tank (gal.)	Cooling System (qts.)
1987	240 DL	140 (2320) B230F	4.0	3.5	—	2.8	15.6	④	15.8	10.0
	240 GL	140 (2320) B230F	4.0	3.5	—	2.8	15.6	④	15.8	10.0
	740 GL	140 (2320) B230F	4.1	3.6	4.8	—	15.6	④	15.8	10.0
	740 GLE	140 (2320) B230F	4.1	3.6	4.8	—	15.6	④	15.8	10.0
	740 Turbo	140 (2320) B230F-Turbo	4.1 ③	3.6 ③	4.8	—	15.6	④	15.8	10.0
	760 GLE	174 (2849) B280F	6.3	5.8	4.8	—	15.8	④	15.8	10.5
	760 Turbo	140 (2320) B230F-Turbo	4.1 ③	3.6 ③	4.8	—	15.8	④	15.8	10.0
	780	174 (2849) B280F	6.3	5.8	4.8	—	15.8	④	15.8	10.5

CAPACITIES

Year	Model	Engine Displacement cu. in. (cc)	Engine Crankcase (qts.) ③ with Filter	Engine Crankcase (qts.) ③ without Filter	Transmission (pts) 4-Spd	Transmission (pts) 5-Spd	Transmission (pts) Auto.	Drive Axle (pts.)	Fuel Tank (gal.)	Cooling System (qts.)
1988	240 DL	140 (2320) B230F	4.0	3.5	—	3.2	15.8	④	15.8	10.0
	240 GL	140 (2320) B230F	4.0	3.5	—	3.2	15.8	④	15.8	10.0
	740 GL	140 (2320) B230F	4.1	3.6	—	3.2	15.8	④	15.8	10.0
	740 GLE	140 (2320) B230F	4.1	3.6	—	3.2	15.8	④	15.8	10.0
	740 Turbo	140 (2320) B230F-Turbo	4.1 ③	3.6 ③	—	4.8	15.8	④	15.8	10.0
	760 GLE	174 (2849) B280F	6.3	5.8	—	—	15.8	④	21.1	10.5
	760 Turbo	140 (2320) B230F-Turbo	4.1 ③	3.6 ③	—	—	15.8	④	21.1	10.0
	780	174 (2849) B280F	6.3	5.8	—	—	15.8	④	21.1	10.5
1989	240 DL	140 (2320) B230F	4.0	3.5	—	3.2	15.8	④	15.8	10.0
	240 GL	140 (2320) B230F	4.0	3.5	—	3.2	15.8	④	15.8	10.0
	740 GL	140 (2320) B230F	4.1	3.6	—	3.2	15.8	④	15.8	10.0
	740 GLE	140 (2320) B234F	4.2	3.7	—	4.8	15.8	④	15.8	10.0
	740 Turbo	140 (2320) B230F-Turbo	4.1 ③	3.6 ③	—	4.8	15.8	④	15.8	10.0
	760 GLE	174 (2849) B280F	6.3	5.8	—	—	15.8	④	21.1	10.5
	760 Turbo	140 (2320) B230F-Turbo	4.1 ③	3.6 ③	—	—	15.8	④	21.1	10.0
	780	174 (2849) B280F	6.3	5.8	—	—	15.8	④	21.1	10.5
	780 Turbo	140 (2320) B230F-Turbo	4.1 ③	3.6 ③	—	—	15.8	④	21.1	10.5
1990-91	240 DL	140 (2320) B230F	4.0	3.5	—	3.2	15.8	④	15.8	10.0
	240 GL	140 (2320) B230F	4.0	3.5	—	3.2	15.8	④	15.8	10.0
	740 GL	140 (2320) B230F	4.1	3.6	—	3.2	15.8	④	15.8	10.0
	740 GLE	140 (2320) B234F	4.2	3.7	—	4.8	15.8	④	15.8	10.0
	740 Turbo	140 (2320) B230F-Turbo	4.1 ③	3.6 ③	—	4.8	15.8	④	15.8	10.0
	760 GLE	174 (2849) B280F	6.3	5.8	—	—	15.8	④	21.1	10.5
	760 Turbo	140 (2320) B230F-Turbo	4.1 ③	3.6 ③	—	—	15.8	④	21.1	10.0

CAPACITIES

Year	Model	Engine Displacement cu. in. (cc)	Engine Crankcase (qts.) ③ with Filter	Engine Crankcase (qts.) ③ without Filter	Transmission (pts) 4-Spd	Transmission (pts) 5-Spd	Transmission (pts) Auto.	Drive Axle (pts.)	Fuel Tank (gal.)	Cooling System (qts.)
1990–91	780	174 (2849) B280F	6.3	5.8	—	—	15.8	④	21.1	10.5
	780 Turbo	140 (2320) B230F-Turbo	4.1 ③	3.6 ③	—	—	15.8	④	21.1	10.5

① Canada only
② Station wagon
③ Models with turbo—add 0.6 qt. if oil cooler has been drained
④ 1030 axle—2.8 pts.
   1031 axle—3.4 pts.

CRANKSHAFT AND CONNECTING ROD SPECIFICATIONS

All measurements are given in inches.

Year	Engine Displacement cu. in. (cc)	Crankshaft Main Brg. Journal Dia.	Crankshaft Main Brg. Oil Clearance	Crankshaft Shaft End-play	Crankshaft Thrust on No.	Connecting Rod Journal Diameter	Connecting Rod Oil Clearance	Connecting Rod Side Clearance
1987	140 (2320) B230F	2.4981–2.4986	0.0011–0.0033	0.0015–0.0058	5	2.1255–2.1260	0.0009–0.0028	0.006–0.014
	140 (2320) B230F-Turbo	2.4981–2.4986	0.0011–0.0033	0.0015–0.0058	5	2.1255–2.1260	0.0009–0.0028	0.006–0.014
	174 (2849) B280F	2.7583	0.0035	0.0106	4	2.0585	0.0031	0.015
1988	140 (2320) B230F	2.4981–2.4986	0.0011–0.0033	0.0015–0.0058	5	2.1255–2.1260	0.0009–0.0028	0.006–0.014
	140 (2320) B230F-Turbo	2.4981–2.4986	0.0011–0.0033	0.0015–0.0058	5	2.1255–2.1260	0.0009–0.0028	0.006–0.014
	174 (2849) B280F	2.7583	0.0035	0.0106	4	2.0585	0.0031	0.015
1989	140 (2320) B230F	2.4981–2.4986	0.0011–0.0033	0.0015–0.0058	5	2.1255–2.1260	0.0009–0.0028	0.006–0.014
	140 (2320) B230F-Turbo	2.4981–2.4986	0.0011–0.0033	0.0015–0.0058	5	2.1255–2.1260	0.0009–0.0028	0.006–0.014
	140 (2320) B234F	1.9640–1.9648	0.0011–0.0033	0.0015–0.0058	5	2.0472–2.0476	0.0009–0.0028	0.006–0.018
	174 (2849) B280F	2.7583	0.0035	0.0106	4	2.0585	0.0031	0.015
1990–91	140 (2320) B230F	2.4981–2.4986	0.0011–0.0033	0.0015–0.0058	5	2.1255–2.1260	0.0009–0.0028	0.006–0.014
	140 (2320) B230F-Turbo	2.4981–2.4986	0.0011–0.0033	0.0015–0.0058	5	2.1255–2.1260	0.0009–0.0028	0.006–0.014
	140 (2320) B234F	1.9640–1.9648	0.0011–0.0033	0.0015–0.0058	5	2.0472–2.0476	0.0009–0.0028	0.006–0.018
	174 (2849) B280F	2.7583	0.0035	0.0106	4	2.0585	0.0031	0.015

VALVE SPECIFICATIONS

Year	Engine Displacement cu. in. (cc)	Seat Angle (deg.)	Face Angle (deg.)	Spring Test Pressure (lbs. @ in.)	Spring Installed Height (in.)	Stem-to-Guide Clearance (in.)		Stem Diameter (in.)	
						Intake	Exhaust	Intake	Exhaust
1987	140 (2320) B230F	45	44.5	158 @ 1.08	1.79	0.0012–0.0024	0.0024–0.0036	0.3132–0.3138	0.3128–0.3134
	140 (2320) B230F-Turbo	45	44.5	158 @ 1.08	1.79	0.0012–0.0024	0.0024–0.0036	0.3132–0.3138	0.3128–0.3134
	174 (2849) B280F	45	44.5	143 @ 1.18	1.85	①	①	②	②
1988	140 (2320) B230F	45	44.5	158 @ 1.08	1.79	0.0012–0.0024	0.0024–0.0036	0.3132–0.3138	0.3128–0.3134
	140 (2320) B230F-Turbo	45	44.5	158 @ 1.08	1.79	0.0012–0.0024	0.0024–0.0036	0.3132–0.3138	0.3128–0.3134
	174 (2849) B280F	45	44.5	143 @ 1.18	1.85	①	①	②	②
1989	140 (2320) B230F	45	44.5	158 @ 1.08	1.79	0.0012–0.0024	0.0024–0.0036	0.3132–0.3138	0.3128–0.3134
	140 (2320) B234F	45	44.5	144 @ 1.04	1.69	0.0012–0.0024	0.0016–0.0028	NA NA	NA NA
	140 (2320) B230F-Turbo	45	44.5	158 @ 1.08	1.79	0.0012–0.0024	0.0024–0.0036	0.3132–0.3138	0.3128–0.3134
	174 (2849) B280F	45	44.5	143 @ 1.18	1.85	①	①	②	②
1990–91	140 (2320) B230F	45	44.5	158 @ 1.08	1.79	0.0012–0.0024	0.0024–0.0036	0.3132–0.3138	0.3128–0.3134
	140 (2320) B234F	45	44.5	144 @ 1.04	1.69	0.0012–0.0024	0.0016–0.0028	NA NA	NA NA
	140 (2320) B230F-Turbo	45	44.5	158 @ 1.08	1.79	0.0012–0.0024	0.0024–0.0036	0.3132–0.3138	0.3128–0.3134
	174 (2849) B280F	45	44.5	143 @ 1.18	1.85	①	①	②	②

NOTE: Exhaust valves for turbo engines (including turbo diesel) are stellite coated and must not be machined. They may be ground against the valve seat.

NA   Not available
① Tapered valve guide ID—0.3150–0.3158
② Tapered valve stem
   Intake
   Base—0.3135–0.3141
   Top—3139–0.3145
   Exhaust
   Base—0.3127–0.3133
   Top—3136–0.3141

PISTON AND RING SPECIFICATIONS

All measurements are given in inches.

Year	Engine Displacement cu. in. (cc)	Piston Clearance	Ring Gap			Ring Side Clearance		
			Top Compression	Bottom Compression	Oil Control	Top Compression	Bottom Compression	Oil Control
1987	140 (2320) B230F	0.0004–0.0012	0.0118–0.0217	0.0118–0.0217	0.0118–0.0236	0.0024–0.0036	0.0016–0.0028	0.0012–0.0026
	140 (2320) B230F-Turbo	0.0004–0.0012	0.0118–0.0217	0.0118–0.0217	0.0118–0.0236	0.0024–0.0036	0.0016–0.0028	0.0012–0.0026
	174 (2849) B280F	0.0007–0.0015	0.0157–0.0236	0.0157–0.0236	0.0157–0.0570	0.0017–0.0029	0.0009–0.0212	0.0003–0.0091

PISTON AND RING SPECIFICATIONS
All measurements are given in inches.

Year	Engine Displacement cu. in. (cc)	Piston Clearance	Ring Gap			Ring Side Clearance		
			Top Compression	Bottom Compression	Oil Control	Top Compression	Bottom Compression	Oil Control
1988	140 (2320) B230F	0.0004–0.0012	0.0118–0.0217	0.0118–0.0217	0.0118–0.0236	0.0024–0.0036	0.0016–0.0028	0.0012–0.0026
	140 (2320) B230F-Turbo	0.0004–0.0012	0.0118–0.0217	0.0118–0.0217	0.0118–0.0236	0.0024–0.0036	0.0016–0.0028	0.0012–0.0026
	174 (2849) B280F	0.0007–0.0015	0.0157–0.0236	0.0157–0.0236	0.0157–0.0570	0.0017–0.0029	0.0009–0.0212	0.0003–0.0091
1989	140 (2320) B230F	0.0004–0.0012	0.0118–0.0217	0.0118–0.0217	0.0118–0.0236	0.0024–0.0036	0.0016–0.0028	0.0012–0.0026
	140 (2320) B234F	0.0004–0.0012	0.0120–0.0220	0.0120–0.0220	0.0120–0.0240	0.0024–0.0036	0.0016–0.0028	0.0012–0.0026
	140 (2320) B230F-Turbo	0.0004–0.0012	0.0118–0.0217	0.0118–0.0217	0.0118–0.0236	0.0024–0.0036	0.0016–0.0028	0.0012–0.0026
1990–91	140 (2320) B230F	0.0004–0.0012	0.0118–0.0217	0.0118–0.0217	0.0118–0.0236	0.0024–0.0036	0.0016–0.0028	0.0012–0.0026
	140 (2320) B234F	0.0004–0.0012	0.0120–0.0220	0.0120–0.0220	0.0120–0.0240	0.0024–0.0036	0.0016–0.0028	0.0012–0.0026
	140 (2320) B230F-Turbo	0.0004–0.0012	0.0118–0.0217	0.0118–0.0217	0.0118–0.0236	0.0024–0.0036	0.0016–0.0028	0.0012–0.0026
	174 (2849) B280F	0.0007–0.0015	0.0157–0.0236	0.0157–0.0236	0.0157–0.0570	0.0017–0.0029	0.0009–0.0212	0.0003–0.0091

TORQUE SPECIFICATIONS
All readings in ft. lbs.

Year	Engine Displacement cu. in. (cc)	Cylinder Head Bolts	Main Bearing Bolts	Rod Bearing Bolts	Crankshaft Pulley Bolts	Flywheel Bolts	Manifold		Spark Plugs
							Intake	Exhaust	
1987	140 (2320) B230F	⑧	80	14 ⑨	43 ⑩	47–54	12	12	18
	140 (2320) B230F-Turbo	⑧	80	14 ⑨	43 ⑩	47–54	12	12	18
	174 (2849) B280F	⑪	④	33–37	177–206	33–37	7–11	7–11	8–11
1988	140 (2320) B230F	⑧	80	14 ⑨	43 ⑩	47–54	12	12	18
	140 (2320) B230F-Turbo	⑧	80	14 ⑨	43 ⑩	47–54	12	12	18
	174 (2849) B280F	⑪	④	33–37	177–206	33–37	7–11	7–11	8–11
1989	140 (2320) B230F	⑧	80	14 ⑨	43 ⑩	47–54	12	12	18
	140 (2320) B234F	⑫	80	15 ⑨	44 ⑩	47–54	12	12	14–22
	140 (2320) B230F-Turbo	⑧	80	14 ⑨	43 ⑩	47–54	12	12	18
	174 (2849) B280F	⑪	④	33–37	177–206	33–37	7–11	7–11	8–11

TORQUE SPECIFICATIONS

All readings in ft. lbs.

Year	Engine Displacement cu. in. (cc)	Cylinder Head Bolts	Main Bearing Bolts	Rod Bearing Bolts	Crankshaft Pulley Bolts	Flywheel Bolts	Manifold Intake	Manifold Exhaust	Spark Plugs
1990-91	140 (2320) B230F	⑧	80	14 ⑨	43 ⑩	47–54	12	12	18
	140 (2320) B234F	⑫	80	15 ⑨	44 ⑩	47–54	12	12	14–22
	140 (2320) B230F-Turbo	⑧	80	14 ⑨	43 ⑩	47–54	12	12	18
	174 (2849) B280F	⑬	④	33–37	177–206	33–37	7–11	7–11	8–11

① Canada only
② Torque head bolts in two stages; first, tighten in sequence to 43 ft. lbs., then to 76–83 ft. lbs.
③ Torque head bolts in sequence to 7 ft. lbs., then 22 ft. lbs., then 44 ft. lbs. Wait 10–15 minutes and slacken the bolts ½ turn. Then torque to 11–14 ft. lbs. and then protractor torque to 116–120° (⅓ of a turn). Finally run to operating temperature, shut off and allow to cool for 30 min. Following the sequence, slacken, torque to 11–14 ft. lbs., and protractor torque to 113–117° each bolt.
④ Torque main bearing nuts to 22 ft. lbs., in sequence. Then slacken 1st nut ½ turn, tighten to 22–26 ft. lbs., and protractor torque to 73–77°. Repeat for remaining nuts following the sequence.

⑤ Torquing these bolts is a 6-step procedure:
A. Torque to 30 ft. lbs.
B. Torque to 44 ft. lbs.
C. Torque to 55 ft. lbs.
D. Tighten 180°, in one movement, without stopping.
E. Run engine until oil temperature is minimum 50°C–120°F.
F. Tighten 90°, in one movement, without stopping. After driving 600–1,000 miles., retorque bolts w/engine cold. DO NOT slacken first.
⑥ Using regular torque wrench. If Volvo tool 5188 is used, torque to 255 ft. lbs.
⑦ Injector: 50 ft. lbs.
⑧ Torque head bolts in three stages; first, tighten in sequence to 15 ft. lbs., then to 44 ft. lbs. Protractor (angle) tighten 90° more in one movement.
⑨ Angle—tighten 90°

⑩ Angle—tighten 60°
⑪ Torque all head bolts in sequence to 44 ft. lbs. (60 Nm), then loosen bolt No. 1 and retorque it to 15 ft. lbs. (20Nm), then tighten it to 106°; repeat for all bolts following number sequence. Loosen and tighten one bolt at a time. Run engine to operating temperature. Then let cool for 2 hours. Finally, tighten each bolt in sequence an additional 45°.
⑫ Torque head bolts in 3 stages; first tighten in sequence to 15 ft. lbs., then to 30 ft. lbs. Protractor (angle) tighten 115° more in one movement.
⑬ Asbestos-free gaskets, fixed-washer bolts Tighten all bolts in stages
1 Tighten bolts to 60 Nm (44 ft. lb.)
2 a Loosen bolts
b Tighten bolts to 40 Nm (30 ft. lb.)
c Angle-tighten bolts 160°–180°
3 Adjust valves

BRAKE SPECIFICATIONS

All measurements in inches unless noted.

Year	Model	Lug Nut Torque (ft. lbs.)	Master Cylinder Bore	Brake Disc Minimum Thickness	Brake Disc Maximum Runout	Standard Brake Drum Diameter	Minimum Lining Thickness Front	Minimum Lining Thickness Rear
1987	240 DL	88	0.878	② (F) 0.330 (R)	0.004 (F) 0.004 (R)	—	0.060	0.060
	240 GL	88	0.878	② (F) 0.330 (R)	0.003 (F) 0.004 (R)	—	0.060	0.060
	740 GL	63	③	④ (F) 0.330 (R)	0.003 (F) 0.004 (R)	—	0.118	0.078
	740 GLE	63	③	④ (F) 0.330 (R)	0.003 (F) 0.004 (R)	—	0.118	0.078
	740 Turbo	63	③	④ (F) 0.330 (R)	0.003 (F) 0.004 (R)	—	0.118	0.078
	760 GLE	63	③	④ (F) 0.330 (R)	0.003 (F) 0.004 (R)	—	0.118	0.078
	760 Turbo	63	③	④ (F) 0.330 (R)	0.003 (F) 0.004 (R)	—	0.118	0.078
	780	63	③	④ (F) 0.330 (R)	0.003 (F) 0.004 (R)	—	0.118	0.078

BRAKE SPECIFICATIONS

All measurements in inches unless noted.

Year	Model	Lug Nut Torque (ft. lbs.)	Master Cylinder Bore	Brake Disc Minimum Thickness	Brake Disc Maximum Runout	Standard Brake Drum Diameter	Minimum Lining Thickness Front	Minimum Lining Thickness Rear
1988	240 DL	88	0.878	② (F) 0.330 (R)	0.004 (F) 0.004 (R)	—	0.060	0.060
	240 GL	88	0.878	② (F) 0.330 (R)	0.003 (F) 0.004 (R)	—	0.060	0.060
	740 GL	63	③	④ (F) 0.330 (R)	0.003 (F) 0.004 (R)	—	0.118	0.078
	.740 GLE	63	③	④ (F) 0.330 (R)	0.003 (F) 0.004 (R)	—	0.118	0.078
	740 Turbo	63	③	④ (F) 0.330 (R)	0.003 (F) 0.004 (R)	—	0.118	0.078
	760 GLE	63	③	④ (F) 0.330 (R)	0.003 (F) 0.004 (R)	—	0.118	0.078
	760 Turbo	63	③	④ (F) 0.330 (R)	0.003 (F) 0.004 (R)	—	0.118	0.078
	780	63	③	④ (F) 0.330 (R)	0.003 (F) 0.004 (R)	—	0.118	0.078
1989	240 DL	88	0.878	② (F) 0.330 (R)	0.004 (F) 0.004 (R)	—	0.060	0.060
	240 GL	88	0.878	② (F) 0.330 (R)	0.003 (F) 0.004 (R)	—	0.060	0.060
	740 GL	63	③	④ (F) 0.330 (R)	0.003 (F) 0.004 (R)	—	0.118	0.078
	740 GLE	63	③	④ (F) 0.330 (R)	0.003 (F) 0.004 (R)	—	0.118	0.078
	740 Turbo	63	③	④ (F) 0.330 (R)	0.003 (F) 0.004 (R)	—	0.118	0.078
	760 GLE	63	③	④ (F) 0.330 (R)	0.003 (F) 0.004 (R)	—	0.118	0.078
	760 Turbo	63	③	④ (F) 0.330 (R)	0.003 (F) 0.004 (R)	—	0.118	0.078
	780	63	③	④ (F) 0.330 (R)	0.003 (F) 0.004 (R)	—	0.118	0.078
1990-91	240 DL	88	0.878	② (F) 0.330 (R)	0.004 (F) 0.004 (R)	—	0.060	0.060
	240 GL	88	0.878	② (F) 0.330 (R)	0.003 (F) 0.004 (R)	—	0.060	0.060
	740 GL	63	③	④ (F) 0.330 (R)	0.003 (F) 0.004 (R)	—	0.118	0.078
	740 GLE	63	③	④ (F) 0.330 (R)	0.003 (F) 0.004 (R)	—	0.118	0.078
	740 Turbo	63	③	④ (F) 0.330 (R)	0.003 (F) 0.004 (R)	—	0.118	0.078
	760 GLE	63	③	④ (F) ⑤ 0.330 (R)	0.003 (F) ⑥ 0.004 (R)	—	0.118	0.078

BRAKE SPECIFICATIONS

All measurements in inches unless noted.

Year	Model	Lug Nut Torque (ft. lbs.)	Master Cylinder Bore	Brake Disc Minimum Thickness	Brake Disc Maximum Runout	Standard Brake Drum Diameter	Minimum Lining Thickness Front	Minimum Lining Thickness Rear
1990–91	760 Turbo	63	③	④ (F) ⑤ 0.330 (R)	0.003 (F) ⑥ 0.004 (R)	—	0.118	0.078
	780	63	③	④ (F) ⑤ 0.330 (R)	0.003 (F) ⑥ 0.004 (R)	—	0.118	0.078

① Station wagon
② Ventilated—0.820
Non-ventilated—0.536
③ Early type—0.878
Late type—0.938
④ Ventilated—0.788
Non-ventilated—0.433
⑤ Multi link rear suspension
0.314
⑥ Multi link rear suspension
0.003

WHEEL ALIGNMENT

Year	Model	Caster Range (deg.)	Caster Preferred Setting (deg.)	Camber Range (deg.)	Camber Preferred Setting (deg.)	Toe-in (in.)	Steering Axis Inclination (deg.)
1987	240 DL	3P–4P	—	1/4P–3/4P	1/2P	1/8	12
	240 GL	3P–4P	—	1/4P–3/4P	1/2P	1/8	12
	740 GL	4 1/2P–5 1/2P	—	3/16N–13/16P	—	9/64	NA
	740 GLE	4 1/2P–5 1/2P	—	3/16N–13/16P	—	9/64	NA
	740 Turbo	4 1/2P–5 1/2P	—	3/16N–13/16P	—	9/64	NA
	760 GLE	4 1/2P–5 1/2P	—	3/16N–13/16P	—	9/64	NA
	760 Turbo	4 1/2P–5 1/2P	—	3/16N–13/16P	—	9/64	NA
	780	4 1/2P–5 1/2P	—	3/16N–13/16P	—	9/64	NA
1988	240 DL	3P–4P	—	1/4P–3/4P	1/2P	1/8	12
	240 GL	3P–4P	—	1/4P–3/4P	1/2P	1/8	12
	740 GL	4 1/2P–5 1/2P	—	3/16N–13/16P	—	9/64	NA
	740 GLE	4 1/2P–5 1/2P	—	3/16N–13/16P	—	9/64	NA
	740 Turbo	4 1/2P–5 1/2P	—	3/16N–13/16P	—	9/64	NA
	760 GLE	4 1/2P–5 1/2P	—	3/16N–13/16P	—	9/64	NA
	760 Turbo	4 1/2P–5 1/2P	—	3/16N–13/16P	—	9/64	NA
	780	4 1/2P–5 1/2P	—	3/16N–13/16P	—	9/64	NA
1989	240 DL	3P–4P	—	1/4P–3/4P	1/2P	1/8	12
	240 GL	3P–4P	—	1/4P–3/4P	1/2P	1/8	12
	740 GL	4 1/2P–5 1/2P	—	3/16N–13/16P	—	9/64	NA
	740 GLE	4 1/2P–5 1/2P	—	3/16N–13/16P	—	9/64	NA
	740 Turbo	4 1/2P–5 1/2P	—	3/16N–13/16P	—	9/64	NA
	760 GLE	4 1/2P–5 1/2P	—	3/16N–13/16P	—	9/64	NA
	760 Turbo	4 1/2P–5 1/2P	—	3/16N–13/16P	—	9/64	NA
	780	4 1/2P–5 1/2P	—	3/16N–13/16P	—	9/64	NA

WHEEL ALIGNMENT

Year	Model	Caster Range (deg.)	Caster Preferred Setting (deg.)	Camber Range (deg.)	Camber Preferred Setting (deg.)	Toe-in (in.)	Steering Axis Inclination (deg.)
1990-91	240 DL	3P-4P	—	1/4P-3/4P	1/2P	1/8	12
	240 GL	3P-4P	—	1/4P-3/4P	1/2P	1/8	12
	740 GL	4 1/2P-5 1/2P	—	3/16N-13/16P	—	9/64	NA
	740 GLE	4 1/2P-5 1/2P	—	3/16N-13/16P	—	9/64	NA
	740 Turbo	4 1/2P-5 1/2P	—	3/16N-13/16P	—	9/64	NA
	760 GLE	4 1/2P-5 1/2P	—	3/16N-13/16P	—	9/64	NA
	760 Turbo	4 1/2P-5 1/2P	—	3/16N-13/16P	—	9/64	NA
	780	4 1/2P-5 1/2P	—	3/16N-13/16P	—	9/64	NA

N – Negative
P – Positive
① Station Wagon
② Manual steering: 2P–3P
③ Manual steering: 13/64

ENGINE ELECTRICAL

NOTE: Disconnecting the negative battery cable on some vehicles may interfere with the functions of the on board computer systems and may require the computer to undergo a relearning process, once the negative battery cable is reconnected.

Distributor

Removal

1. Unsnap the distributor cap clasps and remove the cap.
2. Crank the engine until No. 1 cylinder is at Top Dead Center (TDC) of the compression stroke. At this point, the rotor should point to the spark plug wire socket for No. 1 cylinder and the 0 degree timing mark on the crankshaft damper should be aligned with the pointer. For ease of assembly, scribe a chalk mark on the distributor housing to note the position of the rotor.
3. Disconnect the negative battery terminal. Disconnect the primary lead from the coil at its terminal on the distributor housing. On electronic fuel-injected models, disconnect the plug for the triggering contacts. On all models, except Canadian B21A, remove the retaining screw for the primary voltage wire connector and pull it from the distributor housing.
4. Remove the vacuum hose(s) from the regulator.
5. Remove the distributor attaching screw and lift out the distributor.

Installation

6. When ready to install the distributor, if the engine has been disturbed, find TDC, of the compression stroke, for No. 1 cylinder. If the engine has not been disturbed, install the distributor with the rotor pointing to the No. 1 cylinder spark plug wire socket or the chalkmark made prior to removal. On B21, B27 and B28F engines, the distributor drive gear teeth are beveled, which will cause the rotor to turn counterclockwise as the distributor is installed. For this reason, it is necessary to back off the rotor clockwise, about 60 degrees on the B21 or 40 degrees on the B27 and B28F, to compensate for this. What is necessary is that the rotor aligns with the mark made prior to removal after the distributor is bolted down.
7. Connect the primary lead to its terminal on the distributor housing. On electronic fuel injected models, connect the plug for the triggering contacts. Push the primary voltage wire connector into its slot in the distributor housing and tighten the retaining screw.
8. Connect the vacuum hose(s) to the vacuum regulator, if equipped.
9. If the distributor was disassembled or if the contact point setting was disturbed, proceed to set the point gap and/or dwell angle on B21A (Canadian) engine.
10. Install the distributor cap and secure the clasps. Proceed to set the ignition timing. Tighten the distributor attaching screw.

Ignition Timing

Adjustment

NOTE: On later models, ignition timing is set at the factory and controlled by the ECU. Field adjustment is not possible but timing can be checked.

1. Clean the crankshaft damper and pointer on the water pump housing with a solvent-soaked rag so the marks can be seen.
2. Connect a timing light according to the manufacturer's instructions.
3. Scribe a mark on the crankshaft damper and on the marker with chalk or luminescent (day-glo) paint to highlight the correct timing setting.
4. Disconnect and plug the distributor vacuum line, if equipped, and disconnect the hose between the air cleaner and the inlet duct, if equipped, at the duct.
5. Disconnect and plug the vacuum hose at the EGR valve, if equipped.
6. Attach a tachometer to the engine and set the idle speed to specifications.
7. With the engine running, aim the timing light at the pointer and the marks on the damper.

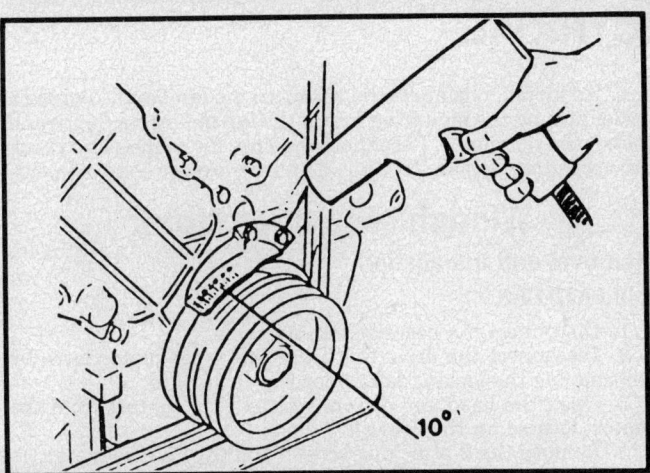

Engine timing marks—B27F and B28F engines

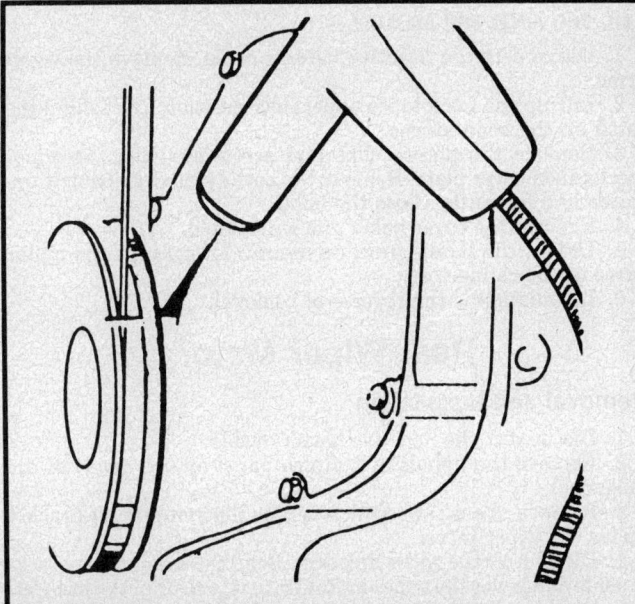

Aim timing light at the pointer and marks on the damper

8. If the marks do not coincide, stop the engine, loosen the distributor pinch bolt and start the engine again. While observing the timing light flashes on the markers, grasp the distributor vacuum regulator and rotate the distributor until the marks coincide.

9. Stop the engine and tighten the distributor pinch bolt, taking care not to disturb the setting.

10. Reconnect all disconnected hoses and remove the timing light and tachometer from the engine.

Alternator

Precautions

Several precautions must be observed with alternator equipped vehicles to avoid damage to the unit.

- If the battery is removed for any reason, make sure it is re-

connected with the correct polarity. Reversing the battery connections may result in damage to the one-way rectifiers.

- When utilizing a booster battery as a starting aid, always connect the positive to positive terminals and the negative terminal from the booster battery to a good engine ground on the vehicle being started.
- Never use a fast charger as a booster to start vehicles.
- Disconnect the battery cables when charging the battery with a fast charger.
- Never attempt to polarize the alternator.
- Do not use test lamps of more than 12 volts when checking diode continuity.
- Do not short across or ground any of the alternator terminals.
- The polarity of the battery, alternator and regulator must be matched and considered before making any electrical connections within the system.
- Never separate the alternator on an open circuit. Make sure all connections within the circuit are clean and tight.
- Disconnect the battery ground terminal when performing any service on electrical components.
- Disconnect the battery if arc welding is to be done on the vehicle.

Belt Tension Adjustment

Accessory drive belt tension is correct when the deflection made with light finger pressure on the belt at a midway point is about ½ in. Any belt that is glazed, frayed or stretched so it cannot be tightened sufficiently must be replaced.

Incorrect belt tension is corrected by moving the driven accessory (alternator, air pump, power steering pump or air conditioning compressor) away from or toward the driving pulley. Loosen the mounting and adjusting bolts on the respective accessory and tighten them, once the belt tension is correct. Never position a metal prybar on the rear end of the alternator, air pump or power steering pump housing, they can be deformed easily.

Removal and Installation

1. Disconnect the negative battery cable.
2. Disconnect the electrical leads to the alternator. Remove all necessary components in order to gain access to the alternator retaining bolts.
3. Remove the adjusting arm-to-alternator bolt and the adjusting arm-to-engine bolt.
4. Remove the alternator mounting bolt.
5. Remove the fan belt and lift the alternator forward and out.
6. Reverse the above procedure to install, taking care to properly tension the fan (drive) belt.

Starter

Removal and Installation

1. Disconnect the negative battery cable.
2. Disconnect the leads from the starter motor. Remove the necessary components in order to gain access to the starter retaining bolts. Raise and safely support the vehicle.
3. Remove the bolts retaining the starter motor brace to the cylinder block (B21 only) and the bolts retaining the starter motor to the flywheel housing and lift it off.
4. To install, position the starter motor to the flywheel housing and install the retaining bolts finger-tight. Torque the bolts to approximately 25 ft. lbs. (34 Nm) and apply locking compound to the threads.
5. Connect the starter motor leads and the negative battery cable.

CHASSIS ELECTRICAL

------------------ CAUTION ------------------
On vehicles equipped with an air bag, the negative battery cable must be disconnected, before working on the system. Failure to do so may result in deployment of the air bag and possible personal injury.

Heater Blower Motor

Removal and Installation
240 MODELS
Without Air Conditioning

1. Disconnect the negative battery cable. Remove the heater unit.
2. Place the unit on its side with the control valve facing upward. Remove the spring clips and separate the housing halves.
3. Lift out the old fan motor and replace it with a new unit, making sure the support leg without the "foot" points to the output for the defroster channel.
4. Assemble the heater housing halves with new spring clips and seal the joint without clips with soft sealing compound.
5. Install the heater unit.

With Air Conditioning

In order to remove the blower motor, both the right and left blower wheels must first be removed. The heater unit does not have to be removed.
1. Disconnect the negative battery cable.
2. Lift the carpet and remove the central unit side panels.
3. Remove the retaining screws for the control panel and move the panel as for back on the transmission tunnel as the electrical cables will permit.
4. Remove the attaching screws for the rear seat heater ducts and disconnect the ducts from the central unit.
5. Remove the instrument cluster.
6. Remove the glovebox by unscrewing the 4 attaching screws, removing the glovebox door stop and disconnecting the wires from the glovebox courtesy light. Remove the molded dashboard padding from under the glovebox.
7. Disconnect the vacuum hoses to the left and right defroster nozzle vacuum motors, then remove the nozzles and the left and right air ducts.
8. Remove the air hoses between the left and right inside air vents.
9. Remove the clamps on the central unit outer ends and remove the ends.
10. Pry off the locking retainer for the turbines (blower wheels) and remove both left and right blower wheels.
11. Position the heater control valve capillary tube aside.
12. Remove the left inner end (blower housing) from the central unit.
13. Unscrew the 3 retaining screws and remove the fan motor retainer.
14. Disconnect the plug contact from the fan motor control panel. Release the tabs of electric cables from the plug contact and removing the rubber grommet and pull the electrical cables down through the central unit right opening.
15. Remove the fan motor from the left opening.
16. Reverse the above procedure to install.

740, 760 AND 780 MODELS

1. Disconnect the negative battery cable. Remove the panel under the glove compartment.
2. Unfasten the screws securing the fan motor and lower the motor. Disconnect the hose for air cooling on the motor and disconnect the wiring.
3. Remove the motor and fan.

4. To install, reconnect the wiring to the fan motor. Spread a sealer around the mounting face of the fan mounting flange and install the fan motor. Reconnect the hose for cooling and check fan operation. Reinstall the panel under the glove compartment.

Windshield Wiper Motor

Removal and Installation
240 MODELS

1. Disconnect the negative battery cable.
2. Disconnect the drive link from the wiper motor lever by unsnapping the locking tab under the dashboard.
3. Open the hood and disconnect the plug contact from the motor, located on the firewall.
4. Remove the 3 attaching screws and lift out the motor.
5. Reverse the above procedure to install, taking care to transfer the rubber seal, rubber damper and spacer sleeves to the new motor.

740, 760 AND 780 MODELS

1. Disconnect the negative battery cable. Remove the wiper arms.
2. Lift up the hood to its uppermost position by pushing the catch on the hood hinges.
3. Remove the plastic clips and screw securing the wiper mechanism cover plate. Remove the cover plate by lifting it upwards and forwards. Close the hood.
4. Remove the cover below the windshield.
5. Unbolt the motor from its mount. Disconnect the motor wires at the connectors.
6. Installation is the reverse of removal.

Rear Wiper Motor

Removal and Installation

1. Disconnect the negative battery cable.
2. Remove the upholstered finish panel on the inside of the tailgate.
3. Remove the screws which retain the reinforcing bracket under the wiper motor.
4. Disconnect the wiper link arm. Bend the reinforcing bracket aside and lower the wiper motor until it is clear of the bracket.
5. Disconnect the electrical wires from the motor and remove the motor.
6. Reverse the above procedure to install.

Instrument Cluster

Removal and Installation

1. Disconnect the negative battery cable. Remove the sound-proofing above the foot pedals.
2. Remove the 2 catches and screws holding the panel.
3. Press the instrument panel forwards. Remove the panel from the dash.
4. Disconnect the connectors and remove the instrument panel completely.

Combination Switch

Removal and Installation

1. Disconnect the negative battery cable.
2. Remove the steering wheel.
3. Remove the upper and lower steering column casings.
4. Unscrew the switch/lever assembly.
5. Disconnect the wires from the switches.

6. Installation is the reverse of the removal procedure.

Ignition Lock/Switch

Removal and Installation

240 MODELS

1. Remove noise insulation panel and center side panel.
2. Disconnect the wires from the switch.
3. Pry out the switch with a suitable tool.
4. Install in reverse of removal.

740, 760 AND 780 MODELS

1. Remove the sound proofing under the instrument panel.
2. Disconnect the connector from the ignition switch.
3. Remove the upper steering column casing and the panel around the ignition switch.
4. Loosen the mounting screw for the switch.
5. Insert the key and turn it to the **START** position. Through the hole under the holder, press in the catch and remove the ignition switch.
6. To install, insert the key and turn and depress the locking tab. Remove the key. Position the switch and release the locking tab by inserting the key. Tighten the mounting screw and reverse the rest of the removal procedure. Test the switch.

Neutral Safety Switch

Adjustment

All models have an adjustable switch, located under the shifter quadrant on the tunnel. To adjust:

1. Remove the shifter quadrant cover.
2. Place the shifter lever in **P**. Check that the round switch contact centers over the indicating line for **P**. If not, loosen the 2 switch mounting screws and align the switch.

3. Place the shifter lever in **N**. Repeat the check and adjust as necessary.
4. Finally check that the engine starts only in **P** or **N** and check that the back-up lights work only in **R**.

Fuses, Circuit Breakers and Relays

Location

On 240 series, the fuse box is located under a protective cover, below the dashboard, in front of the driver's door. On the 740, 760 and 780, the fuses are located under a plastic panel in the center console, behind the ashtray.

On electronic fuel injected models, an additional fuse box is located in the engine compartment on the left wheel well. It houses a single fuse protecting the electric fuel pump.

Computers

Location

The computer for electronic fuel injection is behind the kick panel in front of the right front door. The computer for electronic ignition control is behind the kick panel in front of the driver's door or mounted under the dash near the pedals.

Flashers

Location

On 700 series vehicles, the flasher is the tall one in the center of the relay/fuse panel. On 200 series vehicles, the flasher is also on the fuse/relay panel but its location varies from year-to-year. The owner's manual should indicate the location.

ENGINE COOLING

Electric Cooling Fan

Removal and Installation

1. Disconnect the negative battery cable. Remove the radiator and expansion tank caps, disconnect the lower radiator hose and drain the cooling system.
2. Remove the expansion tank and hose and drain the coolant. Remove the upper radiator hose. On vehicles with automatic transmission, disconnect and plug the transmission oil cooler lines at the radiator.
3. Remove the retaining bolts for the radiator and fan shroud, if equipped, and lift out the radiator.
4. Installation is the reverse of the removal procedure. Start the engine and check for leaks.

Heater Core

Removal and Installation

WITHOUT AIR CONDITIONING

1. Disconnect the negative battery cable. Remove the heater unit.
2. Place the unit on its side with the control valve facing upward. Remove the spring clips and separate the housing halves.
3. Disconnect the capillary tube from the heater core and then lift out the core.
4. Reverse the above procedure to install, being careful to

transfer the foam plastic packing to the new heater core and to install the fragile capillary tube carefully on the core.

WITH AIR CONDITIONING

240 Models

─────── **CAUTION** ───────

Do not disconnect the refrigerant lines from the air conditioning system. These lines carry a dangerous refrigerant, the gas R–12.

1. Disconnect the negative battery cable. Remove the combination heater-air conditioner unit.
2. Remove the left outer end of the central unit. Remove the locking retainer and the turbine (blower wheel).
3. Remove the 2 retaining screws for the left transmission tunnel bracket.
4. Remove the lockring for the left intake shutter shaft.
5. Remove the 3 retaining screws and lift off the inner end.
6. Remove the 3 retaining screws for the fan motor retainer.
7. Disconnect the heater hoses at the heater core.
8. Remove the clamps which retain the central unit halves together, lift off the left half and remove the heater core.
9. Reverse the above procedure to install, taking care to transfer the foam plastic packing to the new heater core.

740, 760 and 780 Models

1. Disconnect the negative battery cable.
2. Pinch the hoses to the heater core near the firewall in the

engine compartment. Use locking pliers. Make sure the hoses are pinched sufficiently so the hose is completely blocked off. Remove the hose clamps on the engine compartment side of the hoses, close to the firewall.

3. Press down the clip under the ashtray and pull the tray out. Remove the cigarette lighter and the storage compartment.

4. Remove the engine console around the shift lever and parking brake. Unplug the connector.

5. Remove the panel under the driver's side dashboard and remove the air duct to the steering column outlet.

6. Pull down the driver's side floor mat and remove the front and rear edge side panel screws. Remove the panels.

7. On the passenger's side, remove the 3 clips that fasten the panel under the glove compartment and remove the panel. Remove the glove compartment and its lighting.

8. Pull down the floor mat on the right side and remove the front and rear edge side panel screws.

9. Remove the radio compartment by pressing forward on the inner wall and removing the screw.

10. Remove the screws inside the center console and remove the side panel screws and the panels.

11. Remove the panel around the heater control. Remove the radio compartment console and remove the control panel. Free the central electrical unit and remove the mounting.

12. Remove the center panel vent and the screw holding the distribution unit. Mark all air ducts to the panel vents and to the distribution unit with tape for later installation and remove the ducts.

13. Remove the vacuum hoses from the vacuum motors.

14. Remove the distribution unit. Remove the heater core retaining clips and remove the heater core.

15. To install, reverse the above procedure taking note of the following vacuum hose connections: On climate unit-equipped vehicles, connect the red hose to the upper shutter for the panel vents and the light brown hose to the lower shutter. Connect the yellow and blue hoses to the floor/defrost shutter, the yellow to the lower one. On automatic climate control-equipped vehicles, connect the red hose to the upper shutter for the panel vent and the blue hose to the defrost vent. Connect the light brown hose to the lower shutter for the panel unit.

Water Pump

Removal and Installation

200 SERIES ENGINES

1. Disconnect the negative battery cable. Remove the overflow tank cap. Drain the cooling system.

2. Remove the fan and fan shroud.

3. Remove the drive belts and the water pump pulley.

4. If necessary, remove the timing belt cover.

5. Remove the lower radiator hose.

6. Remove the retaining bolt for the coolant pipe, beneath exhaust manifold, and pull the pipe rearward.

7. Remove the 6 retaining bolts and lift off the water pump.

8. Clean the gasket contact surfaces thoroughly and use a new gasket and O-rings, especially between the cylinder head and top of water pump.

9. Installation is the reverse of the removal procedure.

B28F AND B280F ENGINES

1. Disconnect the negative battery cable. Remove the front and main sections of the intake manifold.

2. Remove the overflow tank cap and drain the cooling system.

3. Disconnect both radiator hoses. On automatic transmission vehicles, disconnect the transmission cooler lines at the radiator. Disconnect the fan shroud. Remove the radiator and fan shroud.

4. Remove the fan.

Make sure the O-ring around the lower lip of water pump is in good condition. Replace if there is any damage

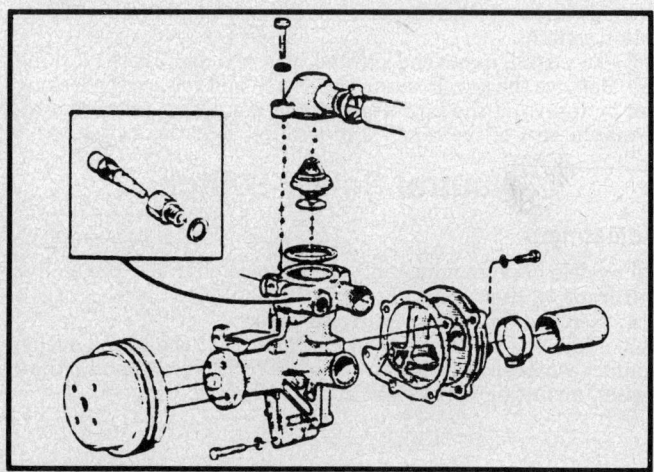

Water pump assembly—B280 engine

5. Remove the hoses from the water pump to each cylinder head.

6. Remove the fan belts. Remove the water pump pulley.

7. Loosen the hose clamps at the rear of the water pump.

8. Remove the water pump from the block (3 bolts).

9. Transfer the thermal time lender and temperature sensor to the new water pump.

10. Transfer the thermostat cover, thermostat and rear pump cover to the new pump.

11. Reverse the removal procedure to install.

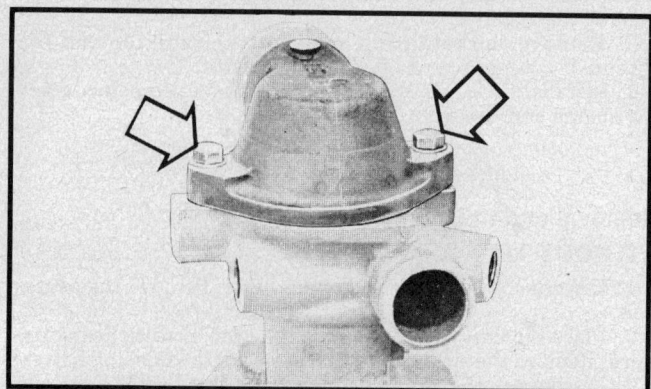

Remove the two top water pump bolts for access to the V6 thermostat

Thermostat

Removal and Installation

1. Disconnect the lower radiator hose and drain the cooling system.
2. Remove the 2 bolts securing the thermostat housing to the cylinder head and carefully lift the housing free.
3. Remove all old gasket material from the mating surfaces and remove the thermostat.
4. Test the operation of the thermostat by immersing it in a container of heated water. Replace any thermostat that does not open at the correct temperature.
5. Place the thermostat, with a new gasket, in the cylinder head. Fit the thermostat housing to the head and hand-tighten the 2 bolts until snug. Do not tighten the bolts more than ¼ turn past snug.
6. Connect the lower radiator hose and replace the coolant.

Cooling System Bleeding

1. Fill the radiator with the proper type of coolant.
2. With the radiator cap off, start the engine and allow it to run and reach normal operating temperature.
3. Run the heater at full force and with the temperature lever in the **HOT** position. Be sure the heater control valve is functioning.
4. Shut the engine off and recheck the coolant level, refill as necessary.

FUEL SYSTEM

Fuel System Service Precautions

Safety is the most important factor when performing not only fuel system maintenance but any type of maintenance. Failure to conduct maintenance and repairs in a safe manner may result in serious personal injury or death. Maintenance and testing of the vehicle's fuel system components can be accomplished safely and effectively by adhering to the following rules and guidelines.

● To avoid the possibility of fire and personal injury, always disconnect the negative battery cable unless the repair or test procedure requires that battery voltage be applied.

● Always relieve the fuel system pressure prior to disconnecting any fuel system component (injector, fuel rail, pressure regulator, etc.), fitting or fuel line connection. Exercise extreme caution whenever relieving fuel system pressure to avoid exposing skin, face and eyes to fuel spray. Please be advised that fuel under pressure may penetrate the skin or any part of the body that it contacts.

● Always place a shop towel or cloth around the fitting or connection prior to loosening to absorb any excess fuel due to spillage. Ensure that all fuel spillage (should it occur) is quickly removed from engine surfaces. Ensure that all fuel soaked cloths or towels are deposited into a suitable waste container.

● Always keep a dry chemical (Class B) fire extinguisher near the work area.

● Do not allow fuel spray or fuel vapors to come into contact with a spark or open flame.

● Always use a backup wrench when loosening and tightening fuel line connection fittings. This will prevent unnecessary stress and torsion to fuel line piping. Always follow the proper torque specifications.

● Always replace worn fuel fitting O-rings with new. Do not substitute fuel hose or equivalent, where fuel pipe is installed.

Relieving Fuel System Pressure

1. Place the proper size wrenches onto the fuel filter fittings.
2. Place a shop towel or rag around the fuel filter fittings and wrenches.
3. Slowly loosen the fuel line at the fuel filter until all pressure is relieved.
4. Tighten fuel filter fittings.

Fuel Filter

Removal and Installation

On earlier models, the fuel filter is mounted under the hood, on or near the air flow sensor. It is also near the battery, so disconnect the negative terminal before changing the filter. Be sure to use the new gaskets provided with the new filter.

On newer models the fuel filter is a "lifetime" filter and only needs to be changed in the event of contamination. It is mounted under the vehicle, in assembly with the pump, accumulator and reservoir but can usually be removed separately.

1. Disconnect the negative battery cable.
2. Raise and safely support the vehicle, if changing under vehicle filter.
3. Relieve the fuel system pressure.

------ CAUTION ------
When relieving the pressure in the fuel system, place a container under the filter to catch the excess fuel.

4. Remove the fuel lines, the mounting bracket nut and the filter.
5. Installation is the reverse of removal. Be sure to use the new sealing rings and torque the fuel lines to the filter to 14 ft. lbs. (20 Nm).

NOTE: Fuel flow direction arrow is marked on the new (and old) filter. Arrow follows direction from fuel tank to engine.

Electric Fuel Pump

Removal and Installation

NOTE: The main fuel pump is located under the vehicle in front of the left rear wheel or at the crossmember. There is also a transfer pump in the tank.

1. Disconnect the negative battery cable.
2. Raise and safely support the vehicle.
3. Disconnect the electrical connector.
4. Relieve the fuel system pressure.

------ CAUTION ------
When relieving the pressure in the fuel system, place a container under the fuel pump to catch the excess fuel.

5. Remove the mounting bolts and the fuel pump.
6. When nstalling, be sure to use new sealing rings and/or gaskets.

Transfer Pump

Removal and Installation

1. Disconnect the negative battery cable.

2. Behind the rear seat in the rear of the vehicle, pull back the carpet and disconnect the electrical connectors from the sending unit.

3. Remove the access plate from the floor.

4. Remove the fuel hoses from the sending unit.

5. Unscrew the cap and carefully lift the sending unit from the fuel tank. Note the direction of the float in the tank.

6. Remove the transfer pump from the sending unit.

7. When installing, be sure the float points the same way and use a new O-ring at the sending unit.

Fuel Injection

For further information, please refer to "Chilton's Electronic Engine Control's Manual" for additional coverage.

Idle Speed and Mixture Adjustment

Fuel injection is set at the factory and controlled by an Electronic Control Unit (ECU). If the measured CO or idle is out of spec, look for other problems under the hood (such as a vacuum leak, bad sensor, loose connection, etc.) and correct any faults before adjusting anything. Idle speed is set with the idle speed adjustment screw on the side of the throttle body. Do not adjust the throttle stop screw. On the CIS engine management systems, idle speed is controlled by the ECU and no adjustment is available. On all systems, air/fuel mixture is sealed at the factory and controlled by the ECU. No adjustment is available.

NOTE: The B28F V6 is equipped with 2 micro-switches actuated by throttle control. This second micro-switch closes a Lambda-Sond (the oxygen sensor) circuit at full throttle to provide richer air/fuel mixture at maximum acceleration. Vehicles sold in high-altitude areas have the switch disconnected.

1. To adjust the switch, loosen the micro-switch retaining screws. Turn the switch sideways. The test light should come on, then go out 0.10 in. (2.5mm) before the pulley touches the full throttle stop. Tighten the retaining screws.

2. To check full throttle enrichment switch operations, disconnect the green wire at the micro-switch. Connect a test light between the micro-switch terminal and the positive battery terminal.

3. Turn the pulley slowly to the full throttle stop. The test light should light up 0.04–0.15 in. (1–4mm) before the pulley touches the stop. Adjust the switch as necessary, following the switch adjustment procedure above.

Fuel Injector

Removal and Installation

On earlier models, the injectors are held in place by rubber rings and can be pried out of their holders one at a time without disconnecting the fuel lines. On the Regina electronic fuel injection, the injectors are mounted with a common rail and must all be removed as a unit with the regulator and cold start injector.

EMISSION CONTROLS

For further information, please refer to "Professional Emission Component Application Guide".

Emission Warning Lamps

Resetting

On most models, there is an "Engine Service" or a "Lamda Sond" light on the instrument panel that lights up at specific intervals or if the on board computer detects a fault. Re-setting this lamp is a simple procedure. Remove the sound proofing above the pedals and remove the screws and catches at the base of the instrument panel. Tilt the panel out and locate the red reset button.

ENGINE MECHANICAL

NOTE: Disconnecting the negative battery cable on some vehicles may interfere with the functions of the on board computer systems and may require the computer to undergo a relearning process, once the negative battery cable is reconnected.

Engine Assembly

Removal and Installation

B23E AND B230F ENGINES

1. If equipped with manual transmission, remove the 4 retaining clips and lift up the shifter boot. Then, remove the snapring from the shifter.

2. Remove the battery.

3. Disconnect the windshield washer hose and engine compartment light wire. Scribe marks around the hood mount brackets on the under-side of the hood for later alignment. Remove the hood.

4. Remove the overflow tank cap. Drain the cooling system.

5. Remove the upper and lower radiator hoses. Disconnect the overflow hoses at the radiator. Disconnect the PCV hose at the cylinder head.

6. If equipped with automatic transmission disconnect the oil cooler lines at the radiator.

7. Remove the radiator and fan shroud.

8. Remove the air cleaner assembly and hoses.

9. Disconnect the hoses at the air pump. Remove the air pump and drive belt, if equipped.

10. Disconnect the vacuum pump hoses and remove the vacuum pump. disconnect the power brake booster vacuum hose.

11. Remove the power steering pump, drive belt and bracket. Position aside.

12. If equipped with air conditioning, remove the crankshaft pulley and compressor drive belt. Then, install the pulley again for reference. Remove the air conditioning wire connector and the compressor from its bracket and position aside. Remove the bracket.

13. Disconnect the vacuum hoses from the engine. Disconnect the carbon canister hoses.

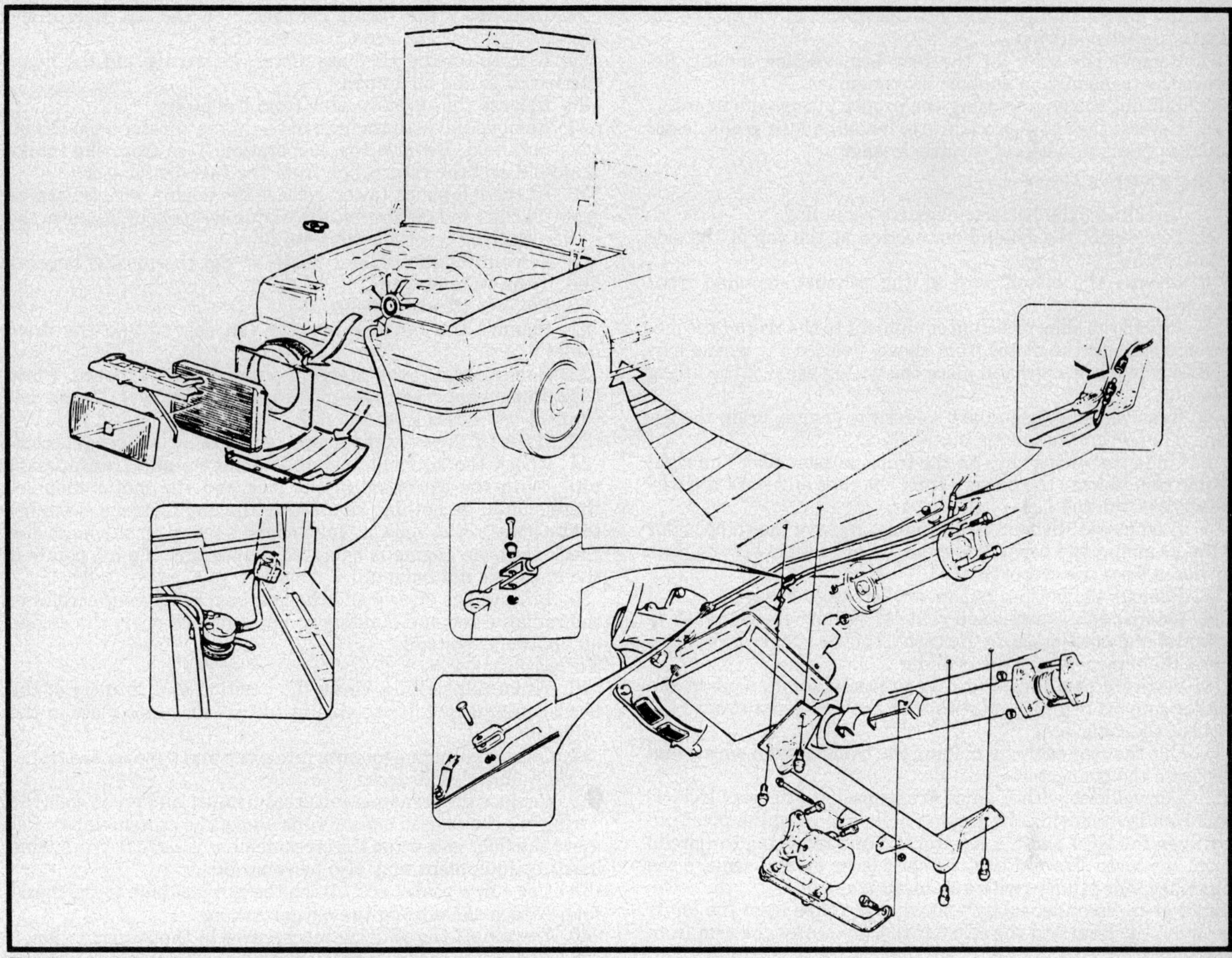

Engine removal preparation—760 shown

14. Disconnect the distributor wire connector, high tension lead, starter cables and the clutch cable clamp.
15. Disconnect the wiring harness at the voltage regulator. Disconnect the throttle cable at the pulley and the wire for the air conditioning at the manifold solenoid.
16. Remove the gas cap. Disconnect the fuel lines at the filter and return pipe.
17. At the firewall, disconnect the electrical connectors for the ballast resistor and relays. Disconnect the heater hoses.
18. Disconnect the micro-switch connectors at the intake manifold and all remaining harness connectors to the engine.
19. Drain the crankcase.
20. Remove the exhaust manifold flange retaining nuts. Loosen the exhaust pipe clamp bolts and remove the bracket for the front exhaust pipe mount. On B21FT (Turbo) models, disconnect the turbo from the intake hose, disconnect the other hoses from the turbo unit and disconnect the turbocharger from the exhaust system.
21. From underneath, remove the front motor mount bolts.
22. If equipped with automatic transmission, place the gear selector lever in **P** and disconnect the gear shift control rod from the transmission.
23. On manual transmission vehicles, disconnect the clutch cable. Then, loosen the set screw, drive out the pivot pin and remove the shifter from the control rod.

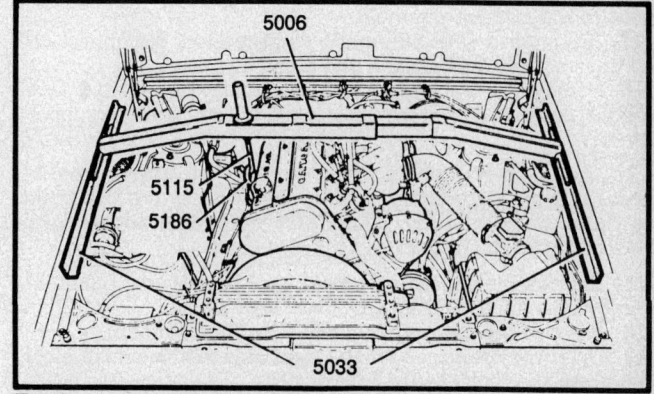

Engine replacement tooling requirement—B234F engine shown, others similar

24. Disconnect the speedometer and the driveshaft from the transmission.
25. On overdrive equipped models, disconnect the control wire from the shifter.
26. Raise and support the vehicle safely. Then, using a floor

jack and a wooden block, support the weight of the engine beneath the transmission.

27. Remove the bolts for the rear transmission mount. Remove the transmission support crossmember.

28. Lift out the engine using the proper lifting equipment.

29. Reverse the above procedure to install. Adjust gear selector linkage, check and adjust throttle linkage.

B234 ENGINE

1. Disconnect the battery, negative cable first.

2. Disconnect the ground connection at the top of the side frame rail.

3. Release the bolted joint at the exhaust manifold front bracket.

4. Attach the sling or lifting equipment to the rear of the motor and support the motor from above. Release any wiring harnesses from their clips and place the wiring aside of the lifting gear.

5. Remove the splash guard under the engine, drain the engine oil and remove the air intake duct.

6. Undo the wiring clips on the front crossmember and right frame rail. Release the battery from the clips and work the wiring free of the roll bar.

7. If equipped with air conditioning, remove the compressor from its mount and position it aside. Do not disconnect any lines or hoses from the compressor.

8. Remove the bottom nut on the left engine mount.

9. On manual transmission vehicles, remove the clutch slave cylinder and position aside. Be careful of the rubber boot; it retains the piston within the cylinder.

10. Separate the front and rear universal joints. Unbolt the center support bearing and withdraw the driveshaft toward the rear of the vehicle.

11. Cut the rear cable tie holding the transmission wiring and separate the connectors.

12. For vehicles with manual transmission, the gear lever is removed by removing the locking bolt, removing the pivot pin between the lever and the selector rod and removing the circlip from the lever sleeve. Push the shift lever up and remove the bushings. For vehicles with automatic transmissions, the selector lever is disconnected by removing the clips from the joints between the lever and the selector rod. Withdraw the arm from the mounting.

13. Release the bolted joint at the front of the catalytic converter and release the oxygen sensor wire from the rear clip.

14. Remove the front exhaust pipe by removing the bolts at its joint to the exhaust manifold.

15. If equipped with automatic transmission, disconnect the oil lines at the transmission and plug the lines.

16. Remove the transmission crossmember. As soon as it is removed, position a floor jack below the transmission to support it.

NOTE: The following steps are in the upper engine area. It may be helpful to temporarily remove the hoist equipment for access. The hoist will need to be reinstalled later in the removal.

17. Remove the upper heat shield from the exhaust manifold. Remove the air hose from the lower heat shield.

18. Remove the top nut from the right motor mount.

19. Open the draincock on the right side of the engine block and drain the coolant into a container.

20. Label and remove the wiring from the distributor cap. Remove the cap and rotor and disconnect the braided engine ground wire.

21. Disconnect the wire to terminal 1 on the coil. Separate the wiring connectors on the right shock tower and release the cable clips on the firewall. Free the wiring from the clips.

22. Disconnect the heater hoses on the left firewall.

23. Release the fuel line connection at the left firewall and attend to any fuel spillage immediately. Plug the fuel lines.

24. Disconnect the wiring connector on the left side of the firewall and free the wires from the clips.

25. Disconnect the air mass meter, its wiring and the hoses connected to the air intake.

26. Release the throttle cable from the pulley.

27. Remove the vacuum hose to the brake booster from the intake manifold. Remove the evaporation hose from the intake manifold and the return line from the fuel distributor.

28. At the left shock tower, release the engine wiring harness from its clips and disconnect the wiring connectors. Remove the power steering reservoir from its clips.

29. Disconnect the coolant hoses at the thermostat housing and at the water pump.

30. Remove the drive belts.

31. Remove the radiator fan, the fan shroud and the drive pulley.

32. Remove the power steering pump from its mount. Place the pump on paper or rags atop the left shock tower. Do not disconnect any hoses from the pump.

33. If the lifting equipment was removed earlier, reconnect it.

34. Check the surroundings of the engine and transmission unit. With the exception of the jack and the motor mounts, there should be nothing connecting the engine/trans assembly to the body of the vehicle. Take slight tension on the hoist and check that the engine is balanced. Reposition the lift points if the engine is not balanced.

35. Lift out the engine and the gearbox, being very careful of the radiator and surrounding components. Support the engine on appropriate stand.

To install:

36. When reinstalling, check the position and security of the hoist equipment. Lift the engine and gearbox into place in the vehicle.

37. Guide the engine mounts into place and support the transmission on the floor jack.

38. Replace the transmission crossmember and make sure the wiring for the oxygen sensor runs above the crossmember. Remove the floor jack when the crossmember is secure. The engine hoisting equipment may also be removed.

39. Use a new gasket and attach the exhaust pipe to the manifold. Attach the wire to the oxygen sensor.

40. Reconnect the shifting mechanism to the transmission.

41. Reconnect the transmission wiring and secure the harness with new wire ties.

42. Install the driveshaft. Tighten the front and rear universal joints and attach the center support bearing.

43. On manual transmission vehicle, connect the clutch slave cylinder. On automatic transmissions, connect the oil cooler lines.

44. Install the lower nut for the left motor mount. On vehicles with air conditioning, remount the compressor on its brackets.

45. Track the wiring between the anti-roll bar and the front crossmember. Install the cable clips on the crossmember and right side frame rail. Install the splash guard under the vehicle. Reconnect the wiring to the ground connection on the right frame rail.

46. Install the nut on the top of the right engine mount. Install the upper heat shield on the manifold and the air tube to the lower heat shield.

47. Reconnect the coolant hoses. The bottom hose connects to the water pump and the upper hose to the thermostat housing.

NOTE: Note the marking on the upper hose. The hose must run at least 1 in. away from the alternator belt.

48. Remount the power steering pump. Install its belt and the air conditioning belt, if equipped, and adjust to the correct tension.

49. Install the fan, pulley and shroud. Secure the wiring below the fan with new wire ties. Install the drive belt and adjust to the correct tension.

50. Reconnect the rear wiring harnesses on the firewall. Plug all connectors carefully and secure harnesses within the clips. Don't forget the wire to terminal 1 on the coil.

51. Reinstall the distributor rotor, cap and wires. Connect the braided engine ground cable.

52. Reconnect the wiring at the left shock tower. Make sure the wiring is secure in its clips. Install the power steering reservoir.

53. At the intake manifold, connect the vacuum line to the brake booster, the evaporation line and the return line for the fuel distributor.

54. At the left side of the firewall, attach the heater hoses and connect the fuel line.

55. Reattach the throttle cable to the pulley.

56. Install the air mass meter with its hoses and connections.

57. Fill the engine with proper coolant, set the heater to its hottest setting and check the system for leaks.

58. Install the engine oil.

59. Reconnect the battery leads (positive first) and the protective cap on the terminals.

60. Double check all installation items, paying particular attention to loose hoses or hanging wires, untightened nuts, poor routing of hoses and wires (too tight or rubbing) and tools left in the engine area.

61. Start the engine and check for leaks. This engine may be somewhat noisy when started; the noise will disappear as the tappets fill with oil.

B28F AND B280F ENGINES

1. If equipped with manual transmission, remove the shifter assembly. From underneath, loosen the set screw and drive out the pivot pin. Then, pull up the boot, remove the reverse pawl bracket, snapring for the shifter and lift out the shifter.

2. Remove the battery.

3. Disconnect the windshield washer hose and engine compartment light wire. Scribe marks around the hood mount brackets on the underside of the hood for later hood alignment. Remove the hood.

4. Remove the air cleaner assembly.

5. Remove the splash guard under the engine.

6. Drain the cooling system.

7. Remove the overflow tank cap. Remove the upper and lower radiator hoses and disconnect the overflow hoses at the radiator.

8. If equipped with automatic transmission, disconnect the transmission cooler lines at the radiator.

9. Remove the radiator and fan shroud.

10. Disconnect the heater hoses, power brake hose at the intake manifold and the vacuum pump hose at the pump. Remove the vacuum pump and O-ring in the valve cover. Remove the gas cap.

11. At the firewall disconnect the fuel lines at the filter and return pipe, disconnect the relay connectors and all other wire connectors. Disconnect the distributor wires.

─────── **CAUTION** ───────

Use caution when disconnecting the fuel lines. The fuel lines may be under high pressure.

12. Disconnect the evaporative control carbon canister hoses and the vacuum hose at the EGR valve.

13. Disconnect the voltage regulator wire connector.

14. Disconnect the throttle cable and kickdown cable, on automatic transmission vehicles, the vacuum amplifier hose at the T-pipe and the hoses at the thermostat.

15. Disconnect the air pump hose at the backfire valve, the solenoid valve wire and the micro-switch wire.

16. Remove the exhaust manifold flange retaining nuts (both sides).

17. If equipped with air conditioning, remove the compressor

and drive belt and place it aside. Do not disconnect the refrigerant hoses.

18. Drain the crankcase.

19. Remove the power steering pump, drive belt and bracket. Position aside.

20. From underneath, remove the retaining nuts for the front motor mounts.

21. Remove, as required, the front exhaust pipe.

22. On 49 states models, remove the front exhaust pipe hangers and clamps and allow the system to hang.

23. If equipped with automatic transmission, place the shift lever in **P**. Disconnect the shift control lever at the transmission.

24. On manual transmission vehicles, disconnect the clutch cylinder from the bell housing. Leave the cylinder connected; secure it to the vehicle.

25. Disconnect the speedometer cable and driveshaft at the transmission.

26. Raise and safely support the vehicle. Place jackstands under the reinforced box member area to the rear of each front jacking attachment. Then, using a floor jack and a thick, wide wooden block, support the weight of the engine under the oil pan.

27. Remove the bolts for the rear transmission mount. Remove the transmission support crossmember.

28. Lift out the engine and transmission as a unit.

29. Reverse the above procedure to install. Adjust gear selector linkage, check and adjust throttle linkage.

Cylinder Head

Removal and Installation

B23 AND B230 ENGINES

1. Disconnect the battery.

2. Remove the overflow tank cap and drain the coolant. Disconnect the upper radiator hose.

3. Remove the distributor cap and wires.

4. Remove the PCV hoses.

5. Remove the EGR valve and vacuum pump.

6. Remove the air pump, if equipped, and air injection manifold. Disconnect and remove all hoses to the turbocharger, if equipped. Plug all open hoses and holes immediately.

7. Remove the exhaust manifold and header pipe bracket.

8. Remove the intake manifold. Disconnect the manifold brace and the hose clamp to the bellows for the fuel injection air-/flow unit. Disconnect the throttle cable and all vacuum hoses and electrical connectors to the fuel injection unit.

9. Remove the fuel injectors.

10. Remove the valve cover.

11. Loosen the fan shroud and remove the fan. Remove the shroud. Remove the upper belts and pulleys.

12. Remove the timing belt cover. Remove the timing belt.

13. Remove the camshaft, if necessary.

14. Remove the cylinder head 10mm Allen head bolts and remove the cylinder head from the vehicle.

15. To install, reverse the removal procedure. Oil the head bolts. Tighten the head bolts in the prescribed torque sequence first to 44 ft. lbs. (60 Nm), then to 81 ft. lbs. (110 Nm). After the engine has been run 30 minutes, slacken the bolts to relieve any pretension and retorque to 81 ft. lbs. (110 Nm). To set the valve timing, follow the steps for timing belt installation.

B234F ENGINE

NOTE: The use of the correct special tools or their equivalent, is required for this procedure.

1. Disconnect the negative battery cable.

2. Remove the heat shield over the exhaust manifold.

3. Remove the cap from the expansion tank and open the draincock on the right side of the motor. Collect the drained coolant in a suitable container.

4. Unbolt the exhaust pipe from the bracket, remove the manifold nuts and remove the manifold from the head.

5. On the left side of the motor, remove the support under the intake manifold. and remove the bottom bolt in the cylinder block.

6. Remove the manifold intact and tie it or support it safely.

7. Disconnect the temperature sensor connectors, the heating hose under cylinders No. 3 and 4 and the upper radiator hose at the thermostat.

8. Remove the upper and lower timing belt covers.

9. Align the camshaft and crankshaft marks. Turn the engine to TDC, of the compression stroke, on cylinder No. 1 and make sure the pulley marks and the crank marks align.

10. Remove the protective cap over the timing belt tensioner locknut. Loosen the locknut, compress the tensioner, to release tension on the belts, and retighten the locknut, holding the tensioner in place.

11. Remove the timing belt from the camshafts. Do not crease or fold the belt.

NOTE: The camshafts and the crankshaft must not be moved when the belt is removed.

12. Remove the timing belt idler pulleys.

13. Remove the camshaft drive pulleys. Use a counterhold wrench to prevent the cam from turning.

14. Remove the plate or panel behind the pulleys. Remove the cover plate for the ignition wires. Label and disconnect the ignition wiring from the spark plugs and the distributor cap; remove the coil wire from the distributor cap.

15. Remove the valve cover and gasket. Clean the surfaces of any gasket remains.

16. Remove the distributor housing from the camshaft carrier. Remove the ignition wire clip next to the left bolt.

17. Plug the spark plug holes with crumpled paper. Remove the center bearing cap for each camshaft. Remove the third nut in the center. Mark the cam bearing caps for proper reinstallation.

18. Install a Volvo camshaft press tool 5021 or similar, on the exhaust side cam in place of the removed bearing cap. When it is securely in place, remove the remaining bearing caps and nuts. Remove the tool and remove the exhaust camshaft.

19. Remove the intake camshaft in identical fashion.

NOTE: Label or identify each cam and its bearing caps. All removed components should be kept in order.

20. Using a magnet or a small suction cup, remove the tappets. Store them upside down, to prevent oil drainage, and keep them in order; they are not interchangeable.

21. Remove the remaining 4 nuts in the center of the cam carrier and detach the carrier from the head. If it is stuck, tap it very gently with a plastic mallet. Remove the O-rings around the spark plug holes.

22. Wipe the remaining oil off the cylinder head and remove the bolts in order. When all the bolts are removed, the cylinder head may be lifted free of the vehicle.

NOTE: The head is aluminum. Support it on clean wood blocks or similar to avoid scoring the face.

23. Clean the camshaft carrier and the head assembly of all gasket material and sealer. Carefully scrape the joint surfaces with a plastic scraper. Do not use metal tools to scrape or clean. Wash the surfaces with a degreasing compound and blow the surfaces completely dry. Inspect the head bolts for any sign of stretching or elongation in the midsection. If this is observed or suspected, discard the bolt. Bolts may not be used more than 5 times.

To install:

24. Install the new head gasket and a new O-ring for the water pump. Carefully place the cylinder head into position; do not damage the gasket.

25. Clean the head bolts and apply a light coat of oil. Install them and tighten, in sequence, in 3 steps: to 15 ft. lbs. (20 Nm), then all to 30 ft. lbs. (41 Nm). Third Step is to tighten each bolt through 115 degree of arc in 1 continuous motion. The use of Volvo protractor fitting tool 5098 is strongly recommended for this task.

26. Install the exhaust manifold with a new gasket. Attach the front exhaust pipe to its bracket and install the heat shields.

27. On the left side of the motor, connect the temperature sensors, the heating hose under cylinders 3 and 4 and the upper coolant hose to the thermostat.

28. Fill the cooling system and check carefully for leaks, particularly around the head to block joint.

29. Install the intake manifold with a new gasket. Tighten the bottom bolts a few turns and place the manifold in position. Tighten all the bolts from the center outwards.

30. Reattach the support under the intake manifold and the cable clip. Double check all connections on and around the intake manifold.

31. Apply Volvo liquid sealing compound to the camshaft carrier. Use a small paint roller and coat the surfaces which match to the head and the bearing cap joint faces.

32. Install the cam carrier on the head and secure it with 4 of the 5 center nuts tightened to 15 ft. lbs. (20 Nm); do not install the middle nut.

33. Oil all matching surfaces on the cam carrier, bearing caps and tappets.

34. Insert the tappets; they must be inserted in their original order and place.

35. Install the exhaust side camshaft by placing it in the carrier with the pulley guide pin facing up. Using the rear bearing cap as a guide, press the cam into place with the press tool. Install the bearing caps in the original order.

36. Install the bearing cap nuts and tighten them in stages to 15 ft. lbs. (20 Nm). Remove the press tool and install the center bearing cap; tighten it in stages to 15 ft. lbs. (20 Nm).

37. Install the intake camshaft in the carrier with the pulley guide pin facing upwards.

38. Turn the distributor shaft to align the driver with the markings on the distributor housing. Install new O-rings on the housing and rotor shaft.

39. Using the rear bearing cap as a guide, press the cam into place with the press tool. Install the bearing caps in the original order.

40. Install the bearing cap nuts and tighten them in stages to 15 ft. lbs. (20 Nm). Remove the press tool and install the center bearing cap; tighten it in stages to 15 ft. lbs. (20 Nm).

41. Install the center nut in the cam carrier and tighten it to 15 ft. lbs. (20 Nm).

42. Double check the tightness of all the camshaft carrier nuts and the bearing cap nuts. All should be 15 ft. lbs.; do not overtighten.

43. Reinstall the distributor, connect the coil wire and install the ignition wire clip at the left bolt. Remove the paper plugs from the spark plug holes.

44. Use a silicone sealer and apply to the front and rear camshaft bearing caps. Install new gaskets for the valve cover and the spark plug wells. Install the spark plug gasket with the arrow pointing towards the front of the vehicle and the word "UP" facing up. Make sure the valve cover gasket is correctly positioned and install the valve cover.

45. Reconnect the ground wire at the distributor.

46. Install the ignition wires and the cover plate.

47. Using a Volvo compression seal driver tool 5025 or similar, install the oil seals for the front of each camshaft. Camshafts must not be allowed to turn during this operation.

48. Install the upper backing plate over the ends of the camshafts and adjust the plate so the cams are centered in the holes.

49. Replace the idler pulleys and tighten their mounts to 18.5 ft. lbs. (25 Nm).

50. Install the camshaft drive pulleys, using a counterhold to prevent the cams from turning.

51. Making sure the camshaft pulleys are properly aligned with the marks on the backing plate, position the timing belt so the double mark on the belt coincides exactly with the top mark on the belt guide plate, at the top of the crankshaft. Place the belt onto the cam pulleys and make sure the single marks on the belt line up exactly with the marks on the pulleys. Fit the belt over the idler pulleys; right side idler first, then the left.

52. Double check that the engine is on TDC, of the compression stroke, for cylinder No. 1 and that all the belt markings line up as they should.

53. Loosen the tensioner locknut. Rotate the crankshaft clockwise 1 full turn until the belt markings again coincide with the pulley markings.

NOTE: The engine must not be rotated counterclockwise while the tensioner is loose.

54. Turn the crankshaft smoothly clockwise until the pulley marks are 1½ teeth beyond the marks on the backing plate.

55. Tighten the tensioner locknut. Install the lower timing belt cover.

56. Install the radiator fan and pulley, the alternator drive belt and the negative battery cable.

57. Double check all installation items, paying particular attention to loose hoses or hanging wires, untightened nuts, poor routing of hoses and wires (too tight or rubbing) and tools left in the engine area.

58. Start the engine and allow it to run until the thermostat opens. Use extreme caution; the timing belt is exposed.

NOTE: This engine may be somewhat noisy when started. The noise will subside as oil reaches the tappets. Do not exceed 2500 rpm while the tappets are noisy.

59. Shut the engine off, rotate the crankshaft to bring the engine to TDC, of the compression stroke, of cylinder No. 1 and use Volvo tool 998 8500 to check the belt tension. Correct deflection is 5.5 ± 0.2 units when measured between the exhaust camshaft pulley and the idler. If the tension is not correct, repeat Steps 51–54, above.

60. Install the upper timing belt cover. Start the engine and final check all functions.

B28F AND B280F ENGINES

1. Disconnect the battery. Drain the coolant.

2. Remove the air cleaner assembly and all attaching hoses.

3. Disconnect the throttle cable. On automatic transmission equipped vehicles, disconnect the kickdown cable.

4. Disconnect the EGR vacuum hose and remove the pipe between the EGR valve and manifold.

5. Remove the oil filler cap and cover the hole with a rag. Disconnect the PCV pipe(s) from the intake manifold.

6. Remove the front section of the intake manifold.

7. Disconnect the electrical connector and fuel line at the cold start injector. Disconnect the vacuum hose, both fuel lines. and the electrical connector from the control pressure regulator.

8. Disconnect the hose, pipe and electrical connector from the auxiliary air valve. Remove the auxiliary air valve.

9. Disconnect the electrical connector from the fuel distributor. Remove the wire loom from the intake manifolds. Disconnect the spark plug wires.

10. Disconnect the fuel injectors from their holders.

11. Disconnect the distributor vacuum hose, carbon filter hose and diverter valve hose from the intake manifold. Also, disconnect the power brake hose and heater hose at the intake manifold.

12. Disconnect the throttle control link from it pulley.

13. If equipped with an EGR vacuum amplifier, disconnect the wires from the throttle micro-switch and solenoid valve.

14. At the firewall, disconnect the fuel lines from the fuel filter and return line.

15. Remove the 2 attaching screws and lift out the fuel distributor and throttle housing assembly.

16. If not equipped with an EGR vacuum amplifier, disconnect the EGR valve hose from under the throttle housing.

17. Remove the cold start injector, rubber ring and pipe.

18. Remove the 4 retaining bolts and lift off the intake manifold. Remove the rubber rings.

19. Remove the splash guard under the engine.

20. If removing the left cylinder head, remove the air pump from its bracket.

21. Remove the vacuum pump and O-ring in the valve cover. Remove the vacuum hose from the wax thermostat.

22. If removing the right cylinder head, disconnect the upper radiator hose.

23. On air conditioned models, remove the air conditioning compressor and secure it aside. Do not disconnect the refrigerant lines.

24. Disconnect the distributor leads and remove the distributor. Remove the EGR valve, bracket and pipe. At the firewall, disconnect the electrical connectors at the relays.

25. On air conditioned models, remove the rear compressor bracket.

26. Disconnect the coolant hose(s) from the water pump to the cylinder head(s). If removing the left cylinder head disconnect the lower radiator hose at the water pump.

27. Disconnect the air injection system supply hose from the applicable cylinder head. Separate the air manifold at the rear of the engine. If removing the left cylinder head, remove the backfire valve and air hose.

28. Remove the valve cover(s).

29. On the left cylinder head, remove the Allen head screw and 4 upper bolts to the timing gear cover. On the right cylinder head, remove the 4 upper bolts to the timing gear cover and the front cover plate.

30. From under the vehicle, remove the exhaust pipe clamps for both header pipes.

31. If removing the right cylinder head, remove the retainer bracket bolts and pull the dipstick tube out of the crankcase.

32. Remove the applicable exhaust manifold(s).

33. Remove the cover plate at the rear of the cylinder head.

34. Rotate the camshaft sprocket, for the applicable cylinder head, into position so the large sprocket hole aligns with the rocker arm shaft. With the camshaft in this position, loosen the cylinder head bolts, in sequence, same sequence as tightening, and remove the rocker arm and shaft assembly.

35. Loosen the camshaft retaining fork bolt, directly in back of sprocket, and slide the fork away from the camshaft.

36. Next, it is necessary to hold the cam chain stretched during camshaft removal. Otherwise, the chain tensioner will automatically take up the slack, making it impossible to reinstall the sprocket on the cam without removing the timing chain cover to loosen the tensioner device. To accomplish this, a Volvo sprocket retainer tool 999 5104 is installed over the sprocket with 2 bolts in the top of the timing chain cover. A bolt is then screwed into the sprocket to hold it in place.

37. Remove the camshaft sprocket center bolt and push the camshaft to the rear, so it clears the sprocket.

38. Remove the cylinder head.

NOTE: Do not remove the cylinder head by pulling straight up. Instead, lever the head off by inserting 2 spare head bolts into the front and rear inboard cylinder head bolt holes and pulling toward the applicable wheel housing. Otherwise, the cylinder liners may be pulled up, breaking the lower liner seal and leaking coolant into the crankcase. If any do pull up, new liner seals must be used and the crankcase completely drained. If the head(s) seem stuck, gently tap around the

edges of the head(s) with a rubber mallet, to break the joint.

39. Remove the head gasket. Clean the contact surfaces with a plastic scraper and lacquer thinner.

40. If the head is going to be off for any length of time, install Volvo liner holders tool 999 5093 or 2 strips of thick stock steel with holes for the head bolts, so the liners stay pressed down against their seals. Install the holders width-wise between the middle 4 head bolt holes.

41. Reverse the above procedure to install, using the following installation notes:

    a. There are a pair of guide dowels at both outboard corners of the head. If they fell down during removal, pull them back out with a puller hammer. They can be propped up with a ⅛ in. drill shank.

    b. Remove the liner holders.

    c. The right and left head gaskets are different.

    d. Check the timing chain cover gasket. If damaged, replace only the upper section.

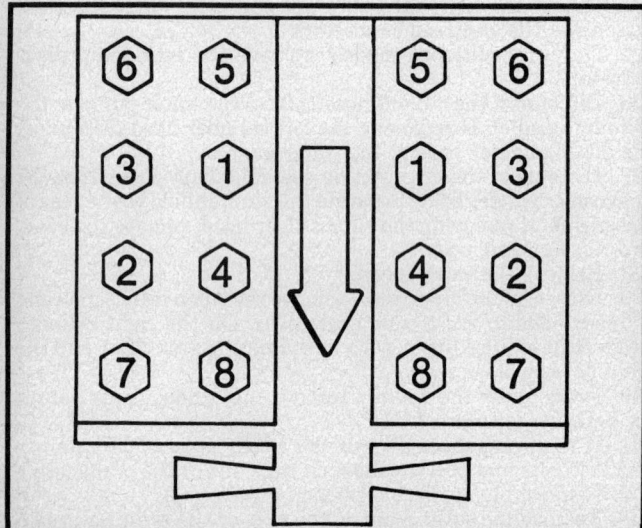

Cylinder head bolt tightening sequence—B21, B23 and B234 engines

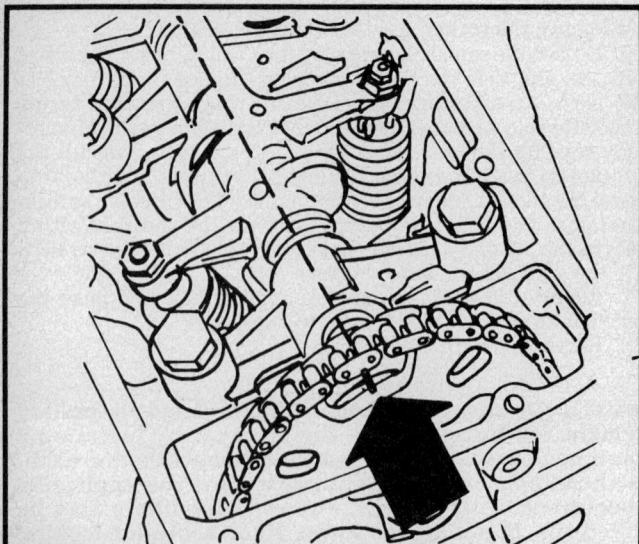

Aligning camshaft for cylinder head removal—B27 and B28 engines

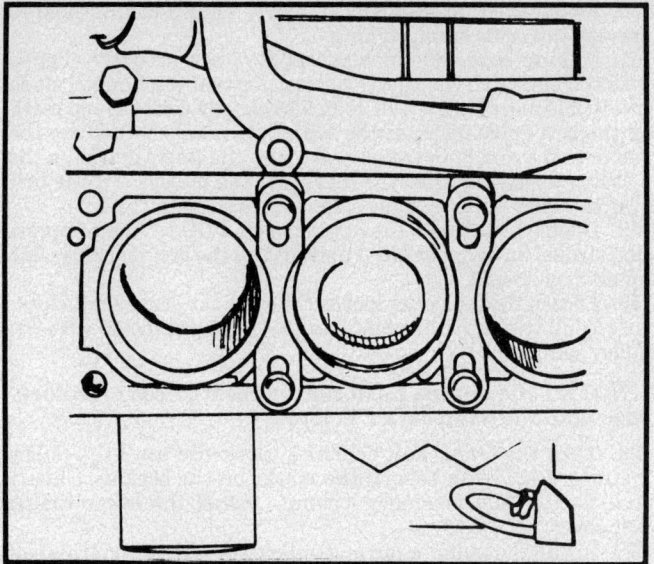

Cylinder liner holders installed

B27, B28 camshaft sprocket retainer tool

    e. Oil the head bolt threads. Position the head on the dowels and install (hand tight) 1 center head bolt. Then, slide the camshaft forward into position against the sprocket and install the sprocket center bolts and remove the retainer tool.

    f. Before installing the head bolts, remove the guide dowel shanks, if used.

    g. On B28F engine, tighten the head bolts to 7 ft. lbs. (9.5 Nm) using the correct tightening sequence, then 22 ft. lbs. (30 Nm) and then 44 ft. lbs. (60 Nm). Next slacken the head bolts, in the tightening sequence, to relieve any pre-tension. Now, tighten the bolts to 11–14 ft. lbs. (15–19 Nm). Finally, tighten the head bolts 116–120 degrees, in the tightening sequence; this is critical for proper piston liner O-ring sealing. If necessary, use a protractor to ensure accuracy.

    h. On 280F engine, tighten all head bolts, in sequence, to 44 ft. lbs. (60 Nm), then loosen bolt No. 1 and retorque it to 15 ft. lbs. (20 Nm), then tighten to 106 degrees. Repeat for all bolts following number sequence and only loosening and tightening 1 bolt at a time. Adjust valves and run engine to operating temperature. Let cool for 2 hours. Tighten each bolt, in sequence, an additional 45 degrees.

   i. Adjust the valves after completing assembly.

   j. After running the engine to operating temperature, allow to cool for 30 minutes and retorquing the head bolts. Following the tightening sequence slacken the bolts to relieve any pre-tension, then tighten to 11–14 ft. lbs. (15–19 Nm) and finally protractor torque them to 113–117 degrees; ⅓ of a full turn.

Valve Lash

Adjustment

B21, B23 AND B230 ENGINES

Valve clearance is checked every 15,000 miles. If necessary to adjust valve clearance, 3 special tools will be needed: 1st, a valve tappet depressor tool used to push down the tappet sufficiently to remove the Volvo adjusting disc (shim) tool 999 5022; 2nd, a specially shaped pliers to actually remove and install the Volvo valve adjusting disc tool 999 5026; and 3rd, a set of varying thickness valve adjusting discs to make the necessary adjustments.

   1. Remove the valve cover. Scribe chalk marks on the distributor body indicating each of the 4 spark plug wire leads in the cap. Remove the distributor cap.

   2. Crank over the engine with a remote starter switch or with a wrench on the crankshaft pulley center bolt (22mm hex) until the engine is in the firing position for No. 1 cylinder. At this point, the **0** degree or TDC mark on the crankshaft pulley is aligned with the timing pointer, the rotor is pointing at the No. 1 spark plug wire cap position and the camshaft lobes for No. 1 cylinder are pointing at the 10 o'clock and 2 o'clock positions. At this point, the clearance between the cam lobe and valve depressor (tappet) may be checked for the intake and exhaust valve of cylinder No. 1, using a feeler gauge. When checking clearance, the wear limit is 0.012–0.018 in. (0.3–0.4mm) for a cold engine and 0.012–0.020 in. (0.3–0.5mm) for a hot one 176°F (80°C).

   3. Repeat Step 2 for cylinders No. 3, 4 and 2, in that order. Each time, rotate the crankshaft pulley 180 degrees so the rotor is pointing to the spark plug wire cap position for that cylinder and the cam lobes are pointing at the 10 and 2 o'clock positions for the valves of that cylinder.

   4. If any of the valve clearance measurements are outside the wear limit, remove the old valve adjusting disc and install a new one to bring the clearance within specifications. First, rotate the

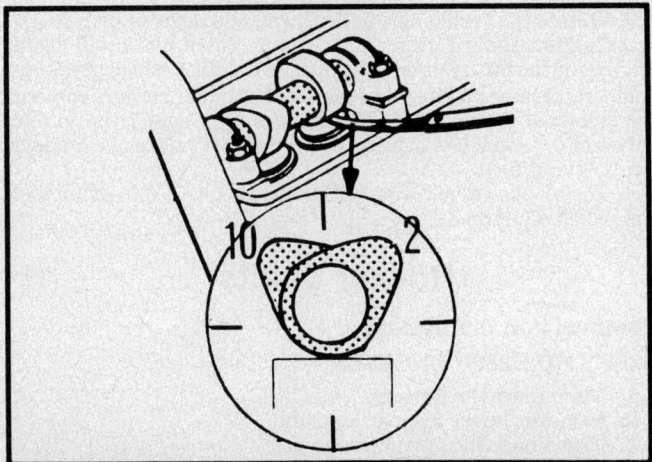

B21, B23, and B230 series camshaft lobes at "10 and 2 o'clock" positions, indicating that subject cylinder is in the firing position and the valves can be adjusted

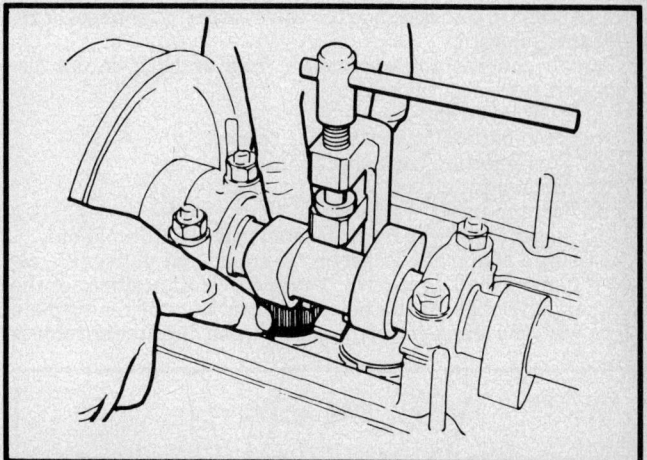

Positioning a new valve adjustment shim in the head. Shim must be oiled

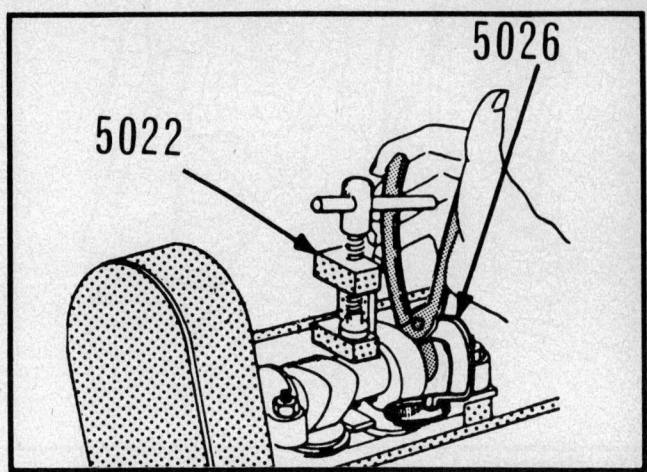

B21, B23 and B230 series valve adjustment tools— tappet depressor is on left, shim pliers on right

valve depressors (tappets) until their notches are at a right angle to the engine center line. Attach valve depressor tool 999 5022 or equivalent, to the camshaft and screw down the tool spindle until the depressor (tappet) groove is just above the edge of its bore and still accessible with the special pliers tool 999 5026.

   5. Remove the valve adjusting disc and measure with a micrometer. The valve clearance should be set to these tolerances: 0.014–0.016 in. (0.35–0.40mm) for a cold engine and 0.016–0.018 in. (0.40–0.45mm) for a hot one. So, if the measured clearance had been 0.019 in. (0.48mm) and the desired clearance 0.016 in. (0.40mm), for a net difference of 0.003 in. (0.076mm), then the new valve adjusting disc should be 0.003 in. (0.076mm) thicker than the old one to take up the clearance. Valve adjusting discs are available from Volvo in sizes 0.130–0.180 in. (3.3–4.6mm), in 0.002 in. (0.050mm) increments. Always oil the new disc and install it with the marks facing down.

   6. Remove the valve tappet depressor tool. Rotate the engine a few times and recheck clearance. Install the valve cover with a new gasket.

B28F AND B280F ENGINES

Valve clearance is checked every 15,000 miles. No special tools are required.

1. In order to gain access to the valve covers, disconnect or remove the following:

a. Air conditioning compressor from bracket; do not disconnect refrigerant hoses

b. EGR valve and hoses

c. Air conditioning compressor bracket

d. Fuel injection control pressure regulator

e. Air pump

f. Vacuum pump

g. Hoses and wires from solenoid valve, California only

2. Using a 36mm hex socket on the crankshaft pulley bolt, rotate the crankshaft to the No. 1 cylinder TDC position, of the compression stroke. At this point the **0** mark on the timing plate aligns with the crankshaft pulley notch, the distributor rotor is

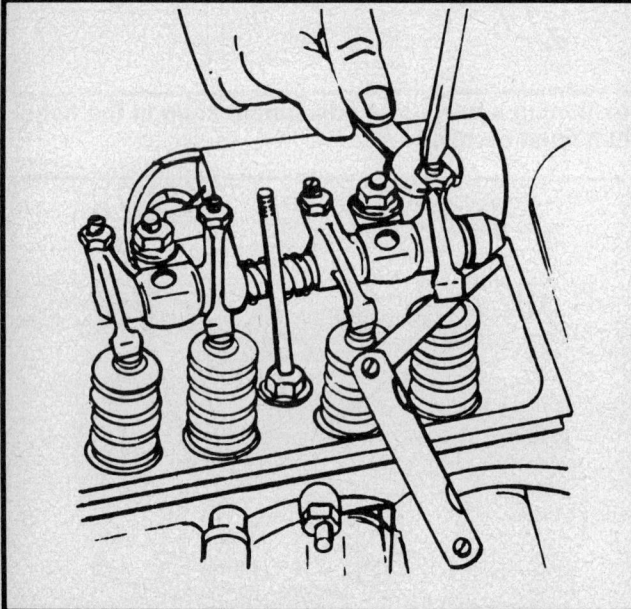

Adjusting valve clearance—B27 and B28 engines

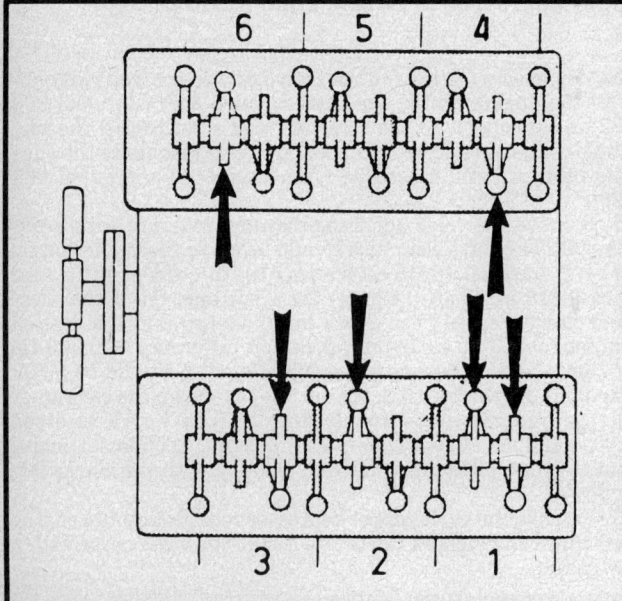

On B27 and B28 engines, on No. 1 cylinder at TDC, adjust these valve (arrows)

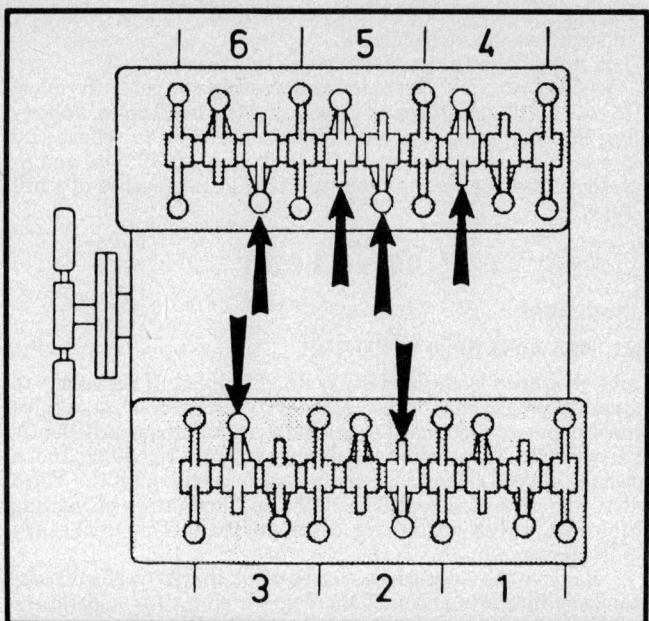

On B27 and B28 engines, rotate the crankshaft 360 degrees and adjust the remaining valve (arrow)

pointing to the No. 1 cylinder spark plug wire cap position and both valves for No. 1 cylinder have clearance. At this position, adjust the intake valves of cylinders No. 1, 2 and 4; the exhaust valves of cylinders No. 1, 3 and 6. Insert a feeler gauge between the rocker arm and valve stem. Loosen the locknut and turn the adjusting screw in the required direction. Tighten the locknut and recheck clearance.

Clearance for B280F should be:

Cold engine
Intake—0.004–0.006 in. (0.10–0.15mm)
Exhaust—0.010–0.012 in. (0.25–0.30mm)

Hot engine
Intake—0.006–0.008 in. (0.15–0.20mm)
Exhaust—0.012–0.014 in. (0.30–0.35mm)

Clearance for B28 should be:

Cold engine
Intake—0.008–0.010 in. (0.20–0.25mm)
Exhaust—0.012–0.014 in. (0.30–0.35mm).

3. Rotate the crankshaft pulley 1 full 360 degrees turn to adjust the remaining valves. At this point, the **0** mark will again align with the pulley notch, the rotor is pointing 180 degrees opposite its former position and the No. 1 cylinder rockers contact the ramps of the camshaft. At this position, adjust the intake valves of cylinders No. 3, 5 and 6; the exhaust valves of cylinders No. 2, 4 and 5.

4. Install the valve covers with new gaskets. Connect all disconnected equipment.

Rocker Shafts

Removal and Installation

B28F AND B280F ENGINES

1. Disconnect the battery.

2. Remove the air cleaner assembly.

3. Disconnect the air pump bracket.

4. Remove the left valve cover, if necessary.

5. Tie the upper radiator hose aside and remove the oil filler cap and carbon canister hose.

6. On air conditioned models, remove the air conditioning compressor from it bracket. Do not disconnect the hoses.

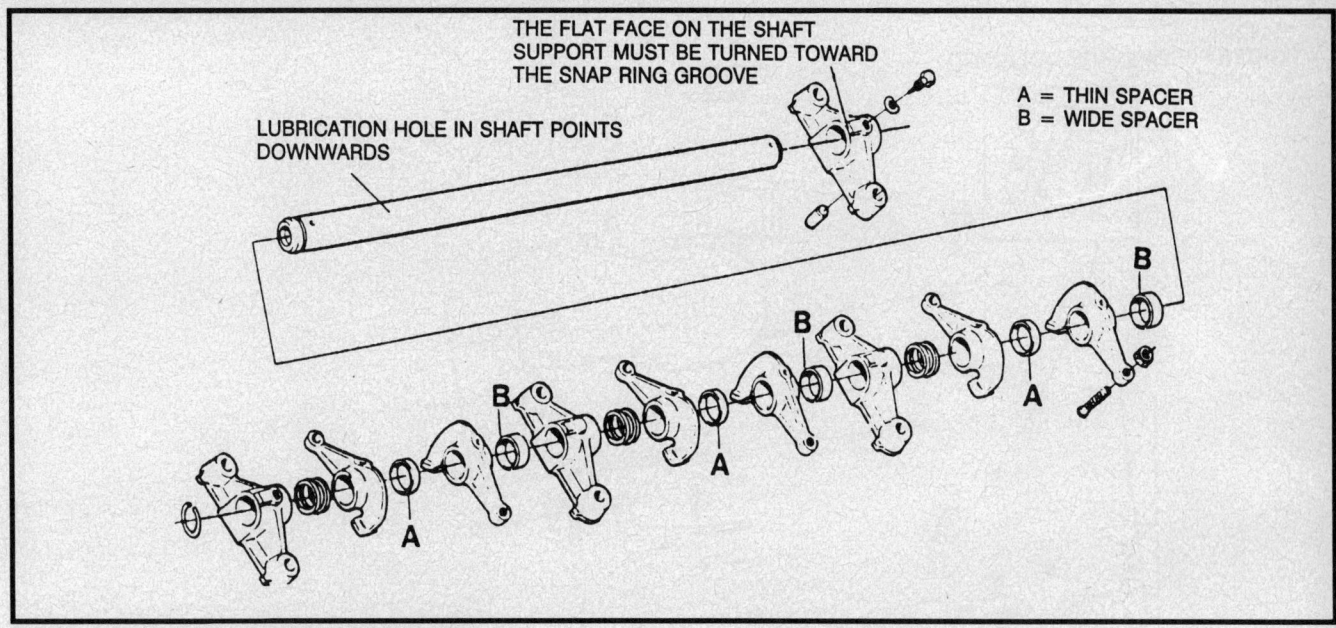

THE FLAT FACE ON THE SHAFT
SUPPORT MUST BE TURNED TOWARD
THE SNAP RING GROOVE

LUBRICATION HOLE IN SHAFT POINTS
DOWNWARDS

A = THIN SPACER
B = WIDE SPACER

Rocker arm shaft assembly—B28 engine

7. Remove the EGR valve.
8. Remove the air conditioning compressor rear bracket.
9. Remove the control pressure regulator.
10. Disconnect any hoses or wires in the way. Remove the right valve cover, if necessary.
11. The rocker arm bolts double as cylinder head bolts. When loosening, follow the cylinder head bolt tightening sequence. If removing both rocker shafts, mark them left and right.

NOTE: Do not jar or strike head while rockers and bolts are out, as cylinder liner O-ring seals may break, necessitating teardown of engine to clean coolant out of crankcase and installation of new seals.

12. To install, reverse removal procedure. Follow cylinder head installation procedure for proper torque sequence.

Intake Manifold

Removal and Installation

INLET DUCT

1. Disconnect the negative battery cable.
2. Disconnect the throttle and downshift linkage. Remove from the inlet duct, the positive crankcase ventilation, distributor advance, pressure sensor for electronic fuel injection models only, and power brake hoses.
3. On electronic fuel injected models (B23F), disconnect the contact for the throttle valve switch and remove the ground cable for the inlet duct.
4. Remove the bolts for the inlet duct stay. Remove the inlet duct-to-cylinder head retaining nuts and slide the inlet duct off the studs. Discard the old gasket.
5. To install, reverse the above procedure. Use a new inlet duct gasket. Torque the nuts to 13–16 ft. lbs. (18–22 Nm).

INTAKE MANIFOLD

B28F and B280F Engines

1. Disconnect the negative battery cable. Remove the air cleaner and all necessary hoses.
2. Drain the radiator coolant.
3. Remove the throttle cable from the pulley and bracket.

4. On automatic transmission vehicles, remove the throttle cable that is connected to the transmission.
5. Remove the EGR pipe from the EGR valve to the manifold.
6. Disconnect the EGR vacuum line.
7. Remove the oil filler cap and PCV valve.

NOTE: Cover the oil cap opening with a rag to keep dirt out.

8. Remove the front manifold bolts and remove the front section of the manifold.
9. Disconnect the cold start connector, fuel line and injector.
10. Disconnect the pressure control regulator vacuum lines, fuel lines and the connector.
11. Remove the auxiliary valve and its necessary piping.
12. Disconnect the electrical connections at the air fuel control unit.
13. Remove all 6 spark plug wires.
14. Remove all 6 injectors.
15. Move the wiring harness to the outside of the manifold.
16. Disconnect the vacuum hose at the distributor and the intake manifold.
17. Disconnect the heater hose at the intake manifold.
18. Disconnect the hose to the diverter valve.
19. Disconnect the vacuum hose to the power brake booster.
20. Disconnect the throttle cable link.
21. Disconnect the wires to the micro-switch.
22. Pull the wires away from the intake manifold.
23. Remove the fuel filter line and the return line.
24. Remove the air control unit.
25. Disconnect the vacuum hose from the throttle valve housing.
26. Remove the pipe and cold start injector assembly.
27. Remove the intake manifold from the vehicle.
28. Installation is the reverse of removal.

NOTE: Always use new gaskets when reinstalling the manifold.

29. Torque the manifold bolts to 7–11 ft. lbs. (10–15 Nm).

B21, B23 and B230 Engines

1. Disconnect the negative battery cable. Remove the air cleaner and all necessary hoses.
2. Remove the PCV valve.

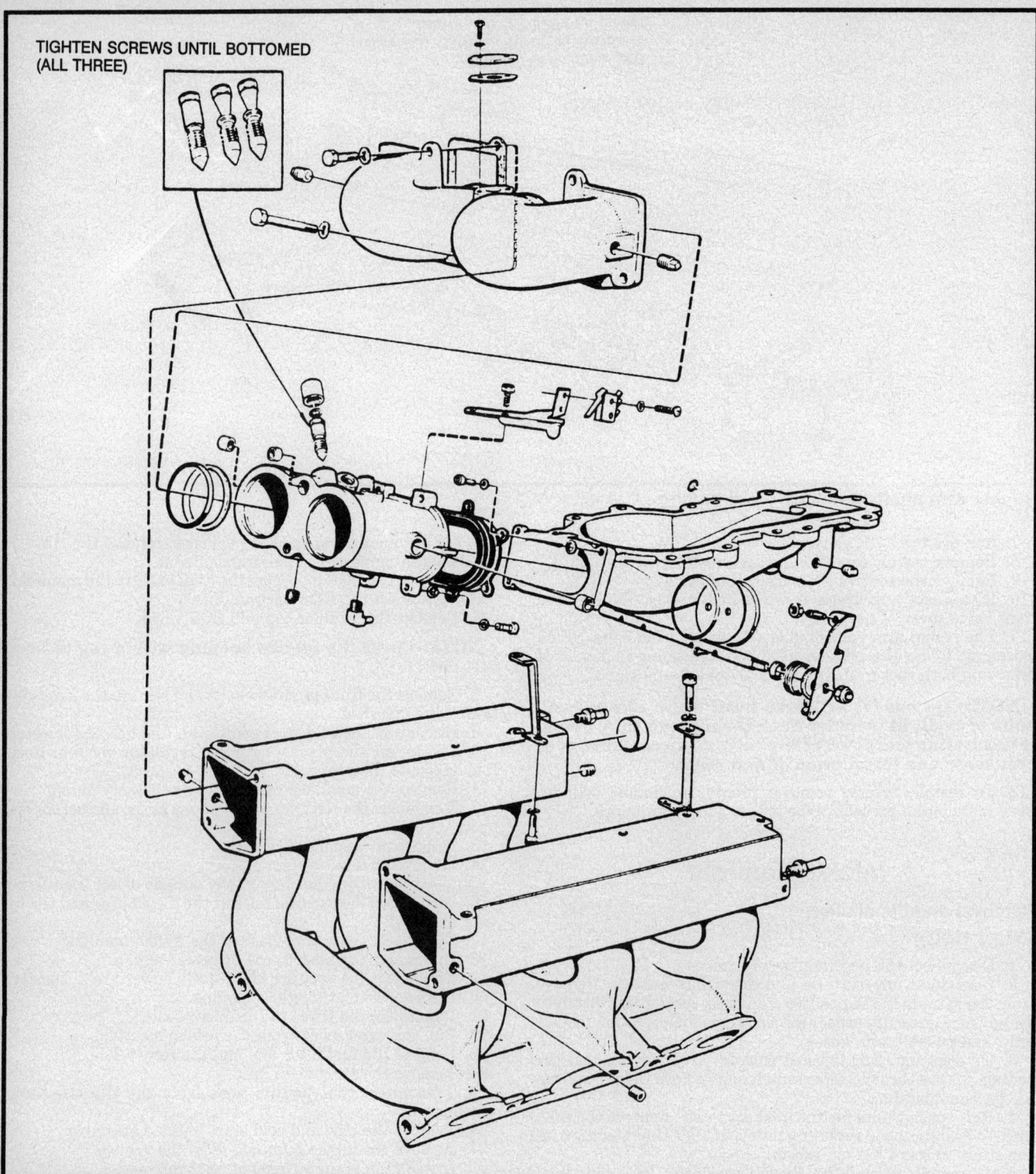

TIGHTEN SCREWS UNTIL BOTTOMED
(ALL THREE)

Intake manifold assembly—B28 engine

3. Remove the connector at the cold start injector.
4. Remove the fuel hose from the cold start injector.
5. Remove the cold start injector.
6. Remove the connector on the auxiliary valve.
7. Disconnect the hoses at the auxiliary valve.
8. Remove the auxiliary valve.

9. On turbocharged models, disconnect the turbocharger inlet hose, between turbo unit and intake manifold. Plug the hose immediately.
10. Remove the intake manifold brace.
11. Disconnect the distributor vacuum hose at the intake manifold.

12. Loosen the clamp for the rubber connecting pipe on the air-fuel control unit.
13. Remove the manifold bolts and remove the manifold.
14. Installation is the reverse of removal.

NOTE: Remember to install new manifold gaskets before replacing the manifold.

15. Torque the manifold bolts to 15 ft. lbs. (20 Nm).

B234F Engine

1. Remove the air mass meter and the air intake hose.
2. Detach the throttle pulley from the intake manifold and remove the link rod from the throttle lever.
3. Separate the throttle housing from the intake manifold and cut the cable tie holding the wiring to the vacuum hose connections.
4. Disconnect the lines and hoses from the manifold, including the brake booster vacuum hose, the evaporation line, the oil trap, the fuel pressure regulator line and the air control valve line. If equipped with a vacuum tank, disconnect its line at the manifold.
5. Disconnect the fuel return line at the distribution pipe. Disconnect the wiring to the injectors and remove the distribution pipe and injectors. Immediately protect these components from the entry of any dirt.
6. Unbolt and remove the intake manifold from the engine.
To install:
7. If installing a new manifold, it is necessary to transfer the various hose nipples and plugs to the new part. Install the manifold with a new gasket. Starting with the center bolts and working outward, tighten the bolts to 15 ft. lbs. (20 Nm).
8. Reconnect the hoses to their proper ports.
9. Position the injector wiring between cylinders 2 and 3 and reinstall the fuel distributor rail and the injectors. Tighten the pipe and the ground wires to the block. Connect the fuel pressure regulator line to the intake manifold.
10. Install the throttle pulley and connect the link rod.
11. Install the throttle housing with a new gasket. Check the operation of the throttle stops and switches.
12. Install the air mass meter and air inlet hose.

Exhaust Manifold

Removal and Installation

B28F AND B280F ENGINES

Depending upon the type of optional equipment the vehicle has, the exhaust manifolds may be removed from under the vehicle.
1. Raise and support the vehicle safely.

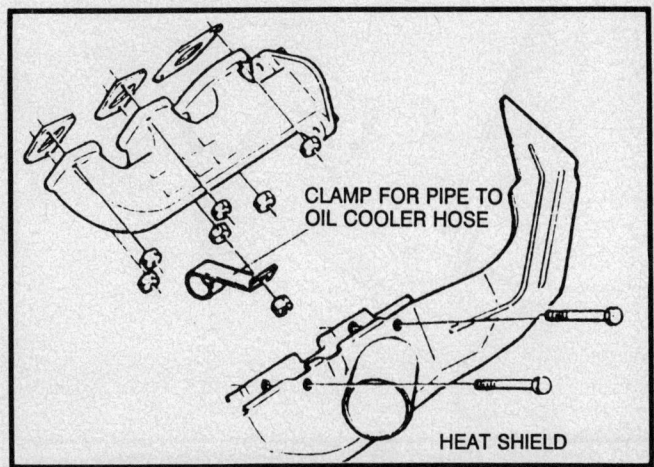

CLAMP FOR PIPE TO OIL COOLER HOSE

HEAT SHIELD

Exhaust manifold assembly—B28 engine

2. Unbolt the crossover pipe from the left and right side of the exhaust manifolds, if equipped.

NOTE: If the vehicle has the Y-type exhaust pipe disconnect this pipe at the left and right manifolds.

3. Remove any other necessary hardware.
4. Remove the left and right side manifolds.
5. Installation is the reverse of removal.

NOTE: Always use new gaskets when reinstalling the manifolds.

6. Torque the manifold bolts to 7–11 ft. lbs. (10–15 Nm).

B21, B23 AND B230 ENGINES

1. Disconnect the negative battery cable. Remove the air cleaner and all necessary hoses.
2. Remove the EGR valve pipe from the manifold.
3. Remove the exhaust pipe from the exhaust manifold. On B21FT, remove the exhaust pipe from the turbocharger.
4. Remove the manifold bolts and remove the manifold.

NOTE: Remember to install new manifold gaskets before installing the manifold.

5. Installation is the reverse of removal.
6. Torque the manifold bolts to 10–20 ft. lbs. (14–27 Nm).

B234F ENGINE

1. Disconnect the front exhaust pipe from the manifold. Disconnect the catalytic converter from the front muffler.
2. Remove the heat shields (top and bottom) from the manifold and remove the air preheat hose.
3. Disconnect the front exhaust pipe from the bracket on the bell housing.
4. Unbolt the exhaust manifold and remove it from the vehicle.
5. Install the manifold with a new gasket and tighten the bolts to 15 ft. lbs. (20 Nm).
6. Install the front exhaust pipe with a new gasket; tighten the joint to the manifold to 20 ft. lbs. (27 Nm). Reattach the catalytic converter to the front muffler.
7. Install the heat shields and the preheat hose.

Turbocharger

Removal and Installation

B230FT ENGINES

1. Disconnect the battery ground cable.
2. Disconnect expansion tank from retainer. Remove expansion tank retainer.
3. Remove preheater hose to the air cleaner. Remove the pipe and rubber bellows between the air/fuel control unit and the turbocharger unit. Pull out the crankcase ventilation hose from the pipe.
4. Remove the pipe and pipe connector between the turbocharger unit and the intake manifold.

NOTE: Cover the turbocharger intake and outlet ports to keep dirt out of the system.

5. Disconnect the exhaust pipe and secure it aside.
6. Disconnect the spark plug wires at the plugs.
7. Remove the upper heat shield. Remove the brace between the turbocharger unit and the manifold.
8. Remove the lower heat shield by removing the 1 retaining screw under the manifold.
9. Remove the oil pipe clamp, retaining screws on the turbo unit and the pipe connection screw in the cylinder block under the manifold. Do not allow any dirt to enter the oilways.
10. Remove the manifold retaining screws and washers. Let 1 nut remain in position to keep the manifold in position.

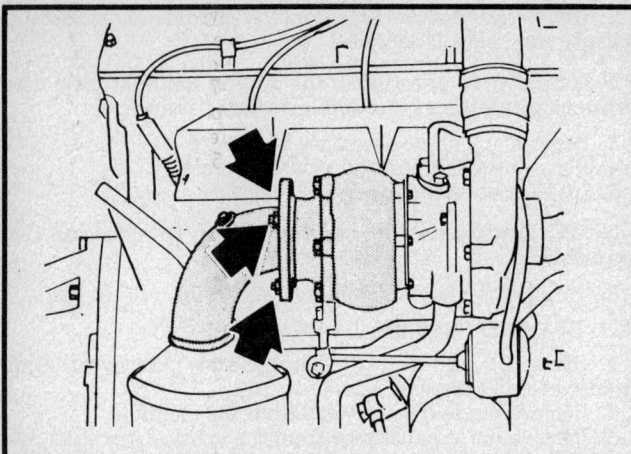

Disconnect the turbocharger unit from the exhaust system

11. Remove the oil delivery pipe. Cover the opening on the turbo unit.

12. Disconnect the air/fuel control unit by loosening the clamps. Move the unit with the lower section of the air cleaner up to the right side wheel housing. Place a cover over the wheel housing as protection.

13. Remove the air cleaner filter.

14. Remove the remaining nut and washer on the manifold. Lift the assembly forward and up. Remove the manifold gaskets. Disconnect the return oil pipe O-ring from the cylinder block.

15. Disconnect the turbocharger unit from the manifold.

16. Installation is the reverse of removal. Be sure to use a new gasket for the exhaust manifold and a new O-ring to the return oil pipe. Keep everything clean during assembly and use extreme care in keeping dirt out of the various turbo inlet and outlet pipes and hoses.

Front Cover

Removal and Installation

B21, B23 AND B230 ENGINES

1. Disconnect the negative battery cable. Loosen the fan shroud and remove the fan. Remove the shroud.

2. Loosen the alternator, power steering pump, if equipped, and air conditioning compressor, if equipped, and remove their drive belts.

3. Remove the water pump pulley.

4. Remove the 4 retaining bolts and lift off the timing belt cover.

5. Reverse the above procedure to install.

Timing Chain Front Cover

Removal and Installation

B28F AND B280F ENGINES

1. Disconnect the negative battery cable. Remove the air cleaner and valve covers.

2. Loosen the fan shroud and remove the fan. Remove the shroud.

3. Loosen the alternator, air pump, power steering pump, air conditioning compressor, if equipped, and remove their drive belts.

4. Block the flywheel from turning, remove the crankshaft pulley nut (36mm) and the pulley.

NOTE: Do not drop the pulley key into the crankcase.

5. Remove the power steering pump and place aside. Remove the pump bracket.

6. Remove the timing chain cover retaining bolts, 25 11mm hex bolts, tap and remove the cover.

To install:

7. Clean the gasket contact surfaces. Place the upper gasket on the cover and the lower gasket on the block. Install the cover and tighten to 7–11 ft. lbs. (10–15 Nm). Trim the gaskets flush with the valve cover.

8. Install a new crankshaft seal.

9. Block the flywheel, install the pulley, key and tighten the 36mm nut to 118–132 ft. lbs. (160–180 Nm).

10. Reverse Steps 1–5 to install.

Timing Chain and Sprockets

Removal and Installation

B28F AND B280F ENGINES

1. Remove the timing chain cover.

2. Remove the oil pump sprocket and drive chain.

3. Slacken the tension in both camshaft timing chains by rotating each tensioner lock ¼ turn counterclockwise and pushing the rubbing block piston.

4. Remove both chain tensioners. Remove the 2 curved and the 2 straight chain damper/runners.

5. Remove the camshaft sprocket retaining bolt, 10mm Allen head, and the sprocket and chain assembly. Repeat for the other side.

To install:

6. Install the chain tensioners and tighten to 5 ft. lbs. (7 Nm). Install the curved chain damper/runners and tighten to 7–11 ft. lbs. (10–15 Nm). Install the straight chain damper/runners and torque to 5 ft. lbs. (7 Nm).

7. First install the left (driver) side camshaft sprocket and chain:

    a. Rotate the crankshaft, using crankshaft nut, if necessary, until the crankshaft key is pointing directly to the left side camshaft and the left side camshaft key groove is pointing straight-up (12 o'clock).

    b. Place the chain on the left side sprocket so the sprocket notchmark is centered precisely between the 2 white lines on the chain.

    c. Position the chain on the crankshaft sprocket (inner), making sure the other white line on the chain aligns with the crankshaft sprocket notch.

    d. While holding the left side chain and sprockets in this position, install the sprocket and chain on the left side cam-

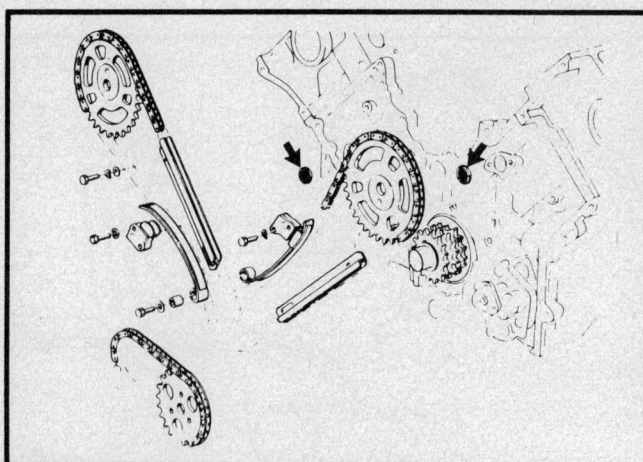

B28 and B280 timing chain tensioner and chain assembly

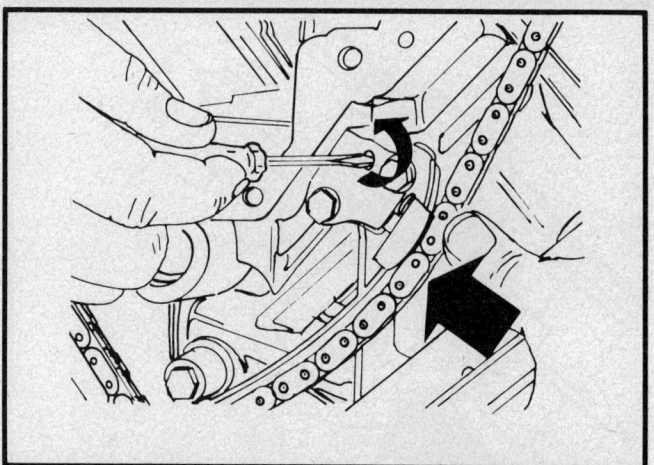

Relieving chain tension

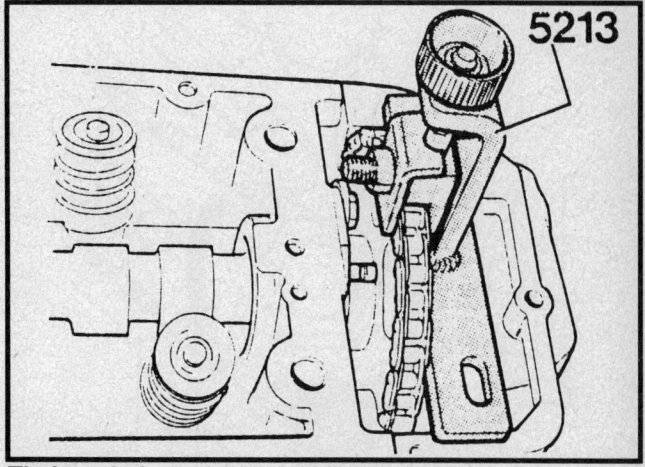

5213

Timing chain and gear holding tool 5213—B28 and B280 engine

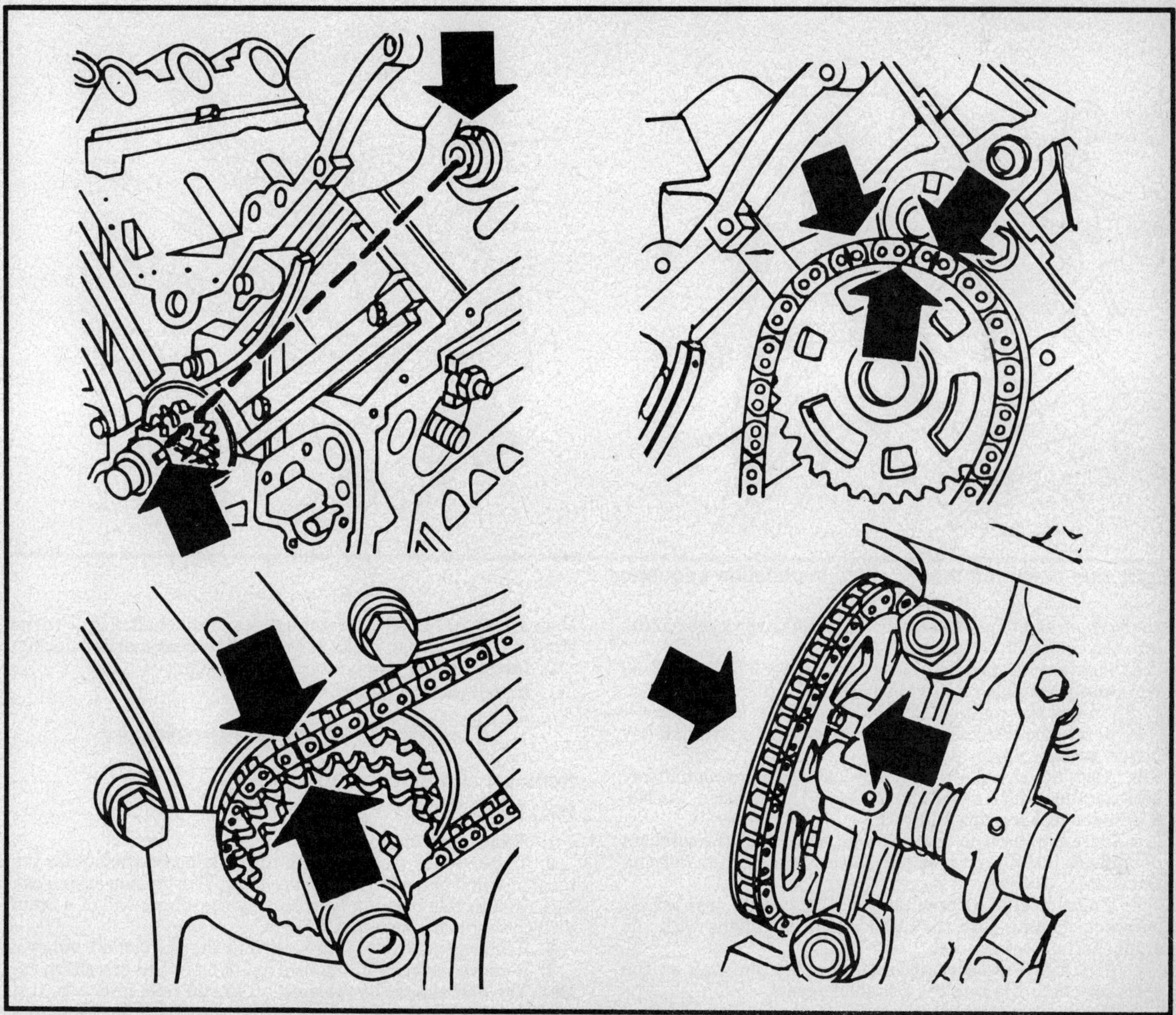

Left side camshaft timing chain installation sequence—V6 engines

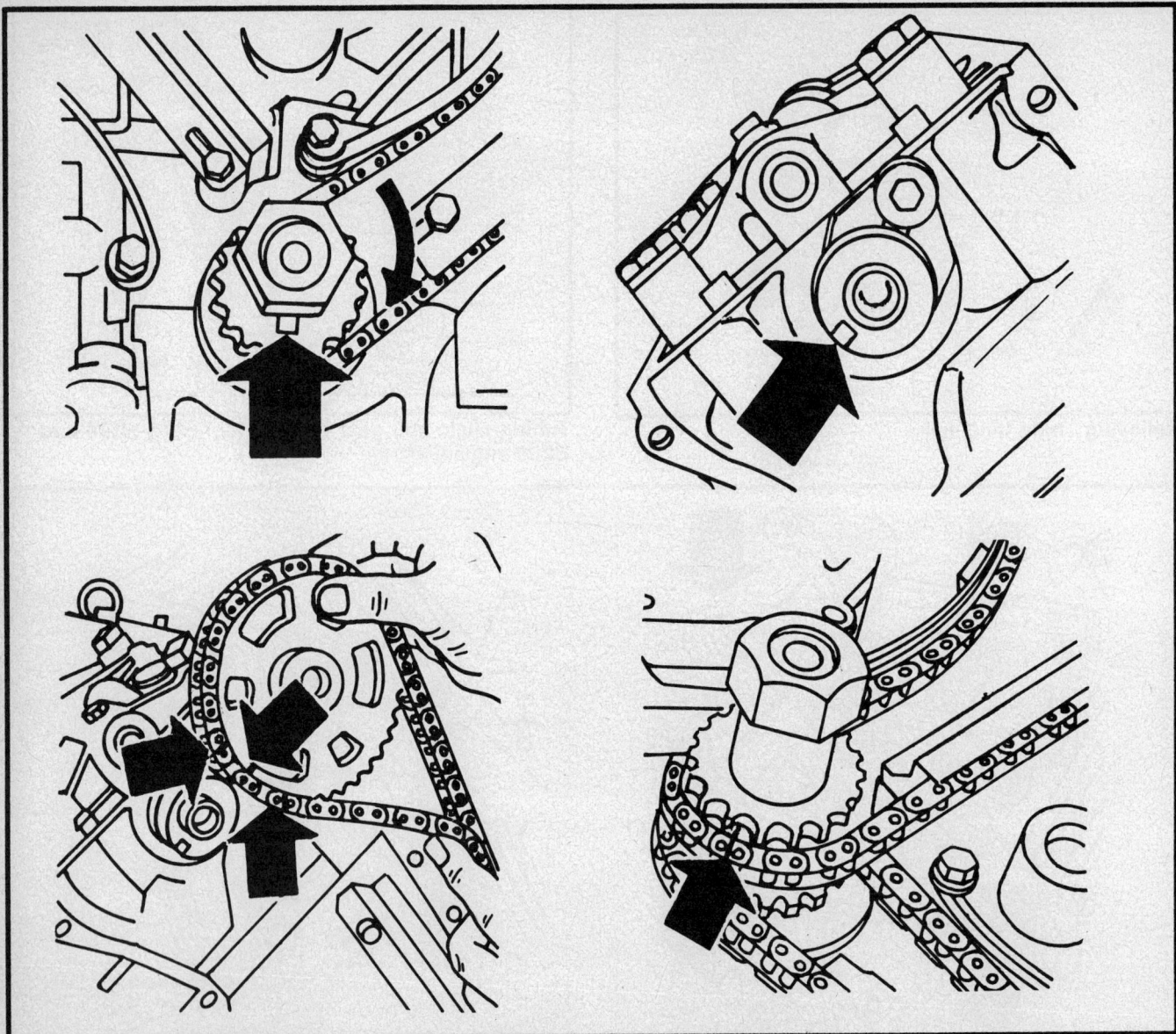

Right side camshaft timing chain installation sequence

shaft, chain stretched on tension side, so the sprocket pin fits into the camshaft recess.

  e. Tighten the sprocket center bolt to 51–59 ft. lbs. (69–80 Nm); use a suitable tool to keep cam from turning.

8. To install the right side camshaft sprocket and chain:

  a. Rotate the crankshaft clockwise until the crankshaft key points straight down (6 o'clock).

  b. Align the camshaft key groove so it is pointing halfway between the 8 and 9 o'clock positions; at this position, the No. 6 cylinder rocker arms will rock.

  c. Place the chain on the right side sprocket so the sprocket notchmark is centered precisely between the 2 white lines on the chain.

  d. Then, position the chain on the middle crankshaft sprocket, making sure the other white line aligns with the crankshaft sprocket notch.

  e. Install the sprocket and chain on the camshaft so the sprocket notch fits into the camshaft recess.

  f. Tighten the sprocket nut to 51–59 ft. lbs. (69–80 Nm).

9. Rotate the chain tensioners ¼ turn clockwise each. The

chains are tensioned by rotating the crankshaft 2 full turns clockwise. Recheck to make sure the alignment marks coincide.

10. Install the oil pump sprocket and chain.

11. Install the timing chain cover.

Timing Belt and Tensioner

Removal and Installation

B21, B23 AND B230 ENGINES

1. Remove the timing belt cover.

2. To remove the tension from the belt, loosen the nut for the tensioner and press the idler roller back. The tension spring can be locked in this position by inserting the shank end of a 3mm drill through the pusher rod.

3. Remove the 6 retaining bolts and the crankshaft pulley.

4. Remove the belt, taking care not to bend it at any sharp angles. The belt should be replaced at 45,000 mile intervals, if it becomes oil soaked or frayed or if it is on a vehicle that has been sitting idle for any length of time.

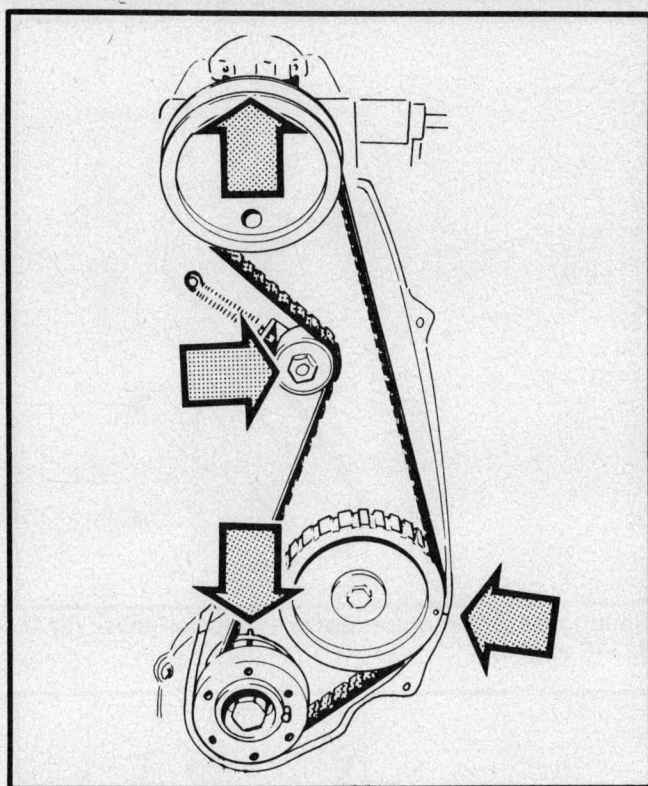

Make sure all timing marks are lined up including marks on the new belt—B23 engine

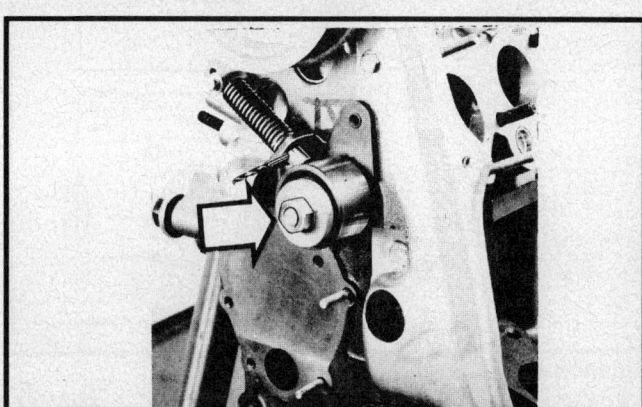

Locking the tensioner spring with drill bit shank

To install:

5. If the crankshaft, idler shaft or camshaft were disturbed while the belt was out, align each shaft with is corresponding index mark to assure proper valve timing and ignition timing, as follows:

   a. Rotate the crankshaft so the notch in the convex crankshaft gear belt guide aligns with the embossed mark on the front cover (12 o'clock position).

   b. Rotate the idler shaft so the dot on the idler shaft drive sprocket aligns with the notch on the timing belt rear cover (4 o'clock position).

   c. Rotate the camshaft so the notch in the camshaft sprocket inner belt guide aligns with the notch in the forward edge of the valve cover (12 o'clock position).

6. Install the timing belt (don't use any sharp tools) over the sprockets and then over the tensioner roller. New belts have yel-

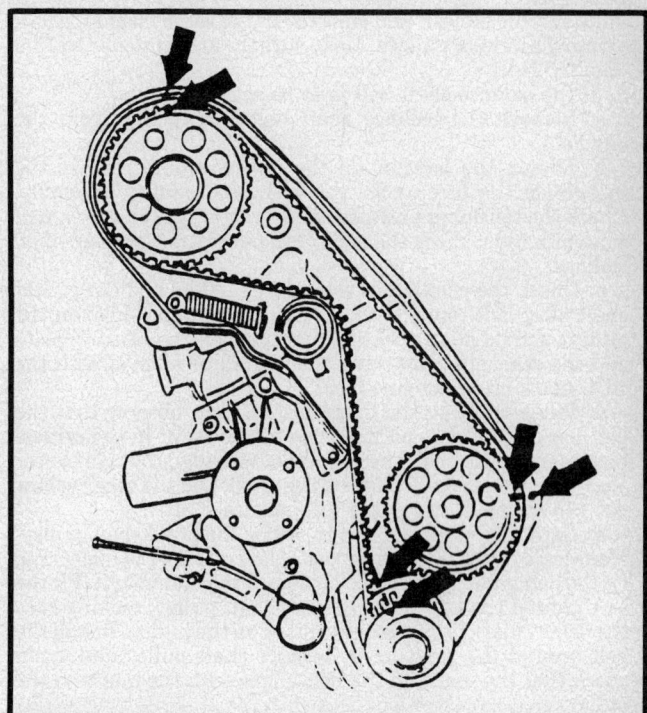

Timing belt alignment—B230 engine

low marks. The 2 lines on the drive belt should fit toward the crankshaft marks. The next mark should then fit toward the intermediate shaft marks, etc. Loosen the tensioner nut and let the spring tension automatically take up the slack. Tighten the tensioner nut to 37 ft. lbs. (51 Nm).

7. Rotate the crankshaft 1 full revolution clockwise and make sure the timing marks still align.

8. Reverse Steps 1–3 to install.

B234F ENGINE

NOTE: The B234 engine has 2 belts, one driving the camshafts and one driving the balance shafts. The camshaft belt may be removed separately; the balance shaft belt requires removal of the cam belt. During reassembly, the exact placement of the belts and pulleys must be observed.

1. Remove the negative battery cable and the alternator belt.

2. Remove the radiator fan, its pulley and the fan shroud.

3. Remove the drive belts for the power steering belts and the air conditioning compressor.

4. Beginning with the top cover, remove the retaining bolts and remove the timing belt covers.

5. Turn the engine to TDC, of the compression stroke, on cylinder No. 1. Make sure the marks on the cam pulleys align with the marks on the backing plate and that the marking on the belt guide plate (on the crankshaft) is opposite the TDC mark on the engine block.

6. Remove the protective cap over the timing belt tensioner locknut. Loosen the locknut, compress the tensioner, to release tension on the belts, and retighten the locknut, holding the tensioner in place.

7. Remove the timing belt from the camshafts. Do not crease or fold the belt.

NOTE: The camshafts and the crankshaft must not be moved when the belt is removed.

8. Check the tensioner by spinning it counterclockwise and listening for any bearing noise within. Check also that the belt

contact surface is clean and smooth. In the same fashion, check the timing belt idler pulleys. Make sure the are tightened to 18.5 ft. lbs. (25 Nm).

9. If the balance shaft belt is to be removed:

a. Remove the balance shaft belt idler pulley from the engine.

b. Loosen the locknut on the tensioner and remove the belt. Slide the belt under the crankshaft pulley assembly. Check the tensioner and idler wheels carefully for any sign of contamination; check the ends of the shafts for any sign of oil leakage.

c. Check the position of the balance shafts and the crankshaft after belt removal. The balance shaft markings on the pulleys should align with the markings on the backing plate and the crankshaft marking should still be aligned with the TDC mark on the engine block.

d. When refitting the balance shaft belt, observe that the belt has colored dots on it. These marks assist in the critical placement of the belt. The yellow dot will align the right lower shaft, the blue dot will align on the crank and the other yellow dot will match to the upper left balance shaft.

e. Carefully work the belt in under the crankshaft pulley. Make sure the blue dot is opposite the bottom (TDC) marking on the belt guide plate at the bottom of the crankshaft. Fit the belt around the left upper balance shaft pulley, making sure the yellow mark is opposite the mark on the pulley. Install the belt around the right lower balance shaft pulley and again check that the mark on the belt aligns with the mark on the pulley.

f. Work the belt around the tensioner. Double check that all the markings are still aligned.

g. Set the belt tension by inserting an Allen key into the adjusting hole in the tensioner. Turn the crankshaft carefully through a few degrees on either side of TDC to check that the belt has properly engaged the pulleys. Return the crank to the TDC position and set the adjusting hole just below the 3 o'clock position when tightening the adjusting bolt. Use the Allen wrench, in the adjusting hole, as a counter hold and tighten the locking bolt to 29.5 ft. lbs. (40 Nm).

h. Use Volvo tool 998 8500 to check the tension of the belt. Install the gauge over the position of the removed idler pulley. The tension must be 1–4 units on the scale or the belt must be readjusted.

To install:

10. Reinstall the camshaft belt by aligning the double line marking on the belt with the top marking on the belt guide plate at the top of the crankshaft. Stretch the belt around the crank pulley and place it over the tensioner and the right side idler. Place the belt on the camshaft pulleys. The single line marks on the belt should align exactly with the pulley markings. Route the belt around the oil pump drive pulley and press the belt onto the left side idler.

11. Check that all the markings align and that the engine is still positioned at TDC, of the compression stroke, for cylinder No. 1.

12. Loosen the tensioner locknut.

13. Turn the crankshaft clockwise. The cam pulleys should rotate 1 full turn until the marks again align with the marks on the backing plate.

NOTE: The engine must not be rotated counterclockwise during this procedure.

14. Smoothly rotate the crankshaft further clockwise until the cam pulley markings are 1½ teeth beyond the marks on the backing plate. Tighten the tensioner locknut.

15. Check the tension on the balance shaft belt; it should now be 3.8 units. If the tension is too low, adjust the tensioner clockwise. If the tension is too high, repeat Step 8g above.

16. Check the belt guide for the balance shaft belt and make sure it is properly seated. Install the center timing belt cover,

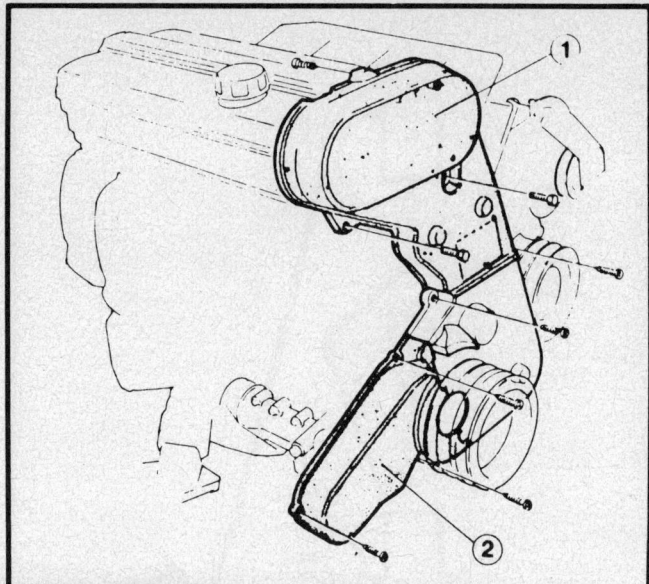

Timing belt cover, upper cover (1), lower cover (2) – B234F engine

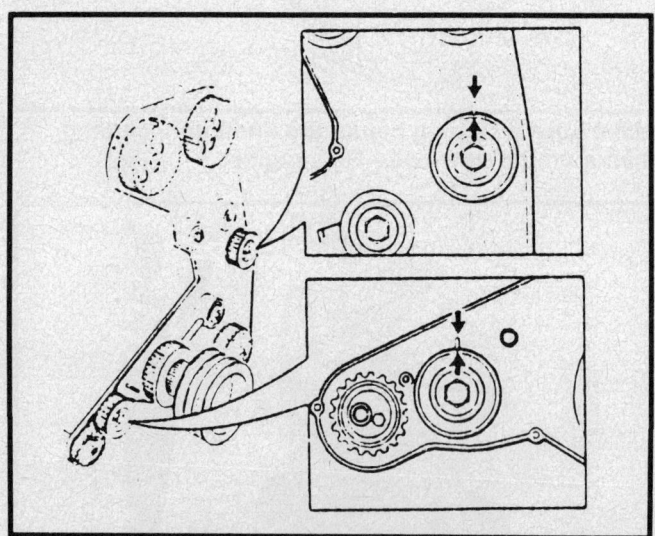

Balance shafts alignment – B234F engine

the one that covers the tensioner, the fan shroud, fan pulley and fan. Install all the drive belts and connect the battery cable.

17. Double check all installation items, paying particular attention to loose hoses or hanging wires, untightened nuts, poor routing of hoses and wires (too tight or rubbing) and tools left in the engine area.

18. Start the engine and allow it to run until the thermostat opens.

— CAUTION —

The upper and lower timing belt covers are still removed. The belt and pulleys are exposed and moving at high speed.

19. Shut the motor off and bring the motor to TDC, of the compression stroke, on cylinder No. 1.

20. Check the tension of the camshaft belt. Position the gauge between the right (exhaust) cam pulley and the idler. Belt tension must be 5.5 ± 0.2 units. If the belt needs adjustment, remove the rubber cap over the tensioner locknut, cap is located on the timing belt cover, and loosen the locknut.

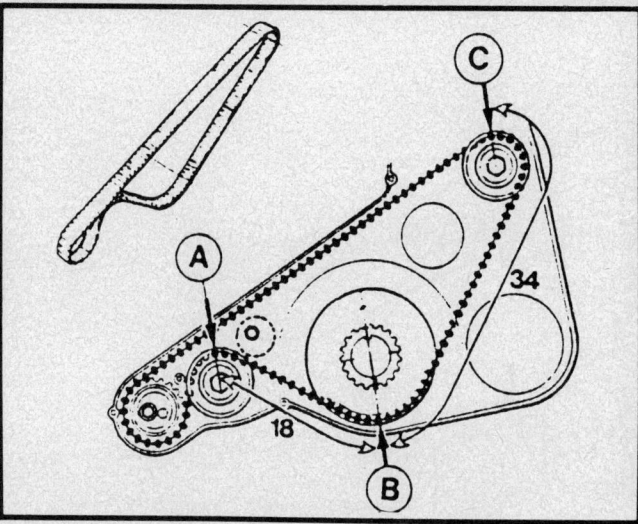

Balance shaft belt markings, 18 teeth between A and B, 34 teeth between B and C — B234F engine

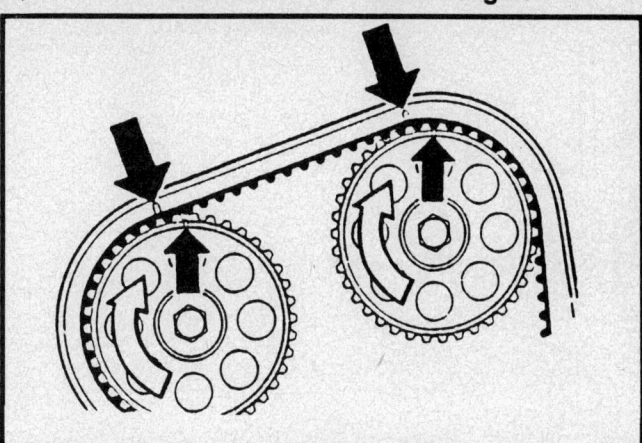

Rotate engine 1½ teeth — B234F engine

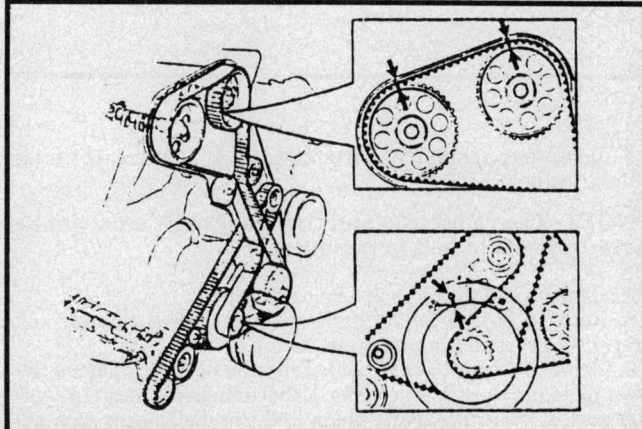

Timing mark alignment — B234F engine

21. Insert a suitable tool between the tensioner wheel and the spring carrier pin to hold the tensioner. If the belt needs to be tightened, move the roller to adjust the tension to 6.0 units. If the belt is too tight, adjust to obtain a reading of 5.0 units on the gauge. Tighten the tensioner locknut.

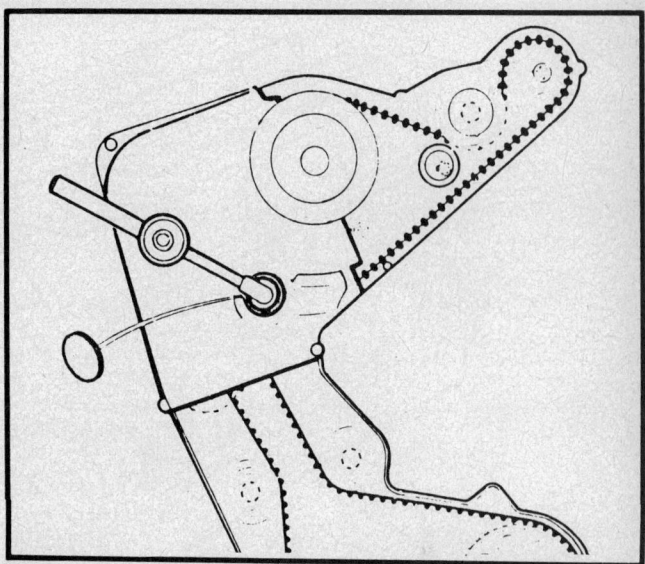

Timing belt tensioner adjustment — B234F engine

22. Rotate the crankshaft so the cam pulleys move through 1 full revolution and recheck the tension on the camshaft belt. It should now be 5.5 ± 0.2 units. Install the plastic plug over the tensioner bolt.

23. Final check the tension on the balance shaft belt by fitting the gauge and turning the tensioner clockwise. Only small movements are needed. After any needed readjustments, rotate the crankshaft clockwise through 1 full revolution and recheck the balance shaft belt. The tension should now be on the final specification of 4.9 ± 0.2 units.

24. Install the idler pulley for the balance shaft belt. Reinstall the upper and lower timing belt covers.

25. Start the engine and final check performance.

Camshaft

Removal and Installation

B21, B23 AND B230 ENGINES

1. Remove the timing belt cover.
2. Remove the valve cover.
3. Remove the camshaft center bearing cap. Install Volvo camshaft press tool 5021 over the center bearing journal to hold the camshaft in place while removing the other bearing caps.
4. Remove the 4 remaining bearing caps.
5. Remove the seal from the forward edge of the camshaft.
6. Release camshaft press tool and lift out the camshaft.

Four cylinder camshaft press tool installed

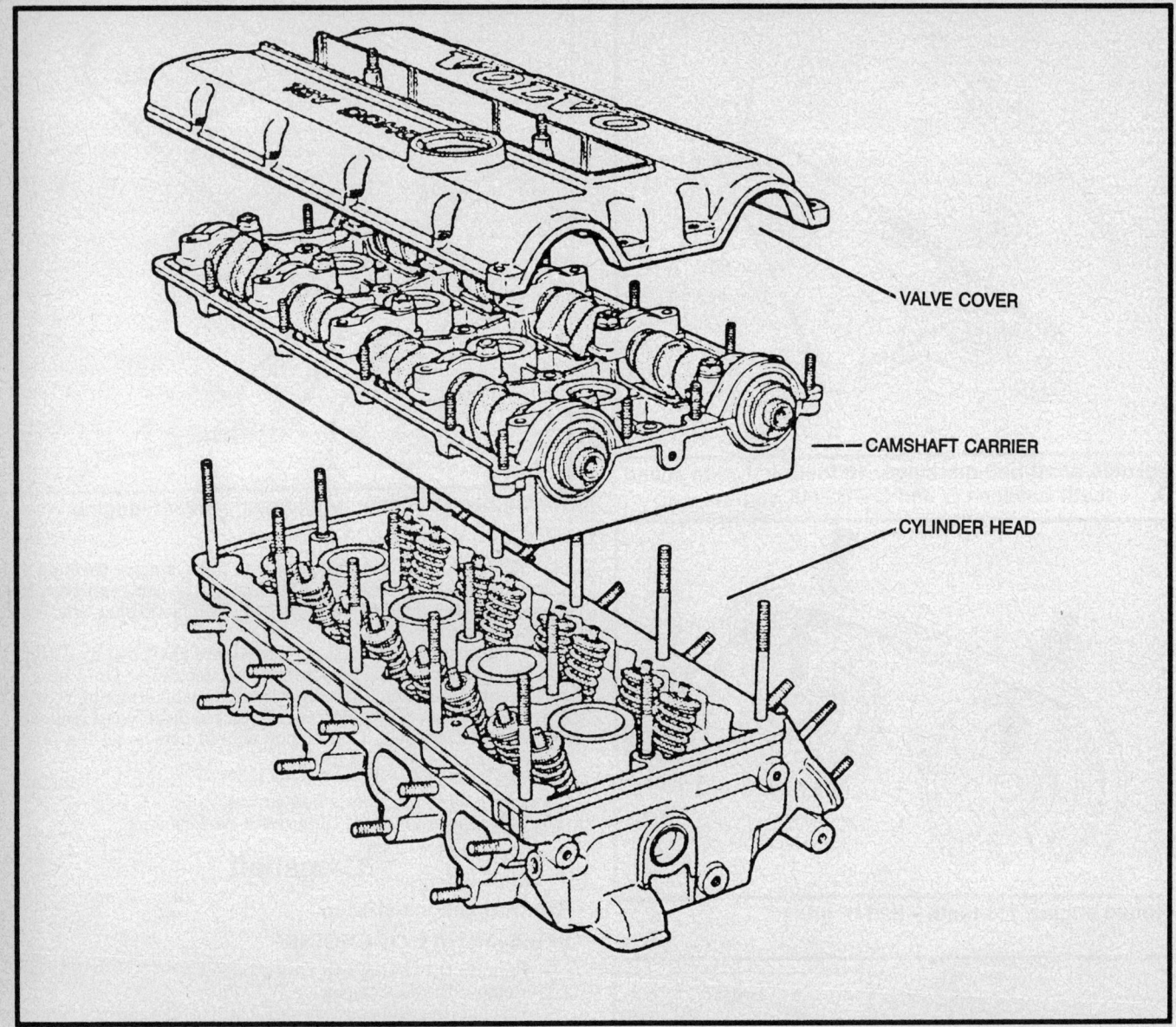

Camshaft carrier assembly—B234F Engine

7. Reverse the above procedure to install. Make sure the camshaft and followers are well oiled before installation.

B234 ENGINE

NOTE: **The use of the correct special tools or their equivalent is required for this procedure.**

1. Disconnect the negative battery cable.
2. Remove the alternator drive belt, the radiator fan and its pulley.
3. Remove the upper and lower timing belt covers.
4. Align the camshaft and crankshaft marks. Turn the engine to TDC, of the compression stroke, on cylinder No. 1 and make sure the pulley marks and the crank marks align with their matching marks on either the backing plate (cam pulleys) or the belt guide plate (crankshaft).
5. Remove the protective cap over the timing belt tensioner locknut. Loosen the locknut, compress the tensioner, to release tension on the belts, and retighten the locknut, holding the tensioner in place.

6. Remove the timing belt from the camshafts; do not crease or fold the belt.

NOTE: **The camshafts and the crankshaft must not be moved when the belt is removed.**

7. Remove the timing belt idler pulleys.
8. Remove the camshaft drive pulleys. Use a counterhold wrench to prevent the cam from turning.
9. Remove the plate or panel behind the pulleys. Remove the cover plate for the ignition wires. Label and disconnect the ignition wiring from the spark plugs and the distributor cap; remove the coil wire from the distributor cap.
10. Remove the valve cover and gasket. Clean the surfaces of any gasket remains.
11. Remove the distributor housing from the camshaft carrier. Remove the ignition wire clip next to the left bolt.
12. Plug the spark plug holes with crumpled paper. Remove the center bearing cap for each camshaft. Mark the cam bearing caps for proper reinstallation.

13. Install a Volvo camshaft press tool 5021 or similar, on the exhaust side cam in place of the removed bearing cap. When it is securely in place, remove the remaining bearing caps and nuts. Remove the tool and remove the exhaust camshaft.

14. Remove the intake camshaft in identical fashion.

NOTE: Label or identify each cam and its bearing caps. All removed components should be kept in order.

15. Using a magnet or a small suction cup, remove the tappets. Store them upside down, to prevent oil drainage, and keep them in order; they are not interchangeable.

To install:

16. Clean and inspect the camshaft carrier and tappet bores for any sign of wear or scoring.

17. Oil all matching surfaces on the cam carrier, bearing caps and tappets.

18. Insert the tappets; they must be inserted in their original order and place.

19. Install the exhaust side camshaft by placing it in the carrier with the pulley guide pin facing up. Using the rear bearing cap as a guide, press the cam into place with the press tool. Install the bearing caps in the original order.

20. Install the bearing cap nuts and tighten them in stages to 15 ft. lbs. (20 Nm). Remove the press tool and install the center bearing cap; tighten it in stages to 15 ft. lbs. (20 Nm).

21. Install the intake camshaft in the carrier with the pulley guide pin facing upwards.

22. Turn the distributor shaft to align the driver with the markings on the distributor housing. Install new O-rings on the housing and rotor shaft.

23. Using the rear bearing cap as a guide, press the cam into place with the press tool. Install the bearing caps in the original order.

24. Install the bearing cap nuts and tighten them in stages to 15 ft. lbs. (20 Nm).

25. Double check the tightness of all the camshaft bearing cap nuts. All should be 15 ft. lbs.; do not overtighten.

26. Reinstall the distributor, connect the coil wire and install the ignition wire clip at the left bolt. Remove the paper plugs from the spark plug holes.

27. Use a silicone sealer and apply to the front and rear camshaft bearing caps. Install new gaskets for the valve cover and the spark plug wells. Install the spark plug gasket with the arrow pointing towards the front of the vehicle and the word "UP" facing up. Make sure the valve cover gasket is correctly positioned and install the valve cover.

28. Reconnect the ground wire at the distributor.

29. Install the ignition wires and the cover plate.

30. Using a Volvo compression seal driver tool 5025 or similar, install the oil seals for the front of each camshaft. Camshafts must not be allowed to turn during this operation.

31. Install the upper backing plate over the ends of the camshafts and adjust the plate so the cams are centered in the holes.

32. Replace the idler pulleys and tighten their mounts to 18.5 ft. lbs. (25 Nm).

33. Install the camshaft drive pulleys, using a counterhold to prevent the cams from turning.

34. Reinstall the camshaft belt by aligning the double line marking on the belt with the top marking on the belt guide plate at the top of the crankshaft. Stretch the belt around the crank pulley and place it over the tensioner and the right side idler. Place the belt on the camshaft pulleys. The single line marks on the belt should align exactly with the pulley markings. Route the belt around the oil pump drive pulley and press the belt onto the left side idler.

35. Check that all the markings align and that the engine is still positioned at TDC, of the compression stroke, for cylinder No. 1.

36. Loosen the tensioner locknut.

37. Turn the crankshaft clockwise. The cam pulleys should rotate 1 full turn until the marks again align with the marks on the backing plate.

NOTE: The engine must not be rotated counterclockwise during this procedure.

38. Smoothly rotate the crankshaft further clockwise until the cam pulley markings are 1½ teeth beyond the marks on the backing plate. Tighten the tensioner locknut.

39. Reinstall the fan pulley and fan. Install all the drive belts and connect the battery cable.

40. Double check all installation items, paying particular attention to loose hoses or hanging wires, untightened nuts, poor routing of hoses and wires (too tight or rubbing) and tools left in the engine area.

41. Start the engine and allow it to run until the thermostat opens.

— **CAUTION** —

The upper and lower timing belt covers are still removed. The belt and pulleys are exposed and moving at high speed.

NOTE: This engine may be somewhat noisy when started. The noise will subside as oil reaches the tappets. Do not exceed 2500 rpm while the tappets are noisy.

42. Shut the motor off and bring the motor to TDC, of the compression stroke, on cylinder No. 1.

43. Check the tension of the camshaft belt. Position the gauge between the right (exhaust) cam pulley and the idler. Belt tension must be 5.5 ± 0.2 units. If the belt needs adjustment, remove the rubber cap over the tensioner locknut and loosen the locknut.

44. Insert a suitable tool between the tensioner wheel and the spring carrier pin to hold the tensioner. If the belt needs to be tightened, move the roller to adjust the tension to 6.0 units. If the belt is too tight, adjust to obtain a reading of 5.0 units on the gauge. Tighten the tensioner locknut and remove the suitable tool.

45. Rotate the crankshaft so the cam pulleys move through 1 full revolution and recheck the tension on the camshaft belt. It should now be 5.5 ± 0.2 units. Install the plastic plug over the tensioner bolt.

46. Reinstall the remaining belt covers. Start the engine and final check performance.

B28F AND B280F ENGINES

1. Remove the cylinder head.

2. Remove the camshaft rear cover plate.

3. Remove the camshaft retaining fork at the front of the cylinder head.

4. Pull the camshaft out the rear of the head.

5. Reverse the above to install. Oil the camshaft and followers before installation.

Balance Shafts

Removal and Installation

B234 ENGINE

NOTE: The use of the correct special tools or their equivalent is required for this procedure.

Left Shaft and Housing

1. Remove the timing and balance shaft belts.

2. Use a Volvo counterhold tool 5362 and remove the left side balance shaft pulley.

3. Remove the air mass meter and inlet hose.

4. Unfasten the bracket under the intake manifold and remove the bracket holding the alternator and power steering pump. These may be swung aside and tied with wire to the left shock tower.

5. Remove the bolts securing the balance shaft housing to the block. Using an Volvo extractor tool 5376 or similar, carefully separate the housing from the block. The housing must be removed evenly from both its front and rear mounts.

To install:

6. Clean the joint faces on the cylinder block. Place new O-rings in the grooves around the oil passages on the housing. The rings can be held in place with a light coating of grease.

7. Install the balance shaft housing. Make absolutely sure the housing is evenly mounted on the front and rear mountings. Tighten the bolts alternately in a diagonal pattern. Tighten each bolt ½ turn at a time; tighten them to 15 ft. lbs. (20 Nm). When all the bolts are at 15 ft. lbs. (20 Nm), loosen them individually and tighten each one to 7.5 ft. lbs. (10 Nm) plug 90 degrees of rotation.

NOTE: Make certain the shaft does not seize within the housing during installation.

8. If the halves of the housing were split apart during the repair, tighten the joint bolts to 6 ft. lbs. (8 Nm).

9. Install the drive pulley. Use a counterholding tool. Note that the pulley has a slot which will align with the guide on the shaft. The shallow side of the pulley faces inward, toward the engine. Tighten the center bolt for the pulley to 37 ft. lbs. (50 Nm).

10. Install the bracket for the alternator and power steering pump. Double check their connections and hoses. Attach the support under the intake manifold and don't forget the wire clamp on the bottom bolt.

11. Install the air mass meter and its intake hose.

12. Install the balance shaft belt and camshaft belt.

Right Shaft and Housing

1. Remove the timing and balance shaft belts.

2. Use a Volvo counterhold tool 5362 and remove the left side balance shaft pulley.

3. Remove the balance shaft belt tensioner and remove the bolt running through the backing plate to the balance shaft housing.

4. Remove the air mass meter and its air inlet hose.

5. Remove the air preheat hose from the bottom heat shield at the exhaust manifold. Remove the nuts holding the right engine mount to the crossmember.

6. Connect a hoist or engine lift apparatus to the top of the engine. Lift the engine at the right side, being careful to maintain clearance between the brake master cylinder and the intake manifold.

7. Remove the complete motor mount from the block, including the pad and lower mounting plate.

8. Remove the bolts securing the balance shaft housing to the block. Using a Volvo extractor tool 5376 or similar, carefully separate the housing from the block. The housing must be removed evenly from both its front and rear mounts.

To install:

9. Clean the joint faces on the cylinder block. Place new O-rings in the grooves around the oil passages on the housing. The rings can be held in place with a light coating of grease.

10. Install the balance shaft housing. Make absolutely sure the housing is evenly mounted on the front and rear mountings. Tighten the bolts alternately in a diagonal pattern. Tighten each bolt ½ turn at a time; tighten them to 15 ft. lbs. (20 Nm). When all the bolts are at 15 ft. lbs. (20 Nm), loosen them individually and tighten each one to 7.5 ft. lbs. (10 Nm) plus 90 degrees of rotation.

NOTE: Make certain the shaft does not seize within the housing during installation.

11. If the halves of the housing were split apart during the repair, tighten the joint bolts to 6 ft. lbs. (8 Nm).

12. Install the drive pulley. Use a counterholding tool. Note that the pulley has a slot which will align with the guide on the shaft. The shallow side of the pulley faces inward, toward the engine. Tighten the center bolt for the pulley to 37 ft. lbs. (50 Nm).

13. Install the engine mount onto the block.

14. Using the studs on the crossmember as a guide, lower the engine into place on the front crossmember. When the engine is correctly seated, the lifting apparatus may be removed.

15. Reinstall the air mass meter and its air intake hose.

16. Reinstall the motor mount bolts and the air preheat tube at the lower part of the exhaust manifold.

17. Install the bolt through the backing plate and into the balance shaft housing. Reinstall the belt tensioner, tightening the bolt so the pulley is movable when the belt is in position.

18. Reinstall the balance shaft and camshaft belts.

Piston and Connecting Rod

Positioning

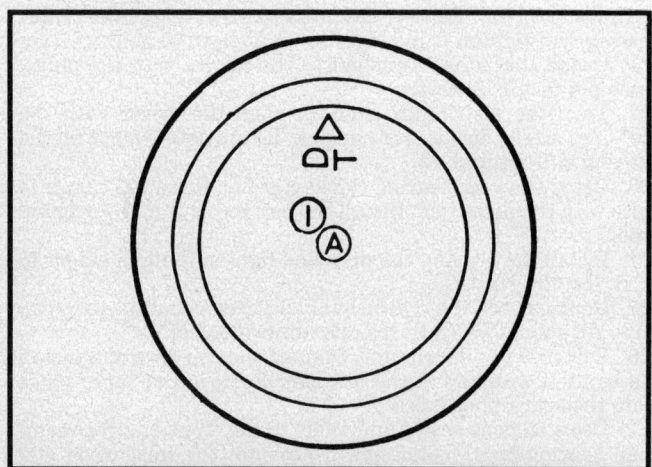

B27 and B28 engine piston positioning. Arrowhead faces forward

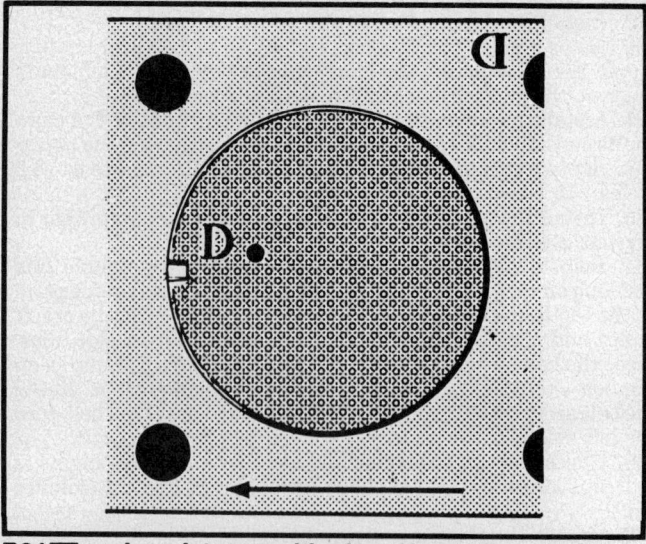

B21FT series piston positioning. Notch faces forward

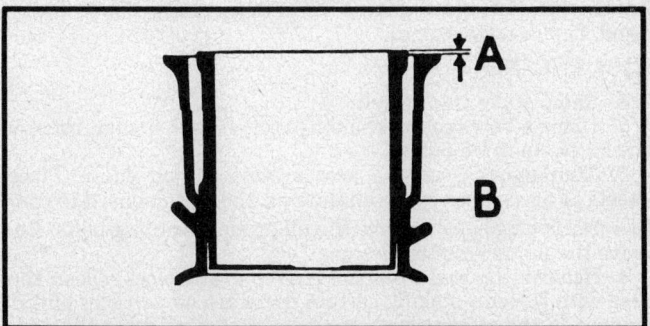

Correct B27 and B28 piston liner height "A" above block face is 0.0091 in. Shims are available for installation at point "B" and should be uniform for all cylinders

When installing B27 and B28 liner shims, color marking "A" must face up and be positioned where shown. Inside tabs "B" fit into liner groove

ENGINE LUBRICATION

Oil Pan

Removal and Installation

B21, B23 AND B230 ENGINES

1. Disconnect the negative battery cable. Raise and support the vehicle safely.
2. Drain the engine oil.
3. Remove the splash guard.
4. Remove the engine mount retaining nuts.
5. Remove the lower bolt and loosen the top bolt on the steering column yoke.
6. Slide the yoke assembly up on the steering shaft.
7. Raise and safely support the front of the engine.
8. Remove the retaining bolts for the front axle crossmember.
9. Remove the crossmember.
10. Remove the left engine mount.
11. Remove the pan support bracket.
12. Remove the pan bolts and remove the pan.

To install:

13. Installation is the reverse of removal.

NOTE: Always use a new pan gasket when reinstalling the pan.

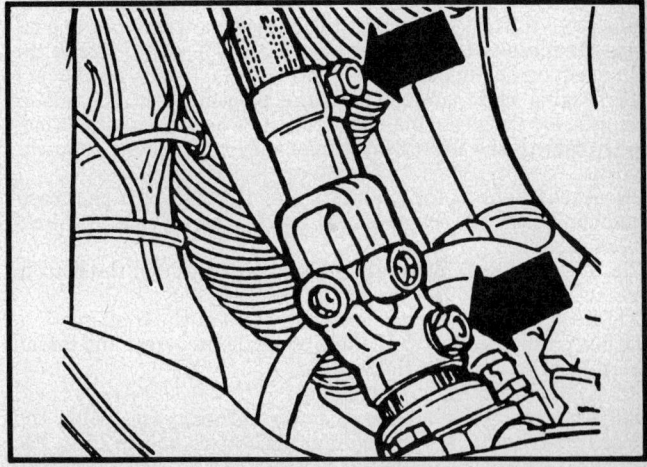

Steering yoke removal; arrows indicate retaining nuts

14. The following torque specifications are needed:
Pan bolts—8 ft. lbs. (11 Nm)
Steering yoke lower bolt—18 ft. lbs. (24 Nm)

B234 ENGINE

1. Raise and safely support the vehicle. Disconnect the negative battery cable and remove the engine oil dipstick.
2. Remove the air mass meter and air inlet hose. Loosen the fan shroud.
3. Remove the bolts at both ends of the crossmember.
4. Fit a chain hoist or lifting apparatus to the top of the engine and relieve the weight of the engine by lifting the at the front.
5. At the right motor mount, unbolt the bottom mounting plate from the crossmember. At the left motor mount, unbolt the upper mounting plate from the cylinder block.
6. Drain the engine oil and replace the drain bolt when the pan is empty. Use a new washer and tighten the bolt to 44 ft. lbs. (60 Nm).
7. Remove the splash guard from under the engine, the bottom nut for the left motor mount and the wiring harness bracket from the transmission cover.
8. At the steering shaft, remove the lower clamping bolt and

Pan support bracket—B21 and B23 series engines (view from under car)

loosen the upper bolt. Matchmark the position of the splined joint and slide the fitting up the steering shaft.

9. Remove the rubber bump-stop on the front crossmember and remove the reinforcing bracket between the engine and transmission.

10. Disassemble the bolted joint at the front of the catalytic converter.

11. Carefully elevate the engine with the hoist. Make very certain that no hoses or wires are strained and that clearance is maintained at the firewall. Raise the motor only enough to perform the next Steps of the procedure.

12. Remove the left motor mount.

13. Unbolt and remove the oil pan. It will need to be lifted and turned during removal.

To install:

14. Clean the gasket surfaces and install the new gasket (always!) so the small tab on the gasket is on the same side as the starter. Lift the pan into place, install the retaining bolts and tighten them to 8 ft. lbs. (11 Nm).

15. Install the reinforcing bracket between the engine and transmission. Attach it first to the transmission and then to the engine block. Tighten the bracket in stages so all the bolts pull up evenly.

16. Install the bump-stop on the front crossmember. Lift the crossmember into position against the side rails, install the bolts and tighten only a few turns to hold it in place.

17. When all the bolts are installed, tighten the crossmember bolts to 70 ft. lbs. (95 Nm). Install the left motor mount and secure the plate to the cylinder block. Don't forget to attach the cable clip on the upper bolt.

18. Paying close attention to the placement of the motor mounts, lower the engine into position. When the engine is correctly seated, the lifting equipment may be removed from the vehicle.

19. At the right motor mount, tighten the plate onto the crossmember. Check the connection of the air preheat tube at the exhaust manifold.

20. Tighten the fan shroud. Adjust the position of the bottom bracket as needed.

21. Reconnect the wiring harness bracket at the transmission, the bolted joint at the front of the catalytic converter and install the splashguard under the engine.

22. Tighten the left motor mount.

23. Observing the markings made earlier, reassemble the steering shafts. Insert and tighten the bottom bolt to 15 ft. lbs. (20 Nm). Tighen the upper bolt the same. Don't forget to install the small spring clips on the bolts.

24. Install the air mass meter and its hoses and connectors.

25. Fill the engine with the correct amount of oil and reinstall the dipstick.

26. Lower the vehicle, reconnect the battery cable and start the engine. Check for leaks.

B28F AND B280F ENGINES

1. Disconnect the negative battery cable. Remove the splash guard.

2. Drain the crankcase.

3. Remove the oil pan retaining bolts. Swivel the pan past the stabilizer bar and remove.

4. Reverse the above to install.

Oil Pump

Removal and Installation

B21, B23 AND B230 ENGINES

1. Remove the oil pan.

2. Remove the 2 oil pump retaining bolts and pull the delivery tube from the block.

3. When installing, use new sealing rings at either end of the delivery tube. Also, make sure to prime the pump, remove all air by filling it with clean engine oil and operating the pump by hand, before installation.

B234 ENGINE

1. Remove the timing belt.

2. Using a Volvo counterholding tool 5039 or similar, remove the oil pump drive pulley.

3. Thoroughly clean the area around the oil pump. Place sheets of newspaper or a container on the splash guard to contain any spillage and remove the oil pump mounting bolts. Remove the pump from the engine.

4. Remove the seal from the groove in the block. Clean the area with solvent, making certain there are no particles of dirt trapped in the pump area.

To install:

5. Install the new seal in the groove and install the new oil pump. Lubricate the pump with clean engine oil before installation. Tighten the mounting bolts to 7.5 ft. lbs. (10 Nm).

6. Using the counterhold, install the drive pulley and tighten the center bolt to 15 ft. lbs. (20 Nm) plug 60 degrees of rotation.

7. Clean the area of any oil spillage; remove the paper or container from the splash guard.

8. Install the timing belt.

B28F AND B280F ENGINES

The oil pump body is cast integrally with the cylinder block. It is chain driven by a separate sprocket on the crankshaft and is lo-

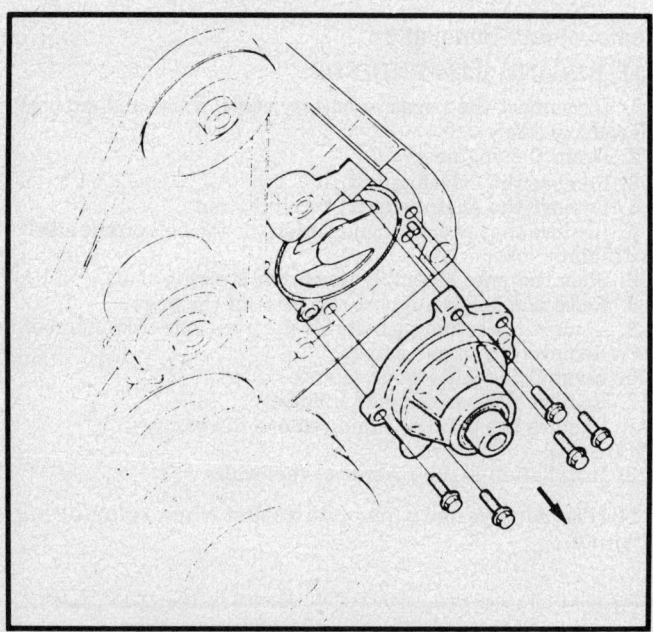

Oil pump assembly—B234F engine

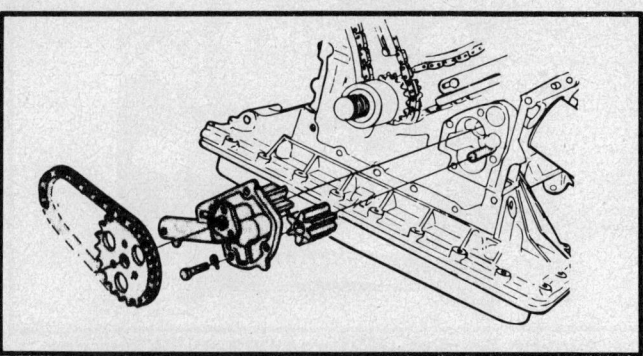

B28F and B280F oil pump installation—B27 similar

cated behind the timing chain cover. The pick-up screen and tube are serviced by removing the oil pan. To check the pump gears or remove the oil pump cover:

1. Disconnect the negative battery cable. Remove the air cleaner and valve covers.

2. Loosen the fan shroud and remove the fan. Remove the shroud.

3. Loosen the alternator, air pump, power steering pump, air conditioning compressor, if equipped, and remove their drive belts.

4. Block the flywheel from turning and remove the 36mm bolt and the crankshaft pulley.

NOTE: Do not drop key into crankcase.

5. Remove the timing gear cover (25 bolts).
6. Remove the oil pump drive sprocket and chain.
7. Remove the oil pump cover and gears.
8. Reverse the removal procedure to install. Prime the pump, remove all air by filling it with clean engine oil and operating the pump by hands, before installation.

Rear Main Bearing Oil Seal

Removal and Installation

B28F AND B280F ENGINES

1. Disconnect the negative battery terminal.
2. Remove the transmission.
3. Remove the clutch and pressure plate, if equipped.
4. Remove the flywheel or driveplate, on automatic transmissions.

NOTE: On automatic transmissions remove the crankshaft spacer.

5. Remove the 2 rear pan bolts.
6. Remove the bolts in the seal housing and then the housing.

NOTE: Gently remove the housing so as not to damage the oil pan gasket.

7. Use Volvo tool 5107 to remove the old seal and install the new one.
8. Installation is the reverse of removal. The following torque specifications are needed: flywheel 33–37 ft. lbs. (45–50 Nm), seal housing 7–11 ft. lbs. (10–15 Nm).

B21, B23, B230 AND B234 ENGINES

1. Disconnect the negative battery terminal.
2. Remove the transmission.
3. Remove the clutch and pressure plate, if equipped.
4. Remove the pilot bearing snapring and remove the bearing.
5. Remove the flywheel or driveplate which ever is applicable.

NOTE: Be careful not to press in the activator pins for the timing device.

6. Remove the rear oil pan brace.
7. Remove the 2 center bolts from the pan that bolt into the seal housing.
8. Loosen 2 bolts on either side of the 2 in the seal housing.
9. Remove the 6 seal housing bolts and remove the seal housing.

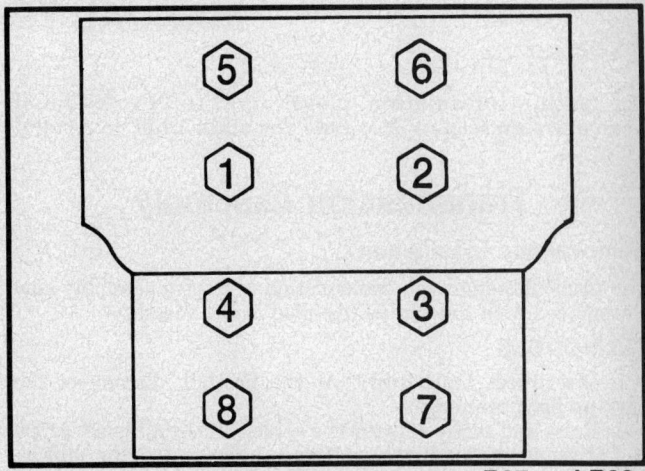

Main bearing nut tightening sequence—B27 and B28 engines

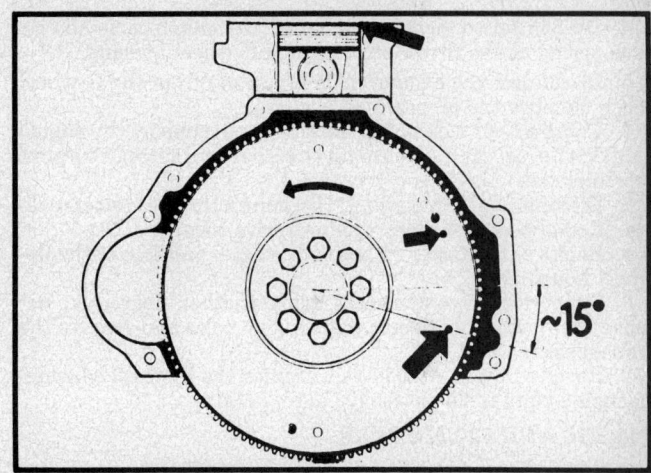

Flywheel installation—B23, B230 and B234 engines

NOTE: Be careful not to damage the oil pan gasket when removing the seal housing.

10. Remove the seal using special tool 2817 or a suitable replacement.
To install:
11. Installation is the reverse of removal.

NOTE: Use a new gasket on the seal housing and coat the seal with oil prior to installation.

12. Torque the flywheel to 47–54 ft. lbs. (64–73 Nm). When installing the flywheel turn the crankshaft to bring the No. 1 piston to TDC. The lower flywheel pin should be installed approximately 15 degrees from the horizontal and opposite the starter. Install the bolts.

MANUAL TRANSMISSION

For further information, please refer to "Professional Transmission Repair Manual" for additional coverage.

Transmission Assembly

Removal and Installation

The transmission or the transmission overdrive assembly may be removed with the engine installed in the vehicle.

240 MODELS

1. Disconnect the battery. At the firewall, disconnect the back-up light connector.
2. Raise and safely support the vehicle. Loosen the set screw and drive out the pin for the shifter rod. Disconnect the shift lever from the rod.
3. Inside the vehicle, pull up the shift boot. Remove the fork for the reverse gear detent. Remove the snapring and lift up the shifter. If overdrive-equipped, disconnect the engaging switch wire.
4. On 240 series models, disconnect the clutch cable and return spring at the throw-out fork and flywheel housing.
5. Disconnect the exhaust pipe bracket(s) from the flywheel cover. Remove the oil pan splash guard.
6. Using a floor jack and a block of wood, support the engine under the oil pan. Remove the transmission support crossmember.
7. Disconnect the driveshaft. Disconnect the speedometer cable. If equipped, disconnect the overdrive wire.
8. Remove the starter retaining bolts and pull free of the flywheel housing.
9. Support the transmission using another floor jack. Remove the flywheel bellhousing-to-engine bolts and remove the transmission.
10. Reverse Steps 1–9 to install. Tighten the flywheel housing-to-engine bolts to 25–35 ft. lbs. (34–47 Nm).

740, 760 AND 780 MODELS

1987–90

1. Disconnect the negative battery cable.
2. Attach a Volvo lifting beam tool 5006, to the rear of the engine. This will support the engine once the transmission is removed.
3. Raise and support the vehicle safely.
4. disconnect the driveshaft at the transmission flange.

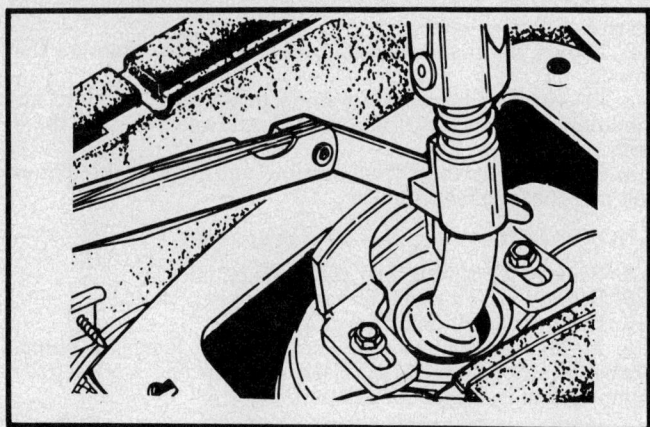

Reverse gear detent clearance adjustment—manual transmission models

5. Disconnect the support bearing for the driveshaft at the crossmember.
6. Remove the driveshaft from the vehicle.
7. Disconnect the exhaust system at the muffler.
8. Loosen the lock screw at the shifter assembly. Remove the pin through the gear shift lever. Remove the lock pin ring. Push the gear shift lever up.
9. Remove the transmission crossmember and bracket. Cut the wire straps and disconnect the wires at the transmission.
10. Disconnect the clutch cable at the clutch slave cylinder.
11. Disconnect the exhaust system attachment at the transmission cover.
12. Position a transmission jack under the transmission assembly. Remove the transmission to engine retaining bolts. Remove the transmission from the vehicle.
13. Installation is the reverse of the removal procedure.
14. Be sure to fill the unit with the proper type fluid. Adjust the clutch as required.

Linkage Adjustment

Reverse gear detent clearance is the only adjustment that can be made to the shift linkage. Remove the shift lever cover, trim frame and ash tray assembly. Engage 1st gear and adjust the clearance between the detent plate and the gear shift lever. Also check clearance should be 0.004–0.06 in. (0.1–1.5mm).

OVERDRIVE

Removal and Installation

To facilitate removal, the vehicle should first be driven in 4th gear with the overdrive engaged, then coasted for a few seconds with the overdrive disengaged and the clutch pedal depressed.

1. Remove the transmission from the vehicle.
2. Disconnect the solenoid cables.
3. If the overdrive unit has not already been drained, remove the 6 bolts and the overdrive oil pan.
4. Remove the bolts which retain the overdrive unit to the transmission intermediate flange. Pull the unit straight to the rear until it clears the transmission mainshaft.
5. Reverse the above procedure to install. Install the overdrive oil pan with a new gasket. After installation of the trans-

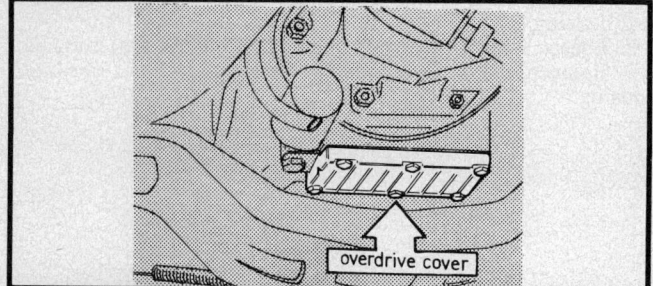

M46 overdrive bottom cover

mission, which automatically fills the overdrive, to the proper level with Automatic Transmission Fluid type F or G. Check the lubricant level in the transmission after driving 6–9 miles. The oil level should be up to the filler plug hole.

CLUTCH

Clutch Assembly

Removal and Installation

1. Remove the transmission.
2. Scribe alignment marks on the clutch and flywheel. In order to prevent warpage, slowly loosen the bolts which retain the clutch to the flywheel diagonally in rotation. Remove the bolts and lift off the clutch and pressure plate.
3. Inspect the clutch assembly.
4. When ready to install, wash the pressure plate and flywheel with solvent to remove any traces of oil and wipe them clean with a cloth.
5. Position the clutch assembly, the longest side of the hub facing backwards, to the flywheel and align the bolt holes. Insert a pilot shaft (centering mandrel or drift) or an input shaft from an old transmission of the same type, through the clutch assembly and flywheel so the flywheel pilot bearing is centered.
6. Install the 6 bolts which retain the clutch assembly to the flywheel and tighten them diagonally in rotation, a few turns at a time. After all the bolts are tightened, remove the pilot shaft (centering mandrel).
7. Install the transmission.
8. On the 760 GLE, bleed the clutch hydraulic system, if necessary.

Clutch Adjustment

240, DL, GL, GLT MODELS

The play in the manually-operated clutches in these 4 cylinder Volvos can be adjusted. Clutch play is adjusted under the at the clutch fork. Loosen the locknut on the fork side of the cable bracket, then turn the adjust nut until the proper play is achieved. Tighten the locknut. Clutch play for all 4 cylinder engines except Turbo is 0.12–0.2 in. (3–5mm) Turbo clutch play (free movement rearward) is 0.04–0.12 in. (1–3mm).

Clutch Master Cylinder

Removal and Installation

760 MODEL WITH B28F AND B280F V6 ENGINE

1. Remove the panel under the instrument panel. Remove the locking spring and pin from the clutch pedal assembly.
2. Disconnect the hose from the clutch fluid reservoir.
3. Unscrew the nipple from the cylinder housing. Place a container under the cylinder to catch the fluid that will spill out. Unbolt and remove the cylinder housing.
4. Reverse the above procedure to install. Make sure there is 0.04 in. (1mm) clearance between the pushrod and the pistons and adjust, if necessary. Fill the reservoir with DOT 4 brake fluid and bleed the system.

Clutch Slave Cylinder

Removal and Installation

760 MODELS WITH B28 AND B280 V6 ENGINES

The slave cylinder is unbolted from the flywheel housing after its fluid tube is disconnected and plugged. Be sure to bleed the system after installation.

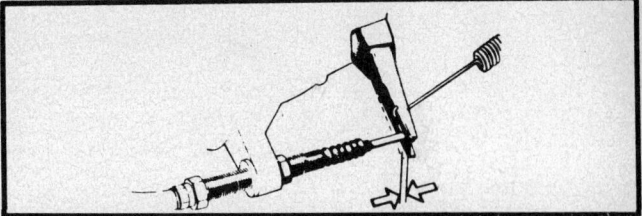

Clutch fork play adjustment, manual (non-hydraulic) clutches. Locknut at center, adjusting nut at left

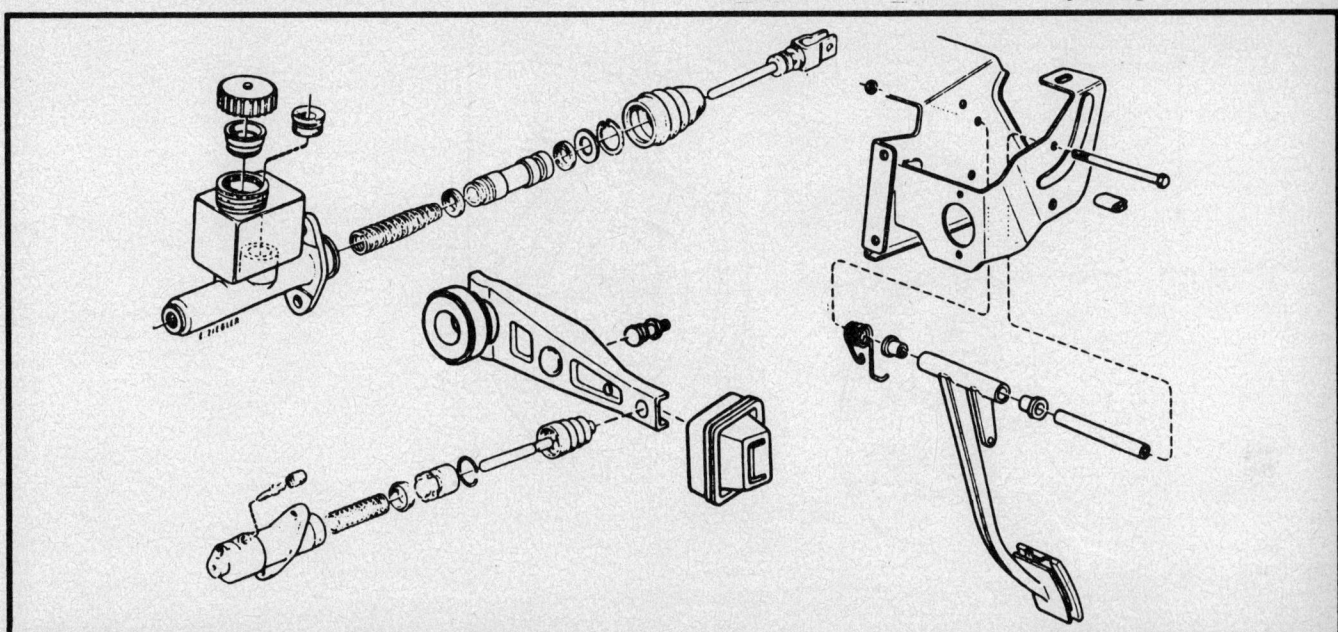

260 series clutch linkage—GLE (all V6) similar

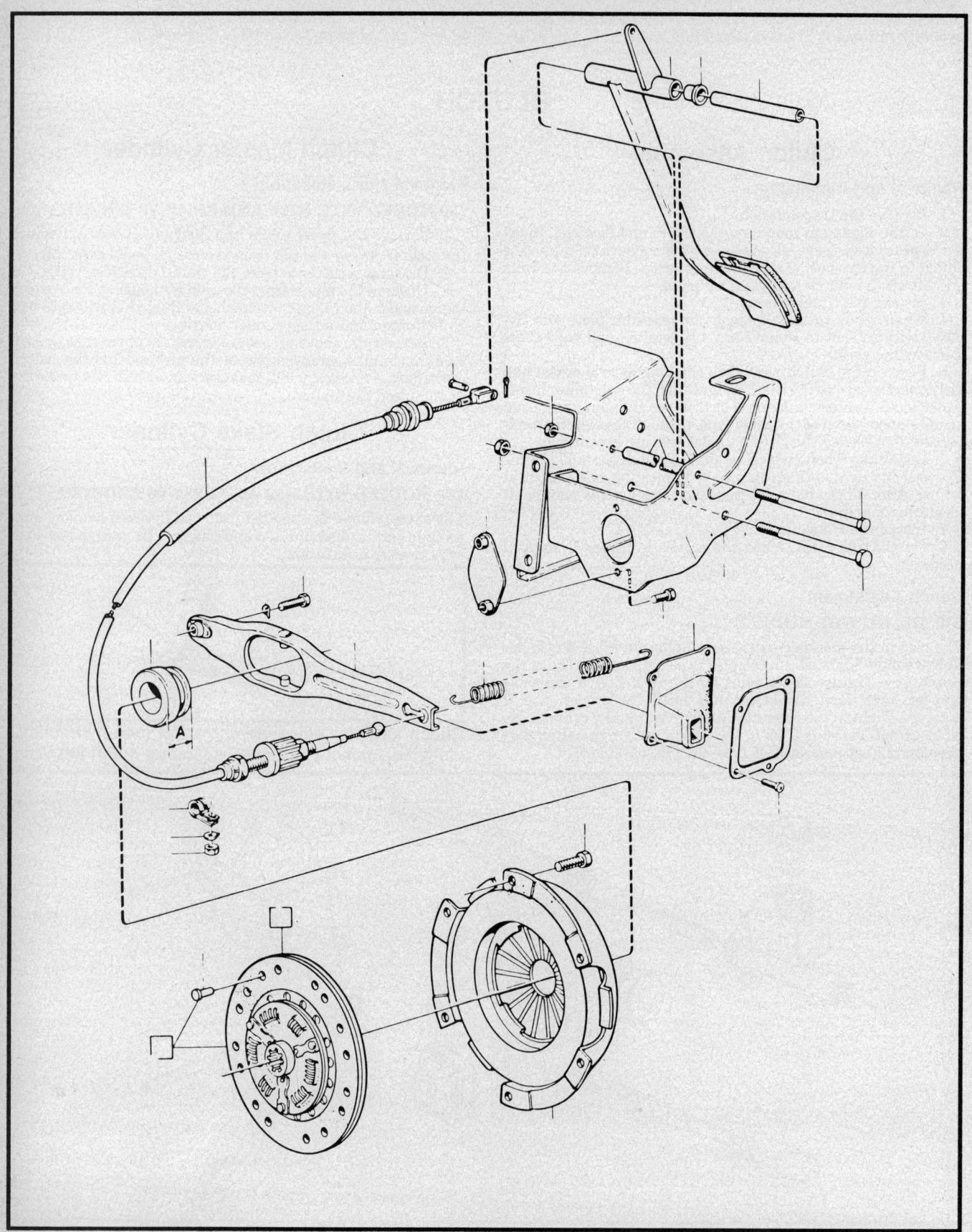

240 series—clutch linkage

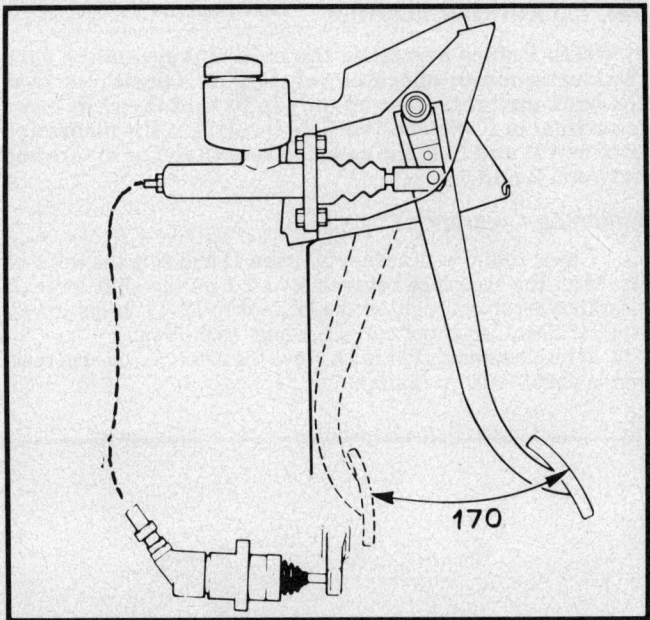

Clutch master cylinder and slave cylinder location—V6 models. Clutch travel is about 6.7 in. (170mm)

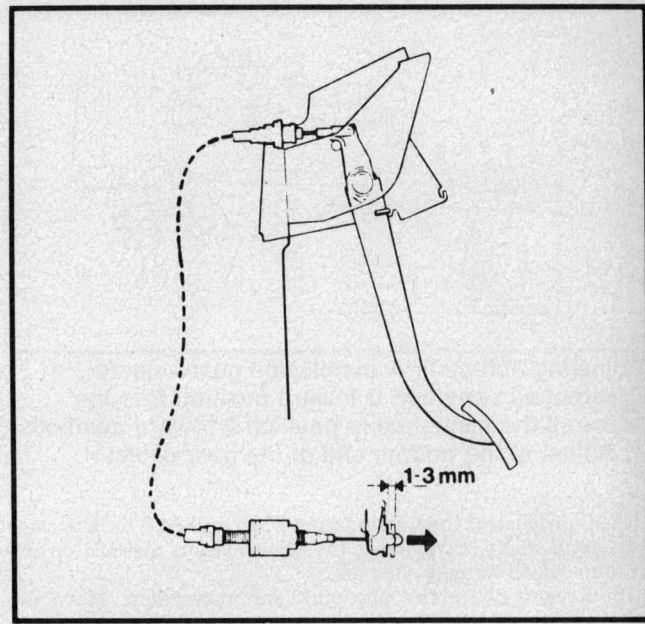

Clutch free-play clearance—B21F Turbo

AUTOMATIC TRANSMISSION

For further information, please refer to "Professional Transmission Repair Manual" for additional coverage.

Transmission Assembly

Removal and Installation

240 MODELS

1. Disconnect the negative battery cable. Remove the dipstick and filler pipe clamp.
2. Remove the bracket and throttle cable from the dashboard and throttle control, respectively.
3. Disconnect the exhaust pipe at the manifold.
4. Raise and safely support the vehicle.
5. Drain the fluid into a clean container.
6. Disconnect the driveshaft from the transmission flange.
7. Disconnect the selector lever controls and remove the reinforcing bracket from the pan.
8. Remove the torque converter attaching bolts.
9. Support the transmission with a jack equipped with a holding fixture.
10. Remove the crossmember.
11. Disconnect the exhaust pipe brackets and remove the speedometer cable form the case.
12. Remove the filler pipe.
13. Place a wooden block between the engine and firewall and lower the jack until the engine is against the block.

NOTE: If the battery cable appears to stretch to much, remove it.

14. Disconnect the starter wires, remove the converter housing bolts and pull the transmission backwards to clear the guide pins.
15. Install in the reverse of removal. Torque all 14mm bolts to 35 ft. lbs. (47 Nm).

740, 760 AND 780 MODELS

1. Disconnect the negative battery cable. Place the gear selector in the **P** position.
2. Disconnect the kickdown cable at the throttle pulley on the engine. Disconnect the battery ground cable.
3. Disconnect the oil filler tube at the oil pan and drain the transmission oil.

— CAUTION —

The oil will be scalding hot if the vehicle was recently driven.

4. Disconnect the control rod at the transmission lever and disconnect the reaction rod at the transmission housing.
5. On AW 71 transmissions, disconnect the wire at the solenoid; slightly to the rear of the transmission-to-driveshaft flange.
6. Matchmark the transmission-to-driveshaft flange and unbolt the driveshaft.
7. Remove the transmission crossmember assembly.
8. Disconnect the exhaust pipe at the joint and remove the exhaust pipe bracket from the exhaust pipe. Remove the rear engine mount with the exhaust pipe bracket.
9. On B28F and B280F V6 models, remove the bolts retaining the starter motor.
10. Remove the cover for the alternate starter motor location on B28F and B280F models. Remove the cover plate at the torque converter housing bottom on B28F and B280F models.
11. Disconnect the oil cooler lines at the transmission.
12. Remove the 2 upper screws at the torque converter cover. Remove the oil filler tube.
13. Place a transmission jack or a standard hydraulic floor jack under the transmission.
14. Remove the screws retaining the torque converter to the driveplate. Pry the torque converter back from the driveplate with a small prybar.

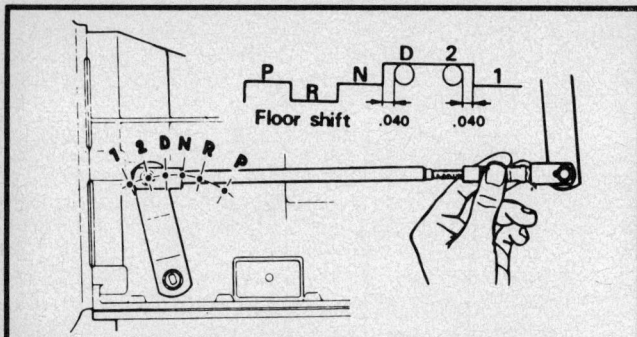

Adjusting automatic transmission gear selector. Clearance in position D toward position N is the same as the clearance in position 2 toward position 1. Adjust at the bottom end of the gear selector

15. Slowly lower the transmission when pulling it back to clear the input shaft. Do not tilt the transmission forward or the torque converter may slide off.

16. Reverse the above procedure for installation. Move the gear selector to the **P** position before attaching the control rod. Adjust the gear shift linkage and connect and adjust the kickdown cable.

Shift Linkage Adjustment

240 MODELS EXCEPT BW55 TRANSMISSION

NOTE: The gear selector shift console has been moved forward, if equipped with the AW70/AW71 transmissions. The shift linkage is also shortened on these vehicles.

1. Disconnect the shift rod from the transmission lever. Place both the transmission lever and the gear selector lever in the **2** position.

2. Adjust the length of the shift control rod so a small clearance of 0.04 in. (1mm) is obtained between the gear selector lever inhibitor and the inhibitor plate, when the shift control rod is connected to the transmission lever.

3. Position the gear selector lever in **D** and make sure a similar small clearance of 0.04 in. (1mm) exists between the lever inhibitor and the inhibitor plate. Disconnect the shift control rod from the transmission lever and adjust, if necessary.

4. Lock the control rod bolt with its safety clasp and tighten the locknut. Make sure the control rod lug follows with the transmission lever.

5. After moving the transmission lever to the **P** and **1** positions, make sure the clearances remain the same. In addition, make sure the output shaft is locked with the selector lever in the **P** position.

MODELS WITH BW55 TRANSMISSION

1. With the engine off, check that the distance between the **D** position and its forward stop is equal to the distance between the **2** position and its rearward stop, when the gear selector is moved. If not sure, remove the gear quadrant cover and measure.

2. If adjustment is necessary, a rough setting is made by loosening the locknut and rotating the clevis on the control rod to the transmission. A fine adjustment can be made by rotating the knurled sleeve between the control rod locknut and the pivot for the gear selector lever. Increasing the rod length will decrease clearance between the **D** position and its forward stop and vice-versa. Maximum permissible length of exposed thread between the locknut and the control rod is 1.1 in. (28mm).

740, 760 AND 780 MODELS

NOTE: Before adjusting the shift linkage, make sure the starter motor operates only in P or N positions; that the back-up lights light up only in R; that the shift lever is vertical in P with the vehicle level; that the clearance between D and N is the same or less than the clearance between 2 and 1.

Adjusting Clearance

1. Check that the clearance between **D** and **N** is the same or less than the clearance between **2** and **1** on the shift lever. If clearance is correct, tighten the locknut to 12–17 ft. lbs. 16–23 Nm). If clearance is not correct, adjust as follows:

2. If no clearance is felt in **D**, move the reaction rod arm rearwards about 0.08 in. (2mm).

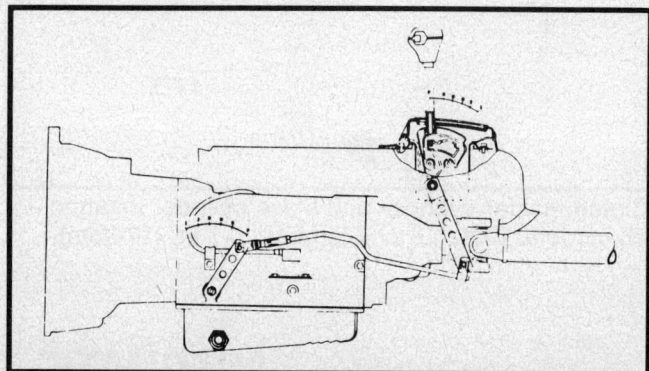

Shortened shaft linkage and closer control console— AW70/AW71 automatics

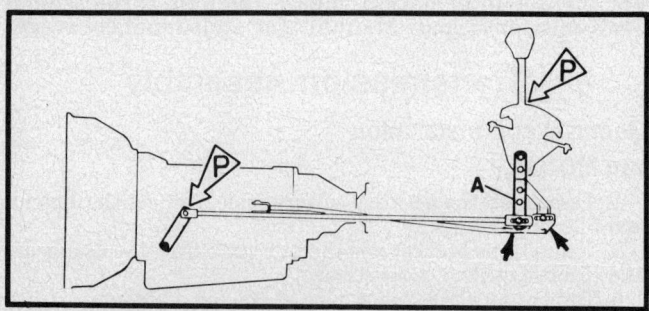

740 and 760 automatic transmission gear linkage. "A" is adjusting rod arm; arrows point to locknuts on adjustment (left) and reaction rod (right) arms

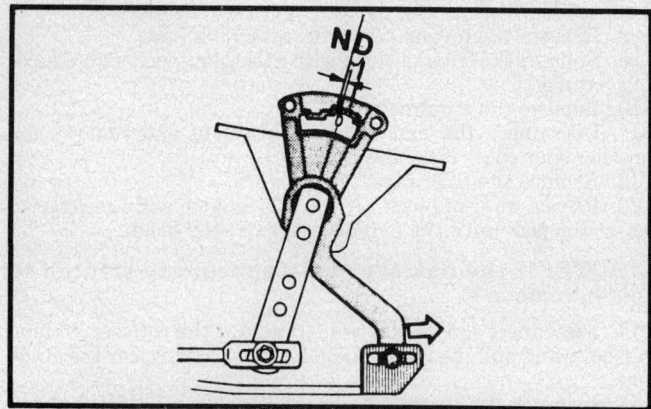

Checking clearance between D and N, and 1 and 2

3. If no clearance is felt in position **2**, move the reaction rod arm forwards about 0.12 in. (3mm). Tighten the locknut.

4. After adjustment, check that the vehicle starts only in **P** or **N** and that the back-up light does not light in **R**, reduce clearance in **D** by moving the rod arm forward slightly.

Throttle and Downshift Cable Adjustment

1. First, adjust the throttle plate angle and throttle cable. Disconnect the cable at the control pulley and the linkage rod at the throttle shaft. Set the throttle plate angle by loosening the adjusting screw locknut and backing off the screw. Then, turn in the screw until it just makes contact and then 1 additional turn. Tighten the locknut. Adjust the linkage rod so it fits onto the throttle shaft pulley ball without moving the cable pulley. Attach the throttle cable to the pulley and adjust the cable sheath so the cable is stretched but does not move the cable pulley. Finally, fully depress the gas pedal and check that the pulley contacts the full throttle abutment.

2. With the transmission cable hooked up, check that there is 0.010–0.040 in. (0.25–1.0mm) clearance between the cable clip and the adjusting sheath. The cable should be stretched at idle. Pull out the cable about ½ in. and release. A distinct click should be heard from the transmission as the throttle can returns to its initial position. Depress the gas pedal again to wide open throttle. Check that the transmission cable moves about 2 in. (50mm). Adjust as necessary at the adjusting sheath.

DRIVE AXLE

Driveshaft and U-Joints

Removal and Installation

1. Raise and safely support the vehicle.

2. Mark the relative positions of the driveshaft yokes and transmission and differential housing flanges for purposes of assembly. Remove the nuts and bolts which retain the front and rear driveshaft sections to the transmission and differential housing flanges, respectively. Remove the support bearing housing from the driveshaft tunnel and lower the driveshaft and universal joint assembly as a unit.

3. Pry up the lock washer and remove the support bearing retaining nut. Pull off the rear section of the driveshaft with the intermediate universal joint and splined shaft of the front section. The support bearing may now be pressed off the driveshaft.

4. Remove the support from it housing.

5. Inspect the driveshaft sections for straightness. Using a dial indicator or rolling the shafts along a flat surface, make sure the driveshaft out-of-round does not exceed 0.010 in. (0.25mm). Do not attempt to straighten a damaged shaft. Any shaft exceeding 0.010 in. (0.25mm) out-of-round will cause substantial vibration and must be replaced. Also, inspect the support bearing by pressing the races against each other by hand and turning them in opposite directions. If the bearing binds at any point, it must be discarded and replaced.

To install:

6. Install the support bearing into its housing.

7. Press the support bearing and housing onto the front driveshaft section. Push the splined shaft of the front section, with the intermediate universal joint and rear driveshaft section, into the splined sleeve of the front section. Install the retaining nut and lock washer for the support bearing.

8. Taking note of the alignment marks made prior to removal, position the driveshaft and universal joint assembly to its flange connections and install but do not tighten its retaining nuts and bolts. Position the support bearing housing to the driveshaft tunnel and install the retaining nut. Tighten the nuts which retain the driveshaft sections to the transmission and differential housing flanges to a torque of 25–30 ft. lbs. (34–40 Nm).

9. Lower the vehicle. Road test the vehicle and check for driveline vibrations and noise.

Solid Rear Axle Shaft

Removal and Installation

1. Raise and safely support the vehicle.

2. Remove the applicable wheel and tire assembly.

3. Place a wooden block under the brake pedal, plug the master cylinder reservoir vent hole; remove and plug the brake line from the caliper. Be careful not to allow any brake fluid to spill onto the disc or pads. Remove the 2 bolts which retain brake cal-

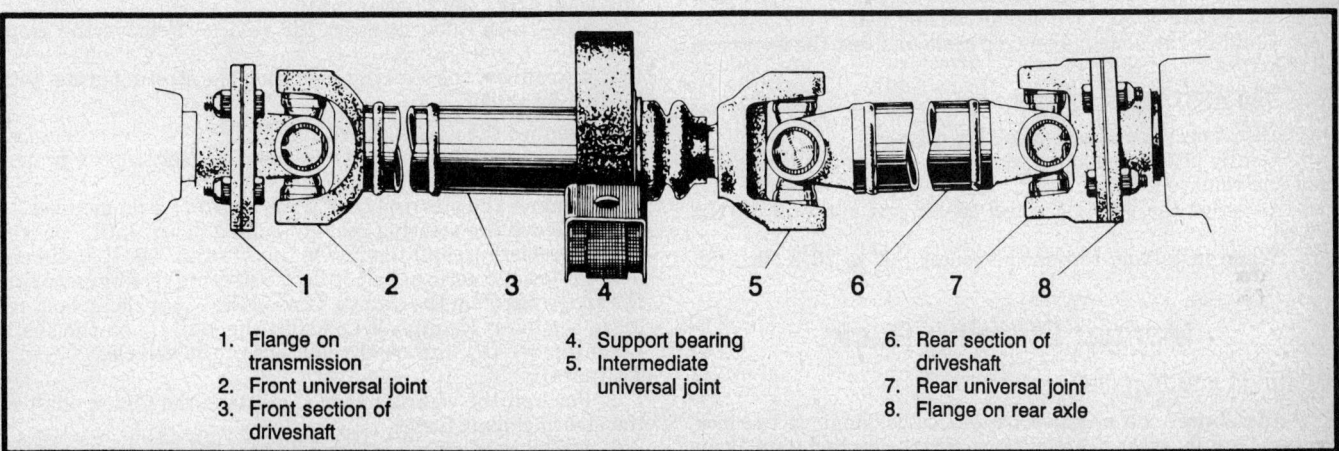

1. Flange on transmission
2. Front universal joint
3. Front section of driveshaft
4. Support bearing
5. Intermediate universal joint
6. Rear section of driveshaft
7. Rear universal joint
8. Flange on rear axle

Driveshaft with support bearing

iper to the axle housing and lift off the caliper. Lift off the brake disc.

4. Remove the thrust washer bolts through the holes in the axle shaft flange. Using a slide hammer, remove the axle shaft, bearing and oil seal assembly. If possible, pull out the shaft by temporarily reinstalling the brake disc and using this to grab on to while pulling out the axle shaft.

5. Using an arbor press, remove the axle shaft bearing and its locking ring from the axle shaft. Remove and discard the old oil seal.

To install:

6. Fill the space between the lips of the new oil seal with wheel bearing grease. Position the new seal on the axle shaft.

Using an arbor press, install the bearing with a new locking ring, onto the axle shaft.

7. Thoroughly pack the bearing with wheel bearing grease. Install the axle shaft into the housing, rotating it so it indexes with the differential. Install the bolts for the thrust washer and tighten to 36 ft. lbs. (50 Nm).

8. Install the brake disc. Position the brake caliper to its retainer on the axle housing and install the 2 retaining bolts. Torque the caliper retaining bolts to 45–50 ft. lbs. (61–68 Nm).

9. Unplug the brake line and connect it to the caliper. Bleed the caliper of all air trapped in the system.

10. Position the wheel and tire assembly on its lugs and hand-tighten the lug nuts. Remove the jack stands and lower the vehicle. Torque the lug nuts to 70–100 ft. lbs. (95–135 Nm).

STEERING

Steering Wheel

CAUTION

On vehicles equipped with an air bag, the negative battery cable must be disconnected, before working on the system. Failure to do so may result in deployment of the air bag and possible personal injury.

Removal and Installation

NOTE: The use of a knock-off type steering wheel puller or the use of a hammer may damage the collapsible column and is not recommended.

240 MODELS

1. Disconnect the negative battery cable.
2. Remove the retaining screws for the upper half of the molded turn signal housing and lift off the housing.
3. Pry off the steering wheel impact pad.
4. Disconnect the horn plug contact.
5. Remove the steering wheel nut.
6. With the front wheels pointing straight-ahead and the steering wheel centered, install a steering wheel puller. Use a universal type puller, such as SVO 2263.

To install:

7. To install, make sure the front wheels are pointing straight ahead, then place the centered steering wheel on the column with the plug contact to the left. Install the nut and tighten to 20–30 ft. lbs. (27–40 Nm).
8. Connect the horn plug contact and install the impact pad.
9. Install the upper turn signal housing half.
10. Connect the negative battery cable and test the operation of the horn.

740, 760 AND 780 MODELS

1. Disconnect the negative battery cable.
2. Gently pry up the lower edge of the steering wheel center pad and remove it.
3. Unscrew the steering wheel center nut and pull off the wheel.
4. When installing, torque the center nut to 26 ft. lbs. (35 Nm).

Manual Steering Rack

Removal and Installation

1. Disconnect the negative battery cable. Remove the lock bolt and nut from the column flange, at the steering gear. Bend apart the flange slightly with a suitable tool.

2. Raise and safely support the vehicle. Remove the front wheels.
3. Disconnect the steering rods from the steering arms, using a ball joint puller.
4. Remove the splash guard.
5. Disconnect the steering gear from the front axle member.
6. Disconnect the steering gear from the steering gear flange. Remove steering gear.

To install:

7. Install rubber spacers and plates for the steering gear attachment points.
8. Position the steering gear and guide the pinion shaft into the steering shaft flange. The recess on the pinion shaft should be aligned towards the lock bolt opening in the flange.
9. Attach the steering gear to the front axle member. Check that the U-bolts are aligned in the plate slots. Install flat washers and nuts.
10. Install the splash guard.
11. Connect the steering rods to the steering arms.
12. Install the front wheels and lower the vehicle.
13. Install the lock bolt for the steering shaft flange.

Power Steering Rack

Removal and Installation

1. Disconnect the negative battery cable. Loosen the steering column shaft flange from the pinion shaft. Remove the lock bolt and bend apart the flange slightly.
2. Raise and safely support the vehicle. Remove the front wheels.
3. Disconnect the steering rods from the steering arms, with a ball joint puller.
4. Remove the splash guard.
5. Disconnect the hoses at the steering gear. Install protective plugs in the hose connections.
6. Remove the steering gear from the front axle member.
7. Remove the steering gear by pulling down until it is free from the steering shaft flange. On the 740 and 760 GLE, disconnect the lower steering shaft from the steering gear by removing the snaprings from the clamps. Loosen the upper clamp bolt, remove the lower clamp bolt and slide the joint up on the shaft. Then remove the unit on the left side of the vehicle.

To install:

8. Position the steering gear and attach the pinion shaft to the steering shaft flange.
9. Install right side U-bolt and bracket but do not tighten the nuts.

10. Install left side retaining bolts and tighten. Tighten the U-bolt nuts.

11. Connect the steering rods to the steering arms.

12. Install the lock bolt on the steering column flange.

13. Connect the return and pressure hoses to the steering gear.

Power Steering Pump

Removal and Installation

1. Disconnect the negative battery cable. Remove all dirt and grease from around the suction line connections and from around the delivery line of the pump housing.

2. Using a container to catch any power steering fluid that might run out, disconnect the lines and plug them to prevent dirt from entering the system.

3. Remove the tensioning bolt and the attaching bolts.

4. Clear the pump free of the fan belt and lift it out.

To install:

5. If a new pump is to be used, the old brackets, fitting and pulley must be transferred from the old unit. The pulley may be removed with a puller and pressed on the pump shaft with a press tool. Under no circumstances should the pulley be hammered on, as this will damage the pump bearings.

6. To install, place the pump in position and loosely fit the attaching bolts. Connect the lines to the pump with new seals.

7. Place the fan belt onto the pulley and adjust the fan belt tension.

8. Tighten the tensioning bolt and the attaching bolts.

9. Fill the reservoir with Type A automatic transmission fluid and bleed the system.

System Bleeding

1. Fill the reservoir up to the edge with Automatic Transmission Fluid Type A. Raise and safely support the vehicle. Place the transmission in neutral and apply the parking brake.

2. Keeping a can of ATF Type A within easy reach, start the engine and fill the reservoir as the level drops.

3. When the reservoir level has stopped dropping, slowly turn the steering wheel from lock to lock several reservoir, if necessary.

4. Locate the bleeder screw on the power steering gear. Open the bleeder screw ½–1 turn and close it when oil starts flowing out.

5. Continue to turn the steering wheel slowly until the fluid in the reservoir is free of air bubbles.

6. Stop the engine and observe the oil level in the reservoir. If the oil level rises more than ¼ in. past the level mark, air still remains the system. Continue bleeding until the level rise is correct.

7. Lower the vehicle.

Tie Rod Ends

Removal and Installation

The ball joints of the tie rod may be replaced individually. After the ball joint is disconnected, the locknut on the tie rod is loosened and the clamp bolt released. The ball joint is then screwed out of the tie rod, taking note of the number of turns. The new ball joint is screwed in the same number of turns, the clamp bolt and locknut tightened. The ball joint is locked to the rod with 55–65 ft. lbs. (75–88 Nm) of torque. The new ball joint is pressed into its connection and the ball stud not tightened to 23–27 ft. lbs. (31–37 Nm).

After reconditioning of the rods and joints, the wheel alignment must be adjusted.

BRAKES

Master Cylinder

Removal and Installation

1. Disconnect the negative battery cable. To prevent brake fluid form spilling onto and damaging the paint, place a protective cover over the fender apron and rags under the master cylinder.

2. Disconnect and plug the brake lines from the master cylinder.

3. Remove the nuts which retain the master cylinder and reservoir assembly to the vacuum booster and lift the assembly forward, being careful not to spill any fluid on the fender. Empty out and discard the brake fluid.

NOTE: Do not depress the brake pedal while the master cylinder is removed.

4. In order for the master cylinder to function properly when installed to the vacuum booster, the adjusting nut for the thrust rod of the booster must not prevent the primary piston of the master cylinder from returning to its resting position. A clearance (C) of 0.004–0.04 in. (0.1–1.0mm) is required between the thrust rod and primary piston with the master cylinder installed. The clearance may be adjusted by rotating the adjusting nut for the booster thrust rod in the required direction. To determine what the clearance (C) will be when the master cylinder and booster are connected, first measure the distance (A) between the face of the attaching flange and the center of the primary piston on the master cylinder, then measure the distance (B) that the thrust rod protrudes from the fixed surface of the booster, making sure the thrust rod is depressed fully with a partial vacuum existing in the booster. When measurement is subtracted from measurement (A), clearance (C) should be obtained. If not, adjust the length of the thrust rod by turning the adjusting screw to suit. After the final adjustment is obtained apply a few drops of locking compound, such as Loctite®, to the adjusting nut.

5. Position the master cylinder and reservoir assembly onto the studs for the booster and install the washers and nuts. Tighten the nuts to 17 ft. lbs. (23 Nm).

6. Remove the plugs and connect the brake lines.

7. Bleed the entire brake system.

Proportioning Valve

Removal and Installation

Sophisticated pressure testing equipment is required to troubleshoot the dual hydraulic system in order to determine if the proportioning valve(s) are in need of replacement. However, if the vehicle demonstrates signs of rear wheel lock-up under moderate to heavy braking pressure and other variables such as tire pressure, tread depth, etc., have been ruled out, the valve(s) may be at fault. The valves are not rebuildable and must be replaced as a unit.

1. Unscrew, disconnect and plug the brake pipe from the master cylinder, at the valve connection.
2. Slacken the connection for the flexible brake hose to the rear wheel a maximum of ¼ turn.
3. Remove the bolt(s) which retain the valve to the underbody and unscrew the valve from the rear brake hose.
4. To install the valve, place a new seal on it and screw the valve onto the rear brake hose and hand tighten. Secure the valve to the underbody with the retaining bolt(s).
5. Connect the brake pipe and tighten both connections, making sure there is no tension on the flexible rear hose.
6. Bleed the brake system.

Brake System Warning Valve

Valve Resetting

1. Disconnect the plug contact and screw out the warning switch so the pistons inside the valve may return to their normal position.
2. Repair and bleed the faulty hydraulic circuit.
3. Screw in the warning switch and tighten it to a torque of 10–14 ft. lbs. (14–19 Nm). Connect the plug contact.

Removal and Installation

1. Placing a rag under the valve to catch the brake fluid, loosen the pipe connections and disconnect the brake lines. Disconnect the electrical plug contact and lift out the valve.
2. Connect the new warning valve in the reverse order of removal and connect the plug contact.
3. Bleed the entire brake system.

Power Brake Booster

Removal and Installation

1. Disconnect the negative battery cable.
2. Remove the master cylinder to power booster retaining bolts and position the master cylinder aside. Be careful not to damage the brake lines.
3. Disconnect the vacuum assist hose, from the booster.
4. From inside the vehicle, disconnect the brake pedal rod.
5. Remove the power booster retaining bolts. Remove the power booster from the vehicle.
6. Installation is the reverse of the removal procedure.

Disc Brake Pads

Removal and Installation

240 AND 260 MODELS

NOTE: The brake pads should be replaced when there is approximately 0.12 in. (3mm) of the lining left. The linings should under no circumstances be less than 0.06 in. (1.5mm).

Front Brakes—ATE Type

1. Raise the vehicle and support safely.
2. Mark the position of the wheels on the hubs and remove the front wheels.
3. Remove the retaining pins using a punch.
4. Remove the retaining spring.
5. Remove the brake pads and identify the pads, if they are to be reused.
To install:
6. To install, compress the pistons using a pair of pliers of special tool 2809 or equivalent.
7. Install the brake pads.
8. Install 1 retaining pin and a new retaining spring.

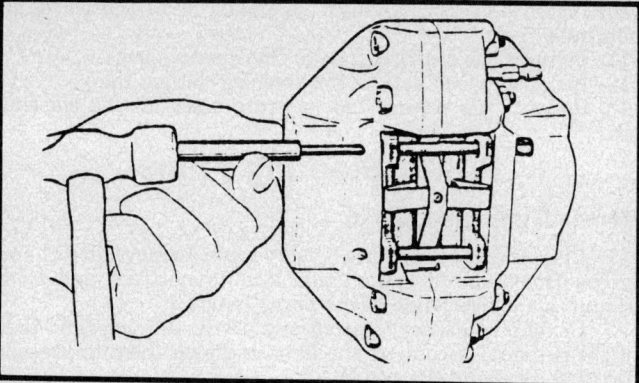

Retaining pin removal—200 series ATE type shown, Girling type similar

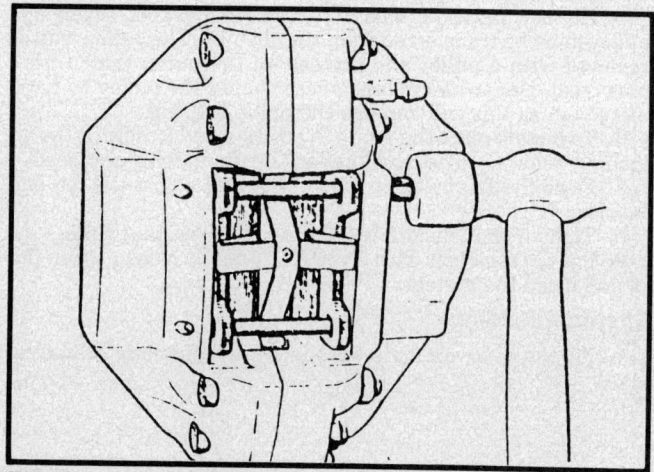

Retaining pin installation—200 series ATE type shown, Girling type similar

9. Install the other retaining pin.
10. Check the brake fluid level and pump the brake pedal.
11. Install the front wheel assemblies and lower the vehicle.

───────── **CAUTION** ─────────
Check the brake pedal operation prior to driving the vehicle.
─────────────────────────────

Front Brakes—Girling Type

1. Raise the vehicle and support safely.
2. Mark the position of the wheels on the hubs and remove the front wheels.
3. Remove the spring clips.
4. Remove the retaining pins.
5. Remove the retaining springs.
6. Remove the brake pads and identify the pads if they are to be reused.
To install:
7. To install, compress the pistons using a pair of pliers of special tool 2809 or equivalent.
8. Install the brake pads.
9. Install the retaining springs.
10. Install the retaining pins.
11. Install the spring clips.
12. Check the brake fluid level and pump the brake pedal.
13. Install the front wheel assemblies and lower the vehicle.

───────── **CAUTION** ─────────
Check the brake pedal operation prior to driving the vehicle.
─────────────────────────────

Rear Brakes—ATE Type

1. Raise the vehicle and support safely.
2. Mark the position of the wheels on the hubs and remove the rear wheels.
3. Remove the retaining pins using a punch.
4. Remove the retaining spring.
5. Remove the brake pads and identify the pads if they are to be reused.

To install:

6. To install, compress the pistons using a pair of pliers of special tool 2809 or equivalent.
7. Install the brake pads.
8. Install 1 retaining pin and a new retaining spring.
9. Install the other retaining pin.
10. Check the brake fluid level and pump the brake pedal.
11. Install the rear wheel assemblies and lower the vehicle.

—————— **CAUTION** ——————

Check the brake pedal operation prior to driving the vehicle.

Rear Brakes—Girling Type

1. Raise the vehicle and support safely.
2. Mark the position of the wheels on the hubs and remove the rear wheels.
3. Remove the retaining spring.
4. Remove the spring clips.
5. Remove the retaining pins.
6. Remove the retaining springs.
7. Remove the brake pads and identify the pads if they are to be reused.
8. Remove any shims or damper washers fitted between the pads and the caliper pistons.

To install:

9. To install, compress the pistons using a pair of pliers of special tool 2809 or equivalent.
10. Install any shims or damper washers.
11. Install the brake pads.
12. Install the springs.
13. Install the retaining pins.
14. Install the spring clips.
15. Install the retaining spring.

NOTE: If damper washers have been fitted, make sure the large flat side faces the piston. A feeler gauge can be used to fit the washers.

16. Check the brake fluid level and pump the brake pedal.
17. Install the rear wheel assemblies and lower the vehicle.

—————— **CAUTION** ——————

Check the brake pedal operation prior to driving the vehicle.

740 AND 760 MODELS

NOTE: The brake pads should be replaced when there is approximately 0.12 in. (3mm) of the lining left. The linings should under no circumstances be less than 0.06 in. (1.5mm).

Parking Brake Cable

Adjustment

1. Remove the rear ashtray, between the front seat backs, or the rear of the center console on the 740 and 760.
2. Tighten the parking brake cable adjusting screw so the brake is fully applied when pulled up 2–3 notches.
3. If one cable is stretched more than the other, they can be individually adjusted by removing the parking brake cover (2 screws) and turning the individual cable adjusting nut at the front of each yoke pivot.
4. Install the ashtray and parking brake cover, if equipped.

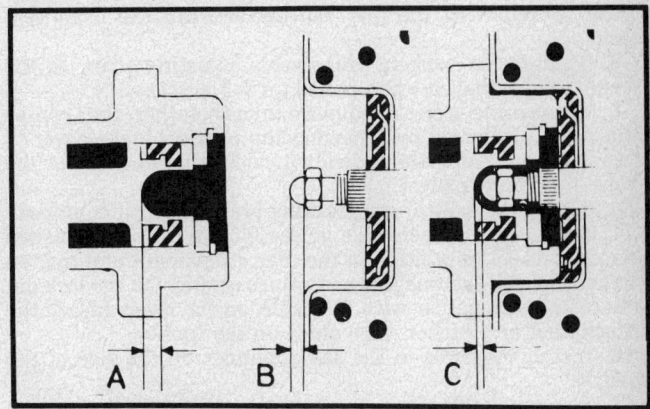

Adjusting thrust rod

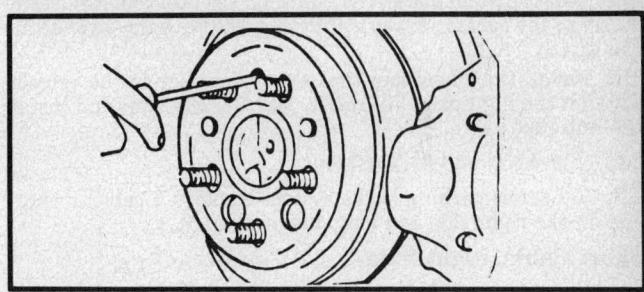

Adjusting the parking brake through the access hole in the rear hub

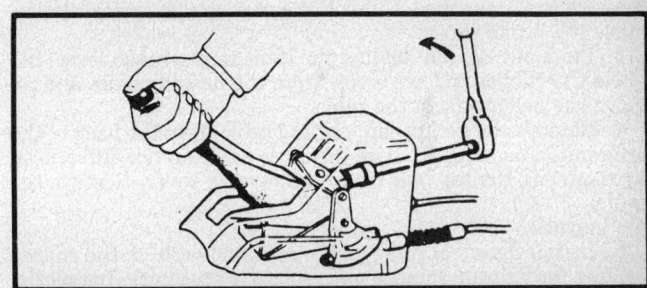

Adjust the parking brake if it is not fully applied after pulling the lever 10–11 notches. After adjusting, good braking power should be obtained after pulling the lever 2–3 notches

Removal and Installation

240 MODELS

1. Apply the parking brake. Remove the hub caps for the rear wheels and loosen the lug nuts a few turns.
2. Raise and safely support the vehicle. Remove the wheel and tire assembly. Release the parking brake.
3. Remove the bolt and the wheel from the pulley.
4. Remove the rubber cover for the front attachment of the cable sleeve and nut, as well as the attachment for the rubber suspension ring on the frame. Remove the cable from the other side of the attachment in the same manner.
5. Hold the return spring in position. Pry up the lock and remove the lock pin so the cable releases form the lever.
6. Remove the return spring with washers. Loosen the nut for the rear attachment of the cable sleeve. Lift the cable forward after loosening both side of the attachments and remove it.

To install:

7. To install, first adjust the rear brake shoes of the parking

brake by removing the rear ashtray between the front seat backs.

8. Tighten the parking brake cable adjusting screw so the brake is fully applied when pulled up 2–3 notches.

9. If one cable is stretched more than the other, they can be individually adjusted by removing the parking brake cover (2 screws) and turning the individual cable adjusting nut at the front of each yoke pivot.

10. Install the ashtray and parking brake cover, if equipped.

11. Install new rubber cable guides for the cable suspension. Place the cable in position in the rear attachment and tighten the nut. Install the washers and return spring. Oil the lock pin and install it, together with the cable, on the lever. Install the attachment and rubber cable guide on the frame.

12. Install the cable in the same manner on the side of the vehicle.

13. Place the cable sleeve in position in the front attachments and install the rubber covers.

14. Lubricate and install the pulley on the pull rod. Adjust the pulley so the parking brake is fully engaged with the lever at the 3rd or 4th notch.

15. Install the wheel and tire assemblies. Lower the vehicle. Tighten the lug nut to 70–100 ft. lbs. (95–135 Nm) and install the hub caps.

740, 760 AND 780 MODELS

The 700 series parking brake system employs 2 cable, a short one on the right side and long one on the left.

Short Cable, Right Side

1. Raise and safely support the vehicle.

2. Remove the right brake caliper rear wheel. Remove the right brake caliper and hang it from the coil spring with a wire. Remove the brake disc. Unhook the rear return spring and remove the brake shoes.

3. Push out the pin holding the cable to the brake lever. Remove the rubber bellows (boot) from the backing plate and remove the bellows from the cable.

4. Remove the spring clip, pin and cable from the back of the differential housing. Remove the cable guide on the differential by removing the top bolt from the housing cover. Remove the cable.

To install:

5. Install the cable guide on the new cable. Check the rubber bellows for wear or damage and replace if necessary. Install the bellows and position it through the hole in the backing plate. Make sure the bellows sits correctly on the backing plate.

6. Smear the contact surfaces of the brake levers with a thin layer of heat resistant graphite grease. Connect the cable to the lever and install the pin.

NOTE: The arrow stamped on the lever should point upward and outwards.

7. Push the cable through and place the lever in position behind the rear axle flange.

8. Install the cable guide on the axle. Connect the cable to the equalizer using the pin and spring clip.

9. Install the brake shoes and rear return spring. Install the brake disc and caliper. Use new bolts. and torque to 43 ft. lbs. (58 Nm). Make sure the disc rotates freely. Adjust the parking brake. Install the wheel and lower the vehicle.

Long Cable, Left Side

1. Remove the center console.

2. Slacken the parking brake adjusting screw. Remove the cable lock ring and remove the cable. Pull out the cable from the spring sleeve.

3. Raise and safely support the vehicle. Remove the left rear wheel.

4. Remove the left rear brake caliper and hang it from the coil spring with a piece of wire. Remove the brake disc and rear return spring. Remove the brake shoes.

5. Push out the pin holding the cable to the lever. Remove the rubber bellows from the backing plate and remove the bellows from the cable.

6. Pull out the cable from the backing plate and the equalizer on top of the rear axle.

7. Remove the cable clamp on the sub-frame, above the driveshaft, and the cable.

To install:

8. Install the new cable through the grommet in the floor; check that the grommet sits correctly. Clamp the cable to the sub-frame.

9. Smear the contact surfaces of the brake levers with a thin layer of heat resistant graphite grease. Connect the cable to the lever and install the pin.

NOTE: The arrow stamped on the lever should point upward and outwards.

10. Push the cable through and place the lever in position behind the rear axle flange.

11. Install the cable guide on the axle. Connect the cable to the equalizer using the pin and spring clip.

12. Install the brake shoes and rear return spring. Install the brake disc and caliper. Use new bolts. and torque to 43 ft. lbs. (58 Nm). Make sure the disc rotates freely. Adjust the parking brake. Install the wheel and lower the vehicle.

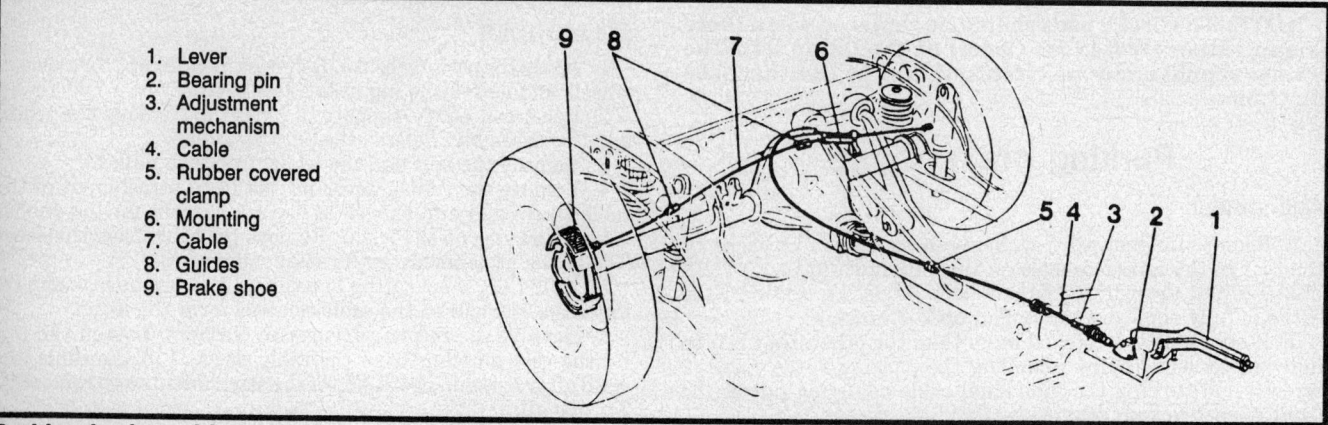

1. Lever
2. Bearing pin
3. Adjustment mechanism
4. Cable
5. Rubber covered clamp
6. Mounting
7. Cable
8. Guides
9. Brake shoe

Parking brake cable assembly—760 models

FRONT SUSPENSION

MacPherson Strut

Removal and Installation

1. Remove the hub cap and loosen the lug nuts a few turns.
2. Firmly apply the parking brake and place blocks in back of the rear wheels.

3. Raise and safely support the vehicle or using a floor jack at the center of the front crossmember. When the wheels are 2–3 in. (50–76mm) off the ground, the vehicle is high enough. Place jackstands under the front jacking points. Then, remove the floor jack from the crossmember, if used, and reposition it under

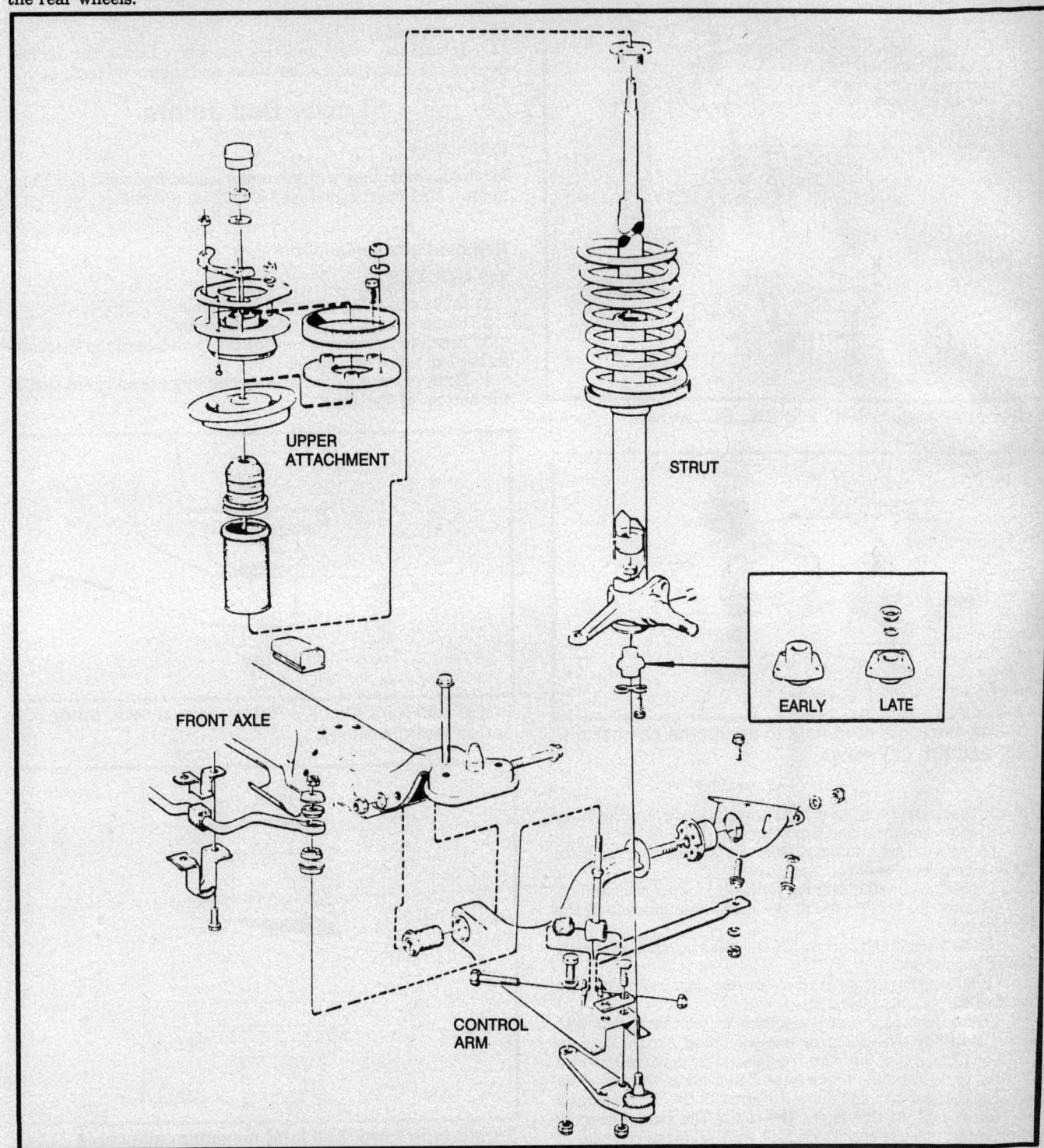

UPPER ATTACHMENT

STRUT

EARLY   LATE

FRONT AXLE

CONTROL ARM

Front suspension assembly—240 and 260 models

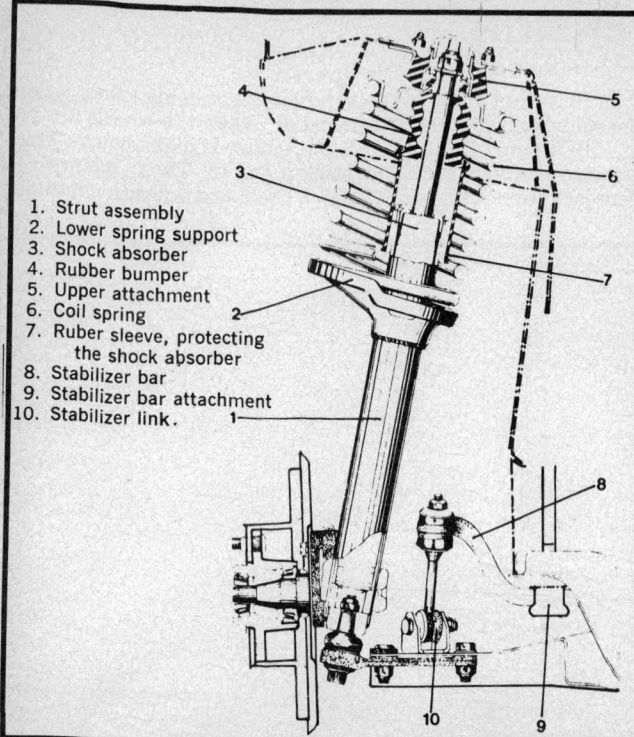

1. Strut assembly
2. Lower spring support
3. Shock absorber
4. Rubber bumper
5. Upper attachment
6. Coil spring
7. Ruber sleeve, protecting the shock absorber
8. Stabilizer bar
9. Stabilizer bar attachment
10. Stabilizer link.

Front suspension—240, 260 (DL, GL) series

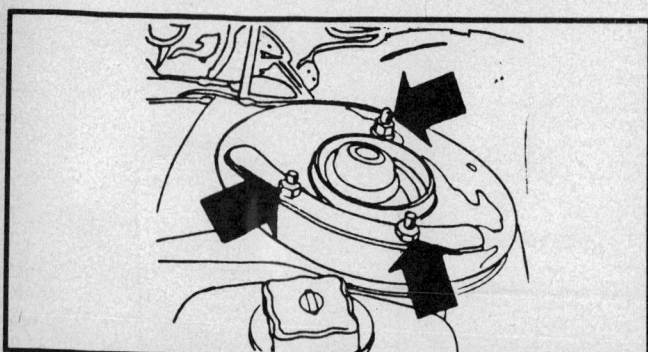

Loosen the upper strut nuts to adjust the camber on 240, 260 (DL, GL) series

the applicable lower control arm to provide support at the outer end. Remove the wheel and tire assembly.

4. Using a ball joint puller, disconnect the steering rod from the steering arm.

5. Disconnect the stabilizer bar at the link upper attachment.

6. Remove the bolt retaining the brake line bracket to the fender well.

7. Open the hood and remove the cover for the strut assembly upper attachment.

8. While keeping the strut from turning, loosen and remove the nut for the upper attachment.

9. Before lowering the strut assembly, wire or tie the strut to some stationary component or use a holding fixture such as SVO 5045, to prevent the strut from traveling down too far and damaging the hydraulic brake lines. Then lower the jack supporting the lower arm and allow the strut to tilt out to about a 60 degree angle. At this angle, the top of the strut assembly should just protrude past the wheel well, allowing removal of the strut from the top.

To install:

10. Carefully lift and guide the strut assembly into its upper attachment in the spring tower. Connect the stabilizer bar to the stabilizer link. Guide the shock absorber spindle into the upper attachment and raise the jack under the lower control are. Install the washer and nut on top of the shock absorber spindle. While holding the spindle from turning, tighten the nut to 15–25 ft. lbs. (20–34 Nm). Install the cover.

11. Attach the brake line bracket to its mount. Tighten the nut retaining the stabilizer bar to the link. Connect the steering rod at the steering arm.

12. Install the wheel and tire assembly. Lower the vehicle. Jounce the suspension a few times and then road test.

Lower Ball Joints

Inspection

Maximum axial play with normally loaded front end is 0.12 in. (3mm). Maximum radial play is 0.02 in. (0.5mm).

Removal and Installation
240 MODELS

1. Raise and safely support the vehicle.
2. Remove the tire and wheel assembly.
3. Reach in between the spring coils and loosen the shock absorber cap nut a few turns.
4. Remove the 4 bolts (12mm) retaining the ball joint seat to the bottom of the strut.

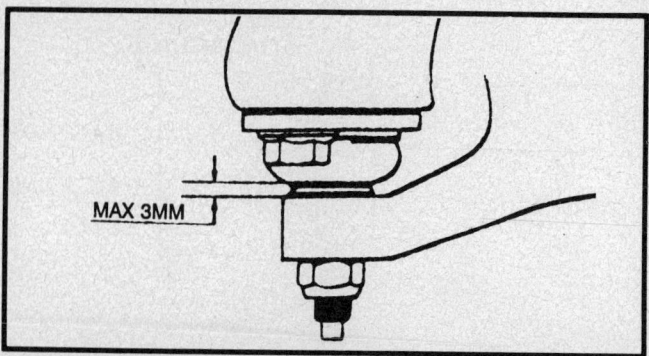

Lower ball joint check—760 models shown, other 700 series models similar

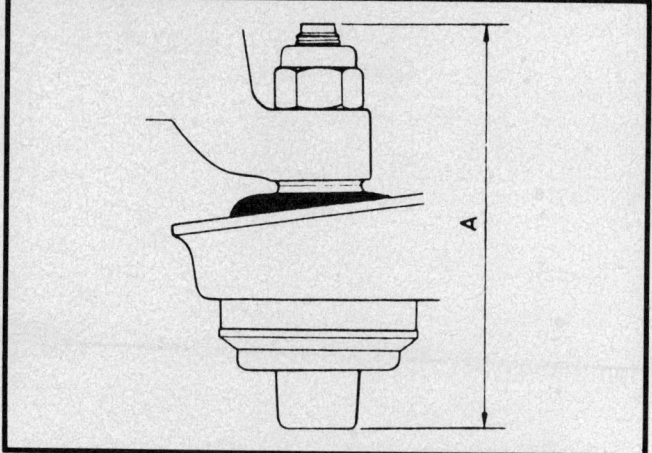

Spring-type lower ball joint maximum allowable length

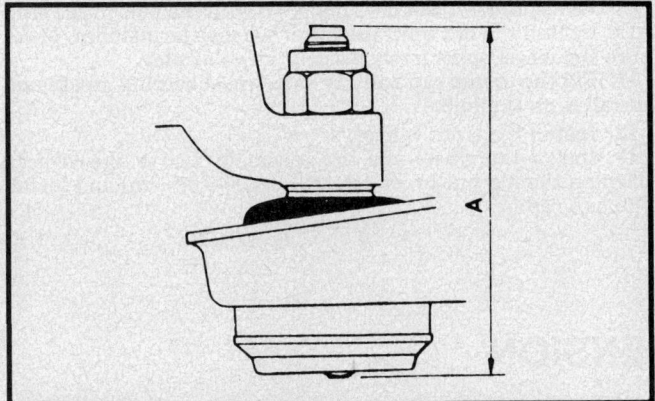

Non-spring type lower ball joint maximum allowable length

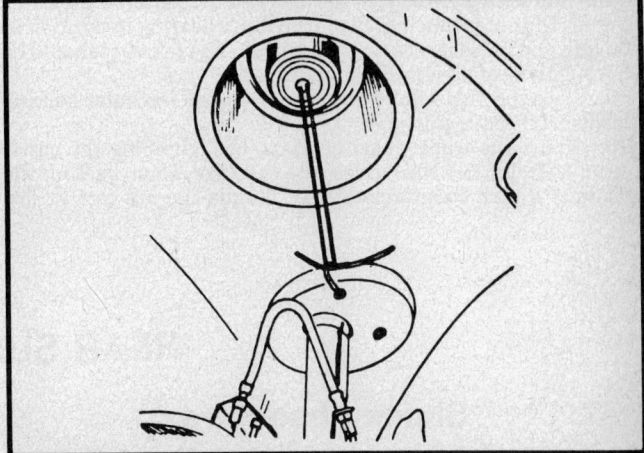

Suspending the top of the strut from the body with a wire while removing the lower ball joint

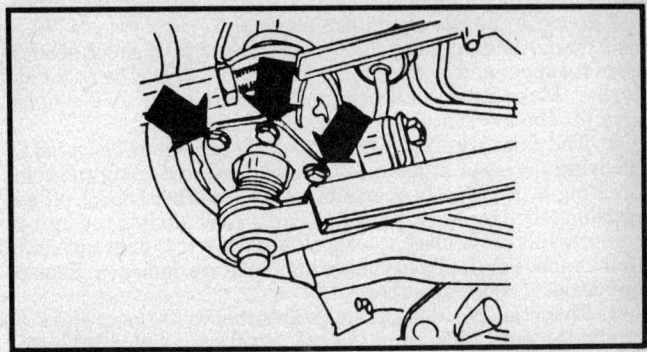

Late type lower ball joint-to-strut retaining bolts

5. Remove the 3 nuts (19mm) retaining the ball joint to the lower control arm.

6. Place the ball joint and attachment assembly in a vise and remove the 19mm nut from the ball joint stud. Then, drive out the old ball joint.

To install:

7. Install the new ball joint in the attachment and tighten the stud nut to 35–50 ft. lbs. (47–68 Nm).

8. Attach the ball joint assembly to the strut. Tighten to 15–20 ft. lbs. (20–27 Nm).

9. Attach the ball joint assembly to the control arm. Tighten to 70–95 ft. lbs. (95–130 Nm).

10. Tighten the shock absorber cap nut. Install the wheel and tire. Lower the vehicle and road-test.

NOTE: On models with power steering, the ball joint are different for the left and right side.

Compared to previous years, the ball joint is 0.393 in. (1mm) forward in control rod attachment. It is therefore most important that these ball joints are installed on the correct side.

740, 760 AND 780 MODELS

1. Raise and safely support the vehicle. Remove the wheel.

2. Remove the bolt connecting the anti-roll bar link to the control arm.

3. Remove the cotter pin for the ball joint stud and remove the nut.

4. Using a ball joint puller, press out the ball joint from the control arm. Make sure the puller is located directly in line with the stud and that the rubber grease boot is not damaged by the puller.

5. Remove the bolts holding the ball joint to the spring strut. Press the control arm down and remove the ball joint.

6. Reverse the above procedure for installation. When installing the new ball joint, always use new bolts and coat all threads with a liquid thread sealer. Torque bolts to 22 ft. lbs. (30 Nm), checking that the bolt heads sit flat on the ball joint, then angle-tighten (protractor-torque) 90 degrees torque the nut holding the control arm ball joint stud to 44 ft. lbs. (60 Nm). Use a new cotter pin on the ball joint stud and install the anti-roll bar link.

Lower Control Arms

Removal and Installation

1. Raise and safely support the vehicle. Remove the front wheels.

2. Remove stabilizer bar.

3. Remove ball joint from control arm.

4. Remove control arm front retaining bolt.

5. Remove control arm rear attachment plate.

6. Remove attachment plate from control arm.

7. Remove stabilizer link from control arm.

8. Install in reverse of removal.

NOTE: Right and left bushings are not interchangeable. The right side bushing should be turned so the small slots point horizontally when installed. Torque the retaining bolt to 55 ft. lbs. (75 Nm), the rear bushing to 4 ft. lbs. and the rear attachment bolts to 30 ft. lbs. (40 Nm).

Front Wheel Bearings

Replacement and Adjustment

1. Remove the hub cap and loosen the lug nuts a few turns.

2. Firmly apply the parking brake. Raise and safely support the vehicle. Support the lower control arms. Remove the wheel and tire assembly.

3. Remove the front caliper.

4. Pry off the grease cap from the hub. Remove the cotter pin and castle nut. Use a hub puller to pull off the hub. On the 760, remove the brake disc. If the inner bearing remains lodged on the stub axle, remove it with a puller.

5. Using a drift, remove the inner and outer bearing rings.

To install:

6. Thoroughly clean the hub, brake disc and grease cap.

7. Press in the new inner and outer bearing rings with a drift.

8. Press grease into both bearing with a bearing packer. If one is not available, pack the bearings with as much wheel bearing grease as possible by hand. Also coat the outsides of the bearings and the outer rings pressed into the hub. Fill the recess

in the hub with grease up to the smallest diameter on the outer ring for the outer bearing. Place the inner bearing in position in the hub and press its seal in with a drift. The felt ring should be thoroughly coated with light engine oil.

9. Place the hub onto the stub axle. Install the outer bearing washer and castle nut.

10. Adjust the front wheel bearings by tightening the castle nut to 45 ft. lbs. (60 Nm) to seat the bearings. Then, back off the nut ⅓ of a turn counterclockwise. Torque the nut to 1 ft. lbs.

(1.5 Nm). If the nut slot does not align with the hole in the stub axle, tighten the nut until the cotter pin may be installed. Make sure the wheel spins freely without any side play.

11. Fill the grease cap halfway with wheel bearing grease and install it on the hub.

12. Install the front caliper.

13. Install the wheel and tire assembly. Lower the vehicle. Tighten the lug nut to 70–100 ft. lbs. (95–135 Nm) and install the hub cap.

REAR SUSPENSION

Shock Absorbers

Removal and Installation

1. Remove the hub cap and loosen the lug nuts a few turns. Raise and safely support the vehicle to unload the shock absorbers. Remove the wheel and tire assembly.

2. Remove the nuts and bolts which retain the shock absorber to its upper and lower attachments and remove the shock absorber. Make sure the spacing sleeve, inside the axle support arm for the lower attachment, is not misplaced.

3. The damping effect of the shock absorber may be tested by securing the lower attachment in a vise and extending and compressing it. A properly operating shock absorber should off approximately 3 times as much resistance to extending the unit as compressing it. Replace the shock absorber if it does not function as above or if it fixed rubber bushings are damaged. Replace any leaking shock absorber.

4. To install, position the shock absorber to its upper and lower attachments. Make sure the spacing sleeve is installed inside the axle support (trailing) arm and is aligned with the lower attachment bolt hole. Install the retaining nuts and bolts and torque to 63 ft. lbs. (85 Nm). On 240 and 760 series models, the shock fits inside the support arm.

5. Install the wheel and tire assembly. Lower the vehicle. Tighten the lug nuts to 70–100 ft. lbs. (95–135 Nm) and install the hub cap.

Coil Springs

Removal and Installation

1. Remove the hub cap and loosen the lug nuts a few turns.

Raise and safely support the vehicle. Remove the wheel and tire assembly.

2. Place a hydraulic jack under the rear axle housing and raise the housing sufficiently to compress the spring. Loosen the nuts for the upper and lower spring attachments.

CAUTION
Due to the fact that the spring is compressed under several hundred pounds of pressure, when it is freed from its lower attachment, it will attempt to suddenly spring back to its extended position. It is therefore imperative that the axle housing be lowered with extreme care until the spring is fully extended. As an added safety measure, a chain may be attached to the lower spring coil and secured to the axle housing.

---

3. Disconnect the shock absorber at its upper attachment. Carefully lower the jack and axle housing until the spring is fully extended. Remove the spring.

4. To install, position the retaining bolt and inner washer, for the upper attachment, inside the spring and then, while holding the outer washer and rubber spacer to the upper body attachment, install the spring and inner washer to the upper attachment (sandwiching the rubber spacer) and tighten the retaining bolt.

5. Raise the jack and secure the bottom of the spring to its lower attachment with the washer and retaining bolt.

6. Connect the shock absorber to its upper attachment. Install the wheel and tire assembly.

7. Lower the vehicle. Tighten the lug nuts to 70–100 ft. lbs. (95–135 Nm) and install the hub cap.

MAINTENANCE REMINDER LIGHT RESET PROCEDURES

ACURA

1988–91 LEGEND

The Legend is equipped with a **SCHEDULED SERVICE DUE** warning light. This maintenance light will illuminate every 7500 miles to indicate that an oil and filter change is needed. However, if a shorter oil change interval is desired, there are 7 different intervals to choose, from 7500 to 1500 miles. To choose a new interval, push the **SERVICE RESET** button and the **ARROW** button for approximately 3 seconds, then push the **ARROW** button until the interval desired appears. Then push the **SET** button. After completing the necessary maintenance service, the maintenance light must be reset.

In order to reset the maintenance light, the **SERVICE RESET** button must be depressed. With the ignition switch in the **ON** position, hold the reset button in for at least 3 seconds. To verify that the reset is complete, turn the ignition switch **OFF** and **ON**, the light should not come on.

ALFA ROMEO

Oxygen Sensor Maintenance Reminder Light

A maintenance reminder light used on all of the Alfa Romeo models. The light will illuminate every 30,000 miles on the Graduate, Quadrifoglio and the Spider equipped with the 2.0L engine. The light will illuminate every 60,000 miles on the GTV-6 models equipped with the 2.5L engine. This reminder light is used as a preventive maintenance indicator in regards to the emission system and the oxygen sensor used on that vehicle. After the light has come on, the oxygen sensor replaced and the emission maintenance has been taken care of, reset the light as follows:

GRADUATE, QUADRIFOGLIO AND SPIDER WITH 2.0L ENGINE

1. Locate the mileage counter that is located on the left side of the engine compartment.
2. To remove the plastic cover on the mileage counter, drill through the shank of the cover retaining screws and remove the cover.
3. Rotate the reset button and depress it to reset the reminder light. Reinstall the cover by using new retaining screws.

GTV-6 WITH 2.5L ENGINE

1. On the GTV-6 models equipped with the 2.5L engine, it will be necessary to remove the ECU cover panel and the lower right side parcel shelf.

2. Locate the mileage counter usually located under the right side of the dash. Depress the white reset button to reset the reminder light. Turn the ignition switch to the **ON** position to be sure the light has been reset.

164 SERIES

The front brake pads wear and the level and temperature of the engine coolant are continuously monitored an electronic control unit, that in case of malfunction alerts th driver by turning on the appropriate warning light on the instrument panel.

Severe wear of the front brake pads causes opening of the contacts of the right and left front brake switches, consequently opening the circuit to pins 9B and 10B of the control unit.

The engine coolant level sensor contacts open when the engine coolant level decreases below the minimum, and disconnect pin 4B of the control unit from the ground point.

The warning lights will go out when the pads are replaced or the coolant is filled to the correct level.

AUDI

EGR Warning Light

Some models use an EGR maintenance light that will come on every 15,000 miles of operation. This indicates the need to inspect the EGR system and make any repairs as necessary. After the EGR system has been inspected and is found in proper working condition, push the EGR reset button located on the mileage counter that is attached to the speedometer cable, located in the engine cowl area.

Oxygen Sensor Maintenance Light

Most models are equipped with an oxygen sensor light that will illuminate every 30,000 miles; 60,000 miles on the 1989–90 100/200. This light indicates that the emission system and components should be checked for proper operation and the oxygen sensor should be replaced. Once the sensor has been replaced and the emission system checked, reset the maintenance light as follows:

1980–84 4000, 5000 AND 5000S

The oxygen sensor light is reset by pushing a white reset button on the in-line mileage counter. The in-line mileage counter on the 4000 models is attached to the speedometer cable, located in the engine cowl area.

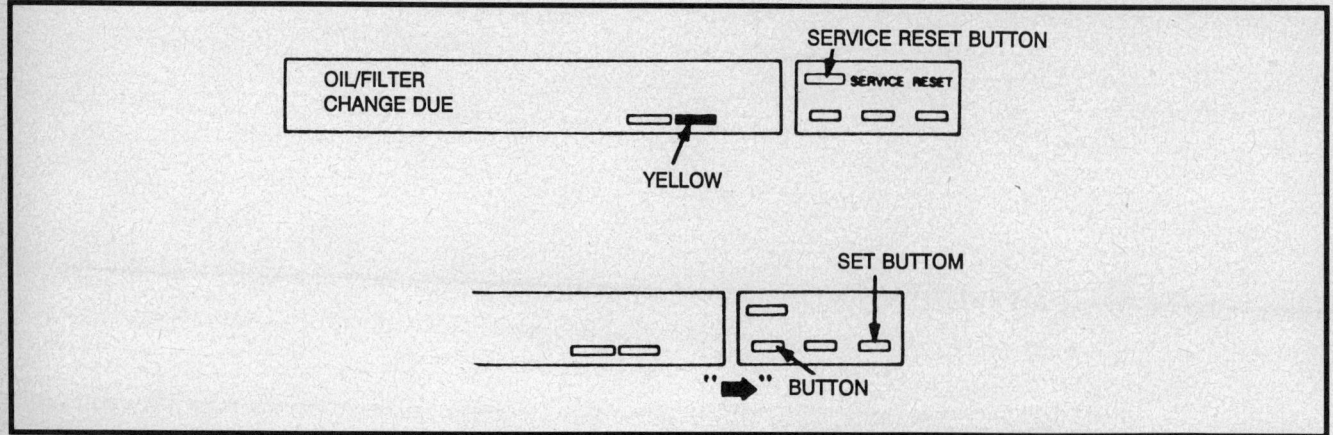

Resetting the service interval light—Legend

The in-line mileage counter on the 5000 models, is mounted under the dash panel, to the left of the steering column, near the pedal assembly. It is recommended to remove the driver's side lower dash cover to reveal the in-line mileage counter. It may be possible to reach the reset button without removing the lower dash cover by using an appropriate bent rod. Whichever procedure is used, the white reset button must be depressed to reset the maintenance reminder light.

1984–90 4000, 5000 AND 5000S

1. To reset the counter on these models, disconnect the negative battery cable and remove the upper and lower instrument cluster cover screws.
2. Pull the cluster cover towards the steering wheel and lift the upper instrument cluster cover of the cluster. On some models, it may be necessary to remove the instrument cluster to gain access to the switch. If so, remove the cluster as follows:

    a. Disconnect the speedometer cable at the transmission and the instrument panel cluster.

NOTE: Use care when removing the speedometer from the instrument panel due to the fragility of the instrument panel cluster.

    b. Disconnect electrical connectors from the cluster and remove the cluster. It may be to the technicians' advantage to remove the steering wheel, allowing more room to work on the cluster.
3. At the top left hand center of the cluster, there should be the initials **OXS** imprinted on the cluster panel.

4. Locate the plastic breakaway box near the **OXS** initials and using a suitable tool, pull the box away from the cluster panel.
5. Insert a suitable tool into the **OXS** opening and push the cancel switch over to the opposite side in order to reset the reminder light.

1984–91 5000 TURBO AND 1989–91 100/200 TURBO MODELS

The in-line mileage counter is used on these models and is located under the rear seat. After checking the emission system and replacing the oxygen sensor, reset the reminder light as follows:
1. Push the rear seat cushion toward the rear of the vehicle, then lift the front of the seat cushion to release the cushion retainers.
2. Place the seat cushions out of the way. The counter is usually located on the left side of the vehicle.
3. Depress the button marked **OXS** and turn the ignition switch to the **ON** position.
4. Turn the ignition switch to the **OFF** position and then **ON** and **OFF** again to be sure the reminder light is reset and does not illuminate any longer.

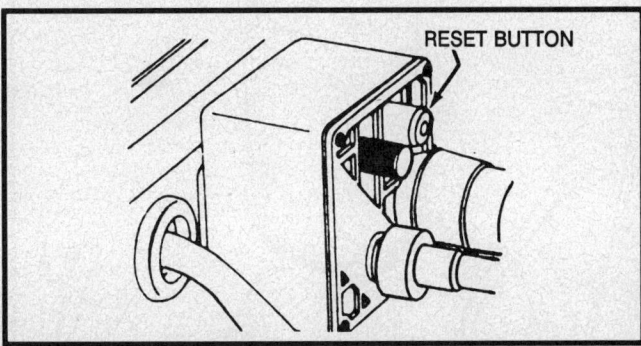

Typical in-line mileage counter and reset mechanism—Audi

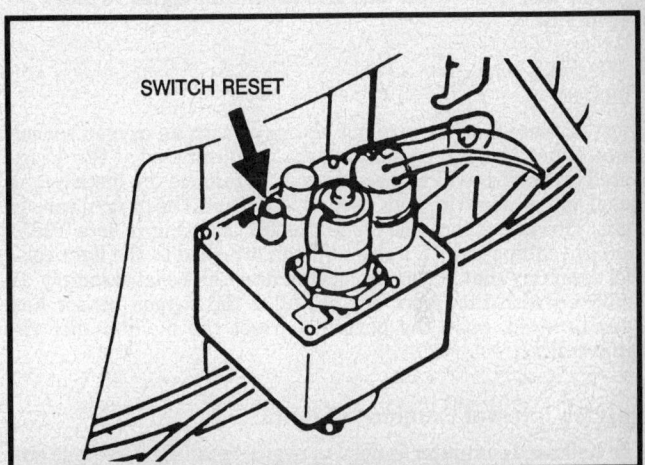

Location of the mileage counter and reset mechanism located under the rear seat—Audi

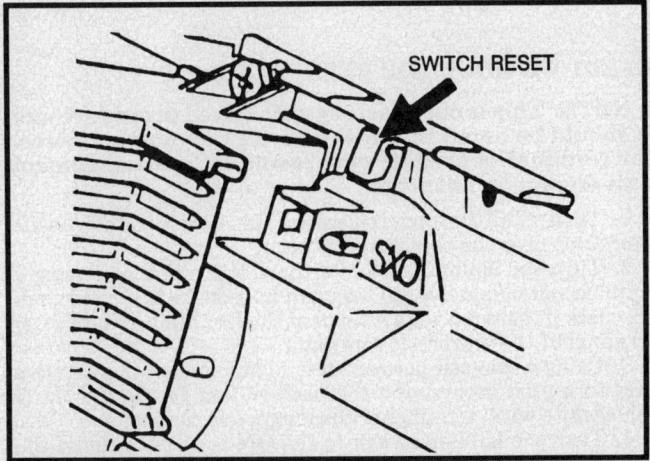

Location of the reset button incorporated into the instrument panel—Audi

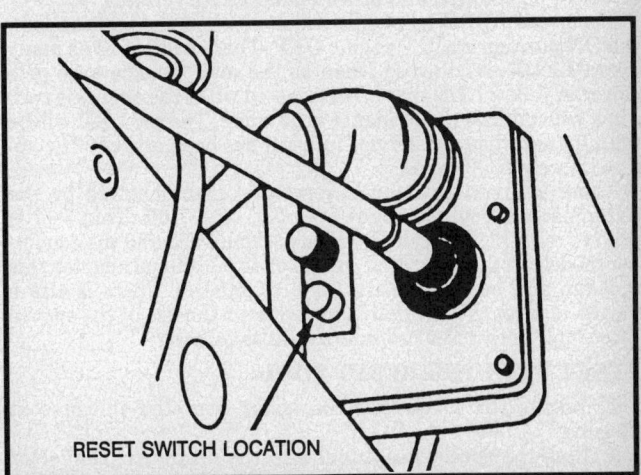

Typical in-line mileage counter and reset mechanism—1980–83 BMW models

BMW

Oxygen Sensor Maintenance Light

Most models are equipped with an oxygen sensor light that will illuminate every 30,000 miles; 25,000 miles on the 528i models. This light indicates the emission system and components should be checked for proper operation and the oxygen sensor should be replaced. After the oxygen sensor has been replaced and the emission system checked, reset the maintenance light as follows:

1980-83 MODELS

The BMW 528E and 633 CSi models do not use a reset switch. On these models, it is necessary to remove the instrument panel and remove the bulb used to illuminate the oxygen sensor light.

1. Locate the in-line mileage counter which is usually placed above the left frame rail, near the transmission.
2. Locate the white reset button on the in-line mileage counter and depress this button to reset the maintenance reminder light.

NOTE: Due to the location of the in-line mileage counter, it is exposed road dirt and moisture. Therefore, when pushing the reset button, be sure to get it to click or the reminder light will remain illuminated. If the switch will not cancel out the reminder light, it must be replaced.

1983-91

Most of these models were not equipped with an oxygen sensor reset. When the oxygen sensor light is illuminated at the designated mileage, it will be necessary to to remove the instrument panel and remove the bulb used to illuminate the oxygen sensor light. However there are some models (starting in late 1985) that are equipped with a reset button attached to the light control assembly that is usually located near the pedal assembly. If equipped with this reset button, after the oxygen sensor has been serviced, push the button to reset the maintenance reminder light.

Service Interval Reminder Lights

The on-board computer is used to evaluate mileage, average engine speed, engine and coolant temperatures, as well as other computer input factors that determine maintenance intervals. There are 5 green, 1 yellow and 1 red **LED** used to remind the driver of oil changes and other maintenance services.

The green **LEDS** will be illuminated when the ignition is in the **ON** position and the engine **OFF**. There will not be as many green **LEDS** illuminated when as the maintenance time gets closer. A yellow **LED** that is illuminated when the engine is running, will indicate maintenance is now due. The red **LED** will be illuminated when the service interval has been exceeded by approximately 1000 miles.

There is a service interval reset tool manufactured by the Assenmacher Tool Company tool No. 62-1-100. This tool is used to reset BMW 6 cylinder models from 1983 and the 4 cylinder models from 1984. With the aid of an additional adapter this tool can also be used on the 1988-91 models. There is also a means to reset the interval lights without the use of the special reset tool. Both reset procedures are as follows:

RESET WITH THE RESET TOOL

1. Locate the diagnostic connector near the thermostat housing.
2. Plug the special reset tool into the diagnostic connector and place the ignition switch in the **ON** position.
3. Depress the reset button on the tool until all 5 green **LEDS** are illuminated, showing that the reset has occurred.

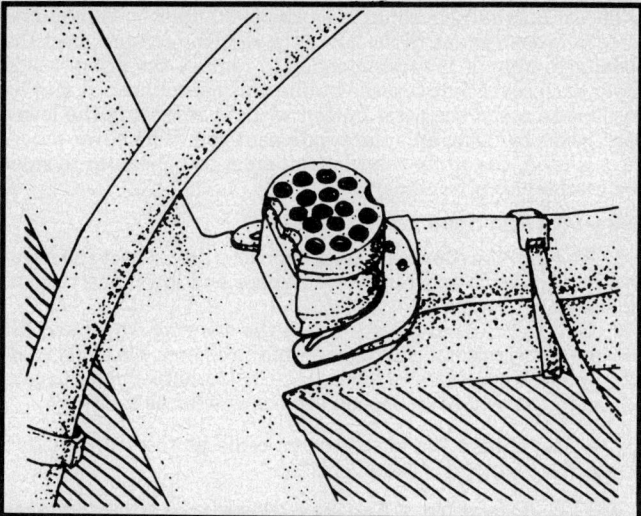

BMW diagnostic test terminal

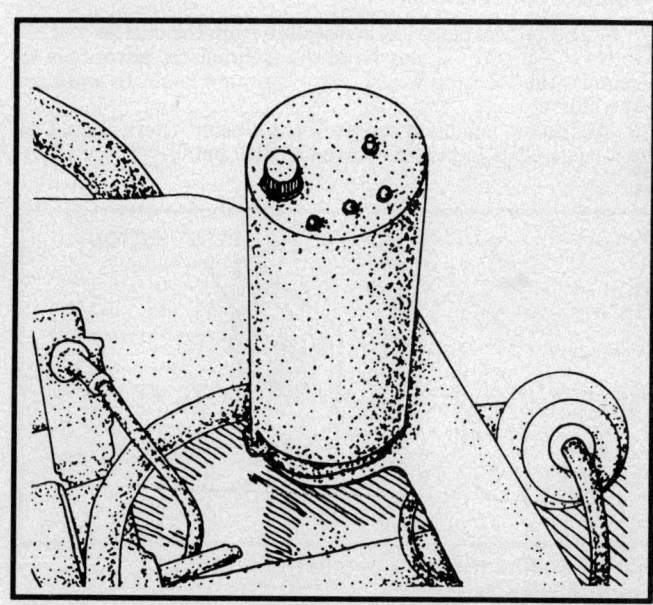

BMW maintenance reminder light reset tool

RESET WITHOUT THE RESET TOOL

NOTE: This is not a factory authorized procedure and it should be noted that if the wrong diagnostic connector terminal is used, it may result in internal control unit (computer) damage.

1. Turn off all the electrical accessories. Locate the diagnostic connector near the thermostat housing.
2. Turn the ignition switch to the **ON** position and using a suitable volt/ohmmeter, 10 megohm impedance is recommended, check if there is 5 volts present at the No. 7 (blue/white wire) terminal of the diagnostic connector.
3. Using a non-self powered test light, connect the negative lead to a good ground and the positive lead to the the No. 7 (blue/white wire) terminal of the diagnostic connector.
4. Turn the ignition switch to the **ON** position. Ground the terminal through the volt/ohmmeter for 12 seconds. All 5 green **LEDS** should be illuminated, showing that the reset has occurred.

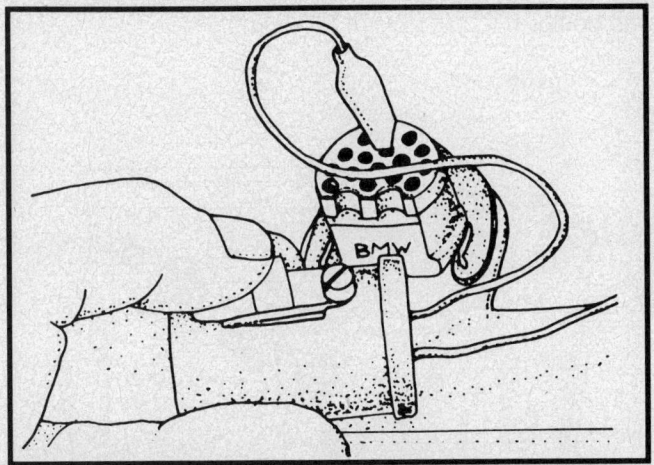

Equivalent version of the BMW maintenance reminder light reset tool

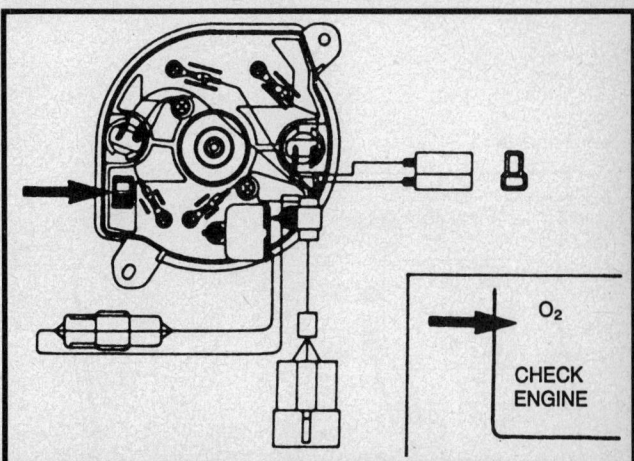

Resetting the oxygen sensor reminder light—Trooper II

NOTE: There is also a means to make a self made version of the reset tool. This version is made by soldering a small momentary contact switch to 2 ten foot lengths of 20 gauge standard wire. Install the switch into a small canister, such as a film canister. Solder 2 small probe connectors to the opposite ends of the wire. To use this tool, plug it into the proper diagnostic connector terminal (No. 7 blue/white wire) and use it just as the real reset tool is used. It must be noted that this is not a factory authorized procedure and if the wrong diagnostic connector terminal is used, it may result in internal control unit (computer) damage.

HONDA

Service Interval Flags

Some 1982–85 Honda models use oil change service interval flags that will appear below the odometer every 7,500 miles. To reset the flags, insert the ignition key into each slot below the indicator flags, at the lower right hand corner of the instrument panel, until the reminder flags turn from red back to green.

ISUZU

Oxygen Sensor Maintenance Light

The 1988–91 Pick-up and Trooper II are equipped with an oxygen sensor maintenance light, located in the dash panel, that will illuminate every 90,000 miles, indicating that the oxygen sensor must be replaced. After the sensor has been replaced and the emission system checked, reset the maintenance light as follows:

1. Reset the reminder light on the Trooper models by removing the speedometer and then sliding the reset switch on the back of the speedometer to the opposite end of its slot.
2. To reset the reminder light on the Pick-up models, proceed as follows:
   a. Remove the instrument cluster assembly.
   b. Working on the backside of the instrument cluster, remove the masking tape over hole **B** in the instrument cluster.
   c. Remove the screw from hole **A** of the instrument cluster and place that screw in hole **B** of the instrument cluster.
   d. After switching the screw from hole **A** to hole **B**, be sure to place a piece of masking tape over hole **A** of the instrument cluster.

NOTE: At the next 90,000 mile interval the screw hole positions will be the opposite of the previous replacement.

JAGUAR

Oxygen Sensor Maintenance Light

All fuel injected Jaguar models are equipped with an oxygen sensor maintenance light, located in the dash panel, that will illuminate every 30,000 miles, indicating that the oxygen sensor must be replaced. After the sensor has been replaced and the emission system checked, reset the maintenance light as follows:

1. The reset switch will be located in the following position on these models:
   a. The 1980–83 XJ6 has the maintenance reminder reset mileage counter located on the right side of the engine, in front of the firewall in the engine compartment.

NOTE: On some of the 1980–83 models, the maintenance reminder reset mileage counter may be hidden either side of the engine or behind the glove box.

   b. The 1983–91 XJ6 and XJS models use a motorized maintenance reminder reset mileage counter, which is located inside the trunk compartment behind the trim panel.
2. Reset the mileage counter on the 1980–83 models by using the special key No. BLT–5007 or using 2 small pins to turn the reset disc on the mileage counter. Start the engine and check to see if the light has been turned off.
3. Reset the mileage counter on the 1983–91 XJ6 models by removing the trim panel at the head of the trunk to uncover the mileage counter. With the ignition switch in the **ON** position, depress the white button to reset the light.
4. Reset the mileage counter on the 1983–91 XJS models, by removing the trim panel from the left rear quarter panel in front of the wheel well to uncover the mileage counter. With the ignition switch in the **ON** position, depress the white button to reset the light.

MAZDA

Timing Belt Warning Light
DIESEL PICK-UPS

Early model diesel pick-ups were equipped with a timing belt warning light. This light would illuminate at approximately

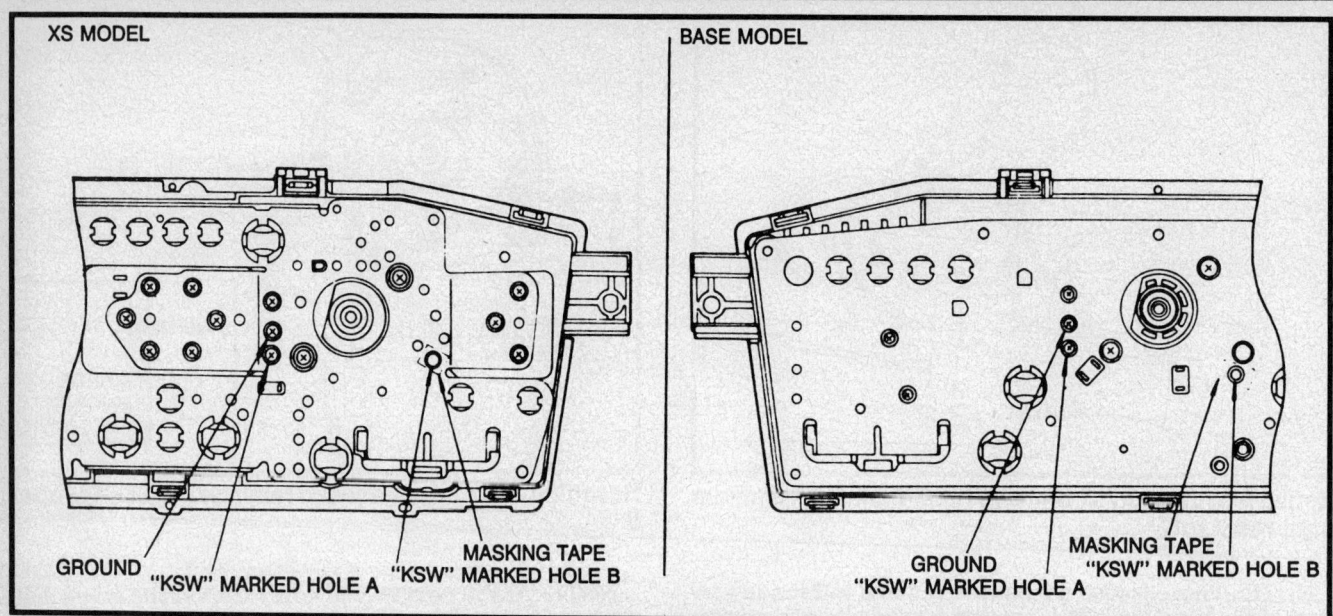

XS MODEL

BASE MODEL

GROUND "KSW" MARKED HOLE A   "KSW" MARKED HOLE B   MASKING TAPE

GROUND "KSW" MARKED HOLE A   MASKING TAPE "KSW" MARKED HOLE B

Resetting the oxygen sensor reminder light—Pick-Up models

60,000 miles to indicate that a new timing belt should be installed. After the belt had been inspected or replaced, the warning light would be reset as follows:

1. Locate the 3 wires used to reset the timing belt warning light.

    a. Black wire located near the intermittent wiper control relay.

    b. Black wire with a white tracer located near the intermittent wiper control relay.

    c. Black wire with a yellow tracer located near the intermittent wiper control relay.

NOTE: The intermittent wiper control relay is located under the left side of the instrument panel.

2. Remove the single black wire from the connector of the black wire with the white tracer.

3. Plug the single black wire into the connector of the black wire with the yellow tracer.

NOTE: Which ever connector the single black wire was connected to originally, it must be removed and reconnected to the opposite connector from which it was removed, in order to reset the light.

EGR Warning Light
1986 B2000 FEDERAL PICK-UPS

The EGR warning light illuminates at the first 60,000 miles to inform the operator that the emission components should be replaced and/or inspected. The suggested replacement components are the oxygen sensor, EGR control valve along with the hose and tube. The suggested inspected components are the PCV system and the ignition timing. The light can be reset as follows:

1. Located above the left side kick panel, there will be a single terminal green wire that is connected to a single terminal black wire. In order to reset the warning light, disconnect the black wire from the green wire and leave it disconnected. Be sure to tape the disconnected wire to prevent shorting.

NOTE: These connectors are sometimes located on the rear of the combination meter.

Check Engine Light
1988–91 PICK–UP

These pick-up models, in addition to displaying computer system malfunction codes, codes used on California models only, the **CHECK** light on the B2200 and B2600 pick-ups will act as an emission maintenance warning light. The **CHECK** engine warning light will come on at 60,000 miles for the EGR system and 80,000 miles for the oxygen sensor system. Once the emission system has been checked and/or the oxygen sensor replaced, reset the warning light as follows:

1. To reset warning light it will be necessary to locate the brown wire with the white tracer, the black wire and the green wires, which are usually under the left side of instrument panel taped to the wiring harness, above the fuse/relay block.

2. When the 60,000 mile interval arrives and the light is illuminated, unplug the black wire connector from the brown and white wire connector and plug it into the green wire connector. When the 80,000 mile interval arrives, return the black wire connector to the brown and white wire connector.

1989–91 MVP

The MVP models, in addition to displaying computer system malfunction codes used on California models only, the **CHECK** light on the instrument cluster will act as an emission mainte-

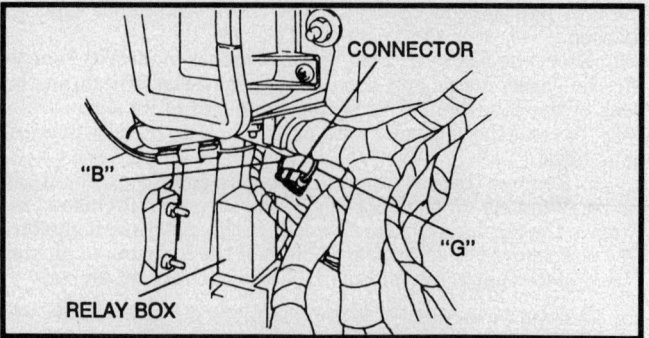

CONNECTOR

"B"

"G"

RELAY BOX

Reset connector location—1986 B2000

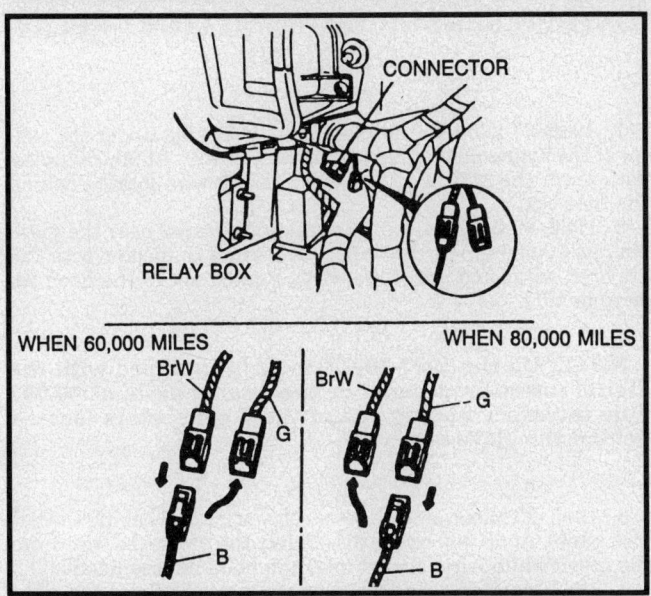

Reset connector location—1988–91 Pick-ups

nance warning light. The **CHECK** engine warning light will come on at 80,000 miles for the oxygen sensor system maintenance. After the emission system has been checked and the oxygen sensor replaced, reset the warning light as follows:

1. Disconnect the negative battery cable. Remove the instrument panel cluster assembly.
2. Locate the lettered reset holes **NO** and **NC** on the rear of instrument cluster.
3. Remove the screw from the **NO** lettered reset hole and install it into the **NC** lettered hole. After an additional 80,000 miles, return the screw to the original lettered hole.

MERCEDES-BENZ

Oxygen Sensor Warning Light

1980–85 MODELS

These models are equipped with an oxygen sensor maintenance warning light that works in junction with the mileage reset counter. The warning light will illuminate when the mileage counter reaches approximately 30,000 miles. The warning light is used as a reminder to check the emission system and to replace the oxygen sensor. After the emission system maintenance has been completed, the mileage counter must be reset. To reset the mileage counter, use the following procedure:

1. On the 280 series vehicles, the mileage counter is usually located in-line with the speedometer cable, under instrument panel. Disconnect the wiring plug from counter and leave it disconnected. No reset switch is provided.
2. To reset the counter on all other series, the instrument cluster must be partially removed. Insert a suitable hooked tool between the right side of cluster and the dash panel.
3. Turn the hook to engage the cluster and pull the cluster out of the spring retaining clips.
4. Remove the bulb from the lower corner of the instrument cluster. Press the instrument cluster back into position. There is no reset switch provided.

1986–89 MODELS

The oxygen sensor light on these models is used as a malfunction indicator for the oxygen sensor circuit. A mileage counter is not used on these models and there is no reset procedure required. Servicing and repairing the oxygen sensor circuit should turn light off. Removing and discarding the oxygen sensor

warning light bulb from the warning light in the instrument cluster, will not resolve the emission system problems and may lead to other problems as well.

MITSUBISHI

EGR And Oxygen Sensor Maintenance Warning Light

The Mistubishi car line does not use a maintenance warning light but some of the light trucks, van/wagons and the Montero vehicles do use a maintenance warning light. This warning light will illuminate at approximately 50,000 miles for the EGR system and 80,000 miles for the oxygen sensor system. On the truck and Montero models, the light is used as a reminder to inspect the EGR emission systems. On the van/wagon models, the light used as a reminder to check and replace the oxygen sensor. After completing the necessary emission service, the maintenance light can be reset as follows:

1. The maintenance reminder reset switch is located in 1 of 2 places.
   a. On some models, the reset switch is located on the back of the instrument cluster near the speedometer junction. After the switch is located, slide the switch knob to the other side to reset the maintenance warning light.
   b. On the other models, the reset switch is located on the lower right corner of the instrument cluster, behind the instrument cluster face panel. After the switch is located, slide the switch knob to the other side to reset the maintenance warning light.

NOTE: There will be some Chrysler import models using this same maintenance warning light system. The procedures are the same.

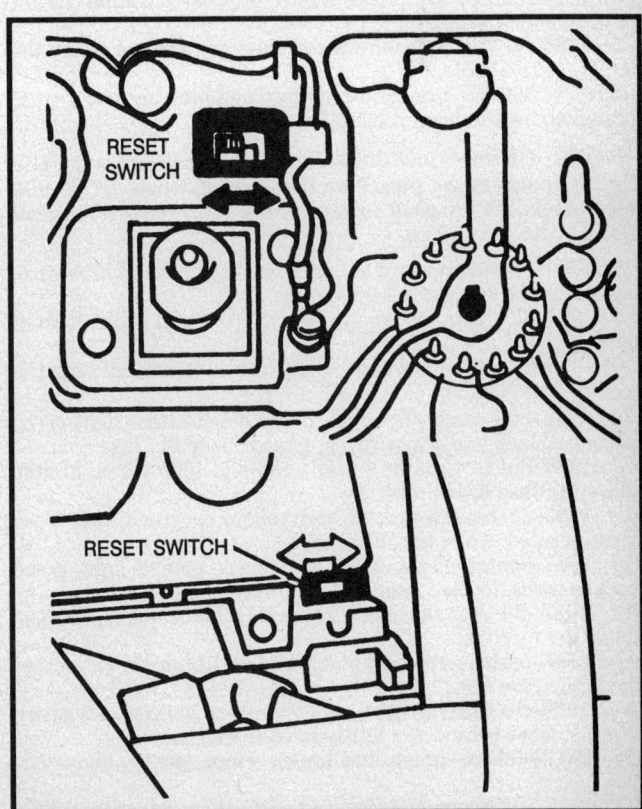

Reset connector locations—Mitsubishi

NISSAN/DATSUN

Oxygen Sensor Light

1980–88 ALL MODELS

These models are equipped with a oxygen sensor maintenance reminder warning light that is located in the instrument cluster. This light will illuminate at approximately 30,000 miles. At this time, the oxygen sensor should be inspected and/or replaced and the entire emission system should be inspected. After the oxygen sensor and emission system have been serviced and repaired as necessary, the maintenance warning light must be reset. On the 1980–84 and some 1985 models, the maintenance warning light is reset by disconnecting the sensor light connector and no further maintenance is required.

On the 1985 Maxima and most 1986–88 models, a warning light hold relay must be located and reset at 30,000 and 60,000 mile intervals. At 90,000 miles, the sensor warning light is disabled by disconnecting the sensor light connector. Use the following chart to locate the reset warning relay and/or warning light electrical connectors.

NOTE: It should be noted that some models may be equipped with either means of resetting the maintenance warning light.

OXYGEN SENSOR WARNING LIGHT CONNECTOR LOCATIONS:

1. 1980–84 200SX—green and white wire, located under the far right side of the instrument panel.
2. 1985–87 200SX—pink and purple wire, located behind the fuse box.
3. 1982–83 280ZX—green and yellow wire, located under the far right side of the instrument panel.
4. 1984 300ZX—white wire connector, located behind the left hand side kick panel.
5. 1985–86 300ZX—white wire connector, located above the hood release handle.
6. 1987 300ZX—gray and red, gray and blue or yellow wire, located above the hood release handle.

NOTE: On the 1987 300ZX models equipped with the digital instrument panel or the analog dash, at 30,000 mile intervals, unplug one of the 3 connectors located behind the glove box.

7. 1980–84 Maxima and 810 Maxima—yellow and blue wire, located near the hood release handle.
8. 1985–87 Maxima—green and red, green and white, located near the hood release handle.
9. 1980–84 Pick-up—yellow and white wire, located near the hood release handle.
10. 1983–86 Pulsar—light green and black with a light green tracer or black and white wires, located near the fuse box.
11. 1987 Pulsar—red and black, red and blue wires, located above the fuse box.
12. 1982–83 Sentra—green and yellow or green and black wires, located above the fuse box.
13. 1984 Sentra—light green and black with a light green tracker wires, located near the hood release handle.
14. 1985–86 Sentra—light green and black wires, located above the fuse box.
15. 1987 Sentra—red and black, red and blue wires, located above the fuse box.
16. 1984–86 Stanza—yellow and red or yellow and green wires, located behind the left hand side kick panel.
17. 1987 Stanza—green and brown wires, located above the fuse box.
18. 1986–87 Stanza Wagon—red and yellow or red and blue wires, located behind the instrument panel.

OXYGEN SENSOR WARNING LIGHT RELAY LOCATIONS

1. 1985–87 200SX—the reset relay is located under the center of the instrument panel behind the console. At 90,000 miles, disconnect the pink wire from the purple wire located behind the fuse box.
2. 1986–87 300ZX—the reset relay is located near the glove box. At 90,000 miles, disconnect the white connector with the gray/red wires and gray/blue wires located above the hood release handle.

NOTE: On the 1987 300ZX models equipped with the digital instrument panel or the analog dash, at 30,000 mile intervals, unplug one of the 3 connectors located behind the glove box.

3. 1985–86 Maxima—the reset relay is located behind the left kick panel. At 90,000 miles, disconnect the green/red wire from the green/white wire located near the hood release handle.
4. 1987 Maxima—the reset relay is located behind the right kick panel. At 90,000 miles, disconnect the green/red wire from the green/white wire located near the hood release handle.
5. 1986 Pick-Up California—the reset relay is located behind the right kick panel. At 90,000 miles, disconnect the connector with the yellow/white wire located above the hood release handle.
6. 1986 Pulsar—the reset relay is located behind the right kick panel. At 90,000 miles, disconnect the connector with the red/black wire and red/blue wire located above the fuse box.
7. 1987 Pulsar—the reset relay is located behind the left kick panel. At 90,000 miles, disconnect the connector with the red/black wire and red/blue wire located above the fuse box.
8. 1985–86 Sentra—the reset relay is located behind the right kick panel. At 90,000 miles, disconnect the connector with the light green and black wire located near the hood release handle.
9. 1987 Sentra—the reset relay is located behind the right kick panel. At 90,000 miles, disconnect the connector with the red/black wire and red/blue wire located above the fuse box.
10. 1986–87 Stanza—the reset relay is located behind the right kick panel. At 90,000 miles, disconnect the white connector on the inside of the left kick panel on the 1986 models. On the 1987 models, disconnect the connector with the green and brown wire located above the fuse box.

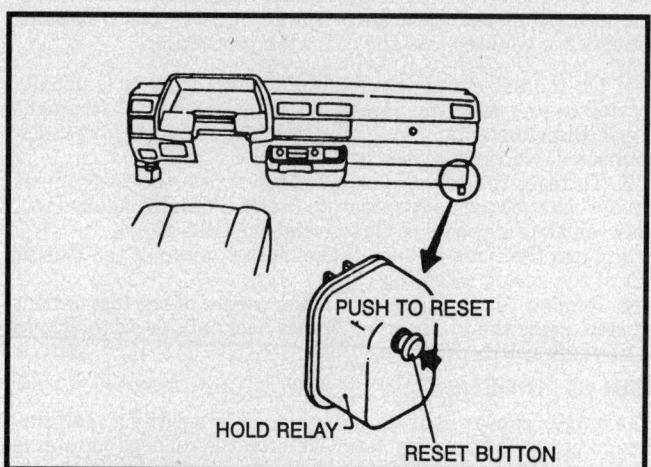

Resetting the oxygen sensor warning light relay— 1985 Pulsar and Sentra

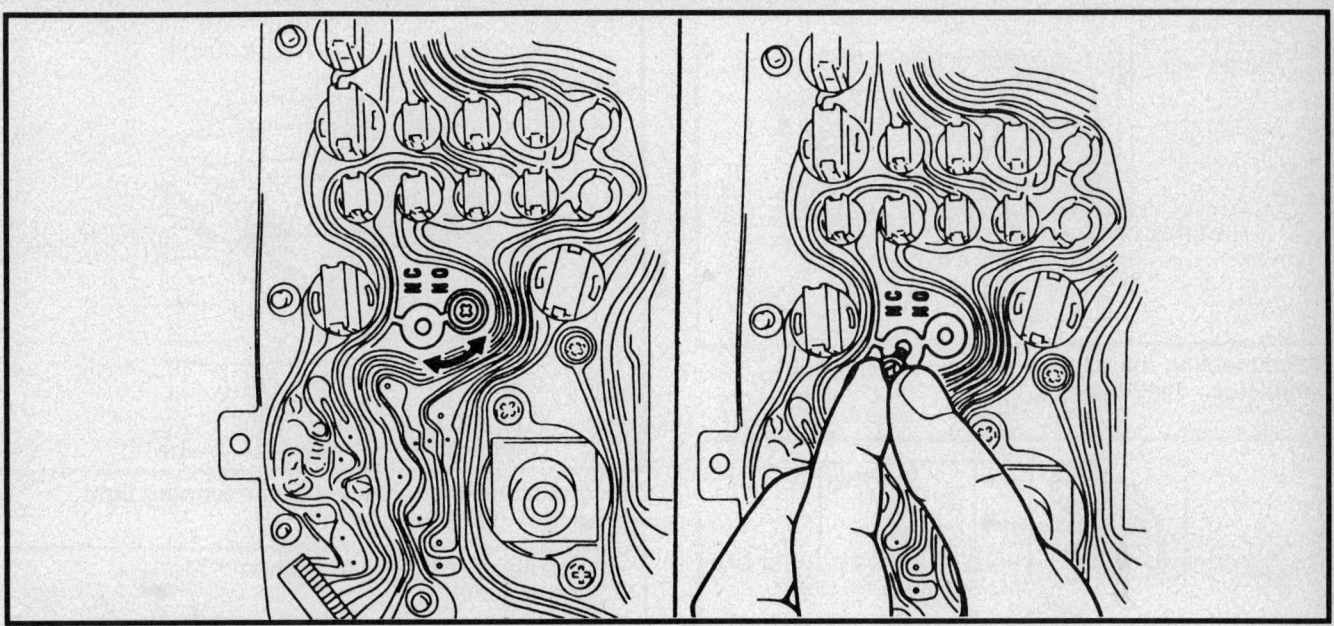

Reset lettered hole locations—1989–91 MVP models

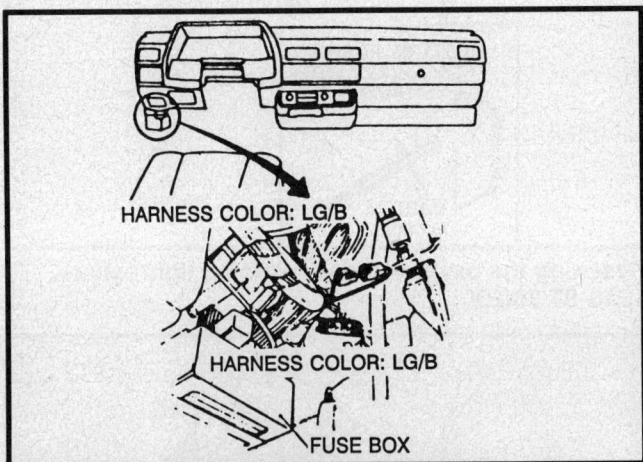

Disconnecting the oxygen sensor warning light connector—1983–86 Pulsar and Sentra

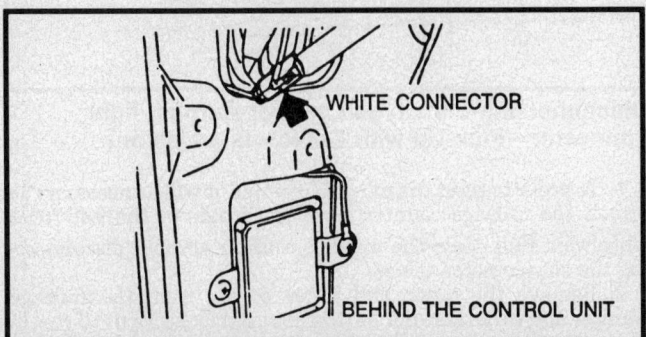

Disconnecting the oxygen sensor warning light connector—1984–87 Stanza

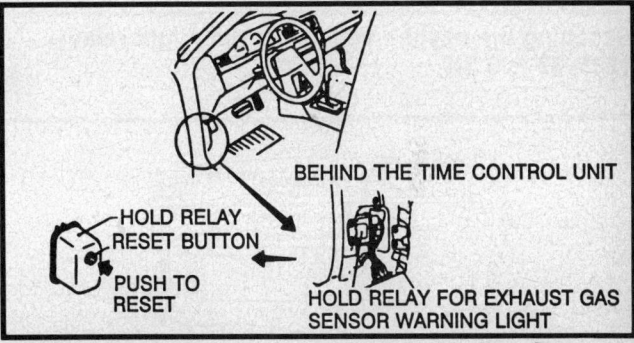

Resetting the oxygen sensor warning light relay— 1985–86 Maxima

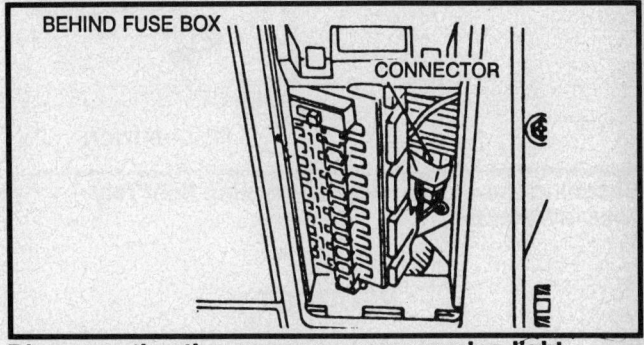

Disconnecting the oxygen sensor warning light connector—1985–87 200SX

11. 1986–867 Stanza Wagon—the reset relay is located under the right side passenger seat. At 90,000 miles, disconnect the red wire from the yellow wire or the red wire from the red/blue wire located behind the instrument panel.

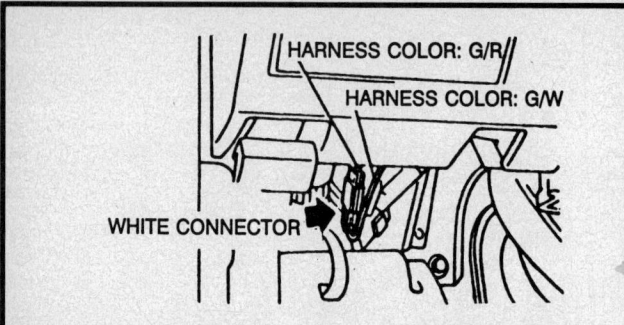

Disconnecting the oxygen sensor warning light connector—1987 Maxima

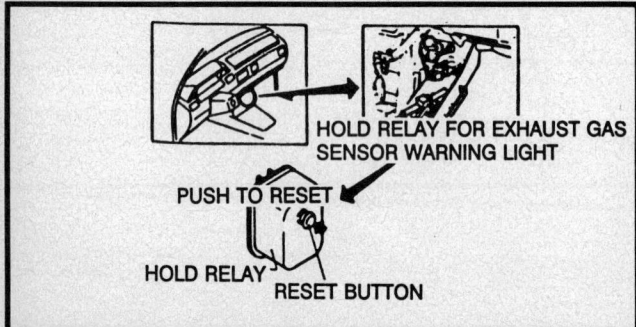

Resetting the oxygen sensor warning light relay—1985–87 200 SX

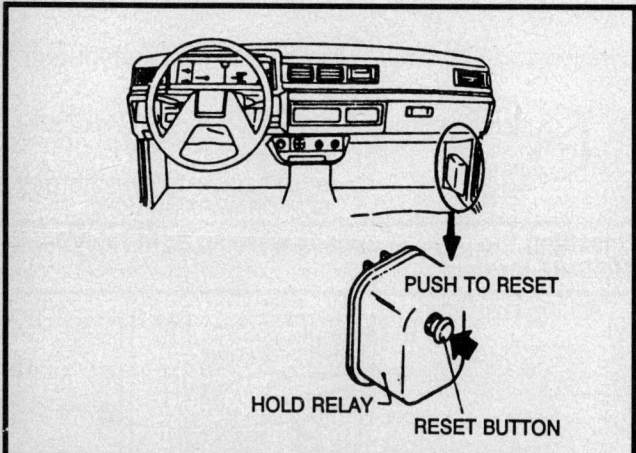

Resetting the oxygen sensor warning light rely—1986–87 Stanza

PEUGEOT

EGR Warning Light

All 1980 604 models are equipped with an **EGR** warning light. This light will illuminate approximately 12,500 mile intervals as determined by a in-line mileage counter. When the light illuminates, it will be necessary to perform maintenance on the EGR system. After completing the necessary maintenance on the EGR system, it will be necessary to reset the mileage counter in order to reset the warning light. The mileage counter can be reset as follows:

Disconnecting the oxygen sensor warning light connector—1985–87 300ZX

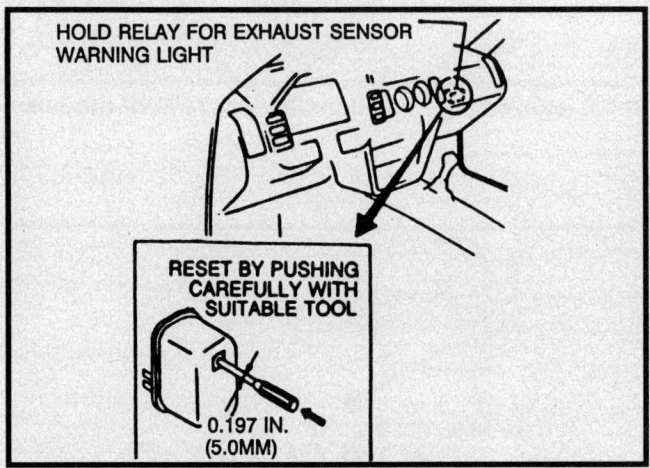

Resetting the oxygen sensor warning light relay—1986–87 300ZX

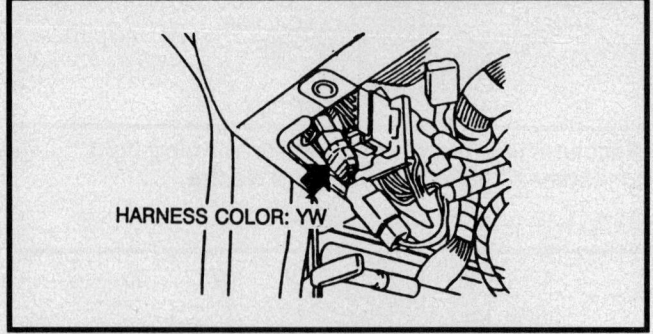

Disconnecting the oxygen sensor warning light connector—Pick-Up with California emissions

1. In order to reset the mileage counter, it will be necessary to unbolt the mileage counter from the inside of the left front wheelwell. Pull down the mileage counter without disconnecting the speedometer cables.

2. Remove the outer and inner covers from the mileage counter and turn the reset button counterclockwise until reaching a stopping point. This will reset the counter to 0.

3. Be sure the warning light is out. Replace the covers and reinstall the mileage counter.

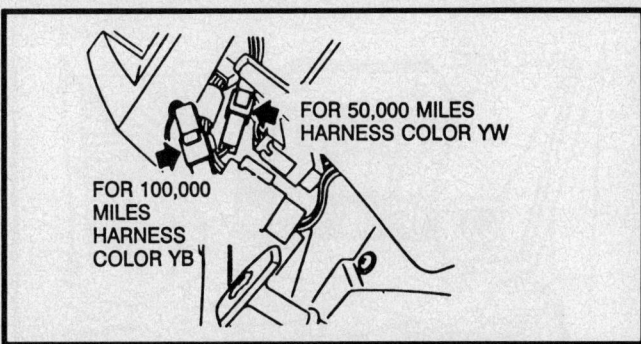

FOR 50,000 MILES
HARNESS COLOR YW

FOR 100,000 MILES
HARNESS COLOR YB

Disconnecting the oxygen sensor warning light connector—Pick-Up with Federal emissions

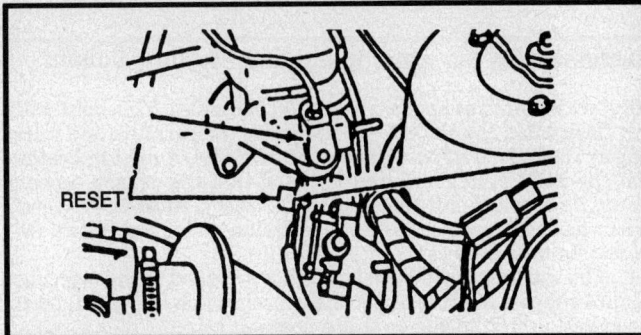

RESET

Resetting the mileage counter—Peugeot

Oxygen Sensor Warning Light

1981–85 505 MODELS

All the 505 models equipped with gasoline engines have an oxygen sensor warning light. This warning light will illuminate at approximately 30,000 mile intervals. When the warning light is illuminated, it is an indication that the oxygen sensor must be replaced and that the mileage counter must be reset. By resetting the mileage counter the warning light will be turned off. The mileage counter can be reset as follows:

1. The mileage counter is located below the brake master cylinder. In order to gain access to the reset button, the white plastic cover must be removed and then unscrew the reset plug.

2. After the reset plug has been removed, use a suitable small punch or rod to press the reset button. Be sure the warning light is out, then replace the reset plug and cover.

PORSCHE

Oxygen Sensor Warning Light

All Porsche models are equipped with an oxygen sensor circuit. All models except the 928S with the LH Jetronic system and the 944S models, are equipped with an **OXS** light that will illuminate at approximately 30,000 mile intervals as a reminder to replace the oxygen sensor. The 928S with the LH Jetronic system and the 944S models do not use a warning light system. It should be noted that even though this models do not use this system, it is recommended that oxygen sensor be replaced every 60,000 miles. On all other models, after replacing the oxygen sensor and checking the emission systems, reset the warning lights as follows.

NOTE: The 1980–83 911 models also used an EGR maintenance reminder warning light system. This light is reset in the same manner as the OXS light.

1. On the 911 models, The **EGR** and **OXS** reset buttons were

both mounted behind the speedometer. Disconnect the negative battery cable and remove the speedometer.

NOTE: On the 1980–83 911 models, the speedometer head is held in place by a ribbed rubber collar. Use caution and gently pry the speedometer head loose in order to gain access to the reset buttons. On the later models, the reset button is visible through the speedometer mounting hole.

2. Use a suitable piece of wire or rod to press the white reset button. Push the reset button all the way in against its stop. Reconnect the battery cable and check that the warning light is out.

NOTE: This procedure also applies to the early 930S models.

3. On the 924 models, after replacing oxygen sensor and with the vehicle still raised and supported safely, located the mileage counter which is usually located on the left engine mount.

NOTE: On the 1980–82 924S turbo models, the mileage counter is located on the engine compartment side of the left strut tower. It may be necessary to follow the speedometer cable from the firewall downward, to be able to locate the mileage counter.

4. Use a suitable piece of wire or metal rod to push in the reset button. Be sure to push the button in all the way to its stop. Make sure the **OXS** light is out. Lower the vehicle.

5. On the 928 and 928S models with the CIS system, the mileage counter is usually located at the right of the passenger seat floor panel under a trim plate between the seat and the step plate.

6. Remove the mileage counter cover retaining screw and the cover. Press the reset button in all the way in against its stop. Make sure the warning light is out.

RENAULT

Oxygen Sensor Warning Light

The Renault 18is and Fuego models, are equipped with a mileage counter and have a dash mounted warning light that will illuminate at approximately 30,000 mile intervals as a reminder to replace the oxygen sensor. After replacing the oxygen sensor and performing any other emission system maintenance, reset the warning light, by resetting the mileage counter as follows:

1. Locate the mileage counter which is located near the firewall and in-line with the speedometer cable. Cut the retaining wires and remove the cover by disengaging the retaining clips.

2. Turn the reset button a ¼ turn counterclockwise toward the **0** mark to reset the mileage counter. Make sure the warning light is out. Replace the cover and secure it with new wires.

SAAB

Oxygen Sensor Warning Light

All Saab models, except the 1985–87 turbo models are equipped with a mileage counter and have a dash mounted **EXS** (EXH on some models) warning light that will illuminate at approximately 30,000 mile intervals as a reminder to replace the oxygen sensor. It should be noted that even though the 1985–87 turbo models do not use this system, it is recommended that oxygen sensor be replaced every 60,000 miles. After replacing the oxygen sensor and performing any other emission system maintenance, reset the warning light, by resetting the mileage counter as follows:

1. Locate the mileage counter which is located under the instrument panel to the left of the steering column, next to the flasher relay.

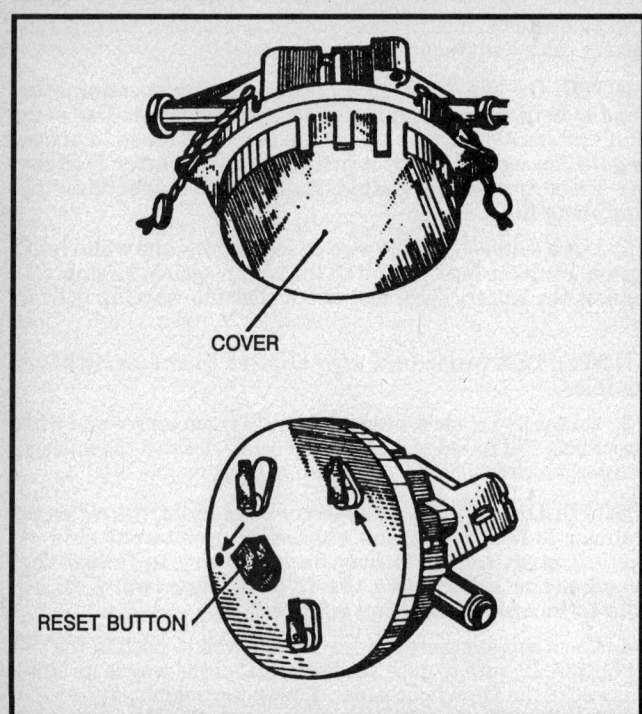

Resetting the mileage counter—Renault

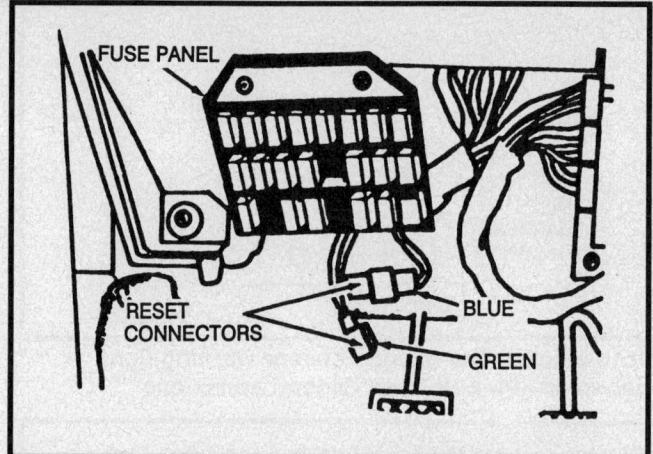

Disconnecting the warning light connector—Subaru

NOTE: Even though the mileage counter is hard to see, there should be no problem in reaching under the instrument panel and locating the mileage counter by feeling it out by hand. It is also possible to reach the mileage counter by reaching under the knee panel or going through the left defrost outlet duct.

2. After the mileage counter has been located, push in the reset button, located on the mileage counter and make sure the warning light has gone out.

SUBARU

EGR Warning Light

The 1981–87 models are equipped with an **EGR** warning light located in the instrument cluster that will illuminate at approximately 30,000–50,000 miles. When this **EGR** light is lit, it is indicating that the EGR system should be checked and with the possibility of an EGR valve replacement.

It should be noted that the 1985–87 turbocharged California models do not use a warning light system. After the EGR system has been checked and all necessary maintenance performed, reset the warning light as follows:

1. Remove the left cover under the instrument panel. Pull down the warning light connectors from behind the fuse panel.
2. Locate the single pin blue connector that is connected to another single pin blue connector. Near the blue connectors is a single green connector that is not connected to any wire terminal.
3. Unplug the connector from the **BLUE** connector and plug it into the **GREEN** connector. This will reset the warning light.

SUZUKI

Oxygen Sensor Warning Light

The Samurai models are equipped with a **SENSOR** light that

will start flashing at approximately 60,000 miles. This light will only flash when the engine is at operating temperature and running at 1500–2000 RPM. This flashing **SENSOR** light indicates that the ECM is in good condition and that the oxygen sensor should be checked and replaced as necessary. After the oxygen sensor has been replaced and the emission systems checked, reset the light as follows:

1. The warning light cancel switch is attached to the steering column support bracket. After the cancel switch is located, turn the cancel switch to the opposite position.
2. Start the engine and drive vehicle to be sure the light does not flash any longer.

TOYOTA

Oxygen Sensor Warning Light

The 1980 Celica, Supra and Cressida models and all the 1981 models with gasoline engines, except Starlet, are equipped with an oxygen sensor. These vehicles are all equipped with a mileage counter that activates a warning light in the instrument cluster at approximately 30,000 miles. When the warning light is illuminated it is an indication that the oxygen sensor must be serviced at this time. After the oxygen sensor and emission systems have been serviced and repaired as required, reset the warning light as follows:

1. All models except the Supra, Land Cruiser and 1980 Celica models: In order to reset the warning light, remove the white cancel switch from top of the left kick panel. It should be noted that this cancel switch has been known to be taped to the main instrument panel wiring harness under the left side of the instrument panel. After the cancel switch has been located, open the switch cover and move the switch slide to the opposite position.
2. On the 1980 Celica, to reset the warning light, remove the black box which is usually located on the top of the bracket above the brake pedal. After the cancel switch has been located, open the switch cover and move the switch slide to the opposite position. It should be noted that some of these Celica models have the cancel switches positioned at the top of the left side kick panel.
3. On the Supra models, it is necessary to remove the small panel next to the steering column in order to gain access to the cancel switch. After the cancel switch has been located, open the switch cover and move the switch slide to the opposite position. It should be noted that some Cressida models have their cancel switch located in this position also.
4. On the Land Cruiser models, the cancel switch is located under the hood in the engine compartment near the firewall. Af-

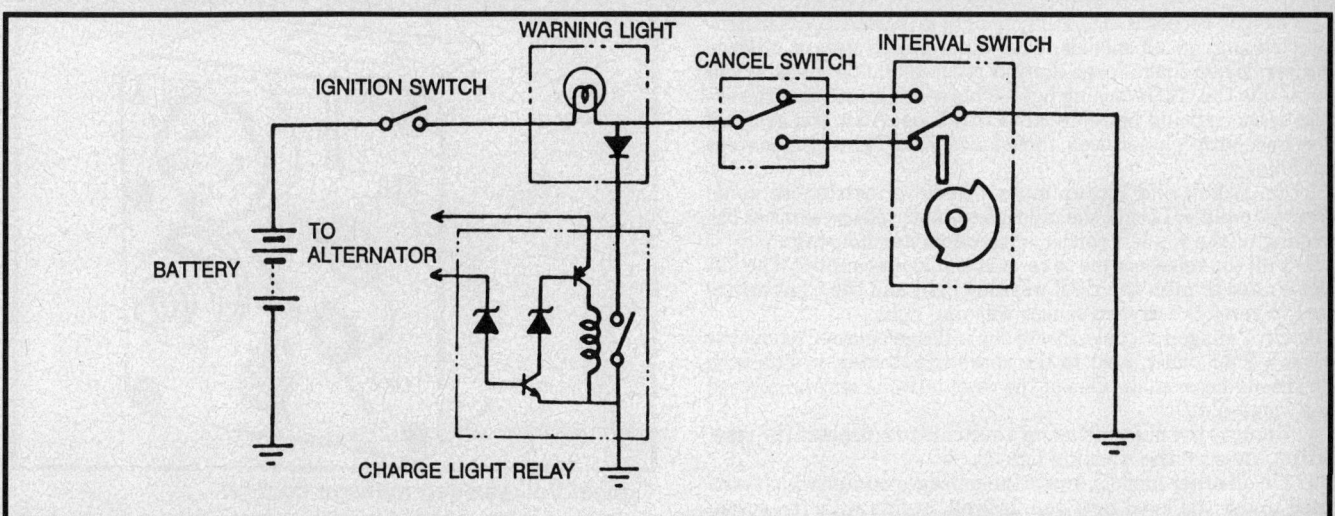

Typical Toyota oxygen sensor maintenance reminder warning light wiring schematic

ter the cancel switch has been located, open the switch cover and move the switch slide to the opposite position.

Timimg Belt Warning Light
DIESEL PICKUPS

The Toyota diesel pickups have a maintenance reminder light that is located in the instrument cluster that will illuminate every 50,000 miles; 60,000 miles on the 1982–83 models. When this light is illuminated, it is indicating that the timing belt should be replaced at this time. After belt has been replaced, reset the warning light as follows:

1. Remove the rubber grommet from the speedometer bezel and reset the speedometer counter by pressing the reset switch.

TRIUMPH/MG

Oxygen Sensor Warning Light

All fuel injected models are equipped with an oxygen sensor. These models also are equipped with a mileage counter and have a dash mounted warning light that will illuminate at approximately every 30,000 mile intervals as a reminder to replace the oxygen sensor. After the oxygen sensor has been replaced, reset the warning light as follows:

1. Locate the mileage counter which is in the engine compartment near the left inner fender panel, in-line with the speedometer cable.

2. After the mileage counter is located, reset the counter by using special key (BLT–5007) supplied in the kit with a new sensor, to turn the reset switch to the opposite position.

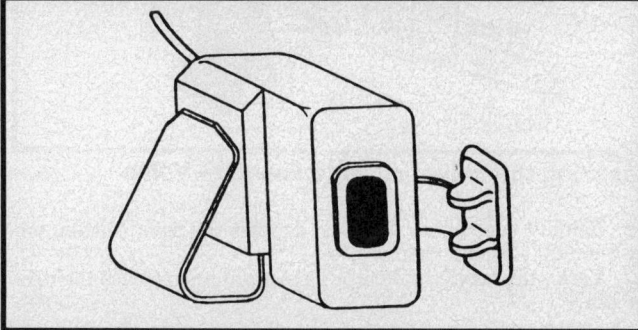

Typical Toyota cancel switch

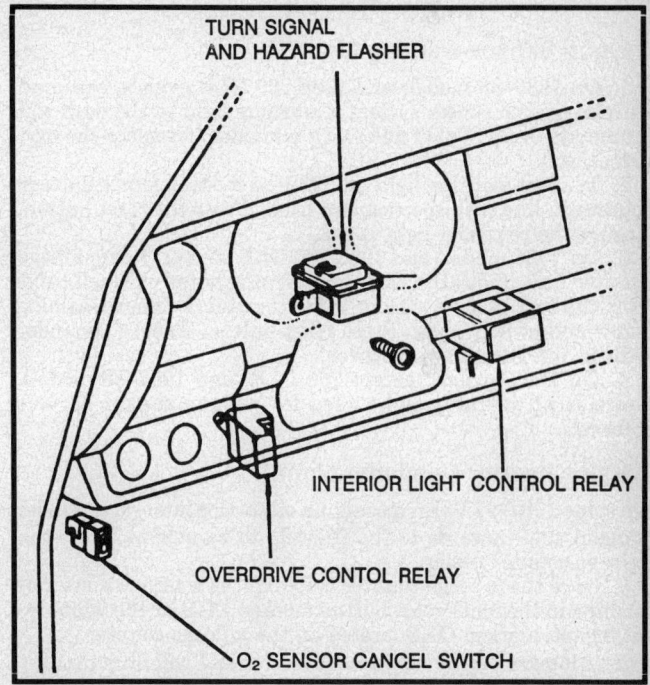

Typical location of a Toyota oxygen sensor cancel switch

3. The mileage counter can also be reset by using 2 small pins that will fit into the reset key holes.

VOLKSWAGEN

EGR And Oxygen Sensor Maintenance Warning Lights

On all models there is an EGR warning light that is located in the instrument cluster. This system also uses a mileage counter. When the mileage counter reaches 15,000 miles, it will illuminate the EGR warning light. This will indicate that the EGR and emission system should be checked for proper operation.

An oxygen sensor (OXS) warning light is located in the instrument cluster on all models. This system also uses a mileage counter. When the mileage counter reaches 30,000 miles, it will illuminate the OXS warning light. This will indicate that the oxygen sensor should be replaced at this time. After the systems have been properly serviced, the maintenance lights can be reset has follows:

1. On Rabbit and Pickup models, remove instrument panel cover trim plate. Locate the mileage counter release arms at the opening of the top left corner of speedometer housing.

2. Pull the release arms to reset the mileage counter. The left arm is used to reset the EGR warning light and the right arm is used to reset the oxygen sensor warning light.

3. On Vanagon models, locate the mileage counter below the driver's floor panel, next to the spare tire carrier, in-line with the speedometer cable. One of the reset buttons may be covered by a small plug.

4. Remove the plug and using a suitable rod, depress the reset button. Be sure the warning light is out.

5. On all other models, locate the mileage counter which is located under the hood near the firewall, in-line with the speedometer cable. It is best to follow the speedometer cable from the

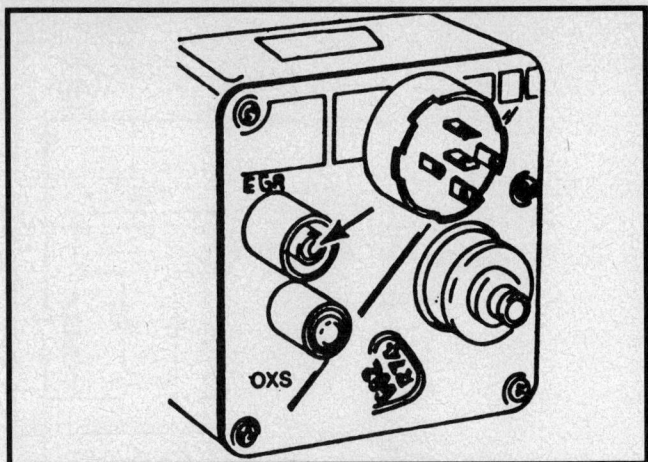

Typical Volkswagen mileage counter

VOLVO

Oxygen Sensor Warning Light

1. On 1980–85 models and 1986 760 GLE models, equipped with an oxygen sensor system, a warning light in the dash will illuminate every 30,000 miles as a reminder to replace the oxygen sensor.

2. To reset warning light on 1980–84 models, locate mileage counter in-line with speedometer cable. Press the reset button. Ensure the reminder light is out.

3. On 1985 models and 1986 760 GLE models, locate milage counter unit under the dash by following wires or small cable from the back of the speedometer to the unit. Remove retaining screw and switch cover. Press reset button. Ensure reminder light is out. Install switch cover.

4. On 1986 models (except 760 GLE) and 1987–89 models, there is no warning light used for oxygen sensor service intervals.

Service Interval Reminder Light

On some 1987–91 Volvo models, an oil service interval reminder transmission upwards to the firewall, to be able to locate the mileage counter easier.

6. Once the mileage counter is found it is a simple matter of pushing in the black reset button marked **EGR** or the white reset button marked **OXS** located on the mileage counter.

light is located on the instrument cluster and will illuminate at 5000 mile intervals. The light will continue to illuminate for 2 minutes after each engine start or until the counter is reset. After completing the necessary service, reset the mileage counter as follows:

740 MODELS

1. To reset the mileage counter, remove the instrument cluster.

2. Locate the button behind the right center of the instrument cluster and press it in too reset the counter. Verify the light is out.

3. Reinstall the instrument cluster.

760 MODELS

1. To reset the mileage counter, remove the rubber plug located between the speedometer and the clock.

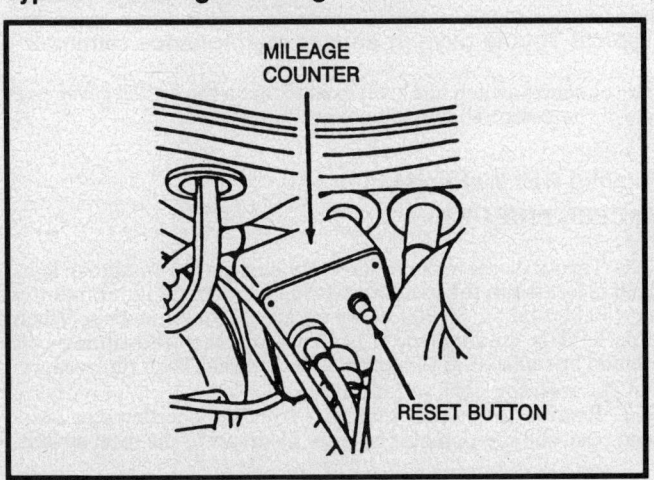

Locating and resetting the in-line mileage counter— Volkswagen

Resetting the in-line mileage counter—Volvo

2. Remove the rubber plug and depress the reset button, using a small, suitable rod.

3. Verify the service indicator light is out and replace the rubber plug.

GENERAL INFORMATION

ALTERNATOR FUNCTION

An alternator makes voltage that alternates between positive and negative current flow, forming a sine wave. These waves must be rectified to DC voltage before the vehicle can use it. A diode does this by acting as an electronic check valve, allowing only ½ of the wave to pass and blocking the other ½. With a diode circuit set up to rectify both phases of the wave, both the positive and negative halves of the wave form can be added together and the full output of the alternator can be used.

An automotive alternator has 3 or more sets of windings in the stator and an equal number in the rotor, meaning there will be 3 or more wave forms (phases) with each rotation of the rotor. Therefore in every standard alternator there will be one diode for each winding, in sets called a rectifier bridge. One rectifier bridge controls the positive part of the wave and one bridge controls the negative part. Usually both rectifiers are mounted on the same plate with a single connector terminal to the battery, and the plate goes to ground. There is usually a third set of diodes called the diode trio, which taps some of the current for the alternator's own internal exciter circuit.

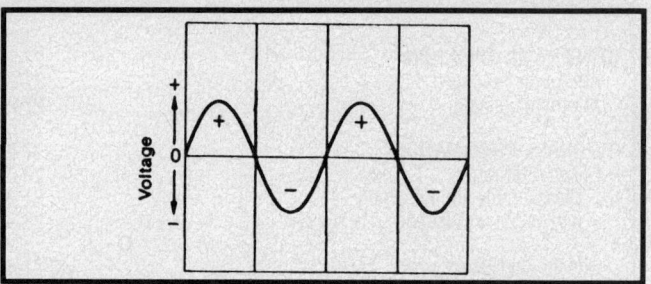

Raw alternator output is both positive and negative voltage

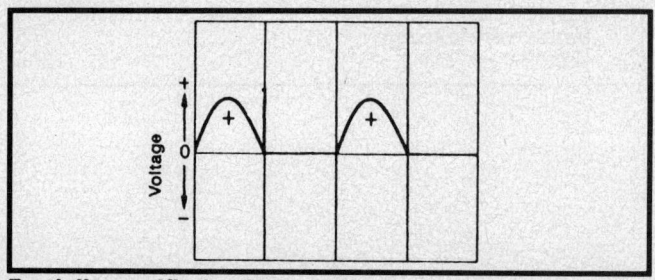

Partially rectified voltage output: the negative half of the wave has been surpressed

ALTERNATOR TESTING

Testing the rectifiers means looking for continuity (current flow) at each diode in that group of diodes in one direction only. Using an ohmmeter with 1 ohm resolution, touch the positive probe to the rectifier connector and the negative probe to each of the diodes, or to each stator connection on the bridge. On one rectifier, there should be infinite resistance at each diode. On the other rectifier, there should be continuity at each diode. Switch the probes and touch the positive probe to each diode. The readings should be reversed. If any diode or bridge shows any continuity in both directions or no continuity in either direction, that rectifier is not functioning properly. Usually individual diodes or rectifier bridges are not available and the whole assembly must be replaced.

To test the wire coils, use an ohm meter with at least a 1 ohm resolution to look for the proper resistance in the stator and rotor coils. Some manufacturers specify the resistance should be measured in the rotor coils but 3–4 ohms is normal. The typical failure mode in any coil is a short circuit or an open circuit. If continuity exists between a coil and the metal body of the rotor or stator, the coil is shorted to ground and probably cannot be repaired.

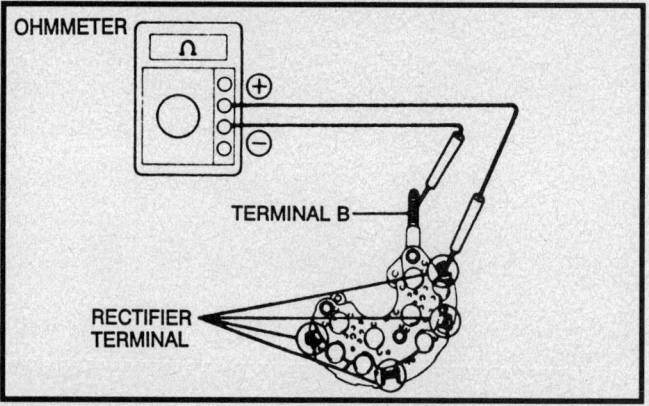

Using an ohmmeter to check each diode in the rectifiers

OVERHAUL INFORMATION

Bosch Alternators

Disassembly and Assembly

1. Remove the pulley nut, pulley and fan. If there are bearing retaining screws on the housing behind the pulley fan, remove them. Mark the front and rear housings so they can be reassembled correctly.

2. On the rear housing, remove the voltage regulator with the brushes.

3. Screw the nut on the shaft and clamp it in a vice. Remove the through screws and at the screw holes, carefully pry the stator away from the front housing. Insert the pry tools no more than ¼ in. (2mm).

4. To separate the rear housing from the stator, remove the nuts from the B+ and D+ terminals and the screws that hold the rectifier bridge to the rear housing.

5. To test the rectifiers, the 3 wires connecting the rectifier bridge to the stator must be unsoldered at the bridge assembly. Work quickly and use only as much heat as needed to avoid damaging the diodes.

6. Both bearings can be removed from the rotor with a bearing puller. They should not be reused. After unsoldering the slip ring terminals, both the slip rings can also be removed with the puller.

To assemble:

7. When installing new slip rings, insert the ends of the coils in the recess and press the rings to 0.138 in. (3.5mm) in from the step in the shaft. Carefully solder the connections and make sure the rings are clean and smooth.

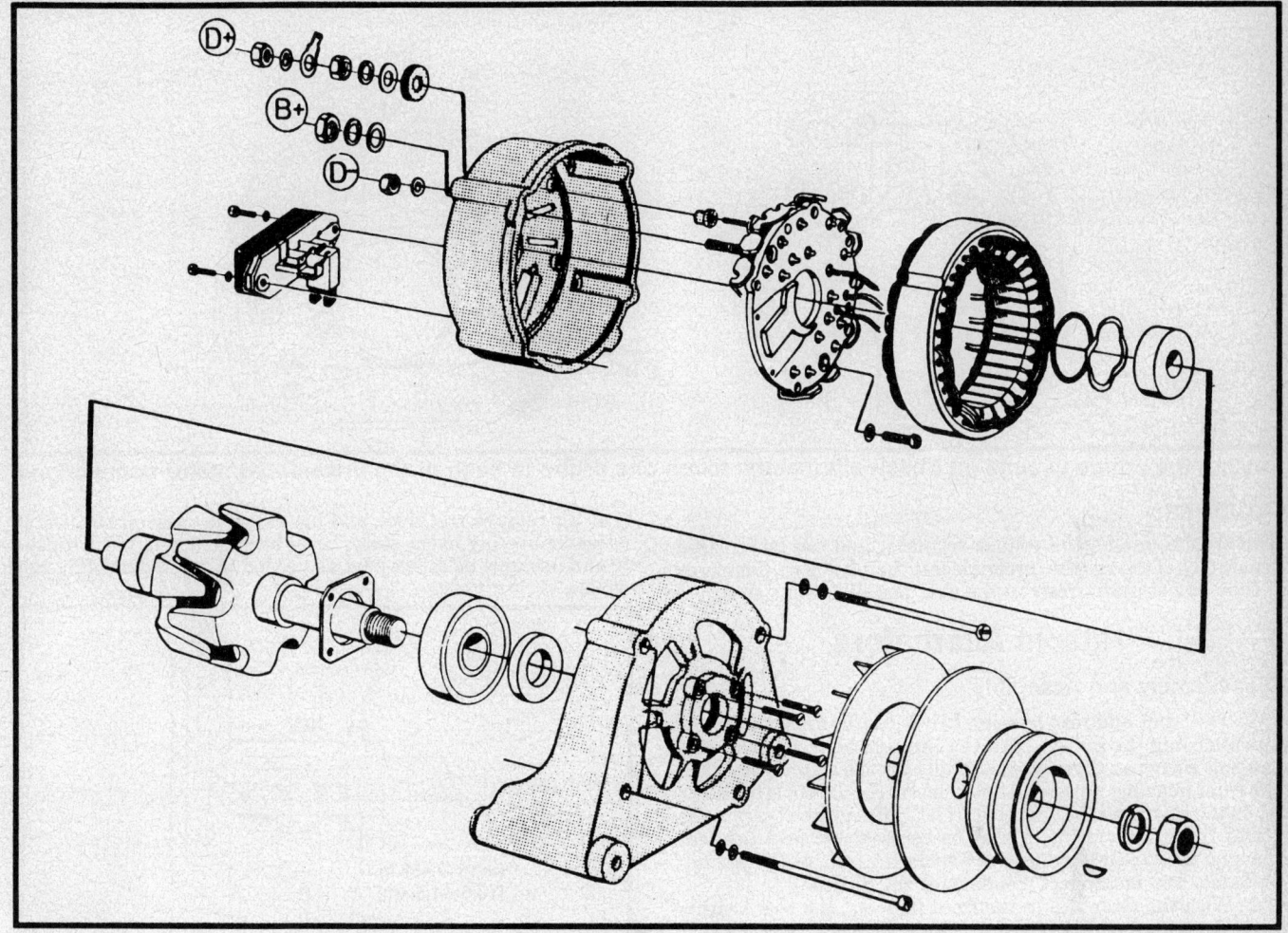

Typical Bosch alternator with removable voltage regulator: Units with a connection labled "W" are for Diesel engines

8. When pressing on a new bearing, make sure to press only on the inner race.

9. When soldering the stator connections to the rectifier bridge, apply the heat quickly and use only as much heat as needed.

10. Install the bearing retainer screws to the front housing before assembling the stator and rear housing. Check to see the matchmarks are aligned.

11. If the brushes are less than 0.200 in. (5mm) long, replace the brushes before installing the voltage regulator.

Inspection and Testing

DIODES

1. To test the positive rectifier diodes, connect the meter probes across the B+ terminal and each stator connection one at a time. Reverse the probes and repeat the test. There should be continuity in one direction only.

2. To test the negative rectifier diodes, connect the meter probes across D- (bridge ground) and each stator connection one at a time. Reverse the probes and repeat the test. There should be continuity in one direction only.

3. To test the exciter diodes, connect the meter probes across the D+ terminal and each stator connection. Reverse the probes and repeat the test. There should be continuity in one direction only.

4. In each test there will be 6 readings. Each diode in a triplet

should read exactly the same as the others. If there is any deviation, the entire bridge assembly should be replaced.

ROTOR

1. Read the resistance between the unpainted portion of the rotor claws and the slip rings. There should be infinite resistance at each ring.

2. Check the physical condition of the slip rings. They should be smooth and clean, not grooved, pitted or corroded. Fine sand paper can be used to clean the surface, or the rings can be machined. Starting at the outer edge away from the rotor body, cut no more than 0.787 in. (20mm) across the face of the rings. This will leave a step at the inner edge of the rings where the wire connections are. The minimum outside diameter of the slip rings is 1.055 in. (26.8mm). If necessary, the slip rings can be replaced.

3. Read the resistance across the slip rings. A reading of less than 2.8 ohms means a short, a reading of more than about 4 ohms means an open circuit. If the reading falls outside this range, the rotor cannot be repaired and must be replaced.

STATOR

1. Read the resistance between the stator body and each wire end. Anything less than infinite resistance means the coil is shorted to ground and the stator must be replaced.

2. Read the resistance between each of the wires. The reading should be less than 1 ohm and the same for each coil.

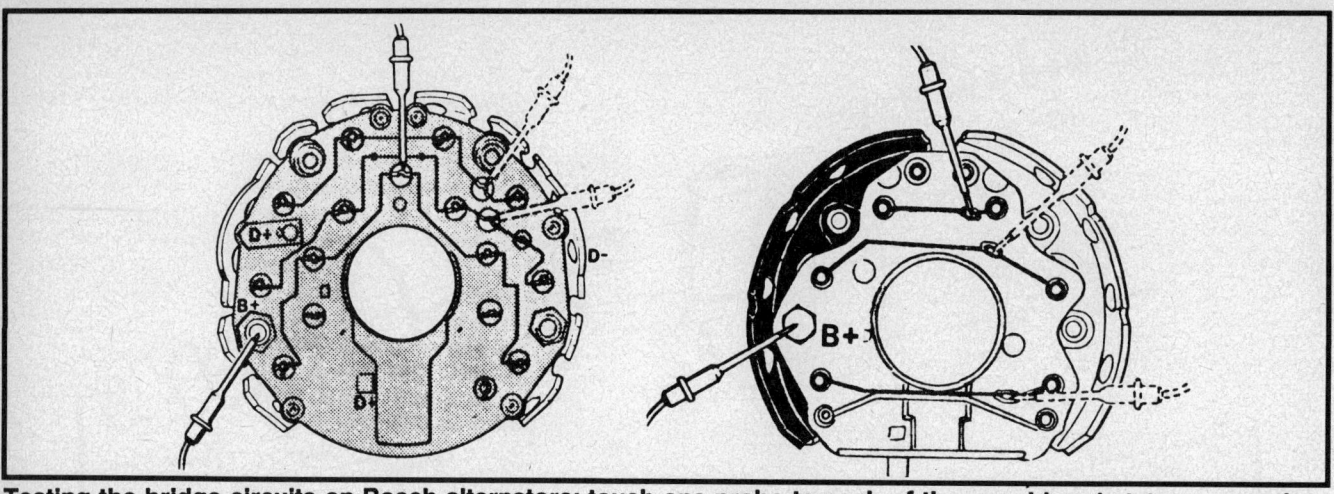

Testing the bridge circuits on Bosch alternators: touch one probe to each of the unsoldered stator connections

BRUSHES

The brushes are on the voltage regulator and can be replaced separately. If the brushes protrude less than 0.200 in. (5mm), or if they do not move freely in the slot, install new brushes.

Hitachi Alternators

Disassembly and Assembly

1. The front and rear housing halves can be separated without removing the pulley. With the through bolts removed and the unit sitting on the pulley, carefully pry the stator away from the front housing. Be careful not to insert the pry tools too deeply, or the stator will be damaged. If it is difficult to separate the stator from the housing, it may be necessary to heat the rear housing at the rear bearing. Use a soldering iron, not a heat gun or flame. Too much heat will damage the diodes.

2. With the rotor still in the front housing, the rear bearing can be removed with a puller

3. With the housings separated, the pulley can be removed by holding the rotor in a soft jaw vice. This must be done to remove the front bearing.

4. To remove the diode and brush holder assemblies, the 3 wires connecting to the stator must be unsoldered. Work quickly and use only as much heat as needed to avoid damaging the diodes.

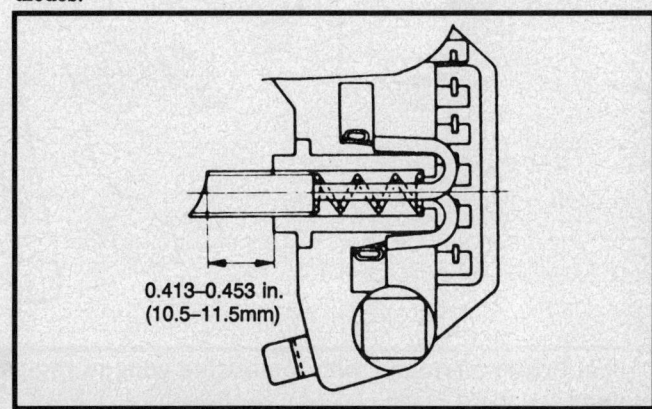

0.413–0.453 in. (10.5–11.5mm)

Position for soldering Hitachi brushes

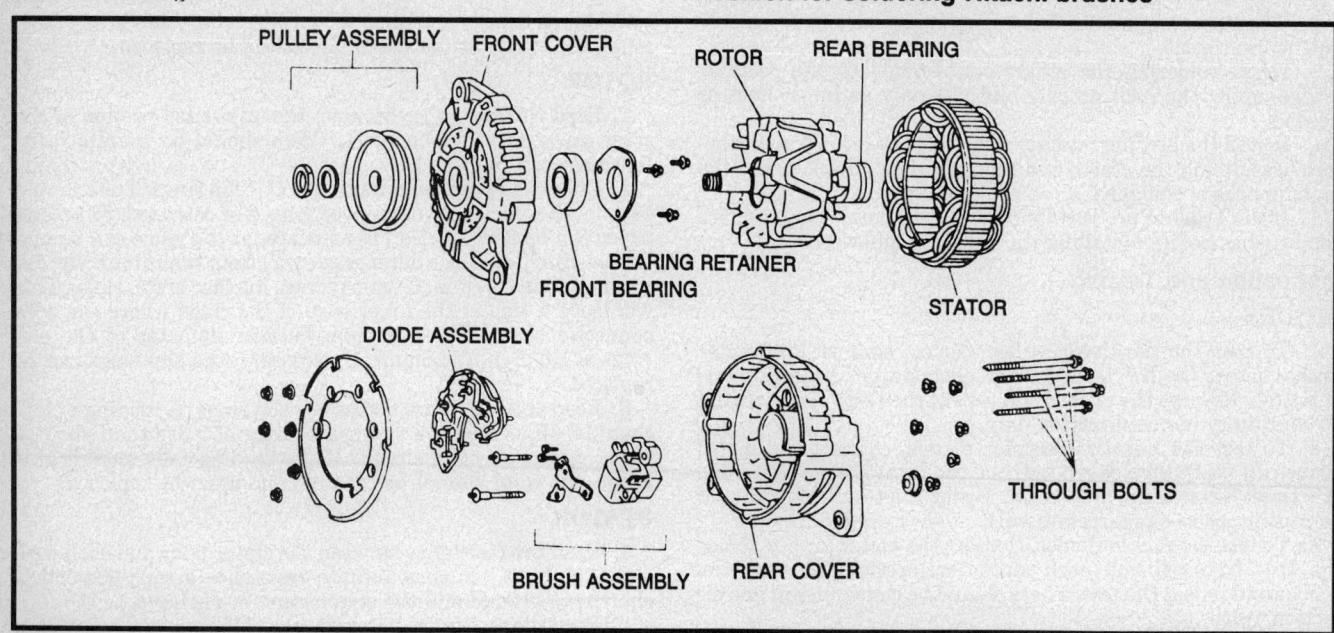

PULLEY ASSEMBLY FRONT COVER ROTOR REAR BEARING

BEARING RETAINER

FRONT BEARING

STATOR

DIODE ASSEMBLY

THROUGH BOLTS

BRUSH ASSEMBLY REAR COVER

Exploded view Hitachi alternator

To assemble:

5. When pressing on a new bearing, make sure to press only on the inner race.

6. When soldering the stator and brush holder connections, apply the heat quickly and use only as much heat as needed to avoid damaging the diodes.

7. If the brushes have worn down to the limit line, new brushes must be installed. Unsolder the pig tail to remove the old brush and spring.

8. The wire loop determines maximum travel of the brush in the holder. Insert the new spring and brush and hold the brush with no more than 0.453 in. (11.5mm) showing, then carefully solder the pig tail.

9. When installing the rear housing, the brushes must be held away from the commutator. With the brush holder installed, push the brushes into the holder. Insert a stiff wire or small Allen wrench into the hole near the rear bearing and across the face of the brushes. After the alternator has been reassembled, remove the tool.

Inspection and Testing

DIODES

1. To check the positive rectifier, check for continuity between the positive diode plate and the diode terminals in both directions. Touch the positive probe of the ohm meter to the plate and the negative probe to each terminal, then switch the probes.

2. To check the negative rectifier, check for continuity between the negative diode plate and the diode terminals in both directions.

3. To check the sub diodes, touch the probes to each end of each diode, then switch the probes.

4. In each test, there should be continuity for each diode in one direction only. If there is continuity in both directions on none in either direction, the rectifier assembly must be replaced.

ROTOR

1. Check each coil for grounding. There should be infinite resistance between the metal core and each slip ring. The rotor cannot be repaired, faulty units must be replaced.

2. Check the physical condition of the slip rings. They should be smooth and clean, not scored or corroded. The outside diameter should be no less than 1.205 in. (30.6mm). Slip rings cannot be replaced.

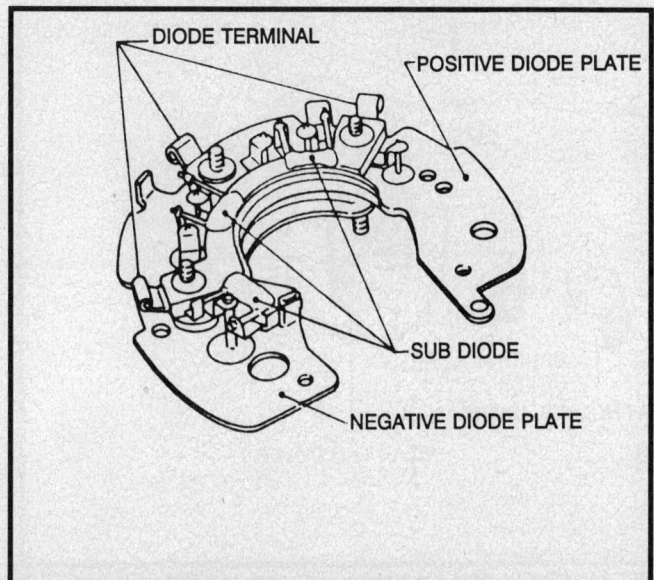

Testing the diodes on Hitachi rectifiers

3. Read the resistance across the slip rings. A reading of less than 2.8 ohms means a short, a reading of more than about 4 ohms means an open circuit. If the reading falls outside this range, the rotor cannot be repaired and must be replaced.

STATOR

1. Check the continuity between the coil leads that were unsoldered from the diode assembly. There should be less than 1 ohm resistance.

2. Check for coil grounding. There should be infinite resistance between each lead and the core. The stator cannot be repaired, faulty units must be replaced.

BRUSHES

The brushes must be more than 0.280 in. (7mm) total length. If the brush has worn to less than this, new brushes must be installed.

Lucas Alternators

Disassembly and Assembly

1. With the front pulley removed, remove the radio capacitor and rear cover. Under the cover is a surge protection diode which can be removed separately from the rectifier diode pack.

2. Tag the leads for the voltage regulator and remove the regulator and brush box assemblies.

3. Carefully unsolder the stator leads from the rectifier pack. Work quickly and use a heat sink to avoid damage to the diodes. Remove the screws to lift out the rectifier pack.

4. Remove the through bolts to split the housing. If necessary, use a mallet to help get the housings apart, do not pry. Mark the position of the stator in the housing and lift the stator out.

5. The rotor must be pressed out of the front bearing, then the bearing can be removed from the housing. To remove the rear bearing from the rotor, the slip rings must be removed first. Unsolder the rings and use a puller to remove the rings and the bearing.

To assemble:

6. Reassembly is basically the reverse of disassembly. Press on the bearings first, making sure to press the outer race of the front bearing, and the inner race of the rear bearing. When installing the slip rings, be careful not to let solder build up on the upper face of the inner ring. Check the rotor for continuity or short-to-ground after soldering the rings.

7. When assembling the housing, make sure the stator is installed with the matchmarks aligned. Tighten the through bolts evenly and spin the rotor by hand to make sure it moves smoothly.

8. When installing the rectifier pack, solder quickly and use a heat sink to minimize the heat on the diodes.

9. Install the remaining parts in order, making sure the volt-

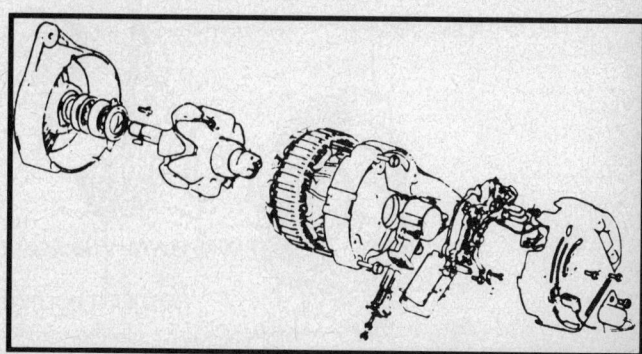

Typical Lucas alternator assembly with internal surge protector diode

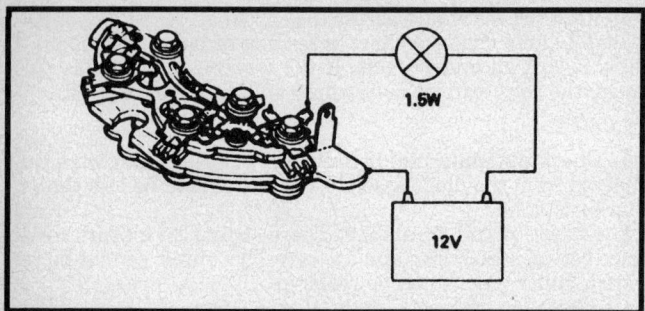

Lucas diode rectifier assembly testing can also be done with a 12 volt test light

age regulator and surge protector are properly connected. Turn the shaft by hand to make sure the brushes are properly seated.

Inspection and Testing

DIODES

1. To check the diodes, check for continuity between the diode plate and each diode terminal in both directions. Touch the positive probe of the ohm meter to the plate and the negative probe to each soldered diode terminal, then switch the probes.

2. In each test, there should be continuity for each diode in one direction only. If there is continuity in both directions on none in either direction, the rectifier assembly must be replaced.

ROTOR

1. Check each coil for grounding. There should be infinite resistance between the metal core and each slip ring. The rotor cannot be repaired, faulty units must be replaced.

2. Check the physical condition of the slip rings. They should be smooth and clean, not scored or corroded. If necessary, use extremely fine sand paper to clean the rings. Slip rings can be replaced, but be careful not to damage the insulator and do not let solder build up at the inner ring.

3. Read the resistance across the slip rings. A reading of less than about 2.5 ohms means a short, a reading of more than about 4 ohms means an open circuit. If the reading falls outside this range, the rotor cannot be repaired and must be replaced.

STATOR

1. Read the resistance between the stator body and each wire end. Anything less than infinite resistance means the coil is shorted to ground and the stator must be replaced.

2. Read the resistance between each of the wires. The reading should be no more than 1 ohm and the same for each coil. If there is any variation from one coil to the next, the stator must be replaced.

Nippondenso Alternators

Disassembly and Assembly

1. The voltage or IC regulator and rectifier assembly are under the rear end cover. Remove the 3 nuts on the back of the al-

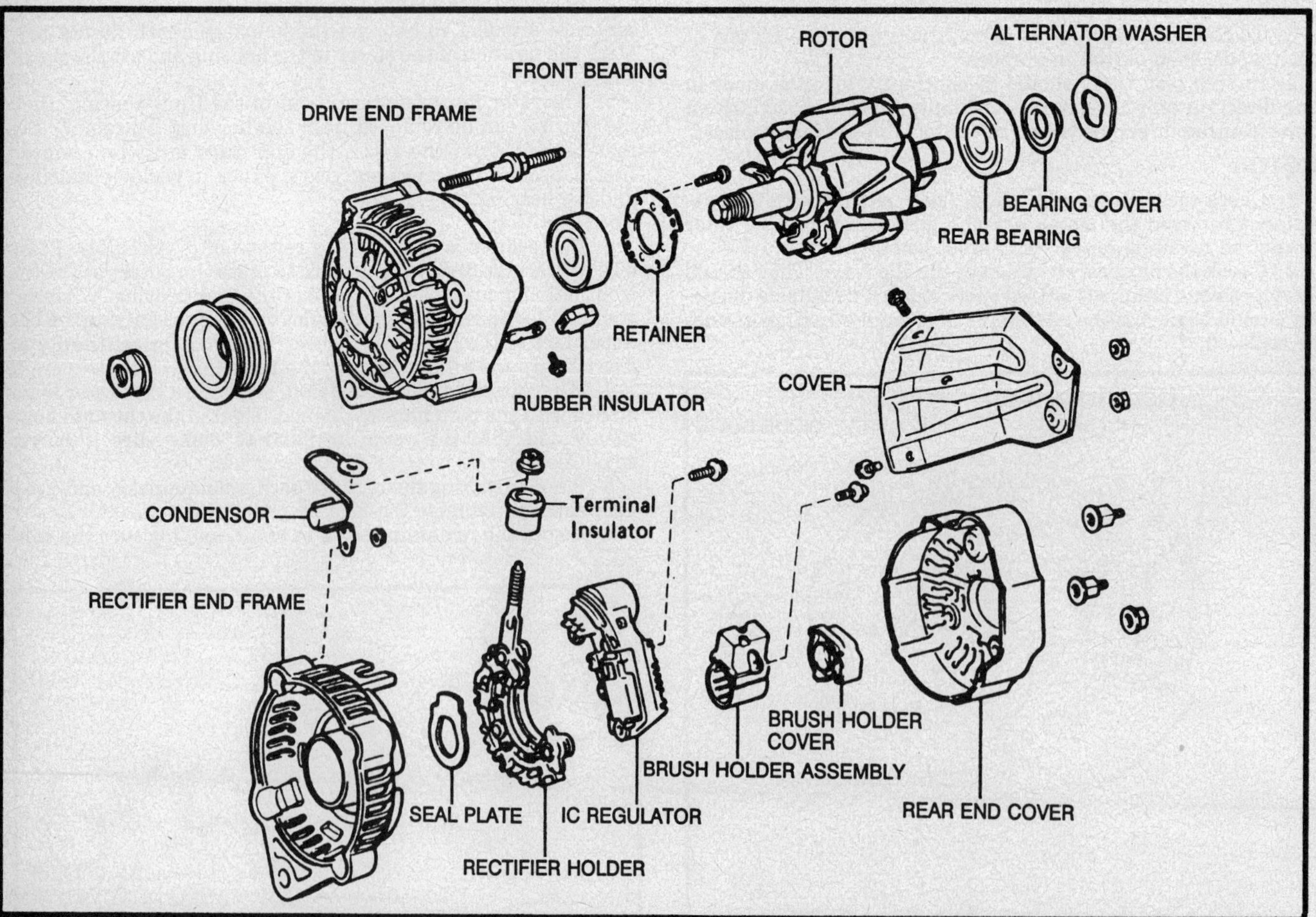

Typical Nippondenso alternator assembly: the rectifier and IC regulator can be removed and tested without disassembling the end frames

ternator to remove the cover and pull off the brush holder cover.

2. Remove the brush holder and IC regulator, then remove the rectifier holder and the 4 rubber insulators. If so equipped, lift off the seal plate.

3. The pulley is held in place with a 22mm nut. Hold the flats on the shaft with a socket and use a box wrench to remove the nut and pulley.

4. To remove the end frames, remove the 4 nuts from the rear of the alternator and use a puller to remove the rectifier end frame from the shaft. The stator is part of the end frame and should not be separated. The rotor should lift out of the drive end frame.

5. The front bearing must be pressed out of the drive end frame after the retainer has been removed. The rear bearing can be remove from the rotor shaft with a puller.

To assemble:

6. When installing new bearings in the drive end frame, be sure to press on the outer race. When installing bearings on the rotor, press on the inner race.

7. With the rotor, retainer and bearing cover installed, carefully fit the rectifier end frame making sure the stator connectors line up with the slots in the frame. Tap the rectifier end frame onto the rear rotor bearing with a plastic or wood hammer, then install the 4 nuts.

8. When installing the pulley, hold the shaft and torque the nut to 81 ft. lbs.

9. Slip the rubber insulators over the stator connectors and install the rectifier bridge, IC regulator, brush holder and cover. Check that the alternator turns freely before installing the remaining covers and terminal insulator.

Inspection and Testing

DIODES

1. To test the positive rectifier diodes, connect the meter probes across the B terminal and each rectifier terminal one at a time. Reverse the probes and repeat the test. At each terminal, there should be continuity in one direction only.

2. To test the negative rectifier diodes, connect the meter probes across each rectifier terminal and each negative terminal one at a time. Reverse the probes and repeat the test. There should be continuity in one direction only.

3. If there is continuity in both directions or no continuity in either direction, the entire rectifier assembly must be replaced.

ROTOR

1. Read the resistance between the unpainted portion of the rotor claws and the slip rings. There should be infinite resistance at each ring.

2. Check the physical condition of the slip rings. They should be smooth and clean, not scored or pitted. Fine sand paper can be used to clean the surface, or the rings can be machined. The minimum outside diameter of the slip rings is 0.504 in. (12.8mm). New slip rings are not available, if necessary, replace the rotor.

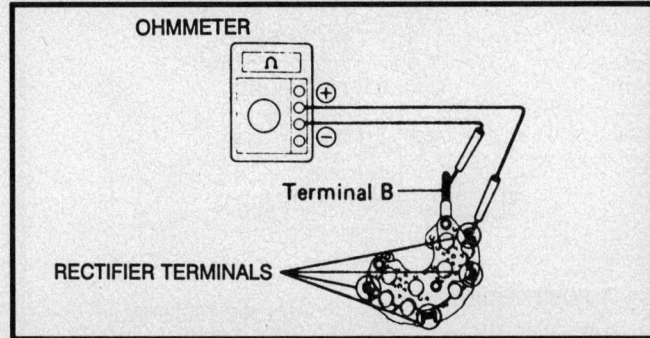

OHMMETER

Terminal B

RECTIFIER TERMINALS

Testing the positive diodes—Nippondenso rectifier

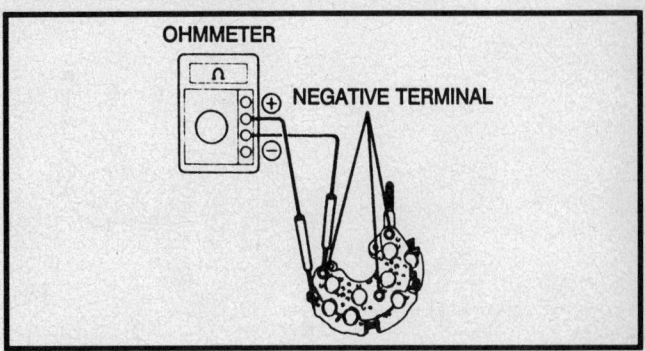

OHMMETER

NEGATIVE TERMINAL

Testing the negative diodes—Nippondenso rectifier

3. Read the resistance across the slip rings. A reading of less than 2.8 ohms means a short, a reading of more than about 4 ohms means an open circuit. If the reading falls outside this range, the rotor cannot be repaired and must be replaced.

STATOR

1. Read the resistance between the end frame and each connector. Anything less than infinite resistance means the coil is shorted to ground and the stator must be replaced.

2. Read the resistance between each of the connectors. The reading should be less than 1 ohm and the same for each coil. The stator cannot be repaired, if necessary, replace the end frame.

BRUSHES

It is easiest to measure the brushes with a caliper, check only the exposed length. The length of new brushes is 0.413 in. (10.5mm). If the brushes are less than 0.059 in. (1.5mm), they must be replaced. On some models, new brushes are available separately. On others it may be necessary to replace the holder assembly.

Mitsubishi Alternators

Disassembly and Assembly

1. The front and rear housing halves can be separated without removing the pulley. With the through bolts removed and the unit sitting on the pulley, carefully pry the stator away from the front housing. Be careful not to insert the pry tools too deeply, or the stator will be damaged. If it is difficult to separate the stator from the housing, it may be necessary to heat the rear housing at the rear bearing. Use a soldering iron, not a heat gun or flame. Too much heat will damage the diodes.

2. With the rotor still in the front housing, the rear bearing can be removed with a puller

3. With the housings separated, the pulley can be removed by holding the rotor in a soft jaw vice. This must be done to remove the front bearing.

4. To remove the rectifier and voltage regulator/brush holder as an assembly, the 3 wires connecting the rectifier bridge to the stator must be unsoldered at the bridge assembly. Work quickly and use only as much heat as needed to avoid damaging the diodes.

5. To remove the voltage regulator/brush holder, 2 solder joints must be melted at the rectifier assembly.

To assemble:

6. When pressing on a new bearing, make sure to press only on the inner race.

7. When soldering the stator or voltage regulator/brush holder connections to the rectifier bridge, apply the heat quickly and use only as much heat as needed.

8. The brushes in the voltage regulator have the Mitsubishi logo stamped into the side. If the brush has worn down to the

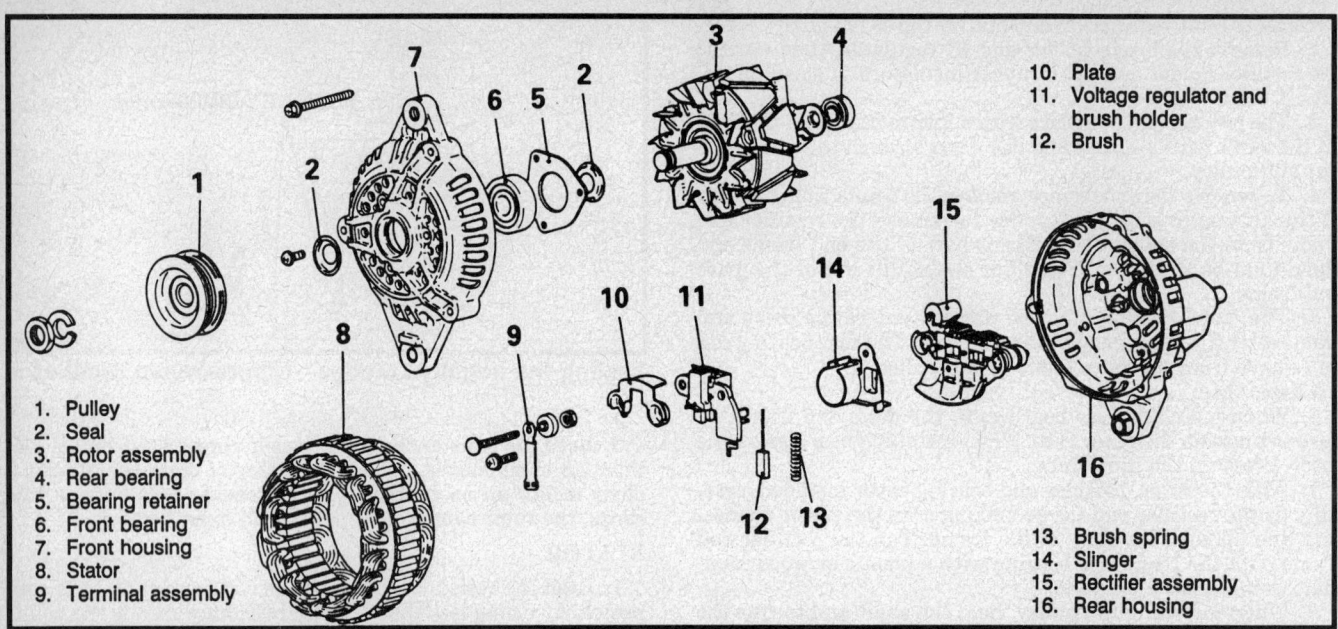

1. Pulley
2. Seal
3. Rotor assembly
4. Rear bearing
5. Bearing retainer
6. Front bearing
7. Front housing
8. Stator
9. Terminal assembly
10. Plate
11. Voltage regulator and brush holder
12. Brush
13. Brush spring
14. Slinger
15. Rectifier assembly
16. Rear housing

Typical Mitsubishi alternator

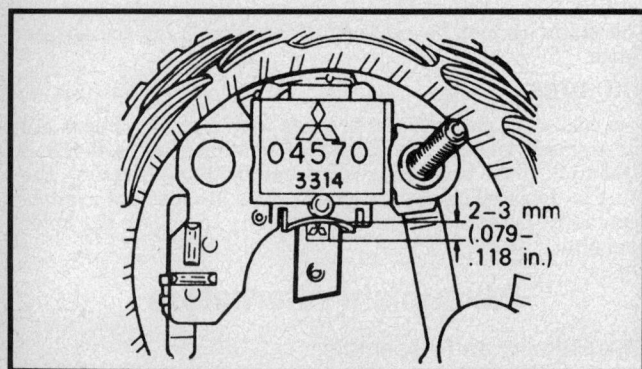

2-3 mm (.079 – .118 in.)

On Mitsubishi alternators, hold the new brush in position to make the solder joint

stamping, new brushes must be installed. Unsolder the pig tail to remove the old brush and spring.

9. Insert the spring and new brush and hold the brush with no more than 0.118 in. (3mm) of the logo showing, then carefully solder the pig tail.

10. When installing the rear housing, the brushes must be lifted up. Insert a stiff wire or small Allen wrench into the hole near the rear bearing and through the hole in the brushes. After the alternator has been reassembled, remove the tool.

Inspection and Testing

DIODES

1. To check the positive rectifier, check for continuity between the positive diode plate and the diode terminals in both directions. Touch the positive probe of the ohm meter to the plate and the negative probe to each terminal, then switch the probes.

2. To check the negative rectifier, check for continuity between the negative diode plate and the diode terminals in both directions.

3. To check the diode trio, or sub diodes, touch the probes to each end of each diode, then switch the probes.

4. In each test, there should be continuity for each diode in one direction only. If there is continuity in both directions on none in either direction, the rectifier assembly must be replaced.

ROTOR

1. Check each coil for grounding. There should be infinite resistance between the metal core and each slip ring. The rotor cannot be repaired, faulty units must be replaced.

2. Check the physical condition of the slip rings. They should be smooth and clean, not grooved, pitted or corroded. The outside diameter should be no less than 0.875 in. (22.2mm). Slip rings cannot be reconditioned or replaced separately.

3. Read the resistance across the slip rings. A reading of less than 2.8 ohms means a short, a reading of more than about 4 ohms means an open circuit. If the reading falls outside this range, the rotor cannot be repaired and must be replaced.

STATOR

1. Check the continuity between the coil leads that were unsoldered from the diode assembly. There should be less than 1 ohm resistance.

2. Check for coil grounding. There should be infinite resistance between the leads and the core. The stator cannot be repaired, faulty units must be replaced.

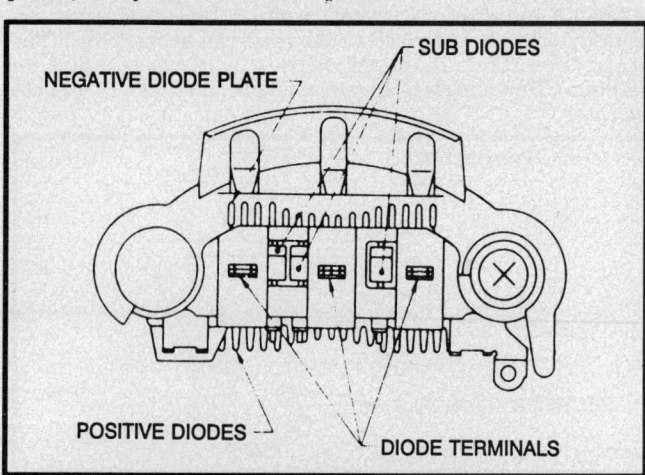

SUB DIODES

NEGATIVE DIODE PLATE

POSITIVE DIODES

DIODE TERMINALS

Testing the diodes on Mitsubishi rectifiers

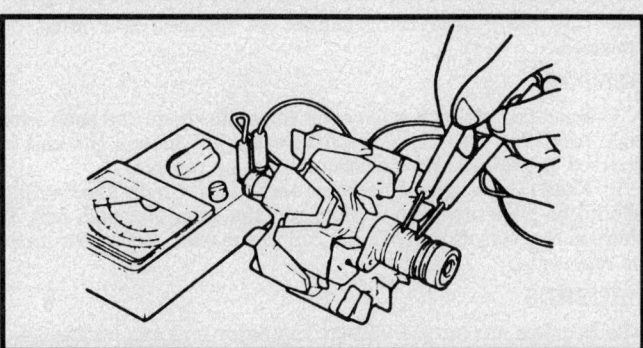

Checking a rotor for correct resistance, there should be infinite resistance between the core and the slip rings

BRUSHES

The brushes in the voltage regulator have the Mitsubishi logo stamped into the side. If the brush has worn down to the stamping, or if the total length is less than 0.310in. (8mm), new brushes must be installed.

Paris-Rhone Alternators

Disassembly and Assembly

1. Remove the pulley and fan from the front of the shaft. Make a matchmark on the front and rear halves of the housing to aid in reassembly.

2. On the rear of the housing, disconnect the output wire and pry off the rear cover. Disconnect the voltage regulator ground wire and remove the screws and regulator.

3. To remove the diode assemblies, remove the screws and nuts and unsolder the connections. Use a heat sink when unsoldering the connections and work quickly to avoid overheating damage to the diodes.

4. To split the housing, remove the through bolts and lift the front housing away from the rotor. If this is difficult, avoid prying the housing at the stator.

5. The rotor and stator can now be lifted out.

To assemble:

6. Mount the rectifier bridge and stator to the rear housing, carefully solder the connections, using a heat sink to avoid overheating the diodes. Install the bridge mounting screws and nuts.

7. Install the rotor and assemble the housing, making sure the matchmarks are aligned. Install the voltage regulator and slowly spin the rotor to make sure the brushes seat properly.

8. Install the fan and pulley and the rear cover, then reconnect the output wire.

Inspection and Testing
DIODES

1. To test the positive diodes, touch one probe to the B+ terminal and the other probe to each diode. Reverse the probes and repeat the test.

2. To test the negative diodes, touch one probe to the B- ter-

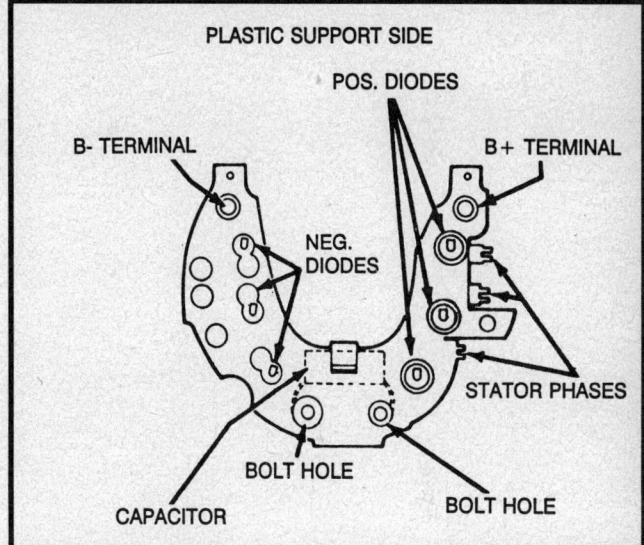

Paris-Rhone rectifier assembly: each diode can be check separately

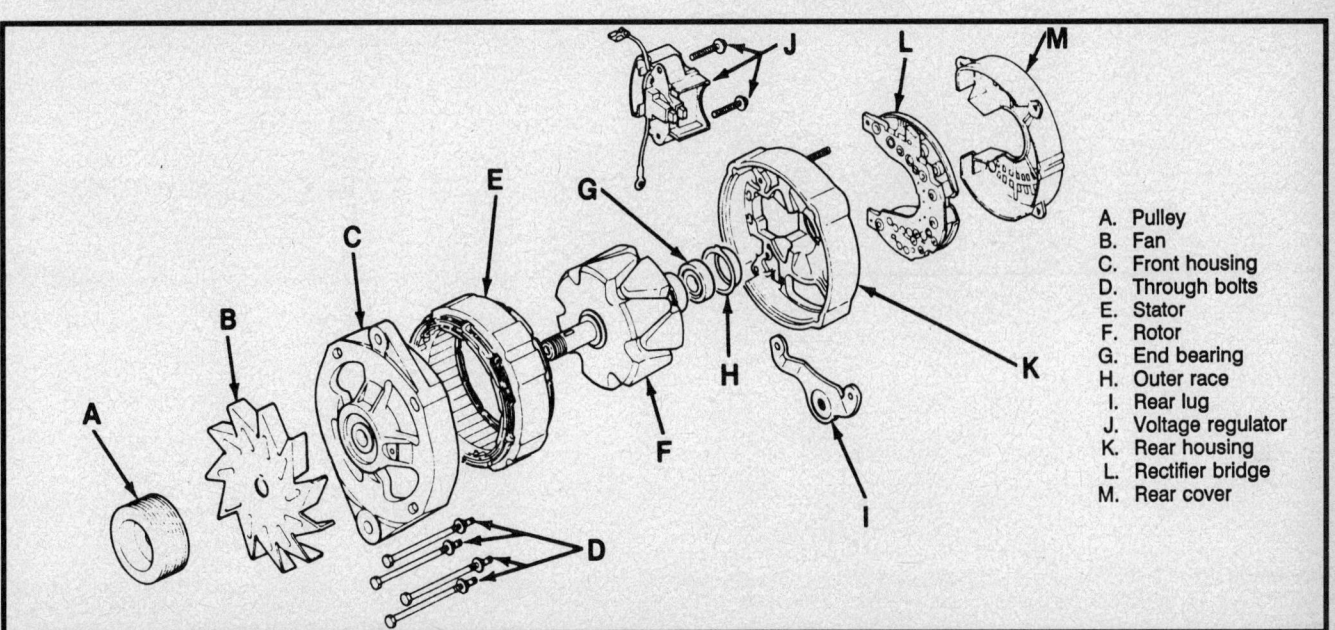

A. Pulley
B. Fan
C. Front housing
D. Through bolts
E. Stator
F. Rotor
G. End bearing
H. Outer race
I. Rear lug
J. Voltage regulator
K. Rear housing
L. Rectifier bridge
M. Rear cover

Typical Paris-Rhone alternator: the regulator and diodes can be removed without splitting the housing

27–9

minal and the other probe to each diode. Reverse the probes and repeat the test.

3. In each test there will be 6 readings. Each diode in a triplet should read exactly the same as the others. If there is any deviation, the entire bridge assembly should be replaced.

ROTOR

1. Check each coil for grounding. There should be infinite resistance between the shaft and each slip ring. The rotor cannot be repaired, faulty units must be replaced.

2. Check the physical condition of the slip rings. They should be smooth and clean, not scored or corroded. The rings can be cleaned with fine sand paper, but machining is not recommended.

3. Read the resistance across the slip rings. A reading of less than about 2.7 ohms means a short, a reading of more than about 3.5 ohms means an open circuit. If the reading falls outside this range, the rotor cannot be repaired and must be replaced.

STATOR

1. Read the resistance between the stator body and each wire end. Anything less than infinite resistance means the coil is shorted to ground and the stator must be replaced.

2. Read the resistance between each of the wires. The reading should be no more than 1 ohm and the same for each coil. If there is any variation from one coil to the next, the stator must be replaced.

BRUSHES

The brushes are on the voltage regulator and can be accessed without disassembling the alternator. Check on parts availability before removing the brushes from the regulator. Brushes cannot be removed separately on some models.

HYDRAULIC BRAKE SYSTEM SERVICE

Braking systems have changed dramatically over the last few years, especially on high performance cars. All systems still operate on hydraulic pressure transmitted by a non-compressable fluid, but now there is more than one type of fluid in service. Most manufacturers now offer Anti-lock Braking Systems (ABS) in at least part of their model align, and service for these systems also includes electronic testing procedures. On most ABS systems, the master cylinder has been augmented or replaced with a hydraulic unit that cannot be repaired in the field, only replaced. System pressures on the vehicle can be quite high, up to 2600 psi, so it is extremely important to follow all safety precautions.

This section describes repair and service procedures done with the component already removed from the vehicle. A clean work area is absolutely essential, and some jobs cannot be done properly without compressed air. Using the correct brake fluid as an assembly lube is equally important. In most cases, wheel cylinder and master cylinder kits are available, but rebuilding these items is only recommended if the cylinder bore is already completely free of corrosion and distortion. Resurfacing the cylinder bore will make it too large for the parts available and is therefore not a part of the repair procedure. When rebuilding calipers, light corrosion or deposits in the bore can be removed, but the piston and bore cannot be resurfaced. In general, if a metal part slides against a rubber part, the size or coated surface of the metal part must remain the same or a positive seal will not be possible.

ACURA

Master Cylinder Service

EXCEPT ANTI-LOCK BRAKES

Disassembly and Assembly

1. Use either DOT 3 or DOT 4 brake fluid for cleaning and assembly.
2. With the cylinder drained and clamped in a soft jaw vice, remove the reservoir cap and filter, then remove the screws holding the reservoir to the cylinder.
3. Using a blunt tool such as a hammer handle, push the piston in just enough to take up the spring tension and remove the snapring.
4. Remove the stop bolt from the side of the cylinder and remove both the secondary and primary piston assemblies. Be careful to not damage the bore when removing the primary piston.

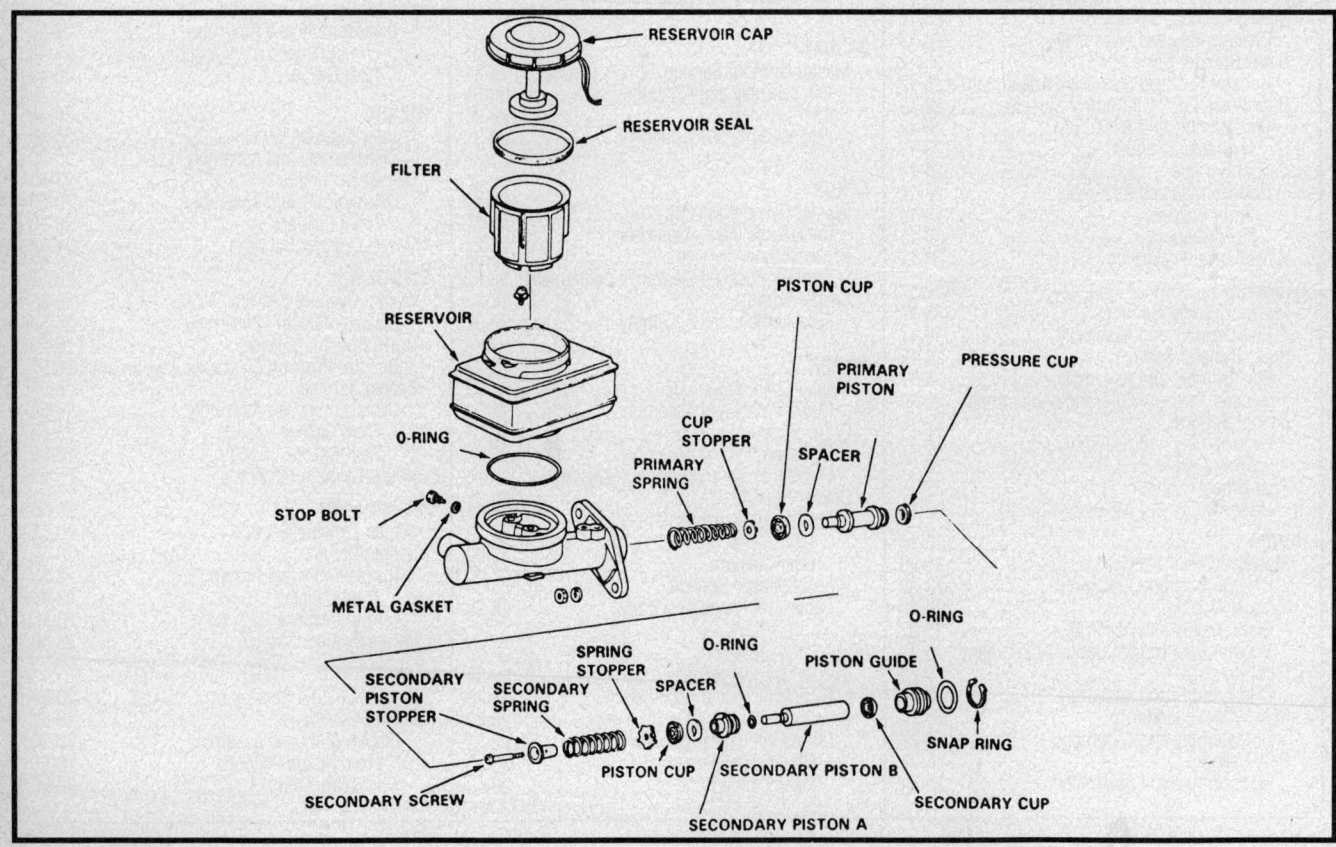

Acura master cylinder without anti lock brakes

CAUTION

When using compressed air to remove a piston, the piston could fly out like a projectile and brake fluid will be sprayed. Personal injury could result. Secure a block of wood in front of the bore, cover the bore with a shop rag and apply pressure gradually. Never use more pressure than needed.

5. Use only clean brake fluid or a brake parts cleaner to clean the master cylinder and carefuly examine the bore. If there is any corrosion or distortion, do not attempt to rebuild the cylinder, replace the entire assembly.

To assemble:

6. When inserting the new pistons, lubricate all parts with clean brake fluid and rotate the pistons while gently pushing them into the bore. Lubricate the inside of the secondary piston guide with a light silicone grease.

7. With both pistons installed, push in on the secondary piston while installing the stop bolt and new gasket. Torque the bolt to 6 ft. lbs.

8. Hold the secondary piston in to install the snapring.

9. Make sure the reservoir and its' sealing surfaces are clean and dry, then install the reservoir with a new O-ring. The cylinder is now ready for installation and testing on the vehicle.

ANTI-LOCK BRAKES

Disassembly and Assembly

1. Use either DOT 3 or DOT 4 brake fluid for cleaning and assembly.

2. With the cylinder drained and clamped in a soft jaw vice, remove the reservoir cap and filter, then remove the screws holding the reservoir to the cylinder.

3. Using a blunt tool such as a hammer handle, push the piston in just enough to take up the spring tension and remove the snapring.

4. Remove the stop bolt from the side of the cylinder and remove both the secondary and primary piston assemblies. Be careful to not damage the bore when removing the primary piston.

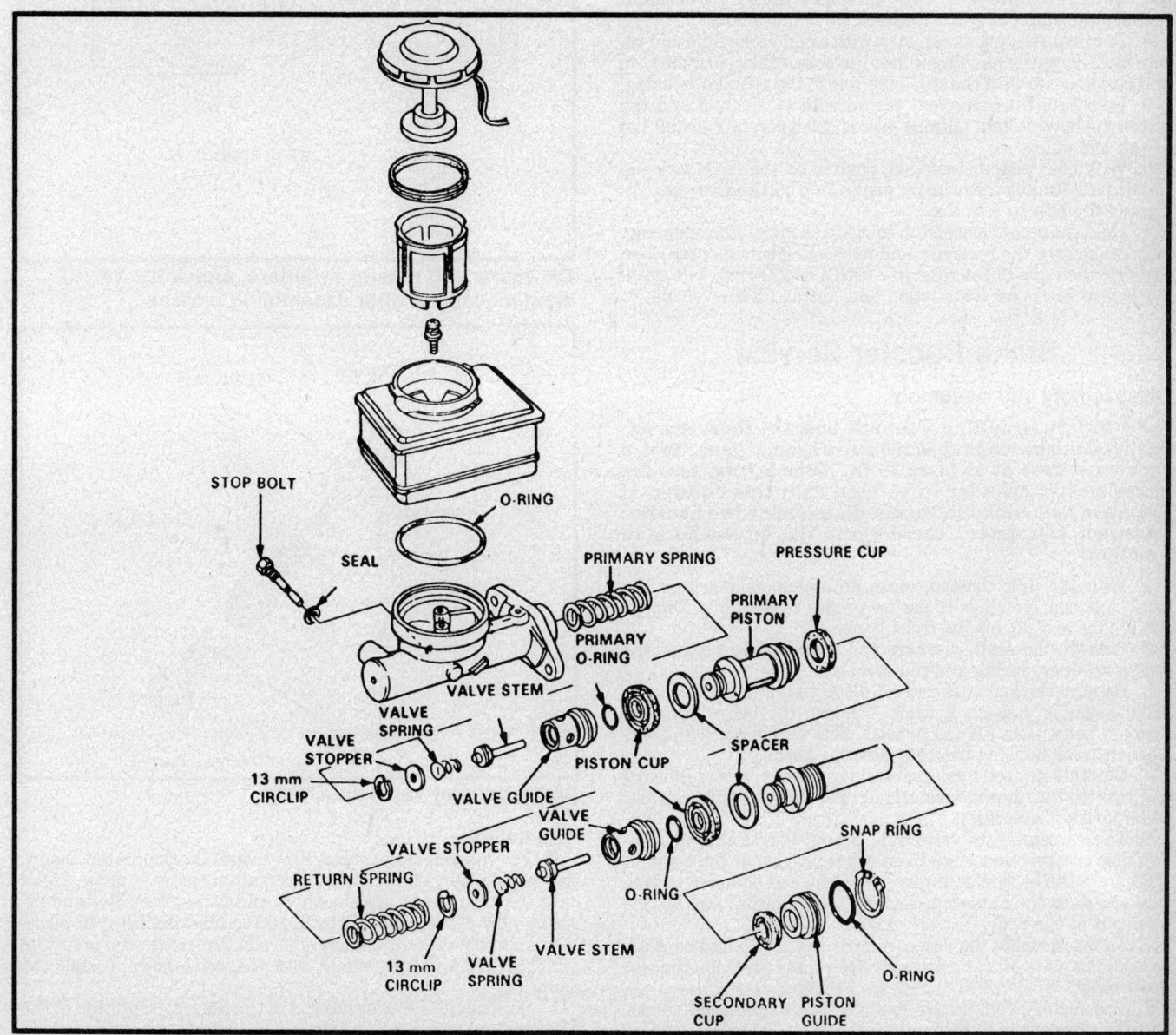

Acura master cylinder with anti lock brake system

CAUTION

When using compressed air to remove a piston, the piston could fly out like a projectile and brake fluid will be sprayed. Personal injury could result. Point the bore at a block of wood up against a wall, cover the bore with a shop rag and apply pressure gradually. Use caution and be prepaired.

5. Use only clean brake fluid or a brake parts cleaner to clean the master cylinder and carefully examine the bore. If there is any corrosion or distortion, do not attempt to rebuild the cylinder, replace the entire assembly.

To assemble:

6. When reassembling the pistons, there is a special tool which should be used for installing the cups, Acura tool 07965-5790300. This is a cone shaped cup guide, and equivalent tools are available. Lubricate the guide with brake fluid and install the cups, O-rings and spacers onto the pistons.

7. Build up each valve assembly using new valve stems and install them onto the pistons. On the primary piston, insert a small tool into the stop bolt slot and gently move the valve stem to check that it moves smoothly. On the secondary piston, gently move the stop pin guide to check valve movement.

8. Lubricate the primary piston with clean brake fluid and rotate it while gently pushing it into the bore. Make sure the stop bolt slot lines up with the stop bolt hole in the cylinder housing.

9. Lubricate the secondary piston with clean fluid and the piston guide with light silicone grease, then carefully install the piston and guide.

10. With both pistons installed, push in on the secondary piston while installing the primary piston stop bolt and new gasket. Torque the bolt to 6 ft. lbs.

11. Hold the secondary piston in again to install the snapring.

12. Make sure the reservoir and its' sealing surfaces are clean and dry, then install the reservoir with a new O-ring. The cylinder is now ready for installation and testing on the vehicle.

Brake Booster Service

Disassembly and Assembly

Note: Before installing a rebuilt booster, there are adjustments to be made that require a special gauge tool, a vacuum source of at least 20 in. (500mm) Hg, and the brake master cylinder to be used with this booster. If these are not available, do not disassemble the booster. Incorrect adjustment could cause the brakes to malfunction.

1. With the unit cleaned, make an alignment mark on the front and rear housings to assure proper reassembly. Remove the E-clips and lift off the front housing.

2. Remove the seals, washers and snaprings to remove the spring retainer, spring and rod stopper.

3. Remove the locknuts and set plate, then remove the valve body assembly and set it aside. Remove the boots from the through bolts, then lift the booster plate and diaphragm away from the rear housing before seperating them.

4. Carefully pry the bushing retainer out of the rear housing to access the bushing and piston seal. The through bolts can also be removed, if necessary.

5. To disassemble the valve body, lift out the output rod, reaction disc and reaction plate from the front side of the body.

6. From the back side, remove the yoke and adjuster nuts to gain access to the snapring. Remove the snapring and lift the valve out of the body.

7. To disassemble the valve, remove the E-clip and carefully slide all the parts off the push rod. Keep these parts in order for reassembly.

8. The factory rebuild kit includes the diaphragm, filters, snaprings and parts to recondition the valve. Be sure to use all the parts in the kit, especially the clips and snaprings.

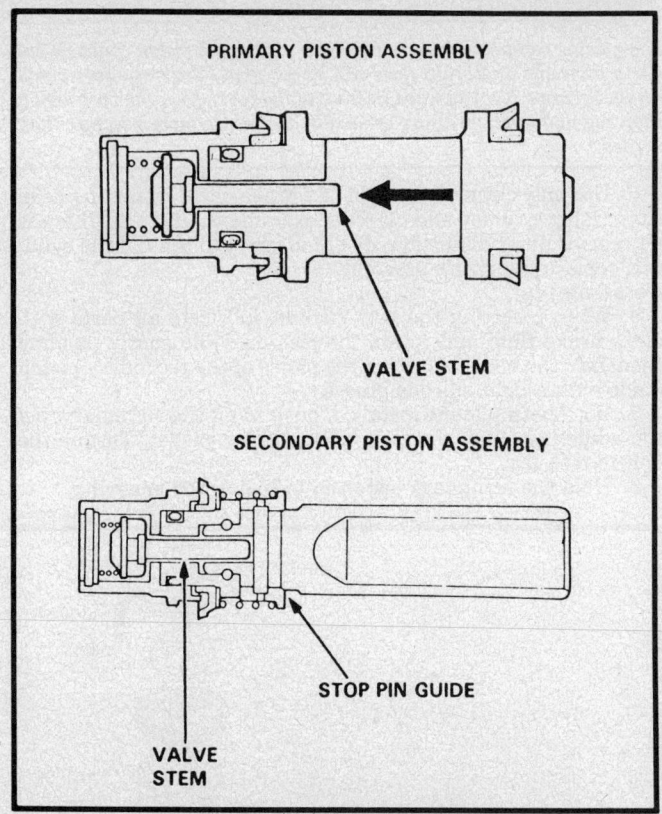

On Acura ABS master cylinders, check the valve stem movement after assembling pistons

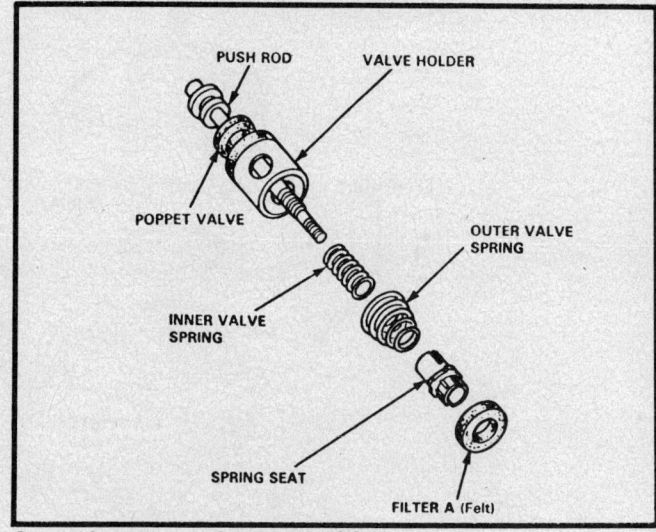

Acura booster valve assembly

To assemble:

9. To reassemble the valve, first install the poppet valve onto the valve holder, then install the remaining parts in order. Make sure the spring seat has the short end facing the filter and install a new E-clip onto the push rod to hold the filter in place.

10. Lubricate the valve body with silicone grease and press the pushrod and valve assembly into the valve body. Install the snapring.

11. Slip the filter B over the end of the push rod and thread the adjuster and star locknut onto the rod but do not tighten them yet. Do not install the yoke yet.

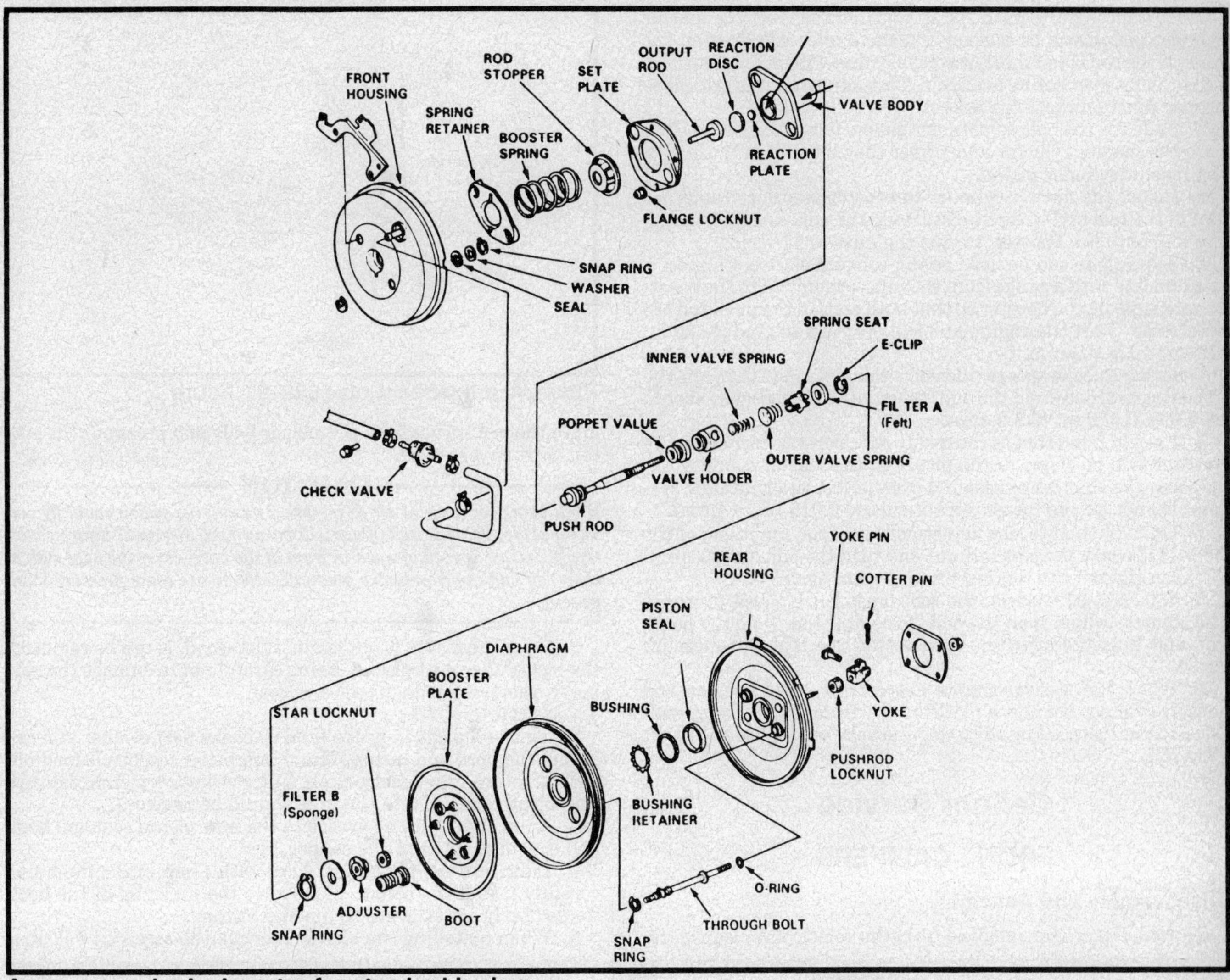

FRONT HOUSING
ROD STOPPER
SET PLATE
OUTPUT ROD
REACTION DISC
VALVE BODY
SPRING RETAINER
BOOSTER SPRING
REACTION PLATE
FLANGE LOCKNUT
SNAP RING
WASHER
SEAL
SPRING SEAT
E-CLIP
INNER VALVE SPRING
FIL TER A (Felt)
POPPET VALUE
OUTER VALVE SPRING
VALVE HOLDER
CHECK VALVE
PUSH ROD
REAR HOUSING
YOKE PIN
COTTER PIN
PISTON SEAL
DIAPHRAGM
BOOSTER PLATE
BUSHING
YOKE
STAR LOCKNUT
PUSHROD LOCKNUT
FILTER B (Sponge)
BUSHING RETAINER
SNAP RING
ADJUSTER
BOOT
O-RING
SNAP RING
THROUGH BOLT

Acura power brake booster for standard brakes

12. On the rear housing, lube the piston seal with silicone grease and install the seal and bushing, with the lip of the seal facing away from the bushing.

13. Set the retainer in place and carefully drive it in evenly with a socket till the retainer is recessed no more than ¼ inch (6mm). Driving the retainer too far will distort the seal.

14. Attach the diaphragm to the booster plate. When installing the plate to the rear housing, be sure to align the plate slot with the housing tab. Slip the new boots onto the through bolts.

15. Lubricate the outer surface of the valve body with the silicone grease and slide the assembly through the seal on the rear housing. Lightly grease the reaction plate and disc and the output rod and install them into the valve body bore.

16. Install the set plate that holds the valve body in place and torque the locknuts to 4 ft. lbs.

17. Install the rod stopper, booster spring, spring retainer and snaprings.

18. Install the washers and seals over the snaprings and press the front housing onto the rear housing with the matchmark aligned. Install new E-clips to hold the housings together. If the valve body was disassembled, adjust the pushrod clearance.

Booster Pushrod Clearance Adjustment

This procedure is for adjusting the static clearance between the push rod on the output end of the booster and the piston on the

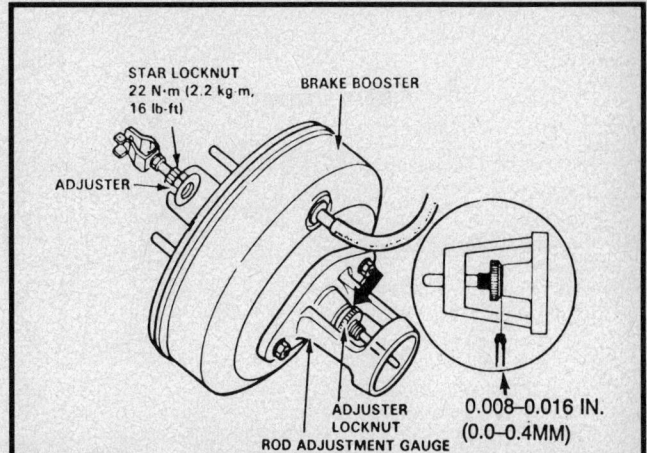

STAR LOCKNUT
22 N·m (2.2 kg·m, 16 lb·ft)
BRAKE BOOSTER
ADJUSTER
ADJUSTER LOCKNUT
ROD ADJUSTMENT GAUGE
0.008–0.016 IN. (0.0–0.4MM)

Use a feeler gauge to check booster pushrod-to-adjuster locknut clearance on Acura and Honda

master cylinder. This needs to be done any time a booster or master cylinder is changed or rebuilt. With the booster installed and the engine running, the diaphragm is pulled part way towards the front housing at all times, moving the push rod the same distance. If the push rod is adjusted too long, the master cylinder piston will be pushed and the brakes will drag all the time. If the rod is too short, the pedal travel will be very long and full braking may not be available. This adjustment is critical to proper functioning of the brakes.

1. Slide the rod bolt adjustment gauge, tool 07JAG-SD40100, onto the master cylinder and adjust the bolt so it is flush with the master cylinder piston.

2. Install the master cylinder-to-booster seal onto the other end of the tool and without disturbing the adjuster bolt, install the tool onto the booster, torque the nuts to 11 ft. lbs.

3. The engine can be used as the vacuum source. Connect a vacuum line with a gauge from the intake manifold to the booster, and support the booster so that both ends of the push rod are accessible. Start the engine and run it at idle to produce 20 in. (500mm) Hg vacuum.

4. Using a feeler gauge, measure the clearance between the adjusting tool body and the adjusting nut. The clearance should be 0.008–0.016 in. (0.2-0.4mm).

5. Keep in mind that as the measured clearance increases, the pushrod will be closer to the piston in the master cylinder, increasing the chances of residual pressure in the hydraulic system. Do not let the measurement exceed 0.016 in. (0.4mm).

6. On 1987 models, the adjustment is at the input end of the booster. Loosen the star locknut and turn the adjuster as needed, then tighten the locknut and measure again.

7. On 1988–91 models, the tool must be removed to access the adjuster which is on the end of the pushrod. Hold the pushrod and turn the adjuster, then install the tool and measure again.

8. When the measurements are correct, that booster and master cylinder are now a matched set. Pedal height is set with the booster installed by adjusting the yoke on the booster input pushrod.

Caliper Service

FRONT CALIPERS

Disassembly and Assembly

1. With the caliper removed from the vehicle and cleaned, re-

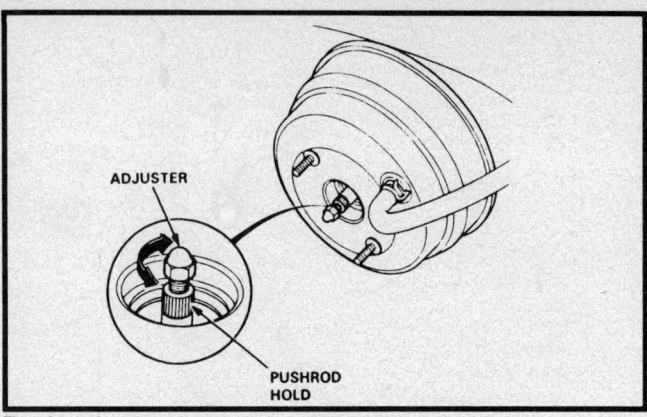

Pushrod adjustment on 1988–91 Acura

move the pad spring from the caliper body and press out the piston with air pressure.

CAUTION
When using compressed air to remove a piston, the piston could fly out like a projectile and brake fluid will be sprayed. Personal injury could result. Secure a block of wood in front of the bore, cover the bore with a shop rag and apply pressure gradually. Never use more pressure than needed.

2. Once the piston is out against the wood, it can be removed the rest of the way by hand. Being careful not to damage the cylinder, remove the dust boot and seal.

To assemble:

3. Clean all parts in brake fluid or brake part cleaner and examine the bore and piston. Minor corrosion can be cleaned off with steel wool or emery cloth, but scoring or piston damage cannot be repaired and the unit should be replaced.

4. Apply light silicone grease to the new piston seal and boot and install them onto the caliper.

5. Lubricate the piston and bore with clean brake fluid and carefully install the piston. Make sure the inner lip of the boot fits properly into the groove on the piston.

6. When installing the bleeder, torque the screw to 6 ft. lbs.

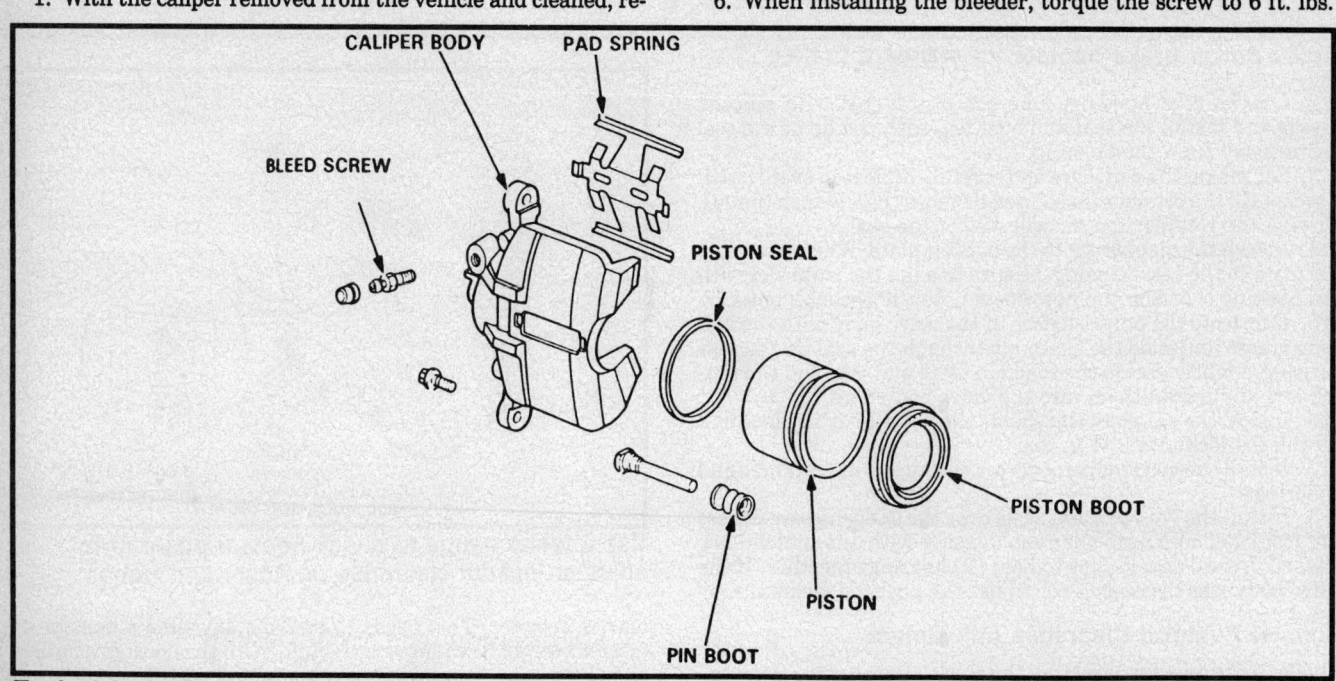

Typical Acura front caliper assembly

REAR CALIPER

Disassembly and Assembly

Two special tools are required; 07GAE-SD40100 spring compressor and on 1987–88 models, 07GAE-SD40200 guide tool. These are used for removing and installing the adjuster mechanism spring and its' upper seat inside the caliper.

1. With the caliper removed and cleaned, rotate the piston to remove the piston and boot. Do not press the piston out with air.

2. From the inside of the piston, remove the snapring and carefully lift out all the parts, keeping them in order for reassembly.

3. Remove the piston seal from inside the bore, being careful not to damage the bore.

4. Install spring compressor 07GAE-SD40100 or equivalent and press the spring down to unload the snapring. Then remove the snapring and lift out the parts.

5. Remove the next snapring and lift the parts out, keeping them in order for reassembly.

6. On the side of the caliper, the parking brake cam and lever assembly can now be removed and disassembled for cleaning. Don't forget to remove the cam boot to gain access to the needle bearing.

To assemble:

7. Clean all parts in brake fluid or brake part cleaner and examine the bore, piston, bearing and cam. Minor corrosion can be cleaned off with steel wool or emery cloth, but scoring or piston damage cannot be repaired and the entire assembly should be replaced.

8. When reinstalling the cam, use an assembly lube such as moly grease to pack the needle bearings and cam boot. Install the boot first, then lube the cam and install it with the slot facing towards the cylinder bore.

9. Install the parking brake lever, lockwasher and nut onto the cam, then install the return spring. Torque the nut to 20 ft. lbs.

10. Support the caliper with the bore facing up and install the small rod or pin into the slot in the cam. The grease should help hold it in place.

11. On 1987–88 models, with a new O-ring on the pushrod, install the pushrod and key plate so that the plate fits on the square part of the pushrod and the hole in the plate lines up with the hole in the cylinder. Then install the snapring.

12. On 1989–91 models, install the sleeve piston so the hole in the bottom lines up with the pin in the cam and the 2 pins on the piston fit in the holes in the caliper.

13. On 1987–88 models, slide the spring seat, spring and upper cover onto the pushrod and place the guide tool onto the cover. Align the slit in the guide tool with the groove in the cover.

14. On 1989–91 models, install a new cup onto the adjusting bolt. Lightly lube the bearing and install the bearing, spacer, spring and cover onto the bolt and set the assembly into the caliper.

15. Install the spring compressor and press the spring all the way down. On 1987–88 models the guide tool should also move down to keep the spring and cover straight in the bore.

16. With the spring compressed, remove the guide tool and see that the spring cover is down far enough so the snapring can be installed.

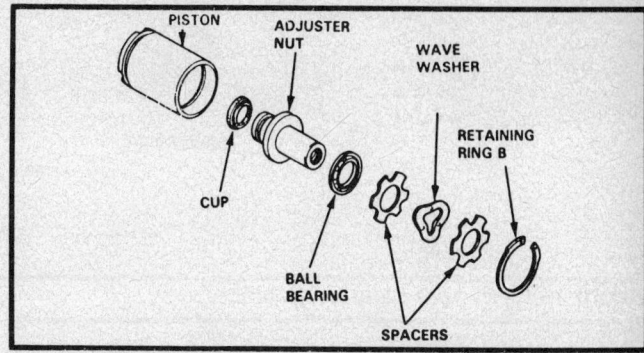

Acura 1987–88 rear caliper piston assembly

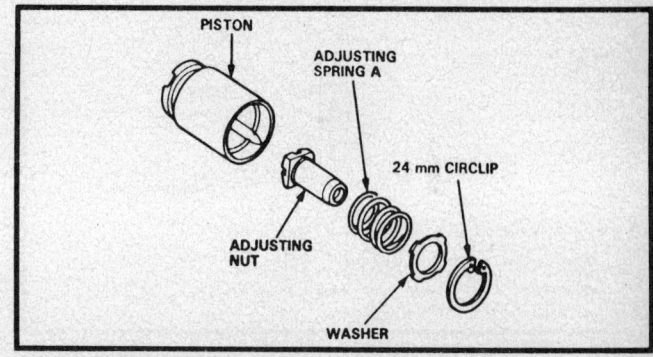

Acura 1989–91 rear caliper piston assembly

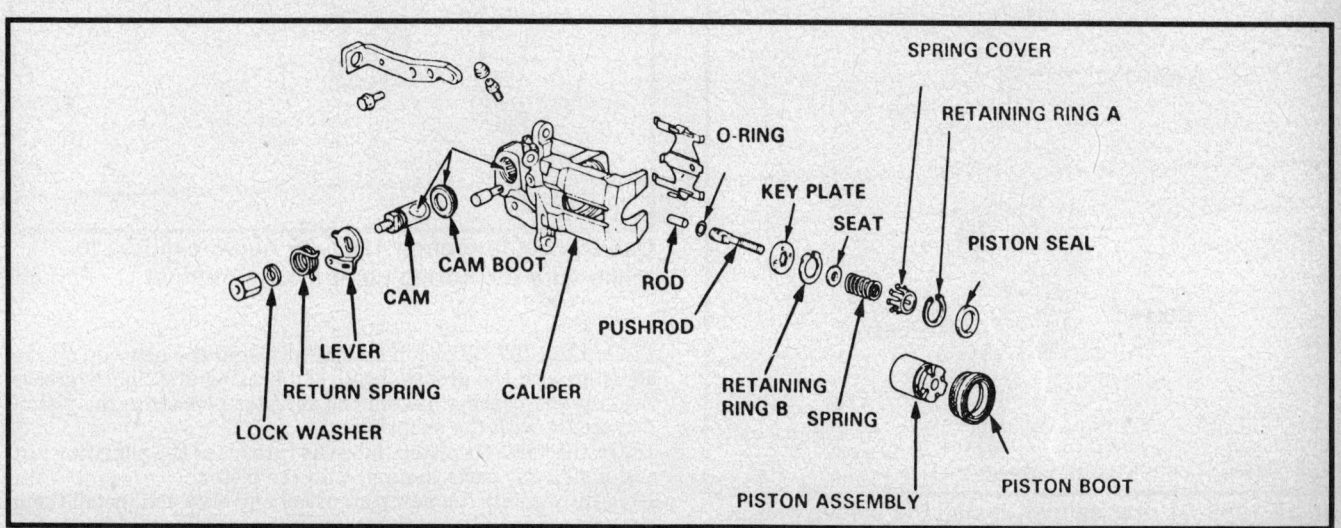

Acura 1987–88 rear caliper assembly

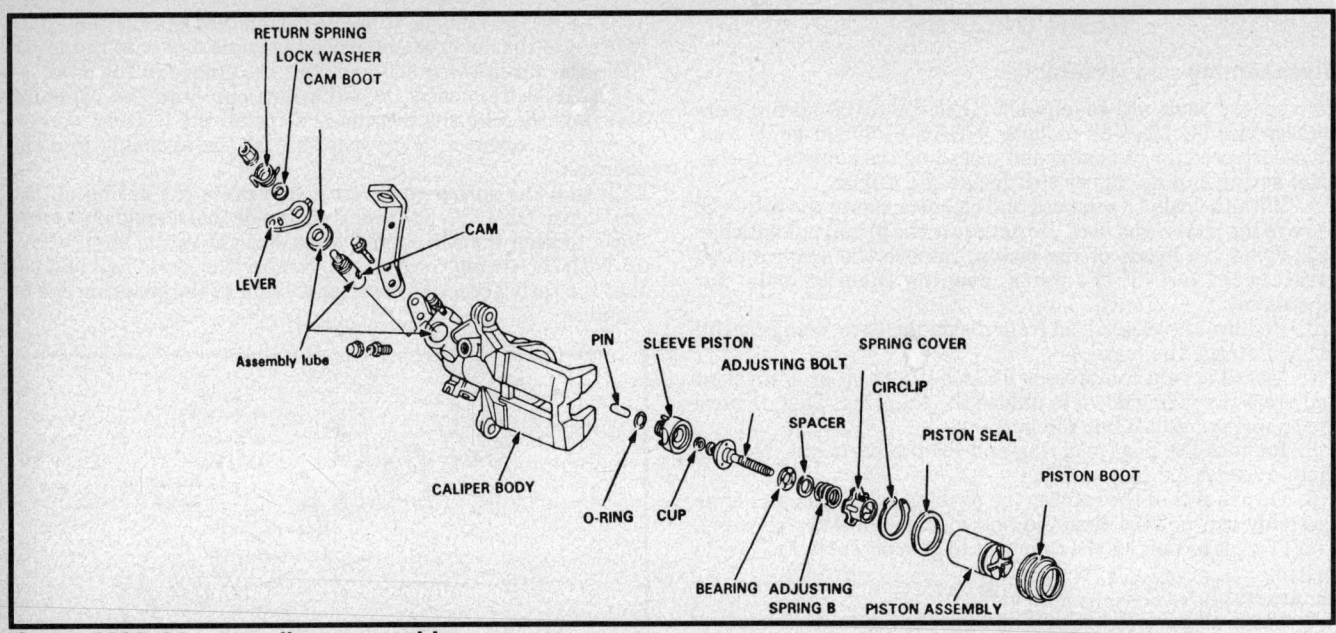

Acura 1989–91 rear caliper assembly

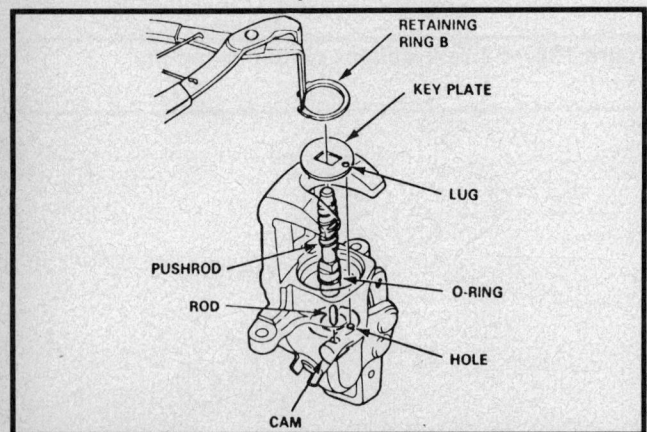

Acura 1987–88 rear caliper, install the key plate so the holes align

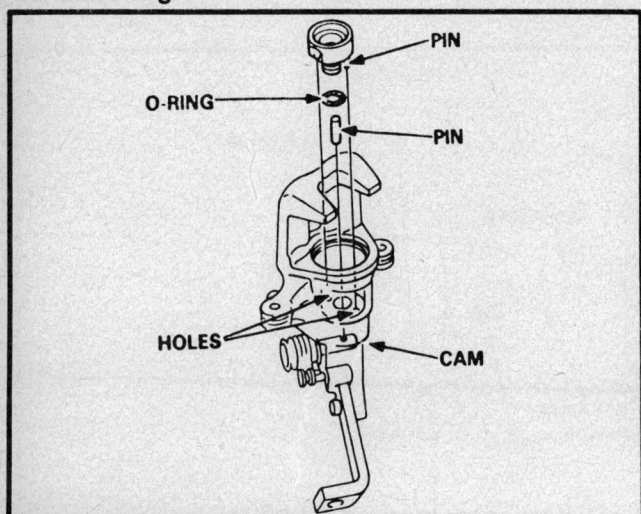

Acura 1989–91 rear caliper, install the sleeve piston so the pins align with the holes

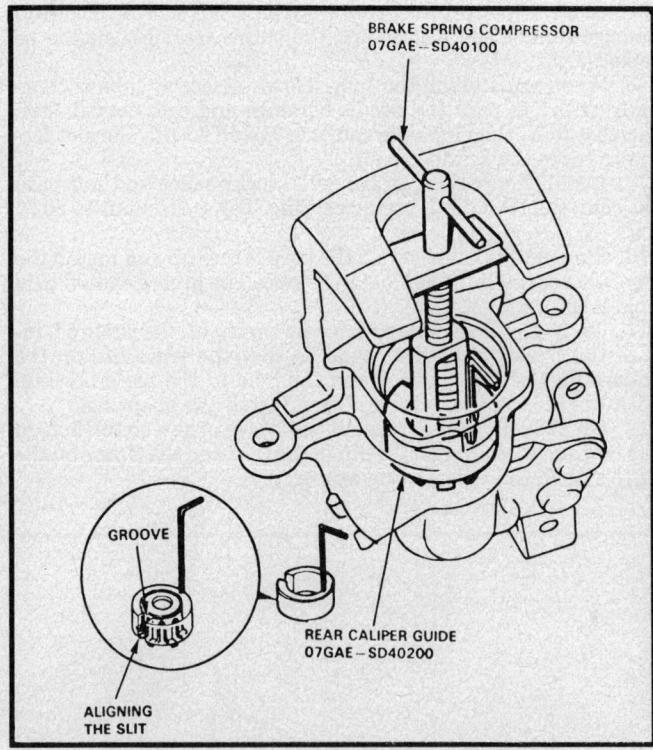

Use the guide tool on 1987–88 Acura calipers to make sure the spring compresses straight

17. On the 1987–88 piston assembly, install the new cup on the adjuster with the groove facing the bearing and lightly grease the cup and bearing. Install the adjuster parts into the piston and secure with the snapring.

18. On the 1989–91 piston, lube the threads of the adjusting nut and install the parts in order into the piston.

19. Lightly grease the new piston seal and boot and install them into the caliper. Grease the piston and carefully start it into the bore through the boot.

20. Rotate the piston clockwise to bottom it on the pushrod threads. Install the bleeder screw and torque it to 6 ft. lbs. The caliper is now ready for installation on the vehicle.

Rear Wheel Cylinder

Disassembly and Assembly

1. The wheel cylinders on vehicles with rear drum brakes are fairly simple units and no special tools are required for service.

Loosen the bleeder screw first, and if it doesn't break off, continue with the rebuild procedure.

2. With the cylinder apart, clean all parts in brake fluid or brake part cleaner and inspect the bore and pistons. Minor corrosion can be cleaned off with steel wool or emery cloth, but scoring or piston damage cannot be repaired and the entire assembly should be replaced.

3. When reassembling, lubricate all parts with brake fluid, not grease. When installing the cylinder, use a silicone sealer between the cylinder and the back plate.

AUDI

Master Cylinder and Booster Service

These vehicles use DOT 4 brake fluid. On some vehicles with power assisted anti-lock brakes, the booster is not vacuum operated but is powered by the same central hydraulic pump used for the power steering. Do not service this booster with brake fluid.

Hydraulic boosters are not field serviceable and no service kits are available. The master cylinder cannot be field serviced on any model. Each unit can be replaced seperately, and gaskets and O-rings are available for installing new assemblies. On some models, both the front and rear calipers can be rebuilt, but check on parts availability before starting the disassembly.

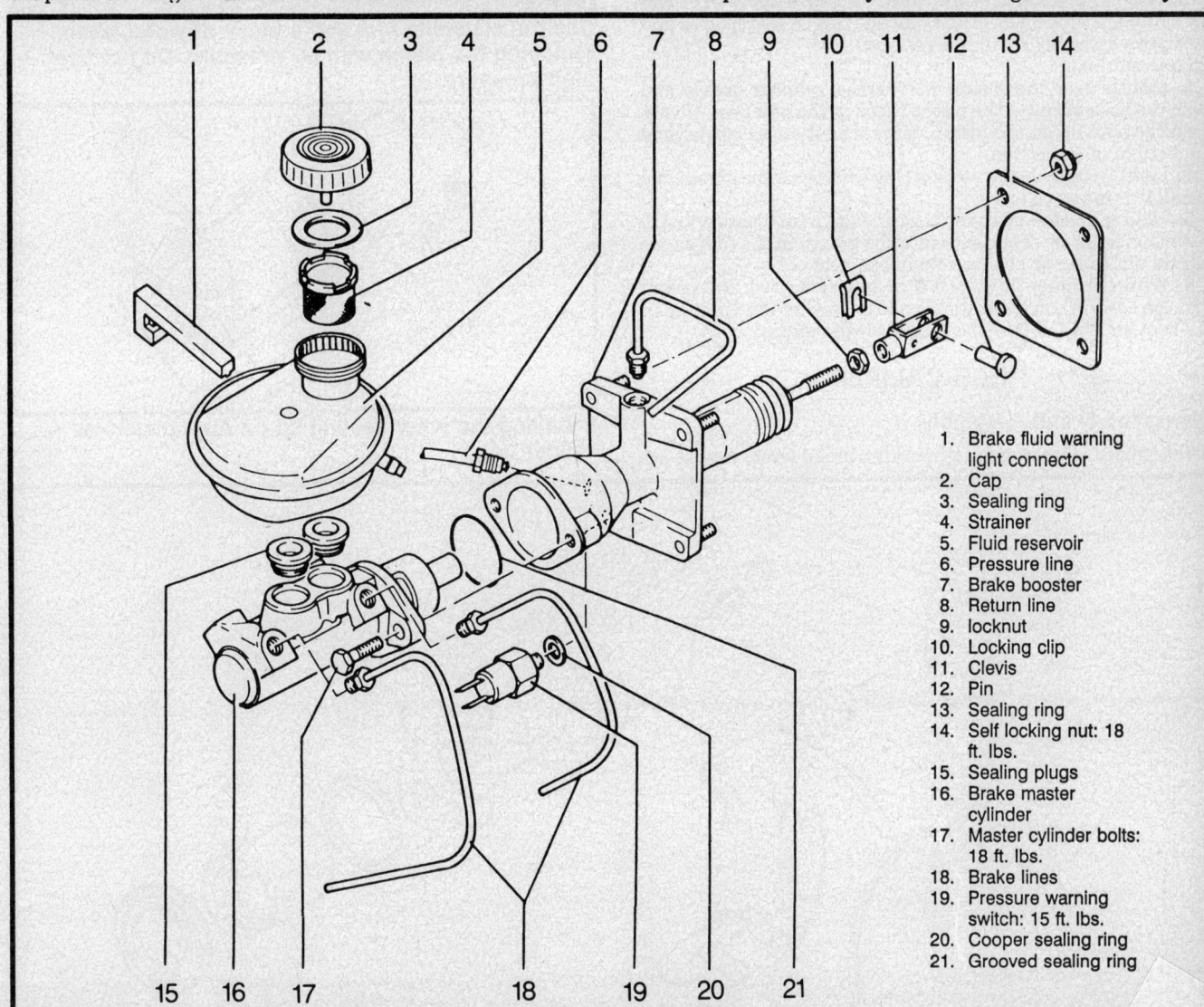

1. Brake fluid warning light connector
2. Cap
3. Sealing ring
4. Strainer
5. Fluid reservoir
6. Pressure line
7. Brake booster
8. Return line
9. locknut
10. Locking clip
11. Clevis
12. Pin
13. Sealing ring
14. Self locking nut: 18 ft. lbs.
15. Sealing plugs
16. Brake master cylinder
17. Master cylinder bolts: 18 ft. lbs.
18. Brake lines
19. Pressure warning switch: 15 ft. lbs.
20. Cooper sealing ring
21. Grooved sealing ring

Audi hydraulic booster and master cylinder can be replaced seperately

Caliper Service

FRONT CALIPERS

The front caliper on hydraulicly boosted systems cannot be repaired and no service kit is available. A leaky or seized caliper must be replaced.

Disassembly and Assembly

1. If the caliper has 2 pistons, remove them one at a time. Secure one piston with tool No.1023/4 or equivalent, and carefully press the other piston out with air pressure.

CAUTION

When using compressed air to remove a piston, the piston could fly out like a projectile and brake fluid will be sprayed. Personal injury could result. Secure a block of wood to the caliper, cover the bore with a shop rag and apply pressure gradually. Never use more pressure than is needed.

---

2. Carefully remove the boot and sealing ring. Clean all parts in brake fluid or brake part cleaner and inspect the bore and pistons. Minor corrosion can be cleaned off with steel wool or emery cloth, but scoring or piston damage cannot be repaired and the entire assembly should be replaced.

To assemble:

3. Lightly coat the piston with brake cylinder grease and push the bottom end of the piston through the new boot. Do not push the boot up on the piston, leave it so it sticks out beyond the bottom of the piston.

4. Lightly coat the new sealing ring with the same grease and install it into the caliper.

5. Hold the piston up to the bore and use a small probe tool to insert the inner lip of the boot into the groove in the caliper. Be careful not to rip or poke a hole in the boot.

6. With the inner lip of the boot installed, push the piston into the bore. When the piston is all the way in, the outer lip of the boot should fall into the groove on the piston.

REAR CALIPER

Disassembly and Assembly

If the caliper is leaking at the parking brake lever, repairs are not possible and the unit must be replaced. On some calipers, special tool 3131 or equivalent is needed to remove and install the piston. This tool is a large pin wrench that fits into the notches in the piston, so that the piston can be easily turned on the threads. Other calipers need only an Allen wrench to remove the piston.

1. With the caliper clamped in a soft jaw vice, use tool # 3131 or equivalent to unscrew the piston and remove it from the caliper.

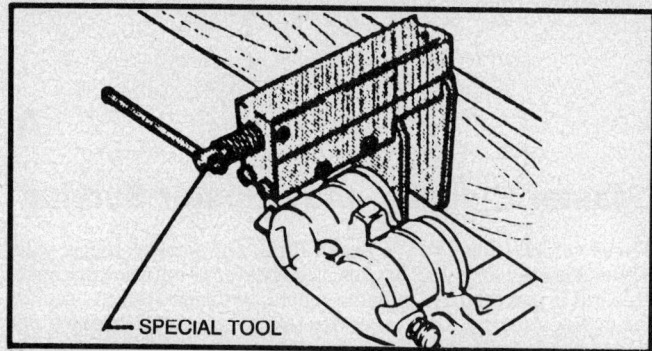

Use the clamping tool and a block of wood when removing the piston with air pressure. Do not use high pressure.

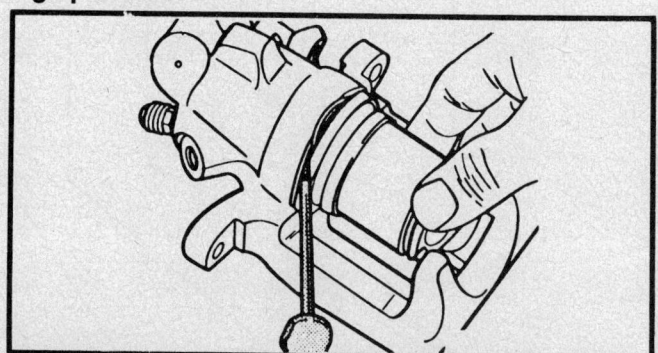

Installing the inner sealing lip on Audi piston-to-caliper boot

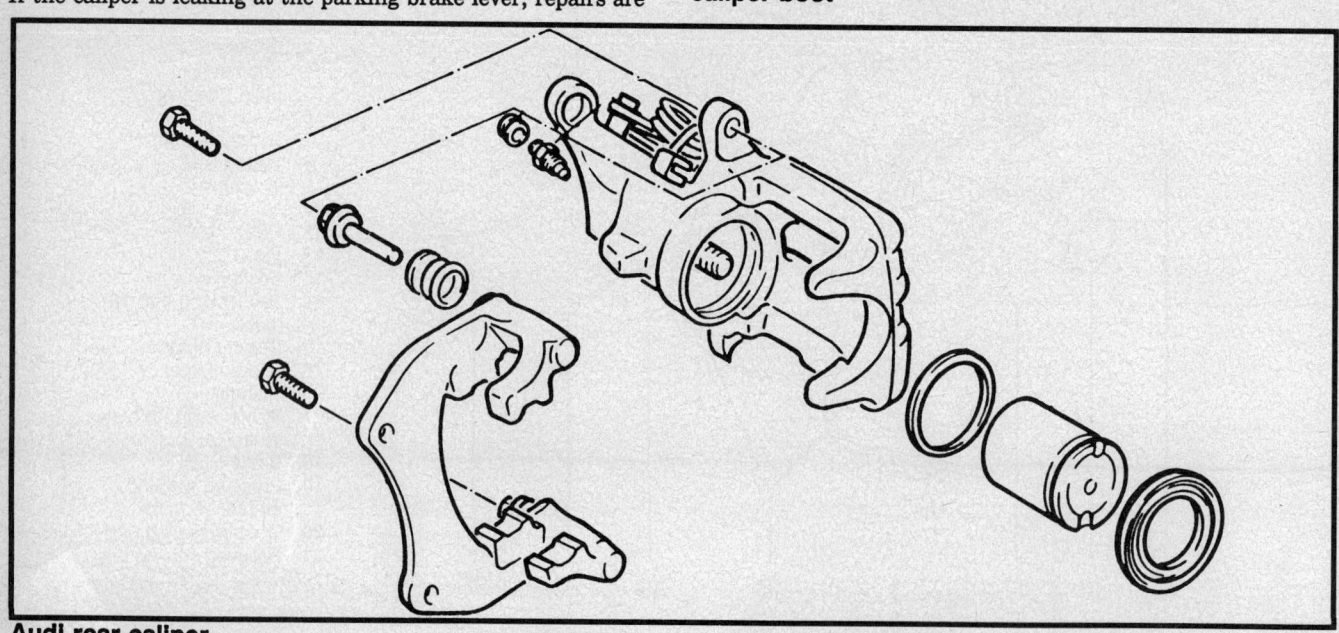

Audi rear caliper

2. carefuly remove the boot and sealing ring. Clean all parts in brake fluid or brake part cleaner and inspect the bore and pistons. Minor corrosion can be cleaned off with steel wool or emery cloth, but scoring or piston damage cannot be repaired and the entire assembly should be replaced.

To assemble:

3. Lightly coat the piston with brake cylinder grease and push the bottom end of the piston through the new boot. Do not push the boot up on the piston, unfold it so it sticks out beyond the bottom of the piston.

4. Lightly coat the new sealing ring with the same grease and install it into the caliper.

5. Hold the piston up to the bore and use a small probe to insert the inner lip of the boot into the groove in the caliper. Be careful not to rip or poke a hole in the boot.

6. Push the piston into the caliper and carefully screw it into place. A little more lubrication should help the outer lip of the boot fall into the groove in the piston.

BMW

Master Cylinder Service

EXCEPT ANTI-LOCK BRAKES

Disassembly and Assembly

1. These vehicles use DOT 4 brake fluid. Only on certain 3-Series vehicles can the master cylinder be rebuilt. Check on parts availability before disassembling the unit. With the cylinder in a soft jaw vice, lightly push in on the piston to take up the spring tension and remove the stop screw from the bottom of the cylinder, then the snapring.

2. With the primary piston out of the bore, tap the cylinder on a block of wood to remove the secondary piston. Do not use air pressure to remove the pistons.

3. Use only clean brake fluid or a brake parts cleaner to clean the master cylinder and carefully examine the bore. If there is any corrosion or distortion, do not attempt to rebuild the cylinder, replace the entire assembly.

To assemble:

4. The factory rebuild kit comes with an assembly sleeve with the new springs and some of the cups already assembled. Remove the plugs from the ends of the sleeve and remove the stop washer, secondary cup, plastic bushing, circlip, O-ring, aluminum seal and silicone grease.

5. Lightly coat the bore with the grease, insert the sleeve into the bore and push the contents of the sleeve all the way into the cylinder. Hold the piston there while installing the stop screw with the new aluminum ring. Torque the screw to 5 ft. lbs., then slowly release the piston.

6. Lightly grease the secondary cup and use the sleeve to install it in the cylinder.

7. Grease the plastic bushing and install it and the snapring. Put the new O-ring on the cylinder before installing it onto the booster.

ANTI-LOCK BRAKES

The master cylinder on all BMW ABS brakes cannot be field serviced and no parts are available from BMW. Faulty units can be replaced without removing the booster.

Brake Booster Service

Two types of booster are used, vacuum and hydraulic. The vacuum unit is similar to other manufacturers' vacuum operated brake boosters, while the hydraulic booster gets its' pressure from the power steering pump. Do not service the hydraulic

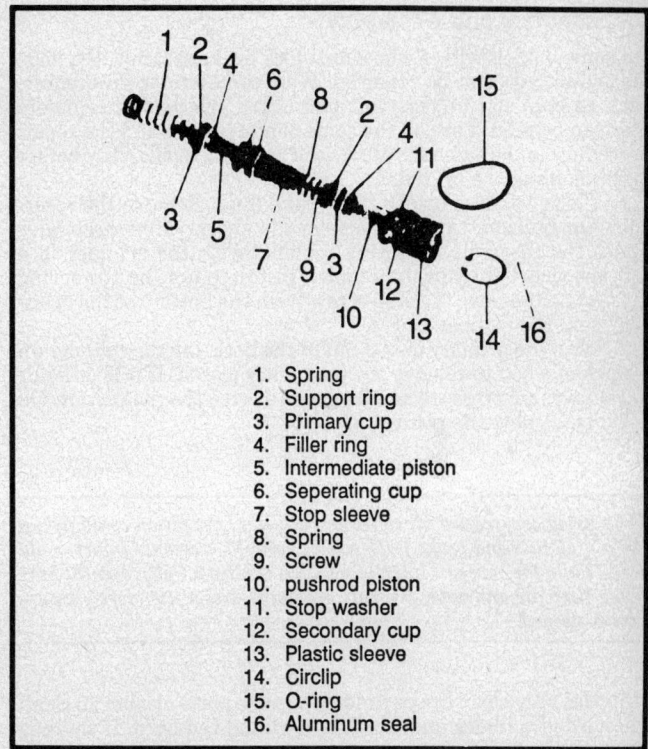

1. Spring
2. Support ring
3. Primary cup
4. Filler ring
5. Intermediate piston
6. Seperating cup
7. Stop sleeve
8. Spring
9. Screw
10. pushrod piston
11. Stop washer
12. Secondary cup
13. Plastic sleeve
14. Circlip
15. O-ring
16. Aluminum seal

BMW 3-Series master cylinder parts for standard brakes. A plastic assembly sleeve comes with the factory rebuild kit and makes the job much easier.

booster with brake fluid. Neither unit can be rebuilt, and factory service parts are not available. Faulty units can be replaced without replacing the master cylinder.

Caliper Service

FRONT AND REAR CALIPERS

Disassembly and Assembly

1. Do not, under any circumstances, split a 2 piece caliper. If the caliper is damaged or leaking at the seam, replace the entire unit. If the caliper has multi pistons, remove them one side at a time. Secure one set with a clamp and carefully press the other out with air pressure. Also be sure not to mix up the left and right side parts.

─────── **CAUTION** ───────

When using compressed air to remove a piston, the piston could fly out like a projectile and brake fluid will be sprayed. Personal injury could result. Secure a block of wood to the caliper, cover the bore with a shop rag and apply pressure gradually. Never use more pressure than is needed.

2. Carefully remove the boot and sealing ring. Clean all parts in brake fluid or brake part cleaner and inspect the bore and pistons. Minor corrosion can be cleaned off with steel wool or em-ery cloth, but scoring or piston damage cannot be repaired and the entire assembly should be replaced.

To assemble:

3. Lightly coat the new sealing ring(s) with brake cylinder grease and install into the caliper.

4. Lightly coat the piston with brake cylinder grease and put the new boot onto the piston. Then carefully start the piston into the bore.

5. Press the piston evenly into the caliper, then pull the boot over the edge of the cylinder and install the clamping ring.

CHRYSLER IMPORTS AND MITSUBISHI

Master Cylinder Service

Disassembly and Assembly

On some models with 4 wheel anti-lock brake systems, the master cylinder cannot be repaired. With some minor differences, such as bore size or reservoir mounting, the master cylinders that can be rebuilt are all the same configuration and the repair procedure is the same for all. Check on parts availability before disassembling the cylinder.

1. These vehicles use DOT 3 brake fluid. Remove the reservoir. On Starion, carefully remove the check valve assemblies under the reservoir mounting nipples. With the cylinder in a soft jaw vice, lightly push in on the piston to take up the spring tension and remove the stop screw from the bottom of the cylinder, then the stopper ring.

2. With the primary piston out of the bore, tap the cylinder on a block of wood to remove the secondary piston. If it is difficult to remove, air pressure can be used to force the piston out. Do not disassemble the pistons.

─────── **CAUTION** ───────

When using compressed air to remove a piston, the piston could fly out like a projectile and brake fluid will be sprayed. Personal injury could result. Point the bore at a block of wood up against a wall, cover the bore with a shop rag and apply pressure gradually. Never use more pressure than is needed.

3. Use only clean brake fluid or a brake parts cleaner to clean the master cylinder and carefully examine the bore. If there is any corrosion or distortion, do not attempt to rebuild the cylinder, replace the entire assembly.

To assemble:

4. The service kit should come with pistons already assembled. Lubricate the cups and cylinder with clean brake fluid and carefully insert the pistons into the bore.

5. While holding the pistons in, install the stop screw with new gasket, new stopper plate and new stopper ring.

6. On Starion, lubricate the new check valve parts and reassemble the valves. Torque the front valve case to 29–36 ft. lbs., and the rear case to 18–25 ft. lbs.

7. Before installing the cylinder onto the booster, the clearance between the pushrod and primary piston must be adjusted.

Brake Booster Service

The vacuum booster can not be repaired, only replaced as a unit. The only part available for booster service is the check valve. Before installing the booster or master cylinder, check the pushrod clearance.

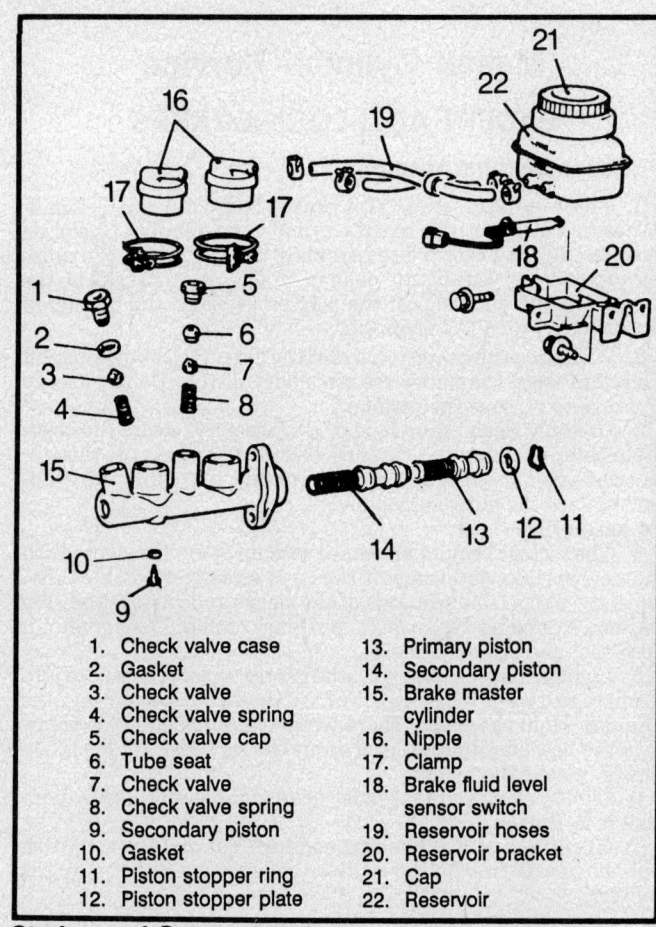

1. Check valve case	13. Primary piston
2. Gasket	14. Secondary piston
3. Check valve	15. Brake master
4. Check valve spring	cylinder
5. Check valve cap	16. Nipple
6. Tube seat	17. Clamp
7. Check valve	18. Brake fluid level
8. Check valve spring	sensor switch
9. Secondary piston	19. Reservoir hoses
10. Gasket	20. Reservoir bracket
11. Piston stopper ring	21. Cap
12. Piston stopper plate	22. Reservoir

Starion and Conquest master cylinder rebuild kit comes with assembled pistons and new check valve parts

BOOSTER PUSHROD CLEARANCE ADJUSTMENT

When installing a booster or master cylinder, the clearance between the booster pushrod and primary piston in the cylinder must be set. With the booster installed and the engine running, the diaphragm is pulled part way towards the master cylinder at all times, moving the pushrod the same distance. If the pushrod is adjusted too long, the master cylinder piston will be pushed and the brakes will be on all the time. If the rod is too short, the pedal travel will be very long and full braking may not be available. This adjustment is critical to proper functioning of the brakes.

1. With a depth caliper, measure dimension **B** between the primary piston and the end of the master cylinder. If using a straight–edge to aid in caliper use, don't forget to subtract its' thickness from the total.

2. Measure dimension **C** between the cylinder mounting face and the end of the cylinder.

3. Measure dimension **D**, how far the pushrod sticks out beyond the mounting face on the booster. Remember the subtract straight–edge thickness.

4. Dimension **A** is the pushrod clearance. **A = B − C − D**. Adjust the screw on the booster pushrod as required.

Pushrod clearance dimension A

Galant 0.059–0.075 in. (1.5–1.9mm)
Sigma V6 0.059–0.075 in. (1.5–1.9mm)
Starion and Conquest 0.028–0.043 in. (0.0–1.1mm)
Precis 0.016–0.031 in. (0.4–0.8mm)
Cordia and Tredia 0.016–0.031 in. (0.4–0.8mm)
Eclipse with 7 and 8 inch booster 0.020–0.028 in. (0.5–0.7mm)
Eclipse with 9 inch booster 0.031–0.039 in. (0.8–1.0mm)
Mirage with 7 inch booster 0.020–0.028 in. (0.5–0.7mm)
Mirage and Colt with 8 inch booster 0.024–0.031 in. (0.6–0.8mm)

Rear Brake Lock-up Control System

Some vehicles all have a rear brake lock-up control system, which is an electronically controlled anti-lock system acting on the rear wheels only. When the brake light switch on the brake pedal is turned activated, a controller is activated which, if necessary, activates the hydraulic modulator to limit rear braking action. The modulator is vacuum powered but like the booster, the vacuum unit cannot be repaired, only replaced. A service kit is available for the hydraulic portion of the modulator. When removing seals and O-rings, use soft tools or fingers whereever possible and pay close attention to their orientation so they can be installed properly.

HYDRAULIC CYLINDER

Disassembly and Assembly

1. With the cylinder cleaned and held upside down, carefully lift the plunger straight out. Use a soft tool such as an aluminum probe or wood stick to remove the dust seal.

2. Remove the snapring, being careful not to damage the bore.

3. Make an L shape at the end of a piece of stiff wire and remove the rest of the parts from the bottom of the cylinder. Be careful not to damage the bore.

4. Clamp the black part of the cylinder in a soft jaw vice and loosen the 2 caps. Take it out of the vice and remove the bleeder and check valve parts.

5. Remove the choke valve cap, spring and seals. carefully reach into the cylinder with long nose pliers and remove the choke valve and bushing. The valve can be pushed out of the bushing with fingers.

6. With the cylinder apart, clean all parts in brake fluid or brake part cleaner and inspect the bores, valves and springs. Minor corrosion can be cleaned off with steel wool or emery cloth, but scoring or heavy wear cannot be repaired and the entire assembly should be replaced.

To assemble:

7. Be sure to use all the new parts in the service kit. Lubricate the O-rings and seals with brake fluid.

8. Push the choke valve into the bushing and install the valve/bushing and cap with a new gasket. With the valve cap

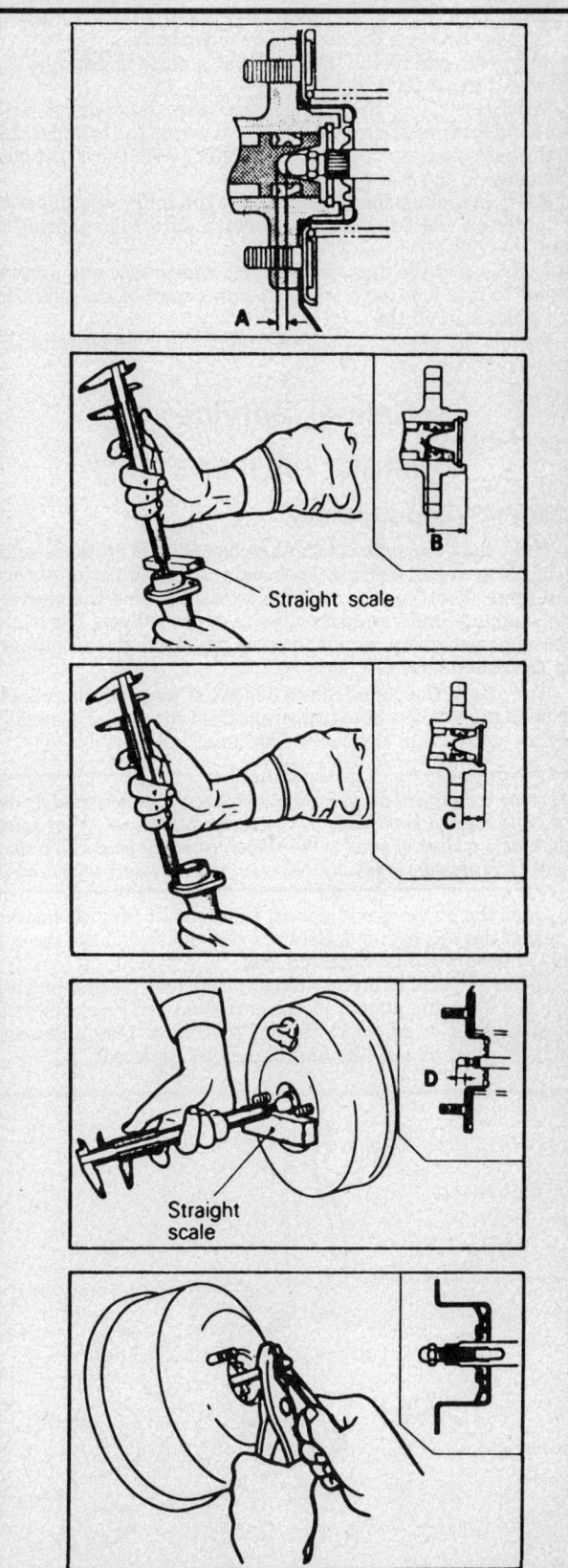

Measuring the pushrod clearance on vacuum booster used in several vehicles

torqued to 22–29 ft. lbs., there should be a gap of 0.020–0.040 in. (0.5–1.0mm) between the cap and cylinder body.

9. Lubricate and install the check valve parts and torque the bleeder cap to 14–22 ft. lbs.

10. When installing the plunger seal cup, lubricate it with brake fluid and make sure the lip is in towards the cylinder. Install the back-up ring, then the cup retainer with the larger outer diameter in towards the cylinder.

11. After installing the snapring, use the long nose pliers to tug lightly on the cup retainer to make sure the snapring is seated.

12. Lightly coat the dust seal with silicone grease and press it by hand so it is just flush with the outer edge of the cylinder. Don't push it in all the way.

13. Install the plunger when installing the cylinder onto the vacuum cylinder.

Caliper Service

FRONT CALIPERS

Disassembly and Assembly

1. More than one make of front caliper is used on these vehicles, but they are all floating types and the procedure for service is the same. Remove the pin bolts to disassemble the sleeves, boots, bushings and torque member from the caliper. The bushing can be pushed out by pushing the pin through the support from the other side.

2. To remove the piston, place a block of wood in the caliper, lay a shop rag over the bore to prevent fluid spray, and gradually apply air pressure to the brake fluid inlet hole.

─ CAUTION ─

When using compressed air to remove a piston, the piston could fly out like a projectile and brake fluid will be sprayed. Personal injury could result. Clamp a block of wood to the caliper, cover the bore with a shop rag and apply pressure gradually. Never use more pressure than needed.

3. Once the piston is out against the wood, it can be removed the rest of the way by hand. Being careful not to damage the cylinder, remove the dust boot and seal.

4. Clean all parts in brake fluid or brake part cleaner and examine the bore and piston. Minor corrosion can be cleaned off with steel wool or emery cloth, but scoring or piston damage cannot be repaired and the unit should be replaced.

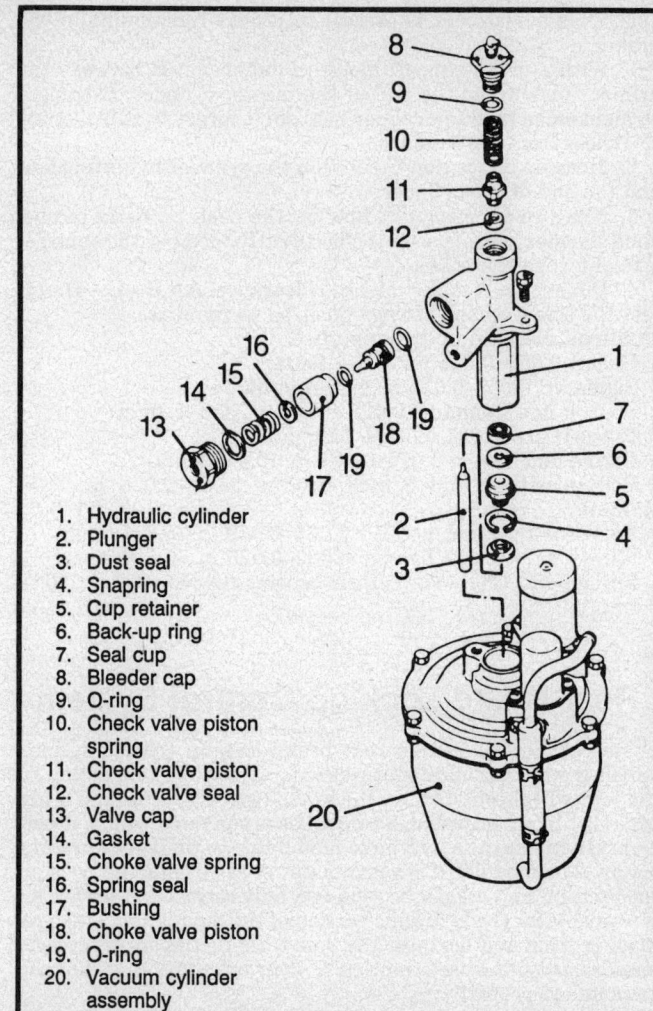

1. Hydraulic cylinder
2. Plunger
3. Dust seal
4. Snapring
5. Cup retainer
6. Back-up ring
7. Seal cup
8. Bleeder cap
9. O-ring
10. Check valve piston spring
11. Check valve piston
12. Check valve seal
13. Valve cap
14. Gasket
15. Choke valve spring
16. Spring seal
17. Bushing
18. Choke valve piston
19. O-ring
20. Vacuum cylinder assembly

Mitsubishi rear brake lock-up control hydraulic valve assembly; the vacuum assembly cannot be repaired

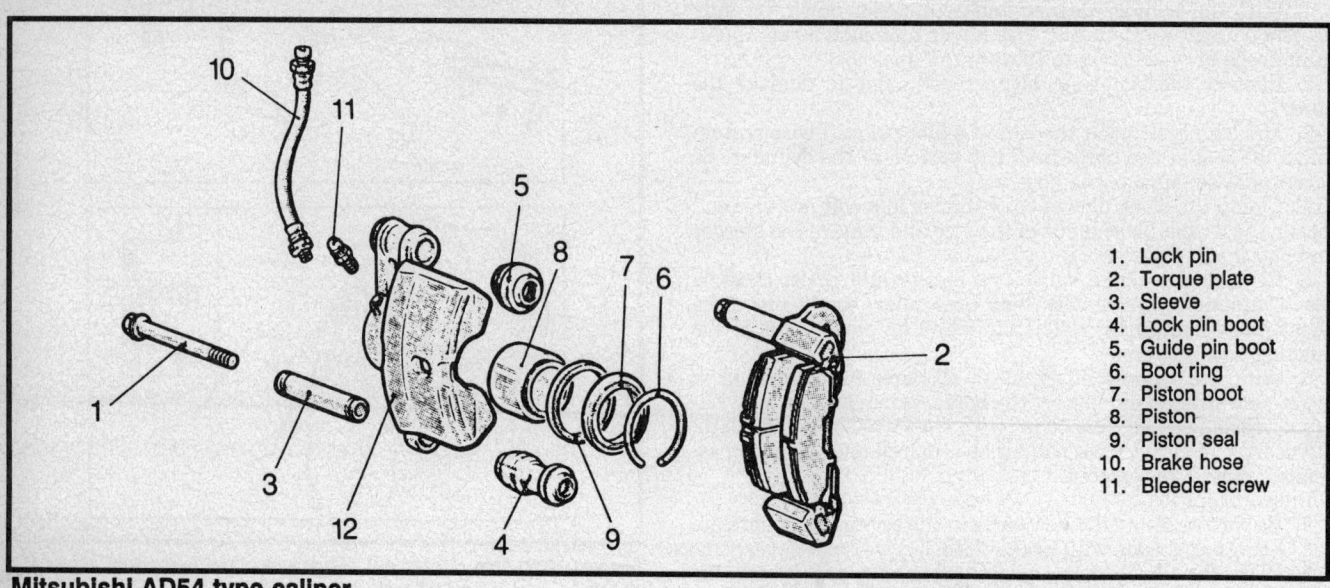

1. Lock pin
2. Torque plate
3. Sleeve
4. Lock pin boot
5. Guide pin boot
6. Boot ring
7. Piston boot
8. Piston
9. Piston seal
10. Brake hose
11. Bleeder screw

Mitsubishi AD54 type caliper

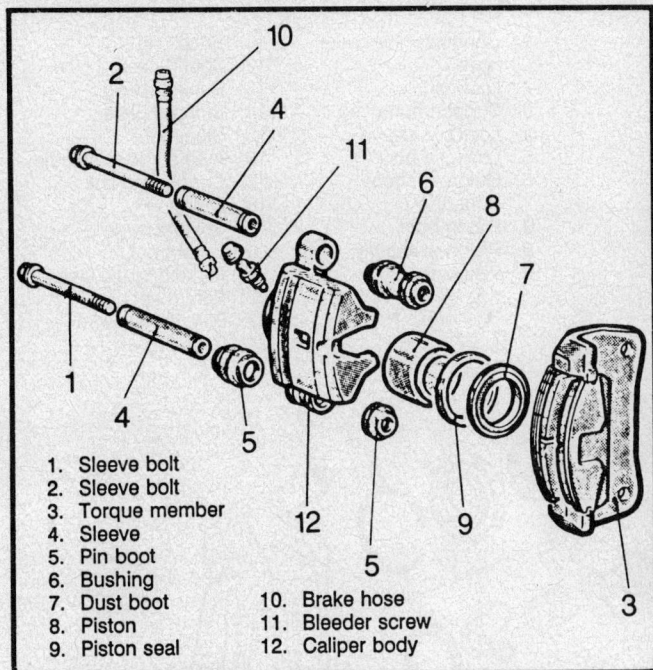

Mitsubishi PFS15 type caliper

1. Sleeve bolt
2. Sleeve bolt
3. Torque member
4. Sleeve
5. Pin boot
6. Bushing
7. Dust boot
8. Piston
9. Piston seal
10. Brake hose
11. Bleeder screw
12. Caliper body

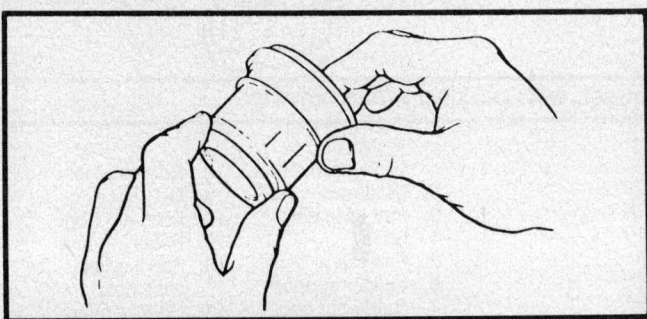

Installing the seal onto the caliper piston

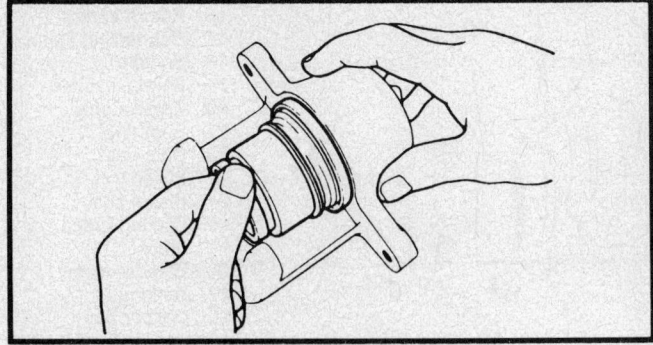

Installing the piston into the caliper

To assemble:

5. Apply the light silicone grease that comes with the kit to the new piston seal and install it into the caliper.

6. Lubricate the piston with clean brake fluid and carefully install the boot onto the bottom end of the piston.

7. Fit the outer lip of the boot into the caliper and carefully push the piston through the boot and all the way into the caliper bore.

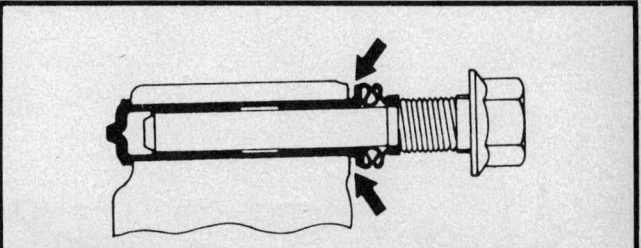

Reassembling the Starion and Conquest caliper. Wipe away excess adhesive after installing the bushing, lightly grease the pin bolt

8. On Starion, the new bushing must be glued into the caliper support with the adhesive supplied in the kit. Lightly grease the pin bolt and slide the bushing onto it. Apply a light coating of the adhesive to the length of the bushing and push it into the caliper support. Remove the pin bolt and wipe off any excess adhesive.

9. On all other models, make sure the pin bolts and sleeves are clean and lightly grease them for reassembly, using the new bushings and boots supplied in the kit.

REAR CALIPERS

Disassembly and Assembly

Some models with rear disc brakes use a floating caliper similar to those used on the front. The repair procedure is the same as for front calipers. This procedure is for calipers with parking brakes.

EXCEPT STARION

1. Remove the lock pins, guides, sleeves and support mounting.

2. Use special tool # MB990652 or equivalent to unscrew the piston from the caliper. carefully remove the piston seal.

3. Use a piece of tube or a socket to compress the spring case, then remove the snapring. Remove the adjuster parts for cleaning and inspection.

4. With the caliper apart, clean all parts in brake fluid or brake part cleaner and inspect the bore and piston. Minor corrosion can be cleaned off with steel wool or emery cloth, but scoring or piston damage cannot be repaired and the entire assembly should be replaced.

To assemble:

5. With the grease supplied in the rebuild kit, lightly lubricate all the parking brake and adjuster parts and install them into the caliper. Hold the spring case down with the tube or socket to install the snapring.

6. Lightly coat the piston seal with grease and install it into the groove in the bore. Grease the piston and push it into the bore, don't thread it.

7. Turn the piston so that the pins on the back of the brake pads fit into the notches. Then grease the piston boot and install it.

8. Lightly grease the lock pin boot and sleeve and the lock pin shaft, not the threads. Install these parts and torque the pin bolt to 16–23 ft. lbs.

STARION

1. Remove the lever cap and the snapring and slide the parking brake lever out of the bearings. Be careful not to let the return spring fly away.

2. Unscrew the spindle and remove it with the spring washers and seal from the caliper. Pay close attention to how the spring washers fit onto the spindle.

3. Remove the piston dust boot ring and boot, insert a blunt

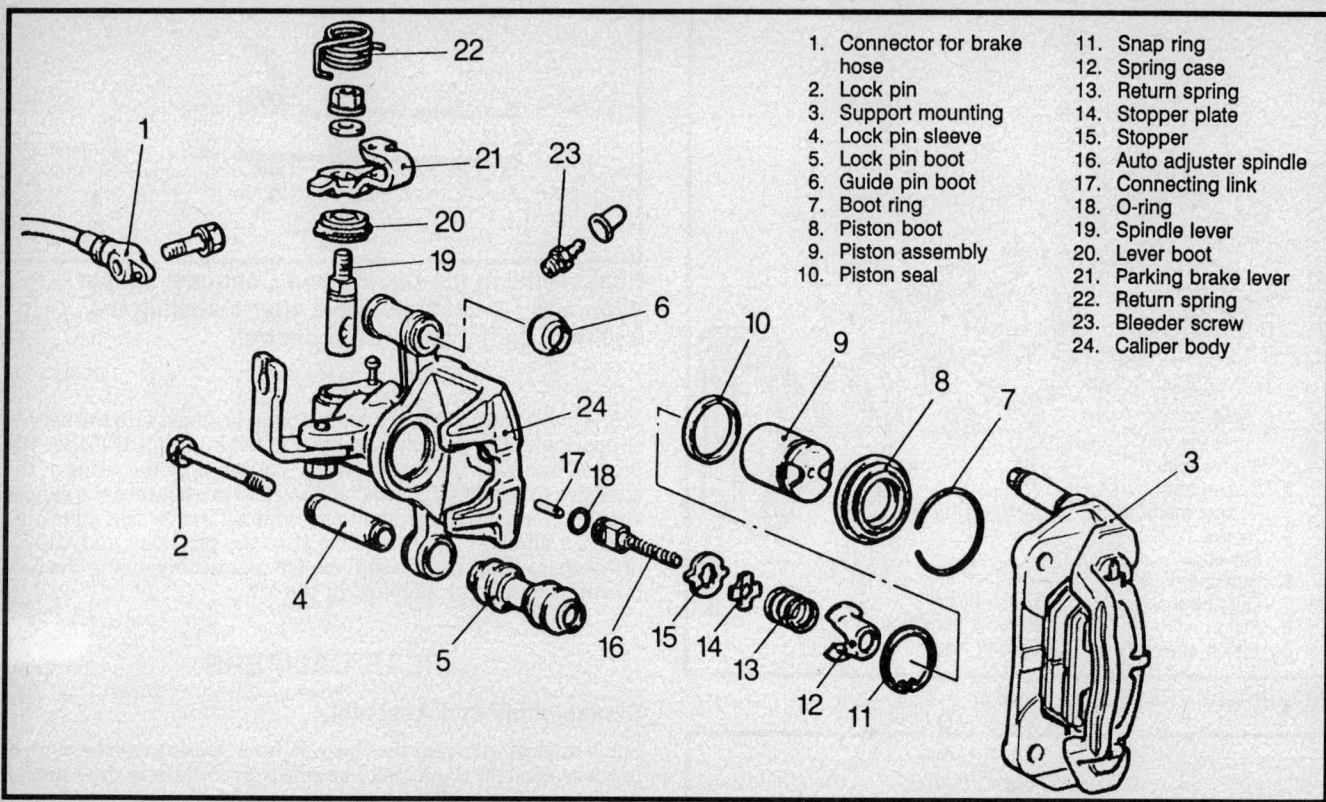

1. Connector for brake hose
2. Lock pin
3. Support mounting
4. Lock pin sleeve
5. Lock pin boot
6. Guide pin boot
7. Boot ring
8. Piston boot
9. Piston assembly
10. Piston seal
11. Snap ring
12. Spring case
13. Return spring
14. Stopper plate
15. Stopper
16. Auto adjuster spindle
17. Connecting link
18. O-ring
19. Spindle lever
20. Lever boot
21. Parking brake lever
22. Return spring
23. Bleeder screw
24. Caliper body

Mitsubishi rear caliper assembly, except Starion and Conquest, with parking brake adjuster

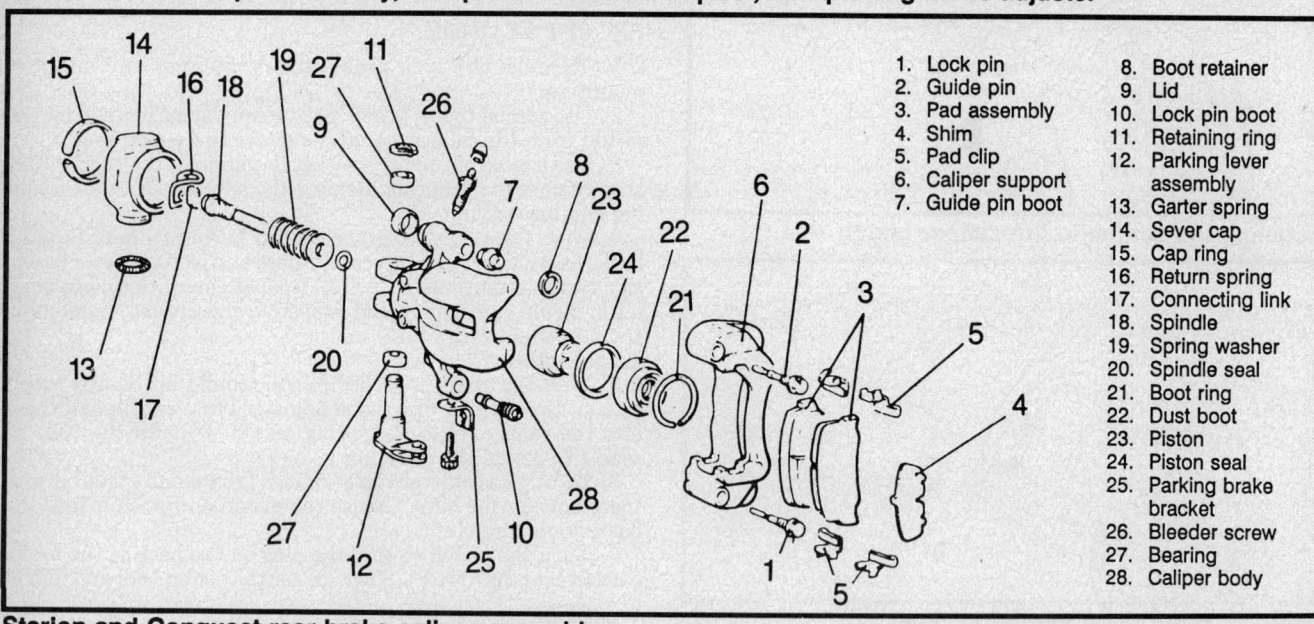

1. Lock pin
2. Guide pin
3. Pad assembly
4. Shim
5. Pad clip
6. Caliper support
7. Guide pin boot
8. Boot retainer
9. Lid
10. Lock pin boot
11. Retaining ring
12. Parking lever assembly
13. Garter spring
14. Sever cap
15. Cap ring
16. Return spring
17. Connecting link
18. Spindle
19. Spring washer
20. Spindle seal
21. Boot ring
22. Dust boot
23. Piston
24. Piston seal
25. Parking brake bracket
26. Bleeder screw
27. Bearing
28. Caliper body

Starion and Conquest rear brake caliper assembly

tool through the spindle hole and push the piston out of the bore. carefully remove the piston seal.

4. If necessary, the bearings can be easily pressed out with press tool MB990665 or equivalent.

To assemble:

5. With the caliper apart, clean all parts in brake fluid or brake part cleaner and inspect the bore and piston. Minor corrosion can be cleaned off with steel wool or emery cloth, but scoring or heavy wear cannot be repaired and the entire assembly should be replaced. Be sure to use all the new parts in the repair.

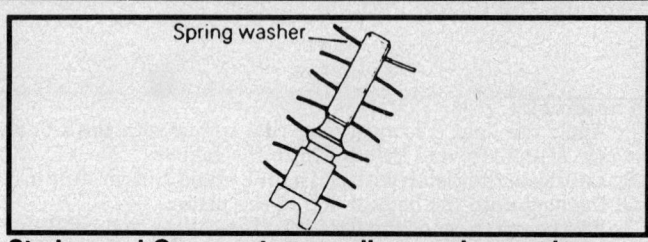

Spring washer

Starion and Conquest rear caliper spring washer orientation on the spindle

6. Grease the bearings and install with the depression facing outward till the press tool is flush with the caliper body.

7. Lubricate the piston and seal with brake fluid and install them into the caliper, without twisting the piston. The depressions in the piston should align with the bumps in the pads.

8. Lightly grease the dust boot groove in the caliper body and install the boot and ring.

9. Lubricate the spindle seal with brake fluid and install it. Lubricate the spring washers with silicone grease and install them as shown.

10. Screw the spindle in till it turns freely, then push it in against the spring washers and screw it in the rest of the way.

11. Install the connecting link and return spring. Push the parking brake lever through the cap and use plenty of the silicone grease to lubricate the whole assembly. Then install the lever with the snapring and the cap.

12. Lubricate the lock pins with silicone grease and install the caliper support to the caliper. Torque the pin bolts to 36–43 ft. lbs.

WHEEL CYLINDER SERVICE

1. The wheel cylinders on vehicles with rear drum brakes are fairly simple units and no special tools are required for service. Loosen the bleeder screw first, and if it doesn't break off, continue with the rebuild procedure.

2. With the cylinder apart, clean all parts in brake fluid or brake part cleaner and inspect the bore and pistons. Minor corrosion can be cleaned off with steel wool or emery cloth, but scoring cannot be repaired and the entire assembly should be replaced.

3. When reassembling, lubricate all parts with brake fluid, not grease. When installing the cylinder, use a silicone sealer between the cylinder and the back plate.

DAIHATSU

Master Cylinder Service

Disassembly and Assembly

1. These vehicles use DOT 3 brake fluid.

2. With the cylinder drained and the flange clamped in a soft jaw vice, remove the reservoir cap, diaphragm and float, then remove the clamp holding the reservoir to the cylinder.

3. Using a blunt tool such as a hammer handle, push the piston in just enough to take up the spring tension and remove the snapring.

4. Remove the stop bolt from the side of the cylinder and remove both the secondary and primary piston assemblies. Be careful to not damage the bore when removing the primary piston.

─────── **CAUTION** ───────

When using compressed air to remove a piston, the piston could fly out like a projectile and brake fluid will be sprayed. Personal injury could result. Hold the bore close to a block of wood up against a wall, cover the bore with a shop rag and apply pressure gradually. Never use more pressure than necessary.

5. Use only clean brake fluid or a brake parts cleaner to clean the master cylinder and carefully examine the bore. If there is any corrosion or distortion, do not attempt to rebuild the cylinder, replace the entire assembly.

To assemble:

6. When inserting the pistons, lubricate all parts with silicone rubber grease and gently push them into the bore.

7. With both pistons installed, push in all the way on the secondary piston while installing the stop bolt and new gasket. Torque the bolt to 6 ft. lbs.

8. Hold the secondary piston in to install the snapring.

9. Clean and install the reservoir assembly making sure the diaphragm is in correctly. Before installing the cylinder, the pushrod clearance on the booster must be adjusted.

Brake Booster Service

Disassembly and Assembly

1. Remove the clevis and locknut from the pushrod.

2. Install the booster into the special tool # 09753–87701–000 or equivalent. This is a fixture which attaches to the studs on each half of the booster and provides the means for twisting the two halves apart.

3. Make reference marks on the halves and twist the lower

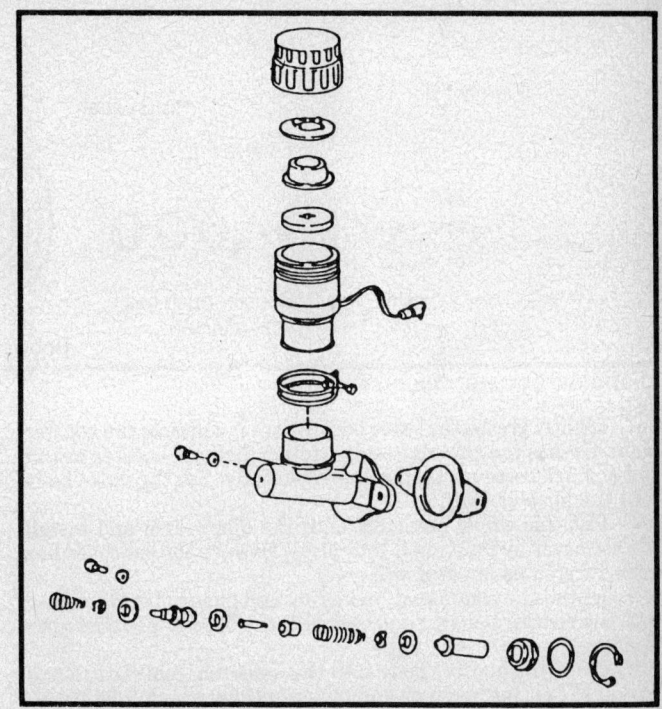

Diahatsu master cylinder kit includes new piston assemblies

half to disassemble the booster. Then take it out of the tool.

4. With the unit apart, completely disassemble the booster. The set cover is removed by prying it in a twisting direction. Inspect all parts for damage or wear. Only the pushrod seal retainer is strictly not reusable, but all parts in the rebuild kit should be installed.

To assemble:

5. Starting with the valve assembly, insert the poppet valve into the air valve spring retainer. Lube the booster valve rod with silicone grease and slide all of the parts onto it. Secure the assembly with the E–ring.

6. Install the valve assembly into the valve body and secure with the piston return spring retainer. Install the element B, adjusting nut and locknut onto the pushrod, but don't torque the nut yet.

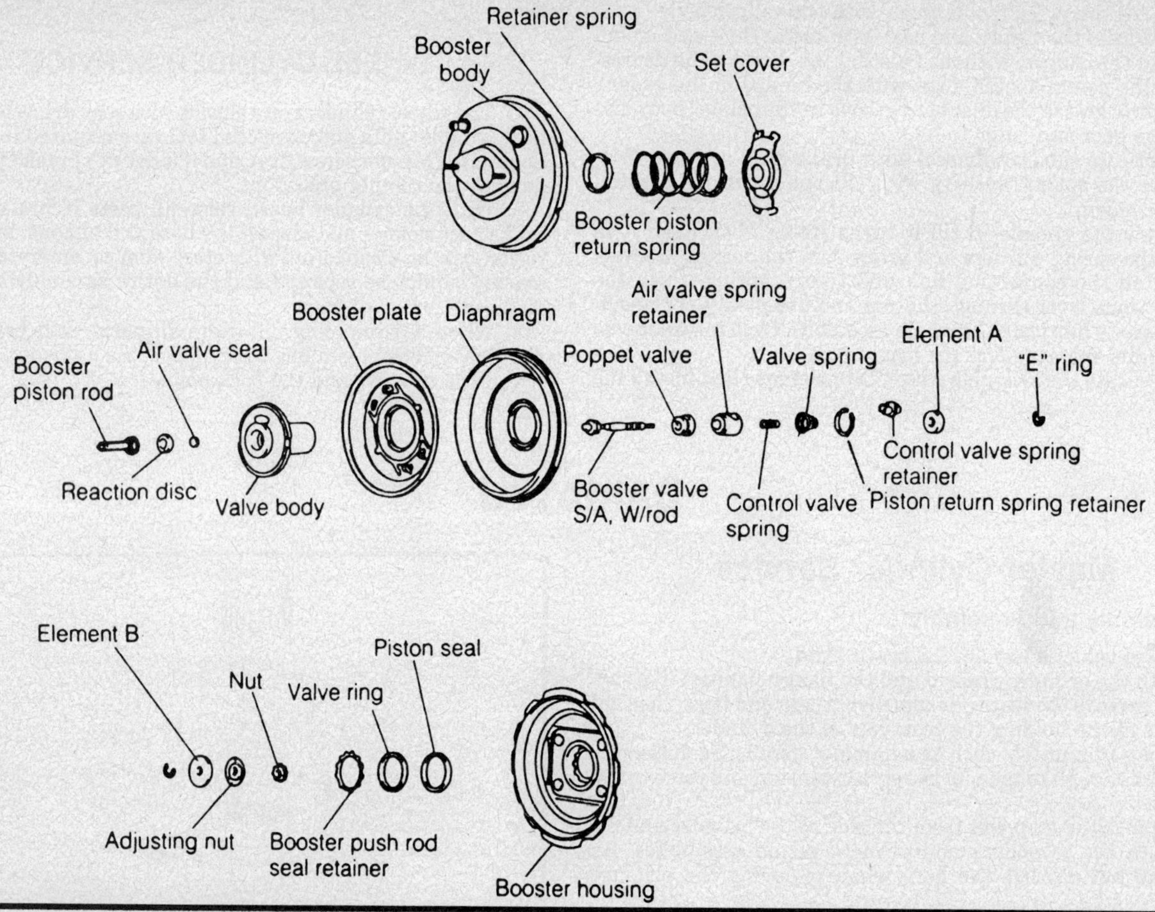

Retainer spring
Booster body
Set cover
Booster piston return spring

Booster piston rod
Air valve seal
Booster plate
Diaphragm
Air valve spring retainer
Element A
"E" ring
Reaction disc
Valve body
Poppet valve
Valve spring
Control valve spring retainer
Booster valve S/A, W/rod
Control valve spring
Piston return spring retainer

Element B
Nut
Valve ring
Piston seal
Adjusting nut
Booster push rod seal retainer
Booster housing

Diahatsu booster disassembly

7. Lightly grease the valve body where it contacts the booster plate. Grease the air valve seal, reaction disc and booster piston rod and set these parts into the valve body. Set the valve body into the booster plate.

8. Put this whole assembly onto the diaphragm and install the set cover by twisting it into place. Be sure the set cover has been twisted as far as it will go.

9. Install the piston seal, valve ring and pushrod seal retainer into the booster housing and assemble the booster plate into the housing.

10. Place the booster body into the assembly tool fixture and install the spring retainer and piston return spring. Lightly lubricate the body where it meets the housing and place the housing onto the body. Make sure everything is a nice square fit, especially the diaphragm so it won't be pinched when the body and housing are twisted together.

11. Turn the tool screw as required to bring the reference marks together.

12. Remove the booster from the fixture and install the rod seal and pushrod clevis and nut. Before installing the booster, the pushrod clearance must be adjusted.

Booster Pushrod Clearance Adjustment

This procedure is for adjusting the static clearance between the pushrod on the output end of the booster and the piston on the master cylinder. This needs to be done any time a booster or master cylinder is changed or rebuilt. If the pushrod is adjusted too long, the master cylinder piston will be pushed and the brakes will drag. If the rod is too short, the pedal travel will be very long and full braking may not be available. This adjust-

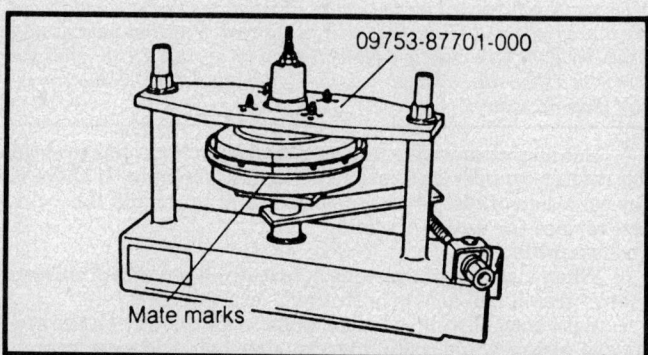

09753-87701-000

Mate marks

Special tool for disassembling Daihatsu booster

ment is critical to proper functioning of the brakes.

1. With a depth caliper, measure dimension **B** between the primary piston and the end of the master cylinder. If using a straight–edge to aid in caliper use, don't forget to subtract its' thickness from the total.

2. Measure dimension **C** between the cylinder mounting face and the end of the cylinder, with the gasket in place.

3. Measure dimension **D**, how far the pushrod sticks out beyond the mounting face on the booster. Remember the subtract straight–edge thickness.

4. Dimension **A** is the pushrod clearance. $\mathbf{A} = \mathbf{B} - \mathbf{C} - \mathbf{D}$. Adjust the pushrod adjusting nut on the booster so that dimension **A** is zero.

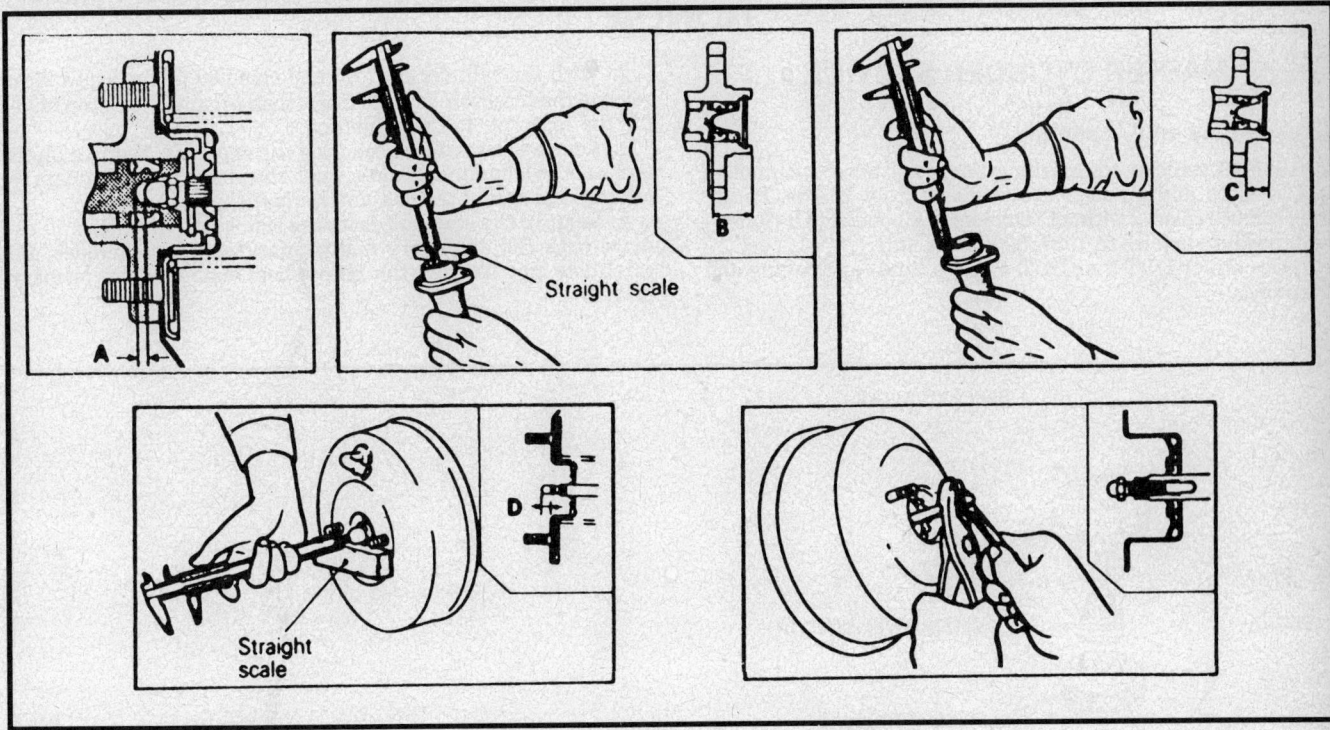

Measuring the pushrod clearance on Diahatsu booster

Caliper Service

FRONT CALIPERS

Disassembly and Assembly

1. Remove the piston boot retainer ring, caliper slide boots and bushings.
2. To remove the piston, place a block of wood in the caliper, lay a shop rag over the bore to prevent fluid spray, and gradually apply air pressure to the brake fluid inlet hole.

――――――――――― **CAUTION** ―――――――――――
When using compressed air to remove a piston, the piston could fly out like a projectile and brake fluid will be sprayed. Personal injury could result. Clamp a block of wood to the caliper, cover the bore with a shop rag and apply pressure gradually. Never use more pressure than needed.
――――――――――――――――――――――――――――――

3. Once the piston is out against the wood, it can be removed the rest of the way by hand. Being careful not to damage the cylinder, remove the dust boot and seal.
4. Clean all parts in brake fluid or brake part cleaner and examine the bore and piston. Minor corrosion can be cleaned off with steel wool or emery cloth, but scoring or piston damage cannot be repaired and the unit should be replaced.
5. Lightly coat the piston and seal with silicone grease and install the seal into the groove in the bore. carefully install the piston and push it part way in.
6. Grease the boot and install it into the caliper, being careful not to poke a hole in it. Make sure the boot is properly seated in the groove in the piston and install the retainer ring. Push the piston in all the way.

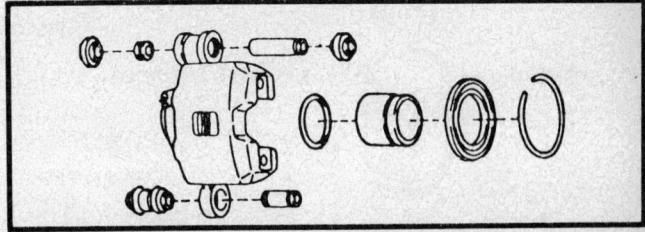

Dalhatsu front brake caliper slide bushings should be lightly greased

7. Lightly grease the slide bushings and install the bushings, retainers and boots.

REAR WHEEL CYLINDER

Disassembly and Assembly

1. The wheel cylinders on these vehicles are fairly simple units and no special tools are required for service. Loosen the bleeder screw first, and if it doesn't break off, continue with the rebuild procedure.
2. With the cylinder apart, clean all parts in brake fluid or brake part cleaner and inspect the bore and pistons. Minor corrosion can be cleaned off with steel wool or emery cloth, but scoring or piston damage cannot be repaired and the entire assembly should be replaced.
3. When reassembling, lubricate all parts with silicone grease, not brake fluid. When installing the cylinder, use a silicone sealer between the cylinder and the back plate.

HONDA

MASTER CYLINDER SERVICE

Disassembly and Assembly

For 1990–91 vehicles, the master cylinder and booster cannot be field serviced and no parts are available from Honda. Faulty units can be replaced without removing the booster. The following procedure applies to 1987–89 models only.

1. Use either DOT 3 or DOT 4 brake fluid for cleaning and assembly.

2. With the cylinder drained and clamped in a soft jaw vice, remove the reservoir cap and filter, then remove the clamp holding the reservoir to the cylinder.

3. Remove the rod seal covering the snapring. Using a blunt tool such as a hammer handle, push the piston in just enough to take up the spring tension and remove the snapring.

4. Remove the stop bolt from the side of the cylinder and remove both the secondary and primary piston assemblies. Be careful to not damage the bore when removing the primary piston.

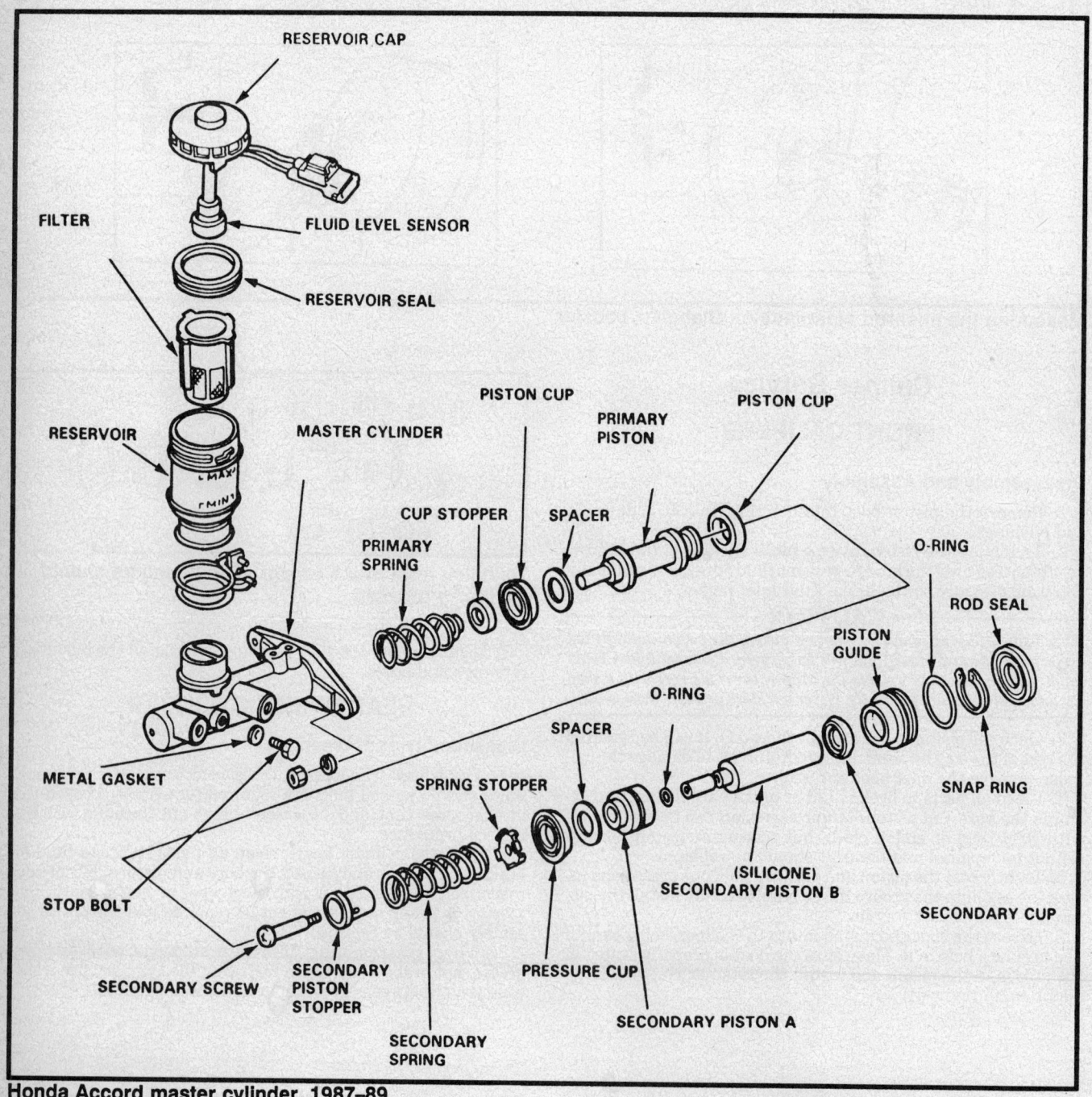

Honda Accord master cylinder, 1987–89

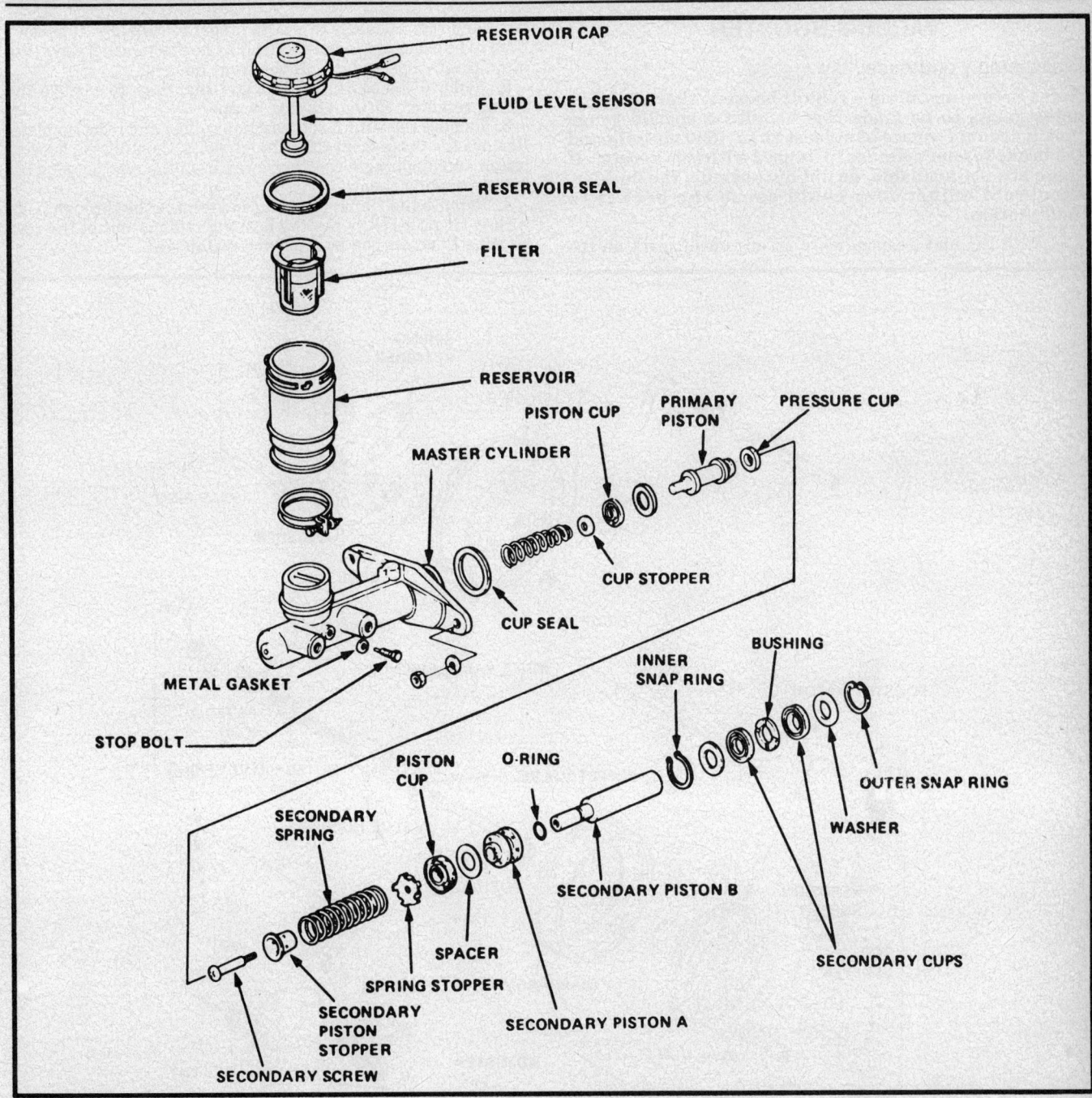

Honda Civic master cylinder

CAUTION

When using compressed air to remove a piston, the piston could fly out like a projectile and brake fluid will be sprayed. Personal injury could result. Point the bore at a block of wood up against a wall, cover the bore with a shop rag and apply pressure gradually. Never use more pressure than needed.

5. Remove the screw from the secondary piston and disassemble both pistons for inspection. Use only clean brake fluid or a brake parts cleaner to clean the master cylinder and carefully examine the bore. If there is any corrosion or distortion, do not attempt to rebuild the cylinder, replace the entire assembly.

To assemble:

6. When reassembling the pistons, use a thread sealer on the secondary screw. Be sure to use all parts in the rebuild kit.

7. When inserting the pistons, lubricate all parts with clean brake fluid and rotate the pistons while gently pushing them into the bore. Lubricate the inside of the secondary piston guide with a light silicone grease.

8. With both pistons installed, push in on the secondary piston while installing the stop bolt and new gasket. Torque the bolt to 6 ft. lbs.

9. Hold the secondary piston in again to install the snapring, then install the new rod seal.

VACUUM BOOSTER

Disassembly and Assembly

Note: Before installing a rebuilt booster, there are fine adjustments to be made that require a special gauge tool, a vacuum source of at least 20 in. (500 mm) Hg and the brake master cylinder to be used with this booster. If these are not available, do not disassemble the booster. Incorrect adjustment could cause the brakes to malfunction.

1. With the unit cleaned, make an alignment mark on the front and rear housings to assure proper reassembly. It doesn't need to be exact as the halves can only be assembled 2 ways. Remove the E-clips and lift off the front housing.

2. Remove the seals, washers and snaprings to remove the spring retainer, spring and rod stopper.

3. Remove the output rod, reaction rubber and reaction plate. Remove the boots from the through bolts, then lift the booster piston and diaphragm together away from the rear housing before separating them.

4. Remove the 19mm snapring and remove the through bolts with O-rings. carefully pry the bushing retainer out of the rear housing to access the bushing and piston seal.

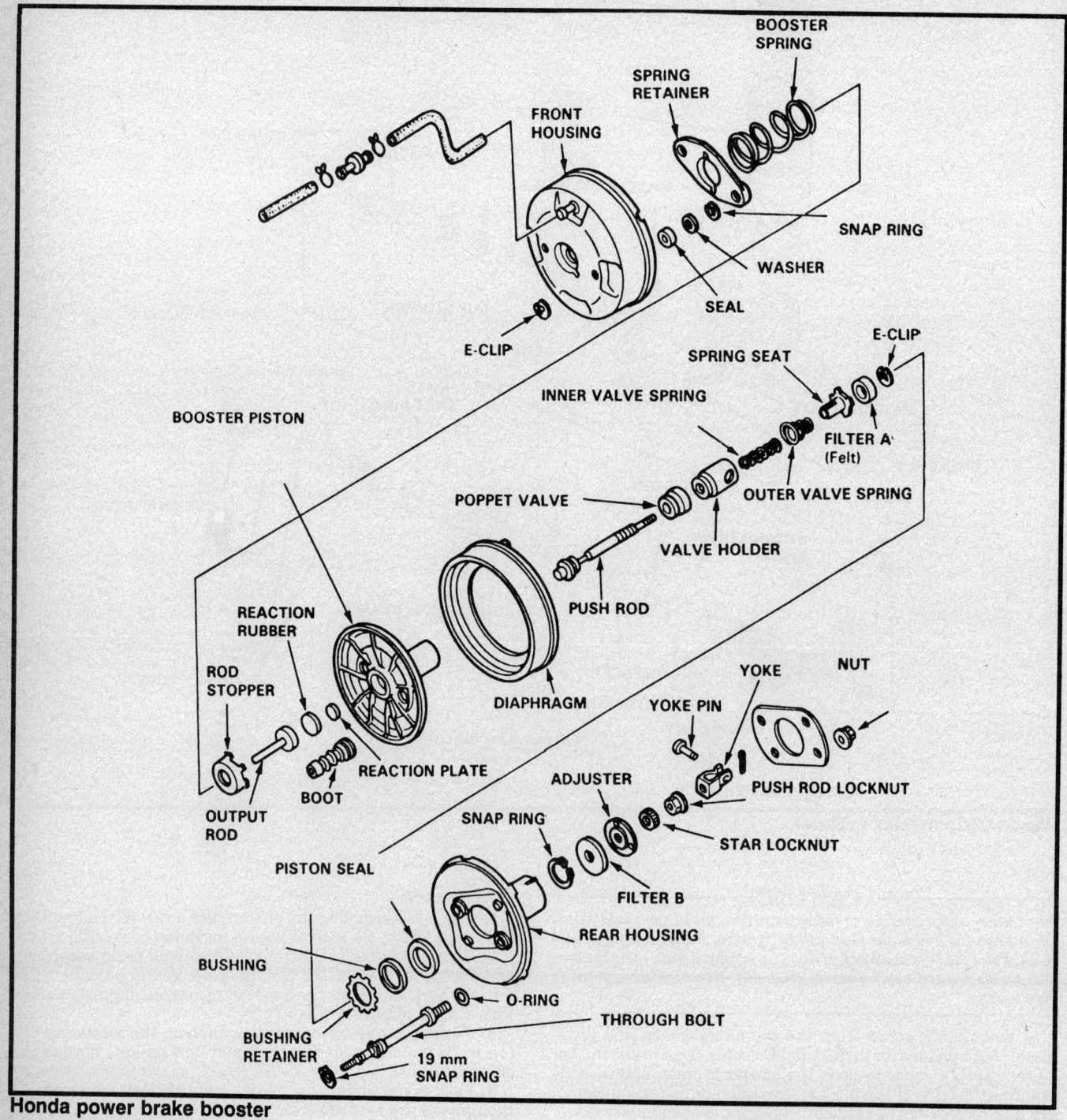

Honda power brake booster

Note: Disassemble the valve body only if the gauge tool and vacuum source are available.

5. To disassemble the valve body, remove the yoke and adjuster nuts to gain access to the snapring. Remove the snapring and lift the valve out of the body.

6. To disassemble the valve, remove the E-clip and carefully slide all the parts off the pushrod. Keep these parts in order for reassembly.

7. The factory rebuild kit includes the diaphragm, filters, snaprings and parts to recondition the valve. Be sure to use all the parts in the kit, especially the clips and snaprings.

To assemble:

8. To reassemble the valve, first lubricate the poppet valve with silicone grease and install it into the valve holder, then install the remaining parts in order. Make sure the spring seat has the short end facing the filter and install a new E-clip onto the pushrod to hold the filter in place.

9. Lubricate the valve body with silicone grease and press the pushrod and valve assembly into the valve body. Install the snapring.

10. Slip the filter B over the end of the pushrod and thread the adjuster and star locknut onto the rod but do not tighten them yet. Do not install the yoke yet.

11. On the rear housing, lube the piston seal with silicone grease and install the seal and bushing, with the lip of the seal facing away from the bushing.

12. Set the retainer in place and carefully drive it in evenly with a socket till the retainer is recessed no more than ¼ inch (6mm). Driving the retainer too far will distort the seal.

13. Install the O-rings and through bolts on the rear housing and secure with the 19mm snapring.

14. Attach the diaphragm to the booster piston. When installing the piston to the rear housing, lubricate the outer surface of the valve body with the silicone grease and be sure to align the slot with the tab.

15. Slip the new boots onto the through bolts. Lightly grease the reaction plate and rubber and them and the output rod and and rod stopper into the booster piston.

16. Install the booster spring and spring retainer on the through bolts and secure with the 10mm snaprings.

17. Install the washers and seals over the snaprings, making sure the flat side of the seal faces the spring retainer.

18. Press the front housing onto the rear housing with the matchmark aligned. Install new E-clips to hold the housings together. If the valve body was disassembled, adjust the pushrod clearance.

Booster Pushrod Clearance Adjustment

This procedure is for adjusting the static clearance between the pushrod on the output end of the booster and the secondary piston on the master cylinder. This needs to be done any time a booster or master cylinder is changed or rebuilt. With the booster installed and the engine running, the diaphragm is pulled part way towards the front housing at all times, moving the pushrod the same distance. If the pushrod is adjusted too long, the master cylinder piston will be pushed and the brakes will drag all the time. If the rod is too short, the pedal travel will be very long and full braking may not be available. This adjustment is critical to proper functioning of the brakes.

1. Slide the rod bolt adjustment gauge tool # 07JAG-SD40100, onto the master cylinder and adjust the bolt so it is flush with the master cylinder piston.

2. Install the master cylinder-to-booster seal onto the other end of the tool and without disturbing the adjuster bolt, install the tool onto the booster, torque the nuts to 11 ft. lbs.

3. The engine can be used as the vacuum source. Connect a vacuum line with a gauge from the intake manifold to the booster, and support the booster so that both ends of the pushrod are accessible. Start the engine and run it at a speed that produces 20 in. (500mm) Hg vacuum.

4. Using a feeler gauge, measure the clearance between the adjusting tool body and the adjusting nut. The clearance should be 0–0.016 in. (0-0.4mm).

5. Keep in mind that as the measured clearance increases, the pushrod will be closer to the piston in the master cylinder, increasing the chances of residual pressure in the hydraulic system. Do not let the measurement exceed 0.016 in. (0.4mm).

6. The tool must be removed to access the adjuster which is on the end of the pushrod. Hold the pushrod and turn the adjuster, then install the tool and measure again.

7. When the measurements are correct, that booster and master cylinder are now a matched set. Pedal height is set with the booster installed by adjusting the yoke on the booster input pushrod.

FRONT CALIPERS

Disassembly and Assembly

1. With the caliper removed from the vehicle and cleaned, remove the pad spring from the caliper body.

2. To remove the piston, place a block of wood in the caliper, lay a shop rag over the bore to prevent fluid spray, and gradually apply air pressure to the brake fluid inlet hole.

───────── **CAUTION** ─────────

When using compressed air to remove a piston, the piston could fly out like a projectile and brake fluid will be sprayed. Personal injury could result. Secure a block of wood in front of the bore, cover the bore with a shop rag and apply pressure gradually. Never use more pressure than needed.

3. Once the piston is out against the wood, it can be removed the rest of the way by hand. Being careful not to damage the cylinder, remove the dust boot and seal.

To assemble:

4. Clean all parts in brake fluid or brake part cleaner and examine the bore and piston. Minor corrosion can be cleaned off

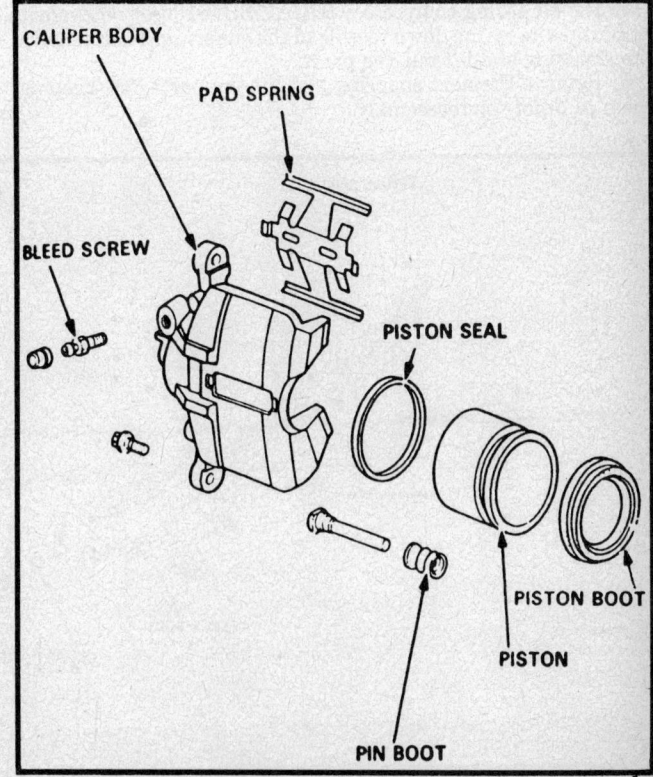

Honda floating caliper assembly

with steel wool or emery cloth, but scoring or piston damage cannot be repaired and the unit should be replaced.

5. Apply light silicone grease to the new piston seal and boot and install them onto the caliper.

6. Lubricate the piston and bore with clean brake fluid and carefully install the piston. Make sure the inner lip of the boot fits properly into the groove on the piston.

7. When installing the bleeder, torque the screw to 6 ft. lbs.

REAR WHEEL CYLINDER

Disassembly and Assembly

1. On 1990–91 vehicles, the wheel cylinders cannot be repaired, faulty units must be replaced. The wheel cylinders on earlier vehicles are fairly simple units and no special tools are required for service. Loosen the bleeder screw first, and if it doesn't break off, continue with the rebuild procedure.

2. With the cylinder apart, clean all parts in brake fluid or brake part cleaner and inspect the bore and pistons. Minor corrosion can be cleaned off with steel wool or emery cloth, but scoring or piston damage cannot be repaired and the entire assembly should be replaced.

3. When reassembling, lubricate all parts with brake fluid, not grease. When installing the cylinder, use a silicone sealer between the cylinder and the back plate.

REAR CALIPERS

Disassembly and Assembly

1. With the caliper removed and cleaned, rotate the piston to remove the piston and boot. Do not blow the piston out with air.

2. From the inside of the piston, remove the snapring and carefuly lift out all the parts, keeping them in order for reassembly.

3. Remove the piston seal from inside the bore, being careful not to damage the bore.

4. Install spring compressor 07GAE-SD40100 or equivalent and press the spring down to unload the snapring. Then remove the snapring and lift out the parts.

5. Remove the next snapring and lift the parts out, keeping them in order for reassembly.

6. On the side of the caliper, the parking brake cam and lever assembly can now be removed and disassembled for cleaning. Don't forget to remove the cam boot to gain access to the needle bearing.

To assemble:

7. Clean all parts in brake fluid or brake part cleaner and examine the bore, piston, bearing and cam. Minor corrosion can be cleaned off with steel wool or emery cloth, but scoring or piston damage cannot be repaired and the entire assembly should be replaced.

8. When reinstalling the cam, use an assembly lube such as moly grease to pack the needle beraings and cam boot. Install the boot first, then lube the cam and install it with the slot facing towards the cylinder bore.

9. Install the parking brake lever, lockwasher and nut onto the cam, then install the return spring. Torque the nut to 20 ft. lbs.

10. Support the caliper with the bore facing up and install the small rod or pin into the slot in the cam. The grease should help hold it in place.

11. On later models, install the sleeve piston so the hole in the bottom lines up with the pin in the cam and the 2 pins on the piston fit in the holes in the caliper.

12. Install a new cup onto the adjusting bolt. Lightly lube the bearing and install the bearing, spacer, spring and cover onto the bolt and set the assembly into the caliper.

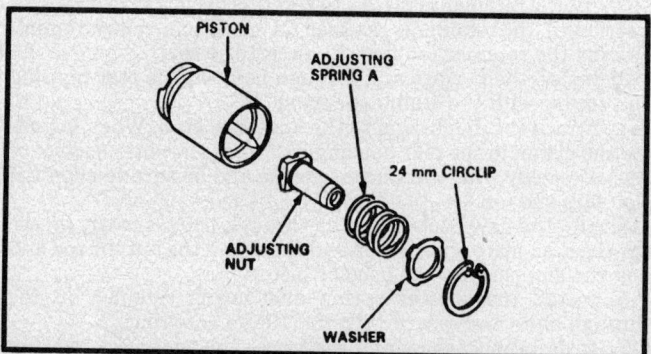

Piston assembly on Honda rear caliper

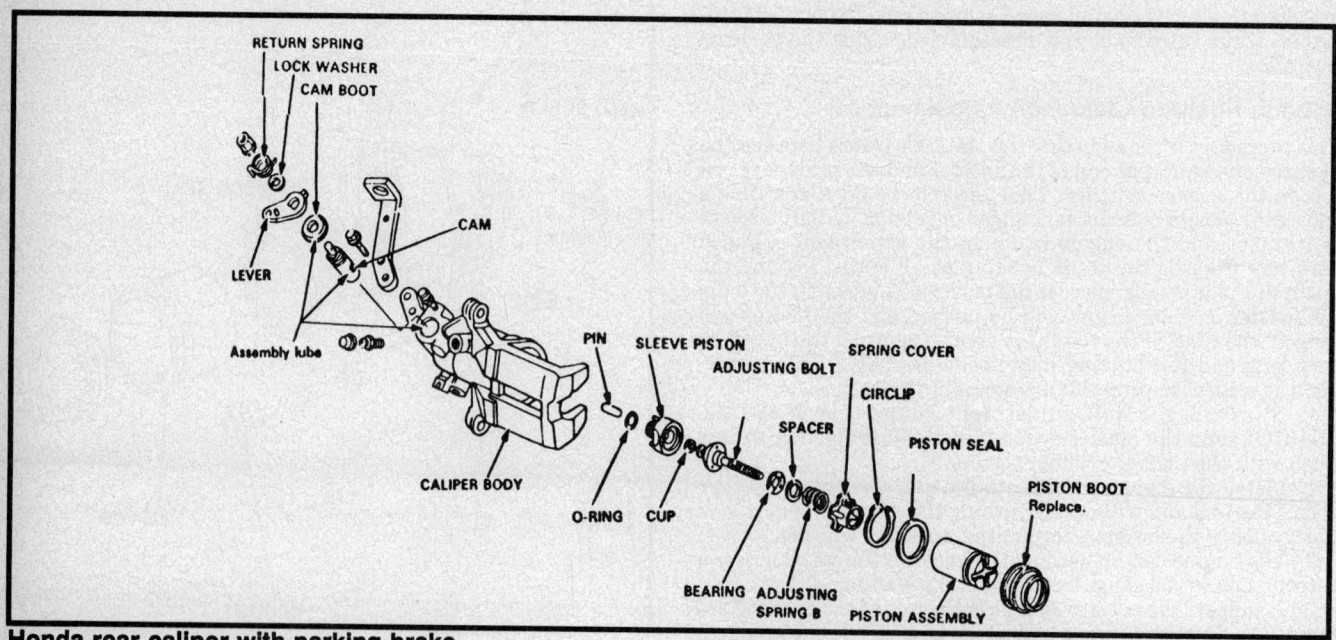

Honda rear caliper with parking brake

13. Install the spring compressor and press the spring all the way down. On early models the guide tool should also move down to keep the spring and cover straight in the bore.

14. With the spring compressed, remove the guide tool and see that the spring cover is down far enough so the snapring can be installed.

15. On the piston assembly, lube the threads of the adjusting nut and install the parts in order into the piston.

16. Lightly grease the new piston seal and boot and install them into the caliper. Grease the piston and carefully start it into the bore through the boot.

17. Rotate the piston clockwise to bottom it on the pushrod threads. Install the bleeder screw and torque it to 6 ft. lbs. The caliper is now ready for installation on the vehicle.

HYUNDAI

Master Cylinder Service

Disassembly and Assembly

On Sonata V6, the master cylinder cannot be repaired and no service parts are available. Faulty units must be replaced.

1. These vehicles use DOT 3 brake fluid. With the cylinder in a soft jaw vice, lightly push in on the piston to take up the spring tension and remove the stop screw from the side of the cylinder, if equipped, then the snapring.

2. With the primary piston out of the bore, tap the cylinder on a block of wood to remove the secondary piston. Do not use air pressure to remove the pistons.

3. On Scoupe, there are proportioning valves at the cylinder outlet ports which can be removed for cleaning. Be sure to use new O-rings when reassembling them to the cylinder.

4. Use only clean brake fluid or a brake parts cleaner to clean the master cylinder and carefully examine the bore. If there is any corrosion, distortion, scoring or piston damage, do not attempt to rebuild the cylinder, replace the entire assembly.

To assemble:

5. The factory rebuild kit comes with with the new springs and pistons already assembled. Lightly coat the bore and pistons with brake fluid, insert the secondary piston into the bore and gently work it all the way into the cylinder. Hold the piston

there while installing the stop screw with the new gasket. Torque the screw to about 2 ft. lbs., then slowly let the piston out against the stop screw.

6. Install the primary piston the same way and install the stopper ring.

7. Before installing a new or rebuilt cylinder, the booster pushrod clearance must be adjusted.

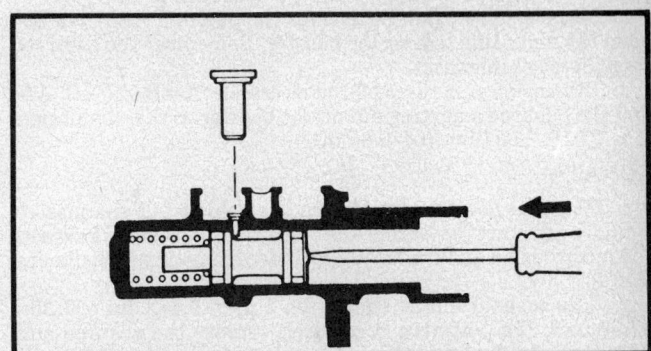

Removing stop pin on Sonata master cylinder

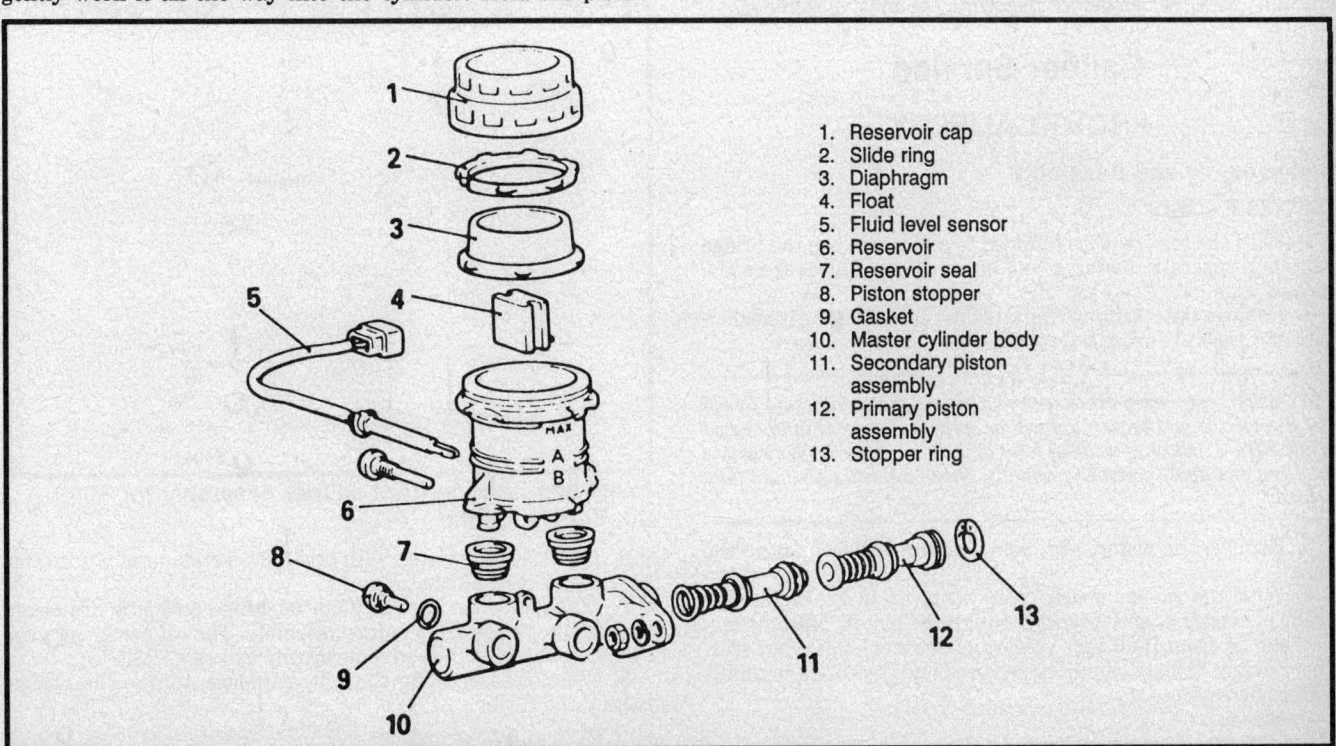

1. Reservoir cap
2. Slide ring
3. Diaphragm
4. Float
5. Fluid level sensor
6. Reservoir
7. Reservoir seal
8. Piston stopper
9. Gasket
10. Master cylinder body
11. Secondary piston assembly
12. Primary piston assembly
13. Stopper ring

Hyundai Excel master cylinder, Sonata and Scoupe similar

Brake Booster Service

Vacuum boosters on these vehicles cannot be rebuilt. The only service parts available are mounting gaskets and check valves. Faulty units must be replaced.

Booster Pushrod Clearance Adjustment

This procedure, required on 1987–89 Excel, is for adjusting the static clearance between the pushrod on the output end of the booster and the piston on the master cylinder. On the noted vehicles, this needs to be done any time a booster or master cylinder is changed or rebuilt. If the pushrod is adjusted too long, the master cylinder piston will be pushed and the brakes will drag. If the rod is too short, the pedal travel will be very long and full braking may not be available. This adjustment is critical to proper functioning of the brakes.

1. With a depth caliper, measure dimension **B** between the primary piston and the end of the master cylinder. If using a straight–edge to aid in caliper use, don't forget to subtract its' thickness from the total.

2. Measure dimension **C** between the cylinder mounting face and the end of the cylinder, with the gasket in place.

3. Measure dimension **D**, how far the pushrod sticks out beyond the mounting face on the booster. Remember the subtract straight–edge thickness.

4. Dimension **A** is the pushrod clearance. **A = B − C − D**. Adjust the pushrod adjusting nut on the booster so that dimension **A** is 0.016–0.031 in. (0.4–0.8mm).

SONATA

1. With the booster installed on the vehicle but the master cylinder off, start the engine and measure the distance between the pushrod end and the master cylinder mounting face; dimension **A**.

2. The measurement should be 1.470–1.482 in. (37.35–37.65mm). If adjustment is required, remove the pushrod and turn the adjuster nut on the end.

3. When reinstalling the pushrod, hold it in place with glue or silicone gasket sealer before installing the master cylinder.

Caliper Service

FRONT CALIPERS

Disassembly and Assembly

1987–88 EXCEL

1. With the torque plate clamped in a vice, remove the bridge bolts and seperate the inner and outer caliper halves from the torque plate.

2. Remove the retaining ring and dust seal from the inner caliper and carefully press the piston out with air pressure.

—————— **CAUTION** ——————

When using compressed air to remove a piston, the piston could fly out like a projectile and brake fluid will be sprayed. Personal injury could result. Secure a block of wood in front of the bore, cover the bore with a shop rag and apply pressure gradually. Never use more pressure than needed.

3. Remove the piston seal, being careful not to damage the bore.

4. With the caliper apart, clean all parts in brake fluid or brake part cleaner and inspect the bore and piston. Minor corrosion can be cleaned off with steel wool or emery cloth, but scoring or piston damage cannot be repaired and the entire assembly should be replaced.

To assemble:

5. Be sure to use all the parts in the rebuild kit. Lightly coat the new seal with silicone grease and install it into the bore.

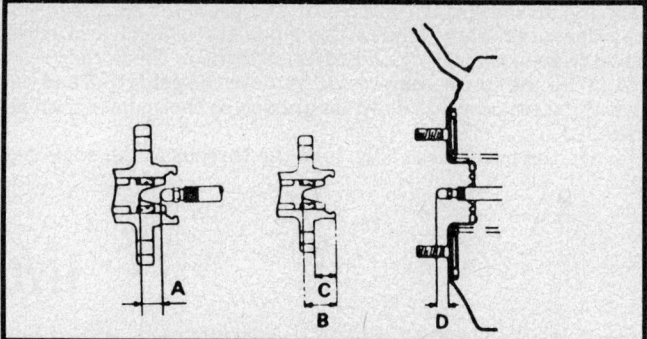

Booster pushrod clearance adjustment

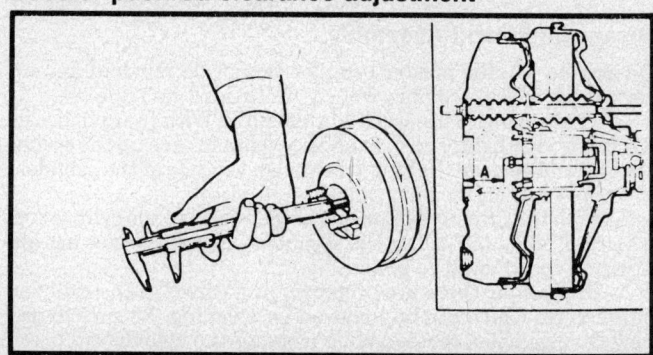

Sonata booster pushrod clearance adjustment, 1989–90

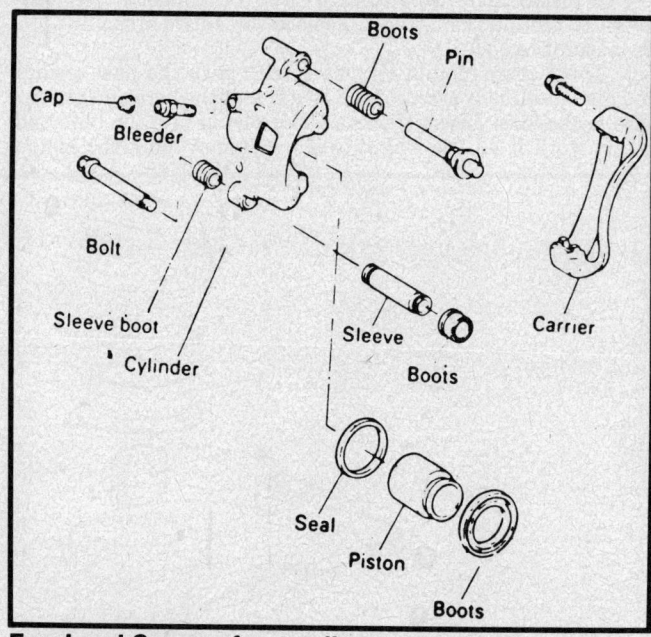

Excel and Scoupe front caliper assembly for 1989–90, Sonata similar

6. Lubricate the piston with brake fluid and install it into the bore. Push it in all the way.

7. Make sure the torque plate bushings and pins are clean and lightly grease them before assembly. The caliper must slide easily on the pins, but wipe away any excess grease.

8. When reassembling the caliper halves, torque the bridge bolts to 64 ft. lbs.

EXCEPT 1987–88 EXCEL

1. Remove the bolt holding the cylinder to the carrier, along

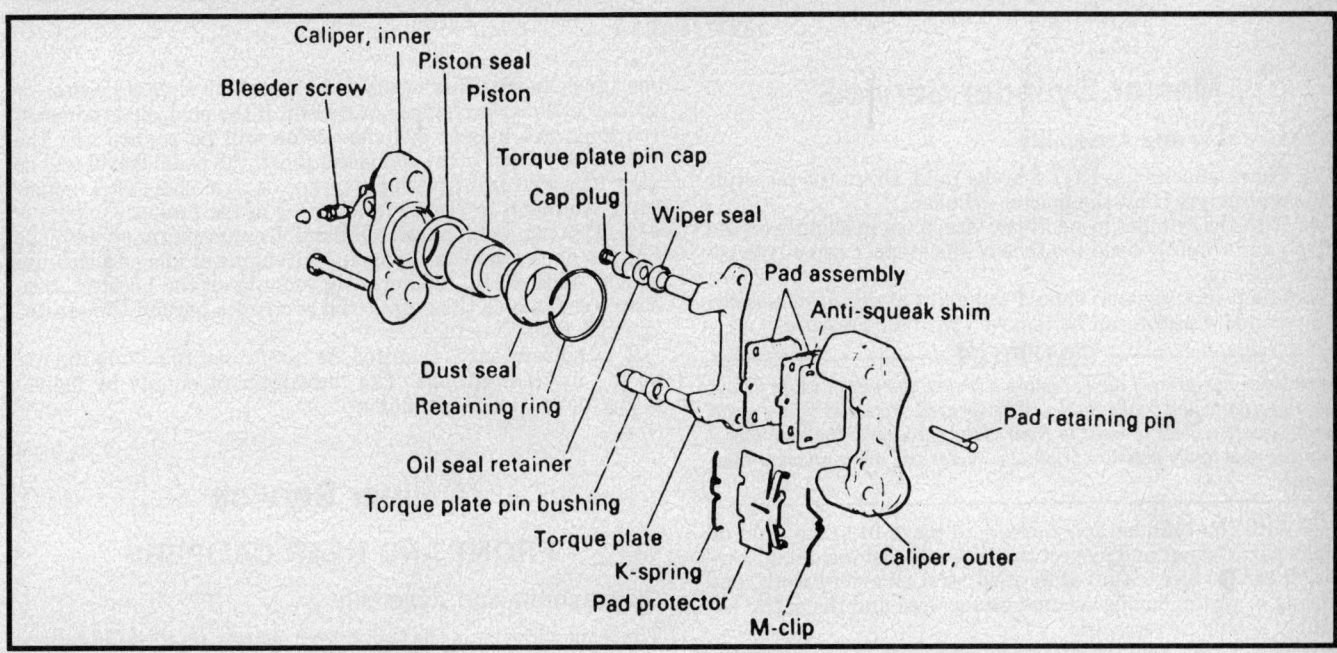

Excel front caliper assembly, 1987–88

with the dust boots, pin, sleeve and bleeder. Pay close attention to how the boots fit onto the caliper.

2. Remove the dust boot from the piston and carefully press the piston out with air pressure.

— **CAUTION** —

When using compressed air to remove a piston, the piston could fly out like a projectile and brake fluid will be sprayed. Personal injury could result. Secure a block of wood in front of the bore, cover the bore with a shop rag and apply pressure gradually. Never use more pressure than needed.

3. Remove the piston seal, being careful not to damage the bore.

4. With the caliper apart, clean all parts in brake fluid or brake part cleaner and inspect the bore and piston. Minor corrosion can be cleaned off with steel wool or emery cloth, but scoring or piston damage cannot be repaired and the entire assembly should be replaced.

To assemble:

5. Be sure to use all the parts in the rebuild kit. Lightly coat the new seal with silicone grease and install it into the bore.

6. Lightly coat the piston with grease and slip the boot onto the bottom of the piston. Extend the boot and fit the outer diameter lip into the groove in the bore, then carefully push the piston all the way into the bore. When this is done properly, the boot will fall into the groove in the piston and be neatly folded into place.

7. Install the pin boots onto the caliper, then install the sleeves onto the boots. Grease the pin and bolt and assemble the carrier to the cylinder. On Excel, torque the long bolt to 16–23 ft. lbs., the short bolt to 47–54 ft. lbs., and the pin to 25–32 ft. lbs. Wipe off any excess grease before installing the caliper.

REAR CALIPER

Disassembly and Assembly

SONATA V6

1. With the caliper cleaned and on the bench, carefully pry the outer ring of the dust boot out of the bore.

2. Remove the dust boot from the piston and carefuly press the piston out with air pressure.

— **CAUTION** —

When using compressed air to remove a piston, the piston could fly out like a projectile and brake fluid will be sprayed. Personal injury could result. Secure a block of wood in front of the bore, cover the bore with a shop rag and apply pressure gradually. Never use more pressure than needed.

3. Remove the piston seal, being careful not to damage the bore.

4. With the caliper apart, clean all parts in brake fluid or brake part cleaner and inspect the bore and piston. Minor corrosion can be cleaned off with steel wool or emery cloth, but scoring or piston damage cannot be repaired and the entire assembly should be replaced.

5. Lubricate the bore and new seal with brake fluid and install the seal.

6. Push the piston through the boot, making sure the boot seats in the groove of the piston. Then lube the piston with brake fluid and carefully slide the piston all the way into the bore.

7. The boot flange must be pressed into the caliper housing, much like installing a wheel bearing seal. One of the old brake pads and a clamp can be used for this job. Make sure it goes in evenly, being careful not to rip the boot.

WHEEL CYLINDER

Disassembly and Assembly

1. The wheel cylinders on vehicles with rear drum brakes are fairly simple units and no special tools are required for service. Loosen the bleeder screw first, and if it doesn't break off, continue with the rebuild procedure.

2. With the cylinder apart, clean all parts in brake fluid or brake part cleaner and inspect the bore and pistons. Minor corrosion can be cleaned off with steel wool or emery cloth, but scoring or piston damage cannot be repaired and the entire assembly should be replaced.

3. When reassembling, lubricate all parts with brake fluid, not grease. When installing the cylinder, use a silicone sealer between the cylinder and the back plate.

INFINITI

Master Cylinder Service

Disassembly and Assembly

1. These vehicles use DOT 3 brake fluid. Drain the reservoir and carefuly pry it off the master cylinder.

2. With the cylinder in a soft jaw vice, push in slightly on the piston and carefuly bend the tabs of the stopper cap out to remove the cap.

3. The primary piston should come out easily. If necessary, the secondary piston can be removed with air pressure.

———— CAUTION ————

When using compressed air to remove a piston, the piston could fly out like a projectile and brake fluid will be sprayed. Personal injury could result. Secure a block of wood in front of the bore, cover the bore with a shop rag and apply pressure gradually. Never use more pressure than needed.

4. With the cylinder apart, clean all parts in brake fluid or brake part cleaner and inspect the bore and pistons. Minor corrosion can be cleaned off with steel wool or emery cloth, but scoring or piston damage cannot be repaired and the entire assembly should be replaced.

5. The factory rebuild kit comes with with the new springs and pistons already assembled. Lightly coat the bore and pistons with brake fluid and carefuly insert both pistons, then install the stopper cap. It may be necessary to bend the tabs on the cap in a little to assure a good grip.

6. Install the reservoir with new seals and before installing the master cylinder, check the booster pushrod length.

Vacuum Booster Service

The booster on these vehicles cannot be repaired and no service parts are available from Nissan. Faulty units must be replaced.

Booster Pushrod Clearance Adjustment

This procedure is for adjusting the static clearance between the pushrod on the output end of the booster and the piston on the master cylinder. This needs to be done any time a booster or master cylinder is changed or rebuilt. If the pushrod is adjusted too long, the master cylinder piston will be pushed and the brakes will drag. If the rod is too short, the pedal travel will be very long and full braking may not be available. This adjustment is critical to proper functioning of the brakes.

1. This can be done with a hand vacuum pump or with the booster on the vehicle and using the engine at idle as a vacuum source. With 20 in. (500mm) Hg vacuum on the booster, measure the distance the output rod protrudes beyond the master cylinder mounting face.

2. If adjustment is required, be careful not to distort the rod or the internal springs. The measurement should be 0.404–0.414 inch (10.275–10.525mm).

Caliper Service

FRONT AND REAR CALIPERS

Disassembly and Assembly

The front calipers on the Q45 have 2 pistons, on the M30 caliper there is only a single piston. The rear calipers are similar on both models and the rebuild procedure for all units is the same. Be sure to use all the parts in the rebuild kit.

1. To remove the piston, place a block of wood in the caliper, lay a shop rag over the bore to prevent fluid spray, and gradually apply air pressure to the brake fluid inlet hole.

———— CAUTION ————

When using compressed air to remove a piston, the piston could fly out like a projectile and brake fluid will be sprayed. Personal injury could result. Secure a block of wood in front of the bore, cover the bore with a shop rag and apply pressure gradually. Never use more pressure than needed.

2. Once the piston is out against the wood, it can be removed the rest of the way by hand. Being careful not to damage the cylinder, remove the dust boot and piston seal.

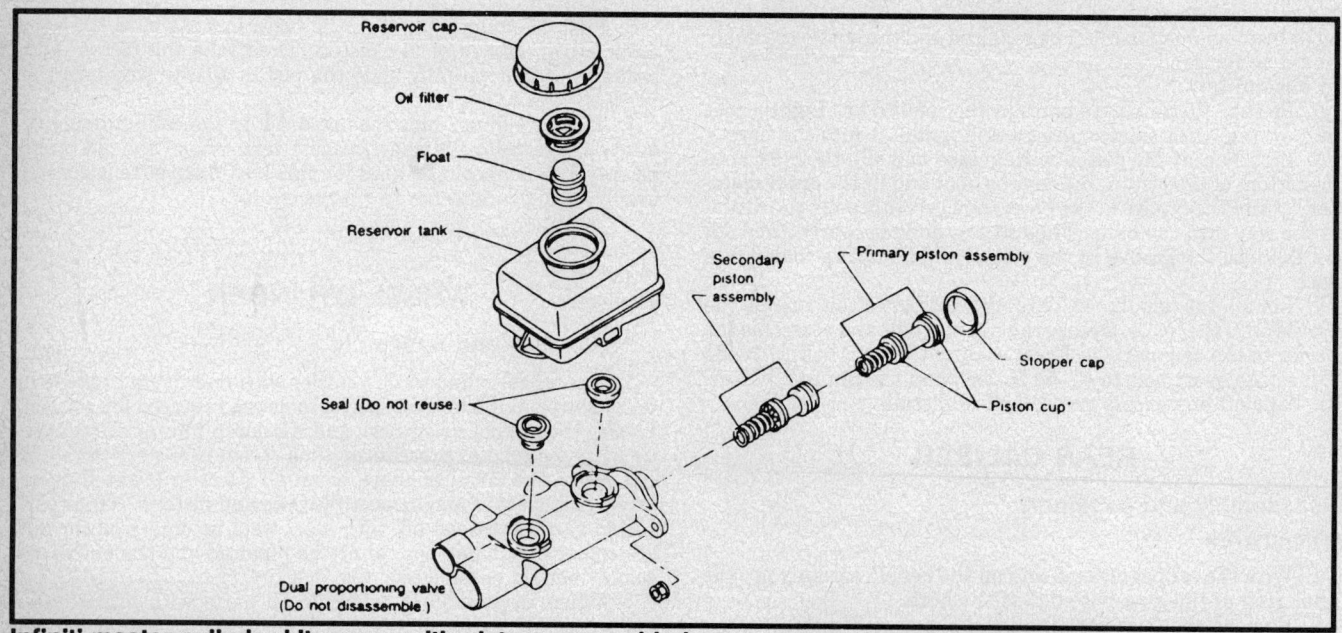

Infiniti master cylinder kit comes with pistons assembled

To assemble:

3. Clean all parts in brake fluid or brake part cleaner and examine the bore and piston. Minor corrosion can be cleaned off with steel wool or emery cloth, but scoring or piston damage cannot be repaired and the unit should be replaced.

4. Apply light silicone grease to the new piston seal and install it onto the groove in the caliper. This seal is directional, with the larger outside diameter towards the open end of the bore.

5. Assemble the boot to the piston, then fit the boot into the groove in the caliper, then push the piston carefully into the bore.

6. Clean and lubricate the sliding pins and bolts and observe the following torques:
   a. Q45 front caliper sliding pin bolts—61–69 ft. lbs.
   b. Q45 rear caliper sliding pin bolts—23–30 ft. lbs.
   c. M30 front caliper sliding pin bolts—53–72 ft. lbs.
   d. M30 rear caliper sliding pin bolts—23–30 ft. lbs.

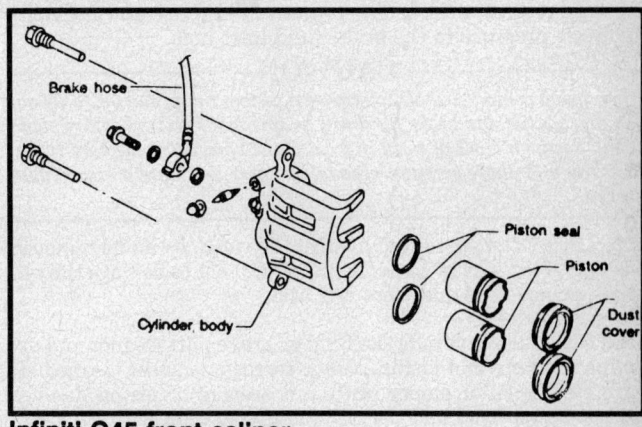

Infiniti Q45 front caliper

ISUZU

Master Cylinder Service

Disassembly and Assembly

1. These vehicles use DOT 3 brake fluid. With the cylinder in a soft jaw vice, lightly push in on the piston to take up the spring tension and remove the stop screws from the side of the cylinder, then the dust seal and snapring.

2. With the primary piston out of the bore, tap the cylinder on a block of wood to remove the secondary piston. Do not use air pressure to remove the pistons.

3. Use only clean brake fluid or a brake parts cleaner to clean the master cylinder and carefuly examine the bore. If there is any corrosion, distortion or scoring, do not attempt to rebuild the cylinder, replace the entire assembly.

To assemble:

4. The factory rebuild kit comes with with the new springs and pistons already assembled. Lightly coat the bore and pistons with silicone grease and insert both pistons, then install the snapring.

5. Push in all the way on the primary piston and install both stop screws with new gaskets. Torque them to 6 ft. lbs. Install the new dust seal with the notch at the bottom. Before installing onto the booster, the pushrod clearance must be adjusted.

Booster Service

Vacuum boosters on these vehicles cannot be repaired and no service parts are available from Isuzu. Faulty units must be replaced.

Booster Pushrod Clearance Adjustment

This procedure is for adjusting the static clearance between the pushrod on the output end of the booster and the piston on the master cylinder. This needs to be done any time a booster or master cylinder is changed or rebuilt. If the pushrod is adjusted too long, the master cylinder piston will be pushed and the brakes will drag. If the rod is too short, the pedal travel will be very long and full braking may not be available. This adjustment is critical to proper functioning of the brakes.

1. With a depth caliper, measure dimension **B** between the primary piston and the end of the master cylinder. If using a straight–edge to aid in caliper use, don't forget to subtract its' thickness from the total.

2. Measure dimension **C** between the cylinder mounting face and the end of the cylinder, with the gasket in place.

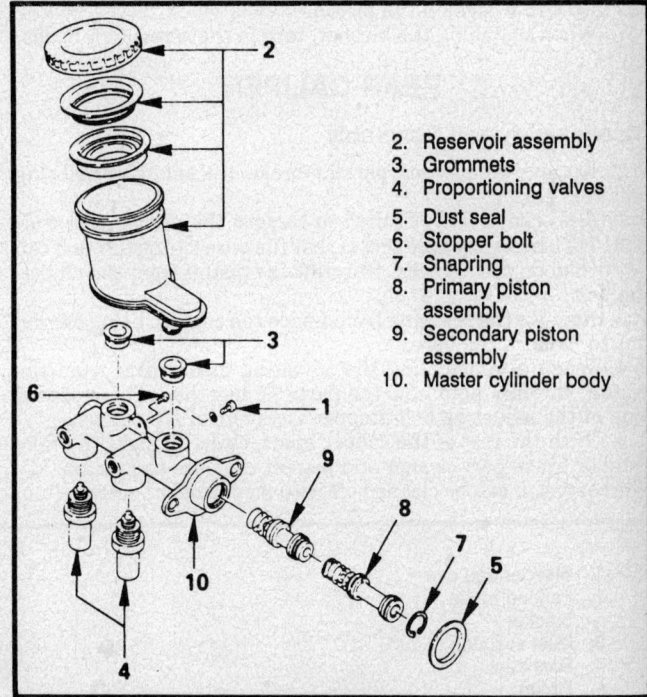

2. Reservoir assembly
3. Grommets
4. Proportioning valves
5. Dust seal
6. Stopper bolt
7. Snapring
8. Primary piston assembly
9. Secondary piston assembly
10. Master cylinder body

Isuzu master cylinder with proportioning valves

3. Measure dimension **D**, how far the pushrod sticks out beyond the mounting face on the booster. Remember the subtract straight–edge thickness.

4. Dimension **A** is the pushrod clearance. $A = B - C - D$. Adjust the pushrod adjusting nut on the booster so that dimension **A** is zero.

Caliper Service

FRONT CALIPERS

Disassembly and Assembly

1. To remove the piston, place a block of wood in the caliper,

lay a shop rag over the bore to prevent fluid spray, and gradually apply air pressure to the brake fluid inlet hole.

CAUTION

When using compressed air to remove a piston, the piston could fly out like a projectile and brake fluid will be sprayed. Personal injury could result. Secure a block of wood in front of the bore, cover the bore with a shop rag and apply pressure gradually. Never use more pressure than needed.

2. Once the piston is out against the wood, it can be removed the rest of the way by hand. Being careful not to damage the cylinder, remove the dust boot and seal.

To assemble:

3. Clean all parts in brake fluid or brake part cleaner and examine the bore and piston. Minor corrosion can be cleaned off with steel wool or emery cloth, but scoring or piston damage cannot be repaired and the unit should be replaced.

4. Apply light silicone grease to the new piston seal and install it onto the groove in the caliper.

5. Unfold the new boot, lubricate the piston with clean silicone grease and carefully slide the bottom of the piston into the boot.

6. Fit the inner lip of the boot properly into the groove in the caliper and push the piston into the bore. Make sure the boot fits into the groove on the piston.

7. When installing the bleeder, torque the screw to 6 ft. lbs.

REAR CALIPER

Disassembly and Assembly

1. Remove the bleeder, parking brake bracket, dust seal ring and dust seal.

2. A special tool is required to remove the piston, tool # J-37617. This is a key type socket that fits onto the piston so it can be turned on the threads. Unscrew the piston from the adjusting bolt.

3. Remove the seal ring from inside the caliper, being careful not to damage the bore.

4. When disassembling the adjusting mechanism from the piston, carefully note how the parts fit together. The embosed side of the adjusting bolt stopper faces out of the caliper.

5. With the rest of the caliper apart, clean all parts in brake fluid or brake part cleaner and inspect the bore and piston. Minor corrosion can be cleaned off with steel wool or emery cloth,

but scoring or piston damage cannot be repaired and the entire assembly should be replaced. Be sure to use all the parts in the rebuild kit when reassembling the caliper.

To assemble:

6. Lightly lubricate the piston seal ring with the silicone grease in the kit and install the ring into the caliper. Lube the boot and install it onto the piston.

7. When installing the parking brake lever, grease the boot and internal parts and torque the nut to 17 ft. lbs.

8. Before installing the adjusting bolt assembly, the spring should be fully compressed using the auto-adjusting spindle on the piston side. Align the adjusting bolt stopper in the bore and install the snapring.

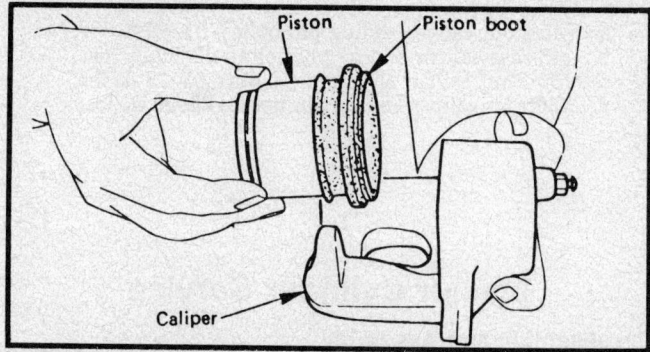

Installing the boot and piston on Isuzu front caliper assembly

Use the auto-adjusting spindle to compress the spring for assembly into the piston

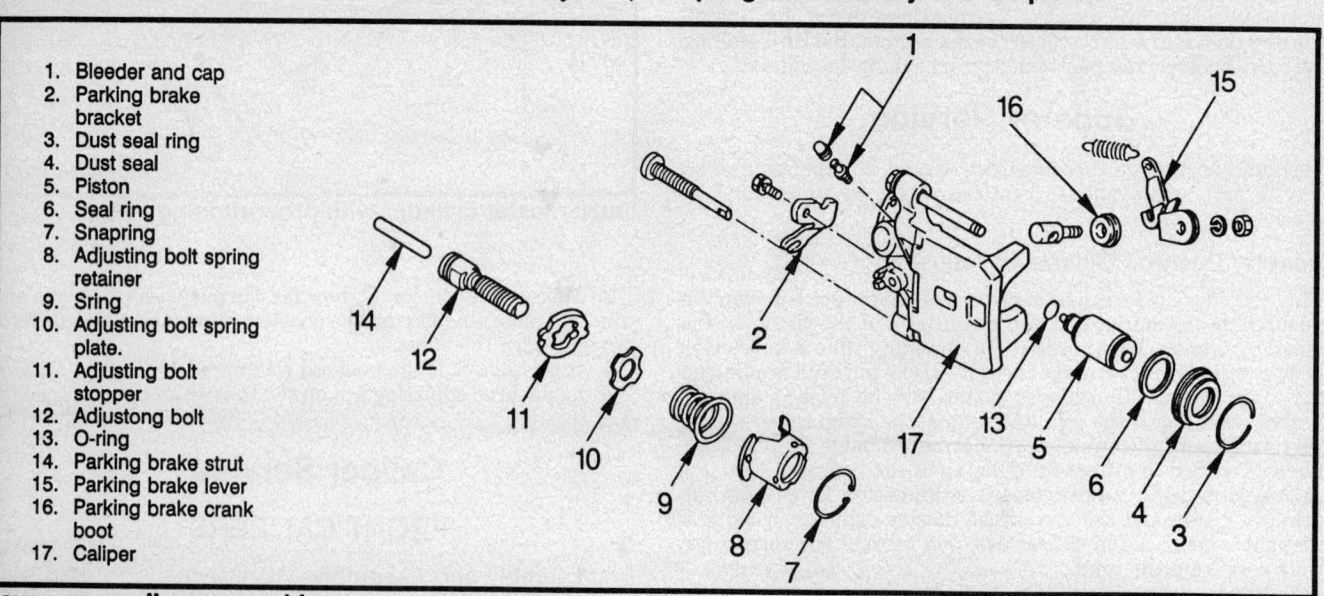

1. Bleeder and cap
2. Parking brake bracket
3. Dust seal ring
4. Dust seal
5. Piston
6. Seal ring
7. Snapring
8. Adjusting bolt spring retainer
9. Sring
10. Adjusting bolt spring plate
11. Adjusting bolt stopper
12. Adjustong bolt
13. O-ring
14. Parking brake strut
15. Parking brake lever
16. Parking brake crank boot
17. Caliper

Isuzu rear caliper assembly

9. Lightly grease the piston before screwing it into the caliper. Make sure the indents in the piston properly align with the back of the brake pad.

REAR WHEEL CYLINDER

Disassembly and Assembly

1. The wheel cylinders on vehicles with rear drum brakes are fairly simple units and no special tools are required for service.

Loosen the bleeder screw first, and if it doesn't break off, continue with the rebuild procedure.

2. With the cylinder apart, clean all parts in brake fluid or brake part cleaner and inspect the bore and pistons. Minor corrosion can be cleaned off with steel wool or emery cloth, but scoring or piston damage cannot be repaired and the entire assembly should be replaced.

3. When reassembling, lubricate all parts with brake fluid, not grease. When installing the cylinder, use a silicone sealer between the cylinder and the back plate.

JAGUAR

Master Cylinder Service

Disassembly and Assembly

These vehicles have no vacuum booster, the power assist is fully hydraulic. Like all anti-lock brake systems, the pressure modulator is not field servicable, faulty units must be replaced. However the master cylinder and calipers are familiar units and rebuild kits are available from Jaguar.

1. These vehicles use DOT 4 brake fluid. Drain the reservoir and remove it by removing the roll pin.

2. carefuly pry the end cap off the master cylinder and remove the primary piston. If the secondary piston is difficult to remove, it can be pressed out with air pressure.

CAUTION
When using compressed air to remove a piston, the piston could fly out like a projectile and brake fluid will be sprayed. Personal injury could result. Secure a block of wood in front of the bore, cover the bore with a shop rag and apply pressure gradually. Never use more pressure than needed.

3. With the cylinder apart, clean all parts in brake fluid or brake part cleaner and inspect the bore and pistons. Minor corrosion can be cleaned off with steel wool or emery cloth, but scoring or piston damage cannot be repaired and the entire assembly should be replaced.

4. A new primary piston is included as an assembly in the manufacturer's rebuild kit, but the secondary piston cups and springs must be fitted to the original piston. Be sure to use all parts in the kit.

5. Liberly lubricate the cylinder and piston cups with new brake fluid and carefully install the secondary spring, rebuilt secondary piston and new primary piston.

6. When installing the new end cap, make sure the gap in the

rim lines up with the space in the cylinder flange. The new cap must be crimped in place. Lube the new reservoir seals and install the reservoir.

Caliper Service

Disassembly and Assembly

1. The front and rear calipers are the same, but there is a right and left. The repair procedures are the same. With the caliper cleaned, carefully press the piston out with air pressure.

CAUTION
When using compressed air to remove a piston, the piston could fly out like a projectile and brake fluid will be sprayed. Personal injury could result. Secure a block of wood in front of the bore, cover the bore with a shop rag and apply pressure gradually. Never use more pressure than needed.

2. With the caliper apart, clean all parts in brake fluid or brake part cleaner and inspect the bore and pistons. Minor corrosion can be cleaned off with steel wool or emery cloth, but scoring or piston damage cannot be repaired and the entire assembly should be replaced. Guide pins cannot be reconditioned. If the pin is rusted or seized, replace it.

3. Lubricate the new piston seal with brake fluid and install it into the groove in the bore.

4. Lubricate the piston with brake fluid and install the new boot into the groove in the piston. Unfold and extend the boot all the way to the bottom of the piston and fit the boot into its' groove in the caliper. With the boot properly fitted, carefuly push the piston all the way into the bore.

5. When installing the pins and boots, lubricate the pins with Molycoat® 111 grease, supplied in the rebuild kit. Do not use any other type of grease.

LEXUS

Master Cylinder Service

Disassembly and Assembly

1. These vehicles use DOT 3 brake fluid. With the cylinder drained and clamped in a soft jaw vice, remove the reservoir set screw and the reservoir. Then remove the boot at the mounting flange.

2. Using a blunt tool, push the piston in just enough to take up the spring tension and remove the 2 piston stopper screws and the snapring.

3. Remove both the secondary and primary piston assemblies

by tapping them out on a block of wood. Do not use air pressure and be careful to not damage the bore.

4. Use only clean brake fluid or a brake parts cleaner to clean the master cylinder and carefuly examine the bore. If there is any corrosion or distortion, do not attempt to rebuild the cylinder, replace the entire assembly. Be sure to use all the parts in the rebuild kit.

To assemble:

5. When inserting the pistons, lubricate all parts with a rubber grease and rotate the pistons while gently pushing them into the bore.

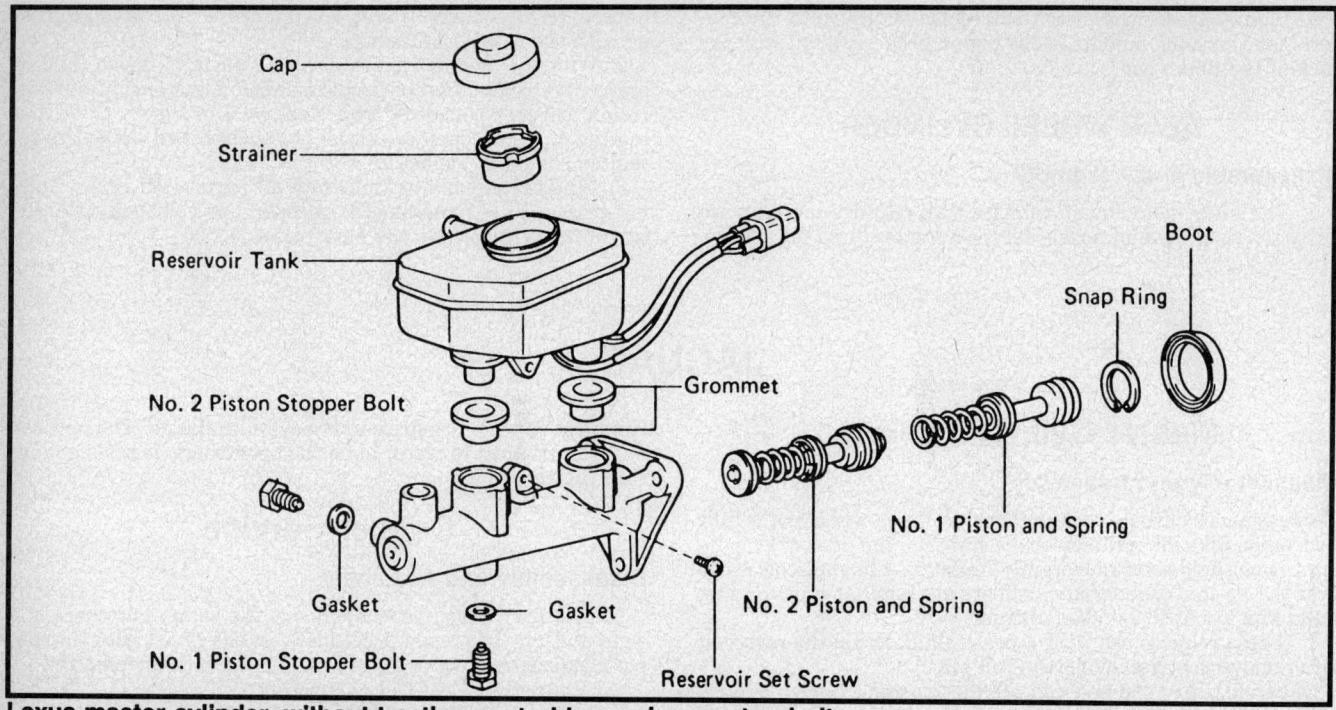

Lexus master cylinder, without traction control has only one stop bolt

6. With both pistons installed, push in on the primary piston while installing the stop bolts and snapring. Torque the bolts to 7 ft. lbs.

7. Install the flange boot and, when installing the reservoir, lubricate the grommets with brake fluid. Before installing the master cylinder, the booster pushrod clearance must be adjusted.

Brake Booster Service

The vacuum booster on these vehicles cannot be repaired and no service parts are available from the factory. Faulty units must be replaced, but the pushrod length must be adjusted before installing the master cylinder.

BOOSTER PUSHROD CLEARANCE ADJUSTMENT

This procedure is for adjusting the static clearance between the pushrod on the output end of the booster and the piston on the master cylinder. This needs to be done any time a booster or master cylinder is changed or rebuilt. If the pushrod is adjusted too long, the master cylinder piston will be pushed and the brakes will drag. If the rod is too short, the pedal travel will be very long and full braking may not be available. This adjustment is critical to proper functioning of the brakes.

1. A special tool is available to make this job much faster and more acurate, special service tool SST 09737-00010. With the new gasket on the master cylinder mounting flange, set the tool on the flange and adjust the pin to touch the piston.

2. Turn the tool over and set it on the booster. The clearance between the pin and the pushrod should be zero. Turn the adjusting nut as needed.

Caliper Service

Disassembly and Assembly

The front and rear caliper on the LS 400 are similar to each other. The front and rear caliper on the ES 250 are similar to each other. This means the parking brake is seperate from the rear

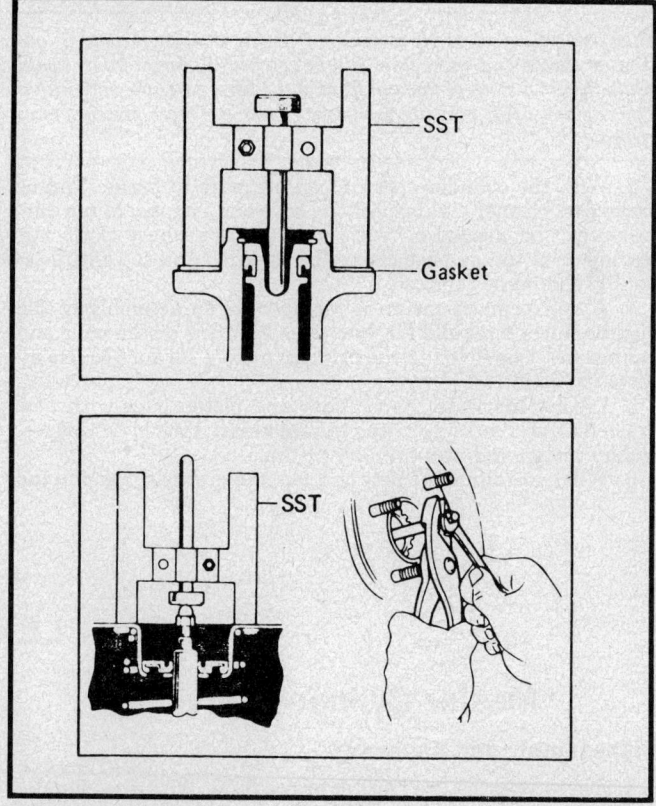

Adjusting the pushrod clearance in the power brake booster assembly

caliper on both vehicles. Even though the calipers are different on each vehicle, the service procedure is the same.

1. Remove the boot set ring and boot, then carefully press the piston out with air pressure and remove the piston seal.

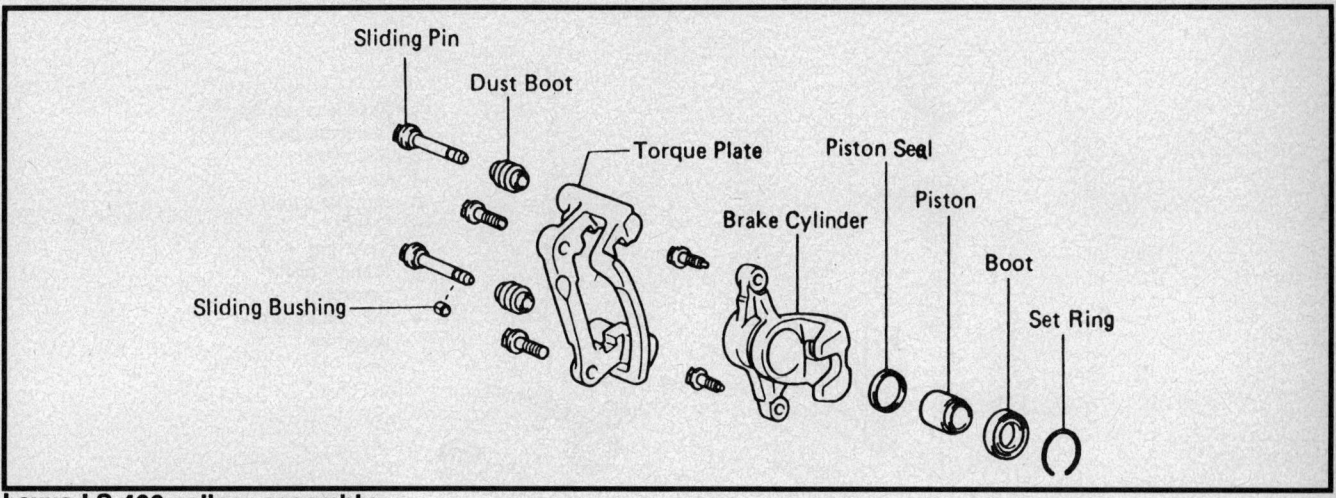

Lexus LS 400 caliper assembly

CAUTION

When using compressed air to remove a piston, the piston could fly out like a projectile and brake fluid will be sprayed. Personal injury could result. Secure a block of wood in front of the bore, cover the bore with a shop rag and apply pressure gradually. Never use more pressure than needed.

---

2. On LS 400, remove the sliding pins and boots from the torque plate.

3. On ES 250, remove the sliding pins and boots from the caliper.

4. With the caliper apart, clean all parts in brake fluid or brake part cleaner and inspect the bore and piston. Minor corrosion can be cleaned off with steel wool or emery cloth, but scoring or piston damage cannot be repaired and the entire assembly should be replaced. Don't forget to clean the sliding pins too.

To assemble:

5. Use a lithium base rubber grease to lubricate the sliding pins and boots and install the boots and bushings. On the LS 400, the boots can be pressed in with a 19mm socket and a light hammer.

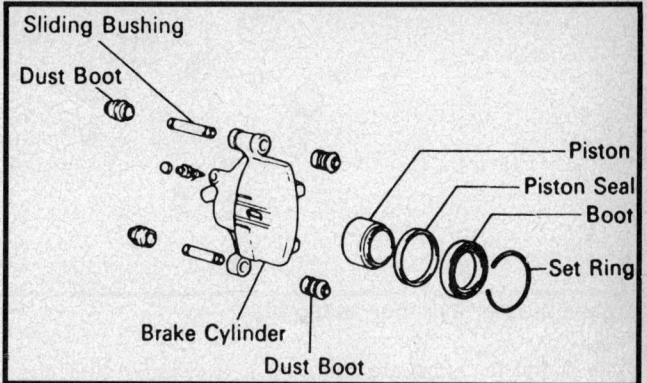

Lexus ES 250 caliper assembly

6. Lightly grease the piston and piston seal and install them into the caliper.

7. Lightly grease the dust boot and install the boot and set ring.

8. Be sure the sliding pins move freely before installing the caliper.

MAZDA

Master Cylinder Service

Disassembly and Assembly

323, 626, AND RX–7

1. These vehicles use DOT 3 or DOT 4 brake fluid. Remove the reservoir assembly and the bushings that hold it in place.

2. With the cylinder in a soft jaw vice, lightly push in on the piston to take up the spring tension and remove the stop screw from the bottom of the cylinder, then the stop ring.

3. With the secondary piston out of the bore, tap the cylinder on a block of wood to remove the primary piston. If it is difficult to remove, air pressure can be used to force the piston out. Do not disassemble the pistons.

CAUTION

When using compressed air to remove a piston, the piston could fly out like a projectile and brake fluid will be sprayed. Personal injury could result. Point the bore at a block of wood up against a wall, cover the bore with a shop rag and apply pressure gradually. Never use more pressure than is needed.

---

4. Use only clean brake fluid or a brake parts cleaner to clean the master cylinder and carefully examine the bore. If there is any corrosion or distortion, do not attempt to rebuild the cylinder, replace the entire assembly.

To assemble:

5. For 1987–89 vehicles, the service kit should come with the primary piston already assembled. For 1990–91, both pistons

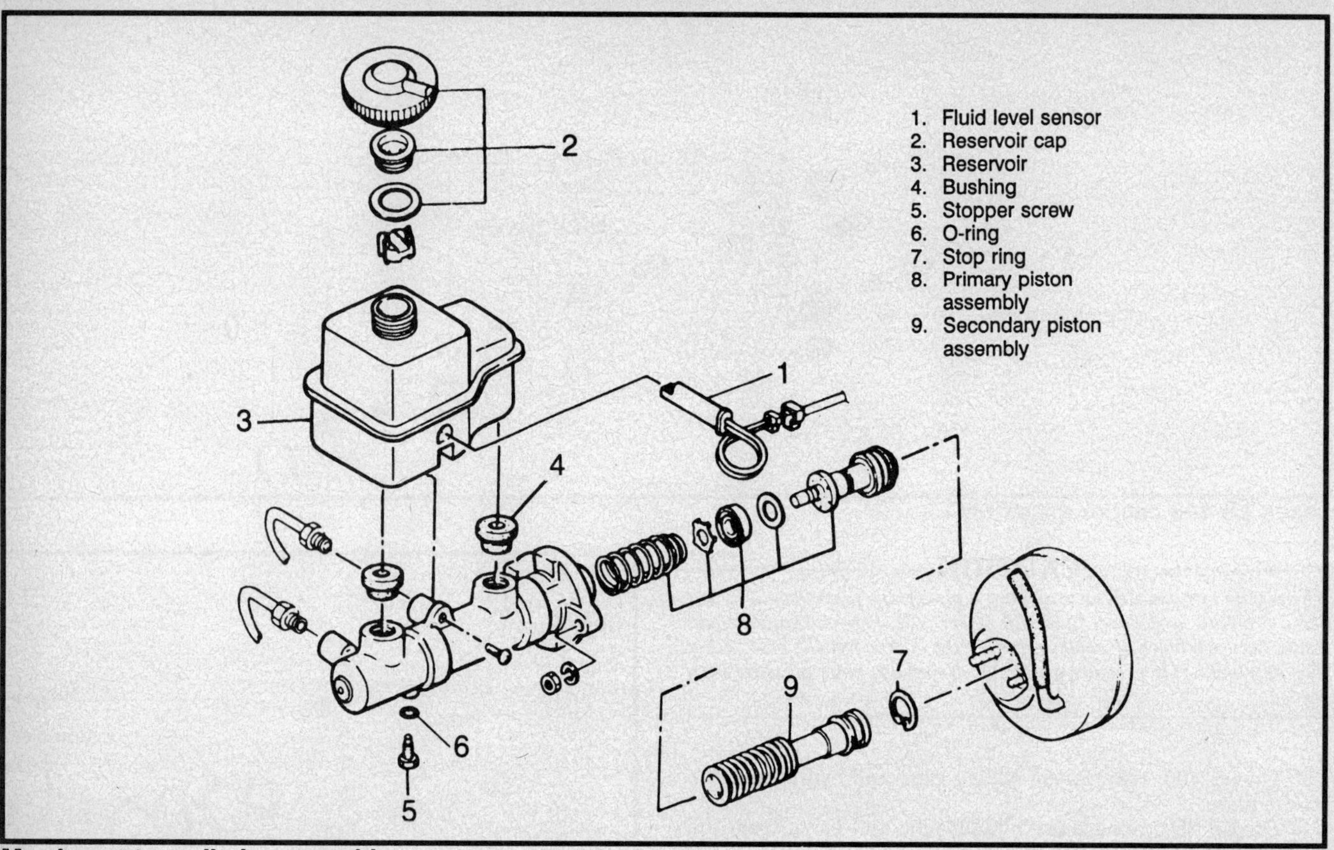

1. Fluid level sensor
2. Reservoir cap
3. Reservoir
4. Bushing
5. Stopper screw
6. O-ring
7. Stop ring
8. Primary piston assembly
9. Secondary piston assembly

Mazda master cylinder assembly

come complete. Lubricate the cups and cylinder with clean brake fluid and carefully insert the pistons into the bore. Install the stop screw, stop ring, and reservoir.

6. Before installing the cylinder onto the booster, the clearance between the pushrod and secondary piston must be adjusted.

Brake Booster Service

Disassembly and Assembly

EXCEPT MIATA

1. Screw 2 nuts onto each master cylinder mounting stud on the booster and clamp the studs in a vice. Install the special wrench that fits onto the 4 studs on the rear housing and torque the nuts evenly. Make a matchmark on each housing half and unscrew the rear housing from the booster. The assembly is spring loaded, so be careful not to let it fly apart.

2. To disassemble the valve assembly, push in on the valve rod and remove the retainer key.

To assemble:

3. Be sure to use all the parts in the rebuild kit. When reassembling, use silicone grease to lubricate the reaction disc (13), dust seal lip (5), pushrod (15), diaphragm where it contacts the housing (9), power piston (10), and valve plunger oil seal (12).

4. When reassembling the housing halves, be sure to carefully align the matchmarks. Wipe away any excess grease and install the dust boot on the rear housing.

MIATA

The booster on these vehicles cannot be repaired, faulty units must be replaced. Before installing the booster, set the pushrod clearance.

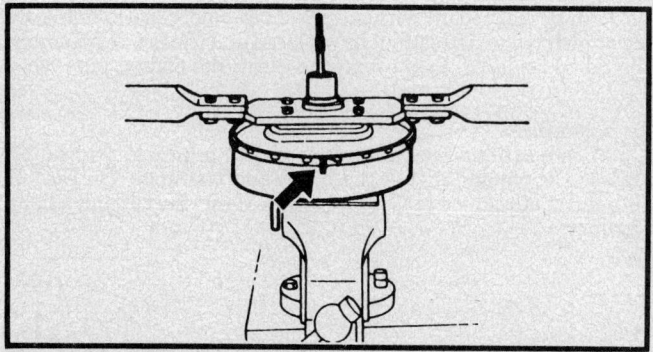

Removing the rear housing with special wrench, be sure to mark both halves

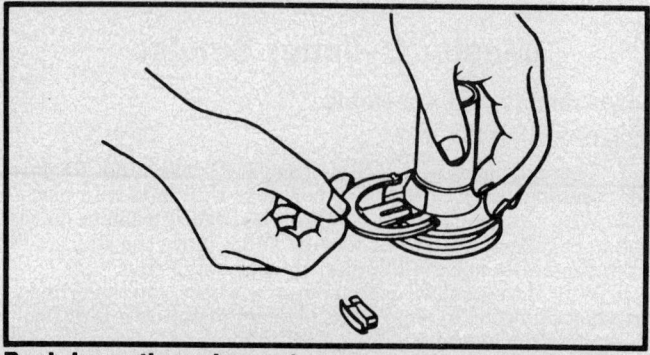

Push in on the valve rod to remove the retainer key

1. Dust boot
2. Rear housing assembly
3. Retainer
4. Bearing
5. Dust seal
6. Retainer
7. Air filter
8. Air silencer
9. Diaphragm and plate
10. Power piston assembly
11. Retainer key and stopper
12. Valve rod and plunger assembly
13. Reaction disc
14. Spring
15. Pushrod
16. Front housing assembly
17. Retainer
18. Seal

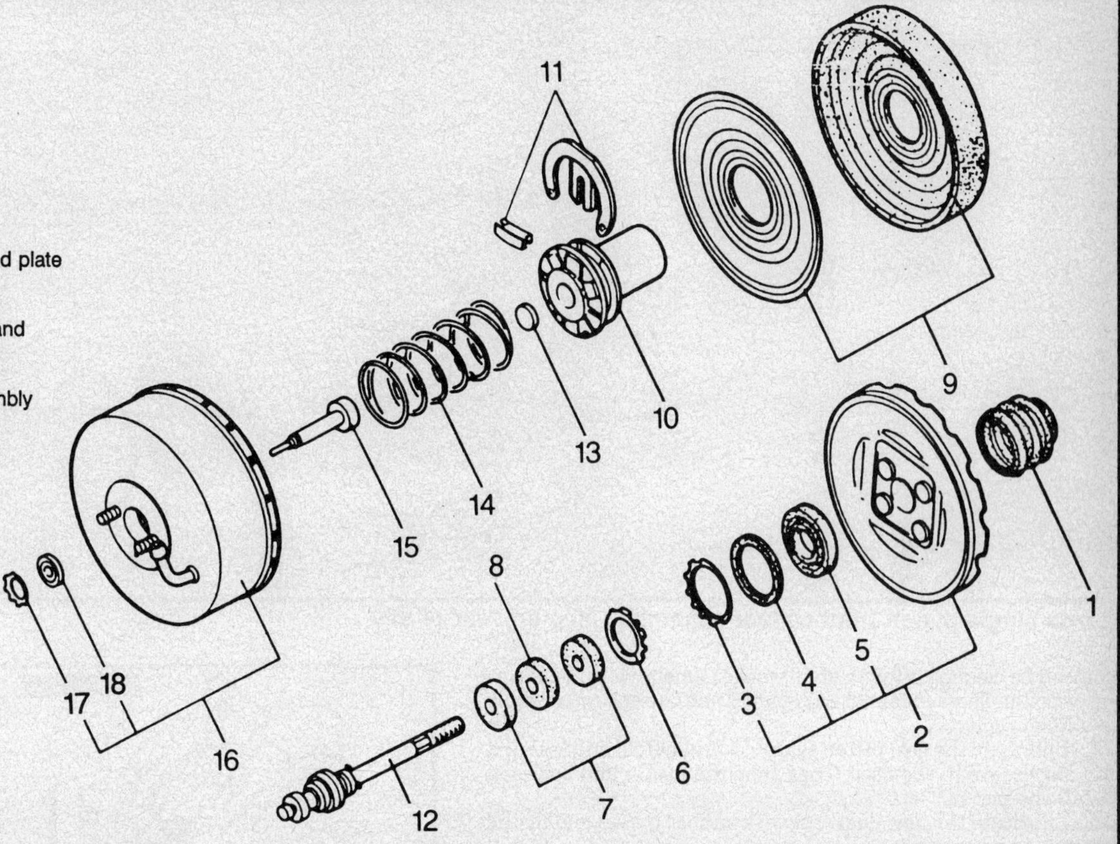

Mazda vacuum booster assembly

Booster Pushrod Clearance Adjustment

This procedure is for adjusting the static clearance between the pushrod on the output end of the booster and the piston on the master cylinder. This needs to be done any time a booster or master cylinder is changed or rebuilt. If the pushrod is adjusted too long, the master cylinder piston will be pushed and the brakes will drag. If the rod is too short, the pedal travel will be very long and full braking may not be available. This adjustment is critical to proper functioning of the brakes.

1. A special tool is available to make this job much faster and more acurate, special service tool SST 49 FO43 001. With the new gasket on the master cylinder mounting flange, set the tool on the flange and adjust the pin to touch the piston.

2. The booster must be under 20 in. (500mm) Hg vacuum. This can be done with a hand pump or the engine manifold vacuum.

3. Turn the tool over and hold it on the booster. The clearance between the pin and the pushrod should be zero. Turn the adjusting nut as needed. When the booster and master cylinder are installed and the booster is under vacuum, the total clearance will be 0.004–0.012 inch (0.1–0.3mm).

Caliper Service

FRONT CALIPERS

Disassembly and Assembly

EXCEPT RX–7

1. This caliper is also used on the rear of the 929. With the caliper cleaned, remove the dust boots and sleeves.

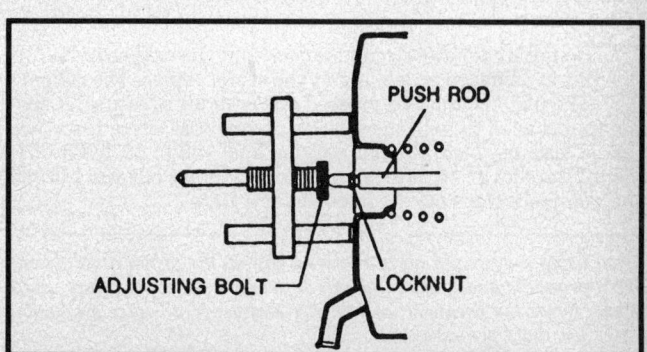

Adjusting Miata booster pushrod clearance

2. Remove the snapring and carefully press the piston out with air pressure. Then remove the piston seal, being careful not to damage the bore.

--- **CAUTION** ---

When using compressed air to remove a piston, the piston could fly out like a projectile and brake fluid will be sprayed. Personal injury could result. Secure a block of wood in front of the bore, cover the bore with a shop rag and apply pressure gradually. Never use more pressure than needed.

To assemble:

3. With the caliper apart, clean all parts in brake fluid or brake part cleaner and inspect the bore and piston. Minor corro-

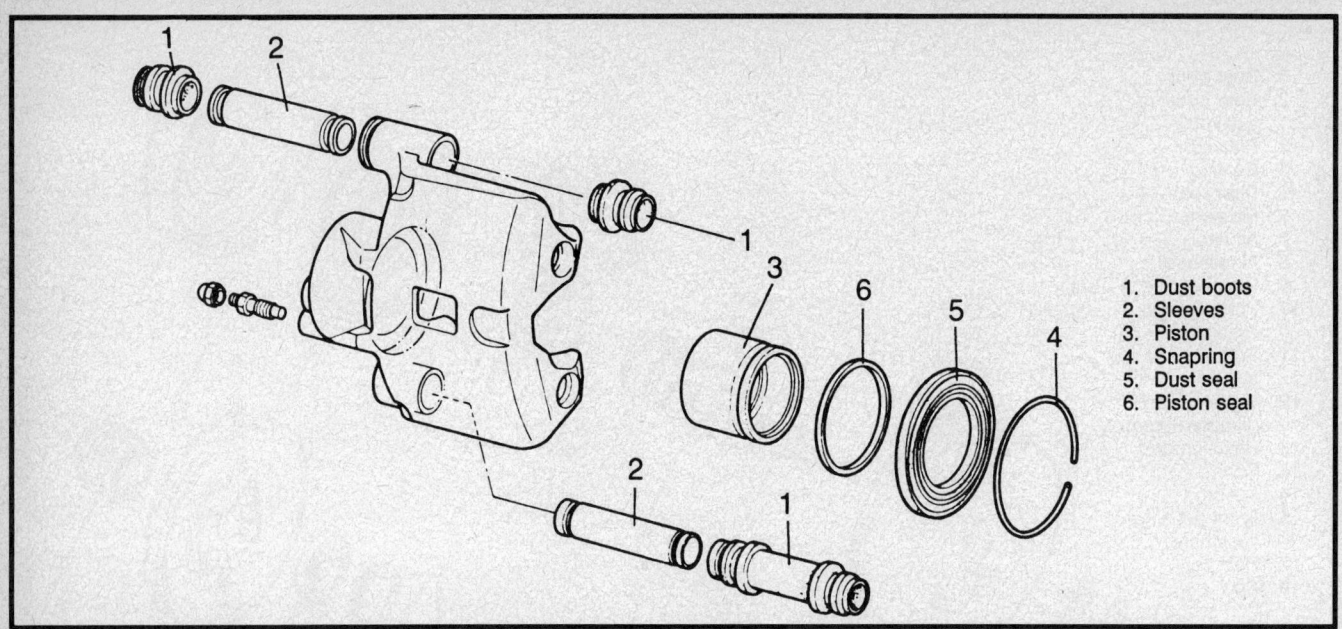

Mazda single piston front caliper assembly, also on rear of 929

1. Dust boots
2. Sleeves
3. Piston
4. Snapring
5. Dust seal
6. Piston seal

sion can be cleaned off with steel wool or emery cloth, but scoring or piston damage cannot be repaired and the entire assembly should be replaced.

4. Lubricate the new piston seal with brake fluid and install it into the groove in the bore. Then lube the piston and bore and install the piston.

5. Lubricate the new dust seal with rubber grease and install the seal and snapring.

6. Make sure the sleeves move easily in the caliper, then lube the sleeves with brake fluid and install with new boots.

RX–7

1. Do not under any circumstances split the caliper in half. If the unit is damaged or leaking at the seam, replace the caliper.

2. The pistons must be pressed out with air pressure. A special tool is used to hold the pistons on one side while the other side is disassembled, Special Service Tool (SST) 49 F033 001. Install the tool or an equivalent, carefully press out the pistons and complete the work on one side at a time.

--- **CAUTION** ---

When using compressed air to remove a piston, the piston could fly out like a projectile and brake fluid will be sprayed. Personal injury could result. Cover the bore with a shop rag and apply pressure gradually. Never use more pressure than needed.

To assemble:

3. With the pistons of one side out, clean all parts in brake fluid or brake part cleaner and inspect the bore and pistons. Minor corrosion can be cleaned off with steel wool or emery cloth, but scoring or piston damage cannot be repaired and the entire assembly should be replaced.

4. Lightly lubricate the new rubber parts with rubber grease and carefully reassemble the piston seals, pistons and dust boots with rings. Install the piston holding tool and repeat the procedure for the other side.

REAR CALIPERS

Disassembly and Assembly

323 AND MIATA

1. Remove the piston dust boot. At the rear of the caliper, in-

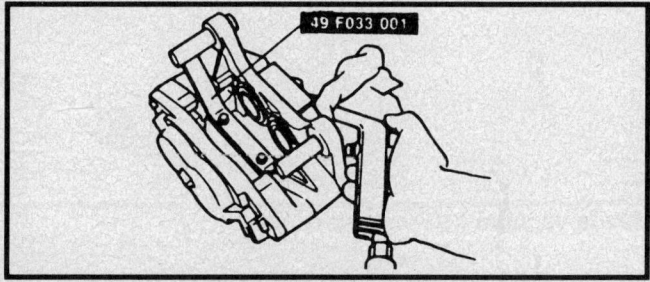

Mazda 4 piston caliper piston removal

sert an Allen wrench into the manual adjuster and unscrew it all the way. The piston can then be pressed out with air pressure.

--- **CAUTION** ---

When using compressed air to remove a piston, the piston could fly out like a projectile and brake fluid will be sprayed. Personal injury could result. Secure a block of wood in front of the bore, cover the bore with a shop rag and apply pressure gradually. Never use more pressure than needed.

2. Remove the adjuster parts and the piston seal, being careful not to damage the bore.

3. With the caliper apart, clean all parts in brake fluid or brake part cleaner and inspect the bore and piston. Minor corrosion can be cleaned off with steel wool or emery cloth, but scoring or piston damage cannot be repaired and the entire assembly should be replaced.

To assemble:

4. When reassembling the caliper, lubricate the rubber and adjuster parts and the piston with rubber grease and reinstall. Turn the manual adjuster screw until it stops to draw the piston into the bore. Install the dust seal last.

5. Make sure the caliper slides easily on the mounting bolts. Lightly lube the bolts when installing the caliper.

626, MX–6, AND RX–7

1. Remove the guide pin, boot, bushing, retaining ring and piston dust seal.

2. Using special service tool 49 FA18 602 or equivalent, un-

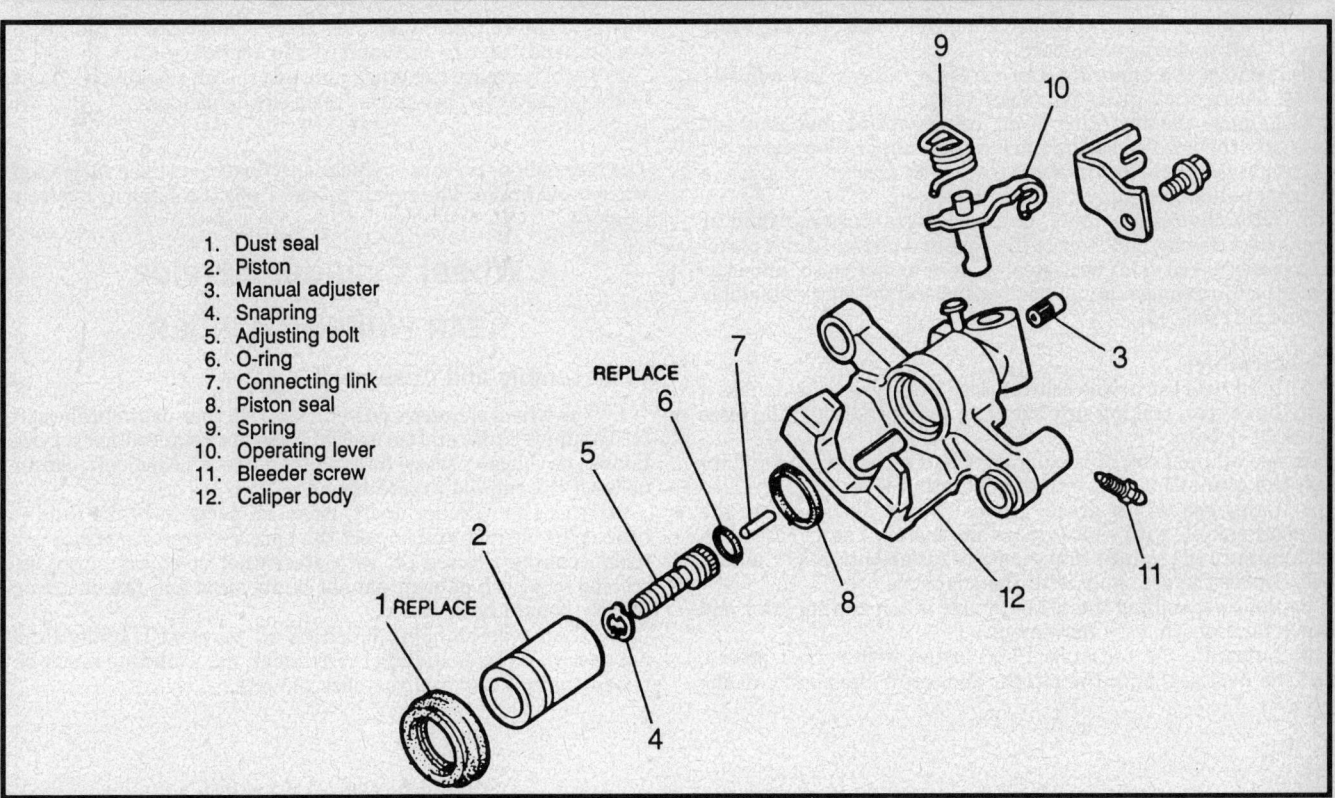

1. Dust seal
2. Piston
3. Manual adjuster
4. Snapring
5. Adjusting bolt
6. O-ring
7. Connecting link
8. Piston seal
9. Spring
10. Operating lever
11. Bleeder screw
12. Caliper body

REPLACE

REPLACE

Mazda 323 and Miata rear caliper assembly

1. Guide pin
2. Pin boot
3. Bushing
4. Retaining ring
5. Dust seal
6. Piston
7. Piston seal
8. Snapring
9. Adjuster spindle
10. Stopper
11. O-ring
12. Connecting link
13. Return spring
14. Operating lever
15. Boot
16. Boot clip
17. Needle beraing
18. Cable bracket

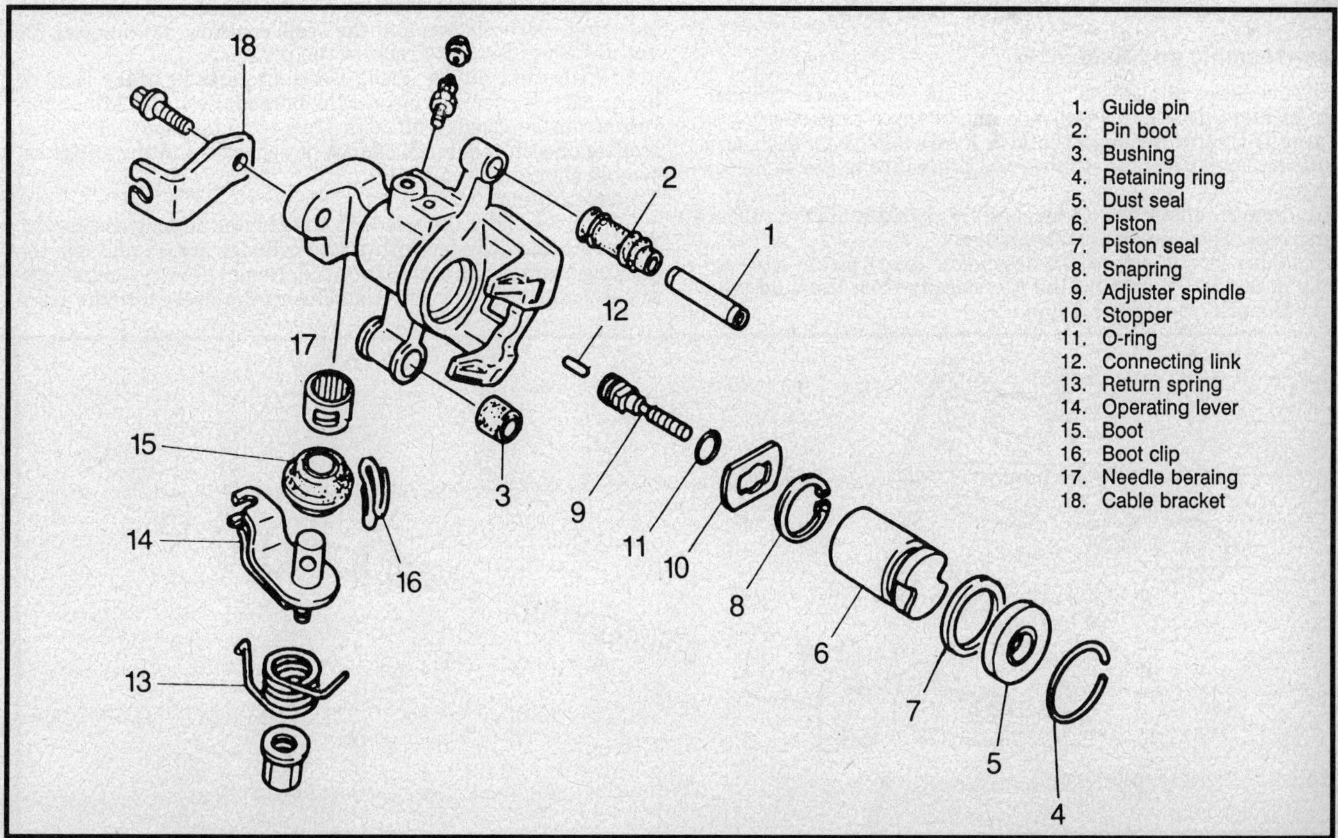

Mazda rear caliper assembly

screw the piston from the caliper. Remove the piston seal, being careful not to damage the bore.

3. Remove the snapring and carefully remove the adjuster parts, noting their order for reassembly.

4. Remove the operating lever, return spring and boot and note how the needle bearing fits into the caliper. The slot in the bearing cage must face the same way when reassembling. Use a bearing puller to remove the needle bearing.

5. With the caliper apart, clean all parts in brake fluid or brake part cleaner and inspect the bore and piston. Minor corrosion can be cleaned off with steel wool or emery cloth, but scoring or piston damage cannot be repaired and the entire assembly should be replaced.

To assemble:

6. Lubricate the needle bearing with white grease and press it into the caliper, making sure the slot in the needle bearing faces the caliper bore.

7. Install the boot, operating lever and return spring and insert the connecting link into the operating lever.

8. Using the rubber grease on the O-ring, lightly grease the adjuster spindle with white grease and install it as an assembly, making sure the pins fit into the holes in the bottom of the caliper. Secure the assembly with the snapring.

9. Before installing the piston, move the operating lever and check for smooth, easy movement.

10. Lubricate the piston seal and piston with rubber grease, put the dust seal onto the piston, and screw the piston all the

way into the caliper. Make sure the indentations in the piston are perpendicular to the shaft of the operating lever.

11. Lightly grease the guide pins and install the pins with new boots. Make sure they move freely in the caliper.

929

The rear caliper on these vehicles is a floating caliper with a separate hand brake. The repair procedure is the same as for front calipers.

Wheel Cylinder Service

REAR WHEEL CYLINDER

Disassembly and Assembly

1. The wheel cylinders on vehicles with rear drum brakes are fairly simple units and no special tools are required for service. Loosen the bleeder screw first, and if it doesn't break off, continue with the rebuild procedure.

2. With the cylinder apart, clean all parts in brake fluid or brake part cleaner and inspect the bore and pistons. Minor corrosion can be cleaned off with steel wool or emery cloth, but scoring or piston damage cannot be repaired and the entire assembly should be replaced.

3. When reassembling, lubricate all parts with brake fluid, not grease. When installing the cylinder, use a silicone sealer between the cylinder and the back plate.

MERCEDES-BENZ

Master Cylinder Service

Disassembly and Assembly

These vehicles all use DOT 4 brake fluid. The master cylinder on all Mercedes-Benz vehicles is one of three manufacturers: Teves, Girling or Bendix. Rebuild kits are available for each, and with minor differences, the service procedure is the same for each.

1. Remove the reservoir by carefully prying it off the rubber bushings. Then remove the bushings.

2. Push in slightly on the secondary (rear) piston and use long nose pliers to remove the cylinder pin from the fluid inlet over the primary (front) piston.

3. Push in on the primary piston again and remove the snapring. Both pistons and the seals can now be removed. Do not use air pressure to remove the pistons.

4. With the cylinder apart, clean all parts in brake fluid or brake part cleaner and inspect the bore and pistons. Minor corrosion can be cleaned off with steel wool or emery cloth, but scoring or piston damage cannot be repaired and the entire assembly should be replaced.

To assemble:

5. The rebuild kits come with the pistons already assembled. Lubricate the cylinder with brake cylinder grease and use the packing sleeve as an installation aid. Remove the secondary piston assembly from the sleeve and insert the sleeve into the cylin-

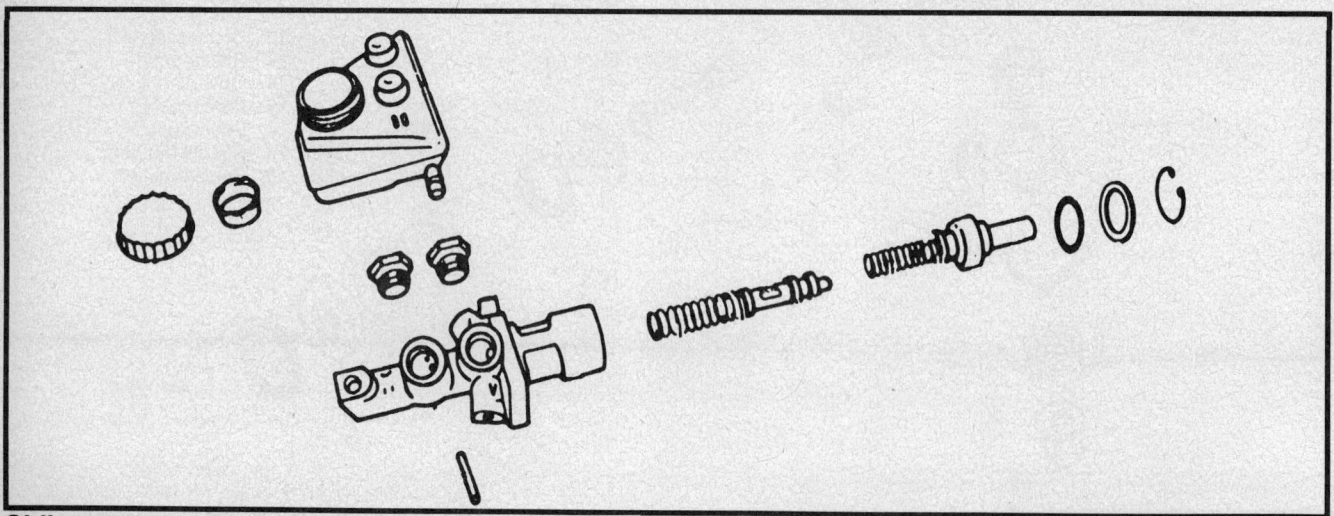

Girling master cylinder in Mercedes-Benz

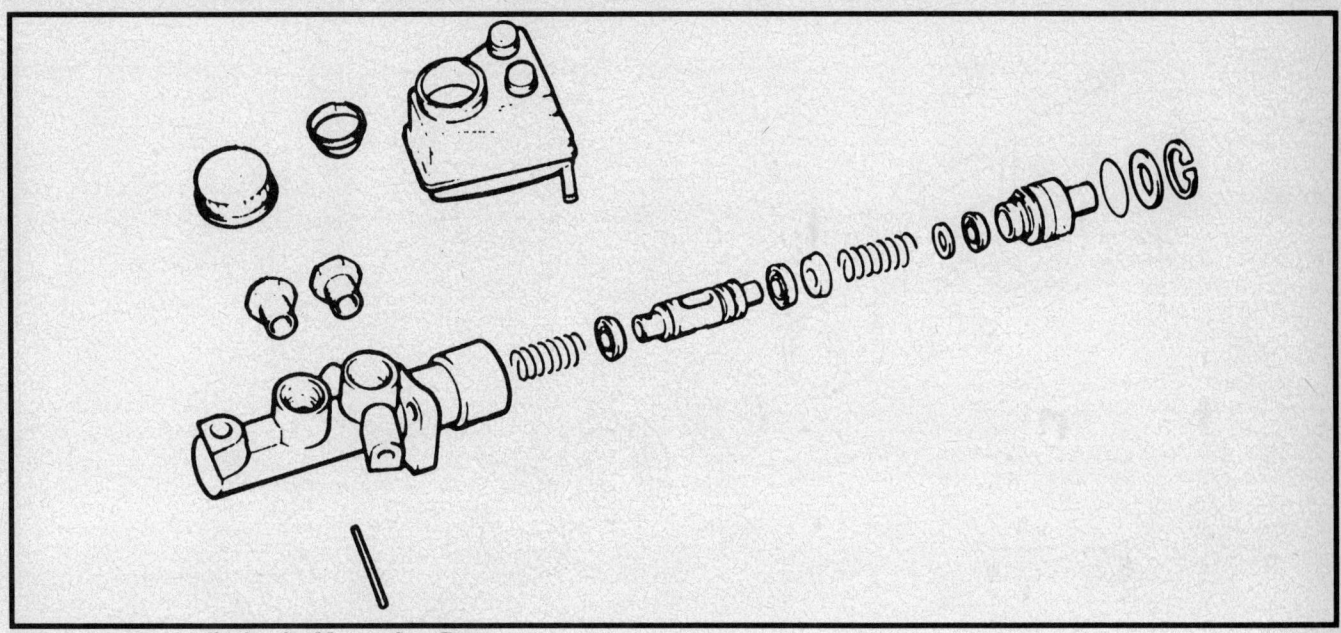

Teves master cylinder in Mercedes-Benz

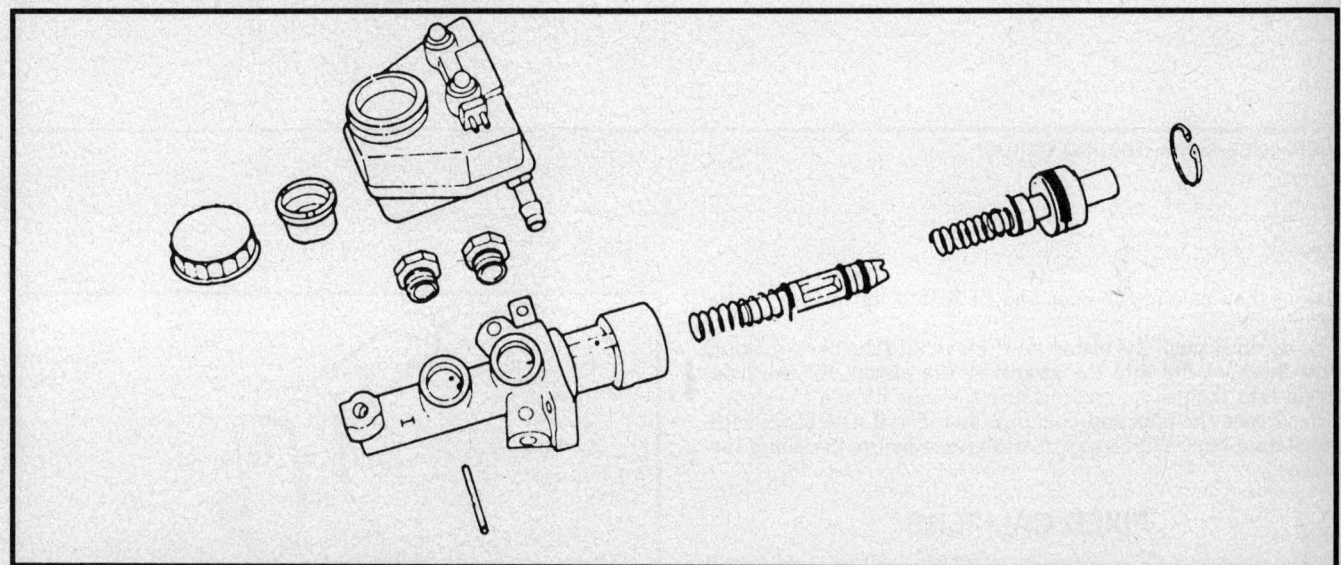

Bendix master cylinder in Mercedes-Benz

der. carefully push the primary piston out of the sleeve and into the cylinder. Make sure the guide slot in the piston is verticle.

6. Remove the sleeve and push in on the piston to insert the cylinder pin that holds the piston in place. The pin should stick out about 2–3 mm.

7. Lubricate the secondary piston and carefully insert it and the spring. Hold it in while installing the snapring.

8. Lubricate the reservoir bushings and press them into place. Insert one of the reservoir nipples, then rotate the reservoir and insert the other nipple.

Caliper Service

FLOATING CALIPERS

Disassembly and Assembly

1. Remove the heat shield plate and carefully press out the piston with air pressure.

CAUTION

When using compressed air to remove a piston, the piston could fly out like a projectile and brake fluid will be sprayed. Personal injury could result. Secure a block of wood in front of the bore, cover the bore with a shop rag and apply pressure gradually. Never use more pressure than needed.

---

2. With the caliper apart, clean all parts in brake fluid or brake part cleaner and inspect the bore and piston. Minor corrosion can be cleaned off the bore with steel wool or emery cloth, but scoring or piston damage cannot be repaired and the entire assembly should be replaced. This also applies to the sliding pins and bushings in the caliper body.

To assemble:

3. Use only the special Mercedes brake caliper grease as an assembly lube. Grease the piston seal and install it in the groove in the caliper. Install the new piston boot onto the bottom of the

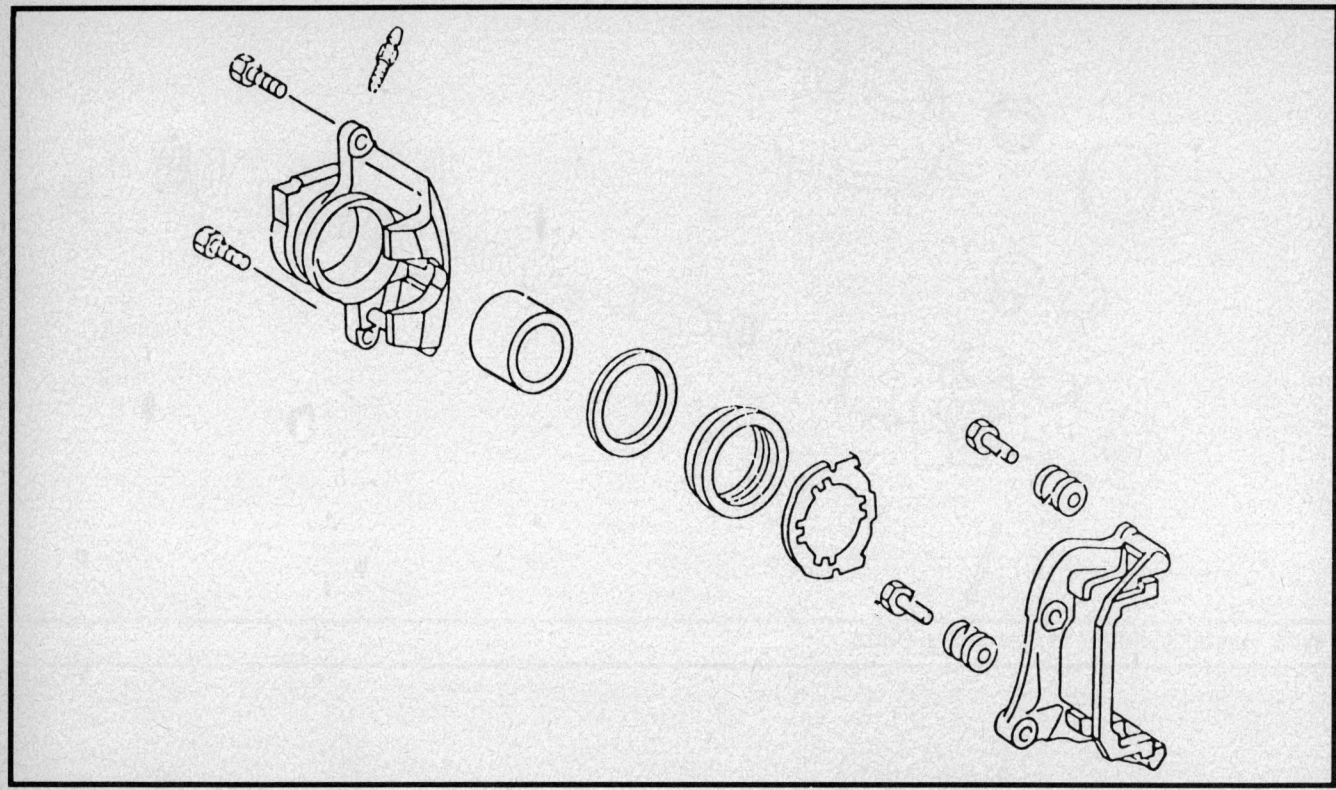

Mercedes-Benz floating caliper

piston, then extend the boot and fit it into its' groove in the caliper.

4. carefully push the piston all the way into the bore, making sure the boot fits into the groove in the piston. Fit the heat shield into the piston, making sure the tabs fit into the slots.

5. Grease the pins and bushings and install new boots with the sliding pins. Wipe away excess grease before installing the caliper.

FIXED CALIPERS

Disassembly and Assembly

1. Do not under any circumstances split the caliper in half. If the unit is damaged or leaking at the seam, replace the caliper.

2. The pistons must be pressed out with air pressure. A special clamping tool can be used to hold the pistons on one side while the other side is disassembled. As an alternate method, insert a block of wood or an old brake pad between the pistons and press out with air as far as possible. Then remove the pistons on one side at a time using expanding pliers to grip the inside of the piston, or by hand. Be careful not to damage the piston or bore.

────────── CAUTION ──────────

When using compressed air to remove a piston, the piston could fly out like a projectile and brake fluid will be sprayed. Personal injury could result. Secure a block of wood in front of the bore, cover the bore with a shop rag and apply pressure gradually. Never use more pressure than needed.

To assemble:

3. With the pistons and seals removed, clean all parts in brake fluid or brake part cleaner and inspect the bore and pis-

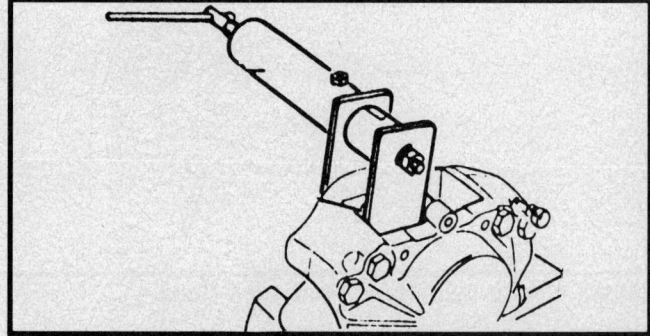

Holding one piston with the clamp tool on Mercedes-Benz two piston fixed caliper

ton. Minor corrosion can be cleaned off the bore with steel wool or emery cloth, but scoring or piston damage cannot be repaired and the entire assembly should be replaced.

4. Lightly lubricate the new rubber parts with Mercedes brake rubber grease and install the new piston seals. Grease the piston and install the new piston boot onto the bottom of the piston.

5. Extend (unfold) the boot and, on 2 piston calipers, hold the piston so that the raised black mark will point up when the caliper is on the vehicle. carefully fit the boot into its' groove in the caliper.

6. carefully push the piston all the way into the bore, making sure the boot falls into the groove in the piston.

MERKUR

Master Cylinder Service

Disassembly and Assembly

XR4Ti

1. These vehicles use DOT 3 or DOT 4 brake fluid. With the cylinder drained, carefuly pry the reservoir off and remove the seals that the reservoir presses into.

2. With the cylinder in a soft jaw vice, push in on the primary piston with a blunt tool and remove the snapring and washer. The primary piston should easily come out. To remove the secondary piston, tap the cylinder on a block of wood. Note how the cups fit onto the pistons before removing them.

3. With the cylinder apart, clean all parts in brake fluid or brake part cleaner and inspect the bore and pistons. Minor corrosion can be cleaned off with steel wool or emery cloth, but scoring or piston damage cannot be repaired and the entire assembly should be replaced.

To assemble:

4. Be sure to use all the parts in the kit. Lubricate the rubber parts and the cylinder with clean brake fluid and carefully fit the new cups to the pistons. With a gentle twisting motion, insert the pistons into the bore.

5. Hold the pistons in with a blunt tool and install the washer and snapring. Lubricate and install new reservoir seals and push the reservoir into place.

Brake Booster Service

The booster on all models cannot be field serviced and no service parts are available. When installing a new unit, adjustment of the pushrod length is not required, however pedal height and travel in the vehicle should be checked.

Caliper Service

FRONT CALIPERS

Disassembly and Assembly

1. Remove the caliper anchor pin bushings and seals. carefully press out the piston with air pressure and remove the piston seal.

------ **CAUTION** ------

When using compressed air to remove a piston, the piston could fly out like a projectile and brake fluid will be sprayed. Personal injury could result. Secure a block of wood in front of the bore, cover the bore with a shop rag and apply pressure gradually. Never use more pressure than needed.

2. With the caliper apart, clean all parts in brake fluid or brake part cleaner and inspect the bore and piston. Minor corrosion can be cleaned off the bore with steel wool or emery cloth, but scoring or piston damage cannot be repaired and the entire assembly should be replaced. Be sure to examine the pins and bushings.

To assemble:

3. Use only clean brake fluid as an assembly lube. Wet the piston seal and install it in the groove in the caliper. Install the new piston boot onto the bottom of the piston, then extend the boot and fit it into its' groove in the caliper.

4. carefully push the piston all the way into the bore, making sure the boot folds and falls into the groove in the piston.

5. Lubricate the pin bushings and seals and press the seals into the caliper. Use the pin to aid installation of the bushings.

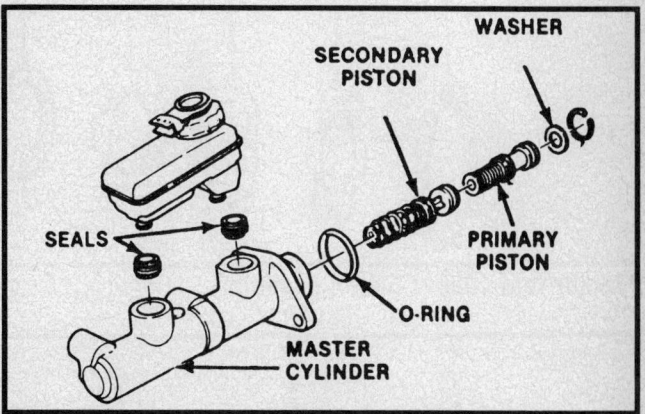

Merkur XR4Ti master cylinder assembly

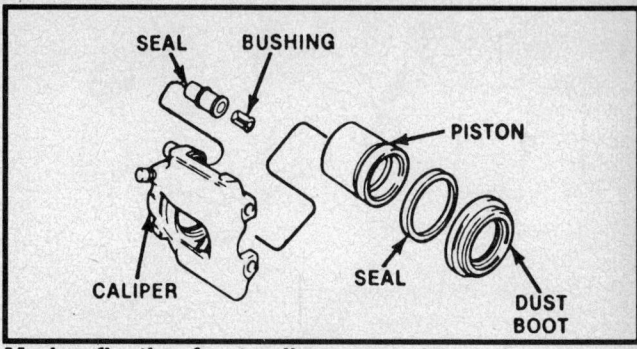

Merkur floating front caliper assembly

REAR CALIPERS

Disassembly and Assembly

1. Using special tool T87P-2588A or equivalent, unscrew the piston far enough to disengage the boot from its' groove, then unscrew the piston the rest of the way.

2. Remove the snapring from inside the piston and carefully remove the adjuster parts, noting which way the seal lip faces.

3. Remove the piston seal from the caliper bore, then push in slightly on the spring cover to remove the snapring. Remove the cover, spring and seat washer. Remove the next snapring and lift out the washer, self-adjusting screw and the pin under the screw.

4. Disengage the return spring from the parking brake lever and remove the spring, bolt, lever assembly and seal. If the shaft of the lever is scored or corroded, the shaft bushing inside the caliper should also be replaced.

5. With the caliper apart, clean all parts in brake fluid or brake part cleaner and inspect the bore and piston. Minor corrosion can be cleaned off with steel wool or emery cloth, but scoring or piston damage cannot be repaired and the entire assembly should be replaced.

To assemble:

6. If the lever shaft bushing is being replaced, press the new bushing with the slot lined up with the caliper bore. Do not press the bushing in all the way, or the bottom will be distorted. The top of the bushing should be 0.295 in. (7.5mm) below the shoulder for the shaft seal.

7. Install the new shaft seal and lightly lube the bushing and seal with brake grease. Insert the lever shaft and install the stop bolt and return spring.

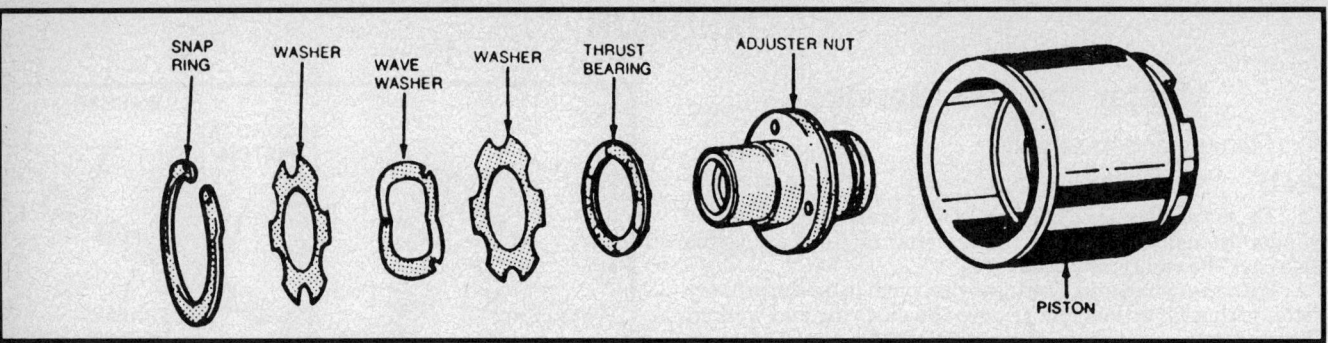

Merkur rear caliper piston assembly

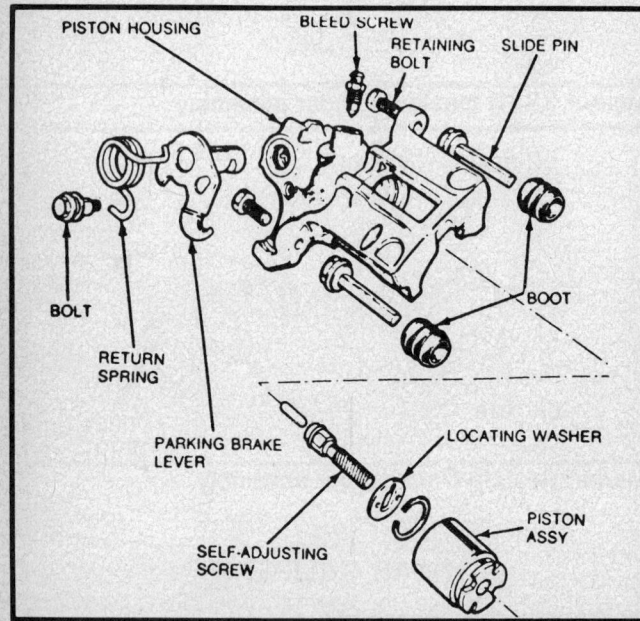

Merkur rear caliper assembly

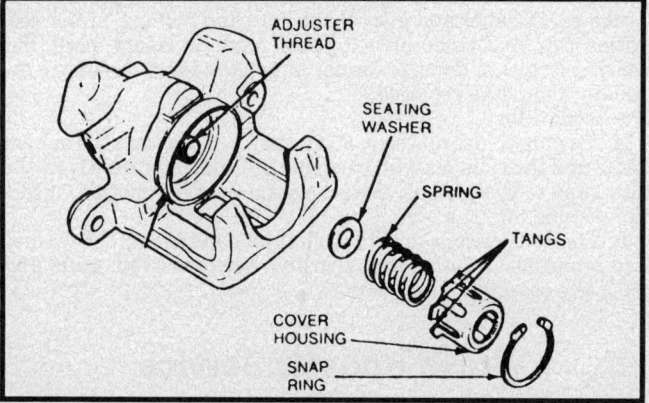

When installing snapring, be careful not to damage bore

boot, and that the boot properly seats in the groove in the piston.

13. Grease the caliper slide pins before installing the caliper.

REAR WHEEL CYLINDER

Disassembly and Assembly

1. The wheel cylinders on vehicles with rear drum brakes are fairly simple units and no special tools are required for service. Loosen the bleeder screw first, and if it doesn't break off, continue with the rebuild procedure.

2. With the cylinder apart, clean all parts in brake fluid or brake part cleaner and inspect the bore and pistons. Minor corrosion can be cleaned off with steel wool or emery cloth, but scoring or piston damage cannot be repaired and the entire assembly should be replaced.

3. When reassembling, lubricate all parts with brake fluid, not grease. When installing the cylinder, use a silicone sealer between the cylinder and the back plate.

8. Inside the bore, install the pin into the parking brake lever shaft. Lightly grease the new O-ring and install the self adjusting screw with the locating washer properly keyed into the caliper. Install the snapring.

9. Install the seating washer, spring, spring cover and snapring, being careful not to damage the caliper bore.

10. Lubricate the adjuster nut, bearing and washers with brake fluid and install them into the piston. Install the snapring.

11. Lube the new piston seal with brake fluid and install it into the groove in the bore. Install the dust boot and lubricate the boot and piston with brake fluid.

12. Stretch the boot over the piston and screw the piston all the way into the caliper. Make sure the turns smoothly in the

NISSAN

Master Cylinder Service

Disassembly and Assembly

1. These vehicles all use DOT 3 Brake fluid. With minor differences, all Nissan vehicles use the same master cylinder, which incorporates the proportioning valve in the same body. The proportioning valve cannot be repaired and no service parts are available. Do not disassemble this valve.

2. With the cylinder drained of fluid, remove the reservoir by gently prying it out of the seals.

3. With the cylinder in a soft jaw vice, push in slightly on the

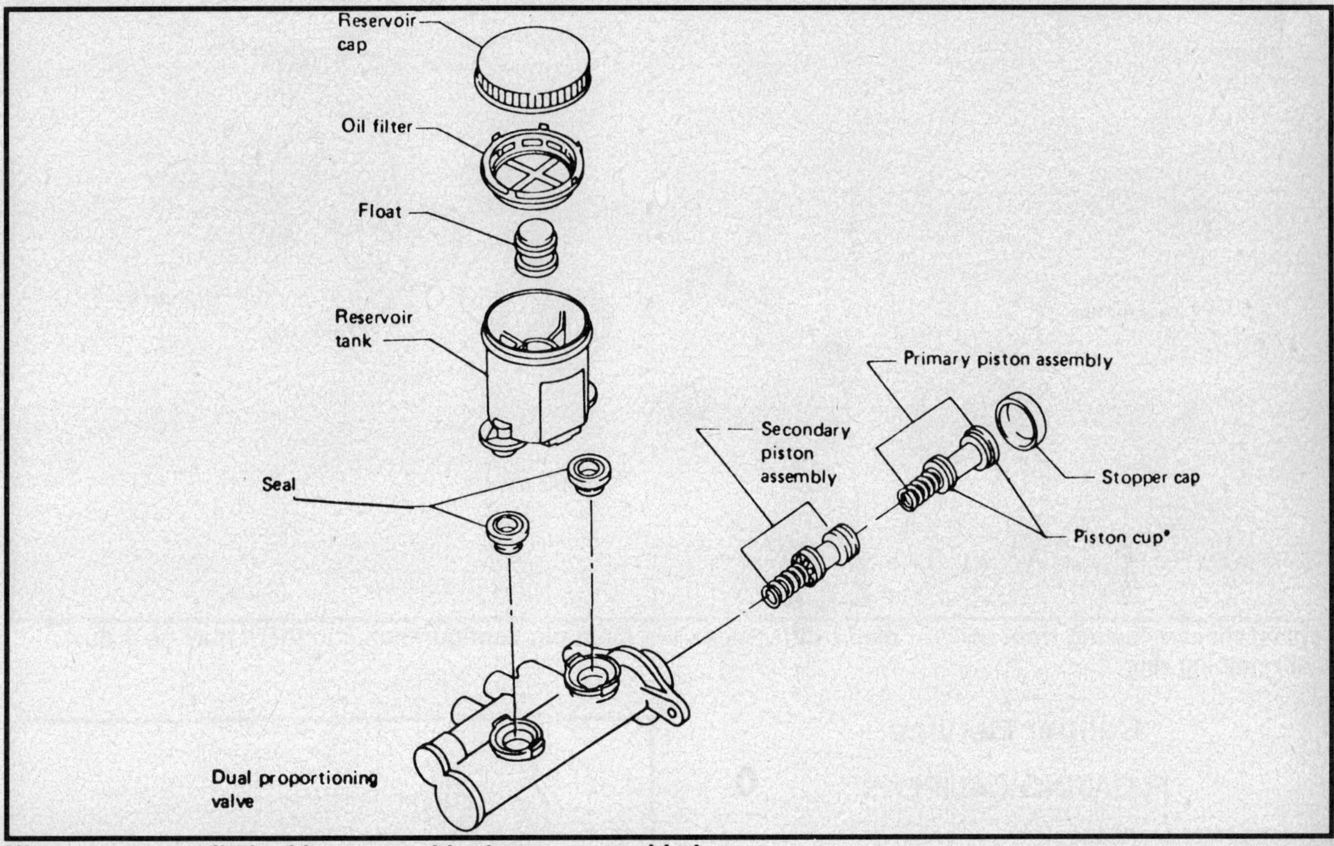

Reservoir cap

Oil filter

Float

Reservoir tank

Seal

Dual proportioning valve

Primary piston assembly

Secondary piston assembly

Stopper cap

Piston cup

Nissan master cylinder kit comes with pistons assembled

piston and carefully bend the tabs of the stopper cap out to remove the cap.

4. The primary piston should come out easily. If necessary, the secondary piston can be removed with air pressure.

------------------ **CAUTION** ------------------

When using compressed air to remove a piston, the piston could fly out like a projectile and brake fluid will be sprayed. Personal injury could result. Secure a block of wood in front of the bore, cover the bore with a shop rag and apply pressure gradually. Never use more pressure than needed.

5. With the cylinder apart, clean all parts in brake fluid or brake part cleaner and inspect the bore and pistons. Minor corrosion can be cleaned off with steel wool or emery cloth, but scoring cannot be repaired and the entire assembly should be replaced.

To assemble:

6. The factory rebuild kit comes with with the new springs and pistons already assembled. Lightly coat the bore and pistons with brake fluid and carefully insert both pistons, then install the stopper cap. It may be necessary to bend the tabs on the cap in a little to assure a good grip.

7. Install the reservoir with new seals and before installing the master cylinder, check the booster pushrod rod length.

Vacuum Booster Service

The booster on these vehicles cannot be repaired and no service parts are available from Nissan. Faulty units must be replaced.

Booster Output Rod Clearance Adjustment

EXCEPT SENTRA, 200SX AND 240SX

On the noted vehicles, do not adjust the output rod clearance.

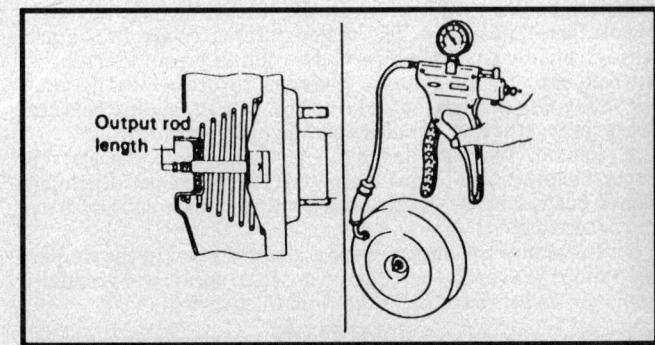

Output rod length

Checking Nissan booster output rod length

This procedure is for adjusting the static clearance between the otuput rod on the output end of the booster and the piston on the master cylinder. This needs to be done any time a booster or master cylinder is changed or rebuilt. If the rod is too long, the brakes will drag. If the rod is too short, the pedal travel will be very long and full braking may not be available. This adjustment is critical to proper functioning of the brakes.

1. This can be done with a hand vacuum pump or with the booster on the vehicle and using the engine at idle as a vacuum source. With 20 in. (500mm) Hg vacuum on the booster, measure the distance the output rod protrudes beyond the master cylinder mounting face.

2. If adjustment is required, be careful not to distort the rod or the internal springs. The measurement should be 0.404–0.414 inch (10.275–10.525mm).

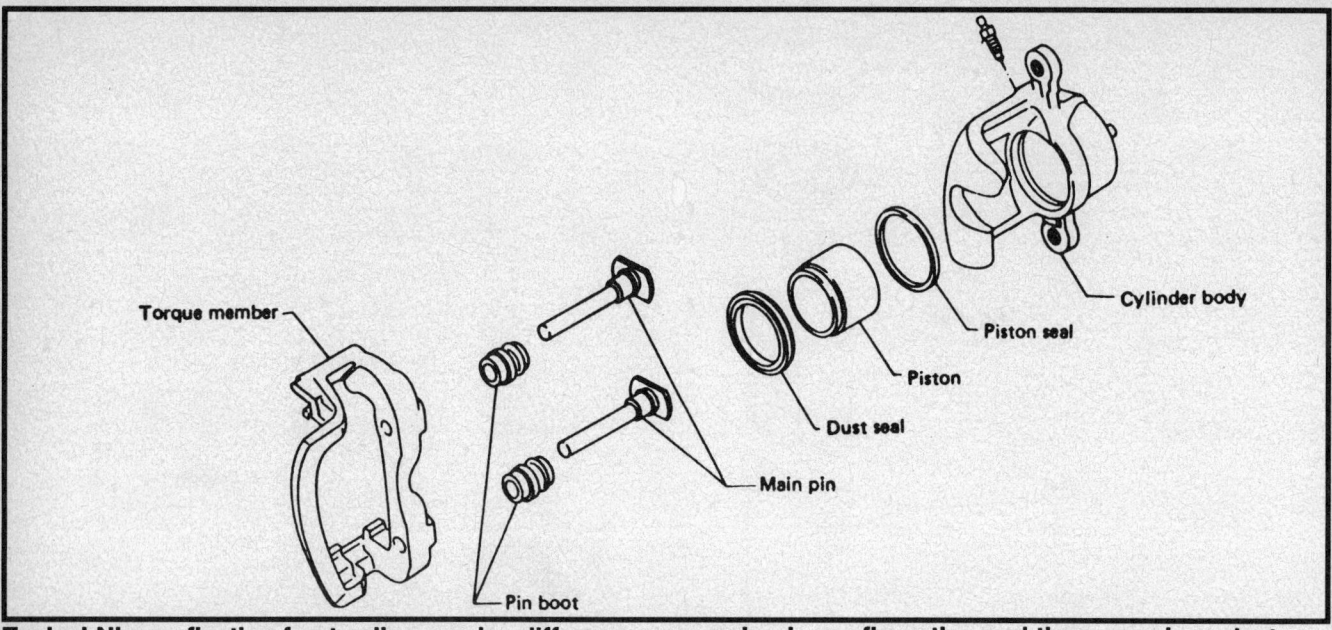

Typical Nissan floating front caliper: major differences are main pin configuration and there may be a dust seal retaining ring

Caliper Service

FLOATING CALIPERS

Disassembly and Assembly

Nissan uses several different front calipers through out their product line. Except for those on the 300ZX, they are all single piston floating calipers. The major differences are in the pad springs, sliding pin assemblies and torque members which carry the caliper on the suspension. The repair procedure is the same for all floating calipers, but take note of how the sliding pins and boots go together before disassembling the caliper.

1. Remove the pins and bolts to disassemble the sleeves, boots, bushings and torque member from the caliper. Bushings can be pushed out by pushing the pin through the support from the other side.

2. To remove the piston, place a block of wood in the caliper, lay a shop rag over the bore to prevent fluid spray, and gradually apply air pressure to the brake fluid inlet hole.

— CAUTION —

When using compressed air to remove a piston, the piston could fly out like a projectile and brake fluid will be sprayed. Personal injury could result. Clamp a block of wood to the caliper, cover the bore with a shop rag and apply pressure gradually. Never use more pressure than needed.

3. Once the piston is out against the wood, it can be removed the rest of the way by hand. Being careful not to damage the cylinder, remove the dust boot and seal.

4. Clean all parts in brake fluid or brake part cleaner and examine the bore and piston. Minor corrosion can be cleaned off with steel wool or emery cloth, but scoring or piston damage cannot be repaired and the unit should be replaced.

To assemble:

5. Apply light silicone grease to the new piston seal and install it onto the groove in the caliper. This seal is directional, with the larger outside diameter towards the open end of the bore.

6. Assemble the dust boot to the bottom of the piston, then fit the boot into the groove in the caliper, then push the piston carefully all the way into the bore. Make sure the dust boot falls

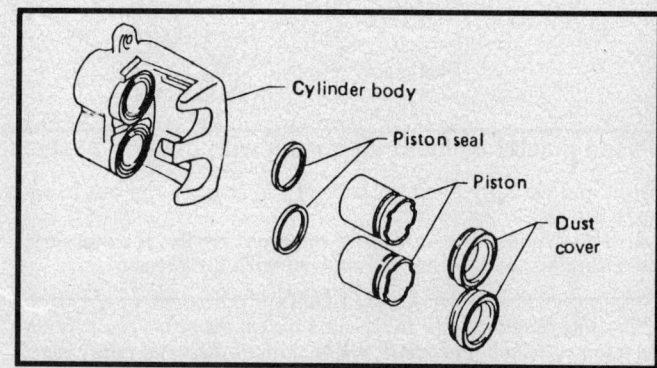

Two piston caliper from 1987–89 300ZX

into the groove in the piston. If the dust boot has a retainer ring, install it and wipe away any excess grease.

7. Clean and lubricate the sliding pins and bolts and make sure the caliper moves freely on the pins.

FIXED CALIPERS

Disassembly and Assembly

1. Do not under any circumstances split the caliper in half. If the unit is damaged or leaking at the seam, replace the caliper. Remove the dust seal retaining ring.

2. The pistons must be pressed out with air pressure. Insert a block of wood or an old brake pad between the pistons and press out with air as far as possible. Then remove the pistons on one side at a time using expanding pliers to grip the inside of the piston, or by hand. Be careful not to damage the piston or bore.

— CAUTION —

When using compressed air to remove a piston, the piston could fly out like a projectile and brake fluid will be sprayed. Personal injury could result. Secure a block of wood in front of the bore, cover the bore with a shop rag and apply pressure gradually. Never use more pressure than needed.

To assemble:

3. With the pistons and seals removed, clean all parts in brake fluid or brake part cleaner and inspect the bore and pistons. Minor corrosion can be cleaned off the bore with steel wool or emery cloth, but scoring or piston damage cannot be repaired and the entire assembly should be replaced.

4. Lightly lubricate the new rubber parts with brake rubber grease and install the new piston seals. Grease the piston and install the new dust seal boot onto the bottom of the piston.

5. Extend (unfold) the dust seal boot and, carefully fit the boot into its' groove in the caliper.

6. carefully push the piston all the way into the bore, making sure the dust boot falls into the groove in the piston. Wipe away any excess grease and install the retaining ring.

CALIPER WITH PARKING BRAKE

Disassembly and Assembly

1. With the caliper cleaned and in a soft jaw vice, use long nose pliers to unscrew the piston from the caliper bore. Remove

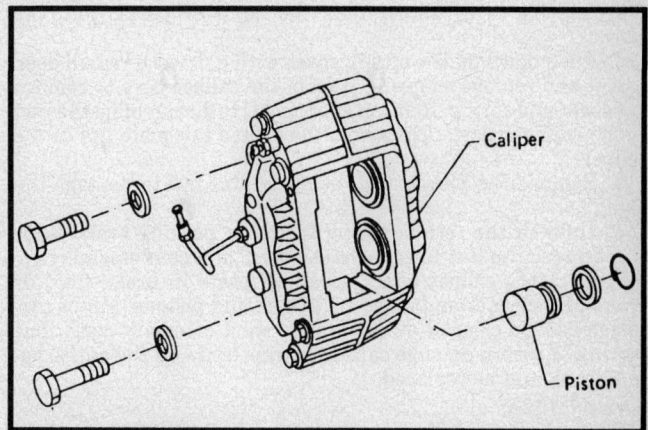

Four piston caliper from the 300ZX, two piston caliper similar

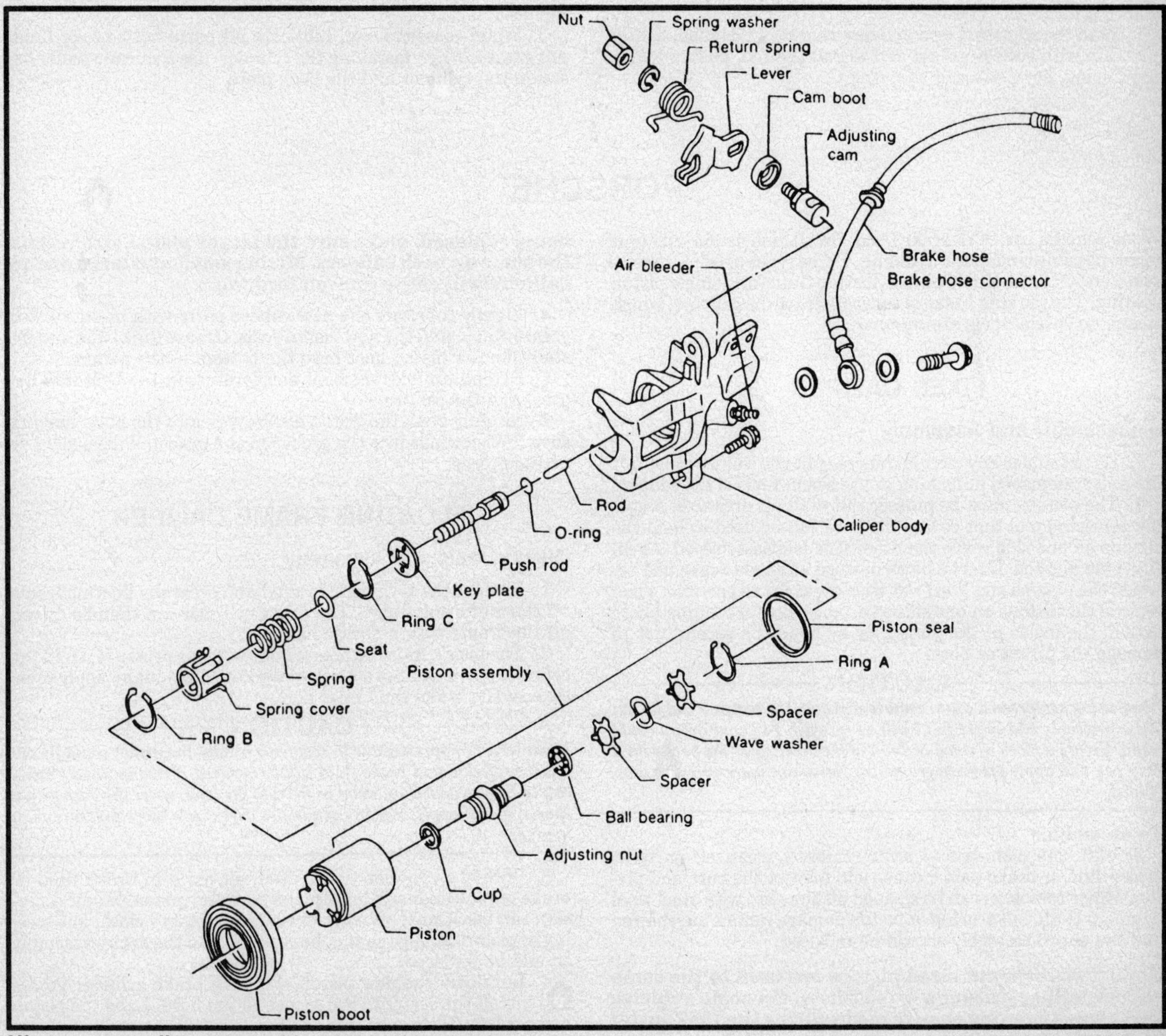

Nissan rear caliper assembly with parking brake

the snapring A to disassemble the adjuster parts from the piston.

2. Push down on the spring cover with a dowel or small deep socket and remove snapring B from the caliper bore to remove the cover and spring. Remove snapring C to disassemble the rest of the adjuster parts. Note how the dished key plate fits in the caliper.

3. Remove the piston seal, being careful not to damage the bore.

4. Unlatch the return spring from the parking brake lever and remove the nut to remove the lever and cam assembly.

5. With the caliper apart, clean all parts in brake fluid or brake part cleaner and inspect the bore and pistons. Minor corrosion can be cleaned off with steel wool or emery cloth, but scoring or piston damage cannot be repaired and the entire assembly should be replaced.

To assemble:

6. Be sure to use all the parts in the rebuild kit. When installing the new cup onto the adjusting nut, make sure the lip diameter faces the large part of the nut. Lightly grease the cup and bearing, assemble the adjuster parts into the piston and install snapring A.

7. With the adjusting cam and new cam boot installed, lightly lubricate with rubber grease and install the rod, pushrod with new O-ring, key plate and snapring C.

8. Install the spring seat and spring and hold the cover down to install the snapring B. Be careful not to damage the bore.

9. Lightly grease the new piston seal and install it in the bore. Grease the piston and fit the new piston boot into the groove in the piston.

10. Unfold the boot down over the piston and fit the boot into the caliper. Screw the piston into place in the caliper and make sure the boot seats properly. Wipe away any excess grease.

11. Make sure the sliding pins are clean and move freely, lightly grease them and install with new boots.

WHEEL CYLINDER SERVICE

1. The wheel cylinders on vehicles with rear drum brakes are fairly simple units and no special tools are required for service. Loosen the bleeder screw first, and if it doesn't break off, continue with the rebuild procedure.

2. With the cylinder apart, clean all parts in brake fluid or brake part cleaner and inspect the bore and pistons. Minor corrosion can be cleaned off with steel wool or emery cloth, but scoring cannot be repaired and the entire assembly should be replaced.

3. When reassembling, lubricate all parts with brake fluid, not grease. When installing the cylinder, use a silicone sealer between the cylinder and the back plate.

PORSCHE

These vehicles use DOT brake fluid. On all models the only unit repair possible is caliper rebuilding. Three types of caliper are in use, 4 piston fixed, single piston floating frame and single piston floating. The parking brake is separate from the calipers, which means no special tools are required.

FIXED CALIPER

Disassembly and Assembly

1. Do not under any circumstances split the caliper in half. If the unit is damaged or leaking at the seam, replace the caliper.

2. The pistons must be pressed out with air pressure. A special clamping tool that covers the bore can be used to hold the pistons on one side while the other side is disassembled. As an alternate method, insert a block of wood or an old brake pad between the pistons and press out with air as far as possible. Then remove the pistons on one side at a time using expanding pliers to grip the inside of the piston, or by hand. Be careful not to damage the piston or bore.

--- CAUTION ---

When using compressed air to remove a piston, the piston could fly out like a projectile and brake fluid will be sprayed. Personal injury could result. Secure a block of wood in front of the bore, cover the bore with a shop rag and apply pressure gradually. Never use more pressure than needed.

To assemble:

3. With the pistons and seals removed, clean all parts in brake fluid or brake part cleaner and inspect the bore and piston. Minor corrosion can be cleaned off the bore with steel wool or emery cloth, but scoring or piston damage cannot be repaired and the entire assembly should be replaced.

Note: Two different sized pistons are used in the same caliper; either 42/36mm or 44/36mm. On some vehicles there was a running change made during the 1987 model year to the larger 44mm leading piston. If the caliper is being replaced, make sure the larger piston size will be the same on both calipers. Mixing small and large piston calipers will cause uneven braking.

4. Lightly lubricate the new rubber parts with brake rubber grease and install the new piston seals. Grease the piston and install the new piston boot onto the bottom of the piston.

5. Extend (unfold) the boot and carefully fit the boot into its' groove in the caliper.

6. carefully push the piston all the way into the bore, making sure the boot falls into the groove in the piston. Wipe away any excess grease.

FLOATING FRAME CALIPER

Disassembly and Assembly

1. Remove the spring guide and hand press the floating frame off the mounting frame. The brake cylinder can then be driven off the frame with a plastic hammer.

2. The piston must be pressed out with air pressure. Hold the cylinder down against a block of wood and gradually apply pressure to the brake fluid inlet port.

--- CAUTION ---

When using compressed air to remove a piston, the piston could fly out like a projectile and brake fluid will be sprayed. Personal injury could result. Secure a block of wood in front of the bore, cover the bore with a shop rag and apply pressure gradually. Never use more pressure than needed.

3. With the cylinder apart, clean all parts in brake fluid or brake part cleaner and inspect the bore and piston. Minor corrosion can be cleaned off with steel wool or emery cloth, but scoring or piston damage cannot be repaired and the entire assembly should be replaced.

4. Lubricate the new piston seal with brake cylinder grease and install the seal into the groove in the bore. Lube the piston and push it all the way into the bore. Install the new dust boot and clamping ring.

5. When installing the cylinder into the frame, do not use any lubrication. Make sure all parts are clean and drive the cylinder onto the frame with a brass or wood drift pin. Reassemble the mounting frame.

FLOATING CALIPER

Disassembly and Assembly

1. Remove the housing retaining spring, guide pin plugs and pins. Remove the caliper housing from the holder.

2. Use air pressure to carefully press the piston our far enough to remove the dust boot, then remove the piston completely. Remove the piston seal.

--- **CAUTION** ---

When using compressed air to remove a piston, the piston could fly out like a projectile and brake fluid will be sprayed. Personal injury could result. Secure a block of wood in front of the bore, cover the bore with a shop rag and apply pressure gradually. Never use more pressure than needed.

3. With the cylinder apart, clean all parts in brake fluid or brake part cleaner and inspect the bore and pistons. Minor corrosion can be cleaned off with steel wool or emery cloth, but scoring or piston damage cannot be repaired and the entire assembly should be replaced.

To assemble:

4. Lightly lubricate the new rubber parts with brake rubber grease and install the new piston seal. Grease the piston and install the new piston boot onto the bottom of the piston.

5. Extend (unfold) the boot and carefully fit the boot into its' groove in the caliper. carefully push the piston all the way into the bore, making sure the boot falls into the groove in the piston. Wipe away any excess grease.

6. Before bolting the holder back in place, make sure the guide pins move smoothly in the slides. Replace them if necessary.

SAAB

Master Cylinder Service

Disassembly and Assembly

1. These vehicles use DOT 4 brake fluid. With the cylinder in a soft jaw vice, remove the reservoir and sealing rings.

2. Push in slightly on the piston and remove the secondary piston stop pin from the front fluid inlet, under the front reservoir sealing ring. On the 900, remove the lock ring. Both pistons can now be removed.

3. With the cylinder apart, clean all parts in brake fluid or brake part cleaner and inspect the bore and pistons. Minor corrosion can be cleaned off with steel wool or emery cloth, but scoring or piston damage cannot be repaired and the entire assembly should be replaced.

To assemble:

4. Be sure to use all the new parts in the rebuild kit. Lubricate the parts with clean brake fluid and carefuly insert the pistons with a twisting motion.

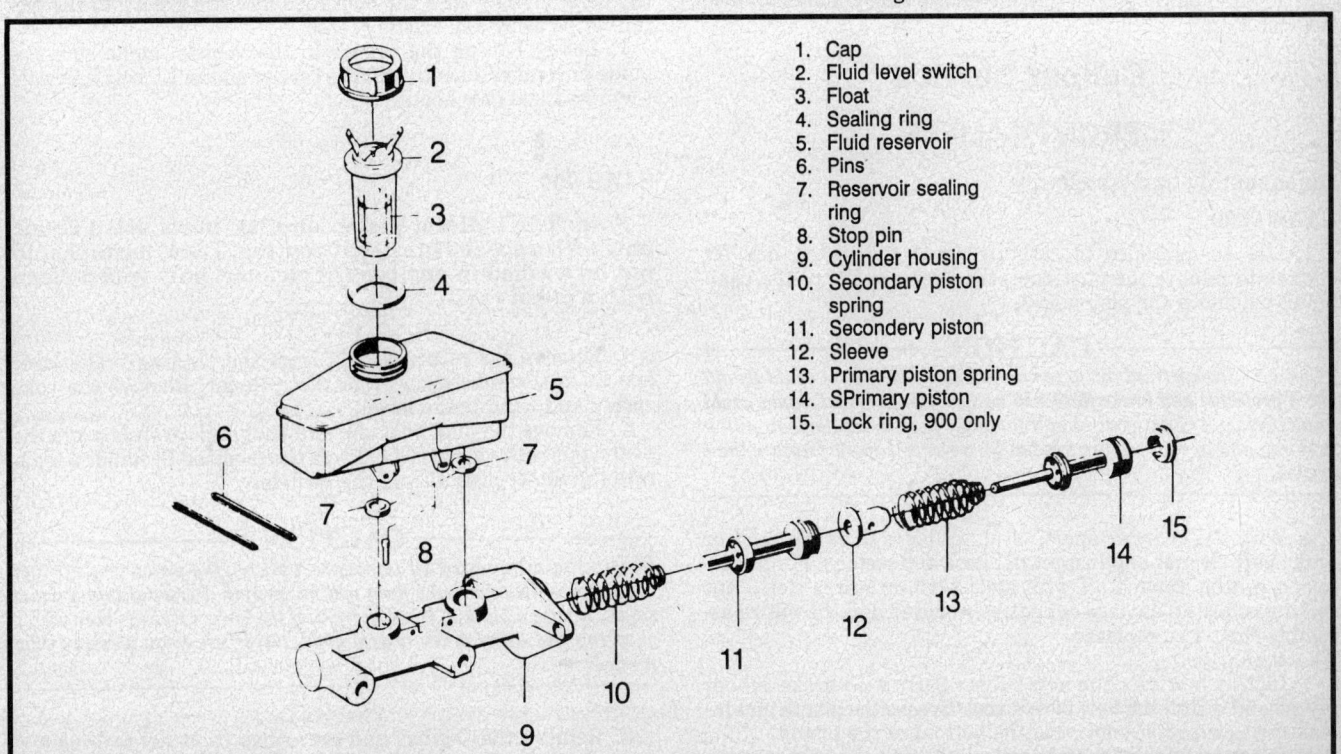

1. Cap
2. Fluid level switch
3. Float
4. Sealing ring
5. Fluid reservoir
6. Pins
7. Reservoir sealing ring
8. Stop pin
9. Cylinder housing
10. Secondary piston spring
11. Secondery piston
12. Sleeve
13. Primary piston spring
14. SPrimary piston
15. Lock ring, 900 only

Saab 900 master cylinder, 9000 similar

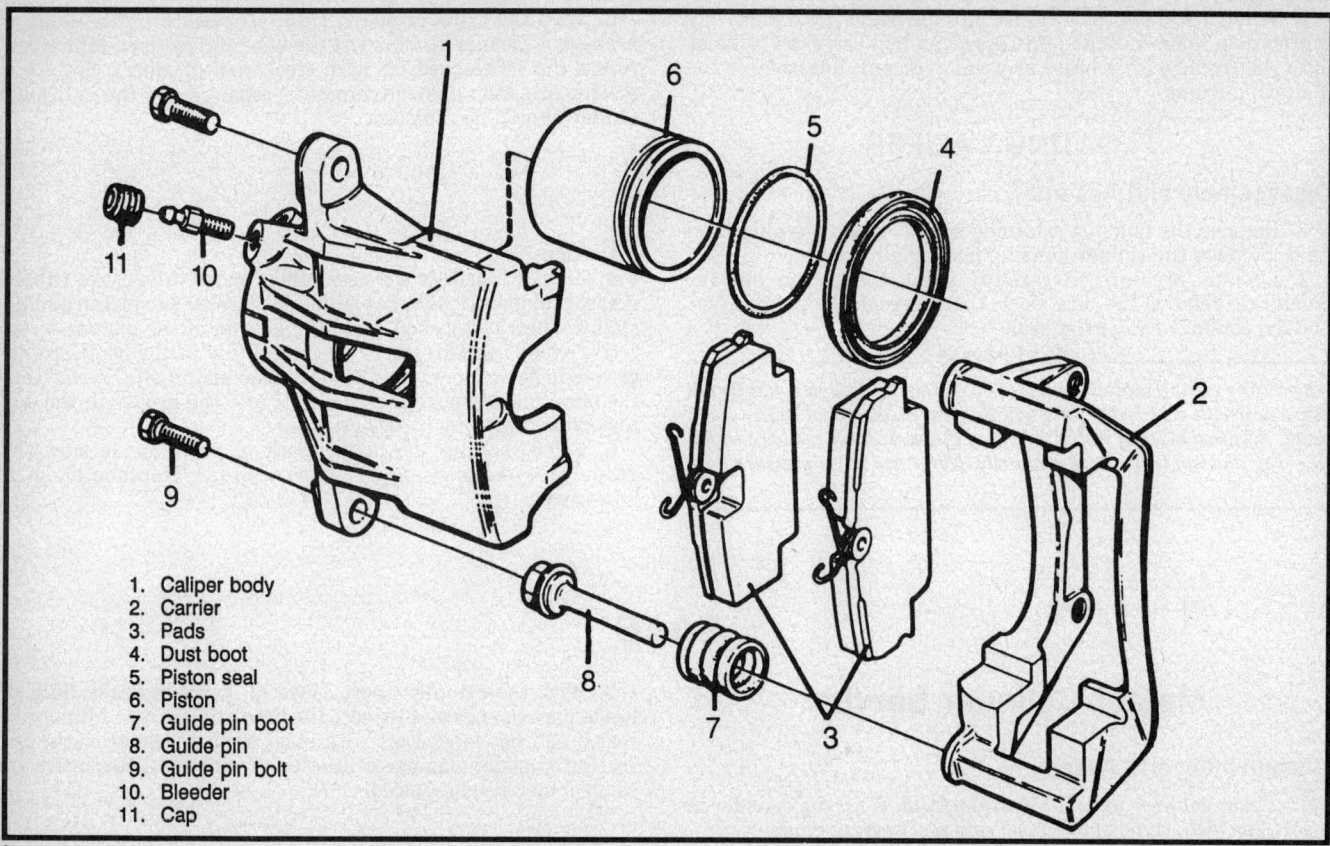

1. Caliper body
2. Carrier
3. Pads
4. Dust boot
5. Piston seal
6. Piston
7. Guide pin boot
8. Guide pin
9. Guide pin bolt
10. Bleeder
11. Cap

Exploded view of the caliper assembly—9000 Saab

5. Push in on the piston and install the stop pin and, on 900, the lock ring.

Caliper Service

FRONT CALIPER

Disassembly and Assembly

SAAB 9000

1. Use air pressure to carefully press the piston our far enough to remove the dust boot, then remove the piston completely. Remove the piston seal.

─── **CAUTION** ───

When using compressed air to remove a piston, the piston could fly out like a projectile and brake fluid will be sprayed. Personal injury could result. Secure a block of wood in front of the bore, cover the bore with a shop rag and apply pressure gradually. Never use more pressure than needed.

2. With the cylinder apart, clean all parts in brake fluid or brake part cleaner and inspect the bore and pistons. Minor corrosion can be cleaned off with steel wool or emery cloth, but scoring or piston damage cannot be repaired and the entire assembly should be replaced.

To assemble:

3. Lightly lubricate the new rubber parts with brake rubber grease and install the new piston seal. Grease the piston and install the new piston boot onto the bottom of the piston.

4. Extend (unfold) the boot and carefully fit the boot into its' groove in the caliper. carefully push the piston all the way into

the bore, making sure the boot falls into the groove in the piston. Wipe away any excess grease.

5. Before bolting the caliper to the vehicle, make sure the guide pins move smoothly in the carrier slides. Lightly lubricate them and use new boots.

SAAB 900

Note: The indirect piston and its' parts are a single unit with a special lubricant coating. These parts should not be washed in any type of cleaner, only wiped clean with a clean rag.

1. Remove the return spring from the parking brake lever and push the yoke away from the cylinder. Remove the yoke spring and hand brake lever.

2. Remove the dust boot clip and boot and carefully press the piston out with air pressure. Press the pushrod by hand to separate the direct piston from the cylinder.

─── **CAUTION** ───

When using compressed air to remove a piston, the piston could fly out like a projectile and brake fluid will be sprayed. Personal injury could result. Secure a block of wood in front of the bore, cover the bore with a shop rag and apply pressure gradually. Never use more pressure than needed.

3. Remove the O-rings and seal rings from the pistons and from the bore. Remove the retainer O-rings from the hole for the hand brake lever.

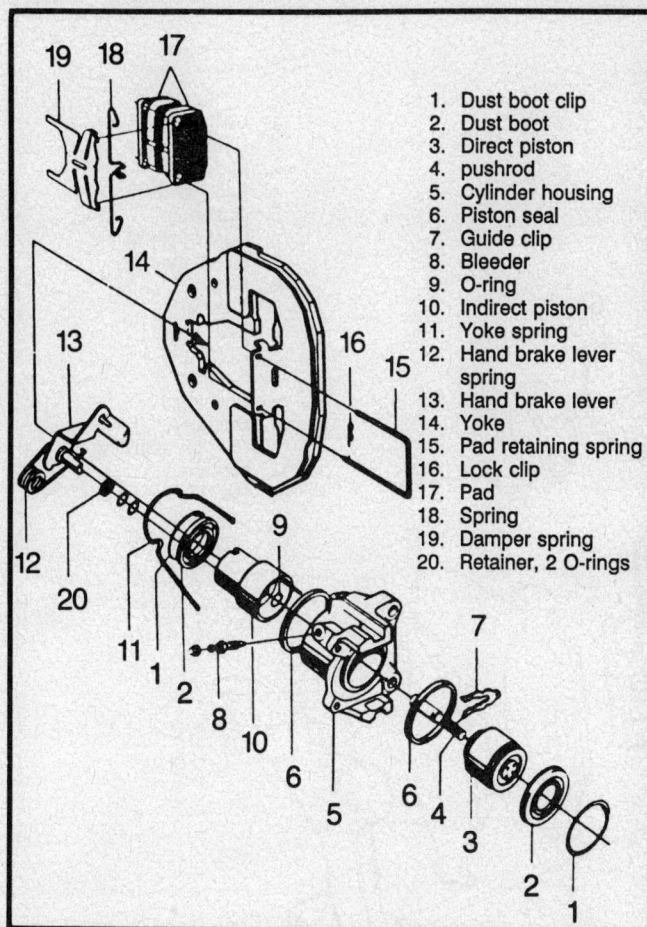

1.	Dust boot clip
2.	Dust boot
3.	Direct piston
4.	pushrod
5.	Cylinder housing
6.	Piston seal
7.	Guide clip
8.	Bleeder
9.	O-ring
10.	Indirect piston
11.	Yoke spring
12.	Hand brake lever spring
13.	Hand brake lever
14.	Yoke
15.	Pad retaining spring
16.	Lock clip
17.	Pad
18.	Spring
19.	Damper spring
20.	Retainer, 2 O-rings

Saab 900 front caliper assembly with hand brake mechanism

To assemble:

4. With the caliper apart, clean all parts except the indirect piston assembly in brake fluid or brake part cleaner and inspect the bore and pistons. Minor corrosion can be cleaned off with steel wool or emery cloth, but scoring or piston damage cannot be repaired and the entire assembly should be replaced.

5. Before assembling anything, fit the cylinder housing into the yoke and measure the clearance between their sliding surfaces. With the bleeder side of the cylinder pushed all the way up against the yoke, there should be 0.006–0.012 in. clearance between the yoke and the other side of the cylinder. Excess clearance will cause vibration and noise when the brake is in use.

6. Be sure to use all the new parts in the rebuild kit. Lubricate the piston seals and O-rings with brake fluid and install them. When installing the indirect piston assembly, make sure the groove lines up with the grooves for the yoke.

7. To install the direct piston, use a pin wrench to screw the two pistons together. Use plenty of brake fluid as lubrication. Both pistons are properly placed when the dust boot grooves are flush with the cylinder housing. Install the new dust boots and clips.

8. Fit the yoke spring and hand brake lever into the yoke and lightly lubicate the sliding edges of the yoke with brake grease. Lift the hand brake lever and make sure the pin fits properly into the cylinder when assembling it onto the yoke.

9. When installing the caliper, hook up the hand brake cable and make sure the clearance between the lever and yoke is no more than 0.019 in. (0.5mm) with the brake off.

REAR CALIPER

Disassembly and Assembly
SAAB 9000

1. Remove the dust boot clip, the hand brake return spring, and the plug for the adjusting screw.

2. Use an Allen wrench to unscrew the piston adjuster and force the piston out of the bore. Remove the piston and seal.

3. With the caliper apart, clean all parts in brake fluid or brake part cleaner and inspect the bore and piston. Minor corrosion can be cleaned off with steel wool or emery cloth, but scoring or piston damage cannot be repaired and the entire assembly should be replaced. If the guide pins did not move freely in the bushings, replace the bushings and pins.

To assemble:

4. Lubricate the piston seal with brake caliper grease and install the seal. Grease the piston, pack the boot with grease and install the boot into the groove in the piston.

5. Install the piston and screw it partially into place with the adjusting screw. Fit the boot into the caliper, install the retainer clip and screw the piston in the rest of the way.

6. Install the hand brake return spring. If the guide pins do not move freely in the bushings, replace the bushings. Be sure the hand brake is properly adjusted when installing the caliper.

SAAB 900

1. Do not under any circumstances split the caliper in half. If the unit is damaged or leaking at the seam, replace the caliper.

2. The pistons must be pressed out with air pressure. A special clamping tool that covers the bore can be used to hold the pistons on one side while the other side is disassembled. As an alternate method, insert a block of wood or an old brake pad between the pistons and press out with air as far as possible. Then remove the pistons on one side at a time using expanding pliers to grip the inside of the piston, or by hand. Be careful not to damage the piston or bore.

--- **CAUTION** ---

When using compressed air to remove a piston, the piston could fly out like a projectile and brake fluid will be sprayed. Personal injury could result. Secure a block of wood in front of the bore, cover the bore with a shop rag and apply pressure gradually. Never use more pressure than needed.

To assemble:

3. With the pistons and seals removed, clean all parts in brake fluid or brake part cleaner and inspect the bore and piston. Minor corrosion can be cleaned off the bore with steel wool or emery cloth, but scoring or piston damage cannot be repaired and the entire assembly should be replaced.

4. Lightly lubricate the new rubber parts with brake rubber grease and install the new piston seals. Grease the piston and install the new piston boot onto the bottom of the piston.

5. Extend (unfold) the boot and carefully fit the boot into its' groove in the caliper.

6. carefully push the piston all the way into the bore, making sure the boot falls into the groove in the piston. Wipe away any excess grease.

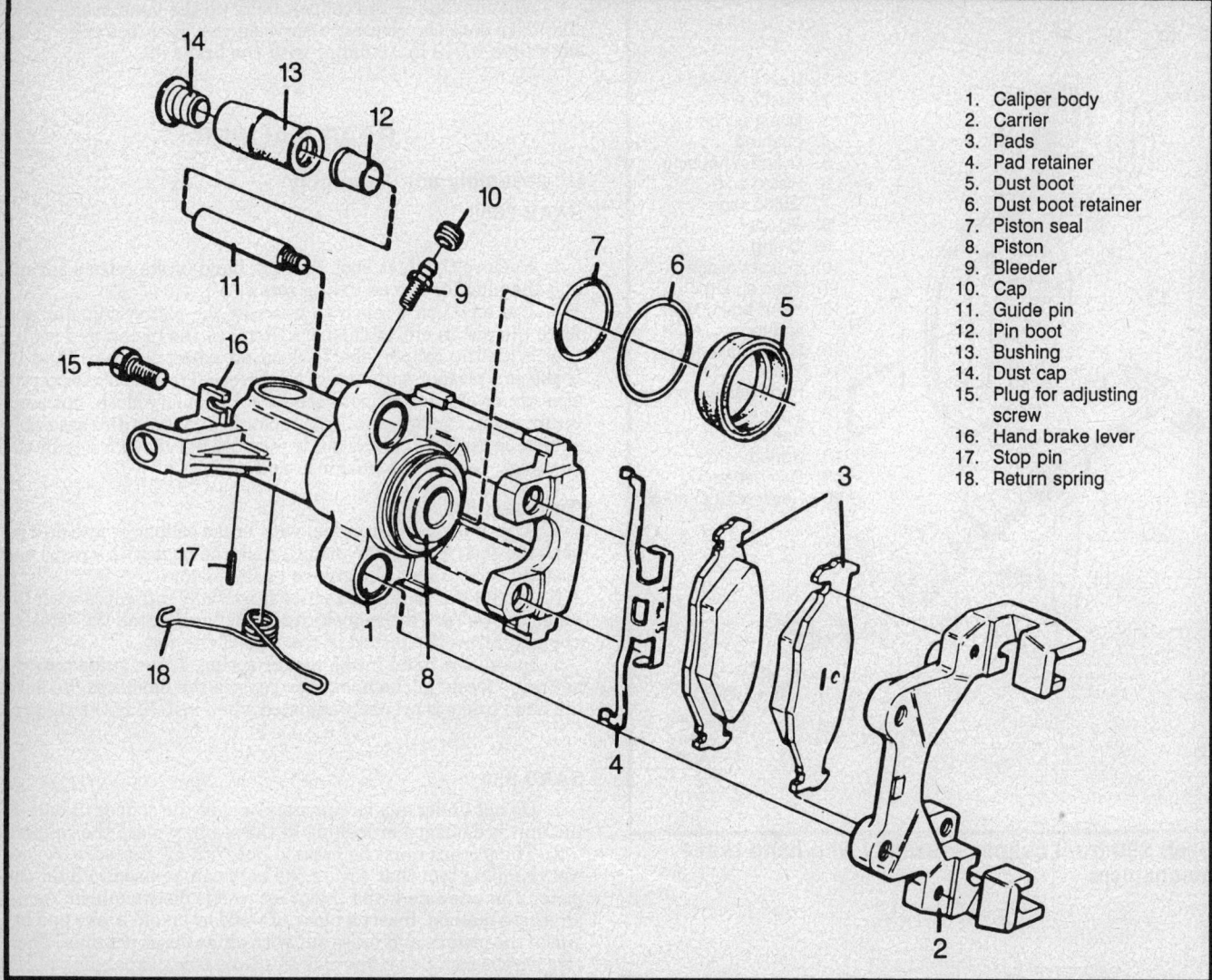

1. Caliper body
2. Carrier
3. Pads
4. Pad retainer
5. Dust boot
6. Dust boot retainer
7. Piston seal
8. Piston
9. Bleeder
10. Cap
11. Guide pin
12. Pin boot
13. Bushing
14. Dust cap
15. Plug for adjusting screw
16. Hand brake lever
17. Stop pin
18. Return spring

Saab 9000 rear caliper with hand brake assembly

SUBARU

Master Cylinder Service

Disassembly and Assembly

1. These vehicles use DOT 3 or 4 brake fluid. With the cylinder in a soft jaw vice, remove the reservoir and sealing rings.

2. Push in slightly on the primary piston and on Justy, remove the secondary piston stop bolt from below the front reservoir sealing ring. Still holding in on the piston, remove the snapring or locking cap. Both pistons can now be removed. Do not disassemble the pistons.

3. With the cylinder apart, clean all parts in brake fluid or brake part cleaner and inspect the bore and pistons. Minor corrosion can be cleaned off with steel wool or emery cloth, but scoring or piston damage cannot be repaired and the entire assembly should be replaced.

To assemble:

4. The new pistons come as an assembly, be sure to use all the new parts in the rebuild kit. Lubricate the parts with clean brake fluid and carefuly insert the pistons with a twisting motion.

5. Push in on the primary piston and install the snapring ro retainer cap and, on Justy, the stop bolt.

Caliper Service

FRONT CALIPERS

Disassembly and Assembly

WITHOUT PARKING BRAKE

1. Remove the bolts to disassemble the pins, sleeves, boots, and caliper support member from the caliper.

2. To remove the piston, place a block of wood in the caliper, lay a shop rag over the bore to prevent fluid spray, and gradually apply air pressure to the brake fluid inlet hole.

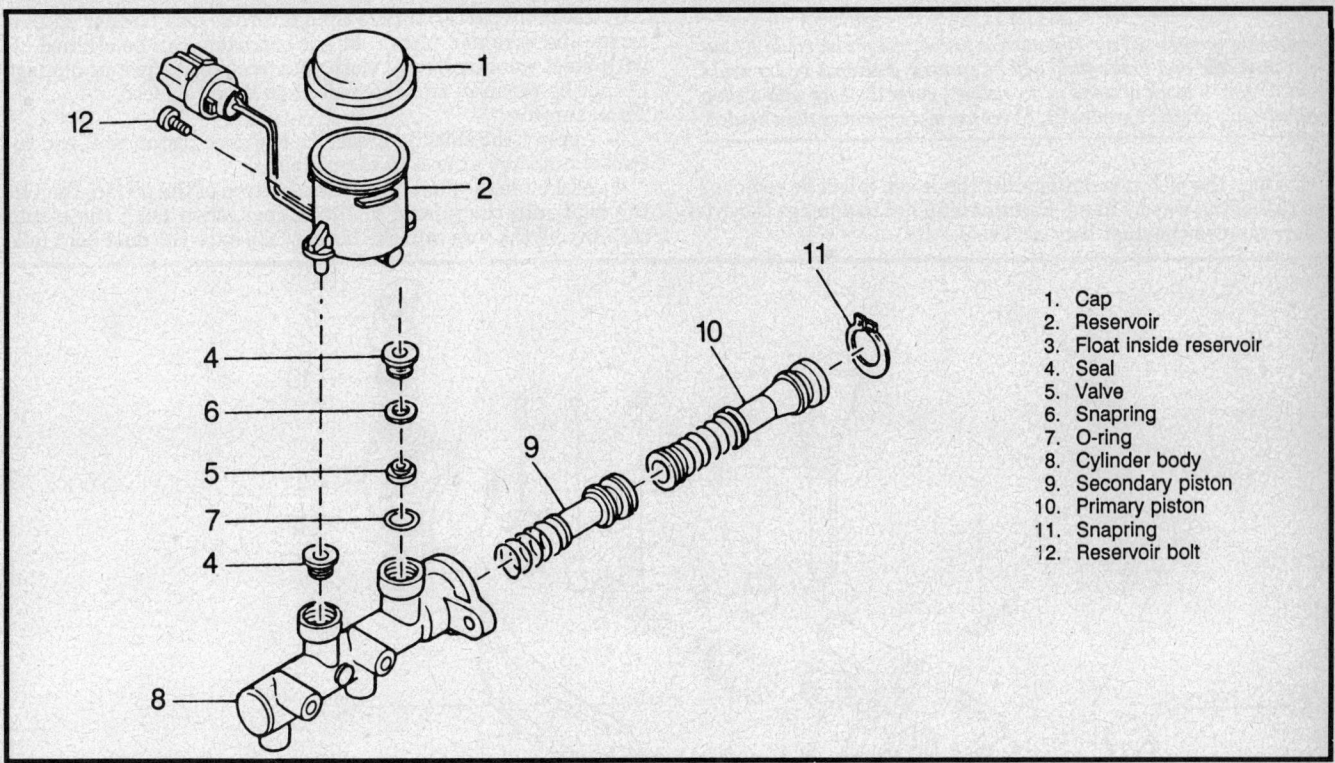

1. Cap
2. Reservoir
3. Float inside reservoir
4. Seal
5. Valve
6. Snapring
7. O-ring
8. Cylinder body
9. Secondary piston
10. Primary piston
11. Snapring
12. Reservoir bolt

Subaru master cylinder; Justy has a stop bolt below the front reservoir seal

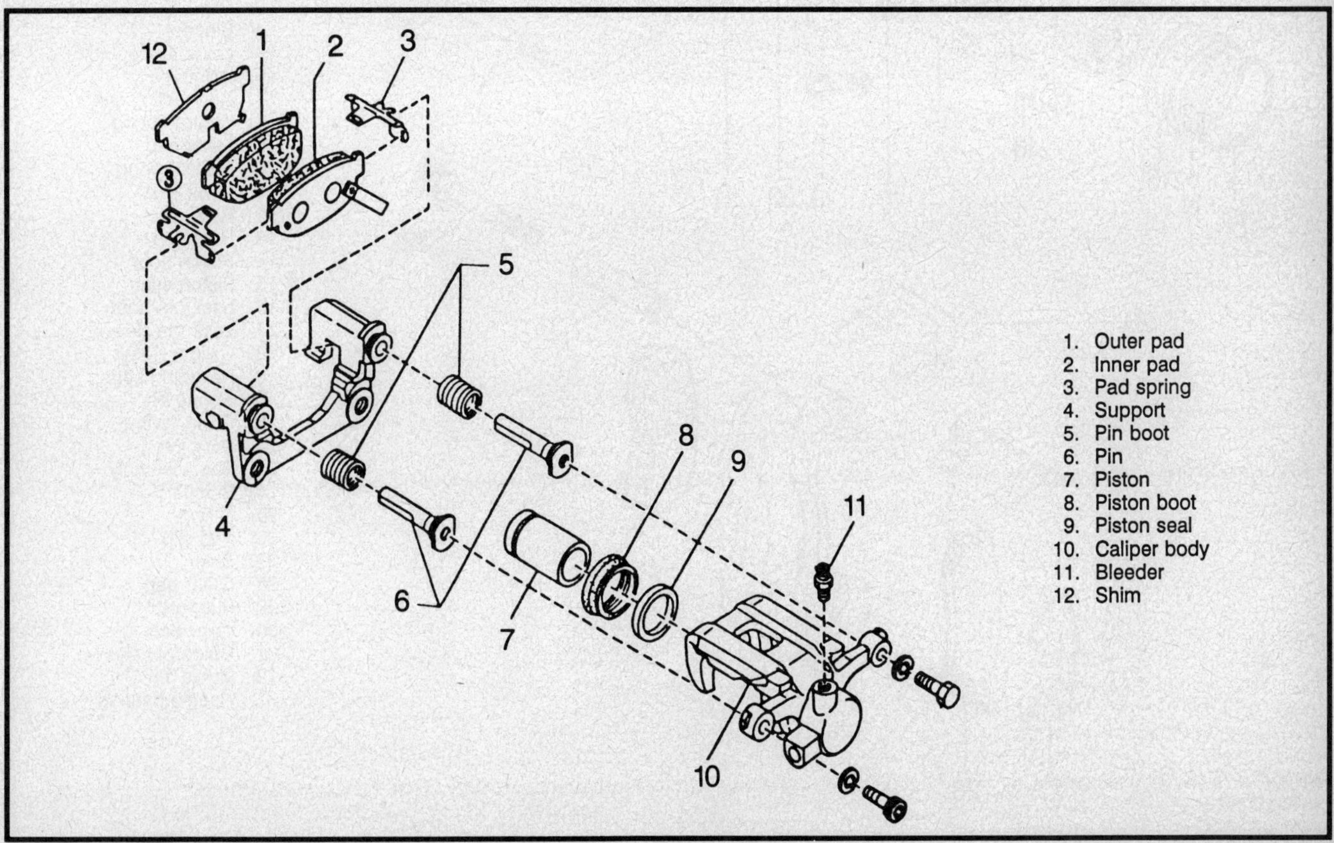

1. Outer pad
2. Inner pad
3. Pad spring
4. Support
5. Pin boot
6. Pin
7. Piston
8. Piston boot
9. Piston seal
10. Caliper body
11. Bleeder
12. Shim

Subaru floating caliper without parking brake, 1990 Loyale shown

---

CAUTION

When using compressed air to remove a piston, the piston could fly out like a projectile and brake fluid will be sprayed. Personal injury could result. Clamp a block of wood to the caliper, cover the bore with a shop rag and apply pressure gradually. Never use more pressure than needed.

---

3. Once the piston is out against the wood, it can be removed the rest of the way by hand. Being careful not to damage the cylinder, remove the dust boot and seal.

4. Clean all parts in brake fluid or brake part cleaner and examine the bore and piston. Minor corrosion can be cleaned off with steel wool or emery cloth, but scoring or piston damage cannot be repaired and the unit should be replaced.

To assemble:

5. Apply light silicone grease to the new piston seal and install it onto the groove in the caliper.

6. Assemble the dust boot to the bottom of the piston, then fit the boot into the groove in the caliper, then push the piston carefully all the way into the bore. Make sure the dust boot falls

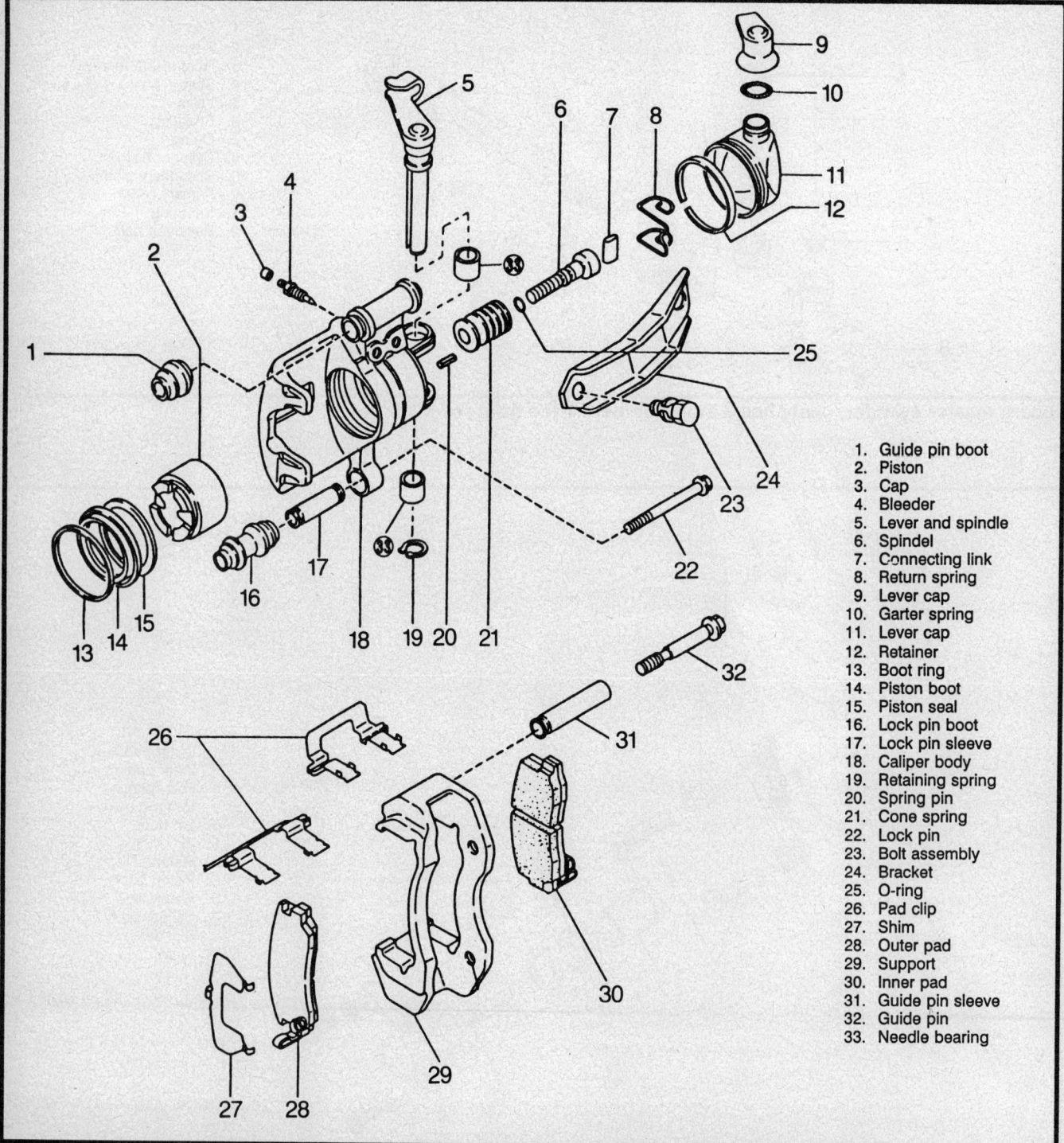

1. Guide pin boot
2. Piston
3. Cap
4. Bleeder
5. Lever and spindle
6. Spindel
7. Connecting link
8. Return spring
9. Lever cap
10. Garter spring
11. Lever cap
12. Retainer
13. Boot ring
14. Piston boot
15. Piston seal
16. Lock pin boot
17. Lock pin sleeve
18. Caliper body
19. Retaining spring
20. Spring pin
21. Cone spring
22. Lock pin
23. Bolt assembly
24. Bracket
25. O-ring
26. Pad clip
27. Shim
28. Outer pad
29. Support
30. Inner pad
31. Guide pin sleeve
32. Guide pin
33. Needle bearing

Subaru caliper with parking brake: compress the cone spring to remove the lever and spindle

into the groove in the piston. If the dust boot has a retainer ring, install it and wipe away any excess grease.

7. Clean and lubricate the sliding pins and bolts and, with new boots installed, make sure the caliper moves freely on the pins.

WITH PARKING BRAKE

1. With the caliper removed from the support, remove the guide pin sleeves and boots and the piston dust boot. carefully press the piston out with air pressure.

─────────── **CAUTION** ───────────

When using compressed air to remove a piston, the piston could fly out like a projectile and brake fluid will be sprayed. Personal injury could result. Secure a block of wood in front of the bore, cover the bore with a shop rag and apply pressure gradually. Never use more pressure than needed.

2. carefully remove the piston seal without damaging the bore.

3. Remove the retaining ring from the lever cap, fold the cap back out of the way and remove the snapring from the bottom end of the lever. There is a special tool available to press the cone spring, tool # 925471000. Press in on the cone spring to unload lever and draw the lever and remaining parts out of the caliper.

To assemble:

4. With the caliper apart, clean all parts in brake fluid or brake part cleaner and inspect the bore and piston. Minor corrosion can be cleaned off with steel wool or emery cloth, but scoring or piston damage cannot be repaired and the entire assembly should be replaced. Be sure to check the needle bearing, replace it if necessary.

5. Apply light silicone grease to the new piston seal and install it onto the groove in the caliper.

6. Grease the piston and assemble the dust boot to the bottom of the piston. Fit the boot into the groove in the caliper, then push the piston carefully all the way into the bore. Make sure the dust boot falls into the groove in the piston. Install the boot ring and wipe away any excess grease.

7. With a new O-ring installed, lightly grease the spindle and install it and the cone spring pin and spring. Install the spring press tool to hold the spring in place.

8. Grease the lever spindle and install it with the connecting link. Install the return spring to hold the connecting link in

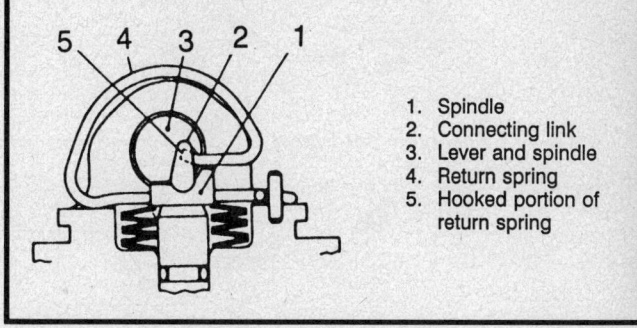

1. Spindle
2. Connecting link
3. Lever and spindle
4. Return spring
5. Hooked portion of return spring

On Subaru caliper with parking brake, the return spring hook holds the connecting link in place

place, then remove the press tool. Install the snapring at the bottom of the lever.

9. When installing the lever cap, pack the lever assembly with grease and carefully clamp the cap in place. Wipe away and excess grease.

10. Make sure the guide pins move freely in the sleeves and lightly lubricate them before installing the new boots.

WHEEL CYLINDER SERVICE

1. The wheel cylinders on vehicles with rear drum brakes are fairly simple units and no special tools are required for service. Loosen the bleeder screw first, and if it doesn't break off, continue with the rebuild procedure.

2. With the cylinder apart, clean all parts in brake fluid or brake part cleaner and inspect the bore and pistons. Minor corrosion can be cleaned off with steel wool or emery cloth, but scoring cannot be repaired and the entire assembly should be replaced.

3. When reassembling, lubricate all parts with brake fluid, not grease. When installing the cylinder, use a silicone sealer between the cylinder and the back plate.

TOYOTA

Master Cylinder Service

Disassembly and Assembly

1. These vehicles use DOT 3 brake fluid. With the cylinder drained and clamped in a soft jaw vice, remove the reservoir set screw and the reservoir. Then remove the boot at the mounting flange.

2. Using a blunt tool, push the piston in just enough to take up the spring tension and remove the piston stopper bolt and the snapring.

3. Remove both the secondary and primary piston assemblies by tapping them out on a block of wood. Do not use air pressure and be careful to not damage the bore.

4. Use only clean brake fluid or a brake parts cleaner to clean the master cylinder and carefully examine the bore. If there is any corrosion or distortion, do not attempt to rebuild the cylinder, replace the entire assembly. Be sure to use all the parts in the rebuild kit.

To assemble:

5. When inserting the pistons, lubricate all parts with a rubber grease and rotate the pistons while gently pushing them into the bore.

6. With both pistons installed, push in on the primary piston while installing the stop bolts and snapring. Torque the bolts to 7 ft. lbs.

7. Install the flange boot and, when installing the reservoir, lubricate the grommets with brake fluid. Before installing the master cylinder, the booster pushrod clearance must be adjusted.

Brake Booster Service

The vacuum booster on these vehicles cannot be repaired and no service parts are available from the factory. Faulty units must be replaced, but the pushrod length must be adjusted before installing the master cylinder.

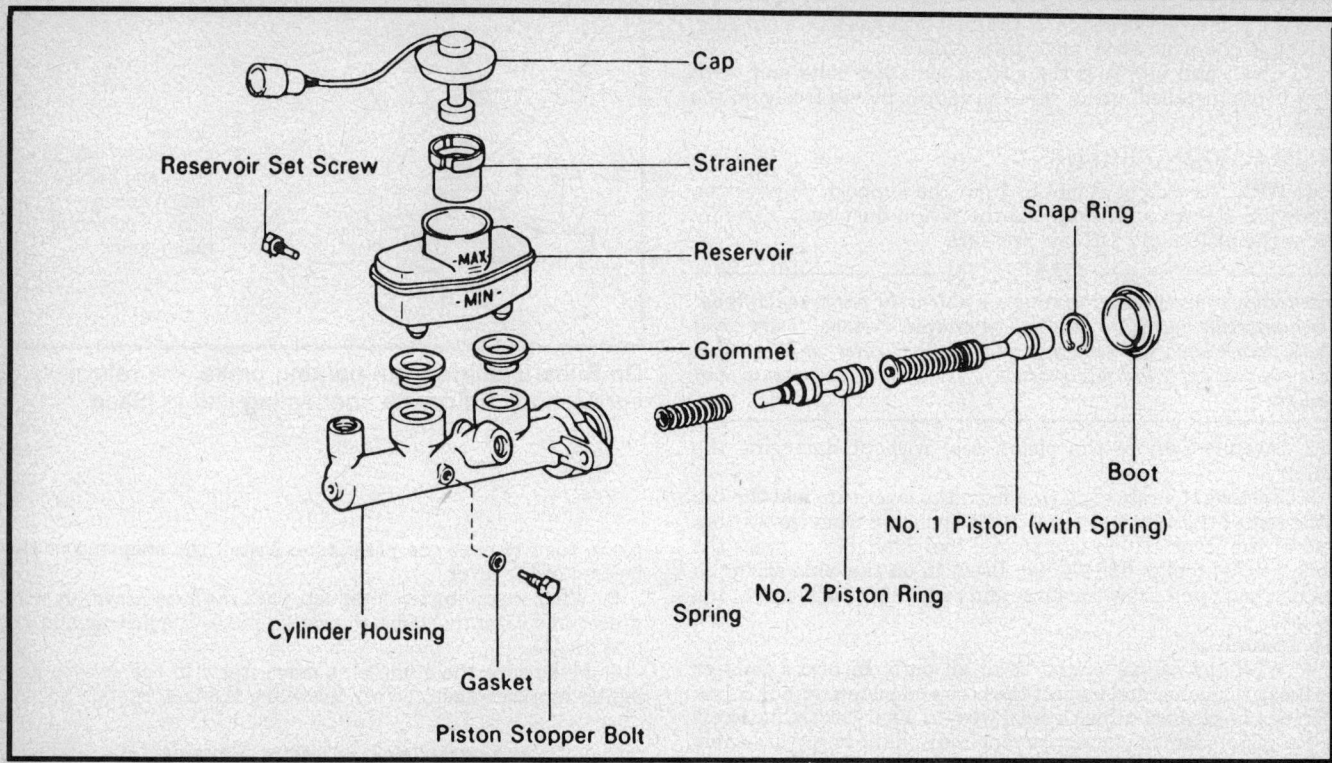

Typical Toyota master cylinder, Tercel shown

BOOSTER PUSHROD CLEARANCE ADJUSTMENT

This procedure is for adjusting the static clearance between the pushrod on the output end of the booster and the piston on the master cylinder. This needs to be done any time a booster or master cylinder is changed or rebuilt. If the pushrod is adjusted too long, the master cylinder piston will be pushed and the brakes will drag. If the rod is too short, the pedal travel will be very long and full braking may not be available. This adjustment is critical to proper functioning of the brakes.

1. A special tool is available to make this job much faster and more acurate, special service tool SST 09737-00010. With the new gasket on the master cylinder mounting flange, set the tool on the flange and adjust the pin to touch the piston.

2. Turn the tool over and set it on the booster. The clearance between the pin and the pushrod should be zero. Turn the adjusting nut as needed.

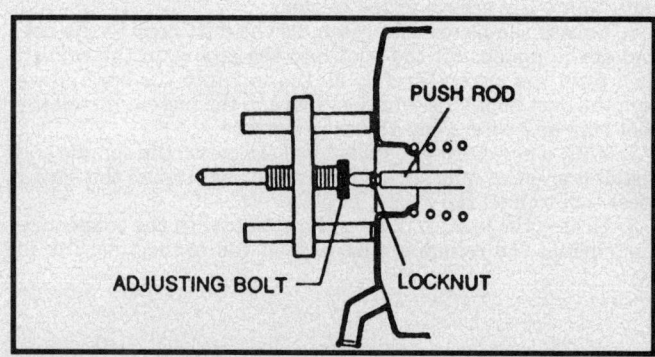

Using the special tool to set pushrod clearance on Toyota

Caliper Service

FRONT CALIPERS

Disassembly and Assembly

1. More than one make of front caliper is used on these vehicles, but they are all floating types and the procedure for service is the same. Remove the pin bolts to disassemble the sleeves, boots, bushings and torque plate from the caliper.

2. To remove the piston, place a block of wood in the caliper, lay a shop rag over the bore to prevent fluid spray, and gradually apply air pressure to the brake fluid inlet hole.

─────────── **CAUTION** ───────────

When using compressed air to remove a piston, the piston could fly out like a projectile and brake fluid will be sprayed. Personal injury could result. Clamp a block of wood to the caliper, cover the bore with a shop rag and apply pressure gradually. Never use more pressure than needed.

3. Once the piston is out against the wood, it can be removed the rest of the way by hand. Being careful not to damage the cylinder, remove the dust boot and seal.

4. Clean all parts in brake fluid or brake part cleaner and examine the bore and piston. Minor corrosion can be cleaned off with steel wool or emery cloth, but scoring or piston damage cannot be repaired and the unit should be replaced.

To assemble:

5. Apply the light silicone grease that comes with the kit to the new piston seal and install it into the caliper.

6. Lubricate the piston with clean brake fluid and carefully install the boot onto the bottom end of the piston.

7. Unfold the boot and fit the lip into the caliper. carefully push the piston through the boot and all the way into the caliper bore, making sure the boot falls into the groove in the piston.

8. Make sure the pin bolts and sleeves are clean and move freely. Lightly grease them for reassembly and use the new bushings and boots supplied in the kit.

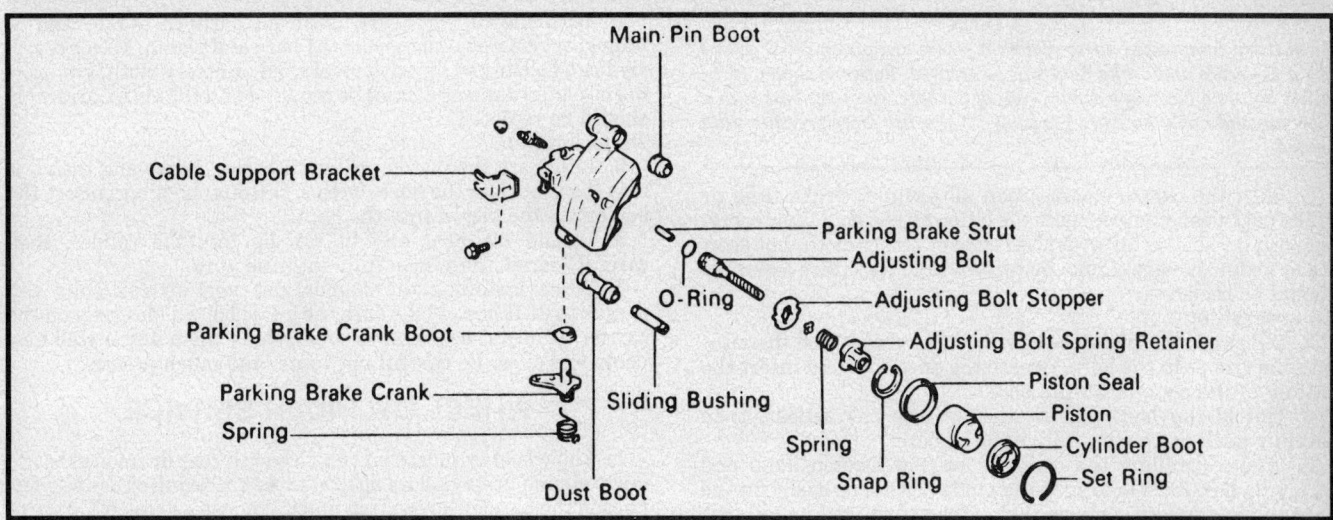

Toyota rear caliper with parking brake

REAR CALIPER

Disassembly and Assembly

1. Remove the lock pins, guides, sleeves and support mounting.

2. Use special tool SST 09719 14020 or equivalent to unscrew the piston from the caliper. carefully remove the piston seal.

3. Use a piece of tube or a socket to compress the adjusting bolt spring retainer, then remove the snapring. Remove the adjuster parts for cleaning and inspection.

4. With the caliper apart, clean all parts in brake fluid or brake part cleaner and inspect the bore and piston. Minor corrosion can be cleaned off with steel wool or emery cloth, but scoring or piston damage cannot be repaired and the entire assembly should be replaced.

To assemble:

5. With the grease supplied in the rebuild kit, lightly lubricate all the parking brake and adjuster parts and install them into the caliper. When installing the snapring, make sure the open end is towards the bleeder. Operate the lever by hand to see that the adjusting bolt moves smoothly.

6. Lightly coat the piston seal with grease and install it into the groove in the bore. Grease the piston and screw it all the way in till it moves freely. Then align the indentations so they will be perpendicular with the axle. Grease the piston boot and install it.

7. Make sure the guide pins move freely in the sleeves and lightly lubricate them before installing the new boots.

WHEEL CYLINDER SERVICE

1. The wheel cylinders on vehicles with rear drum brakes are

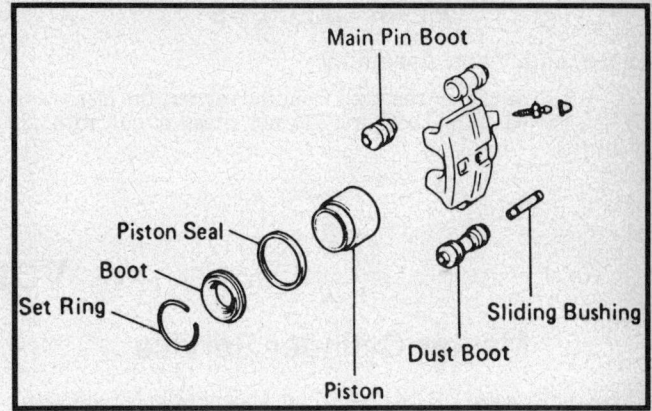

Toyota floating caliper, 1990 Supra shown

fairly simple units and no special tools are required for service. Loosen the bleeder screw first, and if it doesn't break off, continue with the rebuild procedure.

2. With the cylinder apart, clean all parts in brake fluid or brake part cleaner and inspect the bore and pistons. Minor corrosion can be cleaned off with steel wool or emery cloth, but scoring cannot be repaired and the entire assembly should be replaced.

3. When reassembling, lubricate all parts with brake fluid, not grease. When installing the cylinder, use a silicone sealer between the cylinder and the back plate.

VOLKSWAGEN

Master Cylinder Service

These vehicles use DOT 4 brake fluid. Master cylinder and vacuum boosters cannot be repaired and no service parts are available from Volkswagen. Faulty units can be replaced separately, but make sure to use a new gasket or O-ring between them.

Caliper Service

FRONT CALIPERS

Disassembly and Assembly

1. With the caliper removed from the carrier, the piston must be pressed out with air pressure. carefully remove the piston seal.

─────────── CAUTION ───────────
When using compressed air to remove a piston, the piston could fly out like a projectile and brake fluid will be sprayed. Personal injury could result. Secure a block of wood in front of the bore, cover the bore with a shop rag and apply pressure gradually. Never use more pressure than needed.

2. With the caliper apart, clean all parts in brake fluid or brake part cleaner and inspect the bore and piston. Minor corrosion can be cleaned off with steel wool or emery cloth, but scoring or piston damage cannot be repaired and the entire assembly should be replaced.
To assemble:
3. Lubricate the piston seal with brake grease and install it into the groove in the bore. Grease the dust boot and insert the bottom of the piston into the boot.
4. Unfold the boot and fit the lip into the caliper, then carefully push the piston fully into the bore.
5. When installing the caliper, use new stretch bolts and torque to 6 ft. lbs. Make sure the guide bolts slide easily on the carrier. If necessary, remove them, clean them and install new boots and caps. Be careful not to use too much grease.

REAR CALIPERS

Disassembly and Assembly

1. With the caliper removed from the carrier, the piston can be unscrewed from the bore. Do not press it out with air pressure.

2. With the caliper apart, clean all parts in brake fluid or brake part cleaner and inspect the bore and piston. Minor corrosion can be cleaned off with steel wool or emery cloth, but scoring or piston damage cannot be repaired and the entire assembly should be replaced.
To assemble:
3. Lubricate the piston seal with brake grease and install it into the groove in the bore. Grease the dust boot and insert the bottom of the piston into the boot.
4. Unfold the boot and fit the lip into the caliper, then carefully screw the piston fully into the bore.
5. When installing the caliper, use new stretch bolts and torque to 26 ft. lbs.. Make sure the guide bolts slide easily on the carrier. If necessary, remove them, clean them and install new boots and caps. Be careful not to use too much grease.

WHEEL CYLINDER SERVICE

1. The wheel cylinders on vehicles with rear drum brakes are fairly simple units and no special tools are required for service. Loosen the bleeder screw first, and if it doesn't break off, continue with the rebuild procedure.
2. With the cylinder apart, clean all parts in brake fluid or brake part cleaner and inspect the bore and pistons. Minor corrosion can be cleaned off with steel wool or emery cloth, but scoring cannot be repaired and the entire assembly should be replaced.
3. When reassembling, lubricate all parts with brake fluid, not grease. When installing the cylinder, use a silicone sealer between the cylinder and the back plate.

VOLVO

Master Cylinder Service

These vehicles use DOT 4 brake fluid. Master cylinder and vacuum boosters cannot be repaired and no service parts are available from Volvo. On vehicles with a vacuum pump, a kit is available for replacing the diaphragm and check valves. Faulty units can be replaced separately, but make sure to use a new gaskets or O-rings.

Caliper Service

FIXED PISTON CALIPERS

Disassembly and Assembly

1. Do not under any circumstances split the caliper in half. If the unit is damaged or leaking at the seam, replace the caliper.
2. The pistons must be pressed out with air pressure. Insert a block of wood or an old brake pad between the pistons and apply air pressure to one of the brake fluid inlet ports, pressing out two pistons as far as possible. Then remove the pistons one at a time using expanding pliers to grip the inside of the piston, or by hand. Be careful not to damage the piston or bore.

─────────── CAUTION ───────────
When using compressed air to remove a piston, the piston could fly out like a projectile and brake fluid will be sprayed. Personal injury could result. Secure a block of wood in front of the bore, cover the bore with a shop rag and apply pressure gradually. Never use more pressure than needed.

To assemble:
3. With the pistons and seals removed, clean all parts in brake fluid or brake part cleaner and inspect the bore and pistons. Minor corrosion can be cleaned off the bore with steel wool or emery cloth, but scoring or piston damage cannot be repaired and the entire assembly should be replaced.
4. Lightly lubricate the new rubber parts with brake rubber grease and install the new piston seals. Grease the piston and install the new piston boot onto the bottom of the piston.
5. Extend (unfold) the boot and carefuly fit the boot into its' groove in the caliper.
6. carefully push the piston all the way into the bore, making sure the boot falls into the groove in the piston. Wipe away excess grease and install the caliper.

FLOATING CALIPERS

The procedure for rebuilding these calipers is the same as for fixed calipers except for servicing the guide pins and boots. Before installing the caliper to the vehicle, make sure the pins move freely in the carrier and that light grease is used on the pins. Make sure the boots are in good condition. When installing the caliper, replace the bolts that hold the caliper to the carrier. These are stretch bolts and are designed to be used only one time. Torque the stretch bolts to 22–28 ft. lbs.

GENERAL INFORMATION

Wheel Alignment

Wheel alignment refers to the angular relationship between the wheels, suspension and the ground alignment.

For safe steering control with a minimum of tire wear, certain established factors must coexist. The use of planes, angles and radii relative to each other and to vehicle and tire dimensions. Some factors are built in, with no provision for adjustment; others are adjustable within limits. The entire system depends upon all value factors, separately and combined. It is therefore difficult to change some of the established settings without influencing others.

This system is called steering geometry or wheel alignment and requires a complete check of all the factors involved.

WHEEL POSITIONING

Always check steering wheel alignment in conjunction with and at the same time as toe-in. In fact, the steering wheel spoke position, with the vehicle on a straight section of highway, may be the first indication of front end misalignment.

If the vehicle has been been wrecked or indicates any evidence of steering gear or linkage disturbance, the steering linkage at the steering gear, should be disconnected from the shaft. The steering wheel or gear should be turned from extreme right to the extreme left to determine the halfway point in its turning scope. This will be the spot on the gear that is in action during straight-ahead driving and in which position the steering gear should be adjusted. With the steering wheel in the straight-ahead position and the steering gear adjusted to 0 lash status, reconnect the pitman arm.

STEERING AXIS INCLINATION

Steering Axis Inclination (SAI) is the inward tilt, top of the steering axis from the vertical. The inclination angle, is the angle between true vertical and a line passing through the center of upper mount and lower ball joint, as viewed from the front of the vehicle. Steering Axis Inclination (SAI) helps the vehicle track straight down the road and assists the wheel back into the straight-ahead position. Steering Axis Inclination (SAI) on front wheel drive vehicles should be negative.

INCLUDED ANGLE

The included angle is the angle measured from the camber angle to the line passes through the upper mount and lower ball joint as viewed from the front of the vehicle. Included angle is calculated in degrees, however most alignment racks will not measure the included angle directly. To determine the included angle, subtract negative or add positive camber readings to the Steering Axis Inclination (SAI).

SCRUB RADIUS

Ideally, this measurement is as small as possible. Normally, the Steering Axis Inclination (SAI) angle and the centerline of the wheel and tire intersect below the road surface, causing a positive scrub radius. With MacPherson struts, the Steering Axis Inclination (SAI) angle is much larger than with a Long Arm Short Arm (LASA) type suspension. This allows the Steering Axis Inclination (SAI) angle to intersect the camber angle above the rod surface, forming a negative scrub radius. The smaller the scrub radius, the better the directional stability.

Scrub radius is dramatically increased when aftermarket wheels and tires that have additional offset are installed. They

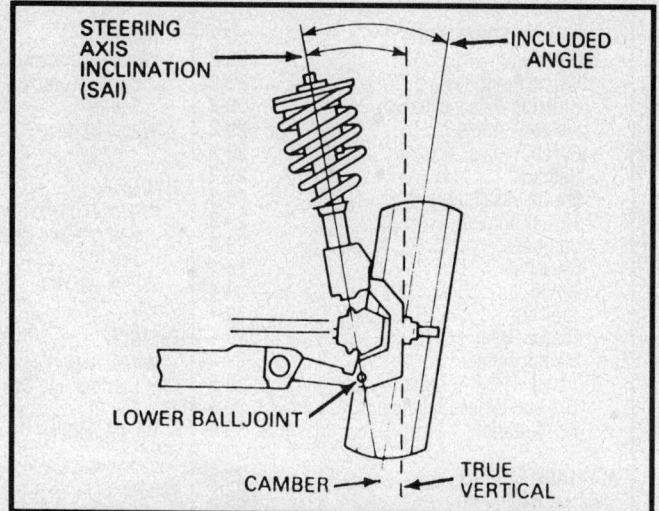

Steering Axis Inclination (SAI) in relationship to the upper mount and ball joint

may cause the centerline of the tires to move further away from the spindle. This will increase the scrub radius, which in turn reduces directional stability. A large amount of scrub radius can cause severe shimmy after hitting a bump.

Scrub radius is not directly measurable by the conventional methods. It is projected geometrically by engineers during the design phase of the suspension.

SETBACK

Setback applies to both front and rear wheels and is the amount 1 wheel may be rearward of the other wheel spindle. Setback may be caused by a road hazard or collision. The first clue will be a caster difference from side-to-side of more than 1 degree.

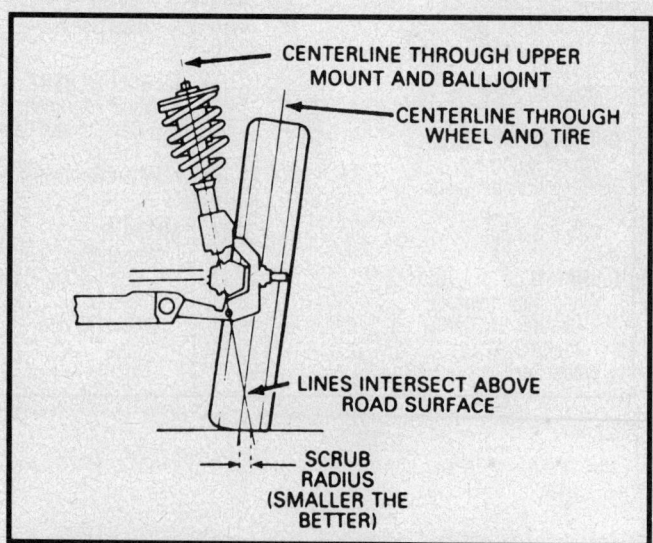

View of the scrub radius, relative to road surface contact

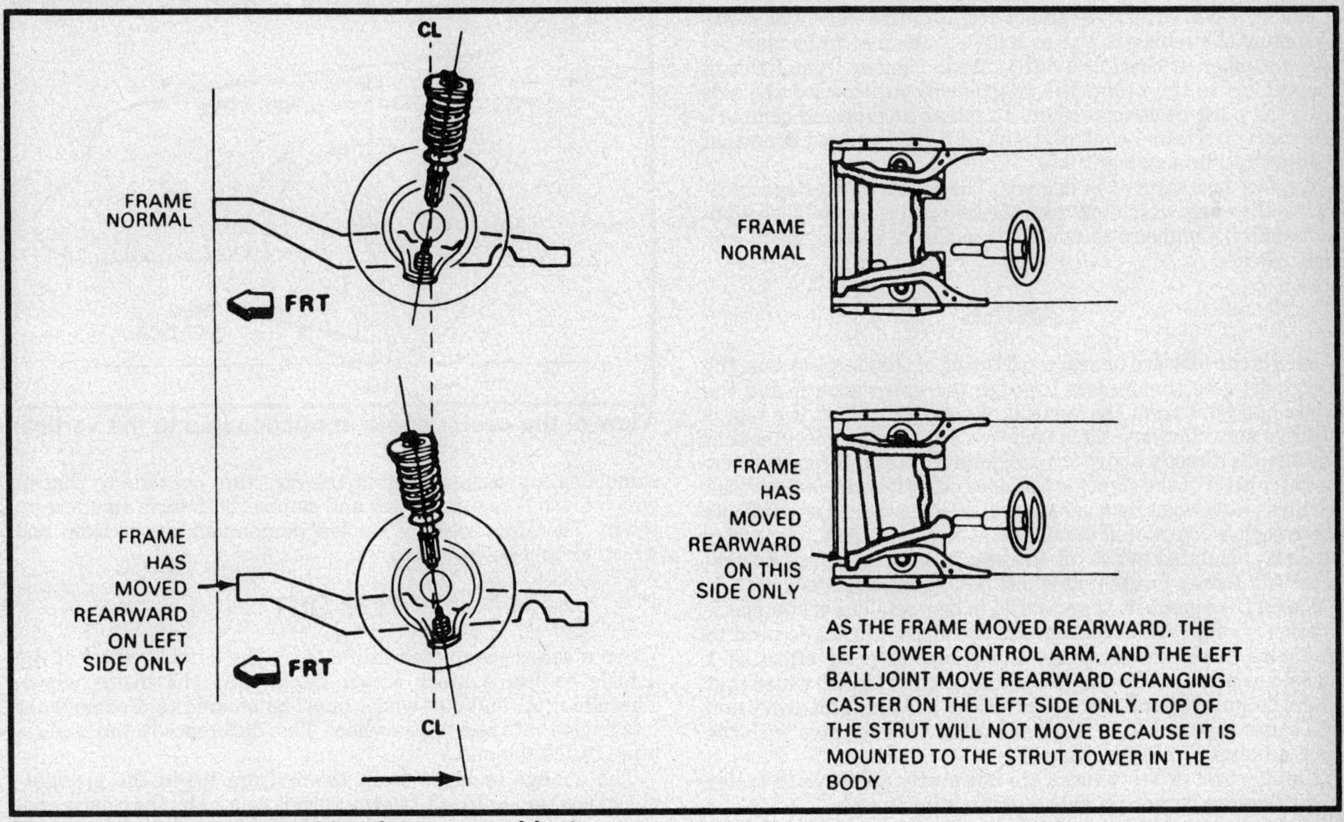

FRAME NORMAL

FRT

FRAME HAS MOVED REARWARD ON LEFT SIDE ONLY

FRT

CL

FRAME NORMAL

FRAME HAS MOVED REARWARD ON THIS SIDE ONLY

AS THE FRAME MOVED REARWARD, THE LEFT LOWER CONTROL ARM, AND THE LEFT BALLJOINT MOVE REARWARD CHANGING CASTER ON THE LEFT SIDE ONLY. TOP OF THE STRUT WILL NOT MOVE BECAUSE IT IS MOUNTED TO THE STRUT TOWER IN THE BODY.

Frame misalignment resulting from an accident

FRAME MISALIGNMENT

The frame supports the engine and transaxle and provides the mounting point for the front suspension lower control arms. Any misalignment of the frame will cause a misalignment of the front wheels. Movement of the frame will usually cause an increase in caster on 1 side of the vehicle and a decrease in caster on the other. It can bind the exhaust system, cause problems with control cables and create unacceptable noises and sounds. Check for any obvious visual damage.

THRUST ANGLES

The front wheels aim or steer the vehicle, but the rear wheels control tracking. This tracking action is relative to thrust angle. Thrust angle is defined as the path that the rear wheels will take. Ideally, the thrust angle would be geometrically aligned with the body centerline.

Front wheel drive vehicles introduced another dimension to the thrust angles. Due to minor accidents, hitting curbs, holes and other related ocurrances, 1 of the rear wheels may change. This directly affects the thrust angle by keeping the rear wheels from tracking properly. Other obvious problems may also occur, such as severe wheel scrubbing, causing unusual and accelerated tire wear, a decrease in fuel economy and less that optimum handling stability. Prior to performing wheel alignment, the following should be observed:

　　a. If an excessive load, such as a tool box, is normally carried in the vehicle, it should remain in the vehicle during alignment checks.

　　b. If the excess load affects the steering or handling safety, the customer must be advised.

　　c. A temporary excess load may cause a temporary change in alignment, but the vehicle should recover with in 500 miles (800 km). Check that the suspension components have not been damaged.

CAMBER

Camber is an important wheel alignment angle, because it is both a tire wear angle and a directional control angle. Camber is the inward or outward tilt of the top of the tires when they are viewed from the front of the vehicle. If the center line of a tire is perfectly vertical, the tire will have 0 camber. Positive camber means the top of the wheels tilt outward. Negative camber means the top of the wheels tilt inward. An excessive amount of positive camber will cause outside shoulder wear on the tires. Likewise, an excessive amount of negative camber will cause inside shoulder wear.

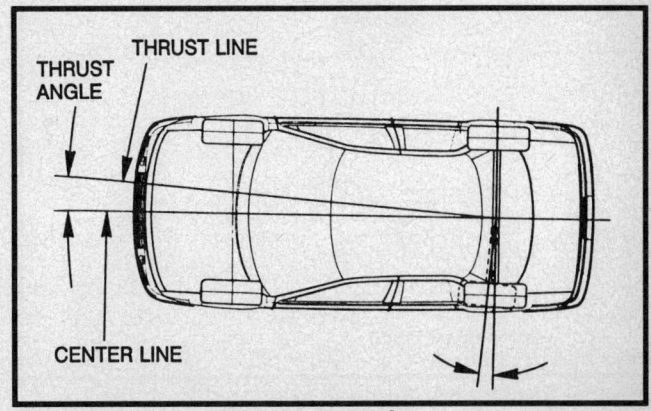

THRUST LINE

THRUST ANGLE

CENTER LINE

Checking the vehicles trust angle

Not only will excessive camber result in tire wear, but it will also cause the vehicle to pull or lead to the side with the most position camber. If there is a difference in camber from 1 side of the vehicle to the other, the vehicle will pull toward the side with the most positive camber. To better understand camber's effect on directional control, think of it as a tapered cone that will not roll in a straight line.

Camber is measured in degrees. The actual camber specification is the angle which provides the best tire wear and directional stability. Camber adjustment is available at both front and rear wheels.

CASTER

Caster is the forward or rearward tilting of the steering axis, the imaginary line that passes through the upper mount and the lower ball joint from the vertical. A rearward tilt at the top, is positive and a forward tilt is negative. Zero caster indicates that the strut is directly above the ball joint. Caster influences directional control of the steering but does not affect tire wear. Weak springs or overloading a vehicle will affect caster. Caster affects the vehicle's directional stability and steering effort. The caster angle is calculated to deliver the best in steering effort, normal wheel returning forces and wheel pulling sensitivity.

Caster, like camber, is measured in degrees. The caster specification, along with Steering Axis Inclination (SAI), is used to give good directional stability and reduce steering effort. If 1 wheel has more positive caster than the other, it will cause that wheel to pull toward the center of the vehicle. This condition will cause the vehicle to move or lead toward the side with the least amount of positive caster.

Front wheel drive vehicles are not overly sensitive to caster and therefore do not provide a caster adjustment.

TOE-IN

Toe-in is the distance that the front wheels are closer together at the front than they are at the rear. This dimension is usually measured, in inches or fractions of an inch.

Generally speaking, the wheels are toed-in because they are cambered. When a vehicle operates with 0 degrees camber, it will be be found to operate with 0 toe-in. As the required camber increases, so does the toe-in. The reason for this is that the cambered wheel tends to steer in the direction in which it is cambered. Therefore, it is necessary to over come this tendency by

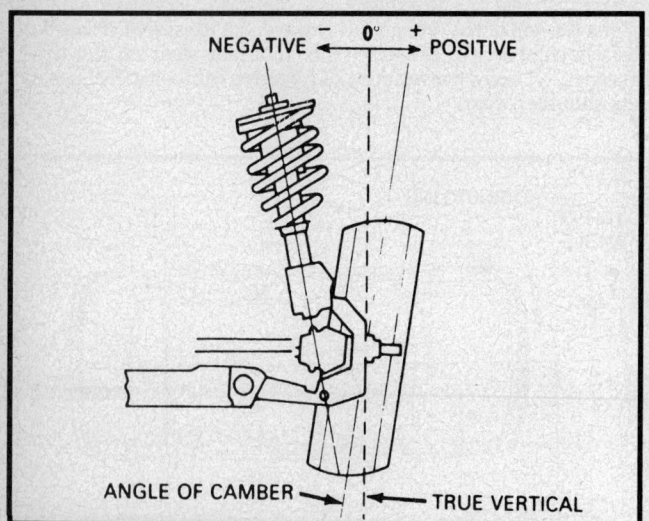

View of the camber angle in relationship to the vertical

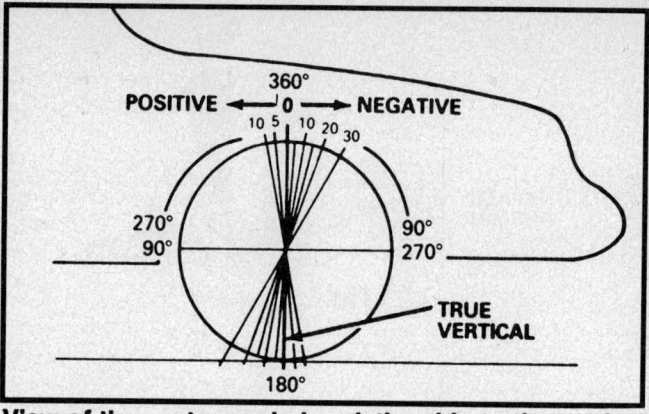

View of the caster angle in relationship to the vertical

compensating very slightly in the direction opposite to that in which it tends to roll. Caster and camber both have an effect on toe-in. Therefore toe-in is the last component on the front end which should be corrected.

TOE-OUT

When a vehicle is steered into a turn, the outside wheel of the vehicle scribes a much larger circle than the inside wheel. Therefore, the outside wheel must be steered to a some what less angle thatn the inside wheel. This difference in the angle is often called toe-out.

The change in angle from toe-in from toe-in the straight-ahead position to toe-out in the turn is caused by the relative position of the steering arms to the ball joint and to each other.

If a line were drawn from the center of the ball joint, through the center of the steering arm tie rod attaching hole at each wheel, the lines would be found to cross almost exactly in the center of the rear axle.

If the front end angles, including toe-in, are set correctly and the toe-out is found to be incorrect, 1 or both of the steering arm are bent.

TORQUE STEER

Torque steer is when a vehicle will pull and lead in 1 direction, when under hard acceleration and will pull and lead in the opposite direction during deceleration. This condition may be apparent on front wheel drive vehicles that utilize a transaxle with different length axle shafts. As a result, both axles tend to twist, but the longer axle will twist sightly more than the shorter one. This causes 1 wheel to start rolling quicker than the other, resulting in very slight pull.

MEMORY STEER

Memory steer is a condition encountered after making a turn in 1 direction, the vehicle will tend to lead or pull in that direction. After turning in the other direction, the vehicle will tend to lead or pull in that direction. This condition is not common, however it is usually the result of a bent steering gear or spool valve and housing wear problem.

While tracking is more a function of the rear axle and frame, it is difficult to align the front suspension when the vehicle does not track straight. Tracking means that the centerline of the rear axle follows exactly the path of the centerline of the front axle when the vehicle is moving in a straight line.

On vehicles that have equal tread, front and rear, the rear tires will follow in exactly the thread of the front tires, when moving in a straight line. However, there are many vehicles whose rear tread is wider than the front tread. On such vehicles, the rear axle tread will straddle the front axle tread an equal amount on both sides, when moving in a straight line.

The easiest way to check a vehicle for tracking is to stand directly in back of it while the vehicle is driven in a straight line. If the observer will stand as near to the center of the vehicle as possible, he can readily observe any difference in perspective between the front and rear wheels, whether or not they are tracking properly. If the vehicle is found to track incorrectly, the difficulty will be found in either the frame or in the rear axle alignment.

A more accurate method to check tracking is to park the vehicle on a level floor and drop a plump line from the extreme outer edge of the front suspension lower A-frame. Use the same drop point on each side of the vehicle. Make a chalk line where the plumb line strikes the floor. Do the same with the rear axle, selecting a point on the rear axle housing for the plumb line.

Measure diagonally from the left rear mark to the right front mark and from the right rear mark to left front mark. These diagonal measurements should be the same but a ¼ in. variation is acceptable.

If the diagonal measurements taken are different, measure from the right rear mark to the right front mark and from the left rear to the left front. These measurements should also be the same within ¼ in.

If the diagonal measurements are different, but the longitudinal measurements are the same, the frame is swayed or diamond shaped.

However, in the event that the diagonal measurements are unequal and the longitudinal measurements are also unequal and the vehicle is tracking incorrectly, the rear axle is misaligned.

Tire and Wheel Service

TIRE AND WHEEL BALANCE

There are are 2 types of tire and wheel balancing procedures. They are the dynamic balance and the static balance.

The dynamic balance is the equal distribution of the weight on each side of the centerline, so when the tire and wheel assembly spins there is no tendency for the assembly for the assembly to move from side to side. The tire and wheel assemblies that are dynamically unbalanced may cause wheel shimmy.

The static balance is the equal distribution of weight around the wheel. Tire and wheel assemblies that are statically unbalanced cause a bouncing action called wheel tramp. This condition will eventually cause uneven tire wear.

Before the tire and wheel assembly can be properly balanced, all deposits of mud, etc, must be be removed from the inside of

the rim area. Stones and other foreign matter should be removed from the tire tread area. The tire and wheel assembly should be inspected for any signs of external damage. Once these conditions have been met, the tire and wheel assembly is ready to be balanced according to manufacturers instructions.

TIRE ROTATION

To ensure that all tires wear evenly tire rotation should be done periodically according to manufacture's specifications. If a tire shows excessive wear, the wear problem should be corrected before rotating the tires. If the vehicle is equipped with a temporary spare tire, do not include it in the the tire rotation procedure.

Specialized tools and equipment have been designed for use in the replacement off tire and rim assemblies. The manufacturers instructions should be followed in the use of these machines in the mounting and dismounting of tires to avoid personal injury.

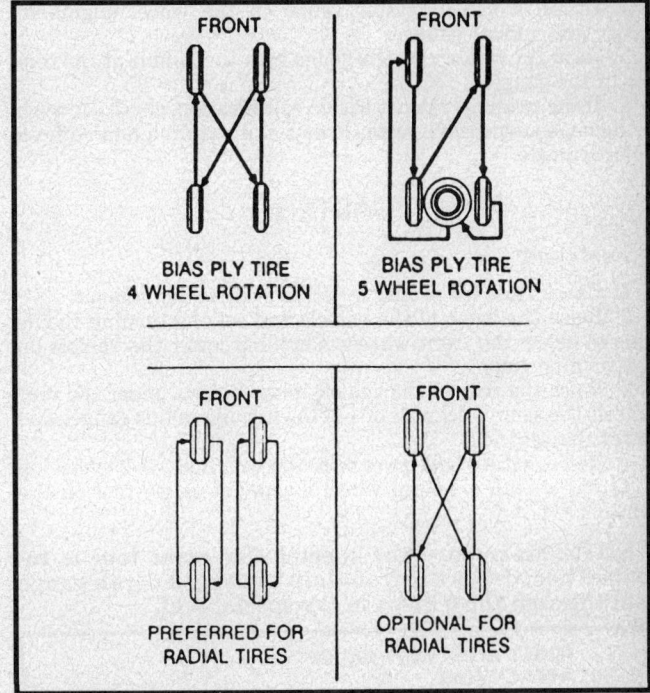

Tire rotation—typical

ACURA/STERLING

Wheel Alignment

Measure the wheel alignment with the vehicle parked on a level ground and with the front wheels place in a straight-ahead position. The front suspension, steering system, tires and wheels should be serviced to the proper condition prior to the measurement of the wheel alignment. Use approved wheel alignment equipment for checking the wheel alignment.

FRONT CAMBER

Camber cannot be adjusted. However, camber angle can be checked by means of and inspection procedure. If camber or kingpin angle is incorrect or front end parts are damaged or

worn, appropriate repairs must be made before alignment is performed.

Inspection

1. Check tires for proper inflation prior to inspection.
2. With the wheels in a straight-ahead position, remove the wheel cover or center cap.
3. Remove 2 wheel lug nuts and install a special wheel alignment gauge tool on the wheel.

NOTE: Make sure the special alignment tool is installed parallel to the front hub by using a depth gauge tool through the 3 holes in the special tool.

4. Install a camber/caster gauge on the wheel alignment gauge attachment gauge.

5. Read the camber on the gauge with the bubble at the center of the gauge.

6. If the readings are not within specification, check for worn or damage suspension parts. Repair and required and recheck camber angle.

REAR CAMBER

1. Check tires for proper inflation prior to inspection.

2. With the wheels in a straight-ahead position, remove the wheel cover or center cap.

3. Remove 2 wheel lug nuts and install a special wheel alignment gauge tool on the wheel.

NOTE: Make sure the special alignment tool is installed parallel to the front hub by using a depth gauge tool through the 3 holes in the special tool.

4. Install a camber/caster gauge on the wheel alignment gauge attachment gauge.

5. Read the camber on the gauge with the bubble at the center of the gauge.

6. If the readings are not within specification, check for worn or damage suspension parts. Repair and required and recheck camber angle.

CASTER

Adjustment

1. Check tires for proper inflation prior to adjustment.

2. Raise the front of the vehicle and set the turning radius gauges below the front wheels. Carefully lower the vehicle on the turning gauges.

3. Raise the rear of the vehicle, place boards under the rear wheels the same thickness of 1 of the turning radius gauges and lower the vehicle.

4. Remove the wheel cover or center cap. Remove 2 wheel lug nuts and install a special wheel alignment gauge tool on the wheel.

NOTE: Make sure the special alignment tool is installed parallel to the front hub by using a depth gauge tool through the 3 holes in the special tool.

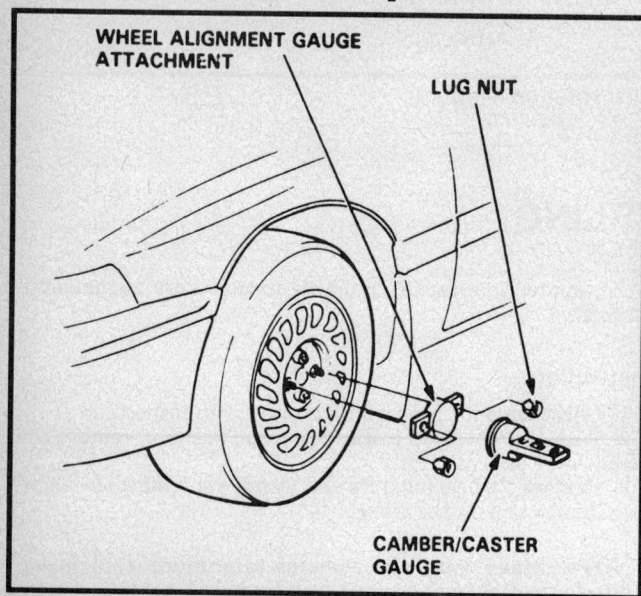

Performing camber inspection

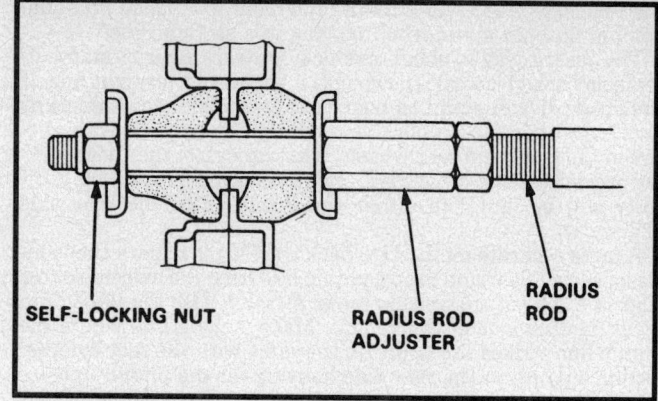

View of the caster adjustment—Legend

5. Install a camber/caster gauge on the wheel alignment gauge attachment and apply the front brake.

6. Turn the wheel 20 degrees inward.

7. Turn the adjustment screw so the bubble in the caster gauge is at 0 degrees.

8. Turn the wheel 20 degrees outward and read the caster on the the gauge with the bubble at the center of the gauge.

9. If the caster angle is not within specifications, proceed to the next step.

10. Loosen the radius rod attaching bolts at the lower arm.

11. Loosen the radius rod adjuster locknut and the self locking nut on the end of the radius rod.

12. Adjust the caster by turning the radius rod adjuster as required. To increase caster, turn the adjuster in. To decrease caster, turn the adjuster out.

13. Tighten the radius rod adjusting bolts and radius rod adjuster locknut to 60 ft. lbs. (83 Nm). Tighten the self locking nut to 32 ft. lbs. (44 Nm).

14. Recheck the caster adjustment.

SPRING HEIGHT

Inspection

1. Check tires for proper inflation prior to inspection. Adjust pressure, as required.

2. Remove any excessive weight from the trunk area.

3. Oscillate the suspension up and down several times before taking height measurement.

4. Spring height is measured from the top of the wheel arch to the ground.

View of the height adjustment—Integra

TORSION BAR

The front suspension height is is adjustable on Integra by means of a torsion bar adjustment. The Legend and Sterling are equipped with MacPherson strut suspension and therefore has no provision for height adjustment.

Adjustment

INTEGRA

1. Raise the vehicle and support it safely.
2. Adjust the height by turning the height adjusting nut.
3. Lower the vehicle and oscillate the suspension up and down.
4. Recheck the suspension height and confirm it is within specifications.

FRONT TOE

Adjustment

1. Check tires for proper inflation prior to adjustment.
2. Center the steering wheel.

NOTE: The turning radius gauges should be in in place from the caster inspection. In that the toe adjustment is affected by camber and caster, it should be adjusted last.

3. Measure the difference in toe measurements with the wheels pointed straight-ahead.
4. If the toe in not within specifications, proceed to the following step.
5. Make toe adjustment by loosing the tie rod locknuts. Turn both tie rods in the same direction until the front wheels are in straight position.
6. Turn both tie rods equally until the toe reading on the turning radius gauge is correct.
7. After completing the adjustment, tighten both locknuts to 33 ft. lbs. (45 Nm). Recheck tie rod measurement.
8. Reposition the tie rod boot if twisted or displace after the adjustment is made.
9. Remove all alignment equipment. Install lug nuts and wheel covers.

REAR TOE

The rear toe is not adjustable in the Integra, if the rear toe is not within specifications, check the suspension for damage and replace parts, as required.

Adjustment

LEGEND AND STERLING

1. Check tires for proper inflation prior to inspection.
2. Release the parking brake.

NOTE: If the parking brake is not engage, an incorrect reading may be obtained.

3. Measure the difference in toe measurements with the wheels pointed straight-ahead.
4. If the toe in not within specifications, proceed to the following step.
5. Hold the adjusting bolt on the rear lower A arm and loosen the locknut.
6. Adjust the rear toe by turning the adjusting bolt until the toe is correct.

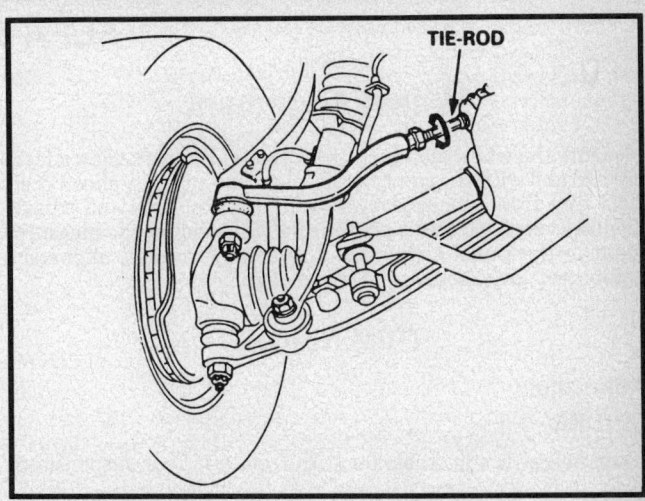

Front toe adjustment—Acura and Sterling

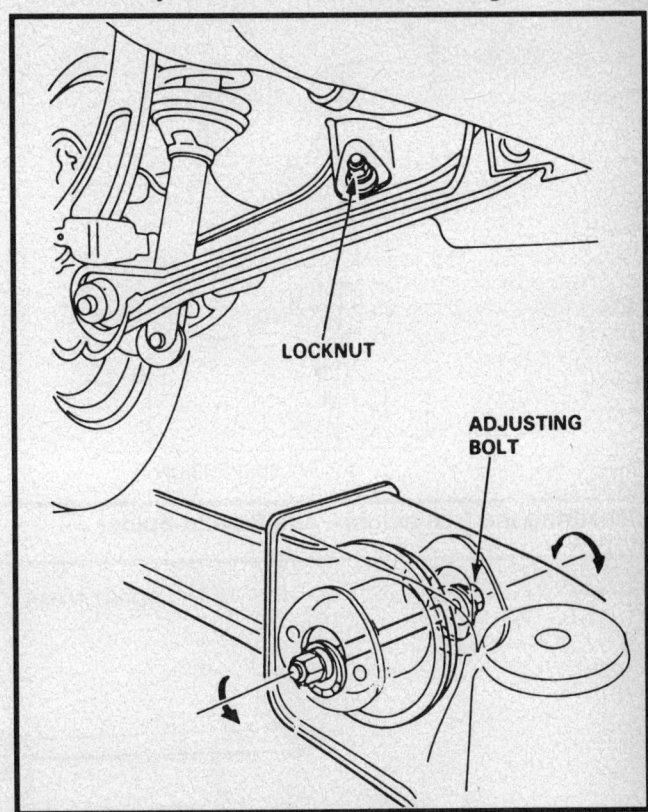

Rear toe adjustment—Acura and Sterling

7. Install a new locknut and tighten while holding the adjusting bolt.

Wheel Service

Tire Rotation

Rotate the tires periodically to ensure uniform wear of the tires. If the spare wheel is of a different type from the other 4 wheels, the 4 wheel rotation method should be used.

ALFA ROMEO

Wheel Alignment

Measure the wheel alignment with the vehicle parked on a level ground and with the front wheels place in a straight-ahead position. The front suspension, steering system, tires and wheels should be serviced to the proper condition prior to the measurement of the wheel alignment. Use approved wheel alignment equipment for checking the wheel alignment.

TRIM HEIGHT

Adjustment
SPIDER

Trim height is adjustable for both front and rear suspensions.

The adjustment is accomplished by fitting the appropriate shim between the coil spring and lower spring seat cup, for front suspensions and between the spring and upper seat cup for rear suspensions. Trim height should be checked and adjusted before alignment procedures.

MILANO

Trim height is accomplished by means of a torsion bar adjustment for the front suspension. The rear trim height is adjusted by shimming the rear coil springs.

Trim height should be checked and adjusted before alignment procedures.

CAMBER

SPIDER

Camber is preset at the factory. If the camber angle is not within

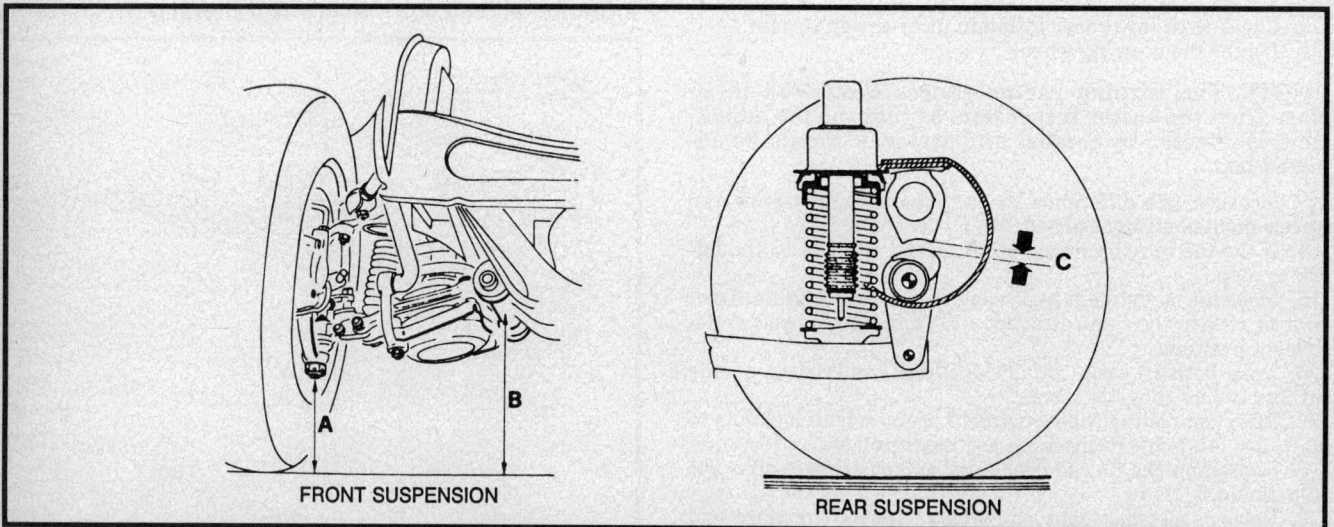

Measuring the trim height—Alfa Romeo Spider

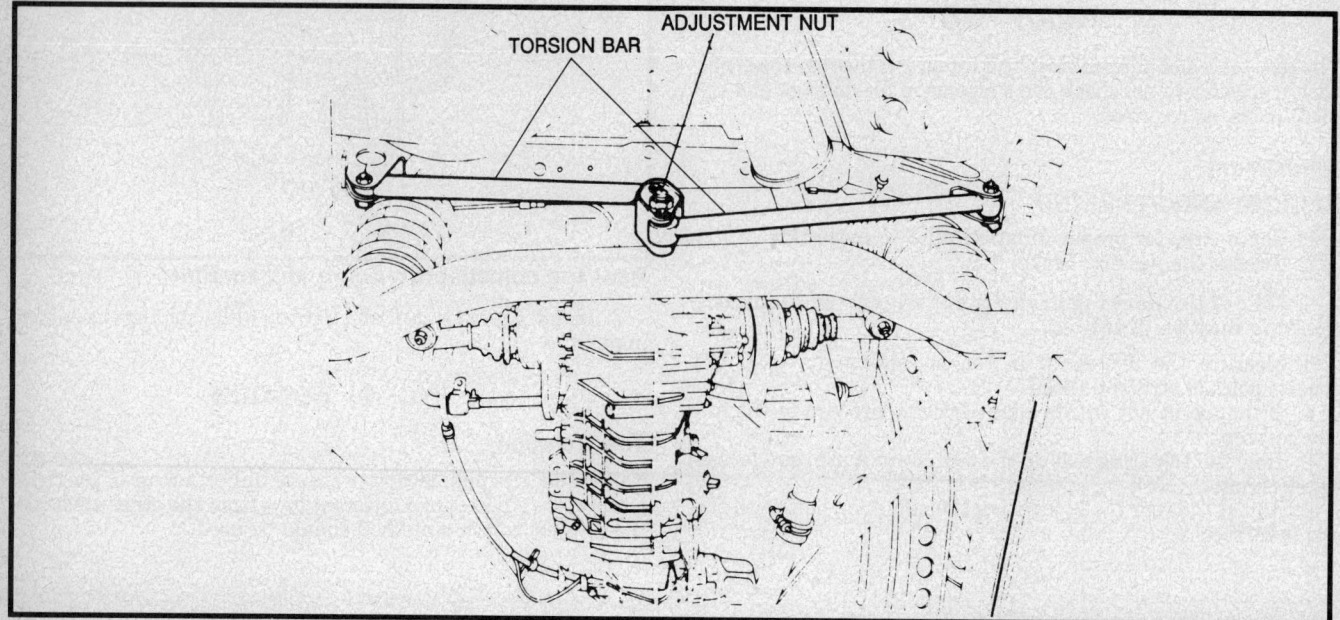

Front torsion bar adjustment—Alfa Romeo Milano

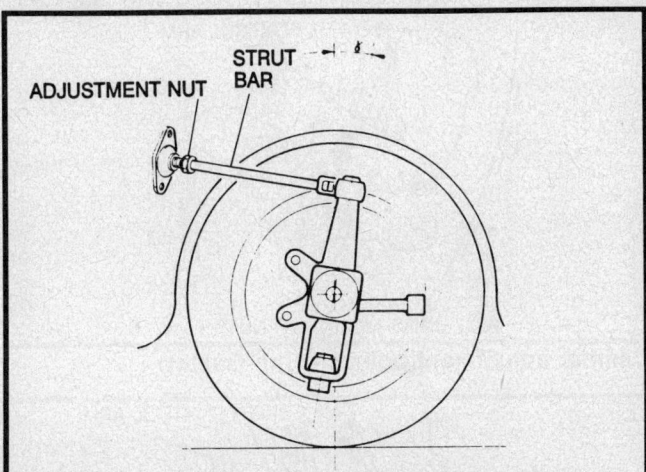

Caster adjustment location—Alfa Romeo

specifications, this would indicate damage suspension parts or possible frame distortion. Inspect and replace the any suspension parts and recheck the camber angle.

MILANO

Camber is adjustable on the Milano. It is accomplished by adding or subtracting shims located between the lower control arm

and frame attachment. Each shim will vary the camber angle by ± 15 minutes.

CASTER

Adjustment

SPIDER AND MILANO

Caster is changed by turning the adjusting nut on the strut bar. To adjust the length of the strut bar. Loosen the locknut and turn the adjustment nut in or out, as required.

TOE-IN

Adjustment

SPIDER AND MILANO

Toe-in is accomplished by adjusting the tie rod. To adjust the toe-in setting loosen the nuts at the steering knuckle end of the tie rod. Rotate the rod as required to adjust the toe-in. Retighten the cover and locknuts, check that the rubber bellows is not twisted.

Wheel Service

Tire Rotation

Rotate the tires periodically to ensure uniform wear of the tires. If the spare wheel is of a different type from the other 4 wheels, the 4 wheel rotation method should be used.

AUDI

Wheel Alignment

Measure the wheel alignment with the vehicle parked on a level ground and with the front wheels place in a straight-ahead position. The front suspension, steering system, tires and wheels should be serviced to the proper condition prior to the measurement of the wheel alignment. Use approved wheel alignment equipment for checking the wheel alignment.

CAMBER

Adjustment

4000, 80 AND 90 EXCEPT QUATTRO

1. Loosen both ball joint flange mounting bolts on the control arm. Check and make sure the ball joint breaks loose from the control arm. If not, joist the vehicle lightly and the wheel should move to the negative camber position.
2. Install special camber gauge and adapter tools to the wheels.
3. Calibrate the camber gauge. Move the wheel in or out until the correct camber is achieved.
4. Torque the outboard ball joint mounting nut to 47 ft. lbs. (64 Nm). Recheck the camber and readjust, as necessary.
5. Torque the inboard ball joint mounting nut to 47 ft. lbs. (64 Nm) and remove all tools.

5000, 100 AND 200 SERIES

1. Loosen the 4 spring strut plate mounting bolts. Attach a socket wrench to the top shock absorber piston rod nut.
2. Move the assembly in the mounting plate slots, until the camber is correct.
3. Tighten all bolts and recheck the camber. Readjust as necessary.

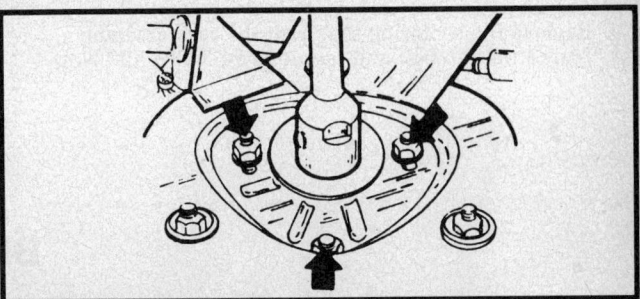

Camber adjustment location—Audi 5000

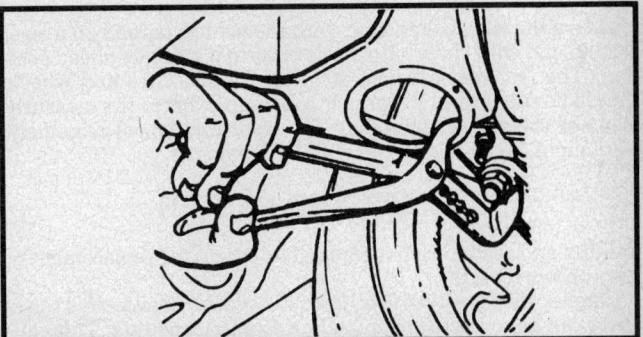

Adjusting the camber on the Audi 4000

QUATTRO

1. Raise the vehicle and support it safely.
2. Loosen the front and and center ball joint mounting nuts, until the washer can be be moved back and forth.

3. Position a special camber adjustment tool in place over the lower ball joint. The hole of the tool, must be positioned over the center ball joint nut.

4. Turn the adjustment spindle knob, so the knurled pin on top of the tool engages the hole in the ball joint. Tighten the tool side nut in this position.

5. Place the top of the tool clamp over the head of the center ball joint bolt and tighten with knurled knob.

6. Loosen the rear ball joint nut until the washer can be removed. Turn the adjustment spindle knob, until the desired camber angle is obtained.

7. Pull the front end of the tool lever inward as far as possible while pushing the rear end of the lever outward, with equal force. Hold the lever in this position.

8. Tighten 2 outer ball joint mounting nuts. Remove the special tool.

9. Tighten the center ball joint mounting nuts to 48 ft. lbs. (65 Nm). Recheck the camber angle.

TOE-IN

Adjustment

1. Turn the steering gear to the center position.

2. Remove the lower pinion rack cap bolt and attach a special centering tool with a tool bracket, into the bolt hole and over the mounting nut of the left tie rod.

3. Insert a bolt in the hole marked L of the centering tool, to lock the steering.

4. Measure and divide the total toe in half.

5. Loosen the clamps and outer locknut on both rods.

6. Adjust each tie rod until the specified setting for toe is reached.

7. Tighten the clamps and locknuts, on the tie rods.

8. Reposition the steering wheel if necessary to obtain horizontal spokes.

9. Remove the centering tool from the rack assembly.

10. Install the cap bolt and torque to 14 ft. lbs. (20 Nm).

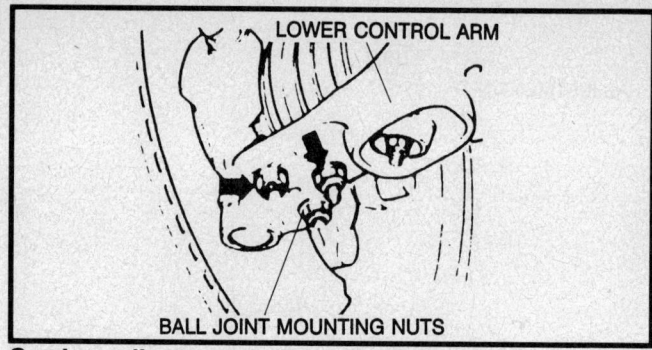

Camber adjustment points—Audi Quattro

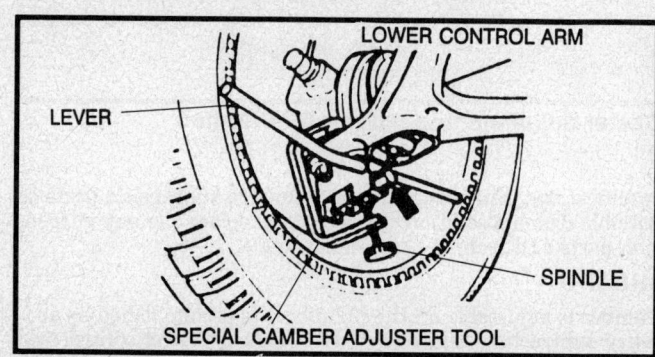

Adjusting the camber on the Audi Quattro

Wheel Service

Tire Rotation

Rotate the tires periodically to ensure uniform wear of the tires. If the spare wheel is of a different type from the other 4 wheels, the 4 wheel rotation method should be used.

BMW

Wheel Alignment

Measure the wheel alignment with the vehicle parked on a level ground and with the front wheels place in a straight-ahead position. The front suspension, steering system, tires and wheels should be serviced to the proper condition prior to the measurement of the wheel alignment. Use approved wheel alignment equipment for checking the wheel alignment.

CAMBER AND CASTER

Camber and caster are not adjustable, except for replacement of bent or worn parts.

Camber that is out of specification because of excessive tolerances can be corrected by installing eccentric mounts. This cannot be done to correct misalignment caused by a collision, however.

TOE-IN

Toe-in is adjusted by changing the length of the tie rod and tie rod end assembly. Center the steering by aligning marks on the steering shaft and the steering housing. Then, loosen the clamp bolt on either end of each tie rod and turn the tie rod, using a wrench on the flats. When adjusting the tie rod ends, adjust each by equal amount, by turning in the opposite direction, to increase or decrease the toe-in measurement.

Wheel Service

Tire Rotation

Rotate the tires periodically to ensure uniform wear of the tires. If the spare wheel is of a different type from the other 4 wheels, the 4 wheel rotation method should be used.

CHRYSLER IMPORTS

Wheel Alignment

Measure the wheel alignment with the vehicle parked on a level ground and with the front wheels place in a straight-ahead position. The front suspension, steering system, tires and wheels should be serviced to the proper condition prior to the measurement of the wheel alignment. Use approved wheel alignment equipment for checking the wheel alignment.

CAMBER AND CASTER

Camber and caster is preset at the factory. It requires adjustment only if the suspension and steering linkage components are damaged, in which case, repair is accomplished by replacing the damaged part. A slight caster adjustment can be made by moving the nuts on the front the nuts on the front anchors of the strut bars.

TOE-IN

Adjustment

Toe-in is the difference in the distance between the front wheels, as measured at both the front and rear of the front tires.

Toe-in is adjusted by turning the tie rod clamps as necessary. The clamps should always be tightened or loosened the same amount for both tie rods; the difference in length between the 2 tie rods should not exceed 2 in.

Wheel Service

Tire Rotation

Rotate the tires periodically to ensure uniform wear of the tires. If the spare wheel is of a different type from the other 4 wheels, the 4 wheel rotation method should be used.

DAIHATSU

Wheel Alignment

Measure the wheel alignment with the vehicle parked on a level ground and with the front wheels place in a straight-ahead position. The front suspension, steering system, tires and wheels should be serviced to the proper condition prior to the measurement of the wheel alignment. Use approved wheel alignment equipment for checking the wheel alignment.

CAMBER AND CASTER

Camber and caster are preset a the factory. Adjustment is required only if the suspension and steering linkage components are damaged. In this case, adjustment is accomplished by replacing the damaged part.

TOE-IN

Adjustment

Toe-in is adjusted by loosening the locknuts on the tie rods and turning the tie rods.

Before adjusting toe-in adjustment, park the vehicle on a level solid surface, inflate the tires to the specification. Be sure the steering gear is centered by aligning the marks on it and that the wheels are straight-ahead.

1. Position the steering wheel in the straight-ahead position. Raise and support the vehicle safely.
2. Use a scribing block to hold a piece of chalk at the center of each tire tread while rotating the wheels by hand. Lower the vehicle and bounce the suspension once or twice.
3. Using a toe gauge, measure and record the toe-in.
4. Remove the boot clip from the tie rod end, if equipped.
5. Turn the left and right tie rod ends equal amounts until the toe-in is within specification.
6. Tighten the tie rod locknuts after the toe-in adjustment is completed. Lower the vehicle.

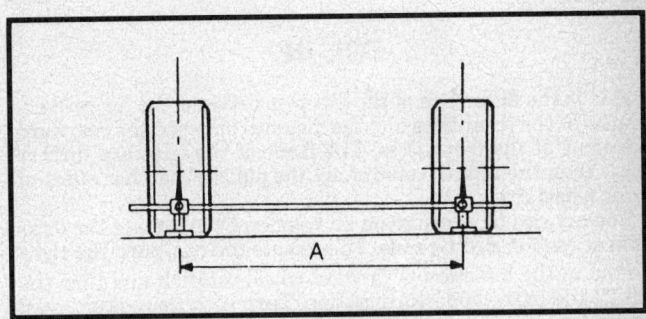

Measuring the front toe—Daihatsu

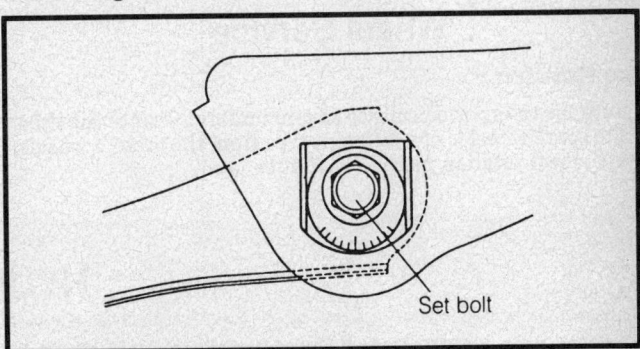

Rear toe adjustment—Daihatsu

Wheel Service

Tire Rotation

Rotate the tires periodically to ensure uniform wear of the tires. If the spare wheel is of a different type from the other 4 wheels, the 4 wheel rotation method should be used.

HONDA

Wheel Alignment

Measure the wheel alignment with the vehicle parked on a level ground and with the front wheels place in a straight-ahead position. The front suspension, steering system, tires and wheels should be serviced to the proper condition prior to the measurement of the wheel alignment. Use approved wheel alignment equipment for checking the wheel alignment.

Torsion bar adjustment—Honda

CAMBER AND CASTER

NOTE: When adjusting the wheel alignment, the adjustments must be performed in the following order: camber, caster and then toe-in.

The camber adjustment can be made by loosening the 2 nuts on the upper control arm and sliding the ball joint until the camber meets specifications. The caster adjustment can be made by loosening the l6mm nuts on the front beam radius rods and then turning the locknut to make the adjustment.

Turning the nut clockwise decreases the caster and turning it counterclockwise increases the caster. After adjusting to sprecifications, hold the nylon locknut and lightly tighten the adjuster. Tighten the 16mm nut to 58 ft. lbs. (79 Nm), then tighten the locknut to 32 ft. lbs. (43 Nm) while holding the 16mm nut.

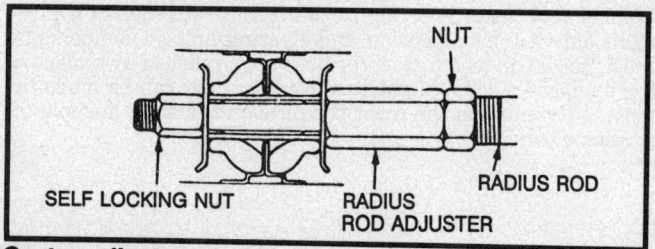
Caster adjustment—Honda

TOE-IN

Toe-in is the difference of the distance between the forward extremes of the front tires and the distance between the rearward extremes of the front tires. The front of the tires are further apart than the rear to counter act the pulling together effect of front wheel drive.

Toe-out can be adjusted on all vehicles by loosening the locknuts at each end of tie rods. To increase toe-out, turn the right tie rod in the direction of forward wheel rotation and turn the left tie rod in the opposite direction. Turn both tie rods an equal amount until toe-out meets specifications.

Wheel Service

Tire Rotation

Rotate the tires periodically to ensure uniform wear of the tires. If the spare wheel is of a different type from the other 4 wheels, the 4 wheel rotation method should be used.

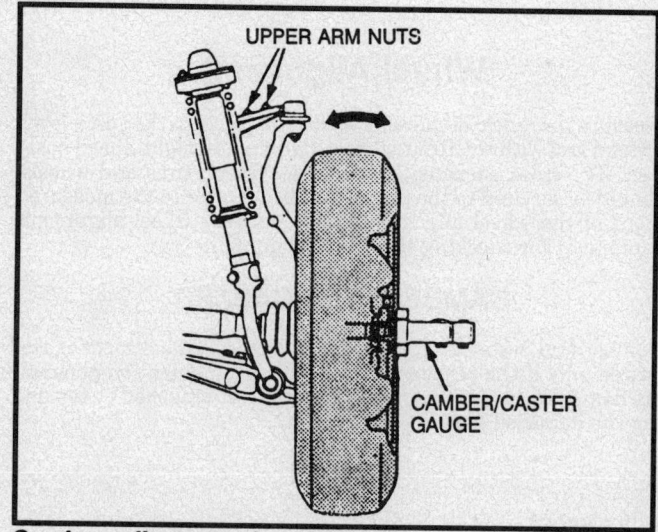
Camber adjustment location—Honda

HYUNDAI

Wheel Alignment

Measure the wheel alignment with the vehicle parked on a level ground and with the front wheels place in a straight-ahead position. The front suspension, steering system, tires and wheels should be serviced to the proper condition prior to the measurement of the wheel alignment. Use approved wheel alignment equipment for checking the wheel alignment.

CAMBER AND CASTER

Caster and caster are preset at the factory. They require service only if the suspension and steering linkage components are

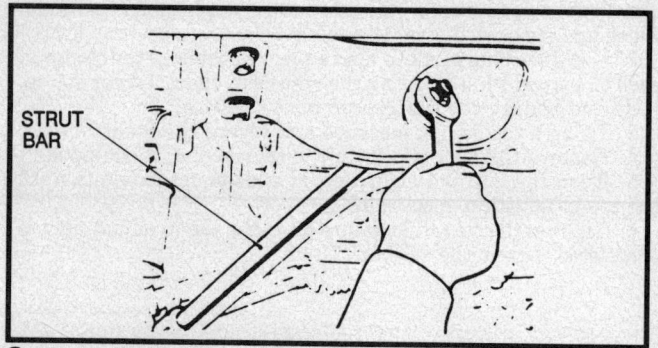
Caster adjustment—Hyundai

damaged, in which case, repair is accomplished by replacing the damaged part. Caster, however, can be adjusted slightly by moving the strut bar nut.

TOE-IN

Toe-in is the difference in the distance between the front wheels, as measured at both the front and rear of the front tires.

Adjustment

1. Raise the vehicle so the front wheels just clear the ground.
2. Use a scribing block to hold a piece of chalk at the center of each tire tread while rotating the wheels by hand.
3. Measure the distance between the marked lines at both the front and rear.
4. Toe-in is equal to the difference between the front and rear measurements.
5. Toe-in is adjusted by screwing the tie rod turn buckle in or out. Left side toe-in may be reduced by turning the tie rod turnbuckle toward the front of the car and the right side toe-in by turning the turn buckle toward the rear of the care. The clamps should always be tightened or loosened the same amount for both tie rods; the difference is length between the tie rods should not exceed 0.2 in. (5mm). Tighten the locknuts to 36–40 ft. lbs. (49–54 Nm).

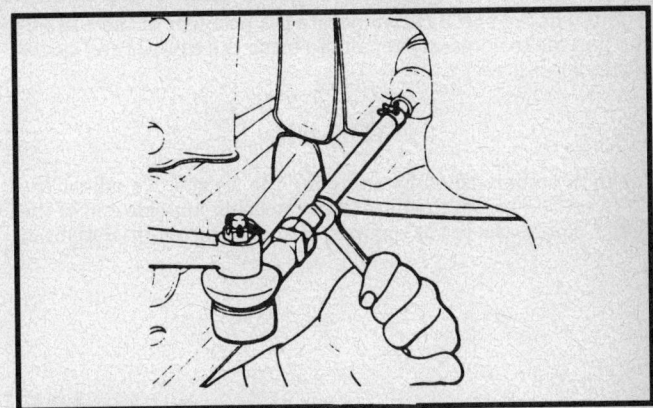

Toe adjustment—Hyundai

Wheel Service

Tire Rotation

Rotate the tires periodically to ensure uniform wear of the tires. If the spare wheel is of a different type from the other 4 wheels, the 4 wheel rotation method should be used.

INFINITI

Wheel Alignment

Measure the wheel alignment with the vehicle parked on a level ground and with the front wheels place in a straight-ahead position. The front suspension, steering system, tires and wheels should be serviced to the proper condition prior to the measurement of the wheel alignment. Use approved wheel alignment equipment for checking the wheel alignment.

CAMBER AND CASTER

Adjustment

Camber and caster are not adjustable. If either of these specifications are not within factory recommendations, this would indicate bent or damaged parts that must be replaced.

TOE-IN

Adjustment

Toe-in is adjusted by loosening the locknuts on the tie rods and turning the tie rods.

Before adjusting toe-in adjustment, park the vehicle on a level solid surface, inflate the tires to the specification. Be sure the steering gear is centered by aligning the marks on it and that the wheels are straight-ahead.

1. Position the steering wheel in the straight-ahead position. Raise and support the vehicle safely.
2. Use a scribing block to hold a piece of chalk at the center of each tire tread while rotating the wheels by hand. Lower the vehicle and bounce the suspension once or twice.
3. Using a toe gauge, measure and record the toe-in.
4. Remove the boot clip from the tie rod end, if equipped.
5 Turn the left and right tie rod ends equal amounts until the toe-in is within specification.
6. Tighten the tie rod locknuts after the toe-in adjustment is completed. Lower the vehicle.

Wheel Service

Tire Rotation

Rotate the tires periodically to ensure uniform wear of the tires. If the spare wheel is of a different type from the other 4 wheels, the 4 wheel rotation method should be used.

ISUZU

Wheel Alignment

Measure the wheel alignment with the vehicle parked on a level ground and with the front wheels place in a straight-ahead position. The front suspension, steering system, tires and wheels should be serviced to the proper condition prior to the measurement of the wheel alignment. Use approved wheel alignment equipment for checking the wheel alignment.

CAMBER AND CASTER

Camber and caster can not be adjusted. Should camber or caster be found out of specification, locate the problem in the suspension and make necessary repairs to bring the camber and caster within specifications.

TOE-IN

Toe-in is accomplished by adjusting the tie rod. To adjust the toe-in setting loosen the nuts at the steering knuckle end of the tie rod. Rotate the rod as required to adjust the toe-in. Retighten

the cover and locknuts, check that the rubber bellows is not twisted.

Wheel Service

Tire Rotation

Rotate the tires periodically to ensure uniform wear of the tires. If the spare wheel is of a different type from the other 4 wheels, the 4 wheel rotation method should be used.

JAGUAR

Wheel Alignment

Measure the wheel alignment with the vehicle parked on a level ground and with the front wheels place in a straight-ahead position. The front suspension, steering system, tires and wheels should be serviced to the proper condition prior to the measurement of the wheel alignment. Use approved wheel alignment equipment for checking the wheel alignment.

CAMBER AND CASTER

Camber and caster are preset a the factory. Adjustment is required only if the suspension and steering linkage components are damaged. In this case, adjustment is accomplished by replacing the damaged part.

TOE-IN

Adjustment

Toe-in is the difference of the distance between the forward ex-

tremes of the front tires and the distance between the rearward extremes of the front tires. The front of the tires are further apart than the rear to counter act the pulling together effect of the front wheels.

Toe-out can be adjusted on by loosening the locknuts at each end of tie rods. To increase toe-out, turn the right tie rod in the direction of forward wheel rotation and turn the left tie rod in the opposite direction. Turn both tie rods an equal amount until toe-out meets specifications. Toe-in must be checked at the suspension ground clearance of 6 in. (150.8mm), measured from the underside of the crossmember to the ground.

Wheel Service

Tire Rotation

Rotate the tires periodically to ensure uniform wear of the tires. If the spare wheel is of a different type from the other 4 wheels, the 4 wheel rotation method should be used.

LEXUS

Wheel Alignment

Measure the wheel alignment with the vehicle parked on a level ground and with the front wheels place in a straight-ahead position. The front suspension, steering system, tires and wheels should be serviced to the proper condition prior to the measurement of the wheel alignment. Use approved wheel alignment equipment for checking the wheel alignment.

CAMBER

Camber is preset at the factory. If the camber angle is not within specifications, this would indicate damage suspension parts or possible frame distortion. Inspect and replace the any suspension parts and recheck the camber angle.

CASTER

The caster is adjusted by means of increasing or decreasing spacers between the stabilizer strut bar and lower control arm. Each spacer changes caster by 30 minutes. Do not install more than 2 spacers per side.

TOE-IN

Adjustment

1. Using a toe-in gauge, position it between the front wheel rims level with the axles. Mark the measurement points with charlk. Roll the vehicle forward until the chalk marks are level with, but behind the axles. Observe the reading on the gauge. If adjustment is required, lengthen or shorted the tie rod to adjust the toe-in to specifications.

2. Remove the nut on the outer end of the tie rod end and the outer clip on the steering gear rubber bellows.

3. Using the proper tool, rotate the tie rod right or left and adjust it until the toe-in is within specification. Hold the tie rod bellows while rotating the tie rod to prevent it from twisting.

4. Lock the locking nut when adjustment is complete.

Wheel Service

Tire Rotation

Rotate the tires periodically to ensure uniform wear of the tires. If the spare wheel is of a different type from the other 4 wheels, the 4 wheel rotation method should be used.

MAZDA

Wheel Alignment

Measure the wheel alignment with the vehicle parked on a level ground and with the front wheels place in a straight-ahead position. The front suspension, steering system, tires and wheels should be serviced to the proper condition prior to the measurement of the wheel alignment. Use approved wheel alignment equipment for checking the wheel alignment.

CAMBER AND CASTER

Camber and caster are preset a the factory. Adjustment is required only if the suspension and steering linkage components are damaged. In this case, adjustment is accomplished by replacing the damaged part.

Some vehicles, the caster and camber may be changed by rotating the shock absorber support. If alignment cannot be brought within specification, replace or repair suspension parts, as necessary.

TOE-IN

To adjust the toe-in, loosen the tie rod locknuts and turn both tie rods an equal amount, until the proper specification is obtained. Both tie rod ends use right hand threads, so to increase the toe-in, turn the right tie rod end towards the front of the ve-

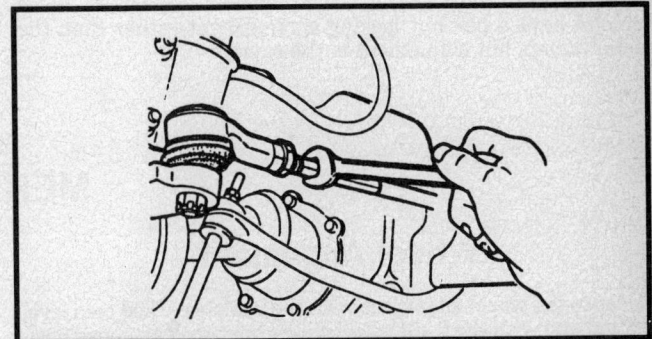

Toe adjustment—Mazda

hicle and turn the left tie rod end toward the rear of the vehicle the same number of turns. One turn of the tie rod end changes the toe-in approximately 0.24 in.

Wheel Service

Tire Rotation

Rotate the tires periodically to ensure uniform wear of the tires. If the spare wheel is of a different type from the other 4 wheels, the 4 wheel rotation method should be used.

MERCEDES-BENZ

Wheel Alignment

Measure the wheel alignment with the vehicle parked on a level ground and with the front wheels place in a straight-ahead position. The front suspension, steering system, tires and wheels should be serviced to the proper condition prior to the measurement of the wheel alignment. Use approved wheel alignment equipment for checking the wheel alignment.

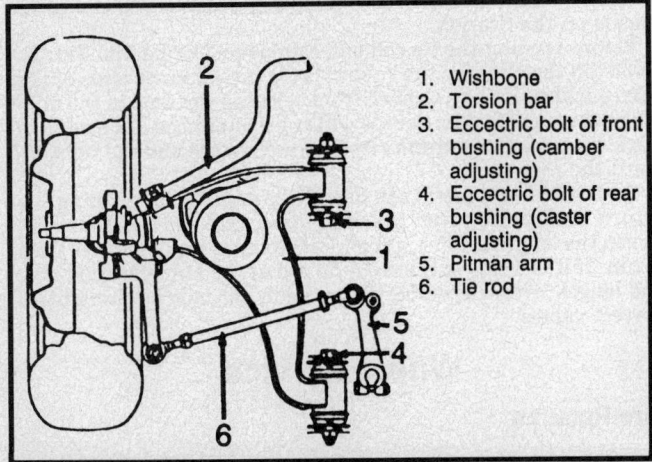

1. Wishbone
2. Torsion bar
3. Eccectric bolt of front bushing (camber adjusting)
4. Eccectric bolt of rear bushing (caster adjusting)
5. Pitman arm
6. Tie rod

Camber and caster adjustment points—190D, 190E, 260E, 300CE, and 300TE

CAMBER AND CASTER

Adjustment
EXCEPT 380SL AND 560SL

The front axle provides for camber and caster adjustment, however, both wheel adjustments can only be made together. Adjustments are made with cam bolts on the lower control arm bearings.

380SL AND 560SL

Camber and caster are dependent upon each other and cannot be adjusted independently. They can only be adjusted simultaneously.

Camber is adjusted by turning the lower control arm at the rear mounting, using the eccentric bolt. Keep in mind that caster will be changed accordingly.

When the camber is adjusted in a positive direction, caster is changed in a negative by 0 degrees, 15 minutes, which results in a caster change of approximately 0 degrees, 20 minutes. Adjustment of the caster by 1 degree, results in a camber change of approximately 0 degrees, 7 minutes.

TOE-IN

Toe-in is the difference of the distance between the front edges of the wheel rims and the rear edges of the wheel rims.

To measure the toe-in, the steering should be in the straight-ahead position and the marks on the pitman arm and pitman shaft should be aligned.

Toe-in is adjusted by changing the length of the 2 tie rods or track rods with the wheels in the straight-ahead position. Some vehicles have a hex nut locking arrangement rather than the newer clamp, but adjustment is the same.

Wheel Service

Tire Rotation

Rotate the tires periodically to ensure uniform wear of the tires. If the spare wheel is of a different type from the other 4 wheels, the 4 wheel rotation method should be used.

MERKUR

Wheel Alignment

Measure the wheel alignment with the vehicle parked on a level ground and with the front wheels place in a straight-ahead position. The front suspension, steering system, tires and wheels should be serviced to the proper condition prior to the measurement of the wheel alignment. Use approved wheel alignment equipment for checking the wheel alignment.

CAMBER AND CASTER

Camber and caster are not adjustable. If alignment angles are out of specification, the vehicle should be checked for damaged of suspension parts or frame distortion, repair as required. With all repairs made, recheck the camber and caster angles. The camber and caster should be within specifications.

TOE-IN

To adjust the toe-in, loosen the tie rod clamp nuts at the tie rod ends and release the clips at the small ends of the steering gear boots. Make sure the boots are free on the tie rods so they are not twisted when the tie rods are turned.

Turn the tie rods in or out an equal amount on each side. Turning the tie rods in will increase the toe, while moving the tie rods out decreases toe. When the toe setting is correct, torque the tie rod end locknuts to 42–52 ft. lbs. (57–68 Nm).

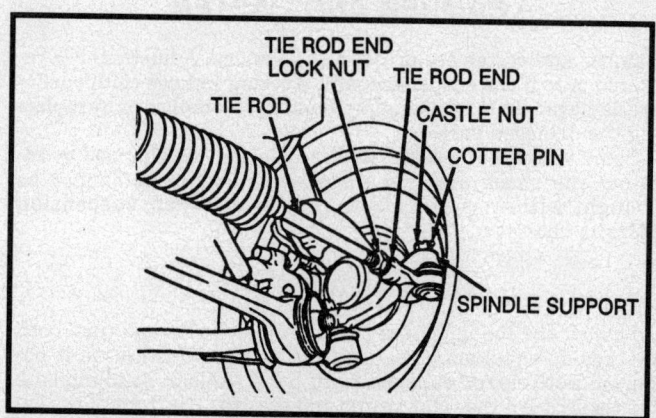

Toe adjustment—Merkur

Wheel Service

Tire Rotation

Rotate the tires periodically to ensure uniform wear of the tires. If the spare wheel is of a different type from the other 4 wheels, the 4 wheel rotation method should be used.

MITSUBISHI

Wheel Alignment

Measure the wheel alignment with the vehicle parked on a level ground and with the front wheels place in a straight-ahead position. The front suspension, steering system, tires and wheels should be serviced to the proper condition prior to the measurement of the wheel alignment. Use approved wheel alignment equipment for checking the wheel alignment.

CAMBER AND CASTER

Camber is preset at the factory and cannot be adjusted. Caster should not require adjustment, although adjustment is possible by adjusting the length of the strut bar. Loosen both nuts and turning in or out, as required.

TOE-IN

Toe is adjusted by loosing both tie rod end clamps equal amounts, on the Cordia and Tredia, or the left tie rod end turnbuckle on the Starion.

Before turning the tie rod end clamps on Cordia and Tredia, unfasten the clips for the rubber boots on the inner ends of the turn buckles. Using a wrench from below on the flats in the middle of the turn buckle, the toe will move out as the left side turn buckle is turned toward the front of the vehicle and the right toward the rear.

On the Starion, toe-in can usually be adjusted by turning the 1 turn buckle. However, check to make sure the difference between the length of the right and left tie rods is not greater than 0.2 in. If it is, remove the right tie rod at the knuckle and bring the length within specifications; toe-in can not be brought to correct values.

Wheel Service

Tire Rotation

Rotate the tires periodically to ensure uniform wear of the tires. If the spare wheel is of a different type from the other 4 wheels, the 4 wheel rotation method should be used.

NISSAN

Wheel Alignment

Measure the wheel alignment with the vehicle parked on a level ground and with the front wheels place in a straight-ahead position. The front suspension, steering system, tires and wheels should be serviced to the proper condition prior to the measurement of the wheel alignment. Use approved wheel alignment equipment for checking the wheel alignment.

CAMBER AND CASTER

Adjustment

EXECPT PULSAR, SENTRA AND 240SX

Camber and caster are not adjustable. If alignment angles are out of specification, the vehicle should be checked for damaged of suspension parts or frame distortion, repair as required. With all repairs made, recheck the camber and caster angles. The camber and caster should be within specifications.

PULSAR, SENTRA AND 240SX

1. Camber is adjusted by means of a pin on the top-most lower strut mounting bolts.
2. The pin is installed with the flat side facing downward at the factory Remove the pin and then reinstall it with the flat side facing up.
3. Turn the pin to adjust camber. Camber changes about 15 minutes with each graduation of the adjusting pin on Pulsar and Sentra. On 240SX, camber changes about 5 minutes with each graduation.
4. Tighten the pin to 72–87 ft. lbs. (98–106 Nm) on 240SX.

TOE-IN

Toe-in is the difference of the distance between the front edges of the wheel rims and the rear edges of the wheel rims.

To measure the toe-in, the steering should be in the straight-ahead position and the marks on the pitman arm and pitman shaft should be aligned.

Toe-in is adjusted by changing the length of the 2 tie rods or track rods with the wheels in the straight-ahead position. Some vehicles have a hex nut locking arrangement rather than the newer clamp, but adjustment is the same.

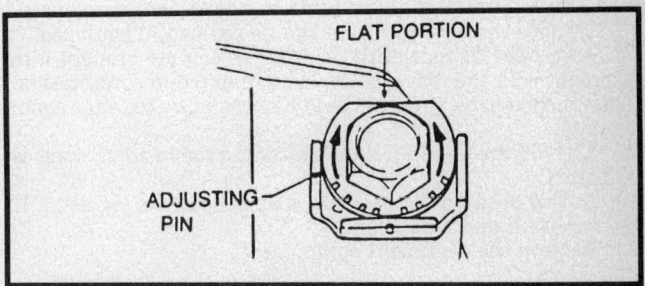

Caster adjustment—Nissan

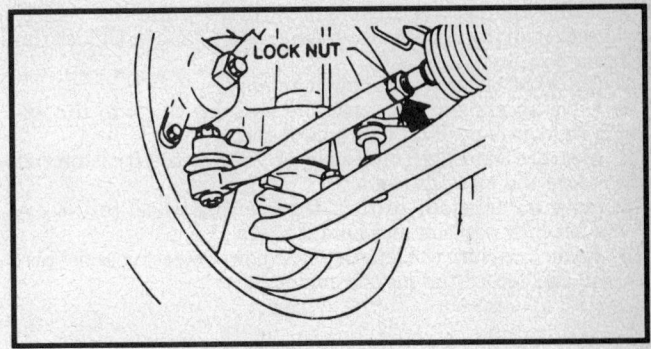

Toe adjustment—Nissan

STEERING ANGLE ADJUSTMENT

The maximum steering angle is adjusted by stopper bolts on the steering arms. Loosen the locknut on the stopper bolt, turn the stopper bolt in or out, as required, to obtain the proper maximum steering angle and retighten the locknut.

Wheel Service

Tire Rotation

Rotate the tires periodically to ensure uniform wear of the tires. If the spare wheel is of a different type from the other 4 wheels, the 4 wheel rotation method should be used.

PEUGEOT

Wheel Alignment

Measure the wheel alignment with the vehicle parked on a level ground and with the front wheels place in a straight-ahead position. The front suspension, steering system, tires and wheels should be serviced to the proper condition prior to the measurement of the wheel alignment. Use approved wheel alignment equipment for checking the wheel alignment.

CAMBER AND CASTER

Camber and caster are not adjustable. If alignment angles are out of specification, the vehicle should be checked for damaged of suspension parts or frame distortion, repair as required. With all repairs made, recheck the camber and caster angles. The camber and caster should be within specifications.

TOE-IN

Prior to making toe-in adjustment, the steering must be centered and the front and rear wheels must be in correct tracking position.

405

1. Using appropriate alignment facilities, raise the vehicle and lower it on the alignment turning radius gauges. Unlock the plates.
2. Turn the steering wheel to the extreme right lock position and hold it in that position.
3. Place a reference mark on the steering wheel with the wheel still at the extreme right lock position.
4. Turn the steering wheel to the extreme left lock position and using the reference mark, count the number of turns and fractions of a turn.

5. Divide the total turns in ½, this will indicate where the steering midpoint should be.

6. Turn the steering wheel to the midpoint. At this point the wheels must be straight-ahead. If not, adjustment is required.

7. Remove the boot clip from the tie rod end, if equipped.

8. Adjust the tie rods until the front wheels are brought into alignment with the rear wheels and within toe-in specification. Adjust the toe-in by, turning the left and right tie rod ends equal amounts.

9. Tighten the tie rod locknuts after the toe-in adjustment is completed.

10. In this position the steering wheel should be centered. If not, remove it and reposition it.

11. Remove the alignment equippment.

505

1. Using appropriate alignment facilities, raise the vehicle and lower it on the alignment turning radius gauges. Unlock the plates.

2. Start the engine and allow it to idle.

3. Have an assistant to turn the steering wheel to the extreme right lock position and hold it there.

4. Measure the length of the power steering assist piston rod and record the measurement.

5. Have an assistant to turn the steering wheel to the extreme left lock position and hold it there.

6. Again, measure the length of the power steering assist piston rod and record the measurement.

7. Add the recorded measurements together and divide by ½. This determines the steering wheel midpoint measurement.

8. Have an turn the steering wheel to the midpoint. Again, measure the power assist piston rod. The measurement should equal the divided measurement.

9. If not, continue to turn the steering wheel until the power assist piston rod equals the mid point measurement, previously recorded.

10. At this position, turn the ignition switch **OFF**.

11. Check to insure that the front wheel are in alignment with the rear wheels. If not, change the length of the tie rods, first on 1 side and then on the other side, to bring the front axle in alignment to the rear wheels.

12. Check the steering wheel position, if not centered, remove and reposition it.

13. Remove the boot clip from the tie rod end, if equipped.

14. Adjust the toe-in by, turning the left and right tie rod ends equal amounts until the toe-in is within specification.

15. Tighten the tie rod locknuts after the toe-in adjustment is completed.

16. Remove the alignment equippment.

Wheel Service

Tire Rotation

Rotate the tires periodically to ensure uniform wear of the tires. If the spare wheel is of a different type from the other 4 wheels, the 4 wheel rotation method should be used.

PORSCHE

Wheel Alignment

Measure the wheel alignment with the vehicle parked on a level ground and with the front wheels place in a straight-ahead position. The front suspension, steering system, tires and wheels should be serviced to the proper condition prior to the measurement of the wheel alignment. Use approved wheel alignment equipment for checking the wheel alignment.

CAMBER

Adjustment

911 AND 911 TURBO

Camber is adjusted at the top of the strut. Pull back the luggage compartment carpet to expose the 3 mounting bolts. Scrape the undercoating from the bolts and plates. Scribe the positions of the 2 plates under the bolts. Loosen the bolts and move the strut in or out, as necessary, to correct the camber angle.

924S AND 928S4

Camber is adjusted at the upper strut-to-steering knuckle retaining bolt.

928, 928S AND 928S

Camber is adjusted by turning the cam bolts on the inner arm bushings.

CASTER

Adjustment

911 AND 911 TURBO

Caster is adjusted in the same manner as camber, except that

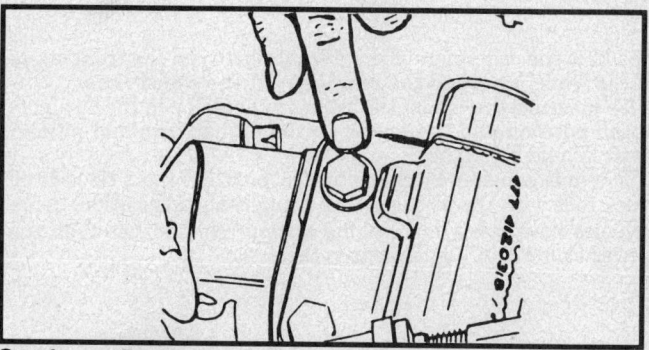
Camber adjustment at the upper strut eccentric–Porsche 944

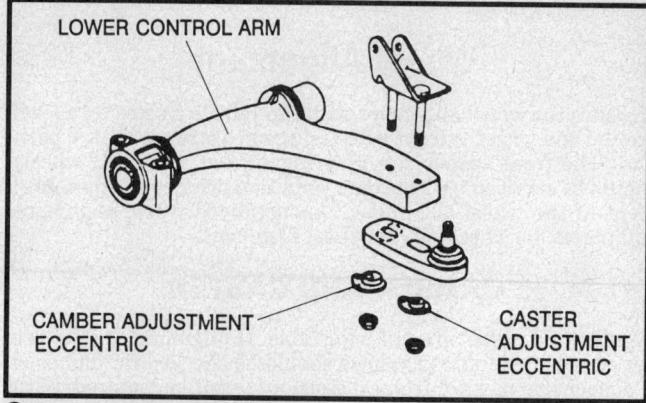
LOWER CONTROL ARM

CAMBER ADJUSTMENT ECCENTRIC

CASTER ADJUSTMENT ECCENTRIC

Caster and camber adjustment location – Porsche 928 and 928S

the strut is moved forward or backward to change the caster angle.

EXCEPT 911 AND 911 TURBO

Caster is adjusted by loosening the 2 control arm-to-crossmember bolts and moving the control arm laterally. 1987–88 928 vehicles, have the slots for adjusting the caster eccentrics. The eccentrics are sealed with an elastic sealing compound. This compound must be removed to make caster adjustment, then resealed after adjustment, to prevent the entry of dirt which could make adjusting difficult.

TOE-IN

Adjustment

911 AND 911 TURBO

Toe-in is set with the front wheels straight-ahead. Tie rod length is adjusted by loosening the tie rod clamps and moving them an equal amount in or out to obtain the correct toe-in.

924S AND 944

Toe-in is set by loosening the locknuts on the tie rod ends and turning them in out, as necessary.

928 AND 928S

Toe-in adjustments are made by turning cam bolts, located at the rear of the front control arm.

Wheel Service

Tire Rotation

Rotate the tires periodically to ensure uniform wear of the tires. If the spare wheel is of a different type from the other 4 wheels, the 4 wheel rotation method should be used.

SAAB

Wheel Alignment

Measure the wheel alignment with the vehicle parked on a level ground and with the front wheels place in a straight-ahead position. The front suspension, steering system, tires and wheels should be serviced to the proper condition prior to the measurement of the wheel alignment. Use approved wheel alignment equipment for checking the wheel alignment.

CAMBER

Adjustment

900 SERIES

Camber is the angle by which the center lines of the wheels lean from the vertical. The camber is position positive if the wheels lean outward and negative if they lean inward.

The camber and king pin angle, can be adjusted with spacers placed under the 2 bearing brackets of the upper control arms. The desired result can thus be obtained by increasing or reducing the number of spacers used. To increase or reduce camber, use the same number of spacers under both brackets.

9000 SERIES

Camber is not adjustable.

CASTER

Adjustment

900 SERIES

The caster is the angle by which the steering knuckle axis departs front the vertical when viewed from the side and the measurement is generally expressed in degrees. If the caster need

adjusting, spacers are inserted under the bearing brackets of the upper control arms.

To increase the caster, transfer spacers from the front bracket to the rear bracket. To reduce the caster, transfer spacers from the rear bracket to the front bracket. In either case, the total spacer thickness removed from 1 bracket must be added to the other one.

9000 SERIES

Caster is not adjustable.

TOE-IN

Adjustment

1. Using a toe-in gauge, position it between the front wheel rims level with the axles. Mark the measurement points with chalk. Roll the vehicle forward until the chalk marks are level with, but behind the axles. Observe the reading on the gauge. If adjustment is required, lengthen or shorted the tie rod to adjust the toe-in to specifications.
2. Remove the nut on the outer end of the tie rod end and the outer clip on the steering gear rubber bellows.
3. Using the proper tool, rotate the tie rod right or left and adjust it until the toe-in is within specification. Hold the bellows during the twisting.
4. Lock the locknut when adjustment is complete.

Wheel Service

Tire Rotation

Rotate the tires periodically to ensure uniform wear of the tires. If the spare wheel is of a different type from the other 4 wheels, the 4 wheel rotation method should be used.

SUBARU

Wheel Alignment

Measure the wheel alignment with the vehicle parked on a level ground and with the front wheels place in a straight-ahead position. The front suspension, steering system, tires and wheels should be serviced to the proper condition prior to the measurement of the wheel alignment. Use approved wheel alignment equipment for checking the wheel alignment.

CAMBER AND CASTER

Adjustment

EXCEPT LEGACY

Camber and caster are not adjustable. If either of these specifications are not within factory recommendations, this would indicate bent or damaged parts that must be replaced.

LEGACY

Caster is none adjustable, but camber can be manually adjusted. Eccentric bolts are located in the joint at the strut and housing.

TOE-IN

Adjustment

Toe-in is adjusted by loosening the locknuts on the tie rods and turning the tie rods.

Before adjusting toe-in adjustment, park the vehicle on a level solid surface, inflate the tires to the specification. Be sure the steering gear is centered by aligning the marks on it and that the wheels are straight-ahead.

1. Position the steering wheel in the straight-ahead position. Raise and support the vehicle safely.
2. Use a scribing block to hold a piece of chalk at the center of each tire tread while rotating the wheels by hand. Lower the vehicle and bounce the suspension once or twice.
3. Using a toe gauge, measure and record the toe-in.
4. Remove the boot clip from the tie rod end, if equipped.
5. Turn the left and right tie rod ends equal amounts until the toe-in is within specification.
6. Tighten the tie rod locknuts after the toe-in adjustment is completed. Lower the vehicle.

Wheel Service

Tire Rotation

Rotate the tires periodically to ensure uniform wear of the tires. If the spare wheel is of a different type from the other 4 wheels, the 4 wheel rotation method should be used.

TOYOTA

Wheel Alignment

Measure the wheel alignment with the vehicle parked on a level ground and with the front wheels place in a straight-ahead position. The front suspension, steering system, tires and wheels should be serviced to the proper condition prior to the measurement of the wheel alignment. Use approved wheel alignment equipment for checking the wheel alignment.

CAMBER

Adjustment

MR2
1987–88 CAMERY, 1987–89 CORROLA FX, CELICA, 1987 TERCEL SEDAN AND 1987–88 TERCEL WAGON

Camber on these vehicles is adjustable by means of a camber adjustment bolt on the lower strut mounting bracket. Loosen the shock absorber set nut and then turn the adjusting bolt until the camber is within specifications. Camber will change about 20 minutes (MR2 18 minutes) for each graduation on the cam.

1989–91 CAMERY, 1988–91 TERCEL SEDAN AND CORROLLA SEDAN/WAGON

Camber is not adjustable.

CASTER

Adjustment

CAMERY AND CRESSISA

Inscrease or decrease the number of spacers on the stabilizer bar (strut bar-1989–90 Cressida). Each spacer changes caster by 30 minutes (20 minutes-1989–90 Cressida). Never install more than 2 spacers.

COROLLA, CELICA AND TERCEL SEDAN

Caster is not adjustable.

MR2

Caster is changed by turning the adjusting nut on the strut bar. Each revolution of the nut changes the caster by 18 minutes.

CASTER AND CAMBER

Adjustment

SUPRA

Camber and caster are adjustable by means of a front and rear adjusting cam on the lower control arm.

TOE-IN

Adjustment

1. Toe can be determined by measuring the distance between the centers of the tire tread, at the front of the tire and the rear. If the tread pattern of the tires make it impossible to make an accurate measurement, the measurement may be taken between the edges of the rims. To avoid the possibility of incorrect readings, due to a bent rim or wheel run out, take measurements at a 3–4 places on the rim.
2. If the measurement is not within specifications, loosen the 4 retaining clamp locknuts on the tie rod ends.
3. Turn the left and right tie rods equal amounts until the measurements are within specifications.
4. Tighten the lock bolts and recheck the measurements. Check to see that the steering wheel is still in the proper position. If not remove it and center it.

Wheel Service

Tire Rotation

Rotate the tires periodically to ensure uniform wear of the tires. If the spare wheel is of a different type from the other 4 wheels, the 4 wheel rotation method should be used.

VOLKSWAGEN

Wheel Alignment

Measure the wheel alignment with the vehicle parked on a level ground and with the front wheels place in a straight-ahead position. The front suspension, steering system, tires and wheels should be serviced to the proper condition prior to the measurement of the wheel alignment. Use approved wheel alignment equipment for checking the wheel alignment.

CAMBER

Adjustment

FOX AND QUANTUM

Camber is adjusted by loosening the ball joint-to-lower control arm bolts and moving the ball joint in or out, as necessary.

GOLF, RABBIT, SCIROCCO, CABRIOLET AND JETTA

Camber is adjusted by loosening the nuts of the 2 bolts holding the top of the wheel bearing housing to the bottom of the strut and turning the top eccentric bolt. The range of adjustment is 2 degrees.

Vehicles using the original bolt can be replaced with a long shank bolt (N903334.01) and adjusted after the new bolt is installed. If adjustment is necessary, the lower bolt can also be replaced with a new one.

TOE-IN

Adjustment

QUANTUM

Toe-in is checked with the wheels straight-ahead. The left tie rod is adjustable. Loosen the nuts and clamps and adjust the length of the tie rod for correct toe-out. If the steering wheel is not centered, remove and reposition it.

FOX

NOTE: A special steering gear tool must be used to adjust the toe, on vehicles equipped with 2 adjustable rods.

1. Turn the steering gear to the center position.
2. Remove the front bolt from the steering gear cover.
3. Attach a special centering tool with the bracket over the mounting nut on the left tie rod.
4. Remove the bolt from the spacer on the chain of the centering tool.
5. Place the spacer under the hole marked with an L and insert a bolt through this hole and the hole in the spacer. Secure it to the steering gear.
6. Measure and divide the total toe in ½.
7. Loosen the clamps and outer locknut on both sides.
8. Turn both tie rods until the specified setting for toe is reached.
9. Tighten the clamps and locknuts on the tie rods.
10. Check and reposition the steering wheel in the center position, if necessary.
11. Remove the centering tool and tighten the front bolt to 15 ft. lbs. (20 Nm).
12. If the steering wheel is still not centered after using the centering tool, remove the steering wheel and reposition it.

GOLF, RABBIT, SCIROCCO, CABRIOLET AND JETTA

Toe-in is checked with the wheels straight-ahead. Only the right tie rod is adjustable, however, replacement left tie rods are available. Replacement left tie rods should be to the same length as the original. Toe-in should be adjusted only with the right tie rod. If the steering wheel off center, remove and reposition it.

Wheel Service

Tire Rotation

Rotate the tires periodically to ensure uniform wear of the tires. If the spare wheel is of a different type from the other 4 wheels, the 4 wheel rotation method should be used.

VOLVO

Wheel Alignment

Measure the wheel alignment with the vehicle parked on a level ground and with the front wheels place in a straight-ahead position. The front suspension, steering system, tires and wheels should be serviced to the proper condition prior to the measurement of the wheel alignment. Use approved wheel alignment equipment for checking the wheel alignment.

CAMBER AND CASTER

Caster angle is fixed by suspension design and cannot be adjusted, If caster is not within specifications, check front end parts for damage and replace, as necessary.

Camber angle, may be adjusted. At the strut upper attachment to the body, 2 of the 3 bolt holes are eccentric, allowing the upper end of the strut to tilt out or in, as necessary. A special pivot lever tool is required to make the adjustment. It is attached to the tops of the strut upper attachment retaining bolt threads.

To adjust, loosen the 3 retaining nuts, install the pivot lever tool and adjust the camber to specifications. After adjusting, torque the nuts to 15–25 ft. lbs. (20–34 Nm).

TOE-IN

Toe-in may be adjusted after performing the caster and camber adjustments. With a wheel spreader tool, measure the distance between the rear of the right and left front tires, at spindle hub height. Next, measure the distance between the front of the right and left front tires, also at spindle hub height. Substract the front distance from the rear distance and compare that to the specifications. If the adjustment is not correct, loosen the locknuts on both sides of the tie rod and rotate the tie rod itself to bring the toe within specification.

Toe-in is increased by turning the tie rod in the normal forward rotation of wheels and reduced by turning it in the opposite direction. After the final adjustment is made, torque the locknuts to 55–65 ft. lbs. (75–88 Nm), be careful not to disturb the adjustment.

Wheel Service

Tire Rotation

Rotate the tires periodically to ensure uniform wear of the tires. If the spare wheel is of a different type from the other 4 wheels, the 4 wheel rotation method should be used.

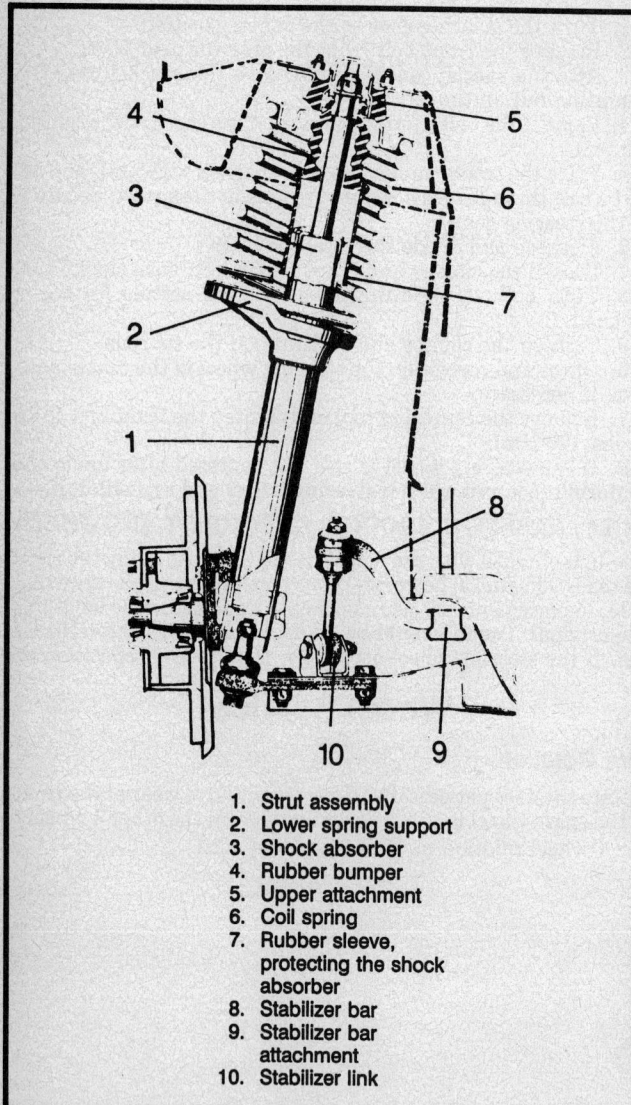

1. Strut assembly
2. Lower spring support
3. Shock absorber
4. Rubber bumper
5. Upper attachment
6. Coil spring
7. Rubber sleeve, protecting the shock absorber
8. Stabilizer bar
9. Stabilizer bar attachment
10. Stabilizer link

Front suspension—240, 260 (DL and GL) Series

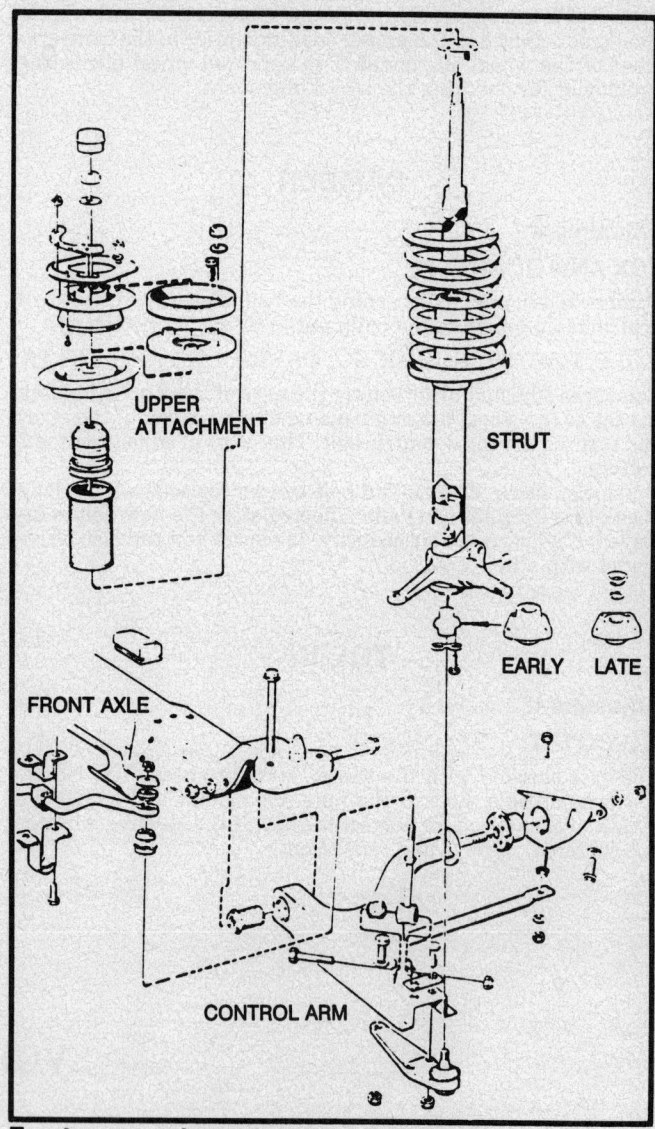

Front suspension assembly—240 and 260 models

STARTERS

General Information

ARMATURE

Inspection and Testing

The only part of the armature that should wear is the commutator, where the brushes make contact. This area must be clean, evenly worn and not burnt or pitted. Most manufacturers specify commutator runout, the amount of uneven or out of round wear as measured with a dial indicator. The commutator surface can be machined in a lathe to make it smooth and to correct the runout, but there is a minimum diameter specified by the manufacturer. This dimension is critical and should be strictly observed. If the wear is not severe, the commutator can be cleaned up with sand paper. Never use emery paper. The grit is an electrical conductor and may cause short circuits.

The gap between each segment of the commutator is partially filled with a non-conducting material such as mica or ceramic. These gaps can be cleaned and deepened with a hack saw blade, and the depth of each gap, called the undercut depth, is usually specified. When cleaning and correcting the undercut,

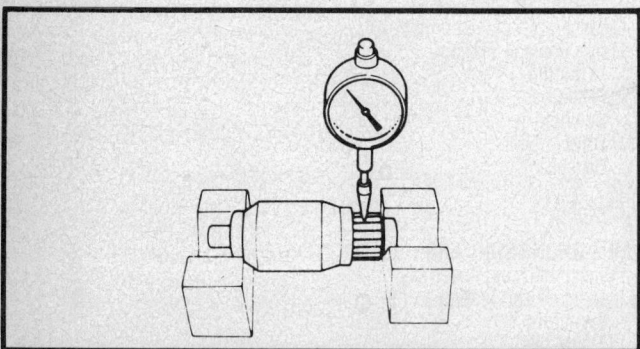

Check that the commutator is clean and round

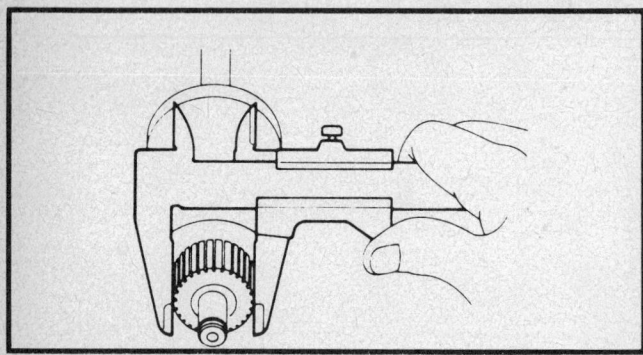

The minimum commutator diameter is critical

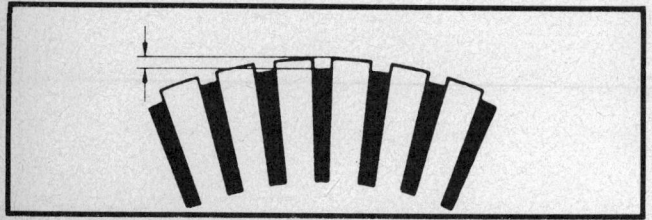

The undercut depth can be set if the commutator diameter is correct

be sure to cut only the insulation material. Removing the metal of the commutator will increase the width of the gap, which will weaken the starter motor.

If the physical condition of the armature is acceptable, then it may be tested for proper electrical performance. A short circuit can be found with a growler, which sets up a magnetic field around the armature. As the armature is slowly rotated in the growler, a hack saw blade held against the core will vibrate or be attracted to the core if there is a short. Other tests are performed with an ohmmeter. To look for grounding, touch one probe to the core and the other probe to each segment on the commutator. There should be no continuity between any segment and the core. There should be continuity between any and all of the segments. If any of these 3 tests shows a bad reading, the armature must be replaced.

FIELD COIL

Inspection and Testing

The field coil should be checked for signs of over heating or contact with the armature. With an ohmmeter or test light, check for continuity between the brush lead(s) and the field coil or battery connection. Also make sure there is no continuity between the coil connections and the field coil housing or starter case. On some starters the field coil can be replaced separately, on others the coil is part of the housing. Damaged, shorted or open field coils cannot be repaired.

SOLENOID

Testing

The solenoid is an electro-magnet with at least one and usually two coils. Some solenoids can be tested with an ohmmeter between the ignition switch terminal and field coil terminal and ground. Others are part of the drive and can only be function tested, using a good battery and jumper wires. Solenoids cannot be repaired, faulty units should be replaced.

STARTER DRIVE

Testing

As an assembly, a pinion drive can usually be checked by hand. It should rotate smoothly in one direction and lock in the other. A little bit of clicking noise may be heard, but rough operation or excess noise indicates a unit about to fail. These drives cannot be repaired, faulty units should be replaced. Some starters use reduction gearing, a clutch or other complex drive system. These will be covered separately.

BRUSHES

Inspection

Brushes are the primary wear part in a starter and should be replaced any time a starter is rebuilt. Some brushes are part of an assembly which makes replacement simple. These assemblies have contact points and insulated portions which must be tested for proper continuity. On many starters, new brushes must be soldered onto a wire. Using too much solder will make the wire stiff and prevent the brush from sliding easily in the holder. This can be avoided by holding the wire near the solder joint with pliers to act as a heat sink. The solder will not run to the cooler wire. Use a hot soldering iron, work quickly and only as much solder as needed.

Note: When servicing starter motors or any rotating electrical device, never use emery cloth. The abrasive material in emery cloth is a conductor and the small particles left behind can cause partial short circuits.

Bosch Starters

Disassembly and Assembly

1. Remove the bushing cap, sealing ring, snapring and spacer shims. By removing the nuts from the through bolts, the bushing and cover can be removed to gain access to the brushes.

2. The brush holder and grounding brushes are removed as an assembly. On some units the holder tabs must be carefully unbent to remove the springs and brushes. On other units, the leaf springs can be carefully lifted out of the way to remove each brush from its' holder separately.

3. To remove the solenoid, disconnect the field coil strap and remove the screws from the front housing. Slide the solenoid straight back and if necessary, unhook it from the shift arm.

4. On direct drive starters, carefully lift off the starter body and remove the nut and screw that hold the shift arm. The armature and shift arm will now lift out of the front housing, but be careful not to loose the steel and rubber washers.

5. On gear drive starters, lift off the starter body and the armature and grease shield. Carefully disassemble the reduction gears before removing the shift arm and drive pinion. Some units have an armature bushing in the planetary gear set. Check its condition before assembling the starter.

6. To remove the drive pinion, tap down on the stop ring using a socket as a sleeve, then remove the snapring.

To assemble:

7. Replacing the front bushing is recommended. Soak the new bushing in motor oil for a half hour, press out the old bushing and clean the hole before pressing in the new bushing.

8. Before assembling the starter, lightly grease both ends of the armature shaft, the shift arm where it contacts the drive pinion, the solenoid where it contacts the shift arm, the armature gear where it fits into the starter drive, and the shift arm bolt. On gear drives, lubricate the gear assembly and armature bushing with moly grease.

9. Install the drive pinion onto the shaft, slide the stop ring on and install the snapring. The stop ring must be moved up to cover the snapring, a bearing puller can be used for this.

10. Install the armature and drive with the shift arm, then install the steel and rubber washers. Install the solenoid to hold the washers in place.

11. Install the starter body and connect the field coil strap. When installing the brushes and holder, make sure the brushes move freely in the holder.

12. Install the rear bushing and cover and tighten the through bolts evenly. Turn the motor by hand to make sure it moves smoothly.

13. The armature shaft end play must be set. With the shims and lock washer installed on the shaft, use a feeler gauge to measure the gap between the shims and the rear bushing. There should be 0.004-0.012 in. (0.1-0.3mm). With the end play correctly set, install the sealing ring and bushing cap and test the starter before installing it on a vehicle.

Inspection and Testing

ARMATURE

1. Check the commutator for wear and damage. If it is burnt, scored or more than 0.002 in. (0.05mm) out of round, it can be reconditioned on a lathe if the core and windings are okay. The minimum commutator diameter on all types is 0.100 in. (2.5mm) less than the original dimension, which can be measured in an area not contacted by the brushes. If a satisfactory original commutator dimension cannot be measured, the armature is already beyond repair.

2. Check the core and windings for grounding and continuity with an ohmmeter. There should be no continuity between any segment and the core. There should be good continuity between all the segments. Use a growler to check for short circuits. If the armature fails any of these tests, it cannot be repaired and must be replaced.

3. With a satisfactory armature condition, recondition the commutator and undercut the space between the segments. The undercut should be 0.015–0.030 in. (0.4–0.8mm). Make sure the undercut is square and do not remove any metal from the segments.

FIELD COILS

1. Some of the smaller Bosch starters have permanent magnet fields which cannot be removed, but most have electric field coils which can be removed for replacement. They need not be removed for testing.

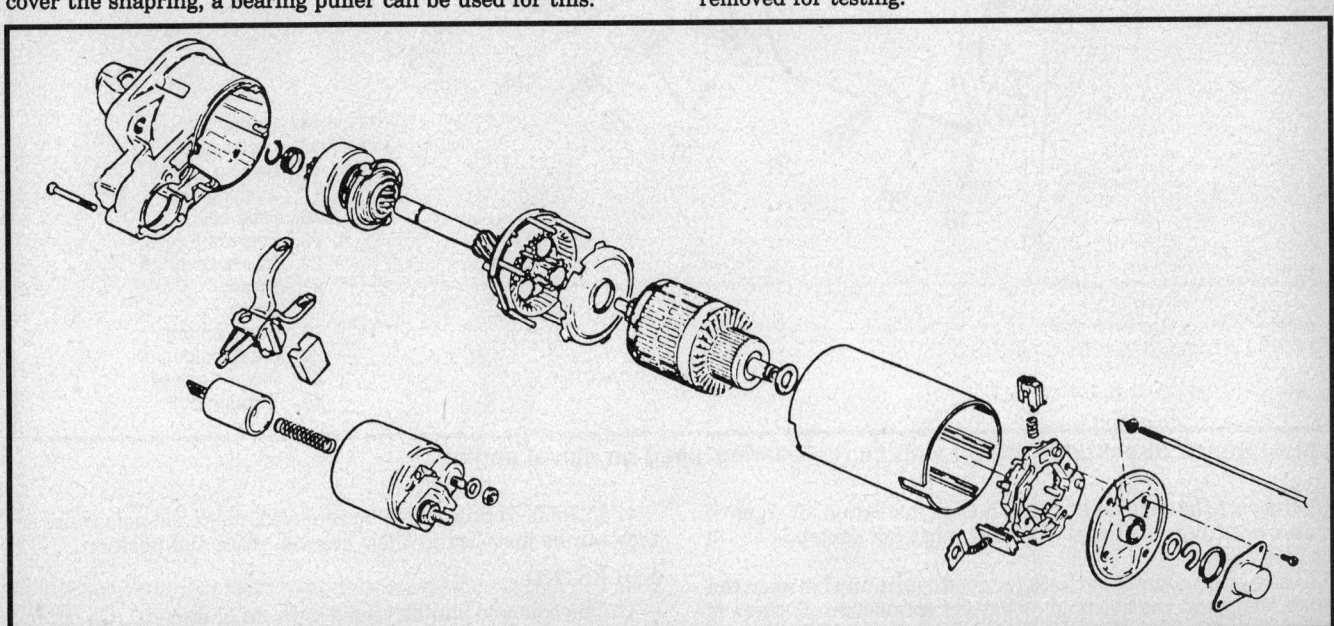

Bosch gear drive starter, lube the gears with moly grease

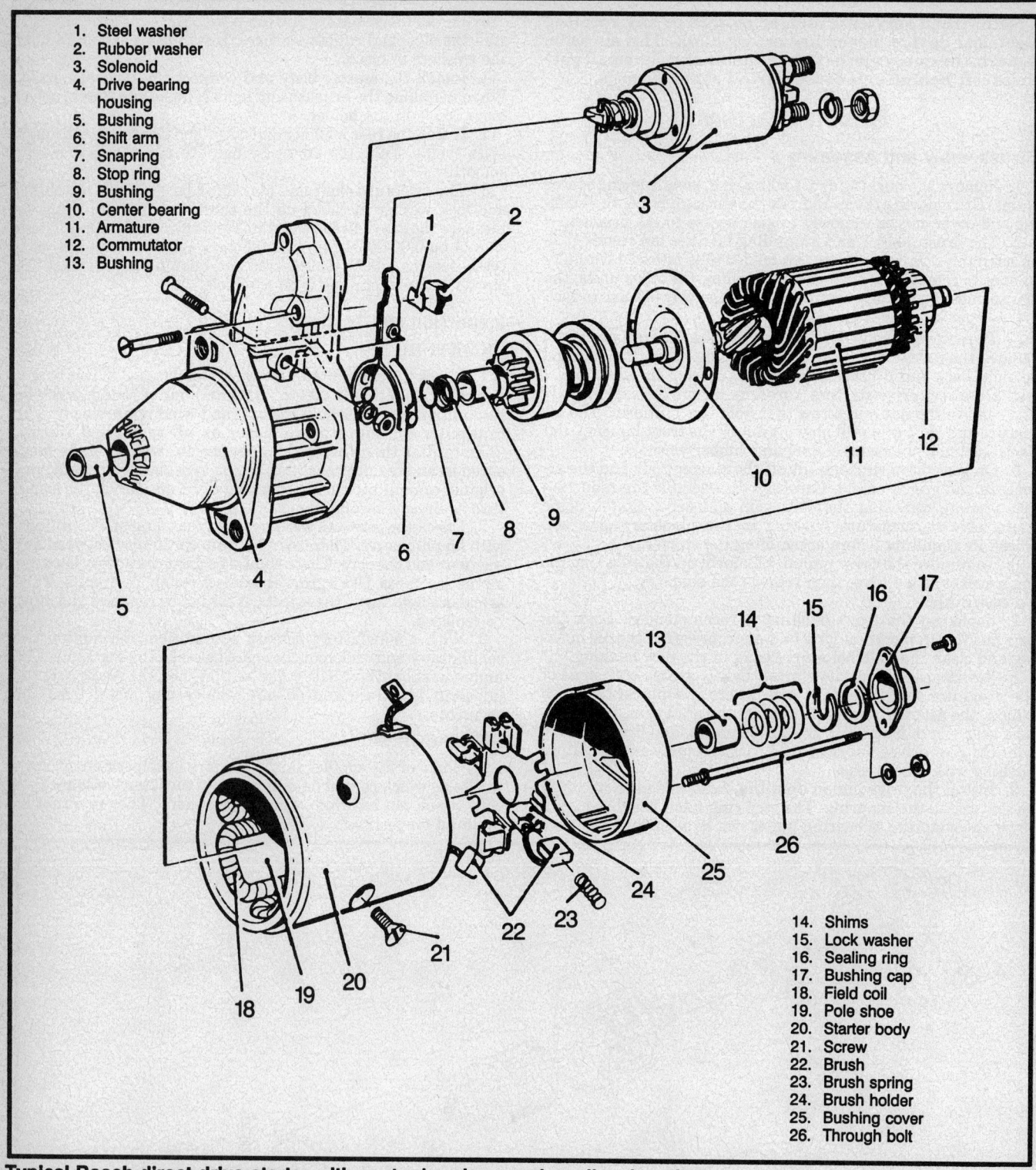

1. Steel washer
2. Rubber washer
3. Solenoid
4. Drive bearing housing
5. Bushing
6. Shift arm
7. Snapring
8. Stop ring
9. Bushing
10. Center bearing
11. Armature
12. Commutator
13. Bushing

14. Shims
15. Lock washer
16. Sealing ring
17. Bushing cap
18. Field coil
19. Pole shoe
20. Starter body
21. Screw
22. Brush
23. Brush spring
24. Brush holder
25. Bushing cover
26. Through bolt

Typical Bosch direct drive starter with center bearing used on diesel engine

2. Inspect the coils for burnt or melted insulation, or signs of contact with the armature. The coils must not protrude above the pole shoe.

3. Use an ohmmeter to check for good continuity between the brush leads and the solenoid or battery connection. If there is continuity between any connection and the starter body, the coil is grounded and must be replaced.

4. If the field coils are to be removed, mark the pole shoes so they can be installed in their original place and position.

SOLENOID

1. The solenoid can be tested with an ohmmeter. Check for continuity between terminal 50 and ground. The shift arm end of the plunger should provide a good ground.

2. Check for continuity between terminal 50 and the field coil connection. Defective solenoids cannot be repaired and must be replaced.

DRIVE

1. Check that the pinion gear teeth are in good condition and evenly worn. If they are not, be sure to check the ring gear on the engine flywheel.

2. Make sure the pinion drive moves freely on the armature or reduction gear shaft and on the shift arm.

3. The pinion drive should rotate smoothly in one direction and lock in the other. A little bit of clicking noise may be heard and felt, but uneven operation or excess noise indicates a faulty unit. Pinion drives cannot be repaired, faulty units should be replaced.

4. If the starter is equipped with reduction gearing, remove the gears and clean all old grease so the gears and bushing can be inspected. The armature bushing can be replaced if necessary, but the gears are an assembly and cannot be replaced separately.

BRUSHES

1. Brushes must be replaced if they are less than ½ in. (13mm) long. Carefully unbend the tabs to remove the springs and brushes from the holder.

2. On some models the brush wire is soldered to the holder assembly. New brushes are installed by soldering the wire to the holder. Work quickly and do not allow solder to flow in the wire. If the wire gets stiff with solder the brush will not move freely in the holder.

3. If the wire is not removable, such as on the field coil brushes, the brush can still be replaced. Break the old brush off the wire by clamping it in a vise or use a hammer to crush the brushes. Do not cut the wire.

4. Hold the wire in the vise or with pliers to act as a heat sink, preventing solder from flowing into the wire. If the wire stiffens with solder, the brush will not move freely in the holder.

5. Clean up the end of the wire, slide it through the hole in the new brush and solder the new brush in place.

Hitachi Starters

Disassembly and Assembly

1. Disconnect the field wire and remove the through bolts to remove the motor. Make sure the armature stays with the field frame.

2. To remove the gear drive housing, remove the screws and hold the starter with the gear housing down so the gears don't fall out. If the steel ball stays with the solenoid housing, retrieve it with a magnet.

3. To remove the clutch assembly on models with a clutch shaft, support the shaft at the inside end and gently tap the stop ring down off the snapring with a small hammer and socket. The snapring is not to be reused once it has been removed.

4. To disassemble the motor, remove the end cover, lift the brush springs to remove the brushes and remove the brush holder. Carefully slide out the armature.

5. Clean all parts for inspection, especially the gear assembly.

To assemble:

6. Carefully inspect the gears and housing for excess wear or damage and repair or replace as required. If there is any gear damage, make sure to check the ring gear on the engine. When reassembling the gears, lubricate the gears and bearings with a high temperature grease.

7. Install the gear drive and clutch assembly into the housing. On models with the clutch shaft, the stop ring can be positioned over the snapring by gently tapping the shaft down with a soft hammer. Assemble the housing to the solenoid switch assembly.

8. Slide the armature into the field frame and install the brush holder and brushes. It may be easier to engage the gears if the motor is assembled to the solenoid before installing the end cover.

9. Make sure the motor is properly positioned on the solenoid, install the cover and through bolts and attach the field wire.

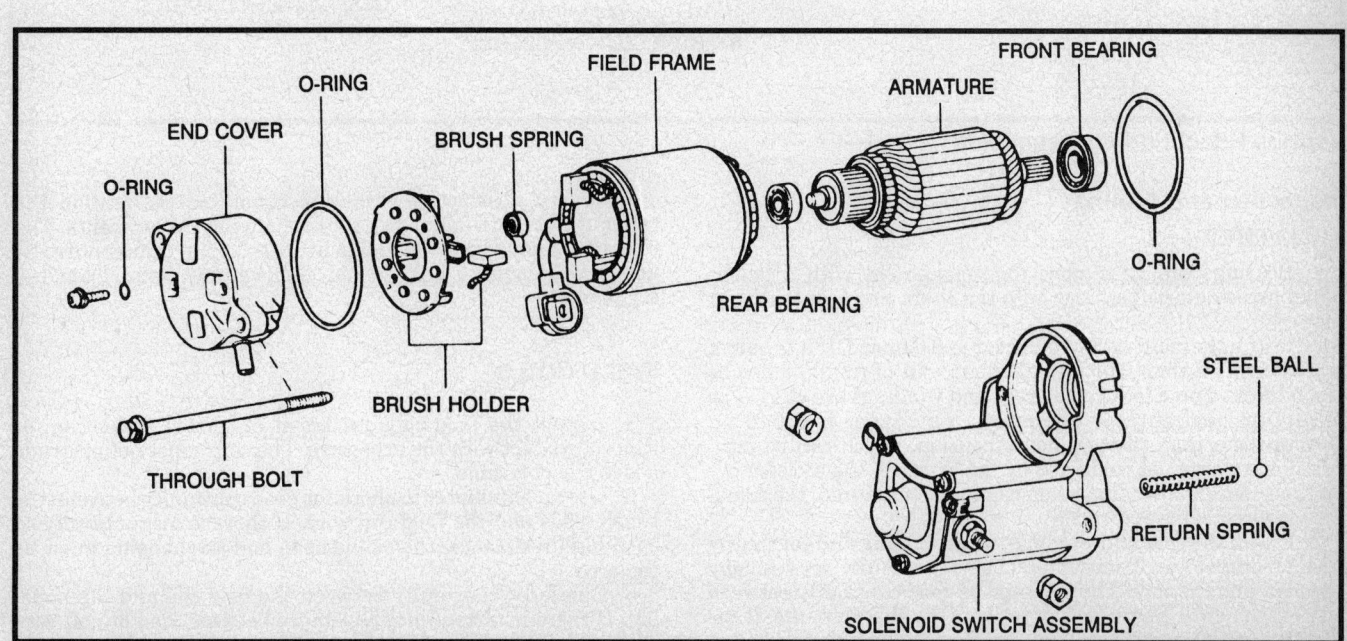

Hitachi starter motor with a variety of drive assemblies

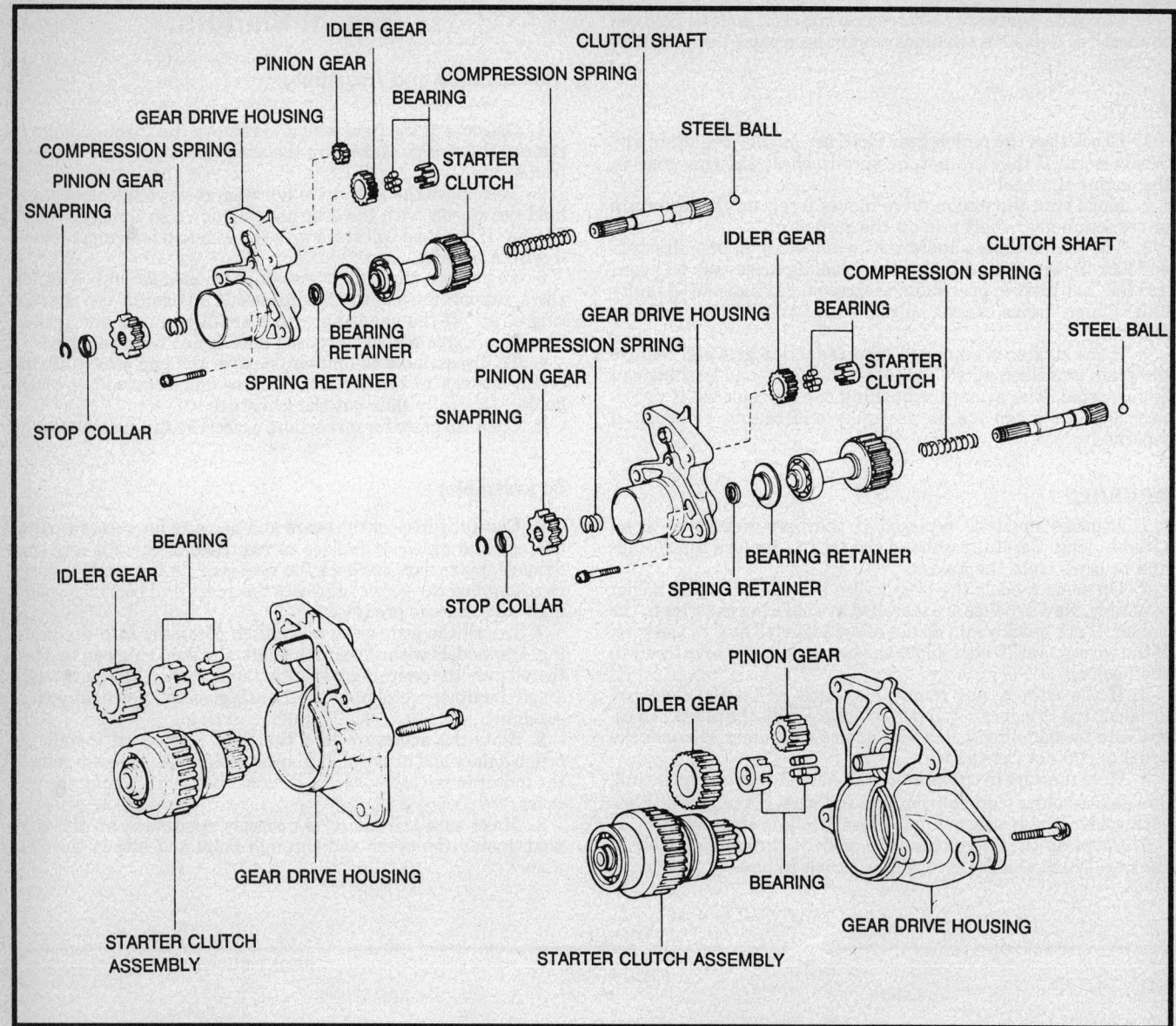

Various Hitachi drive assemblies

Inspection and Testing

ARMATURE

1. Bearings can be remove for replacement with a puller. When pressing new bearings onto the shaft, press on the inner race.

2. Check the commutator for wear and damage. If it is burnt, scored or more than 0.002 in. (0.05mm) out of round, it can be reconditioned on a lathe if the core and windings are okay. The minimum commutator diameter on all types is 0.040 in. (1.0mm) less than the original dimension, which can be measured in an area not contacted by the brushes. If a satisfactory original commutator dimension cannot be measured, the armature is already beyond repair.

2. Check the core and windings for grounding and continuity with an ohmmeter. There should be no continuity between any segment and the core. There should be good continuity between all the segments. Use a growler to check for short circuits. If the armature fails any of these tests, it cannot be repaired and must be replaced.

3. With a satisfactory armature condition, recondition the commutator and undercut the space between the segments. The undercut should be 0.008–0.024 in. (0.2–0.6mm). Make sure the undercut is square and do not remove any metal from the segments.

FIELD COILS

1. Inspect the field coils for burnt or melted insulation, or signs of contact with the armature. The coils must not protrude above the pole shoe.

2. Use an ohmmeter to check for good continuity between the brush leads and the field coil wire. If there is no continuity or even high resistance, the coil is open and the housing must be replaced.

3. Check for continuity between the field coil and the housing. If there is not infinite resistance between lead or coil wire and the housing, the coil is grounded and the housing must be replaced.

SOLENOID

1. The solenoid can be tested with an ohmmeter. Check for continuity between terminal 50 and ground. The housing should provide a good ground.

2. Check for continuity between terminal 50 and the field coil connection. Defective solenoids cannot be repaired and must be replaced.

DRIVE

1. Clean all old grease so the gears and housing can be inspected. If any gear is damaged, check the housing closely for cracks.

2. Check that all the gear teeth are in good condition and evenly worn. If any gear is damaged, replace the whole assembly and be sure to check the ring gear on the engine flywheel.

3. Make sure the clutch moves freely on the shaft. On clutch assemblies without a separate shaft, it should rotate smoothly in one direction and lock in the other. A little bit of clicking noise may be heard and felt, but uneven operation or excess noise indicates a faulty unit. This assembly cannot be repaired, faulty units should be replaced.

4. Before installing the assembly, lubricate the gears and solenoid lever with moly grease.

BRUSHES

1. On starter motors with an O-ring, minimum brush length is 0.395 in. (10mm). On motors without an O-ring, minimum brush length is 0.335 in. (8.5mm).

2. New brushes are installed by soldering. Work quickly and do not allow solder to flow in the wire. If the wire gets stiff with solder the brush will not move freely in the holder.

3. Test the brush holder for continuity. The holders opposite each other are a pair and should have continuity only with each other. If a brush holder has less than infinite resistance with the one next to it, the holder assembly is faulty and must be replaced.

Lucas Starters

Disassembly and Assembly

SOLENOID OPERATED DIRECT DRIVE

1. Disconnect the field wire and remove the solenoid.

2. Remove the cover band and lift the springs to remove the brushes from their holders.

3. Remove the through bolts and remove the end cover and yoke.

4. Loosen the nut on the eccentric pivot pin and remove the pin.

5. Remove the drive end bracket. To remove the drive, press the thrust collar towards the pinion gear with a socket and remove the snapring from the armature shaft extension.

To assemble:

6. Before assembling, check the condition of the bushings in the rear cover and the drive end bracket. If they are to be replaced, soak the new bushing in oil for a half hour before pressing it into place. Trial fit the rear cover with armature brake to the armature to note how they go together.

7. Install the drive assembly, thrust collar, and snapring onto the armature shaft. The thrust ring must be pushed up over the snapring before installing the drive end bracket.

8. When installing the yoke and rear cover, turn the cover to make sure the pin in the shaft properly engages the brake shoes in the cover. Torque the through bolts to 8 ft. lbs.(10.8 Nm).

9. Install the eccentric pivot pin and solenoid, and insert the brushes into their holders.

10. With the starter fully assembled, the pinion movement must be adjusted. With the field wire disconnected so the motor will not run, apply voltage to the solenoid connection and ground the case to activate the solenoid, moving the drive pinion out to full travel.

11. Lightly hold the pinion away from the thrust ring to take up slack in the linkage and measure the gap between the pinion and ring with a feeler gauge. There should be 0.005-0.015 in. (0.13-0.38mm) clearance.

12. To adjust the pinion movement, loosen the engaging lever eccentric pivot pin nut and turn the pin. Full travel occurs over 180 degrees of pin arc.

SOLENOID OPERATED INDIRECT DRIVE

1. Disconnect the field coil wire and remove the solenoid.

2. Remove the front housing to remove the starter drive assembly.

3. Remove the through bolts to remove the motor.

4. When reassembling, use moly grease to lubricate the gear train.

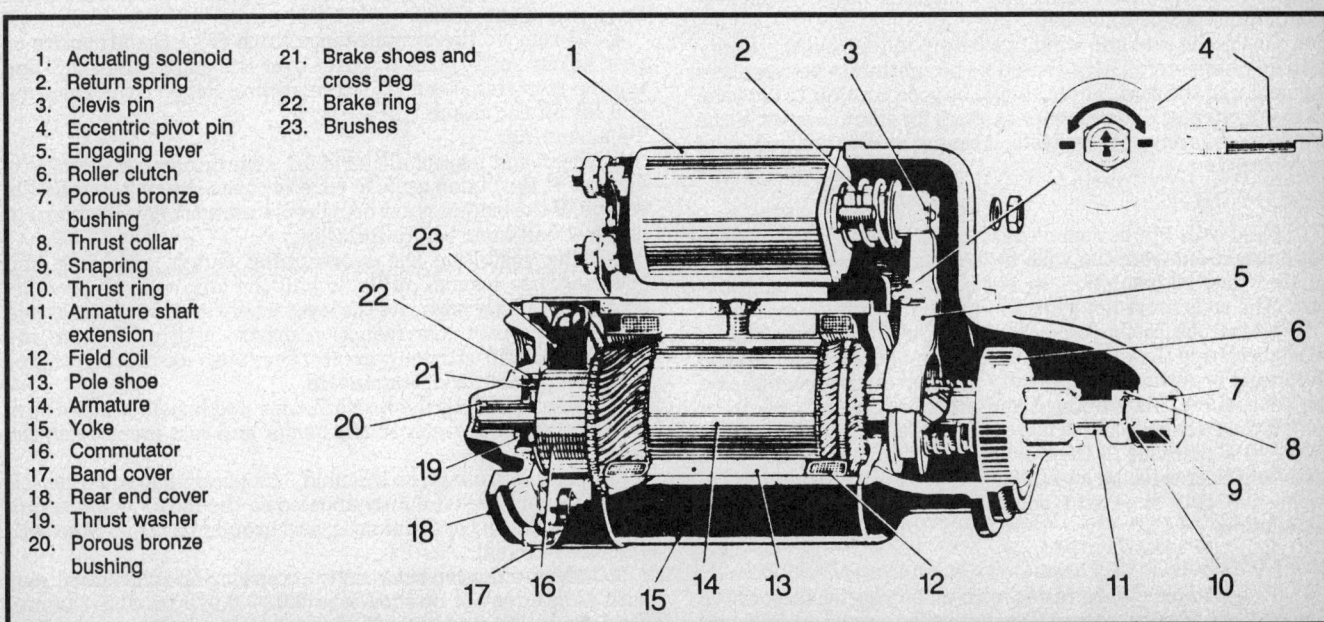

1. Actuating solenoid	21. Brake shoes and cross peg
2. Return spring	22. Brake ring
3. Clevis pin	23. Brushes
4. Eccentric pivot pin	
5. Engaging lever	
6. Roller clutch	
7. Porous bronze bushing	
8. Thrust collar	
9. Snapring	
10. Thrust ring	
11. Armature shaft extension	
12. Field coil	
13. Pole shoe	
14. Armature	
15. Yoke	
16. Commutator	
17. Band cover	
18. Rear end cover	
19. Thrust washer	
20. Porous bronze bushing	

Lucas pre-engaged drive starter has drive pinion end play adjustment and armature brake shoes

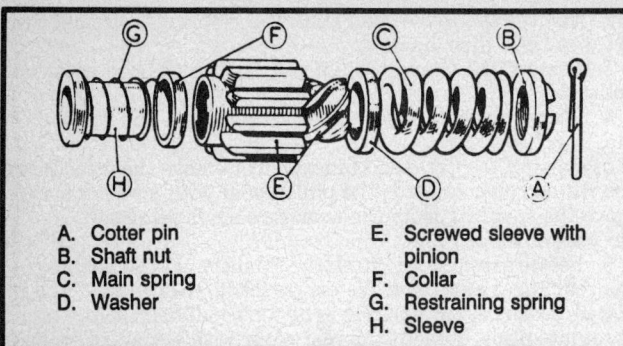

A. Cotter pin
B. Shaft nut
C. Main spring
D. Washer
E. Screwed sleeve with pinion
F. Collar
G. Restraining spring
H. Sleeve

Lucas inertia drive assembly is secured either with a cotter pin or tapered keepers

INERTIA OPERATED DRIVE

1. On models so equipped, remove the cotter pin from the drive end, hold the flats at the brush end of the armature shaft with a wrench and unscrew the shaft nut to remove the drive assembly. Other models secure the main spring with split keepers, like an engine valve. A valve spring compressor can be used to remove the drive assembly.
2. Remove the cover band and lift the springs to remove the brushes from their holders.
3. Remove the through bolts and remove the end covers and yoke.
4. Assembly is the reverse of disassembly. Service to the armature, brushes, bushings and field coils is identical to solenoid equipped starters.
5. When assembling the drive, make sure the screwed sleeve and pinion move freely and are not badly worn or damaged. They can be replaced as a unit, but not separately.

Inspection and Testing

ARMATURE

1. Check the commutator for wear and damage. If it is burnt or scored, it can be reconditioned with sand paper or on a lathe if the core and windings are okay. The minimum commutator diameter 1.531 in. (38.90mm). The insulation between the segments must not be undercut.
2. Check the core and windings for grounding and continuity with an ohmmeter. There should be no continuity between any segment and the core. There should be good continuity between all the segments. Use a growler to check for short circuits. If the armature fails any of these tests, it cannot be repaired and must be replaced.

FIELD COILS

1. Field coils can be removed for replacement, but they need not be removed from the yoke for testing. Inspect the coils for burnt or melted insulation, or signs of contact with the armature. The coils must not protrude above the pole shoe.
2. Use an ohmmeter to check for good continuity between the brush leads and the solenoid or battery connection. If there is no continuity or if there is continuity between any connection and the yoke, the coil is grounded and must be replaced.
3. If the field coils are to be removed, mark the pole shoes so they can be installed in their original place and position. When installing field coils, be careful to not pinch the insulation between the pole shoe and yoke. Retest the field coils after installation.

SOLENOID

1. The solenoid can be tested with an ohmmeter or powered test light. Check for continuity between the small terminal and the case (ground).

2. Check for continuity between the small terminal and the field coil connection.
3. With the plunger pushed in by hand, there should be continuity between the 2 large terminals. Defective solenoids cannot be repaired.

DRIVE

1. Check that the pinion gear teeth are in good condition and evenly worn. If they are not, be sure to check the ring gear on the engine flywheel.
2. Make sure the pinion drive moves freely on the armature shaft splines.
3. The pinion drive should rotate smoothly in one direction and lock in the other. A little bit of clicking noise may be heard and felt, but uneven operation or excess noise indicates a faulty unit. Lubricate the spline and spring loaded operating bushing with grease before installation. Pinion drives cannot be repaired, faulty units should be replaced.

BRUSHES

1. Minimum brush length is $\frac{5}{16}$ in. New brushes can be installed by soldering the wire to the terminals.
2. Before and after soldering new brushes in place, check continuity at the rear cover. Two of the brush boxes are attached directly to the cover for continuity to ground. The other two are insulated from the cover and should show infinite resistance to ground.
3. Make sure the brushes move freely in their boxes.

Mitsubishi Starters

Disassembly and Assembly

DIRECT AND REDUCTION DRIVE TYPES

1. Disconect the field coil wire and remove the solenoid from the motor.
2. Remove the through bolt and screw to remove the rear cover and bushing.
3. Remove the brushes from their holders and remove the holder assembly, yoke assembly and the armature. On reduction drive types, be careful to not loose the steel ball from the drive end of the shaft.
4. To remove the overrunning clutch from the armature or gear holder shaft, place a socket over the end of the shaft and tap the stop ring down off the snapring. Remove the snapring and lift off the clutch.

To assemble:

5. Clean and inspect all parts for wear or damage. If there is damage to the pinion gear, be sure to check the ring gear on the engine. If the bushings are being replaced, soak new bushings in oil for a half hour before installing.
6. After installing the overrunning clutch, stop ring and snapring, use a small puller to pull the stop ring up over the snapring. Lightly lubricate the lever where it contacts the clutch with moly grease. On reduction drives, lightly lubricate the gears and shafts with moly grease. Don't use too much grease or the brushes will be contaminated.
7. After installing the brush holder and brushes, make sure the brushes move freely in the holder and seat properly on the commutator.
8. When installing the solenoid, the pinion gap must be set. With the field coil wire disconnected so the motor will not run, apply 12 volts DC to terminal S, and ground terminal M to activate the solenoid.
9. Measure the gap between the stop ring and the pinion gear with a feeler gauge. It should be 0.020–0.079 in. (0.5–2.0mm). This gap is adjusted by adding or removing gaskets at the solenoid switch mounting.

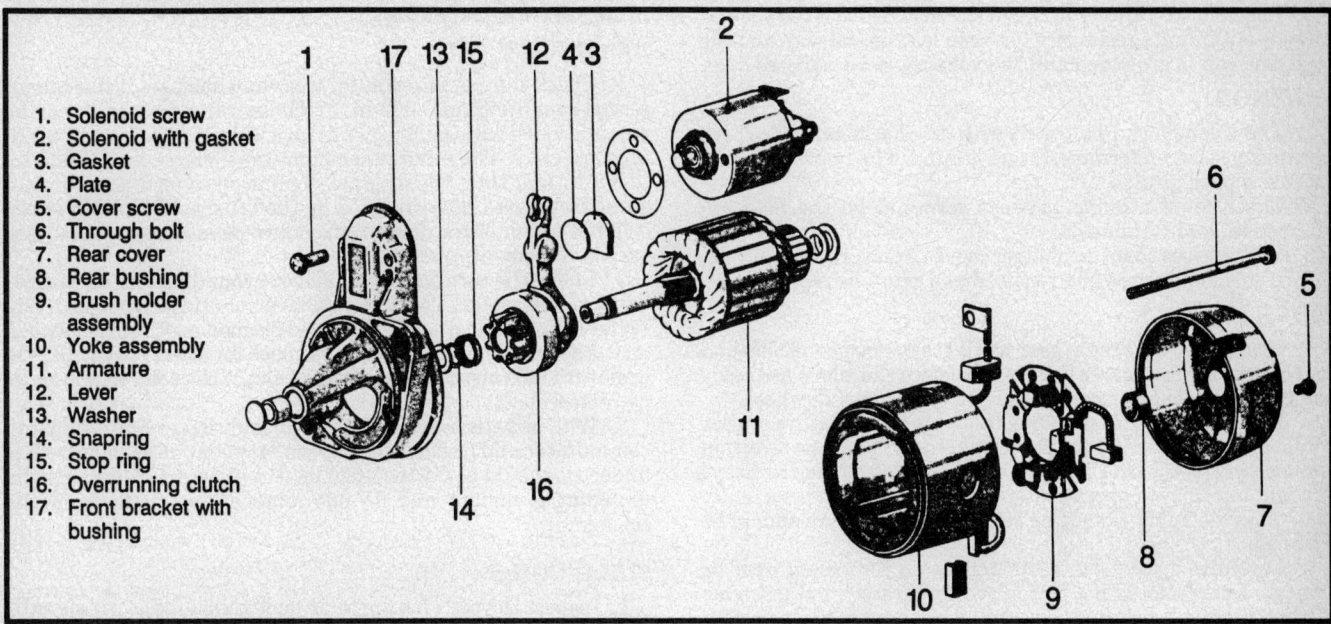

1. Solenoid screw
2. Solenoid with gasket
3. Gasket
4. Plate
5. Cover screw
6. Through bolt
7. Rear cover
8. Rear bushing
9. Brush holder assembly
10. Yoke assembly
11. Armature
12. Lever
13. Washer
14. Snapring
15. Stop ring
16. Overrunning clutch
17. Front bracket with bushing

Mitsubishi direct drive starter assembly

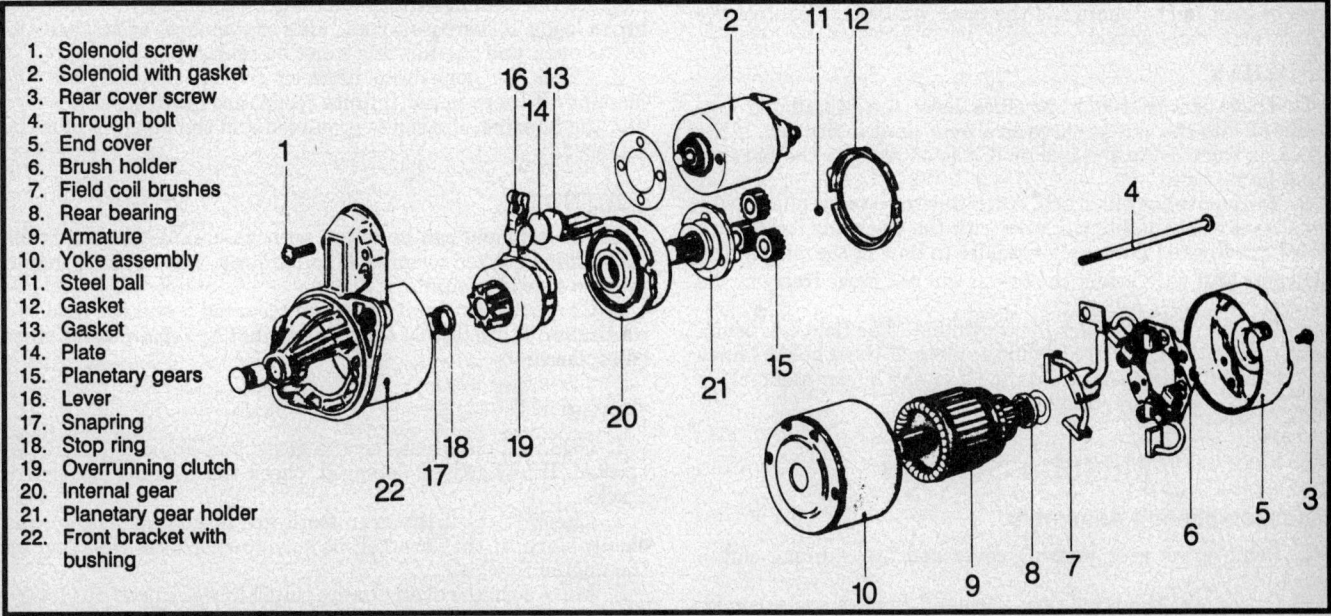

1. Solenoid screw
2. Solenoid with gasket
3. Rear cover screw
4. Through bolt
5. End cover
6. Brush holder
7. Field coil brushes
8. Rear bearing
9. Armature
10. Yoke assembly
11. Steel ball
12. Gasket
13. Gasket
14. Plate
15. Planetary gears
16. Lever
17. Snapring
18. Stop ring
19. Overrunning clutch
20. Internal gear
21. Planetary gear holder
22. Front bracket with bushing

Mitsubishi reduction drive starter assembly

Inspection and Testing

ARMATURE

1. Check the commutator for wear and damage. If it is burnt, scored or more than 0.004 in. (0.1mm) out of round, it can be reconditioned on a lathe if the core and windings are okay. The minimum commutator diameter is 0.040 in. (1.0mm) less than the original dimension, which can be measured in an area not contacted by the brushes. If a satisfactory original commutator dimension cannot be measured, the armature is already beyond repair.

2. Check the core and windings for grounding and continuity with an ohmmeter. There should be no continuity between any segment and the core. There should be good continuity between all the segments. Use a growler to check for short circuits. If the armature fails any of these tests, it cannot be repaired and must be replaced.

3. With a satisfactory armature condition, recondition the commutator and undercut the space between the segments. The undercut should be 0.020 in. (0.5mm). Make sure the undercut is square and do not remove any metal from the segments.

FIELD COILS

1. Inspect the field coils for burnt or melted insulation, or signs of contact with the armature. The coils must not protrude above the pole shoe.

2. Use an ohmmeter to check for good continuity between the brush leads and the field coil wire. If there is no continuity or even high resistance, the coil is open and the housing must be replaced.

3. Check for continuity between the field coil and the yoke. If there is not infinite resistance between lead or coil wire and the yoke, the coil is grounded and the yoke must be replaced.

SOLENOID

1. The solenoid can be tested with an ohmmeter. Check for continuity between terminal S and ground. The housing should provide a good ground.

2. Check for continuity between terminal M, the field coil connection, and terminal S.

3. Check to see that the plunger moves freely. Electrically defective solenoids cannot be repaired and must be replaced.

DRIVE

1. Check that the pinion gear teeth are in good condition and evenly worn. If the gear is damaged, replace the whole assembly and be sure to check the ring gear on the engine flywheel.

2. Make sure the clutch moves freely on the armature or gear holder shaft. The pinion should rotate smoothly in one direction and lock in the other. A little bit of clicking noise may be heard and felt, but uneven operation or excess noise indicates a faulty unit. This assembly cannot be repaired, faulty units should be replaced.

3. Carefully inspect the reduction gears for excess wear or damage. Gears should not be replaced separately, but as an assembly. Lightly lubricate the assembly with moly grease before installation.

4. Before installing the assembly, lightly lubricate the armature or gear holder shaft and the lever where they contact the clutch with moly grease.

BRUSHES

1. These starter motor brushes have the Mitsubishi logo stamped into the side to serve as a wear limit indication. If the brush is worn up to the line or if it is oil soaked, the brushes must be replaced.

2. To remove the old brush, crush it with a vice or pliers. New brushes are soldered to the wire with the wear line facing out. Work quickly and do not allow solder to flow in the wire. If the wire gets stiff with solder the brush will not move freely in the holder.

3. Test the brush holder for continuity. The field coil brush holders should be insulated from the plate. If these holders have less than infinite resistance to the plate, the holder assembly is faulty and must be replaced.

Mitsuba Starters

Disassembly and Assembly

1. Remove the gear housing cover and overrunning clutch assembly.

2. Disconnect the large field wire and remove the solenoid, through bolts, screws and end cover.

3. Remove the field winding brushes from the brush holder and remove the holder.

4. Carefully lift the armature and field winding housing away from the gear housing.

To assemble:

5. Closely check the gear housing for cracks or excess wear. When reassembling the motor, pry the brush spring back and insert the brush half way so when the spring is released it, will wedge the brush against the side of its' holder.

6. After installing the armature and brush holder, push the brushes into place so the springs seat onto the end of the brush. Install the end cover.

7. When installing the solenoid, lightly lubricate the lever with moly grease.

8. Clean and inspect the gears and overrunning clutch assembly. Lubricate with moly grease and install the clutch and housing cover.

Inspection and Testing

ARMATURE

1. Check the commutator for wear and damage. If it is burnt, scored or more than 0.002 in. (0.05mm) out of round, it can be reconditioned with sand paper or on a lathe if the core and windings are okay. The minimum commutator diameter is 0.030 in. (0.6mm) less than the original dimension, which can be measured in an area not contacted by the brushes. If a satisfactory original commutator dimension cannot be measured, the armature is already beyond repair.

2. Check the core and windings for grounding and continuity with an ohmmeter. There should be no continuity between any segment and the core. There should be good continuity between all the segments. Use a growler to check for short circuits. If the armature fails any of these tests, it cannot be repaired and must be replaced.

3. With a satisfactory armature condition, recondition the commutator and undercut the space between the segments. The undercut should be 0.016–0.020 in. (0.4–0.5mm). Make sure the undercut is square and do not remove any metal from the segments.

FIELD COILS

1. Inspect the coils for burnt or melted insulation, or signs of contact with the armature. The coils must not protrude above the pole shoe.

2. Use an ohmmeter to check for good continuity between the brush leads. If there is no continuity or even high resistance, the coil is open and the housing must be replaced.

3. Check for continuity between the brush leads and the housing. If there is not infinite resistance between either lead and the housing, the coil is grounded and the housing must be replaced.

SOLENOID

1. The solenoid can be tested with an ohmmeter. Check for continuity between terminal S and ground. The housing should provide a good ground.

2. Check for continuity between terminal S and the field coil connection M. Defective solenoids cannot be repaired and must be replaced.

DRIVE

1. Clean all old grease so the gears and housing can be inspected. If any gear is damaged, check the housing closely for cracks.

2. Check that all the gear teeth are in good condition and evenly worn. If they are not, be sure to check the ring gear on the engine flywheel.

3. Make sure the overrunning clutch moves in and out freely. It should rotate smoothly in one direction and lock in the other. A little bit of clicking noise may be heard and felt, but uneven operation or excess noise indicates a faulty unit. This assembly cannot be repaired, faulty units should be replaced.

4. Before installing the assembly, lubricate the gears and solenoid lever with moly grease.

BRUSHES

1. Brushes must be replaced if they are 0.370 in. (9.3mm) long or less.

2. New brushes are installed by soldering. Work quickly and do not allow solder to flow in the wire. If the wire gets stiff with solder the brush will not move freely in the holder.

3. Test the brush holder for continuity. The holders opposite each other are a pair and should have continuity only with each other. If a brush holder has less than infinite resistance with the one next to it, the holder assembly is faulty and must be replaced.

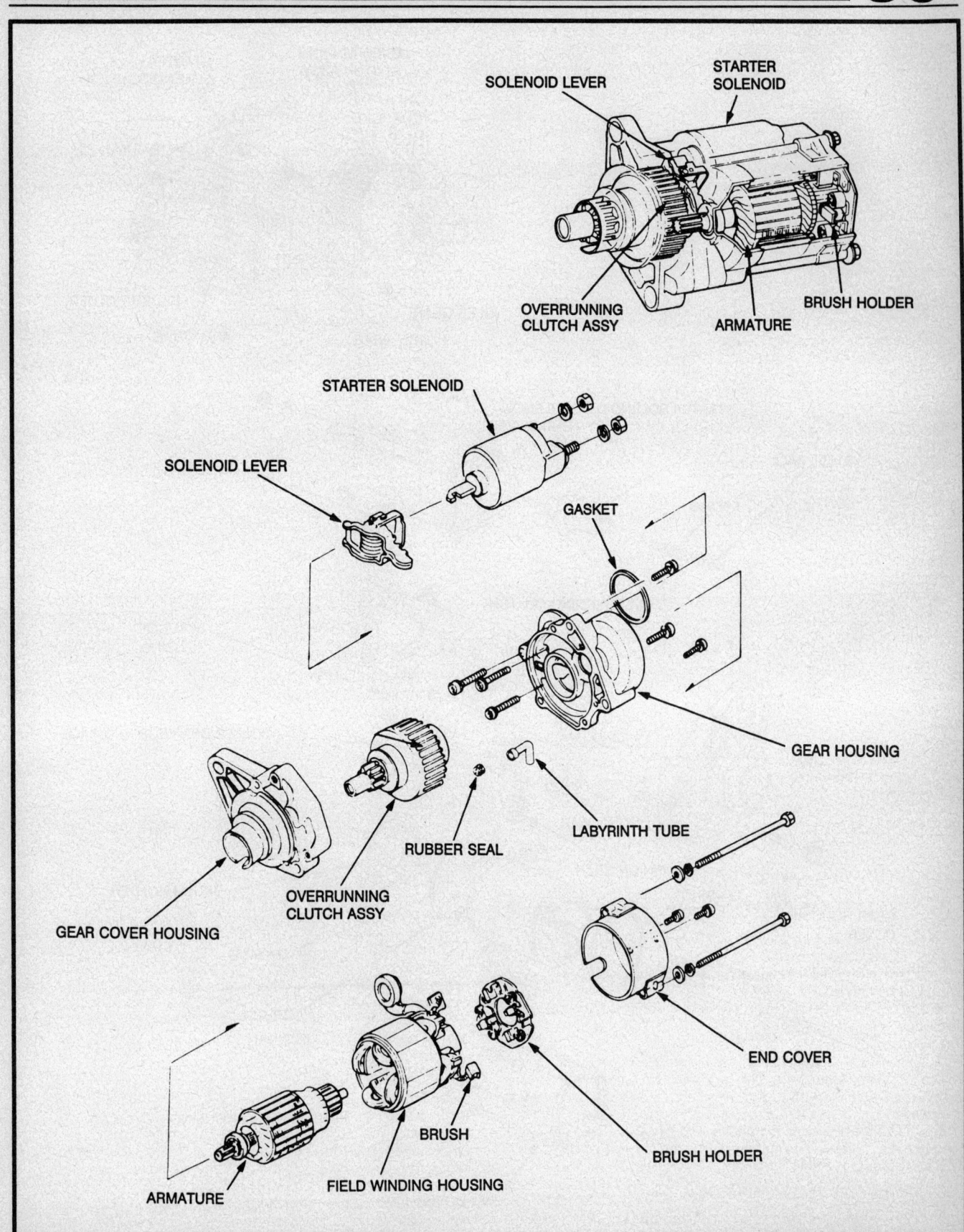

Mitsuba starter assembly with separate solenoid

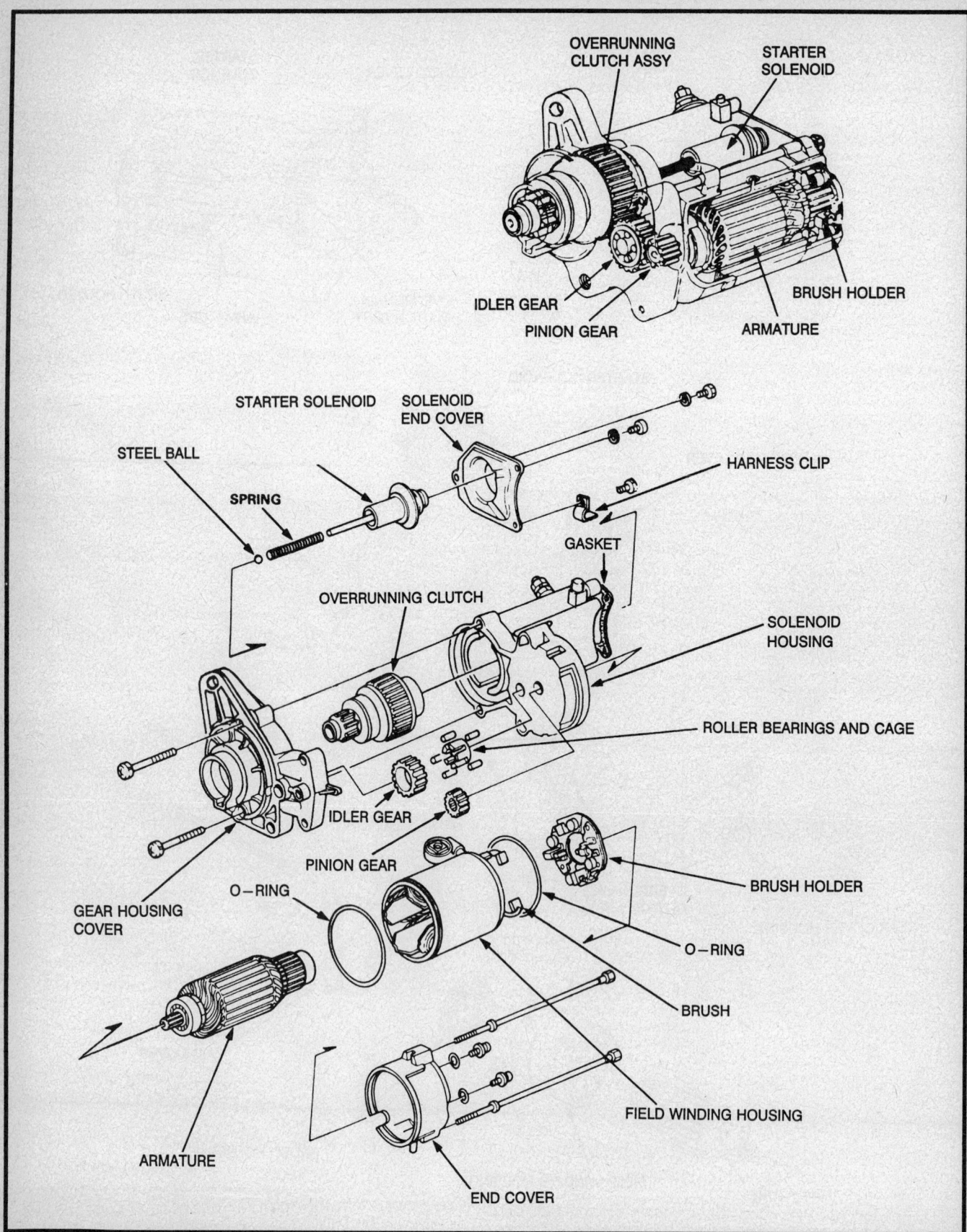

OVERRUNNING CLUTCH ASSY

STARTER SOLENOID

IDLER GEAR

PINION GEAR

BRUSH HOLDER

ARMATURE

STARTER SOLENOID

SOLENOID END COVER

STEEL BALL

SPRING

HARNESS CLIP

GASKET

OVERRUNNING CLUTCH

SOLENOID HOUSING

ROLLER BEARINGS AND CAGE

IDLER GEAR

PINION GEAR

BRUSH HOLDER

GEAR HOUSING COVER

O—RING

O—RING

BRUSH

ARMATURE

FIELD WINDING HOUSING

END COVER

Nippondenso starter with idler gear

Nippondenso Starters

Disassembly and Assembly

1. Disconnect the large field wire, remove the through bolts and screws to remove the end cover.

2. Carefully lift the springs to remove the brushes from the brush holder and remove the brush holder, field winding housing and armature.

3. When disassembling the drive gears, be careful to not let the parts fall out of the housing. Remove the screws that hold the front housing and tilt the housing down while lifting the solenoid housing away from it.

4. Disassemble the gears for cleaning and inspection.

To assemble

5. Clean and inspect the gear drive assembly and replace worn or damaged parts. Don't forget to closely check the housing for cracks or excess wear. The overrunning clutch cannot be repaired and must be replaced as an assembly. Lubricate all parts with moly grease before assembling the system.

6. When reassembling the motor, pry the brush spring back and insert the brush about half way so when the spring is released it, will wedge the brush against the side of its' holder.

7. When installing the armature and brush holder, push the brushes into place so the springs seat onto the end of the brush. Install the end cover and test the starter.

Inspection and Testing

ARMATURE

1. Check the commutator for wear and damage. If it is burnt, scored or more than 0.002 in. (0.05mm) out of round, it can be reconditioned with sand paper or on a lathe if the core and windings are okay. The minimum commutator diameter is 0.040 in. (1.0mm) less than the original dimension, which can be measured in an area not contacted by the brushes. If a satisfactory original commutator dimension cannot be measured, the armature is already beyond repair.

2. Check the core and windings for grounding and continuity with an ohmmeter. There should be no continuity between any segment and the core. There should be good continuity between all the segments. Use a growler to check for short circuits. If the armature fails any of these tests, it cannot be repaired and must be replaced.

3. With a satisfactory armature condition, recondition the commutator and undercut the space between the segments. The undercut should be 0.020–0.030 in. (0.5–0.8mm). Make sure the undercut is square and do not remove any metal from the segments.

FIELD COILS

1. Inspect the coils for burnt or melted insulation, or signs of contact with the armature. The coils must not protrude above the pole shoe.

2. Use an ohmmeter to check for good continuity between the brush leads. If there is no continuity or even high resistance, the coil is open and the housing must be replaced.

3. Check for continuity between the brush leads and the housing. If there is not infinite resistance between either lead and the housing, the coil is grounded and the housing must be replaced.

SOLENOID

1. The solenoid can be tested with an ohmmeter. Check for continuity between terminal S and the ground. The housing should provide a good ground.

2. Check for continuity between terminal S and the field coil connection M. Defective solenoids cannot be repaired and must be replaced.

DRIVE

1. Remove the gears and clean all old grease so the gears and housing can be inspected. If any gear is damaged, check the housing closely for cracks.

2. Check that all the gear teeth are in good condition and evenly worn. If they are not, be sure to check the ring gear on the engine flywheel.

3. Make sure the overrunning clutch moves in and out freely on the gear shaft. It should rotate smoothly in one direction and lock in the other. A little bit of clicking noise may be heard and felt, but uneven operation or excess noise indicates a faulty unit. This assembly cannot be repaired, faulty units should be replaced.

4. Before installing the gear drive assembly, lubricate the gears and bearings with moly grease.

BRUSHES

1. Brushes must be replaced if they are 0.330 in. (8.5mm) long or less.

2. New brushes are installed by soldering. Work quickly and do not allow solder to flow in the wire. If the wire gets stiff with solder the brush will not move freely in the holder.

3. Test the brush holder for continuity. The holders opposite each other are a pair and should have continuity only with each other. If a brush holder has less than infinite resistance with the one next to it, the holder assembly is faulty and must be replaced.

Paris-Rhone Starters

Disassembly and Assembly

1. To remove the solenoid, disconnect the field coil wire and remove the nuts from the front housing. If necessary, unhook the plunger from the shift arm, then slide the solenoid straight back.

2. Disengage the brushes from their holders and remove the through bolts, rear cover and field coil housing.

3. Carefully lift the armature out of the drive end bushing and tilt it to remove it. On some models it may be necessary to disassemble the fork from the housing to remove the armature.

4. To remove the drive pinion from the armature, tap down on the stop ring using a socket as a sleeve, then remove the snapring.

To assemble:

5. Clean all parts for inspection and testing. If the pinion gear shows damage, check the ring gear on the engine. Replacing the

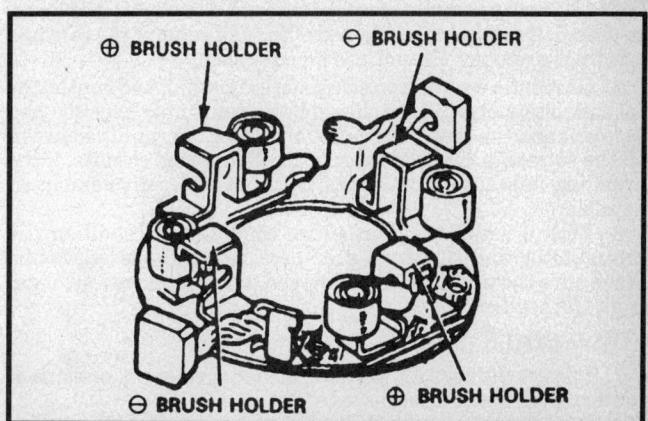

Check brush holder continuity; there should be infinite resistance between positive and negative holders

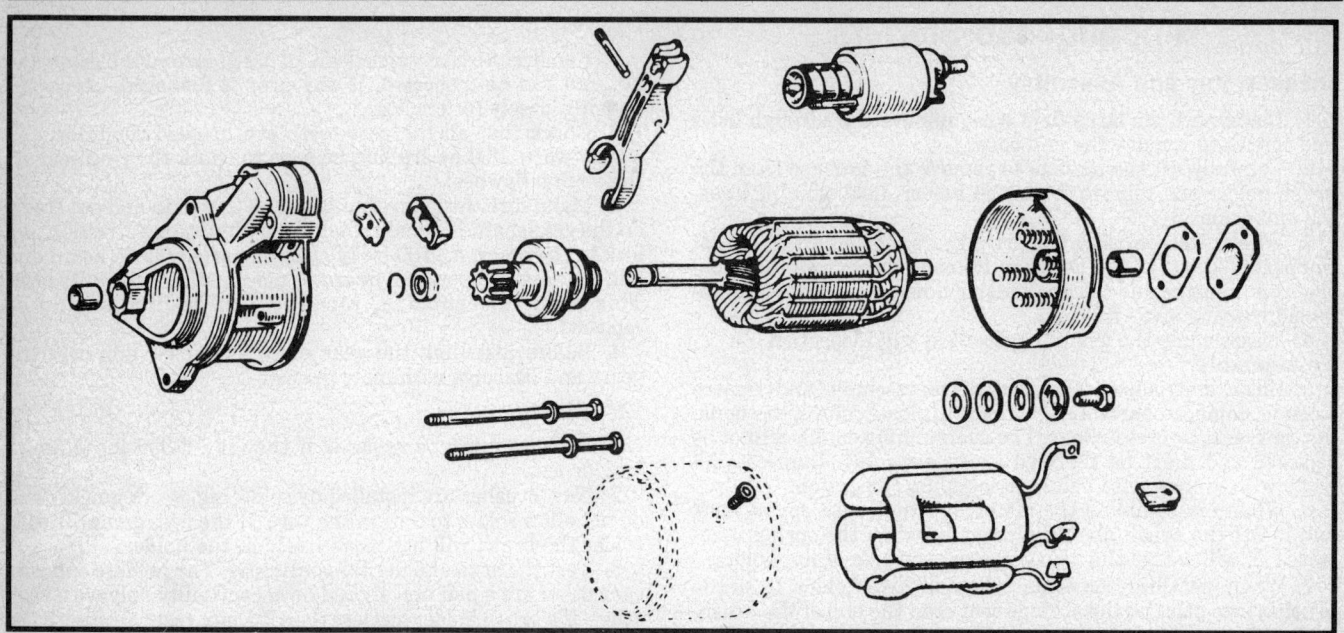

Paris-Rohne starter assembly: some models have an eccentric pin to adjust the pinion-to-stop ring clearance

bushings is recommended. Soak the new bushing in motor oil for about ½ hour, press out the old bushing and clean the hole before pressing in the new bushing.

6. After installing the drive pinion, stop ring and snapring, use a small puller to seat the stop ring over the snapring.

7. Install the field coil housing, end cover and through bolts but do not connect the field coil wire yet. When installing the brushes, make sure they move freely in the holder.

8. On models with the eccentric pin holding the actuating fork, the pinion travel must be set. Connect +12 volts to the small solenoid terminal and the ground to the field coil terminal. The solenoid should be activated but not the motor.

9. With a feeler gauge, measure the gap between the pinion gear and the stop ring. Turn the eccentric pin to adjust the gap to 0.060 in. (1.5mm).

10. Connect the field coil wire and bench test the starter before installation.

Inspection and Testing

ARMATURE

1. Check the commutator for wear and damage. If it is burnt or scored, it can be reconditioned with sand paper if the core and windings are okay. Do not use emery paper.

2. Check the core and windings for grounding and continuity with an ohmmeter. There should be no continuity between any segment and the core. There should be good continuity between all the segments. Use a growler to check for short circuits. If the armature fails any of these tests, it cannot be repaired and must be replaced.

3. With a satisfactory armature condition, recondition the commutator and undercut the space between the segments. Make sure the undercut is square and do not remove any metal from the segments.

FIELD COILS

1. Inspect the coils for burnt or melted insulation, or signs of contact with the armature.

2. Use an ohmmeter to check for good continuity between the brush leads and the solenoid connection. If there is continuity between any connection and the field coil housing, the coil is grounded and must be replaced.

3. If the field coils are to be removed and the starter has pole shoes, mark the pole shoes so they can be installed in their original place and position.

SOLENOID

1. The solenoid can be tested with an ohmmeter. Check for continuity between the switch terminal and ground. The mounting flange should provide a good ground.

2. Check for continuity between the switch terminal and the field coil connection.

3. Activate the solenoid by hand and check for continuity between the field coil and battery connections. Defective solenoids cannot be repaired and must be replaced.

DRIVE

1. Check that the pinion gear teeth are in good condition and evenly worn. If they are not, be sure to check the ring gear on the engine flywheel.

2. Make sure the pinion drive moves freely on the armature and on the actuating fork.

3. The pinion drive should rotate smoothly in one direction and lock in the other. A little bit of clicking noise may be heard and felt, but uneven operation or excess noise indicates a faulty unit. Pinion drives cannot be repaired, faulty units should be replaced.

BRUSHES

Brushes should be replaced whenever the starter is disassembled. New brushes are installed by soldering the wire to the holder or field coil. Work quickly and do not allow solder to flow in the wire. If the wire gets stiff with solder the brush will not move freely in the holder.